RARE RECORD PRICE GUIDE 2024

Over 100,000 listings and values.
Also available online at
www.rarerecordpriceguide.com

OMEGA AUCTIONS

SPECIALIST VINYL & MEMORABILIA AUCTIONEERS

THE BEST PLACE TO SELL YOUR COLLECTION

Rare & Collectable Records | Original Acetates
Stage Clothing | Guitars | Instruments | Posters
Tickets | Programmes | Autographs | Photographs
and much more...

WE DO ALL THE HARD WORK & YOU GET TOP PRICES.
Regular auctions of rare and collectable vinyl & music memorabilia plus one off specialist sales. If you have just one rare item or a collection of thousands then get in touch. We also hold one off sales for musicians or people linked to the music business with a bespoke service to help sell your collection. Contact us for a free no obligation appraisal.

GENRES INCLUDE ROCK, PROG, PSYCH, INDIE, PUNK, ROCK N ROLL, JAZZ, FOLK, BLUES, NORTHERN SOUL, SOUL, DISCO, MOTOWN, FUNK & MORE

WORLDWIDE BEATLES AUCTION EVERY 6 MONTHS

Previous Sales include...

On behalf of Richard Lester (Director of Help & A Hard Days Night)... Ringo's Help! Cape £61,100, George's Help! Jacket £54,000, Piano played by Paul McCartney and John Lennon £59,535

Alan Wilder (Depeche Mode) Collection £300,000
Peter Hook's Joy Division Collection £275,000
Porl Thompson (The Cure) Collection £75,000
The Ian Chapel Record Collection £80,000
Plus sales for Alan McGee, Island Records, BPI Music and many more...

Omega Auctions
Sankey Valley Industrial Estate, Newton-Le-Willows, WA12 8DN
01925 873040 www.omegaauctions.co.uk

PlasticWax**Records**

222 Cheltenham Rd, Bristol BS6 5QU

Serving music lovers since 1978

Plastic Wax Records is Bristol's longest established independent record shop with the largest range of used vinyl and CDs in the South West, including rare collector editions. We cover most genres: Rock, Reggae, Soul, Punk, Hip Hop, Prog, Indie, Electronica, Ska, Funk, African, Country, Jazz, Classical and Soundtracks.

We are the leading stockist for Bristol Archive Records, who showcase music from the diverse Bristol music scene and feature many artists and releases that are rare or have never before been released, and Reggae Archive Records, who feature music from British Reggae labels and artists.

We also offer special discounts for bulk purchases so please enquire for details.

Looking to sell? We are constantly looking to purchase good quality stock so if you are looking to sell your collection or even rare single records or CDs, please contact us.

OPEN 7 DAYS A WEEK:

Mon - Fri: 10am-6pm
Sat: 9.30am-5.30pm
Sun: 12-5pm
Bank hols: 12-5pm
(exc Christmas Day)

Tel: 0117 942 7368

dkellard@plasticwaxrecords.com

plasticwaxrecords.com

Facebook: Plastic Wax Records

222 Cheltenham Rd, Bristol BS6 5QU

SAS

Est. 1991

specialauctionservices.com

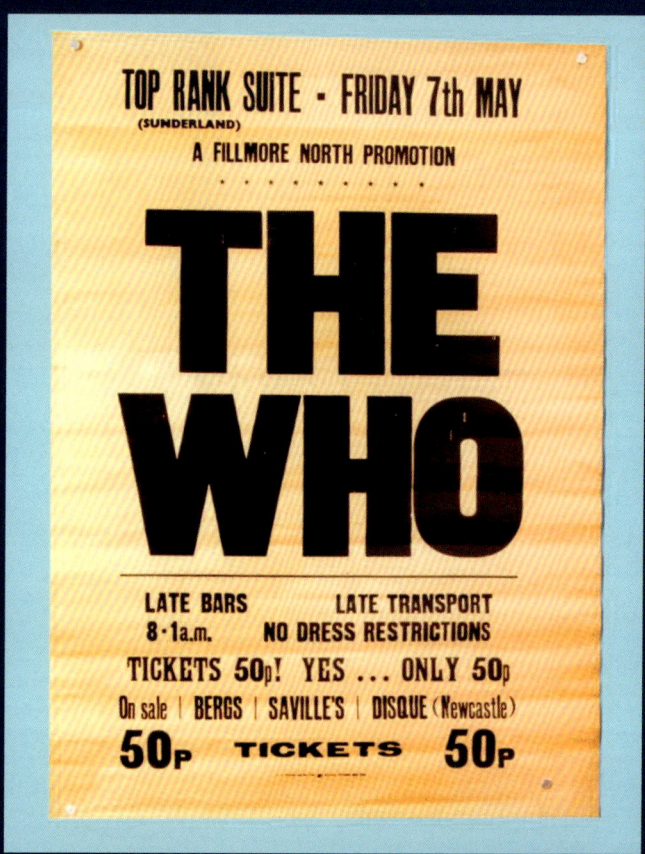

At Special Auction Services we sell many thousands of records in six specialised sales each year and welcome consignments, from fine and rare individual records to very large collections

Sell your records in one of our regular and successful specialised sales

Please contact David Martin or David Howe on + 44 (0)1635 580595
music@specialauctionservices.com

Plenty Close, Off Hambridge Road,
Newbury RG14 5RL
www.specialauctionservices.com

COLLECTORS' VINYL

Established 1976. Quarterly auctions of over 1700 obscure and collectable 45s, EPs, LPs, CDs, DVDs, Print, Ephemera. Printed catalogue or online.

www.collectorsvinyl.co.uk
dhvinyl@gmail.com
18 Grange Road, Camberley GU15 2DH

THE HOME OF VINYL

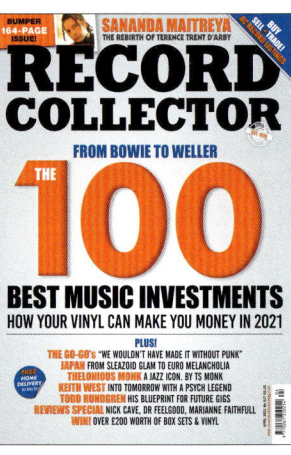

SAVE OVER 38%

13 ISSUES OF RECORD COLLECTOR MAGAZINE

FOR AS LITTLE AS £45.95*

DIGITAL SUBSCRIPTIONS ARE ALSO NOW AVAILABLE

DIGITAL ONLY
- ✓ 13 Issues available on mobile/tablet
- ✓ Save on cover price and international postage price
- ✓ Keep digital copies on your device

PRINT & DIGITAL BUNDLE
- ✓ 13 Issues delivered to your door
- ✓ 13 Issues available on mobile/tablet
- ✓ Unlimited access to the *Rare Record Price Guide* Online

SUBSCRIBER BENEFITS INCLUDE
- ✓ Your magazine delivered to your door, or your device, before it hits the shops
- ✓ SAVE on the cover price – up to 38% off
- ✓ EXCLUSIVE offers and discounts on *Record Collector* products and our vinyl range
- ✓ EXCLUSIVE music calendar at Christmas**
- ✓ FREE gift for new subscribers***

SUBSCRIBE NOW

 020 8752 8193 quote code RC/RRPG OFFER

 shop.recordcollectormag.com/subscriptions

 subscriptions@metropolis.co.uk

*Based on current cover price and for UK Direct Debit only. Call for other rates.** Print and bundle only.
*** Free gift is for new subscribers only. Gift will be posted on receipt of payment. Limited number available. To claim your free gift please contact us on the above number.

RECORD COLLECTOR
RARE RECORD PRICE GUIDE
ONLINE
www.rarerecordpriceguide.com

EXCLUSIVE OFFER!
SUBSCRIBE FOR JUST
£15*

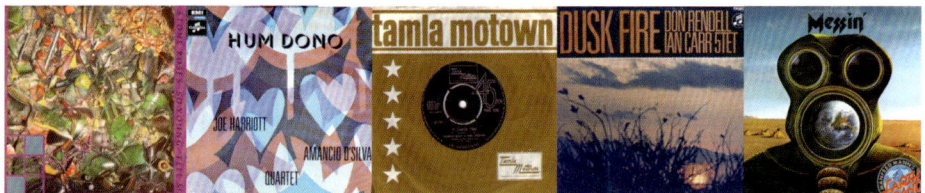

Contains all 100,000 updated entries of the book PLUS...

- **USABLE ON YOUR PC, TABLET, OR YOUR MOBILE PHONE.**
- **THOUSANDS OF ADDITIONAL ENTRIES** not published in the book.
- **INSTANTLY** search by artist, song title, year, label or catalogue number.
- **DAILY** updates of record prices.
- **ILLUSTRATIONS** of sleeves and labels added daily.
- **CURRENCY CONVERSION** to price your records in Pounds, US Dollars, Euros or Japanese Yen.
- **YOUR OWN DATABASE** – our unique 'My Collection' feature allows you to record and eventually value your entire collection with prices updated daily.

***Special offer to purchasers of this book – £45 off an annual subscription!* See opposite for details:**

*Usual price is £60 per year.

SAVE £45!
WHEN YOU SUBSCRIBE TODAY

SAVE £45 on an annual subscription. Use the QR code or Simply visit

www.rarerecordpriceguide.com/offer15

Take a FREE 24 HOUR TRIAL
www.rarerecordpriceguide.com

RECORD COLLECTOR

There are 1,000's of records for sale in each issue of *Record Collector Magazine* – from bargain singles to the cream of collectable LPs and everything in-between...

To advertise in our Record Listings section, please contact:
listings@recordcollectormag.com

SAM HOBDEN RECORDS

Established in 1984 solely a mail-order dealer in vinyl only, no CDs or tapes. With a stock in the region of 75,000-100,000 covering all formats 78s, 45s, EPs, LPs and boxed sets.
Every musical taste catered for from 1950s to the present.

Voted No. 2 Dealer in Record Collector's Annual Poll 2005

For any information on my present stock please write:
Church Farm, Cowbeech, Hailsham, East Sussex BN27 4JH
telephone or fax **01323 832595**, or if you prefer you can e-mail my son Duane as follows – **duanehobden936@hotmail.com**,
or check out our monthly listings in Record Collector magazine.

sounds original
RECORD SHOP

169 SOUTH EALING ROAD, EALING, LONDON W5 4QP
(nr South Ealing Tube Station, Piccadilly Line)
TEL. 020 8560 1155
www.soundsoriginal.co.uk
E-mail: soundsoriginal@aol.com
OPEN WED-SAT 11.00-5.00

50s, 60s and 70s Specialist

Top condition records and pop memorabilia always required

Established 1983
Mail Order since 1978

DISC-COVERY RECORDS

3 KINGSWAY, HUNCOAT, ACCRINGTON LANCS BB5 6LA
TEL: 01254 231387/07739 526262
www.disc-coveryrecords.com
Email us: sales@disc-coveryrecords.com

WE SPECIALISE IN SELLING/ BUYING AND TRADING RARE RECORDS, DVD's, CD's AND ALL MUSIC MEMORABILIA FROM THE UK/EUROPE AND R.O.W.

TRY US FIRST FOR ROCK/PROG ROCK/ POP/INDIE/METAL/PUNK/60's ➔ NOW!!
OVER 20,000 IN STOCK!!
We love to buy and trade so please let us know what you have and we pay top cash and trade prices for clean original vinyl

WE ARE ESTABLISHED SINCE 1986 AND HAVE ATTENDED MAJOR RECORD FAIRS ALL OVER EUROPE THROUGHOUT THAT TIME AND ARE ONE OF THE LAST REMAINING DEALERS DOING SO BUT ARE STILL PICKING UP LOTS OF GREAT UK / EUROPEAN AND REST OF THE WORLD RARITIES ESPECIALLY ON VINYL ON OUR TRAVELS SO ALWAYS HAVE LOTS OF FRESH STOCK IN EVERY WEEK.

WE ALSO HAVE A LARGE COLLECTION OF RECORDS ON & EBAY: SANDYCATRECORDS

CONTENTS

THE ULTIMATE COLLECTOR'S GUIDE 19

ACKNOWLEDGEMENTS 20

HOW TO USE THE GUIDE 21

HISTORY OF THE GUIDE 25

STATE OF THE MARKET 27

USING THE GUIDE: A brief summary 30

ABBREVIATIONS used in this guide 31

IMPORTANT TERMS used in the guide 32

RARE RECORD PRICE GUIDE 34

VARIOUS ARTISTS COMPILATIONS 1400

FILM & TV SOUNDTRACKS 1421

MUSIC LIBRARY LPs 1430

TAX SCAM RECORDS 1445

RECORD COLLECTOR'S
   GRADING SYSTEM 1447

RECORD COLLECTOR'S
   GRADING READY RECKONER 1448

EDITOR
Ian Shirley

DESIGN & PRODUCTION MANAGEMENT
Val Cutts
Yura Surkov

ADVERTISING MANAGER
Bill Edwards

MARKETING MANAGER
Kiran Summan

PUBLISHER
David Saunders

Published in the United Kingdom 2022 by
Diamond Publishing Ltd. 7th Floor, Vantage London,
Great West Road, London TW8 9AG

Copyright © 2022 Diamond Publishing Ltd.

All rights reserved

Founded by Sean O'Mahony in 1987.

No part of this publication may be introduced into or stored in any information retrieval system, or reproduced or transmitted in any form or by any means (electronic or mechanical, photocopying or recording), without permission in writing from the Publisher.

ISBN 978-1-916421-93-6

THE ULTIMATE COLLECTOR'S GUIDE

Welcome to the seventeenth edition of the *Rare Record Price Guide*, the largest and most comprehensive book of its kind. Like its predecessors, this volume has been compiled by the expert research team of *Record Collector*, the world's leading magazine in the field.

The goal of this book is simple: to list and value every collectable pop and rock record issued in the UK since 1950. As regular readers will already know, the *Rare Record Price Guide* doesn't just include vinyl singles, EPs and LPs, although they are still very heavily featured. It also provides information about every other way in which recorded music has been sold to the public over the last 70 years or more, from the brittle 78rpm shellac singles of the 1950s, to the latest permutations of digital sound on compact discs.

Musically, the coverage is equally diverse and thorough. Although the majority of items listed in this book could be at least vaguely described as 'rock' or 'pop', every aspect of music-making outside the specialist classical field is featured in these pages. For over 43 years, record collecting itself has expanded enormously, both in terms of the number of people taking part and the types of music that they are interested in.

Rest assured that no matter how obscure your tastes, you'll find the most sought-after items here whether your particular obsession is 60s MOR, Freakbeat, 80s Post-punk, Disco, House, Lovers Rock, Psychedelia, Hip-Hop, Reggae, NWOBHM, Northern Soul, British jazz, Folk, Shoegaze, Twee-pop, Progressive or today's indie bands. If it's collectable, and it was released in the UK, then you'll find it in the *Rare Record Price Guide*.

WHO SAYS HOW MUCH IT'S WORTH?

The question we're always asked about the prices listed in this book is how we calculate them. The answer is a mix of our 43 years of experience in the field; our ongoing research into the latest prices at record fairs, shops, and sales both via mail order and online; and the invaluable help of a dedicated and extremely knowledgeable team of consultants and experts, who themselves regularly buy and sell items in their specialist areas.

As we always say, however, there is no *fixed* price for a second-hand record, no matter how rare it is. There are still bargains to be found out there, while in other situations like a feverishly competitive online auction particularly sought-after items can fetch prices way above their 'book' value. The price of a rare record is purely determined by what people are prepared to pay for it.

That said, our close scrutiny of the collecting market since the start of the 1980s allows us to make the best possible judgement about the records in this book. Prices may vary from one part of the country to another, or depending whether a disc is being sold in a shop, via an advert in *Record Collector*, at a major international fair, or on internet sites like 991.com, Discogs, Raresoulman or eBay. But we believe that the guide values we list are the most accurate and realistic you'll find anywhere.

The other important point, which can't be repeated often enough, is that anyone selling records to a professional dealer can't expect to raise more than 50% of the prices listed here, except in very unusual cases. It doesn't matter whether you're selling rock'n'roll or jewellery, the same basic mark-up applies right across the collecting field, to cover the dealer's costs and profit margin. If you're selling directly to another collector, however, face-to-face or, as many collectors are now doing, over the internet, you can hope to obtain the prices we list or more, though please remember that all the values in this book are for records in absolutely perfect (or 'Mint') condition. To find out what you should be paying or charging, for a record in less than perfect condition, check the Ready Reckoner printed at the back of this book.

ACROSS THE AGES

Although many of the most valuable items listed in the *Rare Record Price Guide* date back to the 1950s, 1960s, 1970s, 1980s and 1990s record collecting is not all about the distant past. As you turn the pages, you'll find plenty of releases from the last two decades and collectables by major artists like Muse, for example, alongside albums by Paul Weller or new rarities which were on sale one day (especially Record Store Day!) and became fiendishly hard to track down even a few weeks later.

Check the details of those brand-new collectables, and you'll get some idea which of tomorrow's releases are likely to be sought-after in the future. But there are some things you can't predict, like the next 60s, 70s, 80s, 90s or 00s 7" that is worth £6 today but will be worth £60 in three months time. Or bands who were hot and collectable one year and saw their prices tumbling the next. Also, don't forget that virtually every record listed in this book, even the ones worth thousands of pounds, were once available for a few pounds. For all those thousands of releases which have already become collector's items, however, the *Rare Record Price Guide* tells you what they are, what they look like, and how much they're going to cost.

ACKNOWLEDGEMENTS

CONSULTANTS: PAST AND PRESENT. Billy Albert, Keith Ashford, Alan Barndale, John Barnjum, Rob Barrs, Mikael Billborn, Pete Bonner, Marco Bonacchi, Greg Brooks, Andy Brooksbank, Mark Burgess, Colin Carroll, John Coleman, Nigel Cook, Augusto Croce, Peter Croxson, Mark Darby, Brian Davis, Nick Farmer, Les Hare, Herve Denoyelle, Frank Deserto, John Esplen, Mark Evetts, Sean Forbes, Douglas Galloway, Roger Gobell, Kevin Goulding, Tim Greenhall, Steve Guntrip, Marco Henning, Al Hine, Sam Hobden, Jason Hodgeson, John Hodgson, Dizzy Holmes, Justin Huntley, Max Hooley, Dudley Jaynes, Gordon Johnson, Michael Johnson, Sid Johnson, Damien Jones, Mark Jones, Tim Jones, Chris Knight, Freek Kinkelaar, Jake Kennedy, Andrew Lee, Graeme McLagen, John Manship, Haaken Eric Mathiesen, Ian McCann, Joel McIver, Lee Medhurst, Mike at Elista, Howie Moxon, Pol O' Maoleoin, Roscoe Patrol, Chas Pearson, Derek Penny, Stephen Power, Andy Price, Jay Rathbone, Ian Roberts, Barry Smith, Phil Smith, Bob Stoat, Torbjorn Stuhre, Brian Strong, Mitchell Thompson, Jonny Trunk, John Tucker, Peter Vickers, J Walton, Jamie Ward, Ben Watkins, Garry Warren, Martin Webb, Alan Whitaker, Alan Woodburn, Eric White, Robin Wills, Conrad Zimmer. Special thanks to users of the online site, readers of Record Collector and the electronic collecting community worldwide who also submitted corrections, amendments or new additions too numerous to list here.

FINALLY, SPECIAL THANKS to previous editors, contributors and the vast numbers of fanzines (electronic or othwise), websites, forums and fan clubs whose hard work and expertise has helped - and continues - to make the Guide what it is today.

HOW TO USE THE GUIDE

PRICING YOUR RECORDS
Although the *Rare Record Price Guide 2024* contains a comprehensive listing of collectable UK releases, it does NOT list all the recordings made by the artists we've included. More detailed discographies of important artists can be found every month in *Record Collector* magazine.

MINIMUM VALUES FOR INCLUSION
ONLY THOSE RELEASES WHICH ARE CURRENTLY SOLD AT THE MINIMUM VALUES LISTED BELOW HAVE BEEN INCLUDED. Any other releases sell for less than these prices.

> 7" SINGLES, MAXI-SINGLES, CASSETTE SINGLES,
> DOUBLE PACKS £6
> 78s £20
> 10" SINGLES £10
> EPs & 12" SINGLES..£10
> LPs & PICTURE DISCS.......................................£15
> DOUBLE-LPs...£20
> CD SINGLES & CD ALBUMS £30

NOTE: EPs from the 1950s and 1960s usually sold at around twice the retail price of a 7" single. But most so-called EPs released since 1976 actually retailed at the same price as 7" singles. These records have been included in the Guide if they are worth £5 or more.

CURRENT MINT VALUES
The prices listed in this book are for the original issues of records, cassettes and CDs in MINT condition. Bear in mind that most records which turn up from the 1950s, 60s, 70s, 80s, 90s, 00s and 10s are NOT in Mint condition and their value will be affected accordingly. To find out the value of any item which is in less than Mint condition, consult our Grading System and the Ready Reckoner located at the back of this Guide.

ALPHABETICAL ORDER
The artists in this Guide are listed in alphabetical order, from A to Z. After the alphabetical listings, there is a section of Various Artists compilation releases, divided into several sections covering singles and 50s & 60s EPs, 70s, 80s & 90s EPs, LPs, film soundtrack LPs, library music and tax dodge records.

The alphabetical order within the Guide has been determined by the first letter of a group name or an artist's surname. The word 'The' has not been taken into account when placing artists in alphabetical order; for instance, The Beatles' are listed under 'B', rather than 'T'.

The order follows the usual alphabetical principle of 'reading through' an artist's name or title, so that (for example) 'Peter Gabriel' is listed before 'Gabriel's Angels', and 'Generation X' is listed before 'Gen X'. Names and titles which include numbers appear as if the number was spelt out in full; e.g. the band '23 Skidoo' are listed as if their name was 'Twenty Three Skidoo'.

CHRONOLOGICAL ORDER
Within each artist entry, records are listed in chronological order of release. Singles (including 7", 10", 12", CD, cassette, and double packs) are listed first; then EPs; and finally LPs (including cassette and CD albums).

In the case of long entries, different formats of releases have also been grouped together under separate headers to make them easier to find.

PACKAGING AND INSERTS
All prices refer to records with all their original packaging and inserts (where applicable) intact. Wherever possible, we have provided details of inserts and special items of packaging for each entry – pointing out gatefold sleeves, lyric sheets and other bonus items like posters, for example.

Any record with some or all of these additional items missing will obviously be worth less than the values listed here. The level of depreciation depends on the missing items: in some cases, the value of an album can be dramatically reduced without its collectable insert (as in the case of the Who's *The Who Sell Out* LP, for example), while in others, it is the record itself that is desirable, and the insert is only of secondary importance (as with the Picadilly Line LP, *The Huge World Of Emily Small*).

DOUBLE PRICES: PICTURE SLEEVES
Since 1978, most U.K. 7", 10" and 12" singles have been issued in picture sleeves. Before 1978, however, picture covers were the exception rather than the rule.

All those singles which originally appeared in a picture sleeve are listed with the abbreviation '(p/s)'. Where the picture sleeve was only available with the first batch of singles, there are two prices listed: the first refers to the record with its picture sleeve, the second without. If only one price is listed, then the single has to have its picture sleeve intact and in Mint condition to qualify for this value.

Most singles from the 1950s, 1960s and early 1970s were issued in 'company' sleeves, carrying the name and logo of the label which issued the record. Unless a picture sleeve is indicated, the prices listed in this guide are for singles with their company sleeves intact and, like the records themselves, in Mint condition. Many collectors are not too concerned about company sleeves - although in isolated cases (like the cult 60s label Planet), the company sleeves can be harder to find than the records themselves.

Company sleeves don't usually have much effect on a record's value. For example, an original Creation single from 1966, valued at £45, may only be worth £35 without its Planet company sleeve. At the other extreme, no 60s collector is going to be bothered if a copy of a rarity like Allen Pound's Get Rich's *Searchin' In The Wilderness*, valued at £1000 comes in a plain sleeve, or indeed, no sleeve at all - what matters here is that the record is in Mint condition.

DOUBLE PRICES: FREEBIES & INSERTS
Two prices have been listed for those items which were available in more than one form. 'Freebie' singles given away with newspapers and magazines have two values: the first for the record with the publication, the second for the disc itself. Records which were issued only briefly with an insert, like a poster or lyric sheet, are often priced both with and without the extra packaging.

DOUBLE PRICES: CHANGES IN DESIGN

Two or more prices have been given for records which were released more than once with the same catalogue number, but in slightly different form - with a change of label colour or sleeve design (for instance, the substitution of triangular centres by round centres on late 1950s singles), or the manufacture of more recent singles in a variety of different coloured vinyls.

These variations of packaging and presentation can make an enormous difference to the value of a record, which is why we have documented them here. They help collectors identify the first pressing or edition of each release, which is almost always more sought-after than later issues of the same record. One notable example is the first edition of the Beatles' *Please Please Me* LP, which featured the black-and-gold Parlophone label for a few weeks, before the introduction of the more modern-looking yellow-and-black label. Black-and-gold copies of the stereo version of this LP are worth up to £6000, whilst standard yellow and black label later pressings are worth between £3000 and £500.

Occasionally, second pressings can be worth more than the originals, as was the case with early Shadows and Cliff Richard singles. Green label copies of these 45s sold in their millions, while later re-pressings on black labels are much scarcer. So always check which pressing of any record you are buying before parting with your money.

MONO AND STEREO

In the case of EPs and LPs from the 1950s and 1960s, mono and stereo releases often have different values – and different catalogue numbers. Both prices are listed with the separate catalogue numbers for the two versions of each release (mono first, then stereo). Where the mono and stereo editions are worth the same amount, only one price has been listed.

The last few years have seen a polarisation in the prices between mono and stereo pressings – increasingly so for those late mono releases from 1968 to 1970, when the single-channelled format was being phased out in favour of the twin-tracked stereo. Similarly, early stereo copies have proved to be sound investments.

UK RELEASES AND EXPORT ISSUES

Only UK releases are included in the *Rare Record Price Guide*, not overseas issues. The exceptions to this rule are a handful of folk releases and U2 singles, all from the Irish Republic, which were heavily imported into Britain, but not officially issued here. The other exceptions are 'Export Releases'. These were manufactured in the UK in the 1950s and 1960s by companies like EMI and Decca for distribution to countries which didn't have their own pressing plants. Because they were pressed in very small quantities, and then distributed to the furthest corners of the globe, export records by artists like the Beatles, Pink Floyd andthe Rolling Stones are often worth many times the values of similar items pressed for the UK.

UK RELEASES PRESSED OVERSEAS

Although the great majority of the records we've listed were manufactured in the UK, not all UK releases were made in this country – or vice versa. For example, a large proportion of the Rolling Stones' US singles on the London label in the 1960s were actually manufactured in Britain. More recently, many British releases by major labels – notably Warners –

have been made in Europe, and sent in identical form to Britain and many other countries. In these cases, the record sleeves often carry many different catalogue numbers, to cater for every country where the records are being distributed.

The problem of identifying the country where a particular record has been issued has grown more difficult with the advent of CDs. In these cases, it is the packaging that helps you identify the origin of a particular CD, rather than the disc itself.

78 rpm RELEASES

The common misconception about 78s is that they are more valuable than 7" singles. In fact, the opposite is true in most cases, as far more 78s were sold in the 1950s than 45 rpm 7" singles.

The last batches of 78s issued from 1958 to 1960 are the main exception to this rule (see Eddie Cochran's entry, for example). As these were often only available in small quantities (as the public switched to 45s), or even by special order, they can prove to be much harder to find than their 45 rpm equivalents.

COMMERCIAL RELEASES, NOT PROMOS

In general, this Guide only includes records which were manufactured for commercial release, or for distribution in some way to the public – as a freebie with a magazine, for example.

Promotional records, demos, acetates and test pressings have not usually been included, apart from exceptional cases where these items actually reached the public, or where (as with artists like the pre-Iron Maiden act, Urchin) one promo single has become so famous among collectors that it would have been misleading for it not to be mentioned. The major exceptions to this rule are artists like the Beatles, and acts like The Pet Shop Boys, Depeche Mode and Madonna whose promos – often with extended and hard to find remixes – are sometimes more valuable than their commercial releases and highly sought after by their fans. Also, although we have included some CD-R promo releases this market has is no longer vibrant. Some collectors do want them – especially completists – but we should state that the sale of watermarked and numbered CD-R's is still illegal.

Full details of the values of non-commercial rarities like promos, demos, acetates and test pressings can be found in the articles and discographies in *Record Collector* every month.

IMPORTANT NOTE

Every effort has been taken to ensure that the information contained in this Price Guide is as accurate and up-to-date as possible. However, the publishers cannot take any responsibility for any errors or omissions; nor can they be held responsible or liable for any loss or damage to any person acting on the information in this Guide. The publishers welcome any corrections or additions to the Guide, which will be considered for future editions.

ian.shirley@metropolis.co.uk

THE HISTORY OF THE RARE RECORD PRICE GUIDE

RECORD COLLECTOR MAGAZINE

Record Collector was first published in 1979, and the magazine quickly established itself as the bible of pop and rock history. When the magazine was born, record collecting was a small, rather disorganised business, which wasn't making much effort to encourage new people to get involved.

From the start, *Record Collector* set out to provide the information that collectors needed, whether they'd been buying and selling records for years, or were just starting to build up a collection. There were two vital things they wanted to know: what records had been released by their favourite artists, and how much were they worth?

Every issue of *Record Collector* has provided complete discographies (lists of record releases, complete with full catalogue numbers, release dates and current Mint values) for an amazing variety of performers, from pre-rock stars like Frank Sinatra to the latest chart-bound arrivals and cult indie bands, via every imaginable style and genre along the way. Our in-depth features have provided the essential information to help readers get the most out of their music – by explaining the history of the artists and the records.

THE CHANGING FACE OF THE RARE RECORD PRICE GUIDE

In 1987, we published our first price guide - a slim volume which was designed as a quick and easy reference source to records by around 2,000 important artists.

That was only the beginning, though. We soon began work on the first edition of the book you're holding. Published in late 1992, the first *Rare Record Price Guide* filled 960 pages and listed 60,000 rare and collectable records.

The response to that book was tremendous, but we quickly realised that the collecting market was changing so fast that we couldn't rest on our laurels. Every year, thousands of new records reached the shops, in a bewildering variety of formats - everything from 7" singles and cassettes to expensive multi-CD box sets.

A small but sizeable proportion of these new releases became instant collector's items. Over the last 20 years, it's been common for record companies to issue special limited editions – anything from a few hundred to a few thousand copies – which sell out in a few days. The most sought-after of these records can triple or quadruple their value within a few months.

At the same time, interest in vinyl from the past continues to grow. As collectors track down all the records they want in a particular genre, they start to broaden their horizons. As a result, obscure items from the 50s, 60s, 70s and 80s become much-wanted treasures on the collectors' market – and their prices rise to reflect the new demand.

That's why we published a second edition, a year later, which grew to 1152 pages, with 70,000 records listed. And this was expanded again for the 1995 edition (over 75,000 entries and 1252 pages) and 1997/98 edition (85,000 entries and 1440 pages), to take in all the latest collectable releases.

The Millennium Edition ran to 1504 pages, the *Rare Record Price Guide 2002* was bigger than ever, the 2004 edition was 1536 pages the RRPG 2006 1504 pages, RRPG 2008 and 2010 1408 pages RRPG 2012 was 1440 pages, RRPG 2014 1432 pages, RRPG 2016 was 1440 pages, RRPG 2018 1456 pages and RRPG 2020 and 2022 were 1520 pages. Now you're holding the latest edition covering more than 60 years of rare and collectable records.

THE BIRTH OF COLLECTING

When the collecting scene was in its infancy in the 1970s, the market was focused on particular artists or genres. All the early attention was concentrated on 1950s rock'n'roll, and 1960s beat music. In addition, major artists like the Beatles, the Rolling Stones, Elvis Presley and David Bowie began to attract specialist collectors. But the whole collecting scene blossomed during the 1980s and it's now true to say that there aren't any musical styles which *aren't* collectable. Folk, Jazz, Techno, Hip-Hop, Blues, Heavy Metal, Punk, Psychedelia, Progressive Rock, Film Soundtracks, Soul, Funk, Reggae, Disco, Mainstream Rock and Pop, even Library - each genre boasts its share of in-demand rarities.

LIMITED EDITIONS

In the late 1970s, the arrival of punk spawned scores of new, independent record labels, which had fresh views about the way to market their releases. It became common for singles to appear in picture sleeves, as they had done overseas since the 1960s.

Records also began to appear on coloured vinyl or as picture discs, in an attempt to attract more buyers. Never slow to cash in on a marketing trend, the major record companies soon joined in. By the early 1980s, they were issuing a bewildering variety of editions of the same record in slightly different formats.

This sudden change in marketing techniques helped to trigger an entirely new development on the collecting scene. For the first time, records were becoming instant collector's items. A limited-edition single could be released one week, and sell for twice its retail price a fortnight later.

That opened the floodgates. No longer were 1950s and 1960s records the only things you'd find in the collector's shops. Now, it was open season, for anything and everything from Tubby Hayes to U2.

COMPACT DISCS

The arrival of CDs in the mid-1980s was greeted with doom and gloom in some quarters. But extensive remastering and reissue programs on CD have helped to increase the market for old vinyl releases.

If you grew up in the 1960s, you probably remember that it was difficult to find records that had been hits only a few years earlier. Now, you can go online and buy CD or download compilations and original albums with bonus tracks from every era of music history. For thousands of collectors, however, owning the music on CD or via download isn't enough – and they track down the original releases of music made and released before they were born.

The CD is now established as a collectable format especially for some albums which have yet to be remastered on vinyl or a CD issue or reissue is not on iTunes, You Tube or various streaming platforms. Although more music is now sold through digital downloads or experienced through streaming, the CD remains a core physical format alongside resurgent vinyl.

STATE OF THE MARKET

Back in 2005, when I took over as editor of the Rare Record Price Guide the vinyl world was totally different from today.
Internet buying and selling had yet to catch fire and the main driver of sales of second hand vinyl was record shops, independent dealers, fairs, mail order lists and classified adverts in Record Collector magazine. There was no Discogs, 45 Cat and Popsike was an infant and so when it came to compiling Guide prices I managed a large and diverse team of 60 experts who bought and sold records in genres from jazz to new wave. At that time, rock 'n' roll and doo wop were, along with progressive rock, psych, reggae, punk and northern soul top collectable genres. A couple of years later prices for doo wop, rock 'n' roll and early 60s singles had gone soft and fallen. Thus, I had to wrestle with some contributors who dealt in these records and whose business could be affected. They were aghast when I set about reducing prices of what were now over valued records from The Penguins Earth Angel to common Elvis Presley, Bill Haley and Johnny Cash records that had halved in value. At the other end of the scale, other dealers did not want me to add new albums from the 90s by artists like George Michael or Boards Of Canada and adjust upwards of albums by the likes of Blur, Pulp or the Wildhearts that were shooing up in value.

In those days contributors could spend weeks going through hard copies of the previous Guide updating prices manually with a pen or pencil whereas others would send in pages of hand-written lists or meticulously documented 78rpm or 7"singles, EPs and albums on Word documents or Excel spread sheets. In those days, as well as going to record shops and fairs I visited dealers and collectors houses. As stated above, sites like Discogs did not exist and the only was to see a rare private pressing by a band like Grannie or folk singer Ken Saul was to find a copy that someone owned and take a look at it. I could fill this introduction with stories from these travels that would form a nice counterpoint to Graham Jones *Last Shop Standing* book. I vividly recall going into the living room of one dealer's house and asking him where his dog was. He told me that he did not have a dog. At that point I realised that what I though was fur on the carpet was years of accumulated dust. Another dealer was so paranoid about me printing details of the rare singles he was buying and selling not in the Guide that he used to go upstairs and come back with a record in a plastic bag, put it on the turntable, play it and then return the record to the plastic bag. This was to stop me seeing the artist name or song title. Then, plastic bag in hand, he told to me how everyone was after that record and only he knew what it was. The fact that I had just heard it memorised the chorus and could go back to the office and start sleuthing in the forest of reference books used in updating the Guide did not cross his mind. Then there was the story about the collector whose flat was filled with records that extended to the kitchen. The legend goes that when someone went around and opened the oven they discovered it was full of records. I never got to verify that one although for years that collector kept promising to put a date in the diary for me to examine his huge collection.

There was very little vinyl being pressed when I became editor of the Guide. Artists like the White Stripes were vinyl enthusiasts but many albums by independent and mainstream artists were CD only. That means many LPs pressed between 2000 and 2010 are worth money including artists like Corinne Bailey Ray, Aaliyah, Vincent Gallo, The Cure, Muse, Doves, Van Morrison, The Manic Street Preachers, Marilyn Manson, Super Furry Animals, Paul Weller and P.J. Harvey.

As the editor of the Guide I was proud to help establish the Rare Record Club that sought to reissue rare and collectable albums through Record Collector magazine. Those early records by the likes of Pussy, Red Dirt, The Hippy Boys, Agincourt, Grannie and the Backhouse James Blues Band, to name a few, are now in the pages of this current Guide as collectable records in their own right. I'm also proud of the fact that a couple of record dealers (Damian Jones and Rob Henson) and myself put up five grand to pay for rehearsals and hire the Underworld in Camden Town to return collectable progressive rock legends Cressida to the stage. I think, at the end of the night we lost around £33 each, which was well worth it. Suffice to say, the Cressida album Trapped In Time – The Lost Tapes of unreleased demos released by Record Collector sold out within two weeks and is now a collectors item worth £70. Of course, it's got a long way to go to catch up with Cressida (1970) and Asylum (1971) that are both worth £1000.

As readers will know, the last decade has seen a resurgence of vinyl with collectable albums by the likes The Don Rendell Ian Carr Quintet to those wonderful Felt albums being reissued. In fact stepping into any record shops from Dave's in Letchworth Garden City to Rough Trade East is like going back in a time warp to the 60s, 70s or 80s. You can buy brand new repressing's of classic albums by artists as diverse as AC/DC, 10cc, Sparks, Kate Bush, Abba, Fleetwood Mac, King Crimson, the Beatles, Funkadelic, the Ohio Players or Lonnie Liston Smith to name a few. The specialist market has seen most rare albums from genres like British jazz, punk, jazz, metal, folk, new wave and reggae back in print. The same applies to funk, soul and boogie 7" singles from repressing's of Northern Soul classics like The Group (featuring Cecil Washington)'s I Don't Like To Lose to the 12" of Bobbi Humphrey's Baby Don't You Know originally released on Roy Ayers Uno Melodic label stateside in 1982. Indeed, there is so much demand for new vinyl that pressing plants are overwhelmed with orders. As I write, labels big and small have to wait for up to 8 months to for an album to get pressed whether it is the next offering from Wet Leg or another reissue of a classic Pink Floyd album on coloured vinyl.

At a time when fuel bills have doubled and there is a cost of living crisis the price for rare and collectable vinyl has gone through the roof. As always, if you have the right records in the right condition you can make money. Along with dealers who have been in the business for decades there is a new generation making a living selling everything from rare African boogie to collectable singles and albums by the likes of the Sex Pistols, the Rolling Stones, the Beatles, Aphex Twin, Iron Maiden, Queen, Joy Division, Nirvana, The Kinks, Metallica or The Fall. Every dealer still hopes to find that well curated collection they can buy for a thousand pounds and sell for ten thousand. And those collections are still out there. Whilst many people selling their collections are fully aware of what they are worth it still shocks me that I am frequently contacted by people who have inherited collections looking for advice on what they are worth. When you tell them that they have to value each and every record individually they simply cannot be bothered. They don't want to take the time and effort to look online or consult the Guide to get an idea as to what some of the records they have might be worth. They just want to get shot of them. There are dealers and charity shops that have made thousands of pounds from this attitude and practice.

As editor of the Guide since 2005 I have managed to keep up with trends in the market from the increase in prices by collectable artists and genres to the falling prices of others. I have also greatly expanded the coverage of the Guide. Dance and electronic music has been with us for over 50 years and the pages of this Guide now list the most important and collectable records whether they are by Fingers Inc, Andromeda, Plastikman, Electronic Eye, Dillinja, Boards of Canada, Cabaret Voltaire, X-Men, Kraftwerk, Hardnoise, Black Dog, Severe Carnage, Autechre and others. The Guide now features classic and obscure 12" records whether they are techno, drum 'n' bass or pure club bangers. The Coverage of lovers rock has been greatly expanded as has 90s street soul which remains a niche that is criminally overlooked but you try to find an original copy of Gold In The Shade's 1991 Over You for less than £60.

In the year of the Diamond Jubilee it is apt that one of the rarest 7" singles in the Guide is the withdrawn 1977 A&M God Save The Queen by the Sex Pistols valued at £12,000 in mint. The late DJ John Peel actually gave his copy to Jack White as a gift many years ago so we did not get the opportunity to see what that record might have sold for in the recent auction at Bonham's where some of the cream from the Peel collection went under the hammer. This included a copy an acetate of the 1968 Two Virgins LP handed to Peel by John Lennon, a 1976 test pressing of the Sex Pistols Anarchy In The U.K./I Wanna Be Me and the first pressing of Joy Divisions 1978 An Ideal For Living LP with a letter from drummer Stephen Morris.

These records from the John Peel collection were, in many respects, the ultimate collectables from the greatest record collection in the world. Of course, the world has changed a lot since I took over as editor – and the way that the price guide is compiled has also changed. The value of rare and collectable records has never been more transparent with sites like the mature Popsike posting prices realised on eBay. Auction houses from Bonham's to Omega trumpet the hammer price of the latest copy of Dark Round The Edges to surface or a mint black and gold stereo copy of the Beatles Please Please Me LP. 45 Cat are slowly adding prices and Discogs list the lowest, highest and medium price that a record has sold for on their site – although there are plenty of rare records they have never sold. Saying that, Discogs does give collectors and dealers a good indication of what a record is worth as well as, theoretically, how many people are looking to buy a copy. There might be a single copy for sale at an inflated price – or 80 copies listed as cheap as chip.

Sadly, this is the last price guide that I will edit and I am moving onto pastures new. It has been an honour to helm the Guide and I have, during my tenure, endeavoured to do my best to give dealers and collectors an honest and transparent overview as to what rare and collectable UK records are worth from a cracking £100 1968 7" single like Sharon Tandy's Hold On/Daughter Of The Sun to Magazine's seminal 1978 new wave classic Shot By Both Sides/My Mind Ain't So Open (£15). In closing I would like to thank every contributor who assisted me whether their area of expertise was 78rpm singles, soul, funk, punk, junk shop glam, acid folk, ska, dub, library, dance, disco, progressive rock or the best 7" single money could buy for the new entry price of £6. It was also a pleasure to work with editors of Record Collector Ian McCann, Paul Lester and the late Alan Lewis. It was also a pleasure to work with the dedicated staff of Record Collector and the backroom team of designers under the watchful eye of Val Cutts who made sure that every issue of Record Collector – and every Guide I have edited – look amazing.

Although in this digital age everything is available on your phone there is still a need for this printed Guide. It is the ultimate reference resource giving buyers, sellers and the curious an easy to use and comprehensive overview of some of the most collectable and rarest records in the world.

USING THE GUIDE
A BRIEF SUMMARY

ALL PRICES REFER TO RECORDS AND PACKAGING IN MINT CONDITION
(See pages 1447-1448 for Grading System and Ready Reckoner)

ARTISTS AND GROUPS are listed in alphabetical order. Numerical names (e.g. 2.3) are listed as if the numbers are spelt in full (i.e. Two.Three).

ALL RECORDS LISTED ARE U.K. COMMERCIAL RELEASES
with the following exceptions:
- (1) Records pressed in the U.K. for export overseas.
- (2) Important demo or promo releases.
- (3) Records or flexidiscs included as freebies with magazines, books and other records.

In general, promo and demo editions are not included, except when these records contain unique material and/or packaging, or are by major collectable artists.

EACH ENTRY includes:

SINGLES (7" 45s & cassettes) valued at £6 or more

78 rpm singles valued at £20 or more

10" singles & flexidiscs valued at £10 or more

EPs & 12" singles valued at £10 or more

LPs and picture discs valued at £15 or more

DOUBLE-LPs valued at £20 or more

CD SINGLES AND ALBUMS valued at £30 or more

Records worth less than these prices have not been included.

WITHIN EACH ENTRY, records are listed in chronological order of release, within each of the following categories (where applicable): 78s, SINGLES, EPs, LPs, CDs, PROMOS. The exceptions are major artists like the Beatles, the Rolling Stones and Elvis Presley, where the entry is further divided into originals, reissues and label variations.

Where TWO PRICES are listed for a single item, they refer to
- (a) the record with and without a special insert or piece of packaging
- (b) mono and stereo editions of EPs and LPs
- (c) versions of the same record with different artwork, vinyl colour, etc.

ABBREVIATIONS
USED IN THIS GUIDE

act................actually
alt..............alternative
b&w........black and white
cass...............cassette
cat. no.....catalogue number
CD...........compact disc
co................company
d/pack.........double pack
dble................double
diff..............different
edn................edition
EP.....extended-play record
ext...............extended
flexi.............flexidisc
g/f(old)......gatefold sleeve
inst...........instrumental
intl............international
LP......long-playing record
m/s.............mono/stereo

mag.............magazine
no.................number
no'd.............numbered
p/s..........picture sleeve
pic disc........picture disc
pt(s)..............part(s)
sl..................sleeve
st..................stereo
stkr................sticker
t/p............test pressing
vers...............version
vol................volume
w/...................with
w/l...........white label
2-CD or 2xCD....double CD
2-LP or 2xLP......double LP
2 x 45.....two 45rpm singles
3-LP.............triple LP
78............78rpm single

IMPORTANT RECORD COMPANY ABBREVIATIONS

Amalgam.................................Amalgamated
B. Banquet............................Beggars Banquet
B'full/Brains.......................Bucketfull Of Brains
Col....................................Columbia
Elek....................................Elektra
Font...................................Fontana
L.T.T. Slaughter..................Lambs To The Slaughter
M. For Nations.....................Music For Nations
MFP................................Music For Pleasure
M. Minor...........................Major Minor
Parl................................Parlophone
PSI..........................Phil Spector International
Pye Intl...........................Pye International
R. Digest..........................Readers Digest
Regal Zono........................Regal Zonophone
R. Stones..........................Rolling Stones
S'side..............................Stateside
St. Tones..........................Street Tones
Sweet Folk & C...................Sweet Folk And Country
T. Motown..........................Tamla Motown
UA.................................United Artists
W. Bros..........................Warner Brothers
WRC...........................World Record Club

IMPORTANT TERMS
USED IN THIS GUIDE

acetate	one-off disc cut by hand in a mastering studio, used for demonstration purposes
adaptor	plastic outer disc clipped onto 3" CDs to make them compatible with 5" CD players
art sleeve	pictorial cover using graphics rather than photographs or drawings
artwork	original design for sleeves or labels
audiophile pressing	high quality pressing for hi-fi enthusiasts
blister pack	shaped outer PVC packaging, usually for 3" CDs
bonus disc	disc given away free with another disc
bootleg	illegal pressing of material
box set	records or CDs in presentation case
budget release	pressing which retailed below full-price
catalogue number	manufacturer's reference number on record labels and sleeves
CD-R	one-off CD, digital equivalent of acetate
CD-ROM	audio/visual computer-compatible CD
CD Video	5" CD containing several audio tracks and (usually) one video track; now obsolete
company sleeve	standard non-picture sleeve for singles, printed with name or logo of label
counterfeit	illegal reproduction of official release (a.k.a. pirates)
DAT	digital audio tape
deleted	no longer commercially available
demo	record issued for demonstration purposes; not commercially available
die-cut sleeve	sleeve with circular hole cut into the centre
digipak	gatefold CD sleeve with plastic inner tray
DJ-only	record issued for radio airplay only
double groove	record with two grooves pressed concentrically on same side
double pack	two singles issued together as one package
DVDAC	digital versatile disc Audio
DVD	digital versatile disc
8-track cartridge	1970s tape format, popular for in-car entertainment; now obsolete
EP	extended play disc, with four or more tracks, usually in a picture sleeve
EPK	electronic press kit; i.e. short promo-only documentary available on video
envelope p/s	large mailing-type cover with envelope-style foldover flap
etched disc	one-sided vinyl record with laser-etched graphics (e.g. group's signatures) on other side
export issue	record or CD pressed in the UK for sale exclusively overseas
factory custom pressing	unofficial record pressed after hours (usually on coloured vinyl) at official pressing plant
flexidisc	thin, flexible record, usually issued free with magazine, etc.
flipback sleeve	LP or EP cover glued together with card flaps from the front folded over onto the back
foldaround/foldout/ foldover sleeve	sleeve which opens out as a poster, etc.
freebie	record given away free of charge
gatefold sleeve	double-size sleeve opening out like a book
import	record or CD pressed abroad but sold in the UK
inlay	printed paper booklet with CD packaging
inner sleeve	protective sleeve inside main cover
insert	loose item included as part of a record's packaging, e.g. postcard, poster, lyric sheet, etc.
interview album	spoken word record, often used as promo

jewel case	standard clear plastic case for cassettes and CDs
jukebox centre	plastic centre inserted into record with large centre hole
jukebox issue	record issued exclusively to jukebox franchise holders
laminated sleeve	cover with high-gloss plastic coating
large centre hole	1.5 inch (3.8 cm) hole in singles
long box	tall, rectangular outer card packaging for CDs
LP	long playing vinyl record; standard album format superseded by CDs
matrix number	master tape number, scratched into the 'land' or run-off groove area; sometimes also found on the record label
maxi-single	early 70s term for an EP, featuring more than two tracks, often in a picture sleeve
megamix	medley of different tracks, often linked by dance beats
mid-price release	record which retails at a discount
mispressing	record or CD pressed with incorrect material
mono	one-channelled playback system
numbered (no'd)	individually numbered, limited edition release
obi	sealed paper strip wrapped around sleeve of disc; originated in Japan where obis were printed with Japanese translations of foreign titles
one-sided	vinyl record which plays on one side only
picture disc	novelty record made by sealing a picture within clear vinyl
picture sleeve	pictorial paper or card sleeve, used specifically for one particular record
plain sleeve	single sleeve without special printing or artwork
premium	record available via a special offer with another product e.g. food or drink
press kit	information pack with photos and biography, used by record companies to promote new releases
private pressing	record issued and distributed by private individuals rather than a company
promo	promotional record or item sent out to the media for publicity purposes
push-out centre	centre of a single connected to the rest of the disc at 3 or 4 points, so it can be pushed out for use on jukeboxes, etc.
quadrophonic	1970s four-channelled playback system, now obsolete
reel-to-reel tape	1960s tape format, superseded by cassette
reissue	re-release of a deleted disc
remix	different version of existing track created by rearranging its component parts
removeable/ replaceable centre	centre which can be removed from a record without damage and later replaced (not to be confused with jukebox or 'spider' centres)
re-pressing	a second run of a record or CD which hasn't been deleted
run-off groove	groove between end of playing surface and record label
sampler	compilation showcasing an artist or label
sealed/shrinkwrapped	machine-wrapped in cellophane
shaped disc	any non-circular record
shellac	brittle material used for 78s
slipcase	small card cover used for some CDs and cassette singles
solid centre	centre of record which cannot be removed, as on LPs
stickered sleeve	sleeve with sticker as an integral part of its packaging
stereo	two-channelled playback system
test pressing	manufacturer's sample record, pressed for quality control
tri-centre	push-out triangular centre on some 1950s singles/EPs
tri-fold	triple fold-out sleeve
uncut picture disc	shaped disc not yet trimmed to proper shape
unissued/unreleased	disc not made commercially available; may or may not have been pressed
vinyl	material from which records are made
warp	buckle in vinyl caused by heat
white label	usually blank, perhaps printed or handwritten labels, often for promo purposes; term also used for demo, promo or test pressing
withdrawn	record deliberately removed from sale by its manufacturer

AAAH!

MINT VALUE £

AAAH!
81	Flesh Logic EJSP 9863	Slip Away/Duty Calls (p/s)	90
82	Dangerous DRC 8401	Input/Output (p/s)	40

AALIYAH
94	Jive JIVE 357	Back & Forth (LP Version)/(MR Lee & R Kelly's Remix)	30
94	Jive HIP 149	AGE AIN'T NOTHING BUT A NUMBER (2-LP)	100
96	Atlantic 7567 92715-1	ONE IN A MILLION (2-LP)	200
01	Background 724381076712	AALIYAH (2-LP, gatefold sleeve)	200
02	Edel 0146091 ERE	I CARE 4 U (2-LP, gatefold)	100

AARDVARK (1)
70	Deram Nova DN 17	AARDVARK (LP, mono)	325
70	Deram Nova SDN 17	AARDVARK (LP, stereo)	250
85	See For Miles SEE 43	PUT THAT IN YOUR PIPE AND SMOKE IT (LP, reissue of 1970 LP)	18

(see also Home)

AARDVARK (2)
74	Ra 5019	Lonely Sea/Hawaii Five-O	18

AARDVARKS
95	Delerium DELEC LP 029	BARGAIN (LP)	18

A-AUSTR
70	Holy Ground HG 113	A-AUSTR - MUSICS FROM HOLY GROUND (LP, with booklet, 99 only)	500
89	Magic Mixture MM 1	A-AUSTR (LP, reissue, 450 only)	40
95	Holy Ground 010101LP	A-AUSTR (LP, second reissue, foldover gatefold sleeve)	25

ABACUS (1)
71	Polydor 2371 215	ABACUS (LP)	100

ABACUS (2)
74	York YR 207	Indian Dancer/Be That Way	15

ABA SHANTI
94	Aba Shanti ABA 002	Zulu Warrior/Verse II/Verse III/Verse IV (10")	35
95	Aba Shanti ABA12001	Positive Vibration/Verse II/Love & Unity/Verse II (12")	35
13	Sufferahs Choice DUBK 022	Jah Bible/(Dubwise)/(Falasha Style)/(Raw Mix) (12", as Dubkasm meets Aba Shanti)	20
96	Jalasha ABA LP 001	THE WRATH OF JAH (LP)	40
96	Jalasha ABA LP 003	JAH LIGHTNING & THUNDER VERSE II (LP)	60
99	Jalasha ABA LP 004	JERICHO WALLS VERSE THREE HORNS OF JAH (LP)	50
15	Falasha ABA LP 01	THE WRATH OF JAH (LP, reissue)	25

ABBA
73	Epic EPC 1793	Ring Ring/Rock'N'Roll Band (yellow label)	70
74	Epic EPC 2848	So Long/I've Been Waiting For You (yellow label)	15
79	Epic EPC 7499	Voulez Vous/Angel Eyes (red or yellow vinyl, p/s)	300
80	Epic EPC 12-8835	The Winner Takes It All/Elaine (12", gatefold pop-up p/s)	15
83	Epic WA 3894	Thank You For The Music/Our Last Summer (shaped picture disc)	25
84	Epic ABBA 26	ANNIVERSARY BOXED SET (26 x blue vinyl 7", numbered, 2,000 only)	300
84	Epic ABBA 26	ANNIVERSARY BOXED SET (26 x black vinyl 7")	100
99	Polydor 563 286-2	ABBA Singles Collection 1974-1982 (29 CD singles in card sleeves & 1-track CD picture disc, with booklet, in silver tin, 20,000 only)	50
04	Polydor 982054-1	Waterloo/Watch Out (picture disc, 2,000 only, numbered)	25
74	Epic EPC 80179	WATERLOO (LP, yellow label)	15
75	Epic EPC 80835	ABBA (LP, yellow label)	15
76	Epic S EPC 86018	ARRIVAL (LP)	15
79	Epic EPC 11-86086	VOULEZ VOUS (LP, picture disc)	60
80	Epic ABBOX 1	SUPER TROUPER (LP, box set with book & poster)	15
83	Epic ABBOX 11-2/ ABBA-11-10	THE SINGLES - THE FIRST TEN YEARS (2-LP, picture discs, with poster, ticket & booklet in box)	40
92	Polydor 517007	GOLD (2-LP)	20
99	Simply Vinyl SVLP103	ABBA (LP, 180 gram pressing)	15
05	Polar POLS 252	COMPLETE STUDIO RECORDINGS (12-CD box set, 2 booklets)	200

(see also Hep Stars, Hootenanny Singers, Agnetha Faltskog, Frida, Northern Lights)

ABBASANI
91	Roots Rock RR 001	Revelation Time/Version	40
91	Roots Rock RR 009	REVELATION TIME (LP)	30

JOHN ABBEY BAND
77	Duck DUC 101	Lady Mary/Let's Make Up	10

BILLY ABBOTT & JEWELS
63	Cameo Parkway P 874	Groovy Baby/Come On And Dance With Me	12

ABC
91	Parlophone PCS 7355	ABRACADABRA (LP)	15

A BEATBOY
87	Waterloo Sunset RUSS 106	The Honeydripper/Please Please (p/s)	6

ABERDEEN
94	Sarah SARAH 93	Bryon/Toy Tambourine (p/s, insert)	45
95	Sarah SARAH 97	Fireworks/When It Doesn't Matter/Sunny Summer (p/s, insert)	45

A BETTER MOUSETRAP
87	Cuddly SRT 7KS 1178/ CUD001	The Road To Kingdom Come/We Are All Going To Die	10

A.B.H.

MINT VALUE £

A.B.H.
78   Music Bank BECK 694   Geoffrey(Who Wants To Listen To Punk Rock)/Colt 45 Rock (no p/s) 200

SHIRLEY ABICAIR
56   Parlophone MSP 6224   Willie Can/Happy Trails 8
67   Piccadilly 7N 35364   I Will Be There/Am I Losing You 10

A BIGGER SPLASH
82   Mean BIGGER 1   INNOCENT BYSTANDERS EP 15

ABILITY II
90   Bassic BASS 4T   Pressure/Dub Version (12") 70
91   Outer Rhythm FOOT 12   Pressure/Dub Version (12", p/s reissue) 30

ABOVE & BEYOND
04   Anjunabeats ANJ 034   Surrender (Original Mix)/(Filterheadz Remix) (12", p/s as Presents Tranquility Base) 20
05   Anjunabeats ANJ 049   Air For Life (Original Mix)/(Airwave Remix)/(Mirco De Govia Remix) (12", p/ as Above &
                                    Beyond VS Andy Moor) 35
06   Anjunabeats ANJ-059   Alone Tonight (Club Mix)/(Nasty Dub) (12", p/s) 25
07   Anjunabeats ANJ-080   Tri State Remixes - Stealing Time (Deep Club Mix)/(Robert Nickson Mix) (12", p/s) 30
09   Anjunabeats ANJ-138   Anjunabeach (Original Mix)/(Jerome Isma Ae Remix) (12", p/s) 35
14   Anjunabeats ANJLP037   ACOUSTIC (2-LP, 1st pressing) 70
18   Anjunabeats ANJUNLP 024   GROUP THERAPY (2-LP, 1st reissue, gatefold) 50
18   Anjunabeats ANJLP053   ACOUSTIC - LIVE AT THE HOLLYWOOD BOWL (3-LP) 60
19   Anjunabeats ANJLP037   ACOUSTIC (2-LP, repressing, 180gm vinyl) 50
20   Anjunabeats ANJLP096   2000 - 2020 (8-LP) 250

(see also Oceanlab)

MICK ABRAHAMS (BAND)
71   Chrysalis ILPS 9147   (A MUSICAL EVENING WITH) THE MICK ABRAHAMS BAND (LP, g/fold sleeve) 40
72   Chrysalis CHR 1005   AT LAST (LP, first pressing, circular foldout sleeve, Island logo and address in white on
                                    green label) 100
91   Edsel ED 335   AT LAST (LP, repressing with standard sleeve) 25

(see also Blodwyn Pig, Jethro Tull, Mighty Flyers)

ABRASIVE WHEELS
81   Abrasive ABW 1   Army Song/Juvenile/So Low (p/s, 3000 copies) 15
81   Riot City RIOT 4   Vicious Circles/Attack/Voice Of Youth (p/s) 15
82   Riot City RIOT 9   Army Song/Juvenile/So Slow (p/s, reissue, red vinyl) 6
82   Riot City RIOT 16   Burn 'Em Down/Urban Rebels/Burn 'Em Down (p/s) 6
82   Riot City CITY 001   WHEN THE PUNKS GO MARCHING IN (LP) 20
84   Clay CLAY 9   BLACK LEATHER GIRL (LP) 18
95   Captain Oi! AHOY LP 5   WHEN THE PUNKS GO MARCHING IN (LP, reissue, green vinyl) 15
96   Captain Oi! AHOY LP 51   THE PUNK SINGLES COLLECTION (LP) 15

ABS
87   Shed 001   GREASE YOUR RALPH (EP, fold-out p/s) 12
89   Link MLP 100   MENTAL ENENA (LP) 15
90   Blasting Youth   NAIL IT DOWN (LP, with insert) 15

MIKE ABSALOM
65   Sportsdisc ILP 1081   THE MIGHTY ABSALOM SINGS BATHROOM BALLADS (LP) 20
69   Saydisc SDL 162   SAVE THE LAST GHERKIN FOR ME (LP) 90
71   Vertigo 6360 053   MIKE ABSALOM (LP, swirl label, poster sleeve) 400
72   Philips 6308 131   HECTOR AND OTHER PECCADILLOS (LP) 60
74   Sportsdisc ILP 1081   MIKE ABSALOM SINGS BATHROOM BALLADS (LP) 20

ABSENT FRIENDS
85   Zebra 1   Stand Up And Fight/Drift Apart (p/s) 30

ABSENTEES
83   Awol AWOL 1   If You Don't Want Me/AWOL (no p/s) 25

ABSOLUTE
85   Reset 7 REST 5   TV Glare/At The Third Stroke (p/s) 10
85   Reset 12 REST 5   TV Glare/At The Third Stroke (12", p/s) 20
87   Reset 7 REST 8   Can't You See/Love In My Heart (release cancelled) 60

(see also Erasure)

ABSOLUTE ALBERT
82   Completely A MAD 1   Noises/In Flight (p/s) 20

ABSOLUTE BEGINNERS
84   Roundabout RDA BS 1   Dream In A Haze/Southern Beat (hand-made p/s) 25

ABSOLUTE ELSEWHERE
76   Warner Bros K 256192   IN SEARCH OF ANCIENT GODS (LP, gatefold, die-cut, with booklet, quadrophonic) 18

(see also Bill Bruford)

ABSOLUTE ZERO
85   Hotwire HWS 856   You Will Fall/I Want To See Your Face (Irish pressing imported into U.K. p/s) 8

ABSTRAC & LADY PENELOPE
97   Confetti Records COEP 03   Love In Dub/Dub In Love/Deeper (Part 1) (12") 30
97   Confetti Records COEP 04   Love Devotion/Feel The Sunshine/Mind Games (12") 20
97   Confetti Records COEP 12   10 TIMES A DAY E.P. (12", Promo) 12

(see also Lady Penelope)

ABYSSINIA
00   Ital Lion IL 001   Good Vibrations (Original Mix)/(Ecoshock Mix)/(Mental Steppas Mix) (12") 12

ABYSSINIANS
73   Harry J. HJ 6652   Yim Mas Gan/JOHN CROW GENERATION: Crank Shaft 20
75   Grounation GR 2029   Love Comes And Goes/(Version) 12
75   2nd Tracs SK1   Tenayistillin Wandimae/Tenayistillin 10
76   Tropical S'tracks TST 109   African Race/Satta A Massagana 15
76   Nationwide NW009   Sweet Feelings/Version (actually by Carlton & The Shoes) 15
77   Klik KL 631   Forward On To Zion/Satta A Massagana 10
78   Different HAVED 7   Satte A Massagana/I & I (12") 30

ACADEMY

			MINT VALUE £
79	Different HAVE 18	Declaration Of Rights/African Race	8
78	Different GETL 100	FORWARD ON TO ZION (LP)	50
78	Virgin Front Line FL1019	ARISE (LP, with lyric sheet)	25

ACADEMY
69	Morgan Bluetown BTS 2	Rachel's Dream/Munching The Candy (as Academy featuring Polly Perkins)	30
69	Morgan Bluetown BT 5001	POP-LORE ACCORDING TO THE ACADEMY (LP)	200

(see also Polly Perkins)

ACCENT (1)
67	Decca F 12679	Red Sky At Night/Wind Of Change	225

(see also Rick Hayward)

ACCENT (2)
84	Motion 1111	We Are Lost/Blue And Royal Line (p/s with insert)	30

ACCENTS
59	Coral Q 72351	Wiggle Wiggle/Dreamin' And Schemin'	12

ACCESS
81	Ellie Jay EJSP 9674 STA001-7	AUDACITY EP (EP, p/s)	25

ACCIDENT
84	Flicknife SHARP 016	A CLOCKWORK LEGION (LP)	25
87	Link LP 12	CRAZY! (LP)	20

(see also Major Accident)

ACCIDENT ON THE EAST LANCS
80	Roach RR 1	The Back End Of Nowhere/Rat Race (p/s)	75
80	Roach SPLIFF 001	We Want It Legalised/Tell Me What Ya Mean (no p/s)	50
81	Cargo 001	SHOTGUNS AND HOTSHOTS (cassette)	30
14	Ozit Dandelion	RAINY CITY PUNK VOLUME 2: ACCIDENT ON THE EAST LANCS (2-LP, purple vinyl, 500 only, numbered)	20

ACCIDENTS
80	H. Line 'n' Sinker HOOK 1	Blood Spattered With Guitars/Curtains For You (p/s)	20
80	H. Line 'n' Sinker	KISS ME ON THE APOCALYPSE (LP, unreleased; test pressings only)	150
96	Detour DRLP04	KISS ME ON THE APOCALYPSE (LP reissue of unissued album)	20

ACCOLADE
70	Columbia DB 8688	Natural Day/Prelude To A Dawn	35
70	Columbia SCX 6205	ACCOLADE (LP)	100
72	Regal Zono. SLRZ 1024	ACCOLADE 2 (LP)	150

(see also Gordon Giltrap, Wizz Jones, Pauline Filby, Don Partridge)

ACCURSED
83	Wrek 'EM ACC 2	Going Down/I Didn't Mean It (p/s)	8
83	Wrek 'EM ACC 1	AGGRESSIVE PUNK (LP)	20
83	Wrek 'EM ACC 3	UP WITH THE PUNKS (LP)	15
84	Wrek 'EM ACC 4	LAUGHING AT YOU (LP)	15

ACCUSED
87	Children Of The Revolution/Earache GURT 17/MOSH 1	THE RETURN OF MARTHA SPLATTERHEAD (LP, insert)	25

AC/DC
SINGLES
76	Atlantic K 10745	It's A Long Way To The Top (If You Wanna Rock'N'Roll)/Can I Sit Next To You, Girl? (no p/s)	22
76	Atlantic K 10805	Jailbreak/Fling Thing (original issue, running times on dark label, heavy print, no p/s)	22
76	Atlantic K 10860	High Voltage/Live Wire (in p/s)	150
76	Atlantic K 10860	High Voltage/Live Wire (no p/s)	15
77	Atlantic K 10899	Dirty Deeds Done Dirt Cheap/Big Balls/The Jack (maxi-single, 'schoolboy' p/s)	120
77	Atlantic K 11018	Let There Be Rock (edit)/Problem Child (small label lettering & 3.06 timing, no p/s)	12
77	Atlantic K 11018	Let There Be Rock (edit)/Problem Child (no small label lettering & 3.06 timing, no p/s)	7
78	Atlantic K 11142	Rock'N'Roll Damnation/Sin City (initially with small label lettering & 3.05 timing, no p/s)	6
78	Atlantic K 11142T	Rock'N'Roll Damnation/Sin City (12", p/s)	18
78	Atlantic K 11207T	Whole Lotta Rosie (live)/Hell Ain't A Bad Place To Be (live) (12", no p/s)	15
79	Atlantic K 11406	Girl's Got Rhythm/Get It Hot (p/s, initial pressing without 'Elephant Head' motif)	6
79	Atlantic K 11406E	Girl's Got Rhythm/If You Want Blood (You've Got It)/Hell Ain't A Bad Place To Be (live)/Rock'N'Roll Damnation (EP, gatefold envelope p/s)	12
80	Atlantic K 11435	Touch Too Much/Live Wire (live)/Shot Down In Flames (live) (p/s, misprinted back-to-front)	15
80	Atlantic K 10805	Jailbreak/Fling Thing (reissue, light label, fine print; first pressing initially without 'Elephant Head' motif on p/s)	15
80	Atlantic K 10805	Jailbreak/Fling Thing (reissue, light label, fine print; with 'Elephant Head' motif on p/s)	10
80	Atlantic K 11142	Rock'N'Roll Damnation/Sin City (reissue, without 'Elephant Head' motif on p/s)	15
80	Atlantic K 11321	Rock'N'Roll Damnation/Sin City (reissue, with 'Elephant Head' motif on p/s)	10
80	Atlantic HM 1	High Voltage/Live Wire (reissue, p/s)	6
80	Atlantic HM 2	Dirty Deeds Done Dirt Cheap/Big Balls/The Jack (reissue, p/s)	6
80	Atlantic HM 3	It's A Long Way To The Top (If You Wanna Rock'N'Roll)/ Can I Sit Next To You? (p/s, reissue)	6
80	Atlantic HM 4	Whole Lotta Rosie (live)/Hell Ain't A Bad Place To Be (live) (p/s, reissue)	6
80	Atlantic K 11600	You Shook Me All Night Long/Have A Drink With Me (p/s, mispressing, A-side plays "Shake A Leg")	100
82	Atlantic SAM 143	For Those About To Rock (We Salute You)/C.O.D. (12", p/s, promo only)	40
84	Atlantic A 9651P	Nervous Shakedown/Rock'N'Roll Ain't Noise Pollution (live) (shaped picture disc)	15
85	Atlantic A 9532W	Danger/Back In Business (poster p/s)	6
85	Atlantic A 9532P	Danger/Back In Business (fly-shaped picture disc)	20
86	Atlantic A 9474P	Shake Your Foundations/Stand Up (Angus-shaped picture disc)	20
86	Atlantic A 9425P	Who Made Who/Guns For Hire (live) (shaped picture disc)	20
86	Atlantic A 9425TW	Who Made Who (remix)/Guns For Hire (live) (12", stickered p/s & poster)	15
86	Atlantic A 9377P	You Shook Me All Night Long/She's Got Balls (live) (shaped picture disc)	20
88	Atlantic A 9136TP	Heatseeker/Go Zone/Snake Eye (12", picture disc)	15

			MINT VALUE £
90	Atco B8907T	Thunderstruck/Fire Your Guns/DT/Chase The Ace (12" coloured test pressings, white, blue, red, clear, yellow, green & marbled swirl pattern	300
91	Atco B8886T	Money Talks/Mistress For Christmas/Borrowed Time (12" poster p/s)	20
91	Atco 8830W	Are You Ready/Got You By The Balls (numbered 'satchel' p/s)	8
93	Atco B6073T	Dirty Deeds Done Cheap/Shoot To Thrill (live)/Dirty Deeds Done Cheap (live) (12")	10
93	Atco B8396T	Big Gun/Back To Black/For Those About To Rock (12", p/s)	12
95	East West A4368X	Hard As A Rock/Caught With Your Pants Down (p/s, yellow vinyl, numbered)	8

ALBUMS

76	Atlantic K50257	HIGH VOLTAGE (LP, 1st pressing, cartoon sleeve, reissues have barcode)	30
76	Atlantic K50323	DIRTY DEEDS DONE CHEAP (LP)	15
77	Atlantic K50483	LET THERE BE ROCK (LP, etched matrix numbers K50366 A-1/B-2)	30
77	Atlantic K50366	LET THERE BE ROCK (LP, mispressing, both sides play Side 1)	200
78	Atlantic K50483	POWERAGE (LP)	30
78	Atlantic K50366	IF YOU WANT BLOOD YOU'VE GOT IT (LP)	20
79	Atlantic K50625	HIGHWAY TO HELL (LP)	30
79	Atlantic K50628	HIGHWAY TO HELL (LP, test pressing in alternative "live" proof sleeve)	300
80	Atlantic K50735	BACK IN BLACK (LP, embossed sleeve, with inner, A1/B1 Matrixes)	35
81	Atlantic K50851	FOR THOSE ABOUT TO ROCK (LP, gatefold)	20
81	Atlantic SAM 155	JAPAN TOUR ' 81 (LP, picture disc, promo only, clear rim)	150
81	Atlantic SAM 155	JAPAN TOUR ' 81 (LP, picture disc, promo only, black rim)	120
81	Atlantic 60149	BOX SET (3-LP, including "High Voltage", "Dirty Deeds Done Cheap" & Powerage, promo 7" & poster; export issue)	45
83	Atlantic 780100-1	FLICK OF THE SWITCH (LP)	20
88	Atlantic WX 144	BLOW UP YOUR VIDEO (LP, black inner sleeve)	15
91	Atco WX 364P	THE RAZOR'S EDGE (LP, picture disc with inlay card)	15
95	East West 7559 61780-1	BALLBREAKER (LP)	60
00	Elektra 7559-62494-1	STIFF UPPER LIP (LP)	60
03	Epic 509298-7	ACDCROCKS.com BOX (15 x CD box set)	150
09	Columbia 38377	BLACK ICE (2-LP, gatefold, inner sleeves)	20

(see also Geordie, A II Z, Home)

ACE

71	Decca F13216	Speed Freak/Ace Of Spades	8

BUDDY ACE

68	Action ACT 4504	Got To Get Myself Together/Darling Depend On Me	30
64	Vocalion VEP 1-70164	BUDDY ACE (EP)	100

CHARLIE ACE

70	High Note HS 051	Creation (Version)/GAYTONES: Creation (Version Three)	12
70	Punch PH 49	Silver And Gold/PHILL PRATT ALLSTARS: Bump And Bore	30
70	Punch PH 53	Book Of Books/WINSTON HARRIS: Musical Dove	10
70	Punch PH 62	Love I Madly/Especially For You (A-side by Charley & Lloyd)	10
70	Punch PH 67	Do Something/MAYTONES: Run Babylon	15
71	G.G. GG 4507	Ontarius Version/G.G. ALL STARS: Ontarius Version 2	10
71	G.G. GG 4518	Do Something/MAYTONES: Groove Me	10
71	Upsetter US 359	The Creeper/UPSETTERS: The Creeper (Version)	20
71	Smash SMA 2325	Need No Whip/Grine Grine	10
72	Camel CA 92	The Commandments Of Joshua/GABY AND WILTON: Only Love	15
73	Ackee ACK 519	Country Boy (as Charley Ace)/IMPACT ALL STARS: Country Boy Version	8
74	Tropical AL 026	Hot Butter Dub/Pits And Pieces	25

(see also Charles, Paulette & Gee, Gaytones, Phil Pratt Allstars, Maytones, G.G. Allstars, Upsetters, Gaby Wilton & Charlie Ace)

JOHNNY ACE

61	Vogue V 9180	Pledging My Love/Anymore	50
62	Vogue VE 1-70150	JOHNNY ACE (EP)	60
61	Vocalion VA 160177	THE MEMORIAL ALBUM (LP)	150

MARTIN ACE

81	CJS CJS 1	Eating/Sad Party (p/s)	10

(see also Man)

RICHARD ACE (& SOUND DIMENSIONS)

67	Coxsone CS 7031	Don't Let The Sun Catch You Crying/VICEROYS: Maga Down	130
67	Studio One SO 2022	I Need You/SOUL VENDORS: Cool Shade	120
69	Studio One SO 2072	More Reggae (with Sound Dimensions)/GLADIATORS: Hello Carol	50
69	Trojan TR 654	Hang 'Em High/BLACK & GEORGE: Candy Lady	150
70	Sugar SU 104	Sound Of The Reggae/Got To Build A Wall	50
78	Ice GUY 13	Julie/Stalemate	8

(see also Viceroys, Soul Vendors, Gladiators, Ken Boothe)

ACE LANE

83	Expulsion EXIT3	SEE YOU IN HEAVEN (LP)	15

ACEN

92	Production House PNT 034	Close Your Eyes (XXX Mix)/Close Your Eyes (Vitamin 'E' Mix) (12")	20
92	Production House PNT 034R	Close Your Eyes (Remix I: Optikonfusion!)/Close Your Eyes (Remix II: The Sequel) (12")	30
93	Production House PNT 034 R-A, PNT 051 A-2	Close Your Eyes (Non Beatles Version Mispress) (12")	90
92	Production House PNT 042	Trip II The Moon (Part 1)/Obsessed (12", die-cut p/s)	25
92	Production House PNT 042R	Trip II The Moon (Part 2) (12", Promo 100 copies)	60
92	Production House PNT 042R	Trip II The Moon (Part 2, The Darkside)/The Life And Crimes Of A Ruffneck (12", die-cut	25
92	Production House PNT 042 RX	Trip II The Moon (Part 3, Kaleidoscopiklimax)/Obsessed (Part 2, Pictures Of Silence) (12", die-cut p/s)	25
93	Production House PNT 051R	Window In The Sky (DMS Remix)/Window In The Sky (Nino's Night Remix) (white label 12")	15
93	Production House PNT 051	Krystal Fairground (12", Promo, one-sided)	50
94	FFRR PROXDJ 1	Trip To The Moon (Omar Santana Mix) (10" 1-sided)	200

A CERTAIN RATIO

MINT VALUE £

A CERTAIN RATIO
Year	Label	Cat No.	Description	Value
79	Factory	FAC 5	All Night Party/The Thin Boys (p/s, 5,000 only, 1,000 with sticker stating ltd. edition on poor quality vinyl)	25
79	Factory	FAC 5	All Night Party/The Thin Boys (p/s, 5,000 only, 4,000 without sticker stating ltd. edition on poor quality vinyl)	20
80	Factory	FAC 22	Blown Away/Flight/And Then Again (12", p/s, with inner sleeve)	12
81	Factory	FACT 42	THE DOUBLE 12" (2x12", Flight/And Then Again (Version)/Blown Away//Do The Du/The Fox/Shack Up/Son & Heir)	10
81	Factory	FAC 52	Waterline/Funaezekea (12", p/s)	10
84	Factory	FAC 112P	Life's A Scream (edit)/There's Only This (edit) (promo pack including 7", photo & biography in custom ACR envelope)	10
80	Factory	FACT 16C	THE GRAVEYARD & THE BALLROOM (cassette in plastic wallet, first 400 in orange, then later blue, green, brown, red and grey. 1000 only)	30
81	Factory	FACT 35	TO EACH (LP, gatefold)	20
82	Factory	FACT 55	SEXTET (LP, textured sleeve with insert)	20
82	Factory	FACT 65	I'D LIKE TO SEE YOU AGAIN (LP)	15
85	Factory	FACT 16C	THE GRAVEYARD AND THE BALLROOM (reissue, cassette, in box with insert)	25
86	Factory	FACT 135c	THE OLD AND THE NEW (cassette, in box with insert)	25
86	Factory	FACT 166	FORCE (LP, inner and insert)	15
86	Factory	FACT 166c	FORCE (cassette, in box with insert)	25
92	Robs	LPROB 20	UP IN DOWNVILLE (LP)	25
94	Creation	CRELP 159	LOOKING FOR A CERTAIN RATIO (LP, also as 2 x 12")	25
02	Soul Jazz	SJR 65 10	B-SIDES, SESSIONS AND RARITIES (2 x 10")	20
04	Universal Sound	US LP 70	THE GRAVEYARD AND THE BALLROOM (LP, reissue with free 12")	25
19	Mute	ACRBOX1	ACR:BOX (7-LP box set)	60

(see also Sir Horatio)

ACES (1)
63	Parlophone	R 5094	Wait Till Tomorrow/The Last One	10
64	Parlophone	R 5108	I Count The Tears/But Say It Isn't So	10

ACES (2)
81	Etc	ETC 01	One Way Street/Why Should It Be Mine (p/s)	18

(see also Menace)

A CHOCOLATE MORNING
91	Still	CM 001	WASTED EP (12" p/s)	70
92	What's Happening?	WHAT 001	If You Want Me/This Isn't Mine (p/s)	25

ACID ANGELS
88	Fuel	FUEL 1	Speed Speed Ecstacy/Top Fuel Eliminator (no p/s)	6

(see also Jesus & Mary Chain)

ACID GALLERY
69	CBS	4608	Dance Around The Maypole/Right Toe Blues	100

(see also Christie, Epics, Carl Wayne & Vikings, Roy Wood)

ACID MOTHERS TEMPLE AND THE MELTING PARAISO UFO
01	Staticresonance	2	MONSTER OF THE UNIVERSE (Monster Of The Universe/Wholly Weary Flashback/Surfin' Paris-Texas/Midnight Mountain Dew (EP, 500 only, p/s 2 x 7" sold on tour, 500 only)	15
01	Staticresonance	5	My Guitar Wants To Kiss Your Mother/NISHINIHON: Super Station (Hell In A Cell Version) (red vinyl, p/s)	8
04	Ochre	OCH 057	Hello Good Child/You're My Boy (300 on purple vinyl)	6
01	Staticresonance	1	ABSOLUTELY FREAKOUT, (ZAP YOUR MIND) (LP, 1000 only)	50

(See also Cotton Casino)

ACID HORSE
89	Devotion	12DVN 103	No Name No Slogan/No Name No Slogan (12" p/s)	12

ACIDULANT
18	Balkan	BV 23	BORING KINGDOM EP (12", 200 only)	15

JEWEL ACKAH
84	Jetacks	JA 001	AKARA - CHI SPECIAL (LP)	20
84	Dassi	DRS 1	LONDON CONNECTION (LP)	20
86	Highlife	HW2016	ELECTRIC HI-LIFE (LP)	20
86	Asona	ASR 4010	ELECTRIC HI-LIFE (LP, different cover)	18

ACKEE
86	Heavyweight	HW 003	Call Me Rambo/CHESSE ROOTS: Rambo Gun Salute (12", as Ackie)	25
87	Route One	RO 004	Ragamuffin Boogie Rock/Lick Them (Dance Hall Style) (12")	150
87	Route One	RO 005	Roughneck Time/Version (12")	100

DAVID ACKLES
68	Elektra	EKL 4022	DAVID ACKLES (LP, orange label, mono)	35
68	Elektra	EKS 74022	DAVID ACKLES (LP, orange label, stereo)	25
70	Elektra	EKS 74060	SUBWAY TO THE COUNTRY (LP, orange label)	15
72	Elektra	K 42112	AMERICAN GOTHIC (LP)	15
73	CBS	32466	FIVE AND DIME (LP)	15

BARBARA ACKLIN
68	MCA	MU 1038	Love Makes A Woman/Come And See Me Baby	20
69	MCA	MU 1071	Am I The Same Girl/Be By My Side (DJ Copy)	50
69	MCA	MU 1071	Am I The Same Girl/Be By My Side	10
69	MCA	MU 1102	Love Makes A Woman/Come And See Me Baby (reissue)	10
69	MCA	MU 1103	Am I The Same Girl/Be By My Side (reissue)	6
73	Brunswick	BR 8	I'll Bake Me A Man/I Call It Trouble	10
87	Debut	DEBTX 3024	Am I The Same Girl/Love Makes A Woman/From The Preacher To The Teacher (12")	15
69	MCA	MUP(S) 366	LOVE MAKES A WOMAN (LP)	25
71	MCA	MUPS 410	SEVEN DAYS OF NIGHT (LP)	20
71	MCA	MUPS 416	SOMEONE ELSE'S ARMS (LP)	20
75	Capitol	E-ST 11377	A PLACE IN THE SUN (LP)	15
87	Kent	072	GROOVY IDEAS (LP)	18

ACME ATTRACTIONS
MINT VALUE £

(see also Gene Chandler & Barbara Acklin)

ACME ATTRACTIONS
80   A Trax KICK 007   Anyway/Never Again (p/s) 40
81   Orchid OR1   Eve Of Destruction/It's OK (p/s, with Bonnie Parker) 20

ACOUSTIC LADYLAND
06   V2 VVR1043681   SKINNY GRIN (LP) 18

A CRAZE
83   Respond KOB 706   Wearing Your Jumper/She Is So (p/s, produced by Paul Weller) 8
83   Respond KOBX 706   Wearing Your Jumper/She Is So/Dub, But Not Mute (p/s, produced by Paul Weller) 12

ACRO
95   Lucky Spin STU 10   Superpod/Skylab (12" 1-sided white label) 25

ACROSS THE WATER
75   MCW 001   ACROSS THE WATER (LP, two known acetate copies in finished hand-made sleeves) 3000
20   Seelie Court SCLP 001   ACROSS THE WATER (LP, reissue, gatefold) 20

ACRYLIC TONES
95   Detour DRLP002   THE ACRYLIC TONES (LP) 15

ACT (1)
67   Columbia DB 8179   Cobbled Streets/One Heart 25
67   Columbia DB 8261   Here Come Those Tears Again/Without You 15
68   Columbia DB 8331   Just A Little Bit/The Remedies Of Doctor Brohnicoy 70

ACT (2)
81   Act ACT 001   Dance To Despair/Who Let The Flowers Fall? (p/s and lyric sheet) 7

ACT (3)
87   ZTT CT 01   Snobbery And Decay (Moonlighting Mix)/Instant 1/Instant 2 (12" promo, plain black die-cut sleeve) 30
88   ZTT BET 1   Chance/Winner '88 (p/s, withdrawn) 30
88   ZTT BETT 1   Chance (12 To 1 Mix)/Winner '88/Chance (We Give You Another Chance) (12", p/s, withdrawn) 150

(see also Propaganda, Claudia Brucken, Glenn Gregory & Claudia Brucken, Thomas Leer)

ACTION
65   Parlophone R 5354   Land Of 1000 Dances/In My Lonely Room 100
66   Parlophone R 5410   I'll Keep Holding On/Hey Sah-Lo-Ney 150
66   Parlophone R 5474   Baby You've Got It/Since I Lost My Baby 100
67   Parlophone R 5572   Never Ever/Twenty Fourth Hour 100
67   Parlophone R 5610   Shadows And Reflections/Something Has Hit Me 150
67   Parlophone R 5410   Shadows And Reflections/Something Has Hit Me (p/s for export to Holland) 150
81   Edsel E 5001   I'll Keep Holding On/Wasn't It You? (p/s) 12
81   Edsel E 5002   Since I Lost My Baby/Never Ever/Wasn't It You (p/s) 12
82   Edsel E 5003   Shadows And Reflections/Something Has Hit Me (p/s) 12
84   Edsel E 5008   Hey Sah-Lo-Ney/Come On, Come With Me (p/s) 10
80   Edsel ED 101   THE ULTIMATE ACTION (LP, with inner sleeve, first pressing with extra tracks) 25
85   Castle DOJO LP 3   ACTION SPEAK LOUDER THAN... (mini-LP) 15
95   Dig The Fuzz DIG 005   BRAIN - THE LOST RECORDINGS (LP, insert, booklet) 20
98   Dig The Fuzz DIG 025   ROLLED GOLD (LP) 15
14   Demon ACTIONBOXRSD   THE SINGLES BOXSET (8 x 7", booklet) 60

(see also Boys, Sandra Barry & Boys, Mighty Baby, Reg King, Stone's Masonry)

ACTION PACT
81   Subversive ANARCHO 1   HEATHROW TOUCHDOWN (EP, 1 side by Dead Man's Shadow) 20
82   Fallout FALL 003   Suicide Bag/Stanwell/Blue Blood (p/s) 15
83   Fallout FALL 010   People/Times Must Change/Sixties Flix (p/s) 10
83   Fallout FALL 019   Question Of Choice/Hook Line & Sinker (p/s) 10
84   Fallout FALL 026   Yet Another Dole Queue Song/Rockway Beach (p/s) 10
83   Fallout FALL 013   MERCURY THEATRE ON THE AIR (LP) 15
84   Fallout FALL 030   SURVIVAL OF THE FATTEST (LP) 20

ACTION PAINTING!
90   Sarah SARAH 028   These Things Happen/Boy Meets World (wraparound p/s, with insert) 25
93   Sarah SARAH 73   Classical Music/Sensation No. 5/Hip To Hate (p/s, insert) 25
93   Sarah SARAH 87   Mustard Gas/Art Student/Collapsing Cloud (p/s, insert) 25

ACTION REPLAY
79   Rok ROK XV/XVI   Decisions/ZEROS: What's Wrong With Pop Group (die-cut company sleeve) 30

ACTION TRANSFERS
82   SRTS 82 CUS 1635   Into The House/I Sing You Cry (hand-made fold-out sleeve) 10
84   Rewind REW 17   The Light (Oh Baby)/The Right To Remain Silent (p/s) 6
84   Rewind REW 20   If I Loose It/Colours (p/s) 6

ACTIVE MINDS
98   HC 001   Hobson's Choice/Hobson's Choice (stickered white labels, 500 only) 30
02   VELSH 001   Hobson's Choice (Original Mix)/(Dark Side Remix) (12" reissue, white label) 25

ACTIVE RESTRAINT
82   Sticky PEEL OFF 3   Terror In My Home/Turns Out Roses (p/s) 25

ACTIVES
83   Quiet Records QS 001   RIOT (EP) 80
84   Quiet Records QS 004   WAIT & SEE (EP" 12") 60
84   Quiet Records QLP 4   KICK IT DOWN (LP, with insert) 70
03   Intimidation INT 8   REACTIVATED (LP, splatter vinyl) 25

ACTRESS (1)
69   CBS 4016   It's What You Give/Good Job With Prospects 200

ACTRESS (2)
10   Honest Jons HJRLP 49   SPLAZSH (LP, as 2 x 12", embossed sleeve) 20
12   Honest Jons HJRLP 60   R.I.P. (2-LP, embossed sleeve) 20
14   Ninja Tune WDNT 006   GHETTOVILLE (2-LP) 20
17   Ninja Tune ZEN 241X   AZD (2-LP) 20

ACUTE LOGIC

MINT VALUE £

ACUTE LOGIC
81	Illogical EJSP 9589	Morroccan Nights/The Obsession/The Balcony (p/s, insert)	30

ADAM & THE ANTS
78	Decca F 13803	Young Parisians/Lady (in p/s, original with paper labels)	12
78	Decca F 13803	Young Parisians/Lady (company sleeve)	6
79	Do It DUN 8	Zerox/Whip In My Valise (misprinting with 'Physical' on B-side but 'Whip In My Valise' on label. Matrix DUN 8 B1 or W-1KD DUN 8 B1)	8
79	Want 1	Cartrouble Part 1/Cartrouble Part 2/Kick (1-sided promo)	15
88	Damaged Goods FNARR 7	Young Parisians/Lady/Interviews (12" reissue with fanzine)	20
79	Do It RIDE 3	DIRK WEARS WHITE SOX (LP, 1st pressing with 'Do It' labels)	20
80	CBS 84549	KINGS OF THE WILD FRONTIER (LP, inner with booklet)	15
83	CBS 25361	DIRK WEARS WHITE SOX (LP, reissue with different cover, modified track listing)	15
90	Strange Fruit SFRLP 115	PEEL SESSIONS (LP)	15
00	Sony ANTBOX 5007822	ANTBOX (3-CD with book in 7" sized box)	35
06	Sony 88697009032	ADAM & THE ANTS - REMASTERED (7-CD, box set)	40
14	Blue Back Hussar BBH003LP	DIRK WEARS WHITE SOX (LP, reissue, white vinyl)	25

(see also Adam Ant, Maneaters, Models, Danny & Nogoodniks)

ADAM AND DEE
69	Tangerine DP 0002	Question Of Childhood/Run To Her	120

ADAM F
93	Lucky Spin ADM04	STRONGER THAN EVER: Light Years/Sea Of Destiny (12")	15
93	Lucky Spin ADM01	Pressure (Mix 1)/Pressure (Mix 2) (12")	100
94	Lucky Spin LSR 015	Eclipse/Whiplash (12")	30

ADAM, MIKE & TIM
64	Decca F 12040	Little Baby/You're The Reason Why	25
65	Decca F 12221	Little Pictures/Summers Here Again	10
66	Columbia DB 7836	Flowers On The Wall/Give That Girl A Break	6

(see also Mike Sedgewick)

ARTHUR ADAMS
81	RCA RCAT 146	You Got The Floor/Stay With Me Tonight (12")	12

ARTHUR K. ADAMS
68	Blue Horizon 57-3136	She Drives Me Out Of My Mind/Gimme Some Of Your Lovin'	25

BILLY ADAMS (1)
60	Capitol CL 15107	Count Every Star/Peggy's Party	10

BILLY ADAMS (2)
69	London 10258	I Need Your Love/Why Don't You Believe Me (DJ Copy)	20
69	London HL 10258	I Need Your Love/Why Don't You Believe Me	10

BRYAN ADAMS
96	A&M 540 551-1	18 TIL I DIE (LP, inner)	50

ADAMS (CHRIS AND PAULINE)
75	Charisma CB 244	If Only The Good Die Young/The City At Night	8

DERROLL ADAMS
67	Ace Of Clubs ACL 1227	PORTLAND TOWN (LP)	60
72	Village Thing VTS 17	FEELIN' FINE (LP, with inner sleeve)	70
72	Village Thing VTS 17	FEELIN' FINE (LP, without inner sleeve)	40

(see also Ramblin' Jack Elliott)

FAYE ADAMS
56	London HLU 8339	I'll Be True/Happiness To My Soul (Gold Tri label)	400
56	London HLU 8339	I'll Be True/Happiness To My Soul (78)	25

GAYLE ADAMS
82	Epic A 2167	Baby I Need Your Loving/Don't Jump To Conclusions	12
82	Epic A13 2167	Baby I Need Your Loving/Don't Jump To Conclusions (12")	15
80	Epic EPC 84435	GAYLE ADAMS (LP)	15
82	Epic EPC 85687	LOVE FEVER (LP)	15

GLADSTON ADAMS
69	Trojan TR 659	Dollars And Cents/TOMMY McCOOK: Popcorn Reggay	20

(see also Gladstone Anderson)

GLEN ADAMS
67	Island WI 3072	Silent Lover/I Remember	60
67	Island WI 3083	She (actually titled "I'm Shocking")/SONNY BURKE: Some Other Time	80
67	Island WI 3099	Grab A Girl/DELROY WILSON: This Heart Of Mine	70
67	Island WI 3100	Hold Down Miss Winey/VINCENT GORDON: Sounds And Soul	70
67	Island WI 3120	She's So Fine/ROY SHIRLEY: Girlie	80
68	Trojan TR 621	Rent Too High/Every Time	25
68	Duke DU 58	My Girl/GLADIATORS: You Were To Be	20
68	Bullet BU 414	Cat Woman/PETER TOUCH: Selassie Serenade (B-side actually by Peter Tosh)	20
68	Collins Downbeat CR 006	Cool Cool Rock Steady (as Glen Addams & Collins Band)/OWEN GRAY & COLLINS BAND: Girl I Will Be Leaving	125
68	Collins Downbeat CR 010	King Tubby/I'm Gonna Take You Back (B-side actually by Owen Gray)	90
68	Giant GN 33	Lonely Girl/ROY SHIRLEY: Warming Up The Scene	180
69	Amalgamated AMG 837	She's So Fine/ERNEST WILSON: Private Number	50
69	Crab CRAB 21	Mighty Organ/ERNEST WILSON: Just Once	75
69	Sound Systems SS 105	Down To Earth Reggae/Reggae From Mankind	20
70	Gas GAS 141	Leaving On A Jet Plane/REGGAE BOYS: Phrases	35
70	Junior JR 110	Sound In/Sound & Pleasure	20
71	Big BG 321	Weary Version 3/TONY BREVETT: Hills And Valleys	20
71	Explosion EX 2048	Never Fall In Love/JET SCENE: Jet 747	12
71	Upsetter US 367	Never Had A Dream/UPSETTERS: Version	45

(see also Glen Adams, Reggae Boys, Roy Shirley, Maxie & Glen, Delroy Wilson, Derrick Morgan, Owen Gray, Paul Sinclair)

JOHNNY ADAMS (& GONDOLIERS)
59	Top Rank JAR 192	Come On/Nowhere To Go (as Johnny Adams & Gondoliers)	8

JUNE ADAMS
66	King KG 1038	River Keep Movin'/Heavenly Father	12

LLOYD ADAMS
62	Wasp W001	I Wish Your Picture Was You/Pleading For Love (Possibly unreleased)	35
62	Wasp W009	I Wish Your Picture Was You/Pleading For Love	20

MARIE ADAMS
59	Capitol CL 14963	A Fool In Love/What Do You Want To Make Those Eyes At Me For	40
59	Capitol CL 14964	A Fool In Love/What Do You Want To Make Those Eyes At Me For (promo copy in picture sleeve)	60

(see also Johnny Otis)

PEPPER ADAMS
58	Vogue LAE 12134	CRITICS CHOICE (LP)	40
59	Pye NLP 28007	COOL SOUND (LP)	35
74	Spotlite SPJ PA6	EPHEMERA (LP)	20

RITCHIE ADAMS
60	London HLU 9200	Back To School/Don't Go My Love, Don't Go	20

RYAN ADAMS
03	Lost Highway 9861613	So Alive/Luxury (p/s, numbered edition)	12
04	Lost Highway 602498630990	Wonderwall/One By One (p/s)	20
07	Lost Highway 1735574	Two/Halloween Head (numbered)	12
00	Cooking Vinyl COOK 205	HEARTBREAKER (LP, with inner)	70
03	Lost Highway 986 100 1	ROCK N ROLL (LP)	35
03	Lost Highway 986 100-1	ROCK N ROLL (LP, 'blood' cover)	100
03	Lost Highway 986 136-1	LOVE IS HELL PARTS 1 & 2 (LP, as 2x10")	25
05	Lost Highway B0004707-01	JACKSONVILLE CITY NIGHTS (2-LP as Ryan Adams And The Cardinals)	25
08	Lost Highway 02517872608	CARDINOLOGY (2-LP)	25
05	Lost Highway B0004343-01	COLD ROSES (2-LP, embossed cover, as Ryan Adams And The Cardinals)	50
11	Columbia 88697973101	ASHES AND FIRE (LP)	18
13	Pax Americana 039	RYAN ADAMS (LP)	20
16	Pax Americana 056	HEARTBREAKER (4-LP, DVD, reissue)	40
17	Pax Americana PAX 059	LIVE AT ROUGH TRADE (LP)	30

STEVE ADAMS
77	Mind's Ear MER 2010	STEVE ADAMS (LP)	15

WOODROW ADAMS
65	Blue Horizon BH 1001	Baby You Just Don't Know/Wine Head Woman (99 copies only)	250

ZAYNE ADAMS
69	NEMS 56 4473	Can't You See Me/If You Were My Woman	15
69	NEMS 56-4697	Today/Don't Take My World Away (Demo only)	15

ADAM'S APPLES
77	Brunswick BR 42	Don't Take It Out On This World/Don't You Want To Take Me Home	18
85	Kent Town 101	Don't Take It Out On This World/JACKIE WILSON: I Don't Want To Lose You	12

ADAMS FAMILY
93	Loose LOOSE 02	Frustration/Timewaster (p/s)	6

BARRY ADAMSON
89	Mute STUMM 53	MOSS SIDE STORY (LP, inner)	15
92	Mute STUMM 105	SOUL MURDER (LP, inner)	15
93	Mute STUMM 120	THE NEGRO INSIDE ME (LP, inner)	15
96	Mute STUMM 134	OEDIPUS SCHMOEDIPUS (LP, inner)	25
98	Mute STUMM 161	AS ABOVE SO BELOW (LP)	25
02	Mute STUMM 176	THE KING OF NOTTING HILL (2-LP)	25
08	Central Control CC1007LP	BACK TO THE CAT (LP)	20

A DANCING MIRAGE
82	Wide WIDE 001	BOYS IN COLOUR EP	25

AD ASTRA
83	Sane 45001	Give Me The Girl/Find The Time	25

AD CONSPIRACY
79	Diamond Age AD 22957	AD CONSPIRACY (LP)	70

CANNONBALL ADDERLEY
67	Capitol CL 15489	Mercy Mercy Mercy/Games	10
58	Riverside RLP12 286	THINGS ARE GETTING BETTER (LP, with Milt Jackson)	25
59	Riverside RLP12 303	CANNONBALL TAKES CHARGE (LP)	25
60	Riverside RLP12 322	THEM DIRTY BLUES (LP)	25
61	Riverside RLP 433	KNOW WHAT I MEAN (LP, with BILL EVANS)	25
61	Riverside RLP 377	AFRICAN WALTZ (LP)	25
61	Riverside RLP 388	PLUS (LP)	25
62	Riverside RLP 311	THE CANNONBALL ADDERLEY QUINTET IN SAN FRANCISCO (LP)	25
63	Riverside RLP 444	JAZZ WORKSHOP REVISITED (LP)	20
64	Riverside RLP 477	NIPPON SOUL (LP)	20
67	Capitol ST 2663	MERCY! MERCY! MERCY! (LP)	20
67	Capitol T2617	WHY AM I TREATED SO BAD? (LP)	20
68	Mercury LML/SLML 4022	THEM ADDERLEYS (LP, mono/stereo)	20
73	Fantasy FT 517	INSIDE STRAIGHT (LP)	15
79	Blue Note BNS 540036	SOMETHIN' ELSE (LP, reissue)	18
84	Blue Note BST 81595	SOMETHIN' ELSE (LP, reissue)	20

(see also Nancy Wilson, Miles Davis, John Coltrane)

NAT ADDERLEY
56	London LTZC 15018	THAT'S NAT (LP)	20
62	Riverside RLP 12-318	WORK SONG (LP)	25
62	Riverside RLP 12-330	THAT'S RIGHT! (LP, as Nat Adderley and the Big Sax Section)	25
65	Fontana FJL 118	NATURALLY (LP)	20

ADDICTION

MINT VALUE £

65	Atlantic ATL 5032	AUTOBIOGRAPHY (LP)	20
66	Atlantic 587 023/588 023	SAYIN' SOMETHIN' (LP, Mono/Stereo)	20
68	Mercury LML/SLML 4022	THEM ADDERLEYS (LP, mono/stereo)	20
69	A&M AMLS 947	CALLING OUT LOUD (LP)	18

ADDICTION
92	Vicious Pumpin' OBS 002	ADDICTION EP (12", stamped white label)	20
92	Vicious Pumpin' VIC 003	MIND PENETRATION EP (12", stamped white label)	25
92	Vicious Pumpin' VIC 003R	MIND PENETRATION (THE REMIXES) EP (12", stamped white label)	40
92	Vicious Vinyl VIC 001	THE CREATIVE DUB EP (12")	15
93	Vicious Pumpin' VIC 013	Wildstyle/Untitled (12")	10

ADDICTS
64	Decca F 11902	That's My Girl/Here She Comes	40

ADDIS POSSE
90	Warriors Dance WAFT 14	Let The Warriors Dance (Charge Mix)/(Addis Acid Mix)/(Funky Funky Drum Drum Mix)/(Live & Def Mix) (12")	15
90	Warriors Dance WAFT 14R	Let The Warriors Dance (Remixes) (12")	10

ADDIS ROCKERS
85	Warrior WAR 2	ENTER ADDIS ABABA (LP)	20

ADDIX
79	Zig Zag ZZ 22002	Too Blind To See/(No Such Thing As A) Bad Boy (p/s)	15

ADD N TO X
95	Blow Up 004LP	VERO ELECTRONICS (LP)	18
98	Satellite STL010	ON THE WIRES OF OUR NERVES (2-LP, inners)	20
99	Mute STUMM 170	AVANT HARD (2-LP, gatefold)	30
00	Mute STUMM 187	ADD INSULT TO INJURY (2-LP)	20
02	Mute STUMM 204	LOUD LIKE NATURE (2-LP)	20

ADDRISSI BROTHERS
59	Columbia DB 4370	Back To The Old Salt Mine/It's Love	20

JEAN ADEBAMBO
79	Ade J AJ 101	Say That You Love Me/(Instrumental)/Dance Of Love/(Instrumental) (12")	80
81	Third World TWDIS 46	Reaching For A Goal/I Want To Make It With You (12")	12
81	Santic SAN 0012	Paradise/SANTIC ALL STARS: Version (12")	10
82	Ade J AJ 103	Wake Up/Hardships Of Life (10")	10
84	Ade J AJ 106	Never Before/This Will Be (12", p/s)	30
05	Santic SAN 0012	Paradise/Para Dub (reissue)	8
83	Ade J AJ 0123	FEELINGS (LP)	50
85	Ade J AJ 0124	OFF KEY LOVING (LP)	50

ADELE
07	Pacemaker 1	Hometown Glory/Best For Last (7", 500 only)	15
08	XL XLS S321	Chasing Pavements/That's It I Quit	30
08	XL XLS 374	Hometown Glory - Remixes (12". stickered company sleeve)	12
08	XL XLS 393	Make You Feel My Love/Painting Pictures (p/s, 500 only)	15
12	XL XLS 593	Skyfall/Instrumental (p/s)	40
08	XL XLLP 313	19 (LP, inner)	20
11	XL XLLP 520	21 (LP, inner)	20

ADEM
04	Domino WIGLP 129	HOMESONGS (LP)	25
06	Domino WIGLP 160	LOVE AND OTHER PLANETS (LP)	15

BOBBY ADENO
66	Vocalion V 9279	The Hands Of Time/It's A Sad World (DJ copy)	40
66	Vocalion V 9279	The Hands Of Time/It's A Sad World	25

SEGUN ADEWALE
85	Stern's Africa STERNS1009	OJO JE (LP)	15

ADICTS
81	Dining Out TUX 1	LUNCH WITH THE ADICTS (EP, 1st variation with 'brown' bricks with insert & screen-printed p/s)	125
81	Dining Out TUX 1	LUNCH WITH THE ADICTS (EP, 2nd variation with 'white' bricks with insert & screen-printed p/s)	80
82	Fall Out FALL 002	Viva La Revolution/Steamroller (p/s)	20
82	Razor RZS 101	Chinese Takeaway/You'll Never Walk Alone (p/s)	15
83	Razor RZS 104	Bad Boy/Shake, Rattle, Bang Your Head (p/s)	10
81	Dwed SMT 008	SONGS OF PRAISE (LP)	75
81	Fall Out FALL LP 006	SONGS OF PRAISE (LP, reissue, yellow vinyl, 2,000 only)	60
81	Fall Out FALL LP 006P	SONGS OF PRAISE (LP, reissue, picture disc)	20
82	Razor RAZ 2	SOUND OF MUSIC (LP)	35
85	Razor RAZ 15	SMART ALEX (LP)	20
87	Fall Out FALL LP 021	THIS IS YOUR LIFE (LP)	18
87	Fall Out FALL LP 042	FIFTH OVERTURE (LP)	20
90	Fall Out FALL LP 046	ROCKERS INTO ORBIT (LP, green vinyl, stickered sleeve)	18
17	Razor RAZ 2	AND SO IT WAS! (LP)	15

(see also ADX)

BETH ADLAM WITH BUZZ & BOYS
60	Starlite ST45 024	Seventeen/I'll Walk Into The Sea	10

PETER ADLER
66	Decca 12394	I'm Gonna Turn My Life Around/But I Was Cool	15

ADLIBS (U.K.)
65	Fontana TF 584	Neighbour Neighbour/Lovely Ladies	50

AD-LIBS (U.S.)
66	Red Bird RB 10-102	The Boy From New York City/Kicked Around (DJ Copy)	50
66	Red Bird RB 10-102	The Boy From New York City/Kicked Around	35
69	Deep Soul DS 9102	Giving Up/Appreciation	35

ADMINISTRATORS

MINT VALUE £

75	Contempo CS 9029	The Boy From New York City/Johnny My Boy	10
79	Inferno HEAT 1	New York In The Dark/The Boy From New York City (p/s, coloured vinyl)	7

ADMINISTRATORS
81 Cha Cha CHAD 36 — Say You Love Me/So I Can Love You (12") ... 70

ADMIRAL
85 Jah Tubby's JT 101 — General Governor/(Version)//Black Is My Beauty/(Version) (12", with the Offbeat Posse) ... 50

ADMIRAL SIR CLOUDESLEY SHOVELL
10	Rise Above RISE7 123	Return To Zero/Day After (p/s, 300 only)	10
16	Rise Above RISE7/194	Isabelle/Break Up (p/s, black, clear or purple vinyl)	7
17	Rise Above RISE7/213	Nightmare/In A Damaged Brain (p/s, 500 copies: 100 black, 200 red and 200 blue)	12
13	Rise Above RISE7/175FREE	SHARON TATE EXPERIENCE:Christmas Killer/ADMIRAL SIR CLOUDESLEY SHOVEL: Blow Up The Xmas Tree 300 only: 100 white vinyl, 100 red vinyl and 100 green vinyl)	80
12	Rise Above RISELP142	DON'T HEAR IT...FEAR IT! (LP, with 7", both on clear vinyl)	40
12	Rise Above RISELP142	DON'T HEAR IT...FEAR IT! (LP, red, green or purple vinyl)	20
14	Rise Above RISELP179	CHECK EM BEFORE YOU WRECK EM (LP, with 7", clear vinyl with poster)	25
16	Rise Above RISELP205	KEEP IT GREASY (LP, with 7", clear vinyl)	25
19	Rise Above RISELP235	VERY UNCERTAIN TIMES (LP, with 7")	20

ADMIRALS (1)
65 Fontana TF 597 — Promised Land/Palisades Park ... 30

ADMIRALS (2)
75 Angen ANG 102 — Natty Should Be Free/ANSEL COLLINS: Far East Special ... 10

ADMIRAL TIBET
86	Redman Intl. RED 4	New Tactics/RED DRAGON: Ease Off (12")	20
92	Rix RIZ 006	Permission/Sixth Commandment Dub/Version (12")	50
80s	Live & Love LLD301	Victim of Babylon/GREGORY PECK: Wah Do You (12")	15

(see also Red Dragon)

ADMIRATIONS
02 Soul City 135 — You Left Me/I Want To Be Free (reissue) ... 12

ADMIT YOU'RE SHIT
81	Mortarhate MORT 17	EXPECT NO MERCY (EP)	25
86	Mortarhate MORT 27	12 INCHES OF AYS (12" EP)	10

AD NAUSEUM
83	Flicknife FLS 12	BRAINSTORM (EP, p/s)	10
87	No label or cat no	THE GREATEST SHOW ON EARTH (Mini-LP)	20

A.D. 1984
79	Voyage Intl. VOY 005	The Russians Are Coming/New Moon Falling (p/s)	20
80	Grand Prix 001/002	Race To Nowhere/Leisure Crime (with lyric sheet)	15
81	Grand Prix GP 003	The Clockwork Generation/Melody In The Key Of Time (p/s)	10
83	Grand Prix GP 011	Mushroom Music (& Mayhem)/1984	15
83	Grand Prix GP 014	1984/Mushroom Music	12

ADOLESCENTS
90 Overground OVER 07 — ADOLESCENTS (LP, reissue of original US pressing) ... 15

ADRENALIN
79 Hithouse 12 HIT 2 — Feel The Real/Feel The Real (Instrumental) (12" stamped white label) ... 30

AD2000
80	Eagle EGL 007	Rhythm And Chips/Don't Play The Disco	6
84	Disco Funk Music DF 001B	Love Time Machine/Love Time Machine (Instrumental) (12")	300

ADULT JAZZ
14	Spare Thought SPTH 001	Am Gone/Springful/A Collection Of Recordings (12", p/s)	10
14	Spare Thought SPTHLP 002	GIST IS (LP, as 2 x 12")	60

AD VANCE VS GESCOM
98 Fat Cat 12FAT 009 — Viral/FOEHN: Shrouded/Funeral In Space (12", p/s) ... 10

ADVENTURERS
60 Capitol CL 15108 — Trail Blazer/Rip Van Winkle ... 10

ADVENTURES
61 Philips BBL 7548 — CAN'T STOP TWISTIN' (LP) ... 30

ANTHONY ADVERSE
86	él GPO 13	Our Fairy Tale/Eine Symphonie Des Grauens (p/s)	8
87	él GPO 29	Imperial Violets/Fountain (p/s)	8
85	El ACME 11	RED SHOES (LP)	30
80	ÈL ACME 22	SPIN (LP)	15

ADVERTISING
78 EMI EMC 3253 — ADVERTISING JINGLES (LP) ... 18

(see also Secret Affair, Innocents, Simon Boswell)

ADVERTS
77	Stiff BUY 13	One Chord Wonders/Quickstep (p/s, 1st pressing with push-out centre)	25
77	Stiff BUY 13	One Chord Wonders/Quickstep (p/s, re-pressing with solid centre)	10
77	Anchor ANC 1043	Gary Gilmore's Eyes/Bored Teenagers (p/s)	10
77	Anchor ANC 1047	Safety In Numbers/We Who Wait (p/s)	10
78	Bright BR 1	No Time To Be 21/New Day Dawning (p/s)	8
78	RCA PB 5128	Television's Over/Back From The Dead (p/s)	8
79	RCA PB 5160	My Place/New Church (p/s)	8
79	RCA PB 5191	Cast Of Thousands/I Will Walk You Home (p/s)	6
83	Bright BULB 1	Gary Gilmore's Eyes/We Who Wait/New Day Dawning (p/s)	10
87	Strange Fruit SFPS 034	PEEL SESSIONS (12", metallic finish)	10
78	Bright BRL 201	CROSSING THE RED SEA WITH THE ADVERTS (LP, red vinyl, 5,000 only)	40
78	Bright BULB 1	CROSSING THE RED SEA WITH THE ADVERTS (LP, black vinyl second pressing)	20
79	RCA PL 25246	CAST OF THOUSANDS (LP)	30
81	Butt/Bright ALSO 002	CROSSING THE RED SEA WITH THE ADVERTS (LP, reissue, red vinyl)	15
90	Receiver RRLP 136	LIVE AT THE ROXY CLUB (LP)	15

ADVOCATES

MINT VALUE £

ADVOCATES
73	Dovetail DOVE 1	ADVOCATES (LP)	30
75	Dovetail DOVE 7	HERE I REST MY CASE (LP)	30

ADX
85	Sire U 9070	Falling In Love Again/Come Along (p/s)	10

(see also Adicts)

A-ENO-ACID
17	Chicago Bee CB-1988-01	WHO"S THIS GUY (12" EP)	10

AERIAL FX
80	Square SQS 3	So Hard/It's About Time	10
81	Island WIP 6698	Take It From Here/Somewhere (p/s)	10
82	Kamera ERA 012	Instant Feelings/5:15 (p/s, pressed in France but issued in U.K.)	15
82	Kamera KAM 008	WATCHING THE DANCE (LP, pressed in France but issued in U.K.)	30

AEROPHONE
71	RPM 357	Sweet Sweet Suzie/Of Tomorrow	15

AEROSMITH
73	CBS 1898	Dream On/Somebody	10
73	CBS 32005	AEROSMITH (LP)	20
74	CBS 80015	GET YOUR WINGS (LP)	15
89	Geffen WX 304	PUMP (LP, inner)	18
93	Geffen GEF 24444	GET A GRIP (2-LP, inners)	40

(see also Run DMC)

AEROVONS
69	Parlophone R 5790	The Train/A Song For Jane	70
69	Parlophone R 5804	World Of You/Say Georgia	150

A FAIR SET
65	Decca F 12168	Honey And Wine/Run Around	20

PETER AFENDOULIS
78	Folkland FL 1018	THERE'S ONLY ONE F IN AFENDOULIS (LP, mail-order only)	30

AFEX
67	King KG 1058	She Got The Time/I Never Knew Love Was Like This	250

AFFAIRS OF THE HEART
83	Heartbeat PULSE 100	Waterloo Sunset/Waterloo Version (p/s)	10

AFFINITY
70	Vertigo 6059 007	I Wonder If I Care As Much/Three Sisters	35
70	Vertigo 6360 004	AFFINITY (LP, gatefold sleeve, large swirl label)	700

(see also Linda Hoyle, Jeff Beck Group, Queen, Ice)

AFFLECKS PALACE
19	Spirit Of Spike Island	HELLO. IS ANYONE AWAKE? (12", p/s, 300 only)	40
20	Spirit Of Spike Island SOS12	EVERYTHING IS AN ATTEMPT TO BE HUMAN (12", p/s)	40

AFFLICTED (1)
71	Scott SC 02	Miranda/Stolen Dreams	100

AFFLICTED (2)
81	Bonk AFF 1	I'm Afflicted/Be Aware (rubber-stamped white labels, p/s, with insert)	70
81	Bonk AFF 1	I'm Afflicted/Be Aware (rubber-stamped white labels, p/s, without insert)	30
82	Bonk AFF 2	All Right Boy/Who Can Tell (with p/s, stamped white labels)	60
82	Bonk AFF 2	All Right Boy/Who Can Tell (without p/s, stamped white labels)	10
82	Bonk AFF 4	One Forty Two/Senseless Whale Stalker (untitled single in stamped striped bag)	20
82	Bonk AFF 3	THE AFFLICTED MAN'S MUSICAL BAG (LP, stamped white label in stamped bag sleeve)	25

AFFLICTED MAN
80	Human HUM1	I'M OFF MI HEAD (LP)	20

AFGHAN WHIGS
93	Blast First BFFP 90	GENTLEMEN (LP, with free 12")	30
96	Mute STUMM 143	BLACK LOVE (LP)	40
98	Columbia 491486	1965 (LP)	30
10	Music On Vinyl MOVLP 149	1965 (LP, reissue)	20
14	Music On VInyl MOVLP 821	BLACK LOVE (LP, reissue)	18
14	Sub Pop SP 1061	DO TO THE BEAST (LP, 2 x 12", white vinyl, mispressing, skips on first track on side D (Royal Cream)	15

AFI
99	Nitro ADELINE 002	A FIRE INSIDE EP (ps, insert)	10
03	Nitro 450 460-2	Girl's Not Grey/The Hanging Garden (p/s, grey vinyl)	10
03	Nitro 450 462-6	The Leaving Song Pt. II/The Great Disappointment (Demo) (p/s, green vinyl)	8
09	DGC/Interscope 2721645/7	Medicate/Carcinogen Crush//Medicate/Ether (2 x 7", stickered sleeves, 1000 only, numbered)	7
10	Polydor 2736938	Beautiful Thieves (1-sided 7", etched B-side, p/s, 500 only)	8
03	Nitro 65522300261	SING THE SORROW (2-LP, red vinyl, inner sleeves)	50

A FINAL DISCIPLINE
82	Clock House CH 0504	Empty Pictures/And Still I Miss You	20

A FLEETING GLANCE
70	Private Pressing AS 2324	A FLEETING GLANCE (LP)	3000

AFRICAN
72	Sioux SI 006	Cock Mouth Kill Cock/ERROL T: I Need You Now	30

AFRICAN BEAVERS
65	RCA RCA 1447	Find My Baby/Jungle Fever	20

AFRICAN BROTHERS (ACTUALLY MATUMBI)
77	Mainline ML 1	Gimme Gimme African Love/PURE ROOTS: African Love Dub	15
79	Greensleeves GRED 14	A Di System/Gimme Gimme African Love (12")	12

AFRICAN BROTHERS BAND
70	Afribros PAB 001	AFRICAN DANCE BAND INTERNATIONAL (LP)	50
73	Afribros PAB 003	HIGHLIFE TIME (LP)	50

AFRICAN CONNEXION

MINT VALUE £

73	Leo Mensah PN 06	HIGHLIFE TIME (LP)	35
74	Afribros PAB 003	HIGHLIFE TIME (LP, reissue, different cover)	35

AFRICAN CONNEXION
84	Oval OVALT 28/12	MIDNIGHT PRESSURE (12", p/s)	30

AFRICAN HEAD CHARGE
81	ON-U LP 13	MY LIFE IN A HOLE IN THE GROUND (LP)	40
82	ON-U LP 19	ENVIRONMENTAL STUDIES (LP)	35
83	ON-U LP 27	DRASTIC SEASON (LP)	35
86	ON-U LP 40	OFF THE BEATEN TRACK (LP)	35
90	ON-U LP 50	SONGS OF PRAISE (LP)	35
93	ON-U LP 65	IN PURSUIT OF SHASHAMANE LAND (LP, with free 7")	30

AFRICAN MESSENGERS
64	Page One P04043	Highlife Picadilly/Blues For The Messengers	12

AFRICAN MUSIC MACHINE
72	Mojo 2092 046	Black Water Gold (Pearl)/Making Nassau Fruit Drink	15
73	Contempo CR 13	Tropical/A Girl In France	10
73	Contempo CR 25	Never Name A Baby (Before It's Born)/Dapp	10
74	Contempo CS 2025	Mr Brown/Camel Time	8

AFRICAN PRINCESS
81	Jah Shaka SHAKA 809	Jah Jah Children Cry/Jah Jah Dub (12")	75

AFRICAN STONE
76	Concrete Jungle CJ 600	How Long Must I Wait/4TH STREET ORCHESTRA: Long Wait	25
76	Concrete Jungle CJ 604	Singer Man/Song (as African Stones)	15
78	Tempus TEM 1260	Choose Me/Right Choice	10
76	K & B	Run Rasta Run/Run Rasta Run	25

AFRICANS
81	Lord Koos KLP 2	HAVE A GRAND TIME (LP, compilation)	40

AFRIKA
82	L 100	I Want You Tonight/I Want You Tonight (Remix) (p/s)	200
16	Super Disco Edits SDE 15	Don't Waste Your Time/In My Arms	6

AFRIKAN STAR
80	Black Vinyl BV0 77	Livin' In The System/Run & Hide (DIY p/s)	25

AFRIQUE
73	Pye International 7N 25616	Soul Makossa/Hot Mud	8
74	Mainstream MSL 1018	SOUL MAKOSSA (LP)	20

AFRO
71	Punch PH 89	Lonely World/ALTON ELLIS ALL STARS: Put It On	15

AFRO AKINO
74	Afrodesia 1001	Hwe Anna/Maria	10

AFRO DIMENSIONS
72	Ackee 535	Dance With Me/Lonely Nights	15
72	Jay Boy BOY 84	If You Don't Want My Love/Just Because	20

AFRO ENCHANTERS
63	Island WI 071	Peace And Love/Wayward African	25

AFRO FUNK
75	Kabana KAB 1	Obanya Special/Try And Try	15
75	Kabana BSC 01	BODY MUSIC (LP)	50

AFRO NATIONAL
75	Afro National NO 100	Push Am Forward/Salenotu	20

AFROTONES
69	Trojan TR 655	Things I Love/KEBLE DRUMMOND: Since You've Been Gone (unissued)	0
69	Duke DU 19	Freedom Sound/BOYS: Easy Sound (4-prong centre)	100
69	High Note HS 023	I'm In A Corner/BELTONES: Broken Heart	40
17	Duke DU 19	Freedom Sound/BOYS: Easy Sound (reissue, solid centre)	15

(see also Delroy Wilson)

AFTER DARK
81	After Dark AD 001	Evil Woman/Johnny/Lucy (p/s)	40
83	Lazer PROMO 1	Deathbringer/Call Of The Wild (picture disc, promo only)	30
83	Lazer PROMO 1	Deathbringer/Call Of The Wild (white label test pressing)	60

AFTER EIGHT
81	Airship AP 346	JUST THE WAY WE ARE (LP)	20

AFTERMATH (U.K.)
81	Red Star AFTERMATH 0001	The Freedom Fighter/All The Others/1980 (p/s)	15

AFTERMATH (1)
80	S Records AM 001	For You/Mixed Up Kid	50

AFTERSHAVE
73	Splendid SPS 401	Warmaker/One Of The Best	175

AFTER TEA
68	Ace Of Clubs SCL-R 1251	AFTER TEA (LP)	50

(see also Ray Fenwick)

AFTER THE FIRE
75	Rapid RR 001	SIGNS OF CHANGE (LP, with insert)	25

(see also Narnia, Waiting For The Sun)

A FURTHER ROOM
80	Test Pressing Records TP2	Would You Wanna Die For England/Animals	12

AGAIN AGAIN
80	Do It DUN IT 7	THE WAY WE WERE EP (12", p/s)	12

AGATHOCLES
90	Deaf DEAF 01	SUPPOSE IT WAS YOU (split LP with DRUDGE)	20

Yasuko AGAWA

MINT VALUE £

YASUKO AGAWA
86   Blue Bird BRT 26   L.A. Nights/New York Afternoon (12") 35

AGED IN HARMONY
16   Melodies Int. MEL 002/3/4   YOU'RE A MELODY (box set of 3 x 7") 25

AGENT FINCH & SPECIFIK
12   B-Line 104740H1   I Remember When/Still Der Defiance 6

AGENT ORANGE
92   Dog Tag AO 001   Sounds Flakey To Me (Jungle Mix)/Only You Have The Bass/Sounds Flakey To Me (Original Mix) (12") 18
93   Dog Tag AO 002   TECNOSKA EP: The Nuttiest Ska/Gettin' Rougher (Ska Mix)/Gettin' Rougher (Kaos Remix) (12") 15

AGENTS
79   Grapevine GRP 142   Trouble/The Love I Hold 15

AGGRESSORS
70   Pye 7N 17889   Whisky And Soda/Soul Of The Jungle 15
70   Marble Arch 1260   REGGAE STEADAE GO (LP) 15

AGGROVATORS
70   Jackpot JP 751   Sex Machine/You Left Me And Gone (both act. by Dave Barker & Aggrovators) 20
70   Smash SMA 2302   Big Red Ball Parts 1 & 2 (A-side actually "Big Red Bumble" by Lloyd Tyrell; B-side actually "Big Bumble Version" by Lloyd & Devon) 20
71   Smash SMA 2312   One More Bottle Of Beer/Beer Version 10
73   Smash SMA 2339   Straight To Jackson Head/HORACE ANDY: You Are My Angel 12
73   Downtown DT 500   Dreadlocks Man/Rasta Want Peace (both actually by Rasta Twins) 12
76   Grounation GROL 507   RASTA DUB '76 (LP) 40
78   Live & Love LAP 04   JAMMIES IN A LION STYLE DUB (LP) 35
78   Third World TWS 939   KAYA DUB (LP) 50
78   Conflict COLP 2006   RASTA DUB 2000 (LP) 30
90   Attack ATLP 111   DUB JACKPOT (LP, with King Tubby) 15
(see also Dave Barker, Dennis Alcapone, Jerry Lewis [Jamaica], Delroy Wilson, John Holt, Alton Ellis, Cornell Campbell)

AGGROVATORS AND THE REVOLUTIONARIES
77   Third World TWS 900   THE AGGROVATORS MEET THE REVOLUTIONARIES AT CHANNEL ONE (LP) 30
78   Burning Sounds BS 1028   GUERILLA DUB (LP) 35

AGINCOURT
70   Merlin HF 3   FLY AWAY (LP, with insert) 1000
11   Merlin HF3   FLY AWAY (reissue, lyric insert, with or without certificate, RCLP 001 matrix) 50
(see also Friends, Ithaca, Alice Through The Looking Glass, Tomorrow Come Someday)

AGITATORS
79   Redball RR 028   BOUND AND GAGGED WITH RUBBER TUBING EP 40
80   Rasclaat CLAAT 2   NOT QUITE RIGHT IN THE HEAD (LP) 80

AGNES STRANGE
75   Birdsnest BN 1   Give Yourself A Chance/Clever Fool 12
77   Baal BDN 38048   Can't Make Up My Mind/Johnny B. Goode 10
75   Birdsnest BRL 9000   STRANGE FLAVOUR (LP) 150
00   Thorns 7788   DUST IN THE SUNLIGHT (LP) 15

AGNOSTIC FRONT
85   Rough Justice JUST 3   CAUSE FOR ALARM (LP) 15

AGONY BAG
80   Monza MON 2   Rabies Is A Killer/Never Never Never (p/s) 10
(see also Pesky Gee, Black Widow)

AGONY COLUMN
79   Tyger TYG 2   (I Had It) All Worked Out/Good Grief (p/s) 15
80   Back Door DOOR 8   Love In The Head/Free Of Love (p/s) 8
82   Lightbeat LIGHT 003   Love Is A Blanket Expression/Only U/Missing Person (p/s) 6

AGORA
94   Z Records ZEDD 010   LATIN CONNECTION EP (12") 10

AGRO
95   Epsilon 001   THE ASSOCIATION OF AUTONOMOUS ASTRONAUTS EP (12") 20

AGROS
71   Punch PH 56   What Do You Fall In Love For/SLICKERS: Too Much 20

CHRISTINA AGUILERA
06   RCA 82876 82639   BACK TO BASICS (3-LP, numbered) 150

A GUY CALLED GERALD
88   Rham RS8804   Voodoo Ray/Escape/Rhapsody In Acid/Blow Your House Down (12", p/s) 25
89   Avernus AVERNUS 1   Trip City Mambo/Valentines Theme (12", stamped white labels) 250
90   Columbia XPR 1535   Emotions Electric (Frankie Foncett Remix 1)/Emotions Electric (Frankie Foncett Remix 2) (12", promo in stickered plain sleeve) 15
92   Juice Box JBOX 001   Digital Bad Boy/Let It Move You/A Storm Is Coming/Could You Understand? (12", tracks 1 and 4 vocals by MC Tunes) 12
92   Juice Box JBOX 003   Cops/The Trak/28 Gun Bad Boy/Paranoia (12") 40
92   Juice Box JBOX 004   Ses Makes You Wise/Sunshine/King Of The Jungle/Boase up (12") 15
92   Juice Box JBOX 005   The Musical Magical Midi Machine/Let It Go/Like A Drug/Free Africa (12") 15
92   Columbia XPR 1684   Cops/The Track/Paranoia/28 Gun Bad Boy (12" white label promo) 40
93   Juice Box JBOX 009   Too Fucked to Dance/Darker Than I Should Be/Anything v2.1/Is The Right Time (12") 20
93   Juice Box JBOX 014   The Glok Track/Gerald's Bassline/Ease The Pressure/Take Me (12") 15
94   Juice Box JBOX 019   Darker Than I Should Be (Ladies Mix)/Gloc (Remix) (12") 12
89   Rham! RA 1   HOT LEMONADE (LP) 20
89   Rham! RA 1   HOT LEMONADE (LP, repressing, pink sleeve with Voodoo Ray as 1st track on Side 2) 20
90   CBS 4664820   AUTOMANIKK (LP, with free 12") 20
94   Juice Box JBOX 12   28 GUN BAD BOY (LP, promo) 70
95   Juice Box JBLP 25   BLACK SECRET TECHNOLOGY (2-LP, 1st pressing, black and blue sleeve) 30
96   Juice Box JBLP 30   BLACK SECRET TECHNOLOGY (2-LP, 2nd pressing, full colour sleeve, new design) 25

Eric AGYEMANG

MINT VALUE £

ERIC AGYEMANG
78	Apogee BEBLOP 013	HIGHLIFE SAFARI (LP)	50
85	Thornhill TR- LP 01	METE AWO YI MU (LIVING IN THE COLD) (LP, with Thomas Frimpong)	40
87	Asona ASR 6010EX	NANANOM (LP)	20

A-HA
84	Warner Bros W 9146	Take On Me/And You Tell Me (silver/blue p/s)	40
84	Warner Bros W 9146T	Take On Me (Extended)/And You Tell Me/Stop And Make Your Mind Up (12", silver/blue p/s, with poster & stickers)	150
84	Warner Bros W 9146T	Take On Me (Extended)/And You Tell Me/Stop And Make Your Mind Up (12", silver/blue p/s, without poster & stickers)	80
88	Warner Bros W7749W	Touchy!/Hurry Home ('felt' p/s)	15

(see also Phenomena)

AHAB & WAILERS
63	Pye 7N 15553	Cleopatra's Needle/Neb's Tune	40

A HEADS
82	TW Records HIT 107	Dying Man/Hell Cell/Changing Places (p/s)	18
83	Bluurg FISH 3	Forgotten Hero/Isolated/Love Or Pain (p/s)	10

AIKEN'S DRUM
81	Private Pressing SRTX/CUS 1134	AIKEN'S DRUM (LP)	40

JOSS AIKINS AND THE ENVOYS
65	Volta NO 1	The Founder/The Unity Highlife (with Teddy Osei)	60

(see also Osibisa)

AIL SYMUDIAD
80	Sain 765	Ad Drefnu/Whisgi A Soda (p/s)	10
81	Fflach RF 001	Twristiaid Yn Y Dre/Modur Sanctaiddy/Hyfyed Bingo (500 only, first 100 in dayglo sleeve)	10
81	Fflach RF AS 002	Geiriau/Annwyl Rhywun/Cura Dy Law (p/s)	10
81	Fflach RF AS 003	Garej Paradwys/Ffarwel L'e Fyddin (p/s)	10
82	Fflach RF AS 004	Lleisau O'r Gorffennol/Dilyn Y Sebon (p/s)	10
82	Fflach RF AS 005	Edrych Trwy Y Cameraŭ/ANGYLION STANLI: Emyn Roc A Roi (split single, p/s)	10

AIM (1)
94	Detour DR 018	Call Your Name/Out On The Streets (p/s,1,000 only, 100 on blue vinyl)	8
94	Detour DR 018	Call Your Name/Out On The Streets (p/s,1,000 only, black vinyl)	6

AIM (2)
99	Grand Central GCLP 105	COLD WATER MUSIC (2-LP)	40
02	Grand Central GCLP 112	HINTERLAND (2-LP)	30

AIR (1)
71	Atlantic 2400 148	AIR (LP)	20

AIR (2)
98	Source V 2848	MOON SAFARI (LP, with inner)	40
00	Record Makers V2910	VIRGIN SUICIDES (LP)	60
01	Virgin V 2945	10,000 HZ LEGEND (LP)	30
03	Record Makers REC 09	CITY READING (2-LP, with Alessandro Baricco)	25
05	Virgin 72435 966322 7	TALKIE WALKIE (LP)	20
07	EMI V 3032	POCKET SYMPHONY (LP, white vinyl)	15
10	Vinyl Factory VF 007	LOVE 2 (2-LP, 300 only in box with print, booklet and certificate)	150
12	Vinyl Factory VF 042	LA VOYAGE DANS LA LUNE (2-LP, gatefold with DVD)	30
12	Vinyl Factory VF 043	LA VOYAGE DANS LA LUNE (4-LP, art print, DVD, cloth box)	80
14	Vinyl Factory VF 112	MUSIC FOR MUSEUM (2-LP, clear vinyl, poster)	75
16	Parlophone 0190295990121	TWENTYEARS (2-LP, box set, random coloured LPs, 3-CD and poster)	30

AIRBORNE
83	Clubland SJP 844	Burn In Hell/Lord Satan/Temple Of Metal (p/s)	12

AIRBRIDGE
83	Rattees RATT 001	Words And Pictures/Zero Minus One	15

DEBRAH AIRE
67	Polydor 56180	This Land Is Mine/What The World Needs Now Is Love	10

(see also Sharon Tandy)

AIRHEAD
92	Korova 9030 74679 2	BOING! (LP)	20

AIRKRAFT
79	Lathe TSR1	Here Comes That Sound/Video Romance/White Boys	25
80	Square SQS 5	Move In Rhythm/Pumping Iron	12

AIR LIQUIDE
94	Rising High RSN 79	If There Was No Gravity/Auroral Belt/Stratus Static/THX Is On (12", black or blue vinyl)	15
94	Rising High RSN LP 15	NEPHOLOGY - THE NEW RELIGION (2-LP)	40
95	Rising High RSN LP 38	SONIC WEATHER MACHINE (2-LP, black or blue vinyl)	30

AIRMAIL
79	Graffiti GIT 001	No Human Feeling/In A Moment	8

AIR MIAMI
95	4AD CAD 5011	ME. ME. ME. (LP)	30

AIRPEOPLE
95	Malawi COB 139906	7 Deadlines/(Flaw Mix) (12")	50

AIRSHIP
79	Decca FR 13856	Get Out, Take Your Mother With You/Gimme A Can Of Spray Paint	40

AIRTO
71	Buddah 2318 040	SEEDS ON THE GROUND - THE NATURAL SOUNDS OF AIRTO (LP, gatefold)	20
73	CTI CTL 18	FINGERS (LP)	15
74	CTI CTL 21	IN CONCERT (LP, with Deodato)	15
74	CTI CTL 23	VIRGIN LAND (LP)	15

AIR TRAFFIC CONTROL

MINT VALUE £

AIR TRAFFIC CONTROL
77	Epic S EPC 5665	Gotta Get A Message Back To You/Move On Up	8

AISHA
86	Ariwa ARI 48	Dancing Time/The Creator (12")	35
86	Ariwa ARI 52	That's How Heartaches Are Made/AISHA & BLACKSTEEL: Prophecy Dub (12")	15
86	Ariwa ARI 060	Prophecy/THE ROBOTICS: Dub (12")	25
94	Ariwa ARI 153	Only Jah Works/Crisis (12")	18
87	Ariwa ARILP 029	HIGH PRIESTESS (LP)	40
93	Twinkle NG 538	DAUGHTERS OF ZION (LP)	20
94	Ariwa ARLP 084	TRUE ROOTS (LP)	15
96	Twinkle NG 550	RAISE YOUR VOICE (LP)	20

AITCH
71	Decca F13150	Let It Be Me/Let Me Say This	6

BOBBY AITKEN (& CARIBBEATS)
62	Island WI 028	Baby Baby (actually with Patsy)/Lonely Boy	18
62	Blue Beat BB 93	Never Never (South Virginia)/Isabella (as Bobby Aitken & Buster's Group)	18
63	Blue Beat BB 146	Don't Leave Me/Mom And Dad (as Bobby Aitken & Tinse)	18
63	Rio R 14	I've Told You/Please Go Back	18
63	Rio R 15	It Takes A Friend/LAUREL AITKEN: Sunshine	18
64	Rio R 34	Rolling Stone/LESTER STERLING'S GROUP: Man About Town	40
64	Rio R 40	Garden Of Eden/Whiplash	20
64	Rio R 50	Little Girl/Together	20
65	Rio R 52	Rain Came Tumbling Down/SHENLEY & LUNAN: Something Is On Your Mind	15
65	Rio R 64	Mr Judge/BINZ: Times Have Changed	18
65	Black Swan WI 441	Jerico/LESTER STERLING: Lunch Time	25
66	Ska Beat JB 252	Thunderball/ORIGINATORS: Chelip Chelip	200
67	Doctor Bird DB 1071	Keep On Pushing/You Won't Regret It	80
67	Doctor Bird DB 1072	Let Them Have A Home/Temptation (with Caribbeats)	30
67	Doctor Bird DB 1077	Sweets For My Sweet/How Sweet It Is (with Caribbeats)	50
67	Island WI 3028	Kiss Bam Bam (El Bang Bang)/CYNTHIA RICHARDS: How Could I	130
67	Giant GN 11	What A Fool/Curfew (with Caribbeats)	45

(see also Caribbeats, Laurel Aitken, Frank Cosmo, Lloyd & Glen)

LAUREL AITKEN (& BLUE BEATS)
59	Kalypso XX 15	Sweet Chariot/Nebuchnezer	30
59	Kalypso XX 16	Aitken's Boogie/Cherrie	30
60	Kalypso XX 19	Baba Kill Me Goat/Tribute To Collie Smith	20
60	Starlite ST45 011	Boogie In My Bones/Little Sheila	40
60	Starlite ST45 014	Honey Girl (with Caribs)/Drinkin' Whisky (with Bluebeats)	40
60	Melodisc M 1570	Mary Lee/Lonesome Lover (with Bluebeats)	30
60	Blue Beat B 1	Boogie Rock/Heavenly Angel (with the BOOGIE CATS) (white label)	50
60	Blue Beat BB 1	Boogie Rock/Heavenly Angel (with the BOOGIE CATS) (blue label)	30
60	Blue Beat BB 10	Jeannie Is Back/If It's Money You Need	30
60	Blue Beat BB 14	Judgment Day/Yea Yea Baby	15
60	Blue Beat BB 22	Railroad Track/Tell Me Darling (with the Blue Beats)	20
60	Blue Beat BB 25	More Whisky/LLOYD CLARKE: Parapinto Boogie	20
61	Starlite ST45 034	Love Me Baby/Stars Were Made	30
61	Blue Beat BB 40	Bar Tender/Mash Potato Boogie	30
61	Blue Beat BB 52	Bouncing Woman/Nursery Rhyme Boogie (with Blue Beats)	30
61	Blue Beat BB 70	Mighty Redeemer/Please Don't Leave Me	15
62	Blue Beat BB 84	Brother David/Back To New Orleans (with Blue Beats)	15
62	Blue Beat BB 109	Lucille/I Love You More Everyday	15
62	Blue Beat BB 120	Sixty Days And Sixty Nights/Going To Kansas City (with Les Dawson Trio)	40
62	Blue Beat BB 142	Jenny Jenny/Weary Wanderer (with Bandits and Ruddy & Sketto)	20
62	Dice CC 1	Mabel/You Got Me Rocking (with Hyacinth)	20
63	Dice CC 13	Sweet Jamaica/Bossa Nova Hop	20
63	Blue Beat BB 164	Zion/Swing Low Sweet Chariot	20
63	Blue Beat BB 194	Little Girl/Daniel Saw The Stone (with Ruddy and Sketto)	20
63	Duke DK 1002	Low Down Dirty Girl/Pink Lane Shuffle	30
63	Island WI 092	I Shall Remove/We Got To Move	40
63	Island WI 095	What A Weeping/Zion City Wall	25
63	Island WI 099	In My Soul/One More River To Cross	40
63	Rio R 11	Adam & Eve/BOBBY AITKEN: Devil Woman	20
63	Rio R 12	Mary/Hometown	20
63	Rio R 13	Bad Minded Woman/Life	20
63	Rio R 17	Devil Or Angel/Fire	20
63	Rio R 18	Freedom Train/Peace Perfect Peace	20
64	Rio R 35	Rock Of Ages/The Mule	18
64	Rio R 36	Leave Me Standing/Bagaboo (Bug-A-Boo)	12
64	Rio R 37	John Saw Them Coming/Jericho	20
64	R&B JB 167	Yes Indeed/You Can't Stop Me From Loving You	20
64	R&B JB 170	Pick Up Your Bundle And Go/Let My People Go	20
64	R&B JB 171	Bachelor Life/You Was Up	20
64	Columbia DB 7280	Be Mine/Don't Stay Out Late	15
64	Blue Beat BB 249	This Great Day/I May Never See My Baby	25
64	J.N.A.C. 1	West Indian Cricket Test/3 Cheers For Worrell	25
64	Black Swan WI 401	Lion Of Judah/Remember My Darling (B-side with Cynthia Richards)	40
64	Black Swan WI 411	The Saint/Go Gal Go	40
64	Dice CC 28	Jamaica/I Don't Want No More	25
65	Dice CC 31	We Shall Overcome/You Left Me Standing	25

Laurel AITKEN (& BLUE BEATS)

MINT VALUE £

65	Rio R 53	Mary Don't You Weep/I Believe	20
65	Rio R 54	Mary Lou/Jump And Shout	20
65	Rio R 56	One More Time/Ring Don't Mean A Thing	20
65	Rio R 60	Come And Let Us Go/Lonely Nights	25
65	Rio R 65	Let's Be Lovers/I Need You	25
65	Venus VE 4	How Can I Forget You?/Weeping And Crying	12
65	Island WI 198	Boogie In My Bones/Little Sheila	25
65	Island WI 252	How Can I Forget You/Weeping And Crying (white label, existence unconfirmed)	0
66	Blue Beat BB 340	Clementine/Bongo Jerk	30
66	Blue Beat BB 369	Shame And Scandal/Coconut Woman	40
66	Ska Beat JB 232	Jamboree/Looking For My Baby	40
66	Ska Beat JB 236	Propaganda/Shake	35
66	Ska Beat JB 239	Green Banana/Darling	35
66	Rio R 91	How Can I Forget You/I've Been Weeping And Crying	15
66	Rio R 92	Baby Don't Do It/That Girl	15
66	Rio R 97	We Shall Overcome/Street Of Glory	15
66	Rio R 99	Clap Your Hands/Revival	15
66	Rainbow RAI 101	Don't Break Your Promises/Last Night (with Soulmen)	40
66	Rainbow RAI 106	Voodoo Woman/Bewildered And Blue (B-side with Carols)	40
67	Rainbow RAI 111	Sweet Precious Love/I Want To Love You Forever (with Carols)	40
67	Columbia Blue Beat DB 102	Rock Steady/Blowin' In The Wind	30
67	Columbia Blue Beat DB 106	I'm Still In Love With You Girl/Blue Rhythm	30
67	Fab FAB 5	Never You Hurt/I Need You (as Laurel Aitken & Soulmen)	50
68	Fab FAB 45	For Sentimental Reasons/Last Waltz (as Laurel Aitken & Rainbows)	30
68	Doctor Bird DB 1160	Mr Lee/Birmingham Girl	30
68	Doctor Bird DB 1161	La La La (Means I Love You)/DETOURS: Sunnyside	25
69	Ackee ACK 105	Skinheads Are Wrecking The Town (white label only, unissued)	250
69	Doctor Bird DB 1187	Fire In Your Wire/Quando Quando	30
69	Doctor Bird DB 1190	Rice And Peas/CLASSICS: Worried Over Me	40
69	Doctor Bird DB 1196	Reggae Prayer/Deliverance Will Come	40
69	Doctor Bird/J.J. DB 1197	The Rise And Fall (Of Laurel)/If You're Not Black	40
69	Doctor Bird DB 1202	Haile Haile (The Lion)/SEVEN LETTERS: Call Collect	40
69	Doctor Bird DB 1203	Carolina/Kingston Town	40
69	Junior JR 105	Think Me No Know/RECO: Trombone Man	30
69	Nu Beat NB 024	Woppi King/Mr Soul	30
69	Nu Beat NB 025	Suffering Still (with Girlie)/Reggae '69	30
69	Nu Beat NB 032	Haile Selassie/Blues Dance	25
69	Nu Beat NB 033	Lawd Doctor (with Girlie)/Big Fight In Hell Stadium	30
69	Nu Beat NB 035	Run Powell Run/RICO RODRIGUEZ: A Message To You	30
69	Nu Beat NB 039	Save The Last Dance/Walk Right Back	20
69	Nu Beat NB 040	Don't Be Cruel/John B.	20
69	Nu Beat NB 043	Shoo Be Doo/Babylon Gone	20
69	Nu Beat NB 044	Landlords And Tenants/Everybody Sufferin'	20
69	Nu Beat NB 045	Jesse James/Freedom	30
69	Nu Beat NB 046	Pussy Price Gone Up/Gimme Back Me Dollar	30
69	Junior JR 106	River Nile (existence unconfirmed, white labels only)	40
69	Nu Beat NB 047	Skinhead Train/GRUVY BEATS: Kent People	65
70	Nu Beat NB 048	Skinhead Invasion/Benwood Dick (unissued, blank white label demos only)	125
70	Nu Beat NB 048	Mr Popcorn/GRUVY BEATS: Share Your Popcorn	18
70	Nu Beat NB 049	I've Got Your Love/GRUVY BEATS: Blue Mink	20
70	Nu Beat NB 050	Scandal In Brixton Market/Soul Grinder (both sides with Girlie)	20
70	New Beat NB 054	Nobody But Me/Baby Please Don't Go	12
70	New Beat NB 056	I'll Never Love Any Girl/The Best I Can	12
70	New Beat NB 057	Reggae Popcorn/Take Me Back	20
70	New Beat NB 063	Baby I Need Your Loving/Think It Over	20
70	New Beat NB 065	Sex Machine/Since You Left	20
70	New Beat NB 072	Pachanga/Version	20
70	Ackee ACK 104	Pussy Got Thirteen Life/Single Man	25
70	Ackee ACK 106	Sin Pon You/Everynight	80
70	Bamboo BAM 16	Moon Rock/Cut Up Munno (apparantly, white labels only)	80
70	Pama PM 818	Mary's Boy Child/RUPIE EDWARDS ALLSTARS: Version	12
70	Pama Supreme PS 300	Why Can't I Touch You/Can't Turn Your Back On Me	12
71	Trojan TR 7826	It's Too Late/AITKEN'S BAND: Slow Rock	10
71	New Beat NB 078	True Love/The Best I Can	6
71	New Beat NB 089	I Can't Stop Loving You/El Paso	6
71	Black Swan BW 1408	If It's Hell Below/Just A Little Bit Of Love	40
71	Big Shot BI 595	Dancing With My Baby/Do The Boogaloo	20
72	Big Shot BI 605	Take Me In Your Arms/Two-Timing Woman	8
72	Camel CA 90	Africa Arise/GI GINGRI: Holy Mount Zion	12
72	Columbia DB 8914	Pretty Face In The Market Place/Come Back To My Lonely World	6
75	Camel CA 2007	La Vien En Rose/Spanish Eyes	8
77	Dip DL 5012	For Ever And Ever/None Sweeter Than You	25
78	Ultra PFUL 2005	Hoocihe Coochie Man/Sexy Boogie (12")	60
66	Rio LR 1	SKA WITH LAUREL (LP)	300
67	Doctor Bird DLM 5012	SAYS FIRE (LP)	150
69	Pama PSP 1012	THE HIGH PRIEST OF REGGAE (LP)	100
69	Pama ECO 8	SCANDAL IN BRIXTON MARKET (LP, with Girlie)	100
69	J.J.	RISE AND FALL (LP)	120
73	Count Shelly CSLP 1	SOPHIA (LP)	45

A-JAES

93	GAZ 009	GODFATHER OF SKA (LP)	18

(see also Laurel & Owen, Girlie, King Horror, Lorenzo, Ruts, Bobby Aitken, Classics, Beresford Ricketts, Duke Reid, Tommy McCook)

A-JAES
64	Oak RGJ 132	I'm Leaving You/Kansas City	700

AJAX PROJECT
92	MACH III	MACH III EP (12" white labels only)	15

AJL BAND
76	Baal BDN 38033	Sweet Sticky Thing/Classical Salsa	8

AKA & CHARLATANS
78	Vanity VANE 1	Heroes Are Losers/Lady Of The Night/Perhaps One Day (12", various screen-printed die-cut p/s)	12

AKAPEL
92	Phlange AK001	Pick It Up (Vocal)/(Instrumental)/Stick Your Big Dinky In/Background Beats/Let Me Hear You Say/Keep On/They Won't Believe Me (12")	12

JEWEL AKENS
65	London HLN 9954	The Birds And The Bees/Tic Tac Toe	6
65	London HLN 9969	Georgie Porgie/Around The Corner	6
66	Ember EMB S 219	Dancin' Jenny/A Wee Bit More of Your Lovin'	10
65	London HA-N 8234	THE BIRDS AND THE BEES (LP)	25

AKERCOCKE
05	Earache 7MOSH 322	Eyes Of The Dawn (Demo)/The Fulcrum (translucent red vinyl, no p/s)	15

AK 47
81	Output ORR 202	Stop! Dance!/Autobiography/Hilversum-Ao (p/s)	50
91	Rugger Bugger SEEP 004	DON'T CALL ME VANILLA (LP, with lyric sheet)	30

(see also AK Process, File Under Pop)

TOSHIKO AKIYOSHI
58	Columbia 33CX 101101	NEWPORT JAZZ FESTIVAL 1957 (LP)	15

JAN AKKERMAN
73	Harvest HAR 5069	Blue Boy/Minstrel-Farmers Dance	6
72	Harvest SHSP 4026	PROFILE (LP)	20
73	Atlantic K40522	TABERNAKEL (LP, gatefold)	15

(see also Hunters [Holland], Brainbox, Focus)

AK PROCESS
79	Output OPR 101	Electronic Music: After All Love/Post Town (p/s, white labels)	15

(see also AK 47, File Under Pop)

AKRYLYKZ
80	Double R RED 2	Spyderman/Smart Boy (p/s)	6

AL ET ALL
80	Arny's Shack As 047	STRANGE AFFAIR (LP)	200

AL & VIBRATORS
67	Doctor Bird DB 1062	Cool Water/BABA BROOKS: Roll Call	70
67	Doctor Bird DB 1085	Move Up/Lonesome Lover	35
69	High Note HS 005	Check Up/I'll Come Back (featuring Byron Lee & The Dragonaires)	20
69	High Note HS 007	Move Up Calypso/PATSY: Fire In Your Wire	20

(see also Vibrators, Patsy Todd, Lord Power)

STEVE ALAIMO
63	Pye International 7N 25174	Every Day I Have To Cry/(Please Take A Chance On Me) Little Girl (DJ Copy)	50
63	Pye International 7N 25174	Every Day I Have To Cry/(Please Take A Chance On Me) Little Girl	30
63	Pye International 7N 25199	It's A Long Long Way To Happiness/A Lifetime Of Loneliness	10
66	HMV POP 1531	So Much Love/Truer Than True (DJ Copy)	30
66	HMV POP 1531	So Much Love/Truer Than True	20
68	Atlantic 588 227	Watching The Trains Go By/Thank You For The Sunshine Days	10

ALARM
81	White Cross W 3/4	Unsafe Buildings/Up For Murder (gatefold p/s)	25
84	I.R.S. IRS 103	The Deceiver/Reason 41 (p/s, mispress on mustard vinyl)	45
02	Vinyl Japan ASK LP 135	A FLASHING BLUR OF STRIPPED DOWN EXCITEMENT (LP)	20

(see also Seventeen)

ALARM CLOX
80	Ring RING 1	Protector/Restaurant (no p/s)	7

DAMON ALBARN
02	Honest Jons HJRLP1	MALI MUSIC (2-LP)	25
03	Honest Jons HJP10	DEMOCRAZY (2x10" white vinyl, picture disc, 5,000 only)	15
08	Vinyl Factory VF 001	MONKEY: JOURNEY TO THE WEST (2-LP, signed print, programme, tone generator)	60
14	Parlophone 825646331291	EVERYDAY ROBOTS ((2-LP, with CD)	20

(see also Blur, Gorillaz, Monkey, GB & TQ)

ALBATROSS
74	Mooncrest Moon 36	Anything I Want To/Bournemouth Rock	6

Prices fine

EDDIE ALBERT
55	London HL 8136	I'm In Favour Of Friendship/Come Pretty Little Girl	15
56	London HLU 8241	Little Child (Daddy Dear) (with Sondra Lee)/Jenny Kissed Me	15

MEL ALBERT
59	Top Rank JAR 178	Sugar Plum/Never Let Me Go	10

ALBERTO Y LOST TRIOS PARANOIAS
76	Big T BIG 541	Dread Jaws/De Version	6
77	Stiff LAST 2	SNUFF ROCK EP (12" promo, only 50-100 pressed)	200
78	Logo GO 340	Juan Lopez (The Lonely Goatherd)/Teenage Paradise/Dead Meat Part III	6
76	Transatlantic TRA 316	ALBERTO Y LOST TRIOS PARANOIAS (LP, with insert)	15
77	Transatlantic TRA 349	ITALIANS FROM OUTER SPACE (LP)	15
78	Logo LOGO 1009	SKITE (LP)	15
80	Logo MOGO 4008	THE WORST OF THE BERTS (LP)	15

ALBIANS

MINT VALUE £

(see also Mothmen, Charlie Parkas)

ALBIANS
79	K & K 003	Princess/Princess Dub (12", with Ranking Neville)	12
80	K & K KK 0012	Who Is Going To Love Me/VIN GORDON: Who Is Going To Rock Me Tonight (12")	20

(See also N. McCoy & Albians)

ALBINO GORILLA
72	Ember EMBS321	Shake Me, Wake Me/Going To A Go Go	6

ALBION
09	Ambassador's Reception ABR005	Space Time Continuum/Milky Way/Thunder Strikes/Voodoo Safari (12")	15

ALBION BAND
73	Island HELP 25	BATTLE OF THE FIELD (LP, as Albion Country Band)	20
77	Harvest SHSP 4059	THE PROSPECT BEFORE US (LP, as Albion Dance Band)	15
78	Harvest SHSP 4092	RISE UP LIKE THE SUN (LP, textured sleeve)	15

(see also Shirley Collins, Fairport Convention)

MICHAEL ALBUQUERQUE
69	United Artists UP 35037	Better Men Than Me/Burn Burn Burn	10
70	United Artists UP 35098	Roll Him Over/Blind Man	8

(see also Michael D'Albuquerque, E.L.O.)

DENNIS ALCAPONE
70	Explosion EX 2039	Revelation Version/Marka Version	15
70	Supreme SUP 214	You Must Believe Me (with Niney)/RUPIE EDWARDS ALLSTARS: Funk The Funk	12
70	Big Shot BI 565	Shades Of Hudson/Spanish Amigo	30
71	Treasure Isle TI 7069	The Great Woggie/TOMMY McCOOK & SUPERSONICS: Buttercup Version	20
71	Banana BA 328	Duppy Serenade (as Innkeeper)/Sunshine Version	20
71	Banana BA 341	(Love Me) Forever Version/I Don't Want To See You Cry	30
71	Upsetter US 373	Well Dread/UPSETTERS: Dread Version	12
71	Upsetter US 377	Alpha And Omega/JUNIOR BYLES: Beat Down Babylon	15
71	Duke DU 125	Medley Version/Version Two	8
71	Prince Buster PB 8	Sons Of Zion/ANSELL COLLINS: Short Circuit	12
71	Prince Buster PB 12	Let It Roll (with Max Romeo)/ANSELL COLLINS: Clear Blue	15
71	Jackpot JP 773	Jumping Jack (with John Holt)/AGGROVATORS: King Of The Track	8
71	Jackpot JP 775	Togetherness (Black & White) (with John Holt)/DELROY WILSON: Live Good	8
71	Jackpot JP 776	Tell It Like It Is/DELROY WILSON : Come Along	8
71	Dynamic DYN 421	Horse And Buggy/ROLAND ALPHONSO & DENZIL LAING: Buggy And Horse	12
71	Dynamic DYN 422	Ripe Cherry/INNER CIRCLE: Red Cherry	10
71	Dynamic DYN 427	Alcapones Guns Don't Bark/Alcapones Guns Don't Bark Version	15
71	Camel CA 74	This A Butter/PHIL PRATT ALLSTARS: Version	12
71	Tropical AL 003	False Prophet/MAX ROMEO: Rude Medley	12
72	Downtown DT 496	Swinging along/DELROY WILSON: My Baby Is Gone	20
72	Tropical AL 019	Worldwide Love (with Twinkle Brothers)/CARL MASTERS: Gable Up	12
72	Ackee ACK 146	Power Version/BLUESBLASTERS: Martie (B-side actually titled "Margie")	18
72	Prince Buster PB 24	Giant/PRINCE BUSTER: Science	30
72	Upsetter US 381	Wonderman (with Dave Barker, actually by Dave Barker)/ Place Called Africa (with Dave Barker & Junior Byles)	20
72	Upsetter US 388	Master Key/UPSETTERS: Keyhole	20
72	Grape GR 3035	Rasta Dub/UPSETTERS: Rasta Version	30
72	Attack ATT 8027	Fine Style/WINSTON SCOTLAND: On The Track	15
72	Duke DU 131	The Sky's The Limit/HUDSON'S ALLSTARS: Limit Version	12
72	Duke DU 147	Get In The Groove (with Dennis Brown)/DYNAMITES: Version	12
72	Techniques TE 918	Look Into Yourself/TECHNIQUES ALLSTARS: Yourself Version	15
72	Green Door GD 4041	Rub Up A Daughter/TONY'S ALLSTARS: Daughter Version	15
72	Bullet BU 509	Dub Up A Daughter/PRINCE TONY ALL STARS: Version	15
72	Treasure Isle TI 7069	Great Woggie/Buttercup	25
70	Prince Buster PB31	Kings And Castles/Version	12
73	Downtown DT 508	You Don't Say/TONY'S ALLSTARS: Version	12
73	Treasure Isle TI 7074	Wake Up Jamaica/Version (with Tommy McCook)	25
73	Jackpot JP 808	Cassius Clay/SLIM SMITH: Love And Affection	20
73	Bread BR 1121	Musical Liquidator/Lorna Banana (B-side with Prince Jazzbo)	25
73	G.G. GG 4538	Musical Alphabet/BUCKLEY ALLSTARS: Things Gonna Change (B-side actually by Maytones)	12
73	Pyramid PYR 7008	Belch It Off/Jack Horner	8
74	Harry J HJ 6666	Sorry Harry/Party Time	8
76	Ethnic Fight EF 001	Pressure In A Babylon/ETHNIC FIGHT BAND: Pressure Dub	10
71	Trojan TBL 187	GUNS DON'T ARGUE (LP)	40
73	Magnet MGT 001	KING OF THE TRACK (LP)	50
74	Attack ATLP 1005	BELCH IT OFF (LP)	40
75	Live And Love LALP 104	DREAD CAPONE (LP)	40
77	Third World TWS 801	SIX MILLION DOLLAR MAN (LP)	15
77	Third World TWS 911	INVESTIGATOR ROCK (LP)	30
89	Trojan TRLPS 272	MY VOICE IS INSURED FOR HALF A MILLION DOLLARS (LP)	15

(see also El Paso, Dennis & Lizzy, Mad Roy, D. Smith, Wailing Souls, Innkeepers, GG Allstars, Stranger Cole, Lizzy & Dennis, Lee)

CRAIG ALDEN
60	London HLW 9224	Crazy Little Horn/Goggle-Eye'd	15

STEVE ALDO (& CHALLENGERS)
64	Decca F 12041	Can I Get A Witness/Baby What You Want Me To Do (with Challengers)	50
66	Parlophone R 5432	Everybody Has To Cry/You're Absolutely Right (solo)	200
66	Parlophone R 5432	Everybody Has To Cry/You're Absolutely Right (solo) (DJ Copy)	150

URIE ALDRIDGE
71	Harry J. HJ 6634	Set Me Free/LLOYD WILLIS: Free Version	8

ALEANNA

MINT VALUE £

(see also John Holt)

ALEANNA
78 Inchecronin INC 7241   ALEANNA (LP) 40

ALEEM
84 Streetwave MKHAN 26   Release Yourself/Dub (12") 20
84 Streetwave MKHAN 61   Get Loose/Release Yourself (12") 15

AKI ALEONG (& HIS LICORICE TWISTERS)
61 Reprise R 20042   Moon River (Twist)/Tonight (Twist) 6

ALESSI
76 A&M AMLH 64608   ALESSI (LP, inner) 20

ALETHIANS
72 Myrrh MST 6506   ONE WAY (LP, David Pope and the Right Angle on side 2) 30
73 Myrrh Gold MYR 1002   R.S.V.P. (LP) 40

ALEX G
14 Lucky Number LUCKY071LP   DSU (LP, with CD) 20
15 Lucky Number LUCKY076LP   TRICK (LP. with CD) 30
15 Lucky Number LUCKY076LP   TRICK (LP. with CD, blue vinyl, 300 only) 50
15 Lucky Number LUCKY077LP   RULES (LP, with free CD, 1000 only) 30
15 Domino WIGLP350   BEACH MUSIC (LP, blue vinyl with free 12") 60
17 Domino WIGLP398X   ROCKET (LP. red vinyl) 40
19 Domino WIGLP451   HOUSE OF SUGAR LP, purple vinyl, glitter sleeve) 30
19 Domino WIGLP451   HOUSE OF SUGAR LP, purple vinyl with free 7", glitter sleeve) 40

ARTHUR ALEXANDER
62 London HLD 9523   You Better Move On/A Shot Of Rhythm And Blues 40
63 London HLD 9566   Where Have You Been/Soldier Of Love 30
63 London HLD 9641   Anna/I Hang My Head And Cry 35
63 London HLD 9667   Go Home Girl/You're The Reason 20
64 London HLD 9899   Black Night/Ole John Amos 20
66 London HLU 10023   (Baby) For You/The Other Woman 20
76 Buddah BDS 439   Everyday I Have To Cry/Everybody Needs Somebody To Love 10
63 London RE-D 1364   ALEXANDER THE GREAT (EP) 40
63 London RE-D 1401   ARTHUR ALEXANDER (EP) 40
62 London HA-D 2457   YOU BETTER MOVE ON (LP) 80
82 Ace CH 66   A SHOT OF RHYTHM AND SOUL (LP) 18
87 Ace CH 207   SOLDIER OF LOVE (LP) 15

DAVID ALEXANDER
74 Rare Earth RES112   Love, Love, Love/Missy 6

GOLDIE ALEXANDER
81 Project PRJ 1   Show You My Love/Get Back 7

JEFF ALEXANDER & HIS ORCHESTRA
58 London HA-P 2130   ALFRED HITCHCOCK PRESENTS - MUSIC TO BE MURDERED BY (LP, mono) 20
58 London SH-P 6012   ALFRED HITCHCOCK PRESENTS - MUSIC TO BE MURDERED BY (LP, stereo) 20

LLOYD ALEXANDER REAL ESTATE
68 President PT 157   Gonna Live Again/Watcha Gonna Do 80

LUCIEN ALEXANDER
67 Polydor 56205   Baby, You've Been On My Mind/Play Along (Miss R) 20

ALEXISONFIRE
04 Sorepoint SORE 026S   Counterparts And Number Them/THE BLED: Ruth Buzzi Better Watch Her Back (die-cut
                            sleeve, purple vinyl) 10
05 Sorepoint SORE 0398   Accidents/No Transitory (p/s, green vinyl) 8
06 Hassle HOFF016LP   CRISIS (LP, die-cut sleeve, 500 only) 60

ALFALPHA
75 EMI 2650   If I Can Just Get Through Tonight/Railroad 8

ALFA MIST
17 Pink Bird 002   ANTIPHON (2-LP, 1st pressing, numbered white labels in finished sleeve) 250
17 Pink Bird 002   ANTIPHON (2-LP, 2nd pressing, orange label, 350 copies in sleeve) 100
18 Black Acre ACRELP011   ANTIPHON (2-LP, 3rd pressing, gatefold sleeve, printed labels) 60
18 Black Acre ACRELP011   ANTIPHON (2-LP, 4th pressing, gatefold sleeve, orange vinyl, printed labels) 50
19 Seiko SEKIT 002   STRUCTURALISM (2-LP) 35

ALF AND TEEP
71 Fab FAB 16   Freedom, Justice and Equality/THREE TOPS: Down At The Boneyard (promo only, black
                            label) 100

ALFI & HARRY
56 London HLU 8242   Trouble With Harry/A Little Beauty (triangular centre, gold lettering on label) 15
57 London HLU 8494   Closing Time/Safari 7

(see also David Seville)

ALFIE
01 Regal (no cat. no.)   Zoom (p/s, 1-track square, 300 only) 8

CLEM ALFORD
74 Columbia SCX 6571   MIRROR IMAGE - THE ELECTRONIC SITAR OF CLEM ALFORD (LP) 40
75 KPM KPM 1183   INDIA (LP, music library issue, side 2 only) 40

(see also Magic Carpet)

ALFRED & MELMOTH
68 Island WI 3130   I Want Someone/ALFRED BROWN: One Scotch One Bourbon One Beer 20

SANDRA ALFRED
58 Oriole CB 1408   Rocket And Roll/Six Day Rock 50

(see also Sandra Barry, Slack Alice)

ALIAS
98 V.I.P. 005   WHO'S STORY (12", EP) 25

ALICE THROUGH THE LOOKING GLASS
69 H&F Recording/SNP (no cat. ALICE THROUGH THE LOOKING GLASS (LP, private pressing, handmade sleeve, actually 1000

ALICE IN CHAINS

MINT VALUE £

no.			
97	Tenth Planet TP 032	by Peter Howell & John Ferdinando	
		ALICE THROUGH THE LOOKING GLASS (LP, reissue, no'd, 1,000 only)	20

(see also Ithaca, Friends, Agincourt, Tomorrow Come Someday, BBC Radiophonic Workshop/Peter Howell)

ALICE IN CHAINS

93	Columbia 659 090-6	Them Bones/We Die Young/Got Me Wrong/Am I Inside (12", no'd, blue vinyl)	40
93	Columbia 659 090-7	Them Bones/We Die Young (p/s, numbered poster)	10
93	Columbia 659 365-7	Angry Chair/I Know Somethin' About You (snakeskin wallet sleeve)	10
95	Columbia 662 623-7	Grind/Nutshell (green vinyl, numbered card)	8
91	Columbia 467201-1	FACELIFT (LP)	200
92	Columbia 472330-1	DIRT (LP, inner)	200
94	Columbia 475713-1	JAR OF FLIES/SAP (LP, yellow vinyl with blue vinyl, 1-sided, etched 12" EP)	150
95	Columbia 481114-1	ALICE IN CHAINS (2-LP, gatefold sleeve, inners)	150
96	Columbia 4843001	MTV UNPLUGGED (2-LP)	150
01	Simply Vinyl SVLP 0025	DIRT (LP, reissue 180gm vinyl)	40
10	Music On Vinyl MOVLP 086	JAR OF FLIES/SAP (2-LP, reissue, gatefold, orange and blue vinyl)	25

(see also Mad Season)

ALICE ISLAND BAND

| 74 | Warren WAR 341 | SPLENDID ISOLATION (LP, with insert, allegedly 50 only) .... | 500 |

ALIEN

| 92 | Alien And Monster MDF15 | How'd Ya Feel/Ruff House (12") .... | 20 |

ALIEN KULTURE

| 81 | RAR LRAR 1 | Asian Youth/Culture Crossover (p/s) .... | 40 |

ALIEN SEX FIEND

84	Anagram 11 ANA 25	E.S.T. (Trip To The Moon)/Boneshaker Baby/I Am A Product (live) (11", PVC sleeve with insert)	10
83	Anagram GRAM 10	WHO'S BEEN SLEEPING IN MY BRAIN (LP)	15
90	Windsong 02	ASF BOX (box set, export issue, 4,000 only, with 3 coloured vinyl singles [12", 11" & 10"], poster, T-shirt & imitation dog turd)	35
93	Anagram GRAM 69	LEGENDARY BATCAVE TAPES (LP)	15
94	Anagram GRAM 80	INFERNO - THE ODYSSEY CONTINUES (2-LP)	25

(see also Demon Preacher, Demons)

ALIENS (1)

| 78 | Alien ALI 001 | When The River Runs Dry/Winds Of Time (no p/s) .... | 40 |

ALIENS (2)

| 07 | EMI 9463868181 | ASTRONOMY FOR DOGS (2-LP) .... | 40 |
| 08 | Petrock LP 002 | LUNA (2-LP) .... | 35 |

(see also Beta Band)

NUSRAT FATEH ALI KHAN

86	Womad 004	BEST OF QAWWAL AND PARTY VOLUME ONE (LP)	30
88	Womad 008	QAWWAL AND PARTY VOLUME TWO (LP)	30
89	Real World RWLP3	SHAHEN-SHAH (LP)	30
90	Real World RWLP15	MUSTT MUSTT (LP)	25
91	Star SRLP5130	MAGIC TOUCH (LP)	70

ALIMANTADO (DR.)

73	Atra ATRA 007	Return Of Muhummad Ali/Black Love	15
75	Sun & Star ST 003	Best Dress Chicken/She Wreng-Ep	20
77	Greensleeves GRE 002	Born For A Purpose/Reason For Living (with the Rebels)	10
78	Virgin VOLE 1	Slavery Let I Go/Find The One (12")	10
78	Greensleeves GRE 5	Still Alive/Life All Over (with the Rebels)	6
78	Greensleeves GRE 13	Best Dressed Chicken In Town/Can't Conquer Natty Dreadlocks (yellow vinyl)	15
79	Greensleeves GRED 10	Born For A Purpose/Reason For Living/Still Alive/Life All Over (12", with the Rebels)	25
79	Greensleeves GRED 17	Sitting In The Park/Skanking In The Park (12", with the Rebels)	10
80	Isda SUS 11	It Cold In A Babylon/Version (12")	10
78	Greensleeves GREL 1	BEST DRESSED CHICKEN IN TOWN (LP)	30
79	Ital ISA 5000	KINGS BREAD (LP)	20
81	Greensleeves GREL 22	SONS OF THUNDER (LP)	25

ALKALINE TRIO

03	Vagrant 980 123-9	GOOD MOURNING (LP)	60
05	Vagrant VRUK 012LP	CRIMSON (LP, red vinyl, stickered sleeve, inner)	15
08	V2 VVR1051181	AGONY & IRONY (LP)	25
10	Heart & Skull HOFF092LP	THIS ADDICTION (LP, white vinyl)	20
11	Vagrant VR 353	FROM HERE TO INFIRMARY (LP, reissue, green vinyl)	20
11	Vagrant VR 353	FROM HERE TO INFIRMARY (LP, reissue, blue vinyl, 300 only)	25

ALKATRAZ

| 76 | Rockfield UAS 30001 | DOING A MOONLIGHT (LP) .... | 20 |

(see also Man, Quicksand)

ALL ABOUT EVE

| 85 | Eden EDEN 1 | D For Desire/Don't Follow Me (12", p/s) .... | 15 |

(see also Ghost Dance, Gene Loves Jezebel)

ALL BECAUSE THE LADY LOVES

| 87 | Sweet Release 02 | IF YOU RISK NOTHING (EP, with insert) .... | 10 |

ALL SORTS OF FOLK

| 72 | Private Pressing CH 101 | ALL SORTS OF FOLK (LP) .... | 175 |

ALL SOUNDBWOY OUT

| 07 | ASBO 001 | ASBO (1-sided white label 12") .... | 30 |

(see also Loefa)

ALLAH & MR. LONELY

| 73 | Fab FAB 190 | Hide & Seek/CANCER ALL STARS : Version (actually by Allen & Mr. Lonely) .... | 8 |

JOHNNIE ALLAN

| 74 | Oval 1001 | Promised Land/SHELTON DUNAWAY: Betty And Dupree .... | 7 |
| 78 | Oval Stiff LOT 1 | Promised Land/PETE FOWLER: One Heart, One Song (p/s) .... | 6 |

Richard ALLAN

MINT VALUE £

RICHARD ALLAN
60	Parlophone R 4634	As Time Goes By/Only One	20
60	Parlophone R 4711	Don't Ever Say You're Gonna Leave Me/Poetry In Motion	6

ALL DAY
73	Private pressing	YORK POP MUSIC PROJECT (LP)	150

ANNISTEEN ALLEN
55	Capitol CL 14264	Fujiyama Mama/Wheels Of Love	200
57	Brunswick 05639	Don't Nobody Move/The Money Tree	40

DAEVID ALLEN
75	Virgin VS 123	Fred The Fish/It's The Time Of Your Life (p/s, promo only)	8
79	Charly CY 51056	Much Too Old/I Am A Freud (with New York Gong, p/s with insert)	6
75	Caroline C 1512	BANANA MOON (LP, black and white 'Twins' label, ends in a continuous loop)	40
76	Virgin V 5024	GOOD MORNING! (LP, by Daevid Allen & Euterpe)	30
77	Affinity AFF3	NOW IS THE HAPPIEST TIME OF YOUR LIFE (LP)	20
79	Charly CRL 5015	N'EXISTE PAS! (LP, with lyric insert)	20
79	Charly CR 30165	BANANA MOON (LP, reissue, gatefold)	20
82	Charly CR 30218	DIVIDED ALIEN PLAYBAX 80 (LP)	15
82	Shanghai HAI 201	THE DEATH OF ROCK AND OTHER ENTRANCES (LP)	15
89	Demi Monde DMLP 1019	THE OWL AND THE TREE (LP)	25
90	Demi Monde DMLP 1025	AUSTRALIA AQUIARIA (LP)	25
90	Voiceprint VP 101	THE AUSTRALIAN YEARS (LP)	25
13	Vinyl Lovers 901462	STROKING THE TAIL OF THE BIRD (LP, with free 7", reissue, with Gilli Smythe and Harry Williamson)	20

(see also Gong, Planet Gong, Soft Machine)

DEAN ALLEN
58	London HLM 8698	Rock Me To Sleep/Ooh-Ooh Baby Baby	18

JEFF ALLEN
57	HMV JO 477	That'll Be The Day/Guilty Mind (export issue)	25

LEE ALLEN (& HIS BAND)
58	HMV POP 452	Walkin' With Mr. Lee/Promenade	20
59	Top Rank JAR 265	Cat Walk/Creole Alley	10
59	Top Rank JKR 8020	WALKIN' WITH MR LEE (EP)	20
62	Ember ELR 3312	MOOD MUSIC LIBRARY (LP, uncredited library issue, generic sleeve)	30

(see also Huey 'Piano' Smith & Clowns)

LILY ALLEN
06	No Label LILY 001	LDN/Knock Em Down (500 only, jukebox centre)	6
06	Regal 3694931	ALRIGHT, STILL (LP, approx 200 pressed, black die cut sleeve, stickered)	40
09	Regal REG 151LP	IT'S NOT ME IT'S YOU (LP)	20

MAURICE ALLEN
58	Pye Nixa 7N 15128	Ooh Baby/Rockhearted	15

PATRICK ALLEN
77	Kab KB 5540	Groovy Feeling/Instrumental	20

REX ALLEN
54	Brunswick 05341	This Ole House/They Were Doin' The Mambo (with Tex Williams)	20
62	Mercury AMT 1191	Don't Go Near The Indians/Touched So Deeply	8

(see also Tex Williams, Patti Page)

RODNEY ALLEN
88	Subway 18T	CIRCLE LINE EP (12" p/s)	15
87	Subway SUBORG 2	HAPPYSAD (LP)	15

(Blue Aeroplanes)

STEVE ALLEN
72	M&M FFMS 10021	Life On Mars/Baby I'm A Want You/Everything I Own/Diary (Medley) (demo)	20

TONY ALLEN (1)
00	Strut STRUTAALP001	JEALOUSY (LP, reissue with Africa 70)	25
00	Strut STRUTAALP002	NO DISCRIMINATION (LP, reissue with Afro Messengers)	25
00	Strut STRUTAALP003	NO ACCOMODATION FOR LAGOS (LP, reissue with Africa 70)	25

TONY ALLEN (2)
84	Earthworks MWKS 3001	N.E.P.A. (Never Expect Power Always)/N.E.P.A. Dance Dub/When One Road Close (Another One Go Open)/Road Close Dance Dub (12", p/s)	15

VERNON ALLEN
64	R&B JB 169	Far I Come/Babylon	1250

(VERNON) ALLEN & (MILTON) HAMILTON
66	Blue Beat BB 348	It Is I/Baby What's More	15
66	Blue Beat BB 353	You're The Angel/Someone Like You	15

ALLENS
75	Mowest MW 3029	High Tide/California Music	6

ALLEY
74	Jay Boy BOY 82	Singing In Poverty/Tip Toe	6

ALLEY CATS
59	Vogue V 9155	Last Night/Snap-Crackle And Pop	10

ALL FALL DOWN
83	Confidential KIS 1	Arechibo/A Changing Face (12")	45

ALLIES
79	Harp HSP 1025	Plush Living/Computer (p/s, 500 only despite numbering)	8

ALLISON
94	Twinkle NG 544	WAILING (LP)	15

GENE ALLISON
58	London HLU 8605	Hey, Hey, I Love You/You Can Make It If You Try	125

GEORGE ALLISON
80	Cartridge CR-D 107	Ten To One/Hard Times (12")	150
85	Gibbous GBM 15	EXCLUSIVE (LP)	20

JERRY ALLISON & CRICKETS
65 Liberty LIB 10196 — Now Hear This/Everybody's Got A Little Problem 20

(see also Crickets, Ivan)

LUTHER ALLISON
71 Delmark DS 625 — LOVE ME MAMA (LP, blue label) 25

MOSE ALLISON
61 Fontana H 292 — Baby Please Don't Go/Deed I Do 20
64 Columbia DB 7330 — I Love The Life I Live/Life Is Suicide 8
59 Esquire EP 214 — PARCHMAN FARM (EP) 15
64 Columbia SEG 8353 — ALLISON SINGS THE BLUES (EP) 20
59 Esquire 32-051 — BACK COUNTRY SUITE (LP) 25
59 Esquire 32-071 — LOCAL COLOUR (LP) 25
59 Esquire 32-083 — YOUNG MAN MOSE (LP) 25
60 Esquire 32-094 — CREEK BANK (LP) 20
61 Esquire 32-131 — AUTUMN SONG (LP) 20
62 Esquire 32-171 — RAMBLIN' WITH MOSE (LP) 15
63 London HA-K 8083 — SWINGIN' MACHINE (LP, as Mose Allison Jazz Group) 15
64 Columbia SX 6058 — V-8 FORD (LP) 15

ALLISONS (U.K.)
61 Fontana TFL 5135 — ARE YOU SURE (LP, mono) 20
61 Fontana STFL 558 — ARE YOU SURE (LP, stereo) 30

ALLISONS (U.S.)
64 Stateside SS 289 — Surfer Street/Money (vocal: Darlene Love) 35

(see also Blossoms, Darlene Love)

ALLMAN BROTHERS BAND
69 Atco 228 033 — THE ALLMAN BROTHERS BAND (LP, gatefold sleeve) 100
71 Atco 2400 032 — IDLEWILD SOUTH (LP) 80
71 Atlantic 2402 035 — AT FILLMORE EAST (2-LP, 1st pressing, plum/orange labels, gatefold sleeve) 50
71 Atlantic K60011 — AT FILLMORE EAST (2-LP, 2nd pressing, green/orange labels, gatefold sleeve) 20
72 Capricorn K67501 — EAT A PEACH (2-LP, gatefold sleeve with insert) 30
73 Capricorn K47507 — BROTHERS AND SISTERS (LP, gatefold sleeve with insert) 15
75 Warner Bros. 2659 034 — EAT A PEACH (LP, reissue, gatefold) 15

(see also Gregg Allman, Duane & Gregg Allman, Allman Joys, Hour Glass)

DUANE & GREGG ALLMAN
73 Polydor 2310 235 — DUANE & GREGG ALLMAN (LP, laminated sleeve) 15

(see also Allman Brothers, Gregg Allman)

GREGG ALLMAN
73 Capricorn K 47508/CP0116 — LAID BACK (LP) 15

(see also Allman Brothers, Duane & Gregg Allman)

ALLMAN JOYS
73 Mercury 6398 005 — ALLMAN JOYS (LP) 20

ALL NATION ROCKERS
93 Sound N Presuure SNP 002 — Rockers Arise/Rockers Version/Travelling Version (12") 25
95 Sound N Presuure SNP 004 — Once Inna Dubtime/Talking Dread Version/Ruud Boy Sweeps The Rebound Version (12", as A.N.R.) 20

ALL NIGHT BAND
79 Contact CON 5 — Lovely Ladies/It's My Life 15

ALL THE RAGE
82 Rage RR 001 — Concrete City/Emergency (p/s) 150

JOHNNY ALMOND MUSIC MACHINE
69 Deram DM 266 — Solar Level/To R.K. 35
69 Deram DML/SML 1043 — PATENT PENDING (LP) 70
70 Deram DML 1057 — HOLLYWOOD BLUES (LP, mono) 80
70 Deram SML 1057 — HOLLYWOOD BLUES (LP, stereo) 60

(see also Alan Price Set, Zoot Money, Paul Williams Set, John Mayall & Bluesbreakers, Mark Almond, Jon Mark)

ALMOND LETTUCE
68 Columbia DB 8442 — The Tree Dog Song/To Henry With Hope 6
69 Philips BF 1764 — Magic Circle/Twenty Weary Miles 10

MARC ALMOND
82 Lyntone LYN 12505 — Discipline (as 'Marc Almond & Friends', pink flexidisc with Flexipop issue 23. Friends are Throbbing Gristle) 20
84 Gutter Hearts GH 1 — BITE BACK + BLUES (fan club-only LP, credited to "Raoul & The Ruined") 30
88 Parlophone PSR 500 — Kept Boy (1-sided 7" with etched reverse - intended to be free with THE STARS WE ARE LP - but plans scrapped) 30

(see also Soft Cell, Marc & Mambas, Burmoe Brothers, Vicious Pink Phenomena, Flesh Volcano, Annie Hogan, Sally Timms, Gene Pitney)

ALMOND MARZIPAN
70 Trend TNT 53 — Open Up Your Heart/Summer Love 15
70 Trend TNT 55 — Marie Take A Chance/I'll Forget You 6

ALMOST A DREAM
73 Box BX1 — Something's Moving/The Undead 30

ALMOST ALONE
84 Family FAM 001 — Blue City/It's So Sad (p/s) 20

ALPHA & OMEGA
88 Roaring Lion RL 001 — Gather Together/On It's Way 80
92 Alpha & Omega A&O 501 — Watch And Pray/Yemenite Chant 35
96 Alpha & Omega A&O 1002 — Rastafari/Version/Words Of Thy Mouth/Version (10") 25
96 A&O 1201 — Ancient African Civilisation/DISCIPLES & ALPHA & OMEGA: Eternal Dub (12") 25
90 A&O 001 — DANIEL IN THE LIONS DEN (LP) 60
92 A&O 009 — KING & QUEEN (LP) 70
92 A&O 027 — WATCH AND PRAY (LP) 70
92 A&O 077 — ALMIGHTY JAH (LP, listed as Alpha & Omega Meets Dub Judah) 40

ALPHABET

MINT VALUE £

93	A&O 093	EVERYDAY LIFE (LP)	50
94	A&O 094	SAFE IN THE ARK (LP)	40
96	A&O 096	TREE OF LIFE (LP)	30
96	A&O 097	VOICE IN THE WILDERNESS (LP)	35

ALPHABET
| 81 | No Label or Cat. No | This Strange Love/The Handsome Beast (p/s) | 15 |

ALPHA BETA
| 79 | Magnet MAG 158 | Space Invaders/Innocent (p/s) | 10 |

ORVILLE ALPHANSO
| 65 | Caribou CRC 1 | Bellylick/Inspiration | 40 |

ALPHASTONE
| 90s | Enraptured RAPTLP 33 | LIFE IS A MOTORWAY EP (2 x 12", gatefold sleeve, limited issue) | 10 |
| 90s | Enraptured RAPTLP 18 | ELASTICATED WAVEBAND (LP, clear vinyl, 100 only) | 15 |

CARLTON ALPHONSO
| 67 | Pama PM 700 | Where In This World/Peace Makers | 50 |
| 69 | Grape GR 3000 | Belittle Me/Keep Your Love | 30 |

CLYDE ALPHONSO
| 69 | Studio One SO 2076 | Good Enough/Let The Music Play | 130 |

PANCHO ALPHONSO AND THE REVOLUTIONARIES
| 79 | Attack ATT TACK 8 | Never Give Up In A Babylon/Love Is A Pleasure (12") | 20 |
| 78 | Trojan TRLS 165 | NEVER GET TO ZION (LP) | 18 |

(see also Alphonso Pancho)

ROLAND ALPHONSO (ALIAS ROLAND AL)
61	Blue Beat BB 58	Blackberry Brandy/ALVIN & CECIL: Marjorie	25
62	Blue Beat BB 112	Four Corners Of The World (with Alley Cats)/SHINERS: Romantic Shuffle	30
64	R&B JB 161	Mr President/The MAYTALS: A Man Who Knows	25
64	R&B JB 164	Crime Wave/MAYTALS: Hello Honey	45
65	Island WI 217	El Pussy Cat/LORD BRYNNER: Tiger In Your Tank	25
65	Ska Beat JB 210	Nimble Foot/ANDY & JOEY: Love Is Stronger	70
65	Ska Beat JB 216	Nuclear Weapon (with Baba Brooks)/STRANGER COLE: Love Thy Neighbour	50
65	Rio R 5804	Jazz Ska/HYACINTH: Oh Gee	50
66	Blue Beat BB 356	Just A Closer Walk/Jericho Train	500
66	Island WI 259	James Bond/LEE PERRY: Just Keep It Up	350
66	Doctor Bird DB 1010	From Russia With Love/Cleopatra (with Soul Brothers)	130
66	Doctor Bird DB 1011	Sufferer's Choice (with Soul Brothers)/SOULETTES: I Want To Be	50
66	Doctor Bird DB 1013	WAILERS: Rude Boy/ROLANDO AL & SOUL BROTHERS: Ringo's Theme (This Boy)	90
66	Doctor Bird DB 1017	Sugar And Spice/Get Out Of My Life (with Soul Brothers)	25
66	Doctor Bird DB 1020	Phoenix City (with Soul Brothers)/DEACONS: Men Alone	35
66	Doctor Bird DB 1023	Doctor Ring-A-Ding/FREDDIE & HEARTACHES: Here Is My Heart	80
66	Doctor Bird DB 1035	I Love You/Song Of Love	25
66	Doctor Bird DB 1039	WAILERS: Rasta Put It On/ROLAND AL & SOUL BROTHERS: Ska With Ringo	150
66	Ska Beat JB 231	Rinky Dink (So Good) (with Studio One Orchestra)/ SCRATCH & DYNAMITES: Deacon Johnson	45
67	Pyramid PYR 6003	Middle East/Wise Man	30
67	Pyramid PYR 6005	Women Of The World (& Beverley's Allstars)/SPANISHTONIANS: The Kisses	30
67	Pyramid PYR 6006	On The Move (& Beverley's Allstars)/DESMOND DEKKER & ACES: It's A Shame	50
67	Pyramid PYR 6007	Jungle Bit (& Beverley's Allstars)/NORMAN GRANT: Somebody Please Help Me	25
67	Pyramid PYR 6008	The Cat/DESMOND DEKKER & ACES: Rudy Got Soul	40
67	Pyramid PYR 6009	Guantanamera Ska (& Beverley's Allstars)/SPANISHTONIANS: Suffer Me Not	30
67	Pyramid PYR 6011	Nothing For Nothing/DESMOND DEKKER & ACES: Rude Boy Train	25
67	Pyramid PYR 6018	Sock It To Me (& Beverley's Allstars)/SPANISHTONIANS: Rudie Gets Plenty	100
68	Pyramid PYR 6022	Whiter Shade Of Pale/On The Move	80
68	Pyramid PYR 6030	Dreamland/MAYTALS: 54-46, That's My Number	30
68	Pyramid PYR 6043	Stream Of Life/MAYTALS: Struggle	50
68	Coxsone CS 7077	Reggae In The Grass/ROY RICHARDS: Get Smart	45
69	Gas GAS 112	A Thousand Tons Of Megaton (actually by Derrick Morgan)/Musical Resurrection	40
70	Punch PH 39	Roll On (& Upsetters)/CARL DAWKINS: True Love	65
71	Banana BA 340	Mellow Mood (Way To My Heart)/MAYTALS: Marching On	60
12	Duke Reid's THB 7017	Easter Bonnet/STRANGER AND KEN: Feeling Of Love	15
68	Hi Note BSLP 5001	ABC ROCK STEADY (with the Originals Orchestra)	150

ALPHORAS
| 78 | Junior JR 107 | Running Out Of Love/It Pains Me (actually by LEROY SMART) | 15 |

ALPINES
| 68 | Double D DD 110 | Get Ready/CARIBBEATS: Come Back Charlie | 30 |

ALQUIN
| 73 | Polydor 2480 152 | MARKS (LP) | 15 |

ALSATIANS
| 80 | SRT SRTS/80/CUS-629 | Teen Romance/Our Man In Marrakesh (no p/s, 1000 only) | 40 |

RITA ALSTON
| 70 | Trojan TR 7751 | Popcorn Funky Reggae/NAT COLE: My Love | 25 |
| 70 | Trojan TR 7752 | All Kinds Of Everything/CARL LEVEY: Instrumental Version | 6 |

(see also Rita, Nat Cole)

SHIRLEY ALSTON
| 75 | London HLA 10506 | I'd Rather Not Be Loving You/Can't Stop Singin' (Bout The Boy I Love) | 25 |
| 75 | London SHA 8491 | WITH A LITTLE HELP FROM MY FRIENDS (LP) | 25 |

(see also Shirelles)

ALTECS
| 61 | London HLU 9387 | Easy/Recess | 15 |

(see also The Black Dog)

ALTERATIONS

MINT VALUE £

ALTERATIONS
78	Bead Records BEAD 9	CUSACK/BERESFORD/DAY/TOOP (LP)	30

ALTERED STATES
88	Red Rhino CALC 31	IS ANYONE OUT THERE? (LP)	60

ALTERN 8
92	Network A8 PIC 1	FULL ON...MASK HYSTERIA (LP)	15
92	Network TOP LP1	FULL ON...MASK HYSTERIA (LP & 12")	20

(see also Progressive Logic, Mark Archer)

ALTERNATIVE
82	Crass Records 221984/8	IN NOMINE PATRI (EP)	10
83	Corpus Christi CHRIST 13	IF THEY TREAT YOU LIKE SHIT - ACT LIKE MANURE (LP, insert)	50

ALTERNATIVE BRITISH ARMY
80	Hit HIT 1	Angry - The Killer Was A Cop/Bleak Streets (p/s)	10

ALTERNATIVE TV
77	Sniffing Glue SG 75 RPS	Love Lies Limp (1-sided flexidisc with Sniffing Glue fanzine issue 12)	20
77	Deptford Fun City DFC 002	How Much Longer/You Bastard (p/s)	15
77	Deptford Fun City DFC 02	How Much Longer/You Bastard (p/s, labelled 'alternate versions')	15
78	Deptford Fun City DFC 04	Life After Life/Life After Dub (p/s)	15
78	Deptford Fun City DFC 05	Life/Love Lies Limp (p/s)	15
78	Deptford Fun City DFC 07	Action Time Vision/Another Coke (live p/s)	15
79	Deptford Fun City DFC 10	The Force Is Blind/Lost In Room (Vibing Up The Senile Man) (p/s, last track uncredited)	10
85	Noiseville V001	Welcome To The End Of Fun/Anti/Death Time (12", p/s)	12
86	Noiseville V002	Victory/Repulsion/You Never Know (12", p/s)	12
78	Deptford Fun City DLP 01	THE IMAGE HAS CRACKED (LP)	40
78	Deptford Fun City DLP 02	WHAT YOU SEE IS ... WHAT YOU ARE (LP, 1 side by Here & Now)	20
78	Deptford Fun City DFC 3	VIBING UP THE SENILE MAN (LP)	20
79	Crystal CLP 01	LIVE AT THE RAT CLUB (LP)	18
80	Deptford Fun City DLP 05	ACTION TIME VISION (LP, with inner sleeve)	20
90	Chapter 22 CHAP LP 51	DRAGON LOVE (LP)	15

(see also Mark Perry, Good Missionaries, The Door & The Window, Reflections, Jools Holland, Alex Fergusson, Rat & Whale)

ALTERNATORS
78	Energy NRG 001	No Answers/The Kid Don't Know (no p/s)	60

ALTERNOMEN UNLIMITED
79	Object OM 06	Facade/Connections (p/s)	6

(see also Spherical Objects, Steve Miro & Eyes)

ALTHEA & DONNA
78	Front Line VOLE 7	Going To Negril/The West (12")	12
78	Virgin Frontline FL1012	UPTOWN TOP RANKING (LP)	25
01	Front Line LPFL 2023	UPTOWN TOP RANKING (LP, reissue)	15

ALTON (ELLIS) & EDDY
60	Blue Beat BB 17	Muriel/CLUE J. & HIS BLUES BLASTERS: Silky	15
62	Island WI 009	My Love Divine/Let Me Dream	20

(see also Alton Ellis)

ALVARO
77	Squeaky Shoes SSRM 1	DRINKING MY OWN SPERM (LP)	20
79	Squeaky Shoes SSRM 2	MUMS MILK NOT POWDER (LP)	15

(see also 101'ers)

ALVYN
69	Morgan MR 18S	You've Gotta Have An Image/Mind The Gap	15

ALWAYS
84	Inertial ERT 6A	Late Again/Sounds From Music (p/s)	8
86	El GPO 16T	ARIEL (12", p/s)	15
87	El GPO 27T	METROLAND (12", p/s)	15
88	El GPOT 34	Thames Valley Leather Club/Amateur (10", p/s)	15
88	El ACME 12	THAMES VALLEY LEATHER CLUB (LP)	20

ALY-US
92	Cooltempo 12COOLDJX 266	Follow Me (Remixes) (12")	10

AMALGAM (1)
69	Transatlantic TRA 196	A PRAYER FOR PEACE (LP)	70
73	A Records A 002	PLAY BLACKWELL & HIGGINS (LP)	50

AMALGAM (2)
80	Impetus IMPLP 47901	WIPE OUT (4-LP box set with booklet)	50

GLEN AMAMS
69	Escort ES 804	Rich In Love/WOODPECKERS: Zumbelly	45

(see also Glen Adams)

AMANDA
76	DJM DJS 10730	I'm Gonna Enjoy Christmas/Catch That Boy	7

AMAZIAH
74	Sunrise SR 001	STRAIGHT TALKER (LP, private pressing with insert)	75

AMAZING BLONDEL
70	Bell SBLL 131	THE AMAZING BLONDEL AND A FEW FACES (LP, blue/silver label)	300
70	Island ILPS 9136	EVENSONG (LP, gatefold sleeve)	40
71	Island ILPS 9156	FANTASIA LINDUM (LP, with inner lyric sleeve)	30
71	Island ILPS 9156	FANTASIA LINDUM (LP, without inner lyric sleeve)	20
72	Island ILPS 9205	ENGLAND (LP, gatefold)	25
73	Island ILPS 9257	BLONDEL (LP, gatefold sleeve)	20
74	DJM DJF 20442	MULGRAVE STREET (LP)	15
75	DJM DJF 20446	INSPIRATION (LP)	15
13	Prog Temple PTLP 8008	THE AMAZING BLONDEL AND A FEW FACES (LP, reissue)	15

(see also Dimples, Gospel Garden, Methusilah)

AMAZING DANCING BAND

MINT VALUE £

AMAZING DANCING BAND
- 68   Verve VS 567 — Deep Blue Train/Simon Smith & His Amazing Dancing Bear 10
- 67   Verve VLP/SVLP 9214 — AMAZING DANCING BAND (LP, mono/stereo) 20
- 68   Verve VLP 9214 — VOLUME TWO - THESE BOOTS ARE MADE FOR DANCIN' (LP, mono) 18
- 68   Verve SVLP 9214 — VOLUME TWO - THESE BOOTS ARE MADE FOR DANCIN' (LP, stereo) 15

AMAZING FRIENDLY APPLE
- 69   Decca F 12887 — Water Woman/Magician 100

AMAZING SPACE FROGS
- 79   Ribbett RIB 1 — THE DIRTY HABITS EP 300

(see also Bascsax, Blitzkrieg Bop, No Way)

AMAZON
- 81   Megamusic MEGA 1 — Fallen Angel/Hypnotising You (p/s) 20

AMAZON TRUST
- 70   Polydor 2058065 — Run Baby Run/Sheila Lee 50
- 71   Jade JD 03 — Seeing What I See/Night Of Fear 100

AMAZONS
- 15   Goth Cruise (No Cat. No.) — Junk Food Forever/Something In The Water (p/s) 20

AMAZORBLADES
- 77   NS 20 — Common Truth/Mess Around (p/s) 7

AMBASSADOR 277
- 88   El GPUT37 — Pop Up Man/Malediction (10" p/s) 10

AMBER ASYLUM
- 96   Elfenblut SAG 1 — FROZEN IN AMBER (LP, inner) 15

AMBERGRIS
- 70   Paramount SPFL 262 — AMBERGRIS (LP) 15

AMBER RUN
- 15   RCA 88875069521 — 5AM (LP) 30

AMBER SQUAD
- 80   Sound Of Leicester ST 1 — (I Can't) Put My Finger On You/Tell You A Lie (p/s) 25
- 80   Dead Good DEAD 17 — Can We Go Dancing?/You Should See (What I Do To You In My Dreams) (p/s) 20

AMBOY DUKES (U.K.)
- 68   Polydor 56228 — Judy In Disguise/Who's Foolin' Who 10
- 68   Polydor 56243 — Simon Says/The Marquis 10

(AMERICAN) AMBOY DUKES
- 68   Fontana TF 971 — Let's Go Get Stoned/It's Not True 20
- 67   Fontana (S)TL 5468 — THE AMBOY DUKES (LP) 75
- 69   London HA-T/SH-T 8378 — JOURNEY TO THE CENTER OF THE MIND (LP, as American Amboy Dukes) 80
- 69   London HA-T/SH-T 8292 — MIGRATION (LP, as American Amboy Dukes) 45
- 74   Discreet DS 2203 — TOOTH, FANG AND CLAW (LP) 15

(see also Ted Nugent)

SAMMY AMBROSE
- 65   Stateside SS 385 — This Diamond Ring/Bad Night 100
- 65   Stateside SS 399 — Monkey See Monkey Do/Welcome To Dreamsville (DJ Copy) 400
- 65   Stateside SS 399 — Monkey See Monkey Do/Welcome To Dreamsville 250
- 87   Kent 6T3 — Welcome To Dreamsville/PLATTERS: Not My Girl 25

AMBROSE SLADE
- 69   Fontana TF 1015 — Genesis/Roach Daddy 300
- 69   Fontana STL 5492 — BEGINNINGS (LP, laminated sleeve, black label with silver print; beware of counterfeits with matt sleeve & black & white label) 900
- 75   Contour 6870 678 — BEGINNINGS OF SLADE (LP, reissue, different cover & running order, withdrawn) 70
- 10   Morgan Blue Town BT5006 — BEGINNINGS (LP, reissue, 750 only with insert & signed certificate) 40

(see also Slade, 'N Betweens)

AMEBIX
- 82   Spiderleg SDL 6 — Who's The Enemy/Carnage/No Gods No Masters/Enemies (p/s) 30
- 83   Spiderleg SDL 10 — Winter/Beginning Of The End (p/s) 25
- 82   Spiderleg SDLP 14 — NO SANCTUARY (LP) 30
- 85   Alternative Tentacles VIRUS46 — ARISE (LP) 50
- 87   Heavy Metal HMRLP 99 — MONOLITH (LP) 25
- 10   Back On Black BOBV217LP — MONOLITH (LP, clear vinyl reissue) 18

AMEN CORNER
- 67   Deram DM 136 — Gin House Blues/I Know (early copies entitled "Gin House" on label) 6
- 67   Deram DM 151 — The World Of Broken Hearts/Nema 7
- 68   Deram DM 197 — High In The Sky/Run Run Run 6
- 69   Immediate IM 073 — (If Paradise Is) Half As Nice/Hey Hey Girl 6
- 69   Immediate IM 081 — Hello Susie/Evil Man's Gonna Win 6
- 69   Immediate IM 084 — Get Back/Farewell To The Real Magnificent Seven 6
- 69   Immediate AS 3 — So Fine (promo only 'single sampler' for IMSP 023) 20
- 68   Deram DML/SML 1021 — ROUND AMEN CORNER (LP) 30
- 69   Immediate IMSP 023 — THE NATIONAL WELSH COAST LIVE EXPLOSION COMPANY (LP, g/fold sleeve, pink label) .. 30
- 69   Immediate IMSP 028 — FAREWELL TO THE REAL MAGNIFICENT SEVEN (LP, gatefold sleeve) 30

(see also Fairweather, Mayfield's Mule, Judas Jump)

AMERICAN BREED
- 67   CBS 2888 — Step Out Of Your Mind/The Same Old Thing 10
- 68   Stateside SS 2078 — Bend Me Shape Me/Mindrocker 10
- 68   Dot DOT 101 — Green Light/Don't It Make You Cry 15
- 68   Dot DOT 106 — Ready, Willing And Able/Take Me If You Want Me 8
- 67   Dot DOLP 255 — AMERICAN BREED (LP) 15
- 68   Dot (S)LPD 502 — BEND ME, SHAPE ME (LP) 15
- 68   Dot (S)LPD 507 — NO WAY TO TREAT A LADY (LP, soundtrack) 20
- 68   Dot (S)LPD 518 — PUMPKIN, POWDER, SCARLET AND GREEN (LP) 20

AMERICAN GYPSY

MINT VALUE £

AMERICAN GYPSY
71	CBS 7027	Gypsy Queen Pt 1/Dead & Gone	12
70	CBS 64276	AMERICAN GYPSY (2-LP)	30

AMERICAN JAM (BAND)
72	Parlophone R5971	American Jam/Natures Child	20
74	Young Blood YB 1056	Jam Jam/Back On The Road	18

(see also Kansas Hook)

AMERICAN MUSIC CLUB
87	Zippo ZONG 0202	ENGINE (LP, with inner sleeve)	15
88	Demon FIEND 134	CALIFORNIA (LP)	15
89	Demon FIEND 151	UNITED KINGDOM (LP)	15
93	Virgin V2708	MERCURY (LP)	20

AMERICAN POETS
66	London HLC 10037	She Blew A Good Thing/Out To Lunch (as American Poets) (DJ copy)	200
66	London HLC 10037	She Blew A Good Thing/Out To Lunch (as American Poets)	100
71	United Artists UP 35308	She Blew A Good Thing/Out To Lunch (reissue, as Poets)	20

AMERICAN SPRING
72	United Artists UP 35376	Good Time/Sweet Mountain	15
72	United Artists UP 35421	Mama Said/Tennessee Waltz	15
73	CBS CBS 1590	Shyin' Away/Falling In Love	20
72	United Artists UAG 29363	AMERICAN SPRING (LP, "Tree" cover)	50
72	United Artists UAG 29363	AMERICAN SPRING (LP, "Tree" gatefold cover with picture of group)	60

(see also Beach Boys, Honeys)

AMERICAN YOUTH CHOIR
71	Polydor 2066 013	Together We Can Make It/Keep Your Fine Self Near Me	30

AMES BROTHERS
54	HMV 7M 179	I Can't Believe That You're In Love/Boogie Woogie Maxixe	20
55	HMV 7M 281	The Naughty Lady Of Shady Lane/Addio	10
57	RCA RCA 1015	Rocking Shoes/Tammy	8

NANCY AMES
66	Columbia DB 7809	Friends And Lovers Forever/I've Got A Lot Of Love (Left In Me)	30
66	Columbia DB 8039	Cry Softly/I Don't Want To Talk About It (DJ copy)	200
66	Columbia DB 8039	Cry Softly/I Don't Want To Talk About It	100

AMIGO
76	Lucky LY 6015	Judas A No Rasta/Version	70

AMIN-PECK
82	Connection CON 8201	Love Disgrace/Singing In The Wind (p/s)	40
82	Connection CONT 8204	Girls On Me/Anxiety/Coda (12")	15

AMITY
76	Red Rag RRR 001	AMITY (LP)	150

AMM
66	Incus EP 1	AT THE ROUNDHOUSE (EP)	80
67	Elektra EUKS 7256	AMM MUSIC (LP)	200
78	Matchless MR 03	TO HEAR AND BACK AGAIN (LP)	40
81	Matchless MR 5	THE CRYPT (2-LP first pressing, box set, inserts, no text on front cover)	90
83	Matchless MR 6	GENERATIVE THEMES (LP)	40
87	Matchless MR13	INEXHAUSTABLE DOCUMENT (LP)	30
88	Matchless MR 5	THE CRYPT (2-LP reissue box set, with rotated radio and text, inserts)	60
90	Pogus O201-4	COMBINE AND LAMINATES (LP)	20

(see also Eddie Provost Band)

ALBERT AMMONS
54	Mercury MG 25012	ALBERT AMMONS (10" LP)	20

(see also [Big] Joe Turner)

ALBERT AMMONS, PETE JOHNSON & MEADE 'LUX' LEWIS
55	Columbia SEG 7528	SHOUT FOR JOY (EP)	10

(see also Pete Johnson, Meade 'Lux' Lewis)

GENE AMMONS (BAND)
60	Starlite ST45 017	Echo Chamber Blues/Ammons' Boogie	40
63	Starlite ST45 097	Anna/Cae' Cae'	10
58	Esquire 32-047	HI FI JAM SESSION (LP)	20
59	Esquire 32-077	FUNKY (LP)	30
60	Esquire 32-097	JAMMIN' WITH GENE (LP)	25
62	Esquire 32-147	BLUE GENE (LP)	20
63	Esquire 32-177	BOSS TENOR (LP)	25
63	Esquire 32-178	BAD! BOSSA NOVA (LP)	25
72	Prestige PR 24021	JUG & DODO (LP, with Dodo Marmarosa)	15
73	Prestige PR 10019	YOU TALK THAT TALK (LP)	15
73	Prestige PR 10021	BROTHER JUG (LP)	20

AMON DÜÜL
81	Illuminated JAMS 24	HAWK MEETS PENGUIN (LP)	20

AMON DÜÜL II
70	Liberty LBF 15355	Archangel's Thunderbird/Burning Sister	25
69	Liberty LBS 83279	PHALLUS DEI (LP)	250
70	Liberty LSP 101/LBS 83359	YETI (2-LP, 1st pressing, textured gatefold sleeve)	125
71	United Artists UAD 60003/4	DANCE OF THE LEMMINGS (2-LP, laminated gatefold sleeve)	70
72	United Artists LPS 101	YETI (2-LP, 2nd pressing, matt gatefold sleeve)	80
72	Sunset SLS 50257	PHALLUS DEI (LP, reissue)	25
72	United Artists UAG 23937	CARNIVAL IN BABYLON (LP, gatefold sleeve)	35
72	United Artists UAG 29406	WOLF CITY (LP, gatefold sleeve)	30
73	United Artists USP 102	LIVE IN LONDON (LP)	25

Gladys AMONI

			MINT VALUE £
73	United Artists UAS 29504	VIVE LA TRANCE (LP, with inner sleeve)	20
75	United Artists UA 29723 G	LEMMINGMANIA (LP)	20
74	Atlantic K 50136	HIJACK (LP)	20

(see also Utopia)

GLADYS AMONI
76	Untouchable UT 002	Your Best Friend/Your Best Dub	8

AMORPHOUS ANDROGYNOUS
93	Quigley LPEBV 1	TALES OF EPHIDRINA (LP)	60
02	Future Sound Of London FSOLLP101	THE ISNESS (2-LP)	50
05	Harvest 0946 3 33994 1 9	THE FUTURE SOUND OF LONDON PRESENTS THE AMORPHOUS ANDROGYNOUS - ALICE IN ULTRALAND (2-LP)	80
18	EBV LPRSDTOT74	THE ISNESS (2-LP, reissue, numbered)	30

(see also Future Sound Of London)

AMOS & SARA
82	It's War Boys	Go Home Soldier/Enough Is Enough/Surveillance O.H.M.S. (12", screenprint p/s)	20

(see also Homosexuals)

TORI AMOS
92	East West A7504DJ	Winter (radio edit)/The Pool (promo 7" in p/s)	15
92	East West 7567 82358-1	LITTLE EARTHQUAKES (LP)	40
94	East West 7567-82567-1	UNDER THE PINK (LP)	25
96	East West 7567-82862-1	BOYS FOR PELE (2-LP, clear vinyl)	40
98	East West 7567 83095-1	FROM THE CHOIRGIRL HOTEL (LP)	40
06	Epic (No cat no)	THE ORIGINAL BOOTLEGS (12 CD box set, 6 stickers)	50
07	Epic 86140	AMERICAN DOLL POSSE (2-LP)	20

AMPHETAMEANIES
99	F&J Records SHAG024	Last Night/Suzie The Muppet Ltd (7" p/s 600 pressed)	8

(see also Belle and Sebastian, Franz Ferdinand)

CURTIS AMY
60	Vogue LAE 12277	THE BLUES MESSAGE (LP, with Paul Bryant)	15
61	Vogue LA 12287	GROOVIN' BLUE (LP, with Frank Butler)	30
62	Vogue LAE 12298	MEETIN' HERE (LP, with Paul Bryant)	15
63	Fontana 688136ZL	KATANGA (LP)	30

ANABAS
83	Flame On FLAME 003	Barricades/Dream Dance (p/s)	15

ANACONDA
20	Seelie Court SCLP 003	SYMPATHY FOR THE MADMAN (LP, issue of acetate originally recorded in 1969)	18

ANACOSTIA
75	CBS 3742	All I Need/One Less Morning	6

ANACRUSIS
91	Metal Blade ZORRO 23	MANIC IMPRESSIONS (LP)	18

ANA HAUSEN
81	Human HUM 12	Professionals/Tunnel Vision	8

ANAL FLEAS
82	Rectal FLEA 45	Psych/Over the Edge/Landlord/Go Down (p/s, with insert)	100

ANALYSIS
81	Survival SUR 003	Surface Tension/Connections (p/s)	30

ANAN
68	Pye 7N 17571	Haze Woman/I Wonder Where My Sister's Gone	50
68	Pye 7N 17642	Madena/Standing Still	20

PETER ANATHAN
66	Fontana TF 705	You Can't Stop Me Loving You/Feel I'm Falling	10

ANATHEMA
90	Private Pressing	AN ILLIAD OF WOES EP (4 track demo cassette)	30
91	Private Pressing	ALL FAITH IS LOST EP (4 track demo cassette)	30
92	Peaceville VILE 36T	THE CRESTFALLEN EP (12", p/s)	30
94	Peaceville CC 6	WE ARE THE BIBLE EP (purple vinyl, p/s)	25
93	Peaceville VILE 34	SERENADES (LP)	30
95	Peaceville VILE 52	THE SILENT ENIGMA (LP)	25
96	Peaceville VILE 64	ETERNITY (LP)	25
99	Music For Nations MFN 250	JUDGEMENT (LP)	35
01	Music For Nations MFN 260	A FINE DAY TO EXIT (LP)	25
02	Peaceville VILELP 73	ALTERNATIVE 4 (LP, first issued on CD in 1998)	30
10	Peaceville VILELP 305	A NATURAL DISASTER (2-LP, first issued on CD in 2003)	20
10	K-Scope 812	WE'RE HERE BECAUSE WE'RE HERE (2-LP, 2000 only)	20

ANCIENT GREASE
71	Mercury 6338 033	WOMAN AND CHILDREN FIRST (LP, black/silver labels)	250

(see also Eyes Of Blue, Big Sleep, Man, Gary Pickford-Hopkins, Gentle Giant)

ANCIENT GREEKS
81	Slam! SSM 027	I Am An Island/Yap (no p/s)	30

AND ALSO THE TREES
84	Reflex RE 3	The Secret Sea/Secrecy (p/s)	8
84	Reflex 12 RE 6	The Secret Sea/Secrecy/There Were No Bounds/The Tease The Tear/Midnight Garden/Wallpaper Dying (12", p/s)	10
84	Reflex LEX 1	AND ALSO THE TREES (LP)	18

ERIC ANDERSEN
65	Fontana TFL 6061	TODAY IS THE HIGHWAY (LP)	60
68	Fontana TFL/STFL 6068	'BOUT CHANGES AND THINGS TAKE 2 (LP, black/silver label, mono/stereo)	40
68	Vanguard SVRL 19003	MORE HITS FROM TIN CAN ALLEY (LP)	20
72	CBS 65145	BLUE RIVER (LP)	15

Carol ANDERSON

MINT VALUE £

CAROL ANDERSON
79 Grapevine GRP 133   Sad Girl/I'll Get Off At The Next Stop 30
99 Goldmine GSS GS 035   Sad Girl/VELVET HAMMER: Happy 20
03 Grapevine 2000 141   Taking My Mind Off Love/Sad Girl (reissue) 10

CHRISTIAN ANDERSON
74 DJM DJS 330   Supergirl/My Imagination (DJ Copy) 15
74 DJM DJS 330   Supergirl/My Imagination 6

ERNESTINE ANDERSON
61 Mercury AMT 1137   A Lover's Question/That's All I Want From You 15
64 Sue WI 309   Keep An Eye On Love/Continental Mind 70
65 Stateside SS 455   Somebody Told You/How Many Times 10
65 Mercury MF 912   Jerk & Twine/You Can't Buy Love 20
64 Sue ILP 911   THE NEW SOUND OF ERNESTINE ANDERSON (LP, unissued) 150

GLADSTONE ANDERSON (& FOLLOWERS)
69 Blue Cat BS 172   Judas/The World Come To An End (with Followers) 40
74 Ashanti ASH 413   It May Sound Silly/Gladdy's Workshop 15
79 Love & Inity VG 006   Holly Children/Black Music (12") 30
73 Ashanti SHAN 103   IT MAY SOUND SILLY (LP) 20
83 Seven Leaves SLLP 4   PEACE PIPE (LP) 18
94 Roots RRLP 009   FOREVER DUB (LP) 18

(see also Stranger & Gladdy, Tommy McCook)

HALEY ANDERSON
83 Magnet 12 MID 5   All To Myself (Dance Mix)/(7" Version)/(Instrumental) (12") 40

IAN (A.) ANDERSON
71 Village Thing VTSX 1002   One More Chance/Policeman's Ball 18
69 Saydisc EP SD 134   ALMOST THE COUNTRY BLUES (EP, with Elliot Jackson) 50
68 Saydisc Matchbox SDM 159   THE INVERTED WORLD (LP, with Mike Cooper) 70
69 Liberty LBS 83242E   STEREO DEATH BREAKDOWN (LP, blue label, as Ian Anderson Country Blues Band) 60
70 Fontana STL 5542   BOOK OF CHANGES (LP, black/silver labels) 120
70 Village Thing VTS 3   ROYAL YORK CRESCENT (LP, with lyric insert) 35
72 Village Thing VTS 9   A VULTURE IS NOT A BIRD YOU CAN TRUST (LP, laminated front cover) 40
72 Village Thing VTS 18   SINGER SLEEPS ON AS BLAZE RAGES (LP) 60

(see also Mike Cooper, Anderson Jones Jackson)

JAMES ANDERSON
71 Atlantic 2091-055   Mama Mama/Muskatel Muskatel 20

JON ANDERSON
76 Atlantic K50261   OLIAS OF SUNHILLOW (LP, gatefold, insert) 30

(see also Hans Christian, Warriors, Yes, Mike Oldfield)

KIP ANDERSON
67 President PT 163   You'll Lose A Good Thing/I'm Out Of Love 15

LAURIE ANDERSON
82 Warner Bros.WB K 57 002   BIG SCIENCE (LP) 15

MILLER ANDERSON
71 Deram DM 337   Bright City/Another Time, Another Place 15
71 Deram SDL 3   BRIGHT CITY (LP, gatefold sleeve) 175

(see also Voice, At Last The 1958 Rock'n'Roll Show, Keef Hartley Band, Hemlock, Dog Soldier, Lyn Dobson)

REUBEN ANDERSON
66 Doctor Bird DB 1045   Christmas Time Again/DESMOND TUCKER: Oh Holy Night 25

SONNY ANDERSON
60 London HLP 9036   Lonely Lonely Train/Yes, I'm Gonna Love You 40

UDELL T. ANDERSON
69 Direction 58-4212   Love Ain't Love/Funky Walk 15
69 Direction 58-4459   Keep On Loving Me/Rainmaker 15
69 Direction 58-4645   Don't Go Away/Thank You Darling 8

VICKI ANDERSON
71 Mojo 2001 150   Super Good Part 1/Super Good Part 2 10
73 Mojo 2093 005   I'm Too Tough For Mr Big Stuff (Hot Pants)/Sound Funky 20
74 Mojo 2093 028   Don't Throw Your Love In The Garbage Can/Land Of Milk And Honey/BOBBY BYRD: Sayin' It And Doin' It Are Two Different Things 10
04 Soul Brother LP SBPJ 24   MOTHER POPCORN (2-LP) 40

(see also Bobby Byrd, James Brown)

ANDERSON, JONES, JACKSON
68 Saydisc 33 SD 125   ANDERSON, JONES, JACKSON (EP) 35

(see also Ian A. Anderson)

ANDERSON'S ALLSTARS
68 Blue Cat BS 133   Intensified Girls/Jump And Shout 150

BARBARA ANDREWS
70 Escort ERT 838   Lonesome Feeling/RAINY BOP: Hop Scotch 20

BARRY ANDREWS
80 Virgin VS 378   Rossmore Road (NW1)/Win A Night Out With A Well Known Paranoiac (p/s) 6

(see also XTC, Shriekback, Robert Fripp)

CATHERINE ANDREWS
80 Cat Tracks PURR LP 2   FRUITS (LP, with lyric sheet & poster sleeve) 50

(see also Gordon Giltrap, Inner City Unit)

CHRIS ANDREWS
67 Decca F 22668   Hold On/Easy 25

(see also Chris Ravel & Ravers)

DAVE ANDREWS & SUGAR
68 Jewel JL 04   I'm On My Way/Beatin' Of My Heart 60

(see also Heinz)

ERNIE ANDREWS
			MINT VALUE £
65	Capitol CL 15407	Where Were You/What Do I See In The Girl	25

HARVEY ANDREWS
65	Transatlantic TRAEP 133	HARVEY ANDREWS (EP)	35
75	Transatlantic BIG 525	(I'm Resigning) From Today/Darby And Joan (with Graham Cooper)	6
70	Decca Nova SDN 9	PLACES AND FACES (LP)	50
73	Fly HIFLY 15	FRIENDS OF MINE (LP, gatefold sleeve)	15

INEZ ANDREWS & ANDREWETTES
| 65 | Vogue EDVP 1283 | INEZ ANDREWS & ANDREWETTES (EP) | 40 |

JOHN ANDREWS & LONELY ONES
| 66 | Parlophone R 5455 | A Rose Growing In The Ruins/It's Just Love (DJ copy) | 350 |
| 66 | Parlophone R 5455 | A Rose Growing In The Ruins/It's Just Love | 250 |

LEE ANDREWS (& HEARTS)
57	London HL 7031	Teardrops/Girl Around The Corner (solo, export issue)	100
58	London HLM 8546	Teardrops/Girl Around The Corner (solo)	100
58	London HLU 8661	Try The Impossible/Nobody's Home (as Lee Andrews & Hearts)	150

RUBY ANDREWS
| 76 | ABC 4156 | I Got A Bone To Pick With You/I Don't Know How To Love You | 20 |

TIM ANDREWS
67	Parlophone R 5656	Sad Simon Lives Again/You Won't Be Seeing Me Anymore	20
68	Parlophone R 5695	(Something About) Suburbia/Your Tea Is Strong	20
70	Parlophone R 5824	Tiny Goddess/Josephine	40

(see also Fleur De Lys, Rupert's People)

TIM ANDREWS & PAUL KORDA
| 68 | Parlophone R 5714 | Smile If You Want To/Makin' Love To Him | 10 |
| 68 | Parlophone R5046 | Angel Face/Waiter Get Me A Drink Of Water | 10 |

(see also Paul Korda)

ANDREWS SISTERS
| 53 | Brunswick LA 8599 | SING SING SING (10" LP) | 15 |

ANDROIDS
| 79 | Android AND 001 | Robot Riot/Andwellas Dream (p/s) | 15 |

ANDROIDS OF MU
| 80 | Fuck Off FLP 01 | BLOOD ROBOTS (LP) | 50 |

ANDROMEDA (1)
69	RCA RCA 1854	Go Your Way/Keep Out 'Cos I'm Dying	30
69	RCA SF 8031	ANDROMEDA (LP)	1000
90	Reflection MM 06	SEVEN, LONELY STREET (LP, with numbered & signed booklet, 500 only)	25
95	Kissing Spell KSLP 9497	LIVE 1967 (LP)	15
17	Repertoire V 246	ANDROMEDA (LP, reissue)	15

(see Attack, Five Day Week Straw People, Hard Stuff, Atomic Rooster, John Du Cann, Fuzzy Duck)

ANDROMEDA (2)
| 91 | Intrigue IGE15T | Survival (Urban Mix)/(City Mix)/Savage (12") | 15 |
| 91 | Intrigue IGE AD1 | CONTROL OF THE DANCEFLOOR (LP) | 40 |

AND SO TO BED
| 78 | Stonehouse SH004 | THE EP | 12 |

AND THE INDIAN LOGIC
| 00s | Logic KJR 01 | Beggar Man/The Change (p/s) | 10 |

AND THE NATIVE HIPSTERS
| 79 | Heater Volume HVR 003 | There Goes Concorde Again.../Stands, Still The Building.../I Wanna Be Around (several different coloured photocopied foldaround sleeves with insert in polythene bag) | 30 |
| 82 | Illuminated/Glass HIP 1 | TENDERLY HURT ME (Poor Prince/Hang Ten/Tenderly Hurt Me/Stuck) (12" EP, p/s) | 15 |

ANDWELLA('S DREAM)
69	CBS 4301	Sunday/Midday Sun (as Andwella's Dream)	35
69	CBS 4469	Mrs. Man/Felix (as Andwella's Dream)	80
69	CBS 4634	Mr. Sunshine/Shades Of Grey (as Andwella's Dream)	50
70	Reflection RS 1	Every Little Minute/Michael Fitzhenry (as Andwellas Dream)	15
70	Reflection RS 3	Hold Onto Your Mind/Shadow Of The Night (as Andwella)	30
71	Reflection RS 6	People's People/Are You Ready (as Andwella)	10
69	CBS 63673	LOVE AND POETRY (LP, as Andwella's Dream)	1000
70	Reflection REFL 10	WORLD'S END (LP, as Andwella, stickered sleeve with poster)	150
70	Reflection REFL 10	WORLD'S END (LP, without poster)	80
71	Reflection REF 1010	PEOPLE'S PEOPLE (LP, as Andwella)	100
09	Sunbeam SDR2LP 5063	LOVE & POETRY (2-LP, reissue)	20

(see also David Lewis, David Baxter)

BOB ANDY
67	Island WI 3040	I've Got To Go Back Home/SONNY BURKE: Rudy Girl	70
68	Studio One SO 2063	Too Experienced/Let Them Stay	50
68	Coxsone CS 7074	My Time (miscredited to Alton Ellis)/MARCIA GRIFFITHS: Mark My Word	200
69	Doctor Bird DB 1183	The Way I Feel/ETHIOPIANS: Long Time Now	100
69	Doctor Bird DB 1191	Games People Play/The Sun Shines For Me	25
69	Studio One SO 2075	I'm Going Home/SOUND DIMENSION: Straight Flush	50
70	Harry J. HJ 6612	Peace Of Mine/Weep	8
71	Trojan TR 7809	Green Green Valley/Peace Of Mind	6
71	Trojan TR 7821	One Woman/You Don't Know (B-side actually "Save Me Version" by Bob Andy Band)	6
71	Trojan TR 7840	One Woman/You Don't Know	6
71	London HLJ 7127	Games People Play/GAYLETTES: Son Of A Preacher Man (export issue)	10
72	Sioux SI 019	Baby I Need Your Loving/CIRCLES: Mammy Blue	10
72	Sioux SI 020	Everyday People/HONG GANG: Smoking Wild	10
72	Green Door GD 4047	Life/HARRY J. ALL STARS: Version	16
73	Green Door GD 4059	You Don't Know/The Border Song	100

Horace ANDY

MINT VALUE £

73	Horse HOSS 31	One Woman/Second Hand Love	6
75	Fab FAB 241	Feeling Soul/SOUND DIMENSION: Part 2	40
75	Sound Tracs SK2 8	Nyah/Nyah Dub	8
76	Tropical TST 110	Feeling Soul/Rock It Down	10
76	DEB	War In The City/Version	30
77	Sky Note SKY 1011	The Ghetto Stay In The Mind/Ghetto Dub	15
78	Sky Note SKYLP 15	LOTS OF LOVE AND I (LP)	15

(see also Bob & Marcia, Ethiopians, Larry & Alvin)

HORACE ANDY

72	Count Shelly 2	Cha Cha Children/Version	8
72	Attack ATT 8026	Feel Good All Over/PHIL PRATT ALLSTARS: Feel Good (Version)	10
72	Song Bird SB 1085	Lonely Woman/Lonely Version	20
73	Bread BR 1170	Don't Try To Use Me/Goddess Of Love	12
73	Randy's RAN 533	Don't Think About Me (with Earl Flute)/DINO PERKINS: Skin Him Alive	20
73	Atra ATRA 008	Children Of Israel/Part 2	8
73	RCA TCA 2401	I Stand Before You/Unity Strength And Love	70
74	Harry J HJ 6699	Lonely Woman/Lonely Woman (Instrumental)	15
74	Ackee ACK 530	Til/IMPACT ALLSTARS: Version	6
75	Attack ATT 8117	Nice And Easy/Version	10
75	Fab FAB 260	Oh Lord Why Lord/SOUND DIMENSION: Part 2	25
75	Morpheus MOR 1010	Got To Get You	6
76	Venture VEN 7706	Skylarking/Version	10
76	Terminal TM 105	Thank The Lord/Part Two (actually the SUNSHOT BAND)	10
77	Serious Business SB 02	Rock To Sleep/Version	35
78	Carib Gems CGDD110	Guiding Star (with Tapper Zukie)/Zion Gate (12")	20
79	Sufferer's Height SUFF 005	Pure Ranking/The Return Of Jammy's Hi-Fi (Round One)/TREVOR RANKING: Whip Them Jah Jah (12")	30
79	Star PTP 1024	Tonight/Don't Let Problems Get You Down (12")	35
70s	Terminal TM 101	Roots Of All Evil/I Will Forgive You	15
80	Unity UN 002	This Must Be Hell/If I Wasn't A Man (12", with DEADLY HEADLEY)	15
82	Wackie's WR 5252	Money Money/AL MOODIE: Bull Bay Jumping (12")	25
84	Music Hawk MHD 13	Confusion/Version (12")	40
84	Blacker Dread BD 009	Cus-Cus/S.C.O.M RHYTHM SECTION: Watch Your Step	15
84	Blacker Dread BD 012	Money Money Money/Evil Money (no centre)	15
85	Rough Trade RTT 172	Get Down/RHYTHM POSSE : Get Down Deeper (12")	50
86	Music Hawk MF 16	User/Dub (12")	20
89	Highest Grade HGR 002	Right Saloon/LECTURER: Weapon (12")	30
80s	Solid Groove SGL 014	Serious Thing/Love Hangover (12")	10
95	Blood & Fire BAFT 01	Problems/Problems Dub (12" reissue)	15
72	Trojan TBL 197	YOU ARE MY ANGEL (LP)	45
78	Solid Groove SGL 107	EXCLUSIVELY (LP)	40
84	Music Hawk MHLP001	CONFUSION (LP)	20
87	Tachyon WR 2740	EVERYDAY PEOPLE (LP)	20
95	Blood & Fire BAFLP 007	IN THE LIGHT DUB (LP, reissue)	20
96	Trojan TBL 197	YOU ARE MY ANGEL (LP, reissue)	15
99	Virgin SADLP 9	LIVING IN THE FLOOD (LP)	15

(see also Jon Cuno, Big Youth)

HORACE ANDY & FREDDIE MCKAY

75	Treble 7	Talking Love/Dub	8

PATRICK ANDY

78	Grove Music GMDM 3	Woman, Woman, Woman/TOMMY MCCOOK: Lamb's Bread (12")	35

ANDY & CLYDE

65	Rio R 62	Never Be A Slave/Magic Is Love	12
65	Rio R 69	I'm So Lonesome/WINSTON STEWART: Day After Day	12
66	Rio R 71	We All Have To Part/UPSETTERS: Scandalizing	80

ANDY & JOEY

62	Island WI 056	Have You Ever/Cross My Heart	25
64	Port-O-Jam PJ 4009	I Want To Know/My Love Has Gone	40
64	Ska Beat JB 162	You're Wondering Now/You'll Never (copies also exist on R&B label)	30

(see also Roland Alphonso)

JOHNNY ANGEL

60	Parlophone R 4642	Chinese Butterfly/My Very Good Friend The Milkman	10
60	Parlophone R 4679	Too Young To Go Steady/You're Thrilling	20
61	Parlophone R 4750	What Happens To Love/Luna Luna Luna Lu	10
61	Parlophone R 4795	Web Of Love/Trocadero-Double-Nine-One-O	10
62	Parlophone R 4874	Look, Look Little Angel/Jenny From Missouri	8
62	Parlophone R 4948	Better Luck Next Time/The Power Of You	7
63	Parlophone R 5026	A Touch Of Venus/The Two Together	70

MARIAN ANGEL

65	Columbia DB 7537	It's Gonna Be Alright/Tomorrow's Fool	30
65	Columbia DB 7705	You Can't Buy My Love/One Way Only	25
66	CBS 202181	A Little Bit Of Sunshine/All The Time In The World	20

ANGEL PAVEMENT

69	Fontana TF 1059	Baby You've Gotta Stay/Green Mello Hill	20
70	Fontana TF 1072	Tell Me What I've Got To Do/When Will I See June Again	25

(see also Fortes Mentum, Pussy)

ANGEL STREET

79	Ellie Jay EJSP 9290	Done It Again/Song For You (500 only)	200

ANGEL WITCH

80	EMI EMI 5064	Sweet Danger/Flight Nineteen (p/s, credits Angelwitch)	10

ANGEL (1)

			MINT VALUE £
80	EMI 12EMI 5064	Sweet Danger/Hades Paradise/Flight Nineteen (12", p/s)	20
80	Bronze BRO 108	Angel Witch/Gorgon (p/s)	8
81	Bronze BRO 121	Loser/Suffer/Dr Phibes (p/s)	10
85	Killerwatt KIL 3001	Goodbye/Reawakening (no p/s)	15
80	Bronze BRON 532	ANGELWITCH (LP)	20
85	Killerwatt KILP 4001	SCREAMIN' N' BLEEDIN' (LP)	15
86	Killerwatt KILP 4003	FRONTAL ASSAULT (LP)	18
12	Rise Above RISELP145	AS ABOVE, SO BELOW (2-LP, clear vinyl, 1-sided 7", A2 poster, 100 only)	70
12	Rise Above RISELP145	AS ABOVE, SO BELOW (LP, 2 x white vinyl 12", inners, insert)	30

(see also Tytan)

ANGEL (1)

74	Cube BUG 41	Little Boy Blue/Tragedy Queen	7
74	Cube BUG 51	Good Time Fanny/Who D'Ya Think Your Fooling	7

ANGEL (2)

76	Casablanca CBC 4007	ANGEL (LP, with insert)	15

ANGELA & HER FANS

66	Pye 7N 17108	Love Ya Illya/I Know You	15

(see also Alma Cogan)

ANGELIC UPSTARTS

78	Dead IS/AU/1024	Murder Of Liddle Towers/Police Oppression (p/s, 1,000 only)	300
78	Rough Trade RT/SW 001	Murder Of Liddle Towers/Police Oppression (reissue, p/s)	15
81	Zonophone Z 12	England/Stick's Diary (p/s)	15
83	Anagram ANA 12	The Burglar (p/s, unissued)	0
85	Gas GM 3010	Brighton Bomb/Thin Red Line/Soldier (12", banned 'Maggie Thatcher' p/s)	15
79	Warner Bros K 56717	TEENAGE WARNING (LP)	25
80	Warner Bros K 56806	WE GOTTA GET OUT OF THIS PLACE (LP)	15
81	Zonophone ZEM 102	LIVE (LP, with free live flexidisc: "We're Gonna Take The World"/Leave Me Alone/"The Young Ones"/"White Riot" [no cat. no.])	15
81	Zonophone ZEM 102	LIVE (LP)	15
81	EMI ZONO 104	2,000,000 VOICE (LP)	20
83	Anagram GRAM 007	ANGEL DUST (LP)	15
85	Gas GLP 4012	THE POWER OF THE PRESS (LP)	15
85	Razor RAZM 32	LIVE IN YUGOSLAVIA (LP)	15
85	Anagram GRAM004	REASONS WHY (LP, with inner sleeve)	15
90	Link LP 140	LOST & FOUND (LP)	15

ANGELIQUE

77	Tempus TEM 102	Cry/Crying	12

BOBBY ANGELO & TUXEDOS

61	HMV POP 892	Baby Sitting/Skinny Lizzie	20
61	HMV POP 982	I Gotta Have You/Don't Stop	30

(see also Innocents [UK])

ANGELS

62	Pye International 7N 25150	Everybody Loves A Lover/Blow Joe	10
63	Mercury AMT 1211	My Boyfriend's Back/(Love Me) Now	10
63	Mercury AMT 1215	I Adore Him/Thank You And Goodnight	10
64	Philips BF 1312	Wow Wee Wee/Snowflakes And Teardrops	10

(see also Beach-Nuts)

ANGELS AND EIGHTEEN

72	RAK 137	Midnight Flight/Flight 2	80

ANGELS ONE 5

82	Galaxy GAL 005	Cut And Dried/Countdown (p/s)	10

(see also Justified Ancients Of Mu Mu, Timelords, Disco 2000, KLF, Space)

ANGIE

79	Stiff BUY 51	Peppermint Lump/Breakfast In Naples (p/s)	10

GUY ANGIER

70	(No label or cat no)	GUITAR AND BANANAS (LP, with insert)	80

ANGLIANS

67	CBS 202489	A Friend Of Mine/Daytime Lover	15

(see also Moving Finger)

ANGLOS

65	Brit WI 004	Incense/You're Fooling Me	60
65	Fontana 561	Incense/You're Fooling Me (unissued)	200
65	Fontana TF 589	Incense/You're Fooling Me (reissue)	25
67	Sue WI 4033	Incense/You're Fooling Me (unissued)	200
69	Island WIP 6061	Incense/You're Fooling Me (2nd reissue)	10

(see also Spencer Davis Group, Stevie Winwood)

ANGOR WAT

85	Children Of The Revolution GURT8	GENERAL STRIKE (LP)	15

ANIKA

10	Invada INV099LP	ANIKA (LP, blue vinyl)	15

ANIMAL COLLECTIVE

04	Paw Tracks PAW 003	Wastered/Wastered (12" one side BLACK DICE, 1,000 only)	12
04	Fat Cat 7FAT 5	Who Could Win A Rabbit/Baby Day (p/s)	8
05	Fat Cat 7FAT 19	Grass/Must Be Treeman/Ficle Cycle (p/s)	10
06	No label or Cat. No.	Purple Bottle/Polly (tour 7", white label, plain white die-cut sleeve. Later pressings have track info on sleeve)	15
06	Fat Cat 12FAT 060	People/Tikwid/My Favourite Colours/People (live) (12")	12
07	Domino RUG 270T	Fireworks (1-sided pink vinyl other side etched 10", stickered, die-cut pink sleeve)	15
17	Domino RUG 813T	MEETING OF THE WATERS EP (12")	10
04	Fat Cat FATSPLP 08	SUNG TONGS (2-LP, gatefold)	20

ANIMAL FARM

MINT VALUE £

05	Fat Cat FATSPLP 11	FEELS (2-LP)	40
06	Domino WIGLP 199	STRAWBERRY JAM (2-LP, gatefold with inners)	30
09	Fat Cat FATSP08LPX	SUNG TONGS (2-LP, reissue, 180 gm vinyl)	30
09	Domino WIGLP 216	MERRIWEATHER POST PAVILION (2-LP, gatefold, inners)	25
09	Fat Cat FATSP17LPX	SPIRIT THEY'VE GONE, SPIRIT THEY'VE VANISHED (2-LP)	40
09	Fat Cat FATSP18LPX	DANSE MANATEE (LP)	20
15	Domino WIGLP 364	LIVE AT 9.30 (3-LP boxset, poster, hand numbered with screenprint)	35
15	Domino WIGLP 364	LIVE AT 9.30 (3-LP boxset, poster, hand numbered without screenprint)	25

(see also Avey Tare)

ANIMAL FARM

| 84 | Rot Records ASS 7 | Model Soldier/John And Julie (p/s) | 15 |

ANIMALS

64	Columbia DB 7247	Baby Let Me Take You Home/Gonna Send You Back To Walker	10
65	Columbia DB 7445	Don't Let Me Be Misunderstood/Club-A-Go Go (mispressing, with 'demo' version of A-side, matrix: '1N')	10
66	Decca F 12332	Inside Looking Out/Outcast	10
66	Decca F 12407	Don't Bring Me Down/Cheating	10
63	Graphic Sound ALO 10867	THE ANIMALS (12" EP, 1-sided, 99 only, private pressing, blank white cover, printed label. Some credited to the Animals or The Alan Price Rhythm and Blues Group)	500
64	Columbia SEG 8374	THE ANIMALS IS HERE (EP)	20
65	Columbia SEG 8400	THE ANIMALS (EP)	20
65	Columbia SEG 8439	THE ANIMALS (EP)	20
65	Columbia SEG 8452	THE ANIMALS ARE BACK (EP)	35
66	Decca DFE 8643	IN THE BEGINNING THERE WAS EARLY ANIMALS (EP)	30
66	Columbia SEG 8499	ANIMAL TRACKS (EP)	45
64	Columbia 33SX 1669	THE ANIMALS (LP, blue/black label with "sold in the U.K..." label text)	100
64	Regal SREG 1104	THE ANIMALS (LP, export only. 'stereo' blue labels)	45
65	Columbia 33SX 1708	ANIMAL TRACKS (LP, 1st pressing with 33SX on label)	120
66	Columbia SX 1708	ANIMAL TRACKS (LP, 2nd pressing, SX 1708 on labels)	75
66	Columbia SX 6035	THE MOST OF THE ANIMALS (LP, 1st pressing, blue/black labels, flipback sleeve)	30
66	Decca LK 4797	ANIMALISMS (LP)	150
68	Regal SREG 1104	THE ANIMALS (LP, export only. 'mono' black labels)	65
69	Regal Starline SRS 5006	THE ANIMALS (LP, 'stereo' reissue of 33SX 1669, flipback sleeve)	25
69	Columbia SX 6035	THE MOST OF THE ANIMALS (LP, 2nd pressing, black/silver labels, flipback sleeve)	25
88	See For Miles SEE 244	THE EP COLLECTION (LP)	15

(see also Eric Burdon & Animals, Alan Price, Danny McCullough)

ANIMALS & MEN

| 80 | Strange Days DAYS 1 | The Terraplane Fixation/Shell Shock (p/s) | 7 |

ANIMATED EGG

| 69 | Marble Arch MAL 890 | ANIMATED EGG (LP) | 25 |

ANIMATION

| 82 | Dance Fools Dance DF 2 2 | FRAME ON EP | 20 |

PAUL ANKA

SINGLES

59	Columbia DB 4324	Lonely Boy/Your Love (78)	30
59	Columbia DB 4355	Put Your Head On My Shoulder/Don't Ever Leave Me	10
59	Columbia DB 4355	Put Your Head On My Shoulder/Don't Ever Leave Me (78)	70
68	RCA RCA 1676	Can't Get You Out Of My Mind/When We Get There	40
68	RCA RCA 1676	Can't Get You Out Of My Mind/When We Get There (DJ copy)	60
77	RCA PB 9394	When We Get There/I Can't Help Loving You	40

(see also Micki Marlo & Paul Anka, Neil Sedaka)

BARBARA ANN

| 65 | Piccadilly 7N 35221 | You've Lost That Loving Feeling/Till The Summer Time | 10 |

ANNA

| 82 | RCA RCA 213 | Systems Breaking Down/Dance Version (p/s) | 8 |
| 82 | RCA RCAT 213 | Systems Breaking Down/Dance Version (12", p/s) | 25 |

ANNABEL DREAM

| 60s | Oak (no cat no) | My Last Date With You/Gary, Won't You Marry Me (Unreleased - acetate only) | 50 |

ANNALISE

| 99 | Boss Tunage BOSTAGE 701 | Signposts And Alleyways/Empire Builder (p/s, 1-sided green vinyl with free CD, numbered, 250 copies only) | 10 |

ANNETTE

| 88 | Deconstruction PB 42561 | Dream 17/Nightmare On Dream Street (p/s) | 8 |
| 88 | Deconstruction PT 42562 | Dream 17/Nightmare On Dream Street/Dream Slumber (12", p/s) | 18 |

ANNETTE (& AFTERBEATS)

| 64 | HMV POP 1270 | Muscle Beach Party/I Dream About Frankie | 10 |
| 65 | HMV POP 1447 | The Monkey's Uncle (with The Beach Boys)/How Will I Know My Love | 15 |

ANNIE AND THE AEROPLANES

| 88 | Pipedream PIPE 1 | A Million Zillion Miles/Travelling Song | 15 |

ANNIS

| 79 | GTO GT 266 | Don't Play Your Games/After Me | 15 |

ANNIVERSARY

| 78 | Aerco AERE 102 | GIVE ME A SMILE (EP) | 25 |

ANNO DOMINI

| 71 | Deram SML-R 1085 | ON THIS NEW DAY (LP) | 400 |

ANON

| 93 | Nucleus NUKE 006 | Alright/OK Armando (12") | 20 |
| 93 | Nucleus NUKE 009 | Whistle/Whistlers Brother (12") | 10 |

ANONYMOUSLY YOURS

| 69 | Trojan TR 680 | Get Back/ERNIE SMITH : Not For Sale | 15 |

ANOREXIA

			MINT VALUE £
69	Trojan TR 681	It's Your Thing/69 (B-side actually by Wallace Wilson)	50
69	Duke DU 38	Dream Baby/Staggerlee	15
69	Duke DU 40	Organism/Itch	30

ANOREXIA
80	Slim SJP 812	Rapist In The Park/I'm A Square/Pets	35
82	Slim BRS 011	Softly Quietly Or Shout/Steven/Inanimate Objects/Marching Song (p/s)	25

ANOTHER MAN'S POISON
92	Tick Tock TT 1	Alf Garnet's Heart Attack/Now That's What I Call (hand stamped die cut paper sleeve)	10
92	Tick Tock TT 2	I Spit On My Fist/Wallop (p/s)	7

ANOTHER PRETTY FACE
79	New Pleasure Z1	All The Boys Love Carrie/That's Not Enough (green and white foldout p/s)	25
79	New Pleasure Z2	All The Boys Love Carrie/That's Not Enough (red and white p/s)	15
80	Chicken Jazz JAZZ 1	Heaven Gets Closer Every Day/Only Heroes Live Forever (p/s)	7
80	Chicken Jazz JAZZ 2	I'M SORRY THAT I BEAT YOU, I'M SORRY THAT I SCREAMED, FOR A MOMENT THERE I REALLY LOST CONTROL (8-track cassette with fanzine and badge. Some copies exist with tracks of DNV single taped onto the end)	30
80	Virgin VS 320	Whatever Happened To The West?/Goodbye 1970's (p/s)	10
81	Chicken Jazz JAZZ 3	Soul To Soul/A Woman's Place/God On The Screen (foldout p/s)	15

ANOTHER SUNNY DAY
88	Sarah SARAH 003	Anorak City (flexidisc free with Are You Scared To Get Happy fanzine (SARAH 004, 1,500 only – must be together)	200
88	Sarah SARAH 007	I'm In Love With A Girl Who Doesn't Know I Exist/Things Will Be Nice/The Centre Of My Little World (14" x 10" foldout poster p/s)	60
89	Caff CAFF 7	Genetic Engineering/Kilburn Towers (p/s, with inner)	30
89	Sarah SARAH 016	What's happened?/Can't You Tell It's True?/Impossible (foldover p/s in poly bag, insert)	25
89	Sarah SARAH 022	You Should All Be Murdered/Horseriding/Green (foldover p/s in poly bag, insert)	30
90	Sarah SARAH 035	Rio/The Very Beginning (p/s, insert)	25
92	Sarah SARAH 060	New Year's Honours/I Don't Suppose I'll Get A Second Chance (p/s, insert)	25
92	Sarah SARAH 613	LONDON WEEKEND (LP)	75

ANSEL SCANDAL
76	Dynamic DYN 105	Roots Food/Roots Food - Dub	6

BRETT ANSELL
62	Oriole CB 1701	That's Where Lonesome Lives/The Door Is Open	25

ANSELL (COLLINS) & ELAINE
72	Camel CA 98	Presenting Cheater/RON WILSON: Official Trombone	15

MARK ANSLEY
70	Mother MOT 2	909/Venus	50

ANSWER
05	Albert JAS UK 015	Keep On Believin'/New Day Rising	8
05	Albert JAS UK 017	Never Too Late/Some Unity (stickered p/s)	7

ANSWERS (1)
66	Columbia DB 7847	It's Just A Fear/You've Gotta Believe Me	200
66	Columbia DB 7953	That's What You're Doing To Me/Got A Letter From My Baby	70

(see also Misunderstood, High Tide)

ANSWERS (2)
71	Spark SRL 1058	Give Me All That I Need/Tawny Wood	20

ANT
74	Pye 7N 45332	Banana Pie/No Road Goes Your Way	15

ADAM ANT
95	EMI CDEMS370	Beautiful Dream (single version)/Let's Have A Fight/Billy Boy/Wonderful (acoustic) (CD withdrawn, 7 known copies)	75
95	EMI CDEM370	Beautiful Dream (single version)/Shake Your Hips/Antmusic (Acoustic)/Beautiful Dream (Lucas Full Length Mix) (CD, withdrawn, 2 known copies)	100

(see also Adam & The Ants, Maneaters)

ANT & DDR
05	Stay Up Forever SUF 79:000mg	Acid Techno...All The Time (12")	12

(see also DDR)

ANTEEEKS
66	Philips BF 1471	I Don't Want You/Ball And Chain	200

ANTHEM (1)
71	Buddah 2359017	ANTHEM (LP)	40

ANTHEM (2)
81	EJSP9576	England/Some Like It Hot/Do You Mind (EP, p/s, 500 only)	140

ANTHILL MOB (1)
92	Anthill ANT 1T	Penelope's Theme (12" white label)	35
93	Anthill ANT 2T	Antology/Black Rushin'/The Hooded Claw (Tango Mix) (12")	30
93	Anthill ANT 3T	Antology (The Top Buzz Stonehenge Remix)/Black Rushin' (Anthill Remix) (12")	20

ANTHILL MOB (2)
95	Confetti MK 01	Feel It/Deep Down/Untitled/Untitled (white label 12")	30
95	Confetti MK001	MAKESHIFT EP (12")	90
96	Confetti COEP 01	Promise Of... /Was She Ever Mine?/So In Love/Got To Do It (12")	35
96	Confetti COEP 02	Feel The Groove/ANTHILL MOB FEATURING P. PITSTOP - Do You Know?/P. PITSTOP - I Know How To Love! (12")	25
97	Confetti COEP 05	Why (Inside The Rise)/Things Just Started (12")	25
97	Confetti COEP 06	Cloudy Day/Agitator (12")	15
97	Confetti CODP 0197/0287	Missing/Player/X2C/Flava/Sound/Cuts (2 x 12")	200
97	Confetti COEP 08	Higher/How Ya Feeling (12")	15
97	Love Peace & Unity LOVE 03	Burning (The Original Mix) (10" picture disc, 500 only, same track both sides)	35
97	Makeshift MR 001	Set You Free/In The Name/Shake The House/Heaven Knows (12")	15
98	Makeshift MR 002	Never Ever Time/Time To Move/Don't Know/Give Me (12")	20

Billie ANTHONY

MINT VALUE £

98	Quench QUE 14	Don't Leave Me/Listen (12")	30
00	Confetti COEP 19	ANTHILL MOB EP (12")	25
97	Love Peace & Unity LOVE 04	A SPECIAL COLLECTION OF ENCHANTED RHYTHMS (2 x LP)	250

(see also Mystic matt And The Anthill Mob)

BILLIE ANTHONY
54	Columbia SCM 5143	This Ole House/Oh, What A Dream	20

(see also Big Ben Banjo Band)

DAVID ANTHONY
68	Island WI 3148	All Night/Get Out Of My Mind	40

(see also Dave Anthony's Moods)

LITTLE WAYNE ANTHONY
73	Jay Boy BOY 79	Hey Naw/Freedom To Love (reissue)	10

MALCOLM ANTHONY
70	Nashville 6076 004	Memories/Traces Of Tomorrow (demo)	15
70	Vertigo 6076 004	Memories/Traces Of Tomorrow	50

RAY ANTHONY (1)
55	Capitol CL 14243	Juke Box Special/Heat Wave	10
57	Capitol CL 14689	Rock Around The Rock Pile/The Girl Can't Help It	10
57	Capitol EAP 1-823	THE GIRL CAN'T HELP IT (EP)	12
57	Capitol EAP 1-958	ROCK AND ROLL WITH RAY ANTHONY (EP)	12

(see also Gordon MacRae & Ray Anthony)

RAY ANTHONY (2)
79	Mango Media 23	The Arabian Funk/Time	25

RAYBURN ANTHONY
60	London HLS 9167	Who's Gonna Shoe Your Pretty Little Feet/There's No Tomorrow	15

DAVE ANTHONY'S MOODS
66	Parlophone R 5438	New Directions/Give It A Chance	60

(see also David Anthony)

ANTHRAX (U.K.)
83	Small Wonder SMALL 27	THEY'VE GOT IT ALL WRONG (EP, p/s)	10
83	Crass 221984/9	CAPITALISM IS CANNIBALISM (EP, foldout p/s)	20

ANTHRAX (U.S.)
86	Island 12ISP 285	Madhouse/Air/God Save The Queen (12", picture disc)	20
86	Island 12IS 285	Madhouse/Air/God Save The Queen (12", p/s with patch)	15
87	Island ISX 316	I Am The Law (live)/Bud E.Luvbomm And Satan's Lounge Band/Madhouse (live) (red vinyl, p/s)	20
86	Island ISP 325	Indians/Sabbath Bloody Sabbath (orange vinyl, misspressing, B-side plays Imitation Of Life)	10
89	Island IS 409	Anti Social/Parasite (p/s)	10
86	Music For Nations MFN62	SPREADING THE DISEASE (LP)	20
86	Music For Nations MFN62P	SPREADING THE DISEASE (LP, picture disc)	20
87	Music For Nations MFN14	FISTFUL OF METAL (LP)	15
87	Music For Nations MFN14P	FISTFUL OF METAL (LP, picture disc)	20
87	Island ILPS 9865	AMONG THE LIVING (LP)	20
87	Island PILPS 9865	AMONG THE LIVING (LP, picture disc)	20
90	Island ILPSP 9967	PERSISTENCE OF TIME (LP, picture disc)	15
94	BMG 74321 19259 1	LIVE - THE ISLAND YEARS (LP)	20

ANTI ESTABLISHMENT
80	Charnel House CADAV 1	1980/Mechanical Man (p/s)	10

ANTILLES
83	Creole CR 51	I've Got To Have You/Latin Dream	40
83	Creole CR 12-51	I've Got To Have You/Latin Dream (12")	60

ANTI NOWHERE LEAGUE
81	WXYZ ABCD 1	Streets Of London (1-sided test pressing)	35
82	WXYZ ABCD 1	So What/Streets Of London (p/s, withdrawn)	0
82	WXYZ ABCD 2	I Hate ... People/Let's Break The Law (p/s)	6
87	GWR A1	Crime/Working For The Company (Unreleased Test Pressing)	20
82	WXYZ LMNOP1	WE ARE...THE LEAGUE (LP, 1st pressing, uncensored lyrics)	25
82	WXYZ LMNOP1	WE ARE...THE LEAGUE (LP, 2nd pressing, censored lyrics)	15

ANTI PASTI
80	Dose DOSE1	FORE SORE POINTS (EP, 500 only, clear and black vinyl)	18

ANTI SECT
84	Endangered Music EDR 4	Out From The Void/Hope Future Poisoned By Fear	25
11	Anti Sect ANTI 010	4 Minutes Past Midnight/Out From The Void (Part 2) (10", gig only, 300 copies)	10
83	Spiderleg SDL 16	IN DARKNESS THERE IS NO CHOICE (LP)	30
84	Clown Disc Big Top 1/2	LIVE IN THE DARKNESS (LP, splattered grey vinyl with insert, 1,000 only)	20
94	Discipline DISCLP 03	PEACE IS BETTER THAN A PLACE IN HISTORY (LP)	20
17	Rise Above RISELP 216	THE RISING OF THE LIGHTS (LP, clear vinyl, 100 only)	20

ANTI-SOCIAL WORKERS & MAD PROFESSOR
83	Ariwa ARI008LP	POSITIVE STYLE PUNKY REGGAE PARTY (LP)	20

ANTI SOCIAL (1)
77	Dynamite DRO 1	Traffic Lights/Teacher Teacher (no p/s)	500
82	Beat The System BTS 2	Battle Scarred Skinheads/Sewer Rat/Official Hooligan (p/s)	18
82	Beat The System FIT 2	Too Many People/Let's Have Some (p/s)	10

ANTI SOCIAL (2)
82	Lightbeat SOCIAL 1	MADE IN ENGLAND (EP)	20

ANTI STATE CONTROL
83	Asc Records ASC1	Glue Sniffing Blues/M.U.S.E/Third World Bomb	200

ANTI SYSTEM
83	Reconcilliation RECONCILE 3	Strangelove/So Long As/MORBID HUMOUR: Oh My God (Parts 1 and 2)	30
83	Paragon/Pax PAX 11	DEFENCE OF THE REALM (EP)	25

ANTOINE

			MINT VALUE £
86	Reconcilliation RECONCILE 4	A LOOK AT LIFE (12" EP)	20
85	Reconcilliation RECONCILE 1	NO LAUGHING MATTER (LP)	30
17	Boss Tunage BTRC12-110	AT WHAT PRICE IS FREEDOM? (LP with CD, white vinyl 100 only)	18

ANTOINE
| 66 | Vogue VRL 3024 | ANTOINE (LP) | 20 |
| 67 | Vogue VRL 3032 | ANTOINE (LP) | 15 |

ANTOINETTE
64	Decca F 11820	Jenny Let Him Go/Please Don't Hurt Me Anymore	10
64	Piccadilly 7N 35201	There He Goes (The Boy I Love)/Little Things Mean A Lot	15
65	Piccadilly 7N 35223	Thank You For Loving Me/If You Really Love Me	8
65	Piccadilly 7N 35252	Our House/What's A-Happening To Me	8
66	Piccadilly 7N 35293	Why Don't I Run Away From You/There's No-One In The Whole Wide World	20
66	Piccadilly 7N 35310	Lullaby Of Love/I'm For You	8

(see also Toni Daly)

ANTON
| 75 | Spark 1120 | Shot Down In Action/Mine All Mine | 8 |

REY ANTON
62	Oriole CB 1722	As If I Care/After The Laughter	6
62	Oriole CB 1771	Hey Good Looking/Mary Lou	6
63	Oriole CB 1811	Peppermint Man/Can't Say More Than That (with Batons)	7
63	Oriole CB 1843	How Long Can This Last/If You Don't Want Me Now	7
64	Parlophone R 5132	You Can't Judge A Book By The Cover/It's Cold Outside (with Peppermint Men)	20
64	Parlophone R 5172	Heard It All Before/I Want You (with Peppermint Men)	15
65	Parlophone R 5245	Wishbone/Kingsway (with Peppermint Men)	10
65	Parlophone R 5274	Girl You Don't Know Me/Don't Treat Me Bad (with Peppermint Men)	50
65	Parlophone R 5310	Nothing Comes Easy/Breakout (with Peppermint Men)	10
65	Parlophone R 5358	Premeditation/Now That It's Over (with Pro Form)	30
66	Parlophone R 5420	Don't You Worry Boy/Hold It Babe (with Pro Formula)	10
66	Parlophone R 5487	Things Get Better/Newsboy (with Pro Form)	10

ANTONIO
| 98 | Locked On LOCKED009 | Hyperfunk (New Horizons Mix)/(Vocal Mix)/(Original Mix) (12") | 30 |

ANTONIOU
| 82 | Elite DAZZ 17 | Sound On Sound/Street Sound (12" stickered plain sleeve) | 15 |

(see also Atmosfear)

TONY ANTONIU
| 84 | Spartan 12 SP 12 | Send In The Night/(Extended Version) (12") | 30 |

ANTONY
| 67 | Westleigh WSC 1 | No Ones Caring/Be Aware Of The Dark | 30 |

DAVE ANTONY
| 68 | Mercury MF 1031 | Race With The Wind/Playin' Hide And Seek | 20 |

(see also Dave Anthony['s Moods])

MARK ANTONY & AVENGERS
| 60s | Malconi MCD LP 17 | MARK ANTONY & THE AVENGERS (LP, private pressing, plain sleeve) | 100 |

MIKI ANTONY
70	RCA 1906	Cinnamon/Easy Rider	7
71	Columbia DB 8759	Sally Sunshine/It's Good To See You	8
71	Bell BLL 1179	Simon's Doorstep/Eldorado Gold	7
72	Bell BELL 1243	Funny Sorta Day/Home To Kinoki	6
74	Bradley's BRAD 7414	We Made It Last Summertime/Hey Suzanne	6
77	EMI EMI 2683	Can't Get You (Out Of My Mind)/Hey Friend (p/s)	6
78	EMI EMI 2826	If You Never Had The Chance To Fall In Love/Camouflage	6
78	EMI EMC 3259	CITY OF THE ANGELS (LP)	15

(see also Miki)

ANNIE ANXIETY
| 81 | Crass Records 32984/3 | BARBED WIRE HALO: Cyanide Tears/Hello Horror (gatefold sleeve) | 15 |

(see also Crass, Little Annie)

ANY TROUBLE
| 79 | Pennine PSS 7165 | Yesterdays Love/Nice Girls, (1000 only, 100 with 'sewn' p/s) | 20 |
| 79 | Pennine PSS 7165 | Yesterdays Love/Nice Girls, (1000 only, p/s) | 15 |

ANYWAYS/SHAKE APPEAL
| 88 | Jericho JR 001 | Wall of Hurt/Amphetamine (no sleeve) | 15 |

AOA
85	COR COR 4	WHO ARE THEY TRYING TO CON (EP, 12", comes with 7" sleeve with lyrics)	20
86	COR GURT 12	UNLIMITED GENOCIDE (Split LP with OI POLLOI, insert)	20
88	ENDANGERED EDR LP 2	SATISFACTORY ARRANGEMENT (LP)	30

AOS3
| 94 | Words Of Warning WOWLP28 | GODS SECRET AGENT (LP) | 30 |
| 95 | Inna State ANOKLP001 | DIVERSIONARY TACTICS (LP) | 15 |

APARTMENT
| 80 | Heartbeat PULSE 7 | The Car/Winter (p/s) | 20 |

APATCHI BAND
| 73 | President PT 392 | Issmak/Crashpad | 30 |

APB
| 81 | Oily SLICK 6 | Chain Reaction/Power Crisis (p/s) | 15 |
| 81 | Oily SLICK 7 | Shoot You Down/Talk To Me (blue or black p/s) | 15 |

APES
| 72 | Leicester Rec. Co LRS LS 1 | APES (LP) | 50 |

APEX RHYTHM & BLUES ALLSTARS
| 59 | John Lever AP 100 | Yorkshire Relish/Caravan | 40 |

APHEX TWIN

MINT VALUE £

60s	John Lever JLEP 1	APEX RHYTHM & BLUES ALLSTARS (EP, no p/s)	350

(see also Ian Hunter)

APHEX TWIN
SINGLES : SINGLES AND EPS

91	Mighty Force 01	ANALOGUE BUBBLEBATH VOL. 1 (12" EP, label on 1 side only, other side has white label, some stamped)	40
91	Rabbit City CUT 002	ANALOGUE BUBBLEBATH VOL. 2 (12" EP, stamped white label)	35
92	R&S RSUK 12	Didgeridoo/Analogue Bubblebath 1/Flaphead/Isoprophlex (12", stickered R&S sleeve, 'Isoprophlex' is actually 'Phloam')	20
93	Mighty Force MF 201	ANALOGUE BUBBLEBATH VOL. 1 (12" EP, repressing of 1000 copies, MF201 on label, other side has plain white label)	25
93	Rephlex CAT 008	ANALOGUE BUBBLEBATH VOL. 3 (12" EP, paper bag sleeve)	18
93	Warp WAP 39	ON EP (2x12" in special sleeve)	25
93	Warp WAP 39R	On (D-Scape Mix)/On (Reload Mix)/On (μ-Ziq Mix)/On (28 Mix) (12", p/s)	15
93	Warp WAP 60	VENTOLIN EP (12", p/s)	15
93	Warp WAP 60R	VENTOLIN EP (THE REMIXES) (12", p/s)	15
93	Warp WAP 60/WAP 60R	VENTOLIN EP (2 x 12", includes both above 12"s, stickered gatefold p/s)	25
94	Rephlex CAT 019 EP	ANALOGUE BUBBLEBATH VOL. 4 (12" EP, p/s with insert, as AFX)	15
95	Rephlex CAT 034	ANALOGUE BUBBLEBATH VOL. 5 (as AFX, 12" white label only)	500
95	Warp WAP 63	Donkey Rhubarb/Vaz Deferenz/Icct Hedral (Philip Glass Orchestration)/Pancake Lizard (12", p/s)	12
95	Warp WAP 67	HANGABLE AUTO BULB EP (12",as AFX)	40
95	Warp WAP 69	HANGABLE AUTO BULB 2 EP (12", as AFX)	40
96	Warp WAP 78	Boy/Girl	20
97	Warp WAP 94P/WAP 94RP	Come To Daddy(Pappy Mix)/Flim/Come To Daddy (Little Lord Faulteroy Mix)/Bucephalus Bouncing Ball/To Cure A Weakling Child (Contour Regard)/Funny Little Man/Come To Daddy (Mummy Mix)/IZ-US (2 x 12", 500 only)	40
99	Warp WAP105	Windowlicker/(Impossible to title)/Nanno (12", inner)	25
01	Warp DRUKQS 01 54	Cymru Beats (Argonaut Mix)/Cock 10 (Delco Freedom Mix) (12", stickered black sleeve)	12
05	Rephlex ANALORD 10	Fenix Funk 5/XMD 5a (12" in PVC binder with 12 sleeves for the Analord series)	200
05	Warp WAP 195	46 Analord-Masplid/Naks 11 (Mono) (as AFX)/LFO: Flue Shot (Kringlan)/Pathfinder (12")	20
05	Rephlex ANALORD 01	ANALORD 01 (12" EP, stickered plastic sleeve as AFX)	35
05	Rephlex ANALORD 02	ANALORD 02 (12" EP as AFX)	35
05	Rephlex ANALORD 03	ANALORD 03 (12" EP as AFX)	35
05	Rephlex ANALORD 04	ANALORD 04 (12" EP as AFX)	35
05	Rephlex ANALORD 05	ANALORD 05 (12" EP as AFX)	35
05	Rephlex ANALORD 06	ANALORD 06 (12" EP as AFX)	35
05	Rephlex ANALORD 07	ANALORD 07 (12" EP as AFX)	35
06	Rephlex ANALORD 08	ANALORD 08 (12" EP as AFX)	35
05	Rephlex ANALORD 09	ANALORD 09 (12" EP as AFX)	35
05	Rephlex ANALORD 10	ANALORD 10 (12" EP as AFX)	35
05	Rephlex ANALORD10PIC	ANALORD 10 (12" EP as AFX, picture disc)	45
05	Rephlex ANALORD 11	ANALORD 11 (12" EP as AFX)	30
12	Warp WAP 105	Windowlicker/(Impossible to title)/Nanno (12" reissue)	10
15	Warp WAP381	MARCHROMT30a Edit 2b/XMAS_EVET1 N/MARCHROMT38 Fast (12" white label, hand-stamped)	10
15	Warp WAP384	ORPHANED DEEJAY SELEK 2006-8 (12" EP, p/s, as A.F.X.)	10
17	Warp WAP 400	LONDON 03.06.17 (12", as AFX, stamped white labels in plain lime green sleeve, sold at Field Day Festival 2017)	250

ALBUMS

92	R&S/Apollo AMBLP 3922	SELECTED AMBIENT WORKS 85-92 (2-LP, 1st issue with no barcode)	150
94	Warp WARPLP 21	SELECTED AMBIENT WORKS VOL. 2 (3-LP, brown vinyl, black and white sleeve with numbered sticker)	200
94	Warp WARPLP 21	SELECTED AMBIENT WORKS VOL. 2 (3-LP, black vinyl, stickered colour sleeve)	200
95	Warp WARPLP 30	I CARE BECAUSE YOU DO (2-LP, stickered sleeve)	50
96	Warp WARPLP 43	RICHARD D. JAMES (LP)	50
02	Warp WARPLP 92	DRUKQS (4-LP)	150
02	Warp WARPLP 92	DRUKQS (4-LP, 1st pressing with mispressed side B containing 2 tracks by unknown artist)	150
02	Warp WARPLP 92X	DRUKQS (4-LP in 12" x 17" numbered box, 1,000 only)	300
02	Rephlex CAT 008	ANALOGUE BUBBLEBATH VOL 3 (2-LP, reissue)	30
13	Apollo AMBLP 3922	SELECTED AMBIENT WORKS 85-92 (2-LP, reissue)	40
14	Warp WARPLP 247X	SYRO (3-LP special 'ballot' edition of 200 copies in box with additional track on playable print)	300
14	Warp WARPLP 247	SYRO (3-LP, inners, booklet)	30

(see also Caustic Window, Polygon Window, Q-Chastic, Kosmic Kommando, Tuss, Mike & Rich)

APHRODITE'S CHILD

68	Mercury MF 1039	Rain & Tears/Don't Try To Catch A River	15
69	Mercury MF 1079	End Of The World/You Always Stand In My Way	15
69	Polydor 56769	I Want To Live/Magic Mirror	20
72	Vertigo 6032 900	Break/Babylon	15
68	Mercury SMCL 20140	END OF THE WORLD/RAIN AND TEARS (LP, black/silver label, laminated sleeve)	35
69	Polydor 2384 005	IT'S FIVE O'CLOCK (LP, gatefold sleeve)	40
72	Vertigo 6673 001	666 - THE APOCALYPSE OF JOHN (2-LP, swirl labels, gatefold, red laminated sleeve. Sleeve has cat number 6673 001, albums have 6333500/6333501 on labels)	1000
75	Philips 6483025	RAIN & TEARS (LP)	15
77	Vertigo 6641 581	666 (2-LP, reissue, as Aphrodite's Child with Demis Roussos & Vangelis, different sleeve, 'spaceship' labels)	60

(see also Vangelis, Forminx)

APOCALYPSE

82	Gate GATE 2	Storm Child/Chosen Few (p/s)	125

APOLLO FOUR FORTY

			MINT VALUE £
APOLLO FOUR FORTY			
97	Stealth Sonic Recordings SSX2440LP	ELECTRO GLIDE IN BLUE (2-LP)	20
APOLLO TWO			
93	Good Looking GLR 003	VOLUME 1 (12", EP)	25
APOLLO XI			
91	Wau! Mr. Modo APOLLO 11	Peace (In The Middle East) (7" Mix 2)/Peace (Sea Of Tranquility Mix)/Peace (Is This Really The Orb? Mix) (12")	10
(see also Orb)			
APOLLOS			
60	Mercury AMT 1096	Rockin' Horses/Just Dreaming	10
A POPULAR HISTORY OF SIGNS			
80	Melodia M1	Justice Not Vengeance/Possession (p/s)	12
81	Melodia M2	Crowds/Crossing The Border (p/s, insert)	10
82	Melodia M4	Dancing with Ideas/The Traveller (p/s)	15
APOSTLES			
82	No Label	BLOW IT UP BURN IT DOWN KICK IT TILL IT BREAKS EP (fold out p/s)	15
83	Scum SCUM 3	THE CURSE OF THE CREATURE EP	10
84	Scum SCUM 2	RISING FROM THE ASHES EP	10
84	Scum SCUM 4	THE GIVING OF LOVE COSTS NOTHING EP	10
86	Fight Back FIGHT 9	DEATH TO WACKY POP (Split EP with THE JOY OF LIVING)	8
85	Mortarhate MORT 9	SMASH THE SPECTACLE! EP	10
89	Active Sounds ASP 10	NO FAITH NO FEAR? (EP, 3 A side tracks by STATEMENT, 2 b side tracks by APOSTLES)	10
83	Cause For Concern CFC 2	LIVE AT THE LMC (LP, one side by THE MOB)	25
86	Acid Strings 001	HOW MUCH LONGER? (LP, with inserts)	20
86	Mortarhate MORT 23	PUNK OBITUARY (LP, gatefold, insert, lyric sheet)	15
86	Children Of The Revolution GURT 11	THE LIVES AND TIMES OF THE APOSTLES (LP, inserts)	20
87	Active Sounds AB 001	EQUINOX SCREAMS (LP)	18
88	Acid Strings ASR 002	THE ACTS OF THE APOSTLES IN THE THEATRE OF FEAR (LP)	25
88	Active Sounds ASP 20	SPLIT (LP, with booklet/inserts, one side by STATEMENT)	30
APOSTOLIC INTERVENTION			
67	Immediate IM 043	(Tell Me) Have You Ever Seen Me/Madame Garcia	250
(see also Small Faces, Humble Pie)			
APPALOOSA			
94	Recoil RCL 003	UNPLUGGED EP (12", 3-track, die-cut sleeve)	15
(see also Global Communications)			
APPLE			
68	Page One POF 101	Let's Take A Trip Down The Rhine/Buffalo Billy Can	100
68	Page One POF 110	Doctor Rock/The Other Side	90
69	Page One POLS 016	AN APPLE A DAY (LP, textured sleeve, blue/silver labels with 'apple' insert)	1500
69	Page One POLS 016	AN APPLE A DAY (LP, without 'apple' insert)	1000
APPLE PIE AND CUSTARD			
74	Philips 6006439	Five Sisters/Doctor Fantastic	8
APPLE BOUTIQUE			
87	Creation CRE052T	Love Resistance/Don't Even Believe In You/The Ballad Of Jet Harris (12")	60
18	Option Nerve ON 1	Love Resistance/Don't Even Believe In You/The Ballad Of Jet Harris (reissue, red orange swirl vinyl, postcard, poster and badge p/s)	20
GEOFF APPLEBY			
76	Virgin VS157	Hey Sadie/Move On Down The Road	6
APPLEJACKS (U.K.)			
64	Decca F 11981	Three Little Words/You're The One For Me	7
65	Decca F 12050	Chim Chim Chiree/It's Not A Game Anymore (export, unissued)	25
65	Decca F 12106	It's Not A Game Anymore/Bye Bye Girl	10
65	Decca F 12216	I Go To Sleep/Make Up Or Break Up	20
65	Decca F 12301	I'm Through/We Gotta Get Together	8
67	CBS 202615	You've Been Cheating/Love Was In My Eyes	40
64	Decca LK 4635	THE APPLEJACKS (LP)	100
APPLETREE THEATRE			
68	Verve (S)VLP 6018	PLAYBACK (LP)	70
APPOLINAIRES			
82	Two Tone 20 TT	The Feelings Gone/Feelings Back (paper labels, p/s)	12
82	Two Tone CHS TT 12 20	The Feelings Gone (Dance Mix)/The Feelings Back/The Bongo Medley (Extremely Long Version) (12", p/s)	15
82	Two Tone CHS TT 22	Envy The Love/Give It Up (p/s)	12
82	Two Tone CHS TT 12 22	Envy The Love/Give It Up (12", p/s)	25
APPRECIATIONS			
77	Destiny 1016	I Can't Hide It/Instrumental Version (2 acetates only)	175
80s	Soul City 157	I Can't Hide It/No No No (reissue)	15
APPROACHING FOOTSTEPS			
82	Sanctuary HEH 001	Autumn/Fire And Ashes	25
APRIL & THE PENNIES			
80	Rockelly RKR 10780	Light Of Love/Paradise Walk (no p/s, some with postcard)	75
80	Rockelly RKR 10381	Love And Inspiration/You're So Different From The Rest	50
81	Rockelly RKR 10781	Heroes Of The Night/Comes The Dawn	75
APRIL SHOWERS (1)			
73	Ritual RT2	Nowhere To Hide/Suzy Q	15
APRIL SHOWERS (2)			
84	Chrysalis CHS 2787	Abandon Ship/Everytime We Say Goodbye	50
84	Chrysalis CHS 122787	Abandon Ship/Everytime We Say Goodbye (12", p/s)	120

APRIL WINE

MINT VALUE £

APRIL WINE
72	Pye 7N 45145	You Could Have Been A Lady/Teacher	25
72	Pye 7N 45163	Bad Side Of The Moon/Believe In Me	10
73	Pye 7N 45624	Weeping Widow/Just Like That	6
76	London HLU 10549	You Won't Dance With Me/Shot Down	6

AQUA LEVI & THE ROOTS IMENSION
91	Roots RI 001	His Foundation/His Dub (12")	60
92	Roots RI 003	Gather My Children/Gather My Dub (12")	50
92	Roots RI 7002	Babylon Mus Set Me Free/Freedom Dub	35

AQUA REGIA
88	Irdial Discs AQR 1	HOT LOVE 3 & 5 (12", p/s)	120
88	Irdial Discs AQR 2	Pump Up The LEDS to Red, Take Some Drugs And Shake Your Head!/Version (12")	50
89	Irdial 12 IRD AQR 6 R1	New York City Smile On Me!/Untitled/(George Kelly Baron Remix 1)/(George Kelly Baron Remix II) (12", with free 7")	18

AQUARIAN AGE
68	Parlophone R 5700	10,000 Words In A Cardboard Box/Good Wizard Meets Naughty Wizard	600

(see also Twink, Tomorrow, Clem Cattini Ork, Nicky Hopkins)

AQUARIAN DREAM
76	Buddah BDS 455	Phoenix/Once Again	6
79	Elektra LV 7	You're A Star/Play It For Me (One More TIme)	8
79	Buddah BDSL 488	Phoenix/East 6th Street (12")	20
76	Buddah DISC 008	NORMAN CONNORS PRESENTS AQUARIAN DREAM (LP)	50
78	Elektra K 52109	FANTASY (LP)	15

(see also Norman Connors)

AQUARIANS
71	Ackee ACK 135	Circy Cap/Circy Version	12
71	Ackee ACK 137	Rebel/Invasion Version	35

(see also Augustus Pablo, Herman)

AQUATONES
58	London HLO 8631	You/She's The One For Me	25

AQUILA (1)
70	RCA SF 8126	THE AQUILA SUITE (LP, gatefold sleeve, orange labels)	150

(see also Patrick Campbell-Lyons)

AQUILA (2)
83	Graphic S82 CUS 1486 1982	Fall/Threatened (p/s)	20

(see also 101ers)

AQUIZIM
80	Ariwa ARI 1007	Time Of My Life/Sheila (12")	15
80	Ariwa ARI 1011	GARRET PEPER CROSS: Magnet/AQUIZIM: Electromatic Magnet (12")	15
81	Ariwa ARI 1015	Kunte Kinte/Version (10", stamped white labels)	30
81	Ariwa ARISL 006	Merry Christmas/MAD PROFESSOR : Version (12")	12
82	Ariwa ARI 1005	True True Loving/Concrete Slave Ship/RANKING ANN: Liberated Woman (12")	20
82	Ariwa ARI 1025	African Connection/AQUIZIM & MAD PROFESSOR: African Voyage (12")	50

ARABESQUE
72	Polydor 2058-237	Fairytale/Solace And Jamboree	8

ARABIS
69	Doctor Bird DB 1204	Jump High Jump Low/TONY SHABAZZ: Stool Pigeon	18

ARABS
78	Hit Run APLP 9002	CRY TUFF - DUB ENCOUNTER CHAPTER 1	55

(see also Prince Far I)

ARAB STRAP
96	Chemikal U'nd CHEM 007	The First Big Weekend/Gilded (700 only)	20
97	Chemikal U'nd CHEM 017	Hey! Fever/Girls Of Summer (p/s)	10
97	Chemikal U'nd TWEM 017	THE GIRLS OF SUMMER EP (12", p/s)	15
01	Chemikal U'nd CHEM 049	The Love Detective/Bullseye/We Know Where We Live (12")	10
03	Chemikal U'nd CHEM 0677	THE SHY RETIRER EP : Radio Edit, Dirty Hospital Remix, Why Can't This Be Love, Good Part, New Saturday (12")	10
96	Chemikal U'nd CHEM 010	THE WEEK NEVER STARTS AROUND HERE (LP)	35
98	Chemikal U'nd CHEM 021	PHILOPHOBIA (2-LP, inners)	40
99	Go! Beat 547387	MAD FOR SADNESS (LP, 1000 only)	60
99	Go! Beat 5478251	ELEPHANT SHOE (LP)	40
01	Chemikal U'nd CHEM 050	THE RED THREAD (LP)	30
05	Chemikal U'nd CHEM 082	THE LAST ROMANCE (LP)	25
08	Chemikal U'nd CHEM 065	MONDAY AT THE HUG & PINT (LP)	20
10	Chemikal U'nd CHEM 135	SCENES OF A SEXUAL NATURE (3-CD, CD Rom, 4-LP & cassette, 1000 only, numbered with certificate)	150

ARAGORN
81	Neat NEAT 07	Black Ice/Noonday (p/s)	15

A RAINCOAT
75	EMI EMI 2289	I Love You For Your Mind (Not Your Body)/Vote For Me	8
75	EMI WMI 2331	Nostalgia 75/Sneak Preview From 'Macs By Graves' You Can Heavy Breathe On Me/Morocco/Still Waters (Demo Only)	12
75	EMI EMI 2331	Nostalgia 75/Not Waving But Drowning	10
76	EMI EMI 2393	It Came In The Night/Morocco	10
75	EMI EMC 3090	DIGALONGAMACS (LP)	15

ARANBEE POP SYMPHONY ORCHESTRA
66	Immediate IMLP/IMSP 003	TODAY'S POP SYMPHONY (LP, lilac labels)	125

(see also Andrew Oldham Orchestra, Keith Richard[s])

ARBITRATER
91	Cyclone CYCLONE 1	BALANCE OF POWER (LP)	25
93	Cyclone CYCLONE 2	DARKENED REALITY (CD)	200

ARBORS
69	CBS 4137	The Letter/Most Of It	7
69	CBS 4640	Motel Overture/Touch Me	7

ARBRE
75	DJM DJS 397	Fallin'/Doin' Alright	10
76	DJM DJS 10716	Senorita/Zero To Four (with promo p/s)	12

A.R.C. ROCKBAND
79	Rock Records	Homemade Wine/The Chase (p/s)	80

ARC (1)
71	Decca SKL-R 5077	ARC . . . AT THIS (LP, blue/silver "boxed" Decca labels)	200

(see also Heavy Jelly, Skip Bifferty, Bell & Arc)

ARC (2)
80	Orchrist ORC 1	Tribute To Mike Hailwood/For My Next Kick (p/s)	50
81	Slipped Disc SD001	War Of The Ring/Ice Cream Theme (p/s)	150

ARCADE FIRE
05	Rough Trade RTRADS 252	Rebellion (Lies)/Rebellion (Lies) (Live) (p/s, white vinyl)	8
10	Rough Trade	We Used To Wait (1-sided promo, white label 1000 only)	10
12	Sonovox 2793767	Sprawl II/Ready To Start (12")	10
13	Sonovox 3752123	Reflektor/Reflektor Instrumental (12", as The Reflektors, p/s)	10
14	Transgressive TRANS 183	Afterlife (Flume remix) (12", stamped sleeve, white label)	12
05	Rough Trade RTRADLP 219	FUNERAL (LP)	25
06	Universal 1724447	NEON BIBLE (2-LP, 4th side etched, stickered sleeve)	20
10	Universal 2743427	THE SUBURBS (2-LP, gatefold, inners)	20
13	Sonovox 3752119	REFLEKTOR (2-LP, metallic gatefold, with inners)	20
17	Sonovox 88985447851	EVERYTHING NOW (LP, 'Day' or 'Night' cover)	20

ARCADIUM
69	Middle Earth MDS 102	Sing My Song/Riding Alone	200
69	Middle Earth MDLS 302	BREATHE AWHILE (LP, laminated sleeve)	1250
11	Acne ADLP 1077	BREATHE AWHILE (LP, reissue with free 7")	15

(see also Kingdom Come, 'Middle Earth Sampler' in Various Artists)

ARC ANGELS
92	Geffen 24465	ARC ANGELS (LP)	35

ARCH CRIMINALS
86	Fight Back FIGHT 8	HANG (12" EP, with insert)	10

ELIZABETH ARCHER & THE EQUATORS
77	Lightning TRO 9011	Feel Like Making Love/Version	30

MARK ARCHER
11	Balkan BV 08	FREQUENCY REMIXES (12" yellow vinyl)	15
14	Balkan BV 11	ARMAGEDDON REMIXES (12", red vinyl)	10
14	Balkan BV 11, BV 12 BV 13	RAVE ARMAGEDDON SURVIVAL KIT (3 x 12", limited edition of 101, red, green and blue vinyl hand-numbered. Rave SOS flare, filtration unit, eye, hand and dancefloor protection gear, T-shirt and sticker pack)	75

(see also Altern 8)

YVONNE ARCHER
81	Virgo Stomach VG 003	Ain't Nobody/Checking Out The Way We Feel (12")	80

ARCHIE WHITEWATER
70	Pye Intl. NSPL 28143	ARCHIE WHITEWATER (LP)	100

ARCHITECTURE IN HELSINKI
06	Moshi Moshi MOSHILP07	IN CASE WE DIE (LP)	20

ARCHIVE
96	Island ARKLP 1001	LONDINIUM (2-LP)	100
99	Independiente ISOM 10LP	TAKE MY HEAD (LP, with free 12")	80
99	Independiente ISOM 10LP	TAKE MY HEAD (LP, without free 12")	60

ARCTIC MONKEYS
05	Bang Bang (No Cat no)	FIVE MINUTES WITH EP (7" white label with stickered die-cut sleeve)	60
05	Bang Bang BANGB 71	FIVE MINUTES WITH EP (500 only, p/s)	80
05	Bang Bang BANGBCD	FIVE MINUTES WITH EP (CD, 1000 only)	70
05	Domino RUG 212	I Bet You Look Good On The Dancefloor/Bigger Boys And Stolen Sweethearts (p/s, stickered)	15
06	Domino RUG 216	When The Sun Goes Down/Settle For A Draw (p/s)	12
06	Domino RUG 236	Leave Before The Lights Come On/Baby I'm Yours (p/s)	20
06	Domino RUG 226	WHO THE FUCK ARE ARCTIC MONKEYS? (10" EP, p/s)	15
07	Domino RUG 254	Brianstorm/Temptation Greets You Like A Naughty Friend (p/s)	6
07	Domino RUG 254T	If You Found This It's Probably Too Late/Brianstorm/Temptation Greets You Like Your Naughty Friend Rap/What If You Were Right The First Time (10", p/s)	12
07	Domino RUF 279	Matador/Deframe2r (die-cut p/s, white vinyl, 1000 only)	12
07	Domino RUF 279	Death Ramps/Nettles (As DEATH RAMPS, 250 only, stamped labels)	25
07	Domino RUG 261	Flourescent Adolescent/The Bakery (p/s)	8
07	Domino RUG 261T	Flourescent Adolescent/The Bakery/Plastic Tramp/Too Much To Ask (10", p/s)	15
07	Domino RUG 279T	Teddy Picker/Bad Woman//DEATH RAMPS: Death Ramp/Nettles (10" p/s)	12
07	Domino RUG 279	Teddy Picker/RICHARD HAWLEY AND DEATH RAMPS: Bad Woman (p/s)	8
09	Domino RUG 338	Crying Lightning/Red Right Hand (signed 7", 55 only for Oxfam Charity)	30
09	Domino RUG 349	Cornerstone/Catapult (p/s)	8
09	Domino RUG 349T	Cornerstone/Catapult/Sketchhead/Fright Lined Dining Rooms (10")	35
10	Domino RUG 352	My Propeller/Joining The Dots (p/s)	8
10	Domino RUG 359T	My Propeller/Joining The Dots/The Afternoon's Hat/Don't Forget Who's Legs You're On (10")	15
11	Domino RUG 406T	Don't Sit Down Cause I've Moved Your Chair/The Blond-O-Sonic Shimmer Trap/I.D.S.T. (10")	10
11	Domino RUG 422	The Hellcat Spangled Shalala/Little Illusion Machine (Wirrel Riddler) (p/s, with download code, heavyweight vinyl, most destroyed in PIAS distribution fire, 500 later repressed on thinner vinyl)	7

ARCTIC STRINGS

MINT VALUE £

11	Domino RUG 438	Suck It And See/Evil Twin	8
12	Domino RUG 449	Black Treacle/RICHARD HAWLEY AND THE DEATH RAMPS: You & I	8
12	Domino RUG 468	R U MINE/Electricity (7" purple vinyl, white label with stickered die-cut sleeve, 1750 only)	80
13	Domino RUG 542	Do I Wanna Know/2013 (p/s)	7
13	Domino RUG 561	One For The Road/You're So Dark (p/s)	8
06	Domino WIG 162	WHATEVER PEOPLE SAY I AM THATS WHAT I'M NOT (LP, inner)	20
07	Domino WIGLP 188	FAVOURITE WORST NIGHTMARE (LP)	20
08	Domino DOMDVD005X	AT THE APOLLO (LP, box set DVD & stickered sleeve)	40
09	Domino WIGLP 220	HUMBUG (LP, gatefold, 180gm)	15
11	Domino WIGLP 258	SUCK IT AND SEE (LP, 180gm, download card)	18
13	Domino WIGLP 317	AM (LP, gatefold, insert and free 7")	30

ARCTIC STRINGS
75	Black Magic DEMO 2	Turn Me On/Non Stop	20

ARCTIC FLOW
14	Box Bedroom Rebels BBR15	LOST WISHES EP (p/s, inserts, numbered, 150 copies)	10

ARCTURUS
96	Ancient Lore Creations ALC 002 PLP	ASPERA HIEMS SYMFONIA (LP, picture disc, 1000 only)	40
97	Music For Nations MFN 230	LA MASQUERADE INFENALE (LP, 1000 only)	60

ARCWELDER
92	Duophonic DS 45 03	Favor/Plastic (orange vinyl, p/s, 300 only)	12
92	Duophonic DS 45 03	Favor/Plastic (p/s, 1000 only)	8

NEIL ARDLEY
70	Columbia SCX 6414	GREEK VARIATIONS (LP, with Ian Carr & Don Rendell)	250
72	Regal Zono. SLRZ 1028	A SYMPHONY OF AMARANTHS (LP, red/silver labels)	200
74	Argo ZDA 164/5	WILL POWER (2-LP, with Ian Carr, Stan Tracey & Mike Gibbs)	125
75	Gull GULP 1018	KALEIDOSCOPE OF RAINBOWS (LP)	20
78	Decca TXS-R 133	HARMONY OF THE SPHERES (LP, featuring John Martyn)	20
09	Gull/Pure Pleasure GULP 1018	KALEIDOSCOPE OF RAINBOWS (2-LP, reissue)	18

(see also Don Rendell, New Jazz Orchestra, Michael Gibbs)

AREA CODE 615
70	Polydor 2066 249	Stone Fox Chase/Always The Same (first issue on paper labels)	6

COLIN AREETY
72	Deram DM 370	Holy Cow/Can't Do It For You	8
73	Deram 383	(If Loving You Is Wrong) I Don't Want To Be Right/One Night Affair	20

ARENA TWINS
59	London HL 7071	Mama, Care Mama/Little Pig (export issue)	10

ARGENT
71	Epic EPC 5423	Celebration/Kingdom	10
71	Epic EPC 9135	Hold Your Head Up/Closer To Heaven/Keep On Rollin' (33rpm EP, p/s)	12
72	Epic EPC 8115	Tragedy/Rejoice	7
74	Epic EPC 2147	Thunder And Lightning/Keeper Of The Flame	8
74	Epic EPC 2448	Man For All Reasons/Music From The Spheres	8
74	Epic SEPC 2849	Keep On Rollin'/I Am The Dance Of Ages	10
70	CBS 63781	ARGENT (LP, gatefold sleeve)	60
71	Epic EPC 64190	RING OF HANDS (LP, gatefold sleeve)	30
72	Epic EPC 64962	ALL TOGETHER NOW (LP, gatefold sleeve, with booklet)	25
74	Epic EQ 32195/Q 65475	IN DEEP (LP, quadrophonic)	25
75	RCA RS 1020	COUNTERPOINTS (LP)	15

(see also Zombies, Unit 4 + 2, Roulettes, John Verity Band)

ARGONAUTS
85	Lyntone LYN 18249/50	Apeman/Under My Thumb (signed white label, no p/s)	60

(see also Madness)

ARGOSY
69	DJM DJS 214	Mr. Boyd/Imagine	120

(see also Elton John, Supertramp)

ARGUS
84	ABS SRT 4KS258	Holocaust/The Widow (title sleeve)	100

(see also People Like Us)

ARGYLE SQUAD
74	Ra 5018	Farewell 3rd Division/Promotion '75	8

ARIEL
74	Harvest HAR 5085	Jamaican Farewell/And I'm Blue	7
74	Harvest HAR 5088	Yeah Tonite/Laughing Man	10
75	Harvest HAR 5093	I'll Be Gone/Rock And Roll Scars	10
73	Harvest SHSP 4028	A STRANGE FANTASTIC DREAM (LP, textured sleeve)	20
75	Harvest SHSP 4239	ROCK AND ROLL SCARS (LP)	15

ARIEL M
97	Domino WIGLP 37	ARIEL M (LP)	20

ARIEL PINK'S HAUNTED GRAFFITI
10	4AD AD3X24	Round And Round/Mistaken Wedding (p/s)	6

ARIZONA SWAMP COMPANY
70	Parlophone R 5841	Train Keeps Rollin'/Tennessee Woman	50

(see also Nashville Teens)

ARKITEX
79	Arkitex AKX 1	Only One/Drivin All Night/Big Brother (no p/s)	125

WANDA ARLETTY
72	Columbia 8954	Counting Each Minute/Motor Car	6

Deke ARLON (& OFFBEATS)

MINT VALUE £

DEKE ARLON (& OFFBEATS)
64	Columbia DB 7194	I'm Just A Boy/Can't Make Up My Mind	10

ARMADA ORCHESTRA/ULTRAFUNK
75	Contempo 2089	The Love I Lost (Part 1)/The Love I Lost (Part 2)	7
75	Contempo CLP 528	DISCO ARMADA (LP)	15
76	Contempo CLP 536	PHILLY ARMADA (LP)	15

ARMAGEDDON
75	A&M AMLH 64513	ARMAGEDDON (LP, with lyric inner sleeve, silver labels)	60

(see also Keith Relf, Steamhammer, Captain Beyond)

ARMAGIDEON
93	Armagideon ASLP 001	HORNS ENCOUNTER VOLUME 1 (LP)	20
94	Armagideon ASLP 002	NATURAL ELEMENTS DUB (LP)	15

JOAN ARMATRADING
85	A&M AMLH 64588	JOAN ARMATRADING (LP, 'Nimbus' supercuts repressing)	50

ARMED FORCE
80	Armed Forces AF1	Popstar/Attack (p/s, 500 only)	20

ARMENTA
83	Savoir Faire FAIT 005	I Wanna Be With You/Part 2/Part 3 (12")	15

ARMS & LEGS
76	MAM MAM 140	Janice/She'll Surprise You	6
76	MAM MAM 147	Heat Of The Night/Good Times	6
77	MAM MAM 156	Is There Any More Wine/She'll Surprise You	6

RUSSELL ARMS
57	London HLB 8406	Cinco Robles (Five Oaks)/The World Is Made Of Lisa (gold label)	20

CHUCK ARMSTRONG
73	Action ACT 4620	God Bless The Children/Black Foxy Woman	15

FRANKIE ARMSTRONG (& FRIENDS)
79	Action Against Corrie RRFA 001	We Must Choose/RED RINSE: A Woman's Right To Choose (private pressing)	30
83	Plant Life TPLS 03	Message From Mother Earth/Shall There Be Womanly Times Or Shall We Die?	10
72	Topic 12TS 216	LOVELY ON THE WATER (LP)	30
75	Topic 12TS 273	SONGS AND BALLADS (LP)	18

(see also A.L. Lloyd)

HERBIE ARMSTRONG
80	Avatar 108	Real Real Gone/Blackout	10

LORNA ARMSTRONG
74	Ackee 535	Dance With Me/Lonely Nights	15

LOUIS ARMSTRONG
SINGLES
69	United Artists UP 35059	We Have All The Time In The World/Pretty Little Missy	15

B.J. ARNAU
72	Polydor 2058238	The Big Hurt/Hey Brenda!	8
72	RCA 2284	Every Girl Becomes A Woman/Jubilation	8

(see also Brenda Arnau)

BRENDA ARNAU
74	Bell 1351	A Step In The Right Direction/Superman	7
80	Pye 7P 185	Electra Flash/Dance Electra Flash (p/s)	45

GINNY ARNELL
63	MGM MGM 1217	Dumb Head/How Many Times Can One Heart Break	15
63	MGM MGM 1243	I Wish I Knew What Dress To Wear/He's My Little Devil	15
65	MGM MGM 1270	Just Like A Boy/Portrait Of A Fool	10
65	MGM MGM 1283	A Little Bit Of Love Can Hurt/B-I-I-I-Why	10

CALVIN ARNOLD
68	MGM MGM 1378	Funky Way/Snatchin' Back	20
68	MGM MGM 1449	Mama In Law/Mini Skirt	20

EDDY ARNOLD
54	HMV 7MC 22	Hep Cat Baby/This Is The Thanks I Get (For Loving You) (export issue)	10
66	RCA 1519	I Want To Go With You/Mary Claire Melvina Rebecca Jane	6

KOKOMO ARNOLD
69	Saydisc Matchbox SDR 163	KOKOMO ARNOLD (LP)	30

P.P. ARNOLD
66	Immediate IM 040	Everything's Gonna Be Alright/Life Is But Nothin'	200
66	Immediate IM 040	Everything's Gonna Be Alright/Life Is But Nothin' (DJ copy)	300
67	Immediate IM 047	The First Cut Is The Deepest/Speak To Me	25
67	Immediate IM 055	The Time Has Come/If You See What I Mean	20
68	Immediate IM 061	(If You Think You're) Groovy/Though It Hurts Me Badly	20
69	Polydor 56350	Bury Me Down The River/Give A Hand, Take A Hand	7
70	Polydor 2058 061	Likely Piece Of Work/May The Winds Blow	7
80	Virgin/NEMS SV 103	Angel Of The Morning/Everything's Gonna Be Alright/The First Cut Is The Deepest/Groovy/The Time Has Come (doublepack, gatefold p/s)	10
67	Immediate IMLP/IMSP 011	THE FIRST LADY OF IMMEDIATE (LP, withdrawn)	400
68	Immediate IMSP 017	KAFUNTA (LP, gatefold sleeve)	100
83	See For Miles SEE 235	KAFUNTA - THE BEST OF (LP)	20

(see also Ikettes, Nice, Small Faces, Spectrum, P.P. & Primes)

P.P. ARNOLD & THE JEFF WAYNE SINGERS
60s	Pepsi Lyntone 2498	We've Got Pepsi (1-sided with Pepsi Company sleeve)	15

ARPADYS
77	Polydor 2933802	ARPADYS (LP)	25

ARRIVAL
69	Decca F 12986	Friends/Don't Turn His Love Away	6

ARRIVALS

MINT VALUE £

70	Decca F 13026	I Will Survive/See The Lord	6
71	CBS S 7617	Family Tree/Part Of My Dream	10
70	Decca SKL 5055	ARRIVAL (LP, blue/silver with 'boxed' Decca logo)	20

ARRIVALS
69	Pye 7N 17761	Scooby Doo/She's About A Mover	12

ARROGANT
80	Rocket XPRES 43	Ego/So Near So Far (p/s)	12

ARROWS (2) (U.K.)
75	RAK RAK 205	I Love Rock 'n' Roll/Broken Down Heart	6

CLIVE ARROWSMITH
74	Scratchy CHS 2027	Desire/Almost Gone	8

ARS NOVA
68	Elektra EKSN 45029	Zoroaster/Pavan For My Lady	12
68	Elektra EKSN 45034	Fields Of People/Song To The City	12
68	Elektra EKS 74020	ARS NOVA (LP, orange label, gatefold sleeve)	40
69	Atlantic 588 196	SUNSHINE AND SHADOWS (LP)	40

ART
67	Island WIP 6019	What's That Sound (For What It's Worth)/Rome Take Away Three	20
69	Island WIP 6048	Room With A View/SPOOKY TOOTH: Nobody There At All (promo only)	50
75	Island WIP 6048	What's That Sound (For What It's Worth)/Flying Anchors (with promo Art sleeve)	30
75	Island WIP 6224	What's That Sound (For What It's Worth)/Flying Anchors	7
67	Island ILP 967	SUPERNATURAL FAIRY TALES (LP, first pressing, pink label with black/orange circle logo, laminated sleeve)	400
70	Island ILP 967	SUPERNATURAL FAIRY TALES (LP, second pressing, pink label with 'i' logo and factory stamped matrix numbers, those with hand written matrixes are bootlegs, laminated sleeve)	300
75	Island ILP 967	SUPERNATURAL FAIRY TALES (LP, reissue, matt sleeve, 'palm tree' label)	35
15	Island 47089803	SUPERNATURAL FAIRY TALES (LP, reissue)	20

(see also V.I.P.'s, Baron With His Pounding Piano, Spooky Tooth, Luther Grosvenor, Hapshash & Coloured Coat)

ART ATTACKS
78	Albatross TIT 1	I'm A Dalek/Neutron Bomb (p/s)	20
79	Fresh FRESH 3	First And Last: Punk Rock Stars/Rat City/First And Last (p/s)	20
96	Overground OVER 58	OUTRAGE AND HORROR (LP, 600 only, pressed in U.K. for export to Japan)	30

(see also Monochrome Set, Tagmemics, Kray Cherubs)

ART BEARS
81	Recommended RE 6622	CODA TO "MAN AND BOY" (EP, live, 1-sided clear vinyl, silk-screened p/s, 1,750 only, this price for 500 signed & numbered for subscribers)	12
78	Recommended REC 2188	HOPES AND FEARS (LP, gatefold sleeve with poster & booklet)	35
79	Recommended REC 0618	WINTER SONGS (LP, with booklet)	30
81	Recommended RE 6622	THE WORLD AS IT IS TODAY (LP, 45rpm, with booklet)	25
84	Re RE 2188	HOPES AND FEARS (LP, reissue)	15
10	ReR MegacorpRER VAB1	HOPES AND FEARS (LP, reissue, 180gm)	15

(see also Henry Cow, Slapp Happy)

ART ENSEMBLE OF CHICAGO
72	Freedom FLP 40108	THE SPIRITUAL (LP)	40
74	Freedom FLP 40122	TUTANKAMUN (LP)	35
00	Universal Sound USLP 11	LES STANCES A SOPHIE (LP, reissue)	20
80	Affinity AFF (D) 46	LIVE (2-LP)	20

ARTERY
79	Limited Edition TAKE 1	Mother Moon/Pretends/Heinz (p/s)	10
81	Aardvark AARD 5	Cars In Motion/Life And Death (p/s)	6
81	Armageddon AS 026	Afterwards/Into The Garden (p/s)	6
83	Red Flame RFB25	Alabama Song/A Song For Lena (p/s)	7
83	Red Flame RF 18	ONE AFTERNOON IN A HOT AIR BALOON (LP)	18
84	Golden Dawn GDLP 01	SECOND COMING (LP)	15
85	Golden Dawn GDLP 02	NUMBER FOUR (LP)	15

(see also Mission)

ART FAILURE
79	Vague VOG 1	Scream In Pain/In Vogue (stapled over p/s)	12

DAVE & TONI ARTHUR
70	Trailer LER 1	Bushes And Briars/Lazio Feher	8
67	Transatlantic TRA 154	MORNING STANDS ON TIPTOE (LP)	60
69	Topic 12T 190	THE LARK IN THE MORNING (LP, blue label)	30
71	Trailer LER 2017	HEARKEN TO THE WITCHES' RUNE (LP, red label)	20

ARTHUR'S MOTHER
71	Polydor 2058093	On The Dole/Butterfly	8

ANDY ARTHURS
78	Radar ADA 7	I Can Detect You (For 1000 Miles)/I Am A Machine (p/s, withdrawn)	10
79	TDS TDS 6	I Feel Flat/Play The Music (p/s)	7

ARTICLE 58
81	Rational RATE 4	Event To Come/Echoes/Lost And Found (p/s)	8

ART INTERFACE
83	ART ART 2	Secretaries From Heaven (Radio Vers.)/Secretaries From Heaven (Real Vers.) (p/s)	10

ARTISTICS
66	Coral Q 72488	I'm Gonna Miss You/Hope We Have	80
66	Coral Q 72488	I'm Gonna Miss You/Hope We Have (DJ Copy)	150
67	Coral Q 72492	Girl I Need You/I'm Glad I Met You	60
67	Coral Q 72492	Girl I Need You/I'm Glad I Met You (DJ Copy)	150
70	MCA MU 1117	I'm Gonna Miss You/Hope We Have (reissue)	10
76	Brunswick BR 39	I'm Gonna Miss You/GENE CHANDLER: There Was A Time	15
66	Columbia	GET MY HANDS ON SOME LOVIN' (LP, unconfirmed existence)	250

ART MOVEMENT

MINT VALUE £

ART MOVEMENT
67	Livingston LRL/PR 141	Bitter Suite/Here Today/Blame Yourself/She Was Really Saying Something	30
68	Decca F 12768	I Love Being In Love With You/The Game Of Love	20
68	Decca F 12836	Loving Touch/Happy Song	10
69	Columbia DB 8602	Yes Sir . . . No Sir/Sally Goes Round The Moon	15
70	Columbia DB 8651	For As Long As You Need Me/Nice 'n' Easy	12
70	Columbia DB 8697	The Sooner I Get To You/Morning Girl	35

ART NOUVEAU
79	Gimpy Dak DAK 1	Fear Machine/Animal Instincts (p/s)	50

ART NOUVEAUX
64	Fontana TF 843	Extra Terrestrial Visitations/The Way To Play It	35

ART OBJECTS
80	Heartbeat PULSE 10	Showing Off To Impress The Girls/Our Silver Sister (live) (p/s)	12
81	Fried Egg EGG 007	Hard Objects/Bibliotheque/Fit Of Pique (p/s)	10
81	Heartbeat HB 5	BAGPIPE MUSIC (LP)	18

ART OF NOISE
85	ZTT 12 ZTPS 1	CLOSE TO THE EDIT (12", stamped green label, unreleased)	10
86	China WOKP 9	Paranoimia/Why Me (shaped picture disc)	15

ART SCIENCE TECHNOLOGY
90	Debut DEBTX 3100	A.S.T./Esus Flow (2 mixes) (12", p/s)	12

(see also Future Sound Of London)

ARTWOODS
64	Decca F 12015	Sweet Mary/If I Ever Get My Hands On You	70
65	Decca F 12091	Oh My Love/Big City	60
65	Decca F 12206	Goodbye Sisters/She Knows What To Do	60
66	Decca F 12384	I Take What I Want/I'm Looking For A Saxophonist Doubling French Horn Wearing Size 37 Boots	80
66	Decca F 12465	I Feel Good/Molly Anderson's Cookery Book	90
67	Parlophone R 5590	What Shall I Do/In The Deep End	100
66	Decca DFE 8654	JAZZ IN JEANS (EP)	500
66	Decca LK 4830	ART GALLERY (LP, red/silver label with 'unboxed' Decca logo and 'FFrr' laminated front sleeve)	700
70	Decca Eclipse ECM 2025	ART GALLERY (LP, reissue in different sleeve, also stereo [ECS 2025])	125
73	Spark SRLM 2006	THE ARTWOODS (LP)	60
16	Record Collector RCLP 020	LIVE AT KLOOKS KLEEK (2-LP)	30

(see also St. Valentine's Day Massacre, Keef Hartley Band, Jon Lord, Dog Soldier, Lucas & Mike Cotton Sound)

ARTWORK
02	Big Apple BAM 001	RED EP (12")	15
02	Big Apple BAM 001	RED EP (12", red vinyl)	25

ART ZOYD
82	Recommended RR 14.15	Ménage (12.59) (1-sided, other side printed, foldout sleeve in PVC sleeve, existence unconfirmed)	10
82	Recommended RR 14/15	PHASE IV (2-LP with booklet, inserts and free 1-sided 7")	20

ARZACHEL
69	Evolution Z 1003	ARZACHEL (LP, blue label, laminated front sleeve)	1000

(see also Egg, Steve Hillage, Khan, Hatfield & the North, National Health, Gong)

ARZENBOYS
75	DJM DJS 370	Bump On My Head/Instrumental Version	6

ASGARD
72	Threshold TH 10	Friends/Children Of A New Born Age	6
73	Threshold TH 15	In The Realm Of Asgard/Town Cryer	6
72	Threshold THS 6	IN THE REALM OF ASGARD (LP, white/blue label, gatefold sleeve)	175

DANIEL ASH
90	Beggars Banquet BEGA 114	COMING DOWN (LP)	20
92	Beggars Banquet BBQLP 129	FOOLISH THING DESIRE (LP)	50

(see also Bauhaus, Tones On Tail, Love And Rockets)

VIC ASH QUARTET
56	Tempo A 135	Blue Lou/Doxy	6
56	Tempo A 137	Early Morning/Just One Of Those Things	6
56	Nixa NJE 1032	VIC ASH & FOUR (EP)	15
56	Columbia SEG 7634	CLARINET VIRTUOSO (EP)	15
56	Tempo EXA 44	MODERN JAZZ SCENE (EP)	50

(see also Maxine Sullivan, Jazz Five)

ASH (1)
83	Criminal CRI MLP 137	Chase The Spotlight/Evermore (no p/s)	15

ASH (2)
94	La La Land LA LA 001	Jack Names The Planets/Don't Know (wraparound p/s in poly bag, 5,000 only)	12
94	Infectious INFECT 13S	Petrol/The Little Pond/A Message From Oscar Wilde And Patrick The Brewer (p/s, 500 only)	15
94	Infectious INFECT 16S	Uncle Pat/Different Today (p/s, 1,000 only)	10
95	Infectious INFECT 21J	Kung Fu/Day Of The Triffids (p/s, 'Japanese' wraparound no'd p/s in poly bag)	8
95	Fantastic Plastic FP 004	Get Ready/Zero Zero Zero (red vinyl, 1,000 only, mail order only)	12
95	Infectious INFECT 24S	Girl From Mars/Astral (Conversations With Toulouse Lautrec)/Cantina Band (p/s, numbered)	20
97	Barbie Records KEN 1	I Only Want To Be With You/Kung Fu (Live) (silver speckled vinyl p/s, fan club 7")	40
12	Noyes NR 031	LITTLE INFINITY EP (12", hand-numbered)	15
94	Infectious INFECT 14LP	TRAILER (LP, with yellow vinyl 7", "Silver Surfer"/"Jazz '59" [INFECT 14S])	40
96	Infectious INFECT 40LP	1977 (LP, gatefold, inner)	75
98	Infectious INFECT 60LP	NU-CLEAR SOUNDS (LP, gatefold, clear vinyl)	35
01	Infectious INFECT 100LP	FREE ALL ANGELS (LP, gatefold)	50
04	Infectious 5050467319714	MELTDOWN (LP, laminated sleeve)	25

ASHANTIS

MINT VALUE £

ASHANTIS
76	EMI PSR 393	Addis Abeba/Let's Stay Together/We Can We Can (Demo only)	7
77	Calendar DAY 118	Disco Play/A.S.H.A.N.T.I.S.	6
77	Red Bus EMC 3109	LET'S STAY TOGETHER (LP)	20

DOROTHY ASHBY
65	Atlantic ATL 5047	THE FANTASTIC JAZZ HARP OF DOROTHY ASHBY (LP)	20

HAROLD ASHBY
60	Columbia 33SX 1257	BORN TO SWING (LP)	600
61	Columbia 33SX 1379	TENOR STUFF (LP, with Paul Gonsalves)	100

ASH CAN SCHOOL
86	Unit Two TWO 01	She's Only Sleeping/A Day Out Of Paris (p/s)	30

RICHARD ASHCROFT
00	Virgin 72438 38729 78	A Song For Lovers/Money To Burn	8
00	Hut HUTDLP 63	ALONE WITH EVERYBODY (2-LP)	40
02	Hut HUTDLP 77	HUMAN CONDITIONS (2-LP)	40

DOUG ASHDOWN
66	CBS 202083	Guess I'm Doing Fine/I Sure Ain't Standing Still	8

RAFMRA ASHER
78	Maccabees FG1	Fourth Generation/Version	20

ASHFORD & SIMPSON
74	Warner Bros. K16273	Have You Ever Tried It/Time	7
77	Warner Bros. K17679 (T)	Love Don't Make It Right/Bourgie Bourgie (with incorrect mastering) (12")	20
77	Warner Bros. K17679 (T)	Love Don't Make It Right/Bourgie Bourgie (with correct mastering) (12")	60
78	Warner Bros. 12K 17286	Don't Cost You Nothing/Let Love Use Me (12")	15
74	Warner Bros. K46283	GIMME SOMETHING REAL (LP)	18
74	Warner Bros. K56050	I WANNA BE SELFISH (LP)	18

ASHKAN
70	Decca Nova DN-R 1	IN FROM THE COLD (LP, mono)	250
70	Decca Nova SDN-R 1	IN FROM THE COLD (LP, stereo)	175

(see also Fleetwood Mac)

STEVE ASHLEY
74	Gull GULP 1003	STROLL ON (LP, with lyric inner)	20

TYRONE ASHLEY
76	Tomorrow 004	Feet Start Moving/Movin On (promo only)	8
76	Tomorrow 010	Nothing Short Of A Miracle/Instrumental Version (promo only)	8

MICKEY ASHMAN
60	Pye Jazz NJL 25	TAKING THE MICKEY (LP)	20
61	Pye Jazz NJL 29	THROUGH DARKEST ASHMAN (LP)	50

ASHRA
77	Virgin V 2080	NEW AGE OF EARTH (LP)	15

ASHTON, GARDNER & DYKE
69	Polydor 56306	Maiden Voyage/See The Sun In My Eyes	80
69	Polydor 583 081	ASHTON, GARDNER & DYKE (LP)	25
70	Capitol E-ST 563	THE WORST OF ASHTON, GARDNER AND DYKE (LP)	18
72	Capitol EA-ST 22862	WHAT A BLOODY LONG DAY IT'S BEEN (LP, gatefold sleeve)	20

(see also Ashton & Lord, Remo Four, Creation, Birds, Mike Hurst & Method, Badger, Medicine Head)

MARK ASHTON
72	United Artists UP 353390	Get Up And Groove/Barking Dogs	15

ASHTON ON RIBBLE HIGH SCHOOL MUSIC SOCIETY
74	(No label or cat no)	ASHTON SOUND 74 (LP, with inserts)	100

(TONY) ASHTON & (JON) LORD
72	Purple PUR 109	Celebration/Sloeback	7
74	Purple PUR 121	We're Gonna Make It/Band Of The Salvation Army Band	7
74	Oyster OYR 101	TONY ASHTON: The Resurrection Shuffle/Ballad Of Mr Giver	6
74	Purple TPS 3507	FIRST OF THE BIG BANDS (LP)	25

(see also Ashton Gardner & Dyke, Paice Ashton & Lord, Jon Lord, Deep Purple, Green Bullfrog, Cozy Powell)

ASIA
92	IRS 951.959	AQUA (LP, gatefold sleeve)	40

(see also Yes, Emerson Lake & Palmer, Steve Howe)

ASIA FIELDS
90	Frank FRANK 2	Friction/Jack-knifed (12", test pressing only, plain white die-cut sleeve)	25

ASIAN DUB FOUNDATION
98	FFRR 556 066	RAFI'S REVENGE (2-LP)	30

ED ASKEW
69	Fontana STL 5519	ED ASKEW (LP)	60

ASLAN
76	Profile GMOR 006	PAWS FOR THOUGHT (LP)	70
77	Profile GMOR 144	SECOND HELPINGS (LP)	70

AS ONE
94	New Electronica ELEC 6T	Mihara/Dance Of The Uighurs (12")	12
95	New Electronica Elec 23LP	REFLECTIONS ON REFLECTIONS (2-LP)	35
95	New Electronica Elec 26LP	CELESTIAL SOUL (2-LP)	20

ASPECTS
98	Hombre MEX007	2012 (EP)	10
13	Psycho Boogie BOOGS 002	LEFT HAND PATH (LP)	15

MONICA ASPELUND
77	RCA PB 9044	Lapponia/La-La, Sing A Song	8

RON ASPERY
72	Blakey BLP5989	BACK DOOR (LP)	40

Gary & VERA ASPEY

MINT VALUE £

GARY & VERA ASPEY
76	Topic 12TS 299	A TASTE OF HOTPOT (LP)	25

ASPHALT RIBBONS
88	Tigerlily LILY 002	DOWNSIDE EP (12", p/s)	25
89	In Tape IT 063	THE ORCHARD EP (p/s)	30
89	In Tape ITTI 063	THE ORCHARD EP (12", p/s)	35
89	In Tape ITTI 063	THE ORCHARD EP (12", p/s + T-Shirt insert)	50
89	In Tape ITTI 063	THE ORCHARD EP (12", 200 pressed at 48rpm and withdrawn)	40
89	In Tape IT 068	Good Love/Long Lost Uncle/The Day I Turned Bad (p/s)	35
89	In Tape ITTI 068	Good Love/Long Lost Uncle/The Day I Turned Bad (12", p/s)	25
89	In Tape IT 6545 1	Over Again/EVA: Unquenchable (p/s, promo only)	25
91	Tiger Lily LILY 001	A Time To Go/LIFE WITH PATRICK: Wrong (7" sampler)	15
91	Tiger Lily LILY 002	PASSION, COOLNESS, INDIFFERENCE, BOREDOM, MOCKERY, CONTEMPT, DISGUST EP (12")	30
91	ETT 101-1	OLD HORSE (LP)	80

(see also Tindersticks, Stuart A. Staples)

MARY ASQUITH
78	Mother Earth MUM 1204	CLOSING TIME (LP)	30

ASSAGAI
71	Vertigo 6059 034	Telephone Girl/I'll Wait For You	40
71	Vertigo 6360 030	ASSAGAI (LP, gatefold sleeve, large swirl label)	250
72	Philips 6308 079	ZIMBABWE (LP, black/silver labels)	120
74	Contour 2870 394	ASSAGAI (LP, reissue of Philips 6308 079)	20
75	Sounds Superb SPR 90054	AFRO ROCK (LP) (Same as Vertigo 6360030)	15

ASSAULT N BATTERY
92	Dee Jay DJX 002	Beat Dat System/Come Together (12")	10

ASSEMBLED MULTITUDE
70	Atlantic 2091 022	Overture For Tommy/Mud	7
70	Atlantic 2466 004	THE ASSEMBLED MULTITUDE (LP)	20

ASSOCIATES
79	Double Hip DHR 1	Boys Keep Swinging/Mona Property Girl (no p/s, 500 only)	100
79	MCA MCA 537	Boys Keep Swinging/Mona Property Girl (no p/s, demos more common, £25)	40
82	Beggars Banquet BEG 86	Tell Me Easter's On Friday/Straw Towels (unreleased, white labels only)	12
80	Fiction FIX 05	THE AFFECTIONATE PUNCH (LP)	20
82	Beggars Banquet BEGA 43	FOURTH DRAWER DOWN (LP, gatefold sleeve with poster, label credits SITU 2)	15

ASSOCIATION
66	London HLT 10054	Along Comes Mary/Your Own Love	10
66	London HLT 10074	Cherish/Don't Blame It On Me	10
66	London HLT 10098	Pandora's Golden Heebie Jeebies/Standing Still	10
67	London HLT 10118	No Fair At All/Looking Glass	10
67	London HLT 10140	Windy/Sometime	10
67	London HLT 10157	Never My Love/Requiem For The Masses	8
68	Warner Bros WB 6113	Everything That Touches You/Requiem For The Masses	6
69	Warner Bros WB 7267	Goodbye Columbus/The Time It Is Today	8
69	Warner Bros WB 7119	Windy/Never My Love	7
70	Warner Bros WB 7372	Just About The Same/Look At Me, Look At You	6
72	CBS S 8062	Darling Be Home Soon/Indian Wells Woman	6
67	London HA-T 8305	AND THEN . . . ALONG COMES THE ASSOCIATION (LP)	40
67	London HA-T 8313	RENAISSANCE (LP)	35
67	London HA-T/SH-T 8287	INSIGHT OUT (LP)	35
68	Warner Bros W(S) 1733	BIRTHDAY (LP)	30
69	Warner Bros W(S) 1767	GREATEST HITS (LP)	20
69	Warner Bros W(S) 1786	GOODBYE COLUMBUS (LP, soundtrack)	18
69	Warner Bros W(S) 1800	THE ASSOCIATION (LP)	20
72	CBS S 65009	WATERBEDS IN TRINIDAD! (LP)	15

A STATE OF MIND
85	Mind Matters NO THOUGHT 4	What's The Difference?/Animal Human Exploitation (fold out p/s)	15

ASTERIX
70	Decca F 13075	Everybody/If I Could Fly	20

EDWIN/TED ASTLEY (ORCHESTRA)
65	RCA RCA 1492	Danger Man/The Saint	40
62	Decca F 12389	The Baron/Drop Head (as Ted Astley)	10

VIRGINIA ASTLEY
82	Why Fi WHY 08	A BAO A QU (10" EP)	10
87	Warner Bros. WEA YZ 107	Some Small Hope/A Summer Long Since Passed (P/s, featuring David Sylvian)	6
83	Happy Valley HA 001	FROM GARDENS WHERE WE FEEL SECURE (LP)	35

(see also David Sylvian)

ASTON HALL
80	Tamebeat TAME 001	The Daily Sun/Popular People (p/s)	15

ASTON & YEN
66	Doctor Bird DB 1064	Skillamy/BABA BROOKS & BAND: Party Time	30

ASTORS
65	Atlantic AT 4037	Candy/I Found Out	80
65	Atlantic AT 4037	Candy/I Found Out (DJ Copy)	120
69	Atlantic 584 245	Candy/I Found Out (reissue)	15

ASTRA
10	Rise Above RISE 127 FREE	Empty Spaces/DIAGONAL: Stop (300 only, gig freebie)	12
08	Rise Above RISELP 120	THE WEIRDING (LP, gatefold with poster)	20
12	Rise Above RISELP 137	THE BLACK CHORD (LP, gatefold, booklet, clear vinyl, 100 only)	25

ASTRAL NAVIGATIONS

MINT VALUE £

ASTRAL NAVIGATIONS
- 71 Holyground HG 114/ NSR 172   ASTRAL NAVIGATIONS (LP, actually by Lightyears Away & Thundermother, poster cover & booklet, 250 copies only, some numbered) 500
- 89 Magic Mixture MM 2   ASTRAL NAVIGATIONS (LP, reissue with booklet, 425 copies only) 50

(see also David John & Mood)

ASTRAL PROJECTION
- 96 Tip TIP LP 5   TRUST IN TRANCE (2-LP) 50
- 97 Transient TRANR607 LP   THE ASTRAL FILES (2-LP) 50
- 97 Transient TRANR612 LP   DANCING GALAXY (2-LP) 75
- 99 Transient TRANR621 LP   ANOTHER WORLD (2-LP) 40

ASTRA NOVA ORCHESTRA
- 74 Alaska ALA 26   Ev'ry Little Beat Of Your Heart/Soul Sleeper 30

A STREAM
- 82 SRTS 82 CUS 1294   Hero/Space Invaders 20

ASTROBOTNIA
- 02 Rephlex CAT 123 LP   PART 01 (LP) 15
- 02 Rephlex CAT 125 LP   PART 03 (LP) 15

ASTRONAUTS (U.K.)
- 79 Bugle BLAST 1   THE ASTRONAUTS EP (All Night Party/Back Soon/Everything Stops The Baby/Survivors) (p/s) 15
- 82 Stiff BUY DJ 145   I'm Your Astronaut (Promo only, p/s) 10
- 80 Bugle BLAST 5   PRANKSTERS IN REVOLT (EP) 20
- 81 Bugle GENIUS 001   PETER PAN HITS THE SUBURBS (LP) 50
- 86 All The Madmen MAD 5   IT'S ALL DONE BY MIRRORS (LP) 15
- 87 All The Madmen MADLP005   THE SEEDY SIDE OF (LP) 15

(see also Restricted Hours, Syndicate)

ASWAD
- 76 Island WIP 6312   Back to Africa/Africa 15
- 76 Island WIP 6338   Three Babylon/Ire Woman 8
- 78 Grove Music GMDM 9   It's Not Our Wish (That We Should Fight)/Stranger (green vinyl) 20
- 80 Grove Music 12WIP 6575   Rainbow Culture/Covenant (dub) (12") 18
- 80 Island WIP 6646   Warrior Charge/Dub Charge 8
- 80 Island 12WIP 6646   Warrior Charge/Dub Charge (12") 15
- 81 Grove Music IPR 2037   Warrior Charge/Dub Charge (12", with 'Limited Edition' on labels) 60
- 81 Grove Music 12WIP 6693   Babylon/Behold (12") 20
- 82 CBS XPS 148   Unsatisfied/Oh Jah (Dub) (10") 12
- 84 Simba SIM 014   Hooked On You/Version 8
- 76 Island ILPS 9399   ASWAD (LP, inner) 15
- 79 Grove Music GMLP 6   HULET (LP) 15
- 81 Island ASWAD 1   SHOWCASE (LP) 15
- 82 Island ILPS 9711   NEW CHAPTER OF DUB (LP) 25

ASYLUM CHOIR
- 68 Mercury SMCL 21041   A LOOK INSIDE THE ASYLUM CHOIR (LP) 30

(see also Leon Russell)

ASYLUM (1)
- 74 Wax SR 2073   It's My Destiny - Lazy Love/Suzy's Back (p/s) 100

ASYLUM (2)
- 79 Peeping Tom HRSL 291/EJSP 9280   COMMERCIAL QUEEN EP (p/s) 40

ATACAMA
- 71 Charisma CAS 1039   ATACAMA (LP, pink/white 'scroll' label) 35
- 72 Charisma CAS 1060   THE SUN BURNS UP ABOVE (LP, large 'mad hatter' label) 30

ATAVISTIC
- 87 Peaceville WARP 3   LIFE DURING WARTIME EP (p/s) 10
- 90 Deaf DEAF 3   VANISHING POINT (LP) 15

ATGYFODIAD
- 74 Sain SAIN 41   DISGYN MAE'R GLAW (EP) 12

ATHENIANS
- 64 ESC ESC 1   You Tell Me/Little Queenie (custom sleeve) 50
- 64 Waverley SLP 532   I've Got Love If You Want It/I'm A Lover Not A Fighter (p/s) 150
- 64 Waverley SLP 532   I've Got Love If You Want It/I'm A Lover Not A Fighter 80
- 65 Waverley SLP 533   Thinking Of Our Love/Mercy Mercy (in custom sleeve) 60
- 65 Waverley SLP 533   Thinking Of Our Love/Mercy Mercy (not in custom sleeve) 40

GLENN ATHENS & TROJANS
- 65 Spot 7E 1018   GLENN ATHENS & TROJANS (EP) 200

ATHLETE
- 02 Parlophone 5822 991   VEHICLES AND ANIMALS (LP, stickered sleeve) 20
- 05 Parlophone 560 7401   TOURIST (2-LP) 40
- 07 Parlophone 503 1791   BEYOND THE NEIGHBOURHOOD (LP, with booklet) 40
- 09 Fiction 2714237   BLACK SWAN (LP) 18

JUAN ATKINS
- 91 ULR ULRT 3001   THE FUTURE SOUND EP (12") 75

PETE ATKIN
- 67 MJB BEVLP 1009   WHILE THE MUSIC LASTS (LP, 99 copies, with Julie Covington) 400
- 67 Private pressing   THE PARTY'S MOVING ON (LP, 160 copies, with Julie Covington) 175
- 70 Fontana 6309 011   BEWARE THE BEAUTIFUL STRANGER (LP, black/silver labels) 30
- 71 Philips 6308 070   DRIVING THROUGH MYTHICAL AMERICA (LP) 30

BENNY ATKINS
- 60 Mercury AMT 1113   Lipstick On Your Lips/I'm Following You 10

DAVE ATKINSON
- 76 (No label or cat no)   THE BEGGAR & THE SAND (LP) 50

Steve ATKINSON

MINT VALUE £

STEVE ATKINSON
81 Ellie Jay EJSP 9779 — SMALL BOATS (LP) 200

ATLANTIC BRIDGE
71 Dawn DNX 2507 — I Can't Lie To You/Hilary Dickson/Childhood Room (p/s) 10
70 Dawn DNLS 3014 — ATLANTIC BRIDGE (LP, gatefold sleeve, red/black labels) 70

ATLANTICS (1)
64 Windsor WPS 129 — Don't Say No/Send Him To Me 20

ATLANTIS
72 Fury FY 302 — I Ain't Got Time/Teddy Boyd's Rock 'N' Roll Show 100
73 Vertigo 6360 609 — ATLANTIS (LP, small swirl label, sleeve printed in Germany) 40
(see also Rocking Horse)

ATLANTIS PEOPLE
80 Ice GUY 33 — Stormy Weather/No Such Thing 40
80 Ice GUY 33 12 — Stormy Weather/No Such Thing (12") 80

ATLANTIS RISING
83 CMI CMI700 — Tightrope/Reverie: A Vision 20

ATLAS (1)
78 Emerging WIL 001 — AGAINST ALL THE ODDS (LP, private pressing) 25

ATLAS (2)
94 Dee Jay DJX 021 — Drifting Thru The Galaxy/Second Heaven (12") 30
94 Dee Jay DJX 021X — Drifting Thru The Galaxy/Second Heaven (12", white label test pressing) 25

AT LAST THE 1958 ROCK & ROLL SHOW
68 CBS 3349 — I Can't Drive/Working On The Railroad 25
(see also Ian Hunter, Mott The Hoople, Freddie 'Fingers' Lee, Miller Anderson, Charles Woolfe)

ATMOSFEAR
79 Elite DAZZ 1 — Dancing In Outer Space/Outer Space (Version) (12") 20
79 MCA 12 MCA 543 — Dancing In Outer Space/Outer Space (Version) (12", co. sleeve) 18
79 MCA MCAA 543 — Dancing In Outer Space/Outer Space 6
80 Elite DAZZ 2 — Motivation/Extract (12" die-cut cover) 20
80 MCA MCA 580 — Motivation/Extract (demo only) 20
80 MCA MCAT 580 — Motivation/Extract (12" repressing, p/s) 15
81 MCA — Creators Dream/Dream On (Creators Dream) 8
81 Elite DAZZ 8 — Invasion/Alternative II/Interplay/Untitled/Starburst (Reach For The Stars) (12") 20
82 Elite DAZZ 12-7 — Xtra Special (Dry Mix)/(Wet Mix) 20
82 Elite/City Sounds LDAZZ 12 — Xtra Special (Dry Mix)/(Wet Mix) (12") 15
84 Elite ATM 33-1 — FIRST/FOURMOST (12") 15
81 MCA MCF 3110 — EN TRANCE (LP) 40
99 Disorient SUSHI 17 — ALTERED SLATES (2-LP) 20
05 Discotheque DQFDV013 — EN TRANCE (2-LP reissue) 20
18 Mr Bongo MRBLP180 — EN TRANCE (LP, reissue) 15
(see also Antoniou, Norma Lewis)

ATMOSPHERES
59 London HLW 8977 — Kabalo/The Fickle Chicken 10
60 London HLW 9091 — Telegraph/Caravan 10

ATOM SPIES
87 Cake 12 SLICE 3 — AND THEIR TRECHEROUS POP ON MICRODOT (12", EP) 12

ATOMIC ROOSTER
70 B&C CB 121 — Friday The 13th/Banstead (initial copies in p/s) 15
70 B&C CB 121 — Friday The 13th/Banstead 8
72 Dawn DNS 1027 — Stand By Me/Never To Lose 6
72 Dawn DNS 1029 — Save Me/Close Your Eyes 8
74 Decca FR 13503 — Tell Your Story (Sing Your Song)/O.D. (as Vincent Crane's Atomic Rooster) 8
80 EMI EMI 5084 — Do You Know Who's Looking For You/Throw Your Life Away (p/s) 6
80 EMI 12EMI 5084 — Do You Know Who's Looking For You (Ext.)/Throw Your Life Away (12", p/s) 10
70 B&C CAS 1010 — ATOMIC ROOSTER (LP, Matrix CAS +1010 + A/CAS + 1010 + B (Flute Mix)) 200
70 B&C CAS 1010 — ATOMIC ROOSTER (LP, Matrix CAS +1010 + A2/CAS + 1010 + B2 (Flute Mix)) 150
70 B&C CAS 1010 — ATOMIC ROOSTER (LP, Matrix CAS +1010 + A1U/CAS + 1010 + B1U (Guitar Mix)) 100
70 B&C CAS 1026 — DEATH WALKS BEHIND YOU (LP, gatefold sleeve) 100
71 Pegasus PEG 1 — IN HEARING OF ATOMIC ROOSTER (LP, gatefold sleeve) 50
72 Dawn DNLS 3038 — MADE IN ENGLAND (LP, limited 'denim' cover, gatefold, with poster, lilac label) 100
72 Dawn DNLS 3038 — MADE IN ENGLAND (LP, re-pressing, standard cover, gatefold insert, lilac label) 30
73 Dawn DNLS 3049 — NICE'N'GREASY (LP, lilac label) 40
80 EMI EMC3341 — ATOMIC ROOSTER (LP) 15
83 Towerbell TOW LP 4 — HEADLINE NEWS (LP) 15
(see also Cactus, Crane/Farlowe, Chris Farlowe, Crazy World Of Arthur Brown, Hard Stuff, Leaf Hound, Andromeda, John Du Cann, Bullet. Bernie Torme, David Gilmore)

ATOMS
79 Rinka R 23 — Max Bygraves Killed My Mother/Beatles Jacket (colour silk-screened p/s in poly bag with inserts) 12

ATOMS FOR PEACE
13 XL XLT 584SP — Default (1-sided 12", hand silk-screened cover, 100 only) 20
13 XL XLT 592SP — Judge, Jury & Executioner/S.A.D. (12" hand-printed sleeve, 100 only) 20
13 XL XLT 603SP — Ingenue (1-sided 12", hand silk-screened cover, 100 only) 20
13 XL XLT 605SP — Before Your Very Eyes/Magic Beanz (12" hand-printed sleeve, 100 only) 20
13 XL XLT 612SP — Dropped (1-sided 12", hand silk-screened cover, 100 only) 20
13 XL XLT 613SP — Unless (1-sided, hand silk-screened cover, 100 only) 20
13 XL XLT 614SP — Stuck Together Pieces (1-sided, 12", hand silk-screened cover, 100 only) 20
13 XL XLT 615SP — Reverse Running (1-sided 12", hand silk-screened cover, 100 only) 20
13 XL XLT 615P — Amok (12", 1-sided, only sold at gigs) 12
13 XL XLLP 583X — AMOK (2-LP, hand-printed cover, 50 only) 100

			MINT VALUE £
13	XL (No Cat. No.)	AMOK (9 x 1-sided 12" with hand printed sleeves, box set)	70

(see also Radiohead, Red Hot Chilli Peppers)

ATORIE
89	Conscious CON001	It's My Time/Peace Of Mind (12")	35

A II Z
81	Polydor POSP 243	No Fun After Midnight/Treason (no p/s)	10
81	Polydor POSPX 243	No Fun After Midnight/Treason/Valhalla's Force (12", p/s, red vinyl)	15
81	Polydor POSP 314	I'm The One Who Loves You/Ringside Seat (p/s)	12
80	Polydor 2383 587	THE WITCH OF BERKELEY - LIVE (LP, initially sealed with sew-on patch)	20
80	Polydor 2383 587	THE WITCH OF BERKELEY - LIVE (LP)	15

(see also AC/DC)

A TRIBE CALLED QUEST
90	Jive JIVE 256	Bonita Applebaum (7" Why? Edit)/Bonita Appllebaum (Album Version) (p/s)	20
90	Jive JIVE 265	Can I Kick It? (Boilerhouse Mix)/(Radio Edit) (p/s, paper or injection moulded labels)	15
90	Jive HIP 96	PEOPLES INSTINCTIVE TRAVELS AND THE PATH OF RHYTHM (LP, inner)	40
91	Jive HIP 117	THE LOW END THEORY (LP, inner sleeve)	60
93	Jive HIP 143	MIDNIGHT MARAUDERS (2-LP, inners)	50
96	Jive HIP 170	BEATS RHYTHM AND LIFE (2-LP, gatefold)	50
98	Jive 0521031	LOVE MOVEMENT (3-LP, inners)	50
99	Jive 523841	THE ANTHOLOGY (3-LP)	30
17	Epic 88985377871	WE GOT IT FROM HERE...THANK YOU 4 YOUR SERVICE (2-LP)	20

ATRIX
80	Double D D DEE 8	Treasure On The Wasteland/Graphite Pile (p/s)	8

ATTACK (U.K.)
67	Decca F 12550	Try It/We Don't Know	150
67	Decca F 12578	Any More Than I Do/Hi-Ho Silver Lining	45
67	Decca F 12631	Created By Clive/Colour Of My Mind	100
67	Decca F 12631	Created By Clive/Colour Of My Mind (p/s for export to Holland)	200
68	Decca F 12725	Neville Thumbcatch/Lady Orange Peel	175
72	Decca F 13353	Hi-Ho Silver Lining/Any More Than I Do (reissue, unissued)	0
90	Reflection MM 08	MAGIC IN THE AIR (LP)	25

(see also Andromeda, Five Day Week Straw People, Nice)

ATTACK (U.S.)
67	Philips BF 1585	Washington Square/Please Phil Spector	18

ATTACK WAVE PESTREPELLER
98	Prescription DRUG 4	NUG YAR (LP, hand-made sleeve, label, with insert 99 copies only)	18

ATTAK
82	Oi Oi 7	Today's Generation/Hell/No Escape (p/s)	10
82	No Future OI 17	Murder In The Subway/Future Dreams (p/s)	8
83	No Future PUNK 6	THEY WILL EAT YOU WHEN THEY MEAT YOU (LP)	15

ATTEMPTED MOUSTACHE
78	Skeleton SKL 003	Superman/No Way Out (folded p/s)	8

ATTENDANTS
80	Black & White BW 2	Happy Families/Deadbeats & Knowones (p/s)	20

AT THE DRIVE IN
00	Virgin VUS 189	Rolodex Propaganda (Album Version)/Extracurricular/One Armed Scissor (Lamacq Version) (p/s)	6
00	Virgin VUS 193	Invalid Litter Dept/Initiation (Lamacq Version) (p/s, yellow vinyl)	8
13	Transgressive TRANS 154X	ACROBAT TENEMENT (LP, red vinyl reissue)	18
13	Transgressive TRANS 155X	RELATIONSHIP OF COMMAND (2-LP, 4000 copies, orange vinyl reissue)	80
17	Rise RISE 369-2	IN*TER*A*LI*A (LP, half-blue, half splatter, 150 only)	30

AT THE GATES
94	Peaceville CC 7	Souls Of The Evil Departed/All Life Ends (yellow vinyl, p/s)	30
92	Deaf DEAF 10	THE RED IN THE SKY IS OURS (LP)	25
93	Deaf DEAF 14	WITH FEAR I KISS THE BURNING DARKNESS (LP)	25
94	Peaceville VILE 47	TERMINAL SPIRIT DISEASE (LP, inner)	50
95	Earache MOSH 143	SLAUGHTER OF THE SOUL (LP, no inner)	40
02	Earache MOSH 143	SLAUGHTER OF THE SOUL (LP, reissue, inner)	25
02	Earache MOSH 143	SLAUGHTER OF THE SOUL (LP, orange vinyl reissue)	25
06	Earache MOSH 143 PD	SLAUGHTER OF THE SOUL (LP, 2nd reissue, picture disc)	20

AT THE SIGNE OF THE BULL
72	Guildhall/Boston GHS 7	AT THE SIGNE OF THE BULL (LP)	25

ATTITUDES
75	Dark Horse AMS 5504	Ain't Love Enough/The Whole World's Crazy	10
76	Dark Horse AMS 5508	Sweet Summer Music/If We Want To	10

ATTRACTION
66	Columbia DB 7936	Stupid Girl/Please Tell Me	40
66	Columbia DB 8010	Party Line/She's A Girl	125

ATTRITION
85	Third Mind TMS 04	Shrinkwrap/Pendulum Turns (12", p/s with insert)	10
82	Private AC 001	DEATH HOUSE (cassette)	25
84	Third Mind TMLP 06	THE ATTRITION OF REASON (LP)	15

ATTRIX
78	Attrix RB 01	Lost Lenore/Hard Times (p/s, stamped white labels)	15
81	Scoff DT 011	Procession/11th Hour (p/s)	10

AU GO-GO SINGERS
64	Columbia 33SX 1696	THEY CALL US AU GO-GO SINGERS (LP)	25

(see also Buffalo Springfield, Stephen Stills)

(THE) AU PAIR
69	Mercury MF 1126	Casatschok/Don't Boy	6

AU PAIRS

MINT VALUE £

AU PAIRS
79	021 OTO 2	You/Domestic Departures/Kerb Crawler (rubber stamped labels)	20
80	Human OTO 2	You/Domestic Departure/Kerb Crawler	10
80	Human OTO 4	It's Obvious/Diet	8
81	Human HUM 8	Inconvenience/Pretty Boys (p/s)	8
81	Human HUM 8-12	Inconvenience/Pretty Boys/Headache (For Michelle) (12")	10
81	Human HUMAN 1	PLAYING WITH A DIFFERENT SEX (LP, with iron-on transfer)	30
81	Human HUMAN 1	PLAYING WITH A DIFFERENT SEX (LP, without iron-on transfer)	25
82	Kamera KAM 010	SENSE AND SENSUALITY (LP, with insert)	18

AUBREY SMALL
72	Polydor 2058 204	Loser/Oh What A Day It's Been	15
71	Polydor 2383 048	AUBREY SMALL (LP, with gatefold insert)	125

(see also Sons Of Man)

AUDIENCE
71	Charisma CB 126	Belladonna Moonshine/The Big Spell	6
71	Charisma CB 141	Indian Summer/It Brings A Tear/Priestess (p/s)	12
71	Charisma CB 156	You're Not Smiling/Eye To Eye	10
71	Charisma CB 156	Eye To Eye/Eye To Eye (double B side mispressing)	25
69	Polydor 583 065	AUDIENCE (LP)	300
70	Charisma CAS 1012	FRIEND'S FRIEND'S FRIEND (LP, 1st pressing, pink label with 'scroll' logo, matrix A//2-B//2)	100
70	Charisma CAS 1014	FRIEND'S FRIEND'S FRIEND (LP, 2nd pressing, pink label with 'scroll' logo, matrix A-2u/B-2u)	40
71	Charisma CAS 1032	THE HOUSE ON THE HILL (LP, pink scroll label, gatefold sleeve with lyric inner sleeve)	50
72	Charisma CAS 1032	THE HOUSE ON THE HILL (LP, gatefold, 'Mad Hatter' label)	18
72	Charisma CAS 1054	LUNCH (LP, gatefold sleeve, with lyric inner sleeve)	50
72	Charisma CAS 1054	LUNCH (LP, 'Mad Hatter' label)	18

(see also Stackridge, Hot Chocolate)

AUDIO ARTS
87	Audio Arts AA 004	INTERIM ART: The Difference/Head Low (p/s)	40
89	Audio Arts AA 007	PLACEMENT & RECOGNITION: Vinny/World Service (p/s)	40
84	Audio Arts AA 002	ORCHARD GALLERY (LP)	30
87	New Media NMW 004	ACCENT FOR A START (LP)	50

AUDIO ACTIVE
94	On U Sound ONULP 73	WE ARE AUDIO ACTIVE (TOKYO SPACE COWBOYS) (LP)	18

AUDREY
69	Downtown DT 414	Love Me Tonight/BROTHER DAN ALLSTARS: Shoot Them Amigo	20
69	Downtown DT 418	Lover's Concerto/HERBIE GREY & RUDIES Along Came Roy	25
69	Downtown DT 436	You'll Lose A Good Thing/DESMOND RILEY: If I Had Wings	100
69	Downtown DT 449	Pop Your Corn/Pledging My Love	20
70	Downtown DT 452	Sweeter Than Sugar/The Way You Move	35
70	Downtown DT 454	Oh I Was Wrong/Let's Try It Again (B-side with Dandy)	20
70	Downtown DT 457	Someday We'll Be Together/MUSIC DOCTORS: Sunset Rock	15
70	Downtown DT 463	How Glad I Am/DANDY & AUDREY: I'm So Glad	8
70	Trend 6099 006	Getting Ready For A Heartache/M Y O B: Leave Me Alone	10
81	Jah Shaka 826	English Girl/African Queen (12")	25
84	Ariwa ARI 122	English Girl/English Girl (Dub)/English Girl (Riddim) (12", as Sister Audrey)	15

(see also Dandy)

AUDREY & THE DREAMERS
68	Downtown DT408	I Second That Emotion/THE DREAMERS: Dear Love	20

MIKE AUDSLEY
72	Sonet SNTF 641	DARK AND DEVIL WATERS (LP, with insert)	18

LOREN AUERBACH
84	Christabel CRL 001	AFTER THE LONG NIGHT (LP)	40
85	Christabel CRL 002	PLAYING THE GAME (LP)	40

BRIAN AUGER (&) TRINITY
65	Columbia DB 7590	Fool Killer/Let's Do It Tonight (as Brian Auger Trinity)	60
65	Columbia DB 7715	Green Onions '65/Kiko (as Brian Auger Trinity)	75
67	Columbia DB 8163	Tiger/Oh Baby, Won't You Come Back Home To Croydon, Where Everybody Beedle's And Bo's (solo)	60
67	Marmalade 598 003	Red Beans And Rice Pts 1 & 2	45
68	Marmalade 598 006	I Don't Know Where You Are/A Kind Of Love In (with Julie Driscoll, unissued in favour of "This Wheel's On Fire")	0
69	Marmalade 598 015	What You Gonna Do/Bumpin' On Sunset	18
70	RCA RCA 1947	I Want To Take You Higher/Just Me Just You	10
71	Polydor 2058 119	This Wheel's On Fire/Road To Cairo (as Brian Auger & Julie Driscoll)	8
71	Polydor 2058 133	Marai's Wedding/Tomorrow City (as Brian Auger's Oblivion Express)	6
73	CBS 1444	Inner City Blues/Light Of The Path (as Brian Auger's Oblivion Express)	10
74	CBS 2309	Straight Ahead/Change	8
68	Marmalade 608 004	DON'T SEND ME NO FLOWERS (LP, with Jimmy Page & Sonny Boy Williamson)	120
69	Marmalade 607/608 003	DEFINITELY WHAT! (LP)	100
69	Polydor 2334 004	THE BEST OF BRIAN AUGER, JULIE DRISCOLL & THE TRINITY (LP)	20
70	RCA SF 8101	BEFOUR (LP)	35
71	RCA SF 8170	OBLIVION EXPRESS (LP)	25
71	Polydor 2383 062	BETTER LAND (LP, as Brian Auger's Oblivion Express)	30
72	Polydor 2383 104	SECOND WIND (LP, as Brian Auger's Oblivion Express)	30
73	CBS 65155	CLOSER TO IT (LP)	15
74	CBS 80058	STRAIGHT AHEAD (LP)	20

(see also Julie Driscoll Brian Auger & Trinity, Shotgun Express, Jimmy Page, Sonny Boy Williamson)

NAT AUGUSTIN
83	Debut DEBT 12 6	All Of My Love/Summer Is Here Again (12")	60

AUM
MINT VALUE £

AUM
69 London HA-K/SH-K 8401 BLUESVIBES (LP) 45

CLIFF AUNGIER
68 Polydor 56250 Time/Fisherboy 30
68 RCA RCA 1730 My Love And I/Abigail 10
69 Pye 7N 17753 Lady From Baltimore/Back On The Road Again 10
69 Pye NSPL 18294 THE LADY FROM BALTIMORE (LP) 20
(see also Royd Rivers & Cliff Aungier)

AUNTIE FLO & ESA
15 Highlife HGHLFWS 02 HIGHLIFE IN KENYA (12", p/s) 30

AUNTIEPUS
79 Septic AUNT 1 Half-Way To Venezuela/Marmalade Freak (p/s) 6
(see also Damned)

AUNTIE SOCIAL
83 SRT S83-CUS-2014 Preacher/I Want You Back (p/s) 50

AURORA
83 Aurora RAM 9 I'll Be Your Fantasy/If I Really Knew Her (no p/s) 40
(see also AC/DC)

AURORA BOREALIS
97 Kalevala KALA 006 Aurora Borealis (Part 1)/Aurora Borealis (Part 3) 20

AURRA
82 Battersea BATTL 1 A Little Love/Make Up Your Mind (12") 10

AUSGANG
85 FM WKFM LP 52 MANIPULATE (LP, with booklet) 15

AUSTIN
93 Suburban Base SUBBASE 18 THE AUSTIN EP (12", stamped white label) 30

PATTI AUSTIN
69 United Artists UP 35018 The Family Tree/Magical Boy 7
70 United Artists UP 35097 Your Love Made The Difference In Me/It's Easier To Laugh Than Cry 6
71 CBS 7180 Are We Ready For Love/Now That I Know What Loneliness Is 30
74 Probe PRO 608 Music To My Heart/Love 'Em And Leave 'Em Kind Of Love 15

PETER AUSTIN
68 Caltone TONE 125 Your Love/Time Is Getting Harder 120
75 Terminal 108 When You Are Near/Dub 7
(see also Little Freddy, Mr. Foundation)

REG AUSTIN
65 Pye 7N 15885 My Saddest Day/I'll Find Her 40

SIL AUSTIN
58 Mercury 7MT 220 Don't You Just Know It/Rainstorm 10
58 Mercury 7MT 225 Hey, Eula/The Last Time 10
58 Mercury MEP 9540 THE BAND WITH THE BEAT (EP) 15
58 Mercury MEP 9541 GO SIL GO (EP) 15
58 Mercury MPL 6534 SLOW WALK ROCK (LP) 15

AUSTRALIAN CRICKET TEAM
72 Penny Farthing PEN 739 Bowl, Ball, Swing, Bat/Here Come The Aussies 7

AUSTRALIAN PLAYBOYS
67 Immediate IM 054 Black Sheep R.I.P./Sad 800
(see also Procession, Manfred Mann Earth Band)

AUTECHRE
91 Hardcore HARD 003 Cavity Job/Accelera 1 + 2 (12", 1,000 only) 40
94 Warp WAP 54 ANTI EP (12", p/s sealed with sticker) 50
94 Warp 10WAP 44 BASSCADET EP (3 x 10" p/s in box) 25
95 Warp WAP64r ANVIL VAPRE EP (12") 15
95 Warp WAP 58 GARBAGE EP (12") 20
96 Warp WAP 73 We R Are Why/Are Y Are We (12", p/s, mail order only) 25
97 Warp WAP96r CICHLISUITE EP (12") 12
97 Warp WAP 89X EVANE: Laughing Quarter/Draun Quarter (12") 10
99 Warp WAP 124 SPLTRMX: Weissensee Against Im Gluck/At Drowning In A Sea Of Independence (12", 3000 only) 18
99 Warp WAPEP7.1 EP 7.1 (12") 20
99 Warp WAPE7.2 EP 7.2 (12") 20
99 Warp WAP 112 PEEL SESSION (12") 15
00 Warp WAP 150 PEEL SESSION 2 EP (12") 15
10 Warp WAP 505X MOVE OF TEN (PART 1) (12", p/s) 20
10 Warp WAP 505Y MOVE OF TEN (PART 2) (12", p/s) 20
93 Warp WARPLP 17 INCUNABULA (2-LP set, silver vinyl, 1000 only) 80
93 Warp WARPLP 17 INCUNABULA (2-LP set, standard black vinyl) 50
94 Warp WARPLP 25 AMBER (2-LP, 1st pressing with "FUCK OFF TRAINSPOTTER" on run-out groove of B-side) 100
95 Warp WARPLP 38 TRI REPETAE (2-LP, inners) 80
97 Warp WARPLP 49 CHIASTIC SLIDE (2-LP) 45
98 Warp WARPLP 66 LP5 (2-LP, cardboard sleeve) 40
01 Warp WARPLP 128 CONFIELD (2-LP) 60
01 Warp WARPLP 17 INCUNABULA (2-LP, repressing) 30
01 Warp WARPLP 25 AMBER (2-LP, repressing, without "TRAINSPOTTER" reference on run-out on side B) 50
01 Warp WARPLP 38 TRI REPETAE (2-LP, reissue, inners, not sticker on front of sleeve) 35
03 Warp WARPLP 111 DRAFT 7.30 (2-LP) 40
05 Warp WARPLP 180 UNTITLED (2-LP) 35
08 Warp WARPLP 337 QUARISTICE (2-LP) 40
08 Warp WARPCD 333X QUARISTICE (2-CD metal sleeve) 70
10 Warp WARPLP 210 OVERSTEPS (2-LP box set) 35

AUTEURS

			MINT VALUE £
13	Warp WARPLP 234	EXAI (4-LP box set)	50
18	Warp WARPLP364	NTS SESSIONS (12-LP box set)	150

(see also Gescom)

AUTEURS
91	No Label or cat no	THE DEMO EP (cassette, hand-drawn labels, 6 tracks)	50
92	Hut HUTL 2	She Might Take A Train/Untitled	8
93	Hut HUTFS	ACOUSTIC EP (live 7", not sold but given away)	10
93	Hut PM 264	NEW WAVE (LP with free 7")	60
94	Hut Recordings HUTLPX 16	NOW I'M A COWBOY (LP, with free 1-sided 7")	60
96	Hut HUT LP33	AFTER MURDER PARK (LP)	70
99	Hut HUT LP53	HOW I LEARNED TO LOVE THE BOOTBOYS (LP)	70

AUTO DA FÉ (IRELAND)
82	Auto Dafé A.D.F. 003	November November/For Rich People (p/s)	10
82	Auto Dafé A.D.F. 004	Bad Experience/Lot 3 (Live Instrumental)	10
82	Rewind REWIND 13	November November/For Rich People	8

AUTOGRAPHS
78	RAK RAK 281	While I'm Still Young/Fabulous (p/s)	15
78	Strawberry Mastering	While I'm Still Young (different version, acetate only)	30

AUTOMATIC DLAMINI
92	Big Intl. BOT 04	FROM A DIVA TO A DIVER (LP)	20

AUTOMATIC FINE TUNING
76	Charisma CAS 1122	A.F.T (LP)	25

AUTOMATICS
78	Island WIP 6433	Wakin' With The Radio On/Watch Her Now (unissued)	0
78	Island WIP 6439	When Tanks Roll Over Poland Again/Watch Her Now (p/s)	15

AUTOMATION
84	Jung Rhythm SWE T2	Dancing In Outer Space/Outer Space 84 Rap (featuring Family Quest) (12")	15

AUTOPILOT
79	Merimusic/Ze-La Records JHEPS 2244	LOVE IS A PROCESS EP (oversize card p/s)	40

AUTOPSY
89	Peaceville VILE 12	SEVERED SURVIVAL (LP, with inner)	25
89	Peaceville VILE 12	SEVERED SURVIVAL (LP, picture disc)	30
91	Peaceville VILE 25	MENTAL FUNERAL (LP, green vinyl, inner)	40
91	Peaceville VILE 25	MENTAL FUNERAL (LP, picture disc)	30
92	Peaceville VILE 33	ACTS OF THE UNSPEAKABLE (LP)	15
11	Peaceville VILELP 317	MACABRE ETERNAL (2-LP, blue vinyl with poster)	20

AUTOSALVAGE
88	Edsel ED 286	AUTOSALVAGE (LP, reissue)	25

AUTUMN
71	Pye 7N 45090	My Little Girl/Sun Sunshine	7
72	Pye 7N45144	Stood Up/Not The Way She Looks	20
73	Pye 7N 45249	Down Down Down/October	15

AUTUMN VINE
70	Evolution E 2447	He Ain't No Superman/Maxi Baby	15

AVALANCHE (1)
71	Parlophone R 5890	Finding My Way Home/Rabbits	40

(see also Norman Haines Band)

AVALANCHE (2)
80	Childers AVA 1	The Preacher/Mean Lady (no p/s)	90

AVALANCHES
99	Rex REKD 01T	Undersea Community/Yamaha Superstar/Slow Walking/Thank You Caroline	15
99	Rex REKD 05	Electricity/Information	8
01	XL XLT 134	Frontier Psychiatrist/Frontier Psychiatrist (Mario Caldato's 85% Mix)/Frontier Psychiatrist (85% instrumental) (12")	10
01	XL XLS 128	Since I Left You/Thank You Caroline (Andy Votel Mix) (with tattoo)	20
01	XL Recordings XLLP 138	SINCE I LEFT YOU (2-LP, gatefold)	60
16	XL XLLP 755X	WILDFLOWER (2-LP, with CD)	30
12	XL XLLP 138	SINCE I LEFT YOU (LP, gatefold, reissue marbled vinyl)	40

AVALON
82	SRTS 82/CUS/1296	Going Thru'/Gypsy Secret (not released in p/s)	130

FRANKIE AVALON
58	HMV POP 453	Dede Dinah/Ooh-La-La	10
58	London HL 8636	You Excite Me/Darlin'	25
58	HMV POP 517	Ginger Bread/Blue Betty	15

AVALONS
66	Island WI 263	Everyday/I Love You	15

AVANT-GARDE
68	CBS 3704	Naturally Stoned/Honey And Gall	15

AVENGER
83	Neat NEAT 31	Too Wild To Tame/On The Rocks (p/s, with insert)	10
84	Neat NEAT 1018	BLOOD SPORTS (LP)	15
85	Neat NEAT 1026	KILLER ELITE (LP, with lyric insert)	15

AVENGERS (1)
68	Parlophone R 5661	Everyone's Gonna Wonder/Take My Hand	15

(see also Vanity Fair)

AVERAGE WHITE BAND
73	MCA MUPS 486	SHOW YOUR HAND (LP, black/silver labels)	25

AVIATOR
80	Harvest SHSP 4107	TURBULENCE (LP)	15

AVOCADOS
MINT VALUE £

AVOCADOS
81 Choo Choo Train CHUG 3 — I Never Knew/Television Brought Me Up 35

AVO-8
80 Stroppo STROP 1 — Gone Wrong/Target One/No Hesitation (p/s) 10

ALAN AVON & TOY SHOP
70 Concord CON 005 — These Are The Reasons/Night To Remember 150
(see also Hedgehoppers Anonymous)

VALERIE AVON
67 Columbia DB 8201 — He Knows I Love Him Too Much/To Be Let 8

AWAY FROM THE SAND
73 Beaujangle DV 003 — AWAY FROM THE SAND (LP, allegedly only 50 copies) 100

AWESOME 3
92 Entity NTT 12 07 — Don't Go/Headstrong (12") 15
92 Citybeat CBE 1271 — Don't Go (Kicks Like A Mule Mix)/Don't Go (Second Movement)/(Original Mix)/Headstrong (12". p/s) 15

AXEGRINDER
89 Peaceville VILE 7 — RISE OF THE SERPENT MEN (LP) 30

DAVID AXELROD
06 Stateside SS 2230 — Holy Thursday/Song Of Innocence (reissue) 25
06 Stateside SS 2231 — London/The Poison Tree (reissue) 15
02 Stateside SS 2227 — Holy Thursday/DAVID MCCALLUM: The Edge (reissue) 35
68 Capitol ST 2982 — SONG OF INNOCENCE (LP, 'Sold in the U.K...' on label) 70
71 RCA LSP 4636 — MESSIAH (LP) 40
73 MCA MUPS 472 — THE AUCTION (LP, black/blue hexagon label) 40
99 Stateside 7243 4 99405 12 — 1968 TO 1970 AN ANTHOLOGY (2-LP) 30
01 Mo Wax MWR 141LP — DAVID AXELROD (LP) 50
01 Mo Wax MWR 141LPX — DAVID AXELROD (LP as 2 x 12") 60
02 Stateside 7243537484 1 8 — ANTHOLOGY II (2-LP) 30
06 Capitol 0946 3 11617 11 — THE EDGE: DAVID AXELROD AT CAPITOL RECORDS (2-LP) 50
(see also Electric Prunes)

AXIS
80 Metal Minded ISAX 1047 — Lady/Messiah (p/s) 8
81 Axis AM 001 — When You Hold Me/Galaxy Of Love (p/s) 8

HOYT AXTON
64 Stateside SL 10082 — GREENBACK DOLLAR (LP) 15
64 Stateside SL 10096 — THUNDER 'N' LIGHTNIN' (LP) 15
66 London HA-F/SH-F 8276 — THE BEST OF HOYT AXTON (LP) 15

AXXESS
83 Lamborghini LMGLP 100 — NOVELS FOR THE MOONS (LP) 30

AYERS, CALE, NICO & ENO
74 Island ILPS 9291 — JUNE 1ST, 1974 (LP) 18
(see also Kevin Ayers, John Cale, Nico, Brian Eno)

KEVIN AYERS (& WHOLE WORLD)
70 Harvest HAR 5011 — Singing A Song In The Morning/Eleanor's Cake Which Ate Her 20
70 Harvest HAR 5027 — Butterfly Dance/Puis-Je? (with Whole World) 25
71 Harvest HAR 5042 — Stranger In Blue Suede Shoes/Stars (with Whole World) 10
72 Harvest HAR 5064 — Oh! Wot A Dream/Connie On A Rubber Band 10
73 Harvest HAR 5071 — Caribbean Moon/Take Me To Tahiti (p/s) 20
74 Island WIP 6194 — The Up Song/Everybody's Sometimes & Some People's All The Time Blues 6
74 Island WIP 6201 — After The Show/Thank You Very Much 6
75 Harvest HAR 5100 — Caribbean Moon/Take Me To Tahiti 6
76 Island WIP 6271 — Falling In Love Again/Everyone Knows The Song 6
76 Harvest HAR 5107 — Stranger In Blue Suede Shoes/Fake Mexican Tourist Blues (possibly in p/s) 20
76 Harvest HAR 5109 — Caribbean Moon/Take Me To Tahiti (reissue, in different p/s) 20
77 Harvest HAR 5131 — Star/The Owl 6
80 Harvest HAR 5198 — Money, Money, Money/Stranger In Blue Suede Shoes (p/s) 6
83 Charly/Celluloid CYZ 7107 — My Speeding Heart/Champagne & Valium (p/s) 10
86 Illuminated LEV 71 — Stepping Out/Only Heaven Knows (no p/s) 10
70 Harvest SHVL 763 — JOY OF A TOY (LP, gatefold sleeve, 1st pressing with no EMI box) 150
70 Harvest SHSP 4005 — SHOOTING AT THE MOON (LP, with Whole World) 80
72 Harvest SHVL 800 — WHATEVERSHEBRINGSWESING (LP, textured gatefold sleeve) 60
73 Harvest SHVL 807 — BANANAMOUR (LP, gatefold sleeve, with booklet) 200
73 Harvest SHVL 807 — BANANAMOUR (LP, gatefold sleeve, without booklet) 30
74 Island ILPS 9263 — THE CONFESSIONS OF DR. DREAM AND OTHER STORIES (LP, with inner) 30
75 Island ILPS 9322 — SWEET DECEIVER (LP, with inner sleeve) 15
75 Harvest SHDW 407 — JOY OF A TOY/SHOOTING AT THE MOON (2-LP, reissue, gatefold sleeve) 25
76 Harvest SHSP 2005 — ODD DITTIES (LP) 18
76 Harvest SHSP 4057 — YES WE HAVE NO MAÑANAS (LP, textured sleeve, with inner sleeve) 20
78 Harvest SHSP 4085 — RAINBOW TAKEAWAY (LP) 15
80 Harvest SHSP 4106 — THAT'S WHAT YOU GET BABE (LP) 15
86 Illuminated AMA 25 — AS CLOSE AS YOU THINK (LP) 25
86 Harvest Black EMS 1124 — BANANAMOUR (LP, reissue) 15
92 Permanent PERM LP 5 — STILL LIFE WITH GUITAR (LP) 15
(see also Soft Machine, Lady June, Lol Coxhill, David Bedford, Mike Oldfield, Bridget St. John)

ROY AYERS (UBIQUITY)
75 Polydor 2066 671 — Evolution/Mystic Voyage (as Roy Ayers Ubiquity) 7
80 Polydor POSPX 135 — Running Away/Can't You See Me (12") 10
87 Urban URB 6 — Can't You See Me/Love Will Bring Us Back Together 20
87 Urban URBX 6 — Can't You See Me/Love Will Bring Us Back Together/Sweet Tears (12", p/s) 15
19 Dynamite Cuts DYNAM7027 — He's A Superstar (Part 1)/We Live In Brooklyn Baby/Ain't Got Time/Fire Weaver (reissue, 10

ALBERT AYLER

			MINT VALUE £
19	28	Dynamite Cuts DYNAM7029	2 x 7", p/s ....
			Brother Green (The Disco King)/The Black Five/Life Is But A Moment (Part 1)/(Part 2) (reissue, 2 x 7", p/s) 10
19	30	Dynamite Cuts DYNAM7031	Coffee Is The Colour/Aragon/Brawling Broads/Exotic Dance (reissue, 2 x 7", p/s) 12
	32		
72	Polydor PD 5022	HE'S COMING (LP, as Roy Ayers Ubiquity) 40
75	Polydor PD 6057	MYSTIC VOYAGE (LP) 20
77	Polydor 2391 246	VIBRATIONS (LP, as Roy Ayers Ubiquity) 20
81	Polydor 2391 517	AFRICA, CENTRE OF THE WORLD (LP) 15
83	Uno Melodic UMLP 1	SILVER VIBRATIONS (LP) 100
83	Uno Melodic UMLP 2	DRIVIN' ON UP (LP) 30
88	Urban UMID 1	EVERYBODY LOVES THE SUNSHINE (LP, reissue as Roy Ayers Ubiquity) 50

(see also Jack Wilson Quartet)

ALBERT AYLER
64	Transatlantic TRA 130	SPIRITS (LP) 40
64	Fontana Jazz SFJL 925	GHOSTS (LP) 40
64	Fontana Jazz SFJL 927	MY NAME IS (LP) 45
65	Fontana 933 SFJL	SPIRITUAL UNITY (LP) 50
65	Fontana SFJL 925	GHOSTS (LP, reissue) 30
65	Fontana Jazz SFJL 927	MY NAME IS (LP, reissue) 30
67	Polydor 2383089	WITCHES & DEVILS (LP) 40
68	Impulse IMPL 8022	NEW GRASS (LP, gatefold sleeve) 30
69	Impulse SIPL 519	NEW GRASS (LP, reissue, single sleeve) 20
69	Sonet SNTF 604	FIRST RECORDINGS (LP) 25
70s	Freedom 41000 FLP	VIBRATIONS (LP) 15

DENNIS AYLER
| 16 | 22a 010 | Put It On/Ms.Chambers/Smoke .... 15 |

J AYRES
| 77 | Hawkeye HE 004 | Pretty Looks/THE REVOLUTIONARIES - Ugly (actually by The Jays) .... 6 |

AYRSHIRE FOLK
| 74 | Deroy DER 1052 | AYRSHIRE FOLK (LP, private pressing) .... 70 |

AYSHEA
65	Fontana TF 627	Eeny Meeny/Peep My Love 20
68	Polydor 56276	Celebration Of The Year/Only Love Can Save Me Now 30
69	Polydor 56302	Another Night/Taking The Sun From My Eyes 12
70	Polydor 2001 029	Mr White's White Flying Machine/Ship Of The Line 30
73	Harvest HAR 5073	Farewell/The Best Years Of My Life 8
74	DJM DJS 339	Another Without You Day/Moonbeam 6
70	Polydor 2384 026	AYSHEA (LP) 30

(see also Ayshea Brough, Roy Wood)

AZANYAH
| 12 | Jazzman JMANLP 047 | THE ONE (LP, reissue) .... 15 |

A-ZONE
| 94 | White House WYHS 028 | Calling The People/Safety Zone (12") .... 20 |

AZTEC CAMERA
81	Postcard 81-3	Just Like Gold/We Could Send Letters (die-cut sleeve, with card) 50
81	Postcard 81-3	Just Like Gold/We Could Send Letters (die-cut sleeve, without card) 20
81	Postcard 81-8	Mattress Of Wire/Lost Outside The Tunnel (p/s) 35
83	Rainhill ACFC 1	Oblivious (Langer/Winstanley Remix)/Oblivious (Colin Fairley Remix) (no p/s) 20
83	Rough Trade ROUGH 47	HIGH LAND HARD RAIN (LP) 15
12	Domino REWIG LP 92	HIGH LAND, HARD RAIN (LP, reissue with inner and bonus 7" EP) 25

(see also French Impressionists)

AZUL
| 77 | Venture VEN7778 | Babylon Special/Version .... 10 |

AZYMUTH
| 79 | Milestone MRC 101 | Jazz Carnival/Fly Over The Horizon (12") .... 15 |
| 80 | Milestone MRC 102 | Dear Limmertz/Papasong (12") .... 15 |

B

FRANKIE 'ALROUNDER' B
| 86 | Ital Stuff IS 001 | Scratch Mi Back/Version (12") .... 125 |

IKE B & CRYSTALITES
| 68 | Island WI 3151 | Try A Little Merriness/Patricia .... 25 |

JOHN B
| 72 | Decca F 13362 | Take A Look Around/Run Run Run .... 6 |

MEHER BABA
70	Univ. Spiritual League 1	HAPPY BIRTHDAY (LP, with booklet and lyric sheet 6 Pete Townshend tracks, 100 only) .. 300
70	Univ. Spiritual League 2	I AM (LP, with inserts, features 5 Pete Townshend tracks) 100
76	Univ. Spiritual League 3	WITH LOVE (LP, features 3 Pete Townshend tracks) 100
70s	MBO MBO 1	STAR OF THE SILENT SCREEN . . . MEHER BABA (LP, reissue of "Happy Birthday" without inserts) 20
70s	MBO MBO 2	I AM (LP, reissue, without inserts) 20

(see also Pete Townshend)

BABE RUTH
| 71 | Decca F13234 | Rupert's Magic Feather/Flood .... 6 |

BABES IN TOYLAND

MINT VALUE £

71	Capitol CL 15869	Elusive/Say No More (DJ Copy)	12
72	Harvest SHSP 4022	FIRST BASE (LP, 1st pressing with 'Sympathy Music Ltd' credit for 'Wells Fargo' with lyric insert)	40
72	Harvest SHSP 4022	FIRST BASE (LP, 2nd pressing with 'Tone Music' credit for 'Wells Fargo' with lyric insert)	20
74	Harvest SHVL 812	AMAR CABALLERO (LP, gatefold sleeve)	20
75	Harvest SHSP 4038	BABE RUTH (LP, inner lyric sleeve)	20

(see also Wild Turkey, Elias Hulk, Liquid Gold, Whitesnake)

BABES IN TOYLAND
93	Twin Tone TTR89208	TO MOTHER (EP, insert, booklet & green vinyl)	25
93	Southern 18512-1	PAINKILLERS (12" EP)	25
92	Southern 18591	FONTANELLE (LP)	20

BABLA AND HIS ORCHESTRA
79	Savera SAV 1001	YESTERDAY ONCE MORE (LP)	18

ALICE BABS
63	Fontana TF 409	After You've Gone/St. Louis Blues Twist	8

BABY
69	Spark SRL 1030	Heartbreaker/Michael Blues	20

BABY BERTHA
72	SRT 72183	BABY BERTHA (LP, 50 only)	100

BABY BIRD
96	Echo ECS026	You're Gorgeous/You're Gorgeous Too/Bebe Lemonade (p/s, gold vinyl)	40
96	ECHO LP11	UGLY BEAUTIFUL (2-LP)	35
98	Echo ECHLP 24	THERES SOMETHING GOING ON (LP)	30

BABY D
92	Production House PNT 043RX	Let Me Be Your Fantasy (Acen In Wonderland)/Fantasy (Ray Keith Remix) (12")	15
96	Systematic 828683 1	DELIVERANCE (3-LP)	20

BABY GRUNTING
71	United Artists UP 35258	Keep The Circle Turning/Way Down The Line	6

BABY HUEY
71	Buddah 2365 001	LIVING LEGEND - THE BABY HUEY STORY (LP)	40

BABY JANE & ROCKABYES
63	United Artists UP 1010	How Much Is That Doggie In The Window/My Boy John	15

BABY LAUREL
82	Badger SRTS 82 CUS 1483	Trouble In The Air/Leavin Home	50

BABY LEMONADE
87	Narodnik NRK 004	The Secret Goldfish/Real World (p/s)	8

BABYLON
69	Polydor 56356	Into The Promised Land/Nobody's Fault But Mine (p/s)	40
69	Polydor 56356	Into The Promised Land/Nobody's Fault But Mine (no p/s)	25

(see also Carole Grimes)

BABYLON TIMEWARP
93	Subliminal TENSE 001	Durban Poison/Durban Poison (-32Hz And Dropping Mix)/ Durban Poison (The Kashmir Mix)(12")	40
93	Subliminal TENSE 003	I Come In Peace/Durban Poison (Remix)/Durban Poison (Remix) (12")	30
95	Mistermen MR 2	MISTERMEN VOL. 3: Durban Poison/Changing (12", p/s)	25

BABYSHAMBLES
04	High Society (no cat no)	What Katie Did (Demo) (1,000 numbered copies of clear flexi, with Annelise's Magazine. With magazine)	20
04	High Society (no cat no)	What Katie Did (Demo) (1,000 numbered copies of clear flexi, with Annelise's Magazine. Without magazine)	18
04	High Society HS7IN011	Babyshambles/At The Flophouse (p/s, 1000 only)	18
13	Parlophone R 6905	Nothing Comes To Nothing/Picture Me In A Hospital (Demo) (pink vinyl, p/s)	10
06	Regal 379 9021	BLINDING EP (12")	25
05	Rough Trade RTRADLP240	DOWN IN ALBION (2xLP with side 4 etched)	40
07	Parlophone 508 6201	SHOTTER'S NATION (LP)	30

(see also Libertines, Wolfman)

BABY SUNSHINE
75	Deroy DER 1301	BABY SUNSHINE (LP, with insert)	80

(see also Fairy's Moke)

BACCA
73	Grape GR 3048	George Foreman/Version	10

BURT BACHARACH
65	London HLR 9983	What's New Pussycat/My Little Red Book (B-side with Tony Middleton)	20
67	RCA Victor RD 7874	CASINO ROYALE (LP, soundtrack, mono)	40
67	RCA Victor SF 7874	CASINO ROYALE (LP, soundtrack, stereo)	30

(see also Tony Middleton, Breakaways)

BACHDENKEL
77	Initial IRL 001	LEMMINGS (LP, stickered gatefold sleeve, with bonus EP)	50
77	Initial IRL 001	LEMMINGS (LP)	15
77	Initial IRL 002	STALINGRAD (LP, numbered with lyric insert)	40

JOHNNY BACHELOR
60	London HLN 9074	Mumbles/Arabella Jean	50

BACHELOR PAD
87	Sha La La Ba Ba Ba Ba 003	Girl Of Your Dreams/BABY LEMONADE: Jiffy Neckware Creation (p/s, flexi with Are You Scared To Get Happy or Simply Thrilled 3 fanzines)	10

BACHELORS (U.K.)
58	Parlophone R 4454	Platter Party/Love Is A Two Way Street	20
59	Parlophone R 4547	Please Don't Touch/Ding Dong	20

BACH TWO BACH
71	Mushroom 100 MR 10	BACH TWO BACH (LP)	20

BACK ALLEY CHOIR

MINT VALUE £

BACK ALLEY CHOIR
72	York SYK 517	Smile Born Of Courtesy/Why Are You Here	40
73	York FYK 406	BACK ALLEY CHOIR (LP, 500 only)	600

BACK DOOR
72	Blakey BLP 5989	BACK DOOR (LP, sold at gigs)	80
73	Warner Bros. K46231	BACK DOOR (LP, reissue of Blakey LP)	20
76	Warner Bros. K56243	ACTIVATE (LP)	15

(see also Whitesnake)

BACKHOUSE JAMES BLUES BAND
68	private pressing	BACKHOUSE JAMES BLUES BAND (LP, 30 copies only, white labels in sleeve)	1000
13	RCLP 007	BACKHOUSE JAMES BLUES BAND (LP, reissue with signed and numbered certificate)	20

MIRIAM BACKHOUSE
77	Mother Earth MUM 1203	GYPSY WITHOUT A ROAD (LP)	120

BACKLASH
80	Gargoyle GRGL 777	OFF WITH HIS HEAD (EP)	50

BACK PORCH MAJORITY
65	Columbia DB 7627	Ramblin' Man/Good Time Joe	8

BACKSEAT ROMEOS
80	Future Earth FER 007	Zero Ambition/In The Night (p/s)	35

BACK STREET BAND
69	Ember EMBS 277	This Ain't The Road/Daybreak (p/s)	8

BACK TO ZERO
79	Fiction FICS 004	Your Side Of Heaven/Back To Back	10

BACKTRAX
80	S 80 CUS 842	It's Never Too Late/Be Mine	25

BACKYARD BABIES
98	Bad Afro FROO 12	(Is It) Still Alright To Smile/B. Babylon (p/s, yellow vinyl)	10
09	Spinefarm 2701938	Degenerated/SUPERSHIT 666: Star War Jr. (hand-numbered p/s, blue vinyl, 500 only)	7
98	Coalition COLA 046	Look At You/Powderhead/Can't Find The Door/Wireless Mind (gatefold p/s)	8
98	Coalition COLA 051	Bombed (Out Of My Mind)/Rocker (featuring Michael Monroe) (yellow vinyl, fully-autographed numbered (apart from promos) gatefold p/s, 2000 only)	10
99	Coalition COLA 073	Babylon (featuring "Wildhearted Ginger")/Stars (red vinyl, foldover p/s & insert in poly bag, 1000 copies sold at gigs only)	10

(see also Super$hit666, Wildhearts)

BACKYARD HEAVIES
73	Action ACT 4616	Just Keep On Truckin'/Never Can Say Goodbye	30

BACON FAT
70	Blue Horizon 57-3171	Nobody But You/Small's On 53rd	18
70	Blue Horizon 57-3181	Evil/Blues Feeling	25
70	Blue Horizon 7-63858	GREASE ONE FOR ME (LP)	100
71	Blue Horizon 2431 001	TOUGH DUDE (LP)	100

(see also Dirty Blues Band, George 'Harmonica' Smith)

GAR BACON
58	Felsted AF 107	Mary Jane/Chains Of Love	10
59	Fontana H 196	Marshal, Marshal/Too Young To Love	15

BAD ACTORS
80	Sophist. Noise SONO 1	Strange Love/Energy Society (p/s)	10
80	Plastic Speech PLAS 1	Love Song/Are They Hostile (p/s)	12

BAD BRAINS
82	Alt. Tentacles VIRUS 13	I Luv Jah/Sailin' On/Big Takeover (12", p/s)	18
83	Food For Thought YUMT101	I And I Survive (An' T'ing)/Destroy Babylon (12", insert, p/s)	20
83	Abstract ABT 007	ROCK FOR LIGHT (LP)	30
91	Caroline CARLP 8	ROCK FOR LIGHT (LP, reissue, stickered sleeve with 3 bonus tracks)	15

BAD COMPANY (1)
74	Island ILPS 9279	BAD COMPANY (LP, first pressing, A-1U TG 2/B-1U HR 2, 'Robor Limited' gatefold sleeve, no 'Published by Island Music Ltd')	40
75	Island ILPS 9304	STRAIGHT SHOOTER (LP)	20
76	Island ILSP 9346	RUN WITH THE PACK (LP)	20
77	Island ILPS 9279	BAD COMPANY (LP, later EMI pressing with "Published by Island Music Ltd" credit)	15

BAD COMPANY (2)
98	BC Recordings BCR 001	The Nine/The Bridge (company p/s)	20
99	Prototype PROUK 001	The Pulse/China Cup (12", die-cut p/s)	10
00	BC R'dings BCRUKLPS 001	DIGITAL NATION ALBUM SAMPLER: Flashback (Tumpa)/Spacewalk (promo 12", stickered black die-cut sleeve, A-side with Trace)	12
01	BC R'dings BCRUKEP 001	BOOK OF THE BAD VOL. 1 EP: The Voice/Numbers/Spider/Believe (2 x 12", p/s)	10
01	BC R'dings BCRUKEP 002	BOOK OF THE BAD VOL. 2 EP: Dogs On The Moon/Grunge/Ladies of Spain/The Running Man (2 x 12", p/s)	10
01	BC R'dings BCRUKEP 003	BOOK OF THE BAD VOL. 3 EP: Mindgames/Rodeo/Miami Flashback/Storyteller (2 x 12", p/s)	10
01	Prototype PROUK 003	Planet Dust/Speedball (12", p/s)	10
00	BC R'dings BCRLP 001	INSIDE THE MACHINE (5 x 12")	35
00	BC R'dings BCRUKLP 001	DIGITAL NATION (5 x 12")	25

BAD DREAM FANCY DRESS
88	El GPO 41	The Supremes/Choirboy Gas (p/s)	10
88	El GOPT T33	Curry Crazy/Up The King Of Lumembourg (10", p/s)	15
89	El GPO 42	Flair/You Wind Me Up (p/s)	7
88	El ACME 18	CHOIRBOY GAS (LP)	20

BADFINGER
70	Apple APPLE 20	Come And Get It/Rock Of All Ages (p/s)	10
70	Apple APPLE 31	No Matter What/Better Days (p/s)	15
71	Apple APPLE 35	Name Of The Game/Suitcase (unreleased)	0
72	Apple APPLE 40	Day After Day/Sweet Tuesday Morning (p/s)	15

BADGE

MINT VALUE £

72	Apple APPLE 42	Baby Blue/Flying (unreleased in U.K.)	0
74	Apple APPLE 49	Apple Of My Eye/Blind Owl (Demo)	80
74	Apple APPLE 49	Apple Of My Eye/Blind Owl	40
70	Apple SAPCOR 12	MAGIC CHRISTIAN MUSIC (LP)	70
70	Apple SAPCOR 16	NO DICE (LP, gatefold sleeve)	70
72	Apple SAPCOR 19	STRAIGHT UP (LP)	100
73	Warner Bros K 56023	BADFINGER (LP, with insert)	50
74	Apple SAPCOR 27	ASS (LP, with inner sleeve)	80
74	Warner Bros K 56076	WISH YOU WERE HERE (LP, withdrawn)	150
79	Elektra K52129	AIRWAVES (LP, with lyric inner sleeve)	20
91	Apple SAPCOR 12	MAGIC CHRISTIAN MUSIC (LP, reissue, gatefold sleeve with bonus 12" [Sapcor 121])	30
92	Apple SAPCOR 16	NO DICE (LP, reissue, gatefold sleeve with bonus 12" [SAPCOR 161])	30
93	Apple SAPCOR 19	STRAIGHT UP (LP, reissue, gatefold sleeve with bonus 12" [SAPCOR 191])	30
95	Apple SAPCOR 28	COME AND GET IT - THE BEST OF BADFINGER (2-LP, gatefold sleeve)	30

(see also Iveys, Masterminds, Gary Walker & Rain, Natural Gas, Blue Goose)

BADGE
| 81 | Metal Minded MM 2 | Silver Woman/Something I've Lost (p/s) | 25 |

BADGER (1)
| 73 | Atlantic K 40473 | ONE LIVE BADGER (LP, gatefold pop-up sleeve) | 40 |
| 74 | Epic EPC 80009 | WHITE LADY (LP) | 15 |

(see also Ashton Gardner & Dyke, Jackie Lomax, Yes, Flash, Jeff Beck)

BADGER (2)
| 81 | Noize Gate NG 02 | Over The Wall/Faceless Gang (p/s) | 40 |

BADGER BELL BAND
| 85 | Noize Gate SETT 001 | Nothing Left/Rock The Vicar (no p/s) | 40 |

(see also Badger (2))

BADGEWEARER
| 95 | Amanita AMA LP 05 | A TOY GUN IN SAFE HANDS (LP) | 15 |

BAD INFLUENCE
92	Bi BIR 01	F.U.B.A.R (12" EP stamped white labels)	20
92	Bi BIR 02	Never Too Much/Such A Feeling (12")	20
92	Bi BIR 03	Sudden Impact/Untitled/Untitled (12")	40
93	Metamoprhasis MORPHO 003	UNFAIR INFLUENCE (12" EP)	20

HENK BADINGS
| 60 | Philips SABL 206 | ELECTRONIC MUSIC (LP, gatefold) | 30 |

BAD LIEUTENANT
| 09 | Triple Echo BADLP01LP | NEVER CRY ANOTHER TEAR (2-LP) | 40 |

(see also Joy Division, New Order, Electronic, The Other Two)

BAD LUCK
| 81 | Bad Luck IS/BL/1054 | Mutton Dressed As Lamb/Bad Luck (p/s) | 8 |

BADLY DRAWN BOY
97	Mo Wax (no cat no)	Nursery Rhyme (with UNKLE, 5" promo 150 only)	40
98	Twisted Nerve TNXL001	Roadmovie/My Friend Cubilas (feat. Doves) (die-cut sleeve, with insert)	6
90s	Twisted Nerve (no cat. no.)	I Love You All (one-track musical box, 150 only)	100
98	Twisted Nerve TNXMS1	Donna And Blitzen (1 track on 5 track one-sided red vinyl 7", 195 copies, p/s)	50
97	Twisted Nerve TN 001	EP1 (EP, 500 only)	50
98	Twisted Nerve TN 002	EP2: I Love You All/The Treeclimber/I Love You All (I Loop You All Andy Votel Mix)/Thinking Of You (EP, 1,000 only)	30
11	One Last Fruit BDBX10	LOST FOR WORDS (EP, signed photo insert)	10
00	Twisted Nerve TNXLCD 133	THE HOUR OF THE BEWILDERBEAST (LP, 1st pressing, withdrawn, with version of 'Magic In The Air' with the line "Love Is Contagious", and Woody Allen on sleeve)	30
00	Twisted Nerve TNXLLP133	THE HOUR OF THE BEWILDERBEAST (LP)	20
10	One Last Fruit OLFCDXX 01	IT'S WHAT I'M THINKING (PART 1 PHOTOGRAPHING SNOWFLAKES) (box set, LP, 2-CD, 4 badges, signed)	60
15	Twisted Nerve TNXLLP 695X	THE HOUR OF BEWILDERBEAST (3-LP, reissue, leatherette cover)	30

(see also Doves)

BADOO
| 80 | KG Imperial KG 001 | Rocking Of The Five Thousand/BADOO & TOYAN: Reaching To Be Free (12") | 20 |

HENRY BADOWSKI
| 79 | Deptford Fun City DFC 11 | Making Love With My Wife/Baby Sign Here With Me (p/s) | 6 |

BAD TASTE
| 88 | Newgate SRT8KS 1554 | Rockin' Girl (p/s, with insert) | 30 |
| 88 | Newgate SRT8KS 1554 | Rockin' Girl (p/s, without insert) | 10 |

BAD WEATHER INC.
| 02 | Soul City 132 | You Really Got A Hold On Me/I Never Never Knew (reissue) | 10 |

JOAN BAEZ
63	Fontana TF 564	We Shall Overcome/Don't Think Twice It's All Right	6
65	Fontana TF 639	Farewell Angelina/Queen Of Hearts	6
71	Vanguard 35138	The Night They Drove Old Dixie Down/When Time Is Stolen	6
89	Virgin VGC 9	DIAMONDS AND DUST IN THE BULLRING (LP)	40

(see also Bob Dylan)

BAFFLED
| 96 | Urban Beat URB 002 | Going On/Dreams (12") | 25 |
| 96 | Urban Beat URB 003 | Over U (Big Splash Mix)/(Deep Pan Mix)/The Feeling (Rinsing Mix)/(Bonus Roast Mix) (12", as Baffled 2) | 25 |

BAGGA
| 77 | Matumbi MAT 002 | Daughter Of Zion/Version | 50 |

BAGHDAD FIVE
| 83 | Risky R 2511 | Lovin Affection/Lonely Avenue | 25 |

BAG-O-WIRE

MINT VALUE £

BAG-O-WIRE
75	Klik KLP 9007	BAG-O-WIRE (LP)	40
77	Epic 82133	BAG-O-WIRE (LP)	30

JULIAN BAHULAS JAZZ AFRIKA
82	Tsafrika TSA 001	SON OF THE SOIL (LP)	30

BAHUMUTSI
87	Sounds From Bahumutsi SFB 001A	BUSANG MEROPA/BRING BACK THE DRUMS (LP)	100

BURR BAILEY (& SIX SHOOTERS)
63	Decca F 11686	San Francisco Bay/Like A Bird Without Feathers (with Six Shooters)	20
64	Decca F 11846	Chahawki/You Made Me Cry	30

CLIVE BAILEY & RICO'S GROUP
62	Blue Beat BB 92	Evening Train/Take Me Home (as Recko and his Blues Group)	20
68	Double D DD104	Drink & Drive/Oh Oh Sugar (with Double D band)	35

DEREK BAILEY
70	Incus INCUS 2	SOLO GUITAR (LP)	100
71	Incus INCUS 2R	SOLO GUITAR (LP)	70
74	Incus INCUS 12	LOT 74 (LP)	60
80	Incus INCUS 40	AIDA (LP)	70
85	Incus INCUS 48	NOTES (LP)	25
04	Organ Of Corti 10	TAPS (LP, 220gm vinyl, limited issue)	15

(see also Tony Oxley, Springboard, Steve Lacy & Derek Bailey, Anthony Braxton & Derek Bailey, Jamie Muir & Derek Bailey)

DEREK BAILEY, BARRY GUY & PAUL RUTHERFORD
70	Incus INCUS 3/4	ISKRA 1903 (LP)	50

(see also Barry Guy)

DEREK BAILEY & HAN BENNINK
72	Incus INCUS 9	SELECTIONS FROM LIVE PERFORMANCES AT VERITY'S PLACE (LP)	50
76	Incus INCUS 25	COMPANY 3 (LP)	50

DEREK BAILEY, ANTHONY BRAXTON & EVAN PARKER
76	Incus INCUS 23	COMPANY 2 (LP)	50

DEREK BAILEY & TONY COE
79	Incus INCUS 34	TIME (LP)	50

DEREK BAILEY, HUGH DAVIES, JAMIE MUIR, EVAN PARKER
75	Incus INCUS 17	THE MUSIC IMPROVISATION COMPANY 1968-1971 (LP)	40

DEREK BAILEY & TRISTAN HONSINGER
76	Incus INCUS 20	DUO (LP)	50

DEREK BAILEY & EVAN PARKER
75	Incus INCUS 16	THE LONDON CONCERT (LP)	50
85	Incus INCUS 50	COMPATIBLES (LP)	50

(see also Evan Parker)

DEREK BAILEY, EVAN PARKER & HAN BENNINK
70	Incus INCUS 1	THE TOPOGRAPHY OF THE LUNGS (LP)	150
77	Incus INCUS 1	THE TOPOGRAPHY OF THE LUNGS (LP, reissue)	40

PAUL BAILEY SOUND
80	Scott PSB 001	TAKE A WALK IN THE MOONLIGHT (LP)	50

ROY BAILEY (U.K.)
82	Fuse CF 382	HARD TIMES (LP, with insert)	15

(see also Leon Rosselson)

ROY BAILEY (JAMAICA)
72	Duke DU 146	Run Away Child/Wedding March	7

ZEDDIE BAILEY
73	Grape GR 3037	Babylon Gone/TONY KING: Speak No Evil	20

ELROY BAILY
80	Arawak ARK DD 027	24 Hour Love/Wabadab (12")	30
79	Burning Vibrations RRIG 7789	RED HOT DUB (LP)	40

(see also Ras Elroy)

ARTHUR BAIRD SKIFFLE GROUP
56	Beltona BL 2669	Union Train/Union Maid	15

BAJA MARIMBA BAND
63	London HL 9828	Comin' In The Back Door/December Child	6

BINKY BAKER
78	Stiff BUY 41	Toe Knee Black Burn/Rainy Day In Brighton (p/s)	7

CARROLL BAKER
76	RCA PB 9056	It's My Party/Loves Golden Rule	6
78	RCA PB 9370	I'm Getting High Remembering/If It Wasn't For You	6

CHET BAKER (QUARTET)
54	Vogue LDE 045	CHET BAKER QUARTET (10" LP)	30
55	Philips BBL 7022	CHET BAKER AND STRINGS (LP)	20
55	Vogue LDE 116	CHET BAKER QUARTET (10" LP)	20
56	Vogue LAE 120	CHET BAKER SINGS (LP)	20
56	Vogue LDE 159	CHET BAKER SEXTET (10" LP)	25
56	Vogue LDE 163	CHET BAKER ENSEMBLE (10" LP)	25
56	Vogue LDE 182	CHET BAKER SINGS (10" LP)	20
56	Felsted PDL 85008	CHET BAKER QUARTET VOL. 1 (LP)	25
56	Felsted PDL 85013	CHET BAKER QUARTET VOL. 2 (LP)	20
57	Felsted PDL 85036	I GET CHET (LP, with Bobby Jaspar)	50
57	Vogue LAE 12044	CHET BAKER QUARTET AT ANN ARBOR (LP)	20
57	Vogue LAE 12076	CHET BAKER AND HIS CREW (LP, mono)	25
58	Vogue LAE 12109	CHET BAKER - PHIL'S BLUES (LP)	20
59	Vogue SEA 5005	CHET BAKER AND HIS CREW (LP, stereo)	20

Desmond BAKER & CLAREDONIANS

MINT VALUE £

59	Vogue LAE 12164	CHET BAKER SINGS (LP)	20
59	Vogue LAE 12183	CHET BAKER AND ART PEPPER SEXTET - PLAYBOYS! (LP)	60

(see also Art Pepper, Russ Freeman & Chet Baker Quartet, Gerry Mulligan)

DESMOND BAKER & CLAREDONIANS
66	Island WI 295	Rude Boy Gone Jail/SHARKS: Don't Fool Me	25

(see also Claredonians)

ERNEST BAKER
00	Grapevine 2000 110	Alone Again/Do It With Feeling	15

GEORGE BAKER SELECTION
70	Penny Farthing 717	Little Green Bag/Pretty Little Dreamer	15
79	Penny Farthing PELS 503	LITTLE GREEN BAG (LP)	60

GINGER BAKER('S AIRFORCE)
70	Polydor 2662 001	GINGER BAKER'S AIRFORCE (2-LP, gatefold sleeve)	50
70	Polydor 2383 029	AIRFORCE II (LP, gatefold sleeve, with insert)	30
72	Polydor 2383 133	STRATAVARIOUS (LP)	20

(see also Graham Bond Organisation, Cream, Blind Faith, Fela Ransome-Kuti [& Africa '70], Harold McNair, Griffin, Baker-Gurvitz Army)

GLEN BAKER
85	The Stand THE STAND 3	BRIEF ENCOUNTER (LP)	20

(see also Enid)

HYLDA BAKER
59	Decca F 11186	She Knows Y'know/Makin' Love	7
69	Columbia DB 8936	Nearest And Dearest/The More You Laugh	12

JEANETTE BAKER
59	Vogue Pop V 9143	Everything Reminds Me Of You/Crazy With You	150

JOHN BAKER
08	Trunk JBH 030 LP	THE JOHN BAKER TAPES (LP, 500 only)	20

JULIEN BAKER
17	Matador OLE-1127-7	Funeral Pyre/Distant Solar Systems (p/s)	25
18	Matador OLE 1129 1	TURN OUT THE LIGHTS (LP, screen printed sleeve, 50 only)	80

KENNY BAKER
55	Jazz Today JTL 1	OPERATION JAM SESSION (10" LP, with The Jazz Today Unit)	60
55	Jazz Today JTL 4	KENNY BAKER QUARTET/AFTER HOURS GROUP (10" LP)	30
55	Jazz Today JTL 5	TRIBUTE TO BENNY CARTER (10" LP, with The Jazz Today Unit, one side by Bertie King Jazz Group)	20
59	Columbia 33S1140	BLOWIN' UP A STORM (10" LP)	20
78	77 77S 56	BAKER'S JAM (LP)	20

LAVERN BAKER (& GLIDERS)
55	Columbia SCM 5172	Tweedle Dee/Tomorrow Night (with Gliders)	300
55	London HLA 8199	Play It Fair/That Old Lucky Sun (with Gliders)	150
56	London HLE 8260	My Happiness Forever (with Gliders)/Get Up! Get Up! (You Sleepy Head)	100
57	Columbia DB 3879	Jim Dandy/Tra La La (with Gliders)	150
57	London HLE 8396	I Can't Love You Enough/Still	100
57	London HLE 8442	Game Of Love/Jim Dandy Got Married	100
57	London HLE 8524	Humpty Dumpty Heart/Love Me Right	50
58	London HLE 8638	Learning To Love/Substitute	50
58	London HLE 8672	Whipper Snapper/Harbour Lights	50
59	London HLE 8790	I Cried A Tear/St. Louis Blues	20
59	London HLE 8871	I Waited Too Long/You're Teasing Me	20
59	London HLE 8945	So High So Low/If You Love Me (I Won't Care)	20
60	London HLE 9023	Tiny Tim/For Love Of You	20
60	London HLE 9252	Bumble Bee/My Turn Will Come	20
61	London HLE 9300	You're The Boss/I'll Never Be Free (with Jimmy Ricks)	20
61	London HLK 9343	Saved/Don Juan	30
61	London HLK 9468	Hey, Memphis/Voodoo Voodoo	50
63	London HLK 9640	See See Rider/The Story Of My Love (I Had A Dream)	15
65	Atlantic AET 6009	THE BEST OF LAVERN BAKER (EP)	60
58	London HA-E 2107	ROCK 'N' ROLL WITH LAVERN BAKER (LP, with thin card cover)	200
58	London Jazz LTZK 15139	SINGS BESSIE SMITH (LP)	50
61	London HA-K 2422	SAVED (LP)	30
63	London HA-K 8074	SEE SEE RIDER (LP)	20
64	Atlantic ATL 5002	THE BEST OF LAVERN BAKER (LP, plum label)	20
68	Atlantic 587/588 133	SEE SEE RIDER (LP, reissue)	30
84	Charly CRB 1072	REAL GONE GAL (LP)	15

MICKEY BAKER
70	Major Minor SMLP 67	IN BLUNDERLAND (LP)	50

(see also Mighty Flea, Champion Jack Dupree, MIckey & Sylvia)

SALLY BAKER
70s	Old Dog PUP 1	IN THE SPOTLIGHT (LP)	50

SAM BAKER
68	Monument MON 1009	I Believe In You/I'm Number One	30

TOM BAKER
79	Argo ZDSW 722/3	THE STRANGE CASE OF DR. JEKYLL & MR. HYDE (2-LP)	20

TWO-TON BAKER
55	London HL 8121	Clink, Clank (In My Piggy Bank)/Mr. Froggie (Went A Courtin')	15

VICKY BAKER
64	London HLU 9856	No More Foolish Stories/Darling Say The Word	15

YVONNE BAKER
77	London HLU 10553	You Didn't Say A Word/BOBBY PARIS: Night Owl	10
12	Outta Sight OSV 069	You Didn't Say A Word/HATTIE WINSTON: Pictures Don't Lie	7

(see also Sensations, Bobby Paris)

BAKER-GURVITZ ARMY

MINT VALUE £

BAKER-GURVITZ ARMY
74	Vertigo 9103 201	BAKER-GURVITZ ARMY (LP, with lyric insert)	25

(see also Ginger Baker('s Airforce), Three Man Army, Parrish & Gurvitz, Gun, Sharks)

BAKERLOO
69	Harvest HAR 5004	Driving Backwards/Once Upon A Time	25
69	Harvest SHVL 762	BAKERLOO (LP, gatefold sleeve, no EMI on label)	400

(see also Colosseum, Uriah Heep, Humble Pie)

BAKER TWINS
64	Pye 7N 15628	He's No Good/Words Written On Water	15

BALANCE
81	Portrait PRTA 1477	Breaking Away/It's So Strange	8
73	Incus INCUS 11	BALANCE (LP)	100
73	private pressing	IN FOR THE COUNT (LP)	30

BALCONY
82	Praxis TM2	The Lizard Hunt/Surprise After Surprise (p/s)	6

BALDHEAD GROWLER
67	Jump Up JU 531	Sausage/Bingo Woman	8

CHRIS BALDO
68	Vogue VRS 7029	Living For Your Love/Arretez - Vous A Saint Michel	15

LONG JOHN BALDRY
64	United Artists UP 1056	You'll Be Mine (with Rod Stewart)/Up Above My Head (I Hear Music In The Air)	50
65	United Artists UP 1078	I'm On To You Baby/Goodbye Baby	20
65	United Artists UP 1107	How Long Will It Last/House Next Door	30
66	United Artists UP 1124	Unseen Hands/Turn On Your Lovelight	10
66	United Artists UP 1136	The Drifter/Only A Fool Breaks His Own Heart	50
66	United Artists UP 1158	Cuckoo/Bring My Baby Back To Me	30
67	United Artists UP 1204	Only A Fool Breaks His Own Heart/Let Him Go (And Let Me Love You)	20
65	United Artists UEP 1013	LONG JOHN'S BLUES (EP, with Hoochie Coochie Men)	100
64	United Artists UP 1081	LONG JOHN'S BLUES (LP, with Hoochie Coochie Men)	50
66	United Artists (S)ULP 1146	LOOKING AT LONG JOHN (LP)	40
68	Pye N(S)PL 18228	LET THERE BE LONG JOHN (LP, unissued)	0
69	Pye N(S)PL 18306	WAIT FOR ME (LP)	15

(see also Rod Stewart, Alexis Korner, Bluesology)

BALDWIN
67	Decca F22624	The Land At Rainbows End/Beautiful Butterfly	30

KEITH BALFOUR
69	Studio One SO 2079	Dreaming/Tired Of Waiting	20

BALIL
93	Rising High RSN 72	Parasight/Island/Rosary Pilots/Avidya (12")	20

CANNON BALL (CARL BRYAN) & JOHNNY MELODY (MOORE)
69	Big Shot BI 518	Parapinto/Cool Hand Luke	100

DAVE BALL
83	Some Bizarrre BIZL5	IN STRICT TEMPO (LP)	18

(see also Soft Cell)

FLORENCE BALLARD
68	Stateside SS 2113	It Doesn't Matter How I Say It (It's What I Say That Matters)/Goin' Out Of My Head	75
68	Stateside SS 2113	It Doesn't Matter How I Say It (It's What I Say That Matters)/Goin' Out Of My Head (DJ Copy)	100

(see also Supremes)

HANK BALLARD (& MIDNIGHTERS)
59	Parlophone R 4558	The Twist/Kansas City	15
60	Parlophone R 4682	Finger Poppin' Time/I Love You, I Love You So-o-o	15
60	Parlophone R 4688	The Twist/Teardrops On Your Letter	15
60	Parlophone R 4707	Let's Go, Let's Go, Let's Go/If You'd Forgive Me	15
61	Parlophone R 4728	The Hoochie Coochie Coo/LITTLE WILLIE JOHN: Walk Slow	15
61	Parlophone R 4762	Let's Go Again/Deep Blue Sea	35
61	Parlophone R 4771	The Continental Walk/What Is This I See	15
61	Parlophone PMC 1158	SPOTLIGHT ON HANK BALLARD (LP)	75
63	London HA 8101	THE JUMPIN' HANK BALLARD (LP)	40

(see also Midnighters)

RUSS BALLARD
74	Epic SEPC 4995	Some Kinda Hurricane/You Can Do Voodoo	6

BALLOON BUSTERS
69	Pye 7N 17748	Alcock And Brown/Bluer Than Blue (p/s)	10

BALLOON CORPS
69	Stateside SS8034	Make It Right/Muddy Water	20

BALLOON FARM
68	London HLP 10185	A Question Of Temperature/Hurtin' For Your Love	120

BALLOONS
78	Earwacks WAK 001	Calling All Human Beings/(Love Runs) Through Your Elbow	20
80	Earwacks WAK 002	Jean Paul's Wife/The Slope	8

BALLS
71	Wizard WIZ 101	Fight For My Country/Janie Slow Down	30

(see also Denny Laine, Lemon Tree, Trevor Burton, Uglys, Wizzard)

LORI BALMER
68	Polydor 56293	Treacle Brown/Four Faces West	40

BALTIMORE & OHIO MARCHING BAND
67	Stateside SS 2065	Lapland/Condition Red	60
67	Stateside SS 2065	Lapland/Condition Red (DJ copy)	200
68	Stateside (S)SL 10231	LAPLAND (LP)	20

BAMA WINDS

MINT VALUE £

BAMA WINDS
69 Island ILPS 9096   WINDY (LP) 30
BAM BAM (1)
81 Vox Populi VOP 001   Polka Dot!/Crocodile Tears (p/s) 20
BAM BAM (2)
88 Desire Records WANTX 7P   Where's Your Child/Spend The Night (12", promo) 12
88 Desire WANTX 7   Where's Your Child/(Suck Mix) (12", p/s) 15
BAMBI
76 Sol-Doon SDR 019   Lady Of Lies/Somebody Told Me 15
BAMBIS
64 Oriole CB 1965   Not Wrong/Handle With Care 40
65 CBS 201778   Baby Blue/If This Is Love 40
BAMBOO FRINGE
82 Probe Plus PP 4   Dorian Grey/How Do I Dance To This Music (p/s) 8
BAMBOO SHOOT
68 Columbia DB 8370   The Fox Has Gone To Ground/There And Back Again Lane 200
BAMBOO ZOO
81 Phoney Gram PH 45 01   Ghost Party/Binding Wire (p/s) 12
81 Phoney Gram PHOG 8101   LOOK! LISTEN! CONSUME! (LP) 18
BAMBOOS
06 Tru Thoughts TRULP 092   STEP IT UP (LP) 15
07 Tru Thoughts TRULP 125   RAWVILLE (LP) 20
BAMBOOS OF JAMAICA
70 Pye Intl. 7N 25515   Reggae Man/Candy 8
BANANA BUNCH
70 Page One POF 183   Tra-La-La Song/Funky Hoe 15
71 DJM DJS 252   Tra-La-La Song/Season Of The Rain 10
(see also Nite People)
BANBARRA
76 United Artists UP 36113   Shack Up Parts 1 & 2 10
85 Stateside 12STATES 1   Shack Up (Extended)/Shack Up (Part 1)/Shack Up (Part II) (12" p/s) 15
BANCO DE GAIA
94 Planet Dog BARKLP 003   MAYA (2-LP) 20
94 Planet Dog BARKLP 003   MAYA (3-LP, numbered) 25
95 Planet Dog BARKLP 011 S   LAST TRAIN TO LHASA (4-LP, limited edition) 35
97 Planet Dog BARKLP 025   BIG MEN CRY (2-LP) 20
THE BAND
68 Capitol CL 15559   The Weight/I Shall Be Released (artist credit: Jaime Robbie Robertson. Rick Danko, Richard Manuel, Garth Hudson, Levon Helm (the Band)) (demo) 30
68 Capitol CL 15559   The Weight/I Shall Be Released (artist credit: Jaime Robbie Robertson. Rick Danko, Richard Manuel, Garth Hudson, Levon Helm (the Band)) 20
69 Capitol CL 15613   Up On Cripple Creek/The Night They Drove Old Dixie Down (Demo) 20
69 Capitol CL 15613   Up On Cripple Creek/The Night They Drove Old Dixie Down 15
69 Capitol CL 15629   Rag Mama Rag/The Unfaithful Servant (Demo) 20
69 Capitol CL 15629   Rag Mama Rag/The Unfaithful Servant 12
69 Capitol CL 15767   Ain't Got No Home/Get Up Jake (Demo) 20
73 Capitol CL 15767   Ain't Got No Home/Get Up Jake 12
68 Capitol T 2955   MUSIC FROM BIG PINK (LP, black/rainbow label, mono) 70
68 Capitol ST 2955   MUSIC FROM BIG PINK (LP, black/rainbow label, stereo) 40
69 Capitol EST 132   THE BAND (LP, 1st pressing, lemon yellow label, textured sleeve) 20
70 Capitol EA-SW 425   STAGE FRIGHT (LP, 1st pressing, lemon yellow labels, gatefold sleeve and insert) 15
71 Capitol EA ST 651   CAHOOTS (LP) 15
72 Capitol E-ST 2955   MUSIC FROM BIG PINK (LP, reissue, orange labels) 15
72 Capitol E-ST 132   THE BAND (LP, reissue, orange labels) 15
97 EMI LPCENT 23   THE BAND (LP, reissue, EMI 100 Centenary, etched sleeve) 15
(see also Levon & The Hawks, Bob Dylan, Ronnie Hawkins, Robbie Robertson)
BANDA BLACK RIO
96 Universal Sound US LP3   THE BEST OF BANDA BLACK RIO (LP) 30
B & THE FAMILY
16 Super Disco Edits SDE 19   A Good Time/You're Gonna Love Me 20
BANDITS
85 Hosspig HPG1   Treasure Trove/Right In The Head (p/s) 25
BANDITZ
80 Phaeton SPIN 2   JCB/Damage Your Health (p/s) 15
BAND OF ANGELS
64 United Artists UP 1049   Not True As Yet/Me 15
64 United Artists UP 1066   She'll Never Be You/Gonna Make A Woman Of You 15
66 Piccadilly 7N 35279   Leave It To Me/Too Late My Love 15
66 Piccadilly 7N 35292   Invitation/Cheat And Lie 100
(see also Mike D'Abo, Manfred Mann)
BAND OF HORSES
07 Kids KIDS 014   Funeral/The Ends Not Near (p/s, 750 only, no'd, with download card) 12
BAND OF JOY
78 Poydor 2310588   BAND OF JOY (LP, with lyric insert) 30
BAND OF MERCY & SALVATION
69 Duke DU 20   Suffering Stink/BOB MELODY: The Break (B-side actually by Winston Francis) 200
BANDOGGS
78 Transatlantic LTRA 504   BANDOGGS (LP, cream label) 18
(see also Peter & Chris Coe)
BANDULU
93 Infonet INF003LP   GUIDANCE (2-LP) 25

BANDY LEGS

			MINT VALUE £
94	Infonet INF006LP	ANTIMATTERS (2-LP)	20

BANDY LEGS
| 74 | WWW WWS 01 | Ride Ride/Don't Play Games | 20 |
| 76 | Jet JET 783 | Bet You Can't Dance/Circles | 20 |

(see also Quartz)

BANDYT
| 87 | Setspeed BANDYT 001 | A Different Romance/Roadblocks (no p/s) | 7 |

HONEY BANE
| 79 | Crass 521984/1 | YOU CAN BE YOU EP | 10 |

(see also Crass)

BANG (1)
| 72 | EST 11015 | BANG (LP) | 60 |

(see also Quartz)

BANG (2)
| 72 | Capitol CL15722 | Questions/Future Shock | 20 |

ED BANGER
78	Rabid TOSH 106	Kinnel Tommy/Baby Was A Baby (p/s)	7
78	EMI International INT 571	Kinnel Tommy/Baby Was A Baby (reissue, numbered p/s)	7
81	Spiv DIV 1	I've Just Had My Car Nicked/P.C. Plod/Sponge (p/s, with photo insert)	20
83	Cloud Nine CNS 01	Poor People/Vicars In The Dark (p/s)	7

(see also Nosebleeds, Slaughter & The Dogs, Eddie Fiction)

BANGOR FLYING CIRCUS
| 70 | Stateside-Dunhill SSL 5022 | BANGOR FLYING CIRCUS (LP) | 40 |

BANG THE PARTY
87	Warriors Dance WDT 100	I Feel Good All Over/Jacques Theme (Main Mix)/Jacques Theme (Alternative Mix) (12")	18
89	Warriors Dance WAFT 10	Bang Bang You're Mine - The Remixes (12")	10
89	Warriors Dance WAFT 10R	Bang Bang Attitude Rap (Noisy Mix)/(BTP Mix)/(Confusion Clubwire) (12")	10

DEVENDRA BANHART
| 05 | XL XLLP 185 | REJOICING IN THE HANDS/NINO ROJO (2-LP) | 25 |
| 13 | Nonesuch 534455-1 | MALA (2-LP with poster, CD and 7") | 15 |

BANISHED
| 93 | Peaceville CC 3 | Altered Minds/Cast Out The Flesh (blue vinyl, p/s) | 15 |
| 93 | Deaf DEAF 13 | DELIVER ME UNTO PAIN (LP) | 25 |

(see also Baphomet)

BANKRUPT
| 84 | SG 085 | Joy Of Love/Acapella Version/Untitled/Untitled (12", stamped white labels) | 40 |

BESSIE BANKS
64	Red Bird BC 106	Go Now/Sounds Like My Baby	100
64	Red Bird BC 106	Go Now/Sounds Like My Baby(DJ Copy)	150
67	Verve VS 563	I Can't Make It (Without You Baby)/Need You	120
67	Verve VS 563	I Can't Make It (Without You Baby)/Need You (DJ Copy)	100
68	Soul City SC 105	Go Now/Sounds Like My Baby (reissue)	25
75	Contempo CS 2070	Baby You Sure Know How To Get To Me/Try To Leave Me If You Can	35

DARRELL BANKS
66	London HL 10070	Open The Door To Your Heart/Our Love (Is In The Pocket) (demo only)	1000
66	London HL 10070	Open The Door To Your Heart/Our Love (Is In The Pocket) (1 known stock copy)	12000
66	Stateside SS 536	Open The Door To Your Heart/Our Love (Is In The Pocket) (1st pressing demo with white/red label)	200
66	Stateside SS 536	Open The Door To Your Heart/Our Love (Is In The Pocket) (1st pressing)	40
66	Stateside SS 536	Open The Door To Your Heart/Our Love (Is In The Pocket) (2st pressing demo with green/white label)	100
66	Stateside SS 536	Open The Door To Your Heart/Our Love (Is In The Pocket) (2nd pressing)	20
67	Atlantic 584 120	Angel Baby (Don't You Ever Leave Me)/Look Into The Eyes Of A Fool	70
69	Stax STAX 124	Just Because Your Love Is Gone/I'm The One Who Loves You (Demo)	150
69	Stax STAX 124	Just Because Your Love Is Gone/I'm The One Who Loves You	125
77	Atlantic K 10879	Angel Baby (Don't You Ever Leave Me)/Look Into The Eyes Of A Fool (reissue)	20
78	Contempo 8005	Open The Door To Your Heart/Angel Baby (reissue)	8
10	Outta Sight OSV 001	I'm The One Who Loves You/I'm Knocking At Your Heart (reissue)	6
69	Stax SXATS 1011	HERE TO STAY (LP)	50

HOMER BANKS
66	Liberty LIB 12028	A Lot Of Love/Fighting To Win	30
66	Liberty LIB 12028	A Lot Of Love/Fighting To Win (DJ Copy)	60
67	Liberty LIB 12047	60 Minutes Of Your Love/Do You Know What	30
67	Liberty LIB 12047	60 Minutes Of Your Love/Do You Know What (DJ Copy)	60
67	Liberty LIB 12060	Hooked By Love/Lady Of Stone	40
67	Liberty LIB 12060	Hooked By Love/Lady Of Stone (DJ Copy)	75
68	Minit MLF 11004	Round The Clock Lover Man/Foolish Hearts Break Fast	15
68	Minit MLF 11007	60 Minutes Of Your Love/A Lot Of Love	15
69	Minit MLF 11015	Me Or Your Mama/I Know You Know I Know You Know	10
70	Liberty LBF 15392	60 Minutes Of Your Love/I Know You Know I Know You Know	15

LARRY BANKS
67	Stateside SS 579	I Don't Wanna Do It/I'm Coming Home	60
67	Stateside SS 579	I Don't Wanna Do It/I'm Coming Home (DJ Copy)	75
09	Kent 6T 25	My Life Is No Better/JACKIE DAY: Get To Steppin	20
10	Kent Select City 019	Ooh It Hurts Me/BOBBY PENN: Without Your Love	8

LLOYD BANKS
| 66 | Reaction 591 008 | We'll Meet Again/Look Out Girl | 20 |

PETER BANKS
| 73 | Sovereign SVNA 7256 | PETER BANKS (LP, gatefold sleeve) | 40 |

(see also Syndicats, Syn, Neat Change, Yes, Flash, Jan Akkerman, Steve Hackett)

MINT VALUE £

BANNED
77	Can't Eat EAT 1 UP	Little Girl/CPGJ's (stamped white labels, in handmade p/s)	60
77	Can't Eat EAT 1 UP	Little Girl/CPGJ's (stamped white labels)	25

(see also Gryphon)

BANSHEES
64	Columbia DB 7361	I Got A Woman/Don't Say Goodnight And Mean Goodbye	25
65	Columbia DB 7530	Big Buildin'/Mockingbird	20
65	Columbia DB 7752	I'm Gonna Keep On Loving You/Yes Indeed	15

BANTAM
70	COUN 248	BANTAM (LP, private pressing, white label, hand-made wraparound sleeve)	175

PATO BANTON
85	Ariwa ARI LP 023	MAD PROFESSOR CAPTURES PATO BANTON (LP)	15

STARKY BANTON
97	Dub Organiser DOT 101	I And I Saw Dem Coming/I And I Dub/The Herb/Herbal Dub (10")	15

BAPHOMET
92	Peaceville VILE 31	THE DEAD SHALL INHERIT (LP)	80

(see also Banished)

BAPTEME DU FEU
17	La Vida Es Un Mus MUS 136	RIXE EP (p/s, clear vinyl with extra wraparound sleeve, lyric sheet and sticker)	25

DENISE BAPTISTE
80	Gigi G 001	Weak In The Knees/EXILE BAND: Instrumental	50

SELWYN BAPTISTE
70	Black Swan BW 1402	Mo' Bay/RECO'S ALL STARS: Going West	20

BARBARA & BRENDA
68	Direction 58-3799	Never Love A Robin/Sally's Party	15

BARBARA AND THE BROWNS
08	Kent Select CITY 008	I'm Gonna Start A War/OTIS REDDING: Love By The Pound	10

BARBARA & ERNIE
71	Atlantic 2466 015	PRELUDE TO (LP)	50

BARBARA & WINSTON
64	Island WI 418	The Dream/I Love You	18

BARBARELLA
92	Eye Q 4509 90679 1	THE ART OF DANCE (2-LP)	25

BARBARIANS
65	Stateside SS 449	Are You A Boy Or Are You A Girl/Take It Or Leave It	25
66	Stateside SS 497	Moulty/I'll Keep On Seeing You	30

BARBECUE BOB
67	Kokomo K 1002	GEORGIA BLUES NO. 1 (LP, 99 copies only)	100

BARBED WIRE
86	Oi Records OIR 006	THE AGE THAT DIDN'T CARE (LP)	20

JOHN HENRY BARBEE
65	Storyville 616 013	I AIN'T GONNA PICK NO MORE COTTON (LP)	20
65	Storyville 670 171	PORTRAITS IN BLUES VOLUME 9 (LP)	25

CHRIS BARBER AND HIS BAND
67	Marmalade 598 005	Catcall/Mercy Mercy Mercy	75
69	Marmalade 558 013	Battersea Rain Dance/Sleepy Joe	25
69	Marmalade 608 009	BATTERSEA RAIN DANCE (LP, as Chris Barber & His Band)	50
69	Polydor 2384 020	BATTERSEA RAIN DANCE (LP) (2nd Pressing)	25

CHRIS BARBER SOUL BAND
65	Columbia DB 7461	Finishing Straight/Morning Train	30

(see also Louis Jordan & Chris Barber)

KEITH BARBOUR
69	CBS 4606	Echo Park/Here I Am Losing You	6

EDDIE BARCLAY & QUINCY JONES
58	Felsted PDL 85056	EDDIE AND QUINCY (LP)	15

RUE BARCLAY & PEGGY DUNCAN
54	London HL 8033	Tongue Tied Boy/River Of Tears	15

TIMOTHY BARCLAY
70	Penny Farthing PEN 740	Catch The Wind/The Girl From Indiana	12

BARCLAY JAMES HARVEST
68	Parlophone R 5693	Early Morning/Mr. Sunshine	35
69	Harvest HAR 5003	Brother Thrush/Poor Wages	15
70	Harvest HAR 5025	Taking Some Time On/The Iron Maiden	15
71	Harvest HAR 5034	Mocking Bird/Vanessa Simmons	10
72	Harvest HAR 5051	I'm Over You/Child Of Man	10
72	Harvest HAR 5058	Thank You/Medicine Man	10
73	Harvest HAR 5068	Rock And Roll Woman/The Joker (BJH logo p/s)	12
74	Polydor 2058 474	Poor Boy Blues/Crazy City	7
74	Polydor (matrix: SH 1041/2)	Negative Earth/RARE BIRD: Diamonds (33rpm flexidisc free with Sounds magazine)	10
70	Harvest SHVL 770	BARCLAY JAMES HARVEST (LP, 1st pressing, textured gatefold sleeve, 'The Gramophone Co. Ltd' label text, no EMI box on label)	50
71	Harvest SHVL 788	ONCE AGAIN (LP, gatefold sleeve, no EMI box on label)	30
71	Harvest SHVL 794	BARCLAY JAMES HARVEST AND OTHER SHORT STORIES (LP, gatefold sleeve)	25
72	Harvest Q4SHVL 788	ONCE AGAIN (LP, quadrophonic)	40
73	Harvest SHSP 4023	BABY JAMES HARVEST (LP, inner)	25
76	Harvest SHVL 770	BARCLAY JAMES HARVEST (LP, re-pressing, gatefold sleeve, repressing EMI box on label and 'EMI Records Ltd')	25

(see also Bombadil, John Lees)

PETER BARDENS
70	Transatlantic TRA 222	THE ANSWER (LP, white/lilac label with 't' logo)	100
71	Transatlantic TRA 243	PETER BARDENS (LP, gatefold sleeve, side one label is multi-coloured)	50

BARDO POND

			MINT VALUE £
76	Transatlantic TRASAM 36	VINTAGE '69 (LP, featuring Peter Green, clear vinyl)	20
76	Transatlantic TRASAM 36	VINTAGE '69 (LP, featuring Peter Green)	15

(see also Cheynes, Peter B's, Shotgun Express, Them, Village, Camel, Steve Tilston)

BARDO POND

11	Agitated AGIT 009	Fallen/CARLTON MELTON: Slow Growth (12", clear vinyl, 100 only)	15
11	Agitated AGIT 009	Fallen/CARLTON MELTON: Slow Growth (12", black vinyl, 100 only)	10
13	Fire Blaze 207	RISE ABOVE IT ALL (12" EP)	12
14	Fire Blaze 340	LOOKING FOR ANOTHER PLACE (12" EP)	15
15	Fire Blaze 420	IS THERE A HEAVEN? (12" EP)	18
01	Matador Ole 459-1	DILATE (2-LP)	50
03	ATP ATPRLP6	ON THE ELLIPSE (2-LP, gatefold)	40
12	Latitudes GMT 029V	YNTRA (LP, with insert)	20
13	Fire FV 291	TICKET CRYSTALS (2-LP, reissue)	25

BRIGITTE BARDOT

66	Vogue VRS 7018	Mister Sun/Gang Gang (p/s)	100
66	Vogue VRS 7018	Mister Sun/Gang Gang	30
68	Pye International 7N 25290	Harley-Davidson/Contact (p/s)	100
68	Pye International 7N 25290	Harley-Davidson/Contact	20
63	Philips BL 7561	BRIGITTE BARDOT (LP)	120
64	Philips B 77 984	'BB'	100

BARDS (1)

68	Capitol CL 15536	The Owl And The Pussycat/Light Of Love	15

BARDS (2)

71	Folk Heritage FHR 019M	TIME FOR THE BARDS (LP)	150

BARDS OF BARLEYCORN

77	Beet Music BMR 101	WHEN GRANDMA USED TO CALL (LP)	20

BARE FOOT

71	Pye 7N 45110	Frightened/Girl Are You A Woman Now (Promo copies say "Bear Foot")	20

BAREFOOT BLUES BAND

70	Beacon BEA 163	Can't You See/Sunday Morning Barefoot Blues	25
72	Deram DM 353	The Spirit Of Joe Hill/I Believe In Music	8
73	Deram DM 372	Getting Better All The Time/Half Of Me	6

JOHN BARHAM & ASHISH KHAN

73	Elektra K 42129	JUGALBANDI (LP)	15

MARK BARKAN

66	Stateside SS 2064	A Great Day For The Clown/Pity The Woman	10
67	Stateside SS 2064	A Great Day For The Clown/Pity The Woman (DJ copy)	40

BAR-KAYS

67	Stax 601 014	Soul Finger/Knucklehead	6
68	Stax 601 036	A Hard Day's Night/I Want Someone	6
69	Atlantic 584 244	Soul Finger/Knucklehead (reissue)	8
78	Stax 12 STAX 505	Holy Ghost/Monster (12")	15
69	Atco 228 030	SOUL FINGER (LP)	20
69	Stax SXATS 1009	GOTTA GROOVE (LP)	20
71	Stax 2362 003	BLACK ROCK (LP)	20
73	Stax 2325 087	DO YOU SEE WHAT I SEE? (LP)	20
76	Stax STX 1033	COLD BLOODED (LP)	20
77	Mercury 9100 048	FLYING HIGH ON YOUR LOVE (LP)	15

(see also Otis Redding)

DAVE BARKER

70	Duke DU 74	Funkey Reggae/TOMMY McCOOK & SUPERSONICS: I Love You My Baby (B-side actually by Versatiles)	40
70	Punch PH 20	Prisoner Of Love/BUSTY & UPSETTERS: Soul Juice	25
70	Punch PH 22	You Betray Me/Will You Still Love Me Tomorrow?	30
70	Punch PH 25	Shocks Of Mighty Parts 1 & 2	15
70	Punch PH 42	Reggae Meeting/MARTIN ALL STARS: Soul Bone	20
70	Jackpot JP 736	The Fastest Man Alive/NORMAN GRANT: Bloodshot Eyes	15
70	Jackpot JP 742	Wet Version/I Got To Get Away	30
70	Jackpot JP 745	Girl Of My Dreams/On Broadway	20
70	High Note HS 049	She Want It/FIRST GENERATION: Give Him Up	35
70	Randy's RAN 503	October/RANDY'S ALLSTARS: Time Out	70
70	Unity UN 567	Blessed Are The Meek (with Slim Smith)/JEFF BARNES & UNIQUES: The People's Voice	20
70	Techniques TE915	Karatae/Version	15
70	Upsetter US 331	Shocks Of Mighty/Set Me Free (with Upsetters)	25
70	Upsetter US 344	Some Sympathy/UNTOUCHABLES: Tender Love	30
70	Upsetter US 347	Sound Underground/Don't Let The Sun Catch You Crying (features the Wailers)	50
71	Upsetter US 358	Shocks '71/HURRICANES: You've Got To Be Mine	20
71	Upsetter US 362	Groove Me/UPSETTERS: Screwdriver	30
71	Upsetter US 364	What A Confusion/UPSETTERS: Confusion - Version 2	50
71	Ackee ACK 113	Johnny Dollar/Version	30
71	Ackee ACK 119	Life Of A Millionaire/Version	15
71	Trojan TR 7851	Sex Machine/You Left Me And Gone (both sides with Aggrovators)	20
71	Punch PH 69	What A Confusion/BOB MARLEY: Small Axe	50
71	Supreme SUP 228	Double Heavy/Johnny Dollar	30
71	Downtown DT 482	Only The Strong Survive/Only The Strong - Version	15
72	Jackpot JP 803	You'll Be Sorry/Green Grow The Lilacs	10
72	Big Shot BI 614	Are You Sure/I Don't Know Why (B-side actually by Sensations)	10
72	Fab FAB 25	Green Grow The Lilacs/JIMMY RILEY: Keep An Eye (On Your Closest Friend) (white label)	15
80	Black Jack BJD 4507	Glow Of Love/Version (12")	20

			MINT VALUE £
76	Trojan TRL 127	PRISONER OF LOVE (LP)	60

(see also Glen & Dave, Bobby & Dave, Aggrovators, David Crooks, Dennis Alcapone, Don Drummond, Owen Gary, Lizzy & Dennis, Bob Marley, Lester Sterling, Busty Brown)

RONNIE BARKER
78	EMI EMI 2768	Going Straight/String Bean Queen	6

STAN BARKER
79	Nelson N1001	VOLUME 1 (LP)	40

BARKING MAD
90	Ham West 001	My Cat Is Better Than Your Cat/I Wanna Sleep WIth A Troll	8

BARK PSYCHOSIS
92	3rd Stone STONE 006T	Scum (1-sided etched 12", p/s)	12
94	Circa CIRCA 29	HEX (LP)	100
04	Fire FIRELP 90	CODENAME: DUSTSUCKER (LP, inner)	100

BARLASTON DOWN
73	Decca F13321	Always/Mean Woman Mambo	15

BARLEY BREE
67	Piccadilly 7N 35393	Sometime In The Morning/Save Your Love	15

BARNABY RUDGE
68	CBS 3262	Joe, Organ & Co./Railway Jim	10

(see also Will Malone)

BARNES/ADAMS
60s	Lyntone LYN 1021	When It Comes To The Crunch (It's Smiths Time)/Rhythm And Crunch (flexi, p/s)	15

BARNEY J. BARNES & INTRO.
67	Decca F 12662	It Must Be Love/Can't Stand The Pain	100

BENNY BARNES
60	Mercury AMT 1094	Token Of Love/That-A-Boy Willie	10

DENA BARNES
80	Grapevine GRP 141	If You Ever Walked Out Of My Life/Who Am I	40
16	Outta Site OSV 138	If You Ever Walk Out Of My Life/Who Am I (You Ought To Know) (reissue)	8

JEFF BARNES
70	Jackpot JP 735	Get In The Groove/JOHN HOLT: A Little Tear	12
70	Unity UN 568	1,000 Tons Of Version/Wake The Nation (B-side with Hugh Roy)	50
70	Pama PM 802	Jeff Barnes Thing/LENNOX BROWN: Lover's Mood	20
71	Smash SMA 2313	Wake The Nation (with Hugh Roy)/1,000 Tons Of Version	35
71	Gas 163	Peoples Version (work Out) (with PAT KELLY)/TONY LEE & PAT KELLY: Too Late	30

(see also Hugh Roy, Dave Barker, Darker Shade Of Blue, Delroy Wilson)

J.J. BARNES
67	Polydor 56722	Day Tripper/Deeper In Love	35
69	Stax STAX 130	Baby Please Come Back Home/Easy Living	35
73	Tamla Motown TMG 870	Real Humdinger/Please Let Me In/I Ain't Gonna Do It	12
75	Contempo CLS 2063	Baby Please Come Home/Cloudy Days (reissue)	6
76	Contempo CLS 2111	Sara Smile/Let Me Feel The Funk	6
78	Contempo CLS 2105	She's Mine/Erroll Flynn	20
04	Hayley HR006	Love At First Sight/I Think I Got A Good Chance	6
75	Contempo CLP 520	THE GROOVESVILLE MASTERS (LP)	50
77	Contempo CLP 604	SARA SMILE (LP)	20

J.J. BARNES/STEVE MANCHA
69	Stax SXATS 1012	RARE STAMPS (LP)	60

LLOYD BARNES
64	Blue Beat BB 235	Time Is Hard/BUSTER'S ALLSTARS: Reincarnation	30

ORTHEIA BARNES
12	Kent Select CITY 026	Never Ever Leave Me/DAVID HAMILTON ORCHESTRA: What Should I Do (inst.)	7

RICHARD BARNES
70	Philips BF 1840	Take To The Mountains/But It's Now I Need Your Love	8
79	Philips 6006 039	Go North/So Will I	6
70	Philips 630 8027	RICHARD BARNES (LP, black/silver label)	40

(see also Quiet Five, Tony Hazzard)

SIDNEY BARNES
76	Charly CYS 1007	I Hurt On The Other Side/Good Lovin' (as Sid Barnes)	18

TOWANDA BARNES
78	Grapevine GRP 116	You Don't Mean It/SAM WILLIAMS: Love Slipped Thru' My Fingers	25

BARRY BARNETT
58	HMV POP 487	The Book Of Love/All I Have To Do Is Dream	10
58	HMV POP 511	When/Secretly	8
58	HMV POP 521	My Lucky Love/Too Young To Love	6
58	HMV POP 532	Susie Darlin'/Just A Dream	8
59	HMV POP 579	The Diary/Only A Memory	7
63	HMV POP 1126	The Hit Of The Week/If You Ever Leave Me	6

ERIC BARNET(T)
68	Gas GAS 100	The Horse (actually by Theo Beckford & Group)/Action Line (actually by Versatiles)	30
69	Gas GAS 106	Te Ta Toe (act. by Theo Beckford & Group)/MILTON BOOTHE: Lonely And Blue	20
69	Crab CRAB 37	Quaker City/Double Up (both actually by Theo Beckford & Group)	50
70	Gas GAS 130	Pink Shark/Swing Free (both actually by Theo Beckford & Group, white labels only)	30
70	Gas GAS 147	Bumper To Bumper/Fat Turkey (both actually by Theo Beckford & Group)	20

(see also Theo[philus] Beckford)

H.B. BARNUM
61	Fontana H 299	Lost Love/Hallelujah	15
65	Capitol CL 15391	The Record (Baby I Love You)/I'm A Man	40
65	Capitol CL 15391	The Record (Baby I Love You)/I'm A Man (DJ Copy)	80
76	Capitol CL 15851	Heartbreaker/Searchin' For My Soul	10

Carl BARON & CHEETAHS

MINT VALUE £

79	Capitol CL 16067	Heartbreaker/BOBBY PARIS: I Walked Away	15
64	RCA Victor RCX 7147	THE GREAT H.B. BARNUM (EP)	150
62	RCA Victor RD/SF 7500	THE BIG VOICE OF BARNUM . . . H.B., THAT IS (LP, mono/stereo)	15
63	RCA Victor RD/SF 7543	EVERYBODY LOVES H.B. (LP, mono/stereo)	15

(see also Robins)

CARL BARON & CHEETAHS

63	Columbia DB 7162	This Is Only The Beginning/Beg Borrow Or Steal	15

BARON WITH HIS POUNDING PIANO

65	Sue WI 398	Is A Blue Bird Blue/In The Mood	50

(see also V.I.P.'s)

BARONS (U.K.)

61	Oriole CB 1608	Cossack/Summertime	10
61	Oriole CB 1620	Samurai/Whirlwind	12

BARONS (U.S.)

57	London HLP 8391	Don't Walk Out/Once In A Lifetime	1000
57	London HLP 8391	Don't Walk Out/Once In A Lifetime (78)	40

BARONS OF SOUL

05	Grapevine 2000 151	You Need Love/You Need Love (unissued, demo copies only)	40

BARRABAS

73	RCA RCA 2339	Wild Safari/Woman	12

BARRACUDA

73	EMI EMI 2027	Summer Girls/I Feel So Down	8

BARRACUDAS

79	Cells CELLOUT 1	I Want My Woody Back/Subway Surfin' (p/s)	20
80	Zonophone Z 5	Summer Fun/Chevy Baby (p/s, with stickers)	15
80	Zonophone Z 5	Summer Fun/Chevy Baby (p/s, without stickers)	6
80	Zonophone Z 8	His Last Summer/Barracuda Waver/Surfers Are Back (p/s)	8
80	Zonophone Z 11	(I Wish It Could Be) 1965 Again/Rendezvous (p/s)	8
81	Zonophone Z 17	I Can't Pretend/The KGB (Made A Man Out Of Me) (p/s)	8
80	Zonophone ZONO 103	DROP OUT WITH THE BARRACUDAS (LP)	18
83	Closer CL0001	MEAN TIME (LP)	20

MARTIN BARRE

93	Presshouse MBSBCD 92	A SUMMER BAND (LP, 500 only)	30

(see also Jethro Tull)

DICKIE BARRETT

58	MGM MGM 976	Smoke Gets In Your Eyes/Remember Me	20

RICHARD BARRETT & CHANTELS

59	HMV POP 609	Come Softly To Me/Walking Through Dreamland	20

(see also Chantels)

RICHIE BARRETT

62	London HLK 9552	Some Other Guy/Tricky Dicky	40

SYD BARRETT

SINGLES

69	Harvest HAR 5009	Octopus/Golden Hair	250
69	Harvest HAR 5009	Octopus/Golden Hair (Promo with mispelt 'Barratt' and release date 14.11.69)	350
88	Strange Fruit SFPS 043	THE PEEL SESSIONS (12", EP)	15
15	Parlophone R7 547561	Dark Globe/R.E.M.: Dark Globe (Jukebox centre, PVC sleeve, RSD release)	8

ALBUMS : ORIGINAL HARVEST ALBUMS

70	Harvest SHVL 765	THE MADCAP LAUGHS (LP, laminated sleeve, no EMI box on label)	300
70	Harvest SHVL 765	THE MADCAP LAUGHS (LP, matt gatefold sleeve, no EMI box on label)	150
70	Harvest SHSP 4007	BARRETT (LP, 1st pressing, laminated sleeve, 'Gramophone Co. Ltd' label text with no EMI box on label)	300
70	Harvest SHSP 4007	BARRETT (LP, 1st pressing, textured flipback sleeve, 'Gramophone Co. Ltd' and no EMI logo on label)	150

ALBUMS : REISSUES

71	Harvest SHSP 4007	BARRETT (LP, 2nd pressing, textured flipback sleeve, 'Gramophone Co. Ltd' and one EMI box on label. Some copies with EMI box on B-side only)	100
72	Harvest SHSP 4007	BARRETT (LP, 3rd pressing, textured non-flipback sleeve, 'Gramophone Co. Ltd' and one EMI box on label)	65
73	Harvest SHVL 765	THE MADCAP LAUGHS (2nd pressing, boxed EMI logo)	70
74	Harvest SHSP 4007	BARRETT (LP, 4th pressing, textured non-flipback sleeve, 'EMI Records Ltd' and one EMI box on label. Some copies with EMI box on B-side only)	50
74	Harvest SHDW 404	SYD BARRETT (2-LP, reissue of "Madcap" & "Barrett", gatefold sleeve)	40
82	Harvest SHVL 765	THE MADCAP LAUGHS (LP, 3rd pressing, boxed EMI logo, with "copying and hiring of this record prohibited" at bottom of label)	30
82	Harvest SHSP 4007	BARRETT (LP, 5th pressing, textured sleeve, text at top of label begins. 'All Rights Of The Producer...' One EMI box on label'Gramophone Co. Ltd'. One EMI box)	50
87	Harvest SHVL 765	THE MADCAP LAUGHS (LP, black label)	20
86	Harvest SHVL 765	THE MADCAP LAUGHS (LP, 6th pressing, non-textured sleeve, with or without barcode on back of sleeve with black 'Harvest' label)	30
88	Harvest SHSP 4126	OPEL (LP, gatefold sleeve, black label)	20
97	Harvest 7423 855663 18	THE MADCAP LAUGHS (LP, 180gm reissue, heavy quality sleeve)	20
97	Harvest 7423 821450 11	BARRETT (LP, 180gm reissue, heavy quality sleeve)	25
99	Simply Vinyl SVLP 153	OPEL (LP, 180gm reissue, heavy quality gatefold sleeve)	25
00	Simply Vinyl SVLP 281	BARRETT (LP, 180gm reissue, heavy quality gatefold sleeve)	22
00	Simply Vinyl SVLP 289	THE MADCAP LAUGHS (LP, 180gm reissue, heavy quality gatefold sleeve)	20
10	Harvest 985031	AN INTRODUCTION TO (2-LP)	20

(see also Pink Floyd)

WILD WILLY BARRETT

86	Galvanised DIP 1	ORGANIC BONDAGE (LP, with Stephen Two Names; in wooden sleeve)	15

(see also John Otway/Wild Willy Barrett)

RAY BARRETTO
63	Columbia DB 7051	El Watusi/Ritmo Sabroso	10
65	Columbia DB 7684	El Watusi/Swingin' Shepherd Blues	10
69	London HL 10262	Acid/Mercy Mercy Baby (withdrawn)	100
67	Island ILP 946	EL WATUSI (LP)	40
69	London HA/SH 8383	ACID (LP)	50

BARRIER
68	Eyemark EMS 1013	Georgie Brown/Dawn Breaks Through (in handmade p/s)	450
68	Eyemark EMS 1013	Georgie Brown/Dawn Breaks Through	250
68	Philips BF 1692	The Tide Is Turning/Place In Your Heart	15
68	Philips BF 1731	Spot The Lights/Uh	70

BARRINO BROTHERS
72	Invictus INV 523	I Shall Not Be Moved/When Love Was A Child	15

BARRON KNIGHTS
62	Fontana H 368	Let's Face It/Never Miss A Chance	12
64	Columbia DB 7188	Comin' Home Baby/Peanut Butter	40
67	Columbia DB 8161	Lazy Fat People/In The Night	15
72	Penny Farthing PEN 786	You're All I Need/Nothin' Doin'	15
64	Columbia SEG 8425	GUYING THE TOP POPS (EP)	10
66	Columbia SEG 8526	THOSE VERSATILE BARRON KNIGHTS (EP)	15

AL BARRY
70	Doctor Bird DB 1502	Morning Sun/MARKONIANS: Over And Over	400
71	Creole 1005	Down We Go/It Pays To Do Good	30
11	Creole THB 7006	Treat Me Good/Down We Go	10
12	Doctor Bird DB 1502	Morning Sun/MARKONIANS: Over And Over (reissue, jukebox centre)	25

(see also Desmond Dekker & Aces)

DAVE BARRY & SARA BERNER
56	London HLU 8324	Out Of This World With Flying Saucers Parts 1 & 2 (Tri Gold)	40

DAWN BARRY
71	Phoenix NIX 118	My World Keeps Getting Smaller Evry Day/No Love At All	6

JOE BARRY
62	Mercury ZEP 10130	A FOOL TO CARE (EP)	40

JOHN BARRY (SEVEN)
SINGLES
57	Parlophone R 4363	Zip Zip/Three Little Fishes (as John Barry & The Seven)	40
58	Parlophone R 4394	Every Which Way/You've Gotta Way (as John Barry Seven)	15
58	Parlophone R 4418	Big Guitar/Rodeo (as John Barry Seven)	10
58	Parlophone R 4453	Pancho/Hideaway (as John Barry Seven)	8
58	Parlophone R 4488	Farrago/Bee's Knees (as John Barry Seven)	7
59	Parlophone R 4530	Long John/Snap 'n' Whistle (as John Barry Seven)	8
59	Parlophone R 4582	Twelfth Street Rag/Christella (as John Barry Seven)	6
60	Columbia DB 4414	Hit And Miss/Rockin' Already (as John Barry Seven)	6
61	Columbia DB 4598	The Magnificent Seven/Skid Row (as John Barry Seven)	7
62	Columbia DB 4898	The James Bond Theme/The Blacksmith Blues (with Orchestra) (green or black labels)	10
63	Columbia DB 7003	The Human Jungle/Onward, Christian Spacemen (in p/s)	10
64	Columbia DB 7414	Twenty-Four Hours Ago/Seven Faces	20
63	Ember EMB S 178	Kinky/Fancy Dance	8
63	Ember EMB S 181	007/From Russia With Love (in p/s)	15
63	Ember EMB S 183	Elizabeth/The London Theme	8
63	Ember EMB S 185	Zulu Stamp/Monkey Feathers (mauve/grey or red/yellow label; in p/s)	10
63	Lyntone LYN 378	Theme Music From The Ingersoll Trendsetters T.V. Commercial flexidisc with 8-page A4 promo booklet)	10
64	United Artists UP 1068	Goldfinger/Troubador	7
66	CBS 202390	Vendetta/The Danny Scipio Theme	6
67	Ember EMB S 243	007/The Loneliness Of Autumn (in p/s)	10
69	CBS 4680	On Her Majesty's Secret Service/We Have All The Time In The World	6
71	CBS 7469	Theme From "The Persuaders"/The Girl With The Sun In Her Hair	6

EPs
58	Parlophone GEP 8737	THE BIG BEAT (as John Barry Seven)	40
62	Columbia SEG 8138	BEAT GIRL (as John Barry Seven, with Adam Faith)	20
63	Columbia SEG 8255	JOHN BARRY THEME SUCCESSES	10
63	United Artists UEP 1011	FROM RUSSIA WITH LOVE (soundtrack)	15
64	Ember EMB EP 4544	LONELINESS OF AUTUMN	10
64	United Artists UEP 1012	GOLDFINGER (soundtrack)	15
65	Ember EMB EP 4551	JAMES BOND IS BACK	25
65	United Artists UEP 1015	THUNDERBALL: Thunderball/Death Of Fiona/Bond Below Disco Volante/ Mr Kiss Kiss Bang Bang (soundtrack)	15
67	CBS WEP 1126	THEMES FROM JAMES BOND FILMS (mail order via Carr's Sport biscuits)	10
67	CBS WEP 1129	BIG THEMES FROM THE BIG SCREEN (mail order via Wall's)	10
67	CBS WEP 1131	GREAT SCREEN THEMES (mail order via Lyon's Bakery)	10

ALBUMS
60	Columbia 33SX 1225	BEAT GIRL (soundtrack, with Adam Faith)	40
61	Columbia 33SX 1358	STRINGBEAT (mono)	30
61	Columbia SCX 3401	STRINGBEAT (stereo)	35
63	United Artists (S)ULP 1052	FROM RUSSIA WITH LOVE (soundtrack, mono)	25
63	United Artists (S)ULP 1052	FROM RUSSIA WITH LOVE (soundtrack, stereo)	25
63	Colpix PXL 459	ELIZABETH TAYLOR IN LONDON (mono)	20
63	Colpix PXL 459	ELIZABETH TAYLOR IN LONDON (stereo)	20
64	Ember NR 5012	ZULU (soundtrack, yellow/orange label, flipback sleeve)	20

Len BARRY

			MINT VALUE £
64	Stateside S(S)L 10087	MAN IN THE MIDDLE (soundtrack, with Lionel Bart)	15
64	United Artists (S)ULP 1076	GOLDFINGER (soundtrack, mono)	15
64	United Artists (S)ULP 1076	GOLDFINGER (soundtrack, stereo)	15
65	Ember NR 5025	JOHN BARRY PLAYS 007	20
65	CBS BPG 62530	THE IPCRESS FILE (soundtrack, mono only)	150
65	United Artists ULP 1104	THE KNACK (AND HOW TO GET IT) (soundtrack)	80
65	United Artists (S)ULP 1110	THUNDERBALL (soundtrack, mono)	15
65	United Artists (S)ULP 1110	THUNDERBALL (soundtrack, stereo)	15
66	Fontana STL 5387	THE WRONG BOX (soundtrack, release cancelled)	0
66	CBS (S)BPG 62869	THE QUILLER MEMORANDUM (soundtrack, mono)	25
66	CBS (S)BPG 62869	THE QUILLER MEMORANDUM (soundtrack, stereo)	25
67	United Artists (S)ULP 1168	THE WHISPERERS (soundtrack)	40
67	United Artists (S)ULP 1171	YOU ONLY LIVE TWICE (soundtrack)	15
68	Stateside S(S)L 10263	DEADFALL (soundtrack, Shirley Bassey on 1 track)	20
69	United Artists UAS 29020	ON HER MAJESTY'S SECRET SERVICE (soundtrack, foldout sleeve)	25
69	MCA MUPS 360	BOOM! (soundtrack, with Georgie Fame)	30
71	United Artists UAS 29216	DIAMONDS ARE FOREVER (soundtrack)	20
71	Probe SPB 1027	THE LAST VALLEY (soundtrack, with insert)	15
72	Ember SE 8008	JOHN BARRY REVISITED (foldout sleeve, initial pressing in 'nude' gatefold sleeve)	30

(see also Alan Bown, Chad & Jeremy, Adam Faith, Elizabeth Taylor, Desmond Lane, Johnny Pearson, Jim Lowe, Lyn Paul, Lance Fortune, Alan Haven, Countdowns, Johnny De Little, Marion Ryan, Dick Kallman)

LEN BARRY

65	Cameo Parkway P 969	Hearts Are Trump/Little White House	30
65	Brunswick 05942	1-2-3/Bullseye	6
65	Brunswick 05942	1-2-3/Bullseye (DJ Copy)	30
66	Brunswick 05949	Like A Baby/Happiness (Is A Girl Like You)	8
66	Brunswick 05949	Like A Baby/Happiness (DJ Copy)	30
66	Brunswick 05955	Somewhere/It's A Crying Shame	10
66	Brunswick 05955	Somewhere/It's A Crying Shame (DJ Copy)	30
66	Brunswick 05962	It's That Time Of The Year/Happily Ever After	10
66	Brunswick 05962	It's That Time Of The Year/Happily Ever After (DJ Copy)	30
66	Brunswick 05966	I Struck It Rich/Love Is	20
66	Brunswick 05966	I Struck It Rich/Love Is (DJ Copy)	40
67	RCA RCA 1588	The Moving Finger Writes/Our Love	20
67	RCA RCA 1588	The Moving Finger Writes/Our Love (DJ Copy)	30
68	Bell BLL 1022	4-5-6 Now I'm Alone/Funky Night	10
71	Now! NOW 1003	Now I'm Alone/Funky Night	6
73	Paramount PARA 3031	Heaven And Earth/I'm Marching To The Music	15
66	Cameo Parkway CPE 556	HAVIN' A GOOD TIME (EP)	30
65	Brunswick LAT 8637	1-2-3 (LP)	25
66	Brunswick LAT 8656	IT'S THAT TIME OF YEAR (LP, unreleased, no sleeve)	750
66	Cameo Parkway C 1082	LEN BARRY AND THE DOVELLS (LP)	30
69	Bulldog BDL 1013	MORE FROM THE 1-2-3 MAN (LP)	20

(see also Dovells)

SANDRA BARRY (& THE BOYS)

64	Decca F 11851	Really Gonna Shake/When We Get Married (as Sandra Barry & Boys)	80
65	Pye 7N 15753	The End Of The Line/We Were Lovers	10
65	Pye 7N 15840	Question/You Can Take It From Me	6
66	Pye 7N 17102	Stop! Thief/I Won't Try To Change Your Mind	6

(see also Boys, Sandra Alfred, Slack Alice)

BARRY & THE TAMERLANES

63	Warner Bros WB 116	I Wonder What She's Doing Tonight/Don't Go	20
64	Warner Bros WB 124	Roberta/Butterfly	10
64	Warner Bros WM 8145	I WONDER WHAT SHE'S DOING TONIGHT (LP)	40

(see also Barry De Vorzon)

BARRY SISTERS (U.S.)

56	London HLA 8248	Cha Cha Joe/Baby Come A Little Closer	20
56	London HLA 8304	Till You Come Back To Me/Intrigue	70
60	Columbia 33SX 1309	SIDE BY SIDE (LP)	15

(see also Three Barry Sisters)

LIONEL BART

61	Decca F11405	Give Us A Kiss For Christmas/How Now Brown Cow	6
68	Deram SML 1028	ISN'T THIS WHERE WE CAME IN (LP, stereo, gatefold sleeve)	40

CHRIS BARTLEY

67	Cameo Parkway P 101	The Sweetest Thing This Side Of Heaven/Love Me Baby	70
67	Cameo Parkway P 101	The Sweetest Thing This Side Of Heaven/Love Me Baby (DJ Copy)	125
68	Bell BLL 1031	I Found A Goodie/Be Mine Forever	30
75	Right On RO 105	I See Your Name/I See Your Name (Instrumental)	12
86	Move MIS 4	Baby I'm For Real/I've Found A Goodie/Truer Words Were Never Spoken/The Sweetest Thing This Side Of Heaven (12", p/s)	15

BARTOK

82	On ON 1	Insanity/I Am The Bomb (p/s)	12

(see also Jah Wobble, Damned)

RIA BARTOK

64	Columbia DB 7362	See If I Care/I Don't Wanna Leave You	6

EILEEN BARTON

55	Vogue Coral Q 72075	Fujiyama Mama/I'd've Baked A Cake	100
56	Vogue Coral Q 72122	Cry Me A River/Come Home	10
56	Vogue Coral Q 72148	Teenage Heart/My Social Hot Dog	10

Maria BARTON

MINT VALUE £

MARIA BARTON
80 Airship AP 56   RAINFUL DAYS (LP) 100

BASCZAX
79 Pipeline ICI ONE   Madison Fallout/Auto Mekanik Destruktor (4 single sided 7" pages as sleeve) 25
(see also The Amazing Space Frogs, Blitzkrieg Bop, The Gynaecologists)

BASE
80 Base BASE001   Violent Death/Frenchmen/One-Way Girl (hand-made p/s) 80

BASELINE
81 Extrabit EX 1   Suspended Animation/Truth About The Lies (with p/s) 125
81 Extrabit EX 1   Suspended Animation/Truth About The Lies (without p/s) 50

BASEMENT 5
80 Island WIP 6614   Silicone Chip/Chip Butty 8
80 Island 10 WIP 6214   Silicone Chip/Chip Butty (10") 10
80 Island WIP 6654   Last White Christmas/Traffic Dub 8
80 Island IPR 2038   IN DUB (12") 12
80 Island ILPS9641   1965-80 (LP, with inner, poster and embossed sleeve) 20

BASEMENT JAXX
01 XL XLLP 143   ROOTY (2-LP) 20

BASEMENT PHIL
91 Basement BRSS 001   Take Me Up (Part 1)/(Part 2)/(Part 3) (12" promo) 25
92 Basement BRSS 002   Bachbeat (Part 1)/I Love You/Bachbeat (Part 2) (12" promo) 12
92 Basement BRSS 009   WE CAN ROCK IT EP (12", as Basement Phil And The Engineers) 10

BASES/BASSIES
66 Coxsone DIR CS 2001   Checking Out/NORMA FRASER: Telling Me lies (white labels only) 250
67 Coxsone CS 7030   River Jordan/SOUL VENDORS: Swing Easy 150

BASH STREET KIDS
79 Agenda GM 480   C'mon Kids/Travelling Man (p/s) 40

BASHERS
76 Virgin VS 154   The Womble Bashers/Womble Bashers Wock 20
(see also Mike McGear)

BASHFUL ALLEY
82 Ellie Jay BA 001   Running Blind/My, My, My (p/s, black-and-white or black-and-yellow sleeve) 50
82 Graffiti BA 001   Running Blind/My, My, My (p/s, reissue) 35

BASIC BLACK AND PEARL
75 Bus Stop BUS 1030   There'll Come A Time, There'll Come A Day/Right On Baby 30

BASIC INFLUENCE
95 Hardliners HL 004   Still Water/Rain Forest (12") 30
98 Hardliners HL 32   Still Waters (Remix)/ICE MINUS: Zen (12") 15

COUNT BASIE & HIS ORCHESTRA
67 Coral Q 72497   Green Onions/Hang On Sloopy 15
(see also Joe Williams, Jackie Wilson, Lester Young, Ella Fitzgerald)

BASIL
87 Serpent Sounds CBH 1561   Come Dance With Me/Instrumental Version (12") 20

BASKIN & COPPERFIELD
70 Decca F 13053   The Long And Winding Road/Beautiful Blue Eyes 7
70 Decca F 23079   I Never See The Sun/Stranger On The Ground 7

BASKING SHARKS
83 Fin FON 01   Diamond Age/New Industry (p/s, insert) 15
83 SRR SRR 0013   THRILL OF THE GAME EP 20
83 RS 001   SHARK ISLAND (LP) 35

BILLY BASS
69 Pama PM 761   I Need Your Love So Bad/I'm Coming To 50

FONTELLA BASS
65 Chess CRS 8007   Don't Mess Up A Good Thing (with Bobby McClure)/OLIVER SAIN: Jerk Loose 30
65 Chess CRS 8007   Don't Mess Up A Good Thing/Baby What You Want Me To Do (different B-side, existence unconfirmed) 0
65 Chess CRS 8023   Rescue Me/Soul Of The Man 15
65 Chess CRS 8023   Rescue Me/Soul Of The Man (DJ Copy) 70
66 Chess CRS 8027   Recovery/Leave It In The Hands Of Love 20
66 Chess CRS 8027   Recovery/Leave It In The Hands Of Love (DJ Copy) 35
66 Chess CRS 8032   I Can't Rest/Surrender 30
66 Chess CRS 8032   I Can't Rest/Surrender (DJ Copy) 80
66 Chess CRS 8042   Safe And Sound/You'll Never Know 10
66 Chess CRS 8042   Safe And Sound/You'll Never Know (DJ Copy) 40
69 Chess CRS 8090   Rescue Me/I Can't Rest 10
69 Chess CRS 8090   Rescue Me/I Can't Rest (DJ Copy) 25
73 Contempo CS 2032   It's Hard To Get Back In/Talking About Freedom 8
66 Chess CRE 6015   FONTELLA'S HITS (EP) 25
66 Chess CRE 6020   I CAN'T REST (EP) 50
66 Chess CRE 6025   FONTELLA BASS AND BOBBY McCLURE (EP) 40
66 Chess CRL 4517   THE NEW LOOK (LP) 80
72 Mojo 2916 018   FREE (LP) 30

JEWEL BASS
76 Special Agent 9001   Overflowing (for You)/I Don't Trust Myself 8

JEAN BASSA
15 22a 005   ALL MY PEOPLE (12" EP) 20

BASS BALLISTICS
92 J4M JFM 6   BASS BALLISTICS EP (12") 20

BAS-SHEVA
55 Capitol CL 14218   Flame Of Love/I Just Wanna Be Your Loving Baby 10

BASS SELECTIVE

BASS SELECTIVE
92	No label or cat no	Life And Loves Of A Ruffneck/Don't Stop (12", white label only)	25
92	Dj Only Records DJOR 001	Flat Line/Blow Out/Get A Little Stupid/Make Me Rush (12")	25
92	Dj Only Records DJOR 002	THE EXPANSIONS EP (12")	40
93	Dj Only Records DJOR 003	Jessica's Jaw/We Need Some Love/Drum Thunder (12")	35
93	Sour SOUR 003	THE END OF THE BEGINNING EP (12")	30

BASTILLE
11	Young & Lost Club YALC0059	Flaws/Icarus (p/s)	100
12	Virgin VS 2037	Overjoyed/Sleepsong (p/s)	30
12	Virgin VS 2041	Bad Blood/Hunt (Demo) (p/s, lyric insert)	30
13	Virgin VS 2057	Pompeii/Poet (p/s)	40
13	Virgin VS 2066	Laura Palmer/Thinkin Bout You (p/s, reissue)	40
13	Virgin VS 2077	Things We Lost In The Fire/Icarus (Live) (p/s)	40
13	Virgin VST 2082	Of The Night/(MNEK Remix)/Oblivion (Live)/Of The Night (Icarus Remix) (10" picture disc)	30
14	Virgin VS 2104	Oblivion/Bad News (p/s)	30
16	Virgin VS 2130	Hangin/Overload (p/s, white vinyl)	15
12	Virgin VS 2037	THE SINGLES CLUB (box set 7 x 7")	200
14	Virgin VX 3133	VS (LP, pink vinyl)	60
20	Virgin VX 3097	ALL THIS BAD BLOOD (2-LP, reissue)	35

JOE BATAAN
75	RCA RCA 2457	Latin Strut/Peace, Friendship And Solidarity	12
75	RCA RCA 2553	The Bottle/When You're Down	12
69	London HA/SH 8386	RIOT! (LP)	40

JUNE BATEMAN
64	Sue WI 347	I Don't Wanna/NOBLE 'THIN MAN' WATTS & HIS BAND: Noble's Theme	75

COLLIN BATES TRIO
67	Troubadour No. 265	COLIN BATES TRIO (LP, private pressing)	500
68	Fontana SFJL 913	BREW (LP)	200

MARTYN BATES
82	Cherry Red TRED 38	LETTERS WRITTEN (10" EP)	10

(see also Eyeless In Gaza)

BAT FOR LASHES
04	No label or Cat No.	WHO STOLE PETRETSKI'S THUNDER? (CD-R tour only EP, hand-drawn cover)	35
06	Echo ECS 185	The Wizard/I Saw A Light (demo)	12
07	Parlophone R 6744	What's A Girl To Do/Sarah-Reworked (Live)	12
09	Parlophone R 6768	Daniel/A Forest (p/s)	12
11	Parlophone R 6836	Let's Get Lost (with Beck)/Dark Time (demo)	10
09	Echo 6930191	TWO SUNS (LP, gatefold, inner)	20
12	Echo/Parlophone P915 5402	THE HAUNTED MAN (2-LP, with CD)	20
12	Echo/Parlophone P915 5402	THE HAUNTED MAN (2-LP, white vinyl with CD)	25
16	Parlophone 0190295983901	THE BRIDE (2-LP, magenta vinyl)	20
16	Parlophone 0190295983901	THE BRIDE (2-LP, picture discs with CD, prints and air freshner)	40

(see also Sexwitch, Toy)

BATHORY
84	Under One Flag FLAG 8	BATHORY (LP)	20
85	Under One Flag FLAG 9	THE RETURN... (LP, inner)	40
87	Under One Flag FLAG 11	UNDER THE SIGN OF THE BLACK MARK (LP)	20
88	Under One Flag FLAG 26	BLOOD FIRE DEATH (LP, gatefold sleeve, insert)	30
88	Under One Flag FLAG 26 P	BLOOD FIRE DEATH (LP, picture disc)	35

BATMAN THEME
88	Bam Caruso NRIC 107	Batman Theme/Batman Theme (Instrumental Mix) (p/s)	15

(see also Jan & Dean)

STIV BATORS
79	London/Bomp HLZ 10575	It's Cold Outside/The Last Year (p/s)	15

(see also Dead Boys, Lords Of The New Church, Wanderers)

BATS
64	Columbia DB 7429	Accept It/Lovers Lie Sleeping	10
66	Decca F 22534	Listen To My Heart/Stop Don't Do It	25
67	Decca F 22568	You Will Now, Won't You?/You Look Good Together	25
67	Decca F 22616	Hard To Get Up In The Morning/Take Me As I Am	10

MIKE BATT
68	Liberty LBF 15093	Mister Poem/Fading Yellow	25
68	Liberty LBF 15122	I See Wonderful Things In You/Mary Goes Round	25
69	Liberty LBF 15210	Your Mother Should Know/Suddenly	20
70	Midland Counties Ice Cream RMS1	Liberate A Lolly	10
77	Epic A 3957	Railway Hotel/The Ride To Agadir	8
70	Penny Farthing PAGS 534	BATT TRACKS (LP)	15

(see also Farnborough Fireworks Factory, Hapshash & Coloured Coat, Anderson Harley & Batt, Mad Hatters)

BATTERED ORNAMENTS
70	Harvest HAR 5013	Goodbye We Loved You (Madly)/CHRIS SPEDDING: Rock'n'Roll Band	25
69	Harvest SHVL 758	MANTLE-PIECE (LP, gatefold sleeve, no EMI box on label)	500
82	GI WAX 3	MANTLE-PIECE (LP, reissue)	20

(see also Pete Brown & His Battered Ornaments, Chris Spedding, People Band)

BATTERSEA
78	Rak RK 1013	Born And Bred/Summer Rain (no p/s)	15

SKIP BATTIN
72	Signpost SGP 756	Central Park/St. Louis Browns	6
72	Signpost SG 4255	SKIP (LP)	18

Rose BATTISTE

MINT VALUE £

(see also Skip & Flip, Byrds, Flying Burrito Brothers, Evergreen Blueshoes)

ROSE BATTISTE
11	Outta Sight OSV 036	Hit And Run/I Miss My Baby (reissue)	15

LUCIO BATTISTI
77	RCA PB 6129	To Feel In Love/Only (demo)	30
79	RCA PB 9439	Baby It's You/Lady (demo)	50

BATTLEAXE
82	Guardian GRC 132	Burn This Town/Battleaxe (no p/s)	40
83	Music For Nations MFN8	BURN THIS TOWN (LP)	15

BATTLES
07	Warp WARPLP 156	MIRRORED (2-LP)	20
11	Warp WAP 321D	My Machine (Featuring Gary Numan)/Getalt/My Machine (Instrumental) (12", silver vinyl, most destroyed in PIAS warehouse fire)	10

BATWING CHAPS
84	Full Moon FM 01	I Won't Change/Crave (p/s)	6

BAUHAUS
79	Small Wonder TEENY 2	Bela Lugosi's Dead/Boys/Dark Entries (12", p/s, white vinyl, 5000 only)	60
79	Small Wonder TEENY 2	Bela Lugosi's Dead/Boys/Dark Entries (not listed on sleeve) (12")	10
79	Small Wonder TEENY 2	Bela Lugosi's Dead/Boys/Dark Entries (12", p/s, black vinyl)	10
80	Axis AXIS 3	Dark Entries/Untitled (brown label, p/s)	40
80	Axis AD 3	Dark Entries/Untitled (blue label, p/s)	10
80	4AD BEG 37	Dark Entries/Untitled (p/s, blue 4AD labels, lists BEG 37 on sleeve)	10
80	Beggars Banquet BEG 37	Dark Entries/Untitled (p/s, red Beggars Banquet labels)	15
80	4AD AD 7	Terror Couple Kill Colonel/Scopes/Terror Couple Kill Colonel II (p/s)	10
80	4AD AD 7	Terror Couple Kill Colonel/Scopes/Terror Couple Kill Colonel II (version) (mispressed, 'rejected' version of third track, p/s)	20
81	Beggars Banquet BEG 54	Kick In The Eye/Satori (card sleeve)	6
81	Beggars Banquet BEG 54T	Kick In The Eye/Satori (12", white label in stamped plain sleeve)	15
81	Beggars Banquet BEG 59	The Passion Of Lovers/1.2.3.4 (card sleeve with lyric insert)	6
81	Beggars Banquet BEG 59	The Passion Of Lovers/1.2.3.4 (paper sleeve, mispressing with A side label on both sides)	8
82	Beggars Banquet AD 3	Dark Entries/Untitled (reissue, 'nudes wrestling' label, no contact address on p/s)	10
82	Beggars Banquet BEG 79	Spirit/Terror Couple Kill Colonel (live in Paris) (Beggars logo labels and no sleeve titles)	7
82	Beggars Banquet BEG 74T	Kick In The Eye/Poison Pen/Harry/Earwax (12" mispressing, p/s, matrix: A1)	25
82	Beggars Banquet BEG 79	Spirit/Terror Couple Kill Colonel (live) (p/s, mispressed, A-side plays Gary Numan's "We Take Mystery [To Bed]")	25
82	Lyntone LYN 12106	A God In An Alcove (Early Version) (hard vinyl test pressing)	15
82	Beggars Banquet BEG 83	Ziggy Stardust/Third Uncle (original glossy card sleeve, signed by band for record company staff)	30
82	Beggars Banquet BEG 83	Ziggy Stardust/Third Uncle (Beggars Banquet labels no picture sleeve)	8
82	Beggars Banquet BEG 83T	Ziggy Stardust/Party Of The First Part/Third Uncle/Waiting For The Man, 12" p/s, with stickered poster p/s)	8
82	Beggars Banquet BEG 83T	Ziggy Stardust/Party Of The First Part/Third Uncle/Waiting For The Man, (12", repressing in thin spineless sleeve with reversed artwork)	10
82	Beggars Banquet BEG 83T	Ziggy Stardust/Party Of The First Part/Third Uncle/Waiting For The Man, 12" glossy card p/s, no poster, signed for record company staff)	30
83	Lyntone LYN 13777/8	The Sanity Assassin/Spirit In The Sky (fan club freebie, 320 only)	500
88	Small Wonder TEENY 2P	Bela Lugosi's Dead/Boys/Dark Entries (12", reissue, luminous picture disc in PVC sleeve)	25
89	Small Wonder TEENY 2	Bela Lugosi's Dead/Boys/Dark Entries (12", reissue, green vinyl, p/s)	25
89	Small Wonder TEENY 2	Bela Lugosi's Dead/Boys/Dark Entries (12", reissue, blue vinyl, p/s)	25
90	Beggars Banquet BEG 74T	Kick In the Eye/In Fear Of Dub/Harry/Earwax (Searching For Satori EP) (12", reissue, black sleeve lettering, green/gold labels)	15
91	Small Wonder TEENY 2	Bela Lugosi's Dead/Boys/Dark Entries (12", reissue, pink, clear or purple vinyl, in corresponding coloured p/s)	25
80	4AD CAD 13	IN THE FLAT FIELD (LP, inner, 8 Hogarth Road address on rear sleeve)	30
81	Beggars Banquet BEGA 29	MASK (LP, gatefold, group photo inside, Beggars Banquet labels)	20
82	Beggars Banquet BEGA 38	PRESS THE EJECT AND GIVE ME THE TAPE (LP, with bonus 45 "Satori in Paris" [BH 1] & poster)	20
82	Beggars Banquet BEGA 42	THE SKY'S GONE OUT (LP, with bonus LP "Press The Eject And Give Me The Tape" [BEGA 38] inner sleeves & stickered sleeve)	20
83	Beggars Banquet BEGA 45P	BURNING FROM THE INSIDE (LP, picture disc)	20
83	Beggars Banquet BEGA 45P	BURNING FROM THE INSIDE (LP, with 5" die cut and BEGA 45P cat number on sleeve)	20
85	Beggars Banquet BEGA 64	1979-1983 (2-LP, with inserts, 50,000 copies, numbered)	25
08	Vinyl VIN180LP005	IN THE FLAT FIELD (LP, reissue, with free white vinyl 12")	20
08	Let Them Eat Vinyl LETV013LP	GO AWAY WHITE (LP, gatefold, white vinyl)	100
09	Vinyl 180 VIN180LP020	THIS IS FOR WHEN...(2-LP)	70

(see also Sinister Ducks, Tones On Tail, David J, Bubblemen, Peter Murphy, Daniel Ash)

ART BAXTER
57	Philips BBR 8107	ROCK YOU SINNERS (10" LP)	125

DAVID BAXTER
70	Reflection REFL 9	GOODBYE DAVE (LP, white/brown label)	100

(see also David Lewis)

JOAN BAXTER
58	Parlophone R 4470	Ich Liebe Dich (I Love You)/The Only One For Me	6

LES BAXTER & HIS ORCHESTRA
55	Capitol CL 14239	Earth Angel/Happy Baby (as Les Baxter & Bombers)	30

(see also Leonard Pennario)

RONNIE BAXTER
60	Top Rank JAR 293	I Finally Found You/Is It Because?	6

TODD BAYTEE
86	The White Label WL1	In Your Eyes (12" Mix)/(7" Mix)/(Jazz Mix) (12")	250

B.B. BLUNDER

B.B. BLUNDER
Year	Label	Title	Value £
71	United Artists UP 35203	Sticky Living/Rocky Yagbatee Yagbag	10
71	United Artists UP 35204	Little Boy/10,000 Miles	20
71	United Artists UAG 29156	WORKERS' PLAYTIME (LP, gatefold sleeve)	60

(see also Reg King & B.B. Blunder, Action, Julie Driscoll Brian Auger & Trinity, Kevin Westlake, Mark Charig, Blossom Toes)

BBC RADIOPHONIC WORKSHOP/PETER HOWELL
Year	Label	Title	Value £
64	Decca F 11837	Doctor Who/BRENDA & JOHNNY: This Can't Be Love (unboxed Decca logo)	30
72	Decca F 11837	Doctor Who/BRENDA & JOHNNY: This Can't Be Love (reissue, boxed logo)	10
73	BBC RESL 11	Doctor Who/Reg (blue label, credits 'Delia Derbyshire', 'TARDIS' p/s)	10
73	BBC RESL 11	Doctor Who/Reg (white label, credits 'Delia Derbyshire', 'TARDIS' p/s)	6
76	BBC RESL 11	Doctor Who/Reg (reissue, no p/s, silver label)	6
78	BBC RESL 11	Doctor Who/Reg (2nd reissue, in 'TARDIS' p/s, blue label, white rim)	6
80	PRT RESL 80	Doctor Who/The Astronauts ('Tom Baker' p/s, as 'Peter Howell & BBC Radiophonic Workshop')	8
82	PRT RESL 80	Doctor Who/The Astronauts (reissue, 'Peter Davison' p/s)	8
18	Electronic Sound ES 743	Strange Beacons/Mind The Gap (p/s)	15
68	BBC Enterprises REC 25M	BBC RADIOPHONIC WORKSHOP (LP)	45
72	BBC REC 93S	TEST CARD MUSIC (LP)	25
73	BBC REC 93 S	FOURTH DIMENSION (LP)	15
76	BBC REC 225	OUT OF THIS WORLD (LP)	15
70	BBC REC 25 M	BBC RADIOPHONIC MUSIC - WORK BY DELIA DERBYSHIRE (LP)	30
78	BBC REC 307	THROUGH A GLASS DARKLY (LP)	30
78	BBC REC 316	DOCTOR WHO SOUND EFFECTS No. 19 (LP)	18
83	BBC REH 462	DR. WHO - THE MUSIC (LP)	15
04	Rephlex 147 LP	MUSIC FROM THE BBC RADIOPHONIC WORKSHOP (4 x 10")	30

(see also Dr. Who, Jon Pertwee, Ray Cathode, Radiophonic Workshop, Ithaca, Alice Through The Looking Glass, Agincourt, Blossom Toes, Dudley Simpson & Brian Hodgson)

BEACH BOYS
SINGLES
Year	Label	Title	Value £
62	Capitol CL 15273	Surfin' Safari/409	50
63	Capitol CL 15285	Ten Little Indians/County Fair	100
63	Capitol CL 15305	Surfin' USA/Shut Down	20
64	Capitol CL 15339	Fun, Fun, Fun/Why Do Fools Fall In Love	25
64	Capitol CL 15350	I Get Around/Don't Worry Baby (First pressing with purple labels)	8
64	Capitol CL 15361	When I Grow Up (To Be A Man)/She Knows Me Too Well	8
65	Capitol CL 15370	Dance, Dance, Dance/The Warmth Of The Sun	10
65	Capitol CL 15384	All Summer Long/Do You Wanna Dance	10
65	Capitol CL 15392	Help Me Rhonda/Kiss Me Baby	10
65	Capitol CL 15409	California Girls/Let Him Run Wild	10
65	Capitol CL 15425	The Little Girl I Once Knew/There's No Other (Like My Baby)	15
66	Capitol CL 15432	Barbara Ann/Girl Don't Tell Me	7
66	Capitol CL 15441	Sloop John B/You're So Good To Me	8
66	Capitol CL 15459	God Only Knows/Wouldn't It Be Nice	7
66	Capitol CL 15475	Good Vibrations/Wendy	6
67	Capitol CL 15502	Then I Kissed Her/Mountain Of Love	7
67	Capitol CL 15510	Heroes And Villains/You're Welcome	7
67	Capitol CL 15521	Wild Honey/Wind Chimes	8
68	Capitol CL 15527	Darlin'/Country Air	6
68	Capitol CL 15545	Friends/Little Bird	6
68	Capitol CL 15554	Do It Again/Wake The World	6
68	Capitol CL 15572	Bluebirds Over The Mountain/Never Learn Not To Love	6
70	Stateside SS 2181	Tears In The Morning/It's About Time	7
71	Stateside SS 2190	Long Promised Road/Deirdre	8
71	Stateside SS 2194	Don't Go Near The Water/Student Demonstration Time (demos in p/s £20)	6
72	Reprise K 14173	You Need A Mess Of Help To Stand Alone/Cuddle Up (p/s)	10
72	Capitol CMS 1	Wouldn't It Be Nice/Fun Fun Fun/California Girls (printed sleeve)	6
72	Capitol CMS 2	Barbara Ann/Dance Dance Dance/You're So Good To Me (printed sleeve)	6
76	Reprise K 14411	Child Of Winter/Susie Cincinnati (withdrawn)	125
76	EMI PSR 402	Commercial for "20 Golden Greats"/Good Vibrations/Carl Wilson Interview (promo)	10
77	Capitol CL 15954	Little Saint Nick/Little Saint Nick (Instr.)/Santa Claus Is Coming To Town	7
79	Caribou 12-7204	Here Comes The Night/(Disco Version)/Baby Blue (12", p/s, blue vinyl)	10
79	Capitol BBP 26	SINGLES COLLECTION (26 x 7" box set)	50

EPs
Year	Label	Title	Value £
63	Capitol EAP 1-20540	SURFIN' USA	30
64	Capitol EAP 1-20603	FUN, FUN, FUN	30
64	Capitol EAP 5267	FOUR BY THE BEACH BOYS	25
64	Capitol EAP 4-2198	BEACH BOYS CONCERT	25
64	Capitol EAP 1-20781	THE BEACH BOYS HITS	15
67	Capitol EAP 6-2458	GOD ONLY KNOWS	30

ALBUMS
Year	Label	Title	Value £
62	Capitol T 1808	SURFIN' SAFARI (mono only)	50
63	Capitol T 1890	SURFIN' USA (mono)	35
63	Capitol (S)T 1890	SURFIN' USA (stereo)	50
63	Capitol ST 1981	SURFER GIRL (mono)	35
63	Capitol ST 1981	SURFER GIRL (stereo)	50
63	Capitol ST 1998	LITTLE DEUCE COUPE (mono)	30
63	Capitol ST 1998	LITTLE DEUCE COUPE (stereo)	50
63	Capitol T 2027	SHUT DOWN VOLUME 2 (mono)	30
63	Capitol ST 2027	SHUT DOWN VOLUME 2 (stereo)	50

BEACH HOUSE

MINT VALUE £

64	Capitol T 2110	ALL SUMMER LONG (mono)	30
64	Capitol ST 2110	ALL SUMMER LONG (stereo)	40
64	Capitol T 2164	THE BEACH BOYS' CHRISTMAS ALBUM (mono)	35
64	Capitol ST 2164	THE BEACH BOYS' CHRISTMAS ALBUM (stereo)	40
64	Capitol T 2198	BEACH BOYS CONCERT (mono)	20
64	Capitol ST 2198	BEACH BOYS CONCERT (stereo)	25
65	Capitol T 2269	BEACH BOYS TODAY! (mono)	25
65	Capitol ST 2269	BEACH BOYS TODAY! (stereo)	30
65	Capitol T 2354	SUMMER DAYS (AND SUMMER NIGHTS!!) (mono)	25
65	Capitol ST 2354	SUMMER DAYS (AND SUMMER NIGHTS!!) (stereo)	30
65	Capitol (S)T 2398	BEACH BOYS' PARTY! (mono)	20
65	Capitol (S)T 2398	BEACH BOYS' PARTY! (stereo)	25
66	Capitol T 2458	PET SOUNDS (mono)	150
66	Capitol ST 2458	PET SOUNDS (stereo)	150
66	Capitol T 20856	THE BEST OF THE BEACH BOYS (mono)	15
66	Capitol ST 20856	THE BEST OF THE BEACH BOYS (sterero)	18
67	Capitol T 9001	SMILEY SMILE (mono)	45
67	Capitol ST 9001	SMILEY SMILE (stereo)	35
67	Capitol ST 20956/T 20956	THE BEST OF THE BEACH BOYS VOL. 2 (stereo or mono)	15
68	Capitol T 2859	WILD HONEY (mono)	45
68	Capitol ST 2859	WILD HONEY (stereo)	25
68	Capitol T 2895	FRIENDS (mono)	50
68	Capitol (S)T 2895	FRIENDS (stereo)	40
69	Capitol T 21142	THE BEST OF THE BEACH BOYS VOL. 3 (mono)	15
69	Capitol E-T 133	20/20 (mono, gatefold sleeve)	20
69	Capitol E-ST 133	20/20 (stereo, gatefold sleeve)	18

(The above LPs were originally issued with flipback sleeves & rainbow-rim black labels; later yellow label copies from 1969 and 70s orange label pressings - in stereo - are worth up to half the value.)

70	Stateside SSLA 8251	SUNFLOWER (gatefold sleeve)	22
71	Stateside SSL 10313	SURF'S UP (textured sleeve, with gatefold insert)	20
71	Stateside SSL 10313	SURF'S UP (textured sleeve, without gatefold insert)	15
73	Reprise/Brother K 54008	HOLLAND (with insert & bonus EP "Mount Vernon And Fairway" [K 54008/7] in p/s)	30
75	Capitols ST 2458	PET SOUNDS (LP, reissue, orange label, stereo)	15
79	Caribou CRB 1866081	L.A. LIGHT (LP, picture disc)	18
81	WRC SM 651-657	THE CAPITOL YEARS (7-LP box set)	25
97	EMI LPCENT2	PET SOUNDS (LP, reissue, EMI 100 Centenary, stickered sleeve)	30
99	Simply Vinyl SVLP 149	PET SOUNDS (LP, reissue, 180gm vinyl)	20
00	Simply Vinyl SVLP 219	SMILEY SMILE (LP, reissue 180gm vinyl)	15

(see also Brian Wilson, Dennis Wilson, Legendary Masked Surfers, American Spring, Annette,s, California Music, Rutles, Moon, Murry Wilson, Mike Love, Survivors)

BEACH HOUSE

10	Bella Union Bellav 229	Norway/Baby (red vinyl, p/s)	12
12	Bella Union Bellav 338	Lazuli/Equal Mind (blue/purple vinyl)	6
10	Bella Union BELLAV 225	TEEN DREAM (2-LP, DVD, CD)	20
12	Bella Union BELLAV 144	BEACH HOUSE (LP, white vinyl, with CD)	15
12	Bella Union BELLAV 160	DEVOTION (LP, blue vinyl with CD)	15
12	Bella Union BELLAV 334	BLOOM (2-LP with CD)	20
15	Bella Union BELLA 500VX	DEPRESSION CHERRY (LP, white vinyl, CD, felt cover)	20
15	Bella Union BELLA 500V	DEPRESSION CHERRY (LP, clear vinyl, 200 only)	30
15	Bella Union BELLA 512V	THANK YOUR LUCKY STARS (LP)	20

BEACHCOMBER

70	Parlophone R 5850	Surfin' Soul/Nothing To Say	10

BEACHCOMBERS

63	Columbia DB 7124	Mad Goose/You Can't Sit Down	20
64	Columbia DB 7200	Night Train/The Reel Row	30

(see also Pat Wayne)

BEACH-NUTS

65	London HL 9988	Out In The Sun (Hey-O)/Someday Soon	30

(see also Angels, Strangeloves)

BEACON STREET UNION

68	MGM MGM 1416	Blue Suede Shoes/Four Hundred And Five	25
68	MGM MGM-C(S) 8069	THE EYES OF THE BEACON STREET UNION (LP)	100

BEADS

71	Decca F13244	Eeo Eio/Sweetie Peetie	8

BEADY EYE

10	Beady Eye EYE 1	Bring The Light/Sons Of The Stage (4,000 only)	15
10	Beady Eye EYE 3	Four Letter Word/World Outside My Room (4,000 only)	18
11	Beady Eye EYE 4	The Roller/Two Of A Kind (heavyweight vinyl sold via website, numbered)	8
13	Columbia PG 1922 001	Flick Of The Finger (Remix)/Soul Love (Remix) (p/s only, sold through Pretty Green shop)	20
13	Columbia 88843015257	Soul Love/Iz Rite (p/s)	6
11	Columbia BOX 1	SINGLES BOX SET (5 x 7" in special box)	40
11	Columbia 88883721371	BE (2-LP, pre-order version with poster, signed)	50
11	Columbia 88883721371	BE (CD, pre-order version, signed)	40

(see also Oasis, Liam Gallagher, Ride)

BEAK>

10	Wulfstan Wulfstan 01	Wulfstan/Ham Green (live)/Wulfstan (live)/Blagdon Lake (live) (12")	10
12	Invada INV 112	Mono/Kenn (red vinyl, 300 only)	8
15	Invada INV 149	BEAK> V KAEB EP (12" blue vinyl)	12
09	Invada INV 100LP	BEAK> (2-LP, white vinyl)	25

BEAKS

			MINT VALUE £
10	Invada INV 100LP	BEAK> (2-LP, blue vinyl repressing)	20
10	Invada (No cat no)	BEAK> (2-CD in 12" pizza box, 250 copies)	40
12	Invada INV 100LP	BEAK> (2-LP, red vinyl repressing)	20
12	Invada INV 107LP	>> (2-LP, white signed cover, tour edition, 100 only)	40
12	Invada INV 107LP	>> (2-LP, orange vinyl repressing)	20
12	Invada INV 107LP	>> (2-LP)	20

(see also Portishead)

BEAKS
79	Alien ALIX 004	Doktor X/Intellectual (p/s)	12

CARL BEAN
78	Motown TMG 1108	I Was Born This Way/Instrumental	6
78	Tamla Motown TMG 1108-12	I Was Born This Way (Remix)/Instrumental (12")	12

GEORGE BEAN
63	Decca F 11762	Secret Love/Lonely Weekends	25
65	Decca F 12228	She Belongs To Me/Why Must They Criticise? (as George Bean & Runners)	15
67	CBS 2801	The Candy Shop Is Closed/Smile From Sequin	25
68	CBS 3374	Bring Back Lovin'/Floatin'	35

(see also Trifle, Bean & Loopy's Lot)

BEAN & LOOPY'S LOT
66	Parlophone R 5458	A Stitch In Time/Haywire	50

(see also Alan Bown Set)

BEANO
75	Deram DM 427	Little Cinderalla/Bye And Bye	7
77	Decca F 13690	Everybody Knows/Clowns Painted Smile (p/s)	6

BEAR
68	Verve FTS 3059	GREETINGS CHILDREN OF PARADISE (LP)	35

DEAN BEARD & CREW CATS
57	London HLE 8463	Rakin' And Scrapin'/On My Mind Again	250

BEARDED LADY
74	Young Blood YB 1018	Rock Star/Country Lady	15

BEARS
79	Good Vibrations Intl. GVI 1	Insane/Decisions (p/s)	15
79	Waldo's JS 001	On Me/Wot's Up Mate (p/s, various designs, with insert)	15
86	Tigerbeat GROWL 001	INSANE!! (LP)	20

BEARZ
80	Axis AXIS 2	She's My Girl/Girls Will Do (p/s)	20
84	Occult OCC 1	Darwin/Julie (p/s)	12

BEAS
68	Pama PM 744	Dr. Goldfoot And His Bikini Machine/Where Do I Go From You	50

BEAST
83	I.D. EYE T3	New Moone/Guardian (12". p/s)	10

(see also the Cramps)

BEASTIE BOYS
86	Def Jam TA 7055	Hold It, Now Hit It/Acapulco (12", p/s)	10
86	Def Jam 650 114 7	She's On It/Slow'n'Low (p/s with 3 badges)	12
86	Def Jam 650 114 6	She's On It/Slow'n'Low/Hold On, Now Hit It (12", p/s)	10
87	Rat Cage MOTR 26	COOKY PUSS (12", p/s, reissue)	15
87	Def Jam 650 169 6	It's The New Style/It's The New Style (Instrumental)/Paul Revere/Paul Revere (Instrumental) (12", p/s)	10
87	Def Jam 650 418 6	(You Gotta) Fight For Your Right (To Party)/Time To Get Ill (12", p/s)	10
87	Def Jam BEASTP 1	No Sleep Till Brooklyn/Posse In Effect (plane-shaped picture disc)	25
87	Def Jam BEASTT 1	No Sleep Till Brooklyn/Posse In Effect (12", p/s)	10
89	Capitol 12CL 540	HEY LADIES (LOVE AMERICAN STYLE EP) (12", p/s)	15
92	Capitol 12CLS 665	FROZEN METAL HEADS EP (12", p/s, white vinyl)	15
94	Capitol CL 716	Get It Together/Sabotage/Dope Little Song (green vinyl, p/s)	6
94	Capitol 10CL716	Get It Together/(Buck Wild Remix)/(Intrumental)/Sabotage (10" p/s)	15
94	Capitol 7243 8 8173476	Sure Shot/Mullet Head/Sure Shot (Caldato Mix) (red vinyl, p/s)	6
94	Capitol 10CL726	Sure Shot/Mullet Head/Sure Shot (Caldato Mix) (10" p/s)	12
98	Grand Royal 12 CL 803	INTERGALACTIC EP (12", p/s)	12
87	Def Jam 450 062 1	LICENSED TO ILL (LP, with poster)	30
89	Capitol EST2102	PAUL'S BOUTIQUE (LP)	80
92	Grand Royal EST 2171	CHECK YOUR HEAD (2-LP)	35
94	Grand Royal EST 2229	ILL COMMUNICATION (2-LP, gatefold, numbered)	60
94	Grand Royal GR006	ILL COMMUNICATION (2-LP, gatefold)	50
98	Grand Royal GR062	HELLO NASTY (2-LP, orange vinyl)	40
04	Capitol 7243 4 73397	TO THE 5 BOROUGHS (2-LP)	30
05	Capitol 0946 344667 1 4	SOLID GOLD HITS (2-LP)	20

BEASTS IN CAGES
81	Fresh 34	My Coo Ca Choo/Sandcastles (p/s)	8

(see also Craze)

BEAT
79	2-Tone CHS TT 6	Tears Of A Clown/Ranking Full Stop (paper label, company sleeve)	8
80	Go-Feet BEAT 001	JUST CAN'T STOP IT (LP, with inner)	15

(see also Fine Young Cannibals)

BEAT JUNKIES
96	Ugly UGM 001	THE BEAT JUNKIES EP (12')	15

NICKY BEAT & THE BEATNICKS
78	Rigid IS/BEAT/1033	I Can Hear Voices/Split Second Love/Starstruck (oversized p/s, poster insert)	150

BEAT BOYS
63	Decca F 11730	That's My Plan/Third Time Lucky	25

BEAT BROTHERS
63 Polydor NH 52185 — Nick Nack Hully Gully/Lantern Hully Gully 25

(see also Tony Sheridan & Beat Brothers, Bobby Patrick Big Six)

BEAT CHICS
64 Decca F 12016 — Skinny Minnie/Now I Know 25

BEAT HAPPENING
86 Rough Trade ROUGH 105 — BEAT HAPPENING (LP, reissue) 40
87 53rd and 3rd/K AGAS 2 — JAMBOREE (LP, with free flexi, stickered sleeve) 35
89 Rough Trade ROUGH 145 — BLACK CANDY (LP) 30

BEATHOVEN
88 CBS 651 626-7 — Socrates/Socrates (withdrawn) 30

THE BEATLES

SINGLES : 1962

(Dealers and collectors need to be aware of very specific label information for different pressings of Beatles singles and this is given either at the top of each year or in the body of the entry itself. Thus when it comes to these two pressings of their debut single issued in 1962 labels will have "The Parlophone Co. Ltd." in upper or lower case & "Recording first published 1962," label text, without "Sold in UK ...". Also, please note that all Beatles 7" singles issued before 1967 have a push-out centre: unless otherwise stated)

62 Parlophone 45-R 4949 — Love Me Do/P.S. I Love You (First pressing, red label, 'Ringo on drums & no tambourine' version; with or without "Made In Great Britain" credit, Matrix 7XCE 17144-1N/7XCE 17145-1N, in sleeve Type A, B or C) 150

62 Parlophone 45-R 4949 — Love Me Do/P.S. I Love You (First pressing, red label, 'Ringo on drums & no tambourine' version; label variation with "Made In Great Britain" credit on only one side, Matrix 7XCE 17144-1N/7XCE 17145-1N, in sleeve Type A, B, or C) 130

SINGLES : 1963

(with "The Parlophone Co. Ltd." in either upper or lower case & "Recording first published 1963" label text without "Sold in the UK..." unless otherwise stated)

63 Parlophone 45-R 4983 — Please Please Me/Ask Me Why (First pressing, red label; with or without "Made In Great Britain"credit, Matrix 7XCE 17217-1N/&XCE 17218-1N, in sleeve Type A, B or C) .. 200
63 Parlophone R 5015 — From Me To You/Thank You Girl (First pressing, Matrixes: 7XCE 17329 - 1N/7XCE 17330 - 1N, in Type 1 sleeve) 15
63 Parlophone R 5055 — She Loves You/I'll Get You (First pressing, Matrix numbers: 7XCE 17395-1N/7XCE 17396-1N in Type 1 sleeve) 15
63 Parlophone R 5055 — She Loves You/I'll Get You (First pressing, label variation, with elongated "Northern Songs Ltd" and different typography for "7XCEE. 17395" and "Recording First Published 1963" Matrix numbers: 7XCE 17395-1N/7XCE 17396-1N, in Type 1 sleeve) 15
63 Parlophone R 5055 — She Loves You/I'll Get You (First pressing, second label variation, smaller "She Love You" typography and "Northern Songs Ltd" on three lines; Matrix numbers: 7XCE 17395-1N/7XCE 17396-1N, in Type 1 sleeve) 15
63 Parlophone R 5084 — I Want To Hold Your Hand/This Boy (First pressing, with "The Parlophone Co. Ltd" in upper-case only, Matrixes: 7XCE 17559-1N/7XCE 17560-1N, in Type 1 sleeve) 15
63 Parlophone R 5084 — I Want To Hold Your Hand/This Boy (First pressing, label variation, with "N.C.B." after "Northern Songs Mus Ltd" with "The Parlophone Co. Ltd" in upper-case only, Matrixes: 7XCE 17559-1N/7XCE 17560-1N) 15
63 Parlophone R 4949 — Love Me Do/P.S. I Love You (Second pressing, black label, with The Parlophone Co. Ltd in upper-lower case, matrix suffixed with '1N' indicating 'Ringo on drums & no tambourine' version) 150
63 Parlophone 45-R 4983 — Please Please Me/Ask Me Why (Second pressing, black label, with "The Parlophone Co. Ltd" in upper-lower case, with "45" prefix, Matrixes: 7XCE 17217-1N/7XCE 17218-1N) 20
63 Parlophone R 4983 — Please Please Me/Ask Me Why (Third pressing, black label, with "The Parlophone Co. Ltd" in upper-lower case, without "45" prefix) 20

SINGLES : 1964

(with "The Parlophone Co. Ltd." in either upper or lower case & "Recording first published 1964" label text with "Sold in the UK..." unless otherwise stated)

64 Parlophone R 5114 — Can't Buy Me Love/You Can't Do That (First pressing, with "The Parlophone Co. Ltd" in upper case, in Type 1 sleeve) 20
64 Parlophone R 5114 — Can't Buy Me Love/You Can't Do That (First pressing with label variation, with "The Parlophone Co. Ltd" in upper case but "NCB" added after "Northern Songs") 20
64 Parlophone R 5160 — A Hard Day's Night/Things We Said Today (First pressing in Type 1B sleeve) 20
64 Parlophone R 5200 — I Feel Fine/She's A Woman (First pressing, with "The Parlophone Co. Ltd" in upper case, in Type 1B sleeve) 20
64 Parlophone R 5200 — I Feel Fine/She's A Woman (First pressing, label variation, different "Northern Songs NCB" layout and "Recording First Published 1964" below Maxtrix number) 20
64 Parlophone R 5084 — I Want To Hold Your Hand/This Boy (Second pressing) 60
64 Parlophone R 4949 — Love Me Do/P.S. I Love You (Third pressing, black label, with "The Parlophone Co. Ltd" in upper case, matrix suffixed with 1N' indicating 'Ringo on drums & no tambourine' version) 80

(with "The Parlophone Co. Ltd.", "Recording first published 1962" & Sold in UK ... label text)

64 Parlophone R 4983 — Please Please Me/Ask Me Why (Fourth pressing, with "The Parlophone Co. Ltd" in upper/lower case and "Sold in the U.K." label text) 80

SINGLES : 1965

(with "The Parlophone Co. Ltd." in upper case & "Sold in the UK...". 2nd and other pressings from 1965 have "The Gramophone Co. Ltd" unless otherwise stated)

65 Parlophone DP 562 — If I Fell/Tell Me Why (First U.K. pressing of 1964 export single, Matrixes: &XCE 17756-1N/7XCE 17757-1N, in Type 1B sleeve) 100
65 Parlophone R 5265 — Ticket To Ride/Yes It Is (First pressing, in Type 2 sleeve) 15
65 Parlophone R 5265 — Ticket To Ride/Yes It Is (First pressing, label variation, smaller "Sold In U.K." text, larger "Northern Songs NCB" type and (Lennon-McCartney) credit longer than "Ticket To Ride" song title) 15
65 Parlophone R 5265 — Ticket To Ride/Yes It Is (First pressing, label variation, smaller "Northern Songs NCB" type, brackets around matrix number, larger "Trade Mark" & "Parlophone" logos and "T" in "Gt Britain" is in upper (T), not lower case (t) 15
65 Parlophone R 5305 — Help!/I'm Down (First pressing, in Type 2 sleeve) 20
65 Parlophone R 5305 — Help!/I'm Down (Second pressing, with "The Gramophone Co Ltd" label text) 15
65 Parlophone R 5389 — We Can Work It Out/Day Tripper (First pressing, in Type 3 sleeve) 20
65 Parlophone R 5389 — We Can Work It Out/Day Tripper (Second pressing, with "The Gramophone Co Ltd" label text) 15
65 Parlophone R 5389 — We Can Work It Out/Day Tripper (Second pressing, label variation with different type of 15

The BEATLES

MINT VALUE £

65	Parlophone R 4949	"Sold In U.K...", "Northern Songs NCB", matrix number and date. Comma ",", separates "Lennon, McCartney" rather than a dash "-") .... Love Me Do/P.S. I Love You (Fourth pressing, black label, with "The Parlophone Co. Ltd" in upper case, "T" in "Gt Britain" now upper case but text to read "GT. Britain" "Recorded first published" also now in lower case: matrix suffixed with 1N" indicating 'Ringo on drums & no tambourine' version)	100

SINGLES : 1966
(with "The Gramophone Co. Ltd." in upper case & "Sold in the UK...". label text, unless otherwise stated)

66	Parlophone R 5452	Paperback Writer/Rain (First pressing, in Type 4 or 5 sleeve)	15
66	Parlophone R 5452	Paperback Writer/Rain (First pressing, label variation, with larger "Northern Songs, NCB" credit and larger "P" before "1966")	15
66	Parlophone R 5493	Yellow Submarine/Eleanor Rigby (First pressing, in Type 5 or 6 sleeve)	15
66	Parlophone R 5493	Yellow Submarine/Eleanor Rigby (First pressing, label variation with larger "Northern Songs, NCB", no brackets on Matrix number, larger circled "P" and larger typeface for "Eleanor Rigby")	15
66	Parlophone R 5493	Yellow Submarine/Eleanor Rigby (First pressing, label variation with mid-size "Northern Songs, NCB", no brackets on Matrix number, with comma "," separating "Lennon, McCartney" rather than a "-" "Lennon-McCartney", larger typeface for "Eleanor Rigby" and "Sold In U.K...")	15
66	Parlophone R5493	Yellow Submarine/Eleanor Rigby (Second pressing, solid centre, label variation, larger "Northern Songs, NCB" text, smaller "Lennon-McCartney" credit and larger circled "P")..	20
66	Parlophone R 5493	Yellow Submarine/Eleanor Rigby (Second pressing, solid centre label variation, larger "Northern Songs, NCB" text, no brackets on Matrix number and larger typeface on "Eleanor Rigby")	15
66	Parlophone R 5084	I Want To Hold Your Hand/This Boy (Third pressing, solid centre, "The Parlophone Co" rim text)	250
66	Parlophone R 5114	Can't Buy Me Love/You Can't Do That (Second pressing, solid centre, with "The Parlophone Co. Ltd" label text)	150
66	Parlophone R 5200	I Feel Fine/She's A Woman (Second pressing, solid centre)	150

SINGLES : 1967
(All pressings after 1967 have push-out or solid centres with "The Gramophone Co. Ltd." in upper case & "Sold in the UK..." label text, unless otherwise stated)

67	Parlophone R 5570	Strawberry Fields Forever/Penny Lane (First pressing, 250,000 only in p/s)	75
67	Parlophone R 5570	Strawberry Fields Forever/Penny Lane (Second pressing, in Type 5,6 or 7 sleeve)	15
67	Parlophone R 5620	All You Need Is Love/Baby You're A Rich Man (First pressing, solid or pushout centre, with no reference to "Live World Television Transmission")	70
67	Parlophone R 5620	All You Need Is Love/Baby You're A Rich Man (Second pressing, with reference to "Live World Television Transmission")	15
67	Parlophone R 5620	All You Need Is Love/Baby You're A Rich Man (Second pressing, label variation, push-out/solid centre with reference to "Live World Television Transmission" and "Northern Songs NCB" on three lines rather than two, brackets around matrix number, "1967" above Matrix number and "Recorded during 'Live;..." text starts after Lennon-McCartney credit rather than beneath it)	25
67	Parlophone R 5655	Hello, Goodbye/I Am The Walrus (First pressing, company sleeve, with "7/- to 50/- " on reverse)	12
67	Parlophone R 5655	Hello Goodbye/I Am The Walrus (First pressing, label variation with "Northern Songs NCB" on three lines not two, different typeface and matrix number appearing beneath date of "1967", smaller typeface for "Hello, Goodbye" and ""Lennon, McCartney" separated by a "," rather than a "-", "Lennon-McCartney")	15
67	Parlophone R 5452	Paperback Writer/Rain (Second pressing, solid centre only)	80
67	Parlophone R 5493	Yellow Submarine/Eleanor Rigby (Second pressing, solid centre only)	15
67	Parlophone R5305	Help/I'm Down (Third pressing, solid centre, "The Gramophone Co. Ltd" and "Sold in U.K..." label text)	100
67	Parlophone R5305	Help/I'm Down (Third pressing, solid centre, "The Parlophone Co. Ltd" and "Sold in U.K..." label text)	90

SINGLES : 1968
(All Apple pressings except for early issues of "Let It Be" come in black glossy 'Apple' sleeves)

68	Parlophone R 5675	Lady Madonna/The Inner Light (First pressing, with Fan Club insert; sleeve with 7/- to 50/- on reverse)	60
68	Parlophone R 5675	Lady Madonna/The Inner Light (no fan club insert)	20
68	Apple R 5722	Hey Jude/Revolution (First pressing, push-out or solid centre)	20
68	Parlophone R 5084	I Want To Hold Your Hand/This Boy (Fourth pressing, solid centre, with "The Gramophone Co" rim text)	300

SINGLES : 1969
(All Apple pressings except for early issues of "Let It Be" come in black gloss "Apple" sleeves)

69	Apple R 5777	Get Back/Don't Let Me Down (First pressing, push-out or solid centre, as "The Beatles with Billy Preston")	20
69	Apple R 5777	Get Back/Don't Let Me Down (First pressing, label variation with "Northern Songs/NCB" rather than "Northern Songs" solid centre or push-out centre, as "The Beatles with Billy Preston")	20
69	Apple R 5777	Get Back/Don't Let Me Down (Second pressing, solid centre or push-out centre as "The Beatles with Billy Preston", without "Sold in UK..." label text))	25
69	Apple R 5786	Ballad Of John And Yoko/Old Brown Shoe (First pressing, solid or push-out centre)	25
69	Apple R 5786	Ballad Of John And Yoko/Old Brown Shoe (Second pressing, solid centre or push-out centre without "Sold in UK..." label text)	20
69	Apple R 5814	Something/Come Together (First pressing, solid centre or push-out centre without "Sold in UK..." label text)	45
69	Apple R 5722	Hey Jude/Revolution (Second pressing, without "Sold in UK..." label text)	15
69	Parlophone R 5305	Help/I'm Down (Fourth pressing, with "The Parlophone Co. Ltd" but no "Sold In U.K..." label text)	40
69	Parlophone R 5389	We Can Work It Out/Day Tripper (Third pressing, solid centre, no "sold in u.K..." label text)	80
69	Parlophone R 5452	Paperback Writer/Rain (Third pressing, no "Sold in U.K...." label text)	40
69	Parlophone R 5570	Strawberry Fields Forever/Penny Lane (Third pressing, no "Sold In U.K..." label text)	35
69	Parlophone R 5493	Yellow Submarine/Eleanor Rigby (Third pressing, no "Sold In U.K..." label text)	40
69	Parlophone R 5620	All You Need Is Love/Baby You're A Rich Man (Third pressing, no "Sold In U.K..." label text, push-out centre)	40
69	Parlophone R5675	Lady Madonna/The Inner Light (Third pressing, no "Sold In U.K..." label text)	35

SINGLES : 1970

70	Apple R 5833	Let It Be/You Know My Name (Look Up The Number) (First pressing, scratched-out B-side matrix: APPLES 1002, p/s)	30
70	Apple R 5833	Let It Be/You Know My Name (Look Up The Number) (Second pressing, scratched-out B-side matrix: APPLES 1002, no p/s)	15
70	Apple R 5833	Let It Be/You Know My Name (Look Up The Number) (Third pressing, B-side matrix: 7YCE 21408, no p/s)	15

SINGLES : 70S, 80S, 90S & 00S SINGLES: REISSUES AND PICTURE DISCS

(Please note that 1970s Parlophone copies of Beatles singles with EMI boxed logos are of nominal value. Add £10 to the value for any single with a red & white 'Factory Sample Not For Sale' sticker.)

76	Parlophone R5493	Yellow Submarine/Eleanor Rigby (with boxed EMI logo in green and black p/s)	6
76	Parlophone R 5452	Paperback Writer/Rain (with boxed EMI logo in green and black p/s)	8
76	Parlophone R 6013	Yesterday/I Should Have Known Better (p/s)	8
76	Parlophone R 5655	Hello, Goodbye/I Am The Walrus (with boxed EMI logo in green and black p/s)	8
76	Parlophone R 6016	Back In The USSR/Twist And Shout (p/s)	8
76	Parlophone R5570	Strawberry Fields Forever/Penny Lane (with boxed EMI logo in green and black p/s)	8
76	Parlophone R5786	The Ballad Of John And Yoko/ Old Brown Shoes (issued with light green Apple labels and green and black p/s)	8
76	Parlophone R 5814	Something/Come Together (issued with light green Apple labels and green and black p/s)	10
78	Parlophone R 6022	Sgt. Pepper's Lonely Hearts Club Band/With A Little Help From My Friends/A Day In The Life (p/s)	8
82	Parlophone R 4949	Love Me Do/P.S. I Love You (p/s, red label reissue, with "mono" notice &publishing miscredited to "Ardmore & Beechwood" -4 Matrix, Andy White version)	10
82	Parlophone 12R 4949	Love Me Do/P.S. I Love You/Love Me Do (Original Single Version) (12", p/s)	10
84	Parlophone RP 5160	A Hard Day's Night/Things We Said Today (picture disc)	15
86	Parlophone RP 5452	Paperback Writer/Rain (picture disc)	15
(Issued in PVC sleeve)			
87	Parlophone R 5570	Penny Lane/Strawberry Fields Forever (p/s)	8
87	Parlophone 12R 5620	All You Need Is Love/Baby You're A Rich Man (12", p/s)	10
(Issued in PVC sleeve)			
88	Apple 12R 5722	Hey Jude/Revolution (12", p/s)	30
95	Apple R 6422	Free As A Bird/Christmastime Is Here Again (7", p/s)	8
96	Apple R 6425	Real Love/Baby's In Black (7", p/s)	15
10	Parlophone 5099964163970	Paperback Writer/Rain (jukebox centre)	40
12	Parlophone 45-R 4949	Love Me Do/PS I Love You (reissue, withdrawn as A side has album version with Andy White on drums and Ringo on tambourine, Matrixes: BC88258-01A1 01740174/ BC88258-01B1 0174017 J G i i and incorrect catalogue number R 47414 on B-side)	20
17	Parlophone 0602557385618	Strawberry Fields Forever/Penny Lane (p/s)	20

SINGLES : CONTRACT PRESSINGS: SINGLES

Records were often pressed by rival companies on behalf of one another under contract to meet spikes in demand. Non-EMI companies frequently pressed batches of Beatles' records for Parlophone. Occasionally demand for a record was so strong that more than one company was contracted to press batches simultaneously. Subtle differences indicating the origin of a contract pressing can be identified. Many collectors like to include examples in their collections. EMI Pressings: Pre-1966 EMI pressings have flat push-out centres. Thereafter many records were produced with a mix of push-out and solid centres. EMI always pressed Stamper Letters into the vinyl's run-out area positioned at 3 o'clock to the Matrix Number. Up to three letters from the code 'GRAMOPHLTD' were used, each representing a number from 1 to 0. Mother Plate Numbers using a conventional numbering sequence starting with 1 were pressed into the vinyl at 9 o'clock to the Matrix Number. The edges of EMI pressings are all straight-cut. Non-EMI Pressings: Philips' contract pressings (the 'Hey Jude' single) are the easiest to spot as they alone have three-pronged centres. All the others had four prongs except some ORIOLE pressings of "Can't Buy Me Love" which have solid centres. The centres of Decca and PYE pressings have similar raised sections containing the spindle hole, though PYE's are much less prominent. The outermost edges of records made by CBS, PHILIPS, ORIOLE and PYE are not straight-cut but are slightly tapered-off. The edges of Decca pressings are all straight-cut. EMI Stamper Letters are seldom seen on contract pressings though Mother Plate Numbers almost always appear. Controversy long surrounded one style of Beatles' contract pressing. Previously thought to have been pressed by PYE they are now considered to have been made by ORIOLE before its acquisition by CBS in September 1964. The labels on the essentially flat centres of these pressings are often rough-textured with rough edges. The vinyl is thicker and heavier than other pressings. Some November 1964 pressings of 'I Feel Fine' also have these characteristics and are assumed to have come from this source, CBS by then using the old ORIOLE presses. Some 1968 copies of 'Hey Jude' are identical in appearance but are less heavy. Both are now considered to be CBS contract pressings. PYE is believed to have pressed copies of one Beatles' 45 ('Hey Jude') and one EP ('Million Sellers'). The centres of these two pressings look very similar to those made by Decca but they have a less prominent ridge and the edges of the records are slightly tapered. Beatles fans and collectors worldwide continue to scrutinise the magical mystery tour of Beatles' contract pressings and new information continues to be unearthed. The following details are where we at Record Collector stand at the present time

63	Parlophone R 5055	She Loves You/I'll Get You (Decca pressing)	30
63	Parlophone R 5055	She Loves You/I'll Get You (Decca pressing, variation, "Parlophone Co.Ltd" in upper case, different typography for "Northern Songs" Matrix number and "Recording First Published 1963")	25
63	Parlophone R 5084	I Want To Hold Your Hand/This Boy (Decca pressing)	25
63	Parlophone R 5084	I Want To Hold Your Hand/This Boy (Decca pressing, label variation with "N.C.B." after "Northern Songs Mus. Ltd.")	25
63	Parlophone R 5084	I Want To Hold Your Hand/This Boy (Oriole pressing)	25
63	Parlohone R 5084	I Want To Hold Your Hand/This Boy (Pye pressing, label variant with differnt typography and "N.C.B." after "Northern Songs Mus Ltd.")	25
64	Parlophone R 5114	Can't Buy Me Love/You Can't Do That (Oriole pressing)	25
64	Parlophone R 5114	Can't Buy Me Love/You Can't Do That (Oriole pressing with solid centre)	45
64	Parlophone R5114	Can't Buy Me Love/You Can't Do That (Pye contract pressing with solid centre, side 1, matrix 7XCE 17657-1N)	40
64	Parlophone R 5114	Can't Buy Me Love/You Can't Do That (Pye pressing label variation with "NCB" out of alignment with the "N" and "S" of "Northern Songs")	25
64	Parlophone R 5200	I Feel Fine/She's A Woman (Pye pressing)	25
64	Parlophone R 5200	I Feel Fine/She's A Woman (CBS pressing)	25
64	Parlophone R 5200	I Feel Fine/She's A Woman (Decca pressing)	25
65	Parlophone R 5305	Help!/I'm Down (Decca contract pressing)	25
67	Parlophone R 5655	Hello Goodbye/I Am The Walrus (Decca pressing)	25
67	Parlophone R 5655	Hello Goodbye/I Am The Walrus (Decca contract pressing, label variation, with "Northern Songs NCB" on three lines not two, "1967" above not below matrix number	25

The BEATLES

MINT VALUE £

		and "Lennon, McCartney" separated by a comma "," rather than a "-", "Lennon-McCartney")
68	Apple R 5722	Hey Jude/Revolution (Decca contract pressing) 40
68	Apple R 5722	Hey Jude/Revolution (Pye contract pressing) 40
68	Apple R 5722	Hey Jude/Revolution (CBS contract pressing) 40
68	Apple R 5722	Hey Jude/Revolution (Philips contract pressing, three-pronged push-out centre) 70

SINGLES : DEMO SINGLES

(Beatles demo singles between 1962 and 1966 have a red "A" on the A side unless otherwise stated. Demos from All You Need Is Love (1967) to Something (1969) have a white "A" on a green label. Finally, demos with the centre's missing are worth half these values)

62	Parlophone 45-R 4949	Love Me Do/P.S. I Love You (Demo copy, McCartney misspelt "McArtney", 250 only)... 6000
63	Parlophone 45-R 4983	Please Please Me/Ask Me Why (demo copy) 2000
63	Parlophone (45-)R 5015	From Me To You/Thank You Girl (Demo copy, with or without '45-' prefix) 1000
63	Parlophone R 5055	She Loves You/I'll Get You (Demo copy) 800
63	Parlophone R 5084	I Want To Hold Your Hand/This Boy (Demo copy) 800
64	Parlophone R 5114	Can't Buy Me Love/You Can't Do That (Demo copy) 800
64	Parlophone R 5160	A Hard Day's Night/Things We Said Today (Demo copy, red "A" on both sides) 800
64	Parlophone R 5200	I Feel Fine/She's A Woman (Demo single, existence unconfirmed) 0
65	Parlophone R 5265	Ticket To Ride/Yes It Is (Demo copy) 700
65	Parlophone R 5305	Help!/I'm Down (Demo copy, existence unconfirmed) 0
65	Parlophone R 5389	We Can Work It Out/Day Tripper (Demo copy, red "A" on both sides) 600
66	Parlophone R 5452	Paperback Writer/Rain (Demo copy) 600
66	Parlophone R 5493	Yellow Submarine/Eleanor Rigby (Demo copy, existence unconfirmed) 0
67	Parlophone R 5570	Strawberry Fields Forever/Penny Lane (existence unconfirmed) 0
67	Parlophone R 5620	All You Need Is Love/Baby You're A Rich Man (Demo copy) 450
67	Parlophone R 5655	Hello, Goodbye/I Am The Walrus 500
68	Apple (no cat. no.)	Hey Jude/Revolution (Demo copy, green & white Apple 'custom' label, handwritten details).. 450
69	Apple R 5777	Get Back/Don't Let Me Down (Demo copy, green and white Apple 'custom' label test pressing,typed details) 400
69	Parlophone R 5786	Ballad Of John And Yoko/Old Brown Shoe (Demo copy, existence unconfirmed) 0
68	Parlophone R 5675	Lady Madonna/The Inner Light (Demo copy) 500
69	Parlophone R 5814	Something/Come Together (Demo copy) 600
70	Parlophone R 5833	Let It Be/You Know My Name (Look Up The Number) (existence unconfirmed) 0
76	Parlophone R 6013	Yesterday/I Should Have Known Better (Demo, silver/black paper label with a silver "A", green generic p/s) 25
76	Parlophone R 6016	Back In The U.S.S.R./Twist And Shout (silver/black paper label with a silver "A",green generic p/s).. 25
78	Parlophone R 6022	Sgt. Pepper's Lonely Hearts Club Band/With A Little Help From My Friends/A Day In The Life (silver/black paper label with a silver "A", p/s).. 25

SINGLES : FRENCH PRESSINGS - SINGLES

67	Parlophone R 5655	Hello Goodbye/I Am The Walrus (Pathé Marconi pressing, alleged push-out centre version) 100
67	Parlophone R 5655	Hello Goodbye/I Am The Walrus (Pathé Marconi pressing) 25

SINGLES : POLYDOR RECORDINGS

(With push-out centres & orange labels)

62	Polydor NH 66833	My Bonnie/The Saints (When The Saints Go Marching In) (as Tony Sheridan & The Beatles; 1st pressing, 'broad' title& "Made In England" label text) 100
63	Polydor NH 66833	My Bonnie/The Saints (When The Saints Go Marching In) (as Tony Sheridan & The Beatles; 2nd pressing, push-out or solid centre,'narrow' title & "Made In England" label text)... 70
64	Polydor NH 52275	Cry For A Shadow (A-side credited to 'Beatles')/TONY SHERIDAN & THE BEATLES: Why Can't You Love Me Again) ('scroll' label, with "Made In England" text) 50
64	Polydor NH 52317	Ain't She Sweet (A-side as 'The Beatles, vocal: John Lennon')/If You Love Me, Baby (B-side credited to 'The Beatles with Tony Sheridan, vocal'; 1st pressing, 'scroll' label with "Made In England" text)... 45
64	Polydor NH 52317	Ain't She Sweet/If You Love Me, Baby (2nd pressing, red label, with "Made In England" text)... 20
64	Polydor NH 52906	Sweet Georgia Brown/Nobody's Child (German import only, unissued in U.K.) 40

SINGLES : SINGLES BOX SETS

76	Parlophone/Apple BS 24	THE BEATLES' SINGLES COLLECTION 1962-1970 (24 x 7", each in green p/s, green & white stickered box set) 45
76	Parlophone/Apple/ World Record Club	THE BEATLES' COLLECTION (24 x 7", mail-order black box set; later copies with "Sgt. Pepper's Lonely Hearts Club Band" [R 6022]) 45
78	Parlophone/Apple BSC 1	THE BEATLES SINGLES COLLECTION (26 x 7" blue box set, with insert; some copies include mispressing of "Get Back" [Apple R 5777]).. 40
82	Parlophone/Apple BSCP 1	THE BEATLES SINGLES COLLECTION (27 x 7" blue box set, with bonus picture disc "Love Me Do" [RP 4949], export issue)... 45
82	Parlophone/Apple BSCP 1	THE BEATLES SINGLES COLLECTION (27 x 7" blue box set, with mispressed picture disc Love Me Do/"Love Me Do" [RP 4949], export issue)... 50
89	Parlophone/Apple CDBSC 1	THE BEATLES' SINGLES COLLECTION (22 x 3" CD single box set) 75
89	Parlophone/Apple CDBSCP 1	THE BEATLES' SINGLES COLLECTION (22 x 5" CD single box set) 65
12	Apple 5099968	SINGLES BOX SET (4x7", poster) 25

SINGLES : UNIQUE PROMO SINGLES

68	Apple (no cat. no.)	OUR FIRST FOUR (4 x 7" in presentation pack, including Hey Jude [R 5722] & Those Were The Days by Mary Hopkin [APPLE 2], Sour Milk Sea by Jackie Lomax [APPLE 3] & Thingumybob by Black Dyke Mills Band [APPLE 4]; each mounted in PVC pocket on printed dayglo card insert, in 10" x 12" card in plastic box).. 4000
68	Apple (no cat. no.)	OUR FIRST FOUR (4 x 7" in presentation pack, including Hey Jude [R 5722] & Those Were The Days by Mary Hopkin [APPLE 2], Sour Milk Sea by Jackie Lomax [APPLE 3] & Thingumybob by Black Dyke Mills Band [APPLE 4]; each mounted in PVC pocket on printed dayglo card insert, in 10" x 12" card sleeve)... 2500
76	EMI SPSR 401	Medley Of Songs For "Rock'n'Roll Music" (excerpts)... 600

EXPORT SINGLES

64	Parlophone DP 562	If I Fell/Tell Me Why (First pressing, export single without "Sold in UK..." label text) 100

The Beatles

			MINT VALUE £
65	Parlophone DP 563	Yesterday/Dizzy Miss Lizzy (export single)	100
66	Parlophone DP 564	Michelle/Drive My Car (export single)	175
68	Parlophone DP 570	Hey Jude/Revolution (Export copy with Swedish p/s)	60
68	Parlophone DP 570	Hey Jude/Revolution (Export copy without Swedish p/s)	45
70	Parlophone P-R 5833	Let It Be/You Know My Name (Look Up The Number) (Export copy, no p/s)	60

("Let It Be" was pressed with "Parlophone" label text on one side & "Gramophone" on the other)

70	Apple P-R 5833	Let It Be/You Know My Name (Look Up The Number) (Export copy, no p/s)	300

EPS : 1963

(With "The Parlophone Co. Ltd" and "Recording first published 1963" label text. Unless otherwise stated, all 60s EPs have push-out centres and laminated flipback sleeves.)

63	Parlophone GEP 8882	TWIST AND SHOUT (EP, First pressing)	30
63	Parlophone GEP 8880	THE BEATLES' HITS (EP, First pressing, without "Recording first published 1963" label text)	20
63	Parlophone GEP 8883	THE BEATLES (No. 1) (EP, first pressing, without "Recording first published 1963" label text)	25
63	Parlophone GEP 8880	THE BEATLES' HITS (EP, Second pressing)	20

EPS : 1964

(With "The Parlophone Co. Ltd." & "Recording first published 1964" label text & "Sold in the UK..." unless otherwise stated)

64	Parlophone GEP 8891	ALL MY LOVING (EP, First pressing without "Sold in UK" label text)	35
64	Parlophone GEP 8891	ALL MY LOVING (EP, Second pressing, with "Sold in U.K...." label text)	25
64	Parlophone GEP 8899	GOLDEN DISCS (unreleased, 2 x 1-sided test pressings [matrices: 7TCE-1N & 7TCE-1N] & 1 set of label proofs only;price does not include labels)	2500
64	Parlophone GEP 8913	LONG TALL SALLY (EP, First pressing)	30
64	Parlophone GEP 8920	EXTRACTS FROM THE FILM "A HARD DAY'S NIGHT" (EP)	40
64	Parlophone GEP 8924	EXTRACTS FROM THE ALBUM "A HARD DAY'S NIGHT" (EP)	45
64	Parlophone GEP 8882	TWIST AND SHOUT (EP, Second pressing)	12

EPS : 1965

(With "The Parlophone Co. Ltd", & "Sold in UK.." label text, unless otherwise stated.)

65	Parlophone GEP 8931	BEATLES FOR SALE (EP, First pressing)	40
65	Parlophone GEP 8938	BEATLES FOR SALE (No. 2) (EP, first pressing)	45
65	Parlophone GEP 8946	THE BEATLES MILLION SELLERS (EP, with 'Golden Discs' text on labels)	25
65	Parlophone GEP 8883	THE BEATLES (No. 1) (EP, Second pressing, with "The Gramophone Co Ltd" & "Sold in UK..." label text)	10
65	Parlophone GEP 8880	THE BEATLES' HITS (EP, Third pressing, with "The Gramophone Co Ltd" & "Sold in UK..." label text)	10
65	Parlophone GEP 8882	TWIST AND SHOUT (Third pressing, with "The Gramophone Co Ltd" & "Sold in UK..." label text)	10

EPS : 1966

(With "The Gramophone Co. Ltd" & "Sold in UK..." label text unless otherwise stated.)

66	Parlophone GEP 8948	YESTERDAY (EP, First pressing)	90
66	Parlophone GEP 8952	NOWHERE MAN (EP, first pressing)	125
66	Parlophone GEP 8946	THE BEATLES' MILLION SELLERS (EP, Second pressing, with "Million Sellers" label text)	15

EPS : 1967

(With "The Gramophone Co. Ltd" & "Sold in UK..." label text unless otherwise stated. Please note that any EP titles with "The Gramophone Co Ltd" but without "Sold in UK..." are 70s re-pressing with EMI label text & varnished sleeves.)

67	Parlophone MMT-1	MAGICAL MYSTERY TOUR (2-EP, gatefold sleeve, first pressing with booklet & blue lyric sheet; push-out or solid centre; mono)	75
67	Parlophone SMMT-1	MAGICAL MYSTERY TOUR (2-EP, gatefold sleeve, first pressing with booklet & blue lyric sheet; stereo)	75
67	Parlophone GEP 8931	BEATLES FOR SALE (EP, Second pressing with "The Parlophone Co. Ltd" label text; solid centre)	25
67	Parlophone GEP 8952	NOWHERE MAN (EP, Second pressing solid centre)	35

EPS : CONTRACT PRESSINGS : EPS

66	GEP 8946	THE BEATLES MILLION SELLERS (EP, Pye contract pressing, with 'Golden Discs' text on labels)	30

EPS : EP REISSUES AND BOXED SETS

(EPs reissued in the 70s have EMI label text and come in varnished sleeves with flipbacks. Later 80s reissues are housed in cheaper varnished sleeves without flipbacks are are generally worth £8-£10).

73	Parlophone SMMT-1	MAGICAL MYSTERY TOUR (2-EP, gatefold sleeve, stereo only, with booklet & yellow lyric sheet)	15
81	Parlophone BEP 14	THE BEATLES EP COLLECTION (14-EP box set, with bonus stereo EP [SGE 1])	120
76	Parlophone GEP 8882	TWIST AND SHOUT (reissue, 'EMI' text on label)	15
76	Parlophone GEP 8880	THE BEATLES HITS (reissue with 'EMI' text)	15
76	Parlophone GEP 8883	THE BEATLES NO. 1 (reissue with 'EMI' text)	15
76	Parlophone GEP 8891	ALL MY LOVING (reissue with 'EMI' text)	12
76	Parlophone GEP 8913	LONG TALL SALLY (reissue with 'EMI' text)	15
76	Parlophone GEP 8920	EXTRACTS FROM THE FILM "A HARD DAY'S NIGHT" (reissue with 'EMI' text)	18
76	Parlophone GEP 8924	EXTRACTS FROM THE ALBUM "A HARD DAY'S NIGHT" (reissue with 'EMI' text)	18
76	Parlophone GEP 8931	BEATLES FOR SALE (reissue with 'EMI' text)	20
76	Parlophone GEP 8946	THE BEATLES MILLION SELLERS (reissue with 'EMI' text)	15
76	Parlophone GEP 8948	YESTERDAY (reissue with 'EMI' text)	20
76	Parlophone GEP 8952	NOWHERE MAN (reissue with 'EMI' text)	25
76	Parlophone SMMT-1	MAGICAL MYSTERY TOUR (reissue with 'EMI' text)	30
95	Apple R 6406	BABY IT'S YOU (7" EP)	15

EPS : POLYDOR RECORDINGS : EPS

64	Polydor EPH 21 610	TONY SHERIDAN WITH THE BEATLES (1st pressing, German import in U.K. p/s, orange 'scroll' label; Why songwriting credit as 'Sheridan' or 'Sheridan-Crompton')	125
64	Polydor EPH 21 610	TONY SHERIDAN WITH THE BEATLES (2nd pressing, German import in U.K. p/s, red label;Why songwriting credit as 'Sheridan' or 'Sheridan-Crompton')	50

The BEATLES

MINT VALUE £

ALBUMS : PLEASE PLEASE ME

(First pressings from 1963 have 'The Parlophone Co Ltd' label text but no 'Sold in UK...' label text unless otherwise stated. 1963 pressings come in polythene-lined 'Use Emitex' die-cut inners with flipback sleeves. All later label and sleeve variations are clearly stated in the entry for each repressing)

63	Parlophone PMC 1202	PLEASE PLEASE ME (First pressing, black & gold label, with "Dick James Mus. Co." publishing credit for "I Saw Her Standing There", "Misery", "Do You Want To Know A Secret & "There's A Place"; "Made by Ernest J Day Ltd" sleeve with printers credit on right hand side rear of sleeve; Front photo credited to "Angus McBean" at bottom far right of front cover of sleeve less than 5mm from edge. "A" of Angus starting under second letter "S" in the word "songs" in the album title: large mono in top right corner. Research estimates that around 25,000 pressed)	1200
63	Parlophone PCS 3042	PLEASE PLEASE ME (First pressing, black & gold label, with "Dick James Mus. Co."publishing credit for "Please Please Me", "I Saw Her Standing There", "Misery", Do You Want To Know A Secret & "There's A Place"; E. J. Day sleeve; stereo)	6000
63	Parlophone PMC 1202	PLEASE PLEASE ME (Second pressing, black & gold label, with "Northern Songs" publishing credit for "I Saw Her Standing There", "Misery", Do You Want To Know A Secret & "There's A Place"; Made by Ernest J Day Ltd" sleeve with printers credit on right hand side rear of sleeve; Front photo credited to "Angus McBean" at bottom far right of front cover of sleeve less than 5mm from edge. "A" of Angus starting under second letter "S" in the word "songs" in the album title: large mono in top right corner. Research estimates that around 12,000 pressed)	1200
63	Parlophone PCS 3042	PLEASE PLEASE ME (Second pressing, black & gold label, with "Northern Songs" publishing credit for "Please Please Me", "I Saw Her Standing There", "Misery", Do You Want To Know A Secret & "There's A Place"; E. J. Day sleeve; stereo)	5000
63	Parlophone PMC 1202	PLEASE PLEASE ME (Third pressing, black & yellow label with 33 1/3 RPM on label next to matrix number. Many of these records have LOWER stamper numbers than some black and gold second pressings (with Northern Songs credit) suggesting that these records were being pressed at the same time. Made by Ernest J Day Ltd" sleeve with printers credit on right hand side rear of sleeve; Front photo credited to "Angus McBean" at bottom far right of front cover of sleeve less than 5mm from edge. "A" of Angus starting under second letter "S" in the word "songs" in the album title: large mono in top right corner. Research estimates that around 5,000 pressed)	500
63	Parlophone PCS 3042	PLEASE PLEASE ME (Third pressing, black & yellow label with 33 1/3 on label, stereo)	3000
63	Parlophone PMC 1202	PLEASE PLEASE ME (Fourth pressing, black/yellow label Made by Ernest J Day Ltd" sleeve with printers credit on right hand side rear of sleeve; Front photo credited to "Angus McBean" at bottom far right of front cover of sleeve less than 5mm from edge. "A" of Angus starting under second letter "S" in the word "songs" in the album title: large mono in top right corner. Research estimates that around 25,000 pressed. Please note that there are some in sleeves with the Angus McBean credit around 20mm from the edge with the "A" of Angus starting under the letter "G" in "songs".)	150
63	Parlophone PCS 3042	PLEASE PLEASE ME (Fourth pressing, with large "stereo" on front cover; E. J. Day sleeve; stereo)	250
63	Parlophone PMC 1202	PLEASE PLEASE ME (Fifth pressing, "Recording first published 1963" added below matrix number. Research estimates around 184,000 pressed. E. J. Day sleeve with medium mono and"A" of "Angus" starting under the letter "G" in "Songs" or Garrod & Lofthouse Ltd sleeve with large mono and McBean credit around 20mm from edge with "A" of "Angus" starting under letter "G" in "Songs." Large "mono"on front cover; mono)	100
63	Parlophone PCS 3042	PLEASE PLEASE ME (Fifth pressing, G & L or E. J. Day sleeve, with large "stereo"on front cover; stereo)	150
64	Parlophone PCS 3042	PLEASE PLEASE ME (sixth pressing, with 'The Parlophone Co. Ltd', 'Recording first published 1963' & 'Sold in UK...' label text. G & L sleeve, with large "stereo" on front cover; stereo)	80
65	Parlophone PMC 1202	PLEASE PLEASE ME (sixth pressing, from July 1965 until August 1969 "Sold in U.K. subject to resale price conditions, see price lists." printed on centre of all labels. In February 1965 "Recording first published" replaced with (P) in a circle 1963. Records with (P) 1963 start with side 2 matrix XEX 422 - 2N: Research suggests that 250,000 copies pressed. G & L sleeve, with large or small "mono" with McBean credit around 20mm from edge with "A" of "Angus" starting under letter "G" in "Songs; mono)	70
65	Parlophone PCS 3042	PLEASE PLEASE ME (Seventh pressing, with 'The Gramophone Co Ltd' & 'Sold in UK...' label text, stereo, with small "stereo" on front cover)	60
69	Parlophone PMC 1202	PLEASE PLEASE ME (Seventh pressing, pressed between August to December 1969, "Sold in U.K. ..." text removed mono, with small "mono" on front cover made by Garrod & Lofthouse Ltd. Angus McBean credit 20mm from the edge with the "A" of "Angus" starting under the letter "G" in "Songs". Research estimates than only 1000 copies pressed)	400
69	Parlophone PCS 3042	PLEASE PLEASE ME (Eigth pressing, 'The Gramophone Co Ltd' label text, small "stereo" on front cover; stereo)	60
69	Parlophone PMC 1202	PLEASE PLEASE ME (Re-pressing 1969, mono)	50
69	Parlophone PCS 3042	PLEASE PLEASE ME (1969 re-pressing, stereo, with one boxed EMI logo on label)	100

(with laminated flipback sleeves & silver/black labels with one boxed EMI logo)

70	Parlophone PMC 1202	PLEASE PLEASE ME (Eigth pressing, black and silver label, single boxed EMI logo at 6 'o' clock, with G & L sleeve & sepia "LP advertising" inner. Label has "The Gramophone Co. Ltd." but no "Sold in UK ..."small "mono" on front cover made by Garrod & Lofthouse Ltd. Angus McBean credit 20mm from the edge with the "A" of "Angus" starting under the letter "G" in "Songs". Research suggests that around 1000 copies pressed; mono)	350
73	Parlophone PCS 3042	PLEASE PLEASE ME (French pressing)	15
82	Parlophone PMC 1202	PLEASE PLEASE ME (mono)	15

(lightweight vinyl with yellow/black labels listing "mono")

95	Parlophone PMC 1202	PLEASE PLEASE ME (LP, mono)	20

ALBUMS : WITH THE BEATLES

(First pressings from 1963 have 'The Parlophone Co Ltd' label text but no 'Sold in UK...' label text unless otherwise stated. 1963 pressings come in polythene-lined 'Use Emitex' die-cut inners with flipback sleeves. All later label and sleeve variations are clearly stated in the entry for each repressing)

63	Parlophone PMC 1206	WITH THE BEATLES (First pressing, black & yellow label, with "Recording first published", & "Jobete" publishing credit for "Money"; G&L or E. J. Day sleeve, with large "Mono" on front cover, mono)	200
63	Parlophone PCS 3045	WITH THE BEATLES (First pressing black & yellow label, with "Recording first published", & "Jobete" publishing credit for "Money"; G & L or E. J. Day sleeve, with large "stereo" on front cover; stereo)	250
63	Parlophone PMC 1206	WITH THE BEATLES (Second pressing, black & yellow label, with "Recording first published",& "Dominion, Belinda" publishing credit for "Money"; G & L or E. J. Day sleeve, with large "mono" on front cover; mono)	125
63	Parlophone PCS 3045	WITH THE BEATLES (Second pressing, black & yellow label, with "Recording first published",& "Dominion, Belinda" publishing credit for "Money"; G & L or E. J. Day	200

The BEATLES

MINT VALUE £

65	Parlophone PCS 3045	WITH THE BEATLES (Third pressing, 'The Gramophone Co Ltd' & 'Sold in UK...' label text, small "stereo" on front cover; stereo) 60
69	Parlophone PCS 3045	WITH THE BEATLES (Fourth pressing, with 'The Gramphone Co Ltd' label text but no 'Sold in UK...' label text, G&L sleeve with either plain white or sepia 'LP advertising' inner, small "stereo" on front cover; stereo) 60
69	Parlophone PCS 3045	WITH THE BEATLES (silver/black labels with one boxed EMI logo, stereo only) 30
73	Parlophone PCS 3045	WITH THE BEATLES (French pressing, with 'Made In France' on EMI rim copy) 15
82	Parlophone PMC 1206	WITH THE BEATLES (repressing with yellow/black labels on lightweight vinyl, mono) 15

ALBUMS : A HARD DAY'S NIGHT

(First pressings from 1964 have 'The Parlophone Co Ltd' & 'Sold in UK...' label text. All later label and sleeve variations are clearly stated in the entry for each repressing)

64	Parlophone PMC 1230	A HARD DAY'S NIGHT (First pressing, G & L or E. J. Day sleeve, mid-sized "mono" on front cover; mono) 100
64	Parlophone PCS 3058	A HARD DAY'S NIGHT (First pressing, G & L or E. J. Day sleeve, mid-sized "stereo" on front cover; stereo) 250
65	Parlophone PMC 1230	A HARD DAY'S NIGHT (Second pressing, small "mono" on front cover; mono) 60
65	Parlophone PCS 3058	A HARD DAY'S NIGHT (Second pressing, small "stereo" on front cover; stereo) 75
65	Parlophone PCS 3058	A HARD DAY'S NIGHT (Second pressing, outline "stereo" on front cover; stereo) 200
69	Parlophone PMC 1230	A HARD DAY'S NIGHT (Third pressing, with 'The Gramophone Co Ltd' label text but no 'Sold in UK...' label text, G&L sleeve with plain white or sepia 'LP advertising' inners.Small "mono" on front cover; mono) 60
69	Parlophone PCS 3058	A HARD DAY'S NIGHT (Third pressing, with 'The Gramophone Co Ltd' label text but no 'Sold in UK...' label text, G&L sleeve with plain white or sepia 'LP advertising' inners.Small "stereo" on front cover; stereo) 60
69	Parlophone PCS 3058	A HARD DAY'S NIGHT (stereo only, with laminated flipback sleeves & silver/black labels with one boxed EMI logo 30
73	Parlophone PCS 3058	A HARD DAY'S NIGHT (French pressing, 'Made in France' on EMI rim copy) 15
82	Parlophone PMC 1230	A HARD DAY'S NIGHT (lightweight vinyl with yellow/black labels listing "mono") 15

ALBUMS : BEATLES FOR SALE

(First pressings from 1964 have 'The Parlophone Co Ltd' & 'Sold in UK...' rim text with flipback sleeves)

64	Parlophone PMC 1240	BEATLES FOR SALE (First pressing, G & L gatefold sleeve with visible flaps inside gatefold sleeve, with outline "mono" on front cover; mono) 100
64	Parlophone PCS 3062	BEATLES FOR SALE (First pressing, G & L gatefold sleeve with visible flaps inside gatefold sleeve, with outline "stereo" on front cover; stereo) 200
65	Parlophone PCS 3062	BEATLES FOR SALE (Second pressing, with 'The Gramophone Co Ltd' & 'Sold in UK...' label rim text, outline "stereo" on front cover gatefold sleeve; stereo) 75
69	Parlophone PCS 3062	BEATLES FOR SALE (Third pressing, with The Gramophone Co Ltd' label rim text but no 'Sold in UK...' text, gatefold sleeve; stereo) 60
69	Parlophone PCS 3062	BEATLES FOR SALE (1969 repressing - gatefold sleeve, stereo only, with laminated flipback sleeve & silver/black labels with one boxed EMI logo) 30
73	Parlophone PCS 3062	BEATLES FOR SALE (French pressing with 'Made in France' on EMI rim copy, gatefold sleeve) 15
98	Parlophone PMC 1240	BEATLES FOR SALE (LP, gatefold, mono) 20

ALBUMS : HELP!

65	Parlophone PMC 1255	HELP! (LP, first pressing, G & L sleeve, with outline "mono" on front cover; mono) 100
65	Parlophone PCS 3071	HELP! (LP, first pressing, G & L sleeve, with outline "stereo" on front cover; stereo) 150
66	Parlophone PMC 1255	HELP! (LP, second pressing, G & L sleeve, plain white or sepia "LP advertising" inner sleeves; mono, with small solid black "mono" on front cover) 70
66	Parlophone PCS 3071	HELP! (LP, second pressing, G & L sleeve, plain white or sepia "LP advertising" inner sleeves; stereo, with small solid black "stereo" on front cover) 80
69	Parlophone PMC 1255	HELP! (LP, third pressing, small solid black "mono" on front cover; mono) 60
69	Parlophone PCS 3071	HELP! (LP, third pressing, small solid black "stereo" on front cover; stereo) 60
69	Parlophone PMC 1255	HELP! (LP, 1969 repressing, mono, one EMI boxed logo, with laminated flipback sleeve & silver/black labels with one boxed EMI logo) 400
69	Parlophone PCS 3071	HELP! (LP, 1969 repressing, stereo, with laminated flipback sleeve & silver/black labels with one boxed EMI logo) 30
73	Parlophone PCS 3071	HELP! (French pressing, with 'Made in France' on EMI label rim) 15

ALBUMS : RUBBER SOUL

(First pressings from 1965 have 'The Gramophone Co Ltd' & 'Sold in UK...' label text.)

65	Parlophone PMC 1267	RUBBER SOUL (First pressing, G & L or E. J. Day sleeve; mono, "loud cut" with XEX 579-1 and EXE 580-1 matrixes) 250
65	Parlophone PCS 3075	RUBBER SOUL (First pressing, G & L or E. J. Day sleeve; stereo) 225
65	Parlophone PMC 1267	RUBBER SOUL (Second pressing, matrix: [XEX 579-4 or 5]; mono) 90
69	Parlophone PCS 3075	RUBBER SOUL (Second pressing, with 'The Gramophone Co Ltd' label text but no 'Sold In UK...' label text, some with E. J. Day sleeve; stereo) 60
69	Parlophone PMC 1267	RUBBER SOUL (Third pressing, mono) 60
69	Parlophone PCS 3075	RUBBER SOUL (1969 repressing, with laminated flipback sleeves & silver/black labels with one boxed EMI logo, stereo only) 60
73	Parlophone PCS 3075	RUBBER SOUL (French pressing, with 'Made in France' on EMI rim copy) 15

ALBUMS : REVOLVER

(First pressings from 1966 have 'The Gramophone Co Ltd' & 'Sold in UK...' label text)

66	Parlophone PMC 7009	REVOLVER (First pressing, Side Two matrix [XEX 606-1], (G & L or E. J. Day sleeve; mono) 400
66	Parlophone PMC 7009	REVOLVER (First pressing, G & L or E. J. Day sleeve; mono) 100
66	Parlophone PCS 7009	REVOLVER (First pressing, G & L or E. J. Day sleeve; stereo) 150
66	Parlophone PMC 7009	REVOLVER (Second pressing, G & L or E. J. Day sleeve, plain white or sepia "LP advertising" inner sleeves mono) 100
69	Parlophone PMC 7009	REVOLVER (Third pressing, with 'The Gramophone Co Ltd' label text but no 'Sold in UK...' label text, plain white or sepia 'LP advertising' inners, mono) 75
69	Parlophone PCS 7009	REVOLVER (Second pressing, with 'The Gramophone Co Ltd' label text but no 'Sold in UK...' label text, plain white or sepia 'LP advertising' inners stereo) 50
69	Parlophone PCS 7009	REVOLVER (1969 repressing, with laminated flipback sleeves & silver/black labels with one boxed EMI logo, stereo only) 50
73	Parlophone PCS 7009	REVOLVER (French pressing with 'Made in France' on EMI rim copy) 15

The BEATLES

MINT VALUE £

80	Parlophone PMC 7009	REVOLVER (mono, pressed between 1980 and 1982, Black label with two white-black EMI logos and silver print. Matrix numbers: Side 1: YEX 605-3; Side 2: YEX 606-4) 15

ALBUMS : A COLLECTION OF BEATLES OLDIES
(First pressing from 1966 has 'The Gramophone Co Ltd' & 'Sold in UK...' label text.)

66	Parlophone PMC 7016	A COLLECTION OF BEATLES OLDIES (First pressing, G & L or E. J. Day sleeve; mono) 100
66	Parlophone PCS 7016	A COLLECTION OF BEATLES OLDIES (First pressing, G & L or E. J. Day sleeve; stereo) 100
69	Parlophone PMC 7016	A COLLECTION OF BEATLES OLDIES (Second pressing, with 'The Gramophone Co Ltd' label text but no 'Sold in UK...' label text, plain white or sepia 'LP advertising' inners mono) 40
69	Parlophone PCS 7016	A COLLECTION OF BEATLES OLDIES (Second pressing, with 'The Gramophone Co Ltd' label text but no 'Sold in UK...' label text, plain white or sepia 'LP advertising' inners stereo) 35
69	Parlophone PCS 7016	A COLLECTION OF BEATLES OLDIES (stereo only, with laminated flipback sleeves & silver/black labels with one boxed EMI logo) 25
73	Parlophone PCS 7016	A COLLECTION OF BEATLES OLDIES (LP, French pressing, with 'Made in France' on EMI rim copy) 15

ALBUMS : SGT. PEPPER'S LONELY HEARTS CLUB BAND
(First pressing from 1967 has 'The Gramophone Co Ltd' & 'Sold in UK...' label text)

67	Parlophone PMC 7027	SGT. PEPPER'S LONELY HEARTS CLUB BAND (First pressing, G & L laminated gatefold sleeve, visible flaps inside gatefold sleeve, with red & white inner & cut-out insert; mono) 150
67	Parlophone PCS 7027	SGT. PEPPER'S LONELY HEARTS CLUB BAND (First pressing, G & L laminated gatefold sleeve, visible flaps inside gatefold sleeve, with red & white inner & cut-out insert; stereo) 175
69	Parlophone PCS 7027	SGT. PEPPER'S LONELY HEARTS CLUB BAND (Second pressing, with 'The Gramophone Co Ltd' label text but no 'Sold in UK...' label text, plain white or sepia 'LP advertising' inners gatefold sleeve, with white inner and cut-out insert, stereo) 35
69	Parlophone PMC 7027	SGT. PEPPER'S LONELY HEARTS CLUB BAND (Third pressing, with 'The Gramophone Co Ltd' label text but no 'Sold in UK...' label text, plain white or sepia 'LP advertising' inners laminated gatefold sleeve, & cut-out insert; mono) 60
69	Parlophone PMC 7027	SGT. PEPPER'S LONELY HEARTS CLUB BAND (1969 repressing, laminated gatefold sleeve, with cut-out insert, mono, with laminated flipback sleeves & silver/black labels with one boxed EMI logo) 60
69	Parlophone PCS 7027	SGT. PEPPER'S LONELY HEARTS CLUB BAND (1969 repressing, laminated gatefold sleeve, with cut-out insert, stereo, with laminated flipback sleeves & silver/black labels with one boxed EMI logo) 30
73	Parlophone PCS 7027	SGT. PEPPER'S LONELY HEARTS CLUB BAND (French pressing, gatefold sleeve with cut-out insert, some copies with banded vinyl, with 'Made In France' on EMI rim) 18
84	Parlophone/Nimbus PCS 7027	SGT. PEPPER'S LONELY HEARTS CLUB BAND (mail-order only, from Practical Hi-Fi Magazine, Nimbus pressing) 600

ALBUMS : THE BEATLES (THE WHITE ALBUM)

68	Apple PMC/PCS 7067/8	THE BEATLES (WHITE ALBUM) (First pressing, mono or stereo, numbered below 0000010) 10000
68	Apple PMC/PCS 7067/8	THE BEATLES (WHITE ALBUM) (First pressing, 2-LP, mono or stereo, numbered between 0000011 & 0001000) 3000
68	Apple PMC/PCS 7067/8	THE BEATLES (WHITE ALBUM) (First pressing, 2-LP, mono or stereo, numbered between 0001001 & 0010000) 1000
68	Apple PMC 7067/8	THE BEATLES (WHITE ALBUM) (First pressing, 2-LP, mono, numbered above 0010000) ... 300
68	Apple PCS 7067/8	THE BEATLES (WHITE ALBUM) (First pressing, 2-LP, stereo, numbered above 0010000)... 250
69	Apple PCS 7067/8	THE BEATLES (WHITE ALBUM) (Second pressing, 2-LP, side opening, numbered g/fold sl., poster & 4 colour prints; stereo) 100
73	Apple PCS 7067/8	THE BEATLES (WHITE ALBUM) (2-LP, French pressing, un-numbered, laminated, side-opening gatefold sleeve, with four colour prints & poster, 'Made in France by Pathe Marconi EMI' rim copy) 25
73	Apple PCS 7067/8	THE BEATLES (WHITE ALBUM) (2-LP, un-numbered, laminated, side-opening gatefold sleeve, with poster & 4 soft card colour prints, stereo only) 35
82	Apple PMC 7067/8	THE BEATLES (WHITE ALBUM) (2-LP, un-numbered, side-opening gatefold sleeve, with poster & 4 prints, light green Apple label; mono) 30
95	Apple PCS 7067/8	THE BEATLES (WHITE ALBUM) (2-LP) 20

ALBUMS : YELLOW SUBMARINE

69	Apple PMC 7070	YELLOW SUBMARINE (LP, first pressing with red lines above & below rear sleevenote; mono) 300
69	Apple PCS 7070	YELLOW SUBMARINE (LP, first pressing with red lines above & below rear sleevenote; stereo) 150
69	Apple PCS 7070	YELLOW SUBMARINE (LP, second pressing with red lines above & below rear sleevenote; stereo) 50
73	Apple PCS 7070	YELLOW SUBMARINE (LP, French pressing, with 'Made in France by Pathe Marconi EMI' on rim) 15
99	Apple 521 4811	YELLOW SUBMARINE SONGTRACK (yellow vinyl, gatefold stickered sleeve) 35
99	Apple 521 4811	YELLOW SUBMARINE SONGTRACK (LP, gatefold stickered sleeve) 30

ALBUMS : ABBEY ROAD

69	Apple PCS 7088	ABBEY ROAD (LP, first pressing, black or plain white inner sleeve, with Apple logo aligned to Side 1 track listing on rear sleeve; with "Her Majesty" credit on label) 80
69	Apple PCS 7088	ABBEY ROAD (LP, first pressing Apple logo misaligned to Side 1 track listing on rear sleeve; with or without "Her Majesty" credit on label; black or plain white inner sleeve) 100
73	Apple PCS 7088	ABBEY ROAD (some copies with banded vinyl, French Pressing, with 'Made in France by Pathe Marconi EMI' rim copy) 15

ALBUMS : LET IT BE

70	Apple PXS 1	LET IT BE (LP box set, first pressing dark green label red Apple logo on rear sleeve & white inner, with Get Back book housed in black card tray ['PXS 1' not listed on package], with rare Apple mini poster) 1000
70	Apple PXS 1	LET IT BE (LP box set, first pressing dark green label red Apple logo on rear sleeve & white inner, with Get Back book housed in black card tray ['PXS 1' not listed on package], without rare Apple mini poster) 800
73	Apple PCS 7096	LET IT BE (French pressing with 'Made in France by Pathe Marconi EMI' rim text) 15

ALBUMS : 1969

(Apple LPs have G&L sleeves & black inners. Dark green labels with "Sold in UK..." text unless otherwise stated. Parlophone repressings are in G&L

The BEATLES

MINT VALUE £

sleeves with "The Gramophone Co. Ltd." but without "Sold in UK..." label text unless otherwise stated. These pressings also have plain white or sepia "LP advertising" inners.)

69	Apple PCS 7080	GET BACK (LP, unreleased, acetates only)	0

ALBUMS : 1970
(With G&L sleeves and dark green labels, unless otherwise stated)

70	Apple/Lyntone LYN 2154	FROM THEN TO YOU (The Beatles' Christmas Album)	500

ALBUMS : ALBUM BOX SETS

78	Parlophone BC 13	THE BEATLES COLLECTION (13 x LP, stereo, some with poster)	150
80	World Record Club SM 701/708	THE BEATLES BOX (8-LP, mail order only)	80
82	Parlophone BMC 10	THE BEATLES MONO COLLECTION (10 x LP, red box)	350

ALBUMS : CD ALBUMS AND BOX SETS

87	HMV BEACD 25/1	PLEASE PLEASE ME/WITH THE BEATLES/A HARD DAY'S NIGHT/BEATLES FOR SALE (4 x CD, numbered 12" black box set withBook Of Beatles Lists paperback book)	100
87	HMV BEACD 25/2	HELP!/RUBBER SOUL/REVOLVER (3 x CD, numbered 12" red box set with insert & reprint of Beatles Book Monthly, issue 12)	50
87	HMV BEACD 25/4	THE BEATLES (2-CD, numbered 12" box set with booklet & badge)	30
87	HMV BEACD 25/5	YELLOW SUBMARINE (CD, numbered 12" box set with insert, cut-outs & badge)	50

ALBUMS : CONTRACT PRESSINGS : LPS

(Records were often pressed by non-EMI companies under contract, owing to overwhelming demand for Beatles records. Subtle differences indicating their origin can be detected. Philips pressings (the 'Hey Jude' single only) are the easiest to spot as they alone have three-pronged centres. All the others had four except for the French Pathe-Marconi pressings of 'Hello Goodbye' which have solid centres and 'Made In France' at the foot of the label. The centre of a Decca contract pressing has a ridge 3mm from the perimeter. Pre-1966 EMI pressings have flat push-out centres. Thereafter many records were produced with a mix of push-out and solid centres. EMI always pressed stamper letters into the vinyl, positioned at 3 o' clock to the matrix number. Up to three letters from the code 'GRAMOPHLTD' were used each representing a number. EMI stamper letters are seldom seen on contract pressings. Great controversy has surrounded the origin of the only other known style of pre-1965 Beatles' contract pressings. Previously thought to have been made by Pye they are now believed to have been pressed at the ORIOLE pressing plant before their September 1964 aquisition by CBS. The centres of these pressings have no ridge and are finished with rough edges. They are also thicker and heavier than any of the other pressings. Although released in November 1964 'I Feel Fine' also has these characteristics and is assumed to have come from this source. CBS using the old ORIOLE presses. However, it is thought that PYE actually pressed one Beatles 45 and one EP after 1964. The centres of these two pressings look very similar to those made by DECCA but have a less prominent ridge. The edges of records made by PHILIPS, ORIOLE and PYE are not straight-cut but are tapered off. The edges of EMI, DECCA and Pathe-Marconi pressings are all straight-cut. (Decca contract pressings have no stamper letters (G or D) positioned at 3 o'clock to the matrix number; the label has a circularimpression 15mm from the outer edge. Pye pressings between 1973 and 1979 are a dark, translucent red when held up to a strong light.) Let us hope that the online community of Beatles fans and collectors worldwide will one day solve the magical mystery tour of Beatles contract pressings. Until that day, the following is where we at Record Collector stand at the present time)

63	Parlophone PMC 1202	PLEASE PLEASE ME (Decca contract pressing)	200
63	Parlophone PMC 1206	WITH THE BEATLES (Pye contract pressing)	150
63	Parlophone PMC 1206	WITH THE BEATLES (Decca contract pressing)	150
68	Parlophone P-PCS 7067/8	THE BEATLES (WHITE ALBUM) (2-LP, Decca contract pressing, yellow & black labels)	3000

(Decca contract pressings have no stamper letters (G or D) positioned at 3 o'clock to the matrix number; the label has a circularimpression 15mm from the outer edge. Pye pressings are a dark, translucent red when held up to a strong light.)

69	Parlophone P-PCS 7088	ABBEY ROAD (LP, contract pressing export issue, yellow & black labels, Decca pressing)	1000
69	Parlophone P-PCS 7099	ABBEY ROAD (LP, contract pressing, export issue, silver & black labels, Decca pressing)	500
70s	Apple PCSP 717	THE BEATLES 1962-1966 (2-LP, gatefold sleeve with lyric inners, Pye pressing)	50

ALBUMS : EXPORT LPS : ORIGINALS
(with black/yellow labels unless otherwise stated)

68	Parlophone PCS 3075	RUBBER SOUL (LP, with "Sold in U.K." label text, but silver 'Stereo' on top right hand corner, small batch pressed for export)	400
68	Parlophone PCS 3075	RUBBER SOUL (LP, with "Sold in U.K." label text, but black 'Stereo' on top right hand corner, small batch pressed for export)	150
65	Parlophone CPCS 101	SOMETHING NEW (LP, export 2nd pressing, with "Parlophone Co. Ltd." label text, no "sold in the U.K." label text)	500
65	Parlophone CPCS 101	SOMETHING NEW (LP, export 2nd pressing, with "Gramophone Co. Ltd." label text)	350
66	Parlophone CPCS 103	THE BEATLES' SECOND ALBUM (LP, export, first pressing with yellow/black labels)	450
66	Parlophone CPCS 104	BEATLES VI (LP, first export pressing with yellow/black labels)	500
68	Parlophone P-PCS 7067/8	THE BEATLES (WHITE ALBUM) (2-LP, export pressing, yellow/black labels, numbered, top opening 'mono' gatefold sleeve with "stereo" sticker & black inners, poster & 4 colour prints)	800
69	Odeon PPCS 7070	YELLOW SUBMARINE (LP, export pressing Odeon sticker on rear of Apple sleeve)	2000

(with yellow/black labels)

69	Parlophone P-PCS 7088	ABBEY ROAD (LP, export pressing, Parlophone sticker on rear of Apple sleeve, Apple logo on label)	800
70	Parlophone P-PCS 7096	LET IT BE (LP, First export pressing with silver/black labels, one EMI boxed logo)	1000

(with silver/black labels)

70	Parlophone CPCS 106	HEY JUDE (silver/black label, large boxed Parlophone label at top and small EMI boxed logo at bottom, laminated sleeve)	600

ALBUMS : EXPORT LPS : REISSUES

69	Parlophone P-PCS 7088	ABBEY ROAD (LP, export copy reissue, Parlophone sticker on rear of Apple sleeve; one EMI boxed logo)	125
69	Apple CPCS 106	HEY JUDE (2nd reissue, dark green label)	75
69	Parlophone CPCS 101	SOMETHING NEW (one EMI boxed logo)	150
69	Parlophone CPCS 103	THE BEATLES' SECOND ALBUM (LP, export, second pressing with sliver/black labels, one EMI boxed logo)	150
69	Parlophone CPCS 104	BEATLES VI (LP, second export pressing with silver/black labels, one EMI boxed logo)	250
70	Parl./Apple (P-)PCS 7096	LET IT BE (LP, export pressing second reissue, Apple label [PCS 7096] in Parlophone sleeve)	35

(with silver/black labels)

70	Parlophone CPCS 103	THE BEATLES' SECOND ALBUM (LP, export, 2nd reissue, silver/black labels two EMI boxed logos)	100
73	Apple CPCS 106	HEY JUDE (3rd reissue, light green label)	25

The BEATLES

MINT VALUE £

78	Apple PCS 7067/8	THE BEATLES (WHITE ALBUM) (2-LP, export pressing, white vinyl, gatefold sleeve)	40
78	Parlophone PCTC 255	MAGICAL MYSTERY TOUR (LP, transparent yellow vinyl)	50
(with silver/black labels)			
78	Apple PCS 7088	ABBEY ROAD (LP, green vinyl)	50
78	Apple PCS 7096	LET IT BE (LP white vinyl)	50
70s	Parl./Apple (P-)CPCS 106	HEY JUDE (Apple label [CPCS 106] in Parlophone sleeve [P-CPSC 106])	35

ALBUMS : LPS : 1970S RE-PRESSINGS

(Black and silver labels with 'EMI Records Ltd' on label and 2 EMI boxes. Unless otherwise specified all have front laminated and non-flipback sleeves. Those albums with Apple labels are slightly lighter than those on 60s original pressings)

70s	Parlophone PCS 3042	PLEASE PLEASE ME (LP)	25
70s	Parlophone PCS 3045	WITH THE BEATLES (LP)	20
70s	Parlophone PCS 3058	A HARD DAYS NIGHT (LP)	25
70s	Parlophone PCS 3062	BEATLES FOR SALE (LP)	20
70s	Parlophone PCS 3071	HELP! (LP)	20
70s	Parlophone PCS 3075	RUBBER SOUL (LP)	30
70s	Parlophone PCS 7009	REVOLVER (LP)	30
70s	Parlophone PCS 7016	A COLLECTION OF BEATLES OLDIES (LP)	20
70s	Parlophone PCS 7027	SGT. PEPPER'S LONELY HEARTS CLUB BAND (LP, fully laminated sleeve)	30
70s	Apple PCS 7067/68	THE BEATLES (WHITE ALBUM) (2-LP, fully laminated sleeve)	40
76	Parlophone PCTC 255	MAGICAL MYSTERY TOUR (LP, with booklet)	25
70s	Apple PCS 7070	YELLOW SUBMARINE (LP)	25
70s	Apple PCS 7088	ABBEY ROAD (LP, fully laminated sleeve)	35
70s	Apple PCS 7096	LET IT BE (LP, fully laminated sleeve)	25

ALBUMS : LPS : 1980S RE-PRESSINGS

(These repressings come in non laminated 'varnished' sleeves and have black and silver labels. Most sleeves have barcodes)

88	Parlophone PCTC 255	MAGICAL MYSTERY TOUR (gatefold, with booklet)	18
80s	Parlophone PMC 1202	PLEASE PLEASE ME (LP, mono)	18
80s	Parlophone PMC 1206	WITH THE BEATLES (LP, mono)	15
80s	Parlophone PMC 1230	A HARD DAYS NIGHT (LP, mono)	15
80s	Parlophone PMC 1240	BEATLES FOR SALE (LP, mono)	15
80s	Parlophone PCS 3071	HELP! (LP, stereo)	15
80s	Parlophone PCS 3075	RUBBER SOUL (LP, stereo)	20
80s	Parlophone PCS 7009	REVOLVER (LP, stereo)	20
80s	Parlophone PCS 7016	A COLLECTION OF BEATLES OLDIES (LP, stereo)	15
80s	Parlophone PCS 7027	SGT. PEPPER'S LONELY HEARTS CLUB BAND (LP, stereo)	20
80s	Apple PCS 7067/68	THE BEATLES (WHITE ALBUM) (2-LP, stereo)	25
80s	Apple PCS 7070	YELLOW SUBMARINE (LP, stereo)	18
80s	Apple PCS 7088	ABBEY ROAD (LP, stereo)	20
80s	Apple PCS 7096	LET IT BE (LP, stereo)	18

ALBUMS : LPS : RETROSPECTIVES

73	Apple PCSP 717	THE BEATLES 1962-1966 (2-LP, labels state PCS 7171 and PCS 7172)	40
73	Apple PCSP 718	THE BEATLES 1967-1970 (2-LP, labels state 7181 and 7182)	40
76	Parlophone PCSP 719	ROCK N ROLL MUSIC (2-LP, gatefold)	30
76	Polydor 2683 068	THE BEATLES TAPES (2-LP)	30
77	EMI EMTV 4	THE BEATLES AT THE HOLLYWOOD BOWL (gatefold sleeve, with inner)	15
77	Lingasong LNS 1	LIVE AT THE STAR CLUB 1962 (2-LP)	30
77	Parlophone PCSP 721	LOVE SONGS (2-LP, gatefold)	30
77	EMI HRL 026	HISTORY OF ROCK VOL.26 THE BEATLES (2-LP gatefold sleeve)	30
78	Apple PCSPR 717	THE BEATLES 1962-1966 (2-LP, red vinyl, gatefold stickered sleeve with lyric inners)	20
78	Apple PCSPB 718	THE BEATLES 1967-1970 (2-LP, blue vinyl, gatefold stickered sleeve with lyric inners)	20
79	Parlophone PCM 1001	RARITIES (LP)	30
82	Parlophone EMTVS 34	THE BEATLES' GREATEST HITS (2-LP, unreleased)	0
88	HMV BPM 1	PAST MASTERS VOLUME 1 & 2 (2-LP, gatefold sleeve)	45
94	Apple PCSP 726	LIVE AT THE BBC (2-LP, gatefold sleeve, with inners)	40
95	Apple PCSP 727	ANTHOLOGY 1 (3-LP, gatefold sleeve, with inners)	50
96	Apple PCSP 728	ANTHOLOGY 2 (3-LP, gatefold sleeve, with inners)	50
96	Apple PCSP 729	ANTHOLOGY 3 (3-LP, gatefold sleeve, with inners)	50
00	Apple 529 3251	THE BEATLES 1 (2-LP, gatefold sleeve, with poster & 4 prints)	40
00	Apple 7243 529325 11	THE BEATLES 1 (2-LP, gatefold sleeve, with poster & 4 prints, signed certificate– 5293261 A-100/5293261 B-100/5293261 A-100 and 5293261 B-100 matrixes - 100 only)	500
03	Apple 595 4380	LET IT BE...NAKED (LP, gatefold sleeve PLUS "Fly On The Wall" 7" EP)	40
07	Apple 379 8081	LOVE (2-LP, gatefold sleeve, with inners)	30

ALBUMS : POLYDOR RECORDINGS : LPS

64	Polydor Hi-Fi 46 432	THE BEATLES' FIRST (purple/black sleeve, Germany only, unissued in U.K.)	100
67	Polydor Special 236 201	THE BEATLES' FIRST (as Tony Sheridan & The Beatles, 1st pressing, without 'stereo' on label or sleeve, 'pop art' sleeve)	50
67	Polydor Special 236 201	THE BEATLES' FIRST (later pressings with 'stereo' on label & sleeve, minor label variations, 'pop art' sleeve)	30

ALBUMS : REEL-TO-REEL TAPES: ORIGINALS

(All Beatles Reel-to-Reel tapes up to 1967 (from PLEASE PLEASE ME to SGT. PEPPERS LONELY HEARTS CLUB BAND were issued on 4 inch spools with printed leaders and were housed in card trays in card boxes. From THE BEATLES (WHITE ALBUM) to LET IT BE albums were still 4 inch spools but housed in jewel cases with card inlays)

65	Parlophone TA-PMC 1240	BEATLES FOR SALE (Mono only)	20
65	Parlophone TA-PMC 1255	HELP! (Mono-only)	20
65	Parlophone TA-PMC 1267	RUBBER SOUL (Mono only, reel-to-reel tape)	20
66	Parlophone TA-PMC 7009	REVOLVER (Mono only)	25
70	Apple TD-PCS 7088	ABBEY ROAD (Stereo, jewel case)	70
70	Apple TA-PMC 7088	ABBEY ROAD (Mono, jewel case)	100

			MINT VALUE £
69	Apple DTD-PCS 7067/8	THE BEATLES (WHITE ALBUM) (5 inch spool, Stereo, jewel case)	100
69	Apple DTA-PMC 7067/8	THE BEATLES (WHITE ALBUM) (5 inch spool, Mono, jewel case)	100
67	Parlophone TA-PMC 7027	SGT. PEPPER'S LONELY HEARTS CLUB BAND (Mono only)	30

(All Beatles Reel-to-Reel tapes up to 1967 (from PLEASE PLEASE ME to SGT. PEPPERS LONELY HEARTS CLUB BAND were issued on 4 inch spools with printed leaders and were housed in card trays in card boxes)

67	Parlophone TA-PMC 7016	A COLLECTION OF BEATLES OLDIES (Mono only)	20
63	Parlophone TA-PMC 1202	PLEASE PLEASE ME (Mono only)	25
64	Parlophone TA-PMC 1206	WITH THE BEATLES (Mono only)	25
64	Parlophone TA-PMC 1230	A HARD DAYS NIGHT (Mono only)	20
70	Apple TA-PMC 7096	LET IT BE (Mono, jewel case)	100
70	Apple TD-PCS 7096	LET IT BE (Stereo, jewel case)	80

ALBUMS : REEL-TO-REEL TAPES: REISSUES

(These albums were all reissued on reel-to-reel tape in 1968 and are all on 4 inch tape inside jewel cases with card inserts)

68	Parlophone TA-PMC 1202	PLEASE PLEASE ME (Reissue, Mono, jewel case)	25
68	Parlophone TD-PCS 3042	PLEASE PLEASE ME (Reissue, Stereo, jewel case)	25
68	Parlophone TA-PMC 1206	WITH THE BEATLES (Reissue, Mono, jewel case)	30
68	Parlophone TD-PCS 3045	WITH THE BEATLES (Reissue, Stereo, jewel case)	25
68	Parlophone TA-PMC 1230	A HARD DAY'S NIGHT (Reissue, Mono, jewel case)	25
68	Parlophone TD-PCS 3058	A HARD DAY'S NIGHT (Reissue, Stereo, jewel case)	25
68	Parlophone TA-PMC 1240	BEATLES FOR SALE (Reissue, Mono, jewel case)	30
68	Parlophone TD-PCS 3062	BEATLES FOR SALE (Reissue, Stereo, jewel case)	25
68	Parlophone TA-PCM 1255	HELP! (Reissue, Mono, jewel case)	25
68	Parlophone TD-PCS 3071	HELP! (Reissue, Stereo, jewel case)	25
68	Parlophone TA-PMC 1267	RUBBER SOUL (Reissue, Mono, jewel case)	30
68	Parlophone TD-PCS 3075	RUBBER SOUL (Reissue, Stereo, jewel case)	25
68	Parlophone TA-PMC 7009	REVOLVER (Reissue, Mono, jewel case)	30
68	Parlophone TD-PCS 7009	REVOLVER (Reissue, Stereo, jewel case)	25
68	Parlophone TA-PMC 7016	A COLLECTION OF BEATLES OLDIES (Reissue, Mono, jewel case)	30
68	Parlophone TD-PCS 7016	A COLLECTION OF BEATLES OLDIES (Reissue, Stereo, jewel case)	25
68	Parlophone TA-PMC 7027	SGT. PEPPER'S LONELY HEARTS CLUB BAND (Reissue, Mono, jewel case)	40
68	Parlophone TD-PCS 7027	SGT. PEPPER'S LONELY HEARTS CLUB BAND (Reissue, Stereo, jewel case)	35

MISPRESSINGS

63	Parlophone R 4983	Please Please Me/Ask Me Why (Mispressing, A-side actually plays 'Quiet Morning' by the Brian Fahey Orchestra)	50
64	Parlophone GEP 8882	TWIST AND SHOUT (label error: "Do You Want A Know A Secret")	20
64	Parlophone PCS 3062	BEATLES FOR SALE (label error: "I'm A Loser")	250
65	Parlophone GEP 8946	THE BEATLES' MILLION SELLERS (label error: "Beatles Golden Discs")	20
65	Parlophone PCS 3075	RUBBER SOUL (label error: "Norweigian Wood")	400
65	Parlophone CPCS 101	SOMETHING NEW (LP, 1st pressing, 1G/1G mother stampers, export issue, label misprint error: "Sold in UK")	500
66	Parlophone PMC 7009	REVOLVER (copies with side 2 matrix no.: XEX 606-1 have 'Remix 11' of Tomorrow Never Knows, G & L or E. J. Day sleeve; mono only)	500
66	Parlophone CPCS 106	BEATLES VI (LP, export issue, label error: "Sold in UK")	500
67	Parlophone PMC 7027	SGT. PEPPER'S LONELY HEARTS CLUB BAND (First pressing with label misprint omits "A Day In The Life" credit; G & L laminated gatefold sleeve, with plain white inner & insert,; mono only)	200

With "The Gramophone Co Ltd" & "Sold in the UK..." label text

68	Apple PCS 7067/8	THE BEATLES (WHITE ALBUM) (2-LP label misprinting error: "Rocky Racoon")	200
69	Apple PCS 7088	ABBEY ROAD (label omits "Her Majesty")	35
69	Apple CPCS 106	HEY JUDE (label misprint error: "Revolutions")	300
69	Parlophone PCS 7009	REVOLVER (1969 repressing, stereo only with misprint "I Got To Get You Into My Life" on side 2)	70

(with laminated flipback sleeves & silver/black labels with one boxed EMI logo)

69	Parlophone PMC 7027	SGT. PEPPER'S LONELY HEARTS CLUB BAND (1969 Mispressing, mono; matrix YEX 637/8; plays stereo)	200
99	Parlophone PCS 3075	RUBBER SOUL (label error: pressed on Apple)	100
12	Parlophone 45-R 4949	Love Me Do/PS I Love You (reissue, withdrawn as A side has album version with Andy White on drums and Ringo on tambourine, Matrixes: BC88258-01A1 01740174/ BC88258-01B1 0174017 J G i i and incorrect catalogue number R 47414 on B-side)	20

FLEXIDISCS

(Fan club flexidiscs are worth around £20 less without newsletters and half the listed values without picture sleeves.)

63	Lyntone LYN 492	The Beatles' Christmas Record (Flexidisc, gatefold p/s)	120
64	Lyntone LYN 757	Another Beatles Christmas Record (Flexidisc, p/s, with gatefold newsletter insert)	100
65	Lyntone LYN 948	The Beatles' Third Christmas Record (Flexidisc, p/s, with gatefold newsletter insert)	100
66	Lyntone LYN 1145	Pantomime: Everywhere It's Christmas (Flexidisc, p/s, with 7" x 7" newsletter insert)	100
67	Lyntone LYN 1360	Christmas Time (Is Here Again) (Flexidisc, p/s, with 7" x 7" newsletter insert)	100
68	Lyntone LYN 1743/4	The Beatles' Sixth Christmas Record (Flexidisc, p/s, with 'Superpix' sales insert)	100
68	Lyntone LYN 1743/4	The Beatles' Sixth Christmas Record (Flexidisc, p/s, without 'Superpix' sales insert)	100
69	Lyntone LYN 1970/1-IL	The Beatles' Seventh Christmas Record (Flexidisc, p/s, with 2 x foolscap fan club newsletters)	100
69	Lyntone LYN 1970/1-IL	The Beatles' Seventh Christmas Record (p/s)	75

(see also John Lennon, Paul McCartney/Wings, George Harrison, Ringo Starr, Pete Best Four, Quarry Men, Tony Sheridan, George Martin, Billy Preston, Yoko Ono, Fireman, Twin Freaks)

BEATMEN
64	Pye 7N 15659	You Can't Sit Down/Come On Pretty Babe	20
65	Pye 7N 15792	Now The Sun Has Gone/Please Believe	40

BEAT MERCHANTS
64	Columbia DB 7367	Pretty Face/Messin' With The Man	80
65	Columbia DB 7492	So Fine/She Said Yeah	70

BEAT NECESSITY
81	Newtown NTP 2	Pleasure Pain/VELDT: Ghost Child	15

BEATPUMP

MINT VALUE £

82	Newtown NTP 3	When You're Down On Your Luck/Telephone/Don't Know	15

BEATPUMP
80	Slow Lorries SLOW 1	THE FIVE MONTH PLAN EP (p/s)	25

BEATSTALKERS
65	Decca F 12259	Ev'rybody's Talking 'Bout My Baby/Mr. Disappointed	80
66	Decca F 12352	Left Right Left/You'd Better Get A Better Hold On	60
66	Decca F 12460	A Love Like Yours/Base Line	60
67	CBS 2732	My One Chance To Make It/Ain't No Soul (Left In These Ole Shoes)	80
67	CBS 3105	Silver Treetop School For Boys/Sugar Coated Man	75
68	CBS 3557	Rain Coloured Roses/Everything Is For You	60
69	CBS 3936	Little Boy/When I'm Five	70

PAUL BEATTIE
57	Parlophone R 4385	I'm Comin' Home/Nothing So Strange	30
58	Parlophone R 4468	A House, A Car, And A Wedding Ring/Banana	10
68	Parlophone R 4664	Slick Chick/The Big Bounce	30

E.C. BEATTY
59	Felsted AF 127	Ski King/I'm A Lucky Man	6

BEAU
69	Dandelion S 4403	1917 Revolution/Sleeping Town	10
69	Dandelion S 63751	BEAU (LP, black/red/silver label)	50
71	Dandelion DAN 8006	CREATION (LP, with The Way We Live)	40

(see also Way We Live)

BEAU BRUMMEL
82	Moonlight MNS 004	Hot George/Oscar	15

(see also Paul Roland, Andy Ellison)

BEAU BRUMMELS
66	Pye International 7N 25342	Good Time Music/Sad Little Girl (unissued)	0
65	Pye International NPL 28062	INTRODUCING THE BEAU BRUMMELS (LP, mono only)	20

BEAU-MARKS
60	Top Rank JAR 377	Clap Your Hands/Daddy Said	20

(see also Del-Tones, Milton De Lugg Orchestra)

JIMMY BEAUMONT
66	London HLZ 10059	You Got Too Much Going For You/I Never Loved Her Anyway	100
66	London HLZ 10059	You Got Too Much Going For You/I Never Loved Her Anyway (DJ Copy)	200

BEAUTIFUL SOUTH
92	Go! Discs 828 310-1	0898 BEAUTIFUL SOUTH (LP, inner)	20
94	Go! Discs 828 507-1	MIAOW (LP, withdrawn HMV-style 'dog' sleeve with lyric inner)	80
94	Go! Discs 828 507-1	MIAOW (LP, 'cat' sleeve with lyric inner)	60
94	Go! Discs 828 572-1	CARRY ON UP THE CHARTS (LP)	100
96	Go! Discs 828 845-1	BLUE IS THE COLOUR (LP, with lyric inner)	100
98	Go! Discs 538166	QUENCH (LP, inner)	100
01	Mercury 586 444 1	SOLID BRONZE (2-LP)	100

JACKIE BEAVERS
76	Jay Boy BOY 102	Trying To Get Back To You Girl/Trying To Get Back To You Girl (Version)	12
98	Wigan Casino 202	I Need My Baby/JOE MATTHEWS: She's My Beauty Queen (p/s reissue)	8

BEAZERS
64	Decca F 11827	Blue Beat/I Wanna Shout	45

(see also Chris Farlowe, Little Joe Cook)

BE-BOP DELUXE
73	Smile LAFS 001	Teenage Archangel/Jets At Dawn (mono, 1,000 only)	25
74	Harvest HAR 5081	Jet Silver (And The Dolls Of Venus)/Third Floor Heaven	6
75	Harvest HAR 5091	Between The Worlds/Lights (withdrawn)	50
74	Harvest SHVL 813	AXE VICTIM (LP, gatefold sleeve)	18
75	Harvest SHSP 4045	FUTURAMA (LP)	15
76	Harvest SHSP 4053	SUNBURST FINISH (LP, insert)	15
77	Harvest SHVL 816	LIVE! IN THE AIR AGE (LP, with bonus EP "Live! In The Air Age" [PSR 412])	20
78	Harvest SHDW 410	THE BEST AND THE REST OF BE BOP DELUXE (2-LP)	15

(see also A-Austr, Axe Victim)

BE-BOP PRESERVATION SOCIETY
71	Dawn DNLS 3027	THE BE-BOP PRESERVATION SOCIETY (LP, gatefold sleeve, orange label with insert)	30

BECK
94	Geffen GFS 67	Loser/Alcohol/Fume (p/s)	12
94	Geffen GFSJB 67	Loser/Loser (jukebox issue, no p/s)	8
94	Geffen GFS 73	Pay No Mind (Snoozer)/Special People (withdrawn)	80
94	Geffen GFST 73	Pay No Mind (Snoozer)/Special People/Trouble All My Days/Super Golden (Sunchild) (12", p/s, withdrawn - at least 100 pressed up)	50
94	Geffen GFS 19235	Beercan/Spanking Room (p/s, 1500 copies)	20
96	Geffen GFS 22183	Devil's Haircut/Lloyd Price Express (Remix By John King) (p/s)	10
96	Geffen GFS 22205	The New Pollution/Electric Music And The Summer People (p/s)	10
97	Geffen GFS 22276	Jack-Ass (Butch Vig Mix)/Strange Invitation/Devil Got My Woman/Jack-Ass (Lowrider Mix By Butch Vig)/ Burro Brother (Double 7" gatefold some have Butch Vig Mix with no Lowrider Mix)	10
97	Geffen GFS 22293	Deadweight/Erase The Sun (p/s)	8
09	Matador OLE 865-7	Green Light/SONIC YOUTH: Pay No Mind (green vinyl, very few sold in UK for Record Store Day)	60
94	Geffen GEF 24634	MELLOW GOLD (LP, inner)	30
98	Simply Vinyl SVLP 0051	ODELAY (LP, reissue, 180gm)	40
05	Interscope 9864087	GUERO (2-LP)	20

BECK, BOGERT & APPICE
75	CBS EQ 32140/Q 65455	BECK, BOGERT & APPICE (LP, quadrophonic)	18

(see also Jeff Beck, Vanilla Fudge, Cactus)

Gordon BECK (QUARTET)

MINT VALUE £

GORDON BECK (QUARTET)
67	Major Major MM/SMLP 88	DR. DOOLITTLE LOVES JAZZ (LP, as Gordon Beck + Two)	50
68	M. Minor MMLP/SMLP 21	EXPERIMENTS WITH POPS (LP, as Gordon Beck Quartet)	125
68	M. Minor MMLP/SMLP 22	HALF A JAZZ SIXPENCE (LP, as Gordon Beck + 2)	100
68	Morgan MJ 1	GYROSCOPE (LP, as Gordon Beck Trio)	250
72	Dire FO 341	BECK-MATTHEWSON-HUMAIR TRIO (LP)	30

(see also Seven Ages Of Man)

JEFF BECK
67	Columbia DB 8151	Hi-Ho Silver Lining/Beck's Bolero	10
67	Columbia DB 8227	Tallyman/Rock My Plimsoul	12
68	Columbia DB 8359	Love Is Blue (L'Amour Est Bleu)/I've Been Drinking	12
69	Columbia DB 8590	Plinth (Water Down The Drain)/Hangman's Knee (unissued)	0
68	Columbia S(C)X 6293	TRUTH (LP, 1st pressing, blue/black labels, stereo with "sold in U.K." label text)	150
68	Columbia SX 6293	TRUTH (LP, 1st pressing, blue/black labels, mono with "sold in U.K." label text)	200
68	Columbia SX 6293	TRUTH (LP, 2nd pressing, silver/black labels, boxed Columbia logo, with "sold in U.K." label text mono)	70
69	Columbia SX 6351	BECK-OLA (LP, 1st pressing, blue/black labels, mono)	150
69	Columbia S(C)X 6351	BECK-OLA (LP, 1st pressing, blue/black labels, stereo)	100
69	Columbia SCX 6293	TRUTH (LP, 3rd pressing, silver/black labels, stereo)	15
69	Columbia SX 6351	BECK-OLA (LP, 2nd pressing, silver/black labels, mono)	20
69	Columbia SCX 6351	BECK-OLA (LP, 2nd pressing, silver/black labels, stereo)	15
72	Epic EPC 64619	ROUGH AND READY (LP, yellow label)	30
72	Epic EPC 64899	JEFF BECK GROUP (LP, yellow label)	20
72	Epic EQ 30973	ROUGH AND READY (LP, quadrophonic)	40
74	CBS EQ 31331	JEFF BECK GROUP (LP, quadrophonic)	20
97	EMI LPCENT 3	BECK-OLA (LP, reissue, EMI centenary issue, stickered sleeve)	20

(see also Yardbirds, Beck Bogert Appice, Donovan, Rod Stewart, Cozy Powell, Honeydrippers, Buddy Guy)

ROBIN BECK
79	Mercury BECK !2	Sweet Talk/Shake It Through The Night (12")	12

BECKETT
74	Raft RA 48502	BECKETT (LP, with lyric insert)	20

HAROLD BECKETT
71	Philips 6308 026	FLARE UP (LP)	120
72	RCA SF 8225	WARM SMILES (LP)	100
73	RCA SF 8264	THEME FOR FEGA (LP)	60
75	Cadillac SGC 1004	JOY UNLIMITED (LP)	50
76	Ogun OG 800	MEMORIES OF BACARES (LP, as Harry Beckett's Joy Unlimited)	15

(see also Graham Collier, Galliard, Ninesense)

STUART BECKETT
60s	Sherwood SRS 1001	Kariline/Breakthrough	15

(KEE) LYN BECKFORD
68	Island WI 3144	Combination/Hey Little Girl	40
69	Jackpot JP 707	Kiss Me Quick/MRS. MILLER: Feel It	120
69	Big Shot BI 521	Suzie Wong (as K. Beckford)/SWINGING KINGS: Deebo	50
71	G.G. GG 4514	Groove Me/Groove Version (as Keeling Beckford)	35

THEO(PHILUS) BECKFORD
61	Blue Beat BB 33	Jack And Jill Shuffle/Little Lady (as Theophilus Beckford & Clue J. & His Blues Blasters)	20
61	Blue Beat BB 50	Georgie And The Old Shoe/That's Me (as Theo Beckford & City Slickers)	20
62	Blue Beat BB 87	Walking Down King Street/The Clock (B-side actually by Sir D's Group)	20
62	Blue Beat BB 132	Bringing In The Sheep (song actually "Bringing In The Sheaves")/Run Away	20
62	Island WI 026	I Don't Want You (actually by King Edward's All Stars)/Seven Long Years	15
63	Island WI 106	Daphney/Boller Man	12
63	R & B JB 136	Bullo Man/Daphney	25
64	Blue Beat BB 250	She's Gone/Old Flame (as Cotheo Beckford, B-side act. by Frederick Hibbert)	15
64	Blue Beat BB 257	Don't Worry To Cry/Love Me Or Leave Me (as Theophilus Beckford, B-side actually by Lloyd Clarke)	20
64	Blue Beat BB 256	Glamour Girl/BUSTER'S ALLSTARS: Down Beat Burial	120
64	Blue Beat BB 287	On Your Knees/Now You're Gone (with Yvonne Harrison)	15
65	Blue Beat BB 303	Dig The Dig (as Basil Gabbidon)/Don't Let Me Cry No More	15
65	Black Swan WI 452	Take Your Time/STRANGER COLE: Happy-Go-Lucky	20
65	Island WI 238	Trench Town People/PIONEERS: Sometime	25
65	Island WI 243	You Are The One Girl/Grudgeful People	20
65	Island WI 246	If Life Was A Thing/L. CLARKE: Parro Saw The Light (B-side actually "Pharaoh Saw The Light" by Lloyd Clarke)	18
65	Island WI 248	What A Whoe/Bajan Girl	20
68	Nu Beat NB 009	Easy Snappin'/ERIC MORRIS: My Lonely Days	30
69	Crab CRAB 25	Brother Ram Goat (as T. Beckford)/STARLIGHTS: What A Condition	20

(see also Eric Barnet[t], Maytals, Clue J & His Bluesblasters)

BOB BECKHAM
60	Brunswick 05822	Crazy Arms/Beloved	10

BED BUGS
90	Snake Rattle 01	Haywire/No Safe Haven	15

CHUCK BEDFORD
74	Bell 1378	When I See You Smile/Don't Make Me History	15

DAVID BEDFORD
75	Virgin VDJ 10	An Extract From THE RIME OF THE ANCIENT MARINER - Part Two/An Extract From THE RIME OF THE ANCIENT MARINER - Part 2 (B&W girl and dragon logo)	25
70	Argo ZRG 638	MUSIC FOR ALBION MOONLIGHT (LP, 1 side by Elizabeth Lutyens)	25
72	Dandelion 2310 165	NURSE'S SONG WITH ELEPHANTS (LP, gatefold sleeve)	30
75	Virgin V2020	STAR'S END (LP, stickered)	15

(see also Coxhill/Bedford Trio, Kevin Ayers & Whole World, Mike Oldfield, Roy Harper, Edgar Broughton Band)

BEDLAM

MINT VALUE £

BEDLAM
73	Chrysalis CFB 1	I Believe In You/Whiskey And Wine	8
73	Chrysalis CHR 1048	BEDLAM (LP)	20

(see also Cozy Powell, Ace Kefford Stand, Big Bertha, Youngblood)

BEDROCKS
68	Columbia DB 8516	Ob-La-Di-Ob-La-Da/Lucy	7

EDWIN BEE
68	Decca F 12781	I've Been Loving You/Call For My Baby	12

BEE BEE CEE
77	Rel RE 48-S	You Gotta Know Girl/We Ain't Listening (p/s, 2,000 only)	70

BEECH NUT
70	Pastel PT 1	Send For The Magician/Shot In The Dark	30

JOHNNY BEECHER
63	Warner Bros WB89	Sax Fifth Avenue/Jack Sax The City	8

BEEFEATERS
64	Pye International 7N 25277	Please Let Me Love You/Don't Be Long	100
70	Elektra 2101 007	Please Let Me Love You/Don't Be Long (reissue)	15

(see also Byrds)

BEE GEES
67	Polydor 56727	Spicks And Specks/I Am The World	8
67	Polydor 56161	New York Mining Disaster 1941/I Can't See Nobody	6
69	Polydor 56304	Odessa Parts 1 & 2 (unissued)	0
70	Polydor 56377	I.O.I.O./Sweetheart	8
81	RSO SNF 1	Night Fever (promo only 7" with p/s to coincide with ITV showing 'Saturday Night Fever' on Royal Wedding Day)	20
67	Polydor 582/583 012	BEE GEES 1ST (LP)	30
68	Polydor 582/583 020	HORIZONTAL (LP)	25
68	Polydor 236 221	RARE PRECIOUS AND BEAUTIFUL (LP)	15
68	Polydor 236 513	RARE PRECIOUS AND BEAUTIFUL VOL. 2 (LP)	15
68	Polydor 582/583 036	IDEA (LP)	15
69	Polydor 236 556	RARE PRECIOUS AND BEAUTIFUL VOL. 3 (LP)	15
69	Polydor 582 049/050	ODESSA (2-LP, felt cover, gatefold sleeve, mono)	50
69	Polydor 583 049/050	ODESSA (2-LP, felt cover, gatefold sleeve, stereo)	50
70	Polydor 2383 010	CUCUMBER CASTLE (LP)	20
70	Polydor 2310 069	TWO YEARS ON (LP)	15
71	Polydor 2383 052	TRAFALGAR (LP)	20
72	Polydor 2383 139	TO WHOM IT MAY CONCERN (LP)	15

(see also Barry Gibb, Robin Gibb, Maurice Gibb, Humpy Bong, Fut)

BEEKEEPERS
81	Rundown ACE 40	PLATFORM FIVE EP	10

MARK BEER
78	Waste WAS 001	ISOLATIONS EP	10
81	My China TAO 001	DUST ON THE ROAD (LP)	15

BEES MAKE HONEY
73	EMI EMC 3013	MUSIC EVERY NIGHT (LP)	20

BEES (UK) (1)
67	Columbia Blue Beat DB 101	Jesse James Rides Again/The Girl In My Dreams	35
68	Columbia Blue Beat DB 111	The Prisoner From Alcatraz/The Ska's The Limit	35

(see also Pyramids)

BEES (UK) (2)
80	Paw THF 003	Leave Willie Alone/Mr Gaynor	20

BEES (UK) (3)
04	Virgin VS 1884	Chicken Payback/These Are The Ghosts (Undead Version)	7
04	Virgin BEES 1	I Love You/I Love You (Instrumental)	15
01	We Love You AMOUR 6LP	SUNSHINE HIT ME (LP, inner sleeve)	30
04	Virgin V 2983	FREE THE BEES (2-LP, gatefold, with transfer)	30
07	Virgin V 3024	OCTOPUS (LP, with inner sleeve)	18

BILLY BEETHOVEN
75	DJM DJS 10377	Dreams (Out In The Forest)/We're Free	80

(see also Graham Bonnet)

BEEZ
79	Edible SNACK 001	Easy/Vagrant (gatefold p/s)	200
79	Edible SNACK 002	THE BEEZ EP: Do The Suicide (no p/s, stickered sleeve)	200

B.E.F. (BRITISH ELECTRIC FOUNDATION)
91	Ten TEN 386	Free (Edit)/Secret Life Of Arabia (stickered/unstickered p/s, as B.E.F. Featuring Billy MacKenzie, unissued 200 copies only)	40
81	Virgin BEF 1	MUSIC FOR LISTENING TO (LP)	30

(see also Heaven 17)

SI BEGG MEETS NEIL LANDSTRUMM
01	Mosquito MSQ 017	TOKYO ASSASSIN (12" EP)	10

BEGGARS FARM
84	White Rabbit WR 1001	THE DEPTH OF A DREAM (LP)	25

BEGGARS HILL
76	Moonshine MS 60	BEGGARS HILL (LP, private pressing)	175

BEGGARS OPERA
70	Vertigo 6059 026	Sarabande/Think	20
72	Vertigo 6059 060	Hobo/Pathfinder	20
73	Vertigo 6059 088	Two Timing Woman/Lady Of Hell Fire	8
74	Vertigo 6059 105	Classical Gas/Sweet Blossom Woman	6
70	Vertigo 6360 018	ACT ONE (LP, large swirl label, gatefold sleeve)	200
71	Vertigo 6360 054	WATERS OF CHANGE (LP, small swirl label, gatefold sleeve)	300

BEGINNING OF THE END

MINT VALUE £

72	Vertigo 6360 073	PATHFINDER (LP, small swirl label, foldout poster cover)	300
73	Vertigo 6360 090	GET YOUR DOG OFF ME! (LP, 'spaceship' label)	40

BEGINNING OF THE END
71	Atlantic 2091 097	Funky Nassau Parts 1 & 2 (initial pressing on red label)	15
72	Atlantic 2091 166	Monkey Tamarind/Hey Pretty Girl	15
76	Warner Bros. WEA K10021	Funky Nassau (Full Length Version)/Funky Nassau Parts 1 & 2 (12")	40
71	Atlantic K 40304	FUNKY NASSAU (LP)	40

BEIL TEECS
71	Bullet BU 491	So Far Away/BRUTE FORCE & IGNORANCE: So Far (Version)	8

SVEINBJORN BEINTEINSSON
90	Durtro 005	EDDA (LP, with booklet)	20

BELBURY POLY
10	Ghost Box GBX 701	The Young People/Portals And Parallels (with Moon Wiring Club) (p/s)	12
10	Ghost Box GBX 703	Swingalong/Mordant Music: Inn Ohn The Lake (p/s)	15
12	Ghost Box GBX 708	Now Ends The Beginning/Advisory Circle: Wildspot (p/s)	8
11	Ghost Box GBX 003	THE WILLOWS (LP)	35
12	Ghost Box GBX 016LP	THE BELBURY TAKES (LP)	25

(see also Daphne Oram)

BEL CANTOS
65	R&B MRB 5003	Feel Aw Right Parts 1 & 2	20

BELFAST GYPSIES
66	Island WI 3007	Gloria's Dream/Secret Police	80
77	Sonet SNTF 738	LEGENDARY MASTER RECORDINGS (LP)	25

(see also Them, Jackie McAuley, Freaks Of Nature)

ALEXANDER BELL
67	CBS 2977	Alexander Bell Believes/Hymn ... With Love	30

ANDY BELL
19	Sonic Cathedral SCR114	Plastic Bag/The Commune (poster p/s, clear vinyl, 200 only)	50
20	Sonic Cathedral SCR170LP	THE VIEW FROM HALFWAY DOWN (LP, white/splatter vinyl)	60

(see also Ride, Beady Eye, Motorcycle Ride)

ARCHIE BELL & THE DRELLS
68	Atlantic 584 185	Tighten Up/Dog Eat Dog	15
68	Atlantic 584 217	I Can't Stop Dancing/You're Such A Beautiful Child	15
71	Atlantic 2091 156	Tighten Up/I Can't Stop Dancing/(There's Gonna Be A) Showdown	8
72	Atlantic K 10210	Here I Go Again/A World Without Music	10
73	Atlantic K 10263	There's Gonna Be A Showdown/Tighten Up	6
76	Philly Int. 4803	Where Will You Go When The Party's Over?/I Swear You're Beautiful	15
81	Becket BKS 1	Any Time Is Right/Harder And Harder (as Archie Bell)	100
86	Nightmare MARE 16	Look Back Over Your Shoulder/Look Back Over Your Shoulder (Dub Mix) (12")	25
73	President PT 418	Girls Grow Up Faster Than Boys/Love's Gonna Rain On You	10
86	Portrait 7254	Don't Let Love Get You Down/Where Will You Go When The Party's Over/The Soul City Walk	10
99	Achievement 10006	Look Back Over Your Shoulder/(Instrumental)	8
04	UK Atlantic 504676251	A Thousand Wonders/Here I Go Again (promo only)	15
14	Outta Site OSV 124	Here I Go Again/Tighten Up (reissue)	7
68	Atlantic	TIGHTEN UP (LP)	20
72	Atlantic K 40454	HERE I GO AGAIN (LP)	20

BELINDA BELL
73	Columbia SCXA 9255	STONE VALLEY (LP, gatefold sleeve)	15

CHARLES BELL & CONTEMPORARY JAZZ QUARTET
63	London HA-K/SH-K 8095	ANOTHER DIMENSION (LP)	30

EDDIE BELL
72	Injun 109	Johnny B. Goode In Hollywood/ROYCE PORTER: A Woman Can Make You Blue	10

ERIC BELL BAND
81	Hobo HOS 016	Lonely Man/Anyone Seen My Baby (p/s)	30

(see also Thin Lizzy)

FREDDIE BELL & BELLBOYS
56	Mercury MEP 9508	ROCK WITH THE BELL BOYS (EP)	20
57	Mercury MEP 9512	ROCK WITH THE BELL BOYS VOL. 2 (EP)	30

FREDRICK BELL
68	Nu Beat NB 004	Rocksteady Cool/CARLTON ALPHONSO: I Have Changed	35

GARY BELL
67	CBS 202234	Is This What I Get For Loving You?/To Keep You	15
67	CBS 2646	Anyway That You Want Me/Leave It To Me	10

GRAHAM BELL
66	Polydor 56067	How Can I Say I Don't Love You/If You're Gonna Go	10
72	Charisma CAS 1061	GRAHAM BELL (LP, large 'mad hatter' label)	20

(see also Heavy Jelly, Griffin, Every Which Way, Skip Bifferty, Bell & Arc)

MADELINE BELL
63	HMV POP 1215	I Long For Your Love/Because You Didn't Care	20
64	Columbia DB 7257	You Don't Love Me No More/Don't Cross Over To My Side Of The Street	20
65	Columbia DB 7512	Daytime/Don't Cry My Heart	12
65	Philips BF 1448	What The World Needs Now Is Love/I Can't Wait To See My Baby's Face	30
66	Philips BF 1501	Don't Come Running To Me/I Got Carried Away	25
67	Philips BF 1611	Picture Me Gone/Go Ahead On	30
66	Philips BF 1656	One Step At A Time/You Won't See Me	15
68	Philips BF 1688	I'm Gonna Make You Love Me/I'm Gonna Leave You	15
68	Philips BF 1726	Thinkin'/Don't Give Your Love Away	10
68	Philips BF 1726	Hold It/What Am I Supposed To Do?	6
02	Jazzman JM 021	That's What Friends Are For/ALAN PARKER: That's What Friends Are For	7

William BELL

			MINT VALUE £
67	Philips SBL 7818	BELLS A POPPIN' (LP, stereo)	60
67	Philips SBL 7818	BELLS A POPPIN' (LP, mono)	70
68	Philips SBL 7865	DOIN' THINGS (LP)	60
71	Philips 6308 053	MADELINE BELL (LP)	20
73	RCA RCA 2240	COMING ATCHA (LP)	50
76	Pye NSPL 18483	THIS IS ONE GIRL (LP)	20

(see also Seven Ages Of Man, Underground, Ian Green [Revelation])

WILLIAM BELL

67	Atlantic 584 076	Never Like This Before/Soldier's Goodbye	15
67	Stax 601 019	Eloise (Hang On In There)/One Plus One	8
69	Stax STAX 110	I Forgot To Be Your Lover/Bring The Curtain Down	8
69	Stax STAX 121	My Whole World Is Falling Down/All God's Children Got Soul	8
69	Atlantic 584 259	Everyday Will Be Like A Holiday/Ain't Got No Girl	10
69	Stax STAX 128	Happy/Johnny I Love You	50
70	Stax STAX 143	Bring The Curtain Down/Born Under A Bad Sign	7
71	Stax 2025 025	Winding Winding Road/I Forgot To Be Your Lover	6
72	Stax 2025 123	Lonely For Your Love/Save Us	6
86	Tout Ensemble LUTE 1	Headline News/That's What You Get	10
69	Atco 228 003	A TRIBUTE TO A KING (LP)	40
69	Stax SXATS 1016	BOUND TO HAPPEN (LP)	35
71	Stax 2362 009	WOW . . . WILLIAM BELL (LP)	25
72	Stax 2362 027	PHASES OF REALITY (LP)	35
76	Mercury 9100038	COMING BACK FOR MORE (LP)	18
76	Stax STX 1010	RELATING (LP)	18
76	Stax STX 1050	BOUND TO HAPPEN (LP, reissue)	20
84	Charly R&B CRB 1076	DO RIGHT MAN (LP)	15

(see also Judy Clay & William Bell)

BELLA & ME

67	Columbia DB 8243	Whatever Happened To The Seven Day Week/Help Me Break This Habit	8

GEORGE BELLAMY

65	Parlophone R 5282	Where I'm Bound/How Could I Ever	20

(see also Tornados)

PETER BELLAMY

68	Xtra XTRA 1010	PETER BELLAMY (LP)	25
68	Argo XTRA 1060	MAINLY NORFOLK (LP)	80
69	Xtra XTRA 1075	FAIR ENGLAND'S SHORE (LP)	40
69	Topic 12T 200	THE FOX JUMPS OVER THE PARSON'S GATE (LP, blue label)	20
70	Argo ZFB 11	OAK, ASH AND THORN (LP)	20
72	Argo ZFB 37	WON'T YOU GO MY WAY (LP)	20
72	Argo ZFB 81	MERLIN'S ISLE OF GRAMARYE (LP)	20
74	Trailer LER 2089	TELL IT LIKE IT IS (LP)	15
77	Free Reed 21/22	TRANSPORTS (2-LP, gatefold, booklet)	20
79	Topic 12TS 400	BOTH SIDES THEN (LP)	15

(see also Young Tradition)

BELL & ARC

71	Charisma CB 170	She Belongs To Me/Dawn	6
71	Charisma CAS 1053	BELL & ARC (LP, gatefold sleeve, pink scroll label)	60

(see also Skip Bifferty, Arc, Every Which Way, Graham Bell)

BELL BROTHERS

68	Action ACT 4510	Tell Him No/Throw Away The Key	30

BELLE & SEBASTIAN

97	Jeepster JPR 7001	Dog On Wheels/The State I Am In (p/s, 1,000 only)	6
97	Jeepster JPR 12 001	Dog On Wheels/The State I Am In/String Bean Jim/Belle & Sebastian) (12")	15
97	Jeepster JPR 7002	Lazy Line Painter Jane/You Made Me Forget My Dreams (p/s, 1,000 only)	10
97	Jeepster JPR 12 002	Lazy Line Painter Jane/You Made Me Forget My Dreams/Photo Jenny/A Century Of Elvis (12")	18
10	Rough Trade RTRADS 574	God Help The Girl: Baby You're Blind/A Down And Dusky Blond	7
17	Beggars Banquet (No Cat. No.)	THE NATIONAL: England (Live)/BELLE & SEBASTIAN: The State I Am In (12" p/s, splatter vinyl, booklet)	60
96	Elektric Honey EHRLP 5	TIGERMILK (LP, 1,000 only)	400
96	Jeepster JPRLP001	IF YOU'RE FEELING SINISTER (LP, 1st pressing, gatefold)	50
99	Jeepster JPRLP007	TIGERMILK (LP, reissue)	40
98	Jeepster JPRLP003	THE BOY WITH THE ARAB STRAP (LP, gatefold)	40
00	Jeepster JPRLP010	FOLD YOUR HANDS CHILD, YOU WALK LIKE A PEASANT (LP, gatefold)	40
02	Jeepster JPRLP014	STORYTELLING (LP, gatefold)	40
04	Rough Trade RTRADELP 080	DEAR CATASTROPHE WAITRESS (2-LP)	35
05	Jeepster JRPLP015	PUSH BARMAN TO OPEN OLD WOUNDS (3-LP)	60
06	Rough Trade RTRADELP 280	THE LIFE PURSUIT (2-LP)	30
08	Jeepster JPRLP018	THE BBC SESSIONS (2-LP)	25
09	Jeepster JPRLP001	IF YOU'RE FEELING SINISTER (LP, reissue, with 'Universal Music' credit, gatefold)	20
10	Rough Trade RTRADELP 480	WRITE ABOUT LOVE (LP, with free 7")	25
13	Rough Trade RTRADLP 670	THE THIRD EYE CENTRE (2-LP)	25
14	Jeepster JPRLP003	THE BOY WITH THE ARAB STRAP (LP, reissue, with 'Universal Music' credit, gatefold)	40
14	Jeepster JPRLP015	PUSH BARMAN TO OPEN OLD WOUNDS 3-LP, reissue, with download)	30
15	Matador OLE 1056-8	GIRLS IN PEACETIME WANT TO DANCE (4-LP, with badges and poster)	30

(see also Amphetameanies, Isobel Campbell, Gentle Waves)

BELLES

70	President PT 311	Don't Pretend/Words Can't Explain	15
70	Contempo Rarities CS 9027	Don't Pretend/Words Can't Explain	8
98	Wigan Casino 210	Don't Pretend/BETTY BOO: Say It Isn't So (p/s)	10

BELLFIELD
73	Downtown DT 514	Sugar Plum/Sugar Plum Dub	6

BELLINO
63	Fontana 267259	Boss Bossa Nova/Bossa Rock	50

ERROL BELLOT
82	Jet Sounds JS 001	Don't Joke With Love/Wicked Them (with Militant Mikey, 12")	40
85	Jah Tubbys JT 012	New Kind Of Sound/Version (12", with the Offbeat Posse)	40
86	Jah Tubbys JT 019	Sound In Fury/Trouble Maker (12", with the Offbeat Posse)	45
00	Jah Tubbys JT 7002	Glory Hallalujah/DUB TEACHER: Glory Dub	20
00	Jah Tubbys JT 7004	Jah Creation/DISCIPLES RIDDIM SECTION: Creation Style	20
01	Jah Tubbys JT 7007	Roots Gone International/OFFBEAT POSSE: International Ridim	15
03	Jah Tubbys JT 014	It's War/Don't Judge (10", with the Offbeat Posse)	30
03	Jah Tubbys JT 10016	Praise H.I.M/New Life (10", with the Offbeat Posse)	30

ERROL BELLOT & DIXIE PEACH
03	Jah Tubbys JT 10011	The Warning/THE OFFBEAT POSSE: Dub Warning (10")	30

(see also Dixie Peach)

BELLS
70	Polydor 2058 099	Fly Little White Dove Fly/Follow The Sun	8
71	Philips 6006116	Stay Awhile/Simple Song Of Freedom	6
72	Polydor 2121-109	Oh My Love/You, You. You	8

TONY BELLUS
59	London HL 8933	Robbin' The Cradle/Valentine Girl	40

BELLY
93	4AD CAD 3002	STAR (LP, inner)	20
95	4AD CAD 5044	KING (LP)	30

BELMONTS
61	Pye International 7N 25094	Tell Me Why/Smoke From Your Cigarette	30
62	Stateside SS 128	Come On Little Angel/How About Me?	35

(see also Dion & Belmonts)

BELOVED (1)
88	WEA SAM 481	ACID LOVE EP (12" stamped white labels only)	60
89	WEA YZ414T	THE SUN RISING EP (12", p/s)	12
93	East West WX 500	CONSCIENCE (LP)	50
96	East West 0630-13316-1	X (with free 12")	30

BELOVED ONES
68	CBS 3303	My Year Is A Day/She And I	15

BELT & BRACES ROADSHOW BAND
75	Belt & Braces Roadshow	BELT & BRACES ROADSHOW BAND (LP, with lyric sheet)	15

BELTONES
68	Trojan TR 628	No More Heartaches/I'll Follow You	25
69	Duke DU 17	Home Without You/Why Pretend	50
69	High Note HS 017	Mary Mary/Going Away	25
69	High Note HS 023	A Broken Heart/AFROTONES: All For One	20
72	Ackee ACK 150	Wrapped Up In Love/SOUND DIMENSION: Pasero	25

(see Bop & Beltones, Trevor Shield)

JESSE BELVIN
59	RCA RCA 1119	Guess Who/Funny	10

BEN
71	Vertigo 6360 052	BEN (LP, gatefold sleeve, small swirl label)	1500

(see also Jonathan Kelly)

DAVID BENDETH
82	Sidewalk 12 SID 113	Feel The Real/Breakdown/Feel The Real (12")	12

BENDY DOG
72	Jam JAM 20	I Wanna Hear (Rock 'N' Roll Music)/Carry My Mind	10

BENGA
02	Big Apple BAM 002	Skank/Dose (12", blue vinyl)	25
02	Big Apple BAM 002	Skank/Dose (12")	10
03	Big Apple BAM 003	The Judgement (with Skream)/SKREAM: The Bug/BENGA: Amber (12", green vinyl)	30
03	Big Apple BAM 003	The Judgement (with Skream)/SKREAM: The Bug/BENGA: Amber (12")	30
04	Big Apple BAM 005	Hydro/Walkin' Bass/SKREAM: Elektro/Afrika (12")	20
04	Benga Beats BBV 01	BENGA BEATS VOLUME 1 EP (12")	20
08	Tempa TEMPA LP 010	DIARY OF AN AFRO WARRIOR (LP as 3 x 12")	20

SHARON BENGAMIN
80	Shoc Wave SRP 003	Mr Guy/Version (p/s)	10

BENNY BENGIMAN
81	Negus Roots NERT 010	Health And Sorrow/Love A Dub Song	25

JOE BENJAMIN
69	UPC 106	Good Morning Baby/Tell Me Why	30
70	UPC 111	The Same Old Song And Dance/Let Us Break Bread	25

TONY BENJAMIN & THE SANE INMATES
82	Ariwa ARI 008	Treasures In The World/Psychological Pen (12")	40
83	Ariwa ARILP 009	AFRICAN REBEL (LP)	70

BENJAMIN DELANEY LION
69	Rollick & Taylor	SATORI (LP, 70 only)	1500

BOBBY BENNETT (U.K.)
67	CBS 202511	Just Say Goodbye/She Believes In Me	7
68	Columbia DB 8435	All My Life Is You/To Give (The Reason I Live)	7
69	Columbia DB 8532	Music Mother Made/You're Ready Now	50

BOBBY BENNETT (U.S.)
69	London HL 10274	Big New York/Baby, Try Me	10

BOYD BENNETT & HIS ROCKETS (WITH BIG MOE)

MINT VALUE £

BOYD BENNETT & HIS ROCKETS (WITH BIG MOE)
55	Parlophone MSP 6161	Everlovin'/Boogie At Midnight (with Big Moe)	100
55	Parlophone MSP 6180	Seventeen/Little Ole You-All (as Boyd Bennett & His Rockets)	50
56	Parlophone MSP 6203	My Boy - Flat Top/Banjo Rock And Roll (with Big Moe)	100
56	Parlophone MSP 6233	Blue Suede Shoes/Oo-Oo-Oo (with Big Moe)	100
56	Parlophone R 4214	The Groovy Age/Hit That Jive, Jack (as Big Moe with Boyd Bennett & His Rockets)	80
56	Parlophone R 4252	The Most/Rockin' Up A Storm (as Big Moe with Boyd Bennett & His Rockets)	80
58	Parlophone R 4423	Click Clack/Move (as Boyd Bennett & His Rockets)	80
59	Mercury AMT 1031	Tear It Up/Tight Tights (as Big Moe & His Orchestra)	30

(see also Moon Mullican)

BRIAN BENNETT
67	Columbia DB 8294	Canvas/Slippery Jim De Grize	20
74	Fontana 6007 040	Chase Side Shoot-Up/Pegasus	20
76	DJM DJS 10714	Thunderbolt/Clearing Skies (promo in p/s)	10
77	DJM DJS 10756	Saturday Night Special/Farewell To A Friend (promo in p/s)	10
77	DJM DJS 10791	The Girls Back Home/Jonty Jump (as the Brian Bennett Band)	10
67	Columbia S(C)X 6144	CHANGE OF DIRECTION (LP)	50
69	Col. Studio Two TWO 268	THE ILLUSTRATED LONDON NOISE (LP)	60
77	DJM DJF 20499	ROCK DREAMS (LP, with insert, as the Brian Bennett Band)	20
78	DJM DJF 20532	VOYAGE (LP)	40

(see also Shadows, Thunder Company, Wasp, Marty Wilde, Krewcats, Collage, Alan Skidmore, Big Jim Sullivan, Heat Exchange, Julian [Scott], Mean Machine)

BRUCE BENNETT
71	Big BG 311	If You Don't Mind/Lenore (both actually by Dobby Dobson)	7

CAROLE BENNETT
57	Capitol CL 14692	Play The Music/Miser's Gold	10
57	Capitol CL 14725	Haunted Lover/Let The Chips Fall (Where They May)	20

CLIFF BENNETT & REBEL ROUSERS
61	Parlophone R 4793	You've Got What I Like/I'm In Love With You	30
61	Parlophone R 4836	That's What I Said/When I Get Paid	25
62	Parlophone R 4895	Poor Joe/Hurtin' Inside (Twist)	15
63	Parlophone R 5046	Everybody Loves A Lover/My Old Stand-By	10
63	Parlophone R 5080	You Really Got A Hold On Me/Alright	20
63	Parlophone DP 560	Poor Joe/Hurtin' Inside (Twist) (export issue, black label)	10
63	Parlophone DP 561	When I Get Paid/That's What I Said (export issue, black label)	15
64	Parlophone R 5119	Got My Mojo Working/Beautiful Dreamer	10
64	Parlophone R 5173	One Way Love/Slow Down	8
65	Parlophone R 5229	I'll Take You Home/Do You Love Him?	8
65	Parlophone R 5259	Three Rooms Of Running Water/If Only You'd Reply	10
65	Parlophone R 5317	I Have Cried My Last Tear/As Long As She Looks Like You	7
66	Parlophone R 5406	You Can't Love 'Em All/Need Your Loving Tonight	6
66	Parlophone R 5466	Eyes For You/Hold On I'm Coming	7
66	Parlophone R 5489	Got To Get You Into My Life/Baby Each Day	10
66	Parlophone R 5534	Never Knew Lovin' Could Be So Doggone Good/Don't Help Me Out	6
67	Parlophone R 5565	I'm Sorry/I'll Take Good Care Of You	6
67	Parlophone R 5598	I'll Be There/Use Me	6
69	Parlophone R 5792	Memphis Streets/But I'm Wrong	8
65	Parlophone GEP 8923	CLIFF BENNETT AND THE REBEL ROUSERS (EP)	20
65	Parlophone GEP 8936	TRY IT BABY (EP)	25
66	Parlophone GEP 8955	WE'RE GONNA MAKE IT (EP)	30
64	Parlophone PMC 1242	CLIFF BENNETT AND THE REBEL ROUSERS (LP, yellow/black label)	50
66	EMI Regal REG 1039	CLIFF BENNETT (LP, export issue)	20
67	Parlophone PMC/PCS 7017	GOT TO GET YOU INTO OUR LIFE (LP, yellow/black label)	40

CLIFF BENNETT BAND
68	Parlophone R 5666	Take Your Time/House Of A Thousand Dolls	6
68	Parlophone R 5691	You're Breaking Me Up (And I'm Wasting Away)/I Hear Her Voice	10
68	Parlophone R 5711	Lonely Weekends/Good Times	10
68	Parlophone R 5728	One More Heartache/Nobody Runs Forever	10
68	Parlophone R 5749	Back In The USSR/This Man	10
68	Parlophone PMC/PCS 7054	BRANCHES OUT (LP, yellow/black label, with "sold in the U.K." label text)	40

CLIFF BENNETT'S REBELLION
71	CBS 7231	Amos Moses/Movin' And Travelin' On	10
71	CBS 64487	CLIFF BENNETT'S REBELLION (LP)	20

(see also Charles Hodges, Rebel Rousers, Toefat, Screaming Lord Sutch & Savages)

DUSTER BENNETT
68	Blue Horizon 57-3141	It's A Man Down There/Things Are Changing	25
69	Blue Horizon 57-3148	Raining In My Heart/Jumpin' For Joy	20
69	Blue Horizon 57-3154	Bright Lights, Big City/Fresh Country Jam (with His House Band)	25
69	Blue Horizon 57-3164	I'm Gonna Wind Up Endin' Up Or I'm Gonna End Up Windin' Up With You/ Rock Of Ages, Cleft For Me	25
70	Blue Horizon 57-3173	I Chose To Sing The Blues/If You Could Hang Your Washing Like You Hang Your Lines	15
70	Blue Horizon 57-3179	Act Nice And Gentle/I Want You To Love Me	12
74	Rak RAK 177	Comin' Home/Pretty Little Thing	10
68	Blue Horizon 7-63208	SMILING LIKE I'M HAPPY (LP, mono with His House Band, i.e. Fleetwood Mac)	70
68	Blue Horizon S 7-63208	SMILING LIKE I'M HAPPY (LP, stereo with His House Band, i.e. Fleetwood Mac)	50
69	Blue Horizon S 7-63221	BRIGHT LIGHTS... (LP, gatefold sleeve)	100
70	Blue Horizon 7-63868	12 DB's (LP, with lyric sheet)	50

(see also Fleetwood Mac)

JO JO BENNETT
67	Doctor Bird DB 1097	The Lecture/Cantelope Rock (with Fugitives)	50

Joe BENNETT & SPARKLETONES

MINT VALUE £

67	Doctor Bird DB 1116	Rocksteady/Real Gone Loser (with Fugitives)	60
70	Explosion EX 2029	Groovy Jo Jo/Ten Steps To Soul (both actually with Mudie's All Stars)	30
70	Trojan TR 7774	Leaving Rome/In The Nude (both with Mudie's All Stars)	15
71	Moodisc MU 3514	Snowbird/MUDIE'S ALLSTARS: Change The Tide	12
71	Moodisc HME 108	Poison Ivy/MUDIE'S ALLSTARS: Ivy Poison	12
70	Trojan TBL 133	GROOVY JO JO (LP, with Mudie's Allstars)	50

(see also Fugitives, I Roy)

JOE BENNETT & SPARKLETONES
57	HMV POP 399	Black Slacks/Boppin' Rock Boogie	100
58	HMV POP 445	Rocket/Penny Loafers And Bobby Socks	100

LORNA BENNETT
72	Blue Mountain BM 1013	Breakfast In Bed/Skank In Bed	10
75	Island WIP 6237	Breakfast In Bed/Skank In Bed (reissue)	6

PETER E, BENNETT
71	RCA SF 8190	THE BALLAD OF GALDWAIN (LP, lyric insert, orange/white label)	15

RAY BENNETT
62	Decca DFE 8516	INTRODUCING RAY BENNETT (EP)	30

ROY BENNETT
68	Blue Cat BS 146	I Dangerous/DEE SET: I Know A Place	80

RUDI BENNETT
68	Decca F12729	I'm So Proud/You're My Adee	20

VAL BENNETT
68	Island WI 3113	Jumping With Mr. Lee/ROY SHIRLEY: Keep Your Eyes On The Road	50
68	Island WI 3146	The Russians Are Coming (Take Five)/LESTER STERLING: Sir Lee's Whip	80
68	Trojan TR 611	Spanish Harlem/ROY SHIRLEY: If I Did Know	20
69	Trojan TR 640	Baby Baby/Barbara	30
69	Crab CRAB 6	Reggae City/CANNON KING: Mellow Trumpet (B-side actually by Carl 'King Cannon Ball' Bryan)	80
69	Camel CA 24	Midnight Spin/SOUL CATS: Money Money	60

(see also Roy Shirley, Max Romeo, Derrick Morgan, Clancy Eccles, Harry J Allstars, George A Penny, Lloyd Terrell,

MARC BENNO
71	A & M AMS850	Good Year/Second Story Window	8

JON BENNS
80	Aveda AVA 106	BENNS MEANS LAFFS (LP)	15

(see also The Enid)

BENNY (AKA B.E.N.N.Y THE BUTCHER)
18	Daupe! DM SP 032	BUTCHER ON STEROIDS (12", p/s, with DJ Green Lantern, 187 copies)	100
18	Daupe! DM SP 032	BUTCHER ON STEROIDS (12", p/s, with DJ Green Lantern, red vinyl, 187 copies)	100
18	Daupe! DM SP 032	BUTCHER ON STEROIDS (12", p/s, with DJ Green Lantern, green vinyl, 187 copies)	100
18	Daupe! DM SP 032	BUTCHER ON STEROIDS (12", p/s, with DJ Green Lantern, cream vinyl, 187 copies)	100
18	Daupe! DM SP 032	BUTCHER ON STEROIDS (12", p/s, with DJ Green Lantern, with obi strip 20 copies)	300
19	Daupe! DM SP 041	TANA TALK 3 (2-LP, 500 copies)	200
19	Daupe! DM SP 041	TANA TALK 3 (2-LP, blue vinyl, 333 copies)	300
19	Daupe! DM SP 041	TANA TALK 3 (2-LP, splatter vinyl, 333 copies)	300
19	Daupe! DM SP 041	TANA TALK 3 (2-LP, white vinyl, 333 copies)	300
19	Daupe! DM SP 041	TANA TALK 3 (2-LP, with obi strip, 20 copies)	500

BENNY & TINA
69	Mercury MF 1133	This Love Is Real/Over My Dead Body	10

BARRY BENSON
66	Parlophone R 5446	Stay A Little While/That's For Sure	35
66	Parlophone R 5446	Stay A Little While/That's For Sure (DJ Copy)	50
66	Parlophone R 5484	Not A One Girl Guy/Sunshine Child	25
66	Parlophone R 5544	Always Waitin'/My Friend And I	8
67	Parlophone R 5578	Cousin Jane/Meet Jacqueline	20
67	Page One POF 034	I Can't Wait/Oh No	10

GARY BENSON
73	Birth RAB 1002	The Concert/To Kill Another Day	10
70	Penny Farthing PELS 506	THE REUNION (LP)	50
73	Birth RAB 5	THE CONCERT (LP, gatefold sleeve)	30

GEORGE BENSON (QUARTET)
80	Warner Bros. LV 40	Give Me The Night/The World Is A Ghetto (12")	15
66	CBS (S)BPG 62817	IT'S UPTOWN (LP, flipback sleeve, as George Benson Quartet)	25
67	CBS (S)BPG 62971	THE GEORGE BENSON COOKBOOK (LP)	15
69	A&M AMLS 945	SHAPE OF THINGS TO COME (LP)	30
72	CTI 6015	WHITE RABBIT (LP)	15
73	CTI CTL 20	BODY TALK (LP, gatefold)	15
76	CTI CTI 6063	GOOD KING BAD (LP, gatefold)	15
76	CTI CTI 6069	BENSON & FARREN (LP, with Joe Farrell)	15
76	Warner Bros. K56199	BREEZIN' (LP)	15
77	Warner Bros. K56327	IN FLIGHT (LP)	15
78	CTI CTI 7085	SPACE (LP)	15

SHARON BENSON
95	Leap Of Faith LEAP 002	Anything For You (Remake)/(For The People Mix)/(Original)/(Remake)/(80s Old School)/(Rare Mix) (12")	30
95	Leap Of Faith LEAP 003	Rock Me Down (Full Freddie Mix)/(Sugar Johnson Rare Mix)/(Marvin Gaye Remix)/(Dark Knight Bass Head Remix)/(Lex Mix) (12")	30
95	Leap Of Faith LEAP 001LP	SHARON BENSON (LP, plain die-cut sleeve)	30

BENT
00	Sport SPORTLP 01	PROGRAMMED TO LOVE (2-LP without free 7")	35
00	Sport SPORTLPX 01	PROGRAMMED TO LOVE (2-LP with free 7")	45

Michael BENTINE

MINT VALUE £

MICHAEL BENTINE
62	Parlophone 4927	Football Results/The Astronauts	7
62	Parlophone PMC 1179	IT'S A SQUARE WORLD (LP, also stereo PCS 3031)	15

ACE BENTLEY
81	Traffic Light TL 181	Beat Boys/Sometimes In The Night (p/s)	40

BRIAN BENTLEY & THE BACHELORS
60	Philips PB 1085	Wishing Well/Please Make Up Your Mind	25
62	Salvo SLO 1813	Caramba/Nellie Dean (99 copies only)	10

ED BENTLEY
79	SB SB 1001	Bentley Boogie/Hot E/Walk On High (12")	60

BROOK BENTON & DINAH WASHINGTON
60	Mercury AMT 1083	Baby (You've Got What It Takes)/I Do	12
60	Mercury AMT 1099	A Rockin' Good Way/I Believe	12
61	Mercury ZEP 10120	A ROCKING GOOD WAY (EP, mono)	12
61	Mercury SEZ 19022	A ROCKING GOOD WAY (EP, stereo)	15
64	Mercury 20069 MCL	THE TWO OF US (LP)	15

STEVE BERESFORD
75	Incus INCUS 15	TEATIME (LP)	40

BERETS
70	Avant Garde AVS 116	THE MASS FOR PEACE (LP, with insert)	20

BERKELEY KITES
68	Polydor 56742	Hang Up City/Mary-Go-Round	10
69	Polydor 56770	Alice In Wonderland/What Goes Up Must Come Down	10

BERLIN BLONDES
80	EMI EMC 3346	BERLIN BLONDES (LP)	15

BERLIN RITZ
80	Big Muff BM 001	Crazy Nights/You're Where I Belong (no p/s)	10

BERLIN WALLS
83	La Rondie LK 101	Night And Day/You Can't Do That	10
83	Passport PORT 101	Stop/You Don't Have To Live That Way	8

BERMUDAS
64	London HLN 9894	Donnie/Chu Sen Ling	8

BERNADETTE
67	Rim RIM 2	Come Kiss Me Love/Let Me Do The Talking	20
68	Philips 1725	Toys, Toys, Toys/Kiss And Run Away	10

JACKIE BERNARD
71	Fab FAB 16	Torture And Flames/WESTMORELITES: Longing To Hold You (promo only, black label)	70
72	KSK 001	Tribute To Slim Smith (Soul Dragon)/Version (white label only)	50
76	Grounation GRO 2061	Fantasy Rock/Roots Music	12
78	One Stop OSM 001	Keep Rowing/Version (12")	50

(see also Kingstonians)

KENNY BERNARD (& WRANGLERS)
65	Pye 7N 15920	The Tracker/You Gotta Give (with Wranglers)	20
65	Pye 7N 15920	The Tracker/You Gotta Give (with Wranglers) (DJ Copy)	125
66	Pye 7N 17131	Nothing Can Change This Love/What Love Brings	70
66	Pye 7N 17131	Nothing Can Change This Love/What Love Brings (DJ Copy)	100
67	Pye 7N 17233	Ain't No Soul (Left In These Old Shoes)/Hey Woman	40
67	Pye 7N 17284	I Do/Isn't That A Good Idea	15
67	CBS 2936	Somebody/Pity My Feet	100
67	CBS 2936	Somebody/Pity My Feet (DJ copy)	150
68	CBS 3860	Victim Of Perfume And Lace/A Change Is Gonna Come	25

(see also Kenny & Wranglers, Wranglers, Cat's Pyjamas)

ROD BERNARD
59	London HLM 8849	This Should Go On Forever/Pardon, Mr. Gordon	20
59	Mercury AMT 1070	One More Chance/Shedding Teardrops Over You	10

BERNHARDTS
84	Parlophone 12R 6078	I Hear You Calling (Extended)/Send Your Heart To Me (Extended) (12" p/s)	20
84	Parlophone R6078	I Hear You Calling/Send Your Heart To Me	7

BERNIE & BUZZ BAND
68	Decca F 22829	The House That Jack Built/PETE KELLY'S SOULUTION: Midnight Confessions (export issue)	18
68	Deram DM 181	When Something's Wrong With My Baby/Don't Knock It	35

(see also Pete Kelly's Soulution)

BERNIE & MYSTERIONS
81	Chipping Norton CHIP 5	Another Night/Front Seat Love (no p/s)	8

ELMER BERNSTEIN
59	Capitol CL 15101	Staccato's Theme/The Jazz At Waldo's	7
62	MGM 1164	Walk On The Wild Side/Walk On The Wild Side Jazz	7
63	MGM MGM 1238	Rat Race/Saints & Sinners	20
63	MGM MGM 1238	Rat Race/Saints & Sinners (DJ Copy)	40
56	Brunswick LAT 8101	THE MAN WITH THE GOLDEN ARM (LP, soundtrack)	20
57	Brunswick LAT 8195	SWEET SMELL OF SUCCESS (LP, soundtrack)	20
62	MGM MGM-C 891	WALK ON THE WILD SIDE (LP, soundtrack)	15
63	MGM MGM-C 934	TO KILL A MOCKINGBIRD (LP, soundtrack)	15
63	United Artists ULP 1041	THE GREAT ESCAPE (LP, soundtrack, mono/stereo)	15
67	RCA Victor RD 7792	THE SILENCERS (LP, soundtrack, feat. Vikki Carr)	30

ROCK BERNTSEN
84	Forest Tracks FT 3017	KELPERS AFTER ALL (LP, with insert)	18

Chuck BERRY

MINT VALUE £

CHUCK BERRY
78s
Year	Catalogue	Title	Value
56	London HLU 8275	Down Bound Train/No Money Down	50
57	London HLN 8375	You Can't Catch Me/Havana Moon	35
57	London HLU 8428	Roll Over Beethoven/Drifting Heart	25
58	London HL 8677	Beautiful Delilah/Vacation Time	20
58	London HL 7055	Carol/Hey Pedro (export single)	30
58	London HL 8712	Carol/Hey Pedro	25
58	London HLM 8767	Sweet Little Rock And Roller/Jo Jo Gun	35
59	London HLM 8853	Almost Grown/Little Queenie	50
59	London HLM 8921	Back In The U.S.A./Memphis, Tennessee	50

SINGLES
Year	Catalogue	Title	Value
56	London HLU 8275	No Money Down/Down Bound Train (silver lettering on label, triangular centre)	400
56	London HLU 8275	No Money Down/Down Bound Train (silver lettering on label, round centre)	150
57	London HLN 8375	You Can't Catch Me/Havana Moon (gold lettering on label)	350
57	London HLN 8375	You Can't Catch Me/Havana Moon (silver lettering on label)	100
57	London HLU 8428	Roll Over Beethoven/Drifting Heart	50
57	Columbia DB 3951	School Day (Ring! Ring! Goes The Bell)/Deep Feeling	50
57	London HLM 8531	Rock And Roll Music/Blue Feeling	30
58	London HLM 8585	Sweet Little Sixteen/Reelin' And Rockin'	30
58	London HLM 8629	Johnny B. Goode/Around And Around	25
58	London HL 8677	Beautiful Delilah/Vacation Time	25
58	London HL 8712	Carol/Hey Pedro	25
58	London HL 7055	Carol/Hey Pedro (export issue)	25
58	London HLM 8767	Sweet Little Rock And Roller/Jo Jo Gun	25
59	London HLM 8853	Almost Grown/Little Queenie	25
59	London HLM 8921	Back In The U.S.A./Memphis, Tennessee	25

(Originally issued with triangular centres; later silver top label/round centre pressings are worth half to two-thirds these values.)

Year	Catalogue	Title	Value
60	London HLM 9069	Let It Rock/Too Pooped To Pop	25
60	London HLM 9159	Bye Bye Johnny/Mad Lad	25
61	Pye International 7N 25100	I'm Talkin' 'Bout You/Little Star (blue label)	25
61	Pye International 7N 25100	I'm Talkin' 'Bout You/Little Star (later red/yellow label)	10
63	Pye International 7N 25209	Go Go Go/Come On	10
63	Pye International 7N 25218	Memphis, Tennessee/Let It Rock	6
63	Pye International 7N 25228	Run Rudolph Run/Johnny B. Goode	10
64	Pye International 7N 25236	Nadine (Is It You?)/O Rangutang	10
64	Pye International 7N 25242	No Particular Place To Go/Liverpool Drive	6
64	Pye International 7N 25257	You Never Can Tell/Brenda Lee	7
64	Pye International 7N 25271	Little Marie/Go Bobby Soxer	10
65	Pye International 7N 25285	The Promised Land/The Things I Used To Do	10
65	Chess CRS 8006	I Got A Booking/Lonely School Days	10
65	Chess CRS 8012	Dear Dad/My Little Lovelight	6

EPs
Year	Catalogue	Title	Value
56	London REU 1053	RHYTHM AND BLUES WITH CHUCK BERRY (maroon/gold label, tri-centre)	150
56	London REU 1053	RHYTHM AND BLUES WITH CHUCK BERRY (later pressing, maroon/silver label, round centre)	40
60	London REM 1188	REELIN' AND ROCKIN' (maroon and gold label, tri centre)	250
60	London REM 1188	REELIN' AND ROCKIN' (round centre)	100
63	Pye Intl. NEP 44011	CHUCK BERRY	15
63	Pye Intl. NEP 44013	THIS IS CHUCK BERRY	15
64	Pye Intl. NEP 44018	THE BEST OF CHUCK BERRY	15
64	Pye Intl. NEP 44028	CHUCK BERRY HITS	15
64	Pye Intl. NEP 44033	BLUE MOOD	15
65	Chess CRE 6002	THE PROMISED LAND	15
65	Chess CRE 6005	COME ON	15
66	Chess CRE 6012	I GOT A BOOKING	15
66	Chess CRE 6016	YOU CAME A LONG WAY FROM ST. LOUIS	25

ALBUMS
Year	Catalogue	Title	Value
58	London HA-M 2132	ONE DOZEN BERRYS	150
60	Pye Intl. NPL 28019	NEW JUKE BOX HITS	30
63	Pye Intl. NPL 28024	CHUCK BERRY	20
63	Pye Intl. NPL 28027	CHUCK BERRY ON STAGE	20
63	Pye Intl. NPL 28028	MORE CHUCK BERRY	20
64	Pye Intl. NPL 28031	THE LATEST AND THE GREATEST	20
64	Pye Intl. NPL 28039	YOU NEVER CAN TELL	20
65	Chess CRL 4005	CHUCK BERRY IN LONDON	20
65	Chess CRL 4506	FRESH BERRYS	20

CHUCK BERRY/BO DIDDLEY
Year	Catalogue	Title	Value
63	Pye Intl. NEP 44009	CHUCK AND BO (EP)	10
63	Pye Intl. NEP 44012	CHUCK AND BO, VOL. 2 (EP)	12
64	Pye Intl. NEP 44017	CHUCK AND BO, VOL. 3 (EP)	15
73	Chess 6145 012	BIG DADDIES (LP)	10

(see also Bo Diddley)

DAVE BERRY (& CRUISERS)
Year	Catalogue	Title	Value
64	Decca F 12020	One Heart Between Two/You're Gonna Need Somebody	10
65	Decca F 12103	Little Things/I've Got A Tiger By The Tail	6
65	Decca F 12188	This Strange Effect/Now	6
65	Decca F 12258	I'm Gonna Take You There/Just Don't Know	6

Heidi BERRY

MINT VALUE £

Year	Catalogue	Title	Value
66	Decca F 12337	If You Wait For Love/Hidden	6
66	Decca F 12513	Picture Me Gone/Ann	10
67	Decca F 12579	Stranger/Stick By The Book	7
67	Decca F 12651	Forever/And I Have Learned To Dream	7
68	Decca F 12739	Just As Much As Ever/I Got A Feeling	8
68	Decca F 12771	(Do I Figure) In Your Life/Latisha	8
69	Decca F 12905	Huma Lama Oh What A Life (by Dave Berry & Sponge)	8
70	Decca F 12999	Change Our Minds/Long Walk To D.C.	8
70	Decca F 13080	Chaplin House/Trees	10
72	CBS 7780	Movin' On (Turn Around)/Don't Bring Me Down	10
88	Flagstaff 002	Out Of Time/Serenade To Alice (p/s, 200 only)	10
65	Decca DFE 8625	CAN I GET IT FROM YOU (EP)	15
64	Decca DFE 8601	DAVE BERRY (EP)	15
64	Decca LK 4653	DAVE BERRY (LP)	20
66	Ace Of Clubs ACL 1218	ONE DOZEN BERRIES (LP, also stereo SCL 1218)	15
66	Decca LK 4823	THE SPECIAL SOUND OF DAVE BERRY (LP)	15
68	Decca LK/SKL 4932	DAVE BERRY '68 (LP)	20

(see also Cruisers)

HEIDI BERRY

Year	Catalogue	Title	Value
87	Creation CRELP 023	FIREFLY (LP)	15
89	Creation CRELP 048	BELOW THE WAVES (LP)	20
91	4AD CAD 1012	LOVE (LP)	25
93	4AD CAD 3009	HEIDI BERRY (LP)	30
96	4AD CAD 6011	MIRACLE (LP)	35

LEN & BARBARA BERRY

Year	Catalogue	Title	Value
60s	Greenwich Village GVR 229	THE PORTWAY PEDDLERS (LP)	50

MIKE BERRY (& THE OUTLAWS)

Year	Catalogue	Title	Value
61	Decca F 11314	Will You Love Me Tomorrow/My Baby Doll (with The Outlaws)	10
62	HMV POP 979	It's Just A Matter Of Time/Little Boy Blue (backing group miscredited as Admirals, actually The Outlaws)	8
62	HMV POP 1042	Every Little Kiss/How Many Times	8
63	HMV POP 1194	It Really Doesn't Matter/Try A Little Bit Harder	7
64	HMV POP 1257	This Little Girl/On My Mind	10
64	HMV POP 1284	Lovesick/Letter Of Love	8
64	HMV POP 1314	Who Will It Be/Talk (with Innocents)	8
64	HMV POP 1362	Two Lovers/Don't Try To Stand In My Way	10
65	HMV POP 1449	That's All I Ever Wanted From You/She Didn't Care	10
65	HMV POP 1494	It Comes And Goes/Gonna Fall In Love	12
66	HMV POP 1530	Warm Baby/Just Thought I'd 'Phone	15
63	HMV 7EG 8808	A TRIBUTE TO BUDDY HOLLY (EP)	20

(see also Outlaws, Le Roys, Shepperton Flames, Innocents [U.K], UK Jones)

RICHARD BERRY & PHARAOHS

Year	Catalogue	Title	Value
64	Ember EMB EP 4527	RHYTHM AND BLUES VOL. 3 (EP)	100

CINDY LEE BERRYHILL

Year	Catalogue	Title	Value
89	Awareness AWP 001	Me, Steve, Kirk And Keith/Baby (Should I Have The Baby) (p/s)	6

BERRY STREET STATION

Year	Catalogue	Title	Value
75	Crystal CR 7024	Chocolate Sugar/All I Want Is You	15

BERTY B AND DILLINJA

Year	Catalogue	Title	Value
95	Lionheart BERT1	Lionheart/Art Of Control (12")	15

(see also Dillinja, Cybotron Featuring Dillinja)

BESHARA

Year	Catalogue	Title	Value
82	Home Spun HS 002	Glory Glory/Version (12")	80
84	Mass Media Music MM121004	Men Cry Too/Version (12", purple vinyl)	20

ADAM BEST

Year	Catalogue	Title	Value
70	Fontana SFL 13209	WALL OF SOUND (LP)	20

PETE BEST FOUR

Year	Catalogue	Title	Value
64	Decca F 11929	I'm Gonna Knock On Your Door/Why Did I Fall In Love With You?	60

(see also Beatles, Lee Curtis & All Stars)

BEST EVER

Year	Catalogue	Title	Value
75	Polydor 2001594	Rope A Dope/People's Choice (with Muhammad Ali)	20

RICHARD BESWICK & PHILIPP WACHSMANN

Year	Catalogue	Title	Value
81	Bead Records BEAD 18	HELLO BRENDA! (LP)	25

BETA BAND

Year	Catalogue	Title	Value
97	Regal REG 16	CHAMPION VERSIONS EP: Dry The Rain/I Know/B+A/Dog's Got A Bone (12", p/s, 1,000 only)	80
98	Regal REG 18	THE PATTY PATTY SOUND EP: Inner Meet Me/The House/The Monolith/ She's The One (2 x 12", p/s, 1,000 only)	40
98	Regal REG 20	LOS AMIGOS DEL BETA BANDITOS EP: Push It Out/It's Over/Dr Baker/Needles In My Eyes (12", p/s)	30
13	Regal REGS 16	CHAMPION VERSIONS (12", reissue 750 only)	25
13	Regal REGS 18	THE PATTY PATTY SOUND (12", reissue, 750 only)	25
13	Regal REGS 20	LOS AMIGOS DEL BETA BANDITOS (12", reissue, 750 only)	20
99	Regal REG 30	THE BETA BAND (2-LP)	50
01	Regal REG 59	HOT SHOTS II (2-LP)	50
04	Regal REG 101	HEROS TO ZEROS (LP, gatefold sleeve)	40

(see also Aliens)

BETTERDAYS

Year	Catalogue	Title	Value
65	Polydor BM 56024	Don't Want That/Here 'Tis	175
96	Dig The Fuzz DIG 008	HOWLIN' (LP, with booklet)	15

HAROLD BETTERS
| 65 | Sue WI 378 | Do Anything You Wanna (Parts 1 & 2) | 60 |

AL BETTS
| 73 | Peer Int. PIL 9018 | CONTRASTS IN JAZZ VOLUME 2 (LP) | 15 |

BETWEEN PICTURES
| 81 | A Side AS 002 | Treat Me Like An Equal/Life On Your Own | 15 |
| 81 | Applause CLAP 3 | Birthday Card/Down At The Factory (p/s) | 6 |

BEVERLEY
| 66 | Deram DM 101 | Happy New Year/Where The Good Times Are | 50 |
| 67 | Deram DM 137 | Museum/DENNY CORDELL TEA TIME ENSEMBLE: A Quick One For Sanity | 35 |

(see also John & Beverley Martyn, Levee Breakers)

BEVERLEY SISTERS
| 56 | Decca F 10705 | Willie Can/I've Started Courtin' | 10 |
| 55 | Philips BBR 8052 | A DATE WITH THE BEVS (10" LP) | 20 |

BEVERLEY & DUANE
| 97 | Expansion EXLPM2 | BEVERELY & DUANE (LP, reissue) | 15 |

BEVERLEY'S ALLSTARS
65	Black Swan WI 449	Go Home/THEO BECKFORD: Ungrateful People	25
69	Trojan TR 683	Double Shot/Gimme Gimme Gal (B-side act. "Banana Water" by Mellotones)	50
70	Trojan TR 7729	Moon Dust/Fat Cat (both sides actually by Ansell Collins)	30

(see also Clarendoinians, Gaylads, Ken Boothe, Glen Brown, Desmond Dekker, Bob Marley, Maytals, Melodians, Derrick Morgan, Pioneers, Rockstones, Bruce Ruffin, Delroy Wilson)

FRANK BEVERLY & BUTLERS
| 79 | Inferno HEAT 4 | If That's What You Wanted/Love (Your Pain Goes Deep) (with p/s) | 10 |
| 00 | Goldmine Soul Supply GS002 | If That's What You Wanted/EDDIE FOSTER: I Never Knew (reissue, as Frankie Beverly) | 30 |

BEVERLY HILLS BLUES BAND
| 76 | Warner Bros K 16752 | Just Because/If I Can Just Get Through Tonight | 15 |

(see also Four Seasons)

BEVIS FROND
88	Bucketfull/Brains BOB 21	High In A Flat/DREAM SYNDICATE: Blind Willie McTell (free with Bucketfull Of Brains issue 27, 33rpm, yellow die-cut sleeve)	12
88	Bucketfull/Brains BOB 21	High In A Flat/DREAM SYNDICATE: Blind Willie McTell (without Bucketfull Of Brains)	7
87	Woronzow WOO 3	MIASMA (LP, laminated cover, 500 copies only)	20
87	Woronzow WOO 5 1/2	BEVIS THROUGH THE LOOKING GLASS - THE GREAT MAGNET DISASTER (2-LP, 500 only, originals all signed, with booklet; counterfeits unsigned)	40
88	Woronzow WOO 8	TRIPTYCH (LP)	20
80s	Reckless RECKLP 15	TRIPTYCH (LP, reissue)	15
92	Woronzow WOO 26	SUPERSEEDER (2-LP)	30
93	Woronzow WOO 22	SPRAWL (2-LP, gatefold sleeve, with insert)	30
96	Woronzow WOO28	SON OF WALTER (2-LP)	30
97	Woronzow WOO 406	NORTH CIRCULAR (3-LP, with insert, 750 only, signed & numbered)	75
99	Woronzow WOO 31	VAVONA BURR (2-LP)	35
00	Woronzow WOO 42	VALEDICTORY SONGS (2-LP)	35

(see also Von Trap Family, Room 13)

RODNEY BEWES
| 69 | Revolution REV 1003 | Remember When/Dear Mother Love Albert | 10 |
| 70 | Revolution Pop REVP 1001 | Dear Mother Love Albert/Meter Maid | 10 |

(see also Highly Likely)

BEYOND THE IMPLODE
| 79 | Diverse DIVE 101 | LAST THOUGHTS EP (EP, 250 copies with hand-written labels, numbered, with 'Look Back' Fanzine) | 250 |
| 80 | Diverse DIVE 102 | 11th HOUR BREAKDOWN EP | 75 |

BEYOND THE WIZARD'S SLEEVE
05	3rd Mynd 02	BEYOND THE WIZARD'S SLEEVE (LP)	15
06	3rd Mynd 03	SPRING (LP)	18
07	3rd Mynd 04	GEORGE (LP, red vinyl)	15
07	3rd Mynd 05	WEST (LP, clear vinyl)	15

BEYOND THE QUARRY
| 92 | Flair (No Cat. No) | Comedown/Disappointment/One Way/Relegate (12", purple vinyl) | 70 |

B-52'S
79	PSR 438	Rock Lobster/52 Girls (p/s, reproduction of original US pressing, given away free with The B-52'S LP)	15
79	Island WIP 6506	Rock Lobster/Running Around (glossy p/s)	6
79	Island ILPS 9580	THE B-52's (LP, insert, with bonus single "Rock Lobster"/"52 Girls" [PSR 438])	40
79	Island ILPS 9580	THE B-52's (LP, insert, without bonus single "Rock Lobster"/"52 Girls" [PSR 438])	20
80	Island ILPS 9622	WILD PLANET (LP, in plastic bag with badge)	20

B FILM
| 80 | Plastic Records BEE 001 | Night Running/Danger Man | 20 |

BG AND THE MOUSE
| 82 | Maestro MR 003 | Da Doo Ron Ron/Clever Boy (no p/s) | 10 |

BG FROM BASS INC
| 88 | Black Steel BS002 | Rock The Boat (12") | 10 |

MAURICIO BIANCHI
| 81 | Sterile SR 2 | SYMPATHY FOR A GENOCIDE (LP, 200 only) | 200 |
| 83 | Broken BV 3 | THE PLAIN TRUTH (LP) | 70 |

GENE BIANCO GROUP
| 60 | Vogue V 9167 | Alarm Clock Rock/Harp Rock Boogie | 30 |

BIBBY
| 65 | Blue Beat BB 289 | Rub It Down/Wicked Man (actually by Harris Seaton) | 30 |

(see also B.B. Seaton, Horace Seaton)

BIBIO

MINT VALUE £

BIBIO
09	Warp WARPLP 177	AMBIVALANCE AVENUE (2-LP)	30
09	Warp WARPLP 190	THE APPLE AND THE TOOTH (LP)	25

BICYCLE
92	Warriors Dance WAFT 002T	Bicycle (Vocal Mix)/(Dub Mix) (12")	10

BID
86	El GPO 10	Reach For Your Gun/Sweet Chariots (p/s)	6
86	El GPO 10T	Reach For Your Gun/Love/Sweet Chariots (12", p/s)	12

(see also the Monochrome Set)

BIDDU
67	Regal Zonophone RZ 3002	Daughter Of Love/Look Out Here I Come	15
77	Epic EPC 5416	Soul Coaxing/Nirvana (12", p/s)	15
78	Epic EPCS 6230	Blacker Than Berry/James Bond Disco Theme (12", white label promo only)	15

BIFF BANG POW!
84	Creation CRE 003	Fifty Years Of Fun/Then When I Scream (foldaround sprayed p/s in poly bag)	30
84	Creation CRE 007	There Must Be A Better Life/The Chocolate Elephant Man (foldaway p/s in poly bag)	30
90	Caff CAFF 13	Sleep/TIMES: Extase (p/s, with insert)	20
90	Creation CRELP 058	SONGS FOR THE SAD EYED GIRL (LP)	15
91	Creation CRELP 099	L'AMOUR, DEMURE, STENHOUSEMUIR (LP)	20

(see also Laughing Apple, Times)

BIFFY CLYRO
99	Babi Yaga YAGA 001	Iname/All The Way Down (Chapter 2)/Travis Perkins (CD)	100
00	Electric Honey HER 013 CD	Thekidswhopoptodaywillrocktomorrow (CD, 1000 only)	80
01	Beggars Banquet BBQ 335	Justboy/Unsubtle/Being Gabriel (p/s)	20
01	Beggars Banquet BBQ 352	27/Breatheher/Instructio4 (p/s)	20
02	Beggars Banquet BBQ 358	57/Kill The Old, Torture Their Young (Evening Session Version) (p/s)	20
02	Beggars Banquet BBQ 361	Joy. Discovery. Invention/Toys Toys Toys Choke/Toys Toys Toys/All The Way Down Chapter 2 (p/s)	12
03	Beggars Banquet BBQ 365	The Ideal Height/...And With The Scissorkick Is Victorious (p/s)	10
03	Beggars Banquet BBQ 374	Eradicate The Doubt/The Ideal Height (Live)/Justboy (Live) (p/s, numbered)	10
04	Beggars Banquet BBQ 377	Glitter And Trauma/There's No Such Thing As A Jaggy Snake (Peel Session) (p/s)	8
07	14th Floor 14FLR21V1	Living Is A Problem Because Everything Dies/Loneliness (p/s, blue vinyl, poster)	8
07	14th Floor 14FLR21V2	Living Is A Problem Because Everything Dies/Kittens Cakes And Cuddles (p/s, red vinyl, poster)	8
07	14th Floor 14FR24V1	Folding Stars/Coward (stickered p/s, with poster, blue vinyl)	8
07	14th Floor 14FLR27V1	Machines (Alternative Version)/Classical Machines (gatefold p/s, sky blue vinyl, poster, numbered)	8
02	Beggars Banquet BBQLP226	BLACKENED SKY (LP)	70
03	Beggars Banquet BBQLP233	THE VERTIGO OF BLISS (LP)	75
04	Beggars Banquet BBQLP238	INFINITY LAND (LP)	75
09	14th Floor 5051865629702	ONLY REVOLUTIONS (LP, 2-CD, DVD box set)	250
10	14th Floor 825646789566	LONELY REVOLUTIONS (2-LP, 300 only)	300
12	Beggars Banquet BBQLP2089	BLACKENED SKY (2-LP, reissue, purple vinyl)	30
12	Beggars Banquet BBQLP2091	INFINITY LAND (2-LP, reissue, grey vinyl)	30
13	Beggars Banque tBBQLP 2090	THE VERTIGO OF BLISS (2-LP, reissue, white vinyl, 300 only)	50
13	14th Floor 825646550371	OPPOSITES (2-LP, 3-CD and DVD box set)	70

BIG AFRICA
87	Leopard BALMS 2	I Need You/I Need You Dub	25
87	Leopard BALMT 2	I Need You/I Need You Dub (12")	50

BIG AMONGST SHEEP
83	Rock Solid RSS 01	ASTROPOP (12" EP, p/s)	12
82	Rock Solid RSR 2001	TERMINAL VELOCITY (LP)	60

(see also Inner City Unit, Silverwing)

BIG AUDIO DYNAMITE
86	CBS 6051477	C'mon Every Beatbox/Badrock City (p/s)	6
85	CBS CK 40220	THIS IS BIG AUDIO DYNAMITE (LP, inner)	18
90	CBS 4674661	KOOL-AID (LP, as Big Audio Dynamite II)	25
91	Columbia 4677061	THE GLOBE (LP, as Big Audio Dynamite II)	35
94	Columbia C2S 6214	HIGHER POWER (2-LP as Big Audio)	40

(see also The Clash, Carbon/Silicon)

BIG BARON
60	Top Rank JAR 404	Swinging Bells (Oberon Jump)/Romance	8

BIG BERTHA FEATURING ACE KEFFORD
69	Atlantic 584 298	This World's An Apple/Gravy Booby Jamm	35

(see also Cozy Powell, Ace Kefford Stand, Bedlam, Youngblood)

BIG BIG TRAIN
17	Plane Groovy PLGS 07	Merry Christmas/Snowfalls (p/s, white vinyl)	6
91	Least Peculiar (no cat no)	FROM THE RIVER TO THE SEA (cassette)	30
92	English Peculiar BBTLPT2	FROM THE RIVER TO THE SEA (CD)	70
93	Least Peculiar BBT LPT3	THE INFANT HERCULES (cassette)	60
02	Tree Frog TFCD 001	BARD (CD)	40
04	Tree Frog TFCD 002	GATHERING SPEED (CD)	30
12	Plane Groovy PLG 010	ENGLISH ELECTRIC PART ONE (2-LP, numbered, 500 only)	200
13	Plane Groovy PLG 017	ENGLISH ELECTRIC PART TWO (2-LP, numbered, 500 only)	100
16	Plane Groovy PLG 044	FOLKLORE (2-LP)	70
17	Plane Groovy PLG 050	GRIMSPOUND (2-LP)	40
17	Plane Groovy PLG 044	FOLKLORE (2-LP, reissue, blue vinyl)	45
17	Plane Groovy PLG 056	THE SECOND BRIGHTEST STAR (2-LP, foam green vinyl)	60
18	Plane Groovy PLG 071	MERCHANTS OF LIGHT (3-LP, box set)	50
19	Plane Groovy PLG 074	GRAND TOUR (2-LP, clear vinyl)	40

BIG BLACK

MINT VALUE £

Year	Label/Cat #	Description	Value
19	Plane Groovy PLG 078	ENGLISH ELECTRIC PART ONE (2-LP, reissue, blue vinyl)	40
19	Plane Groovy PLG 017	ENGLISH ELECTRIC PART TWO (2-LP, reissue, orange vinyl)	40

BIG BLACK

Year	Label/Cat #	Description	Value
85	Homestead HMS 007	RACER-X (12" EP, with insert)	12
87	Blast First BFFP 14T	HEADACHE (12" p/s, 1,000 only, free 45, Heartbeat/"Things To Do Today"/"I Can't Believe")	12
86	Homestead HMS 044	HAMMER PARTY (LP)	15
86	Blast First BFFP 11	ATOMIZER (LP)	18
87	Blast First BFFP 19	SONGS ABOUT FUCKING (LP, usually with sticker over 'Fucking')	25
87	Blast First CHAT 2	TALK ABOUT FUCKING (LP, promo interview disc with question sheet insert)	15
87	NOT 2 (BUT 1)	SOUND OF IMPACT (LP, matt sleeve, numbered up to 1,000, with 8-page booklet)	30
87	NOT 2 (BUT 1)	SOUND OF IMPACT (LP, laminated sleeve, numbered from 1,001-1,500, with 8-page booklet)	20
92	Touch & Go TG 24	SONGS ABOUT FUCKING (LP, reissue)	15
92	Touch & Go TG 81	PIGPILE (LP, boxed set with video & T-shirt with insert)	30

(see also Rapeman)

BIG BOB

Year	Label/Cat #	Description	Value
59	Top Rank JAR 185	Your Line Was Busy/What Am I	25

BIG BOPPER

Year	Label/Cat #	Description	Value
58	Mercury AMT 1002	Chantilly Lace/The Purple People Eater Meets The Witchdoctor	20
59	Mercury AMT 1017	Big Bopper's Wedding/Little Red Riding Hood	25
59	Mercury AMT 1046	It's The Truth, Ruth/That's What I Am Talking About	30
59	Mercury ZEP 10004	THE BIG BOPPER (EP)	100
59	Mercury ZEP 10027	PINK PETTICOATS (EP)	100
58	Mercury MMC 14008	CHANTILLY LACE (LP)	150

BIG BOSS MAN

Year	Label/Cat #	Description	Value
01	Blow Up BU017	Sea Groove/Sea Groove (Version)	10

BIG BOY PETE

Year	Label/Cat #	Description	Value
68	Camp 602 005	Cold Turkey/My Love Is Like A Spaceship	80
96	Tenth Planet TP 026	HOMAGE TO CATATONIA (LP)	18

(see also Miller, Pete Miller)

BIG BROTHER & HOLDING COMPANY

Year	Label/Cat #	Description	Value
67	Fontana TF 881	Bye Bye Baby/All Is Loneliness	25
68	CBS 3683	Piece Of My Heart/Turtle Blues (p/s)	25
68	CBS 3683	Piece Of My Heart/Turtle Blues (without p/s)	7
68	London HLT 10226	Down On Me/Call On Me	10
67	Fontana TL 5457	BIG BROTHER & THE HOLDING COMPANY (LP, with Janis Joplin, mono)	60
67	Fontana (S)TL 5457	BIG BROTHER & THE HOLDING COMPANY (LP, with Janis Joplin, stereo)	40
68	CBS 63392	CHEAP THRILLS (LP, 1st pressing, with Janis Joplin, laminated single sleeve with 'Ernest J. Day & Co Ltd' printing credit, mono)	75
68	CBS (S)63392	CHEAP THRILLS (LP, 1st pressing, with Janis Joplin, laminated single sleeve with 'Ernest J. Day & Co' printer credit stereo)	50
69	London HA-T/SH-T 8377	BIG BROTHER & THE HOLDING COMPANY (LP, reissue, mono/stereo)	20
71	CBS S 64118	BE A BROTHER (LP)	25
73	CBS (S)63392	CHEAP THRILLS (LP, reissue, no printer credit on rear of sleeve)	20
82	CBS 32004	CHEAP THRILLS (LP, 'Nice Price' reissue)	15
84	Edsel ED 135	CHEAPER THRILLS (LP)	15
99	Simply Vinyl SVLP 064	CHEAP THRILLS (LP, reissue)	20

(see also Janis Joplin, Nick Gravenites)

BIG CARROT

Year	Label/Cat #	Description	Value
73	EMI EMI 2047	Blackjack/Squint Eye Mangle	50
73	EMI EMI 2047	Blackjack/Squint Eye Mangle (Demo copy)	50

(see also Marc Bolan/T. Rex)

BIG CHARLIE

Year	Label/Cat #	Description	Value
64	Blue Beat BB 241	Red Sea/You May Not Believe	40

BIG CITY BEAT BAND

Year	Label/Cat #	Description	Value
88	Big City Beat BCB 001	Can I Be Your Friend (Radio Mix)/Club Mix (12", white label)	80
88	Big City Beat BCB 001	Can I Be Your Friend (Radio Mix)/(Dub)/(Club Mix) (12")	80

BIG COMBO

Year	Label/Cat #	Description	Value
81	Nothing Shaking SHAD 2	The Man In The Desert/Play For Today (p/s)	20

BIG COUNTRY

Year	Label/Cat #	Description	Value
83	Mercury COUP 4	Chance/The Tracks Of My Tears/The Crossing (12", picture disc)	15
83	Phonogram COUNT 313	In A Big Country (Pure Mix)/Heart And Soul/In A Big Country/All Of Us (12")	15
84	Mercury COUNT 5-5	Wonderland/Giant//Lost Patrol (Live - parts 1 & 2) (2 x 7")	10
84	Mercury MERD 185	Where The Rose Is Sown/Belief In The Small Man//Wonderland (Live)/In A Big Country (Live)/Auld Lang Syne (Live) (2 x 7")	10
84	Mercury (no cat no)	THE BIG COUNTRY 12" COLLECTION (boxed set with 5 x 12")	200
13	Cherry Red CHERRY 505	In A Broken Promise Land/Flower Of Scotland/Strong (Acoustic) (p/s)	20
91	Vertigo 510230-1	NO PLACE LIKE HOME (LP)	15
93	Compulsion NOIS 2	THE BUFFALO SKINNERS (LP)	150
94	Compulsion NOIS 5	WITHOUT THE AID OF A SAFETY NET (LP)	100
95	Transatlantic TRALP109	WHY THE LONG FACE (LP, 3000 only, numbered)	100
11	Track TRALP 1069	DRIVING TO DAMASCUS (2-LP, reissue of LP originally issued on CD in 1999)	75
12	Universal 278 909 1	THE CROSSING (2-LP, 30th anniversary reissue)	125
13	Cherry Red CHERRY 505	THE JOURNEY (LP, die-cut cover, orange vinyl, 250 only, numbered)	150

(see also Skids)

BIG DADDY KANE

Year	Label/Cat #	Description	Value
88	Cold Chillin' W7676	Set It Off/Get Into It (p/s)	40
88	Cold Chillin' W7676	Set It Off (Extended Mix)/Get Into It, Set It Off (12", p/s)	20
88	Cold Chillin' W7953	Word To The Mother (Land)/Raw (p/s, original US issue released in 1987)	40

BIG DAISY

MINT VALUE £

BIG DAISY
80	Ellie Jay 9428	Fever/Footprints (p/s)	250

(see also Wishbone Ash)

BIG DAVE (CAVANAUGH) & HIS ORCHESTRA
54	Capitol CL 14195	Loosely With Feeling/The Cat From Coos Bay (triangular centre)	20
55	Capitol CL 14245	Rock And Roll Party/Your Kind Of Love (triangular centre)	30

BIG DREAD
75	B&C BC 003	Musically Mad/Musical Excursion (white labels only)	30
76	Nice One N002	I Got To Go Girl/Blood & Fire	12

BIG FAYIA AND THE AFRO NATIONAL CALYPSO BAND
75	Afro Disc AD 1004	Rosaline/Blackpool	10

BIG FLAME
84	Laughing Gun PLAQUE 001	Sink/The Illness/Sometimes (p/s, with insert)	10
86	Ron Johnson ZRON 7	Why Popstars Can't Dance/Chanel Samba/Breath Of A Nation (p/s)	8

BIG FRONT YARD
75	Rampant RAM 1	Money Go Round/Mad John's Dream (no p/s)	8

BIG HAIR
80	Fresh FRESH 19	Puppet On A String/Lies (p/s)	8

(see also Disco 2000)

BIG IN JAPAN
77	Eric's ERICS 0001	Big In Japan/CHUDDIE NUDDIES: Do The Chud (p/s)	20
78	Zoo CAGE 1	FROM Y TO Z AND NEVER AGAIN (EP, foldout p/s)	40

(see also Pink Industry/Military, Holly, Holly Johnson, Yachts, Bill Drummond, Siouxsie & Banshees, Lightning Raiders, Justified Ancients of Mu Mu/JAMMS, KLF, Teardrop Explodes)

BIG JOE (JOSEPH SPALDING)
73	Chanan Jah 1003	Natty Love/Musical Air Raid	10
73	Atra ATRA 005	Jah Guide/SWEET HARMONY: Student Dub	15
73	Atra ATRA 010	Down Santic Way/Santic Dub	20
74	Dip DL 5007	Selassie Skank/Version	20
74	Dip DL 5008	Weed Specialist/CHERRY & DUB MASTER: Rub A Daughter	15
74	Dip DL 5027	Hog In A Me Minty/Sweet Melody	30
75	Fab FAB 243	American Pum Pum/Tape White Wash	10
76	Bimbo Music BM 4	Zion Dread/D. MORGAN: What A Disturbance	15
76	Burning Sounds BS 008	Natty Dread Don't Bow/CHANNEL ONE: Natty Dubbing	15
77	ATA ATA 1001	Set Your Face At Ease/Version	30
77	Venture VEN7770	Natty Don't Make War/CHANNEL ONE FLYERS: War Dubbing	15
78	Attack ATT 8136	Tubby At The Controls/Dignity And Principle	10
79	Tribesman TM 013	Respect Jah Word (with Rodney)/The Profit Says (12")	50
77	Live & Love LAP001	KEEP ROCKING AND SWINGING (LP)	50
78	Live & Love LAP 010	AT THE CONTROL (LP)	40
78	Trojan TRLS 152	AFRICAN PRINCESS (LP)	30

BIG JUMP BAND
73	Decca F 13411	All I Want/Utopia	7

BIG LUCKY, BIG AMOS & DONALD HINES
72	London SHU 8425	RIVER TOWN BLUES (LP)	25

BIG MAYBELLE
57	London HLC 8447	I Don't Want To Cry/All Of Me	50
59	London HLC 8854	Baby, Won't You Please Come Home/Say It Isn't So	20
65	London HL 9941	Careless Love/My Mother's Eyes	10
67	CBS 2735	Turn The World Around The Other Way/I Can't Wait Any Longer	20
67	CBS 2926	Mama (He Treats Your Daughter Mean)/Keep That Man	50
68	Direction 58-3312	Quittin' Time/I Can't Wait Any Longer	30
68	Direction 58-3312	Quittin' Time/I Can't Wait Any Longer (DJ Copy)	40
67	CBS 62999	THE PURE SOUL OF BIG MAYBELLE (LP)	30

BIG MOOSE (WALKER)
68	Python PKM 01	Ramblin' Woman/Puppy Howl Blues	50

BIG OUTDOOR TYPE
84	Havasac SAC 01	Call You On Sundays/Seventeen (p/s)	50

BIG PINK
08	House Anxiety HA 001	Too Young To Love/Crystal Visions	12

BIG ROY
76	Rockers 6	In The Desert/Natty Judge	6

BIG SLEEP
71	Pegasus PEG 4	BLUEBELL WOOD (LP, gatefold sleeve)	150

(see also Eyes Of Blue, Ancient Grease, Gentle Giant, Man, Ritchie Francis, Gary Pickford-Hopkins)

BIG SPENDERS
70	Gemini GMS 008	If It Feels Good, Do It/Why Don't Ya Tend To Your Business	12
70	Gemini GMS 010	Who's Making Love/Cum Ba Ye	15

BIG STAR
78	Stax STAX 504	September Gurls/Mod Lang (DJ Copy)	50
78	Stax STAX 504	September Gurls/Mod Lang	50
78	Aura AUS 103	Kizza Me/Dream Lover (p/s)	20
78	Aura AUS 107	Jesus Christ/Big Black Car	20
78	Stax SXSP 302	RADIO CITY/BIG STAR (2-LP)	60
78	Aura AUL 703	THIRD ALBUM (LP)	20
86	Big Beat WIK 53	NO. 1 RECORD (LP, reissue)	30
86	Big Beat WIK 54	RADIO CITY (LP, reissue)	30
11	Omnivore	BIG STAR III (replica test pressing in box, inserts, 2000 only)	35

(see also Alex Chilton, Box Tops)

BIG T
MINT VALUE £

BIG T
73	Avalanche AV 67324	Tea For Two/I Know A Place	25

BIG THREE (U.K.)
63	Decca F 11614	Some Other Guy/Let True Love Begin	10
63	Decca F 11689	By The Way/Cavern Stomp	10
63	Decca F 11752	I'm With You/Peanut Butter	10
64	Decca F 11927	If You Ever Change Your Mind/You've Got To Keep Her Under Hand	12
63	Decca DFE 8552	AT THE CAVERN (EP)	25
73	Polydor 2383 199	RESURRECTION (LP)	15

(see also Escorts, Paddy Klaus & Gibson, Johnny Gustafson, Faron's Flamingos, Johnny & John)

BIG THREE (U.S.)
68	Roulette RCP 5002	THE BIG THREE FEATURING MAMA CASS (LP)	30

(see also Mama Cass [Elliot], Mamas & Papas)

BIG TROUBLE
72	Pye 7N45292	You Said A Bad Word/Cyclone Blues	15

BIG VERN & CHATTERBOX
93	Straight From The Bedroom	Volume 3 (12")	35

BIG WHEEL
73	Bell Bell 1310	Shake-A-Tail Part 1/Shake-A-Tail Part 2	8

BIG YOUTH
72	Blue Beat BB 424	Chi Chi Run/JOHN HOLT: OK Fred	25
73	Downtown DT 497	Dock Of The Bay/CRYSTALITES: Bass And Drums (Version)	20
73	Gayfeet CS 206	Medicine Doctor/Facts Of Life	20
73	Prince Buster PB 46	Chi Chi Run/Drums And Bass (Version)	12
73	Prince Buster PB 48	Leggo Beast/Leave Your Skeng	15
73	Prince Buster PB 50	Cain And Abel/Cain And Abel (Version)	20
73	Grape GR 3040	Foreman Versus Frazier/Foreman Versus Frazier Round Two	20
73	Grape GR 3044	JA To UK/JA To UK (Version)	12
73	Grape GR 3051	Opportunity Rock/Double Attack	25
73	Grape GR 3061	Concrete Jungle/Screaming Target	15
73	Green Door GD 4051	Cool Breeze/CRYSTALITES: Windstorm	25
73	Summit SUM 8542	A So We Say (with Dennis Brown)/WINSTON SCOTLAND: Scarface	8
74	Harry J. HJ 6682	Ride On Ride On/Wild Goose Chase (both with Dennis Brown)	8
75	Action ACT 101	Notty No Jester/Instrumental	8
75	Angem ANG 103	All Nations/ANSEL COLLINS : Stalag 17	20
75	Attack ATT 8096	House Of Dread Locks/GROOVEMASTER: Tangle Locks	8
75	Attack ATT 8104	Mammy Hot And Daddy Cold/GROOVEMASTERS: Some Like It Dread	8
75	Lucky DL 5097	Big Youth Dread/Another Version	10
75	Lucky DL 5103	Natty Warning/Version	8
75	Klik KLP 9001	Dread Locks Dread/Version	15
76	Lucky LY 6001	Get Up Stand Up/Version (with Dennis Brown)	8
77	Eji E 011	Strictly Rockers/AUGUSTUS PABLO : No Entry (12")	40
78	Wildflower WF 538	Jah Jah Love Them/Oven Baking	8
72	Fab MS 8	CHI CHI RUN (LP)	45
73	Trojan TRLS 61	SCREAMING TARGET (LP, orange & white label)	50
75	Klik KLP9001	DREAD LOCKS DREAD (LP)	25
78	Virgin Front Line FL 1011	ISIAH, FIRST PROPHET OF OLD (LP)	18
78	Virgin Front Line FL 1014	DREAD LOCKS DREAD (LP, reissue)	25
76	Trojan TRLS 123	NATTY CULTURAL DREAD (LP, orange/white labels)	30
76	Trojan TRLS 137	HIT THE ROAD JACK (LP)	20
77	Trojan BYD 1	REGGAE PHENOMENON (2-LP, blue labels)	25
80	Trojan TRLS 123	NATTY CULTURAL DREAD (LP, reissue, blue labels)	20
80	Trojan TRLS 189	EVERYDAY SKANK (LP)	15
83	Virgin VX 1009	DREADLOCKS DREAD (LP, reissue)	18

(see also Upsetters)

BIG YOUTH & KEITH HUDSON
73	Pyramid PYR 7055	Can You Keep A Secret/HORACE ANDY & EARL FLUTE: Peter And Judas	35

BIGGA DREAD
02	Chariot Cha 001	Batty Dread/Closet Bwoy/Truck Inna Garage/Special Request (10")	30

EDWINA BIGLET AND THE MIDGETS
72	RCA RCA 2193	Thing/Vanessa's Luminous Coat	10

BIJOUX TOO
86	Apex APE 002	Shadows In My Heart/Come On Back (oversized p/s, Welsh-only release)	30

THEO BIKEL
69	Reprise RS 2344	I Love My Dog/The Great Mandela (The Wheel Of Life)	15

BIKINIS
58	Columbia DB 4149	Bikini/Boogie Rock And Roll	15

BILBO BAGGINS
74	Polydor 2058 479	Saturday Night/Monday Morning Blues	15

(MR.) ACKER BILK (& HIS PARAMOUNT JAZZ BAND)
60	Melodisc 1547	Goodnight Sweet Prince/East Coast Trot	25

(see also Michael London)

BILLIE & EDDIE
59	Top Rank JAR 249	The King Is Coming Back/Come Back, Baby	20

TREVOR BILLMUSS
70	Charisma CB 130	Whoops Amour/Sunday Afternoon In Belgrave Square	15
71	B & C CB 158	English Pastures/Fishing Song	8
70	Charisma CAS 1017	FAMILY APOLOGY (LP)	30

BILL THE MURDERER
78	SRT/78/CUS192	I'd Find You/Spring Rain (no p/s)	100

Eddie BILLUPS

MINT VALUE £

EDDIE BILLUPS
02　Grapevine 2000 126　　　Ask My Heart/A Soldier's Prayer 10

BONNIE 'PRINCE' BILLY
07　No label or Cat. No.　　　BONNY (7" tour EP) 15
12　Spiritual Pyjamas SPIRITUAL 004　Hummingbird/Tribulations/Because Of Your Eyes (10") 20
99　Domino WIGLP 59　　　I SEE A DARKNESS (LP) 25
01　Domino WIGLP 89　　　EASE DOWN THE ROAD (LP) 15
03　Palace/Domino WIGLP121　MASTER & EVERYONE (LP, insert) 15
04　Domino WIGLP 140　　SINGS GREATEST PALACE MUSIC (LP, 1-sided) 15
08　Domino WIGLP 213　　IS IT THE SEA (2-LP with Harum Scarem and Alex Neilson) 20
09　Domino WIGLP 233　　BEWARE (LP) 15
12　Faber And Faber FAB 02EP　WILL OLDHAM ON BONNIE PRINCE BILLY (2 x 10" in box with book, 300 only) 200
17　Domino WIGLP P420　　WOLF OF THE COSMOS (LP) 30

BILLY & ESSENTIALS
63　London HLW 9657　　　Over The Weekend/Maybe You'll Be There 30

BILLY & LILLIE (& BILLY FORD & THUNDERBIRDS)
58　London HLU 8564　　　La Dee Dah/BILLY FORD'S THUNDERBIRDS: The Monster 20
58　London HLU 8630　　　Creepin', Crawlin', Cryin'/Happiness (with Billy Ford & Thunderbirds) 30
59　London HLU 8795　　　I Promise You/Lucky Ladybug 20
59　Top Rank JAR 157　　　Bells, Bells, Bells/Honeymoonin' (as Billie & Lillie) 10

BILLY BARRY BELLY
87　Sidetrack SIDE 001　　　Do They Know/Conversations With... (p/s) 25

(see also Chris Sievey, Frank Sidebottom)

BIM & BAM
70　Crab CRAB 48　　　　　The Pill (with Clover)/TOMMY McCOOK: Spring Fever 15
70　Crab CRAB 49　　　　　Immigrant Plight (w/ Clover)/PETER AUSTIN & HORTENSE: Bang Shangalang 15
73　Gayfeet GS 201　　　　Fatty/Landlord 30

BIM, BAM & CLOVER
70　Trojan TR 7754　　　　Party Time Parts 1 & 2 8

BINGO
79　Polydor 2066365　　　　We Can't Get Enough/Mumblin' Man 20

SONNY BINNS (& RUDIES)
69　Downtown DT 420　　　The Untouchables/Lazy Boy 20
69　Downtown DT 424　　　Wheels/Night Train 25
70　Escort ES 818　　　　　Boss A Moon (as S. Binns)/BUNNY LEE ALLSTARS: Brotherly Love 40

(see also Rudies)

TONY BINNS
71　Explosion EX 2044　　　Love I Madly/Musical Shower 10
71　Explosion EX 2046　　　Humpty Dumpty/Got To Get A Message 8

BINO
81　Upper Class CPS 1　　　Dream (For My Sake)/Tonight (p/s) 15

BINTANGS
70　Decca F22995　　　　　Ridin' On The L And N/Down South Blues 18

BIOME
12　Macabre Unit MUV 001　Persepolis/DCULT: Inner Peace (12") 15
12　Macabre Unit MUV 003　Incubus/DEMON: Symmetry (12") 20
13　Macabre Unit MUV 004　Black Widow/Quasar/Mystery (12") 30
13　Macabre Unit MUV 007　Abyss/Brimstone/Redux (12") 12

BIONIC ECHO
86　Josiah KJ 003　　　　　Digital/Chatty Chatty Mouth (12") 80

BIOTA
85　Recommended DYS 12 & 13　RACKABONES (LP, with inserts) 30
87　Recommended RRC27　BELLOWING ROOM (LP) 30
88　Recommended RRC31　TINCT (LP) 25

KEV BIRD
91　Basement BRSS 003　　Inside Your Mind (Full Length Mix)/En Bass (Original Mix)/En Bass (Crash Mix) (12", promo) 20
92　Basement BRSS 006　　THE VISIT TO 14B EP (12", with The Wax Doctor) 15
92　Basement BRSS 012　　This Is A Trip/Let's Turn It Out/Eloquence (12") 10
94　Basement BRSS 031　　Kano/Sub Zero (12") 10

BIRD LEGS & PAULINE
66　Sue WI 4014　　　　　　Spring/In So Many Ways 40

STANLEY & JEFFREY BIRD
60　HMV POP 702　　　　　Johnny At The Crossheads/Betty, Betty (Go Steady With Me) 10

BIRD CURTIS
67　Tony Pike TPMLP 144　BIRD CURTIS QUINTET (LP) 400

BIRDS
64　Decca F 12031　　　　　You're On My Mind/You Don't Love Me (You Don't Care) 100
65　Decca F 12140　　　　　Leaving Here/Next In Line 100
65　Decca F 12257　　　　　No Good Without You Baby/How Can It Be 90
85　Demon WEST 901　　　THESE BIRDS ARE DANGEROUS (LP) 15

(see also Birds Birds, Ron Wood, Faces, Creation, Ashton Gardner & Dyke)

BIRDS BIRDS
66　Reaction 591 005　　　　Say Those Magic Words/Daddy Daddy 500

(see also Birds, Gods)

BIRDS & BRASS
70　Rediffusion ZS 57　　　SOUNDSATIONAL (LP) 15
74　Rediffusion 0100 171　...ARE BACK (LP) 15

BIRDS OF A FEATHER
69　Page One POF 156　　　Blacksmith Blues/Sing My Song And Pray 10

BIRDS WITH EARS

MINT VALUE £

70	Page One POF 179	All God's Children Got Soul/Get It Together	6
70	Page One POLS 027	BIRDS OF A FEATHER (LP)	100

(see also Chanters)

BIRDS WITH EARS
81	Attrix RB12LP	YOUTH IN ASIA (LP)	15

JANE BIRKIN & SERGE GAINSBOURG
69	Fontana STL 5493	JANE BIRKIN AND SERGE GAINSBOURG (LP)	15

BIRMINGHAM
71	Grosvenor GRS 1011	BIRMINGHAM (LP)	80

(see also Dave Peace Quartet)

BIRTH CONTROL
71	Charisma CAS 1036	BIRTH CONTROL (LP, pink/white 'scroll' label)	150

BIRTHDAY PARTY
80	4AD AD 12	The Friend Catcher/Waving My Arms/Cat Man (p/s)	12
80	Missing Link ML-18	Mr. Clarinet/Happy Birthday	50
81	4AD AD 111	Release The Bats/Blast Off (p/s)	10
81	4AD AD 114	Mr. Clarinet/Happy Birthday (p/s)	12
81	(no cat. no.)	Mr. Clarinet/Missing Link (sold at gigs only)	50
82	4AD BAD 301	THE BAD SEED EP	15
82	4AD JAD 202	DRUNK ON THE POPE'S BLOOD/THE AGONY IS THE ECSTACY (12" EP, with Lydia Lunch)	15
87	Strange Fruit SFSP 020	PEEL SESSIONS 1 (12")	10
88	Strange Fruit SFSP 058	PEEL SESSIONS 2 (12")	10
81	4AD CAD 104	PRAYERS ON FIRE (LP, inner)	20
82	4AD CAD 207	JUNK YARD (LP, with inner)	20
83	Mute MUTE 29	MUTINY (LP, insert)	20
92	4AD DAD 2016	HITS (2-LP)	50

(see also Nick Cave & Bad Seeds, Roland S. Howard & Lydia Lunch, These Immortal Souls)

BISH
80	Rainbow RS 2	Modern Women/He's So Foggy (p/s)	10

BISHOP
74	Purple PUR 122	Gazaroody/The So, So Song	10

DAVE BISHOP
78	Bible COM L	FIRST EP (with The Apostles, fold-out p/s)	15

DICKIE BISHOP & SIDEKICKS
57	Decca F 10869	Cumberland Gap/No Other Baby	10
57	Decca F 10959	The Prisoner's Song/Please Remember Me	8
58	Decca F 10981	Skip To My Lou/No Other Baby	6
58	Decca F 11028	They Can't Take That Away From Me/Jumpin' Judy	8

BITCH (1)
71	B & C CB 151	Laughing/House Where I Live	8
72	Warners K16235	Good Time Coming/At The Party	6

BITCH (2)
79	Hurricane FIRE 5	Big City/Wild Kids (p/s)	20

BITCH (3)
81	Rutland RX 101	First Bite/Maggie (with p/s & promo insert)	20
81	Rutland RX 101	First Bite/Maggie	15

BITCHES SIN
81	Neat NEAT 09	Always Ready For Love/Sign Of The Times (p/s)	8
83	Quiet QT 001	No More Chances/Overnight/Ice Angels (12", p/s)	25
82	Heavy Metal HMRLP 4	PREDATOR (LP, textured sleeve)	20

BITCH MAGNET
91	Caff CAFF 14	Sadie/Ducks And Drakes (p/s, with insert)	12

BITING TONGUES
81	Situation 2 SITU 1	DON'T HEAL (LP)	15

BITSTREAM
99	Signal SIGNAL 01	MONOLITH EP (12")	50

BITTER ALMOND
70	Warner Bros WB 8008	In The Morning/Silver	10
71	United Artists UP35197	Loving Each Other/We Need Someone	12

BITTER END SINGERS
67	Atlantic 584 075	A Taste Of Your Love/Everybody Knows My Name	10

BITTER SUITE
73	Jam 43	Six O' Clock News/Here's Hoping	8

BITTERNESS
74	Brent BR 1	She Flies/Have We Seen Tomorrow	20

BIZ
93	Warp WARP LP 9	ELECTRO SOMA (LP, orange vinyl)	15

BIZARRE
79	Polydor 2383 553	BIZARRE (LP)	20

(see also Alan Hawkshaw)

BIZARRE INC
91	Vinyl Solution STORM 25	Playing With Knives (12")	10
91	Vinyl Solution STORM 25 RT	Playing With Knives (The Climax) (12")	10
89	Blue Chip BLUE TEC. 1	TECHNOLOGICAL (LP)	15

BIZARRE UNIT
81	MRS MRS 004	Dancing/Away From The Screaming Car	20

(see also Paul Nova)

BIZ MARKIE
88	Cold Chillin' W7890	Vapors/The Do Do (p/s)	25
88	Cold Chillin' W7930	Biz Is Goin' Off/The Doo Doo (p/s)	20

BJÖRK

			MINT VALUE £
90	Warners W9823	Just A Friend ('Ard Done By Mix)/Just A Friend (LP version) (p/s)	12

BJÖRK

93	O. L. Indian 112TP12	Human Behavior : Underworld Mix/Close To Human Mix/Dom T Mix (12" p/s)	10
93	O. L. Indian 122TP7	Venus As A Boy : Edit/7" Dream Mix	6
96	O. L. Indian 193TP712TD	Possibly Maybe (Calcutta Cyber Café Mix)/I Miss You (Dobie's Rub Part One (12", 1,000 only)	12
96	O. L. Indian 193TP12DM	Enjoy (Beats Mix)/Possibly Maybe (Lucy Mix) (p/s, 1,000 only, numbered)	15
96	O. L. Indian 193TP12DM	Enjoy/Possibly Maybe (12", 1,000 only, numbered p/s)	18
96	O. L. Indian 193TP12TD	POSSIBLY MAYBE (12" EP, 1,000 only, numbered p/s)	12
97	O. L. Indian TPLP 81	JOGA (12" triple-pack, inner sleeves, p/s)	12
98	Fat Cat 12FAT 022	All Is Full Of Love (FunkstÖrung Remix)/The Shit (12", custom stamped sleeve)	12
08	One L. Indian 805TP12	EARTH INTRUDERS (CD, DVD & 2 x 12")	20
08	One L. Indian 837TP12	DECLARE INDEPENDENCE (CD, DVD & 2 x 12")	20
08	One L. Indian 838TP12	INNOCENCE (CD, DVD & 2 x 12")	20
08	One L. Indian 853TP12	WANDERLUST (CD, DVD & 2 x 12")	20
93	One L. Indian TPLP 31L	DEBUT (LP, 5,000 with 16-page lyric booklet)	100
93	One L. Indian TPLP 31L	DEBUT (LP)	70
94	One L. Indian 152TP 12	THE BEST MIXES FROM THE ALBUM "DEBUT" FOR THOSE PEOPLE WHO DON'T BUY WHITE LABELS (mini-LP)	40
95	One L. Indian TPLP 51L	POST (LP, pink vinyl, with inner sleeve)	75
96	One L. Indian TPLPT51	TELEGRAM (LP)	60
97	One L. Indian TPLP71	HOMOGENIC (LP, with poster)	60
00	One L. Indian TPLP151	SELMA SONGS (LP)	50
01	One L. Indian TPLP101	VESPERTINE (2 x LP, gatefold)	50
02	One L. Indian TPLP359	GREATEST HITS (2 x LP, gatefold)	70
04	One L. Indian TPLP358	MEDULLA (2-LP, 33rpm version)	35
04	One L. Indian TPLP358	MEDULLA (2-LP, 45rpm version)	35
06	One L. Indian TPLP101SACD	SURROUNDED (7 dualdisc box-set of all albums)	60
07	One L. Indian TPLP460H	VOLTA (2-LP fold-out cover, stickered sleeve)	35
08	One L. Indian TPLP31DMM	DEBUT (2-LP, reissue, DMM mastered, stickered sleeve, numbered, 1000 only)	100
08	One L. Indian TPLP51DMM	POST (2-LP, reissue, DMM mastered, stickered sleeve, numbered, 1000 only)	100
08	One L. Indian TPLP71DMM	HOMOGENIC (2-LP, reissue, DMM mastered, stickered sleeve, numbered, 1000 only)	100
08	One L. Indian TPLP151DMM	SELMASONGS (2-LP, reissue, DMM mastered, stickered sleeve, numbered, 1000 only)	100
08	One L. Indian TPLP101DMM	VESPERTINE (2-LP, reissue, DMM mastered, stickered sleeve, numbered, 1000 only)	100
08	One L. Indian TPLP358DMM	MEDULLA (2-LP, reissue, DMM mastered, stickered sleeve, numbered, 1000 only)	100
09	One L. Indian TPLP916	VOLTAIC (2-LP, 2-CD and 2-DVD)	40
11	One L. Indian TPLP1016	BIOPHILIA (LP, 2x12")	35
15	One L. Indian TPLP 1231	VULNICURA (2-LP, yellow vinyl, PVC outer, gatefold sleeve, inners)	30

(see also Sugarcubes, Kukl)

BLACK

81	Rox ROX 17	Human Features/Electric Church (p/s)	20
82	Wonderful World WWW3	More Than The Sun/Jump (no p/s)	20

BILL BLACK'S COMBO

64	London HLU 9925	Little Queenie/Boo-Ray	30
64	London HLU 9925	Little Queenie/Boo-Ray (DJ Copy)	100
60	London REU 1277	BILL BLACK'S COMBO (EP)	12
63	London REU 1369	THE UNTOUCHABLE SOUND OF BILL BLACK (EP)	12
64	London HA-U 8187	PLAYS CHUCK BERRY (LP)	15

(see also Elvis Presley)

CILLA BLACK

63	Parlophone R 5065	Love Of The Loved/Shy Of Love	10
64	Parlophone GEP 8901	ANYONE WHO HAD A HEART (EP)	10
64	Parlophone GEP 8916	IT'S FOR YOU (EP)	12
67	Parlophone GEP 8967	TIME FOR CILLA (EP)	15

FRANK BLACK

93	4AD CADD 3004	FRANK BLACK (LP, die-cut screen-printed sleeve, with lyric inner)	20
96	EPC 481647	THE CULT OF RAY (LP)	25
99	4AD DAD 4009	TEENAGER OF THE YEAR (2-LP)	25
98	PIAS BIAS 370LP	FRANK BLACK AND THE CATHOLICS (LP)	30
03	Diverse DIV 006LP	SHOW ME YOUR TEARS (LP, as Frank Black And The Catholics)	45
10	Vinyl Lovers 7901295	CHRISTMASS (LP, with free 7")	20

(see also Pixies)

IKA BLACK & THE NATIONS CRK

81	I One I IONE 001	Human Life/Better Life (12")	25

LINCOLN BLACK

70	Penny Farthing PEN 712	Famous Last Words/You Built Me Up So High	12

MARY BLACK

89	Grapevine GRALP 009	NO FRONTIERS (LP, with lyric inner sleeve)	25
92	Grapevine GRALP 009	NO FRONTIERS (LP, audiophile pressing, white sleeve)	30
92	Grapevine GRALP 009	NO FRONTIERS (LP, audiophile pressing, red sleeve with different design and inner sleeve)	30
95	Grapevine GRALP 011	THE HOLY GROUND (LP, audiophile pressing)	20
95	Grapevine GRALP 014	CIRCUS (LP, audiophile pressing with lyric inner)	20

MATT BLACK & THE DOODLEBUGS

76	Punk BCS 0005	Punky Xmas/Nightmare (no p/s)	8

SAM BLACK

74	DJM DJS 334	I'm Goin' Left/Take Me With You	50

STEVE BLACK

83	Dudu DAR 001	HAPPY BIRTHDAY TO U (LP)	400

BLACK ABBOTTS

70	Chapter One CH 123	She Looked Away/I Don't Mind	7

BLACK ACE

MINT VALUE £

71	Evolution E 3001	How About Me/Everybody Needs A Little Sunshine	7
71	Evolution E 3004	Love Is Alive/The Painter	25

BLACK ACE
61	XX MIN 701	BLACK ACE (EP)	30
62	Heritage HLP 1006	BLACK ACE (LP, 99 copies only)	75

BLACKALICIOUS
99	Mo Wax MWR 112LP	NIA (2-LP)	25

BLACK AND WHITE LOVERS
86	Guillotine GR 001	Best Years Of Our Lives/Boulevard Of Broken Dreams (p/s)	8

BLACK ARK PLAYERS
80	Black Ark Intl. BALP 4000	BLACK ARK IN DUB (LP, white label, green vinyl)	45
80	Black Ark Intl. BALP 4000	BLACK ARK IN DUB (LP)	40

BLACK AXE
80	Metal MELT 1	Highway Rider/Red Lights (in p/s)	20
80	Metal MELT 1	Highway Rider/Red Lights	6

BLACKBEARD
78	Ballistic LBR 1013	STRICTLY DUB WISE (LP)	30
80	More Cut RDC 2002	I WAH DUB (LP)	30

BLACK BEATLES
70	Pama PM 804	Reggae And Shout/LENOX BROWN: The Green Hornet	30

BLACKBIRDS
68	Saga OPP 3	No Destination/Space (either p/s or company sleeve, possibly promo only)	30
68	Saga FID 2113	NO DESTINATION (LP, black/silver label)	40

BLACK BLOOD
76	Bradleys 1002	Rasteferai/Ewohe Dance	6

TONY BLACKBURN
65	Fontana TF 562	Don't Get Off That Train/Just To Be With You Again	8
69	MGM 1467	It's Only Love/Janie	8
69	Polydor 583 082	TONY BLACKBURN (LP)	15

BLACKBYRDS
78	Fantasy FTCT 194	Rock Creek Park/Don't Know What To Say (12")	20
85	Streetwave SWAVE 3	Rock Creek Park/Walking In Rhythm (12")	15
75	Fantasy FT 9444	BLACKBYRDS (LP)	20
75	Fantasy FT 522	FLYING START (LP)	15
76	Fantasy FTA 3003	CITY LIFE (LP)	15
77	Fantasy FT 534	ACTION (LP)	15
79	Fantasy FT 555	NIGHT GROOVES - THE BEST OF THE BLACKBYRDS (LP)	15

(see also Donald Byrd)

BLACK CAT
81	Gate MS02	Queen Of The Hop/Let's Rock/Rockin Chair/Black Cat Boogie (p/s)	15
81	Cheapskate CHEAP 32	Gonna Type A Letter/Race With The Devil (p/s)	10
83	Underworld BBUW 09	Dance With The Dolly/She's A Rocker (p/s)	40
83	Hot Wax HOT WAX 4501	STROLLING AFTER DARK EP	10

BLACK CAT BONES
68	Sceptre SALR 1216	COME ABOARD QE2 (LP, sold on liner, one track by Black Cat Bones)	25
70	Decca Nova DN 15	BARBED WIRE SANDWICH (LP, mono, blue/silver label)	500
70	Decca Nova SDN 15	BARBED WIRE SANDWICH (LP, stereo, blue/silver label)	600

(see also Leaf Hound, Brian Short, Free, Foghat)

BLACK CLAW
69	Bell BLL 1089	Across The Great Divide/Sally	8

BLACK COCK
94	Black Cock BCOK 069	ON THE NEST EP (12", beware of bootlegs)	70
95	Black Cock BCK 077	FREE RANGE EP (12")	40
97	Black Cock BK 068	Give It Up/Cosmic (12")	25
97	Black Cock BK 068	Give It Up/Cosmic (12", repressing)	25
97	Black Cock BK 076	Luna Parrrrty/Frog Scene (12", white label, stickered sleeve)	25

(see also DH Harvey, Ersatz)

BLACK COUNTRY, NEW ROAD
19	Speedy Wunderground SW026	Athen's France (Part 1)/(Part 2) (die-cut p/s, 250 only)	100
19	Blank Editions BETBC018	Sunglasses/Sunglasses (Cont) (1st pressing, unique individual sleeves, certificate of ownership, stickered p/s)	70
19	Blank Editions BETBC018	Sunglasses/Sunglasses (Cont) (2nd pressing, standard p/s, insert)	40
19	Blank Editions BETBC018	Sunglasses/Sunglasses (Cont) (3rd pressing, 'assembly' p/s)	30

BLACK COUNTRY THREE
66	W.F.C. WS 100	BLACK COUNTRY SONGS (EP)	250
66	Transatlantic TRA 140	BLACK COUNTRY THREE (LP)	50

(see also Jon Raven)

BLACK CROWES
91	Def American 7-17580	HARD TO HANDLE (7 x 7" box set, with 2 bonus tracks)	20
90	Def American 842515	SHAKE YOUR MONEY MAKER (LP)	30
92	Def American 512263	SOUTHERN HARMONY AND MUSICAL COMPANION (LP)	30
94	American 74321 23682 1	AMORICA (LP, white vinyl)	60
99	American 491699 1	BY YOUR SIDE (LP)	60

BLACK DEVIL
04	Rephlex CAT 146EP	DISCO CLUB (12", p/s)	15

BLACK DOG
91	GPR GENP(X) 2	PARALLEL EP (12", p/s)	30
92	Black Dog Prods BDP 001	VIRTUAL EP (12", p/s)	50
92	Black Dog Prods BDP 002	AGE OF SLACK (12", p/s)	50
92	Black Dog Prods BDP 003	BLACK DOG EP (12", p/s, 500 only)	125

92	GPR GENP(X) 3	VIR 2 L (12", custom sleeve) ... 50
92	GPR GENP(R) 03	VIR 2 L/Shout (12" remix with SHIVA) ... 30
92	GPR GENP(X) 9	VANTOOL EP (12", custom sleeve) ... 100
93	GPR GENP(X) 17	COST II (12", custom sleeve) ... 15
93	Rising High RSN 046	BLACK DOG PRODUCTIONS (12", 4-track, p/s) ... 20
99	Warp WAP 115	PEEL SESSION (12") ... 10
07	Soma SOMA 214	VIRTUAL EP (12" reissue) ... 20
91	GPR GPR 004	PARALLEL SQUELCH (LP) ... 30
92	GPR GPRLP 1	TEMPLE OF TRANSPARENT BALLS (2-LP, with poster) ... 45
92	GPR GPRLP 1	TEMPLE OF TRANSPARENT BALLS (2-LP, without poster) ... 30
95	GPR GPRLP 15	PARALLEL (2-LP) ... 35
95	GPR GPRCD 15	PARALLEL (CD) ... 30
95	Warp PUP LP1	SPANNERS (2-LP) ... 40
95	Warp WAP LP 8LTD	BYTES (LP, bronze vinyl) ... 40
96	Warp PUP LP2	MUSIC FOR ADVERTS (AND SHORT FILMS) (2-LP) ... 20

(see also Alter Ego, Plaid, Repeat, Unexplored Beats, Shiva)

BLACK DYKE MILLS BAND
68	Apple APPLE 4	Thingumybob/Yellow Submarine ... 40

BLACK DYNAMITES
60	Top Rank JAR 319	Brush Those Tears/Lonely Cissy ... 15

BLACK EASTER
82	Illuminated KILL 13	READY TO ROT (EP, p/s) ... 10

BLACK-EDS
80	Acne ACNE 1	Isn't It Strange/Living Doll/Jimmy 2 Stroke (p/s) ... 20

BLACK EXOTICS
07	Funk 45 FUNK45 038	Theme Of Blackbyrds/What Am I Waiting For (reissue) ... 12

BLACK FAITH
70	Phillips 6006065	Woman In My Life ... 12
70	Phillips 6007018	Song For A Dollar/Peace In The Family ... 10
74	Fresh Air 6121107	The Vow/Stop The World ... 20

BLACK FANTASY
84	Dingle TIG 001	Evil Places/Fade Away From Me (p/s) ... 100

BLACK FLAG
81	Alt. Tentacles VIRUS 9	Six Pack/I've Heard It All Before/American Waste (p/s) ... 12
84	SST SST 12001	Family Man/I Won't Stick Any Of You Unless And Until I Can Stick All Of You (12", p/s) ... 10

J.D. BLACKFOOT
71	Mercury 6338 031	THE ULTIMATE PROPHECY (LP) ... 70

BLACKFOOT SUE
73	DJM DJS 296	Bye Bye Birmingham/Messiah ... 10
74	DJM DJS 326	You Need Love/Tobago Rose ... 12
73	Jam JAL 104	NOTHING TO HIDE (LP, gatefold sleeve with poster) ... 50
73	Jam JAL 104	NOTHING TO HIDE (LP, gatefold sleeve without poster) ... 20
75	DJM DJLPS 455	GUN RUNNING (LP, withdrawn) ... 65

BLACK GORILLA
77	Response (PYE) SR 502	Gimme Dat Banana/Funky Jungle ... 6

BLACK GRAPE
95	Radioactive RAR 11224	IT'S GREAT WHEN YOU'RE STRAIGHT YEAH (LP) ... 30
97	Radioactive RAR 11716	STUPID STUPID STUPID (LP) ... 15
17	UMC 5757997	POP VOODOO (LP, yellow vinyl, signed) ... 18

(see also Happy Mondays)

BLACK HARMONY
79	Burning Sounds BS 14	I'm Still Waiting/Love Marcus ... 10
79	Laser LAS 9	Don't Let It Go To Your Head/DEB PLAYERS : Don't Let It Go To Your Brain (12") ... 18

BLACK HEAT
72	Atlantic 10270	Streets Of Tears/Chips Funk ... 10

BLACK HONEY
15	(No label or cat. no.)	Corrine/Mothership (p/s, pink vinyl) ... 15
16	Black Honey	HEADSPIN EP (10", p/s, red vinyl) ... 30
16	Black Honey	All My Pride/On Your Time (p/s, blue vinyl) ... 8
17	Black Honey BLK 12	Somebody Better/Cadillac (p/s, orange vinyl) ... 8
17	Black Honey	Hello Today/Ghost (heart-shaped red/white 10") ... 40
20	Foxfire BHRSD001	Corrine/Mothership (green heart-shaped 10") ... 15

BLACK IVORY
74	Kwanza K19500	What Goes Around/No One Else Will Do ... 8
79	Buddah BDLP 4060	HANGIN HEAVY (LP) ... 15

BLACKJACK
80	Polydor POSP 76	Without Your Love/Heart Of Mine (p/s) ... 18
79	Polydor 2391 411	BLACKJACK (LP) ... 18

(see also Michael Bolton)

BLACKJACKS
63	Pye 7N 15586	Woo Hoo/Red Dragon ... 6

(see also Pat Harris & Blackjacks)

BLACK KEYS
03	Fat Possum 111-7	Hard Row/Evil (p/s) ... 15
03	Fat Possum 1130-7	Have Love Will Travel/No Trust (live)/The Moan (live) (p/s, yellow vinyl) ... 10
04	Fat Possum 11747	10AM Automatic/Summertime Blues (p/s) ... 6
06	V2 VVR5043087	Your Touch/The Breaks ... 12
07	V2 VVR5048347	Just Got To Be/Black Door (p/s, no'd) ... 6
08	V2 VVR5051097	I Got Mine/Here I Am I Always Am ... 12
13	Warner Bros. 7559-79592-4	No Fun/THE STOOGES: No Fun (orange vinyl) ... 8

BLACK KNIGHTS

MINT VALUE £

06	V2 VVR1042541	MAGIC POTION (LP)	20
12	Fat Possum FP803713	THICKFREAKNESS (LP, picture disc, 300 only)	15
12	Fat Possum FP80379-3	RUBBER FACTORY (LP, picture disc)	15
12	Nonesuch 530454-1	EL CAMINO (2-LP, CD, numbered)	20

BLACK KNIGHTS
65	Columbia DB 7443	I Gotta Woman/Angel Of Love	25

BLACK LIPS
07	Vice VICE 004LP	GOOD BAD NOT EVIL (LP, gatefold)	15

DON BLACKMAN
82	Arista RIST 30	Hearts Desire/Let Your Conscience Be Your Guide (12", EP)	15

HONOR BLACKMAN
68	CBS 3896	Before Today/I'll Always Be Loving You (in p/s)	30
68	CBS 3896	Before Today/I'll Always Be Loving You	10
64	Decca LK/SKL 4642	EVERYTHING I'VE GOT (LP, mono/stereo)	20
80	Deram 844057-1	KINKY BOOTS (LP)	20

(see also Patrick MacNee & Honor Blackman)

PAUL BLACKMAN
79	Daddy Kool DKR 123	Earth, Wind & Fire/A. Pablo: Ras-Menlik Congo (12")	50

(see also Augustus Pablo)

BLACK MIDI
18	Speedy Wunderground SW005	Bmbmbm/Savage Gary's Dbdbdb (1st pressing of 250, numbered)	35
18	Speedy Wunderground SW024	Bmbmbm/Savage Gary's Dbdbdb (2nd pressing of 250, un-numbered)	25

RITCHIE BLACKMORE (ORCHESTRA)
65	Oriole CB 314	Getaway/Little Brown Jug (Spelt "Richie" on label)	600

(see also Outlaws, Neil Christian & Crusaders, Deep Purple, [Ritchie Blackmore's] Rainbow, Rally Rounders, Green Bullfrog)

BLACK NASTY
79	Grapevine 140	Cut Your Motor Off/Keep On Stepping (reissue)	10

BLACK OAK ARKANSAS
75	Atlantic K 10621	Fancy Nancy/Keep On	7
71	Atlantic 2400 180	BLACK OAK ARKANSAS (LP)	15

BLACK PROPHETZ
91	GTI KICK8	FAX ON WAX (EP)	13

BLACK RADICAL MK II
91	Mango 12 MNG 782DJ	Sign Of The Beast (12" - Grey Vinyl/Promo only)	12

BLACK RADICAL/SIR NOVA
88	Bass Inc B1001 500	B Boys Be Wise/We Outta Here (12")	60

BLACK REBEL MOTORCYCLE CLUB
02	Virgin VUS 245	Spread Your Love/Tonight's With You (p/s)	8
02	Virgin VUSLP 224	BLACK REBEL MOTORCYCLE CLUB (LP)	50
03	Virgin VUSLP 245	TAKE THEM ON YOUR OWN (2-LP, gatefold, with inner sleeves)	50
05	Echo ECHLP 67	HOWL (2-LP, with inner sleeves)	50
10	Cobraside CSDLP 1142	BEAT THE DEVIL'S TATTOO (2-LP, white vinyl 400 copies, tour only)	30
10	Cobraside CSDLP 1142	BEAT THE DEVIL'S TATTOO (2-LP, grey vinyl)	20

BLACK RIDERS
85	Plastic Head GILP 555	CHOSEN FEW (LP)	15

BLACK ROD
73	Phoenix NIX 133	See What You Get Out Of Me/Mad Donkey	15

BLACK ROOTS
81	Nubian NR 0021D	Chanting For Freedom/Confusion/What Them A Do (12")	15
83	Silvertown STST 002	Move On/What Them A Do (12")	12
84	Bullet BOL 9	Boys Will Be Boys/Liar (p/s, some with patch)	35
84	Nubian NR 001	Bristol Rock/Tribal War/The Father/The System (12")	25
83	Kick KIC LP 02	BLACK ROOTS (LP)	30
84	Bullet BULP 3	BOYS WILL BE BOYS (LP)	15
84	BBC REC 555	THE FRONT LINE (LP)	30
84	BBC REC 5570	IN SESSION (LP)	20

BLACK ROSE
82	Teesbeat TB 5	Sucker For Your Love/No Point Runnin' (in p/s)	125
82	Teesbeat TB 5	Sucker For Your Love/No Point Runnin'	35

BLACK SABBATH
SINGLES
70	Fontana TF 1067	Evil Woman/Wicked World (A label promo)	200
70	Fontana TF 1067	Evil Woman/Wicked World	125
70	Vertigo V2	Evil Woman/Wicked World (A label promo)	150
70	Vertigo V2	Evil Woman/Wicked World (reissue, Vertigo 'swirl' sleeve)	35
70	Vertigo V2	Evil Woman/Wicked World (reissue, later silver label)	15
70	Vertigo 6059010	Paranoid/The Wizard (promo)	100
70	Vertigo 6059 010	Paranoid/The Wizard (Vertigo 'swirl' sleeve)	20
72	Vertigo 6059061	Tomorrow's Dream/Laguna Sunrise (promo)	60
72	Vertigo 6059 061	Tomorrow's Dream/Laguna Sunrise (Vertigo 'swirl' sleeve)	25
72	Phonogram DJ 005	Children Of The Grave/STATUS QUO: Roadhouse Blues (100 promo copies only)	500
73	WWA WWS 002	Sabbath Bloody Sabbath/Changes (company sleeve)	10
75	NEMS 6165 300	Am I Going Insane? (Radio)/Hole In The Sky (no p/s)	10
77	NEMS NES 112	Paranoid/Sabbath Bloody Sabbath (p/s)	10
78	Vertigo SAB 001	Never Say Die/She's Gone (p/s)	10
78	NEMS NES 112	Paranoid/Snowblind	10
78	Vertigo SAB 002	Hard Road/Symptom Of The Universe (black vinyl)	6
78	Vertigo SAB 002	Hard Road/Symptom Of The Universe (blue vinyl)	10

BLACK SABBATH

MINT VALUE £

Year	Label/Cat#	Description	Value
78	Vertigo SAB 002	Hard Road/Symptom Of The Universe (purple vinyl with 'Sympton' typo on label)	30
80	Vertigo SAB 3	Neon Knights/Children Of The sea (live) (p/s)	6
81	Vertigo SAB 512	Mob Rules/Die Young (live) (12", p/s)	10
82	NEMS NEP 1	Paranoid/Iron Man (picture disc)	20
86	Vertigo SABDJ 12	In For The Kill/Turn To Stone/Heart Like A Wheel (12", promo only)	15
87	Vertigo SABAF 1	4 SONGS FROM THE ETERNAL IDOL (12", p/s, promo only)	15
89	I.R.S. EIRS CB 107	Headless Cross (Edit)/Cloak And Dagger (signed label, stickered PVC sleeve)	10
89	I.R.S. EIRSB 115	Devil And Daughter (box set, 1-sided disc with stencil, insert & 2 postcards)	20
10	Vertigo 00602527391199	Paranoid (Alternative Lyric Version)/METALLICA: Frantic (UNKLE Remix) (12", 1000 only)	20
14	Secret 7" S715	Age Of Reason (100 only, each with unique art sleeve)	100

ALBUMS

Year	Label/Cat#	Description	Value
70	Vertigo VO 6	BLACK SABBATH (LP, 1st pressing, with black gatefold inner sleeve, no composers/publishers credits on cross; large swirl label with "A Philips record product" text on label and "Copyright subsists in all Stereo recordings" text)	500
70	Vertigo VO 6	BLACK SABBATH (LP, 2nd pressing, with Dunbar credit for 'Warning'; swirl label, without "A Philips record product" on label and without composers/publishers credits, with "Copyright subsists in all Vertigo recordings" text)	300
70	Vertigo 6360 011	PARANOID (LP, 1st pressing with 'Jim Simpson' management credit inside gatefold sleeve, large swirl label)	350
70	Vertigo 6360 011	PARANOID (LP, 2nd pressing, large swirl label, without Jim Simpson credit inside laminated sleeve)	200
70	Vertigo 6360 011	PARANOID (LP, 3rd pressing, small swirl label, gatefold sleeve)	100
70	Vertigo 6360 011	PARANOID (LP, gatefold sleeve, later spaceship label)	100
71	Vertigo 6360 050	MASTER OF REALITY (LP in box cover, swirl label, with poster)	500
71	Vertigo 6360 050	MASTER OF REALITY (LP in box cover, swirl label, without poster)	350
71	Vertigo VO 6	BLACK SABBATH (LP, 3rd pressing, 'Vertigo' lettering beneath small swirl above centre hole, composers/publishers credits in lower case. "Copyright subsists in all Vertigo recordings" credit)	100
72	Vertigo 6360 071	BLACK SABBATH VOL. 4 (LP, 1st pressing, no "Made in England" beneath 1972 on top right hand side" gatefold sleeve with booklet attached, small swirl label, "PORKY/PECKO" hand etched in run out grooves)	250
72	Vertigo 6360 071	BLACK SABBATH VOL. 4 (LP, 2nd pressing, with "Made in England" beneath 1972 on top right hand side" gatefold sleeve with booklet attached, small swirl label, no "PORKY/PECKO" hand etching in run out grooves)	150
72	Vertigo 6360 071	BLACK SABBATH VOL. 4 (LP, gatefold sleeve with booklet attached, 'spaceship' label)	150
73	Vertigo VO6	BLACK SABBATH (LP, 4th pressing, 'spaceship' label)	100
73	WWA WWA 05	SABBATH BLOODY SABBATH (LP, 1st pressing, no ridge around rim, 1 Y 1/ 2 Y 1 matrix numbers, silver WWA logo, gatefold with "Manufactured and printed in England" (no "Howard's Printers" reference), inside image extends to edge of sleeve with no border, textured lyric inner)	60
73	WWA ACB 00166	SABBATH BLOODY SABBATH (LP, reissue, Audio Club of Great Britain pressing)	30
73	WWA 006	BLACK SABBATH (LP, reissue, in Vertigo sleeves with WWA006 sticker on rear)	50
73	WWA 006	BLACK SABBATH (LP, reissue)	20
73	WWA 007	PARANOID (LP, reissue)	40
73	WWA 009	BLACK SABBATH VOL 4 (LP, reissue, gatefold)	40
73	Vertigo 6360 050	MASTER OF REALITY (LP, ' spaceship' label, with poster, reissue)	100
73	WWA WWA 008	MASTER OF REALITY (LP, 'transitional sleeve' with sticker over Vertigo cat no on rear, with poster, reissue)	80
73	WWA 008	MASTER OF REALITY (LP, label, with poster, reissue)	30
73	WWA WWA 005	SABBATH BLOODY SABBATH (LP, reissue)	15
75	NEMS 9119001	SABOTAGE (LP, 1st pressing with "Record and Tapes" logo matrix numbers 1//Y2 S 1 3 5 & 2 Y2 S 1 1 4 with 'Sterling' stamped into dead wax on both sides, textured sleeve made by 'Robert Stace', "Meglomania" typo)	100
75	NEMS 9119001	SABOTAGE (LP, 2nd pressing with no "Record and Tapes" logo matrix numbers 1//Y2 S 1 3 5 & 2 Y2 S 1 1 4 with 'Sterling' stamped into dead wax on both sides, textured sleeve made by 'Robert Stace', "Meglomania" typo)	50
76	Vertigo 9102 750	TECHNICAL ECSTACY (LP, insert)	35
76	NEMS NEL 6003	PARANOID (LP, reissue)	20
76	NEMS NEL 6004	MASTER OF REALITY (LP, reissue, stickered sleeve)	20
76	NEMS NEL 6005	BLACK SABBATH VOL 4 (LP, reissue, gatefold)	20
78	Vertigo 9102 751	NEVER SAY DIE (LP, laminated sleeve, inner)	40
80	Vertigo 9102 752	HEAVEN AND HELL (LP, A1/B2 matrixes)	35
80	NEMS NEL 6018	SABOTAGE (LP, reissue)	15
80	NEMS BS 001	LIVE AT LAST (LP)	30
80	NEMS NEL 6017	SABBATH BLOODY SABBATH (LP, reissue)	15
81	Vertigo 6302 119	MOB RULES (LP)	50
83	Vertigo SAB 10	LIVE EVIL (2-LP, gatefold, inners orange Vertigo label)	35
83	Vertigo VER 8	BORN AGAIN (LP)	30
85	Nems BSBLP 001	THE SABBATH COLLECTION (7-LP box set)	50
86	Vertigo VERH 29	SEVENTH STAR (LP, as Black Sabbath featuring Tony Iommi)	30
87	Vertigo VERH 51	ETERNAL IDOL (LP, lyric inner)	30
88	Castle BSBCD 001	THE BLACK SABBATH CD COLLECTION (6-CD box set with badge & book, numbered, 3,000 only)	40
89	IRS METAL 24 1005	HEADLESS CROSS (LP, poster)	75
89	IRS EIRSAPD 1002	HEADLESS CROSS (LP, picture disc with extra track)	35
90	IRS EIRSA 1038	TYR (LP, inner)	100
90	IRS EIRSAPD 1038	TYR (LP, picture disc with 2 extra tracks)	35
91	Essential ESBLP 142	THE OZZY OSBOURNE YEARS (5-LP box set)	30
92	IRS 713155 1	DEHUMANIZER (LP)	80
94	IRS 07777132221 1	CROSS PURPOSES (LP, with inner)	300
97	Castle ORRLP 004	BLACK SABBATH (LP, reissue, 5000 only with free 7")	20
00	Raw Power RAWLP 145	THE BEST OF BLACK SABBATH (4-LP, gatefold sleeve, numbered and stickered)	50
02	Earmark 41045	PAST LIVES (2-LP)	40
13	Vertigo 602537349593	13 (2-LP, 2-CD, DVD, box set)	45

BLACK SHEEP

MINT VALUE £

(see also Ozzy Osborne, Dio, Elf, Cozy Powell, Quartz, Phenomena, Brian May)

BLACK SHEEP
91	Mercury MER 356	Try Counting Sheep/(Original Sheep LP Mix) (p/s)	60
91	Mercury MER 369	Strobelite Honey (Maybe We Did Mix)/(The Original) (p/s)	50

BLACK SLATE
76	Slate KG 04	Sticks Man/Robber Man In Dub	20
76	King George KG 001	Mixed Up Man/Put Your Head On My Shoulder	8
78	Ted TCDD 003	Mind Your Motion/You Can't Make Us (12")	35
78	Ted TCDD 008	Sticks Man/Version (12")	25
78	Slate KG 008	Live Up To Love/Jah In The Ghetto (12")	12
80	TCD TCDLP1	AMIGO (LP)	15
81	TCD TCDLP 02	OGIMA (DUB SLATE) (LP)	40
82	Top Ranking TRY IT 1	SIX PLUS ONE (LP, with free dub LP)	20

BLACKSTAR
95	Congo Natty RASTA 1	TRIBUTE TO HAILE SELASSIE I (2-LP)	40

BLACK STASH
75	Seville 1004	Mighty Love Man/Mighty Love Man Part 2	15

BLACK STONES
76	Daddy Kool DK 003	We Nah Go Suffer/Unity Dub	10
78	Chanah Jah CJ3026	Punk Rockers/Open The Gates (12" p/s)	15
81	KG Imperial KG 005	Created By One Power/Satisfy Her Soul (12")	12
81	Jah Lion JLDC610	Sweet Feeling/Riding High (12")	12

BLACKSTREET
94	Interscope 6544 92351 1	BLACKSTREET (2-LP, insert)	40
96	Interscope INTLP 90071	ANOTHER LEVEL (2-LP)	30

BLACK SWAN
71	Ember EMBS 303	Echoes And Rainbows/Belong Belong (with p/s)	15
71	Ember EMBS 303	Echoes And Rainbows/Belong Belong (without p/s)	8

BLACK SYMBOL
79	Black Symbol BS 001	Non A Jah Jah Children Passing/Version (12")	50
80	Black Symbol BS 003	Loving Jah/Everything Has Time (12")	70
80	Black Symbol BS 006	My Heart Reveal Dancer/Dub Piano	25
82	Black Symbol BS 008	Solidarity/Tension (12")	30

BLACKTHORN
77	WHM 1921	BLACKTHORN (LP)	60
78	WHM 1922	BLACKTHORN II (LP)	100

BLACK UHURU
77	Carib Gems CG 015	Sun Is Shining/REVOLUTIONARIES : Version	15
77	Third World TWDIS 009	Natural Mystic/Sorry For The Man (12")	20
79	Warrior WAR 140	Bad Girl/African Love/PRINCE HAMMER - Yogi Bear (12")	25
79	DEB DEB 034	Rent Man/Rent Board/ALTON ELLIS - La La Means I Love You/Version (12")	18
79	DEB DEB 036	Wood For My Fire/EARL CUNNINGHAM/JAH THOMAS - Words Of The Father (12")	15
79	D Roy DDR 09	Plastic Smile/Guess Who's Coming To Dinner (12")	25
79	D Roy DRDD 15	Shine Eye (featuring Keith Richards)/D-ROY BAND: Licking Stick (12")	25
80	Island 12WIP 6626	Sinsemilla (Discomix)/Guess Who's Coming To Dinner (Discomix) (12")	10
85	Taxi BUT 1	Fit You Haffe Fit/Fitness (12")	18
77	Third World TWS 925	LOVE CRISIS (LP, as Black Sounds Uhro)	40
79	D-Roy DRLP 1003	SHOWCASE (LP)	25
80	Island ILPS 9593	SINSEMILLA (LP)	20
81	Greensleeves GREL 23	BLACK SOUNDS OF FREEDOM (LP)	15
82	CSA CSLP 2	UHURU IN DUB (LP)	15

(See also Don Carlos)

BLACK VELVET
69	Beacon BEA 129	African Velvet/Whatcha' Gonna Do 'Bout It	8
69	Beacon BEA 137	Peace And Love Is The message/Clown	8
70	Beacon BEA 151	Please Let Me In/Clown	20
70	Beacon BEA 162	What Am I To Do/Coal Mine	12
70	Beacon BEA 170	Thought I Had Me A Good Thing/Love Makes The World Go Round	10
71	Mams MAM 47	Make It Better/Tropicana	15
73	Pye 7N 45338	There Must Be A Way/Domestic Man	12
70	Beacon BEAS 16	THIS IS BLACK VELVET (LP)	25
72	Pye NSPL 18392	PEOPLE OF THE WORLD (LP)	25
73	Seven Sun SUNLP1	CAN YOU FEEL IT? (LP)	80

BLACKWELL
76	Penny Farthing PELS 559	BOOGIE DOWN MESS AROUND (LP)	20

CHARLES BLACKWELL ORCHESTRA
61	HMV POP 977	Taboo/Midnight In Luxembourg	10
60	Triumph TRY 4000	THOSE PLUCKING STRINGS (LP, unreleased, test pressings only)	500

OTIS BLACKWELL
58	London HLE 8616	Make Ready For Love/When You're Around	40

RORY BLACKWELL & HIS BLACKJACKS
57	Parlophone R 4236	Bye Bye Love/Such A Shame	20

SCRAPPER BLACKWELL
63	'77' LA 12/4	BLUES BEFORE SUNRISE (LP)	40
60s	Xtra XTRA 5011	MR SCRAPPER'S BLUES (LP)	25

BLACKWELLS (U.K.)
65	Columbia DB 7442	Why Don't You Love Me/All I Want Is Your Love	15

BLACKWELLS (U.S.)
60	London HLW 9135	Unchained Melody/Mansion On The Hill	10
61	London HLW 9234	Love Or Money/Big Daddy And The Cat	8

BLACK WIDOW

MINT VALUE £

BLACK WIDOW
70	CBS 5031	Come To The Sabbat/Way To Power	20
71	CBS 7596	Wish You Would/Accident	20
70	CBS 63948	SACRIFICE (LP, gatefold sleeve)	100
70	CBS 64133	BLACK WIDOW II (LP, gatefold sleeve)	100
72	CBS 64562	BLACK WIDOW III (LP, with inner)	100

(see also Pesky Gee, Agony Bag)

BLADE
88	Chart Moves 732-1532	Chart Moves (12", not officially released. Intended to be instructions to game of same name but never used in final version of game)	25
89	Raw Bass 1202	Lyrical Maniac/The Comin' Is Near/We're Going Independent (12")	15
89	691 Influential 1203	Mind Of An Ordinary Citizen/Forward (12")	12
91	691 Influential 1204	Rough It Up/Whatcha Waitin' For?/You Better Get Yours (12")	12
93	691 Influential 1206	Clear The Way/They Ain't Shit To Me (12", white vinyl, Blade gave this to fans who paid in advance for his THE LION GOES FROM STRENGTH TO STRENGTH LP)	12
96	691 Influential SURV 1	Survival Of The Hardest Working (12")	25
97	Bomb 2006	Rhyme Bomb/The Way It Has To Be (12")	10
92	691 Influential 1205	SURVIVAL OF THE HARDEST WORKING (LP)	15
93	691 Influential 1202	THE LION GOES FROM STRENGTH TO STRENGTH (LP)	20
95	691 Influential 1208	PLANNED AND EXECUTED (LP, limited edition on red vinyl)	25

ANDY BLADE
80	SMS SMS 001	Break The News/Girl With The Goods (p/s)	25

(see also Eater)

JOYELLA BLADE
78	Front Line FLS108	Cairo/Cairo Dub	8

BLADE RUNNER
84	Ebony EBON 26	Back Street Lady/Too Far Too Late	6
84	Ebony EBON 21	HUNTED (LP)	15

BLADES
81	Reekus RKS005	The Bride Wore White/Animation (p/s)	25
80	Energy NRG 3	Hot For You/The Reunion (p/s; Irish with paper labels)	20
80	Energy NRG 3	Hot For You/The Reunion (p/s; later UK pressing with plastic labels, in plastic sleeve)	15
81	Energy NRG 5	Ghost Of A Chance/Real Emotion (p/s; Irish with paper labels)	20
81	Energy NRG 5	Ghost Of A Chance/Real Emotion (p/s; later UK pressing with plastic labels, in plastic sleeve)	12
84	Reekus RKS 013	The Last Man In Europe/Sadlands (p/s)	12
85	Reekus RKS 15	Those Were The Days (p/s)	10
86	Reekus RKS 017	Downmarket/Truth Don't Hurt (as Blades with Paul Cleary)	10
84	Reekus RKLP 1	THE LAST MAN IN EUROPE (LP)	20
86	Reekus RKLP 3	RAY TOWN REVISITED (LP)	20

(see also Partisans)

BLADES OF GRASS
67	Stateside SS 2040	Happy/That's What A Boy Likes	15
68	Stateside SS 2101	Charlie And Fred/You Won't Find That Girl	10

BLAGGER
70	Mount Clifton MCL 002	Day After Day/The Hunt Is On	30

BLAH BLAH BLAH
81	Some Bizzare	BLAH BLAH BLAH (LP, unreleased, stickered sleeve, white label test pressings only)	40

HAL BLAINE (& YOUNG COUGARS)
64	RCA RD 7624	DEUCES, T'S, ROADSTERS AND DRUMS (LP, mono)	15
64	RCA SF 7624	DEUCES, T'S, ROADSTERS AND DRUMS (LP, stereo)	15

BLAIR
79	Miracle M4	Night Life/Virgo Princess	8
79	Miracle M4-12	Night Life/Virgo Princess (12")	40

ARNOLD BLAIR
76	Curtom NEET 1024	Trying To Get Next To You/I Won The Big Deal/House Party (12" with Fred Wesley)	15
12	Outta Sight MSX 03	Trying To Get Next To You/I Won The Big Deal (reissue)	7
16	Soul Jazz SJR 347-7	Trying To Get Next To You/I Won The Big Deal (reissue)	8
16	Super Disco Edits SDE 20	Finally Made It Home/I Won The Big Deal This Time (Alternative Version)	20

BEVERLEY BLAIR
58	Mercury 7MT 209	With Love We Live/Tony	10

JOYCE BLAIR AND OLIVER REED
63	Picadilly 7N 35083	Baby It's Cold Outside/JOYCE BLAIR: Safe In The Arms Of My Darling	15

VERN BLAIR DEBATE
05	Funk 45 FUNK45 024	Super Funk/Ooh Ah Ee (reissue)	15

BARDI BLAISE
80	Din Disc DIN 8	Trans Siberian Express/Competition Side (p/s)	6

COREY BLAKE
04	Grapevine 2000 G2K 45-144	How Can I Go On Without You/Your Love Is Like A Boomerang	8

DAVID BLAKE
69	SNB 55-4178	We'll Meet Again/Now is The Time	7

ERIC BLAKE
80	Carrere CAR 141	Sin City/Zero 6 (p/s)	10
81	Carrere CAR 179	Born To Be Special/80s Girl/Give Generously (p/s)	10

GARRY BLAKE
66	Columbia DB 7885	Strawberries And Cream/Look Out Now!	8
66	Columbia DB 7977	Wait Until Dark/Jungle Juice	8
66	Columbia DB 8074	The Danny Scipio Theme/Celebration Day	10

KARL BLAKE
83	Glass GLASS 013	THE PREHENSILE TAPES (LP)	20

(see also Lemon Kittens, Shock Headed Peters, Underneath, Gland Shrouds, Fur Fur, Sol Invictus)

Keith BLAKE

MINT VALUE £

KEITH BLAKE
68 Blue Cat BS 102   Musically/I'm Moving On 175
(see also Overtakers, Uniques, Prince Allah)

TIM BLAKE
78 Barclay Towers BAR 711   Generator Laserbeam/Woodland Voice (p/s) 8
78 Barclay Towers CLAY 7005 BLAKE'S NEW JERUSALEM (LP) 15
(see also Gong, Hawkwind)

WINSTON BLAKE & M-SQUAD
69 Crab 40   Big Thing/RUPIE EDWARDS : Exclusively Yours 20
71 Green Door GD 4003   Carrol Street/ANSELL COLLINS & M-SQUAD: Carol St. Version 12

ART BLAKEY JAZZ MESSENGERS
57 Parlophone PMC 1084   HARD DRIVE (LP) 25
58 Parlophone PMC 1099   BIG BAND (LP) 25
59 Vogue LAE 12096   RITUAL (LP) 25
59 London 15157   ART BLAKEY'S JAZZ MESSENGERS WITH THELONIOUS MONK (LP) 20
61 Fontana TFL 5116   OLYMPIA CONCERT (LP) 25
62 HMV CLP 1532   ART BLAKEY JAZZ MESSENGERS (LP, also stereo CSD 1423) 30
62 Fontana TFL 5184   DANGEROUS FRIENDSHIPS (LP, soundtrack) 25
63 RCA Victor RD 7555   A NIGHT IN TUNISIA (LP) 25
63 United Artists (S)ULP 1017 THREE BLIND MICE (LP, mono/stereo) 20
64 Riverside RLP 438   CARAVAN (LP) 20
64 HMV CLP 1760   A JAZZ MESSAGE (LP) 30
64 Riverside RLP 464   UGETSU (LP) 30
65 Limelight (S)LML 4000   'S MAKE IT (LP) 25
66 Limelight (S)LML 4012   SOUL FINGER (LP) 25
66 Limelight (S)LML 4021   BUTTERCORN LADY (LP) 25
66 Fontana FJL 111   SOUL! (LP) 25
67 Limelight (S)LML 4023   HOLD ON, I'M COMIN' (LP) 20
67 Atlantic 590 009   BLUE MONK (LP, with Thelonious Monk) 20
68 Riverside 673013   KYOTO (LP) 25
69 Polydor 545101   DRUM THUNDER (LP) 15
(see also Annie Ross)

ART BLAKEY/MILES DAVIS
66 Fontana FJL 135   L'ASCENSEUR POUR L'ECHAFAUD/FEMME DISPARAISSANTE (LP, soundtrack, 1 side each) 30
(see also Thelonious Monk, Miles Davis)

ALAN BLAKLEY
75 DJM DJS 367   Sorry (Lyn's Song)/Windows Are Nice 8
(see also the Tremeloes)

BLAK TWANG
95 Sound Of Money SNM 005   Queen's Head/Mr Jam Promota (12" with Roots Manuva) 12
02 Bad Magic MAGICT 25   SO ROTTEN EP (12", p/s) 20
96 Sound Of Money SNM 008   DETTWORK SOUTH EAST (LP - unissued) 75
02 Bad Magic MAGIC LP 5   KIK OFF (2-LP, artwork by Banksy) 50

BLANCK MASS
11 Rock Action ROCKACT 58LP BLANCK MASS (2-LP) 20
17 Sacred Bones SBR-174   WORLD EATER (LP, red vinyl, 200 only with print) 50

BLANCMANGE
80 Blaah Music MFT-1   IRENE AND MAVIS (EP, gatefold p/s) 40

BILLY BLAND
60 London HL 9096   Let The Little Girl Dance/Sweet Thing 12

BOBBY BLAND
61 Vogue V 9178   Cry Cry Cry/I've Been Wrong So Long 30
61 Vogue V 9182   Lead Me On/Hold Me Tenderly 30
61 Vogue V 9188   Don't Cry No More/St. James Infirmary 30
62 Vogue V 9190   You're The One (That I Need)/Turn On Your Love Light 30
62 Vogue V 9192   Blue Moon/Who Will The Next Fool Be? 30
64 Vocalion VP 9222   Ain't Nothing You Can Do/Honey Child 30
64 Vocalion VP 9229   After It's Too Late/Share Your Love With Me 30
65 Vocalion VP 9232   Yield Not To Temptation/How Does A Cheating Woman Feel? 30
65 Vocalion VP 9251   These Hands (Small But Mighty)/Today 30
66 Vocalion VP 9262   I'm Too Far Gone (To Turn Around)/ If You Could Read My Mind 25
66 Vocalion VP 9273   Good Time Charlie/Good Time Charlie (Working His Groove Bag) 35
68 Sue WI 4044   That Did It/A Touch Of The Blues 50
69 Action ACT 4524   Rockin' In The Same Old Boat/Wouldn't You Rather Have Me? 30
69 Action ACT 4538   Gotta Get To Know You/Baby I'm On My Way 30
69 Action ACT 4548   Share Your Love With Me/Honey Child 40
69 Action ACT 4553   Chains Of Love/Ask Me 'Bout Nothing But The Blues 30
74 ABC ABC 4014   Ain't No Love In The Heart Of The City/Twenty Four Blues 10
85 Kent Town 108   Shoes/Call On Me/Getting Used To The Blues/Good Time Charlie (EP, p/s) 10
63 Vocalion VEP 170153   BOBBY BLAND (EP) 80
64 Vocalion VEP 170157   BOBBY BLAND SINGS (EP) 100
60 Vogue VA 160183   TWO STEPS FROM THE BLUES (LP) 200
61 Vocalion VA 160183   TWO STEPS FROM THE BLUES (LP) 200
61 Vogue VAP 8027   AIN'T NOTHING YOU CAN DO (LP) 75
64 Vocalion VAP 8027   AIN'T NOTHING YOU CAN DO (LP) 40
63 Vogue VAP 8034   CALL ON ME/ THAT'S THE WAY LOVE IS (LP) 75
64 Vocalion VAP 8034   CALL ON ME/ THAT'S THE WAY LOVE IS (LP) 40
66 Vocalion VAP 8041   HERE'S THE MAN (LP) 50
68 Island ILP 974   A TOUCH OF THE BLUES (LP) 100

Marcie BLANE

MINT VALUE £

69	Action ACLP 6006	A PIECE OF GOLD (LP)	40
74	ABC ABCL 5053	DREAMER (LP)	30
74	Polydor 2383 257	BLUES FOR MR. CRUMP (LP, with tracks by Junior Parker & Howlin' Wolf)	20
85	Kent 044	THE SOULFUL SIDE OF BOBBY BLAND (LP)	15

MARCIE BLANE

62	London HLU 9599	Bobby's Girl/A Time To Dream	10
63	London HLU 9673	What Does A Girl Do/How Can I Tell Him	10
63	London HLU 9744	Little Miss Fool/Ragtime Sound	10
63	London HLU 9787	You Gave My Number To Billy/Told You So	15
63	London REU 1393	MARCIE BLANE (EP)	75

BLANKS

| 79 | Void SRTS/79/CUS/560 | The Northern Ripper/Understand (p/s) | 70 |

(see also Destructors)

BLANK STUDENTS

| 80 | Dexter Discs | We Are Natives/I Want To Be Happy (500 only) | 25 |

BLAPPS POSSE

| 90 | Sex 075 | DON'T HOLD BACK (12" EP) | 12 |
| 92 | Ruff Lick LIKK 002 | SET YOURSELF FREE (12" EP) | 15 |

BLARNEY SISTERS

| 67 | GO AJ11407 | The Greatest Blessing/Golden Band | 15 |

BLAST FURNACE AND THE HEATWAVES

| 78 | HOT 1 | BLUE WAVE (EP) | 8 |

BLAWAN

10	Hessle Audio HES 013	Fram/Iddy (12")	12
11	Down 001	Getting Me Down (1-sided 12")	25
12	Hinge Finger HINF 8674	HIS HE SHE & SHE (12" EP, p/s)	25

BLAZE

| 99 | Slip And Slide SLIP 99 | Wishing You Were Here/(Mixes) (2x12") | 10 |

BLAZE X

| 80 | Fixed Wheel FX 1 | Some Hope/Rippy (Irish pressing, gatefold p/s) | 150 |

BLAZER, BLAZER

| 78 | Logo GO 362 | Cecil B. Devine/Warsaw/Six O'Clock In The Morning (p/s) | 10 |

BLAZERS

| 58 | Fontana TFR 6010 | ROCK AND ROLL (10" LP) | 30 |

BLAZING SONS

| 83 | Cool Ghoul COOL 002 | Chant Down The National Front/N.F. Dub (no p/s) | 10 |

(see also Phantom)

BLEACH BOYS

| 78 | Tramp THF 002 | Chloroform/You've Got Nothing (no p/s, 1,000 only) | 60 |
| 85 | Zombie International ZOMBO 103010 | Stocking-Clad Nazi Death Squad Bitches/Death Before Disco/Gimme That Neutron Taste (12", p/s) | 25 |

BLEAK HOUSE

80s	Buzzard BUZZ 1	Rainbow Warrior/Isandlhwana/Inquisition (in p/s)	100
80s	Buzzard BUZZ 1	Rainbow Warrior/Isandlhwana/Inquisition	30
82	Buzzard BUZZ 2	LIONS IN WINTER (Chase The Wind/No Reply/Down To Zero/ Flight Of The Salamander) (EP, p/s with insert)	90

BLEECHERS

69	Trojan TR 679	Ease Up/You're Gonna Feel It	20
69	Upsetter US 314	Come Into My Parlour/MELOTONES: Dry Up Your Tears	120
70	Col. Blue Beat DB 118	Send Me The Pillow (That You Dream On)/Adam And Eve	20
71	Duke DU 187	Put It Good/J.J. ALLSTARS: Good Good Version	20

(see also Busty Brown, Upsetters)

BLEEDING HEARTS

| 80 | Crazy Plane SP 003 | This Is The Way/OK | 30 |

PETER BLEGVAD

| 77 | Virgin V 2082 | KEW RHONE (LP, with John Greaves) | 15 |

(see also Slapp Happy)

BLENDELLS

64	Reprise RS 20291	La La La La La La/Huggies Bunnies	10
64	Reprise RS 20291	La La La La La La/Huggies Bunnies (DJ Copy)	20
64	Reprise RS 20340	Dance With Me/Get Your Baby	50
64	Reprise RS 20340	Dance With Me/Get Your Baby (DJ Copy)	60

CARLA BLEY

| 72 | JCOA JT 4001 | ESCALATOR OVER THE HILL (3xLP, gatefold with Paul Haines & Jack Bruce) | 25 |
| 74 | Watt WATT 1 | TROPIC APPETITES (LP, gatefold sleeve) | 15 |

(see also Jazz Composers Orchestra, Michael Mantler, Jack Bruce)

PAUL BLEY TRIO

| 69 | Fontana SFJL 929 | TOUCHING (LP) | 100 |

(see also Bley-Peacock Synthesizer Show, Annette Peacock)

BLEY-PEACOCK SYNTHESIZER SHOW

| 72 | Polydor 2425 043 | REVENGE (LP) | 250 |

(see also Annette Peacock, Paul Bley)

ARCHIE BLEYER & HIS ORCHESTRA

54	London HL 8035	Amber/Julie's Jump	8
54	London HL 8111	The Naughty Lady Of Shady Lane/While The Vesper Bells Were Ringing	8
55	London HLA 8176	Hernando's Hideaway/S'il Vous Plait	8
56	London HLA 8243	Nothin' To Do/JANET BLEYER: 'Cause You're My Lover	10
56	London HLA 8263	Bridge Of Happiness/You Tell Me Your Dream, I'll Tell You Mine (Gold Tri)	10

B,L&G

| 71 | Birds Nest BN 3 | Live In The Mountains/Janie Slow Down | 7 |

(see also Trevor Burton, Denny Laine, Steve Gibbons)

BLIND BLAKE

MINT VALUE £

BLIND BLAKE
58 Ristic LP 18 — THE LEGENDARY BLIND BLAKE (10" LP) 35
(see also Paramount Allstars)

BLIND BLAKE/CHARLIE JACKSON
50s Heritage HLP 1011 — BLIND BLAKE AND CHARLIE JACKSON (LP, 99 only) 40

BLIND FAITH
69 Island (no cat. no.) — Change Of Address From June 23rd 1969 (promo issue, 500 only) 500
69 Polydor 583 059 — BLIND FAITH (LP, gatefold sleeve, first pressing with single paper on left gatefold stating distribution by Polydor and Island) 100
69 Polydor 583 059 — BLIND FAITH (LP, gatefold sleeve, later issue without Polydor and Island distribution credit) 40
77 RSO 2394142 — BLIND FAITH (LP, reissue) 15
83 RSO SPELP 14 — BLIND FAITH (LP, reissue) 15
08 RSO 53167 — BLIND FAITH (LP, reissue 180gm vinyl) 15
(see also Stevie Winwood, Ginger Baker, Eric Clapton)

BLIND LEMON CLEGG
80 Pollen PBM 029 — RUN FOR YOUR MONEY EP 50

BLINDERS
17 (No label or Cat. No.) — Swine/Ramona Flowers (p/s) 70
19 Modern Sky — Rat In A Gabe/Nuclear Love (p/s) 30
18 Modern Sky MODERN060LP — COLUMBIA (LP) 15

BLINKERS
69 Pye 7N 17752 — Original Sin/Dreams Secondhand 60

BLINKY & EDWIN STARR
69 Tamla Motown TMG 720 — Oh How Happy/Ooo Baby Baby (unissued, demos only) 375
70 Tamla Motown TMG 748 — Oh How Happy/Ooo Baby Baby 10
70 T. Motown (S)TML 11131 — JUST WE TWO (LP, as Edwin Starr & Blinky) 25
(see also Edwin Starr)

BLISS
69 Chapter One CH 107 — Courtyards In Castile/Lifetime 15

MELVIN BLISS
77 Contempo CS 2013 — Reward/Synthetic Substitution 80

BLITZ
81 No Future OI 1 — ALL OUT ATTACK (EP, rubber-stamped labels, 500 only, fold-out sleeve) 30
81 No Future OI 1 — ALL OUT ATTACK (EP, reissue, initially with white labels, fold-out sleeve) 15
81 No Future OI 1 — ALL OUT ATTACK (EP, reissue, later printed labels) 10
82 No Future OI 6 — Never Surrender/Razor In The Night (p/s) 12
82 No Future OI 16 — Warriors/Youth (p/s) 15
82 No Future PUNK 1 — VOICE OF A GENERATION (LP, with inner sleeve) 35
83 Future FL 1 — SECOND EMPIRE JUSTICE (LP) 35
88 Link LINK LP 029 — BLITZED - AN ALL OUT ATTACK (LP) 15
(see also Rose Of Victory)

BLITZ BOYS
80 Told You So TYS 001 — Eddy's New Shoes/Eddie's Friend/She Told My Friends (foldover p/s) 125

BLITZKREIG (1)
79 Ellie Jay/BRP EJSP 9257 — SURVIVAL (LP) 100

BLITZKRIEG (2)
81 Neat NEAT 10 — Buried Alive/Blitzkrieg (p/s) 60
91 Roadrunner R 09302 — 10 YEARS OF BLITZKRIEG (EP) 10
85 Neat NEAT 1023 — A TIME OF CHANGES (LP) 40

BLITZKRIEG (3)
82 No Future OI 8 — LEST WE FORGET (EP) 10
83 Sexual Phonograph SPH2 — Animals In Lipstick/Land Of Failure/No Compromise (p/s, SPH2 on cover but SPH3 on label) 15

BLITZKRIEG BOP
77 Mortonsound MTN 3172/3 — Let's Go/Nine Till Five/Bugger Off (p/s, 500 only) 100
77 Lightning GIL 504 — Let's Go (re-recorded)/Life Is Just A So-So/Mental Case (p/s) 30
78 Lightning GIL 543 — U.F.O./Bobby Joe (p/s) 20
(see also Basczax, The Gynaecologists, Nicky Beat)

BLIZZARD
71 CBS CBS 7238 — Baby Blue/Mama, The Sparrow And The Tree 8

BLIZZARD KING
97 Kalevala KALA 005 — Break On Through/Strangers In The Night/In The Ghetto 20

BLO
75 Afrodisia DWAPS 2009 — PHASE IV (LP) 40
01 Strut STRUTALP 004 — PHASES 1972-1982 (2-LP) 25

BLOC PARTY
04 Trash Aesthetics TA701 — She's Hearing Voices/The Marshals Are Dead/The Answer (p/s clear vinyl, 500 only) 50
04 Moshi Moshi MOSHI10 — Banquet/Staying Fat (p/s, 500 only) 15
04 Wichita WEBB 067S — Little Thoughts/Storm And Stress (Blue vinyl, p/s) 6
04 Wichita WEBB 070S — Helicopter/Skeleton (green vinyl) 20
05 Wichita WEBB 088S — The Pioneers/The Pioneers (Bloc Party vs Mystery Jets) (numbered pic disc) 10
07 Wichita WEBB 118S — The Prayer/England (1st 7" of 2 and comes in box) 15
08 Wichita WEBB 180T — MERCURY EP (2 x 7", CD in box) 15
12 Transgressive TRANS 137 — She's Hearing Voices/The Marshals Are Dead/The Answer (red vinyl, 500 only) 15
05 Wichita WEBB 075LP — SILENT ALARM (LP) 50
05 Wichita WEBB 075PD — SILENT ALARM (LP, picture disc) 50
05 Wichita WEBB 090LP — SILENT ALARM REMIXED (2-LP) 25
07 Wichita WEBB 120 LP — A WEEKEND IN THE CITY (LP) 15
07 Wichita WEBB 120 PD — A WEEKEND IN THE CITY (LP, picture disc) 30
08 Wichita WEBB 185PD — INTIMACY (LP, picture disc, 500 only) 15

BLOCKHEAD

MINT VALUE £

15	Wichita WEBB250LPTEN	SILENT ALARM (LP, reissue with free 7", 1000 only)	50

BLOCKHEAD
04	Ninja Tune ZEN 88	MUSIC BY CAVELIGHT (2xLP)	25

BLODWYN PIG
69	Island WIP 6059	Dear Jill/Sweet Caroline	15
69	Island WIP 6069	Walk On The Water/Summer Day	15
70	Chrysalis WIP 6078	Same Old Story/Slow Down	10
69	Island ILPS 9101	AHEAD RINGS OUT (LP, 1st pressing, gatefold sleeve, pink label with black/orange circle logo)	100
69	Island ILPS 9101	AHEAD RINGS OUT (LP, 2nd pressing, gatefold sleeve, with block logo)	50
70	Island ILPS 9101	AHEAD RINGS OUT (LP, gatefold sleeve, 3rd pressing with white i' logo)	40
70	Chrysalis ILPS 9122	GETTING TO THIS (LP, gatefold sleeve, island logo and address in white on green label)	70
70s	Island ILPS 9101	AHEAD RINGS OUT (LP, gatefold sleeve, reissue 'pink rim palm tree' label)	15

(see also Mick Abrahams, Jethro Tull)

BLOND
69	Fontana TF 1040	(I Will Bring You) Flowers In The Morning/I Wake Up And Call	12
69	Fontana STL 5515	THE LILAC YEARS (LP, gatefold sleeve)	125

(see also Tages)

BLONDE ON BLONDE
69	Pye 7N 17637	All Day All Night/Country Life	40
70	Ember EMB S 279	Castles In The Sky/Circles (in p/s)	20
70	Ember EMB S 279	Castles In The Sky/Circles (no p/s)	12
72	Ember EMB S 316	Sad Song For An Easy Lady/Happy Families (p/s)	15
69	Pye NSPL 18288	CONTRASTS (LP, gatefold sleeve, blue/black label with logo/banner on top)	175
70	Ember NR 5049	RE-BIRTH (LP, gatefold sleeve)	100
71	Ember NR 5058	REFLECTIONS ON A LIFE (LP, gatefold sleeve)	100
70s	Ember LP 7005	BLONDE ON BLONDE (LP, unissued, test pressings only)	300

BLONDIE
76	Private Stock PVT 90	X Offender/In The Sun (unissued, promos or stock copies, no p/s)	2000
76	Private Stock PVT 105	In The Flesh/X Offender (demo in promo p/s)	50
76	Private Stock PVT 105	In The Flesh/X Offender (no p/s)	20
77	Chrysalis CHS 2180	Rip Her To Shreds/In The Flesh/X Offender (p/s)	12
77	Chrysalis CHS 2180-12	Rip Her To Shreds/In The Flesh/X Offender (12", green or blue/white labels, '75p' strip on p/s)	10
78	Chrysalis CHS 2204	Denis (Denee)/Contact In Red Square/Kung Fu Girls (Contract pressing, paper labels with 'Denis', in red p/s)	8
78	Chrysalis CHS 2204-12	Denis (Denee)/Contact In Red Square/Kung Fu Girls (12", red p/s)	10
78	Chrysalis CHS 2217	(I'm Always Touched By Your) Presence Dear/Poet's Problems/Detroit 442 (p/s)	6
78	Chrysalis CHS 12-2217	(I'm Always Touched By Your) Presence Dear/Poet's Problems/Detroit 442 (12", p/s)	10
78	Chrysalis CHS 2242	Picture This/Fade Away (And Radiate) (p/s, yellow vinyl)	8
78	Chrysalis CHE 2266	Hanging On The Telephone/Will Anything Happen (p/s, export issue)	6
78	Chrysalis CHE 2275	Heart Of Glass/Rifle Range (p/s, export issue with "pain in the ass" lyrics)	8
81	Chrysalis 12-2485	Rapture (Special Disco Mix)/Live It Up (Special Disco Mix) (12", p/s)	15
98	EMI 12 ATOM 150	ATOMIC 98 (Remixes) (12", p/s, withdrawn)	15
76	Private Stock PVLP 1017	BLONDIE (LP)	20
77	Chrysalis CHR 1166	PLASTIC LETTERS (LP)	20
78	Chrysalis CHR 1166-P	PLASTIC LETTERS (LP, picture disc)	20
78	Chrysalis CDL1192	PARALLEL LINES (LP, inner)	20
81	Chrysalis CDL TV1	THE BEST OF BLONDIE (LP, with poster)	15
82	Chrysalis PCDL 1384	THE HUNTER (LP, picture disc)	15
97	Chrysalis 7243821459 1 2	PARALLEL LINES (LP, reissue, part of EMI 100 series, stickered sleeve)	20

(see also Debbie Harry, Wind In The Willows, Rodney & Brunettes)

ALPHA BLONDY
86	Sterns STERNS 1017	APARTHEID IS NAZISIM (LP)	15
87	Stern's STERNS 1019	JESUSALEM (LP, with the Wailers)	18

BLOOBLO
76	Feelgood FLG 104	Please Mister Please/Chaka	12
78	Mother & Son	IS THAT YOU (LP)	25

BLOOD
83	No Future OI 22	Megalomania/Calling The Shots/Parasite In Paradise (p/s)	20
83	Noise NOY 1	Stark Raving Normal/Mesrine (p/s)	18
82	Noise NOYZLP 1	FALSE GESTURES FOR A DEVIOUS PUBLIC (LP, inner)	35
85	Conquest QUEST 3	SE PARARE NEX (LP)	15
89	Link Classics CLINK 5	FALSE GESTURES FOR A DEVIOUS PUBLIC (LP, reissue, red vinyl)	15

BARRY BLOOD
75	Alaska ALA 24	Poor Annie/On The Run	40
82	Wretchord WOO 1	She's The Queen Of My Rock And Roll/What D'Ya Say?	40

BLOOD DIVINE
96	Peaceville VILE 62	AWAKEN (LP)	18

(see also Cradle Of filth, Anathema)

BLOOD DONOR
79	Arista ARIRV 262	Rubber Revolution/Chemical Babies (p/s red vinyl)	8
79	Arista ARIST 269	Rice Harvest/Something Happened (p/s)	10
81	Safari SAFE 29	Doctor/Soap Box Blues (p/s)	10

BLOOD RED SHOES
06	Jonson Family	Bless His Heart/Don't Always Say Yes/Victory For The Magpie (p/s, insert, 500 only)	25
06	Try Harder	Stitch Me Back/Meet Me At Eight (500 only)	30
07	V2 B000PHX186	It's Getting Boring By The Sea/Box Of Secrets (p/s)	8
13	V2 VVR 726627	Red River/Black Distractions/Idle Hands (10" red vinyl)	10
17	Jazz Life JAZZLIFE 09	Eye To Eye (gig only red flexi)	25
08	V2 1763548	BOX OF SECRETS (LP)	25

BLOODROCK

MINT VALUE £

10	V2 VVR736628	FIRE LIKE THIS (LP, silkscreened sleeve)	15
12	V2 VVR795935	IN TIME TO VOICES (LP, silkscreened cover with CD)	20
14	Jazz Life JAZZLIFE 1 BDL	BLOOD RED SHOES (LP, orange/purple vinyl with 2 CDs)	20

BLOODROCK
71	Capitol CL 15670	D.O.A./Children's Heritage	8
71	Capitol E-ST 491	BLOODROCK 2 (LP)	15
71	Capitol E-ST 765	BLOODROCK 3 (LP)	15

BLOOD SHANTI
96	Aba Shanti ABA 12003	Tear Down Babylon/Verse 1/Verse 2/Verse 3/Verse 4 (12")	35
96	Falasha ABA10002	Children Of The Most High/Verse 1/Verse 2/Verse 3 (12")	40
00	Falasha AB12003	What A Gwan/Dub/Banks Of The Nile/Dub (12")	10
00	Falasha AB12004	Jah Liveth (One Love)/Dub/Hail Jah/Dub (12")	30
02	Aba Shanti ABALP 002	PURE SPIRIT (LP)	30
02	Aba Shanti ABALP 005	UNDILUTED (LP)	20

BLOOD SISTERS
79	Sound City SCD 002	Ring My Bell/Dub (12")	20
79	Sound City SCD 004	What About Me/I'd Rather Go Blind (12")	15
79	Sound City SCD 006	My Love Don't Come Easy/My Guy (12")	12
80	King & City KCD001	Be Thankful/What About Me (12")	20
81	Ballistic 12BP314	Don't Say Goodbye Too Loud/Let Me Love You (12", some on clear vinyl)	20

BLOOD, SWEAT & TEARS
68	CBS 3563	I Can't Quit Her/House In The Country	20
74	CBS 2462	Tell Me That I'm Wrong/Rock Reprise	20
68	CBS 63296	CHILD IS THE FATHER TO THE MAN (LP)	20

(see also Al Kooper)

ROGER BLOOM'S HAMMER
| 67 | CBS 202654 | Out Of The Blue/Life's A Gamble | 40 |
| 67 | CBS 2848 | Polly Pan/Fifteen Degree Temperature Rise | 40 |

MIKE BLOOMFIELD
| 69 | CBS 63652 | IT'S NOT KILLING ME (LP) | 20 |

(see also Barry Goldberg Reunion, Stephen Stills, K.G.B.)

MIKE BLOOMFIELD & AL KOOPER
69	CBS 4094	The Weight/59th Street Bridge Song	10
69	CBS 66216	THE LIVE ADVENTURES OF MIKE BLOOMFIELD AND AL KOOPER (2-LP, mono)	60
69	CBS 66216	THE LIVE ADVENTURES OF MIKE BLOOMFIELD AND AL KOOPER (2-LP, stereo)	25

(see also Al Kooper, Paul Butterfield Blues Band, Electric Flag)

BLOOMFIELDS
| 72 | Pye 7N 45114 | The Loner/Homing In On The Next Trade Wind | 15 |

BLOSSOM TOES
67	Marmalade 598 002	What On Earth/Mrs Murphy's Budgerigar/Look At Me I'm You (in p/s)	70
67	Marmalade 598 002	What On Earth/Mrs Murphy's Budgerigar/Look At Me I'm You	30
68	Marmalade 598 009	I'll Be Your Baby Tonight/Love Is	30
68	Marmalade 598 012	Postcard/Everyone's Leaving Me Now	30
69	Marmalade 598 014	Peace Loving Man/Up Above My Hobby Horse's Head	30
69	Marmalade 598 022	New Day/Love Bomb (unissued, existence unconfirmed)	0
67	Marmalade 607 001	WE ARE EVER SO CLEAN (LP, mono)	700
67	Marmalade 608 001	WE ARE EVER SO CLEAN (LP, stereo)	800
69	Marmalade 608 010	IF ONLY FOR A MOMENT (LP)	800
07	Sunbeam SBR2LP5035	WE ARE EVER SO CLEAN (2-LP, reissue)	20
07	Sunbeam SBR2LP5036	IF ONLY FOR A MOMENT (2-LP, reissue)	20

(see also B.B. Blunder, Stud, Kevin Westlake, Solid Gold Cadillac)

BLOSSOMS (1)
58	Capitol CL 14833	Move On/He Promised Me	50
58	Capitol CL 14856	Little Louie/Have Faith In Me	40
58	Capitol CL 14947	No Other Love/Baby Daddy-O	40
68	MGM MGM 1435	Tweedle Dee/You Got Me Hummin'	20
71	Pama PM 814	Stand By/Soul And Inspiration	30

(see also Darlene Love, Allisons [U.S.])

BLOSSOMS (2)
14	RIP 0001	BLOOM EP (CD-R, 100 only)	50
14	Skeleton Key SKL 015	Blow/Winters Kiss (yellow vinyl)	50
15	Skeleton Key SKL 016	Cut Me And I'll Bleed/The Urge (live) (clear vinyl)	18
15	Virgin 4761817	Charlemagne/Across The Moor/Polka Dot Bones/For Evelyn (12")	10
16	Virgin 4771395	You Pulled A Gun On Me/Getting Away With It (live)	20
16	Virgin V 3156	BLOSSOMS (LP)	25

MICHAEL BLOUNT
70	CBS 5248	Ryba Jyba/Acorn Street	15
71	CBS 64230	PATCHWORK (LP)	20
72	York FYK 401	SOUVENIRS (LP)	20
73	York FYK 414	FANTASIES (LP)	20

BLOWZABELLA
| 82 | Plant Life PLR 051 | IN COLOUR (LP) | 30 |
| 90 | Special Delivery SPD 1028 | VANILLA (LP) | 40 |

BLUE
73	RSO 2090 109	Red Light Song/Look Around	6
73	RSO 2090 114	Little Jody/The Way Things Are	6
73	RSO 2394 105	BLUE (LP)	15

(see also Poets, Thunderclap Newman)

BABBITY BLUE
| 65 | Decca F 12053 | Don't Make Me (Fall In Love With You)/I Remembered How To Cry | 8 |

BOBBY BLUE

MINT VALUE £

65	Decca F 12149	Don't Hurt Me/Question	6

BOBBY BLUE
70	Duke DU 86	Going In Circles (actually by Lloyd Charmers)/Doggone Right (actually by Winston Francis)	20

DAVID BLUE
69	Reprise RS20830	Beautiful Susan/You Don't Need A Thing	8
67	Elektra EKL 4003	DAVID BLUE (LP, red label)	50
72	Asylum SYL 9001	STORIES (LP)	20
73	Asylum SYL 9009	NICE BABY AND THE ANGEL (LP)	20
75	Asylum SYL 9025	COMIN' BACK FOR MORE (LP)	20
76	Asylum K 53056	CUPID'S ARROW (LP)	20

PAMELA BLUE
63	Decca F 11761	My Friend Bobby/Hey There Stranger	70

TIMOTHY BLUE
68	Spark SRL 1014	The Room At The Top Of The Stairs/She Won't See The Light	20

BLUE ACES
64	Pye 7N 15672	Land Of Love/Love Song Of The Waterfall	15
64	Pye 7N 15713	I Beat You To It/I Just Can't Help Loving You	15
65	Pye 7N 15821	Ain't What You Say/You Don't Care	15
65	Columbia DB 7755	Tell Me What You're Gonna Do/All I Want	100
66	Columbia DB 7954	That's All Right/Talk About My Baby	100

(see also Riot Squad)

BLUE ANCHOR
79	Workhouse WHR 6	PLENTY LOVE & BACON (LP)	15

BLUE ANGEL
80	Polydor POSP 212	I'm Gonna Be Strong/Anna Blue (no p/s)	6
81	Polydor POSP 241	I Had A Love/Can't Blame Me	8
84	Polydor POSP 212	I'm Gonna Be Strong/Anna Blue (p/s, reissue)	8
80	Polydor 2391 486	BLUE ANGEL (LP)	25

BLUE ANGER
89	Future Art FA 0089	Total Intervention/The Drunken Teenagers (p/s)	8

BLUE AQUARIUS
73	Akashic 998	The Ultimate Train/At The Feet Of The Master	30

BLUE ARSED FLY
95	Ferox FER 012	IN THE BAG EP (12")	15
96	Mosquito MSQ 04	BLUE ARSED FLY EP (12")	20

(see also Christian Vogel, Neil Landstrumm)

BLUE BEARD
71	Ember EMB S 302	Country Man/Sly Willy (in p/s)	30
71	Ember EMB S 302	Country Man/Sly Willy (no p/s)	20
71	Ember LT 7004	BLUE BEARD (LP, unreleased, test pressings only)	200

BLUEBEATERS
64	Piccadilly 7N 35181	Little David/Ain't Got A Care	7

BLUEBEATS
64	Ember EMB EP 4525	THE FABULOUS BLUEBEATS VOL. 1 (EP)	25
64	Ember EMB EP 4526	THE FABULOUS BLUEBEATS VOL. 2 (EP)	25

BLUE BEATS
60	Blue Beat 45/BB 20	Baby What You Done Me Wrong/Go Pretty Baby Go	20

BLUE-BELLES
62	HMV POP 1029	I Sold My Heart To The Junkman/Itty Bitty Twist	15

(see also Patti Labelle)

BLUE BELLS & JAH BERRY
78	Burning Rockers BRD 001	Teacher Teach, Teach The Youth/Golden Rule (12")	30

BLUEBERRIES
66	Mercury MF 894	It's Gonna Work Out Fine/Please Don't Let Me Know	75

BLUE BLOOD
70	Sonet SNTF 615	BLUE BLOOD (LP)	25

BLUE BLUDD
87	Blud Donor no cat. No.	LIQUOR 'N' POKER (EP)	20

BLUEBOY
91	Sarah SARAH 55	Clearer/Alison (p/s, insert)	20
93	Sarah SARAH 70	Cloud Babies (6" one-sided flexi with fanzine)	15
92	Sarah SARAH 65	Popkiss/Chelsea Guitar/Fearon (p/s, insert)	20
93	Sarah SARAH 74	Meet Johnny Rave/Elle/Air France (p/s)	15
93	Sarah SARAH 80	SOME GORGEOUS ACCIDENT EP (wraparound p/s in ply bay, insert)	15
94	Sarah SARAH 88	River/Nimbus/Hit	15
95	Sarah SARAH 99	Dirty Mags/Loony Tunes/Toulouse (p/s)	20
92	Sarah SARAH 612	IF WISHES WERE HORSES (LP)	40
94	Sarah SARAH 620	UNISEX (LP)	40

BLUE CHEER
68	Philips BF 1646	Summertime Blues/Out Of Focus	25
68	Philips BF 1684	Just A Little Bit/Gypsy Ball	12
68	Philips BF 1711	Feathers From Your Tree/Sun Cycle	12
69	Philips BF 1778	West Coast Child Of Sunshine/When It All Gets Old	15
71	Philips 6051 010	Pilot/Babaji (Twilight Raga)	15
68	Philips BL 7839	VINCEBUS ERUPTUM (LP, mono)	75
68	Philips (S)BL 7839	VINCEBUS ERUPTUM (LP, stereo)	50
68	Philips SBL 7860	OUTSIDEINSIDE (LP, gatefold sleeve)	75
69	Philips SBL 7896	NEW! IMPROVED! (LP)	60
69	Philips 6336 001	BLUE CHEER (LP)	60

BLUE CHIPS

MINT VALUE £

| 71 | Philips 6336 004 | B.C. #5 THE ORIGINAL HUMAN BEING (LP) | 60 |

(see also Leigh Stephens, Group B)

BLUE CHIPS
65	Pye 7N 15970	I'm On The Right Side/You're Good To Me	30
66	Pye 7N 17111	Some Kind Of Lovin'/I Know A Boy	20
66	Pye 7N 17155	Tell Her/Good Lovin' Never Hurt	20

BLUE DANUBE
| 80 | EMI EMI 5070 | You Are A Song (Du Bist Musik)/Let Me Hear That Song Again/Du Bist Musik | 8 |

BLUE EPITAPH
| 74 | Holyground HG 117 | ODE (LP, 99 copies only) | 400 |
| 91 | Holyground HG 117 | ODE (LP, reissue, folded gatefold sleeve) | 25 |

(see also Magus)

BLUE EYES
| 91 | Union Hall 001 | Pick Up The Mic On A Soul Tip/The Law (12") | 15 |

BLUE & FERRIS
| 68 | Blue Cat BS 147 | You Stole My Money/Tell Me The Reason | 40 |

BLUE FLAMES
| 63 | R&B JB 114 | J.A. Blues/Orange Street | 60 |
| 63 | R&B JB 126 | Stop Right Here/Rik's Tune | 60 |

(see also Georgie Fame & Blue Flames)

BLUE GOOSE
| 75 | Anchor ANCL 2005 | BLUE GOOSE (LP) | 15 |

(see also Badfinger, Curtis Knight & Zeus, Motorhead)

BLUE HORIZON
| 71 | Folk Heritage FHR 022S | BLUE HORIZON (LP) | 350 |

BLUE ICE
| 82 | Vulcan | Falling Tears/The Rocker/That Place/A Dream Come True | 8 |

BLUE JEANS
| 69 | Columbia DB 8555 | Hey Mrs. Housewife/Sandfly | 50 |

(see also Swinging Blue Jeans, Ray Ennis & Blue Jeans)

BLUE MAXI
| 70 | Major Minor MM 705 | Here Comes Summer/Famous Last Words | 8 |

BLUE MEN
60	Triumph RGXST 5000	I HEAR A NEW WORLD (PART ONE) (EP)	300
60	Triumph RGXST 5001	I HEAR A NEW WORLD (PART TWO) (EP, only sleeves exist, this price is for sleeve)	25
60	Triumph TRX ST 9000	I HEAR A NEW WORLD (LP, unreleased, white label demos only)	800
20	Electronic Sound ES 762	I HEAR A NEW WORLD (PART ONE) (p/s, reissue)	15

(see also Joe Meek, Peter Jay & Blue Men, Rodd-Ken & Cavaliers)

BLUE MINK
70	Philips SBL 7926	MELTING POT (LP)	15
71	Philips 6308 024	OUR WORLD (LP)	15
73	EMI EMA 756	ONLY WHEN I LAUGH (LP, gatefold sleeve)	15
74	EMI EMC3021	FRUITY (LP)	15

BLUE MIST
| 74 | Ice ICE 1 | Riding To The War/Who Are You | 15 |

BLUE MOVIES
| 79 | ROK ROK 9 | Mary Jane/THE NOISE: Criminal (company sleeve) | 15 |

BLUE NILE
81	RSO RSO 84	I Love This Life/The Second Act (p/s)	20
83	Linn LKH 001	A WALK ACROSS THE ROOFTOPS (LP)	20
89	Linn LKH 2	HATS (LP)	40
14	Epstein EPL01	PEACE AT LAST (2-LP, reissue)	70

BLUE NOTES
76	Ogun OGD 001/002	BLUE NOTES FOR MONGEZI (2-LP)	50
78	OGUN OG 220	BLUE NOTES IN CONCERT VOLUME 1 (LP)	25
87	OGUN OG 532	BLUE NOTES FOR JOHNNY (LP)	20

BLUENOTES
| 60 | Top Rank JAR 291 | I Don't Know What It Is/You Can't Get Away From Love | 10 |

BLUE ORCHIDS
| 84 | Rough Trade ROUGH 36 | GREATEST HITS (LP) | 15 |

(see also Nosebleeds, Fall, Fates)

BLUE OX BABES
| 88 | Go! Discs GOLP 14 | APPLES AND ORANGES (LP, unissued, test pressings only) | 50 |

(see also Dexys midnight Runners)

BLUE ÖYSTER CULT
| 76 | CBS 4483 | (Don't Fear) The Reaper/Tattoo Vampire (promo with different B-side) | 10 |
| 73 | CBS 64904 | BLUE ÖYSTER CULT (LP) | 20 |

BLUE PHANTOM
| 72 | Kaleidoscope KAL 101 | DISTORTIONS (LP, laminated front cover, yellow label) | 150 |

BLUE RIDGE RANGERS
73	Fantasy FTC 105	Hearts Of Stone/Somewhere Listening For My Name	6
73	Fantasy FTC 110	You Don't Own Me/Back In The Hills	6
73	Fantasy FT 511	BLUE RIDGE RANGERS (LP)	18

(see also John Fogerty, Creedence Clearwater Revival)

BLUE RONDOS
| 64 | Pye 7N 15734 | Little Baby/Baby I Go For You | 30 |
| 65 | Pye 7N 15833 | Don't Want Your Lovin' No More/What Can I Do | 40 |

BLUES
| 81 | Precious PRE 1 | Aim For The Eyes/Out Of Town | 125 |

BLUES EXPLOSION

MINT VALUE £

BLUES EXPLOSION
04	Mute STUMM 236	DAMAGE (LP, gatefold with booklet)	18

BLUE SAND
67	Saturn HEY 006	Florida Bound/Blue Mama/The Dream/Name Of The Game	35

BLUES BAND
80	Blues Band BBBP 101	OFFICIAL BOOTLEG ALBUM (LP, numbered, with autographs, 3000 only)	18

(see also Paul Jones, McGuinness-Flint, Manfred Mann)

BLUE BENDER
66	Rio R93	Girl Next Door/Leave Me Out	20

BLUES BUSTERS
59	Limbo XL101	Little Vilma/ Early One Morning	20
61	Starlite ST45 031	The Spiritual/ Lost My Baby	40
61	Blue Beat BB55	Donna/You're Driving Me Crazy	15
62	Blue Beat BB73	There's Always Sunshine/ You Had It Wrong	15
62	Starlite ST45 072	Your Love/You Send Me Crazy	25
62	Island WI-023	Behold/ Oh Baby	20
62	Blue Beat BB102	Tell Me Why/ I've Done You Wrong	20
65	Island WI-214	How Sweet It Is/ I Had A Dream	40
65	Island WI-219	Wide Awake In A Dream (actually by Philip James solo)/ MAYTALS: Tell Me The Reason	75
65	Island WI-222	Wings Of A Dove/ BYRON LEE & DRAGONAIRES: Dan Is The Man	25
66	Doctor Bird DB1030	I've Been Trying/ Pretty Girls	50
67	Doctor Bird DB 1078	There's Always Sunshine/ Lovers' Reward	30
71	Dynamic DYN408	Each One Teach One/ Thinking Of You	10
71	Jay Boy BOY 44	I Can't Stop/Inspired To Love You	10
71	Trojan TR7819	Thinking Of You/ Version	10
70s	Spank SP 20	The Closer I Get To You/WILLIE LINDO: Midnight (12")	30
65	Island ILP-923	BEHOLD! (LP)	60
67	Doctor Bird DLM5008	BEST OF THE BLUES BUSTERS (LP)	150
76	Dynamic DYLP 3007	PHILLIP & LLOYD (LP)	20

BLUES BY FIVE
64	Decca F 12029	Boom Boom/I Cried	120

BLUES COUNCIL
65	Parlophone R 5264	Baby Don't Look Down/What Will I Do	100

BLUE SCREAMING
78	Albatross TIT 2	Bland Hotel/Thin X Cinema (p/s)	10

BLUES 5
64	Studio 36 (no cat. no.)	Hey Baby/When You're In Love	150

BLUE SKIES
70	Pendant PN 004	Nightmares/Marigold	50
70	Fontana 6007026	Happy/Nightingale	12

BLUES MAGOOS
66	Mercury MF 954	(We Ain't Got) Nothin' Yet/Gotta Get Away	30
67	Fontana TF 848	One By One/Love Seems Doomed	15
66	Fontana TL 5402	BLUES MAGOOS (LP, mono)	50
66	Fontana (S)TL 5402	BLUES MAGOOS (LP, stereo)	30
71	Probe SPB 1024	GULF COAST BOUND (LP)	20

BLUES MASTERS
63	Island WI 078	5 O'Clock Whistle/African Blood (both sides actually by Baba Brooks)	40

BLUESOLOGY
65	Fontana TF 594	Come Back Baby/Time's Getting Tougher Than Tough	350
66	Fontana TF 668	Mister Frantic/Everyday (I Have The Blues)	350
16	Fontana 476 788-2	Come Back Baby/Time's Getting Tougher Than Tough (reissue)	8

(see also Stu Brown & Bluesology, Elton John, Long John Baldry, Elton Dean, Mark Charig)

BLUES PROJECT
67	Verve Forecast VS 1505	I Can't Keep From Crying/The Way My Baby Walks	35
67	Verve (S)VLP 6004	PROJECTIONS (LP)	75

(see also Al Kooper, Tommy Flanders, Seatrain)

BLUE STARS
65	Decca F 12303	Please Be A Little Kind/I Can Take It	200
94	Dig The Fuzz DIG 020	THE BLUE STARS (LP)	20

BLUE STEAM
78	Rip Off RIP 5	Lizard King/Cortina Cowboys (p/s)	10

BLUETONES
95	Superior Quality TONE 001	Slight Return/The Fountainhead (blue vinyl, plain white sleeve in stickered polythene bag, 2,000 only sold by mail-order or at gigs, some numbered)	6
95	Superior Quality TONE 001	Slight Return/The Fountainhead (red vinyl, foldover p/s in poly bag, 1,000 only, export issue to Japan)	12
96	Superior Quality BLUE 003X	Slight Return/Don't Stand Me Down (red vinyl, export issue to Japan with Japanese text on rear of p/s)	12
96	Superior Quality BLUELP 004	EXPECTING TO FLY (LP, booklet, numbered, 5000 only)	50
96	Superior Quality BLUELP 004	EXPECTING TO FLY (LP)	30
98	Superior Quality BLUE V008	RETURN TO THE LAST CHANCE SALOON (LP, white vinyl)	20
03	Superior Quality BLUE 019LP	LUXEMBOURG (LP)	18

BLUE TRAIN
87	Dreamworld DREAM 007T	LAND OF GOLD (12" EP)	40

BLUE U
72	York SYK 524	I've Been Lonely For So Long/BLUE ME: Melinda Marie	10

BLUE VELVET BAND
69	Warner Bros WS 1802	SWEET MOMENTS WITH THE BLUE VELVET BAND (LP, gatefold sleeve)	20

BLUEWATER FOLK
70	Folk Heritage FHJR 013S	BLUEWATER FOLK (LP)	50

BLUE YOGURT

MINT VALUE £

BLUE YOGURT
70	Penny Farthing PEN 732	Lydia/Umbrella Man	40

BLUNDERBUSS
71	Penny Farthing PEN 762	New Day/Emma	12

COLIN BLUNSTONE
71	Epic EPC 64557	ONE YEAR (LP, textured sleeve)	15
72	Epic EPC 65278	ENNISMORE (LP, textured sleeve)	15

(see also Zombies, Neil MacArthur, Mitchell-Coe Mysteries)

BLUNT INSTRUMENT
78	Diesel DCL 01	No Excuse/Interrogation (p/s)	15

JAMES BLUNT
05	Atlantic ATO 207	You're Beautiful (Edit)/So Long Jimmy (Acoustic)	10
05	Atlantic ATO 230	Goodbye My Lover/Where Is My Mind? (Live In Manchester)	6
07	Atlantic ATO 285	1973/So Happy (pink vinyl, stickered, p/s)	6

BLUR

SINGLES
90	Food FOOD 26	She's So High (Edit)/I Know (p/s)	10
90	Food 12FOOD 26	She's So High (Definitive)/Sing/I Know (Extended) (12", p/s)	12
91	Food 12FOODX 29	There's No Other Way (The Blur Remix)/Won't Do It/ Day Upon Day (live) (12", p/s lists '12 FOODDX 29')	20
91	Food 12FOOD 29	There's No Other Way (Extended)/Inertia/Mr. Briggs/I'm All Over (12", p/s)	10
92	Food FOOD 37	Popscene/Mace (p/s)	15
92	Food 12FOOD 37	Popscene/I'm Fine/Mace/Garden Central (12", p/s)	18
93	Food FOODS 45	Chemical World/Maggie May (red vinyl, paper labels, p/s)	8
92	Food BLUR 6	The Wassailing Song (1-sided gig freebie, as "Gold, Frankinscence and Blur" no p/s, 500 only)	150
93	Food FOODS 46	Sunday Sunday/Tell Me, Tell Me (B-side as "Blur featuring Seymour") (yellow vinyl, p/s)	8
94	Food FOODS 47	Girls And Boys/Magpie/People In Europe (p/s, numbered)	10
94	Food FOOD 56	End Of A Century/Red Necks (p/s, numbered)	6
96	Food FOOD 73	Stereotypes/The Man Who Left Himself/Tame (p/s, pink vinyl)	6
96	Food FOOD 77	Charmless Man/The Horrors (gatefold p/s, sealed with sticker)	6
97	Food FOOD 89	Beetlebum/Woodpigeon Song (p/s, red vinyl)	7
97	Food FOOD 93	Song 2/Get Out Of Cities (p/s. purple vinyl)	20
97	Food FOOD 98	On Your Own/Pop Scene (Live)/Song 2 (Live) (p/s, white vinyl)	7
99	Food FOOD 117	Tender/All We Want (p/s, blue vinyl, numbered)	6
99	Food BLURBOX 10	THE 10 YEAR ANNIVERSARY BOX SET (22xCD singles)	60
03	EMI R 6610	Crazy Beat/The Outsider (p/s, red vinyl 'Banksy' cover)	75
03	EMI R 6619	Good Song/Morricone (p/s, red vinyl)	7
05	Fan Club SGLAD 01	Some Glad Morning (CD, card wallet, fan club issue)	30
10	Parlophone LCO 3098	Fools Day (1-sided 7", jukebox centre, blue Parlophone sleeve, 1000 only)	30
15	Parlophone 08256117833	Y'All Doomed (red vinyl, numbered)	12

ALBUMS : LPS
91	Food FOODLP 6	LEISURE (LP)	25
93	Food FOODLP 9	MODERN LIFE IS RUBBISH (LP, with inner)	60
94	Food FOODLP 10	PARKLIFE (LP, with inner)	70
95	Food FOODLP 14	THE GREAT ESCAPE (LP, with inner)	25
95	Food FOODLP 14	THE GREAT ESCAPE (LP, in 12" box with book and print. Produced by Vinyl Experience, 2000 only)	70
97	Food FOODLP 19	BLUR (2-LP)	50
97	Food FOODLP 19	BLUR (1-LP version)	30
99	Food FOODLP 29	13 (2-LP, stickered, gategold, with inner sleeves)	50
00	Food FOODLPD 33	THE BEST OF (2-LP)	120
03	Parlophone 07243-582887-1-7	THINK TANK (2-LP)	25
12	EMI BLURBOXLP 1	BLUR 21 (6 x 2-LP box set)	150
12	EMI BLURBOX21	BLUR 21 (18 CD, 3 DVD & 7" box set)	70
12	Food 509997942320	PARKLIVE (3-LP, bonus disc version)	20
12	Food FOODLPX 6	LEISURE (LP, reissue, 180gm)	15
12	Food FOODLPX 9	MODERN LIFE IS RUBBISH (LP, reissue, 180gm)	18
13	Food FOODLPX 14	THE GREAT ESCAPE (LP, 180gm reissue)	18
15	Parlophone 0825646141715	MAGIC WHIP (2-LP gatefold, poster in obi)	20

PROMOS
90	no cat. no.	Bad Day/Bad Day (version) (white label)	20
92	Food 12BLUR5	Popscene (1-sided promo 12" in die cut company sleeve. 1000 only)	10
94	Food FOODLP19	PARKLIFE (LP, blue vinyl promo)	40
93	Food 12FOODDJ 40	For Tomorrow (Visit to Primrose Hill Extended Version/Into Another/Hanging Over (12" in company die cut sleeve)	10
93	Food BBLUR1	BASICALLY BLUR (CD, interview disc with 3 tracks from Modern Life Is Rubbish)	80
94	Food CD5 BET BET BET	Girls and Boys/Jubilee/Trouble In The Message Centre/Lot 105 (Live CD promo produced for Mark Radcliffe show)	30
97	Food 12BLURDJ 7	On Your Own (Crouch End Broadway Mix) (12", 1-sided, promo only)	10
91	Food 12BLUR 4	High Cool (Easy Listening Mix)/Bad Day (Leisurely Mix) (12", blue & gold company sleeve, promo, 1,000 only)	25
00	Food 10FOODDJ 135	Music Is My Radar (12" one-sided w/10" cat. No., white die cut sleeve, stamped label)	10
98	Food FOODLH 117	Tender (Radio Edit)/Song 2 (jukebox copy, no centre)	10
99	Food FOOD CDJX 29	13 (in duffelbag with folder, photos, ski-hat and biography, promo only)	80
99	Food 10FOODDJ 117	Tender (10" promo record plays inside to out, foil sealed)	20
02	The Bombo!	(red label, bearing Arabic writing which translates as "Don't bomb when you are the bomb"; large centre hole; 1,000 7" were pressed, but many were blown up)	30

(see also Graham Coxon, Gorillaz, Damon Albarn)

BLUSH

MINT VALUE £

BLUSH
79	Venal Vinyl PMB 117	Everyday/Before We Came Together (no p/s, 200 only)	150

B-MOVIE
80	Dead Good DEAD 9	TAKE THREE (EP)	20
80	Dead Good BIG DEAD 12	NOWHERE GIRL (12" EP, with insert, 800 only)	20
88	Wax 12 WAX 3	Nowhere Girl/Remembrance Day (12", p/s, 250 on orange vinyl, numbered)	15
88	Wax 12 WAX 3	Nowhere Girl/Remembrance Day (12", p/s, pink vinyl, numbered)	15

BMX BANDITS
86	53rd & 3rd AGARR 3	Sad?/E102 (p/s, with comic)	10
87	53rd & 3rd AGARR 6	What A Wonderful World/The Day Before Tomorrow (p/s)	6

(see also Soup Dragons, Boy Hairdressers, Teenage Fanclub, Vaselines)

EDDIE BO
73	Action ACT 4609	Check Your Bucket Parts 1 & 2	30

BO & PEEP
64	Decca F 11968	Young Love/The Rise Of The Brighton Surf	40

(see also Andrew Oldham Orchestra)

BOARDS OF CANADA
94	Music 70 AOMC43	PLAY BY NUMBERS EP (Cassette)	50
94	Music 70 AOCS43	PLAY BY NUMBERS EP (CD)	60
94	Music 70 THS 012	HOOPER'S BAY (12" EP)	100
94	Music 70 THS 012	HOOPER'S BAY (cassette EP)	30
96	Skam SKA 008	Hi Scores/Turquoise Hexagon Sun/Nlogax/June 9th/See Ya Later/Everything You Do Is A Balloon (12", p/s)	10
98	Skam KMAS 1	Aquarius/Chinook (p/s, with insert, 500 only)	60
98	Warp 10WARP LP 55P	Telephasic Workshop/Roygbiv (10" promo, 2000 only)	25
00	Warp Records WAP 144	In A Beautiful Place Out In The Country (12", EP)	40
99	Warp WAP 114	THE PEEL SESSIONS (12", p/s)	15
06	Warp WAP 200	TRANS CANADA HIGHWAY EP (12", white vinyl)	25
13	Warp 37367	------ / ------ / ------ / XXXXXX / ------ / ------ (12" p/s. 6 known copies)	1500
95	Music 70 BOARD 1	TWOISM (LP, 100 copies only)	400
95	Music 70 BOARD 1	TWOISM (Cassette, 100 copies only)	100
98	Warp 10 WARP LP 55 P	MUSIC HAS THE RIGHT TO CHILDREN (10", Promo)	40
98	Warp Skam WARP LP 55, SKALP001	MUSIC HAS THE RIGHT TO CHILDREN (2-LP)	65
02	Warp	GEOGADDI (LP, blue vinyl test pressing - etched - 10 only)	200
02	Warp/Music 70 WARLP LP 101	GEOGADDI (3-LP)	60
02	Warp WARPLP 70	TWOISM (LP, reissue, die-cut sleeve)	20
05	Warp WARPLP 123	CAMPFIRE HEADPHASE (2-LP)	30
13	Warp WARPLP 257	TOMORROW'S HARVEST (2-LP, gatefold, inners)	25
13	Warp WARPLP 70R	TWOISM (LP, reissue in die-cut sleeve with sticker and download code)	15
13	Warp WARPLP 55	MUSIC HAS THE RIGHT TO CHILDREN (2-LP, reissue, gatefold sleeve, sticker, and download code)	20
13	Warp WARPLP 101R	GEOGADDI (3-LP, reissue, 1 side etched, sticker sheet and download code)	20

BOARDWALKERS
60s	own label J.C. 1	A Miracle/Any Man's Girl	200

(see also Warren Davis)

TOOTER BOATMAN
72	Injun 108	Thunder & Lightning/The Will Of Love	10

BOATMEN
70s	Sweet Folk SFA 018	STRAIGHT FROM THE TUNNEL'S MOUTH (LP)	40

BOBALOUIS
81	WEA K18441	Not A Second Chance/City Boys	20

BOB & CAROL
67	CBS 2738	On My Life/Mary Jane	8

BOB (RELF) & EARL (NELSON)
65	Sue WI 374	Harlem Shuffle/I'll Keep Running Back	20
65	Sue WI 393	Baby I'm Satisfied/The Sissy	40
67	Sue WI 4030	Don't Ever Leave Me/Fancy Free	75
69	Warner Bros WB 6059	Everybody Jerk/He's A Playbrother	40
72	Jay Boy BOY 72	I Can't Get Away/I'll Keep Running Back	10
72	Jay Boy BOY 73	My Little Girl/His & Her Shuffle (as Bob & Earl Band)	10
67	Sue ILP 951	HARLEM SHUFFLE (LP)	80
69	B & C BCB 1	BOB & EARL (LP)	15
69	Joy JOYS 199	TOGETHER (LP)	15

(see also Jackie Lee, Earl Nelson, Hollywood Flames)

BOB & JERRY
58	Pye International 7N 25003	Ghost Satellite/Nothin'	10

BOB (ANDY) & MARCIA (GRIFFITHS)
70	Bamboo BAM 40	Always Together/BOB ANDY: Desperate Lover	25
70	Harry J. HJ 6605	Young, Gifted And Black/JAY BOYS: Young, Gifted & Black (Instrumental)	6
70	Escort ES 824	Young, Gifted And Black/BARRINGTON BIGGS: My Cheri Amour (Different version: no strings)	30
70	Trojan TBL 122	YOUNG, GIFTED & BLACK (LP)	30
72	Trojan TRLS 26	PIED PIPER (LP)	15

(see also Bob Andy, Marcia Griffiths)

BOB (ANDY) & TIE (TYRONE EVANS)
69	Coxsone CS 7086	I Don't Care/LASCELLES PERKINS: Little Green Apples	60

BOB(B)ETTES
57	London HLE 8477	Mr. Lee/Look At The Stars	40
58	London HLE 8597	Come-A Come-A/Speedy	40

BOBBSEY TWINS

MINT VALUE £

60	London HLE 9173	I Shot Mr. Lee/Untrue Love	60
60	London HLE 9248	Have Mercy Baby/Dance With Me Georgie	40
60	Pye International 7N 25060	I Shot Mr. Lee/Billy (as Bobettes)	40
72	Action ACT 4603	That's A Bad Thing To Know/All In Your Mind	18

BOBBSEY TWINS
57	London HLA 8474	A Change Of Heart/Part-Time Gal	30

BOBBY & DAVE
71	Ackee ACK 116	Build My World Around You/LIZZY & TONY BOP: Sammy Version	15

(see also Dave Barker, Lizzy & Dennis)

BOBBY & LAURIE
66	Parlophone R 5480	Hitch Hiker/You'll Come 'Round	15

BOBBY & MIDNITES
84	CBS 26046	WHERE THE BEAT MEETS THE STREET (LP)	25

(see also Grateful Dead)

BOBBY (ELLIS) & TOMMY (MCCOOK)
74	Attack ATLP 1004	GREEN MANGO (LP)	35

BOBCATS
67	Pye 7N 17242	Can't See For Looking/Let Me Get By	25

WILLIE BOBO
66	Verve VS 548	Sunshine Super Man/Sockit To Me	12
66	Verve SVLP9134	ELATION (LP)	20
71	A&M AMLS 68034	DO WHAT YOU WANT TO DO (LP)	25

FRIDA BOCCARA
69	Philips BF 1765	Through The Eyes Of A Child/So Fair	10

BOCKY & VISIONS
65	Atlantic AT 4049	I Go Crazy/Good Good Lovin'	40

BODDIKA
12	Swamp 81 SWAMP 019	Acid Jackson/Basement (12")	10

J.P. BODDY
73	Columbia DB 89789	Stop Me Spinning (Like A Spinning Top)/Song Without A Word	8

BODEAN
76	DJM DJS 10697	Saturday Woman/Flying High (promo, p/s)	7

BODGERS
82	SRTS/82/CUS/1484	Stutter/I Hate Phoning Girls (no p/s)	100

BODGER'S MATE
78	Cottage COT 521	BRIGHTER THAN USUAL (LP)	20

BODKIN
72	West CSA 104	BODKIN (LP, private pressing, red label 10-20 in silk screened cover)	1200
72	West CSA 104	BODKIN (LP, private pressing, red label, in posthumously designed sleeve)	800
12	Acme ADLP 1085	BODKIN (LP, reissue)	15

BODY
81	Recession	THE BODY ALBUM (LP, private pressing with booklet)	50

BODY AND SOUL
70	Penny Farthing PEN 720	Here Comes That Feeling/Go Back To School	7

BODYSNATCHERS (1)
80	2-Tone CHS TT 9	Let's Do Rocksteady/Ruder Than You (paper label, company sleeve)	20
80	2-Tone CHS TT 9	Let's Do Rocksteady/Ruder Than You (injection moulded labels)	7
80	2-Tone CHS TT 12	Easy Life/Too Experienced (paper label, company sleeve)	20
80	2-Tone CHS TT 12	Easy Life/Too Experienced (injection moulded labels)	7

BODYSNATCHERS (2)
97	Backbone (No Cat. No)	GENOCIDE (EP, 30 test copies)	100

(see also Icepick)

BOEING DUVEEN & BEAUTIFUL SOUP
68	Parlophone R 5696	Jabberwock/Which Dreamed It (demos without p/s)	100
68	Parlophone R 5696	Jabberwock/Which Dreamed It (demos with p/s)	250
68	Parlophone R 5696	Jabberwock/Which Dreamed It	150

BOFFALONGO
70	United Artists UP 35144	Dancing In The Moonlight/Endless Questions	6
71	United Artists UAG 29290	BEYOND YOUR HEAD (LP)	15

BOG UGLY AND THE WOOFTERS
78	Toadstool GOOD 2	Disco Veteran/I've Seen It Vomit (p/s)	25

DIRK BOGARDE
65	Fontana TF 615	Darling/MOVIE SOUNDS: Pavan For Diane	6
60	Decca LK 4373	LYRICS FOR LOVERS (LP)	15

BOGAZ
83	AGR 7 AGR 2	I've Got Love/I've Got Love (Instrumental)	30
83	AGR 12 AGR 2	I've Got Love/I've Got Love (Instrumental) (12")	45

BOGDAN
81	Black Label GB 3	Oh Eddie/Reet Petite (p/s)	10
81	Brilliant HIT 1	Who Do You Think You Are?/Take Me Back (p/s)	10

(see also Whitesnake)

BOGIES
64	private press (no cat. no.)	THE BOGIES ON CAMPUS (LP)	40
64	private press (no cat. no.)	BYE BYE BOGIES (LP)	40

ERIC BOGLE
77	Autogram ALLP 211	LIVE IN PERSON (LP)	35
81	Plant Life PLR 033	PLAIN AND SIMPLE (LP)	15
83	Plant Life PLR 046	SCRAPS OF PAPER (LP)	15
85	Topic 12TS 437	WHEN THE WIND BLOWS (LP)	15
88	Plant Life PLR 042	NOW I'M EASY (LP)	15

Lee BOGLE

Year	Label/Cat#	Description	MINT VALUE £
LEE BOGLE			
71	Black Swan BW 1406	Tomorrow's Dreams/SWANS: Hot Pants Reggae	15
BOGUS ORDER			
90	Ninja Tune ZEN 01	ZEB BRAKES (LP)	25
BUDDY BOHN			
71	Regal Zonophone RX 3040	Piccalilli Lady/Summer Song	8
71	Purple TPSA 7503	A DROP IN THE OCEAN (LP, gatefold sleeve)	30
BOILER SHOP			
72	Music Box MB 03	Seeing Things In Colour/Darkness	40
HOUSTON BOINES			
66	Blue Horizon 45 BH 1006	Superintendent Blues/Monkey Motion (99 copies only, Ike Turner on piano)	200
BOISTEROUS			
95	Hammer HR 5	SKIP RAIDERS (LP)	15
BOK BOK			
80	Bok Bok BOK 2	Come Back To Me/Misfit (p/s)	10
BOLA			
95	Skam SKA 5	Forcasa 3/Krak Jakomo/Metalurg 2/Ballom (12", custom sleeve)	50
98	Skam KMAS002	KS (500 pressed)	30
00	33 33Shapes	SHAPES (LP, 3x12")	35
MARC BOLAN			
65	Decca F 12288	The Wizard/Beyond The Rising Sun (some as Marc Bölan)	500
65	Decca F 12288	The Wizard/Beyond The Rising Sun (demo copy)	350
66	Decca F 12413	The Third Degree/San Francisco Poet	500
66	Decca F 12413	The Third Degree/San Francisco Poet (demo copy)	350
66	Parlophone R 5539	Hippy Gumbo/Misfit	650
66	Parlophone R 5539	Hippy Gumbo/Misfit (demo copy)	500
72	Track 2094 013	Jasper C. Debussy/Hippy Gumbo/The Perfumed Garden Of Gulliver Smith (p/s, withdrawn)	50
72	Track 2094 013	Jasper C. Debussy/Hippy Gumbo/The Perfumed Garden Of Gulliver Smith (white label demo)	70
81	Rarn MBFS 001C	Sing Me A Song/Endless Sleep (Extended Version)/The Lilac Hand Of Menthol Dan (12", no p/s, clear vinyl, handwritten labels)	10
81	Rarn MBFS 001P	Sing Me A Song/Endless Sleep (Extended Version)/The Lilac Hand Of Menthol Dan (12" picture disc, misprinted with black rim)	15
81	Rarn MBFS 001P	Sing Me A Song/Endless Sleep (Extended Version)/The Lilac Hand Of Menthol Dan (12", picture disc misprinted back-to-front)	15
81	Cherry Red CHERRY 29	You Scare Me To Death/The Perfumed Garden Of Gulliver Smith (initial copies with bronze label, glossy p/s & free flexidisc [Lyntone LYN 10086])	10
72	Track 2406 101	HARD ON LOVE (LP, unreleased, white label test pressing, 3 known copies)	1000
72	Track 2406 009	HARD ON LOVE (LP, unreleased, 2-sided EMIdisc acetate with "swearing intro")	2250
74	Track 2410 201	THE BEGINNING OF DOVES (LP, laminated sleeve, black/silver label)	35
81	Cherry Red PERED 20	YOU SCARE ME TO DEATH (LP, picture disc)	15
89	Media Motion MEDIA 2	THE BEGINNING OF DOVES (LP, reissue, 750 only, withdrawn)	25

(see also Marc Bolan/T. Rex, Marc Bolan & Gloria Jones, Toby Tyler, John's Children, Big Carrot, Dib Cochran & The Earwigs)

Year	Label/Cat#	Description	MINT VALUE £
MARC BOLAN & GLORIA JONES			
77	EMI EMI 2572	To Know Him Is To Love Him/City Port	15

(see also Gloria Jones)

MARC BOLAN/T. REX

SINGLES

Year	Label/Cat#	Description	MINT VALUE £
70	Octopus OCTO 1	Ride A White Swan/Summertime Blues/Jewel (unreleased, handwritten white label, 2/3 test pressings only)	2500
70	Fly BUG 1	Ride A White Swan/Is It Love/Summertime Blues (p/s, purple labels)	20
70	Fly BUG 1	Ride A White Swan/Is It Love/Summertime Blues (p/s, later pressing with mustard labels)	10
71	Fly	Hot Love/Woodland Rock/King Of The Mountain Cometh (IBC Sound Recordings Studios acetate)	250
71	Fly BUG 6	Hot Love/Woodland Rock/King Of The Mountain Cometh (mustard labels)	10
71	Fly BUG 10	Get It On/There Was A Time/Raw Ramp (p/s, black label with silver 'fly' logo)	15
71	Fly BUG 10	Get It On/There Was A Time/Raw Ramp (p/s, 1st pressing, black label with silver fly)	6
71	Fly GRUB 1	Electric Warrior Preview Single: Jeepster/Life's A Gas (gig freebie, in pink envelope sleeve)	200
71	Fly GRUB 1	Electric Warrior Preview Single: Jeepster/Life's A Gas (gig freebie, originally in pink envelope sleeve, this price is for later standard paper sleeve)	145
71	Fly BUG 16	Jeepster/Life's A Gas (scarce issue w/out 'GRUB 1A' ref.)	6
72	EMI T REX 101	Telegram Sam/Cadillac/Baby Strange	6
72	Magni Fly ECHO 102	One Inch Rock/The Woodland Bop/The Throat Of Winter (unreleased, rejected 1-sided test pressing for B-side of "Deborah"/"One Inch Rock", stamped white label)	150
72	Magni Fly ECHO 102	Debora/One Inch Rock/The Woodland Bop/Seal Of Seasons (p/s)	6
72	EMI MARC X	Metal Guru (rejected 1-sided test pressing with Marc's annotation 'bad cut')	300
72	EMI MARC 1	Metal Guru/Thunderwing/Lady	8
72	EMI MARC 2	Children Of The Revolution/Jitterbug Love/Sunken Rags	6
72	EMI MARC 3	Solid Gold Easy Action/(5th Dimension track) (mispressing)	15
72	EMI MARC 3	Solid Gold Easy Action/(Partridge Family track) (mispressing)	15
72	EMI SPRS 346	Chariot Choogle/The Slider (promo only, 'T. Rex' picture label)	425
72	EMI SPRS 346	Chariot Choogle/The Slider (promo only, white label)	375
72	Lyntone	Christmas Time/Wanna Spend My Christmas With You/ Christmas/Everybody Knows It's Christmas (fan club flexi, with letter in brown envelope)	45
72	Lyntone	Christmas Time/Wanna Spend My Christmas With You/ Christmas/Everybody Knows It's Christmas (fan club flexi, without letter in brown envelope)	30
73	EMI MARC 4	20th Century Boy/Free Angel	6
73	EMI MARC 5	The Groover/Midnight	6
73	EMI MARC 6	Truck On (Tyke)/Sitting Here	6
74	EMI MARC 7	Teenage Dream/Satisfaction Pony (credited to 'Marc Bolan & T. Rex')	6

Francy BOLAND

MINT VALUE £

Year	Label/Cat	Title	Value
74	EMI MARC 7	Teenage Dream/Satisfaction Pony (credited to 'Marc Bolan')	8
74	EMI MARC 8	Light Of Love/Explosive Mouth	6
74	EMI MARC 9	Zip Gun Boogie/Space Boss	6
75	EMI MARC 10	New York City/Chrome Sitar	6
75	EMI MARC 11	Dreamy Lady/Do You Wanna Dance?/Dock Of The Bay (as T. Rex Disco Party)	6
75	EMI MARC 12	Christmas Bop/Telegram Sam/Metal Guru (unreleased, A- & B-side paper labels exist, 2 sets only this price is for the labels)	1250
76	EMI MARC 13	London Boys/Solid Baby	6
76	Cube BUG 66	Hot Love/Get It On	6
76	EMI MARC 14	I Love To Boogie/Baby Boomerang	6
76	EMI MARC 15	Laser Love/Life's An Elevator	6
77	EMI MARC 16	The Soul Of My Suit/All Alone	8
77	EMI MARC 17	Dandy In The Underworld/Groove A Little/Tame My Tiger (p/s)	10
77	EMI MARC 18	Celebrate Summer/Ride My Wheels (p/s)	10
78	EMI MARC 19	Crimson Moon/Jason B. Sad (p/s)	10
78	Cube ANT 2	Hot Love/Raw Ramp/Lean Woman Blues (p/s, misprinted Raw Amp, sleeve credits 'Bolan', label credits 'T.Rex')	8
79	Cube ANTS 001	Life's A Gas/Find A Little Wood/Once Upon The Seas Of Abyssinia/ Blessed Wild Apple Girl (12", p/s)	12
82	Marc ABOLAN 2	THE CHILDREN OF RARN (10" EP, p/s, 33rpm, gatefold sleeve with 12-page lyric book)	25
82	Marc SBOLAN 13	Mellow Love/Foxy Box/Lunacy's Back (p/s, blue vinyl, as Marc Bolan)	8
82	Rarn MBFS RAP 2	Deep Summer/Oh Baby/One Inch Rock (unreleased version) (12", p/s, blue vinyl)	10
83	Marc SBOLAN 12EP	CHRISTMAS BOP EP (12", p/s, OMBFS only, extra tracks: acoustic versions of "King Of The Rumbling Spires" & "Savage Beethoven")	10
84	Marc On Wax SPS 1	Mister Motion (1-sided, from "Child Of The Revolution - 14 Greats" LP, p/s)	8
84	Cube BUG 99	Sailor Of The Highway/Do You Remember (7" in plain black sleeve)	15
84	Cube HBUG 99	RARE MAGIC (12" EP)	12
87	Strange Fruit SFPS 031	PEEL SESSIONS (12")	15
94	Edsel MBPROMO 1	T. REX (CD, picture disc, 4-track sampler, tri-fold digipak, promo only)	15
07	Edsel BOLAN 1	Metal Guru/The Slider (Acoustic Demo) (Blue vinyl, numbered, 1,000 only)	15
07	Edsel BOLAN 2	Children Of The Revolution/The Leopards (Electric Demo) (Red vinyl, numbered, 1,000 only)	15
07	Edsel BOLAN 3	20th Century Boy/Teenager In Love (Marc & Gloria acoustic duet) (White vinyl, numbered, 1,000 only)	12
07	Edsel TREXMAS 1	Christmas Bop/The Xmas Riff/Xmas Flexi message (7", promo)	60
12	Universal 533812-3	ELECTRIC SEVENS (4 x 7" box set)	20
14	Secret 7" S721	Get It On (100 only, each with unique art sleeve)	50

ALBUMS

Year	Label/Cat	Title	Value
70	Fly HIFLY 2	T. REX (semi-gatefold sleeve, white label with 'Fly' logo)	50
71	Fly HIFLY 6	ELECTRIC WARRIOR (unreleased version with "Jeepster" on side 2, 1 test pressing copy only, with Marc's annotations on white sleeve)	700
71	Fly HIFLY 6	ELECTRIC WARRIOR (with poster & inner sleeve, stickered sleeve, white label with 'Fly' logo)	150
71	Fly HIFLY 6	ELECTRIC WARRIOR (with poster & inner sleeve, non-stickered sleeve, white label with 'Fly' logo)	60
72	Fly HIFLY 8	BOLAN BOOGIE (1-sided test pressing with "The Visit" instead of "Jewel")	375
72	Fly HIFLY 8	BOLAN BOOGIE	15
72	EMI BLN 5001	THE SLIDER (with lyric inner sleeve, sleeve with 'sniped' spine edges, flipbacks, blue/red T-Rex label)	40
73	EMI BLN 5002	TANX (with poster & inner sleeve)	30
73	EMI BLN 5003	GREAT HITS (with poster)	15
74	EMI BNLA 7751	ZINC ALLOY AND THE HIDDEN RIDERS OF TOMORROW (with 3-way numbered promo fold-out sleeve & inner, given as competition prize with letter from Pink or Mirabelle magazines, 1,000 only)	300
74	EMI BNLA 7751	ZINC ALLOY AND THE HIDDEN RIDERS OF TOMORROW (with 3-way promo fold-out sleeve & inner, without letter; numbered)	300
74	EMI BNLA 7751	ZINC ALLOY AND THE HIDDEN RIDERS OF TOMORROW (with 3-way promo fold-out sleeve & inner, without letter; unnumbered)	250
74	EMI BLNA 7751	ZINC ALLOY AND THE HIDDEN RIDERS OF TOMORROW (commercial gatefold sleeve with lyric inner sleeve)	20
75	EMI BNLA 7752	BOLAN'S ZIP GUN (diamond-cut laminated sleeve & inner sleeve, blue/red T-Rex label)	25
76	EMI BLNA 5004	FUTURISTIC DRAGON (with lyric inner sleeve)	25
77	EMI BLNA 5005	DANDY IN THE UNDERWORLD (with round-cut sleeve & lyric inner sleeve)	25
78	Cube HIFLD 1	MARC: THE WORDS AND MUSIC OF MARC BOLAN 1947-1977 (2-LP, gatefold sleeve, with free single [BINT 1])	20
81	Marc ABOLAN 1P	T. REX IN CONCERT (picture disc, 2 designs)	20
82	Cube/Dakota ICSX 1004	ACROSS THE AIRWAVES (picture disc)	20
82	Marc ABOLAN 3P	ELECTRIC WARRIOR (picture disc)	20
84	Marc ABOLAN 5	T. REXTASY (with 12" "Jam (live)"/Elemental Child (live) [ABOLAN 5F], Official Fanclub only)	18
80	EMI NUT 28	THE UNOBTAINABLE T-REX (LP, initial batch with rejected rear sleeve photo of Bolan with tongue out)	200
86	Marc On Wax WARRIOR 1/4	HISTORY OF T. REX (4-LP, numbered picture disc set, with free fanclub T-shirt)	45
86	Marc On Wax WARRIOR 1/4	HISTORY OF T. REX (4-LP, numbered picture disc set, without free fanclub T-shirt)	35

(see also Marc Bolan, Tyrannosaurus Rex, Dib Cochran & the Earwigs, John's Children, Big Carrot)

FRANCY BOLAND

Year	Label/Cat	Title	Value
75	Freedom FLP40176	PAPILLON NOIR (LP)	18

(see also Kenny Clarke with Francy Boland)

TOMMY BOLIN

Year	Label/Cat	Title	Value
76	Nemperor K 10730/NE 4	The Grind/Homeward Strut	10
75	Atlantic K 50208	TEASER (LP, stickered)	25
75	Atlantic K 50208	TEASER (LP, unstickered)	15
76	CBS S 81612	PRIVATE EYES (LP)	15

(see also James Gang, Deep Purple)

BOLLARD

MINT VALUE £

BOLLARD
72	Satril SAT 1	I Need Your Love/Sunshine In The Morning	6

BOLLARDS
70s	Bumkin Records	BOLLARDS (LP)	15

BOLLWEEVIL
81	Ellie Jay EJSP 9715	Rock Solid/Sands Of Time (p/s)	90

BOLT THROWER
88	Strange Fruit SFPS 056	PEEL SESSIONS (12")	20
91	Strange Fruit SFRLP 116	PEEL SESSIONS 1988-90 (LP)	20
88	Vinyl Solution SOL 11	IN BATTLE THERE IS NO LAW (LP, with insert)	20
89	Earache MOSH 12	REALM OF CHAOS (LP, with booket)	20
89	Earache MOSH 13	REALM OF CHAOS (LP, picture disc)	15
91	Earache MOSH 29	WAR MASTER (LP, booklet)	25

MEL BOLTON'S MIGHTY FIRE
16	Super Disco Edits SDE 16	Love/I Wanna Talk To You About Loving (reissue)	20

BOMAR
68	Flesh FH 01	Suddenly A Dream/Terry O McDonald's Son	18

BOMB AND DAGGER
86	SSR BDSS01	Wake Up/No Real Place (p/s)	40

BOMBADIL
72	Harvest HAR 5056	Breathless/When The City Sleeps (p/s)	8
75	Harvest HAR 5095	Breathless/When The City Sleeps (p/s, reissue)	8

(see also Barclay James Harvest)

BOMBAY DUCKS
80	Complete Control CON 1	Sympathy For The Devil/1-0-6-9 (p/s)	10
80s	United Dairies UD 05	DANCE MUSIC (LP)	15

BON JOVI
84	Vertigo VER 11	She Don't Know Me/Breakout (p/s)	8
84	Vertigo VER 14	Runaway/Breakout (live) (p/s)	8
84	Vertigo VERX 14	Runaway/Breakout (live)/Runaway (live) (12", p/s)	15
85	Vertigo VER 19	In And Out Of Love/Roulette (live) (p/s)	7
85	Vertigo VERP 19	In And Out Of Love/Roulette (live) (picture disc)	30
85	Vertigo VERDP 22	The Hardest Part Is The Night/Always Run To You//Tokyo Road (live)/ Shot Through The Heart (live) (double pack, gatefold p/s)	8
85	Vertigo VERXR 22	Red Hot And Two Parts Live: The Hardest Part Is The Night/ Tokyo Road (live)/In And Out Of Love (live) (12", p/s, red vinyl)	15
88	Vertigo VERHP 38	SLIPPERY WHEN WET (LP, picture disc with poster)	15
88	Vertigo VERHP 62	NEW JERSEY (LP, picture disc, stickered PVC sleeve)	15
95	Mercury 528 248-1	THESE DAYS (2-LP)	60

BONA DISH
82	In Phaze	BONA DISH ON C30 (cassette)	70
82	In Phaze IP 010	EP (cassette)	40
82	In Phaze	CARDBOARD TUBE (cassette in cardboard tube packaging)	50

JOE BONAMASSA
06	Provogue PRD71851	YOU AND ME (LP, pressed in Netherlands)	15

BONA RAYS
81	Mystery EJSP 9614	Catch 22/We're Never Going To Miss You	35

BON-BONS
55	London HL 8139	That's The Way Love Goes/Make My Dreams Come True	20
56	London HLU 8262	Circle/Frog On A Log	20

BOBBY BOND
61	Pye International 7N 25081	Livin' Doll/Sweet Love (as Bonny Bond and the Bandits)	8

BRIGITTE BOND
64	Blue Beat BB 212	Oh Yeah Baby/Blue Beat Baby (with the Bluebeats)	45

GRAHAM BOND (ORGANISATION)
64	Decca F 11909	Long Tall Shorty/Long Legged Baby (as Graham Bond Organization)	50
65	Columbia DB 7471	Wade In The Water/Tammy (as Graham Bond Organisation)	50
65	Columbia DB 7528	Tell Me (I'm Gonna Love Again)/Love Come Shining Through (as Graham Bond Organisation)	50
65	Columbia DB 7647	Lease On Love/My Heart's In Little Pieces (as Graham Bond Organisation)	35
66	Columbia DB 7838	St James Infirmary/Soul Tango (as Graham Bond Organisation)	40
67	Page One POF 014	You've Gotta Have Love Babe/I Love You	50
70	Warner Bros WB 8004	Walking In The Park/Springtime In The City (solo)	15
71	Vertigo 6059 042	Twelve Gates To The City/Water Water (as Graham Bond with Magick)	30
65	Columbia 33SX 1711	THE SOUND OF '65 (LP, 1st pressing, with '33SX' on blue/black label and "sold in the U.K." label text)	400

(N.B, LP has '33SX' on the sleeve, but only the 1st pressings have '33SX' on the label)

65	Columbia 33SX 1750	THERE'S A BOND BETWEEN US (LP, 1st pressing, with '33SX' on blue/black label and "sold in the UK" label text)	400
66	Columbia SX 1711	THE SOUND OF '65 (LP, 2nd pressing, with 'SX' on blue/black label)	200
66	Columbia SX 1750	THERE'S A BOND BETWEEN US (LP, 2nd pressing, with 'SX' on blue/black label)	150
69	Columbia SX 1750	THERE'S A BOND BETWEEN US (LP, 3rd Pressing, black/silver with boxed EMI logol)	60
69	Columbia SX 1711	THE SOUND OF '65 (LP, 3rd pressing, with boxed logo on silver/black label)	60
71	Warner Bros WS 3001	SOLID BOND (2-LP, gatefold sleeve, orange label)	50
71	Vertigo 6360 021	HOLY MAGICK (LP, gatefold sleeve, large swirl label, as Graham Bond & Magick)	150
71	Vertigo 6360 042	WE PUT OUR MAGICK ON YOU (LP, gatefold sleeve, swirl label,	150
72	Philips 6382 010	BOND IN AMERICA (2-LP, solo [individual discs: 6499 200/1], unreleased)	35
72	Philips 6382 010	THIS IS GRAHAM BOND (LP, solo)	20
88	Edsel DED 254	THE SOUND OF '65/THERE'S A BOND BETWEEN US (2-LP, reissue)	30

(see also Jack Bruce, Dick Heckstall-Smith, Ginger Baker, Duffy Power, Who, Don Rendell, Steve York's Camelo Pardalis)

GRAHAM BOND & PETE BROWN
71	Greenwich GSS 104	Lost Tribe/Macumbe/Milk Is Turning Sour In My Shoes (maxi-single)	25
72	Chapter One CHS-R 813	TWO HEADS ARE BETTER THAN ONE (LP)	250

(see also Pete Brown)

ISABEL BOND
68	Major Minor MM 565	Cry/When A Woman Loves A Man (in p/s)	20
68	Major Minor MM 565	Cry/When A Woman Loves A Man	10
69	Major Minor MM 627	Don't Forget About Me/You'll Never Get The Chance Again	10
68	Major Minor MMLP 28	THE HEART AND SOUL OF ISABEL BOND (LP)	50

JACKI BOND
65	Columbia DB 7719	My Sister's Boy/Now I Know	20
66	Strike JH 302	Tell Him To Go Away/Don't You Worry	25
66	Strike JH 320	He Say/Why Can't I Love Him	50

JOHNNY BOND
60	London HLU 9189	Hot Rod Jalopy/Five-Minute Love Affair	10
60	London HL 7100	Hot Rod Lincoln/Five-Minute Love Affair (export issue)	15

JOYCE BOND
66	Island WI 3019	Tell Me What It's All About/Tell Me Right Now	50
67	Airborne NBP 0011	It's Alright/Mrs. Soul	125
67	Island WIP 6010	Do The Teasy/Sugar	20
67	Island WIP 6018	This Train/Not So With Me	20
68	Island WIP 6051	Ob-La-Di, Ob-La-Da/Robin Hood Rides Again (as Joyce Bond Review)	20
68	Pama PM 718	Back To School/They Wish	18
69	Pama PM 771	Mr. Pitiful/Let's Get Married (as Joyce Bond & Little John)	18
70	Upfront UPF 5	Wind Of Change/First In Line	10
71	Trojan TR 7837	Help Me Make It Through The Night/Reconsider Our Love	10
68	Island ILP 968	SOUL AND SKA (LP, mono only)	175
72	Windmill WMD 121	SOUL OF CHANGE (LP)	35

LOUIS BOND
74	Cooltempo 2005	Tell Me When/Instrumental	8

OLIVER BOND
66	Parlophone R 5476	I Saw You All Alone/Let Me Love You	20

(see also Oliver Bone)

PETER BOND
77	Trailer LER 2108	IT'S ALL RIGHT FOR SOME (LP, yellow label)	15

RONNIE BOND (1)
69	Page One POF 123	Anything For You/Carolyn	20

(see also Troggs)

RONNIE BOND (2)
80	Clap CLAP 1	Fly On The Wall/You Can't Expect Miracles To Happen Tonight (p/s)	10

TONY BOND
66	Decca SKL 4776	PRESENTING TONY BOND (LP)	20

(see also Kestrels)

GARY (U.S.) BONDS
60	Top Rank JAR 527	New Orleans/Please Forgive Me (as U.S. Bonds)	10
61	Top Rank JAR 566	Not Me/Give Me One More Chance (as U.S. Bonds)	10
61	Top Rank JAR 575	Quarter To Three/Time Ole Story (as U.S. Bonds)	6
61	Top Rank JAR 581	School Is Out/One Million Tears	7
61	Top Rank JAR 595	School Is In/Trip To The Moon	7
62	Top Rank JAR 602	Dear Lady Twist/Havin' So Much Fun	8
62	Top Rank JAR 615	Twist Twist Senora/Food Of Love	8
62	Stateside SS 111	Seven Day Weekend/Gettin' A Groove	8
62	Stateside SS 125	Copy Cat/I'll Change That Too	6
63	Stateside SS 144	Mixed Up Faculty/I Dig This Station	6
63	Stateside SS 179	Where Did That Naughty Little Girl Go?/Do The Limbo With Me	6
63	Stateside SS 219	What A Dream/I Don't Wanta Wait	6
64	Stateside SS 271	New Orleans/Quarter To Three	6
64	Stateside SS 308	My Sweet Baby Rose/Ella Is Yella	6
67	Stateside SS 2025	Send Her To Me/Workin' For My Baby	10
61	Top Rank 35/114	DANCE 'TIL QUARTER TO THREE WITH U.S. BONDS (LP)	25
62	Stateside SL 10001	TWIST UP CALYPSO (LP)	20

OLIVER BONE & SOUNDS MAXIMUM
66	Parlophone R 5527	Knock On Wood/Jugger Tea	30

(see also Oliver Bond)

MATTHEW BONES
71	Pye 7N 45100	I Am The Pixi/Two Sugars	15

BONESCHI ELECTRONIC COMBO
73	Chappell International CAL 4004	SOUNDS ELECTRONIC (LP)	50

BONESHAKER
71	London HLU 10332	Sweetness/Badman Strikes Again	60

BONES & NATTY
95	BN 001	Pow/Thunder (12", white label only)	80

BONE THUGS-N-HARMONY
95	Ruthless EPC 481038 1	E 1999 ETERNAL (LP, inner)	60

BONGO HERMAN (DAVIS)
70	Songbird SB 1018	True Grit/True Grit Version 2 (both credited with Les Crystalites but actually with Les Crystalites)	35
71	Songbird SB 1060	BONGO HERMAN & LES BUNNY: Know For I/CRYSTALITES: Version (B-side actually titled 'Know Fari')	20
71	Songbird SB 1066	BONGO HERMAN & LES & BUNNY: Salaam (Peace)/CRYSTALITES: Scraper	20

BONGO LES & HERMAN

MINT VALUE £

72	Big BG 332	Eternal Drums/ERROL DUNKLEY: Darling Ooh Wee (both actually by Hugh Roy Junior)	20
72	Green Door GD 4049	African Breakfast/BONGO HERMAN & LES AND BUNNY: Chairman Of The Board	20
72	Songbird SB 1069	We Are Praying/CRYSTALITES: Version	15

BONGO LES & HERMAN
69	Explosion EX 2002	Dr. Who Part 1/Dr. Who Part II	25
71	Songbird SB 1050	Home Sweet Home/Hail I	30

(see also Heptones, Meditators)

JUKE BOY BONNER
69	Blue Horizon 57-3163	Runnin' Shoes/Jackin' In My Plans	40
60s	Jan & Dil JR 451	MORE DOWN HOME BLUES (EP)	50
68	Flyright LP 3501	THE ONE MAN TRIO (LP)	25
69	Liberty LBS 83319	THINGS AIN'T RIGHT (LP)	25

GRAHAM BONNET
72	RCA RCA 2230	Rare Specimen/Whisper In The Night	25
73	RCA RCA 2380	Trying To Say Goodbye/Castles In The Air	15
74	DJM DJS 328	Back Row In The Stalls/Ghost Writer In My Eye	10
77	Ring O' 2017 105	It's All Over Now, Baby Blue/Heroes On My Picture Wall (company sleeve)	8
77	Ring O' 2017 106	Danny/Rock Island Line (promo p/s)	18
77	Ring O' 2017 106	Danny/Rock Island Line (company sleeve)	6
77	Ring O' 2017 110	Goodnight And Goodmorning/Wino Song (company sleeve)	6
78	Ring O' 2017 114/POSP 2	Warm Ride/10/12 Observation (company sleeve)	6
78	Ring O' POSP 002	Warm Ride/10/12 Observation (12", company sleeve)	10
81	Vertigo VER 4	That's The Way That It Is/Don't Tell Me To Go (p/s)	6
81	Vertigo VER 2	Liar/Bad Days Are Gone (p/s)	6
77	Ring O' 2320 103	GRAHAM BONNET (LP, with inner sleeve)	18

(see also Marbles, Rainbow, Cozy Powell, Fut, Michael Schenker Group, Jon Lord)

GRAHAM BONNEY
65	Columbia DB 7773	My Little World Is All Blue/Why Can't We Be Friends	10
66	Columbia DB 7843	Super Girl/Hill Of Lovin'	35
66	Columbia DB 7934	Baby's Gone/Later Tonight	10
66	Columbia DB 8005	No One Knows/Mixed Up Baby Girl	10
69	Columbia DB 8531	Get Ready/Fly Me High Lorelei	10
70	Columbia DB 8648	Sign On The Dotted Line/Words We Said	25
70	Columbia DB 8687	When Evelyn Was Mine/Sunny Has Gone	20
66	Columbia SX/SCX 6052	SUPER GIRL (LP, mono/stereo)	30

(see also Riot Squad)

BONNIE
67	Ska Beat JB 270	Do You Get The Message/A Man Called Dan	20
69	Jolly JY 014	Loving You/Shoo Be Doo	15

BONNIE & SKITTO
63	Island WI 122	Get Ready (actually by Vikings (with Toots Hibbert)/ DON DRUMMOND: The Rocket	30
63	R&B JB 110	Hey Mr. Chauffer/DON DRUMMOND: Jet Stream	30

BONNIE & TREASURES
65	London HLU 9998	Home Of The Brave/Our Song	35

BONOBO
00	Tru Thoughts TRU 004	Terrapin (12")	15
13	Ninja Tune ZEN 12357	Cirrus (12" 1-sided picture disc with Zoetrope viewer, PVC sleeve some with art print)	80
00	Tru Thoughts TRU LP 007	ANIMAL MAGIC (2xLP)	40
01	Ninja Tune ZEN 63	ANIMAL MAGIC (2xLP)	30
02	Tru Thoughts TRU LP 031	ONE OFFS...REMIXES & B SIDES (2xLP)	30
03	Ninja Tune ZEN 80	DIAL M FOR MONKEY (2xLP)	30
06	Ninja Tune ZEN 119	DAYS TO COME (2xLP)	30
10	Ninja Tune ZEN 140	BLACK SANDS (2xLP)	20
13	Ninja Tune ZEN 195X	THE NORTH BORDERS (Box set, 6 x 10", with CD and posters)	30
13	Ninja Tune ZEN 195	THE NORTH BORDERS (2-LP, inners)	20

BONZO DOG (DOO-DAH) BAND
66	Parlophone R 5430	My Brother Makes The Noises For The Talkies/I'm Gonna Bring A Watermelon To My Gal Tonight	20
66	Parlophone R 5499	Alley Oop/Button Up Your Overcoat	20
67	Liberty LBF 15040	Equestrian Statue/The Intro And The Outro	10
68	Liberty LBF 15144	Urban Spaceman/Canyons Of Your Mind (initially pressing with spoken intro to B-side)	10
69	Liberty LBF 15201	Mr. Apollo/Ready Mades	7
69	Liberty LBF 15273	I Want To Be With You/We Were Wrong	7
70	Liberty LBF 15314	You Done My Brain In/Mr. Slater's Parrot	7
73	United Artists UP 35602	The Intro And The Outro/Hello Mabel	7
74	United Artists UP 35662	Mr. Slater's Parrot/Noises For The Leg	7
92	China WOK 2021	No Matter Who You Vote For The Government Always Gets In/ NEIL INNES: Them (promo only)	15
67	Liberty LBL 83056	GORILLA (LP, mono with booklet)	80
67	Liberty LBS 83056	GORILLA (LP, stereo with booklet)	40
67	Liberty LBL/LBS 83056	GORILLA (LP, without booklet, blue label)	20
71	Liberty LBL/LBS 83158E	THE DOUGHNUT IN GRANNY'S GREENHOUSE (LP, gatefold sleeve, with booklet, blue label)	70
71	Liberty LBS 83158E	THE DOUGHNUT IN GRANNY'S GREENHOUSE (LP, gatefold sleeve, without booklet, blue label)	25
69	Liberty LBS 83257	TADPOLES (LP, die-cut sleeve, with insert, blue label)	50
69	Liberty LBS 83257	TADPOLES (LP, die-cut sleeve, without insert, blue label)	25
69	Liberty LBS 83290	KEYNSHAM (LP, gatefold sleeve, blue label)	35
72	United Artists UAS 29288	LET'S MAKE UP AND BE FRIENDLY (LP)	22
74	United Artists UAD 60071/2	THE HISTORY OF THE BONZOS (2-LP, gatefold sleeve with booklet)	25

(see also Vivian Stanshall, Neil Innes, Grimms, Roger Ruskin Spear, Topo D. Bill)

BETTY BOO
79	Grapevine GRP 125	Say It Isn't So/Say It Isn't So (Instrumental)	20
98	Wigan Casino 210	Say It Isn't So/BELLES: Don't Pretend (p/s)	10

BOOGALOOS
69	President PT 253	Rule Britannia/Love Is Blind	12

BOOGIE MAN RCHESTRA
76	Contempo CS 2082	(For Me) (Instrumental)/(Vocal)	6

BOOK EM DANNO
89	Splinter SG 1	Brand New Disease/Eighties Hero/Top Of The Agenda/You'd Better Believe It (12")	80

JAMES BOOKER
61	Vogue V 9177	Cool Turkey/Gonzo	30
63	Vocalion VEP 170154	GONZO (EP)	60

BOOKER T (JAMAICA)
75	Ethnic Fight EF 016	Down Presser/Pressure Dub	25

BOOKER T. & THE M.G.S
62	London HLK 9595	Green Onions/Behave Yourself	20
63	London HLK 9670	Jelly Bread/Aw' Mercy	10
63	London HLK 9784	Chinese Checkers/Plum Nellie	10
65	Atlantic AT 4033	Boot-Leg/Outrage	10
66	Atlantic AT 4063	Be My Lady/Red Beans And Rice	10
66	Atlantic 584 044	My Sweet Potato/Booker Loo	10
67	Atlantic 584 088	Green Onions/Boot-Leg	6
67	Stax 601 009	Hip Hug Her/Summertime (initially dark blue label)	10
69	Stax STAX 119	Time Is Tight/Hang 'Em High	10
69	Stax STAX 127	Soul Clap '69/Mrs. Robinson	10
71	Stax 2025 026	Melting Pot/Kinda Easy Like	8
63	London REK 1367	R&B WITH BOOKER T (EP)	20
64	Atlantic AET 6002	R&B WITH BOOKER T VOL. 2 (EP)	20
64	London HA-K 8182	GREEN ONIONS (LP, plum label)	35
65	Atlantic ATL 5027	SOUL DRESSING (LP, plum label, 1st pressing with green & white sleeve)	30
66	Atlantic 587/588 033	GREEN ONIONS (LP, reissue, mono/stereo)	15
67	Stax 589 002	AND NOW! (LP)	30
68	Stax 589 013	SOUL CHRISTMAS (LP)	15
68	Stax 230 002/231 002	DOIN' OUR THING (LP)	15
68	Stax (S)XATS 1001	SOUL LIMBO (LP)	15
69	Atco 228 004	GET READY (LP)	15
69	Stax (S)XATS 1005	UPTIGHT (LP, soundtrack, with Judy Clay)	15
69	Stax (S)XATS 1015	THE BOOKER T. SET (LP)	15
69	Atco 228 015	THE BEST OF BOOKER T. AND THE M.G.s (LP)	15
70	Stax SXATS 1031	McLEMORE AVENUE (LP)	15
71	Stax 2325 030	MELTING POT (LP)	15

(see also Mar-Keys, Steve Cropper, Albert King, Judy Clay)

BOOMBACK
85	Headphone HP/DC/003	Ghetto Life/Roadblock (12")	125

BOOMERANGS
64	Fontana TF 507	Rockin' Robin/Don't Let Her Be Your Baby	10

BOOMTOWN RATS
13	Mercury RATLIFEDJ1	RATLIFE (10", 100 copies, signed, gig only)	50

PAT BOONE
SINGLES
55	London HLD 8172	Ain't That A Shame/Tennessee Saturday Night ()gold label)	35
55	London HLD 8197	At My Front Door/No Arms Can Ever Hold You	10
56	London HLD 8233	Gee Whittakers/Take The Time	10
56	London HLD 8253	I'll Be Home/Tutti Frutti	10
56	London HLD 8291	Long Tall Sally/Just As Long As I'm With You	10
56	London HLD 8303	I Almost Lost My Mind/I'm In Love With You	10
59	London HLD 8824	There's Good Rockin' Tonight/With The Wind And The Rain In Your Hair	10

EXPORT SINGLES
56	London HL 7007	I'll Be Home/Tutti Frutti	10
56	London HL 7010	Long Tall Sally/Just As Long As I'm With You	10

ALBUMS
63	London SH-D 8109	SINGS ... GUESS WHO? (LP, stereo)	15

(see also Fontane Sisters)

BOONES FARM
72	CBS 8212	If You Can't Be My Woman/Start Today	20

BOO RADLEYS
92	Creation CRELP 120	EVERYTHING'S ALRIGHT FOREVER (LP, first 1000 with free Sunfly 7")	15
93	Creation CRELP 149	GIANT STEPS (2-LP)	30
95	Creation CRELP 179	WAKE UP! (LP, gatefold sleeve)	15
96	Creation CRELP 194	C'MON KIDS (2-LP with free 7')	30
96	Creation CRELP 194	C'MON KIDS (2-LP without free 7')	20

ANTHONY BOOTH
69	Tangerine DP 0008	Till Death Do Us Part/September Days	7

BILL BOOTH REVIVAL MACHINE
75	HEADSRTM/CUS038	FACE TO FACE (LP)	18

KEN BOOTHE
66	Island WI 3020	The Train Is Coming/This Is Me	50
66	Island WI 3035	Don't Want To See You Cry/Baby I Need You (B-side actually by Wailers)	100
66	Ska Beat JB 248	You're No Good/SOULETTES: Don't Care What The People Say	100

BOOTLES

			MINT VALUE £
67	Doctor Bird DB 1210	Say You/LYN TAITT & JETS: Smokey Places	50
67	Coxsone CS 7006	Lonely Teardrops/Oowee Baby	70
67	Coxsone CS 7020	Home Home Home/SOUL BROTHERS: Windell	40
67	Caltone TONE 107	The One I Love/You Left The Water Running	75
67	Studio One SO 2000	Feel Good/Mustang Sally	40
67	Studio One SO 2012	Puppet On A String/ROLAND ALPHONSO: Look Away Ska	25
67	Studio One SO 2014	Fatty Fatty (actually Heptones)/Mother Word (actually by Delroy Wilson)	30
67	Studio One SO 2026	Why Did You Leave (actually by Leroy Sibbles)/Don't Try To Reach Me (actually by Gaylads)	30
68	Studio One SO 2039	When I Fall In Love/HEPTONES: Christmas Time	45
68	Studio One SO 2041	The Girl I Left Behind/TERMITES: My Last Love	90
68	Studio One SO 2053	Tomorrow/Movin' Away	70
68	Fab FAB 63	I Remember Someone/Can't You See?	150
68	Coxsone CS 7041	Everybody Knows/GAYLADS: I'm Free	60
69	Coxsone CS 7094	Sherry/I've Got You	40
69	Studio One SO 2073	You're On My Mind/RICHARD ACE & SOUND DIMENSIONS: Love To Cherish	50
69	High Note HS 003	Lady With The Starlight/LESLIE BUTLER & COUNT OSSIE: Gay Drums	25
69	Bamboo BAM 4	Pleading/COUNT MATCHUKI & SOUND DIMENSION: Call 1143	80
69	Bamboo BAM 8	Be Yourself/SOUND DIMENSION: Rathid	70
70	Trojan TR 7716	Why, Baby Why/Keep My Love From Fading	15
70	Trojan TR 7756	Freedom Street/BEVERLEY'S ALLSTARS: Freedom Version	15
70	Trojan TR 7772	It's Gonna Take A Miracle/Now I Know	25
70	Trojan TR 7780	Drums Of Freedom/BEVERLEY'S ALLSTARS: Version	15
70	Gas GAS 169	Give To Me/Why	8
70	Jackpot JP 748	You Left The Water Running/PHIL PRATT ALL STARS: Cut Throat	30
70	Punch PH 30	Artibella/PRATT ALLSTARS: Version Of Artibella	30
70	Punch PH 33	Morning/Morning (Version)	8
71	Punch PH 70	Stop Your Crying/CONSCIOUS MINDS: Suffering Through The Nation	12
71	Banana BA 352	Original Six (Parts 1 & 2)	12
71	Summit SUM 8518	I Wish It Could Be Peaceful Again/BEVERLEY'S ALLSTARS: Peaceful Version	15
71	Summit SUM 8519	Your Feeling And Mine/BEVERLEY'S ALLSTARS: Your Feeling Version	15
71	Big Shot BI 590	So Nice/So Nice Version	20
71	Green Door GD 4002	Medley Version/Medley Version 2	10
71	Dynamic DYN 411	Hallelujah/Trying To Reach	10
72	Camel CA 91	Ain't No Sunshine/LLOYD & HORTENSE: You Are Everything	25
72	Pama Supreme PS 369	Look What You've Done/LLOYD CHARMERS: Look What You've Done Version	10
72	Ashanti ASH 403	Make Me Feel Alright (with The Incrowd)/INCROWD: Down On The Corner	8
73	Trojan TR 7893	Is It Because I'm Black/Black, Gold And Green	15
73	Green Door GD 4053	Silver Words/Rasta God Version	20
75	Fab FAB 270	Thinking/Moving Away	30
75	Torpedo TOR 35	Lady With The Starlight/Light Version	20
75	Torpedo TOR 54	Say You/You Version	8
78	Trojan TR 9036	Freedom Day/Love Don't Love Nobody	12
79	Attack TACK 6	You're No Good/PRINCE JAMMY: Out Of Order Dub (12")	25
79	Trojan TRO 9036	Who Gets Your Love/Is It Because I'm Black	10
79	Trojan TRO T 9052	Who Gets Your Love/(Version)/Is It Because I'm Black (12")	18
02	Trojan TJH10001	Can't You See (1968 Version)/(1971 Version)/Tears From My Eyes/Ain't No Sunshine (10")	20
67	Studio One SOL 9001	MR. ROCK STEADY (LP)	200
73	Trojan TRLS 58	BLACK, GOLD AND GREEN (LP)	40
74	Trojan TRLS 83	LETS GET IT ON (LP)	25
74	Trojan TRLS 95	EVERYTHING I OWN (LP)	25
75	Trojan TRLS 120	FREEDOM STREET (LP)	40
78	Trojan TRLS 148	BLOOD BROTHER (LP)	20
79	Phil Pratt PP01LP	GOT TO GET AWAY (LP)	40
87	Trojan TRLS 249	EIGHTEEN CLASSIC SONGS (LP)	18

(see also Stranger & Ken, Gaylads, Richard Ace, Lloyd & Ken)

BOOTLES

64	Vocalion VN 9216	I'll Let You Hold My Hand/Never Till Now	25

BOOTS

68	CBS 3550	Even The Bad Times Are Good/The Animal In Me	20
68	CBS 3833	Keep Your Lovelight Burning/Give Me One More Chance	25
70	Youngblood YB 1018	You Better Run/A To D	60

DAVE BOOTS

60s	Solent SM 013	GREEN SATIN AND GOLD (LP)	100

BOOTS FOR DANCING

80	Pop Aural POP 002	BOOTS FOR DANCING EP (12")	15
80	Pop Aural POP 006	Hesitate/Rain Song (p/s)	10
82	Repop X WAY 100	Ooh Bop Sh'bam/Money (p/s)	8

BOOTSY'S RUBBER BAND

76	Warner Bros K 56200	STRETCHIN' OUT IN BOOTSY'S RUBBER BAND (LP)	18
77	Warner Bros K 56302	AHH... THE NAME IS BOOTSY, BABY! (LP, gatefold sleeve)	18
78	Warner Bros K 56424	BOOTSY? PLAYER OF THE YEAR (LP, gatefold sleeve)	15
79	Warner Bros K 56615	THE BOOT IS MADE FOR FONK-N (LP, with inner sleeve)	15
81	Warner Bros K 56998	THE ONE GIVETH, THE COUNT TAKETH AWAY (LP)	15

(see also Parliament, Funkadelic)

BOOVER BOYS

70	Torpedo TOR 22	A.G.G.R.O/Sha La La La Lee	100

RANNY BOP

70	Escort ERT 837	Crock Iron/Memphis Bop	25

BORDER

MINT VALUE £

70	Gas GAS 155	Pipe Dream/Suck Suck	20

(see aso Ranny Williams)

BORDER
78	Pear PEAR 1	Song For J/Easy/Going Away (p/s, 500 only)	40

BORE-TOWN BOP
81	Vital VIS001	Try/Surf's Up (p/s)	15

RICHARD BORIE & PDF
80	Don't Panic PDF 1	On and On/Sorry (p/s)	8

BORZOI
87	CS 2509	It's Called Rincarnation/I'm At War (p/s)	20

BOSCH
80	Trific TRIF 1	The Two Tree/Packing Jean (p/s)	25

BOSS
86	Power House (no cat. no.)	One Good Reason/Wake Up Children (p/s, with lyric sheet)	6

BOSS ATTACK
71	Fab FAB 187	Hell-El/TEARDROPS: Let Me Be Free	15

BOSS COMBO
62	Coral LVA 9205	GOLDEN ROCK AND ROLL INSTRUMENTALS (LP)	20

BOSS GUITARS
65	London HA-R/SH-R 8237	PLAY THE WINNERS (LP)	20

EARL BOSTIC (ORCHESTRA)

SINGLES

54	Parlophone MSP 6075	Off Shore/What! No Pearls	10
54	Parlophone MSP 6089	Deep Purple/Smoke Rings	10
54	Parlophone MSP 6105	Melancholy Serenade/Don't You Do It	10
54	Parlophone MSP 6110	Jungle Drums/Danube Waves	10
54	Parlophone MSP 6119	Mambolino/Blue Skies	10
54	Parlophone MSP 6131	These Foolish Things/Mambostic	10
54	Parlophone CMSP 8	Cherokee/The Song Is Ended (export issue)	10
55	Parlophone MSP 6162	Melody Of Love/Sweet Lorraine	10
56	Vogue V 2145	Flamingo/Sleep	10
56	Vogue V 2148	Moonglow/Ain't Misbehaving	10
56	Parlophone R 4208	The Bo-Do Rock (with Bill Doggett)/Mean To Me	10
56	Parlophone R 4232	For All We Know/Beyond The Blue Horizon	10
57	Parlophone R 4263	I Hear A Rhapsody/Harlem Nocturne	8
57	Parlophone R 4278	Bubbins Rock/Indiana (with Bill Doggett)	8
57	Parlophone R 4305	Avalon/Too Fine For Crying (B-side with Bill Jones)	8
57	Parlophone R 4370	Temptation/September Song	8
58	Parlophone R 4460	Over The Waves Rock/Twilight Time	8
59	Parlophone DP 553	Barcarolle/My Reverie (export single)	8
62	Ember JBS 708	Tuxedo Junction/Air Mail Special	8
66	Island WI 271	Honeymoon Night/PATSY COLE: Disappointed Bride	15

EPs

54	Parlophone GEP 8506	FLAMINGO	10
55	Parlophone GEP 8513	LINGER AWHILE	10
55	Parlophone GEP 8520	EARL BOSTIC AND HIS ALTO SAX	15
55	Vogue EPV 1010	EARL BOSTIC	15
56	Vogue EPV 1111	VELVET SUNSET	10
56	Parlophone GEP 8539	WRAP IT UP	10
58	Parlophone GEP 8701	BOSTIC BEAT	20
58	Parlophone GEP 8741	ROCKING WITH BOSTIC	20

ALBUMS

54	Vogue LDE 100	EARL BOSTIC AND HIS ORCHESTRA (10")	30
54	Parlophone PMD 1016	EARL BOSTIC AND HIS ALTO SAX (10" LP)	25
56	Parlophone PMD 1040	EARL BOSTIC AND HIS ALTO SAX NO. 2	25
58	Parlophone PMD 1054	BOSTIC MEETS DOGGETT (10" LP, with Bill Doggett)	30
58	Parlophone PMD 1068	BOSTIC ROCKS (10" LP)	30

(see also Bill Doggett, Sonny Carter)

BOSTON
76	Epic EPCH 81611	BOSTON (LP, audiophile pressing)	20
86	MCA MCGP 6017	THIRD STAGE (LP, picture disc)	15
94	MCA MCGP 6017	WALK ON (LP, picture disc)	15

BOSTON BOPPERS
74	Penny Farthing PEN 828	Did You Get What You Wanted/Whirlwind Girl	25

BOSTON CRABS
65	Columbia DB 7586	Down In Mexico/Who?	20
65	Columbia DB 7679	As Long As I Have You/Alley Oop	20
66	Columbia DB 7830	Gin House/You Didn't Have To Be So Nice	20

BOSTON DEXTERS
64	Contemporary CR 101	Matchbox/La Bamba	200
64	Contemporary CR 102	You've Been Talking About Me/Nothing's Gonna Change Me	150
64	Contemporary CR 103	What Kind Of Girl Are You/I've Got Troubles Of My Own	150
65	Columbia DB 7498	I Believe To My Soul/I've Got Something To Tell You	50
65	Columbia DB 7641	Try Hard/No More Tears	45

(see also Tam White)

JACK ANGLIN BOSTON AND THE SOULITES
69	Ackee ACK 103	Starvation/Slave	20

BO STREET RUNNERS
64	Decca F 11986	Bo Street Runner/Tell Me	50

Connie BOSWELL

			MINT VALUE £
65	Columbia DB 7488	Tell Me What You're Gonna Do/And I Do Just What I Want	60
65	Columbia DB 7640	Baby Never Say Goodbye/Get Out Of My Way	60
66	Columbia DB 7901	Drive My Car/So Very Woman (featuring Mike [Too Much] Patto)	70
64	Oak RGJ 131	BO STREET RUNNERS (EP, 49 copies only)	1000

(see also [Mike] Patto, Timebox, Chicago Line, Cheynes, Fleetwood Mac)

CONNIE BOSWELL

54	Brunswick 05319	T-E-N-N-E-S-S-E-E (Spells ...)/If I Give My Heart To You	7
55	Brunswick 05397	How Important Can It Be?/Fill My Heart With Happiness	7

EVE BOSWELL

53	Parlophone MSP 6006	Sugar Bush/Moon Above Malaya (China Nights)	15
55	Parlophone MSP 6158	Ready, Willing And Able/Pam-Poo-Dey	10
55	Parlophone MSP 6160	The Heart You Break (May Be Your Own)/Tika Tika Tok	10
56	Parlophone MSP 6208	Young And Foolish/Where You Are	10
56	Parlophone MSP 6220	It's Almost Tomorrow/Cookie	12
56	Parlophone MSP 6250	Saries Marias/Come Back My Love	10
56	Parlophone R 4230	True Love/Where In The World Is Billy?	10
57	Parlophone R 4275	Rock Bobbin' Boats/Tra La La	10
57	Parlophone GEP 8601	THE ENCHANTING EVE (EP)	15
58	Parlophone GEP 8690	EVE BOSWELL'S SHOWCASE (EP)	10
56	Parlophone PMD 1039	SUGAR AND SPICE (10" LP)	75
57	Parlophone PMC 1038	SENTIMENTAL EVE (LP)	200
59	Parlophone PMC 1105	FOLLOWING THE SUN AROUND (LP)	100

SIMON BOSWELL

75	Transatlantic TRA 307	MIND PARASITES (LP)	18

(see also Advertising)

BOTH HANDS FREE (1)

76	Kemp/Pegrum KP 001J	BOTH HANDS FREE (LP)	150

BOTH HANDS FREE (2)

78	Zyzzle ZYZZLE 1	USE FROM THE POCKET (LP)	100

BOTHY BAND

75	Polydor 2383379	THE BOTHY BAND (LP)	18

RAMON BOUCHE

67	Columbia 8257	I Gotta Be With You/The Real Thing (DJ Copy)	200

BOULEVARD

79	Chopper CHOP 5D	MAGIC MAN (12", red vinyl, no p/s)	15
81	Boulevard VARD 1	Dawn Raid/Take It Or Leave It (p/s)	40

BOUNCING FLOWERS

81	Rewind REWIND 8	Fire/Expanding Cases (p/s)	10

DENNIS BOVELL

78	Tempus TEMLP 001	STRICTLY DUBWISE (LP)	25
81	Fontana 6381047	BRAIN DAMAGE (2-LP)	35
93	Arawak ARKLP105	DUB DEM SILLY (LP)	15

(see also Matumbi, Rama)

BOW BELLS

65	Polydor 56030	Not To Be Taken/I'll Try Not To Hold It Against You	6
66	Parlophone R 5520	Belinda/When You're In	6

(see also Nola York)

JIMMY BOWEN

57	Columbia DB 3915	I'm Stickin' With You/Ever Lovin' Fingers	30
57	Columbia DB 3984	Warm Up To Me, Baby/I Trusted You	30
57	Columbia DB 4027	Cross Over/It's Shameful	15
58	Columbia DB 4184	The Two Step/By The Light Of The Silvery Moon	15
65	Reprise RS 23043	The Eagle (demos & some issues list "The Golden Eagle")/Spanish Cricket	15
58	Columbia SEG 7757	MEET JIMMY BOWEN (EP)	30
58	Columbia SEG 7793	MEET JIMMY BOWEN NO. 2 (EP)	30

BOWERY ELECTRIC

00	Beggars Banquet BBQLP 213	LUSHLIFE (LP)	40

DAVID BOWIE

SINGLES : DEMO SINGLES

66	Pye 7N 17020	Can't Help Thinking About Me/And I Say To Myself (Demo copy, push-out centre)	1000
66	Pye 7N 17020	Can't Help Thinking About Me/And I Say To Myself (demo copy, solid centre)	500
66	Pye 7N 17079	Do Anything You Say/Good Morning Girl (Demo copy, push-out centre)	1000
66	Pye 7N 17079	Do Anything You Say/Good Morning Girl (Demo copy, solid centre)	500
66	Pye 7N 17157	I Dig Everything/I'm Not Losing Sleep (Demo copy, push-out centre)	1000
66	Pye 7N 17157	I Dig Everything/I'm Not Losing sleep (Demo copy, solid centre)	500
66	Deram DM 107	Rubber Band/The London Boys (Demo copy)	300
67	Deram DM 123	The Laughing Gnome/The Gospel According To Tony Day (Demo copy)	200
67	Deram DM 135	Love You Till Tuesday/Did You Ever Have A Dream (Demo copy)	200
70	Mercury MF 1135	The Prettiest Star/Conversation Piece (Demo copy)	300
70	Mercury 6052 026	Memory Of A Free Festival Parts 1 & 2 (Demo copy, large centre)	300
70	Mercury 6052 026	Memory Of A Free Festival Parts 1 & 2 (Demo copy, push-out centre)	175
71	Mercury 6052 049	Holy Holy/Black Country Rock (Demo copy)	175
72	RCA 2160	Changes/Andy Warhol (Demo copy)	45
72	RCA 2160	Starman/Suffragette City (Demo copy in p/s)	75
72	RCA 2199	Starman/Suffragette City (Demo copy, not in p/s)	25
72	RCA 2302	The Jean Genie/Ziggy Stardust (Demo copy)	20
72	RCA 2263	John, I'm Only Dancing/Hang Onto Yourself (Demo copy)	25
73	RCA 2316	Life On Mars?/The Man Who Sold The World (Demo copy in p/s)	40
73	RCA 2316	Life On Mars?/The Man Who Sold The World (Demo copy without p/s)	15
73	RCA 2352	Drive-In Saturday/Round And Round (Demo copy)	30

David BOWIE

MINT VALUE £

73	RCA 2424	Sorrow/Amsterdam (Demo copy)	15
74	RCA LPBO 5009	Rebel Rebel/Queen Bitch (Demo copy, label states "Bowie" not "David Bowie")	25
74	RCA LPBO 5009	Rock'N'Roll Suicide/Quicksand (Demo copy)	20
74	RCA APBO 0293	Diamond Dogs/Holy Holy (Demo copy, as "Bowie" not "David Bowie", push-out centre)	25
74	RCA APBO 0293	Diamond Dogs/Holy Holy (as "Bowie" not "David Bowie", solid centre)	35
74	RCA 2466	Knock On Wood/Panic In Detroit (Demo copy)	15
75	RCA 2523	Young Americans (short version)/Young Americans (long version) (Demo copy)	25
75	RCA 2640	Golden Years/Can You Hear Me (Demo copy, solid centre, as "Bowie" not "David Bowie")	60
75	RCA 2640	Golden Years/Can You Hear Me (Demo copy, push-out centre, as "Bowie" not "David Bowie")	15
75	Decca F 13579	The London Boys/Love You Till Tuesday (Demo)	40
75	RCA 2579	Fame/Right (Demo copy)	15
75	RCA 2593	Space Oddity/Velvet Goldmine (Demo copy in p/s)	30
75	RCA 2593	Space Oddity/Velvet Goldmine (Demo copy, no p/s)	15
76	RCA 2682	TVC15/We Are The Dead (Demo copy)	15
76	RCA 2726	Suffragette City/Stay (Demo copy in p/s)	25
76	RCA 2726	Suffragette City/Stay (Demo copy, no p/s)	15
77	RCA PB 0905	Sound And Vision/A New Career In A New Town (Demo copy)	15
77	RCA PB 1017	Be My Wife/Speed Of Life (Demo copy in promo sleeve with titles on front)	500
77	RCA PB 1017	Be My Wife/Speed Of Life (Demo copy not in sleeve)	15
77	RCA PB 1121	Heroes/V-2 Schneider (Demo copy)	20
77	RCA PB 1190	Beauty And The Beast/Sense Of Doubt (Demo copy with p/s)	20
78	RCA BOW 1	Breaking Glass/Art Decade/Ziggy Stardust (Demo copy with p/s)	20
79	RCA BOW 2	Boys Keep Swinging/Fantastic Voyage (Demo copy)	15
79	RCA BOW 3	DJ/Repetition (Demo copy)	15
79	RCA BOW 4	John, I'm Only Dancing (Again)(1975)/John, I'm Only Dancing (1972) (Demo copy p/s)	15
80	RCA BOW 5	Alabama Song/Space Oddity (Demo copy, poster p/s)	20

SINGLES : IRISH PRESSINGS

70	Mercury EMF 1135	The Prettiest Star/Conversation Piece (Irish pressing)	2000
73	RCA 2352	Drive-In Saturday/Round And Round (Irish pressing)	100
73	RCA 2424	Sorrow/Amsterdam (Irish pressing)	30
73	Deram DM(1) 123	The Laughing Gnome/The Gospel According To Tony Day (Irish pressing)	120
73	Deram DM(1) 123	The Laughing Gnome/The Gospel According To Tony Day (Irish pressing)	120
74	RCA LPBO 5009	Rebel Rebel/Queen Bitch (Irish pressing)	100
74	RCA LPBO 5021	Rock'N'Roll Suicide/Quicksand (Irish pressing)	100
75	RCA 2523	Young Americans/Sufragette City (Irish pressing)	100
79	RCA 2316	Life On Mars?/The Man Who Sold The World (Irish pressing)	100
82	RCA BOW 11	Wild Is The Wind/Golden Years (Irish pressing, p/s)	15
83	RCA BOW 503	Rock 'n' Roll Suicide/Quicksand (Irish pressing)	10
83	RCA BOW 502	Life On Mars?/The Man Who Sold The World (Irish pressing)	10
83	RCA BOW 504	Diamond Dogs/Holy Holy (Irish issue)	10
83	RCA BOW 501	Drive-In Saturday/Round And Round (Irish pressing, p/s)	10

SINGLES

66	Pye 7N 17020	Can't Help Thinking About Me/And I Say To Myself (with Lower Third)	300
66	Pye 7N 17079	Do Anything You Say/Good Morning Girl	400
66	Pye 7N 17157	I Dig Everything/I'm Not Losing Sleep	400
66	Deram DM 107	Rubber Band/The London Boys	450
67	Deram DM 123	The Laughing Gnome/The Gospel According To Tony Day (with inverted matrix number on label)	60
67	Deram DM 135	Love You Till Tuesday/Did You Ever Have A Dream	200
69	Philips BF 1801	Space Oddity/Wild Eyed Boy From Freecloud (mono, solid centre)	150
69	Philips BF 1801	Space Oddity/Wild Eyed Boy From Freecloud (mono, push-out centre)	20
69	Philips BF 1801	Space Oddity/Wild Eyed Boy From Freecloud (unreleased p/s, only 2 or 3 copies known to exist)	3000
69	Philips BF 1801	Space Oddity/Wild Eyed Boy From Freecloud (UK pressed stereo 45: unconfirmed)	0
	(is this really a UK pressing or a Dutch pressing as is generally acknowledged?)		
69	Philips BF 1801	Space Oddity/Wild Eyed Boy From Freecloud (mono, large centre)	15
70	Mercury MF 1135	The Prettiest Star/Conversation Piece	250
70	Mercury 6052 026	Memory Of A Free Festival Parts 1 & 2 (large centre)	250
70	Mercury 6052 026	Memory Of A Free Festival Parts 1 & 2 (push-out centre)	200
71	Mercury 6052 049	Holy Holy/Black Country Rock	150
72	RCA RCA 2160	Changes/Andy Warhol	25
72	RCA RCA 2199	Starman/Suffragette City (in p/s)	60
72	Pye 7NX 8002	FOR THE COLLECTOR EP (Do Anything You Say/I Dig Everything//I Can't Help Thinking About Me/I'm Not Losing Sleep (re-issue, blue label with art sleeve)	20
72	Pye 7NX 8002	FOR THE COLLECTOR EP (Do Anything You Say/I Dig Everything//I Can't Help Thinking About Me/I'm Not Losing Sleep (re-issue, pink label with push-out centre)	20
72	Pye PRT 7NX 8002	FOR THE COLLECTOR EP (Do Anything You Say/I Dig Everything//I Can't Help Thinking About Me/I'm Not Losing Sleep (re-issue)	10
72	Pye 7NX 8002	FOR THE COLLECTOR EP (Do Anything You Say/I Dig Everything//I Can't Help Thinking About Me/I'm Not Losing Sleep (re-issue, pink label, solid centre)	6
72	Pye 7NX 8002	FOR THE COLLECTOR EP (Do Anything You Say/I Dig Everything//I Can't Help Thinking About Me/I'm Not Losing Sleep (re-issue, grey label)	6
72	RCA RCA 2263	John, I'm Only Dancing/Hang Onto Yourself (original pressing with slow 'acoustic guitar' version)	6
73	RCA RCA 2316	Life On Mars?/The Man Who Sold The World (in p/s)	20
73	RCA 2263	John, I'm Only Dancing/Hang Onto Yourself (2nd issue, sax version, orange label, MATRIX BGBS 1056 2E)	7
74	RCA LPBO 5009	Rebel Rebel/Queen Bitch (label states "Bowie" not "David Bowie")	15
74	RCA LPBO 5021	Rock'N'Roll Suicide/Quicksand	7

David BOWIE

MINT VALUE £

Year	Catalogue	Title	Value
74	RCA APBO 0293	Diamond Dogs/Holy Holy ("Bowie" not "David Bowie", solid centre)	25
74	RCA APBO 0293	Diamond Dogs/Holy Holy (as "Bowie" not "David Bowie", push-out centre)	10
74	RCA/Mainman	Bowie's Greatest Hits (excerpts from Knock On Wood/ Lyntone LYN 2929 Space Oddity/The Man Who Sold The World/Life On Mars?/Starman/Jean Genie/Sorrow/Diamond dogs) 33rpm 1-sided flexidisc with Record Mirror/Popswop magazines)	35
75	Decca F 13579	London Boys/Love You Till Tuesday (plastic moulded label)	8
75	RCA RCA 2593	Space Oddity/Changes/Velvet Goldmine (p/s)	10
76	RCA RCA 2726	Suffragette City/Stay (p/s)	15
77	RCA PB 0905	Sound And Vision/A New Career In A New Town (re-issue, black label)	7
77	RCA PB 1017	Be My Wife/Speed Of Life (solid centre)	20
77	RCA PB 1121	Heroes/V-2 Schneider (Orange label, solid centre)	10
77	RCA PB 1121	Heroes/V-2 Schneider (plastic moulded label in white sleeve)	10
77	RCA PB 1190	Beauty And The Beast/Sense Of Doubt (sold centre centre with p/s)	20
78	RCA BOW 1	Breaking Glass/Art Decade/Ziggy Stardust (p/s)	8
78	RCA PB 1190	Beauty And The Beast/Sense Of Doubt (push-out centre with p/s)	8
79	RCA BOW 2	Boys Keep Swinging/Fantastic Voyage (p/s)	10
79	RCA BOW 3	DJ/Repetition (p/s)	7
79	RCA BOW 3	DJ/Repetition (p/s, green vinyl)	50
79	RCA LPBO 5009	Rebel Rebel/Queen Bitch (re-issue, black label)	7
79	RCA 2424	Sorrow/Amsterdam (re-issue)	7
79	RCA 2199	Starman/Suffragette City (re-issue, black label solid centre)	7
79	RCA BOW 4	John, I'm Only Dancing (Again)(1975)/John, I'm Only Dancing (1972) (p/s)	7
79	RCA 2263	John, I'm Only Dancing/Hang Onto Yourself (re-issue, sax version, black label)	7
79	RCA 2316	Life On Mars?/The Man Who Sold The World (re-issue, black label, solid centre)	15
79	RCA 2316	Life On Mars?/The Man Who Sold The World (re-issue, black label, push-out centre)	7
80	RCA 2263	John, I'm only Dancing/Hang Onto Yourself (re-issue, original version, black label)	7
80	RCA LPBO 5009	Rebel Rebel/Queen Bitch (re-issue, black label, B-side plays "Song For Bob Dylan")	10
80	RCA BOW 5	Alabama Song/Space Oddity (pink vinyl, custom factory pressing, poster p/s)	500
80	RCA BOW 5	Alabama Song/Space Oddity (poster p/s)	10
80	RCA BOW 6	Ashes To Ashes/Move On (with 3 different p/s & 4 different sheets of 9 stamps)	15
80	RCA BOW 9	Up The Hill Backwards/Crystal Japan (orange label, solid centre, p/s)	8
81	RCA BOW 9	Up The Hill Backwards/Crystal Japan (orange label, push-out centre, p/s)	6
81	RCA BOW 10	Wild Is The Wind/Golden Years (push-out centre. with p/s)	7
81	RCA BOW 10	Wild Is The WInd/Golden Years (solid centre, p/s)	8
82	RCA BOW 11	IN BERTHOLT BRECHT'S "BAAL" (Baal's Hymn/Remembering Marie A//Ballad Of The Adventureres/The Drowned Girl/Dirty Song, EP, foldout p/s)	10
82	RCA BOW 100	FASHIONS (10 x 7" picture discs in plastic wallet [BOWP 101-110], each £8)	100
83	RCA BOW 514	Rebel Rebel/Queen Bitch (Reissue, p/s)	7
83	RCA BOW 514	Rebel Rebel/Queen Bitch (plays Song For Bob Dylan) (Reissue, p/s)	7
84	EMI America EA 187	Tonight/Tumble And Twirl (poster p/s)	6
86	Virgin VSS 906	When The Wind Blows/When The Wind Blows (Instrumental) (shaped pic disc)	8
87	EMI America EAP 237	Time Will Crawl (Single Version)/Girls (Single Edit) (poster p/s)	8
92	Warner Bros W 0127	Real Cool World/Real Cool World (Instrumental) (White label with "Made in the UK", art sleeve)	10
92	Warner Bros W 0127	Real Cool World/Real Cool World (Instrumental) (silver label, art sleeve)	10
93	BMG Arista 136977	Jump They Say (Radio Edit)/Pallas Athena (Don't Stop Praying Mix) (jukebox issue)	6
93	Arista 74321 162267	Miracle Tonight/Looking For Lester (p/s)	7
93	Arista 74321 177057	The Buddah Of Suburbia/Dead Against It (p/s)	7
93	BMG Arista 74321 148287	Black Tie White Noise/You've Been Around (black moulded label, large centre)	15
93	BMG Arista 74321 148287	Black Tie White Noise/You've Been Around (silver moulded label, p/s)	7
95	RCA 329407	Strangers When We Meet (Edit)/The Man Who Sold The World (live) (green vinyl, stickered card p/s)	20
95	RCA 353847	Hallo Spaceboy (Remix)/The Heart's Filthy Lesson (Radio Edit) (pink vinyl, stickered card p/s)	20
95	RCA 74321 353847JB	Hallo Spaceboy (Remix)/The Heart's Filthy Lesson (Radio Edit) (juke box issue, moulded label)	50
97	RCA 7432 1475841	Dead Man Walking (House Mix)/(Vigor Mortis Mix)/(Paradox Mix) (plain sleeve, stickered)	6
97	RCA 512347	Seven Years In Tibet (Edit)/Seven Years In Tibet (Mandarin Version) (p/s, clear vinyl)	8
99	Castle ESBO7 765	I DIG EVERYTHING: THE 1966 PYE SINGLES (box set)	20
02	Columbia COL 672744 7/ 6727447000	Slow Burn/Wood Jackson (orange vinyl, p/s)	15
09	Parlophone LCO 299	DAVID BOWIE : Heroes/TV ON THE RADIO : Heroes	40
13	EMI DBSTAR40	Starman (original version)/Top Of The Pops Version (picture disc, stickered PVC sleeve)	150
13	EMI DBDRIVE 40	Drive In Saturday/(Russell Harty Plus Pop Version) (picture disc in PVC stickered sleeve)	20
13	Sony 88883705557	The Stars (Are Out Tonight)/Where Are We Now (white vinyl, p/s)	10

ALBUMS

Year	Catalogue	Title	Value
67	Deram DML 1007	DAVID BOWIE (1st pressing, brown label, mono)	1000
67	Deram SML 1007	DAVID BOWIE (1st pressing, red label, stereo)	1000
69	Philips SBL 7912	DAVID BOWIE (1st pressing, unlaminated gatefold sleeve, black/silver label)	700
70	Decca PA 58	THE WORLD OF DAVID BOWIE (mono)	40
71	Mercury 6338 041	THE MAN WHO SOLD THE WORLD (LP, 1st pressing, with 'Produced by Tonny Viconti' mis-print on label, black/silver labels with 'dress' cover)	1000
71	Mercury 6338 041	THE MAN WHO SOLD THE WORLD (LP, 2nd pressing, without 'Produced by Tonny Viconti' mis-print on label, black/silver labels with 'dress' cover)	900
71	Mercury 6338 041	THE MAN WHO SOLD THE WORLD (cassette, with 'dress' cover)	50
71	RCA SF 8244	HUNKY DORY (LP, 1st pressing, orange label with lyric sheet, 1st pressing with laminated sleeve, no GEM logo on right hand top corner of rear cover and no Mainman reference on sleeve or labels)	600
71	RCA SF 8244	HUNKY DORY (LP, 2nd pressing, non-laminated sleeve, orange label with 'Chrysalis Music Ltd./Titanic Music' credits, lyric sheet)	75
71	RCA SF 8244	HUNKY DORY (LP, 3rd pressing, non-laminated sleeve, orange label with 'Mainman/	50

David BOWIE

MINT VALUE £

Year	Catalog	Description	Value
72	RCA SF 8287	Chrysalis' credits, lyric sheet) ... THE RISE AND FALL OF ZIGGY STARDUST AND THE SPIDERS FROM MARS (1st pressing, Stamped matrixes: BGBS 0864 1E/0865 1E (with A4S etched into dead wax on side 1, B2K etched into dead wax on side 2) with with 'Gem Productions' and no 'Mainman' logo on rear sleeve, "Victor" under RCA label not "International", glossy orange label with "Titanic/Chrysalis" credits on labels, lyric inner sleeve)	250
72	RCA SF 8287	THE RISE AND FALL OF ZIGGY STARDUST AND THE SPIDERS FROM MARS, 2nd pressing, Gem Production and Mainman on rear of sleeve, 'Mainman/Chrysalis' publishing credits)	70
72	RCA LSP 4813	SPACE ODDITY (LP, reissue of SBL 7912 in different sleeve, orange label with lyric inner sleeve & poster)	75
72	RCA LSP 4816	THE MAN WHO SOLD THE WORLD (first reissue, 'Titanic' credit, 'Ziggy' sleeve glossy orange labels with inner sleeve & foldout poster)	40
73	RCA LSP-486	THE MAN WHO SOLD THE WORLD (second reissue 'Mainman' credit, lyric inner)	20
73	RCA RS 1001	ALADDIN SANE (gloss orange label with 'Victor' on right side, 'Shorewood' gatefold sleeve & lyric inner sleeve, with fan club membership folder. Matrix numbers: CPRY 4543-3T/4544-3T)	100
73	RCA RS 1001	ALADDIN SANE (orange label, 'Dynaflex' pressing, gatefold sleeve & lyric inner sleeve)	35
73	RCA RS 1003	PIN UPS (LP, insert, orange label)	40
74	RCA APL1 0576	DIAMOND DOGS (LP, 1st pressing, gatefold sleeve, orange label, 'Mainman' logo on rear sleeve, ARL1-0576A-1oly/ARL1-0576B-1oly matrixes)	80
74	RCA APL 2-0771	DAVID LIVE (2-LP, 1st pressing, gatefold sleeve, orange label, photos on inners. 1st pressing has July 14th and 15th dates on inside cover, later pressings from 1974 have corrected dates of July 12nd and 13th)	30
75	RCA Victor RS 1006	YOUNG AMERICANS	40
76	RCA APL 1 1327	STATION TO STATION (LP, 1st pressing, 'Garrodprint Ltd' on sleeve with 'ZZ' in top rear right corner, matt orange label, lyric inner with cat no, Matrix numbers: two sets crossed out before APLI-1327-A-1E/B-1E)	60
76	RCA RS 1055	CHANGESONEBOWIE (with 'sax' version of "John I'm Only Dancing")	30
76	RCA APLI 1327	STATION TO STATION (with original colour proof sleeve)	500
77	RCA INTS 5065	LOW (red vinyl, semi-official 'factory custom pressing')	500
77	RCA PL12030	LOW (LP, insert, fan club flyer, sticker on front ('Featuring the hit single Sound & Vision') and back of sleeve (tracklisting))	100
77	RCA PL12030	LOW (LP, insert, sticker on front ('Featuring the hit single Sound & Vision') and back of sleeve (tracklisting))	70
77	RCA PL 12522	HEROES (LP, with insert, laminated sleeve, orange label)	80
78	RCA PL 02913	STAGE (2-LP, gatefold sleeve, yellow vinyl)	35
78	RCA PL 02913	STAGE (2-LP, gatefold sleeve)	25
78	RCA Red Seal RL 12743	DAVID BOWIE NARRATES PROKOFIEV'S PETER AND THE WOLF	20
79	RCA BOW 1	LODGER (gatefold sleeve, insert)	35
80	RCA BOW LP 2	SCARY MONSTERS (AND SUPER CREEPS) (purple vinyl, semi-official 'factory custom pressing')	600
80	RCA BOWLP2	SCARY MONSTERS AND SUPER CREEPS	30
80	RCA International INTS 5066	HEROES (LP, repressing, insert, green label)	25
80	RCA International INS 5063	THE RISE AND FALL OF ZIGGY STARDUST AND THE SPIDERS FROM MARS (LP, reissue, green label)	25
81	EMI America AML 3029	LET'S DANCE (LP, inner)	20
81	RCA International INTS 5067	ALADDIN SANE (LP, reissue, single sleeve, green label)	25
81	RCA Intl. INTS 5068	DIAMOND DOGS (LP, reissue, green label)	20
81	RCA Intl. INTS 5235	PIN UPS (LP, reissue, green label)	15
81	RCA BOWLP3	CHANGESTWOBOWIE (LP, inner)	25
81	RCA Int. RCAPL 12030	LOW (LP, repressing, green label)	25
83	RCA NL 14654	THE MAN WHO SOLD THE WORLD (third reissue, silver on black labels)	20
83	RCA INTS 5237	THE MAN WHO SOLD THE WORLD (fourth reissue, black on green labels)	20
83	RCA International NL 83843	THE RISE AND FALL OF ZIGGY STARDUST AND THE SPIDERS FROM MARS (LP, reissue, black label)	20
83	RCA PL 84862(2)	ZIGGY STARDUST - THE MOTION PICTURE (2-LP)	25
84	RCA BOPIC 3	ZIGGY STARDUST (picture disc with numbered insert)	18
84	RCA BOPIC 5	DIAMOND DOGS (picture disc with numbered insert)	18
84	RCA BOPIC5	DIAMOND DOGS (LP, reissue, picture disc, numbered)	50
84	RCA BOPIC 4	PIN-UPS (picture disc with numbered insert)	18
84	RCA BOPIC 2	HUNKY DORY (picture disc with numbered insert)	50
84	Deram 800 087-1	DAVID BOWIE (reissue)	20
84	RCA BOPIC 1	ALADDIN SANE (picture disc with numbered insert)	18
84	RCA BOPIC 4	PIN UPS (LP, reissue, picture disc, numbered)	40
84	RCA PL 81327	STATION TO STATION (LP, reissue, black label)	18
84	RCA Int. INTS 5212	LODGER (LP, reissue, non gatefold sleeve, green label)	15
90	EMI EMC 3571	SPACE ODDITY (LP, 1990 reissue, gatefold with extra tracks)	25
90	EMI EMC 3573	THE MAN WHO SOLD THE WORLD (LP, reissue, gatefold, 'dress cover', with four bonus tracks)	40
90	EMI WMC 3572	HUNKY DORY (LP, reissue, gatefold with bonus tracks)	20
90	EMI EMC 3577	ZIGGY STARDUST (LP, 1990 reissue, gatefold with unreleased tracks)	20
90	EMI EMC 3584	DIAMOND DOGS (LP, remastered with 2 bonus tracks - Dodo/Candidate)	30
90	EMI DBTV1	CHANGESBOWIE (2-LP, gatefold)	20
91	EMI EMD 1021	YOUNG AMERICANS (remastered with 3 bonus tracks)	25
91	EMI EMD 1020	STATION TO STATION (remastered with 2 bonus tracks, gatefold sleeve)	30
93	BMG 74321 13697 1	BLACK TIE WHITE NOISE (LP, inner)	150
93	EMI EM 1512	THE SINGLES COLLECTION (3-LP)	50
94	MAINMAN GYLP 002	SANTA MONICA LIVE '72 (2xLP, clear vinyl)	40
95	RCA 307021	EXCERPTS FROM OUTSIDE (with 12" booklet & lyric sheet)	50
97	RCA 44949	EARTHLING (gatefold sleeve, stickered sleeve)	200
97	EMI LPCENT 4	THE RISE AND FALL OF ZIGGY STARDUST AND THE SPIDERS FROM MARS (LP, reissue, EMI 100 Centenary, stickered lseeve)	50
97	EMI LPCENT 21	HUNKY DORY (LP, reissue, EMI 100 Centenary edition, stickered sleeve)	30
99	EMI 7243 4 99463 1 6	ALADDIN SANE (LP, reissue, gatefold)	60

David BOWIE AND BING CROSBY

MINT VALUE £

01	Simply Vinyl SVLP 264	THE MAN WHO SOLD THE WORLD (reissue, remaster, 'dress' sleeve)	25
02	Columbia 508222 1	HEATHEN (LP)	100
03	EMI 0724359451121	SOUND AND VISION (4-CD box set with booklet)	30
03	EMI 07243 5 41979 1 8	ZIGGY STARDUST - THE MOTION PICTURE SOUNDTRACK (2-LP, red vinyl, reissue)	40
09	EMI DBSOLP 40	DAVID BOWIE (LP, reissue, gatefold with poster)	20
10	EMI BOWSTSD2010	STATION TO STATION (Reissue, box set 5-CD, DVD, LP)	100
11	Deram 532760-1	DAVID BOWIE (2-LP, reissue, gatefold)	40
11	Music On Vinyl MOVLP 470	HEATHEN (LP, reissue, standard black vinyl, 180gm)	40
12	EMI DBZSX 40	ZIGGY STARDUST AND THE SPIDERS FROM MARS (LP, with DVD)	20
13	Music On Vinyl MOVLP 470	HEATHEN (LP, orange vinyl, 500 only, V&A Exhibition exclusive, numbered stickered sleeve)	150
13	Music On Vinyl MOVLP 500	OUTSIDE (LP, reissue, green vinyl 500 only, V&A Exhibition exclusive, numbered stickered sleeve)	150
13	Music On Vinyl MOVLP 815	EARTHLING (LP, reissue, blue vinyl, inner, numbered)	100
13	Sony Music 88765 461861	THE NEXT DAY (2-LP, CD, 180gram vinyl)	35
14	Music On Vinyl MOVLP 875	REALITY (LP, reissue, 180gm vinyl)	25
15	Parlophone DBXL 1	FIVE YEARS 1969-1973 (box set, 13-LP)	500
16	Sony Music 88875173871	BLACK STAR (LP, Clear vinyl, die-cut sleeve, booklet, download, 5000 pressed)	200
16	Sony Music 88875173871 S1	BLACK STAR (LP, black vinyl, die-cut sleeve, booklet, download, 1st pressing with '(c) & (p) 2015 ISO Records' on back cover and not 2015, 2016 which is repressing)	40
16	ISO 88875173871	BLACK STAR (LP, repressing, black vinyl, die-cut sleeve, booklet, download, 2nd pressing with 2016 copyright info on back)	20
16	Parlophone DBBBCLP6872	BOWIE AT THE BEEB (box set, 4-LP, with 20 page booklet)	50
17	Parlophone DBRSD 6973	BOWPROMO (box set, 1-sided LP with photos and press release)	35
20	Parlophone 0190295198787	METROBOLIST (full cartoon sleeve, gatefold with Keef pics, 50 copies on white vinyl)	1000
20	Parlophone 0190295198787	METROBOLIST (full cartoon sleeve, gatefold with Keef pics, 1970 copies on white vinyl)	100
20	Parlophone 0190295198787	METROBOLIST (full cartoon sleeve, gatefold with Keef pics, black vinyl)	20

ALBUMS : CDS

84	Deram 800 087-2	DAVID BOWIE (withdrawn with white title)	80
84	RCA PD 84202	CHANGESTWOBOWIE (withdrawn)	30
84	RCA PD 89002	STAGE (2-CD, withdrawn)	40
84	RCA PD 94792	GOLDEN YEARS (withdrawn)	30
84	RCA PD 84919	FAME AND FASHION (ALL TIME GREATEST HITS) (withdrawn)	50
85	RCA PD 81732	CHANGESONEBOWIE (withdrawn)	35

PROMOS

71	Gem BOWPROMO 1	BOWPROMO (LP, white label only, also known as HUNKY DORY SAMPLER Some with handwritten sleeve or Gem sticker on A-side, B-side features DANA GILLESPIE, 500 only)	2000
71	None	HUNKY DORY (LP, preview pressing. Green labels with large red G and track listing, Matrixes Side 1: APRS-5947-35-A1A R Side 2: APRS-5948-35-A1A R, white sleeve with typed track listing and handwritten details "David Bowie Hunky Dory Preview Pressing 19 October 1971)	3000
77	RCA BOW-1E	From The New Album 'Low' (1-sided promo, excerpts from Speed Of Life, Breaking Glass, What In The World, Sound And Vision)	1500
83	RCA LIFETIMES 1	LIFETIMES (LP, promo, numbered, with insert)	100
90	BMG BOW 908	SO FAR (CD, 8-track sampler for "Sound & Vision" box set)	40
93	EMI BOWIE 1	SELECTIONS FROM THE SINGLES COLLECTION 10-track sampler,card p/s, promo only	18
93	BMG MEAT 1	Pallas Athena (12", white label, no p/s, includes two exclusive Meat Beat Manifesto remixes)	40
93	Back To Basics HOME 1	Night Flights/(B-side by Moodswings) (12")	18
93	BBC MMCD 0072	BBC SESSIONS 1969-1972 (CD, picture disc, promo-only, withdrawn)	75
95	RCA HALLO 2	Hallo Spaceboy (12" Remix) (12", 1-sided, no p/s)	18
95	BMG SOLO 1	EXCLUSIVE TOUR CD: Strangers When We Meet/MORRISSEY: The Boy Racer (Outside Tour CD)	90
95	RCA OUT 1	The Heart's Filthy Lesson (12", 1-sided promo)	10
96	RCA SPACE 2	Hallo Spaceboy (12" Remix) (1-sided 12", some copies listed as RCA HALLO 2, no p/s)	25
96	RCA SPACE 3	Hallo Spaceboy (Double Click Mix)/Hallo Spaceboy (Instrumental)/ Hallo Spaceboy (Lost In Space Mix) (12", no p/s)	50
99	EMI QUEENWL 28	Under Pressure (Remixes) (with Queen) (12", white label, unreleased mix, promo only)	30

(see also Davie Jones & King Bees, Davy Jones & Lower Third, Manish Boys, Arnold Corns, Spiders From Mars, Mick Ronson, Queen, Tao Jones Index, Bing Crosby, Tin Machine)

DAVID BOWIE AND BING CROSBY

82	RCA BOW 12 (PRO)	Peace On Earth/Little Drummer Boy//Dialogue/Peace On Earth/LDB (Demo copy, p/s)	20
82	RCA BOW 12	Peace On Earth/Little Drummer Boy/Fantastic Voyage (Irish pressing, p/s)	15

(see also David Bowie, Bing Crosby)

CANDY BOWMAN

81	RCA RCAT 148	Since I Found You/I Wanna Feel Your Love (12")	20

BOWMAN-HYDE PLAYERS

61	Ember EMB S 141	I Like A Little Honey/Teenage Kiss	8
61	Parlophone PMC 1155	SING ME A SOUVENIR (LP)	20

ALAN BOWN (SET)

65	Pye 7N 15934	Can't Let Her Go/I'm The One	30
66	Pye 7N 17084	Baby Don't Push Me/Everything's Gonna Be Alright	30
66	Pye 7N 17148	Headline News/Mister Pleasure	50
66	Pye 7N 17192	Emergency 999/Settle Down	60
67	Pye 7N 17256	Gonna Fix You Good (Everytime You're Bad)/I Really Really Care	50
67	Music Factory CUB 1	We Can Help You/Magic Handkerchief (as the Alan Bown!)	12
67	MGM MGM 1355	Toyland/Technicolour Dream	10
68	MGM MGM 1387	Story Book/Little Lesley	25
69	Deram DM 259	Still As Stone/Wrong Idea (as The Alan Bown)	10
69	Deram DM 278	Gypsy Girl/All I Can	6

Alan BOWN SET/JIMMY JAMES & VAGABONDS

MINT VALUE £

Year	Label/Cat #	Title	Value
75	CBS 3721	Rockford Files/I Don't Know	6
75	CBS 3366	Moanin'/Time To Change	6
68	Music Factory CUB LS 1	OUTWARD BOWN (LP, stereo)	100
68	Music Factory LM 1	OUTWARD BOWN (LP, mono)	100
69	Deram SML 1049	THE ALAN BOWN! (LP, stereo)	70
69	Deram DML 1049	THE ALAN BOWN! (LP, mono)	80
70	Island ILPS 9131	LISTEN (LP, with inner sleeve)	30
71	Island ILPS 9163	STRETCHING OUT (LP, gatefold sleeve)	30
96	Tenth Planet TP 027	OUTWARD BOWN FIRST ALBUM (LP, reissue)	20

(see also John Barry Seven, Bronco, Jonesy)

ALAN BOWN SET/JIMMY JAMES & VAGABONDS
Year	Label/Cat #	Title	Value
68	Pye N(S)PL 18156	LONDON SWINGS - LIVE AT THE MARQUEE CLUB (LP, 1 side each)	30

(see also Jimmy James & Vagabonds)

ANDREW BOWN
Year	Label/Cat #	Title	Value
70	Parlophone R 5856	Tarot (Theme From 'Ace Of Wands')/Lulli Rides Again	75

(see also Andy Bown)

ANDY BOWN
Year	Label/Cat #	Title	Value
75	GM GMS 9039	Supersonic/Feeling Better	10
79	EMI EMI 2906	Another Shipwreck/Another Night With You	6
79	EMI EMI 2943	Good Advice/One More Chance (p/s)	15
81	EMI EMI 5245	Say It Was Magic/One Forward Two Back Again (in p/s)	10
72	Mercury 6310 002	GONE TO MY HEAD (LP)	20
73	GM GML 1001	SWEET WILLIAM (LP)	20

(see also Andrew Bown, Herd, Judas Jump, Status Quo, Rossi & Frost, Storyteller)

BRENDAN BOWYER
Year	Label/Cat #	Title	Value
66	HMV POP 1578	One Way Street/Rapparee	10

BENDALLS BOX
Year	Label/Cat #	Title	Value
81	Circus CIRC 004	Nightmares/Games Today (p/s)	25

DAVID BOX
Year	Label/Cat #	Title	Value
64	London HLU 9874	If You Can't Say Something Nice/Sweet Sweet Day	15
64	London HLU 9924	Little Lonely Summer Girl/No One Will Ever Know	15

(see also Crickets)

BOX CLEVER
Year	Label/Cat #	Title	Value
98	Prolific PROHP 003	Talk To Me/Treat Me Right (12")	12

BOXER
Year	Label/Cat #	Title	Value
75	Virgin VDJ 12	All The Time In The World/Don't Wait (12", promo only)	15
75	Virgin V 2049	BELOW THE BELT (LP, gatefold sleeve with uncensored full-frontal back cover)	30
76	Virgin V 2049	BELOW THE BELT (LP, censored sleeve)	15
76	Virgin V 2073	BLOODLETTING (LP, withdrawn)	100

(see also Patto, Timebox, Koobas, May Blitz)

BOXER REBELLION
Year	Label/Cat #	Title	Value
13	Absentee TBR012VL	PROMISES (LP)	50
14	Absentee TBR003VL	EXITS (LP)	30
15	Absentee TBR12BOX 1	THE BOXER REBELLION (3-LP, box set, signed hand-written lyric sheet, 5 art cards and download card, 500 only	150

BOX TOPS
Year	Label/Cat #	Title	Value
67	Stateside SS 2044	The Letter/Happy Times	10
67	Stateside SS 2070	Neon Rainbow/She Knows How	7
68	Bell BLL 1001	Cry Like A Baby/The Door You Closed To Me	6
69	Bell BLL 1068	Soul Deep/The Happy Song	6
68	Stateside (S)SL 10218	THE LETTER/NEON RAINBOW (LP)	15
68	Bell MBLL/SBLL 105	CRY LIKE A BABY (LP)	15
68	Bell MBLL/SBLL 108	NON-STOP (LP)	15
69	Bell SBLL 120	DIMENSIONS (LP)	15

(see also Big Star, Alex Chilton)

JUNIOR BOYCE (ACTUALLY JR. BYLES)
Year	Label/Cat #	Title	Value
77	Observer OB 004	Natty Dreadlocks/Sick-More Tree/What Kind Of World/Sic Easy Stepping (12", with Ranking Buckers)	30

(see also Junior Byles)

TOMMY BOYCE
Year	Label/Cat #	Title	Value
65	MGM MGM 1287	Pretty Thing/I Don't Have To Worry 'Bout You	10

TOMMY BOYCE & BOBBY HART
Year	Label/Cat #	Title	Value
67	A&M AML 907	TEST PATTERNS (LP)	25

(see also Monkees, Tommy Boyce)

EDDIE BOYD
Year	Label/Cat #	Title	Value
66	Blue Horizon 45 BH 1009	It's So Miserable To Be Alone/Empty Arms	150
67	Blue Horizon 57-3137	The Big Boat/Sent For You Yesterday (with Fleetwood Mac) (no Fleetwood Mac credit on label)	40
68	Blue Horizon 57-3137	The Big Boat/Sent For You Yesterday (with Fleetwood Mac) (Fleetwood Mac credit on label)	40
62	Esquire EP 247	BOYD'S BLUES (EP, as Eddie Boyd Blues Combo)	70
65	Fontana SFJL 905	FIVE LONG YEARS (LP)	60
67	Decca LK/SKL 4872	EDDIE BOYD AND HIS BLUES BAND FEATURING PETER GREEN (LP)	120
68	Blue Horizon 7-63202	7936 SOUTH RHODES (LP, with Fleetwood Mac)	100
68	Storyville SLP 4054	IN CONCERT (LP)	25

(see also Fleetwood Mac)

EDDIE BOYD/BUDDY GUY
Year	Label/Cat #	Title	Value
66	Chess CRE 6009	WITH THE BLUES (EP, 2 tracks each)	25

(see also Buddy Guy)

JIMMY BOYD
Year	Label/Cat #	Title	Value
53	Columbia SCM 5072	I Saw Mommy Kissing Santa Claus/Little Train A-Chuggin' In My Heart	10

Moses BOYD EXODUS

MINT VALUE £

MOSES BOYD EXODUS
16	Exodus XODUS 001	Rye Lane Shuffle/Drum Dance (12", p/s)	25
17	Exodus XOEP03	ABSOLUTE ZERO (12" EP, p/s)	15
20	Exodus XOLP001XX	DARK MATTER (2-LP, wrapped in flag, 'dinked' edition, grey vinyl, as Moses Boyd)	40

BOY FRIDAY (& GROOVERS)
70	Downtown DT 470	Version Girl/Grumble Man	20
71	Downtown DT 471	Music So Good/Right Track (both with Groovers)	35
71	Downtown DT 472	Sounds I Remember/JOAN LONG: Reconsider Our Love	18
71	Downtown DT 473	Take A Message Ruby/Second Note	50
71	Downtown DT 476	There'll Always Be Sunshine/Sunshine Track	20
71	Downtown DT 477	Hot Pants Girl/Raunchy	15
71	Downtown DT 481	El Raunchy/Conversation (as Boy Friday & Collins)	15
71	J-Dan JDN 4416	I Don't Want No War/Third Note Swing	7
71	J-Dan JDN 4418	Situation Version/OUR BAND: Keep Tracking	7

(see also Dandy & Superboys)

BOYFRIENDS
78	United Artists UP 36424	I'm In Love Today/Saturday Night (p/s)	10
78	United Artists UP 36442	Jenny/Don't Ask Me To Explain (p/s)	10
78	United Artists UP 36478	Last Bus Home/Romance (p/s)	10

(see also Vibrators)

BOYFRIENDS
| 82 | Plastic PRES 001 | Boyfriend/Give A Little, Take A Little (p/s) | 40 |

BOY HAIRDRESSERS
| 88 | 53rd & 3rd AGARR T12 | Golden Showers/Tidalwave/The Assumption As An Elevator (12", p/s) | 30 |

(see also Teenage Fanclub, BMX Bandits, Clouds)

BILLY BOYLE
| 62 | Decca F 11503 | My Baby's Crazy 'Bout Elvis/Held For Questioning | 15 |
| 70 | UPC UPC112 | Lookin' For Love/Pisces Man | 20 |

(see also Le Roys)

A. BOYNE
| 70 | Punch PH 36 | Oh My Darling (actually Audley Rollins)/DENNIS SMITH: Ball Of Confusion | 10 |

BILLY BOYO
| 82 | Greensleeves GRELD 89 | Righteousness/Itie Title Girl (12") | 15 |

BOYRACER
92	Fluff HONEY 2	Railway/Reverse (p/s)	10
93	Wurlitzer Jukebox WJ 01	Boyracer/SABINE: Painted Portraits (single sided, p/s)	10
93	Sarah SARAH 76	B IS FOR BOYRACER EP (p/s, insert)	20
93	Sarah SARAH 85	FROM PURITY TO PURGATORY EP (p/s, insert)	30
94	Sarah SARAH 96	PURE HATED EP (p/s, insert)	20

BOYS IN DARKNESS
81	Bid For Freedom BID 1	Back To France/A Man An Island (no p/s)	15
81	Champagne BUBL-702	Back To France/A Man An Island (p/s)	10
81	Champagne BUBLY-702	Back To France/A Man An Island (12" p/s)	12

BOYS (JAMAICA)
| 69 | Duke DU 19 | Easy Sound/AFROTONES: Freedom Sound | 20 |

(see also Harry J. Allstars)

BOYS BLUE
| 65 | HMV POP 1427 | You Got What I Want/Take A Heart | 50 |

(see also Jeff Elroy & Boys Blue)

BOYS (U.K.) (1)
| 63 | Parlophone R 5027 | Polaris/Jumpin' | 20 |
| 64 | Pye 7N 15726 | It Ain't Fair/I Want You | 100 |

BOYS (U.K.) (2)
77	NEMS NES 102	I Don't Care/Soda Pressing (p/s)	15
77	NEMS NES 111	First Time/Whatcha Gonna Do/Turning Grey (p/s)	15
78	NEMS NES 116	Brickfield Nights/Teacher's Pet (p/s)	12
79	Safari SAFE 21	Kamikaze/Bad Days (p/s, with booklet)	6
80	Safari SAFE 33	Let It Rain/Lucy (p/s)	6
77	NEMS NES 6001	THE BOYS (LP, 1st pressing with 33 and a thrid on labels)	25
78	NEMS NEL 6015	ALTERNATIVE CHARTBUSTERS (LP, 1st pressing, laminated sleeve. inner, 33 and a third on labels)	30
79	Safari 1-2 BOYS	TO HELL WITH THE BOYS (LP, with songbook & stickered sleeve)	25
80	Safari BOYS 4	BOYS ONLY (LP)	15

(see also Yobs, Rowdies, Hollywood Brats)

BOYS (U.K.) (3)
| 88 | Cleversounds BOYS 1 | Happy Days/Standard Avenue/Learn How To Dance (p/s) | 8 |

(see also Ocean Colour Scene)

BOYS WONDER
| 88 | Boys Wonder BW 1 | Goodbye Jimmy Dean/Hot Rod (p/s) | 10 |

BOYZ II MEN
| 91 | Motown 53000-1 | COOLEYHIGHHARMONY (LP) | 20 |
| 94 | Motown 53043-1 | II (LP) | 25 |

BOZ
66	Columbia DB 7832	You're Just The Kind Of Girl I Want/Isn't That So	30
66	Columbia DB 7889	Meeting Time/No (Ah) Body Knows The Blues	30
66	Columbia DB 7941	Pinocchio/Stay As You Are	10
66	Columbia DB 7972	The Baby Song/Carry On Screaming	20
68	Columbia DB 8406	I Shall Be Released/Dove In The Flood	50
68	Columbia DB 8468	Light My Fire/Back Against The Wall	15

(see also King Crimson, Bad Company)

BOZOS

BOZOS
78 Other BOZ 101   Weekend Girl/Fool Out Of Me 25

JANET BRACE
55 Brunswick 05272   Teach Me Tonight/My Old Familiar Heartache 6

BRACKEN
79 Look LKLP 6438   PRINCE OF THE NORTHLANDS (LP, private pressing, with insert) 60

WILLIE BRACKENRIDGE
79 Burning Vibrations BVD 005   Blood Money/You Are On My Mind (12") 35

BOBBY BRADFORD
73 Emanem 302   LOVE'S DREAM (LP) 25

JAN BRADLEY
63 Pye International 7N 25182   Mama Didn't Lie/Lovers Like Me 35

MARTIN BRADLEY
80 Greenwich Village GVR 205   TIME CAN'T STAND STILL (LP) 15

OWEN BRADLEY (ORCHESTRA/QUINTET)
58 Brunswick 05736   Big Guitar/Sentimental Dream (as Owen Bradley Quintet) 10
60 Brunswick LAT 8327   THE BIG GUITAR (LP) 20

BRADLEY STRYDER
92 Rephlex CAT 001   BRADLEY'S BEAT (12" EP, logo sleeve) 20
96 Rephlex CAT 020   BRADLEY'S ROBOT (12" EP, poster p/s) 10

BUDDY BRADSHAW
59 Capitol CL 15036   Nothing You Can Say/Tonight I Walk Alone 10
(see also Owen Gray)

SONNY BRADSHAW QUINTET
62 Top TD 106   This Is Happiness/Island In The Sun 15

SONNY BRADSHAW (& YOUNG JAMAICA)
61 Duke DK 1003   Yellow Birds/Festival Jump Up 10
71 Big Shot BI 576   Wig Wam/Peace And Love (as Sonny Bradshaw & Young Jamaica) 12

TINY BRADSHAW & HIS ORCHESTRA
54 Parlophone GEP 8507   TRAIN KEPT A ROLLING (EP) 30
56 Parlophone GEP 8552   POMPTON TURNPIKE (EP) 15

TINY BRADSHAW ORCHESTRA/WYNONIE HARRIS
70 Polydor 623 273   KINGS OF RHYTHM AND BLUES (LP, 1 side each) 15
(see also Wynonie Harris)

DON BRADSHAW-LEATHER
72 Distance DIST 101   DISTANCE BETWEEN US (2-LP, gatefold sleeve, private pressing) 400

BOB BRADY & CONCHORDS
68 Bell BLL 1025   Everybody's Goin' To The Love-In/It's Been A Long Time Between Kisses 60
70 Bell BLL 1114   Everybody's Goin' To The Love-In/It's Been A Long Time Between Kisses (reissue) 20

MAJELLA BRADY
65 Rex R11015   Light In My Window/Girl 8

PHIL BRADY & THE RANCH SET
67 Go AJ 11406   Lonesome For You/Please Come Back 18

VICTOR BRADY
70 Polydor 2489010   BROWN RAIN (LP) 40

BRADY BUNCH
73 Paramount SPFL 284   MEET THE BRADY BUNCH (LP) 15

JOHNNY BRAGG
79 Inferno 2   They're Talking About Me/Is It True (p/s, orange vinyl) 8

AL 'TNT' BRAGGS
66 Vocalion VP 9278   Earthquake/How Long (Do You Hold On) 20
66 Vocalion VP 9278   Earthquake/How Long (Do You Hold On) (DJ Copy) 60
68 Action ACT 4506   Earthquake/How Long (Do You Hold On) (reissue) 20
69 Action ACT 4526   I'm A Good Man/I Like What You Do To Me 15
65 Vocalion VFP 170163   AL 'TNT' BRAGGS (EP) 125

ERNEL BRAHAM
66 Rio R 79   Musical Fight/EDWARDS ALLSTARS: Pipeline 35

ROY BRAHAM
64 R&B 166   Believe Me/Red Sea 30

BRAIN
67 Parlophone R 5595   Nightmares In Red/Kick The Donkey 150
87 Bam Caruso OPRA 63   Nightmares In Red/SRC: Black Sheep (jukebox edition, die-cut company sleeve) 10
(see also Giles Giles & Fripp, Trendsetters Ltd, League Of Gentlemen)

BRAINBOX
69 Parlophone R 5775   Woman's Gone/Down Man 20
70 Parlophone R 5842   So Helpless/To You 15
70 Parlophone PCS 7094   BRAINBOX (LP, black/silver/white boxed Parlophone label) 200
(see also Jan Akkerman, Hunters, Focus)

BRAINCHILD
70 A&M AMS 805   Cage/Autobiography 10
70 A&M AMLS 979   HEALING OF THE LUNATIC OWL (LP, brown label) 120

BRAIN DONOR
06 Invada INV031LP   DRAIN'D BONER (12" gatefold, picture disc) 10

BRAINIAC 5
80 Roach RR 5002   Working/Feel (p/s) 10
78 Roach RREP 5001   MUSHY DOUBT (EP, 33rpm, p/s) 15

BRAINKILLERS
93 Vibe Alive VALV 36   Crackhead/Dark Moon/Stupid/This Is Where It Takes Us (12", with Lewi Cifer) 50
93 Vibe Alive VALV 76   On A Different Mission/One Stype/Hurt Me/Girl U Look Good (12", stickered die-cut paper sleeve, with Lewi Cifer) 20
94 3rd Party, Kemet KM3RD#1   BORDER LINE EP (with FAMILY OF INTELLIGENCE) (12") 20

BRAIN KILLERS/FAMILY OF INTELLEGENCE

MINT VALUE £

BRAIN KILLERS/FAMILY OF INTELLEGENCE
94   3rd Party/Kemet KM3Rd 1   Screwface/Jungle Love/Champion Of Champions/Bonus Beats 1 (12") 30

BRAINSTORM
77   Miracle M5   Lovin' Is Really My Game/Stormin 8
79   Miracle M5   Lovin' Is Really My Game/Stormin' (12", red or black vinyl no p/s) 20

BRAINTAX
92   Low Life Low 2   FAT HEAD (EP 12" - 500 pressed) 40
97   Low Life Low 4   FUTURE YEARS (EP, 12") 20
01   Low Life LOW 15   BIRO FUNK (2-LP) 25
06   Low Life LOW 50   PANORAMA (LP) 25
08   Low Life LOW 50   MY LAST AND BEST ALBUM (LP) 25

BRAKES
80   Magnet MAGL   FOR WHY YOU KICKA MY DONKEY? (LP) 15

DELANEY BRAMLETT
64   Vocalion VP 9227   Heartbreak Hotel/You Never Looked Sweeter 15
65   Vocalion VP 9237   Liverpool Lou/You Have No Choice 30
65   Vocalion VP 9237   Liverpool Lou/You Have No Choice (DJ Copy) 50
(see also Delaney & Bonnie, King Curtis with Delaney & Friends)

BRAM STOKER
72   Windmill WMD 117   HEAVY ROCK SPECTACULAR (LP) 30

BRAN
74   Gwawr GWA 104   BRAN EP 50
75   Sain 1038M   AIL-DDECHRA (LP) 300
76   Sain 1070M   HEDFAN (LP) 100
78   Sain 1120M   GWRACH Y NOS (LP) 40

GLENN BRANCA
89   Blast First BFFP 39   SYMPHONY NO 6 (LP) 15

BRAND
64   Piccadilly 7N 35216   I'm A Lover Not A Fighter/Zulu Stomp 100

BRAND NEW
03   Eat Sleep   Jude Law And A Semester Abroad/Am I Wrong (p/s) 30
03   Sore Point SORE 004S   The Quiet Things That No One Ever Knows/Jude Law And A Session Abroad (live in session) (die-cut sleeve, red vinyl) 15
04   Sore Point SORE 0145   The Quiet Things That No One Ever Knows/The No Seatbelt Song (live) (p/s, green vinyl) .. 8
04   Sore Point SORE 011S   Sic Transit Gloria...Glory Fades/Jaws Theme Swimming (Demo) (pink vinyl) 15
07   Interscope 1733030   Jesus/Brothers (picture sleeve, stickered sleeve) 60

BRAND NEW HEAVIES
91   Acid Jazz JAZID 39P   Never Stop (12", company sleeve, withdrawn) 20
90   Acid Jazz JAZID LP 23   THE BRAND NEW HEAVIES (LP) 15
97   FFRR 828 887-1   SHELTER (2-LP) 30
12   Acid Jazz AJLP 293   THE BRAND NEW HEAVIES (LP, reissue) 15

BILL BRANDON
73   Mercury 6052 186   I Am Free Of Your Love/(Take Another Little) Piece Of My Heart 8
(see also John Edwards)

JOHNNY BRANDON
56   Parlophone MSP 6238   Rock-A-Bye Baby/Lonely Lips 40
56   Parlophone R 4207   Shim Sham Shuffle/I Didn't Know 40
56   Decca F 10778   Glendora/Song For A Summer Night 15
57   Decca F 10858   Nothing Is Too Good For You/A Sort-Of-A-Feeling 10
55   Pye NEP 24003   JOHNNY BRANDON HITS (EP) 15

KIRK BRANDON & PACK OF LIES
87   SS SS1N2/SS2N1   KIRK BRANDON AND THE PACK OF LIES (EP) 10
(see also Theatre Of Hate, Spear Of Destiny, Senate, Pack)

VERN BRANDON
62   Decca F 11472   Let Me Be The One/Gotta Know The Reason 20

BRANDY
94   Atlantic 7567 82610-1   BRANDY (LP) 30
98   Atlantic 7567 83039-1   NEVER SAY NEVER (2-LP) 25
02   Atlantic 7567 83110-1   FULL MOON (2-LP) 25
05   Atlantic 7567 83633-1   AFRODISIAC (2-LP) 20

BRANDY BOYS
65   Columbia DB 7507   Gale Winds/Don't Come Knocking At My Door 10

BRANDY WINE BRIDGE
77   Cottage COT 311   THE GREY LADY (LP, as Brandywinebridge) 25
78   Cottage COT 321   AN ENGLISH MEADOW (LP, hand-drawn sleeve with insert) 25

BRANDY WINE SINGERS
68   President PT 204   Mandy/Two Little Boys 6

LINDA BRANNON
63   Columbia DB 7156   Funny Face/Will It Last 10

JOHNNY BRANTLEY'S ALL STARS
58   London HLU 8606   The Place/Pot Luck 20

BRASS ALLEY
73   Alaska ALA 11   You Better Run/Be My Friend 20

BRASS BIRD
68   TP TO 024   Simple Life/A Place To Die 60

BRASS CONSTRUCTION
75   United Artists UP 617   Movin'/Changin' (12") 10
76   United Artists UAS 29923   BRASS CONSTRUCTION (LP) 15

BRASS RAIL
70   Hot Pursuit HP 1   Deep In The Woods/Light Up The Sky 30

André BRASSEUR

MINT VALUE £

ANDRÉ BRASSEUR
65	Pye International 7N 25332	Early Bird Satellite/Special 230	10
67	CBS 202557	The Kid/Holiday	20
67	CBS 202557	The Kid/Holiday (DJ Copy)	50
71	CBS 2557	The Kid/Holiday (reissue)	8
66	CBS 62858	TASTY (LP)	15

BRASS INCORPORATED
70	Pye International 7N 25520	At The Sign Of The Swinging Cymbal/Just Like That	25

BRASS MONKEY
71	Philips 6303 025	BRASS MONKEY (LP)	30
71	Philips 6303 027	NO VISIBLE MEANS OF SUPPORT (LP)	30

BRASS TACKS
68	Big T BIG 110	I'll Keep On Holding On/Let The Sunshine In	35
68	Big T BIG 114	Maxwell Ferguson/Sunshine After The Rain	100

BRATZ
80	A Famous Record AFR 1	The Bratz Are Coming/Coast To Coast/Everyone Wants To Be Elvis (p/s)	6

RICHARD BRAUTIGAN
69	Zapple ZAPPLE 03	LISTENING TO RICHARD BRAUTIGAN (LP, unreleased, acetates exist)	1500

CEDRIC BRAVO
65	Ska Beat JB 229	Merry Christmas/Sugar Baby	15

LOS BRAVOS
66	Decca F 22529	Going Nowhere/Brand New Baby	20
68	Decca F 22765	Bring A Little Lovin'/Make It Last	8
66	Decca LK 4822	BLACK IS BLACK (LP)	15
68	Decca LK/SKL 4905	LOS BRAVOS (LP)	20

(see also Mike Kennedy)

ANTHONY BRAXTON
85	Leo 414/415/416	QUARTET (2-LP box set with insert)	35

ANTHONY BRAXTON & DEREK BAILEY
73	Emanem 601	DUO (2-LP)	30
84	Incus INCUS 43	ROYAL VOLUME 1 (LP)	20

(see also Derek Bailey)

TONI BRAXTON
93	Arista 74321 16268 1	TONI BRAXTON (LP)	40
96	La Face 73008-26020-1	SECRETS (LP)	70
00	La Face 73008-26069-1	THE HEAT (LP)	70

BRAZELIA
82	Broad Star BS100	Everlasting Love/Brazelia	7

PRISCILLA BRAZIER
74	Dovetail DOVE 9	PRISCILLA BRAZIER (LP)	25
76	Key KL 038	SOMETHING BEAUTIFUL (LP)	35

BREAD
69	Elektra EKS 74044	BREAD (LP)	25

(see also David Gates, Pleasure Fair)

BREAD & BEER BAND
69	Decca F 12891	Dick Barton Theme (The Devil's Gallop)/Breakdown Blues	75
72	Decca F 13354	Dick Barton Theme (The Devil's Gallop)/Breakdown Blues (reissue)	40
69	Rubbish (no cat. no.)	THE BREAD AND BEER BAND (LP, 1 copy known to exist)	2000

(see also Elton John, Caleb)

BREAD, LOVE & DREAMS
69	Decca F 12958	Virgin Kiss/Switch Out The Sun	22
69	Decca LK 5008	BREAD, LOVE AND DREAMS (LP, unboxed large Decca on label, mono)	250
69	Decca SKL 5008	BREAD, LOVE AND DREAMS (LP, unboxed large Decca on label, stereo)	200
70	Decca LK 5048	THE STRANGE TALE OF CAPTAIN SHANNON AND THE HUNCHBACK FROM GIGHA (LP, small boxed Decca label, mono)	250
70	Decca SKL 5048	THE STRANGE TALE OF CAPTAIN SHANNON AND THE HUNCHBACK FROM GIGHA (LP, small boxed Decca label, stereo)	200
71	Decca SKL 5081	AMARYLLIS (LP, small boxed Decca label)	800
07	Sunbeam SBRLP 5027	AMARYLLIS (LP, reissue)	15
08	Sunbeam SBRLP 5042	THE STRANGE TALE OF CAPTAIN SHANNON AND THE HUNCHBACK FROM GIGHA (LP, reissue)	20

(see also Human Beast)

BREAKAWAYS
62	Pye 7N 15471	He's A Rebel/Wishing Star	15
63	Pye 7N 15585	That Boy Of Mine/Here She Comes	10
64	Pye 7N 15618	That's How It Goes/He Doesn't Love Me	50
65	Pye 7N 15973	Danny Boy/Your Kind Of Love	10
67	CBS 2833	Sacred Love/Don't Be A Baby	20

(see also Vernons Girls, Burt Bacharach Orchestra, Mike Patto, Ken Cope, Sharades, De Laine Sisters, Dany Chandelle, Nicky James, Russ Loader)

BREAKDOWN
77	MCP 001	MEET ME ON THE HIGHWAY (LP, private pressing with insert)	30

BREAKERS
81	Riot RS 1001	Radio Love/My Momma Told Me (p/s)	20

BREAKFAST BAND
81	Disc Empire DEF 1	LA 14/Dolphin Ride	6

BREAKING THE ILLUSION
92	Lowlife LOW 1	WHERE WILL IT END? (EP, 12" p/s, 1000 pressed)	15
93	Lowlife LOW 3	LOSE YOUR ILLUSION (EP)	12

BREAKOUT
81	Guardian GRC 101	Wall Of Solitude/Get Out Fight Back	100

Danny BREAKS

MINT VALUE £

DANNY BREAKS
93	Droppin Science DS 001	DROPPIN SCIENCE VOLUME 01 (12")	30
94	Droppin Science DS 002	DROPPIN SCIENCE VOLUME 02 (12")	25
94	Droppin Science DS 003	DROPPIN SCIENCE VOLUME 03 (12")	30
94	Droppin Science DS 004	DROPPIN SCIENCE VOLUME 04 (12")	12
95	Droppin Science DS 001R	DROPPIN SCIENCE VOLUME 01 REMIXES (12")	18
95	Droppin Science DS 003R	DROPPIN SCIENCE VOLUME 03 REMIXES (12")	20
95	Droppin Science DS 005	DROPPIN SCIENCE VOLUME 05 (12")	15

BREAKTHRU'
68	Mercury MF 1066	Ice Cream Tree/Julius Caesar	25

BREAKWATER
86	Arista ARIST 12674	Say You Love Me Girl/Work It Out (12", p/s)	15

BREATHERS
80	Diversion DIV 1	Living In The Age Age/Counting On Counting	15

BREATHING AGE
81	Edge EDGE 13	Here We Go/Camera Room (p/s)	10

BREATHLESS
81	Magnum Force MFEP 005	SOCK HOP BOPPIN' (EP)	20

BREEDERS
92	4AD BAD 2003	SAFARI (12, EP, p/s)	12
92	4AD AD 3012	Divine Hammer/Do You Love Me Now Jr? (clear vinyl, p/s)	10
93	4AD BREED 1	Cannonball (12" promo)	30
17	4AD 4AD0036S3	Wait In The Car/Gates Of Steel (p/s, yellow vinyl)	8
17	4AD 4AD0036S2	Wait InThe Car/Joanne (p/s, red vinyl)	10
17	4AD 4AD0036S1	Wait In The Car/Archangel's Thunderbird (p/s, orange vinyl tour only)	20
93	4AD BAD 3011	Cannonball/Cro-Aloha/Lord Of The Thighs/900 (12", p/s)	15
90	4AD CAD 0006	POD (LP)	25
93	4AD CAD 3014	LAST SPLASH (LP, with free 7")	40
02	4AD CAD 2205	TITLE TK (LP, inner)	40
08	4AD CAD 2803	MOUNTAIN BATTLES (LP, inner sleeve and booklet)	20
13	4AD DAD 3308	LSXX (3-LP, 4 x 10" box set)	50
21	4AD CAD 006	POD (LP, reissue, pink vinyl)	40

JIMMY BREEDLOVE
57	London HLE 8490	Over Somebody Else's Shoulder/That's My Baby	100
62	Pye International 7N 25121	You're Following Me/Fabulous	30

(see also Cues)

BOBBY BREEN
62	Fontana 373	When The Lights Go Out/Everybody Twist	10

BRELLO CABAL
67	CBS 3214	Margarine Flavoured Pineapple Chunk/Follow That (as The Brello Cabal)	10

(see also Anita Harris)

BEVERLEY BREMERS
72	Wand WN 18	Get Smart Girl/Don't Say You Don't Remember	15

BRENDA & TABULATIONS
67	London HL 10127	Dry Your Eyes/The Wash	30
67	London HL 10174	When You're Gone/Hey Boy	25
68	Direction 58-3678	Baby You're So Right For Me/To The One I Love	15
69	Action ACT 4541	That's In The Past/I Can't Get Over Her	30
70	London HL 10325	A Child No One Wanted/'Scuse Uz Y'all	15
71	CBS 7279	Right On The Tip of My Tongue/Always And Forever	15
73	Epic EPC 1361	One Girl Too Late/The Magic Of Your Love	10
69	Action ACLP 6003	DRY YOUR EYES (LP)	50
77	Casablanca CAL 2016	I KEEP COMING BACK FOR MORE (LP)	15

ROSE BRENNAN
55	HMV 7M 299	Ding Dong/Sincerely	15
55	HMV 7M 328	Wake The Town And Tell The People/Ten Little Kisses	7

BRENT FORD & NYLONS
78	Brumbeat	19th Nervous Breakdown/Big Rock Candy Mountain (handmade foldout p/s)	50

TONY BRENT & JULIE DAWN
53	Columbia SCM 5029	Ding Dong Boogie/When Are We Gonna Get Married?	15

(see also Julie Dawn)

BRENTFORD ROAD ALLSTARS
70	Bamboo BAM 23	Love At First Sight/MAYTALS: Life Could Be A Dream	30
70	Bamboo BAM 25	Soul Shake/Moon Ride	35

BERNARD BRESSLAW
59	HMV 7EG 8439	I ONLY ARSKED (EP)	10

PAUL BRETT('S SAGE)
70	Pye 7N 17974	Three D Mona Lisa/Mediterranean Lazy Heat Wave	15
71	Dawn DNX 2508	Reason For Your Askin'/Everlasting Butterfly/Savannah Ladies/ To Everyman (Freedom) (p/s)	10
71	Dawn DNS 1010	Goodbye Forever/Good Old Fashioned Funky Kind Of Music	6
72	Dawn DNS 1021	Dahlia/Cottage Made For Two	6
73	Bradley's BRAD 301	Mr. Custer/Good Times, Hard Times	6
73	Bradley's BRAD 305	Summer Driftin'/Clocks (p/s)	7
70	Pye NSPL 18347	PAUL BRETT SAGE (LP, blue/black label with logo banner on top)	75
71	Dawn DNLS 3021	JUBILATION FOUNDRY (LP, gatefold sleeve, as Paul Brett's Sage, orange label)	50
72	Dawn DNLS 3032	SCHIZOPHRENIA (LP, foldout sleeve, as Paul Brett's Sage, lilac label)	50
73	Bradley's BRADL 1001	PAUL BRETT (LP, fully laminate envelope sleeve with inner)	30
73	Bradley's BRADL 1004	CLOCKS (LP)	15
75	Private pressing PF 001	PHOENIX FUTURE (LP, 500 only, numbered on rear sleeve)	30

Steve BRETT & MAVERICKS

MINT VALUE £

70s	Private pressing	MUSIC MANIFOLD (LP, library issue)	25

(see also Elmer Gantry's Velvet Opera, Fire)

STEVE BRETT & MAVERICKS
65	Columbia DB 7470	Wishing/Anything That's Part Of You	85
65	Columbia DB 7581	Sad, Lonely And Blue/Candy	125
65	Columbia DB 7794	Sugar Shack/Chains On My Heart	100

(see also 'N Betweens, Slade)

TONY BREVETT
71	Supreme SUP 224	Don't Get Weary/BREVETT ALLSTARS: Version	20
71	Bullet BU 497	So Ashamed (credited to Tony Bravett)/GREGORY ISAACS: My Only Lover	30
74	Dip DL 5019	From Dusk To Dawn/JAH ALI: Black Snowfall	20
74	Dip DL 5028	You Don't Love Me/Version	20
76	Stop Point SPR 001	Words Of Prophecy/Version	10

(see also Melodians, Glen Adams)

BREW
60s	Oak LONDON	Crossroads/Play Your Tune (acetate, unreleased, handwritten labels)	150

(see also Camel)

TERESA BREWER
SINGLES
54	Vogue Coral Q 2011	Skinny Minnie (Fishtail)/I Had Someone Else Before I Had You	10
54	Vogue Coral Q 2029	Au Revoir/Danger Signs	12
55	Vogue Coral Q 72043	Let Me Go, Lover (with Lancers)/Baby, Baby, Baby	12
55	Vogue Coral Q 72065	How Important Can It Be?/What More Is There To Say?	10
55	Vogue Coral Q 72066	Tweedlee Dee/Rock Love	20
55	Vogue Coral Q 72077	Pledging My Love/I Gotta Go Get My Baby	10
55	Vogue Coral Q 72083	You're Telling Our Secret/Time	8

ALBUMS
51	London H-APB 1006	SHOWCASE (10")	15

(see also Snooky Lanson)

BREWER'S DROOP
72	RCA RCA 2216	Sweet Thing/Heart Of Stone/It Ain't The Meat - It's The Motion (p/s)	6
72	RCA SF 8301	OPENING TIME (LP, gatefold sleeve, orange label)	25

(see also McGuinness Flint)

BRIAR
82	Happy Face MM 142	Rainbow (To The Skies)/Crying In The Rain (p/s)	12
87	UK UKALP 002	CROWN OF THORNS (LP)	15

DICK BRICE
80s	Sylvan SYL 101R	A FEW ON 'IMS OWN (LP)	50

BRICK COCKTAIL
84	SRT4KS130	Borderline/Sunday Afternoon (p/s)	12

BRICKS
79	Trans Galactic TGR 801	Startrekker/Smash And Grab	10

BRIDGE
85	Atlantic 9565(T)	Baby, Don't Hold Your Love Back/(Instrumental Version) (12")	20
00	First Direction FER LP1	CRYING FOR LOVE (2-LP, compilation)	150

BOBBY BRIDGER
70	Beacon BEA 149	The World Is Turning On/Why Do I Love You	10
70	Beacon BEA 159	Sugar Shaker/You're In Love	15

(see also Errol Sobers)

PHOEBE BRIDGERS
20	Dead Oceans DOC254	COPYCAT KILLER (12", p/s)	50
20	Dead Oceans DOC200LP-C3	PUNISHER (LP, blue and green swirly coloured vinyl)	50
20	Dead Oceans DOC200LP-C8	PUNISHER (LP, green and black galaxy coloured vinyl)	60
20	Dead Oceans DOC200LP-C9	PUNISHER (LP, galaxy blue and blue vinyl)	50
21	Dead Oceans DOC200LP-C9	PUNISHER (LP, repressing, red vinyl with booklet)	50

SLIM BRIDGES & THE WILD FLOWERS
81	Cricus CIRC 0006	Rocking Goose/Mole At The Circus (p/s)	20

DEE DEE BRIDGEWATER
78	Elektra K 52067	JUST FAMILY (LP)	15

BRIEF ENCOUNTER
10	Jazzman JMANLP 038	THE BRIEF ENCOUNTER (LP, reissue)	30

MARC BRIERLEY
68	CBS 3857	Hold On, Hold On, The Garden Sure Looks Good Spread On The Floor/Autograph Of Time	15
69	CBS 4191	Stay A Little Longer Merry Ann/Flaxen Hair	10
69	CBS 4632	Lady Of The Light/Sunny Weather	10
70	CBS 5266	Be My Brother/If You Took The Bandage Off	8
60s	Transatlantic TRAEP 147	MARC BRIERLEY (EP)	50
68	CBS 63478	WELCOME TO THE CITADEL (LP, orange label with textured surface)	400
69	CBS 63835	HELLO (LP, gatefold sleeve, stickered sleeve, orange label)	100
69	CBS 63835	HELLO (LP, gatefold sleeve, no sticker, orange label)	90

(see also Tractor)

ANNE BRIGGS
63	Topic TOP 94	THE HAZARDS OF LOVE (EP, with leaflet)	150
14	Topic TOP 94	THE HAZARDS OF LOVE (EP, reissue, insert)	10
71	Topic 12T 207	ANNE BRIGGS (LP)	300
71	CBS 64612	THE TIME HAS COME (LP)	500
15	Topic 12T2207	ANNE BRIGGS (LP, reissue)	18
17	Earth EARTHLP 019	THE TIME HAS COME (LP, reissue with obi)	15

(see also A.L. Lloyd)

BRIAN BRIGGS

MINT VALUE £

BRIAN BRIGGS
80	Bearsville ILPS 9644	BRIAN DAMAGE (LP)	20
81	Avatar AALP/BRK 6996	BRIAN DAMAGE (LP, reissue)	15

DUGGIE BRIGGS
78	It IT 3	Punk Rockin' Granny/I'm A Flasher (p/s)	12
78	It ITEP 5	THE DUGGIE BRIGGS FLASHES ON IT AGAIN (EP)	18

ANNIE BRIGHT
70	Columbia DB 8717	Peaceful Mountain/Heartbreak House	12
69	Columbia DB 8587	Concerning Love/Sneakin' Up On You	15

GREGORY BRIGHT
69	Private Pressing	ROOM BY GREG (LP)	400

LEN BRIGHT COMBO
86	Empire LEN 1	Someone Must've Nailed Us Together/Mona (p/s)	18
86	Empire NICE 1	THE LEN BRIGHT COMBO (LP)	20
86	Ambassador AMBAS 1	COMBO TIME! (LP)	20

(see also Wreckless Eric, Milkshakes)

BRIGHT LIGHT
73	Warm WM 01	Hold Out For Love/Inbetween Dreams	15

BRIGHTER
89	Sarah SARAH 019	Around The World In 80 Days (p/s, with inserts)	25
90	Sarah SARAH 27	Noah's Ark/I Don't Think It Matters/Does Love Last Forever? (foldover p/s, postcard insert)	25
91	Sarah SARAH 56	Poppy Day/Half-Hearted/So You Said (p/s, insert)	25
92	Sarah SARAH 69	DISNEY EP (10", p/s)	30
91	Sarah SARAH 404	LAUREL (LP, 10")	40

BRIGHT EYES (1)
77	Wild Dog DOG 14	Miss In Betweener/Way of The Bow (500 only, no p/s)	10

BRIGHT EYES (2)
00		The Calendar Hung Itself/HER SPACE HOLIDAY :The Doctor And The DJ	6
04	Saddle Creek SCE 68	Lua/I Woke Up With This Song In My Head This Morning (p/s)	8
05	Saddle Creek SCE 79V	First Day Of My Life/When The President Talks To God (p/s)	20
02	Wichita WEBB 034	LIFTED OR THE STORY IS IN THE SOIL, KEEP YOUR EAR TO THE GROUND (LP)	15
05	Saddle Creek SCE 72	I'M WIDE AWAKE IT'S MORNING (LP)	15
10	Wichita WEBB 001 LPTEN	FEVERS AND MIRRORS (LP, reissue)	15

SARAH BRIGHTMAN
79	Ariola Hansa AHA 585	Love In a UFO/Illusions Of Love	6
81	Whisper WSP 104	Not Having That/Echo 4	12
83	Polydor POSP 659	Rhythm Of The Rain/Action Man (p/s)	20
87	Polydor POSP 862	Theme From 'A Room With A View'/O Mio Babbino Caro (p/s)	10

IAN BRIGHTON
77	Bead Records BEAD 3	MARSH GAS (LP)	50

BRIGHTON HORNS
66	Stateside SS 526	Surf Dell'amore/High Midnight	8

BRIGHTWINTER
70s	Myrrh MYR 1030	A BAND FOR ALL SEASONS (LP)	25

BRILLIANT CORNERS
84	SS20 SS21	She's Got Fever/Black Water (red p/s)	15
84	SS20 SS21	She's Got Fever/Black Water (pink p/s)	30
84	SS20 SS22	Big Hip/Tangled Up In Blue (p/s)	10
88	McQueen MCQ2T	Why Do You Have To Go Out With Him?/Shangri La (12" p/s)	10
86	McQueen MCQLP2	WHAT'S IN A WORD (LP)	18
88	McQueen MCQLP	SOMEBODY UP THERE LIKES ME (LP, with inner)	15
00	Vinyl Japan ASKLP 117	THE BBC SESSIONS (LP)	15

JOHN BRIMACOMBE
72	Pye 7N 45159	Try A Little Harder/Four Sad Men	8

CHARLES BRIMMER
80	Special Agent 9005	I Stand Accused/God Bless Our Love	10
80	Hayley HR 001	Show And Tell (1-sided white label test pressings only)	80

BRIMSTONE (1)
71	Deram DM 322	Keyhole Jake/The Monkey Song	6

BRIMSTONE (2)
78	Grove Music GM 9	Final Judgement/Final Dub	12

LOS BRINCOS
67	Page One POF 023	Lola/Passport (1st 5,000 in p/s)	40
67	Page One POF 023	Lola/Passport (no p/s)	15
67	Page One POF 031	Nobody Wants You Now/Train (as Brincos)	70

BRINDLEY BRAE
73	Harmony DB 0002	VILLAGE MUSIC (LP, 50 copies only, private pressing with insert)	150

(see also Bev Pegg, Away From The Sand)

BRING ME THE HORIZON
10	Let Them Eat Vinyl LETV027LP	THERE IS A HELL BELIEVE ME I'VE SEEN IT, THERE IS A HEAVEN LET'S KEEP IT A SECRET (LP, translucent vinyl)	40
11	Let Them Eat Vinyl LETV026LP	COUNT YOUR BLESSINGS (LP, reissue, blue vinyl, 1000 only)	40
11	Let Them Eat Vinyl LETV028LP	SUICIDE SEASON (LP, reissue, red vinyl)	40

BRINSLEY SCHWARZ
70	United Artists UP 35118	Shining Brightly/What Do You Suggest	10
71	Liberty LBY 15419	Country Girl/Funk Angel	15
72	United Artists UP 35312	Country Girl/Funk Angel (reissue)	6
74	United Artists UP 35700	(What's So Funny 'Bout) Peace, Love And Understanding/ Ever Since You're Gone	6

Lloyd BRISCO

MINT VALUE £

75	United Artists UP 35768	Everybody/I Like You, I Don't Love You	6
75	United Artists UP 35812	There's A Cloud In My Heart/I Got The Real Thing	6
70	United Artists UAS 29111	BRINSLEY SCHWARZ (LP, gatefold sleeve, orange/pink label)	50
70	Liberty LBG 83427	DESPITE IT ALL (LP, gatefold sleeve)	40
72	United Artists UAS 29217	SILVER PISTOL (LP, with poster)	35
72	United Artists UAS 29374	NERVOUS ON THE ROAD (LP)	15
73	United Artists UAS 29489	PLEASE DON'T EVER CHANGE (LP)	20
78	United Artists UAK 30177	FIFTEEN THOUGHTS OF BRINSLEY SCHWARZ (LP, poster)	20

(see also Kippington Lodge, Hitters, Knees, Limelight, Nick Lowe, Ernie Graham, Rumour, Chilli Willi & Red Hot Peppers, Ducks Deluxe)

LLOYD BRISCO
64	Rio R42	Fabulous Eyes/What You See	20
64	Island WI 187	Jonah The Master/Mr. Cleveland	20

JOHNNY BRISTOL
80	Ariola AHA 567	Love No Longer Has A Hold On Me/Till I See You Again	10

BRITISH LIONS
78	Vertigo 9102 019	BRITISH LIONS (LP, with inner sleeve)	15
80	Cherry Red ARED 7	TROUBLE WITH WOMEN (LP)	15

(see also Mott The Hoople, Medicine Head)

BRITISH SEA POWER
01	Rough Trade RTRADE S032	Remember Me/A Lovely Day Tomorrow (p/s, 1264 only)	6
02	Rough Trade RTRADE 048	The Lonely/Spirit Of St. Louis	6
02	Rough Trade RTRADES 069	Childhood Memories/Favours In The Beetroot Fields (p/s, 1000 only)	6
03	Rough Trade RTRADE S092	Carrion/Apologies To Insect Life (handdrawn, textured sleeve, 2003 only)	12
03	Rough Trade RTRADES 125	Remember Me/The Scottish Wildlife Experience (hand-drawn name on 2003 copies)	8
05	Rough Trade RTRADS302	Remember Me/I Am A Cider Drinker (7" limited edition. 1,966 copies)	10
12	Golden Chariot GOLDEN CHARIOT 006-011	BSP EP BOX SET (6 x CD box set)	120
02	Rough Trade RTRADLP 090	THE DECLINE OF BRITISH SEA POWER (2-LP, insert)	25
05	Rough Trade RTRADLP 200	OPEN SEASON (LP)	18
08	Rough Trade RTRADLP 300	DO YOU LIKE ROCK MUSIC? (LP)	18
11	Rough Trade RTRADLP 549	VALHALLA DANCEHALL (2-LP)	18
13	Rough Trade RTRADLP 666	MACHINERIES OF JOY (LP, with CD EP)	15

(see also The Wurzels)

BRITISH SHOES
79	NWJ SRTS/79/CUS 542	Running From Mummy/Where Would We Be Without Shoes (p/s)	100
79	NWJ SRTS/79/CUS 542	Running From Mummy/Where Would We Be Without Shoes (no p/s)	50

BRITISH WALKERS
65	Pye International 7N 25298	I Found You/Diddley Daddy	25

BRITT
66	Piccadilly 7N 35273	You Really Have Started Something/Leave My Baby Alone	30

MEL BRITT
00	Goldmine Soul Supply GS 003	She'll Come Running Back/ANDERSON BROTHERS: I Can See Him Loving You (reissue)	20

TINA BRITT
65	London HLC 9974	The Real Thing/Teardrops Fell	70
65	London HLC 9974	The Real Thing/Teardrops Fell (DJ Copy)	100

BUDDY BRITTEN & REGENTS
62	Piccadilly 7N 35075	My Pride, My Joy/Long Gone Baby	15
62	Decca F 11435	Don't Spread It Around/The Beat Of My Heart	15
63	Oriole CB 1827	If You Gotta Make A Fool Of Somebody/Money	15
63	Oriole CB 1839	Hey There/I'll Cry No More	15
63	Oriole CB 1859	My Resistance Is Low/When I See You Smile	12
63	Oriole CB 1889	Money/Sorrow Tomorrow	20
64	Oriole CB 1911	I Guess I'm In The Way/Zip-A-Dee-Doo-Dah	10
65	Piccadilly 7N 35241	She's About A Mover/Since You've Gone	10
65	Piccadilly 7N 35257	Right Now/Jailer Bring Me Water	8

(see also Regents)

TERRY BRITTEN
69	Columbia DB8580	2000 Weeks/Bargain Day	100

CHRIS BRITTON
69	Page One POLS 022	AS I AM (LP, gatefold sleeve, blue/silver label)	400

(see also Troggs)

JEFF BRITTON & THE SPITFIRES
76	Decca F13643	Rub Out/Breakwood	20

MAGGIE BRITTON
80	Piccadilly 7P191	Goodship Earth/No Secrets	6

BRIXTON MARKET
69	Beacon BEA 138	Children Get Ready/Bangarang	15
69	Beacon SBEAB 8	BLACK FUNK (LP)	15

JO BROADBERY & THE STANDOUTS
80	Revenge REV-S-1	Out Of The Real/Breaking Down (no p/s)	10
80	Revenge REVLP-1	JO BROADBERRY AND THE STANDOUTS (LP)	20

BROADCAST
96	Wurlitzer Jukebox WJ 6	Accidentals/We've Got Time (p/s, with sticker)	40
96	Wurlitzer Jukebox WJ 6	Accidentals/We've Got Time (p/s, without sticker)	10
96	Duophonic DS 45-14	Living Room/Phantom (wraparound p/s, 1,500 only)	12
96	Duophonic DS 45-16	THE BOOK LOVERS EP (12", p/s, 2,000)	25
99	Warp 7WAP 125	Echo's Answer/Test Area	15
00	Warp 7WAP 132	Come On Let's Go/Distant Call (p/s)	12
00	Warp WAP 129	EXTENDED PLAY (12" EP)	10
00	Warp WAP 141	EXTENDED PLAY TWO EP (12", p/s)	15

BROADSIDE

			MINT VALUE £
03	Warp WAP 162	Pendulum/Small Song IV/One Hour Empore/Still Feel Like Tears/Violent Playground/Minus Two (12" p/s)	15
05	Warp 7WAP 193	America's Boy/Tender Buttons (p/s)	8
09	Warp WARPCD 189T	MOTHER IS THE MILKY WAY (Tour CD in card sleeve)	35
97	Warp WARPLP 52	WORK & NON WORK (LP)	40
00	Warp WARPLP 65	THE NOISE MADE BY PEOPLE (LP, gatefold sleeve, insert)	40
03	Warp WARPLP 106	HAHA SOUND (LP)	30
05	Warp WARPLP 136	TENDER BUTTONS (LP)	30
06	Warp WARPLP 146	THE FUTURE CRAYON (2-LP)	30
09	Warp WARPLP 189	INVESTIGATES WITCH CULTS OF THE RADIO AGE (LP, with the Focus Group)	30
13	Warp WARPLP 233	BERBERIAN SOUND STUDIO (LP)	15

BROADSIDE

71	Lincolnshire Ass. LA 4	THE GIPSY'S WEDDING DAY (10" LP)	50
73	Topic 12TS 228	THE MOON SHONE BRIGHT (As The Broadside From Grimsby) (LP, blue label)	40
75	Guildhall GHS 5	SONGS FROM THE STOCKS (LP)	80
75	Guildhall GHS 12	DRIVE THE DARK AWAY (LP)	50

BROADSIDE OUTCASTS

78	Profile GMOR 154	ABO EP	20

PETER BROGGS

79	Hit Run HITDD 13	Higher Field Marshall (Feat. Prince Far I)/I And I A The Chosen One/PRINCE FAR I & BRIGADIER JAM DOWN : Loved By Everyone (12")	50
80	Cha Cha CHAD 25	Never Forget Jah/CORNELL CAMBELL: Rainbow (12")	70
80	Selena SO 006	Jah Golden Throne/DEXTER MCKINTYRE : 144.00 Saints	60
79	Shashamane IMF 004	PROGRESSIVE YOUTH (LP)	50

BROKEN BONES

84	Fall Out FALL 025	Crucifix/Fight The Good Fight	10
85	Fall Out FALL 10034	Seeing Through My Eyes/The Point Of Agony/It's Like/Decapitated/Part 2/Death Is Imminent (10", p/s)	8
83	Fall Out FALL LP 028	BROKEN BONES (LP)	15
84	Stoned Spliff 1	LIVE AT THE 100 CLUB (LP)	20

(see also Discharge)

BROKEN BOW

87	Sodium	Vagrant/Bite Back	25

BROKEN GLASS (1)

75	Capitol E-ST 11510	BROKEN GLASS (LP, with insert)	18

(see also Chicken Shack, Warhorse, Miller Anderson, Bronco)

BROKEN GLASS (2)

84	Streetwave MKHAN 17	Style Of The Street (12")	20

BROKEN ROSE

86	Exhibit 1 EXL 006	WAR TEARS (LP)	100

(see also Bizarre Unit, Paul Nova)

JOHN BROMLEY

68	Polydor 56244	What A Woman Does/My My	30
68	Polydor 56287	And The Feeling Goes/Sweet Little Princess	20
69	Polydor 56305	Melody Fayre/Sugar Love	40
69	Polydor 56340	Hold Me Woman/Weather Man	30
69	Atlantic 584 289	Kick A Tin Can/Wonderland Avenue U.S.A.	30
69	Polydor 583 048	SING (LP)	100

(see also Fleur De Lys, Three People)

BILLY BRIMSTONE

05	YNR YNR 021	Keep It Live (Vocal)/Keep It Live (Instrumental)	10

(see also Jehst)

BRONCO

70	Island WIP 6096	Lazy Now/A Matter Of Perspective	20
73	Polydor 2058 395	The Traveller/Steal That Gold	6
70	Island ILPS 9124	COUNTRY HOME (LP, gatefold sleeve, pink 'i' label)	40
70	Island ILPS 9124	COUNTRY HOME (LP, gatefold sleeve, 'pink rim palm tree' label)	20
71	Island ILPS 9161	ACE OF SUNLIGHT (LP, gatefold sleeve, 'pink rim palm tree' label)	25
73	Polydor 2383 215	SMOKIN' MIXTURE (LP, gatefold sleeve)	20

(see also Alan Bown Set)

BRONNT INDUSTRIES

05	Static Caravan	KAPITAL BROCKEN (EP (8" lathe cut, clear vinyl, hand-stamped bag, 100 only)	10

BRONX

06	Wichita WEBB 113S	History's Stranglers/Venice (p/s, translucent vinyl)	10
06	Wichita WEBB 114S	White Guilt/Rockers NYC (red vinyl, p/s)	15
07	Wichita WEBB 116S	Shitty Future/Dirty Leaves (Demo) (p/s)	6

BRONX CHEER

70	Parlophone R 5865	Drive My Car/Foxtrot	8
71	Dawn DNX 2512	Barrelhouse Player/Surprising Find/Whether Or Not/Party For One (p/s)	8
72	Dawn DNS 1019	Hold On To Me/Late Date	6
72	Dawn DNLS 3034	GREATEST HITS VOLUME 3 (LP, gatefold sleeve with insert, lilac label)	20

DAVID BROOK

68	President PT 196	Witchfinder General/Janie	10

MICHAEL BROOK

92	4AD CAD 2007	COBALT BLUE (LP, featuring Brian Eno)	40

TONY BROOK & BREAKERS

64	Columbia DB 7279	Meanie Genie/Ooh Poo Pah Doo (in p/s)	200
64	Columbia DB 7279	Meanie Genie/Ooh Poo Pah Doo	80
65	Columbia DB 7444	Love Dances On/I Won't Hurt You	15

BROOK BROTHERS

60	Top Rank JAR 349	Green Fields/How Will It End?	10

Gary BROOKER

MINT VALUE £

60	Top Rank JAR 409	Please Help Me, I'm Falling/When Will I Be Loved	10
61	Pye NEP 24140	BROOK BROTHERS HIT PARADE (EP)	10
61	Pye NEP 24148	BROOK BROTHERS HIT PARADE VOLUME 2 (EP)	10
62	Pye NEP 24155	BROOK BROTHERS (EP)	15
61	Pye NPL 18067	BROOK BROTHERS (LP)	20

GARY BROOKER

81	Chrysalis CHS 2396	Leave The Candle/Chasing The Chop (Eric Clapton guest appearance)	100

PAUL BROOKES

78	State ETAT 21	STEPS FROM BEYOND (LP)	20

HOWARD S BROOKING

82	H.S.B. S82/CUS/1596	In The Autumn Gold/Checkmate (no p/s)	15

BROOKLYN

80	Rondelet ROUND 3	I Wanna Be A Detective (p/s)	30
81	Rondelet ROUND 6	Hollywood/Late Again (p/s)	20
80	Rondelet ABOUT 3	YOU NEVER KNOW WHAT YOU'LL FIND (LP)	30

BROOKLYN BRIDGE

68	Pye International 7N 25473	From My Window I Can See/Little Red Boat By The River	8
69	Buddah 201 029	The Worst That Could Happen/Your Kite, My Kite	10
70	Buddah 2011 010	Free As The Wind/He's Not A Happy Man	6
70	Buddah 2011 034	Down By The River/Look Again	6

(see also Johnny Maestro, Crests)

BABA BROOKS

63	Island WI 078	5 O'Clock Whistle/African Blood (by Blues Masters)	50
63	Island WI 096	Bank To Bank (Parts 1 & 2)	35
63	Island WI 127	Three Blind Mice/BILLY & BOBBY: We Ain't Got Nothing	30
63	R&B JB 125	Water Melon Man/STRANGER COLE: Things Come To Those Who Wait	40
64	Black Swan WI 137	Portrait Of My Love/STRANGER COLE: Goodbye Peggy	20
64	Black Swan WI 412	Jelly Beans/ERIC MORRIS: Sampson	30
64	Black Swan WI 414	Key To The City/ERIC MORRIS: Solomon Grundie	40
64	Black Swan WI 434	Spider/Melody Jamboree	30
64	Black Swan WI 438	Cork Foot/HERSANG COMBO: B.B.C. Channel 2	30
65	Black Swan WI 442	Musical Workshop/DUKE WHITE: Be Wise	40
65	Black Swan WI 444	Bus Strike/DUKE WHITE: Sow Good Seeds	40
65	Black Swan WI 451	Ethiopia/ARCHIBALD TROTT: Promised Land	40
65	Black Swan WI 456	Dreadnaught/PLAYGIRLS: Looks Are Deceiving	65
65	Black Swan WI 466	Baby Elephant Walk/DON DRUMMOND: Don's Special	30
65	Ska Beat JB 189	Dr. Decker/OWEN & LEON SILVERA : Woman	30
65	Ska Beat JB 220	One Eyed Giant (with His Band)/DYNAMITES: Walk Out On Me	40
65	Island WI 229	Guns Fever/DOTTY & BONNIE: Don't Do It	35
65	Island WI 233	Independent Ska/STRANGER & CLAUDETTE: Seven Days	30
65	Island WI 235	Duck Soup/ZODIACS: Renegade	150
65	Island WI 239	Vitamin A/ALTON ELLIS: Dance Crasher	50
65	Island WI 241	Teenage Ska/ALTON ELLIS: You Are Not To Blame	70
65	Rio R 061	Shenk I Sheck (& Band)/SHENLEY & HIACYNTH: Set Me Free	50
66	Doctor Bird DB 1042	The Clock (& Band)/LYN TAITT & COMETS & SILVERTONES: Raindrops	40
66	Doctor Bird DB 1046	Jam Session (with His Band)/CONQUERORS: What A Agony	40
67	Ska Beat JB 268	One Eyed Giant (with His Band)/DYNAMITES: Walk Out On Me (reissue)	20

(see also Blues Masters, Eric Brooks, Stranger & Patsy, Riots, Joey Smith, Saints, Richard Brothers, Derrick Morgan, Lord Tanamo, Lord Brisco, Hippy Boys, Roy Panton, Higgs & Wilson, Vinley Gayle, Joe White, Stranger & Patsy)

CEDRIC 'IM' BROOKS

75	Tropical AL046	South African Reggae/Part 2	12
78	Water Lily ARCO LP 009	UNITED AFRICA (LP)	25

CHUCK BROOKS

69	Soul City SC 116	Black Sheep/I've Got To Get Myself Together	20
69	Soul City SC 116	Black Sheep/I've Got To Get Myself Together (DJ Copy)	75

D. BROOKS

70	Big BG 304	Oh Me Oh My (actually "Every Time" by Hi-Tals)/ANSEL COLLINS: Staccato (actually "Every Time Version" by Rupie Edwards Allstars)	12

DALE BROOKS

65	King KG 1025	Army Green/Reminds Me Of You	10
66	Stateside SS 553	I Wanna Be Your Girl/Like Other Girls Do	30

DONNIE BROOKS

61	London HA-N 2391	THE HAPPIEST DONNIE BROOKS (LP)	20

ELKIE BROOKS

64	Decca F 11928	Something's Got A Hold On Me/Hello Stranger	40
64	Decca F 11983	Nothing Left To Do But Cry/Strange Though It Seems	40
65	Decca F 12061	The Way You Do The Things You Do/Blue Tonight	40
65	HMV POP 1431	He's Gotta Love Me/When You Appear	40
65	HMV POP 1431	He's Gotta Love Me/When You Appear (DJ Copy)	80
65	HMV POP 1480	All My Life/Can't Stop Thinking Of You	20
66	HMV POP 1512	Baby Let Me Love You/Stop The Music	30
66	HMV POP 1512	Baby Let Me Love You/Stop The Music (DJ Copy)	80
69	NEMS 56-4136	Come September/If You Should Go	7
74	Chrysalis CHS 2069	Sacrifice/ALICE COOPER: I'm Flash (p/s, unissued, promo only)	35
84	A & M SCREEN 1	SCREEN GEMS (CD, beware of copies!)	50

(see also Dada, Vinegar Joe, Steve York's Camelo Pardalis, Elki & Owen)

JOE BROOKS COLLECTIVE

71	CBS 7234	Messing Up The Mind Of A Young Girl/Before The Sand Has Run Out Of The Hour Glass	12

JULIAN BROOKS

70	Pye 7N17996	Justine/Lazy Guy	25

Merlyn BROOKS

MINT VALUE £

MERLYN BROOKS
76	Jama JAMA 0012	Perfect Love/CONSCIOUS MINDS: Dub To Remember	6
76	Jama JAMA 0027	I've Been Down/CONSCIOUS MINDS: I've Been Dubbing	25
76	Pacific PAC 002	Mechanical Body/Mechanical Dub	25

MIKE BROOKS
79	Hit Run HIT DD 9	Love Is Like A Password/Feeling Of Reggae (12")	25
79	Hit Run HIT DD 23	Long Long Time/Dub In Time	30
76	Burning Sounds BSLP 1026	WHAT A GATHERING (LP)	15

NORMAN BROOKS & G-BOYS
54	London L 1166	Hello Sunshine/You're My Baby	15
54	London L 1202	Somebody Wonderful/You Shouldn't Have Kissed Me The First Time	15
54	London L 1228	A Sky-Blue Shirt And A Rainbow Tie/This Waltz With You	15
54	London HL 8015	I'm Kinda Crazy/I'd Like To Be In Your Shoes, Baby	15
54	London HL 8041	I Can't Give You Anything But Love (solo)/GO-BOYS: Johnny's Tune	15
54	London HL 8051	Candy Moon/My 3-D Sweetie	10
55	London HL 8115	Back In Circulation/Lou Lou Louisiana	10
54	London RE-P 1004	PRESENTING NORMAN BROOKS VOLUME 1 (EP)	10
55	London RE-P 1021	BABY MINE (EP)	10

PAM BROOKS
70	Big BG 307	Oh Me Oh My/ANSELL COLLINS: Staccato	18

RAY BROOKS
72	Polydor 2001334	Pictures/On My Own	10

ROY BROOKS AND THE ARTISTIC TRUTH
10	Jazzman JMANLP 034	ETHNIC EXPRESSIONS (LP, reissue)	20

WES BROOKS
77	ATA ATA 1003	Lay Down Your Arms/Version	70

BROOKS & JERRY
68	Direction 58-3267	I Got What It Takes Parts 1 & 2	15
68	Direction 58-3267	I Got What It Takes Parts 1 & 2 (DJ Copy)	30

BIG BILL BROONZY/CHICAGO BILL
52	Melodisc 1203	Five Foot Seven/Plough Hand Blues (78, as Chicago Bill)	10
58	Vogue V 2351	Guitar Shuffle/When Did You Leave Heaven	30
61	Storyville A 44053	Midnight Special/Black Brown And White	10
55	Vogue EPV 1024	HEY BUD BLUES (EP)	20
56	Vogue EPV 1074	SINGS THE BLUES (EP)	20
56	Vogue EPV 1107	GUITAR SHUFFLE (EP)	20
56	Pye Jazz NJE 1005	MISSISSIPPI BLUES VOLUME 1 (EP)	20
56	Pye Jazz NJE 1015	MISSISSIPPI BLUES VOLUME 2 (EP)	20
56	Melodisc EPM7 65	KEEP YOUR HANDS OFF (EP)	15
57	Pye Jazz NJE 1047	SOUTHERN SAGA (EP)	10
57	Vogue LAE 12009	BIG BILL BLUES (LP)	25
57	Philips BBL 7113	BIG BILL BROONZY (LP)	25
58	Vogue LAE 12063	THE BLUES (LP)	25
58	Pye Nixa Jazz NJL 16	TRIBUTE TO BIG BILL (LP)	25
59	Tempo TAP 23	AN EVENING WITH BIG BILL BROONZY (LP)	25

BIG BILL BROONZY & PETE SEEGER
64	Xtra XTRA 1006	IN CONCERT (LP)	20
66	Verve Folkways VLP 5006	IN CONCERT (LP, reissue, also stereo SVLP 506)	15

(see also Pete Seeger)

BIG BILL BROONZY/SONNY BOY WILLIAMSON [I]
65	RCA Victor RD 7685	BIG BILL AND SONNY BOY (LP)	30

(see also Sonny Boy Williamson [I])

BIG BILL BROONZY, SONNY TERRY & BROWNIE MCGHEE
64	Xtra XTRA 1004	BIG BILL BROONZY/SONNY TERRY/BROWNIE McGHEE (LP)	30

(see also Sonny Terry & Brownie McGhee, Washboard Sam)

BROTH
71	Mercury 6338 032	BROTH (LP)	60

BROTHER BARON
70s	Fab FAB 281	Your Love/Your Love Version	6

BROTHER BONES & HIS SHADOWS
60	orile CB 1030	Sweet Georgia Brown/Margie	6

BROTHER BUNG
68	Avenue BEV 1054	BLUES CRUSADE (EP)	15

(see also Bob Pearce)

BROTHER D & THE COLLECTIVE EFFORT
80	Island IPR 2005	How We Gonna Make The Black Nation Rise (12")	10

BROTHER DAN ALLSTARS
68	Trojan TR 601	Donkey Returns/Tribute To Sir K.B.	20
68	Trojan TR 602	Eastern Organ/JIVERS: Our Love Will Last	40
68	Trojan TR 603	Hold Pon Them/OWEN GRAY: Answer Me	18
68	Trojan TR 607	Read Up/Gallop	15
68	Trojan TR 608	Another Saturday Night/Bee's Knees	10
68	Trojan TBL 101	LET'S CATCH THE BEAT (LP)	100
69	Trojan TRL 1	FOLLOW THAT DONKEY (LP)	100

(see also Pooch Jackson)

BROTHER SUSAN
74	EMI EMI 2117	See My Fingers Fly/Full Blooded Natural Man	18
74	EMI EMI 2174	Ride Ride Ride/Flash	18

BROTHER TREVOR & U BROWN
78	Matumbi Music MM005	Skip Away/Selassi I (12")	25

BROTHER (1)

MINT VALUE £

(see also Matumbi)

BROTHER (1)
92	Tribal Bass TRIBE 10	Ghettogedden	7

BROTHER (2)
11	Chess Club CC 035	Darling Buds Of May/Homesick (Demo) (p/s, 500 only)	7

BROTHERHOOD (1)
69	Philips BF 1756	Paper Man/Give It To Me Now	15

BROTHERHOOD (2)
91	Bite It BITE 1	DESCENDANTS OF THE HOLOCAUST (EP)	30
91	Bite It BITE 2	DESCENDANTS OF THE HOLOCAUST (remix 12")	15

BROTHERHOOD OF BREATH
74	Ogun OG 100	LIVE AT WILLISAU (LP, with Chris McGregor)	20

(see also Chris McGregor's Brotherhood Of Breath, Mark Charig)

BROTHERHOOD OF LIZARDS
89	Deltic DELT LP5	LIZARDLAND (LP)	20

(see also Gypp, Martin Newall, Cleaners From Venus)

BROTHERHOOD OF MAN
69	Deram DM 276	Love One Another/A Little Bit Of Heaven	6
70	Deram DM 317	This Boy/You Can Depend On Me	6
71	Deram DM 327	Reach Out Your Hand/Better Tomorrow	15
74	Dawn DNS 1055	When Love Catches Up With You/How Can You Love (p/s)	6

(see also Sue & Sunny, Sue & Sunshine, Stockingtops)

BROTHERLY LOVE
67	CBS 2978	Ocean Of Tears/Mr Average Man	15

BROTHERS & SISTERS (U.K.)
68	Private pressing	ARE WATCHING YOU (LP)	90

BROTHERS & SISTERS (U.S.)
69	CBS 63746	DYLAN'S GOSPEL (LP)	15

BROTHERS GRIMM
65	Decca F 12224	Lost Love/Make It Or Break It	10
66	Ember EMB 222	A Man Needs Love/Looky Looky	50

BROTHERS KANE
66	Decca F 12448	Walking In The Sand/Won't You Stay Long	25

(see also Sarstedt Brothers, Peter Lincoln, Peter Sarstedt, Clive Sands, Wes Sands, Eden Kane)

BROTHERS TWO
68	Action ACT 4513	Here I Am, In Love Again/I'm Tired Of You Baby	30

BROTHERS WILLIAM
65	Parlophone R 5293	Honey Love/Linda James Blues	8

(see also Maureeny Wishful)

BROTHERS (1)
67	London HLU 10158	Love Story/The Girl's Alright	7

BROTHERS (2)
89	BASL 007T	Brothers Groove/Funky Paella (12", p/s)	15

BROTHERS SEVEN
02	Funk 45 001	Funky Smunk/Evil Ways (reissue)	8

BROTHERS (U.S.)
75	RCA 2618	Are You Ready For This/Everybody Loves A Winner	6

AYSHEA BROUGH
71	RCA RCA 2105	Master Jack/Both Sides Now	7

(see also Ayshea)

EDGAR BROUGHTON BAND
69	Harvest HAR 5001	Evil/Death Of An Electric Citizen	15
70	Harvest HAR 5015	Out Demons Out/Momma's Reward	7
70	Harvest HAR 5021	Up Yours!/Officer Dan	8
70	Harvest HAR 5032	Apache Drop Out/Freedom	7
71	Harvest HAR 5040	Hotel Room/Call Me A Liar	10
72	Harvest HAR 5049	Gone Blue/Someone/Mr. Crosby	8
69	Harvest SHVL 757	WASA WASA (LP, 1st pressing, gatefold sleeve, no EMI box on label with "the Gramophone Co" and "sold in U.K." label text)	170
69	Harvest SHVL 757	WASA WASA (LP, 1st pressing, gatefold sleeve, no EMI box on label without "the Gramophone Co" and "sold in U.K." label text)	100
69	Harvest SHVL 757	WASA WASA (LP, 2nd pressing, gatefold sleeve, later issue with EMI box on label)	50
69	Harvest SHVL 757	WASA WASA (LP, 2nd pressing variation, gatefold sleeve, no EMI box on label or "the Gramophone Co" and "sold in U.K." label text)	40
70	Harvest SHVL 772	SING BROTHER SING (LP, gatefold sleeve, with lyric insert, no EMI on label)	100
71	Harvest SHVL 791	THE EDGAR BROUGHTON BAND (LP, 1st pressing, textured gatefold)	100
71	Harvest SHVL 791	THE EDGAR BROUGHTON BAND (LP, 2nd pressing with EMI boxed logo on side 1 only, textured gatefold)	40
72	Harvest SHTC 252	IN SIDE OUT (LP, multifold gatefold sleeve with lyric sheet, some copies come with Harvest "Letter of introduction".)	100
73	Harvest SHVL 810	OORA (LP, wraparound card sleeve in clear artwork plastic bag, inner sleeve)	80
74	Harvest SHVL 772	SING BROTHER SING (LP, reissue gatefold, EMI box on label)	25
74	Harvest SHVL 791	THE EDGAR BROUGHTON BAND (LP, reissue, boxed EMI on label)	25
75	Harvest SHSM 2001	A BUNCH OF 45s (LP)	18
76	Nems NEL 6006	BANDAGES (LP with lyric inner sleeve)	20
88	BGO BBOLP 7	SING BROTHER SING (LP, reissue, gatefold sleeve)	18

AL BROWN (JAMAICA)
71	Banana BA 360	No Soul Today/RUFFIANS: Where Did I Go Wrong (B-side actually "Bang Shang Alang" by Peter Austin & Hortense Ellis)	25
71	Fab FAB 186	Ain't Got No Soul/TEARDROPS: I Got A Feeling	20

AL BROWN'S TUNETOPPERS (U.S.)
60	Top Rank JAR 374	The Madison/Mo' Madison	6

Arthur BROWN (CRAZY WORLD OF)

MINT VALUE £

ARTHUR BROWN (CRAZY WORLD OF)

Year	Label/Cat#	Title	£
65	Lyntone LYN 770/1	You Don't Know (as Arthur Brown & Diamonds)/DIAMONDS: You'll Be Mine (Reading University Rag Week flexidisc)	60
67	Track 604 008	Devil's Grip/Give Him A Flower	12
68	Track 604 022	Fire!/Rest Cure (push-out centre)	6
68	Track 604 026	Nightmare/What's Happening (some copies list "Music Man" as B-side)	6
68	Track 612 005	THE CRAZY WORLD OF ARTHUR BROWN (LP, mono, black/silver label)	120
68	Track 613 005	THE CRAZY WORLD OF ARTHUR BROWN (LP, stereo, black/silver labels)	80
74	Gull GULP 1008	DANCE (LP)	15
77	Gull GUD 2003/4	THE LOST EARS (2-LP, gatefold sleeve, as Arthur Brown's Kingdom Come)	22
88	Reckless 2 RECK	STRANGELANDS (LP, unreleased)	0

(see also Kingdom Come, Nick Greenwood, Atomic Rooster, Crane/Farlowe)

BARRY BROWN

Year	Label/Cat#	Title	£
78	Justice JUDIS 104	Step It Up/Youthman Version (12", with SHORTY THE PRESIDENT)	20
78	Tribesman TM 008	Unity Is Strength/DRUMMIE BENJI: Higher Region (12")	35
79	D Roy DRDD 12	Conscious Girl/School Days (12")	10
79	Justice JUDIS 126	Big Big Politician/No Wicked Shall Enter (12")	30
79	Justice JUDIS 135	We Can't Live Like This/From Creation I Man There (12")	30
79	Sufferer's Heights SUFF 003	I Love Sweet Jah Jah/RANKING JOE : Youthman Promotion (12")	40
80	Daddy Kool DKR 124	Peace And Love (with Ranking Toyan) JAH THOMAS & ROOTS RADICS: Adapter Chapter (12")	50
80	Strong Like Sampson SLSD 07	Natty Dread Nah Run/ANTHONY JOHNSON: Life Is Not Easy (12")	40
80	Strong Like... SLSD 010	Don't You Try/ANTHONY JOHNSON: Hey Mr Rich Man (12")	40
80	Attack TACK 17	Mr. CID/SCIENTIST AND ROOTS RADICAL BAND: King Tubby's Rockers (12")	35
80	Black Roots BR 009	Things And Time/Time Dub (12")	25
80	Attack TACK 21	Separation/Scientist In A Fine Style (12")	50
80	JB JBD 022	Jealous Lover/Seven To One (12" with Jah Thomas)	12
80	Attack TACK 23	Living As A Brother/SCIENTIST: Second Hand Girl (12")	30
80	Justice JUDIS 135	We Can't Live Like This/From Creation I Man Free (12")	40
81	City Sounds CSD 003	Warmonger/ROOTS RADICS BAND: Radical Style (12", green vinyl)	50
81	Greensleeves GRED 68	Give Israel Another Try/Sweet Sixteen (12")	30
82	Selena SD004	Them Ha Fi Get A Beatin'/ROOTS RADICS BAND : Stop The Fighting (12")	40
82	Selena SD008	Physical Fitness/HEPTONES : Lovers Feeling (12", blue vinyl)	35
83	Downbeat DBD 004	Belly Full (with General Saint)/WAYNE WADE: Little Suzie (12")	40
84	Greensleeves GRED 150	Belly Move/Why The World Stay So (12")	20
03	Trojan TACK 23	Living As A Brother/Caring For My Sister (12")	15
79	Paradise PDL 006	STEP IT UP YOUTHMAN (LP)	25
80	Trojan TRLS 191	COOL PON YOUR CORNER (LP)	50
80	Black Roots BRLP 1000	I'M NOT SO LUCKY (LP)	18
80	Third World TWS 937	SHOWCASE (LP)	40
84	Uptempo UT 003	ROOTS & CULTURE (LP)	35

BEN BROWN

Year	Label/Cat#	Title	£
67	Polydor 56198	Ask The Lonely/Sidewinder	50

BOOTS BROWN & HIS BLOCKBUSTERS

Year	Label/Cat#	Title	£
58	RCA RCA 1078	Cerveza/Juicy	10
59	RCA RCA 1102	Jim Twangy/Trollin'	10

(see also Shorty Rogers)

BUSTER BROWN

Year	Label/Cat#	Title	£
60	Melodisc 1559	Fannie Mae/Lost In A Dream	70
65	Sue WI 368	Fannie Mae/Lost In A Dream (reissue)	40
67	Island WI 3031	My Blue Heaven/Two Women	20
69	Blue Horizon 57-3147	Sugar Babe/I'm Going, But I'll Be Back	45
60s	No Cat No	B. AND BUSTER BROWN (EP, with B. Brown)	20

BUSTY BROWN

Year	Label/Cat#	Title	£
68	Doctor Bird DB 1158	Here Comes The Night/Don't Look Back	40
69	Upsetter US 304	What A Price/How Can I Forget?	40
69	Upsetter US 308	To Love Somebody/BLEECHERS: Farmer's In The Den	40
69	Punch PH 10	Broken Heart/Tribute To A King	40
70	Punch PH 38	Greatest Love/I Love You Madly	15
70	Escort ES 822	Fight For Your Right/MEDITATORS: Soul Fight (Busty Top A Pop) (B-side actually "Soul Fight" by Busty Brown)	25
70	Escort ES 845	Man Short (with Gaytones)/DAVE BARKER: She Want It	12
70	Gas GAS 154	I Love You Madly/Greatest Love	10
70	High Note HS 048	Man Short (with Gaytones)/GAYTONES: Another Version	12
71	Bullet BU 476	Never Love Another/Version	8
71	Punch PH 72	You Inspire Me/UPSETTERS: Version	35
71	Pama Supreme PS 356	Throw Away Your Gun/TWINKLE BROTHERS: Sad Song	30

CHARLES BROWN (BAND)

Year	Label/Cat#	Title	£
56	Vogue V 9061	I'll Always Be In Love With You/Soothe Me	400
57	Vogue V 9065	Confidential/Trouble Blues	300
61	Parlophone R 4848	It's Christmas All Year Round/Christmas Question	7

(see also Brown Brothers)

CLARENCE 'GATEMOUTH' BROWN

Year	Label/Cat#	Title	£
65	Vocalion VE 170161	CLARENCE 'GATEMOUTH' BROWN (EP)	90
72	Python PLP 26	CLARENCE 'GATEMOUTH' BROWN VOL. 1: 1948-1953 (LP)	25
72	Python PLP 27	CLARENCE 'GATEMOUTH' BROWN VOL. 2: 1956-1965 (LP)	25

CLIFFORD BROWN (& HIS GROUP)

Year	Label/Cat#	Title	£
55	Vogue EPV 1027	GIGI GRYCE - CLIFFORD BROWN ORCHESTRA (EP)	10
55	Vogue EPV 1041	CONCEPTION (EP)	10
56	Vogue EPV 1119	CLIFFORD BROWN ENSEMBLE (EP)	10

Clyde BROWN

MINT VALUE £

54	Vogue LDE 042	CLIFFORD "BROWNIE" BROWN QUARTET (10" LP)	40
55	Vogue LDE 121	THE CLIFFORD BROWN SEXTET (10" LP)	40
58	Emarcy EJL 1278	STUDY IN BROWN (LP)	35

(see also Art Farmer, Sonny Rollins, Max Roach)

CLYDE BROWN
73	Atlantic 10362	Ghetto Cowboy/You've Gone Too Far	6

DANNY BROWN
16	Warp WARPLP 276X	ATROCITY EXHIBITION (2-LP, electric blue vinyl)	40

DENNIS BROWN
70	Bamboo BAM 56	Love Grows/SOUND DIMENSION: Less Problem	50
70	Banana BA 309	No Man Is An Island/SOUL SISTERS: Another Night	35
71	Banana BA 336	Never Fall In Love/Make It With You	25
71	Ocean OC 001	Little Green Apples/SOUND DIMENSION: Version	18
72	Duke DU 139	What About The Half/What About The Half Version	30
72	Explosion EX 2068	Black Magic Woman/PHILL PRATT ALL STARS: Black Magic Woman Pt 2	20
72	Pressure Beat PR 5513	Money In My Pocket/JOE GIBBS ALLSTARS: Money Love	25
72	Randy's RAN 526	Cheater/TOMMY McCOOK & IMPACT ALLSTARS: Harvest In The East	25
72	Randy's RAN 528	Meet Me On The Corner (actually unknown instrumental)/IMPACT ALLSTARS: Version	10
72	Songbird SB 1074	Silhouettes/CRYSTALITES: Version	12
73	Ashanti ASH 402	It's Too Late/Song My Mother Used To Sing	18
73	Jackpot JP 813	He Can't Spell/CRYSTALITES: Acid Version	15
73	Smash SMA 2327	Concentration/Version	18
74	Sydna SYD 5027	No More Shall I Roam/Coming Home	10
76	Doctor DR 03	Out In The Rain/Version	8
76	Hawkeye HE 01	Whip Them Jah/Version	12
77	Observer OBS 999	Jah Is Watching/Hustling/Rock On/Murder Observer Style (12" with DILLINGER)	40
77	Observer OB 003	Tenement Yard/Kill Landlord/HORACE ANDY: Them Never Fall I/Teacher Gal (12", with Ranking Buckers)	25
77	DEB 0002	Half/Troubled World (12")	20
77	Deb DBR102	Emanuel/Wolfs And Leopards	10
78	DEB DDDEB 010	Oh What A Day/Man Next Door (12")	20
78	Diamond DM DC 702	Children Of Israel/Version (12", p/s)	25
79	Laser LAS 20	Slave Driver/Version	20
79	Laser LAS 20(T)	Slave Driver/Dub Driver (12")	15
79	Observer OBS 902	Blessed Are The Men (The Pill)/JUNIOR DELGADO : Cry Cry (12")	20
79	3 in 1 SKLP 001	Tribulation (with Jah Bop)/JUNIOR BYLES: Can You Feel It (12")	25
80	High Times HT 001	Blood City/FREDDIE McGREGOR : Natural Collie (12")	35
80	Pratt PP 30	Black Magic Woman/Version (12")	40
80	DEB DEB 039	I Don't Want To Be No General/General (Version) (12" with Ranking Dread)	25
83	Tad's TRD 21483	Easy Take It Easy/Easy Version (12")	25
83	Natty Congo NCDM 020	Breaking Down The Barriers/Dubbing The Barriers (12")	40
83	Taxi IPR 2059	Revolution/Dub Revolution (12")	15
84	Tad TRD 111585	Here I Come/Version	10
84	Blue Moon BMS 1002	Slave Driver/Version (12")	15
84	Greensleeves GRED 167	It's Magic/PAD ANTHONY: Crazy Love (12")	25
85	Greensleeves GRED 175	Slow Down Woman/Lord Is My Shepherd (12")	12
86	Jakki JM 468	Rebel With A Cause/JACKIE MITTOO: Trade Mark (12")	25
80s	Live & Love LLD 117	Little Village/Version (12")	15
73	Trojan TRLS 57	SUPER REGGAE & SOUL HITS (LP)	30
75	Trojan TRLS 107	JUST DENNIS (LP)	20
77	DEB DEBLP 01	WOLF AND LEOPARDS (LP)	25
77	Pioneer PIO LP2	MEETS HARRY HIPPY (LP)	50
78	Lightning LIP 7	VISIONS OF (LP)	20
78	Laser LASL 1	WORDS OF WISDOM (LP, stickered sleeve with free 12" Money In My Pocket)	25
78	Laser LASL 1	WORDS OF WISDOM (LP)	20
80	Laser LASL 6	JOSEPH'S COAT OF MANY COLOURS (LP)	18
86	Trojan TRSL 238	THE EXIT (LP)	15

(see also Big Youth & Dennis Brown, Hugh Roy, Big Youth, Sound Dimension)

DENNIS BROWN & ASWAD
80	Simba SM003	Promised Land/More Dub (12")	20

DUSTY BROWN
61	Starlite ST45 058	Please Don't Go/Well You Know	15

ERROL BROWN & CHOSEN FEW
72	Songbird SB 1082	People Make The World Go Round/People Make The World Go Round (Version)	12

ERROL BROWN
73	Count Shelly CS 008	Time Is My Love/SOUL REBEL: I Don't Want To Lose You	6

FAY BROWN
55	Columbia SCM 5185	Unchained Melody/I Was Wrong	15

FUNKY BROWN
72	Sioux SI 018	African (Indian Reservation)/JUMBO STERLING: Elizabethan Reggae	10

GABRIEL BROWN
77	Policy Wheel PW 4592	GABRIEL BROWN AND HIS GUITAR (LP, withdrawn)	15

GEORGIA BROWN
72	Bug 18	Turn Out The Light/I Scare Myself	10

GLEN BROWN
68	Blue Cat BS 131	Way Of Life (with Joe White & Trevor Shield)/ KARL BRYAN & LYN TAITT: I'm So Proud	175
70	Summit SUM 8502	Collie And Wine/BEVERLEY'S ALLSTARS: Version	40
70	Songbird SB 1021	Love I/CRYSTALITES: Heavy Load	25
72	Songbird SB 1081	Smokey Eyes (with Crystalites)/Smokey Eyes (Version)	20
73	Downtown DT 5072	Wedden Skank/BERRY SIMPSON: Daughter A Whole Lotta Sugar	25

Glenmore BROWN & HOPETON LEWIS

MINT VALUE £

79	Kingley Sounds REX 4	Marcus Garvey Words/SLYFORD WALKER: Africa (12")	35
96	Blood & Fire BAFLP 015	TERMINATION DUB (LP, as Glen Brown & King Tubby)	25

GLENMORE BROWN & HOPETON LEWIS
68	Fab FAB 42	Girl You're Cold/Soul Man	130

(see also Hopeton Lewis & Glenmore Brown)

GREGG BROWN
84	Beau-Jolly BJ 1004	Baby Talk/Baby Talk (Edit) (p/s)	20
84	Beau-Jolly 12 BJ 1004	Baby Talk (Club Mix)/Extended Mix (12", p/s)	40

HENRY BROWN
61	'77' LA 12-5	HENRY BROWN BLUES (LP)	30

HUX BROWN & SCOTTY
71	High Note HS 056	Unbelievable Sounds/GAYTONES: Unbelievable Sounds Version	25

IAN BROWN
00	Polydor 561 908-1	Thriller/Billie Jean (12", p/s)	10
01	Polydor 5872847	F.E.A.R./F.E.A.R. (Instrumental) (stickered p/s)	8
09	Fiction 2717752	Stellify/Crowning Of The Poor (red vinyl, 1000 only, numbered)	10
98	Polydor 539 916-1	UNFINISHED MONKEY BUSINESS (LP, gatefold, booklet)	45
99	Polydor 543 141-1	GOLDEN GREATS (LP, yellow vinyl, p/s)	40
01	Polydor 589 126-1	MUSIC OF THE SPHERES (LP)	60
02	Polydor SPHERE2	REMIXES OF THE SPHERES (2x12" Promo Sampler)	30
02	Polydor 065 927-1	REMIXES OF THE SPHERES (2-LP)	30
05	Fiction 987289	GREATEST (2-LP)	25
07	Polydor 174 341-4	THE WORLD IS YOURS (2-LP)	60
09	Fiction 2717470	MY WAY (LP)	100
12	Fiction (No Cat No)	COLLECTED (10-CD, LP, DVD boxed set, 1000 only)	80
16	Fiction SOLARIZED LP 1	SOLARIZED (LP, reissue)	25

(see also Stone Roses)

IRVING BROWN
70	Bamboo BAM 36	Today/SOUND DIMENSION: Young Gifted And Black Version	15
70	Bamboo BAM 58	I'm Still Around/Run Come	18
70	Bamboo BAM 61	Let's Make It Up (actually by Larry Marshall)/BURNING SPEAR: Free	35
71	Bamboo Now BN 1003	Now I'm Alone/Funky Night	18

(see also Larry Marshall)

JACKIE BROWN
72	High Note HS 057	One Night/GAYTONES: One Night Version	8
72	High Note HS 060	Last Dance/GAYTONES: Last Dance Version	8
75	Black Wax 10	Send Me The Pillow/MIGHTY TWO: Pillow With Strings	6

JAMES BROWN (& FAMOUS FLAMES)
SINGLES

60	Parlophone R 4667	Think/You've Got The Power (with Famous Flames)	50
60	Fontana H 273	This Old Heart/Wonder When You're Coming Home	35
62	Parlophone R 4922	Night Train/Why Does Everything Happen To Me (with Famous Flames)	40
62	Parlophone R 4952	Shout And Shimmy/Come Over Here (with Famous Flames)	30
63	London HL 9730	Prisoner Of Love/Choo-Choo (Locomotion) (with Famous Flames)	20
63	London HL 9775	These Foolish Things/(Can You) Feel It (Part 1) (with Famous Flames)	20
64	Philips BF 1368	Out Of Sight/Maybe The Last Time (& His Orchestra)	25
64	Sue WI 360	Night Train/Why Does Everything Happen To Me (with Famous Flames)	35
65	London HL 9945	Have Mercy Baby/Just Won't Do Right (with Famous Flames)	18
65	London HL 9990	Papa's Got A Brand New Bag Parts 1 & 2 (with Famous Flames)	20
65	Ember EMB S 216	Tell Me What You're Gonna Do/Lost Someone (p/s)	40
65	Ember EMB S 216	Tell Me What You're Gonna Do/Lost Someone	20
65	Philips BF 1458	Try Me/Papa's Got A Brand New Bag	20
66	Philips BF 1481	New Breed Parts 1 & 2	20
66	Pye International 7N 25350	I Got You (I Feel Good)/I Can't Help It (I Just Do-Do-Do) (with Famous Flames)	15
66	Pye International 7N 25367	Ain't That A Groove Parts 1 & 2 (with Famous Flames)	10
66	Pye International 7N 25371	It's A Man's Man's Man's World/Is It Yes Or Is It No? (with Famous Flames)	8
66	Pye International 7N 25379	Money Won't Change You Parts 1 & 2 (with Famous Flames)	15
66	Pye International 7N 25394	Don't Be A Drop-Out/Tell Me That You Love Me (with Famous Flames)	10
67	Pye International 7N 25411	Bring It Up/Nobody Knows (with Famous Flames)	10
67	Pye International 7N 25418	Kansas City/Stone Fox (with Famous Flames)	10
67	Pye International 7N 25423	Let Yourself Go/Good Rockin' Tonight (with Famous Flames)	10
67	Pye International 7N 25430	Cold Sweat Parts 1 & 2 (with Famous Flames)	10
67	Pye International 7N 25441	Get It Together Parts 1 & 2 (with Famous Flames)	15
68	Polydor 56740	I Can't Stand Myself/There Was A Time	15
68	Polydor 56752	Say It Loud, I'm Black And I'm Proud Parts 1 & 2	8
68	Polydor 56540	That's Life/Please, Please, Please (with Famous Flames)	15
69	Polydor 56776	Mother Popcorn Parts 1 & 2	6
69	Polydor 56780	The World Parts 1 & 2	6
69	Polydor 56783	Let A Man Come In And Do The Popcorn/Sometimes	10
69	Polydor 56787	There Was A Time/I Can't Stand Myself (When You Touch Me)	12
70	Polydor 56793	Ain't It Funky Now Parts 1 & 2	6
70	Polydor 2001 018	It's A New Day/Georgia On My Mind	6
70	Polydor 2001 071	Get Up, I Feel Like Being A Sex Machine Parts 1 & 2 (paper label)	6
70	Polydor 2001 097	Call Me Super Bad Parts 1, 2 & 3	6
71	Polydor 2001 163	Soul Power Parts 1, 2 & 3	6
71	Polydor 2001 190	I Cried/Get Up, Get Into It, Get Involved	6
71	Polydor 2001 213	Hot Pants (She Got To Use What She Got To Get What She Wants) Parts 1, 2 & 3	6
71	Polydor 2001 223	Make It Funky Parts 1 & 2	6
71	Mojo 2093 006	Hey America!/Brother Rapp (Part 1)	6

James BROWN (Jamaica)

MINT VALUE £

Year	Catalogue	Title	Value
71	Polydor 2066 153	I'm A Greedy Man Parts 1 & 2	6
72	Polydor 2066 185	King Heroin/Theme From King Heroin	20
72	Polydor 2066 210	There It Is Parts 1 & 2	7
72	Polydor 2066 216	Honky Tonk Parts 1 & 2	10
72	Polydor 2066 231	Get On The Good Foot Parts 1 & 2	10
72	Polydor 2066 283	What My Baby Needs Now Is A Little More Lovin'/ This Guy's In Love With You (with Lyn Collins)	15
73	Polydor 2066 285	I've Got A Bag Of My Own/I Know It's True	7
74	Polydor 2066 411	Stone To The Bone/Sexy, Sexy, Sexy	6
74	Polydor 2066 485	My Thang/The Payback	6
79	Polydor POSP 24	For Goodness Sakes, Look At Those Cakes/Get Up, I Feel Like Being A Sex Machine (red label)	8
79	Polydor POSPX 24	Get Up, I Feel Like Being A Sex Machine/For Goodness Sakes, Look At Those Cakes (12")	10
79	Polydor POSPX 68	It's Too Funky In Here/Are We Really Dancing? (12")	10

EPs

Year	Catalogue	Title	Value
64	London RE 1410	JAMES BROWN AND THE FAMOUS FLAMES	90
64	Ember EMB EP 4549	I DO JUST WHAT I WANT	40
66	Pye Intl. NEP 44059	I GOT YOU	40
66	Pye Intl. NEP 44068	I'LL GO CRAZY	40
67	Pye Intl. NEP 44072	PRISONER OF LOVE	40
67	Pye Intl. NEP 44076	HOW LONG DARLING	40
67	Pye Intl. NEP 44088	BRING IT UP	45
70	Polydor 580 701	TURN IT LOOSE	30

ALBUMS

Year	Catalogue	Title	Value
64	London HA 8177	PURE DYNAMITE! (as James Brown & Famous Flames)	80
64	London HA 8184	LIVE AT THE APOLLO (as James Brown & Famous Flames)	60
64	Ember EMB 3357	TELL ME WHAT YOU'RE GONNA DO	45
64	Philips BL 7630	SHOWTIME	30
65	London HA 8203	UNBEATABLE 16 HITS	45
65	London HA 8231	PLEASE, PLEASE, PLEASE (as James Brown & Famous Flames)	80
65	Philips BL 7664	GRITS AND SOUL	60
65	London HA 8240	JAMES BROWN TOURS THE U.S.A. (with Famous Flames)	50
66	London HA 8262	PAPA'S GOT A BRAND NEW BAG (as James Brown & Famous Flames)	50
66	Philips BL 7697	JAMES BROWN PLAYS JAMES BROWN TODAY AND YESTERDAY	40
66	Pye Intl. NPL 28074	I GOT YOU (I FEEL GOOD)	50
66	Philips BL 7718	JAMES BROWN PLAYS NEW BREED	20
66	Pye Intl. NPL 28079	IT'S A MAN'S MAN'S WORLD	30
66	Pye Intl. NPL 28097	THE JAMES BROWN CHRISTMAS ALBUM	40
67	Pye Intl. NPL 28093	MIGHTY INSTRUMENTALS	40
67	Philips (S)BL 7761	HANDFUL OF SOUL	25
67	Pye Intl. NPL 28099	PAPA'S GOT A BRAND NEW BAG (reissue)	20
67	Pye Intl. NPL 28100	MR. EXCITEMENT	30
67	Polydor 582 703	THE JAMES BROWN SHOW (live)	20
67	Pye Intl. NPL 28103	SINGS RAW SOUL	30
67	Pye Intl. NPL 28104	LIVE AT THE GARDEN	35
68	Philips (S)BL 7823	JAMES BROWN PLAYS THE REAL THING	25
68	Polydor 184 136	I CAN'T STAND MYSELF	20
69	Polydor 184 148	SOUL FIRE	15
69	Mercury 20133 SMCL	JAMES BROWN SINGS OUT OF SIGHT	25
69	Polydor 583 741	SAY IT LOUD - I'M BLACK AND I'M PROUD	20
69	Polydor 583 768	IT'S A MOTHER	20
69	Polydor 643 317	THIS IS ... JAMES BROWN	15
70	Polydor 583 742	GETTIN' DOWN TO IT	20
70	Polydor 184 319	THE POPCORN	20
70	Polydor 2343 010	AIN'T IT FUNKY	25
71	Polydor 2625 004	SEX MACHINE (2-LP)	20
71	Polydor 2310 022	SOUL ON TOP	20
71	Polydor 2310 029	IT'S A NEW DAY	20
71	Polydor 2310 089	SUPER BAD	20
72	Polydor 2659 011	REVOLUTION OF THE MIND: RECORDED LIVE AT THE APOLLO VOL. III (2-LP)	20
72	Polydor 2391 033	THERE IT IS	20
73	Polydor 2659 018	GET ON THE GOOD FOOT (2-LP)	25
73	Polydor 2490 117	BLACK CAESAR (soundtrack)	35
73	Polydor 2391 084	SLAUGHTER'S BIG RIP-OFF (soundtrack)	30
74	Polydor 2659 030	THE PAYBACK (2-LP)	35
74	Polydor 2659 036	IT'S HELL (2-LP)	25
75	Polydor 2391 175	SEX MACHINE TODAY	15
75	Polydor 2391 197	EVERYBODY'S DOIN' THE HUSTLE AND DEAD ON THE DOUBLE BUMP	15
77	Polydor 2391 300	MUTHA'S NATURE (by James Brown & the New J.B.'s)	15

(see also Lyn Collins, JBs, Maceo & All King's Men, Nat Kendrick & Swans)

JAMES BROWN (JAMAICA)

Year	Catalogue	Title	Value
71	Punch PH 76	Don't Say/TRANS AM ALLSTARS: Don't Say Version	8
72	Ashanti ASH 408	Mama Don't Want To See You/Mama Don't Want To See You Version	7
75	Mango MAN 1001	Stop The War In Babylon/Dub In Peace	15

JIM EDWARD (BROWN) & MAXINE BROWN

Year	Catalogue	Title	Value
55	London HL 8123	Itsy Witsy Bitsy Me/Why Am I Falling?	30
55	London HLU 8166	Your Love Is Wild As The West Wind/Draggin' Mainstreet	30
55	London HLU 8200	You Thought I Thought/Here Today And Gone Tomorrow (B-side with Bonnie)	30

Joe BROWN (& BRUVVERS)

MINT VALUE £

JOE BROWN (& BRUVVERS)
| 59 | Decca F 11185 | People Gotta Talk/Comes The Day (solo, triangular centre) | 15 |
| 60 | Pye 7N 15322 | Shine/The Switch | 7 |

(see also Vicki Brown, Browns Homebrew)

JOHNNY BROWN
| 61 | Philips PB 1119 | Walkin' Talkin' Kissin' Doll/Sundown | 10 |

KENT BROWN & RAINBOWS
| 68 | Fab FAB 53 | When You Going To Show Me How/Come Ya Come Ya | 15 |

(see also Kent & Jeannie, Sir D's Group)

LAWRENCE BROWN
| 56 | Columbia 33CX 10246 | SLIDE TROMBONE (LP) | 35 |

LENNOX BROWN
| 72 | Green Door GD 4023 | High School Serenade/WINSTON SCOTLAND: On The Track (1st issue) | 7 |
| 72 | Bullet BU 501 | High School Serenade/WINSTON SCOTLAND: On The Track (2nd issue) | 7 |

(see also Jeff Barnes, Peter Tosh)

LEROY BROWN
| 78 | Revue REVD 10 | Blood A Go Run/Taxi (12") | 40 |
| 79 | Jah Lion JL DC 606 | Gone Gone/TRISTAN PALMER: Gone Clear (12") | 60 |

LES BROWN (JR)
| 60s | Vocalion VA 8011 | WILDEST DRUMS YET (LP) | 15 |

MARION BROWN
| 69 | Polydor 583724 | PORTO NOVO (LP) | 60 |

MATT BROWN
| 01 | Grapevine 2000 G2K 45-107 | Thank You Baby/Sweet Thing | 8 |
| 03 | Grapevine 2000 G2K 45-133 | Everyday (I Love You Just A Little Bit More)/Baby I'm A Want You | 8 |

MAXINE BROWN
61	London HLU 9286	All In My Mind/Harry, Let's Marry	40
62	HMV POP 1102	Am I Falling In Love/Promise Me Anything (DJ Copy)	250
62	HMV POP 1102	Am I Falling In Love/Promise Me Anything	150
63	Stateside SS 188	Ask Me/Yesterday's Kisses	40
64	Pye International 7N 25272	Oh No Not My Baby/You Upset My Soul	30
65	Pye International 7N 25299	It's Gonna Be Alright/You Do Something To Me	30
65	Pye International 7N 25317	One Step At A Time/Anything For A Laugh	40
67	Pye International 7N 25410	I've Got A Lot Of Love Left In Me/Hold On (I'm Comin') (B-side with Chuck Jackson)	30
67	Pye International 7N 25434	Since I Found You/Gotta Find A Way	25
70	Major Minor MM 709	Reason To Believe/I Can't Get Along Without You	25
73	Avco 6105 022	Picked Up, Packed Up And Put Away/Bella Mia	10
75	Pye Disco Demand DDS 117	One In A Million/Let Me Give You My Lovin'	10
90s	Kent TOWN 110	It's Torture/I Got Love	12
85	Kent 047	LIKE NEVER BEFORE (LP)	15

(see also Chuck Jackson & Maxine Brown)

NAPPY BROWN (& HIS BAND)
55	London HL 8145	Don't Be Angry/It's Really You	300
55	London HLC 8182	Pitter Patter/There'll Come A Day	250
57	London HLC 8384	Little By Little/I'm Getting Lonesome (& His Band) (gold lettering on label)	250
57	London HLC 8384	Little By Little/I'm Getting Lonesome (& His Band) (silver lettering on label)	100
58	London HLC 8760	It Don't Hurt No More/My Baby	50

NOEL BROWN
68	Island WI 3149	Man's Temptation/Heartbreak Girl	80
69	Songbird SB 1012	By The Time I Get To Phoenix/Heartbreak Girl	20
70	Bullet BU 423	Phoenix (actually by "By The Time I Get To Phoenix")/Heartbreak Girl	20

(see also Bunny Brown)

PAMELA BROWN
| 70 | Joe JRS 8 | People Are Running/CRITICS: School Days | 15 |

PATRICK BROWN
| 82 | Kufe EB 003 | Fantasy/On The Right Track (12") | 40 |

PETE BROWN (& PIBLOKTO)
69	Parlophone R 5767	The Week Looked Good On Paper/Morning Call (as Pete Brown & His Battered Ornaments, promo p/s)	65
69	Parlophone R 5767	The Week Looked Good On Paper/Morning Call (as Pete Brown & His Battered Ornaments)	22
69	Harvest HAR 5008	Living Life Backwards/High Flying Electric Bird (as Pete Brown & Piblokto!)	20
70	Harvest HAR 5023	Can't Get Off The Planet/Broken Magic (with His Battered Ornaments)	15
70	Harvest HAR 5028	Flying Hero Sandwich/My Last Band (as Pete Brown & Piblokto!)	25
69	Harvest SHVL 752	A MEAL YOU CAN SHAKE HANDS WITH IN THE DARK (LP, as Pete Brown & His Battered Ornaments, with "Sold in U.K" label text on 4 lines, stereo)	350
69	Harvest SHVL 752	A MEAL YOU CAN SHAKE HANDS WITH IN THE DARK (LP, as Pete Brown & His Battered Ornaments, without "Sold in U.K" label text on 4 lines, stereo)	100
70	Harvest SHVL 768	THE ART SCHOOL DANCE GOES ON FOREVER (LP, as Pete Brown & Piblokto!, gatefold sleeve, no EMI on label)	350
70	Harvest SHVL 782	THOUSANDS ON A RAFT (LP, as Pete Brown & Piblokto!, gatefold sleeve, no EMI on label)	300
73	Deram SML 1103	THE NOT FORGOTTEN ASSOCIATION (LP, with Graham Bond)	120
77	Harvest SHSM 2017	MY LAST BAND (LP, as Pete Brown & Piblokto)	20
82	Discs Intl. INTLP 1	PARTY IN THE RAIN (LP, with Ian Lynn, private pressing)	15
12	Pure Pleasure PPAN SHVL 752	A MEAL YOU CAN SHAKE HANDS WITH IN THE DARK (2-LP, reissue)	20

(see also Battered Ornaments, Graham Bond & Pete Brown, Deke Leonard, Cream)

PETER BROWN
| 77 | T.K TKR 82514 | DO YOU WANNA GET FUNKY WITH ME? (LP) | 15 |

POLLY BROWN
| 72 | Pye 7N 45197 | I'll Cry My Heart Out For You/Teardrops WIll Fall | 10 |

Year	Label & Cat#	Title	Mint Value £
72	Pye 7N 45148	The Feeling's Right/I Can't Do Without You	10
75	GTO GT 14	Dial L For Love/Love Lovin' You	6
76	GTO GT 61	Love Bug/Love Bug Buzzin'	6
77	GTO GT 88	Beautiful Things For You/MY Heart Keeps Breaking Over You	6
73	Pye NSPL 18396	POLLY BROWN (LP)	20

RANDY BROWN
87	Threeway WAYLP 1	WELCOME TO MY ROOM (LP)	20

ROY BROWN
57	London HLP 8398	I'm Sticking With You/Party Doll (gold label print)	400
57	London HLP 8398	I'm Sticking With You/Party Doll (later silver print pressing)	150
57	London HLP 8448	Saturday Night/Everybody	500

RUTH BROWN (& HER RHYTHMAKERS)
55	London HL 8153	Mambo Baby/Mama (He Treats Your Daughter Mean) (with Rhythmakers)	250
55	London HLE 8210	As Long As I'm Moving/R.B. Blues (with Her Rhythmakers)	250
56	London HLE 8310	I Want To Do More/Sweet Baby Of Mine	150
57	London HLE 8401	Mom Oh Mom/I Want To Be Loved (But Only By You)	150
57	Columbia DB 3913	Lucky Lips/My Heart Is Breaking Over You	250
57	London HLE 8483	When I Get You Baby/One More Time	80
58	London HLE 8552	A New Love/Look Me Up	80
58	London HLE 8645	Just Too Much/Book Of Lies	80
58	London HLE 8757	This Little Girl's Gone Rockin'/Why Me	60
58	London HL 7061	This Little Girl's Gone Rockin'/Why Me (export issue)	60
59	London HLE 8887	Jack O' Diamonds/I Can't Hear A Word You Say	25
59	London HLE 8946	I Don't Know/Papa Daddy	25
59	London HLE 8946	I Don't Know/Papa Daddy (78)	35
60	London HLE 9093	Don't Deceive Me/I Burned Your Letter	25
61	London HLK 9304	Sure 'Nuff/Here He Comes	25
64	Brunswick 05904	Yes Sir That's My Baby/What Happened To You	10
76	President PT 457	Sugar Babe/Stop Knocking	10
55	London REE 1038	THE QUEEN OF R&B (EP)	150
63	Philips BE 12537	GOSPEL TIME (EP)	50
60	London Jazz LTZ-K 15187	LATE DATE WITH RUTH BROWN (LP)	60
62	Philips 652 012 BL	ALONG COMES RUTH (LP)	50
63	Philips 652 020 BL	GOSPEL TIME (LP)	40
64	Atlantic ATL 5007	THE BEST OF RUTH BROWN (LP, plum label)	100
76	President PTLS 1067	SUGAR BABE (LP)	20
84	Charly CRB 1069	ROCKIN' WITH RUTH (LP)	15

RUTH BROWN/JOE TURNER
56	London REE 1047	THE KING AND QUEEN OF R&B (EP, 2 tracks each)	200

SAMMI BROWN
68	Fontana TF 947	Daydream/Stop The Music	7

SANDY BROWN('S JAZZ BAND)
53	Esquire EP 28	SANDY BROWN'S JAZZ BAND (EP)	10
55	Tempo EXA 13	SANDY BROWN'S JAZZ BAND (EP)	10
55	Tempo EXA 33	SANDY BROWN'S JAZZ BAND (EP)	10
56	Tempo EXA 49	TRADITIONAL JAZZ SCENE '56 (EP)	10
57	Nixa NJE 1054	BLUE McJAZZ (EP)	10
57	Nixa NJE 1056	AFRO McJAZZ (EP)	10
53	Esquire 20-022	SANDY BROWN (10" LP, with Bobby Mickleburgh)	20
56	Tempo TAP 3	SANDY'S SIDEMEN PLAYING COMPOSITIONS BY AL FAIRWEATHER (LP)	25
57	Nixa Jazz Today NJL 9	McJAZZ (LP)	15
66	Fontana TE1 7473	SANDY BROWN ALL STARS (LP)	15
69	Fontana SFJL 921	HAIR AT ITS HAIRIEST (LP, as Sandy Brown & His Gentlemen Friends)	15

(see also Wally Fawkes)

SHIRLEY BROWN
75	Stax STXS 2019	Woman To Woman/Yes Sir, Brother	6
75	Stax STXS 2032	I Can't Give You Up/It Ain't No Fun	20
77	Arista 102	Blessed Is The Woman (With A Man Like Mine)/Lowdown Dirty Good Lover	8
75	Stax STX 1031	WOMAN TO WOMAN (LP)	20
79	Stax STX 2014	FOR THE REAL FEELING (LP)	15

(see also Oliver Sain)

STU BROWN & BLUESOLOGY
67	Polydor 56195	Since I Found You Baby/Just A Little Bit	300

(see also Bluesology, Elton John)

TEDDY BROWN
70	Trojan TR 7793	What Greater Love/Lady Love	6
71	Trojan TR 7827	Walk The World Away/Senorita Rita	6

U BROWN
75	Fay FM 606	Jah Jah Whip Them/Skanking in Dub	30
76	Fay Music FM 608	Wet Up Your Pant/Ringo Don't Take Your Gun To Town (with Little Youth)	20
78	Cancer CAN 702	Starsky And Hutch/Version	6
77	Klik KLP 9018	SATTA DREAD (LP)	60
78	Virgin Frontline FL 1003	MR. BROWN SOMETHING (LP)	18
79	Virgin Frontline FL 1030	CAN'T KEEP A GOOD MAN DOWN (LP)	15
84	VSLP 5005	SUPERSTAR (LP)	15

VICKI BROWN
77	Power Exchange PXL 012	FROM THE INSIDE (LP)	15

VINCENT BROWN
70	Gas GAS 128	Look What You're Going To Do/Hold On To What You Have Got	8

Watson T. BROWN (& EXPLOSIVE)

MINT VALUE £

WATSON T. BROWN (& EXPLOSIVE)
68	President PT 207	Some Lovin'/Home Is Where Your Heart Lies	6
68	President PT 221	Crying All Night/I Close My Eyes	10
70	Bell BLL 1109	Will You Still Love Me Tomorrow/Save The Last Dance For Me (solo)	6
71	MAM MAM 16	I'm On The Road Again/Feeling Bad	6

(see also Explosive)

WILLIAM BROWN
| 71 | Ackee ACK 128 | I'm Alone/BELTONES: Soul People | 10 |

BROWN BROTHERS
| 59 | Vogue V 9131 | Let The Good Times Roll/You're Right, I'm Left | 150 |

(see also Charles Brown)

CHARLEY BROWNE
| 78 | Hurry! LT1113 | Feeling Under The Weather/Sez Lez (no p/s) | 15 |

DUNCAN BROWNE
68	Immediate IM 070	On The Bombsite/Alfred Bell	25
70	Bell BLL 1119	Resurrection Joe/Final Asylum	12
73	Rak RAK 162	Send Me The Bill/My Only Son	6
78	Logo GO 329	Wild Places/Camino Real (p/s)	6
68	Immediate IMSP 018	GIVE ME, TAKE YOU (LP, with insert, lilac label with "sold in U.K." label text)	600
73	RAK SRKA 6754	DUNCAN BROWNE (LP, gatefold sleeve)	50

FRIDAY BROWN(E)
66	Parlophone R 5396	Getting Nowhere/And (To Me He Meant Everything) (as Friday Browne)	25
66	Fontana TF 736	32nd Love Affair/Born A Woman	150
69	Fontana TF 996	Stand By Your Man/I Want To Rain	6
71	Philips 6308 074	FRIDAY BROWN (LP)	40

(see also Marianne & Mike, High Society, Manchester Mob, Graham Gouldman)

GEORGE BROWNE
| 54 | Parlophone CMSP 6 | Calypso Mambo/The Peanut Vendor (export issue) | 10 |
| 54 | Parlophone CMSP 17 | Somebody Bad Stole De Wedding Bell (Who's Got De Ding Dong?)/ Matilda, Matilda! (export issue) | 7 |

(see also Humphrey Lyttleton)

JACKSON BROWNE
| 74 | Asylum K2 43007 | LATE FOR THE SKY (LP, quadrophonic) | 15 |
| 85 | Asylum K53070 | RUNNING ON EMPTY (LP, Nimbus Supercut, mail order only via through Hi Fi Today) | 50 |

SANDRA BROWNE (& BOYFRIENDS)
63	Columbia DB 4998	By Hook Or By Crook/Johnny Boy (as Sandra Browne & Boyfriends)	15
63	Columbia DB 7109	You'd Think He Didn't Know Me/Mama Never Told Me	15
65	Columbia DB 7465	Knock On Any Door/I Want Love	15

THOMAS F. BROWNE
| 71 | Vertigo 6325 250 | WEDNESDAY'S CHILD (LP, gatefold sleeve, small swirl label) | 400 |

(see also Gary Wright, The Gladiators)

TOBY BROWNE
| 64 | Parlophone 5192 | Play The Music, Keep On Dancing/Child | 15 |

TOM BROWNE
| 80 | Arista ARIST 12357 | Funkin' For Jamaica (N.Y.)/Her Silent Smile (12") | 10 |

DUKE BROWNER
| 79 | Grapevine GRP 145 | Crying Over You/Crying Over You (Instrumental) | 20 |

(see also Kaddo Strings)

BROWNHILL'S STAMP DUTY
| 69 | Columbia DB 8625 | Maxwell's Silver Hammer/My Woman's Back | 10 |

BILL BROWNING
| 80s | Roller Coaster RRC 2003 | Wash Machine Boogie/Ramblin' Man (p/s) | 8 |

BROWNS
59	RCA RCA 1140	The Three Bells/Heaven Fell Last Night (tri centre)	7
59	RCA RD 27153	SWEET SOUNDS BY THE BROWNS (LP, mono)	20
59	RCA RD 27153/SF 5052	SWEET SOUNDS BY THE BROWNS (LP, stereo)	20

(see also Jim Edward & Maxine Brown)

BROWN'S FERRY FOUR
| 54 | Parlophone CMSP 11 | I Need The Prayers/Through The Pearly Gates (with Clyde Moody, export issue) | 15 |

(see also Grandpa Jones, Merle Travis)

BROWNS HOME BREW
| 72 | Bell BELLS 208 | BROWN'S HOME BREW (LP) | 100 |
| 74 | Vertigo 6360 114 | TOGETHER (LP, spaceship label) | 15 |

(see also Joe Brown)

BROWN SUGAR (1)
77	Lovers Rock CJ 613	I'm In Love With A Dreadlocks/Version	30
77	Lovers Rock CJ 614	Hello Stranger/Version	25
77	Lovers Rock CJ 619	Black Pride/Version (p/s)	25
77	Lovers Rock CJ 624	Do You Really Love Me/Version	20
77	Lucky LY 6041	For All Eternity/For All Eternity (Version)	18
78	Lovers Rock LR DIS 07	Forever My Darling/Free/Albatross (12")	100
79	Studio 16 WE 014	You And Your Smiling Face/Version (12")	20
79	Decca F 13857	Our Reggae Music/Our Reggae In Dub	12
79	Studio 16 WE 017	Our Reggae Music/Dub (12")	15
80	African Drums AF 002	Hello Stranger/Black Is The Colour (12")	12
80	Studio 16 WE 092	Dreaming Of Zion/Version (12")	40
80	Studio 16 WE 106	Confession Hurts/Version (12")	30
80	Studio 16 WE 113	Runaway Love/Version (12")	30
04	Lovers Rock LOVERS001	I'm In Love With A Dreadlocks/Black Pride (reissue)	8
80	Black Roots BRLP 1000	NOT SO LUCKY (LP)	15

Annette (Reis) & VICTOR BROX
MINT VALUE £

(see also Kofi)

ANNETTE (REIS) & VICTOR BROX
65	Fontana TF 536	I've Got The World In A Jug/Wake Me And Shake Me	10
74	Sonet SNTF 663	ROLLIN' BACK (LP)	15

(see also Aynsley Dunbar Retaliation)

DAVE BRUBECK (QUARTET)
54	Vogue LDE 090	DAVE BRUBECK TRIO (10" LP)	20
54	Vogue LDE 095	DAVE BRUBECK QUARTET (10" LP)	20
54	Vogue LDE 104	DAVE BRUBECK QUARTET VOL. 2 (10" LP)	20
55	Vogue LDE 114	DAVE BRUBECK QUARTET VOL. 3 (10" LP)	15
57	Fontana TFL 5017	DAVE DIGS DISNEY (LP)	15
59	Vogue LAE 12008	THE FABULOUS DAVE BRUBECK TRIO AND OCTET (LP)	15
59	Fontana STFL 523	TIME OUT (LP, stereo)	60
59	Fontana TFL 5085	TIME OUT (LP, mono)	50
59	CBS BPG 62068	TIME OUT (LP)	40
59	Fontana TFL 5071	GONE WITH THE WIND (LP, also stereo STFL 501)	15
60	Vogue LAE 12114	DAVE BRUBECK QUARTET FEATURING PAUL DESMOND (LP)	15
60	Fontana (S)TFL 532	THE RIDDLE (LP)	18
60	Fontana (S)TFL 530	SOUTHERN SCENE (LP)	15
61	CBS BPG 62078	TIME FURTHER OUT (LP)	20
61	Fontana TFL 5160	TIME FURTHER OUT (LP)	20
62	CBS BDG 62013	COUNTDOWN TIME IN OUTER SPACE (LP)	18
64	CBS SPBG 62431	JAZZ IMPRESSIONS OF JAPAN (LP)	20

(see also Jimmy Rushing, Carmen McRae)

JACK BRUCE
65	Polydor BM 56036	I'm Getting Tired (Of Drinking And Gambling)/Rootin' Tootin'	100
71	Polydor 2058 153	The Consul At Sunset/Letter Of Thanks	15
69	Polydor 583 058	SONGS FOR A TAILOR (LP, laminated gatefold sleeve)	18
70	Polydor 2343 033	THINGS WE LIKE (LP)	18
71	Polydor 2310 070	THINGS WE LIKE (LP, reissue)	15
71	Polydor 2310 107	HARMONY ROW (LP, gatefold sleeve)	20

(see also Alexis Korner's Blues Incorporated, Cream, Manfred Mann, Graham Bond Organisation, John Mayall, West Bruce & Laing, Lifetime, Rocket 88, Carla Bley, Duffy Power, Cozy Powell)

TOMMY BRUCE (& BRUISERS)
64	Columbia DB 7387	Over Suzanne/It's Drivin' Me Wild	15
65	Polydor BM 56006	Boom Boom/Can Your Monkey Do The Dog (with Bruisers)	20
66	RCA RCA 1535	Monster Gonzales/I Hate Getting Up In The Morning	20
61	Columbia SEG 8077	KNOCKOUT (EP)	50

HEIDI BRÜHL
60	Philips PB 1095	Ring Of Gold/I'll Belong To You Forever (in p/s)	10
69	Philips BF 1768	The Drifter/Berlin	200
69	Philips BF 1768	The Drifter/Berlin (DJ Copy)	250

BRUISERS
63	Parlophone R 5042	Blue Girl/Don't Cry	10
63	Parlophone R 5092	Your Turn To Cry/Give It To Me	10

(see also [Peter] Lee Stirling & Bruisers)

BRUMBEATS
64	Decca F 11834	Cry Little Girl, Cry/I Don't Understand	15

BRUNNING (HALL) SUNFLOWER BLUES BAND
68	Saga FID 2118	BULLEN STREET BLUES (LP, as Brunning Sunflower Blues Band, with black/silver label)	30
69	Saga EROS 8132	TRACKSIDE BLUES (LP, black/silver labels)	45
70	Saga EROS 8150	I WISH YOU WOULD (LP, as Brunning Sunflower Blues Band, with black/silver labels)	75
71	Gemini GM 2010	THE BRUNNING/HALL SUNFLOWER BLUES BAND (LP, with white/red labels)	120

(see also Five's Company, Fleetwood Mac, Leaf Hound)

BRUNO
66	Parlophone R5450	Wonderboy/Window In My Room	20
66	Parlophone R5507	The English Girl/The Driver	20

TONY BRUNO
68	Capitol CL 15534	What's Yesterday/Small Town, Bring Down	50

BRUTE FORCE
69	Apple APPLE 8	King Of Fuh/Nobody Knows (unissued)	2000

BRUTUS
75	Purple PUR 126	Payroll/New Deal Princess	7

TONY BRUTUS
82	Intense INT 013	Water Pistol/Shooting Water (12")	100
13	Intense/Pressure Sounds PST110	Water Pistol/Water Pistol (Alt Vocal)/Water Pistol (Dub) (12")	25

CARL BRYAN
69	Trojan TR 673	Red Ash/SILVERTONES: Bluebirds Flying Over	30
69	Duke DU 13	Soul Pipe/Overproof	30
69	Camel CA 22	Run For Your Life/TWO SPARKS: When We Were Young	25
69	Gas GAS 133	Stagger Back/The Creeper	50
69	Gas GAS 134	Walking The Dead/TREVOR & KEITH: Got What You Want	30

(see also Cannon Ball & Johnny Melody, King Cannon, Vincent Foster, Hugh Malcolm, King Cannonball, Glen Brown, Shenley Duffas, Alton Ellis, Kid Gungo, Jackie Mittoo, Johnny Moore, Joe White, Royals)

RAD BRYAN
71	Techniques TE 909	Jumping Jack/ANSELL COLLINS: Point Blank	30
71	Bullet BU 463	Shock Attack/Cuban Waltz	30
71	Big Shot BI 559	Just Do The Right Things/Corporal Jones	20
71	Big Shot BI 591	I'll Be Right There (actually by Techniques)/PLAYBOYS: Hot Pants Rock	30

Tim BRYAN

MINT VALUE £

71	Big Shot BI 592	My Best Girl/My Best Girl Version	20
71	Black Swan BW 1410	Girl You Rock My Soul/Version	35
72	Attack ATT 8040	Standing In The Rain (actually by Neville Grant)/Standing In The Rain Version	10
75	Love 1	Rock Children/Version	7

TIM BRYAN
| 71 | Phillips 6006026 | Mary Anne/It's So Easy | 8 |

WES BRYAN
| 58 | London HLU 8607 | Lonesome Love/Tiny Spaceman | 40 |
| 59 | London HLU 8978 | Honey Baby/So Blue Over You | 50 |

BRYAN & BRUNELLES
| 65 | HMV POP 1394 | Jacqueline/Louie Louie | 45 |

ANITA BRYANT
66	CBS 202026	Another Year, Another Love/My Mind's Playing Tricks On Me Again	50
62	CBS AAG 20005	KISSES SWEETER THAN WINE (EP)	10
61	London HA-L 2381	IN MY LITTLE CORNER OF THE WORLD (LP)	30

BOUDLEAUX BRYANT
| 60 | Polydor NH 66952 | Hot Spot/Touché (with Sparks) | 6 |

(see also Bood & Fileece Bryant)

DON BRYANT
| 70 | London HA-U/SH-U 8409 | PRECIOUS SOUL (LP) | 40 |

JAY DEE BRYANT
| 76 | Island WIP 6273 | Standing Ovation For Love/I Want To Thank You Baby | 10 |

JOHN BRYANT (1)
| 65 | Fontana H 625 | Tell Me What You See/Poor Unfortunate Me | 15 |
| 71 | Polydor 2383069 | JOHN BRYANT (LP, gatefold sleeve) | 20 |

JOHN BRYANT (2)
69	Decca 12894	She's In Need Of Love	25
68	MCA MU 1020	Columbine/I Bring The Sun	20
71	Polydor 2058-145	Back On The Road/I Won't Sleep Tonight/Ain't Got No Woman	6

LAURA K. BRYANT
| 58 | London HLU 8551 | Bobby/Angel Tears | 20 |

MARIE/MARGARET BRYANT
61	Kalypso XX 27	Water Melon/Tomato	6
61	Kalypso XX 28	Don't Touch Me Nylons/Little Boy	6
60s	Melodisc MLP 12 132	DON'T TOUCH ME NYLONS (LP, with sleeve)	25

MATT BRYANT & LINDA JOYCE
| 60 | Embassy WB 420 | Goodness Gracious Me/STEVE STANNARD & HIS GROUP: Man Of Mystery | 6 |

(see also Maureen Evans)

RUSTY BRYANT
| 57 | London HB-D 1066 | RUSTY BRYANT (10" LP) | 30 |

SANDRA BRYANT
| 67 | Major Minor MM 523 | Girl With Money/Golden Hours | 10 |
| 68 | Major Minor MM 553 | Out To Get You/There's No Lock Upon My Door | 30 |

GAVIN BRYARS
75	Obscure OBS 1	THE SINKING OF THE TITANIC (LP, 1st pressing with grey labels)	70
76	Obscure OBS 1	THE SINKING OF THE TITANIC (LP, 2nd pressing with red labels)	60
78	Obscure OBS 8	MACHINE MUSIC (split LP with John White)	20
87	EG EGED 21	THE SINKING OF THE TITANIC (LP, reissue)	20

(see also Brian Eno)

CALUM BRYCE
| 68 | Condor PS 1001 | Lovemaker/I'm Glad | 475 |

BERYL BRYDEN('S BACK-ROOM SKIFFLE)
56	Decca F 10823	Casey Jones/Kansas City Blues	20
57	Decca (no cat. no.)	Rock Me/This Train (test pressing, with Alexis Korner & Cyril Davies)	60
63	Columbia DB 4860	I'm Movin' On/Moanin'	10
63	Columbia DB 7010	I'm Living With The Blues/Big Daddy	10

(see also Alexis Korner, Cyril Davies)

BETSY BRYE
| 59 | Columbia DB 4350 | Sleep Walk/Daddy Daddy (Gotta Get A Phone In My Room) | 25 |

BRYGADA KRYZYS
| 82 | Fresh Records FRESH 13 | BRYGADA KRYZYS (LP) | 25 |

B'S
| 70s | private pressing | IN YOUR BONNET (LP) | 35 |

B SIDE
| 93 | B Promo B Side | Rip Piece Off/Can't Slow Me Down (12") | 20 |

B.T.B.
| 68 | Liberty LBF 15067 | Do It To 'Em/Sparrows And Daisies | 15 |

B.T. EXPRESS
| 75 | Pye Intl. NSPL 28207 | DO IT (TIL YOU'RE SATISFIED) (LP) | 15 |
| 75 | EMI International INA 1501 | NON-STOP (LP) | 15 |

B.T.P. FOLDERS
| 80 | Future Earth FER 005 | Radio/All Of A Sudden (p/s) | 50 |

B TROOP
| 81 | Illuminated JAMS 6 | EUROPEANS (LP) | 15 |

B12
94	B12 15	B12 (12", 4-track promo only, 10 copies pressed)	40
93	Warp WAPLP 9LTD	ELECTRO - SOMA (2-LP, orange vinyl)	40
96	Warp WARPLP 37	TIME TOURISTS (2-LP)	20
07	B12 B1215	Practopia (12")	20

(see also Redcell, Musicology)

BUBA & SHOP ASSISTANTS
| | MINT VALUE £ |

BUBA & SHOP ASSISTANTS
85 Villa 21 002 — Something To Do/Dreaming Backwards (p/s, with insert in poly bag) 75

(see also Shop Assistants, Pastels)

BUBBLEGUM
68 Philips BF1677 — Little Red Bucket/With The Sun In Your Hair 45

BUBBLEGUM SPLASH
87 Bonk On 001 — If Only/THE DARLING BUDS: Spin (flexidisc free with So Naive fanzine) 10
88 Subway 13 — SPLASHDOWN EP 10

BUBBLEMEN
88 Beggars Banquet BUB1 — The Bubblemen Are Coming/B Side (p/s, comic included) 6

(see also Bauhaus)

BUBBLES & CO
65 Pye 7N 15875 — Underneath My Pillow/Just One Girl 8

BUBBLES (1)
63 Duke DK 1001 — The Wasp/Bopping In The Barnyard (matrix: DK 1001A-1, plays Rocking Crickets by Hot Toddy's) 18

BUBBLES (2)
72 Bumble GE 117 — Hazy Hazy Crazy Crazy/Audrey 8
75 Decca F 13583 — This Is Where The Hurdie Gurdie Heebie Geebie Greenie Meenie Man Came In/Zap N' Cat 35
78 Rainbow RS 611 — Jamais/Night Life 8

BUCCA
82 Plant Life PLR 039 — THE HOLE IN THE HARPERS HEAD (LP) 20

BUCHANAN BROTHERS
69 Page One POF 139 — Medicine Man Part 1/Part 2 8
70 Penny Farthing PEN 725 — Rosianna/The Feeling That I Get When Your Near 6

GILLY BUCHANAN
80 Toe TOE 002 — Me No Mix/PATRICK ANDY: Ain't No Me (12") 80

LINDSEY BUCKINGHAM
84 Mercury MERX 168 — Go Insane (Extended Remix)/(Go Insane (Dub Mix)/Play In The Rain Part 1 (12" white label promo with 1 on side 1 and 2 on side 2) 100
13 Back On Black RCV078LP — SEEDS WE SOW (2-LP, reissue, clear red vinyl) 80

(see also Fleetwood Mac)

BUCKINGHAM-NICKS
74 Polydor 2066 398 — Don't Let Me Down Again/Races Are Run 15
76 Polydor 2066 700 — Don't Let Me Down Again/Crystal 10
73 Polydor 2391 013 — BUCKINGHAM-NICKS (LP, with insert, with stickered sleeve) 40
73 Polydor 2391 093 — BUCKINGHAM-NICKS (LP, with insert, without stickered sleeve) 35
81 Polydor 2482 378 — BUCKINGHAM-NICKS (LP, reissue with insert) 25

(see also Lindsay Buckingham, Fleetwood Mac)

BUCKINGHAMS (U.S.)
67 Stateside SS 588 — Kind Of A Drag/You Make Me Feel So Good 12
67 CBS 2859 — Mercy Mercy Mercy/You Are Gone 12
67 CBS 2995 — Hey Baby/And Our Love 15
68 CBS 2640 — Don't You Care/Why Don't You Love Me 25
68 CBS 3559 — Back In Love Again/You Misunderstand Me 6
69 CBS 3195 — Susan/Foreign Policy 10

BOB BUCKLE
73 Ash ALP 107 S — COME LISTEN TO (LP) 50

BUCKLEY
72 CBS 58303 — My My My/Goodbye Wurzel Gummage 12

JEFF BUCKLEY
93 Big Cat ABB 61XCD — LIVE AT SIN-E EP (Mojo Pin/Eternal Life/Je N'en Connais Pas La Fin/The Way Young Lovers Do (CD) 30
95 Columbia 662042 1 — Last Goodbye (Edit)/Lover, You Should've Come Over (Live And Acoustic In Japan)/Tongue (Live) (10", p/s, 5000 only) 30
95 Columbia 661498 — Last Goodbye/Last Goodbye (Full)/So Real (Live)/Dream Brother (Live) (12") 30
95 Columbia 88697098847 — Hallelujah/I Know It's Over (Live 1995) (p/s, numbered sleeve, 2,700 only, blue/black vinyl) 20
13 Music On Vinyl MOV 7017 — Hallelujah/LEONARD COHEN: Hallelujah (numbered 7") 6
04 Big Cat ABB 61X — LIVE AT SIN-E (12" reissue) 40
94 Columbia 475928 — GRACE (LP, with insert) 60
98 Columbia 3C 67229 — SKETCHES FOR MY SWEETHEART THE DRUNK (3-LP) 40
99 Simply Vinyl SVLP 077 — GRACE (LP, reissue, insert) 25
07 Columbia 4979721 — MYSTERY WHITE BOY LIVE 95-96 (LP) 20

SEAN BUCKLEY & BREADCRUMBS
65 Stateside SS 421 — It Hurts Me When I Cry/Everybody Knows 70

TIM BUCKLEY
67 Elektra EKSN 45008 — Aren't You The Girl/Strange Street Affair Under Blue 15
67 Elektra EKSN 45018 — Morning Glory/Knight-Errant 10
68 Elektra EKSN 45023 — Once I Was/Phantasmagoria In Two 7
68 Elektra EKSN 45031 — Wings/I Can't See You 7
68 Elektra EKSN 45041 — Pleasant Street/Carnival Song 10
70 Straight S 4799 — Happy Time/So Lonely 20
91 Strange Fruit SFPS082 — THE PEEL SESSIONS: Morning Glory/Coming Home To You/ Sing A Song For You/Hallucinations/Troubadour/Once I Was (12", p/s) 10
66 Elektra EKL 4004 — TIM BUCKLEY (LP, dark orange label, black lettering, mono) 75
67 Elektra EKS 74004 — TIM BUCKLEY (LP, dark orange label, black lettering, stereo) 75
67 Elektra EKL 318 — GOODBYE AND HELLO (LP, dark orange label, gatefold sleeve, mono) 70
67 Elektra EKS 7318 — GOODBYE AND HELLO (LP, dark orange label, gatefold sleeve, stereo) 75
68 Elektra EKS 74045 — HAPPY SAD (LP, light orange label, silver lettering) 70
69 Straight STS 1060 — BLUE AFTERNOON (LP) 80

Vernon BUCKLEY

MINT VALUE £

70	Elektra 2410 005	LORCA (LP)	50
71	Straight STS 1064	STARSAILOR (LP)	100
74	Warner Bros K 46176	GREETINGS FROM L.A. (LP, gatefold sleeve, postcard)	25
74	Elektra K42072	HAPPY SAD (LP, reissue, butterfly label)	20
74	Discreet K 49201	SEFRONIA (LP)	25
74	Discreet K 59204	LOOK AT THE FOOL (LP)	25
76	Elektra K42079	GOODBYE AND HELLO (LP, reissue, inside loading gatefold sleeve, Butterfly label)	20
84	Elektra ELK 42079	GOODBYE AND HELLO (LP, reissue, red label)	15
90	Demon DFIEND 200	DREAM LETTER - LIVE IN LONDON 1968 (2-LP)	25

VERNON BUCKLEY
73	Grape GR 3057	Mr Softhand/G.G. ALLSTARS: Dub	10
73	Grape GR 3058	Ital Queen/G.G. ALLSTARS: Dub	10

SID BUCKNOR PRODUCTIONS
76	Lyntone/Tropical Sounds DSR SB1008/1009	DUB SENSATION (LP, 50 copies, promo only in stamped white card sleeve)	250

BUCKY & STRINGS
62	Salvo SLO 1807	Lolita's On The Loose/Lonely Island (99 copies only)	20

BILLY BUDD
69	Page One POF 138	Alice Long (You're Still My Favourite Girlfriend)/The Straight Life	20
70	Pye 7N 45010	You're Sailing Away/I'm Gonna Change It	12

HAROLD BUDD
78	Obscure OBS 10	PAVILLION OF DREAMS (LP)	20

HAROLD BUDD & BRIAN ENO
80	Editions EG EGAMB 002	AMBIENT 2 (THE PLATEAUS OF MIRRORS) (LP)	40
87	Editions EG EGED 18	AMBIENT 2 (THE PLATEAUS OF MIRRORS) (LP, reissue)	15

(see also Brian Eno)

ROY BUDD
65	Pye 7N 15807	Birth Of The Budd/M'Ghee M'Ghee	15
67	Pye 7N 17279	Mr Rose/Summer Rain	10
70	Pye 7N 45051	Carter (Theme)/Plaything (in p/s)	70
70	Pye 7N 45051	Carter (Theme)/Plaything	50
19 34	Dynamite Cuts DYNAM7033	Main Title Theme Get Carter/Gettin' Nowhere In A Hurry/Love Is A Four Letter Word/Hallucinations (reissue, 2 x 7", p/s)	12
68	Pye NPL 18212	AT NEWPORT (LP)	18
71	Pye NSPL 18348	PLAYS SOLDIER BLUE AND OTHER THEMES (LP)	20
72	Polydor 2383 102	KIDNAPPED (Roy Budd/Mary Hopkin)	25
72	Pye NSPL 18389	CONCERTO FOR HARRY - SOMETHING TO HIDE (Roy Budd)	25
73	Pye NSPL 18398	FEAR IS THE KEY (LP, soundtrack)	50
76	Bradley's BRADS 8002	DIAMONDS (LP, soundtrack)	50
70s	Pye NSPL 19494	EVERYTHING'S COMING UP (LP)	15
99	Cinephile CINLP001	GET CARTER (LP, gatefold)	25
00	Cinephile CINLP004	THE BLACK WINDMILL (LP, gatefold)	30

BUDDY & SKETTO
62	Dice 45/CC 7	Little Schoolgirl/Hush Baby	25

(see also Ruddy & Sketto, Sketto Rich)

BUDGIE
71	MCA MK 5072	Crash Course In Brain Surgery/Nude Disintegrating Parachutist Woman	20
72	MCA MK 5085	Whisky River/Guts	8
74	MCA MCA 133	Zoom Club (Edited Version)/Wondering What Everyone Knows	6
75	MCA MCA 175	I Ain't No Mountain/Honey	6
78	A&M AMS 7342	Smile Boy Smile/All At Sea	6
80	Active BUDGE	Wildfire/Wildfire (promo only)	10
80	Active BUDGE 1	IF SWALLOWED DO NOT INDUCE VOMITING (12" EP)	10
80	Active BUDGE 2	Crime Against The World/Hellbender (p/s)	8
71	MCA MKPS 2018	BUDGIE (LP, pink/red label, initial pressing with laminated sleeve and poster)	150
71	MCA MKPS 2018	BUDGIE (LP, pink/red label, with no poster)	100
71	MCA MKPS 2018	BUDGIE (LP, later pressing with blue/black label)	15
72	MCA MKPS 2023	SQUAWK (LP, 1st pressing, Matrix numbers: 7-LNMG-216-1l/262-1L, blue/black hexagon label, matt sleeve)	50
72	MCA MKPS 2023	SQUAWK (LP, 2nd pressing, black label, matt sleeve)	40
73	MCA MDKS 8010	NEVER TURN YOUR BACK ON A FRIEND (LP, black label, gatefold sleeve)	100
74	MCA MDKS 8010	NEVER TURN YOUR BACK ON A FRIEND (LP, reissue, rainbow label, gatefold sleev	40
74	MCA MCF 2546	IN FOR THE KILL (LP, rainbow label, black background)	40
75	MCA MCF 2723	BANDOLIER (LP)	30
75	MCA MCF 2766	THE BEST OF BUDGIE (LP)	15
76	A&M AMLH 68277	IF I WAS BRITANNIA I'D WAIVE THE RULES (LP, silver/green label)	15
78	A&M AMLH 64675	IMPECKABLE (LP)	15
80	Active ACTLP 1	POWER SUPPLY (LP, with insert)	15
80	RCA RCALP 3046	POWER SUPPLY (LP, reissue, with different back sleeve)	20
81	RCA RCALP 6003	NIGHT FLIGHT (LP)	15
82	RCA RCALP 6054	DELIVER US FROM EVIL (LP)	15

(see also Tredegar, Phenomena, George Hatcher Band)

NANA BUDJEI
88	Asona ARLP 015	AFRIKAMAN (LP)	20
90	KBN 0248	YONKO PA (LP)	18

DENNIS BUDLIMAR
67	Fontana TL 5307	THE CREEPER (LP)	20

BUENA VISTAS
66	Stateside SS 525	Hot Shot/T.N.T.	25

BUFFALO
81	Heavy Metal HEAVY 3	Battle Torn Heroes/Women Of The Night (p/s)	30

BUFFALO SPRINGFIELD

BUFFALO SPRINGFIELD

Year	Label/Cat No	Title	Mint Value £
82	Heavy Metal HEAVY 15	Mean Machine/The Rumour (p/s)	25
67	Atlantic 584 077	For What It's Worth (Stop Hey What's That Sound)/Do I Have To Come Right Out And Say It	25
67	Atlantic 584 145	Rock'n'Roll Woman/A Child's Claim To Fame	15
68	Atlantic 584 165	Expecting To Fly/Everydays	15
68	Atlantic 584 189	Uno-Mundo/Merry-Go-Round	15
69	Atco 226 006	Pretty Girl Why/Questions	10
72	Atlantic K 10237	Bluebird/Mr Soul/Rock'n'Roll Woman/Expecting To Fly (p/s)	6
67	Atlantic 587 070	BUFFALO SPRINGFIELD (LP, plum label, mispressing, lists "For What It's Worth" but plays "Baby Don't Scold Me"; matrix no. ends '1' mono)	120
67	Atlantic 588 070	BUFFALO SPRINGFIELD ((LP, plum label, mispressing, lists "For What It's Worth" but plays "Baby Don't Scold Me"; matrix no. ends '1' stereo)	70
67	Atlantic 587 070	BUFFALO SPRINGFIELD (LP, plum label, plays "For What It's Worth", mono)	50
67	Atlantic 588 070	BUFFALO SPRINGFIELD (LP, plum label, plays "For What It's Worth", stereo)	40
68	Atlantic 587 091	BUFFALO SPRINGFIELD AGAIN (LP, plum label, mono)	70
68	Atlantic 588 091	BUFFALO SPRINGFIELD AGAIN (LP, plum label, stereo)	50
69	Atco 228 024	LAST TIME AROUND (LP, plum label, gatefold sleeve)	40
69	Atco 228 012	RETROSPECTIVE (LP, plum label)	25
70	Atlantic 2464 012	EXPECTING TO FLY (LP, plum label)	25
72	Atlantic K 40014	BUFFALO SPRINGFIELD AGAIN (LP, reissue, green & orange label)	15
72	Atlantic K 40077	LAST TIME AROUND (LP, reissue, green & orange label, gatefold sleeve)	15
73	Atlantic K 30028	BUFFALO SPRINGFIELD - ATLANTIC MASTERS: THE BEGINNNING (LP)	15

(see also Neil Young, Stephen Stills, Au-Go-Go Singers, Crosby Stills Nash & Young)

BUFFALO TOM

Year	Label/Cat No	Title	Mint Value £
89	Caff CAFF 6	Enemy/Deep In The Ground (p/s)	20
92	Situation 2 SITU 36	LET ME COME OVER (LP)	15
93	Beggars Banquet BBQLP 142	BIG RED LETTER DAY (LP)	15

BUFF MEDWAYS

Year	Label/Cat No	Title	Mint Value £
00	Friends Of...FOBMFA 2	Fire/Manic Depression (die-cut sleeve)	8
01	Vinyl Japan PAD 74	Into Your Dreams/Highway Chile (p/s)	8
01	Hangman 004	Sally Sensation/Dawn Said What Have I Done	8
02	Transcopic TRAN 012	A Strange Kind Of Happyness/BILLY CHILDISH: Hound Dog (p/s, 500 only)	8
02	Transcopic TRAN 015	Troubled Mind/BILLY CHILDISH: Leave My Kitten Alone (p/s, 500 only)	10
02	Transcopic TRAN 017	Strood Lights/You Make Me Die (p/s)	10
01	Vinyl Japan ASKLP 132	THIS IS THIS (LP)	25
02	Transcopic TRANLP 016	STEADY THE BUFFS (LP)	25
03	Transcopic TRANLP 026	1914 (LP, as the Buffs)	20

(see also Billy Childish, Wild Billy Childish & Buff Medways, Nilkshakes, Thee Headcoats)

BUFFOONS

Year	Label/Cat No	Title	Mint Value £
67	Columbia DB 8217	My World Fell Down/Tomorrow Is Another Day	18

BUG

Year	Label/Cat No	Title	Mint Value £
08	Ninja Tune ZEN 132	LONDON ZOO (3-LP, gatefold)	20

BUG CENTRAL

Year	Label/Cat No	Title	Mint Value £
99	Dole Office/DHSS 1	Gotta Get A Real Job/No Free Records (Unreleased, white label test pressings only)	35
99	Helen Of Oi HOO 48	THE MEEK WILL INHERIT NOTHING (LP, with inserts)	15

JAKE BUGG

Year	Label/Cat No	Title	Mint Value £
12	Kitchenware JAKE 01	Trouble Town/Someone Told Me (p/s)	50
13	EMI (No Cat/ No.)	What Doesn't Kill You (1-sided, die-cut sleeve)	20
14	Secret 7" S717	Strange Creatures (100 only, each in unique art sleeve)	20
12	Mercury 3717304	JAKE BUGG (LP)	15

THE BUGGER ALL STARS

Year	Label/Cat No	Title	Mint Value £
81	Bead Records BEAD 19	THE BUGGER ALL STARS (LP)	20
83	Bead Records BEAD 21	BONZO BITES BACK (LP)	20

BUGGIS

Year	Label/Cat No	Title	Mint Value £
75	Third World TW 031	Duggis Is Mood/GENE RONDO: Declaration Of Rights	20

BUGGY

Year	Label/Cat No	Title	Mint Value £
70	Parlophone R5832	The Rolly Pole Coaster/Harry The Keeper	15

BUKKSHEE

Year	Label/Cat No	Title	Mint Value £
86	Lyntone BUK 13	In The Country/Sting In The Tail	10

SANDY BULL

Year	Label/Cat No	Title	Mint Value £
69	Vanguard 19040	E PLURIBUS UNUM (LP)	25

BULLAMAKANKA

Year	Label/Cat No	Title	Mint Value £
83	BBC REL 454	Dr Who Is Gonna Fix It/Harlequin	10

BULLDOG BREED

Year	Label/Cat No	Title	Mint Value £
69	Deram DM 270	Portcullis Gate/Halo In My Hair	150
70	Deram Nova DN 5	MADE IN ENGLAND (LP, mono)	350
70	Deram Nova SDN 5	MADE IN ENGLAND (LP, stereo)	300
02	Acme ADLP 1036	MADE IN ENGLAND (LP, reissue with free 7")	15

(see also Flies)

BULLDOGS

Year	Label/Cat No	Title	Mint Value £
64	Mercury MF 808	John, Paul, George And Ringo/What Do I See	20

BULLET TRAIN

Year	Label/Cat No	Title	Mint Value £
79	Sidewalk 12YSID 109	Don't Hold Back My Bullets/Bang Bang (12")	39

BULLET (1)

Year	Label/Cat No	Title	Mint Value £
71	Purple PUR 101	Hobo/Sinister Minister	20
75	Polydor 2058 548	Hanged Man/The Contract Man	10
75	Contour 2870 437	THE HANGED MAN (LP, TV soundtrack)	40

(see also Hard Stuff, Quatermass, Atomic Rooster)

BULLET (2)

Year	Label/Cat No	Title	Mint Value £
78	Pennine PSS 138	Don't Go/Streetcrawler (500 only)	20

BULLETS

MINT VALUE £

BULLETS
78   Big Bear BB 16   Girl On Page 3/Grammar School Girls (p/s) 15

BULLFROG
74   Cube BUG 44   Clancy/In The City 8

JOHN BULL BREED
66   Polydor BM 56065   Can't Chance A Breakup/I'm A Man 375

BULL MINSTRELS
73   Boston /Guildhall GHS 9   HORNCASTLE FAYRE (LP) 20

BULLRING
70   CBS 4881   Birmingham Brass Band/Lady Of The Morning Sun 15

BULLSEYE
80   Kennet K1   No. 10,553/Why Don't You Let Me Know 8

BULLY BOYS BAND
70   Stateside SSL 5232   MOVIE SCENE - HEAVY SOUNDS FROM TODAY'S FILMS (LP) 20

BULLY WEE (BAND)
75   Folksound FS 102   BULLYWEE (LP) 20
76   Red Rag RRR 007   THE ENCHANTED LADY (LP) 15
78   Red Rag RRR 017   SILVERMINES (LP, as Bullywee Band, with insert) 15
80   Jigsaw SAW 1   THE MADMAN OF GOTHAM (LP) 20

B. BUMBLE & STINGERS
61   Top Rank JAR 561   Bumble Boogie/School Day Blues 6
62   Stateside SE 1001   THE PIANO STYLINGS OF B. BUMBLE (EP) 12
(see also Kim Fowley)

BUMBLE BEE SLIM
60s Fontana 688 138ZL   BEE'S BACK IN TOWN (LP) 25

BUMBLEBEE UNLIMITED
79   Sky SKY1004   Love Bug/Disco Version 15
14   Groove Line GLR12 003   Lady Bug (Disco Mix)/Lady Bug (Disco Remix) (12" reissue) 15

BUMBLES
72   Purple PUR 107   Beep Beep/Buzz Off (promo only p/s) 25
72   Purple PUR 107   Beep Beep/Buzz Off 8
(see laos Hard Stuff, Atomic Rooster, Curtis Muldoon)

BUNCH
67   CBS 202506   We're Not What We Appear To Be/You Never Came Home 70
67   CBS 2740   Don't Come Back To Me/You Can't Do This 25
67   CBS 3060   Looking Glass Alice/Spare A Shilling 200
68   CBS 3692   Birthday/Still 30
68   CBS 3709   Birthday/Still (reissue) 15
69   Beacon BEA 128   Red Rover, Red Rover/Happy Like This 10
72   Island WIP 6130   When Will I Be Loved/Willie And The Hand Jive 10
72   Island ILPS 9189   ROCK ON (LP, with 1-sided flexi attached to die-cut sleeve: "Let There Be Drums" [WI 4002]) 75
72   Island ILPS 9189   ROCK ON (LP, without 1-sided flexi: "Let There Be Drums" [WI 4002]) 25
(see also Peter & The Wolves, Sounds Around, John Pantry)

BUNCH OF FIVES
66   Parlophone R 5494   Go Home Baby/At The Station 120
(see also Viv Prince, Egg, Hullaballoos, Junior's Eyes, Outsiders [U.K.])

BUNDLE
70   Polydor 2058 029   Dirty La Rue/Progressive Underground 15

ROGER BUNN
70   Major Minor SMLP 70   PIECE OF MIND (LP, red/white/black label) 200
(see also Pete Browns Pitlokto, Roxy Music)

BUNNIES (OF LONDON)
68   Decca LK4951   CAUGHT LIVE AT THE PLAYBOY CLUB (LP) 20
69   Decca SKL5026   THE BUNNIES AGAIN SINGIN' AND SWINGIN' AT THE LONDON PLAYBOY CLUB (LP) 20

BUNNY & RICKY
75   Attack ATT 8107   Two Bad Bull (as Bunnie And Rickey)(actually by Pat Simpson)/UPSETTERS: Bad Cow 30
75   Attack ATT 8109   Bushwood Contrash/UPSETTERS: Callying Butt 30
75   Locks LOX 11   Freedom Fighter/UPSETTERS: Iron Wolf 15

BUNNY & RUDDY
68   Nu Beat NB 007   Rhythm & Soul/BOBBY KALPHAT: True Romance 80
68   Nu Beat NB 011   On The Town/MONTY MORRIS: Simple Simon 40

BINGY BUNNY
82   Cha Cha CHAD 46   Keep It In The Family (with MORWELLS/SCIENTIST : Extended Dub/Me & Jane (with MORWELLS/SCIENTIST : Extended Dub (12") 40
82   Cha Cha CHAD 48   Street Lover (with MORWELLS/NICODEMUS : How You Look Girl 'Pon The Street (12") ... 30
82   Cha Cha CHALP 015   ME & JANE (LP) 50

BINGY BUNNY & BONGO LES
73   Ackee ACK 506   International Scout/International Scout Version 12
(see also Bongo Les, Mediators)

BUNNY BROWN
72   Songbird SB 1073   Fat Boy/Fat Boy - Version 15
78   JCB JCB 002   I Love The Way You Love/Version 18
(see also Noel Brown, Winston Scotland)

BUNNY LION
77   M&M MM03   Introducing Bunny Lion/REVOLUTIONARIES: Version (12", as Linval Thompson) 20
79   Starlight SLP 900   RED (LP) 25

BUNNY MACK
80   Rokel MACK 1   Let Me Love You/Love You Forever (12") 20

BOB BUNTING
68   Transatlantic TRA 166   YOU'VE GOT TO GO DOWN THIS WAY (LP) 50

VASHTI BUNYAN
70	Philips 6308 019	JUST ANOTHER DIAMOND DAY (LP)	1500
00	Spinney SPINNEY 001	JUST ANOTHER DIAMOND DAY (LP, reissue, gatefold)	20
05	Fat Cat FATLP 38	LOOKAFTERING (LP)	20
07	Fat Cat FATLP 59	SOME THINGS JUST STICK IN YOUR MIND (SINGLES AND DEMOS 1964-1967) (2-LP)	25

(see also Vashti, Fairport Convention, Dave Swarbrick, Robin Williamson)

BUOYS
70	Wand WN7	Timothy/It Feels Good	20
71	Wand MSW 8296	Give Up Your Guns/The Prince Of Thieves	15

VERNON BURCH
75	United Artists UAS 29743	I'LL BE YOUR SUNSHINE (LP)	15

DONI BURDICK
10	Outta Sight/Ron's OSV006	Candle (In The Window)/Whatcha Gonna Do (reissue)	10

ERIC BURDON (BAND)
75	Capitol E-ST 11426	STOP (LP, as Eric Burdon Band)	15
78	Polydor 2302 078	SURVIVOR (LP, with 5 inserts with lyrics and drawings)	25

ERIC BURDON & THE ANIMALS
66	Decca F 12502	Mama Told Me Not To Come/See See Rider (unreleased)	0
66	Decca F 12502	Help Me Girl/See See Rider (amended issue with new A-side)	8
67	MGM MGM 1340	When I Was Young/A Girl Named Sandoz	8
67	MGM MGM 1344	Good Times/Ain't That So	8
67	MGM MGM 1359	San Franciscan Nights/Gratefully Dead	10
68	MGM MGM 1373	Sky Pilot (Parts 1 & 2)	10
68	MGM MGM 1412	Monterey/Anything	8
69	MGM MGM 1461	Ring Of Fire/I'm An Animal	8
69	MGM MGM 1481	River Deep Mountain High/Help Me Girl	8
67	MGM C(S) 8052	WINDS OF CHANGE (LP, yellow/black label with "sold in the U.K." label text)	80
68	MGM C(S) 8074	THE TWAIN SHALL MEET (LP, yellow black labels with "sold in the U.K." text)	80
68	MGM C(S) 8105	LOVE IS (LP, blue/gold labels with "sold in the U.K." text)	100
71	MGM 2619 002	LOVE IS (2-LP; individual LP nos.: 2354 006/7)	50

(see also Animals, Stud, Zoot Money's Big Roll Band)

ERIC BURDON & WAR
70	Polydor 2001 072	Spill The Wine/Magic Mountain	7
70	Polydor 2310 041	ERIC BURDON DECLARES WAR (LP)	35
70	Liberty LDS 8400 3/4	BLACKMAN'S BURDON (2-LP, gatefold, with banned track "P.C. 3")	45
70	Liberty LDS 8400	BLACKMAN'S BURDON (2-LP, gatefold, without banned track "P.C. 3")	20

(see also War)

ERIC BURDON & JIMMY WITHERSPOON
71	United Artists UP 35287	Soledad/Headin' For Home	6
71	United Artists UAG 29251	GUILTY! (LP, gatefold sleeve)	18

(see also Jimmy Witherspoon)

DAVID BURGE
69	Vox STGBY 637	AVANT GARDE PIANO MUSIC (LP)	15

DAVE BURGESS (TRIO)
55	London HLB 8175	I Love Paris/Five Foot Two, Eyes Of Blue (Has Anybody Seen My Girl)	10
58	Oriole CB 1413	I'm Available/Who's Gonna Cry?	20

LEROY BURGESS
01	Soul Brother LP SBPJ 6	ANTHOLOGY 1 - THE VOICE (2-LP)	35
07	Soul Brother LP SBPJ 34	THROWBACK HARLEM 79-83 (2-LP, compilation)	25

MARK BURGESS AND THE SONS OF GOD
93	Imaginary ILLUSION 44	ZIMA JUNCTION (LP)	40

(see also Chameleons)

SONNY BURGESS
60	London HLS 9064	Sadie's Back In Town/A Kiss Goodnight	200

TIM BURGESS
03	PIAS B099LP	I BELIEVE (LP)	25

(see also Charlatans (U.K.))

JIM BURGETT
61	Philips PB 1133	Let's Investigate/The Living Dead	40

BURGUNDY BLOOD
13	Chopped Herring CHBURG 001	THE CORDIAL STANCE EP (black vinyl)	15
13	Chopped Herring CHBURG 001	THE CORDIAL STANCE EP (burgundy vinyl)	35
13	Chopped Herring CHBURG 001	THE CORDIAL STANCE EP (white vinyl)	20
14	Chopped Herring FHBURGLP01	SUEDE COMET (LP)	18
14	Chopped Herring FHBURGLP01	SUEDE COMET (LP, burgundy vinyl)	25
14	Chopped Herring FHBURGLP01	SUEDE COMET (LP, clear vinyl)	30
14	Chopped Herring FHBURGLP01	SUEDE COMET (LP, Instrumental version)	20

ELPEDO BURKE
75	Black Wax WAX 3	Madgie/MIGHTY CLOUD: Madgie Dub	15

KEVIN BURKE
78	Rockburgh ROC 105	IF THE CAP FITS (LP)	15

SOLOMON BURKE
61	London HLK 9454	Just Out Of Reach/Be Bop Grandma	40
62	London HLK 9512	Cry To Me/I Almost Lost My Mind	50
62	London HLK 9560	Down In The Valley/I'm Hanging Up My Heart For You	20

Sonny BURKE (U.K.)

MINT VALUE £

Year	Catalogue	Title	Value
63	London HLK 9715	If You Need Me/You Can Make It If You Try	20
63	London HLK 9763	Can't Nobody Love You/Stupidity	40
64	London HLK 9849	He'll Have To Go/Rockin' Soul	20
64	London HLK 9887	Goodbye Baby (Baby Goodbye)/Someone To Love Me	20
64	Atlantic AT 4004	Everybody Needs Somebody To Love/Looking For My Baby	30
64	Atlantic AT 4014	The Price/More Rockin' Soul	15
65	Atlantic AT 4022	Got To Get You Off My Mind/Peepin'	20
65	Atlantic AT 4030	Maggie's Farm/Tonight's The Night	20
65	Atlantic AT 4044	Someone Is Watching/Dance, Dance, Dance	18
65	Atlantic AT 4061	Only Love (Can Save Me Now)/Little Girl That Loves Me	22
66	Atlantic AT 4073	Baby Come On Home/No, No, No, I Can't Stop Lovin' You Now	18
66	Atlantic 584 005	I Feel A Sin Comin' On/Mountain Of Pride	10
66	Atlantic 584 026	Keep Lookin'/Suddenly	10
67	Atlantic 584 100	Keep A Light In The Window Till I Come Home/Time Is A Thief	10
67	Atlantic 584 122	Take Me (Just As I Am)/I Stayed Away Too Long	10
68	Atlantic 584 191	I Wish I Knew (How It Would Feel To Be Free)/It's Just A Matter Of Time	10
68	Atlantic 584 204	Save It/Meet Me In Church	10
68	Bell BLL 1047	Uptight Good Woman/I Can't Stop (No No No)	10
69	Bell BLL 1062	Proud Mary/What Am I Living For	10
63	London REK 1379	TONIGHT MY HEART SHE IS CRYING (EP)	70
65	Atlantic AET 6008	ROCK'N'SOUL (EP)	60
63	London HA-K 8018	SOLOMON BURKE'S GREATEST (LP)	70
64	Atlantic ATL 5009	ROCK'N'SOUL (LP)	50
66	Atlantic 587/588 016	THE BEST OF SOLOMON BURKE (LP)	30
68	Atlantic 587 105	KING SOLOMON (LP)	35
68	Atlantic 587/588 117	I WISH I KNEW (LP)	30
69	Bell MBLL/SBLL 118	PROUD MARY (LP)	20
72	MGM 2315 048	THE ELECTRONIC MAGNETISM (LP)	15

(see also Soul Clan)

SONNY BURKE (U.K.)

Year	Catalogue	Title	Value
62	Island WI 155	Let And Let Live/Our Love Is True	25
64	Black Swan WI 457	I Love You Still/It's Always A Pleasure	15
64	Black Swan WI 458	City In The Sky/Everyday I Love You More	15
65	Black Swan WI 469	Glad/Jeanie	15
65	Black Swan WI 470	Dance With Me/My Girl Can't Cook	15
65	Black Swan WI 471	Wicked People/Good Heaven Knows	15
66	Blue Beat BB 363	Blue Island/You Came And Left	40
67	Blue Beat BB 371	Look In Her Eyes/LLOYD CLARKE: Love Is Strange	40
67	Ska Beat JB272	Have Faith/Guinea Pig	40
68	Island ILP 972	THE SOUNDS OF SONNY BURKE (LP, mono only)	125

(see also Bob Andy, Gaylads, Ken Parker, Eddie Thornton Outfit, Glen Adams, Stranger Cole, Gaylads, Sonny & Yvonne)

SONNY BURKE OUTFIT

Year	Catalogue	Title	Value
68	Instant IN 003	Baby Be My Girl/All You	120

(see also Sonny Burke)

DAVE BURLAND

Year	Catalogue	Title	Value
71	Trailer LER 2029	A DALESMAN'S LITANY (LP, red label)	25
72	Trailer LER 2082	DAVE BURLAND (LP)	20
75	Rubber RUB 012	SONGS AND BUTTERED HAYCOCKS (LP)	18
79	Rubber RUB 036	YOU CAN'T FOOL THE FAT MAN (LP)	15

BURLITZ

Year	Catalogue	Title	Value
84	Spartan SP 13	Sleep Softly Mary/In The Dead Of The Night (p/s)	8

PETER BURMAN

Year	Catalogue	Title	Value
62	Columbia 33SX 1452	JAZZ TETE A TETE (LP)	200

BURMOE BROTHERS

Year	Catalogue	Title	Value
85	Wild Blue Yonder WBY 121	Skin/Leber Oder Lippenstift/Under The Blanket Of Love (12", p/s)	15

(see also Marc Almond, Nick Cave)

BURN

Year	Catalogue	Title	Value
00s	Virgin HUTCDP 146	Facing The Music (1-sided, numbered gold-embossed p/s, 1000 only)	20

CHRIS BURN & JOHN BUTCHER

Year	Catalogue	Title	Value
85	Bead Records BEAD 24	FONETIKS (LP)	20

JEAN-JACQUES BURNEL

Year	Catalogue	Title	Value
80	United Artists BP 361	Girl From The Snow Country/Ode To Joy (live)/Do The European (live) (p/s, unissued)	500
79	United Artists UAG 30214	EUROMAN COMETH (LP, inner)	15

BURNER

Year	Catalogue	Title	Value
84	High Roller 7HRR0132007	Hammer Of The Gods/Time Is On My Side/Old Enough To Know Better (EP, p/s)	10

JOHN BURNESS

Year	Catalogue	Title	Value
69	Columbia DB8536	Theresa/I Don't Want You Anymore	10

CHARMAINE BURNETT

Year	Catalogue	Title	Value
79	Hawkeye HD 21	Make It With You/Let's Get Started (12")	10
81	Pro PROD 001	(Am I The) Same Girl/Direct Response (12")	25
82	Dread At The Controls DATC 007	Dancing Shoes/Congo Dubba (12")	30

FRANCES BURNETT

Year	Catalogue	Title	Value
59	Coral Q 72374	Please Remember Me/How I Miss You So (triangular centre)	60
59	Coral Q 72374	Please Remember Me/How I Miss You So (round centre)	30

KING BURNETT

Year	Catalogue	Title	Value
75	Dip DL 5056	I Man Free/UPSETTERS: Version	20
75	Dip DL 5073	Key Card/UPSETTERS: Domino Game	25

(see also Congos)

Dorsey BURNETTE

MINT VALUE £

DORSEY BURNETTE
60	London HLN 9047	Juarez Town/(There Was A) Tall Oak Tree	10
60	London HLN 9160	Hey Little One/Big Rock Candy Mountain	10
61	London HLN 9365	(It's No) Sin/Hard Rock Mine	10
65	Tamla Motown TMG 534	Jimmy Brown/Everybody's Angel	225
65	Tamla Motown TMG 534	Jimmy Brown/Everybody's Angel (DJ copy)	250
63	London RE-D 1402	DORSEY BURNETTE SINGS (EP)	40
63	London HA-D 8050	DORSEY BURNETTE (LP)	70

(see also Johnny & Dorsey Burnette)

HANK C. BURNETTE
74	Southern Sound SSR 500	Slow Down/Here Comes That Train	8
74	Southern Sound SSRLP 400	SPINNIN ROCK BOOGIE (LP)	30
76	Sonet SNTF 693	DONT'T MESS WITH MY DUCKTAIL (LP)	15
78	Sonet SNTF 750	ROCKABILLY GASSEROONIE (LP)	15

JOHNNY BURNETTE (TRIO)
SINGLES
56	Vogue Coral Q 72177	Tear It Up/You're Undecided (as Johnny Burnette & Rock'N'Roll Trio)	500
56	Vogue Coral Q 72177	Tear It Up/You're Undecided (as Johnny Burnette & Rock'N'Roll Trio) (78)	60
57	Vogue Coral Q 72227	Honey Hush/Lonesome Train (as Johnny Burnette Trio)	500
57	Vogue Coral Q 72227	Honey Hush/Lonesome Train (as Johnny Burnette Trio) (78)	70
57	Vogue Coral Q 72283	Touch Me/Eager Beaver Baby (as Johnny Burnette Trio)	200
57	Vogue Coral Q 72283	Touch Me/Eager Beaver Baby (as Johnny Burnette Trio) (78)	60
60	London HLG 9172	Dreamin'/Cincinnati Fireball	10
60	London HLG 9172	Dreamin'/Cincinnati Fireball (78)	250
61	London HLG 9453	God Country And My Baby/Honestly I Do (withdrawn)	50
62	Pye International 7N 25158	I Wanna Thank Your Folks/The Giant	10
63	Pye International 7N 25187	Remember Me/Time Is Not Enough	10
63	Capitol CL 15322	All Week Long/It Isn't There	20
64	Capitol CL 15347	Sweet Suzie/Walking Talking Doll	35
96	Cruisin' The 50s CASB 003	The Train Kept A Rollin'/Sweet Love On My Mind (300 copies only) (78)	20

EPs
60	London RE-G 1263	DREAMIN'	25
61	London RE-G 1291	LITTLE BOY SAD	25
61	London RE-G 1309	BIG BIG WORLD	25
61	London RE-G 1327	GIRLS	25
63	Liberty LEP 2091	HIT AFTER HIT	25
64	Capitol EAP 20645	FOUR BY BURNETTE	60

ALBUMS
56	Coral LVC 10041	ROCK AND ROLL TRIO (10", as Johnny Burnette Trio)	800
61	London HA-G 2306	DREAMIN'	40
61	London HA-G 2349	YOU'RE SIXTEEN	40
61	London HA-G 2375	JOHNNY BURNETTE SINGS (mono)	40
61	London SAH-G 6175	JOHNNY BURNETTE SINGS (stereo)	60
62	Liberty LBY 1006	BURNETTE'S HITS AND OTHER FAVOURITES	20
64	Liberty LBY 1231	THE JOHNNY BURNETTE STORY	20
66	Ace Of Hearts AH 120	ROCK AND ROLL TRIO (reissue, as Johnny Burnette Trio)	20
68	Coral CP 10	TEAR IT UP (as Johnny Burnette Trio)	20

(see also Johnny & Dorsey Burnette)

JOHNNY & DORSEY BURNETTE
63	Reprise R 20153	Hey Sue/It Don't Matter Much	70

(see also Johnny Burnette, Dorsey Burnette)

SMILEY BURNETTE
54	London HL 8071	Lazy Locomotive/That Long White Line	25
54	London HL 8085	Chuggin' On Down "66"/Mucho Gusto	25

ALAN BURNHAM
80	Cherry Red CHERRY 15	Music To Save The World/Science Fiction (p/s)	12

BURNIN' RED IVANHOE
70	Warner Bros WS 3013	BURNIN' RED IVANHOE (LP, green label)	70
72	Dandelion 2310 145	W.W.W. (LP, gatefold sleeve)	70

BURNING BUSH
84	Kongo DP 001	Go To School/School/Jah Is Coming?Hail The Emperor (12")	20

BURNING SAVIORS
06	Rise Above RISE 7/084	The Giant/The Clown	10

BURNING SKIES OF ELYSIUM
87	Crisis EL 3	THE LAST REVOLVING DOOR (LP)	25

BURNING SOUND
82	Right Track BURN 001	Shining Through/Fit To Burn	6

BURNING SPEAR
70	Bamboo 50	SOUND DIMENTION: Soul Food/BURNING SPEAR: Door Peeper	80
71	Fab FAB 18	Creation Rebel/ERROL DUNKLEY: Get Up Now (black label, promo only)	30
75	Fab FAB 240	Foggy Road/Version	45
76	Island WIP 6346	Lion/Door Peep	18
76	Island WIP 6294	Black Wa-Da-Da (Invasion (Dub Version))/I And I Survive (Slavery Days) (Dub Version)	15
78	Island Pre IPR 2027	Civilised Reggae/Social Living (12")	20
79	Burning Spear BS 001	Free The Whole Wide World/Jah Jah No Dead (12")	30
79	Tribesman TM 20	Free The Whole Wide World/Jah Jah No Dead (12")	60
82	Radic 12RIC114	Jah Is My Driver/Driver Dub/Distance/Forever	15
75	Island ILPS 9377	MARCUS GARVEY (LP, 1st pressing has stickered sleeve)	40
76	Island ILPS 9377	GARVEY'S GHOST (LP)	35

Jan BURNNETTE

MINT VALUE £

76	Island ILPS 9412	MAN IN THE HILLS (LP, gatefold)	18
77	Island MPLS 9431	DRY AND HEAVY (LP)	15
77	Island ILPS 9513	LIVE (LP)	15
78	1 Stop STOP 1001	SOCIAL LIVING (LP)	18
79	Island PRELP 3	LIVING DUB VOL 1 (LP)	25
79	Island ILPS 9567	HARDER THAN THE BEST (LP)	15
80	EMI RDC 2003	HAIL H.I.M (LP, inner)	15
82	Island SVLP 191	MARCUS GARVEY/GARVEY'S GHOST (2-LP, reissue)	20
01	Pressure Sounds PSLP 33	SPEAR BURNING (2-LP)	35
04	Soul Jazz SJRLP 101	SOUNDS FROM BURNING SPEAR (2-LP)	20

(see also Irving Brown, King Cry Cry)

JAN BURNNETTE

62	Oriole CB 1716	I Could Have Loved You So Well/The Miracle Of Life	15
62	Oriole CB 1742	All At Once/Does My Heartache Show?	10
62	Oriole CB 1761	Teddy/Trust In Me	12
63	Oriole CB 1807	The Boy I Used To Know/Unimportant Things	15
63	Oriole CB 1841	Till I Hear The Truth From You/Fool In Love	15
64	Oriole CB 1905	Let Me Make You Smile Again/No Regrets	12
64	Oriole CB 1920	Too Young/The Four Winds And The Seven Seas	15
64	Oriole CB 1949	Love, Let Me Not Hunger/The One I Love (Belongs To Somebody Else)	10

CLARKIE BURNS
| 78 | Jungle Beats JBCD 805 | Troubles (with I ROY)/I ROY: Worries (12") | 80 |

EDDIE 'GUITAR' BURNS
| 72 | Action ACMP 100 | BOTTLE UP AND GO (LP) | 30 |
| 75 | Big Bear BEAR 7 | DETROIT BLACKBOTTOM (LP) | 20 |

GILLIAN BURNS
| 69 | Fontana TF 1044 | Hop Skip And Jump/Merry Go Round | 10 |

JACKIE BURNS & BELLES
| 63 | MGM MGM 1226 | He's My Guy/I Do The Best I Can | 100 |

JIMMY BURNS
| 79 | Grapevine GRP 118 | I Really Love You/I Love You Girl | 25 |
| 79 | Grapevine GRP 118 | I Really Love You/I Love You Girl (DJ Copy) | 30 |

LISA BURNS
| 78 | MCA MCF 2849 | LISA BURNS (LP) | 15 |

RANDY BURNS
| 68 | Fontana STL 5520 | EVENING OF THE MAGICIAN (LP) | 50 |

(see also Blue Cheer)

RAY BURNS
| 56 | Columbia DB 3811 | Condemned For Life (With A Rock And Roll Wife)/The Mare Piccola | 35 |
| 55 | Columbia SEG 7594 | RAY BURNS (EP) | 20 |

(see also Ruby Murray, Ronnie Harris, Diana Decker, Ray Martin)

HAROLD BURRAGE
65	Sue WI 353	I'll Take One/A Long Ways Together	50
68	President PT 130	You Made Me So Happy/Take Me Now	10
81	Flywright FLY 579	SHE KNOCKS ME OUT - ORIGINAL COBRA BLUES (LP)	15

KENNY BURRELL
61	Esquire 32-140	ALL NIGHT LONG (LP, as Kenny Burrell All Stars)	40
64	Verve VLP 9058	BLUE BLASH (LP, with Jimmy Smith)	25
65	Verve VLP 9099	GUITAR FORMS (LP)	20
67	Transatlantic PR 7215	SOUL CALL (LP)	15
66	Stateside SL 10163	CRASH! (LP, with Brother Jack McDuff)	30
68	Verve (S)VLP 9217	BLUES, THE COMMON GROUND (LP)	20
69	Verve SVLP 9246	NIGHT SONG (LP)	18
79	Blue Note BNS 40015	MIDNIGHT BLUE (LP, reissue, blue label with black 'b')	18

(see also Brother Jack McDuff, Jimmy Smith)

ROLAND BURRELL
| 84 | C&E CEDI 105 | Rip Off/Version (12") | 80 |

WILLIAM S. BURROUGHS
| 80 | Industrial IR 0016 | NOTHING HERE NOW BUT THE RECORDINGS (LP) | 80 |

TONY BURROWS
| 70 | Bell BLL 1124 | Every Little Move She Makes/I've Still Got My Heart, Joe | 8 |

CHINA BURTON
79	Logo GO 354	You Don't Care (About Our Love)/(Instrumental Version)	100
79	Logo GO 354	You Don't Care (About Our Love)/(Instrumental Version) (DJ Copy)	100
79	Logo GO(T) 354	You Don't Care (About Our Love) (Long Version)/(Short Version)/(Instrumental Version) (12")	300

GARY BURTON (QUARTET)
68	RCA Victor SF 7923	LOFTY FAKE ANAGRAM (LP)	20
69	RCA SF 7980	IN CONCERT (LP)	15
69	RCA Victor SF 8015	GENUINE TONGUE FUNERAL (LP)	18
71	Atlantic 2400 107	GOOD VIBES (LP)	18

(see also Michael Gibbs)

HAL BURTON
| 58 | Embassy WB 308 | Move It/Susie Darling | 8 |

JAMES BURTON
| 71 | A&M AMLS 64293 | THE GUITAR SOUNDS OF JAMES BURTON (LP) | 50 |

(see also Jim & Joe, Shindogs)

JOHNNY BURTON
| 72 | Philips 60006 238 | Polevault Man/The Polythene Doll | 25 |

MINT VALUE £

TOMMY BURTON COMBO
64	Blue Beat BB 237	Lavender Blue/I'm Walking 25

TREVOR BURTON
71	Wizard WIZ 103	Fight For My Country/Janie Slow Down 30
85	Bluebar BARLP 1	DOUBLE ZERO (LP) 20

(see also B,L&G; Uglys, Move, Balls, Denny Laine, Danny King's Mayfair Set, Magic Christians, Idle Race)

BURU
83	CSA CSALP 04	BURO (LP) 30

BURZUM
93	Misanthropy Amazon 001	HVIS LYSET TAR OSS (LP, marbled vinyl, with poster) 200
94	Misanthropy Amazon 002	DET SOM ENGANG VAR (LP, with stickered sleeve, inner sleeve and poster) 200
95	Misanthropy Amazon 003	BURZUM/ASKE (2-LP, gatefold sleeve) 100
96	Misanthropy Amazon 009	FILOSOFEM (2-LP, 1 side etched, stickered gatefold sleeve, booklet) 200
97	Misanthropy Amazon 013	DAUOI BALDRS (LP, with postcards and booklet, 1,000 only) 25
99	Misanthropy Amazon 021	HILOSKJALF (LP, booket and insert, 1,000 only) 50
08	Back On Black BOBV 087LP	HVIS LYSET TAR OSS (LP, reissue) 25
08	Back On Black BOBV 089LP	FILOSOFEM (LP, reissue, gatefold) 25
10	Back On Black BOBV 215LP	BELUS (LP, white vinyl) 50
10	Back On Black BOBV 215LP	BELUS (LP, black vinyl) 20
11	Back On Black BOBV 293LP	FALLEN (LP, clear vinyl) 20

ERNIE BUSH
75	Contempo CS 2060	Breakaway/(Version 2) 6
76	Contempo CX 12	Breakaway/BANZAI: Chinese King Fu 15

KATE BUSH
78	EMI EMI 2719	Wuthering Heights/Kite (p/s) 30
78	EMI EMI 2806	The Man With The Child In His Eyes/Moving (p/s) 15
79	EMI PSR 442/3	KATE BUSH ON STAGE (EP, double pack, gatefold sleeve, promo only) 60
82	EMI IEMI 9001	Night Of The Swallow/Houdini (pressed in England for export to Ireland, p/s) 100
84	EMI KBS 1	THE SINGLE FILE (13 x 7" box set with lyric booklet) 70
85	EMI KB 1	Running Up That Hill/Under The Ivy (gatefold p/s) 10
90	EMI TRIB02	Rocket Man/Candle In The Wind (poster p/s) 8
93	EMI EM 280	Eat The Music/Big Stripey Lie (p/s, picture labels, release cancelled, 17 copies only) 1600
93	EMI 12EMPD 280	Eat The Music/Eat The Music (Madagascan Remix)/Big Stripey Lie (12", picture disc, unissued) 0
93	EMI CDEM 280	Eat The Music/(Madagascan Remix)/Big Stripey Lie (CD, unissued) 0
93	EMI MUSIC 1	Eat The Music (CD, 1-track promo for unissued single, no inlay, withdrawn) 150
78	EMI EMA 787	LIONHEART (LP, gatefold with gold embossed titles, inner) 20
78	EMI EMC 3223	THE KICK INSIDE (LP, laminated sleeve) 20
79	EMI EM CP 3223	THE KICK INSIDE (LP, picture disc, stickered sleeve) 60
79	EMI EM CP 3223	THE KICK INSIDE (LP, picture disc, stickered sleeve, second pressing with "manufactured in the U.K. by EMI Records Ltd" wording) 30
79	EMI EM CP 3223	THE KICK INSIDE (LP, picture disc, mispress with same picture both sides) 150
80	EMI EMA 794	NEVER FOR EVER (LP, gatefold) 15
82	EMI EMC 3419	THE DREAMING (LP, inner) 20
85	EMI KAB 1	THE HOUNDS OF LOVE (LP, with inner and insert) 25
86	EMI KBTV1	THE WHOLE STORY (LP, gatefold) 20
89	EMI EMD 1010	THE SENSUAL WORLD (LP) 20
90	EMI KBBX 1	THIS WOMAN'S WORK (9-LP, box set) 250
90	EMI CDKBBX 1	THIS WOMAN'S WORK (CD, box set) 80
93	EMD 1047	THE RED SHOES (LP, lyric inner) 100
93	EMI (No Cat. No)	THE RED SHOES (CD, video, slide transparency, fountain pen, parchment discography & red ribbon box set, promo) 200
97	EMI LPCENT5	THE KICK INSIDE (LP, reissue, EMI 100 Centenary, stickered sleeve) 40
97	EMI CENT 34	THE HOUNDS OF LOVE (LP, reissue, EMI 100 Centenary, stickered sleeve) 40
05	EMI 343960 1	AERIAL (2 LP, gatefold, booklet, stickered sleeve) 125
11	Fish People FPLP 007	50 WORDS FOR SNOW (2-LP, booklet, CD) 40
16	Fish People 0190295920166	BEFORE THE DAWN (4-LP, box set) 50
21	Fish People 0190296729041	HOUNDS OF LOVE (LP, reissue, obi, recycled vinyl) 60

(see also Lesley Duncan)

RAY BUSH & AVON CITIES' SKIFFLE
56	Tempo A 146	Hey Hey Daddy Blues/Green Corn 25
56	Tempo A 149	Fisherman's Blues/This Little Light Of Mine 25
57	Tempo A 156	How Long, How Long, Blues/Julian Johnson 25
57	Tempo A 157	Lonesome Day Blues/I Don't Know 25
57	Tempo EXA 40	RAY BUSH & AVON CITIES' SKIFFLE (EP) 25
57	Tempo EXA 50	RAY BUSH & AVON CITIES' SKIFFLE NO. 2 (EP) 25

(see also Avon Cities Jazz Band)

CLEMENT BUSHAY
75	Summertime BUS 10 LP	DREAD IN SESSION (LP) 85

BUSH CHEMISTS
98	Conscious Sounds DNC 1203	Collie Weed/Collie Dub/Earth Rocker/Rocker Dub (12") 40
06	Jah Tubbys JT10025	Star Dub/Waters Edge (10") 18
94	JKPD JKPD 001	MEETS THE BUSH CHEMISTS AT CONSCIOUS SOUNDS (LP, with Jonah Dan) 25
94	Conscious Sounds DNC 003	STRICTLY DUBWISE (LP) 20
96	Conscious Sounds DNC 005	LIGHT UP YOUR SPLIFF (LP) 40
98	Dubhead DBHD 009LP	CULTURE FREEMAN MEETS THE BUSH CHEMISTS (LP) 20
99	Dubhead DBHD 010LP	LIGHT UP YOUR CHALICE (LP) 18
01	Dubhead DBHD 023LP	DUB FIRE BLAZING (LP) 20

(see also King General, King General & Bush Chemists)

BUSHKILLER

MINT VALUE £

BUSHKILLER
92	Danger 001	92 Salute/Bushkiller Draw (12")	12
94	Danger 002	TROUBLEMAKERS (EP)	25

BUSH TETRAS
81	Fetish FET 007	Things That Go Boom In The Night/Das Ah Riot (p/s)	10
82	Fetish FE 15	Can't Be Funky (unissued, stamped white label only, custom plain sleeve)	10
82	Fetish FET 16EP	RITUALS (12" EP)	15

BUSINESS
81	Secret SHH 123	Harry May/National Insurance Blacklist (p/s)	12
82	Secret SHH 132	SMASH THE DISCOS EP: Day-O (The Banana Boat Song)/Disco Girls/Smash The Disco (p/s)	10
83	Secret SHH 150	OUT OF BUSINESS (12" EP, unissued, white label promo, 10 copies only)	100
85	Wonderful World Of... 121	Get Out Of My House/All Out Tonight/Foreign Girl/Outlaw (12", p/s)	25
85	Diamond DIA 001	Drinking N Driving/H-Bomb (live) (p/s)	15
85	Diamond DIA 001T	Drinking N Driving/H-Bomb (live)/Hurry Up Harry/Drinking 'N' Driving (original version) (12", p/s)	25
80s	Link LINK 1201	DO A RUNNER (12" EP)	12
83	Secret SEC 11	SUBURBAN REBELS (LP)	40
83	Syndicate SYNLP 2	1980-81 OFFICIAL BOOTLEGS (LP)	15
83	Wonderful WOWDLP 4	OFFICIAL BUSINESS 1980-81 (LP)	20
84	Syndicate SYNLP 6	LOUD, PROUD 'N' PUNK, LIVE (LP)	20
85	Harry May SE 13	SATURDAY HEROES (LP)	20
86	Dojo DOJO LP 35	SINGALONGABUSINESS (LP)	15
90	Link LRMO 1	IN AND OUT OF BUSINESS (LP, mail-order, 550 only)	20
91	Wonderful WOWDLP 5	SUBURBAN REBELS/SMASH THE DISCOS - BACK TO BACK VOL 2. (2xLP)	25

BUSKERS
73	Rubber RUB 007	LIFE OF A MAN (LP)	18
75	Hawk HALPX 142	THE BUSKERS (LP)	15

GEORGE HENRY BUSSEY/JIM BUNKLEY
71	Revival RVS 1003	GEORGE HENRY BUSSEY/JIM BUNKLEY (LP)	15

BUSTER
71	Parlophone R5881	Pasadena/Priscilla	8
73	Bradleys BRAD 310	Motor Machine/Ring Around	25
74	Bradleys BRAD 7401	Superstar/Rainbows & Colours	20

BUSTERS
63	Stateside SS 231	Bust Out/Astronauts	25

BUSTER('S) ALLSTARS
64	Blue Beat BB 244	Prince Royal/COSMO: One God	40
64	Blue Beat BB 269	The Tickler/COSMO: Rice And Badge	40
65	Blue Beat BB 294	Eye For Eye/South Virginia	35
65	Blue Beat BB 322	Happy Independence 65/STRANGER COLE: When The Party Is Over	25
65	Blue Beat BB 325	Congo Revolution/Little Darlin' - No One	150
65	Blue Beat BB 333	When The Party Is Over/Matilda (with Stranger Cole)	30
66	Blue Beat BB 342	Cincinnatti Kid/Sammy Dead	75
67	Blue Beat BB 372	Sounds And Pressure/My Darling (both actually by Hopeton Lewis)	45
67	Blue Beat BB 384	Take It Easy/Why Must I Cry (both actually by Hopeton Lewis)	25
69	Fab FAB 101	Pum Pum A Go Kill You/Oh Lady Oh	15
70	Fab FAB 124	The Rebel/The Preacher	15

(see also Prince Buster, Teddy King, Little Darling, Khandars, Higgs & Wilson, Owen Gray, Charmers, Fitzroy D Long, Maytals, Derrick Morgan, Eric Morris, Personalities, Roy & Millie, Zoot Simms, Spanish Boys, Spanish Town Skabeats)

BUSTER'S GROUP
61	Starlite ST45 052	Buster's Shack/ERIC MORRIS: Search The World	40
65	Blue Beat BB 395	This Gun For Hire/Yes Daddy	60

(see also Prince Buster, Rico, Owen Gray)

BUSTY & COOL
62	Blue Beat BB 144	Mr Policeman/What A World	20

TONY BUTALA
62	Salvo SLO 1801	Long Black Stockings/Rumors (99 copies only)	40

STAN BUTCHER
66	CBS SS62838	HIS BIRDS AND BRASS (LP)	20
67	CBS 63072	SWING LIKE A BASTARD (LP)	35

SAM BUTERA (& WITNESSES)
58	HMV POP 476	Good Gracious Baby/It's Better Than Nothing At All	50
58	Capitol CL 14913	Bim Bam/Twinkle In Your Eye (as Sam Butera & Witnesses)	250
59	Capitol CL 14988	Handle With Care/French Poodle	20
64	Prima PR 1003	Skinnie Minnie/Little Liza Jane	18
81	Capitol CL 16179	Bim Bam/Twinkie In Your Eyes (reissue)	10
56	HMV 7EG 8087	SAX SERENADE (EP)	15
60	London HA-D 2288	THE RAT RACE (LP, as Sam Butera & Witnesses)	20

(see also Louis Prima)

BILLY BUTLER (& ENCHANTERS)
69	Soul City SC 113	The Right Track/Boston Monkey	15
74	Epic S EPC 2508	The Right Track/Can't Live Without Her (Yellow label)	10
78	Epic S EPC 2508	The Right Track/Can't Live Without Her (Orange label)	8
85	SMP SKM 9	Right Track (Vocal)/Right Track (Instrumental) (reissue)	6
12	Outta Sight OSV 063	Right Track/Right Track (Instrumental) (reissue)	6

HAROLD BUTLER
77	Charmers 3	GOLD CONNECTION (LP)	150

JERRY BUTLER
58	London HL 8697	For Your Precious Love/Sweet Was The Wine (as Jerry Butler & the Impressions)	200

Leslie BUTLER (& FUGITIVES)

MINT VALUE £

58	London HL 8697	For Your Precious Love/Sweet Was The Wine (as Jerry Butler & the Impressions) (78 rpm)	100
60	Top Rank JAR 389	I Found A Love/A Lonely Soldier	45
60	Top Rank JAR 531	He Will Break Your Heart/Thanks To You	55
61	Top Rank JAR 562	Find Another Girl/When Trouble Calls	40
61	Columbia DB 4743	Moon River/Aware Of Love	25
62	Stateside SS 121	Make It Easy On Yourself/It's Too Late	25
63	Stateside SS 158	You Can Run But You Can't Hide/I'm The One	30
63	Stateside SS 170	You Go Right Through Me/The Wishing Star	20
63	Stateside SS 195	Whatever You Want/You Won't Be Sorry	20
64	Stateside SS 252	Need To Belong/Give Me Your Love	25
64	Stateside SS 300	Giving Up On Love/I've Been Trying	20
65	Fontana TF 553	Good Times/I've Grown Accustomed To Her Face	20
65	Fontana TF 588	I Can't Stand To See You Cry/Nobody Needs Your Love	15
65	Mercury MF 932	Love (Oh, How Sweet It Is)/Loneliness	15
66	Sue WI 4003	I Stand Accused/I Don't Want To Hear Anymore	50
66	Sue WI 4009	Just For You/Believe In Me	50
67	Mercury MF 964	I Dig You Baby/Some Kinda Magic	8
67	Mercury MF 1005	Mr. Dream Merchant/'Cause I Love You So	8
68	Mercury MF 1035	Never Give You Up/Beside You	10
68	Mercury MF 1058	Hey Mr Western Union Man (Send A Telegram)/Just Can't Forget About You	10
69	Mercury MF 1078	Are You Happy/Strange I Still Love You	8
69	Mercury MF 1094	Only The Strong Survive/Just Because I Really Love You	10
69	Mercury MF 1122	Moody Woman/Go Away And Find Yourself	20
69	Mercury MF 1122	Moody Woman/Go Away And Find Yourself (DJ copy)	100
69	Mercury MF 1132	What's The Use Of Breaking Up/A Brand New Me	10
70	President PT 299	Make It Easy On Yourself/Moon River	8
72	Mercury 6052 036	One Night Affair/What's So Good About It (You're My Baby)	8
72	Mercury 6052 119	Moody Woman/A Brand New Me	15
63	Stateside SL 10032	HE WILL BREAK YOUR HEART (LP)	100
63	Stateside SL 10050	FOLK SONGS (LP)	40
68	Fontana (S)TL 5246	LOVE ME (LP)	45
68	Mercury 20118 (S)MCL	MR. DREAM MERCHANT (LP)	30
69	Mercury 20144 (S)MCL	SOUL GOES ON (LP)	35
69	Mercury SMCL 20175	ICE ON ICE (LP)	20
69	Mercury 20154 (S)MCL	THE ICE MAN COMETH (LP)	35
70	Joys JOYS 171	MAKE IT EASY ON YOURSELF (LP)	15
72	Mercury 6338 102	SPICE OF LIFE (LP)	15
76	Tamla Motown STML 12032	LOVES ON THE MENU (LP)	15

(see also Betty Everett & Jerry Butler, Impressions)

LESLIE BUTLER (& FUGITIVES)

67	Island WI 3069	Hornpipe Rock Steady/You Don't Have To Say You Love Me	35
67	Doctor Bird DB 1083	Winchester Rocksteady (with Fugitives)/ASTON CAMPBELL & CONQUERORS : Ramona	35
68	High Note HS 008	Top Cat/WEBBER SISTERS: Stars Above	25
68	High Note HS 009	Revival/GAYLADS: Over The Rainbow's End	12
75	Trojan TRLS 112	JA-GAN (LP)	40

(see also Ken Boothe, Fugitives, Gaylads)

BUTTERCUPS

68	Pama PM 742	If I Love You/Loving You	15
69	Pama PM 760	Come Put My Life In Order/If I Love You	15

BILLY BUTTERFIELD & HIS ORCHESTRA

55	London HLF 8181	The Magnificent Matador/Sugar Blues Mambo	35

PAUL BUTTERFIELD BLUES BAND

66	London HLZ 10100	Come On In/I Got A Mind To Give Up Living	35
67	Elektra EKSN 45007	All These Blues/Never Say No	10
67	Elektra EKSN 45020	Run Out Of Time/One More Heartache	20
68	Elektra EKSN 45047	Get Yourself Together/Mine To Love	12
69	Elektra EKSN 45069	Where Did My Baby Go/In My Own Dream	10
70	Elektra 2101 012	Love March/Love Disease	6
65	Elektra EKL/EKS 294	PAUL BUTTERFIELD BLUES BAND (LP, with rare gold 'guitar player' label)	200
65	Elektra EKL/EKS 294	PAUL BUTTERFIELD BLUES BAND (LP, orange label)	50
66	Elektra EKL/EKS 315	EAST - WEST (LP, orange label)	50
67	Elek. EKL 4015/EKS 74015	THE RESURRECTION OF PIGBOY CRABSHAW (LP, orange label)	35
68	Elektra EKL 4025	IN MY OWN DREAM (LP, orange label, also stereo EKS 74025)	40
69	Elektra EKS 74053	KEEP ON MOVIN' (LP)	20
71	Elektra EKD 2001	LIVE (2-LP)	20
72	Elektra K 62011	GOLDEN BUTTER (LP, gatefold sleeve)	18

(see also John Mayall's Bluesbreakers, Mike Bloomfield)

BUTTERFLIES

68	President PT 192	Love Me Forever/He's Got Everything	15

BUTTERFLYS

64	Red Bird RB 10009	Goodnight Baby/The Swim	22

BUTTERSCOTCH

70	RCA 1937	Don't You Know (She Said Hello)/The Closer To You	7
70	RCA 1983	Surprise, Surprise/In This World Of Loving You	6
72	Jam 15	Can't You Hear A Song/All I Ever Wanna Do	7
70	RCA LSA 5000	BUTTERSCOTCH (LP, with insert and music book)	20

BUTTERSCOTCH CABOOSE

68	Bell BLL 1023	Melinda/Let A Little Sunshine In	8

BUTTHOLE SURFERS

MINT VALUE £

BUTTHOLE SURFERS
85	Fundamental SAVE 5	PSYCHIC...POWERLESS...ANOTHER MAN'S SAC (LP)	20
86	Red Rhino Europe RRELP 2	REMBRANDT PUSSYHORSE (LP)	20
88	Blast First BFFP 29	HAIRWAY TO STEVEN (LP)	20
87	Blast First BFFP 15	LOCUST ABORTION TECHNICIAN (LP)	25
91	Rough Trade R 2081 2601	PIOUGHD (LP, with bonus 12")	15
93	Capitol 0777 7 98798 1 6	INDEPENDENT WORM SALOON (LP)	25
96	Capitol EST 2285	ELECTRIC LARRYLAND (2-LP, one disc etched on one side, poster)	20

BUTTONDOWN BRASS
68	Fontana TF 950	March Of The Little Brown Jugs/Frere Jacques	7
67	Fontana LPS 16255	HA HA HA (HEE-HEE-HEE) (LP)	15
76	DJM DJS 22046	FUNK IN HELL (LP)	40
76	DJM DJSLM2023	FIREDOG (LP)	15
77	DJM DJS 22076	COPS N'ROBBERS (LP)	15

BUTTS BAND
75	ABC ABC4050	Get Up, Stand Up/Mike's Blues	12

BUY OFF THE BAR
88	Bi-Joopiter BIJOOP 023	PARBOILED (LP, screen printed sleeve with insert)	20

BUZZ AND THE FLYERS
80	Hot Rock HR45 007	Go Cat Wild/Dance To The Bop (p/s)	15

BUZZ & BUCKY
65	Stateside SS 428	Tiger A Go Go/Bay City	50

(see also Ronny & The Daytonas)

BUZZ (1)
66	Columbia DB 7887	You're Holding Me Down/I've Gotta Buzz	250

(see also Boston Dexters, Tam White)

BUZZ (2)
79	Redball RR 06	Insanity/Him Not Me/Sick At Heart (p/s)	30

BUZZARD
85	PTO MSPT01	Catch Me Alone/Raven Eyed Queen	45

BUZZCOCKS
77	New Hormones ORG 1	SPIRAL SCRATCH (EP, 1st pressing, plastic labels, p/s doesn't credit Howard Devoto on front of sleeve beneath band name)	75
77	United Artists UP 36316	Orgasm Addict/Whatever Happened To...? (p/s)	18
77	United Artists UP 36316	Whatever Happened To? (1-sided, promo only)	50
77	United Artists UP 36348	What Do I Get? (1-sided, promo)	60
78	United Artists UP 36348	What Do I Get?/Oh Shit (p/s)	10
78	United Artists UP 36348	What Do I Get?/Oh Shit (Mispress, plays Stranglers Peaches) (p/s)	75
78	United Artists UP 36386	I Don't Mind/Autonomy (p/s)	12
78	United Artists UP 36433	Love You More/Noise Annoys (p/s)	10
78	United Artists UP 36455	Ever Fallen In Love (With Someone You Shouldn't've?)/Just Lust (p/s)	10
78	United Artists UP 36455	Ever Fallen In Love (With Someone You Shouldn't've?)/Just Lust (p/s mispressed with Gerry Rafferty track Island on B-side)	25
78	United Artists UP 36471	Promises/Lipstick (p/s)	8
78	United Artists UALP 15	Moving Away From The Pulsebeat (12", 1-sided, die-cut co. sl., promo only)	25
79	United Artists UP 36499	Everybody's Happy Nowadays/Why Can't I Touch It? (p/s, available in 3 different colours)	8
79	New Hormones ORG 1	SPIRAL SCRATCH (EP, reissue, p/s credits Howard Devoto, paper label)	15
79	United Artists UP 36541	Harmony In My Head/Something's Gone Wrong Again (red or blue p/s)	8
79	United Artists BP 316	You Say You Don't Love Me/Raison D'etre (p/s)	8
80	United Artists BP 365	Why She's A Girl From The Chainstore/Are Everything (p/s, two different designs - double A side)	8
80	United Artists BP 365 DJ	Why She's A Girl From The Chainstore/Are Everything (DJ promo)	20
80	United Artists BP 371	Strange Thing/Airwaves Dream (p/s, two different designs as double A side)	8
80	United Artists BP 382	Running Free/What Do You Know (two different p/s)	8
87	Strange Fruit SFPS044	PEEL SESSION EP (12")	12
89	EMI EM104	THE FAB FOUR: Ever Fallen In Love/Promises/Everybody's Happy Nowdays/Harmony in My Head (p/s)	10
91	Document DPRO-1	SPIRAL SCRATCH (EP, 2nd reissue, promo only 7")	18
91	New Hormones DV1T	SPIRAL SCRATCH (12" EP, reissue, numbered)	12
91	Planet Pacific PPAC3	Alive Tonight/Serious Crime (p/s)	7
95	United Artists ESP001	What Do I Get?/Mad Mad Judy/Raison D'Etre (Demo) (Fan Club only, no p/s)	20
95	One Stop ONE 7001	Isolation/Noise Annoys (p/s)	6
00	Mute SCRATCH 1	SPIRAL SCRATCH (EP) (3rd reissue, p/s)	10
78	United Artists UAG 30159	ANOTHER MUSIC IN A DIFFERENT KITCHEN (LP, black inner sleeve, in printed carrier bag)	40
78	United Artists UAG 30159	ANOTHER MUSIC IN A DIFFERENT KITCHEN (LP, black inner sleeve)	30
78	United Artists UAG 30159	ANOTHER MUSIC IN A DIFFERENT KITCHEN (LP, black inner, mispressing without "I Need")	50
78	United Artists UAG 30197	LOVE BITES (LP, embossed sleeve with insert, 'Buzzcocks' logo on labels)	30
78	United Artists UAG 30197	LOVE BITES (LP, mispressing, Side A plays first side of Maxine Nightingales's LOVE LINE LP, with insert & embossed sleeve)	45
79	United Artists UAG 30260	A DIFFERENT KIND OF TENSION (LP, with inner sleeve)	25
80	United Artists UAK 30279	SINGLES - GOING STEADY (LP)	25
80	Liberty UAG 30159	ANOTHER MUSIC IN A DIFFERENT KITCHEN (LP, reissue with b/w photo on sleeve, black inner)	20
85	Liberty UAG 30197	LOVE BITES (LP, reissue, non embossed sleeve, no 'Buzzcocks' logo on label)	15
89	Strange Fruit SFRLP 104	PEEL SESSIONS (LP)	20
89	EMI LP PRODT 1	PRODUCT (5xLP boxed set with booklet)	80
89	Absolutely Free FREELP 02	LIVE AT THE ROXY (LP)	15
91	Document DLP 2	TIME'S UP (LP, mock bootleg, with bonus 33rpm interview single [FDLP 2])	20
93	Castle ESSLP 195	TRADE TEST TRANSMISSIONS (LP)	20

BUZZIN CUZZINS

MINT VALUE £

17	Domino REWIG113X	MK.1 (Box set, LP, 7" 2-CD, fanzine, booklet, postcards, photos, badges and posters)	80

(see also Pete Shelley, Things, Stevie's Buzz)

BUZZIN CUZZINS
94	Azuli Records AZNY 024	Let Me Show You Love (12")	60

JAKI BYARD
67	Transatlantic PR 7419	LIVE! VOL 1 (LP, white purple label)	20
68	Transatlantic PR 7463	FREEDOM TOGETHER! (LP)	20
68	Transatlantic PR 7550	SUNSHINE OF MY SOUL (LP)	20

DON BYAS & HIS RHYTHM
56	Vogue V 2390	On The Way To Your Heart/The Portuguese Washerwomen	10
64	Realm RM 230	ON 52ND STREET (LP)	15

BYE LAWS
68	Pye 7N 17481	Then You Can Tell Me Goodbye/Come On Over To My Place	8
69	Pye 7N 17701	Run Baby Run/To Sir With Love	20

TREVOR BYFIELD
80	Ethnic Fight EF 086	Jah Guide/TREVOR & CLIVE: Sea Of Love (12")	45

ANTHONY BYGRAVES
74	Pye 7N 45429	Painted Lady/Love Star Ship	15

JUNIOR BYLES
71	Bullet BU 499	Beat Down Babylon/UPSETTERS: Version	20
71	Upsetter US 365	Place Called Africa/UPSETTERS: Earthquake	35
72	Upsetter US 387	Festival Da Da/UPSETTERS: Version	25
72	Pama PM 857	Fever/GROOVERS: Soul Sister (B-side actually by Heptones)	60
72	Dynamic DYN 432	Pharaoh Hiding/UPSETTERS: Hail To Power	15
72	Randy's RAN 523	King Of Babylon/UPSETTERS: Nebuchadnezzer	20
72	Punch PH 109	Pharaoh Hiding/UPSETTERS: Hail To Power	20
73	Pama PM 878	Education Rock/KEN McKAY: Nobody Knows	10
73	Count Shelley CS 31	Break Up To Make Up (with Heptones)/YOUTH MAN (DILLINGER): Plat Skank	25
74	Magnet MAG 27	Curly Locks/Now Generation	8
74	Dip DL 5035	Curly Locks/Now Generation	20
75	Dip DL 5074	Long Way/All The Way	20
75	Ethnic Fight ETH 26	Mumbling And Grumbling/King Size Mumble	15
76	Jessus JI 006	Know Where You Are Going/JESSUS EXPERIENCE: Going To Zion	12
76	Ethnic Fight EF 042	Bury O Boy/THE THING MUSIC CO: Version	12
76	Black Wax WAX 17	Pitchy Patchy/THE JA-MAN ALL STARS: 129 Beat Street	8
72	Trojan TRL 52	BEAT DOWN BABYLON (LP, beware of Canadian imports)	60
87	Trojan TRLS 253	BEAT DOWN BABYLON: THE UPSETTER YEARS (LP)	15
88	Trojan TRLS 269	WHEN WILL BETTER COME (LP)	15

(see also King Chubby, Lloyd Terrell, Dennis Alcapone, Upsetters, Bob Marley, Lee & Junior)

JUNIOR BYLES & RUPERT REID
76	Black Wax WAX 15	Chant Down Babylon/THE JA-MAN ALL STARS: Version	20

JAMES BYNUM
79	Grapevine GRP 117	Time Passes By/Love You	10

BOBBY BYRD
71	Mojo 2001 118	I Need Help Parts 1 & 2	12
71	Mojo 2027 003	I Know You Got Soul/If You Don't Work You Can't Eat	10
71	Mojo 2093 004	Hot Pants ... I'm Coming, I'm Coming, I'm Coming/Hang It Up	10
72	Mojo 2093 013	Keep On Doin' What You're Doin'/Let Me Know	8
72	Mojo 2093 017	If You Got A Love You'd Better Keep Hold Of It/ You've Got To Change Your Mind	8
72	Mojo 2093 020	Never Get Enough/My Concerto	8
73	Warner Bros K 16291	Try It Again/I'm On The Move	6
73	Mojo 2093 028	Saying It And Doing It Are Two Different Things/VICKI ANDERSON: Don't Throw Your Love In Garbage/In The Land Of Milk & Honey	15
87	Urban URB 8	I Know You Got Soul/Hot Pants	7
87	Urban URBX 8	I Know You Got Soul/Hot Pants ... I'm Coming, I'm Coming, I'm Coming/I Know You Got Soul (Version) (12", die-cut company sleeve)	10
71	Mojo 2918 002	I NEED HELP (LIVE ON STAGE) (LP)	40

(see also JB's, James Brown, Anna King & Bobby Byrd, Vicki Anderson)

C. BYRD & SIR D.'S GROUP
60	Blue Beat BB 49	Baa Baa Black Sheep/LLOYD & CECIL: Come Over Here	12

CHARLIE BYRD
84	Riverside RLP 9451	THE GUITAR ARTISTRY OF CHARLIE BYRD (LP, Nimbus Supercut, mail oder only through Practical Hi Fi magazine)	40

DONALD BYRD
65	Verve VS 532	Boom Boom/See See Rider	10
73	Blue Note 35564	Black Byrd/Slop Jar Blues	7
80	United Artists UP 622	Dominoes/Wind Parade	7
80	Blue Note 12 UP 622	Dominoes/Wind Parade (12")	30
81	Elektra K 12559	Love Has Come Around/Loving You (12")	15
55	Esquire 32-013	BYRD'S EYE VIEW (LP)	50
55	Esquire 32-019	BYRD JAZZ (THE MOTOR CITY SCENES) (LP, as Donald Byrd Sextet)	100
56	Esquire 32-032	JAZZ FOR THE CARRIAGE TRADE (LP)	50
60s	Esquire 32-039	INFORMAL JAZZ (LP)	25
75	Blue Note BN-LA047	BLACK BYRD (LP, reissue)	25
75	Blue Note UAG 20001	PLACES AND SPACES (LP)	40
76	Blue Note UAG 20008	CARICATURES (LP)	15
78	Elektra K52097	THANK YOU FOR F.U.M.L. (FUNKING UP MY LIFE) (LP)	20
78	Elektra K52199	DONALD BYRD & 125th STREET (LP)	15
82	Elektra K 52427	WORDS, SOUNDS, COLOURS AND SHAPES (LP)	20
92	Blue Note 7844661	BLACK BYRD (LP, reissue)	20
92	Blue Note B1 98638	THE BEST OF DONALD BYRD (2-LP)	30

Russell BYRD

			MINT VALUE £
95	Blue Note 31875	KOFI (LP)	40
97	Blue Note 7243 8 53923 1 3	STREET LADY (LP, reissue)	25
97	Blue Note 72438 54326 1 3	PLACES AND SPACES (LP, reissue)	20

(see also Blackbyrds, Art Farmer)

RUSSELL BYRD
64	Sue WI 305	Hitch Hike Parts 1 & 2	50

ESTHER BYRDE
79	Survival SUR 1	Touch Me Take Me/Tracks Of Love	50

BYRDS
SINGLES

65	CBS 201765	Mr. Tambourine Man/I Knew I'd Want You	8
65	CBS 201796	All I Really Want To Do/Feel A Whole Lot Better	8
65	CBS 202008	Turn! Turn! Turn! (To Everything There Is A Season)/ She Don't Care About Time	8
66	CBS 202037	Set You Free This Time/It Won't Be Wrong	12
66	CBS 202067	Eight Miles High/Why	15
66	CBS 202259	5D (Fifth Dimension)/Captain Soul	10
66	CBS 202295	Mr Spaceman/What's Happening?!?!	20
67	CBS 202559	So You Want To Be A Rock'n'Roll Star/Everybody's Been Burned	12
67	CBS 2648	My Back Pages/Renaissance Fair	12
67	CBS 2924	Lady Friend/Don't Make Waves	20
67	CBS 3093	Goin' Back/Change Is Now	12
68	CBS 3411	You Ain't Goin' Nowhere/Artificial Energy	8
68	CBS 3752	I Am A Pilgrim/Pretty Boy Floyd	8
69	CBS 4055	Bad Night At The Whiskey/Drug Store Truck Drivin' Man	12
69	CBS 4284	Lay Lady Lay/Old Blue (p/s)	12
69	CBS 4572	Wasn't Born To Follow/Child Of The Universe	8
70	CBS 4753	Jesus Is Just Alright/It's All Over Now Baby Blue	8
71	CBS 5322	Chestnut Mare/Just A Season	7
71	CBS 7253	I Trust/This Is My Destiny	10
72	CBS 7712	America's Great National Pastime/Farther Along (unreleased)	0
73	Asylum AYM 516	Things Will Be Better/For Free (promos in p/s)	12
73	Asylum AYM 516	Things Will Be Better/For Free (promos without p/s)	6
73	Asylum AYM 517	Full Circle/Long Live The King	6

EPs
66	CBS EP 6069	THE TIMES THEY ARE A' CHANGIN' (EP)	25
66	CBS EP 6077	EIGHT MILES HIGH (EP)	30

ALBUMS
65	CBS BPG 62571	MR TAMBOURINE MAN (LP, mono)	45
65	CBS (S)BPG 62571	MR TAMBOURINE MAN (LP, stereo)	35
66	CBS BPG 62652	TURN! TURN! TURN! (LP, mono)	45
66	CBS (S)BPG 62652	TURN! TURN! TURN! (LP, stereo)	40
66	CBS BPG 62783	FIFTH DIMENSION (LP, mono)	45
66	CBS (S)BPG 62783	FIFTH DIMENSION (LP, stereo)	40

(All of the above LPs originally issued with textured orange labels and front laminated flipback sleeves)

67	CBS BPG 62988	YOUNGER THAN YESTERDAY (LP, mono)	45
67	CBS (S)BPG 62988	YOUNGER THAN YESTERDAY (LP, stereo, with large white 'stereo' sticker on back sleeve)	40
68	CBS BPG 63107	THE BYRDS GREATEST HITS (LP, mono)	25
68	CBS SBPG 63107	THE BYRDS GREATEST HITS (LP, stereo)	20
68	CBS BPG 63169	THE NOTORIOUS BYRD BROTHERS (LP, mono, 'Ernest J, Day' on rear)	50
68	CBS (S)BPG 63169	THE NOTORIOUS BYRD BROTHERS (LP, stereo)	35
68	CBS 63353	SWEETHEART OF THE RODEO (LP, mono, no 'M' or 'mono' on label but lacks 'S' prefix found on stereo copies)	45
68	CBS 63353	SWEETHEART OF THE RODEO (LP, stereo, large white 'stereo' sticker on black sleeve)	45

(The above LPs were issued with textured orange labels and front laminated non-flipback sleeves)

69	CBS 63545	DR BYRDS & MR HYDE (LP, mono)	40
69	CBS S 63545	DR BYRDS & MR HYDE (LP, stereo)	25
69	CBS S 63795	BALLAD OF EASY RIDER (LP, stereo only)	25
69	CBS SBPG 62571	MR TAMBOURINE MAN (LP, 2nd stereo issue)	25
70	CBS SPBG 62783	FIFTH DIMENSION (LP, 2nd stereo issue)	25
70	CBS SBPG 62988	YOUNGER THAN YESTERDAY (LP, 2nd stereo issue, small gold 'stereo' sticker on rear)	25

(The above LPs were originally issued with smooth orange labels and front laminated non-flipback sleeves)

70	CBS 66253	UNTITLED (LP, discs have S 64094 and S 64095 on labels as well as main cat no.)	25
71	Bumble GEXP 8001	PRE-FLYTE (LP)	25
71	CBS S 64389	BYRDMANIAX (LP)	18
72	CBS 64676	FARTHER ALONG (LP)	15
72	CBS S 64650	THE BYRDS GREATEST HITS VOL. 2 (LP)	15
73	Asylum SYLA 8754	THE BYRDS (LP, gatefold sleeve)	20
73	CBS 63169	NOTORIOUS BYRD BROTHERS (LP, 2nd stereo issue)	25
73	CBS S 63353	SWEETHEART OF THE RADIO (LP, 2nd stereo issue, 'stereo' printed on label)	25
73	CBS SBPG 63107	THE BYRDS GREATEST HITS (LP, 2nd stereo reissue, slightly altered sleeve design)	15
73	CBS 68252	HISTORY OF THE BYRDS (2-LP)	15
75	CBS 63353	SWEETHEARTS OF THE RODEO (LP, reissue)	15
82	CBS 32284	FIFTH DIMENSION (LP, reissue)	15
87	Edsel ED 227	YOUNGER THAN YESTERDAY (LP, stereo reissue)	15
87	Edsel ED 234	SWEETHEART OF THE RODEO (LP, stereo reissue)	18
88	Edsel ED 262	NOTORIOUS BYRD BROTHERS LP, stereo reissue)	18
91	BGO BGOLP 106	FIFTH DIMENSION (LP, stereo reissue)	15
98	Simply Vinyl 0037/492519 1	TURN! TURN! TURN! (LP, stereo reissue)	18

Packie BYRNE (& BONNIE SHALJEAN)

MINT VALUE £

98	Simply Vinyl SVLP 032/62571	MR TAMBOURINE MAN (LP, stereo reissue)	18
98	Simply Vinyl SVLP 0006/63169	NOTORIOUS BYRD BROTHERS (LPs, stereo reissue)	18
99	Simply Vinyl SVLP 007/62988	YOUNGER THAN YESTERDAY (LP, stereo reissue)	18
00	Simply Vinyl SVLP0057/63353	SWEETHEART OF THE RODEO (LP, stereo reissue)	18
02	Simply Vinyl SVLP 375	THE VERY BEST OF (2-LP)	18

(see also Beefeaters, Roger McGuinn, David Crosby, Gene Clark, Gram Parsons, Gene Parsons, Skip Battin, Flying Burrito Brothers, Evergreen Blueshoes, Dillard & Clark, Kentucky Colonels)

PACKIE BYRNE (& BONNIE SHALJEAN)
69	EFDSS LP 1009	PACKIE BYRNE (LP)	20

MARTIN BYRNES
70	Leader LEA 2004	BYRNES (LP)	15

DAVID BYRON
75	Bronze ILPS 9342	TAKE NO PRISONERS (LP, lyric inner sleeve)	15
78	Arista SPART 1077	BABY FACED KILLER (LP)	25
81	Creole CRX 2	ON THE ROCKS (LP, as BYRON BAND)	20

(see also Uriah Heep)

SOL BYRON & IMPACTS
60s	Flamingo PR 5027	Pride And Joy/Thou Shall Not Steal	15

BYSTANDERS (1)
65	Pylot WD 501	That's The End/This Time	150
66	Piccadilly 7N 35330	(You're Gonna) Hurt Yourself/Have I Offended The Girl	25
66	Piccadilly 7N 35351	My Love - Come Home/If You Walk Away	30
67	Piccadilly 7N 35363	98.6/Stubborn Kind Of Fellow	20
67	Piccadilly 7N 35382	Royal Blue Summer Sunshine Day/Make Up Your Mind	30
67	Piccadilly 7N 35399	Pattern People/Green Grass	15
68	Pye 7N 17476	When Jezamine Goes/Cave Of Clear Light	50
68	Pye 7N 17540	This World Is My World/Painting The Time	15

(see also Man)

BYSTANDERS (2)
81	Uncle Robert UR 001	Nowhere To Hide/Sweet Fanny Adams/True Blue/I Wonder (EP)	20

BYZANTIUM
73	A&M AMS 7064	What A Coincidence/My Seasons Changing With The Sun	7
72	Private pressing	LIVE AND STUDIO ('BLACK AND WHITE') (LP, 100 only with insert)	300
72	A&M AMLH 68104	BYZANTIUM (LP, with poster, brown label)	100
72	A&M AMLH 68104	BYZANTIUM (LP, without poster)	50
73	A&M AMLH 68163	SEASONS CHANGING (LP, poster sleeve, brown labels)	100

(see also Ora)

B.Z.N.
73	Birth RAB 1003	Rolling Round The Band/Superman	12

C

ANDY C
92	RAM RAMM 001	SOUR MASH EP (12")	50
93	RAM RAMM 003	BASS LOGIC EP (12")	35
93	RAM RAMM 006	Slip 'N' Slide/Bass Constructor (Sonz Of A Loop Da Loop Era Remix) (12")	25
95	RAM RAMM 012	Cool Down/Roll On (12")	15

(See also Randall and Andy C.)

ERROL C
76	Concrete Jungle CJ 601	Jah For I/4TH STREET ORCHESTRA: Version	35

FANTASTIC JOHNNY C
67	London HL 10169	Boogaloo Down Broadway/Look What Love Can Make You Do	15
68	London HL 10212	Hitch It To The Horse/Cool Broadway	15
69	Action ACT 4543	Is There Anything Better Than Making Love/New Love	18
75	Island USA 8	Don't Depend On Me (Parts 1 & 2)	8
69	Action ACLP 6001	BOOGALOO DOWN BROADWAY (LP)	40

ROY C
66	Island WI 273	Shotgun Wedding/I'm Going To Make It	20
66	Island WI 273	Shotgun Wedding/High School Dropout (different B-side)	12
67	Ember EMB S 230	Twistin' Pneumonia/Tear Avenue	30
66	Ember NR 5035	THE SHOTGUN WEDDING MAN (LP)	30
75	Mercury 9100 017	SEX AND SOUL (LP)	15

CABARET VOLTAIRE
78	Rough Trade RT 003	EXTENDED PLAY EP (paper p/s)	15
79	Rough Trade RT 018	Nag Nag Nag/Is That Me (p/s)	15
79	Rough Trade RT 035	Silent Command/Chance Versus Causality (p/s)	10
80	Rough Trade RT 060	Seconds Too Late/Control Addict (p/s)	10
80	Rough Trade RT 038	THREE MANTRAS (12", p/s)	15
81	Rough Trade RT 096	Eddie's Out/Walls Of Jericho (12" p/s with free 7" Jazz The Glass/Burnt To The Ground (RT 095)	30
82	Rough Trade ROUGH 42	2 x 45 (2 x 12")	18
83	Factory FAC 82	Yashar (7.20)/Yashar (5.00) (12")	15
85	Virgin CVDJS1	Big Funk/Kino (white label, 500 only)	18

CABINET

			MINT VALUE £
86	Doublevision DVR 21	THE DRAIN TRAIN EP (2 x 12")	12
91	Plastex EXL 1	COLOURS (12" EP. p/s)	20
79	Rough Trade ROUGH 4	MIX UP (LP)	25
80	Rough Trade ROUGH 7	LIVE AT THE Y.M.C.A 27.10.79 (LP)	15
80	Rough Trade ROUGH 11	VOICE OF AMERICA (LP)	25
80	Industrial IRC 35	1974-1976 (LP, cassette)	30
81	Rough Trade ROUGH 27	RED MECCA (LP)	25
83	Some Bizarre CV1	THE CRACKDOWN (LP, with free 12")	20
83	Doublevision DVR 1	JOHNNY YESNO (LP, soundtrack)	15
84	Some Bizarre CV2	MICROPHONIES (LP)	20
85	Some Bizzare CV3	THE COVENANT, THE SWORD AND THE ARM OF THE LORD (LP)	20
85	Some Bizarre CVM 1	DRINKING GASOLINE (LP as 2 x 12")	15
87	Parlophone PCS 7312	CODE (LP)	15
90	Parlophone PCSX 7338	GROOVY, LAIDBACK AND NASTY (LP, with free 12")	25
90	Parlophone PCSX 7338	GROOVY, LAIDBACK AND NASTY (LP, without free 12")	18
90	Mute CABS 5	LISTEN UP WITH CABARET VOLTAIRE (2-LP)	20
90	Mute CABS 6	THE LIVING LEGENDS (2-LP)	25
92	Plasticity EXL LP03	PLASTICITY (2-LP)	80
92	Virgin CV 4	TECHNOLOGY: WESTERN REWORKS 1992 (2-LP)	70

(see also Acid Horse,, Chemical Agent, Citrus, Cold Warrior, Richard H. Kirk, Hafler Trio,, Stephen Mallinder, Multiple Transmission, Papadoctrine, Pressure Co, Robot and Humanoids, Wicky Wacky, Sandoz, Sweet Exorcist, Wranger)

CABINET
83	Sharp CAL 2	Language And Words/Language And Words (Extended) (p/s)	6

CABLES
68	Coxsone CS 7072	What Kind Of World?/My Broken Heart	70
68	Coxsone CS 7082	Soul Power/HEPTONES: Love Me Alway	125
68	Studio One SO 2060	Baby Why?/Be A Man	50
68	Studio One SO 2071	Love Is A Pleasure/Cheer Up	80
68	Studio One SO 2085	Got To Find Someone/ALEXANDER HENRY: Please Be True	50
69	Bamboo BAM 12	So Long/PRESSURE BOYS: More Love	40
69	Bamboo BAM 19	How Can I Trust You?/SOUND DIMENSIONS: How Can I Trust You? (Inst.)	40
70	Trojan TR 7792	Salt Of The Earth/Ring A Bell	10
70	Harry J. HJ 6614	Didn't I/JAY BOYS: Tilly	20
70	Harry J. HJ 6620	Feel Alright/Equal Rights	10
71	Big Shot BI 598	A Sometime Girl/IN CROWD BAND: A Sometime Girl Version	10
71	Duke DU 124	Mixing/IN CROWD BAND: In Orbit	8
72	Jackpot JP 787	Come On/Come On Version	6
73	Attack ATT 8053	Give Me A Chance/JAH FISH: King Of Zion	8
86	Studio One PSOL 002	WHAT KIND OF WORLD (LP, repressing, red and white labels)	35

(see also Dingle Brothers, Alton Ellis)

CABOOSE
70	Stax STAX 151	Black Hands, White Cotton/In My Hour Of Need	6

CACHE
81	Groove GP 111	Where Is My Sunshine/Jazzin' And Crusin'	6
81	Groove GP 111 T	Where Is My Sunshine/Jazzin' And Crusin' (12")	30

CACTUS
70	Atco 2400 020	CACTUS (LP)	50
71	Atco 2400 114	ONE WAY ... OR ANOTHER (LP)	30
72	Atlantic K 40307	RESTRICTIONS (LP)	20
72	Atlantic K 50013	'OT AND SWEATY (LP)	18

(see also Vanilla Fudge, Leaf Hound, Beck Bogert Appice, Atomic Rooster)

ALAN CADDY
64	HMV POP 1286	Tornado/Workout	35

(see also Tornados)

CADETS (U.K.)
65	Pye 7N 15852	Jealous Heart/Right Or Wrong	20
65	Pye 7N 15947	Baby Roo/Raining In My Heart	10

CADETS (U.S.)
56	London HLU 8313	Stranded In The Jungle/I Want You (gold label lettering)	500
56	London HLU 8313	Stranded In The Jungle/I Want You (silver label lettering)	250
56	London HLU 8313	Stranded In The Jungle/I Want You (78)	20

CADILLAC
86	CBS A 7180	Valentino/Valentino (p/s)	8

CADILLACS (1)
59	London HLJ 8786	Peek-A-Boo/Oh, Oh, Lolita	40

CADILLACS (2)
80	Red Eye	Billy/Who Dat Man (p/s)	8

BOBBY CADMAN
74	Regal Zonophone RZ3008	A Magic Spell/Own Up Time	25

CADO BELLE
76	Anchor 1033	Got To Love/Paper In The Rain	15
76	Anchor 1038	Stone Throw From Nowhere/Airport Shutdown	8

SUSAN CADOGAN
74	Dip DL 5030	Hurt So Good/UPSETTERS: Loving Is Good	15
75	Lucky LY 5078	Feeling Right/Congratulations	7
75	Black Wax WAX 2	Love My Life/MR. VIBES: Love Vibes	8
75	Magnet MAG 23	Hurt So Good/Hurt So Good (Instrumental)	10
77	Trojan TR9028	Nice And Easy/If You Need Me	10
75	Upsetter UP 121	SEXY SUZY (LP, white label pre-release, 500 only, 'Upsetter Records Sexy Suzy' in white type, die-cut sleeve)	70

CAEDMON

MINT VALUE £

76	Trojan TRLS 122	SUSAN CADOGAN (LP)	40

CAEDMON
78	Private pressing	CAEDMON (LP, with insert, with bonus 7": Beyond The Second Mile/Give Me Jesus)	750
78	Private pressing	CAEDMON (LP, with insert, without bonus 7": Beyond The Second Mile/Give Me Jesus)	600
97	English Garden ENG 1014	CAEDMON (LP, reissue)	25

CAESAR & CLEO
65	Reprise R 20419	Love Is Strange/Let The Good Times Roll (in p/s)	25
65	Reprise R 30056	CAESAR AND CLEO (EP, 2 tracks each by Caesar & Cleo and Sonny & Cher)	20

(see also Sonny & Cher)

CAESARS
65	Decca F 12251	On The Outside Looking In/Can You Blame Me?	15
66	Decca F 12462	Five In The Morning/It's Superman	10

CAFE SOCIETY
75	Konk KOS 5	Whitby Two-Step/Maybe It's Me	6
75	Konk KONK 102	CAFE SOCIETY (LP, with inner sleeve)	20

(see also Tom Robinson Band, Claire Hamill)

BUTCH CAGE/MABEL LEE WILLIAMS
60s	Storyville SLP 129	COUNTRY BLUES (LP)	20

CAGES PLAY
81	SSM 031	Midnight In Katowice/Abstraction (p/s)	10

AUBREY CAGLE
62	Starlite ST 45 082	Come Along Little Girl/Blue Lonely World	75
77	Starlite ST 45 082	Come Along Little Girl/Blue Lonely World (reissue)	10
78	Glee GLEE 10012	Rock A Billy Boy/Bop And Stroll (p/s, reissue)	8

CAGLIOSTRA
86	él GPO 22	Libera Me/Madmen And Lovers (p/s)	8

JEREMY CAHILL
70s	Solent	September Blues/Yesterday	15

(see also Shide & Acorn)

PATRICIA CAHILL
70	Deram Nova SDN 22	SUMMER'S DAUGHTER (LP)	30

DAVID CAIN
69	BBC RESR7	THE SEASONS (LP)	50

CAIN (1)
68	Page One POF 054	Her Emotion/Take Me Back One Time	35
78	SHP 103	VISITOR 2035 (2-LP, fold-out lyric sheet)	20

CAIN (2)
80s	private pressing	CAIN (2-LP)	30

DAVID CAIN & RONALD DUNCAN
12	Trunk JBH 043 LP	THE SEASONS (LP, 750 only)	15

CHRISTOPHER CAINE
67	Decca F12586	Saturday Night People/Turn The World Around The Other Way	10

MARTI CAINE
81	BBC RESL 90	I'll Never See You Again/Bitch Is Love (p/s)	10
82	BBC RESL 130	Can I Speak To The World Please?/Tin Heart And The Rebel (p/s)	15
81	BBC REB 408	POINT OF VIEW (LP)	150

TUBAL CAINE
70	Attack ATT 8023	I'm A Drifter Part 1/CIMARONS: I'm A Drifter Part 2	30

AL CAIOLA (ORCHESTRA)
56	London HLC 8285	Flamenco Love/From The Heart	15
61	London HLT 9294	The Magnificent Seven/The Lonely Rebel	8
61	London HLT 9325	Bonanza/Bounty Hunter	10
62	United Artists UP 1003	Big Guitar/Guns Of Navarone	8
66	United Artists (S)ULP 1115	SOUNDS FOR SPIES AND PRIVATE EYES (LP)	20

(see also Hugo Montenegro)

CAIRO (2)
83	Tunnel TUN 01	Seconds & Hours/Green Light (p/s)	6

CAIROS
03	Shrine 101	Stop Overlooking Me/Don't Fight It	8
03	Shrine L2AS	Stop Overlooking Me/CAUTIONS: Watch Your Step (reissue)	7

CAIR PARAVEL
76	Koala KOA PO 16	SOME OTHER MORNING (LP, insert)	600

CAJUN MOON
76	Polydor 2058 801	No Honey No Love/Version	6

(see Allan Taylor)

CAKE
68	MCA MUPS 303	THE CAKE (LP)	30
69	MCA MUPS 390	A SLICE OF CAKE (LP)	30

J.J. CALE
66	Liberty LIB 55881	Outside Lookin' In/In Our Time	18
79	Shelter ISA 5018	FIVE (LP, with bonus single "Katy Cool"/"Juan And Maria Juarez Blues" [JJ-1])	15
92	Silvertone ORE 532	NUMBER TEN (LP)	20

(see also Leathercoated Minds)

JOHN CALE
74	Island WIP 6202	The Man Who Couldn't Afford To.../Sylvia Said (Demo copy)	15
74	Island WIP 6202	The Man Who Couldn't Afford To Orgy/Sylvia Said	10
77	Illegal IL 006	Jack The Ripper In The Moulin Rouge/Memphis (unissued, test pressings only)	25
77	Illegal IL 003	ANIMAL JUSTICE (12" EP)	12
83	Ze IS 113	Close Watch/I Keep A Close Watch (p/s)	6
84	Ze IS 157	Caribbean Sunset/(same) (unissued, promo only)	10

CALEB (Quaye)

MINT VALUE £

85	Beggars Banquet BEG 145	Dying On The Vine/Every Time The Dog's Bark (p/s)	8
12	Double Six DS059T	EXTRA PLAYFUL: TRANSITIONS (12", p/s)	10
71	CBS 64256	VINTAGE VIOLENCE (LP, dark orange labels)	35
71	CBS 64259	CHURCH OF ANTHRAX (LP, with Terry Riley, dark orange labels)	35
73	Reprise K 44239	PARIS 1919 (LP, with lyric insert)	35
74	Island ILPS 9301	FEAR (LP, pink rim)	25
75	Island ILPS 9317	SLOW DAZZLE (LP, pink rim with picture inner sleeve)	15
75	Island ILPS 9350	HELEN OF TROY (LP, orange palm tree label, inner sleeve, withdrawn A1/B1 matrix includes 'Leaving It Up To You')	30
75	Island ILPS 9350	HELEN OF TROY (LP, orange palm tree label, inner sleeve, A1/B2 matrix includes 'Coral Moon' in place of 'Leaving It Up To You')	20
77	Island ILPS 9459	GUTS (LP)	20
77	Island ILPS 9350	HELEN OF TROY (LP, repressing, orange palm tree label, inner sleeve, A1/B3 matrix reinstates 'Leaving It Up To You')	15
82	Ze ILPS 7019	MUSIC FOR A NEW SOCIETY (LP)	15
84	Ze ILPS 7026	COMES ALIVE (LP)	15
89	Land LAND 09	WORDS FOR THE DYING (LP)	15
07	EMI 37760	CIRCUS LIVE (3-LP with free 7", sealed)	90
12	Double Six DS047LPX	SHIFTY ADVENTURES IN NOOKIE WOOD (LP, lyric insert and 1-sided 7")	22
16	Domino REWIGLP 107X	FRAGMENTS OF A RAINY SEASON (3-LP reissue, inners)	40

(see also Velvet Underground, Nico, Terry Riley, Ayers Cale Nico & Eno, Judy Nylon, Eno & Cale)

CALEB (QUAYE)
67	Philips BF 1588	Baby Your Phrasing Is Bad/Woman Of Distinction (300-500 pressed)	950
00s	Philips BF 1588	Baby Your Phrasing Is Bad/Woman Of Distinction (limited edition reissue)	7

(see also Mirage, Hookfoot, Bread & Beer Band, Elton John)

CALEDONIANS
69	Fab FAB 103	Funny Way Of Laughing/Don't Please	40

(see also Clarendonians, Prince Buster)

CALENDAR CROWD
82	Romantic RR002	Perfect Hideaway/Perfect Hideaway Dub (p/s)	20

CALIBAN
84	Caliban CLB 001	Digital Reggae/Open Mind (no p/s)	50

CALIBRE
09	Signature SIG 015	Let Me Hold You/Love's Too Tight To Mention (12")	30
01	Creative Source CRSE002LP	MUSIQUE CONCRETE (LP as 5 x 12")	25
05	Signature SIGLP001	SECOND SUN (LP as 4 x 12")	40
07	Signature SIGLP002	SHELFLIFE (LP as 4 x 12")	30
08	Signature SIGLP003	OVERFLOW (LP as 5 x 12")	30
09	Signature SIGLP004	SHELFLIFE VOL. 2 (LP as 4 x 12")	35
10	Signature SIGLP006	EVEN IF... (LP as 3 x 12")	30
11	Signature SIGLP007	CONDITION (LP as 3 x 12" with CD)	30
14	Signature SIGLP010	SHELFLIFE VOL. 3 (LP as 3 x 12" with CD)	35

CALIFORNIA IN-CROWD
66	Fontana TF 779	Questions And Answers/Happiness In My Heart	70

CALIFORNIA MUSIC
74	RCA RCA 2488	Don't Worry Baby/Ten Years Harmony	12
76	RCA RCA 2661	Jamaica Farewell/California Farewell	12
78	RSO 014	I Can Hear Music/Love's Supposed To Be That Way (as California)	10

(see also Beach Boys)

CALIFORNIA PINES
67	CBS 3074	Two Weeks In September Part 1/Part 2	10

CALIFORNIAN LICENSE
70	Philips 6006052	The Cage/Easter Song	12

CALIFORNIANS
67	CBS 2263	Golden Apples/Little Ship With A Red Sail	75
67	Decca F 12678	Follow Me/What Love Can Do	20
67	Decca F 12712	Sunday Will Never Be The Same/Can't Get You Out Of My Mind	10
68	Decca F 12758	Congratulations/What Is Happy, Baby?	10
68	Decca F 12802	Out In The Sun/The Sound	20
69	Fontana TF 991	Mandy/The Cooks Of Cake And Kindness	100
69	Fontana TF 1052	Sad Old Song/Weep No More	15
69	Chapter One CH 112	You've Got Your Troubles/Early Morning Sun	7

(see also Warren Zevon)

CALLAN & JOHN
69	CBS 4447	House Of Delight/Long Shadow Day	40

CALL GIRLS
88	53rd & 3rd AGAR 001	Primal World/VATICAN SHOTGUN SCARE: Thick Fat Heat Source (p/s)	8

CALLICOTT, (MISSISSIPPI) JOE
68	Blue Horizon 7-63227	PRESENTING THE COUNTRY BLUES (LP)	110
71	Revival RVS 1002	DEAL GONE DOWN (LP, as Joe Callicott)	25

TERRY CALLIER
90	Acid Jazz JAZID 27T	I Don't Want To See Myself (Without You)/(If I Could Make You) Change Your Mind (12")	10
78	Elektra K 52096	FIRE ON ICE (LP)	15
79	Elektra K 52140	TURN YOU TO LOVE (LP)	15
98	Verve/Talkin Loud 539 249 1	TIMEPEACE (LP)	30

CALLIES
71	Rubber RUB 002	ON YOUR SIDE (LP, gatefold sleeve)	15

CALLINAN-FLYNN
72	Mushroom 50 MR 17	We Are The People (The Road To Derry Town)/The Old Man And The Flower	30
72	Mushroom 150 MR 18	FREEDOM'S LAMENT (LP)	200

CALLING HEARTS

MINT VALUE £

CALLING HEARTS
91	Illuminated ILL 6	Return To Base/In The Jungle (p/s)	15

CALLIOPE
69	Uni UN 514	Clear Mud/Wiser	15
68	Buddah 203 016	STEAMED (LP)	25

CALOOGIE
68	CBS 1095	Bleeker Street/Benedictus	10

GEORGE CALSTOCK
78	Hit Run DD2	The Ungodly (Feat. U Black)/DOCTOR PABLO: Righteous Melody (12")	35

EDDIE CALVERT
55	Columbia SCM 5168	Cherry Pink And Apple Blossom White/Roses Of Picardy	10

ROBERT CALVERT
72	United Artists UP 35543	Ejection/Catch A Falling Starfighter (p/s)	25
79	Wake Up WUR 5	Cricket Star (p/s, 33rpm flexidisc, as Robert Calvert & 1st XI)	10
80	Flicknife FLS 204	Lord Of The Hornets/The Greenfly & The Rose (purple print p/s)	10
74	United Artists UAS 29507	CAPTAIN LOCKHEED AND THE STARFIGHTERS (LP, embossed gatefold sleeve, with attached booklet and inner sleeve)	40
75	United Artists UAS 29852	LUCKY LIEF AND THE LONGSHIPS (LP, gatefold sleeve)	20
81	A-Side IF 0311	HYPE (SONGS OF TOM MAHLER) (LP)	15
88	Beat Goes On BGOLP 2	LUCKY LIEF AND THE LONGSHIPS (LP, gatefold sleeve, reissue)	20
88	Beat Goes On BGOLP 5	CAPTAIN LOCKHEED AND THE STARFIGHTERS (LP, gatefold sleeve with booklet, reissue)	15
89	Clear BLACK 1	ROBERT CALVERT AT THE QUEEN ELIZABETH HALL (LP, mail order only, with badge, poster & T-shirt, gatefold sleeve)	40

(see also Hawkwind, Imperial Pompadours, Catapilla, Adrian Wagner, John Stevens Away)

TABBY CALVIN & ROUNDERS
56	Capitol CL 14620	False Alarm/I Came Back To Say I'm Sorry	10

CALYPSO JOE
69	Escort ES 801	Adults Only/Calalue	30

CAMALEONTI
68	CBS 3968	Applause/Applausi	20

CAMARATA
59	Top Rank JAR 160	Love Theme Sleeping Beauty/Medley Sleeping Beauty (as Walt Disney Studio Orchestra)	10

CAMARQUE
83	Clubland SJP 848	Howl Of The Pack/Someone Just Like You (in p/s)	75
83	Clubland SJP 848	Howl Of The Pack/Someone Just Like You	30

CAMBERWELL NOW
83	Duplicate 0011	MERIDIAN (12", p/s)	20
87	Ink 1224	GREENFINGERS (12", p/s)	15
86	Ink 19	GHOST TRADE (LP)	30

(see also This Heat, Camberwell Now)

CAMBODIANS
70	Duke DU 101	Coolie Man/J.J. ALLSTARS: Coolie Version	25

CAMEL
73	MCA MUPS 1177	Never Let Go/Curiosity	8
80	Decca FR 13871	Your Love Is Stranger Than Mine/Neon Magic (p/s)	6
73	MCA MUPS 473	CAMEL (LP, 1st pressing, black/blue hexagon label)	175
73	MCA MUPS 473	CAMEL (LP, 2nd pressing, black label)	50
74	Deram SML 1107	MIRAGE (LP, with insert, red/white label, small Deram logo)	60
73	MCA MCF 6265	CAMEL (LP, later rainbow label with black background)	30
75	Decca SKL-R 5207	THE SNOW GOOSE (LP, laminated sleeve, insert)	40
76	Decca TXS-R 115	MOON MADNESS (LP, 1st pressing with textured gatefold sleeve and P1 matrixes)	30
77	Decca TXS-R 124	RAIN DANCES (LP, with inner)	20
78	Decca TXS R 132	BREATHLESS (LP, insert)	20
78	Decca DBC-R 7/8	A LIVE RECORD (2-LP, gatefold)	20
79	Decca TXS R 137	I CAN SEE YOUR HOUSE FROM HERE (LP, insert)	15
06	Tapestry TPT 227	CAMEL (LP, repressing, 500 only)	18

(see also Pete Bardens, Gong, Camel, Caravan, Hatfield & The North)

CAMEL DRIVERS
68	Pye International 7N 25271	Sunday Morning 6 O'Clock/Give It A Try	15

CAMEOS (1)
63	Columbia DB 7092	Powercut/High Low And Lonesomely	30
64	Columbia DB 7201	My Baby's Coming Home/Where E'er You Walk	30

CAMEOS (2)
67	Toast TT 503	A Pretty Shade Of Blue/You Didn't Have To Be So Nice	8
68	Toast TT 508	On The Good Ship Lollipop/The Love Of A Boy	8

CAMERA OBSCURA (1)
80	Small Wonder SMALL 28	Destitution/Race In Athens (p/s)	12

CAMERA OBSCURA (2)
98	Andmoresounds AND 0945	Park And Ride/Swimming Pool	25
98	Andmoresounds AND 1145	Your Sound/Autumn Tides/Annawaltzerpose	25
01	Andmoresounds AND 1645	Eighties Fan/Shine Like A New Pin/Let's Go Bowling	10
01	Andmoresounds AND 1733	BIGGEST BLUEST HI-FI (LP)	35
03	Elefant ER-1104LP	UNDERACHIEVERS PLEASE TRY HARDER (LP, gatefold sleeve)	20
06	Elefant ER-1123LP	LET'S GET OUT OF THIS COUNTRY (LP)	18

CAMERA 3
79	Service SER 001	Russians In Space/The Solution To All Our Problems (p/s)	20

CAMERAS IN CARS
80	In Cinc CINC 1	Time Room/Avoid A Void/Bright Boy/The Author (p/s)	15

DION CAMERON & THREE TOPS
66	Rio R 111	Lord Have Mercy/Get Ready	30

G.C. CAMERON

MINT VALUE £

(see also Dion & Three Tops)

G.C. CAMERON
76	Tamla Motown TMG 1033	Me And My Life/Act Like A Shotgun	10
80	Flamingo FM-11	Live For Love/If I Love You	50
80	Flamingo FM T-11	Live For Love/If I Love You (12")	60
89	Ardent ADS 9002	Wait Until Tomorrow/Shadows	18
76	Tamla Motown ATML12029	G.C. CAMERON (LP)	15

(see also Detroit Spinners)

ISLA CAMERON
64	Transatlantic TRAEP 109	LOST LOVE (EP)	12

(see also Ewan MacColl)

JOHN CAMERON (QUARTET)
67	Columbia DB 8120	You Owe Me/Walk Small (solo)	8
69	Deram DM 256	Troublemaker/Off Centre	60
67	Columbia SCX 6116	COVER LOVER (LP)	30
68	Columbia Studio Two 197	WARM & GENTLE (LP)	20
69	Deram DML/SML 1044	OFF CENTRE (LP)	100
01	Trunk KES 001 LP	KES (1-sided LP, 500 only)	20
03	Trunk JBH 002	PSYCHOMANIA (LP, 1000 only, as John Cameron & Frog)	60

(see also Frog)

JOHNNY CAMERON
60	Top Rank JAR 396	I Double Dare You/Fantasy	8

KEN CAMERON
73	DJM DJS 5281	Land Of Love/Don't Bring Me Down	10

RAY CAMERON
67	Island WIP 6003	Doin' My Time/Gateway, Getaway Car	12

AL CAMPBELL
73	Magnet MA 023	When Spring Is Around/It Wouldn't Be Fair	30
74	Faith FA 003	When The Grass Is Green/Where Were You	12
75	Sunshot SS 008	Can't Get No Peace/REVOLUTIONARIES: Peace & Love	20
78	Phil Pratt SS 1009	Gee Baby/Where Were You (12")	20
78	Deb DEB 018	Love The Way It Should Be/Version (12")	40
79	Saferno SOF 004	Gone Down The Drain/One More Chance (12")	30
79	Nigara NADD 103	La-La Means I Love You (12")	40
70s	Ethnic ETH DD 2244	Down In A Babylon/Babylon Dub (12")	30
80	Strong Like Sampson SLSD 14	Jah Shine On Me/SUGAR MINOTT: Hall Of Love (12")	35
80	JB JBD 019	You Jamming/You Jamming (Part 2) (12")	30
80	JB Music JBD 004	Late Night Blues/Shower Me With Blessings (12")	15
81	Greensleeves GRED 51	Unfaithful Children/WAILING SOULS: Who No Waan Come (12")	60
81	JB JBD 029	Feed Back/Part 2 (12")	30
81	Greensleeves GRED 63	Your Love Means So Much To Me/Got To Love You (12")	10
82	Greensleeves GRED 94	Dance Hall Stylee/Fight I Down (12")	20
82	Silver Camel SC 014	Lambs Bread/I Was Born A Loser (10", p/s)	15
78	Sunshot SS 1002	GEE BABY (LP)	85
78	Terminal TMLP 1002	NO MORE RUNNING (LP)	100
78	ITAL IT001	LOVING MOODS OF (LP)	50
78	Jamaica Sounds JSLP 015	AIN'T THAT LOVING YOU (LP)	50
78	Manic PFULP 8551	MR. MUSIC MAN (LP)	30
78	D.E.B. DBLP07	SHOWCASE (LP)	100
79	Burning Sounds BS 1036	DIAMONDS (LP)	30
79	Hawkeye HLD 03	RAINY DAYS (LP)	35
80	Ethnic Fight ETH 2236	MORE SHOWCASE (LP)	60
80	JB JBLP 002	LATE NIGHT BLUES (LP)	100
80	JB JBLP 005	WORKING MAN (LP)	60
83	Vista Sounds VSLP 4033	AIN'T THAT LOVING YOU (LP, reissue)	25
84	CSA CSLP 14	BAD BOY (LP)	20

AL CAMPBELL & TRINITY
78	Deb DEB 013	Reggae Dance/Dragon Dance/AL CAMPBELL: Roots Man Style (12")	30

ALEX CAMPBELL
65	Transatlantic TRASP 4	Been On The Road So Long/The Night Visiting Song (in p/s)	10
68	Saga OPP 2	Victoria Dines Alone/Pack Up Your Sorrows	30
64	Xtra XTRA 1014	ALEX CAMPBELL (LP, with Martin Carthy)	25
65	Polydor 623 035	IN COPENHAGEN (LP)	18
67	Saga ERO 8021	ALEX CAMPBELL AND HIS FRIENDS (LP, with Sandy Denny)	15
71	Ad-Rhythm/Tepee ARPS 1	THIS IS ALEX CAMPBELL VOL. 1 (LP)	15
71	Ad-Rhythm/Tepee ARPS 2	THIS IS ALEX CAMPBELL VOL. 2 (LP)	15

(see also Sandy Denny)

AMBROSE CAMPBELL
66	Columbia SX 6081	HIGH LIFE TODAY (LP)	60

BILL & PETE CAMPBELL
71	Duke DU 123	Come On Home Girl/You Are Mine	7

CAT CAMPBELL & NICKY THOMAS
72	Pressure Beat PB 5511	Hammering/PETER TOSH: Medicine Man	20

CHOKER CAMPBELL
65	Tamla Motown TMG 517	Mickey's Monkey/Pride And Joy (as Choker Campbell's Big Band)	140
65	Tamla Motown TMG 517	Mickey's Monkey/Pride And Joy (as Choker Campbell's Big Band) (DJ copy)	250
65	Tamla Motown TML 11061	HITS OF THE SIXTIES (LP, as Choker Campbell & His 16-Piece Band)	125

CORNELL CAMPBELL (AKA CORNEL CAMPBELL)
63	Island WI 039	Rosabelle/Turndown Date (B-side actually "Under The Old Oak Tree")	30

David CAMPBELL

MINT VALUE £

63	Island WI 083	Each Lonely Night/ROLAND ALPHONSO: Steamline	20
64	Port-O-Jam PJ 4008	Jericho Road (with Dimple Hinds)/DON DRUMMOND & GROUP: Roll On Sweet Don	80
64	Rio R 38	Gloria/I'll Be True	25
72	Dynamic DYN 446	My Confession/AGGROVATORS: Version	20
72	Green Door GD 4042	Dearest Darling/Star Dust	20
72	Jackpot JP 801	Queen And The Minstrel/Put Yourself In My Place	30
72	Bullet BU 515	For Once In My Life/Didn't I?	25
73	Jackpot JP 809	Pity The Children/You're No Good	35
73	Jackpot JP 814	Harry Hippy/Just One Kiss	12
73	Green Door GD 4057	Give Me Love/Help Them O Lord	70
73	Duke DU 158	Shotgun Wedding/Girl Of My Dreams	15
73	Duke DU 159	The Very Best I Can/Heading For The Mountains	15
73	Ackee ACK 513	Give Me A Love/SHORTY PERRY: Message Of Love	10
73	Gayfeet GS 209	My Baby Just Care For Me/Jah Jah Me Horn Ya	20
75	Action ACT 102	Natty In A Greenwich Farm/Natty Version	15
75	Angen ANG 101	Talking Love/AGGROVATORS: Gorgon Dub	12
75	Angen ANG 105	The Gorgon Speaks/AGGROVATORS: Version	12
76	Angen ANG 122	A Tear Fell/My True Destination	12
76	Attack ATT 8125	I Will Never Change/Version	12
76	Daddy Kool DK001	I Heart Is Clean/KING TUBBY AND THE OBSERVERS : Zinc Fence	10
77	Third World TW57	The Investigator/Version	15
70s	Rocket VR 001	Many Rivers To Cross/Many Dub	10
77	Nationwide 1018	Let Me Go Girl/Version	7
77	Terminal TM 104	I Am A King/Watch And Peep	10
78	Cactus CT 118	My Country/ Part 2	30
78	D-Roy 3	Listen Dread/Version	10
78	Third World 7529	Blessed Are They/New York City (With I ROY)	10
79	Lord Koos EQ 1001	Mash You Down/Sweet Talking (12")	15
80	Cha Cha CHAD25	Rainbow/PETER BROGGS: Never Forget Jah (12")	70
70s	Wambesi TW 004	I'm A Man/Jah Jah GIve Us Love (12")	15
80s	Live & Love LLDIS0022	Nothing Don't Come Easy/Version (12")	20
80	Papa D PD0167	Rasta Come From Jail (with SASSAFRASS)/100 Pounds of Collie (with PAPA TULLO)	18
87	Live & Love LLDIS0022	Nothing Don't Come Easy/Version/SUPER BLACK: Bad Boys/Version (12")	15
04	Trojan/Jackpot TJGSE013	You're No Good/Pity The Children (reissue)	25
72	Trojan TBL 199	CORNELL CAMPBELL (LP)	50
75	Groundnation GROL 503	DANCE IN A GREENWICH FARM (LP)	50
76	Angen ANGL 03	GORGON (LP)	50
76	Third World TWS 301	STALOWATT (LP)	40
78	Justice JUSLP 09	ROPIN (LP)	30
79	Striker Lee TSL 104	NATTY DREAD IN A GREENWICH FARM (LP)	40
79	Burning Sounds BS 1034	SWEET BABY (LP)	25
82	Starlight SDLP 908	BOXING (LP)	25
83	Vista Sounds VSLP 4020	FIGHT AGAINST CORRUPTION (LP)	20
00	Simply Vinyl SVLP 391	I SHALL NOT REMOVE (2-LP)	20

(see also Eternals, Don Cornel & Eternals, Clarendonians, Charmers, Stranger & Patsy, GG Allstars, Flames)

DAVID CAMPBELL

67	Transatlantic TRA 141	DAVID CAMPBELL (LP)	30
67	Transatlantic TRA 153	YOUNG BLOOD (LP)	20
72	Decca SKL 5139	SUN WHEEL (LP)	25

ERROL CAMPBELL

77	Tempus 103	Jah Man/Jah	20
76	Shebazz SHE 001	Wolves/Follow	30

ETHNA CAMPBELL

64	Mercury MF 804	What's Easy For Two Is Hard For One/Again	20
64	Mercury MF 816	Girls Like Boys/Five Minutes More	10
74	Philips 6382138	FOR THE GOOD TIMES (LP)	15

GLEN CAMPBELL

61	Top Rank JAR 596	Turn Around, Look At Me/Brenda	12
69	Ember EMB S 263	Galveston/Everytime I Itch I Wind Up Scratching You (p/s)	7

(see also Sagittarius, Jimmy Slade)

IAN CAMPBELL (FOLK) GROUP

65	Transatlantic TRASP 5	The Times They Are A-Changin'/Across The Hills (in p/s)	15
68	Transatlantic TRA 263	THE CIRCLE GAME (LP)	15
71	Acorn CF 233	HOPE IS A STAR (LP)	30
71	Argo ZFB 13	THE SUN IS BURNING (LP)	15

(see also Dave Swarbrick)

ISOBEL CAMPBELL

04	Snowstorm STORM 026	Time Is Just The Same/Why Does My Head Hurt So?/Bordello Queen/Bang Bang/The Breeze Whispered Your Name Pt II/Argomenti (12" clear vinyl)	10
03	Snowstorm STORM 024LP	AMORINO (LP, 1500 only)	50
06	V2 VVR1043451	MILKWHITE SHEETS (LP)	15

(see also Belle & Sebastian, Gentle Waves, Isobel Campbell & Mark Lanegan)

ISOBEL CAMPBELL & MARK LANEGAN

06	V2 VVR5036037	Ramblin Man/Further Into The Night	12
08	V2 VVR5050637	Who Built The Road/Wild Is The Night	12
10	V2 VVR749786	You Won't Let Me Down Again/Hawk (Extended)	12
06	V2 VVR1635821	BALLAD OF THE BROKEN SEAS (LP)	70
08	V2 VVR1050621	SUNDAY AT DEVIL DIRT (LP)	100
10	V2 VVR745755	HAWK (LP)	120

(see also Mark Lanegan, Solusavers, Belle & Sebastian)

Jimmy CAMPBELL

MINT VALUE £

JIMMY CAMPBELL
69	Fontana TF 1009	On A Monday/Dear Marge (in p/s)	35
69	Fontana TF 1009	On A Monday/Dear Marge	25
70	Fontana TF 1076	Lyanna/Frankie Joe	6
70	Fontana 6007 025	Don't Leave Me Now/So Lonely Without You	6
69	Fontana STL 5508	SON OF ANASTASIA (LP, black/silver label)	120
70	Vertigo 6360 010	HALF BAKED (LP, gatefold sleeve, large swirl label)	150
72	Philips 6308 100	JIMMY CAMPBELL'S ALBUM (LP, black/silver label)	150

(see also Kirkbys, 23rd Turnoff, Rockin' Horse)

JO-ANN CAMPBELL
58	London HLU 8536	Wait A Minute/It's True	50
60	HMV POP 776	Bobby, Bobby, Bobby/A Kookie Little Paradise	25
61	HMV POP 873	Motorcycle Michael/Puka Puka Pants	20
62	HMV POP 1003	You Made Me Love You/I Changed My Mind Jack	20
62	Columbia DB 4889	I'm The Girl From Wolverton Mountain/Sloppy Joe	10
62	Cameo Parkway CP 237	Mr Fix It Man/Let Me Do It My Way	15
63	Cameo Parkway CP 249	Mother Please/Waitin' For Love	15

JUNIOR CAMPBELL
73	Deram 387	Sweet Illusion/Ode To Karen	6
74	Deram SML 1206	SECOND TIME AROUND (LP)	18

(see also Marmalade, Clan, Dean Ford & Gaylords)

LLOYD CAMPBELL
76	Love LOV 2	FIGHTING DUB (LP, artist commonly listed as Skin, Flesh & Bone)	50

MARTIN CAMPBELL
90	Jah Works JW 002T	Who Can We Run To?/SISTER NETIFA: Woman Determined (12")	20
91	Jah Works JW 015	Got To Pray/Praying Dub (12")	20
95	Raghga Delic LIC 1	Wicked Rule/Dub/Version/Drums (12")	25
97	Channel 1 (UK) NXTB 007	Wicked Rule/Remix Next Vs/Wicked Dub/Everywhere/I Walk/Next Version/Dub (12")	18
98	Channel 1 TBX 010	ROOTSMAN - THE REAL THING (LP)	25
90	Jah Works JW008P	THE DREAM IS OVER (LP)	30
02	Channel 1 LOGLP 015	HISTORICAL TRACKS (1978-1981) THE FOUNDATION (LP)	15

PETE CAMPBELL
79	Union UND1016	Does She Have A Friend For Me/CARLTON HUNTER: You Know Why (12")	40

ROY CAMPBELL (& JAZZBO JASPERS)
68	Giant GN 41	Another Saturday Night/Wonderful World (with Jazzbo Jaspers)	12
68	Jolly JY 003	Suzette/Engine Engine Number Nine	15

PATRICK CAMPBELL-LYONS
73	Sovereign SOV 115	Everybody Should Fly A Kite/I Think I Want Him Too	15
73	Sovereign SOV 119	Out On The Road/Me And My Friend	15
73	Sovereign SVNA 7258	ME AND MY FRIEND (LP, gatefold sleeve)	250
81	Public PUBL 1	THE ELECTRIC PLOUGH (LP)	20

(see also Nirvana [U.K.], Pica, Hat & Tie, Aquila, Informants)

CAMPER VAN BEETHOVEN
86	Rough Trade RT 161	TAKE THE SKINHEADS BOWLING (12" EP)	15
86	Rough Trade ROUGH 95	TELEPHONE FREE LANDSLIDE VICTORY (LP, with insert)	18
87	Rough Trade ROUGH 109	CAMPER VAN BEETHOVEN (LP)	15

RAY CAMPI
74	Injun EP 200	ROCK 'N' ROLL (EP)	10

CAN
73	United Artists UP 35596	Moonshake/Future Days (Edit)	20
73	United Artists UP 35506	Spoon/I'm So Green	20
74	United Artists UP 35749	Dizzy Dizzy (Edit)/Splash (Edit)	10
76	Virgin VS 153	I Want More/... And More	6
83	Cherry Red CHERRY 57	Moonshake/Turtles Have Short Legs/One More Night (12")	20
69	United Artists UAS 29094	MONSTER MOVIE (LP, burgundy label)	175
70	United Artists UAS 29283	SOUNDTRACKS (LP)	50
71	United Artists UAS 29094	MONSTE MOVIE (LP, repress by 'the can', sleeve has laminated front)	50
71	United Artists UAD 60009/10	TAGO MAGO (2-LP, flip-top sleeve)	150
72	United Artists UAS 29414	EGE BAMYASI (LP, with inner sleeve)	100
73	United Artists UAS 29505	FUTURE DAYS (LP)	80
74	United Artists UAG 29673	SOON OVER BABALUMA (LP, original silver sleeve)	50
74	United Artists USP 103	LIMITED EDITION (LP)	50
75	Virgin V 2041	LANDED (LP)	40
76	Caroline CAD 3001	UNLIMITED EDITION (2-LP, gatefold sleeve)	40
76	Sunset SLS 50400	OPENER (LP)	20
76	Virgin V 2071	FLOW MOTION (LP, some stickered stating "featuring the hit single I Want More")	18
77	Virgin V 2079	SAW DELIGHT (LP, with insert)	30
78	Lightning LIP 4	OUT OF REACH (LP)	15
78	United Artists UDM 105/6	CANNABALISM (2-LP, gatefold sleeve)	35
81	Virgin OVED 195	INCANDESCENCE (LP)	15
89	Mercury 838883	RITE TIME (LP)	20
97	Mute SPOON39/40	SACRILEGE (3-LP, gatefold)	30
07	Mute SPOON 008	EGE BAMYASI (LP, reissue)	15
12	Mute SPOON 55	THE LOST TAPES (5-LP box set, booklet)	100
12	Spoon CDSPOON5	THE LOST TAPES (3-CD boxed set, booklet)	25
14	Spoon XSPOON 4	MONSTER MOVIE (LP, reissue, inner with download card)	15
14	Spoon XSPOON 5	SOUNDTRACKS (LP, reissue, inner with download card)	15
14	Spoon XSPOON 6/7	TAGO MAGO (2-LP, reissue, download card)	20
14	Spoon XSPOON 8	EGE BAMYASI (LP, reissue, inner, download card)	15
14	Spoon XSPOON 9	FUTURE DAYS (LP, inner, download card)	15

CANAAN

MINT VALUE £

14	Spoon XSPOON 10	SOON OVER BABALUMA (LP, reissue, inner with download card)	15
14	Spoon XSPOON 25	LANDED (LP, reissue, inner with download card)	15
14	Spoon XSPOON 23/24	UNLIMITED EDITION (2-LP reissue)	20
17	Spoon SPOON 60	THE SINGLES (3-LP)	25

CANAAN
73	Dovetail DOVE 3	CANAAN (LP)	25
76	Myrrh MYR 1042	OUT OF THE WILDERNESS (LP, with inner sleeve)	20

LOS CANARIOS
67	Major Minor MM 502	Three Two One Ah/What Can I Do For You	50
67	Major Minor MM 532	Get On Your Knees/Keep On The Right Side	35

CANCER
90	Vinyl Solution SOL 22	TO THE GORY END (LP)	25
91	VInyl Solution SOL 28	DEATH SHALL RISE (LP)	20
93	Vinyl Solution SOL 35	THE SINS OF MANKIND (LP)	25

CANDIDO
79	Salsoul SSOL 121	Jingo/Rock And Shuffle (DJ Copy)	7
79	Salsoul Sa 8520	DANCIN AND PRANCIN (LP)	18

CANDLE FACTORY
77	CAVS 020	NIGHTSHIFT (LP, private pressing)	80

CANDLELIGHT
67	CBS 2002507	That's What I Want/The Happy Days Of Summer	25

CANDLEMASS
87	Active ATV 3	NIGHTFALL (LP)	15
89	Music For Nations MFN 95	TALES OF CREATION (LP)	15
88	Active Records ACT LP7	ANCIENT DREAMS (LP, insert)	20
03	Powerline PRLP 010	DIAMONDS OF DOOM (2-LP, white vinyl, gatefold sleeve with iron-on transfer)	20

ICHO CANDY
88	Selah DEX 007	Cool Down Sufferer/FISH CLARKE: Carry You Woman Go A Dance (12")	20
93	Jah Shaka SHAKA 948	GLORY TO THE KING (LP)	18

PENNY CANDY
60	Top Rank JAR 328	Come On Over/They Said	7

CANDY (1)
69	Emerald MD 1119	Little Bit Of Soul/Signs Of Love	20

CANDY (2)
69	Grape GR 3017	Ace Of Hearts/BILLY JACK: Bet Yer Life I Do	20
70	Big Shot BI 599	Ace Of Hearts/BILLY JACK: Bet Your Life	10

CANDY CHOIR
66	Parlophone R 5472	Silence Is Golden/Shake Hands (And Come Out Crying)	15
67	CBS 3061	Children And Flowers/Marianne	10
68	CBS 3305	Alexander's Ragtime Band/No Grey Skies	10

(see also Summer Set, Barry Ryan)

CANDY DATES
65	Pye 7N 15944	A Day Just Like That/Well I Do	12

CANDY FLOSS
72	Polydor 2041360	Delta Queen/Looking Over My Shoulder	8

CANDY & KISSES
65	Cameo Parkway C 336	The 81/Two Happy People	150
65	Cameo Parkway C 336	The 81/Two Happy People (DJ copy)	200
85	Kent TOWN 104	Mr Creator/CHUCK JACKSON: Hand It Over (withdrawn)	40

CANDYLAND
91	Yes 1	Bitter Moon/I'm A Good Girl (p/s)	6

CANDYMEN
67	HMV POP 1612	Georgia Pines/Movies In My Mind	10

CANDY ROCK
75	Phillps 6006 442	Captain Captain/Pocahontas (some with photo)	12

CANE
78	Lightning GIL 31	3 BY 3 EP (p/s)	25

CANIS MAJOR
80	Gem GEMLP 109	BUTTERFLY QUEEN (LP)	30

(see also Girlschool)

JAMES CANN BAND
82	LJS LJS 001	Love Don't Know Your Name/Hush Hush We Can Boogie	15

CANNED HEAT
68	Liberty	Rollin' And Tumblin'/Bullfrog Blues (unreleased)	0
68	Liberty LBF 15090	On The Road Again/The World In A Jug	8
69	Liberty LBF 15169	Going Up The Country/One Kind Favour	6
69	Liberty LBF 15200	Time Was/Low Down	8
69	Liberty LBF 15255	Poor Moon/Sic 'Em Pigs	8
69	Liberty LBF 15302	Let's Work Together/I'm Her Man	6
70	Liberty LBF 15350	Sugar Bee/Shake It And Break It	8
70	Pye International 7N 25513	Spoonful/Big Road Blues	12
70	Liberty LBF 15395	Future Blues/Skat	8
70	Liberty LBF 15429	Christmas Blues/Do Not Enter	6
71	Liberty LBF 15439	Wooly Bully/My Time Ain't Long	6
72	United Artists UP 35348	Rockin' With The King (with Little Richard)/I Don't Care What You Tell Me	6
73	United Artists UP 35562	Keep It Clean/You Can Run But You Sure Can't Hide	6
67	Liberty LBL/LBS 83059E	CANNED HEAT (LP)	100
68	Liberty LBL/LBS 83103	BOOGIE WITH CANNED HEAT (LP)	50
69	Liberty LDS 84001E	LIVING THE BLUES (2-LP, gatefold sleeve)	40
69	Liberty LBS 83239	HALLELUJAH (LP, gatefold sleeve)	25

CANNIBAL & HEADHUNTERS

			MINT VALUE £
70	Pye Intl. NSPL 28129	VINTAGE HEAT (LP)	30
70	Liberty LBS 83303	CANNED HEAT COOKBOOK (LP)	15
70	Liberty LBS 83364	FUTURE BLUES (LP, gatefold sleeve)	20
71	Liberty LPS 103/4	HOOKER'N'HEAT (2-LP, gatefold sleeve, with John Lee Hooker)	50
72	United Artists UAG 29304	HISTORICAL FIGURES AND ANCIENT HEADS (LP, gatefold sleeve)	15
73	United Artists UAS 29455	THE NEW AGE (LP)	15
76	United Artists REM 407	CANNED HEAT (EP)	10

(see also Harvey Mandel, John Lee Hooker)

CANNIBAL & HEADHUNTERS

65	Stateside SS 403	Land Of A Thousand Dances/I'll Show You How To Love Me	30
67	CBS 62942	LAND OF A 1000 DANCES (LP)	40

CANNIBAL CORPSE

93	Metal Blade MZORRO 57	HAMMER SMASHED FACE EP (12")	10
90	Metal Blade ZORRO 12	EATEN BACK TO LIFE (LP, inner)	25
91	Metal Blade ZORRO 26	BUTCHERED AT BIRTH (LP)	40
92	Metal Blade ZORRO 49	TOMB OF THE MUTILATED (LP, inner)	45
94	Metal Blade ZORRO 67	THE BLEEDING (LP)	45

CANNIBALS

85	Hit Records REEBEE 2	Christmas Rock 'n' Roll/New Year's Eve Song (doublepack in stocking)	6

(see also Count Bishops)

PHIL CANNING

79	Woodbine St. WSR 002	Sell Out/Underground (p/s)	40

FREDDY CANNON

59	Top Rank JAR 135	Tallahassee Lassie/You Know	15
59	Top Rank JAR 135	Tallahassee Lassie/You Know (78)	25
59	Top Rank JAR 207	Okefenokee/Kookie Hat	10
60	Top Rank JAR 518	Humdinger/My Blue Heaven	7
61	Top Rank JAR 568	Buzz Buzz A Diddle It/Opportunity	20
61	Top Rank JAR 579	Transistor Sister/Walk To The Moon	6
62	Top Rank JAR 609	Teen Queen Of The Week/Wild Guy	7
62	Stateside SS 101	Palisades Park/June July And August	7
62	Stateside SS 118	What's Gonna Happen When Summer's Done/Broadway	7
62	Stateside SS 134	If You Were A Rock & Roll Record/The Truth Ruth	10
63	Stateside SS 155	Come On And Love Me/Four Letter Man	6
63	Stateside SS 183	The Ups And Downs Of Love/It's Been Nice	10
63	Stateside SS 201	Patty Baby/Betty Jean	20
64	Warner Bros WB 123	Abigail Beecher/All American Girl	8
64	Stateside SS 298	Sweet Georgia Brown/What A Party	7
65	Warner Bros WB 5645	Action/Beechwood City	10
66	Warner Bros WB 5693	The Dedication Song/Come On Come On	6
60	Top Rank JKP 2058	THE EXPLOSIVE FREDDY (BOOM! BOOM!) CANNON (EP)	15
60	Top Rank JKP 2066	FOUR DIRECT HITS (EP)	15
61	Top Rank JKP 3010	ON TARGET (EP)	15
62	Stateside SE 1002	BLAST OFF WITH FREDDY CANNON (EP)	20
60	Top Rank 25/018	THE EXPLOSIVE FREDDY CANNON (LP)	20
61	Top Rank 35/106	FREDDY CANNON SINGS HAPPY SHADES OF BLUE (LP)	30
61	Top Rank 35/113	FREDDY CANNON FAVOURITES (LP)	25
63	Stateside SL 10013	BANG ON (LP)	35
64	Stateside SL 10062	STEPS OUT (LP)	40
64	Warner Bros WM/WS 8153	FREDDY CANNON (LP)	25

(see also Danny & Juniors)

JUDY CANNON

65	Pye 7N 15900	The Very First Day I Met You/Hello Heartache	50

SEAN CANNON

77	Cottage COT 411	ROVING JOURNEYMAN (LP)	30

CONROY CANNON

69	Pama PM 769	Oh Happy Day/Can't Get Along Without You (as Conroy Cannon Mission)	8
69	Atlantic 584 305	My Bunny/Good Boy	8

CANNON BALL & JOHNNY MELODY

69	Big Shot BI 518	Parapinto/Cool Hand Luke	100

(see also Carl Bryan, King Cannon, Johnny Moore, Jackie Mittoo, Royals)

CANNONBALLS

61	Coral Q 72428	Cannonball Caboose/New Orleans Beat	10
61	Coral Q 72431	Lullaby Of Birdland/Calliope Boogie	8

CANNON BROTHERS

65	Brit WI 1003	Turn Your Eyes To Me/Don't Stop Now	18

CANNONS

60	Decca F 11269	I Didn't Know The Gun Was Loaded/My Guy's Come Back	15
61	Columbia DB 4724	Bush Fire/Juicy	20

CANNY FETTLE

75	Tradition TSR 023	VARRY CANNY (LP)	30
77	Tradition TSR 027	TRIP TO HARROGATE (LP)	18

CAN'T STOP

80	Can't Stop CAN 1	IT'S GETTING DARK AGAIN EP	10

CANYON

75	RCA RCA 2112	Top Of The World/Boogie Down Broadway	15

CAPABILITY BROWN

72	Charisma CB 193	Wake Up Little Sister/Windfall	6
73	Charisma CB 207	Midnight Cruiser/Silent Sounds	6
72	Charisma BCP 7	Liar/SPREADEAGLE: Nightingale Lane (demo in p/s)	10

Jim CAPALDI

			MINT VALUE £
73	Charisma CB 217	Liar/Keep Death Off The Road (Drive On The Pavement)	6
70s	Charisma BCP 7	War (p/s)	6
72	Charisma CAS 1056	FROM SCRATCH (LP, lyric inner sleeve, pink 'scroll' label)	50
73	Charisma CAS 1068	VOICE (LP, gatefold sleeve, large 'Mad Hatter' label)	40
74	Charisma Perspective CS 5	LIAR (LP)	15

(see also Unit 4+2, Tony Rivers & Castaways, Fuzzy Duck)

JIM CAPALDI
72	Island ILPS 9187	OH HOW WE DANCED (LP, gatefold sleeve, pink rim label)	20
74	Island ILPS 9254	WHALE MEAT AGAIN (LP, pink rim label)	15
77	Island ILPS 9497	PLAY IT BY EAR (LP)	15

(see also Hellions, Traffic)

CAPDOWN
00	Peter Bower PBR 006	CIVIL DISOBEDIENTS (LP, blue vinyl)	35
03	Rugger Bugger SEEP35LP	POUND FOR THE SOUND (LP)	25

DEE CAPE
84	GroovATron GAI 1	TIC TOC (12" EP p/s)	40

CAPE KENNEDY CONSTRUCTION CO.
69	President PT 265	First Step On The Moon/Armageddon	70

CAPES & MASKS
65	Fontana TL 5339	COMIC BOOK HEROES (LP)	50
65	Nevis NEV R005	COMIC BOOK HEROES (LP)	18

CAPES OF GOOD HOPE
66	Stateside SS 577	Winter's Children/If My Monique Could Only Dance	15

CAPITAL LETTERS
77	Greensleeves GRED 2	Smoking My Ganja/Natty Walk (12")	30
79	Greensleeves GRED 16	UK Skanking/Run Run Run (12")	30
79	Greensleeves GREL 7	HEADLINE NEWS (LP)	28

CAPITOL K
99	Planet Mu ZIQ 015	Postcard/JEGA: Untitled (100 in numbered p/s, those un-numbered = £4)	10

CAPITOLS (U.K.)
66	Pye 7N 17025	Honey And Wine/Boulavogue	15

CAPITOLS (U.S.)
66	Atlantic 584 004	Cool Jerk/Hello Stranger	25
72	Atlantic 10205	Ain't That Terrible/Zig-Zagging	8

(see also Three Caps)

CAPLO BANAAL
83	Rambert RAM THREE	She Loves The Money/Is This Love (p/s)	45

CAPOEIRA TWINS
99	Blowpop BLOWP 001	4 x 3 (12", with hand-sprayed Banksy artwork, beware of bootlegs)	3000
99	Blowpop BLOWP 001	4 x 3 (12")	15

CAPONE
98	Hardleaders HL 028	Friday/Alaska (12")	30

EDDIE CAPONE'S TREATMENT
85	Treatment SOB 004	I Won't Give You Up/We Would Like To Spend Some Time With You (12", p/s featuring Diane Jones)	80
85	Treatment SOB 0045P	I Won't Give You Up/We Would Like To Spend Some Time With You (p/s featuring Diane Jones)	20

ANDY CAPP
69	Treasure Isle TI 7052	Pop-A-Top/RICO: The Lion Speaks	25
70	Duke DU 69	The Law Parts 1 & 2	25
70	Duke DU 71	Poppy Show/Pop-A-Top (Part 2)	12

CAPPO
99	Son Records SON011	CAP 3000 (EP)	10
00	Son Records SON016	CODEX (EP)	10
00	Blunted Astronaut BAR 12 TWE 0007	THOUSAND WORD EXODUS (EP)	10
14	Boot BEP 011	THE BOOT (EP, 100 copies only)	35
14	Boot BEP 012	UN:PROGRAMMABLE RAW EP (12", p/s)	12
10	Son Records 047	GENGHIS (LP, 200 only)	20

CAPPO & NAPPA
15	King Underground KU0-13	REBEL BASS (2-LP)	20

CAPPO & STYLY CEE
11	SON 050	FALL OUT (LP, 200 only hand-sprayed sleeve)	25

AL CAPPS
73	Stateside SS 2214	Shangri-La/Magician	7

CAPREEZ
79	Grapevine 113	How To Make A Sad Man Glad/It's Good To Be Home Again	8

DANNY CAPRI
55	Capitol CL 14265	Desirable/I Do, I Do	7
55	Capitol CL 14302	Don't Make A Liar Out Of Me/Angelica	7

CAPRICORN
70	MCA MK 5050	Liverpool Hello/How Did You Find Me	6

(see also Marty Wilde)

CAPRIS
61	Columbia DB 4605	There's A Moon Out Tonight/Indian Girl	80

CAPTAIN BEEFHEART & HIS MAGIC BAND
SINGLES
68	Pye International 7N 25443	Yellow Brick Road/Abba Zabba	40
68	A&M AMS 726	Moonchild/Who Do You Think You're Fooling	30
73	Reprise K 14233	Too Much Time/My Head Is My Only House Unless It Rains	12
78	Buddah BDS 466	Sure 'Nuff 'N Yes I Do/Electricity	7

CAPTAIN BEYOND

MINT VALUE £

78	MCA MCA 366	Hard Workin' Man (Jack Nitzsche featuring Captain Beefheart)/ JACK NITZSCHE: Coke Machine	6
82	Virgin VS 534	Ice Cream For Crow/Light Reflected Off The Oceans Of The Moon	7

EPs

71	A&M AME 600	DIDDY WAH DIDDY (EP promo only in p/s)	250
79	Virgin SIXPACK 1	SIX-PACK/SIX TRACK (picture disc, die-cut p/s with stand, 5,000 only)	15
82	Virgin VS 534 12	LIGHT REFLECTED OFF THE OCEANS OF THE MOON (12" EP, p/s)	12
84	A&M AMY 226	THE LEGENDARY A&M SESSIONS (12" EP/mini-LP, Diddy Wah Diddy EP plus "Here I Am, I Always Am")	15
86	Edsel BLIMP 902	THE LEGENDARY A&M SESSIONS (12" EP, reissue)	15

ALBUMS

68	Pye Intl. NPL 28110	SAFE AS MILK (mono, flipback sleeve)	150
68	Liberty LBL 83172	STRICTLY PERSONAL (gatefold sleeve, mono)	120
68	Liberty LBS 83172	STRICTLY PERSONAL (gatefold sleeve, stereo)	80
69	Straight STS 1053	TROUT MASK REPLICA (2-LP, gatefold sleeve)	200
69	Buddah 623171	SAFE AS MILK (LP, reissue, stereo)	40
69	Pye/Marble Arch MAL 1117	SAFE AS MILK (LP, reissue, mono, 10 tracks not 12)	40
70	Straight STS 1063	LICK MY DECALS OFF, BABY	100
70	Buddah 2349 002	DROPOUT BOOGIE (stereo reissue of "Safe As Milk")	30
71	Buddah 2365 002	MIRROR MAN (gatefold die-cut sleeve)	50
71	Sunset SLS50208	STRICTLY PERSONAL (LP, reissue)	20
72	Reprise K 44162	THE SPOTLIGHT KID (tan 'riverboat' label, with lyric card insert)	40
72	Reprise K 44162	THE SPOTLIGHT KID (tan 'riverboat' label, without lyric card insert)	15
72	Reprise K 54007	CLEAR SPOT (PVC sleeve with card insert)	40
73	Reprise K 44244	LICK MY DECALS OFF, BABY (reissue)	18
74	Virgin V 2015	UNCONDITIONALLY GUARANTEED ('two virgins' label)	35
74	Buddah BDLP 4004	MIRROR MAN	20
74	Virgin V 2023	BLUEJEANS & MOONBEAMS ('two virgins' label)	30
75	Reprise K 64026	TROUT MASK REPLICA (2-LP, gatefold sleeve, tan 'riverboat' label, matt sleeve, 'Captain Beefhart' on labels)	50
76	Reprise K 84006	TWO ORIGINALS OF CAPTAIN BEEFHEART (2-LP, reissue of Lick My Decals Off, Baby & "The Spotlight Kid")	20
77	Pye FILD 008	THE FILE SERIES (2-LP, reissue of "Safe As Milk" & "Mirror Man", die-cut sleeve with inners)	25
78	Reprise K 64026	TROUT MASK REPLICA (2-LP, gatefold sleeve, 2nd re-pressing, tan 'riverboat' label, soft laminated sleeve)	30
79	Virgin V 2149	SHINY BEAST (BAT CHAIN PULLER) (LP, inner)	20
80	Virgin V 2172	DOC AT THE RADAR STATION	25
81	PRT NCP 1004	SAFE AS MILK (LP, reissue, 10 track version omits 'I'm Glad' and 'Grown So Ugly')	15
82	Virgin OVED 19	BLUEJEANS AND MOONBEAMS (LP, reissue, Green/Red labels)	15
82	Virgin V 2237	ICE CREAM FOR CROW (with inner sleeve)	18
84	PRT NCP 1004	SAFE AS MILK (LP, reissue)	20
85	Virgin OVED 66	UNCONDITIONALLY GUARANTEED (LP, reissue, green/red labels)	15
85	Virgin OVED 67	SHINY BEAST (BAT CHAIN PULLER) (LP, reissue, green/red labels)	15
85	Virgin OVED 68	DOC AT THE RADAR STATION (LP, reissue)	15
85	Virgin OVED 121	ICE CREAM FOR CROW (LP, reissue, green/red labels)	15
99	Buddah 91751	SAFE AS MILK (2-LP reissue)	20
08	Oz It Morpheus OZITLP 8006	DUST SUCKER (2-LP)	20

(see also Mu, Frank Zappa, Jack Nitzsche)

CAPTAIN BEYOND

72	Capricorn K 47503	CAPTAIN BEYOND (LP)	30

(see also Deep Purple, Iron Butterfly)

CAPTAIN JESUS AND THE SUNRAY TEAM

92	Criminal Jesus 2	ALL THANKS TO THE LORD JESUS CHRIST AMEN (LP)	40
94	Criminal (No Cat. No.)	THE DAY THAT NEBULON EXPLODED (LP)	40

(see also Hawkwind)

CAPTAIN LOCKHEED & THE STARFIGHTERS

73	United Artists UP 35524	Ejection/Catch A Falling Starfighter (p/s)	25
73	United Artists UP 35524	Ejection/Catch A Falling Starfighter (different mix of A-side, no p/s)	10

(see also Robert Calvert)

CAPTAIN MARRYAT

74	Thor THOR 1007 S	CAPTAIN MARRYAT (LP, 200 only)	2000
10	Shadoks S114	CAPTAIN MARRYAT (LP, reissue)	35

CAPTAIN ROCK & SKYRIDERS

72	Crystal CR 7028	Luppy Lu/Together	8

CAPTAIN SINBAD

83	Rusty Intl. RI 006	Sister Maracle/ASHANTI WAUGH: Funny Love (Version) (12")	18
83	Oak Sound OSLP 002	AGAIN (LP)	25
84	Greensleeves GREL 34	THE SEVEN VOYAGES OF SINBAD (LP)	25

CAPTAIN ZERO

75	Gull GULS 23	Space Walk/I'm Only An Elf	6

CAPTAIN ZORRO

79	Gem GEM 12 11	Phantasm/Sure Can Boogie (12", yellow vinyl)	12

C.A. QUINTET

83	Psycho PSYCHO 12	TRIP THROUGH HELL (LP, reissue of U.S. 60s LP)	15

CARAVAN

69	Verve VS 1518	A Place Of My Own/Ride	60
70	Decca F 13063	If I Could Do It All Over Again, I'd Do It All Over You/Hello, Hello	20
71	Decca F 23125	Love To Love You (And Tonight Pigs Will Fly)/Golf Girl	20
76	BTM SBT 104	All The Way (With John Wayne's Single-Handed Liberation Of Paris)/ Chiefs And Indians (p/s)	6

CARAVELLES

MINT VALUE £

Year	Label/Cat	Title	Value
80	Kingdom KV 8009	Heartbreaker/It's Never Too Late (p/s)	6
68	Verve VLP 6011	CARAVAN (LP, 'pillar' sleeve, mono, brown/white label, with "sold in the U.K." text)	500
68	Verve SVLP 6011	CARAVAN (LP, 'pillar' sleeve, stereo)	400
70	Decca SKL 5052	IF I COULD DO IT ALL OVER AGAIN, I'D DO IT ALL OVER YOU (LP, boxed logo)	80
71	Deram SDL-R 1	IN THE LAND OF GREY AND PINK (LP, gatefold sleeve, 1st pressing with brown/white label)	120
71	Deram SDL-R 1	IN THE LAND OF GREY AND PINK (LP, gatefold sleeve, later pressing with red/white label)	40
72	Deram SDL 8	WATERLOO LILY (LP, gatefold sleeve, 1st pressing brown/white large Deram labels. SDL8 on sleeve and label)	150
72	Deram SDL 8	WATERLOO LILY (LP, gatefold sleeve later pressing with red/white labels and SDL-R 8 on labels and sleeves)	20
72	MGM 2353 058	CARAVAN (LP, reissue, blue/gold label)	25
73	Deram SDL-R 12	FOR GIRLS WHO GROW PLUMP IN THE NIGHT (LP, gatefold sleeve, red/white label)	30
74	Deram SML-R 1110	CARAVAN AND THE NEW SYMPHONIA (LIVE AT DRURY LANE) (LP, red/white label)	20
75	Decca SKL-R 5210	CUNNING STUNTS (LP)	20
76	BTM BTM 1007	BLIND DOG AT ST. DUNSTAN'S (LP)	15
80	Kingdom KVL 9003	THE ALBUM (LP, laminated sleeve)	20
11	Music On Vinyl MOVLP 385	CARAVAN (LP, reissue)	18
11	Decca 375 069-3	IF I COULD DO IT ALL OVER AGAIN, I'D DO IT ALL OVER YOU (LP, reissue)	18
11	Deram 533 420	IN THE LAND OF GREY AND PINK (2-LP reissue, 'splatter pink' vinyl)	20

(see also Gringo, Matching Mole, Hatfield & The North, Spiro Gyra)

CARAVELLES

Year	Label/Cat	Title	Value
66	Polydor 56137	Hey Mama You've Been On My Mind/New York	10
67	Polydor 56156	I Want To Love You Again/I Had To Walk Home Myself	8
68	Pye 7N 17654	The Other Side Of Love/I Hear A New Kind Of Music	25
63	Decca LK 4565	THE CARAVELLES (LP)	25

(see also Lois Lane)

CARAVELLI
| 69 | CBS 4275 | Theme From The Film Z/Isadora | 8 |

GUY CARAWAN
58	Topic 10T 24	MOUNTAIN SONGS AND BANJO TUNES (10" LP)	20
57	77 Records LP8	GUY CARAWAN, HIS BANJO AND GUITAR (10" LP)	30
67	Columbia SX 6065	A GUY CALLED CARAWAN (LP)	20

(see also Peggy Seeger & Guy Carawan)

CARBARETTA
| 78 | Ignition IR 1 | You Must Be Kidding Me/Scat (die-cut sleeve) | 20 |

CARBON COPIES
| 02 | Grapevine 125 | Just Don't Love You/Baby I'm Coming Home | 8 |

CARBON/SILICON
| 08 | Carbon/Silicon CS 7004 | Why Do Men Fight?/Be Good To Yourself (p/s) | 12 |

(see also Big Audio Dynamite, Clash)

CARCASS
89	Strange Fruit SFPS073	PEEL SESSION (12")	20
94	Earache MOSH 108T	THE HEARTWORK EP (12")	15
88	Earache MOSH 06	REEK OF PUTREFACTION (LP)	40
89	Earache MOSH 18	SYMPHONIES OF SICKNESS (LP, picture disc)	30
91	Earache MOSH 42	NECROTICISM - DESCANTING THE INSALUBRIOUS (LP)	30

CARDBOARD ORCHESTRA
| 69 | CBS 4176 | Zebady Zak/Mary Tell Me Why | 8 |
| 69 | CBS 4633 | Nothing But A Sad Sad Song/Yes I Heard A Little Bird | 8 |

(see also Zior, Monument)

CORNELIUS CARDEW
71	Deutsche Grammaphon 2538 216	THE GREAT LEARNING (LP, with the Scratch Orchestra)	40
85	Impetus IMP 28204	MEMORIAL CONCERT (2-LP)	45
86	Matchless MR 10	THALMANN VARIATIONS (LP)	25

CARDIAC ARREST (1)
| 79 | Tortch TOR 002 | A BUS FOR A BUS ON A BUS (EP) | 200 |

(see also Cardiacs)

CARDIAC ARREST (2)
| 79 | Another AN 1 | Running In The Street/TV Friends (p/s) | 50 |

CARDIACS
86	Alphabet ALPH 002	SEASIDE TREATS (12" EP, with poster & lyric insert)	50
87	Alphabet ALPH 006	THERE'S TOO MANY IRONS IN THE FIRE (12" EP, with poster)	40
88	Alphabet ALPH 008	Is This The Life/I'm Eating In Bed (p/s)	12
88	Alphabet ALPHT 008	Is This The Life/Loosefish Goosegash/I'm Eating In Bed (12", p/s)	20
88	Alphabet ALPH 009	Susannah's Still Alive/Blind In Safety And Leafy In Love (p/s)	10
88	Alphabet ALPH 009T	Susannah's Still Alive/Blind In Safety And Leafy In Love/All His Geese Are Swans (12", p/s)	15
88	Strange Fruit SFNT 013	RADIO 1 SESSIONS/THE EVENING SHOW (12", p/s)	25
89	Alphabet ALPH 011	Baby Heart Dirt/I Hold My Love In My Arms (p/s)	10
89	Alphabet ALPH 011T	Baby Heart Dirt/I Hold My Love In My Arms/Horse Head/The Safety Bowl (12", p/s)	15
91	Alphabet ALPH 015	Day Is Gone/No Bright Side/Ideal/Joining The Plankton (12" EP, with lyric sheet)	25
81	private label	THE OBVIOUS IDENTITY (cassette, as Cardiac Arrest)	100
81	private label	TOY WORLD (cassette)	100
84	Alphabet ALPH 001	THE SEASIDE (cassette)	80
87	Alphabet ALPH 004	BIG SHIP (mini LP, with lyric insert)	50
88	Night Tracks SFNT 013	RADIO ONE EVENING SESSION: R.E.S./ Buds And Spawn/In A City Lining/Is This The Life/Cameras (12" EP)	20
87	Alphabet ALPH 005	RUDE BOOTLEG - LIVE AT READING '86 (LP, stamped sleeve with insert)	80
87	Alphabet ALPH MC005	RUDE BOOTLEG - LIVE AT READING '86 (cassette)	35

CARDIGANS

MINT VALUE £

88	Alphabet ALPHLP 010	CARDIACS LIVE (LP)	30
88	Alphabet ALPH 007	A LITTLE MAN AND A HOUSE AND THE WHOLE WORLD WINDOW (LP)	60
88	Alphabet ALPH 012	ON LAND AND IN THE SEA (LP)	40
89	Alphabet ALPH 000	ARCHIVE CARDIACS (cassette, fan club issue, compilation of "Toy World" & "The Obvious Identity")	40
90	Alphabet ALPH 013	THE SEASIDE (LP)	50
91	Alphabet ALPHLP 014	SONGS FOR SHIPS AND IRONS (LP)	60
92	Alphabet ALPHLP 017	HEAVEN BORN AND EVER BRIGHT (LP)	40
14	Alphabet Business Concern ALPH DLP 022	SING TO GOD (2-LP, 1st pressing, 200 copies only)	40
15	Alphabet Business Concern ALPH DLP 027	GUNS (2-LP, 200 only)	30

(see also Cardiac Arrest 1, Mr and Mrs Smith and Mr Drake)

CARDIGANS

95	Trampoliene 523 556-1	LIFE (LP)	25
96	Stockholm 533117-1	FIRST BAND ON THE MOON (LP)	40
03	Stockholm 067 101-1	LONG GONE BEFORE DAYLIGHT (LP)	80
00	Stockholm/Simply Vinyl SVLP 175	GRAN TURISMO (LP, with inner sleeve)	80

CARDINAL

94	Dedicated DEDLP 018	CARDINAL (LP)	25

CARDINALS

71	Nelmwood Audio NWA 1	SWEET & REFRESHING (LP)	30
72	Nelmwood Audio NWA 012	ON TOP OF THE WORLD (LP)	22

JACK CARDWELL

54	Parlophone CMSP 24	Whiskey, Women And Loaded Dice/Slap-Ka-Dab (export issue)	20
54	Parlophone CMSP 27	Blue Love/Diddle Diddle Dumpling (export issue)	20

CARE

83	Arista KBIRD 122	Flaming Sword/Misericorde (12" p/s)	10

(see also Wild Swans, Lightning Seeds)

CAREFREES

63	Oriole CB 1916	We Love You Beatles/Hot Blooded Lover	25
64	Oriole CB 1931	Aren't You Glad You're You/Paddy Whack	15

CARELESS HANDS

81	Flying Kite FKR 001	Looking For A Secret/New Lamps For Old (p/s)	6
81	Flying Kite FKR 002	Lawrence/Other (p/s)	8

THE CARETAKER

01	V/VM Test Record OFFAL 07	A STAIRWAY TO THE STARS (2-LP, blue vinyl)	50
11	History Always Favors The Winners HAFTW008-LP	AN EMPTY BLISS BEYOND THIS WORLD (LP, blue vinyl)	45
11	History Always Favors The Winners HAFTW008-LP	AN EMPTY BLISS BEYOND THIS WORLD (LP, repressing, clear vinyl)	35
12	History Always Favors The Winners HAFTW 013	PATIENCE (AFTER SEBALD) (LP, blue vinyl, 300 only)	30
12	History Always Favors The Winners HAFTW 013	PATIENCE (AFTER SEBALD) (LP, black vinyl)	20

CARETAKER/ELLIS BAND

80s	Stonehouse 2	Majority Rules/Two Steps Forward	8

(see also Alton Ellis)

DAVE CAREY (JAZZ BAND)

56	Tempo EXA 51	DAVE CAREY JAZZ BAND (EP)	10
55	Tempo LAP 4	JAZZ IN THE TRADITIONAL SPIRIT (10" LP)	20
58	Tempo TAP 16	JAZZ AT THE RAILWAY ARMS NO. 2 (LP)	20

CAREY & LLOYD

72	Attack ATT 8032	Do It Again (as Carey/Lloyd)/GARY RANGLIN: Watch It	15
72	Grape GR 3025	Come Down Part 1/DYNAMITES: Come Down Part 2	15

(see also Carey Johnson, Lloyd Young, Lloyd & Carey)

MARIAH CAREY

94	Columbia 661070 7	All I Want For Christmas Is You/Miss You Most (At Christmas Time) (jukebox issue)	50
98	Columbia MARIAH 1	12s (10x12" in box)	70
93	Columbia 474270 1	MUSIC BOX (LP)	50
94	Columbia 477342 1	MERRY CHRISTMAS (LP)	100
95	Columbia 481367 1	DAYDREAM (LP)	100
97	Columbia 488537-1	BUTTERFLY (LP)	100
98	Columbia 4926041	#1's (2-LP)	80
99	Columbia 495065-1	RAINBOW (2-LP)	50
01	Virgin VUSLP 201	GLITTER (2-LP)	30

TONY CAREY

84	MCA MCA 873	Fine Fine Day/Say It's Over (p/s)	6

(see also Rainbow)

HENSON CARGILL

68	Monument MON 1015	Skip A Rope/A Very Well-Travelled Man	6

CARGO (1)

70	No Label, LS 1674	Killing Time/Love Will Turn You Round (Unissued, white labels only)	300

CARGO (2)

82	Cargo Z38	Holding On/It's Your Love	6

CARIBBEANS (1)

69	Doctor Bird DB 1181	Let Me Walk By/AMBLINGS: Tell Me Why	50
69	Crab CR 14	Please Please/MATADORS: The Destroyer	35

CARIBBEANS (2)

68	Group One G1 501	A Trembling Feeling/Hoping	40

Rare Record Price Guide 2024

CARIBBEATS
			MINT VALUE £
66	Ska Beat JB 246	The Bells Of St. Mary's/WINSTON RICHARDS: Loki	20
67	Double D DD 101	Highway 300/I Think Of You (actually by Marlene McKenzie and Caribbeats)	75
67	Double D DD 103	I'll Try/If You Did Look	60
68	Double D DD 111	One Step/HAZEL WRIGHT: Please Help Me	60

(see also Bobby Aitken, Itals)

CARIBBENN (THE)
65	Pye 7N 15961	Inside Out/Up My Street	8

CARIBOES
71	Bullet BU 479	Let It Be Me/All I Have To Do Is Dream	15

CARIBOU
14	Jialong JIALONG 012	Can't Do Without You (Extended MIx) (12" 1-sided)	15
05	Leaf BAY 42V	THE MILK OF HUMAN KINDNESS (LP)	20
07	City Slang SLANG 1047981	ANDORRA (LP)	15
10	City Slang SLANG 9550055	SWIM (2-LP)	20
14	City Slang SLANG 500070LP	OUR LOVE (LP, CD)	20

(see also Manitoba)

CARIBS
60	Starlite ST45 012	Taboo/Mathilda Cha Cha Cha!	25

CARIFTA ALLSTARS
72	Green Door GD 4040	The Harder They Come (actually by Charlie Ace)/Time Is Still Here	8

CARL & COMMANDERS
61	Columbia DB 4719	Farmer John/Cleanin' Up	20

DONOVAN CARLESS
71	Tropical ALO31	How Can I Tell Her About It/Be Thankful For What You Got	15

CARLEW CHOIR
69	Spark SRL 1028	Huma-Lama/Give A Hand To This Clown	7

TOM CARLILE
67	CBS 3249	I Saw The Light/Nightingale	7

BILL CARLISLE & CARLISLES
59	Mercury AMT 1063	Down Boy/Union Suit	30

JIM CARLISLE
78	Billy Goat 001	Don't Start Crying Now/She Knows How To Rock Me	15
79	Billy Goat 003	Train Whistle Boogie/Hillbilly Boogie	15

CARLISLE BROTHERS
59	Parlophone GEP 8799	FRESH FROM THE COUNTRY (EP)	20

DON CARLOS
78	Dove 511	Plantation/Version	20
80	Pirate PIR 001	Nice Time/Get Up (12")	20
80	Negus Roots NERT 003	I Love Jah/I Don't Care (12", as Don McCarlos)	40
80	Ethnic ETH 2236	Grief My Heart/Spread Out (12")	15
81	Negus Roots NERT 004	Gimme Gimme Your Love/PAPA TULLO: Gimme More Love (12")	30
82	Negus Roots NERT 015	Magic Man/Magic Dub (12")	15
82	Cha Cha CHAD 52	Can't Waste Time/PAPA BRUCE : No Time To Waste (10")	20
83	Shuttle SH 008	Money & Women (with John Wayne)/CORNELL CAMPBELL/PURPLEMAN: Keep On Working (12")	20
83	Blacker Dread SCOM 003	From Creation/Versions (12")	30
83	Youth In Progress YP001	Jordan River/LITTLE JOHN: Reasons/LADY ANNE AND SANTANA; Love Life (12")	20
85	Blacker Dread SCOM 020	Strictly Culture (Love We Culture Version)/MIKEY DREAD: Dubuling Mix (12")	30
80s	Rusty International RI 001	Isabel/BILLY BOYO: One Morning/CAPTAIN SINBAD & ROOTS RADICALS: Radication Dehbout (12")	20
81	Blue Moon BM 001	PROPHET (LP)	40
82	Negus Roots NERLP 001	SUFFERING (LP)	40
82	Greensleeves GREL 45	DAY TO DAY LIVING (LP)	15
82	Negus Roots NERLP 005	HARVEST TIME (LP)	60
83	Burning Sounds BRD 1053	SPREAD OUT INA DANCEHALL STYLE (LP)	20
84	Real Authentic Sound RAS 3008	JUST A PASSING GLANCE (LP)	15
84	Saxon International 5550	SAMMY DREAD MEETS DON CARLOS (LP, not released in sleeve)	25

(see also Black Uhuru)

DAVE CARLSEN
73	Spark SRLP 110	A PALE HORSE (LP, yellow/blue label)	40

MAGNUS CARLSON
11	Acid Jazz AJX268S	From Now On/Barbajagel (with the Ray Moon Quintet)	30

RAY CARLSON
67	MGM MGM 1362	Speak No Sorrow/It's Getting Me Down Girl	6

CARL CARLTON (LITTLE)
68	Action ACT 4501	Competition Ain't Nothin'/Three Way Love	50
68	Action ACT 4514	46 Drums 1 Guitar/Why Don't They Leave Us Alone	35
69	Action ACT 4537	Look At Mary Wonder/Bad For Each Other (as Carl Carlton)	20
75	ABC ABC 4040	Smokin' Room/Signed, Sealed, Delivered, I'm Yours (as Carl Carlton)	6
85	Kent TOWN 105	Competition Ain't Nothin'/HESITATIONS: I'm Not Built That Way	12

EDDIE CARLTON
76	Cream CRM 5001	It Will Be Done (Parts 1 & 2)	10

CARLTON & HIS SHOES
68	Coxsone CS 7065	Love Me Forever/Happy Land	175
68	Studio One SO 2062	This Feeling/You And Me (Love Is A Treasure)	100
80s	Live & Love LLDIS 116	What A Day/Version (12")	40
79	Studio One PSOL 003	LOVE ME FOREVER (LP, laminated sleeve, 1st UK press through Peckings)	80
85	Studio One PSOL 002	LOVE ME FOREVER (LP, reissue, Peckings)	30

(see also Lee 'Scratch' Perry, Roy & Enid, Abyssinians)

MINT VALUE £

PAUL CARMAN
74 DJM DJS 317   In My World/School Love 6

CARMEN
74 Regal Zonophone RZ 3086   Flamenco Fever/Lonely House 10
74 Regal Zonophone RZ 3090   Bulerias/Stepping Stone 6
73 R. Zonophone SRZA 8518   FANDANGOS IN SPACE (LP, gatefold sleeve, red/silver label) 35
75 R. Zonophone SLRZ 1040   DANCING ON A COLD WIND (LP, with inner sleeve, red/silver label) 45

(see also Jethro Tull)

ROGER CARMEN, ROCK KEELING, MO THOMAS & ANN & STEVE MITCHELL
71 Mosart Music MM 1   FROST LAND (LP) 25

JEAN CARN
79 Philadelphia Int. S PIR 13 8840   Was That All It Was/Whats On Your Mind (12") 15

CARNABY
65 Piccadilly 7N 35272   Jump And Dance/My Love Will Stay 120

CARNABY STREET POP ORCHESTRA & CHOIR
69 Carnaby CNLS 6003   THE LONDON THEME (LP) 40

CARNAGE
84 Creative Reality REAL 07   FACE THE FACTS (LP) 20

CARNATIONS
65 Blue Beat BB 285   Mighty Man/What Are You Selling 22

JUDY CARNE
69 Reprise RS 20680   Right, Said Fred/Sock It To Me 8

CARNEGY HALL
68 Polydor 56224   The Bells Of San Francisco/Slightly Cracked 6

CARNIVAL
67 Columbia DB 8255   The Big Bright Green Pleasure Machine/Silver Dreams And Scarlet Memories 10
70 Liberty LBF 15252   Son Of A Preacher Man/Walk On By 6
70 Liberty LBS 83305   THE CARNIVAL (LP) 20

SASHA CARO
67 Decca F 12687   Grade 3 Section 2/Little Maid Song 12
68 Decca F12744   Molotov Molotov/Never Play A B Side 15

BOBBI CAROL
63 Fontana 267 260TF   Will You Love Me Tomorrow/It Doesn't Matter 8

CAROL & MEMORIES
66 CBS 202086   Tears On My Pillow/Crying My Eyes Out 22

CAROLINA SLIM
72 Flyright LP 4702   CAROLINA BLUES AND BOOGIE (LP) 20

CAROLINES
65 Polydor BM 56027   Love Made A Fool Of Me/Believe In Me 20

CAROLLS
65 Polydor BM 56046   Give Me Time/Darling I Want You So Much 20

(see also Carrols)

CAROLS
70 Revolution REV 013   Everyday I Have To Cry Some/FIRE SESSION: Sleeping Reggae 10

(see also Carolls)

CAROUSELS
67 Pye 7N 17353   Holiday Romance/The Run Run 15

CAR PARK
81 Carrrere CAR 202T   Let's Do What You Do So Well/Fun City (12") 15

BOB CARPENTER
76 Celtic Music CM 027   SILENT PASSAGE (LP) 20

CARPENTER JOE
87 Solo SOLO 2   MAVERICK GENIUS (EP) 20

(See also Doubt)

THELMA CARPENTER
61 Coral Q 72422   Yes, I'm Lonesome Tonight/Gimme A Little Kiss Will Ya, Huh? 10
61 Coral Q 72442   Back Street/I Ought To Know 10

CARPENTER'S APPRENTICE
72 SRS 12107   CHANGES (LP, with insert) 200

CARPET BAGGERS
67 Spin SP 2006   Flea Teacher/On Sunday 30

CARPETTES
77 Small Wonder SMALL 3   THE CARPETTES (EP) 15
78 Small Wonder SMALL 9   Small Wonder?/2 Ne 1 (p/s, 2,000 only) 35
79 Beggars Banquet BEG 27   I Don't Mean It/Easy Way Out (p/s) 10
80 Beggars Banquet BEG 32   Johnny Won't Hurt You/Frustration Paradise//Keys To Your Heart/Total Insecurity (double pack) 10
80 Beggars Banquet BEG 47   Nothing Ever Changes/You Never Realise/Frustration Paradise (live) (p/s) 10
80 Beggars Banquet BEG 49   The Last Lone Ranger/Love So Strong/Fan Club (p/s) 12
79 Beggars Banquet BEGA 14   FRUSTRATION PARADISE (LP) 18
80 Beggars Banquet BEGA 21   FIGHT AMONGST YOURSELVES (LP) 20

CATHY CARR
56 London HLH 8274   Ivory Tower/Please, Please Believe Me 15
56 Vogue Coral Q 72175   Heartbroken/I'll Cry At Your Wedding 6
63 Stateside SS 147   Sailor Boy/The Next Time The Band Plays A Waltz 12

DEREK CARR
01 Trident 001   COPPER BEECH EP (12") 40
02 Digital Soul DS 04   INITIAL TRANSMISSIONS EP (12") 45
03 Geek GEEK 006   DESTINY EP (12") 40
03 Nice & Nasty DB3 008T   FUTURISTIC OVERTONES EP (12") 40

04	Headspace HS 015	PLANET JUMP EP (12")	35
17	Revoke REVOKE 001	WARM MACHINES EP (12" white labels, 150 only)	40

JAMES CARR
66	Stateside SS 507	You've Got My Mind Messed Up/That's What I Want To Know	80
66	Stateside SS 507	You've Got My Mind Messed Up/That's What I Want To Know (DJ Copy)	150
66	Stateside SS 535	Love Attack/Coming Back To Me Baby	40
66	Stateside SS 535	Love Attack/Coming Back To Me Baby (DJ copy)	70
66	Stateside SS 545	You're Pouring Water On A Drowning Man/Forgetting You	20
67	Stateside SS 2001	The Dark End Of the Street/Loveable Girl	30
67	Stateside SS 2038	Let It Happen/A Losing Game	15
67	Stateside SS 2052	I'm A Fool For You/Gonna Send You Back To Georgia	25
68	Bell BLL 1004	A Man Needs A Woman/Stronger Than Love	20
69	B&C CB 101	Freedom Train/That's The Way Love Turned Out For Me	12
69	B&C CB 101	Freedom Train/That's The Way Love Turned Out For Me (DJ Copy)	50
72	Mojo 2092 053	Freedom Train/That's What I Want To Know	8
11	Goldwax ITDEP 012	IN MUSCLE SHOALS EP (p/s)	10
67	Stateside SL 10205	YOU GOT MY MIND MESSED UP (LP)	100
69	Bell MBLL/SBLL 113	A MAN NEEDS A WOMAN (LP)	60

JOE 'FINGERS' CARR
55	Capitol CL 14372	Give Me A Band And My Baby/Zag-A-Zig (with Joy-Riders)	6

(see also Lou Busch, Vicki Young)

JOHNNY CARR (& CADILLACS)
64	Decca F 11854	Remember That Night/Respectable	20
65	Fontana TF 600	Do You Love That Girl?/Give Him A Little Time	15
66	Fontana TF 681	Then So Do I/I'm Just A Little Bit Shy (solo)	10
67	Fontana TF 823	Things Get Better/You Got Me Baby (solo)	35

LEROY CARR
63	CBS BPG 62206	BLUES BEFORE SUNRISE (LP)	50

LINDA CARR
67	Stateside SS 2058	Everytime/Trying To Be Good For You	40

LODY CARR
60	Top Rank 35-111	LADYBIRD (LP)	15

MIKE CARR
62	Decca F11448	That Certain Something/The Girl In The Mountains	10
68	Columbia SCX 6248	UNDER PRESSURE (LP)	20
73	Ad-Rhythm ARPS 1020	MIKE CARR (LP)	18

PETER CARR
69	DJM DJS213	Angel And The Woman/Imagine Yourself	20

ROMEY CARR
70	Columbia DB 8710	These Things Will Keep Me Loving You/Stand Up And Fight	30
70	Columbia DB 8710	These Things Will Keep Me Loving You/Stand Up And Fight (DJ Copy)	50

VIKKI CARR
67	Liberty LBF 15022	There I Go/One More Mountain	10
68	CBS 5161	Ain't No Mountain High Enough/Call My Heart Your Home	10

WYNONA CARR
61	Reprise R 20033	I Gotta Stand Tall/My Faith	8
85	Ace CH 130	HIT THAT JIVE, JACK! (LP)	15

CARRAIG AONAIR
77	Gwerin	CARRAIG AONAIR (LP, insert)	25

CARRIAGE COMPANY
70	CBS 5209	In Your Room/Feel Right	30
71	CBS 7059	Paint The City Red/Jubilee	12

ANDREA CARROLL
63	London HLX 9772	It Hurts To Be Sixteen/Why Am I So Shy (some copies have Why Am I So Sorry as the B-side)	25

BARBARA CARROLL
59	London HLR 8981	North By Northwest/Far Away	8

BERNADETTE CARROLL
64	Stateside SS 311	Party Girl/I Don't Wanna Know	20

BOB CARROLL
55	MGM SP 1132	I Love You So Much It Hurts/My Dearest, My Darling, My Love	10
56	London HLU 8299	Red Confetti, Pink Balloons And Tambourines/Handwriting On The Wall	25
58	London HLT 8724	Hi Yo Silver/Tonto The Brave	15
59	London HLT 8888	I Can't Get You Out Of My Heart/Since I'm Out Of Your Arms	10

CATH CARROLL
91	Factory FACT 210	ENGLAND MADE ME (LP)	18

CATHY CARROLL
62	Warner Bros WB 72	Poor Little Puppet/Love And Learn	10

DON CARROLL
57	Capitol CL 14812	At Your Front Door/The Gods Were Angry With Me	10

GINA CARROLL
65	Decca F 12297	Bye Bye Big Boy/Down The Street	20

JOHNNY CARROLL & HOT ROCKS
56	Brunswick 05580	Corrine Corrina/Wild Wild Women	600
56	Brunswick 05580	Corrine Corrina/Wild Wild Women (78)	70
56	Brunswick 05603	Crazy, Crazy Lovin'/Hot Rock	600
56	Brunswick 05603	Crazy, Crazy Lovin'/Hot Rock (78)	70
74	UK USA 1	Black Leather Rebel/Be-Bop-A-Lula (as Johnny Carroll & Blue Caps)	10

LISA CARROLL
69	CBS 4428	You Made Me What I Am/Don't Count The Days	6

Toni CARROLL

MINT VALUE £

TONI CARROLL
| 58 | MGM MGM 987 | Dreamsville/I've Never Felt This Way Before | 10 |
| 58 | MGM EP 689 | THIS ONE IS TONI (EP) | 15 |

VIVIAN CARROLL
| 12 | Goldmine Soul Supply GS 051 | Oh Yeah Yeah Yeah/Instrumental Version | 6 |

CARROLLS
66	Polydor BM 56081	Surrender Your Love/The Folk I Love	25
66	Polydor BM 56081	Surrender Your Love/The Folk I Love (DJ Copy)	50
68	CBS 3875	A Lemon Balloon And A Blue Sky/Make Me Belong To You	20
69	CBS 4401	We're In This Thing Together/We Know Better	15
67	CBS 3414	So Gently Falls The Rain/Nice To See You Darling	15
67	CBS 3414	So Gently Falls The Rain/Nice To See You Darling (DJ Copy)	25

(see also Carols, Carolls, Brotherly Love)

BEN CARRUTHERS & DEEP
| 65 | Parlophone R 5295 | Jack O' Diamonds/Right Behind You | 50 |

CHAD CARSON
| 63 | HMV POP 1156 | They Were Wrong/Stop Picking On Me | 50 |

JOE CARSON
| 63 | Liberty LIB 55178 | I Gotta Get Drunk (And I Shore Do Dread It)/Who Will Buy My Memories | 25 |

KEN CARSON
| 55 | London HLF 8213 | Hawkeye/I've Been Working On The Railroad | 70 |
| 56 | London HLF 8237 | Let Her Go, Let Her Go/The Song Of Daniel Boone (The Daddy Of Them All) | 60 |

KIT CARSON
| 56 | Capitol CL 14524 | Band Of Gold/Cast Your Bread Upon The Waters | 10 |

MINDY CARSON & GUY MITCHELL
| 53 | Columbia SCM 5022 | That's A Why/Train Of Love | 15 |

(see also Guy Mitchell)

CARSTAIRS
| 79 | Inferno Heat 7 | It Really Hurts Me Girl (Re-mix 1)/It Really Hurts Me Girl (Re-mix 2) (reissue) | 8 |
| 12 | Inferno 1001 | It Really Hurts Me Girl (Unreleased Mix)/Original Mix (reissue) | 8 |

CARTE BLANCHE
| 79 | Pye 7NL46193 | Get Up On Your Feet/Do It Like You Like It (p/s) | 15 |

ANITA CARTER
| 58 | London HLA 8693 | Blue Doll/Go Away Johnnie | 10 |
| 60 | London HLW 9102 | Moon Girl/Mama Don't Cry At My Wedding | 10 |

BENNY CARTER
| 62 | HMV CLP 1624/CSD1480 | FURTHER DEFINITIONS (LP, mono/stereo) | 20 |

(see also Helen Humes)

BETTY CARTER
| 63 | London HLK 9748 | The Good Life/Nothing More To Look Forward To | 7 |

(see also Ray Charles)

CAROLINE CARTER
| 65 | Decca F 12239 | The Ballad Of The Possibilities/We Want Love | 20 |

CAROLYN CARTER
| 65 | London HL 9959 | It Hurts/I'm Thru | 40 |

CHRIS CARTER
81	Industrial IRC 32	THE SPACE BETWEEN (cassette)	30
85	Conspiracy International CTILP3	MONDO BEAT (LP)	25
10	Optimo OM CC01	THE SPACES BETWEEN (LP, reissue)	15

(see also Throbbing Gristle, Chris & Cosey)

CLARENCE CARTER
68	Atlantic 584 154	Thread The Needle/Don't Make My Baby Cry	18
68	Atlantic 584 176	Looking For A Fox/I Can't See Myself (Crying About You)	20
68	Atlantic 584 187	Funky Fever/Slip Away	15
68	Atlantic 584 223	Too Weak To Fight/Let Me Comfort You	15
69	Atlantic 584 248	Snatchin' It Back/Making Love (At The Dark End Of The Street)	15
69	Atlantic 584 272	The Feeling Is Right/You Can't Miss When You Can't Measure	10
70	Atlantic 584 309	Take It Off Him And Put It On Me/The Few Troubles I've Had	10
70	Atlantic 2091 030	Patches/I Can't Leave Your Love Alone	10
71	Atlantic 2091 045	It's All In Your Mind/Willie And Laura Mae Jones	10
71	Atlantic 2091 093	The Court Room/Getting The Bills (But No Merchandise)	10
71	Atlantic 2091 139	Slipped, Tripped And Fell In Love/I Hate To Love And Run	10
74	ABC 4037	Warning/On Your Way Down	8
83	Certain ACERT 1	Messin' With My Mind/Messin' (Instrumental Version)	15
68	Atlantic 588 152	THIS IS CLARENCE CARTER (LP)	30
69	Atlantic 588 172	THE DYNAMIC CLARENCE CARTER (LP)	25
69	Atlantic 588 191	TESTIFYIN' (LP)	20
70	Atlantic 2400 027	PATCHES (LP)	20

ERROL CARTER
| 73 | Cactus CT 71 | Hold Up Your Head/SUCCESS ALL STARS: Tank Skank | 30 |
| 76 | Cactus CT 96 | Ram Goat Malish Water/Ranking Dub | 60 |

HAL CARTER FIVE
| 62 | Oriole CB 1709 | Come On And Twist Me/Twistin' Time Is Here | 10 |

HERBIE CARTER
| 68 | Duke DU 4 | Happy Time (actually by Keble Drummond)/BOYS: Smashville | 50 |

JACK CARTER
| 70 | Penny Farthing PEN 739 | Morning/Fanny | 8 |

JEAN CARTER & CENTREPIECES
| 68 | Stateside SS 2114 | No Good Jim/And None | 15 |

John CARTER & RUSS ALQUIST

MINT VALUE £

68	Stateside SS 2114	No Good Jim/And None (DJ Copy)	30

JOHN CARTER & RUSS ALQUIST
68	Spark SRL 1017	The Laughing Man/Midsummer Dreaming	30

(see also Carter-Lewis & Southerners, Ivy League, Flowerpot Men)

JOHN CARTER
72	Spark SRL 1069	One More Mile To Freedom/The Saddest Word I Know	6

LYNDA CARTER
73	EMI 2005	It Might As Well Stay Monday/I Believe In Music	6
80	Motown TMG 1207	The Last Song/What's A Little Love Between Friends (p/s)	7
78	CBS EPC 83052	LYNDA CARTER (LP, as aka WONDER WOMAN)	18

MARTIN CARTER
71	Tradition TSR 008	SOMEONE NEW (LP)	30
72	Tradition TSR 012	UPS & DOWNS (LP)	25

MEL CARTER
63	Pye International 7N 25212	When A Boy Falls In Love/So Wonderful	50
66	Liberty LIB 66113	Hold Me, Thrill Me, Kiss Me/Sweet Little Girl	20
65	Liberty LIB 66138	(All Of A Sudden) My Heart Sings/When I Hold The Hand Of The One I Love	10
66	Liberty LIB 66148	Love Is All We Need/I Wish I Didn't Love You So	10
66	Liberty LIB 66165	Band Of Gold/Detour	10
66	Liberty LIB 66183	You You You/If You Lose Her	10

MIKE CARTER (& DRAGONFLY)
84	Button BTN 117	My True Love/Talk To Me	6

See also Dragonfly

NELL CARTER
74	RCA 2503	Dreams/Send Him Back To Me	15
74	RCA 2503	Dreams/Send Him Back To Me (DJ Copy)	25

NICK CARTER
79	NC 001	ABSTRACTS & EXTRACTS (LP, insert 250 only)	150

SHEILA CARTER & EPISODE SIX
66	Pye 7N 17194	I Will Warm Your Heart/Incense	30

(see also Episode, Episode Six)

SONNY CARTER WITH EARL BOSTIC & HIS ORCHESTRA
55	Parlophone MSP 6167	There Is No Greater Love/Oh Baby	20

(see also Earl Bostic)

CARTER STEPHENS CHORALE
68	Fontana TF 936	Peace! (Dream Of The Common Man)/The Promised Land	15

CARTERHALL
76	Thor 1010S	I WISH YOU COULD SEE (LP, 200 only)	700

CARTER-LEWIS & SOUTHERNERS
61	Piccadilly 7N 35004	So Much In Love/Back On The Scene	30
61	Ember EMB S 145	Two Timing Baby/Will It Happen To Me?	50
62	Piccadilly 7N 35085	Here's Hopin'/Poor Joe	30
62	Ember EMB S 165	Tell Me/My Broken Heart	50
63	Oriole CB 1835	Sweet And Tender Romance/Who Told You?	20
63	Oriole CB 1868	Your Momma's Out Of Town/Somebody Told My Girl	20
64	Oriole CB 1919	Skinny Minnie/Easy To Cry	40

(see also Ivy League, Flowerpot Men, White Plains, John Carter & Russ Alquist, Jimmy Page, Dawn Chorus)

CARTER TUTTI VOID
12	Mute STUMM 340	TRANSVERSE (LP, CD)	18
15	Industrial IRCTVLP 01	f(x) (LP, white vinyl)	20

(see also Chris & Cosey, Factory Floor, Nik Colk Void)

MARTIN CARTHY
65	Fontana (S)TL 5269	MARTIN CARTHY (LP, black/silver label)	30
71	Philips 6308 049	LANDFALL (LP, black/silver label)	30
72	Peg PEG 12	SHEARWATER (LP, with insert, purple label)	25
74	Deram SML 1111	SWEET WIVELSFIELD (LP, red/white label)	15

MARTIN CARTHY & DAVE SWARBRICK
67	Fontana TE 17490	NO SONGS (EP)	30
66	Fontana STL 5362	SECOND ALBUM (LP, black/silver label)	30
67	Fontana STL 5434	BYKER HILL (LP)	30
68	Fontana STL 5477	BUT TWO CAME BY (LP)	30
70	Fontana STL 5529	PRINCE HEATHEN (LP, black/silver label)	35
71	Pegasus PEG 6	SELECTIONS (LP, gatefold sleeve)	30

(see also Dave Swarbrick, Three City Four, Steeleye Span, Leon Rosselson, Alex Campbell, Nigel Denver)

CARTOONE
69	Atlantic 584 240	Knick Knack Man/A Penny For The Sun	12
69	Atlantic 588 174	CARTOONE (LP)	25

(see also Jimmy Page)

CARTOONS (1)
80	Hot HOT 001	Lunchtime Love Affair/Dark Alleys (p/s)	15
81	Hot HOT 002	Beep Beep Love/Thomas Cadillac (p/s)	10

CARTOONS (2)
84	Cage CAGE 2	Once The Victor/Instrumental Version (p/s)	10

CARTOONS (3)
83	Stiletto SO 1	Gee George/Love Is The Drug (p/s)	7

DAVE CARTWRIGHT
73	DJM DJS 10750	Band Of Hope/Queen Of The May (promo)	10
70	Harmony DB 0001	MIDDLE OF THE ROAD (LP, private pressing, 99 only, with insert)	200
72	Transatlantic TRA 255	A LITTLE BIT OF GLORY (LP, with inner sleeve)	20
73	Transatlantic TRA 267	BACK TO THE GARDEN (LP, with lyric inner sleeve)	20

Mike CARVER

MINT VALUE £

74	Transatlantic TRA 284	DON'T LET YOUR FAMILY DOWN (LP, with lyric insert)	20

(see also Bev Pegg, Away From The Sand)

MIKE CARVER
79	Venom SRTS/79/CUS 396	THE MURDER OF BLAIR PEACH	8
81	SRTS/CUS1139	Ordinary People/Brixton (p/s)	7

TRISTRAM CARY
70	Galliard GAL 4006	3 4 5 (LP, with booklet)	100
70	Galliard GAL 4007	NARCISSIS (LP, gatefold, with insert)	100
71	EMS (No Cat No)	TRIOS (2-LP, with booklet/instructions, warped copies worth half this price)	400
10	Trunk JBH 035 LP	IT'S TIME FOR TRISTRAM CARY (LP, 500 only, black vinyl)	18
10	Trunk JBH 035 LP	IT'S TIME FOR TRISTRAM CARY (LP, reissue, 300 only, clear vinyl)	20

CASABLANCA
74	Rocket PIGL 7	CASABLANCA (LP, die-cut sleeve with inner lyric sleeve)	20

(see also Trees, Ginger Bakers Airforce)

JULIAN CASABLANCAS
09	Rough Trade RTRADS 563	I Wish It Was Christmas Today/Old Hollywood (p/s, 500 only, white vinyl)	50

(see also Strokes)

CASANOVAS
00s	Singles Society 7STAS 3320	Nasty/Too Cool (numbered die-cut p/s, 500 only)	10

CASCADES
63	Warner Bros WB 88	Rhythm Of The Rain/Let Me Be	7
63	Warner Bros WB 98	Shy Girl/The Last Leaf	7
63	Warner Bros WB 103	I Wanna Be Your Lover/My First Day Alone	7
63	RCA Victor RCA 1358	Cinderella/A Little Like Loving	6
64	RCA Victor RCA 1378	Jeannie/For Your Sweet Love	6
65	Liberty LIB 55822	I Bet You Won't Stay/She'll Love Again	8
66	Stateside SS 515	Cheryl's Goin' Home/Truly Julie's Blues	10
63	Warner Bros WEP 6106	RHYTHM OF THE RAIN (EP, mono)	20
63	Warner Bros WSE 6106	RHYTHM OF THE RAIN (EP, stereo)	25
63	Warner Bros WM 8127	RHYTHM OF THE RAIN (LP, mono)	30
63	Warner Bros WM 8127	RHYTHM OF THE RAIN (LP, stereo)	35

AL CASEY & K.C. ETTES
63	Pye International 7N 25215	Surfin' Hootenanny/Easy Picking	12

(see also Sanford Clark, Duane Eddy)

HOWIE CASEY & SENIORS
62	Fontana H 364	Double Twist/True Fine Mama	25
62	Fontana H 381	I Ain't Mad At You/Twist At The Top	20
63	Fontana TF 403	The Boll Weevil Song/Bony Moronie	20
62	Fontana TFL 5180	TWIST AT THE TOP (LP, mono)	80
62	Fontana STFL 592	TWIST AT THE TOP (LP, stereo)	100

(see also Freddie Starr)

ALVIN CASH (& REGISTERS)
65	Stateside SS 386	Twine Time/The Bump (as Alvin Cash & Crawlers)	30
65	Stateside SS 386	Twine Time/The Bump (as Alvin Cash & Crawlers) (DJ Copy)	60
66	Stateside SS 543	Philly Freeze/No Deposits, No Returns (as Alvin Cash & Registers)	25
66	Stateside SS 543	Philly Freeze/No Deposits, No Returns (as Alvin Cash & Registers) (DJ Copy)	50
68	President PT 119	Alvin's Boo-Ga-Loo/Let's Do Some Good Timing (as Alvin Cash & Registers)	10
68	President PT 129	Doin' The Ali Shuffle/Feel So Good	10
68	President PT 147	Charge/Diff'rent Strokes For Diff'rent Folks	10
71	President PT 351	Twine Time/Twine Awhile	8
72	President PT 383	Barracuda/Do It One More Time (as Alvin Cash & Crawlers)	8
67	President PTL 1000	THE PHILLY FREEZE (LP)	35

JOHNNY CASH (SOLO & WITH TENNESSEE TWO)
78s
57	London HL 8358	I Walk The Line/Get Rhythm	20
57	London HLS 8427	Train Of Love/There You Go	20
57	London HLS 8461	Next In Line/Don't Make Me Go	20
57	London HLS 8514	Home For The Blues/Give My Love To Rose	20
58	London HLS 8586	Ballad Of A Teenage Queen/Big River (with Tennessee Two)	20
58	London HLS 8656	Guess Things Happen That Way/Come In, Stranger	20
59	Philips PB 874	All Over Again/What Do I Care	20
59	Philips PB 897	Don't Take Your Guns To Town/I Still Miss Someone	20
59	London HLS 8789	It's Just About Time/I Just Thought You'd Like To Know	20
59	London HLS 8847	Luther Played The Boogie/Thanks A Lot	40
59	Philips PB 928	Frankie's Man, Johnny/You Dreamer You	20
59	London HLS 8928	Katy Too/I Forgot To Remember To Forget	40
59	Philips PB 953	I Got Stripes/Five Feet High And Rising	40
59	London HLS 8979	You Tell Me/Goodbye, Little Darlin', Goodbye	40
59	Philips PB 979	The Little Drummer Boy/I'll Remember You	40

SINGLES
57	London HL 8358	I Walk The Line/Get Rhythm (gold label lettering)	80
57	London HL 8358	I Walk The Line/Get Rhythm (silver label lettering)	20
57	London HLS 8427	Train Of Love/There You Go	30
57	London HLS 8461	Next In Line/Don't Make Me Go	50
57	London HLS 8514	Home For The Blues/Give My Love To Rose	40
58	London HLS 8586	Ballad Of A Teenage Queen/Big River (with Tennessee Two)	20
58	London HLS 8656	Guess Things Happen That Way/Come In, Stranger (with Tennessee Two)	20
58	London HLS 8709	The Ways Of A Woman In Love/You're The Nearest Thing To Heaven (with Tennessee Two)	15

CASHMAN, PISTILLI & WEST

MINT VALUE £

59	Philips PB 874	All Over Again/What Do I Care	10
59	Philips PB 897	Don't Take Your Guns To Town/I Still Miss Someone	10
59	London HLS 8789	It's Just About Time/I Just Thought You'd Like To Know (with Tennessee Two)	20
59	London HLS 8847	Luther Played The Boogie/Thanks A Lot	20
59	Philips PB 928	Frankie's Man, Johnny/You Dreamer You	10
59	London HLS 8928	Katy Too/I Forgot To Remember To Forget	20
59	Philips PB 953	I Got Stripes/Five Feet High And Rising	6
59	London HLS 8979	You Tell Me/Goodbye, Little Darlin', Goodbye	8
59	Philips PB 979	The Little Drummer Boy/I'll Remember You	6
60	London HLS 9070	Straight A's In Love/I Love You Because	10
60	Philips PB 1017	Seasons Of My Heart/Smiling Bill McCall	8
60	London HLS 9182	Down The Street To 301/Story Of A Broken Heart	15
60	Philips PB 1075	Going To Memphis/Loading Coal	15
61	London HLS 9314	Oh Lonesome Me/Life Goes On	10
61	Philips PB 1148	Forty Shades Of Green/he Rebel - Johnny Yuma	7
61	Philips PB 1200	Tennessee Flat-Top Box/Tall Man	6
63	CBS AAG 159	Ring Of Fire/I'd Still Be There	10
63	CBS AAG 173	The Matador/Still In Town	10

EXPORT SINGLES
57	London HL 7020	Next In Line/Don't Make Me Go	30
57	London HL 7023	Home For The Blues/Give My Love To Rose	30
58	London HL 7032	Ballad Of A Teenage Queen/Big River	25
58	London HL 7053	The Ways Of A Woman In Love/You're The Nearest Thing To Heaven	20
57	London HL 7131	Folsom Prison Blues/I Walk The Line	40

EPs
58	London RES 1120	JOHNNY CASH (triangular centre)	25
58	London RES 1120	JOHNNY CASH (round centre)	15
59	London RES 1193	JOHNNY CASH SINGS HANK WILLIAMS (triangular centre)	25
59	London RES 1193	JOHNNY CASH SINGS HANK WILLIAMS (round centre)	15
59	London RES 1212	COUNTRY BOY (triangular centre)	25
59	London RES 1212	COUNTRY BOY (round centre)	15
59	London RES 1230	JOHNNY CASH NO. 2 (triangular centre)	25
59	London RES 1230	JOHNNY CASH NO. 2 (round centre)	15
60	Philips BBE 12377	THE TROUBADOR	20
60	Philips BBE 12318	GRANDFATHER'S CLOCK	15
60	Philips BBE 12395	SONGS OF OUR SOIL	15
61	Philips BBE 12494	STRICTLY CASH	12

ALBUMS
59	London HA-S 2157	SINGS THE SONGS THAT MADE HIM FAMOUS	40
59	London HA-S 2179	WITH HIS HOT AND BLUE GUITAR	40
59	Philips BBL 7298	THE FABULOUS JOHNNY CASH (mono)	20
59	Philips SBBL 554	THE FABULOUS JOHNNY CASH (stereo)	20
59	Philips BBL 7353	SONGS OF OUR SOIL	15
60	Philips BBL 7358	NOW THERE WAS A SONG! (mono)	15
60	Philips SBBL 580	NOW THERE WAS A SONG! (stereo)	20
60	Philips BBL 7417	RIDE THIS TRAIN	15
61	CBS (S)BPG 62042	THE FABULOUS JOHNNY CASH (mono/stereo)	15
62	CBS (S)BPG 62073	THE SOUND OF JOHNNY CASH (mono/stereo)	15
63	CBS BPG 62119	BLOOD SWEAT AND TEARS	15
63	CBS (S)BPG 62171	RING OF FIRE (mono/stereo)	15
68	CBS LP 63308	LIVE AT FOLSOM PRISON (LP)	20
69	CBS LP 63629	LIVE AT SAN QUENTIN (LP)	20
84	Charly SUN BOX-105	THE SUN YEARS (5-LP box set)	25
94	American 0731458679028	AMERICAN RECORDINGS (LP, inner)	30
96	American 51011 2793-1	UNCHAINED (LP, inner)	30
00	American 51011 279-14	AMERICAN III: SOLITARY MAN (LP)	25
06	American 0602517005099	AMERICAN V: A HUNDRED HIGHWAYS (LP)	25

CASHMAN, PISTILLI & WEST
70	Capitol CL 15633	Goodbye Jo/She Never Looked Better	6

CASHMERES
90s	Soul City 133	Showstopper/Let The Door Hit Your Back (reissue)	8

CASH PUSSIES
79	The Label TLR 010	99% Is Shit/Cash Flow ('Sid Vicious' p/s)	8

(see also Sex Pistols)

CASINO
81	Ellie Jay EJSP 9609	More Than Ever/Tonight (p/s)	10

CASINO ROYALE
72	Nest NRS 125	Come On Down To The Beach/Jig-A-Jag	10

CASINO ROYALES
67	London HLU 10122	When I Tell You That I Love You/Love In The Open Air	6

CASINOS
67	Ember EMB S 241	That's The Way/Too Good To Be True	30
67	President PT 123	Then You Can Tell Me Goodbye/I Still Love You	10
68	President PT 140	To Be Loved/Tailor Made	10
68	President PT 156	When I Stop Dreaming/Please Love Me	10
68	President PTL 1007	THEN YOU CAN TELL ME GOODBYE (LP)	25

CASPAR
79	Rock Steady MICK 007	Messin' Around/Make You Feel Like You're Mine (p/s)	20

(see also 10cc)

MINT VALUE £

PAUL CASS
75 Rainbow Records RBW 2000 Mini Marianne/Riverboat Rock 30

CASSANDRA
76 Lucky LY 6034 Love Me Sweeter Tonight/Albatross 30
79 D Roy DRDD 19 Sitting In The Park/D ROY BAND: Hyde Park Dub 30
80 D Roy DRDD 29 My Angel Baby/Thank You For The Many Things You've Done (12") 30
80 D Roy DRDD 31 I Must Be Dreaming/Trading Dub (12") 30
(see also Johnny Clarke)

TOMMY CASSELL
70 Injun 114 Rockin' Rock A Rollin' Stone/Go Ahead On 10

CASSETTE
79 1 track CAS 001 THE FAST FORWARD EP: What's The Point/Product/All The Rage 35

CASSETTES (1)
81 Zip ZIP 101 Reverberate/Don't Label Me (die-cut sleeve) 50

CASSETTES (2)
82 X-Ray X 001 Call On Me/Fast Forward 20

CASSIBER
84 Recommended RE 0110 BEAUTY AND THE BEAST (LP) 18
86 Recommended RE 0000 PERFECT WORLDS (LP) 18

DITCH CASSIDY
71 Decca F13240 Pisces Apple Lady/Hamburger Midnight 20

TED CASSIDY
65 Capitol CL 15423 The Lurch/Wesley 30
65 Capitol CL 15423 The Lurch/Wesley (DJ Copy) 40

CAST
93 No label or cat no Sandstorm/Follow Me Down/Tell It Like It Is (10", white label sold at gigs) 20
95 Polydor INV137 LP COL ALL CHANGE (2-LP, gatefold, inners, postcard) 60
97 Polydor 537567 1 MOTHER NATURE CALLS (LP) 40
99 Polydor 547 176-1 MAGIC HOUR (2-LP) 50
01 Polydor 589096 1 BEETROOT (LP) 25
(see also La's)

CASTANARC
74 Peninsula PENCIL 10 JOURNEY TO THE EAST (LP, private pressing) 18

CASTAWAYS
65 London HL 10003 Liar Liar/Sam 50
65 London HL 10003 Liar Liar/Sam (DJ Copy) 80

CASTE
68 President PT 211 Don't Cast Aside/One Step Closer 6

JOEY CASTELL
57 Decca F 10966 I'm Left, You're Right, She's Gone/Tryin' To Get To You 200
57 Decca F 10966 I'm Left, You're Right, She's Gone/Tryin' To Get To You (78) 25

LACKSLEY CASTELL
79 Sufferers Heights SUFF 01 What A Great Day/PRINCE JAMMY: Slaughter House 5 (12") 50
79 Sound Off SOFD 003 My Collie Tree/RISING SUN: Stop Cheating (12") 50
80 Negus Roots NERT 001 African Queen/Queen In Dub (12") 25
80 Negus Roots NERT 003 I Love Jah/Version 40
80 Black Joy DH 805 Jah Love Is Sweeter/ROCKERS BAND: Sweeter Rockers (12") 60
81 Negus Roots NERT 005 Jah Is Watching You/PAPA TULLO: Sweet Reggae Music (12") 30
81 Negus Roots NERT 008 Government Man/P. TULLO: Straight To The Government (12" blue/black vinyl) 40
82 Negus Roots NERT 013 Speak Softly/Money A The Remedy (with PAPA TULLO/Take This Message To My Woman (12") 30
83 Negus Roots NERT 019 Johnny Brown/Mrs Brown (12") 20
83 Csa SPCSA 12006 Tug A War Game/EARL SIXTEEN: Rise In The Morning (12") 50
82 Negus Roots NERT LP 002 MORNING GLORY (LP) 100
83 Negus Roots NERT LP 008 AFRICAN LADY (LP) 50

CASTELLS
61 London HLN 9392 Sacred/I Get Dreamy 20
62 London HLN 9551 So This Is Love/On The Street Of Tears 25
67 Masquerade MA 500 Two Lovers/Jerusalem 8

BEBETO CASTILHO
02 What Music WMLP 0016 BEBETO (LP) 15

CASTLE FARM
72 Farm FARM 1 Hot Rod Queen/Mascot (p/s, lyric insert) 60

LEE CASTLE & BARONS
64 Parlophone R 5151 A Love She Can Count On/Foolin' 10

ROY CASTLE
60 Philips PB 1087 Little White Berry/Crazy Little Thorn 8
65 CBS 201736 Doctor Terror's House Of Horrors/Voodoo Girl (with Tubby Hayes) 50

CASTLE SISTERS (JAMAICA)
66 Ska Beat JB 257 Stop Your Lying/Don't Be A Fool 40

CAST OF THOUSANDS
66 Stateside SS 546 My Jenny Wears A Mini/Girl Do What You Gonna Do 40

CASTON & MAJORS
75 Tamla Motown TMG 938 Child Of Love/No One Will Know 15
(see also Radiants)

JIMMY CASTOR (BUNCH)
66 Philips BF 1543 Hey Leroy, Your Mama's Callin'/Ham Rock's Espanol 20
67 Philips BF 1590 Magic Saxophone/Just You Girl 25
73 RCA Victor APD1 0103 DIMENSION III (LP, quadrophonic) 20

MARIO CASTRO NEVES & HIS ORCHESTRA
73 Decca PFS 4294 BRAZILIAN MOOD (LP) 15

CASUAL FOUR

CASUAL FOUR
70s Specially Made For Us 102   I Can Tell/Love Potion No. 9 20
CASUALEERS
74   Pye Disco Demand DDS 103   Dance Dance Dance/Something About This Girl 6
CASUALS
65   Fontana TF 635   If You Walk Out/Please Don't Hide 10
68   Decca F 12737   Adios Amor (Goodbye My Love)/Don't Dream Of Yesterday 8
68   Decca F 22852   Toy/Touched (p/s) 10
69   Decca F 22900   Fools Paradise/7 X 7 7
69   Decca F 22943   Sunflower Eyes/Never My Love 7
69   Decca F 22969   Caroline/Naughty Boy 7
70   Decca F 23027   My Name Is Love/I Can't Say 7
71   Decca F 23112   Someday Rock 'n' Roll Lady/A Letter Every Day 7
72   Parlophone R 5959   Tara Tiger Girl/Nature's Girl 10
74   Dawn DNS 1069   Witch/Good Times 20
69   Decca LK-R/SKL-R 5001   HOUR WORLD (LP, large unboxed logo on label) 50
(see also American Jam, Kansas Hook)

JOHNNY CASWELL
85   Kent TOWN 106   You Don't Love Me No More/STEINWAYS: You've Been Leading Me On 20
CATACOMB
13   Macabre Unit MUV 005   Music Mi Luv/Badman Culture Pt 2/Cursed (12") 20
CATAPILLA
71   Vertigo 6360 029   CATAPILLA (LP, gatefold sleeve, small swirl label) 600
72   Vertigo 6360 074   CHANGES (LP, die-cut gatefold sleeve, small swirl label) 1500
(see also Jon Stevens, Liar)
CATAPULT
75   Box BOX 7   Put On The Lights/Linda 15
CATATONIA
96   Blanco Y Negro 16305-1   WAY BEYOND BLUE (LP, deleted after one week, with free 7") 40
98   Blanco Y Negro 20834-1   INTERNATIONAL VELVET (LP, 1,000 only, with free 12") 80
99   Blanco Y Negro 3984270941   EQUALLY CURSED AND BLESSED (LP, with free 1-sided 7") 50
01   Blanco Y Negro 8573888481   PAPER SCISSORS STONE (LP) 35
CATCH
77   Logo GO 103   Borderline/Black Blood (company sleeve) 40
(see also Tourists, Eurythmics)
CAT CLUB
87   Jive 155   One Last Kiss/Wild (p/s) 60
87   Jive JIVE T 155   One Last Kiss/(Extended Version)/Wild (12", p/s) 200
CATE BROTHERS
76   Asylum 13062   Where Can We Go/Instrumental 15
CATFISH
70   CBS 64006   GET DOWN (LP, orange label) 15
71   Epic 64408   LIVE CATFISH (LP) 15
CATHEDRAL
92   Earache MOSH 40T   Soul Sacrifice/Autumn Twilight/Frozen Rapture/Golden Blood (Flooding) 12
94   Earache MOSH 106T   STATIK MAJIK EP (12", p/s) 10
95   Earache MOSH 152   HOPKINS (THE WITCHFINDER GENERAL) EP (12", p/s) 12
11   Rise Above ROSE 12 141   A NEW ICE AGE EP: Open Mind Surgery/Sabbadaius Sabbatim (12", poster 100 clear/
                                                       100 white or 100 translucent blue vinyl, sold at farewell gig) 60
91   Earache MOSH 43   FOREST OF EQUILIBRIUM (LP, gatefold) 40
93   Earache MOSH 77C   THE ETHEREAL MIRROR (LP, blue vinyl, 1000 copies) 80
94   Rise Above RISE 8   IN MEMORIAM (LP, purple vinyl) 25
95   Earache MOSH 130   THE CARNIVAL BIZARRE (2 x 10" LP, gatefold sleeve) 20
96   Earache MOSH 156   SUPERNATURAL BIRTH MACHINE (2 x 10" test pressings, 10 copies only, release
                                                       cancelled) 350

CATHERINE WHEEL
92   Fontana 510903-1   FERMENT (LP, initially with free 12") 50
92   Fontana 510903-1   FERMENT (LP, without free 12") 40
93   Fontana 518 039-1   CHROME (LP with inner sleeve) 150
97   Chrysalis 7243 4 93099 1 3   ADAM & EVE (2-LP) 80
00   Chrysalis 7243526776 1 0   WISHVILLE (LP) 40
17   Music On Vinyl MOVLP1880   FERMENT (LP, reissue, numbered, orange vinyl) 35
17   Music On Vinyl MOVLP1880   FERMENT (LP, reissue, 180gm) 30
17   Music On Vinyl MOVLP1881   CHROME (LP, reissue, numbered, silver vinyl) 40
17   Music On Vinyl MOVLP1881   CHROME (LP, reissue, 180gm) 30
19   Music On Vinyl MOVLP2288   ADAM AND EVE (2-LP, reissue) 20

RAY CATHODE (BBC RADIOPHONICS)
62   Parlophone R 4901   Time Beat/Waltz In Orbit 20
(see also BBC Radiophonic Workshop, George Martin)
CATHY LA CREME
80   Ovation OVS 12   I Married A Cult Figure From Salford/CROTONES: Tea Machine Dub 6
CAT IRON
69   Xtra XTRA 1087   CAT IRON (LP) 25
CAT MOTHER & ALL NIGHT NEWSBOYS
69   Polydor 56543   Good Old Rock'N'Roll/Bad News 8
70   Polydor 2066 026   I Must Be Dreaming/Last Go Round 6
69   Polydor 184 300   THE STREET GIVETH AND THE STREET TAKETH AWAY (LP) 30
70   Polydor 2425 021   ALBION DOO-WAH (LP, gatefold sleeve) 15
72   United Artists UAG 29313   CAT MOTHER & ALL NIGHT NEWS BOYS (LP, gatefold sleeve) 20
73   United Artists UAG 29381   LAST CHANCE DANCE (LP) 15
(see also Jimi Hendrix)

CATS 'N' JAMMER KIDS

MINT VALUE £

CATS 'N' JAMMER KIDS
77	Ebony EYE 3	Disco Drum/Disco Drum (Part 5)	6
77	Ebony EYEC 3	Disco Drum/Disco Drum (Part 5) (12")	30

CATS EYES (1)
68	Deram DM 190	Smile Girl For Me/In A Fantasy World	10
68	Deram DM 209	I Thank You Marianne/Turn Around	10
69	Deram DM 251	Where Is She Now?/Tom Drum	25
70	MCA MK 5028	The Loser/Circus	12
70	MCA MK 5056	The Wizard/Hey (Open Your Eyes)	20

CAT'S PYJAMAS
68	Direction 58-3235	Virginia Water/Baby I Love You	40
68	Direction 58-3482	Camera Man/House For Sale	40

(see also Kenny Bernard)

CATS (1)
67	Parlophone R 5558	What A Crazy Life/Hopeless Try	7
68	Parlophone R 5663	What Is The World Coming To/How Could I Be So Blind?	10
69	Columbia DB 8524	I Gotta Know What's Going On/Lea	10

CATS (2)
69	Baf BAF 1	Swan Lake/Swing Low	12
69	Baf BAF 2	My Girl/The Hog	10
69	Baf BAF 3	The Hig/Blues For Justice	10
69	Baf BAF 4	William Tell/Love Walk Right In	10
70	Crystal CR 7009	Sherman/What Can I Do	40
75	Groove GVE 1001	Swan Lake/Swan Lake (Disco Version) (reissue)	15

CATS EYES (2)
11	Polydor 2763913	BROKEN GLASS EP (2 x 7")	20
11	Polydor 2766263	CAT'S EYES (LP)	20

(see also Horrors)

CLEM CATTINI ORK
65	Decca F 12135	No Time To Think/Impact	50

(see also Tornados, Aquarian Age, Rumplestiltskin, Spaghetti Head, Sounds Nice)

NADIA CATTOUSE
66	Reality RY 1001	NADIA CATTOUSE (LP)	40
70	RCA Victor SF 8070	EARTH MOTHER (LP, orange/white label)	30

CATWAX AXE CO
81	Waxwalk CAT 001	Waxwalk/Jumbo Jet (Hey! I Wany Your Crazy Wild)	10
81	Waxwalk CAT 001	Waxwalk/Jumbo Jet (Hey! I Wany Your Crazy Wild) (reissue)	6

THE CAUSE
82	Rising Sun RS 001	METRO POLICE EP (original copies with insert sleeve)	30
82	Rising Sun RS 001	METRO POLICE EP (without insert sleeve)	15

CAUSE N EFFECT
90	Foxadelic JTF1	Hype/That's What It Is	60
91	Foxadelic JTF2	Some Bite The Bullet (EP)	50

CAUSTIC WINDOW
92	Rephlex CAT 004	JOYREX J4 EP (12", 6-track)	40
92	Rephlex CAT 005	JOYREX J5 EP (12, 4-track, black vinyl)	40
92	Rephlex CAT 005	JOYREX J5 EP (12, 4-track, white vinyl)	30
93	Rephlex CAT 009 i	JOYREX J9 EP (10", picture disc, with bonus track "HMNA", 300 only)	100
93	Rephlex CAT 009 ii	JOYREX J9 EP (12" 4-track, initial 100 in card mailer with bag of "space dust")	70
93	Rephlex CAT 009 ii	JOYREX J9 EP (12" 4-track)	50
94	Rephlex CAT 023	CAUSTIC WINDOW (2-LP, test pressing only, 10 pressed, 5 known copies)	5000

(see also Aphex Twin)

CAVALIERS
86	él GPO 11	It's A Beautiful Game/The I.T. Man (p/s)	10

EDDIE CAVE & FYX
66	Pye 7N 17161	Fresh Out Of Tears/It's Almost Good	35

NICK CAVE (& BAD SEEDS)
84	Mute 7 MUTE 32	In The Ghetto/The Moon Is In The Gutter (p/s)	8
85	Mute 7 MUTE 38	Tupelo/The Six Strings That Drew Blood (p/s)	8
86	Mute MUTE 47	The Singer/Running Scared/Black Betty	6
86	Lyntone LYN 18038	Scum (green vinyl flexidisc, with poster, concert freebie)	18
86	Lyntone LYN 18038	Scum (green vinyl flexidisc, without poster, concert freebie)	12
88	Mute MUTE 52	The Mercy Seat/New Day	8
88	Muite 12MUTE 52	The Mercy Seat (Full Length Version)/New Day/The Mercy Seat (Video Mix) (12", p/s)	15
88	Mute MUTE 86	Oh Deanna/The Girl At The Bottom Of My Glass (no p/s, DJ-only)	12
88	Mute 12MUTE 86	Deanna/The Girl At The Bottom Of My Glass (12". with poster and postcard)	10
90	Mute MUTE 118	The Weeping Song/Cocks 'n' Asses	8
92	Mute LMUTE 140	Straight To You/Jack The Ripper (Acoustic Version) (limited issue, p/s)	8
92	Mute MUTE 148	I Had A Dream, Joe/The Good Son (live) (numbered p/s, 7,000 only)	8
94	Mute PMUTE 172	Red Right Hand (1-sided promo, with postcard and press release)	20
94	Mute MUTE 160	Do You Love Me? (Single Version)/Cassiel's Song/Sail Away (silver vinyl, p/s, 1,000 copies)	10
94	Mute MUTE 172	Red Right Hand/That's What Jazz Is To Me (red vinyl, p/s, with 2 different stickers & labels, 2,000 only)	15
97	Mute MUTE 192	Into My Arms/Little Empty Boat	10
01	Mute 10MUTE 262	Fifteen Feet Of Pure Snow/God Is In The House/And No More Shall We Part (10", p/s numbered)	20
04	Mute MUTE 329	Breathless (Alternative Mix)/These She Goes, My Beautiful World (Edit)/She's Leaving You	6
05	Mute MUTE 339	Get Ready For Love (Edit)/Hiding All Away (Live) (p/s)	10
08	Mute MUTE 403	Midnight Man/Hey Little Firing Squad	10

Stuart & SANDY CAVE

MINT VALUE £

12	Bad Seed Ltd. 7SEED001	Needle Boy/Lightning Bolts (p/s)	10
84	Mute STUMM 17	FROM HER TO ETERNITY (LP, with inner sleeve)	40
85	Mute STUMM 21	THE FIRSTBORN IS DEAD (LP, with inner sleeve)	40
86	Mute STUMM 28	KICKING AGAINST THE PRICKS (LP)	40
86	Mute STUMM 34	YOUR FUNERAL...MY TRIAL (2-LP, gatefold sleeve, with inner sleeves)	30
88	Mute LSTUMM 52	TENDER PREY (LP, with bonus spoken word 12" And The Ass Saw The Angel [P STUMM 52]: "Autumn"/Animal Static/Mah Sanctum/Lamentation, 5,000 only)	60
88	Mute STUMM 52	TENDER PREY (LP, without bonus spoken word 12")	40
90	Mute LSTUMM 76	THE GOOD SON (LP, with bonus 7" "Acoustic Versions From Tender Prey" [P STUMM 76]: "The Mercy Seat"/"City Of Refuge"/"Deanna")	60
90	Mute STUMM 76	THE GOOD SON (LP, inner sleeve, without free 7")	40
92	Mute STUMM 92	HENRY'S DREAM (LP, with inner sleeve and art print)	70
94	Mute LSTUMM 123	LET LOVE IN (LP, inner, with set of postcards or poster)	100
96	Mute STUMM 138	MURDER BALLADS (LP, with insert)	100
97	Mute STUMM 142	THE BOATMANS CALL (LP)	100
98	Mute MUTEL4	THE BEST OF NICK CAVE AND THE BAD SEEDS (2-LP, inners)	75
01	Mute STUMM 164	NO MORE SHALL WE PART (2-LP, with inner sleeves)	75
03	Mute STUMM 207	NOCTURAMA (2-LP, inners)	60
04	Mute STUMM 233	ABBATOIR BLUES/THE LYRE OF ORPHEUS (2-LP, inner sleeves and insert)	80
08	Mute STUMM 277	DIG LAZARUS DIG (LP, inners, booklet, and free 7")	50
13	Bad Seed Ltd. BS001 DLX	PUSH THE SKY AWAY (2-LP, 2x7", DVD, book numbered and signed box set)	150
13	Bad Seed Ltd. BS001 DLX	PUSH THE SKY AWAY (2-LP, 2x7", DVD, book numbered and unsigned box set)	100
13	Bad Seed Ltd. DSC001CE	PUSH THE SKY AWAY (LP, with free 7")	25
16	Bad Seed Ltd. BS009V	SKELETON TREE (LP, mispressing, A-side plays on both sides, labels correct)	30

(see also Birthday Party, Annie Hogan, Burmoe Brothers)

STUART & SANDY CAVE

77	Profile GMOR 143	DAWN ON SUNDAY (LP)	60

ANDY CAVELL

62	HMV POP 1024	Hey There Cruel Heart/Lonely Soldier Boy	40
62	HMV POP 1080	Always On Saturday/Hey There, Senorita	40
63	Pye 7N 15539	Andy/There Was A Boy	30
64	Pye 7N 15610	Shut Up/Tell The Truth	30

JIMMY CAVELLO & HIS HOUSE ROCKERS

57	Vogue Coral Q 72226	Rock, Rock, Rock/The Big Beat	250
57	Vogue Coral Q 72240	Foot Stompin'/Ooh-Wee	250

(see also Alan Freed)

CAVE OF THE LIVING STREAMS

74	Indigo Sound Studios UHC 1	SIXTEEN SONGS (LP, private pressing with booklet)	20

CAVERN OF ANTI MATTER

13	Associated Electronic AER-2	YOU'RE AN ART SOUL EP (12")	40
14	Deep Distance DD19	Interlude Music 1/Interlude Music 2 (12")	25
14	Peripheral Conserve PH24	Total Availability And The Private Future/Cluster Of Rainbows (12")	20
15	Ghost Box GBX 716	Pulsing River Velvet Phase/Photones	15
16	Duophonic DUHFLP33RT	VOID BEATS/INVOCATION TREX (3-LP, hand-made sleeve, 80 only)	80
17	Duophonic DUHFLP 35	BLOOD DRUMS (3-LP reissue, clear vinyl)	25

(see also Stereolab)

MONTE CAZAZZA

79	Industrial IR 0005	To Mom On Mother's Day/Candy Man (p/s, with outer polystyrene sleeve & insert, 2,500 only)	20
80	Industrial IR 0010	SOMETHING FOR NOBODY (EP)	20

(see also Psychic TV)

C.C.S. (COLLECTIVE CONSCIOUSNESS SOCIETY)

71	Rak 119	Tap Turns On The Water/Save The World	6
70	Rak SRAK 6751	C.C.S. (LP, gatefold sleeve)	25
72	Rak SRAK 503	C.C.S. (LP)	25
73	Rak SRAK 504	THE BEST BAND IN THE LAND (LP)	15

(see also Alexis Korner)

CEDARS

68	Decca F 22720	For Your Information/Hide If You Want To Hide	50
68	Decca F 22772	I Like The Way/I Don't Know Why	50

(see also Seaders)

TONY CEE

81	Cheeseman CT 1	Holiday/One Way Street	30

CELEBRATION FEATURING MIKE LOVE

73	MCA 365	Almost Summer/Lookin' Good	8

(see also Beach Boys)

ADRIANO CELENTANO

72	Epic EPC 1886	Prisencohnensinaincusol/Disc Jockey	6

CELIA & THE MUTATIONS

77	United Artists UP 36262	Mony Mony/Mean To Me (p/s)	6
77	United Artists UP 36318	You Better Believe Me/Round And Around (p/s)	10

(see also Stranglers, Tonight)

CELIBATES

81	ALPLP 1001	A SHAMELESS FASHION (LP)	40

CELITIA

96	Diesel DES LP 03	CELITIA (LP)	15

CELTIC F.C.

67	Thistle	Celtic Celtic (p/s)	12

CELTIC FROST

84	Noise N 0017	MORBID TALES (mini LP, with poster)	40
84	Noise N 0017	MORBID TALES (mini LP, without poster)	25

CENET ROX

MINT VALUE £

86	Combat MX 8091	TO MEGA THERION (LP, gatefold, with inner sleeve)	25
87	NOISE NOISE 065	INTO THE PANDEMONIUM (LP, gatefold sleeve, with insert)	25
06	Century Media 9979951	MONOTHEIST (2-LP, gatefold, brown marbled vinyl, 100 only)	50

CENET ROX
| 80 | ROX OFF 1 | Sonny/French Tutor (no p/s) | 8 |

CENOTAPH CORNER
| 76 | Cottage COT 501 | UPS AND DOWNS (LP) | 20 |
| 79 | Cottage COT 031 | EVERY DAY BUT WEDNESDAY (LP) | 25 |

CENTIPEDE
| 71 | RCA Neon NE 9 | SEPTOBER ENERGY (2-LP, gatefold sleeve, black inner sleeve) | 80 |
| 74 | RCA DPS 2054 | SEPTOBER ENERGY (2-LP, reissue, different cover) | 25 |

(see also Mark Charig, Elton Dean, Zoot Money, Alan Skidmore, Keith Tippett, Julie Tippetts, Mike Patto, Robert Wyatt)

CENTRY
80s	Conscious Sounds DPS 001	Stepping Time/Stepping Dub (12")	10
93	Conscious Sounds DNC 002	THUNDER MOUNTAIN : CENTRY IN DUB (LP)	25
95	Conscious Sounds DNC 005	RELEASE THE CHAINS (LP)	15

CENTURION
| 82 | Centurion 0001 | Two Wheels/Bitch (private pressing) | 50 |
| 82 | Centurion 0001 | Two Wheels/Bitch (private pressing, mislabelled 'Nikki') | 30 |

CENTURY 21 (GERRY ANDERSON TV SPIN-OFFS)
65	Century 21 MA 100	JOURNEY TO THE MOON (EP)	15
65	Century 21 MA 101	INTO ACTION WITH TROY TEMPEST (EP)	12
65	Century 21 MA 102	A TRIP TO MARINEVILLE (EP)	15
65	Century 21 MA 103	INTRODUCING THUNDERBIRDS (EP)	15
65	Century 21 MA 104	MARINA SPEAKS (EP)	15
65	Century 21 MA 105	TV CENTURY 21 THEMES (EP)	15
66	Century 21 MA 106	THE DALEKS (EP)	50
66	Century 21 MA 107	F.A.B. (EP)	18
66	Century 21 MA 108	THUNDERBIRD 1 (EP)	18
66	Century 21 MA 109	THUNDERBIRD 2 (EP)	18
66	Century 21 MA 110	THE STATELY HOME ROBBERIES (EP)	25
66	Century 21 MA 111	LADY PENELOPE & OTHER TV THEMES (EP)	25
66	Century 21 MA 112	THUNDERBIRD 3 (EP)	25
66	Century 21 MA 113	THUNDERBIRD 4 (EP)	25
66	Century 21 MA 114	THE PERILS OF PENELOPE (EP)	25
66	Century 21 MA 115	TOPO GIGIO IN LONDON (EP)	40
67	Century 21 MA 116	GREAT THEMES FROM GERRY ANDERSON'S THUNDERBIRDS (EP)	30
67	Century 21 MA 117	SPACE AGE NURSERY RHYMES (EP)	30
67	Century 21 MA 118	LADY PENELOPE AND PARKER (EP)	30
67	Century 21 MA 119	BRAINS AND TIN TIN (EP)	30
67	Century 21 MA 120	INTERNATIONAL RESCUE (EP)	30
67	Century 21 MA 121	THUNDERBIRDS (EP)	30
67	Century 21 MA 122	LADY PENELOPE (EP)	30
67	Century 21 MA 123	BRAINS (EP)	30
67	Century 21 MA 124	BRINK OF DISASTER (EP)	30
67	Century 21 MA 125	ATLANTIC INFERNO (EP)	30
67	Century 21 MA 126	RICOCHET (EP)	30
67	Century 21 MA 127	TINGHA & TUCKER & THE WOMBAVILLE BAND (EP)	30
67	Century 21 MA 128	ONE MOVE & YOU'RE DEAD (EP)	30
67	Century 21 MA 129	30 MINUTES AFTER NOON (EP)	30
67	Century 21 MA 130	TINGHA & TUCKER IN NURSERY RHYME TIME (EP)	30
67	Century 21 MA 131	INTRODUCING CAPTAIN SCARLET (EP)	25
67	Century 21 MA 132	CAPTAIN SCARLET AND THE MYSTERONS (EP)	25
67	Century 21 MA 133	CAPTAIN SCARLET IS INDESTRUCTIBLE (EP)	20
67	Century 21 MA 134	CAPTAIN SCARLET OF SPECTRUM (EP)	20
67	Century 21 MA 135	CAPTAIN SCARLET VS. CAPTAIN BLACK (EP)	20
67	Century 21 MA 136	THEMES FROM GERRY ANDERSON'S CAPTAIN SCARLET (EP)	20
65	Century 21 LA 100	JOURNEY TO THE MOON (LP)	50
66	Century 21 LA 1	THE WORLD OF TOMORROW (LP)	40
66	Century 21 LA 2	LADY PENELOPE PRESENTS (LP)	40
66	Century 21 LA 3	JEFF TRACY INTRODUCES INTERNATIONAL RESCUE (LP)	40
66	Century 21 LA 4	LADY PENELOPE INVESTIGATES (LP)	40
66	Century 21 LA 5	THE TINGHA & TUCKER CLUB SONG BOOK (LP)	40
67	Century 21 LA 6	FAVOURITE TELEVISION THEMES (LP)	40
68	Marble Arch MAL 770	TV FAVOURITES VOL. 1 (LP)	20
68	Marble Arch MAL 771	TV FAVOURITES VOL. 2 (LP)	20

(see also Barry Gray, Dr. Who)

CEOLBEG
| 90 | Ceolbeg Music CB 001 | NOT THE BUNNY HOP (LP) | 20 |

CEREBRAL FIX
| 88 | Vinyl Solution SOL 15 | LIFE SUCKS AND THEN YOU DIE! (LP) | 15 |

CERTAIN LIONS & TIGERS
| 70 | Polydor 2344 002 | SOUL CONDOR (LP) | 40 |

CESSMAN
| 17 | System SYSTM 018 | Higher Rising/Deadly Serpent (12") | 12 |

CEYLEIB PEOPLE
| 68 | Vocalion SAVL 8072 | TANYET (LP) | 200 |

CHAD (STUART) & JEREMY (CLYDE)
| 64 | Ember EMB EP 4543 | YESTERDAY'S GONE (EP) | 12 |
| 65 | United Artists UEP 1008 | CHAD STUART AND JEREMY CLYDE (EP) | 20 |

(see also John Barry)

ERNIE CHAFFIN
57	London HLS 8409	Feelin' Low/Lonesome For My Baby	80

CHAIN OF STRENGTH
91	First Strike FS010	WHAT HOLDS US APART (EP, blue vinyl)	30
91	First Strike FS010	WHAT HOLDS US APART (EP, white vinyl)	40

CHAIN REACTION
77	Gull GULS 77	Never Lose Never Win/Chase A Miracle	15
77	Gull GULS 53	Why Can't We Be Lovers/Hogtied	40
77	Gull GULS 43	This Eternal Flame/Never Lose, Never Win	15
77	Gull GULP 1021	INDEBTED TO YOU (LP)	100
80	Congress CPLPS1	CHANGE OF ACTION (LP)	15
81	Congress CPLPS2	CHASE A MIRACLE (LP)	15
12	Vocalion VOCLP 3302	INDEBTED TO YOU (LP, reissue)	15

CHAINSAW
80	Square SQSP 2	Police And Politicians/Hole In The Road (p/s)	45
80	Pot Belly EJSP 9462	Lonely Without You/On The Highway	35
84	GMC CS 001	Long Legged Woman/Midnight Blue	30

CHAIRMAN YOUTH
81	Last Ditch TRENCH 1	Uncertainty/Business Partners (p/s)	6

CHAIRMEN OF THE BOARD
70	Invictus INV 501	Give Me Just A Little More Time/Since The Days Of Pigtails	8
70	Invictus INV 501	Give Me Just A Little More Time/Since The Days Of Pigtails (DJ Copy)	20
70	Invictus INV 504	You've Got Me Dangling On A String/Patches	6
70	Invictus INV 504	You've Got Me Dangling On A String/Patches (DJ Copy)	20
71	Invictus INV 507	Everything's Tuesday/Bless You	6
71	Invictus INV 507	Everything's Tuesday/Bless You (DJ Copy)	15
71	Invictus INV 511	Pay To The Piper/When Will She Tell Me She Needs Me? (DJ Copy)	15
70	Invictus SVT 1002	CHAIRMEN OF THE BOARD (LP)	20
71	Invictus SVT 1003	IN SESSION (LP)	20
72	Invictus SVT 1006	BITTERSWEET (LP)	15
74	Invictus SVT 65868	SKIN I'M IN (LP)	15

(see also Showmen, General Johnson, Norman Johnson)

CHAKA KHAN
81	Warner Bros. LV 48	Wha'cha Gonna Do For Me/We Got The Love/I'm Every Woman (12", p/s)	12
80	Warner Bros. 17617T	Clouds/What You Did (12")	10
18	Diary	Like Sugar (Extended)/(Switch Remix) (12", 100 only, hand-numbered)	150

(see also Rufus, Rufus & Chaka Khan)

CHAKACHAS
72	Polydor 2121 064	Jungle Fever/Chaka Cha	10
72	Polydor 2489 050	JUNGLE FEVER (LP)	20
73	Young Blood SYB 3003	CHAKACHAS (LP)	20

GEORGE CHAKIRIS
60	Triumph RGM 1010	Heart Of A Teenage Girl/I'm Always Chasing Rainbows	30

CHALAWA
78	Skynote SKYLP 14	EXODUS DUB (LP)	40

CHALICE
80	Galactic GALD 002	I'm Gonna Get You/Oi Nayga (12")	12

CHALK GIANTS
91	SRT 91 LS 2856	THROW IT ALL AWAY EP (12", p/s)	10

BRYAN CHALKER('S NEW FRONTIER)
70	Amity OTS 502	Ned Kelly/Four Girls From The Town Of Boston	6
72	Columbia DB 8883	Daddy Sang Bass/Lot 69	6
77	Chapter One SCH 179	Help Me Make It Through The Night/Eskimo Song	6
73	Chapter One SCH 185	Daisy A Day/Life Gets Tee-jus, Don't It	6
71	Avenue AVE 071	THE HANGING OF SAMUEL HALL (LP, textured sleeve, as Bryan Chalker's New Frontier)	15

CHALLENGER
81	CMC CM 0001	So Sure Of Yourself/Out To Kill	40

CHALLENGERS (U.K.)
61	Parlophone R 4773	Cry Of The Wild Goose/Deadline	10

CHALLENGERS (U.S.)
63	Stateside SS 177	Torquay/Bulldog	10
65	Vocalion V 9253	The Man From U.N.C.L.E./The Streets Of London	20
66	Vocalion V 9270	Walk With Me/How Could I	10
63	Stateside SL 10230	SURFBEAT (LP)	50
67	Vocalion VA-N 8069	WIPE OUT (LP, mono)	50
67	Vocalion SAV-N 8069	WIPE OUT (LP, stereo)	55

CHAMBERPOT
76	Bead Records BEAD 2	CHAMBERPOT (LP)	50

JAMES CHAMBERS
71	Summit SUM 8523	Bongo Man/KEN BOOTHE: Now I Know	10

(see also Jimmy Cliff)

CHAMBERS BROTHERS
66	Vocalion VL 9267	Love Me Like The Rain/Pretty Girls Everywhere	20
66	Vocalion VL 9276	Call Me/Seventeen	20
67	CBS 202565	All Strung Out Over You/Falling In Love	10
68	Direction 58-3215	Up Town/Love Me Like The Rain	7
68	Direction 58-3671	Time Has Come Today/Dinah	12
68	Direction 58-3760	Time Has Come Today/Dinah (reissue)	8
68	Direction 58-3865	I Can't Turn You Loose/Do Your Thing	8

CHAMELEON

MINT VALUE £

69	Direction 58-4098	Are You Ready/You Got The Power To Turn Me On	6
69	Direction 58-4318	People Get Ready/No, No, No, Don't Say Goodbye	6
69	Direction 58-4367	Wake Up/Everybody Needs Someone	10
70	Direction 58-4846	Love Peace And Happiness/If You Want Me To	7
70	Direction 58-5033	Let's Do It (Do It Together)/To Love Somebody	7
71	CBS 5389	Funky/Love, Peace And Happiness	15
71	CBS 7689	By The Hair On My Chinny Chin Chin/Heaven	6
66	Vocalion VA-L/SAV-L 8258	PEOPLE GET READY (LP)	60
68	Liberty LBS 83272	SHOUT! (LP, blue label)	30
68	Direction 8-63407	THE TIME HAS COME (LP)	30
69	Direction 8-63451	A NEW TIME - A NEW DAY (LP)	30
70	Direction 8-66228	LOVE PEACE AND HAPPINESS (Live At Bill Graham's Fillmore West) (2-LP)	30
70	Liberty LBS 83276	FEELIN' THE BLUES (LP)	15
71	CBS 64156	A NEW GENERATION (LP)	15

CHAMELEON
71	CBS 5428	Who Am I/Coogans Keep	20

CHAMELEONS
82	Epic EPCA 2210	In Shreds/Less Than Human (p/s)	15
83	Statik STAT 30	As High As You Can Go/Pleasure And Pain (p/s)	6
83	Statik STAT 3012	As High As You Can Go/Pleasure And Pain/Paper Tigers (12", p/s)	10
83	Statik TAK 6	A Person Isn't Safe Anywhere These Days/Thursday's Child (p/s)	7
83	Statik TAK 6/12	A Person Isn't Safe Anywhere These Days/Thursday's Child/Prisoners Of The Sun (12", p/s)	15
83	Statik TAK 11/12	Up The Down Escalator/Monkeyland/Prisoner Of The Sun (12", p/s)	15
85	Statik TAK 29	In Shreds/Nostalgia (p/s)	15
85	Statik TAK 29/12	In Shreds/Less Than Human/Nostalgia (12", p/s)	10
86	Geffen GEF 4F/SAM 287	Tears/Paradiso//Swamp Thing/Inside Out (double pack, gatefold p/s)	15
86	Geffen GEF 10	Swamp Thing/John, I'm Only Dancing	6
90	Glass Pyramid EMC 1	TONY FLETCHER WALKED ON WATER (12" EP)	40
90	Strange Fruit SFRLP 114	PEEL SESSIONS (LP)	15
83	Statik STATLP 17	SCRIPT OF THE BRIDGE (LP, 1st pressing, textured sleeve, insert)	40
85	Statik STATLP 17	SCRIPT OF THE BRIDGE (LP, picture disc)	20
85	Statik STATLP 22	WHAT DOES ANYTHING MEAN? BASICALLY (LP, gatefold sleeve, with insert)	20
86	Geffen 924119	STRANGE TIMES (LP, pink or blue sleeves)	20
90	Glass Pyramid EMC 2	TRIPPING DOGS (LP)	25
93	Imaginary ILLUSION 042	AUFFUHRUNG IN BERLIN (LP)	45

(see also Reegs, Mark Burgess and the Sons Of God)

TEDDY CHAMES
68	Blue Cat BS 141	I Want It Girl/She Is Gone (actually by Teddy Charmes)	100

DES CHAMP ORCHESTRA
70	Page One POF 172	It Takes A Thief/My Own Thing	10

CHAMPAGNE BUBBLER PART 1
97	Strictly Limited SHQ 4	RUMP FUNK EP (12")	25

CHAMPIONS OF NATURE
00	White FOFF 1	The Fuck Off Song/An Undercurrent/360/Carpe Diem (EP)	30
00	White FOFF 2	Finalisation/Cold Dessert/Breakfast Of Champions (EP)	30
01	White SALSA001	Salsa Smurph/Jazzy Styles (12")	12

CHAMPS (JAMAICA)
64	Blue Beat BB 267	Walk Between Your Enemies/Do What I Say	20

CHAMPS (U.S.)
58	London HLU 8580	Tequila/Train To Nowhere	10
58	London HL 8655	Midnighter/El Rancho Rock	12
58	London HL 8715	Chariot Rock/Subway	10
59	London HLH 8811	Beatnik/Gone Train	10
59	London HLH 8864	Caramba/Moonlight Bay	10
60	London HLH 9052	Too Much Tequila/Twenty Thousand Leagues	8
59	London RE 1176	FOUR BY THE CHAMPS (EP)	20
59	London RE-H 1209	ANOTHER FOUR BY THE CHAMPS (EP)	20
59	London RE-H 1223	STILL MORE BY THE CHAMPS (EP)	20
61	London RE-H 1250	KNOCKOUTS! (EP)	20
58	London HA-H 2152	GO CHAMPS GO! (LP)	40
59	London HA-H 2184	EVERYBODY'S ROCKIN' WITH THE CHAMPS (LP)	40
62	London HA-H 2451	GREAT DANCE HITS (LP, early issue with flipback cover)	30

BOB CHANCE
12	Trunk JBH 044	IT'S BROKEN (LP, 1000 only)	35

ROB CHANCE & CHANCES-R
67	CBS 3130	At The End Of The Day/I've Got The Power	15

(see also Chances-R)

CHANCES ARE
67	Columbia DB 8144	Fragile Child/What Went Wrong	40

CHANCES-R
67	CBS 202614	Talking Out The Back Of My Head/I Aimed Too High	20
67	CBS 2940	Do It Yourself/Turn A New Leaf Over	12

(see also Rob Chance & Chances-R)

CHANCIS
64	Decca F 11860	Everybody's Laughing/Tell Me	15

CHANDELIERS
73	Penny Farthing PEN 809	Can't You Hear My Heartbreak/One Way Street	6

TIM CHANDELL
78	Orbitone 05	Keep Me/Let's Make Love	20

DANY CHANDELLE
65	Columbia DB 7540	Lying Awake/I Love You	30

KERRI CHANDLER
96	Freetown FTILP2	HEMISPHERE (LP as 2 x 12")	30

BARBARA CHANDLER
63	London HLR 9823	Do You Really Love Me Too?/I Live To Love You	30
64	London HLR 9861	I'm Going Out With The Girls/Lonely New Year	30

GENE CHANDLER
62	Columbia DB 4793	Duke Of Earl/Kissing In The Kitchen	25
63	Stateside SS 185	Rainbow/You Threw A Lucky Punch	40
64	Stateside SS 331	Just Be True/A Song Called Soul	25
64	Stateside SS 364	Bless Our Love/London Town	25
65	Stateside SS 388	What Now/If You Can't Be True (Find A Part Time Love)	35
65	Stateside SS 401	You Can't Hurt Me No More/Everybody Let's Dance	25
65	Stateside SS 425	Nothing Can Stop Me/The Big Lie	60
65	Stateside SS 425	Nothing Can Stop Me/The Big Lie (DJ copy)	150
65	Stateside SS 458	Good Times/No One Can Love You (Like I Do)	35
66	Stateside SS 500	(I'm Just A) Fool For You/Buddy Ain't It A Shame	35
66	Chess CRS 8047	I Fooled You This Time/Such A Pretty Thing	40
66	Chess CRS 8047	I Fooled You This Time/Such A Pretty Thing (DJ copy)	100
67	Coral Q 72490	The Girl Don't Care/My Love	20
68	Soul City SC 102	Nothing Can Stop Me/The Big Lie (reissue)	15
69	Action ACT 4551	I Can't Save It/I Can Take Care Of Myself	60
69	President PT 234	Duke Of Earl/Stand By Me	8
70	Mercury 6052 033	Groovy Situation/Not The Marrying Kind	6
71	Mercury 6052 098	You're A Lady/Stone Cold Feeling	15
76	Brunswick BR 39	There Was A Time/ARTISTICS: I'm Gonna Miss You	15
65	Fontana TL 5247	DUKE OF EARL (LP)	80
67	Coral LVA 9236	THE GIRL DON'T CARE (LP)	60
69	MCA MUPS 367	THERE WAS A TIME (LP)	30
69	Action ACLP 6010	LIVE ON STAGE (LP)	50
71	Mercury 6338 037	SITUATION (LP)	20
74	Joy JOYS 136	A GENE CHANDLER ALBUM (LP)	15
86	Kent 049	60s SOUL BROTHER (LP)	15

GENE CHANDLER & BARBARA ACKLIN
74	Brunswick BR 30	From The Teacher To The Preacher/Little Green Apples	8

(see also Barbara Acklin)

GEORGE CHANDLER
82	Polydor 436	This Could Be The Night/Can't Go Back No More	15

JEFF CHANDLER
54	Brunswick 05264	I Should Care/More Than Anyone	7
58	London HA-U 2100	JEFF CHANDLER SINGS TO YOU (LP)	20

KAREN CHANDLER
55	Vogue Coral Q 72091	The Price You Pay For Love/The Man In The Raincoat	6
56	Brunswick 05570	Love Is The $64,000 Question/(I'm Just A) Beginner	10
56	Brunswick 05596	Tonight You Belong To Me/Crazy Arms (with Jimmy Wakely)	10
57	Brunswick 05662	Your Wild Heart/It's An International Language	6
62	Salvo SLO 1803	My Own True Love/You Made Me Love You (99 copies only)	10

(see also Jimmy Wakely)

KENNY CHANDLER
63	Stateside SS 166	Heart/Wait For Me	15
68	Stateside SS 2110	Beyond Love/Charity	40
68	Stateside SS 2110	Beyond Love/Charity (DJ Copy)	60

LEN CHANDLER
67	CBS 62931	TO BE A MAN (LP)	20

LORRAINE CHANDLER
75	Black Magic BM 105	Love You Baby/What Can I Do	8
97	Kent 6T 13	You Only Live Twice/METROS: My Imagination	30
11	Outta Sight OSV 032	I Can't Change/You Only Live Twice	6

CHANDONS
68	RCA RCA 1704	Timber/Never Been Loved Before	6

ALLEN CHANEY
82	Albion ION 1027	The Sound Of Musak/It Is Nowhere (p/s)	12

CHANG AND VOYLE
86	Cottage Industry CIR 001	Chinese Eyes/If You Were Here	8

CHANGE (1)
73	Orange OAS 221	Lazy London Lady/Arkmaker	40
73	Orange OAS 222	Sunshine/Get Your Gun	25
73	Orange OAS 210	Yaketty Yak, Smacketty Smack/When The Morning Comes	8
74	EMI EMI 2354	Wildcat/Hold On	10

CHANGE (2)
80	WEA K 79141	A Lovers Holiday/The Glow Of Love (12")	15
80	Warner Bros. K99107	THE GLOW OF LOVE (LP)	15

CHANGIN' TIMES
65	Phillips BF 1442	Pied Piper/Thank You Babe	25
68	Bell BLL 1009	When The Good Sun Shines/Show Me The Way To Go Home	6

BRUCE CHANNEL
62	Mercury AMT 1171	Hey! Baby/Dream Girl	8
62	Mercury AMT 1177	Number One Man/If Only I Had Known	10
62	Pye International 7N 25137	Run Romance Run/Don't Leave Me	15

CHANNEL 4

MINT VALUE £

63	London HLU 9776	I Don't Wanna/Blue And Lonesome	15
64	London HLU 9841	Going Back To Louisiana/Forget Me Not	15
67	Stateside SS 2066	Mr. Bus Driver/It's Me	10
68	Bell BLL 1010	Keep On/Barbara Allen	7
68	Bell BLL 1030	Try Me/Water The Family Tree	6
68	Bell BLL 1038	Mr. Bus Driver/Trouble With Sam	6
62	Mercury MMC 14104	HEY! BABY! (LP)	50
68	Bell MBLL/SBLL 110	KEEP ON (LP)	20

CHANNEL 4

79	Ripping RIP 1	Vampire/Channel 4 (numbered p/s with insert)	6

CHANNEL 3

82	No Future OI 11	I've Got A Gun/Manzanar/Mannequin (p/s)	10
82	No Future PUNK 2	I'VE GOT A GUN (LP)	18

CHANTAYS

63	London HLD 9696	Pipeline/Move It	6
64	King KG 1018	Beyond/I'll Be Back Someday	15
63	London RED 1397	PIPELINE (EP)	35
63	London HA-D 8087	PIPELINE (LP, mono)	40
63	London SH-D 8087	PIPELINE (LP, stereo)	50

CHANTELLES

65	Parlophone R 5271	I Want That Boy/London My Home Town	25
65	Parlophone R 5303	The Secret Of My Success/Sticks And Stones	15
65	Parlophone R 5350	Gonna Get Burned/Gonna Give Him Some Love	15
66	Parlophone R 5431	I Think Of You/Please Don't Kiss Me	15
66	Polydor 56119	There's Something About You/Just Another Fool	20
67	CBS 2777	Blue Mood/The Man I Love	25

(see also Lana Sisters)

CHANTELLS

76	Treble C CCC 012	Eva/JAH MIKE: Eva Rockers	10
78	Phase 1 PRF 1	Waiting In The Park/Desperate Times (12")	12
78	Sagittarius SUS 6A	Man In Love/Natty Supper (12")	15
82	Phase 1 SUS 4	Children Of Jah/Desperate Time (12")	20

CHANTELS

58	London HLU 8561	Maybe/Come My Little Baby	250
58	London HLU 8561	Maybe/Come My Little Baby (78)	35
62	London HLL 9428	Look In My Eyes/Glad To Be Back	50
62	London HLL 9480	Well I Told You/Still	50
62	London HLL 9532	Here It Comes Again/Summertime	30
63	Capitol CL 15297	Swamp Water/Eternally	30

(see also Richard Barrett)

CHANTERS (1)

66	CBS 202454	Every Night (I Sit And Cry)/Where	30
67	CBS 202616	You Can't Fool Me/All Day Long	20
68	CBS 3400	What's Wrong With You/Right By Your Side	6
68	CBS 3668	My Love Is For You/Mississippi Paddleboat	8

(see also Birds Of A Feather)

CHANTERS (2)

79	Burning Rockers BRD 011	Mash Down Babylon/I Told You So (12")	25

CHANTS (U.K.)

63	Pye 7N 15557	I Don't Care/Come Go With Me	15
64	Pye 7N 15591	I Could Write A Book/A Thousand Stars	15
64	Pye 7N 15643	She's Mine/Then I'll Be Home	15
64	Pye 7N 15691	Sweet Was The Wine/One Star	15
66	Fontana TF 716	Come Back And Get This Loving Baby/Love Light	20
67	Decca F 12650	A Lover's Story/Wearing A Smile	20
67	Page One POF 016	Ain't Nobody Home/For You	15
68	RCA Victor RCA 1754	A Man Without A Face/Baby I Don't Need Your Love	100
68	RCA Victor RCA 1754	A Man Without A Face/Baby I Don't Need Your Love (DJ Copy)	130
69	RCA Victor RCA 1823	I Get The Sweetest Feeling/Candy	25
76	Chipping Norton CHIP 2	I've Been Trying/Lucky Old Me	30

(see also Real Thing)

CHANTS (U.S.)

58	Capitol CL 14876	Close Friends/Lost And Found	25

CHAOS & JULIA SET

93	Recoil RCL 001	VOL. 1 ATMOSPHERE EP (12", plain sleeve)	10
93	Recoil RCL 002	VOL. 2 - FEAR OF THE FUTURE (12", plain sleeve)	12

(see also Global Communications)

CHAOS U.K.

79	Chaotic Records VD 1	Summer Of Hate/I Wanna To Be Left Alone (p/s, 500 only)	200

CHAOS U.K. (BRISTOL)

82	Riot City RIOT 6	BURNING BRITAIN (EP)	10
82	Riot City RIOT 12	LOUD, POLITICAL AND UNCOMPROMISING (EP)	10
83	Riot City CITY 002	CHAOS U.K. (LP)	30
85	C.O.R. GURT 1	SHORT SHARP SHOCK (LP)	20
86	Manic Ears ACHE 1	RADIOACTIVE (LP, with inner, split with EXTREME NOISE TERROR)	20

CHAOTIC DISCHORD

81	Riot City 12 ROT 30	Don't Throw It Away (12")	15
83	Riot City RIOT RIOT 22	Never Trust A Friend/Are Students Safe? (p/s)	12
82	Riot City RIOT 10	FUCK THE WORLD (EP)	10
83	Riot City CITY 004	FUCK RELIGION, FUCK POLITICS, AND FUCK THE LOT OF YOU (LP)	18

CHAOTIC YOUTH

MINT VALUE £

84	Syndicate SYNLP 12	FUCK OFF YOU CUNT WHAT A LOAD OF BOLLOCKS (LP)	15

CHAOTIC YOUTH
83	Beat The System YOUTH 1	SAD SOCIETY (EP)	50

PAUL CHAPLAIN & HIS EMERALDS
60	London HLU 9205	Shortnin' Bread/Nicotine	15

CHARLIE CHAPLIN
82	Kingdon KVL 9012	PRESENTING CHARLIE CHAPLIN (LP)	18
82	Tamoki Wambesi TWLP 1014	RED POND (LP)	15
82	Tamoki Wambesi TWLP 1020	CHAPLIN CHANT (LP)	15
83	Trojan TRLS 216	ONE OF A KIND (LP)	30
84	Vista VSLP 4063	ROOTS & CULTURE (LP)	25

CHAPMAN AND WHITNEY
74	Reprise K54017	STREETWALKERS (LP, with inner)	20

(see also Streetwalkers)

GENE CHAPMAN
63	Starlite ST45 102	Oklahoma Blues/Don't Come Crying	25

GRADY CHAPMAN
60	Mercury AMT 1107	Sweet Thing/I Know What I Want	30

MICHAEL CHAPMAN
74	Deram DM 407	The Bento Song/Dumplings	7
69	Harvest HAR 5002	It Didn't Work Out/Mozart Lives Upstairs	18
69	Harvest SHVL 755	RAINMAKER (LP, gatefold sleeve, with "Sold in U.K..." label text on 4 lines, No EMI on label)	100
69	Harvest SHVL 755	RAINMAKER (LP, gatefold sleeve, later pressing with EMI on label)	40
69	Standard ESL 146	SOLO GUITAR (LP, library issue)	60
70	Harvest SHVL 764	FULLY QUALIFIED SURVIVOR (LP, gatefold sleeve, 1st pressing with no EMI on label)	90
70	Harvest SHVL 764	FULLY QUALIFIED SURVIVOR (LP, gatefold sleeve, later pressing with EMI on label)	30
70	Harvest SHVL 786	WINDOW (LP, gatefold sleeve, with no EMI on label)	80
70	Harvest SHVL 786	WINDOW (LP, gatefold sleeve, with EMI on label)	25
71	Harvest SHVL 798	WRECKED AGAIN (LP, gatefold sleeve, EMI on label)	60
73	Deram SML 1105	MILLSTONE GRIT (LP, red/white label)	20
74	Deram SML 1114	DEAL GONE DOWN (LP)	20
76	Decca SKL-R 5242	SAVAGE AMUSEMENT (LP, with lyric sheet, blue/silver label)	20
77	Decca SKL-R 5290	THE MAN WHO HATED MORNINGS (LP)	15
78	Criminal STEAL 2	PLAYING GUITAR THE EASY WAY (LP)	15
79	Criminal TAKE 3	FULLY QUALIFIED SURVIVOR (LP, reissue)	15

CHAPS
62	Parlophone R 4979	Poppin' Medley (Parts 1 & 2)	10

(see also Outlaws)

CHAPTER FIVE
66	CBS 202395	Anything You Do Is Alright/You Can't Mean It	800
67	CBS 2696	One In A Million/Hey Hey (unissued, demos only)	250
00s	Goldmine Soul Supply GS 009	You Can't Mean It/One In A Million (reissue)	15

CHAPTER FOUR (U.K.)
60s	GSP 11009/10	CHAPTER FOUR (EP, no p/s)	90

CHAPTER FOUR (U.K.)
80	Bridge BR 001	HANGING AROUND STERLING (LP)	35

CHAPTER FOUR (U.S.)
66	United Artists UP 1143	In My Life/In Each Other's Arms	250

(see also Jay & Americans)

CHAPTER ONE
84	Wag 4	I Know That She Knows/Take My Advice (p/s)	6
86	Wag 5	When The Summer Comes/Stephanie Powers/Girl On The Phone	6

CHAPTER THREE (U.K.)
67	CBS 2971	Cold And Lonely Hours/Wrecking Crew	7
67	CBS BPG 63007	RAMBLE AWAY (LP)	25

CHAPTERHOUSE
91	Chapterhouse HOUSE 002	Losing Touch With My Mind/It Won't Be Wrong (flexi)	12
91	Dedicated DEDLP 001	WHIRLPOOL (LP with bonus 12")	30
91	Dedicated DEDLP 001	WHIRLPOOL (LP, without free 12")	20
93	Dedicated DEDLP 011D	BLOOD MUSIC (2-LP)	35

(see also Slowdive)

CHAPTERS
65	Pye 7N 15815	Can't Stop Thinking About Her/Dance Little Lady	60

CHARACTERS
86	BEM BEM 101	Love Talk/Where Has All The Love Gone (500 only)	30

ERIC CHARDON
69	Major Minor MM596	One Love One Life/Sorrow Is My Name	8

CHARGE (1)
73	SRT private pressing	CHARGE (LP, 1 known copy)	1500
92	Kissing Spell KSLP 9205	CHARGE (LP, reissue, revised sleeve, 500 only)	20

CHARGE (2)
70	Private pressing	Zeugma/Boring Song (art sleeve)	20

CHARGE (3)
80	YCAFO Records	You Get What You Deserve/Rather B Crazy/Angel Deceast (foldout p/s)	65
81	Test Pressing	You Deserve More Than A Maybe (p/s, 500 only, existence unconfirmed)	30
82	Test Pressing TP 3	Kings Cross/Brave New World (p/s)	12

CHARGERS
84	Charge BCSK 01	Desperaroes/Are You Out There (p/s)	60

Mark CHARIG

MINT VALUE £

MARK CHARIG
77	Ogun OG 710	PIPEDREAM (LP)	15

(see also Bluesology, B.B. Blunder, Reg King, Centipede, Keith Tippett, Julie Tippett, Brotherhood Of Breath, Elton Dean, Ninesense)

CHARIOT
84	Shades SHADE 2	ALL ALONE AGAIN (EP)	12
84	Shades SHADE 1	THE WARRIOR (LP)	15
86	Shades SHADE 4	BURNING AMBITION (LP)	15

CHARIOTS
62	Piccadilly 7N 35061	Problem Girl/Song Of A Broken Heart	10

CHARLATANS (U.K.)
90	Situation Two SITU 30L	SOME FRIENDLY (LP, 'some friendly edition' in white PVC sleeve with inner)	25
90	Situation Two SITU 30	SOME FRIENDLY (LP)	20
92	Situation Two SITU 37	BETWEEN 10TH AND 11TH (LP)	25
91	Live Live Good CB 2	ISOLATION 21.2.91 (LP, official live bootleg, sold via fan club, 1,000 only)	25
94	Beggars Banquet BBQLP 147	UP TO OUR HIPS (LP, textured sleeve)	25
95	Beggars Banquet BBQLP 174	THE CHARLATANS (2-LP, inners)	80
97	Beggars Banquet BBQLP 190	TELLIN' STORIES (LP)	40
98	Beggars Banquet BBQLP 198	MELTING POT (2-LP)	40
99	Universal 1538650-1	US & US ONLY (LP)	50
01	Universal 014911-1	WONDERLAND (2-LP)	30
04	MCA MCA 60093	UP AT THE LAKE (LP)	20
08	Cooking Vinyl COOK 462	YOU CROSS MY PATH (LP)	25
10	Music On Vinyl MOVLP 185	WHO WE TOUCH (LP)	20
15	BMG 538014171	MODERN NATURE (2-LP, gold vinyl)	20
15	BMG 538014171	MODERN NATURE (2-LP, signed, gold vinyl with CD)	35
17	Beggars Banquet BBQLP 147E	UP TO OUR HIPS (LP, reissue, green vinyl, 250 only)	80

(see also Electric Crayons, Makin' Time, Tim Burgess)

CHARLATANS (U.S.)
69	Philips SBL 7903	THE CHARLATANS (LP)	90

(see also Mike Wilhelm, Tongue & Groove, Dan Hicks & His Hot Licks)

BOBBY CHARLES
56	London HLU 8247	See You Later, Alligator/On Bended Knee	1000
56	London HLU 8247	See You Later, Alligator/On Bended Knee (78)	150

CHILLI CHARLES
74	Virgin V2009	BUSY CORNER (LP)	15
75	Virgin V2028	QUICKSTEP (LP)	15

DON CHARLES
62	Decca F 11424	Walk With Me My Angel/Crazy Man, Crazy	8
62	Decca F 11464	The Hermit Of Misty Mountain/Moonlight Rendezvous	8
62	Decca F 11528	It's My Way Of Loving You/Guess That's The Way It Goes	10
63	Decca F 11602	Angel Of Love/Lucky Star	10
63	Decca F 11645	Heart's Ice Cold/Daybreak	7
64	HMV POP 1307	If You Don't Know I Ain't Gonna Tell Ya/Voice On The Phone	7
63	HMV POP 1271	Tower Tall/Look Before You Love	7
64	HMV POP 1332	Big Talk From A Little Man/She's Mine	10
68	Parlophone R 5688	The Drifter/Great To Be Livin'	150
68	Parlophone R 5688	The Drifter/Great To Be Livin' (DJ Copy)	200
68	Parlophone R 5712	Your Name Is On My Heart/How Can I	15
63	Decca DFE 8530	DON CHARLES (EP)	50
67	Parlophone PMC/PCS 7021	HAVE I TOLD YOU LATELY (LP, mono/stereo)	25

EVAN CHARLES
82	Naive NAV 2	Ask Yourself/Flowers Of England (p/s)	8
83	Naive NAV 6	Intimacy/Ask Yourself (Revisited) (p/s)	80

GARY CHARLES
71	B & C CB 159	You've Been Away Too Long/Lovely Linda	6

JIMMY CHARLES
60	London HLU 9206	A Million To One/Hop Scotch Hop	25
63	Windsor WPS 120	Pitter Pitter Patter/How You Gonna Treat Me Now	10

LEON CHARLES
80	Rokel ROK 15	Disco Carnival/Instrumental (12")	20

RAY CHARLES

78s
58	London HLE 8768	Rockhouse (Parts 1 & 2)	25
59	London HLE 8917	What'd I Say (Parts 1 & 2)	30
59	London HLE 9009	I'm Movin' On/I Believe To My Soul	40
60	HMV POP 792	Georgia On My Mind/Carry Me Back To Old Virginny	50

SINGLES
58	London HLE 8768	Rockhouse (Parts 1 & 2)	30
59	London HLE 8917	What'd I Say (Parts 1 & 2)	25
59	London HLE 9009	I'm Movin' On/I Believe To My Soul	20
60	London HLE 9058	Let The Good Times Roll/Don't Let The Sun Catch You Cryin'	20
60	HMV POP 774	Sticks And Stones/Worried Life Blues	15
60	London HLK 9181	Tell The Truth/You Be My Baby	15
61	HMV POP 838	Them That Got/I Wonder	25
61	London HLK 9364	Early In The Mornin'/A Bit Of Soul	15
61	HMV POP 862	One Mint Julep/Let's Go	15
61	HMV POP 935	Hit The Road Jack/The Danger Zone	10
61	London HLK 9435	I Wonder Who/Hard Times	10

Roger CHARLES

MINT VALUE £

62	HMV POP 969	Unchain My Heart/But On The Other Hand Baby	7
62	HMV POP 1017	Hide Nor Hair/At The Club	10
63	HMV POP 1133	Don't Set Me Free/The Brightest Smile In Town	10
63	HMV POP 1221	Busted/Making Believe	7
64	HMV POP 1315	My Baby Don't Dig Me/Something's Wrong	10
66	HMV POP 1502	Crying Time/When My Dreamboat Comes Home	6
66	HMV POP 1519	Together Again/You're Just About To Lose Your Clown	20
66	HMV POP 1537	Let's Go Get Stoned/The Train	20
66	HMV POP 1551	I Chose To Sing The Blues/Hopelessly	25
66	HMV POP 1566	Please Say You're Fooling/I Don't Need No Doctor	50
66	HMV POP 1566	Please Say You're Fooling/I Don't Need No Doctor (DJ Copy)	80
67	Atlantic 584 093	What'd I Say/I Got A Woman	8
67	HMV POP 1607	In The Heat Of The Night/Something's Got To Change	6

EPs

59	London Jazz EZK 19043	THE GREAT RAY CHARLES	15
59	London Jazz EZK 19048	SOUL BROTHERS (with Milt Jackson)	15
61	London REK 1306	WHAT'D I SAY	20
61	London REK 1317	RAY CHARLES AT NEWPORT	15
62	HMV 7EG 8729	HIT THE ROAD JACK	15
62	HMV 7EG 8781	I CAN'T STOP LOVING YOU	15
63	HMV 7EG 8783	THE BALLAD STYLE OF RAY CHARLES	10
63	HMV 7EG 8801	THE SWINGING STYLE OF RAY CHARLES	10
63	HMV 7EG 8807	BABY IT'S COLD OUTSIDE (with Betty Carter)	10
63	HMV 7EG 8812	TAKE THESE CHAINS FROM MY HEART	10
63	London REB 1407	THE ORIGINAL RAY CHARLES VOLUME ONE	10
63	London REB 1408	THE ORIGINAL RAY CHARLES VOLUME TWO	10
63	London REB 1409	THE ORIGINAL RAY CHARLES VOLUME THREE	10
64	HMV 7EG 8841	BUSTED	10
64	HMV 7EG 8861	RAY CHARLES SINGS	10
64	Realm REP 4001	THE YOUNG RAY CHARLES	10
66	HMV 7EG 8932	RAY CHARLES LIVE IN CONCERT	10
66	HMV 7EG 8951	RAY CHARLES SINGS SONGS OF BUCK OWENS	10

ALBUMS

58	London Jazz LTZ-K 15134	THE GREAT RAY CHARLES	50
59	London Jazz LTZ-K 15146	SOUL BROTHERS (with Milt Jackson, mono)	25
59	London Jazz SAH-K 6030	SOUL BROTHERS (with Milt Jackson, stereo)	25
59	London Jazz LTZ-K 15149	RAY CHARLES AT NEWPORT (mono)	25
59	London Jazz SAH-K 6008	RAY CHARLES AT NEWPORT (stereo)	25
59	London HA-E 2168	YES INDEED	50
59	London HA-E 2226	WHAT'D I SAY	40
60	London Jazz LTZ-K 15190	THE GENIUS OF RAY CHARLES	40
60	HMV CLP 1387/CSD 1320	THE GENIUS HITS THE ROAD (mono)	15
60	HMV CLP 1387/CSD 1320	THE GENIUS HITS THE ROAD (stereo)	18
60	London HA-K 2284	RAY CHARLES IN PERSON	30
61	HMV CLP 1449/CSD 1362	DEDICATED TO YOU (mono)	15
61	HMV CLP 1449/CSD 1362	DEDICATED TO YOU (stereo)	20
61	HMV CLP 1475/CSD 1384	GENIUS + SOUL = JAZZ (mono)	15
61	HMV CLP 1475/CSD 1384	GENIUS + SOUL = JAZZ (stereo)	20
62	HMV CLP 1520/CSD 1414	RAY CHARLES AND BETTY CARTER (mono)	15
62	HMV CLP 1520/CSD 1414	RAY CHARLES AND BETTY CARTER (stereo)	18
62	London Jazz LJZ-K 15238	THE GENIUS SINGS THE BLUES	25
62	HMV CLP 1580/CSD 1451	MODERN SOUNDS IN COUNTRY & WESTERN (mono)	15
62	HMV CLP 1580/CSD 1451	MODERN SOUNDS IN COUNTRY & WESTERN (stereo)	18
63	HMV CLP 1613/CSD 1477	MODERN SOUNDS IN COUNTRY & WESTERN VOL. TWO (mono)	15
63	HMV CLP 1613/CSD 1477	MODERN SOUNDS IN COUNTRY & WESTERN VOL. TWO (stereo)	15
63	London HA-K 8022	THE ORIGINAL RAY CHARLES	15
63	London HA-K 8035	THE GENIUS AFTER HOURS	15
63	London HA-K/SH-K 8045	SOUL MEETING (with Milt Jackson)	15
63	HMV CLP 1678	INGREDIENTS IN A RECIPE FOR SOUL	20

(see also Raelets, Milt Jackson)

ROGER CHARLES

73	Dawn DNS 1038	Understand Each Other/Can't Forget	6

SONNY CHARLES (& CHECKMATES LTD)

67	Ember EMB S 240	Mastered The Art Of Love/Please Don't Take My World Away	40
69	A&M AMS 752	Black Pearl/Lazy Susan	10
70	A&M AMS 787	It Takes A Little Longer/Welfare Man	6

TINA CHARLES

69	CBS 4015	Nothing In The World/Millions Of Hearts	15
69	CBS 4307	In The Middle Of The Day/Rich Girl	40
69	CBS 4658	Good To Be Alive/Same Old Story	50

CHILI CHARLES

75	Virgin V 2028	QUICKSTEP (LP)	15

CHARLES, PAULETTE & GEE

71	G.G. GG 4515	Shock And Shake (Version 3)/WINSTON WRIGHT: Roll On (Version 2) (as Charlie, Paulette & Gee)	
71	G.G. GG 4517	Rock And Shake (Version 3) (actually "Lover's Affair" by Charlie Ace & Maytones)/Roll On (Version 2) (actually "My Love And I" by Winston Wright)	10

(see also Charlie Ace)

Dick CHARLESWORTH (& HIS CITY GENTS)

MINT VALUE £

DICK CHARLESWORTH (& HIS CITY GENTS)
61	Top Rank 35-104	MEET THE GENTS (LP)	15
62	HMV CLP 1495	YES INDEED IT'S THE GENTS (LP)	15

CHARLIE
72	Bumble GE 111	Dream Hero/Lament	15
73	Decca F 13451	I Need Your Love/I'm So Happy	20

CHARLIE BOY
71	Trojan TR 7823	Funky Strip/UPSETTERS: Mellow Mood	25

(see also Lee Perry/Upsetters)

CHARLIE & FAY
72	Pama 853	Big Seven (Punnany)/YOUTH PROFESSIONAL BAND : Version	12

CHARLIE PARKAS
80	Paranoid Plastics PPS 1	The Ballad Of Robin Hood/Space Invaders (mock 2-Tone die cut p/s)	30

(see also Alberto Y Lost Trios Paranoias)

CHARLIES BROTHER
84	Lost Moment LMO 100	Wishing Tree/Further Adventures Of	25

CHARLY & THE BOURBON FAMILY
71	Decca F 23164	Acapulco Gold/Boogachi	15

CHARMAINES
98	Kent 6T 18	I Idolize You/M&M & THE PEANUTS: Can't Say No	25

CHARMERS (JAMAICA)
61	Blue Beat BB 42	Lonely Boy/I Am Going Back Home	20
62	Blue Beat BB 114	Crying Over You/Now You Want To Cry	20
63	Blue Beat BB 157	Time After Time/Done Me Wrong (with Prince Buster's Band)	15
60s	Blue Beat	How Could I Forget/Why Won't You Come Home? (with Prince Buster's Band) (white label only)	75
63	R&B JB 118	Angel Love/My Heart	20
63	R&B JB 121	Oh Why Baby/ROLAND ALPHONSO: Perhaps	30
64	R&B JB 151	What's The Use/I Am Through	20
64	R&B JB 156	In My Soul/Beware	20
64	Blue Beat BB 204	I'm Back/It's A Dream	20
64	Blue Beat BB 238	Waiting For You/You Are My Sunshine	20
64	Blue Beat BB 251	Dig Then Prince (actually Dip Them Prince)/Girl Of My Dreams (as The Charmer)	25
65	Blue Beat BB 279	Nobody Takes My Baby Away From Me/ BUSTER ALLSTARS: Mules Mules Mules	75
66	Blue Beat BB 345	Oh My Baby/STRANGER COLE: When The Party Is Over	20
66	Ska Beat JB 237	Best Friend/MAYTALS: My Darling	25
66	Rio R 78	You Don't Know/CORNELL CAMPBELL & ROY PANTON: Sweetest Girl	20
68	Coxsone CS 7043	Things Going Wrong/KEN BOOTHE: You Keep Me Hanging On	300
68	Treasure Isle TI 7036	Keep On Going (actually by Lloyd Charmers)/SILVERTONES: Don't Say No	20
70	Duke DU 87	Colour Him Father/Version	30
70	Trojan TR 7773	Sweeter She Is (actually by Lloyd Charmers, Dave Barker & Slim Smith)/ Fire Fire (actually by Lloyd Charmers)	12
70	Explosion EX 2026	Can I Get Next To You?/Big Five	10
70	Explosion EX 2035	Sweet Back/Music Talk (actually by Lloyd Charmers)	12
71	Bullet BU 473	Reggae In Wonderland/Wonder (Version)	10
71	Explosion EX 2045	Skinhead Train/TONY & CHARMERS: Everstrong (B-side with Tony Binns)	125
71	Explosion EX 2055	Reggae In Wonderland/Wonder - Version (both actually by Byron Lee & Dragonaires)	7
71	Supreme SUP 220	Just My Imagination/Gotta Get A Message To You (actually by Dave Barker)	25
71	Green Door GD 4000	Rasta Never Fails (actually by Lloyd Charmers & Ken Boothe)/CHARMERS ALL STARS: Rasta Version	7
71	Green Door GD 4001	One Big Unhappy Family/CONSCIOUS MINDS: Africa Is Paradise	15
71	Pama Supreme PS 340	Red Head Duck/Jingle Jangle	6

(see also Spanishtown Skabeats, Lloyd & Ken, Lloydie & Lowbites, Lloyd Terrell)

LLOYD CHARMERS
67	Coxsone CS 7023	Time Is Getting Hard/TONY GREGORY: I Sit By The Shore	100
69	Duke DU 15	Cooyah/UNIQUES: Forever	30
69	Duke DU 16	Follow This Sound/Why Pretend	30
69	Duke DU 25	5 To 5/SOUL STIRRERS: Come See About Me	35
69	Duke DU 36	Safari (The Far East)/Last Laugh	40
69	Songbird SB 1001	Ling Ting Tong/LLOYD ROBINSON: Sweet Sweet	20
69	Songbird SB 1007	Duckey Luckey/In The Spirit	50
69	Camel CA 30	Confidential/TOMMY COWAN: House In Session	35
69	Explosion EX 2001	Death A Come/Zylon	50
70	Explosion EX 2034	Ready Talk/There Is Something About You	18
70	Trojan TR 7788	Oh Me Oh My/I Did It	20
70	Bullet BU 435	Dollars And Bonds/Sounds Familiar	35
70	Bullet BU 442	Reggae A Bye Bye/DAVE BARKER:Doctor Jekyll	40
70	Escort ES 820	Soul Of England/Shang I	30
70	Escort ES 836	Hi Shan/Soul At Large	30
70	Smash SMA 2302	Big Red Bum Ball/BUNNIE LEE ALLSTARS: Big Bum Ball Version	7
71	Black Swan BW 1405	Love You The Most/LOW BITES:Version	15
71	Expolsion EX 2054	Going In Circles/Doggone Right (actually by Winston Francis)	20
73	Green Door GD 4064	Save The People (as L. Charmers)/SCOTTY: Salvation Train	10
74	Harry J. HJ 6662	I'm Gonna Love You Just A Little Bit More/Have I Sinned	50
71	Pama Supreme PS 339	Shaft/Harry's Mood	10
71	Pama Supreme PS 346	Show Business/DEBBY & LLOYD: Gloria	8
72	Pama Supreme PS 355	Desiderata/Desiderata Music	10
11	Explosion THB 7009	The Premises/JOKERS: Brixton	50
70	Trojan TTL 25	REGGAE IS TIGHT (LP, orange/white label)	40
70	Trojan TTL 30	REGGAE CHARM (LP)	30

CHARMERS (U.S.)

MINT VALUE £

Year	Label/Cat#	Title	Value
70	Pama SECO 25	HOUSE IN SESSION (LP, with Hippy Boys)	175
72	Trojan TRLS 86	BEST OF (LP)	20
73	Trojan TBL 201	IN SESSION (LP)	20

(see also Charmers, Lloyd Tyrell/Terrell, Ken Boothe, Hippy Boys, Wayne Howard, Martia Riley, Eric Donaldson)

CHARMERS (U.S.)
58	Vogue V 9095	He's Gone/Oh! Yes	200
58	Vogue V 9095	He's Gone/Oh! Yes (78)	20

CHARMETTES
63	London HLR 9820	Please Don't Kiss Me Again/What Is A Tear	40

CHARMS (JAMAICA)
64	Island WI 154	Carry, Go, Bring Home (actually by Justin Hinds & Dominoes)/Hill And Gully (actually by L. Reid's Group)	20
66	Rio R 98	Everybody Say Yeah/This World Is Yours	20

CHARMS (U.S.)
55	Parlophone MSP 6155	Hearts Of Stone/Ko Ko Mo (I Love You So)	250
55	Parlophone R3988	Hearts Of Stone/Ko Ko Mo (I Love You So) (78)	20
55	Parlophone DP 412	Hearts Of Stone/Bazoom, I Need Your Lovin' (78) (export issue)	20
55	Parlophone DP 423	Two Hearts/The First Time We Met (78) (export issue)	20

(see also Otis Williams & Charms, Harmonizing Four)

CHARTBUSTERS
64	London HLU 9906	She's The One/Slippin' Thru Your Fingers	15

CHARTERED HURRICANE
83	SRTS 83 CUS 1695	Cathy Come Home/All Smashed Up (stamped plain white sleeve)	25

CHARTZ
83	Digital ZELSPS 404	Girls World/Girls World (Dance Mix)	20

CHASE
71	Epic EPC 7301	Get It On In The Morning/River	6
71	Epic EPCS 7506	Handbags And Gladrags/Open Up Wide	10

LINCOLN CHASE
57	London HLU 8495	Johnny Klingeringding/You're Driving Me Crazy (What Did I Do)	20
61	Philips PB 1103	Miss Orangutang/Walking Slowly	20

CHASERS
65	Decca F 12302	Hey Little Girl/That's What They Call Love	50
66	Parlophone R 5451	Inspiration/She's Gone Away	150
67	Philips BF 1546	The Ways Of A Man/Summer Girl	15

CHASERS
84	SRT SRT4KS 304	Raiders/Final Stand (300 only)	60

CHATEAUX
82	Ebony EBON 9	Young Blood/Fight To The Last	20
83	Ebony EBON 13	CHAINED AND DESPERATE (LP)	20
84	Ebony EBON 18	FIRE POWER (LP)	15
85	Ebony EBON 31	HIGHLY STRUNG (LP)	15

CHEAP BOOTS
70	Fontana 6001 020	Baby I Do Need You/Come And Stay With Me	6

CHEAP TRICK
78	Epic S EPC 6199	So Good To See You/You're All Talk (withdrawn)	20
79	Epic S EPC 7258	I Want You To Want Me (live)/I Want You To Want Me (studio) (DJ only)	6
79	Epic CT-1	Dream Police/Voice/I'll Be With You Tonight (sampler, promo only)	10

CHEATERS
80	Pre Fab Z 01	I Wanna Be A Policeman/Baby What Do You Want Me To Do/From The Hip (foldout p/s)	8

OLIVER CHEATHAM
83	MCA MCAT 828	Get Down Saturday Night/Something About You (12")	18
83	MCA MCF 3179	SATURDAY NIGHT (LP)	30

CHEATIN' HEARTS
66	Columbia DB 8048	Zip-Tease/The Bad Kind	10

CHUBBY CHECKER
59	Top Rank JAR 154	The Class/Schooldays, Oh, Schooldays	30
60	Columbia DB 4503	The Twist/Toot	8
60	Columbia DB 4541	The Hucklebuck/Whole Lotta Shakin' Goin' On	15
61	Columbia DB 4591	Pony Time/Oh Susannah	8
61	Columbia DB 4652	Good Good Loving/Mess Around	15
61	Columbia DB 4728	The Fly/That's The Way It Goes	10
62	Columbia DB 4876	Dancin' Party/Gotta Get Myself Together	6
62	Cameo Parkway P 849	Limbo Rock/Hitch Hiker	7
63	Cameo Parkway P 873	Black Cloud/Birdland	6
63	Cameo Parkway P 890	Loddy Lo/Hooka Tooka	8
64	Cameo Parkway P 907	Hey Bobba Needle/Spread Joy	10
64	Cameo Parkway P 922	She Wants T'Swim/You Better Believe It Baby	15
65	Cameo Parkway P 936	Lovely, Lovely/The Weekend's Here	20
65	Cameo Parkway P 949	(At The) Discotheque/Do The Freddie (DJ copy)	150
65	Cameo Parkway P 949	(At The) Discotheque/Do The Freddie	50
65	Cameo Parkway P 959	Everything's Wrong/Cu Ma La Be Stay (DJ copy)	120
65	Cameo Parkway P 959	Everything's Wrong/Cu Ma La Be Stay	50
65	Cameo Parkway P 965	Two Hearts Make One Love/You Just Don't Know (What You Do To Me) (DJ Copy)	400
65	Cameo Parkway P 965	Two Hearts Make One Love/You Just Don't Know (What You Do To Me)	300
65	Cameo Parkway P 989	Hey You Little Boogaloo/Pussy Cat	30
65	Cameo Parkway P 989	Hey You Little Boogaloo/Pussy Cat (DJ Copy)	60
73	Pye Int 25620	Reggae My Way/Gypsy	25
78	London HLU 10557	You Just Don't Know (What You Do To Me)/ Two Hearts Make One Love (reissue) (DJ Copy)	35

CHUBBY CHECKER & DEE DEE SHARP

			MINT VALUE £
78	London HLU 10557	You Just Don't Know (What You Do To Me)/ Two Hearts Make One Love (reissue)	20
93	Kent 6T 9	You Can't Lose Something You've Never Had/TEARDROPS: Here Comes The Lonliness	10
71	London SHZ 8419	CHEQUERED (LP)	20

CHUBBY CHECKER & DEE DEE SHARP
| 62 | Cameo Parkway C 1029 | DOWN TO EARTH (LP) | 20 |

(see also Dream Lovers, Bobby Rydell, Dee Dee Sharp)

CHECKERBOARD SQUARES
| 11 | Outta Sight OSV 041 | Double Cookin'/A Day In Saulsalito | 8 |

CHECKMATES
61	Piccadilly 7N 35010	Rockin' Minstrel/Pompeii	8
63	Decca F 11603	You've Gotta Have A Gimmick Today/Westpoint	10
64	Decca F 11844	Sticks And Stones/Please Listen To Me	15
65	Decca F 12114	Around/I've Got To Know Now	10
65	Parlophone R 5337	Stop That Music/I've Been In Love Before	10
66	Parlophone R 5402	(You Got) The Gamma Goochie/It Ain't Right	10
66	Parlophone R 5495	Every Day Is Just The Same/I'll Be Keeping The Score	15
61	Pye NPL 18061	THE CHECKMATES (LP)	30

(see also Original Checkmates, Emile Ford)

CHEEKY
| 80 | Woodbine St. WSR 005 | Don't Mess Around/Get Outa My 'Ouse (no p/s) | 40 |

CHEERS
54	Capitol CL 14189	Bazoom (I Need Your Lovin')/Arrivederci	15
55	Capitol CL 14248	Bernie's Tune/Whadaya Want?	10
55	Capitol CL 14280	Blueberries/Can't We Be More Than Friends	10
55	Capitol CL 14337	I Must Be Dreaming/Fancy Meeting You Here	10
55	Capitol CL 14377	Black Denim Trousers And Motorcycle Boots/Some Night In Alaska	30
55	Capitol CL 14377	Black Denim Trousers And Motorcycle Boots/Some Night In Alaska (78)	8
56	Capitol CL 14561	Chicken/Don't Do Anything	20
56	Capitol EAP1 584	THE CHEERS (EP)	15

(see also Bert Convy [& Thunderbirds])

CHEETAHS (1)
64	Philips BF 1362	Mecca/Goodnight Kiss	15
65	Philips BF 1383	Soldier Boy/Johnny	15
65	Philips BF 1412	Goodbye Baby (Baby Goodbye)/That's How It Goes	10
65	Philips BF 1453	Whole Lotta Love/The Party	12
66	Philips BF 1499	The Russian Boat Song/Gamble	10

(see also Carl Wayne & Cheetahs)

CHEETAHS (2)
| 79 | Zoom ZUM 14 | RADIO-ACTIVE EP (p/s) | 6 |

CHEFS (1)
| 80 | Attatrix RB 10 | SWEETIE EP | 15 |
| 81 | Graduate GRAD 11 | 24 Hours/Thrush | 15 |

CHEFS (2)
| 02 | Funk 45 FUNK45.003 | Mr. Machine Part I/Mr. Machine Part II (reissue) | 10 |

CHELMSFORD COUNTY HIGH SCHOOL FOLK GROUP
| 70 | Private Pressing | CHELMSFORD COUNTY HIGH SCHOOL FOLK GROUP (LP) | 20 |

CHELSEA
77	Step Forward SF 2	Right To Work/The Loner (p/s, original pressing in card p/s)	15
77	Step Forward SF 2	Right To Work/The Loner (p/s)	8
77	Step Forward SF 5	High Rise Living/No Admission (p/s)	10
78	Step Forward SF 8	Urban Kids/No Flowers (p/s)	8
80	Step Forward SF 14	No One's Coming Outside/What Would You Do (p/s)	6
80	Step Forward SF 15	Look At the Outside/Don't Get Me Wrong (p/s)	6
80	Step Forward SF 16	No Escape/Decide (p/s)	6
79	Step Forward SFLP 2	CHELSEA (LP, with inner sleeve)	30
81	Step Forward SFLP 5	ALTERNATIVE HITS (LP)	20
82	Step Forward SFLP 7	EVACUATE (LP)	15

CHEMICAL AGENT
| 96 | Alphaphone ALPHA 003 | Waterfall/Shock (12") | 15 |

(see also Cabaret Voltaire, Richard H. Kirk)

CHEMICAL ALICE
| 81 | Acidic GNOME 1 | The Judge/Goodnight Vienna/Lands Of Home/Henry The King (12", p/s) | 40 |

(see also Marillion)

CHEMICAL BROTHERS
91	Eastern Bloc	Sea Of Beats/Sea Of Beats (Justin Robertson Mix) (12", p/s, as Ariel)	80
91	Deconstruction PT 44888	Rollercoaster/Mustn't Grumble/Mustn't Grumble (God's Grumble Mix) (12", as Ariel)	45
93	Dust Brothers DB's 333	Song To The Siren (12", as Dust Brothers, no p/s, 500 only)	60
93	Junior Boys Own JBO 10	Song To The Siren/Song To The Siren (Sabres Of Paradise Mixes) (12", p/s)	30
94	Boys Own COLLECT 004	14TH CENTURY SKY EP (12", no p/s, as Dust Brothers)	20
94	Junior Boys Own JBO 20	MY MERCURY MOUTH EP (12", JBO sleeve, as Dust Brothers)	30
95	Junior Boys Own CHEMS TI	Leave Home/Leave Home (Sabres Of Paradise)/Let Me In Mate (12", p/s)	15
95	Junior Boys Own	Leave Home (Underworld Mix One)/Leave Home (Underworld Mix Two) (12", p/s)	15
15	Secret 7" S722	Let Forever Be (100 only, each with unique art sleeve)	45
95	Junior Boys Own XDUSTLP1	EXIT PLANET DUST (2-LP, inners)	35
97	Freestyle Dust XDUST LP2	DIG YOUR OWN HOLE (2-LP)	50
99	Freestyle Dust XDUST LP4	SURRENDER (2-LP, gatefold)	50
02	Virgin XDUST LP5	COME WITH US (2-LP)	30
03	Freestyle Dust XDUSTLP 6	SINGLES 93-03 (4-LP box set)	50
04	Virgin XDUST LP7	PUSH THE BUTTON (2-LP)	30

CHEMICAL (1)

MINT VALUE £

CHEMICAL (1)
92	Head Press SRT 92LS 3170	Distrurbance/Paranoia (12")	10
92	Head Press HP 002	THE VIRUS EP (12")	12
92	Basement BRSS 017	Hex/Sub Sector (12")	10

(see also Two Dark Troopers, DJ Chemistry Meets Jack Smooth)

CHEMICAL (2)
96	Acme AC 8014LP	CHEMICAL (LP, 500 only)	15

CHEMISTRY SET
11	Fruits De Mer Winkle1	Impossible Love/We Luv You (folded p/s, inserts)	15
12	Regal Crambone Winkle 8	Time To Breathe/Come Kiss Me Vibrate And Smile/Hallucinations (p/s, blue vinyl)	7

CLIFTON CHENIER
69	Action ACT 4550	Black Gal/Frogs Legs	15
70	Specialty SNTF 5012	BAYOU BLUES (LP)	20
70	Harvest MHSP 4002	CLIFTON CHENIER'S VERY BEST (LP)	50
79	Flyright FLY 539	ZYDECO BLUES (LP, with other artists)	20

CHEQUERED PAST
85	Heavy Metal America	CHEQUERED PAST (LP, picture disc, 1,000 only)	30

(see also Steve Jones)

CHEQUERS (1)
72	Rhino RNO 112	Everyday/Butler's Cross	10
73	Rhino RNO 119	Rudi's In Love/Ask For Reggae	8
76	Creole CRLP 504	CHECK US OUT (LP)	40

CHEQUERS (2)
80	Matthias MT 101	Midnight Hour/Move Up	15
83	Matthias MT 102	Hard Times/If You Want My Love (no p/s)	200

CHER
69	Atlantic 584 278	Walk On Gilded Splinters/Tonight I'll Be Staying Here With You	15
66	Liberty LEP 4047	THE HITS OF CHER (EP)	12
66	Liberty LBY 3081	CHER (LP, mono)	15
66	Liberty (S)LBY 3081	CHER (LP, stereo)	15

(see also Sonny & Cher, Caesar & Cleo, Nilsson)

VIVIENNE CHERING
66	Decca F 12360	I'll Do My Crying Tomorrow/Make My Dreams Come True	10

(see also Flip & Dateliners)

CHEROKEE
71	Probe PRO 550	Girl, I've Got News For You/Write To You	10

CHEROKEES (U.K.)
64	Decca F 11915	You've Done It Again Little Girl/Girl Girl Girl	7
64	Columbia DB 7341	Seven Daffodils/Are You Back In My World Now	8
65	Columbia DB 7473	Wondrous Place/Send Me All Your Love	40
65	Columbia DB 7704	I Will Never Turn My Back On You/Dig A Little Deeper	10
66	Columbia DB 7822	Land Of A 1000 Dances/Everybody's Needs	20

(see also Lee Diamond)

CHEROKEES (U.S.)
61	Pye International 7N 25066	Cherokee/Harlem Nocturne	15

CHERRY
80s	Crashed Records CAR 91	He's A Bum/He Rides With Me	10

CHERRY BOYS
81	Open Eye OE5	Man To Man/So Much Confusion (p/s)	6

DON CHERRY (1)
56	Brunswick 05538	Wanted Someone To Love/The Thrill Is Gone	6
57	Philips JK 1013	The Last Dance/Don't You Worry (jukebox edition)	7

DON CHERRY (2)
16	Cacophony CACK4506	Don/Jon (p/s with Jon Appleton)	6
73	JCOA/Virgin J2001	RELATIVITY SUITE (LP)	25
74	Sonet SNTF 653	ETERNAL NOW (LP)	50
75	DJM DJSLM 2008	KAWAIDA (LP, with Herbie Hancock)	30
77	Blue Note BNS 40027	WHERE IS BROOKLYN? (LP, reissue)	35
78	Sonet SNFF 669	LIVE IN ANKARA (LP)	50
78	Affinity AFF 8	MU: FIRST PART (LP, reissue)	15
78	Affinity AFF 17	MU: SECOND PART (LP, reissue)	15
82	Affinity AFFD 82	ORIENT (2-LP, reissue)	25
89	A&M 395 258-1	ART DECO (LP)	25
15	Bue Note ST 84225	COMPLETE COMMUNION (LP, reissue)	18

JIMMY CHERRY
76	Gull GULS 36	Capella/Slow Burning	8

CHERRY ORCHARD
88	Red Honey (No Cat. No)	So Blind (p/s, 1-sided flexi)	15
89	Red Honey ORCHARD 1	SING SISTER GLORY (12" EP)	18
90	Red Honey ORCHARD 3	For What It's Worth/For What It's Worth (Version) (12", no p/s, promo only)	18
90	Red Honey ORCHARD 2	HEALING FAITH LIKE FIRE (LP)	15

CHERRY PEOPLE
68	MGM MGM 1438	And Suddenly/Imagination	40
68	MGM MGM 1438	And Suddenly/Imagination (DJ copy)	60
69	MGM MGM 1472	Gotta Get Back/I'm The One Who Loves You	15
69	MGM MGM 1489	Light Of Love/On To Something New	8
69	MGM MGM 1489	Light Of Love/I'm The One Who Loves You	8
75	Black Magic BM 112	And Suddenly/Imagination (reissue)	8

CHERRY PIES
64	Black Swan WI 448	Do You Keep Dreaming/Sweeter Than Cherry Pie	25

CHERRY POPPERS

MINT VALUE £

CHERRY POPPERS
80   Hiroshima HRH 1   Money In My Pocket/Hiroshima 20
CHERRY SMASH
67   Track 604 017   Sing Songs Of Love/Movie Star 20
68   Decca F 12838   Goodtime Sunshine/Little Old Country Home Town 25
69   Decca F 12884   Fade Away Maureen/Green Plant 60
VIC CHESNUTT
96   PLR 005-1   ABOUT TO CHOKE (LP) 15
PETE CHESTER
60   Pye 7N 15305   Ten Swinging Bottles/Whole Lotta Shakin' On The Range (with Consulates) 10
61   Pye International 7N 25074   Three Old Maids/Forest Fire (as Pete Chester & Group) 15
(see also Five Chestnuts)
VIC CHESTER
57   Decca F 10882   Rock-A-Billy/First Date, First Kiss, First Love 12
CHESTERFIELD KINGS
85   Ligget & Mayers   THE CHESTERFIELD KINGS (LP) 18
CHESTERFIELDS (2)
03   Grapevine 45-134   Think It Over/Why Did You Leave Me Baby? (reissue) 15
MORRIS CHESTNUT
79   Grapevine GRP 128   Too Darn Soulful/You Don't Love Me Anymore 20
79   Grapevine GRP 128   Too Darn Soulful/You Don't Love Me Anymore (DJ Copy) 35
CHEVRONS (2)
79   Shy Talk   Sindy's Got An Action Man/No More Tears (p/s) 25
CHEVY
80   Avatar AAA 104   Too Much Loving/See The Light (company sleeve) 15
80   Avatar AAA 107   The Taker/Life On The Run (p/s) 15
81   Avatar AAA 114   Just Another Day/Rock On 12
80   Avatar AALP 5001   THE TAKER (LP, with inner sleeve) 18
CHEYNES (1)
63   Columbia DB 7153   Respectable/It's Gonna Happen To You 125
64   Columbia DB 7368   Going To The River/Cheyne-Re-La 125
65   Columbia DB 7464   Down And Out/Stop Running Around 125
(see also Peter Bardens, Peter B's, Fleetwood Mac, Mark Leeman Five, Bo Street Runners)
CHEYNES (2)
71   Bell BLL 1144   April Fool/Gotta Get Back 6
CHIC
78   Atlantic K 11209   Le Freak/Savoir Faire (12") 10
79   Atlantic K11385T   My Forbidden Lover/What About Me? (12") 10
78   Atlantic K 50441   CHIC (LP) 20
78   Atlantic K 50565   C'EST CHIC (LP, inner) 20
79   Atlantic K 50634   RISQUE (LP) 15
79   Atlantic K 50686   GREATEST HITS (LP) 15
13   Rhino/Atlantic 8122796497   THE 12" SINGLES COLLECTION (Box set, 5 x 12") 35
CHICAGO
69   CBS 4381   Questions 67 And 68/Listen 6
69   CBS 4503   I'm A Man (Parts 1 & 2) (withdrawn) 20
69   CBS 4715   I'm A Man/Does Anyone Really Know What Time It Is? (promo p/s) 20
69   CBS 66221   CHICAGO TRANSIT AUTHORITY (2-LP, orange label) 20
70   CBS 66233   CHICAGO (2-LP) 20
71   CBS 66405   IV (AT CARNEGIE HALL) (4-LP, orange label) 20
CHICAGO LINE
66   Philips BF 1488   Shimmy Shimmy Ko Ko Bop/Jump Back 200
(see also Mike Patto, Bo Street Runners, Viv Prince)
CHICAGO LOOP
66   Stateside SS 564   (When She Needs Good Lovin') She Comes To Me/This Must Be The Place (DJ Copy) 40
66   Stateside SS 564   (When She Needs Good Lovin') She Comes To Me/This Must Be The Place 15
CHICAGO UNDERGROUND COUNCIL
96   Peacefrog PF 060   2 DAYS (12" EP) 15
CHICANES
81   Dinosaur Discs DD 003   Cry A Little/Further Thoughts (p/s) 20
88   Bam Caruso NRIC 039   Cry A Little/Further Thoughts (p/s) 20
CHICK WITH TED CAMERON & D.J.'S
60   Pye 7N 15292   Early In The Morning/Cool Water 40
CHICKEN SHACK
67   Blue Horizon 57-3135   It's OK With Me Baby/When My Left Eye Jumps 20
68   Blue Horizon 57-3143   Worried About My Woman/Six Nights In Seven 20
68   Blue Horizon 57-3146   When The Train Comes Back/Hey Baby 15
69   Blue Horizon 57-3153   I'd Rather Go Blind/Night Life 8
69   Blue Horizon 57-3160   Tears In The Wind/The Things You Put Me Through 10
70   Blue Horizon 57-3168   Maudie/Andalucian Blues 10
70   Blue Horizon 57-3176   Sad Clown/Tired Eyes 15
73   Deram DM 381   Time Goes Passing By/Poor Boy 10
73   Deram DM 396   You Know You Could Be Right/The Loser 10
68   Blue Horizon 7-63203   FORTY BLUE FINGERS FRESHLY PACKED AND READY TO SERVE (LP, 1st pressing with 'stereo' sticker on sleeve) 100
68   Blue Horizon 7-63203   FORTY BLUE FINGERS FRESHLY PACKED AND READY TO SERVE (LP, 1st pressing, mono) 40
69   Blue Horizon 7-63209   O.K. KEN? (LP, gatefold sleeve, 1st pressing with 'stereo' sticker on sleeve) 100
69   Blue Horizon 7-63209   O.K. KEN? (LP, gatefold sleeve, 1st pressing, mono) 60
69   Blue Horizon 7-63218   100 TON CHICKEN (LP, gatefold, 1st pressing with 'stereo' sticker on sleeve) 100
70   Blue Horizon 7-63861   ACCEPT CHICKEN SHACK (LP, gatefold sleeve) 75

CHICKEN SHED

MINT VALUE £

71	Deram SDL 5	IMAGINATION LADY (LP, gatefold sleeve, brown/white label with large Deram label)	75
71	Deram SDL 5	IMAGINATION LADY (LP, gatefold sleeve, later pressing with red/white label)	30
73	Deram SML 1100	UNLUCKY BOY (LP)	40

(see also Errol Dixon, Fleetwood Mac, Christine Perfect, Carmen Macrae, Broken Glass)

CHICKEN SHED
| 77 | Colby AJ 370 | ALICE (LP, hand-made sleeves) | 120 |

CHICKS
| 63 | Oriole CB 1828 | What Are Boys Made Of?/Over The Mountain | 20 |

CHICORY TIP
| 71 | CBS 7118 | My Girl Sunday/Doctor Man | 15 |
| 71 | CBS 7595 | I Love Onions/Don't Hang Jack | 12 |

CHIEF
| 81 | Swamp WAM 114 | Don't Touch The Receiver/Icebreaker (not released in p/s) | 25 |

CHIEF CHECKER
| 79 | Original WBA 102 | Impossibilities/Possibility (dub) (12", die cut sleeve) | 40 |
| 79 | Original WBL 101 | THE SOUND OF CHIEF CHECKER (LP) | 100 |

CHIEFS
| 58 | London HLU 8624 | Apache/Dee's Dream | 20 |
| 58 | London HLU 8720 | Enchiladas!/Moments To Remember | 20 |

CHIFFONS
63	Stateside SS 172	He's So Fine/Oh! My Lover	7
63	Stateside SS 202	One Fine Day/Why Am I So Shy	10
63	Stateside SS 230	A Love So Fine/Only My Friend	15
64	Stateside SS 254	I Have A Boyfriend/I'm Gonna Dry Your Eyes	15
64	Stateside SS 332	Sailor Boy/When Summer's Through	20
65	Statside SS 437	Nobody Knows What's Going On (In My Mind But Me)/The Real Thing (DJ copy)	60
65	Stateside SS 437	Nobody Knows What's Going On (In My Mind But Me)/The Real Thing	40
66	Stateside SS 512	Sweet Talkin' Guy/Did You Ever Go Steady	10
66	Stateside SS 533	Out Of This World/Just A Boy	15
66	Stateside SS 559	Stop, Look And Listen/March	30
67	Stateside SS 578	My Boyfriend's Back/I Got Plenty Of Nuttin'	22
64	Stateside SE 1012	THEY'RE SO FINE (EP)	60
63	Stateside SL 10040	THE CHIFFONS - HE'S SO FINE (LP)	80
66	Stateside S(S)L 10190	SWEET TALKIN' GUY (LP)	80
85	Impact ACT 007	FLIPS FLOPS & RARITIES (LP)	15

(see also Four Pennies)

ANTHONY CHILD/ANDREW READ
| 99 | Fat Cat 12FAT 031 | Speedranch/Jansky Noise (12" EP, 'bullet hole' sleeve) | 12 |

ALAN CHILDE
| 76 | Epic SEPC 4183 | Rainmaker/Mind Blowing Love | 6 |

SONNY CHILDE (& T.N.T.)
65	Decca F 12218	Giving Up On Love/Mighty Nice (Of You To Call)	150
65	Decca F12218	Giving Up On Love/Mighty Nice (Of You To Call) (DJ Copy)	300
66	Polydor 56108	Two Lovers/Ain't That Good News	15
66	Polydor 56141	Heartbreak/I Still Love You (as Sonny Childe & T.N.T.)	30
66	Polydor 582 003	TO BE CONTINUED (LP)	40

CHILD HAROLDS
| 68 | Trident TRA 201 | Diary Of My Mind/Loophole | 30 |

BILLY CHILDISH
93	Damaged Books DAMBOOK 1	TREMBLING OF LIFE (3 x 7" box set with book & 2 postcards)	20
87	Hangman HANG 9-UP	THE 1982 CASSETTES (LP, blue & white sleeve, with poster)	30
87	Hangman HANG 9-UP	THE 1982 CASSETTES (LP, blue & white sleeve, without poster)	30
88	Hangman HANG 16 UP	POEMS OF LAUGHTER & VIOLENCE (LP)	30
91	Hangman HANG 37 UP	50 ALBUMS GREAT (LP)	30
08	Aquarium AQU 000I-13	LIVE AT THE AQUARIUM (2-LP, 150 only, numbered and signed)	100

WILD BILLY CHILDISH & HIS FAMOUS HEADCOATS
| 00 | Buff Medway COCK 1-UP | I AM THE OBJECT OF YOUR DESIRE (LP) | 15 |

BILLY CHILDISH & THE BLACKHANDS
| 93 | Hangman 53 UP | LIVE IN THE NETHERLANDS (LP) | 20 |

BILLY CHILDISH & THE NATURAL BORN LOVERS
| 89 | Hangman 30 UP | LONG LEGGED BABY (LP) | 20 |

BILLY CHILDISH & SEXTON MING
87	Hangman HANG 05 UP	WHICH DEAD DONKEY DADDY (LP, poster)	15
87	Hangman HANG 10 UP	PLUMP PRIZES & LITTLE GEMS (LP)	15
87	Hangman HANG 12 UP	YPRES 1917 OVERTURE(LP)	20
98	Damaged Goods DAMGOOD 159LP	THE CHEEKY CHEESE (LP)	15

BILLY CHILDISH & THE SINGING LOINS
| 93 | Hangmans Daughter SCRAG 1 | AT THE BRIDGE (LP) | 20 |

WILD BILLY CHILDISH & THE BLACKHANDS
| 88 | Hangman HANG-21 UP | PLAY CAPT'N CALYPSO'S HOODOO PARTY | 20 |

(see also Milkshakes, Thee Mighty Caesars and Billy Childish & entries)

WILD BILLY CHILDISH & BIG RUSS WILKINS
| 87 | Empire CPO 195 | LAUGHING GRAVY (10" LP) | 20 |

WILD BILLY CHILDISH & BUFF MEDWAYS
03	Aquarium (No Cat. No)	You Are All Phonys (p/s, 1-sided, white label other side etched, 100 numbered and signed by Childish)	50
03	Aquarium (No Cat. No)	You Are All Phonys (p/s, 1-sided, white label other side etched, 400 unsigned)	20
04	Aquarium (No Cat. No)	(I'm Not Going To Your Boring) Private View (p/s, 1-sided other side etched, 100	50

Wild BILLY CHILDISH

			MINT VALUE £
		numbered and signed by Childish)	
04	Aquarium (No Cat. No)	(I'm Not Going To Your Boring) Private View (p/s, 1-sided other side etched, 400 unsigned)	20
05	Damaged Goods DAMGOOD 239LP	MEDWAY WHEELERS (LP, 50 copies with numbered 'The Poundlands Poets' booklet	30
05	Damaged Goods DAMGOOD 239LP	MEDWAY WHEELERS (LP, without booklet)	15

(see also Buff Medways)

WILD BILLY CHILDISH
87	Hangman HANG 2 UP	I'VE GOT EVERYTHING INDEED (LP)	35
87	Hangman HANG 13 UP	I REMEMBER (LP)	20

CHILDREN
82	C391/1	Demon Blues/Nightland (promo version - different catalogue number)	15
82	INT 002	Nightland/Demon Blues	10

CHI-LITES
69	Beacon BEA 119	Pretty Girl/Love Bandit..	70
71	MCA 1143DJ	What Do I Wish For (1-sided DJ copy)	15
72	Brunswick 55489	We Need Order/Living In The Footsteps Of Another Man	6
70	MCA MUPS 397	GIVE IT AWAY (LP)	20
71	MCA MUPS 437	(FOR GOD'S SAKE) GIVE MORE POWER TO THE PEOPLE (LP)	30

(see also Jackie Wilson)

CHILLIWACK
71	London SHU 8418	CHILLIWACK (LP, U.K. issue of US 1970 issue)	25
71	A&M AMLH 63509	CHILLIWACK (LP)	15

(see also Collectors, Electric Prunes)

CHILLI WILLI & RED HOT PEPPERS
75	Mooncrest MOON 40	Breathe A Little/Friday Song	6
72	Revelation REV 002	KINGS OF THE ROBOT RHYTHM (LP, with lyric insert, inner sleeve and sticker)	60
72	Revelation REV 002	KINGS OF THE ROBOT RHYTHM (LP, with lyric insert, but without inner sleeve and sticker)	30
74	Mooncrest CREST 21	BONGOS OVER BALHAM (LP, with inner sleeve)	25

(see also Brinsley Schwarz, Jo-Ann Kelly, Mighty Baby, Hapshash And The Coloured Coat, Attractions, Action)

CHILLS
85	Normal 43	LOST EP (12")	15
84	Flying Nun Europe FNE 13	KALEIDOSCOPE WORLD (LP, with free 7")	30
84	Flying Nun Europe FNE 13	KALEIDOSCOPE WORLD (LP, without free 7")	20
90	Slash 828191	SUBMARINE BELLS (LP, with inner sleeve)	15

CHILLUM
71	Mushroom 100 MR 11	CHILLUM (LP, with photo insert)	250

(see also Secondhand)

ALEX CHILTON
80	Aura AUS 117	Hey! Little Child/No More The Moon Shines Lorena (p/s)	8

(see also Box Tops, Big Star)

CHIMES FEATURING DENISE (U.K.)
63	Decca F 11783	Say It Again/Can This Be Love?	7
64	Decca F 11885	I'll Be Waiting, I'll Be Here/Hello Heartache..	7

(see also Little Frankie)

CHIMES (U.S.)
61	London HLU 9283	Once In A While/Summer Night	15

CHIMNEYS
80	Tagmemics 45-003	Do The Big Baby/Take Your Brain Out For A Walk (p/s, 500 only)	15

CHINA DOLL
80	Wessex WEX 273	Oysters And Wine/Past Tense (p/s)	150

CHINA DOLLS
82	Speed FIRED 1	One Hit Wonder/Ain't Love Ain't Bad (p/s)	35

(see also Slade, Dummies)

CHINA DRUM
93	No label or Cat. No.	Simple/On My Way/Meaning (Acoustic) (p/s, 550 only gig freebie)	12
96	Mantra MNTLP1002	GOOSE FAIR (LP)	15
97	Mantra MNTLP1009	SELF MADE MANIAC (LP)	15

CHINA SOUL
09	Foofar FF 001	Cold/Be My Husband (signed sleeve)	15
09	Foofar FF 001	Cold/Be My Husband (unsigned sleeve)	10

CHINA STREET
78	Criminal CRM 1	You're A Ruin/(I Wanna Be) Your M.P. (foldout lyric p/s in poly bag & badge)	10

CHINATOWN
81	Airship AP 138	Short And Sweet/How Many Times (p/s)	60
81	Airship AP 343	PLAY IT TO DEATH (LP)	85

CHINAWITE
83	Future Earth FER 014	Blood On The Streets/Ready To Satisfy (p/s)	30

CHINNER
77	Third World TWS 924	STICKY FINGERS (LP)	40

KES CHINS
62	Starlite ST45 089	Annie/Moody	8

CHIPS
75	Decca FR 13604	Twice A Week/Reelin In The Years	8

CHISEL
70	Ariel AR 003	Turn To The Sun/Nightingale	35

GEORGE CHISHOLM & BLUENOTES
56	Beltona BL 2671	Honky Tonk/D.R. Rock (with Bert Weedon)	10

(see also Bert Weedon)

CHITINIOUS ENSEMBLE

MINT VALUE £

CHITINIOUS ENSEMBLE
71   Deram SML 1093   CHITNOUS ENSEMBLE (LP) 300

!!! (CHK CHK CHK)
07   Warp WARLP154   MYTH TAKES (2-LP) 30
13   Warp WARPLP236   THR!!!LER (LP) 15
15   Warp WARLP260   AS IS (2-LP) 18

CHOC
70   Decca F23106   Way Of Life/I Want You To Be My Girl 30

CHOC ICE
71   Polydor 2056189   Groovy Situation/Look At It My Way 20

CHOCOLATE BOYS
74   Decca F 13556   El Bimbo/Voltaire Pier 25
74   Decca F 13556   El Bimbo/Voltaire Pier (DJ Copy) 35

CHOCOLATE FROG
68   Atlantic 584 207   Butchers And Bakers/I Forgive You 45
(see also Fleur De Lys)

CHOCOLATE MILK
75   RCA RCA 2592   Action Speaks Louder Than Words/Ain't Nothing But A Thing 10
79   RCA RCAT 2592   I'm Your Radio/Actions Speak Louder Than Words (12") 15
77   RCA PL 11830   COMIN' (LP) 15

CHOCOLATE WATCH BAND
67   Decca F 12649   The Sound Of The Summer/The Only One In Sight 50
67   Decca F 12704   Requiem/What's It To You 40
84   Big Beat WIK 25   44 (LP) 15

CHOCOLATS
76   Aquarius AQ 1   Voltaire Pier/Brasilia Carnival 40
(see also chocolate Boys)

CHOICE OF COLOUR
00   Goldmine G2K 45 102   Your Love/Love Is Gone (with Ron Henderson) (no p/s) 8

CHOIR
68   Major Minor MM 537   It's Cold Outside/I'm Going Home 40
68   Major Minor MM 557   When You Were With Me/Changin' My Mind 30

HENRI CHOPIN
99   Hot Air AIRMILE 73   Alphabe Et Glotter: 1/2 (die cut sleeve) 10
71   Tangent TGS 106   AUDIOPOEMS (LP) 80

CHOPPER
71   Decca F 13161   Singer Wihout A Song/Think I'm A Man 50

CHOPYN
75   Jet LPO 8   GRAND SLAM (LP) 20
(see also Ann Odell, Ray Russell, Simon Phillips, C.M.U)

CHORDETTES
54   Columbia SCM 5158   Mr. Sandman/I Don't Wanna See You Cryin' 100
55   London HLA 8169   Humming Bird/Lonely Lips 15
56   London HLA 8217   Dudelsack Polka/I Told A Lie 25
56   London HLA 8264   Eddie My Love/Our Melody (triangular centre) 25
56   London HLA 8264   Eddie My Love/Our Melody (round centre) 10
56   London HLA 8302   Born To Be With You/Love Never Changes 10
56   London HA 7011   Born To Be With You/Love Never Changes (export issue) 10
56   London HLA 8323   Lay Down Your Arms/Teenage Goodnight 10
57   London HLA 8473   Echo Of Love/Just Between You And Me 10
57   London HLA 8497   Like A Baby/Soft Sands 10
58   London HLA 8566   Baby Of Mine/Photographs 10
58   London HLD 8584   Lollipop/Baby, Come-A-Back-A 10
58   London HLA 8654   Love Is A Two-Way Street/I Don't Know, I Don't Care 7
59   London HLA 8809   We Should Be Together/No Other Arms, No Other Lips 7
59   London HLA 8926   A Girl's Work Is Never Done/No Wheels (B-side with Jeff Crom & Jackie Ertel) 10
61   London HLA 9400   Never On Sunday/Faraway Star 6
62   London HLA 9519   The White Rose Of Athens/Adios (Goodbye My Love) 6
60   London RE-A 1228   THE CHORDETTES (EP) 30
58   London HA-A 2088   THE CHORDETTES (LP) 60
62   London HA-A 2441   THE CHORDETTES SING NEVER ON SUNDAY (LP) 25
83   Ace CH 82   THE CHORDETTES (LP, compilation) 20

CHORDS (U.K.)
80   Polydor POSP 101   Maybe Tomorrow/I Don't Wanna Know/Hey Girl (p/s) 6
80   Polydor 2059 258   The British Way Of Life/The Way It's Got To Be (p/s) 6
80   Polydor POSP 185   In My Street/I'll Keep On Holding On (p/s) 6
81   Polydor POSP 270   One More Minute/Who's Killing Who (p/s) 6
81   Polydor POSP 288   Turn Away Again/Turn Away Again (Again) (p/s) 8
80   Polydor Super POLS 1059   SO FAR AWAY (LP, stickered sleeve & 7" Now It's Gone/Things We Said [KRODS 1]) 30
80   Polydor Super POLS 1019   SO FAR AWAY (LP, without free 7') 20
86   Unicorn PHZA-1   NO ONE IS LISTENING ANYMORE (LP) 20
(see also Rage)

CHORDS (U.S.)
54   Columbia SCM 5133   Sh-Boom (Life Could Be A Dream)/Little Maiden 1500
54   Columbia DB 3512   Sh-Boom (Life Could Be A Dream)/Little Maiden (78) 60

CHORDS FIVE
67   Island WI 3044   I'm Only Dreaming/Universal Vagrant 100
68   Polydor 56261   Same Old Fat Man/Hold On To Everythin' You've Got 40
69   Jay Boy BOY 6   Some People/Battersea Fair 80
(see also Smoke)

CHOSEN FEW (Jamaica)

MINT VALUE £

CHOSEN FEW (JAMAICA)
70	Songbird SB 1031	Time Is Hard/CRYSTALITES: Time Is Hard Part Two	15
70	Songbird SB 1032	Going Back Home/CRYSTALITES: Going Back Home Part Two	10
70	Songbird SB 1046	Why Can't I Touch You/INNER CIRCLE BAND: Touch You Version	15
71	Fab FAB 14	Babylon/VIN GORDON: Red Blood (promo only, black label)	50
71	Songbird SB 1061	Shaft/Shaft (Version)	18
71	Songbird SB 1067	Everybody Just A Stall/Everybody (Version)	10
72	Songbird SB 1070	Do Your Thing/Your Thing (Version)	20
72	Trojan TR 7864	Ebony Eyes/Ebony Eyes (Version)	10
72	Trojan TR 7882	Everybody Plays The Fool/You're A Big Girl Now	12
72	Grape GE 3033	You're A Big Girl Now/Version	12
73	Trojan TR 7894	Am I Black Enough For You/Message From A Blackman	12
73	Duke DU 162	Children Of The Night/LLOYD CHARMERS: For The Good Times	20
73	Duke DU 163	Stoned In Love/MIKE CHUNG & NOW GENERATION: Stoned In Love (Version)	12
73	Duke DU 164	It's Too Late/MIKE CHUNG & NOW GENERATION: It's Too Late (Version)	12
73	Trojan TRLS 56	HIT AFTER HIT (LP)	40
75	Trojan TRLS 106	EVERYBODY PLAYS THE FOOL (LP)	60
76	Trojan Records TRLS 131	IN MIAMI (LP, blue labels)	60

CHOSEN FEW (U.K.) (1)
65	Pye 7N 15905	It Won't Be Around You Anymore/Big City	20
65	Pye 7N 15942	So Much To Look Forward To/Today, Tonight & Tomorrow	20

(see also Alan Hull, Lindisfarne, Skip Bifferty)

CHOSEN FEW (U.K.) (2)
74	Action ACT 4623	Funky Butter/Wondering	70
76	Polydor 2058 721	I Can Make Your Dreams Come True/Pretty Face	20
76	Miami MIA401	Night And Day/Funky Buttercup	60
78	Polydor 2058 975	You Mean Everything To Me/It Won't Be Long	30
77	Polydor 2058 752	Miracle Worker/Young And Foolish	25

CHOSEN PEOPLE
69	Royalty RT 01	When A Dream Ends/Firefly	35

CHOU PAHROT
79	Klub KEP 101	Buzgo Tram Chorus/Gwizgweela Gwamhnoo/Lemons (p/s)	10

CHRIS AND MAXINE
67	Philips BF 1587	Only A Thousand Times A Day/I've Made You My Mind	15

CHRIS & COSEY/CREATIVE TECHNOLOGY INSTITUTE/CARTER TUTTI
81	Rough Trade RT 078	October (Love Song)/Little Houses (p/s)	30
81	Rough Trade RTT 078	October (Love Song)/Little Houses (12", p/s)	20
84	Conspiracy International CTI 1	CONSPIRACY INTERNATIONAL ONE (12", p/s, as CTI)	25
85	Conspiracy International CTI 2	CONSPIRACY INTERNATIONAL TWO (12", p/s, as CTI)	25
85	Rough Trade RTT 148	Sweet Surprise 1 (1984)/2 (1985) (12", p/s, with Annie Lennox & Dave Stewart)	15
87	Play It Again Sam BIAS 54	Obsession/Obsession (Short Mix)/47 Sound/Metroeme (12", p/s)	12
87	Play It Again Sam BIAS 75	Exotika (Remix)/Workout/Beatbeatbeat (live) (12", p/s)	15
91	Play It Again Sam BIAS 186	Synaesthesia (Daniel Miller Mix)/Chris & Cosey Mix/D.M. Instrumental Mix (12", p/s)	20
13	Conspiracy International CTIV045	Coolican A/Coolican Fusion (10", green vinyl, p/s, as Carter Tutti)	20
81	Rough Trade ROUGH 34	HEARTBEAT (LP, with insert)	35
82	Rough Trade ROUGH 44	TRANCE (LP)	40
84	Rough Trade ROUGH 64	SONGS OF LOVE AND LUST (LP)	40
84	Doublevision DVR3	ELEMENTAL 7 (LP, as CTI)	75
84	Doublevision DVR8	EUROPEAN RENDEZVOUS CTI LIVE 1983 (LP, as CTI)	20
85	Rough Trade ROUGH 84	TECHNO PRIMATIV (LP)	20
87	Play It Again Sam BIAS 69	EXOTIKA (LP)	20
91	Play It Again Sam BIAS 179	PAGAN TANGO (LP)	20
95	T&B TBLP 003	TWIST (2-LP)	20
10	Conspiracy International CTILP016	EXOTICA (LP, reissue)	15
15	Conspiracy International CTILP012014	PLAYS CHRIS & COSEY (2-LP as Carter Tutti)	25

(see also Throbbing Gristle, Chris Carter, Eurythmics, Cosey Fanni Tutti)

PETER CHRIS & OUTCASTS
66	Columbia DB 7923	Over The Hill/The Right Girl For Me	40

CHRIST CHILD
78	Barak BAR 5	Let Them Eat Rock/Five Finger Exercise	8

CHRISTEL & THE GOLDMASTER
98	Goldmaster GM 002	Government Man/Version	25

CHRISTIAN
71	Decca F 23137	Other Side Of Life/She	15

CHARLIE CHRISTIAN
57	Philips BBL 7172	CHARLIE CHRISTIAN (LP)	20

FUD CHRISTIAN ALL STARS
71	Big Shot BI 571	Never Fall In Love (actually by Winston Heywood)/Never Fall In Love Version	15

HANS CHRISTIAN
68	Parlophone R 5676	All Of The Time/Never My Love	80
68	Parlophone R 5698	(The Autobiography Of) Mississippi Hobo/Sonata Of Love	100

(see also Jon Anderson, Yes)

JOHN CHRISTIAN DEE
68	Pye 7N 17566	Take Me Along/The World Can Pack Its Bags And Go Away	15
69	Decca F12901	The World Can Pick Up Its Bags And Go Away/Stick To Your Guns	15

Liz CHRISTIAN

MINT VALUE £

LIZ CHRISTIAN
67	CBS 202520	Suddenly You Find Love/Make It Work Out	90
67	CBS 202520	Suddenly You Find Love/Make It Work Out (DJ copy)	120
69	Spark SRL 1004	Call My Name/Think Of You Baby	8

(see also James Royal)

MARIA CHRISTIAN
85	MCA MCA 974	Wait Until The Weekend Comes/(Instrumental) (p/s)	15

NEIL CHRISTIAN (& CRUSADERS)
61	Private Pressing	Restless/Red Sails In The Sunset/Your Cheating Heart/Danny (1-sided 4 track 12" demo acetate, 6 made, Jimmy Page's first studio recording)	3000
62	Columbia DB 4938	The Road To Love/The Big Beat Drum	40
63	Columbia DB 7075	A Little Bit Of Someone Else/Get A Load Of This (with Crusaders)	20
66	Strike JH 301	That's Nice/She's Got The Action	15
66	Strike JH 313	Oops/She Said Yeah	10
66	Strike JH 319	Two At A Time/Wanna Lover	10
67	Pye 7N 17372	You're All Things Bright And Beautiful/I'm Gonna Love You Baby	15
73	Youngblood YB 1044	That's Nice/She's Got The Action	6
76	Satril SAT 106	She's Got The Power/Someone Following Me Around	20
66	Columbia SEG 8492	A LITTLE BIT OF SOMETHING ELSE (EP)	80

(see also Christian's Crusaders, Guy Hamilton, Jimmy Page, Nicky Hopkins, Miki Dallon, Screaming Lord Sutch)

CHRISTIAN DEATH
83	Future FL 2	ONLY THEATRE OF PAIN (LP, with insert)	25

CHRISTIAN'S CRUSADERS
64	Columbia DB 7289	Honey Hush/One For The Money	75

(see also Neil Christian & Crusaders)

CHRISTIE
71	CBS 9130	Everything's Gonna Be Alright/Freewheelin' Man/Magic Highway (p/s)	6
72	CBS S 8403	Fools Gold/Born To Lose	10
70	CBS 64108	CHRISTIE (LP)	15
71	CBS 64397	FOR ALL MANKIND (LP, gatefold sleeve, orange label)	20

(see also Acid Gallery, Epics)

DAVE CHRISTIE
68	Mercury MF1028	Love And The Brass Band/Penelope Breedlove	15

JOHN CHRISTIE
74	Polydor 2058 441	Everybody But Me/Childhood	7
74	Polydor 2058 496	4th Of July (written by Paul McCartney)/Old Enough To Know Better (in p/s)	30
74	Polydor 2058 496	4th Of July (written by Paul McCartney)/Old Enough To Know Better	15
74	Polydor 2058 528	Everybody Knows/How Does It Feel (p/s)	6

KEITH CHRISTIE
54	Esquire 20-047	HOMAGE TO THE DUKE (LP)	20

LOU CHRISTIE
63	Columbia DB 4983	The Gypsy Cried/Red Sails In The Sunset	10
63	Columbia DB 7031	Two Faces Have I/All That Glitters Isn't Gold	10
63	Columbia DB 7096	How Many Teardrops/You And I (Have A Right To Cry)	10
66	MGM MGM 1297	Lightnin' Strikes/Cryin' In The Streets	15
66	MGM MGM 1297	Lightnin' Strikes/Cryin' In The Streets (DJ Copy)	50
66	MGM MGM 1317	Painter/Du Ronda	6
66	MGM MGM 1325	If My Car Could Only Talk/Song Of Lita	20
66	Colpix PX 735	Merry Go Round/Guitars And Bongos	10
67	King KG 1036	Outside The Gates Of Heaven/All That Glitters Isn't Gold	8
67	CBS 2718	Shake Hands And Walk Away Cryin'/Escape	15
67	CBS 2922	Gina/Back To The Days Of The Romans	10
66	MGM MGM-C(S) 8008	LIGHTNIN' STRIKES (LP)	25
66	Colpix PXL 551	STRIKES AGAIN (LP)	25

SUSAN CHRISTIE
66	CBS 202261	I Love Onions/Take Me As You Find Me	15
06	Finders Keepers FKR45 001	Paint A Lady/Ghost Riders In The Sky (p/s)	10
06	Finders Keepers FKR007LP	PAINT A LADY (LP)	60

TONY CHRISTIE (& TRACKERS)
66	CBS 202097	Life's Too Good To Waste/Just The Two Of Us	8
67	MGM MGM 1365	Turn Around/When Will I Ever Love Again?	8
68	MGM MGM 1386	I Don't Want To Hurt You Anymore/Say No More	8
68	MGM MGM 1440	My Prayer/I Need You	8

CHRISTIEN BROTHERS
69	Major Minor MM 628	I Reached For You/Answer Me	7

DEREK CHRISTIEN
70	Major Minor MM 676	When A Woman Has A Baby/Please Don't Go Away	30
70	Major Minor MM 713	Suddenly There's A Valley/I'll Be Coming Home	100

(see also Christien Brothers)

CHRISTINES'S CAT
89	Sarah SARAH 13	Your Love Is.... (5" flexi with two fanzines 'Lemonade: A Fanzine' and 'Cold: A Lie')	50

KEITH CHRISTMAS
69	RCA Victor SF 8059	STIMULUS (LP, with Mighty Baby, orange/white label)	200
70	B&C CAS 1015	FABLE OF THE WINGS (LP)	80
71	B&C CAS 1041	PIGMY (LP, gatefold sleeve)	70
74	Manticore K 53503	BRIGHTER DAY (LP, with inner sleeve)	20
76	Manticore K 53509	STORIES FROM THE HUMAN ZOO (LP, with insert)	20

(see also Mighty Baby, Magic Muscle)

CHRISTOPHER
70	Chapter One CH121	Sharkey/The Race	20

Jordan CHRISTOPHER

MINT VALUE £

JORDAN CHRISTOPHER
66   United Artists UP 1140 — Hello Lover/What That I Was 20
LYN CHRISTOPHER
73   Paramount PARA 3037 — Is Everybody Happy/She Used To Wanna Be A Ballerina (promo only) 10
73   Paramount SPFL 288 — LYN CHRISTOPHER (LP) 100
CHARA CHRISTOU
71   Somerville SVL 1 — CELEBRATE HIS LOVE (LP) 25
JUNE CHRISTY
55   Capitol CL 14355 — Pete Kelly's Blues/Kicks 6
(see also Stan Kenton)
CHROME
80   Red RS 12007 — READ ONLY MEMORY (12" EP, with poster) 40
80   Red RS 12007 — READ ONLY MEMORY (12" EP, without poster) 25
80   Beggars Banquet BEG 36 — New Age/Information (p/s) 15
81   D. F. O. T. Mountain Y3 — INWORLDS (12") 15
82   D. F. O. T. Mountain Z17 — Firebomb/Shadows Of A Thousand Years (p/s) 15
80   Beggars Banquet BEGA 15 — RED EXPOSURE (LP, with inner sleeve) 25
80   Beggars Banquet BEGA 18 — HALF MACHINE LIP MOVES (LP, reissue, with poster insert) 30
80   Beggars Banquet BEGA 18 — HALF MACHINE LIP MOVES (LP, reissue, without poster insert) 20
81   D. F. O. T. Mountain X6 — BLOOD ON THE MOON (LP, blue, green or purple labels, with inner sleeve) 20
82   D. F. O. T. Mountain X18 — 3RD FROM THE SUN (LP, with insert) 20
CHEETAH CHROME
85   Children Of The Revolution GURT 3 — I REFUSE IT! (Split LP with MOTHERFUCKERS) 35
CHROME & ILLINSPIRED
13   B-Line Recordings BLN 004 — You Should Know/Big Dreams (p/s) 10
14   B-Line Recordings BLN 009 — No Messin' (DJ Format Remix)/Shock The Place (Part 1) (p/s) 8
15   B-Line Recordings BLN 012 — THE ALL C N I (LP) 30
CHROMEO
07   Back Yard BACK22LPC1 — FANCY FOOT WORK (LP) 60
CHRON GEN
81   Gargoyle GRGL 780 — PUPPETS OF WAR (EP, with sticker) 15
82   Secret SHH 139 — Outlaw/Behind Closed Doors/Disco (p/s) 6
84   Picasso PIK 002 — NOWHERE TO RUN (12' EP) 40
83   Secret SEC 3 — CHRONIC GENERATION (LP, with free 7") 15
CHRYSTAL BELLE SCRODD
86   United Dairies — BELLE DE JOUR (LP with insert) 40
(see also Nurse With Wound)
CHUBBY & HONEYSUCKERS
65   Venus VE 3 — Come On Home/What Shall I Do? 12
66   Rio R 75 — Emergency Ward/LEN & HONEYSUCKERS: One More River 12
CHUCK & BETTY
59   Brunswick 05815 — Sissy Britches/Come Back Little Girl 20
CHUCK (JOSEPHS) & DOBBY (DOBSON)
60   Blue Beat BB 19 — Til The End Of Time (as Chuck & Darby)/DUKE REID & HIS GROUP: What Makes Honey ... 20
60   Blue Beat BB 23 — Cool School/DUKE REID & HIS GROUP: Joker 20
61   Starlite ST45 043 — Sad Over You/Sweeter Than Honey 20
61   Starlite ST45 044 — Lovey Dovey/Sitting Square 20
61   Blue Beat BB 39 — Du Du Wap/I Love My Teacher (with Aubrey Adams & Du Droppers) 18
61   Blue Beat BB 59 — Oh Fanny/Running Around 18
64   Blue Beat BB 246 — Tell Me/I'm Going Home 15
CHUCK & GARY
58   HMV POP 466 — Teenie Weenie Jeanie/Can't Make Up My Mind 40
CHUCKA
74   Lemmy LMY2 — Switch On The Heat/My Oh My 30
CHUCKLES (1)
69   Bullet BU 416 — Run Nigel Run/Come On Home 30
CHUCKLES (2)
72   Duke DU 144 — Reggae Limbo/ZAP POW: Broken Contract 30
CHUCKS
64   Decca DFE 8562 — THE CHUCKS (EP) 25
CHUMBAWAMBA
88   Agit Prop AGIT 3 — Smash Clause 28/Fight The Alton Bill (with booklet) 6
86   Agit Prop PROP 1 — PICTURES OF STARVING CHILDREN SELL RECORDS (LP, with inner) 30
87   Agit Prop PROP 2 — NEVER MIND THE BALLOTS... (LP, gatefold) 15
88   Agit Prop PROP 3 — ENGLISH REBEL SONGS 1381-1914 (10" LP, with die-cut sleeve) 15
90   Agit Prop PROP 7 — SLAP! (LP, with poster) 15
94   One Little Indian TPLP 46 — ANARCHY (LP) 40
95   One Little Indian TPLP 56 — SHOWBUSINESS (LP) 25
MIKIE CHUNG & NOW GENERATION
73   Duke DU 163 — Stoned In Love/CHOSEN FEW: Stoned In Love 7
73   Duke DU 164 — It's Too Late/CHOSEN FEW: It's Too Late 7
CHUNKY
73   Orange OAS 214 — Albatross Baby/Road Runner Girl 30
CHURCH
82   Carrere CAR EP 257 — Unguarded Moment/Interlude/Golden Dawn/Sisters (10", p/s) 8
83   Carrere CHURCH R5A — Different Man/I Am A Rock (no p/s) 7
83   Carrere CHURCH 5 — SING SONGS (12" EP) 10
86   EMI EMC 3508 — HEYDAY (LP) 15
88   Arista 208895 — STARFISH (LP, with bonus 5-track numbered 12") 15

EUGENE CHURCH
59	London HL 8940	Miami/I Ain't Goin' For That (round centre)	50

MARK CHURCHER
95	Emote MOTE 001	Nowhere Man/Blue Depression/3D Thought Of Life (12")	40

(see also SEND/RETURN)

CHICK CHURCHILL
73	Chrysalis CHR 1051	YOU AND ME (LP)	20

(see also Ten Years After, Cozy Powell, Jethro Tull)

CHVRCHES
12	National Anthem ANTHEM 003	The Mother We Share/(AJD Optimo Remix)/(Miaoux Miaoux Remix) (10" 500 only)	60
13	Goodbye GR001V	Recover/ZVVL/Recover (Cim Rim Remix)/Recover Curxes 1996 Remix) (12" orange vinyl)	20
14	Virgin 3780474	We Sink/It's Not Right But It's OK (green vinyl)	12
15	Virgin VS 2116	Get Away/Dead Air	15
15	Secret 7 S729	Clearest View (1-sided, 100 only)	50
13	Virgin V3116	THE BONES OF WHAT YOU BELIEVE (LP)	15

SUZANNE CIANI
20	Electronic Sound ES 766	Chase Excerpt From Festival Antigen/Jungle Excerpt from Festival Antigen (p/s)	10
91	Private Music 21 1973	HOTEL LUNA (LP)	15
12	Dead Cert VCR 001	VOICES OF PACKAGED SOULS (LP, reissue, play at 45rpm)	25
12	Bird 015EGGSLP	SEVEN WAVES (LP, reissue)	25
14	Disposable Music DIM 009	LOGO PRESENTATION REEL 1985 (LP)	15
16	Finders Keepers FKR082LP-A	BUCHLA CONCERTS (LP, turquoise leatherette sleeve, inserts, 200 only)	40
16	Finders Keepers FKR082LP	BUCHLA CONCERTS 1975 (LP)	15
19	Finders Keepers FKR099LP	FLOWERS OF EVIL (LP)	15

CICPEN
86	SRT 6KS/826/FFACH F	CYMER FI (EP, p/s)	25

CIGARETTES
78	Dead Good KEVIN 1	THE CIGARETTES (EP, unreleased)	0
79	Company CIGCO 008	They're Back Again, Here They Come/I've Forgot My Number/All We Want Is Your Money (gatefold p/s, initial pressing with red labels)	100
79	Company CIGCO 008	They're Back Again, Here They Come/I've Forgot My Number/All We Want Is Your Money (gatefold p/s, later pressing with black labels)	60
80	Dead Good DEAD 10	Can't Sleep At Night/It's The Only Way To Live (Die) (p/s)	40
02	Detour DRLP 029	WILL DAMAGE YOUR HEALTH (2-LP)	30

CIM(M)AR(R)ONS
70	Hot Rod HR 105	Grandfather Clock/Kick Me Or I Kick You (as Cimarrons)	100
70	Reggae REG 3003	Bad Day At Black Rock (with Cimmaron Kid)/Fragile	70
71	Big Shot BI 562	Funky Fight/You Turned Me Down	30
71	Spinning Wheel SW 107	Soul For Sale/Bogus-ism	30
71	Downtown DT 486	Oh Mammy Blue/Oh Mammy Blue - Version	15
71	Downtown DT 487	Holy Christmas/Silent Night/White Christmas	12
71	Bullet BU 457	Call Me/Call Me (Part 2)	8
71	Bullet BU 458	Leave Me A Little Love/My Baby	8
74	Trojan TR7919	Over The Rainbow/We Are Not The Same	15
75	Vulcan VUL 1005	Tradition/Wicky Wacky	15
78	Cimarak CR002	Paul Bogle/Greedy Man (12")	30
83	MPL/Cimarons CIM 001	Love And Affection	12
83	MPL/Cimarons 12CIM 001	Love And Affection (12", less than 1000 pressed)	30
74	Trojan TRLS 77	IN TIME (LP)	20
76	Vulcan VULA 501	ON THE ROCKS (LP)	40
78	Polydor 2383512	MAKA (LP, green vinyl)	15

(see also Reaction, Winston Groovy)

CINCH
80	SRTS/80/CUS 622	SELL OUT EP	20

CINDERELLAS (1)
59	Brunswick 05794	Mister Dee-Jay/Yum Yum Yum	10
60	Philips PB 1012	The Trouble With Boys/Puppy Dog	25

CINDERELLAS (2)
64	Colpix PX 11026	Baby, Baby (I Still Love You)/Please Don't Wake Me	60
64	Colpix PX 11026	Baby, Baby (I Still Love You)/Please Don't Wake Me (DJ Copy)	100

(see also Cookies)

CINDERS
63	Warner Bros WB 86	The Cinnamon Cinder/C'mon Wobble	10

(see also Darlene Love)

CINDI AND THE BARBI DOLLS
79	A Not Major Production NOTEM 1	ISN'T SHOWBIZ WONDERFUL EP (hand-made p/s)	15

CINEMA
82	Floppy FLOPPY 1	Donor Donor/Cinema Star (p/s)	8

CINEMATIC ORCHESTRA
99	Ninja Tune ZEN12 084	Channel 1 Suite/Ode To The Big Sea (12")	15
99	Ninja Tune ZEN 45	MOTION (2xLP)	30
00	Ninja Tune ZEN 50	REMIXES 98 - 2000 (2xLP)	20
02	Ninja Tune ZEN 59	EVERY DAY (2xLP)	35
03	Ninja Tune ZEN 78	MAN WITH A MOVIE CAMERA (2xLP)	40
07	Ninja Tune ZEN 122	MA FLEUR (2xLP)	25

CINEMATICS
82	Pulsebeat CINE 001	FAREWELL TO THE PLAYGROUND (EP, foldover p/s)	30

(see also Razorcuts)

CINNAMON
69	Beacon BEA 111	You Won't See Me Leaving/Leaves Of Love	6
69	President PT 258	So Long Sam/Broken Hearted Me, Evil Hearted You	6

CINNAMON QUILL
69	Morgan MRS 17	Girl On A Swing/Take It Or Leave It	20
69	Morgan MRS 21	Candy/Hello, It's Me	50

CIRCLE (1)
60s	Circle GR 1	IN AID OF THE MILLFIELD BUILDING FUND (EP, private pressing)	150

CIRCLE (2)
02	Static Caravan/Resonance Staticresonance 6	PROSPEKT (2-LP, gatefold sleeve, black vinyl and green vinyl, 1000 only)	30

CIRCLES (1)
66	Island WI 279	Take Your Time/Don't You Love Me No More	100

(see also Plastic Penny, Savages, Tony Dangerfield & Thrills, Screaming Lord Sutch)

CIRCLES (2)
72	Sioux SIOUX 017	Mammy Blue/POOCH JACKSON & HARRY J. ALLSTARS: King Of The Road	12

(see also Bob Andy)

CIRCLES (3)
79	Graduate GRAD 4	Opening Up/Billy (p/s)	20
80	Vertigo ANGRY 1	Angry Voices/Summer Nights (p/s)	20
80	Chrysalis CHS 2418	Opening Up/Billy (p/s, reissue)	8
85	Graduate GRAD 17	Circles/Summer Nights (p/s)	40

CIRCUIT 7
84	Micro Rapp MIC 1 RAPP 023459	Video Boys/The Force (p/s red vinyl)	40
84	Rapp 023462	Modern Story/Eastern Dream (p/s, blue vinyl)	25

CIRCULUS
05	Rise Above RISE 7/064	Mirl It Is (Moog Up Mix)/WITCHCRAFT: Chylde Of Fire	18
06	Rise Above RISE 7/094	Song Of Our Despair/Honeycomb (clear or purple vinyl)	6
05	Rise Above RISELP 063	THE LICK ON THE TIP OF MY ENVELOPE YET TO BE SENT (LP, clear vinyl gatefold sleeve, poster, 100 only)	30
06	Rise Above RISELP 093	CLOCKS ARE LIKE PEOPLE (LP, white vinyl, free 1-sided 7", "Tapestry", 500 only)	25
06	Rise Above RISELP 093	CLOCKS ARE LIKE PEOPLE (LP, 700 on blue vinyl, 500 on black vinyl)	18

CIRCUS
67	Parlophone R 5633	Gone Are The Songs Of Yesterday/Sink Or Swim	25
68	Parlophone R 5672	Do You Dream/House Of Wood	45
69	Transatlantic TRA 207	CIRCUS (LP, gatefold sleeve, white/lilac label with 'T' logo)	125

(see also Philip Goodhand-Tait, King Crimson)

CIRCUS MAXIMUS
67	Vanguard VSD 79260	CIRCUS MAXIMUS (LP)	20
68	Vanguard VSD 79274	NEVERLAND REVISITED (LP)	20

CIRKUS
80	Guardian GRCA 4	Melissa/Amsterdam/Pick Up A Phone (EP)	20
73	RCB 1	CIRKUS ONE (LP, private pressing with gatefold sleeve, black/white label)	300
77	Shock SHOCK 1	FUTURE SHOCK (LP)	90

CITATIONS
63	Columbia DB 7068	Moon Race/Slippin' And Slidin'	30

CITIZEN FISH
90	Bluurg FISH 24	FREE SOULS IN A TRAPPED ENVIRONMENT (LP, with cartoon insert)	15
91	Bluurg FISH 26	WIDER THAN A POSTCARD (LP)	15

CITIZENS
80	Cavalcade CAV 1	Satisfy The Citizens/TV Woman (p/s)	6

CITIZENS OF ROME
82	Someone Elses Music SOM 1	Someone Elses World/St Malo (p/s)	15

CITRUS
92	Pork PORK 010	Adrenachrome/Decoder/Narcosynthesis (12")	20

CITY GENTS
73	Triumph TR02	Shake/Turn It Down	15

CITY GIANTS
87	Give It A Blast BLA 001	Little Next To Nothing/Where Love's Concerned/Have You Got Any Idea? (p/s)	15

CITY LIMITS
79	Luggage RRP 1003	Morse Code Signals/If I Had Time/I Just Can't Say (EP)	125

CITY RAMBLERS SKIFFLE GROUP
57	Tempo A 158	Ella Speed/2.19 Blues	15
57	Tempo A 161	Mama Don't Allow/Tom Dooley	15
57	Tempo A 165	Delia's Gone/Boodle-Am Shake	15
57	Storyville SEP 327	I WANT A GIRL (EP)	25
57	Storyville SEP 345	I SHALL NOT BE MOVED (EP)	25
57	Tempo EXA 59	I WANT A GIRL (EP)	25
57	Tempo EXA 71	GOOD MORNING BLUES (EP)	25
57	Tempo EXA 77	DELIA'S GONE (EP)	25

(see also Henrik Johansen)

CITY SMOKE
66	Mercury MF 971	Sunday Morning/A Little Bit Of Love	7

CITY TALK
80	PAD PAD 001	Trick Of The Light/Nightmare	12

CITY WAITES
74	EMI EMC 3012	A GORGEOUS GALLERY OF GALLANT INVENTIONS (LP)	20
76	Decca SKL 5264	THE CITY WAITES (LP)	20
81	Hyperion A 66008	HOW THE WORLD WAGS (LP, gatefold sleeve, some with Hyperion insert)	40

CIVILIANS

CIVILIANS
79 Arista ARIST 318   MADE FOR TELEVISION EP 60

CIVILISED SOCIETY?
86 Manic Ears ACHE 2   SCRAP METAL (LP, with inner) 15
87 Manic Ears ACHE 6   VIOLENCE SUCKS (LP, with lyric inner) 15

C-JAM BLUES
66 Columbia DB 8064   Candy/Stay At Home Girl 40

CLAGGERS
71 DJM DJS 235   Train Song/Mr Sun 6
71 DJM DJS 242   Ania/Primo 6
71 DJM DJS 260   Some One/Umber Rag 15
73 Jam 57   Primo/Ania (reissue) 8

CLAGUE
69 Dandelion S 4493   Mandy Lee/Bottle Up And Go (with Kevin Coyne) 12
69 Dandelion 4494   The Stride/I Wonder Where 12

(see also Coyne-Clague, Kevin Coyne, Claque, Siren)

CLAIM
89 Esurient Comms PACE 4   Wait & See/Business Boy/God, Cliffe & Me 12
89 Esurient Comms PACE 7   Picking Up The Bitter Little Pieces/Losers Corner (p/s, with postcard) ... 15
90 Caff CAFF 008   Birth Of A Teenager/Mike The Bike 20
91 Esurient Comms PACE 10   Sunday/Sporting Life 12
92 A Turntable Friend TURN 08 Say So/Plastic Grip/Waiting For Jesus 12
87 Trick Bag CU 0388   THIS PENCIL WAS OBVIOUSLY SHARPENED BY A LEFT-HANDED INDIAN KNIFE THROWER (EP) 18
85 Trick Bag TBR 001   ARMSTRONG'S REVENGE AND ELEVEN OTHER SHORT STORIES (LP) 30
88 Esurient Comms PACE 003 BOOMY TELLA (LP) 30

CLAIR OBSCUR
86 Cathexi CRC 69   SMURF IN THE GULAG (12" EP p/s) 12
86 All The Madmen MAD 10   THE PILGRIM'S PROGRESS (LP) 15

CLAMS CASINO
11 Tri Angle TRIANGLE 06   RAINFOREST (12" EP. p/s) 18

CLAN (1)
70 Bullet BU 419   Copycats/BUNNY LEE ALLSTARS: Hot Lead 30
70 Bullet BU 430   Na Na Hay Hay Goodbye/KING STITT: Musical Bop 40

CLAN (2)
72 Deram DM 356   Pretty Belinda/Ode To Karen 7

(see also Junior Campbell)

CLANCY'S ALLSTARS
68 Pama PM 722   C.N. Express Parts 1 & 2 (B-side actually "You Were Meant For Me" by Lee Perry) 40

(see also Clancy Eccles)

CLANDESTINE
86 Market Trader PITCH 1   I'm All Over You (Like Jam On A Scone)/The Valley Of The Larne 6

CLAN OF XYMOX
85 4AD BAD 504   A Day/Stranger (12") 10
85 4AD CAD 503   CLAN OF XYMOX (LP) 15

JIMMY CLANTON
58 London HLS 8699   Just A Dream/You Aim To Please (as Jimmy Clanton & His Rockets) 20
58 London HL 7066   A Letter To An Angel/A Part Of Me (as Jimmy Clanton & Aces) (export issue) ... 20
59 London HLS 8779   A Letter To An Angel/A Part Of Me (as Jimmy Clanton & Aces) 20
59 Top Rank JAR 189   My Own True Love/Little Boy In Love 15
60 Top Rank JAR 269   Go, Jimmy, Go/I Trusted You 15
60 Top Rank JAR 382   Another Sleepless Night/I'm Gonna Try 12
60 Top Rank JAR 509   Come Back (To Me)/Wait 10
61 Top Rank JAR 544   What Am I Gonna Do/If I 10
62 Stateside SS 120   Venus In Blue Jeans/Highway Bound 10
63 Stateside SS 159   Darkest Street In Town/Dreams Of A Fool 8
65 Stateside SS 410   Hurting Each Other/Don't Keep Your Friends Away 20
65 Stateside SS 140   Hurting Each Other/Don't Keep Your Friends Away (DJ Copy) 40
59 London RES 1224   JUST A DREAM (EP) 50

CLAP
79 SRTS SRTS/79/CUS   Hey Little Girl/20 Watts Of Power (p/s) 20

CLAPHAM SOUTH ESCALATORS
81 Upright UP YOUR 1   Get Me To The World On Time/Leave Me Alone/Cardboard Cut Outs (p/s) ... 15

(see also Meteors, Escalators, Tall Boys)

ERIC CLAPTON
66 Purdah 45-3502   Lonely Years/Bernard Jenkins (with John Mayall, 500 copies only) 400
70 Polydor 2001 096   I Am Yours (unissued) 0
70 Polydor 2001 096   After Midnight/Easy Now 10
76 RSO 2090 208   Hello Old Friend/All Our Pastimes (p/s) 8
80 RSO JON 1   Wonderful Tonight (live)/Further On Up The Road (live) (promo only) .. 10
80 RSO JONX 1   Wonderful Tonight (live)/Further On Up The Road (live) (12", numbered p/s) ... 10
87 Duck W 8461F   Behind The Mask/Grand Illusion//Crossroads (live)/White Room (live) (double pack, gatefold p/s) 10
87 Duck W 8397F   It's In The Way That You Use It/Bad Influence//Behind The Mask/Grand Illusion (double pack, shrinkwrapped with sticker) 8
89 Duck W 2644B   Bad Love/I Shot The Sheriff (live) (box set with family tree & 2 colour prints) 6
70 Polydor 2383 021   ERIC CLAPTON (LP, laminated sleeve, red label) 25
73 RSO 2479 702   CLAPTON (LP, withdrawn) 60
74 RSO QD 4801   461 OCEAN BOULEVARD (LP, quadrophonic) 20
82 RSO RSDX 3   TIME PIECES (2-LP, unissued) 0
84 Aston PD 20118   TOO MUCH MONKEY BUSINESS (LP, picture disc, with Yardbirds) 15

Eric CLAPTON & STEVE WINWOOD

MINT VALUE £

99	Reprise 9362-47564-1	CHRONICLES (2-LP)	60

(see also Yardbirds, John Mayall, Cream, Blind Faith, Delaney & Bonnie, Derek & The Dominos, Viv Stanshall, King Curtis, Randy Crawford)

ERIC CLAPTON & STEVE WINWOOD

09	Resprise 9362 497985	LIVE FROM MADISON SQUARE GARDEN (3-LP)	40

ALAN CLARE GROUP

56	Decca DFE 6368	THE IMPROVISATIONS OF... (EP)	20
56	Decca DFE 6391	ALAN CLARE TRIO WITH BOB BURNS (EP)	20
58	Decca LK 4260	JAZZ AROUND THE CLOCK (LP)	50

KENNY CLARE & RONNIE STEPHENSON

67	Columbia SCX 6168	DRUM SPECTACULAR (LP, with Tubby Hayes, stereo)	40
67	Columbia SX 6168	DRUM SPECTACULAR (LP, with Tubby Hayes, mono)	30
72	Sounds Superb SPR90057	DRUM SPECTACULAR (LP, reissue with Tubby Hayes and Stan Tracey)	18

CLARENDONIANS

65	Ska Beat JB 219	Muy Bien (My Friend)/You Are A Fool	40
66	Ska Beat JB 261	Doing The Jerk/You Won't See Me	45
66	Island WI 284	Try Me One More Time/Can't Keep A Good Man Down	40
66	Island WI 3005	I'll Never Change/Rules Of Life	40
67	Island WI 3032	Shoo-Be-Doo-Be (I Love You)/Sweet Heart Of Beauty	40
67	Island WI 3041	You Can't Be Happy/Goodbye Forever	40
67	Studio One SO 2004	The Table's Going To Turn/I Can't Go On	40
67	Studio One SO 2007	He Who Laughs Last/GAYLADS: Just A Kiss From You	50
67	Studio One SO 2017	Love Me With All Your Heart/Love Don't Mean Much To Me	40
67	Rio R 112	Rudie Bam Bam/Be Bop Boy	30
67	Rio R 115	Musical Train/Lowdown Girl	40
68	Caltone TONE 114	Baby Baby/Bye Bye Bye	80
69	Duke DU 97	Come Along/Try To Be Happy	20
69	Gas GAS 131	When I Am Gone/She Brings Me Joy	20
70	Trojan TR 7714	Lick It Back/BEVERLEY'S ALLSTARS: Busy Bee	20
70	Trojan TR 7719	Baby Don't Do It/BEVERLEY'S ALLSTARS: Touch Down	50
71	Green Door GD 4009	Seven In One (Medley) (both sides)	12
72	Attack ATT 8039	Bound In Chains/STUD ALLSTARS: Version	12
72	Pama PM 847	This Is My Story/VAL BENNETT: Caledonia	25
73	Pama PM 856	Good Hearted Woman/CORNELL CAMPBELL: What Happens	25
73	Techniques TE 925	Just One Look/Sinner Man	12
73	Dragon DRA 1006	Walking Up A One Way Street/DYNAMITES: Instrumental	30

(see also Lee & Clarendonians, Desmond Baker & Clarendonians, Four Aces, Prince Buster, Dennis Walks)

CLARITY

85	Bpop BPOB T02	The Way U Make Me Feel/Turning Over (12")	75

ALICE CLARK

69	Action ACT 4520	You Got A Deal/Say You'll Never	60
04	Acid Jazz 01716	Don't You Care/Never Did I Stop Loving You	20
16	Kent TOWN 162	You Hit Me (Right Where It Hurt)/THE DEVONNES: I Couldn't Build A World (With You On The Outside)	7
16	BGP HIQLP045	THE COMPLETE STUDIO RECORDINGS 1968-72 (LP, white vinyl)	20

CHRIS CLARK (1)

67	Tamla Motown TMG 591	Love's Gone Bad/Put Yourself In My Place	200
67	Tamla Motown TMG 591	Love's Gone Bad/Put Yourself In My Place (DJ Copy)	250
67	Tamla Motown TMG 624	From Head To Toe/The Beginning Of The End	45
67	Tamla Motown TMG 624	From Head To Toe/The Beginning Of The End (DJ Copy)	80
68	Tamla Motown TMG 638	I Want To Go Back There Again/I Love You	30
68	Tamla Motown TMG 638	I Want To Go Back There Again/I Love You (DJ Copy)	60
68	T. Motown STML 11069	SOUL SOUNDS (LP, stereo)	90
68	T. Motown TML 11069	SOUL SOUNDS (LP, mono)	100

CHRIS CLARK (2)

01	Warp WARPLP86	CLARENCE PARK (LP)	18
03	Warp WARPLP107	EMPTY THE BONES OF YOU (2-LP)	20
06	Warp WARLP149	BODY RIDDLE (LP as 2 x 12")	18
09	Warp WARPLP185	TOTEMS FLARE (LP as 2 x 12")	25
12	Warp WARPLP222	IRELDELPHIC (LP)	15

CLAUDINE CLARK

62	Pye International 7N 25157	Party Lights/Disappointed	20
63	Pye International 7N 25186	Walk Me Home From The Party/Who Will You Hurt?	20
67	Sue WI 4039	The Strength To Be Strong/Moon Madness	75

DAVE CLARK FIVE

62	Ember EMB S 156	Chaquita/In Your Heart (grey/pink labels)	40
62	Ember EMB S 156	Chaquita/In Your Heart (red/yellow labels)	30
62	Piccadilly 7N 35088	First Love/I Walk The Line	30
62	Piccadilly 7N 35500	That's What I Said/I Knew It All The Time	30
63	Columbia DB 7011	The Mulberry Bush/Chaquita	20
63	Columbia DB 7112	Do You Love Me/Doo-Dah	10
64	Columbia DB 7335	Thinking Of You Baby/Whenever You're Around	6
64	Columbia DB 7377	Any Way You Want It/Crying Over You	7
65	Columbia DB 7453	Everybody Knows/Say You Want Me	10
65	Columbia DB 7503	Reelin' And Rockin'/Little Bitty Pretty One	6
65	Columbia DB 7580	Come Home/Mighty Good Loving (in p/s)	18
65	Columbia DB 7580	Come Home/Mighty Good Loving	6
65	Columbia DB 7625	Catch Us If You Can/Move On	6
65	Columbia DB 7744	Over And Over/I'll Be Yours	10
66	Columbia DB 7863	Try Too Hard/All Night Long	6
66	Columbia DB 7909	Look Before You Leap/Please Tell Me Why	6

Dee CLARK

MINT VALUE £

Year	Catalogue	Title	Value
66	Columbia DB 8028	Nineteen Days/I Need Love	7
67	Columbia DB 8194	Tabatha Twitchit/Man In A Pin-Striped Suit (in export p/s)	20
67	Columbia DB 8194	Tabatha Twitchit/Man In A Pin-Striped Suit	6
68	Columbia DB 8465	The Red Balloon/Maze Of Love	7
69	Columbia DB 8591	Get It On Now/Maze Of Life (unreleased, acetates exist)	0
70	Columbia DB 8681	Julia/Five By Five	10
72	Columbia DB 8963	All Time Greats Medley (Glad All Over/Do You Love Me/Bits & Pieces/ Glad All Over)/Wild Weekend (p/s)	15
64	Columbia SEG 8289	THE DAVE CLARK FIVE (EP)	10
65	Columbia SEG 8381	THE HITS OF THE DAVE CLARK FIVE (EP)	15
65	Columbia SEG 8447	WILD WEEKEND (EP)	20
64	Columbia 33SX 1598	SESSION WITH THE DAVE CLARK FIVE (LP, blue/black label, with "sold in the U.K..." label text)	20
64	Ember FA 2003	DAVE CLARK FIVE AND THE WASHINGTON D.C.'s (LP)	20
65	EMI Regal REG 2017	IN SESSION (LP, export issue)	20
65	Columbia SX 1756	CATCH US IF YOU CAN (LP, soundtrack, blue/black label)	30
67	Columbia SX 6105	THE DAVE CLARK FIVE'S GREATEST HITS (LP, blue/black label)	20
68	Columbia SX 6207	EVERYBODY KNOWS (LP, blue/black label)	20
69	Columbia SX 6309	5 BY 5 1964-69: 14 TITLES BY THE DAVE CLARK FIVE (LP, blue/black label)	30
70	Columbia SCX 6437	IF SOMEBODY LOVES YOU (LP)	30
72	Columbia SCX 6494	DAVE CLARK AND FRIENDS (LP, boxed logo on label)	30

(see also Dave Clark & Friends, Smith D'Abo, Mike Smith, Washington D.C.s)

DEE CLARK

Year	Catalogue	Title	Value
59	London HL 8802	Nobody But You/When I Call On You	30
59	London HL 8915	Just Keep It Up (And See What Happens)/ Whispering Grass(Don't Tell The Trees)	20
59	Top Rank JAR 196	Hey, Little Girl/If It Wasn't For Love	15
60	Top Rank JAR 284	How About That/Blues Get Off My Shoulder	12
60	Top Rank JAR 373	At My Front Door/Cling-A-Ling	25
60	Top Rank JAR 501	Gloria/You're Looking Good	10
61	Top Rank JAR 551	Your Friends/Because I Love You	10
61	Top Rank JAR 570	Raindrops/I Want To Love You	15
62	Columbia DB 4768	Don't Walk Away From Me/You're Telling Our Secrets	40
63	Stateside SS 180	I'm A Soldier Boy/Shook Up Over You	25
64	Stateside SS 355	Heartbreak/Warm Summer Breeze	15
65	Stateside SS 400	T.C.B./It's Impossible	20
70	Liberty LBF 15334	Where Did All The Good Times Go?/24 Hours Of Loneliness	10
60	Top Rank BUY 044	HOW ABOUT THAT! (LP)	30
70	Joy JOYS 130	YOU'RE LOOKING GOOD (LP)	20

DUANE CLARK
77	Spark SRL 1152	Stop Come Down Come Around/Gettin It	15

GAVIN CLARK
14	Club AC30 AC 301 1061	BEAUTIFUL SKELETONS (2-LP, CD and DVD)	100

GENE CLARK
67	CBS 202523	Echoes/I Found You	50
74	Asylum AYM 536	No Other/The True One	6
74	Asylum AYM 540	Life's Greatest Fool/From A Silver Phial	6
67	CBS 62934	GENE CLARK WITH THE GOSDIN BROTHERS (LP)	60
72	A&M AMLS 64297	WHITE LIGHT (LP)	30
74	Asylum SYL 9020	NO OTHER (LP)	35

(see also Byrds, Dillard & Clark)

J. CLARK
80	Cha Cha CHAD 17	Babylon/One Man Live (12")	40

JIMMY 'SOUL' CLARK
76	Black Magic BM 115	Sweet Darlin'/Sweet Darlin' (Instrumental)	20

LARENA CLARK
66	Topic 12T 140	A CANADIAN GARLAND (LP)	15

MICHAEL CLARK
66	Liberty LIB 5893	None Of These Girls/Work Out	15

MICKY CLARK
65	HMV POP 1400	You Want My Love Again/Do You Ever Feel Lonely?	7

NOBBY CLARK
76	Epic S EPC 4381	Steady Love/Give Me The Heart	10
78	Mercury 6007164	Shake It Down/Lifes Long Highway	10

PAUL CLARK & FRIENDS
77	Myrrh MYR 1054	GOOD TO BE HOME (LP, with inner sleeve)	20
78	Myrrh MYR 1059	HAND TO THE PLOUGH (LP)	20

PETULA CLARK
ALBUMS
56	Pye Nixa NPT 19002	PETULA CLARK SINGS (10")	60
56	Pye Nixa NPT 19014	A DATE WITH PET (10")	60
57	Pye Nixa NPL 18007	YOU ARE MY LUCKY STAR	60
59	Pye Nixa NPL 18039	PETULA CLARK IN HOLLYWOOD	50
62	Pye NPL 18070	IN OTHER WORDS - PETULA CLARK	15
63	Pye NPL 18098	PETULA	15
64	Pye-Vogue VRL 3001	LES JAMES DEAN	25

ROBIN CLARK
61	Capitol CL 15230	It's Love/The Butterfly Tree	6

ROY CLARK
59	HMV POP 581	Please Mr. Mayor/Puddin'	100
63	Capitol CL 15288	In The Mood/Texas Twist	15

Sanford CLARK

MINT VALUE £

63	Capitol CL 15417	Tips Of My Fingers/Spooky Movies	15
62	Capitol (S)T 1780	THE LIGHTNING FINGERS OF ROY CLARK (LP)	30

SANFORD CLARK

56	London HLD 8320	The Fool/Lonesome For A Letter (with Al Casey) (gold label print)	100
56	London HLD 8320	The Fool/Lonesome For A Letter (with Al Casey) (later silver print label)	30
56	London HL 7014	The Fool/Lonesome For A Letter (with Al Casey) (export issue)	20
59	London HLW 8959	Run, Boy Run/New Kind Of Fool (triangular centre)	15
59	London HLW 8959	Run, Boy Run/New Kind Of Fool (round centre)	8
59	London HLW 8959	Run, Boy Run/New Kind Of Fool (78)	20
60	London HLW 9026	Son-Of-A-Gun/I Can't Help It (If I'm Still In Love With You) (tri centre)	20
60	London HLW 9026	Son-Of-A-Gun/I Can't Help It (If I'm Still In Love With You) (round centre)	15
60	London HLW 9095	Go On Home/Pledging My Love	15
57	London RED 1205	PRESENTING SANFORD CLARK (EP)	25
60	London REW 1256	LOWDOWN BLUES (EP)	25

(see also Al Casey)

TERRY CLARK

70	Myrrh MYR 1071	WELCOME (LP)	15

ALLAN CLARKE

72	RCA RCA 2244	You're Losing Me/A Coward By Name	10
72	RCA SF 8283	MY REAL NAME IS 'AROLD (LP, lyric insert, orange/white label)	20
73	EMI EMA 752	HEADROOM (LP, gatefold sleeve, lyric inner sleeve)	15

(see also Hollies)

ANNETTE CLARKE

73	Techniques TE 925	Just One Look/Sinner Man	18
73	Black Ark BAR 102	Just One Look/Dub Power (white labels more common)	25

AUGUSTUS 'GUSSIE' CLARKE

77	Burning Sounds BS 1023	BLACK FOUNDATION DUB (LP)	60
78	Hawkeye HALP 001	DREAD AT THE CONTROLS DUB (LP)	25

BOB CLARKE

70	CBS 7435	Haunted/Run Colorado	30
72	CBS 17741	Sad/Some Ones Slipping Into My Mind	10

BRYAN CLARKE

75	Safari SF 1107	What Am I to Do/So Good To See You	12

BUNNY CLARKE

75	Dip DL 5064	Be Thankful/UPSETTERS: Dubbing In The Back (Mr. Chang)	50

DAVE CLARKE

94	Bush 1012	Red 1 (of 3) (Protective Custody)/Zeno Xero (12", p/s, red vinyl)	15
94	Bush 1015	Red 2 (of 3) (Wisdom To The Wise)/Gonk (12", p/s, red vinyl)	12

ERIC CLARKE

75	Torpedo TOR 40	Fight Against Babylon/Babylon Dub (as Eric Clark)	20
78	Baal BAL 89004	LOVE THAT GROWS AND GROWS (LP)	60

FREDDIE CLARKE

81	Main Line MLD6	Home We Wanna Go/THE CIRCLE: Legend (12")	50

FREDDY CLARKE

78	Jungle Beat JBDC 805	Troubles/I Man (12" with I ROY)	80
81	Jungle Beat JBDC801	Fight I Down/VIN GORDON: Fire Horns (12", red vinyl)	40
82	Live & Love LLDIS 205	Are We Gonna Make It Up/Mash It Up (Dub Version) (12")	15

(see also Freddie Clarke)

JAMES CLARK(E) + SOUNDS

68	Fontana TF 918	A Man Of Our Times T.V. Series Theme/Spring Bossa	8
68	Fontana SFJL 966	A MAN OF OUR TIMES (LP)	40

JOHN COOPER CLARKE

79	Epic S EPC 12 7009	¡Gimmix!/I Married A Monster From Outer Space (Third Version) (p/s, triangular disc, orange vinyl)	6
78	CBS 83132	DISGUISE IN LOVE (LP)	20
80	Epic EPC 84083	SNAP, CRACKLE [&] BOP (LP, with 48-page book in sleeve pocket)	20
81	Epic EPC 84979	ME AND MY BIG MOUTH (LP)	15

JOHNNY CLARKE

73	Pep PEP 001	Don't Go/SUCCESS ALL STARS: Version	25
74	Explosion EX 2089	None Shall Escape The Judgement/Every Rasta Is A Star	15
74	Pyramid PYR 7013	My Desire/Lemon Tree	15
74	Lord Koos KOOS42	Enter Into This Gate With Praise/KING TUBBY & THE AGGROVATORS : This Is The Hardest Version	15
74	Atra ATRA019	Everyday Wondering/Julie	12
74	Cactus CTEP2	Jump Back Baby	15
74	Harry J HJ6706	Move Out A Babylon/Move Out A Babylon (Instrumental)	10
75	Horse HOSS86	Move out Of Babylon/AGGROVATORS : Version	7
75	Horse HOSS100	Too Much War/AGGROVATORS : Version	10
75	Vulcan VUL 1001	I'm Gonna Put It On/KING TUBBY AND THE AGGROVATORS - Version	6
75	Attack ATT 8100	Rock With Me Baby/KING TUBBYS AND THE AGGROVATORS: A Crabit Version	6
75	Attack ATT 8118	Cold I Up/Cold I Up (Version)	15
76	Virgin VS159	Crazy Baldhead/Version	8
77	Virgin VS173	Roots, Natty Roots, Natty Congo/Version	20
77	Third World TW 70	Age is growing/Version	20
77	Paradise PDIS 002	Empty Chair/Can't Go On Without You (12", p/s with Dillinger)	15
78	Star PTP1009	Every Knee Shall Bow/Version (With U Roy) (12")	25
78	Justice JUDIS 109	Pity Fool Fe Get Wise/Satisfaction (12")	40
78	Third World TW 76	Peace And Love In The Ghetto/Version	15
78	Third World TW 92	Riding For A Fall/CLINT EASTWOOD AND THE AGROVATORS: Version	8
79	Justice JUDIS 109	Play Fool Fe Get Wise/Version/Satisfaction/Version (12")	25

Kenny CLARKE

MINT VALUE £

79	Greensleeves GRED20	Jah Love Is With I/Bad Days Are Going (12")	35
80	Jah Shaka 842	Got To Be Strong/Babylon (12")	30
80	Cha Cha CHAD17	Babylon/One Man Live (as J. Clark) (12")	100
81	Chrysalis 122849	Babylon/Than You For The Many Things You've Done - Cassandra (12")	50
81	Art & Craft ACD 007	Can't Get Enough/Version (12')	20
81	Art & Craft ACD 014	Guide Us Jah/Version (12")	40
81	Art & Craft ACD 015	Rude Boy/Version (12")	20
82	Art & Craft ACD 018	You Better Try/Version (12")	20
82	Black Joy DH822	Stop Them Jah/Too Much War	15
82	Cha Cha CHAD 49	Give Me Love/Version (10")	20
82	Red Nail RN 039	Guidance/DUB BAND: Protection (12")	30
83	Top Notch TOP005	Young Rebel/Version (10")	25
84	Ariwa ARISL002	Nuclear Weapon/Reggae Music (12")	20
89	Jah Shaka SHAKA 876	Rosie/Rosie Dub (12")	12
90	Justice JS 008	Give Up The Badness/Version	8
03	Attack Gold ATT10 001	Jah Love Is With I/KING TUBBY: Dub/LEROY SMART: I Don't Like It/DILLINGER: Jah Show Them The Way (10")	12
04	Trojan TJHTE 011	Blood Dunza/Version/Blood Sweat & Dunza Dub/Don't Trouble Trouble/A Ruffer Version (10" die-cut Trojan sleeve)	20
13	Attack Gold ATT10 010	Dem A Say/Dub Version/Two Face Rasta/Extended Dub (10")	18
75	Attack ATLP 1015	ENTER INTO HIS GATES WITH PRAISE (LP)	60
75	Vulcan VULP 001	PUT IT ON (LP)	40
76	Virgin V2076	AUTHORISED VERSION (LP, mono)	20
76	Virgin V2058	ROCKERS TIME NOW (LP, mono credits on label)	35
77	Justice JUSLP 001	GIRL I LOVE YOU (LP)	40
77	Paradise PDLP 001	DON'T STAY OUT LATE (LP)	25
77	Third World TWS 914	SWEET CONVERSATION (LP)	30
78	Third World TWS 932	KING IN A ARENA (LP, as Johnie Clark)	40
79	Paradise PDLP 008	SHOWCASE (LP)	35
79	Third World TDWD 4	SATISFACTION (LP)	20
82	Art & Craft ACDLP001	CAN'T GET ENOUGH (LP)	50
83	Ariwa ARI 007 LP	YARD STYLE (LP)	30
83	Vista VSLP 4016	MEETS CORNEL CAMPBELL (LP)	30
85	Ariwa ARI LP 022	GIVE THANKS (LP)	15
89	Attack ATLP 105	ENTER INTO HIS GATES WITH PRAISE (LP, reissue)	15
89	Attack ATLP 107	DON'T TROUBLE TROUBLE (LP)	15

KENNY CLARKE

56	London LTZC 15004	KENNY CLARKE SEXTET (LP)	25
56	London LTZC 15008	KENNY CLARKE AND ERNIE WILKINS (LP)	20
57	London LTZC 15038	KENNY CLARKE (LP)	25
57	London LTZC 15047	KENNY CLARKE (LP)	20
57	Vogue LAE 12029	JAZZ INTERNATIONAL (LP)	25

KENNY CLARKE (WITH FRANCY BOLAND BIG BAND)

56	London LTZ C 15047	BOHEMIA AFTER DARK (LP)	15
57	Columbia SEG 7830	KENNY CLARKE QT. (EP)	10
63	London HA-K 8085	JAZZ IS UNIVERSAL (LP, with Francy Boland Big Band)	20
66	CBS SBPG 62567	NOW HEAR OUR MEANIN' (LP)	18
68	Polydor 583726	LATIN KALEIDOSCOPE (LP)	20
69	Polydor 583727	ALL SMILES (LP)	20
69	Polydor 583738	FELLINI 712 (LP)	20
69	Polydor 583054	LIVE AT RONNIE SCOTT'S - THE FIRST SET (LP)	20
69	Polydor 583055	LIVE AT RONNIE SCOTT'S - THE SECOND SET (LP)	20
70	Polydor 583739	FACES (LP)	15
70	Polydor 2310 147	OFF LIMITS (LP, reflective sleeve)	30

(see also Francey Boland, Kenny Clarke)

LINDA CLARKE

67	Decca F 12709	Your Hurtin' Kinda Love/Send Me The Pillow You Dream On	15
68	Decca F 12787	Society's Child/Rain In My Heart	20

LLOYD CLARKE

62	Blue Beat BB 99	Good Morning/Now I Know A Reason (with Smithie's Sextet)	12
62	Blue Beat BB 104	Fool's Day/You're A Cheat (with Reco's All Stars)	15
62	Island WI 007	Love You The Most/LLOYD ROBINSON: You Said You Loved Me	20
62	Island WI 045	Japanese Girl/He's Coming	20
63	Rio R 16	Love Me/Half As Much	20
64	Rio R 23	Stop Your Talking/A Penny	20
64	Rio R 24	Fellow Jamaican/PATRICK & GEORGE: My Love	20
68	Island WI 3116	Summertime/VAL BENNETT: Soul Survivor	130
68	Blue Cat BS 136	Young Love/UNTOUCHABLES: Wall Flower	60
70	Escort ERT 849	Chicken Thief/STRANGER COLE: Tomorrow	15

(see also Derrick & Lloyd, Theo Beckford, Soulettes, Delroy Wilson, Laurel Aitken, Sonny Burke, Uniques)

MICKEY CLARKE

66	HMV 1483	Help Me/For Me	20

PAULA CLARKE

83	Oak Sound OSD 013	University/Didn't I Blow Your Mind (12")	40

RICK CLARKE

81	KR 1001	Potion (Vocal)/(Instrumental) (12" white label only)	30
85	Local LR 11	Love With A Stranger/Dub With A Stranger (12" p/s)	20
88	Raven RAVLP 1	TIME KEEPS MOVING ON (LP)	30

RONA CLARKE

67	Westwood WRS 067	UTOPIAN DREAM (LP)	30

Terry CLARKE

MINT VALUE £

TERRY CLARKE
72	Polydor 2058191	Lady/Army Captains Daughter	10

TONY CLARKE
64	Pye International 7N 25251	Ain't Love Good, Ain't Love Proud/Coming Back Strong	22
65	Chess CRS 8011	The Entertainer/This Heart Of Mine	30
65	Chess CRS 8011	The Entertainer/This Heart Of Mine (DJ Copy)	50
69	Chess CRS 8091	The Entertainer/Ain't Love Good, Ain't Love Proud	8
74	Chess 6145 030	Landslide/The Entertainer	8

CLARK-HUTCHINSON
68	Decca LK-R 5006	CLARK-HUTCHINSON (LP, red Decca labels, no sleeve Matrix: ARL-8968.P-1A/1B	500
70	Decca Nova DN-R 2	A = MH2 (LP, dark green label, mono)	150
70	Decca Nova DN-R 2	A = MH2 (LP, turquoise label, stereo)	100
70	Deram SML 1076	RETRIBUTION (LP)	100
71	Deram SML 1090	GESTALT (LP, laminated sleeve)	100
71	Deram SML 1090	GESTALT (LP, non-laminated sleeve)	80

(see also Vamp, Upp)

CLARK OF THE COURT
85	Clark 1	Only The Strong Survive/Instrumental (p/s)	8

CLARO INTELECTO
02	Ai Ai 003	PEACE OF MIND (12", first pressings in blue p/s)	15

CLASH
SINGLES
77	CBS S CBS 5058	White Riot/1977 (p/s, 'The Clash' or 'The CLASH' on label, 'copyright control' publishing credit)	30
77	CBS S 5058	White Riot/1977 (p/s, 'The Clash' or 'The CLASH' on label, 'Nineden/Riva' publishing credits)	20
77	CBS CL 1	CAPITAL RADIO (EP, NME freebie, p/s)	150
77	CBS S CBS 5293	Remote Control/London's Burning (p/s with 'live version...in mono...for the first time' on rear, 'copyright control' and 'Dunstable' publishing credit)	20
77	CBS CBS 5293	Remote Control/London's Burning (p/s, with 'Nineden/Riva' publishing credits)	15
77	CBS S CBS 5664	Complete Control/The City Of The Dead (p/s, 'copyright control' publishing credits)	20
77	CBS S CBS 5664	Complete Control/The City Of The Dead (p/s, 'Nineden/Riva publishing credits')	10
78	CBS CBS 5834	Clash City Rockers/Jail Guitar Doors (p/s)	15
78	CBS S CBS 6383	(White Man) In Hammersmith Palais/The Prisoner (initially green, then pink, blue or yellow die-cut sleeve)	15
78	CBS S CBS 6788	Tommy Gun/1 - 2 Crush On You (p/s)	10
78	CBS S CBS 7082	English Civil War/Pressure Drop (p/s)	15
79	CBS S CBS 7324	THE COST OF LIVING (EP, gatefold p/s & inner sleeve)	15
79	CBS S CBS 8087	London Calling/Armagideon Time (p/s, green or red shaded sleeve, white or yellow/orange label)	15
79	CBS 12 8087	London Calling/Armagidion Time/Armagidion Time (Version) (12")	40
79	CBS S CBS 5058	White Riot/1977 (reissue, LC0149 on labels, some in p/s)	8
79	CBS CBS 5664	Complete Control/The City Of The Dead (reissue, LC0149 on labels, some in p/s)	10
79	CBS S CBS 5834	Clash City Rockers/Jail Guitar Doors (reissue, LC0149 on labels, some in p/s)	10
80	CBS 8323	Bankrobber/Rockers Galore (p/s)	10
80	CBS S CBS 9339	The Call Up/Stop The World (p/s, solid or push-out centre)	8
81	CBS A 1133	The Magnificent Seven/The Magnificent Dance (die cut sleeve)	8
81	CBS A12 1133	The Magnificent Seven/The Magnificent Dance (12", p/s, with stickers)	20
81	CBS S CBS 9480	Hitsville U.K./Radio One (die cut sleeve)	6
81	CBS A 1797	This Is Radio Clash/Radio Clash (p/s)	6
81	CBS CBS A 131797	This Is Radio Clash/Radio Clash/Outside Broadcast/Radio 5 (12", p/s)	10
81	CBS S 2309	Know Your Rights/First Night Back In London (p/s, with free sticker)	15
82	CBS A 2479	Rock The Casbah/Long Time Jerk (p/s, with free stickers)	15
82	CBS A 11 2479	Rock The Casbah/Long Time Jerk (picture disc)	15
82	CBS A 13 2479	Rock The Casbah/Mustapha Dance (12", p/s)	18
82	CBS A 2646	Should I Stay Or Should I Go/Straight To Hell (p/s, with dragon sticker)	15
82	CBS A 11 2646	Should I Stay Or Should I Go/Straight To Hell (picture disc)	15
82	CBS A 12 2646	Should I Stay Or Should I Go/Straight To Hell (12", p/s with stencil)	30
85	CBS A 6122	This Is England/Do It Now (p/s)	8
85	CBS A 6122	This Is England/Do It Now (poster p/s)	15
85	CBS TA 6122	This Is England/Do It Now/Sex Mad Roar (12", p/s, with 6 sticker postcard)	30
85	CBS S CBS 7082	English Civil War/Pressure Drop (reissue, red label with LC0149 on labels, some in p/s)	40
88	CBS CLASH 1	I Fought The War/City Of The Dead/1977 (p/s)	15
88	CBS CLASH T1	I Fought The Law/City Of The Dead/Police On My Back/48 Hours (12", p/s)	15
88	CBS CLASH B 2	London Calling/Brand New Cadillac/Rudie Don't Fail (box set)	40
88	CBS CLASH T2	London Calling/Brand New Cadillac/Rudie Can't Fail/Street Parade (p/s)	20
90	CBS 656072-1	Return To Brixton/Guns Of Brixton (p/s)	20
91	Columbia 6568147	Rock The Casbah/Mustapha Dance (p/s, reissue)	12
91	Columbia 6568146	Rock The Casbah/Mustapha Dance/The Magnificent Dance (12", p/s)	12
91	Columbia 6569467	London Calling/Brand New Cadillac (p/s, reissue)	12
91	Columbia 6569466	London Calling/Brand New Cadillac/Return To Brixton (12", p/s)	10
91	Columbia 6569466	London Calling/Brand New Cadillac/Return To Brixton (12", poster p/s)	20
91	Columbia 6574307	Train In Vain/The Right Profile (p/s)	12
91	Columbia 6574306	Train In Vain/The Right Profile/Groovy Times/Gates Of The West (12", p/s)	20
06	Sony 82876 876287	THE SINGLES (Box set 19 x 7" singles)	200
11	Columbia 88697890297	The Magnificent Seven/The Cool Out (red vinyl, numbered, die-cut sleeve)	30
12	Columbia 88691959140	London Calling (2012 Mix)/London Calling (2012 Instrumental) (p/s)	15
18	Secret S 736	I'm Not Down (1-sided, 100 only, each with unique p/s)	75

ALBUMS
77	CBS 82000	THE CLASH (LP, 10,000 only with sticker on inner sleeve for free NME Capital Radio EP	100

CLASS ACTION

MINT VALUE £

		freebie, orange/yellow labels with 'made in England' at bottom)	
77	CBS 82000	THE CLASH (LP, 1st issue with orange/yellow labels with 'made in England' at bottom, 'Copyright Control' publishing credits)	50
77	CBS CBS 82000	THE CLASH (LP, 1st issue with orange/yellow labels with 'made in England' at bottom, 'Nineden/Riva' publishing credits)	40
78	CBS 82431	GIVE 'EM ENOUGH ROPE (LP, promo-only package with poster in folder)	1500
78	CBS 82431	GIVE 'EM ENOUGH ROPE (LP)	40
79	CBS CLASH 3	LONDON CALLING (2-LP, stickered, with inner sleeves, 1st issue with black & white labels, no Train In Vain)	250
79	CBS CBS CLASH 3	LONDON CALLING (2-LP, stickered, with inner sleeves, 2nd issue with black & white labels, Train In Vain on side 4 but not listed on sleeve or labels, 'Track 5 is Train In Vain' etched in run-out groove on side 4). 'Stagger Lee' reference on rear sleeve after Wrong Em Boyo)	80
79	CBS CBS CLASH 3	LONDON CALLING (2-LP, stickered, with inner sleeves, 2nd issue with black & white labels, Train In Vain on side 4 but not listed on sleeve or labels, 'Track 5 is Train In Vain' etched in run-out groove on side 4)	80
79	CBS CBS 32232	THE CLASH (LP, reissue, LC0149 on labels, some with 'Nice Price £2.99' sticker on sleeve)	15
80	CBS FSLN 1	SANDINISTA (3-LP, stickered sleeve with 'Armagideon Times' insert)	75
82	CBS FMLN2	COMBAT ROCK (LP, 1st pressing, inner sleeve and poster of band sitting in bar)	60
82	CBS FMLN2	COMBAT ROCK (LP, 2nd pressing, inner sleeve and poster of front cover artwork)	50
84	CBS 32444	GIVE 'EM ENOUGH ROPE (LP, reissue, red labels)	15
85	CBS 26601	CUT THE CRAP (LP, with inner)	15
85	CBS 4601141	LONDON CALLING (2-LP, reissue, red labels)	25
85	CBS 4601141	COMBAT ROCK (LP, reissue, red labels)	15
88	CBS 460244 1	THE STORY OF THE CLASH (2-LP)	20
91	Columbia 4689461	THE SINGLES (LP, with poster)	40
92	CBS 32787	COMBAT ROCK (LP, reissue, has barcode on sleeve)	15
93	Columbia 4745461	SUPER BLACK MARKET CLASH (LP as 3 x 10" with inners, 'police' labels)	60
99	CBS 49 5344-1	THE CLASH (LP, reissue)	20
99	Simply Vinyl SVLP 134	GIVE 'EM ENOUGH ROPE (LP, reissue)	20
99	CBS 495347-1	LONDON CALLING (2-LP, reissue)	30
99	CBS 495348-1	SANDINISTA (3-LP, reissue)	25
99	CBS 495349-1	COMBAT ROCK (LP, 2nd reissue)	20
99	Columbia 4953511	THE STORY OF THE CLASH (2-LP, reissue)	40
99	Sony 496183-1	FROM HERE TO ETERNITY (2-LP, gatefold with inners)	100
99	Columbia 4953521	SUPER BLACK MARKET CLASH (LP as 3 x 10" with inners, reissue, labels replicate front cover artwork)	50
08	Epic 88697348801	LIVE AT SHEA STADIUM (LP)	30
13	Columbia 88883725981	THE CLASH (8-LP box set, stencil and badge)	180
13	Columbia 88725460002	SOUND SYSTEM (Box set, 11 x CD, DVD, book, 5 badges, 3 stickers, notebook, booklet & poster)	100
16	Columbia 88985316611	LONDON CALLING (2-LP, reissue, green and pink vinyl, 'Tesco' exclusive)	80
16	Columbia 88985316581	THE CLASH LP, reissue, green vinyl, HMV exclusive)	40
17	Columbia 88985431091	GIVE EM ENOUGH ROPE (LP, reissue, blue vinyl, HMV exclusive)	35
19	Columbia 19075978671	LONDON CALLING (2-LP, reissue, 40th anniversary edition with plastic outer sleeve)	30
19	Sony 88985391771	COMBAT ROCK (LP, reissue, green vinyl, HMV exclusive)	35

PROMOS

77	CBS S CBS 5058	White Riot/1977 (A label promo, The Clash on label, p/s)	70
77	CBS S CBS 5293	Remote Control/London's Burning (Studio Version) ('A' Label Promo)	50
77	CBS S 5664	Complete Control/The City Of The Dead (A label promo, p/s)	50
78	CBS S CBS 5834	Clash City Rockers/Jail Guitar Doors (A label promo, p/s)	50
78	CBS S CBS 6383	(White Man) In Hammersmith Palais/The Prisoner (A label demo - small black A - in die-cut sleeve)	60
78	CBS S CBS 6788	Tommy Gun/1 - 2 Crush On You (A label promo, p/s)	60
78	CBS S CBS 7082	English Civil War/Pressure Drop (A label promo, p/s)	50
79	CBS S CBS 7324	I Fought The Law/Gates Of The West (2-track promo for COST OF LIVING EP)	40
80	CBS S CBS 9339	The Call Up/Stop The World (A label promo, p/s)	50
80	CBS S CBS 9480	Hitsville U.K./Radio One (A label promo, die cut sleeve)	60
81	WEA SAM 144	4 Track White label EP featuring London Calling and tracks by the Beat, Bad Manners and the Jam)	200
82	CBS A2309	Know Your Rights/First Night Back In London ("promo copy not for sale", no A, p/s)	30
82	CBS A2479	Rock The Casbah/Long Time Jerk (promo with small "A", p/s)	30
82	CBS A 2646	Should I Stay Or Should I Go/Straight To Hell (edit) (A label promo, p/s)	40

(see also 101'ers, Janie Jones & Lash, Tymon Dogg, Ellen Foley, Futura 2000, Joe Strummer, Carbon/Silicon, Havana 3AM, The Good The Bad And The Queen)

CLASS ACTION

83	Jive JIVE T 35	Weekend (Vocal)/(Acapella)/(Vocal)/(Dub) (12")	12

CLASS 50

77	Electric WOT 13	Freerider/Time Machine	12

CLASSICS IV

66	Capitol CL 15470	Pollyanna/Cry Baby (issued as if by the "Classics")	40
68	Liberty LBF 15051	Spooky/Poor People	8
69	Liberty LBF 15177	Stormy/Twenty Four Hours Of Loneliness	15

(see also Dennis Yost & Classics IV)

CLASSICS (JAMAICA)

69	Doctor Bird DB 1190	Worried Over Me/LAUREL AITKEN: Rice And Peas	40
70	New Beat NB 061	Same Old Feeling/So Much Love	12
70	New Beat NB 071	History Of Africa/Honeybee	12
70	Pama PM 830	Sex Education/POWER: Soul Flash	12
71	Punch PH 79	Cheerio Baby/Civilization	80
71	Banana BA331	Mr Fire Coal Man/SOUND DIMENSION: Version (actually by Wailing Souls)	40

CLASSICS (U.S.)

MINT VALUE £

CLASSICS (U.S.)
61	Mercury AMT 1152	Life Is But A Dream/That's The Way	75
63	Stateside SS 215	Till Then/Enie Minie Mo	30

CLASSIC SULLIVANS
74	Kwanza K19501	Paint Yourself Into A Corner/I Don't Want To Loose You	10

CLASSIFIED INFO
84	Dead Dog DOG 02	Drug Called Love/Drug Called Love Dub (p/s)	12

CLAUDETTE (& CORPORATION)
69	Jackpot JP 712	Let's Fall In Love/PROPHETS: Purple Moon	30
70	Grape GR 3020	Skinheads A Bash Them (with Corporation)/ CORPORATION: Walkin' Thru Jerusalem	200
12	Grape THB 701	Hot Bread And Butter/Ashes To Ashes	25

(see also Corporation)

CLAUDIA
84	Rhythmic RMIC5	Don't Give Up (Your Love) (Club Mix)/Don't Give Up (Your Love)/Do You Wanna Dance With Me (12", p/s)	15
84	Rhythmic 7RMIC5	Don't Give Up (Your Love) (Club Mix)/Don't Give Up (Your Love) (p/s)	10
85	Rhythmic RMIC9	Hold On/(Radio Mix)/(Instrumental) (12")	12

CASSIUS CLAY
64	CBS AAG 190	Stand By Me/I Am The Greatest	20
63	CBS BPG 62274	I AM THE GREATEST! (LP)	40

JUDY CLAY
67	Stax 601 022	You Can't Run Away From Your Heart/It Takes A Lotta Good Love	10

(see also Billy Vera & Judy Clay, Booker T. & M.G.'s)

JUDY CLAY & WILLIAM BELL
69	Stax STAX 115	My Baby Specialises/Left Over Love	8

(see also William Bell, Billy Vera & Judy Clay)

OTIS CLAY
67	President PT 121	It's Easier Said Than Done/Flame In Your Heart	8
68	President PT 132	I'm Satisfied/I Testify	8
68	President PT 148	That's How It Is/Show Place	10
68	President PT 176	A Lasting Love/Got To Find A Way	10
69	Atlantic 584 282	Baby Jane/You Hurt Me For The Last Time	80
72	London HLU 10397	Trying To Live My Life Without You/Let Me Be The One	15
74	London HLU 10467	You Did Something To Me/It Was Jealousy	12
76	President PT 456	All I Need Is You/Special Kind Of Love	12
73	London SH-U 8446	TRYING TO LIVE MY LIFE WITHOUT YOU (LP)	30

TOM CLAY
72	Tamla Motown TMG 801	What The World Needs Now Is Love/The Victors	12

CLAY FAV
79	Own label	CONSIGNMENT STOCK (EP, 200 stamped "consignment Stock' sleeve)	150
79	Own label	CONSIGNMENT STOCK (EP, 800 without stamped 'consignment Stock' sleeve)	50

ALASDAIR CLAYRE
67	Elektra EUK 255	ALASDAIR CLAYRE (LP, some with mail order insert)	60
76	Acorn CF 252	ADAM AND THE BEASTS (LP)	30

DOCTOR CLAYTON
65	RCA Victor RCX 7177	RCA RACE SERIES VOLUME 6 (EP)	10
70	RCA Intl. INTS 1176	PEARL HARBOUR BLUES (LP)	15

MERRY CLAYTON
70	A&M AMS 802	Gimme Shelter/Good Girls	20
70	A&M AMS 802	Gimme Shelter/Good Girls (DJ Copy)	30
73	Ode ODS 66301	Acid Queen/Underture (p/s)	10
75	Ode 66110	Keep Your Eye On The Sparrow/Love Creeps Up Slowly	6
70	A&M AMLS 995	GIMME SHELTER (LP)	30
72	A&M AMLS 67012	MERRY CLAYTON (LP)	35

(see also Raelets)

PAUL CLAYTON
61	London REU 1276	PAUL CLAYTON (EP)	30

VIKKI CLAYTON
88	Dambuster DAM 021	LOST LADY FOUND (LP)	20

(see also Fairport Convention)

CLAYTON SQUARES
65	Decca F 12250	Come And Get It/And Tears Fell	40
66	Decca F 12456	There She Is/Imagination	175

(see also Liverpool Scene, Andy Roberts, Mike Hart)

CLAYTOWN TROUPE
92	EMI 12 88007)	SKYBOUND (LP, withdrawn)	20

CLEAN
94	Dark Beloved Cloud DBC 020	Late Last Night/Psychedelic Clown (p/s)	8
86	Flying Nun FNE 29	COMPILATION (LP)	25
89	Flying Nun Europe FNE 29	IN-A-LIVE (Mini-LP)	20
90	Rough Trade ROUGH 143	VEHICLE (LP)	25

CLEANERS FROM VENUS
87	Ammunition JANGLE 1	Illya Kurayakin Looked At Me/Black And White And Blue All Over (p/s)	25
87	Ammunition JANGLE 1T	Illya Kurayakin Looked At Me/Albion's Daughter/Black And White And Blue All Over/Illya Kurayakin Looked At Me (Full Version) (12", p/s)	15
87	Ammunition JANGLE 2	Living With Victoria Grey/Sunday Afternoon (p/s)	20
87	Ammunition JANGLE 2T	Living With Victoria Grey/Sunday Afternoon/She's Checking You Out (12", p/s)	15
88	Ammunition JANGLE 3	Mercury Girl/Gamma Ray Blues	20
88	Ammunition JANGLE 3T	Mercury Girl/Gamma Ray Blues/The Iceberg Unicorn (12", p/s)	15
87	Ammunition CLEAN LP 1	GOING TO ENGLAND (LP)	30
88	Ammunition CLEAN LP 2	TOWN AND COUNTRY (LP)	30

CLEAN LOOKING BOYS

(see also Gypp, Martin Newall, Brotherhood of Lizards)

CLEAN LOOKING BOYS
83	DJW 001	Sent To Coventry/I Like Your Feel (no p/s)	12

CLEAR BLUE SKY
70	Vertigo 6360 013	CLEAR BLUE SKY (LP, gatefold sleeve, large swirl label)	500
90	Saturn SRLP 101	DESTINY (LP)	15

CLEAR LIGHT
67	Elektra EKSN 45019	Black Roses/She's Ready To Be Free	10
68	Elektra EKSN 45027	Night Sounds Loud/How Many Days Have Passed	30
67	Elektra EKL 4011	CLEAR LIGHT (LP, orange label, mono)	150
67	Elektra EKS 74011	CLEAR LIGHT (LP, orange label, stereo)	100
87	Edsel ED 245	BLACK ROSES (LP, reissue of original Clear Light LP with 1 bonus track)	15

CLEARLIGHT
75	Virgin V 2029	SYMPHONY (LP, stickered sleeve)	20
75	Virgin V 2039	FOREVER BLOWING BUBBLES (LP)	20

(see also Gong, Steve Hillage)

CLEAR LIGHT SYMPHONY
75	Virgin V 2039	CLEAR LIGHT SYMPHONY (LP)	15

CLEARWAYS
64	Columbia DB 7333	I'll Be Here/I've Just Got A Letter	10

JOHN CLEESE (& 1948 CHOIR)
67	Pye 7N 17336	The Ferret Song - From 'At Last The 1948 Show'/The Rhubarb Tart Song	8

(see also Monty Python)

CLEFS
62	Salvo SLO 1810	Don't Cry/The Dream Train Special (99 copies only)	20

CLEFS OF LAVENDER HILL
66	CBS 202230	Stop, Get A Ticket/First Tell Me Why	20

CLEFTONES
56	Columbia SCM 3801	You Baby, You/Little Girl Of Mine	250
61	Columbia DB 4678	Heart And Soul/How Do You Feel	100
61	Columbia DB 4720	(I Love You) For Sentimental Reasons/Deed I Do	100
63	Columbia DB 4988	Lover Come Back To Me/There She Goes	50

JACK CLEMENT
58	London HLS 8691	Ten Years/Your Lover Boy	150
58	London HLS 8691	Ten Years/Your Lover Boy (78)	40

SOUL JOE CLEMENTS
69	Plexium PXM 10	Smoke And Ashes/Ever, Ever	400

CLEO
64	Decca F 11817	To Know Him Is To Love Him/ANDREW OLDHAM ORCHESTRA: There Are But Five Rolling Stones	25

(see also Andrew Oldham Orchestra, This 'N' That)

CLERKS
79	Rok ROK VIII/VII	No Good For Me/HAZARD: Gotta Change My Life (company sleeve)	15

CLICHE
80	Carrere CAR 133	I Know Your Name/Drawing The Line	100

CLIENTELE
98	Pointy POINT 001	What Goes Up/Five Day Morning (p/s)	15
99	Johnny Kane KANE 002	Reflections After Jane/An Hour Before The Light (p/s)	15
99	Pointy POINT 002	I Had To Say This/Monday's Rain (p/s)	15
00	Pointy POINT 004LP	SUBURBAN LIGHT (LP, insert)	40
03	Pointy POINT 011LP	THE VIOLET HOUR (LP)	40
05	Pointy POINT 017LP	STRANGE GEOMETRY (LP)	20
17	Tapete TR 385	MUSIC FOR THE AGE OF MIRACLES (LP, CD and 7")	20

CLIENTELLE
79	Quest BRS 003	Can't Forget/Skyline (p/s)	125
81	Banana BANANA 505	DESTINATION UNKNOWN (LP, with insert)	100

JIMMY CLIFF
62	Blue Beat BB 78	I'm Sorry (with Cavaliers Combo)/BLUE BEATS: Roarin' (with Red Price)	30
62	Island WI 012	Hurricane Hatty/Dearest Beverley	18
62	Island WI 016	Miss Jamaica/Gold Digger	25
62	Island WI 025	Since Lately/I'm Free	25
63	Island WI 062	My Lucky Day/One-Eyed Jacks	25
63	Island WI 070	King Of Kings/SIR PERCY: Oh Yeah	30
63	Island WI 112	Miss Universe/The Prodigal	18
63	Black Swan WI 403	The Man (vocal version)/You Are Never Too Old	20
63	Black Swan WI 403	The Man (Instrumental version)/You Are Never Too Old	20
64	Stateside SS 342	One Eyed Jacks/King Of Kings	20
66	Fontana TF 641	Call On Me/Pride And Passion	15
67	Island WIP 6004	Aim And Ambition/Give And Take	15
67	Island WIP 6011	I Got A Feeling/Hard Road To Travel	15
67	Island WIP 6024	That's The Way Life Goes/Thank You	10
68	Island WIP 6039	Waterfall/Reward	35
69	Trojan TR 690	Wonderful World, Beautiful People/Hard Road To Travel (in p/s)	7
68	Island ILP 962	HARD ROAD TO TRAVEL (LP)	60
69	Trojan TRLS 16	JIMMY CLIFF (LP)	30
71	Island ILPS 9159	ANOTHER CYCLE (LP)	18
72	Island ILPS 9202	THE HARDER THEY COME (LP, pink rim palm tree label)	20

(see also Jackie Edwards & Jimmy Cliff, James Chambers)

CLIFF DWELLERS
66	Polydor BM 56707	Hang On Stupid/I'm A Superman For You	15

CLIFFORD

MINT VALUE £

CLIFFORD
73　Satril SAT 10　　Drink Wine Susan/Looking Upon The Day 7

BUZZ CLIFFORD
61　Fontana H 297　　Baby Sittin' Boogie/Driftwood 6
61　Fontana H 312　　Three Little Fishes/Simply Because 8
62　Columbia DB 4903　More Dead Than Alive/Nobody Loves Me Like You 12
61　Fontana TFL 5147　BABY SITTIN' WITH BUZZ CLIFFORD (LP, mono) 30
61　Fontana STFL 567　BABY SITTIN' WITH BUZZ CLIFFORD (LP, stereo) 40

JOHN & JULIA CLIFFORD
77　Topic 12TS 311　　THE HUMOURS OF LISHEEN (LP) 20

LINDA CLIFFORD
74　Paramount PARA 3051　After Loving You/Check Out Your Heart 30
78　Curtom K17078　　From Now On/You Can Do It 8
78　Curtom K 17163T　If My Friends Could See Me Now/Runaway Love (12") 12

MIKE CLIFFORD
62　United Artists UP 1006　Close To Cathy/She's Just Another Girl 7

PAUL CLIFTON
09　Kent Select CITY 029　She Wobbles When She Walks/BOYCE CUNNINGHAM: Too Young 10

CLIMAX (CHICAGO) BLUES BAND
69　Parlophone R 5809　Like Uncle Charlie/Loving Machine 30
70　Harvest HAR 5029　Reap What I've Sowed/Spoonful 12
71　Harvest HAR 5041　Towards The Sun/Everyday (as Climax Chicago) 10
72　Harvest HAR 5065　Mole On The Dole/Like Uncle Charlie 12
69　Parlophone PMC 7069　CLIMAX CHICAGO BLUES BAND (LP, yellow/black label, with "sold in the UK.." text, mono) 150
69　Parlophone PCS 7069　CLIMAX CHICAGO BLUES BAND (LP, yellow/black label, with "sold in the UK.." text, stereo) 90
70　Parlophone PCS 7084　PLAYS ON (LP, yellow/black labels) 250
70　Parlophone PCS 7084　PLAYS ON (LP, later issue with boxed Parlophone logo) 70
70　Harvest SHSP 4009　A LOT OF BOTTLE (LP, no EMI logo on label, fully laminated sleeve) 60
71　Harvest SHSP 4015　TIGHTLY KNIT (LP, with EMI logo on label, flipback sleeve) 40
71　Harvest SHSP 4009　A LOT OF BOTTLE (LP, repressing, with EMI logo on label, fully laminated sleeve) 30
72　Harvest SHSP 4024　RICH MAN (LP) 25
74　Polydor 2383259　　LIVE (LP) 18
75　BTM 1004　　　　　STAMP ALBUM (LP) 20
76　BTM 1009　　　　　GOLD PLATED (LP, gatefold) 18
(see also Hipster Image)

CLIMAX INVASION
77　Top Secret TS1　　The Advertiser (one-sided) 30

CLIMAX (1)
71　Voice VC1　　　　I'm A Man/I'm A Man Part 2 45

CLIMAX (2)
72　Bell 1219　　　　　Precious And Few/Park Preserve 6

CLIMB
81　Pinnacle PIN 510　I Can't Forget/Only A Human (p/s) 8
81　Pinnacle 12 PIN 510　I Can't Forget (A Mother's Crime)/Your Hell (12", p/s) 15
82　Pinnacle PIN 511　Touch Me (Heaven)/A Lower Class Of Heaven (p/s) 7
84　Second Vision SV 004　Poacher Is (As Poacher Does)/The Woodcutter (p/s) 20

PATSY CLINE
57　Brunswick 05660　A Poor Man's Roses (Or A Rich Man's Gold)/Walkin' After Midnight 20
61　Brunswick 05855　I Fall To Pieces/Lovin' In Vain 10
61　Brunswick 05861　Crazy/Who Can I Count On 15
62　Brunswick 05866　She's Got You/Strange 10
63　Brunswick 05888　Sweet Dreams/Back In My Baby's Arms 10
63　Decca 31262　　　Blue Moon Of Kentucky/Faded Love (export) 20
62　Brunswick OE 9490　SWEET DREAMS (EP) 15
62　Brunswick LAT 8394　SHOWCASE (LP) 15

CLINIC
97　Aladdin's Cave Of Golf GOLF001　IPC Subeditors Dictate Our Youth/Porno/D.I.Y. (p/s, 500 copies only) 12
98　Aladdin's C.O.G. GOLF002　Monkey On Your Back/D.T. (p/s, 500 copies only) 8
98　Aladdin's C.O.G. GOLF003　Cement Mixer/Kimberley (p/s, 1,000 copies only) 8
99　Domino WIGLP 64　CLINIC (LP) 25
00　Domino WIGLP 78　INTERNATIONAL WRANGLER (LP) 30
01　Domino WIGLP 100　WALKING WITH THEE (LP) 20
04　Domino WIGLP 144　WINCHESTER CATHEDRAL (LP) 18
06　Domino WIGLP 181　VISITATIONS (LP) 15
10　Domino WIGLP 261X　BUBBLEGUM (2-LP, pink vinyl, transfer, sticker, poster & badge) 20

BUDDY CLINTON
60　Top Rank JAR 287　Across The Street From Your House/How My Prayers Have Changed 15

DAVY CLINTON
68　NEMS 56-3855　　Can I Bring Back Yesterday/The Girl With The Sun In Her Hair 35
68　President PT 290　House Of The Rising Sun/On A Rooftop In Memphis 6

GEORGE CLINTON
79　ABC ABC 4053　　Please Don't Run From Me/Life And Breath (DJ Copy) 15
(do not see also Parliament, Funkadelic)

LARRY CLINTON
79　Grapevine GRP 120　She's Wanted In Three States/If I Knew 40
79　Grapevine GRP 120　She's Wanted In Three States/If I Knew (DJ Copy) 50

CLINTONES
73　Ackee ACK 515　　Equal Rights/Version 6

CLIQUE (U.K.) (1)

MINT VALUE £

CLIQUE (U.K.) (1)
65	Pye 7N 15786	She Ain't No Good/Time Time Time	100
65	Pye 7N 15853	We Didn't Kiss, Didn't Love, But Now We Do/You've Been Unfair	175
	60s private pressing	THE CLIQUE (EP, no p/s)	550
95	Dig The Fuzz DIG 003	THE COMPLETE RECORDINGS 1964/1965 (LP)	20

(see also Hammersmith Gorillas)

CLIQUE (U.K.) (2)
91	Guild GUIEP 001	INTRODUCING...THE CLIQUE (EP)	20
94	Detour DR 014	Reggie/She Doesn't Need You Anymore (p/s, red vinyl)	10
94	Detour DR 014	Reggie/She Doesn't Need You Anymore (pic disc, 200 only)	15
93	Detour DR 006	THE EARLY DAYS (EP)	15

CLIQUE (U.S.)
69	London HLU 10286	Sugar On Sunday/Superman	20

JIMMY CLITHEROE
65	Parlophone R 5387	They All Blame Jim/Jim Plays Hookie	8

CLIVE & DOREEN
68	Treasure Isle TI 7033	What Can I Do/TOMMY MCCOOK: Black Power	45

CLIVE & GLORIA
63	R&B JB 113	Change Of Plan/Little Gloria	20
64	R&B JB 173	Money Money Money/Have I Told You Lately	20
64	King KG 1004	Do The Ska/You Made Me Cry	20

CLIVE & NAOMI
65	Ska Beat JB 181	You Are Mine/Open The Door	20

(see also Desmond Dekker)

CLOCK DVA
81	Fetish FET 008	Four Hours (Re-mixed)/Sensorium (p/s)	10
82	Polydor POSP 499	High Holy Disco Mass/The Voice That Speaks From Within (p/s, as DVA)	7
81	Fetish FR 2002	THIRST (LP, with insert)	25
81	Industrial IRC 31	WHITE SOULS IN BLACK SUITS (cassette, with booklet)	30
83	Polydor POLS 1082	ADVANTAGE (LP)	20

CLOCKHOUSE
83	Picturesque PIC 1	Vanishing Point/Everyman (p/s)	7

CLOCKWORK CRIMINALS
82	Ace ACE 38	YOUNG AND BOLD (EP)	150

CLOCKWORK ORANGES
66	Ember EMB S 227	Ready Steady/After Tonight	40

CLOCKWORK SOLDIERS
84	Rot ASS 5	Wet Dreams/Suicide/In The Name Of Science (p/s)	15

CLONE 81
81	FMR 058	Product Of Society/Into The Recess (hand-made p/s)	25

CLOR
05	Regal REG 122	CLOR (LP as 2 x 12")	25

CLOSE LOBSTERS
89	Caff CAFF 4	Just Too Bloody Stupid/All The Little Boys And Girls (fold-out, p/s, insert)	20
15	Fire FIRELP 397	FIRESTATION TOWERS (3-LP compilation)	20

CLOSE SHAVE
99	Helen Of Oi! H 003	Attack/We Hate You (p/s, first pressing, 200 numbered copies)	8

CLOSE RIVALS
81	Hyped BMRB 52	Short Sharp Kick In The Teeth/You've Got To Make Mistakes	6

CLAUDE CLOUD
55	MGM MGM 820	Cloudburst/One Bone (78, as Claude Cloud & Thunderclaps)	10
57	MGM MGM 946	The Beat/Around The Horn (as Claude Cloud & His Orchestra)	15
55	MGM MGM-EP 517	LET'S GO CATSTATIC NO. 1 (EP, as Claude Cloud & Thunderclaps)	15
56	MGM MGM-D 142	ROCK 'N' ROLL (10" LP)	80

(see also Sonny Thompson, Sam 'The Man' Taylor)

CLOUD CONTROL
11	Infectious INFECT127LP	BLISS RELEASE (LP)	30
12	Infectious INFECT163LP	DREAM CAVE (LP)	18

CLOUD NINE
93	Acid Jazz JAZID 87P	I Feel It (12", p/s, promo-only, withdrawn)	18
93	Acid Jazz JAZID 78	MILLENNIUM (LP, withdrawn)	30

CLOUD ONE
77	Contempo CS 2119	Atmosphere Strut (Part 1)/Atmosphere Strut (Part 2)	6

CLOUD (1)
75	Kingsway DOVE 16	FREE TO FLY (LP)	20
77	Kingsway DOVE 44	WATERED GARDEN (LP, gatefold sleeve)	30
78	Kingsway DOVE 62	THE RESTING PLACE (LP)	20
82	Kingsway KMR 369	HALLOWED GROUND (LP, with insert)	15
85	Songs Of Fellow SFR103	THE PROMISE (LP)	15

CLOUD (2)
80	Flashback FLASH 001	All Night Long (Vocal)/All Night Long (Instrumental) (12", white labels most with sticker on one side)	100
81	Flashback FLASH 002	Take It To The Top/All Night Long (Remix) (12")	50
81	Flashback FLASH 003	Party Life/The Rio (12")	80
83	Rygel RYG 7	Steppin' Out With You/Rico Rico/Steppin' Out Jam (12")	20

(see also Style X)

CLOUDS (1)
69	Island WIP 6055	Heritage/Make No Bones About It	20
69	Island WIP 6067	Scrapbook/Carpenter	20
69	Island ILPS 9100	THE CLOUDS SCRAPBOOK (LP, gatefold sleeve, first pressing with black/orange circle logo)	250

CLOUT

			MINT VALUE £
69	Island ILPS 9100	THE CLOUDS SCRAPBOOK (LP, second pressing, circle logo)	100
69	Island ILPS 9100	THE CLOUDS SCRAPBOOK (LP, later pressing 'pink rim palm tree')	25
71	Chrysalis ILPS 9151	WATERCOLOUR DAYS (LP, gatefold sleeve, green label with Island logo and Island address in white)	50

CLOUT
90	Mooncrest JWL 1000	We'll Bring The House Down/Jim Jam (p/s)	7

(see also Slade)

CLOVEN HOOF
82	Elemental EM 001	OPENING RITUAL (12" EP)	80
84	Neat NEAT 1013	CLOVEN HOOF (LP)	20
86	Trojan CH 002	FIGHTING BACK (LP, with poster)	25
86	Trojan CH 002	FIGHTING BACK (LP, without poster)	20

CLOVER
70	Liberty LBF 15341	Wade In The Water/Stealin'	10
69	Liberty LBS 83340	CLOVER (LP)	30
71	Liberty LBS 83487	FORTY-NINER (LP)	30

(see also Huey Lewis & News)

CLOVERLEAFS
56	MGM MGM 933	Step Right Up And Say Howdy/With Plenty Of Money And You (Gold Digger's Lullaby)	8

(see also Art Mooney)

CLOVERS
56	London HLE 8229	Nip Sip/If I Could Be Loved By You (gold label lettering)	400
56	London HLE 8229	Nip Sip/If I Could Be Loved By You (silver label lettering)	150
56	London HLE 8229	Nip Sip/If I Could Be Loved By You (78)	20
56	London HLE 8314	Love, Love, Love/Hey, Doll Baby	250
56	London HLE 8314	Love, Love, Love/Hey, Doll Baby (78)	20
56	London HLE 8334	From The Bottom Of My Heart/Your Tender Lips	150
56	London HLE 8334	From The Bottom Of My Heart/Your Tender Lips (78)	20
58	London HL 7048	Wishing For Your Love/All About You (export issue)	150
58	HMV POP 542	In The Good Old Summertime/Idaho	30
59	London HLT 8949	Love Potion No. 9/Stay Awhile (triangular centre)	50
59	London HLT 8949	Love Potion No. 9/Stay Awhile (round centre)	35
60	London HLT 9122	Lovey/One Mint Julep	30
60	London HLT 9154	Easy Lovin'/I'm Confessin' (That I Love You)	40
61	HMV POP 883	Honey Dripper/Have Gun	25
68	Atlantic 584 160	Your Cash Ain't Nothin' But Trash/I've Got My Eyes On You	15
69	Atlantic 587 162	LOVE BUG (LP)	50

CLOWN
72	CBS 7906	Lord Of The Ringside/Rumania	40

CLOX ITALIA
82	B Flat FLAT 2	LookingThe Part/Leave It In (p/s, as Clox)	15
84	B Flat FLAT 3	Ageing Agent/You Belong To Me	8
84	B Flat FLAT 4	Follow Me Into The Water/This (p/s, as Clox)	7

CLUES
81	Clues CLU 001	NO VACANCIES (EP)	10

CLUTCH
73	EMI 2010	Black Angel/The Frightners	8

CLUTHA (FOLK GROUP)
71	Argo ZFB 18	SCOTIA! (LP, as Clutha Folk Group)	15

CMETRIC
94	B12 B1210	Cmetric (12", pink vinyl, 300 only)	35
94	B12 B1210	Cmetric (12")	30

C.M.J.
68	Impression IMP 102	I Can't Do It All By Myself/Nothing At All	45
71	Mother MOT 3	La La La/Step Around It	50
65	Impression EPIM 501	THE C.M.J. TRIO (EP)	50
69	Impression IMPL 1001	C.M.J. LIVE AT THE BANKHOUSE (LP, private pressing)	80

C.M.U. (CONTEMPORARY MUSIC UNIT)
72	Transatlantic BIG 508	Heart Of The Sun/Doctor Am I Normal?	15
71	Transatlantic TRA 237	OPEN SPACES (LP, gatefold sleeve, clear plastic with foam inner, this price for mint record that has not reacted and been marked by plastic/foam inner)	150
71	Transatlantic TRA 237	OPEN SPACES (LP, gatefold sleeve, clear plastic with foam inner, this price for mint sleeve with record that has been marked by chemical reaction to the plastic/foam inner)	50
72	Transatlantic TRA 259	SPACE CABARET (LP, with lyric insert)	100

(see also Chopyn)

COACHMEN
66	Columbia DB 8057	Gabrielle/Seasons In The Sun	8

COACHOUSE RHYTHM SECTION
77	Ice ICE 3 12	Nobody's Got Time/Nobody's Got Time	20
77	Ice ICE 3 12	Nobody Got Time/Time Warp (12")	80

(see also Eddy Grant)

COASTERS
57	London HLE 8450	Searchin'/Young Blood	75
57	London HL 7021	Searchin'/Young Blood (export issue)	30
58	London HLE 8665	Yakety Yak/Zing! Went The Strings Of My Heart	15
58	London HLE 8729	The Shadow Knows/Sorry But I'm Gonna Have To Pass	50
59	London HLE 8819	Charlie Brown/Three Cool Cats	10
59	London HL 7073	Charlie Brown/Three Cool Cats (export issue)	10
59	London HLE 8882	Along Came Jones/That Is Rock And Roll (silver top label)	15
59	London HLE 8938	Poison Ivy/I'm A Hog For You	15

(The above 45s were originally issued with triangular centres, later round centre copies are worth half to two-thirds these values.)

COASTERS (Jamaica)

MINT VALUE £

60	London HLE 9020	What About Us/Run Red Run	20
60	London HLK 9111	Besame Mucho (Parts 1 & 2)	50
60	London HLK 9111	Besame Mucho (Parts 1 & 2) (78)	50
60	London HLK 9151	Wake Me, Shake Me/Stewball	20
60	London HLK 9208	Shoppin' For Clothes/The Snake And The Bookworm	25
61	London HLK 9293	Wait A Minute/Thumbin' A Ride	15
61	London HLK 9349	Little Egypt/Keep On Rolling	15
61	London HLK 9413	Girls! Girls! Girls! (Parts 1 & 2)	15
62	London HLK 9493	(Ain't That) Just Like Me/Bad Blood	15
64	London HLK 9863	T'Ain't Nothin' To Me/Speedo's Back In Town	15
66	Atlantic 584 033	She's A Yum Yum/Saturday Night Fish Fry	12
67	Atlantic 584 087	Searchin'/Yakety Yak	10
67	CBS 2749	Soul Pad/Down Home Girl	15
68	Direction 58-3701	She Can/Everybody's Woman	10
72	Stateside SS 2201	Cool Jerk/Talkin' 'Bout A Woman	30
59	London REE 1203	THE COASTERS (EP)	25
60	London HA-E 2237	GREATEST HITS (LP)	50
63	London HA-K 8033	COAST ALONG WITH THE COASTERS (LP)	50
66	Atlantic 588 134	COAST ALONG WITH THE COASTERS (LP, reissue)	15
67	Atlantic 590 015	ALL TIME GREATEST HITS (LP)	15
71	Joy JOYS 189	HUNGRY (LP)	15

COASTERS (JAMAICA)

69	Doctor Bird DB 1182	Stoney Hill/RICK RODRIGUES & JOHNNY MOORE : Continental Shuffle	100

COAST ROAD DRIVE

74	Deram SML 1113	DELICIOUS AND REFRESHING (LP)	60

COAST TO COAST

79	Yorkie JB 102	The Hucklebuck/Telephone Baby (special die-cut sleeve)	10
82	Polydor POSP 451	The Bell/How Can I Be Sure	8

(see also Status Quo)

C.O.B. (CLIVE'S ORIGINAL BAND)

72	Polydor 2058 260	Blue Morning/Bones	15
71	CBS 69010	SPIRIT OF LOVE (LP, gatefold sleeve, orange label)	200
72	Polydor Folk Mill 2383 161	MOYSHE McSTIFF & THE TARTAN LANCERS OF THE SACRED HEART (LP, gatefold sleeve, red label)	400
06	Sunbeam SBRL2LP 5029	MOYSHE McSTIFF & THE TARTAN LANCERS OF THE SACRED HEART (2-LP, reissue)	20

(see also Famous Jug Band, Incredible String Band)

JIMMY COBB

00	Expansion EXP 76	So Nobody Else Can Hear/Pistachio	10

COBBLERS

70	Emblem JDR 314	WARM ARE THE SOUNDS (LP)	30

COBBLERS LAST

79	Banshee BAN 1012	BOOT IN THE DOOR (LP, with insert)	80

COBBS

69	Amalgamated AMG 845	Hot Buttered Corn/COUNT MACHUKI: It Is I	40
69	Amalgamated AMG 849	Space Doctor/LLOYD & DEVON: Baby Reggae	100

BILLY COBHAM

74	Atlantic K50037	CROSSWINDS (LP)	15
73	Atlantic K40506	SPECTRUM (LP, gatefold)	20

COBRA (1)

78	Rip Off RIP 3	Looking For A Lady/Graveyard Boogie (p/s)	35

(see also Speed)

COBRA (2)

85	Criminal Response COBRA 2	WARRIORS OF THE DEAD (LP)	18
87	Ebony EBON 39	BACK FROM THE DEAD (LP)	18

OODWCD

71	Private Pressing SJP 762	You'll Go far/Broken Web	10

COCHISE

70	United Artists UP 35134	Watch This Space/59th St. Bridge Song	6
70	Liberty LBS 15425	Love's Made A Fool Of You/Words Of A Dying Man	6
71	Liberty LBF 15460	Why I Sing The Blues/Jed Colider	6
70	United Artists UAS 29117	COCHISE (LP, gatefold sleeve, orange/pink label)	30
70	Liberty LBS 83428	SWALLOW TALES (LP, black label)	20
72	United Artists UAS 29286	SO FAR (LP)	25

(see also B.J. Cole, Mick Grabham)

DIB COCHRAN & EARWIGS

70	Bell BLL 1121	Oh Baby/Universal Love	500

(see also Marc Bolan, Tyrannosaurus Rex, Tony Visconti, Rick Wakeman)

EDDIE COCHRAN

78s

57	London HLU 8386	20 Flight Rock/Dark Lonely Street	50
57	London HLU 8433	Sittin' In The Balcony/Completely Sweet	60
58	London HLU 8702	Summertime Blues/Love Again	70
59	London HLU 8792	C'mon Everybody/Don't Ever Let Me Go	90
59	London HLU 8880	Teenage Heaven/I Remember	100
59	London HLU 8944	Somethin' Else/Boll Weevil Song	250
60	London HLW 9022	Hallelujah, I Love Her So/Little Angel	200
60	London HLG 9115	Three Steps To Heaven/Cut Across Shorty	400
95	Cruisin' The 50s CASS 001	Three Steps To Heaven/Cut Across Shorty (reissue, 300 only)	40
96	Cruisin' The 50s CASB 004	Week-End/Cherished Memories (reissue, 400 only)	30

Hank COCHRAN

MINT VALUE £

SINGLES
57	London HLU 8386	20 Flight Rock/Dark Lonely Street (silver writing, triangular centre)	100
57	London HLU 8386	20 Flight Rock/Dark Lonely Street (silver-top label with triangular centre)	125
57	London HLU 8386	20 Flight Rock/Dark Lonely Street (round centre)	50
57	London HLU 8433	Sittin' In The Balcony/Completely Sweet	350
58	London HLU 8702	Summertime Blues/Love Again	25
59	London HLU 8792	C'mon Everybody/Don't Ever Let Me Go	25
59	London HLU 8880	Teenage Heaven/I Remember	25
59	London HL 7082	Teenage Heaven/Boll Weevil Song (export issue)	20
59	London HLU 8944	Somethin' Else/Boll Weevil Song	30
60	London HLW 9022	Hallelujah, I Love Her So/Little Angel (triangular centre)	30

(The above 45s were originally issued with triangular centres, later round centre copies are worth half these values unless otherwise stated.)

60	London HLW 9022	Hallelujah, I Love Her So/Little Angel (round centre)	15
60	London HLG 9115	Three Steps To Heaven/Cut Across Shorty	10
60	London HLG 9196	Sweetie Pie/Lonely	40
61	London HLG 9362	Weekend/Cherished Memories	20
61	London HLG 9460	Jeannie, Jeannie, Jeannie/Pocketful Of Hearts	25
61	London HLG 9464	Pretty Girl/Teresa	35
61	London HLG 9467	Undying Love/Stockin's 'n' Shoes	50
62	Liberty LIB 10049	Never/Think Of Me	20
63	Liberty LIB 10088	My Way/Rock And Roll Blues	15
63	Liberty LIB 10108	Drive-In Show/I Almost Lost My Mind	15
64	Liberty LIB 10151	Skinny Jim/Nervous Breakdown (black label)	60
66	Liberty LIB 10233	C'mon Everybody/Summertime Blues	10
66	Liberty LIB 10249	Three Stars/Somethin' Else	20
67	Liberty LIB 10276	Three Steps To Heaven/Eddie's Blues	20
68	Liberty LBF 15071	Summertime Blues/Let's Get Together	10
68	Liberty LBF 15109	Somethin' Else/Milk Cow Blues	10
70	Liberty LBF 15366	C'mon Everybody/Mean When I'm Mad	10

EPs
59	London REU 1214	C'MON EVERYBODY (orange sleeve, triangular centre)	30
59	London REU 1214	C'MON EVERYBODY (orange sleeve, round centre)	20
59	London REU 1214	C'MON EVERYBODY (yellow sleeve, silver-top label)	30
59	London REU 1214	C'MON EVERYBODY (yellow sleeve, round centre)	20
60	London REU 1239	SOMETHIN' ELSE (triangular centre)	30
60	London REU 1239	SOMETHIN' ELSE (round centre)	20
60	London REG 1262	EDDIE'S HITS	30
61	London REG 1301	CHERISHED MEMORIES OF EDDIE COCHRAN	30
62	Liberty LEP 2052	NEVER TO BE FORGOTTEN	30
63	Liberty LEP 2090	CHERISHED MEMORIES (VOL.1)	20
63	Liberty LEP 2111	C'MON EVERYBODY (reissue)	15
63	Liberty LEP 2122	SOMETHIN' ELSE (reissue)	15
63	Liberty LEP 2123	CHERISHED MEMORIES OF EDDIE COCHRAN (reissue)	15
63	Liberty LEP 2124	EDDIE'S HITS (reissue)	15
64	Liberty LEP 2165	C'MON AGAIN	60
64	Liberty LEP 2180	STOCKIN'S 'N' SHOES	25

ALBUMS
58	London HA-U 2093	SINGIN' TO MY BABY (initial pressing with laminated rear sleeve)	250
58	London HA-U 2093	SINGIN' TO MY BABY (without laminated rear sleeve)	100
60	London HA-G 2267	THE EDDIE COCHRAN MEMORIAL ALBUM	80
62	Liberty LBY 1109	CHERISHED MEMORIES	50
63	Liberty LBY 1127	THE EDDIE COCHRAN MEMORIAL ALBUM (reissue)	15
63	Liberty LBY 1158	SINGIN' TO MY BABY (reissue)	20
64	Liberty LBY 1205	MY WAY	40
88	Liberty ECB 1	THE EDDIE COCHRAN BOX SET (6-LP box set with booklet)	40

HANK COCHRAN
68	Monument LMO 5020	HEART OF HANK (LP)	15

JACKIE LEE COCHRAN
57	Brunswick 05669	Ruby Pearl (with Jimmy Pruett)/Mama Don't You Think I Know	2000
57	Brunswick 05669	Ruby Pearl (with Jimmy Pruett)/Mama Don't You Think I Know (78)	250

COCK & WOODPECKERS
71	Newbeat 93	Every Day And Every Night/I Fall In Love Everyday	15

BRUCE COCKBURN
71	True North WTN 003	HIGH WINDS WHITE SKY (LP)	15
71	True North TNX 7	SUNWHEEL DANCE (LP)	15

JARVIS COCKER
06	Rough Trade RTRADLP 340	THE JARVIS COCKER RECORD (LP, with bonus one-sided 7")	35
09	Rough Trade RTRADLP 540	FURTHER COMPLICATIONS (LP with free 12")	25

(see also Pulp, Relaxed Muscle)

JOE COCKER
64	Decca F 11974	I'll Cry Instead/Precious Words	250
68	Regal Zonophone RZ 3006	Marjorine/New Age Of The Lily	8
68	Regal Zonophone RZ 3013	With A Little Help From My Friends/Something's Coming On	6
70	Regal Zonophone RZ 3027	The Letter/Space Captain	6
83	Island WIP 6818	Ruby Lee/Talking Back To The Night (export issue)	7
60s	Oak	JOE COCKER (EP, existence unconfirmed)	500
67	Action ACT 002 EP	RAG GOES MAD AT THE MOJO (33rpm EP, 2 tracks by Joe Cocker's Blues Band, in conjunction with Sheffield University rag magazine Twikker)	50
69	Regal Zono. LRZ 1006	WITH A LITTLE HELP FROM MY FRIENDS (LP, mono, red/silver label with "sold in the	120

COCKERSDALE

MINT VALUE £

69	Regal Zono. SLRZ 1006	WITH A LITTLE HELP FROM MY FRIENDS (LP, stereo, red/silver label with "sold in the U.K..." text)	70
69	Regal Zono. SLRZ 1011	JOE COCKER! (LP, red/silver label)	30
70	A&M AMLS 6002	MAD DOGS & ENGLISHMEN (2-LP, multifold gatefold sleeve, brown label)	20
71	Fly HIFLY 3	COCKER HAPPY (LP, gatefold sleeve)	20

(see also Grease Band, Made In Sheffield)

COCKERSDALE
85	EFDSS ESLP 001	PROSPECT PROVIDENCE (LP)	20

COCKNEY REJECTS
79	Small Wonder SW 19	Flares'N'Slippers/Police Star/I Wanna Be A Star (p/s)	15
79	EMI EMI 5008	I'm Not A Fool/East End (p/s)	6
80	EMI EMI 5035	Bad Man!/The New Song (p/s)	6
80	Zonophone Z 2	The Greatest Cockney Rip-Off/Hate Of The City (p/s, yellow vinyl)	7
80	Zonophone Z 4	I'm Forever Blowing Bubbles/West Side Boys (p/s)	8
80	Zonophone Z 6	We Can Do Anything/15 Nights (p/s)	6
80	Zonophone Z 10	We Are The Firm/War On The Terraces (p/s)	8
81	Zonophone Z 20	Easy Life/Motorhead/Hang 'Em High (p/s)	6
80	Zonophone ZONO 101	GREATEST HITS VOLUME 1 (LP)	20
80	Zonophone ZONO 102	GREATEST HITS VOLUME 2 (LP, with inner sleeve & poster)	20
81	Zonophone ZEM 101	GREATEST HITS VOLUME 3 (LIVE AND LOUD) (LP, gatefold)	15
85	Wonderful World WOW LP 2	UNHEARD REJECTS (LP)	15

COCKNEYS
64	Philips BF 1303	After Tomorrow/I'll Cry Each Night	10
64	Philips BF 1360	I Know You're Gonna Be Mine/Oh No You Won't	10

COCK SPARRER
77	Decca FR 13710	Runnin' Riot/Sister Suzie (demos in p/s)	200
77	Decca FR 13710	Runnin' Riot/Sister Suzie (no p/s)	40
77	Decca FR 13732	We Love You/Chip On My Shoulder (no p/s)	20
77	Decca LFR 13732	We Love You/Chip On My Shoulder (12" p/s, with photo insert, 7,500 only)	25
82	Carrere CAR 255	England Belongs To Me/Argy Bargy (p/s, beware of bootlegs With "fuzzy" looking label logo on sleeve)	40
83	Razor RAZ 9	SHOCK TROOPS (LP)	30
84	Syndicate SYNLP 7	RUNNIN' RIOT IN 84 (LP)	35
86	Razor RAZ 26	TRUE GRIT (LP)	35
87	Link LP 005	LIVE AND LOUD (LP)	15

(see also Little Roosters, Guttersnipes)

COCKTAIL CABINET
67	Page One POF 046	Puppet On A String/Breathalyser	40

COCOA TEA
88	Live And Love LLD 87	Lonesome Side/ADMIRAL TIBET: Reality Time (12")	30

COCONUT DOGS
80	Mongrel Music MM 001	Lipstick On The Glass/The Neighbours/Mannequin (no p/s, 1000 only)	50
81	Rialto TREB 136	Officers Mess/Germinate (p/s)	7

COCO STEEL AND LOVEBOMB
89	Instant INST 10	Frenzy/Version	20
91	Instant VU 004	Feel It/Discotechno/Discodub (12")	15
91	Instant VU 005	Touch It (African Plain Mix)/(Butch Mix)/(Sandeed Shore Mix) (12")	20

COCTEAU TWINS
82	4AD AD 303	LULLABIES EP (Feathers Oar Blades/Alas DIes Laughing/It's All But An Ark-Lark) (12")	10
83	4AD BAD 314	SUNBURST AND SNOWBLIND EP: Sugar Hiccup (extended Version)/From The Flagstones/Hitherto/Because Of Whirl-Jack (12")	10
83	4AD AD 303	PEPPERMINT PIG EP (Peppermint Pig (7" Version)/Laugh Lines/Hazel/Pepperment Pig (12" Extended Version) (12")	10
83	4AD AD 303	Peppermint Pig/Laugh Lines (p/s)	10
84	4AD BAD 405	THE SPANGLE MAKER EP (The Spangle Maker/Pearly Dewdrops Drops (12" Version)/Pepper Tree/Pearly Dedrops Drops (7" Version) (12")	10
85	4AD BAD 501	AIKEA GUINEA EP (Aikea Guinea/Kookaburra/Quisquose/Rococo) (12")	10
85	4AD BAD 510	TINY DYNAMITE EP (Pink Orange Red/Ribbed And Veined/Sultitan Itan/Plain TIger) (12")	10
85	4AD BAD 511	ECHOES IN A SHALLOW BAY EP (Great Spangled Fritillary/Melonella/Pale Clouded White/Eggs And Their Shells) (12")	10
86	4AD BAD 610	LOVES EASY TEARS EP (Loves Easy Tears/Those Eyes, That Mouth/Sighs Smell Of Farewell/Orange Applied) (12")	10
93	Fontana CT 1	Evangeline/Mud & Dark (p/s, numbered)	8
93	Fontana CTX 1	Evangeline/Mud & Dark/Summer Blink (12", p/s, numbered, insert)	20
94	Fontana CT 2	Bluebeard/Three Swept (p/s)	7
94	Fontana CTX 2	Bluebeard/Three Swept/Ice-Pulse (12", gatefold p/s)	15
95	Fontana CT 3	Rilkean Heart/Golden Vein/Pink Orange Red/Half Gifts (2 x 7", p/s)	20
96	Fontana CTX 4	OTHERNESS EP (12", p/s, inner)	20
96	Fontana CTX 6	Violaine/Alice/Tranquil Eye (12", p/s)	20
91	4AD CT BOX 1	COCTEAU TWINS - SINGLES COLLECTION (9-CD box set)	40
82	4AD CAD 411	GARLANDS (LP)	30
83	4AD CAD 313	HEAD OVER HEELS (LP)	30
84	4AD CAD 412	TREASURE (LP, inner)	30
86	4AD CAD 602	VICTORIALAND (LP, inner)	30
88	4AD CAD 807	BLUE BELL KNOLL (LP, tri-foldout sleeve, inner)	30
90	4AD CAD 0012	HEAVEN OR LAS VEGAS (LP, with inner)	35
91	4AD CT BOX 1	SINGLES COLLECTION (10-CD box set)	50
93	Fontana 518259-1	FOUR CALENDAR CAFE (LP)	125
96	Fontana 514-501-1	MILK AND KISSES (LP, inner)	125
05	4AD CTBOX 2	LULLABIES TO VIOLAINE (4-CD box set, tactile cover)	40

Bill CODAY

			MINT VALUE £
10	Vinyl 180 VIN180LP024	BOX SET ONE (5-LP, 1 x 12", box set)	125
14	4AD CAD 3420	HEAVEN OR LAS VEGAS (LP, 180 gm reissue, inner, download card)	18
15	4AD CAD 3509	THE PINK OPAQUE (LP, compilation, reissue)	15
17	Mercury 5735405	FOUR CALENDAR CAFE (2-LP reissue, purple/blue vinyl)	25
17	Mercury 5735401	MILK AND KISSES (2-LP reissue, white vinyl)	25

(see also This Mortal Coil, Felt, Massive Attack, Harold Budd, Lonely Is An Eyesore, The Future Sound Of London, Elizabeth Fraser, Drowning Craze)

BILL CODAY
01	Grapevine G2K 45 117	A Man Can't Be A Man (Without A Woman)/SANDRA WRIGHT: A Man Can't Be A Man (Without A Woman)	10

CODE BLUE
94	Dee Jay DJX 018	Angels In Dub/Angels In Rhythm (12")	12

CODEK
80	MCA MCA 550	Me Me Me/Demo (p/s)	6
80	MCA MCAT 550	Me Me Me (Full Length Version)/Demo (12", p/s)	25
82	Island 12WIP 6764	Tim Toum/Closer (12", p/s)	40

CODENAME JOHN
94	Prototype PRO 001	Deep Inside Of Me/(Inta) The Anthem (12")	12
94	Prototype PRO 002	Kindred/Dreams Of Heaven (Shorty's Mix) (12", as John)	10

CODE OF PRACTICE
95	Certificate 18 CERT 1813	Can We Change The Future/Remix (12")	10

CODE 071
92	Reinforced RIVET 1213	A London Sumtin' (12")	20

C.O.D.S
66	Stateside SS 489	Michael (The Lover)/Cry No More	25
66	Stateside SS 489	Michael (The Lover)/Cry No More (DJ copy)	60

CODY
71	Polydor 2058-100	I Belong With You/Wanna Make You Happy	6

TONY CODY
72	Pye 7N 45153	Walk On By/(Ain't It) Funny How Time Slips By	30
72	Pye 7N 45153	Walk On By/(Ain't It) Funny How Time Slips By (DJ Copy)	50

JAMIE COE
59	Parlophone R 4600	Summertime Symphony/There's Gonna Be A Day	150
60	Parlophone R 4621	School Day Blues/I'll Go On Loving You	100
61	HMV POP 991	How Low Is Low/Little Dear Little Darling	25
63	London HLX 9713	The Fool/I've Got That Feeling Again	20

PETER & CHRIS COE
72	Trailer LER 2077	OPEN THE DOOR AND LET US IN (LP)	25
76	Trailer LER 2098	OUT OF SEASON, OUT OF RHYME (LP, yellow label)	20
79	Highway SHY 7007	GAME OF ALL FOURS (LP)	15

(see also Bandoggs)

TONY COE (QUINTET)
61	Philips B 10784L	SWINGIN' TILL THE GIRLS COME HOME (LP)	50
67	Columbia SCX 6170	TONY'S BASEMENT (LP)	100
78	Lee Lambert LAM100	COE-EXISTENCE (LP)	20

TONY COE & BRIAN LEMON TRIO
68	'77' SEU 12/41	TONY COE AND BRIAN LEMON TRIO (LP)	30

(see also Robert Farnon & Tony Coe)

JACK & CHARLIE COEN
77	Topic 12TS 337	THE BRANCH LINE (LP)	22

CARLTON COFFE
78	Justice JUS 110	Chant Away/Version (12")	45

COFFEE BAR SKIFFLERS
58	Embassy WEP 1008	SKIFFLE SESSION (EP)	10

(see also Chas McDevitt Skiffle Group)

CARLTON COFFEE
78	Shebazz FME 003	Music Revoluion/Music Revolution Part 2	25

COFFEE SET
69	Mercury MF 1113	Happy Birthday/Our Anniversary	6
69	Fontana LPS 16503	SAY IT WITH MUSIC (LP)	15

DENNIS COFFEY
72	A&M AMS 7010	Getting It On/Ride Sally Ride	8
71	A&M AMS 875	Scorpio/Sad Song (with Detroit Guitar Band)	20
70	A&M AMLS 68035	EVOLUTION (LP)	25
71	A&M AMLS 68072	GOIN' FOR MYSELF (LP)	20
74	Sussex LPSX 9	INSTANT COFFEY (LP)	20

ALMA COGAN
53	HMV 7M 106	I Went To Your Wedding/You Belong To Me	15
53	HMV 7M 107	To Be Loved By You/The Homing Waltz (B-side with Larry Day)	15
53	HMV 7M 166	Over And Over Again/Isn't Life Wonderful (with Les Howerd)	15
54	HMV 7M 173	Ricochet (Rick-O-Shay)/The Moon Is Blue	15
54	HMV 7M 188	Bell Bottom Blues/Love Me Again	25
54	HMV 7M 196	Make Love To Me/Said The Little Moment	15
54	HMV 7M 219	The Little Shoemaker/Chiqui-Chaqui (Chick-ee Chock-ee)	20
54	HMV 7M 228	Little Things Mean A Lot/Canoodlin' Rag	15
54	HMV 7M 239	Skinnie Minnie (Fishtail)/What Am I Going To Do, Ma (The Doo-Ma Song)	20
54	HMV 7M 269	This Ole House/Skokiaan	20
54	HMV 7M 271	I Can't Tell A Waltz From A Tango/Christmas Cards	20
55	HMV 7M 286	Paper Kisses/Softly, Softly	10
55	HMV 7M 293	Chee-Chee-Oo-Chee (Sang The Little Bird)/Tika Tika Tok	10
55	HMV 7M 301	Tweedlee-Dee/More Than Ever Now	15

Don COGAN

MINT VALUE £

55	HMV 7M 316	Got'n Idea/Give A Fool A Chance	15
55	HMV 7M 337	Never Do A Tango With An Eskimo/Twenty Tiny Fingers	15
56	HMV 7M 367	Love And Marriage/Sycamore Tree	15
56	HMV 7M 415	Why Do Fools Fall In Love?/ (The Same Thing Happen With) The Birds And The Bees?	20
56	HMV POP 239	Mama Teach Me To Dance/I'm In Love Again	20
56	HMV POP 261	In The Middle Of The House/Two Innocent Hearts	20
57	HMV POP 284	You, Me And Us/Three Brothers	15
57	HMV POP 317	Whatever Lola Wants (Lola Gets)/Lucky Lips	30
57	HMV POP 367	Fabulous/Summer Love	10
57	HMV POP 415	Party Time/Please Mister Brown (Mister Jones, Mister Smith)	10
59	HMV POP 670	We Got Love/I Don't Mind Being All Alone	8
64	Columbia DB 7390	It's You/I Knew Right Away	20
65	Columbia DB 7652	Snakes And Snails (And Puppy Dog Tails)/How Many Days, How Many Nights	20
65	Columbia DB 7786	Eight Days A Week/Help!	10
55	HMV 7EG 8122	THE GIRL WITH A LAUGH IN HER VOICE (EP)	10
55	HMV 7EG 8151	THE GIRL WITH A LAUGH IN HER VOICE NO. 2 (EP)	10
56	HMV 7EG 8169	THE GIRL WITH A LAUGH IN HER VOICE NO. 3 (EP)	10
57	HMV 7EG 8437	SHE LOVES TO SING (EP)	10
58	HMV CLP 1152	I LOVE TO SING (LP)	30
61	Columbia 33SX 1345	ALMA SINGS WITH YOU IN MIND (LP, mono)	20
62	Columbia 33SX 1469	HOW ABOUT LOVE! (LP, mono)	20
61	Columbia SCX 3391	ALMA SINGS WITH YOU IN MIND (LP)	30
62	Columbia SCX 3459	HOW ABOUT LOVE! (LP, stereo)	30
67	Columbia SX 6130	ALMA (LP)	30

(see also Ronnie Hilton, Angela & Fans)

DON COGAN

58	MGM MGM 984	The Fountain Of Youth/I'm Takin' Over	25

SHAYE COGAN

58	Columbia DB 4055	Billy Be Sure/Doodle Doodle Doo	10
60	MGM MGM 1063	Mean To Me/They Said It Couldn't Be Done	30

(see also Buddy Morrow)

ALAN COHEN BAND

72	Argo ZDA 159	BLACK, BROWN AND BEIGE (LP)	80

LEONARD COHEN

68	CBS 3337	Suzanne/So Long, Marianne	7
69	CBS 4245	Bird On The Wire/Seems So Long Ago, Nancy	7
71	CBS 7292	Joan Of Arc/Diamonds In The Mine	7
74	CBS 2494	Bird On The Wire (live)/Tonight Will Be Fine (live)	7
74	CBS 2699	Lover Lover Lover/Who By Fire	6
76	CBS 4306	Suzanne/Take This Longing	6
77	CBS 5882	Memories/Don't Go Home With Your Hard-On	6
78	CBS 6095	True Love Leaves No Traces/I Left A Woman Waiting	6
68	CBS BPG 63241	SONGS OF LEONARD COHEN (LP, orange label, with stickered sleeve; mono)	35
68	CBS (S)BPG 63241	SONGS OF LEONARD COHEN (LP, orange label, with stickered sleeve; stereo)	30
68	CBS 63241	SONGS OF LEONARD COHEN (LP, orange label, re-pressing w/out prefix)	15
69	CBS M 63587	SONGS FROM A ROOM (LP, laminated sleeve, mono)	45
69	CBS 63587	SONGS FROM A ROOM (LP, laminated sleeve, stereo)	35
71	CBS S 69004	SONGS OF LOVE & HATE (LP, orange label, with booklet)	25
73	CBS 65224	LIVE SONGS (LP)	15
74	CBS 69087	NEW SKIN FOR THE OLD CEREMONY (LP)	20
75	CBS 69161	GREATEST HITS (LP, inner and insert, orange/yellow vinyl)	20
77	CBS 86042	DEATH OF A LADIES MAN (LP, gatefold)	20
79	CBS 86097	RECENT SONGS (LP)	18
84	CBS 465569	VARIOUS POSITIONS (LP)	20
88	CBS 460642	I'M YOUR MAN (LP)	15
92	Columbia COL 472498 1	THE FUTURE (LP)	40
97	Simply Vinyl SVLP 008	SONGS FROM A ROOM (LP, reissue, 180gm vinyl)	20
10	Music On Vinyl MOVLP 193	SONGS FROM THE ROAD (2-LP)	20
12	Columbia C 79871	OLD IDEAS (LP)	20

PHILIP COHRAN AND THE ARTISTIC HERITAGE ENSEMBLE

10	Jazzman JMAN 077	THE ZULU 45S COLLECTION (3 x 7" box set)	35

COIL (1)

79	North'ton Wood H. HAV 1	Motor Industry/Alcoholic Stork (p/s)	25

COIL (2)

85	F & F/K.422 FFK 512	Panic/Tainted Love/Aqua Regis (12", red vinyl, 'hair'-textured p/s)	25
85	F & F/K.422 FFK 512	Panic/Tainted Love/Aqua Regis (12", black vinyl, 'hair'-textured p/s)	25
86	Force & Form/K.422	The Anal Staircase/Blood From The Air/Ravenous (12", p/s, on clear vinyl)	25
86	Force & Form/K.422 ROTA 121	The Anal Staircase/Blood From The Air/Ravenous (12", p/s)	15
87	Solar Lodge 001	HELLRAISER (10" EP, coloured vinyl [clear or pink, 500 each])	25
90	Shock SX 002	Wrong Eye/Scope (pink p/s, signed & lettered A-Z, 26 only)	45
90	Shock SX 002	Wrong Eye/Scope (974 with numbered white p/s)	15
90	Shock SX 002	Wrong Eye/Scope (1,000 with un-numbered yellow p/s)	10
90	Shock SX 002	Wrong Eye/Scope (green p/s, 300 only, some with gold/black sticker)	25
92	Clawfist 22	Airborne Bells/Is Suicide A Solution (p/s, 1,250 only)	25
94	Loci S1	Themes From Blue (p/s, 23 on yellow vinyl)	60
94	Loci S1	Themes From Blue (p/s, 1,000 on blue vinyl)	20
94	Eskaton 001	Nasa Arab/First Dark Ride (12", stickered plain black sleeve, 2,500 only)	15
95	Eskaton 003	PHILM (10" EP, with poster, 50 on clear vinyl in handmade p/s)	60
95	Eskaton 003	PHILM (10" EP, with poster, 2,000 only)	12

COINS

			MINT VALUE £
84	FFK1	SCATOLOGY (LP, with pasted anal staircase postcard, some with poster)	200
86	Threshold ROTA 1	HORSE ROTORVATOR (LP, with A5 card insert & stickers)	20
87	Threshold House LOCI 1	GOLD IS THE METAL (LP, red vinyl; with bonus 7": "The Wheel"/The Wheal, unfinished proof sleeve without writing, 25 only)	200
87	Threshold House LOCI 1	GOLD IS THE METAL (LP, box set with 7", "The Wheel"/"The Wheal", poster & booklet in black linen folder, embossed sleeve, autographed, 55 only)	300
87	Threshold House LOCI 1	GOLD IS THE METAL (LP, red vinyl [150 only] with inner sleeve; with bonus 7": "The Wheel"/"The Wheal")	70
87	Threshold House LOCI 1	GOLD IS THE METAL (LP, clear vinyl [500 only], with inner sleeve; with bonus 7": "The Wheel"/"The Wheal")	50
90	Normal NORMAL 77	GOLD IS THE METAL (LP, black vinyl re-pressing with 7": The Wheel/"Keel Hauler")	18
95	Eskaton 007	WORSHIP THE GLITCH (2 x 10" LP, as Coil Vs. Elph, with insert, 50 with white optical plastic cover)	100
95	Eskaton 007	WORSHIP THE GLITCH (2 x 10" LP, as Coil Vs. Elph, with insert, 2,000 only)	50
99	Acme/Prescription DRUG8	ASTRAL DISASTER (LP, 99 copies signed and numbered by Balance And Christopherson, with insert, artwork in plastic bag)	100
99	Chalice GRAAL LP002	MUSICK TO PLAY IN THE DARK VOL 1 (LP, 500 only, white vinyl)	200
00	Threshold House LOC114	ASTRAL DISASTER (LP re-issue, 100 copies, grey vinyl signed lyric sheet and art	60
00	Chalice GRAAL LP004	MUSICK TO PLAY IN THE DARK VOL 2 (2 x LP, white vinyl, one side etched)	200
00	Chalice GRAAL LP004	MUSICK TO PLAY IN THE DARK VOL 2 (2 x LP, 100 copies with blue/green vinyl)	250
00	Chalice GRAAL LP004	MUSICK TO PLAY IN THE DARK VOL 2 (2 x LP, translucent purple, 4th side etched with picture of moon and has 'gold leaf' attached, art print on cover, 2 part print inserts – signed – 60 copies only)	300
00	Chalice GRAAL LP004	MUSICK VOL 2 (26 copy "trauma edition" lettered A-Z white sleeves smeared with Balance's blood.)	70
02	Eskaton 28	TIME MACHINES (Coil as Time Machines) (2 x LP, 1,000 55 clear, signed)	50
02	Eskaton 28	TIME MACHINES (Coil as Time Machines) (2 x LP, 1,000 only)	40

(see also Psychic TV, Throbbing Gristle, Current 93)

COINS
69	Toast TT 513	Love Power/You Can't Get Away From It	8
69	Toast TT 515	Don't You Know It's Just A Game, Love? (actually by Miss White & Mr. Green)/Crying Over You	6

ALVADEAN COKER
55	London HLU 8191	Do Dee Oodle De Do I'm In Love/We're Gonna Bop	750
55	London HLU 8191	Do Dee Oodle De Do I'm In Love/We're Gonna Bop (78)	60

SANDY COKER & HIS BAND
54	London HL 8109	Meadowlark Melody/Toss Over	40

COKI
05	DMZ DMZ 004	Officer/Mood Dub (12")	20
06	Tempa TEMPA 024	Tortured/Shattered (12")	15
07	Big Apple BAM 009	Red Eye/Beep/The Sign/Hidden Treasure (12")	18
07	SMZ DMZ 013	Spongebob/The End (12")	20

RIC COLBECK QUARTET
70	Fontana 6383 001	THE SUN IS COMING UP (LP)	75

COLD BLOOD
70	Atlantic 584 319	You Got Me Hummin'/If You Will	10
70	Atlantic 588 218	COLD BLOOD (LP, plum/red label)	50
71	Atlantic 2400 102	SISYPHUS (LP, gatefold sleeve, plum/red label)	18
74	Warner Bros K 56247	LYDIA (LP)	15

COLD CAVE
11	Matador OLE 921 1	CHERISH THE LIGHT YEARS (LP)	20

COLDCUT
91	Ninja Tune ZEN12 004	Jade (12")	15
94	Ninja Tune ZEN 12	PHILOSOPHY (2xLP, promo, different mixes to commercial release)	20
97	Ninja Tune ZEN 30	LET US PLAY (2-LP)	30

COLD FISH
82	CBS A2779	Love Me Today/Strange Boy (p/s)	6

COLD FLY
73	Bus Stop BUS 1007	Caterpillar/Yesterday Started For Judy	15

COLD HAND BAND
82	BK BK 12	Tropicana/Instrumental	12

COLDPLAY

SINGLES
98	private pressing HGCD 633	SAFETY EP: Bigger, Stronger/No More Keeping My Feet On The Ground/Such A Rush (CD, 500 only)	400
99	Fierce Panda NING 68	Brothers And Sisters/Easy To Please (wraparound p/s, 1000 only)	30
99	Fierce Panda NING 68CD	Brothers And Sisters/Easy To Please/Only Superstition	8
99	EMI EMI CDR 6528	THE BLUE ROOM EP (Bigger, Stronger/Don't Panic/See You Soon/High Speed/Such A Rush) (CD, digipak)	30
99	EMI EMI 12R 6528	THE BLUE ROOM EP (Bigger, Stronger/Don't Panic/See You Soon/High Speed/Such A Rush) (12", numbered sleeve)	100
00	Parlophone R 6536	Shiver/For You/Careful Where You Stand (p/s)	8
00	Parlophone R 6538	Yellow/Help Is Around The Corner (7" ltd edn. Numbered single p/s)	25
00	Parlophone R 6549	Trouble/Brothers And Sisters (p/s, numbered, stickered poly outer)	10
01	COLDXMAS01	Mince Spies/Have Yourself A Merry Little Christmas/Yellow (Alpha Mix) (CD EP, 1000 only, given away with Coldplayground fanzine)	150
01	Parlophone 07243 879080-6-2	Don't Panic/You Only Live Twice (live)/Bigger Stronger (live) (12" p/s, withdrawn)	60
02	Parlophone R 6588	The Scientist/1:36/I Ran Away (p/s)	7
03	Parlophone R 6594	Clocks/Crest Of Waves (p/s)	7
03	Parlophone 12 R 6594	Clocks (Roykoopp Trembling Heart Mix)/Roykoopp Trembling Heart Instrumental Mix/God Put A Smile Upon Your Face (Def Inc. Remix feat. Mr. Thing) (12", die-cut sleeve, 1000 only)	10
05	Parlophone R 6671	Fix You/The World Turned Upside Down	8

COLD TURKEY

MINT VALUE £

08	Parlophone 5099926473710	PROSPEKT'S MARCH EP (12")	12
07	Parlophone 3883247	THE SINGLES 1999 - 2006 (15 x 7" box set)	50
09	Parlophone R 676	Life In Technicolour II/The Goldrush	10
12	Parlophone R6851	Up With The Birds/UFO (die-cut sleeve)	8
13	Parlophone R6901	Hurts Like Heaven/Up Against The World (live) (picture disc with comic)	8

ALBUMS

00	Parlophone 5277831	PARACHUTES (LP, inner)	20
02	Parlophone 540 5041	A RUSH OF BLOOD TO THE HEAD (LP, gatefold sleeve, with inner)	18
05	Parlophone 474 7861	X&Y (LP, gatefold sleeve with slip case and poster)	18
11	Parlophone P 729 7262	MYLO XYLOTO (LP in pop up sleeve with 12" picture disc and stencil)	25
11	EMI 087 5531	MYLO XYLOTO (LP with poster)	18

PROMOS

98	None	Ode To Deodorant/Brothers And Sisters (2-track cassette sent to concert promoters and radio DJ's. White label, attributed to The Coldplay with "contact Phil" and 0777 mobile no.)	400
99	Parlophone CDRDJ 6528	THE BLUE ROOM EP (Bigger, Stronger/Don't Panic/See You Soon/High Speed/ Such A Rush) (CD digipak)	40
99	Parlophone 12RDJ 6528	THE BLUE ROOM EP (Bigger, Stronger/Don't Panic/See You Soon/High Speed/ Such A Rush) (12", blue cover)	60
00	Parlophone 12RDJ 6538	Yellow/Help Is Round The Corner/No More Keeping My Feet On The Ground (12")	15
06	Parlophone (No cat no)	Talk (FK Dub Mix) 12" one-sided acetate 10 only DJ copies)	40
06	Parlophone (No cat. no)	Clocks (Royksopp remixes) (12" promo. die-cut sleeve)	10
08	Parlophone VIVA 001	VIVA LA VIDA (OR DEATH AND ALL HIS FRIENDS) (LP, promo, 300 only)	80

COLD TURKEY

| 72 | Pye 7N 45142 | Nobody's Fool/Sesame Street .... | 15 |

COLD WAR

| 83 | Namedrop NR 4 | The Machinist/Illusion (p/s) .... | 15 |

COLD WARRIOR

| 96 | Alphaphone ALPHA 006 | Yellow Square/Walk East/Witch Hunt/Modern Art (12") .... | 40 |

(see also Cabaret Voltaire, Richard H. Kirk)

ANN COLE

| 84 | Krazy Kat KK 782 | GOT MY MOJO WORKING (LP) .... | 15 |

BILLY COLE

| 75 | Power Exchange 104 | Extra Careful/Bump All Night .... | 20 |

B.J. COLE

| 73 | United Artists UAS 29418 | NEW HOVERING DOG (LP, laminated front sleeve) .... | 30 |

(see also Cochise)

CINDY COLE

| 65 | Columbia DB 7519 | A Love Like Yours/He's Sure The Boy I Love .... | 25 |
| 66 | Columbia DB 7973 | Just Being Your Baby (Turns Me On)/Lonely City Blue Boy .... | 30 |

(see also Jeannie & Big Guys)

CLAY COLE

| 62 | London HLP 9499 | Twist Around The Clock/Don't Twist (With Anyone Else But Me) .... | 10 |

KEITH COLE

| 71 | Big BG 315 | Musical Attack/RUPIE EDWARDS ALLSTARS: Shack Attack .... | 8 |
| 71 | Big BG 316 | Music Alone Version 3/RUPIE EDWARDS ALLSTARS: Behold Another Version .... | 8 |

LLOYD COLE & COMMOTIONS

84	Welcome To L. Vegas LC 1	Are You Ready To Be Heartbroken?/Down At The Mission (p/s, withdrawn)	30
85	Polydor COLET 5	Lost Weekend (extended)/Big World/Lost Weekend - (7" version) (10" p/s)	8
84	Polydor LCLP 1	RATTLESNAKES (LP)	15
85	Poldyor LCLP 2	EASY PIECES (LP)	15
93	Phonogram 518318-1	BAD VIBES (LP, as Lloyd Cole)	20

MJ COLE

| 00 | Talkin Loud 542 591-1 | SINCERE (4-LP) .... | 25 |

NAT COLE

70	Jackpot JP 717	Pack Of Cards/RITA & NAT COLE: Spread Joy	10
70	Jackpot JP 718	Love Making/SONNY BINNS & RITA: My Love	20
70	Jackpot JP 722	Sugar Sugar/SONNY BINNS & RITA: Sign Off	10
70	Explosion EX 2022	In The Summertime/Apollo Moon Walk	12
70	Creole CR 1002	Me And My Life/Instrumental	10

(see also Rita Alston)

NIKKI COLE

| 70s | Dance Centre 023 | ELEMENTARY MODERN DANCE (LP) .... | 40 |
| 70s | Dance Centre DC020 | CONTEMPORARY DANCE - BEGINNERS VOL 1. (LP) .... | 40 |

PATSY COLE

| 66 | Island WI 271 | Disappointed Bride/EARL BOSTIC: Honeymoon Night .... | 45 |

STRANGER COLE

63	R&B JB 133	Out Of Many/Nothing Tried	25
63	Island WI 110	Stranger At The Door/Conqueror	25
63	Island WI 114	Last Love/STRANGER & KEN: Hush Baby	25
63	Island WI 126	We Are Rolling/Millie Maw	25
64	Island WI 137	Goodbye Peggy (actually plays "Goodbye Peggy Darling" by Roy Panton)/ BABA BROOKS: Portrait Of My Love	25
64	R&B JB 129	Morning Star/Beat Up Your Gum	18
64	Island WI 133	Til My Dying Days/STRANGER & PATSY: I Need You	20
64	Black Swan WI 413	Uno Dos Tres (act. with Ken Boothe)/Look (B-side actually by unknown artist)	20
64	Black Swan WI 415	Summer Day/Loving You Always (both actually by Dottie & Bonnie)	20
64	Black Swan WI 435	Little Boy Blue/ERIC MORRIS: Words Of Wisdom	20
65	Ska Beat JB 192	Pussy Cat/MAYTALS: Sweet Sweet Jenny	25
65	Island WI 169	Koo Koo Doo (with Owen & Leon)/GLORIA & DREAMLETTS: Stay Where You Are	30
65	Island WI 177	Run Joe (with Baba Brooks)/Make Believe	40

Tony COLE

MINT VALUE £

65	Blue Beat BB 322	When The Party Is Over/BUSTER'S ALLSTARS: Happy Independence '65	30
65	Blue Beat BB 333	Matilda (actually with Prince Buster)/BUSTER'S ALL STARS: When The Party Is Over	35
66	Doctor Bird DB 1025	We Shall Overcome/Do You Really Love Me (as Stranger Cole & Seraphines)	40
66	Doctor Bird DB 1040	Drop The Ratchet/Oh Yee Mahee (as Stranger Cole & Conquerors)	45
67	Doctor Bird DB 1066	You Took My Love (actually by Patsy Todd)/FUGITIVES: Living Soul	300
68	Island WI 3154	Jeboza Macoo/Now I Know (B-side actually with Gladdy Anderson)	70
68	Amalgamated AMG 801	Just Like A River (as Stranger Cole & Gladdy)/LEADERS: Hope Someday	30
69	Amalgamated AMG 838	What Mama Na Want She Get/We Two	30
69	Duke DU 27	Glad You're Living/Help Wanted	40
69	Unity UN 501	Last Flight To Reggae City (w/ Tommy McCook)/JUNIOR SMITH: Watch Dem Go	30
69	Unity UN 514	When I Get My Freedom/Life Can Be Beautiful	40
69	Escort ES 810	Pretty Cottage/To Me	40
69	Escort ES 811	Why Did You/Do You Remember	25
69	Escort ES 819	Leana Leana/Na Na Na	25
69	Escort ES 826	Loneliness/Remember	25
70	Escort ES 830	Little Things/Till The Well Runs Dry	15
70	Escort ES 831	Everything With You/Picture On The Wall	10
70	Escort ES 832	Pussy/Let Me In	10
70	Camel CA 54	Everyday Tomorrow/Let Your Head Up High	40
70	Pama PM 790	Come Dance With Me/Dance With Me	10
71	Bullet BU 488	Soul Sop/Stranger Cole Medley	15
71	Camel CA 72	Crying Every Night/DENNIS ALCAPONE & DELROY WILSON: It Must Come	15
71	Escort ERT 849	Tomorrow/SONNY BURKE: Chicken Thief	12
72	Tropical AL 0011	Mail Man (with Charlie Ace)/Mail Man (Version)	15
72	Jackpot JP 791	My Confession/LASCELS & HORTENSE: The Might Organ	15
72	Pama PM 848	The House Where Bombo Lives/Our High School Dance	19

(see also Stranger, Stranger & Gladys, Stranger & Patsy, Stranger & Ken, Rob Walker, Charmers, Lloyd Clarke, Don Drummond, Tommy McCook, Delroy Wilson, Lester Sterling, Baba Brooks, Roland Alphonso, Roy Richards)

TONY COLE
69	Columbia DB 8604	If I Were A Cat/Magdalena	10

BOBBY COLEMAN
66	Pye International 7N 25365	(Baby) You Don't Have To Tell Me/Pleasure Girl	70
66	Pye International 7N 25365	(Baby) You Don't Have To Tell Me/Pleasure Girl (DJ Copy)	100

LONNIE COLEMAN & JESSE ROBERTSON
56	London HLU 8335	Dolores Diane/Oh Honey, Why Don'tcha	40

ORNETTE COLEMAN
60	Contemporary LAC 12228	TOMORROW IS THE QUESTION (LP)	50
61	London Jazz LTZ-K 15199	CHANGE OF THE CENTURY (LP, mono)	50
61	London Jazz SAH-K 5099	CHANGE OF THE CENTURY (LP, stereo)	60
61	London Jazz LTZ-K 15228	THIS IS OUR MUSIC (LP, mono)	50
62	London Jazz LTZ-K 15241	THE ORNETTE COLEMAN QUARTET (LP, mono)	40
62	London Jazz SAH-K 6235	THE ORNETTE COLEMAN QUARTET (LP, stereo)	45
62	Atlantic 588121	ORNETTE ON TENOR (LP)	40
65	Fontana SFJ 923	TOWN HALL DECEMBER 1962 (LP)	30
66	Atlantic 588022	THE SHAPE OF JAZZ TO COME (LP, mono/stereo)	40
67	CBS 66023	CHAPPAQUA SUITE (2-LP)	50
68	Polydor 623 246/7	AN EVENING WITH ORNETTE COLEMAN (2-LP)	40
69	Impulse SIPL 518	ORNETTE AT 12 (LP)	35
71	Atlantic 2400 109	THE AT OF THE IMPROVISERS (LP)	20
72	Atlantic K 40278	TWINS (LP)	25
77	Blue Note BNS 40021	AT THE GOLDEN CIRCLE STOCKHOLM (LP, reissue)	20
82	CBS 85934	BROKEN SHADOWS (LP)	20
82	Antilles AN2001	OF HUMAN FEELINGS (LP)	20

COLETTE & BANDITS
65	Stateside SS 416	A Ladies Man/Lost Love	20

COLEY
70s	Coley (Private Pressing)	GOODBYE BRAIN (LP)	35

NORMAN 'STAR' COLIN & MYSTIC MURPHY
81	Awawak ARK DD 037	You Never Know/Studio 80 Shank (12")	20

NIK COLK VOID
12	O Genesis OGEN 007	Gold E (7", with playable sleeve)	15

(see also Factory Floor)

COLLAGE
73	Studio Two TWO 410	MISTY (LP)	30

(see also Brian Bennett)

COLLECTIVE HORIZONTAL
79	Dolmen DO 1	COLLECTIVE HORIZONTAL EP (gatefold p/s, stickered white labels)	20

COLLECTORS (CANADA)
70	London HLU 10304	I Must Have Been Blind/The Beginning	6
69	Warner Bros WS 1774	GRASS AND WILD STRAWBERRIES (LP)	22

(see also Chilliwack, Electric Prunes)

COLLECTORS (U.K.)
80	Central Collection COL 1	Different World/Talking Hands (p/s)	15

COLLEGE
11	Valerie (No Cat. No.)	A Real Hero/Instrumental Version (p/s, 300 only)	60
13	Invada INV113LP	SECRET DIARY (LP)	15
13	Invada INV 126	HERITAGE (LP)	15
13	Invada INV 126	HERITAGE (box set, LP, CD and cassette)	35
14	Invada INV131LP	NORTHERN COUNCIL (LP, clear vinyl, 300 only)	15

COLLEGE BOYS (Jamaica)

MINT VALUE £

COLLEGE BOYS (JAMAICA)
64　Blue Beat BB 202　Love Is A Treasure/Someone Will Be There 25

COLLEGE BOYS (U.K.)
64　Columbia DB 7306　I Just Don't Understand/I'm Gonna Cry 20
67　Pye 7N 17294　Good Times/San Antonio Rose 10

KEITH COLLEY
63　Stateside SS 234　Enamorado/No Joke.. 8

GRAHAM COLLIER SEXTET/SEPTET
67　Deram DML/SML 1005　DEEP DARK BLUE CENTRE (LP) 150
69　Fontana SFJL 922　DOWN ANOTHER ROAD (LP).. 100
70　Fontana 6309 006　SONGS FOR MY FATHER (LP, as Graham Collier Music featuring Harry Beckett) 80
71　Philips 6308 051　MOSAICS (LP, live, as Graham Collier Music featuring Harry Beckett) 80
72　Saydisc SDL 244　PORTRAITS (LP) 25
74　Mosaic GMC 741　DARIUS (LP)... 20
75　Mosaic GCM 751　MIDNIGHT BLUE (LP)... 20
75　Cambridge Univ 521205638　JAZZ LECTURE CONCERT (LP) 40
12　Whatmusic WMLP 017　DEEP DARK BLUE CENTRE (LP, reissue) 20
(see also Harry Beckett)

MITTY COLLIER
64　Pye International 7N 25275　I Had A Talk With My Man/Free Girl 20
64　Pye International 7N 25275　I Had A Talk With My Man/Free Girl (DJ Copy)... 40
69　Peachtree P122　I'd like To Change Places/Share What You Got 20
15　Outta Sight RSV 059　Don't Let Her Take My Baby/BABY JEAN: If You Wanna 6

ALBERT COLLINS
69　Liberty LBS 585275　TRASH TALKIN (LP) 30
69　Liberty LBS 83238　LOVE CAN BE FOUND ANYWHERE (LP) 40
73　Tumbleweed TW 3501　THERE'S GOTTA BE A CHANGE (LP) 30

ANSEL(L) COLLINS
69　Trojan TR 699　Night Of Love/DERRICK MORGAN: Copy Cat.. 15
69　Trojan TR 7712　Cotton Dandy/CARL DAWKINS: Don't Get Weary.. 20
70　Trojan TR 7729　Moon Dust/Fat Cat.. 30
70　Trojan TR 7730　Monkey (Version I)/(Version II) (plays "High Voltage"/"High Voltage Version"; B-side actually by Beverley All Stars) 15
70　J-Dan JDN 4401　Cock Robin/KING DENNIS: Seven Zero... 12
70　Techniques TE 907　Top Secret/Crazy Rhythm (both actually by Winston Wright) 15
71　Techniques TE 913　Nuclear Weapon/TECHNIQUES ALL STARS: La, La, La 15
11　Techniques THB 7011　Double Or Nothing/DANDY: Double Barrel Man 18
(see also Conquerors, Lloyd Young, Prince Buster, Les Foster, Ethiopians, Eternals, Pam Brooks, Dennis Alcapone, Rad Bryan, Immortals)

CLANCY COLLINS ALL STARS (ACTUALLY, LLOYD CHALMERS)
71　Smash SMA 2321　Sir Collins Special/Conqueror (Actually, LENNOX BROWN : Heart of Knights) 40

DAVE COLLINS
72　Rhino RNO 103　Shackatac/Smooths And Sorts 15

DAVE & ANSELL COLLINS
72　Techniques TE 915　Karate/Doing Your Own Thing 20
73　Rhino RNO 111　Hot Line/Sunshine Rock (label credits 'Dave Collins') 15
75　Jama JAMA 002　Heavy Boomerang/Version 12
03　Lave LV1　Heavy Boomerang/DYNAMIC ALLSTARS: It's Not Possible 12
71　Trojan TBL 162　DOUBLE BARREL (LP) 25
75　Trojan TRLS12　IN THE GHETTO (LP) 18
(see also Dave Barker)

DONIE COLLINS SHOWBAND
68　Pye 7N 17682　Get Down With It/I Can't Help Myself (Sugar Pie Honey Bunch) 10

DOROTHY COLLINS
55　Vogue Coral Q 72111　My Boy - Flat Top/In Love.. 30
56　Vogue Coral Q 72193　Love Me As Though There Were No Tomorrow/Rock And Roll Train 15
56　Vogue Coral Q 72198　The Italian Theme/Cool It, Baby 15
57　Vogue Coral Q 72232　Baby Can Rock/Would You Ever 15
55　London REP 1025　DOROTHY COLLINS SINGS (EP) 10

EDWYN COLLINS
87　Creation CRE 047T　Don't Shilly Shally/If Ever You're Ready (7" white label test pressing only) 40
87　Creation CRE 047T　Don't Shilly Shally/If Ever You're Ready (12", white label test pressing only) 35
87　Elevation ACIDB 6　My Beloved Girl/50 Shades Of Blue (Acoustic Version)/Clouds (Fogging Up My Mind)/What's The Big Idea? (box set with 3 postcards) 6
08　Heavenly HVN 180　Home Again/Searching For The Truth (7", 1500 copies in sealed brown envelope in PVC sleeve) 8
08　Heavenly HVN 180　Home Again/Searching For The Truth (7" one of 25 copies with hand decorated insert by 25 different people including John Squire, Nicky Wire, Billy Childish and Jarvis Cocker).... 50
94　Setanta SETLP14　GORGEOUS GEORGE (LP, inner) 25
97　Setanta SETLP039　I'M NOT FOLLOWING YOU (LP, inner) 35
(see also Orange Juice, Paul Quinn & Edwyn Collins)

GLENDA COLLINS
60　Decca F 11280　Take A Chance/Crazy Guy 15
61　Decca F 11321　Oh How I Miss You Tonight/Age For Love 15
61　Decca F 11417　Head Over Heels In Love/Find Another Fool 15
63　HMV POP 1163　I Lost My Heart In The Fairground/I Feel So Good 60
63　HMV POP 1233　If You Gotta Pick A Baby/In The First Place 80
64　HMV POP 1283　Baby It Hurts/Nice Wasn't It.. 65
64　HMV POP 1323　Lollipop/Everybody's Got To Fall In Love 50
65　HMV POP 1439　Johnny Loves Me/Paradise for Two 50
65　HMV POP 1475　Thou Shall Not Steal/Been Invited To A Party 50
66　Pye 7N 17044　Something I've Got To Tell You/My Heart Didn't Lie 75

Honey BOY COLLINS

MINT VALUE £

| 66 | Pye 7N 17150 | It's Hard To Believe It/Don't Let It Rain On Sunday | 75 |
| 90 | Document CSAP LP 108 | BEEN INVITED TO A PARTY (LP) | 20 |

HONEY BOY COLLINS
| 73 | Sir Collins SCMW 004 | Better Must Come/Lola | 30 |
| 73 | Sir Collins SCMW 005 | Let Me In/GENE RONDO: I May Flay Again | 10 |

JOHNNY COLLINS
| 75 | Tradition TSR 020 | JOHNNY'S PRIVATE ARMY (LP) | 18 |

JOHNNY COLLINS & FRIENDS
| 73 | Tradition TSR 014 | THE TRAVELLER'S REST (LP, dark blue label, laminated sleeve) | 18 |

JUDY COLLINS
| 66 | London HLZ 10029 | I'll Keep It With Mine/Thirsty Boots | 12 |
| 65 | Elektra EKL 209 | MAID OF CONSTANT SORROW (LP) | 15 |

KEANYA COLLINS
| 77 | Grapevine 105 | Barnabus Collins - Love Bandit/I Call You Daddy (reissue) | 8 |

LYN COLLINS
64	Sabre SA 0002	What Am I Gonna Do Without You?/When A Girl Meets A Bad, Bad Boy	20
74	Polydor 2066 490	Rock Me Again And Again And Again And Again And Again And Again/Wide Awake In A Dream	15
74	Mojo 2093 029	Think (About It)/Me And My Baby Got Our Own Thing Going	10
88	Urban URBX 15	THINK (ABOUT IT) (12" EP p/s)	12
72	Polydor 2918 006	THINK (ABOUT IT) (LP)	40
88	Urban URBLP 7	CHECK ME OUT IF YOU DON'T KNOW ME BY NOW (LP, reissue)	15

(see also James Brown)

PETER COLLINS
| 70 | Decca F 13048 | Get In A Boat/Girl By The Sea | 6 |
| 70 | Decca Nova SDN 21 | PETER COLLINS (LP, blue/silver label) | 60 |

RODGER COLLINS
| 67 | Vocalion VF 9285 | She's Looking Good/I'm Serving Time | 40 |
| 67 | Vocalion VF 9285 | She's Looking Good/I'm Serving Time (DJ copy) | 70 |

SHIRLEY COLLINS
60	Collector JEI 1508	SINGS IRISH (EP)	70
60	Collector JEB 3	THE FOGGY DEW (EP)	70
60	Collector JEB 5	ENGLISH SONGS (EP)	70
64	Collector JEB 9	ENGLISH SONGS VOL. 2 (EP, with Robin Hall)	70
63	Topic TOP 95	HEROES IN LOVE (EP)	70
59	Folkways FG 3564	FALSE TRUE LOVERS (LP)	200
60	Argo RG 150	SWEET ENGLAND (LP, blue/silver label)	300
64	Decca LK 4652	FOLK ROOTS, NEW ROUTES (LP, insert, with Davy Graham)	320
67	Topic 12T 170	THE SWEET PRIMROSES (LP, original pressing with blue label)	50
67	Topic 12T 170	THE SWEET PRIMROSES (LP)	25
68	Polydor 583 025	THE POWER OF THE TRUE LOVE KNOT (LP, with Incredible String Band)	250
71	Pegasus PEG 7	NO ROSES (LP, gatefold sleeve, with Albion Country Band)	55
74	Topic 12T 238	ADIEU TO OLD ENGLAND (LP, original pressing with blue label)	40
74	Topic 12T 238	ADIEU TO OLD ENGLAND (LP)	25
75	Deram SML 1117	A FAVOURITE GARLAND (LP)	50
76	Harvest SHSM 2008	AMARANTH (LP, textured sleeve)	35
76	Mooncrest CREST 011	NO ROSES (LP, reissue, gatefold sleeve)	25
78	Topic 12T 380	FOR AS MANY AS WILL (LP)	20
81	Righteous GDC 001	FOLK ROOTS, NEW ROUTES (LP, reissue, with Davy Graham)	20
83	Hannibal HNBL 1327	THE POWER OF THE TRUE LOVE KNOT (LP, reissue)	20
87	See For Miles SEE 212	SWEET ENGLAND (LP, reissue)	25
91	Mooncrest CREST 011	NO ROSES (LP, reissue)	15
05	Boweavil WEAVIL 05	FALSE TRUE LOVERS (LP, reissue)	20
05	Boweavil WEAVIL 06	THE POWER OF THE TRUE LOVE KNOT (LP, reissue)	20
06	Boweavil WEAVIL 09	THE SWEET PRIMROSES (LP, reissue)	15
09	6 Spices 6S 229005	ADIEU TO OLD ENGLAND (LP, reissue)	15
14	Decca 379 616 3	FOLK ROOTS, NEW ROUTES (LP, reissue, with Davy Graham)	18
16	Domino WIGLP 389	LODESTAR (LP and CD)	15

SHIRLEY & DOLLY COLLINS
69	Harvest SHVL 754	ANTHEMS IN EDEN (LP, gatefold sleeve, with "Sold in U.K..." text on 4 lines)	175
69	Harvest SHVL 754	ANTHEMS IN EDEN (LP, gatefold sleeve, later issue with EMI logo on label)	100
70	Harvest SHVL 771	LOVE, DEATH AND THE LADY (LP, gatefold sleeve, no EMI logo on label)	140
78	Topic 12T 5380	FOR AS MANY AS WILL (LP)	30
87	See for Miles SEE57	ANTHEMS IN EDEN (LP, reissue)	20
87	Beat Goes On BGOLP1	LOVE, DEATH AND THE LADY (LP, reissue, gatefold)	25

(see also Davy Graham, Albion Country Band, Conundrum)

STEVE COLLINS
| 73 | Big Shot BI 620 | Ding A Ling Ting A Ling/Run Rhythm Run | 15 |

TERRY COLLINS
| 74 | Warner Bros. K16426 | I L.O.V.E. You/Action Speaks Louder | 7 |

COLLINS BAND & BOB STACKIE
| 68 | Collins Downbeat | Bob Stackie In Soho/LORD CHARLES & HIS BAND: Jamaican Bits And Pieces | 45 |

COLLOCUTOR
| 14 | On The Corner OTCLP001 | INSTEAD (LP) | 60 |

COLLUSION
| 71 | SRT 71114 | COLLUSION (LP, private pressing, plain sleeve, 99 copies only) | 1500 |
| 15 | Audio Archives AALP 101 | COLLUSION (LP, reissue) | 18 |

JOE COLMAN
| 90 | Blast First FU10 | INFERNAL MACHINE (LP, picture disc, 1,000 only) | 18 |

COLONEL ELLIOTT & THE LUNATICS

MINT VALUE £

COLONEL ELLIOTT & THE LUNATICS
73 Rhino SRNP 9001   INTERSTELLAR REGGAE DRIVE (LP) 30

COLONEL (1)
75 Ring O' 2017 104   Cokey Cokey/Away In A Manger (company sleeve) 10

COLONEL (2)
80 Virgin VS 380   Too Many Cooks (In The Kitchen)/I Need Protection (p/s) 6
(see also XTC)

COLONEL BAGSHOT
71 Parlophone R 5893   Georgia Fireball/Look In Her Eyes 15

JERRY COLONNA
54 Brunswick 05243   Ebb Tide/The Velvet Glove 10
55 Brunswick LA 8711   MUSIC FOR SCREAMING (10" LP) 15

COLORADOS
64 Oriole CB 1972   Lips Are Redder Than You/Who You Gonna Hurt? 30

COLOR TAPES
79 Wavelength HURT 4   Cold Anger/Leaves Of China (p/s) 6

COLOSSEUM
69 Fontana TF 1029   Walking In The Park/Those About To Die 15
69 Fontana STL 5510   THOSE WHO ARE ABOUT TO DIE SALUTE YOU (LP, laminated gatefold sleeve, black/silver labels) 150
69 Vertigo VO 1   VALENTYNE SUITE (LP, gatefold sleeve, large swirl label with 'A Philips Record Product' credit & inner bag) 175
69 Vertigo VO 1   VALENTYNE SUITE (LP, 2nd pressing, gatefold sleeve, large swirl label without 'A Philips Record Product' credit & inner bag) 80
70 Vertigo 6360 017   DAUGHTER OF TIME (LP, gatefold sleeve, with large swirl label & bag) 200
70 Vertigo 6360 017   DAUGHTER OF TIME (LP, gatefold sleeve, small swirl label) 60
71 Bronze ICD 1   COLOSSEUM LIVE (2-LP, gatefold, plastic inner) 40
71 Bronze ILPS 9173   THE COLLECTORS COLOSSEUM (LP) 20
72 Bronze HELP 4   VALENTYNE SUITE (LP, reissue with rarer HELP 4 cat no, 'Tinsley-Robor Group Ltd' sleeve printing credit) 20
72 Bronze BRNA 214   VALENTYNE SUITE (LP, reissue) 15
16 Music On Vinyl MOVLP 1684 THOSE WHO ARE ABOUT TO DIE SALUTE YOU (LP, reissue, gatefold) 15
(see also Bakerloo, Dick Heckstall-Smith, Chris Farlowe, Greenslade, Humble Pie, John Mayall, Howard Riley Trio, Tempest, Mogul Thrash)

COLOSSEUM II
77 Mercury MCF 2800   ELECTRIC SAVAGE (LP) 15

COLOURBOX
82 4AD AD 215   Breakdown/Tarantula (p/s) 6
85 4AD CAD 508   COLOURBOX (LP, stickered sleeve, 10,000 only, with bonus LP MAD 509) 18

COLOURED RAISINS
70 Trojan TR 7700   One Way Love/No More Heartaches 7
(see also Raisins)

COLOURFUL SEASONS
68 MGM MGM 1433   Out Of The Blue/It's Gonna Break My Heart 6

COLO(U)RS OF LOVE
68 Page One POF 060   I'm A Train/Up On A Cotton Cloud 8
68 Page One POF 086   Just Another Fly/Twenty Ten 8
69 Page One POF 124   Mother Of Convention/Music Mother Made 8
75 DJM DJS 625   I Can Dream Can't I?/I'll Be Seeing You 6

COLOURS (1)
68 Dot 113   Bad Day At Black Rock, Baby/Love Heals 6

COLOURS (2)
80 See Saw Sounds SAW 1   Dierdre Is An Artist/Over My Head/Facts Of Live (p/s) 12

COLOURS OUT OF TIME
81 Minsters In Orbit TVEYE 1 Dancing With Joy/Rock Section/Mambo Girls Mambo (hand-made pasted sleeve) 10
82 TVEYE 007   She Spins/The Ocean Monsters In Orbit 10

CHRISTOPHER COLT
68 Decca F 12726   Virgin Sunrise/Girl In The Mirror 40

TONY COLTON('S BIG BOSS BAND)
64 Decca F 11879   Lose My Mind/So Used To Loving You (solo) 30
65 Pye 7N 15886   I Stand Accused/Further On Down The Track (with Big Boss Band) 200
66 Pye 7N 17046   You're Wrong There Baby/Have You Lost Your Mind 100
66 Pye 7N 17117   I've Laid Some Down In My Time/Run Pony Rider 150
68 Columbia DB 8385   In The World Of Marnie Dreaming/Who Is She? (solo) 25
(see also Poet & One Man Band, Head Hands & Feet, Real McCoy, Peter B's)

ALICE COLTRANE
76 Impulse! AS 9156   A MONASTIC TRIO (LP, reissue) 20

JOHN COLTRANE
58 Esquire 32-079   THE FIRST TRANE (LP) 60
58 Esquire 32-089   SOUL TRANE (LP) 100
59 Esquire 32-091   TRANEING IN (LP) 40
60 Esquire 32-101   CATTIN' (LP) 40
60 London Jazz LTZ-K 15197   GIANT STEPS (LP) 200
61 Esquire 32-129   LUSH LIFE (LP) 100
61 London Jazz LTZ-K 15219   COLTRANE JAZZ (LP, also stereo SAH-K 6162) 35
62 London Jazz LTZ-K 15232   BAGS AND TRANE (LP, also stereo SAH-K 6192) 30
62 Columbia 33SX 1399   THE BIRDLAND STORY VOL. 1: ECHOES OF AN ERA (LP) 20
62 London Jazz LTZ-K 15239   OLE COLTRANE (LP, mono) 35
62 London Jazz SAH-K 6223   OLE COLTRANE (LP, stereo) 40
62 HMV CLP 1548   AFRICA/BRASS (LP, mono) 40
62 HMV SCD 1431   AFRICA/BRASS (LP, stereo) 45
62 HMV CLP 1590   LIVE AT THE VILLAGE VANGUARD (LP, mono) 25

COLUMBIA BOYS

MINT VALUE £

62	HMV CSD 1456	LIVE AT THE VILLAGE VANGUARD (LP, stereo)	30
63	United Artists (S)ULP 1018	COLTRANE TIME (LP)	26
63	London HA-K/SH-K 8017	COLTRANE PLAYS THE BLUES (LP, as John Coltrane Group)	30
63	Esquire 32-179	STANDARD COLTRANE (LP)	35
63	HMV CLP 1629	COLTRANE (LP, also stereo CSD 1483)	40
63	HMV CLP 1647	BALLADS (LP, also stereo CSD 1496)	25
63	HMV CLP 1657	DUKE ELLINGTON & JOHN COLTRANE (LP, mono)	40
63	HMV CSD 1502	DUKE ELLINGTON & JOHN COLTRANE (LP, stereo)	70
64	HMV CLP 1695	IMPRESSIONS (LP, mono)	30
64	HMV CSD 1509	IMPRRESSIONS (LP, stereo)	40
64	HMV CLP 1700	JOHN COLTRANE WITH JOHNNY HARTMAN (LP)	30
64	Realm RM 157	ON WEST 42ND STREET (LP)	25
64	Realm RM 181	TRANE RIDE (LP)	25
64	HMV CLP 1741	LIVE AT BIRDLAND (LP, also stereo CSD 1544)	30
65	HMV CLP 1799	CRESCENT (LP, mono)	40
65	HMV SCD 1567	CRESCENT (LP, stereo)	45
65	Stateside SL 10124	BLACK PEARLS (LP)	40
65	HMV CLP 1869	A LOVE SUPREME (LP, mono)	80
65	HMV CSD 1605	A LOVE SUPREME (LP, stereo)	100
65	Atlantic ATL/SAL 5022	MY FAVOURITE THINGS (LP)	25
65	Realm RM 52226	TANGANYIKA STRUT (LP)	25
65	HMV CLP 1897	COLTRANE PLAYS (LP, also stereo CSD 1619)	30
66	Stateside SL 10162	BAHIA (LP)	30
66	HMV CLP/CSD 3543	ASCENSION (LP, as John Coltrane Orchestra)	50
66	HMV CLP/CSD 3551	NEW THING AT NEWPORT (LP, with Archie Shepp)	40
66	Atlantic 587/588 004	THE AVANT-GARDE (LP, with Don Cherry)	40
66	HMV CLP 3575	MEDITATIONS (LP, mono)	35
66	HMV CSD 3575	MEDITATIONS (LP, flipback sleeve stereo)	40
67	Atlantic 587/588 039	COLTRANE'S SOUND (LP)	40
67	HMV CLP/CSD 3599	COLTRANE LIVE AT THE VILLAGE VANGUARD AGAIN! (LP)	30
67	HMV CLP/CSD 3617	OM (LP, withdrawn)	60
67	HMV CLP/CSD 3617	KULU SE MAMA (LP)	30
68	Transatlantic PR 7280	DAKAR (LP)	30
68	Transatlantic PR 7378	LAST TRANE (LP)	30
68	Impulse MIPL 502	EXPRESSION (LP, mono)	30
68	Impulse SIPL 502	EXPRESSION (LP, stereo)	20
69	Atlantic 588 139	THREE LITTLE WORDS (LP)	30
69	Impulse MIPL/SIPL 515	COSMIC MUSIC (LP, by Alice & John Coltrane)	50
70	Impulse SIPL 522	SELFLESSNESS (LP)	30
71	Probe SPB 1025	AFRO BLUE (LP)	30
72	Prestige PR 24003	JOHN COLTRANE (2-LP)	25
74	CBS PR 24037	BLACK PEARLS (2-LP)	25
76	Atlantic ATL 50239	GIANT STEPS (LP, reissue, gatefold)	15
77	Blue Note BNS 40009	BLUE TRAIN (LP, reissue)	18
91	MCA MCL 1648	A LOVE SUPREME (LP, reissue)	18

(see also Miles Davis, Thelonious Monk, Cannonball Adderley, Archie Shepp)

COLUMBIA BOYS
68	Pye 7N 17513	Baby Come Back/Born To Lose	8
69	Pye 7N 17763	That's My Pa/She Thinks I Still Care	7

COLUMBUS
70	Deram DM 294	Ev'rybody Loves The U.S. Marshall/So Tired	10

RAY COLUMBUS INVADERS
60s	Zodiac AZ/1009	She's A Mod/INVADERS : Cruel Sea	20

STEVE COLYER
75	Polydor 2058 647	Hey Mary/I Found My Sunshine	6

KEN COLYER'S SKIFFLE GROUP
55	Decca F 10631	Down By The Riverside/Take This Hammer	20
56	Decca FJ 10711	Streamline Train/Go Down Old Hannah	20
56	Decca FJ 10751	Down Bound Train/Mule Skinner	20
56	Decca FJ 10772	Old Riley/Stack O'Lee Blues	10
55	Decca DFE 6286	KEN COLYER'S SKIFFLE GROUP (EP, various coloured sleeves)	20

(see also Crane Skiffle Group)

VEE COMA
62	Pun PUN 001	Piccadilly/Independence Day	15

COMBAT 84
82	Victory VIC 1	ORDERS OF THE DAY (EP, wraparound p/s)	20
83	Victory VIC 2	Rapist/The Right To Choose/Barry Prudom (p/s)	20

PETER COMBE
78	Voyage VOY 001	Music Of The Day (Sing Birds Sing)/You Baby On My Mind	6

COMBE RALEIGH COUNTRY FOLK
76	MJB Recording BEV LP 1334	COMBE RALEIGH COUNTRY FOLK (LP)	250

COMBINATIONS
72	Punch PH 99	1 2 3 A B C/Zee	15

COMBO A
80	Broderick BROD 1	Smalltown/Lead By The Neck	8

COME
81	Come Org. WDC 883012	Come Sunday (cassette)	60
79	Come Org. WDC 88001	Come Sunday/Shaved Slits (p/s)	40
79	Come Org. WDC 883001	COME PRESENT RAMPTON (cassette)	60
79	Come Org. WDC 88203	PRESENT RAMPTON (LP)	100

COME ON

MINT VALUE £

| 81 | Come Org. WDC 881012 | I'M JACK (LP, orange vinyl with insert) | 80 |

COME ON
| 80 | Aura AUS 120 | Housewives Play Tennis/Howard After 6 (p/s) | 10 |

COMET GAIN
94	Soul Static SOUL 5	HOLLOWAY SWEETHEARTS EP	10
96	Wiiija WIJ 50V	SAY YES TO INTERNATIONAL SOCIALISM EP	10
97	Wiiija WIJ 66	Strength/A Film By Kenneth Anger/Letting Go (p/s)	8
98	Mei Mei MEI 001	Jack Nance Hair/We Are All Rotten/Record Prayer (p/s)	8
01	Fortuna Pop! FPOP 26	You Can't Hide Your Love Forever/Beatnik (p/s)	10
95	Wiiija WIJ 042V	CASINO CLASSICS (LP)	25
99	Fortuna Pop! FPOP 17	TIGERTOWN PICTURES (LP, insert, with free 7")	18
02	Milou Studios 2MILLP	REALISTES (LP)	20

COMETS SHOWGROUP
| 70 | LRC SCG 1 | COMETS ON LOCATION (LP, private pressing, handmade sleeve) | 50 |

COMING UP ROSES
| 89 | Utility UTIL 5 | I SAID BALLROOM (LP) | 30 |

(see also Dolly Mixture)

COMMANCHES
| 64 | Pye 7N 15609 | Tomorrow/Missed Your Loving | 10 |

(see also Bobby Allen)

COMMENDABLES
| 78 | Lip CC 1 | London E1/Decaying House | 10 |

COMMERCIAL ACROBATS
| 81 | Teesbeat TB1 | LITTLE MIXED UP (EP, front and back insert p/s with photo inside) | 10 |

COMMERCIALS
| 81 | Fast Product COM 1 | Sixteen Again And Again/The Heroine Dies/Simon (p/s) | 8 |

COMMITTED
| 79 | Ace ACE 006 | Crash Victim/British Crimes/Fast Lane/Advertising (500 only) | 100 |

COMMITTEE (1)
| 68 | Liberty LBF 15154 | The Hard Way/Hey You | 15 |

COMMITTEE (2)
| 69 | Pye 7N 17826 | Sleep Tight Honey/Memories Of Melinda | 6 |

COMMIX
| 07 | Metalheadz METH LP 09 | CALL TO MIND (LP as 3 x 12", gatefold sleeve) | 30 |

COMMODORES (1)
| 55 | London HLD 8209 | Riding On A Train/Uranium | 200 |
| 56 | London HLD 8251 | Speedo/Whole Lotta Shakin' Goin' On | 200 |

COMMODORES (2)
| 69 | Atlantic 584 273 | Keep On Dancing/Rise Up | 30 |

COMMOTION UPSTAIRS
| 89 | Saucy SAUCY TT 17 | Lift Me Up/Not Like That/Too Bad/Fake (p/s) | 100 |

PERRY COMO
53	HMV 7M 102	The Ruby And The Pearl/My Love And Devotion	8
53	HMV 7M 110	Some Enchanted Evening/Bali Ha'i	8
53	HMV 7M 118	Don't Let The Stars Get In Your Eyes/To Know You (Is To Love You) (B-side with Fontane Sisters)	25
54	HMV 7M 200	Idle Gossip/Look Out The Window	12
54	HMV 7M 263	There Never Was A Night So Beautiful/Papa Loves Mambo	20
55	HMV 7M 296	Ko Ko Mo (I Love You So)/You'll Always Be My Lifetime Love	15
55	HMV 7M 326	There's No Place Like Home For The Holidays/Tina Marie	10
56	HMV 7M 404	Hot Diggity (Dog Ziggity Boom)/My Funny Valentine	8

(see also Fontane Sisters, Betty Hutton)

COMPANY OF COWARDS
| 87 | Company Of Cowards COC 1 | 18 AGAIN EP (12") | 70 |

COMPANY (1)
| 79 | United Artists BP 326 | We Wish You Well/Right Time For Love | 30 |

(see also Whitesnake)

COMPANY (2)
80	Incus INCUS 36	FABLES (LP)	50
80	Incus INCUS 38	FICTIONS (LP)	50
82	Incus INCUS 46	EPIPHANY (LP)	50
82	Incus INCUS 47	EPIPHANIES (LP)	50
83	Incus INCUS 51	TRIOS (LP)	50

COMPAQ
| 98 | X System X SYS 3 | JUICY EP (12") | 15 |

COMPASS (1)
| 74 | MAM 115 | No More Whiskey/Maybe She Will | 7 |

COMPASS (2)
| 70 | Modello MHMS 136 | Don't Let The Sun Catch You Crying/Stepping Stone (no p/s) | 8 |

COMPLETE CYCLE
| 70 | Jay Boy BOY 23 | I'm On The Road Again/Back On The Road Again | 6 |

COMPLETE CONTROL
| 85 | Oi! OIR 1 | BRICKS BLOOD N GUTS (mini-LP) | 20 |

COMPLEX
70	CLPM 001	COMPLEX (LP, private pressing, 99 copies only)	4000
71	Deroy	THE WAY WE FEEL (LP, private pressing, 99 copies only)	1000
98	Tenth Planet TP 038	COMPLEX (LP, reissue, 1000, no'd)	30

(see also Monsoon, Misfits)

COMPLEXXION
| 79 | UK Records INT 584 | So Much In Love/Weekend (in p/s with bonus floppy gold disc) | 8 |

COMPROMISE

			MINT VALUE £
COMPROMISE			
66	CBS 202050	You Will Think Of Me/Love Minus Zero	7
COMSAT ANGELS			
79	Junta JUNTA 1	Red Planet/I Get Excited/Specimen No. 2 (1st pressing, black vinyl, 2000 copies p/s)	6
79	Junta JUNTA 1	Red Planet/I Get Excited/Specimen No. 2 (p/s, later reissue on red vinyl)	8
81	Polydor POLS 1038	SLEEP NO MORE (LP)	15
BOBBY COMSTOCK (& COUNTS)			
59	Top Rank JAR 223	The Tennessee Waltz/Sweet Talk (with Counts)	10
60	London HLE 9080	Jambalaya/Let's Talk It Over (as Bobby Comstock & Counts)	10
63	Stateside SS 163	Let's Stomp/I Want To Do It	15
63	Stateside SS 221	Susie Baby/Take A Walk	15
65	United Artists UP 1086	I'm A Man/I'll Make You Glad	10
COMUS			
71	Dawn DNX 2506	Diana/In The Lost Queen's Eyes/Winter Is A Coloured Bird (p/s)	100
71	Dawn DNLS 3019	FIRST UTTERANCE (LP, gatefold sleeve with lyric sheet, orange label)	1000
74	Virgin V 2018	TO KEEP FROM CRYING (LP, twin Virgin label)	60
10	Rise Above Relics RARLP 006	FIRST UTTERANCE (LP, reissue, limited edition with 10" and A2 poster, 300 only, black vinyl)	50
12	Rise Above RISELP 144	OUT OF THE COMA (LP, clear vinyl, 100 only)	30
12	Rise Above RISELP 144	OUT OF THE COMA (LP, white splatter vinyl)	20
12	Rise Above RISELP 144	OUT OF THE COMA (LP)	15

(see also Gong, Henry Cow, Esperanto Rock Orchestra)

CON-CHORDS			
65	Polydor BM 56059	You Can't Take It Away/Let Me Walk With You	25
CONCORDE			
70	Attack ATT 8020	Let Me Out/I Belong To You	12
CONCORDS (1)			
66	Emblem JDR 303	SOUL PURPOSE (LP)	30
CONCORDS (2)			
69	Blue Cat BS 170	Buttoo/I Need Your Loving	50
CONCORDS (3)			
70	Pye 7N17902	Robin/Hello Memories	10
CONCRETE			
81	Concrete CON 001	GHOULISH PRACTICES EP	15
CONCRETE GOD			
87	Phlox CGOD1	FLOOR EP (12" p/s)	15
87	Phlox CGOD2	TOYTOWN EP (12" p/s)	25
CONCRETE JUNGLIST			
94	Lloyd Crucial LC12 002	Ribbon In The Sky/Just Kick It/Pick A Sound/Screw Face (12")	20
94	Lloyd Crucial LC12 005	Southern California (Concrete Mix)/(Suburban Mix)/Crucial Archive (Dub Mix) (12")	35
94	Lloyd Crucial LC12 007	Lick Him Ina Him Head/India Posie Pan De Map (12")	40
CONCRETE SOX			
89	Big Kiss KISS 1	SEWERSIDE (LP, with inner)	15
87	Manic Ears ACHE 11	WHOOPS, SORRY VICAR! (LP)	15
88	C.O.R GURT 10	YOUR TURN NEXT (LP, with insert)	15
CONCRETES			
04	EMI LFLP 012	CONCRETES (LP, stickered sleeve)	20
CONDEMNED			
79	Rock Against Racism TRAR 1	Soldier Boys/Endless Revolution/PROLES: Stereo Love/Thought Crime (p/s)	45
CONDEMNED 84			
86	RFB SIN 2	Oi Ain't Dead!/Under Her Thumb/Follow The Leader/The Nutter (12", p/s, blue vinyl)	25
86	RFB SIN 2	Oi Ain't Dead!/Under Her Thumb/Follow The Leader/The Nutter (7", p/s, blue vinyl)	20
87	RFB SIN 3	IN SEARCH OF THE NEW BREED (12" EP)	30
88	Oi! OIR 003	BATTLE SCARRED (LP)	22
88	Grade 1	FACE THE AGGRESSION (LP)	22
CONEY ISLAND KIDS			
55	London HLJ 8207	Baby, Baby You/Moonlight Beach	30
CONFESSOR			
91	Earache MOSH 44	CONDEMNED (LP)	40
CONFIDENTIAL/PRIMEA FACEY			
90	Catt CATT 013	Jam The Frequency/Jet Black At Birth (12")	25
CONFLICT			
82	Crass 221984/1	THE HOUSE THAT MAN BUILT (EP, foldout poster p/s)	15
83	Corp. Christi CHRIST IT'S 4	A Nation Of Animal Lovers/Liberate (fold-out poster p/s)	8
83	Mortarhate MORT 1	The Serenade Is Dead EP ('Pay no more than 99p' on cover, with insert)	8
83	Mortarhate MORT EX001	The Serenade Is Dead (12" with insert)	15
85	Mortarhate MORT 15	The Battle Continues (both sides) (p/s, black or white sleeve, with lyric sheet)	8
85	Mortarhate MORT 20	Custom Rock/Statement (Ungovernable Force Promo, white label)	30
83	Corpus Christi CHRIST IT'S 3	IT'S TIME TO SEE WHO'S WHO (LP, gatefold, inner)	15
86	Mortarhate MORT 20	THE UNGOVERNABLE FORCE (LP, inner)	20
87	Mortarhate MORT 30	TURNING REBELLION INTO MONEY (LP)	20
88	Mortarhate LPMORT 50	THE FINAL CONFLICT (LP, gatefold)	20
15	Jungle FREUS LP 068	THERE MUST BE ANOTHER WAY - THE SINGLES (LP)	18
CON FUNK SHUN			
80	Mercury MERX 14	Got To Be Enough (Think About It - Don't You Doubt It)/Early Morning Sunshine (12")	15
CONGO ASHANTI ROY			
82	On-U Sound DP 08	Hands & Feet/African Blood (10")	15
80	Pre PREX 8	SIGN OF THE STAR (LP)	30
DAHWEH CONGO			
94	Soljie SOLJ 703	Most Naturally/In These Times (with Anthony John)	18

CONGOS

MINT VALUE £

CONGOS
77	Black Swan BS 1	Congo Man/Congo Man Chant (12")	40
78	Go Feet FEET 5	Fisherman/Can't Come In	15
80	Go-Feet BEAT 2	HEART OF THE CONGOS (LP)	40
96	Blood & Fire BAFLP 009	HEART OF THE CONGOS (2-LP, reissue)	45
00	Simply Vinyl SVLP 247	HEART OF THE CONGOS (2-LP, reissue, 180gm vinyl)	40

CONGREGATION
73	Columbia DB 9006	Jubilation/Love Is The Sweetest Thing I know	12

ARTHUR CONLEY
67	Atlantic 584 083	Sweet Soul Music/Let's Go Steady	10
67	Atlantic 584 143	Whole Lotta Woman/Love Comes And Goes	10
68	Atlantic 584 175	Funky Street/Put Our Love Together	10
68	Atlantic 584 197	People Sure Act Funny/Burning Fire	10
68	Atlantic 584 224	Aunt Dora's Love Soul Shack/Is That You Love	10
69	Atco 226 004	Star Revue/Love Sure Is A Powerful Thing	7
71	Atlantic 2091 106	Sweet Soul Music/Shake, Rattle And Roll	8
67	Atlantic 587 069	SWEET SOUL MUSIC (LP)	35
68	Atlantic 587 084	SHAKE, RATTLE AND ROLL (LP)	20
68	Atlantic 587/588 128	SOUL DIRECTIONS (LP)	20
69	Atco 228 019	MORE SWEET SOUL (LP)	15

(see also Soul Clan)

CONNARD
68	Spot JW 11	Amadhan/Desdemona	70

CONNECTION
92	Spare Beat SBRR 006	THE CONNECTION EP (12")	30
93	Spare Beat SBRR 008	THE CONNECTION EP VOL II (12")	30

BRIAN CONNELL & ROUND SOUND
66	Mercury MF 956	Just My Kind Of Loving/Something You've Got	10
66	Mercury MF 991	The Same Thing's Happened To Me/Mister Porter	10
68	Philips BF 1661	What Good Am I/Just Another Wedding Day	10
68	Philips BF 1718	I Know/Mister Travel Company	45

RAY CONNIFF & ROCKIN' RHYTHM BOYS
55	Vogue Coral QW 5001	Piggy Bank Boogie/Short Stuff	6

TERRY CONNOLLY & THE TRIXONS
67	King KG 1069	You're Gonna Wonder About Me/Mama, I'm Not The Boy I Used To Be	20

BRIAN CONNOLLY
82	Carrere CAR 231	Hypnotised/Fade Away (p/s)	18

(see also Sweet)

CHRIS CONNOR
60	London LZ-N 14036	THIS IS CHRIS (10" LP)	15

EDRIC CONNOR
53	Argo RG 33	SONGS FROM JAMAICA (LP, with the Caribbeans)	15
55	Argo RG 57	SONGS FROM TRINIDAD (LP, with the Southlanders)	15
55	Argo RG 58	CALYPSO (LP)	15

PAUL CONNOR
71	Polydor 2121045	Little Sparrow/I Don't Love You Any More	35
71	Polydor 2480072	EASY TO REMEMBER (LP)	40

CAROL CONNORS
62	London HLN 9619	Big Big Love/Two Rivers	20

(see also Teddy Bears)

NORMAN CONNORS
18	Dynamite Cuts DYNAM7015/Slewfoot/Back On The Streets/Chuka/Mother Of The Future (reissue, 2 x 7", p/s)		10
74	Buddah BDS 5611	SLEWFOOT (LP)	20
77	Buddah BDLP 4043	YOU ARE MY STARSHIP (LP)	20
77	Buddha BDLP 4053	THIS IS YOUR LIFE (LP)	18
79	Pye DISC 06	INVITATION (LP, as 2 x 12")	20

(see also Aquarian Dream)

CONQUERING LION
93	X Project DUBPLATE 2	Inah Sound/Outasound/King David Dub (12")	25
93	X Project DUBPLATE 3	Lion Of Judah/Inah Sound/Dub Plate Special (12")	20

CONQUERORS
67	Doctor Bird DB 1119	Won't You Come Home Now?/Oh That Day	50
67	Treasure Isle TI 7035	Lonely Street/I Fell In Love	40
69	Amalgamated AMG 832	Secret Weapon (actually by Ansell Collins)/Jumpy Jumpy Girl	75
69	High Note HS 016	If You Can't Beat Them/Anywhere You Want To Go	50
69	High Note HS 025	National Dish/Mr D.J.	50
72	Fab FAB 22	You Hold The Handles/SOUL REBELS : Bongo Skank	150

(see also Stranger Cole & Conquerors, Baba Brooks)

JESS CONRAD
61	Decca F 11412	Twist My Wrist/Hey Little Girl (p/s)	8
60	Decca DFE 6666	JESS CONRAD (EP)	10
62	Decca DFE 6702	TWIST MY WRIST (EP)	10
63	Decca DFE 8524	THE HUMAN JUNGLE (EP, with Rhet Stoller)	20
61	Decca LK 4390	JESS FOR YOU (LP)	30

(see also Guvners)

TONI CONRAD & FAUST
73	Caroline C 1501	OUTSIDE THE DREAM SYNDICATE (LP, as Tony Conrad)	80

(see also Faust)

CONSCIOUS MINDS

MINT VALUE £

CONSCIOUS MINDS
71	Big BG 318	Jamaican Boy/Brainwash	25
71	Ackee ACK 141	Paul, Marcus And Norman/Version	15
71	Punch PH 97	Paul, Marcus And Norman/Version (reissue)	6
71	Escort ERT 857	Peace Treaty/Brainwash	20

(see also Ken Boothe, Jamaicans, B.B.Seaton, Charmers)

CONSOLERS
67	President PT165	Someone Must Answer/Lord Bring Me Down	8

CONSORTIUM
68	Pye 7N 17635	All The Love In The World/Spending My Life Saying Goodbye	10
69	Pye 7N 17725	When The Day Breaks/Day The Train Never Came	30
69	Pye 7N 17797	Beggar Man/Cynthia Serenity	20
69	Pye 7N 17841	I Don't Want Her Anymore/The House Upon The Hill	7
70	Trend TNT 52	Melanie Cries Alone/Copper Coloured Years	7

CONSTRUCTION
90	White SDT17	Sudden Impact - In A State Of Experimentation	35
90	White SDT30	Transmission/Revenge Of The Dragon (12")	250
91	White SDT37	Change Your Attitude/Time To Get Raw (12")	50

CONSUMATES
68	Coxsone CS 7054	What Is It/SOUL VENDORS: Musical Happiness	70

CONSUMER RAPPORT
75	Atlantic K 10614	Ease On Down The Road/Go On With Your Bad Self	7
76	Atlantic K 10684	Everybody Join Hands/Love Takes Tears	8

CONTACT
79	Object OM 11	FUTURE/PAST EP	18

CONTACTS
81	Small Operations S0001	Young Girls/Boyfriends (p/s)	12

CONTINENTALS (1)
62	Oriole 1569	Bye Bye Blackbird/Everybody Loves My Baby	15
62	Island WI 010	Going Crazy/Give Me All Your Love	25

CONTINENTAL UPTIGHT BAND
71	Columbia SCX 6454	BEAUTIFUL FRIENDSHIP (LP, black/silver/white boxed Columbia label)	30

CONTINUUM (1)
70	RCA Victor SF 8157	CONTINUUM (LP, gatefold, orange labels)	30
71	RCA Victor SF 8196	AUTUMN GRASS (LP, gatefold sleeve, orange label)	50

CONTINUUM (2)
14	Tonefloat TF 134	CONTINUUM I & 2 (3-LP)	60

(see also Steven Wilson, Porcupine Tree, No Man, Blackfield)

CONTOURS
62	Oriole CB 1763	Do You Love Me/Move Mister Man (DJ Copy)	100
62	Oriole CB 1763	Do You Love Me/Move Mister Man	40
63	Oriole CB 1799	Shake Sherry/You Better Get In Line	60
63	Oriole CB 1831	Don't Let Him Be Your Baby/It Must Be Love	75
64	Stateside SS 299	Can You Do It/I'll Stand By You	60
64	Stateside SS 299	Can You Do It/I'll Stand By You (DJ Copy)	100
65	Stateside SS 381	Can You Jerk Like Me/That Day She Needed Me	60
65	Stateside SS 381	Can You Jerk Like Me/That Day She Needed Me (DJ Copy)	100
65	Tamla Motown TMG 531	First I Look At The Purse/Searching For A Girl	60
65	Tamla Motown TMG 531	First I Look At The Purse/Searching For A Girl (DJ Copy)	120
66	Tamla Motown TMG 564	Determination/Just A Little Misunderstanding	60
66	Tamla Motown TMG 564	Determination/Just A Little Misunderstanding (DJ Copy)	150
67	Tamla Motown TMG 605	It's So Hard Being A Loser/Your Love Grows More Precious Every Day	35
67	Tamla Motown TMG 605	It's So Hard Being A Loser/Your Love Grows More Precious Every Day (DJ Copy)	70
70	Tamla Motown TMG 723	Just A Little Misunderstanding/First I Look At The Purse	15
70	Tamla Motown TMG 723	Just A Little Misunderstanding/First I Look At The Purse (DJ Copy)	40
74	Tamla Motown TMG 886	Baby Hit And Run/Can You Jerk Like Me	25
65	Tamla Motown TME 2002	THE CONTOURS (EP)	120
63	Oriole PS 40043	DO YOU LOVE ME (LP)	250

CONTRABAND
74	Transatlantic BIG 518	Lady For Today/On The Road	6
74	Transatlantic TRA 278	CONTRABAND (LP, with lyric insert)	20

CONTRAST (1)
69	Orange OAS 202	Hey That's No Way To Say Goodbye/We Can Make It If We Try	10

CONTRAST (2)
70	Rs LP 6002	A GOOD YEAR (LP)	25

CONTRASTS FEATURING BOB MORRISON
68	Monument MON 1018	What A Day/Lonely Child	6

(see also Bill Forbes)

CONTROLLED BLEEDING
86	Sterile SR 11	HEADCRACK (LP)	20

CONTROLLERS
75	President PT 448	Is That Long Enough For You/Pictures And Memories	6
86	MCA 1052	Stay/Undercover Lover (p/s)	6

CONUNDRUM & RICHARD HARVEY
78	Streetsong No. 1	Black Birds Of Brittany/SHIRLEY COLLINS & ANNIE POWER: The Mariners Farewell (poster p/s)	18

(see also Bert Jansch, Shirley Collins)

BERT CONVY & THUNDERBIRDS
55	London HLB 8190	C'mon Back/Hoo Bop De Bow	50

(see also Cheers, Thunderbirds)

CONWAY

MINT VALUE £

CONWAY
16	Daupe! DM SP 016	GRISELDA GHOST (12", p/s, 250 copies, with Westside Gunn)	300
16	Daupe! DM SP 016	GRISELDA GHOST (12", p/s, aqua marine vinyl, 150 copies, with Westside Gunn)	400
16	Daupe! DM SP 016	GRISELDA GHOST (12", p/s, with obi strip, 20 copies, with Westside Gunn)	500
16	Daupe! DM SP 017	HALL & NASH (12", p/s, 230 only, with Westside Gunn)	250
16	Daupe! DM SP 017	HALL & NASH (12", p/s, liquor coloured vinyl, 150 only, with Westside Gunn)	300
16	Daupe! DM SP 017	HALL & NASH (12", p/s, 20 only, with Westside Gunn)	300
17	Daupe! DM SP 027	REJECT ON STEROIDS (12", p/s, white vinyl, 187 copies)	100
17	Daupe! DM SP 027	REJECT ON STEROIDS (12", p/s, red vinyl, 187 copies)	150
17	Daupe! DM SP 027	REJECT ON STEROIDS (12", p/s, grey vinyl, 187 copies)	150
17	Daupe! DM SP 027	REJECT ON STEROIDS (12", p/s, with obi strip, 20 copies)	120
18	Daupe! DM SP 034	DEATH BY MISADVENTURE (12", p/s, with Sonny Jim, 250 copies)	40
18	Daupe! DM SP 034	DEATH BY MISADVENTURE (12", p/s, with Sonny Jim, white vinyl, 250 copies)	40
18	Daupe! DM SP 034	DEATH BY MISADVENTURE (12", p/s, with Sonny Jim, picture disc, 250 copies)	50
18	Daupe! DM SP 034	DEATH BY MISADVENTURE (12", p/s, with Sonny Jim, red vinyl, 250 copies)	40
18	Daupe! DM SP 034	DEATH BY MISADVENTURE (12", p/s, with Sonny Jim, with obi strip, 20 copies)	150
16	Daupe! DM SP 015	REJECT 2 (LP, white vinyl, 100 only)	400
16	Daupe! DM SP 015	REJECT 2 (LP, numbered, 250 only)	400
16	Daupe! DM SP 015	REJECT 2 (LP, with obi strip, 20 only)	500
18	Daupe! DM SP 033	G.O.A.T. (LP, orange vinyl, 333 copies)	100
18	Daupe! DM SP 033	G.O.A.T. (LP, green vinyl, 333 copies)	100
18	Daupe! DM SP 033	G.O.A.T. (LP, grey vinyl, 333 copies)	100

MIKE CONWAY
66	Plexium PXM 1	I'm Gonna Get Me A Woman/Reign Of King Sadness	15

PAUL CONWAY
64	Piccadilly 7N 35215	Come A Little Bit Closer/Be Lonely Little Girl	7

JIMMY CONWELL
72	Jay Boy BOY 64	Cigarette Ashes/Second Hand Happiness	15
72	Jay Boy BOY 64	Cigarette Ashes/Second Hand Happiness (DJ Copy)	35
74	Contempo Raries CS 9001	Cigarette Ashes/Second Hand Happiness (reissue)	6

RY COODER
71	Reprise RS 23497	How Can A Poor Man Stand Such Times And Live/Goin' To Brownsville	7
71	Reprise RSLP 6402	RY COODER (LP)	15

(see also Captain Beefheart)

LITTLE JOE COOK (U.K.)
65	Sue WI 385	Stormy Monday Blues (Parts 1 & 2)	50

(see also Chris Farlowe, Beazers)

LITTLE JOE COOK (U.S.)
68	Sonet SON 2002	Don't You Have Feelings?/Hold On To Your Money	20
74	Sonet SON 2041	Hold On To Your Money/Don't You Have Feelings? (reissue, sides reversed)	10

PETER COOK (1)
65	Pye 7N 15847	Georgia/There And Bach Again	20

(see also Peter London)

PETER COOK (2)
66	Lyntone LYN 776	Watney's Pale Ale (Flexi, p/s)	15

PETER COOK & DUDLEY MOORE
62	Parlophone R 4969	Excerpts From "Beyond The Fringe": Sitting On The Bench/The End Of The World (with Alan Bennett & Jonathan Miller)	8
66	Decca F 12380	Isn't She A Sweetie/Bo Duddley	6
67	Decca F 12551	The L.S. Bumble Bee/The Bee Side	25
67	Decca F 12710	Bedazzled/Love Me	70
68	Decca SKL 4923	BEDAZZLED (LP, stereo, soundtrack)	100

(see also Dudley Moore Trio)

ROGER NOEL COOK
73	Dart ART 2039	Slick Go Getter/I Mean It You Know It	8

COOK COUNTY
77	Barak BAR 5	Space Dancin'/Star Wars	15

PAUL COOKE
71	Ackee ACK 129	That Girl Was Mine/No Harm	12

ROGER (JAMES) COOKE
68	Columbia DB 8458	Skyline Pigeon/I'm Burning	7
69	Columbia DB 8510	Not That It Matters Anymore/Paper Chase	6
69	Columbia DB 8556	Stop/Someday	6
69	Columbia DB 8596	Smiling Through My Tears/Ain't That A Wonderful Thing (with Eve Graham)	8
70	Columbia DB 8729	Jubilation/Anticipation Grows	6
71	Columbia DB 8761	If You Would Stay/Mama Packed A Picnic Tea	6
71	Columbia DB 8806	People I've Gotta Dream/Today I Killed A Man I Didn't Know	6
70	Regal Zonophone RZ 3005	We Will Get By/My Home City (as Roger Cook)	6
73	Regal Zonophone RZ 3074	She/Stay With Me (as Roger Cook)	6
76	Polto DR 2058 857	Please Get My Name Right/Alright	6
70	Columbia SCX 6388	STUDY (LP, boxed logo on label)	25
72	Regal Zono. SRZA 8258	MEANWHILE ... BACK AT THE WORLD (As Roger Cook, LP, gatefold sleeve, red/silver label)	30
73	Regal Zono. SLRZ 1035	MINSTREL IN FLIGHT (LP)	20

(see also David & Jonathan)

SAM COOKE
57	London HLU 8506	You Send Me/Summertime	40
57	London HLU 8506	You Send Me/Summertime (78)	20
58	London HLU 8615	That's All I Need To Know/I Don't Want To Cry	40
58	London HLU 8615	That's All I Need To Know/I Don't Want To Cry (78)	20

COOKIE MONSTER

MINT VALUE £

58	HMV POP 568	Love You Most Of All/Win Your Love For Me	40
58	HMV POP 568	Love You Most Of All/Win Your Love For Me (78)	20
59	HMV POP 610	Everybody Likes To Cha Cha Cha/The Little Things You Do	40
59	HMV POP 610	Everybody Likes To Cha Cha Cha/The Little Things You Do (78)	25
59	HMV POP 642	Only Sixteen/Let's Go Steady Again	10
59	HMV POP 642	Only Sixteen/Let's Go Steady Again (78)	30
59	HMV POP 675	There, I've Said It Again/One Hour Ahead Of The Posse	30
60	London HLU 9046	Happy In Love/I Need You Now	25
60	RCA RCA 1184	Teenage Sonata/If You Were The Only Girl	20
60	HMV POP 754	Wonderful World/Along The Navajo Trail	10
60	RCA RCA 1202	Chain Gang/I Fall In Love Everyday	7
61	RCA RCA 1221	Sad Mood/Love Me	10
61	RCA RCA 1230	That's It, I Quit, I'm Movin' On/What Do You Say	15
61	RCA RCA 1242	Cupid/Farewell, My Darling	7
61	RCA RCA 1260	Feel It/It's Alright	10
62	RCA RCA 1296	Bring It On Home To Me/Having A Party	8
62	RCA RCA 1310	Nothing Can Change This Love/Somebody Have Mercy	8
63	RCA RCA 1327	Send Me Some Loving/Baby Baby Baby	20
63	RCA RCA 1341	Another Saturday Night/Love Will Find A Way	7
63	RCA RCA 1361	Frankie And Johnny/Cool Train	10
63	RCA RCA 1367	Little Red Rooster/Shake Rattle And Roll	10
64	RCA RCA 1386	Good News/Basin Street Blues	6
64	RCA RCA 1405	Good Times/Tennessee Waltz	6
64	RCA RCA 1420	Cousin Of Mine/That's Where It's At	10
65	RCA RCA 1436	Shake/A Change Is Gonna Come	30
65	RCA RCA 1452	It's Got The Whole World Shakin'/Ease My Troublin' Mind	20
65	RCA RCA 1476	Sugar Dumpling/Bridge Of Tears	40
65	RCA RCA 1476	Sugar Dumpling/Bridge Of Tears (DJ Copy)	70
68	RCA RCA 1701	Another Saturday Night/DUANE EDDY: Dance With The Guitar Man (w/drawn)	10
63	RCA RCX 7117	HEART AND SOUL (EP)	20
64	RCA RCX 7128	SWING SWEETLY (EP)	25
58	HMV CLP 1261	SAM COOKE (LP, with Bumps Blackwell Orchestra)	100
59	HMV CLP 1273	ENCORE (LP)	70
61	RCA RD 27190	COOKE'S TOUR (LP, mono)	35
61	RCA SF 5076	COOKE'S TOUR (LP, stereo)	45
61	RCA RD 27215	HITS OF THE FIFTIES (LP, mono)	25
61	RCA RD SF 5098	HITS OF THE FIFTIES (LP, stereo)	40
61	RCA RD 27222	SWING LOW (LP)	35
62	RCA RD 27245	MY KIND OF BLUES (LP, mono)	30
62	RCA SF 5120	MY KIND OF BLUES (LP, stereo)	30
62	RCA RD 27263	TWISTIN' THE NIGHT AWAY (LP, mono)	30
62	RCA RD SF 5133	TWISTIN' THE NIGHT AWAY (LP, stereo)	40
63	RCA RDF 7539	MR. SOUL (LP, mono)	40
63	RCA SF 7539	MR. SOUL (LP, stereo)	45
63	RCA RD/SF 7583	NIGHT BEAT (LP)	40
63	RCA RD/SF 7583	NIGHT BEAT (LP)	45
64	RCA RD 7635	AIN'T THAT GOOD NEWS (LP, mono)	25
64	RCA SF 7635	AIN'T THAT GOOD NEWS (LP, stereo)	30
65	RCA RD 7674	AT THE COPA (LP, mono)	25
65	RCA SF 7674	AT THE COPA (LP, stereo)	30
65	RCA RD 7730	SHAKE (LP, mono)	40
65	RCA SF 7730	SHAKE (LP, stereo)	55
65	London HA-U 8232	THE SOUL STIRRERS FEATURING SAM COOKE (LP)	70
66	RCA RD/SF 7764	TRY A LITTLE LOVE (LP)	30
66	Immediate IMLP 002	THE WONDERFUL WORLD OF SAM COOKE (LP)	80
74	BBC	SAM COOKE AND OTHERS (LP, for radio use)	70

COOKIE MONSTER

03	Ninja Tune ZEN 12241	C Is For Cookie (Funky)/DJ Food Edit/Sweet Version (12" reissue, p/s)	20

COOKIES

62	London HLU 9634	Chains/Stranger In My Arms	30
63	London HLU 9704	Don't Say Nothin' Bad About My Baby/Softly In The Night	25
63	Colpix PX 11012	Will Power/I Want A Boy For My Birthday	30
64	Colpix PX 11020	Girls Grow Up Faster Than Boys/Only To Other People	30

(see also Earl-Jean, Cinderellas, Dorothy Jones)

COOKIN SOUL

19	No label or cat no	DOOM XMAS (LP, picture disc)	100

(see also MF Doom, Madvillian)

COOL BREEZE

71	Patheway PAT 103	People Ask What Love Is/There'll Be No More Sad Tomorrows	20
72	Decca F 13324	Summertime Sunshine/Sing Out Your Love	6
75	Bus Stop BUS 1023	Do It Some More/Citizen Jones	6
75	Bus Stop BUS 1027	You Gotta Love Me More/Turn On The Sun	6

COOL CATS

68	Jolly JY 007	What Kind Of Man/HEMSLEY MORRIS: Little Things	125
69	Jolly JY 009	Hold Your Love/ALVA LEWIS: Hang My Head And Cry	100

COOLERS

73	Bread BR 1112	The Youth Of Today/TYRONE TAYLOR: Close Observation	6

EDDIE COOLEY & DIMPLES

57	Columbia DB 3873	Priscilla/Got A Little Woman	150

			MINT VALUE £
57	Columbia DB 3873	Priscilla/Got A Little Woman (78)	30

COOL HAND FLEX

92	De Underground UG 08	Your Risk/Untitled/Untitled (12", white label)	12
92	Ruff Groove HN 05	Lock Me Up/I Don't Want No (12", stamped white label)	10
92	Ruff Groove UG 10	Welcome/Way Back Then/Woman (12")	10
92	In Touch INT 001	On The Strength/Your Risk/Go Insane (12")	25

COOLIES

77	Electric WOT 14	Geisha Girl/Calling Out Your Name	25

JOE COOL & KILLERS

77	Ariola ARO 165	I Just Don't Care/My Way	6

(see also Killers)

COOL MEN

58	Parlophone GEP 8739	COOL FOR CATS NO. 1 (EP)	25
58	Parlophone GEP 8752	COOL FOR CATS NO. 2 (EP)	25

COOL NOTES

77	Circle Int. CIR 003	After Tonight/Jah Lovely Wonderful Marvellous	15
80	Gem GEMS 32	Sugar Sugar/No No No No	6
80	Jama JADC 0008	Billy The Kid/Kidnap My Baby (12")	12
80	Jama JADC 0024	My Tune (Re-Mix)/Version (12")	30
81	Jama JA 017	Just Girls/Sweet Vibes	7
81	Mass Media Music MMM 12 1006	Meant To Be/Why Can't We Be Friends (Instrumental)	12
82	Mass Media Music MMM 12 1008	I Forgot How To Love/Why Can't We Be Friends (12")	60
82	Mass Media Music MMM 12 1008	I Forgot How To Love/Why Can't We Be Friends	15
82	Mass Media Music MMM 12 1011	Morning Child (Radio Mix)/Morning Child (Radio Mix)	25
82	Cool Notes 12CN 1001	It's Not Unusual/People Make The World Go Round (12")	15
84	Sour Grapes SG 116	I Wanna Dance/Blowin It	25
84	Sour Grapes SGR 116	I Wanna Dance (Extended)/Blowin It (12")	80
85	Abstract Dance 12AD 001	You're Never Too Young/Sound Of Summer (12")	15
84	Mass Media MMLP 2	DOWN TO EARTH (LP)	60
85	Abstract Dance AD LP1	HAVE A GOOD FOREVER (LP)	15

COOL RUNNERS

82	MCA MCAT 760	Play The Game (So You Think It Funny)/Hawaiian Dream (12", p/s)	20
82	MCA MCAT 893	Checking Out/High On A Feeling (12", p/s)	40
84	Tai Wan TWD 1949	Checking Out/High On A Feeling (12", p/s, reissue as Nat King Cool & Cool Runners)	25

COOL SPOON (JEFF DIXON & ALTON ELLIS)

67	Coxsone CS 7031	Yakety Yak/SOUL VENDORS: Drum Song	50

COOL STICKY

68	Amalgamated AMG 825	Train To Soulsville/ERIC MONTY MORRIS: Cinderella (actually by Errol Dunkley)	50

CHRIS COOMBES

65	Holyground HG 110	WHERE IT'S AT (EP, 99 only)	35

CHRIS COOMBS

75	Guildhall GHS 11	CHRIS COOMBS WITH THE GALLERY (LP)	100

NIGEL COOMBES & STEVE BERESFORD

80	Bead Records BEAD 16	IMPROVISED VIOLIN AND PIANO DUETS (LP)	25

ALICE COOPER

71	Straight W 7209	Eighteen/Body	100
71	Warner Bros K 16127	Under My Wheels/Desperado	6
72	Warner Bros K 16188	School's Out/Gutter Cat (p/s)	7
72	Warner Bros K 16214	Elected/Luney Tune (p/s)	8
73	Warner Brothers K16262	No More Mr. Nice Guy/Raped And Freezin' (possibly export only)	20
74	Chrysalis CHS 2069	I'm Flash/ELKIE BROOKS: Sacrifice (p/s, promo only)	35
75	Anchor ANC 1012	Department Of Youth/Cold Ethyl (p/s)	6
75	Anchor ANE 12001	Welcome To My Nightmare/Department Of Youth/Black Widow/ Only Women Bleed (12" EP, p/s)	10
80	Warner Bros K 17598	Clones (We're All)/Model Citizen (p/s)	8
86	MCA MCA 1090	He's Back (The Man Behind The Mask)/Billion Dollar Babies (poster p/s)	10
89	Epic ALICE 3	Bed Of Nails/I'm Your Gun (p/s, with poster)	8
69	Straight STS 1051	PRETTIES FOR YOU (LP, purple label, gatefold sleeve)	100
69	Straight STS 1061	EASY ACTION (LP, purple label, gatefold sleeve)	100
71	Straight STS 1065	LOVE IT TO DEATH (LP, purple label, gatefold sleeve)	80
71	Warner Bros K 56005	KILLER (LP, olive green label, A1/B1 Matrix numbers, gatefold sleeve with perforated foldout calendar that must have '1972' in bottom left hand corner. Any with '1973' are repressings)	70
72	Warner Bros K 56007	SCHOOL'S OUT (LP, green label, 'desktop' gatefold sleeve, with 'paper panties' inner)	60
73	Warner Bros K 56013	BILLION DOLLAR BABIES (LP, 1st pressing, A1/B1 matrixes, 'Pil' etched into dead wax side 2, olive green label, gatefold embossed sleeve with round corners and K56013 in top right corner, 'WEA records printed in England' in bottom right on rear, attached perforated cards, with $ billion note & inner sleeve with large thumb notch)	40
73	Warner Bros K 46177	LOVE IT TO DEATH (LP, reissue, green label, gatefold sleeve)	15
74	Warner Bros K 56018	MUSCLE OF LOVE (LP, 'cardboard box' sleeve, with insert & inner sleeve)	15

BO COOPER

74	Bell 1373	Don't Call It Love/Christian	15
74	Bell 1373	Don't Call It Love/Christian (DJ Copy)	30

GARNELL COOPER & KINFOLKS

63	London HL 9757	Green Monkey/Long Distance	20

HENRY COOPER

76	DJM DJS 10734	Knock Me Down With A Feather/Knocked Out For Your Love (p/s)	6

Les COOPER & SOUL ROCKERS

LES COOPER & SOUL ROCKERS
62	Stateside SS 142	Wiggle Wobble/Dig Yourself	20

LINDSAY COOPER
83	Re RE 1851	PICTURES FROM THE GREAT EXHIBITION (EP, p/s)	8
80	Arc ARC 1	RAGS (LP)	30
82	Sync Pulse 1789	LIVE AT THE BASTILLE (LP, with Maggie Nichols and Joelle Leandre)	20
83	Sync Pulse 0617	MUSIC FROM THE GOLD DIGGERS (LP)	15
86	Sync Pulse SP3	MUSIC FOR OTHER OCCASIONS (LP)	15

MARTY COOPER CLAN
63	RCA Victor RD 7596	NEW SOUNDS - OLD GOODIES (LP)	15

MIKE COOPER
70	Dawn DNX 2501	Your Lovely Ways (Parts 1 & 2)/Watching You Fall (Parts 1 & 2) (p/s)	7
71	Dawn DNX 2511	Too Late Now/The Ballad Of Fulton Allen/Good Times (p/s)	7
72	Dawn DNS 1022	Time In Hand/Schwabisch Hall	6
60s	Saydisc SD 137	UP THE COUNTRY BLUES (EP)	80
68	Matchbox SDM 159	THE INVERTED WORLD (LP, with Ian A. Anderson)	70
69	Pye NSPL 18281	OH REALLY!? (LP, blue/black label with logo banner on top)	40
70	Dawn DNLS 3005	DO I KNOW YOU? (LP, gatefold sleeve, orange label)	30
70	Dawn DNLS 3011	TROUT STEEL (LP, with poster insert, gatefold sleeve, orange label)	50
71	Dawn DNLS 3026	PLACES I KNOW (LP, with insert, lilac label)	40
72	Dawn DNLS 3031	THE MACHINE GUN COMPANY (LP, lilac label)	25
74	Fresh Air 6370 500	LIFE AND DEATH IN PARADISE (LP)	20
81	Matchless MR 4	'AVE THEY STARTED YET? (LP, with Joanna Pyne)	15

(see also Ian A. Anderson, Heron)

TOMMY COOPER
61	Palette PG 9019	Don't Jump Off The Roof Dad/How Come There's No Dog Day?	15
67	Pye 7N 17259	Happy Tommy/Tom Tom The Piper's Son	8
78	Pye 7N 46061	We'll Meet Again/The Sheik Of Araby (p/s)	8

COOPERETTES
75	Brunswick BR22	Shing A Ling/Don't Trust Him (DJ Copy)	20
75	Brunswick BR22	Shing A Ling/Don't Trust Him	10

COOPER TEMPLE CLAUSE
00s	private pressing	The Crayon Demos/Who Needs Enemies?/Let's Kill Music/Devil Walks In The Sand Demos (CD-R, in hand-crayoned sleeve, 120 only)	40
01	Morning MORNING 2	THE HARDWARE EP (Way Out West/Sister Soul/The Devil Walks In The Sand/ Solitude) (2 x 7", 1 black and 1 white vinyl, poly sleeves in box, 500 only)	10
02	Morning MORNING 20	SEE THIS THROUGH AND LEAVE (6 x 7", limited, numbered box set)	12

JULIAN COPE
87	Antar 4503	Interview/Christmas Mourning/Transmitting (fan club box set, with card, biography, membership card, letter, photos & stickers)	30
91	Island JC 1	Safesurfer/If You Love Me At All (33rpm, sold at gigs, stickered white sleeve)	6
94	K.A.K. (no cat. no.)	Paranormal In The West Country (Original Version)/(String Quartet Version)/ (Acoustic Version)/(Krankenhausmusik Version)/(Acoustic Version)/(Krankenhausmusik Version) (Mail-order only via offer with "Queen Elizabeth" LP)	10
84	Mercury MERL 48	FRIED (LP, with poster & promo 12" [MADOX 5])	20
87	Island ILPS 9861	SAINT JULIAN (LP, with free 12" interview LP [JCCLP 1])	15
89	CopeCo JULP 89	SKELLINGTON (LP, mail order only)	25
90	Mofoco MOFOCO 90	DROOLIAN (LP, mail order only)	20
91	Island ILPSD 9977	PEGGY SUICIDE (2-LP)	20
92	Island ILPSD 9997	JEHOVAHKILL (2-LP, 4th side etched)	25
93	Ma-Gog MA-GOG 2	THE SKELLINGTON CHRONICLES (LP, mail order only)	25
94	Echo ECHLP 1	AUTOGEDDON (LP, gatefold sleeve)	35
95	Echo ECHLP 5	20 MOTHERS (2-LP, black or purple vinyl)	45
96	Echo ECHLP 12	INTERPRETER (LP, with poster)	40
01	Head Heritage HH12	DISCOVER ODIN (CD, mail order only, 10" x 5" package with booklet, signed & numbered, 1000 only)	40

(see also Teardrop Explodes, Brain Donor, Elizabeth, L.A.M.F.)

SUZY COPE
61	HMV POP 941	Teenage Fool/Juvenile Delinquent	25
62	HMV POP 1047	Not Never Not Now/Kisses And Tears	25
63	HMV POP 1167	Biggity Big/Doing What You Know Is Wrong	25
65	CBS 201792	You Can't Say I Never Told You/And Now I Don't Want You	25

AL(L)AN COPELAND
57	Vogue Coral Q 72237	Feeling Happy/You Don't Know	10
57	Vogue Coral Q 72277	How Will I Know?/Will You Still Be Mine	7
59	Pye International 7N 25007	Flip Flop/Lots More Love (as Allan Copeland)	25

JOHNNY COPELAND
69	Atlantic 10242	Sufferin' City/It's My Own Tears That's Being Wasted	12

KEN COPELAND
57	London HLP 8423	Pledge Of Love/MINTS: Night Air	100

BOB & RON COPPER
63	EFDSS 1002	BOB & RON COPPER (LP)	35

COPPER FAMILY
71	Leader LED 2067	A SONG FOR EVERY SEASON (LP, sampler, tracks from 4-LP set)	40
71	Leader LEAB 404	A SONG FOR ALL SEASONS (4xLP)	50

COPPERFIELD
69	Instant IN 004	Any Old Time/I'm No Good For Her	15
69	Parlophone R 5818	I'll Hold Out My Hand/Far Away Love	10

(see also Quartz)

JOHNNY COPPIN
87	Rola RO 15	FOREST & VALE (LP)	20

COPS 'N ROBBERS

MINT VALUE £

COPS 'N ROBBERS
64	Decca F 12019	St. James Infirmary/There's Gotta Be A Reason	50
65	Pye 7N 15870	I Could Have Danced All Night/Just Keep Right On	25
65	Pye 7N 15928	It's All Over Now Baby Blue/I've Found Out	25

(see also Fairies)

COPY CATS
69	Bullet BU 419	Copy Cat (with Derrick Morgan)/BUNNY LEE ALL STARRS: Hot Lead	20

C (COPYRIGHT SIGN)
93	Transglobal GLOBAL 1	WITCH (LP)	60

CORAL
02	Deltasonic DLTLP 006	THE CORAL (LP)	40
04	Deltasonic DLTLP 014	MAGIC AND MEDICINE (2-LP, orange vinyl)	45
04	Deltasonic DLTLP 018	NIGHTFREAK AND THE SONS OF BECKER (mini-LP, gatefold)	20
05	Deltasonic DLTLP 036	THE INVISIBLE INVASION (2-LP, gatefold)	35
07	Deltasonic DLTLP 069	ROOTS & ECHOES (2-LP)	50
08	Deltasonic DLTLP 083	SINGLES COLLECTION (3-LP)	30
10	Deltasonic DLTBX 08	BUTTERFLY HOUSE (LP, 2-CD, DVD, box set)	25
10	Deltasonic DLTLP 086	BUTTERFLY HOUSE (LP)	30
14	Skeleton SKL 006	THE CURSE OF LOVE (LP, CD)	25

CORBAN
78	Acorn AC 002	A BREAK IN THE CLOUDS (LP, with insert)	18

HARRY CORBETT
61	Fontana TFE 17367	SOOTY AND SWEEP (EP)	10
61	Fontana TFE 17368	SOOTY AND SWEEP (EP, side 1 - Double Cross Quiz side 2 - The Music Lesson)	10

HARRY H. CORBETT
67	Decca F 12714	Flower Power Fred/(I'm) Saving All My Love (with Unidentified Flower Objects)	15

(see also & Harry H. Corbett, Faraway Folk)

MIKE CORBETT & JAY HIRSH
71	Atlantic 2091-126	Gypsy Child/Butterfly Day	6
71	Atlantic 2400 141	MIKE CORBETT & JAY HIRSH (LP, gatefold sleeve)	20

(see also Mr. Flood's Party)

JERRY CORBITT
69	Polydor 583 576	CORBITT (LP)	25

MANNY CORCHADO
06	Jazzman JM 049	Pow Wow/Chicken And Booze	8

JASON CORD
69	Chapter One CH 102	I've Got My Eyes On You/I Can't Take No More Of Your Lies	6
69	Chapter One CH 110	Why Shouldn't I/Spring Never Came Twice	6

FRANK CORDELL & HIS ORCHESTRA
61	HMV POP 824	The Black Bear/Darling Charlie	7
68	National (No cat. no.)	Theme One/Theme Two (with John Meyer Group)	8

PHIL CORDELL
69	Warner Bros WB 8001	Pumping The Water/Red Lady	35

(see also Thursday's Children)

CORDES
65	Cavern Sound IMSTL 1	Give Her Time/She's Leaving	70

LOUISE CORDET
62	Decca F 11476	I'm Just A Baby/In A Matter Of Moments	8
62	Decca F 11476	I'm Just A Baby/In A Matter Of Moments (export copy in p/s)	15
62	Decca F 11524	Sweet Enough/Someone Else's Fool	10
62	Decca F 11524	Sweet Enough/Someone Else's Fool (export copy in p/s)	15
63	Decca F 11673	Around And Around/Which Way The Wind Blows	15
64	Decca F 11824	Don't Let The Sun Catch You Crying/Loving Baby	15
64	Decca F 11875	Don't Make Me Over/Two Lovers	20
62	Decca DFE 8515	THE SWEET BEAT OF LOUISE CORDET (EP)	50

CORDUROYS
66	Planet PLF 122	Tick Tock/Too Much Of A Woman	60

CHICK COREA (& RETURN TO FOREVER)
74	People PLEO 9	SUNDANCE (LP)	15

PADDY COREA
72	Explosion EX 2066	Soul And Inspiration/STAGS: You Must Be Trying My Faith	6

CORKSCREW
79	Highway SHY 7005	FOR OPENERS (LP)	25

CORNBREAD & JERRY
61	London HLG 9352	L'il Ole Me/Loco Moto	10

DON CORNEL & ETERNALS
70	Moodisc MU 3506	Christmas Joy/WINSTON & RUPERT: Musically Beat	18

CORNELIUS
98	Matador OLE 3000	FANTASMA (LP)	20
02	Matador OLE 3321	POINT (LP)	40

EDDIE CORNELIUS
80	GB Records GB 001	That's Love Making In Your Eyes/Hurry Up	15

DON CORNELL
54	Vogue Coral Q 2013	Hold My Hand/I'm Blessed	15
54	Vogue Coral Q 2037	S'Posin'/I Was Lucky	10
55	Vogue Coral Q 72058	No Man Is An Island/All At Once	8
55	Vogue Coral Q 72070	Give Me Your Love/When You Are In Love	8
55	Vogue Coral Q 72071	Athena/Size 12	8
55	Vogue Coral Q 72073	Stranger In Paradise/The Devil's In Your Eyes	8
55	Vogue Coral Q 72080	Unchained Melody/Most Of All	8

Jerry CORNELL

MINT VALUE £

55	Vogue Coral Q 72104	Love Is A Many Splendored Thing/The Bible Tells Me So	6
56	Vogue Coral Q 72132	There Once Was A Beautiful/Make A Wish	6
56	Vogue Coral Q 72144	Teenage Meeting (Gonna Rock It Right)/I Still Have A Prayer	30
57	Vogue Coral Q 72234	Let's Be Friends/Afternoon In Madrid	6

JERRY CORNELL
| 55 | London HL 8157 | Please Don't Talk About Me When I'm Gone/St. Louis Blues | 25 |

LYN CORNELL
60	Decca F 11227	Like Love/Demon Lover	20
60	Decca F 11260	Teaser/What A Feeling	7
62	Decca F 11469	I Sold My Heart To The Junkman/Step Up And Rescue Me	15
63	Decca F 11750	Sally Go Round The Roses/You Can Kiss Me If You Like	10

CORNFLAKES
| 62 | Fontana 267 227TF | Oh, Listen To The Band/Moonstruck | 10 |

BARRY CORNISH
| 73 | Jam 60 | Questions/Stones From The Wishing Well | 8 |

ARNOLD CORNS
71	B&C CB 149	Moonage Daydream/Hang Onto Yourself (Demo copy as 'The Arnold Corns')	150
71	B&C CB 149	Moonage Daydream/Hang Onto Yourself (as 'The Arnold Corns')	125
72	B&C CB 189	Hang Onto Yourself/Man In The Middle (Demo copy)	80
72	B&C CB 189	Hang Onto Yourself/Man In The Middle (reissue)	75
74	Mooncrest MOON 25	Hang Onto Yourself/Man In The Middle (Demo copy)	40
74	Mooncrest MOON 25	Hang Onto Yourself/Man In The Middle (reissue)	35

(see also David Bowie)

CORONADOS
| 64 | London HL 9895 | Love Me With All Your Heart/Querida | 10 |
| 67 | Stateside SS 2043 | Johnny B. Goode/Shook Me Down | 10 |

CORONETS (1)
| 54 | Columbia SCM 5117 | Do, Do, Do, Do, Do, Do It Again/I Ain't Gonna Do It No More | 15 |

(see also Chris Sandford & Coronets, Ronnie Harris, Benny Hill, Eric Jupp, Lee Lawrence)

CORONETS (2)
| 68 | Stresa BEV SP 1104/1105 | I Wonder Why/You're Leaving Tomorrow | 45 |

CORPORATION (JAMAICA)
| 70 | Grape GR 3022 | Sweet Musille/Walking Thru' Jerusalem | 22 |

(see also Claudette & Corporation, Billy Jack)

CORPORATION (U.S.)
| 69 | Capitol E-T/E-ST 175 | THE CORPORATION (LP) | 25 |

CORRIE FOLK TRIO/CORRIES
| 63 | Waverley SLP 530 | Love Is Teasing/O, Waly Waly (p/s) | 8 |

CORROSION OF CONFORMITY
85	Toxic Shock TXLP 4	EYE FOR AN EYE (LP)	18
91	Roadrunner RO9236 1	BLIND (LP)	40
96	Columbia 484328 1	WISEBLOOD (2-LP)	35

JAY C CORRY
| 76 | Decca FR 13680 | Love Me Or Leave Me/House Of Truth | 12 |

CORSAIRS (JAMAICA)
| 70 | Unity UN 558 | Goodnight My Love/Lover Girl | 8 |

CORSAIRS (U.K.)
| 67 | CBS 202624 | Pay You Back With Interest/I'm Going To Shut You Down | 20 |

CORSAIRS (U.S.)
| 62 | Pye International 7N 25142 | I'll Take You Home/Sitting On Your Doorstep (with Jay 'Bird' Uzzel) | 15 |

BOB CORT (SKIFFLE GROUP)
57	Decca FJ 10831	It Takes A Worried Man To Sing A Worried Blues/ Don't You Rock Me Daddy-O	10
57	Decca F 10892	Six-Five Special/Roll Jen Jenkins	10
57	Decca F 10899	Maggie May/Jessamine (with Liz Winters)	10
57	Decca F 10905	Schoolday (Ring! Ring! Goes The Bell)/Ain't It A Shame (To Sing Skiffle On Sunday)	12
58	Decca F 10989	The Ark (Noah Found Grace In The Eyes Of God)/Yes! Suh!	15
60	Decca F 11256	Mule Skinner Blues/The Ballad Of Walter Williams (solo)	10
57	Decca LK 4222	AIN'T IT A SHAME (LP)	20

(see also Liz Winters & Bob Cort)

DAVE 'BABY' CORTEZ
59	London HLU 8852	The Happy Organ/Love Me As I Love You	10
60	London HLU 9126	Deep In The Heart Of Texas/You're Just Right	15
62	Pye International 7N 25159	Rinky Dink/Getting Right	15
60	London RE-U 1233	DAVE 'BABY' CORTEZ (EP)	20
64	London HA-U 8142	THE GOLDEN HITS OF DAVE 'BABY' CORTEZ (LP)	30

CORTINAS (1)
| 68 | Polydor 56255 | Phoebe's Flower Shop/Too Much In Love | 15 |

CORTINAS (2)
77	Step Forward SF 1	Fascist Dictator/Television Families (p/s, first 1,000 in card sleeve)	25
77	Step Forward SF 1	Fascist Dictator/Television Families (p/s)	15
78	Step Forward SF 6	Defiant Pose/Independence (p/s)	12
78	Step Forward SF 6	Defiant Pose/Independence (12", pink die-cut sleeve)	12
78	CBS CBS 6759	Heartache/Ask Mr. Waverley (p/s)	8
78	CBS CBS 82831	TRUE ROMANCES (LP, with photo insert)	20

LEE CORVETTE
| 62 | Decca F11481 | The Heart You Break (May Be Your Own)/Tender Love | 10 |

CORVETTES
| 82 | Bitchin BIT 100 | Surf, Don't Walk/She'll Be Blonde (p/s) | 15 |
| 84 | Bitchin BIT 101 | Girls Cars Girls Sun Girls Surf Girls Fun Girls/The Beach Is Not Enough (p/s) | 18 |

Larry CORYELL

MINT VALUE £

LARRY CORYELL
69	Vanguard SVRL 19051	LADY CORYELL (LP)	18
69	Vanguard SVRL 19059	CORYELL (LP)	18
70	Vanguard 6359 005	SPACES (LP)	25
85	Nimbus/Novus AN 3024	STANDING OVATION (LP, NImbus Supercut, mail order only sold via Practical Hi Fi magazine)	40

(see also Jazz Composers Orchestra)

BILL COSBY
67	Warner Bros WB 7272	Little Ole Man (Uptight! Everything's Alright)/Don'cha Know (in p/s)	10

COSMETICS
81	Panic SEC 31	Closures/The Chain (p/s)	8

COSMIC BABY/VANGELIS
94	East West SAM 1484	A TRIBUTE TO BLADERUNNER (12", double pack, promo only)	20

(see also Vangelis)

COSMIC DEAD
13	Cardinal Fuzz CFUL 010	THE COSMIC DEAD (2-LP gatefold, 1st press, black vinyl, 300 only)	30
13	Cardinal Fuzz CFUL 010	THE COSMIC DEAD (2-LP gatefold, 1st press, orange vinyl, 200 only)	35

COSMIC EYE
72	Regal Zono. SLRZ 1030	DREAM SEQUENCE (LP)	250

COSMIC PSYCHOS
88	What Goes On GOES ON 23	COSMIC PSYCHOS (LP)	15

COSMO
63	Blue Beat BB 175	Gypsy Woman/Do Unto Others	10
64	Blue Beat BB 244	One God/BUSTER'S ALL STARS: Prince Royal (actually "Reincarnation")	50
64	Blue Beat BB 269	Rice And Badgee/BUSTER'S ALL STARS: The Tickler	50

(see also Cosmo & Dennis, Denzil Dennis)

COSMO & DENNIS (ALIAS DENZIL)
62	Blue Beat BB 145	Bed Of Roses/Tonight And Evermore (as Cosmo & Denzil)	10
65	Blue Beat BB 296	Sweet Rosemarie/Lollipop I'm In Love	12
65	Blue Beat BB 312	Come On Come On/I Don't Want You (As COSMO & DENZIL)	12

(see also Cosmo)

FRANK COSMO
63	Island WI 058	Revenge/Laughin' At You (B-side actually with Bobby Aitken)	15
63	Island WI 073	Dear Dreams/Go Go Go	15
63	Island WI 100	Merry Christmas/Greetings From Beverley's	20
63	R&B JB 119	I Love You/DON DRUMMOND: Close Of Play	22
64	Island WI 135	Better Get Right/Ameletia	20
64	Black Swan WI 446	Alone/Beautiful Book	20

(see also Two Kings)

COSMOTHEKA
74	Highway SHY 6002	A LITTLE BIT OFF THE TOP (LP)	20
77	Shy SHY 7001	WINES & SPIRITS (LP)	35
81	Highway SHY 7015	A GOOD TURN OUT (LP)	15
85	Dambuster DAM 1	COSMOTHEKA (LP)	18

DON COSTA, HIS ORCHESTRA & CHORUS
55	London HLF 8186	Love Is A Many Splendoured Thing/Safe In The Harbour	10
59	London HLT 8992	I Walk The Line/Cat Walk	7

JACK COSTANZO & TUBBY HAYES
62	Fontana TFL 5190	COSTANZO PLUS TUBBS - EQUATION IN RHYTHM (LP, mono)	50
62	Fontana STFL 598	COSTANZO PLUS TUBBS - EQUATION IN RHYTHM (LP, stereo)	40

(see also Tubby Hayes)

CELIA COSTELLO
75	Leader LEE 4054	CELIA COSTELLO (LP, with insert)	20

DAY COSTELLO
71	Spark SRL 1042	The Long And Winding Road/Free (Unlimited Horizons)	10

(see also Ross McManus)

ELVIS COSTELLO (& ATTRACTIONS)
77	Stiff BUY 11	Less Than Zero/Radio Sweetheart (p/s)	10
77	Stiff Buy 14	Alison/Welcome To The Working Week (p/s)	10
77	Stiff Buy 14	Alison/Welcome To The Working Week (p/s, A-side mispress on white vinyl)	300
77	Stiff BUY 15	(The Angels Wanna Wear My) Red Shoes/Mystery Dance (push-out centre)	6
77	Stiff BUY 15	Red Shoes/Mystery Dance (p/s, mispress, plays "Dream Tobacco" by Max Wall)	8
77	Stiff BUY 20 DJ	Watching The Detectives (short version)/Blame It On Cain (live)/Mystery Dance (live) (promo copy)	40
77	Stiff BUY 20	Watching The Detectives/Blame It On Cain (live)/Mystery Dance (live) (phone book p/s)	8
78	Radar ADA 24	Radio Radio/Tiny Steps (12", promo-only, 500 pressed)	15
78	Radar RG 1	Talking In The Dark/Wednesday Week (p/s, gig freebie)	8
80	2-Tone CHS TT 7	I Can't Stand Up For Falling Down/Girls Talk (unreleased, later a gig freebie, more common issue (see other price) has XX1 in run-off groove, 13,000 pressed)	50
80	2-Tone CHS TT 7	I Can't Stand Up For Falling Down/Girls Talk (unreleased, gig freebie, more common issue with XX1 in run-off groove, 13,000 pressed)	20
80	Stiff GRAB 3	STIFF SINGLES FOUR PACK (BUY 11, 14, 15 & 20 in clear plastic wallet)	20
81	F-Beat XX 17	A Good Year For The Roses/Your Angel Steps Out Of Heaven (withdrawn p/s)	10
77	Stiff SEEZ 3	MY AIM IS TRUE (LP, 1st pressing, b/w front photo, red lettering with 'Help us hype Elvis' promo insert)	150
77	Stiff Seez 3	MY AIM IS TRUE (LP, 1st pressing, b/w front photo, red lettering)	30
78	Radar RAD 3	THIS YEAR'S MODEL (LP, with free 7" "Stranger In The House"/"Neat Neat Neat" (live) [die-cut company sleeve, SAM 83], 50,000 pressed; 1st 5,000 shrinkwrapped and stickered)	25
79	Radar RAD 15	ARMED FORCES (LP, foldout stickered sleeve with free EP Live At Hollywood High [p/s, SAM 90] & postcards)	20
79	Radar RAD 15	ARMED FORCES (LP, mispress, plays "[What's So Funny 'Bout] Peace, Love &	25

COTERIE

			MINT VALUE £
		Understanding" instead of "Two Little Hitlers"; sticker on insert)	
82	F-Beat EC CHAT 2	A CONVERSATION WITH ELVIS COSTELLO (2-LP)	20

(see also Nick Lowe, George Jones, Coward Brothers)

COTERIE
69	Emerald GEM 1026	A SWING TO FOLK (LP)	40

COTTI & CLUEKID
06	$N Format EPV 001	4N EXCHANGE EP (12", stickered white label)	35

JAMES COTTON (BLUES BAND)
68	Vanguard SVRL 19035	CUT YOU LOOSE! (LP, as James Cotton Blues Band)	25

JIMMY COTTON
62	Columbia SEG 8141	CHRIS BARBER PRESENTS JIMMY COTTON (EP)	20
62	Columbia SEG 8189	CHRIS BARBER PRESENTS JIMMY COTTON NO. 2 (EP)	20

(see also James Cotton Blues Band, Alexis Korner)

JOSEPH COTTON
77	Observer OB 001	Fit And Ready/OBSERVER: Iron Fist (12")	40

MIKE COTTON (SOUND)
62	Columbia DB 4910	The Tinker/Zulu Warrior (as the Mike Cotton Jazz Men)	10
63	Columbia DB 7029	Swing That Hammer/Heartaches (as Mike Cotton Jazzmen)	8
63	Columbia DB 7134	Midnite Flyer/One Mint Julep (as Mike Cotton Band)	10
64	Columbia DB 7267	I Don't Wanna Know/This Little Pig	60
64	Columbia DB 7382	Round And Round/Beau Dudley	50
65	Columbia DB 7623	Make Up Your Mind/I've Got My Eye On You	50
66	Polydor BM 56096	Harlem Shuffle/Like That	40
62	Columbia SEG 8144	COTTON PICKING (EP)	40
63	Columbia SEG 8190	THE WILD AND THE WILLING (EP)	40
64	Columbia 33SX 1647	MIKE COTTON SOUND (LP)	500

(see also Lucas & Mike Cotton Sound, Satisfaction)

COTTON CASINO
03	Riot Season REPOSE 701	Fly High/Open The Shine (white vinyl, p/s)	8

(See also Acid Mothers Temple and the Melting Paraiso UFO)

COUGARMAN AND GENERAL Z
12	Golden Hole GH001	When Sally Met Mandingo/Afro Symphony	15
13	Golden Hole GH002	Seaman Level/Susan Loves To Jack (12" p/s)	15

COUGARS
63	Parlophone R 4989	Saturday Night At The Duckpond/See You In Dreamland	10
63	Parlophone R 5038	Red Square/Fly-By-Nite	10
64	Parlophone R 5115	Caviare And Chips/While The City Sleeps	10
63	Parlophone GEP 8886	SATURDAY NIGHT WITH THE COUGARS (EP)	30

ROGER COULAM QUARTET
67	CBS 52399	ORGAN IN ORBIT (LP)	20
70	Fontana 16009	BLOW HOT, BLOW COLD (LP)	20

DENIS COULDRY (& SMILE)
68	Decca F 12734	James In The Basement (solo)/DENIS COULDRY & NEXT COLLECTION: I Am Nearly There	40
68	Decca F 12786	Penny For The Wind/Tea And Toast, Mr. Watson? (as Denis Couldry & Smile)	20

(see also Felius Andromeda)

COULSON, DEAN, McGUINNESS, FLINT
72	DJM DJS 267	Lay Down Your Weary Tune/Tiny Montgomery/I Wanna Be Your Lover	6
72	DJM DJLPS 424	LO AND BEHOLD (LP, gatefold sleeve)	18

(see also Manfred Mann, McGuinness Flint, Dennis Coulson, Lyle McGuinness Band)

DENNIS COULSON
73	Elektra K 42148	DENNIS COULSON (LP, gatefold sleeve)	15

PHIL COULTER ORCHESTRA
68	Pye 7N 17511	Congratulations/Gold Rush	20

COUNCIL COLLECTIVE
84	Polydor MINEX 1	Soul Deep (Club Mix)/Soul Deep (12", stickered black die-cut sleeve)	12

(see also Style Council, Jimmy Ruffin)

COUNT BISHOPS
77	Chiswick S12	Baby You're Wrong/Stay Free (p/s)	8
78	Chiswick NS 35	Mr Jones/Human Bean/Route 66/Too Much Too Soon (unissued, test pressings only, as Bishops)	40
77	Chiswick WIK 1	THE COUNT BISHOPS (LP)	18

(see also Cannibals)

COUNT BUSTY & RUDIES
68	Melody MRC 003	You Like It/The Reggay	200

COUNT DOWNE & ZEROS
64	Ember EMB S 189	Hello My Angel/Don't Shed A Tear	40

(see also Peter & Headlines)

COUNT FIVE
66	Pye International 7N 25393	Psychotic Reaction/They're Gonna Get You	75
87	Edsel ED 225	PSYCHOTIC REACTION (LP)	20

COUNT HALA
69	Rude Boy RBH 005	Cut Price Pussy/THE ATTACKERS : Police In Z Cars Blues	50
70	Rude Boy RBH 006	Gems Of Christies/Cut Price Meow	25

COUNT HOUSE FOLK MUSIC CLUB
65	Own label MSCH 2	MORE SINGING AT THE COUNT HOUSE (LP, private pressing)	150

COUNT LASHER
59	Caribou 106	Caribou Calabash/Dalvey Girl	20

COUNT MACHUKI
10	Randys THB 7002	Pepper Pot/WINSTON SAMUELS: Lick It Back	30

COUNT OSSIE & HIS MYSTIC REVELATION
71	Ashanti ASH 404	Rasta Reggae/Samia	15

COUNT OSSIE & THE REVOLUTIONARIES

			MINT VALUE £
71	Moodisc MU 3515	Whispering Drums/SLIM SMITH & UNIQUES: Give Me Some More Loving	20
74	Ashanti NTI 1301	GROUNATION (3-LP, booklet, with Mystic Revelation Of Rastafari)	100
76	Dynamic DVLS 1001	TALES OF MOZAMBIQUIE (LP)	30

(see also Jackie Estick, Gaylads, Soul Defenders)

COUNT OSSIE & THE REVOLUTIONARIES
| 78 | Charmers CH 0012 | Hog Head/TRINITY: Dog Meat (12") | 40 |
| 05 | Hot Pot HPLP1014 | LEGGO DUB (LP, reissue) | 18 |

COUNT SUCKLE
| 70 | Q 2200 | Lavender Blues/Humpty Dumpty | 15 |
| 70 | Q 2201 | Please Don't Go/FREDDIE & THE NOTES: Bread On The Table | 15 |

COUNT VICTORS
| 62 | Coral Q 72456 | Peepin' 'N' Hidin'/Don't Laugh At Me ('Cos I'm A Fool) | 8 |
| 63 | Coral Q 72462 | Road Runner/Lorie | 8 |

COUNTDOWNS
| 63 | United Artists UP 1024 | Mouse On The Moon/The Big Safari | 10 |

(see also John Barry)

COUNTING CROWS
| 94 | Geffen GFS 69 | Mr Jones/Raining In Baltimore/Mr Jones (live) (p/s) | 10 |
| 93 | Geffen GEF 24528 | AUGUST AND EVERYTHING AFTER (LP, inner) | 80 |

COUNTRY BOY
| 64 | Blue Beat BB 236 | I'm A Lonely Boy (actually by Shenley Duffas)/EDWARD'S ALL STARS: He's Gone Ska | 35 |

COUNTRY EXPRESS
| 70 | Lucky LU 104 | Watching Trains Go By/Blue Against Grey | 8 |

COUNTRY FEVER
| 69 | Bell BLL 1052 | Too Much Of Nothing/Tears Of Rage | 8 |
| 71 | Lucky LU 106 | Mental Revenge/My World Has Ended | 10 |

COUNTRY FOLK
| 70s | Thule SLP 101 | THE COUNTRY FOLK (LP, private pressing) | 180 |

COUNTRY FUNK
| 70 | Polydor 248 2018 | COUNTRY FUNK (LP) | 18 |

COUNTRY GAZETTE
| 72 | United Artists UAG 29404 | TRAITOR IN OUR MIDST (LP) | 15 |

(see also Flying Burrito Brothers)

COUNTRY GENTLEMEN
| 63 | Decca F 11766 | Greensleeves/Baby Jean | 10 |

(see also High Society, Peter Cowap)

COUNTRY HAMS
| 74 | EMI EMI 2220 | Walking In The Park With Eloise/Bridge On The River Suite (p/s, red & brown label) | 50 |
| 82 | EMI EMI 2220 | Walking In The Park With Eloise/Bridge On The River Suite (p/s, reissue, beige label) | 15 |

(see also Paul McCartney/Wings, Floyd Cramer)

COUNTRY JOE & THE FISH
67	Fontana TF 882	Not So Sweet Martha Lorraine/Love	15
69	Vanguard VA 3	Here I Go Again/It's So Nice To Have Love	7
70	Vanguard 6076 250	I-Feel-Like-I'm-Fixin'-To-Die Rag/Maria	10
67	Fontana TFL 6081	ELECTRIC MUSIC FOR THE MIND AND BODY (LP, flipback sleeve, also Stereo STFL 6087)	40
68	Fontana TFL 6086	I-FEEL-LIKE-I'M-FIXIN'-TO-DIE (LP, flipback sleeve)	40
68	Vanguard SVRL 19006	TOGETHER (LP)	20
69	Vanguard SVRL 19026	ELECTRIC MUSIC FOR THE MIND AND BODY (LP, reissue)	30
69	Vanguard SVRL 19029	I-FEEL-LIKE-I'M-FIXIN'-TO-DIE (LP, reissue)	15
69	Vanguard SVRL 19048	HERE WE ARE AGAIN (LP)	20
70	Vanguard 6359 002	C.J. FISH (LP)	25
72	Vanguard VSD 79244	ELECTRIC MUSIC FOR THE MIND AND BODY (LP, reissue, 'West Brothers' printing credit)	20
73	Vanguard VSD 27/28	THE LIFE AND TIMES OF (2-LP, gatefold sleeve, quadraphonic)	20
75	Vanguard VSD 79244	ELECTRIC MUSIC FOR THE MIND AND BODY (LP, reissue)	15
80	Piccadilly PIC 3009	THE EARLY YEARS (LP, private pressing, withdrawn)	40

(see also Country Joe McDonald)

COUNTRY JUG
| 72 | Decca F 13270 | I'm Sorry/Do You Wanna?/Flying | 8 |

(see also Ray Dorset)

WAYNE/JAYNE COUNTY (& ELECTRIC CHAIRS)
77	Illegal IL 002	Stuck On You/Paranoia Paradise/The Last Time (p/s)	10
77	Sweet F.A. WC 1	Fuck Off/On The Crest (p/s)	12
78	Safari SAFE 1	Eddie And Sheena/Rock And Roll Cleopatra (p/s, with cartoon insert)	15
78	Safari SAFE 1	Eddie And Sheena/Rock And Roll Cleopatra (p/s, without cartoon insert)	10
78	Safari SAFE 6	I Had Too Much To Dream Last Night/Fuck Off (unissued)	0
78	Safari WC 2	BLATANTLY OFFENZIVE (EP, gold vinyl)	10
79	Illegal IL 005	Thunder When She Walks/What You Got (p/s)	6
79	Safari SAFE 18	So Many Ways/J'Attends Les Marines (p/s, as Electric Chairs)	20
78	Safari LONG 1	ELECTRIC CHAIRS (LP)	20
78	Safari GOOD 1	STORM THE GATES OF HEAVEN (LP, multicoloured or grey marbled vinyl)	20
79	Safari GOOD 2	THINGS YOUR MOTHER NEVER TOLD YOU (LP)	18

COURIERS
| 66 | Ember EMB S 218 | Take Away/Done Me Wrong (with p/s) | 80 |
| 66 | Ember EMB S 218 | Take Away/Done Me Wrong | 25 |

(see also William E. Kimber)

COURIERS
| 69 | Ash ALP 201 | PACK UP YOUR SORROWS (LP) | 30 |

COURTEENERS
| 07 | Loog LOOG 022 | Cavorting/No You Didn't, No You Don't (p/s, 750 only) | 50 |
| 07 | Loog 174 971-7 | Acrylic/An Ex Is An Ex For A Reason (7") | 12 |

COURTIERS OF FASHION

MINT VALUE £

07	COURT 2	Bide Your Time (1-sided, in white die-cut sleeve)	75
08	Loog 1764282	Not Nineteen Forever/If It Wasn't For Me (Demo) (p/s)	15
08	Loog 175 691 3	What Took You So Long?/Not One Could I Give (p/s, numbered)	10
10	Polydor 2758403	ELECTRIC LICK (EP, 10", numbered)	10
13	V2 VVR726589	Lose Control/Chipping Away	6
08	Polydor 1767024	ST. JUDE (LP)	200
10	Polydor 2729354	FALCON (LP)	200
13	V2 VVR724852	ANNA (LP, CD)	150
16	Ignition IGNLP82	MAPPING THE RENDEZVOUS (LP, white/cream vinyl, some signed)	35
16	Ignition IGNLP82	MAPPING THE RENDEZVOUS (LP)	25
18	A&M 6729515	ST. JUDE (LP, reissue, red vinyl)	150
18	Ignition IGNLP127	ST. JUDE REWIRED (LP)	60
18	Ignition IGNLP127	ST. JUDE REWIRED (LP, picture disc)	75
19	Polydor 7730574	FALCON (LP, reissue, hate vinyl)	20
20	Ignition IGNLP186	MORE. AGAIN. FOREVER (LP, clear vinyl)	20
20	Ignition IGNLP186	MORE. AGAIN. FOREVER (LP, pop-up sleeve)	30

COURTIERS OF FASHION
83	Sonar SON 1	Courtiers Of Fashion/The Discussion (p/s)	6

COURT MARTIAL
82	Riot City RIOT 11	NO SOLUTION (EP)	20
82	Riot City RIOT 5	GOTTA GET OUT EP (p/s)	10

LOU COURTNEY
99	Soul Brother SBCS2	I'M IN NEED OF LOVE (LP, reissue)	20

DEAN COURTNEY
96	Kent 6T 12	Today Is My Day/SHARON SCOTT: (Putting My Heart) Under Lock And Key	35

COURTSHIPS
72	UK USA 6	Oops It Just Slipped Out/Love Ain't Love (Until You Give It To Somebody)	10

COURTYARD MUSIC GROUP
74	Deroy	JUST OUR WAY OF SAYING HELLO (LP, private pressing)	1500
15	No Label or Cat no	JUST OUR WAY OF SAYING GOODBYE (LP, reissue, with 48 page booklet, 300 only)	100

DAVE COUSINS
72	A&M AMS 7032	Going Home/Ways And Means	6
72	A&M AMLS 68118	TWO WEEKS LAST SUMMER (LP, brown label)	35
79	Old School SLURP 1	OLD SCHOOL SONGS (LP, private pressing with Brian Willoughby)	35

(see also The Strawbs)

COUSTEAU
00	Palm PALMLP-58-1	COUSTEAU (LP, numbered)	18

DON COVAY (& GOODTIMERS)
61	Pye International 7N 25075	Pony Time/Love Boat	30
61	Philips PB 1140	Shake Wid The Shake/Every Which Way	30
62	Cameo Parkway C 239	The Popeye Waddle/One Little Boy Had Money	30
64	Atlantic AT 4006	Mercy, Mercy/Can't Stay Away	20
65	Atlantic AT 4016	Take This Hurt Off Me/Please Don't Let Me Know	20
65	Atlantic AT 4056	See Saw/I Never Get Enough Of Your Love	20
66	Atlantic AT 4078	Sookie Sookie/Watching The Late Late Show	15
66	Atlantic 584 025	You Put Something In Me/Iron Out The Rough Spots	15
66	Atlantic 584 059	See Saw/Somebody's Got To Love You	15
67	Atlantic 584 082	Shingaling '67/I Was There	10
67	Atlantic 584 094	Sookie Sookie/Mercy Mercy	10
67	Atlantic 584 114	40 Days - 40 Nights/The Usual Place	10
65	Atlantic ATL 5025	MERCY! (LP, plum label)	80
67	Atlantic 587 062	SEE-SAW (LP)	40
69	Atlantic K 50225	HOUSE OF BLUE LIGHT (LP)	25

(see also Soul Clan)

DAVID COVERDALE
90	Epic 656 292 7	Last Note Of Freedom/HANS ZIMMER: Car Building (poster p/s)	8
77	Purple TPS 3509	DAVID COVERDALE'S WHITESNAKE (LP, with inner)	25
77	Purple TPS 3509TC	DAVID COVERDALE'S WHITESNAKE (LP, white label promo, plain sleeve, with insert)	40
78	Purple TPS 3513	NORTHWINDS (LP, with inner sleeve)	20

(see also Whitesnake, Deep Purple, Wizard's Convention, Roger Glover, Jimmy Page)

COVERDALE PAGE
93	EMI EMD 1041	COVERDALE PAGE (LP, inner)	50

(see also David Coverdale, Jimmy Page, Led Zeppelin, Deep Purple, Whitesnake)

COVERS
79	Decca FR 13880	Modern Girls/Head Out On The Road	30
80	Small Operations SO 001	Young Girls/Boyfriend (p/s)	20
81	Polydor POSP 233	Too Hot To Handle/Tinted Windows (p/s)	6
81	Polydor POSP 320	Lonely Diamond/Shoot Shoot	12

JULIEN COVEY & MACHINE
67	Island WIP 6009	A Little Bit Hurt/Sweet Bacon	50
78	Island WIP 6442	A Little Bit Hurt/Sweet Bacon (reissue, with inner)	15
87	Sunset	A Little Bit Hurt/Sweet Bacon (reissue)	12

JULIE COVINGTON
70	Columbia DB 8649	The Magic Wasn't There/The Way Things Ought To Be	15
70	Columbia DB 8705	Tonight Your Love Is Over/If I Had My Time Again	15
72	RCA RCA 2181	Day By Day/With Me It Goes Deeper	6
67	MJB BEVLP 1009	WHILE THE MUSIC LASTS (LP, 99 copies, with Pete Atkin)	400
71	Columbia SCX 6466	THE BEAUTIFUL CHANGES (LP)	150

(see also Rock Follies)

COWBOY

MINT VALUE £

COWBOY
71	Atlantic 2466 022	REACH FOR THE SKY (LP)	15
72	Atlantic K 40312	5'LL GETCHA TEN (LP, with insert)	20

COWBOY COPAS
54	Parlophone CMSP 10	I Can't Go On/A Wreath On The Door Of My Heart (export issue)	10
54	Parlophone MSP 6079	Tennessee Senorita/If You Will Let Me Be Your Love	10
55	Parlophone MSP 6164	I'll Waltz With You In My Dreams/Return To Sender	10
60	Melodisc M 1566	Alabam/I Can	6

(see also Johnny Bond)

COWBOY JUNKIES
88	Cooking Vinyl COOK 011	THE TRINITY SESSIONS (LP)	20

COWBOYS INTERNATIONAL
79	Virgin VS 253	Aftermath/Pt. 2 (orange vinyl, p/s)	10
79	Virgin V2136	THE ORIGINAL SIN (LP, stickered PVC outer sleeve)	15

(see also Public Image Ltd.)

STANLEY COWELL
72	Freedom FLP40204	BRILLIANT CIRCLES (LP)	25

ELLERY COWLES
18	Revoke REVOKE 005	RELEASED TOXINS (12", stamped white labels, 300 only)	20

COWSILLS
67	MGM MGM 1353	The Rain, The Park And Other Things/River Blue	30
68	MGM MGM 1383	We Can Fly/A Time For Remembrance	15
68	MGM MGM 1400	In Need Of A Friend/Mr. Flynn	6
68	MGM MGM 1424	Indian Lake/Newspaper Blanket	6
67	MGM C/CS 8059	THE COWSILLS (LP)	25
68	MGM CS 8077	WE CAN FLY (LP)	20
68	MGM CS 8095	CAPTAIN SAD AND HIS SHIP OF FOOLS (LP)	15

BILLY COX
71	Pye Intl. NSPL 25158	NITRO FUNCTION (LP, blue/black label with logo-banner on left)	100

(see also Jimi Hendrix)

HARRY COX
65	EFDSS LP 1004	ENGLISH FOLK SINGER (LP)	25
65	DTS Records LFX 4	ENGLISH FOLK SINGER (LP)	15

IDA COX
54	London AL 3517	SINGS THE BLUES (10" LP)	30

(see also Ma Rainey)

IDA COX/ETHEL WATERS
50s	Poydras 104	IDA COX AND ETHEL WATERS (EP)	25

MICHAEL COX
59	Decca F 11166	Boy Meets Girl/Teenage Love	20
59	Decca F 11182	Too Hot To Handle/Serious	20
60	Triumph RGM 1011	Don't Want To Know/Angela Jones	12
60	Ember EMB S 103	Angela Jones/Don't Want To Know (export issue)	50
60	HMV POP 789	Along Came Caroline/Lonely Road	15
61	HMV POP 830	Teenage Love/Linda	15
61	HMV POP 905	Sweet Little Sixteen/Cover Girl	25
62	HMV POP 972	Young Only Once/Honey Cause I Love You	8
62	HMV POP 1065	Stand Up/In April	10
63	HMV POP 1220	Gee What A Party/See That Again	10
64	HMV POP 1293	Rave On/Just Say Hello	15
65	HMV POP 1417	Gypsy/It Ain't Right	10
66	Parlophone R 5436	I Hate Getting Up In The Morning/Love 'Em And Leave 'Em	10
67	Parlophone R 5580	I'll Always Love You/You Never Can Tell (Till You Try)	10

SONNY COX
70	Pama PM 815	Choking Kind/Chocolate Candy	12

WALLY COX
61	Vogue V 9175	I Can't Help It/The Heebie Jeebees	15
74	Pye Disco Demand DDS 105	This Man/I've Had Enough	8
74	Pye Disco Demand DDS 105	This Man/I've Had Enough (DJ Copy)	15
89	Kent 6T 5	This Man Wants You/SIX TEASERS: Doing The Hundred	15

LOL COXHILL
78	Chiltern Sound CS 100	MURDER IN THE AIR (12" EP)	35
71	Dandelion DSD 8008	EAR OF BEHOLDER (2-LP, gatefold sleeve)	90
72	Mushroom 150 MR 23	TOVERBAL SWEET (LP)	80
73	Caroline C 1503	COXHILL MILLER (LP, with Stephen Miller)	20
74	Caroline C 1507	THE STORY SO FAR ... OH REALLY? (LP, with Stephen Miller)	25
75	Caroline C 1514	LOL COXHILL & WELFARE STATE (LP)	20
75	Caroline C 1515	FLEAS IN THE CUSTARD (LP)	20
76	Ogun OG 510	DIVERSE (LP)	15
78	Ogun OG 525	THE JOY OF PARANOIA (LP)	25
78	Incus 0008	MOOT (LP)	25
80	Pipe PIPE 1	SLOW MUSIC (LP)	30

(see also Stephen Miller & Lol Coxhill, Kevin Ayers, Steve York's Camelo Pardalis)

COXHILL BEDFORD DUO
71	Polydor 2001 253	Pretty Little Girl (Parts 1 & 2)	25
72	Dandelion 2058 214	Mood/WILL DANDY & DANDYLETTES: Sonny Boy/Oh Mein Papa	20

(see also David Bedford, Lol Coxhill)

GRAHAM COXON
00	Transcopic 10 RDJ 6541	Oochy Woochy/That's When I Reach For My Revolver (10" promo p/s)	6
06	Parlophone R 6721	What Ya Gonna Do Now?/Bloody Annoying	6

Kevin COYNE

			MINT VALUE £
98	Transcopic TRANLP 005	THE SKY IS TOO HIGH (LP, inner sleeve, 4 postcards)	45
01	Transcopic TRANLP 010	CROW SIT ON BLOOD TREE (2-LP, with inners & print, signed, 1,000 only)	50
01	Transcopic TRANLP 010	CROW SIT ON BLOOD TREE (2-LP, with inners & print, 1,000 only)	40
02	Transcopic TRANLP 018	THE KISS OF MORNING (2-LP, 10" x 10" picture book)	30
04	EMI 5775191	HAPPINESS IN MAGAZINES (LP)	50
06	Parlophone 350 5191	LOVE TRAVELS AT ILLEGAL SPEEDS (2-LP)	45
09	Transcopic TRANS 102X	THE SPINNING TOP (2-LP)	50
12	Parlophone 5099960278418	A+E (LP)	18
18	Graham Coxon Records GC1	THE END OF THE F****ING WORLD (LP, gatefold)	60

(see also Blur)

KEVIN COYNE

72	Dandelion 2001 357	Cheat Me/Flowering Cherry	7
72	Dandelion 2310 228	CASE HISTORY (LP)	150
73	Virgin VD 251/2	MARJORY RAZORBLADE (2-LP, gatefold sleeve with "130 Notting Hill Gate" credit, black/white label)	25
73	Virgin VD 2501	MARJORY RAZORBLADE (2-LP, gatefold sleeve, later pressing without "130 Notting Hill Gate" credit)	15
74	Virgin V 2012	BLAME IT ON THE NIGHT (LP, lyric insert, coloured 'twin Virgin' label)	25
75	Virgin V 2033	MATCHING HEAD AND FEET (LP, laminated sleeve, lyric poster, coloured "twin-Virgin" label)	15
79	Virgin V 2128	BABBLE (LP, with Dagmar Krause)	20
80	Dandelion BUTBOX 1	DANDELION YEARS (3-LP, re-issue of Siren LP's Siren, Strange Locomotion and Coynes Case History)	25

(see also Clague, Coyne-Clague, Siren, Gordon Smith)

COYNE-CLAGUE
69	Dandelion S 4494	The Stride/I Wonder Where	8

CRABBY APPLETON
70	Elektra 2101 006	Go Back/Try	12
71	Elektra EK 45716	Grab On/Can't Live My Life	8
70	Elektra EKS 74067	CRABBY APPLETON (LP)	20
71	Elektra EKS 74106	ROTTEN TO THE CORE (LP)	20

CRACK (1)
80	JSO EAT 4	Making The Effort/Easy Street	8

CHRIS CRACK
18	Daupe! DM SP 043	THANKS UNCLE TRILL (LP, 125 copies)	30
18	Daupe! DM SP 043	THANKS UNCLE TRILL (LP, blue, marbled or white vinyl, 125 copies of each)	35
18	Daupe! DM SP 043	THANKS UNCLE TRILL (LP, with obi strip, 20 copies)	80

CRACK (3)
82	RCA RCA 214	Don't You Ever Let Me Down/I Can't Take It (die-cut 'Battle of the Bands' sleeve)	25
82	RCA RCA 255	Going Out/The Troops Have Landed (p/s)	15
83	RCA CRACK 1	All Or Nothing/I Caught You Out (p/s)	30
83	Link LP073	IN SEARCH OF THE CRACK (LP)	20

CRACKED MIRROR
83	CMLP 001	CRACKED MIRROR (LP, private pressing, 200 only)	80

CRACKERS
69	Fontana TF 995	Honey Do/It Happens All The Time	15

(see also Merseys)

CRACKLES
74	Filo FL2	Keep Shaking/Hey Hey Little Girl	20

SARAH CRACKNELL
87	3 Bears TED 001	Love Is All You Need/Coastal Town (p/s)	100

(see also St. Etienne, 50 Year Void, Lovecut D.B.)

CRACK THE SKY
76	Lifesong ELS 45016	We Want Mine/Invaders From Mars	8
76	Lifesong LSLP 6005	ANIMAL NOTES (LP, with inner sleeve)	15

(BILLY) 'CRASH' CRADDOCK
59	Philips PB 966	Boom Boom Baby/Don't Destroy Me (as 'Crash' Craddock)	30
60	Philips PB 1006	Since She Turned Seventeen/I Want That (as 'Crash' Craddock)	30
60	Philips PB 1092	Good Time Billy (Is A Happiness Fool)/Heavenly Love	15
61	Mercury AMT 1146	How Lonely He Must Be/Truly True	8

CRADLE OF FILTH
94	Cacophonous NIHIL1	THE PRINCIPLE OF EVIL MADE FLESH (LP)	25
96	Cacophonous NIHIL 6LP	VEMPIRE (mini-LP)	30
96	Music For Nations MFN 108	DUSK AND HER EMBRACE (LP, with poster)	30
98	Music For Nations MFN 242	CRUELTY AND THE BEAST (LP, stickered sleeve)	25
00	Music For Nations MFN 666	MIDIAN (2-LP)	20
01	AbraCadaver COF 001LP	BITTER SUITES TO SUCCUBI (LP)	15

CARL CRAIG
94	Open OPENT-001	Throw/Remake Uno (as CARL CRAIG PRESENTS PAPERCLIP PEOPLE) (12")	15
94	Open OPENT-004	Throw (The Remixes) (as CARL CRAIG PRESENTS PAPERCLIP PEOPLE) (12")	12
04	Carl Craig (White) CCR002	Volume Two (2x12")	25
95	Blanco Y Negro 509-99865-1	LANDCRUISING (2xLP)	25
01	Obsessive EVSLP20	ABSTRACT FUNK THEORY (as CARL CRAIG PRESENTS...) (2xLP)	20

DESMOND CRAIG
78	Jah Lion HLDC 602	African Children/Coming From Jamaica/Jack The Ripper (12")	12

PAUL CRAIG
66	CBS 202406	Midnight Girl/Autumn	10

CRAIG (1)
65	King KG 1022	Ain't That A Shame/International Blues	18
66	Fontana TF 715	I Must Be Mad/Suspense	250

CRAIG (2)
Year	Label/Cat#	Title	Mint Value £
66	Fontana TF 665	A Little Bit Of Soap/Ready Steady Let's Go	80

(see also Galliard)

DON CRAINE'S NEW DOWNLINERS SECT
Year	Label/Cat#	Title	Mint Value £
67	Pye 7N 17261	I Can't Get Away From You/Roses	250

(see also Downliners Sect)

FLOYD CRAMER
Year	Label/Cat#	Title	Mint Value £
54	London HL 8012	Fancy Pants/Five Foot Two Eyes Of Blue	20
54	London HL 8062	Jolly Cholly/Oh! Suzanna	20
55	London HLU 8195	Rag-A-Tag/Aunt Dinah's Quiltin' Party	30
58	RCA RCA 1050	Flip Flop And Bop/Sophisticated Swing	40
60	RCA RCA 1211	Last Date/Sweetie Baby	7
61	RCA 1241	San Antonio Rose/I Can Just Imagine	6
55	London REP 1023	PIANO HAYRIDE (EP, with Louisiana Hayride Band)	30

(see also Country Hams)

CRAMP
Year	Label/Cat#	Title	Mint Value £
78	Rip Off RIP 7	She Doesn't Love Me/Suzy Lie Down (p/s)	10

CRAMPS
Year	Label/Cat#	Title	Mint Value £
79	Illegal ILS 12013	GRAVEST HITS (12" EP, blue vinyl)	30
79	Illegal ILS 12013	GRAVEST HITS (12" EP, black vinyl)	15
80	Illegal ILS 0017	Fever/Garbage Man (withdrawn 1st 'full band' p/s)	20
80	Illegal ILS 0017	Fever/Garbage Man (p/s; re-pressing in different p/s with 4 separate shots)	15
80	Illegal ILS 0017	Garbage Man/Mystery Plane (Unreleased test pressing)	150
80	Illegal ILS 021	Drug Train/Love Me/I Can't Hardly Stand It (p/s)	15
81	IRS PFS 1003	Goo Goo Muck/She Said (p/s, yellow vinyl)	15
81	IRS PFSX 1008	The Crusher/Save It/New Kind Of Kick (12", p/s)	15
85	Big Beat NS 110	Can Your Pussy Do The Dog?/Blue Moon Baby (p/s, orange see-through vinyl)	8
86	Big Beat NS 115	What's Inside A Girl/Give Me A Woman (p/s, purple vinyl)	10
86	Big Beat NS 115	What's Inside A Girl/Get Off The Road/Give Me A Woman (12", p/s, white vinyl)	12
90	Enigma 12ENV22	Creature From The Black Leather Lagoon/Jailhouse Rock/Beat Out My Love (12")	15
80	Illegal ILP 005	SONGS THE LORD TAUGHT US (LP, white label with "Drug Train" in place of "T.V. Set")	175
80	Illegal ILP 005	SONGS THE LORD TAUGHT US (LP, with "T.V. Set")	30
81	IRS SP 70016	PSYCHEDELIC JUNGLE (LP)	25
83	Illegal ILP 012	OFF THE BONE (LP, white label, with different mix of "Drug Train", around 50 copies pressed, unreleased)	100
83	Illegal ILP 012	OFF THE BONE (LP, with 3-D sleeve & glasses)	35
83	Illegal ILP 012	OFF THE BONE (LP, picture disc with extra track)	15
84	Big Beat NED 6	SMELL OF FEMALE (LP, red see-through vinyl)	20
84	Big Beat BEDP 6	SMELL OF FEMALE (LP, picture disc)	20
84	Big Beat NED 6	SMELL OF FEMALE (LP, 2nd issue, black vinyl)	15
86	Big Beat WIKA 46	A DATE WITH ELVIS (LP, with poster)	20
86	Big Beat WIKA 46	A DATE WITH ELVIS (LP, blue vinyl)	25
90	Enigma ENVLP 1001	STAY SICK (LP, inner)	18
91	Big Beat WIKDP 101	LOOK MOM NO HEAD (LP)	15
91	Big Beat WIKPD 101	LOOK MOM NO HEAD (LP, picture disc)	18
90	Illigal ILP 5	SONGS THE LORD TAUGHT US (LP, reissue)	15
91	Windsong WINDSONG 4	LUX (3 x 12" box set, with poster, T-shirt & book, numbered, withdrawn)	50

(see also Beast)

CRANBERRIES
Year	Label/Cat#	Title	Mint Value £
91	Xeric XER 014	Uncertain/Nothing Left At All (p/s)	15
91	Xeric XER 014T	Uncertain/Nothing Left At All/Pathetic Senses/Them (12", p/s)	20
91	Xeric XER 014CD	Uncertain/Nothing Left At All/Pathetic Senses/Them (CD)	40
92	Island IS 548	Dreams/What You Were (p/s)	15
92	Island 12IS 548	Dreams/What You Were/Liar (12")	20
94	Island IS 600	Zombie/Away (p/s)	15
94	Island IS 559	Linger/Pretty (p/s, 2nd issue with b/w picture)	6
94	Island ILPS 8003	EVERYBODY ELSE IS DOING IT... (LP, audiophile edition, black cover, numbered)	125
92	Island ILPS 8003	EVERYBODY ELSE IS DOING IT... (LP)	100
94	Island ILPS 8029	NO NEED TO ARGUE (LP)	100
96	Island ILPS 8048	TO THE FAITHFUL DEPARTED (LP, yellow vinyl, poster)	100
99	Mercury/Island 524 644 1	BURY THE HATCHET (2-LP)	100
12	Cooking Vinyl COOK 552	ROSES (LP, CD)	40
17	BMG 538274061	SOMETHING ELSE (LP)	60

CRANE/FARLOWE
Year	Label/Cat#	Title	Mint Value £
73	Dawn DNS 1034	Can't Find A Reason/Moods	7

(see also Atomic Rooster, Crazy World Of Arthur Brown, Chris Farlowe)

LES CRANE
Year	Label/Cat#	Title	Mint Value £
71	Warner Bros K16119	Desiderata/A Different Drummer	7

TONY CRANE
Year	Label/Cat#	Title	Mint Value £
65	Polydor BM 56008	Ideal Love/Little You	15
66	CBS 202022	Even The Bravest/I Still Remember	20
67	Pye 7N 17337	Anonymous Mr Brown/In This World	15
68	Pye 7N 17517	Scratchin' Ma Head/Patterns In The Sky	20

(see also Bob Miller, Merseys/Merseybeats)

CRANES
Year	Label/Cat#	Title	Mint Value £
89	Bite Back! BB! 017	SELF NON SELF (LP)	15
91	Dedicated DEDLP 003S	WINGS OF JOY (LP with free 12")	15
93	Dedicated DEDLP 009S	FOREVER (LP, with free 12")	15
94	Dedicated DEDLP 016	LOVED (LP)	20

CRANIUM PIE

MINT VALUE £

CRANIUM PIE
09		Fruits De Mer Crustacean 08 Baby You're A Rich Man/Madman Running Through The Fields (poster p/s, 300 only	60
11	Regal Crabmophone WINKLE	MECHANISMS (PART 1) LP, red vinyl card inserts)	30
	002		
11	Regal Crabmophone WINKLE	MECHANISMS (PART 1) (LP, black vinyl, 100 only)	80
	002		
12	Lunartica LUNAR LP 001	THE GEOMETRY OF THISTLES (LP, 'down under' edition, 25 copies, hand-numbered, hand-painted/decorated insert and slightly different cover to standard issue)	60
12	Lunartica LUNAR LP 001	THE GEOMETRY OF THISTLES (LP)	30

CRANNOG
76	Crannog CR 1	CRANNOG (LP)	25

CRASH
82	Crash EJSP 9819	FIGHT FOR YOUR LIFE (EP, no p/s)	30

CRASH ACTION WINNERS
80	Sonic International SI 4281	Texas Girls/Two Trains (p/s)	10

CRASH COURSE IN SCIENCE
79	Go Go ROO1	Kitchen Motors/Mechanical Breakdown/Cakes In The Home (p/s)	15

CRASHERS
69	Amalgamated AMG 834	Hurry Come Up/Off Track	100

CRASS
78	Small Wonder WEENY 2	THE FEEDING OF THE 5000 (12" EP, with 4-page insert with 621984 on front & poster).....	80
78	Small Wonder WEENY 2	THE FEEDING OF THE 5000 (12" EP, reissue, please note that booklet has 621984 on front with the 6 crossed out)	40
79	Crass 521984/1	Reality Asylum/Shaved Women (brown cardboard gatefold p/s)	20
79	Crass 521984/1	Reality Asylum/Shaved Women (later pressing in white newspaper foldout sleeve)	10
80	Crass/Xntrix 421984/1	Bloody Revolutions/POISON GIRLS: Persons Unknown (foldout p/s)	20
80	Crass 421984/5	Nagasaki Nightmare/Big A Little A (foldout p/s, with patch)	25
80	Crass 421984/5	Nagasaki Nightmare/Big A Little A (foldout p/s, without patch)	15
81	Crass 421984/6	Rival Tribal Rebel Revel/Bully Boys Out Fighting (flexidisc with Toxic Graffiti fanzine)	20
81	Crass 421984/6	Rival Tribal Rebel Revel/Bully Boys Out Fighting (flexidisc without Toxic Graffiti fanzine)..	10
81	Crass 421984/6	Rival Tribal Rebel Revel/Bully Boys Out Fighting (hard vinyl promo, p/s)	60
81	Crass COLD TURKEY 1	Merry Crassmass/Merry Crassmass - Have Fun (p/s)	15
81	Crass 321984/IF flexi	Our Wedding (free flexi sent to readers of Loving -'for the price of a Stamp'. By Creative Recording And Sound Services – CRASS' with mailer envelope)	300
81	Crass 621984	THE FEEDING OF THE 5000 (12" EP, reissue)	25
82	Crass 221984/6	How Does It Feel (To Be The Mother Of 1000 Dead?)/The Immortal Death/Don't Tell Me You Care (foldout p/s)	20
83	Crass 121984/3	Sheep Farming In The Falklands/Gotcha! (p/s with lyric insert)	15
83	(no label)	Gotcha! (clear flexidisc)	10
83	Crass 121984/4	Who Dunnit? (Parts 1 & 2) (p/s, brown vinyl)	6
84	Crass 1984	YOU'RE ALREADY DEAD EP	7
79	Crass 521984	STATIONS OF THE CRASS (2-LP, fold-out sleeve, black and white inners, original issue with "Pay no more than £3.00" on sleeve)	40
81	Crass 321984/1	PENIS ENVY (LP, original pressing with "pay no more than £2.25 on sleeve)	40
82	Crass BOLLOX 2U2	CHRIST THE ALBUM (2-LP, box set with poster and booklet, with "pay no more than 5.00" on spine of box)	50
83	Crass 121984	YES SIR, I WILL (LP, fold-out sleeve, original issue with "Pay no more than £2.75" on sleeve)	25
83	Crass 521984	STATIONS OF THE CRASS (2-LP reissue)	25
84	Crass CAT 5	BEST BEFORE 1984 (2-LP, gatefold, 2 inners)	20
11	Crass 321984	PENIS ENVY (LP, reissue)	25
12	Crass 121994/2	YES SIR, I WILL (LP, reissue)	20
17	Crass 621984	FEEDING OF THE 5000 (SECOND SITTING) (LP, reissue, white vinyl)	15

(see also Anne Anxiety, Joy De Vivre, Eve Libertine, Poison Girls)

CRATOR
79	Recordiau Lloer SEL 0001	Blas Da/Fy Mreuddwyd I/Gelyn Yr Awyr (EP, 1000 only, no p/s)	20

CRAVATS
78	The Cravats CH 004	Gordon/Situations (p/s)	25
79	Small Wonder SMALL 15	The End/Burning Bridges/I Hate The Universe (p/s)	10
80	Small Wonder SMALL 25	You're Driving Me Mad/I Am The Dregs (p/s)	10
81	Small Wonder SMALL 26	Off The Beach/And The Sun Shone On (p/s)	8
82	Crass 221984/2	RUB ME OUT (EP, 21" x 14" poster p/s)	12
85	Reflex 12 RE 10	THE LAND OF THE GIANTS (12" EP)	12
80	Small Wonder CRAVAT 1	THE CRAVATS IN TOYTOWN (LP, with inner sleeve)	25

(see also Very Things)

CAROLINE CRAWFORD
78	Mercury 6167 753	Coming On Strong/A Nice Feeling	6
79	Mercury 9198 055	Coming On Strong/A Nice Feeling (12")	18
19	Kent 6T 35	Ready Or Not Here Comes Love/MIKEY STEVENSON: I Stand Blue	40
90	Motorcity MOTCLP 42	HEARTACHES (LP)	15

CAROLYN CRAWFORD
65	Stateside SS 384	When Someone's Good To You/My Heart	250
65	Stateside SS 384	When Someone's Good To You/My Heart (DJ copy)	300

HANK CRAWFORD
76	Kudu KU 26	I HEAR A SYMPHONY (LP)	15

JAMES 'SUGARBOY' CRAWFORD
73	Chess 6145 024	BOBBY CHARLES: See You Later, Alligator/Jock-o-mo (Iko Iko)	6

JIMMY CRAWFORD
60	Columbia DB 4525	Long Stringy Baby/Unkind	70

JOHNNY CRAWFORD
62	London RE 1343	JOHNNY CRAWFORD (EP)	12
64	London RE 1416	WHEN I FALL IN LOVE (EP)	12

Michael CRAWFORD

MINT VALUE £

63	London HA 8060	RUMORS (LP)	35
64	London HA 8197	JOHNNY CRAWFORD - HIS GREATEST HITS (LP)	30

MICHAEL CRAWFORD
65	United Artists UP 1095	The Knack/Oh That Girl	6

CRAWFORD BROTHERS
57	Vogue V 9077	Midnight Mover Groover/Midnight Happenings	200
57	Vogue V 9077	Midnight Mover Groover/Midnight Happenings (78)	50
59	Vogue V 9140	It Feels Good/I Ain't Guilty (triangular or round centre)	150
59	Vogue V 9140	It Feels Good/I Ain't Guilty (triangular or round centre) (78)	50

CRAWLING CHAOS
80	Factory FAC 17	Sex Machine/Berlin (1st pressing, 3000 copies in embossed p/s)	25
80	Factory FAC 17	Sex Machine/Berlin (repressing, p/s)	15
84	Foetus FOETUS 3	THE BIG C (LP)	20
85	Foetus FOETUS 4	WAQQAZ (LP)	15

PEE WEE CRAYTON
71	Vanguard VSD 6566	THINGS I USED TO DO (LP)	15

CRAZE
79	Cobra COB 3	Motions/Spartans (p/s)	6
80	Harvest HAR 5205	Lucy/Stop Living In The Past (p/s)	6
80	Harvest SHSP 4114	SPARTANS (LP, unissued, test pressings only)	50

(see also Skunks, Hard Corps, Beasts In Cages)

CRAZY CAVAN AND THE RHYTHM ROCKERS
73	Crazy Rhythm CR 01	Teddy Boy Boogie/Bop Little Baby	30
74	Crazy Rhythm CR 02	Teddy Boy Rock'N'Roll/Rockabilly Star/Wildest Cat In Town/Little Teddy Girl	30

CRAZY ELEPHANT
69	Major Minor MM 609	Gimme Gimme Good Lovin'/Dark Part Of My Mind	6
69	Major Minor SMLP 62	CRAZY ELEPHANT (LP, red/white/black label)	60

CRAZY ENGLISH
82	Crazy English CH 001	Crazy English/Lose Or Win	40

CRAZY FEELINGS
67	Polydor NH 56723	Please Lie/Time Is Running Out	6

CRAZY HORSE
72	Reprise RSLP 6438	CRAZY HORSE (LP)	25
72	Reprise K 44171	LOOSE (LP, gatefold sleeve)	15

(see also Neil Young, Jack Nitzsche)

CRAZY HOUSE
82	T.W. PROP 2	THEY DANCE LIKE THIS FROM AS FAR OFF AS THE CRAZY HOUSE (LP, insert)	15

CRAZY PAVING
70	MCA KM55057	Anytime Sunshine/Sweet Brandy	12

CREAM
66	Reaction 591 007	Wrapping Paper/Cat's Squirrel	20
66	Reaction 591 011	I Feel Free/N.S.U.	12
67	Reaction 591 015	Strange Brew/Tales Of Brave Ulysses	15
68	Polydor 56258	Anyone For Tennis (The Savage Seven Theme)/Pressed Rat And Warthog	10
68	Polydor 56286	Sunshine Of Your Love/SWLABR	10
68	Polydor 56300	White Room/Those Were The Days	8
69	Polydor 56315	Strange Brew/Wrapping Paper (unissued)	0
69	Polydor 56315	Badge/What A Bringdown	7
71	Polydor 2058 120	I Feel Free/Wrapping Paper	6
72	Polydor 2058 285	Badge/What A Bringdown (reissue)	6
66	Reaction 593 001	FRESH CREAM (LP, mono)	150
66	Reaction 594 001	FRESH CREAM (LP, stereo)	120
67	Reaction 593 003	DISRAELI GEARS (LP, 1st pressing, with label miscredits to 'Windfall Music' and 'Apple Publishing' , '1967' on side 2 label, A1/B1 matrix, sleeve laminated on front & back, mono)	250
67	Reaction 694 003	DISRAELI GEARS (LP, 1st pressing, with 'Windfall Music' and 'Apple publishing' label miscredits.Sleeve laminated on front only, stereo)	120
67	Reaction 594 003	DISRAELI GEARS (LP, 1st pressing, with 'Windfall Music' and 'Apple publishing' label miscredits.Sleeve laminated on front & back, stereo)	120
67	Reaction 593 003	DISRAELI GEARS (LP, 2nd pressing, with label credits of 'Immediate Music' and 'Apple publishing', sleeve laminated on front & back, mono)	150
68	Reaction 593 003	DISRAELI GEARS (LP, 3rd pressing, with 'Immediate' and 'Copyright Control' label credits, sleeve laminated on front only, white box with text in top right corner of back sleeve, mono)	75
68	Reaction 594 003	DISRAELI GEARS (LP, DISRAELI GEARS (LP, 3rd pressing, with 'Immediate' and 'Copyright Control' label credits, sleeve laminated on front only, white box with text in top right corner of back sleeve, stereo)	60
68	Polydor 582 031/2	WHEELS OF FIRE (2-LP, gatefold sleeve, mono)	100
68	Polydor 583 031/2	WHEELS OF FIRE (2-LP, gatefold sleeve, stereo)	80
68	Polydor 582 033	WHEELS OF FIRE - IN THE STUDIO (LP, mono)	50
68	Polydor 583 033	WHEELS OF FIRE - IN THE STUDIO (LP, stereo)	40
68	Polydor 582 040	WHEELS OF FIRE - LIVE AT THE FILLMORE (LP, mono)	50
68	Polydor 583 040	WHEELS OF FIRE - LIVE AT THE FILLMORE (LP, stereo)	40
69	Polydor 583 033	WHEELS OF FIRE - IN THE STUDIO (LP, 2nd pressing, matt sleeve, stereo)	30
69	Polydor 583 053	GOODBYE (LP, gatefold sleeve, with poster)	25
69	Polydor 583 053	GOODBYE (LP, gatefold sleeve, without poster)	20
69	Polydor 583 060	THE BEST OF CREAM (LP, 1st pressing, red labels)	18
70	Polydor 2612 001	WHEELS OF FIRE (2-LP, 2nd pressing, matt sleeve, stereo. New catalogue number features on sleeve, spine and labels)	40
70	Polydor 2383 016	LIVE CREAM (LP)	18
71	Polydor 2855 002	CREAM ON TOP (LP, mail-order compilation)	20
72	Polydor 2383 119	LIVE CREAM VOL. 2 (LP)	18

CREAMERS

MINT VALUE £

73	Reaction 594 003	DISRAELI GEARS (LP, 4th pressing, unlaminated sleeve, printed inner, stereo)	35
77	RSO 2394 178	GOODBYE (LP, 2nd pressing)	15
77	RSO 2479 160/1	WHEELS OF FIRE (2-LP reissue, 'set no. 2671 109' on back sleeve and labels)	20
80	RSO 2658 142	CREAM (7-LP set including "Fresh Cream", "Disraeli Gears", "Wheels Of Fire", Goodbye, "Live Cream" & "Live Cream Vol. 2")	40
83	RSO SPDLP 2	WHEELS OF FIRE (2-LP reissue, black labels)	20
88	RSO 18MW 0068	DISRAELI GEARS (LP, 5th pressing, unlaminated sleeve, stereo)	15
97	Polydor/Simply Vinyl SVLP 087	DISRAELI GEARS LP, reissue)	20
97	Polydor/Simply Vinyl SVLP 106	FRESH CREAM (LP, reissue with extra track I Feel Free)	15
97	Polydor/Simply Vinyl SVLP 202	WHEELS OF FIRE (2-LP, reissue)	25
97	Polydor/Simply Vinyl SVLP 211	GOODBYLE (LP, reissue)	15
14	Polydor/Back To Black 0600753548417	CREAM 1966 - 1972 (7-LP box set)	100
17	Polydor 572 266-9	FRESH CREAM (6-LP box set)	60

(see also Eric Clapton, Jack Bruce, Ginger Baker, Blind Faith)

CREAMERS
89	Fierce FRIGHT 045	Sunday Head/Think I'm Gonna Be Sick (p/s)	10

JOAN CREARY
71	Fab FAB 181	Your Best Friend/Version	7

CREATION (U.K.)
66	Planet PLF 116	Making Time/Try And Stop Me (with Planet sleeve)	80
66	Planet PLF 116	Making Time/Try And Stop Me (without Planet sleeve)	50
66	Planet PLF 119	Painter Man/Biff Bang Pow (with Planet sleeve)	80
66	Planet PLF 119	Painter Man/Biff Bang Pow (without Planet sleeve)	50
67	Polydor 56177	If I Stay Too Long/Nightmares	50
67	Polydor 56207	Life Is Just Beginning/Through My Eyes	100
68	Polydor 56230	How Does It Feel To Feel/Tom Tom	75
68	Polydor 56246	Midway Down/The Girls Are Naked	50
73	Charisma CB 213	Making Time/Painter Man	8
77	Raw RAW 4	Making Time/Painter Man (reissue, p/s)	10
84	Edsel E 5006	Making Time/Uncle Bert (p/s)	10
73	Charisma Perspective CS 8	THE CREATION '66-67 (LP)	50
82	Edsel ED 106	HOW DOES IT FEEL TO FEEL (LP, with foldout insert)	15

(see also Mark Four, Birds, Ashton Gardner & Dyke, Kennedy Express, Eddy Phillips, Smiley, Spectrum)

CREATION (U.S.)
72	Stateside SS 2205	I Got The Fever/Soul Control	12

(see also Prophets)

CREATION REBEL
79	Hit Run HIT DD8	Beware/Natty Conscience Free (12")	50
81	On-U Sound DP3	Independent Man Dub/CREATION REBEL : Dub (10")	30
82	Cherry Red CHERRY 41	Love I Can Feel/Read And Learn (p/s)	18
78	Hit Run APLP 9001	DUB FROM CREATION (LP)	80
79	Hit Run APLP 9004	REBEL VIBRATIONS (LP)	70
79	Hit Run APLP 9008	CLOSE ENCOUNTERS OF THE THIRD WORLD (LP)	45
81	4D Rhythms 4DLP1	STARSHIP AFRICA (LP)	40
81	Static STATLP 04	PSYCHOTIC JONKANOO (LP)	30
82	On-U Sound ON-U LP08	STARSHIP AFRICA (LP)	30
82	Cherry Red BRED 21	THREAT TO CREATION (LP, with the New Age Steppers)	25
82	Cherry Red/On-U BRED 33	LOWS & HIGHS (LP)	25

CREATIONS
67	Rio R 133	Meet Me At Eight/Searching	35
68	Amalgamated AMG 818	Holding Out/Get On Up	50
69	Punch PH 2	Mix Up Girl/Qua Kue Shut	400

(see also Little Roys)

CREATION STEPPER
79	Tribesman TM 006	Stormy Night (with Ranking Jahman)/Stepper Now (12", p/s as Creation Stoppers)	70
79	Tribesman TM 22	What You Are Not Supposed To Do/Children Obey Your Parents (12")	18
80	Nationwide NWD 015	Homeward Bound/Version (12")	80
81	Moa Anbassa MA005	Treat Me Unkind/Unkind Dub (12")	15
04	Jah Tubbys JT 10019	King Nebuchadnezzar (with the Disciples Riddim Section)/The Nebuchadnezzar Skarock (with the Dread-UK Crew) (12")	30

(see also Fred Locks)

CREATIVE SOURCE
75	Polydor 2066680	Don't Be Afraid (Take My Love)/Pass The Feelin' On	30
73	Sussex LPSX6	CREATIVE SOURCE (LP, gatefold)	20
74	Sussex LPS X7	MIGRATION (LP)	15
75	Polydor 2391196	PASS THE FEELIN ON (LP)	15
76	Polydor 2391221	CONSIDER THE SOURCE (LP)	15

CREATOR
80	Seven Leaves SLPP 001	Such Is Life/PRODIGAL CREATOR: Such Is Life (12")	75

(see also Lord Creator)

CREATOR & NORMA
63	Island WI 105	We Will Be Lovers/Come On Pretty Baby	15

(see also Lord Creator)

CREATORS
96	Blind Side BS002	HAVE A MASTER PLAN (EP)	12

CREATURE BEAT
80	Puritan PUR 1	She Won't Dance/Creature Beat (p/s)	8

CREATURES
66	CBS 202048	Turn Out The Light/It Must Be Love	12
66	CBS 202350	String Along/Night Is Warm	12
67	CBS 2666	Looking At Tomorrow/Someone Needs You	12

MARTIN CREED AND BOX CODAX
11	Telephone/Vinyl Factory VF 031	Where You Go/Dawning (12", 100 only labels hand-painted by Martin Creed)	100

CREEDENCE CLEARWATER REVIVAL
69	Liberty LBF 15223	Proud Mary/I Put A Spell On You (withdrawn)	20
69	Liberty LBF 15223	Proud Mary/Born On The Bayou	6
69	Liberty LBF 15230	Bad Moon Rising/Lodi	7
69	Liberty LBF 15250	Green River/Commotion	6
70	Liberty LBF 15283	Down On The Corner/Fortunate Son	7
70	Liberty LBF 15310	Travellin' Band/Who'll Stop The Rain	8
70	Liberty LBF 15354	Up Around The Bend/Run Through The Jungle (in p/s)	10
70	Liberty LBF 15354	Up Around The Bend/Run Through The Jungle	6
70	Liberty LBF 15384	Long As I Can See The Light/Lookin' Out My Back Door (in p/s)	10
69	Liberty LBS 83259	CREEDENCE CLEARWATER REVIVAL (LP, blue label)	80
69	Liberty LBS 83261	BAYOU COUNTRY (LP, blue label)	40
69	Liberty LBS 83273	GREEN RIVER (LP, blue label)	40
70	Liberty LBS 83338	WILLY AND THE POORBOYS (LP, 1st pressing, blue labels, textured sleeve)	40
70	Liberty LBS 83338	WILLY AND THE POORBOYS (LP, 2nd pressing, blue labels, front laminated sleeve)	35
70	Liberty LBS 83388	COSMO'S FACTORY (LP, 1st pressing, black labels, front laminated sleeve)	40
71	Liberty LBG 83400	PENDULUM (LP, gatefold sleeve)	20
73	Fantasy FT 506	CREEDENCE CLEARWATER REVIVAL (LP, reissue)	15
73	Fantasy FT 507	BAYOU COUNTRY (LP, reissue)	15
73	Fantasy FT 503	WILLY AND THE POORBOYS (LP, reissue)	15

(see also Golliwogs, John Fogerty, Blue Ridge Rangers)

CREEPERS
66	Blue Beat BB 366	Beat Of My Soul/LLOYD ADAMS: I Wish Your Picture Was You	40

CREEPIES
75	Penny Farthing PEN 875	Teach Me How To Rock N Roll/Legend Of The Creepies	12

CREERY SISTERS
70	High Note BSLP 5004	OH WHAT A GLORY (LP)	20

CREME CARAMEL
69	Pye International 7N 25495	My Idea/Excursion	6

CREPSOLES
71	Ackee ACK 136	The World Gonna Be A Better Place/Invasion	75

CRESCENDOS
58	London HLU 8563	Oh Julie/My Little Girl	60

CRESCENTS (1)
58	Columbia DB 4093	Wrong/Baby, Baby, Baby	100

CRESCENTS (2)
64	London HLN 9851	Pink Dominos/Breakout	15

CRESSIDA
70	Vertigo VO 7	CRESSIDA (LP, gatefold sleeve, large swirl label)	1000
71	Vertigo 6360 025	ASYLUM (LP, gatefold sleeve, large swirl label)	1000
11	Record Collector RCLP 002	TRAPPED IN TIME - THE LOST TAPES (LP)	70
14	Reportoire REP 2224	ASYLUM (LP, reissue)	20
14	Repertoire REP 2225	CRESSIDA (LP, reissue)	20

(see also Uriah Heep, Black Widow)

CRESTAS
65	Fontana TF 551	To Be Loved/When I Fall In Love	25

CRESTERS
64	HMV POP 1249	I Just Don't Understand/I Want You	25
64	HMV POP 1296	Put Your Arms Around Me/Do It With Me	10

(see also Mike Sagar & Cresters, Richard Harding)

CRESTS
59	London HL 8794	Sixteen Candles/Beside You	25
59	Top Rank JAR 150	Flower Of Love/Molly Mae	20
59	Top Rank JAR 168	Six Nights A Week/I Do	25
59	London HL 8954	The Angels Listened In/I Thank The Moon	30
60	Top Rank JAR 302	A Year Ago Tonight/Paper Crown	20
60	Top Rank JAR 372	Step By Step/Gee (But I'd Give The World)	20
60	HMV POP 808	Isn't It Amazing/Molly Mae	20
60	HMV POP 768	Always You/Trouble In Paradise	20
61	HMV POP 848	Model Girl/We've Got To Tell Them	15
62	HMV POP 976	Little Miracles/Baby I Gotta Know	20
63	London HLU 9671	Guilty/Number One With Me	20

(see also Johnny Maestro)

CREW
69	Plexium PXM 12	Marty/Danger Signs	10
70	Decca F 13000	Cecilia/1970	7

CREW-CUTS
56	Mercury 7MT 2	Angels In The Sky/Seven Days (export issue)	10
58	RCA RCA 1075	Hey, Stella!/Forever, My Darling	12
56	Mercury MEP 9002	PRESENTING THE CREW-CUTS (EP)	40
56	Mercury MPT 7501	THE CREW-CUTS ON PARADE (10" LP)	50

BOB CREWE (GENERATION)
64	Stateside SS 356	Maggie Maggie May/We Almost Made It	6

CREWSKY FIXERS

MINT VALUE £

67	Stateside SS 582	Music To Watch Girls By/Girls On The Rocks	8
67	Stateside SS 2032	You Only Live Twice/A Lover's Concerto	10
67	Philips BL 7788	PLAY THE FOUR SEASONS HITS (LP, as Bob Crewe Generation)	25
67	Stateside SL 10210	MUSIC TO WATCH GIRLS BY (LP)	35
68	Stateside S(S)L 10260	BARBARELLA (LP, soundtrack)	75

CREWSKY FIXERS
80	Big Mix ACE 22	CREWSKY FIXERS EP (hand-made p/s, stamped white labels)	12

BERNARD CRIBBINS
67	Parlophone R 5603	When I'm Sixty-Four/Oh My Word	20
62	Parlophone PMC 1186	A COMBINATION OF CRIBBINS (LP, also stereo [PCS 3035])	15

THE CRIBS
03	Squirrel No 5	Baby Don't Sweat/You and I (other 2 tracks by JEN SCHANDE)	80
03	Wichita WEBB 051S	Baby Don't Sweat/Another Number (p/s, yellow vinyl)	6
04	Wichita WEBB 059S	You Were Always The One/Song From Practice 1 (p/s)	20
04	B-Unique KAISER	Plays Kaiser Chiefs (gig only 7" given away free, stickered sleeve)	15
04	Wichita WEBB 061S	What About Me/Feelin' It (yellow vinyl, p/s)	12
05	Wichita WEBB 074 s	Hey Scenesters!/North Of England (p/s, clear vinyl)	7
05	Wichita WEBB 074 SX	Hey Scenesters!/You're Gonna Loose Us (p/s, clear vinyl)	7
05	Wichita WEBB 097S	COLLECTORS BOX SET (8 x 7" box set, coloured vinyl)	45
10	Wichita WEBB 271S	Housewife (1-sided)	8
12	Wichita WEBB 337S	Come On Be A No One/Don't Believe In Me (red vinyl)	8
12	Wichita WEBB 338S	Glitters Like Gold/On A Hotel Wall (clear vinyl)	15
12	Wichita WEBB 344S	Chi-Town/Better Than Me (purple vinyl)	8
13	Roots ROOTS 3	Jaded Youth (Live)/THE BLACK BELLES: Leave You With A Letter (Live) (10" only sold in Jumbo Records, Leeds)	15
17	Sonic Blew 247 CRIBS 001	Year Of Hate (1-sided white label, 247 copies)	20
06	Wichita WEBB 082LP	THE NEW FELLAS (LP)	100
07	Wichita WEBB 126LP	MEN'S NEEDS, WOMAN'S NEEDS, WHATEVER (LP)	40
09	Wichita WEBB 220LP	IGNORE THE IGNORANT (LP)	30
10	Wichita WEBB 058 LPTEN	THE CRIBS (LP, reissue with CD)	100
12	Wichita WEBB 335LP	IN THE BELLY OF THE BRAZEN BULL (2-LP, one side etched with free 7")	25
13	Wichita WEBB 360LP	PAYOLA (2-LP)	40
15	Sony 88875052921	FOR ALL MY SISTERS (2-LP, CD)	25

(see also The Smiths)

CRICKETS FEATURING BUDDY HOLLY
SINGLES
57	Vogue Coral Q 72279	That'll Be The Day/I'm Lookin' For Someone To Love	25
57	Coral Q 72298	Oh Boy!/Not Fade Away	20
58	Coral Q 72279	That'll Be The Day/I'm Lookin' For Someone To Love (2nd issue)	10
58	Coral Q 72307	Maybe Baby/Tell Me How	20
58	Coral Q 72329	Think It Over/Fool's Paradise	20
58	Coral Q 72343	It's So Easy/Lonesome Tears	20

(Originally issued with triangular centres; later round centre copies are worth around half these values.)

68	Decca AD 1012	Oh, Boy/That'll Be The Day (export issue)	75

EPs
58	Coral FEP 2003	THE SOUND OF THE CRICKETS (triangular or round centre)	30
59	Coral FEP 2014	IT'S SO EASY (triangular or round centre)	30
60	Coral FEP 2060	FOUR MORE BY THE CRICKETS	30
60	Coral FEP 2062	THAT'LL BE THE DAY	30

ALBUMS
58	Vogue Coral LVA 9081	THE CHIRPING CRICKETS (Vogue-Coral labels & Coral sleeve)	150
58	Coral LVA 9081	THE CHIRPING CRICKETS (re-pressing with Coral labels & sleeve)	100

(see also Buddy Holly)

CRICKETS
SINGLES
59	Coral Q 72365	Love's Made A Fool Of You/Someone, Someone	15
59	Coral Q 72382	When You Ask About Love/Deborah	15
60	Coral Q 72395	More Than I Can Say/Baby My Heart	15
61	Coral Q 72417	Peggy Sue Got Married/Don'tcha Know	15
61	Coral Q 72440	I Fought The Law/A Sweet Love	15
61	London HLG 9486	He's Old Enough To Know Better/I'm Feeling Better	15
62	Liberty LIB 55495	Little Hollywood Girl/Parisian Girl	8
64	Liberty LIB 55696	(They Call Her) La Bamba/All Over You	7
64	Liberty LIB 10174	I Think I've Caught The Blues/We Gotta Get Together	8
66	Liberty LIB 55603	April Avenue/Don't Say You Love Me	10

EPs
60	Coral FEP 2053	THE CRICKETS (initial triangular centre)	40
61	Coral FEP 2064	THE CRICKETS DON'T EVER CHANGE	15
63	Liberty (S)LEP 2094	STRAIGHT NO STRINGS (mono/stereo)	25
64	Liberty LEP 2173	COME ON	25

ALBUMS
61	Coral LVA 9142	IN STYLE WITH THE CRICKETS	30
62	Liberty LBY 1120	SOMETHING OLD, SOMETHING NEW, SOMETHING BLUE, SOMETHING ELSE! (mono)	15
62	Liberty (S)LBY 1120	SOMETHING OLD, SOMETHING NEW, SOMETHING BLUE, SOMETHING ELSE! (stereo)	20

(see also Buddy Holly, Jerry Allison & Crickets, Ivan, Sonny Curtis, Earl Sinks, Sinx Mitchell, David Box)

JIMMY CRIKIT
70	MCA MK 5047	Isabella/Love Is A See Saw	8

CRIME

MINT VALUE £

CRIME
80	Punk Products PP 1	Johnny Come Home/Generation Gap (p/s, beware of bootlegs)	100

CRIME (U.S.)
90	Solar Lodge DOOMED 2	SAN FRANCISCO'S DOOMED (LP)	15

CRIMEAPPLE
18	Daupe! DM SP 035	AGUARDIENTE (12", p/s, 230 copies)	80
18	Daupe! DM SP 035	AGUARDIENTE (12", p/s, picture disc, 250 copies)	80
18	Daupe! DM SP 035	AGUARDIENTE (12", p/s, aquamarine vinyl, 250 copies)	80
18	Daupe! DM SP 035	AGUARDIENTE (12", p/s, with obi strip, 20 copies)	150
19	Daupe! DM SP 044	WET DIRT (LP, with DJ Skizz, white, pink or yellow vinyl, 125 copies of each)	50
19	Daupe! DM SP 044	WET DIRT (LP, with DJ Skizz, with obi strip, 20 copies)	100
20	Daupe! DM SP 059	JAGUAR ON PALISADE (LP, 200 copies)	40
20	Daupe! DM SP 059	JAGUAR ON PALISADE (LP, picture disc, 250 copies)	50
20	Daupe! DM SP 059	JAGUAR ON PALISADE (LP, white vinyl, 100 copies)	40
20	Daupe! DM SP 059	JAGUAR ON PALISADE (LP, red vinyl, 100 copies)	40
20	Daupe! DM SP 059	JAGUAR ON PALISADE (LP, with obi strip, 20 copies)	125

THE CRIMEWATCH PROJECT
92	Strategic Dance Initiative SDI 004	Boomzabang/Kis My Neck/Friday Night Style (white label 12", stickered paper sleeve)	80

CRIMINAL CLASS
82	Inferno HELL 7	Fighting The System/Soldier (p/s)	15

CRIMINAL JUSTICE
85	Endangered Music EDR 2	HIERARCHY OF HELL (EP)	35

THE CRIMINAL MINDS
90	TCM SRT90L2748	GUILTY AS CHARGED (EP)	180
91	TCM EP002	TALES FROM THE WASTELAND (EP)	80
03	Vinylstore Records VSR001	BREAK SHIT UP (EP)	30
01	UK Rap Records UKR001	WIDOWMAKER (LP)	25

CRIMINALS
81	Crush CR 1	No Pleasure/The Criminals Of This World (no p/s)	100

CRIMINAL SEX
85	Flexi Tits Disc	CRIMINAL SEX EP (white label inside p/s)	20

CRIMSON BRIDGE
72	Myrrh Ms 6224	FILL YOUR HEAD WITH (LP)	25

CRINKS
67	Softspot SPO 1	Pure And Simple/You Can't Cheat	35

CRISIS (1)
79	Peckham Action NOTH 1	No Town Hall (Southwark)/Holocaust/P.C. One Nine Eight Four (p/s)	20
79	Ardkor CRI 002	UK '79/White Youth (p/s)	20
80	Ardkor CRI 003	HYMNS OF FAITH (12" EP)	20
81	Ardkor CRI 004	Alienation/Brückwood/Hospital (p/s, with insert)	20
82	Crisis NOTH 1/CRI 002	HOLOCAUST UK (12" EP)	15

(see also Death In June, Current 93, Theatre Of Hate)

CRISIS (2)
70s	private pressing	ANOTHER FINE MESS (LP)	35

MARILYN CRISPELL
83	Leo LR 118	RHYTHMS HUNG IN UNDRAWN SKY (LP)	15
85	Leo LR 126	AND YOUR IVORY VOICE SINGS (LP)	15

CRISPY AMBULANCE
79	Aural Assault AAR 001	From The Cradle To The Grave/4 Minutes From The Frontline (glossy p/s)	15
79	Aural Assault AAR 001	From The Cradle To The Grave/4 Minutes From The Frontline (matt p/s)	8
81	Factory FAC 32	Unsightly And Serene: Not What I Expected/Deaf (10", p/s)	12

GARY CRISS
62	Stateside SS 104	Our Favourite Melodies/Welcome Home To My Heart	12
62	Stateside SS 123	My Little Heavenly Angel/The Girl That I Told You About	8
63	Stateside SS 164	Long Lonely Nights/I Still Miss You So	8
63	Stateside SS 265	Sweet, Warm And Soft/Little Joe	8
65	Stateside SS 427	Hands Off Buddy/If This Is Goodbye	8

PETER CRISS
79	Casablanca CAN 139	You Matter To Me/Hooked On Rock And Roll (p/s, green vinyl with mask)	20

(see also Kiss)

CRISTINA
78	ZE 12 ZE 001	Disco Clone (Disco Mix)/(Original Mix)/(Instrumental Mix) (12", p/s)	15
80	Ze 12WIP 6560	Is That All There Is/Jungle Love	15
80	Island/Ze 12WIP 6560	Is That All There Is?/Jungle Love (12", p/s)	15
80	Ze ILPS 7004	CRISTINA (LP)	15

BOBBY CRISTO & REBELS
64	Decca F 11913	The Other Side Of The Track/I've Got You Out Of My Mind	45

MARY CRISTY
76	Polydor 2056 513	Thank You For Rushing Into My Life/We Can't Hide This Time	10

CRITICS
81	Moody Music 80C1	Town Girl/Without You/Plastic Valentine (foldout p/s)	35

CRITICS & NYAH SHUFFLE
70	Joe JRS 1	Behold/SEXY FRANKIE: Tea, Patty, Sex And Ganja	50

CRITICS GROUP
66	Argo ZDA 46	A MERRY PROGRESS TO LONDON (LP, with insert)	25
68	Argo ZDA 82	THE FEMALE FROLIC (LP, with insert)	20
68	Argo DA 86	WATERLOO PETERLOO (LP, yellow label with insert)	20
71	Argo ZDA 138	YE MARINERS ALL (LP)	15

CRITTERS

MINT VALUE £

CRITTERS
66	London HLR 10047	Younger Girl/Gone For Awhile	15
66	London HLR 10071	Mr. Dieingly Sad/It Just Won't Be That Way	15
66	London HLR 10101	Bad Misunderstanding/Forever Or No More	25
67	London HLR 10119	Marryin' Kind Of Love/New York Bound	25
67	London HLR 10149	Don't Let The Rain Fall Down On Me/Walk Like A Man Again	15
67	London HA-R 8302	THE CRITTERS (LP)	40

JIM CROCE
72	Vertigo 6073 251	Operator/Rapid Roy	6
72	Vertigo 6360 700	YOU DON'T MESS AROUND WITH JIM (LP, gatefold sleeve, swirl label)	40
73	Vertigo 6360 701	LIFE & TIMES (LP, laminated sleeve, with small spiral label)	200
70s	Life Song 135004	LIFE & TIMES (LP)	15
70s	Life Song 135004	GREATEST CHARATOR (LP)	15

CROCHETED DOUGHNUT RING
67	Polydor 56204	Two Little Ladies (Azalea And Rhododendron)/Nice	40
67	Deram DM 169	Havana Anna/Happy Castle	40
68	Deram DM 180	Maxine's Parlour/Get Out Your Rock And Roll Shoes	25

(see also Force Five, Doughnut Ring, Daddy Lindberg)

TONY CROCKET
82	Alternative ALT 010	Queen Of Hearts/Plane Jane (12", p/s)	50

CROCODILE RIDE
88	CROC 1	Kiss And Tell/Ride	8

CROCODILES
81	Aura AUS 126	New Wave Goodbye/Ribbons Of Steel	10

CROFT
71	Maple MP 1	The Dream/Henry And His Friends	200

CROFTERS
69	Say Disc SD 113	PILL FERRY (EP)	10
69	Beltona SBE 103	CROFTERS (LP)	15

NICOLE CROISILLE
68	Polydor 56746	We Got A Thing/It's All Over	6
77	Decca F13708	The Loving Song/Tell Me What I Want To Hear/Telephone Moi	6

TONY CROMBIE
56	Columbia DB 3822	Teach You To Rock/Short'nin' Bread Rock (as Tony Crombie & Rockets)	40
56	Columbia DB 3859	Sham Rock/Let's You And I Rock (as Tony Crombie & Rockets)	30
57	Columbia DB 3881	Lonesome Train (On A Lonesome Track)/We're Gonna Rock Tonight (78, as Tony Crombie & Rockets)	20
57	Columbia DB 3921	London Rock/Brighton Rock (as Tony Crombie & Rockets)	30
57	Columbia SEG 7676	ROCK ROCK ROCK (EP)	50
57	Columbia SEG 7686	LET'S YOU AND I ROCK (EP)	50
61	Decca DFE 6670	FOUR FAVOURITE FILM THEMES (EP)	10
59	Columbia SEG 7882	SWINGIN' DANCE BEAT NO. 1 (EP)	10
59	Columbia SEG 7896	SWINGIN' DANCE BEAT NO. 2 (EP)	10
59	Columbia SEG 7918	ATMOSPHERE (EP, as Tony Crombie & His Men)	10
54	Decca LK 4087	MODERN JAZZ AT THE FESTIVAL HALL (LP, also features Ken Moule Seven and Don Rendell)	50
56	Columbia 33S 1117	TONY CROMBIE & HIS SWEETBEAT (10" LP)	40
57	Columbia 33S 1108	ROCKIN' WITH TONY CROMBIE & ROCKETS (10" LP)	150
58	Columbia SCX 3262	ATMOSPHERE (LP)	30
59	Top Rank 35/043	MAN FROM INTERPOL (LP, TV series music, by Tony Crombie & Band)	20
61	Tempo TAP 30	JAZZ INC. (LP)	175
60	Top Rank BUY 027	DRUMS! DRUMS! DRUMS! (LP, as Tony Crombie & His Band)	30
61	Decca SKL 4114	SWEET WIDE AND BLUE (LP)	30
61	Ember EMB 3336	WHOLE LOTTA TONY (LP)	40

(see also Annie Ross, Ray Ellington, London Jazz Quartet)

CROMWELL
75	Cromwell WELL 006	First Day	20
75	Cromwell WELL 005	AT THE GALLOP (LP, private pressing)	120

(see also Establishment)

LINK CROMWELL (LENNY KAYE)
66	London HLB 10040	Crazy Like A Fox/Shock Me	25

(see also Patti Smith Group)

ANDREW CRONSHAW
77	Trailer LREP 1	CLOUD VALLEY (EP)	10
77	Trailer LER 2104	EARTHED IN CLOUD VALLEY (LP)	15

CROOKED OAK
76	Folkland FL 0102	FROM LITTLE ACORNS GROW (LP, 500 only)	200
79	Eron ERON 019	THE FOOT O'WOR STAIRS (LP)	25

CROOKS
79	Blue Print BLU 2002	Modern Boys/The Beat Goes On (die-cut p/s)	6
80	Blue Print BLU 2006	All The Time In The World/Bangin' My Head (p/s)	10

DAVID CROOKS
70	Jackpot JP 759	I Won't Hold It Against You (actually by Dave Barker)/ BOBBY JAMES: King Of Hearts	20

(see also Dave Barker)

STEVE CROPPER
70	Stax STAX 147	Funky Broadway/Crop Dustin'	10
69	Stax SXATS 1008	WITH A LITTLE HELP FROM MY FRIENDS (LP)	30

STEVE CROPPER & ALBERT KING
69	Stax SXATS 1020	JAMMED TOGETHER (LP, with Pops Staples)	20

(see also Booker T. & M.G.'s, Albert King)

Bing CROSBY

MINT VALUE £

BING CROSBY
54	Brunswick 03384	White Christmas/Let's Start The New Year Right	10
67	Reprise RS 20645	What Do We Do With The World/Step To The Rear	15

(see also Gary Crosby, Louis Armstrong, Bob Hope, Peggy Lee)

DAVID CROSBY
71	Atlantic 2401 005	IF I COULD ONLY REMEMBER MY NAME (LP, gatefold sleeve, red/plum label)	50

(see also Byrds, Crosby [Stills] Nash [& Young])

GARY CROSBY
58	HMV POP 550	Judy, Judy/Cheatin' On Me	60
57	Vogue VA 160118	GARY CROSBY (LP)	15

(see also Bing Crosby, Louis Armstrong)

CROSBY & NASH
72	Atlantic K 10192	Southbound Train/Whole Cloth	7
72	Atlantic K 50011	GRAHAM NASH & DAVID CROSBY (LP, foldout sleeve)	20

CROSBY, STILLS & NASH
69	Atlantic 584 283	Marrakesh Express/Helplessly Hoping	10
69	Atlantic 584 304	Suite: Judy Blue Eyes/Long Time Gone	10
91	Atlantic 7567-87513-7	Carry On/Questions (p/s)	10
69	Atlantic 588 189	CROSBY, STILLS & NASH (LP, gatefold sleeve, with lyric sheet, plum/orange labels)	30
72	Atlantic K40033	CROSBY, STILLS & NASH (LP, reissue, green/orange labels)	15
91	Atlantic 7567804871	CARRY ON (3-LP, compilation)	80

CROSBY, STILLS, NASH & YOUNG
70	Atlantic 2091 002	Teach Your Children/Country Girl	7
70	Atlantic 2091 010	Woodstock/Helpless	8
70	Atlantic 2091 023	Ohio/Find The Cost Of Freedom	7
70	Atlantic 2091 039	Our House/Deja Vu	10
70	Atlantic 2401 001	DÉJA VU (LP, 1st pressing, 'copyright control/Warner Bros.' publishing credits, gatefold sleeve, pasted-on photo on front, plum/red label)	80
70	Atlantic 2401001	DÉJA VU (LP, 2nd pressing 'Goldhill/Giving Room/Guerilla/Kinney & Flamingo' publishing credits, gatefold sleeve, pasted-on photo on front, plum/red label)	30
71	Atlantic 2657 004	FOUR WAY STREET (2-LP, gatefold sleeve with lyric sheet)	25
72	Atlantic K50001	DÉJA VU (LP, reissue, green/orange labels)	15
99	Atlantic 9362474261	LOOKING FORWARD (2-LP)	50

(see also David Crosby, Stephen Stills [Manassas], Graham Nash, Neil Young)

CROSS
90	Parlophone PCS 7342	MAD, BAD AND DANGEROUS TO KNOW (LP)	15

(see also Roger Taylor, Queen)

JIMMIE CROSS
66	Red Bird RB 10042	Super Duper Man/Hey Little Girl	30

(see also T2)

SANDRA CROSS (1)
85	Ariwa ARILP 026	COUNTRY LIFE (LP)	18
87	Ariwa ARILP 031	STEPPING IN DUBWISE COUNTRY (LP)	18
88	Ariwa ARILP 034	COMET IN THE SKY (LP)	15
91	Ariwa ARILP 066	THIS IS SANDRA CROSS (LP)	18

SANDRA CROSS (2)
11	Trunk JBH 040 LP	THE MMS BAR RECORDINGS (LP, 300 only)	30

CROSS SECTION
74	Private Pressing AAMA/B	Loving Song/Rock N Roll Queen	50

CROSS & ROSS
71	Decca F 13224	Can You Beleive It/Blind Willie Johnson	30
72	Decca F 13316	Peace In The End/Prophets Guiders	15
72	Decca EPS1	CROSS & ROSS (EP) (in demo only p/s)	75
72	Decca EPS 1	CROSS & ROSS (EP)	60
72	Decca SKL 5129	BORED CIVILIANS (LP, blue/silver labels)	300

CROSS COUNTRY
72	Atlantic K 10353	In The Midnight Hour/A Smile Song	6

(see also Tokens)

CROSSTALK A/V
82	Tufty Club TC 1	The Queue/No Earthly Reason/Dear Peter, As You Are A Nice Person... (p/s)	6

CROSS TOWN TRAFFIC
83	Cross Town Traffic CTT 001	No For An Answer/Hanging On To You	50

ANDRAE CROUCH (& DISCIPLES)
70s	Light LS 7019	KEEP ON SINGING (LP)	10

CROW (1)
70	Stateside SS 2159	Evil Woman, Don't Play Your Games With Me/Gonna Leave A Mark	6
70	Stateside SS 2171	Slow Down/Cottage Cheese	10
70	Stateside SS 2180	Don't Try To Lay No Boogie Woogie On The King Of Rock And Roll/Satisfied	6
70	Stateside SSL 10301	CROW MUSIC (LP)	25
70	Stateside SSL 10310	CROW BY CROW (LP)	20

CROW (2)
78	Inferno HEAT 14	Uncle Funk/Your Autumn Of Tomorrow	20

CROWBAR
84	Skinhead SKIN 1	Hippie Punks/White Riot (p/s)	45

CROWD (1)
76	Tropical TST 108	Mango Walk/Beefy Dub	15

CROWD (2)
79	SRT SRTS/79/CUS 377	Ronnie (Is A Headbanger)/A Little Of What I Fancy/Let's Fly Together (p/s)	6

CROWDED HOUSE
88	Capitol EST 2064	TEMPLE OF LOW MEN (LP)	20
91	Capitol 064-793559-1	WOODFACE (LP)	35

Don CROWN & HIS BUSKING BUDGIES

MINT VALUE £

93	Capitol SVLP 282	TOGETHER ALONE (LP)	35
96	Capitol EST 2283	RECURRING DREAM - THE VERY BEST OF CROWDED HOUSE (2-LP)	75
97	EMI LPCENT 6	WOODFACE (LP, reissue EMI 100 Centenary, stickered sleeve)	25

(see also Liam Finn)

DON CROWN & HIS BUSKING BUDGIES
- 70 Orange OA 5507 — Budgerigar Man/Piper Call A Tune 15
- 71 President PT 340 — Mrs Wilson's Budgie/Flying Machines 10

JUDITH CROWNE
- 73 Dart ART 2034 — Steam Hammer/I Will Need Your Love 10

CROWNS
- 68 Pama PM 725 — I Know, It's Alright/I Surrender 25
- 68 Pama PM 736 — Jerking The Dog/Keep Me Going 35
- 68 Pama PM 745 — She Ain't Gonna Do Right/I Need Your Loving 25
- 68 Pama PM 759 — Since You Been Gone/Call Me 25
- 68 Pama PMLP 6 — MADE OF GOLD (LP) 45

CROWS (1)
- 54 Columbia SCM 5119 — Gee/I Love You So 1000
- 54 Columbia DB 3478 — Gee/I Love You So (78) 150

CROWS (2)
- 16 Telharmonium HARM 0005 — UNWELCOME LIGHT (12", p/s) 60

STEVE CROWTHER BAND
- 82 SMK Records SRTS 82 CUS 1584 — Red Herring/My Machine 100

TREVOR CROZIER'S BROKEN CONSORT
- 72 Argo AFB 60 — PARCEL OF OLD CRAMS (LP) 35

CRUCIAL BUNNY
- 79 Star PT LP 1008 — CRUCIAL BUNNY VERSUS PRINCE JAMMYS (LP) 40
- 82 Hawkeye HLP 008 — DUB DUAL (LP, as Crucial Bunny Vs Scientist) 50

(see also Prince Jammy)

CRUCIFIX
- 83 Corpus Christi CHRIST ITS 11 — DEHUMANISATION (LP, poster sleeve) 25

CRUCIFIXION
- 80 Miramar MIR 4 — The Fox/Death Sentence (no p/s) 80
- 82 Neat NEAT 19 — Take It Or Leave It/On The Run (p/s) 10
- 84 Neat NEAT 37 — Green Eyes/Moon Rising/Jailbait (p/s) 10
- 84 Neat NEAT 3712 — Green Eyes/Jailbait/Moon Rising (12", p/s, purple or green vinyl) ... 20

ARTHUR 'BIG BOY' CRUDUP
- 64 RCA RCA 1401 — My Baby Left Me/I Don't Know It 40
- 64 RCA RCX 7161 — RHYTHM AND BLUES VOL. 4 (EP) 15
- 69 Blue Horizon 7-63855 — MEAN OLE FRISCO (LP) 100
- 70 Delmark DS 614 — LOOK ON YONDERS WALL (LP) 25
- 71 Delmark DS 621 — CRUDUP'S MOOD (LP) 25
- 72 RCA RD 8224 — THE FATHER OF ROCK 'N' ROLL (LP) 30
- 74 United Artists UAS 29092 — ROEBUCK MAN (LP) 35

CRUELLA DE VILLE
- 83 EMI 12 EMI 5412 — Gypsy Girl/Blue Blue Blues/Gyspy Girl (Edit) (12") 10

JULEE CRUISE
- 89 Warner Bros. 925 859 — FLOATING INTO THE NIGHT (LP) 25

CRUISERS (1)
- 65 Decca F 12098 — It Ain't Me Babe/Baby What You Want Me To Do 30

(see also Dave Berry, Godley & Creme)

CRUISERS (2)
- 73 EMI 2202 — Schoolgirls/College Collage 6

CRUIZE (1)
- 83 Wait WAIT 1 — Strange Little Girl/Standing In The Rain 35

CRUIZE (2)
- 89 TSR TSCRT 2 — Get Your Lovin/Donyx Soula Muffin Mix (12") 30

SIMON CRUM
- 58 Capitol CL 14965 — Stand Up, Sit Down, Shut Your Mouth/Country Music Is Here To Stay .. 8

(see also Ferlin Husky)

RAY CRUMLEY
- 77 Magnet MAG 103 — It's Uncanny/All The Way In Love With You 10

CRUNCH (1)
- 72 Youngblood YB 1064 — Let's Do It Again/Not Tonight Josephine 7

CRUNCH (2)
- 80 Bridgehouse BHS 7 — 2 (b) By The C Side/Makin Out (no p/s) 8

CRUSADERS
- 71 Rare Earth SRE 3001 — OLD SOCKS NEW SHOES (LP) 15

(see also Jazz Crusaders)

CRUSH
- 80 Carrere CAR 150 — JFC 105/He's A Rebel 12

CRUSHED BUTLER
- 69 EMIDISC — Love Is All Around Me/Factory Grime (acetate) 150

CRUSTATION
- 97 Jive HIP 184 — BLOOM (LP) 50

BETTYE CRUTCHER
- 75 Stax STXS 2031 — Sugar Daddy/As Long As You Love Me 6
- 74 Stax STX 1035 — LONG AS YOU LOVE ME (LP) 18

CRUX/CRASH
- 82 No Future OI 18 — KEEP ON RUNNING (12" EP) 15

CRY (1)

MINT VALUE £

CRY (1)
Year	Label/Cat	Title	Value
80	Sayonara S-3221083	Looking To The Future/Alone (p/s)	35

CRY (2)
| 81 | DATO DAT 1A | Love Is Necessary/Ends Are Split (no p/s) | 80 |

CRY (3)
87	Crazy Flowerpot CFP 001	Party After Dark (with p/s)	80
87	Crazy Flowerpot CFP 001	Party After Dark	15
87	Crazy Flowerpot CFP 002	Give Her An Ice Cream (no p/s)	20

CRYER
| 80 | Happy Face MM 124 | The Single/Hesitate (p/s, with 2 inserts) | 65 |

BARRY CRYER
58	Fontana H 139	The Purple People Eater/Hey! Eula	8
58	Fontana H 151	Nothin' Shakin'/Seven Daughters	10
59	Fontana H 177	Angelina/Kissin'	8

CRYIN' SHAMES
| 66 | Decca F 12340 | Please Stay/What's News Pussycat | 20 |
| 66 | Decca F 12435 | Nobody Waved Goodbye/You | 30 |

(see also Paul & Ritchie & Cryin' Shames, Gary Walker & Rain)

CRYING SHAMES
| 80 | Logo GO 385 | That's Rock'n'Roll/Too Late (p/s) | 12 |

CRY OF THE INNOCENT
| 82 | Pagan CUS 1436 | The Haunting/Still Forever (p/s) | 25 |

CRYPTIC SLAUGHTER
| 90 | Metal Blade ZORRO 6 | SPEAK YOUR PEACE (LP, inner) | 15 |

CRYSBAS
| 79 | Sain 66S | Draenog Marw/Y Nhw (p/s) | 25 |
| 79 | Sain 72E | Mae'di Bwrw/Blws Ty Golchi//Mor Gryg wr Morgrug/Amser (p/s) | 25 |

CRY SHARK
| 81 | Radical Wallpaper RD 002 | Protect And Survive/One Phone Call (p/s) | 20 |

CRYSTAL CASTLES
07	Merok ME 002	Alice Practice/Air War/Love And Caring (p/s)	60
07	Trouble TROUBLE 1	XxzxcuZx Me/HEALTH: Crimewave (200 only, green vinyl white label promo)	10
07	Trouble TROUBLE 1	XxzxcuZx Me/HEALTH: Crimewave (500 only, gig freebie, die-cut stamped sleeve)	12
07	Trouble TROUBLE 001	XxzxcuZx Me/HEALTH: Crimewave (1000 only, p/s)	8
07	Trouble DUDE 003	Air War/Air War (David Wolf Remix) (7" p/s)	10
07	Rough Trade	Pre Untrust/S&MSMS (demo)/Fuck Nicole/And Prolapse (7" given away as 'ticket' to Rough Trade In-Store appearance, 500 only)	25
08	PIAS 451 1092 140	Courtship Dating/Trash Hologram (Demo) (p/s)	7
10	Polydor/Fiction LC06444/2735690	Doe Deer/Mother Knows Best/Insectica/Seed (12" EP, 500 only, p/s)	25
08	Different DIFB 1200PLP	CRYSTAL CASTLES (2-LP)	70
10	Fiction 2740406	CRYSTAL CASTLES (2-LP, gatefold)	40

CRYSTAL CLEAR
| 75 | Crystal Clear CC 1 | Buena Sera/I Want To Make Clear To You | 15 |

CRYSTAL JOY
| 70 | Wren 0346 | Little Dreamer/Bite Hard | 30 |

CRYSTAL MANSION
| 70 | Polydor 2058-070 | Carolina in My Mind/If I Live | 6 |

CRYSTAL METHOD
| 97 | S3 VEGLP 1 | VEGAS (2-LP) | 35 |

CRYSTAL SET
| 81 | Heart & Soul HSCS 001 | Know How/Critical Town | 15 |

(see also Al Foulcer)

CRYSTALITES
69	Big Shot BI 510	Biafra/Drop Pan	40
69	Nu Beat NB 036	Splash Down/Finders Keepers	150
69	Songbird SB 1015	Musical Madness Parts 1 & 2	20
69	Songbird SB 1016	The Bad Parts 1 & 2	40
69	Explosion EX 2002	Doctor Who (Parts 1 & 2)	30
69	Explosion EX 2005	Bombshell/Bag-A-Wire (B-side actually by Bobby Ellis & Crystalites)	70
69	Explosion EX 2006	A Fistful Of Dollars/The Emperor (B-side actually by Bobby Ellis & Crystalites)	50
70	Explosion EX 2010	The Bad/The Bad Version	35
70	Bullet BU 424	A Fistful Of Dollars/BOBBY ELLIS: Crystal	35
70	Songbird SB 1017	The Undertaker/Stop That Man (B-side actually "Easy Ride" by Ike Bennett & Crystalites)	30
70	Songbird SB 1020	Lady Madonna/Ghost Rider	35
70	Songbird SB 1024	Isies/Isies (Version 2)	20
70	Songbird SB 1025	Stranger In Town/Stranger In Town (Version 2)	30
70	Songbird SB 1030	Sic Him Rover/Drop Pon	25
70	Songbird SB 1034	Overtaker (Version I)/Overtaker (Version II)	15
70	Songbird SB 1035	Undertaker's Burial/Ghost Rider	20
70	Songbird SB 1036	Short Story/No Baptism (Version 2)	45
71	Songbird SB 1057	Earthly Sounds/Version	15
72	Songbird SB 1072	Trinity/SCOTTY: Monkey Drop	20
73	Grape GR 3050	Blacula/Version	35

(see also Chosen Few, Ramon & Crystalites, Kingstonians, Bongo Herman, Denzil Laing, Derrick Harriot, Ethiopians, Dennis Brown, Glen Brown, Big Youth)

CRYSTALS
62	Parlophone R 4867	There's No Other Like My Baby/Oh Yeah Maybe Baby	150
62	London HLU 9611	He's A Rebel/I Love You Eddie	10
63	London HLU 9661	He's Sure The Boy I Love/Walking Along (La-La-La)	15

CRYTUFF & THE ORIGINALS

63	London HLU 9732	Da Doo Ron Ron/Git It	8
63	London HLU 9773	Then He Kissed Me/Brother Julius	8
64	London HLU 9837	Little Boy/Uptown (withdrawn)	150
64	London HLU 9852	I Wonder/Little Boy	50
64	London HLU 9909	All Grown Up/PHIL SPECTOR GROUP: Irving (Jaggered Sixteenths)	15
65	United Artists UP 1110	My Place/You Can't Tie A Girl Down	50
63	London RE-U 1381	DA DOO RON RON (EP)	50
63	London HA-U 8120	HE'S A REBEL (LP)	70

(see also Darlene Love, Bob B. Soxx & Blue Jeans, Phil Spector)

CRYTUFF & THE ORIGINALS
79	Hit Run APLP 9006	DUB TO AFRICA (LP) (Pre-release)	45

CSA
78	Goat GOAT 001	STOCKADE (LP)	40

C.S.A.
96	Squariel Records SQ003	Don't/'Till I Waltz Again With You (p/s)	6

C-SAIM
83	Summit SUM 3 T	Night Air/Give And Take (p/s)	15

C.S.L.
93	Nucleus NUKE 008	Work It Tough Bitch/Work It (Tough Mix)/Run Free (Original Jump Mix)/(Dark Black Mix) (12")	40

C. STAR
73	Jam JAM 56	Bad Boy/Alex	10

C.U.B.
73	Dart ART 2033	I'm Going Home/You Have Come My Way	8

JOE CUBA SEXTET
66	Pye International 7N 25401	Bang! Bang!/Push, Push, Push	20

CUBAN HEELS
78	Housewives' Choice JY 1/2	Downtown/Do The Smoke Walk (p/s)	30

CUBY & BLIZZARDS
68	Philips BF 1638	Distant Smile/Don't Know Which Way To Go	15
68	Philips BF 1719	Windows Of My Eyes/Checkin' Up On My Baby	10
69	Philips BF 1827	Apple Knocker's Flophouse/Go Down Sunshine	25
69	Philips (S)BL 7874	DESOLATION (LP, black/silver labels)	80
69	Philips SBL 7918	APPLE KNOCKERS FLOPHOUSE (LP)	45

'CUDDLY' DUDLEY (HESLOP)
59	HMV POP 586	Lots More Love/Later	20
60	HMV POP 725	Too Pooped To Pop/Miss In-Between	25
61	Ember EMB S 136	Sitting On A Train/One Thing I Like	10
62	Piccadilly 7N 35090	Monkey Party/The Ferryboat Ride (as Cudley Dudley)	10
64	Oriole International ICB 9	Blarney Blues/Peace On Earth	10
64	Oriole International ICB 10	Way Of Life/When Will You Say You'll Be Mine	15

CUDDLY TOYS
80	Fresh FRESH 10	Madman/Join The Girls (p/s)	12
81	Parole PURLE 9	Astral Joe/Slowdown (p/s)	12
81	Fresh FRESH 20	Astral Joe/Slowdown (p/s, reissue)	12
81	Fresh FRESH 25	Someone's Crying/Bring On The Ravers (p/s)	8
82	Fresh LP 6	TRIALS AND CROSSES (LP)	15

(see also Raped)

CUES
56	Capitol CL 14501	Burn That Candle/O My Darlin'	250
56	Capitol CL 14651	Crackerjack/The Girl I Love (featuring Jimmy Breedlove)	200
57	Capitol CL 14682	Prince Or Pauper/Why	150

(see also Jimmy Breedlove)

CUFF-LINKS
70	MCA MU 1112	When Julie Comes Around/Sally Ann (You're Such A Pretty Girl)	6
70	MCA MU 1128	Robin's World/Lay A Little Love On Me	6
70	MCA MUP(S) 398	TRACY (LP)	20

XAVIER CUGAT
63	Mercury AMT 1202	Watermelon Man/Swinging Shepherd Blues	10

CLIVE CULBERTSON
79	Rip Off RIP 9	Time To Kill/Busy Signal (initially came in brown paper bag sleeve)	75
79	Logo GO 364	Time To Kill/Busy Signals (reissue)	25
82	Mint CHEW 66	Kill Me/The Night's No Friend Of Mine	30
84	Mint CHEW 89	Just A Little Bit/The Last Laugh	30
85	Mint CHEW 101	I Can't Fight It/You Don't Have A Dream	20

(see also No Sweat (1))

ELI CULBERTSON
74	EMI 2207	I Need Your Love Tonight/Boogie Queen	25

CHRIS CULLEN
82	Zim Zam Z1	Coincidence/I'll See You Later (p/s)	15

CULPEPPER'S ORCHARD
72	Polydor 2480 123	SECOND SIGHT (LP)	175

CULT FIGURES
79	Rather GEAR 4/RT 020	Zip Nolan (Highway Patrolman)/P.W.T. (Playing With Toys)/ Zip Dub (gatefold p/s)	8
80	Rather GEAR 8	In Love/Laura Kate/Almost A Love Song (p/s)	8

(see also Swell Maps)

CULT HERO
79	Fiction FICS 006	I'm A Cult Hero/I Dig You (p/s, 2,000 only)	60

(see also Cure)

CULT MANIAX

82	Elephant Rock ROCK 001	Blitz/Lucy Looe (p/s, with A3 lyric poster)	30
82	Elephant Rock ROCK 002	American Dream/Elephant Rock	15
82	Next Wave NXT 2/BAK 1	Frenzie/The Russians Are Coming/Black Horse/Death March (p/s, withdrawn most have band-inflicted scratch through Black Horse)	60
84	Xcentric SIXTH 1	FULL OF SPUNK! (EP, fold-over p/s in polythene bag)	6
84	Xcentrix EIGTH 1	THE AMAZING ADVENTURES OF JOHNNY THE DUCK AND THE BATH TIME BLUES (EP)	6

CULT (1)

80	Anti-Hype DL 001	It'll Take Time/Frontier/I Always Lose My Temper (p/s)	100

CULT (2)

84	Situation Two SIT 33	Spiritwalker/A Flower In The Desert (p/s)	6
94	Beggars Banquet BBQ 45T	Star/Breathing Out/The Witch (Full Version) (12", p/s)	20
84	Beggars Banquet BEGA 57	DREAMTIME (white label test pressing, with unique version of "Go West")	45
84	Beggars Banquet BEGA 57	DREAMTIME (LP, with free live LP)	30
84	Beggars Banquet BEGA 57P	DREAMTIME (LP)	20
84	Beggars Banquet BEGA 57P	DREAMTIME (LP, picture disc)	20
85	Beggars Banquet BEGA 65	LOVE (LP, gatefold)	25
87	Beggars Banquet BEGA 80	ELECTRIC (LP, gatefold)	25
87	Beggars Banquet BEGA 80	ELECTRIC (LP, gatefold sleeve gold vinyl, 5,000 only)	35
89	Beggars Banquet BEGA 90	SONIC TEMPLE (LP)	25
91	Beggars Banquet CBOX 1	SINGLES COLLECTION (10-CD box set, picture discs with booklet)	30
91	Beggars Banquet BEGA 122	CEREMONY (LP)	40
93	Beggars Banquet BEGA 1230B	PURE CULT (4-LP box set)	100
94	Beggars Banquet BBQLP 164	THE CULT (2-LP)	100
09	Vinyl 180 VIN180LP013	LOVE (LP, reissue, with 12")	60
09	Vinyl 180 VIN180LP014	LOVE (LP, reissue)	25
12	Cooking Vinyl COOKLP548	CHOICE OF WEAPON (LP, with 12")	25
16	Cooking Vinyl COOKLP621	HIDDEN CITY (2-LP, white vinyl)	35
18	Music On Vinyl MOVLP2322	BORN INTO THIS (LP, reissue, pink vinyl, insert)	25
21	Beggars Banquet BBL 65 LP	LOVE (LP, reissue, platinum vinyl)	40

(see also Death Cult, Southern Death Cult, Lonesome No More, Theatre Of Hate, Studio Sweethearts)

CULT MOUNTAIN

15	No label or Cat. No.	CULT MOUNTAIN (LP, repressing, white vinyl, p/s)	60
15	No label or Cat. No.	CULT MOUNTAIN (LP, stamped and signed white labels)	100
16	Daupe! DM SP 013	CULT MOUNTAIN 2 (LP, with OBI strip 20 only)	200
16	No label or Cat. No.	CULT MOUNTAIN 2 (LP, 100 only)	50

CULTS PERCUSSION ENSEMBLE

79	HS 001	CULTS PERCUSSION ENSEMBLE (LP)	100
12	Trunk JBH 046 LP	CULTS PERCUSSION ENSEMBLE (LP, reissue 803 only)	35

CULTURAL ROOTS

82	Reggae REG 01	Ghetto Running/Version (12")	25
83	Music Works MW 007	Whole Heap A Daughter/(Version) (12")	20
80s	Up Front EX 718	Mr Liar Man/People Com A Dance (12", with HUGH CHRIS)	20
82	Germain GLP 002	DRIFT AWAY FROM EVIL (LP)	30
84	Greensleeves GREL 62	HELL A GO POP (LP)	15

CULTURE

77	Sky Note DD 003	The Cultures Trod On/THE REVOLUTIONARIES, CULTURE AND RANKING TREVOR: Trod On In Dub (A-side as "The Cultures") (12" white pasted sleeve)	25
78	Lightning LIG 1978	Two Sevens Clash/I'm Not Ashamed	10
87	Strange Fruit SFPS 042	PEEL SESSIONS (12")	10
78	Sky Note SKY LP 016	IN DUB (LP)	45
78	Lightning LIP 1	TWO SEVENS CLASH (LP)	25
78	Virgin FL 1016	HARDER THAN THE REST (LP)	18
79	Virgin Frontline FL1047	INTERNATIONAL HERB (LP)	15
81	Virgin VX1001	VITAL SELECTION (LP)	15
83	Blue Moon BMLP 004	TWO SEVENS CLASH (LP, reissue)	15

BOBBY CULTURE

82	Leggo LG 003	Health And Strength/Buenos Dias (12")	40

CULTURE CLUB

84	Virgin VSY 694	The War Song/La Cancion De Guerra (picture disc, withdrawn)	30

(see also The Edge)

CULTURE PAUL

80s	Music House MH 2	Mini Van Man (12")	40

PETER CULTURE

84	Ariwa ARI 38	The Counsel Of The Father/BLACK STEEL: Grooving In Love (12")	20
84	Ariwa ARILP 018	FACING THE FIGHT (LP)	15

CULTURE SHOCK

82	Bluurg FISH 20	ONWARDS & UPWARDS (LP)	15
87	Bluurg FISH 19	GO WILD (LP)	15

CULTURED FEW

76	Feelgood FLG 102	Better No Come/Better Dub	25

CULVER STREET PLAYGROUND

68	President PT 145	Alley Pond Park/A Decent Sort Of Guy	12

ANDREW CULVERWELL

71	Polydor 2343 035	WHERE IS THE LOVE? (LP)	15

CUMBERLAND THREE

61	Columbia 33SX 1302	FOLK SCENE, U.S.A. (LP, also stereo SCX 3364)	15
61	Columbia 33 SX 1325	CIVIL WAR ALABAMA VOL 2 (LP)	15
64	Parlophone PMC 1223	INTRODUCING (LP)	15

(see also John Stewart)

David CUMMING

MINT VALUE £

DAVID CUMMING
67 Philips BF 1545 — Rubber Rabbit/The Parrots Of Simple Street 6

BARBARA CUMMINGS
67 London HLU 10110 — She's The Woman/There's Something Funny Going On 7

JON CUNDO
72 Bamboo BAM 69 — Love Is Strange/When We Were Children 10

(see also Joncuno)

ROGER CUNLIFFE
79 Voix VOX 1 — Rebecca Part 1/Slow Dazzle 1 8

DAVID CUNNINGHAM
80 Piano PIANO 001 — GREY SCALE (LP) 40

EARL CUNNINGHAM
70s One Top OSM 002 — Got To Know That Place/Gates Are Wide Open (12") 100
79 Freedom Sounds FSD 016 — Vanity Woman/Best Things (12") 15
80 Freedom Sounds FSD 017 — Never Give Up/Follow Fashion (12") 25
81 Rusty International RI 012 — Cool Profile/School Girl (12") 80
79 Vista Sounds VSLP 4021 — EARL CUNNINGHAM (LP) 25
84 Time TRLP 002 — JOHN TOM (LP, insert) 25

CUPIDS
58 Vogue V 9102 — Now You Tell Me/Lillie Mae 900
58 Vogue V 9102 — Now You Tell Me/Lillie Mae (78) 100

CUPID'S INSPIRATION
68 NEMS 56-3500 — Yesterday Has Gone/Dream 15
68 NEMS 56-3702 — My World/Everything Is Meant To Be 7
69 Bell BLL 1069 — The Sad Thing/Look At Me 7
69 CBS 4509 — Boat Trip/Time Only Knows 20
70 CBS 4722 — Without Your Love/Different Guy 8
70 CBS 4994 — Are You Growing Tired Of My Love/Sunshine 8
74 DJM DJS 300 — Yesterday Has Gone/My World 6
69 NEMS 6-63553 — YESTERDAY HAS GONE (LP, gatefold, as Cupid's Inspiration Featuring T. Rice-Milton) 20

(see also Gordon Haskell, Paper Blitz Tissue)

CUPOL
80 4AD BAD 9 — Like This For Ages/Kluba Cupol (12", p/s, 45/33rpm) 20

(see also Wire, Dome, Gilbert & Lewis, Bruce Gilbert, P'o)

CUPPA T
67 Deram DM 144 — Miss Pinkerton/Brand New World 25
68 Deram DM 185 — Streatham Hippodrome/One Man Band 20

(see also Overlanders)

CUPS
68 Polydor 56777 — Good As Gold/Life And Times 40

(see also Gallagher & Lyle)

CURE
SINGLES
78 Small Wonder SMALL 11 — Killing An Arab/10.15 Saturday Night (p/s, 15,000 only, beware of counterfeits) 80
79 Fiction FICS 001 — Killing An Arab/10.15 Saturday Night (p/s, reissue) 20
79 Fiction FICS 002 — Boys Don't Cry/Plastic Passion ('soldier' p/s, typed matrix, 'but Bill does' on A side runout and 'land of 1000 motorhomes' on B) 20
79 Fiction FICS 005 — Jumping Someone Else's Train/I'm Cold (p/s, typed matrix) 25
80 Fiction FICS 010 — A Forest/Another Journey By Train (p/s) 30
80 Fiction FICS 010 — A Forest/Another Journey By Train (2nd pressing, "radiophonic' sleeve) 15
80 Fiction FICS 010 — A Forest/Another Journey By Train ('radiophonic' die-cut sleeve) 10
80 Fiction FICSX 010 — A Forest (Extended Version)/Another Journey By Train (12", p/s) 200
81 Fiction FICS 012 — Primary/Descent (p/s) 15
81 Fiction FICSX 012 — Primary (Extended)/Descent (12", p/s) 25
81 Fiction FICS 014 — Charlotte Sometimes/Splintered In Her Head (p/s) 15
81 Fiction FICSX 014 — Charlotte Sometimes/Splintered In Her Head/Faith (live) (12", p/s) 18
82 Fiction FICS 015 — The Hanging Garden/Killing An Arab (live) (p/s) 10
82 Fiction FICG 015 — The Hanging Garden/100 Years//A Forest/Killing An Arab (double pack, gatefold p/s, 5,000 only) 18
82 Lyntone LYN 12011 — Lament (1-sided flexidisc, red vinyl) 40
82 Lyntone LYN 12011 — Lament (1-sided flexidisc, green vinyl) 15
82 Lyntone LYN 12011 — Lament (1-sided flexidisc, red vinyl with Flexipop issue 22) 50
82 Lyntone LYN 12011 — Lament (1-sided flexidisc, green vinyl, with Flexipop issue 22) 18
82 Fiction FICS 17 — Let's Go To Bed/Just One Kiss (p/s) 8
82 Fiction FICSX 017 — Let's Go To Bed (Extended)/Just One Kiss (Extended) (12", p/s) 12
83 Fiction FICS 018 — The Walk/The Dream (paper labels, poster p/s) 20
83 Fiction FICSP 018 — The Walk/The Dream (picture disc) 35
83 Fiction FICSX 018 — Upstairs Room/The Dream/The Walk/Lament//Let's Go To Bed (Extended)/ Just One Kiss (Extended) (12" double pack, shrinkwrapped with sticker) 30
83 Fiction FICSP 019 — The Lovecats/Speak My Language (picture disc, PVC sleeve) 35
84 Fiction FIXSP 020 — The Caterpillar/Happy The Man (picture disc, printed PVC sleeve) 30
85 Fiction 080182-2 — In Between Days/The Exploding Boy/A Few Hours After This/ Six Different Ways (live)/Push (live) (CD Video) 40
85 Fiction FICSG 23 — Close To Me (Remix)/A Man Inside My Mouth (poster p/s; some copies with blue & white 'Head On The Door' sticker) 15
85 Fiction FICST 23 — HALF AN OCTOPUS: Close To Me (Remix)/A Man Inside My Mouth/New Day/ Stop Dead (10" EP, p/s) 18
85 Fiction 080180-2 — Close To Me (12" Remix)/A Man Inside My Mouth/Stop Dead/ New Day (CD Video) 45
87 Fiction FICSG 25 — Why Can't I Be You?/A Japanese Dream//Six Different Ways (live)/ Push (live) (numbered double pack, gatefold p/s) 12
87 Fiction FICS 26 — Catch/Breathe (p/s, in carrier bag) 8

Rare Record Price Guide 2024

Martin CURE & PEEPS

MINT VALUE £

Year	Cat #	Description	Value
87	Fiction FICSP 26	Catch/Breathe (clear vinyl, printed PVC sleeve)	18
87	Fiction 080186-2	Catch/Breathe/A Chain Of Flowers/Icing Sugar (Remix) (CD Video)	45
87	Fiction FICS 27	Just Like Heaven/Snow In Summer (p/s, numbered, white vinyl)	8
87	Fiction FICS 27	Just Like Heaven/Snow In Summer (p/s, mispress, A-side plays both sides)	20
87	Fiction FICSP 27	Just Like Heaven/Snow In Summer (picture disc in custom PVC sleeve)	20
88	Strange Fruit SFPS 050	PEEL SESSIONS EP (12")	12
89	Fiction FICSG 29	Lullaby (Remix)/Babble (gatefold p/s, numbered with sticker)	8
89	Fiction FICSP 29	Lullaby (Remix)/Babble (clear vinyl, numbered printed 'spider web' PVC sleeve)	18
89	Fiction FICVX 29	Lullaby (Remix)/Babble/Out Of Mind (12", pink vinyl, numbered with stickers)	18
89	Fiction FICSG 30	Lovesong/2 Late ('The Love Box' set with linen print)	12
90	Fiction FICPA 34	Pictures Of You (Remix)/Last Dance (live) (p/s, green vinyl, no'd sticker)	6
90	Fiction FICPA 34	Pictures Of You (Remix)/Last Dance (live) (p/s, green vinyl, mispress, plays "Last Dance" both sides)	30
90	Fiction FICPB 34	Pictures Of You (Remix)/Prayers For Rain (p/s, purple vinyl, numbered sticker)	10
90	Fiction FICXA 34	Pictures Of You (Extended Remix)/Last Dance (Live)/Fascination Street (Live) (12")	18
90	Fiction 080184-2	Why Can't I Be You? (12" Remix)/A Japanese Dream (5.40 Remix)/Hey You!!! (CD Video)	45
92	Fiction FICCD 42	Friday I'm In Love/Halo/Scared Of You/Friday I'm In Love (Strangelove Mix) (12", p/s, different coloured or marbled vinyl)	25
12	Secret 7 S74	Friday I'm In Love (1-sided RSD 7" in unique individual art sleeve, 100 only)	150

ALBUMS

Year	Cat #	Description	Value
79	Fiction FIX 1	THREE IMAGINARY BOYS (with inner sleeve, postcard & badge)	50
79	Fiction FIX 1	THREE IMAGINARY BOYS (LP, with inner sleeve and "Limited edition special price" stamped in gold on cover)	20
80	Fiction FIXD 004	SEVENTEEN SECONDS (LP, textured sleeve, 1st pressing has FIX 004 on rear of sleeve)	25
80	Fiction FIXD 4	SEVENTEEN SECONDS (LP, reissue)	18
81	Fiction FIX 6	FAITH (LP, inner)	30
82	Fiction FIX D7	PORNOGRAPHY (LP, with inner sleeve)	20
83	Fiction SPELP 26	BOYS DON'T CRY (LP)	20
83	Fiction FIXM 8	JAPANESE WHISPERS (LP)	18
84	Fiction FIXS 9	THE TOP (with badge & poster, green inner sleeve)	20
84	Fiction FIXS 9	THE TOP (with promo plastic snake & top)	35
84	Fiction FIXH 14	CONCERT (LP)	18
85	Fiction FIXH 11	HEAD ON THE DOOR (LP, inner)	20
86	Fiction 815 011-2	BOYS DON'T CRY (CD, original non-picture disc, with "Object" & "World War" & without "So What")	30
86	Fiction FIXH 12	STANDING ON A BEACH - THE SINGLES (LP, gatefold with inner sleeve)	30
87	Fiction FIXH 13/FIXHA 13	KISS ME, KISS ME, KISS ME (with bonus orange vinyl 6-track 12" [FIXHA 13], in custom PVC sleeve)	50
87	Fiction FIXH 13	KISS ME, KISS ME, KISS ME (LP, 2-LP)	30
89	Fiction FIXH 14	DISINTEGRATION (LP, snakeskin effect sleeve, with inner)	35
89	Fiction FIXHP 14	DISINTEGRATION (picture disc, printed PVC sleeve)	30
90	Fiction FIXLP 18	MIXED UP (2-LP, inners)	35
92	Fiction FIXH 20	WISH (2-LP, inners)	100
92	Fiction 513 600-0	LIMITED EDITION CD BOX (15 x CD hinged box set, 2,500 only)	200
96	Fiction FIXLP 28	WILD MOOD SWINGS (2-LP)	125
97	Fiction FIXLP 30	GALORE (2-LP, inners)	150
00	Fiction FIX 31	BLOODFLOWERS (2-LP)	175
04	Geffen 0602498628461	THE CURE (2-LP)	125

PROMOS

Year	Cat #	Description	Value
79	Fiction FICS 002	Boys Don't Cry/Plastic Passion	45
79	Fiction CUR 1	Grinding Halt/Meat Hook (12", stickered sleeve)	150
81	Fiction FICS 12	Primary (1-sided, no p/s)	25
82	Fiction CURE 1	One Hundred Years/The Hanging Garden (12", p/s, promo/gig freebie)	70
82	Lyntone LYN 12011	Lament (hard vinyl test pressing, no p/s)	400
84	Fiction KAREN 1	THE TOP (12", 1-sided, 3-track sampler)	55
88	Fiction FICSDJ 28	Hot Hot Hot!!! (Remix)/Hey You!!! (Remix) (die-cut title p/s)	15
89	Fiction CIFCD 3	STRANGER THAN FICTION (CD, 6-track sampler, 1000 only)	100
80s	Fiction FICS DJ 42	Friday I'm In Love (Promo in die-cut fiction sleeve)	20
96	Fiction FICSTX 53	Gone! (Ultraliving Mix) (12", same track both sides, with 'DJ' insert)	12
97	Fiction FICSX 54	Wrong Number (Single Mix)/(ISDN Mix)/(Digital Exchange Mix)/(Dub Analogue Exchange Mix)/(Crossed Line Mix)/(Engaged Mix)/(P2P Mix) (12", double pack, p/s promo only)	25
97	Fixtion FIXCD.COM 1	FIVE SWING LIVE (CD, 5-track sampler, available via the internet, 5,000 only)	30

(see also Cult Hero, Siouxsie & Banshees, Glove, Fools Dance, Tim Pope, Lockjaw, Obtainers)

MARTIN CURE & PEEPS

Year	Cat #	Description	Value
67	Philips BF 1605	It's All Over Now/I Can Make The Rain Fall Up	40

(see also Peeps, Rainbows)

CURFEW

Year	Cat #	Description	Value
70	Brent BN 001	Visions/Look Behind You	200

CURIOSITY SHOPPE

Year	Cat #	Description	Value
68	Deram DM 220	Baby I Need You/So Sad	100

JOHNNY CURIOUS & STRANGERS

Year	Cat #	Description	Value
78	Illegal IL 009	In Tune/Road To Cheltenham/Pissheadsville/Jennifer (p/s)	20
79	Bugle BLAST 2	Someone Else's Home/Backwards In The Night (p/s)	12

CURLY

Year	Cat #	Description	Value
75	EPIC EPC 3145	High Flying Bird/Breakout	6
71	Pye 25570	Funky Yeah/Shelly's Rubber Band	12

TERRY CURRAN

Year	Cat #	Description	Value
80	Norwood NR 2004	Singing The Blues/Wednesday Chant	6

CURRANT KRAZE

			MINT VALUE £
	CURRANT KRAZE		
70	Deram DM 292	Lady Pearl/Breaking The Heart Of A Good Man	6
	CURRENT 93		
83	L.A.Y.L.A.H. L.A.Y. 1	Lashtal/Salt/Caresse (12", white p/s)	22
83	L.A.Y.L.A.H. L.A.Y. 1	Lashtal/Salt/Caresse (12", white p/s [reissue from in 1988 with dark p/s and "1988" on label])	18
85	L.A.Y.L.A.H. L.A.Y. 14	NIGHTMARE CULTURE (12" EP, with Sickness Of Snakes [i.e. Coil feat. Boyd Rice]; matt black & red sleeve)	22
87	L.A.Y.L.A.H. L.A.Y. 18	HAPPY BIRTHDAY PIGFACE CHRISTUS (12" EP)	22
87	Maldoror MAL 108	Crowleymass/Christmassacre/Crowleymass (Mix Mix Mix) (12", p/s)	28
88	Yangki 002	FAITH'S FAVOURITES EP (Ballad Of The Pale Girl/NURSE WITH WOUND: Swamp Rat) (12", laminated p/s)	28
88	Maldoror MAL 088	The Red Face Of God/The Breath And The Pain Of God (12", p/s, with insert, 666 only)	40
89	Yangki 003	DEATH OF THE CORN (12" EP, with Sol Invictus; 'art' sleeve)	18
90	Harbinger 001	No Hiding From The Blackbird/NURSE WITH WOUND: Burial Of The Stoned Sardine (p/s, remixed reissue of giveaway 7")	12
90	Shock SX 003	She Is Dead And All Fall Down/God Has Three Faces And Wood Has No Name (folded sleeve in bag, 1,000 only, this price for 26 copies that were signed/lettered)	45
90	Shock SX 003	She Is Dead And All Fall Down/God Has Three Faces And Wood Has No Name (folded sleeve in bag, 1,000 only)	22
90	Cerne 004	This Ain't The Summer Of Love (live) (with Sol Invictus, gig freebie, printed labels, this price for 93 copies with ticket)	30
90	Cerne 004	This Ain't The Summer Of Love (live) (with Sol Invictus, gig freebie, printed labels)	20
92	Durtro DURTRO 004	LOONEY RUNES (12", live EP, 2,000 only, with poster)	20
94	Ptolemaic Terrascope POT6	Broken Birds Fly/RANDY CALIFORNIA: The American Society/The Whale Song (free with Ptolemaic Terrascope mag)	10
94	Ptolemaic Terrascope POT6	Broken Birds Fly/RANDY CALIFORNIA: The American Society/The Whale Song (without Ptolemaic Terrascope mag)	8
94	Durtro DURTRO 022	THE FIRE OF THE MIND (CD EP, free with book 'Simply Being')	55
95	Durtro DURTRO 025	Tamlin/How The Great Satanic Glory Faded (12", numbered with insert, 2,000 only)	28
95	Durtro DURTRO 028	Where The Long Shadows Fall (12", 1-sided clear vinyl with insert, 2,000 only)	18
84	L.A.Y.L.A.H. LAY 008	DOGS BLOOD RISING (LP)	25
86	Maldoror UDO 22M	IN MENSTRUAL NIGHT (LP, 25 with handmade inserts & cover)	100
86	Maldoror UDO 22M	IN MENSTRUAL NIGHT (LP)	20
86	United Dairies UD 022	IN MENSTRUAL NIGHT (LP, picture disc)	20
87	L.A.Y.L.A.H. LAY 20	SWASTIKAS FOR NODDY (LP, with insert)	25
88	Maldoror MAL 666	CHRIST AND THE PALE QUEENS MIGHTY IN SORROW (3-sided LP, with inserts, 93 copies only)	100
88	Maldoror MAL 777	IMPERIUM (LP, black label, with insert)	28
88	Maldoror MAL 777	IMPERIUM (LP, later pressing with white label)	18
89	Maldoror MAL 093	DAWN (LP)	60
89	Durtro DURTRO 001	LIVE AT BAR MALDOROR (LP, white label, 1,000 only)	55
80s	Maldoror MAL 123	NATURE UNVEILED (LP, with insert & free 7": "No Hiding From The Blackbird/NURSE WITH WOUND: Burial Of The Sardine")	30
80s	Maldoror MAL 123	NATURE UNVEILED (LP, with insert)	20
88	United Dairies UD 029	EARTH COVERS EARTH (mini-LP)	35
90	Dutro 048	I HAVE A SPECIAL PLAN FOR THIS WORLD (LP, limited edition on red vinyl)	50
90	Dutro 048	I HAVE A SPECIAL PLAN FOR THIS WORLD (LP, limited edition on clear vinyl)	30
90	Cerne 00123	THE CERNE BOX SET (3-LP set, includes "Horse"; other LPs by Sol Invictus & Nurse With Wound, 2,000 only)	70
90	NER BADVC 693	1888 (LP, split with Death In June, 500 each on clear & red vinyl)	35
90	NER BADVC 693	1888 (LP, split with Death In June, black vinyl)	25
92	Durtro DURTRO 006	ISLAND (LP, with insert, 2,000 only)	25
92	Durtro DURTRO 011	THUNDER PERFECT MIND (2-LP, with insert)	25
94	Durtro DURTRO 018	OF RUINE, OR SOME BLAZING STARRE (LP, blue vinyl w/insert, 2,000 only)	25
94	Durtro DURTO 019	LUCIFER OVER LONDON (LP, red vinyl with insert, 2,000 only)	30
96	Durtro DURTRO 026	ALL THE PRETTY LITTLE HORSES (LP, clear vinyl with insert, 2,000 only)	35
98	Durtro DURTRO 042	SOFT BLACK STARS (LP, clear vinyl with free 12" and insert, 2000 only)	25

(see also Nurse With Wound, 23 Skidoo, Psychic TV, Crisis, Death In June, Sol Invictus, Steven Stapleton & David Tibet, Tibet & Stapleton)

	DAVID CURRIE		
71	Philips 6006165	I Don't Want To Talk About It/The Question	10
	CLIFFORD CURRY		
69	Action ACT 4549	She Shot A Hole In My Soul/We're Gonna Hate Ourselves In The Morning	10
69	Pama PM 793	You Turn Out The Light/Good Humour Man	10
69	Pama PM 797	I Can't Get A Hold Of Myself/Ain't No Danger	50
	TIM CURRY		
74	Ode ODE 66103	Sweet Transvestite/Time Warp (in p/s)	8
	TED CURSON QUARTET		
64	Fontana 688310 ZL	TEARS FOR DOLPHY (LP)	35
	CURTAINS		
95	Detour DR 025	In My Street/Family Affair (p/s, blue vinyl, 100 only)	7
	DAN CURTIN		
94	Peacefrog PF 018X	PARALLEL EP (12", sampler, plain sleeve)	10
95	Peacefrog PF 023	PURVEYORS OF FINE FUNK - HEIGHTS TRAX VOL 1 EP (12", plain sleeve)	15
95	Peacefrog PF 024	DREAMS NOT OF TODAY EP (12", plain sleeve)	10
95	Peacefrog PF 032	PURVEYORS OF FINE FUNK - HEIGHTS TRAX VOL 2 EP (12", plain sleeve)	10
96	Peacefrog PF 058	PURVEYORS OF FINE FUNK VOL 3 EP (12", plain sleeve)	10
94	Peacefrog PF 018	THE SILICON DAWN (2-LP)	50
	CHRIS CURTIS		
66	Pye 7N 17132	Aggravation/Have I Done Something Wrong	35

(see also Searchers)

	CLEM CURTIS & FOUNDATIONS		
72	Pye 7N 45150	I've Never Found A Girl (To Love Me Like You)/Point Of No Return	20

Denny CURTIS

MINT VALUE £

75	Riverdale RS 105	Sweet Happiness/Lady Luck	20

(See also the Foundations)

DENNY CURTIS
68	Plexium PXM 2	Crying Over You/You Don't Love Me No More	6
69	Plexium PXM 6	Message/You Gotta Be Mine	6

EDDIE CURTIS
63	Oriole CB 1852	Leavin Town/Faithful Kind (with Hellions)	10

JOE CURTIS
72	Spiral DIT 4	Black Is Beautiful/This Is Love	8

JOHNNY CURTIS
66	Parlophone R 5529	Our Love's Disintegrating/(I'd Be) A Legend In My Time	70
67	Parlophone R 5582	Jack And The Beanstalk/Go On Back	30
68	Major Minor MM 564	Pickin' Up Pebbles/Gentle On My Mind	7

LEE CURTIS (& ALL STARS)
63	Decca F 11622	Little Girl/Just One More Dance (solo)	10
63	Decca F 11690	Let's Stomp/Poor Unlucky Me	15
64	Decca F 11830	What About Me/I've Got My Eyes On You	15
64	Philips BF 1385	Ecstasy/A Shot Of Rhythm And Blues	15

(see also Pete Best Four)

LYNNE CURTIS
64	Decca F11869	House For Sale/My Little Boy	8

MAC CURTIS
57	Parlophone R 4279	The Low Road/You Ain't Treatin' Me Right	1500
57	Parlophone R 4279	The Low Road/You Ain't Treatin' Me Right (78)	200
74	Polydor 2310 293	ROCKABILLY KINGS (LP, with Charlie Feathers)	30

SONNY CURTIS
60	Coral Q 72400	The Red Headed Stranger/Talk About My Baby	40
64	Colpix PX 11024	A Beatle I Want To Be/So Used To Loving You	12
64	Liberty LIB 55710	I Pledged My Love To You/Bo Diddley Bach	15

(see also Crickets)

T.C. CURTIS
82	Romantic RR 0001	Party Down/Party Down (Instrumental)	6
82	Romantic RR 0001/12	Party Down/Party Down (Instrumental) (12")	10
86	Hot Melt CURTIS 1	STEP BY STEP (LP)	15

WINSTON CURTIS
79	Supreme SUP DC 1001	You're Mine/My Desire/Mine Part II/Desire Part II (with Samantha Rose) (12")	30
84	World Intl. WIR12D503	Be Thankful (For What You've Got)/This Magic Monent (12")	50
77	Empire EMP 901	WINSTON'S GREATS (LP)	60
77	Diamond DMLP 401	INSTRUMENTAL EXPLOSION (LP)	100
81	Empire EMP 906	PORTRAIT (LP)	100

DAVE CURTISS & TREMORS
63	Philips BF 1257	You Don't Love Me Any More/Sweet Girl Of Mine	10
63	Philips BF 1285	What Kind Of Girl Are You?/Dreamer's Funfair	10
64	Philips BF 1330	Summertime Blues/I'm A Hog For You Baby	10

CURTISS MALDOON
72	Purple PUR 106	One Way Ticket/Next Time	7
71	Purple TPS 3501	CURTISS MALDOON (LP)	30
73	Purple TPS 3502	MALDOON (LP)	15

ROCKY CURTISS & HARMONY FLAMES
59	Fontana TFE 17172	U.S.A. HIT PARADE (EP)	40

BOBBY CURTOLA (& MARTELLS)
61	Columbia DB 4672	Don't You Sweetheart Me/My Heart's Tongue-Tied (solo)	15
62	London HL 9577	Fortune Teller/Johnny Take Your Time (solo)	15
62	London HL 9639	Aladdin/I Don't Want To Go On Without You (solo)	15
63	Decca F 11670	Gypsy Heart/I'm Sorry	15
63	Decca F 11725	Three Rows Over/Indian Giver	15

CURVE
93	Anxious	FALLING FREE - APHEX TWIN REMIX (12", 1-sided promo only, 500 only)	15
92	Anxious ANXLP 77	DOPPELGANGER (LP, with poster)	30
93	Anxious ANXLP 81	CUCKOO (LP)	30

CURVED AIR
71	Warner Bros WB 8023	It Happened Today/What Happens When You Blow Yourself Up/Vivaldi	7
72	Warner Bros K 16164	Sarah's Concern/Phantasmagoria	6
84	Pearl Key PK 07350	Renegade/We're Only Human (p/s)	15
70	Warner Bros K 56004	AIR CONDITIONING (LP, picture disc, with booklet, 10,000 only)	70
70	Warner Bros K 56004	AIR CONDITIONING (LP, picture disc)	30
70	Warner Bros WSX 3012	AIR CONDITIONING (LP, green label, laminated sleeve)	40
71	Warner Bros K 46092	SECOND ALBUM (LP, die-cut 'leaves' fold-out sleeve, green label)	40
72	Warner Bros K 46158	PHANTASMAGORIA (LP, green label, with inner lyric card)	20
73	Warner Bros K 46224	AIR CUT (LP, green label, gatefold sleeve)	25
75	Deram SML 1119	LIVE (LP, red/white label)	20

(see also Kirby, Sonja Kristina, [Darryl Way's] Wolf, Trace, Legs, Stretch, Police)

PETER CUSACK
77	Bead Records BEAD 5	AFTER BEING IN HOLLAND FOR TWO YEARS (LP)	40
84	Bead Records BEAD 22	BIRD JUMPS INTO WOOD (LP, with Clive Bell)	20

SUE CUSS
79	Orchid OR 101	You Really Got Me/Physical Love (no p/s)	10

CUSTERS TRACK
70	Major Minor MM698	On The Run/Hello Heaven	12

Ivor CUTLER TRIO

MINT VALUE £

IVOR CUTLER TRIO
Year	Label	Title	Value
67	Parlophone R 5624	I Had A Little Boat/A Great Grey Grasshopper	12
59	Fontana TFE 17144	OF Y'HUP (EP)	20
61	Decca DFE 6677	GET AWAY FROM THE WALL (EP)	20
89	Strange Fruit SFPS 068	PEE SESSIONS (12")	15
61	Decca LK 4405	WHO TORE YOUR TROUSERS? (LP)	100
67	Parlophone PCS 7040	LUDO (LP)	100
74	Virgin V2021	DANDRUFF (LP, as Ivor Cutler)	30
75	Virgin V2037	VELVET DONKEY (LP)	20
76	Virgin V2056	JAMMY SMEARS (LP)	20
78	Harvest SHSP4084	LIFE IN A SCOTCH SITTING ROOM VOL 2 (LP)	20
84	Rough Trade ROUGH 59	PRIVILEGE (LP with Linda Hirst)	25
85	Virgin OVED 12	JAMMY SMEARS (LP, reissue)	15
86	Virgin OVED 34	VELVET DONKEY (LP, reissue)	15
86	Rough Trade ROUGH 89	PRINCE IVOR (2-LP)	25
86	Rough Trade ROUGH 98	GRUTS (LP)	20

L CUTMORE
| 90 | Fast Forward CUT 1 | Subsonic Mix 1/Subsonic Mix 2 (12") | 25 |

T. TOMMY CUTRER (& GINNY WRIGHT)
| 54 | London HL 8093 | Mexico Gal/Wonderful World (B-side with Ginny Wright) | 40 |

(see also Ginny Wright)

CUTTERS
| 59 | Decca F 11110 | I've Had It/Rockaroo | 10 |

(see also Neville Taylor & Cutters)

CYAN THREE
| 66 | Decca F 12371 | Since I Lost My Baby/Face Of A Loser | 20 |

CYANIDE
78	Pye 7N 46048	I'm A Boy/Do It (p/s)	25
78	Pye 7N 46094	Mac The Flash/Hate The State (demo copies in p/s)	60
78	Pye 7N 46094	Mac The Flash/Hate The State (demo copies no p/s)	15
79	Pinnacle PIN 23	Fireball/Your Old Man (p/s)	40
78	Pye NSPL 18554	CYANIDE (LP)	40

CYBERMEN
78	Rockaway AERE 101	THE CYBERMEN (EP, available in 2 different sleeves with info sheet)	100
78	Rockaway AERE 101	THE CYBERMEN (EP, available in 2 different sleeves without info sheet)	40
79	Rockaway LUV 002	You're To Blame/It's You I Want (with inserts)	45

CYBERNETIC SERENDIPITY GROUP
| 68 | ICA ICA 1/2 | CYBERNETIC SERENDIPITY MUSIC (LP, private pressing) | 150 |

CYBERSONIK
| 90 | Champion CHAMP 264 | Technarchy/Algorhythm (p/s) | 18 |

CYBERTRON & DC SAVAGE
| 88 | Warriors Dance WAF 07T | Climax (Radio Club Mix Vocal)/(Real Deal Acid Mix)/(Fingers Jazz Mix) (12") | 10 |

CYBOTRON FEATURING DILLINJA
96	Prototype PRO 004	Threshold/Hot To (12")	10
98	Prototype PRO 010	Light Years/Revelations (12")	10
00	Valve CYBX 001	NASTY WAYZ (EP)	15

(see also Dillinja)

CYCLE
70	S.R.T. 71143	CYCLE (LP, 99 copies only)	1000
20	Rise Above Relics RARLP 21	COSMIC CLOUDS (2-LP, with 7" and booklet)	40
20	Rise Above Relics RARLP 21	COSMIC CLOUDS (2-LP, silver vinyl)	20

CYCLONE
| 79 | Magnet MAG 159 | Palisades Park/Crazy Haze (p/s) | 8 |

(see also Matchbox)

CYCLONES (1)
| 64 | Oriole CB 1898 | Nobody/Little Egypt | 60 |

CYCLONES (2)
| 71 | Banana BA 338 | My Sweet Lord/DENNIS BROWN: Silky (B-side actually by Monty Alexander & Cyclones) | 15 |

CYCLOP'S EYE
| 72 | Phoenix PHO12 | Rolling Thunder/Kentucky Freeway | 12 |

CYGNUS
| 78 | Greensleeves GRED 4 | Jah Man/Babylon (12") | 25 |

CYLOB
| 95 | Rephlex CAT 015 | INDUSTRIAL FOLKSONGS (12", initially in polystyrene sleeve) | 12 |
| 96 | Rephlex CAT 033 LP | CYLOBIAN SUNSET (LP) | 35 |

CYMANDE
73	Alaska ALA 4	The Message/Zion I	20
73	Alaska ALA 10	Bra/Ras Tafarian Folk Song	18
74	Contempo CS 2019	Brothers On The Slide/Pon De Dungle	80
76	Alaska ALA1021	Friends/One More	8
99	Sequel NEET 1008	The Message/Brothers On The Slide/Bra/Dove (12")	25
18	Mr. Bongo MRB7143	Bra/The Message (p/s, reissue)	8
18	Mr. Bongo MRB7144	Fug/Brothers On The Slide (p/s, reissue)	8
73	Alaska ALKA 100	CYMANDE (LP)	100
74	Contempo CLP 508	PROMISED HEIGHTS (LP)	80
93	Sequel NEXLP 202	CYMANDE (LP, reissue, actually The Best Of)	40
99	Sequel NEMLP 428	CYMANDE (LP, reissue)	20
99	Sequel NEMLP 429	SECOND TIME AROUND (LP, reissue)	20
99	Sequel NEMLP 430	PROMISE HEIGHTS (LP, reissue)	20
15	Cherry Red BRED 668	A SIMPLE ACT OF FAITH (LP)	15

Johnny CYMBAL

MINT VALUE £

18	Mr. Bongo MRBLP 159	SECOND TIME AROUND (LP, reissue, 180gm)	20
18	Mr. Bongo MRBLP 160	PROMISED HEIGHTS (LP, reissue, 180gm)	20

JOHNNY CYMBAL

60	MGM MGM 1106	It'll Be Me/Always, Always	10
63	London HLR 9682	Mr Bass Man/Sacred Lovers Vow	7
63	London HLR 9731	Teenage Heaven/Cinderella Baby	8
63	London HLR 9762	Dum Dum Dee Dum/Surfing At Tijuana	8
64	London HLR 9911	Mitsou/Robinson Crusoe On Mars	6
65	United Artists UP 1093	Go V.W. Go/Sorrow And Pain	10
63	London RER 1375	MISTER BASS MAN (EP)	25
64	London RER 1406	CYMBAL SMASHES (EP)	15

(see also Derek)

CYMBALINE

65	Pye 7N 15916	Please Little Girl/Coming Home Baby	35
65	Mercury MF 918	Top Girl/Can You Hear Me?	25
66	Mercury MF 961	I Don't Want It/Where Did Love Go Wrong	8
66	Mercury MF 975	Peanuts And Chewy Macs/Found My Girl	10
67	Philips BF 1624	Matrimonial Fears/You Will Never Love Me	70
68	Philips BF 1681	Down By The Seaside/Fire	25

CYMERONS

64	Decca F 11976	I'll Be There/Making Love To Another	15
66	Polydor 56098	Everyday (Will Change)/I Can See You	7

CYNIC

83	Cynic CYN 1	Suicide/No Time At All (no p/s)	75

CYNICS

85	Sounds Cynical CYNIC 1	Don't Give In (Fight to Win)/Breaking Out/One Way Out (foldout p/s)	8

CYNTHIA & ARCHIE

64	R&B JB 168	Every Beat/DELROY WILSON: Sammy Dead	25

CYPRESS HILL

91	Columbia 468893 1	CYPRESS HILL (LP)	20
93	Columbia 474075	BLACK SUNDAY (2-LP, gatefold, inners)	35
95	Columbia 478127-1	CYPRESS HILL III (TEMPLES OF BOOM) (2-LP, gatefold)	25

NOHELANI CYPRIOANO

14	Athens Of The North ATH 007	Lihue/Playing With Fire (reissue)	15
15	Be With BEWITH008LP	NOHELANI (LP, reissue)	25

CYRKLE

66	CBS 202064	Red Rubber Ball/How Can I Leave Her	8
66	CBS 202246	Turn Down Day/Big Little Woman	8
67	CBS 202516	Bony Maronie/Please Don't Ever Leave Me	8
67	CBS 202577	I Wish You Could Be There/The Visit (She Was Here)	8
67	CBS 2790	We Had A Good Thing Goin'/Two Rooms	8
67	CBS 2917	Penny Arcade/Words	8
67	CBS 62977	NEON (LP)	40

CZAR

70	Philips 6006 071	Oh Lord I'm Getting Heavy/Why Don't We Be A Rock'n'Roll Band	40
70	Fontana 6309 009	CZAR (LP, black/silver label, laminated sleeve)	1500
11	Sunbeam SBR2LP5040	CZAR (2-LP, reissue)	40

(see also Hungry Wolf)

HOLGER CZUKAY

79	EMI 5005	Cool In The Pool/Oh Lord Give Us More Money (p/s)	12
79	EMI EMC 3319	MOVIES (LP)	20
81	EMI EMC 3384	ON THE WAY TO THE PEAK OF NORMAL (LP)	15
84	Virgin V 2307	DER OSTEN IST ROT (LP)	15

(see under Jah Wobble, Can)

D

KIM D

65	Pye 7N 15953	The Real Thing/Come On Baby	30

(see also Kim Davis)

ROB D

95	Mo' Wax MW 037	Clubbed To Death/(Mixes) (12", p/s)	25

SCHOOLLY D

86	Flame MELT LP 1	SCHOOLLEY D (LP)	15

TONY D & SHAKEOUTS

64	Piccadilly 7N 35168	Is It True/Never Let Her Go	25

DA BAND

78	Rip Off RIP 2	I Like It/Pirate's Lullaby (p/s)	20

DA BIZ

80	Small Operations SO 002	On The Beach/This Is No Audition (p/s)	10
80	Sire SIR 4045	On The Beach/This Is No Audition (p/s, reissue)	6

DA REBELS

97	Ugly UGM 009	HOUSE NATION UNDER A GROOVE EP (12")	30
97	Ugly UGM 012	HOUSE NATION UNDER A GROOVE (12", reissue, promo)	18

DAB HAND

MINT VALUE £

DAB HAND
85 Celtic Music CM 025   HIGH ROCK AND LOWATER (LP) 18

MIKE D'ABO
69 Immediate IM 075   See The Little People — Gulliver's Travels/Anthology Of Gulliver's Travels Part 2
                                (withdrawn) 30
70 Uni UNS 525   Let It Roar/California Line 7
70 Bell BLL 1134   Miss Me In The Morning/Arabella, Cinderella 6
72 A&M AMS 7016   Belinda/Little Miss Understood 6
74 A&M AMS 7121   Fuel To Burn/Hold On Darlin' 6
70 Uni UNLS 114   D'ABO (LP, gatefold sleeve) 40
72 A&M AMLH 68097   DOWN AT RACHEL'S PLACE (LP, with lyric insert) 15
74 A&M AMLH 63634   BROKEN RAINBOWS (LP) 15

(see also Manfred Mann, Band Of Angels, Gulliver's Travels, Smith & D'Abo)

TERESA D'ABREAU BAND
80 Miss Chief MC 1   Sister Revoluton/Carry It Through 7

KAREN D'ACHE
89 SRT KDA 2   Spin And Cry/Divide And Rule 6

RITA DACOSTA
75 Contempo CS 2060   Don't Bring Me Down/No! No! No! 10

DADA
71 Atco 2400 030   DADA (LP, mustard/blue label) 50

(see also Elkie Brooks, Paul Korda, Vinegar Joe)

DADDY COLONEL
85 Bubblers UKMC7   Take A Tip From Me/Lyric Banton (12") 20

DADDY DEWDROP
71 Stateside SS2192   Foxhunting On The Weekend/March Of The White Corpuscles 8

DADDY FREDDY
89 Fashion FAD 7707   Yes We A Blood/Version 25

DADDY JUNGLE
80s Daddy Jungle DJ001   Flash It Operator/Jungle Dub 20

DADDY LONGLEGS
70 Warner Bros WS 3004   DADDY LONGLEGS (LP) 40
71 Vertigo 6360 038   OAKDOWN FARM (LP, gatefold sleeve, swirl label) 250
72 Polydor 2371 261   THREE MUSICIANS (LP) 15
73 Polydor 2371 323   SHIFTING SANDS (LP) 25

(see also Daylight)

DADDY MAXFIELD
73 Pye 7N 45266   Rave 'N' Rock/Smilin' Again 50

DADDY TAR
90 Umbra   Zigawya/Full Up The Style (12" with Aytonbridge) 15

DADDY'S ACT
67 Columbia DB 8242   Eight Days A Week/Gonna Get You 18

DAD'S ARMY PLATOON
71 Columbia DB 8766   Dad's Army March/What Did You Do In The War? 6
72 Columbia DB 8952   We Stood Alone/Down Our Way (AS DAD'S ARMY CHOIR) 6

DAEMION
82 SiJenn MSP1001   Dizzy/Human Arcade (p/s) 50

D.A.F. (DEUTSCHE AMERIKANISCHE FREUNDSCHAFT)
80 Mute MUTE 005   Kebabtraume/Gewalt (p/s) 8
81 Mute MUTE 011   Der Rauber Und Der Prinz/Tanz Mit Mir (p/s) 6
81 Virgin VS 418   Der Mussolini/Der Räuber Und Der Prinz (co. sleeve) 8
81 Virgin VS 418-12   Der Mussolini/Der Räuber Und Der Prinz (12", p/s, original issue) 10
80 Mute STUMM 1   DIE KLEINEN UND DIE BOSEN (LP) 20
81 Virgin V2202   ALLES IST GUT (LP) 20
81 Virgin V2218   GOLD UND LIEBE (LP) 20

CALVIN DAFOS
66 Blue Beat BB 347   Brown Sugar/I'm Gone 22
69 Doctor Bird DB 1174   Lash Them/CDs: Medicine Master 35

DAFT PUNK
94 Soma 014   Alive/The New Wave (12" EP, company sleeve) 12
95 Soma 025   Da Funk/Rollin' And Scratchin' (12" EP, company sleeve) 10
13 Columbia 88883746911   Get Lucky (Daft Punk Remix)/(Album Version)/(Radio Edit) (12", p/s) ... 15
96 Virgin V 2821   HOMEWORK (2-LP, emobossed sleeve, inners) 80
01 Virgin V 2940   DISCOVERY (2-LP) 75
01 Virgin V 2952   ALIVE 1997 (LP) 50
05 Virgin V 2996   HUMAN AFTER ALL (2-LP, gatefold) 60
10 Warner Bros.   TRON LEGACY (2-LP, soundtrack) 100
    5099909792012

DAGABAND
83 MHM A-M 094   Second Time Around/Reds Under The Beds/I Can See For Miles (p/s) ... 25

DAGGERMEN
86 Empire UPW 258J   INTRODUCING THE DAGGERMEN (EP, die-cut company sleeve) 10
86 Own Up DAG 001   DAGGERS IN MY MIND (LP) 15

(see also James Taylor Quartet)

DAGGERS (1)
74 Scotty SC 003   Live Your Life Alone/Circles Of Dust 50

DAGGERS (2)
07 Fandango/Galagos 18   Money/Magazine (die cut sleeve) 12

(see also Hurts)

DAILY FLASH
84 Psycho PSYCHO 32   I FLASH DAILY (LP) 20

DAISY CLAN
70	Pye Intl. 7N 25532	Love Needs Love/Glory Be	30
71	Decca F23169	San Francisco China Town/Ridin' A Rainbow	30

DAISY HILL
88	Lakeland LKND 006	POPPY FARM EP	10

DAISY PLANET
60s	Oak (no cat. no.)	DAISY PLANET (EP, no p/s)	70

DAKOTA JIM
66	Blue Beat BB 358	Only Soul Can Tell (actually by Slim Smith)/DAKOTA'S ALLSTARS: Call Me Master (actually by Prince Buster All Stars)	150

(see also Slim Smith)

DAKOTAS
63	Parlophone R 5044	The Cruel Sea/The Millionaire	10
63	Parlophone R 5064	Magic Carpet/Humdinger	12
64	Parlophone R 5203	Oyeh/Hello Josephine	30
67	Page One POF 018	I'm 'N 'Ardworkin' Barrow Boy/Seven Pounds Of Potatoes	35
68	Philips BF 1645	I Can't Break The News To Myself/The Spider And The Fly	200
63	Parlophone GEP 8888	MEET THE DAKOTAS (EP)	40

(see also Billy J. Kramer & Dakotas)

ALAN DALE
55	Vogue Coral Q 72105	Rockin' The Cha-Cha/Wham! (There I Go In Love Again)	12
57	Vogue Coral Q 72225	Don't Knock The Rock/Your Love Is My Love	25
57	Vogue Coral Q 72231	The Girl Can't Help It/Lonesome Road	25

(see also Johnny Desmond)

DICK DALE & HIS DELTONES
63	Capitol CL 15296	Peppermint Man/Surf Beat	20
63	Capitol CL 15320	The Scavenger/Wild Ideas	20
63	Capitol T 1886	SURFERS' CHOICE (LP)	30
63	Capitol T/ST 1930	KING OF THE SURF GUITAR (LP, mono/stereo)	30

GLEN DALE
66	Decca F 12475	Good Day Sunshine/Make Me Belong To You	8
68	Page One POF 059	I've Got You On My Mind/Now I See You	10

(see also Fortunes)

JACKIE DALE
78	Freedom Sounds FSD 020	Stop And Think Me Over/Bucket Bottom (12", with Prince Allah)	15

JIM DALE
57	Parlophone R 4329	Piccadilly Line/I Didn't Mean It	6
57	Parlophone R 4343	Be My Girl/You Shouldn't Do That	7
57	Parlophone R 4356	All Shook Up/Wandering Eyes (with Vipers & King Brothers)	10
57	Parlophone GEP 8656	JIM DALE (EP)	20
58	Parlophone PMD 1055	JIM (10" LP)	40

PAUL DALE BAND
82	KA KA 6/PAUL 1	Alright On The Night/Hold On (p/s, clear vinyl)	12
82	KA KA 6/PAUL 1	Alright On The Night/Hold On (p/s)	6

SYD DALE ORCHESTRA
65	Decca F 22300	C'mon In/Disc A Go Go	10
01	Trunk JBH 01	Theme To Screen Test (Marching There & back) (1-sided 7", 500 only)	60

DALE & GRACE
63	London HL 9807	I'm Leaving It Up To You/That's What I Like About You	15
64	London HL 9857	Stop And Think It Over/Bad Luck	15
69	London HL 10249	I'm Leaving It Up To You/Love Is Strange	10
64	London RE 1428	DALE AND GRACE NO. 1 (EP)	30
64	London RE 1429	DALE AND GRACE NO. 2 (EP)	30
64	London RE 1430	DALE AND GRACE NO. 3 (EP)	35

DALEK I LOVE YOU
79	Vertigo DALEK 1	Freedom Fighters/Two Chameleons (p/s, as Dalek I)	6
83	Korova KOW 31	Horrorscope/These Walls We Build	7

DALEKS
80	Exterminated EXPS 1	Rejected/Man Of The World/This Life (fold-out, p/s)	15

DALES
75	Deroy 953	LUCKY THIRTEEN (LP)	30

DALE SISTERS
61	Ember EMB S 140	My Sunday Baby/All My Life	15
62	Ember EMB S 151	Secrets/Road To Love	10

DÄLEX
81	Dodgy DODGY 1	Juvenile/Action Man/Touched (p/s)	30

BASIL DALEY
68	Studio One SO 2054	Hold Me Baby/HEPTONES: I Got A Feeling	60

JIMMY DALEY & DING-A-LINGS
57	Brunswick 05648	Rock, Pretty Baby/Can I Steal A Little Love	100

GRAHAM DALLEY
66	Hollick & Taylor HT/LP 1068	GRAHAM DALLEY AT THE BARN (LP)	15

SALVADOR DALI
62	Decca SET/MET 230	DALI IN VENICE (LP, mono/stereo, gatefold sleeve with booklet)	60

DALIDA
60	HMV POP 793	Never On A Sunday/MILKO PAPAYAKI: Parle Doucement	7
57	Felsted ESD 3043	DALIDA IS HER NAME (EP)	20
59	Felsted ESD 3077	PARDON MY ENGLISH (EP)	25
57	Felsted SDL 86053	THE GLAMOUROUS DALIDA (10" LP)	50
66	Fontana TL 5348	DALIDA (LP)	18

Cynthia DALL

			MINT VALUE £
CYNTHIA DALL			
96	Domino WIGLP 23	UNTITLED (LP)	20
DALLIONS			
62	Oriole CB 1794	Teardrops In The Rain/Loop De Loop	6
MIKI DALLON			
65	RCA RCA 1438	Do You Call That Love?/Apple Pie	20
65	RCA RCA 1478	I Care About You/I'll Give You Love	40
66	Strike JH 306	Cheat And Lie/(I'm Gonna Find A) Cave	40
66	Strike JH 318	What Will Your Mama Say Now?/Two At A Time	8
(see also Neil Christian & Crusaders)			
DAVID & MARIANNE DALMOUR			
65	Columbia 33SX 1715	INTRODUCING (LP)	20
66	Columbia SCX 6005	STRANGE ENCHANTMENT (LP)	25
KAREN DALTON			
71	Paramount SPFL 271	IN MY OWN TIME (LP)	60
DALTONS			
67	Fab FAB 30	Never Kiss You Again/RIGHTEOUS FLAMES: When A Girl Loves A Boy	150
(see also Prince Buster)			
ROGER DALTREY			
73	Track 2094 014	Thinking/There Is Love	6
75	A&M AMS 7206	Orpheus Song/Love's Dream	6
77	Polydor 2058 896	One Of The Boys/You Better Put Something Inside Me (p/s)	6
77	Polydor 2058 948	Say It Ain't So Joe/Satin And Lace (withdrawn, existence unconfirmed)	20
77	Polydor 2121 319	Written On The Wind/Dear John	8
78	Polydor 2058 986	Say It Ain't So Joe/The Prisoner	8
73	Track 2406 107	DALTREY (LP, gatefold sleeve)	15
80	Polydor POLD 5034	McVICAR (LP, soundtrack, clear vinyl)	15
80	Polydor POLD 5034	McVICAR (LP, soundtrack)	15
(see also Who, High Numbers, McEnroe & Cash)			
TONI DALY			
66	Columbia DB 8043	Like The Big Man Said/You Can't Get No Water	7
(see also Antoinette)			
DALYS			
67	Fontana TF 841	A Fistful Of Dollars/Man With No Name	6
DAMARIS			
83	CBS 4172	What About My Love/Hooray For Love	12
83	CBS 4172	What About My Love/Hooray For Love (12")	30
DAMASCUS			
80s	Private pressing	OPEN YOUR EYES (12" EP, with insert)	100
80s	Private pressing	OPEN YOUR EYES (12" EP, later with different back sleeve, with insert)	75
(see also Thin End Of The Wedge)			
DAMBALA			
78	Isis ISIS 001	Rebel/MILITANT BARRY : Version	20
78	Music Hive MH001	Zimbabwe/GUS ANYIA : Visions Of War	40
79	Radic RIC 107	Babylon/No Go (As Dambala featuring Gus Anyia)	40
81	Blank IS 1002	Rally Round/Version (12" p/s)	40
83	Dada Music DLP 1	AZANIA (LP)	40
DAMITA JO			
61	Mercury AMT 1155	I'll Be There/Love Laid Its Hands On Me	10
DAMNED (1)			
74	Youngblood YB 1067	Morning Bird/Theta	40
DAMNED (2)			
SINGLES			
76	Stiff BUY 6	New Rose/Help! (first pressing with push-out centre, 'Street music co' credit on label, 'is this a record' & 'a bilbo boppa' on A side run out, 'Damned Beatles & 'Bilbo master room' on B. 'Delga' credit on p/s)	50
76	Stiff BUY 6	New Rose/Help! (p/s, 2nd pressing, with Rock Music Co Ltd/Street Music Co credit on A side, push-out centre)	12
76	Stiff BUY 6	New Rose/Help! (3rd pressing, solid centre)	7
77	Stiff BUY 10	Neat Neat Neat/Stab Yor Back/Singalongascabies (glossy p/s, no 'Island' logo on sleeve, first pressing solid centre)	25
77	Stiff BUY 10	Neat Neat Neat/Stab Yor Back/Singalongascabies (glossy p/s, no 'Island' logo on sleeve, second pressing push-out centre)	25
77	Stiff BUY 10	Neat Neat Neat/Stab Yor Back/Singalongascabies (glossy p/s, 'Island' logo on rear, later pressing, push-out/solid centre)	12
77	Stiff DAMMED 1	Stretcher Case Baby/Sick Of Being Sick (p/s, NME competition & gig freebie)	125
77	Stiff BUY 18	Problem Child/You Take My Money (p/s, originally with press-out centre)	15
77	Stiff BUY 18	Problem Child/You Take My Money (p/s)	7
77	Stiff BUY 24	Don't Cry Wolf/One Way Love (promo grey label with small "A")	30
77	Stiff BUY 24	Don't Cry Wolf/One Way Love (20,000 on pink vinyl, no p/s)	12
77	Stiff BUY 24	Don't Cry Wolf/One Way Love (push-out centre, black vinyl)	15
78	Dodgy Demo Co. SGS 105	Love Song/Burglar (mail order issue/gig freebie, plain sleeve, stickered labels)	60
79	Chiswick CHIS 112	Love Song/Noise Noise Noise/Suicide (red vinyl, 4 different sleeves)	8
79	Chiswick CHIS 120 ADJ-1	I Just Can't Be Happy Today/Ballroom Blitz ('A' Label DJ promo copy)	200
80	Chiswick CHIS 130	White Rabbit/Rabid (Over You)/Seagulls (unissued in U.K., Europe-only, 2 x 1-sided white-label test pressings exist, hand-written labels)	400
80	Chiswick CHIS 139 DJ	There Ain't No Sanity Clause/Hit Or Miss (double A side demo)	30
81	Stiff GRAB 2	Four Pack (4 x 7" [BUY 6, 10, 18 & 24], in a plastic wallet)	50
82	Big Beat NS 75	Love Song/Noise Noise Noise/Suicide (3 different sleeves, blue vinyl)	6
82	Big Beat NS 75	Love Song/Noise Noise Noise/Suicide (3 different sleeves, black vinyl with black and white labels)	25
82	Big Beat NS 76	Smash It Up/Burglar (p/s, red vinyl)	6

Kenny DAMON

MINT VALUE £

82	Big Beat NS 80	Lively Arts/Teenage Dream (p/s, green vinyl)	10
82	Bronze BRO 149	Lovely Money/Lovely Money (Disco Mix)/I Think I'm Wonderful (p/s)	6
82	Bronze BRO 156	Dozen Girls/Take That/Mine's A Large One, Landlord/Torture Me (p/s)	6
82	Bronze BRO 159	Generals/Disguise/Citadel Zombies (p/s)	8
84	Plus One DAMNED 1	Thanks For The Night/Nasty (p/s, 1,000 each on red, white & blue vinyl)	10
84	Plus One DAMNED 1T	Thanks For The Night/Nasty/Do The Blitz (12", no'd p/s, multicoloured vinyl)	15
84	Plus One DAMNED 1T	Thanks For The Night/Nasty ('woman'-shaped pic disc w/ plinth, 1,000 only)	25
85	MCA GRIM 1	Grimly Fiendish/Edward The Bear (autographed gatefold p/s, 1,000 only)	8
85	MCA GRIMT 1	Grimly Fiendish (Spic'n'Span Mix)/Edward The Bear (12", autographed p/s)	10
85	Stiff BUY DJ 238	New Rose/Help!/I'm So Bored (promo reissue)	20
86	Stiff BUY DJ 238	New Rose/Neat Neat Neat (promo)	12
86	Stiff BUY 6/BUY DJ 6A	New Rose/Help!/I'm So Bored (1-sided) (double pack, stickered PVC sleeve with insert, 1st disc on white vinyl, 2nd disc actually plays "I Fall" [live])	20
86	Stiff BUY 6	New Rose/Help! (reissue, red vinyl, PVC sleeve, with card insert)	8
86	Stiff BUYIT 6	New Rose/Neat Neat Neat/Help/Stretcher Case/Sick Of Being Sick (12", p/s)	20
86	Strange Fruit SFPS002	PEEL SESSIONS (12")	10
87	Strange Fruit SFPS040	PEEL SESSIONS 2 (12")	10
88	Sugar & Spite SS 01	History Of The World Part 1 (Psychedelic Mix) (1-sided flexi credited to 'The Dimmed' wraparound p/s free with Sugar & Spite fanzine)	35
88	Sugar & Spite SS 01	History Of The World Part 1 (Psychedelic Mix) (1-sided flexi credited to 'The Dimmed' wraparound p/s free without Sugar & Spite fanzine)	20
89	Sugar and Spite SS02	No Fun (1-sided flexi)	20
90	Deltic DELT 7T	Fun Factory/CAPTAIN SENSIBLE: Freedom/Pasties/A Riot On Eastbourne Pier (p/s)	15
90	Deltic DELT 7T	Fun Factory/CAPTAIN SENSIBLE: Freedom/Pasties/A Riot On Eastbourne Pier (12", p/s, blue vinyl, mail-order only, 2000 only)	20
02	Stiff FBUPC 004	New Rose/Help! (reissue with free CD single)	15
05	Lively Arts LADAM 1	Little Miss Disaster/Anti-Pope (live) (p/s, red splatter vinyl)	30
08	Devil's Jukebox DJB66619PRO	WHITE EP (p/s, white vinyl)	40
09	Devil's Jukebox DJB66630PRO7	MACHINE GUN ETIQUETTE (p/s, promo single, blue vinyl, 300 only)	30
10	Devil's Jukebox DJB66644	A Nation Fit For Heroes/Time (p/s, blue, white or red vinyl)	20
11	Devil's Jukebox DJBSAMP02	NOT FOR SALE EP (p/s, green vinyl)	40
16	Sanctuary BMG CATS V190	New Rose/Amen (Live) (40th Anniversary picture disc)	30
17	Union Square SALVOS V17	New Rose/Help (40th Anniversary picture disc)	30

ALBUMS

77	Stiff SEEZ 1	DAMNED DAMNED DAMNED (LP)	75
77	Stiff SEEZ 1	DAMNED DAMNED DAMNED (LP, 2,000 with Eddie & Hot Rods photograph on rear sleeve; shrinkwrapped with title sticker)	400
77	Stiff SEEZ 1	DAMNED DAMNED DAMNED (LP, 2,000 with Eddie & Hot Rods photograph on rear sleeve; not shrinkwrapped with title sticker)	200
77	Stiff SEEZ 2	MUSIC FOR PLEASURE (LP)	25
79	Chiswick CWK 3011	MACHINE GUN ETIQUETTE (LP, with inner sleeve)	35
80	Chiswick CWK 3015	THE BLACK ALBUM (2-LP)	30
81	Ace DAM 1	ANOTHER GREAT RECORD FROM THE DAMNED: THE BEST OF THE DAMNED (LP, red or blue vinyl)	15
82	Bronze BRON 542	STRAWBERRIES (LP, with scratch and sniff insert)	20
82	Ace DAM 3	THE BLACK ALBUM (LP, single reissue, 12,000 with lyrics & poster)	15
82	Ace DAM 2	MACHINE GUN ETIQUETTE (LP, reissue, blue or clear vinyl with inner)	25
83	Stiff MAIL 2	DAMNED DAMNED DAMNED/MUSIC FOR PLEASURE (2-LP, reissue, gatefold sleeve, mail-order only, 5000 only)	25
83	Damned DAMU 2	LIVE IN NEWCASTLE (LP, 5,000 by mail-order only)	15
83	Damned PDAMU 2	LIVE IN NEWCASTLE (LP, picture disc, 5,000 only)	15
85	MCA MCFW 3275	PHANTASMAGORIA (LP, white vinyl, with inner)	15
86	Stiff MAIL 2	DAMNED, DAMNED, DAMNED/MUSIC FOR PLEASURE (2-LP, reissue, yellow vinyl, 4000 by mail-order only)	25
86	Duju DOJOPD 46	STRAWBERRIES (LP, reissue picture disc)	15
86	Stiff GET 4	THE CAPTAIN'S BIRTHDAY PARTY — LIVE AT THE ROUNDHOUSE (mini-LP, 45rpm, blue vinyl, stickered plain white sleeve)	15
86	MCA MCG 6015	ANYTHING (LP, gatefold with band pop-up)	15
87	Demon FIEND 91	DAMNED DAMNED DAMNED (LP, reissue)	15
87	Demon PFIEND 91	DAMNED DAMNED DAMNED (LP, reissue picture disc)	15
87	Demon FIEND 108	MUSIC FOR PLEASURE (LP, reissue, orange vinyl)	15
89	Essential ESCLP 008	FINAL DAMNATION (LP, green vinyl, with poster)	20
89	Essential ESSLP 008	FINAL DAMNATION (LP)	15
92	Receiver RRLP 159	LIVE AT THE LYCEUM (LP, clear vinyl)	15
10	Devil's Jukebox DJB66643LP	SO, WHO'S PARANOID? (2-LP, numbered)	30
18	Spinefarm SPINE 734043	EVIL SPIRITS (LP, white vinyl, signed, postcard and Damned plectrum)	50
16	Live Here Now LHN014LP	40TH ANNIVERSARY TOUR - LIVE IN MARGATE (3-LP)	35

(see also Bartok, Brian James (2), Captain Sensible, Rat Scabies, Rat & Whale, Edge, Maxim's Thrash, Naz Nomad & Nightmares, Auntiepus, Phantom Chords, Tank, Eddie & Hot Rods, U.F.O., Tanz Der Youth, Motordam)

KENNY DAMON

65	Mercury MF 907	While I Live/Fountain In Capri	8

(see also Kenny Roberts)

RUSS DAMON

64	Stateside SS 258	Hip Huggers/Heaven Sent	12

STUART DAMON

70	Reflection REF L7	STUART 'CHAMPION' DAMON (LP)	20

DAMON & NAOMI

97	Earworm WORM 3	The Navigator/Awake In A Muddle (p/s)	8

(see also Galaxie 500)

Vic DAMONE

MINT VALUE £

VIC DAMONE
57   Mercury MPT 7514   ALL-TIME SONG HITS (10" LP) 15

DAN
89   Meantime COX 013c   KICKING ASS AT TJ'S (LP, with flexi) 15

RUPIE DAN
82   Flag FLG 101   My Black Race/Black Race Dub (12") 40

JONAH DAN
96   Inner Sanctuary ACT10-004   Meditation Rock/Dub 1/Dub 2 (10") 20
89   Conscious Sounds JKPD 001   MEETS THE BUSH CHEMISTS AT CONSCIOUS SOUNDS (LP) 25

DANCE CHAPTER
80   4AD AD 18   Anonymity/New Dance (p/s, with card insert) 10
80   4AD AD 18   Anonymity/New Dance (p/s) 6
81   4AD BAD 115   CHAPTER II (12" EP, most with mismatched A&B-side labels) 10

DANCE CONSPIRACY
92   Metamorphosis MORPHO 001   DUB WAR EP 12" (die cut sleeve) 15

DANCELAND ROCK GROUP
62   Danceland Y 2032   Anytime/Because They're Young 15
63   Danceland Y 2043   William Tell/Last Night Was Made For Love 15

DANCE PEOPLE
79   Satril SATLP 4013   FLY AWAY (LP) 15

DANCER
75   Dawn DNS 1118   Hate Generator/Love Seeds 12

DANCE SQUAD
93   Mendoza MEN 0026   Everybody (Vocal Mix)/Everybody (Instrumental)/Bad Boy (Hard Mix) (12", as Dance Squad featuring Camilla) 25
94   Wicked Sounds WS 02   Yu-a Raggamuffin/Ganjaman (12") 25

DANCETTE
83   Bel BEL 45   Going Green/He's Clever 30

GRAHAM PHILIP D'ANCEY
81   Blue September BSEP 005   Sacred Heart/Lament Of The Winged Warrior (p/s) 40
83   Shibui SHS 001   Freedom/False Prophet (p/s) 30
83   Shibui SHS 001   ALLUMA (LP) 30

DANCING DID
79   Fruit & Veg F&V 1   Dancing Did/Lorry Pirates (p/s, insert) 20
80   Fruit & Veg F&V 2   The Haunted Tearooms/Squashed Things On The Road (p/s) 10
82   Stiff BUY 136   The Lost Platoon/The Human Chicken (withdrawn 'cavalry' p/s) 15
82   Kamera Records KAM 009   AND DID THOSE FEET (LP, with insert) 25

DANDO SHAFT
70   Youngblood YB 1012   Cold Wind/Cat Song 15
72   RCA RCA 2246   Sun Clog Dance/This Gift 10
70   Youngblood SSYB 6   AN EVENING WITH DANDO SHAFT (LP, white/red label) 120
71   RCA Neon NE 5   DANDO SHAFT (LP, gatefold sleeve, black inner sleeve) 175
72   RCA Victor SF 8256   LANTALOON (LP, with poster, orange label) 175
72   RCA Victor SF 8256   LANTALOON (LP, without poster, orange label) 80
77   Rubber RUB 034   KINGDOM (LP) 60

(see also Hedgehog Pie)

DANDY (& SUPERBOYS)
64   Dice CC 21   Rudie Don't Go/It's Just Got To Be 15
65   Dice CC 24   You Got To Pray/I Got To Have You (as Dandy & Barbara) 15
65   Blue Beat BB 308   To Love You/I'm Looking For Love 15
65   Blue Beat BB 319   Hey Boy Hey Girl/So Long Baby (as Dandy & Del) 15
65   Blue Beat BB 327   My Baby/I'm Gonna Stop Loving You 15
65   Blue Beat BB 336   I Found Love/You've Got Something Nice 15
66   Dice CC 29   The Operation/A Little More Ska 20
66   Ska Beat JB 247   The Fight/Do You Know 15
67   Ska Beat JB 269   One Scotch One Bourbon One Beer/Maximum Pressure 25
67   Ska Beat JB 273   Rudie A Message To You/Til Death Do Us Part 20
67   Ska Beat JB 279   You're No Hustler/No No 15
67   Giant GN 3   My Time Now/East Of Suez (with Superboys) 35
67   Giant GN 5   Puppet On A String/Have Your Fun (with Superboys) 15
67   Giant GN 7   We Are Still Rude/Let's Do Rocksteady (with Superboys) 15
67   Giant GN 10   Somewhere My Love/My Kind Of Love (with Superboys) 15
67   Giant GN 15   There Is A Mountain/This Music Got Soul (with Superboys) 15
68   Giant GN 20   Charlie Brown/Groovin' At The Cue 40
68   Giant GN 23   Propagandist/Giant March 20
68   Giant GN 27   Sweet Ride/Up The Hill (with Superboys) 10
68   Giant GN 30   Tears On My Pillow/Mad Them (with Superboys) 10
68   Giant GN 36   I'm Back With A Bang Bang/Jungle Walk (with Superboys) 80
68   Trojan TR 618   The Toast/Kicks Out 12
69   Columbia Blue Beat DB 112   Play It Cool/Rude With Me 8
68   Downtown DT 401   Move Your Mule/Reggae Me This 25
69   Downtown DT 402   Come Back Girl/Shake Me Wake Me 20
68   Downtown DT 404   Tell Me Darling/Cool Hand Luke 30
68   Downtown DT 405   Copy Your Rhythm/BROTHER DAN ALL STARS: Lovely Lady 20
69   Downtown DT 406   Doctor Sure Shot/Put On Your Dancing Shoes 20
69   Downtown DT 410   Reggae In Your Jeggae/DREAMERS: Reggae Shuffle 25
69   Downtown DT 411   You Don't Care/Tryer (both sides with Audrey) 20
69   Downtown DT 415   Rocksteady Gone/Walking Down 20
69   Downtown DT 416   I'm Your Puppet/Water Boy 30

DANDY & AUDREY

MINT VALUE £

Year	Label/Cat#	Title	Value
69	Downtown DT 421	Games People Play/AUDREY: One Fine Day	7
69	Downtown DT 429	People Get Ready/RUDIES: Near East	50
69	Downtown DT 434	Be Natural, Be Proud/Who Do You Want To Run To	15
69	Downtown DT 437	Come On Home/Love Is All You Need	20
69	Downtown DT 442	Everybody Loves A Winner/Try Me One More Time	20
69	Downtown DT 445	Let's Come Together (with Israelites)/JAKE WADE: Music Fever	20
69	Downtown DT 453	Won't You Come Home/Baby Make It Soon	20
70	Downtown DT 456	Raining In My Heart/First Note	15
70	Downtown DT 458	Build Your Love (On Solid Foundation)/Let's Talk It Over (p/s)	15
70	Downtown DT 458	Build Your Love (On Solid Foundation)/Let's Talk It Over	8
70	Downtown DT 462	Morning Side Of The Mountain (as Dandy & Audrey)/AUDREY: Show Me Baby	15
70	Downtown DT 468	How Glad I Am/I'm So Glad (as Dandy & Audrey)	12
70	Trojan TR 7800	Take A Letter Maria/You're Coming Back	6
71	Downtown DT 483	Could It Be True/Your Eyes Are Dreaming (as Dandy & Jackie)	15
71	Downtown DT 484	Daddy's Home/Everyman	10
71	Trojan TR 7816	Same Old Fashioned Way/Out Of Many, One People	6
72	Trojan TR 7857	What Do You Want To Make Those Eyes At Me For/Talking About Sally	6
67	Giant GNL 1000	ROCKSTEADY WITH DANDY (LP)	100
68	Trojan TRL 2	DANDY RETURNS (LP)	75
69	Trojan TRL 17	I NEED YOU (LP, with Audrey)	40
69	Trojan TTL 26	YOUR MUSICAL DOCTOR (LP)	50
70	Trojan TBL 118	MORNING SIDE OF THE MOUNTAIN (LP, with Audrey)	40

(see also Bobby Thompson, Sugar & Dandy, Rub A Dubs, Don Martin,, Little Sal with Dandy & Superboys, Dandy Livingtsone)

DANDY & AUDREY

Year	Label/Cat#	Title	Value
69	Downtown DT 411	You Don't Care/Tryer (both sides with Audrey)	20
70	Downtown DT 462	Morning Side Of The Mountain (as Dandy & Audrey)/AUDREY: Show Me Baby	15
69	Downtown TRLS 17	I NEED YOU (LP)	40
70	Downtown TBL 118	MORNING SIDE OF THE MOUNTAIN (LP)	40

CHRIS DANE
| 55 | London HLA 8165 | Cynthia's In Love/My Ideal | 30 |

JERRY DANE
| 63 | Windsor WPS 127 | Everybody Go Wild/Watcha Want (p/s) | 10 |

D'ANGELO
95	Cooltempo CTLP46	BROWN SUGAR (LP)	60
00	EMI 523373 1	VOODOO (2-LP)	30
15	Virgin/Back To Black 00602547240811	BROWN SUGAR (LP, reissue)	18

CAL DANGER
| 62 | Fontana 267 225 TF | Restless/Teenage Girlie Blues | 100 |

(see also Tony Dangerfield)

DANGERDOOM
| 05 | Lez LEX 036LP | MOUSE AND THE MASK (2-LP, printed plastic sleeve, inner & insert) | 50 |

A.P. DANGERFIELD
| 68 | Fontana TF 935 | Conversations (In A Station Light Refreshment Bar)/Further Conversations | 30 |

KEITH DANGERFIELD
| 68 | Plexium P 1237 | No Life Child/She's A Witch | 200 |

TONY DANGERFIELD & THRILLS
| 64 | Pye 7N 15685 | I've Seen Such Things/She's Too Way Out | 100 |

(see also Savages, Circles, Cal Danger)

DANGEROUS BROTHERS
| 80 | Sheep Worrying TMS 002 | False Nose/County Councillor (p/s) | 15 |

DANGEROUS GIRLS
78	Happy Face MM 115	Dangerous Girls/I Don't Want To Eat (With The Family) (p/s)	10
80	Human HUM 1	Man In The Glass/MO75 (p/s)	6
81	Human HUM 6	Step Out/Sidekick Phenomenon/Men In Suits (p/s)	6

PINO D'ANGIO
| 82 | System 12 STEM 2 | Ma Quale Idea/Lezione D'Amore (12") | 20 |

DANI
| 74 | Pye International 7N 25664 | La Vie A 25 Ans/Pour Que Ça Dure (p/s) | 6 |
| 74 | Pye International 7N 25667 | That Old Familiar Feeling/Pour Que Ça Dure | 12 |

ERROLL DANIEL
| 69 | Paradox PAR 45902 | No Excuses/Go Back | 20 |

DANIEL IN THE LION'S DEN
| 70 | Trojan TR 7797 | Dancing In The Sun/LION'S DEN: Chick A Bow | 6 |

DANIELLE
| 66 | Philips BF 1532 | I'm Gonna Marry The Boy/Magic Carpet Of Love | 8 |
| 67 | Philips BF 1574 | Oh Mama/Come A Little Closer | 7 |

JULIUS DANIELS
| 65 | RCA RCX 7175 | R.C.A. VICTOR RACE SERIES VOL. 4 (EP) | 15 |

MAXINE DANIELS
| 57 | Oriole CB 1366 | Coffee-Bar Calypso/Cha-Cha Calypso | 8 |

MIKE DANIELS & HIS BAND
| 57 | Parlophone R 4285 | Hiyawatha/Don't You Think I Love You | 8 |
| 57 | Columbia 33SX 1256 | MIKE ON MIKE (LP) | 40 |

ROLY "YO YO" DANIELS
| 60s | Stardisc SD 101 | Yo Yo Boy/The Teacher (p/s, features Don Rendell) | 50 |
| 62 | Decca F 11501 | Yo Yo Boy/The Teacher (reissue) | 10 |

SAM DANIELS
| 63 | Sway SW 003 | Tell Me Baby/ERNIE FAULKENER: Beautiful Girl (both with Planets) | 8 |

JOHNNY DANKWORTH ORCHESTRA

MINT VALUE £

JOHNNY DANKWORTH ORCHESTRA

Year	Label & Cat No	Title	Value
53	Parlophone MSP 6026	Honeysuckle Rose (with Cleo Laine)/Swingin'	10
53	Parlophone MSP 6032	Moon Flowers/Two Ticks	10
53	Parlophone MSP 6037	I Get A Kick Out Of You (with Frank Holder)/Easy Living (with Cleo Laine)	10
54	Parlophone MSP 6067	S' Wonderful/Younger Every Day	10
54	Parlophone MSP 6077	The Slider/It's The Talk Of The Town	10
54	Parlophone MSP 6083	The Jerky Thing/My Buddy	10
54	Parlophone MSP 6092	Runnin' Wild/Oo-Be-Doop	10
54	Parlophone MSP 6113	Perdido/Four Of A Kind	10
54	Parlophone MSP 6139	Bugle Call Rag/You Go To My Head	10
55	Capitol CL 14285	Singin' In The Rain/Non-Stop London	10
56	Parlophone MSP 6255	Experiments With Mice/Applecake	15
61	Columbia DB 4695	The Avengers/Chano	15
62	No label 19517	Music For The New Prestige Film (1-sided white label)	15
62	Fontana TF 396	Hoe Down/Sing Sing Sing	6
63	Fontana TF 422	The Avengers/Off The Cuff	15
64	Fontana TF 512	Beefeaters/Down A Tone	35
65	Fontana TF 643	Sands Of The Kalahari/Night Thoughts	6
66	Fontana TF 700	Modesty Blaise Theme/The Frost Report	10
67	Fontana TF 805	(Ain't That) Just Like A Woman/Accident	10
73	Philips 6006 337	Tomorrows World/Bitter Lemons	10
78	BBC RESL 63	Telford's Change/Serenade For Sylvia (p/s)	8
58	Parlophone GEP 8653	DANKWORTH WORKSHOP NO. 1 (EP)	20
58	Parlophone GEP 8697	DANKWORTH WORKSHOP NO. 2 — EXPERIMENTS WITH DANKWORTH (EP)	15
60	Columbia SEG 8037	THE CRIMINALS (EP, soundtrack; also stereo ESG 7825)	15
56	Parlophone PMD 1042	JOURNEY INTO JAZZ (10" LP)	20
58	Parlophone PMC 1076	THE VINTAGE YEARS (LP)	20
59	Parlophone PMC 1043	FIVE STEPS TO DANKWORTH (LP)	20
60	Top Rank 30/019	LONDON TO NEWPORT (LP)	40
61	Columbia 33SX 1280	JAZZ ROUTES (LP, also stereo SCX 3347)	30
64	Encore ENC 165	FROM 7 ON (LP)	20
65	Fontana TL 5229	THE ZODIAC VARIATIONS (LP, mono)	25
65	Fontana STL 5229	THE ZODIAC VARIATIONS (LP, stereo)	30
67	Stateside S(S)L 10213	FATHOM (LP, soundtrack)	40
68	Fontana TL 5445	THE $1,000,000 COLLECTION (LP)	15
69	Fontana LPS 16261	OFF DUTY (LP)	18

(see also Cleo Laine, Philip Green, Tony Mansell, Kenny Wheeler & Johnny Dankworth)

DANLEERS

58	Mercury AMT 1003	One Summer Night/Wheelin' And A-Dealin'	200
58	Mercury AMT 1003	One Summer Night/Wheelin' And A-Dealin' (78)	40

DAN LE SAC VS SCROOBIUS PIP

07	Lex Records LEX 044 SVN	Thou Shalt Always Kill/Thou Shalt Always Kill (Knifehandchop Remix) (p/s)	15
08	Sunday Best SBESTLP24	ANGLES (2-LP, CD)	40

DANNY & NOGOODNIKS

82	Chrysalis CHS 2667	Bike/Spaghetti (p/s)	10

(see also Adam Ant, Adam & The Ants)

DANNY BOYS

89	Ugly Man UG 1	Days Of The Week (12" EP)	15

DANNY & THE JUNIORS

58	HMV POP 436	At The Hop/Sometimes (When I'm All Alone)	15
58	HMV POP 467	Rock And Roll Is Here To Stay/School Boy Romance	40
58	HMV POP 504	Dottie/In The Meantime	30
60	Top Rank JAR 510	Twistin' U.S.A./Thousand Miles Away	15
61	Top Rank JAR 552	Pony Express/Daydreamer	15
61	Top Rank JAR 587	Back To The Hop/The Charleston Fish	15
62	Top Rank JAR 604	Twistin' All Night Long/Twistin' England (with Freddy Cannon)	15
63	London HL 9666	Oo-La-La-Limbo/Now And Then	10

(see also Freddie Cannon)

DANNY & JOE/TOMMY MCCOOK'S BAND

12	Jackpot THB 7018	Please Be Mine/More Strings	8

DANSE MACABRE

88	Wild West/Alchemy 1	THINK ABOUT DEATH EP	20

DANSE SOCIETY

81	Society SOC 3-81	The Clock/Continent (brown, black & white foldout p/s)	15
81	Pax PAX 2	There Is No Shame In Death/Dolphins/These Frayed Edges (12", p/s, blue vinyl)	20
82	Pax SOC 5	Woman's Own/We're So Happy (p/s)	8
82	Pax PAX 5	Woman's Own/Continent/We're So Happy/Belief (12", with spined p/s)	10
84	Society SOC V 127	2,000 Light Years From Home (12" blue vinyl, 50-150 pressed)	60

DANSETTE DAMAGE

78	Shoestring LACE 001	New Musical Express/The Only Sound (p/s, Robert Plant on backing vocals)	150
79	Pinnacle PIN 30	20013/4 Approximately/Must Be Love (p/s)	8
94	Shoestring BLOO 2LP	SOLD AS SEEN (LP, gatefold sleeve, 500 only)	30

DANTA

72	Epic EPC 7776	Freeway/Mau Mau	15
73	Epic SEPC 1466	Crossfire/Daddy's Gone	15

DANTALIAN'S CHARIOT

67	Columbia DB 8260	The Madman Running Through The Fields/Sun Came Bursting Through My Cloud	120
95	Tenth Planet TP 015	CHARIOT RISING (LP, numbered, 1,000 only)	25

(see also Zoot Money's Big Roll Band)

DANTE (1)

MINT VALUE £

DANTE (1)
| 61 | Brunswick 05857 | Bye Bye Baby/That's Why | 12 |

DANTE (2)
| 71 | CBS 7382 | Queen Of Sheba/Feelin' The Heat | 15 |

RON DANTE
| 68 | MCA MK5003 | It's About Time/Behold | 8 |
| 70 | RCA 1992 | Let Me Bring You Up/How Do You Know | 8 |

TROY DANTE (& INFERNOS)
63	Decca F 11639	The Face/Give Me Some More	7
63	Decca F 11746	It's Alright/Tell Me (as Troy Dante & Infernos)	7
64	Fontana TF 445	Tell Me When/It Had To Be (as Troy Dante & Infernos)	7
64	Fontana TF 477	This Little Girl/Loving Eyes (as Troy Dante & Infernos)	8

DANTE & EVERGREENS
| 60 | Top Rank JAR 402 | Alley-Oop/The Right Time | 15 |

DANZIG
88	Def American 838 487-1	DANZIG (LP, gatefold sleeve)	50
90	Def American 846 374-1	DANZIG II - LUCIFUGE (LP, with inner)	40
92	Def American 512 270-1	DANZIG III - HOW THE GODS KILL (LP, gatefold, stickered sleeve)	80

DAPHINE
| 79 | My Records MY 12 | The World Is Moving On/Just Another Flirt (p/s) | 8 |

DAPHNI
| 12 | Jialong JIA 05V | JIALONG (2-LP) | 20 |

STEVE DARBYSHIRE
65	Decca F12261	That's The Reason Why/She's Got Quality	10
66	Decca F 12512	Trains Trains/Alma Jones (as Steve Darbishire)	7
67	Decca F 12553	Just A Little Lovin' Changes Things/Holiday In Waikiki	6

DARIEN SPIRIT
| 73 | Charisma CAS 1065 | ELEGY TO MARILYN (LP, large "Mad Hatter" label, with lip intact!) | 40 |

BOBBY DARIN

78s
56	Brunswick 05561	Rock Island Line/Timber (as Bobby Darin & Jaybirds)	40
58	London HLE 8737	Queen Of The Hop/Lost Love	25
59	London HLE 8793	Mighty Mighty Man/You're Mine (as Bobby Darin with Rinky Dinks)	30
59	London HLE 8815	Plain Jane/While I'm Gone	30
59	London HLE 8867	Dream Lover/Bullmoose	20
59	London HLK 8939	Mack The Knife/Was There A Call For Me	25
60	London HLK 9034	La Mer (Beyond The Sea)/That's The Way Love Is	40
60	London HLK 9086	Clementine/Down With Love	50
60	London HLK 9142	Bill Bailey Won't You Please Come Home/Tall Story	60

SINGLES
56	Brunswick 05561	Rock Island Line/Timber (as Bobby Darin & Jaybirds)	30
58	London HLE 8666	Splish Splash/Judy Don't Be Moody	25
58	London HLE 8679	Early In The Morning/Now We're One (as Rinky-Dinks featuring Bobby Darin)	25
58	London HLE 8737	Queen Of The Hop/Lost Love	30
58	London HL 7060	Queen Of The Hop/Lost Love (export issue)	20
59	London HLE 8793	Mighty Mighty Man/You're Mine (as Bobby Darin with Rinky Dinks)	25
59	London HLE 8815	Plain Jane/While I'm Gone	30
59	London HL 7078	Plain Jane/Dream Lover (export issue)	25

EPs
59	London REE 1173	BOBBY DARIN (tri centre)	25
59	London REE 1173	BOBBY DARIN (round centre)	10
59	London REE 1225	BOBBY DARIN NO. 2 (tri centre)	25
59	London REE 1225	BOBBY DARIN NO. 2 (round centre)	10
60	London REK 1243	THAT'S ALL	10
61	London REK 1286	FOR TEENAGERS ONLY	20
61	London REK 1290	UP A LAZY RIVER	10
61	London REK 1310	TWO OF A KIND (with Johnny Mercer)	10
61	London REK 1321	THE 25TH DAY OF DECEMBER	10
61	London REK 1334	LOVE SWINGS	10
62	London REK 1338	TWIST WITH BOBBY DARIN	10
62	London REK 1342	THINGS!	10
65	Atlantic AET 6013	MILORD	10

ALBUMS
58	London HA-E 2140	BOBBY DARIN	30
59	London HA-E 2172	THAT'S ALL	15
59	London HA-K 2235	THIS IS DARIN (mono)	15
59	London SAH-K 6067	THIS IS DARIN (stereo)	18
60	London HA-K 2311	FOR TEENAGERS ONLY	40
61	London SAH-K 6194	LOVE SWINGS (stereo)	15
62	London SAH-K 6243	DARIN SINGS RAY CHARLES (stereo)	15
64	Capitol (S)T 2007	GOLDEN FOLK HITS (stereo)	15
67	Atlantic 587 073	SOMETHING SPECIAL	20
69	Bell SBLL 128	COMMITMENT (LP, as Bob Darin)	30

(see also Rinky Dinks)

DARK (1)
| 72 | SIS 0102 | DARK ROUND THE EDGES (LP, private pressing, test pressing with colour gatefold sleeve & booklet) | 6000 |
| 72 | SIS 0102 | DARK ROUND THE EDGES (LP, private pressing, test pressing in white sleeve with 'doodles' by Steve Giles) | 6000 |

DARK (2)

			MINT VALUE £
72	SIS 0102	DARK ROUND THE EDGES (LP, private pressing, 12 copies with colour gatefold sleeve & booklet)	15000
72	SIS 0102	DARK ROUND THE EDGES (LP, private pressing, 12 copies with black & white gatefold sleeve)	6000
72	SIS 0102	DARK ROUND THE EDGES (LP, private pressing, 38 copies with single black & white sleeve)	4000
90	Swank/Darkside 001	DARK ROUND THE EDGES (LP, reissue, U.K. pressing marketed in U.S.)	50
91	Swank/Darkside 001	DARK ROUND THE EDGES (LP, as above, with different insert, 225 only)	50
95	Acme AC 8009LP	ARTEFACTS FROM THE BLACK MUSEUM (LP, 500 only, with insert)	40

DARK (2)
79	Fresh FRESH 2	My Friends/John Wayne (p/s)	8
80	Fresh FRESH 13	Hawaii Five O/Don't Look Now (/s)	20

DARK ANGEL
86	Under One Flag FLAG 6	DARKNESS DESCENDS (LP)	15
91	Under One Flag FLAG 54	TIME DOES NOT HEAL (2-LP)	20

JOHNNY DARKE
79	Carrere CAR 130	I'm Not A Believer/What She Knows (p/s)	20

DARKER SHADE OF BLACK
71	Jackpot JP 758	War/JEFF BARNES: People's Version	10

DARK & MOODY
93	Dark & Moody DARK T 001	VOLUME 1 (12")	12

DARKNESS
03	Must Destroy DESTROYER 6	Get Your Hands Off My Woman (Clean Version)/(Dirty Version)/Best Of Me (p/s)	10
03	Atlantic 745217	PERMISSION TO LAND (LP, gatefold, poster)	80

(see also Hot Leg)

DARK SAND
72	Dark DK001	Visions Of Tomorrow/Sad Affair	30

DARK STAR
81	Avatar AAA 105	Lady Of Mars/Rock 'N' Romancin' (company sleeve)	12
81	Steel Strike no cat. no.	Lady Of Mars/Rock 'N' Romancin' (12", 250 pressed)	90
81	Avatar AALP 5003	DARK STAR (LP, with patch)	20
81	Avatar AALP 5003	DARK STAR (LP)	15
87	FM WKFMLP 97	REAL TO REEL (LP)	15

DARKTHRONE
91	Peaceville VILE 22	SOULSIDE JOURNEY (LP, picture disc)	50
92	Peaceville VILE 28	A BLAZE IN THE NORTHERN SKY (LP)	50
93	Peaceville VILE 35	UNDER A FUNERAL MOON (LP)	50
94	Peaceville VILE 43	TRANSILVANIAN HUNGER (LP)	80

DARLETTES
70	President PT 317	Lost/Sweet Kind Of Loneliness	15

DARLING BUDS
87	Darling Buds DAR 1	If I Said/Just To Be Seen (p/s, with insert, 2,000 only)	12
87	Darling Buds DAR 1	If I Said/Just To Be Seen (p/s, without insert, 2,000 only)	6
87	Bonk On 001	Spin/BUBBLEGUM SPLASH: If Only (flexidisc free with So Naive fanzine)	10
90	Native NTV 54	Shame On You/Valentine//It's All Up To You/Spin/Think Of Me/That's The Reason (triple-pack in envelope sleeve)	6

DARLINGS
67	CBS 2932	Saturday Town/Wish You Were Here	20

BILL DARNEL
55	London HLU 8204	My Little Mother/Bring Me A Bluebird (with Frank Weir & His Orchestra)	15
56	London HLU 8234	The Last Frontier/Rock-A-Boogie Baby	25
56	London HLU 8267	Guilty Lips/Ain't Misbehavin'	10
56	London HLU 8292	Tell Me More/Satin Doll	10

(see also Frank Weir & His Orchestra)

DARONDO
12	Kent Select CITY 027	Didn't I/Saving My Love (reissue)	8

GUY DARRELL (& MIDNIGHTERS)
63	Oriole CB 1932	Go Home Girl/You Won't Come Home (as Guy Darrell & Midnighters)	15
64	Oriole CB 1964	Sorry/Sweet Dreams (as Guy Darrell & Midnighters)	15
65	CBS 201806	Stupidity/One Of These Days	10
66	CBS 202033	Somewhere They Can't Find Me/It Takes A Lot To Laugh	10
66	CBS 202082	I've Been Hurt/Blessed	40
66	CBS 202082	I've Been Hurt/Blessed (demo)	45
67	CBS 202510	Hard Lovin'/I've Never Had A Love Like That	10
67	Piccadilly 7N 35406	Evil Woman/What You Do About That	30
73	Santa Ponsa PNL 502	I'VE BEEN HURT (LP)	15

JEANNIE DARREN & SECOND CITY SOUND
69	Major Minor MM 611	River Deep, Mountain High/Julie	7

MAXINE DARREN
65	Pye 7N 15796	How Can I Hide It From My Heart/Don't You Know	10

EARL DARREN SOUND
77	GTKTEP 1003	EARL DARREN SOUND EP (no p/s)	15

CHRIS DARROW
73	United Artists UAG 29453	CHRIS DARROW (LP, gatefold)	20
74	United Artists UAG 29634	UNDER MY OWN DISGUISE (LP)	20

(see also Kaleidoscope, Nitty Gritty Dirt Band)

DARRYL RAYNER STEVE
77	Clubland SJP 776	LET THE GOOD STONES ROLL 4 BY 3 77 EP (fold out, p/s)	40

DARTELLS
63	London HLD 9719	Hot Pastrami/Dartell Stomp	20

BARRY DARVELL
60	London HL 9191	Geronimo Stomp/How Will It End?	50

DARWIN'S THEORY
67	Major Minor MM 503	Daytime/Hosanna	50

DAS EFX
92	East West 7567 91827-1	DEAD SERIOUS (LP, inner)	30

NITAE DASGUPTA
72	Mushroom 100 MR 22	SONGS OF INDIA (LP)	35

DAS KABINETTE
83	Klosette PL0026	The Cabinet/Fudge It (p/s, 500 only)	100

DAS SCHNITZ
79	Ellie Jay EJSP 9249	4 AM (EP, custom sleeve)	70

DATE WITH SOUL
67	Stateside SS 2062	Yes Sir, That's My Baby/PRISCILLA: He Noticed Me	50

(see also Jack Nitzsche, Brian Wilson, Sonny & Cher, Darlene Love/Blossoms, Jackie De Shannon, the Paris Sisters)

DAT POLITICS
04	Chicks On Speed COSR 15	GO PET GO (LP)	15

DAUGHTERS OF ALBION
69	Fontana STL 5486	DAUGHTERS OF ALBION (LP)	30

DAVANI & RYAN
72	Philips 6308 132	FUNKY COUNTRY (LP)	20

DAVE
89	Linkway DAVE 1	WHATEVER HAPPENED TO... (LP, insert, 50 copies only)	300

DAVE DAVANI & D MEN
63	Columbia DB 7125	Don't Fool Around/She's The Best For Me	15
64	Decca F 11896	Midnight Special/Sho' Know A Lot About Love	20

(see also Davani & Ryan)

DAVE DAVANI (FOUR)
65	Parlophone R 5329	Top Of The Pops/Workin' Out	40
66	Parlophone R 5490	Tossin' And Turnin'/Jupe	50
66	Parlophone R 5525	One Track Mind/On The Cooler Side	35
72	Philips 6006 195	King Kong Blues/Come Back Baby (solo)	12
65	Parlophone PMC 1258	FUSED (LP)	100

(see also Davani & Ryan)

DAVE & DIAMONDS
65	Columbia DB 7692	I Walk The Lonely Night/You Do Love (p/s)	35
65	Columbia DB 7692	I Walk The Lonely Night/You Do Love	15

DAVE & DON
67	Polydor 56212	What A Feeling/That's My Way	6

BOB DAVENPORT (& RAKES)
60	Collector JEB 4	GEORDIE SONGS (EP)	10
62	Topic TOP 83	WOR GEORDIE (EP, with Rakes)	10
66	Columbia SX 1786	BOB DAVENPORT AND THE RAKES (LP, with Rakes)	40
71	Trailer LER 3008	BOB DAVENPORT & THE MARSDEN RATTLERS (LP, red label)	22
73	Trailer LER 2088	PAL OF MY CRADLE DAYS (LP, red label)	18
77	Topic 12TS 318	POSTCARDS HOME (LP, with lyric sheet)	15

D.A.V.E. THE DRUMMER
90s	Yolk YOLK 05	Steamliner/Jaws (12", with Jerome Hill)	40
00	Smitten SMT 46	DIG YOUR OWN GRAVE EP (2x12", p/s)	10
00	Smitten SMTLTD 02	Effective Therapy (1-sided EP, green vinyl)	15

ALAN DAVEY
87	Hawkfan HWFB 3/4	THE ELF EP (double pack, 2 x 7" with insert in wraparound p/s in poly bag)	20

(see also Hawkwind)

DAMIEN DAVEY
87	Pashion PASH 12 71	I'm A Man/Sounds So Fine (12", p/s)	30

(SHAUN) DAVEY & (JAMES) MORRIS
73	York FYK 417	DAVEY AND MORRIS (LP, with insert)	400

(see also Strawbs)

DAVID
69	Philips BF 1776	Light Of Your Mind/Please Mister Policeman	200
69	President PT286	The Who The Why/President	6
70	Fontana TF 1081	I'm Going Back/Selppin	60

ALAN DAVID
64	Decca F 11956	I Want So Much To Know You/I Can't Go Wrong	10
65	Decca F 12084	Hurt/I Found Out Too Late	50
65	Decca F 12130	Crazy 'Bout My Baby/A Thousand Tears Ago	10
67	Polydor BM 56201	Flower Power/Completely Free	30
69	Page One POF116	Oh What A Naughty Man/I've Got To Know	10
65	Decca LK 4674	ALAN DAVID (LP)	40

DAVID & DAVID
70	Columbia DB8678	In The City/Good Morning Morning	10

DAVID & GIANTS
68	Capitol CL 15915	Ten Miles High/Super Love	10

DAVID & GOLIATH
71	Concord CON 025	Why Do You Pretend/I Wonder Where	8

DAVID & JONATHAN
67	Columbia S(C)X 6031	DAVID AND JONATHAN (LP)	20

(see also Roger Cook, Edison Lighthouse, White Plains)

JUSTIN DAVID
95	Ugly UGM 003	GEEKS 'N' FREAKS EP (12')	20

DAVID & ROZAA

DAVID & ROZAA
70	Philips 6006 040	Time Of Our Life/We Can Reach An Understanding	20
71	Philips 6006 094	The Spark That Lights The Flame/Two Can Share	20

(see also David Essex, Rozaa & Wine)

DIANNE DAVIDSON
72	Janus 6146 019	Sympathy/All I Wanted	8
72	Janus 6310 209	BACKWOODS WOMAN (LP)	18

TOMMY DAVIDSON
56	London HLU 8219	Half Past Kissing Time/I Don't Know Yet But I'm Learning	20

ALAN DAVIE
70	ADMW ADMW 001	THE ALAN DAVIE MUSIC WORKSHOP (LP)	300
71	ADMW ADMW 002	SUITE FOR PREPARED PIANO AND MINI DRUMS (LP)	200
71	ADMW ADMW 003	BIRD THROUGH THE WALL (LP)	100
71	ADMW ADMW 004	PHANTOM IN THE ROOM (LP)	100

(see also Tony Oxley and Alan Davie)

HUTCH DAVIE
58	London HLE 8667	At The Woodchopper's Ball/Honky Tonk Train Blues (& Honky Tonkers)	7

ALUN DAVIES
65	Parlophone R 5384	Girls Were Made To Love And Kiss/Rose Marie	6
68	Mercury MF 1043	One Day Soon/Pretend You Don't See Her	6
72	CBS 58302	Waste Of Time/Portobello Road	6
72	CBS 65108	DAYDO (LP, gatefold sleeve)	30

(see also Cat Stevens, Sweet Thursday)

BARRY DAVIES
70	Beacon BEA 114	I Wish It Would Rain/Strange Days	30
71	Beacon BEA 185	Strange Days/My Song My Whisky and Me (different A-side version)	40

BAZ DAVIES
80	BAT EJSP 9397	Back In 1969/Easy On My Mind	8

BOB DAVIES
63	London HLU 9767	Rock'N'Roll Show/With You Tonight	25

CYRIL DAVIES (R&B ALLSTARS)
63	Pye International 7N 25194	Country Line Special/Chicago Calling	25
63	Pye International 7N 25221	Preachin' The Blues/Sweet Mary	40
69	Pye 7N 17663	Country Line Special/Sweet Mary	15
64	Pye Intl. NEP 44025	THE SOUND OF CYRIL DAVIES (EP)	75
57	'77' LP 2	THE LEGENDARY CYRIL DAVIES (10" LP, 99 only, with Alexis Korner)	300
70	Folklore F-LEAT 9	THE LEGENDARY CYRIL DAVIES (LP, reissue)	50

(see also Alexis Korner, Beryl Bryden)

DAVE DAVIES
67	Pye 7N 17356	Death Of A Clown/Love Me Till The Sun Shines	8
67	Pye 7N 17429	Susannah's Still Alive/Funny Face	10
68	Pye 7N 17514	Lincoln County/There's No Life Without Love	20
69	Pye 7N 17678	Hold My Hand/Creeping Jean	25
68	Pye NEP 24289	DAVE DAVIES HITS (EP)	300

(see also Kinks)

GLYN DAVIES
89	Eyewitness SRT 9KS 1968	Everyone Will Benefit In The End/Building Bridges To Another World	8

MARION DAVIES
69	Columbia DB 8589	Walk Out Of My Mind/This Is My Lonely Life	7

(see also Ladybirds)

MIAR DAVIES
64	Decca F 11805	Ten Good Reasons/I Won't Remember You	10
64	Decca F 11894	I Hear You Knocking/Navy Blue	10

NICOLA DAVIES
68	SNB 55-3627	Infatuation/My Boy	10

RON DAVIES
70	A&M AMS 799	It Ain't Easy/Silent Song Through The Land	6
70	A&M AMLS 993	SILENT SONG THROUGH THE LAND (LP, green label)	30

BARRINGTON DAVIS
72	Montague MONS 2	TRACKS OF MIND (LP, with lyric inner sleeve)	60

BETTE DAVIS (& DEBBIE BURTON)
63	London HLU 9711	Whatever Happened To Baby Jane?/DEBBIE BURTON:I've Written A Letter To Daddy	8
76	EMI EMA 778	MISS BETTE DAVIS (LP)	15

BETTY DAVIS
75	Island USA 2011	Shut Off The Light/He Was A Big Freak	6
75	Island ILPS 9329	NASTY GAL (LP)	60
93	Vinyl Experience UFOXY1LP	NASTY GAL (LP, reissue)	30
93	Vinyl Experience UFOXY 2LP	BETTY DAVIS (LP, reissue)	40
93	Vinyl Experience UFOXY 3LP	THEY SAY I'M DIFFERENT (LP, reissue)	40

BILLIE DAVIS
63	Decca F 11572	Tell Him/I'm Thankful	10
63	Decca F 11572	Tell Him/I'm Thankful (export copies with p/s)	20
63	Decca F 11658	He's The One/V.I.P.	10
63	Decca F 11658	He's The One/V.I.P. (export copies with p/s)	15
63	Columbia DB 7115	Bedtime Stories/You And I	15
64	Columbia DB 7195	That Boy John/Say Nothin' Don't Tell	15
64	Columbia DB 7246	School Is Over/Give Me Love	15
64	Columbia DB 7346	Whatcha Gonna Do/Everybody Knows (as Billie Davis & Le Roys)	35
65	Piccadilly 7N 35227	Last One To Be Loved/You Don't Know	10
65	Piccadilly 7N 35266	No Other Baby/Hands Off	18

Blind GARY DAVIS/REVEREND GARY DAVIS

MINT VALUE £

66	Piccadilly 7N 35308	Heart And Soul/Don't Take All Night	10
66	Piccadilly 7N 35350	Just Walk In My Shoes/Ev'ry Day	100
67	Decca F 12620	Wasn't It You?/Until It's Time For You To Go	10
67	Decca F 12696	Angel Of The Morning/Darling Be Home Soon	15
68	Decca F 12823	I Want You To Be My Baby/Suffer	10
69	Decca F 12870	Make The Feeling Go Away/I'll Come Home	10
69	Decca F 12923	I Can Remember/Nobody's Home To Go Home To	20
69	Decca F 12977	Nights In White Satin/It's Over	18
70	Decca F 13049	Venid Con Migo/Love (Spanish export issue)	7
70	Decca F 13085	There Must Be A Reason/Love	20
72	Regal Zonophone RZ 3050	I Tried/Touch My Love	8
70	Decca LK 5029	BILLIE DAVIS (LP, mono)	50
70	Decca SKL 5029	BILLIE DAVIS (LP, stereo)	45

(see also Le Roys, Mike Sarne)

BLIND GARY DAVIS/REVEREND GARY DAVIS

63	'77' LA 12-14	PURE RELIGION AND BAD COMPANY (LP)	30
60s	Fontana 688 303 ZL	HARLEM STREET SINGER (LP)	45
64	Xtra XTRA 1009	REV. GARY DAVIS/SHORT STUFF MACON (LP, 1 side each)	22
66	Xtra XTRA 5014	SAY NO TO THE DEVIL (LP)	25
67	Xtra XTRA 5042	A LITTLE MORE FAITH (LP)	25
69	Fontana SFJL 914	BRING YOUR MONEY HONEY (LP)	25
71	Transatlantic TRA 244	RAGTIME GUITAR (LP)	15
71	Transatlantic TRA 249	CHILDREN OF ZION (LP)	15
77	Kicking Mule SNKF 103	LET US GET TOGETHER (LP)	18

BOBBY DAVIS (JAMAICA)

71	Banana BA 342	Got To Get Away/We'll Cry Together (with BARBARA DUNKLEY)	20
71	Banana BA 344	Return Your Love/RILEY'S ALLSTARS: Version	20
71	Beacon 114	Strange Days/I Wish It would Rain	12

(see also Barbara Dunkley)

BOBBY DAVIS (U.S.)

| 61 | Starlite ST45 056 | I Was Wrong/Hype You Into Selling Your Head | 50 |

BONNIE DAVIS

| 55 | Brunswick 05507 | Pepper-Hot Baby/For Always, Darling | 40 |

CLIFFORD DAVIS

| 69 | Reprise RS 27003 | Before The Beginning/Man Of The World | 20 |
| 70 | Reprise RS 27008 | Come On Down And Follow Me/Homework | 15 |

DANNY DAVIS ORCHESTRA (U.S.)

| 65 | MGM MGM 1277 | Main Theme From "The Saint"/Little Bandits Of Juarez | 10 |
| 64 | London HAR 8204 | THEY'RE PLAYING OUR SONG (LP, with Ruby & Romantics) | 20 |

(see also Ruby & Romantics, Byron Lee)

DANNY DAVIS & BYRON LEE

| 64 | MGM 1256 | Night Train From Jamaica/Ska Dee Dah | 18 |

DANNY DAVIS (U.K.)

60	Parlophone R 4657	Love Me/You're My Only Girl	20
60	Parlophone R 4796	Talking In My Sleep/Lullaby Of Love	15
61	Pye 7N 15391	Tell All The World/Rumours	10

(see also Marauders)

DEL DAVIS

71	Bread BR-1105	Baby Don't Wake Me/Wishing And Hoping	150
72	Trojan 7870	Baby Don't Wake Me/Sugarloaf Hill	200
72	Horse HOSS 13	Love Sweet Love/Open The Door	7
73	Horse HOSS 26	World Without Love/Bucket	7

EDDIE ('LOCKJAW') DAVIS

56	Parlophone GEP 8587	EDDIE 'LOCKJAW' DAVIS TRIO (EP)	10
57	Parlophone GEP 8678	LOCKJAW (EP)	10
58	Parlophone GEP 8685	EDDIE 'LOCKJAW' DAVIS TRIO (EP)	10
59	Esquire EP 217	EDDIE 'LOCKJAW' DAVIS (EP)	10
61	Esquire EP 237	EDDIE 'LOCKJAW' DAVIS QUARTET (EP)	10
60	Esquire 32-104	THE EDDIE 'LOCKJAW' DAVIS COOK BOOK (LP)	35
60	Esquire 32-117	VERY SAXY (LP, with Coleman Hawkins, Arnett Cobb & Bobby Tate)	35
61	Esquire 32-128	JAWS IN ORBIT (LP)	30
64	Stateside SL 10201	THE FIRST SET — LIVE AT MINTONS (LP, with Johnny Griffin)	20

(see also Coleman Hawkins, Johnny Griffin)

EDWARD H. DAVIS

| 74 | Sain SAIN 1016M | HEN FFORDD GYMREIG O FYW (LP) | 20 |
| 76 | Sain SAIN 1053M | SNEB YN BECSO DAM (LP, gatefold) | 15 |

JESSE DAVIS

| 71 | Atlantic 2400 106 | JESSE DAVIS (LP, features Gram Parsons and Eric Clapton) | 18 |

JESSE (ED) DAVIS

71	Atlantic 2091 076	Every Night Is Saturday Night/Washita Love Child (as Jesse Davis)	6
71	Atco 2400 106	JESSE 'ED' DAVIS (LP)	18
72	Atlantic K 40329	ULULU (LP)	15

JIMMY DAVIS

| 66 | Bounty BY 6009 | MAXWELL STREET (LP) | 25 |

KIM DAVIS

66	Decca F 12387	Don't Take Your Lovin' Away/Feelin' Blue	20
67	CBS 202568	Tell It Like It Is/Losing Kind	25
68	CBS 3260	Until It's Time For You To Go/I Hold No Grudge	7
69	CBS 4210	Are You Ready For Love/Taste Of Excitement	7

(see also Kim D, Kim & Kinetics)

Larry DAVIS/FENTON ROBINSON

MINT VALUE £

LARRY DAVIS/FENTON ROBINSON
72	Python PLP 24	LARRY DAVIS AND FENTON ROBINSON (LP, 99 copies only)	90

LESLIE A DAVIS
83	Sea View SV2	If I Told You A Live I Am Sorry/Me Nah Tun No Informer (12")	40

MAXWELL DAVIS
66	Ember FA 2040	BATMAN THEME AND OTHER BAT SONGS (LP)	30

MELVIN DAVIS
69	Action ACT 4531	Save It/This Love Was Meant To Be	35

MILES DAVIS
70	CBS S 5104	Miles Runs The Voodoo Down/Spanish Key	12
53	Esquire 20-017	MILES DAVIS PLAYS (10")	75
53	Esquire 20-021	MILES DAVIS ALL STARS (10")	75
53	Vogue LDE 028	MILES DAVIS ALL STARS (10")	75
54	Esquire 20-041	MILES DAVIS BLOWS (10")	75
54	Esquire 20-052	MILES DAVIS ALL STARS (A HIFI MODERN JAZZ JAM SESSION) (10")	75
54	Esquire 20-056	MILES DAVIS ALL STARS (A SECOND HIFI MODERN JAZZ JAM SESSION) (10")	75
54	Vogue LDE 064	MILES DAVIS AND HIS ORCHESTRA (10")	75
54	Capitol LC 6683	CLASSICS IN JAZZ (10")	40
55	Esquire 20-062	DIG (10")	100
55	Esquire 20-072	MILES DAVIS QUINTET (10")	100
56	Esquire 32-012	THE MUSINGS OF MILES	70
56	Esquire 32-021	HIS NEW QUINTET (10")	100
56	Philips BBL 7140	'ROUND ABOUT MIDNIGHT	50
57	Esquire 32-028	CHANGES	50
57	Esquire 32-030	BIRTH OF THE COOL	50
57	Vogue LDE 191	NATURE BOY	40
57	Fontana TFL 5007	MILES AHEAD	50
58	Fontana TFL 5035	MILESTONES	50
58	Esquire 32-048	COOKIN'	100
58	Esquire 32-068	RELAXIN' WITH THE MILES DAVIS QUARTET	100
59	Esquire 32-090	BAGS' GROOVE	40
59	Fontana TFL 5056	PORGY AND BESS (mono)	30
59	Fontana STFL 507	PORGY AND BESS (stereo)	40
60	Fontana TFL 5081	JAZZ TRACK — "L'ANSCENSEUR POUR L'ECHAFAUD"	20
60	Fontana TFL 5089	THE MOST OF MILES	20
60	Fontana TFL 5072	KIND OF BLUE (mono)	100
60	Fontana STFL 513	KIND OF BLUE (stereo)	100
60	CBS SBPG 62066	KIND OF BLUE (stereo)	60
60	CBS BPG 62066	KIND OF BLUE (mono)	60
60	Esquire 32-088	BLUE HAZE	25
60	Esquire 32-098	WALKIN'	80
60	Esquire 32-100	MILES DAVIS AND THE MODERN JAZZ GIANTS VOL. 2	40
60	Esquire 32-108	WORKIN' WITH THE MILES DAVIS QUINTET	80
61	Fontana TFL 5100/STFL 531	SKETCHES OF SPAIN	40
61	Esquire 32-118	EARLY MILES	20
61	Esquire 32-138	STEAMIN' WITH THE MILES DAVIS QUINTET	50
61	Fontana TFL 5163	FRIDAY NIGHT AT THE BLACKHAWK, SAN FRANCISCO (VOL. 1) (with Cannonball Adderley & John Coltrane; also stereo STFL 580)	35
61	Fontana TFL 5164	SATURDAY NIGHT AT THE BLACKHAWK, SAN FRANCISCO (VOL. 2) (with Cannonball Adderley & John Coltrane; also stereo STFL 581)	35
62	Fontana TFL 5172	SOMEDAY MY PRINCE WILL COME (also stereo STFL 587)	40
62	Transatlantic PR 7254	THE ORIGINAL QUINTET	20
63	CBS CL 2106	QUIET NIGHTS (LP)	35
63	CBS BPG 62389	MILES AND MONK AT NEWPORT (with Thelonious Monk, also stereo SBPG 62389)	30
64	Vocalion LAEF 584	BLUE MOODS	20
65	Stateside SL 10111	MILES DAVIS AND JOHN COLTRANE	35
65	CBS BPG 62510	MY FUNNY VALENTINE - MILES DAVIS IN CONCERT (LP)	30
66	CBS 62577	E.S.P.	50
66	CBS SPBG 85560	FOUR & MORE (LP)	20
66	Stateside SL 10168	MILES DAVIS PLAYS FOR LOVERS	20
66	Fontana FJL 135	BACK TO BACK	25
66	Transatlantic PR 7044	COLLECTORS ITEMS (LP, reissue)	20
67	CBS 62933	MILES SMILES (LP, stereo/mono)	50
67	CBS 963097	SORCERER (LP)	50
67	CBS 63248	NEFERTITI (LP)	50
68	CBS 63352	MILES IN THE SKY (LP)	50
69	CBS 63551	FILLES DE KILIMANJARO (stereo)	50
69	CBS 63630	IN A SILENT WAY	50
70	CBS 64010	BITCHES BREW (2-LP, gatefold)	50
70	CBS 70089	A TRIBUTE TO JACK JOHNSON	40
71	CBS 66257	MILES DAVIS AT FILLMORE (2-LP)	40
72	CBS 64575	LIVE-EVIL (2-LP, gatefold)	40
72	CBS 65246	ON THE CORNER	40
72	Prestige PR 24001	MILES DAVIS (2-LP)	20
72	Prestige PR 24012	TALLEST TREES (2-LP)	35
73	CBS CQ 30997/Q 66236	BITCHES BREW (2-LP, quadrophonic)	40
73	CBS GQ 30954/Q 67219	LIVE-EVIL (2-LP, quadrophonic)	40
73	CBS 68222	IN CONCERT (2-LP)	30
74	Columbia 88024	BIG FUN (LP, gatefold)	40
74	CBS S80476	GET UP WITH IT (2-LP)	35

Miles DAVIS/ART BLAKEY

MINT VALUE £

79	CBS 88471	CIRCLE IN THE ROUND (2-LP)	20
85	CBS 62066	KIND OF BLUE (LP, Nimbus Supercut, mail order from Practical Hi Fi magazine)	125
85	Columbia 451126	BITCHES BREW (2-LP, reissue, single sleeve)	30
87	CBS 4606031	KIND OF BLUE (LP, remastered CBS Jazz masterpieces series)	18
87	CBS 450982-1	IN A SILENT WAY (LP, reissue, CBS Jazz masterpieces series)	18
89	CBS 463351-1	AURA (2-LP)	15
91	Beat Goes On BGO LP 30	ON THE CORNER (LP, reissue, gatefold)	18
92	Warner Bros. WB 7599 26938-1	DOO-BOP (LP)	50
96	Columbia 67219	LIVE-EVIL (LP, reissue, gatefold)	25
97	Columbia 069897-1	PANTHALASSA: THE REMIXES (2-LP)	30
98	Sony C4K 65570	COMPLETE BITCHES BREW SESSIONS (5-CD box set)	40
01	Columbia S3K 65362	COMPLETE IN A SILENT WAY SESSIONS (3-CD box set in book sleeve)	30
05	Columbia COL 516253 2	COMPLETE JACK JOHNSON SESSIONS (5-CD box set, booklet)	35
06	Columbia C6K 93674	COMPLETE CELLAR DOOR SESSIONS (6-CD box set, booklet)	80
07	Legacy 88697062392	COMPLETE ON THE CORNER SESSIONS (6-CD, Metal box sleeve)	100

MILES DAVIS/ART BLAKEY
66	Fontana FJL 135	L'ASCENSEUR POUR L'ECHAFAUD/LA FEMME DISPARAISSANTE (LP, soundtrack, 1 side each)	30

(see also Art Blakey, Thelonius Monk, Dizzy Gillespie, Milt Jackson, Cannonball Adderley, Charlie Parker)

NATHAN DAVIS
09	Universal Sound USLP 29	IF (LP, reissue)	20

PAT DAVIS
75	Black Wax WAX 8	I'm Just A Girl/SKIN, FLESH & BONES: Girl Version	10

RONNIE DAVIS
75	Angen ANG 104	The Good News/AGGROVATORS: Version	8
75	Angen ANG 110	Maga Lion/AGGROVATORS: Version	8
75	Attack ATT 8088	I Lost My Lover/MATADOR ALL STARS: Bula Dub	8
75	Attack ATT 8116	Tradition/Tradition (Version)	10
75	Live & Love LAL 04	Jah Jah Jehovah/Version	15
77	Third World TWDIS 005	Anywhere Don't Watch Your Woman (with Dillinger)/BARRY BROWN : Mr Money Man (12")	25
77	Hawkeye HE 011	Used To Be My Girl/HAWKEYE IN SESSION - My Dub	10
76	Dip DLP 5028	BEAUTIFUL PEOPLE FROM JAMAICA (LP)	100
77	Third World TWS 917	HARD TIMES (LP)	20

ROY DAVIS JR
97	XL XLT 88	GABRIEL (12" EP p/s, featuring Peven Everett)	20

SAMMY DAVIS (JNR.)
63	Reprise R 20227	The Shelter Of Your Arms/Falling In Love With You	15
64	Reprise R 20289	Not For Me/Bang Bang	10
69	MCA MK 1072	Rhythm Of Life/Pompeii Club/Rich Man's Frug	30
76	20th Century BTC 2292	Baretta's Theme/I Heard A Song	10
70	Tamla Motown STML 11160	SOMETHING FOR EVERYONE (LP)	30

(see also Dean Martin)

SANDY DAVIS
75	EMI EMC 3070	BACK ON MY FEET AGAIN (LP)	15

SANGIE DAVIS & LEE PERRY
03	Black Art TJITW006	Words/DEVON IRONS & DR ALIMANTADO: Vampire (12" reissue)	50

SILKIE DAVIS
70	Torpedo TOR 2	Conversations/TWIZZLE & HOT ROD ALL-STARS: Peace & Tranquility	70
70	Torpedo TOR 12	When I Was A Little Girl/I'm So Lonely	40

SKEETER DAVIS
63	RCA Victor RCA 1328	The End Of The World/Somebody Loves You	7
65	RCA Victor RCA 1474	Sun Glasses/He Loved Me Too Little	10
64	RCA Victor RCX 7153	SILVER THREADS AND GOLDEN NEEDLES (EP)	12

SKEETER DAVIS & BOBBY BARE
65	RCA RD 7711	TUNES FOR TWO (LP)	15

SMILEY DAVIS
53	London L 1189	Big Mamou/Play Girl (78, actually by Smiley Lewis)	80

SPENCER DAVIS (GROUP)
64	Fontana TF 471	Dimples/Sittin' And Thinkin'	30
64	Fontana TF 499	I Can't Stand It/Midnight Train	25
65	Fontana TF 530	Every Little Bit Hurts/It Hurts Me So	15
65	Fontana TF 571	Strong Love/This Hammer	20
65	Fontana TF 632	Keep On Running/High Time Baby	7
66	Fontana TF 679	Somebody Help Me/Stevie's Blues	7
66	Fontana TF 739	When I Come Home/Trampoline	10
66	Fontana TF 762	Gimme Some Loving/Blues In F	7
67	Fontana TF 785	I'm A Man/I Can't Get Enough Of It	12
67	Fontana TF 854	Time Seller/Don't Want You No More	15
67	United Artists UP 1203	Mr. Second Class/Sanity Inspector	10
68	United Artists UP 2213	After Tea/Moonshine	10
68	United Artists UP 2226	Short Change/Picture Of Heaven	10
73	Vertigo 6059 076	Catch Me On the Rebop/The Edge	10
73	Vertigo 6059 087	Livin' In A Back Street/Sure Need A Helping Hand	10
65	Fontana TE 17444	YOU PUT THE HURT ON ME (EP)	25
65	Fontana TE 17450	EVERY LITTLE BIT HURTS (EP)	25
66	Fontana TE 17463	SITTIN' AND THINKIN' (EP)	40
65	Fontana TL 5242	THEIR FIRST LP (LP, laminated front, black/silver label)	90
66	Fontana TL 5295	THE SECOND ALBUM (LP, laminated front cover, flipbacks, island) label on rear)	80
66	Fontana TL 5359	AUTUMN '66 (LP, laminated front sleeve, flipbacks. black/silver label)	60

Steve DAVIS

			MINT VALUE £
67	United Artists ULP 1186	HERE WE GO ROUND THE MULBERRY BUSH (LP, soundtrack, with Traffic, mono)	50
67	United Artists (S)ULP 1186	HERE WE GO ROUND THE MULBERRY BUSH (LP, soundtrack, with Traffic, stereo)	40
68	United Artists ULP 1192	WITH THEIR NEW FACE ON (LP, mono, blue/silver label)	60
68	United Artists (S)ULP 1192	WITH THEIR NEW FACE ON (LP, stereo)	50
68	Wing WL 1165	EVERY LITTLE BIT HURTS (LP, reissue of "Their First LP")	15
68	Island ILP 970 9070	THE BEST OF THE SPENCER DAVIS GROUP FEATURING STEVIE WINWOOD (LP, plain pink label, flipback sleeve; sleeve lists "Please Do Something" but plays "Together Till The End Of Time", mono)	30
68	Island ILPS 9070	THE BEST OF THE SPENCER DAVIS GROUP FEATURING STEVIE WINWOOD (LP, plain pink label, flipback sleeve; sleeve lists "Please Do Something" but plays "Together Till The End Of Time", stereo)	15
69	CBS 63842	LETTERS FROM EDITH (LP, unissued, 50 white label test pressings only)	500
71	United Artists UAS 29177	IT'S BEEN SO LONG (LP, solo with Peter Jameson, 'envelope' cover)	20
72	United Artists UAS 29361	MOUSETRAP (LP, solo)	20
73	Vertigo 6360 088	GLUGGO (LP, die cut, gatefold sleeve, 'spaceship' label)	30
74	Vertigo 6360 105	LIVIN' IN A BACK STREET (LP)	15

(see also Stevie Winwood, Traffic, Anglos, Blind Faith, Ray Fenwick, Pete York, Hardin & York, Murgatroyd Band, Mirage, Portobello Explosion, Shotgun Express)

STEVE DAVIS

68	Fontana TF 922	Take Time To Know Her/She Said Yeah	75

TYRONE DAVIS (1)

68	Stateside SS 2092	What If A Man/Bet You Win	45
69	Atlantic 584 253	Can I Change My Mind/A Woman Needs To Be Loved	20
69	Atlantic 584 265	Is It Something You've Got?/Undying Love	15
69	Atlantic 584 288	All The Waiting Is Not In Vain/Need Your Lovin' Everyday	15
70	Atlantic 2091 003	Turn Back The Hands Of Time/I Keep Coming Back	15
71	Atlantic 2091 078	Could I Forget You/Just My Way Of Loving You	15
71	Atlantic 2091 131	One Way Ticket/We Got A Love	12
72	Atlantic K 10207	Can I Change My Mind/Turn Back The Hands Of Time/One Way Ticket	12
73	Brunswick BR 4	Without You In My Life/How Could I Forget You	10
73	Brunswick BR 6	There It Is/You Wouldn't Believe	10
74	Brunswick BR 10	I Wish It Was Me/You Don't Have To Beg To Stay	10
76	Brunswick BR 31	Turning Point/Don't Let It Be Too Late	10
77	Brunswick BR 40	Ever Lovin' Girl/Forever	10
70	Atlantic 588 209	CAN I CHANGE MY MIND (LP)	30
71	Atlantic 2465 021	TURN BACK THE HANDS OF TIME (LP)	40
73	Brunswick BRLS 3002	I HAD IT ALL THE TIME (LP)	35
73	Brunswick BRLS 3005	GREATEST HITS (LP)	18

TYRONE DAVIS (2) (ACTUALLY TYRONE EVANS)

69	Trojan TR 677	If This World Were Mine/You Done Me Wrong (label miscredit: this is Tyrone Evans)	300
16	Trojan TR677	If This World Were Mine/You Done Me Wrong (reissue)	20

WALTER DAVIS

64	RCA RCX 7169	R.C.A. VICTOR RACE SERIES VOL. 3 (EP)	15
70	RCA Intl. INTS 1085	THINK YOU NEED A SHOT (LP)	15

WARREN DAVIS MONDAY BAND

60s	Island WI 353	How Can You Forget/Best News (test pressings only)	50
60s	Island WIP 354	Strain On My Heart/Question (test pressings only)	50
67	Columbia DB 8190	Wait For Me/I Don't Wanna Hurt You	30
67	Columbia DB 8270	Love Is A Hurtin' Thing/Without Fear	20

(see also Boardwalkers)

ALFIE DAVISON

00	Philly Groove PG2	Love Is A Serious Business/FLASHLIGHT: Beware She's Pulling My Strings (reissue)	20

BRIAN DAVISON

70	Charisma CAS 1021	BRIAN DAVISON'S EVERY WHICH WAY (LP, pink 'scroll' label)	40

(see also Habits, Nice, Every Which Way, Refuge)

DAVISON BROTHERS

60	Philips PB 1053	Journey Of Love/Seven Days A Week	60

WILD BILL DAVISON

55	Melodisc MLP 501	WILD BILL DAVISON (LP)	15

TIM DAWE

69	Straight ST(S) 1058	PENROD (LP)	70

CARL DAWKINS

67	Rio R 136	All Of A Sudden/Running Shoes	20
67	Rio R 137	Baby I Love You/Hard Time	20
68	Blue Cat BS 114	I Love The Way You Are/DERMOTT LYNCH: I Can't Stand It	100
68	Duke DU 3	I'll Make It Up/J.J. ALL STARS: One Dollar Of Music	70
69	Nu Beat NB 030	Rodney's History/DYNAMITES: Tribute To Drumbano	80
70	Duke DU 93	Get Together/FAMILY MAN: Instalment Plan	12
70	Duke DU 95	This Land/J.J. ALL STARS: Land Version	15
70	Trojan TR 7765	Satisfaction/Things A Get Bad To Worse	12
71	Big Shot BI 570	Perseverance/J.J. ALL STARS: Perseverance (Version)	12
71	Explosion EX 2051	I Feel Good/J.J. ALL STARS: I Feel Good Version Two	10
71	Explosion EX 2059	Make It Great/STONE: What A Day	10
71	New Beat NB 086	Walk A Little Prouder/YOUTH PROFESSIONALS: Walk (Version)	10
72	Duke DU 133	My Whole World/Men A Broken Heart	10
73	Lord Koos KOO 18	I'd Rather Go Blind/DEROY WASHINGTON: Jah Man A Come	70

(see also Rass Dawkins, Untouchables, Winston Wright, Ansell Collins, Roland Alphonso, West Indians)

HORRELL DAWKINS

66	Ska Beat JB 240	Cling To Me/Butterfly	25

JIMMY DAWKINS

73	Mojo 2027 011	The Things I Used To Do/Put It On The Hawg	8

Rass DAWKINS (& WAILERS)

MINT VALUE £

71	Delmark DS 623	FAST FINGERS (LP)	30
78	Sonet SNTF 758	TRANSATLANTIC 770 (LP)	15
82	JSP 1042	PLAY MY BLUES (LP)	18
86	JSP 1102	ALL BLUES (LP)	15
88	JSP 1085	FEEL THE BLUES (LP)	15

RASS DAWKINS (& WAILERS)
71 Upsetter US 368   Picture On The Wall/UPSETTERS: Picture Version 50

(see also Bob Marley/Wailers, Carl Dawkins)

DAWN AND CHRISTINE
78 Burning Rockers BRD 002   We Love Collie Weed (with Clint Eastwood)/LAWES ROCKERS: Version (12") 30

JULIE DAWN
53 Columbia SCM 5035   Wild Horses/A Whistling Kettle And A Dancing Cat 10

(see also Tony Brent & Julie Dawn, Cyril Stapleton)

DAWN TRADER
80 AFE 1980   NO ONE GONNA BETTER ME (EP, private pressing) 40

DAWNBREAKERS
65 Decca F 12110   Let's Live/Lovin' For You 15

DAWN CHORUS (1)
69 MCA MK 5004   A Night To Be Remembered/Crying All Night 15

(see also Carter-Lewis)

DAWN CHORUS (2)
85 Dawn DAWN 1   Teenage Kicks/Dream Lover (p/s) 18

DAWN & DEEJAYS
65 RCA RCA 1470   These Are The Things About You/I Will Think Of You 18

DAWNWATCHER
80 Dawnwatcher DWS 001   Spellbound/Hall Of Mirrors 75
82 Dawnwatcher DWS 002   Salvadors Dream/Backlash 20

DAWNWIND
76 Amron ARN 5003   LOOKING BACK ON THE FUTURE (LP, private pressing) 80

DONNA DAWSON
73 Trojan TR 7892   You Can't Buy Me Love/First Cut Is The Deepest 10

LESLEY DAWSON
67 Mercury MF 946   Just Say Goodbye/Just A Passing Phase 8
67 Mercury MF 965   Run For Shelter/I'll Climb On A Rainbow 35

DANIELLE DAX
83 Initial IRC 009   POP-EYES (LP, with 'Meat Harvest' cover & lyric sheet) 40

(see also Lemon Kittens)

DAY
94 Detour DR 019   Another Country/Gospel (p/s, 100 on green vinyl) 7

BING DAY
59 Mercury AMT 1047   I Can't Help It/Mama's Place 60

BOBBY DAY (& SATELLITES)
57 HMV POP 425   Little Bitty Pretty One/When The Swallows Come Back To Capistrano (as Bobby Day & Satellites) 150
57 HMV POP 425   Little Bitty Pretty One/When The Swallows Come Back To Capistrano (as Bobby Day & Satellites) (78) 25
58 London HL 8726   Rockin' Robin/Over And Over 10
59 London HL 8800   The Bluebird, The Buzzard And The Oriole/Alone Too Long 40
59 London HL 8964   Love Is A One Time Affair/Ain't Gonna Cry No More 10
60 London HLY 9044   My Blue Heaven/I Don't Want To 15
61 Top Rank JAR 538   Over And Over/Gee Whiz 20
65 Sue WI 388   Rockin' Robin/Over And Over (reissue) 15

DORIS DAY & JOHNNIE RAY
53 Columbia SCM 5033   Ma Says, Pa Says/A Full Time Job 20

(see also Johnnie Ray)

HELEN DAY
76 Philips 6006 503   You Can Do It Better Than Me/I Got The Catch (with Catch) 7
76 Philips 6006 531   Butter Wouldn't Melt In Your Mouth/Posessed (p/s) 7

JACKIE DAY
67 Sue WI 4040   Before It's Too Late/Without A Love 250
09 Kent 6T 25   Get To Steppin/LARRY BANKS: My Life Is No Better 20
09 Kent TOWN 145   Naughty Boy/Get To Steppin (reissue) 15

JILL DAY
55 Parlophone MSP 6169   Sincerely/Chee-Chee-Oo Chee (Sang The Little Bird) 8
55 Parlophone MSP 6177   Promises/Whistlin' Willie 8
56 HMV 7M 362   I Hear You Knocking/Far Away From Everybody 8
56 HMV 7M 391   A Tear Fell/Holiday Affair 10

JOHNNY DAY
69 Stax STAX 111   Stay Baby Stay/I Love Love (listed as Johnny Daye on demos) 20

KENNY DAY
60 Top Rank JAR 339   Teenage Sonata/My Love Doesn't Love Me At All (p/s) 10
61 Top Rank JAR 400   Why Don't We Do This More Often/The Sheik Of Morocco (p/s) 10

MURIEL DAY
66 Pye 7N 17197   A Petal From A Faded Rose/I Wear His Heart 10
69 CBS 4115   The Wages Of Love/Thinking Of You 15
69 Page One POF 151   Optimistic Fool/Nine Times Out Of Ten 60
69 Page One POF 151   Optimistic Fool/Nine Times Out Of Ten (DJ copy) 100

SYLVIA DAY
68 SNB 55-3859   You Don't Understand/Show A Little Love 10

TANYA DAY & NU-NOTES
64 Polydor NH 52331   His Lips Get In The Way/I Get So Lonely 8

Terry DAY

MINT VALUE £

TERRY DAY
62 CBS AAG 104 That's All I Want/I Waited Too Long 20

(see also Rip-Chords, Rogues)

DAYBREAKERS
67 John Hassell 814/5 DAYBREAKERS (LP) 60
67 John Hassell HAS LP 1126 VOL 2 (LP) 60

DAY BROTHERS
60 Oriole CB 1575 Angel/Just One More Kiss 20

JOEL DAYDE
71 Barclay BAR 7 Mammy Blue/You've Got Freedom 25

JENNIFER DAYE
80 Arawak ARK DD 018 Together/Version (12") 10

DAYLIGHT
71 RCA RCA 2106 Lady Of St. Clare/Wednesday People 10
71 RCA SF 8194 DAYLIGHT (LP, gatefold sleeve, orange label) 80

(see also Daddy Longlegs)

DAYLIGHTERS
64 Sue WI 343 Oh Mom! (Teach Me How To Uncle Willie)/Hard-Headed Girl 45

DAY N NIGHT
70 DJM DJS 220 I Just Need Somebody/Such A Lot To Talk About 12

DAY OF THE PHOENIX
70 Greenwich GSLP 1002 WIDE OPEN N-WAY (LP) 100
72 Chapter One CHS-R 812 THE NEIGHBOUR'S SON (LP, red/silver label) 70

DAYSHIFT
80 Wot WOT 1 Living In The UK/Cedric Wazza Superstar/Yeah Eh Oh Yeah (p/s) 20

DAYS OF GRACE
82 DJM DJS 10988 My Life Is A Video/21st Century (p/s) 6

DAYS OF 29
85 Trigger Happy TH 271284AA DESTINATION D-DAY EP (12", p/s) 12

DAYTON
83 Capitol 12 CL 318 The Sound Of Music/Eyes On You/Love You Anyway (12", p/s) 12
84 Capitol 12CLX 318 The Sound Of Music (X-Tended Remix)/Eyes On You/Love You Anyway (12", p/s) 15

DAYTONAS
97 Kalevala KALA 004 Faster Gimpo Faster Kill! Kill! Kill!/Faster Gimpo Faster Kill! Kill! Kill! (version) 20

DAZE (1)
79 Motor City Rhythm MCR10S I Wanna Be A Star/At The Seaside 300

DAZE (2)
83 Mynah SDM 001 Deep South/Made In America 20

DAZZLE (3)
89 Jam Today 12 CHIL 16 Dazzle You/Only You (12", p/s) 20
89 Jet Star 12 CHIL 11 Don't Want Your Love/Don't Want Your Love (12" white label) 20
89 Jam Today CHIL LP 7 SOUL SISTERS (LP) 20
90 Jam City CHIL LP 10 ON SECOND THOUGHTS (LP, white labels, hand-made sleeve, 500 only) 30

BOBBY DAZZLER
76 Bigbear BB1 Dance Dance Dance/Easy Lovin' Lady 8

DAZZLERS
78 Charisma CB 325 Phonies/Kick Out (5,000 copies in fold-out p/s with poly bag) 8
79 Charisma CB 330 Lovely Crash/Feeling In Your Heart (p/s) 7
79 Charisma CB 338 Feeling Free/No One Ever Knows (p/s) 10

D BASE
99 D Base DR 1 Dreaming/Dreaming/(Dream Dub)/(Nightmare Dub) (12") 50
99 D Base BASE 1 Can't Stop/Believe In Yourself/Still Can't Stop (12") 30
99 D Base BASE 2 The Fight (South Central Remix 1)/(Original Mix)/(South Central Remix 2) (12") 30
00 D Base BASE 3 Drop The Bomb/Good Body Girlz (12") 15
00 D Base BASE 4 Dark Riddumx: What's The Time/Base Theory (12") 15

DBX
93 Peacefrog PF 015 Alien EP (12", plain sleeve) 40
94 Peacefrog PF 022 Losing Control/Beat Phreak/Live Wire/Spock's Brain (12", plain sleeve) 22
95 Peacefrog PR 025 Losing Control Remixes (12", plain sleeve) 20

DC 10'S
80 A Certain Euphoria ACE 451 Bermuda/I Can See Through Walls 20

D DASTARDLEY & P PERFECT
97 Confetti Dubs CO DB01 Tear It Up/Da Beats/Party Time (12") 30
97 Confetti Dubs CO DB02 THE BEATS AND BREAKS EP (12") 20

DDR
90s Smitten SMTLTD 05 The Gift (12", 1-sided yellow vinyl, 500 only) 60

CHRISTOPH DE BABALON
97 Digital Hardcore DHR LP8 IF YOU'RE INTO IT. I'M OUT OF IT (2-LP) 40

DE BLANC
75 Arista 35 Oh No, Not My Baby/Guava Jelly 6

BOBBY DEACON
60 Pye 7N 15270 A Fool Was I/Where's My Love? 10
60 Pye 7N 15299 I Love You So/Your Kisses Are Fine 6

GEORGE DEACON & MARION ROSS
73 Xtra XTRA 1130 SWEET WILLIAM'S GHOST (LP, with lyric insert) 60

DEAD PARROTS SOCIETY
92 Private Press MDNLP 001 MUSIC OF A BYGONE AGE (LP) 20

DEAD SKELETONS
10 A Records AUKDS 001-10 Dead Mantra (1-sided 10" other side etched) 30
12 Too Pure PURE 277S Om Mani Peme Hung/Yarna (p/s, blue vinyl) 12

DEADBEATS

MINT VALUE £

12	Fuzz Club Dead 12 12 12	Buddha Christ/Kundalini Eyes (12", p/s Silk Screened B side, 300 only)	40
11	A Records AUK103LP	DEAD MAGICK (2-LP, burgundy/blue vinyl)	60

DEADBEATS
80	Red Rhino RED 3	Choose You/Julie's New Boyfriend (p/s)	10

DEAD BOYS
77	Sire SRE 1004	Sonic Reducer/Down In Flames (no p/s)	25
77	Sire 6078 609	Sonic Reducer/Little Girl/Down In Flames (12", p/s)	15
78	Sire SRE 1029	Tell Me/Not Anymore/Ain't Nothin' To Do (p/s)	25
77	Sire 9103 329	YOUNG, LOUD & SNOTTY (LP)	30
78	Sire SRK 6054	WE HAVE COME FOR YOUR CHILDREN (LP)	25
87	Line LILP 400200	NIGHT OF THE LIVING DEAD BOYS (LP)	15
99	Rude LP00010	3RD GENERATION NATION (LP, clear vinyl, mail order only)	15

(see also Stiv Bators, Lords Of The New Church, Wanderers)

DEAD CAN DANCE
96	4AD DCD 2	Nierika/Dedicace Outo/The Snake And The Moon (12", promo red vinyl, PVC sleeve)	12
84	4AD CAD 404	DEAD CAN DANCE (LP)	25
85	4AD CAD 512	SPLEEN AND IDEAL (LP)	25
87	4AD CAD 705	WITHIN THE REALM OF A DYING SUN (LP)	25
88	4AD CAD 808	THE SERPENT'S EGG (LP)	25
90	4AD CAD 0007	AION (LP, inner)	40
93	4AD DAD 3013	INTO THE LABYRINTH (2-LP)	60
94	4AD DAD 4015	TOWARDS THE WITHIN (2-LP)	60
96	4AD DAD 608	SPIRITCHASER (2-LP)	60
05	The Show (No Cat. No.)	CHICAGO: 12th OCTOBER 2005 (3-LP, 500 only, signed and numbered)	125
08	Vinyl 180 VIN180LP003	DEAD CAN DANCE (LP, reissue on 180gm vinyl, with free 12" on black or clear vinyl)	20
08	Vinyl 180 VIN180LP007	SPLEEN AND IDEAL (LP, reissue 180gm vinyl)	20
09	Vinyl 180 VIN180LP011	WITHIN THE REALMS OF A DYING SUN (LP, reissue, 180gm vinyl)	20
09	Vinyl 180 VIN180LP016	THE SERPENTS EGG (LP, reissue 180gm vinyl)	30
10	Vinyl 180 VIN180LP029	DEAD CAN DANCE (2-LP, 2 x 12" reissue, insert)	150
11	Vinyl 180 VIN180LP028	AION (LP, reissue 180gm vinyl)	20
12	PIAS PIAS R3313LP	IN CONCERT (3-LP box set)	70
12	PIAS PIASR311DLP	ANASTASIS (2-LP)	25

DEAD FINGERS TALK
79	Pye 46156	This Crazy World/The Boyfriend (p/s)	20

DEAD FLOWERS
87	Lout 001	TV/Fallout	10
91	Mystic Stones RUNE 2	SMELL THE FRAGRANCE, FREE YOUR MIND (LP)	15
92	Mystic Stones RUNE 12	MOONTAN (LP)	15
94	Delerium DELEC LP 022	ALTERED STATE CIRCUS (LP)	15

DEAD KENNEDYS
80	Fast Products FAST 12	California Uber Alles/Man With The Dogs (p/s, moulded or paper labels)	6
81	Statik STAT EP 2	IN GOD WE TRUST (12" EP, with insert)	10
81	Cherry Red CHERRY 13	Holiday In Cambodia/Police Truck ('burning man' p/s, with lyric sheet)	6
81	Cherry Red CHERRY T13	Holiday In Cambodia/Police Truck (12")	10
81	Cherry CHERRY 16	Kill The Poor/In-Sight (p/s)	8
82	Statik STAT 24	Nazi Punks Fuck Off/Moral Majority (p/s)	7
82	Statik STAT 22	Bleed for Me/Life Sentence (p/s)	7
82	Statik STAT 27	Halloween/Saturday Night Holocaust (p/s)	7
81	Cherry Red B RED 10	FRESH FRUIT FOR ROTTING VEGETABLES (LP, with insert & 'Heads' pic on rear)	40
80	Cherry Red B RED 10	FRESH FRUIT FOR ROTTING VEGETABLES (LP, with insert & without 'Heads' pic on rear)	20
85	Statik/Alternative Tentacles VIRUS 45	FRANKENCHRIST (LP, with poster)	20
86	Statik/Alternative Tentacles VIRUS 50	BEDTIME FOR DEMOCRACY (LP)	18
87	Alternative Tent. VIRUS 57	GIVE ME CONVENIENCE... (LP, with booklet and "Buzzbomb From Pasadena" flexidisc)	18

(see also Lard)

DEADLINE
60s	Hollick & Taylor HT 137	Glass Man/I'm In My Element	300

DEADLY HEADLEY
82	On-U Sound ONULP 14	35 YEARS FROM ALPHA (LP)	30

DEADLY TOYS
79	Bonhard/Hunt DT 1	Nice Weather/Roll On Doomsday/I'm Logical/Deadly Mess Around (EP, in hand-made sleeve)	125
79	Bonhard/Hunt DT 1	Nice Weather/Roll On Doomsday/I'm Logical/Deadly Mess Around (EP)	50

DEAD MANS SHADOW
81	Pig Records HOG 1	Neighbours/Morons With Power/Poxy Politics/War Ploys (p/s and sticker)	20
81	Subversive Anarcho 1	HEATHROW TOUCHDOWN (Shared EP with ACTION PACT)	20
82	Rondelet ROUND 16	Bomb Scare/Another Hiroshima/Fighting For Reality (p/s)	10

DEAD MEADOW
03	Matador OLE 566-1	SHIVERING KING AND OTHERS (2-LP)	35
05	Matador OLE 625-1	FEATHERS (2-LP)	25
08	Matador OLE 750-1	OLD GROWTH (2-LP)	20

DEAD OR ALIVE
80	Inevitable INEV 005	I'm Falling/Flowers (foldout p/s)	12
81	Inevitable INEV 008	Number Eleven/Name Game (live) (p/s)	8
82	Black Eyes BE 1	It's Been Hours Now/Whirlpool/Nowhere To Nowhere/ It's Been Hours Now (Alternative Mix) (12", p/s)	20
82	Black Eyes BE 2	The Stranger/Some Of That (p/s)	8
83	Epic A 3399	Misty Circles/Misty Circles (Instrumental) (p/s)	8
83	Epic TA 3399	Misty Circles (Dance Mix)/Misty Circles (Dub Mix)/Selfish Side (12", p/s)	10
83	Epic A 3676	What I Want/The Stranger (Remix) (white 'floppy hat' p/s, withdrawn)	35

DEAD PREZ

MINT VALUE £

83	Epic TA 3676	What I Want (Dance Mix)/The Stranger (12", p/s, with poster)	15
84	Epic XPR 1257	MIGHTY MIX: Wish You Were Here/What I Want/Do It/Misty Circles/ Absolutely Nothing/Sit On It/You Make Me Wanna/That's The Way (I Like It) (12", white label, promo only)	15
85	Epic A 6086	Lover Come Back To Me/Far Too Hard (blue p/s, withdrawn)	150
87	Epic XPR 1328	CLEAN AND DIRTY: Something In My House (Mortevicar Mix)/Something In My House (Naughty XXX Mix) (12", white label, plain white sleeve)	40
88	Epic BURNSQ 4	Turn Around And Count 2 Ten (I Had A Disco Dream Mix)/Something In My House (Instru-Mental)/Then There Was You/Come Inside (12", p/s autographed)	15

(see also Nightmares In Wax, Sisters Of Mercy, Pauline Murray & Invisible Girls, International Chrysis, Mission)

DEAD PREZ
99	Epic 668986	Hip Hop (Real Version)/It's Bigger Than Hip Hop (Real Version)/Selling DOPE (12", p/s)	12
00	Epic 496864-1	LET'S GET FREE (2-LP)	35

DEAD RESIDENTS
04	Sin Nombre SIN 003	POLTERGEIST FREQUENCY (12" EP)	15

DEAD SEA FRUIT
67	Camp 602 001	Kensington High Street/Put Another Record On	20
68	Camp 602 004	Love At The Hippiedrome/My Naughty Bluebell	20
67	Camp 603 001	DEAD SEA FRUIT (LP)	150

DEAD WEATHER
09	Third Man TMR 001	Hang You From The Heavens/Are Friends Electric? (luminous vinyl, 'Halloween' cover, 100-only)	200

(see also The Kills, White Stripes, Raconteurs)

DEADWOOD
71	Decca F13109	The Turning Of Them All/They Don't Help Me None	45
71	Decca F13179	Me And My Friends/Little Joe	12

DEAD WRETCHED
82	Tempest HELL 2	NO HOPE FOR ANYONE EP	20

DEAF AIDS
79	Regana REG 1	DO IT AGAIN EP (250 copies only)	100
80	Conspiracy CONS1	Heroes/Bored Christine (p/s)	15

BILL DEAL & RHONDELLS
69	MGM MGM 1466	May I/Day By Day My Love Grows Stronger	6
69	MGM MGM 1479	I've Been Hurt/I've Got My Needs	15
69	MGM MGM 1488	What Kind Of Fool Do You Think I Am/Are You Ready For This	10

MICHAEL DE ALBUQUERQUE
74	RCA SF 8383	WE MAY BE CATTLE BUT WE ALL HAVE NAMES (LP, with lyric sheet)	35
76	Warner Bros K 56276	STALKING THE SLEEPER (LP)	20

(see also E.L.O., Michael Albuquerque, Ricotti & Albuquerque)

DEALER (1)
79	MCA NCA 517	Buffalo Bill/Star Dance	20

DEALER (2)
83	Windrush WR 1030	Better Things To Do/Suspected Foul Play (p/s)	100

DEALERS
76	Private Stock PVT 73	Midnight Dog/Higher Than God's Hat	6

ALAN DEAN
57	Columbia DB 3932	Rock 'n' Roll Tarantella/Life Is But A Dream	10

ALAN DEAN & HIS PROBLEMS
64	Decca F 11947	The Time It Takes/Dizzy Heights	40
65	Pye 7N 15749	Thunder And Rain/As Time Goes By	60

LITTLE BILLY DEAN
67	Strike JH 325	That's Always Like You/Tic Toc	20

ELTON DEAN
71	CBS 64539	ELTON DEAN (LP)	60
77	Ogun OG 610	THE CHEQUE IS IN THE MAIL (LP, with Joe Gallivan & Kenny Wheeler)	20
78	Ogun OG 530	THE BOLOGNA TAPE (LP)	25

(see also Bluesology, Soft Machine, Centipede, Ninesense, Julie Tippetts, Hugh Hopper, Mike Hugg, Reg King, Keith Tippett)

EMIL DEAN
67	CBS 3106	Ave Maria/Now You're Gone	6
68	Island WIP 6033	This Is Our Anniversary/Lonely Boy	12
69	Mercury MF 1071	It's Only Make Believe/One Broken Heart For Sale	6

(see also Nirvana [UK])

HAZEL DEAN
75	Decca F 13613	Our Day Will Come/Instrumental	6
76	Decca F 13668	Got You Where I Want You/You Were There	6
77	Decca F 13683	Look What I've Found At The End Of A Rainbow/Where Are We Going	6
77	Decca F 13736	No One's Ever Gonna Love You (The Way That I Love You)/Just One More Time	6
77	Decca F 13751	Who Was That Lady (I Saw You With)/One Bad Mistake	6
81	Carlin CMC 1004	THE SOUND OF BACHARACH & DAVID (LP, promo only)	25

JIMMY DEAN
61	Philips BBE 12501	JIMMY DEAN (EP)	12
61	Philips BBL 7537	BIG BAND JOHN AND OTHER FABULOUS SONGS AND TALES (LP)	15

NORA DEAN
69	Upsetter US 322	The Same Thing You Gave To Daddy/UPSETTER PILGRIMS: A Testimony	90
70	Trojan TR 7735	Barbwire/BRONS: Calypso Mama	50
71	Randy's RAN 508	Want Man/RANDY'S ALL STARS: Man	25
71	High Note HS 050	I Must Get A Man/The Valet	20
71	Bullet BU 472	Peace Begins Within/SLICKERS: Go Back Home	400
71	Gas GAS 165	Greedy Boy/KEITH: Please Stay (B-side actually by Slim Smith)	20
72	Big Shot BI 611	Night Food Reggae/PROPHETS: Jaco	20
73	Bread BR 1117	Mama/Man A Walk And Talk	20

Paul DEAN (& SOUL SAVAGES)

MINT VALUE £

74	Harry J HJ6668	Eddie My Love/What Is Your Plan (with Jackie Brown)	12
76	Attack ATT 8126	Scorpion/Version	20
11	Harry J THB 7013	Mama/SOUL SYNDICATE: Natty In Hong Kong	25
79	Nationwide NWLP 007	PLAY ME A LOVE SONG (LP)	50

(see also Hugh Roy, Ebony Sisters)

PAUL DEAN (& SOUL SAVAGES)
65	Decca F 12136	You Don't Own Me/Hole In The Head (as Paul Dean & Thoughts)	18
66	Reaction 591 002	She Can Build A Mountain/A Day Gone By (as Paul Dean & Soul Savages)	15

(see also Oscar, Thoughts)

PAULA DEAN & NYAH SHUFFLE
70	Joe's JRS 2	Since I Met You Baby/Jug Head	20

ROGER DEAN'S LYSIS
77	Mosaic GCM 762	LYSIS LIVE (LP)	15
77	Mosaic GCM 774	CYCLE (LP)	15

TERRI DEAN
59	Top Rank JAR 141	I'm Confessin' (That I Love You)/I Blew Out The Flame	7

TRACEY DEAN
74	Decca FR 13497	Moonshiner/Boy On The Ball	20

DEAN & JEAN
64	Stateside SS 249	Tra La La La Suzy/I Love The Summertime	20
64	Stateside SS 283	Hey Jean Hey Dean/Please Don't Tell Me How	20
64	Stateside SS 313	Thread Your Needle/I Wanna Be Loved	25

(see also Brenda Lee Jones)

DEAN & MARK
64	Hickory 45-1227	With Tears In My Eyes/Kissin' Games	10
64	Hickory 45-1249	When I Stop Dreaming/There Oughta Be A Law	10
65	Hickory 45-1294	Just A Step Away/Fallen Star	10

(see also Newbeats, Larry Henley)

JASON DEANE
66	King KG 1049	Make Believe/Don't Ever Want To See You No More	30
67	King KG 1060	Down In The Street/Ain't Got No Love	40

(see also Jason Dene)

DEANO
65	Columbia DB 7728	Just A Child In This World/Little Miss With-It	10
66	Columbia DB 7898	Starlight, Starbright/I'm So Happy	10
67	Columbia DB 8233	What's The Matter With The Matador?/Baby, Let Me Be Your Baby	10
65	Columbia SEG 8470	DEANO (EP)	25

BLOSSOM DEARIE
66	Fontana TF 719	I'm Hip/Wallflower Lonely, Cornflower Blue	8
67	Fontana TF 788	Sweet Georgie Fame/One Note Samba	8
67	Fontana TF 886	Once I Loved/Sunny	8
67	Fontana TF 934	The Music Played/Discover Who I Am	8
68	Fontana TF 986	Hey John/59th Street Bridge Song	8
67	Fontana TL 5399	SWEET BLOSSOM DEARIE (LP)	45
67	Fontana TL 5352	BLOSSOM TIME AT RONNIE'S (LP)	50
67	Fontana STL 5454	SOON IT'S GONNA RAIN (LP)	40
70	Fontana 6309 015	THAT'S THE WAY I WANT IT TO BE (LP)	80

DEAR MR. TIME
70	Square SQ 3	Prayer For Her/Light Up A Light	50
71	Square SQA 101	GRANDFATHER (LP, black/white label)	200

DEATH
87	Under One Flag FLAG 12	SCREAM BLOODY GORE (LP, with inner sleeve)	60
88	Under One Flag FLAG 24	LEPROSY (LP, inner)	50
90	Under One Flag FLAG 38	SPIRITUAL HEALING (LP)	35
90	Under One Flag FLAG 38	SPIRITUAL HEALING (LP, picture disc)	30
92	Under One Flag FLAG 71	FATE (LP)	35
07	Back On Black BOBV 055	SCREAM BLOODY GORE (2-LP, reissue, orange vinyl, 500 only)	20
07	Back On Black BOBV 056	LEPROSY (LP, reissue, red and white splatter vinyl, gatefold p/s)	15
07	Back On Black BOBV 058	HUMAN (LP, reissue, red splatter vinyl)	15
07	Back On Black BOBV 059	INDIVIDUAL THOUGHT PATTERNS (LP, reissue, red splatter vinyl)	15
07	Back On Black BOBV 059	INDIVIDUAL THOUGHT PATTERNS (LP, reissue, clear vinyl)	15

DEATH ADDICT
83	Stench STN 1	Killing Time/Dead And Buried (p/s)	12

DEATH ANGEL
87	Under One Flag FLAG 14	THE ULTRA-VIOLENCE (LP)	30

DEATH CAB FOR CUTIE
02	Fierce Panda NING 116	I Was A Kaleidoscope/405 (Acoustic) (p/s)	6
02	Fierce Panda NING 126	We Laugh Indoors (New Mix)/Debate Exposed Doubt (Acoustic SBN Session) (p/s)	8
03	Fierce Panda NING 149	The New Year/TV Trays (p/s)	8
04	Fierce Panda NING 158	The Sound Of Settling/This Charming Man (p/s)	10
98	Sonic Boom SBR 002	SOMETHING ABOUT AIRPLANES (LP)	35
03	Sonic Boom SBR 012	TRANSATLANTICISM (2-LP)	35

DEATH CULT
83	Situation 2 SIT 23T	BROTHERS GRIMM EP (12", p/s)	10

(see also Cult, Southern Death Cult)

DEATH FROM ABOVE 1979
05	679 679LP100P	YOU'RE A WOMAN, I'M A MACHINE (2-LP, pink vinyl limited edition)	50

DEATH IN JUNE
84	New European SA 29634	Heaven Street/We Drive East/In The Night Time (12", 2,000 with brown/gold embossed/textured sleeve)	60

DEATH IN VEGAS

			MINT VALUE £
84	New European SA 29634	Heaven Street/We Drive East/In The Night Time (12", later pressing of 2,000 with blue/white sleeve)	50
84	New European SA 30634	State Laughter/Holy Water (p/s)	50
84	New European BADVC 6	She Said Destroy/The Calling (p/s)	25
84	New European 12BADVC 6	The Calling/She Said Destroy/Doubt To Nothing (12", p/s with insert)	35
85	New European BADVC 69	Born Again/The Calling (Mk II)/Carousel (Bolt Mix) (12", p/s)	25
85	New European BADVC 73	...And Murder Love/A.M.L. (Instrumental) (p/s)	25
85	New European 12BADVC73	Come Before Christ And Murder Love/Torture By Roses (12", p/s)	25
87	New European BADVC 10	To Drown A Rose/Zimmerit/Europa/The Gates Of Heaven (10", p/s)	20
88	Cenaz CENAZ 09	Born Again/The Calling (Mk II)/Carousel (Remix) (12" picture disc, 1st pressing with silver print & rim, 970 only)	25
88	Cenaz CENAZ 09	Born Again/The Calling (Mk II)/Carousel (Remix) (12" picture disc, 2nd pressing bronze print & rim)	20
94	Twilight Command NERO I	SUNDOGS (Rose Clouds Of Holocaust/13 Years Of Carrion) (p/s with sticker)	7
92	New European BADVC 8	CATHEDRAL OF TEARS (12" EP, picture disc with sticker)	25
93	New European BADVC 63	PARADISE RISING (12" EP)	18
96	Twilight. Command NERO XIII	Kapo!/Occidental Martyr (p/s)	18
85	New European BADVC 3	THE GUILTY HAVE NO PRIDE (LP)	75
92	Leprosy UBADVC 4	BURIAL (LP, standard sleeve, green vinyl)	40
80s	Leprosy UBADVC 4	BURIAL (LP, 'quilted' sleeve, brown, pink, white & other coloured vinyl)	60
90s	Leprosy UBADVC 4	BURIAL (LP, textured sleeve, various coloured vinyl)	35
85	New European BADVC 13	NADA (LP, blue sleeve)	50
85	New European BADVC 13	NADA (LP, brown sleeve)	35
85	New European BADVC 13	NADA (LP, picture disc)	15
86	New European BADVC 726	LESSON ONE: MISANTHROPY (LP, embossed sleeve with insert)	25
87	New European BADVC 11	BROWN BOOK (LP, textured sleeve with inner & insert; export copies with extra inserts & postcards)	50
87	New European BADVC 11	BROWN BOOK (LP, textured sleeve with inner & insert)	30
88	New European BADVC 9	THE WORLD THAT SUMMER (2-LP, gatefold textured sleeve)	30
88	New European BADVC 88	WALL OF SACRIFICE (LP, red sleeve)	70
88	New European BADVC 88	WALL OF SACRIFICE (LP, green/yellow sleeve)	40
89	New European BADVC 93	93 DEAD SUN WHEELS (mini-LP, with Current 93)	50
92	Leprosy LEPER 2	NIGHT AND FOG (LP, red vinyl, 1,000 only)	30
93	New European BADVC 36	BUT WHAT ENDS WHEN THE SYMBOLS SHATTER (LP, with inner & insert, 500 on purple vinyl)	150
93	New European BADVC 36	BUT WHAT ENDS WHEN THE SYMBOLS SHATTER (LP, with inner & insert, 3,000 on black vinyl)	20
95	New European BADVC 39	BLACK WHOLE OF LOVE (box set with 12", 10", 7" & CDs with inserts)	30
99	New European BAD VC44	OPERATION HUMMINGBIRD (LP, with inner and postcards)	25

(see also Crisis, Current 93, Boyd Rice & Friends, Sol Invictus)

DEATH IN VEGAS

03	Concrete HARD 550	So You Say You've Lost Your Baby (7", pink vinyl, white labels featuring Paul Weller)	25
97	Concrete HARD 22 LP 12	DEAD ELVIS (2-LP)	60
99	Concrete HARD 41 LP	CONTINO SESSIONS (2-LP)	40
02	Concrete HARD 5312	SCORPIO RISING (2-LP, gatefold sleeve with inners)	35
04	Drone DRONELP ONE	SATAN'S CIRCUS (3-LP)	35
05	Concrete 82876672671	MIX IT - THE BEST OF DEATH IN VEGAS (2-LP)	30

DEATH SENTENCE

82	Beat The System DEATH 1	DEATH & PURE DESTRUCTION (EP)	30

DEB MUSIC PLAYERS

78	Deb DEB LP 003	UMOJA - LOVE AND UNITY (LP)	45

DEBONAIRES (U.S.)

70	Track 604 035	I'm In Love Again/Headache In My Heart	50

DEBRIS

78	Kelly DEB-1	THE FIRST ONE EP (no p/s)	50

DEBS

65	Mercury MF 888	Sloopy's Gonna Hang On/Under A Street Light	10

DEB-TONES

59	RCA RCA 1137	Knock, Knock — Who's There?/I'm In Love Again	25

DEBUTANTES

80	Rok ROK XVII/XVIII	Man In The Street/INNOCENT BYSTANDERS: Where Is Johnny (company sleeve)	6

DECADES BY NIGHT

81	Slip 001	Life Spiral/SONS OF MONKEYS: Me And Mr. Suzuki	50

DECAMERON

73	Vertigo 6360 097	SAY HELLO TO THE BAND (LP)	18
73	Mooncrest CREST 19	MAMMOTH SPECIAL (LP, lyric insert)	30
75	Transatlantic TRA 304	THIRD LIGHT (LP)	20
76	Transatlantic TRA 325	TOMORROW'S PANTOMIME (LP)	25

DECAPITATED

02	Earache MOSH 255	NIHILTY (LP, embossed sleeve, 500 only)	75
10	Earache WICK 011LP	WINDS OF CREATION (LP, reissue)	25

YVONNE DE CARLO

55	Capitol CL 14380	Take It Or Leave It/Three Little Stars	8

PAULO DE CARVALHO

74	Pye International 7N 25647	(And Then) After Love/E Depois Do Adeus (p/s)	10

DE CASTRO SISTERS

54	London HL 8104	Teach Me Tonight/It's Love	20
55	London HL 8137	Boom Boom Boomerang/Let Your Love Walk In	20
55	London HL 8158	I'm Bewildered/To Say You're Mine	15
55	London HLU 8189	If I Ever Fall In Love/Cuckoo In The Clock	20
55	London HLU 8212	Christmas Is A-Comin'/Snowbound For Christmas	15

			MINT VALUE £
56	London HLU 8228	Give Me Time/Too Late Now	15
56	London HLU 8296	No One To Blame But You/Cowboys Don't Cry	15

DECEMBER
96	Elfenblut SAG 44	River Of Blood/Venus In Chains (red vinyl, p/s, 1000 only)	10

DECISION
68	MCA MU 1027	In The Shade Of Your Love/Constable Jones	7

DECISIONS
71	A&M 844	It's Love That Really Counts In The Long Run/I Can't Forget About You	18

DIANA DECKER
54	Columbia SCM 5083	Oh, My Papa/Crystal Ball	15
54	Columbia SCM 5096	The Happy Wanderer/Till We Two Are One	15
54	Columbia SCM 5120	Jilted/The Man With The Banjo	10
54	Columbia SCM 5123	Kitty In The Basket/Never Never Land	10
54	Columbia SCM 5130	Mama Mia/Percy The Penguin	10
54	Columbia SCM 5145	Sisters/Abracadabra	15
55	Columbia SCM 5166	Open The Window Of Your Heart/The Violin Song	6
55	Columbia SCM 5173	Apples, Peaches And Cherries/Paper Valentine	6
56	Columbia SCM 5246	Rock-A-Boogie Baby/Willie Can	30

(see also Ray Burns, Ruby Murray)

DECLINO
85	Children Of the Revolution GURT 7	MUCCHIO SELVAGGIO (split LP with NEGAZIONE)	75

GAT DECOR
92	Effective EFFS 1	Passion (Naked Mix)/(D Emerson Mix) (p/s)	10
92	Effective 12 EFFS 1	Passion (Naked Mix)/(D Emerson Mix) (12", p/s)	25
92	Tag TAGO 1	Passion (1-sided white label 12")	20

NINA DECOSTA
80	Rokel ROK 12	Don't Want To Lose You/Instrumental Version (12")	40

DECOYS
64	Studio 36 KEP 108	DECOYS (EP, 500 only)	30

DE DANAAN
75	Polydor 2904 005	DE DANAAN (LP)	15
77	Decca SKL-R 5287	DE DANAAN — SELECTED JIGS AND REELS (LP)	18

DEDRINGER
80	DinDisc DIN 11	Maxine/Innocent 'Till Proven Guilty//Took A Long Time/We Don't Mind (double pack)	8
81	DinDisc DID 7	DIRECT LINE (LP)	15
83	Neat NEAT 1009	SECOND RISING (LP, with inner sleeve)	15

DAVE DEE, DOZY, BEAKY, MICK & TICH
65	Fontana TF 531	No Time/Is It Love	25
65	Fontana TF 586	All I Want/It Seems A Pity	25
65	Fontana TF 630	You Make It Move/I Can't Stop	10
67	Fontana TE 17488	LOOS OF ENGLAND (EP)	10
66	Fontana TL 5350	DAVE DEE, DOZY, BEAKY, MICK & TICH (LP)	20
66	Fontana TL 5388	IF MUSIC BE THE FOOD OF LOVE PREPARE FOR INDIGESTION (LP, mono)	20
66	Fontana STL 5388	IF MUSIC BE THE FOOD OF LOVE PREPARE FOR INDIGESTION (LP, stereo)	25
67	Fontana (S)TL 5441	GOLDEN HITS OF DAVE DEE, DOZY, BEAKY, MICK & TICH (LP)	15
68	Fontana (S)TL 5471	IF NO-ONE SANG (LP)	15

(see also Dozy Beaky Mick & Tich [D,B,M & T])

JAY DEE
74	Warner Bros. 7798	Strange Games And Funky Things/Intrumental	7

JEANNIE DEE
69	Beacon BEA 115	Come Into My Arms/Sun Shine On Me	7
69	Beacon BEA 142	Don't Go Home My Little Darling/Come See About Me	15

JOEY DEE
74	Alaska ALA 14	Baby Don't You Know (I Need You)/Half Moon	20

JOEY DEE & STARLI(GH)TERS
62	Columbia DB 4842	Shout (Parts 1 & 2)	7
62	Columbia DB 4905	What Kind Of Love Is This?/Wing Ding	10
63	Columbia DB 7055	Hot Pastrami With Mashed Potatoes (Parts 1 & 2)	8
63	Columbia DB 7102	Dance, Dance, Dance/Let's Have A Party (features Ronettes uncredited)	12
63	Columbia DB 7277	Down By The Riverside/Getting Nearer (features Ronettes uncredited)	12
61	Columbia 33SX 1406	DOIN' THE TWIST LIVE AT THE PEPPERMINT LOUNGE (LP)	15
62	Columbia 33SX 1461	BACK AT THE PEPPERMINT LOUNGE (LP)	15
62	Columbia 33SX 1502	ALL THE WORLD IS TWISTIN' (LP)	15
63	Columbia 33SX 1532	JOEY DEE (LP)	15
63	Columbia 33SX 1607	DANCE DANCE DANCE (LP, with Starlighters, also with Ronettes uncredited)	15

(see also Young Rascals)

JOHNNIE DEE
65	Columbia DB 7612	Frankie's Angel/Everything's Upside Down	7

JOHNNY DEE
57	Oriole CB 1367	Sittin' In The Balcony/A-Plus Love	150
57	Oriole CB 1367	Sittin' In The Balcony/A-Plus Love (78)	20

(see also John D. Loudermilk)

KIKI DEE
63	Fontana TF 394	Early Night/Lucky High Heels	25
63	Fontana TF 414	Don't Put Your Heart In His Hand/I Was Only Kidding	12
64	Fontana TF 443	Miracles/That's Right, Walk On By	18
64	Fontana TF 490	(You Don't Know) How Glad I Am/Baby I Don't Care	15
65	Fontana TF 596	Runnin' Out Of Fools/There He Goes	10
66	Fontana TF 669	Why Don't I Run Away From You?/Small Town	30

Lenny DEE

MINT VALUE £

67	Fontana TF 792	I'm Going Out (The Same Way I Came In)/We've Got Everything Going For Us	20
67	Fontana TF 833	I/Stop And Think	10
67	Fontana TF 870	Excuse Me/Patterns	10
68	Fontana TF 926	Can't Take My Eyes Off You/Hungry Heart	10
68	Fontana TF 983	Now The Flowers Cry/On A Magic Carpet Ride	400
70	Tamla Motown TMG 739	The Day Will Come Between Sunday And Monday/My Whole World Ended (The Moment You Left Me)	25
72	Philips 6006 352	Excuse Me/Patterns	8
73	Rocket PIG 2	Lonnie And Josie/The Last Good Man In My Life	7
65	Fontana TE 17443	KIKI DEE (EP)	40
66	Fontana TE 17470	KIKI DEE IN CLOVER (EP)	30
68	Fontana (S)TL 5455	I'M KIKI DEE (LP)	50
70	Tamla Motown STML 11158	GREAT EXPECTATIONS (LP)	45

(see also Elton John)

LENNY DEE
55	Brunswick 05440	Plantation Boogie/Birth Of The Blues	7

RICKY DEE & EMBERS
62	Stateside SS 136	Workout/JOHN MOBLEY: Tunnel Of Love	15

SANDRA DEE
61	Brunswick 05858	Tammy Tell Me True/Let's Fall In Love	10

TAMMI DEE
71	Downtown DT 479	Val/MUSIC DOCTORS: Bank Raid	12

TOMMY DEE
59	Melodisc 1516	Three Stars/TEEN JONES (TONES): I'll Never Change (tri centre)	20
59	Melodisc 1516	Three Stars/TEEN JONES (TONES): I'll Never Change (round centre)	10

DEE AND THE CHEETAHS
80	MG MO 001	You To Me/Touch Me (ps)	40

DEE AND THE QUOTIUM
69	Jay Boy Boy 8	Someday You'll Need Someone/Send Some Flowers To Jule	45

MAURICE DEEBANK
84	Cherry Red MRED 61	INNER THOUGHT ZONE (LP)	25

(see also Felt)

DEEE LITE
90	Elektra EKR 114T	Groove Is In The Heart/(Peanut Butter Mix)/What Is Love? (Holographic Goatee Mix)/(Rainbow Beard Mix) (12" original pressing with "EW" in centre of label)	10

DEEJAY FRIENDLY
96	Deejay Friendly PK 01	Piano Me Softly (12" promo)	8

DEEJAYS
65	Polydor BM 56034	Dimples/Coming On Strong	60
65	Polydor BM 56501	Blackeyed Woman/I Just Can't Go To Sleep	110

ANTHONY DEELEY
68	Pama PM 728	Anytime Man/Don't Change Your Mind About Me	20

ANGELA DEEN
64	Fontana TF 491	There's So Much About My Baby That I Love/Gotta Hand It To The Boy	8

CAROL DEENE
61	HMV POP 922	Sad Movies (Make Me Cry)/Don't Forget	10
62	HMV POP 1027	Johnny Get Angry/Somebody's Smiling (While I'm Crying)	7
62	HMV POP 1058	Some People/Kissin'	7
62	HMV POP 1086	James(Hold The Ladder Steady)/It Happened Last Night	7
64	HMV POP 1337	Very First Kiss/Hard To Say Goodnight	8
65	HMV POP 1405	Most People Do/I Can't Forget Someone Like You	7
65	Columbia DB 7743	He Just Don't Know/Up In The Penthouse	30
66	Columbia DB 7890	Dancing In Your Eyes/Please Don't Be Unfaithful Again	8
67	Columbia DB 8107	Love Not Have I/Time	8
68	CBS 3206	When He Wants A Woman/I'm Not Crying	15
69	Conquest CXT 102	One More Chance/Invisible Tears	7
70	World Records ST 1031	A LOVE AFFAIR (LP)	20

DEEPART
04	Deepart DEEPART LP	ELECTRIC BATTLE FIELD (LP, test pressings only)	60

DEEP END
78	Private pressing	BEGGED AND BORROWED (LP, listed as CPLP 016)	15

DEEP FEELING
69	Page One POF 160	Oh Darlin'/Feelin'	40
70	DJM DJS 231	Do You Wanna Dance/The Day My Lady Cried	6
70	Page One POF 165	Do You Love Me/Move On	6
70	Page One POF 177	Skyline Pigeon/We've Thrown It All Away	6
71	DJM DJS 237	Sweet Dust And Red Wine/Turn Around	6
74	Santa Ponsa PN 512	Lets Spend The Night Together/Avalon	8
71	DJM DJLPS 419	DEEP FEELING (LP)	200

(see also Raw Material)

DEEP FREEZE MICE
86	Cordelia ERICAT 002	Zoology/These Floors Are Smooth (500 copies, no sleeve)	15
86	Cordelia ERICAT 016	NEURON MUSIC (12" EP, also featuring Mr. Concept, Yung Analysts and Rimarimba)	20
93	Farce 042	Slow Shiny Bricks/George Bailey Lassoes A Refrigerator (Remix) (300 numbered copies)	10
79	Mole Embalming MOLE 1	MY GERANIUMS ARE BULLETPROOF (LP, 1st 250 copies with paste-on sleeve, 8-page booklet & various A4 inserts)	120
79	Mole Embalming MOLE 1	MY GERANIUMS ARE BULLETPROOF (LP, printed sleeve, 1500 only)	70
81	Mole Embalming MOLE 2	TEENAGE HEAD IN MY REFRIGERATOR (LP, 400 copies with red cover)	45
81	Mole Embalming MOLE 2	TEENAGE HEAD IN MY REFRIGERATOR (LP, 800 printed)	50
81	Inedible MOLE 3	GATES OF LUNCH (LP, 1,000 pressed, various inserts)	40
82	Mole Embalming MOLE C1	TEENAGE HEAD IN MY REFRIGERATOR/LED ZEPPELIN 2 (cassette, around 30 copies)	50

DEEP POCKETS

MINT VALUE £

83	Mole Embalming MOLE 4	SAW A RANCH BURNING LAST NIGHT (LP, 120 in wraparound sleeve)	40
83	Mole Embalming MOLE 4	SAW A RANCH BURNING LAST NIGHT (LP, 1000 copies)	40
84	Inedible MOLE 3	GATES OF LUNCH (LP, 1,000 pressed, these 150 copies with wraparound poster sleeve with insert)	55
84	Cordelia ERICAT 001	I LOVE YOU LITTLE BOBO WITH YOUR DELICATE GOLDEN LIONS (2 x LP)	60
84	Cordelia ERICAT 004	HANG ON CONSTANCE, LET ME HEAR THE NEWS (LP, 120 wraparound poster sleeve with insert)	20
84	Cordelia ERICAT 004	HANG ON CONSTANCE, LET ME HEAR THE NEWS (LP, 1000 copies)	20
84	Mole Embalming MOLE C2	MY GERANIUMS ARE BULLETPROOF (cassette, 30 copies only)	50
84	Mole Embalming MOLE C3	TEENAGE HEAD IN MY REFRIGERATOR (cassette, around 30 copies)	50
86	Cordelia/Unlikely CERICAT 001	I LOVE YOU LITTLE BOBO WITH YOUR DELICATE GOLDEN LIONS (double cassette, around 25 copies)	25
87	Cordelia ERICAT 013	RAIN IS WHEN THE EARTH IS TELEVISION (LP, 1000 copies only)	20
87	Cordelia ERICAT 024	WAR, FAMINE, DEATH, PESTILENCE & MISS TIMBERLAKE (LP, 1000 copies)	20
88	Cordelia ERICAT 027	THE TENDER YELLOW PONIES OF INSOMNIA (LP, 1000 copies)	20
89	Logical Fish 1	LIVE IN SWITZERLAND (LP, 500 copies)	15

DEEP POCKETS

| 74 | Stadium S77 | Loose Change/Run Back To Me | 30 |

DEEP PURPLE

SINGLES

68	Parlophone R 5708	Hush/One More Rainy Day (in promo-only p/s)	400
68	Parlophone R 5708	Hush/One More Rainy Day	40
68	Parlophone R 5745	Kentucky Woman/Wring That Neck (withdrawn)	65
69	Parlophone R 5763	Emmaretta/Wring That Neck	40
69	Harvest HAR 5006	Hallelujah (I Am The Preacher)/April Part 1 (in promo-only p/s)	275
69	Harvest HAR 5006	Hallelujah (I Am The Preacher)/April Part 1	35
70	Harvest PSR 325	Concerto, 1st Movement (edit)/Concerto, 2nd Movement (edit) (promo, possibly some commercial)	40
70	Harvest HAR 5020	Black Night/Speed King	6
71	Harvest HAR 5033	Strange Kind Of Woman/I'm Alone	6
71	Harvest HAR 5045	Fireball/Demon's Eye	6
72	Purple PUR 102	Never Before/When A Blind Man Cries	6
74	Purple PUR 117	Might Just Take Your Life/Coronarias Redig	8
76	Purple PUR 130	You Keep On Moving/Love Child	8
77	Purple PUR 132	Smoke On The Water/Woman From Tokyo/Child In Time (10,000 with p/s)	8
85	Harvest 12 HAR 5233	Black Night/Speed King/Into The Fire (12", p/s)	10
85	Harvest 12 HAR 5234	Strange Kind Of Woman/I'm Alone/Highway Star (12", p/s)	10
85	Harvest 12 HAR 5235	Fireball/Demon's Eye/Anyone's Daughter (12", p/s)	10
85	Harvest PSR 474	Smoke On The Megamix/Mixed Alive	10
87	Polydor POSPX 843	Call Of The Wild/Strangeways (12", p/s with sew-on patch)	12
88	Polydor POC 4	Hush ('88 Re-recording)/Dead Or Alive (Live) (black vinyl, p/s)	7
88	Polydor POC 4	Hush ('88 Re-recording)/Dead Or Alive (Live) (blue vinyl, p/s)	8
90	RCA PT 49224	King Of Dreams (Edit)/Fire In The Basement (shaped picture disc, insert)	7
11	EMI 266987 8 HAR 5304	Hush (1969 BBC Session)/Speed King (1969 BBC Session) (p/s)	20
12	EMI PURRSD 138	Smoke On The Water/Smoke On The Water (p/s, purple vinyl)	15
13	Ear Music 0208665 ERE	Hell To Pay/All The Time In The World (Edit) (p/s, red vinyl)	15
13	Ear Music 0210271 ERE	Out Of Hand/Apres Vous (Instrumental)/Laze (live)/Hell To Pay (Instrumental) (10", white vinyl)	25
13	Ear Music 0208943 ERE	Above And Beyond/Space Truckin' (live) (p/s, purple vinyl)	10
17	Ear Music 0211854 EMU	Time For Bedlam/Uncommon Man (Instrumental)/Paradise Bar/Hi Boots (rehearsal) (10", p/s)	18

EPs

77	Purple PUR 135	NEW LIVE AND RARE VOL. 1 (EP, 15,000 on purple vinyl)	12
78	Purple PUR 137	NEW LIVE AND RARE VOL. 2 (EP)	10
80	Harvest SHEP 101	NEW LIVE AND RARE VOL. 3 (EP)	10

ALBUMS : PARLOPHONE

68	Parlophone PMC 7055	SHADES OF DEEP PURPLE (LP, yellow/black label, mono, with "sold in U.K..." text)	600
68	Parlophone PCS 7055	SHADES OF DEEP PURPLE (LP, yellow/black label, stereo, with "sold in U.K..." text)	400
69	Parlophone PCS 7055	SHADES OF DEEP PURPLE (LP, stereo repressing, laminated sleeve, white/black label)	40

ALBUMS : HARVEST

69	Harvest SHVL 751	THE BOOK OF TALIESYN (LP, laminated gatefold sleeve, first pressing with "sold in U.K." text spread over 4 lines, no EMI logo on label)	200
69	Harvest SHVL 751	THE BOOK OF TALIESYN (LP, laminated sleeve, second pressing with "sold in U.K." text spread over 5 lines)	75
69	Harvest SHVL 751	THE BOOK OF TALIESYN (LP, laminated sleeve, third pressing without "sold in U.K." text)	40
69	Harvest SHVL 759	DEEP PURPLE (LP, laminated gatefold sleeve, no EMI logo on label)	150
69	Harvest SHVL 759	DEEP PURPLE (LP, laminated gatefold sleeve, later pressing with EMI logo on label)	25
70	Harvest SHVL 767	CONCERTO FOR GROUP AND ORCHESTRA (LP, laminated gatefold sleeve, no EMI logo on label)	75
70	Harvest SHVL 767	CONCERTO FOR GROUP AND ORCHESTRA (LP, laminated gatefold sleeve, later pressing with EMI logo on label)	25
70	Harvest SHVL 777	IN ROCK (LP, laminated gatefold sleeve with "file under popular: pop groups", "Printed and Made by Garrod & Lofthouse Ltd." A2, B1 matrix, "The Gramophone Co" text around label rim not "EMI Records" no EMI logo on label, advertising inner sleeve with "Patent no's 1,125,555 & 1,072,844" at bottom)	100
70	Harvest SHVL 777	IN ROCK (LP, laminated gatefold sleeve, later pressing with EMI logo on label)	25
71	Harvest SHVL 759	DEEP PURPLE (LP, laminated gatefold sleeve, non EMI pressing with indented circular groove around spindle hole)	20
71	Harvest SHVL 793	FIREBALL (LP, textured gatefold sleeve, with lyric insert)	125
71	Harvest SHVL 793	FIREBALL (LP, gatefold sleeve, with light or no texture, lyric insert)	20
71	Harvest SHVL 751	THE BOOK OF TALIESYN (LP, laminated gatefold sleeve with 'Ernest J. Day' printing credit	40

DEEP PURPLE

MINT VALUE £

75	Harvest SHVL 751	THE BOOK OF TALIESYN (LP, laminated gatefold sleeve, fifth pressing with EMI logo)	15
76	Harvest SHVL 751	THE BOOK OF TALIESYN (LP, laminated gatefold sleeve with 'Garrod & Lofthouse Ltd' printing credit, sixth pressing with EMI logo on slightly more yellow label)	15
78	Harvest SHSM 2026	THE SINGLES A's AND B's (LP, purple vinyl)	20
80	Harvest SHSM 2016	SHADES OF DEEP PURPLE (LP, 'dismembered doll-limb' sleeve, withdrawn)	200
80	Harvest SHDW 412	IN CONCERT (2-LP)	22
82	Harvest SHSP 4124	LIVE IN LONDON (LP)	15
99	Harvest 7243 4 99469 10	BOOK OF TALIESYN (LP, 180gm vinyl, gatefold sleeve in stickered PVC outer)	20

ALBUMS : PURPLE

75	Purple TPSM 2002	24 CARAT PURPLE (LP, with "woman From Tokyo" mis-spelling on label)	15
72	Purple TPSP 3511/12	MADE IN JAPAN 2-LP, First pressing, "Gramophone Co" on label rim, MATRIX TPS 3511 A-1U/B-1U/TPS 3512 A-1U/B1-U, "Porky" (side 1), "Delta Pork" (side 2), "Pecko" (side 3), "Peckie" (Side 4) etched into dead wax, double gatefold sleeve, many originals with £3.25 price sticker)	100
72	Purple TSPS 3511/12	MADE IN JAPAN 2-LP, Contract pressing, no mother or stamper details at 3 and 9 'o' clock, (just number "3" at 9 "o" clock. Ridge around inside of label half an inch from the rim, no "Made in Gt. Britain" at foot of label, no brackets on "Made In Japan" on labels,double gatefold sleeve)	80
72	Purple TPSA 7504	MACHINE HEAD (LP, laminated gatefold sleeve, with fold-out lyric insert, date code 7204 on sleeve, no EMI credit on label, outer rim of label has 'The Gramophone Co. Ltd' at 11 o clock and 'Made in Great Britain' at 6 o clock on label)	100
73	Purple TPSA 7508	WHO DO WE THINK WE ARE (LP, 1st pressing with 'The Gramophone Co' on rim of label, -1U matrix numbers on both sides, laminated gatefold sleeve with 'File under popular: pop groups', with lyric insert)	50
74	Purple Q4TPS 7504	MACHINE HEAD (LP, laminated gatefold sleeve, quadrophonic)	60
74	Purple TPS 3505	BURN (LP, First Pressing: "The Gramophone Co" on rim, MATRIX TPS 3505 A-1U/B-1U, "Porky & Mel * Trish" etched into dead wax side 1/"Pecko" etched into dead wax on side 2. Spine wording on top edge as well as spine)	40
74	Purple TPS 3505	BURN (LP, Second Pressing: "EMI Records" on rim, -1U Matrixes)	25
74	Purple TPS 3505	BURN (LP, hybrid pressing with: "The Gramophone Co" on one label and "EMI Records" on the other)	30
74	Purple TPS 3505	BURN (LP, later pressings with "EMI Records" on both labels)	15
74	Purple TPS 3508	STORMBRINGER (LP, 1st pressing, matrixes TPS3508 A-1U/B-1U, 'Kendun' stamped in dead wax, "EMI Records Ltd" on label rim, spine wording on top edge and spine, "7411 Garrod & Lofthouse Ltd" on bottom right corner of sleeve)	40
75	Purple TPSA 7515	COME TASTE THE BAND (LP, laminated gatefold sleeve with inner)	30
78	Purple TPS 3510	POWERHOUSE (LP)	15
79	Purple TPS 3514	THE MARK 2 PURPLE SINGLES (LP, purple vinyl)	18
04	EMI 7243 4 73592	BURN (2-LP, remastered anniversary edition)	30
09	EMI/Purple TPSD 3508	STORMBRINGER (2-LP, reissue, extra tracks, gatefold sleeve, inners)	20
10	EMI/Purple TPSD 7515	COME TASTE THE BAND (2-LP, reissue, gatefold sleeve)	20
12	EMI 50999 463275 1 2	MACHINE HEAD (LP, gatefold sleeve, 180gm 40th anniversary edition, bonus 7")	20
12	EMI TPSAD 7504	MACHINE HEAD (4-CD/DVD, 40th Anniversary edition)	40
14	Purple 3769654	MADE IN JAPAN (9-LP boxed set)	200
18	Purple/Universal TPSA 7504	MACHINE HEAD (LP, purple vinyl)	20
18	Purple/Universal TPS 3505	BURN (LP, reissue, purple vinyl)	20
18	Purple/Universal TPSA 7508	WHO DO WE THINK WE ARE? (LP, gatefold sleeve, purple vinyl)	20
18	Purple/Universal TPSA 7515	COME TASTE THE BAND (LP, reissue, purple vinyl, gatefold sleeve)	20
18	Purple/Universal TPSA 7515	MADE IN JAPAN (2-LP, purple vinyl)	18
18	Purple/Universal TPSA 7517	MADE IN EUROPE (LP, purple vinyl)	18
20	Purple/Universal TPS 3505	BURN (LP, reissue, orange vinyl)	20

ALBUMS : OTHER LPS

84	Polydor POLH 16	PERFECT STRANGERS (LP, inner)	15
84	Polydor POLHP 16	PERFECT STRANGERS (LP, picture disc, with extra track & die-cut sleeve)	15
84	Polydor DEEP 1A	DEEP PURPLE INTERVIEW (LP, 1-sided, promo-only, stickered white sleeve)	20
85	EMI EJ 26 0343 0	IN ROCK (LP, picture disc with poster)	25
85	EMI EJ 34 0344 0	FIREBALL (LP, picture disc with poster)	25
85	EMI EG 26 0345 0	MACHINE HEAD (LP, picture disc with poster)	25
85	EMI PUR 1/E 2606131	DEEP PURPLE — ANTHOLOGY (2-LP, blue vinyl)	25
86	Polydor DEEP 2A	HOUSE OF BLUE LIGHT (interview LP, promo-only, plays same both sides, stickered black sleeve)	20
87	Polydor POLH 32	HOUSE OF BLUE LIGHT (LP, inner)	15
88	Connoisseur VSOP 125	SCANDINAVIAN NIGHTS (2-LP, gatefold sleeve, with booklet)	25
90	RCA PL 90535	SLAVES AND MASTERS (LP)	15
91	Connoisseur DPVSOPLP 163	IN THE ABSENCE OF PINK – KNEBWORTH 85 (2-LP gatefold)	50
91	EMI 96129	ANTHOLOGY (3-LP, gatefold sleeve)	30
93	BMG 74321 15420-1	THE BATTLE RAGES ON (LP, with inner sleeve)	50
95	EMI 7243 8 34019 18	DEEP PURPLE IN ROCK (2-LP, purple vinyl, gatefold sleeve with inners)	35
97	EMI DEEPP 3	MACHINE HEAD (2-LP, 'EMI 100' remixed anniversary edition, purple vinyl, gatefold sleeve, with insert)	40
97	EMI LPCENT 25	SHADES OF DEEP PURPLE (LP, 'EMI 100', 180gm vinyl edition, yellow/black label)	40
97	EMI DEEPP 2	FIREBALL (2-LP, gatefold sleeve with inners & limited edition print)	30
98	EMI PP 074	30: THE VERY BEST OF (2-LP, purple vinyl)	30
98	EMI 7243 8 57864 19	MADE IN JAPAN (2-LP, numbered, purple vinyl, gatefold sleeve with inners)	35
03	EMI 7243 5 91048 12	BANANAS (LP, gatefold sleeve, inner)	50
11	Music On Vinyl MOVLP 361	PURPENDICULAR (2-LP, black vinyl)	25
11	Music On Vinyl MOVLP 361	PURPENDICULAR (2-LP, purple vinyl)	35
11	EMI/BBC DPBBC 6870	THE BBC SESSIONS (2-LP)	30
12	Back On Black RCV083LP	TOTAL ABANDON, AUSTRALIA '99 (2-LP)	25
13	Music On Vinyl MOVLP 668	THE BATTLE RAGES ON (LP, reissue, 180gm)	20
13	Eagle Vision ERDVLP 080	PERFECT STRANGERS (2-LP, 2-CD & DVD)	40
13	Ear Music 0208578 ERE	NOW WHAT? (2-LP, gatefold, inner)	20

DEEP RIVER BOYS

MINT VALUE £

14	Edel 0209815 ERE	RAPTURE OF THE DEEP (2-LP, reissue, gatefold sleeve)	20
14	Ear Music 0209764 ERE	LIVE IN PARIS 1975 (3-LP)	20
14	Ear Music 0209658 ERE	PHOENIX RISING (2-LP)	20
14	Ear Music 0209624 ERE	LIVE IN GRAZ 1975 (2-LP, gatefold, inners)	20
15	Ear Music 0210539	FROM THE SETTING SUN...LIVE AT WACKEN (3-LP)	20
15	Ear Music 0210534 EMU	...TO THE RISING SUN IN TOKYO (3-LP)	20
15	Ear Music 0210221 EMU	LIVE IN LONG BEACH 1971 (2-LP, gatefold sleeve)	20
16	Ear Music 0210976 EMU	LONG BEACH 1976 (3-LP, gatefold)	20
17	Sony 88985438451	THE BATTLE RAGES ON (LP, reissue, 180gm)	15
17	Ear Music 0214725 EMU	INFINITE (2-LP)	18
17	Ear Music 0212506 EMU	INFINITE LIVE RECORDS VOLUME 1 (3-LP, black or purple vinyl)	20
19	Ear Music 0213901 EMU	LIVE IN NEWCASTLE, AUSTRALIA (3-LP)	20
19	Ear Music 0214547 EMU	LIVE IN ROME, ITALY (3-LP)	20

(see also Rainbow, Gillan, [David Coverdale's] Whitesnake, Tommy Bolin, [Sheila Carter &] Episode Six, Jon Lord, Roger Glover, Green Bullfrog, Wizard's Convention, Elf, M.I. Five, Warhorse, Captain Beyond, John Lawton, Hell Preachers Inc., Glen Hughes, Trapeze, Leading Figures, Paice Ashton & Lord, Silverhead, Pete York Percussion Band)

DEEP RIVER BOYS

54	HMV 7M 174	Sweet Mama Tree Top Tall/A Kiss And Cuddle Polka	10
54	HMV 7M 280	Shake, Rattle And Roll/St. Louis Blues	40
56	HMV 7M 361	Rock-A-Beatin' Boogie/Just A Little Bit More!	40
56	HMV POP 263	That's Right/Honey Honey	20
57	HMV POP 395	Whole Lotta Shakin' Goin' On/There's A Goldmine In The Sky	30
58	HMV POP 449	Not Too Old To Rock And Roll/Slow Train To Nowhere	15
58	HMV POP 537	Itchy Twitchy Feeling/I Shall Not Be Moved	10
60	Top Rank 35/108	THE BLUE DEEPS (LP)	15

(see also Fats Waller, Harry Douglass & Deep River Boys)

DEEP SET

68	Pye 7N 17594	That's The Way Life Goes/Hello Amy	60
69	Major Minor MM 607	I Started A Joke/Spicks And Specks	8
70	Target 7N 45018	Cinnamon Girl/You'll Never Know	100

DEEP SIX

66	Liberty LIB 55282	Counting/When Morning Breaks	8

DEEP SWITCH

86	SWITCH 1	NINE INCHES OF GOD (LP, private pressing)	40

DEEP THOUGHTS

73	Accute ACC 1	Send Her Away/Waterfall Woman	10

DEEP THROATS

78	Limp LMP 1	Rock N Roll Discharge/Miami Connection	15

DEEP TIMBRE

72	Westwood WR 5006	DEEP TIMBRE (LP)	40

DEEP WATER

70	Pye 7N 17946	Take A Look Around/Poor Little Me	6

DEERHUNTER

07	4AD CAD 2822	MICROCASTLE/WEIRD ERA CONT. (LP, CD)	25

SAM DEES

69	Major Minor MM 655	If It's All Wrong (It's All Right)/Don't Keep Me Hangin' On	50
75	Atlantic K 10676	Fragile, Handle With Care/Save The Love At Any Cost	100
89	RCA PB 43129	After All/Always Something (p/s)	10
80s	Soul City 137	Lonely For You Baby/I Need You Girl (reissue)	8
97	Soul Supply GS0002	Lonely For You Baby/SAM FLETCHER: I'd Think It Over (promos [GS 0002X] £12)	10
10	Outta Sight OSV 008	Lonely For You Baby (original version)/Lonely For You Baby (alternative version) (reissue)	6

SAM DEES & BETTYE SWANN

76	Atlantic K 10719	Storybook Children/Just As Sure	15

(see also Bettye Swann)

DEE SET

68	Blue Cat BS 146	I Know A Place/ROY BENNETT: I Dangerous	80

DEF J

92	Kold Sweat KS122	Just Save It (12")	15

(see also Encona Coarse)

DEF LEPPARD

79	Bludgeon Riffola SRT/CUS/232	THE DEF LEPPARD EP: Ride Into The Sun/Getcha Rocks Off/The Overture (red label, p/s with lyric insert, 150 only)	400
79	Bludgeon Riffola SRT/CUS/232	THE DEF LEPPARD EP: Ride Into The Sun/Getcha Rocks Off/The Overture (red label, with p/s, 850 only)	300
79	Bludgeon Riffola SRT/CUS/232	THE DEF LEPPARD EP: Ride Into The Sun/Getcha Rocks Off/The Overture (red label, /without p/s, 850 only)	100
79	Bludgeon Riffola MSB 001	Ride Into The Sun/Getcha Rocks Off/The Overture (reissue, yellow label, 15,000 pressed, no p/s)	35
79	Phonogram 6059 240	Getcha Rocks Off/Ride Into The Sun/The Overture (2nd reissue, no p/s)	10
79	Phonogram 6059 240	Getcha Rocks Off/Ride Into The Sun/The Overture (mispressing, both sides play "The Overture")	40
79	Phonogram 6059 247	Wasted/Hello America (p/s)	12
80	Phonogram LEPP 1	Hello America/Good Morning Freedom (p/s)	12
81	Phonogram LEPP 2	Let It Go/Switch 625 (p/s, 10,000 shrinkwrapped with patch)	15
81	Phonogram LEPP 2	Let It Go/Switch 625 (p/s)	12
82	Phonogram LEPP 3	Bringin' On The Heartbreak/Me And My Wine (p/s)	35
82	Phonogram LEPP 312	Bringin' On The Heartbreak/Me And My Wine/You Got Me Runnin' (12", p/s)	18
83	Phonogram VER 5	Photograph/Bringin' On The Heartbreak (p/s)	10
83	Phonogram VERP 5	Photograph/Bringin' On The Heartbreak (camera-shaped fold-out/pop-up sleeve, 500 only)	25
83	Phonogram VERX 5	Photograph/Bringin' On The Heartbreak/Mirror, Mirror (12", p/s)	20

DEF TEX

			MINT VALUE £
83	Phonogram VER 6	Rock Of Ages/Action! Not Words (p/s)	7
83	Phonogram VERP 6	Rock Of Ages/Action! Not Words (guitar-shaped picture disc)	35
83	Phonogram VERQ 6	Rock Of Ages/Action! Not Words (foldout 'rock box' cube sleeve, 500 only)	40
83	Phonogram VERX 6	Rock Of Ages/Action! Not Words (12", p/s)	18
83	Phonogram VERDJ 8	Too Late/Foolin' (p/s, DJ-only promo with rear band photo in football kit)	150
83	Phonogram VER 8	Too Late For Love/Foolin' (p/s)	12
83	Phonogram VERX 8	Too Late For Love/Foolin'/High And Dry (12", p/s)	20
83	Phonogram VER 9	Photograph/Bringin' On The Heartbreak (reissue, 'wallet' p/s)	10
84	Phonogram VERG 9	Photograph/Bringin' On The Heartbreak (g/fold printed 'wallet' p/s, 500 only)	35
84	Phonogram VERX 9	Photograph/Bringin' On The Heartbreak/Mirror, Mirror (12", p/s)	15
87	Phonogram LEPC 1	Animal/Animal (Extended Mix)/Tear It Down (12", p/s, red vinyl)	15
87	Phonogram LEPPX 2	Pour Some Sugar On Me (Extended Version)/Pour Some Sugar On Me (Extended)/I Wanna Be Your Hero (12", picture disc, unissued)	0
87	Phonogram LEPS 3	Hysteria/Ride Into The Sun (1987 Version) (p/s, shrinkwrapped with patch)	10
87	Phonogram LEPX 313	Hysteria/Ride Into The Sun (1987 Version)/Love And Affection (live) (12", envelope box sleeve with poster & international discography, 5,000 only)	15
88	Phonogram LEPP 4	Armageddon It! (The Atomic Mix)/Ring Of Fire (poster p/s)	7
88	Phonogram LEPXB 4	Armageddon It!/Armageddon It! (The Atomic Mix)/Ring Of Fire (12", numbered box set with poster, enamel badge & 5 postcards, 5,000 only)	18
88	Phonogram LEPG 5	Love Bites/Billy's Got A Gun (live) (no'd gatefold p/s with 8-page lyric book)	8
88	Phonogram LEPXB 5	Love Bites/Billy's Got A Gun (live)/Excitable (Orgasmic Mix) (12", box set with 4 cardboard inserts, 5,000 only)	15
89	Phonogram LEPC 6	Rocket/Release Me (foldout 'Brit' pack, envelope sleeve with 3 inserts)	8
89	Phonogram LEPXP 6	Rocket (The Lunar Mix)/(Radio Edit)/Release Me (12", picture disc, numbered)	15
89	Phonogram LEPXC 6	Rocket (The Lunar Mix)/Release Me/Rock Of Ages (live) (12", calendar pack)	10
80	Vertigo 9102 040	ON THROUGH THE NIGHT (LP)	15
81	Vertigo 6359 045	HIGH 'N' DRY (LP)	15
83	Vertigo VERS 2	PYROMANIA (LP)	20
87	Phonogram HYSLP 1	HYSTERIA (LP, Jack Adams cut. A side Matrix HYSLP 1 A 2U 1 1)	35
87	Bludgeon Riffolla HYSLP 1	HYSTERIA (LP, Dennis Blackham cut A side matrix: HYSLP 1 A - 3U - 1)	25
87	Phonogram HYSPD 1	HYSTERIA (LP, picture disc)	15
92	Bludgeon Riffola 510 978 1	ADRENALIZE (LP, inner)	30
92	Phonogram 510 978-1	ADRENALIZE (LP, picture disc, 5,000 only, numbered, die-cut sleeve)	15
93	Bludgeon Riffola 518 305 1	RETRO ACTIVE (LP)	50
94	Phonogram (no cat. no.)	ADRENALIZE — MAHOGANY BOX SET (CD, picture disc, with interview picture CD, 3 booklets, signed/no'd certificate, signed photo & plectrum, 1,000 only)	200
95	Mercury 528 656-1	VAULT 1980 - 1995 (2-LP, inners)	100
96	Mercury 532 486-1	SLANG (LP, inner)	60

(see also Lucy, Gogmagog, Johnny Kalendar Band)

DEF TEX

91	Sound Clash SCR 003	MASTER BLASTER (EP)	70
92	Sound Clash CLASH001	TUTORIAL SESSIONS (EP)	10
94	Sound Clash CLASH003	HERBS & VERBS (EP)	10
95	Sound Clash SCR007	MOON MEDITATION (EP)	10
99	Son SON008	Poetic Speech Techniques (12")	12
01	Monkey Face MF01	Sing Sad Songs (7")	8
11	Son SON049	Stop, Pause, Reflect/Get Respect (with Chrome, 10", 150 copies only)	10
01	Son SONCD018	SERENE BUG (LP)	15

DEFECTS

81	Casualty CR 001	Dance 'Til You Drop/Guilty Conscience/Brutality (p/s)	20
85	WXYZ LMNOP2	DEFECTIVE BREAKDOWN (LP, with insert)	25

DEFENDANTS

80s	Edible EAT 001	Headmaster/Such A Spiv (stickered insert cover & stickered labels)	12

DEFENDERS

68	Doctor Bird DB 1104	Set Them Free/Don't Blame The Children (actually by Lee Perry & Sensations)	50

(see also Lee Perry)

DEFIANT

77	Angry LIG 1	L.S.D./Social-Climber (unissued and both tracks unrecorded, 20 sets of labels stuck on pre-existing singles by other artists)	50

DEFIANT POSE

81	Groucho Marxist WH 4	Someone Else's War/After The Bang (p/s)	15

ZION DE GALLIER

68	Parlophone R 5686	Me/Winter Will Be Cold	25
68	Parlophone R 5710	Dream Dream Dream/Geraldine	20

(see also Mark Wirtz)

GLORIA DE HAVEN

55	Brunswick 05457	Red Hot Pepper Pot/Won't You Save Me?	10

DE-HEMS

72	President PT 388	Don't Cross That Line/Lover Let Me Go	20

DEIGHTON TASK FORCE

89	White REACT1	Neighbourhood (12")	50

(see also Unique 3)

JACK DE JOHNETTE

70	CBS 64076	COMPLEX (LP)	20

RICK DE JONGH

83	Challenge TALL 3	So Easy/So Easy (Bonus Beats) (12")	15

DEK & JERRY

66	Philips BF 1494	What's The Matter With Me?/Don't Waste Your Time	8

DESMOND DEKKER (& ACES)

63	Island WI 054	Honour Your Mother And Father (as Desmond Decker & Beverley's Allstars)/ Madgie ('63) (with Beverley's Allstars)	20
63	Island WI 111	Parents/Labour For Learning (solo)	30

George DEKKER

			MINT VALUE £
64	Island WI 158	Jeserine/King Of Ska (as Desmond Dekkar & His Cherry Pies)	30
64	Black Swan WI 455	Dracula (as Desmond Dekkar)/DON DRUMMOND: Spitfire	50
65	Island WI 181	Get Up Adine (as Desmond Dekkar, actually with Four Aces)/Be Mine Forever (as Patsy & Desmond; song is act. "Down Down Down" by Clive & Naomi)	50
65	Island WI 202	This Woman (as Desmond Dekkar & Four Aces)/UPSETTERS: Si Senora (B-side actually by Ossie & Upsetters)	25
67	Pyramid PYR 6003	Wise Man/ROLAND ALPHONSO: Middle East	30
67	Pyramid PYR 6004	007 (Shanty Town)/ROLAND ALPHONSO: El Torro	12
67	Pyramid PYR 6006	It's A Shame/ROLAND ALPHONSO: On The Move	25
67	Pyramid PYR 6008	Rudy Got Soul/ROLAND ALPHONSO: The Cat	40
67	Pyramid PYR 6011	Rude Boy Train/ROLAND ALPHONSO: Nothing For Nothing	25
67	Pyramid PYR 6012	Mother's Young Girl/SOUL BROTHERS: Confucious	35
67	Pyramid PYR 6017	Unity/Sweet Music	20
67	Pyramid PYR 6020	Sabotage/Pretty Africa	20
67	Pyramid PYR 6020	Sabotage/It Pays	15
67	Pyramid PYR 6026	It Pays/Young Generation	15
68	Pyramid PYR 6031	Beautiful And Dangerous/I've Got The Blues	25
68	Pyramid PYR 6035	Bongo Gal/Shing A Ling	15
68	Pyramid PYR 6037	To Sir, With Love/Fu Manchu	175
68	Pyramid PYR 6044	Mother Pepper/Don't Blame Me	18
68	Pyramid PYR 6045	Try Me/I'm Leaving	15
68	Pyramid PYR 6047	Hey Grandma/Young Generation	15
68	Pyramid PYR 6051	Music Like Dirt (Intensified)/Coconut Water	15
68	Pyramid PYR 6054	It Mek/Writing On The Wall	10
68	Pyramid PYR 6058	Israelites/BEVERLEY'S ALLSTARS: The Man	7
68	Pyramid PYR 6059	Christmas Day/I've Got The Blues	10
70	Trojan TR 7777	You Can Get It If You Really Want/Perseverance	10
80	Stiff BUY 70	Israelite/Why Fight?	6
10	Trojan THB 7001	Sugar & Spice/Sentimental Reasons	15
10	Trojan THB 7005	Dancing Time/Beverley's Special (Nothing For Nothing)	15
13	Island WI 3161	007/Wise Man	10
67	Doctor Bird DLM 5007	007 SHANTY TOWN (LP)	150
69	Doctor Bird DLM 5013	THE ISRAELITES (LP, solo)	130
69	Trojan TTL 4	THIS IS DESMOND DEKKAR (LP, label credits Dekker)	30
70	Trojan TBL 146	YOU CAN GET IT IF YOU REALLY WANT (LP)	30
80	Stiff SEEZ 26	BLACK AND DEKKER (LP)	15
85	Trojan TRLS 226	ORIGINAL REGGAE HITSOUND (LP)	15
91	Trojan TRLS 292	KING OF SKA (LP)	18
93	Trojan TRLS 324	KING OF KINGS (LP, with the Specials)	15

(see also Al Barry, Skatalites, Maytals)

GEORGE DEKKER

71	Trojan TR 7879	Time Hard/SYDNEY, GEORGE & JACKIE: Fall In Love	6

HOWARD DEKKER

74	A Rover AR 01	Me Throw Me Corn/On The Fire	12

DEL

73	Uk UK 40	Motorbike Annie/Gypsy Girl (some in p/s)	20

DELACARDOS

61	HMV POP 890	Hold Back The Tears/Mister Dillon	30

SIMON DE LACY

68	Spark 1001	Baby Come Back To Me/Goodbye Love	25

JUNIOR DELAHAYE

80	Solid Groove SG 015	Love/I Love You (12")	20

DE LAINE SISTERS

62	Piccadilly 7N 35070	It Might As Well Rain Until September/Puppet On A String	10

(see also Ladybirds, Breakaways)

DEL AMITRI

83	No Strings NOSP 1	Sense Sickness/The Difference Is (p/s)	30
89	A&M AM 527	Stone Cold Sober/The Return Of Maggie Brown/Talk It To Death (p/s)	6
90	A&M AMX 589	Spit In The Rain/Scared To Love/The Return Of Maggie Brown/Talk It To Death (10", in box with lyric insert)	8
95	A&M 540 311-1	TWISTED (LP, with poster)	60
97	A&M 540 705-1	SOME OTHER SUCKER'S PARADISE (LP)	70

DELANEY & BONNIE (& FRIENDS)

69	Elektra EKSN 45066	Get Ourselves Together/Soldiers Of The Cross (withdrawn)	20
69	Atlantic 584 308	Comin' Home/Groupie (Superstar)	8
70	Stax 139	Just Plain Beautiful/Hard To Say Goodbye	6
69	Apple SAPCOR 7	THE ORIGINAL DELANEY & BONNIE (LP, unreleased, no sleeve)	1500
69	Elektra EKS 74039	THE ORIGINAL DELANEY & BONNIE — ACCEPT NO SUBSTITUTE (LP, commercial release of above LP)	25
69	Stax SXATS 1029	HOME (LP)	20
70	Atlantic 2400 013	ON TOUR WITH ERIC CLAPTON (LP)	25
71	Atco 2400 029	TO BONNIE FROM DELANEY (LP)	15

(see also Eric Clapton, Delaney Bramlett, King Curtis with Delaney & Friends, Shindogs)

ERIC DELANEY BAND

57	Pye Nixa NEP 24066	AT THE BBC FESTIVAL (EP)	10
56	Pye NIAX NP 19218	HI-FI DELANEY (10" LP)	20

SIMON DELANO

70	Jay Boy JSX2001	BANGARANG REGGAE (LP, with the Gassers)	20

DELAYS

06	Rough Trade RTRADLP 214	YOU SEE COLOURS (LP)	20

DEL-BYZANTEENS

			MINT VALUE £

DEL-BYZANTEENS
82 Don't Fall Off The Mountain Draft Riot/Sally Go Round The Roses (p/s) 6
    Z 16

DEL-CAPRIS
79 Grapevine GRP 112 Hey Little Way Out Girl (actually by Construction)/EULA COOPER: Beggars Can't Be Choosey (p/s) 10

DELEGATION
77 State STAT 25 The Promise Of Love/It Only Happens 25
78 State STAT 82 Oh Honey/Love Is Like A Fire (12") 40
78 State STAT 82 Oh Honey/Love Is Like A Fire 15

DELFONICS
68 Bell BLL 1005 La La Means I Love You/Can't Get Over Losing You 7
68 Bell BLL 1028 Break Your Promise/Alfie 6
68 Bell BLL 1042 Ready Or Not Here I Come/Somebody Loves You 8
69 Bell BLL 1066 You Can't Be Loving Him/Let It Be Me 10
69 Bell BLL 1073 You Got Yours And I'll Get Mine/Funny Feeling 6
70 Bell BLL 1467 With These Hands/Let It Be Me 20
68 Bell SBLL 106 LA-LA MEANS I LOVE YOU (LP) 25
69 Bell SBLL 121 THE SOUND OF SEXY SOUL (LP) 20
70 Bell SBLL 137 THE DELFONICS (LP) 20
72 Bell SBLL 217 TELL ME THIS IS A DREAM 20
74 Bell BELLS 245 ALIVE AND KICKING (LP) 15

TERESA DEL FUEGO
81 Satril HH 155 Don't Hang Up/Wonder Wonder (no p/s) 8

DELGADOS
96 Boa HISS 4 Liquidation Girl/VAN IMPE: Piranha (hand-painted brown paper bag p/s, 500 only) 12
96 Chemikal Underground CHEM 009 DOMESTIQUES (LP, inner) 20
98 Chemikal Underground CHEM 024 PELOTON (LP, inner) 25
00 Chemikal Underground CHEM 040 THE GREAT EASTERN (LP) 25

DELICATES
59 London HLT 8953 Ronnie Is My Lover/Black And White Thunderbird 50
60 London HLT 9176 Too Young To Date/The Kiss 30

DELICATESSAN
67 Vocalion VN 9286 The Red Baron's Revenge/The Dog Fight (Der Hundtkampf) 10

DE LITE
89 Circa YRTPRX 35 Wild Times (12") 30

DE-LITES
79 Destiny 1022 Lover/Do The Zombie 20
80 Grapevine GRP 127 Lover/Tell Me Why 20

JOHNNY DE LITTLE
61 Columbia DB 4578 Not Guilty/They 10
62 Columbia DB 4907 Lover/You Made Me Love You 8
65 CBS 201790 The Knack/What To Do With Laurie 6
(see also John Barry)

DELIVERANCE
92 European Rhyme ERR001 Serious Public Disorder/Do Not Disturb (12") 20
94 Nut Cracker NUT001 Dead Funny/Up And Down The Country (12") 20
95 Nut Cracker NUT002 INJECT INTELLECT (EP) 10
96 Nut Cracker NUT003 Twisted Mystics/Sedating Your Aims (12") 8

DELKOM
91 Wau! Mr Modo MWS 034R Superjack — Orbital Infusion 2000/Neutron 9000 Mix (12", 500 only) 12

ANNA DELL
66 Hollick & Taylor HT/LP S 1166 CRUISIN WITH ANNA DELL (LP) 40

DENNIS D'ELL
67 CBS 202605 It Breaks My Heart In Two/Better Use Your Head (withdrawn) 400
67 CBS 202605 It Breaks My Heart In Two/Better Use Your Head (withdrawn: DJ copy) 300
67 Decca F 12647 A Woman Called Sorrow/The Night Has A Thousand Eyes (as Denny D'ell) 15
76 Polydor 2058 715 Home Is Home/Morning Without You (as Denis D'ell) 7
(see also Honeycombs)

JIMMY DELL
58 RCA RCA 1066 Teeny Weeny/BARRY DE VORZON: Barbara Jean 50
58 RCA RCA 1066 Teeny Weeny/BARRY DE VORZON: Barbara Jean (78) 20

DELL-VIKINGS
57 London HLD 8405 Come Go With Me/How Can I Find A True Love (gold label lettering) 100
57 London HLD 8405 Come Go With Me/How Can I Find A True Love (silver label lettering) 20
57 London HLD 8464 Whispering Bells/Little Billy Boy 30
58 Mercury 7MT 199 The Voodoo Man/Can't Wait 10
59 Mercury AMT 1027 Flat Tyre/How Could You 40
62 HMV POP 1072 Kilimanjaro/Confession Of Love 10
63 HMV POP 1145 An Angel Up In Heaven/The Fishing Chant 10
(see also Chuck Jackson)

DELLINGER
77 Carib Gems GG 004 Melting Pot/Version 7
(see also Dillinger)

PETE DELLO & FRIENDS
71 Nepentha 6437 001 INTO YOUR EARS (LP, gatefold sleeve) 750
89 See For Miles 257 INTO YOUR EARS....PLUS (2-LP, reissue) 40
(see also Honeybus, Lace, Red Herring, Leah, John Killigrew, Magic Valley, Grant Tracy & Sunsets, Sunsets)

DELLS

MINT VALUE £

DELLS
63	Pye International 7N 25178	The (Bossa Nova) Bird/Eternally	25
67	Chess CRS 8066	O-O I Love You/There Is	15
68	Chess CRS 8071	Wear It On Our Face/Please Don't Change Me Now	20
68	Chess CRS 8079	Stay In My Corner/Love Is So Simple	8
68	President PT 223	It's Not Unusual/Stay In My Corner	15
68	Chess CRS 8084	Always Together/I Want My Momma	8
69	Chess CRS 8099	I Can Sing A Rainbow/Love Is Blue-Hallelujah Baby	6
69	Chess CRS 8102	Oh What A Night/Believe Me	7
69	President PT 270	Oh What A Night/Moving On	7
69	Chess CRS 8105	On The Dock Of The Bay/When I'm In Your Arms	7
71	Chess 6145 001	The Love We Had Stays On My Mind/Freedom Means	7
72	Chess 6145 008	It's All Up To You/Oh, My Dear	6
73	Chess 6145 022	Give Your Baby A Standing Ovation/Run For Cover	20
74	Philips 6145037	Bring Back The Love Of Yesterday/Learning To Love You Was Easy	10
80	20th Century TC 2403	All About The Paper/I Touched A Dream	10
80	20th Century TC 2478	Your Song/Look At Us Now	40
68	Chess CRLS 4554	GREATEST HITS (LP)	25
69	Chess CRLS 4555	LOVE IS BLUE/OH, WHAT A NIGHT (LP)	25
71	Joy JOYS 186	OH WHAT A NIGHT (LP)	15

ELAINE DELMAR
63	Columbia DB 7101	Hum Drum Blues/Amor Amor	30
68	CBS 63511	Sneakin' Up On You/Very Slowly	40
60	Columbia SEG 8060	A SWINGING CHICK (EP)	20
68	EMI SX6222	LA BELLE ELAINE (LP)	20
68	CBS 63511	SNEAKIN' UP ON YOU (LP)	35

DEL MONAS
85	Empire JLM 14	Sally Sue Brown/Dangerous Charms (7" die cut sleeve)	15
84	Big Beat SW 101	COMIN' HOME BABY - VOLUME ONE (7" EP)	12
84	Big Beat SW 102	HELLOW WE LOVE YOU - VOLUME TWO (7" EP)	12
85	Big Beat WIK 35	DANGEROUS CHARMS (LP)	20
85	Empire SYF 95	5 (LP)	25
88	Hangman HANG 20 UP	5 (LP, reissue)	15
89	Hangman HANG 28 UP	DEL MONAS (LP)	18
99	Vinyl Japan ASKLP 107	DANGEROUS CHARMS (LP, reissue)	15

DELMONTES
| 80s | Rational RATE 3 | Don't Cry Your Tears/So It's Not To Be (yellow or blue p/s) | 8 |

DELMONTS
| 71 | Spiral DIT 1 | A Ra Chicera/Sorry For My Jealousy | 6 |
| 72 | Spiral DIT 2 | Gimmie Gimmie Your Loving/Now Is The Time For Love | 15 |

JOEY DELORENZO
| 02 | Fab-U-Lus FBU07007 | Wake Up To The Sunshine Girl/Lost My Sense Of Direction (reissue) | 15 |

AL DE LORY
| 65 | London HLU 9999 | Yesterday/Traffic Jam | 20 |

LANA DEL REY
| 11 | Stranger 2783433 | Video Games/Blue Jeans (picture disc, 100 copies signed) | 20 |
| 12 | Polydor 2793424 | BORN TO DIE (2-LP) | 18 |

DELROY & SPORTY
| 71 | Banana BA 322 | Lovers Version/DUDLEY SIBLEY: Having A Party | 25 |

DELROY & TENNORS
| 71 | Camel CA 62 | Donkey Shank/MURPHY'S ALL STARS: Donkey Track | 50 |

DELTA 5
79	Rough Trade RT 31	Mind Your Own Business/Now That You've Gone (p/s)	20
80	Rough Trade RT 41	Anticipation/You (p/s)	10
81	Rough Trade RT 61	Try/Colour (p/s)	10
81	Pre PRE 16	Shadow/Leaving (p/s)	7
82	Pre PRE 24	Powerlines/The Heart Is A Lonely Hunter (p/s)	7
81	PRE PREX 6	SEE THE WHIRL (LP)	20

DELTA CATS
| 69 | Bamboo BAM 3 | I Can't Re-Live (song actually "I Can't Believe")/I've Been Hurt | 75 |

(see also Thrillers)

DELTA RHYTHM BOYS
| 54 | Brunswick 05353 | Mood Indigo/Have A Hope, Have A Wish, Have A Prayer | 10 |
| 52 | Esquire 15-001 | DELTA RHYTHM BOYS WITH THE METRONOME ALLSTARS (10" LP) | 15 |

DELTAS
| 64 | Blue Beat BB 265 | Georgia/The Party | 20 |
| 65 | Blue Beat BB 275 | The Visitor/SKATALITES: Hanging The Beam | 40 |

DELTA SKIFFLE GROUP
| 58 | Esquire EP 162 | DELTA SKIFFLE GROUP (EP) | 40 |

DELTONES (JAMAICA)
| 71 | Green Door GD 4010 | Chopsticks/DES BRYAN: Belmont Street | 8 |
| 72 | Trojan TRM 9001 | Chopsticks/I Got It/Put It On | 6 |

DELTONES (U.K.)
| 70 | Columbia DB 8719 | Gimme Some Lovin'/Have A Little Talk With Myself | 20 |

DEL-TONES (U.S.)
| 59 | Top Rank JAR 171 | Moonlight Party/Rockin' Blues | 100 |
| 59 | Top Rank JAR 171 | Moonlight Party/Rockin' Blues (78) | 20 |

(see also Beau-Marks)

MILTON DE LUGG ORCHESTRA
| 65 | Columbia DB 7474 | The Addams Family Theme/The Alfred Hitchcock Theme | 8 |

DELUSION

MINT VALUE £

66	Columbia DB 7762	The Munsters Theme/The Addams Family Theme	8

(see also Beau-Marks)

DELUSION
79	Wizzo WIZZO 2	Pessimists Paradise/Desert Island (gatefold p/s)	8

DELUSIONS OF GRANDEUR
86	Music Factory GRAND 1	We Are The Humans/Colour Me/Destiny (12", p/s)	10

DELUXE
90	Heaven Sent HSX 001	Love Forever/1-2-1 (12")	15
89	Unyque UNQ LP1	JUST A LITTLE MORE (LP)	25
96	Leap Of Faith LEAP 004LP	SHOW ME (LP)	80

LEO DE LYON
54	MGM SP 1087	The Band Played On/Say It Isn't So	7

DEM 2
94	New York Soundclash NYSC001	REACH (12")	25
97	New York Soundclash NYSC004	BOSTON EXPERIMENTS EP (12")	30
97	New York Soundclash NYSC005	24 SEVEN EP (12")	30
03	New York Soundclash NYSC010	Luv's Hard/Luv's Hard In Destiny's Bed (12")	25

ARIN DEMAIN
90s	Goldmine/Soul Supply GS 028	Silent Treatment/PARIS: Sleepless Nights	8

RALPH DE MARCO
59	London HLL 9010	Old Shep/More Than Riches	7

DEMENSIONS
60	Top Rank JAR 505	Over The Rainbow/Nursery Rhyme Rock	40
61	Coral Q 72437	Count Your Blessings Instead Of Sheep/Again	10

(see also Wheels, James Brothers, Fox)

DEMENTED ARE GO
86	ID NOSE 9	IN SICKNESS AND IN HEALTH (LP)	20
88	ID NOSE 21	KICKED OUT OF HELL (LP)	20
89	Link MLP 084	THE DAY THE EARTH SPAT BLOOD (LP, as the Demon Teds)	15
90	Link LRM 05	GO GO DEMENTED (LP, blue vinyl)	15
91	Fury F 3016	ORGASMIC NIGHTMARE (LP, blue vinyl)	15
93	Fury DAGLP 1	TANGENTAL MADNESS ON A PLEASANT SIDE OF HELL (LP, white vinyl)	15

(ROD) DEMICK & (HERBIE) ARMSTRONG
70	Decca F 13056	We're On The Right Track/Dreaming (as Demick-Armstrong)	6
71	Mam MAM-AS 1001	LITTLE WILLY RAMBLE (LP, black/silver labels)	25
72	A&M AMLH 68908	LOOKIN' THROUGH (LP, inner sleeve, brown label)	50

DEMOB
81	Round Ear ROUND 1	Anti Police/Teenage Adolescence (foldout p/s)	15
81	Round Ear ROUND 1	Anti Police/Teenage Adolescence (later standard p/s)	10
81	Round Ear EAR 3	No Room For You/Think Straight/New Breed (p/s)	18

DEMOLISHED MEN
84	Anthem ANTHEM 2	Ghost Train/Yours In Haste	15

DEMOLITION
81	Demolition ZEL SPS 296	Hooker Hater/Axeman (p/s)	250

DEMON BOYZ
88	Music Of Life NOTE 13	Northside/Rougher Than An Animal	10
90	Mango 12 MNS 738	International Karate (12")	8
92	Tribal Bass Tribe4	DETT (12")	10
92	Tribal Bass Tribe9	Glimity Glamity/Junglist (12")	12
89	Music Of Life DEMON1	RECOGNITION (LP)	25
92	Tribal Bass Tribe11	ORIGINAL GUIDANCE – THE SECOND CHAPTER (LP)	40

DEMON D
95	Voyager VOD 94	Let The Jazz Take You/Together (12")	20

DEMON FUZZ
70	Dawn DNX 2504	I Put A Spell On You/Message To Mankind/Fuzz Oriental Blues (p/s)	50
70	Dawn DNX 2504	I Put A Spell On You/Message To Mankind/Fuzz Oriental Blues	10
70	Dawn DNLS 3013	AFREAKA! (LP, gatefold sleeve, orange label)	200

DEMON OF (EAST CO)
04	FL FLAS 001	Gansta Style/Instrumental (12" featuring Kano)	12

(see also Kano)

DEMON PACT
81	Slime PACT 1	Eaten Alive/Raiders (p/s)	50
81	Slime PACT 2	Escape/Demon Pact (unreleased, labels only)	0

DEMON PREACHER
78	Illegal SRTS/CUS/78110	Royal Northern (N7)/Laughing At Me/Steal Your Love/Dead End Kidz (numbered p/s)	125
78	Small Wonder SMALL TEN	Little Miss Perfect/Perfect Dub (p/s)	20

(see also Demons, Alien Sex Fiend, Fenzyx)

DEMON ROCKA
82	Unity UN 001	Iron Lady/Stick Together	12

DEMON (1)
81	Clay CLAY 4	Liar/Wild Woman (p/s, red vinyl)	8
83	Clay CLAY 25	The Plague/The Only Sane Man (p/s)	6
84	Clay CLAY 41	Wonderland/Blackheath (p/s)	6
81	Carrere CA 651	NIGHT OF THE DEMON (LP, pressed in France)	20
83	Clay CLAYLP 6	THE PLAGUE (LP, gatefold sleeve, with insert)	15
83	Clay CLAYLP 6P	THE PLAGUE (LP, picture disc)	20

			MINT VALUE £
90	Sonic SONICLP 1	NIGHT OF THE DEMON (LP, reissue)	15

DEMON (2)
12	Macabre Unit MUV 003	Frostbite/DCULT: Sliver (12")	20
13	Macabre Unit MUV 008	Physics/Morning Glory (12")	12

DEMONS (JAMAICA)
69	Big Shot BI 523	You Belong To My Heart/Bless You	20

DEMONS (U.K.)
80	Crypt Music DEM 1	Action By Example/I Wish I Was A Dog (p/s)	12

(see also Alien Sex Fiend, Demon Preacher)

DEMONSTRATORS
64	Warner Bros WB 132	Sweet Violets/Ultra Violet	12

JASON DENE
66	Parlophone R 5485	Opportunity/It's Me	8

(see also Jason Deane)

TERRY DENE
57	Decca F 10895	A White Sport Coat/The Man In The Phone Booth	12
57	Decca F 10914	Start Movin'/Green Corn	10
57	Decca F 10938	Come And Get It/Teenage Dream	10
57	Decca F 10964	Lucky Lucky Bobby/Baby, She's Gone	25
58	Decca F 10977	The Golden Age/C'Min And Be Loved	10
58	Decca F 11016	Stairway Of Love/Lover, Lover!	7
58	Decca F 11037	Seven Steps To Love/Can I Walk You Home	7
58	Decca F 11076	Who Baby Who/Pretty Little Pearly	7
59	Decca F 11100	I've Got A Good Thing Going/Bimbombey	7
60	Oriole CB 1562	Geraldine/Love Me Or Leave Me	10
61	Oriole CB 1594	Like A Baby/Next Stop Paradise	15
63	Aral PS 107	The Feminine Look/Fever (all in p/s)	15
57	Decca DFE 6459	THE GOLDEN DISC (EP)	20
57	Decca DFE 6507	TERRY DENE NO. 1 (EP)	30
66	Herald ELR 107	TERRY DENE NOW (EP)	30

DENE BOYS
57	HMV POP 374	Bye Bye Love/Love Is The Thing	20
58	HMV POP 455	Skylark/I Walk Down The Street	8

DENE FOUR
59	HMV POP 666	Hush-a-bye/Something New	25

(see also Dene Boys)

DENIGH
80	Ace ACE 16	No Way/Running (no p/s)	50

DENIM
92	Boys Own BOI 12	Middle Of The Road/Ape Hangers	8
92	Boys Own BOIX 12	Middle Of The Road/Ape Hangers/Robin's Nest/The Great Grape Ape Hangers (12")	10
97	EMI RADIODJ 1	Summer Smash (promo, withdrawn)	20
97	Emidisc DISC009	Summer Smash/Sun's Out (p/s, yellow vinyl)	60
92	Boys Own 828349	BACK IN DENIM (LP)	50
96	Echo ECH LP8	DENIM ON ICE (LP)	45
97	EMI ADISC 001	NOVELTY ROCK (LP)	75
97	EMI ADISCCD 001	NOVELTY ROCK (CD)	30

(see also Felt, Go-Kart Mozarts, Supermarket)

DENIMS
65	CBS 201807	I'm Your Man/Ya Ya	70

ROGER DENISON
66	Parlophone R 5545	I'm On An Island/I'm Running Out Of Time	12
67	Parlophone R 5566	It Just Doesn't Seem To Be My Day/She Wanders Through My Mind	50

DENIZENS
79	Big SOLD 5	People Of The Night/Ammonia Subway (p/s)	10
80	Citizen	IN THE CROWD EP (with 16-page booklet)	12

SUE DENNING
65	Columbia DB 7246	Kiss Me Once Again/Goodtime Johnny	20

WADE DENNING & PORT WASHINGTONS
67	MGM MGM 1339	Tarzan's March/Batman	15

D.D. (DENZIL) DENNIS
70	Crab CRAB 53	Rain Is Ginna Fall/This Game Ain't Free	25
70	Crab CRAB 60	Having A Party/Man With Ambition	25
70	Pama Supreme PS 301	My Way/Happy Days	25
71	Punch PH 93	Christmas Message/Cool It Girl	15
71	Pama Supreme PS 330	I'm A Believer/I'll Make The Way Easy	15
74	Pama Supreme PS 391	Women And Money/UPSETTERS: Ten Cent Skank	15

(see also Denzil Dennis)

D D DENNIS - BROTHER LLOYD'S ALL STARS
68	Mercury MF 1064	Save The Last Dance For Me/Will You Still Love Me Tomorrow	15

DENZIL DENNIS
63	Blue Beat BB 181	Seven Nights In Rome/Love Is For Fools (as DENZIL)	15
68	Trojan TR 614	Donkey Train/Down By The Riverside	15
68	Trojan TR 615	Me Nah Worry/Hush Don't You Cry	15
68	Jolly JY 011	Oh Carol/Where Has My Little Girl Gone	15
70	Mary Lyn ML 100	I Guess I'd Better Start Believing/When Will You Ever Learn	15
70	Pama Supreme PS 304	Painful Situation/Nothing Has Changed	8
71	Pama Supreme PS 350	South Of The Border/GRAHAM: Long Island	15
72	Pama Supreme PS 375	Mama We're All Crazy Now/ROY SHIRLEY: A Lady's A Man's Best Friend	7
74	Arrow AR 003	If/How Can I Touch You	8

Jackie DENNIS

MINT VALUE £

(see also D.D. Dennis, Cosmo & Dennis, Denzil & Pat, Denzil & Jennifer, Les & Silkie)

JACKIE DENNIS
58	Decca F 10992	La Dee Dah/You're The Greatest	8
58	Decca F 11011	Miss Valerie/My Dream	7
58	Decca F 11033	The Purple People Eater/You-Oo	10
58	Decca F 11060	More Than Ever (Come Prima)/Linton Addie	7
58	Decca F 11090	Gingerbread/Lucky Ladybug	7
59	Top Rank JAR 129	Summer Snow/Night Bird	6
58	Decca DFE 6513	JACKIE DENNIS NO. 1 (EP)	25

DENNIS & LIZZY
| 70 | Camel CA 56 | Everybody Bawlin'/Mr Brown | 10 |
| 73 | Pyramid PYR 7002 | Ba-Ba-Ri-Ba-Shank/TOMMY McCOOK ALL STARS: Buck And The Preacher | 15 |

(see also Dennis Alcapone, Lizzy & Dennis)

DENNISONS
63	Decca F 11691	(Come On) Be My Girl/Little Latin Lupe Lu	10
64	Decca F 11880	Walkin' The Dog/You Don't Know What Love Is	15
64	Decca F 11990	Nobody Like My Babe/Lucy (You Sure Did It This Time)	20

SANDY DENNY
72	Island WIP 6141	Here In Silence/Man Of Iron (theme from Pass Of Arms film, in p/s)	50
72	Island WIP 6141	Here In Silence/Man Of Iron (theme from Pass Of Arms film)	25
72	Island WIP 6142	Listen Listen/Tomorrow Is A Long Time	8
73	Island WIP 6176	Whispering Grass/Friends (p/s)	8
74	Island WIP 6195	Like An Old Fashioned Waltz (unissued)	0
76	Mooncrest MOON 54	Make Me A Pallet On Your Floor/This Train	6
77	Island WIP 6391	Candle In The Wind/Still Waters Run Deep (unissued, promo only)	30
11	Island 276-797-3	I'm A Dreamer (Second Demo)/Who Knows Where The Time Goes? (First Demo)	8
67	Saga EROS 8041	SANDY AND JOHNNY (LP, with Johnny Silvo, black/silver label)	30
70	Saga EROS 8153	SANDY DENNY (LP)	30
71	Island ILPS 9165	THE NORTH STAR GRASSMAN AND THE RAVENS (LP, gatefold sleeve, 'pink rim palm tree' label)	60
72	Island ILPS 9207	SANDY (LP, gatefold sleeve, original pressing with 'pink rim palm tree' label)	50
72	Island ILPS 9207	SANDY (LP, reissue, gatefold sleeve)	15
73	Island ILPS 9258	LIKE AN OLD FASHIONED WALTZ (LP, gatefold sleeve, 'pink rim palm tree' label)	40
73	Hallmark SHM 813	ALL OUR OWN WORK (LP, with Strawbs)	20
77	Island ILPS 9433	RENDEZVOUS (LP, with lyric inner sleeve)	25
78	Mooncrest CREST 28	THE ORIGINAL SANDY DENNY (LP)	25
97	Strange Fruit SFRSCD 006	THE BBC SESSIONS 1971-73 (CD, limited edition, withdrawn – beware of bootlegs)	30
85	Island SDSP 100	WHO KNOWS WHERE THE TIME GOES (4-LP, box set with booklet)	60

(see also Fairport Convention, Strawbs, Fotheringay, Alex Campbell, Trevor Lucas, Richard Thompson)

SUSAN DENNY
| 65 | Melodisc MEL 1596 | Don't Touch Me/Johnny | 35 |

DENNY & WILSON
| 72 | Hillcrest HCT 6 | Hey Hey Girl/CARLTON ALPHONSO: Girl I Love You | 6 |

DENTISTS
85	Spruck SP 003	Strawberries Are Growing In My Garden (And It's Wintertime)/Burning The Thoughts From My Skin/Doreen (p/s, with folded insert)	30
85	Spruck SP 004	YOU AND YOUR BLOODY ORANGES (12" EP, p/s)	10
86	Tambourine SP 006	DOWN AND OUT IN PARIS AND CHATHAM (12" EP, brown/white or group p/s)	10
87	Tambourine URINE 3	Writhing On The Shagpile/Just Like Oliver Reed/A Strange Way To Go About Things/Calm You Down/The Turquoise Castle (12", p/s)	10
85	Spruck SPR 001	SOME PEOPLE ARE ON THE PITCH THEY THINK IT'S ALL OVER IT IS NOW (LP)	30

MICKEY DENTON
| 61 | London HLX 9398 | The Steady Kind/Now You Can't Give Them Away | 8 |

NIGEL DENVER
64	Decca DFE 8580	FOLK SINGER (EP)	15
66	Decca LK 4728	MOVIN' ON (LP, featuring Martin Carthy)	40
67	Decca LK 4844	REBELLION (LP)	20

DENYM
| 82 | Occult S 82 CUS 1351 | Beauty/Selassie Hi | 30 |
| 83 | Real Wax RW003 | Why Boy/Why Dub (12") | 50 |

DENZIL & JENNIFER
| 70 | Escort ES 824 | Young, Gifted And Black/OWEN GRAY: I Am Satisfied | 100 |

DENZIL (DENNIS) & PAT (RHODEN)
| 69 | Downtown DT 403 | Dream/Sincerely | 15 |

DEPECHE MODE
| 84 | Mute L12BONG 5 | People Are People (On-U-Sound Remix)/In Your Memory/ People Are People (12", numbered in die-cut p/s) | 15 |

SINGLES
81	Lyntone LYN 10209	Sometimes I Wish I Was Dead/FAD GADGET: King Of The Flies (test pressing)	150
81	Lyntone LYN 10209	Sometimes I Wish I Was Dead/FAD GADGET: King Of The Flies (red flexidisc free with Flexipop magazine, issue 11)	25
81	Lyntone LYN 10209	Sometimes I Wish I Was Dead/FAD GADGET: I Wish I Was Dead (red vinyl flexidisc free without Flexipop magazine, issue 11)	15
81	Mute MUTE 013	Dreaming Of Me/Ice Machine (p/s)	15
81	Mute MUTE 014	New Life/Shout (p/s)	8
81	Mute 12MUTE 014	New Life (Remix)/Shout! (Rio Mix) (12", p/s)	12
81	Mute MUTE 016	Just Can't Get Enough/Any Second Now (p/s)	8
81	Mute 12MUTE 016	Just Can't Get Enough (Schizo Mix)/Any Second Now (12", p/s)	12
82	Mute 12MUTE 018	See You (Extended)/Now, This Is Fun (Extended) (12", p/s)	10
82	Mute 12MUTE 022	The Meaning Of Love (Fairly Odd Mix)/Oberkorn (Development Mix) (12", p/s)	10
82	Mute BONG 1	Leave In Silence/Excerpt From My Secret Garden (p/s)	7

DEPECHE MODE

MINT VALUE £

82	Mute 12 BONG 1	Leave In Silence (Longer)/Excerpt From My Secret Garden/Leave In Silence (Quieter) (12", p/s)	10
83	Mute L12BONG 2	Get The Balance Right/My Secret Garden (live)/See You (live)/Satellite (live) (12", numbered p/s)	20
83	Mute 12 BONG 2	Get The Balance Right (Combination Mix)/The Great Outdoors/Tora! Tora! Tora! (Live) (12, p/s)	10
83	Mute BONG 3	Everything Counts/Work Hard (p/s)	6
83	Mute L12 BONG 3	Everything Counts/Boys Say Go (live)/New Life (live)/Nothing To Fear (live)/The Meaning Of Love (live) (12", numbered p/s)	20
84	Mute BONG 5	People Are People/In Your Memory (p/s)	6
84	Mute L12BONG 6	Master And Servant (On-U-Sound Science Fiction Dancehall Classic)/Are People People?/(Set Me Free) Remotivate Me (12", numbered p/s)	20
84	Mute BONG 6	Master And Servant/Set Me Free (Remotivate Me) (p/s)	7
84	Mute BONG 7	BLASPHEMOUS RUMOURS EP (p/s)	8
85	Mute BONG 8	Shake The Disease/Flexible (p/s)	7
85	Mute L 12 BONG 8	Shake The Disease (Edit The Shake)/Master And Servant (Live)/Flexible (Pre-Deportation Mix)/Something To Do (Metalmix) (12", p/s)	15
85	Mute BONG 9	It's Called A Heart/Fly On The Windscreen (p/s, with poster)	10
85	Mute D12BONG 9	It's Called A Heart (Mixes)/Fly On The Windscreen (Mixes) (12", p/s, dbl-pack)	15
86	Mute BONG 10	Stripped/But Not Tonight (p/s)	8
86	Mute 12 BONG 10	Stripped (Highland Mix)/But Not Tonight (Extended Mix)/Breathing In Fumes/Fly On The Windscreen (Quiet MIx)/Black Day (12", p/s)	12
86	Mute BONG 11	A Question Of Lust/Christmas Island (p/s)	8
86	Mute 12 BONG 11	A Question Of Lust/Christmas Island (Extended)/People Are People (Live)/It Doesn't Matter Two (Instrumental)/A Question Of Lust (Minimal) (12", p/s)	10
86	Mute CBONG 11	A Question Of Lust/Christmas Island/If You Want (Live)/Shame (Live)/Blasphemous Rumours (live) (Cassette)	35
87	Mute BONG 13	Strangelove/Pimpf (p/s)	7
87	Mute BONG 14	Never Let Me Down Again/Pleasure, Little Treasure (p/s)	10
87	Mute P12 BONG 14	Never Let Me Down Again (7" Mix)/Pleasure Little Treasure (7" Mix)/Never Let Me Down Again (12" Split Mix) (p/s)	50
88	Mute LITTLE 15	Little 15/Stjarna (p/s)	10
88	Mute 12 LITTLE 15	Little 15/Stjarna/Sonata 14 IN CM - MOONLIGHT SONATA (12", p/s)	15
87	Mute L12BONG 15	Behind The Wheel (Beatmasters Remix)/Route 66 (Casuality Mix) (12", p/s)	12
89	Mute 10BONG 16	Everything Counts (Absolute Mix)/(1983 12" Mix)/Nothing (US 7" Mix) (10", envelope p/s, with 2 postcards & window sticker)	30
89	Mute LCDBONG 16	Everything Counts (Tim Simenon & M. Saunders Remix)/Nothing (Justin Strauss Remix)/Strangelove (Tim Simenon & M. Saunders Remix) (3" CD 'filofax' page- p/s)	15
89	Mute GBONG 17	Personal Jesus/(Acoustic)/Dangerous (Hazchemix) (gatefold p/s with photos)	12
89	Mute L12BONG 17	Personal Jesus (Mixes)/Dangerous (Hazchemix) (12", p/s)	15
90	Mute BONG 18	Enjoy The Silence/Memphisto (p/s)	12
90	Mute 12 BONG 18	Enjoy The Silence/Enjoy The Silence (Hands And Feet Mix)/(Ecstatic Dub)/Sibeling (12", p/s)	30
90	Mute BONG 19	Policy Of Truth/Kaleid (p/s)	6
90	Mute XL12BONG 18	Enjoy The Silence (The Quad: Final Mix) (12", 1-side etched, p/s)	30
90	Mute BONG 20	World In My Eyes/Happiest Girl (Jack Mix)/Sea Of Sin (Tonal Mix) (p/s)	10
90	Mute L12BONG 20	World In My Eyes (Dub In My Eyes)/(Mode To Joy)/Happiest Girl (The Pulsating Orbital Mix) (12", p/s with inner, in sealed blue PVC pack)	25
93	Mute BONG 21	I Feel You/One Caress (p/s)	6
93	Mute 12 BONG 21	I Feel You (Throb Mix)/(Seven Inch Mix)/(Babylon Mix)/One Caress (12", p/s)	20
93	Mute L12 BONG 21	I Feel You (Life's Too Short MIx)/(Swamp Mix)/(Renegade Soundwavwe Afgham Surgery Mix)/(Helmet At The Helm Mix) (12", gatefold p/s)	40
93	Mute 12 BONG 22	Walking In My Shoes (Grungy Gonads Mix)/(Seven Inch Mix)/My Joy (Seven Inch Mix)/(Slow Slide Mix) (12", p/s)	80
93	Mute L12 BONG 22	Walking In My Shoes (Extended)/(Random Carpet Mix)/(Anadamidic Mix)/(Ambient Whale Mix) (12", p/s, gatefold) Mix	40
93	Mute 12 BONG 22	Walking In My Shoes (Grungy Gonads Mix)/(Seven Inch Mix)/My Joy (Seven Inch Mix)/(Slow Slide Mix) (12", p/s, repressing with 'Olympus Studios' misprint))	60
93	Mute 12 BONG 63	Condemnation (Paris MIx)/Death's Door (Jazz Mix)/Rush (Spiritual Guidance Mix)/Rush (Amylnitrate Mix)/Rush (Wild Panet Mix) (12", p/s)	60
94	Mute 12 BONG 25	In Your Room (Zephyr Mix)/(Apex Mix)/(Jeep Rock Mix)/Higher Love (Adrenaline Mix)/In Your Room (Extended Zephyr Mix) (12", p/s, black inner sleeve)	100
94	Mute L12 BONG 24	In Your Room/Policy Of Truth/World In My Eyes/Fly On The Windscreen/Never Let Me Down Again/Death's Door (12", p/s, black inner)	100
97	Mute L12 BONG 25	Painkiller (Plastikman Mix)/Painkiller/Barrel Of A Gun (One inch Punch Mix) (United Mix) (12", p/s)	20
97	Mute 12 BONG 25	Barrel Of A Gun/(Underworld Hard Mix)/(3 Phase Mix)/(One Inch Punch Mix 2)/(Underworld Soft Mix) (12", p/s, gatefold)	15
97	Mute 12 BONG 26	It's No Good (Hardfloor Mix)/(Speedy J Mix)/(Motor Bass Mix)/(Andrea Parker Mix)/(Dom T Mix) (12", p/s)	20
97	Mute 12 BONG 27	Home (Jedi Knights Remix)/(Air Remix)/(LFO Mix)/(Grantby Remix) (12", p/s)	30
97	Mute 12 BONG 28	Useless (Kruder Dorfmeister Session)/(CJ Bolland Funky Sub Mix)/(Air 20 Mix) (12", p/s)	35
98	Mute 12 BONG 29	Only When I Lose Myself (Subsonic Legacy Remix)/(Dan The Automator Remix)/(LUke Slater Remix) (12", p/s)	20
98	Mute L BONG 29	Only When I Lose Myself (Gus Gus Long Play Mix)/Painkiller (DJ Shadow Mix)/Surrender (Catalan FC Out Of Reah Mix) (12", p/s)	40
01	Mute 12 BONG 30	Dream On (Bushwacka Tough Guy Mix)/(Dave Clarke Remix)/(Bushwacka Blunt Mix) (12", p/s)	15
01	Mute 12 BONG 32	Freelove (Console Remix)/(Schlammpeitziger Remix)/Zenstation (Atom's Stereonerd Remix)/Freelove (Bertrand Burgalat Version)/(DJ Muggs Remix) (12", p/s)	30
01	Mute L12 BOONG 31	I Feel Love (Umek Mix)/(Thomas Brinkmann Remix)/(Chamber's Remix) (12", p/s)	25
01	Mute 12 BONG 31	I Feel Loved (Danny Tenaglia Labor Of Love Edit)/(Danny Tenaglia Labour Of Dub Edit) (12", p/s)	15
02	Mute MUTE 12BONG 33	Goodnight Lovers (ISAN Falling Leaf Mix)/When The Body Speaks (Acoustic Version)/The Dead Of Night (Electronicat Remix) (12", red vinyl, p/s)	40
04	Mute 12 BONG 34	Enjoy The Silence (Timo Maas Extended Remix)/(Ewan Pearson Extended Remix) (12", p/s)	20

DEPECHE MODE

MINT VALUE £

Year	Cat No	Title	Value
05	Mute 12 BONG 35	Precious (Sasha's Spooky Mix)/(Sasha's Gargantuan Vocal Mix) (12", p/s)	20
05	Mute BONG 35	Precious/(Michael Mayer Ambient Mix) (picture disc)	20
05	Mute 12 BONG 36	A Pain That I'm Used To (Jacques Lu Cont Remix)/(Jacques Lu Cont Dub) (12", p/s)	25
05	Mute L12 BONG 36	A Pain That I'm Used To (Bitstream Threshold Mix)/(Bistream Spansule Mix) (12", p/s)	25
05	Mute BONG 36	A Pain That I'm Used To (Goldfrapp Remix)/Newborn (Foster Remix) (picture disc)	10
06	Mute BONG 38	John The Revelator (UNKLE Dub)/Lilian (Robag Wruhme Slomoschen Killer) (Picture disc in sealed PVC band, stickered)	15
06	Mute 12 BONG 38	John The Revelator (Dave Is In The Disco Tiefschwartz Remix)/(Tiefschwartz Dub)/Lilian (Chab Dub) (12", p/s)	20
06	Mute L12 BONG 38	John The Revelator (Murk Mode Dub)/(Boosta Club Remix)/Lilian (Chab Vocal Remix) (12", p/s)	25
06	Mute BONG 37	Suffer Well (Metope Vocal Remix)/The Darkest Star (Monolake Remix) (picture disc)	20
06	Mute 12 BONG 37	Suffer Well (Tiga Remix)/(Tiga Dub)/(Narcotic Thrust Vocal Dub (12", p/s)	25
06	Mute L12 BONG 36	Suffer Well (Metope Remix)/(Metope Vocal Remix)/(M83 Remix)/Better Days (12", p/s)	35
06	Mute 12 BONG 37	The Darkest Star (Holden Remix)/(Holden Dub) (12", p/s)	30
06	Mute BONG 39	Martyr/Never Let Me Down Again (Digitalism Remix) (picture disc)	10
06	Mute 12 BONG 39	Martyr (Booka Shade Dub Mix)/(Dreher and Smart BN Reload Mix)/(Alex Smoke Gravel Mix (12", embossed or non-embossed p/s)	15
09	Mute BONG 40	Wrong/Oh Well (p/s)	12
09	Mute 12 BONG 40	Wrong/(Thin White Duke Remix)/(Trentmoller Club Remix)/(Caspa Remix) (12", p/s)	30
09	Mute BONG 41	Peace/Come Back (Jonsi Remix) (p/s, grey marbled vinyl)	8
09	Mute 12 BONG 42	Fragile Tension/Hole To Feed/Perfect/Peace (Mixes) (2x12", p/s)	60
11	Mute 12 BONG 43	Personal Jesus (Alex Metric Remix)/MAN Remix)/(Stargate Mix)/(Eric Prydz Remix)/(Sie-Medway Smith Remix) (12", purple vinyl, p/s)	40
13	Mute 88765 49171 1	Heaven (Blawan Dub)/(Owlle Remix)/(Steps To Heaven Voxdub)/(Matthew Dear V Audion Remix) (12", p/s)	12
13	Mute 88883 73070 1	Soothe My Soul (Steve Angello Vs Jacques Lu Cont Remix)/(Matador Remix)/(Destructo Remix)/(Gregor Tresher Remix) (12", p/s)	12
13	Mute 88883 75834 1	Should Be Higher (Truss Remix)/(MP3IA Definition)/(Koen Groenveveld Massive Remix)/(Pangea Dub Remix)/(Uberzone Remix)/(DJMREX Remix) (12", p/s)	25

ALBUMS

Year	Cat No	Title	Value
82	Mute STUMM 5	SPEAK AND SPELL (LP)	30
82	Mute STUMM 9	A BROKEN FRAME (LP)	30
83	Mute STUMM 13	CONSTRUCTION TIME AGAIN (LP)	30
84	Mute STUMM 19	SOME GREAT REWARD LP, lyric inner)	30
85	Mute MUTEL1	SINGLES 81-85 (LP, gatefold, inner)	35
86	Mute STUMM 26	BLACK CELEBRATION (LP, embossed cover, lyric inner)	40
87	Mute STUMM 47	MUSIC FOR THE MASSES (LP, clear vinyl)	200
87	Mute STUMM 47	MUSIC FOR THE MASSES (LP, with bonus 12" "Strangelove (Maximix)"/"Never Let Me Down Again (Split Mix)" [HMV1])	60
89	Mute STUMM 101	101 (2-LP, stickered gatefold sleeve, inner sleeves and 16-page booklet)	60
89	Mute STUMM 101	101 (2-LP, envelope sleeve, inner sleeves and 16-page booklet)	70
90	Mute STUMM 64	VIOLATOR (LP, inner)	80
90	Mute STUMM 47	MUSIC FOR THE MASSES (LP, reissue, withdrawn, 'budget' sleeve)	3000
93	Mute STUMM 106	SONGS OF FAITH AND DEVOTION (LP, inner)	80
93	Mute STUMM 106	SONGS OF FAITH AND DEVOTION LIVE (LP)	150
97	Mute STUMM 148	ULTRA (LP, inner sleeve with transfer)	200
98	Mute P12MUTEL5	REMIXES 86-98 (3-LP)	40
98	Mute MUTEL 5	THE SINGLES 86-98 (3 x LP, box set with booklet, numbered)	250
01	Mute STUMM 190	EXCITER (2-LP)	100
05	Mute STUMM 260	PLAYING THE ANGEL (2-LP)	100
04	Mute MUTEL 8	MUTE REMIXES 81-04 (6 x LP box set, numbered)	250
07	Mute MUTEL 15	THE BEST OF (3-LP)	150
09	Mute STUMM 300	SOUNDS OF THE UNIVERSE (2-LP)	60
09	Mute BXSTUMM300	SOUNDS OF THE UNIVERSE (4-CD/DVD set)	40
11	Mute MUTEL 18	REMIXES 2: 81-11 (6-LP, box set)	175
13	Mute 88765460631	DELTA MACHINE (2-LP)	30
17	Mute 88985 41165 1	SPIRIT (2-LP, 1 side etched)	20

PROMOS

Year	Cat No	Title	Value
82	Mute 12MUTE 018	See You/This Is Fun (12", white label promo)	40
82	Mute 12 BONG 1	Leave In Silence (Stripped Mix)/Instrumental (12" white label promo)	50
84	Mute 12 BONG 8	Blasphemous Rumours/Somebody (Live)/Two Minute Warning (Live)/Everything Counts (Live)/Ice Machine (Live) (12" white label promo)	60
85	Mute BONG 9	It's Called A Heart/Fly On The Windscreen (12" white label promo with stamped labels)	100
86	Mute BONG 10	Stripped/But Not Tonight (white label test pressing)	250
86	Mute RR BONG 10	Breathing In Fumes/Stripped (Highland Mix) (12", white labels, some stamped)	80
86	Mute 7BONG 12	A Question Of Time (Edited)/Black Celebration (Live) (white label)	100
86	Mute L12 BONG 12	A Question Of Time (New Town Mix)/A Question Of Time (Live)/Black Celebration (Black Tulip Mix)/More Than A Party (Live) (12", printed labels with stamped number, plain black die-cut sleeve)	150
87	Mute CLUB BONG 13	Strangelove (12 Inch Maxi Mix)/(7 Inch Mix) (12" promo)	100
87	Mute DANCE BONG 13	Strangelove (Blind Mix)/(Fresh Ground Mix) (12" promo)	100
87	Mute R BONG 13	Strangelove (Radio Edit)/Strangelove (p/s)	200
87	Mute DANCE BONG 13	Strangelove (Blind Mix)/(Fresh Ground Mix) (12", promo-only remix some on blue vinyl)	80
87	Mute CLUB BONG 13	Strangelove (12 Inch Maxi Mix)/Strangelove (Pain Mix) (12", promo)	80
87	Mute BONG 14	Never Let Me Down Again/Pleasure Little Treasure	125
87	Mute P 12 BONG 14	Never Let Me Down Again (7" Mix)/Pleasure, Little Treasure (7" Mix)/Never Let Me Down Again (12" Split Mix) (12" promo)	100
87	Mute 12BONG 14	Never Let Me Down Again (Split Mix)/Pleasure Little Treasure (Glitter Mix)/Never Let Me Down Again (Aggro Mix) (12")	100

DEPECHE MODE

MINT VALUE £

Year	Cat. No.	Title	Value
87	Mute DJBONG 15	Behind The Wheel (DJ Remix)/Behind The Wheel (LP Mix) ('DJ Bong' ethed in A-side run out groove)	1000
87	Mute D BONG 15	Behind The Wheel (Shep Mix)/Behind The Wheel (LP Mix)/Route 66 (7" Mix) (12")	80
87	Mute (no cat. no.)	THE B-SIDES (4-LP test pressings in title box)	800
87	Mute (no cat. no.)	THE B-SIDES (4-cassette set)	200
87	Mute L 12 BONG 15	Behind The Wheel (Beatmasters Mix)/Route 66 (Casualty Mix) (12" promo stamped white labels)	60
89	Mute S BONG 13	Strangelove (12 Inch Maxi Mix)/(7 Inch Mix)/Pimpf (12" promo)	100
89	Mute BONG 16R	Everything Counts (Live – Radio Edit)/Nothing (Live Mix) (stickered p/s)	100
89	Mute P12 BONG 16	Everything Counts (Tim Simenon/Mark Saunders Remix)/(Alan Moulder Remix) (12", black die-cut sleeve)	80
89	Mute P12 BONG 17	Personal Jesus (Pump Mix)/Dangerous (Hazchemix) (12", black die-cut sleeve)	60
89	Mute BONG 17	Personal Jesus/Dangerous (censored black rear p/s)	200
89	Mute PP 12 BONG 16	Strangelove (Hijack Mix)/Nothing (12", promo)	80
89	Mute CD BONG !7	Personal Jesus (Holier Than Thou Approach)/Dangerous (Sensual Mix)/Personal Jesus (Acoustic) (Promo Cd with censored artwork)	300
90	Mute BONG 18	Enjoy The Silence/Memphisto ('A' label)	200
90	Mute P12 BONG 18	Enjoy The Silence (Bass Line)/(Ricki Tik Tik Mix)/(7" Mix) (12", die-cut Mute sleeve)	70
90	Mute R7 BONG 19	Policy Of Truth (Radio Edit)/Kaleid (p/s)	50
90	Mute BONG 19R	Policy Of Truth (7" Version)/Kaleid (Remix) (CD)	30
90	Mute P12 BONG 19	Policy Of Truth (Capitol Mix)/(Pavlov's Dub) (Trancentral)/Kaleid (Remix) (12", die-cut Mute sleeve)	80
90	Mute 12BONG 20	World In My Eyes (Oil Tank Mix)/Happiest Girl (Kiss-A-Mix)/Sea Of Sin (Sensoria) (12", white label, numbered, stickered sleeve)	100
90	Mute BONG 20R	World In My Eyes (7" Version)/Happiest Girl (Jack Mix)/Sea Of Sin (Tonal Mix) (p/s, 33rpm)	60
90	Mute PSTUMM 64	VIOLATOR (12" EP, 4-track sampler)	30
90	Mute (no cat. no.)	VIOLATOR (LP, CD & cassette in 12" x 12" picture box with insert)	1000
90	Mute P12 BONG 20	World In My Eyes (Mayhem Mode Mix)/Happiest Girl (The Pulsating Orbital Mix) (12", die-cut Mute sleeve)	80
93	Mute P12 BONG 21	I Feel You (Throb Mix)/(Seven Inch Mix)/(Babylon Mix)/One Caress (12", die-cut Mute sleeve)	30
93	Mute BONG 22	Walking In My Shoes/My Joy (large centre hole)	60
93	Mute BONG 23	Condemnation (Paris Mix)/Death's Door (Jazz Mix) (large centre hole)	60
93	Mute PL12BONG 23	Rush (Spiritual Guidance Mix)/Rush (Amylnitrate Mix)/Rush (Wild Planet Vocal Mix) (12")	80
93	Mute P12 BONG 22	Walking In My Shoes (Grungy Gonads Mix)/(Seven Inch Mix)/(Slow Slide Mix) (12", die-cut Mute sleeve)	60
93	Mute P 12 BONG 23	Condemnation (Paris Mix)/Death's Door (Jazz Mix)/Rush (Spiritual Guidance Mix) (12". die-cut Mute sleeve)	50
93	Mute VERBONG 1	SONGS OF FAITH & DEVOTION (interview CD)	50
93	Mute (no cat. no.)	SONGS OF FAITH & DEVOTION (4-CD box set)	300
94	Mute P12 BONG 24	In Your Room (The Jeep Rock Mix)/Higher Love (Adrenaline Mix)/In Your Room (Extended Zephyr Mix) (12", die-cut Mute sleeve)	50
94	Mute DEPRO 1	DEPRO 1 (13-track compilation CD)	50
97	Mute P 12 BONG 25	Barrel Of A Gun/(Underworld Hard Mix)/Painkiller (Plastikman Mix)/(Orignal Edit)/Barrel Of A Gun (Underworld Hard instrumental) (12" promo)	30
97	Mute PL 12 BONG 25	Barrel Of A Gun (One Inch Punch Mix [Version 2])/Painkiller (Original Mix)/Barrel Of A Gun (3 Phase Mix)/Barrel Of A Gun (Original Mix) (12", p/s)	30
97	Mute P 12 BONG 26	It's No Good (Club 69 Future Mix)/It's No Good (Club 69 Future Dub)/It's No Good (Club 69 Funk Dub) (12")	35
97	Mute PL12BONG 26	It's No Good (Club 69 mixes) (12")	40
97	Mute P12BONG26	It's No Good (Hardfloor Mix)/(Speedy J Mix)/(Motor Bass Mix)/(Andrea Parker Mix)/(Dom T Mix) (12")	8
97	Mute XLCDBONG 26	It's No Good (Live) (CD)	70
97	Mute P12 BONG 27	Home (Jedi Knights Remix [Drowning In Time])/(Air "Around The Golf" Remix)/(Meant To Be)/(Grantby Mix) (12", 33rpm, die-cut p/s)	25
97	Mute P12BONG 28	Useless (CJ Bolland Funky Sub Mix)/Useless (the Kruder & Dorfmeister Session™) (12", die-cut p/s)	20
97	Mute BXSTUMM 148	ULTRA (box set, with CD, T-shirt, stickers & EPK video, soap box pack)	250
98	Mute PL 12 BONG 29	Headstar (Luke Slater Remix)/Surrender (Catalan FC Out Of Reach Mix)/Only When I Lose Myself (Gus Gus Mix) (12", promo)	40
98	Mute P12 BONG 29	Only When I Lose Myself (Dan The Automator Mix)/Only When I Lose Myself (Subsonic Legacy Mix)/Painkiller (Kill The Pain — DJ Shadow Vs Depeche Mode)/Headstar (12", die-cut p/s)	50
98	Mute (no cat. no.)	THE SINGLES 86>98 (15" x 6" box set, with 3 CDs, video tape & cards)	120
01	Mute P12BONG 30	Dream On (Bushwacka Tough Guy mixes) (12", p/s)	16
01	Mute PL12 BONG 30	Dream On (Dave Clarke Club Mix)/Dream On (Bushwacka Blunt Mix) (12", p/s)	25
01	Mute PXL12 BONG 30	Dream On (Octagon Man Mix)/(Octagon Man Dub)/(Dave Clarke Acoustic Mix)/(Kid 606 Mix) (12" p/s)	30
01	Mute P 12BONG 31	I Feel Loved (Danny Tenaglia Mixes) (12", p/s)	25
01	Mute P 12 BONG 34	Freelove (Console Remix)/(Schlammpeitziger Remix)/Zenstation (Atom's Stereonerd Remix)/Freelove (Bertrand Burgalat Version)/(DJ Muggs Remix) (12", p/s)	30
01	Mute PL12 BONG 32	Freelove (Deep Dish Freedom Mix)/Freelove (Josh Wink Vocal Interpretation)/Freelove (Deep Dish Freedom Dub)/Freelove (Power Productions Remix) (12", doublepack, p/s)	40
01	Mute PXL12 BONG 31	I Feel Loved (Umek Mix)/(Thomas Brinkman Remix)/(Chamber's Remix) (12", p/s)	30
01	Mute IPKSTUMM 190	EXCITER (interview CD with bonus multimedia disc)	30
01	Mute BCDSTUMM 190	EXCITER (interview CD with bonus multimedia disc, in long box)	60
04	Mute P12BONG 34	REMIXES 81 – 04 SAMPLER : Enjoy The Silence (Richard X Extended Mix)/(Ewan Pearson Extended Instrumental)/Timo Maas Extended Remix)/Ewan Pearson Extended Remix) (2 x 12")	80
04	Mute ACD MUTEL8	REMIXES 81 – 04 (3 x CD, insert & press release)	30
05	Mute PL 12 BONG 35	Precious (Full Vocal Mix)/(Michael Mayer Balearic Mix)/(Motor Mix)/(Crunch Mix) (12", promo)	30
05	Mute P 12 BONG 35	Precious (Sasha's Spooky Mix)/(Sasha's Gargantuan Vocal Mix) (12", promo)	30
05	Mute P12 BONG 36	A Pain That I'm Used To (Jacques Lu Cont Remix)/(Jacques Lu Cont Dub) (12", promo)	50
05	Mute PL 12 BONG 36	A Pain That I'm Used To (Bitstream Threshold Mix)/(Bistream Spansule Mix (12",	50

DEPRAVED

MINT VALUE £

06	Mute PL BONG 37	Suffer Well (Metope Remix)/(Metope Vocal Remix)/(M83 Remix)/Better Days (12", promo)	30
06	Mute P 12 BONG 37	Suffer Well (Tiga Remix)/(Tiga Dub)/(Narcotic Thrust Vocal Dub (12", promo)	30
06	Mute P 12 BONG 39	Martyr (Booka Shade Dub Mix)/(Dreher and Smart BN Reload Mix)/(Alex Smoke Gravel Mix (12", embossed or non-embossed p/s)	20
06	Mute PXL 12 BONG 37	The Darkest Star (Holden Remix)/(Holden Dub) (12", promo)	40

(see also Martin L. Gore, David Gahan)

DEPRAVED
| 86 | Children Of the Revolution GURT 14 | STUPIDITY MAKETH THE MAN (LP, insert) | 15 |

DEPRESSIONS
77	Barn 2014 112	Living On Dreams/Family Planning (p/s)	10
78	Barn 2014 119	Messing With Your Heart/Street Kid (p/s)	10
78	Barn 2014 122	Get Out Of This Town/Basement Daze (p/s)	10
78	Barn 2314 105	THE DEPRESSIONS (LP)	30

DEPTFORD GOTH
| 13 | Merok V2 | LIFE AFTER DEFO (LP, with CD) | 25 |

DEPUTIES
| 66 | Strike JH 305 | Given Half A Chance/Where Do People Go | 12 |

DEPUTY DAWG
| 96 | Peacefrog P F053 | GUN SLINGER EP (12", plain sleeve) | 10 |

(see also Luke Slater)

DELIA DERBYSHIRE
14	Trunk TTT 008	Moogies Bloogies/I Decoded You (Moogies Bloogies Part 2) (p/s, with Anthony Newley, clear vinyl, 500 only)	10
14	Silva Screen SIL 71458	The Delian Mode/Blue Veils And Golden Sands (p/s)	10
19	Electronic Sound ES 759	Doctor Who Theme/Strange Lines And Distances (p/s, yellow vinyl)	15

(see also BBC Radiophonic Workshop)

DEREK
| 68 | London HLZ 10230 | Cinnamon/This Is My Story | 12 |

(see also Johnny Cymbal)

DEREK & THE DOMINOES
70	Polydor 2058 057	Tell The Truth/Roll It Over (withdrawn)	80
70	Polydor 2058 130	Layla/Bell Bottom Blues (original, red paper label)	6
71	Polydor 2625 005	LAYLA AND OTHER ASSORTED LOVE SONGS (2-LP, gatefold sleeve)	40
11	Universal 0600753314326	LAYLA AND OTHER ASSORTED LOVE SONGS (box set, 4-CD, DVD, Book, art print and badge)	45

(see also Eric Clapton, Bobby Whitlock)

DEREK & FRESHMEN
| 65 | Oriole CB 305 | Gone Away/I Stand Alone | 15 |

FRANK DE ROSA & HIS ORCHESTRA
| 58 | London HLD 8576 | Big Guitar/Irish Rock | 10 |

DERRICK (MORGAN) & JENNIFER
| 70 | Crab CRAB 47 | Need To Belong/Let's Have Some Fun | 20 |
| 70 | Crab CRAB 54 | Rocking Good Way/Wipe These Tears | 20 |

(see also Derrick Morgan)

DERRICK (MORGAN) & LLOYDS (CLARKE)
| 62 | Blue Beat BB 135 | Love And Leave Me (actually by Lloyd Clarke)/Merry Twist (actually "Whistle Stop Tour" by Roy Richards) | 15 |

(see also Derrick Morgan, Lloyd Clarke)

DERRICK (MORGAN) & NAOMI (CAMPBELL)
65	Island WI 193	Two Of A Kind/I Want A Lover (credited to Derrick Morgan)	20
65	Ska Beat JB 185	Heart Of Stone/DERRICK MORGAN: Let Me Go	18
65	Ska Beat JB 188	I Wish I Were An Apple/DERRICK MORGAN: Around The Corner	18

(see also Derrick Morgan, Naomi, Don Drummond)

DERRICK (MORGAN) & PATSY (TODD)
61	Blue Beat BB 57	Feel So Fine/ROLAND ALPHONSO & GROUP: Mean To Me	18
61	Blue Beat BB 65	Baby Please Don't Leave Me/Let The Good Times Roll	20
62	Blue Beat BB 97	Love Not To Brag/DRUMBAGO'S ALL STARS: Duck Soup	20
62	Blue Beat BB 100	In My Heart (actually by Derrick Morgan)/BELL'S GROUP: Kingston 13	30
62	Blue Beat BB 106	Oh Shirley/BASIL GABIDON'S GROUP: Sam The Fisherman (B-side actually by Roland Alphonso)	18
62	Blue Beat BB 121	Crying In The Chapel/Come Back My Love	15
62	Blue Beat BB 123	Oh My Love/Let's Go To The Party	15
62	Island WI 018	Housewife's Choice/Gypsy Woman	25
63	Blue Beat BB 152	Little Brown Jug/Mow Sen Wa (with Lloyd Clarke)	15
63	Blue Beat BB 160	Trying To Make You Mine (actually "Baby Please Don't Leave Me" by Derrick Morgan)/Hold Me	15
63	Island WI 055	Sea Wave/Look Before You Leap	20
64	Blue Beat BB 207	Lover Boy/The Moon	15
64	Blue Beat BB 224	Steal Away/Money	15
64	Blue Beat BB 247	Troubles/Right (B-side actually "Baby Face")	15
65	Blue Beat BB 291	You I Love/Let Me Hold Your hand (song actually "Steal Away")	15
65	Blue Beat BB 318	Eternity/Want My Baby	15
65	Island WI 224	The National Dance/DESMOND DEKKER & FOUR ACES: Mount Zion	25
66	Island WI 288	I Found A Queen/It's True My Darling	18
68	Nu Beat NB 008	Hey Boy, Hey Girl/Music Is The Food Of Life	30

(see also Derrick Morgan, Patsy Todd)

DERRICK (MORGAN) & PAULETT
| 69 | Nu Beat NB 027 | I'll Do It/Give You My Love | 20 |

(see also Derrick Morgan, Paulette)

DERRICK (Morgan) & PAULINE (Morgan)
MINT VALUE £

DERRICK (MORGAN) & PAULINE (MORGAN)
68	Pyramid PYR 6027	You Never Miss Your Water/DERRICK MORGAN: Got You On My Mind	18
68	JJ PYR 6063	Don't Say/DERRICK MORGAN: Johnny Pram Pram	85

(see also Derrick Morgan, Patsy Todd, Basil Gabbidon)

DERRICK & SOUNDS
69	Pye 7N 17801	Morning Papers And Margarine/Winter Of Your Love	12

DERRINGERS
61	Capitol CL 15189	(If You Cry) True Love, True Love/Sheree	10

DES ALLSTARS
79	Black Joy DH807	Gone West/West Side (12", yellow/green vinyl)	10

DES (BRYAN) ALLSTARS
70	Grape GR 3014	Night Food Reggae/Walk With Des	80
70	Grape GR 3015	If I Had A Hammer/Hammer Reggae	20
70	Grape GR 3016	Henry The Great/Black Scorcher	125

(see also Rudies (Fanatics))

HENRI DES
70	United Artists UP 35109	Return/Retour	18

SUGAR PIE DE SANTO
64	Pye International 7N 25249	Soulful Dress/Use What You Got	25
64	Pye International 7N 25267	I Don't Wanna Fuss/I Love You So Much	30
66	Chess CRS 8034	There's Gonna Be Trouble/In The Basement (B-side with Etta James)	30
69	Chess CRS 8093	Soulful Dress/There's Gonna Be Trouble	20

(see also Etta James & Sugar Pie De Santo)

MICHAEL DES BARRES
74	Purple PUR 123	Leon/New Moon Tonight	8

(see also Silverhead)

DESCENDANTS
67	CBS 202545	Garden Of Eden/Lela	50

LIZZY MERCIER DESCLOUX
79	Ze ILPS 7001	PRESS COLOUR (LP)	35
83	CBS 25936	LIZZY MERCIER DESCLOUX (LP)	15

DESECTORS
70	GAS GAS 137	King Kong/Please Stay	6

DESERT SESSIONS (JOSH HOLME)
03	Island IS 835	Crawl Home/The Whores Hustle And The Hustlers Whore (p/s)	20

(see also P J Harvey)

DESERT WOLVES
87	Ugly Man UGLY 6	Love Scattered Lives/Stopped In My Tracks (p/s)	20
87	Ugly Man UGLY 6T	Love Shattered Lives/Stopped In My Tracks/Desolation/Sunday Morning (12", p/s)	25
88	Ugly Man UGLY 9	Speak To Me Rochelle/Besotted (p/s)	15
88	Ugly Man UGLY 9T	Speak To Me Rochelle/Mexico/Besotted/La Petite Rochelle (12", p/s)	20

JACKIE DE SHANNON
62	Liberty LIB 55497	You Won't Forget Me/I Don't Think So Much	20
63	Liberty LIB 55563	Needles And Pins/Did He Call Today Mama?	20
64	Liberty LIB 55645	When You Walk In The Room/Till You Say You'll Be Mine	20
64	Liberty LIB 10165	Dancing Silhouettes/Hold Your Head High	15
64	Liberty LIB 10175	Don't Turn Your Back On Me/Be Good Baby	18
65	Liberty LIB 10192	She Don't Understand Him Like I Do/The Prince	12
65	Liberty LIB 10202	What The World Needs Now Is Love/It's Love Baby	7
65	Liberty LIB 12019	A Lifetime Of Loneliness/I Remember The Boy	10
66	Liberty LIB 66224	Come On Down/Find Me Love	20
68	Liberty LBF 15133	The Weight/Effervescent Blue	6
69	Liberty LBF 15238	Put A Little Love In Your Heart/Always Together	8
65	Liberty LEP 2233	JACKIE (EP)	40
64	Liberty LBY 1182 (S)	JACKIE DE SHANNON (LP)	25
65	Liberty LBY 1245	DON'T TURN YOUR BACK ON ME (LP)	25
65	Liberty LBY 3063	THIS IS JACKIE DE SHANNON (LP)	20
66	Liberty SLBY 3085	ARE YOU READY FOR THIS? (LP)	25
68	Liberty LBS 83117E	GREAT PERFORMANCES (LP)	20
69	Liberty LBS 83148E	ME ABOUT YOU (LP)	20
70	Liberty LBS 83304	PUT A LITTLE LOVE IN YOUR HEART (LP)	20
72	Atlantic K 40396	JACKIE (LP)	15

(see also Date With Soul)

DESIGN FOR LIVING
84	Anthem 3	Hold Me Closer/The Girl Who Knew Too Much	18

DESIGN (1)
70	CBS 5112	Willow Stream/Coloured Mile	7
71	Epic EPC 7119	Jet Song/Minstrel's Theme	15
72	Regal Zonophone RZ 3044	Colour All The World/Lazy Song	7
72	Regal Zonophone RZ 3060	Mayday/Yellow Bird (Have You No Home)	6
73	Regal Zonophone RZ 3082	One Sunny Day/End Of The Party	6
76	EMI 2430	Michaelangelo/Never Need Another Love	6
71	Epic EPC 64322	DESIGN (LP)	15
71	Epic EPC 64651	TOMORROW IS SO FAR AWAY (LP, with lyric insert, stickered sleeve)	20
73	Regal Zono. SLRZ 1037	DAY OF THE FOX (LP, textured sleeve, red/silver label)	15

DESIGN (2)
86	Dental 12DENT001	I Want You I Need You/Never Gonna Give You Up (12")	40

DESIRE
79	Carrere CAR 124	Boogie Airlines/Lifting Off	7

DESI ROOTS

MINT VALUE £

DESI ROOTS
79	Hawkeye HD 018	Hung-Up/Up-Town Rebel (12")	50
80	Hawkeye HD 025	Weed Fields/Hawkeye All Stars – Burning (12")	40
80	Hawkeye HD 029	One In A Million/CAROL COOL: Upside Down (12")	25
80	Hawkeye HD 033	Go Deh Right/Revolutionaries Go Right Deh (12", blue vinyl)	30
80	Hakweye HD 037	Youth Attack/TALENT INC: Mobilization/Victory (12")	25
80	Hawkeye HLP 007	DO IT RIGHT (LP)	75
82	Hawkeye HLP 009	CHILDREN IN EXILE (LP)	75

(see also Desi Young)

ANDY DESMOND
75	Konk KONK 103	LIVING ON A SHOESTRING (LP)	40

(see also Gothic Horizon)

JOHNNY DESMOND
55	Vogue Coral Q 72099	Yellow Rose Of Texas/You're In Love With Someone	12
56	Vogue Coral Q 72115	Sixteen Tons/Ballo Italiano	10
57	Vogue Coral Q 72261	A White Sports Coat (And A Pink Carnation)/Just Lookin'	10
60	Philips PB 1044	Hawk/Playing The Field	25
62	Top Rank JAR 612	Twistin' Rose Of Texas/ Hello Honey	7
67	Stateside SS 373	Rio Conchos/Fate In The Hunter	7

LORRAE DESMOND (& REBELS)
54	Decca F 10375	Hold My Hand/On The Waterfront	10
54	Decca F 10398	Far Away (My Love Is Far Away)/No One But You	10
54	Decca F 10404	I Can't Tell A Waltz From A Tango/For Better, For Worse (with Johnston Brothers)	10
55	Decca F 10461	A Boy On Saturday Night/Why — Oh Why?	10
55	Decca F 10510	Don't/Where Will The Baby's Dimple Be?	10
55	Decca F 10533	Stowaway/Heartbroken (B-side with Johnston Brothers)	10
55	Decca F 10612	You Should Know/Wake The Town And Tell The People	6
56	Parlophone R 4239	Written On The Wind/A House With Love In It	6
57	Parlophone R 4287	You Won't Be Around/Play The Music (as Lorrae Desmond & Rebels)	8
57	Parlophone R 4320	Kansas City Special/Preacher, Preacher (as Lorrae Desmond & Rebels)	6
57	Parlophone R 4361	Ding-Dong Rock-a-billy Weddin'/Cabin Boy (as Lorrae Desmond & Rebels)	15
58	Parlophone R 4400	Two Ships/Little David	8
58	Parlophone R 4430	Down By The River/The Secret Of Happiness	6
58	Parlophone R 4463	Soda Pop Hop/Blue, Blue Day	20
59	Parlophone R 4534	Tall Paul/Wait For It	10
60	Parlophone R 4670	Tell Me Again/Get Your Daddie's Car Tonight	10

MIKE DESMOND
57	Columbia DB 3954	Young And In Love/Two Loves (as Michael Desmond)	6
57	Columbia DB 4018	Chances Are/If You're Not Completely Satisfied (as Michael Desmond)	6

PAUL DESMOND
65	RCA RS 7701	BOSSA ANTIGUA (LP, label with red spot)	20
65	RCA Victor SF 7761	GLAD TO BE HAPPY (LP, with Jim Hall)	20

(see also Gerry Mulligan, Dave Brubeck)

DESOLATION ANGELS
84	AM AM 266	Valhalla/Boadicea (p/s)	40
85	Thameside TRR 111	DESOLATION ANGELS (LP)	50

DESPERATE BICYCLES
77	Refill RR 1	Smokescreen/Handlebars (p/s, same tracks both sides)	40
77	Refill RR 2	The Medium Was Tedium/Don't Back The Front (p/s, same tracks both sides)	40
78	Refill RR 3	NEW CROSS NEW CROSS (EP)	40
78	Refill RR 4	Occupied Territory/Skill (p/s)	20
78	Refill RR 7	Grief Is Very Private/Obstructive/Conundrum	20
80	Refill RR 6	REMORSE CODE (LP)	60

DESSIE & JOHN
69	Downtown DT 440	Boss Sound/Everything Is Alright	30

DESSUS
81	Ellie Jay EJSP 9710	Ghetto Children/Dessus Jammin' (with p/s)	25
81	Ellie Jay EJSP 9710	Ghetto Children/Dessus Jammin' (without p/s)	12

DESTINY
80	VLM LP VLM 001	I CAN FEEL HIM (LP)	200

DESTROY ALL MONSTERS
79	Cherry Red CHERRY 3	Bored/You're Gonna Die (p/s, red vinyl)	7
79	Cherry Red CHERRY 7	Meet The Creeper/November 22nd 1963 (p/s)	7
79	Cherry Red CHERRY 9	Nobody Knows/What Do I Get? (p/s)	7

(see also MC5)

DESTROYER (1)
81	Clean Kill SJP 829	Evil Place/Stand And Deliver (no p/s)	50

DESTROYER (2)
13	Dead Oceans DOC 088	FIVE SPANISH SONGS EP (12")	10
14	Dead Oceans DOC 046	KAPUTT (2-LP, white vinyl reissue)	20

DESTROYERS
70	Amalgamated AMG 856	Niney Special/Danger Zone	40
70	Pressure Beat PR 5505	Pressure Tonic/Machuki's Cooking (B-side actually with Count Machuki)	35

(see also Soul Brothers, Nicky Thomas)

DESTRUCTORS
82	KILL 3	Electronic Church/Khymer Rouge Boogie (rubber-stamped white label, 500 only given away with copies of Trees And Flowers punkzine)	50
82	Illuminated ILL 14	Jailbait/Kalgsnocov/Sewage Worker/Image (p/s)	10
82	Carnage Records BOOK 2	SENSELESS VIOLENCE (EP)	10
82	Death DEATH 1	MERRY XMAS & FUCK OFF (LP)	20

Frank DETAILS
MINT VALUE £

83	Radical Change RCLP 2	ARMAGEDDON IN ACTION (LP)	20

(see also Blanks)

FRANK DETAILS
80	Buzz Bomb BB 1	False Pretences/Stranger On A Train (p/s)	10

DETENTE
82	SRTS 82 CUS 1411	Feel Like Crying/On My Own	6

DETERGENTS
65	Columbia DB 7513	Leader Of The Laundromat/Ulcers	12
65	Columbia DB 7591	I Don't Know/The Blue Kangaroo	6

DETONATORS (1)
78	Local LR 1	Need Love Tonight/Great Big Ghetto/Shoob Shooby Do/Give Me A Helping Hand (p/s)	6

DETONATORS (2)
79	Burning Rockers BR 1008	GANGSTER (LP)	20

DETOURS (1)
68	CBS 3213	Run To Me Baby/Hangin' On	50
68	CBS 3401	Whole Lotta Lovin'/Pieces Of You	200

(see also Gene Latter)

DETRIUS
90	Under One Flag FLAG 55	PERPETUAL DEFIANCE (LP, with inner sleeve)	15

DETROIT WITH MITCH RYDER
72	Paramount SPFL 277	DETROIT (LP)	20

(see also Mitch Ryder)

DETROIT EMERALDS
71	Pye International 7N 25544	Do Me Right/Just Now And Then	6

DETROIT ESCALATOR CO.
96	Ferox FERLP 2	SOUNDTRACK (313) (LP)	20

DETROIT MAGNIFICENTS
06	Grapevine GRP 161	Is This A Woman's Way/Where Can I Find Love	10

DETROIT SPINNERS
65	Tamla Motown TMG 514	Sweet Thing/How Can I? (demo credited to 'Spinners')	425
65	Tamla Motown TMG 514	Sweet Thing/How Can I? (demo credited to 'Detroit Spinners')	250
65	Tamla Motown TMG 514	Sweet Thing/How Can I? (stock copies credited to 'Spinners')	425
65	Tamla Motown TMG 523	I'll Always Love You/Tomorrow May Never Come (as 'Spinners')	110
65	Tamla Motown TMG 523	I'll Always Love You/Tomorrow May Never Come (as 'Detroit Spinners')	75
65	Tamla Motown TMG 523	I'll Always Love You/Tomorrow May Never Come (as 'Spinners' or 'Detroit Spinners' DJ Copy)	250
67	Tamla Motown TMG 627	For All We Know/I'll Always Love You (1st pressing with tall, narrow print)	25
67	Tamla Motown TMG 627	For All We Know/I'll Always Love You (2nd pressing)	18
70	Tamla Motown TMG 755	It's A Shame/Together We Can Make Such Sweet Music (unissued)	0
70	Tamla Motown TMG 755	It's A Shame/Sweet Thing (as Motown Spinners)	7
71	Tamla Motown TMG 766	Together We Can Make Such Sweet Music/Truly Yours (as Motown Spinners)	7
75	Atlantic K10571	Living A Little, Laughing A Lot/I've Got To Make It On My Own	20
80	Atlantic K 11558	Split Decision/Now That You're Mine Again (12")	12
82	Atlantic 9891	I'll Be Around/City Full Of Memories	6
68	T. Motown TML 11060	THE DETROIT SPINNERS (LP, mono)	50
68	T. Motown STML 11060	THE DETROIT SPINNERS (LP, stereo)	60
71	T. Motown STML 11182	SECOND TIME AROUND (LP, as Motown Spinners)	20

(see also G.C. Cameron)

DEUCE
86	1986 Powermetal VB004	Backs To The Ball/Queen Of The Night/Jealousy	10

DEUCE COUP
67	Mercury MF 1013	A Clown In One Town/Angela (in p/s)	12
67	Mercury MF 1013	A Clown In One Town/Angela (no p/s)	6

DEUCE OF HEARTS
66	CBS 202345	Closer Together/The Times They Are A Changin'	10

JIMMY DEUCHAR
54	Esquire EP 53	JIMMY DEUCHAR (EP)	50
55	Tempo EXA 18	JIMMY DEUCHAR ENSEMBLE (EP)	50
56	Esquire EP 93	JIMMY DEUCHAR QUARTET (EP)	50
56	Esquire EP 103	JIMMY DEUCHAR QUARTET (EP)	50
58	Tempo EXA 79	OPUS DE FUNK (EP, as Jimmy Deuchar Sextet)	50
58	Tempo EXA 81	SWINGIN' IN STUDIO TWO (EP)	50
59	Tempo EXA 88	WAIL (EP, with Victor Feldman Quintet)	50
54	Esquire 20-059	DIG DEUCHAR, DON'T DANCE (10", LP)	125
55	Tempo LAP 2	JIMMY DEUCHAR ENSEMBLE (10" LP)	275
56	Tempo TAP 4	TOP TRUMPETS (LP)	250
56	Vogue LDE 023	SHOWCASE (LP)	80
58	Tempo TAP 20	PAL JIMMY (LP)	750

(see also Victor Feldman)

BIG PETE DEUCHAR/DUKER
63	Fontana 267 278 TF	Google Eye/There's A Hand Leading Me (as Big Pete Deuchar)	8
63	Fontana TF 423	It Comes And Goes/Married By The Bible	8
65	Columbia DB 7763	Goin' In Training/I Saw Your Face In The Moon (as Big Pete Duker)	8

DEUS
94	Island 155981854 018-7	Suds & Soda/Secret Hell (limited edition, numbered)	25
94	Island 1215598854-019-7	Suds And Soda (Extended Version)/Texan Coffee/Secret Hell/Furniture In The Far West (12")	20
94	Island 15599/854 150 7	Via/Violins And Happy Endings	12
95	Island 15603/854 188-7	Hotel Lounge (Be The Death Of Me)/Jigsaw You (Live) (limited edition, die-cut sleeve)	8
96	Island 1015630/854 682-0	Theme From Turnpike/Overflow/My Little Contessa (10", gatefold sleeve)	10
99	Island 15750/562-109-7	Sister Dew (Album Version)/Thirteen (Live) (with poster)	6

DEUX

			MINT VALUE £
99	Island IS 714	Instant Street/Dream Sequence 1 (Demo) (p/s)	6
94	Island ILPS 8028/524-0451	WORST CASE SCENARIO (LP, limited edition with postcard and CD booklet)	70
96	Island ILPS 8052/52429-1	IN A BAR UNDER THE SEA (LP, with inner sleeve)	60
99	Island ILPS 8082/524 643-1	THE IDEAL CRASH (LP)	60
05	V2 VVR 1034711	POCKET REVOLUTION (2-LP)	40
08	V2 VVR 1050471	VANTAGE POINT (LP)	30

DEUX
19	Electronic Sound ES 751	Europe/Paris/Orly (p/s, reissue)	15

DEUX FILLES
82	Papier Mache PULP 81	SILENCE & WISDOM (LP)	80
83	Papier PULP 32	DOUBLE HAPPINESS (LP)	25

DEVASTATING AFFAIR
73	Mowest 3010	That's How It Was (Right From The Start)/It's So Sad	10
73	Mowest 3010	That's How It Was (Right From The Start)/It's So Sad (DJ copy)	20

WILLIAM DEVAUGHN
74	Chelsea 2306 002	BE THANKFUL FOR WHAT YOU'VE GOT (LP)	40
89	Start CHELV 1001	BE THANKFUL FOR WHAT YOU'VE GOT (LP, reissue)	20

DEVASTATION
84	Creative Reality REAL 8	DRAG YOU DOWN EP	20

DEVIANTS
68	Stable STA 5601	You Got To Hold On/Let's Loot The Supermarket	20
67	Underground Imp. IMP 1	PTOOFF! (LP, foldout sleeve, private pressing via IT magazine)	400
68	Stable SLP 007	DISPOSABLE (LP, gatefold sleeve, red/black label)	300
69	Transatlantic TRA 204	THE DEVIANTS (LP, with booklet, white/lilac label with 't' logo)	300
69	Transatlantic TRA 204	THE DEVIANTS (LP, without booklet, white/lilac label with 't' logo)	150
69	Decca LK-R/SKL-R 4993	PTOOFF! (LP, reissue, large unboxed logo on label)	90
78	Logo MOGO 4001	THE DEVIANTS (LP, reissue)	15
84	Psycho PSYCHO 25	HUMAN GARBAGE (LIVE AT DINGWALLS '84) (LP)	15

(see also Mick Farren, Pink Fairies, Larry Wallis)

DEVIATED INSTINCT
86	Peaceville WARP 2	WELCOME TO THE ORGY EP	15
88	Peaceville VILE 3	ROCK 'N' ROLL CONFORMITY (LP, inner)	25
90	Prophecy PRO 004	NAILED EP (12", p/s)	20
90	Peaceville VILE 16	GUTTURAL BREATH (LP)	20

ROLAND DEVILLE
80	Dummy DUMB 1	Come Dancing/Dial 9 (p/s)	10

DEVIL'S HOLE GANG
70s	Slow Burning Fuse SSSS 1	Free The People/Isn't It/Something To Look Forward To (p/s, with insert)	12

JOHNNY DEVLIN (& DETOURS)
64	Pye 7N 15598	Sometimes/If You Want Someone (as Johnny Devlin & Detours)	6

DEVO
78	Stiff DEV 1	Jocko Homo/Mongoloid (foldout p/s)	15
79	Elevator NICE 1	Mechanical Man/Blockhead/Blackout/Auto-Modern (official bootleg, red/yellow stamped sleeves)	8
18	Electronic Sound ES 744	Uncontrollable Urge/Sloppy (I Saw My Baby Gettin') (p/s)	20
20	Electronic Sound ES 767	Whip It/Snowball (p/s, reissue, white vinyl)	10
78	Virgin V 2106	Q: ARE WE NOT MEN? (LP, various coloured vinyl)	30
78	Virgin VP 2106	Q: ARE WE NOT MEN? (LP, picture disc, with 'Flimsy Wrap' 33rpm 1-sided flexidisc [VDJ 27/Lyntone LYN 6260])	15
79	Stiff ODD 1	B-STIFF (Mini-LP, 6 tracks released as Stiff singles)	15
79	Virgin V2125	DUTY NOW FOR THE FUTURE (LP, promo version with stock LP but different sleeve from official release)	20
79	Virgin V2125	DUTY NOW FOR THE FUTURE (LP, with red or blue band on front sleeve, card insert)	20
80	Virgin V2162	FREEDOM OF CHOICE (LP, stickered sleeve with poster)	20
81	Virgin V2191	NEW TRADITIONALISTS (LP)	15
82	Virgin V2241	OH NO. IT'S DEVO! (LP)	15
90	Enigma ENVLP 1006	SMOOTH NOODLE MAPS (LP)	18

DEVON (RUSSELL) & SEDRIC (MYTON)
69	Blue Cat BS 158	What A Sin Thing/Short Up Dress	60

(see also Congos)

DEVON (RUSSELL) & TARTANS
68	Nu Beat NB 021	Let's Have Some Fun/Making Love	25

(see also Tartans)

DEVONNES
06	Kent 6T 21	Doin The Gittin' Up/MAYBERRY MOVEMENT: I See Him Making Love To You	20

BARRY DE VORZON
58	RCA RCA 1066	Barbara Jean/JIMMY DELL: Teeny Weeny	50
60	Philips PB 993	Betty Betty (Go Steady With Me)/Across The Street	25

(see also Barry & Tamerlanes, Jimmy Dell)

DEVOTED
68	Page One POF 076	I Love George Best/United (p/s)	35
68	Page One POF 076	I Love George Best/United	15

DEVOTION
79	Sapphire	Devotion/Acid/Energy For The Universe (no p/s)	50

DEVOTIONS
64	Columbia DB 7256	Rip Van Winkle/(I Love You) For Sentimental Reasons	100

DEWDROPS
67	Blue Beat BB 381	Somebody's Knocking/By And By	25

BRIAN DEWHURST
75	Folk Heritage FHR 075	THE HUNTER & THE HUNTED (LP, black label and laminated sleeve)	20

Harry DE WIT

MINT VALUE £

HARRY DE WIT
| 79 | Bead Records BEAD 11 | APRIL '79 (LP) .... | 25 |
| 79 | Bead Records BEAD 12 | FOR HARM (LP, with Philipp Wachsmann) .... | 25 |

DANNY DEXTER
| 63 | London HLU 9690 | Sweet Mama/Go On .... | 8 |

LEVI DEXTER (AND THE RIPCHORDS)
| 80 | Mistral BLOW 1 | IN THE BEGINNING... (EP) .... | 10 |

RAY DEXTER & LAYABOUTS
| 62 | Decca F 11538 | The Coalman's Lament/Lonely Weekend .... | 30 |

DEXYS MIDNIGHT RUNNERS
80	Oddball R 6028	Dance Stance/I'm Just Looking (p/s)	6
80	Late Night Feelings R 6042	Keep It Part Two (Inferiority Part One)/One Way Love (p/s)	6
14	Absolute 7DEXY 1	Nowhere Is Home/I Love You (Listen To This) (die-cut cover)	15
80	Parlophone/Late Night Feelings PCS 7213	SEARCHING FOR THE YOUNG SOUL REBELS (LP, 1st issue with inner)	20
85	Mercury MERH 56	DON'T STAND ME DOWN (LP)	20
14	Absolute DEXLP1	NOWHERE IS HOME (4-LP)	60

(see also Killjoys)

TRACEY DEY
| 64 | Stateside SS 287 | Go Away/Gonna Get Along Without You Now .... | 18 |

DEZIGN
| 84 | EN AY DZ 256 | Love Myth/Let's Go (no p/s) .... | 10 |

DEZZI D
| 05 | Vibes House VH008 | Judas/Dub Version .... | 15 |

BOBBY D'FANO
| 63 | Palette PG 9038 | Message Of Love/The Kiss That Broke My Heart .... | 10 |

DHAIMA
| 77 | Paradise PD 006 | Jah Jah I/Version .... | 10 |
| 78 | Lightning LIG 528 | Ina Jah Children/MIGHTY TWO: Save The Children .... | 60 |

DHARMA BLUES BAND
| 69 | Major Minor SMCP 5017 | DHARMA BLUES (LP, yellow/white/black label) .... | 125 |

(see also Hawkwind)

ALI BEN DHOWN
| 67 | Piccadilly 7N 35395 | Musapha/Turkish Delight .... | 30 |

DIABOLIKS
| 00 | Vinyl Japan ASKLP P116 | THREE FUR BURGERS...AND A HOT CHILLI DOG TO GO! (LP) .... | 15 |

DIAGONAL
| 10 | Rise Above 127 FREE | Stop/ASTRA: Empty Spaces (300 only, gig freebie) .... | 12 |

DIAGRAM BROTHERS
80	Construct CON 1	We Are All Animals/There Is No Shower/Would I Like To Live In Prison	15
81	New Hormones ORG 9	Bricks/Postal Bargains (p/s)	8
82	New Hormones ORG 21	DISCORDO EP	10

DIALS (JAMAICA)
| 69 | Duke DU 48 | Bye Bye Love/It's Love .... | 12 |
| 69 | Duke DU 49 | Love Is A Treasure/DIAMONDS: I Want To Be .... | 12 |

DIALS (U.K.)
| 79 | Wessex WEX 266 | Maxine/Hey Denise (p/s) .... | 7 |
| 79 | Scene ACT1 | All I Hear/Running (p/s) .... | 10 |

BRIAN DIAMOND & THE CUTTERS
63	Decca F 11724	Jealousy Will Get You Nowhere/Brady Brady	15
64	Fontana TF 452	Shake, Shout And Go/Wotcha Gonna Do Now Pretty Baby	150
65	Pye 7N 15779	Big Bad Wolf/See If I Care	15
65	Pye 7N 15952	Bone Idol/Sands Of Time	15

GREGG DIAMOND'S BIONIC BOOGIE
79	Urban URBX 16	Hot Butterfly/Mess Up The Boogie/When The Shit Hits The Fan (12", p/s)	10
79	Polydor POSPX 50	Chains/Hot Butterfly (12")	15
79	Polydor 2391322	BIONIC BOOGIE (LP)	15
78	Polydor 2391373	HOT BUTTERFLY (LP)	15

JERRY DIAMOND
| 57 | London HLE 8496 | Sunburned Lips/Don't Trust Love .... | 20 |

LEE DIAMOND (& CHEROKEES)
| 61 | Fontana H 310 | I'll Step Down/Josephine (as Lee Diamond & Cherokees) .... | 10 |
| 61 | Fontana H 345 | Stop Your Crying/You'll Want Me .... | 10 |

(see also Cherokees)

NEIL DIAMOND
66	London HLZ 10049	Solitary Man/Do It	10
66	London HLZ 10072	Cherry, Cherry/I'll Come Running	10
66	London HA-Z 8307	THE FEEL OF NEIL DIAMOND (LP)	20

DIAMOND BOYS
| 62 | Parlophone GIB 102 | Fool In Love/New Orleans (export issue) .... | 25 |
| 63 | RCA RCA 1351 | Hey Little Girl/What'd I Say .... | 15 |

(see also Albert Ammons)

DIAMOND HEAD
80	Happy Face MMDH 120	Shoot Out The Lights/Helpless (p/s)	15
80	Media SCREEN 1	Sweet And Innocent/Streets Of Gold (p/s)	15
81	DHM DHM 004	Waited Too Long/Play It Loud (p/s)	7
81	DHM DHM 005	DIAMOND LIGHTS EP (Diamond Lights/We Won't Be Back/I Don't Got/It's Electric) (12", p/s)	20
82	MCA DHMT 101	FOUR CUTS (12" EP, with insert)	12
83	MCA DHM 103	Makin' Music/(Andy Peebles Interview)/To The Devil His Due (p/s)	8
83	MCA DHMT 103	Makin' Music/(Andy Peebles Interview) (12", p/s)	15

DIAMONDS (JAMAICA)

MINT VALUE £

83	MCA DHMT 104	Out Of Phase/The Kingmaker/Sucking My Love (live) (12", p/s)	25
80	DHM MMDHLP 105	LIGHTNING TO THE NATIONS (LP, plain or printed white labels, plain white sleeve, sold at gigs, signed in blue ink & available via Sounds)	100
80	DHM MMDHLP 105	LIGHTNING TO THE NATIONS (LP, plain or printed white labels, plain white sleeve, sold at gigs)	50
81	MCA DH 1001	LIVING ON BORROWED TIME (LP, gatefold sleeve with inner sleeve, with poster & fan club insert)	25
81	MCA DH 1001	LIVING ON BORROWED TIME (LP, gatefold sleeve with inner sleeve)	15
82	MCA DH1001	BORROWED TIME (LP, with poster)	25
83	MCA DH 1002	CANTERBURY (LP, with lyric and tour dates sheet, first pressing faulty and jumps)	15
86	Metal Masters METALP 110	BEHOLD THE BEGINNING (LP, remixed reissue of 1st LP)	20
87	FM WKFMLP 92	AM I EVIL (LP, with inner sleeve)	20

DIAMONDS (JAMAICA)

72	Songbird SB 1079	Mash Up/DYNAMITES: Mash Up (Version)	10
75	Attack ATT 8108	Jah Jah Bless Your Dreadlocks/Version	15
75	Attack ATT 8113	Just Can't Figure Out/Just Can't Figure Out (Version)	12
75	Black Wax WAX 5	Country Living/A Living Version	12
78	Virgin V2102	PLANET EARTH (LP)	20

(see also Dymonds, Mighty Diamonds)

DIAMONDS (U.K.)

63	Philips BF 1264	The Lost City/Chasey Chasey (John Peel)	10

DIAMONDS (U.S.)

55	Vogue Coral Q 72109	Black Denim Trousers And Motorcycle Boots/Nip Sip	30
58	Mercury 7MT 187	Silhouettes/Honey Bird	25
58	Mercury 7MT 195	The Stroll/Land Of Beauty	10
58	Mercury 7MT 207	Don't Let Me Down/High Sign	10
58	Mercury 7MT 208	Straight Skirts/Patsy	50
59	Mercury AMT 1024	She Say (Oom Dooby Doom)/From The Bottom Of My Heart	6
60	Mercury AMT 1086	Tell The Truth/Real True Love	30
61	Mercury AMT 1156	One Summer Night/It's A Doggone Shame	15
57	Mercury MEP 9515	PRESENTING THE DIAMONDS (EP)	20
57	Mercury MEP 9523	THE DIAMONDS VOL. 1 (EP)	20
58	Mercury MEP 9527	THE DIAMONDS VOL. 2 (EP)	20
58	Mercury MEP 9530	THE DIAMONDS VOL. 3 (EP)	20
59	Mercury ZEP 10003	DIG THE DIAMONDS (EP)	20
59	Mercury ZEP 10020	THE DIAMONDS MEET PETE RUGOLO (EP)	15
60	Mercury ZEP 10053	STAR STUDDED DIAMONDS (EP)	15
59	Mercury ZEP 10026	DIAMONDS ARE TRUMPS (EP)	15
61	Mercury ZEP 10097	PETE RUGOLO LEADS THE DIAMONDS (EP, mono)	10
61	Mercury SEZ 10912	PETE RUGOLO LEADS THE DIAMONDS (EP, stereo)	10
57	Mercury MPT 7526	THE DIAMONDS (10" LP)	40

(see also Pete Rugolo)

DIAMOND TWINS

66	HMV POP 1508	Crying The Night Away/Start The World Spinning Again	6

(see also Sonia Kent)

DIANA

82	Oak Sounds OSD 003	When Music Hits You/Feel No Pain Combination (12")	60
83	A1 A1002	Flowers/A1 Dub (12")	15
83	A1 A1003	The Feeling/Dubbing Feeling (12")	15

ALENA DIANE

06	Names NAMES 25	SONGS WHISTLED THROUGH WHITE TEETH (EP, 10", 500 only)	12

DIANE & JAVELINS

66	Columbia DB 7819	Heart And Soul/Who's The Girl	55

(PAUL) DI'ANNO

84	FM VHF 1	Heart User/Road Rat (p/s)	8
84	FM WKFM LP1	DI'ANNO (LP, blue vinyl, stickered sleeve)	15
84	FM WKFM PD1	DI'ANNO (LP, picture disc)	18

(see also Gogmagog, Iron Maiden)

DIATONES

61	Starlite ST45 057	Ruby Has Gone/Oh Baby Come Dance With Me	100

DIATRIBE

84	Criminal Damage CRI 12 123	DIATRIBE EP	15

DANNY DIAZ & THE CHECKMATES

69	Pye 7N 17690	Solomon Grundy/Goodbye Baby	15

MANU DIBANGO

73	London HL 10423	Soul Makossa/Lily	10
73	London SH 8451	O BOSO (LP)	25
75	Creole CRLP 503	MAKOSSA MUSIC (LP)	15
78	Decca SKL-R 5296	AFROVISION (LP)	15
78	Decca SKL-R 5303	SUN EXPLOSION (LP)	15
86	Gallo GSL 289	SUPER KUMBA (LP, reissue)	15

BILLY DICE & SHENLEY DUFFUS

73	Pama 874	Women Smarter/Standing On The Hill (B-side with uncredited Silvertones)	12

(see also Billy Dyce)

DICE THE BOSS

69	Joe DU 50	Brixton Cat Big And Fat/JOES ALL STARS : Solitude	55
69	Duke/Joe DU 51	Gun The Man Down/JOE MANSANO: The Thief	50
69	Duke/Joe DU 52	But Officer/JOE'S ALL STARS: Reggae On The Shore	50
70	Duke/Joe DU 57	Your Boss D.J./TITO SIMON: Read The News	80
70	Joe's JRS 17	The Informer/Cool It	40
70	Explosion EX 2017	Funky Monkey/JOE'S ALL STARS: Funky Monkey Version	15

70	Explosion EX 2020	Funky Duck/Dunkier Than Duck	15

(see also Joe The Boss, Ray Martel)

LLOYD DICE
70	Joe JRS 5	Trial Of Pama Dice/JOE: Jughead Returns	25

(see also Trevor Lloyd)

PAMA DICE
70	Reggae 3002	Brixton Pum Pum Wrecker/JOE ALLSTARS: Version (White label, possibly unreleased)	100
69	Jackpot JP 715	Honky Tonk Popcorn/Bongo Man	40
69	Jackpot JP 715	Bongo Man/Bear De Pussy	30
69	Jackpot JP 716	Sin, Sun And Sex/Reggae Popcorn	30
70	Reggae REG 3001	Brixton Fight/OPENING: Tea House	150

(see also Dice The Boss, Joe The Boss)

DICEMEN
83	Random MCPS RR1	Number 19/A Year Without You/Sunrise/Today	15

DICK & DEE DEE
61	London HLG 9408	The Mountain's High/I Want Someone	8
62	London HLG 9483	Goodbye To Love/Swing Low	10
65	Warner Bros WB 156	Be My Baby/Room 404	10
63	Warner Bros WM 8132	YOUNG AND IN LOVE (LP, mono)	25
63	Warner Bros WS 8132	YOUNG AND IN LOVE (LP, stereo)	25

CHARLES DICKENS
65	Pye 7N 15887	That's The Way Love Goes/In The City	25
65	Pye 7N 15938	I Stand Alone/Hey Little Girl	10
66	Immediate IM 025	So Much In Love/Our Soul Brothers	40

(see also Habits)

DOLES DICKEN'S BAND
58	London HLD 8639	Piakukaungchung (Pie-ah-coo-ka-ung-chung)/Our Melody	10

LITTLE JIMMY DICKENS
54	Columbia DC 670	Then I Had To Turn Around/Hot Diggity Dog (78, export issue)	8

DICKIES
78	A&M AMS 7403	Silent Night/The Sounds Of Silence (p/s, white vinyl)	6
79	A&M AMS 7491	Manny, Moe And Jack/She Loves Me Not (p/s, black vinyl only)	8
80	A&M AMS 7504	Fan Mail/Tricia Toyota (I'm Stuck In A Pagoda) (opaque or translucent red vinyl, poster p/s)	6
80	A&M AMS 7544	Gigantor/Bowling With Bedrock Barney (yellow vinyl, p/s with full colour or b&w reverse)	8
90	Overground OVER 12	Just Say Yes/Ayatollah You So (p/s with lyric sheet, mauve, blue or white vinyl, 2,000 of each colour)	7
79	A&M AMLE 64742	THE INCREDIBLE SHRINKING DICKIES (LP, black or yellow vinyl)	20
79	A&M AMLE 64742	THE INCREDIBLE SHRINKING DICKIES (LP, blue vinyl, with black or red-and-black on sleeve)	20
79	A&M AMLE 64742	THE INCREDIBLE SHRINKING DICKIES (LP, orange vinyl, with black or red-and-black on sleeve)	20
79	A&M AMLH 68510	DAWN OF THE DICKIES (LP, blue vinyl)	25
79	A&M AMLH 68510	DAWN OF THE DICKIES (LP, black vinyl)	15

(see also Chuck Wagon)

BRUCE DICKINSON
90	EMI EMPD 138	Tattooed Millionaire/Ballad Of Mutt (uncut shaped picture disc)	40
90	EMI EMPD 142	All The Young Dudes/Darkness Be My Friend (uncut shaped picture disc)	25
94	EMI EMD 1057	BALLS TO PICASSO (LP, gatefold sleeve)	50
95	Raw DV 102	ALIVE IN STUDIO (2-LP, gatefold with inners)	60
96	Raw Power RAWLP 106	SKUNKWORKS (LP, gatefold, inner)	80
97	Raw Power RAWLP 124	ACCIDENT OF BIRTH (LP)	75

(see also Iron Maiden, Samson, Xero, Speed)

BARBARA DICKSON
70	Decca SKL 5041	THRO' RECENT YEARS (LP, with Archie Fisher)	50
71	Decca SKL 5058	DO RIGHT WOMAN (LP)	40
72	Decca SKL 5116	FROM THE BEGGAR'S MANTLE FRINGED WITH GOLD (LP)	35
74	RSO 2394 141	JOHN, PAUL, GEORGE, RINGO AND BERT (LP, with London cast)	30

DICK TURPIN
70	Evolution E 2446	If You've Got The Time/Madeline	180

DICTATORS WITH TONY & HOWARD
63	Oriole CB 1934	So Long Little Girl/Say Little Girl	20

(see also Tony & Howard)

DICTATORS
75	Epic S EPC 80767	GO GIRL CRAZY (LP)	20
77	Asylum K 53061	MANIFEST DESTINY (LP, lyric inner)	15
78	Asylum K 53083	BLOOD BROTHERS LP, inner)	15

BO DIDDLEY
59	London HLM 8913	The Great Grandfather/Crackin' Up	50
59	London HLM 8913	The Great Grandfather/Crackin' Up (78)	20
59	London HLM 8975	Say Man/The Clock Strikes Twelve	70
59	London HLM 8975	Say Man/The Clock Strikes Twelve (78)	20
60	London HLM 9035	Say Man, Back Again/She's Alright	80
60	London HLM 9112	Road Runner/My Story	50
62	Pye Intl. 7N 25165	You Can't Judge A Book By The Cover/I Can Tell	15
63	Pye Intl. 7N 25193	Who Do You Love?/The Twister	20
63	Pye Intl. 7N 25210	Bo Diddley/Detour	20
63	Pye Intl. 7N 25216	You Can't Judge A Book By The Cover/I Can Tell (reissue)	10
63	Pye Intl. 7N 25217	Pretty Thing/Road Runner	10
63	Pye Intl. 7N 25227	Bo Diddley Is A Lover/Doin' The Jaguar	12

Year	Label/Cat#	Title	Value £
64	Pye Intl. 7N 25235	Memphis/Monkey Diddle	12
64	Pye Intl. 7N 25243	Mona/Gimme Gimme	15
64	Pye Intl. 7N 25258	Mama Keep Your Big Mouth Shut/Jo-Ann	12
65	Chess CRS 8000	Hey Good Lookin'/You Ain't Bad (As You Claim To Be)	10
65	Chess CRS 8014	Somebody Beat Me/Mush Mouth Millie	12
65	Chess CRS 8021	Let The Kids Dance/Let Me Pass	10
66	Chess CRS 8026	500% More Man/Stop My Monkey	10
66	Chess CRS 8036	We're Gonna Get Married/Easy	10
67	Chess CRS 8053	Ooh Baby/Back To School	12
67	Chess CRS 8057	Wrecking My Love Life/Boo-Ga-Loo Before You Go	20
68	Chess CRS 8078	Another Sugar Daddy/I'm High Again	10
69	Chess CRS 8088	Bo Diddley 1969/Soul Train	10
56	London RE-U 1054	RHYTHM AND BLUES WITH BO DIDDLEY (EP, gold label lettering)	200
63	Pye Intl. NEP 44014	HEY! BO DIDDLEY (EP)	20
64	Pye Intl. NEP 44019	THE STORY OF BO DIDDLEY (EP)	20
64	Pye Intl. NEP 44031	BO DIDDLEY IS A LUMBERJACK (EP)	20
64	Pye Intl. NEP 44036	DIDDLING (EP)	20
65	Chess CRE 6008	I'M A MAN (EP)	20
66	Chess CRE 6023	ROOSTER STEW (EP)	20
59	London HA-M 2230	GO BO DIDDLEY (LP)	350
62	Pye Jazz NJL 33	BO DIDDLEY IS A GUNSLINGER (LP)	50
63	Pye Intl. NPL 28025	HEY! BO DIDDLEY (LP)	25
63	Pye Intl. NPL 28026	BO DIDDLEY (LP)	25
63	Pye Intl. NPL 28029	BO DIDDLEY RIDES AGAIN (LP)	25
63	Pye Intl. NPL 28032	BO DIDDLEY'S BEACH PARTY (LP)	25
64	Pye Intl. NPL 28034	BO DIDDLEY IN THE SPOTLIGHT (LP)	25
64	Pye Intl. NPL 28049	16 ALL-TIME HITS (LP)	15
64	Chess CRL 4002	HEY GOOD LOOKIN' (LP)	20
65	Chess CRL 4507	LET ME PASS (LP)	25
67	Chess CRL 4525	THE ORIGINATOR (LP)	25
68	Chess CRL 4529	SUPER BLUES (LP, with Muddy Waters & Little Walter)	20
68	Chess CRL 4537	THE SUPER SUPER BLUES BAND (LP, with Muddy Waters & Howlin' Wolf)	20
71	Chess 6310107	ANOTHER DIMENSION (LP)	20

(see also Chuck Berry & Bo Diddley)

DIDO
00	Cheeky 74321 86823 1	NO ANGEL (LP, gatefold)	75

DIE ELECTRIC EELS
78	Rough Trade RT 008	Agitated/Cyclotron (p/s)	15

DIE LAUGHING
80	Ocean OC 003	Hard Living Man/You Got The Power (p/s)	50

DIESEL M
94	Choci's Chewns CCB 001	M for Multiple (12", blue vinyl, 666 only)	25
95	Choci's Chewns DDL 001	M For Mangoes (12", red vinyl, 666 only)	25

DIF JUZ
81	4AD BAD 109	HU/RE/MI/CS (12" EP)	10
81	4AD BAD 116	VIBRATING AIR: Heset/Diselt/Gunet/Soarn (12" EP)	15

DIFFERENT EYES
79	Tuzmadoner TUZMADONER 001	Open The Box/Uncomfortable//ROYSTON: Snake's Song/Gerald's Eyes (stapled photocopied cover, rubber-stamped labels)	100

DIGA RHYTHM BAND
76	United Artists UAG 29975	DIGA RHYTHM BAND (LP)	25

(see also Grateful Dead, Mickey Hart, Jerry Garcia)

DIGABLE PLANETS
93	Pendulum 7243 8-3-654 1 7	REACHIN' (A NEW REFUTATION OF TIME AND SPACE) (LP)	50
94	Pendulum 7243 8 30654 1 7	BLOWOUT COMB (2-LP, inners)	35

DIG DIG DIG
81	No Cure DIG 001/DIG 002	Our Money/625 Lines/Four Five	8

DIGGA
97	Groove Yard GYARD 14	DIG A GROOVE EP (12")	20

STEVE DIGGLE
80	Faulty Products FEP 7000	Fifty Years Of Comparative Wealth/Shut Out The Light/Here Comes The Fire Brigade (unreleased)	0

(see also Buzzcocks, Flag Of Convenience)

DIGITAL MYSTIKZ
04	Big Apple BAM 004	Pathways/Ugly/Mawo Dub/Da Wrath (12")	20
05	DMZ DMZ 005	Neverland/Struck (12")	25
06	DMZ DMZ 005	Haunted/Anti War Dub (12")	100
06	DMZ DMZ 008	Ancient Memories/Ancient Memories (Skream Remix) (12")	25
10	DMZ DMZLP 001	RETURN II SPACE (3-LP, picture discs, 200 only but no indication on sleeve if you get picture discs or black vinyl!)	40

DIGITAL MYSTIKZ & LEOFAH
04	DMZ DMZ 001	Twisup/B/Chainba (with Loefah) (12" white labels)	45
04	DMZ DMZ 002	Lost City/Jah Fire/Horror Show/Dread Commands (EP)	25

DILATED PEOPLES
00	Capitol 7243 5 23310 1 7	THE PLATFORM (2-LP)	25
01	Capitol 531477	EXPANSION TEAM (3-LP)	30

DILLARD & CLARK
69	A&M AMS 764	Radio Song/Why Not Your Baby	40
69	A&M AMLS 939	THE FANTASTIC EXPEDITION OF DILLARD & CLARK (LP)	18
69	A&M AMLS 966	THROUGH THE MORNING, THROUGHTHENIGHT (LP)	18

(see also Gene Clark, Byrds, Dillards)

Moses & JOSHUA (DILLARD)

MINT VALUE £

MOSES & JOSHUA (DILLARD)
67	Stateside SS 2059	My Elusive Dreams/What's Better Than Love (as Moses & Joshua Dillard)	25
67	Stateside SS 2059	My Elusive Dreams/What's Better Than Love (as Moses & Joshua Dillard) (DJ Copy)	40
68	Bell BELL 1018	Get Out Of My Heart/They Don't Want Us Together (as Moses & Joshua)	25
72	Mojo 2092 054	My Elusive Dreams/Get Out Of My Heart	15

DILLARDS
65	Capitol CL 15420	Nobody Knows/Ebo Walker	8
69	Elektra EKSN 45048	Reason To Believe/Nobody Knows	6
66	Bounty BY 6019	BACK PORCH BLUEGRASS (LP)	20
68	Elektra EKS 7265	LIVE!!! ALMOST!!! (LP)	15
72	United Artists UAG 29366	ROOTS AND BRANCHES (LP, textured gatefold sleeve)	15

(see also Dillard & Clark)

DILLINGER
73	Duke DU 149	Headquarters (as Dellenger)/CHENLEY DUFFAS: Black Girl In My Bed	15
73	Downtown DT 512	Tighten Up Skank/Middle East Rock (actually by Dillinger)	45
76	Black Swan WIP 6355	Bionic Dread/Eastman Skank	10
77	Black Swan WIP 6380	Natty BSc/Buckingham Palace	10
77	Black Swan WIP 6416	Cokane In My Brain/Buckingham Palace/Ragnampiza	10
77	Black Swan BS 7	Cocaine In My Brain/Buckingham Palace/Ragnampiza (12")	20
77	Third World TW 65	Flat Foot Hustling/Under Tight Wraps	15
76	Black Swan ILPS 9385	CB200 (LP)	20
76	Black Swan ILPS 9455	BIONIC DREAD (LP)	25
76	Island ILPS 9385	CB200 (LP, reissue)	15
77	Magnum DEAD 1001	TALKIN' BLUES (LP)	30
77	Magnum BB27	TALKIN' BLUES (LP, reissue)	20
77	Third World TWS 919	TOP RANKING (LP)	30
78	Third World TWS 928	ANSWER ME QUESTION (LP)	30
79	Jamaica Sound JSLP 002	MARIJUANA IN MY BRAIN (LP)	15
79	Jamaica Sound JSLP 009	FUNKY PUNK/ROCK TO THE MUSIC (LP)	18

(see also David Isaacs)

DILLINGER, TRINITY, WAYNE WADE. AL CAMPBELL & JUNIOR TAMLIN
82	Oak OSD 002	Five Man Army/Send Another Moses/Five Man Dub (12")	30

DILLINGER V TRINITY
78	Burning Sounds BSLP 1003	CLASH (LP)	30

DILLINJA
93	Cybotron DILL 01	Steal The Way/Forever Fierce (1-sided 12")	20
93	Cybotron DILL 03	From Beyond/Ride It Hard (1-sided 12")	20
93	Cybotron DILL 04	Sinewave/Dark Science (1-sided 12")	100
93	Tough Toonz TT 02	DILLINJA EP (12", promo only, four untitled tracks)	40
93	Wave Form DIL 08	TEST [2] EP (12", as Dillinger)	15
94	Deadly Vinyl D2	Deadly Ceremonies/Soverign Melody (12")	100
94	Deadly Vinyl D3	Deadly Deep Subs/Calculus Beats (12")	30
94	Logic Productions DM 003	You Don't Know (Remix)/Heavenly Bass (12")	15
94	Deadly Vinyl DIL 06	MAJESTIC B-LINE EP (12")	12
94	IQ IQ 001	3.01 In The Morning/Catch The Vibe (12", as Dillinja And Mr E)	10
94	Logic Productions DM 001	Moods/Deep Love (Remix) (12", as Dillinja And Mystery)	12
94	Logic Productions DM 002	You Don't Know/Warrior (12")	12
94	Heavyweight HW 003	VOL 3 (10", two untitled tracks, as Dillinja And Ruffkut)	12
94	JA 1	South Side (Riffin Mix)/Stompers Delight (12")	15
95	Deadly Vinyl D4	Deadly Deep Subs (Remix)/Perfect Match (12")	15
95	Philly Blunt PB 005	Muthaf*cka/Sky (12")	15
95	Metalheadz MET 006	The Angel Fell/Ja Know Ya Big/Brutal Bass (12")	18

(See also Cybotron featuring Dillinja)

LEONARD DILLON
66	Island WI 285	Beggars Have No Choice (by Leonard Dillon & Wailers)/ MARCIA GRIFFITHS: Funny	120

(see also Ethiopians)

PHYLLIS DILLON
66	Doctor Bird DB 1061	Don't Stay Away (as Phillis Dillon)/TOMMY McCOOK & SUPERSONICS: What Now	70
67	Trojan TR 006	This Is A Lovely Way/Thing Of The Past (as Phyllis Dellon)	70
67	Treasure Isle TI 7003	This Is A Lovely Way/Thing Of The Past	40
67	Treasure Isle TI 7015	Perfidia/It's Rocking Time	40
68	Treasure Isle TI 7041	I Wear This Ring/Don't Touch Me Tomato	15
69	Trojan TR 651	Love Is All I Had/Boys And Girls Reggae (as Phillis Dylon)	50
69	Trojan TR 671	Get On The Right Track/TOMMY McCOOK & SUPERSONICS: Moonshot	60
69	Trojan TR 686	Lipstick On Your Collar (as Phillis Dillon)/TOMMY McCOOK & SUPERSONICS: Tribute To Rameses	25
70	Duke Reid DR 2508	This Is Me/Skabuvie (act. "If Your Name Is Andy"/"Ska Vovi" by Dorothy Reid)	12
70	Duke DU 76	Walk Through This World/The Rooster	40
71	Treasure Isle TI 7058	One Life To Live, One Love To Give/TOMMY McCOOK: My Best Dress	20
71	Treasure Isle TI 7070	Midnight Confession/TOMMY McCOOK & SOUL SYNDICATE: Version	30
72	Sioux SI 009	In The Ghetto (actually by Judy Mowatt)/NYAH EARTH: Knight Of The Long Knives	60
72	Trojan TRL 41	ONE LIFE TO LIVE (LP)	60
91	Treasure Isle LG2 1014	ONE LIFE TO LIVE (LP, reissue)	20

DIMENSIONS
65	Parlophone R 5294	Tears On My Pillow/You Don't Have To Whisper	25

DIMPLES & EDDIE WITH RICO'S COMBO
62	Planetone RC 3	Fleet Street/Good Bye World	20

DIMPLES (1)
66	Decca F 12537	The Love Of A Lifetime/My Heart Is Tied To You	40

(see also Gospel Garden, Amazing Blondel)

DIMPLES (2)

MINT VALUE £

DIMPLES (2)
76	Hybrid HB09	Doctor Dark Eyes/Devil You	20

D'INFLUENCE
97	Echo ECHLP 16	LONDON (2-LP, gatefold, inners)	30

DINGER
85	Face Value FVRA 221	Air Of Mystery/I Love To Love (no p/s)	35

(see also Erasure)

DINGLE BROTHERS
71	Dynamic DYN 418	You Don't Know/CABLES: Rich Man, Poor Man	6

MARK DINNING
60	MGM MGM 1053	Teen Angel/Bye Now Baby	10
60	MGM MGM 1069	You Win Again/A Star Is Born (A Love Is Dead)	7
60	MGM MGM 1101	The Lovin' Touch/Come Back To Me (My Love)	6
61	MGM MGM 1125	Top Forty, News, Weather And Sport/Suddenly	15
62	MGM MGM 1155	All Of This For Sally/The Pickup	10

DINNING SISTERS
55	London HLF 8179	Drifting And Dreaming/Truly	20
56	London HLF 8218	Hold Me Tight/Uncle Joe	20

(see also Tennessee Ernie Ford)

DINO
65	RCA 1494	Now I Know/Loeeg Negli Occhi	6

DINO, DESI & BILLY
65	Reprise R 20367	I'm A Fool/So Many Ways	8
66	Reprise R 23047	Not The Loving Kind/Chimes Of Freedom	8

KENNY DINO
61	HMV POP 960	Your Ma Said You Cried In Your Sleep Last Night/Dream A Girl	15

DINOSAUR JR
92	Warner Bros. NEG61TEP	START CHOPPIN' (10" EP numbered picture disc)	12
06	Blast First PIL 0713	Been There All The Time/Back To Your Heart	6
89	Blast First BFFP 31	BUG (LP)	20
91	Blanco Y Negro BYN 24	GREEN MIND (LP)	30
93	Blanco Y Negro BYN 28	WHERE YOU BEEN (LP)	35
94	Blanco Y Negro 4509 96933-1	WITHOUT A SOUND (LP)	40
97	Blanco Y Negro 0630183121	HAND IT OVER (LP)	45
01	Strange Fruit SFRSLP078	IN SESSION (LP)	30
07	Play It Again Sam PIL070LP	BEYOND (LP, with 7")	20
09	PIAS 110LP	FARM (2-LP, white vinyl 7")	20
12	PIAS PIASR575LP	I BET ON SKY (LP, purple vinyl)	15

DINOSAUR L
78	Sire SRE 1034	Kiss Me Again/Instrumental Version (as Dinosaur)	10
78	Sire SRE 1034 (T)	Kiss Me Again/(Version) (12", as Dinosaur)	30
86	City Beat CBE 1205	Go Bang! 5/Clean On Your Bean 1 (12", p/s)	15

(see also Arthur Russell)

DIO
75	Purple PUR 128	Sitting In A Dream (as Ronnie Dio featuring Roger Glover & Guests)/JOHN LAWTON: Little Chalk Blue	15
83	Vertiho VERS 5	HOLY DIVER (LP, inner)	30
93	Vertigo 518486-1	STRANGE HIGHWAYS (LP, on 'swirl' label, with inner sleeve)	80

(see also Elf, Rainbow, Roger Glover, Black Sabbath, John Lawton)

DION (& BELMONTS)
78s
58	London HL 8646	I Wonder Why/Teen Angel (as Dion & Belmonts)	20
58	London HL 8718	I Can't Go On (Rosalie)/No One Knows (as Dion & Belmonts)	20
59	London HL 8799	Don't Pity Me/Just You (as Dion & Belmonts)	20
59	London HLU 8874	A Teenager In Love/I've Cried Before (as Dion & Belmonts)	20
59	Pye International 7N 25038	A Lover's Prayer/Every Little Thing I Do (as Dion & Belmonts)	40
60	London HLU 9030	Where Or When/That's My Desire (as Dion & Belmonts)	50

SINGLES
58	London HL 8646	I Wonder Why/Teen Angel (as Dion & Belmonts)	40
58	London HL 8718	I Can't Go On (Rosalie)/No One Knows (as Dion & Belmonts)	40
59	London HL 8799	Don't Pity Me/Just You (as Dion & Belmonts)	40
59	London HLU 8874	A Teenager In Love/I've Cried Before (mispressing as Dion & Delmonts)	30
59	London HLU 8874	A Teenager In Love/I've Cried Before (as Dion & Belmonts)	30

(The above 45s were originally issued with triangular centres, round-centre re-pressings are worth half to two-thirds of these values.)

59	Pye International 7N 25038	A Lover's Prayer/Every Little Thing I Do (as Dion & Belmonts)	50
60	London HLU 9030	Where Or When/That's My Desire (as Dion & Belmonts)	25
60	Top Rank JAR 368	When You Wish Upon A Star/My Private Joy (as Dion & Belmonts)	20
60	Top Rank JAR 503	In The Still Of The Night/Swinging On A Star (as Dion & Belmonts)	20
60	Top Rank JAR 521	Lonely Teenager/Little Miss Blue	20
61	Top Rank JAR 545	Havin' Fun/North-East End Of The Corner	15
61	Top Rank JAR 586	Runaround Sue/Runaway Girl	10
62	HMV POP 971	The Wanderer/The Majestic	10
62	HMV POP 1020	Lovers Who Wander/(I Was) Born To Cry	10
62	Stateside SS 115	Little Diane/Lost For Sure	10
62	Stateside SS 139	Love Came To Me/Little Girl	10
63	CBS AAG 133	Ruby Baby/He'll Only Hurt You	10
63	Stateside SS 161	Sandy/Faith	20
63	CBS AAG 145	This Little Girl/The Loneliest Man In The World	6
63	Stateside SS 209	Come Go With Me/King Without A Queen	15

DION (Cameron) & THREE TOPS

MINT VALUE £

63	CBS AAG 161	Be Careful Of Stones That You Throw/I Can't Believe (That You Don't Love Me Anymore) .. 6
63	CBS AAG 169	Donna, The Prima Donna/You're Mine (credited to Dion) 10
63	CBS AAG 177	Drip Drop/No One's Waiting For Me 10
64	CBS AAG 188	I'm Your Hoochie Coochie Man/The Road I'm On (Gloria) 7
64	CBS AAG 224	Johnnie B. Goode/Chicago Blues 10
65	CBS 201728	Sweet, Sweet Baby/Unloved, Unwanted Me (as Dion Di Mucci) 10
65	CBS 201780	Spoonful/Kickin' Child 10
66	HMV POP 1565	Berimbau (as Dion & Belmonts)/My Girl The Month Of May 10
67	HMV POP 1586	Movin' Man/For Bobbie (as Dion & Belmonts) 10

EPs
62	HMV 7EG 8745	SWINGALONG WITH DION 40
63	Stateside SE 1006	DION'S HITS 20

ALBUMS
59	London HA-U 2194	PRESENTING DION AND THE BELMONTS (as Dion & Belmonts) 150
60	Top Rank 25-027	THE TOPPERMOST — VOL. 1 (as Dion & Belmonts, with others) 40
61	HMV CLP 1539	RUNAROUND SUE 50
63	Stateside SL 10034	LOVERS WHO WANDER 40
63	CBS (S) BPG 62137	RUBY BABY (mono/stereo) 25
64	CBS (S) BPG 62203	DONNA THE PRIMA DONNA (mono/stereo) 25
67	HMV CLP 3618	TOGETHER AGAIN (as Dion & Belmonts, also stereo CSD 3618) 20

(see also Belmonts)

DION (CAMERON) & THREE TOPS
67	Doctor Bird DB 1101	Miserable Friday/This World Has A Feeling 50
72	Big BG 331	Three Tops Time/UNDERGROUND PEOPLE: Tops (Version) 10

(see also Three Tops)

CELINE DION
| 93 | Columbia 474743 | COLOUR OF MY LOVE (LP) .... 25 |

DIOS MALOS
| 06 | Full Time Hobby FTH 012S | I Want It All/Asshole (p/s, 500 only) .... 8 |

DIPLOMATS (1)
67	Caltone TONE 108	Meet Me At The Corner/Do It To Me Baby (by Lloyd & Groovers) 50
68	Caltone TONE 109	Going Alone/My Heart My Soul (by Lloyd & Groovers) 60
68	Caltone TONE 112	Strong Man/Listen To The Music (by Lloyd & Groovers) 60
68	Direction 58-3899	I Can Give You Love/I'm So Glad I Found You 20

DIPLOMATS (2)
| 82 | Exchange EX 1 | Memories Of You/I'll Keep Holding On (p/s) .... 7 |

(see also Scene)

DIPLOMATS (3)
| 98 | Kent 6T 19 | I Really Love You/DEBRA JOHNSON: To Get Love .... 30 |

DIRECT ACTION
| 85 | Second Coming SCP 78501 | THE ALBUM (LP, with booklet) .... 18 |

DIRECT CURRENT MCS
| 90 | Underground TUBE1 | Keep In Step/Gangland Rap (12") .... 30 |

DIRECT HITS
82	Whaam! WHAAM 007	Modesty Blaise/Sunny Honey Girl (p/s) 60
85	Direct POP 001	Christopher Cooper/She Really Didn't Care (p/s) 7
80	Bootleg BOOT 004	COLLISIONS AT TEEN JUNCTION (LP, white card sleeve with home made printed front and back, lyric insert) 30
84	Whaam! BIG 7	BLOW UP (LP) 30

(see also Exits)

DIRECTION
| 93 | Detour DR 003 | Yesterday/The Kids Wanna New Direction (p/s, 1,000 only) .... 6 |

DIRECTIONS
79	Tortch TOR 004	Three Bands Tonite/On The Train (p/s, with badge) 80
79	Tortch TOR 004	Three Bands Tonite/On The Train (p/s) 75

(see also Big Sound Authority)

DIRECTIONS IN JAZZ UNIT
| 64 | Philips BL 7625 | DIRECTIONS IN JAZZ (LP) .... 50 |

DIRE STRAITS
85	Vertigo DSTRD 11	Brothers In Arms/Going Home — Theme From 'Local Hero' with free copy of Sultans Of Swing/Earthbound Train (live) in stickered PVC pack) 7
78	Vertigo 9102 021	DIRE STRAITS (LP) 20
82	Vertigo HS 6359 034	MAKING MOVIES (LP, half-speed master recording) 30
82	Vertigo HS 9102 021	DIRE STRAITS (LP, half-speed master recording) 30
85	Vertigo VERH 25	BROTHERS IN ARMS (LP, insert) 25
91	Vertigo 510 160-1	ON EVERY STREET (LP) 30
93	Vertigo 514 766-1	ON THE NIGHT (2-LP) 60
95	Vertigo 528 323 2	LIVE AT THE BBC (LP) 100

(see also Mark Knopfler, Notting Hillbillies)

DIRK & STIG
78	Ring O' 2017 109/DIB 1	Ging Gang Goolie/Mr. Sheene (unissued) 0
79	EMI EMI 2852	Ging Gang Goolie/Mr. Sheene (p/s, khaki vinyl) 18
79	EMI EMI 2852	Ging Gang Goolie/Mr. Sheene (p/s, black vinyl) 10

(see also Rutles, Neil Innes)

DIRT
82	Crass 221984/7	NEVER MIND THE DIRT HERE'S THE BOLLOCKS (LP, inner) 25
85	Dirt DIRT 1	JUST AN ERROR (LP) 25
95	Dirt DIRT 3	DRUNKS IN RUSTY TRANSITS (LP) 15

DIRTY BLUES BAND
| 68 | Stateside S(S)L 10234 | DIRTY BLUES BAND (LP) .... 100 |

DIRTY DOG

MINT VALUE £

69	Stateside S(S)L 10268	STONE DIRT (LP)	100

(see also Bacon Fat and Juicy Lucy)

DIRTY DOG
78	Lightning GIL 511	Let Go Of My Hand/Shouldn't Do It/Gonna Quit/Guitar In My Hand (p/s)	25

DIRTY HARRY
73	Unity UN 573	Big Haire/YOUNG DOUG: Skank In Skank	12
76	Treble C CCC 015	Djamballa (with Bobby Ellis)/BIG JOE: Rock Up A Zion	8

DIRTY PRETTY THINGS
06	Mercury 9856418	WATERLOO TO ANYWHERE (LP, with free 7")	25
08	Vertigo 177 236-7	ROMANCE AT SHORT NOTICE (LP)	18

(see also Libertines)

DIRTY STRANGERS
89	Thrill TH 3	Bathing Belles/Oh Yeah/Hands Up (p/s, featuring Keith Richards)	8

(see also Rolling Stones)

DIRTY THREE
96	big Cat ABB 107	SAD AND DANGEROUS (LP)	30

DIRTY TRICKS
75	Polydor 2383351	DIRTY TRICKS (LP, red label)	30

DIRTY BEACHES
10	Italian Beach Babes IBB 006	Golden Desert Sun/Night Drive (p/s, 300 only)	20
10	Italian Beach Babes IBB 010	No Fun/No Where Fast (100 hand-numbered copies, risograph cover)	20
10	Italian Beach Babes IBB 010	No Fun/No Where Fast (p/s, 500 only)	10
13	A Records AUK 104LP	WATER PARK OST EP (10" white vinyl)	15
11	Zoo ZM 010	BADLANDS (LP)	20

DIRTY FUNKER
06	Spirit DF006	Let's Get Dirty (Vocal)/Let's Get Dirty (Dirty Dub) (12", p/s, Unofficial Banksy artwork, without headband)	800
06	Spirit DF006	Let's Get Dirty (Vocal)/Let's Get Dirty (Dirty Dub) (12", p/s, Unofficial Banksy artwork, with headband)	400
08	Spirit DF008	Future (Remixes) (12", white/grey or brown sleeve with Banksy artwork)	200

DIRTY PROJECTORS
11	Domino RUG 418T	MOUNT WITTENBERG (LP, with Bjork, 3D sleeve, insert, first 500 hand-numbered with signed print)	20

DISASTER
91	Tone Deaf TONE DEAF 1	WAR CRY (LP)	50

DISCHARGE (1)
80	Clay CLAY 1	Realities Of War/They Declare It/But After The Gig/Society's Victim (p/s)	12
80	Clay CLAY 3	Fight Back/War's No Fairy Tale/Always Restrictions/You Take Part In Creating This System/Religion Instigates (p/s)	12
80	Clay CLAY 5	Decontrol/It's No TV Sketch/Tomorrow Belongs To Us (p/s)	12
81	Clay CLAY 6	Never Again/Death Dealers/Two Monstrous Nuclear Stock-Piles (p/s)	9
81	Clay PLATE 2	WHY (12" EP)	15
82	Clay CLAY 14	State Violence, State Control/Doomsday (p/s)	10
83	Clay PLATE 5	WARNING: HER MAJESTY'S GOVERNMENT CAN SERIOUSLY DAMAGE YOUR HEALTH (12")	15
83	Clay CLAY 29	Price Of Silence/Born To Die In The Gutter (p/s)	7
84	Clay CLAY 34	The More I See/Protest And Survive (p/s)	8
85	Clay CLAY 45	Ignorance/No Compromise (p/s)	6
82	Clay CLAYLP 3	HEAR NOTHING, SEE NOTHING, SAY NOTHING (LP, original issue has "Pay no more than £3.99" on top right of sleeve)	40
84	Clay CLAYLP 12	NEVER AGAIN (LP, red vinyl)	20
86	Clay CLAY LP 19	GRAVE NEW WORLD (LP)	15
87	Clay CLAY LP 24	1980-1986 (LP)	20
89	Clay CLAY LP 103	LIVE AT THE CITY GARDEN NEW JERSEY (LP, red vinyl)	18
90	Clay CLAY 107	THE NIGHTMARE CONTINUES...LIVE (LP)	20
91	Clay CLAY LP 110	MASSACRE DIVINE (LP)	15
03	Earmark 40024	DISCHARGE (LP)	15

(see also Broken Bones)

DISCHARGE (2)
80	Go Round ROUND 001	DISCHARGE/THE FILTH (split 7, wraparound p/s)	175

(not the Discharge that punks know and love!)

DISCIPLE (1)
69	Parlophone R 5760	Cherie Alamayonaika/Caucasoid Junkie	45

DISCIPLES
93	Boom Shacka Lacka BSL 001	Prowling Lion/Downbeat Rock (12")	35
94	Boom Shacka Lacka BSL 002	Return To Addis Ababa/Africa Macka (12")	30
94	Boom Shacka Lacka BSL 003	Dub Revolution/(Innovation Mix)/(Chamber Of Echoes Mix) (10")	20
94	Topatop TOP 001	Prowling Lion (Original Cut)/Fourth Cut (Unreleased)/Return To Addis Ababa (Original Cut)/Next Cut (Unreleased) (10")	12
95	Boom Shacka Lacka BSL 004	Chant Of Freedom/Unshackled Version (10")	20
95	Boom Shacka Lacka BSL 005	Sunrise/Message (12")	45
02	Boom Shacka Lacka BSL 006	Ilodica Theme Pt.1/Ilodica Theme Pt.2/Fearless Dub Pt.1/Fearless Dub Pt.2 (12")	15
04	Boom Shacka Lacka BSL 009	Almighty Dub/Zion Rock Dub (12")	20
95	Cloak & Dagger NLX5 004	RESONATIONS (LP)	20
96	Boom Shacka Lacka BSL 101	FOR THOSE WHO UNDERSTAND (LP)	30

DISCIPLES OF BELIAL
95	Praxis PRAXIS 17	GOAT OF MENDES EP (12")	40
97	Praxis PRAXIS 7	Lucifer We Praise Thee/Sell Your Soul To The Devil/One God (p/s)	50

DISCIPLES RIDDIM SECTION
03	Jah Tubbys JT 10018	Roots Workout/Mission Of Dub (10")	25

DISCO DREAD
93	Dub Jockey DJ 023	Ancient Vibrations/Modern Dub	10

DISCO DREAM AND ANDROIDS

MINT VALUE £

DISCO DREAM AND ANDROIDS
79	Wake Up WUR 3 7	Love Dance/Android Love (p/s)	8
79	Wake Up WUR 3	Love Dance/Android Love (12" p/s)	15
79	Wake UP WUR 2	DISCO DREAM AND THE ANDROIDS (LP)	50

DISCO DUB BAND
76	Movers MO 1	For the Love Of Money/For The Love Of Money Part 2	40

DISCO INFERNO
91	Che CHE 2	OPEN DOORS (LP)	18
94	Rough Trade R 3071	D.I. GO POP (LP)	40

DISCORDS
91	Hangman 41 UP	SECOND TO NO-ONE (LP)	15

DISCO STUDENTS
79	Yeah Yeah Yeah UHHUH 1	South Africa House/Kafkaesque (no p/s)	15
80	Yeah Yeah Yeah UHHUH 2	A Boy With A Penchant For Open-Necked Shirts/Pink Triangles/Credit (no p/s)	15

DISCO 2000
87	KLF Comms. D2000	I Gotta CD/I Love Disco 2000 (12", p/s)	10

(see also Angels One 5, Big Hair, KLF, Timelords, Bill Drummond, Space)

DISCO/VERY
79	Pinnacle PIN 15	Get It On/Part 2	8
79	Pinnacle PIN 15 12	Get It On/Part 2 (12")	20

DISCO VOLANTE
84	Catalyst Box CBR 001	No Motion/Click Punishment Tank Live! (p/s)	50

DISCO ZOMBIES
79	South Circular SGS 106	Drums Over London/Heartbeats Love (black, white & pink or black, white & green handmade wraparound p/s)	40
79	Uptown/Wizzo WIZZO 1	THE INVISIBLE (EP)	25
81	Dining Out TUX 2	Here Come The Buts/Mary Millington (p/s)	15

(see also Fifty Fantastics)

DISCS
65	Columbia DB 7477	Not Meant To Be/Come Back To Me	10

BABA DISE
69	Gas GAS 118	Wanted/SENSATIONS: I'll Always Love You	35

DISGUISE
78	Chiswick CHIS 107	Hey Baby/Juvenile Delinquent	30

DISORDER (1)
80	Ace ACE 12	Air Raid/Law And Disorder (1st 100 in custom 'War Book' p/s)	200
80	Ace ACE 12	Air Raid/Law And Disorder	70
80	Durham Book Centre BOOK 1	Reality Crisis/1984 (over sized p/s)	30

DISORDER (2)
81	Disorder ORDER 1	Complete Disorder/Insane Youth/Today's World/Violent Crime (p/s)	8
81	Disorder ORDER 2	Distortion To Deafness/More Than Fights/Daily Life/You've Got To Be Someone (p/s)	8
84	Disorder AARGH 1	UNDER THE SCALPEL BLADE (LP, with poster)	15
84	Disorder 12 ORDER 5	THE SINGLES COLLECTION (12" EP)	10
85	Disorder AARGH 2	GI FAEN I NASJONALITENTEN DIN (LP)	15
86	Disorder AARGH 3	ONE DAY SON ALL THIS WILL BE YOURZ (split LP with KAFKA PROCESS)	15

DISQUES DU LIVRES
97	Noid NOID 0101	MAD SEX EP (12")	10

DISRUPTERS
81	Radical Change RC 1	Young Offender/U.K. Solider/No Place For You (p/s)	8
82	Radical Change RC 2	Shelters For The Rich/Animal Farm/Self Rule (p/s)	10
83	Radical Change RC 6	Bomb Heaven/Die With Mother (p/s)	8
85	Radical Change 12 RC 8	ALIVE IN THE ELECTRIC CHAIR (12" EP, with insert)	20
83	Radical Change RCLP1	UNREHEARSED WRONGS (LP)	30
84	Radical Change RCLP3	PLAYING WITH FIRE (LP)	20

TOM DISSEVELT
62	Philips 430 736 PE	ELECTRONIC MOVEMENTS (EP)	20
65	Philips BL 7681	FANTASY IN ORBIT (LP)	60

DISTAINERS
79	Beck 885	Say Goodbye/Spies In Your Eyes (no p/s, 300 copies)	60

DISTANT COUSINS
66	CBS 202352	She Ain't Loving You/Here Today, Gone Tomorrow	18
67	CBS 2800	Mister Sebastian/Empty House	10

DISTANT DRUMS
82	Rhythmic RMNS 3	Perfect Eyes/Halloween (p/s)	25

DISTANT MEMORIES
72	N&G 01	Someone Who Knows/Escape From Reality	60

DISTINCTION
80	En Ay AM 262	Destiny/Destiny (Dub) (12", p/s)	70

DISTINCTIVE DRONE
79	No label, no cat no	DISTINCTIVE DRONE (cassette LP, 20 only)	60

(see also Guardians Of The Ancient Wisdom)

DISTORHAUS
94	Mystic MRD 99401	PLASTIC ANGEL EP (12")	20

DISTORTED WAVES OF OHM
94	Eurk 12EK 001	ZYRCON (12" EP)	50
95	Eurk 12EK 002	STRANGE ROTATION (12" EP)	30
95	Eurk 12EK 003	WITH INTENT TO DISTORT (12" EP)	20
96	Eurk 12EK 004	SURREAL SKETCH SHOW (12" EP)	10

DISTRACTIONS
79	TJM TJM 2	YOU'RE NOT GOING OUT DRESSED LIKE THAT (12" EP)	12

DISTRAINERS

MINT VALUE £

Year	Label	Title	Value
79	Factory FAC 12	Time Goes By So Slow/Pillow Fight (p/s)	18
80	Island WIP 6533	It Doesn't Bother Me/One Way Love	10
80	Island WIP 6568	Boys Cry (Where No One Can See Them)/Paracetamol Paralysis (p/s)	6
80	Island ILPS 9604	NOBODY'S PERFECT (LP, sleeve designed by Peter Saville)	15

DISTRAINERS
79	DJ Records BECK 885	Say Goodbye/Spies In Your Eyes (no p/s, 300 only)	125

DISTRIBUTORS
80	Tap TAP 1	TV Me/Wireless (various foldover p/s)	8

DISTURBED
79	Parole PURL: 3	I Don't Believe/Betrayed (p/s)	10

DIVINE COMEDY
92	Setanta SET 011	Europop: New Wave/Intifada/Monitor/Timewatch/Jerusalem/The Rise And Fall (12", p/s)	15
93	Setanta CAO 008	Lucy/The Pop Singer's Fear Of The Pollen Count/I Was Born Yesterday (mail order, p/s)	8
93	Setanta DC 001	Indulgence No. 1: Hate My Way/Untitled Melody/Europe By Train (picture disc)	8
94	Setanta DC 002	Indulgence No. 2: A Drinking Song/When The Lights Go Out All Over Europe/Tonight We Fly (handfinished wraparound p/s, stamped labels)	15
96	Setana SET 27-7	Becoming More Like Alfie/Your Daddy's Car (p/s)	8
90	Setanta SETLPM 002	FANFARE FOR THE COMIC MUSE (LP, with inner sleeve)	40
93	Setanta SET LP 11	LIBERATION (LP)	40
94	Setanta SETLP 13	PROMENADE (LP)	45
96	Setanta SETLP 25	CASSANOVA (LP)	35
97	Setanta SETLP 36	A SHORT ALBUM ABOUT LOVE (LP)	50
98	Setanta SETLP 57	FIN DE SIECLE (LP)	80
10	Divine Comedy DCRP 101LP	BANG GOES THE KNIGHTHOOD (LP)	30

DIVISION
72	Wren WR1	Under Your Influence/Dark Dreams	35

DIVORCE BROTHERS
87	Separation	To Understand/That First Kiss/Walk Out Of The Door/The Divorce/The Liquidator (12")	20

DIXIEBELLES
63	London HLU 9797	(Down At)Papa Joe's/Rock, Rock, Rock	8
64	London HLU 9842	Southtown, U.S.A./Why Don't You Set Me Free?	7
64	London REU 1434	THE DIXIE BELLES (EP)	25
64	London HA-U/SH-U 8152	DOWN AT PAPA JOE'S (LP, with Cornbread & Jerry)	30

DIXIE CUPS
64	Pye International 7N 25245	Chapel Of Love/Ain't That Nice	15
64	Red Bird RB 10006	People Say/Girls Can Tell (some copies on Pye label)	10
64	Red Bird RB 10012	You Should Have Seen The Way He Looked At Me/No True Love	15
64	Red Bird RB 10017	Little Bell/Another Boy Like Mine	15
65	Red Bird RB 10024	Iko Iko/Gee Baby Gee	15
65	Red Bird RB 10032	Gee The Moon Is Shining Bright/I'm Gonna Get You Yet	20
65	HMV POP 1453	Two Way Poc A Way/That's Where It's At	15
66	HMV POP 1524	What Kind Of Fool/Danny Boy	25
66	HMV POP 1557	Love Ain't So Bad (After All)/Daddy Said No	25
65	Red Bird RB 20100	CHAPEL OF LOVE (LP)	60
66	HMV CLP 1916	RIDING HIGH (LP)	50
79	Charly CRM 2004	TEEN ANGUISH (LP)	15

DIXIE DRIFTER
65	Columbia DB 7710	Soul Heaven/Three Chairs Theme	12

DIXIE FOUR
60s	Rarities RA 3	THE DIXIE FOUR (EP)	25

DIXIE HUMMINGBIRDS
64	Vogue V 2422	Have A Talk With Jesus/In The Morning	10
64	Vogue LAE-P 588	PRAYER FOR PEACE (LP)	20

DIXIELANDERS
63	Vocalion V 9209	Cyclone/Mardyke	35

DIXIELAND JUG BLOWERS
54	HMV 7M 223	Memphis Shake/Boodle-Am-Shake	10
54	HMV 7M 233	Hen Party Blues/Carpet Alley Breakdown	10

DIXIE PEACH
85	Jah Tubbys JT 005	Just Worries/Pure Worries (12")	60
85	Jah Tubbys JT 014	Spin Spin/Spin Style (12", with the Offbeat Posse)	40
86	Jah Tubbys JT 018	Slaughter/Slaughter Mix (12")	45
86	Y&D YDD 0102	Raggamuffin And Rambo/Ragamuffin Style (12")	40
87	Y&D YDD 0106	Get Up And Skank/LONG MAN AND THE OFFBEAT POSSE: Skank With Me/OFFBEAT POSSE: The Skank (12")	40
87	Y&D YDD 0112	Hold Onto Your Man/Tonight Is The Night (12")	30
88	Y&D YDD 0119	Running Around/Run Come Follow Me Now (12")	30
00	Jah Tubbys JT 7003	Every Step/DISCIPLES RIDDIM SECTION: Step Dub	20
01	Jah Tubbys JT 7008	I Heard Them Bawling/OFFBEAT POSSE: Bawling For Riddim	18
03	Jah Tubbys JT 10013	Sufferers Time/What Am I to Do? (10", with the Offbeat Posse)	30
03	Jah Tubbys JT 10017	Jah Jah Army/Who's Gonna Stop Us? (10", with the Offbeat Posse)	30
06	Jah Tubbys JT 10027	Roots Vibration (with the Roots Squad)/Got To Be Humble (with WD Production)	20

THE DIXIES
64	Parlophone R 5223	Love Made A Fool/Valley Of Tears	10

DONALD DIXON
71	Fab FAB 19	Trouble A Fe You/CORNELL CAMPBELL: Just Can't Find Love (unissued, white label only. Beware: this is not the only Fab 45 with this cat. no))	350

ERROL DIXON
60	Blue Beat BB 27	Midnight Track/Anytime Anywhere	15
61	Blue Beat BB 46	Mama Shut Your Door/Too Much Whisky	15

Jeff DIXON

Year	Label/Cat	Title	MINT VALUE £
62	Blue Beat BB 86	Bad Bad Woman/Early This Morning	15
62	Island WI 017	Morning Train/Lonely Heart	20
63	Island WI 069	I Love You/Tell Me More	20
63	Carnival CV 7001	Oo Wee Baby/Twisting And Shaking	10
63	Carnival CV 7004	Mean And Evil Woman/Tutti Frutti	10
64	Oriole CB 1945	Rocks In My Pillow/Give Me More Time (as Errol Dixon & Bluebeaters)	70
66	Blue Beat BB 337	Gloria/Heavy Shuffle	15
66	Blue Beat BB 344	You're No Good/Midnight Bus	20
66	Rainbow RAI 104	I Need Someone To Love/I Want (as Errol Dixon & Goodtime Band)	30
66	Fab EP 1	I Need Someone To Love/I Want (reissue)	20
67	Ska Beat JB 271	Midnight Party/It Makes No Difference	18
67	Direct DS 5002	I Don't Want/The Hoop	60
67	Decca F 12613	Six Questions/Not Again	15
67	Decca F 12717	True Love Never Runs Smooth/What Ya Gonna Do (B-side with Judy Kay)	8
68	Decca F 12826	Back To The Chicken Shack (as Big City Blues Of Errol Dixon)/ I Done Found Out	20
69	Doctor Bird DB 1197	Why Hurt Yourself/She Started To Scream	20
60s	Carnival CU 7002	Crazy Baby/Our First Love (with Maynell Wilson)	10
70	Gas GAS 148	Something On Your Mind/I Need Love	8
72	Transatlantic BIG 503	Let The Love Shine into Your Heart/In A Moment Of Weakness	10
65	Decca DFE 8626	SINGS FATS (EP, with Honeydrippers)	60
68	Decca LK/SKL 4962	BLUES IN THE POT (LP, with Chicken Shack)	100
70	Transatlantic TRA 225	THAT'S HOW YOU GOT KILLED BEFORE (LP)	30

(see also Chicken Shack)

JEFF DIXON

Year	Label/Cat	Title	MINT VALUE £
67	Coxsone CS 7015	The Rock/HAMBOYS: Harder On The Rock	60
68	Studio One SO 2051	Tickle Me/ENFORCERS: Forgive Me	60

WILLIE DIXON & ALLSTARS

Year	Label/Cat	Title	MINT VALUE £
56	London HLU 8297	Walking The Blues/Crazy For My Baby	1500
56	London HLU 8297	Walking The Blues/Crazy For My Baby (78)	150
64	Pye International 7N 25270	Crazy For My Baby/Walkin' The Blues (reissue)	25

TEX DIXSON

Year	Label/Cat	Title	MINT VALUE £
70	Ackee ACK 111	Funky Trombone/Crying Horn	10
70	Ackee ACK 112	My Ring/Here I Am	10

DIXXY SISTERS

Year	Label/Cat	Title	MINT VALUE £
54	Columbia SCM 5105	Spin The Bottle Polka/The Game Of Broken Hearts	10

DJ ASSASSIN

Year	Label/Cat	Title	MINT VALUE £
96	Ugly UGM 007	THE STALKER EP (12")	20
96	Groove Yard GYARD 009	14 SPLIFFS OF INSPIRATION (12" white label with Lab 79)	10

DJ ASSAULT

Year	Label/Cat	Title	MINT VALUE £
00	Mo Wax MWR 115LP	BELLE ISLE TECH (LP as 3 x 12")	30

DJ B AND EZM.

Year	Label/Cat	Title	MINT VALUE £
92	Industrial Noize DE 001	Can't Beat Ruff Beats/Shockin' To The Break Of Dawn (12", stamped white label)	35

DJ CHEMISTRY MEETS JACK SMOOTH

Year	Label/Cat	Title	MINT VALUE £
94	Homegrown HG 015	Alchemy/Freefall (12")	12

(see also Chemistry, Jack Smooth)

DJ CRYSTL

Year	Label/Cat	Title	MINT VALUE £
92	Lucky Spin LSR 001	Suicidal/Drop XTC (12")	20
93	Dee Jay Recordings DJX 008	Crystalize/Deep Space (12")	30
93	Dee Jay Recordings DJX 010	Meditation/Warpdrive (12")	50
93	Force Ten FTR 001	The Dark Cryst/Inna Year 3000 (12")	15
93	Lucky Spin STU-1	LIVE EP (12" 1-sided white label)	45
94	Lucky Spin STU-2	Give It Up (12" 1-sided white label)	50
94	Dee Jay Recordings DJX 016	Your Destiny/Sweet Dreamz (12")	25
94	Dee Jay Recordings DJX 020	Let It Roll/Paradise (12")	25
94	Dee Jsy DJX 019	Meditation/Warpdrive (Remixes) (12")	15
94	Lucky Spin STU 5	Let It Roll (Remix) (12" 1-sided white label)	20

DJ CRYSTL & SLIPMASTER J

Year	Label/Cat	Title	MINT VALUE £
92	Lucky Spin LSR 004	Frantic Situation/Drop XTC (12")	25

DJ CYCLONE

Year	Label/Cat	Title	MINT VALUE £
96	Acid Fever MDMA 9612	909 TRAX EP: Trak 101/Trak 3/4/Trak 303/Trak 23 (12")	20
96	Acid Fever MDMA 9613	Innersense (Halfcore Remix)/Innersense (Original Hardcore Mix)/Mushroom Of Fire/Non-sense (12")	20
96	Acid Fever MDMA 9614 303	Joy Ride/Cycloid Spiral Motion/Circular Motion/Cycloid Spiral Slow Motion (12")	20
97	Acid Fever MDMA 9703	STATE OF THE PLANET EP (12" two tracks, other two tracks by OCTODRED)	15

DJ DADO

Year	Label/Cat	Title	MINT VALUE £
96	Steppin' Out IAN 045T	Face It (Club Mix)/(Radio Edit)/(Alternative Mix)/(Status Mix) (12")	15

DJ DEVICE & DEVIBES

Year	Label/Cat	Title	MINT VALUE £
95	Stronghouse STR12 006	POSITIVE INFLUENCES 2 (12" EP)	35

DJ DEXTROUS & H PEE

Year	Label/Cat	Title	MINT VALUE £
95	Subversive SUBVR 001	Hot Flame/Junglist (12")	40

DJ DM

Year	Label/Cat	Title	MINT VALUE £
08	PC2	LAUGH NOW EP (12". gold, silver, bronze or green p/s, artwork by Banksy)	1500

DJ EXCEL

Year	Label/Cat	Title	MINT VALUE £
91	(No company) EDUC 2	Just When You Thought It Was Safe/Breakbeat 1/Breakbeat 2/Breakbeat 3 /Breakbeat 4 (12")	30

DJ FOKUS

Year	Label/Cat	Title	MINT VALUE £
95	Lucky Spin LSR 022	I Want/Pulse (12")	50

DJ FOOD

Year	Label/Cat	Title	MINT VALUE £
00	Ninja Tune ZEN12 015/021	Classic House Tracks From The Vaults (12")	10
90	Ninja Tune ZEN 02	JAZZ BRAKES VOL. 1 (LP)	15

DJ FORCE & EVOLUTION

MINT VALUE £

91	Ninja Tune ZEN 03	JAZZ BRAKES VOL. 2 (LP)	20

DJ FORCE & EVOLUTION
93	Knifeforce KF 003	Fall Down On Me/The Force Will Be With You/Escape The Feeling/Mine All Mine (12")	30
93	Knifeforce KF 003	Fall Down On Me/The Force Will Be With You/Escape The Feeling/Mine All Mine (12", red vinyl, 200 only)	35
93	Knifeforce KF 011	Twelve Midnight/Lost It (12")	20
93	Knifeforce KF 16	Poltergeist/Perfect Dreams (10", some on clear vinyl)	20
93	Knifeforce KF 019	Perfect Dreams (Citadel Of Kaos Remix)/Perfect Dreams (Original Mix)/Fall Down On Me (Remix) (12")	10

DJ FORMAT
03	Genuine GEN 005 DLP	MUSIC FOR THE MATURE B-BOY (2-LP)	30

DJ GIL'R
98	U Star USR 003	Espece Funk (Part 1)/(Part 2)/(Original Mix)/(Drums Mix) (12")	10

DJ GOLLUM
96	UK44 UK44 07	Pleasant Experience/Mystic Fusion (12")	30
98	UK44 UK44 15	The Energy (Trance Mix)/The Energy (Rave Mix)/The Energy (Mix Mix) (12", p/s)	10

(see also Gollum & Gary D, M-Zone & DJ Gollum)

DJ GUNSHOT
93	GOD 1	Untitled/Untitled (White label with Dread Or Dead stamp) (12")	15
94	No U Turn NUT 009	Wheel N Deal/Marble Mix (10")	15
95	No U Turn NUT 010	Soundboy/Soundtest (12")	12
95	DAT II DISC D2D 001	Bad Boy/(Smooth Mix) (12")	15

DJ GWANGE
94	Legend LEG 007	Motionless/Adrenalin (12")	60

DJ HARVEY
96	Noid Recordings NOID 0066	I Am A Man/MONSIEUR D: Hot Love (12", black or green vinyl)	30
98	Black Cock Records BK 016	LOVE HOTEL EP (12", with Gerry Rooney)	15
98	Black Cock Records BC 0017	LOVE HOTEL EP 2 (12")	10
98	Black Cock Records BK 017	LOVE HOTEL EP 2 (12")	20
00	Weekend Inc WKD 069	Done Turn Me/Protect And Survive (Fuck Loop) (12")	20

(see also Black Cock, Ersatz)

DJ ILEAGLE
93	Dee Jsy DJX 005	Crazy/Testify (12")	50

DJ JINX
92	Music Madness MM 003	Devotion/Paradise Project/Paradise Project (Bounty Remix) (12")	40

DJ KRUSH
94	Mo' Wax MWLP 025	STRICTLY TURNTABLIZED (2-LP)	25
98	Mo' Wax MW 088 LP	HOLONIC (LP)	15

(see also DJ Shadow)

DJ LEWI
95	Jet Star ELT1	You Better Run/After Hours/Ganja (12", white label)	200

DJ LJT
93	KIN 2	Untitled/Untitled (stamped white labels "DJ LJT FEATURING KINETIC") (12")	20

DJ MAYHEM
92	Basement BRSS 008	Damage/Metrix: The Remix/Signal Generator (12")	15
92	Basement BRSS 016	Storm Trooper/Cold Acid (12")	15

(see also Two Dark Troopers)

DJ MINK FEAT. 2WICE THE TROUBLE
89	FON T18	Hey Hey Can You Relate (4 Mixes) (12")	12

DJ NUT NUT
93	Virtual Motion VM 001	Forbidden Planet/Set My Mind Free (12")	12
94	Production House PNT 058 R	The Rumble (Remixes) (12")	25
94	Babylon BR 001	Press Up (VIP Mix)/Press Up (Dub Mix) (12", stamped white labels)	15
94	Hard Step HRD 001	Special Dedication (Ladies Mix)/Bloodclart Hour (12")	20
96	London Some 'ting LS 006	Special Dedication (DJ Ron Remix)/Special Dedication (The Dream Team Remix) (12")	10

DJ PHANTASY
95	Dee Jay DJX 024	Ruff N Ready/Remix (12")	10

DJ POOCH
93	LUcky Spin LSR 014	LUCKY SPIN EP (12")	30

DJ RON
92	Pure BR001	Crackman (Mix 1)/Crackman (Mix 2)/Bad Boy/Untitled (12", stamped white label)	15
93	Rough Tone RT007	Crackman The Return (Remix D.J. Ron)/Crackman The Return (Booyaka Mix) (E.Q.P. Mix) (12")	40

DJ SHADOW
93	Mo' Wax MW 014	In/ Flux/Hindsight (12", plain sleeve, with obi sticker, with the Groove Robbers)	12
93	Mo' Wax MW 014	In/ Flux/Hindsight (12" picture disc, plastic sleeve, with the Groove Robbers)	25
94	Mo' Wax MW 027 P1/2/3	What Does Your Soul Look Like (3 x 10" forming DJ Shadow tag)	70
94	Mo' Wax MW 027	What Does Your Soul Look Like (Parts 1, 3 & 4) (12" p/s)	10
97	Mo' Wax MW 063s	High Noon/Organ Donor (Extended Overhaul) (stickered p/s)	8
02	none	Monosylabik/First Letter From Home (acetate, with letter, 10 copies only)	100
06	Gabacradabra CT 010	Gabracadabra/Acappella Version (7", 500 only hand-stamped white label given away at door of London Indig02 gig 2007)	50
10	TNF-1	Def Surrounds Us/I've Been Trying (100 only, hand-made cover)	70
10	New Futility TNF2	Def Surrounds Us/Def Surrounds US (Neil Landstrumm Remix) (12" promo, 100 only electric blue sleeve, green vinyl)	40
12	A&M/Talenthouse S75	Come On Riding (Through The Cosmos) (1-sided, 100 only, each with unique art sleeve)	70
96	Mo' Wax MW059LP	ENDTRODUCING (2-LP, gatefold, centre opening sleeve)	40
98	Mo' Wax MW059LP	ENDTRODUCING (2-LP, gatefold, spine opening sleeve)	40
12	Island 3708138	RECONSTRUCTED (6-CD, DVD, 12" in perspex box with signed certificate, 500 only)	80
02	Island ILPSD8118586981-1	THE PRIVATE PRESS (2-LP, gatefold)	45
02	none	PRESS CUTTINGS ('The Private Press' Compacted, 5 copies only)	200

DJ SIDE PHONE/DJ CYDER CLONE

MINT VALUE £

06	Island 1704960	THE OUTSIDER (2-LP)	25

(see also Q-Bert, U.N.K.L.E.)

DJ SIDE PHONE/DJ CYDER CLONE
97	Acid Fever MDMA 9705	ACID FLUFF EP (12", three tracks each)	20

DJ TOKEN PACE & TOXIC KEV
92	Face The Bass FBR 001	Losing You/Dreamers Revenge (12")	40

DJ TRACE
91	Orbital 12 ORBIT 11	Inception/Ain't Gonna Wait No More/Love Dove Sound (12")	20
92	(No company, no number)	Rudeboy Hardcore/Untitled/Untitled (white label 12" with 'DJ Trace' and phone number stamped on labels. A-side samples 'Orinoco flow')	10
92	Orbital 12OUT 997	Teach Me To Fly/Inception (After Dark Remix) (12")	18
93	Lucky Spin LSR 003	Lost Entity (London side)/Lost Entity (New York side) (12")	20
93	Dee Jay Recordings DJX 007	Never Felt This Way (One Step Ahead)/Never Felt This Way (Intel Mix)	18
94	Lucky Spin LSR 017	Coffee (Full Of Flavour Mix)/Coffee (Bonus Beat Mix) (12")	40
95	Dee Jay DJX 023	Final Chapta (Rollers)/Final Chapta (Chronic) (12", black, red, yellow or purple vinyl)	40
95	Dee Jay DJX 027	By Any Means Necessary (Speed)/By Any Means Necessary (Original) (12")	30

DJ TRACE & ED RUSH
93	Lucky Spin LSR 008	Don Bad Man/Clean Gun (12")	25

DJ TRACE/DEFENDER
94	Lucky Spin LSR/BM01	Inside Information/DEFENDER: Feel It (12")	20

DJ TREMA & THE AVENGER
93	DBS 22	Untitled/Untitled (12", white label, "DBS 22" etched in run-out groove)	45

DJ VADIM
98	Ninja Tune ZEN 31/2	U.S.S.R. RECONSTRUCTION (2 x 12")	15

DJAGO
72	Duke DU 134	Rebel Train/Babylon Version	10

DJANGO DJANGO
09	Shadazz SHAD 09	Storm/Love's Dart	15
10	Bonhour Branch BONBRA 002	WOR/Skies Over Cairo	10
13	Because ILMVF004	Love's Dart (Sal P Liquid Liquid Remix) (12" 1-sided, 50 copies only)	25
15	Because BEC 5156060	BORN UNDER SATURN (2-LP, orange vinyl with bonus CD)	25

RICHIE D-JAY
79	Arawak ARK DD 004	Grooving In Love/Grooving Version (12")	25

DJD
99	Noid NOID 007	Ginger Tree/Feelin The Party Groove (12")	15

D'JURANN JURANN
74	Dawn DNS 1068	Streakin'/Oh! Janine	10

(see also Paul King, King Earl Boogie Band, Mungo Jerry)

D-LIVIN
92	D-Livin DL01	Why/Up Their Head/Make A Joyful Noize/Yard An Gorage (12")	25

JED(RZEZ) DMOCHOWSKI
83	Whaam! WHAAM 009	Sha-La-La-La (Dance With Me)/Ruined City (with 'Jed' on p/s)	8
83	Whaam! WHAAM 009	Sha-La-La-La (Dance With Me)/Ruined City (without 'Jed' on p/s)	10

(see also V.I.P.'s)

DMS
91	Production House PNT 032	Exterminate (12")	15
92	Production House PNT 039	Vengeance/Love Overdose (Remix) (12")	15

DMX KREW
07	Revoke REVOKE 004	SYNTHE SOUND EP (12", test pressing)	50
96	Rephlex CAT 029LP	SOUND OF THE STREET (2-LP)	30
97	Rephlex CAT 053LP	FFRESSSHH! (2-LP)	30
98	Rephlex CAT 061LP	NU ROMANTIX (LP)	25
99	Rephlex CAT 086LP	WE ARE DMX (LP)	35

D.N.A.
80	CPEP 002	SHOCK ROCK EP	30

DNA (1)
81	Rough Trade RTO 86	A TASTE OF DNA (12" EP, p/s)	15

DNA (2)
81	DNA 1	Do The Shopping/Zoo Tango (p/s)	6
82	DNA 2	Atlantic Flyer/What A Way To Go (p/s)	6
81	DNA 3	The Road To Kong Kong/Praying Mantis (p/s)	6

DNA (3)
83	Confidential FILE 001	EXTENDED PLAY	15

DNV
79	New Pleasures Z2	Mafia/Death In Venice/Goodbye 70s (foldout p/s)	20

(see also Another Pretty Face, Funhouse, Waterboys, TV21)

D.O.A.
83	Alt. Tentacles VIRUS 31	BLOODIED BUT UNBOWED — THE DAMAGE TO DATE 1978-84 (LP)	15

CARL DOBKINS JNR.
59	Brunswick 05804	My Heart Is An Open Book/My Pledge To You	10
59	Brunswick 05811	If You Don't Want My Lovin'/Love Is Everything	15
60	Brunswick 05817	Lucky Devil/(There's A Little Song A-Singing) In My Heart	10
60	Brunswick 05832	Exclusively Yours/One Little Girl	10
60	Brunswick LAT 8329	CARL DOBKINS JNR. (LP)	21

BOBBY DOBSON
69	Punch PH 4	Strange/Your New Love	10

(see also Dobby Dobson)

BONNIE DOBSON
69	RCA RCA 1901	I'm Your Woman/I Got Stung	8
70	RCA SF 8079	BONNIE DOBSON (LP)	35

DOBBY DOBSON (& DELTAS)

MINT VALUE £

| 72 | Argo ZFB 79 | BONNIE DOBSON (LP) | 30 |
| 76 | Polydor 2383 400 | MORNING DEW (LP) | 15 |

DOBBY DOBSON (& DELTAS)

65	King KG 1008	Cry A Little Cry/Diamonds And Pearls (as Dobby Dobson & Deltas)	15
67	Trojan TR 011	Loving Pauper/TOMMY McCOOK & SUPERSONICS: Sir Don	35
68	Studio One SO 2068	Walking In The Footsteps/SOUL VENDORS: Studio Rock	70
68	Coxsone CS 7058	Seems To Me I'm Losing You/GAYLADS: Red Rose	40
69	Blue Cat BS 171	Strange/Your New Love	25
69	Punch PH 12	The Masquerade Is Over/Love For Ambition	10
70	Success RE 906	Crazy/RUPIE EDWARDS ALL STARS: Your New Love	6
70	Big BG 303	That Wonderful Sound/I Wasn't Born Yesterday	6
69	Pama SECO 33	STRANGE (LP)	80
70	Trojan TBL 145	THAT WONDERFUL SOUND (LP)	50

(see also Bobby Dobson, Chuck & Dobby, Bruce Bennett, Ernest Wilson & Freddy)

LYN DOBSON

| 74 | Fresh Air 6370 501 | JAM SANDWICH (LP) | 40 |

(see also Manfred Mann, Soft Machine, Miller Anderson)

DOC SCOTT

91	Absolute 2 ABS 001DJR	Surgery (Remix) (12")	8
92	Absolute 2 ABS 006DJ	The N.H.S. EP Vol 2 - The Second Chapter EP (12")	10
92	Absolute 2 ABS 006DJR	The N.H.S. EP Vol 2 - The Second Chapter (Remix) EP (12")	60
94	Metalheadz MET 004	Far Away (Fourteen Flavors Of Funk)/It's Yours (12")	18
95	Metalheadz METH 015	Drumz '95 (Nasty Habits Remix)/Blue Skies (12")	15
94	Reinforced RIVET 1256	Last Action Hero EP (12")	15
94	Metalheadz MH 001	Doc Scott/GOLDIE : Unreleased Metal (12")	20

ROY DOCKER

68	Domain D3	Mellow Moonlight/MUSIC THROUGH SIX: Riff Raff	30
69	Pama PM 750	When/Go	15
69	Pama PM 756	Everyday Will Be Like A Holiday/I'm An Outcast	8

DR. ATOMIC

| 93 | Guerilla GRRR42 | Schudelfloss (12") | 20 |

DOCTOR BIRDS

| 77 | JS JSM 001 | Smoking (Smoking My Ganja)/Rock With Me (12") | 30 |

DOCTOR BROWN

| 95 | Magic Gnome | ANOTHER REALM (LP, 500 only) | 15 |

DOCTOR DARK

| 76 | Target TGT 102 | Red Hot Passion/Instrumental (no p/s) | 7 |

(see also Snivelling Shits)

DOCTOR FATHER

| 70 | Pye 7N 17977 | Umbopo/Roll On | 10 |

(see also 10cc, Godley & Creme, Hotlegs)

DR. FEELGOOD & THE INTERNS (U.S.)

62	Columbia DB 4838	Dr. Feelgood/Mister Moonlight	25
64	Columbia DB 7228	Blang Dong/The Doctor's Doogie	25
66	CBS 202099	Don't Tell Me No Dirty/Where Did You Go	20
68	Capitol CL 15569	Sugar Bee/You're So Used To It	20
64	Columbia SEG 8310	DR. FEELGOOD AND THE INTERNS (EP)	70

(see also Piano Red)

DR. FEELGOOD (U.K.)

77	United Artists UP 36332	Baby Jane/Looking Back (p/s)	6
75	United Artists UAS 29727	DOWN BY THE JETTY (LP, mono only)	35
75	United Artists UAS 29880	MALPRACTICE (LP)	25
76	United Artists UAS 29990	STUPIDITY (LP, with stickered covers & bonus 7": "Riot In Cell Block No. 9"/"Johnny B. Goode" [FEEL 1])	20
77	United Artists UAS 30075	SNEAKIN SUSPICION (LP)	15
79	United Artists UAK 30239	AS IT HAPPENS (LP, with inner sleeve & bonus 7" "Encore EP": "Riot In Cell Block No. 9"/"The Blues Had A Baby And They Named It Rock'N'Roll"/"Lights Out"/"Great Balls Of Fire" [p/s, FEEL 2], with inner sleeve)	20
85	Edsel ED 160	DOWN BY THE JETTY (LP, reissue)	15

(see also Wilko Johnson, Lew Lewis, Oil City Sheiks)

DR. HOOK

| 73 | CBS 1037 | The Cover Of "Radio Times" (1-sided, promo only, by Dr. Hook & Friends) | 10 |

DR. JOHN (THE NIGHT TRIPPER)

70	Atco 2091 019	Wash Mama Wash/Mama Roux	12
72	Atlantic K 10158	Iko Iko/Huey Smith Medley	6
73	Atlantic K 10291	Right Place, Wrong Time/I Been Hoodooed	10
73	Atlantic K 10329	Such A Night/Life	6
68	Atlantic 587/588 147	GRIS GRIS (LP, plum label, mono/stereo)	80
69	Atco 228 018	BABYLON (LP, plum label)	40
70	Atco 2400 015	REMEDIES (LP, plum label)	40
71	Atlantic 2400 161	THE SUN, MOON AND HERBS (LP, plum label, gatefold sleeve with insert)	40
72	Atlantic K 40384	GUMBO (LP, green & orange label, gatefold sleeve)	30
72	Atlantic K 40168	GRIS GRIS (LP, reissue, green & orange label)	25
72	Atlantic K 40250	THE SUN, MOON AND HERBS (LP, reissue, green & orange label, gatefold sleeve with insert)	30
73	Atco K 50017	IN THE RIGHT PLACE (LP, U.K. disc in U.S. stickered 3-way gatefold sleeve)	40
73	CBS 65659	TRIUMVIRATE (LP, with John Hammond & Mike Bloomfield)	20
74	Atlantic K 50035	DESITIVELY BONNAROO (LP)	20
75	DJM DJSLM 2019	CUT ME WHILE I'M HOT (LP)	22
75	United Artists UAG 29902	HOLLYWOOD BE THY NAME (LP, with inner sleeve)	20

DR. K'S BLUES BAND
68	Spark SRLP 101	DR. K'S BLUES BAND (LP, red/silver label)	120

DR. MARIGOLD'S PRESCRIPTION
68	Pye 7N 17493	My Old Man's A Groovy Old Man/People Get Ready	6
69	Pye 7N 17832	You've Got To Build Your Love/My Picture Of Love	6
70	Bell BLL 1096	Breaking The Heart Of A Good Man/Night Hurries On By	6
70	Bell BLL 1126	Sing Along, Sing Along, Sing Along/Father Jim	6
71	Bell BLL 1149	Muddy Water/Come With Me	6

DR. MIX & THE REMIX
79	Rough Trade ROUGH 6	Wall Of Noise (12")	20

DR. OCTAGON
96	Mo' Wax MW 046LP	DR OCTAGON (3-LP)	30
96	Mo' Wax MW064LP	INSTRUMENTALYST (OCTAGON BEATS) (LP)	25

DOCTOR PABLO
84	On U-Sound ON U 30	NORTH OF THE RIVER THAMES (LP, with Dub Syndicate)	25

DOCTOR ROCKIT
96	Clear CLR 416	D For Doktor EP (12", p/s)	12

DR. STRANGELY STRANGE
69	Island CIR 15006	KIP OF THE SERENES (cassettte promo)	50
69	Island ILPS 9106	KIP OF THE SERENES (LP, pink label, with black/orange circle logo)	400
69	Island ILPS 9106	KIP OF THE SERENES (LP, pink label, with white 'i' logo)	200
69	Island ILPS 9106	KIP OF THE SERENES (LP, later 'palm-tree' label with remix)	100
70	Vertigo 6360 009	HEAVY PETTING (LP, gatefold sleeve, large swirl label; original pressing has machine etched matrix in the run out grooves, beware of counterfeits)	600
86	Timeless TIME 702	KIP OF THE SERENES (LP, reissue)	20

(see also Sweeney's Men, Gary Moore)

DR. TECHNICAL & MACHINES
83	Hawkfan HWFB 1	Zones/Processed (1-sided with insert, mail-order issue, no p/s)	25

(see also Hawkwind)

DR. WEST'S MEDICINE SHOW & JUNK BAND
67	CBS 202492	The Eggplant That Ate Chicago/You Can't Fight City Hall Blues	10
67	CBS 202658	Gondoliers, Shakespeares, Overseers/Daddy I Know	8
68	Page One POF 061	Bullets La Verne/Jigsaw	50
70	Page One POF 176	Gondoliers, Shakespeares, Overseers/Daddy I Know (reissue)	6
69	Page One POLS 017	THE EGGPLANT THAT ATE CHICAGO (LP)	25

(see also Norman Greenbaum)

DR. WHO
76	Argo ZSW 564	DR. WHO AND THE PESCATONS (LP, spoken word, read by Tom Baker & Elizabeth Sladen)	18
79	BBC REC 364	GENESIS OF THE DALEKS (LP, spoken word)	15
81	RNIB	TALKING BOOK (reel-to-reel tape, read by Gabriel Wolf)	20
82	BBC 2LP-22001	DOCTOR WHO COLLECTOR'S EDITION (2-LP, includes "Genesis Of The Daleks" [BBC 22364], "Sound Effects" [BBC 22316], & bonus 7" "Doctor Who"/"The Astronauts" [RESL 451], with poster)	30

(see also BBC Radiophonic Workshop, Century 21, Jon Pertwee)

DR. Z
70	Fontana 6007 023	Lady Ladybird/People In The Street	100
71	Vertigo 6360 048	THREE PARTS TO MY SOUL (LP, gatefold sleeve, small swirl label)	2000

(see also Gorilla Grip)

DOCTORS OF MADNESS
77	Polydor 2058 921	Bulletin/Waiting (p/s)	6

DODD'S ALLSTARS
69	Coxsone CS 7096	Mother Aitken (actually by Lord Power)/What A Love (actually by Denzil Laing)	70

NELLA DODDS
65	Pye 7N 25281	Come See About Me/You Don't Love Me Anymore	50
65	Pye 7N 25281	Come See About Me/You Don't Love Me Anymore (DJ Copy)	75
65	Pye 7N 25291	Finders Keepers, Losers Weepers/A Girl's Life	35
65	Pye 7N 25291	Finders Keepers, Losers Weepers/A Girl's Life (DJ Copy)	60

DODGEMS
79	Attrix RB/07/DGM	Science Fiction (Baby You're So)/Hard Shoulder (p/s)	8
80	Criminal SWAG 12	Lord Lucan Is Missing/Gotta Give It Up	8

DODGERS (1)
60	Downbeat CHA 2	Let's Make A Whole Lot Of Love/You Make Me Happy	25

DODGERS (2)
70	S & S SC 002	True Love/TONY SEXTON: Baby I Will Be Yours	12

DODGERS (3)
76	Island WIP 6342	Just Wanna Love You/Don't Know What You're Doing	8
78	Polydor 2059028	Love On The Rebound/Come Out Fighting	8
78	Polydor 2059046	Don't Let Me Be Wrong/Come Out Fighting	8

DODGY
93	A&M 540 0821	THE DODGY ALBUM (LP)	25
94	A&M 540 02821	HOMEGROWN (LP)	35

DODO'S
67	Polydor BM 56153	I Made Up My Mind/Can't Make It Out	30

DOES IT OFFEND YOU, YEAH?
07	Private Pressing	LIVE AT THE FEZ CLUB (12" white label)	20

DOGFEET
71	Reflection HRS 7	Sad Story/On The Road	15
71	Reflection HRS 12	Since I Went Away/Evil Woman	35
70	Reflection REFL 8	DOGFEET (LP, white/brown label)	1000
94	Kissing Spell CA 36001	DOGFEET (LP, reissue)	25

Tymon DOGG

MINT VALUE £

TYMON DOGG
81	Ghost Dance GHO 1	Lose This Skin (featuring the Clash)/Indestructible (p/s)	10

(see also Timon, Clash)

DOGGEREL BANK
73	Charisma CAS 1079	SILVER FACES (LP, gatefold sleeve, large "Mad Hatter" label)	25
75	Charisma CAS 1102	MISTER SKILLCORN DANCES (LP, small "Mad Hatter" label)	30

BILL DOGGETT
56	Parlophone CMSP 39	Honky Tonk (Parts 1 & 2) (gold label lettering, export issue)	25
56	Parlophone R 4231	Honky Tonk (Parts 1 & 2) (gold label lettering, later silver)	15
57	Parlophone R 4265	Slow Walk/Peacock Alley	10
57	Parlophone R 4306	Ram-Bunk-Shush/Blue Largo	10
61	Warner Bros WB 46	You Can't Sit Down (Parts 1 & 2)	15
58	Parlophone PMD 1067	DAME DREAMING (10" LP)	15
59	Parlophone PMD 1073	DANCE AWHILE WITH DOGGETT (10" LP)	20

(see also Ella Fitzgerald, Earl Bostic)

DOGHEAD
73	Sacred SC 01	Come Out Shooting/Passing The Buck	20

DOGMA CATS
80	Leisure Sounds SRS 33	Experts/Choke (p/s)	20

DOGMATIC ELEMENT
82	Cattle Company CC001/562CUS 1412	Strange Passion/Just Friends (p/s, 1000 only)	15
84	Cattle Company CC002/SRT4KS128	False Emotions/Not Now (p/s, 1000 only)	10

DOG ON A ROPE
98	Chase Out DAN 1	SPIKE (LP)	15

DOGROSE
72	Satril SAT 2	Paradise Row/Sunday Morning	15
73	Satril SAT 6	All For The Love Of City Lights/All Of The Love Of Each Other	20
72	Satril SATL 4002	ALL FOR THE LOVE OF DOGROSE (LP)	30

DOGS D'AMOUR
88	China WOL 7	THE (UN)AUTHORISED BOOTLEG (LP)	30

DOG SOLDIER
75	United Artists UA 29769	DOG SOLDIER (LP)	25

(see also Miller Anderson, Keef Hartley)

THE DOG THAT BIT PEOPLE
71	Parlophone R 5880	Lovely Lady/Merry-Go-Round	45
71	Parlophone PCS 7125	THE DOG THAT BIT PEOPLE (LP, black/silver label with boxed logo)	800

(see also Norman Haines, Locomotive)

DOGWATCH
79	Bridgehouse BHLP 002	PENFRIEND (LP, with insert)	20

NED DOHENY
81	CBS 9481	To Prove My Love/On The Swing Shift (p/s)	8
81	CBS 13-9481	To Prove My Love/On The Swing Shift (12", p/s)	10

JIM DOHERTY TRIO
65	Decca LK 4684	EXECUTIVE SUITE (LP)	60

DAVE DOLBY
73	Bell 1418	Shine A Light/Your Weight Is Your Mind	6

DOLE
78	Ultimate ULT 402	New Wave Love/Hungry Men No Longer Steal Sheep But Are There Hanging Judges? (die-cut p/s)	30

MICKY DOLENZ
67	London HLH 10152	Huff Puff/OBVIOUS: Fate	8

(see also Monkees)

ANDY DOLL
62	Starlite ST45 068	Wild Desire/Wyat	10
63	Starlite STLP II	ON STAGE (LP, by Andy Doll Band & Guests)	15

LINDA DOLL & SUNDOWNERS
64	Piccadilly 7N 35166	Bonie Maronie/He Don't Want Your Love Anymore	15

DOLLIES
65	CBS 201788	You Touch Me Baby/I Can't Go On	10

DOLLY MIXTURE
80	Chrysalis CHS 2459	Baby It's You/New Look Baby (p/s)	30
81	Respond RESP 1	Been Teen/Honky Honda/Ernie Ball (p/s)	25
82	Respond RESP 4	Everything And More/You And Me On The Sea Shore (p/s)	20
83	Dead Good Dolly Platters DMS 1	Remember This/Listening Pleasure/Borinda's Lament (p/s)	40
84	Cordelia ERICAT 017	FIRESIDE EP (12" p/s)	30
84	DM 1	DEMONSTRATION TAPES (2-LP, rubber stamped, hand-numbered signed sleeves with insert)	150
10	DMBOX 1	EVERYTHING AND MORE (3-CD box set)	90
10	Germs Of Youth GERMOS 08	DEMONSTRATION TAPES (2-LP, rubber stamped, hand-numbered signed sleeves with poster, 300 only)	100
11	For Us FU 043	REMEMBER THIS: THE SINGLES 1980-1984 (LP, black vinyl)	80
11	For Us FU 043	REMEMBER THIS: THE SINGLES 1980-1984 (LP, white vinyl)	100
19	Sealed SEAL 005	OTHER MUSIC (LP)	20
19	Sealed SEAL 005	OTHER MUSIC (LP, yellow vinyl)	30
19	Spa Green SPA 001	DEMONSTRATION TAPES (2-LP, red vinyl)	50
19	Spa Green SPA 001	DEMONSTRATION TAPES (2-LP)	35

(see also Coming Up Roses)

DOLPHIN
76	Private Stock PVT 52	Then I Kissed Her/The Glyderes	6

			MINT VALUE £
76	Private Stock PVT 67	Goin' Back/Think Ahead	10
77	Private Stock PVT 122	Imagination Dancing/The Actress	6
78	Private Stock PVT 154	Carry Me Away/Linda Lovelace	6

DOLPHINS
65	Stateside SS 375	Hey Da Da Dow/I Don't Want To Go On Without You	15

ERIC DOLPHY
60	Esquire 21-123	OUTWARD BOUND (LP)	150
61	Esquire 32-153	OUT THERE (LP)	100
61	Esquire 32-173	AT THE 5 SPOT VOL. 1.(LP)	150
64	Fontana TL5284	LAST DATE (LP)	60
65	Fontana 688521XL	MEMORIAL ALBUM (LP)	35
69	Transatlantic PR 7311	OUTWARD BOUND (LP)	20
67	Xtra 5039	SCREAMING THE BLUES (LP, with Oliver Nelson Sextet)	25

ERIC DOLPHY & BOOKER LITTLE
66	Stateside SL 10160	ERIC DOLPHY AND BOOKER LITTLE MEMORIAL ALBUM (LP)	15

BILLY DOLTON
61	Parlophone R 4733	Winkie Doll/Girls	10

DO MAKE SAY THINK
99	Resonant RES 001	BESIDES (12" EP)	12

DOME
80	Dome DOME 1	DOME (LP)	25
80	Dome DOME 2	DOME 2 (LP)	25
81	Dome DOME 3	DOME 3 (LP)	25

(see also Wire, Gilbert & Lewis, Cupol, Bruce Gilbert, P'o, Duet Emmo)

DOMESTIC BLISS
80	Woodbine ST WSR 004	Child Battery/Life (p/s)	15

DOMINANT FORCE
91	Gangster GAGR001	Criminals/Raptivity (12")	10

DOMINIC WAXING LYRICAL
86	Neptune LPPIE 020	DOMINIC WAXING LYRICAL (LP)	15

ANNA DOMINO
86	Factory FAC 158	Summer/The Summer Gets Captured By The Game (p/s)	12

FATS DOMINO
78s
54	London HL 8007	Rose Mary/You Said You Love Me	40
54	London HL 8063	Little School Girl/You Done Me Wrong	40
54	London HL 8096	Don't Leave Me This Way/Something's Wrong	30
55	London HL 8124	Love Me/Don't You Hear Me Calling You	30
55	London HL 8133	Thinking Of You/I Know	25
59	London HLP 8822	When The Saints Go Marching In/Telling Lies	20
59	London HLP 8865	Margie/I'm Ready	20
59	London HLP 8942	I Want To Walk You Home/I'm Gonna Be A Wheel Some Day	20
59	London HLP 9005	Be My Guest/I've Been Around	40
60	London HLP 9073	Country Boy/If You Need Me	40
60	London HLP 9163	Walking To New Orleans/Don't Come Knockin'	60

SINGLES
55	London HL 8124	Love Me/Don't You Hear Me Calling You	175
55	London HL 8133	Thinking Of You/I Know	125
55	London HLU 8173	Ain't That A Shame/La La	80
56	London HLU 8256	Bo Weevil/Don't Blame It On Me	100
56	London HLU 8280	I'm In Love Again/My Blue Heaven	100
56	London HLU 8309	When My Dream Boat Comes Home/So Long	50
56	London HLU 8330	Blueberry Hill/I Can't Go On (Rosalie)	50
57	London HLU 8356	Honey Chile/Don't You Know	100
57	London HLP 8377	Blue Monday/What's The Reason I'm Not Pleasing You	50

(Originally issued with triangular centres & gold lettering labels; later silver-label re-pressings are worth around half these values.)

57	London HLP 8407	I'm Walkin'/I'm In The Mood For Love	15
57	London HLP 8449	The Valley Of Tears/It's You I Love	15
57	London HLP 8471	What Will I Tell My Heart/When I See You	12
57	London HLP 8519	Wait And See/I Still Love You	15
58	London HLP 8575	The Big Beat (From The Film)/I Want You To Know	20
58	London HLP 8628	Sick And Tired/No, No	20
58	London HLP 8663	Little Mary/The Prisoner's Song	20
58	London HLP 8727	Young School Girl/It Must Be Love	30
58	London HLP 8759	Whole Lotta Loving/Coquette	20
59	London HLP 8822	When The Saints Go Marching In/Telling Lies	10

(HLP 8407 through to 8822 45s were issued with triangular centres & silver lettering on all-black labels; later copies are worth around half these values.)

59	London HLP 8865	Margie/I'm Ready (triangular centre & silver-top)	12
59	London HLP 8865	Margie/I'm Ready (later round centre)	6
59	London HLP 8942	I Want To Walk You Home/I'm Gonna Be A Wheel Some Day (round)	10
59	London HLP 9005	Be My Guest/I've Been Around (triangular centre)	20
59	London HLP 9005	Be My Guest/I've Been Around (round centre)	7

(All subsequent London 45s for Fats Domino after London HLP 9005 were issued with round centres & silver-top labels.)

60	London HLP 9073	Country Boy/If You Need Me	10
60	London HLP 9133	Tell Me That You Love Me/Before I Grow Too Old	10
60	London HLP 9163	Walking To New Orleans/Don't Come Knockin'	10
60	London HLP 9198	Three Nights A Week/Put Your Arms Around Me, Honey	10
60	London HLP 9244	My Girl Josephine/Natural Born Lover	10

DOMINOES (Jamaica)

MINT VALUE £

Year	Label/Cat #	Title	Value
61	London HLP 9301	What A Price/Ain't That Just Like A Woman	10
61	London HLP 9327	Fell In Love On Monday/Shu-Rah	10
61	London HLP 9374	It Keeps Rainin'/I Just Cry	20
61	London HLP 9415	Let The Four Winds Blow/Good Hearted Man	10
61	London HLP 9456	What A Party/Rockin' Bicycle	10
62	London HLP 9520	Jambalaya/You Win Again	8
62	London HLP 9557	My Real Name/My Heart Is Bleeding	10
62	London HLP 9590	Dance With Mr. Domino/Nothing New (Same Old Thing)	10
62	London HLP 9616	Did You Ever See A Dream Walking/Stop The Clock	10
63	London HLP 9738	You Always Hurt The One You Love/Trouble Blues	10
63	HMV POP 1164	There Goes My Heart Again/Can't Go On Without You	10
63	HMV POP 1197	When I'm Walkin'/I've Got A Right To Cry	8
63	HMV POP 1219	Red Sails In The Sunset/Song For Rosemary	8
63	HMV POP 1265	Just A Lonely Man/Who Cares	8
64	HMV POP 1281	I Don't Want To Set The World On Fire/Lazy Lady	7
64	HMV POP 1303	If You Don't Know What Love Is/Something You Got Baby	40
64	HMV POP 1324	Mary Oh Mary/Packin' Up	8
64	HMV POP 1370	Kansas City/Heartbreak Hill	8
65	Mercury MF 869	(I Left My Heart) In San Francisco/I Done Got Over It	6
65	Mercury MF 873	What's That You Got?/It's Never Too Late	6
65	HMV POP 1421	Why Don't You Do Right?/Wigs	6
67	HMV POP 1582	I'm Livin' Right/I Don't Want To Set The World On Fire	6
67	Liberty LBF 12055	It Keeps Rainin'/Blue Monday	15
67	Liberty LBF 12055	It Keeps Rainin'/Blue Monday (DJ Copy)	30
68	Reprise RS 20696	Honest Mamas Love Their Papas Better/One For The Highway	20
68	Reprise RS 20763	Lady Madonna/One For The Highway	10
69	Reprise RS 20810	Everybody's Got Something To Hide Except Me And My Monkey/ So Swell When You're Well	10
69	Mercury MF 1104	What's That You Got?/Jambalaya (On The Bayou)	8
78	Sonet SON 2168	Sleeping On The Job/After Hours	8

EXPORT SINGLES

Year	Label/Cat #	Title	Value
57	London HL 7028	Wait And See/I Still Love You	30
58	London HL 7040	Sick And Tired/No, No	30
58	London HL 7054	The Big Beat (From The Film)/Little Mary	30

EPs

Year	Label/Cat #	Title	Value
55	London RE-P 1022	BLUES FOR LOVE (1st pressing with gold lettering label)	30
55	London RE-P 1022	BLUES FOR LOVE (2nd pressing with silver lettering label)	20
56	London RE-U 1062	BLUES FOR LOVE VOL. 2 (1st pressing with gold label)	30
56	London RE-U 1062	BLUES FOR LOVE VOL. 2 (2nd pressing with silver label)	20
57	London RE-U 1073	FATS (export issue, plain sleeve)	40
57	London RE-P 1079	HERE COMES FATS VOL. 1	30
58	London RE-P 1080	HERE COMES FATS VOL. 2	30
58	London RE-P 1115	CARRY ON ROCKIN' PART 1	60
58	London RE-P 1116	CARRY ON ROCKIN' PART 2	60
58	London RE-P 1117	BLUES FOR LOVE VOL. 3	30
58	London RE-P 1121	BLUES FOR LOVE VOL. 4	30
58	London RE-P 1138	HERE COMES FATS VOL. 3	30
59	London RE-P 1206	THE ROCKIN' MR. D VOL. 1	30
59	London RE-P 1207	THE ROCKIN' MR. D VOL. 2	30

(The above EPs were originally issued with triangular centres; round-centre re-pressings are worth two-thirds these values.)

Year	Label/Cat #	Title	Value
60	London RE-P 1261	BE MY GUEST	30
60	London RE-P 1265	THE ROCKIN' MR. D VOL. 3	30
62	London RE-P 1340	WHAT A PARTY	30
64	HMV 7EG 8862	RED SAILS IN THE SUNSET	15
65	Liberty LEP 4026	MY BLUE HEAVEN	20
66	Liberty LEP 4045	ROLLIN'	20

ALBUMS

Year	Label/Cat #	Title	Value
56	London HA-U 2028	FATS' ROCK AND ROLLIN'	90
56	London HA-P 2041	CARRY ON ROCKIN'	100
57	London HA-P 2052	HERE STANDS FATS DOMINO	90
56	London HA-P 2073	THIS IS FATS DOMINO	60
58	London HA-P 2087	THIS IS FATS	60
58	London HA-P 2135	THE FABULOUS "MR. D"	50
59	London HA-P 2223	LET'S PLAY FATS DOMINO	50
60	London HA-P 2312	A LOT OF DOMINOES!	40
61	London HA-P 2364	I MISS YOU SO	40
61	London HA-P 2420	LET THE FOUR WINDS BLOW	40
61	London HA-P 2426	WHAT A PARTY	40
62	London HA-P 2447	TWISTIN' THE STOMP	40
63	London HA-P 8039	JUST DOMINO	40
63	London HA-P 8084	WALKING TO NEW ORLEANS	40
63	HMV CLP 1690	HERE COMES FATS DOMINO (also stereo CSD 1520)	25
63	HMV CLP 1740	FATS ON FIRE (also stereo CSD 1543)	25
65	HMV CLP 1821	GETAWAY WITH FATS DOMINO (also stereo CSD 1580)	18
65	Mercury (S)MCL 20070	DOMINO '65 (mono/stereo)	15
68	Stateside (S)SL 10240	FANTASTIC FATS	15

DOMINOES (JAMAICA)

Year	Label/Cat #	Title	Value
68	Melody MRC 001	Tears In Your Eyes/Johnny Darling	30
68	Melody MRC 002	A Tribute (actually by Ann Reid)/Hooray (actually by Uniques)	110

DOMINOES (U.K.)

MINT VALUE £

DOMINOES (U.K.)
60	Reading Rag LYN 545	Bye Bye Johnny/Yakety Yak	15

DOMINOES (U.S.)
51	Vogue V 9012	Sixty Minute Man/I Can't Escape From You (78)	50
52	Vogue V 2135	Have Mercy, Baby/That's What You're Doing To Me (78)	40
67	Vogue V 212	Sixty Minute Man/I Can't Escape From You	30

(see also Billy Ward & Dominoes, Clyde McPhatter, Jackie Wilson)

DON DAVID AND DEAN
64	United Artists UP 1064	No Need to Cry/Fairy Tales	10

DON, DICK & JIMMY
54	Columbia SCM 5210	Brand Me With Your Kisses/Angela Mia	12
55	London HL 8117	You Can't Have Your Cake And Eat It Too/That's What I Like	20
55	London HL 8144	Make Yourself Comfortable/(Whatever Happened To The) Piano Players (That Played Like This)	10
56	HMV POP 280	That's The Way I Feel/Two Voices In The Night	6
56	London RE-U 1043	DON, DICK AND JIMMY (EP)	20

SAM DONAHUE & HIS ORCHESTRA
55	Capitol CL 14349	Saxaboogie/September In The Rain	10

TROY DONAHUE
63	Warner Bros WB 111	Live Young/Somebody Loves Me	7

MIKE DONALD & BOB SIDDALL
74	Tradition Century TSC 2	A BUG'S EYE VIEW (LP, 100 copies only)	30

(see also Mike Donald)

MIKE DONALD
71	Folk Heritage FHR 021	YORKSHIRE SONGS OF THE BROAD ACRES (LP, first pressing, textured sleeve with black and white photo)	25
71	Folk Heritage FHR 021	YORKSHIRE SONGS OF THE BROAD ACRES (LP, second pressing, laminated sleeve with colour photo)	15
72	Galliard GAL 4020	NORTH BY NORTH EAST (LP)	15

ERIC DONALDSON
71	Dynamic DYN 420	Cherry Oh Baby/LLOYD CHARMERS: Sir Charmers Special	6
71	Dynamic DYN 423	Love Of The Common People/DRAGONAIRES: The Dragon's Net	10
71	Dynamic DYN 425	Just Can't (Happen This Way)/Just Can't (Happen This Way) Version	7
72	Dynamic DYN 431	I'm Indebted/I'm Indebted (Version)	7
72	Dynamic DYN 439	Miserable Woman/The Lion Sleeps	7
72	Dynamic DYN 445	Blue Boot/Blue Boot (Version)	7
72	Dynamic DYN 452	Little Did You Know/Little Did You Know (Version)	7
73	Dragon DRA 1017	What A Festival/I ROY & ERIC: Festival Version	7
73	Dragon DRA 1018	The Way You Do The Things You Do/Version	7
73	Dragon DRA 1020	Watch What You're Doing To Me/You Must Believe Me	7
73	Dragon DRA 1027	A Weh We A Go Go/SOUL DEFENDERS: Version	7
70s	Serengeti SGTI 01	Penny Farthing/Evil Eyes (12")	60
05	Black Art/Trojan TJLBX 244/6	Stand Up (with the Keystones)/UPSETTERS: Dub Fo Yo Right (reissue)	20
72	Trojan TRL 42	ERIC DONALDSON (LP)	20

(see also Prunes, Satchmo)

DON & DENNY
60s	Loop LOO 504	(Ain't That)Just Like Me/Feeling Groovy	40

DON & DEWEY
64	London HL 9897	Get Your Hat/Annie Lee	20
66	Cameo Parkway CP 750	Soul Motion/Stretchin' Out	50
67	Sue WI 4032	Soul Motion/Stretchin' Out (reissue)	30
71	Specialty SNTF 5006	DON AND DEWEY (LP)	15

(see also Dewey Terry)

DON & GOODTIMES
67	Columbia DB 8199	I Could Be So Good To You/And It's So Good	12
67	Columbia DB 8266	Happy And Me/If You Love Her, Cherish Her And Such	8

DON & JUAN
62	London HLX 9529	What's Your Name?/Chicken Necks	15

DONAVAN/FULLWOOD
76	Stop Point	Deeper And Deeper/Hit After Hit	35

DONAYS
62	Oriole CBA 1770	Devil In His Heart/Bad Boy	150

DON CABALLERO
93	City Slang 04929-08	FOR RESPECT (LP)	15

LONNIE DONEGAN

SINGLES
55	Decca F 10647	Rock Island Line/John Henry (as Lonnie Donegan Skiffle Group) (tri-centre)	15
56	Decca FJ 10695	Diggin' My Potatoes/Bury My Body (as Lonnie Donegan Skiffle Group) (tri-centre)	15
56	Columbia DB 3850	On A Christmas Day/Take My Hand, Precious Lord (as Lonnie Donegan with Chris Barber's Jazz Band)	20
57	Pye Nixa 7N 15116	Jack O' Diamonds/Ham 'N' Eggs	8
58	Pye Jazz 7NJ 2006	Midnight Special/When The Sun Goes Down	25
58	Pye Nixa 7N 15148	Sally, Don't You Grieve/Betty, Betty, Betty	8
62	Pye 7N 3109	The Comancheros/Medley (export, p/s)	10

ALBUMS
56	Pye Nixa NPT 19012	LONNIE DONEGAN SHOWCASE (10")	15
57	Pye Nixa NPTs19027	LONNIE (10" LP, stereo)	20
58	Pye Nixa NPT 19027	LONNIE (10" LP)	15
62	Pye NPL 18073	SING HALLELUJAH (LP)	15
65	Pye NPL 18126	THE LONNIE DONEGAN FOLK ALBUM	18

DONKEYS

(see also Chris Barber)

DONKEYS
Year	Label/Cat	Title	MINT VALUE £
80	Rhesus GO APE 102	What I Want/Four Letters (yellow or orange label, p/s)	12
80	Rhesus GO APE 3	No Way/You Jane (p/s)	10
80	Rhesus GO APE 105	Don't Go/Living Legends (p/s)	10
80	Back Door DOOR 006	No Way/You Jane (reissue, p/s)	7
81	MCA MCA 721	Let's Float/Watched By Everyone (p/s)	10
81	MCA MCA 737	Listen To Your Radio/Watched By Everyone (as Donkees) (p/s)	10

JIMMY DONLEY
Year	Label/Cat	Title	£
57	Brunswick 05715	South Of The Border/The Trail Of The Lonesome Pine	20
59	Brunswick 05807	The Shape You Left Me In/What Must I Do	100
59	Brunswick 05807	The Shape You Left Me In/What Must I Do (78)	20

DONNA & FREEDOM SINGERS
Year	Label/Cat	Title	£
70	Bamboo BAM 53	Oh Me Oh My (actually by Jerry Jones)/JACKIE MITTOO: Gold Mine	25

PAUL DONNER
Year	Label/Cat	Title	£
78	Wildfire WRP 22	Yesterday's Roses - No More Baby/Carolina Feel It Burning (p/s)	6

RAL DONNER
Year	Label/Cat	Title	£
61	Parlophone R 4820	You Don't Know What You've Got/So Close To Heaven	10
61	Parlophone R 4859	Please Don't Go/I Didn't Figure On Him (To Come Back)	15
62	Parlophone R 4889	I Don't Need You/She's Everything (I Wanted You To Be)	15
62	Stateside SS 109	Bells Of Love/Loveless Life	20
63	Reprise R 20141	I Got Burned/A Tear In My Eye	30

DONNIE & DREAMERS
Year	Label/Cat	Title	£
61	Top Rank JAR 571	Count Every Star/Dorothy	50

DON & OLLIE
Year	Label/Cat	Title	£
79	Cartridge CR D 106	Superman/Have A Party (12")	100

DO NOTHING
Year	Label/Cat	Title	£
19	No label or Cat no	Gangs/Handshakes (p/s)	20
20	Exact Truth DNLJ00212	ZERO DOLLAR BILL EP (12", p/s)	20

DONOVAN
Year	Label/Cat	Title	£
65	Pye 7N 15984	Turquoise/Hey Gyp (Dig The Slowness)	8
66	Pye 7N 17067	Josie/Little Tin Soldier	10
66	Pye 7N 17088	Remember The Alamo/The Ballad Of A Crystal Man	15
66	Pye 7N 17241	Sunshine Superman/The Trip	7
67	Pye 7N 17267	Mellow Yellow/Preachin' Love	6
67	Pye 7N 17403	There Is A Mountain/Sand And Foam	6
68	Pye 7N 17457	Jennifer Juniper/Poor Cow	6
68	Pye 7N 17537	Hurdy Gurdy Man/Teen Angel	10
68	Pye 7N 17660	To Susan On The West Coast Waiting/Atlantis (unreleased)	0
68	Pye 7N 17660	Atlantis/I Love My Shirt	6
69	Pye 7N 17778	Goo Goo Barabajagal (Love Is Hot)/Bed With Me (with Jeff Beck Group)	12
69	Pye 7N 17778	Barabajagal/Trudi (shortened A-side title & retitled B-side)	10
70	Dawn DNS 1006	Ricki Ticki Tavi/Roots Of Oak (as Donovan with Open Road)	6
70	Dawn DNS 1007	Celia Of The Seals (with Danny Thompson)/Mr. Wind	6
72	private pressing	The Music Makers (one-sided, paper sleeve, 50 only)	50
73	Epic EPC 1644	Maria Magenta/Intergalactic Laxative (p/s)	6
73	Epic EPC 1960	Sailing Homeward/Lazy Daze (p/s)	6
74	Epic EPC 1960	Sailing Homeward/Yellow Star (p/s, reissue with different B-side; some copies list both Donovan & Andrew Oldham as producers)	6
75	Epic EPC 2661	Rock'n'Roll With Me/Divine Daze Of Deathless Delight (in p/s)	20
75	Epic EPC 2661	Rock'n'Roll With Me/Divine Daze Of Deathless Delight	6
77	Rak RAK 265	The Light/The International Man (p/s)	8
81	Luggage LUG 03	Lay Down Lassie/Love Is Only A Feeling (p/s)	7
65	Pye NEP 24229	COLOURS (EP)	15
66	Pye NEP 24239	DONOVAN VOL. 1 (EP)	15
68	Pye NEP 24287	CATCH THE WIND (EP)	15
68	Pye NEP 24299	HURDY GURDY DONOVAN (EP)	20
65	Pye NPL 18117	WHAT'S BIN DID AND WHAT'S BIN HID (LP, some with misprinted Side 2 label)	35
65	Pye NPL 18128	FAIRYTALE (LP, some copies with blank rear sleeve)	50
66	World Records ST 951	DONOVAN (LP)	18
67	Pye NPL 18181	SUNSHINE SUPERMAN (LP)	50
68	Pye NPL 20000	A GIFT FROM A FLOWER TO A GARDEN (2-LP, black or navy blue box set, separate halves with taped hinge; with 12 inserts in folder, mono)	125
68	Pye N(S)PL 20000	A GIFT FROM A FLOWER TO A GARDEN (2-LP, black or navy blue box set, separate halves with taped hinge; with 12 inserts in folder, stereo)	100
68	Pye NPL 18237	DONOVAN IN CONCERT (LP, mono)	20
68	Pye N(S)PL 18237	DONOVAN IN CONCERT (LP, stereo)	18
70	Dawn DNLS 3009	OPEN ROAD (LP, gatefold sleeve)	30
71	Dawn DNLD 4001	H.M.S. DONOVAN (2-LP, First pressing, orange label, MATRIX: DNLP 4001 A-1 *T/B-1 *T/C-1*T/D-1*T :gatefold sleeve, with foldout poster)	150
72	Dawn DNLD 4001	H.M.S. DONOVAN (2-LP, Second pressing, lilac label, gatefold sleeve, with foldout poster)	60
72	Dawn DNLD 4001	H.M.S. DONOVAN (2-LP, Second pressing, lilac label, gatefold sleeve, without foldout poster)	20
73	Dawn DNLD 4001	H.M.S. DONOVAN (2-LP, Third pressing, white label with pink and blue sunrise, gatefold sleeve)	40
71	Dawn DNLD 4001	H.M.S. DONOVAN (2-LP, gatefold sleeve, without foldout poster)	25
73	Pye 11PP 102	FOUR SHADES ("H.M.S. Donovan"/"Greatest Hits"/"Open Road") (4-LP box set)	50
73	Epic EPC 69050	ESSENCE TO ESSENCE (LP, gatefold sleeve, lyric insert, with sticker)	15

(see also Jeff Beck, Open Road)

DONTELLS

MINT VALUE £

DONTELLS
65	Fontana TF 566	In Your Heart/Nothing But Nothing	50
74	President PT 373	In Your Heart/Nothing But Nothing (reissue)	10

DICKY DOO & DON'TS
58	London HLU 8589	Click Click/Did You Cry	20
58	London HLU 8754	Leave Me Alone/Wild, Wild Party (with Orchestra)	25
60	Top Rank JAR 318	Wabash Cannonball/WEST TEXAS MARCHING BAND: The Drums Of Richard A Doo	10

DOOF
80	Namedrop NR1	EXIST (10" mini-LP, with booklet)	25

(see also Exhibit A)

DOOKIE SQUAD
94	Dookie DS 001	6FT Under/Mad Shit (12")	15
13	1st Bass DS002	Deep Rising (12" red vinyl)	10

DOOLEY SISTERS
55	London HL 8128	Ko Ko Mo (I Love You So)/Heart Throb	30

DOOM/CRESS
98	Flat Earth FE 27	SPLIT 10" LP (with insert)	10

DOOM (1)
89	Discard DISC 001	POLICE BASTARD EP	15
88	Peaceville VILE 4	WAR CRIMES INHUMAN BEINGS (LP, white vinyl)	35
89	Strange Fruit SFPMA 203	DOUBLE PEEL SESSIONS (LP, with insert)	15
89	Peaceville VILE 11	BURY THE DEBT NOT THE DEAD (split LP with NO SECURITY)	18

DOOM (2)
93	Discipline DISCLP10	THE GREATEST INVENTION (mini-LP)	20

JOHN DOONAN
72	Leader LEA 2043	FLUTE FOR THE FEIS (LP)	15

DOONICANS
87	Probe Plus PP 23T	THE FISHERMAN'S WAY (12" EP)	10

DOOR & THE WINDOW
79	NR NR 1	Subculture/Fashion Slaves/Nostradamus/Don't Kill Colin/Wurst Ban	25
80	NB Records NB 5	DETAILED TWANG (LP, blank labels)	18
80	NB Records NB 9	MUSIC AND MOVEMENT (live cassette)	15

(see also Alternative TV)

DOORS

SINGLES
67	Elektra EKSN 45009	Break On Through (To The Other Side)/End Of The Night	50
67	Elektra EKSN 45012	Alabama Song (Whisky Bar)/Take It As It Comes	25
67	Elektra EKSN 45014	Light My Fire/The Crystal Ship	20
67	Elektra EKSN 45017	People Are Strange/Unhappy Girl	20
67	Elektra EKSN 45022	Love Me Two Times/Moonlight Drive	15
68	Elektra EKSN 45030	We Could Be So Good Together/The Unknown Soldier	15
68	Elektra EKSN 45037	Hello, I Love You, Won't You Tell Me Your Name/Love Street	10
69	Elektra EKSN 45050	Touch Me/Wild Child	10
69	Elektra EKSN 45059	Wishful Sinful/Who Scared You?	10
69	Elektra EKSN 45065	Tell All The People/Easy Ride	10
70	Elektra 2101 004	You Make Me Real/The Spy	10
70	Elektra 2101 008	Roadhouse Blues/Blue Sunday	10
71	Elektra EK 45726	Love Her Madly/(You Need Meat) Don't Go No Further	6
71	Elektra K 12021	Riders On The Storm/The Changeling	6
72	Elektra K 12036	Tightrope Ride/Variety Is The Spice Of Life	8
79	Elektra K 12215/SAM 94	Love Me Two Times/Hello, I Love You// Ghost Song/Roadhouse Blues (double pack)	10
83	Elektra E 9974T	Gloria/Love Me Two Times (12", p/s with poster)	10
92	Final Vinyl FV 1/2	INTERVIEW TAPES (2 x 7" box set, with 7 inserts, numbered, 500 only)	10

ALBUMS
67	Elektra EKL 4007	THE DOORS (1st mono pressing, orange labels with black lettering, 'manufactured by Elektra records' on label, in U.S. printed sleeve, mono)	200
67	Elektra EKL 4007	THE DOORS (2nd mono pressing, orange labels with black lettering, 'manufactured by Polydor' on label records' on label in fully laminated UK printed sleeve, mono)	150
67	Elektra EKS 4007	THE DOORS (1st stereo pressing, orange labels with black lettering, 'manufactured by Elektra records' on label, in U.S. sleeve, stereo)	140
67	Elektra EKS 74007	THE DOORS (2nd stereo pressing, orange labels with black lettering, 'manufactured by Polydor' on label, in fully laminated UK printed sleeve)	80
68	Elektra EKL 4014	STRANGE DAYS (1st mono pressing, orange labels with black lettering, 'THE DOORS' in regular typeface and 'manufactured by Polydor' on label, with printed inner sleeve, fully laminated UK printed sleeve)	200
68	Elektra EKL 4014	STRANGE DAYS (2nd mono pressing, lighter orange labels with black lettering, 'THE DOORS' as logo and 'manufactured by Polydor' on label, with printed inner sleeve, fully laminated UK printed sleeve)	150
68	Elektra EKS 4014	STRANGE DAYS (1st stereo pressing, orange labels with black lettering, 'THE DOORS' in regular typeface and 'manufactured by Polydor' on label, with printed inner sleeve, fully laminated UK printed sleeve)	180
68	Elektra EKS 74014	STRANGE DAYS (2nd stereo pressing, lighter orange labels with black lettering, 'THE DOORS' as logo and 'manufactured by Polydor' on label, with printed inner sleeve, full laminated UK printed sleeve)	120
68	Elektra EKL 4024	WAITING FOR THE SUN (1st - and only - mono pressing, orange labels with black lettering, 'Polydor Records Ltd' on label, in non laminated gatefold sleeve, with or without 'Ernest J. Day' credit)	200
68	Elektra EKS 4024	WAITING FOR THE SUN (1st stereo pressing, orange labels with black lettering. 'Polydor Records Ltd' on label, in non laminated gatefold sleeve)	120
69	Elektra EKS 75005	THE SOFT PARADE (1st pressing, orange labels with silver lettering, with lyric insert, non laminated gatefold sleeve)	150
69	Elektra EKS 74007	THE DOORS (3rd stereo pressing, orange labels with silver lettering, 'manufactured by Polydor' on label, in fully laminated UK printed sleeve)	80
70	Elektra EKS 74014	STRANGE DAYS (3rd stereo pressing, red labels, white 'E' logo, in fully laminated UK	60

DOORS OF PERCEPTION

MINT VALUE £

		printed sleeve)	
70	Elektra EKS 75007	MORRISON HOTEL (1st pressing, red labels, white 'E' logo, in laminated gatefold sleeve)	100
70	Elektra 2665 002	ABSOLUTELY LIVE (2-LP, 1st pressing, red labels, white 'E' logo, in non laminated gatefold sleeve. Early copies have 2409-004 & 2409-004 on the respective discs, both with SET NO 2665 002 beneath in brackets. Some also have a white sticker with EKS 9002 on the back sleeve)	80
70	Elektra EKS 74007	THE DOORS (4th stereo pressing, red labels, white 'E' logo in fully laminated sleeve)	50
71	Elektra EKS 74079	13 (1st pressing, 'butterfly' labels, p.1970* on labels, non laminated sleeve)	35
71	Elektra K 42090	L.A. WOMAN (1st pressing, Butterfly labels, embossed round-cornered, die-cut PVC 'window' sleeve & yellow and black inner sleeve)	80
71	Elektra K 42012	THE DOORS (5th stereo pressing, Butterfly labels, non laminated sleeve)	35
71	Elektra K 42104	OTHER VOICES (Butterfly labels, gatefold sleeve)	15
71	Elektra K 42016	STRANGE DAYS (4th stereo pressing. Butterfly labels, non laminated sleeve)	35
71	Elektra K 42012	WAITING FOR THE SUN (2nd stereo pressing, Butterfly labels, non laminated gatefold sleeve)	40
72	Elektra K 62009	WEIRD SCENES INSIDE THE GOLDMINE (1st pressing, 2-LP, Butterfly labels, gatefold sleeve)	40
72	Elektra K 62005	ABSOLUTELY LIVE (2-LP, 2nd pressing, Butterfly labels, 'EMI records Ltd' on back sleeve)	40
72	Elektra K 62116	FULL CIRCLE (Butterfly labels, gatefold sleeve)	15
73	Ekektra K 42090	L.A. WOMAN (2nd pressing, Butterfly labels, embossed round-cornered die cut acetate window sleeve with yellow and black inner sleeve. 'EMI' Records Ltd' in label copyright text)	60
74	Elektra K 42090	LA WOMAN (3rd pressing, Butterfly labels, non embossed, 'round cornered' burgundy, black and white sleeve, no window. Yellow and black inner sleeve. 'EMI Records Ltd' on label copyright text)	35
74	Elektra K 62009	WEIRD SCENES INSIDE THE GOLDMINE (2nd pressing, 2-LP set, 'EMI Records Ltd' in copyright text on label and on back cover)	35
74	Elektra K 75007	MORRISON HOTEL (2nd pressing, Butterfly labels, non laminated gatefold sleeve)	40
74	Elektra K 42062	13 (2nd pressing, Butterfly labels, p.1970 on labels, 'EMI records Ltd' on label copyright text, some with 'EMI Records Ltd' sticker on back sleeve)	20
76	Elektra K 42062	13 (3rd pressing, Butterfly labels, WEA pressing, p.1971 and 'W' Warner logo added to copyright text on label, non laminated sleeve)	20
76	Elektra K42012	THE DOORS (6th stereo pressing, Butterfly labels, p.1971 and 'W' Warners logo added to copyright text on label, non laminated sleeve)	20
76	Elektra K42016	STRANGE DAYS (5th stereo pressing, Butterfly labels, 'W' Warner logo added to copyright text on label, non laminated sleeve)	20
76	Elektra K42080	MORRISON HOTEL (3rd pressing, Butterfly labels, 'W' Warner logo added to copyright text on label, non laminated gatefold sleeve)	15
76	Elektra K42079	THE SOFT PARADE (2nd pressing, Butterfly labels, 'W' Warner logo added to copyright text on label, non laminated gatefold sleeve)	25
76	Elektra K42041	WAITING FOR THE SUN (3rd stereo pressing, 'Butterfly' labels, p.1971 and 'W' Warner logo added to copyright text on label, non laminated gatefold sleeve)	25
76	Elektra K 62009	WEIRD SCENES INSIDE THE GOLDMINE (3rd pressing, 2-LP set WEA pressing, 'W' added to label copyright text)	25
76	Elektra K42090	L.A. WOMAN (4th pressing, Butterfly labels, standard 'square' burgundy, black and yellow sleeve. No inner sleeve. WEA pressing with 'W' Warner logo in copyright text on label)	25
76	Elektra K 42143	THE BEST OF THE DOORS (Butterfly labels)	20
78	Elektra K52111	AN AMERICAN PRAYER ('Butterfly' label, gatefold sleeve, with 8-page booklet)	20
76	Elektra K 62005	ABSOLUTELY LIVE (2-LP, 3rd pressing, Butterfly labels, 'W' Warner logo added to copyright text on label)	25
83	Elektra 96-0269-1	ALIVE SHE CRIED (cream labels, with inner sleeve)	20

(see also Ray Manzarek)

DOORS OF PERCEPTION
| 91 | Lizard Nation LN 001 | SO JOIN MR. DREAMS (LP, with inner sleeve and booklet) | 15 |

D.O.P.E.
| 92 | Spare Beat SBRR 002 | When I Was Young (Original Mix)/RIchard's First Trip (12") | 12 |
| 93 | Rugged Vinyl RUGGED 1 | THE DOPE ON PLASTIC EP (12") | 10 |

DOPE ON PLASTIC
| 94 | Wave DJC 001 | Wave Dub/Out Of Time/East A Bit/It's A Dream (12") | 70 |

M.J. DORANE
74	Dip DL 5023	Loving You/Medley	10
76	Rockers RRLP 2	AVONMORE DUB (LP, pre-release, white labels only)	400
76	Rockers RRLP 3	REGGAE TIME (LP)	150

MIKE DORANE & CIMARONS
| 71 | Ackee ACK 144 | Penguin Funk/Ad-Lib | 12 |

DOREEN (CAMPBELL) & ALL STARS
| 67 | Rainbow RAI 114 | Rude Girls/Please Stay | 20 |

DOREEN (SHAFFER) & JACKIE (OPEL)
| 65 | Ska Beat JB 208 | Welcome Home/You And I | 35 |

(see also Jackie & Doreen)

DORIAN
| 70 | Ember EMB S 285 | Psychedelic Lipstick/Help For My Waiting | 8 |

DORIS
81	ABCD ABCD 1	Sitting Here Waiting (no p/s)	10
82	ABCD ABCD 3	GYPSY LADY (LP, actually credited to A Band Called Doris)	250
98	EMI/Mr. Bongo MRBLP 010	DID YOU GIVE THE WORLD SOME LOVE TODAY, BABY? (LP, reissue of Swedish 60s LP)	15

HAROLD DORMAN
| 60 | Top Rank JAR 357 | Mountain Of Love/To Be With You | 25 |
| 61 | London HLS 9386 | There They Go/I'll Stick By You | 15 |

DOROTHY
| 80 | Industrial IR 0014 | I Confess/Softness (p/s) | 15 |

RALPH DORPER
| 83 | Operation Twilight OPT 18 | THE ERASERHEAD EP (12") | 20 |

(see also Propaganda)

CHRIS DORS
			MINT VALUE £
61	Fontana H 329	That's When Your Heartaches Begin/They Called It Love	6

DIANA DORS
60	Pye 7N 15242	April Heart/Point Of No Return	10
64	Fontana TF 506	So Little Time/It's Too Late	50
66	Polydor BM 56111	Security/Gary	10
60	Pye NPL 18044	SWINGIN' DORS (LP, foldout sleeve, red vinyl)	100

RAY DORSET (WITH MUNGO JERRY)
79	Satellite RAY 001	Forgotten Land/New Way Of Life (solo, unreleased; 100 promos only)	6
72	Dawn DNLS 3033	COLD BLUE EXCURSION (LP, solo; gatefold sleeve with lyric inner, lilac label)	50

(see also Mungo Jerry, Good Earth, County Jug,, Insiders, Panache, Made In England)

DORSETS
65	Sue WI 391	Pork Chops/Cool It	50

GERRY DORSEY
59	Decca F 11108	Mister Music Man/Crazy Bells	25
59	Parlophone R 4595	I'll Never Fall In Love Again/Every Day Is A Wonderful Day	10
61	Parlophone R 4739	Big Wheel/The Sentimental Joker	10
64	Pye 7N 15622	Baby I Do/Take Your Time	10
65	Hickory 45-1337	Baby Turn Around/Things I Wanna Do	35

JACK DORSEY ORCHESTRA
64	Pye 7N 15730	Ringo's Dog/March Of The Gonks (as BIG BAND)	10
65	Polydor 56020	Dance Of The Daleks/Likely Lads	10
66	Polydor 56090	Alfie's Theme/Alfie's Theme Too	15
68	Pye 7N 17501	Soul Coaxing/Elizabeth's Waltz	10

LEE DORSEY
62	Top Rank JAR 606	Do-Re-Mi/People Gonna Talk	25
65	Sue WI 367	Do-Re-Mi/Ya Ya	40
65	Stateside SS 441	Ride Your Pony/The Kitty Cat Song	12
65	Stateside SS 465	Work Work Work/Can You Hear Me	12
66	Sue WI 399	Messed Around/When I Meet My Baby	40
66	Stateside SS 485	Get Out Of My Life, Woman/So Long	10
66	Stateside SS 506	Confusion/Neighbour's Daughter	8
66	Stateside SS 528	Working In A Coalmine/Mexico	10
66	Stateside SS 528	Working In A Coalmine/Mexico (yellow vinyl)	50
66	Stateside SS 552	Holy Cow/Operation Heartache	7
67	Stateside SS 2017	My Old Car/Why Wait Until Tomorrow	6
67	Stateside SS 2055	Go-Go Girl/I Can Hear You Callin'	10
69	Bell BLL 1074	Everything I Do Gonna Be Funky/There Should Be A Book	15
66	Stateside SE 1038	RIDE YOUR PONY (EP)	30
66	Stateside SE 1043	YOU'RE BREAKING ME UP (EP)	30
65	Sue ILP 924	THE BEST OF LEE DORSEY (LP)	60
66	Stateside S(S)L 10177	LEE DORSEY — RIDE YOUR PONY (LP)	30
66	Stateside S(S)L 10192	THE NEW LEE DORSEY (LP)	25
71	Polydor 2489 006	YES WE CAN (LP, black/red/white Polydor logo on bottom left of front sleeve)	50
84	Polydor 2482 280	YES WE CAN (LP, reissue, 'Special Polydor' in top right hand corner)	20

LEE DORSEY & BETTY HARRIS
69	Buffalo BFS 1002	Love Lots Of Lovin'/Take Care Of Your Love	20

(see also Betty Harris)

D.O.S.E.
95	Colosseum TOGA 001TJX	Plug Myself In (with Mark E. Smith) (p/s, numbered, 1-sided, 500 only)	10

(see also Fall)

DOSSERS
83	Secret SHH 168-12	Red Night/Punk Rocker/Running Running/Armada (12" in Secret records house bag)	25

JOHNNY DOT & DASHERS
62	Salvo SLO 1805	I Love An Angel/Just For You (99 copies only)	50

DOTTY & BONNIE
64	Rio R 43	I'm So Glad/DOUGLAS BROTHERS: Got You On My Mind	12
64	Island WI 143	Your Kisses/Why Worry	18
64	Island WI 148	Dearest/Tears Are Falling	15
65	Ska Beat JB 183	Foul Play/ROLAND ALPHONSO & GROUP: Yard Broom	30
67	Ska Beat JB 274	I'll Know/Love Is Great	15
70	Ackee ACK 110	I'm So Glad/Lonely Road	20

(see also Bonnie Frankson, Eric Morris, Don Drummond, Skatalites, Baba Brooks)

DOUBLE EXPOSURE
76	Salsoul SZS 5503	TEN PERCENT (LP)	18

DOUBLE FEATURE
67	Deram DM 115	Baby Get Your Head Screwed On/Come On Baby	70
67	Deram DM 165	Handbags And Gladrags/Just Another Lonely Night	10

DOUBLE VISION
97	Big Drum BDRUM 01	HOW SHOULD I START EP (12")	25

DOUBLES WITH GAY BLADES
59	HMV POP 613	Hey Girl!/Little Joe	100

DOUBT
80	Solo SOLO 1	Fringes/Lookaway/Contrast Disorder/Time Out (EP, with no p/s but insert)	20

(See also Carpenter Joe)

SUZANNE DOUCET
68	Liberty LBF 15150	Swan Song/Cry My Heart	12

DOUGHNUT RING
68	Deram DM 215	Dance Around Julie/The Bandit	35

(see also Crocheted Doughnut Ring)

Johnny DOUGHTY

MINT VALUE £

JOHNNY DOUGHTY
77	Topic 12TS 324	ROUND RYE BAY FOR MORE (LP, with insert)	15

CARL DOUGLAS (& BIG STAMPEDE)
66	Go AJ 11401	Crazy Feeling/PETER PERRY SOUL BAND: Keep It To Myself	35
67	Go AJ 11408	Let The Birds Sing/Something For Nothing	50
67	United Artists UP 1206	Nobody Cries/Serving A Sentence Of Life	250
67	United Artists UP 1206	Nobody Cries/Serving A Sentence Of Life (DJ Copy)	300
68	United Artists UP 2227	Sell My Soul To The Devil/Good Hard Worker	30
68	Pye 7N 45551	Witchfinder General/Crazy Feeling	20
71	CBS 7101	Do You Need My Love (To Get Better)/Lean On Me	70
72	Blue Mountain BM 1007	Somebody Stop This Madness/Ain't No Use (as Karl Douglas)	10
79	Pye 7N 46155	Choose Between Two Lovers/Shame (red vinyl)	6

CHIC DOUGLAS
58	Fontana H 121	I'm Not Afraid Anymore/Jo-Ann	6

CRAIG DOUGLAS
58	Decca F 11055	Nothin' Shakin'/Sitting In A Tree House	10
58	Decca F 11075	Go Chase A Moonbeam/Are You Really Mine	10
59	Top Rank TR 5004	Battle Of New Orleans/Dream Lover/SHEILA BUXTON: Personality/ Where Were You On Our Wedding Day/BERT WEEDON: I Need Your Love Tonight ('King-Size' 7", special sleeve)	10
61	Top Rank JAR 556	A Hundred Pounds Of Clay (censored version)/Hello Spring (p/s)	10
62	Top Rank JAR 603	Another You/A Change Of Heart	10
63	Decca F 11763	Counting Up The Kisses/From Russia With Love	7
64	Fontana TF 458	Silly Boy/Love Leave Me Alone	7
64	Fontana TF 475	Come Closer/She's Smiling At Me (as Craig Douglas & Tridents)	8
65	Fontana TF 525	Across The Street/Party Girl	7
69	Pye 7N 17746	How Do You Feel About That/Then	12
59	Top Rank JKR 8033	CRAIG SINGS FOR 'ROXY' (EP)	15
60	Decca DFE 6633	CRAIG (EP)	15
62	Decca DFE 8509	CUDDLE UP WITH CRAIG (EP)	15
63	Columbia SEG 8219	CRAIG MOVIE SONGS (EP)	20
60	Top Rank BUY 049	CRAIG DOUGLAS (LP)	25
61	Top Rank 35-103	BANDWAGON BALL (LP)	25
62	Columbia 33SX 1468	OUR FAVOURITE MELODIES (LP)	40

(see also Bert Weedon)

DEV DOUGLAS
65	Parlophone R 5237	I Don't Know/How Does It Feel	6
66	Parlophone R 5462	What Am I Doing Here With You/I've Got Lovin'	12

DONNA DOUGLAS
62	Piccadilly 7N 35031	The Message In A Bottle/If This Is Love	7
62	Piccadilly 7N 35042	Matelot/All The Other Girls	6
64	Pye 7N 15654	Blue Star/Java Jones	6

JACK DOUGLAS
68	Columbia DB 8393	Swanee River/Call Alf (Why Does Love Pass Me By)	8

JAN DOUGLAS
64	Vocalion V 9226	More And More/Walkin' In The Rain	10

JOHNNY DOUGLAS (& HIS ORCHESTRA/COMBO)
65	RCA 1444	Crack In The World/Time	10

KEITH DOUGLAS
84	Zip ZIP001	Frontline/Dub Version (12")	40

KIRK DOUGLAS & MELLOMEN
55	Brunswick 05408	A Whale Of A Tale/And The Moon Grew Brighter And Brighter	10

LEW DOUGLAS & HIS ORCHESTRA
54	MGM SP 1093	Caesar's Boogie/Turn Around Boy	10

MARK DOUGLAS
62	Ember EMB S 166	It Matters Not/Upside Down	75

NORMA DOUGLAS
57	London HLZ 8475	Be It Resolved/Joe He Gone	15

ROBB & DEAN DOUGLAS
67	Deram DM 132	I Can Make It With You/Phone Me	50

DOUGLAS BROTHERS
66	Rio R 57	Valley Of Tears/CHARMERS: Where Do I Turn	15
66	Rio R 63	Down And Out/RONALD WILSON: Lonely Man	125

(see also Dotty & Bonnie)

HARRY DOUGLASS & DEEP RIVER BOYS
60	Top Rank JAR 352	Dum Dum De Dum/Go Galloway, Go	7

(see also Deep River Boys)

RONNIE DOVE
64	Stateside SS 314	Sweeter Than Sugar/I Believed In You	8
64	Stateside SS 346	Say You/Let Me Stay Today	8
64	Stateside SS 366	Right Or Wrong/Baby, Put Your Arms Around Me	6
65	Stateside SS 392	Hello Pretty Girl/Keep It A Secret	6
65	Stateside SS 412	One Kiss For Old Times' Sake/Bluebird	7
65	Stateside SS 436	A Little Bit Of Heaven/If I Live To Be A Hundred	7
65	Stateside SS 462	I'll Make All Your Dreams Come True/I Had To Lose You To Find That I Need You	6
65	Stateside SS 480	Kiss Away/Where In The World	6
66	Stateside SS 492	When Liking Turns To Loving/I'm Learning How To Smile Again	6
66	Stateside SS 510	Let's Start All Over Again/That Empty Feeling	6
66	Stateside SS 524	Happy Summer Days/Long After	6
66	Stateside SS 542	I Really Don't Want To Know/Years Of Tears	6
66	Stateside SS 571	Cry/Autumn Rhapsody	6

DOVELLS

MINT VALUE £

Year	Label & Cat No	Title	Value
70	Stateside SS 2003	One More Mountain To Climb/All	6
67	Stateside SS 2018	My Babe/Put My Mind At Ease	6
68	Stateside SS 2119	Mountain Of Love/Never Gonna Cry (The Way I'll Cry Tonight)	10
70	Stateside SS 2047	I Want To Love You For What You Are/I Thank You For Your Love	6
70	Stateside SS 2086	Dancin' Out Of My Heart/Back From Baltimore	6
65	Stateside SL 10149	RONNIE DOVE (LP)	40

DOVELLS
Year	Label & Cat No	Title	Value
61	Columbia DB 4718	The Bristol Stomp/Out In The Cold Again	20
62	Columbia DB 4810	Do The New Continental/Mopitty Mope Stomp	20
62	Columbia DB 4877	Bristol Twistin' Annie/The Actor	20
62	Cameo Parkway P 845	Hully Gully Baby/Your Last Chance	10
63	Cameo Parkway P 861	You Can't Run Away From Yourself/Save Me Baby	10
63	Cameo Parkway P 867	You Can't Sit Down/Stompin' Everywhere	25
63	Cameo Parkway P 882	Betty In Bermudas/Dance The Froog	10
63	Cameo Parkway P 901	Be My Girl/Dragster On The Prowl	25
79	London HAU 8515	CAMEO PARKWAY SESSIONS (LP)	15

(see also Len Barry)

DOVES
Year	Label & Cat No	Title	Value
98	Manchester MANC 9	Seven Day Smile (with Jane Weaver)/ANDY VOTEL & JANE WEAVER: Gutter Girl (p/s)	6
99	Casino CHIP 003	Here It Comes/Meet Me At The Pier/(Acoustic Version) (10", p/s)	10
98	Casino CHIP 001	CEDAR EP: Cedar Room/Rise/Zither (10", wraparound p/s)	35
99	Casino CHIP 002	SEA EP (10", p/s)	20
02	Heavenly HVN115-10	Pounding/Satellites (Soulsavers Remix)/M62 (Four Tet Remix) (10")	12
00	Heavenly HVNLP 26	LOST SOULS (2-LP, gatefold)	100
02	Heavenly HVNLP 35	THE LAST BROADCAST (2-LP)	50
05	Heavenly HVNLP 50	SOME CITIES (2-LP)	50
09	Heavenly HVNLP 67	KINGDOM OF RUST (2-LP)	30

(see also Badly Drawn Boy, Sub Sub, Jane Weaver v Doves)

NICK DOW
Year	Label & Cat No	Title	Value
79	Dingles DIN 306	BURD MARGARET (LP)	15

BRENT DOWE
Year	Label & Cat No	Title	Value
71	Summit SUM 8521	Knock Three Times/GAYLADS: This Time I Won't Hurt You	6
71	Summit SUM 8525	Put Your Hand In The Hand/Miracle (B-side actually "It Took A Miracle Version" by Beverley's All Stars)	6
71	Summit SUM 8530	Freedom Train/BEVERLEY'S ALL STARS: Freedom Train (Version)	6
73	Green Door GD 4061	Reggae Makossa/No Nola (B-side actually by Melodians)	12
75	Torpedo TOR 42	No Sweeter Way/Sweeter Version	8
76	Student STU 1006	It was Love/Version	8
74	Trojan TRLS 76	BUILD ME UP (LP)	15

(see also Melodians)

JOE DOWELL
Year	Label & Cat No	Title	Value
62	Mercury AMT 1180	Little Red Rented Rowboat/The One I Left For You	7

JOHN DOWIE
Year	Label & Cat No	Title	Value
81	Factory FAC 19	It's Hard To Be An Egg/Mind Sketch (white vinyl, clear sleeve, with white feather)	15

DOWLANDS
Year	Label & Cat No	Title	Value
62	Oriole CB 1748	Little Sue/Julie (as Dowlands & Soundtracks)	50
62	Oriole CB 1781	Big Big Fella/Don't Ever Change	100
63	Oriole CB 1815	Break Ups/A Love Like Ours	50
63	Oriole CB 1892	Lonely Johnny (song actually titled "Lucky Johnny")/Do You Have To Have Me Blue?	500
64	Oriole CB 1897	All My Loving/Hey Sally (as Dowlands & Soundtracks)	15
64	Oriole CB 1926	I Walk The Line/Happy Endings	40
64	Oriole CB 1947	Wishing And Hoping/You Will Regret It	80
65	Columbia DB 7547	Don't Make Me Over/Someone Must Be Feeling Sad	40

DOWNBEATS
Year	Label & Cat No	Title	Value
61	Starlite ST45 051	Thinkin' Of You/Midnight Love	200

BRUCE DOWNER
Year	Label & Cat No	Title	Value
71	Summit SUM 8524	Free The People (actually by Bruce Ruffin)/BEVERLEY'S ALL STARS: Free The People (Version)	6

ROLAND DOWNER & COUNT OSSIE
Year	Label & Cat No	Title	Value
68	Doctor Bird DB 1130	Ethiopian Kingdom/A Ju Ju Wah	90

BOB DOWNES
Year	Label & Cat No	Title	Value
70	Vertigo 6059 011	No Time Like The Present/Keep Off The Grass	35
70	Philips SBL 7922	BOB DOWNES' OPEN MUSIC (LP)	200
70	Vertigo 6360 005	ELECTRIC CITY (LP, gatefold sleeve, large swirl label)	300
70	Music For Pleasure MFP 1412	DEEP DOWN HEAVY (LP, red/silver label)	25
73	Ophenian BDOM 001	DIVERSIONS (LP)	25
74	Ophenian BDOM 002	EPISODES AT 4AM (LP, with insert)	22
75	Ophenian BDOM 003	HELLS ANGELS (LP)	30

(see also Rock Workshop)

DOWNHILL
Year	Label & Cat No	Title	Value
79	Bead Records BEAD 8	DOWNHILL (LP)	30

BIG AL DOWNING
Year	Label & Cat No	Title	Value
64	Sue WI 341	Yes I'm Loving You/Please Come Home	45

DOWNLINERS SECT
Year	Label & Cat No	Title	Value
64	Columbia DB 7300	Baby What's Wrong/Be A Sect Maniac	30
64	Columbia DB 7347	Little Egypt/Sect Appeal	15
64	Columbia DB 7415	Find Out What's Happening/Insecticide	35
65	Columbia DB 7509	Wreck Of The Old '97/Leader Of The Sect	30
65	Columbia DB 7597	I Got Mine/Waiting In Heaven Somewhere	35
65	Columbia DB 7712	Bad Storm Coming/Lonely And Blue	35

DOWN TO EARTH

			MINT VALUE £
66	Columbia DB 7817	All Night Worker/He Was A Square	30
66	Columbia DB 7939	Glendora/I'll Find Out	70
66	Columbia DB 8008	The Cost Of Living/Everything I've Got To Give	25
64	Contrast Sound RBCSP 1	NITE IN GREAT NEWPORT STREET (EP)	300
65	Columbia SEG 8438	THE SECT SING SICK SONGS (EP)	100
64	Columbia 33SX 1658	THE SECT (LP)	200
65	Columbia 33SX 1745	THE COUNTRY SECT (LP)	150
66	Columbia SX 6028	THE ROCK SECT'S IN (LP, mono, black/blue label with "sold in the U.K..." text)	200
66	Columbia S(C)X 6028	THE ROCK SECT'S IN (LP, stereo, blue/black label with "sold in the U.K..." text)	250
93	Hangman HANG 42 UP	BIRTH OF SUAVE (LP)	15

(see also Don Crane's Downliners Sect)

DOWN TO EARTH
71	Downtown DT 485	Under The Boardwalk/Under The Boardwalk (Version) (B-side actually "Double Barrel Version")	10

DOWNTOWN ALL STARS
69	Downtown DT 426	Everybody Feel Good/RUDIES: Downtown Jump	30

GENE DOZIER & UNITED FRONT
74	Mercury 6167 007	Give The Women What They Want/The Best Girl I Ever Had	10

LAMONT DOZIER
77	Warner Bros K 16942	Going Back To My Roots/Going Back To My Roots (Version)	8
81	CBS A 1235	Cool Me Out/Starting Over (We've Made The Necessary Changes)	10
74	ABC ABCL 5042	OUT HERE ON MY OWN (LP)	20
75	ABC ABCL 5096	BLACK BACH (LP)	15
76	Warner Bros. K56225	RIGHT THERE (LP)	15
99	Sequel NEMLP 989	LOVE AND BEAUTY (LP)	18

(see also Holland & Dozier)

DOZY, BEAKY, MICK & TICH (D.B.M.&T.)
70	Fontana 6007 022	Mr. President/Frisco Annie (as D.B.M.&T)	6
70	Fontana 6006 066	Festival/Leader Of A Rock 'N' Roll Band	6
70	Philips 6308 029	FRESH EAR (LP, gatefold sleeve, credited to D.B.M&T)	25

(see also Dave Dee Dozy Beaky Mick & Tich)

DP'S
78	Barn 2314107	IF YOU KNOW WHAT I MEAN (LP)	15

(see also The Depressions)

DR. DOG
05	Rough Trade RTRADLP 258	EASY BEAT (LP, textured sleeve, inner)	15

DRACULAS DAUGHTER
97	Kalevala KALA 001	Candy/Candy (version)	20

DRAGON
76	Acorn CF 268	DRAGON (LP, gatefold sleeve)	60

DRAGONFLY
74	Retreat RTS 257	Gondola/Almost Abandoned (demo)	15
75	Retreat RTS 261	Driving Around The World/Since I Left My Home	8
74	Retreat RTL 6002	ALMOST ABANDONED (LP)	25
80s	Dragonfly DF 001	SILENT NIGHTS EP (p/s, private pressing)	150

DRAGONS
69	Page One	Heart Transplantation/Hello I Love Maria	40

DRAGONSFIRE
82	Belltree BTR 001	RISING PHOENIX (LP, with insert)	20

(see also Spinning Wheel)

DRAGONSLAYER
83	Cavalier CAV 017	Broken Hearts/Satan Is Free/I Want Your Life (Early copies with band name as 'Slayer'. NO STICKER)	120
83	Cavalier CAV 017	Broken Hearts/Satan Is Free/I Want Your Life (Early copies had band name as 'Slayer', these later copies have sticker with new name – Dragonslayer – covering it)	80

DRAG SET
66	Go AJ 11405	Get Out Of My Way/Day And Night	250

(see also Open Mind)

DRAGSTER
81	Heavy Metal HEAVY 4	Ambition/Won't Bring You Back (p/s)	30

CHARLES DRAIN
75	RCA 2750	Is This Really Love/Only You	15

CHARLIE DRAKE
59	Parlophone R 4552	Sea Cruise/Starkle, Starkle Little Twink	8
64	Parlophone R 5209	Charles Drake 007/Bumpanology (Bump Head Blues)	8
67	Pye 7N 17269	Who Is Sylvia/I Wanna Be In A Group	6
73	EMI 2079	Someone Opened Watergate And They All Got Wet/'Ello Erf	6
75	Charisma CB 270	You Never Know/I'm Big Enough For Me (produced by Peter Gabriel)	10
76	Sol Doon SDRO 24S	Super Punk/Someone	8
58	Parlophone GEP 8720	HELLO MY DARLINGS (EP)	10
60	Parlophone GEP 8812	NAUGHTY CHARLIE DRAKE (EP)	12
64	Parlophone GEP 8903	HITS FROM THE MAN IN THE MOON (EP)	12

NICK DRAKE
79	Island RSS 7	Introduction/Hazy Jane II/Time Has Told Me/Fruit Tree/Rider On The Wheel ("Fruit Tree" sampler, 1-sided promo only)	200
04	Island IS 854	Magic/Northern Sky	12
04	Island IS 871	River Man/River Man (1968 Recording)	12
12	Antar 11	Plaisir D'Amour (1-sided, die cut sleeve)	50
13	Secret 7 S713	Rider On The Wheel (1-sided, 100 only, each sleeve decorated by different artist)	80
14	Antar ANTARSP012	Cello Song (Peel session version, 1-sided, p/s, booklet)	25
69	Island ILPS 9105	FIVE LEAVES LEFT (LP, 1st pressing, pink label, black 'circle' logo, matrix numbers ILPS 1000

Pete DRAKE

MINT VALUE £

Year	Label/Cat	Description	Value
		9105 A//2/ILPS 9105 B//2, gatefold sleeve printed by Ernest J. Day, track order of Day Is Done and Way To Blue reversed)	
69	Island ILPS 9105	FIVE LEAVES LEFT (LP, gatefold sleeve, 2nd pressing, 'pink rim label', 'palm tree' logo)	100
70	Island ILPS 9134	BRYTER LAYTER (LP, 1st pressing, 'pink rim label', 'palm tree' logo, 'stereo' on label and Joe Boyd credit on one line, Matrixes: ILPS 9134 A-1U/ILPS 9134 B-1U)	400
71	Longman (no cat. No.)	INTERPLAY ONE (2xLP, educational recording for schools, Drake plays guitar on three tracks, 2 booklets of 'teachers' notes)	450
72	Island ILPS 9134	BRYTER LAYTER (LP, 2nd pressing 'pink rim label', 'palm tree' logo, no 'stereo' on right hand side of label and Joe Boyd credit on two lines)	150
72	Island ILPS 9184	PINK MOON (LP, 'pink rim label', 'palm tree' logo, gatefold sleeve)	400
76	Island ILPS 9184	PINK MOON (LP, reissue, blue rim, palm tree logo)	50
76	Island ILPS 9134	BRYTER LATER (LP, reissue, 3rd pressing, blue rim palm tree label, textured sleeve)	50
78	Island ILPS 9134	BRYTER LATER (LP, reissue, blue label)	30
78	Island ILPS 9184	PINK MOON (LP, reissue)	25
76	Island ILPS 9105	FIVE LEAVES LEFT (LP, reissue, 3rd pressing blue rim palm tree label)	50
79	Island NDSP 100	FRUIT TREE (3-LP, box set with booklet)	70
85	Island ILPS 9826	HEAVEN IN A WILD FLOWER (THE BEST OF NICK DRAKE) (LP)	20
86	Hannibal HNBX 5302	FRUIT TREE (4-LP, expanded reissue with booklet)	90
86	Hannibal HNBL 1318	TIME OF NO REPLY (LP)	20
89	Island ILPS 9105	FIVE LEAVES LEFT (LP, reissue, 'blue with white palm tree' label)	35
89	Island ILPS 9134	BRYTER LAYTER (LP, reissue, 'blue with white palm tree' label)	35
89	Island ILPS 9184	PINK MOON (LP, reissue, 'blue with white palm tree' label)	35
91	Hannibal HNCD 5402	FRUIT TREE (4-CD, with booklet in 12" x 12" box)	70
00	Simply Vinyl SVLP 163	FIVE LEAVES LEFT (LP, Simply Vinyl 180gm repressing)	20
99	Simply Vinyl SVLP 094	BRYTER LAYTER (LP, Simply vinyl 180gm repressing)	25
00	Simply Vinyl SVLP 172	PINK MOON (LP, Simply Vinyl 180gm repressing)	20
04	Island 8141	MADE TO LOVE MAGIC (LP, gatefold with inner sleeve)	30
07	Sunbeam SBR2LP 5041	FAMILY TREE (2-LP)	20

PETE DRAKE
63	Philips BF 1332	Forever/Sleep Walk	8

DRAMA
82	Orbit TRIP 1	Been Too Long/Do You Love Me (no p/s)	10

DRAMATICS
72	Stax 2025 053	Whatcha See Is Whatcha Get/Thankful For Your Love	8
72	Stax 2025 101	In The Rain/Get Up And Get Down	6
73	Stax 2025 117	Toast To A Fool/Your Love Was Strange	12
73	Stax 2025 181	Hey You, Get Off My Mountain/Devil Is Dope	6
76	ABC ABC 4101	You're Fooling You/I'll Make It So Good	6
82	Capitol CL 252	I Can't Stand It/It's Dramatic Music	7
72	Stax 2362 025	WHATCHA SEE IS WHATCHA GET (LP)	25
74	Stax STX 1021	A DRAMATIC EXPERIENCE (LP)	15
75	ABC ABCL 5121	DRAMATIC JACKPOT (LP, gatefold sleeve)	15
75	ABC ABCL 5150	DRAMA V (LP, gatefold sleeve)	15

BARRY DRANSFIELD
72	Polydor Folk Mill 2383 160	BARRY DRANSFIELD (LP, red label)	350
78	Topic 12TS 386	BOWIN' AND SCRAPIN' (LP)	25
02	Spinney SPINNEY 003	BARRY DRANSFIELD (LP, reissue)	20
20	Glass Modern GLAMLP 020	BARRY DRANSFIELD (LP, reissue, green vinyl)	15

(see also Robin & Barry Dransfield)

ROBIN DRANSFIELD
80	Topic 12TS 414	TIDEWAVE (LP)	15

(see also Robin & Barry Dransfield)

ROBIN & BARRY DRANSFIELD
70	Trailer LER 2011	THE ROUT OF THE BLUES (LP, first pressing, white Trailer 'test' label)	50
70	Trailer LER 2011	THE ROUT OF THE BLUES (LP, second pressing, dark red label/silver logo and text)	40
71	Trailer LER 2026	LORD OF ALL I BEHOLD (LP)	40
73	Trailer LER 2026	LORD OF ALL I BEHOLD (LP, red/black labels)	25
73	Trailer LER 2011	THE ROUT OF THE BLUES (LP, red and black labels)	30
75	Trailer LER 2011	THE ROUT OF THE BLUES (LP, yellow labels)	20
75	Trailer LER 2026	LORD OF ALL I BEHOLD (LP, yellow labels)	15
82	Highway	THE ROUT OF THE BLUES (LP, 80s repressing, black and white 'Highwayman' labels)	20
82	Highway/Trailer LER 2011	THE ROUT OF THE BLUES (LP, Trailer labels and sleeves with 'Highway Records' stickers over 'Trailer' logo on sleeve)	15

(see also Robin Dransfield, Barry Dransfield)

RUSTY DRAPER
58	Mercury 7MT 211	Gamblin' Gal/That's My Doll	10
58	Mercury 7MT 229	Chicken-Pickin' Hawk/June, July And August	15
59	Mercury AMT 1019	Shoppin' Around/With This Ring	30
60	Mercury AMT 1101	Mule Skinner Blues/Please Help Me, I'm Falling	10
61	Mercury AMT 1127	Jealous Heart/Ten Thousand Years Ago	7
56	Mercury MEP 9506	PRESENTING RUSTY DRAPER (EP)	40
59	Mercury ZEP 10016	RUSTY DRAPER (EP)	20
60	Mercury ZEP 10059	RUSTY IN GAMBLING MOOD (EP)	20
60	Mercury ZEP 10095	MULE SKINNER BLUES (EP)	25
64	London RE-U 1431	RUSTY DRAPER NO. 1 (EP)	20
64	London RE-U 1432	RUSTY DRAPER NO. 2 (EP)	20

MIKEY DREAD (AKA MICHAEL CAMPBELL)
79	Do It DUNE 24	Heavyweight Style/Rub A Dub (12")	20
79	Warrior WAR 125	Barber Saloon/CARLTON PATTERSON: Wash Wash (12")	20
80	Dread At The Controls DREAD 1	Break Down The Walls/Jumping Master (12")	15

DREAD AND THE BALDHEAD

MINT VALUE £

81	Dread At The Controls DATC 003	Warrior Stylee/Israel Stylee (12")	25
82	Dread At The Controls DATCD 008	Roots & Culture/Jungle Dread (12")	40
82	Dread At The Controls DATCD10	Warning/Death Squad/Manslaughter (12")	10
83	Earthquake EQ 001	RAINBOW STEPPER: And Behold/MIKEY DREAD: Paradise (12")	50
77	Hawkeye HALP 001	DUB (LP)	15
79	Dread At The Controls DTCLP 002	AFRICAN ANTHEM – THE MIKEY DREAD SHOW DUBWISE (LP)	40
79	Trojan TRLS178	DREAD AT THE CONTROLS (LP)	30
80	Dread At The Controls DTCLP 006	WORLD WAR III (LP)	30
80	Dread At The Controls DTLP 001	MASTER SHOWCASE (LP)	30
82	Dread At The Controls DATCD 005	DUB CATALOGUE VOLUME 1 (LP)	20
82	Dread At The Controls DATCLP 008	JUNGLE SIGNAL (LP)	30
82	Dread At The Controls RIDE 19	SWALK (LP)	15
83	Dread At The Controls DTLP 009	DUB MERCHANT (LP)	30

DREAD AND THE BALDHEAD
94	Slam SLM5	I The Conqueror/Ganja Plant (Drum & Bass Mix)/Ganja Plant (Hard Step Mix) (12")	50
95	Slam SLM7	Wicked Piece A Tune/Twenty Four Seven (12")	120

DREAD & FRED
89	Jah Shaka SHAKA 870	Warriors Stance/Warriors Advance (12")	12
92	Ironworks D&F 001	Down Too Long/CREATIVE STEPPERS: Creative Version (12")	30
89	Jah Shaka SHAKA 875	IRON WORKS (LP)	20
89	Jah Shaka SHAKA 937	AFRICAN CHANT (LP)	30
93	Jah Shaka SHAKA 937	IRON WORKS PART 3 (LP)	15

DREADZONE
93	Creation CRELP 162	360 DEGREES (LP)	40
94	Totem TTPLP 002	PERFORMANCE (LP)	30
95	Virgin V 2778	SECOND LIGHT (2-LP)	70

DREAMBOYS
80	St Vitus SV1	Bela Lugosi's Birthday/Outer Limits/Shall We Dance	25

DREAM CYCLE 7
82	SRT 82 CUS 1041	I'll Please Myself/Who's To Blame	10

DREAMERS (1)
68	Columbia DB 8340	The Maybe Song/The Long Road	10

(see also Freddie & Dreamers)

DREAMERS (2)
69	Downtown DT 407	Sweet Chariot/Let's Go Downtown	20
69	Downtown DT 408	I Second That Emotion/Dear Love (as Audrey and the Dreamers)	10

DREAMLETS
65	Ska Beat JB 182	Really Now/SKATALITES: Street Corner	85

DREAMLOVERS
61	Columbia DB 4711	When We Get Married/Just Because	200

(see also Chubby Checker)

DREAM MERCHANTS
67	Decca F 12617	Rattler/I'll Be With You In Apple Blossom Time	10

DREAM POLICE
70	Decca F 12998	I'll Be Home (In A Day Or So)/Living Is Easy	10
70	Decca F 13078	Our Song/Much Too Much	8
70	Decca F 13105	I've Got No Choice/What's The Cure For Happiness?	8

(see also Average White Band)

DREAMS
68	United Artists UP 2249	I Will See You There/A Boy Needs A Girl	35
69	CBS 4247	Baby I'm Your Man/Softly, Softly	25
69	Dolphin 4432	Casatschok/Don't You Ask Me	7
70	CBS 64203	DREAMS (LP)	20
72	CBS 64597	IMAGINE MY SURPRISE (LP)	20

DREAM SYNDICATE
82	Rough Trade ROUGH 53	THE DAYS OF WINE AND ROSES (LP)	15

DREAM THEATER
94	East West A 5835	Lie/Space-Dye Vest/To Live Forever/Another Day (live) (p/s)	8
94	East West A 5835 T	Lie/Take The Time (Demo)/Space-Dye Vest (12", p/s)	10
89	MCA MCF 3445	WHEN DREAM AND DAY UNITE (LP)	30
92	Atco 7567 92148 1	IMAGES AND WORDS (LP)	15

DREAMTIMERS
61	London HLU 9368	The Dancin' Lady/An Invitation	20

DREAM WEAVERS
56	Brunswick 05515	It's Almost Tomorrow/You've Got Me Wondering (gold label lettering)	30
56	Brunswick 05515	It's Almost Tomorrow/You've Got Me Wondering (silver label lettering)	15
56	Brunswick 05568	A Little Love Can Go A Long, Long Way/Into The Night (featuring Wade Buff)	12
56	Brunswick 05607	You're Mine/Is There Somebody Else? (featuring Wade Buff)	8

MIKE DRED
90	Machine Codes DH VOL 1	THE MIGHTY DRED EP (12")	12
93	Machine Codes CODE A	FU-CHIN-RA EP (12")	10

DREGS
79	Disturbing DRO 1	THE DREGS EP (p/s, numbered, stamped sleeve, 500 only)	50

D-REN

D-REN
97	Ugly UGM 011	BROTHERS AND SISTERS EP (12")	25

LEN DRESSLAR
56	Mercury 7MT 3	Chain Gang/These Hands (export issue)	10

JOHN DREVAR('S EXPRESSION)
67	MGM MGM 1367	The Closer She Gets/When I Come Home	200
67	MGM MGM 1367	The Closer She Gets/When I Come Home (DJ Copy)	300
68	Polydor BM 56290	What Greater Love/I've Decided (solo)	10

KENNY DREW
14	Blue Note MMBST 84059	UNDERCURRENT (LP, reissue, gatefold)	20

PATTI DREW
68	Capitol CL 15557	Workin' On A Groovy Thing/Without A Doubt	15
68	Capitol CL 15215	Hard To Handle/Just Can't Forget About You	8

DREXCIYA
96	Warp WP 57	JOURNEY DOWN EP (12", p/s)	18
93	Rephlex Cat 017	3 - MOLECULAR ENHANCEMENT EP (12", 4-track)	25

DRIFTERS (U.K.)
59	Columbia DB 4263	Feelin' Fine/Don't Be A Fool (With Love)	50
59	Columbia DB 4263	Feelin' Fine/Don't Be A Fool (With Love) (78)	50
59	Columbia DB 4325	Driftin'/Jet Black	45

(see also Shadows, Cliff Richard, Jet Harris, Tony Meehan)

DRIFTERS (U.S.)
78s
56	London HLE 8344	Soldier Of Fortune/I Gotta Get Myself A Woman	50
58	London HLE 8686	Moonlight Bay/Drip-Drop	50
59	London HLE 8892	There Goes My Baby/Oh, My Love	70
59	London HLE 8988	Dance With Me/True Love, True Love	80
60	London HLE 9081	This Magic Moment/Baltimore	100

SINGLES
56	London HLE 8344	Soldier Of Fortune/I Gotta Get Myself A Woman	1000
58	London HLE 8686	Moonlight Bay/Drip-Drop	150
59	London HLE 8892	There Goes My Baby/Oh, My Love	30
59	London HLE 8988	Dance With Me/True Love, True Love	10
60	London HLE 9081	This Magic Moment/Baltimore	18
60	London HLK 9145	Lonely Winds/Hey Senorita	18
61	London HLK 7114	Save The Last Dance For Me/This Magic Moment (export issue)	10
61	London HLK 7115	I Count The Tears/Dance With Me (export issue)	20
61	London HLK 9287	I Count The Tears/Sadie My Lady	25
61	London HLK 9326	Some Kind Of Wonderful/Honey Bee	15
61	London HLK 9382	Please Stay/No Sweet Lovin'	15
61	London HLK 9427	Sweets For My Sweet/Loneliness Or Happiness	12
62	London HLK 9500	Room Full Of Tears/Somebody New Dancin' With You	10
62	London HLK 9522	When My Little Girl Is Smiling/Mexican Divorce	10
62	London HLK 9554	Stranger On The Shore/What To Do	8
62	London HLK 9626	Up On The Roof/Another Night With The Boys	10
63	London HLK 9699	On Broadway/Let The Music Play	15
63	London HLK 9750	Rat Race/If You Don't Come Back	15
63	London HLK 9785	I'll Take You Home/I Feel Good All Over	8
64	London HLK 9848	Vaya Con Dios/In The Land Of Make Believe	8
64	London HLK 9886	One Way Love/Didn't It	10
64	Atlantic AT 4001	Under The Boardwalk/I Don't Want To Go On Without You	12
64	Atlantic AT 4008	I've Got Sand In My Shoes/He's Just A Playboy	15
64	Atlantic AT 4012	Saturday Night At The Movies/Spanish Lace	12
65	Atlantic AT 4019	At The Club/Answer The Phone	15
65	Atlantic AT 4023	Come On Over To My Place/Chains Of Love	12
65	Atlantic AT 4034	Follow Me/The Outside World	15
65	Atlantic AT 4040	I'll Take You Where The Music's Playing/Far From The Maddening Crowd	12
66	Atlantic AT 4062	We Gotta Sing/Nylon Stockings	15
66	Atlantic AT 4084	Memories Are Made Of This/My Island In The Sun	15
66	Atlantic 584 020	Up In The Streets Of Harlem/You Can't Love 'Em All	15
67	Atlantic 584 065	Baby What I Mean/Aretha	20
68	Atlantic 584 152	I'll Take You Where The Music's Playing/On Broadway	12
68	Atlantic 584 195	Still Burning In My Heart/I Need You Now	10
69	Atlantic 584 246	Saturday Night At The Movies/Under The Boardwalk	6
71	Atlantic 2091 064	A Rose By Any Other Name/Be My Lady	7
75	Atlantic K10700	You Gotta Pay Your Dues/One Way Love	10
77	Arista 94	I'll Know When True Love Really Passes By/A Good Song Never Dies	18
78	Arista 202	Closely Guarded Secret/I Can't Believe It's Over	10
79	Epic EPC 7806	Pour Your Little Heart Out Parts 1 & 2	50

EPs
61	London RE-K 1282	THE DRIFTERS' GREATEST HITS	20
63	London RE-K 1355	THE DRIFTERS	20
63	London RE-K 1385	DRIFTIN'	20
64	Atlantic AET 6003	DRIFTIN' VOL. 2	25
65	Atlantic AET 6012	TONIGHT	25

ALBUMS
60	London HA-K 2318	THE DRIFTERS' GREATEST HITS	50
62	London HA-K 2450	SAVE THE LAST DANCE FOR ME	30

DRIFTING SLIM

			MINT VALUE £
65	Atlantic ATL 5015	OUR BIGGEST HITS	20
65	Atlantic ATL/STL 5023	THE GOOD LIFE WITH THE DRIFTERS (mono/stereo)	20
66	Atlantic ATL/STL 5039	I'LL TAKE YOU WHERE THE MUSIC'S PLAYING (mono/stereo)	20
67	Atlantic 587 038	BIGGEST HITS	15
67	Atlantic 590 010	SOUVENIRS	18
68	Atlantic 587 123	ROCKIN' AND DRIFTIN'	35
68	Atlantic 587 144	GOOD GRAVY (as Clyde McPhatter & Drifters)	45
69	Atlantic 587/588 160	UP ON THE ROOF	15

(see also Clyde McPhatter, Ben E. King, Bobby Hendricks)

DRIFTING SLIM
| 66 | Blue Horizon 45-1005 | Good Morning Baby/My Sweet Woman (99 copies only) | 175 |

DRIFTWOOD
70	Decca F 13084	Shylock Bay/The Wind Cries Above You	6
71	Decca F 13139	Say The Right Things/Still I'll Stay With You	6
70	Decca SKL 5069	DRIFTWOOD (LP, blue/silver label with boxed logo)	100

(see also Neil Harrison)

DRINKING ELECTRICITY
80	Pop Aural POP 005	Shake Some Action/Shake Some Action (Cheap Version)	8
80	Pop Aural POP 008	Cruising Missiles/Shaking All Over (Dub) (p/s)	8
81	Survival SUR 001	Subliminal/Random Particles	8
82	Survival SUR 122	Subliminal/Breakout (12")	10
82	Survival SUR LP 001	OVERLOAD (LP)	20

JULIE DRISCOLL
63	Columbia DB 7118	Take Me By The Hand/Stay Away From Me	30
65	Parlophone R 5296	Don't Do It No More/I Know You	30
66	Parlophone R 5444	I Didn't Want To Have To Do It/Don't Do It No More	25
67	Parlophone R 5588	I Know You Love Me Not/If You Should Ever Leave Me	20
67	Marmalade 598 005	Save Me Pts 1 & 2	30
71	Polydor 2383077	JULIE DRISCOLL — 1969 (LP)	60

JULIE DRISCOLL, BRIAN AUGER & TRINITY
68	Marmalade 598 006	This Wheel's On Fire/A Kind Of Love In (3-print push out or large centre, Marmalade sleeve)	8
68	Marmalade 598 011	Road To Cairo/Shadows Of You	8
69	Marmalade 598 018	Take Me To The Water/Indian Rope Man	60
67	Marmalade 607002	OPEN (mono, first pressing, with 1-sided insert and non laminated cover produced by "Upton Printing")	175
67	Marmalade 607 002	OPEN (LP, mono)	125
67	Marmalade 608 002	OPEN (LP, stereo)	100
68	M. For Pleasure MFP 1265	JOOLS/BRIAN (LP, tracks shared by Julie Driscoll & Brian Auger)	20
69	Marmalade 608 005/6	STREET NOISE (2-LP, gatefold sleeve)	300
69	Marmalade 608 014	STREET NOISE PART 1 (LP)	35
69	Marmalade 608 015	STREET NOISE PART 2 (LP)	35
70	Polydor 2334004	BEST OF (LP, 99p series)	20

(see also Brian Auger & Trinity, Working Week, Julie Tippetts, B.B. Blunder)

DRIVE
| 77 | NRG NE 467 | Jerkin'/Push'N'Shove (no p/s) | 50 |

DRIVER
79	Rods ROD 1	Like A Mirror/Here I Am (p/s)	20
79	Rods ROD 2	I'm Not Dreaming/So They Say	15
80	Rods HOT 1	YOU BETTER TAKE IT (LP, 300 only)	60

DRIVERS
| 83 | Greyhound GRK 701 | Talk All Night/Sister (p/s) | 6 |
| 84 | Nouveau NMS 5 | Things/Stolen Treasure (p/s) | 6 |

(see also Nick Van Eede)

DRIVESHAFT
| 80 | Undercover DC 02 | Cold As Ice/I Know What You Are After (features Noel Redding) | 50 |
| 82 | Undercover DC 03 | Heartbreaker/Now That It's Over (p/s) | 25 |

DRIZABONE
| 94 | 4th & Broadway 12 BRW 264 | Pressure (Roger's Soul Sensation Mix)/Pressure (Album Version)/Pressure (Bonus Beats Mix)/Pressure (Bone Idol Remix)/Pressure (Nu Solution Mix)/Pressure (Underground Network Mix) (12", p/s) | 30 |

D-ROK
| 91 | Warhammer DROK 08722 | Get Out Of My Way (D-Mix)/Renegade/Get Out Of My Way (Airmix) (12", p/s) | 10 |

(see also Brian May)

FRANK D'RONE
60	Mercury AMT 1223	Strawberry Blonde (The Band Rocked On)/Time Hurries By	6
59	Mercury ZEP 10033	FRANK D'RONE SINGS (EP)	10
59	Mercury ZEP 10083	BLUE SERENADE (EP)	10
59	Mercury ZEP 10116	THE BAND ROCKED ON (EP)	10
60	Mercury MMC 14253	AFTER THE BALL (LP)	15

DRONES (1)
77	Valer VRS 1	Bone Idol/I Just Wanna Be Myself (gatefold p/s, made in France)	12
77	Valer VRS 1	Bone Idol/I Just Wanna Be Myself (gatefold p/s, made in England)	6
77	Fifth Avenue CAS 107	Bone Idol/I Just Wanna Be Myself (cassette, flip-open 'cigarette box' sleeve)	30
77	Valer VRSP 1	Be My Baby/Lift Off The Bans (12", white label, unreleased)	50
77	Valer	Be My Baby (Take Two)/The Clique (white label, unreleased, many autographed)	20
77	Ohms GOOD MIX 1	TEMPTATIONS OF A WHITE COLLAR WORKER (EP, different coloured sleeves, some with writing on inner sleeve)	20
80	Fabulous JC 4	Can't See/Fooled Today (p/s)	7
77	Valer VRLP 1	FURTHER TEMPTATIONS (LP)	35

DRONES (2)

			MINT VALUE £

DRONES (2)
06   ATP ATPRLP 22   GALA MILL (2-LP) 30

DRONGOS FOR EUROPE
81   Kite DFE 001   ADVERSE CHORUS EP 40
82   Inferno HELL 3   DEATH'S A CAREER (EP, p/s with insert) 10
82   Inferno HELL 6   ETERNITY EP (p/s) 8

DROP
81   Dropped SRTS/81/CUS 929   He Doesn't Know He's Trendy/Death In The Afternoon/I'm Wearing An Appliance 20

DROP NINETEENS
92   Hut HUTLP 4   DELAWARE (LP) 40
93   Hut HUTLP 14   NATIONAL COMA (LP, clear vinyl) 25
93   Hut HUTLP 14   NATIONAL COMA (LP) 20

DROWNING CRAZE
81   Situation 2 SIT 3   Storage Case/Damp Bones (p/s) 15
81   Situation 2 SIT 13   Trance/I Love The Fjords (foldout p/s) 15
82   Situation 2 SIT 16   Heat/Replays (p/s) 15

DRUDGE
90   Deaf DEAF 01   SUPPOSE IT WAS YOU (split LP with Agathocles) 20

DRUG ADDIX
78   Chiswick SW 39   MAKE A RECORD (EP) 12

(see also Kirsty MacColl)

DRUID
76   EMI SPSR 395   Barnaby- Kestrel/Nothing But Morning 12
75   EMI EMC 3081   TOWARDS THE SUN (LP, textured, with inner sleeve) 20
76   EMI EMC 3128   FLUID DRUID (LP, with inner sleeve) 20

DRUID CHASE
67   CBS 3053   Take Me In Your Garden/I Wanna Get My Hands On You 30

DRUIDS (1)
63   Parlophone R 5097   Long Tall Texan/Love So Blue 20
64   Parlophone R 5134   It's Just A Little Bit Too Late/See What You've Done 20

DRUIDS (2)
71   Argo ZFB 22   BURNT OFFERING (LP) 80
73   Argo ZFB 39   PASTIME WITH GOOD COMPANY (LP) 60

(see also Giles Farnaby's Dream Band)

DRUM CLUB
93   Butterfly BFLT10A   Sound System Volume 1 (12") 10
93   Big Life DC PROMO 2   Big Life (2 x 12" promo) 15

DRUMBAGO
63   Island WI 085   I Am Drunk (actually by Raymond Harper & Drumbago's Group)/Sea Breeze (actually by Sammy & Drumbago's Group) 20
68   Blue Cat BS 145   Reggae Jeggae (with Blenders)/TYRONE TAYLOR: Delilah 100
69   Trojan TR 638   Dulcemania (with Dynamites)/CLANCY ECCLES: China Man 40

(see also Derrick Patsy, Dennis Walks)

BILL DRUMMOND
87   Creation CRE 039T   King Of Joy/The Manager (12", p/s) 20
86   Creation CRELP 014   THE MAN (LP) 20

(see also Big In Japan,, KLF, Disco 2000, Timelords)

DON DRUMMOND
62   Island WI 021   Schooling The Duke/Bitter Rose (as Don Drummond Orchestra; B-side is actually by Shenley Duffus) 30
63   Black Swan WI 406   Scrap Iron/DRAGONAIRE: Prevention 25
63   Blue Beat BB 179   Reload/Far East 30
63   Island WI 094   Scandal/My Ideal (B-side actually by W. Sparks) 25
63   R&B JB 103   Royal Flush/MAYTALS: Matthew Mark 30
63   R&B JB 105   The Shock/TONETTES: Tell Me You're Mine 25
64   Ska Beat JB 178   Silver Dollar/TOMMY McCOOK: My Business 30
64   Island WI 149   Eastern Standard Time/DOTTY & BONNIE: Sun Rises 25
64   Island WI 153   Musical Storeroom/STRANGER COLE: He Who Feels 25
64   Island WI 162   Garden Of Love/STRANGER COLE: Cherry May 40
65   Island WI 192   Stampede (with Drumbago)/JUSTIN HINDS & DOMINOES: Come Bail Me 30
65   Island WI 204   Coolie Baby/LORD ANTICS: You May Stray 30
65   Island WI 208   Man In The Street/RITA & BENNY: You Are My Only Love 40
65   Island WI 242   University Goes Ska/DERRICK & NAOMI: Pain In My Heart 40
69   Studio One SO 2078   Heavenly/GLEN BROWN & DAVE BARKER: Lady Lovelight 55
69   Trojan TR 678   Memory Of Don/JOHN HOLT: Darling I Love You 20
69   Coxsone CSL 8021   IN MEMORY OF DON DRUMMOND (LP) 150
69   Studio One SO 9008   THE BEST OF DON DRUMMOND (LP) 200
69   Trojan TTL 23   MEMORIAL ALBUM (LP) 50

(see also Joe White, Rhythm Aces, Roy & Millie, Movers, Desmond Dekker, Shenley Duffas, Hi-Tones, Duke Reid, Soul Brothers, Baba Brooks, Bonnie & Skitto, Eric Morris, Pioneers, Stranger & Patsy, Techniques, Winston Wright)

DON DRUMMOND JUNIOR
67   Caltone TONE 104   Sir Pratt Special/HEMSLEY MORRIS: Love Is Strange 90
68   Caltone TONE 124   Dirty Dozen/PHIL PRATT: Reach Out 90
70   Jackpot JP 710   Memory Of Don Drummond/TOBIES: Resting 20
82   Rush NIBZ 001   The Clash And The Specials Go To Jail/Jailbird Dub/Rudies Ska (12", p/s) 25

(see also Vincent Gordon)

JOHN DRUMMOND
68   Page One POF 084   Break My Mind/Molly Bye Bye 7

KEITH DRUMMOND
82   Bengad   Love Grows/(Version) (12") 20

Lee DRUMMOND

MINT VALUE £

LEE DRUMMOND
66   Fontana TF 728 — Messrs Lindsay, Parker & Flynn/Sitting And Drinking Alone 8

PETE DRUMMOND & THE VHF BAND
72   Warner Bros K 16232 — Rocking At The BBC/Goodbye (vinyl 78) 20

DRUNKEN MASTER
93   Kold Sweat KSEP209 — DEVIL IN DISGUISE (EP) 12

(see also SLR/Dashy D & Cue Tips)

DRY CLEANING
18   It's OK — SWEET PRINCESS (cassette) 60
21   4AD 4AD0415MCE — Bug Eggs/Tony Speaks! (cassette) 50
21   4AD – 4AD0334SE — Scratchcard Lanyard/Bug Eggs (p/s, yellow vinyl) 15
19   It's OK OK 002 — BOUNDARY ROAD SNACKS AND DRINKS (LP) 150
21   4AD 4AD0254LP — NEW LONG LEG (LP, yellow vinyl, some with free 7") 25
21   4AD 0254LPE2 — NEW LONG LEG (LP, clear vinyl, with CD) 25

DRY FRUIT
70   Staple ST 004 — Magic Thimble/The Die Is Cast 40

DRY ICE
69   B&C CB 115 — Running To The Convent/Nowhere To Go 25

(see also Pluto)

DRY RIB
79   Clockwork COR 001 — THE DRY SEASON (EP, 33rpm, photocopied foldover p/s, screen-printed labels) 30

(see also Television Personalities, Times, L'Orange Mechanik)

DRY THE RIVER
12   RCA 88691934251 — SHALLOW BED (2-LP) 60

DRY WATERS
72   Denby DEN 003 — Crystal Ball/The Magic Valley 150

AMANCIO D'SILVA
69   Columbia S(C)X 6322 — INTEGRATION (LP) 1000
71   Columbia SCX 6465 — REFLECTIONS (LP) 30
17   Pheon PHE 003 — INTEGRATION (LP, reissue) 15

(see also Cosmic Eye, Joe Harriott)

D.S.K.F.
92   WG 001 — NEW SCIENCE EP (12", stickered white label) 100

D.S.P.
92   FX FXUKT 10 — Obsession/Revenge Attack/Intravenus/Kebab (12") 20

D TO THE K
88   BPM BP12004 — Hard But Live/Ease Up Your Mind (12") 25

DTS
81   Marvo MVO 002 — Bsa Rocket 111/Lonesome 10
84   Marvo AM 130 — Willy & The Hand Jive/Roadrunner 10

D12
01   Shady 493080-1 — DEVILS NIGHT (2-LP) 30

DUALS
61   London HL 9450 — Stick Shift/Cruising 25

DUBBING IN THE U.K.
81   Star Light SDLP 902 — DUBBING IN THE U.K.(LP) 30

DUB FACTORY
95   Dub Factory GEMCD 001 — VOYAGE INTO DUB - THE 1st JOURNEY (LP) 18

DUB JUDAH
90   Dub Jockey DJ012 — No Tresspassers/FOUNDATION PLAYERS: Version (12") 15
92   Dub Jockey DJ021 — Babylon Is A Trap/Version 15
93   Dub Jockey DJ024 — Fishers Of Men/Dub Fisher 12
94   Dub Jockey DJ030 — Revolution Revelation/Rev Dub 12
95   Dub Jockey DJ031 — Never Slumber/Ever Alert Dub 10
92   Dub Jockey DJLP 002 — BABYLON IS A TRAP (LP) 40
93   Dub Jockey DJLP 003 — DUBTECH DUB (LP) 30
94   Dub Jockey DJLP 004 — BETTER TO BE GOOD (LP) 30

DUBKASM
04   Sufferah's Choice DUBK02 — Displaced African/Higher Judgement (12") 20
05   Sufferah's Choice DUBK03 — Deh Inna De Lion's Den/Iration Steppas MIx (12" featuring Iration Steppas) 20

DUB PLATE VIBE CREW
96   Solar Dub SOLD 12003 — Respect Jah/Dub/Jah Putting On The Press (12") 12

DUBS
57   London HLU 8526 — Could This Be Magic/Such Lovin' 250
57   London HLU 8526 — Could This Be Magic/Such Lovin' (78) 40
58   London HL 8684 — Gonna Make A Change/Beside My Love 200
58   London HL 8684 — Gonna Make A Change/Beside My Love (78) 30

DUB SYNDICATE
84   On-U Sound ON-U LP 18 — POUNDING SYSTEM (LP) 30
86   On-U Sound ON-U LP 38 — TUNES FROM THE MISSING CHANNEL (LP) 30
89   On-U Sound ON-U LP 47 — STRIKE THE BALANCE (LP) 30
91   On-U Sound ON-U LP 56 — STONED IMMACULATE (LP) 30
93   On-U Sound ON ULP 64 — ECHOMANIA (LP, with free 7") 30

DUBTRONIX
94   QDance DUBTLP 1 — INTERFAZE - JUNGLISM VOL 1 (LP) 20

DIANE DUCANE
79   Contact WN 2 — Better Late Than Never/One Day 30

JOHNNY DU CANN
77   Arista ARIST 128 — Throw Him In Jail/Street Stutter 25
77   Arista ARIST 145 — Where's The Show/Hang Around 30

DUCHESS OF BEDFORD

(see also Attack, Andromeda, Five Day Week Straw People, Atomic Rooster, Hard Stuff, Status Quo)

DUCHESS OF BEDFORD
56	HMV POP 361	Luck's In Love With You/MRS GERALD LEGGE: I'm In Love	8

DUCKS DELUXE
73	RCA RCA 2438	Coast To Coast/Bring Back That Packard Car	6
74	RCA 2477	Love's Melody/Two Times Twister	6
75	RCA RCA 2531	I Fought The Law/Cherry Pie	6
74	RCA LPL1 5008	DUCKS DELUXE (LP)	15
74	RCA SF 8402	TAXI TO THE TERMINAL ZONE (LP)	15

(see also Tyla Gang, Brinsley Schwarz)

DUDLEY
60	Vogue V 9171	Lone Prairie Rock/El Pizza	10

DAVE DUDLEY
63	United Artists UP 1029	Six Days On The Road/I Feel A Cry Coming On	10

DUET EMMO
81	Mute MUTE 25	OR SO IT SEEMS (12" EP)	18

(see also Dome, Wire)

DU-ETTES
72	President PT 382	Every Beat Of My Heart/Sugar Daddy	8
72	President PT 398	Please Forgive Me/Lonely Days	8

D DUFFUS
79	Jay Dee JD 009	Is It Just A Dream/Cheaters (12")	50

SHENLEY DUFFAS
62	Island WI 036	Give To Get/What You Gonna Do (as S. Duffas; B-side actually with Millie Small)	18
63	Island WI 063	Fret Man Fret/Doreen	20
63	Island WI 093	What A Disaster/I Am Rich	20
63	Island WI 115	Know The Lord/TOMMY McCOOK: Ska Ba	45
63	Island WI 125	Easy Squeal/Things Ain't Going Right	20
63	R&B JB 134	No More Wedding Bells/Let Them Fret	15
64	R&B JB 146	Big Mouth/FRANKIE ANDERSON: Peanut Vendor	25
64	R&B JB 152	Christopher Columbus/CARL BRYAN ORCHESTRA: Barber Chair	18
64	R&B JB 154	Mother-In-Law/DON DRUMMOND & GROUP: Festival	22
64	Black Swan WI 440	Digging A Ditch/He's Coming Down	18
64	Black Swan WI 443	Gather Them In/Crucifixion	20
64	Rio R 41	I Will Be Glad/Heariso (as Shandly Duffus)	18
65	Island WI 182	La La La/UPCOMING WILLOWS: Jonestown Special	40
65	Island WI 184	You Are Mine/UPCOMING WILLOWS: Red China	50
65	Island WI 186	Rukumbine/One Morning	35
72	Upsetter US 380	Bet You Don't Know/UPSETTERS: Ring Of Fire	35
72	Dynamic DYN 451	Peace (with Soul Avengers)/UPSETTERS: Peace — Version	12
72	Pama PM859	At The End/Good Night My Love	20
72	Grape GR 3031	Sincerely/Sincerely — Version (with Upsetters)	10

(see also Chenley Duffus, Billy Dyce)

CHRIS DUFFIN
76	Deroy ADM LP 864	HEY SANDY (LP)	250

CHENLEY DUFFUS
72	Upsetter US-386	To Be A Lover/Baby Lose Burning	20

(see also Shenley Duffas)

DUFFY (1)
73	Chapter One SCHR 184	The Joker/Running Away	18
70	Chapter One CHS-R 814	SCRUFFY DUFFY (LP, red/silver label)	300

DUFFY (2)
07	A&M 175 410-6	Rockferry/Oh Boy (p/s, 1,500 only)	10
08	A&M Records 176 178-2	Mercy/Save It For Your Prayers	10

CHRIS DUFFY
68	SNB 55-3681	Mr Jones Mr Brown Mr Smith And Not Forgetting Charlie Green/Something For Now	10

STEPHEN 'TIN TIN' DUFFY
85	10	She Loves Me/She Loves It (p/s, withdrawn)	40
85	10	Baby Impossible (p/s, withdrawn)	40

(see also Hawks, Lilac Time)

DUFFY'S NUCLEUS
67	Decca F 22547	Hound Dog/Mary Open The Door	50

(see also Duffy Power, Pentangle, John McLaughlin)

DON DUGGAN
68	Pye 7N 17633	Let Her Dance/Westmeath Bachelor (with Savoys)	6

DUGZ
14	Time and Matter T&M 015	The Berlin Lights : Caught In A War/Hit The Floor	20

DENVER DUKE & JEFFREY NULL BLUEGRASS BOYS
63	Starlite STEP 33	DENVER DUKE & JEFFREY NULL BLUEGRASS BOYS (EP)	15

DORIS DUKE
71	Mojo 2092 005	To The Other Woman/I Don't Care Anymore	8
71	Mojo 2092 017	If She's Your Wife Who Am I?/It Sure Was Fun	15
73	Mainstream MSS 302	Business Deal/Nobody But You	8
74	Contempo CS2037	Grasshopper/Please Come Back	8
71	Mojo 2916 001	I'M A LOSER (LP)	30
71	Mojo 2916 006	A LEGEND IN HER OWN TIME (LP)	30
75	Contempo CRM 211	A LEGEND IN HER OWN TIME (LP, reissue)	20
75	Contempo CLP 519	WOMAN (LP)	30

GEORGE DUKE
75	MPS MC 25671	I LOVE THE BLUES SHE HEARD MY CRY (LP)	15

James DUKE

			MINT VALUE £
75	MPS BAP 5064	THE AURA WILL PREVAIL (LP)	25

JAMES DUKE
86	Creole CR 93	Hold On/Zyzafon (p/s)	150
86	Creole CRT 93	Hold On/Zyzafon (12", p/s)	250

PATTY DUKE
65	United Artists UP 1103	Don't Just Stand There/Everything But Love	10
66	United Artists UP 1131	Whenever She Holds You/Nothing But You	10
65	United Artists (S)ULP 1123	DON'T JUST STAND THERE (LP, mono/stereo)	50

DUKE ALL STARS
68	Blue Cat BS 111	Letter To Mummy And Daddy (Parts 1 & 2)	80

DUKE & DUCHESS
55	London HLU 8206	Borrowed Sunshine/Get Ready For Love (with Sir Hubert Pimm)	40

(see also Sir Hubert Pimm)

DUKE OF BURLINGTON
71	Decca F23120	Flash/Slot Machine	15

AGGIE DUKES
57	Vogue V 9090	John John/Well Of Loneliness	250
57	Vogue V 9090	John John/Well Of Loneliness (78)	40

DUKES NOBLEMEN
69	Philips BF 1691	City Of Windows/Thank You For Your Loving	25

DUKES OF ILLYRIA
70	IAMBIG 0001	Food Of Love/Come Away Death	20

DUKES OF STRATOSPHEAR
85	Virgin VS 763	The Mole From The Ministry/My Love Explodes	10
87	Virgin VSY 982	You're A Good Man Albert Brown/Vanishing Girl (p/s, 5,000 on multi-coloured vinyl)	20
87	Virgin VS 982	You're A Good Man Albert Brown/Vanishing Girl (p/s)	10
85	Virgin WOW 1	25 O'CLOCK (LP)	20
87	Virgin VP 2440	PSONIC PSUNSPOT (LP, gatefold sleeve, 5,000 on multi-coloured vinyl)	30
87	Virgin VP 2440	PSONIC PSUNSPOT (LP, gatefold)	20
10	Ape House APELPP023	25 O'CLOCK (LP, reissue)	20
10	Ape House APELPP024	PSONIC PSUNSPOT (LP, reissue)	25
10	Ape House APEBOX 002	THE COMPLETE AND UTTER DUKES (Box set, LP, 12", 7" and 2-CD)	200

(see also XTC)

DUKE SPIRIT
05	Loog 987099	CUTS ACROSS THE LAND (LP, textured gatefold sleeve)	20
12	Fiction 3700883	DRESDEN LIVE (LP, 300 only)	30

DULCIMER
71	Nepentha 6437 003	AND I TURNED AS I HAD TURNED AS A BOY (LP, gatefold sleeve)	300
80	Happy Face MMLP 1021	A LAND FIT FOR HEROES (LP, private pressing)	15

LIZA DULITTLE
68	Pye 7N 17590	I've Got To Get A Grip Of Myself/Did You Hear A Heart Break Last Night?	8

(see also Margo & Marvettes)

DUM
74	RAK RAK 179	In The Mood/Watching The Clock	8

(see also Mud)

DUM DUM
72	Phillips 6414-318	Peter Gunn/Cosa Nostra	15

MARTIN DUMAS JR
15	BBE 304SLP	Attitude Belief And Determination/Non-Stop To The Top (12", p/s reissue)	20

DUMB ANGELS
88	Fierce FRIGHT 033	Love And Mercy/Love And Mercy (p/s, numbered)	55

(see also Pooh Sticks)

DUMBELLES
80	Polydor POSP 209/EGO 3	Giddy Up/A Christmas Dream (no p/s)	10

(see also Roxy Music)

JOHN DUMMER (BLUES BAND)
68	Mercury MF 1040	Travelling Man/40 Days (as John Dummer Blues Band)	20
69	Mercury MF 1119	Try Me One More Time/Riding At Midnight (as John Dummer Blues Band)	15
70	Fontana 6007 027	Happy/Nightingale (unissued in U.K.; France-only)	0
70	Philips 6006 111	Nine By Nine/Going In The Out (credited to either Famous Music Band or John Dummer Band)	8
69	Mercury SMCL 20136	CABAL (LP, black/silver label)	200
69	Mercury SMCL 20167	JOHN DUMMER BAND (LP, black/silver label)	200
70	Philips 6309 008	FAMOUS MUSIC BAND (LP, gatefold sleeve, black/silver labels)	150
72	Philips 6382 039	THIS IS THE JOHN DUMMER BLUES BAND (LP)	20
73	Philips 6382 040	VOLUME II — TRY ME ONE MORE TIME (LP)	20
72	Vertigo 6360 055	BLUE (LP, gatefold sleeve, small swirl label)	600
73	Vertigo 6360 083	OOBLEEDOOBLEE JUBILEE (LP, as John Dummer Oobleedooblee Band, small swirl label)	250

(see also Nick Pickett, Dave Kelly, Famous Music Band, Tony McPhee)

DUMMIES
79	Cheapskate FWL 001	When The Lights Are Out/She's The Only Woman (no p/s)	8
80	Cheapskate CHEAP 003	Didn't You Used To Use To Be You?/Miles Out To Sea (p/s)	8
81	Cheapskate CHEAP 014	Maybe Tonite/When I'm Dancin' I Ain't Fightin' (p/s)	10

(see also China Dolls, Slade)

DUMMY RUN
97	Hot Air BSE LP 002	ICE CREAM HEADACHE (LP)	15

(see also Stock, Hausen & Walkman)

DUNAMIS
79	Daybreak DB 2602	I CAN FLY (LP, signed)	60
79	Daybreak DB 2602	I CAN FLY (LP, un-signed)	15

AYNSLEY DUNBAR (RETALIATION)

MINT VALUE £

67	Blue Horizon 3109	Warning/Cobwebs (in p/s)	60
67	Blue Horizon 3109	Warning/Cobwebs	30
68	Liberty LBF 15132	Watch 'N' Chain/Roamin' And Ramblin'	15
68	Liberty LBL/LBS 83154	AYNSLEY DUNBAR RETALIATION (LP, mono/stereo)	130
68	Liberty LBL/LBS 83177	DR. DUNBAR'S PRESCRIPTION (LP, mono/stereo)	150
69	Liberty LBS 83223	TO MUM FROM AYNSLEY AND THE BOYS (LP)	150
70	Liberty LBS 83316	REMAINS TO BE HEARD (LP)	150
71	Warner Bros WS 3010	BLUE WHALE (LP, green label)	70

(see also John Mayall & Bluesbreakers, Heavy Jelly, Annette & Victor Brox, Excheckers)

SCOTT DUNBAR

71	Ahura Mazda AMS SDS 1	FROM LAKE MARY (LP)	30

JOHNNY DUNCAN (& BLUE GRASS BOYS)

57	Columbia DB 3925	Kaw-Liga/Ella Speed (gold label lettering)	20
57	Columbia DB 3959	Last Train To San Fernando/Rock-A-Billy Baby (gold label lettering)	20
57	Columbia DB 4029	Footprints In The Snow/Get Along Home, Cindy	6
57	Columbia SEG 7708	JOHNNY DUNCAN AND HIS BLUE GRASS BOYS (EP)	10
57	Columbia SEG 7733	JOHNNY DUNCAN AND HIS BLUE GRASS BOYS NO. 2 (EP)	10
58	Columbia SEG 7753	FOOTPRINTS IN THE SNOW (EP)	12
58	Columbia SEG 7850	TENNESSEE SING SONG (EP)	10
57	Columbia 33S 1122	TENNESSEE SONG BAG (10" LP)	30
58	Columbia 33S 1129	JOHNNY DUNCAN SALUTES HANK WILLIAMS (10" LP)	30
61	Columbia 33SX 1328	BEYOND THE SUNSET (LP)	15

LESLEY DUNCAN (& JOKERS)

63	Parlophone R 5034	I Want A Steady Guy/Movin' Away (as Lesley Duncan & Jokers)	15
64	Parlophone R 5206	Tell Me/You Kissed Me Boy	15
64	Mercury MF 830	When My Baby Cries/Did It Hurt?	10
65	Mercury MF 847	Just For The Boy/See That Guy	20
65	Mercury MF 876	Run To Love/Only The Lonely And Me	20
65	Mercury MF 939	Hey Boy/I Go To Sleep	60
68	RCA 1746	Lullaby/I Love You, I Love You	6
69	CBS 4585	Sing Children Sing/Exactly Who Are You	7
79	CBS 8061	Sing Children Sing/Rainbow Games (p/s, with Kate Bush)	10
71	CBS 64202	SING CHILDREN SING (LP, gatefold sleeve, orange labels)	20
72	CBS 64807	EARTH MOTHER (LP, gatefold sleeve, orange labels)	15
74	GM GML 1007GM	EVERYTHING CHANGES (LP)	15

(see also Mitchell/Coe Mysteries, Pete Townshend, Phil Lynott, Madeline Bell, Joe Brown & Vicki Brown)

TOMMY DUNCAN

66	Sue WI 4002	Dance, Dance, Dance/Let's Try It Over Again	40

DIANE DUNCANE

79	Contact 2	Better Late Than Never/One Day (We're Gonna Do It Again)	15

DUNCANS

81	Impact IMP 3	Too Damn Hot/Communication (12")	12

DUNDEEVILLE PLAYERS

65	Stateside SS451	Wheels/Woodpecker	7

BARBARA DUNKLEY

71	Banana BA 342	We'll Cry Together/BOBBY DAVIS: Got To Get Away	7

DELROY DUNKLEY

70	Hot Rod HR 109	I Wish You Well/TONY & DELROY: Impossible Love	20

ERROL(L) DUNKLEY

67	Rio R 109	Love Me Forever/VIETNAM ALLSTARS: The Toughest	100
67	Rio R 131	You're Gonna Need Me/Seek And You'll Find	35
68	Island WI 3150	Once More/I'm Not Your Man	45
68	Amalgamated AMG 800	Please Stop Your Lying/Feel So Fine (B-side actually by Tommy McCook & Band)	35
68	Amalgamated AMG 805	I'm Going Home/I'm Not Your Man	30
68	Amalgamated AMG 807	The Scorcher/Do It Right Tonight	80
68	Amalgamated AMG 820	Love Brother/I Spy	20
69	Fab FAB 117	I'll Take You In My Arms/KING CANNON: Daphney Reggae	30
70	Unity UN 554	My Special Prayer/Never Hurt The One You Love	7
70	Banana BA 302	Satisfaction/CECIL LOCKE: Sing Out Loud	15
71	Big BG 324	Deep Meditation/RUPIE EDWARDS ALL STARS: Meditation Version	25
71	Big BG 327	Three In One/RUPIE EDWARDS ALL STARS: One In Three	8
71	Nu Beat NB 091	Three In One/RUPIE EDWARDS ALL STARS: One In Three	10
71	Explosion EX 2053	O Lord/KEITH with IMPACT ALL STARS: Raindrops (B-side actually "My Baby" by Lloyd Charmers)	8
72	Camel CA 87	Black Cinderella/PHIL PRATT ALLSTARS: Our Anniversary (B-side actually Tropic Shadows)	20
73	Grape GR 3039	Why Did You Do It/One Love	10
73	Count Shelley CS 3039	Girl You Cried/Where Must I Go	10
73	Ackee 507	Keep The Pressure Down/Version	55
75	Kiss KISS 11	Praise Jah All The Time/KISS ALLSTARS : Jah Rockers (12")	25
76	Daddy Kool DK 002	Eunoch Power/INTIMIDATORS: Straight To Him Chest	6
77	Aries ARI 001	Hard Luck Story/To Hell And Forward (p/s both with Jah Steach, actually Jah Stitch)	100
78	Arawak ARK DD 002	Little Way Different/Differentiah (with Dreadful Julio) (12")	25
79	Success SRLD 004	Down Below/The End/Untitled (12")	12
79	Burning Sounds BDS 022	Holding On/Ranking Dub (12" with Ranking Dread)	12
80	Third World TW DIS 01	Little Angel/GENE RONDO: Rebel Woman (12")	25
81	Natty Congo NCDM 005	Happiness Forgets/Happy Dub (12", some on yellow vinyl)	12
81	Natty Congo NCDM007	Jah Apple/Little Green Apple/Hell And Sorrow (12")	10
82	Success SRLD 014	If You Say So/AFRICAN BROTHERS: Mystery Or Nature	15

George DUNN

MINT VALUE £

80s	PC Music PCDD 006	You Have Been Bad/Militant Man (12")	20
73	Attack ATLP 1003	DARLING OOH! (LP)	60
79	Black Joy DH 802	DISCO SHOWCASE (LP)	30
76	Third World TWLP 101	SIT AND CRY OVER YOU (LP)	40
79	Trojan TR 179	DARLING OOH! (LP, reissue)	25
91	Attack ATLP 116	DARLING OOH! (LP, reissue)	15

(see also Errol & His Group, Gaynor & Erroll), Mister Versatile, Don Lee, Ken Parker, Bongo Herman)

GEORGE DUNN

73	Leader LEE 4042	GEORGE DUNN (LP, with insert)	18

MIKE DUNN

90	Desire LUVLP 8	FREE YOUR MIND (LP, die-cut front)	20

TONY DUNNING (& TREMELOS)

60	Palette PG 9006	Seventeen Tomorrow/Be My Girl	10
61	Palette PG 9018	Pretend/Don't Bother To Call	12
61	Palette PG 9027	Under Moscow Skies/Sixteen Candles	10

DUNNO

71	M&M FFMS 100013	Sunday Girl/Magic Beat	20

BLIND WILLIE DUNN'S GIN BOTTLE FOUR WITH KING OLIVER

54	Columbia SCM 5100	Jet Black Blues/Blue Blood Blues	25

(see also Eddie Lang & Lonnie Johnson)

PETE DUNTON

73	Rockfield ROC3	Taking Time/Still Confused	12

DUPARS

76	Contempo 2104	Love Cookin'/Instrumental	30

CHAMPION JACK DUPREE

51	Jazz Parade B 16	Fisherman's Blues/County Jail Special (78)	30
62	Storyville A 45051	Whiskey Head Woman/Shirley May	20
67	Decca F 12611	Barrelhouse Woman/Under Your Hood	25
67	Blue Horizon 45-1007	Get Your Head Happy/Easy Is The Way (with T.S. McPhee)	120
68	Blue Horizon 57-3140	I Haven't Done No-One No Harm/How Am I Doing It (with Stan Webb)	20
69	Blue Horizon 57-3152	Ba'la Fouche/Kansas City	30
69	Blue Horizon 57-3158	I Want To Be A Hippy/Goin' Back To Louisiana	25
61	Storyville SEP 381	BLUES ANTHOLOGY VOL. 1 (EP)	15
64	RCA RCX 7137	RHYTHM AND BLUES VOL. 1 (EP)	15
64	Decca DFE 8586	LONDON SPECIAL (EP, with Keith Smith Climax Band)	60
65	Ember EMB 4564	JACK DUPREE (EP)	25
59	London Jazz LTZ-K 15171	BLUES FROM THE GUTTER (LP)	50
61	London Jazz LTZ-K 15217	CHAMPION JACK'S NATURAL AND SOULFUL BLUES LP, mono)	65
61	London Jazz SAH-K 6150	CHAMPION JACK'S NATURAL AND SOULFUL BLUES LP, stereo)	75
65	Storyville SLP 145	TROUBLE TROUBLE (LP)	25
65	Xtra XTRA 1028	CABBAGE GREENS (LP)	25
65	Storyville SLP 161	PORTRAITS IN BLUES (LP)	40
66	Decca LK/SKL 4747	FROM NEW ORLEANS TO CHICAGO (LP)	100
67	Storyville 670 194	CHAMPION JACK DUPREE (LP)	25
67	Decca SKL 4871	CHAMPION JACK DUPREE AND HIS BIG BLUES BAND (LP)	125
68	Blue Horizon 7-63206	WHEN YOU FEEL THE FEELING YOU WAS FEELING (LP)	90
69	Blue Horizon 7-63214	SCOOBYDOOBYDOO (LP)	120

(see also T.S. McPhee)

CHAMPION JACK DUPREE/JIMMY RUSHING

64	Ember CJS 800	TWO SHADES OF BLUE (LP)	18

(see also Jimmy Rushing)

SIMON DUPREE & BIG SOUND

66	Parlophone R 5542	I See The Light/It Is Finished	10
67	Parlophone R 5574	Reservations/You Need A Man	15
67	Parlophone R 5594	Day Time, Night Time/I've Seen It All Before	10
67	Parlophone R 5646	Kites/Like The Sun Like The Fire (with Jacqui Chan)	6
68	Parlophone R 5670	For Whom The Bell Tolls/Sleep	10
68	Parlophone R 5697	Part Of My Past/This Story Never Ends	10
68	Parlophone R 5727	Thinking About My Life/Velvet And Lace	10
69	Parlophone R 5757	Broken Hearted Pirates/She Gave Me The Sun	12
69	Parlophone R 5816	The Eagle Flies Tonight/Give It All Back	12
67	Parlophone PMC/PCS 7029	WITHOUT RESERVATIONS (LP, yellow & black label, with "sold in the U.K..." text, laminated sleeve)	125

(see also Moles, Gentle Giant, Shape Of The Rain)

DUPREES

62	HMV POP 1073	You Belong To Me/Take Me As I Am	25
62	Stateside SS 143	My Own True Love/Ginny	15
63	London HLU 9678	I'd Rather Be Here In Your Arms/I Wish I Could Believe You	15
63	London HLU 9709	Gone With The Wind/Let's Make Love Again	15
63	London HLU 9774	Why Don't You Believe Me?/My Dearest One	15
63	London HLU 9813	Have You Heard?/Love Eyes	15
64	London HLU 9843	It's No Sin/The Sand And The Sea	15
65	CBS 201803	Around The Corner/They Said It Couldn't Be Done	15
66	CBS 202028	She Waits For Him/Norma Jean	15
68	MGM MGM 460	My Special Angel/Ring Of Love	10
70	Polydor 2058 077	Check Yourself/The Sky's The Limit	35
75	State 22	Delicious/The Skys The Limit	10

DURAN DURAN

87	EMI TRADEX 1	Skin Trade/We Need You (poster p/s)	8
89	EMI DDC 12	Do You Believe In Shame?/Drug (It's Just A State Of Mind) (p/s, with 3 postcards)	8

Allison DURBIN

MINT VALUE £

93	Parlophone DD 16	Ordinary World/My Antarctica (p/s)	15
93	Parlophone DD 17	Come Undone/Ordinary World (Acoustic Version) (p/s)	20
95	Parlophone DD 20	Perfect Day/Femme Fatale (p/s)	10
90	Parlophone PCSD 112	LIBERTY (LP, inner)	30
93	Parlophone 7988761	THE WEDDING ALBUM (LP, inner)	150
95	Parlophone 72438518981	THANK YOU (LP, with poster)	100
11	Tape Modern DURANLP01	ALL YOU NEED IS NOW (2-LP)	150
14	EMI DDLIVEX82	LIVE 2011 (2-LP, screen printed sleeve)	80
15	Warner Bros. 9362 49251 5	PAPER GODS (2-LP)	30
15	Vinyl Factory VF 212	PAPER GODS (box set, 2 x 12", prints, booklet, magnets, signed, 350 only)	250
18	Warner Bros. 9362 49078 8	BUDOKAN (LP)	25
19	Parlophone DDRSD2019	AS THE LIGHTS GO DOWN (2-LP, one side etched)	40
21	BMG 4050538693669/3652	FUTURE PAST (LP, red or white vinyl)	20

ALLISON DURBIN
69	Decca LK-R/SKL-R 4996	I HAVE LOVED ME A MAN (LP)	40

JUDITH DURHAM
67	Columbia DB 8290	Again And Again/Memories	8
70	A&M AMS 777	The Light Is Dark Enough/Wander Love	6
74	Pye 7N 45312	I Wanna Dance To Your Music/Mama's Got The Blues	6
74	Pye NSLP 18431	THE HOTTEST BAND IN TOWN (LP)	15

(see also Seekers, Keith Potger)

TERRY DURHAM
69	Deram DML/SML 1042	CRYSTAL TELEPHONE (LP, with insert, red/white label with large logo)	40

(see also Storyteller)

LAWRENCE DURRELL
70	Turret TRT 102	ULYSSES COME BACK (LP)	40

DURUTTI COLUMN
82	Factory FAC 64	I Get Along Without You Very Well/Prayer (p/s)	7
80	Factory FACT 14	THE RETURN OF THE DURUTTI COLUMN (LP, with sandpaper sleeve, with Martin Hannett's "Testcard" flexidisc [FACT 14C])	500
80	Factory FACT 14	THE RETURN OF THE DURUTTI COLUMN (LP, with sandpaper sleeve, without Martin Hannett's "Testcard" flexidisc [FACT 14C])	400
80	Factory FACT 14	THE RETURN OF THE DURUTTI COLUMN (reissue, different sleeve)	20
82	Factory FACT 44	LC (LP, 1st pressing with misspelt 'Durrutti Column' on spine, with inner)	30
83	Factory FACT 74	ANOTHER SETTING (LP, with perfumed cut-out insert)	30
83	VU VINI 1	LIVE AT THE VENUE LONDON (LP)	25
84	Factory FACT 84	WITHOUT MERCY (LP, pasted on picture)	20
86	Factory FACT 164c	VALUABLE PASSAGES (cassette in box with insert)	35
86	Factory FACT 14C	THE RETURN OF THE DURUTTI COLUMN (reissue, cassette in box with insert)	35
86	Factory FACT 44c	LC (reissue, cassette in box with insert)	35
86	Factory FACT 74c	ANOTHER SETTING (reissue, cassette in box with insert)	35
86	Factory FACT 84c	WITHOUT MERCY (reissue, cassette in box with insert)	35
87	Factory FACT 204	THE GUITAR AND OTHER MACHINES (LP, inner)	30
88	Factory FACT 244	VINI REILLY (LP, with free p/s 7" "I Know Very Well How I Got My Note Wrong" [FAC 244++] by Vincent Gerard & Steven Patrick)	50
88	Factory FACD 244	VINI REILLY (CD, with 3" CD "I Know Very Well How I Got My Note Wrong" [FAC CD 244++] by Vincent Gerard & Steven Patrick)	45
88	Factory FACT 244	VINI REILLY (LP, without 7")	20
90	Factory FACT 274	OBEY THE TIME (LP)	35
19	Factory FBN 274	OBEY THE TIME (2-LP, reissue. yellow/purple vinyl)	20
20	Demon DEMREC743	REBELLION (LP, reissue, blue vinyl)	15
20	Factory Benelux FBN 244	VINI REIILLY (2-LP, clear vinyl, 7", reissue)	35

(see also Nosebleeds, Morrissey)

IAN DURY (& THE BLOCKHEADS)
77	Stiff BUY 23	Sweet Gene Vincent/You're More Than Fair (solid centre)	30
77	Stiff BUY 23	Sweet Gene Vincent/You're More Than Fair (promo pressing small "A" on label)	10
78	Stiff BUY 2712	What A Waste/Wake Up (12", plain white sleeve, 100 only)	100
78	Stiff BUY 38	Hit Me With Your Rhythm Stick/There Ain't Half Been Some Clever Bastards (red vinyl, p/s, one copy known)	300
78	Stiff FREEBIE 1	Sex And Drugs And Rock And Roll/England's Glory/Two Steep Hills (p/s, free at NME party/competition, 1500 only)	10
80	Stiff BUY 90	I Want To Be Straight/That's Not All (Band photo p/s)	7
85	MT1	Fuck Off Noddy/SUN RA: Nuclear War (white label, 500 only)	50
77	Stiff SEEZ 4	NEW BOOTS AND PANTIES!! (LP, with bonus track 'Sex And Drugs And Rock And Roll')	20
77	Stiff SEEZ 4	NEW BOOTS AND PANTIES!! (LP, limited edition gold vinyl)	25

(see also Kilburn & The High Roads, Greatest Show On Earth, Loving Awareness, Davey Payne)

ANDREW DURYER
75	Real RR 2003	BALLADS OF A WANDERER (LP)	25

JEAN DUSHON
65	Chess CRL 4000	MAKE WAY FOR JEAN DUSHON (LP)	40

DUSK
71	Bell BLL 1167	I Hear Those Church Bells Ringing/I Cannot See To See You	12

PAT DUSKY AND MARINES
67	Stardust STP 1	I Fall To Pieces/This Can Be The Night	6

LA DÜSSELDORF
78	Radar ADA 5	La Düsseldorf/Silver Cloud (unissued, white label promo only)	25
81	Albion ION 1025	Tintarella Di/Dampfriemen (some might have p/s)	10
78	Radar RAD 7	DUSSELDORF (LP)	25
78	Radar RAD 10	VIVA (LP, with lyric inner)	25
80	Albion ALB 207	INDIVIDUELLOS (LP)	25

(see also Neu!)

DUST (1)

MINT VALUE £

DUST (1)
68	Full Stop FS 039	Before Time/There You Are	45

DUST (2)
75	20th Century BTC 1009	Rebound/Pieces	7
72	Kama Sutra 2319	DUST (LP)	20

DUST BROTHERS
93	Diamond DBS 333	Song To The Siren (12" single sided)	40
93	Diamond DBS 333	Song To The Siren (12", no p/s, 500 only)	40
93	Junior Boys Own JBO 10	Song To The Siren/Song To The Siren (Sabres Of Paradise Mixes) (12", p/s)	15
94	Dust Up Beats NS 1	Loops Of Fury (12")	25
94	Boys Own COLLECT 004	14TH CENTURY SKY EP (12", no p/s)	15
94	Junior Boys Own JBO 20	MY MERCURY MOUTH EP (12", JBO sleeve)	15

(see also Chemical Brothers)

DUSTY LEDGE
71	Axes AX 114	Sign Here/Look To The Sun	50

DUSTY SHELF
74	Sprint SP 2	Jacobs Ladder/You Don't Realise	25

SLIM DUSTY
57	Columbia DB 4212	A Pub With No Beer/Once When I Was Mustering (with His Country Rockers)	6
60	Columbia SEG 8009	SLIM DUSTY AND HIS COUNTRY ROCKERS (EP)	15

DUTCH
68	Phillips BF 1673	What Is Soul/Down Here	12

DUTCHESS
81	B'kreig Waxworks EJSP 9580	Your Love/Dead And Gone	150

JACQUES DUTRONC
66	Vogue VRS 7015	Et Moi, Et Moi, Et Moi/Mini-Mini-Mini	15
66	Vogue VRS 7021	Les Cactus/L'Espace D'Une Fille	12
66	Vogue VRS 7024	J'Aime Les Filles/L'Idole	12
67	Vogue VRS 7027	Le Plus Difficile/Les Rois De La Reforme	12
67	Vogue VRL 3029	JACQUES DUTRONC (LP)	60

JOSE DUVAL
57	London HLR 8458	Message Of Love/That's What You Mean To Me	25

D&V
83	Crass 121984/1	Jekyll And Hyde/Wake Up/High Above/Today's Conclusion/Step Inside/DignityS21RN (fold-out sleeve)	15
85	Crass CATNO 1	INSPIRATION GAVE THEM THE MOTIVATION TO MOVE OUT OF THEIR ISOLATION (LP, inner)	15

DYAKS
78	Bonaparte BONE 2	Gutter Kids/It's A Game (p/s)	7

JOHNNY MBIZO DYANI
87	Cadillac SGC 1016	WITCHDOCTORS SON TOGETHER (LP)	18
88	Cadillac SCG 1017	REJOICE (LP)	20

JUDY DYBLE
06	Fungus 006	SONGS FROM THE SPINDLE AND THE WHORL (LP, hand-made sleeves, 250 only, numbered)	30

BILLY DYCE
72	G.G. GG 4532	Be My Guest/HUGH ROY: Way Down South	15
72	G.G. GG 4534	Take Warning/TYPHOON ALL STARS: Warning (Version)	8
72	G.G. GG 4537	Time Is Still Here/G.G. ALL STARS: Time — Version	7
72	Pama PM 835	Be My Guest/HUGH ROY: Way Down South	15
73	Pama PM 874	Woman Smarter/SHENLEY DUFFAS: Standing On The Hill (with the (uncredited) Silvertones)	12
73	Bread BR 1115	You Need Love (with Millions)/G.G. ALL STARS: Love — Dub	6

DYKE & BLAZERS
67	Pye International 7N 25313	Funky Broadway (Parts 1 & 2)	20

MICHAEL DYKE
70s	Attack ATT 8112	Saturday Night Special/CHINNA : Saturday Night Version	20

BOB DYLAN

SINGLES
65	CBS 201751	The Times They Are A-Changin'/Honey, Just Allow Me One More Chance	10
65	CBS 201753	Subterranean Homesick Blues/She Belongs To Me	10
65	CBS 201781	Maggie's Farm/On The Road Again	10
65	CBS 201811	Like A Rolling Stone/Gates Of Eden	10
65	CBS 201824	Positively 4th Street/From A Buick 6	10
66	CBS 201900	Can You Please Crawl Out Your Window/Highway 61 Revisited	15
66	CBS 202053	One Of Us Must Know (Sooner Or Later)/Queen Jane Approximately	20
66	CBS 202307	Rainy Day Women Nos. 12 & 35/Pledging My Time	10
66	CBS 202258	I Want You/Just Like Tom Thumb's Blues (live)	15
66	CBS 2700	Leopard-Skin Pill-Box Hat/Most Likely You Go Your Way And I'll Go Mine (p/s)	45
66	CBS 2700	Leopard-Skin Pill-Box Hat/Most Likely You Go Your Way And I'll Go Mine	10
67	CBS 2476	Mixed Up Confusion/Corrine Corrina (unissued in U.K.)	0
69	CBS 4219	I Threw It All Away/The Drifter's Escape	6
71	CBS SS 7092	If Not For You/New Morning	8
71	CBS 7688	George Jackson (Acoustic)/George Jackson (Big Band Version)	8
73	CBS 1158	Just Like A Woman/I Want You (p/s, 'Hall Of Fame Hits' series)	6
74	CBS 2006	A Fool Such As I/Lily Of The West	6
75	CBS 3160	Tangled Up In Blue/If You See Her, Say Hello	6
75	CBS 3665	Million Dollar Bash/Tears Of Rage	6
76	CBS SCBS 3878	Hurricane (Part 1)/(Full Version) (some list 'Pt 1'/'Pt 2'; with p/s)	8
76	CBS 4859	Stuck Inside Of Mobile With The Memphis Blues Again/Rita May (p/s; demos have "Rita May" as A-side, p/s)	12

Bob DYLAN

MINT VALUE £

76	CBS 4859	Rita May/Stuck Inside Of Mobile With The Memphis Blues Again (demos with "Rita May" as A-side)	8
84	CBS A 4055	Jokerman (Special Faded Radio Version)/Licence To Kill (p/s, promo only)	15
85	CBS GA 5020	Highway 61 Revisited (live)/It Ain't Me Babe (live) (gatefold p/s)	8
88	CBS 6514066	Silvio/When Did You Leave Heaven? (p/s)	6
89	CBS 6553588	Everything Is Broken/Dead Man, Dead Man/I Want You (Live) (12" with limited edition album sleeve print)	20
89	CBS 6553587	Everything Is Broken/Death Is Not The End (p/s)	6
90	CBS 6556436	Political World/Ring Them Bells/Silvio/ All Along The Watchtower (Live) (12" p/s)	6
90	CBS 6563047	Unbelievable/10,000 Men (p/s grey shaded not laminated/brown shaded laminated)	6
00	Columbia 6693797	Things Have Changed/Blind Willy McTell (numbered p/s)	6

EPs

64	CBS 6051	DYLAN (Bob Dylan below song titles, solid/push-out centre, designer credits in bottom right corner, p/s)	60
64	CBS 6051	DYLAN (Bob Dylan vertically on left: 'EXTENDED PLAY' on 1 line above 'EP 6051', push out centre – no designer credits, p/s)	45
65	CBS 6051	DYLAN (Bob Dylan vertically on left: 'EXTENDED PLAY' on 2 lines above 'EP 6051', solid centre, no designer credits, p/s)	45
66	CBS 6070	ONE TOO MANY MORNINGS (Only EP in Europe with five songs, p/s)	50
66	CBS 6070	MR. TAMBOURINE MAN (length of EP on both sides: 27mm 'EXTENDED PLAY' on 1 line, 'Blossom Music LTD' on both sides. Solid/push-out centre, p/s)	50
66	CBS 6078	MR. TAMBOURINE MAN (length of EP on side 1, 'EXTENDED PLAY' divided over 2 lines, 'Bossom Music' (side 1) 'Bossom Music Ltd' (Side 2),	50
65	Fontana TFE 18009	WITH GOD ON OUR SIDE (Joan Baez and Bob Dylan title track)/PETE SEEGER: The Bells of Rhymney/JOAN BAEZ: Waggoner's Lad, p/s)	75
65	Fontana TFE 18010	BLOWIN' IN THE WIND (BOB DYLAN: Blowin' In The Wind/JOAN BAEZ: Oh Freedom/ PETE SEEGER: Careless Love, p/s)	75
65	Fontana TFE 18011	YE PLAYBOYS AND PLAYGIRLS (Bob Dylan and Pete Seeger title track/JOAN BAEZ: Te Ador, Te Manha/PETE SEEGER: This Land Is Mine, p/s)	75

ALBUMS

62	CBS BPG 62022	BOB DYLAN (mono)	75
62	CBS SBPG 62022	BOB DYLAN (stereo)	75
63	CBS BPG 62193	THE FREEWHEELIN' BOB DYLAN (mono)	60
63	CBS SBPG 62193	THE FREEWHEELIN' BOB DYLAN (stereo)	50
63	CBS BPG 62251	THE TIMES THEY ARE A-CHANGIN' (mono)	60
63	CBS SBPG 62251	THE TIMES THEY ARE A-CHANGIN' (stereo)	50
64	CBS BPG 62429	ANOTHER SIDE OF BOB DYLAN (mono)	60
64	CBS SBPG 62429	ANOTHER SIDE OF BOB DYLAN (stereo)	50
65	CBS BPG 62515	BRINGING IT ALL BACK HOME (mono, flipback sleeve)	60
65	CBS SBPG 62515	BRINGING IT ALL BACK HOME (stereo, flipback sleeve)	50
65	CBS BPG 62572	HIGHWAY 61 REVISITED (mono)	80
65	CBS SBGP 62572	HIGHWAY 61 REVISITED (stereo)	70
66	CBS DDP 66012	BLONDE ON BLONDE (2-LP, 8 or 9 photos on inside gatefold sleeve, mono)	100
66	CBS (S)BPG 66012	BLONDE ON BLONDE (2-LP, 8 or 9 photos on inside gatefold sleeve, stereo)	70
67	CBS BPG 62847	BOB DYLAN'S GREATEST HITS (mono)	18
68	CBS BGP 63252	JOHN WESLEY HARDING (mono)	40

(The above LPs were originally issued with rough textured orange labels & flipback sleeves, without 'CBS Records' credit on rear sleeve & with inner sleeves advertising other CBS LPs. First pressings of Bob Dylan, The Freewheelin Bob Dylan, The Times They Are A-Changin', Another Side Of Bob Dylan, Bringing It All Back Home and Blond On Blond have '33' on the labels rather than 33 and a third which denote later 60s repressings. These copies are worth around half the value of the above LPs.)

68	CBS (S)BGP 63252	JOHN WESLEY HARDING (stereo)	20
69	CBS (M) 63601	NASHVILLE SKYLINE (mono)	30
69	CBS (S) 63601	NASHVILLE SKYLINE (stereo)	15
71	CBS S 67239	MORE BOB DYLAN GREATEST HITS	15
73	CBS S 69049	DYLAN	15
73	CBS 69042	PAT GARRETT & BILLY THE KID	20
74	Island ILPS 9261	PLANET WAVES ('pink rim palm tree' label, with inner sleeve)	15
74	Island IDBD-1	BEFORE THE FLOOD (2-LP, gatefold)	20
75	CBS 69097	BLOOD ON THE TRACKS (orange label, red inner with painting on rear sleeve)	20
75	CBS 69097	BLOOD ON THE TRACKS (orange label, red inner with liner notes on rear sleeve)	25
75	CBS S 88147	THE BASEMENT TAPES	35
76	CBS S 86003	DESIRE (LP, inner)	25
76	CBS CBS 86016	HARD RAIN (LP, with inner)	15
78	CBS CBS 86067	STREET LEGAL (LP)	15
79	CBS CBS 96004	AT BUDOKAN (with poster and 16 page booklet)	25
83	CBS 25539	INFIDELS (LP, inner)	15
91	Columbia 468086	THE BOOTLEG SERIES VOLUMES 1-3 (5-LP box set, booklet)	125
92	Columbia 472710	GOOD AS I BEEN TO YOU (LP, inner)	30
93	Columbia 4748571	WORLD GONE WRONG (LP)	100
95	Columbia 478374 1	MTV UNPLUGGED (2-LP)	80
98	Columbia CK265759-1	LIVE 1966 (2-LP)	40
01	Columbia COL 504364 1	LOVE AND THEFT (2-LP, inners)	40
12	Sony No Cat No	THE 50th ANNIVERSARY COLLECTION (4xCD-R, barcode 88765460722, 100 copies only, beware of bootlegs)	600
13	Sony 88883799701	50th ANNIVERSARY COLLECTION (6-LP box set)	200

ALBUMS : REISSUES

64	CBS BPG 62066	BOB DYLAN (LP, mono repressing)	25
67	CBS SBGP 62572	HIGHWAY 61 REVISITED (LP, reissue, flipback sleeve, stereo with 33 and a third on the label)	25
68	CBS S BPG 62022	BOB DYLAN (LP, stereo, repressing)	20
68	CBS BPG 62193	THE FREEWHEELIN' BOB DYLAN (LP, reissue, not flipback sleeve with 33 and a third on the label)	18

DYMONDS

			MINT VALUE £
68	CBS 62515	BRINGING IT ALL BACK HOME (LP, reissue, non-flipback sleeve, orange label)	18
69	CBS 66012	BLONDE ON BLONDE (2-LP, stereo, smooth label, gatefold with no flipback, 9 photos)	25
70	70s	BOB DYLAN (LP, reissue, orange/yellow labels)	15
70	CBS SBPG 62251	THE TIMES THEY ARE A-CHANGIN' (LP, reissue, orange/yellow labels)	15
70	CBS 62515	BRINGING IT ALL BACK HOME (LP, 70s reissue, non-flipback sleeve, orange/yellow label)	15
70	CBS SBGP 62572	HIGHWAY 61 REVISITED (LP, 2nd reissue, orange/yellow labels, stereo)	20
75	CBS S62429	ANOTHER SIDE OF BOB DYLAN (LP, reissue, orange/yellow labels)	15
75	CBS 66012	BLONDE ON BLONDE (2-LP, gatefold, stereo reissue, orange/yellow labels, 7 photos)	20
85	CBS 66509	BIOGRAPH (5-LP, box set, 2 booklets)	35
98	Simply Vinyl SVLP 063	BLONDE ON BLOND (2-LP, reissue)	20

(see also Dick Farina, Band, George Harrison, Traveling Wilburys, Doug Sahm)

DYMONDS

71	Big BG 326	Girl You Are Too Young/RUPIE EDWARDS ALL STARS: Version	6

(see also Diamonds)

DYNAMIC

92	Dee Jay DJX 002	Rule The Dancefloor/Your Son Is Back (12")	10

DYNAMIC CORVETTES

75	Contempo CS 2059	Funky Music Is The Thing (Parts 1 & 2)	7

DYNAMIC GANG (BOB ANDY & MARCIA GRIFFITHS)

71	Moodisc MU 3511	I'll Never Believe In You/LLOYD WILLIS: Black Attack	12

DYNAMIC MCS

87	Tuff Groove TUFF002	I Feel Dynamic (12")	60

DYNAMIC SUPERIORS

77	Motown PSLP 233	Nowhere To Run/MANDRE: Solar Flight (Opus 1) (12")	80
76	Tamla Motown STNL 12007	PURE PLEASURE (LP)	15

DYNAMICS (JAMAICA)

68	Blue Cat BS 104	My Friends/NEVILLE IRONS: Soul Glide	70
69	Punch PH 1	The Burner/Juckie Juckie (B-side actually by Tommy McCook & Carl Bryan)	150

DYNAMICS (U.S.)

63	London HLX 9809	Misery/I'm The Man	50
64	King KG 1007	So In Love With Me/Say You Will	25
69	Atlantic 584 270	Ice Cream Song/The Love That I Need	20

DYNAMITES

69	Duke DU 30	John Public/CLANCY ECCLES: Fire Corner (B-side actually by King Stitt)	30
69	Duke DU 31	I Don't Care (actually by Dingle Brothers)/CLANCY ECCLES: Shoo-Be-Do	40
69	Clandisc CLA 200	Mr. Midnight (Skokiaan)/KING STITT: Who Yeah	15
70	Clandisc CLA 212	Black Beret/BARRY & AFFECTIONS: Love Me Tender	12
70	Clandisc CLA 219	Sha La La La/Pop It Up	8
72	Duke DU 147	Get In The Groove/Version	6
69	Trojan/Clandisc TTL 21	FIRE CORNER (LP, with King Stitt)	60

(see also Clancy Eccles & Dynamites, Baba Brooks, Dennis Alcapone, Diamonds, Joe Higgs, Silvertones, Carl Dawkins, Chris Leon, Hopeton Lewis, Melodians, Cynthia Richards, Soul Twins, Stranger & Gladys, Carey & Lloyd)

DYNASTY

72	Top Nix 134	Tutankhamen/Let's Boogie	15

DYNATONES

59	Top Rank JAR 149	Steel Guitar Rag/The Girl I'm Searching For	10
59	Top Rank JAR 149	Steel Guitar Rag/The Girl I'm Searching For (78)	20
66	Pye International 7N 25389	The Fife Piper/And I Always Will	50

ALAN DYSON

68	Pye NPL 18218	THE STILL SMALL VOICE OF...(LP)	20

RONNIE DYSON

70	CBS 5285	She's Gone/I Don't Wanna Cry	6
71	CBS 7449	When You Get Right Down To It/Sleeping Sun	6
73	CBS 1659	Just Don't Want To Be Lonely/Point Of Mo Return	7
74	CBS 2430	We Can Make It Last Forever/Just A Little Love From Me	8
76	CBS 4462	The More You Do It/You And Me	6
71	CBS S 64779	WHEN YOU GET RIGHT DOWN TO IT (LP)	30

E

VINCE EAGER (& THE VAGABONDS)

58	Decca F 11023	Tread Softly Stranger & Yea Yea (as Vince Eager & The Vagabonds; unissued, 2 x 1-sided demos only)	30
58	Parlophone R 4482	Five Days, Five Days/No More	30
59	Parlophone R 4531	When's Your Birthday, Baby?/The Railroad Song	10
59	Parlophone R 4550	This Should Go On Forever/No Other Arms, No Other Lips	10
59	Top Rank JAR 191	Makin' Love/Primrose Lane	7
60	Top Rank JAR 307	Lonely Blue Boy/No Love Have I	7
61	Top Rank JAR 539	(I Wanna) Love My Life Away/I Know What I Want	7
61	Top Rank JAR 593	The World's Loneliest Man/Created In A Dream	6
63	Piccadilly 7N 35110	Any Time Is The Right Time/Heavenly	7
63	Piccadilly 7N 35157	I Shall Not Be Moved/It's Only Make Believe	7
11	Stateside SS 2242	MORRISSEY: Glamorous Glue (2011 remaster)/VINCE EAGER: The World's Loneliest Man (Retro A label 'Stateside' promo in die-cut 'Stateside' sleeve, 150 only)	250
58	Decca DFE 6504	VINCE EAGER AND THE VAGABONDS NO. 1 (EP)	100

EAGLE

			MINT VALUE £
70	Pye International 7N 25530	Kickin' It Back To You/Come In, It's All For Free	15
69	Pye Intl. NSPL 28138	COME UNDER NANCY'S TENT (LP)	40

EAGLES (JAMAICA)
69	Songbird SB 1006	Rudam Bam/Prodigal Boy (B-side actually "Any Little Bit" by Crystals)	8
72	Duke Reid DR 2522	Your Enemies Can't Hurt You/Version	7
73	Techniques TE 927	Rub It Down/TOMMY McCOOK ALL STARS: Rub It Down — Version	12

(see also Roy Richards)

EAGLES (U.K.)
62	Pye 7N 15451	Bristol Express/Johnny's Tune	10
62	Pye 7N 15473	Exodus: The Main Theme/March Of The Eagles	8
62	Pye 7N 15503	The Desperados/Special Agent	8
63	Pye 7N 15550	Come On Baby (To The Floral Dance)/Theme From Station Six Sahara	6
63	Pye 7N 15571	Eagles Nest/Poinciana (unreleased)	0
64	Pye 7N 15613	Andorra/Moonstruck	8
64	Pye 7N 15650	Write Me A Letter/Wishin' And Hopin'	10
62	Pye NEP 24166	NEW SOUND T.V. THEMES (EP)	12
63	Pye NPL 18084	SMASH HITS (LP)	30

(see also Valerie Mountain)

EAGLES (U.S.)
72	Asylum AYM 505	Take It Easy/Get You In The Mood (promo only p/s)	8
75	Asylum K 53003	DESPERADO (LP, audiophile pressing, mail-order via Hi-Fi Today mag)	100
98	Simply Vinyl SVLP 050	HELL FREEZES OVER (2-LP, reissue)	100

EAGLES OF DEATH METAL
04	AntAcidAudio AAA 999	PEACE LOVE AND DEATH METAL (LP)	35

SNOOKS EAGLIN
60s	Storyville A 45056	Country Boy/Alberta (some with p/s)	15
60s	Storyville SEP 386	BLUES ANTHOLOGY VOL. 6 (EP)	20
61	Heritage HLP 1002	SNOOKS EAGLIN (LP, 99 only)	100
63	Storyville SLP 119	NEW ORLEANS STREET SINGER (LP)	25
64	Storyville SLP 140	VOL. 2 — BLUES FROM NEW ORLEANS (LP)	15
70s	Storyville 670 146	PORTRAITS IN BLUES VOLUME 1 (LP)	18

JIM EANES
59	Melodisc 1530	Christmas Doll/It Won't Seem Like Christmas	10

EARCANDY
93	Poor Person Prod. PPPR 1	SPACE IS JUST A PLACE (LP, handmade sleeve, 500 only)	20
94	Poor Person Prod. PPPR 2	TIME IS JUST A STATE OF MIND (LP, handmade sleeve)	20
95	Poor Person Prod. PPPR 5	SOUND IS JUST THE WAY YOU EAR IT (LP, handmade sleeve with insert, numbered, 600 only)	20
95	Poor Person Prod. PPPR 8	TASTING 1,2,3, TASTING (LP, handmade sleeve & insert, numbered, 500 only)	20

JON EARDLEY SEVEN
56	Esquire 32040	DOWN EAST (LP)	150

EARGASM
81	Venture EAR 26	This Is Lovers Rock/Name That Tune (as Eargasm, P Pop & Beagle)	20
80	Venture CUT 007	LOVERS DUB (LP)	40

CHARLES EARLAND
78	Mercury 9199831	Let The Music Play/Broken Heart (12")	15
80	CBS 84815	COMING TO YOU LIVE (LP)	15

EARL & DEAN
66	Strike JH 323	Slowly Goin' Out Of My Head/Little Buddy	7

KENNETH EARLE
60	Decca F 11205	The New Frankie And Johnny/40-30-40	10

EARL-JEAN
64	Colpix PX 729	I'm Into Somethin' Good/We Love And Learn	30
64	Colpix PX 748	Randy/They're Jealous Of Me	30

(see also Cookies)

JOSEPH EARLOCKS
80s	Freedom Sounds FSD014	Free Up The Blackman/JAMAICANS & I DAUGHTER : Country Life (12")	20

EARLS
63	Stateside SS 153	Remember Then/Let's Waddle	40
63	London HL 9702	Never/I Keep-A Tellin' You	50
71	Atlantic 2091 129	Remember Then/I Believe	10

EARLY B
82	Black Solidarity BSI 001	Imitator/Mi Huh Know (with Papa San)	40

EARLY MORNING
72	Philips 6006240	Rainbow/Song To The Dawn	8

EARTH (1)
69	CBS 4671	Resurrection City/Comical Man	40
69	Decca F 22908	Everybody Sing The Song/Stranger Of Fortune	15

EARTH (2)
15	Record Collector RCLP 019	ELEMENTAL (LP, silver sleeve)	30

EARTH & FIRE
70	Polydor 56790	Seasons/Paradise	15
71	Nepentha 6129 001	Invitation/Wild And Exciting	15
72	Polydor 2001 356	Memories/From The End To The Beginning	8
73	Polydor 2001-435	Maybe Tomorrow, Maybe Tonight/Theme From Atlantis	8
71	Nepentha 6437 004	EARTH AND FIRE (LP, gatefold sleeve, artwork by Roger Dean)	1000
73	Polydor 2310 262	ATLANTIS (LP, laminated sleeve)	30

EARTH & STONE
78	Different HAED 5	Back To Africa/Still In Slavery (12")	20

EARTHBOUND

MINT VALUE £

79	Cha Cha CHAD 09	Sweet Africa/Dance With Me (12")	35
79	Cha Cha CHAD 013	False Ruler/Don't Let Them Fool You (12")	50
79	Cha Cha CHAD 015	Slave Driver/Magic Woman (12")	30
77	Different DIFF 105	BACK TO AFRICA (LP)	50
79	Cha Cha CHADLP 007	KOOL ROOTS (LP, gatefold)	80

EARTHBOUND
78	Archway S/79/CUS 308	The Robot/Liberated Lady (7", different p/s)	10
79	Archway AR 17945	The Robot/Liberated Lady/Song For South Kensington (12" p/s with inserts)	25

EARTH BOYS
59	Capitol CL 14979	Barbara Ann/Space Girl	25

EARTH LEAKAGE TRIP
91	Moving Shadow SHADOW 1	PSYCHOTRONIC EP (12", p/s)	15

EARTHLING SOCIETY
11	Fruits De Mer Crustacean 19	The Green Manalishi (With The Two-Prong Crown)/And I Heard The Fire Sing (orange vinyl, folded p/s, inserts)	15

EARTHLINGS
65	Parlophone R 5242	Landing Of The Daleks/March Of The Robots	50

EARTH MAN
80	Feast	Life Is For Living/Love Is For Giving	100

EARTH OPERA
68	Elektra EKSN 45035	Close Your Eyes And Shut The Door/Dreamless	8
69	Elektra EKSN 45049	American Eagle Tragedy/When You Were Full Of Wonder	7
69	Elektra EKSN 45061	Home To You/Alfie Finney	7
68	Elektra EKS 74016	EARTH OPERA (LP, stereo, gatefold sleeve)	35
68	Elektra EKL 4016	EARTH OPERA (LP, mono, gatefold sleeve)	40
69	Elektra EKS 74038	GREAT AMERICAN EAGLE TRAGEDY (LP)	30

(see also Rowan Brothers)

EARTHQUAKE
74	Cloud One HIT 4	Friday On My Mind/Madness (p/s)	10

EARTHQUAKERS
67	Stateside SS 2050	Whistling In The Sunshine/Dreaming In The Moonlight	10

EARTHQUAKES
69	Duke DU 54	Pair Of Wings/I Can't Stop Loving You	50
69	Duke DU 56	Earthquake/Simmering	25

(see also Sir Collins & Earthquakes)

EARWIG
74	DJM DJS 310	Sun Comes Up/Water It Down	7

TIM EASLEY
68	Bell BLL 1036	Susie Q (Parts 1 & 2)	10

EASTBOUND EXPRESSWAY
76	Pye 7N 45628	Danger Zone/Danger Zone - Long Disco Version	7
78	Pye 7NL 25798	Never Let Go/Soundburst (12")	10

EAST COAST ANGELS
77	Ruby RUB 207	Punk Rockin'/To Nite's The Nite (Irish pressing, no p/s)	60

EASTER AND THE TOTEM
88	TOTEM III	Co-Conspirator/Chasing The Whale (p/s)	10
88	TOTEM IV	Act Of Faith/Tomb Of The Kings (p/s)	10
82	Ark Music (No Cat. No.)	HIP REPLACEMENT (LP)	25
86	Ideologically Sound ET 1	THE SUM IS GREATER THAN ITS PARTS (LP)	15

EASTER MONDAY
89	SRT TTWW001	EASTER MONDAY EP (numbered foldover p/s, 500 only)	15

EASTERN VARIATION
86	Cartridge CRD 15	Baby I Love You/Version (12")	30
86	XL 180	Creation/V.A.R.I.O.U.S. (12", p/s)	40

EAST MAIN ST. EXPLOSION
69	Fontana TF 1039	Hop, Skip And Jump/Little Jackie Horner	6

EAST OF EDEN
68	Atlantic 584 198	King Of Siam/Ballad Of Harvey Kaye	150
69	Deram DM 242	Northern Hemisphere/Communion	10
70	Deram DM 297	Jig-A-Jig/Marcus Junior	8
71	Deram DM 338	Ramadhan/In The Snow For A Blow/Better Git It In Your Soul/ Have To Whack It Up A Bit	10
72	Harvest HAR 5055	Boogie Woogie 'Flu/Last Dance Of The Clown (p/s)	8
69	Deram DML 1038	MERCATOR PROJECTED (LP, mono, red/white label with large logo)	200
69	Deram SML 1038	MERCATOR PROJECTED (LP, stereo, red/white label with large logo)	100
70	Deram SML 1050	SNAFU (LP, mono, red/white label with small logo)	200
70	Deram SML 1050	SNAFU (LP, stereo, red/white label with small logo)	100
71	Decca SPA 157	WORLD OF EAST OF EDEN (LP, credited on sleeve and blue/silver label as a Deram release)	15
71	Harvest SHVL 792	EAST OF EDEN (LP, gatefold sleeve, early copies with EMI box on side 1 label but no EMI box on side 2)	80
71	Harvest SHVL 792	EAST OF EDEN (LP, gatefold sleeve)	50
72	Harvest SHVL 792	EAST OF EDEN (LP, gatefold sleeve, non EMI 2nd pressing with indented centre perimeter)	50
71	Harvest SHVL 796	NEW LEAF (LP, gatefold sleeve, with EMI on label)	70

EAST RIVER PIPE
93	Sarah SARAH 75	Helmet On/Happytown/Axl Or Iggy (foldover p/s, insert)	20
93	Sarah SARAH 78	She's A Real Good Time/My Life Is Wrong/Times Square Go-Go Boy (foldover p/s in poly bag, insert)	20
93	Sarah SARAH 405	GOODBYE CALIFORNIA (10" LP)	50
94	Sarah SARAH 621	POOR FRICKY (LP)	60
95	Sarah SARAH 407	EVEN THE SUN WAS AFRAID (10" LP)	45

EASTWOOD

MINT VALUE £

EASTWOOD
70	SRT SRTS7332	Little Miss Lucy/Living To Learn	200
71	CBS 7076	I Am Free/Gypsy	45
72	CBS 7325	Orphan/Another Day In My Life	25

ALAN EASTWOOD
73	President PT 403	Moonchild/Red Shoe Truckin'	8

(see also Alan James Eastwood, Eastwood & Powell)

ALAN JAMES EASTWOOD
68	President PT 209	Blackbird Charlie/My Sun (as Bugsy Eastwood)	6
71	President PT 320	Seeds/Boston	6
72	President PT 379	Closer To The Truth/Strange News	20
71	President PTLS 1037	SEEDS (LP)	40

(see also Alan Eastwood, Eastwood & Powell)

CLINT EASTWOOD (1)
62	Cameo Parkway C 240	Rowdy/Cowboy Wedding Song (in p/s)	10
62	Cameo SC 1056	COWBOY FAVOURITES... (LP)	30

CLINT EASTWOOD (2)
79	Greensleeves GRED 25	True True Love/Me Go Deh Already (12")	15
77	Jamaica Sounds JSLP 0010	JAH LIGHTS SHINING (LP)	15
78	Live & Love LAP 011	STEP IT IN A ZION! (LP)	15
78	Cha Cha CHALP003	DEATH IN THE ARENA (LP)	45
78	Third World TWS933	AFRICAN YOUTH (LP)	35
79	Burning Vibrations BV 1001	LOVE AND HAPPINESS (LP)	20
80	Greensleeves GREL 17	SEX EDUCATION (LP)	15

EASTWOOD & POWELL
71	President PT 352	Beautiful/Opal Blue Sunday	8

(see also Alan James Eastwood, Alan Eastwood)

EASYBEATS
66	United Artists UP 1144	Come And See Her/Make You Feel Alright (Women)	20
66	United Artists UP 1157	Friday On My Mind/Made My Bed, Gonna Lie In It	8
66	United Artists UP 1175	Who'll Be The One?/Saturday Night	10
67	United Artists UP 1183	Heaven And Hell/Pretty Girl	10
67	United Artists UP 1201	The Music Goes Round My Head/Come In, You'll Get Pneumonia	12
68	United Artists UP 2219	The Land Of Make-Believe/We All Live Happily	8
68	United Artists UP 2209	Hello, How Are You?/Falling Off The Edge Of The World	6
68	United Artists UP 2243	Good Times/Lay Me Down And Die	6
69	Polydor 56335	St. Louis/Can't Find Love	6
70	Polydor 2001 028	(Who Are My) Friends?/Rock'n'Roll Boogie	6
67	United Artists (S)ULP 1167	GOOD FRIDAY (LP)	175
68	United Artists (S)ULP 1193	VIGIL (LP)	100
70	Polydor Special 2482 010	FRIENDS (LP)	80

(see also Paintbox, Haffy's Whisky Sour, Harry Vanda, Grapefruit)

EASY LIFE
18	Chess Club CC089	RINGTONES (10". p/s, teal coloured vinyl)	100
18	Universal 6787818	CREATURE HABITS (12", p/s)	80
19	Island 6789085	SPACESHIPS (12", p/s, flow in the dark vinyl)	80
19	Island 6789085	Frank/Ojpl (10", p/s, white vinyl)	40
20	Island 0848479	JUNK FOOD (LP, red or mustard vinyl)	40

EASY STREET
76	Polydor 2058807	Feels Like Heaven/Shadows On The Wall (no p/s)	10
70s	Muscle Music AP 591	Person To Person/Easy Come Easy Go	30
77	Polydor 2058873	Flying/Blame The Love	12

EATER
77	The Label TLR 001	Outside View/You (p/s)	10
77	The Label TLR 003	Thinkin' Of The USA/Space Dreamin'/Michael's Monetary System (p/s)	10
77	The Label TLR 004	Lock It Up/Jeepster (p/s)	10
78	The Label TLR 007	GET YOUR YO-YO'S OUT (12" EP, white vinyl; blue, green or red p/s)	10
78	The Label TLR 009	What She Wants She Needs/Reaching For The Sky (p/s)	6
78	The Label TLRLP 001	THE ALBUM (LP, with inner sleeve)	40
85	De Lorean EAT 1	THE HISTORY OF EATER (LP, 1,000 each on red, white & blue vinyl, with bonus 7" [EAT FREEBIE 1])	15
85	De Lorean EAT 1	THE HISTORY OF EATER (LP, green vinyl)	15

(see also Andy Blade)

EATHOPIANS
69	Nu Beat NB 038	Buss Your Mouth (actually "Contention" by Ethiopians)/REGGAE BOYS: Rough Way Ahead (B-side actually by Keith Blake & Hi-Tals)	45
68	Crab 4	Reggie Hit The Town/Ding Dong Bell	40

(see also Ethiopians)

KOOKIE EATON
68	Condor PS 1002	Cream Machine/Joke B Side	15

EAT STATIC
91	Alien HAB 1	Monkey Man/Habi Beep (12")	30
91	Alien AR 1	Inanna/Medicine Wheel (12")	20
92	Alien AR 2	ALMOST HUMAN EP (12")	20
93	Planet Dog BARK 002T	LOST IN TIME EP (12", p/s)	20
95	Planet Dog BARK 581 023-1	EYSYLON EP (2x12", p/s)	15
93	Planet Dog BARK LP 001	ABDUCTION (2-LP)	25
95	Planet Dog BARK LP 005	IMPLANT (2-LP)	25
97	Planet Dog BARK LP 029	SCIENCE OF THE GODS (3-LP)	25

EAZIE RYDER

MINT VALUE £

EAZIE RYDER
78 Graduate GRAD 1   Motorbikin'/City Lights (p/s) 15
EAZYSTREET
84 Private Pressing   Quest For Glory/Let 'Em Rock (no p/s) 100
EBONIES
68 Philips BF 1648   Never Gonna Break Your Heart Again/Shoeshine Boy 10
EBONY
84 Touched TOUCH 1   Dream Girl/We'll Fight Back (p/s) 15
EBONY DUBSTERS
03 Ebony EBR 028   EBONY DUBS VOL. 2 (12", p/s one side etched) 20
EBONY SISTERS
69 Bullet BU 401   Let Me Tell You Boy/RHYTHM RULERS: Mannix 30
70 Bullet BU 420   Each Time/BUNNY LEE ALLSTARS: Boss Walk 35
(see also Sister)
EBONY DIAMONDS
16 Super Disco Edits EDI 101   I'm So Lucky/I'm So Lucky (p/s) 15
EBONY STEEL BAND
82 TJ ESBLP 001   A TOUCH OF CLASS (LP) 40
19 OM Swagger OMSLP 001   PAN MACHINE (LP, gatefold) 15
19 OM Swagger OMSLP 001   PAN MACHINE (LP, gatefold, red vinyl, 100 only) 35
KATJA EBSTEIN
70 Liberty LBF 15317   No More Love For Me/Without Love 25
ECCENTRICS
65 Pye 7N 15850   What You Got/Fe Fi Fo Fum 45
CLANCY ECCLES (& DYNAMITES)
61 Blue Beat BB 34   River Jordan/I Live And I Love (with Hersan & His City Slickers) 15
61 Blue Beat BB 67   Freedom/More Proof 25
63 Island WI 044   Judgement/Baby Please (B-side actually with Paulette) 25
63 Island WI 098   Glory Hallelujah/Hot Rod (B-side actually by Roland Alphonso) 25
65 Ska Beat JB 194   Sammy No Dead/Roam Jerusalem 20
65 Ska Beat JB 198   Miss Ida/KING ROCKY: What Is Katty 20
67 Doctor Bird DB 1156   Feel The Rhythm/Easy Snapping (B-side actually by Theo Beckford) .. 35
67 Pama PM 701   What Will Your Mama Say/Darling Don't Do That 25
67 Pama PMB 703   Western Organ/Mother's Advice (actually by The Clancy Set) 25
68 Pama PM 712   The Fight/Great 20
68 Nu Beat NB 006   Festival '68/I Really Love You 25
69 Trojan TR 639   Sweet Africa/Let Us Be Lovers 30
69 Trojan TR 647   Bangarang Crash/DYNAMITES: Rahthid 100
69 Trojan TR 648   Constantinople/Deacon Sun 40
69 Trojan TR 649   Demonstration/VAL BENNETT: My Girl 30
69 Trojan TR 658   Fattie Fattie/SILVERSTARS: Last Call 50
69 Duke DU 9   Auntie Lulu/SLICKERS: Bag A Boo 100
69 Duke DU 31   Shoo-Be-Do/DYNAMITES: I Don't Care (B-side actually by Dingle Brothers) 40
69 Clandisc CLA 201   The World Needs Loving/DYNAMITES: Dollar Train (B-side actually by Clancy Eccles) 20
69 Clandisc CLA 206   Dance Beat/KING STITT: The Ugly One 45
70 Clandisc CLA 209   Open Up/HIGGS & WILSON: Agane (B-side actually "Again") 20
70 Clandisc CLA 211   Promises/Real Sweet (both sides with Dynamites) 8
70 Clandisc CLA 212   Black Beret (with Dynamites)/BARRY & AFFECTIONS: Love Me Tender 12
70 Clandisc CLA 213   Phantom/Skank Me (both sides with Dynamites) (B-side actually by Barry & Affections) . 25
70 Clandisc CLA 214   Africa/Africa Part Two (both sides with Dynamites) 6
70 Clandisc CLA 221   Unite Tonight/Uncle Joe 10
70 Clandisc CLA 227   Credit Squeeze/DYNAMITES: Credit Squeeze 10
71 Clandisc CLA 231   Sweet Jamaica/DYNAMITES: Going Up West 6
71 Clandisc CLA 232   Rod Of Correction/Rod Of Correction Version 6
71 Clandisc CLA 235   John Crow Skank/KING STITT: Merry Rhythm 15
71 Clandisc CLA 236   Power For The People/DYNAMITES: Power For The People — Version .. 8
71 Pama Supreme PS 332   What Will Your Mama Say/TIGER: United We Stand 25
72 Clandisc CLA 239   Hallelujah, Free At Last/DYNAMITES: Sha-La-La 8
72 Attack ATT 8037   Ganja Free/DYNAMITES: Ganja (Version) 12
69 Clandisc TTL 22   FREEDOM (LP) 60
69 Trojan TTL 22   FREEDOM (LP) 60
70 Clandisc TBL 124   HERBSMAN REGGAE (LP) 60
73 Big Shot BILP 101   TOP OF THE LADDER (LP) 30
88 Trojan TRLS 262   FATTY FATTY (LP) 15
(see also Dynamites, Drumbago, Marlene Webber, Westmorelites)
JIMMY ECHO
65 Columbia DB 7629   After Tonight/Practise What You Preach 6
ECHO & BUNNYMEN
79 Zoo CAGE 004   Pictures On My Wall/Read It In Books (p/s, 4000 only) 8
88 WES YZ175TW   People Are Strange/Paint It Black (live)/Run Run Run (live)/Friction (live) (12", p/s with free poster, in shrinkwrap) 60
80 Korova KODE 1   CROCODILES (LP, with bonus 7", "Do It Clean"/"Read It In Books" [SAM 128] & inner sleeve) 30
80 Korova KODE 1   CROCODILES (LP, with inner) 20
81 Korova KODE 2   HEAVEN UP HERE (LP) 20
83 Korova KODE 6   PORCUPINE (LP, with bonus Peel Session [KOW 26C]) 20
83 Korova KODE 6   PORCUPINE (LP, with inner) 15
84 Korova KODE 8   OCEAN RAIN (LP, inner) 20
85 Korova KODE 13   SONGS TO LEARN AND SING (LP, with lyric booklet & 7": "The Pictures On My Wall"/"Read It In Books" [p/s, yellow/blue labels, CAGE 004], no "Voodoo Billy" run-off groove message; signed) 30

Year	Label & Cat. No.	Title	Mint Value £
85	Korova KODE 13	SONGS TO LEARN AND SING (LP)	20
01	Cooking Vinyl COOK 208	FLOWERS (LP)	60
06	Let Them Eat Vinyl LEN 007LP	SIBERIA (2-LP)	80
13	Vinyl 180 VIN180LP063	CROCODILES (2-LP, reissue, hardback cover)	40
13	Vinyl 180 VIN180LP068	HEAVEN UP HERE (2-LP, reissue, hardback cover)	40
13	Vinyl 180 VIN180LP068	HEAVEN UP HERE (LP, reissue, blue vinyl)	30
13	Vinyl 180 VIN180LP068	HEAVEN UP HERE (LP, reissue,180gm)	20
14	Vinyl 180 VIN180LP070	PORCUPINE (LP. reissue, white vinyl)	25
14	Vinyl 180 VIN180LP071	PORCUPINE (2-LP, reissue, harback cover)	40
14	Vinyl 180 VIN180LP075	OCEAN RAIN (LP, reissue)	20
14	Vinyl 180 VIN180LP075	OCEAN RAIN (LP, reissue, silver vinyl)	25
14	Vinyl 180 VIN180LP075R	OCEAN RAIN (LP, reissue, blue vinyl)	30
14	Vinyl 180 VIN180LP076	OCEAN RAIN (2-LP, reissue, hardback cover)	40
15	Vinyl 180 VIN180LP082	ECHO & THE BUNNYMEN (LP, reissue, clear vinyl)	25
15	Vinyl 180 VIN180LP082	ECHO & THE BUNNYMEN (LP, reissue)	18

(see also Will Sergeant)

ECHO BASE
Year	Label & Cat. No.	Title	Mint Value £
84	DEP International DEP 14	Out Of My Reach/Splash Down (p/s)	12
85	DEP International DEP 19	Puppet At The Go Go/Genius + Soul = Jazz (p/s)	12
85	DEP International LPDEP 9	BUY ME (LP)	15

(see also Ocean Colour Scene)

ECHOBELLY
Year	Label & Cat. No.	Title	Mint Value £
94	Fauve FAUV3LP	EVERYONES GOT ONE (LP)	25
95	Rhythm King FAUV 6LX	ON (LP, with free 7")	40

ECHOES (U.K.)
Year	Label & Cat. No.	Title	Mint Value £
68	Philips BF 1687	Searchin' For You Baby/Listen To Me Baby	10

ECHOES (U.S.)
Year	Label & Cat. No.	Title	Mint Value £
60	Top Rank JAR 399	Born To Be With You/My Guiding Light	15
61	Top Rank JAR 553	Baby Blue/Boomerang	15

ECHOES & CELESTIALS (JAMAICA)
Year	Label & Cat. No.	Title	Mint Value £
61	Hornet H 1004	Are You Mine/I'll Love You Forever	18
62	Blue Beat BB 89	Are You Mine/I'll Love You Forever (reissue)	10

CHUCK E
Year	Label & Cat. No.	Title	Mint Value £
94	White House WYHS 038	THE CHUCK EP (12")	20

BILLY ECKSTINE
Year	Label & Cat. No.	Title	Mint Value £
54	MGM SP 1101	No One But You/I Let A Song Go Out Of My Heart	10
65	Tamla Motown TMG 533	Had You Been Around/Down To Earth	100
65	Tamla Motown TMG 533	Had You Been Around/Down To Earth (DJ copy)	150
57	Parlophone GEP 8672	A DATE WITH RHYTHM (EP, with His All Star Band)	10
66	T. Motown TML 11025	THE PRIME OF MY LIFE (LP, mono)	55
66	T. Motown STML 11025	THE PRIME OF MY LIFE (LP, stereo)	65
67	T. Motown TML 11046	MY WAY (LP, mono)	50
67	T. Motown STML 11046	MY WAY (LP, stereo)	60
69	T. Motown (S)TML 11101	GENTLE ON MY MIND (LP, mono/stereo)	45

ECLECTION
Year	Label & Cat. No.	Title	Mint Value £
68	Elektra EKSN 45033	Nevertheless/Mark Time	12
68	Elektra EKSN 45040	Another Time, Another Place/Betty Brown	12
68	Elektra EKSN 45042	Please/Saint George And The Dragon	12
68	Elektra EKSN 45046	Please (Mark II)/In The Early Days	10
68	Elektra EKL 4023	ECLECTION (LP, gatefold sleeve, also stereo EKS 74023)	100

(see also Fotheringay, Dorris Henderson, Trevor Lucas, Mogul Thrash)

ECLIPSE
Year	Label & Cat. No.	Title	Mint Value £
78	Baal BAL 89005	ECLIPSED (LP)	50

ECOLOGY
Year	Label & Cat. No.	Title	Mint Value £
92	Vicious Pumpin'	THE COMMUNAL MIND EP (12", stamped white label)	20
92	Vicious Pumpin' OBS 004	ECOLOGY EP (12", stamped white label)	30
92	Vicious Pumpin' VIC 002	THE SMOKIN' JAM EP (12", stamped white label)	20
93	Vicious Pumpin' VIC 010	Vicious House/Take Me Higher (12", stamped white label)	15

ECSTACY OF SAINT THERESA
Year	Label & Cat. No.	Title	Mint Value £
94	FREE LP FRE4	FREE D (LP)	80

ECSTASY CLUB
Year	Label & Cat. No.	Title	Mint Value £
88	Swordfish DROP 1	JESUS LOVES THE ACID (EP, 12")	15
88	Flim Flam FFR1207	JESUS LOVES THE ACID (EP, 12")	20
88	Flim Flam FFR1207	JESUS LOVES THE ACID (EP, 12" picture disc)	20
89	LD Records	JESUS LOVES THE ACID (EP, 12")	20

ECSTASY, PASSION & PAIN
Year	Label & Cat. No.	Title	Mint Value £
74	Pye International 7N 25660	Good Things Don't Last Forever/Born To Lose You	8

ECTOMORPH
Year	Label & Cat. No.	Title	Mint Value £
90s	Woronzow WOO 15	THE FURIOUS SLEEPER (LP, with poster & inserts, 500 only)	20

EDAN
Year	Label & Cat. No.	Title	Mint Value £
02	Lewis LEWISLP001	PRIMITIVE PLUS (2-LP)	35
05	Lewis LEWISLP 007	BEAUTY & THE BEAT (LP)	25

EDDIE
Year	Label & Cat. No.	Title	Mint Value £
82	PC PCDD 001	I Don't Wamnt To Lose You/I Don't Lost In Dub You (12")	30

EDDIE & THE CRAZY JETS
Year	Label & Cat. No.	Title	Mint Value £
64	King KG 1000	Come On Let's Slop/Down By The Riverside	6

EDDIE & THE HOT RODS
Year	Label & Cat. No.	Title	Mint Value £
76	Island WIP 6270DJ	Writing On The Wall/Cruisin' (In The Lincoln) (promos in generic title p/s)	25
76	Island WIP 6270	Writing On The Wall/Cruisin' (In The Lincoln) (in black & white p/s)	15

Jason EDDIE & THE CENTREMEN

MINT VALUE £

76	Island WIP 6306	Wooly Bully/Horseplay (Weary Of The Schmaltz) (p/s)	8
76	Island WIP 6333	Get Out Of Denver/96 Tears (with 'Collectors item' and 'jukebox special' on label)	80
76	Island WIP 6354	Teenage Depression/Shake (p/s)	10
77	Island WIP 6388	I Might Be Lying/Ignore Them (p/s)	10
77	Island 12WIP 6438	Life On The Line/Do Anything You Wanna Do (live)/(I Don't Know) What's Really Going On (live)/Why Can't It Be (live) (12", p/s)	10
76	Island ILPS 9457	TEENAGE DEPRESSION (LP, with poster)	25
76	Island ILPS 9457	TEENAGE DEPRESSION (LP, without poster)	15
77	Island ILPS 9509	LIFE ON THE LINE (LP, gatefold)	20

(see also Engineers, Lew Lewis)

JASON EDDIE & THE CENTREMEN

65	Parlophone R 5388	Whatcha Gonna Do Baby/Come On Baby (as Jason Eddie & the Centremen)	175
66	Parlophone R 5473	Singing The Blues/True To You (as Jason Eddy & the Centremen)	175
69	Tangerine DP 0010	Heart And Soul/Playing The Clown (solo)	50

EDDIE & JERRY

| 72 | Hillcrest HCT 4 | Hail Rasta Man Hail/UPSETTERS: Scorcher | 12 |

EDDIE'S CROWD

| 66 | CBS 202078 | Baby Don't Look Down/Take It Easy Baby | 90 |

DUANE EDDY (& THE REBELS)

78s

59	London HLW 8821	The Lonely One/Detour	20
59	London HLW 8879	Peter Gunn/Yep!	40
59	London HLW 8929	Forty Miles Of Bad Road/The Quiet Three	30
59	London HLW 9007	Some Kind-A Earthquake/First Love, First Tears	30
60	London HLW 9050	Bonnie Came Back/Movin 'N' Groovin'	40
60	London HLW 9104	Shazam!/The Secret Seven	60
60	London HLW 9162	Because They're Young/Rebel Walk	80

SINGLES

58	London HL 8669	Rebel-Rouser/Stalkin' (initially with triangular centre)	15
58	London HL 8723	Ramrod/The Walker (as Duane Eddy & Rebels, actually by Al Casey tri-centre centre)	10
58	London HL 8764	Cannonball/Mason-Dixon Lion (as Duane Eddy & Rebels, tri centre)	10
59	London HLW 8821	The Lonely One/Detour (triangular centre)	10
60	London HLW 9050	Bonnie Came Back/Movin 'N' Groovin' (tri centre)	15
59	London HLW 8821	The Lonely One/Detour (round centre)	8
59	London HLW 8879	Peter Gunn/Yep! (triangular centre)	8
59	London HLW 8929	Forty Miles Of Bad Road/The Quiet Three (triangular centre)	10
59	London HLW 9007	Some Kind-A Earthquake/First Love, First Tears (tri centre)	15
61	London HLW 9324	Theme From Dixie/The Battle	6
61	London HLW 9406	Drivin' Home/My Blue Heaven	7
61	London HLW 9477	The Avenger/Londonderry Air	6
61	Parlophone R 4826	Caravan (Parts 1 & 2) (actually by Al Casey)	10
62	RCA RCA 1288	Deep In The Heart Of Texas/Saints And Sinners	6
62	RCA RCA 1300	The Ballad Of Paladin/Wild Westerner	7
63	RCA RCA 1329	Boss Guitar/Desert Rat (with Rebelettes)	7
63	RCA RCA 1344	Lonely Boy, Lonely Guitar/Joshin'	7
63	RCA RCA 1357	You're Baby's Gone Surfin'/Shuckin'	10
63	RCA RCA 1369	My Baby Plays The Same Old Song On His Guitar All Night Long/ Guitar'd And Feather'd	8
64	RCA RCA 1389	The Son Of Rebel Rouser/The Story Of Three Loves	8
64	RCA RCA 1425	Guitar Star/The Iguana	15
65	Colpix PX 779	Trash/South Phoenix	15
65	Colpix PX 788	The House Of The Rising Sun/Don't Think Twice, It's All Right	15
66	Reprise RS 20504	Daydream/This Guitar Was Made For Twangin'	10
67	Reprise RS 20557	Monsoon/Roarin'	10
68	Reprise RS 20690	Niki Hoeky/Velvet Nights (Theme From "Elvira Madigan")	10
68	RCA RCA 1701	Dance With The Guitar Man/SAM COOKE: Another Saturday Night (withdrawn)	10
69	CBS 3962	Break My Mind/Loving Bird	10

EXPORT SINGLES

58	London HL 7057	Ramrod/The Walker (as Duane Eddy & Rebels)	20
59	London HL 7072	The Lonely One/Detour	20
59	London HL 7076	Yep!/Three-30-Blues	30
59	London SLW 4001	Peter Gunn/Yep! (stereo)	90
59	London HL 7080	Forty Miles Of Bad Road/The Quiet Three	15
60	London HL 7090	Bonnie Come Back/Lost Island	15
60	London HL 7096	Because They're Young/Rebel Walk	15

EPs

58	London RE 1175	REBEL ROUSER (as Douane Eddy)	20
59	London RE-W 1216	THE LONELY ONE	20
59	London RE-W 1217	YEP!	15
60	London RE-W 1252	BECAUSE THEY'RE YOUNG	10
60	London RE-W 1257	TWANGY	15
61	London RE-W 1287	PEPE	15
61	London RE-W 1303	DUANE EDDY PLAYS MOVIE THEMES	15
61	London RE-W 1341	TWANGY NO. 2	15
63	RCA RCX 7115	A COUNTRY TWANG	15
63	RCA RCX 7129	MR. TWANG	15
64	RCA RCX 7146	TWANGIN' UP A SMALL STORM	15
65	Colpix PXE 304	COTTONMOUTH	30

Pearl EDDY

MINT VALUE £

ALBUMS

			MINT VALUE £
58	London HA-W 2160	HAVE 'TWANGY' GUITAR, WILL TRAVEL	40
59	London HA-W 2191	ESPECIALLY FOR YOU (mono)	20
59	London SAH-W 6045	ESPECIALLY FOR YOU (stereo with different version of "Tuxedo Junction")	25
60	London HA-W 2236	THE "TWANG'S" THE "THANG!" (mono)	20
60	London SAH-W 6068	THE "TWANG'S" THE "THANG" (stereo)	30
60	London HA-W 2285	SONGS OF OUR HERITAGE (gatefold sleeve, mono)	20
60	London SAH-W 6119	SONGS OF OUR HERITAGE (gatefold sleeve, stereo)	20
61	London HA-W 2325	A MILLION DOLLARS' WORTH OF TWANG	25
61	London HA-W 2373	GIRLS, GIRLS, GIRLS (mono)	25
61	London SAH-W 6173	GIRLS, GIRLS, GIRLS (stereo)	30
62	London HA-W 2435	A MILLION DOLLARS' WORTH OF TWANG VOL. 2	25
62	RCA RD 27264/SF 5134	TWISTIN' AND TWANGIN' (mono/stereo)	25
62	RCA RD/SF 7510	TWANGY GUITAR — SILKY STRINGS (mono)	15
62	RCA SF 7510	TWANGY GUITAR — SILKY STRINGS (stereo)	20
63	RCA RD/SF 7545	DANCE WITH THE GUITAR MAN (mono)	20
63	RCA SF 7545	DANCE WITH THE GUITAR MAN (stereo)	25
63	RCA RD/SF 7560	TWANG A COUNTRY SONG (mono)	20
63	RCA SF 7560	TWANG A COUNTRY SONG (stereo)	25
63	RCA RD/SF 7568	TWANGIN' UP A STORM (mono)	20
63	RCA SF 7568	TWANGIN' UP A STORM (stereo)	25
64	RCA RD/SF 7621	LONELY GUITAR (mono)	20
64	RCA SF 7621	LONELY GUITAR (stereo)	20
64	RCA RD/SF 7656	WATER SKIING (mono)	25
64	RCA SF 7656	WATER SKIING (stereo)	30
65	RCA RD/SF 7689	TWANGIN' THE GOLDEN HITS (mono)	15
65	RCA SF 7689	TWANGIN' THE GOLDEN HITS (stereo)	15
65	RCA RD/SF 7754	TWANGSVILLE (mono)	20
65	RCA SF 7754	TWANGSVILLE (stereo)	20
65	Colpix PXL 490	DUANE A-GO-GO-GO	20
66	Colpix PXL 494	DUANE EDDY DOES BOB DYLAN	20
67	Reprise R(S)LP 6218	THE BIGGEST TWANG OF THEM ALL (mono)	15
67	Reprise R(S)LP 6218	THE BIGGEST TWANG OF THEM ALL (stereo)	18
67	Reprise RLP 6240	THE ROARIN' TWANGIES (mono only)	25

(see also Lee Hazlewood)

PEARL EDDY

54	HMV 7M 262	Devil Lips/That's What A Heart Is For	12

EDDY & TEDDY

61	London HLU 9367	Bye Bye Butterfly/Star Crossed Lovers	15

EDDYSONS

68	Olga OLE 010	Ups And Downs/Sweet Memories	7

DAVID EDE BAND

60	Pye 7N 15280	Easy Go/The Blue Bird (as David Ede & Rabin Rock)	15
61	Pye 7N 15329	Obsession/Bootnik (& Go Man Go, Men)	10
61	Pye 7N 15370	Last Night/Ding Dong John (as David Ede & Go Man Go Men)	20
62	Pye 7N 15417	Twistin' Those Meeces To Pieces/Twistin' The Trad (as David Ede & Rabin Band)	15

(see also Oscar Rabin)

EDEN

87	Den 3DEN	FORM FOLLOWS FUNCTION EP	35

EDEN STREET SKIFFLE GROUP

57	Headquarter & General Stores	SKIFFLE ALBUM NO. 1 (10 x 7" 78rpm clear flexidiscs in p/s)	35

TONI EDEN

60	Columbia DB 4409	Teen Street/No One Understands (My Johnny)	25
60	Columbia DB 4458	Grown Up Dreams/Whad'ya Gonna Do	20
60	Columbia DB 4527	Will I Ever/The Waitin' Game	10
61	Decca F 11342	Send Me/Interesting Facts	10

EDEN'S CHILDREN

68	Stateside (S)SL 10235	EDEN'S CHILDREN (LP)	80

EDGE BROS

82	Edge EDGE 1	Video/Instrumental	8

EDGE (1)

78	Albion ION 4	Macho Man/I'm Cold (p/s)	8
79	Hurricane FIRE 3	Downhill/American Excess (p/s, white vinyl)	8
79	Hurricane FIRE 6	Watching You/Overtaking (p/s)	7
96	Volume VOL 19	Little Girl Blue/The Hopeless Dreams Of Neville Been (p/s)	8
80	Hurricane FLAK 102	SQUARE 1 (LP, some on white vinyl)	15

(see also Damned, Culture Club)

EDGE (2)

78	Chiltern Sound CSLP 1	UNEASY PEACE (LP)	20

EDIKANFO

81	Editions EG EGED 12	THE PACE SETTERS (LP)	20

EDISON LIGHTHOUSE

71	Bell BLL 1153	What's Happening/Take A Little Time	6
72	Bell BLL 1206	Find Mr. Zebedee?/Reconsider, My Belinda	6
81	Greenstone GRS 3441	Endearing Young Charms/Livin' On A Roller	6

(see also Flowerpot Men, White Plains, David & Jonathan, First Class)

EDITORS

05	Kitchenware SKX 77	Bullet/You Are Fading	20
05	Kitchenware SKCD77	Bullets/You Are Fading/Dust In The Sunlight (CD, 500 only)	35

Lada EDMUND JR

MINT VALUE £

05	Kitchenware SKX77	You Are Fading/Dust In The Sunlight (500 only)	35
05	Kitchenware SKX78	Munich/Disappear (Numbered, p/s)	6
07	Kitchenware SKX 973	Escape The Nest (Demo)/When Anger Shows (Demo) (Fan club 7", 1,000 only)	10
13	Independent Label Market ILMVF008	A Ton Of Love (Acoustic) (12" 1-sided, 50 only)	60
15	PIAS (No Cat. No.)	Life Is A Fear/Marching Orders (Michael Price Rework) (picture disc free with Sonic Seducer magazine)	15
16	PIAS (No Cat. No.)	Dream Dark As Your Heaven (numbered, 2 copies only)	100
05	Kitchenware KWX 34	THE BACK ROOM (LP, gatefold sleeve)	30
07	Kitchenware KWX 37	AN END HAS A START (LP, CD)	30
09	Kitchenware KWX 43	IN THIS LIGHT AND ON THIS EVENING (LP)	20
11	PIAS PIASR 250 BOX	UNEDITED (7-LP, 7-CD, book, box set 200 with hand-written insert)	200
11	PIAS PIASR 250 BOX	UNEDITED (7-LP, 7-CD, book, box set without hand-written insert)	125
15	Play It Again Sam PIASR830LP	IN DREAM (LP, gold vinyl)	20

LADA EDMUND JR

75	MCA MU 172	The Larue/Soul Au Go-Go	10
75	MCA MU 172	The Larue/Soul Au Go-Go (DJ Copy)	20

DAVE EDMUNDS (& ROCKPILE)

71	Regal Zonophone RZ 3032	I'm Comin' Home/Country Roll	10
71	Regal Zonophone RZ 3037	Blue Monday/I'll Get Along	10
72	Regal Zonophone RZ 3059	Down, Down, Down/It Ain't Easy	10
77	Swan Song SSK 19411	I Knew The Bride/Back To Schooldays	6
90	Capitol 10CL 568	King Of Love/Stay With Me Tonight (45rpm)/King Of Love (78 rpm) (10", p/s)	30
90	Capitol 12CL 568	King Of Love/Stay With Me Tonight/Every Time I See Her (12", p/s)	10
71	Regal Zono. SRZA 8503	ROCKPILE COLLECTION (LP, unreleased)	0
72	Regal Zono. SLRZ 1026	ROCKPILE (LP)	60
75	Rockfield RRL 101	SUBTLE AS A FLYING MALLET (LP)	20
82	Arista SPART 1184	DE 7TH (LP, with bonus EP "Live At The Venue" [JUKE 1])	15

(see also Image, Human Beans, Love Sculpture, Rockpile)

EDOUARD

66	CBS 202200	My Name Is Edouard/N'aie Pas Peur Antoinette (p/s)	8

EDQ

77	Ogun OG 410	THEY ALL BE ON THIS OLD ROAD (LP)	30

EDSELS

61	Pye International 7N 25086	Rama Lama Ding Dong/Bells	60

EDWARD & HARDING

71	Stateside SS 2196	Mr. Sunlight/Blackbird	10

J VINCENT EDWARD

69	CBS 4388	Run To The Sun/I Never Thought I'd Fall In Love	15

ADINA EDWARDS

72	Dynamic DYN 454	Talk About Love/Don't Forget To Remember	6
60s	Tabernacle TLP 1005	JESUS IS MINE (LP)	15

(see also Coxsone Dodd)

BOBBY EDWARDS

61	Top Rank JAR 584	You're The Reason/I'm A Fool Loving You	10

BRENT EDWARDS

63	Pye International 7N 25197	Pride/Over The Weekend	8

C EDWARDS & SYMBOLIC

80	Symbolic BS 02	Loving Jah/Loving One & All (12")	80

CHUCK EDWARDS

68	Soul City SC 104	Downtown Soulville/I Need You	30
68	Soul City SC 104	Downtown Soulville/I Need You (DJ Copy)	100

DEE EDWARDS

98	Goldmine Soul Supply GS 208	All The Way Home/DONI BURDICK: Bari Track (reissue)	10

DEVON EDWARDS

82	CF 12	Bad Boy Lay Down Flat/JAH RUBAL : Burst Shot	35

DICK EDWARDS

71	Ra 5003	Torquay United's War Cry/Around You	8

GARY EDWARDS (COMBO)

62	Oriole CB 1700	Twist Or Bust/The Franz Liszt Twist (as Gary Edwards Combo)	10
62	Oriole CB 1717	The Method/Twistful Thinkin'	12
62	Oriole CB 1733	Africa/One Fifteen A.M.	10
62	Oriole CB 1759	Hopscotch/Theme For A Broken Dream	10

IDIATER EDWARDS

85	Pressure HAVE 2	Loving Sweet Devotion/Version (12")	200

(WILFRED) JACKIE EDWARDS

60	Starlite ST45 016	We're Gonna Love/Your Eyes Are Dreaming (as Wilfred Edwards & Caribs)	25
60	Starlite ST45 026	I Know/Tell Me Darling (as Wilfred Edwards)	25
61	Starlite ST45 046	Whenever There's Moonlight/Heaven Just Knows (as Wilfred Edwards)	25
61	Starlite ST45 062	More Than Words Can Say/I Love You No More (as Wilfred Edwards)	25
62	Starlite ST45 076	Little Bitty Girl/Never Go Away (as Wilfred Edwards)	25
62	Island WI 008	All My Days/Hear Me Cry (as Wilfred Jackie Edwards)	18
62	Island WI 019	One More Week/Tears Like Rain (as Wilfred Edwards)	18
62	Decca F 11547	Lonely Game/Suddenly	15
63	Black Swan WI 404	Why Make Believe/Do You Want Me (as Wilfred Jackie Edwards & Velvetts)	15
64	Black Swan WI 416	The Things You Do/Little Smile (as Wilfred Jackie Edwards)	20
64	Black Swan WI 426	Why Make Believe/Do You Want Me Again	22
64	Fontana TF 465	Sea Cruise/Little Princess	15
64	Sue WI 329	Stagger Lee/Pretty Girl	40

Jackie EDWARDS & JIMMY CLIFF

MINT VALUE £

65	Aladdin WI 601	He'll Have To Go/Gotta Learn To Love Again	25
65	Aladdin WI 605	Hush/I Am In Love With You No More (p/s)	12
65	Aladdin WI 611	The Same One/I Don't Know	15
65	Island WI 255	White Christmas/My Love And I	20
66	Island WI 270	Sometimes/Come On Home	40
66	Island WI 274	L-O-V-E/What's Your Name	40
66	Island WI 287	Think Twice/Oh Mary	20
66	Island WI 3006	I Feel So Bad/I Don't Want To Be Made A Fool Of	300
66	Island WI 3018	Royal Telephone/It's No Secret	15
67	Island WI 3030	Only A Fool Breaks His Own Heart/The End	15
67	Island WIP 6008	Come Back Girl/Tell Him You Lied	25
68	Island WIP 6026	Julie On My Mind/If This Is Heaven	15
68	Island WI 3157	You're My Girl/Heaven Only Knows	15
69	Direction 58-4096	Why Must I Be Alone/I'm Gonna Make You Cry	6
69	Direction 58-4402	Too Experienced/Someone To Love	10
69	Direction 58-4630	Oh Manio/Here We Go Again	6
70	CBS 5147	Tell Me Why Say Goodbye/Walter Walter	6
71	Horse HOSS 1	I Must Go Back/Baby I Want To Be Near You (in p/s)	20
71	Horse HOSS 1	I Must Go Back/Baby I Want To Be Near You	15
71	Bread BR 1107	Johnny Gunman/JACKIE'S BOYS: Johnny Gunman Version	15
72	Bread BR 1108	I Do Love You/Who Told You So?	8
76	Island WIP 6285	I Feel So Bad/Come On Home (reissue)	15
76	Grounation GRO 2056	Invasion/JACKIE EDWARDS & THE AGGROVATORS: Version	25
11	Island 009	I Feel So Bad/JULIAN COVEY: Little Bit Hurt	5
66	St. Mary's IEP 701	SACRED HYMNS VOL. 1 (EP, in p/s)	40
66	St. Mary's IEP 701	SACRED HYMNS VOL. 1 (EP)	15
66	St. Mary's IEP 702	SACRED HYMNS VOL. 2 (EP, with St. Mary's label, in p/s)	40
66	St. Mary's IEP 702	SACRED HYMNS VOL. 2 (EP, with St. Mary's label)	15
66	St. Mary's IEP 702	SACRED HYMNS VOL. 2 (EP, with red-and-white Island label; in p/s)	40
66	St. Mary's IEP 702	SACRED HYMNS VOL. 2 (EP, with red-and-white Island label)	15
66	Island IEP 708	HUSH! (EP)	45
64	Island ILP 906	THE MOST OF WILFRED JACKIE EDWARDS (LP)	50
64	Island ILP 912	STAND UP FOR JESUS (LP)	50
66	Island ILP 931	COME ON HOME (LP)	50
66	Island ILP 936	THE BEST OF JACKIE EDWARDS (LP)	50
66	Island ILP 940	BY DEMAND (LP)	50
67	Island ILP(S) 960	PREMATURE GOLDEN SANDS (LP)	40
69	Island IWPS 4	PUT YOUR TEARS AWAY (LP)	40
69	Direction 8-63977	LET IT BE ME (LP)	20
70	Trojan TTL 40	THE MOST OF WILFRED JACKIE EDWARDS (LP, as Wilfred Jackie Edwards)	25
70	Trojan TTL 45	COME ON HOME (LP)	25
70	Trojan TTL 46	BY DEMAND (LP)	25
70	Trojan TTL 57	PREMATURE GOLDEN SANDS (LP, reissue)	25
72	Trojan TRLS 47	I DO LOVE YOU (LP)	30
78	Trojan TRLS 47	SINCERELY (LP)	15
82	Black Music BMLP 801	KING OF THE GHETTO (LP)	60

(see also Wilfred & Millicent, Wilfred & Millie, Jackie & Millie, Jackie's Boys)

JACKIE EDWARDS & JIMMY CLIFF

68	Island WIP 6036	Set Me Free/Here I Come	20
68	Island WIP 6042	You're My Girl/Heaven Only Knows	10

(see also Jackie & Millie, Millie, Jimmy Cliff, Wilfred & Millie, Jackie's Boys)

JIMMY EDWARDS (& PROFILE)

79	Warner Bros K 17415	Nora's Diary/Call Me A Fraud (features Sham 69) (p/s)	20
79	Warner Bros K 17464	Twentieth Century Time/Seven Hail Marys (features Pretenders) (p/s)	6

(see also Time U.K., Pretenders, Sham 69)

JIMMY EDWARDS (U.S.)

58	Mercury 7MT 193	Love Bug Crawl/Honey Lovin' (demo - hand-written label)	700
58	Mercury 7MT 193	Love Bug Crawl/Honey Lovin'	500
58	Mercury MT 193	Love Bug Crawl/Honey Lovin' (78)	50

JOHN EDWARDS

95	Kent 6T 11	Ain't That Good Enough/LOLEATTA HOLLOWAY: This Man's Arms	25
08	Kent TOWN 115	Tin Man/BILL BRANDON: The Streets Got My Lady	45
14	Kent Select CITY 34	Cold Hearted Woman/Ain't That Good Enough	8

MILL EDWARDS

73	Action ACT 4617	I Found Myself/Don't Forget About Me	25

NOKIE EDWARDS

77	Cream CR 9006	NOKIE (LP)	15

(see also Ventures)

O.G. EDWARDS

88	Dance Yard YARDT 4	Only You (Know What I Like)/Only You (Know What I Like) (Extended Version) (12")	40

PAUL EDWARDS

76	Cottage COT 301	LONGSTONE FARM (LP)	40
77	Cottage COT 021	BUTTERFLY DAYS (LP)	30

R. EDWARDS & SOCIAL EAGLES

73	Dip DL 5014	One Sunday Morning/Version Sunday Morning (with Allstars)	6
73	Dip DL 5014	One Sunday Morning/AFRICAN BROTHERS: Mysterious Nature (2nd issue, different B-side)	10

RUPIE EDWARDS (ALL STARS)

62	Blue Beat BB 90	Guilty Convict/Just Because (as Rupert Edwards & Smithie's Sextet)	25
68	Doctor Bird DB 1163	I Can't Forget/I'm Writing Again	25

Samuel EDWARDS

MINT VALUE £

69	Crab CRAB 35	Long Lost Love/Uncertain Love	60
70	Crab CRAB 41	Sharp Pan Ya Machete/Redemption	20
70	Explosion EX 2030	Full Moon/Baby	20
70	Explosion EX 2031	Love At First Sight/I Need Your Care	8
70	Success RE 902	Grandfather Clock/Promoter's Grouse	25
70	Success RE 905	Handicap/If You Can't Beat Them	25
70	Success RE 909	Pop Hi (as Rupie Edwards All Stars)/VAL BENNETT AND BUNNY LEE ALL STARS: High Tide	15
71	Bullet BU 494	I'm Gonna Live Some Life/RUPIE EDWARDS ALLSTARS: Rock 'In'	6
71	Nu Beat NB 082	Black Man/Tell The People	10
71	Nu Beat NB 091	One In Three/ERROLL DUNKLEY: Three In One	8
71	Big BG 320	Soulful Stew/Soulful Stew — Version Two (as Rupie Edwards Allstars)	15
71	Big BG 324	Deep Meditation (version)/ERROLL DUNKLEY: Deep Meditation	25
71	Big BG 327	One In Three/ERROLL DUNKLEY: Three In One	6
71	Bullet BU 462	My Love (actually by Gaylads)/Stronger Love (both as Rupie Edwards All Stars)	8
72	Big BG 333	Press Along/Press Along — Version (as Rupie Edwards Allstars)	6
72	Big BG 335	Jimmy As Job Card (actually titled "Jimmy Has A Job Card")/ Riot (as Rupie Edwards Allstars)	50
78	Success SLD 016	Oh Black People/NOEL TEMPO : It's Time To Be Free (12")	65
75	Cactus CTLP 106	IRE FEELING (LP)	20
75	Cactus CTLP 107	DUB BASKET (LP)	80
76	Cactus CTLP 117	DUB BASKET CHAPTER 2 (LP)	40
76	Cactus CTLP 120	JAMAICA SERENADE (LP)	40
77	Success SUCLP	101 DUB CLASSICS (LP)	60

(see also R. Edwards & Social Eagles, Gaylads, Heptones, Ethiopians, Dymonds, Dobby Dobson, Keith Cole, Country Boy, Keith Cole, Laurel Aitken, Dennis Alcapone, Gregory Isaacs, Itals, Hugh Roy, Kingstonians, Little George, Winston Blake, Mediators, Max Romeo, I Roy)

SAMUEL EDWARDS
| 69 | Blue Cat BS 159 | Want It Want It/SPARKERS: Israel | 35 |

SANDRA EDWARDS
| 85 | Soultown SAND 001 | Give Me Some Emotion/I Love You (p/s) | 20 |
| 85 | Sir George SG034 | Give Me Some Emotion/Reggae Give Me Some Emotion/Georgie Rock (12") | 20 |

SIMON EDWARDS
| 70 | Jayboy JSX 2001 | NO RETURN (LP) | 30 |

TOM EDWARDS
| 57 | Vogue Coral Q 72236 | What Is A Teen Age Girl?/What Is A Teen Age Boy? | 6 |

TOMMY EDWARDS
| 53 | MGM SP 1030 | (Now And Then, There's) A Fool Such As I/Take These Chains From My Heart | 8 |
| 56 | MGM SP 1168 | Baby, Let Me Take You Dreaming/MARION SISTERS: Life Could Not Be Better | 8 |

VINCE EDWARDS (U.K.)
| 67 | United Artists UP 1179 | I Can't Turn Back Time/The Lively One | 20 |
| 68 | United Artists UP 2230 | County Durham Dream/It's The Same Old Song | 6 |

VINCE EDWARDS (U.S.)
58	Capitol CL 14825	Widget/Lollipop	10
62	Brunswick 05872	Don't Worry About Me/And Now	8
64	Colpix PX 771	No Not Much/See That Girl (p/s)	10
62	Brunswick LT 8515	VINCE EDWARDS SINGS (LP)	15

WINSTON EDWARDS
| 75 | Studio 16 WE 0010 | DUB CONFERENCE (with BLACKBEARD) | 50 |

EDWARDS HAND
70	RCA 2019	Death Of A Man/Please Mister Man	8
71	RCA SF 8154	STRANDED (LP, orange label)	20
73	Regal Zono. SRZA 8513	RAINSHINE (LP, unissued, demos only)	150

(see also Picadilly Line)

WINSTON EDWARS
| 75 | Fay FLP 2004 | NATTY LOCKS DUB (LP) | 200 |

EDWICK RUMBOLD
| 66 | CBS 202393 | Specially When/Come Back | 120 |
| 67 | Parlophone R 5622 | Shades Of Grey/Boggle Woggle | 300 |

EEK A MOUSE
80	Greensleeves GRED 42	Noah's Ark/FLICK WILSON: My Lady (12", green vinyl)	20
81	Love Linch LL019	No Wicked/Trying To Be Free (12")	50
81	Greensleeves GRED 58	Wa-Do-Dem/Wild Inna Eighty-One Style (12", with ERROL SHORTER)	10
81	Greensleeves GRED 74	Christmas A Come/LEE VAN CLEEF: Water Gone (12")	15
82	Greensleeves GRED 88	Do You Remember/TOYAN : Strictly The Dread (12")	15
82	Echo 12 008	Georgie Porgie (with LUI LEPKI)/Version (12")	15
83	Greensleeves GRED 98	Anarexol/Teacher (12")	15
91	Mango 12MNG790	Rude Boys A Foreign/Version/Gangster Chronicles/Version (12")	50
81	Greensleeves GREL 31	WA-DO-DEM (LP)	25
82	Greensleeves GREL 41	SKIDIP! (LP)	20
83	Greensleeves GREL 86	ASSASSINATOR (LP)	15
84	Greensleeves GREL 65	MOUSEKETEER (LP)	20

EELS
96	Dreamworks DRMS 22174	Novocaine For The Soul/Fucker (p/s)	20
97	Dreamworks DRMS 22277	Your Lucky Day In Hell/Altar Boy (p/s)	10
97	Dreamworks DRMS 22238	Susan's House/Stepmother (p/s)	10
98	Dreamworks DRMS 22346	Last Stop: This Town/Funeral Parlour (p/s)	10
98	Dreamworks DRMS 22373	Cancer For The Cure/Everything's Gonna Be Cool This Christmas (p/s)	6
96	Dreamworks DRLP 50001	BEAUTIFUL FREAK (LP)	100
01	Dreamworks 450 335-1	SOULJACKER (LP)	40
10	Eworks CSDLP 1145	TOMORROW MORNING (LP and free 7")	18

14	Dreamworks 533 771	BEAUTIFUL FREAK (LP, reissue)	20

EERIE SUMMER
15	Box Bedroom Rebels BBR21	EERIE SUMMER EP (p/s, inserts, numbered, 20 only)	10

E.F. BAND
80	Rok ROK XI/XII	Another Day Gone/SYNCHROMESH: October Friday (die-cut co. sleeve)	40
80	Aerco/EF Band EF 1	Night Angel/Another Day Gone (p/s)	30
80	Aerco/EF Band EF 1	Night Angel/Another Day Gone	15
80	Redball RR 026	Self Made Suicide/Sister Syne (with wraparound p/s)	30
80	Redball RR 026	Self Made Suicide/Sister Syne	7
80	Redball RR 036	The Devil's Eye/Comprende (with wraparound p/s)	25
80	Redball RR 036	The Devil's Eye/Comprende	7
82	Bullet CULP 2	DEEP CUT (LP)	15

WILLIE EGANS
70s	Flyright LP 6000	ROCKS, BOOGIES AND ROLLS (LP)	15

JULIE EGE
71	CBS 5431	Love/In One Of Your Weaker Moments	6

JOSEPH EGER
70	Charisma CAS 1008	CLASSICAL HEADS (LP, gatefold sleeve, "pink scroll" label)	25

EGG
69	Deram DM 269	Seven Is A Jolly Good Time/You Are All Princes	40
70	Deram Nova SDN 14	EGG (LP, stereo, 1st pressing, red/silver labels, with sticker on rear sleeve correcting credits)	175
70	Deram Nova DN 14	EGG (LP, mono, 1st pressing, blue/silver labels, with sticker on rear sleeve correcting credits)	300
70	Deram Nova SDN 14	EGG (LP, stereo, 2nd pressing, orange label with black print)	80
70	Deram Nova DN 14	EGG (LP, mono, 2nd pressing, blue/silver labels)	150
71	Deram SML 1074	THE POLITE FORCE (LP, 1st pressing, red/white label)	150
71	Deram SML 1074	THE POLITE FORCE (LP, 2nd pressing, red/white label with small 'r' in circle to right of 'M' in 'Deram' at top of label)	70
74	Caroline C 1510	THE CIVIL SURFACE (LP, 1st pressing, red/white/red "twin" label with 'E.J.D' printers text on rear)	80
76	Caroline C 1510	THE CIVIL SURFACE (LP, 2nd pressing)	40
85	See For Miles SEE 47	SEVEN IS A JOLLY GOD TIME (LP)	18

(see also Hatfield & The North, Arzachel, Bunch Of Fives, Khan)

EGGS OVER EASY
86	Edsel ED 199	GOOD 'N' CHEAP (LP, reissue)	15

EGGY
69	Spark SRL 1024	Hookey/You're Still Mine	40

EG OBLIQUE GRAPH
82	Recloose LOOSE 2	TRIPTYCH EP	30

(see also Muslim Gauze)

EGYPT
88	HTD 7HTD 1	Crazy Horses /Got No Fear (p/s)	10
88	HTD HTD LP 1	EGYPT (LP, with inner)	15

(see also Paul Samson)

EGYPTIAN EMPIRE
91	Fokus FKFR 1	The Horn Track (Original Mix)/The Horn Track (Mickey Finn Fog Horn Mix) (12")	20
92	FFRR TABX 115	The Horn Track (Original Mix)/The Horn Track (Foghorn Mix)/The Horn Track (Toxic 2 Mix) (12")	15

8-EYED SPY
82	Fetish FE 19	Diddy Wah Diddy/Dead You Me B Side (p/s)	12
81	Fetish FR 2003	8-EYED SPY (LP, with inner sleeve)	20

(see also Lydia Lunch)

808 STATE
88	Creed STATE 003	Let Yourself Go (303 Mix)/Let Yourself Go (D50 Mix)/Deepville (12", plain stickered sleeve)	12
19	Electronic Sound ES 758	Ozawa/Cubik 80830 (p/s)	10
88	Creed STATE 002	NEWBUILD (LP)	25
89	Creed STATE 004	QUADRASTATE (LP)	20
89	ZTT ZTT 2	90 (LP)	15
91	ZTT ZTT6D	EX:EL (2-LP)	20
96	ZTT 0630 14356-1	DON SOLARIS (LP)	18
99	Rephlex CAT 080 LP	NEWBUILD (LP, reissue as 3 x 12")	30

(see also Hit Squad)

EIGHTH WONDER
88	CBS SCARE Y1	I'm Not Scared/I'm Not Scared (Disco Mix)/J'ai Pas Peur (10", p/s, with Pet Shop Boys)	15

(see also Pet Shop Boys)

EIGHTIES LADIES
86	Music Of Life MOLIF 6	Turned On To You/Sing Me/And I Knew That Love (12", p/s)	20
16	Expansion X7037	Turned On To You/Ladies Of The Eighties (Instrumental Version) (reissue)	6
10	Universal Sound USLP 33	LADIES OF THE EIGHTIES (LP, reissue)	20

(see also Roy Ayers)

EINSTEIN & CHEWY
96	Groove Yard GYARD 007	KUTZ FROM THE LAB VOL. I (12")	15
96	Groove Yard GYARD 12	KUTZ FROM THE LAB VOL. 2 (12", white label)	20

EINSTÜRZENDE NEUBAUTEN
85	Some Bizzare BART 12	Yü-Gung/Seelebrennt/Sand (12", p/s)	10
83	Mute STUMM 14	STRATEGIES AGAINST ARCHITECTURE (LP)	15
85	Some Bizarre BART 331	HALBER MENSCH (LP)	25
87	Some Bizarre BART 332	FUENF AUF NACH OBEN OFFEN RICHTERSKALA (LP)	15
89	Some Bizarre BART 333	HAUS DER LUEGE (LP)	15
92	Mute BETON 106	TABULA RASA (LP)	40

EIRE APPARENT

			MINT VALUE £
96	Mute BETON 504	ENDE NEU (LP)	35
04	Mute STUMM 221	PERPETUUM MOBILE (2-LP)	30

EIRE APPARENT
67	Track 604 019	Follow Me/Here I Go Again	25
69	Buddah 201 039	Rock'N'Roll Band/Yes I Need Someone	20
72	Buddah 2011 117	Rock'N'Roll Band/Yes I Need Someone (reissue)	10
69	Buddah 203 021	SUN RISE (LP, featuring Jimi Hendrix, black/silver labels)	200

(see also Ernie Graham, Henry McCulloch)

EJECTED
82	Riot City RIOT 14	HAVE YOU GOT 10p? (EP)	10
82	Riot City RIOT 19	NOISE FOR THE BOYS (EP)	10
82	Riot City CITY 003	A TOUCH OF CLASS (LP)	20
83	Riot City CITY 007	THE SPIRIT OF REBELLION (LP)	25

LIVY EKEMEZIE
17	Odion Livingstone ODILIV001LP	FRIDAY NIGHT (LP, reissue, blue vinyl)	30

EKSEN TRICK BRICK BAND
78	Aerco AERL 17	SKY STORY (LP, with insert)	30

EKSEPTION
69	Philips 6314 001	BEGGAR JULIAN'S TIME TRIP (LP)	15
70	Philips 6314 005	EKSEPTION (LP)	18
71	Philips 6423 005	EKSEPTION III (LP, laminated sleeve)	15
72	Philips 6423 019	00.04 (LP)	15
72	Philips 6423 042	V (LP, gatefold sleeve)	15

EL PAS(S)O
71	Big Shot BI 572	Out De Light, Baby/Mosquito I (both actually by Dennis Alcapone)	15
71	Punch PH 61	Mosquito One/Out De Light (reissue)	12

(see also Dennis Alcapone)

ELAINE
63	Columbia DB 7091	I Never Wonder Where My Baby Goes/Look But Don't Touch	12

ELAINE & DEREK
61	Parlophone PMC 1160	ELAINE & DEREK (LP)	20

ELANO B
81	Ellie Jay EJSP 9639	Diane/Too Late (p/s, insert)	20

ELASTICA
93	Deceptive BLUFF 003	Stutter/Pussycat (numbered die-cut sleeve, 1,500 only)	12
93	Deceptive BLUFF 003	Stutter/Pussycat (White label test pressing)	6
94	Deceptive BLUFF 004	Line Up/Vaseline (numbered die-cut sleeve, 1,500 only)	8
95	Deceptive BLUFF 014LP	ELASTICA (LP, with flexidisc & booklet, no'd & stickered sleeve, 5,000 only, misprinted labels)	60
95	Deceptive BLUFF 014LP	ELASTICA (LP)	40
00	Deceptive BLUFF 075LP	THE MENACE (LP, inner, poster, stickered sleeve)	25

(see also Suede)

ELASTIC BAND
68	Decca F 12763	Think Of You Baby/It's Been A Long Time Baby	45
68	Decca F 12815	Do Unto Others (From "Mr. Rose" T.V. Series)/81/2 Hours Of Paradise	60
69	Decca Nova (S)DN 6	EXPANSIONS ON LIFE (LP, mono)	300
69	Decca Nova (S)DN 6	EXPANSIONS ON LIFE (LP, stereo)	200

(see also Mayfield's Mule, Sweet, Andy Scott, Love Affair, Northwind)

ELASTICK BAND
67	Stateside SS 2056	Spazz/Papier Mache (unissued, demos only)	300

EL-B
00	Scorpion SCORPION 001	Ghetto Girl/Show A Little Love (12")	20
00	Locked On LOCKED 25	Digital/Alternative Mix/Bonus Mix (12")	10
00	Shelflife 001	South West/Reality (12")	15
00	Scorpion SCORPION 003	Bubble/Bubble (Dub) (12")	20
00	777 001	When I Fall In Love (Vocal)/(Dub Mix) (12", white label with J DA FLEX)	35
00	BD009	El-Brand (Vocal)/El-Brand (Dub) (12" white labels only)	30
00	El Breaks ELB 001	EL BREAKS VOL. 1 (12" white label, some with sticker)	35
00	Bison B001	Breakbeat Science/Cuba (12" as Roxy Vs El-B)	15
09	Tempa TEMPALP 012	THE ROOTS OF EL-B (2-LP)	40

DONNIE ELBERT
58	Parlophone R 4403	Let's Do The Stroll/Wild Child	100
58	Parlophone R 4403	Let's Do The Stroll/Wild Child (78)	40
65	Sue WI 377	A Little Piece Of Leather/Do Wat'cha Wanna	35
65	Sue WI 396	You Can Push It (Or Pull It)/Lily Lou	30
67	CBS 2807	Get Ready/Along Came Pride	30
68	Polydor BM 56234	In Between The Heartaches/Too Far Gone	20
68	Polydor BM 56265	This Old Heart Of Mine (Is Weak For You)/Run Little Girl	10
68	New Wave NW 001	Baby Please Come Home/Without You	8
69	Deram DM 235	Without You/Baby Please Come Home (reissue)	45
69	R&B UP 2000	Without You/(different B-side) (white label test pressing only)	8
73	London HLU 10370	A Little Piece Of Leather/If I Can't Have You	6
79	Echo EC 7001	Are You Ready (Willing And Able)/You Keep Me Crying (With Your Lying)	8
97	Joe Boy JBV 1	So Soon/Can't Get Over Losing You (p/s with numbered certificate, 300 only)	20
69	Polydor 236 560	TRIBUTE TO A KING (LP)	50
73	Ember EMB 3421	THE ROOTS OF DONNIE ELBERT (LP)	20

ELBOW
98	Soft Records Softrec001	NOISEBOX EP: Powder Blue/Red/George Lassoes The Moon (Original version)/Theme From Munroe Kelly/Can't Stop (CD, 200 copies – 150 numbered)	100
98	Soft Records Softrec001	NOISEBOX EP: Powder Blue/Red/George Lassoes The Moon (Original version)/Theme	50

EL CAMINO

MINT VALUE £

		From Munroe Kelly/Can't Stop (CD, 200 copies – 50 un-numbered)	
08	Fiction 1767731	One Day Like This/Every Bit The Little Girl	15
08	Fiction 1773700	One Day Like This/L'il Pissed Charmin' Tune	15
14	Secret 7" S716	Grounds For Divorce (100 only, each with unique art sleeve)	50
01	V2 VVR 101588-1	ASLEEP IN THE BACK (2-LP)	50
03	V2 VVR 102181-1	CAST OF THOUSANDS (LP)	60
05	V2 VVR 103255-1	LEADERS OF THE FREE WORLD (LP)	40
08	Fiction 1764728	THE SELDOM SEEN KID (LP as 2 x 12", gatefold)	30
11	Fiction 2763747	BUILD A ROCKET BOYS! (2-LP, mispressing side B and D have same labels)	30
11	Fiction 2763747	BUILD A ROCKET BOYS! (2-LP)	25
12	Fiction 3711518	THE DEFINITIVE VINYL ALBUM BOX SET (7 x 2-LP, USB stick box set)	200

EL CAMINO

20	Daupe! DM SP 058	MARTYR'S PRAYER (LP, with 38 Spesh, 100 copies)	40
20	Daupe! DM SP 058	MARTYR'S PRAYER (LP, with 38 Spesh, orange vinyl, 100 copies)	40
20	Daupe! DM SP 058	MARTYR'S PRAYER (LP, with 38 Spesh, blue vinyl, 100 copies)	40
20	Daupe! DM SP 058	MARTYR'S PRAYER (LP, with 38 Spesh, yellow vinyl, 100 copies)	40
20	Daupe! DM SP 058	MARTYR'S PRAYER (LP, with 38 Spesh, splatter vinyl, 100 copies)	50
20	Daupe! DM SP 058	MARTYR'S PRAYER (LP, with 38 Spesh, with obi strip, 20 copies)	80

EL CHICANO

72	MCA MUPS 445	REVOLUCION (LP)	15

ELCORT

66	Parlophone R 5447	Tammy/Searchin'	20

ELDORADOS (JAMAICA)

70	Bullet BU 428	Savage Colt/The Clea Hog	25

ELDORADOS (RHODESIA)

63	Decca DFE 8543	THE ELDORADOS (EP)	100

ELDORADOS (U.S.)

72	Mojo 2092 050	Loose Booty (Parts 1 & 2)	10

ROY ELDRIDGE QUINTET

55	Columbia/Clef 33C 9005	ROY ELDRIDGE QUINTET (LP)	15

ROY ELDRIDGE & CLAUDE BOLLING

56	Vogue V 2373	Wild Man Blues/Fireworks	10

ELECAMPANE

75	Dame Jane ODJ 1	WHEN GOD'S ON THE WATER (LP, private pressing with insert)	50
78	Dame Jane ODJ 2	FURTHER ADVENTURES OF MR PUNCH (LP, private pressing with booklet)	20

ELECKTROIDS

95	Warp WARPLP 35	ELEKTROWORLD (2-LP)	100

ELECTRIC EXPRESS

71	Atlantic 2091 165	It's The Real Thing Part 1/Part 2	12
00	Grapevine 2000 G2K 45	Hearsay (Vocal)/Hearsay (Instrumental)	10

ELECTRIC BANANA

67	De Wolfe DW/LP 3040	ELECTRIC BANANA (LP, 10", original issue, tricolour label)	100
67	De Wolfe DWLP 3040	ELECTRIC BANANA (LP, second issue, with other artists)	50
68	De Wolfe DWLP 3069	MORE ELECTRIC BANANA (LP)	200
69	De Wolfe DWLP 3123	EVEN MORE ELECTRIC BANANA (LP)	60
73	De Wolfe DWLP 3284	HOT LICKS (LP)	60
76	De Wolfe DWLP 3381	THE RETURN OF THE ELECTRIC BANANA (LP)	50
79	Butt NOTT 001	THE SEVENTIES (LP)	20
80	Butt NOTT 003	THE SIXTIES (LP)	20
97	Tenth Planet TP 031	THE ELECTRIC BANANA BLOWS YOUR MIND (LP, numbered, 1,000 only)	35

(see also Pretty Things)

ELECTRIC CIRCUS

90	White Label Only	Rhythm & Rhyme/Time	10

ELECTRIC CRAYONS

89	Emergency MIV 3	Hip Shake Junkie/Happy To Be Hated (p/s)	20

(see also Charlatans)

ELECTRIC DOLLS

73	DJM 345	Dr. Love/Love A Little Longer	8
73	Jam JAM 52	Dr. Love/Love A Little Longer	8

ELECTRIC FLAG

68	CBS 3584	Groovin' Is Easy/Over-Lovin' You	10
69	CBS 4066	Sunny/Soul Searchin'	7
68	CBS 62394	A LONG TIME COMIN' (LP, mono)	30
68	CBS S 63294	A LONG TIME COMIN' (LP, stereo)	35
69	CBS 63462	THE ELECTRIC FLAG — AN AMERICAN MUSIC BAND (LP)	15

(see also Mike Bloomfield, Buddy Miles, Barry Goldberg)

ELECTRICIANS

67	Columbia DB 8228	Champion House Theme/DON HARPER & ELECTRICIANS: Shin Bone	7

(see also Don Harper)

ELECTRIC JOHNNY

61	London HLU 9384	Black-Eyes Rock/Johnny On His Strings	25

ELECTRIC LIGHT ORCHESTRA (E.L.O.)

72	Harvest HAR 5053	10538 Overture/1st Movement (Jumping Biz)	6
72	Harvest HAR 5063	Roll Over Beethoven/Manhattan Rumble (49th Street Massacre) (with withdrawn B-side)	10
73	Harvest HAR 5077	Showdown/In Old England Town (Boogie 2) (Instrumental)	8
81	Jet ELO 2	Mr Blue Sky/Across The Border/Telephone Line/Don't Bring Me Down (withdrawn, in p/s)	8
71	Harvest SHVL 797	ELECTRIC LIGHT ORCHESTRA (LP, gatefold sleeve, with inner sleeve & lyric insert)	150
71	Harvest SHVL 797	ELECTRIC LIGHT ORCHESTRA (LP, gatefold sleeve, without inner sleeve & lyric insert)	100
72	Harvest SHVL 806	ELO 2 (LP, 1st pressing, gatefold sleeve with EMI box but no 'stereo' on label)	50

ELECTRIC PRUNES

MINT VALUE £

73	Harvest SHVL 806	ELO 2 (LP, 2nd pressing, gatefold sleeve with EMI box with 'stereo' on label)	30
73	Harvest Q4SHVL 797	ELECTRIC LIGHT ORCHESTRA (LP, quadrophonic, promo only)	100
74	Harvest SHSP 4037	SHOWDOWN (LP)	20
76	Jet JETLP 19	OLE ELO (LP, withdrawn)	15
77	Jet UAG 30091	ON THE THIRD DAY (LP, new mix, new sleeve & inner sleeve)	15
78	Jet JETLP 200	A NEW WORLD RECORD (LP, red vinyl, with inner sleeve)	15
78	Jet JETLP 201	FACE THE MUSIC (LP, green vinyl, with inner sleeve)	20
78	Jet JETLP 202	ON THE THIRD DAY (LP, clear vinyl, with inner sleeve)	15
78	Jet JETLP 203	ELDORADO (LP, yellow vinyl, with inner sleeve)	15
78	Jet JETDP 400	OUT OF THE BLUE (2-LP, clear or dark blue vinyl, with inner sleeves, with cut-out spaceship, poster & insert)	40

(see also Idle Race, Move, Roy Wood, Michael D'Albuquerque, Wilson Gale & Co., Tandy-Morgan)

ELECTRIC PRUNES

66	Reprise RS 20532	I Had Too Much To Dream (Last Night)/Luvin'	35
67	Reprise RS 20564	Get Me To The World On Time/Are You Lovin' Me More (But Enjoying It Less)	30
67	Reprise RS 20607	The Great Banana Hoax/Wind-Up Toys	20
67	Reprise RS 23212	A Long Day's Flight/The King Is In His Counting House	18
67	Reprise RS 20652	Everybody Knows You're Not In Love/You Never Had It Better	30
73	Elektra K 12102	I Had Too Much To Dream (Last Night)/KNICKERBOCKERS: Lies	7
79	Radar ADA 16	I Had Too Much To Dream (Last Night)/Luvin' (p/s)	8
67	Reprise R(S)LP 6248	THE ELECTRIC PRUNES (LP, mono/stereo)	200
68	Reprise R(S)LP 6275	MASS IN F MINOR (LP, mono/stereo)	120
68	Reprise RSLP 6316	RELEASE OF AN OATH (LP)	120
86	Edsel ED 179	LONG DAY'S FLIGHT (LP)	15
97	Heartbeat HB 67	STOCKHOLM '67 (LP, gatefold sleeve with booklet)	20

ELECTRIC SIX

02	XL XLS 151	Danger! High Voltage/I Lost Control (Of My Rock And Roll) (p/s)	10
03	XL XLS 158	Gay Bar/The Living End (p/s)	10
03	XL XLLP 169	FIRE (LP)	100

ELECTRIC TOILET

83	Psycho PSYCHO 8	IN THE HANDS OF KARMA (LP, reissue of U.S. LP)	15

ELECTRIC WIZARD

95	Rise Above RISE 11	Demon Lung/OUR HAUNTED KINGDOM: Aquatic Fanatic (blue vinyl, p/s)	60
98	Bad Acid TRIP 1	Supercoven/Burnout (12", p/s)	80
08	Rise Above RISE 12/116	The Processean (Procession) (1-sided 12", 500 only sold at Rise Above 20th Anniversary Gig, ULU London 13th December 2008)	60
08	Rise Above RISE 12/116	The House On The Border/REVEREND BIZARRE: The Gates Of Nanna (12", 500 clear, 500 purple, 500 silver and 500 black vinyl, censored p/s)	20
08	Rise Above RISE 12/116	The House On The Border/REVEREND BIZARRE: The Gates Of Nanna (12", 350 red vinyl, uncensored p/s, poster)	50
95	Rise Above RISE 009	ELECTRIC WIZARD (LP, green vinyl)	50
04	Rise Above RISELP 48	WE LIVE (2-LP, purple vinyl)	70
04	Rise Above RISELP 52	DOPETHRONE (2-LP, white vinyl, reissue, first issued on CD in 2000)	70
04	Rise Above RISELP 52	DOPETHRONE (2-LP, black vinyl, reissue, first issued on CD in 2000)	40
06	Rise Above RISELP 48	WE LIVE (2-LP, gatefold sleeve, reissue on green vinyl with 1-sided 7" "The Living Dead At Manchester Morgue")	60
06	Rise Above RISELP 072	COME MY FANATICS... (2-LP, reissue, with balck vinyl 7", black/dark red/violet space dust vinyl)	50
06	Rise Above RISELP 072	COME MY FANATICS... (2-LP, reissue, with coloured 7", violet space dust vinyl, 100 only)	100
07	Rise Above RISELP 74	LET US PREY (2-LP, 100 clear vinyl, reissue first issued on CD in 2002)	60
07	Rise Above RISELP 74	LET US PREY (2-LP, 500 dark red, 500 black vinyl, reissue first issued on CD in 2002)	40
07	Rise Above RISELP 100	WITCHCULT TODAY (2-LP, 200 green vinyl, foil gatefold sleeve, poster, patch)	50
07	Rise Above RISELP 100	WITCHCULT TODAY (2-LP, 500 silver vinyl, foil gatefold sleeve, poster, patch)	40
07	Rise Above RISELP 52	DOPETHRONE (2-LP, reissue, purple sink vinyl, 50 only)	80
07	Rise Above RISELP 52	DOPETHRONE (2-LP, reissue, transparent amber or clear, 100 only of each)	40
07	Rise Above RISELP 52	DOPETHRONE (2-LP, reissue, black vinyl, reissue)	25
10	Rise Above RISELP 130 BOX	BLACK MASSES (2-LP, gatefold p/s, poster, comic, embroidered patch in box, clear vinyl, 100 only)	350
10	Rise Above RISELP 130	BLACK MASSES (2-LP, gatefold p/s, poster, comic, embroidered patch in box, 400 only)	120
11	Rise Above RISELP 072	COME MY FANATICS... (2-LP, reissue, green or black 195 gram vinyl)	35
14	Spinefarm SPINE 788083	TIME TO DIE (2-LP, with poster)	20
15	Rise Above RISELP 073	DOPETHRONE (2-LP, reissue, clear vinyl)	50
17	Witchfinder W004	WIXARD BLOODY WIZARD (LP)	20

ELECTRIX

79	ELX 001	HOLLAND (EP)	30

ELECTRO HIPPIES

87	Strange Fruit SFPS 042	PEEL SESSIONS (12", metallic finish with insert)	15
88	Peaceville VILE 02	THE ONLY GOOD PUNK... IS A DEAD ONE (LP)	15
89	Peaceville VILE 13	LIVE (LP, clear vinyl)	15
89	Necrosis NECR 0001	PLAY FAST OR DIE (LP)	15

ELECTRONIC

91	Factory FAC 287r/7	Get The Message (Edit) (DNA Groove Mix)/(DNA Sin Mix) (promo only)	50
99	Parlophone 12R651	Late At Night/Make It Happen (Original Version)/Make It Happen (Darren Price Mix) (12" withdrawn)	20
91	Factory FACT 290	ELECTRONIC (LP, inner)	25
96	Parlophone PCS 7382	RAISE THE PRESSURE (LP)	100

(see also New Order, Smiths, Pet Shop Boys, Joy Division)

ELECTRONIC CIRCUS

81	Scratch SCR 002	Direct Lines/Le Chorale (p/s)	50

ELECTRONIC EXPERIENCED

93	Basement BRSS 025	V-10 Overload/No. 303 (12")	25

ELECTRONIC DUB

MINT VALUE £

94	Basement BRSS 032	I.Q./I.Q. More (12")	25

ELECTRONIC DUB
94	Rising High RSN LP 21	ELECTRONIC DUB (2-LP)	70

ELECTRONIC EYE
94	Beyond RBADLP8	CLOSED CIRCUIT (4-LP)	50
95	Beyond RBADLP14	THE IDEA OF JUSTICE (2-LP)	30

(see also Cabaret Voltaire, Sandoz, Richard H. Kirk, Sweet Exorcist)

ELEGANTS
58	HMV POP 520	Little Star/Getting Dizzy	15
58	HMV POP 551	Please Believe Me/Goodnight	40

ELEKTRAS
63	United Artists UP 1027	All I Want To Do Is Run/It Ain't Easy	30

ELEKTRIC MUSIC
93	East West YZ 755	TV/Television (p/s)	8
93	East West SAM 1252	Lifestyle (Edit-Style Mix)/(Club-Style Mix)/(Phoneme-Style Mix) (10", promo)	20

(see also Kraftwerk)

ELEMENTS
81	Look LK/LP 6649	ELEMENTARY (LP)	30

ELENA
65	Columbia DB 7598	Evening Time/Road Of Love	20

ELEPHANT BAND
72	Mojo 2092 036	Stone Penguin/Groovin' At The Apollo	45

ELEPHANT NOISE
91	Own Label	This Song Is Our Friend/Halloween Day/Remember The Big Time/Cactus Talk (12" EP)	100

ELEPHANT'S MEMORY
69	Buddah 201055	Crossroads Of The Stepping Stones/Yoghurt Song	6
69	Buddah 201067	Old Man Willow/Jungle Gym At The Zoo	25
70	CBS 5207	Mongoose/I Couldn't Dream	25
72	Apple APPLE 45	Power Boogie/Liberation Special	20
69	Buddah 203 022	ELEPHANT'S MEMORY (LP)	30
72	Apple SAPCOR 22	ELEPHANT'S MEMORY (LP, gatefold sleeve with inner sleeve)	40

(see also John Lennon, Yoko Ono)

ELERGY
94	Applied Rhythmic Technology ART 6	ENSEMBLE EP (12")	15

ELERI, JANET & DIANE
70s	Fanfare FR 2196	THE ANSWER (LP)	100

ELEVATORS
80	Koala KOA 401	Your I's Are Too Close Together/That's My Baby	60

11.59
74	Dovetail DOVE 4	THIS IS OUR SACRIFICE OF PRAISE (LP, with insert)	40

11 PARANOIAS
14	Ritual RITE 028	SPECTRALBEASTIARIES (LP)	20
14	Ritual RITE 31	STEALING FIRE FROM HEAVEN (2-LP)	20

ELEVENTH HOUR (2)
93	Big Music HOUR 1	Wish It Was You/Can't Stand Being Alone (p/s)	8

ELF
74	Purple PUR 118	L.A. 59/Ain't It All Amusing	10
74	Purple TPS 3506	CAROLINA COUNTRY BALL (LP)	30

(see also Roger Glover, Dio, Rainbow, Deep Purple, Black Sabbath)

ELFLAND ENSEMBLE
77	Chrysalis CHS 2151	Too Much Magic (feat. Derek Brimstone)/Lizarel (featuring Mary Hopkin) (p/s)	6
77	Chrysalis CHS 2193	Beyond The Fields We Know/Alveric's Journey (featuring Mary Hopkin)	6

(see also Mary Hopkin)

STEVE ELGIN
74	Dawn DNS 1093	Don't Leave Your Lover Lying Around (Dear)/Seductress	10

ELGINS
66	Tamla Motown TMG 551	Put Yourself In My Place/Darling Baby	130
66	Tamla Motown TMG 551	Put Yourself In My Place/Darling Baby (DJ Copy)	150
66	Tamla Motown TMG 583	Heaven Must Have Sent You/Stay In My Lonely Arms	80
66	Tamla Motown TMG 583	Heaven Must Have Sent You/Stay In My Lonely Arms (DJ Copy)	120
67	Tamla Motown TMG 615	It's Been A Long Long Time/I Understand My Man	35
67	Tamla Motown TMG 615	It's Been A Long Long Time/I Understand My Man (DJ Copy)	50
68	Tamla Motown TMG 642	Put Yourself In My Place/Darling Baby (reissue)	25
71	Tamla Motown TMG 771	Heaven Must Have Sent You/Stay In My Lonely Arms (reissue)	7
71	Tamla Motown TMG 787	Put Yourself In My Place/It's Gonna Be Hard Times	7
68	T. Motown (S)TML 11081	DARLING BABY (LP, mono/stereo)	100

ELIAS HULK
70	Youngblood SSYB 8	UNCHAINED (LP, laminated front cover, red/white label)	1000

(see also Babe Ruth)

ELIFFANT
79	Macym MACYM 1	Seren I Seren/Lisa Lan (no p/s)	6
79	Sain 1130M	M.O.M. (LP)	20

ELIJAH
71	Ackee ACK 121	Selassie High/Mount Zion	20

ELIMINATORS (1)
66	Pye NPL 18210	GUITARS AND PERCUSSION (LP, pink black label)	25

ELIMINATORS (2)
99	Soul Brother SBC 54	LOVING EXPLOSION (LP, reissue)	20

ELITE
79	Aerco LAS 102	Take Away/Part Of My Life (no p/s)	8

ELIXIA

MINT VALUE £

79	L&S	ANY PORT IN A STORM (LP, 500 only)	20

ELIXIA
83	Record Shack SOHO 4	Soho Phase/Soho Nights (p/s)	15
83	Record Shack SOHOT 4	Soho Phase/Soho Nights (12")	30

ELIXIR
85	Elixir ELIXIR 1	Treachery (Ride Like The Wind)/Winds Of Time (folded p/s with insert)	80
86	Elixir ELIXIR 2	THE SON OF ODIN (LP, private pressing with insert)	60
90	Sonic SONICLP 9	LETHAL POTION (LP, features Clive Burr)	15

(see also Iron Maiden)

ELIZABETH (1)
73	Paramount PARA 3032	Stop Killing Me With Kindness/Oh Bird	6
68	Vanguard SVRL 19010	ELIZABETH (LP)	150

ELIZABETH (2)
77	Creole CR 139	God Save The Sex Pistols/Silver Story	15

ELIZABETH (3)
94	Echo Special Prods ESPLP2	QUEEN ELIZABETH (LP, mail order only, with inner sleeve)	18
97	Head Heritage HH2	QUEEN ELIZABETH 2 - ELIZABETH VAGINA (2-CD mail order, 1000 only)	30

(see also Julian Cope)

ELKI & OWEN & RIM RAM BAND
69	Revolution REV 004	Groovie Kinda Love	8

(see also Elkie Brooks, Owen Gray)

JIMMY ELLEDGE
62	RCA RCA 1274	Swanee River Rocket/Funny How Time Slips Away	15
65	Hickory 45-1363	Pink Dally Rue/(I'd Be) A Legend In My Time	10
64	RCA RCX 7132	FUNNY HOW TIME SLIPS AWAY (EP)	20

ELLI
67	Parlophone R 5575	Never Mind/I'll Be Looking Out For You	20
99	Dig The Fuzz DIG 038	ELLI (LP, 500 only)	18

ELLIE
74	Fresh Air 6121111	Tip Of My Tongue/Someones Stolen My Marbles	8
74	Fresh Air 6121123	My Love Is Your Love/Let Me Shout It Out	8

YVONNE ELLIMAN
73	Purple PUR 114	I Can't Explain/Hawaii	25
73	Purple TPS 3504	FOOD OF LOVE (LP)	15

DUKE ELLINGTON & HIS (FAMOUS) ORCHESTRA
60	Philips SBBL 514	ANATOMY OF A MURDER (soundtrack)	25

MARC ELLINGTON
68	Philips BF 1665	I Shall Be Released/Mrs. Whittle	8
69	Philips BF 1742	DId You Give The World Some Love Today Baby/Bless The Executioner	8
69	Philips BF 1779	Four In The Morning/Peggy Day	8
71	Charisma CB 161	Alligator Man/Song For A Friend	8
69	Philips (S)BL 7883	MARC ELLINGTON (LP, black/silver labels)	100
71	B&C CAS 1033	RAINS, REINS OF CHANGES (LP, envelope cover with lyric insert)	100
72	Philips 6308 120	A QUESTION OF ROADS (LP, gatefold sleeve, black/silver label)	100
72	Xtra XTRA 1154	MARC TIME (LP, with Fairport Convention)	40
73	Philips 6308 143	RESTORATION (LP, blue/silver label)	80

(see also Fairport Convention, Matthews Southern Comfort)

RAY ELLINGTON QUARTET
53	Columbia SCM 5050	The Little Red Monkey/Kaw-Liga	20
54	Columbia SCM 5088	All's Going Well (My Lady Montmorency) (with Marion Ryan)/Ol' Man River	20
54	Columbia SCM 5104	Rub-A-Dub-Dub/The Owl Song	15
54	Columbia SCM 5147	A.B.C. Boogie/Christmas Cards	20
55	Columbia SCM 5177	Ko Ko Mo (I Love You So)/Woodpecker	20
55	Columbia SCM 5187	Play It Boy, Play/The Irish Were Egyptians Long Ago	20
55	Columbia SCM 5199	Cloudburst/Pet	15
56	Columbia SCM 5250	Hold Him Tight/Who's Got The Money?	10
56	Columbia SCM 5274	Keep The Coffee Hot/Lucky 13	10
56	Columbia DB 3821	Stranded In The Jungle/Left Hand Boogie	20
56	Columbia DB 3838	Giddy-Up-A Ding Dong/The Green Door	20
57	Columbia DB 3905	Marianne/That Rock 'N' Rollin' Man	20
57	Columbia DB 4013	Don't Burn Me Up/Swaller-Tail Coat	10
58	Columbia DB 4057	Living Doll/Long Black Nylons (solo)	20
59	Pye Nixa 7N 15189	Chip Off The Old Block/Charlie Brown	10
60	Ember EMB S 102	The Madison/Jump Over (with Tony Crombie Orchestra) (p/s with insert)	10
60	Ember EMB S 114	Très Jolie/Dracula's Three Daughters	10
59	Pye Nixa NPL 83011	THAT'S NICE (LP, with Judd Proctor, mono)	20
59	Pye Nixa NPL 18032	THAT'S NICE (LP, with Judd Proctor, stereo)	20

(see also Tony Crombie, Marion Ryan)

ELLINGTONS
79	Grapevine GRP 114	(I'm Not) Destined To Become A Loser/MILLIONAIRES: You've Got To Love Your Baby	10
79	Grapevine GRP 114	(I'm Not) Destined To Become A Loser/MILLIONAIRES: You've Got To Love Your Baby (DJ Copy)	20

BILL ELLIOT & ELASTIC OZ BAND
71	Apple APPLE 36	God Save Us/Do The Oz (initially with p/s)	60
71	Apple APPLE 36	God Save Us/Do The Oz	20

(see also Splinter, John Lennon/Yoko Ono)

DEREK & DOROTHY ELLIOT
72	Trailer LER 2023	DEREK & DOROTHY ELLIOT (LP)	15
76	Tradition TSR 025	YORKSHIRE RELISH (LP)	15

Mama CASS (ELLIOT)

MINT VALUE £

MAMA CASS (ELLIOT)
68	Stateside S(S)L 5004	DREAM A LITTLE DREAM (LP)	20
69	Stateside S(S)L 5014	BUBBLEGUM, LEMONADE AND SOMETHING FOR MAMA (LP)	18
72	RCA SF 8306	THE ROAD IS NO PLACE FOR A LADY (LP)	15

(see also Mamas & Papas, Big Three, Dave Mason & Cass Elliot, Mugwumps)

N. ELLIOT & N. BAILEY
71	Moodisc HME 111	People Let Love Shine/MUDIES ALL STARS: Too Much	80

ELLIOT MANSIONS
71	President PT 323	Float On Up/Shades And Shadows	12
72	President PT 361	Don't Want To Live Inside Myself/Three Score And Ten	6

BERN ELLIOTT (& FENMEN)
63	Decca F 11770	Money/Nobody But Me	10
64	Decca F 11852	New Orleans/Everybody Needs A Little Love	10
64	Decca F 11970	Good Times/What Do You Want With My Baby (as Bern Elliott & Klan)	12
65	Decca F 12051	Guess Who/Make It Easy On Yourself (solo)	12
65	Decca F 12171	Lipstick Traces/Voodoo Woman (solo)	20
64	Decca DFE 8561	BERN ELLIOTT AND THE FENMEN (EP)	30

(see also Fenmen)

DAVID ELLIOTT
72	Atlantic K40374	DAVID ELLIOTT (LP, with lyric insert)	20

JACK ELLIOTT
69	Leader LEA 4001	JACK ELLIOTT OF BIRTLEY (LP, with booklet)	20

(see also Elliotts Of Birtley)

(RAMBLIN') JACK ELLIOTT
56	Topic TRC 98	Talking Miner Blues/Pretty Boy Floyd (78)	20
57	Topic TRC 103	Old Blue/Rambling Blues (78)	20
57	Topic TRC 104	Streets Of Laredo/Boll Weevil (78)	20
65	Columbia DB 7593	Rusty Jigs And Sandy Sam/Rocky Mountain Belle (as Ramblin' Jack Elliott)	6
58	77 Records EP/1	JACK ELLIOTT SINGS Vol 1. (EP)	100
58	77 Records EP/2	JACK ELLIOTT SINGS Vol. 2. (EP)	100
60	Columbia SEG 8046	KID STUFF (EP)	10
61	Collector JEA 5	RAMBLING JACK ELLIOTT (EP)	20
64	Collector JEA 6	BLUES AND COUNTRY (EP)	20
55	Topic T 5	WOODY GUTHRIE'S BLUES (8" mini-LP)	40
57	Topic 10T 15	JACK TAKES THE FLOOR (10" LP)	40
59	Columbia 33SX 1166	RAMBLIN' JACK ELLIOT IN LONDON (LP)	20
62	Encore ENC 194	IN LONDON (LP, reissue of Columbia 33SX 1166)	20
60	Columbia 33SX 1291	RAMBLIN' JACK ELLIOTT SINGS WOODY GUTHRIE & JIMMIE RODGERS (LP)	40
61	77 LP 1	JACK ELLIOT SINGS (10" LP, spelt 'Elliot' on sleeve)	175
65	Fontana TFL 6044	JACK ELLIOTT (LP)	20
65	Stateside SL 10143	JACK ELLIOTT COUNTRY STYLE (LP)	20
66	Stateside SL 10167	SINGS THE SONGS OF WOODY GUTHRIE (LP)	20
57	Topic 10T 14	THE RAMBLING BOYS (10" LP, stickered Topic sleeve, insert)	60
63	Topic 12T 105	THE RAMBLING BOYS (LP, reissue of above with 2 extra tracks)	50
64	Topic 12T 106	MULESKINNERS (LP)	30
67	Bounty BY 6036	ROLL ON BUDDY - THE JACK ELLIOTT AND DERROLL ADAMS STORY VOL. 1 (LP)	50

KEN ELLIOTT
79	RCA PL 25262	BODY MUSIC (LP)	30

MARI ELLIOTT
76	GTO GT 58	Silly Billy/Half Past One	30

(see also Poly Styrene, X Ray Spex)

MIKE ELLIOTT
72	Ackee ACK 151	Milk And Honey/Burst A Shirt	7

PETER ELLIOTT
61	Top Rank JAR 390	Waiting For Robert E. Lee/Toot Toot Tootsie	6
61	Fontana 325	Three Little Peggies/The Devil's Workshop	6
66	Strike JH 311	Thinking/Song Is Love	7

SHAWN ELLIOTT
63	Stateside SS 174	Sincerely And Tenderly/Why Don't You Love Me Anymore	8
64	Rio R 51	Shame And Scandal In The Family/My Girl	8
64	Columbia DB 7418	My Girl/Shame And Scandal In The Family (reissue)	8
71	London HLK 10247	Child Is Father To The Man/Any Dream Will Do	12

SIDNEY ELLIOTT
69	Spark SRL 1021	Who Dat Girl In The Mini Skirt/Strawberry Blonde	12
71	CBS 7448	Man And Woman/Stolen Fruit	8
71	CBS 7683	Desperation/Came To See Me Yesterday	12

VERNON ELLIOTT ENSEMBLE
07	Trunk JBH029 LP	IVOR THE ENGINE & POGLES WOOD (LP)	15

ELLIOTTS OF BIRTLEY
69	Xtra XTRA 1091	A MUSICAL PORTRAIT OF A DURHAM MINING FAMILY (LP)	15

(see also Jack Elliott)

ELLIOTT'S SUNSHINE
68	Philips BF 1649	Is It Too Late/'Cos I'm Lonely	10

ELLIS
72	Epic S EPC 64878	RIDING ON THE CREST OF A SLUMP (LP)	20
72	Epic SEPC 1052	El Doomo/Your Game	6
73	Epic SEPC 1627	Open Road/Leaving In The Morning	6

(see also Steve Ellis)

ALTON ELLIS (& FLAMES)
65	Island WI 239	Dance Crasher (with Flames)/BABA BROOKS: Vitamin A	50

Alton ELLIS (& FLAMES)

MINT VALUE £

65	Island WI 241	You Are Not To Blame/BABA BROOKS: Teenage Ska	70
66	Doctor Bird DB 1044	Blessings Of Love/Nothing Sweeter (as Alton & Flames)	60
66	Doctor Bird DB 1049	The Preacher (as Alton & Flames)/LYNN TAITT & COMETS: Tender Loving Care	40
66	Doctor Bird DB 1055	Shake It (with Flames)/SILVERTONES: Whoo Baby	45
66	Doctor Bird DB 1059	Girl I've Got A Date (with Flames)/LYNN TAITT & TOMMY McCOOK: The Yellow Basket	40
67	Island WI 3046	Cry Tough (with Flames)/TOMMY McCOOK & SUPERSONICS: Mr Solo	150
67	Treasure Isle TI 7004	Rocksteady (with Flames)/TOMMY McCOOK & SUPERSONICS: Wall Street Shuffle	40
67	Treasure Isle TI 7010	Duke Of Earl/All My Tears (with Flames)	35
67	Treasure Isle TI 7016	Ain't That Loving You/TOMMY McCOOK/SUPERSONICS: Tommy's Rocksteady	35
67	Treasure Isle TI 7030	Oowee Baby/How Can I (with Flames)	35
67	Treasure Isle TI 7044	Willow Tree/I Can't Stop Now	25
67	Trojan TR 004	Ain't That Loving You (with Flames)/TOMMY McCOOK & SUPERSONICS: Comet Rocksteady	30
67	Trojan TR 009	Wise Birds Follow Spring/TOMMY McCOOK & SUPERSONICS: Soul Rock	25
67	Studio One SO 2028	I Am Just A Guy/SOUL VENDORS: Just A Bit Of Soul	120
67	Studio One SO 2033	Only Sixteen/Baby (both actually by Heptones)	20
68	Studio One SO 2037	Live And Learn/HEPTONES: Cry Baby Cry	40
68	Trojan TR 630	I Can't Stand It/Trying To Reach My Goal	25
68	Trojan TR 642	Breaking Up/Party Time	18
68	Nu Beat NB 010	I Can't Stand It/Tonight	45
68	Nu Beat NB 013	Bye Bye Love/MONTY MORRIS: My Lonely Days	50
68	Nu Beat NB 014	La La Means I Love You/Give Me Your Love	25
68	Pama PM 707	The Message/Some Talk	50
68	Pama PM 717	My Time Is The Right Time/JOHNNY MOORE: Tribute To Sir Alex	45
68	Coxsone CS 7071	A Fool/SOUL VENDORS: West Of The Sun	150
69	Studio One SO 2084	Change Of Plans/CABLES: He'll Break Your Heart (B-side act. by Mad Lads)	160
69	Gas GAS 105	Diana/English Talk	60
69	Bamboo BAM 2	Better Example/DUKE MORGAN: Lick It Back	70
69	Duke DU 14	Diana/Personality	30
70	Duke DU 72	Remember That Sunday/TOMMY McCOOK & SUPERSONICS: Last Lick	40
70	Gas GAS 151	Suzie/Life Is Down In Denver (some copies credit Alton Ellis & Flames)	15
70	Gas GAS 161	Deliver Us/NEVILLE HINDS: Originator	10
70	Duke Reid DR 2501	What Does It Take To Win Your Love/TOMMY McCOOK: Reggae Meringue	18
70	Duke Reid DR 2512	You Made Me So Very Happy/TOMMY McCOOK & SUPERSONICS: Continental	25
70	Bamboo BAM 29	Tumbling Tears/SOUND DIMENSION: Today Version	22
70	Techniques TE 903	It's Your Thing/TECHNIQUES ALL STARS: Get Left	25
70	Techniques TE 905	I'll Be Waiting/TECHNIQUES ALL STARS: I'll Be Waiting Version	25
71	Banana BA 318	Sunday Coming/CARL BRYAN: Sunday Version	20
71	Banana BA 330	Bam Bye/Keep On Yearning	22
71	Banana BA 347	Hey World/Harder And Harder	25
71	Gas GAS 164	Back To Africa/NEVILLE HINDS: Originator	12
71	Fab FAB 165	Good Good Loving/Since I Fell For You	40
71	Bullet BU 466	Black Man's Pride/LEROY PALMER: Groove With It	18
71	Bullet BU 485	Don't Care/True Born African	35
71	Smash SMA 2319	A Little Loving/DELROY WILSON & ALTON ELLIS: Loving Version	12
71	Smash SMA 2320	I'll Be There/ITALS: Rude Boy Train	12
71	Big Shot BI 589	Be True/Be True — Version	20
72	Big Shot BI 602	I'm Trying/Luna's Mood	15
72	Count Shelly CS 004	Follow My Heart/KOOS ALL STARS: Sincerely	10
72	Spur SP 3	All That We Need Is Love/KEITH HUDSON: Better Love	30
72	Grape GR 3029	Big Bad Boy/HUDSON'S ALLSTARS: Big Bad Version	12
72	Ackee ACK 145	Oppression/Oppression Version (both with Zoot Simms)	45
72	Ackee ACK 148	Let's Stay Together/Version	35
72	Ackee ACK 502	Too Late To Turn Back Now/IMPACT ALLSTARS: Version	15
72	Jackpot JP 796	Play It Cool/AGGROVATORS: King Of The Zozas	10
72	Camel CA 94	Wonderful World/FAB DIMENSION: Wonderful Version	6
72	Pama Supreme PS 347	Moon River/I Can't Find Out	7
72	Pama Supreme PS 361	Working On A Groovy Thing/HARLESDEN SKANKERS: Version	20
73	Ackee ACK 511	Alton's Official Daughter/Aquarius Dub (both with Herman)	15
73	Pyramid PYR 7003	Truly/LLOYD COXSONE SIX: Cruising	25
73	A&M AMS 7093	Shoo BeDoo Be Doo/I Love You True	25
75	Bam Bam BAM 02	I'm Still In Love With You/Version	25
75	Atra ATRA 26	Rasta Spirit/WILD BUNCH: Jal Dub	40
77	Venture VEN7709	Confusion/Version	10
77	Grove GMDM 13	It's Hard To Be A Lover/Love Like Mine (12")	10
79	Cha Cha	Children Are Crying/Mr. Ska Beana	20
83	Fashion FAD 013	Too Late To Turn Back Now/Party Mix (12")	12
83	Body Music BMDIS 8	Love On Top/Tops Version (12")	12
12	Doctor Bird THB 7022	Honey I Love/Don't Trouble People	10
67	Coxsone CSL 8008	SINGS ROCK AND SOUL (LP)	200
69	Coxsone CSL 8019	THE BEST OF ALTON ELLIS (LP)	100
71	Bamboo BDLPS 214	SUNDAY COMING (LP)	100
80	Cha Cha	MR. SKABEANA (LP)	30
77	Trojan HRLP 708	STILL IN LOVE (LP)	30
73	Count Shelly SSLO 02	ALTON ELLIS'S GREATEST HITS (LP)	45
84	Jet Star SKYLP 246	25TH SILVER JUBILEE (LP)	15
95	Horse HRLP 708	STILL IN LOVE (LP, reissue)	25

(see also Alton & Eddy, Hortense Ellis, Hortense & Alton, Flames [Jamaica], Righteous Flames, Tony Gordon, Soul Flames)

Alton ELLIS & THE HEPTONES

MINT VALUE £

ALTON ELLIS & THE HEPTONES
80   Cha Cha CHAD 21   Mr. Ska Beana/ALTON ELLIS: Ain't No Music (12") 25

ALTON ELLIS & DENNIS ALCAPONE
72   Lord Koos KOO 21   Big Bad Boy Version/TAPPER ZUKIE: Ira Lion 35
(see also Tapper Zukie)

BOBBY ELLIS
68   Island WI 3136   Dollar A Head (with Crystalites)/RUDY MILLS: I'm Trapped 55
74   Dragon DRA 1033   Up Park Camp/Verse 4 6
77   Third World TWS 9   MEET THE REVOLUTIONARIES (LP) 40
(see also Jerry Lewis, Derrick Harriot, Rudy Mills, Crystalites, Keith & Tex, Eric Morris, Roy Richards, Soul Vendors)

DAVE ELLIS
72   Sonet SNTF 646   ALBUM (LP) 25

ELLIS DEE PROJECT
92   Ellis Dee Project LSD 001   Do You Want Me/Rock To The Max (12") 20
92   Ellis Dee Project LSD 003   Dance Factor (1-sided 12") 20
92   Ellis Dee Project LSD 004   Dance Factor (Rennie P Remix)/Don't Stop Rocking (12") 10
92   Ellis Dee Project LSD 005   Desire/Renegade (12") 10

DON ELLIS (ORCHESTRA)
68   Liberty LBL 83060E   LIVE IN THREE QUARTER TIME (LP) 20
68   CBS 63230   ELECTRIC BATH (LP) 25
68   CBS 63356   SHOCK TREATMENT (LP) 15
69   CBS 63680   THE NEW DON ELLIS BAND GOES UNDERGROUND (LP) 15

HERB ELLIS-JIMMY GIUFFRE ALL STARS
60   HMV POP 721   Goose Grease/My Old Flame 6
59   HMV CLP 1337   HERB ELLIS MEETS JIMMY GIUFFRE (LP) 18

HORTENSE ELLIS
63   R&B JB 101   I'll Come Softly/I'm In Love (with Alton Ellis) 20
65   Blue Beat BB 295   I've Been A Fool/Hold Me Tenderly 25
67   Fab FAB 20   Somebody Help Me (with Buster's All Stars)/ PRINCE BUSTER & ALL STARS: Rock & Shake 80
68   Coxsone SC 7033   A Man Of Chances(as Tree Tops)/HORTENSE ELLIS: A Groovy Kind Of Love 300
70   Bullet BU 427   Last Date/PAT SATCHMO: Cherry Pink 50
70   Gas GAS 160   To The Other Man/MUSIC BLENDERS: Raindrops 7
70   Techniques TE 908   To The Other Man/TECHNIQUES ALL STARS: To The Other Man Version 7
71   Gas 166   I Shall Sing/Stand By Your Man 40
72   Green Door GD 4035   Bringing In The Sheaves (with Stranger Cole)/Version 6
73   Tropical AL020   Woman in The Ghetto/Instrumental Version 25
77   Hawkeye HE 02   Superstar/Superstick 12
78   Hawk Eye HE 007   Unexpected Places/Lovers Places 10
76   Third World TWS 918   JAMAICA'S FIRST LADY OF SONG (LP) 20
(see also Hortense & Alton, Hortense & Delroy, Hortense & Jackie, Alton Ellis, Duke Reid, Three Tops, Jackie Opal)

JAMES ELLIS
62   Philips PB 1230   Johnny Todd/Trottin' To The Fair 6

JOANNE ELLIS
82   RCA 247   Self Service Love/Bye Baby 15

JO-JO ELLIS
72   Fury FY 302   The Fly/Perdona Mia 30

LARRY ELLIS
58   Felsted AF 110   Buzz Goes The Bee/Nothing You Can Do 15

LARRY ELLIS AND THE BLACK HAMMER
03   Jazzman JMANLP 014   Funky Thing 1/Funky Thing 2 (reissue) 18

MATTHEW ELLIS
71   Regal Zonophone RZ 3033   Avalon/You Are 15
71   Regal Zonophone RZ 3039   Birthday Song/Salvation 10
72   Regal Zonophone RZ 3045   Palace Of Plenty/Two By Two 12
71   Regal Zono. SRZA 8501   MATTHEW ELLIS (LP, gatefold sleeve, red/silver labels) 40
72   Regal Zono. SRZA 8505   AM I...? (LP, gatefold sleeve, red/silver labels) 50
(see also Procol Harum, Chris Spedding)

SHIRLEY ELLIS
63   London HLR 9824   The Nitty Gritty/Give Me A List 10
65   London HLR 9946   The Name Game/Whisper To Me Wind 10
65   London HLR 9961   The Clapping Song/This Is Beautiful 10
65   London HLR 9973   The Puzzle Song/I See It, I Like It, I Want It 8
66   London HLR 10021   Ever See A Diver Kiss His Wife While The Bubbles Bounce About Above The Water?/Stardust 8
67   CBS 202606   Soul Time/Waitin' (DJ copy) 75
67   CBS 202606   Soul Time/Waitin' 40
67   CBS 2817   Sugar Let's Shing-A-Ling/How Lonely Is Lonely 15
71   CBS 7463   Soul Time/Waitin' (reissue) 20
77   CBS 4901   Soul Time/Waitin' (2nd reissue, blue coloured vinyl) 10
67   CBS (S)BPG 63044   SOUL TIME WITH SHIRLEY ELLIS (LP) 70

(STEVE) ELLIS
70   CBS 4992   Loot/More More More 70
72   Epic EPC 64878   RIDING ON THE CREST OF A SLUMP (LP, as Ellis) 20
73   Epic EPC 65650   WHY NOT? (LP, as Ellis) 20
(see also Ellis, Love Affair)

ANDY ELLISON
68   Track 604 018   It's Been A Long Time/JOHN'S CHILDREN: Arthur Green 70
68   CBS 3357   Fool From Upper Eden/Another Lucky Lie 45
68   S.N.B. 55-3308   You Can't Do That/Casbah 75

Lorraine ELLISON

MINT VALUE £

| 68 | S.N.B. 55-3308 | You Can't Do That/Cornflake Zoo (second issue, different B-side) .... 85 |

(see also John's Children, Jet, Radio Stars, Beau Brummel)

LORRAINE ELLISON
66	Warner Bros WB 5850	Stay With Me/I Got My Baby Back 15
70	Warner Bros WB 7394	You've Really Got A Hold On Me/You Don't Know Anything About Love 10
71	Mercury 6052 073	Call Me Anytime You Need Some Lovin'/Please Don't Teach Me To Love You ... 30
70	Warner Bros WS 1821	STAY WITH ME (LP) 40

ELMER HOCKETT'S HURDY GURDY
| 68 | Parlophone R 5716 | Fantastic Fair/MOOD MOSAIC: The Yellow Spotted Capricorn .... 15 |

(see also Mood Mosaic, Mark Wirtz)

IAN ELMS
| 82 | Squid Marks SMT 013 | GOOD NIGHT (LP, with insert) .... 180 |

ELOY
83	Heavy Metal HMPD 1	Fools/Heartbeat (clear vinyl) 6
82	Heavy Metal HMILP 1	PLANETS (LP, clear vinyl with inner sleeve) 15
82	Heavy Metal HMIPD 1	PLANETS (LP, picture disc) 18
82	Heavy Metal HMIPD 3	TIME TO TURN (LP, picture disc) 18
83	Heavy Metal HMIPD 12	PERFORMANCE (LP, picture disc) 15
84	Heavy Metal HMIPD 21	METROMANIA (LP, picture disc) 18
89	FM Revolver REV PD120	RA (LP, picture disc) 15

RAS ELROY
| 81 | Arawak DD 030 | Stepping/Walking On (12") .... 30 |

(see also Elroy Baily)

JEFF ELROY & BOYS BLUE
| 66 | Philips BF 1533 | Honey Machine/Three Woman .... 30 |

(see also Boys Blue)

EL 7
| 80 | Pop 000 | MAGNIFICO EP .... 7 |

ELTI-FITS
| 80 | Worthing Street WSEF 1 | GOING STRAIGHT (EP, various foldover picture sleeves) .... 10 |

ELVES
| 70 | MCA MU 1114 | Amber Velvet/West Virginia .... 7 |

CAROL ELVIN
| 63 | Columbia DB 7095 | 'Cos I Know/C'mon Over .... 10 |
| 65 | Parlophone R 5228 | Don't Leave Me/'Cos I Love You .... 10 |

LEE & JAY ELVIN
| 59 | Fontana H 191 | So The Story Goes/When You See Her .... 20 |

(see also Jerry Lordan)

ELVIS HITLER
| 90 | GWR GWLP 37 | DISGRACELAND (LP) .... 20 |

EMANON
| 77 | Clubland SJP 777 | Raging Pain/Rip A Bough (stamped sleeve) .... 30 |

ROBERT EMANUEL
80	Black Roots BRD 1	Illiteracy/RANKING SIMEON: Cultural Dread/Unknown Artist: Progress Road Dub/Don't Get Weary/RANKING SIMEON: Don't Get Jumpy/Unknown Artist: Strictly Rub-A-Dub (12") 20
81	Black Roots BR 25	Never Get Away/Jah Is My Light (12" as Robert Emanuel & Ranking Simeon) 45
85	CF CMF 02	Fashion Dread/No Beggy Beggy (12") 50
84	Black Roots BR 181262	Leave Natty Business/BARRINGTON LEVY & DARBAZ: Jah Black (12") 20

EMBASSY
| 90 | Impact SRT 90LS 2554 | You Can't Poison Me/Take Me Back/How Loud Is Too Loud/She's Got The Mind (12") ... 10 |

BOBBIE EMBER
| 65 | Polydor BM 56062 | Why Can't You Bring Me Home/When Love Isn't There .... 10 |

EMBERS
| 63 | Decca F 11625 | Chelsea Boots/Samantha .... 20 |

(see also Three's A Crowd)

EMBRACE
96	Fierce Panda NING 29	All You Good Good People/My Weakness Is None Of Your Business (p/s, 1,300 only, numbered) 10
98	BBC BOX SET	EMBRACE EP'S (6 x 12"s in black box, numbered, 100 only) 60
98	Hut HUTLP 46	THE GOOD WILL OUT (2-LP) 50
00	Hut HUTLP 60	DRAWN FROM MEMORY (LP) 50
01	Hut HUTLP 68	IF YOU'VE NEVER BEEN (LP) 50
04	Independiente ISOM 45LP	OUT OF NOTHING (LP) 60
06	Independiente ISOM 60LP	THIS NEW DAY (LP) 30

EMBRYO
| 80 | Rampant RAM 001 | I'm Different/You Know He Did (p/s) .... 15 |

(see also Jump Squad)

EMCEE 5
| 62 | Columbia SEG 8153 | LET'S TAKE FIVE (EP) .... 175 |
| 62 | Alpha International DB 92 | VOLUME ONE (EP) .... 150 |

(see also Rendell-Carr, Ian Carr's Nucleus)

EMERALD
| 78 | Look LK/SP 6365 | The Tempter/Rolling Stone (no p/s) .... 20 |

EMERALDS (U.K.)
| 65 | Decca F 12096 | Don't Listen To Your Friends/Say You're Mine .... 7 |
| 65 | Decca F 12304 | King Lonely The Blue/Someone Else's Fool .... 40 |

EMERALDS (U.S.)
| 64 | London HL 9839 | Donkey Kick Back/Sittin' Bull .... 10 |

E-MERGE
| 96 | Groove Yard GYARD 006 | I NEED YOUR LOVIN (12") .... 12 |

Avalon EMERSON

MINT VALUE £

AVALON EMERSON
16	Whities WHYT006	WHITIES 006 (12", p/s)	40

KEITH EMERSON
76	Manticore K 13513	Honky Tonk Train Blues/Barrel House Shake Down (p/s)	6
80	Atlantic K 11612	Taxi Ride (Rome)/Mater Tenebrarum (p/s)	6
81	MCA MCA 697	I'm A Man/Nighthawks Main Title Theme (p/s)	7
15	Record Collector RCLP015	THE KEITH EMERSON TRIO (10", brown die-cut sleeve, with certificate, 750 only)	15

(see also Emerson Lake & Palmer, Nice, V.I.P.'s)

EMERSON, LAKE & PALMER
74	Manticore K 13503	Jerusalem/When The Apple Blossoms Bloom In The WIndmills Of Your Mind, I'll Be Your Valentine (with p/s)	8
70	Island ILPS 9132	EMERSON, LAKE AND PALMER (LP, pink label)	150
70	Island ILPS 9123	EMERSON, LAKE AND PALMER (LP, later 'pink rim palm tree')	40
71	Island ILPS 9155	TARKUS (LP, 1st pressing, gatefold sleeve, 'pink rim palm tree' label with 'side 1' and 'side 2' on labels)	100
71	Island ILPS 9155	TARKUS (LP, 2nd pressing, gatefold sleeve, 'pink rim palm tree' label with 'A' and 'B' on label	50
71	Island HELP 1	PICTURES AT AN EXHIBITION (LP, gatefold sleeve, black label and pink "i")	75
72	Island ILPS 9186	TRILOGY (LP, gatefold sleeve. pink rim label)	50
73	Manticore K 53501	BRAIN SALAD SURGERY (LP, fold-out die cut sleeve with poster)	40
73	Epic S EPC 65450	WELCOME BACK MY FRIENDS TO THE SHOW THAT NEVER ENDS (3-LP, trifold sleeve)	30
73	Manticore K 43503	EMERSON, LAKE AND PALMER (LP, reissue)	20
73	Manticore K 443504	TARKUS (LP, reissue)	20
73	Manticore K 33501	PICTURES AT AN EXHIBITION (LP, repressing)	20
73	Manticore K 43505	TRILOGY (LP, repressing)	20
92	Victory 828 318-1	BLACK MOON (LP)	30

(see also Emerson Lake & Powell, Nice, Keith Emerson, Shame, Asia, King Crimson, Stray Dog, Atomic Rooster)

DICK EMERY
69	Pye NPL (NSPL) 18277	DICK EMERY SINGS (LP)	15

KATHLEEN EMERY
97	Jazzman JM001	Sometimes I Feel Like A Motherless Child/Evil Ways (hand numbered sticker on paper sleeve, 500 only)	20

ÉMIGRÉ
79	Chrysalis CHS 2291	Poison/Trouble Shooter	6

EMILY (1)
74	Emily (No cat no)	If All The World/Long Tall Glasses/Smoke On The Water (p/s)	70

EMJAYS
59	Top Rank JAR 145	All My Love All My Life/Cross My Heart	50

ENDAF EMLYN
71	Wren WRL 537	HIRAETH (LP)	300
74	Sain 1012M	SALEM (LP)	50

DAVID EMMANUEL
83	White Lodge WLT 1	Giving It Up For Love/Stir It Around (p/s)	10
83	White Lodge WLT 1	Giving It Up For Love/Stir It Around (12")	50

EMMET SPICELAND
68	Page One POF 089	Lowlands Low/Bunclody	7
69	Page One POF 143	So Long Marianne/In Search Of Franklin	7
68	Page One POLS 011	THE FIRST (LP, with stickered sleeve, blue/silver labels)	60
68	Page One POLS 011	THE FIRST (LP, without sticker on sleeve, blue/silver labels)	50
77	Hawk HALP 166	THE EMMET SPICELAND ALBUM (LP, reissue of above LP)	35

FRED EMNEY
58	Decca TRI DFE 6554	FRED EMNEY (EP)	20

E-MOTIONS
90s	Slammin 1	E-MOTIONS (EP)	20

EMOTIONS
69	Downtown DT 446	Give Me Love/HORACE FAITH: Daddy's Home	20

EMOTIONS (JAMAICA)
66	Ska Beat JB 263	Rude Boy Confession/Heartbreaking Gypsy	40
67	Caltone TONE 100	A Rainbow/TONY & DOREEN: Just You And I	40
68	Caltone TONE 118	Soulful Music/No Use To Cry	45
68	Caltone TONE 120	Careless Hands/TOMMY McCOOK & SUPERSONICS: Caltone Special	60
69	High Note HS 018	The Storm/Easy Squeeze	15
69	High Note HS 026	Rum Bay/PATSY: Find Someone	8
70	Supreme SUP 209	Halleluiah/MATADOR ALLSTARS: Boat Of Joy	15
71	Prince Buster PB 22	Walking Along/Sometimes	15
11	Big Shot THB 7010	You Are The One/PHIL PRATT ALL STARS: Girls Like Dirt Stars	25

(see also Romeo & Emotions, Horace Faith, Max Romeo)

EMOTIONS (U.K.)
62	London HLR 9640	Echo/One Dance Baby	40
63	London HLR 9701	L-O-V-E/A Million Reasons	30
63	Stateside SS 237	A Story Untold/One Life One Love One You	20

EMOTIONS (U.S.)
69	Stax STAX 123	So I Can Love You/Got To Be The Man	7
69	Stax STAX 134	I Like It/Best Part Of A Love Affair	8
69	Deep Soul DS 9104	Somebody New/Brushfire	30
75	Stax STXS 2020	Baby I'm Through/I Wanna Come Back	6
70	Stax SXATS 1030	SO I CAN LOVE YOU (LP)	20

EMPEROR (NORWAY)
93	Candlelight 002	EMPEROR (LP)	20
95	Candlelight 008	IN THE NIGHTSIDE ECLIPSE (LP)	20
98	Candlelight 023	ANTHEMS TO THE WELKIN AT DUSK (LP, gatefold sleeve)	20

EMPERORS

MINT VALUE £

99	Candlelight 035	IX : EQUILIBRIUM (LP, gatefold sleeve)	20
01	Candlelight 052	EMPERIAL VINYL PRESENTATION (Numbered box set with 5 picture disc LPs and booklet)	60

EMPERORS

66	Stateside SS 565	Karate/I've Got To Have Her	30
68	Pama 786	I've Got To Have Her/Karate	25

EMPHASIS

76	Jaycee JC 002	EMPHASIS (LP)	40

EMPIRE

81	Dinosaur DE 004	Hot Seat/All These Things (p/s)	10

(see also Generation X)

EMPIRE OF THE SUN

09	Capitol 50999	WALKING ON A DREAM (LP)	60
13	EMI 3748461	ICE ON THE DUNE (LP)	60

EMPIRES

02	Goldmine Soul Supply GS 038	You're On Top Girl/DE-LITES: Lover (reissue)	7

EMPTY POCKETS

83	S 83 CUS 1990	Caroline/You Made It Right/Oh Sussanah/Go With The Crowd	8

EMPTY VESSELS

79	Empty Vessel SRTS/79/CUS 361	Too Much Trouble/Loony (p/s)	8

EMS STUDIOS

72	(No label or cat no)	SOUNDS FROM EMS (7" flexi in printed sleeve)	120
72	EMS	EMS SYNTHI AND THE COMPOSER (LP)	500

EN ROUTE

79	Barn BARN 006	Break Down Your Defences/Rusty Capri	30

ENCHANTED FOREST

68	Stateside SS 2080	You're Never Gonna Get My Lovin'/Suzanne	15

ENCHANTERS

67	Warner Bros WB 2054	We Got Love/I've Lost All Communications	25

ENCONA COURSE (FEATURING DEF J)

91	Edutainment EDUT001	Rhyme Grenade/Taste Of The Future/Hit Men (EP)	40
92	White (No Cat. No.)	VIA COARSEVILLE (EP)	41

END RESULT

73	Priory PRY 1	Towards The Sun/Please Go	175

THE END

65	Philips BF 1444	I Can't Get Any Joy/Hey Little Girl	30
68	Decca F 22750	Shades Of Orange/Loving, Sacred Loving	50
69	Decca LK 5015	INTROSPECTION (LP, large unboxed logo on label, mono)	700
69	Decca SKL-R 5015	INTROSPECTION (LP, large unboxed logo on label, stereo)	500
96	Tenth Planet TP 025	IN THE BEGINNING ... THE END (LP, gatefold sleeve, numbered, 1,000 only)	20
97	Tenth Planet TP 033	RETROSPECTION (LP, numbered, 1,000 only)	15

(see also Tucky Buzzard, Bill Wyman, Innocents, Bobby Angelo, Tuxedo)

END (THE)

81	No label or cat no	I Can't Take Any More/Take A Look (no p/s)	30

ENDEAVOURS

75	Bradleys BRAD 7510	Baby's Comin' Home/First Price To The Winner	12

ENDEVERS

68	Decca F 12817	Remember When We Were Young/Taking Care Of Myself	30
68	Decca F 12859	She's My Girl/She's That Kind Of Girl	30
69	Decca F 12939	Sunny And Me/I Really Hope You Do	10

ENDGAMES

83	Virgin VS 640	Miracle In My Heart/Miracle In My Heart (Instrumental)	6
83	Virgin VS 640	Miracle In My Heart/Ecstacy (Centurion MIx) (12")	20

END PHENOMENA

70	Hollick And Taylor	END PHENOMENA (LP)	50

SERGIO ENDRIGO

68	Pye International 7N 25502	Marianne/Il Dolce Paese	10

MELVIN ENDSLEY

57	RCA RCA 1004	I Like Your Kind Of Love/Is It True?	25
58	RCA RCA 1051	I Got A Feelin'/There's Bound To Be	20

END TO END

87	T.S. TS3	Are You Gonna Be/Version/We Can Work It Out/Verion (12")	60
88	Sure Delight SDT 7	Confusion/(7" Mix)/(Instrumental Version) (12") white label)	40
88	TS 7TS 1	Confuzzion/Confuzzed	40

ENEMY (1)

81	Tin Tin NM 1	50,000 Dead/Society's Fool/Neutral Ground (p/s)	8
82	Fallout FALL 001	Fallen Hero/Tomorrow's Warning/Prisoner Of War (p/s, with inner)	7
82	Fallout FALL 004	Punks Alive/Piccadilly Sidetracks/Twist And Turn (p/s, orange vinyl)	7
84	Rot ASS 9	Last But Not Least/Images (live) (p/s)	6
83	Fallout FALL LP 015	THE GATEWAY TO HELL (LP)	20

ENERGETIC KRUSHER

89	Vinyl Solution SOL 17	PATH TO OBLIVION (LP, with insert, features Danny McCormack)	20

(see also Wildhearts)

ENERGY

81	GRN 1	CONQUER THE WORLD: Conquer The World/Make It/Law Breaker (EP, no p/s)	75
80	BIPS BECK 927	ENERGISED (EP)	50
83	Aros AROS 11233	Nowhere To Hide/Fight For Your Freedom (no p/s)	50

SCOTT ENGEL

58	Vogue V 9125	Blue Bell/Paper Doll	150

Scott ENGEL & JOHN STEWART

MINT VALUE £

58	Vogue V 9125	Blue Bell/Paper Doll (78)	80
59	Vogue V 9145	The Livin' End/Good For Nothin' (with Count Dracula & Boys)	400
59	Vogue V 9145	The Livin' End/Good For Nothin' (with Count Dracula & Boys) (78)	60
59	Vogue V 9150	Charlie Bop/All I Do Is Dream Of You	200
59	Vogue V 9150	Charlie Bop/All I Do Is Dream Of You (78)	40
66	Liberty LEP 2261	SCOTT ENGEL (EP)	35

(see also Scott Walker, Walker Brothers)

SCOTT ENGEL & JOHN STEWART
| 66 | Capitol CL 15440 | I Only Came To Dance With You/Greens | 40 |

(see also Scott Walker, Walker Brothers)

ENGINEERS
| 78 | Beserkley BZZ 16 | You Baby/Easy Street (p/s) | 6 |

(see also Eddie & Hot Rods)

ENGINEERS WITHOUT FEARS
| 94 | Dee Jay DJX 015 | Spiritual Aura/Rhythm (12") | 25 |

ENGLAND (1)
| 76 | Deroy DER 1356 | ENGLAND (LP, private pressing) | 1000 |

ENGLAND (2)
77	Arista ARISTA 88	Pariffinalea/Nanagram	6
77	Arista ARTY 153	GARDEN SHED (LP, allegedly with booklet)	60
77	Arista ARTY 153	GARDEN SHED (LP, without alleged booklet)	40

ENGLAND FOOTBALL SQUAD
70	Pye 7N 17920	Back Home/Cinnamon Stick (some with 'football centre')	6
70	Pye 7N 17920	Back Home/Cinnamon Stick (with 'football centre and p/s)	15
70	Pye 7N 17920	Back Home/Cinnamon Stick (in promo 'BOAC' sleeve)	50

ENGLAND'S GLORY
| 73 | Venus VEN 105 | ENGLAND'S GLORY (LP, private pressing, pink label, 25 copies only, Venus VEN 105 in run-out groove; beware of white label counterfeits) | 1000 |

(see also Only Ones)

ENGLAND SISTERS
| 60 | HMV POP 710 | Heartbeat/Little Child | 30 |

ENGLISH
| 81 | Albion ION 1008 | Hooray For The English/When You Fly (p/s) | 10 |

BARBARA JEAN ENGLISH
| 73 | Contempo CLP 507 | BARBARA JEAN ENGLISH (LP) | 25 |

ENGLISH COUNTRY BLUES BAND
| 83 | Rogue FMSL 2004 | HOME AND DERANGED (LP) | 15 |

ENGLISH DOGS
83	Clay PLATE 6	MAD PUNX AND ENGLISH DOGS (12")	25
84	Ros ASS 17	TO THE ENDS OF THE EARTH (12" EP, p/s)	20
86	Under One Flag 12 FLAG 101	METALMORPHOSIS (12" EP, p/s)	10
83	Clay LP 10	INVASION OF THE PORKY MEN (LP, inner)	20
85	Rot ASS 20	FORWARD INTO BATTLE (LP)	15
86	Under One Flag FLAG 4	WHERE LEGEND BEGAN (LP)	15

ERROL(L) ENGLISH
70	Big Shot BI 547	I Don't Want To Love You/Love Is Pure	6
70	Big Shot BI 548	Once In My Life/Rabbit In A Cottage	10
70	Torpedo TOR 8	Open The Door To Your Heart/That Will Do	30
70	Torpedo TOR 9	Where You Lead Me/Hitchin' A Ride	30
70	Torpedo TOR 16	Sad Girl/Welcome Me Back Home	30
70	Torpedo TOR 22	Sha La La La Lee/BOVVER BOYS: A.G.G.R.O	100
71	Duke DU 99	Sometimes (with Champions)/Sugar Cane	6

(see also Junior English, Errol & Champions)

MR JOE ENGLISH
| 69 | Fontana TF 3034 | Lay Lady Lay/Two Minute Silence | 15 |

JUNIOR ENGLISH
69	Camel CA 35	Nobody Knows (with Tony Sexton)/Somewhere	25
71	Pama PM 828	Jesamine/SYDNEY ALL STARS: The Flash	8
72	Pama PM 841	Miss Playgirl/Once In My Life	8
72	Pama PM 866	I Don't Want To Die/Land Of Sea And Sand	8
72	Pama PM 869	Daniel/Perfidia	8
72	Banana BA 368	Anniversary/Girls Like You	8
73	Pama Supreme PS 381	Garden Party/Version	8
78	Ethnic Fight ETH 1228	Keep On Trying/HORSE MOUTH WALLACE: Herb Vendor (12")	35
79	Burning Rockers BRD 004	Love And Key/Key Down (12", red vinyl)	20
79	Burning Rockers BRD 009	Natural High/In Loving You (12")	12
81	Cha Cha CHAD 35	We Can Work It Out/Love Me Tonight (12")	12
74	Cactus CTLP 102	THE DYNAMIC (LP)	25
75	Horse HRLP 707	THE GREAT (LP)	15
80	Burning Rockers BR 1010	LOVERS KEY (LP)	25
83	Sunsplash SNSLP01	TWO OF A KIND (LP)	40

(see also Errol English, Tony Sexton)

ENGLISH ROSE
| 70 | Polydor 2058 040 | Yesterday's Hero/To Jackie | 10 |

(see also Neat Change, Love Affair)

ENGLISH SUBTITLES
| 79 | Small Wonder SMALL 22 | Time Tunnel/Sweat/Reconstruction (p/s) | 7 |
| 82 | Glass 007/10 SEC 21 | Tannoy/Cars On Fire (folded p/s in bag with insert) | 7 |

ENGLISH MCCOY
| 88 | Nowyertalkin' 7TALK 2 | Give Me Something To Believe In/Breaking Down (p/s) | 100 |

ENID

			MINT VALUE £
88	Nowyertalkin' 12TALK 2	GIVE ME SOMETHING TO BELIEVE IN (12" EP)	200

ENID

76	Buk BUK 3002	The Lovers/In The Region Of The Summer Stars	8
77	EMI International INT 540	Golden Earrings/Omega (p/s)	6
79	Pye 7P 106	Dambusters March — Land Of Hope And Glory/The Skye Boat Song (p/s, blue vinyl)	6
80	Pye 7P 187	Fool/Tito (p/s)	6
80	EMI EMI 5109	Golden Earrings/665 The Great Bean (p/s)	6
81	Bronze BRO 127	When You Wish Upon A Star/Jessica (p/s)	6
81	Bronze BRO 134	Heigh Ho/Twinkle Twinkle Little Star (p/s)	6
76	Buk BULP 2014	IN THE REGION OF THE SUMMER STARS (LP, 1st issue, white label, with insert, without mention of "Enid" on front cover; distributed by Decca)	35
77	Buk BULP 2014	IN THE REGION OF THE SUMMER STARS (2nd issue, black label, with "Enid" on front cover)	20
77	honeybee INS 3005	IN THE REGION OF THE SUMMER STARS (3rd pressing, brown label with poster)	18
84	The Stand LE 1	"THE LIVERPOOL ALBUM" (untitled mini-album, sold at gigs, 800 only)	20
84	The Stand THE STAND 1	THE STAND (fan club issue, 5,000 only, autographed)	25
84	The Stand THE STAND 1	THE STAND (fan club issue, 5,000 only, some autographed)	15
85	The Stand THE STAND 2	THE STAND 1985-1986 (fan club issue, 2,000 only, autographed)	15
85	The Stand THE STAND 2	THE STAND 1985-1986 (fan club issue, 2,000 only)	15

(see also Robert John Godfrey, Godfrey & Stewart, William Arkle, Glen Baker)

ETHEL ENNIS

64	RCA SF 7654	ONCE AGAIN (LP)	15

RAY ENNIS & BLUE JEANS

68	Columbia DB 8431	What Have They Done To Hazel?/Now That You've Got Me (You Don't Seem To Want Me)	25

(see also Swinging Blue Jeans, Blue Jeans)

BRIAN ENO

74	Island WIP 6178	Seven Deadly Finns/Later On	15
75	Island WIP 6233	The Lion Sleeps Tonight (Wimoweh)/I'll Come Running	6
78	Polydor 2001 762	The King's Lead Hat/R.A.F. (B-side with Snatch)	10
83	EG EGO 12	Silver Morning/Deep Blue Day (with Daniel Lanois & Roger Eno, with wraparound promo p/s with Eno notes on back)	8
86	EG ENODJ1	Backwater/On Some Faraway Beach (promo only)	10
73	Island ILPS 9268	HERE COME THE WARM JETS (LP, pink rim, palm tree label, MATRIX A-1E/B-1E)	50
74	Island ILPS 9309	TAKING TIGER MOUNTAIN (BY STRATEGY) (LP, gatefold sleeve, pink rim, Island label)	50
75	Island ILPS 9351	ANOTHER GREEN WORLD (LP, 1st pressing, blue rim, palm tree label)	75
75	Island HELP 22	EVENING STAR (LP, as Fripp & Eno)	30
75	Obscure OBS 3	DISCREET MUSIC (LP, 1st pressing with grey labels)	75
75	Obscure OBS 3	DISCREET MUSIC (LP, 2nd pressing, red labels)	40
76	Editions EG EGM 1	MUSIC FOR FILMS (LP, private pressing)	250
77	Polydor 2302 071	BEFORE AND AFTER SCIENCE (LP, with 4 Peter Schmidt prints)	80
77	Polydor 2302 071	BEFORE AND AFTER SCIENCE (LP, without prints)	35
77	Polydor 2683082	HERE COME THE WARM JETS/BEFORE & AFTER SCIENCE (2-LP reissue)	30
77	Polydor 2302 063	HERE COME THE WARM JETS (LP, reissue)	25
77	Polydor 2302 668	TAKING TIGER MOUNTAIN (BY STRATEGY) (LP, reissue, red label)	25
77	Polydor 2302 069	ANOTHER GREEN WORLD (LP, reissue, red label)	25
78	Polydor 2310623	MUSIC FOR FILMS (LP, textured sleeve)	35
78	EG AMB 001	AMBIENT 1 - MUSIC FOR AIRPORTS (LP, inner)	50
82	EG EGED 20	AMBIENT 4 (LP)	30
82	Editions EG EGED 17	AMBIENT 1 - MUSIC FOR AIRPORTS (LP, reissue)	25
82	EG EGED 5	MUSIC FOR FILMS (LP, reissue)	20
83	EG EGLP 53	APOLLO (LP)	40
83	EG EGBS 002	WORKING BACKWARDS 1983-1973 (9-LP box set with "Music For Films, Vol. 2" LP & "Rarities" 12")	200
84	EG EGLP 17	TAKING TIGER MOUNTAIN (BY STRATEGY) (LP, reissue)	15
86	EG EGLP 65	MORE BLANK THAN FRANK (LP)	20
87	Editions EG EGED 23	DISCREET MUSIC (LP, reissue)	20
87	EG EGLP 32	BEFORE AND AFTER SCIENCE (LP, reissue)	20
87	Editions EG EGED 20	AMBIENT 4 (LP. reissue, barcode on rear of sleeve)	20
89	Standard Music Library ESL 168	TEXTURES (LP)	400
89	Standard Music Library SML ESL 003CD	TEXTURES (CD)	50
92	Opal 9362 45010-1	SHUTOV ASSEMBLEY (LP)	40
93	Virgin ENOBOX1	INSTRUMENTAL (box set 3-CD, booklet)	35
95	All Saints AS 23	SPINNER (LP, with Jah Wobble as Eno/Wobble)	35
11	Warp WARPLP207R	SMALL CRAFT ON A MILK SEA (2-LP)	20

(see also Ayers Cale Nico & Eno, Roxy Music, Passengers, Robert Fripp, Lady June, David Toop, Gavin Bryars, Toto, Eno & Cale, Brian Eno & David Byrne, Harold Budd & Brian Eno)

BRIAN ENO & DAVID BYRNE

81	EG EGO 1	The Jezebel Spirit/Regiment (p/s)	10
81	EG ECOX 1	The Jezebel Spirit/Regiment/Very Very Hungry (12", p/s)	18
81	EG EGLP 48	MY LIFE IN THE BUSH OF GHOSTS (LP, 1st pressing, later pressings have barcode on sleeve)	30

(see also David Byrne, Talking Heads)

BRIAN ENO & JOHN CALE

90	Land LAND 12	WRONG WAY UP (LP)	20

(see also Brian Eno. John Cale)

ENOS & SHEILA

68	Blue Cat BS 138	Tonight You're Mine/UNTOUCHABLES: Your Love	60

(see also Enos McLeod)

ENOUGH'S ENOUGH

MINT VALUE £

ENOUGH'S ENOUGH
| 68 | Tattoo TT 101 | Please Remember/Look Around You Baby | 700 |

ENSEMBLE
| 82 | Stiff WIN 1 | Viva Scotland, England, Ireland/Viva Scotland, England, Ireland ("A" label promo) | 15 |

ENSLAVED
| 90s | Candlelight 001MLP | HORDANES LAND (EP) | 60 |

ENTER SHIKARI
09	Ambush Reality LPAMBR006V	COMMON DREADS (LP)	150
12	Ambush Reality LPAMBR015	A FLASH FLOOD OF COLOUR (LP, blue, transparent pink or white vinyl)	30
13	Ambush Reality LPAMBR001	TAKE TO THE SKIES (2-LP reissue, with CD, green/beige vinyl)	60
13	Ambush Reality LPAMBR001	TAKE TO THE SKIES (2-LP reissue, with CD, orange/blue vinyl)	50
13	Ambush Reality ESBS002LP	LIVE AT ROCK CITY 2009 (LP, grey vinyl)	20
13	Ambush Reality EBS004LP	LIVE IN LONDON (LP/DVD)	20
15	Ambush Reality AMBR031	THE MINDSWEEP (LP)	15
15	Ambush Reality PIASR835DLP	THE MINDSWEEP: HOSPITALIZED (2-LP, orange vinyl)	20
15	Ambush Reality LPAMBR001	TAKE TO THE SKIES (2-LP reissue, with CD, clear vinyl)	40
17	Ambush Reality LPAMBR001	TAKE TO THE SKIES (2-LP reissue, with CD, violet vinyl)	35
17	Ambush Reality PIASR990CP	THE SPARK (LP, silver vinyl)	20
19	Ambush Reality LPAMBR006V	COMMON DREADS (LP, repressing, splatter vinyl, with 7")	60

ENTICERS
| 72 | Atlantic 2091 136 | Calling For Your Love/Storyteller | 40 |

JIMI ENTLEY SOUND
| 02 | Espionage Disk ESP 001 | Apache/Charlie's Theme | 25 |

(see also Portishead)

ENTOMBED
91	Earache 7 MOSH 38	Crawl/Forsaken (p/s)	10
91	Earache MOSH 38T	Crawl/Forsaken/Bitter Loss (12" p/s)	12
92	Earache MOSH 52 T	Stranger Eons/Dusk/Shreds Of Flesh (12", p/s)	10
93	Earache 7 MOSH 114	Out Of Hand/God Of Thunder/Black Breath (p/s)	12
93	Earache MOSH 114 T	Out Of Hand/God Of Thunder/Black Breath (12", p/s)	12
93	Earache MOSH 94 T	HOLLOWMAN EP (6 track 12", p/s)	15
95	Earache 7 MOSH 132	Night Of The Vampire/NEW BOMB TURKS: I Hate People (p/s)	8
89	Earache MOSH 21P	LEFT HAND PATH (LP, picture disc)	20
90	Earache MOSH 21	LEFT HAND PATH (LP, insert)	25
91	Earache MOSH 21	LEFT HAND PATH (LP, white vinyl, stickered sleeve, 2000 only)	30
91	Earache MOSH 37	CLANDESTINE LP, embossed sleeve, insert)	20
93	Earache MOSH 82	WOLVERINE BLUES (LP, lyric insert)	50
97	Music For Nations MFN 216	TO RIDE, SHOOT STRAIGHT AND SPEAK THE TRUTH (LP, with "Family Favourites" 12")	50
98	Music For Nations MFN 244	SAME DIFFERENCE (LP)	40
07	Back On Black BOBV 067 LP	SERPENT SAINTS/THE TEN AMENDMENTS (LP, red vinyl)	15

JOHN ENTWISTLE('S OX)
71	Track 2094 008	I Believe In Everything/My Size	10
75	Decca FR 13567	Mad Dog/Cell No.7 (as John Entwistle's Ox)	8
71	Track 2406 005	SMASH YOUR HEAD AGAINST THE WALL (LP, gatefold, black/silver label)	30
72	Track 2406 104	WHISTLE RYMES (LP, gatefold sleeve, black/silver labels)	25
73	Track 2406106	RIGOR MORTIS SETS IN (LP, gatefold, inner)	15
75	Decca TXS 114	MAD DOG (LP, as John Entwistle's Ox, with poster, lyric insert)	25
75	Decca TXS 114	MAD DOG (LP, as John Entwistle's Ox, without poster, lyric insert)	15

(see also Who, Rigor Mortis)

ENYA
87	BBC RESL 201	I Want Tomorrow/The Celts Theme (p/s)	7
91	WEA YZ 635 T	How Can I Keep From Singing/O'che Chi'n (Silent Night) (12", metallic p/s)	10
87	BBC REB 605	ENYA (LP)	20

EPEE MD
| 87 | Cooltempo COOL 156 | It's My Thing (Club)/You're A Customer (Club) (p/s) | 50 |

EPICS (JAMAICA)
| 70 | Bamboo BAM 37 | Your Love/Driving Me Crazy | 30 |

EPICS (U.K.)
65	Pye 7N 15829	There's Just No Pleasing You/My Little Girl	10
66	Pye 7N 17053	Just How Wrong Can You Be/Blue Turns To Grey	10
68	CBS 3564	Travelling Circus/Henry Long	20

(see also Acid Gallery, Christie)

EPIDEMIC
| 89 | Metalcore CORE 4 | THE TRUTH OF WHAT WILL BE (LP) | 20 |

EPILEPTICS
80	Stortbeat/Mirror BEAT 8	1970'S EP (black & white p/s, stencilled white labels)	20
81	Spiderleg SDL 1	1970'S EP (re-recorded, printed labels, folded different printed b&w p/s)	15
81	Spiderleg SDL 2	LAST BUS TO DEBDEN (EP, hand-written labels & photocopied p/s)	12
81	Spiderleg SDL 2	LAST BUS TO DEBDEN (EP, printed labels & different photocopied p/s)	8

(see also Licks, Flux Of Pink Indians)

EPISODE
| 68 | MGM MGM 1409 | Little One/Wide Smiles | 30 |

(see also Episode Six)

EPISODE FOUR
| 86 | Lenin & McCarthy LENM 001T | STRIKE UP MATCHES EP (p/s with insert, 500 only, many destroyed) | 150 |

(see also East Village)

EPISODE SIX

MINT VALUE £

EPISODE SIX
66	Pye 7N 17018	Put Yourself In My Place/That's All I Want	25
66	Pye 7N 17110	I Hear Trumpets Blow/True Love Is Funny That Way	20
66	Pye 7N 17147	Here, There And Everywhere/Mighty Morris Ten	20
67	Pye 7N 17244	Love, Hate, Revenge/Baby Baby Baby	40
67	Pye 7N 17330	Morning Dew/Sunshine Girl	25
67	Pye 7N 17376	I Can See Through You/When I Fall In Love	40
68	Chapter One CH 103	Lucky Sunday/Mr. Universe	20
69	Chapter One CH 104	Mozart Versus The Rest/Jak D'Or	20
87	PRT PYL 6026	PUT YOURSELF IN MY PLACE (LP)	15

(see also Episode, Sheila Carter & Episode Six, Neo Maya, Roger Glover, Jon Lord, Gillan, Deep Purple, Quatermass)

EPITOME OF SOUND
10	Go Ahead TICK 1	You Don't Love Me/Where Were You (reissue)	10

EPMD
88	Sleeping Bag SBUK LP 1	STRICTLY BUSINESS (LP)	20
89	Sleeping Bag SBUK LP 8	UNFINISHED BUSINESS (LP)	20
90	Def Jam 467697 1	BUSINESS AS USUAL (LP)	20
92	Def Jam 471963 1	BUSINESS NEVER PERSONAL (LP)	25

MINNIE EPPERSON
68	Action ACT 4503	Grab Your Clothes (And Get On Out)/No Love At All	75

KAT EPPLE AND BOB STOHL
13	Dead Cert VCR 004	SANCTUS SPIRITUS (LP)	18

PRESTON EPPS
59	Top Rank JAR 140	Bongo Rock/Bongo Party	12
59	Top Rank JAR 180	Bongos In Pastel/Doin' The Cha Cha Cha	8
60	Top Rank JAR 345	Bongo Boogie/Flamenco Boogie	10
60	Top Rank JAR 413	Bongo Bongo Bongo/Hully Gully Bongo	10
60	Top Rank JKP 2060	RUSHING FOR PERCUSSION (EP, with Sandy Nelson)	20

(see also Sandy Nelson)

EQUA
83	Mr Fox FOX 1	In The Red/City Dub	20
83	Mr Fox FOX 1	In The Red/City Dub/City Lights (12")	60

EQUALS
67	President PT 117	I Won't Be There/Fire	8
67	President PT 135	Baby, Come Back/Hold Me Closer	6
67	President ZAM 2	I'm A Poor Man/Can't Find A Girl To Love Me (Export only)	30
67	President PT 158	Give Love A Try/Another Sad And Lonely Night	7
68	President PT 180	I Get So Excited/The Skies Above	6
68	President PT 200	Laurel And Hardy/The Guy Who Made Her A Star	6
68	President PT 222	Softly Softly/Lonely Rita	6
69	President PT 240	Michael And The Slipper Tree/Honey Gum	6
69	President PT 260	Viva Bobby Joe/I Can't Let You Go	6
69	President PT 275	Rub A Dub Dub/After The Lights Go Down Low	6
70	President PT 288	Soul Brother Clifford/Happy Birthday Girl	6
70	President PT 303	I Can See But You Don't Know/Gigolo Sam	40
70	President PT 345	Help Me Simone/Love Potion	6
70	Presiden ZAM 1	Let's Go To The Moon/Watching The Girls (export)	25
72	CBS 7874	Stand Up And Be Counted/What Would You Do To Survive	12
73	President PT 405	Honey Bee/Put Some Rock & Roll In Your Soul	6
73	President PT 414	Diversion/Here Today Gone Tomorrow	15
74	President PT 422	Hang Up My Rock & Roll Shoes/She Lives For Today	6
75	President PT 436	Georgetown Girl/We've Got It All Worked Out	6
76	Mercury 6007 104	Kaiwana Sunshine Girl/Soul Mother	6
76	Mercury 6007 106	Funky Like A Train/If You Didn't Miss Me	15
76	Mercury 6007 107	Funky Like A Train/If You Didn't Miss Me (12")	12
76	Phonogram EQUAL 001	EQUALS PARTY (12", promo only)	100
77	Mercury 6007 139	Irma La Douce/Ar'e Harry	6
77	President PT 464	Beautiful Clown/Daily Love	6
78	Ice GUY 5	Red Dog/Something Beautiful	6
88	Club JAB 58	Funky Like A Train/Born Ya!/Funky Like A Train (extended) (reissue)	7
88	Club JABX 58	Funky Like A Train/Born Ya!/Funky Like A Train (extended) (12", reissue)	20
68	President PTE 1	BABY COME BACK (EP)	20
68	President PTE 2	THE EQUALS (EP)	25
67	President PTL 1006	UNEQUALLED EQUALS (LP)	30
68	President PTL 1015	EQUALS EXPLOSION (LP)	30
68	President PTL(S) 1020	SENSATIONAL EQUALS (LP)	30
68	President PTL(S) 1025	SUPREME (LP)	30
69	President PTLS 1030	THE EQUALS STRIKE AGAIN (LP)	30
69	President PTLS 1050	BEST OF THE EQUALS (LP)	20
70	President PTLS 1038	AT THE TOP (LP, gatefold, poster)	20
76	Mercury 9109 601	BORN YA! (LP)	35
78	Ice ICEL 1002	MYSTIC SISTER (LP)	80

(see also Little Grants & Eddie, Pyramids, Hickory, Little Brother Grant, Zappata Schmitt, Seven Letters/Syramip, Thirty-Second Turn-Off)

EQUATION
80	Dash 850101	Arcacia Avenue/Down The Avenue	10

EQUATIONS
69	Fontana TF 1235	Waiting On The Shores Of Nowhere/You Stood Beside Me	10

EQUATORS
76	Klik KL 620	Father Oh Father/Version	25

EQUINOX
73	Boulevard BLVD 4118	HARD ROCK (LP, black/silver labels)	25

EQUIPE 84
67	Major Minor MM 517	Auschwitz/Twenty Ninth Of September	20

ERAMUS HALL
96	Westbound SEWD 112	YOUR LOVE IS MY DESIRE (LP, reissue)	35
16	Expansion ERAMUS LP !	YOUR LOVE IS MY DESIRE (LP, reissue)	20
16	Expansion ERAMUS LP !	YOUR LOVE IS MY DESIRE (LP, reissue, with free 7")	35

ERASMUS CHORUM
72	Chapter 1 SCM 173	Oh Lord, The Holy House On Sunday/Mary Jane	20
73	Alaska 19	I Don't Want Our Loving To Die/That Is Why	10
73	Alaska ALA 13	Jungle/That Is Why	40

ERASURE
SINGLES
85	Mute L12MUTE 40	Who Needs Love (Like That) (Mexican Mix)/Push Me Shove Me (Tacos Mix) (12", p/s)	20
85	Mute L12MUTE 42	Heavenly Action (Yellow Brick Mix)/Don't Say No (Ruby Red Mix) (12", p/s, L12 cat. no. must be listed on sleeve & label)	40
85	Mute DMUTE 42	Heavenly Action/Don't Say No (Ruby Red Mix)//Who Needs Love (Like That) (Mexican Mix)/Push Me Shove Me (Tacos Mix) (12" shrinkwrapped double pack)	15
86	Mute 12MUTE 45	Oh L'Amour/March On Down The Line/Gimme! Gimme! Gimme! (12", 'Thomas The Tank Engine' p/s, withdrawn)	12
94	Mute MUTE 166	I Love Saturday/Dodo/Because You're So Sweet (unreleased, p/s only)	30

ALBUMS
91	Mute STUMM 95	CHORUS (LP)	20
92	Mute L2	POP! - THE FIRST 20 HITS (2-LP)	80
94	Mute STUMM 115	I SAY I SAY I SAY (LP, with booklet)	30
95	Mute STUMM 145	ERASURE (2-LP, inners)	40
97	STUMM 155	COWBOY (LP)	35

PROMOS
86	Mute P12MUTE 45	Oh L'Amour/March On Down The Line/Gimme! Gimme! Gimme! (12", plain white sleeve, dark blue vinyl)	20
89	Mute (no cat. no.)	WILD (CD, promo-only box set, with LP, 12", stickers, postcard, photo & info sheet)	80
90s	Mute P12MUTE 195	Don't Say Your Love Is Killing Me (Tall Paul Mix)//(John Pleased Wimmin Flashback Vox) Oh L'Amour (Tin Tin Out Remix)/(Matt Darey Mix) (12", white label test pressing with press release & release sheet, 10 copies only)	70
91	Mute CDSTUMM 95	CHORUS (promo CD, with and booklet)	60
92	Mute (no cat. no.)	POP! THE FIRST 20 HITS (CD, promo-only box set, with T-shirt, info sheets, 2-LP, video tape, & CD)	70
94	Mute PL12 MUTE 166	Ghost (12", 1-sided)	8
20	Mute FSTUMM455	Welcome To The Neon - 1-track promo with Hey Now (Think I Got A Feeling) (500 only)	35

(see also Depeche Mode, Dinger)

ERIC (SYKES) & HATTIE (JACQUES)
63	Decca LK 4507	ERIC, HATTIE AND THINGS (LP)	15

ERIC & THE VIKINGS
86	Kool Kat 5	Hurting/My Baby Ain't No Play Thing (red vinyl)	25

ROKY ERICKSON (& THE ALIENS)
77	Virgin VS 180	Bermuda/The Interpreter (p/s)	10
80	CBS 8888	Creature With The Atom Brain/The Wind And More (with The Aliens)	8
80	CBS 9055	Mine Mine Mind/Bloody Hammer (Acoustic Version) (p/s, with The Aliens)	8
80	CBS SCBS 84463	ROKY ERICKSON & THE ALIENS (LP)	20
86	Demon FIEND 66	GREMLINS HAVE PICTURES (LP)	15
87	5 Hours Back TOCK 007	CASTING THE RUNES (LP)	15
87	5 Hours Back TOCK 7P	CASTING THE RUNES (LP, picture disc)	25
92	Swordfish SFMD LP 1	MAD DOG (LP)	25
92	Swordfish SFMD LP 2	LOVE TO SEE YOU BLEED (LP)	25

(see also 13th Floor Elevators)

ROLF ERICSON
59	Pye NIxa NJL 14	SESSION IN STOCKHOLM (LP, with Freddie Redd)	100

ERIN PERYGLUS
87	OFN OFN 3	Bronson/Y Dyn Newydd (p/s)	30
88	OFN OFN 6	Dafydd Yn Gwneud Teisen/Merthyr (p/s)	20
89	OFN OFN 07B	Y LLOSG (12" picture disc)	20

ERNIE & ED
72	Jay Boy BOY 58	Beautiful World/Indication	50

ERROL (ENGLISH) & CHAMPIONS
70	Jackpot JP 732	Lonely Boy/Da Boo	7
70	Jackpot JP 738	Lonely Boy/TONY & CHAMPIONS: All Of My Life	8

(see also Errol English)

ERROL (DUNKLEY) & HIS GROUP
65	Blue Beat BB 284	Gypsy/Miss May (actually by Errol Dunkley & Roy Shirley)	25

(see also Errol Dunkley)

ERROL (DUNKLEY) & U ROY
72	Punch PH 105	Darling Ooh Wee/GOD SONS: Merry Up Version	12

E.R. & THE ROUGH RIDERS
69	Polydor 56361	Heya/I'm Alive	15

ERSATZ
81	Raw RAW 35	Motorbody Love/One Good Reason/Gimme A Chance (poster p/s)	35
81	Leisure Sounds SRS 32	Smile In Shadow/House Of Cards (p/s)	12

(see also DJ Harvey)

BOOKER ERVIN
61	Parlophone PMC 1170	THE BOOK (LP)	80

Dee ERVIN

MINT VALUE £

DEE ERVIN
72 Signpost SG 4356 — DEE ERVIN SINGS (LP) 20

ESCALATORS
83 Big Beat NS 86 — Something's Missing/The Edge (p/s) 8
83 Big Beat NS 87 — The Munsters Theme/Monday (p/s) 8
83 Big Beat WIKM15 — MOVING STAIRCASES (LP) 25
(see also Clapham South Escalators, The Meteors)

ESCAPE FROM NEW YORK
84 Rollerball BALL 1 — Fire In My Heart/Won't Be Your Fool/Fire In My Heart (Instrumental) (12") 50

ESCORTS (JAMAICA)
70 Big Shot BI 535 — I'm So Afraid/Mother Nature 40
74 Fab FAB 245 — Sixpense/Loving Feeling 15
(see also Sensations)

ESCORTS (U.K.)
64 Fontana TF 453 — Dizzy Miss Lizzy/All I Want Is You 25
64 Fontana TF 474 — The One To Cry/Tell Me Baby 25
64 Fontana TF 516 — I Don't Want To Go On Without You/Don't Forget To Write 25
65 Fontana TF 570 — C'Mon Home Baby/You'll Get No Lovin' That Way 25
66 Fontana TF 651 — Let It Be Me/Mad Mad World 25
66 Columbia DB 8061 — From Head To Toe/Night Time 45
(see also Big Three, Paddy Klaus & Gibson, Swinging Blue Jeans)

ESCORTS (U.S.)
63 Coral Q 72458 — Submarine Race Watching/Somewhere 25

ESCORTS & KAY JUSTICE
54 Columbia SCM 5132 — If You Took Your Love From Me/Yes, Indeed 15

ESCOURTS
76 Alaska ALA 1014 — Disrespect Can Wreck/Bam A Lam A Boogie 8

ESG
81 Factory FAC 34 — You're No Good/UFO (p/s) 25
93 C.T. CTT42 — Moody (Original Mix)/(Spaced Out Mix)/(CT Remix 1)/CT Remix 2) (12") 20
15 Fire BLAZE 221 — MOODY EP (12" splatter green vinyl) 20
00 Universal Sounds USLP 10 — ESG: A SOUTH BRONX STORY (2-LP, insert) 50
02 Soul Jazz SJR LP 65 — STEP OFF (2-LP) 20
06 Soul Jazz SJR LP 150 — COME AWAY WITH ESG (2-LP reissue) 30
07 Soul Jazz SJR LP 167 — ESG: A SOUTH BRONX STORY VOLUME 2 (2-LP, insert) 30
10 Fire FIRELP 156 — DANCE TO THE BEST OF ESG (3-LP) 45
11 Fire F222 — ESG (LP, reissue) 25

ESKIMOS & EGYPT
81 Village VILS 102 — The Cold/A Year/Screams And Whispers (EP, p/s) 60

ESOTERIC/ESOTERIK
96 Club Craft OR 100 — Dancing With The Devil/Esoteric Vs. Hybrid (12") 50
96 Club Craft OR 200 — Ultimate Straightness/Playing With Voices (12") 40
96 Club Craft OR 300 — Elegant Panning/3 After That One (12") 30
96 Club Craft OR 400 — Odd Sins/Odd Sins (12") 80
96 Crowd Control CROWD 005T — Desert Planet/Mayhem (12", as Esoterik) 80
96 Utmostfear UTMOST 1301 — Falling, Floating, Flying/Ultimate Straightness (12") 40
96 Utmostfear UTMOST 1302 — Curley And Ramon/Mad Strings (12") 40
97 Crowd Control CROWD 006 — Mayhem/Purdey's Effect/In The Hills (12", as Esoterik) 80
98 Utmostfear UTMOST 1303 — Untitled/Untitled (12", label bears legend "Curley Truly Unique 1973-1998") ... 40
(See also Spiral Tribe)

ESOTERIC (2)
11 Aesthetic Death ADLP 003 — EPISTEMOLOGICAL DESPONDENCY (2-LP, reissue of 1994 CD release, numbered gatefold sleeve, insert, 350 only) 25

ESP
89 Radical DJ INT 14 — It's You (12", p/s) 40

ESPERANTO ROCK ORCHESTRA
73 A&M AMLH 68175 — ESPERANTO ROCK ORCHESTRA (LP, gatefold sleeve, brown label) 20
74 A&M AMLH 63624 — DANSE MACABRE (LP, as Esperanto, silver/gold labels) 15
75 A&M AMLS 68294 — LAST TANGO (LP, as Esperanto, silver/brown labels) 20
(see also Keith Christmas, Comus)

ESPERS
05 Wichita WEBB084LP — ESPERS (LP) 60

ESPRIT DE CORPS (1)
73 Jam JAM 24 — If (Would It Turn Out Wrong)/Picture On The Wall 15
73 Jam JAM 32 — Lonely/Do You Remember Me (Like I Remember You) 10
(see also David Ballantyne, Just Plain Smith, Just Plain Jones)

ESPRIT DE CORPS (2)
81 Come COME 1 — Anxiety/The Tea Cup Song (hand-made silk-screened sleeve) 30

ESQUERITA
58 Capitol CL 14938 — Rockin' The Joint/Esquerita And The Voola 100
72 Specialty SPE 6603 — WILDCAT SHAKEOUT (LP) 30

ESQUIRES
67 Stateside SS 2048 — Get On Up/Listen To Me 20
68 Stateside SS 2077 — And Get Away/Everybody's Laughing 20
73 Action ACT 4618 — My Sweet Baby/Henry Ralph 50
68 London HA-Q/SH-Q 8356 — GET ON UP AND GET AWAY (LP) 40

ESQUIVEL
63 Reprise R 6046 — MORE OF OTHER WORLDS, OTHER SOUNDS (LP) 15

ESSENTIAL LOGIC
78 Cells SELL ONE — Aerosol Burns/World Friction (p/s) 8

ESSER
MINT VALUE £

79	Rough Trade RT29	Popcorn Boy/Flora Force (p/s)	12
80	Rough Trade RT50	Eugene/Tame The Neighbours (p/s)	10
81	Rough Trade RT74	Fanfare In The Garden/The Captain (p/s)	7
79	Rough Trade ROUGH 5	BEAT RHYTHM NEWS (LP)	20

(see also X-Ray Spex, Lora Logic)

ESSER
| 09 | Transgressive TRANS094X | BRAVEFACE (LP, 300 only, numbered) | 30 |

ESSEX
63	Columbia DB 7077	Easier Said Than Done/Are You Going My Way	15
63	Columbia DB 7122	A Walkin' Miracle/What I Don't Know Won't Hurt Me (with Anita Humes)	20
63	Columbia DB 7178	She's Got Everything/Out Of Sight, Out Of Mind	20
63	Columbia 33SX 1593	EASIER SAID THAN DONE (LP)	50
64	Columbia 33SX 1613	A WALKIN' MIRACLE (LP)	50

DAVID ESSEX
65	Fontana TF 559	And The Tears Came Tumbling Down/You Can't Stop Me Loving You	50
65	Fontana TF 620	Can't Nobody Love You/Baby I Don't Mind	45
66	Fontana TF 680	This Little Girl Of Mine/Brokenhearted	45
66	Fontana TF 733	Thigh High/De Boom Lay Boom	40
68	Uni UN 502	Love Story/Higher Than High	20
68	Pye 7N 17621	Just For Tonight/Goodbye	20
69	Decca F 12935	That Takes Me Back/Lost Without Linda	40
69	Decca F 12967	The Day The Earth Stood Still/Is It So Strange?	30
79	Vertigo 6059 233	M.O.D./M.O.D. (2) (as M.O.D., songwriting credited to D. Cook, p/s, allegedly mispressed on 2-Tone label)	75
79	Vertigo 6059 233	M.O.D./M.O.D. (2) (as M.O.D., songwriting credited to D. Cook, p/s)	7

(see also David & Rozaa, Us)

ESSJAY
| 71 | DJM DJS 254 | Twins Of Evil/Fastback | 35 |

ASTON ESSON
| 80 | Studio 16 STD 01 | Woman Of My Dreams/Version (12") | 30 |

NEVILLE ESSON
| 61 | Blue Beat BB 37 | Lover's Jive/Wicked And Dreadful (with Clue J. & His Blues Busters) | 18 |

ESTABLISHMENT
| 81 | Foetain | BAD CATHOLICS (LP) | 30 |

(see also Cromwell)

'SLEEPY' JOHN ESTES
66	Delmark DJB 3	SLEEPY JOHN'S GOT THE BLUES (EP)	40
63	Esquire 32-195	THE LEGEND OF SLEEPY JOHN ESTES (LP)	60
63	'77' LA 12-27	TENNESSEE JUG BUSTERS — BROKE AND HUNGRY (LP)	40
65	Storyville SLP 172	PORTRAITS IN BLUES VOLUME 10 (LP)	22
72	Delmark DS 619	ELECTRIC SLEEP (LP)	20
71	Delmark DS 613	BROWNSVILLE BLUES (LP)	25

JOHN ESTES/FURRY LEWIS/WILL SHADE
| 71 | Revival RVS 1008 | OLD ORIGINAL TENNESSEE BLUES (LP) | 20 |

JACKIE ESTREK
61	Blue Beat BB 64	Boss Girl/COUNT OSSIE & GROUP: Cassavubu	30
63	Island WI 042	Since You've Been Gone/Daisy I Love You	15
66	Ska Beat JB 256	The Ska/Daisy I Love You	18

ETCETERAS
| 64 | Oriole CB 1950 | Where Is My Love/Bengawan Solo | 15 |
| 64 | Oriole CB 1973 | Little Lady/Now I Know | 20 |

ETERNAL
| 90 | Sarah SARAH 031 | Sleep/Breathe/Take Me Down (p/s) | 30 |

(see also Slowdive)

ETERNAL BASS
| 93 | Volatile VILE 003 | Way Of The Future/Deep Sensation (12") | 40 |

ETERNALS (JAMAICA)
69	Coxsone CS 7091	Queen Of The Minstrels/Stars	60
71	Moodisc MU 3507	Push Me In The Corner/MUDIE'S ALL STARS: Mudie's Madness (B-side actually by Ansell Collins)	35
71	Moodisc MU 3508	Keep On Dancing/HAZEL WRIGHT: My Jealous Eyes	30

(see also Don Cornel & Eternals, Cornel Campbell)

ETERNALS (U.S.)
59	London HL 8995	Rockin' In The Jungle/Rock 'N' Roll Cha-Cha (triangular centre)	150
59	London HL 8995	Rockin' In The Jungle/Rock 'N' Roll Cha-Cha (round centre)	50
59	London HL 8995	Rockin' In The Jungle/Rock 'N' Roll Cha-Cha (78)	35

ETERNAL SCREAM
| 81 | Eternal 01 | Hypocrite/Action In My Life (p/s) | 15 |
| 81 | Eternal 02 | How I Wish/Child (p/s) | 20 |

ETERNAL TRIANGLE
| 69 | Decca F 12979 | I Guess The Lord Must Be In New York City/Perfumed Candle | 6 |
| 69 | Decca F 12954 | Turn To Me/Window | 7 |

ETERNITY'S CHILDREN
| 68 | Capitol CL 15558 | Mrs Bluebird/Little Boy | 25 |

ETHEL THE FROG
80	Best SRTSFMR 014	Eleanor Rigby/Whatever Happened To Love	60
80	EMI EMI 5041	Eleanor Rigby/Fight Back (reissue)	10
80	EMI EMC 3329	ETHEL THE FROG (LP, with Terry Hopkinson & Doug Sheppard)	22

ETHIOPIAN IRATION BLOOD RELATIVE & IDREN
| 79 | Greensleeves GRED 21 | This Foundation/Elders and Deacons/How Can A Man/Jah Children Come (12") | 40 |

ETHIOPIANS

			MINT VALUE £
ETHIOPIANS			
66	Coxsone DIR 2003	Let The Light Shine/Let's Get Together (white labels only)	200
66	Ska Beat JB 260	Live Good (credited to the Etheopians)/SOUL BROTHERS: Soho	70
66	Island WI 3015	I Am Free/SOUL BROTHERS: Shanty Town	70
67	Rio R 110	Owe Me No Pay Me/SHARKS: I Wouldn't Baby	30
67	Rio R 114	I'm Gonna Take Over Now/JACKIE MITTOO: Home Made	70
67	Rio R 123	What To Do/JACKIE MITTOO: Got My Bugaloo	225
67	Rio R 126	Dun Dead A'Ready/BOB ANDY: Stay In My Lonely Arms	60
67	Rio R 130	Train To Skaville/You Are The Girl (B-side actually by Gladiators)	30
67	Doctor Bird DB 1092	I Need You/Do It Sweet	100
67	Doctor Bird DB 1096	The Whip/Cool It, Amigo	25
67	Doctor Bird DB 1103	Stay Loose, Mama/The World Goes Ska	50
68	Doctor Bird DB 1141	Come On Now/Sh'Boom	45
68	Doctor Bird DB 1147	Engine 54/Give Me Your Love	150
68	Doctor Bird DB 1148	Train To Glory/You Got The Dough	75
68	Doctor Bird DB 1169	Everything Crash/I'm Not Losing You	22
68	Crab CRAB 2	Fire A Muss Tail/Blacker Black (B-side actually by Count Ossie)	45
68	Crab CRAB 5	Reggie Hit The Town/Ding Dong Bell	40
69	Crab CRAB 7	I Am A King/What A Big Surprise	50
69	Doctor Bird DB 1172	Not Me/Cut Down	200
69	J J Records DB 1185	Hong Kong Flu/Clap Your Hands	18
69	J J Records DB 1186	What A Fire/You	20
69	Doctor Bird DB 1199	Everyday Talking/Sharing You	25
69	Trojan TR 666	Woman Capture Man/One	20
69	Trojan TR 697	Well Red/J.J. ALLSTARS: R.F.K.	30
69	Nu Beat NB 031	My Testimony (credited to the Maytals)/J.J. ALL STARS: One Dollar Of Soul	30
69	Nu Beat NB 038	Buss Your Mouth/GLEN ADAMS (Actually REGGAE BOYS) Rough Way Ahead	60
69	Duke DU 35	My Girl/ANSELL COLLINS: Bigger Boss	60
70	Duke DU 61	Mek You Go On So/WINSTON WRIGHT & J.J. ALL STARS: Neck Tie	50
70	Duke Reid DR 2507	Mother's Tender Care/TOMMY McCOOK: Soldier Man	15
70	Bamboo BAM 26	Walkie Talkie/SOUND DIMENSION: Moan And Groan	25
70	Bamboo BAM 38	You'll Want To Come Back/JACKIE MITTOO: Baby Why (Instrumental) (B-side actually by Sound Dimension)	35
70	J.J. JJ 3302	Wreck It Up/Don't Go	90
70	J.J. JJ 3303	Hong Kong Flu/Everything Crash	20
70	Gas GAS 142	Satan Girl/MATADORS: The Pum	8
70	High Note HS 042	Praise For I (actually "Praise Fari")/GAYTONES: Charrie Part II	12
70	Songbird SB 1040	No Baptism/CRYSTALITES: No Baptism (Version Two)	15
70	Songbird SB 1047	Good Ambition/CRYSTALITES: Ambition Version	10
71	Randy's RAN 509	Mi Want Girl/RANDY'S ALL STARS: Girl — Version	10
71	Randy's RAN 510	True Man, Free Man/RANDY'S ALL STARS: Truthful — Version	10
71	Randy's RAN 512	Mr. Tom/Sad News	10
71	Fab FAB 180	Monkey Money/Version	20
71	Treasure Isle TI 7067	Pirate/TOMMY McCOOK & SOUL SYNDICATE: Depth Charge	10
71	Songbird SB 1059	What A Pain/CRYSTALITES: Pain Version	12
71	Songbird SB 1062	Lot's Wife/DERRICK HARRIOTT: Slave	12
71	Songbird SB 1064	Best Of Five (Parts 1 & 2)	12
71	Big Shot BI 569	He's Not A Rebel/J.J. ALL STARS: He's Not A Rebel — Version	15
71	Big Shot BI 574	The Selah/Don't Let Me Go	18
71	Duke DU 102	Drop Him/J.J. ALL STARS: Drop Him Version	15
71	Duke DU 108	Rim Bim Bam/RANDY'S ALL STARS: Rim Bim Bam Version	10
71	Explosion EX 2050	Starvation/TROJAN ALL STARS: Starvation Version	10
71	G.G. GG 4519	Love Bug/Sound Of Our Forefathers	10
71	Supreme SUP 221	Love Bug/Sound Of Our Forefathers	12
71	Supreme SUP 226	Starvation/MAXIE & GLEN: Jordan River	15
71	Big BG 330	Solid As A Rock/RUPIE EDWARDS ALL STARS: Solid As A Rock Version	6
71	Punch PH 96	Solid As A Rock/RUPIE EDWARDS ALL STARS: Solid As A Rock Version	6
72	G.G. GG 4533	Israel Want To be Free/TYPHOON ALL STARS: Israel (Version)	15
72	Prince Buster PB 38	You Are For Me/Playboy	20
72	Techniques TE 919	Promises/TIVOLIS: Promises — Version	6
73	Harry J. HJ 6646	The Word Is Love/The Word Is Love — Version	10
74	Cactus CT 37	Better Man/Skanking Man	10
74	Cactus CT 46	Conquering Lion/Lion Head	8
75	Tropical ALO54	Another Moses/Moses	10
76	Attack ATT 8131	Another Moses/SYLFORD WALKER: I Can't Understand	15
78	Sensation SSD015	Hail Rasta/Version (12")	15
78	Treasure Isle TRE 010	The Whip/Cool It, Omigo/BOBBY ELLIS: Shank I Sheck (12")	15
86	Trojan TROT 9085	Pirate/Version (12")	10
11	Smash THB 7012	I'm Shocking/Sign The Cheque	20
68	Doctor Bird DLM 5001	THE ETHIOPIANS GO ROCK STEADY/ENGINE 54 (LP, this is a UK pressing in a Jamaican sleeve)	400
69	Trojan TTL 10	REGGAE POWER (LP)	75
70	Trojan TBL 112	WOMAN CAPTURE MAN (LP)	80
77	Third World TWS 15	SLAVE CALL (LP)	35
86	Trojan TRLS 228	ORIGINAL REGGAE HITSOUND (LP)	20
92	Trojan TRLS 312	THE WORLD GOES SKA (LP)	15

(see Eathopians, Soul Brothers, Soul Vendors, Hamliins)

ETHNIC FIGHT BAND

75	Ethnic Fight EF 4416	OUT OF ONE MAN COMES MANY DUBS (LP)	80
77	Ethnic Fight EF 4444	MUSIC EXPLOSION DUB (LP)	100

ETIVES
MINT VALUE £

ETIVES
81	Ayrespin AYRC 106	A BREATH OF FRESH AIR (LP)	20
84	Ayrespin AYRC 015	AN GAOL A THUG MI OG (MY LOVE OF EARLY DAYS) (LP)	20

ETTA (JAMES) & HARVEY (FUQUA)
60	London HLM 9180	If I Can't Have You/My Heart Cries	50

(see also Etta James, Moonglows, Harvey & Moonglows)

E-TYPES
83	Banana 507	Don't Wanna Do Those Things	6

JACK EUBANK'S ORCHESTRA
61	London HLU 9312	What'd I Say/Chiricahua	10

EUGENE & BURST
71	Supreme SUP 225	Let It Fall/DENZIL & BURST: Can't Change	6

EUGENIUS
92	Paperhouse PAPLP 011	OOMALAMA (LP)	15
94	August Rust 008	MARY QUEEN OF SCOTS (LP)	15

(see also Teenage Fanclub)

EUROPEAN TOYS
83	SUBVERSIVE SUB 008	I Am The Creator/Keep It All/So Look At Me Now (p/s)	10
84	Backs 12NCH 009	KOREA EP (12")	15

EURYTHMICS
81	RCA RCAT 68	Never Gonna Cry Again (Extended)/Le Sinistre (Extended) (12", p/s)	15
81	RCA RCA 115	Belinda/Heartbeat, Heartbeat (p/s)	10
82	RCA RCA 199	This Is The House/Home Is Where The Heart Is (p/s)	10
82	RCA RCAT 199	This Is The House/Your Time Will Come (live)/Never Gonna Cry Again/4/4 In Leather (live)/Take Me To Your Heart (live) (12", p/s)	25
82	RCA RCA 230	The Walk/Step On The Beast/The Walk (Part 2) (p/s)	10
82	RCA RCAT 230	The Walk/Invisible Hands/Dr Trash/The Walk (Part 2) (12", printed die-cut sleeve)	25
83	RCA DA 4/EUC 001	Right By Your Side/Right By Your Side (Party Mix) (stickered p/s with free shrinkwrapped (RCA EUC 001)	25
84	RCA PLP 70109	TOUCH (LP, picture disc)	20

(see also ACatch, Tourists, Chris & Cosey, Stewart & Harrison, Vegas)

JOHN EVAN BAND
90	A New Day NRS/CD 1	THE JOHN EVAN BAND LIVE '66 (CD, 500 only)	30

(see also Jethro Tull)

ADRIANA EVANS
97	RCA 07863 66958-1	ADRIANA EVANS (2-LP)	25

BARBARA EVANS
59	RCA RCA 1122	Souvenirs/Pray For Me, Mother (triangular centre)	25
61	Mercury AMT 1151	Charlie Wasn't There/Nothing You Can Do	7

BILL EVANS
59	Fontana FJL 104	DIG IT (LP)	20
59	Riverside 12-315	PORTRAIT IN JAZZ (LP)	150
60	Riverside 291	EVERYBODY DIGS BILL EVANS (LP)	150
61	Riverside RLP 9399	WALTZ FOR DEBBY (LP)	200
61	Riverside RLP 351	EXPLORATIONS (LP)	100
61	Riverside RLP 376	SUNDAY AT THE VILLAGE VANGUARD (LP)	80
62	Riverside RLP 428	MOONBEAMS (LP)	80
63	Verve VLP 9054	CONVERSATIONS WITH MYSELF (LP)	40
64	Riverside RLP 473	HOW MY HEART SINGS (LP)	50
67	Verve VLP 9161	A SIMPLE MATTER OF CONVICTION (LP)	30
64	Verve VLP 9077	TRIO 64 (LP)	50

BRIAN EVANS
71	CBS 5392	We're Going Wrong/Paradise Lost	50
71	CBS 7293	This Is My Woman/If You Still Want Me (as Bryan Evans)	10

BRYAN EVANS
72	Columbia DB 8911	Turnaround Sunday/Re-United	8

CHRISTINE EVANS
66	Philips BF 1496	Somewhere There's Love/Right Or Wrong	6
67	Melodisc MEL 1620	I'm Gonna Tell Tony/Someone In Love	10

DAVE EVANS
71	Village Thing VTS 6	THE WORDS IN BETWEEN (LP)	40
72	Village Thing VTS 14	ELEPHANTASIA (LP)	45
74	Kicking Mule SNKF 107	SAD PIG DANCE (LP, with booklet)	20
76	Kicking Mule SNKF 122	TAKE A BITE OUT OF LIFE (LP)	18

GIL EVANS ORCHESTRA
60	Vogue LAE 12234	GREAT JAZZ STANDARDS (LP)	20
61	HMV CLP 1456	OUT OF THE COOL (LP)	20

JOHN EVANS
62	Palette PG 9040	Melodie Pour Madame/Cry Me A River	10

LARRY EVANS
56	London HLU 8269	Crazy 'Bout My Baby/Henpecked	750
56	London HLU 8269	Crazy 'Bout My Baby/Henpecked (78)	75

MAUREEN EVANS
58	Embassy WB 300	Carolina Moon/Stupid Cupid	10
58	Embassy WB 303	Fever/Born Too Late	10
58	Embassy WB 309	The Hula Hoop Song/Hoopa Hoola	6
58	Embassy WB 313	I'll Get By/Someday (You'll Want Me To Want You)	6
58	Embassy WB 316	The Day The Rains Came/You Always Hurt The One You Love	6
58	Embassy WB 319	To Know Him Is To Love Him/Kiss Me, Honey Honey, Kiss Me	10
59	Embassy WB 344	Goodbye Jimmy, Goodbye/May You Always	6
59	Embassy WB 348	Lipstick On Your Collar/What A Diff'rence A Day Made	10

Mill EVANS

MINT VALUE £

59	Embassy WB 356	Broken-Hearted Melody/Plenty Good Lovin'	6
59	Embassy WB 371	Among My Souvenirs/Happy Anniversary	10
59	Oriole CB 1517	Don't Want The Moonlight/The Years Between	6
60	Oriole CB 1533	The Big Hurt/I Can't Begin To Tell You	10
60	Oriole CB 1540	Love, Kisses And Heartaches/We Just Couldn't Say Goodbye	10
60	Oriole CB 1550	Paper Roses/Please Understand	10
61	Oriole CB 1563	Mama Wouldn't Like It/My Little Corner Of The World	8
61	Oriole CB 1578	As Long As He Needs Me/Where Is Love?	8
61	Oriole CB 1581	Till/Why Don't You Believe Me	8
61	Oriole CB 1613	My Foolish Heart/Oh Gypsy Oh Gypsy	8
62	Oriole CB 1743	Never In A Million Years/We Had Words	10
63	Oriole CB 1804	Pick The Petals/Melancholy Me	8
63	Oriole CB 1806	Tomorrow Is Another Day/Acapulco Mexico	10
63	Oriole CB 1875	Like You Used To Do/As You Love Her	7
64	Oriole CB 1906	I Love How You Love Me/John John	8
64	Oriole CB 1939	He Knows I Love Him Too Much/Don't Believe Him	8
64	Oriole CB 1969	Get Away/I've Often Wondered	10
65	CBS 201733	All The Angels Sing/Speak Sugar Speak	8
65	CBS 201752	Never Let Him Go/Poco Sole	12
67	CBS 202621	Somewhere There's Love/It Takes A Little Time	8
67	CBS 3222	I Almost Called Your Name/Searching For Home (Demo copy)	50
68	CBS 3222	I Almost Called Your Name/Searching For Home	40
63	Oriole EP 7076	MELANCHOLY ME (EP)	30
63	Oriole PS 40046	LIKE I DO (LP)	30

(see also Matt Bryant & Linda Joyce)

MILL EVANS
01	Kent 6T 17	Ain't You Glad/MILLIONAIRES: I'm The One Who Loves You	20

PAUL EVANS (& CURLS)
59	London HLL 8968	Seven Little Girls Sitting In The Back Seat/Worshipping An Idol (with Curls)	6
60	London HLL 9045	Midnite Special/Since I Met You, Baby	30
60	London HLL 9129	Happy-Go-Lucky Me/Fish In The Ocean	7
60	London HLL 9183	Brigade Of Broken Hearts/Twins	7
60	London HLL 9239	Hushabye Little Guitar/Blind Boy	20
62	London HLR 9636	The Bell That Couldn't Jingle/Gilding The Lily	6
63	London HLR 9770	Even Tan/Ten Thousand Years	6
63	London RE-R 1349	PAUL EVANS (EP)	40
60	London HA-L 2248	PAUL EVANS SINGS THE FABULOUS TEENS (LP)	100

RICHARD EVANS
78	A&M AMSP 7438	Burning Spear/Do Re Me For Soul	10
78	AMS 7438	Burning Spear/Do Re Me For Soul (12")	20

ROGER EVANS & SWANSEA CITY FOOTBALL CLUB
79	Rotor Pro 001	Swansea City/The Ballad Of Swansea Jack	8

RUSSELL EVANS & NITEHAWKS
66	Atlantic 584 010	Send Me Some Cornbread/The Bold	30

TONY EVANS BAND
71	Polydor 2058 101	Hot Pants/Beach Bird	15

VIC EVANS & THE HASTINGS
64	Airborne NBP 006	Caribbean Child/Hurry Along Belinda	20

EVEN AS WE SPEAK
90	Sarah SARAH 37	Nothing Ever Happens/Blue Suburban Skies/Bizarre Love Triangle/ Goes So Slow/A Stranger Calls (p/s, insert)	15
91	Sarah SARAH 49	One Step Forward/Must Be Something Else/Best Kept Secret (p/s, insert)	15
91	Sarah SARAH 59	Beautiful Day/Nothing Much At All (p/s, insert)	15
93	Sarah SARAH 79	(All You Find Is) Air/Getting Faster/Blue Eyes Deceiving Me (p/s, insert)	15
93	Sarah SARAH 614	FERAL POP FRENZY (LP)	40

EVEN DOZEN JUG BAND
66	Bounty BY 6023	THE EVEN DOZEN JUG BAND (LP)	25

(see also Lovin' Spoonful, John Sebastian)

EVENING OUTS
80	Refill RR5	Channel/Stammer (no p/s, hand stamped labels)	100

EVENSONG
73	Philips 6006 276	I Was Her Cowboy/Gypsy	15

EVER RED
88	Supertone STR 007	Dem No Ruff Like We/Hot Number (12")	40

BETTY EVERETT
64	Stateside SS 259	You're No Good/Chained To Your Love	20
64	Stateside SS 280	It's In His Kiss (The Shoop Shoop Song)/Hands Off	20
64	Stateside SS 321	I Can't Hear You/Can I Get To Know You	25
64	Fontana TF 520	Getting Mighty Crowded/Chained To A Memory	20
64	King KG 1002	Happy I Long To Be/Your Loving Arms	20
65	Sue WI 352	I've Got A Claim On You/Your Love Is Important To Me	60
68	President PT 215	It's In His Kiss (The Shoop Shoop Song)/Getting Mighty Crowded	8
69	President PT 251	You're No Good/Hands Off	8
69	MCA Soul Bag BAG 3	I Can't Say No To You/Better Tomorrow Than Today	10
69	MCA MU 1055	There'll Come A Time/Take Me	8
70	Uni UN 517	Sugar/Hold On	8
71	Liberty LBF 15428	I Got To Tell Somebody/Why Are You Leaving Me	15
72	President PT 372	Trouble Over The Weekend/The Shoe Doesn't Fit	10
65	Fontana TL 5236	IT'S IN HIS KISS (LP)	60
68	Joy JOYS 106	IT'S IN HIS KISS (LP, reissue)	15

Betty EVERETT & JERRY BUTLER

MINT VALUE £

| 69 | Uni UNLS 109 | THERE'LL COME A TIME (LP) | 25 |

BETTY EVERETT & JERRY BUTLER
64	Stateside SS 339	Let It Be Me/Ain't That Lovin' You Baby	10
65	Fontana TF 528	Smile/Love Is Strange	8
68	President PT 214	Let It Be Me/Smile	8
69	President PT 252	Our Day Will Come/Just Be True	6
65	Fontana TL 5237	DELICIOUS TOGETHER (LP)	50

(see also Jerry Butler)

KENNY EVERETT
| 68 | MGM 1421 | It's Been So Long/Without Her | 10 |
| 69 | Deram DM 245 | And Now For A Little Train Number/Nice Time | 8 |

ROY EVERETT
| 70 | Parlophone R 5857 | Turn On You Own Heat/Look At That Old Bird | 10 |

VINCE EVERETT
65	Fontana TF 606	Bless You/'Til I Lost You	10
67	Fontana TF 818	Endlessly/Who's That Girl?	10
68	Fontana TF 915	Every Now And Then/Barbarella	10

EVERGREEN BLUES
67	Mercury MF 1012	Midnight Confessions/(Yes) That's My Baby	10
68	Mercury MF 1025	Laura (Keep Hangin' On)/Yesterday's Coming	6
68	Mercury 20122 SMCL	7 DO ELEVEN (LP)	20

EVERGREEN BLUESHOES
| 69 | London HA-U/SH-U 8399 | THE BALLAD OF THE EVERGREEN BLUESHOES (LP) | 20 |

(see also Skip Battin, Byrds)

EVERLY BROTHERS

78s
59	London HLA 8863	Poor Jenny/Take A Message To Mary	20
59	London HLA 8934	('Til) I Kissed You/Oh, What A Feeling	30
60	London HLA 9039	Let It Be Me/Since You Broke My Heart	60
60	Warner Bros WB 1	Cathy's Clown/Always It's You	100
60	London HLA 9157	When Will I Be Loved/Be-Bop-A-Lula	60
60	Warner Bros WB 19	Lucille/So Sad (To Watch Good Love Go Bad)	200

SINGLES
57	London HLA 8440	Bye Bye, Love/I Wonder If I Care As Much (triangular centre)	10
57	London HLA 8498	Wake Up Little Susie/Maybe Tomorrow (triangular centre)	10
58	London HLA 8554	Should We Tell Him/This Little Girl Of Mine (triangular centre)	20
60	London HLA 9039	Let It Be Me/Since You Broke My Heart (triangular centre)	10
61	Warner Bros WB 50	Muskrat/Don't Blame Me	6
63	Warner Bros WB 99	It's Been Nice/I'm Afraid	7
63	Warner Bros WB 109	The Girl Sang The Blues/Love Her	6
64	Warner Bros WB 129	Ain't That Lovin' You Baby/Hello Amy	7
64	Warner Bros WB 135	The Ferris Wheel/Don't Forget To Cry	6
64	Warner Bros WB 143	You're The One I Love/Ring Around My Rosie (withdrawn)	20
64	Warner Bros WB 146	Gone, Gone, Gone/Torture	6
65	Warner Bros WB 154	You're My Girl/Don't Let The Whole World Know	6
65	Warner Bros WB 158	That'll Be The Day/Give Me A Sweetheart	6
65	Warner Bros WB 5628	The Price Of Love/It Only Costs A Dime (reissue)	7
65	Warner Bros WB 5639	I'll Never Get Over You/Follow Me	8
65	Warner Bros WB 5649	Love Is Strange/Man With Money	7
66	Warner Bros WB 5682	It's All Over/I Used To Love You (unissued)	0
66	Warner Bros WB 5743	(You Got) The Power Of Love/Leave My Girl Alone	10
66	Warner Bros WB 5754	I've Been Wrong Before/Hard Hard Year	10
67	Warner Bros WB 7520	Bowling Green/I Don't Want To Love You	10
67	Warner Bros WB 7062	Mary Jane/Talking To The Flowers	10
67	Warner Bros WB 7088	Love Of The Common People/A Voice Within	10
68	Warner Bros WB 7192	It's My Time/Empty Boxes	10
68	Warner Bros WB 7226	Milk Train/Lord Of The Manor	10
70	Warner Bros WB 6074	Good Golly, Miss Molly/Oh, Boy!	8
70	Warner Bros WB 7425	Yves/Human Race	15
72	RCA Victor RCA 2232	Ridin' High/Stories We Could Tell	10
73	RCA Victor RCA 2286	Not Fade Away/Lay It Down	7

EPs
58	London RE-A 1113	THE EVERLY BROTHERS	15
58	London RE-A 1148	THE EVERLY BROTHERS — NO. 2	15
58	London RE-A 1149	THE EVERLY BROTHERS — NO. 3	15
59	London RE-A 1174	THE EVERLY BROTHERS — NO. 4	15
59	London RE-A 1195	SONGS OUR DADDY TAUGHT US PART 1	15
59	London RE-A 1196	SONGS OUR DADDY TAUGHT US PART 2	15
59	London RE-A 1197	SONGS OUR DADDY TAUGHT US PART 3	15
60	London RE-A 1229	THE EVERLY BROTHERS — NO. 5	15

(The above EPs were originally issued with triangular centres, later round-centre editions are worth half to two-thirds of these values.)

61	Warners WEP 6034	ESPECIALLY FOR YOU (mono)	20
61	Warners W(S)EP 6034	ESPECIALLY FOR YOU (stereo)	20
61	London RE-A 1311	THE EVERLY BROTHERS — NO. 6	15
62	Warners WEP 6049	FOREVERLY YOURS (mono)	15
62	Warners W(S)EP 6049	FOREVERLY YOURS (stereo)	15
62	Warners WEP 6056	IT'S EVERLY TIME (mono)	15
62	Warners W(S)EP 6056	IT'S EVERLY TIME (stereo)	15
63	Warners WEP 6107	A DATE WITH THE EVERLY BROTHERS VOL. 1 (mono)	15

EVERREADY'S

MINT VALUE £

63	Warners W(S)EP 6107	A DATE WITH THE EVERLY BROTHERS VOL. 1 (stereo)	15
63	Warners WEP 6109	A DATE WITH THE EVERLY BROTHERS VOL. 2 (mono)	15
63	Warners W(S)EP 6109	A DATE WITH THE EVERLY BROTHERS VOL. 2 (stereo)	18
63	Warners WEP 6111	INSTANT PARTY VOL. 1 (mono)	15
63	Warners W(S)EP 6111	INSTANT PARTY VOL. 1 (stereo)	20
63	Warners WEP 6113	INSTANT PARTY VOL. 2 (mono)	15
63	Warners W(S)EP 6113	INSTANT PARTY VOL. 2 (stereo)	20
63	Warners WEP 6115	BOTH SIDES OF AN EVENING — FOR DANCING VOL. 1 (mono)	15
63	Warners W(S)EP 6115	BOTH SIDES OF AN EVENING — FOR DANCING VOL. 1 (stereo)	18
64	Warners WEP 6117	BOTH SIDES OF AN EVENING — FOR DREAMING VOL. 2 (mono)	15
64	Warners W(S)EP 6117	BOTH SIDES OF AN EVENING — FOR DREAMING VOL. 2 (stereo)	18
64	Warners WEP 6128	THE EVERLY BROTHERS SING GREAT COUNTRY HITS VOL. 1	15
64	Warners WEP 6131	THE EVERLY BROTHERS SING GREAT COUNTRY HITS VOL. 2	15
64	Warners WEP 6132	THE EVERLY BROTHERS SING GREAT COUNTRY HITS VOL. 3	15
65	Warner Bros WEP 6138	BOTH SIDES OF AN EVENING — FOR FUN VOL. 3	12
65	Warner Bros WEP 604	THE PRICE OF LOVE	10
65	Warner Bros WEP 608	ROCK'N'SOUL VOL. 1	15
65	Warner Bros WEP 609	ROCK'N'SOUL VOL. 2	15
66	Warner Bros WEP 610	LOVE IS STRANGE	15
66	Warner Bros WEP 612	PEOPLE GET READY	15
66	Warner Bros WEP 618	WHAT AM I LIVING FOR?	20
67	Warner Bros WEP 622	LEAVE MY GIRL ALONE	20
67	Warner Bros WEP 623	SOMEBODY HELP ME	20

ALBUMS

58	London HA-A 2081	THE EVERLY BROTHERS	40
58	London HA-A 2150	SONGS OUR DADDY TAUGHT US	30
60	Warner Bros WM 4012	IT'S EVERLY TIME (Mono)	30
60	Warner Bros WS 8012	IT'S EVERLY TIME (Stereo)	30
60	London HA-A 2266	THE FABULOUS STYLE OF THE EVERLY BROTHERS	30
60	Warner Bros WM 4028	A DATE WITH THE EVERLY BROTHERS (mono)	30
60	Warner Bros WS 8028	A DATE WITH THE EVERLY BROTHERS (stereo)	35
61	Warner Bros WM 4052	BOTH SIDES OF AN EVENING (Mono)	20
61	Warner Bros WS 8052	BOTH SIDES OF AN EVENING (stereo)	25
62	Warner Bros WM 4061	INSTANT PARTY (also stereo WS 8061)	20
62	Warner Bros WM 4061	INSTANT PARTY (also stereo WS 8061)	25
62	Warner Bros WM 8116	CHRISTMAS WITH THE EVERLY BROTHERS AND THE BOYS TOWN CHOIR (mono)	20
62	Warner Bros WS 8116	CHRISTMAS WITH THE EVERLY BROTHERS AND THE BOYS TOWN CHOIR (stereo)	25
63	Warner Bros WM 8138	SING GREAT COUNTRY HITS (mono)	20
63	Warner Bros WS 8138	SING GREAT COUNTRY HITS (stereo)	25
65	Warner Bros WM 8169	GONE GONE GONE (mono)	20
65	Warner Bros WS 8169	GONE GONE GONE (stereo)	25
65	Warner Bros WM 8171	ROCK 'N' SOUL (mono)	20
65	Warner Bros WS 8171	ROCK 'N' SOUL (stereo)	25
65	Warner Bros W(S) 1605	BEAT 'N' SOUL	15
65	Warner Bros W 1620	IN OUR IMAGE (mono)	15
65	Warner Bros W(S) 1620	IN OUR IMAGE (stereo)	18

EVERREADY'S
| 80 | Taaga TAG 3 | Don't Do It Again/Martian Girl (gatefold p/s) | 15 |

LENNY EVERSONG
| 57 | Vogue Coral Q 72255 | Jezebel/Jealousy | 6 |

EVERVESSENCE
| 69 | Priory 02 | Strange One/My Illusive Life | 50 |

EVERYBODY
| 70 | Page One POF 163 | The Shape Of Things To Come/Do Like The Little Children Do | 15 |

EVERY MOTHER'S SON
67	MGM MGM 1341	Come And Take A Ride In My Boat/I Believe In You	25
67	MGM MGM 1350	Put Your Mind At Ease/Proper Four Leaf Clover	25
67	MGM MGM 1372	Pony With The Golden Mane/Dolls In The Clock	10
67	MGM C(S) 8044	EVERY MOTHER'S SON (LP)	40
68	MGM C(S) 8061	EVERY MOTHER'S SON'S BACK (LP)	35

EVERYONE
| 71 | B&C CAS 1028 | EVERYONE (LP, gatefold sleeve, attached envelope with booklet) | 50 |

(see also Andy Roberts)

EVERYONE ELSE
| 79 | Woodbine St WSR 001 | Schooldays/Brainwashed/Out Of My Mind/Don't Call Us (p/s) | 100 |

EVERYONE INVOLVED
| 72 | Arcturus ARC 3 | The Circus Keeps On Turning/Motor Car Madness | 30 |
| 72 | Arcturus ARC 4 | EITHER OR (LP, private pressing, embossed plain white sleeve with inserts) | 250 |

EVERYTHING BUT THE GIRL
96	Virgin V 2803	WALKING WOUNDED (LP)	80
99	Virgin V 2892	TEMPERAMENTAL (LP)	80
01	DMC BACKLP06	BACK TO MINE (3-LP, compilation - non EBG tracks)	60

(see also Ben Watt, Marine Girls, Tracey Thorn)

EVERYTHING EVERYTHING
08	Saliva TIC 008	Suffragette Suffragette/Luddites & Lambs (with poster)	15
09	Young & Lost YALC 0044	My Keys, Your Boyfriend/Nasa Is On Your Side (12")	12
09	Another AMAK 014	Photoshop Handsome/DNA Dump!	10
10	Gaffe 2743110	Schoolin/Lee Zero Dub	12
10	Gaffe 2748166	My Kz, Yr Bf/Clock Opera Remix)	12

EVERYTHING IS EVERYTHING

MINT VALUE £

11	Polydor 2758306	MAN ALIVE (LP)	80
13	RCA Victor 88725473731	ARC (LP, gatefold with booklet)	40
15	RCA 88875061171	GET TO HEAVEN (LP)	30

EVERYTHING IS EVERYTHING
69	Vanguard VA 1	Witchi Tai To/Oooh Baby	15
68	Vanguard SVRL 19286	EVERYTHING IS EVERYTHING (LP)	25

EVERY WHICH WAY
70	Charisma BD 1	Go Placidly/The Light	12

(see also Brian Davison, Griffin, Heavy Jelly, Skip Bifferty, Graham Bell, Bell & Arc)

EVIL ED
01	YNR YNR4	THE TOURNAMENT ROUND 1 (12", EP stickered black die-cut sleeve)	16
02	Hidden Identity HID1	THE TOURNAMENT ROUND 2 (12" EP)	15

EVOLUTION
90	Positive Vinyl PV 001	Came Outa Nowhere (12")	20
91	Positive Vinyl PV 002	Metropolis (12")	20

EWAN (MCDERMOTT) & DENVER
67	Giant GN 17	I Want You So Bad/ERIC McDERMOTT: I'm Gonna Love You	12

EWAN (MCDERMOTT) & JERRY (MCCARTHY)
67	Blue Beat BB 385	Oh Babe/Dance With Me (with Carib Beats)	18
67	Giant GN 5	The Right Track/We Got To Be One	18
67	Giant GN 10	Rock Steady Train/My Baby Is Gone	40
67	Giant GN 14	Tennessee Waltz/You've Got Something	18

EX
86	Ron Johnson ZRON 11	'1936' THE SPANISH REVOLUTION (double pack with book)	20

EX/ALERTA
84	CNT CNT 017	THE RED DANCE PACKAGE (12", split EP)	15

EXCALIBUR
88	Clay PLATE 1	HOT FOR LOVE (Hot For Love/Early In The Morning/Come On And Rock/Death's Door (12" EP)	15
85	Conquest QUEST 5	THE BITTER END (mini-LP)	20

EXCEL
79	ARSS XL1	If It Rains/Rolling Home/She's One Of The Boys/Rock Show (EP, p/s)	100
80	Polydor POSP 110	What Went Wrong?/Junita (p/s)	8

EXCELS
67	Atlantic 584 133	California On My Mind/The Arrival Of Mary	25

EXCELSIOR SPRING
69	Instant IN 002	Happy Miranda/It	35

EXCEPTIONS
65	Decca F 12100	What More Do You Want?/Soldier Boy	25

(see also Orchids)

EXCEPTION(S)
67	CBS 202632	The Eagle Flies On Friday/Girl Trouble	70
67	CBS 2830	Gaberdine Saturday Night Street Walker/Sunday Night At The Prince Rupert	30
68	President PT 181	Rub It Down/It's Snowing In The Desert	6
68	President PT 205	Helicopter/Back Room	6
68	President PT 218	Tailor Made Babe/Turn Over The Soil	6
69	President PT 236	Jack Rabbit/Keep The Motor Running	8
69	President PT 271	Pendulum/Don't Torture Your Mind	12
69	President PTLS 1026	THE EXCEPTIONAL EXCEPTION (LP, yellow/black labels)	40

(see also Fotheringay, Fairport Convention)

EXCHANGE AND MART
72	President PT 385	Yeah My Friend/I Know That I'm Dreaming	15

EXCHECKERS
64	Decca F 11871	All The World Is Mine/It's All Over	25

(see also Aynsley Dunbar Retaliation)

EXCITER
85	Music For Nations MFN 47	LONG LIVE THE LOUD (LP, inner)	15
86	Music For Nations MFN 61	UNVEILING THE WICKED (LP, with inner)	15

EXCITERS
63	United Artists UP 1011	Tell Him/Hard Way To Go	15
63	United Artists UP 1017	He's Got The Power/Drama Of Love	15
63	United Artists UP 1026	Get Him/It's So Exciting	20
64	United Artists UP 1041	Do-Wah-Diddy/If Love Came Your Way	25
65	Columbia DB 7479	I Want You To Be My Boy/Tonight, Tonight	25
65	Columbia DB 7544	Just Not Ready/Are You Satisfied	20
65	Columbia DB 7606	Run Mascara/My Father	20
66	London HLZ 10018	A Little Bit Of Soap/I'm Gonna Get Him Someday	20
66	London HLZ 10038	You Better Come Home/Weddings Make Me Cry	40
69	United Artists UP 2274	Do Wah Diddy Diddy/Hard Way To Go	10
71	Jay Boy BOY 38	Soul Motion/You Know It Ain't Right	20
74	Contempo CS 2033	Blowing Up My Mind (Vocal)/Blowing Up My Mind (Instrumental)	20
75	20th Century BTC 1005	Reaching For The Best/Keep On Reaching	6
65	United Artists UEP 1005	DO WAH DIDDY DIDDY (EP)	60
64	United Artists ULP 1032	THE EXCITERS (LP)	100

(see also Jerry Allen)

EXCURSION
68	Morgan MX 7001	NIGHT TRAIN (LP)	30
69	Gemini GMX 5029	NIGHT TRAIN (LP, reissue)	18

(see also Jerry Allen)

EXECUTE/INFERNO

MINT VALUE £

EXECUTE/INFERNO
86 Pusmort 0012-06   SPLIT LP 20

EXECUTIVE(S) (1)
64 Columbia DB 7323   March Of The Mods/Why, Why, Why 10
64 Columbia DB 7393   Strictly For The Beat/No Room For Squares 10
65 Columbia DB 7573   It's Been So Long/You're For Me (as Executives) 10
65 Columbia DB 7770   Return Of The Mods/How Sad 10
66 Columbia DB 7919   Lock Your Door/In My Arms (as Executives) 8

EXECUTIVE(S) (2)
67 CBS 202652   Smokey Atmosphere/Sensation 30
67 CBS 3067   Ginza Strip/I'll Always Love You 25
68 CBS 3431   Tracy Took A Trip/Gardena Dreamer (as Executive, with promo only p/s) 40
68 CBS 3431   Tracy Took A Trip/Gardena Dreamer (as Executive) 30
69 CBS 4013   I Ain't Got Nobody/To Kingdom Come (as Executive) 30

EXECUTIVES (3)
80 Attrix RB 05   Shy Little Girl/Never Go Home/JONNIE & LUBES: I Got Rabies/Terror In The Parking Lot (p/s) 15

EXECUTIVE SUITE
74 Cloud One HIT 1   When The Fuel Runs Out/You Got It 7
74 Polydor 2310400   EXECUTIVE SUITE 1 (LP) 50

EXHIBIT A
80 Irrelevant Wombat DAMP 1   NO ELEPHANTS THIS SIDE OF THE WATFORD GAP (EP, with insert) 25
80 Irrelevant Wombat DAMP 2   DISTANCE (EP) 15
(see also Doof)

EXILE
77 Boring BO 1   DON'T TAX ME (EP, 1,000 only p/s) 30
78 Charly CYS 1033   The Real People/Tomorrow Today/Disaster Movie (p/s) 18

EXILES
66 Topic 12T 143   FREEDOM, COME ALL YE (LP) 15
67 Topic 12T 164   THE HALE AND THE HANGED (LP) 15

EXILES INTACT
86 Chri$ Dixon EX 1 (T)A Who Is There/On Broadway/Who''s Dub (12" p/s) 30
86 Chri$ Dixon EX 1A   Who Is There/On Broadway 15
(see also Royal Blood (1))

EXIT (1)
80 Kik KIK 010   Look Inside/Three In A Bed 20

EXIT (2)
83 Red Beret REB 1   Planetoid Passion/Social Graces 50

EXITS (1)
78 Way Out WOO 1   YODELLING (EP, numbered, gatefold p/s, hand-stamped labels) 60

EXITS (2)
78 Red Lightning GIL 519 The Fashion Plague/Cheam (p/s, labels on wrong sides) 100
(see also Direct Hits)

EXIT STANCE (1)
84 Mortarhate MORT 11   WHILE BACKS ARE TURNED (LP, with insert) 20
84 Fight Back FIGHT 4   CRIME AGAINST HUMANITY (EP) 15

EXIT STANCE (2)
84 Exit Stance ES 002   Esthetics/Conspiracy Of Silence 30

EXIT 13
82 Artlos Music LOS 001 CELIA'S LAST WEDNESDAY (LP) 25

EXOCET
86 Exocet EXO 1PS12   STALEMATE (EP) 50

EXODUS
85 Music For Nations MFN 44   BONDED BY BLOOD (LP) 20

EXODUS (JAMAICA)
71 Duke DU 103   Pharoah's Walk/Little Caesar 12
72 Sioux SI 001   Pharoah's Walk No. 9/SAMMY JONES: Worried Over You 10
72 Sioux SI 010   Julia Sees Me/LLOYD THE MATADOR: The Train (Engine 54) 50

EXORDIUM
72 Face To Face FTF 1001 TROUBLE WITH ADAM (LP, private pressing) 30

EXOTICS (1)
64 Decca F 11850   Cross My Heart/Ooh La La 10
68 Columbia DB 8418   Don't Lead Me On/You Can Try 25

EXOTICS (2)
70 Pye 7N 17925   I Don't Want Nobody (To Lead Me On)/Driftaway 6

EXPELAIRES
79 Zoo CAGE 007   To See You/Frequency (p/s) 6
(see also Mission)

EXPELLED
82 Riot City RIOT 8   Dreaming/No Life, No Future/What Justice (p/s) 6
82 Riot City RIOT 17   Government Policy/Make It Alone (p/s) 6

EXPERIMENTAL AUDIO RESEARCH
99 Ochre OCH 009LV   PESTREPELLER EP 10

EXPERIMENTAL GARDENS
83 Attic ATT 001   The One That Got Away/People Will Be People (p/s) 10

EXPERIMENTS WITH ICE
81 United Dairies EX 001 EXPERIMENTS WITH ICE (LP) 25

EX PISTOLS
84 Cherry Red/Virgina Pistol 76p   Land Of Hope And Glory/The Flowers of Romansk (Picture disc) 10

EXPLICIT CORPSE

EXPLICIT CORPSE
81	Corpse 1	That Day Before.../I Gotta Gistol (stickered white labels, plastic gatefold p/s)	8

EXPLOITED
81	Exploited EXP 1001	Army Life/Fuck The Mods/Crashed Out (p/s)	10
81	Exploited EXP 002	Exploited Barmy Army/I Believe In Anarchy/What You Gonna Do? (p/s)	8
83	Blurg/Pax PAX 15	Rival Leaders/Army Style/Singalongabushell (p/s)	6
83	Secret SHH145-12	Troops Of Tomorrow (DJ Edit)/Troops Of Tomorrow (12", promo, no p/s)	25
81	Exploited EXP 1001	PUNK'S NOT DEAD (LP)	20
81	Exploited EXP 1002	ON STAGE (LP, some on yellow vinyl)	20
82	Secret SEC 8	TROOPS OF TOMORROW (LP)	20
83	Pax PAX 18	LET'S START A WAR (LP)	20
86	Dojo DOJOLP 37	HORROR EPICS (LP)	15
87	Rough Justice JUST 6	DEATH BEFORE DISHONOUR (LP, inner)	15
90	Rough Justice JUST 15	THE MASSACRE (LP)	15
96	Rough Justice JUST 22	BEAT THE BASTARDS (LP, inner)	25

EXPLORER
84	Rock Shop RSR 006	EXPLODING (LP)	50

EXPLOSIVE
68	President PT 221	Crying All Night/I Close My Eyes	6
69	President PT 244	Cities Make The Country Colder/Step Out Of Line	20
69	President PT 262	Who Planted Thorns In Miss Alice's Garden?/I Get My Kicks From Living	15
70	President PT 286	I'm Gonna Use What I Got To Get What I Need/Am I A Fool? (with Del Taylor)	6
70	President PT 302	This Ain't The Road To Freedom/Today Is Today	6
71	Plexium PXM 20	Hey Presto, Magic Man/Get It Together	300
71	Plexium PXM 24	Love Doesn't Come Easy/See You In The Morning	6

(see also Watson T. Browne & Explosive)

EXPORT
79	Atlantic K 11344	Julie Bitch/Nice To Know You	15
80	His Master's Vice VICE 2	You've Got To Rock/Wheeler Dealer (title sleeve)	18
80	His Master's Vice VICE 1	EXPORT (LP)	18

EXPOSE
79	A&M AMS 7473	Teenage Girls/If You See Kay (red vinyl, p/s)	6
79	A&M AMS 7490	Pretty Women Walk All Over Me/Isn't Life A Mystery (withdrawn, A label promos only)	10

EXPOSURE
80	Angular Music ACUTE 1	Style & Fashion/Video Eyes (p/s)	10

EXPOZER
80	Hit Hard HARD 1	Rock Japan/On My Knees (p/s)	12

EXPRESSION
82	A&M AM 149	With Closed Eyes/Nothing Changes (p/s)	6

EXTERNAL MENACE
82	Beat The System!! MENACE 1	YOUTH OF TODAY (EP)	15
83	Beat The System!! MENACE 2	NO VIEWS (EP)	15

EXTREEM
66	Strike JH 326	On The Beach/Don't You Ignore Me	20

EXTREME NOISE TERROR
88	Strange Fruit SFPS 048	PEEL SESSION (12" EP p/s)	18
15	Quagga Curious QCS 039	Chained And Crazed/Nih Nightmare (lathe cut 7", 31 copies only)	30
88	Head Eruption HURT 1	A HOLOCAUST IN YOUR HEAD (LP, with inner)	20
91	Vinyl Japan/Discipline DISC1T	PHONOPHOBIA (LP, insert)	15

EXTREME NOISE TERROR/CHAOS U.K.
86	Manic Ears ACHE 01	EAR SLAUGHTER — RADIOACTIVE (LP)	15

EXTREMES
87	SRT 6KS 1082	Eat My Dust/Salome	10

EXTRO 2
80	Friendly Street FSR 100	Cruciform Man/Fast Car	10

EXUMA
70	Mercury 6052 071	Exuma The Obeah Man/Junanoo	6
71	Mercury 6052 080	Damn Fool/You Don't Know What's Going On	6
72	Kama Sutra 2013 053	Monkberry Moon Delight/Obeah Man Come Back	8
70	Mercury 6338 018	EXUMA (LP, gatefold)	35
71	Kama Sutra 2319 010	DU WAH NANNY (LP, gatefold)	20

EYE DO IT
84	No Rip Off YAW 2	I Lost My MInd/Hold Back (p/s)	10

EYE FULL TOWER
67	Polydor BM 56734	How About Me?/Carol Cartoon	7

EYE WITNESS
81	Pro PRO 002	Tax Exile/Boys In Blue (p/s)	8

EYEHATEGOD
00	People Like You 772521	SOUTHERN DISCOMFORT (LP, white vinyl with inner)	20

EYELESS IN GAZA
80	Ambivalent Scale ASR 2	Kodak Ghosts Run Amok/China Blue Vision/The Feeling's Mutual (wraparound p/s)	20
82	Cherry Red CHERRY 47	Veil Like Calm/Taking Steps (p/s)	8
81	Cherry Red BRED 18	CAUGHT IN THE FLUX (LP, with bonus 12" EP [12 BRED 18], with inner)	15

(see also Martyn Bates)

EYES OF BLUE
66	Deram DM 106	Heart Trouble/Up And Down	60
67	Deram DM 114	Supermarket Full Of Cans/Don't Ask Me To Mend Your Broken Heart	70
68	Mercury MF 1049	Largo/Yesterday	15

EYES (1)

			MINT VALUE £
69	Mercury SMCL 20134	THE CROSSROADS OF TIME (LP, black/silver labels with 'Mercury' logo)	200
69	Mercury SMCL 20164	IN FIELDS OF ARDATH (LP, black/silver label with Mercury logo)	250

(see also Ancient Grease, Big Sleep, Man, Ritchie Francis, Gary Pickford-Hopkins, Gentle Giant)

EYES (1)
65	Mercury MF 881	When The Night Falls/I'm Rowed Out	200
66	Mercury MF 897	The Immediate Pleasure/My Degeneration	150
66	Mercury MF 910	Man With Money/You're Too Much	175
65	Mercury MF 934	Good Day Sunshine/Please Don't Cry	100
66	Mercury 10035 MCE	THE ARRIVAL OF THE EYES (EP)	350
84	Bam Caruso KIRI 028	BLINK (LP, 2 different sleeves)	18
87	Bam Caruso MARI 038	SCENE BUT NOT HEARD (mini-LP)	15

(see also Pupils)

EYES (2)
78	Raw RAW 29	Once In A Lifetime/Hello I Love You (1000 only in p/s)	8

(see also Doug Kane)

EYNESBURY GIANT
78	Ultimate URL 602	FROM THE CASK (LP, with insert)	20

EZRA COLLECTIVE
16	EZCOLCHP7	CHAPTER 7 (12", p/s)	100

EZY MEAT
84	Electric Storm ES 0001	NOT FOR WIMPS (LP, with insert, Irish only)	50
86	Electric Storm ES 0002	ROCK YOUR BRAINS OUT (LP, with insert, Irish only)	40

EZY RIDER
82	English Steel	POWER (LP)	150

F

SHELLEY FABARES
62	Pye International 7N 25132	Johnny Angel/Where's It Gonna Get Me? (blue label, later yellow label)	8
62	Pye International 7N 25133	She Can't Find Her Keys/Very Unlikely (with Paul Peterson)	8
62	Pye International 7N 25151	Johnny Loves Me/I'm Growing Up	8
62	Pye International 7N 25166	The Things We Did Last Summer/Breaking Up Is Hard To Do	8
63	Pye International 7N 25184	Telephone (Won't You Ring)/Big Star	8
63	Pye International 7N 25207	Ronnie Call Me When You Get A Chance/I Left A Note To Say Goodbye	8
65	Fontana TF 592	My Prayer/Pretty Please	10

(see also Paul Peterson & Shelley Fabares)

FAB FOOD
80	Smile SR 021	Never Alone/Holiday	10

FABIAN
59	HMV POP 587	I'm A Man/Hypnotized	20
59	HMV POP 587	I'm A Man/Hypnotized (78)	20
59	HMV POP 612	Turn Me Loose/Stop Thief!	20
59	HMV POP 643	Tiger/Mighty Cold (To A Warm, Warm Heart)	12
59	HMV POP 659	Got The Feeling/Come On And Get Me	12
60	HMV POP 695	Hound Dog Man/This Friendly World	12
60	HMV POP 724	String Along/About This Thing Called Love	10
60	HMV POP 778	I'm Gonna Sit Right Down And Write Myself A Letter/Strollin' In The Springtime	8
60	HMV POP 800	Tomorrow/King Of Love	10
60	HMV POP 810	Kissin' And Twistin'/Long Before	10
61	HMV POP 829	You Know You Belong To Somebody Else/Hold On	10
61	HMV POP 869	Grapevine/David And Goliath	12
61	HMV POP 934	You're Only Young Once/The Love That I'm Giving To You	10
59	HMV CLP 1301	HOLD THAT TIGER (LP)	40
60	HMV CLP 1345	THE FABULOUS FABIAN (LP)	40
61	HMV CLP 1433	YOUNG AND WONDERFUL (LP, mono)	30
61	HMV CSD 1352	YOUNG AND WONDERFUL (LP, stereo)	30

FABIAN (JAMAICA)
77	Tribesman TM 004	Prophecy/Prophecy Dub	30
77	Black Swan BS 8	Prophecy/JIMMY LINDSAY : Easy (12")	15
78	Tribesman TM 08	Prophecy/JIMMY LINDSAY : Easy (12")	35
78	Island 12 WIP 6431	Prophecy/JIMMY LINDSAY : Easy (12")	25
96	Tribesman TM 01	Prophecy/Prophecy Dub (12" reissue)	40

FABIONS
69	Bullet BU 410	V. Rocket/Smile (B-side actually "My Baby" by Tennors)	200

FABLE
73	Magnet MAG 5002	FABLE (LP, gatefold sleeve, white/red labels)	20

(see also Trapeze, Uriah Heep)

BENT FABRIC
61	Columbia DB 4753	The Alleycat/Markin' Time	6

GREGORY FABULOUS
03	Jah Tubbys JT 10015	Get Up/Moving To Zion (10", with the Offbeat Posse)	20
04	Jah Tubbys JT 10022	Love Jah/Tra-La-La (10", with Prof. Natty)	20
06	Jah Tubbys JT 10026	Jah Lead I Forward/Bless We Oh Jah (12")	15
11	Jet Star TK 107	Give Your Face A Rest/(Jungle Mix) (12" white label)	18

FABULOUS COUNTS
71	Mojo 2092 021	Get Down People/Lunar Funk	8

FABULOUS DIALS

MINT VALUE £

FABULOUS DIALS
63   Pye International 7N 25200   Bossa Nova Stomp/Forget Me Not 25

FABULOUS ECHOES
73   Contempo CON 002   Don't You Know I Love You/If You Move It You Lose It 8

FABULOUS FIVE INC.
73   Ahanti SHAN 104   FABULOUS FIVE INC. (LP) 25

FABULOUS FLAMES
70   Clandisc CLA 224   Holly Holy/LORD CREATOR: Kingston Town... 15
71   Trojan TR 7822   Growing Up/Lovitis 6
(see also Dynamites)

FABULOUS IMPACT
90   Kent 6T 6   Baby Baby, I Want You/HAMPTONS: No No No No No No Not My Girl (100 Club 6T's All-nighter anniversary disc) 30

FABULOUS JADES
04   Soul City 140   Come On And Live/Planning The Moment... 8

FABULOUS MARK III
02   Funk 45 FUNK45.004   Psycho Part 1/Psycho Part 2 7

FABULOUS ORIGINALS
02   Funk 45 FUNK45 006   It Ain't Fair But It's Fun Parts I and II (reissue) 15

FABULOUS SHADES
71   Tropical AL 005   Lonely Man/Version 2 12

FABULOUS SWINGTONES
58   HMV POP 471   Geraldine/You Know Baby.. 250
58   HMV POP 471   Geraldine/You Know Baby (78).. 50

FABULOUS TALBOT BROTHERS
50s   Melodisc M 1507   Bloodshot Eyes/She's Got Freckles 20

FACES
70   Warner Bros WB 8005   Flying/Three-Button Hand-Me-Down 10
70   Warner Bros WB 8014   Wicked Messenger/Nobody Knows (unissued) 0
70   Warner Bros WB 8018   Had Me A Real Good Time/Rear Wheel Skid 8
73   Warner Bros K 16247   Cindy Incidentally/Skewiff (Mend The Fuse) (with lyric insert, no p/s)............... 8
73   Warner Bros K 16281   Borstal Boys (withdrawn, any pressed?)... 0
73   NME SF1 139   Dishevelment Blues/Ooh La La Preview (flexidisc free with NME) 10
74   Warner Bros K 16494   You Can Make Me Dance, Sing Or Anything/As Long As You Tell Him (credited to Rod Stewart and the Faces, p/s)... 8
70   Warner Bros WS 3000   FIRST STEP (LP, orange label, gatefold sleeve) 100
71   Warner Bros WS 3011   LONG PLAYER (LP, blue & silver label, stitched die-cut '78rpm' style sleeve)....... 50
71   Warner Bros K 46053   FIRST STEP (LP, reissue, green label, gatefold sleeve) 20
71   Warner Bros K 56006   A NOD IS AS GOOD AS A WINK ... TO A BLIND HORSE (LP, green label, with poster) 40
72   Warner Bros K 46064   LONG PLAYER (LP, reissue, blue & silver label, stitched die-cut '78rpm'-style sleeve) 20
73   Warner Bros K 56011   OOH-LA-LA (LP, green label, die-cut fold out 'Faces' sleeve with lyric poster, 'can can' picture label)... 80
74   Warner Bros K 56011   OOH-LA-LA (LP, 'Burbank' label, 'Faces' sleeve, with lyric poster) 20
74   Warner Bros K 56006   A NOD IS AS GOOD AS A WINK ... TO A BLIND HORSE (LP, reissue, 'Burbank' label) 15
75   Warner Bros K 66027   TWO ORIGINALS OF . . . (2-LP, reissue of "First Steps" & "Long Player", gatefold sleeve) ... 20
(see also Small Faces, Rod Stewart, Ronnie Lane & Slim Chance, Ron Wood, Jeff Beck Group, Kenney Jones)

FACE TO FACE
71   Face To Face FTF 1000   FACE TO FACE (LP, 1000 only) 150

FACTION
81   Inevitable INEV 007   Faction/Wrong Again 7

FACTOR FICTION
81   TKS 001   FACTOR FICTION EP (Pressed in Ireland but imported into U.K) 15

FACTORY FLOOR
08   Outside OUT 0015   Bipolar/You Were Always Wrong (p/s, orange vinyl, 500 only) 30
08   One Of One ON 01   PLANNING APPLICATION EP (12" p/s, 500 only) 25
10   Blast First Petite PTYT 035 V   Lying/16-16-9-2--1-14-9-7/A Wooden Box/Solid Sound (10" clear vinyl with DVD, 2000 only) 10
10   Blast First Petite PTYT 048   Lying (Stephen Morris Mix)/Lying (Original)/Lying (Chris Carter Mix)/A Wooden Box (Original) (2x12" in plastic sleeve, 200 only) 15
11   DFA DAF 2318   Two Different Ways/Second Way (12", limited edition screen printed sleeve, numbered and signed by one member of the band) 20
14   Vinyl Factory VF 079   o/o/o/o/o/o/o/o/o (NVC Remix) (12" signed, numbered, 100 only) 20
13   DFA DFA 2392   FACTORY FLOOR (2-LP, yellow vinyl, with CD and CD-R, 300 only) 30
13   DFA DFA 2392   FACTORY FLOOR (2-LP, white vinyl, with CD and CD-R)................................. 25
18   H/O/D HOD003COL   A SOUNDTRACK FOR A FILM (4-LP, grey vinyl) 30
(see also Nik Colk Void)

FACTORY (1)
68   MGM MGM 1444   Path Through The Forest/Gone 1000
69   CBS 4540   Try A Little Sunshine/Red Chalk Hill 1400
(see also Peter & Wolves, Norman Conquest, John Pantry, Velvet Hush)

FACTORY (2)
70   OAK RGJ718   Time Machine/Castle On The Hill (99 copies only) 450

FACTORY (3)
82   Future Earth FER 011   You Are The Music/History Of The World (silver die-cut sleeve) 20

FACTORY (4)
86   Strike Back SBR10   Hold Out/Burn Me Up (p/s) 20
86   Strike Back SBR 10T   Hold Out (Extended)/Burn Me Up/Outcast (12", p/s) 25

FACTOTUMS
65   Immediate IM 009   In My Lonely Room/Run In The Green And Tangerine Flaked Forest 40
65   Immediate IM 022   You're So Good To Me/Can't Go Home Anymore My Love 30
66   Piccadilly 7N 35233   Here Today/In My Room 30
66   Piccadilly 7N 35333   I Can't Give You Anything But Love/Absolutely Sweet Marie 20

FADED TAPES

MINT VALUE £

67	Pye 7N 17402	Cloudy/Easy Said, Easy Done	25
69	CBS 4140	Mr And Mrs Regards/Driftwood	20

FADED TAPES
13	Box Bedroom BBR 2	5 TRACK EP (p/s, numbered, 100 only)	20

FADELA
88	Factory FAC 197	N'sel Fik/Ateni Bniti (12")	10

FADERS
79	Rip Off RIP 8	Cheatin'/Library Book (in bag p/s)	75

FAD GADGET
81	Lyntone LYN 10209	King Of The Flies/DEPECHE MODE: Sometimes I Wish I Was Dead (red vinyl flexidisc free with Flexipop magazine, issue 11)	25
81	Lyntone LYN 10209	King Of The Flies/DEPECHE MODE: Sometimes I Wish I Was Dead (red vinyl flexidisc free without Flexipop magazine, issue 11)	15
80	Mute STUMM 3	FIRESIDE FAVOURITES (LP)	25
81	Mute STUMM 6	INCONTINENT (LP)	20
82	Mute STUMM 8	UNDER THE FLAG (LP)	20
84	Mute STUMM 15	GAG (LP)	15

FADING COLOURS
66	Ember EMB S 229	(Just Like) Romeo And Juliet/Billy Christian	20
67	Ember EMB S 237	Be With Me/You're No Use	10

(see also Orange Seaweed)

FAERIE SYMPHONY
77	Decca F13735	Dance Of The Enashee (Da Oine Sidhe)/The Unseelie Court	8

DONALD FAGEN
93	Resprise 9362 45230-1	KAMAKIRIAD (LP)	40
05	Reprise 9362-49975-1	MORPH THE CAT (2-LP)	60
17	Reprise 081227932824	CHEAP XMAS: DONALD FAGEN COMPLETE (7-LP box set)	150

(see laos Steely Dan)

BRIAN FAHEY (& HIS ORCHESTRA)
59	Parlophone R 4655	Street Of A Thousand Bongos/Waltz For Beatniks	8
60	Parlophone R 4686	At The Sign Of The Swingin' Cymbal/The Clanger	20
62	Parlophone R 4909	At The Sign Of The Swingin' Cymbal/The Clanger (reissue, as Brian Faye & His Orchestra)	10
65	Parlophone R 5262	Gidian's Way/Love Theme From "In Harm's Way"	8
65	United Artists UP 1115	Twang/You Can't Catch Me	8
67	Parlophone R 5615	The Plank/Stay On the Island	15
67	Parlophone R 5639	With A Song In My Heart/Swinging Choice	6
68	Columbia DB 8447	Late Night Extra/Oh The Pity Of It All	8
69	Major Minor MM 656	Open House/Countdown	25
67	Studio Two TWO 175	TIME FOR TV (LP)	20

JOHN FAHEY
67	Transatlantic TRA 173	THE TRANSFIGURATION OF BLIND JOE DEATH (LP, with booklet)	40
67	Transatlantic TRA 173	THE TRANSFIGURATION OF BLIND JOE DEATH (LP, without booklet)	20
68	Vanguard SVRL 19033	YELLOW PRINCESS (LP)	25
68	Vanguard SVRL 19055	REQUIA (LP)	30
69	Takoma SNTF 607	BLIND JOE DEATH (LP)	20
69	Sonet SNTF 608	VOLUME 2 DEATH CHANTS,BREAKDOWNS AND MILITARY WALTZES(LP)	20
72	Sonet SNTF 628	AMERICA (LP)	25
72	Reprise K 44213	OF RIVERS AND RELIGION (LP)	20
73	Reprise K 44246	AFTER THE BALL (LP)	20
74	Takoma SNTF 675	JOHN FAHEY, PETER LANG AND LEO KOTTKE (LP)	15
74	Sonet SNTF 656	FARE FORWARD VOYAGERS (LP)	20
76	Sonet SNTF 702	THE NEW POSSIBILITY (LP)	20
77	Transatlantic TRA 173	THE TRANSFIGURATION OF BLIND JOE DEATH (LP, reissue, picture label)	25

MIATTA FAHNBULLEH
79	EMI EMC 3294	MIATTA (LP)	80
80	Pan African PAF 001	THE MESSAGE OF THE REVOLUTION (LP)	75

JAD FAIR
80	Armageddon AEP 003	THE ZOMBIES OF MORA-TAU (EP, die-cut p/s with insert)	12

(see also Half Japanese)

JAD FAIR & PASTELS
91	Paperhouse PAPER 013T	THIS COULD BE THE NIGHT EP (12", p/s)	15
92	Paperhouse PAPER 018	HE CHOSE HIS COLOURS WELL (12" EP)	10

(see also Pastels)

YVONNE FAIR
74	Tamla Motown TMG 913	Funky Music Sho Nuff Turns Me On/Let Your Hair Down	7
75	Tamla Motown TMG 1025	It's Bad For Me To See You/Walk Out The Door If You Wanna	7
75	Tamla Motown STML 12008	THE BITCH IS BLACK (LP)	25

WERLY FAIRBURN & DELTA BOYS
56	London HLC 8349	I'm A Fool About Your Love/All The Time	1000
56	London HLC 8349	I'm A Fool About Your Love/All The Time (78)	150

JOHNNY FAIRE
58	London HLU 8569	Bertha Lou/Till The Law Says Stop	500
58	London HLU 8569	Bertha Lou/Till The Law Says Stop (78)	150

FAIRFIELD PARLOUR
70	Vertigo 6059 003	Bordeaux Rosé/Chalk On The Wall	20
70	Vertigo 6059 008	Just Another Day/Caraminda/I Am All The Animals/Song For You	40
76	Prism PRI 1	Bordeaux Rosé/Baby Stay For Tonight (as Fairfield Parlor)	10
70	Vertigo 6360 001	FROM HOME TO HOME (LP, textured gatefold sleeve, large swirl label)	400
91	UFO BFTP 003	FROM HOME TO HOME (LP, reissue)	30
03	Circle CPWL 104	PLEASE LISTEN TO THE PICTURES (2-LP, BBC sessions, split release with Kaleidoscope)	20

FAIRIES

MINT VALUE £

(see also Kaleidoscope [U.K.], I Luv Wight)

FAIRIES
64	Decca F 11943	Don't Think Twice, It's Alright/Anytime At All	125
65	HMV POP 1404	Get Yourself Home/I'll Dance	200
65	HMV POP 1445	Don't Mind/Baby Don't	175

(see also Twink, Cops 'N Robbers)

FAIRPORT CONVENTION

SINGLES
67	Track 604 020	If I Had A Ribbon Bow/If (Stomp)	75
68	Island WIP 6047	Meet On The Ledge/Throwaway Street Puzzle (pink label)	20
69	Island WIP 6064	Si Tu Dois Partir/Genesis Hall	8
70	Island WIP 6089	Now Be Thankful/Sir B. McKenzie's Daughter's Lament	10
70	Polydor 2058 014	If (Stomp)/Chelsea Morning	12
71	Island WIP 6128	John Lee/The Time Is Near (in p/s)	12
71	Island WIP 6128	John Lee/The Time Is Near	6
73	Island WIP 6155	Rosie/Knights Of The Road	6
75	Island WIP 6241	White Dress/Tears (in p/s)	12
75	Island WIP 6241	White Dress/Tears	6
78	Hawk HASP 423	Jam's O'Donnell's Jig/The Last Waltz (Irish-only)	15
79	Simons PMW 1	Rubber Band/The Bonny Black Hare	12
86	Sunrise Bong 1	Quazi B Goode/MIKE SILVER: Where Would You Rather Be Tonight	10
87	Island 12IF 324	Meet On The Ledge (Re-recorded)/John Barleycorn (live)/Sigh Bheg Sigh Mhor (live) (12", p/s, with poster)	10

ALBUMS : POLYDOR ALBUMS
68	Polydor 582 035	FAIRPORT CONVENTION (mono, laminated sleeve)	300
68	Polydor 582/583 035	FAIRPORT CONVENTION (stereo, laminated sleeve)	250
76	Polydor Special 2384 047	FAIRPORT CONVENTION (LP, reissue)	15

ALBUMS : ISLAND ALBUMS
69	Island ILPS 9092	WHAT WE DID ON OUR HOLIDAYS (1st pressing, laminated front cover, pink label with orange/black 'circle')	250
69	Island ILPS 9092	WHAT WE DID ON OUR HOLIDAYS (2nd pressing, pink label with black 'block' logo)	100
69	Island ILPS 9092	WHAT WE DID ON OUR HOLIDAYS (3rd pressing, pink label with 'i' logo)	60
70	Island ILPS 9092	WHAT WE DID ON OUR HOLIDAYS (4th pressing, pink rim label with 'palm tree' logo)	20
69	Island ILPS 9102	UNHALFBRICKING (1st pressing, pink label with black 'block' logo)	250
69	Island ILPS 9102	UNHALFBRICKING (2nd pressing, pink label with 'i' logo)	100
70	Island ILPS 9102	UNHALFBRICKING (3rd pressing, pink rim label with 'palm tree' logo)	40
69	Island ILPS 9115	LIEGE AND LIEF (gatefold sleeve, 1st pressing, pink label with 'i' logo)	150
70	Island ILPS 9115	LIEGE AND LIEF (gatefold sleeve, 2nd pressing, pink label with 'palm tree' logo)	20
70	Island ILPS 9130	FULL HOUSE (white label test pressing, with "Poor Will & The Jolly Hangman")	300
70	Island ILPS 9130	FULL HOUSE (1st pressing, pink 'i' label, gatefold sleeve lists "Poor Will & The Jolly Hangman")	60
70	Island ILPS 9130	FULL HOUSE (2nd pressing, with pink 'i' label, gatefold sleeve without reference to "Poor Will & The Jolly Hangman")	30
70	Island ILPS 9130	FULL HOUSE (gatefold sleeve, 3rd pressing, pink rim label with 'palm tree' logo)	15
71	Island ILPS 9162	ANGEL DELIGHT (gatefold sleeve with 'stuck-on' photos, pink rim label)	20
71	Island ILPS 9176	BABBACOMBE LEE (gatefold sleeve, with innersleeve and booklet, with sticker, pink rim label)	35
71	Island ILPS 9176	BABBACOMBE LEE (gatefold sleeve, with innersleeve and booklet, without sticker)	20
72	Island ICD 4	THE HISTORY OF FAIRPORT CONVENTION (2-LP, with 12-page booklet & blue ribbons)	20
73	Island ILPS 9208	ROSIE	15
73	Island ILPS 9246	FAIRPORT NINE (gatefold sleeve)	18
74	Island ILPS 9285	LIVE CONVENTION (with insert)	15
75	Island ILPS 9313	RISING FOR THE MOON (with insert, 'palm tree' label)	15
75	Island ISS 2	FAIRPORT TOUR SAMPLER (free in NME competition, 500 only)	150
76	Island HELP 28	LIVE AT THE L.A. TROUBADOR 1974	30
00	Simply Vinyl SVLP 164	UNHALFBRICKING (LP, reissue)	15

ALBUMS : OTHER ALBUMS
77	Vertigo 9102 015	BONNY BUNCH OF ROSES (gatefold sleeve)	18
78	Vertigo 9102 022	TIPPLER'S TALES (with lyric insert)	15
79	Woodworm BEAR 22	FAREWELL FAREWELL (gatefold sleeve)	20
79	Simons GAMA 1	FAREWELL FAREWELL (reissue, gatefold sleeve)	18
83	Woodworm WRC 1	AT 2 (AIRING CUPBOARD TAPES 2)	15

(see also Richard Thompson, Ian Matthews, Dave Swarbrick, Sandy Denny, Ashley Hutchings, Trevor Lucas, Albion Band. Bunch, Fotheringay. Vashti Bunyan, Trader Horne, Allan Taylor, Krysia, Marc Ellington, Brian Maxine, Steeleye Span, Vikki clayton)

FAIRUZ
61	Parlophone 45 VDL 309	Am Betdawui Eshams/Shatty Ya Deney (export only)	15
61	Parlophone 45 VDL 322	Lwayn Rayheem/Medwiyyeh (export only)	15
57	Parlophone LPVD 1	FAIRUZ SINGS (10" LP, Export)	50
58	Parlophone LPVD 4	FAIRUZ SINGS AGAIN (10" LP, Export)	60
66	Parlophone LPVDX 106	DAMASCUS FESTIVAL (LP)	30

FAIR WARNING
87	Areba ERA 2	Rocking At The Speed Of Light EP (12", p/s)	30

FAIRWAYS (FEATURING GARY STREET)
69	Mercury MF 1116	Yoko Ono/I Don't Care	8

FAIR WEATHER
70	RCA RCA 1977	Natural Sinner/Haven't I Tried (To Be A Good Man)	6
70	RCA RCA 2040	Road To Freedom/Tutti Frutti	8
71	RCA Neon NE 1000	Lay It On Me/Looking For The Red Label Pt 2	15
70	RCA Victor SF 8155	BEGINNING FROM AN END (LP, withdrawn, different cover and one less track than Neon issue)	175

FAIRY'S MOKE

MINT VALUE £

71	RCA Neon NE 1	BEGINNING FROM AN END (LP, gatefold sleeve, black inner sleeve)	125

(see also Amen Corner, Wynder K. Frog)

FAIRY'S MOKE
75	Deroy 1175	FAIRY'S MOKE (LP, private pressing, actually various artists LP)	80

(see also Baby Sunshine)

FAIRYTALE
67	Decca F 12644	Guess I Was Dreaming/Run And Hide	125
67	Decca F 12665	Lovely People/Listen To Mary Cry	70

ADAM FAITH (& ROULETTES)
SINGLES
58	HMV POP 438	(Got A) Heartsick Feeling/Brother Heartache And Sister Tears	80
58	HMV POP 438	(Got A) Heartsick Feeling/Brother Heartache And Sister Tears (78)	30
58	HMV POP 557	High School Confidential/Country Music Holiday	100
58	HMV POP 557	High School Confidential/Country Music Holiday (78)	30
59	Top Rank JAR 126	Ah, Poor Little Baby!/Runk Bunk (blue label)	25
59	Top Rank JAR 126	Ah, Poor Little Baby!/Runk Bunk (blue label) (78)	40
59	Parlophone R 4591	What Do You Want?/From Now Until Forever (78)	30
60	Parlophone R 4623	Poor Me/The Reason (78)	30
60	Parlophone R 4665	Made You/When Johnny Comes Marching Home (78, existence unconfirmed)	0
67	Parlophone R 5635	Cowman Milk Your Cow/Daddy, What'll Happen To Me	30

EPs
62	Columbia SEG 8138	BEAT GIRL (2 Faith tracks, with John Barry Orchestra)	20
64	Parlophone GEP 8893	TOP OF THE POPS (with Roulettes)	12
64	Parlophone GEP 8904	FOR YOU — ADAM	15
65	Parlophone GEP 8929	A MESSAGE TO MARTHA — FROM ADAM	15
65	Parlophone GEP 8939	SONGS AND THINGS	15

ALBUMS
60	Parlophone PMC 1128	ADAM (mono)	15
60	Columbia 33SX 1225	BEAT GIRL (soundtrack, with John Barry Orchestra)	40
64	Parlophone PMC 1228	ON THE MOVE (with Roulettes)	30
65	Parlophone PMC 1249	FAITH ALIVE! (with Roulettes)	30

(see also Roulettes, John Barry)

AUSTIN FAITH
71	Dynamic DYN 407	634 5789/DYNAMIC BOYS: Warm And Tender Love	7

(see also Austin Faithful)

GEORGE FAITH
77	Island IPR 2034	Diana/To Be A Lover (12")	15
77	Black Swan BS 2	To Be A Lover/UPSETTERS: Rastaman Shuffle (12")	25
77	Black Swan BS 3	I've Got The Groove/Diana (12")	20
77	Black Swan BS 4	Midnight Hour/Turn Back The Hands Of Time (12")	20
77	Black Swan BS 5	All The Love I've Got/So Fine (12")	20
79	Warrior WAR 134	Don't Be Afraid/BUNNY SCOTT : What's The Use/Never Had It So Good (act. Jimmy Riley) (12")	25
77	Black Swan ILPS 9504	TO BE A LOVER (LP)	30

(see also Earl George, George Ferris. Winston Reedy)

HORACE FAITH
69	B&C CB 104	Spinning Wheel/Like I Used To Do	10
69	Downtown DT 446	Daddy's Home/EMOTIONS: Give Me A Love	10
70	Trojan TR 7790	Black Pearl/Help Me Help Myself	7
70	A&M AMS 817	Shame And Scandal In The Family/REGGAE STRINGS: Reggae Strings	6
76	DJM DJS 10687	I Can't Understand It/Gimme Good Lovin'	30
78	Ultra PFU 7501	Rich Man Poor Man/No More	15

PALOMA FAITH
12	RCA 88725412231	FALL TO GRACE (2-LP)	40
14	RCA 88843043981	A PERFECT CONTRADICTION (2-LP)	100

FAITH BROTHERS
67	Tabernacle TS 1002	I Am Saved Now/Too Near My Heavenly Home	20

AUSTIN FAITHFUL
68	Blue Cat BS 140	Uncle Joe/Can't Understand	250
68	Pyramid PYR 6016	I'm In A Rocking Mood/ROLAND ALPHONSO: Stream Of Life	80
69	Pyramid PYR 6028	Eternal Love/ROLAND ALPHONSO: Goodnight My Love	80
69	Pyramid PYR 6042	Ain't That Peculiar?/Miss Anti-Social	40

(see also Austin Faith)

FAITHFUL DAWN
94	Dawn 001	The Sequel (Original mix)/Dark Beat Mix (12", white label – 300 only)	20

MARIANNE FAITHFULL
64	Decca F 11923	As Tears Go By/Greensleeves	7
64	Decca F 12007	Blowin' In The Wind/The House Of The Rising Sun	8
65	Decca F 12075	Come And Stay With Me/What Have I Done Wrong?	8
65	Decca F 12162	This Little Bird/Morning Sun	6
65	Decca F 12193	Summer Nights/The Sha La La Song	7
65	Decca F 12268	Yesterday/Oh Look Around You	7
66	Decca F 12408	Tomorrow's Calling/That's Right Baby	10
66	Decca F 12443	Counting/I'd Like To Dial Your Number	20
66	Decca F 22524	Is This What I Get For Loving You?/Tomorrow's Calling	12
69	Decca F 12889	Something Better/Sister Morphine (withdrawn)	50
75	NEMS NES 004	Dreamin' My Dreams/Lady Madalaine	10
76	NEMS NES 013	All I Wanna Do In Life/Wrong Road Again	10
77	NEMS NES 014	Wrong Road Again/The Way You Want Me To Be	10

FAITH NO MORE

MINT VALUE £

78	NEMS NES 117	The Way You Want Me To Be/That Was The Day (Nashville)	10
79	Island WIP 6491	The Ballad Of Lucy Jordan/Brain Drain (p/s)	7
80	Island 12WIP 6542	Broken English/Why D'Ya Do It? (12", p/s)	10
80	Decca F 13890	As Tears Go By/Come And Stay With Me/This Little Bird/Summer Nights (p/s)	6
65	Decca DFE 8624	GO AWAY FROM MY WORLD (EP)	35
65	Decca LK 4688	COME MY WAY (LP)	100
65	Decca LK 4689	MARIANNE FAITHFULL (LP)	80
66	Decca LK 4778	NORTH COUNTRY MAID (LP)	75
67	Decca LK/SKL 4854	LOVEINAMIST (LP)	120
69	Decca PA 17	THE WORLD OF MARIANNE FAITHFULL (LP, mono)	20
69	Decca SPA 17	THE WORLD OF MARIANNE FAITHFULL (LP, stereo)	15
76	NEMS NEL 6007	DREAMIN' MY DREAMS (LP)	15
78	NEMS NEL 6012	FAITHLESS (LP)	15
92	Island ILPM 9570	BROKEN ENGLISH (LP)	15

FAITH NO MORE

88	Slash LASH 17	We Care A Lot/Spirit (p/s)	10
88	Slash LASH 18	Annie's Song (Remix)/Greed (p/s)	10
88	Slash LASHX 18	Anne's Song (Remix)/Greed (12", p/s)	10
92	London LASH 44	I'm Easy/Be Aggressive (red vinyl, p/s)	8
90	London/Slash 850 228	KING FOR A DAY, FOOL FOR A LIFETIME (7 x 7" box set)	40
89	Slash 828154	THE REAL THING (LP)	35
89	Slash 828 217-1	THE REAL THING (LP, picture disc)	25
92	Slash LASHP18	ANGEL DUST (LP, insert with free 12")	30
95	Slash 828 560-1	KING FOR A DAY FOOL FOR A LIFETIME (2-LP, red vinyl)	50
97	Slash 828 901	ALBUM OF THE YEAR (LP)	40

FAKES

79	Deep Cuts DEEP TWO	Production/Look-Out/Tony Blackburn/Sylvia Clark (p/s)	15

FALCON

80	Ellie Jay EJSP 9344	FALCON EP (12", p/s, 500 only)	10

EDDIE FALCON

60	Columbia DB 4420	The Young Have No Time To Lose/My Thanks To You	6
61	Columbia DB 4646	Linda Rose/If Ever I Should Fall In Love	6

FALCONS (U.K.)

64	Philips BF 1297	Stampede/Kazutzka	20

FALCONS (U.S.)

59	London HLT 8876	You're So Fine/Goddess Of Angels	100
59	London HLT 8876	You're So Fine/Goddess Of Angels (78)	70
62	London HLK 9565	I Found A Love/Swim (some labels credit B-side as "Swin")	50

(see also Wilson Pickett, Eddie Floyd)

FALL OUT BOY

04	Sorepoint SORE 010S	Dead On Arrival/Dead On Arrival (acoustic) (blue vinyl, die-cut sleeve)	10
05	Sorepoint SORE 038S	Grand Theft Autumn/Where Is Your Boy/MY AWESOME COMPILATION: As Always (yellow vinyl, die-cut sleeve)	8

THE FALL
SINGLES

78	Step Forward SF 7	Bingo-Masters' Breakout! (EP)	50
78	Step Forward SF 9	It's The New Thing/Various Times (p/s)	25
79	Step Forward SF 11	Rowche Rumble/In My Area (p/s)	25
80	Step Forward SF 13	Fiery Jack/Second Dark Age/Psykick Dancehall 2 (black-and-white p/s)	35
80	Step Forward SF 13	Fiery Jack/Second Dark Age/Psykick Dancehall 2 (yellow p/s)	30
80	Rough Trade RT 048	How I Wrote Elastic Man/City Hobgoblins (p/s)	25
80	Rough Trade RT 056	Totally Wired/Putta Block (p/s)	25
81	Rough Trade RT 071	SLATES (10" EP, 33rpm)	30
81	Kamera ERA 001	Lie Dream Of A Casino Soul/Fantastic Life (p/s)	20
82	Kamera ERA 004	Look, Know/I'm Into C.B. (p/s)	20
82	Rough Trade RT 133	The Man Whose Head Expanded/Ludd Gang (p/s)	25
82	Kamera ERA 014	Marquis Cha Cha/Papal Visit (p/s, B-side plays "Room To Live", withdrawn)	100
83	Rough Trade RT 143	Kicker Conspiracy/Wings//Container Drivers/New Puritan (g/fold double pack)	30
84	Beggars Banquet BEG 110	Oh! Brother/God Box (p/s)	15
84	Beggars Banquet BEG 116	C.R.E.E.P./Pat-Trip Dispenser (p/s)	20
84	Beggars Banquet BEG 116T	C.R.E.E.P./(Extended Version)/Pat-Trip Dispenser (12", p/s, green vinyl)	25
84	Beggars Banquet BEG 116TP	C.R.E.E.P./(Extended Version)/Pat-Trip Dispenser (12", p/s, with art print)	25
84	Beggars Banquet BEG 120E	CALL FOR ESCAPE ROUTE (7"/12" double pack EP)	15
85	Beggars Banquet BEG 150	Cruiser's Creek/LA (p/s)	15
85	Beggars Banquet BEG 150T	Cruiser's Creek/Vixen/LA (12", p/s)	12
86	Beggars Banquet BEG 168	Mr. Pharmacist/Lucifer Over Lancashire (p/s)	7
87	Beggars Banquet BEG 200	Hit The North Part 1/Hit The North Part 2 (p/s)	10
87	Beggars Banquet BEG 200T	Hit The North (Parts 1 & 2) (12", gatefold sleeve)	12
87	Beggars Banquet BEG 206B	Victoria/Tuff Life Boogie (box set with inserts & badge)	15
88	Beggars Banquet BEG 206	Victoria/Tuff Life Boogie (p/s)	8
88	Beggars Banquet FALL 2B	Jerusalem/Acid Priest 2088/Big New Prinz/Wrong Place, Right Time No 2 (as 2 x 7" in box with postcard, numbered)	10
89	Beggars Banquet BEG 226	Cab It Up/Dead Beat Descendant (p/s)	6
90	Cog Sinster SIN 4	Telephone Thing/British People In Hot Weather (p/s)	12
90	Cog Sinister SINR 5	Popcorn Double Feature/Zandra (p/s)	6
90	Cog Sinister SIN 6	White Lightning/Blood Outta Stone (p/s)	6
91	Cog Sinister FALL 1	So What About It/Edinburgh Man (promo only)	20
92	Cog Sinister SINS 8	Free Range/Everything Hurtz (p/s)	6
93	Permanent PERM 9	Why Are People Grudgeful?/Glam Racket (p/s)	8
94	Permanent 10SPERM 14	15 Ways (10", p/s)	10

FALLEN ANGELS (U.S.)

MINT VALUE £

Year	Label/Cat#	Title	Value
96	Jet JET 500	The Chiselers/Chilinist (p/s)	8
01	Flitwick MK45 1FG	I Wake Up In The City/Rude (All The Time) (500 only)	50
03	Action TAKE 20	The Fall Vs 2003: Susan vs Youthclub/Janet vs Johnny (p/s)	8
03	Action TAKE 22	(We Wish You) A Protein Christmas/(We Are) Mock Goth/(Birtwistles) Girl In Shop/Recovery Kit 2 (as 2 x 7")	10
04	Action TAKE 25	Theme From Sparta F.C. 2/My Ex Classmates Kids (live) (p/s)	8
05	Slogan SLOS 005	I Can Hear The Grass Grow/Clasp Hands (p/s)	15
09	Action ACTOUT 01V	Slippy Floor/Hot Cake Part 2 (tour-only 7")	6
11	Cherry Red CHERRY 500	Laptop Dog/Cosmos 7/Monocard (p/s)	6
12	Cherry Red CHERRY 501	Night Of The Humerons: Victoria Time/Taking Off (live) (p/s)	6
13	Cherry Red CHERRY 502	Sir William Wray/Jetplane/Hittite Man (p/s)	6

ALBUMS

Year	Label/Cat#	Title	Value
79	Step Forward SFLP 1	LIVE AT THE WITCH TRIALS (LP, 1st pressing)	45
79	Step Forward SFLP 4	DRAGNET (LP, 1st pressing, with insert. Lyntone version with LYN 7552/3 and SFLP 4 in run-out groove)	45
79	Step Forward SFLP4	DRAGNET (LP, 1st pressing, with insert. Non-Lyntone version with SFLP 4 in run-out groove)	40
80	Rough Trade ROUGH 10	TOTALE'S TURNS (IT'S NOW OR NEVER) (LP)	30
80	Rough Trade ROUGH 18	GROTESQUE (AFTER THE GRAMME) (LP)	30
81	Step Forward SFLP 6	THE EARLY YEARS 1977-79 (LP)	30
82	Kamera KAM 005	HEX EDUCATION HOUR (LP)	50
82	Kamera KAM 011	ROOM TO LIVE (LP)	40
83	Rough Trade ROUGH 062	PERVERTED BY LANGUAGE (LP)	40
84	Beggars Banquet BEGA 58	WONDERFUL AND FRIGHTENING WORLD OF (LP)	35
85	Beggars Banquet BEGA 67	THIS NATIONS SAVING GRACE (LP, gatefold with inner sleeve)	35
85	Situation 2 SITU 13	HIP PRIEST AND KAMERADAS (LP)	20
86	Beggars Banquet BEGA 75	BEND SINISTER (LP)	35
88	Beggars Banquet BEGA 91	THE FRENZ EXPERIMENT (LP, with free 7")	40
88	Beggars Banquet BEGA 91	THE FRENZ EXPERIMENT (LP)	20
88	Beggars Banquet BEGA 96	I AM A KURIOUS ORANJE (LP, gatefold)	40
90	Cog Sinister 842204	EXTRICATE (LP)	30
90	Beggars Banquet BEGA 111	458489 - A SIDES (LP)	30
90	Beggars Banquet BEGA 116	458489 - B SIDES (LP)	50
91	Cog Sinister COG 1	PALACE OF SWORDS REVERSED - COMPILATION 1980-83 (LP)	20
91	Cog Sinister 848594	SHIFT-WORK (LP)	20
92	Fontana 512162-1	CODE: SELFISH (LP)	60
93	Permanent PERMLP 12	THE INFOTAINMENT SCAN (LP)	80
94	Permanent PERMLP 16	MIDDLE CLASS REVOLT (LP)	80
95	Cog Sinister PERMLP 36	TWENTY SEVEN POINTS (2-LP, gatefold)	80
95	Cog Sinister PERMLP 30	CEREBRAL CAUSTIC (LP)	70
96	Receiver RRLP 209	SINISTER WALTZ (LP)	18
96	Receiver RRLP 211	FIEND WITH A VIOLIN (LP)	20
96	Receiver RRLP 213	OSWALD DEFENCE LAWYER (LP)	25
96	Jet JETLP 1012	THE LIGHT USER SYNDROME (LP)	80
97	Artful ARTFUL LP 9	LEVITATE (LP)	100
99	Artful ARTFUL LP 17	THE MARSHALL SUITE (2-LP)	100
02	Cog Sinister COGVP 131	ARE YOU ARE MISSING WINNER (LP, picture disc)	50
03	Action TAKE 21	THE REAL NEW FALL LP (LP)	60
05	Slogan SLOLP 003	FALL HEADS ROLL (LP)	150
05	BBC CMXBX982	COMPLETE PEEL SESSIONS (6-CD box set)	40
07	Slogan SLODV 007	REFORMATION POST TLC (LP)	30
07	Castle CMXBX1558	THE FALL BOX SET 1976-2007 (5-CD box set)	40
08	Sanctuary 1766796	IMPERIAL WAX SOLVENT (LP)	80
10	Domino WIGLP 245	YOUR FUTURE OUR CLUTTER (2-LP)	30
11	Cherry Red BRED 500	ERSATZ GB (LP)	40
13	Cherry Red BRED 580	RE-MIT (LP)	20
13	Ozit Morpheus OZITDALP 8014	LIVE IN SAN FRANCISCO (LP)	25
14	Secret SECLP 104	YARBLES (LP)	20
14	Cherry Red BRED 559	LIVE (2-LP, as The Fall Group)	25
15	Cherry Red BRED 660	SUB-LINGUAL (2-LP)	30
17	Cherry Red BRED 706	NEW FACTS EMERGE (LP, as 2 x 10")	20

ALBUMS : REISSUES

Year	Label/Cat#	Title	Value
85	Step Forward SFLP1	LIVE AT THE WITCH TRIALS (LP, repressing, with 'Made in France' on bottom of labels)	15
85	Step Forward SFLP4	DRAGNET (LP, reissue, with insert. 'Made in France' on bottom of labels)	15
02	Turning Point TPM 02208	LIVE AT THE WITCH TRIALS (LP, reissue)	15
02	Turning Point TPM 02209	DRAGNET (LP, reissue)	15
02	Turning Point TPM 02210	GROTESQUE (AFTER THE GRAMME) (LP, reissue)	15
05	Earmark 40040	HEX EDUCATION HOUR (2-LP, reissue)	25
14	Let Them Eat Vinyl LETV109LP	THE UNUTTERABLE (2-LP, reissue)	50
15	Beggars Banquet BBQLP 2136	WONDERFUL AND FRIGHTENING WORLD OF (2-LP reissue)	20
19	Cherry Red BRED 752	LIVE AT THE WITCH TRIALS (LP, reissue, red vinyl, some with badge)	20
19	Cherry Red BRED 744	DRAGNET (LP, reissue, splatter vinyl, with 7", some with badge)	30
19	Cherry Red BRED 781	ROOM TO LIVE (2-LP, reissue, brown marbled vinyl)	20

(see also D.O.S.E., Fates, Von Sudenfed)

FALLEN ANGELS (U.S.)

Year	Label/Cat#	Title	Value
67	London HL 10166	I Don't Want To Fall/Most Children Do	10
68	London HA-Z/SH-Z 8259	THE FALLEN ANGELS (LP)	50

Johnny FALLIN

MINT VALUE £

JOHNNY FALLIN
| 59 | Capitol CL 15043 | Party Kiss/The Creation Of Love | 60 |
| 59 | Capitol CL 15091 | Wild Streak/If I Could Write A Love Song | 60 |

FALLING LEAVES (1)
| 65 | Parlophone R 5233 | She Loves To Be Loved/Not Guilty | 75 |

FALLING LEAVES (2)
| 66 | Decca F 12420 | Beggar's Parade/Tomorrow Night | 50 |

FALLOUT (1)
81	No label or Cat. No.)	Conscription/Democracy?/Nuclear Power/Them & Us/Laughable Attack/Sign Away (fold-out sleeve)	15
83	Mouth Too Small To F. F2	SALAMI TACTICS (EP)	12
83	Own Label F3 LP 1	HOME COOKED MEAT (LP, with 2 inserts)	30

FALLOUT (2)
| 90 | Azuli AZ001 | The Morning After (12") | 20 |

FALLOUT CLUB
80	Secret SHH104	The Falling Years/The Beat Boys (p/s)	15
81	Happy Birthday UR 7	Wanderlust/Desert Song (p/s)	10
81	Happy Birthday UR 3	Dream Soldiers/Pedestrian Walk Way (p/s)	15

FALSE IDOLS (1)
| 78 | Old Knew Wave BOG 005 | Broken Judy/Marbled Hands/H-Brain (tri-fold p/s) | 12 |
| 78 | Old Knew Wave BOG 007 | Ego Wino/Good Night (p/s, pink vinyl) | 7 |

FALSE IDOLS (2)
| 81 | Caveman CM 02 | Ten Seconds To Midnight/American Nightmare | 12 |

AGNETHA FALTSKOG
82	Epic EPC A 2824	Never Again/Just For The Fun (p/s, with Tomas Ledin)	12
83	Epic EPC A 3436	The Heat Is On/Man (p/s)	6
83	Epic EPC WA 3436	The Heat Is On/Man (picture disc)	30
83	Epic EPC A 3622	Wrap Your Arms Around Me/Take Good Care Of The Children (p/s)	6
83	Epic EPC TA 3622	Wrap Your Arms Around Me/The Heat Is On/ Take Good Care Of The Children (Extended) (12", p/s)	12
83	Epic EPC A 3812	Can't Shake Loose/To Love (p/s)	6
83	Epic EPC A 3812	Can't Shake Loose/To Love (poster p/s)	15
83	Epic EPC WA 3812	Can't Shake Loose/To Love (picture disc)	25
85	Epic EPC A 6133	I Won't Let You Go/You're There (p/s)	6
85	Epic EPC TA 6133	I Won't Let You Go (Extended)/You're There (12", p/s)	12
86	Sonet SON 2317	The Way You Are/Fly Like The Eagle (p/s, with Ola Hanansson)	10
88	WEA YZ 170	The Last Time/Are You Gonna Throw It All Away (p/s)	6
88	WEA YZ 170T	The Last Time (Extended Remix)/The Last Time/ Are You Gonna Throw It All Away (12", p/s)	12
88	WEA YZ 177	I Wasn't The One (Who Said Goodbye)/If You Need Somebody Tonight (p/s, with Peter Cetera)	6
88	WEA YZ 177T	I Wasn't The One (Who Said Goodbye) (Extended Version)/(Yo No Fui [Quien Dijo Adios])/If You Need Somebody Tonight (12", p/s, with Peter Cetera)	12
88	WEA YZ 300	Let It Shine/Maybe It Was Magic (p/s)	8
88	WEA YZ 300T	Let It Shine (Extended)/('Bright' Mix)/Maybe It Was Magic (12", p/s)	12
98	Polydor POLPROCD 2	The Queen Of Hearts (Nar Du Tar Mej I Din Fam) (CD, promo only)	30
74	Embassy EMB 31094	AGNETHA (LP)	40

(see also Abba)

GEORGIE FAME (& THE BLUE FLAMES)

SINGLES
64	Columbia DB 7193	Do The Dog/Shop Around	25
64	Columbia DB 7255	Green Onions/Do-Re-Mi	18
64	Columbia DB 7328	Bend A Little/I'm In Love With You (solo)	20
65	Columbia DB 7494	In The Meantime/Telegram	10
65	Columbia DB 7633	Like We Used To Be/It Ain't Right	8
65	Columbia DB 7727	Something/Outrage	8
66	Columbia DB 7946	Getaway/El Bandido	8

(The above 45s were credited to Georgie Fame & Blue Flames)

66	Columbia DB 8015	Sunny/Don't Make Promises	7
66	Columbia DB 8096	Sitting In The Park/Many Happy Returns	8
67	CBS 202587	Because I Love You/Bidin' My Time (p/s)	8
67	CBS 5946/7	Knock On Wood/Didn't Want To Have To Do It (promo only)	20
67	CBS 2945	Try My World/No Thanks (p/s)	7
69	CBS 4659	Seventh Son/Fully Booked	7
70	CBS 5035	Entertaining Mr. Sloane/Somebody Stole My Thunder (DJ Copy)	175
70	CBS 5035	Entertaining Mr. Sloane/Somebody Stole My Thunder	150
77	Island WIP 6384	Daylight/Three Legged Mule	40
77	Island WIP 6384	Daylight/Three Legged Mule (12")	30

EPs
64	Columbia SEG 8334	RHYTHM AND BLUE BEAT	60
64	Columbia SEG 8382	RHYTHM AND BLUES AT THE FLAMINGO	50
64	Columbia SEG 8393	FAME AT LAST	25
65	Columbia SEG 8406	FATS FOR FAME	25
65	Columbia SEG 8454	MOVE IT ON OVER	25
66	Columbia SEG 8518	GETAWAY	25
67	CBS EP 6363	KNOCK ON WOOD	25
80	RSO 2252 136	BLUE BEAT	10

ALBUMS
| 64 | Columbia 33SX 1599 | RHYTHM AND BLUES AT THE FLAMINGO | 90 |
| 64 | Columbia 33SX 1638 | FAME AT LAST | 35 |

Georgie FAME & ANNIE ROSS

MINT VALUE £

Year	Catalogue	Title	Value
66	Columbia SX 6043	SWEET THINGS	25
66	Columbia SX 6076	SOUND VENTURE	40
67	Columbia SX 6120	HALL OF FAME	20
67	CBS (S)BPG 63018	TWO FACES OF FAME	20
68	CBS (S) 63293	THE THIRD FACE OF FAME (mono/stereo)	15
69	CBS S 63786	SEVENTH SON	15
69	Regal Starline SRS5002	GEORGIE FAME AND THE BLUE FLAMES	15
71	CBS S 64350	GOING HOME	15
72	Reprise K 44183	ALL ME OWN WORK (LP, gatefold sleeve)	20
74	Island ILPS 9293	GEORGIE FAME	20

(see also Blue Flames, Jimmy Nicol, Perry Ford & Sapphires, Annie Ross)

GEORGIE FAME & ANNIE ROSS

Year	Catalogue	Title	Value
81	Bald Eagle	Drip Drop/One Morning In May (12" p/s 50 copies only)	40

FAMILY

Year	Catalogue	Title	Value
67	Liberty LBF 15031	Scene Through The Eye Of A Lens/Gypsy Woman (misspress, B-side plays "Let Me Be Good To You" by Otis Redding)	150
67	Liberty LBF 15031	Scene Through The Eye Of A Lens/Gypsy Woman	200
68	Reprise RS 23270	Me My Friend/Hey Mr. Policeman	20
68	Reprise RS 23315	Second Generation Woman/Home Town	15
69	Reprise RS 27001	No Mule's Fool/Good Friend Of Mine (p/s)	15
70	Reprise RS 27005	Today/Song For Lots (p/s)	15
70	Reprise RS 27009	The Weaver's Answer/Strange Band/Hung Up Down (first pressing with 'cream' label in p/s)	8
71	Reprise SAM 1	Larf And Sing/Children (promo only)	15
73	Raft RA 18501	Boom Bang/Stop This Car	7
73	Raft RA 18503	Sweet Desiree/Drink To You	7
88	Strange Fruit SFPS 061	PEEL SESSIONS (12")	10
68	Reprise RLP 6312	MUSIC IN A DOLL'S HOUSE (LP, 1st pressing with 'Steamboat' label, insert, mono)	250
68	Reprise R(S)LP 6312	MUSIC IN A DOLL'S HOUSE (LP, 1st pressing, with 'Steamboat' label, insert, stereo)	150
69	Reprise RLP 6340	FAMILY ENTERTAINMENT (LP, 1st pressing, with 'Steamboat' label mono, with poster)	150
69	Reprise RSLP 6340	FAMILY ENTERTAINMENT (LP, 1st pressing with 'Steamboat' label, stereo, with poster)	90
70	Reprise RSLP 9001	A SONG FOR ME (LP, 1st pressing with 'Steamboat' label, with lyric sheet)	90
70	Reprise RSX 9005	ANYWAY (LP, custom polythene sleeve)	35
71	Reprise RMP 9007	OLD SONGS NEW SONGS (LP)	30
71	Reprise K 54003	FEARLESS (LP, multi gatefold sleeve, lyric insert)	50
72	Reprise K 54006	BANDSTAND (LP, 'window' die-cut sleeve, lyric inner)	30
73	Raft RA58501	IT'S ONLY A MOVIE (LP, lyric inner and 'banger' insert)	40
73	Raft RA 58501	IT'S ONLY A MOVIE (LP, lyric inner and no 'banger' insert)	15

(see also Farinas, Stud, Mogul Thrash, Hellions, Ashton Gardner & Dyke, Revolution, Streetwalkers)

FAMILY AFFAIR

Year	Catalogue	Title	Value
68	Saga STFID 2124	THE FAMILY AFFAIR (LP)	15

FAMILY CHOICE

Year	Catalogue	Title	Value
78	Union UN 005	Used To Be My Girl/Long Time	10
78	Union UND 1003	I'm Still Waiting/Don't Give Up Your Right (12")	35
77	S-Fa SOLP 001	DO IT AGAIN (LP)	40
78	BB BBL1R	LET'S DO IT TOGETHER (LP)	30

FAMILY CIRCLE

Year	Catalogue	Title	Value
69	Attack AT 8001	Phoenix Reggae/BIG L: Music Box	35
69	Attack AT 8002	Reggae Krishna/Official	40
69	JJ DB 1300	Give Peace A Chance/GEORGE LEE: Reggae Groove	30

FAMILY DOGG

Year	Catalogue	Title	Value
67	MGM MGM 1360	The Storm/Family Dogg	20
68	Fontana TF 921	I Wear A Silly Grin/Couldn't Help It	15
68	Fontana TF 968	Brown-Eyed Girl/Let It Rain	7
69	Bell BLL 1055	A Way Of Life/Throw It Away	7
69	Bell BLL 1077	Arizona/The House In The Heather	6
72	Buddah 2011-143	Sweet America/Rikers Island	10
70	Bell BLL 1100	When Tomorrow Comes Tomorrow/This Unhappy Heart Of Mine	6
69	Bell SBLL 122	A WAY OF LIFE (LP, with members of Led Zeppelin, gatefold)	30
72	Buddah 2318 061	THE VIEW FROM ROWLAND'S HEAD (LP, gatefold, lyric insert)	20

(see also Steve Rowland, Christine Holmes)

FAMILY FODDER

Year	Catalogue	Title	Value
79	Fresh Records FRESH 9	SUNDAY GIRLS (12")	15
80	Fresh FRESH 15	Debbie Harry/Version (p/s)	10
80	Fresh FRESH 22	Savoir Faire/Carnal Knowledge (p/s)	10
81	Fresh FRESH 37	ScHiZoPhReNiA pArTy! (12" EP)	10
82	Fresh FRESH 42	The Big Dig/Plant Life (p/s)	10
80	Fresh LP 3	MONKEY BANANA KITCHEN (LP)	25
83	Jungle FREUD 2	ALL STYLES (2-LP)	20

FAMILY MAN (ASTON BARRETT)

Year	Catalogue	Title	Value
70	Escort ERT 834	Midnight Sunshine/GREGORY ISAACS & STICKY: You Are My Sunshine	10
72	Downtown DT 491	Herb Tree/STUDIO SOUND: Holy Poly (reissue)	12

(see also Hippy Boys, Upsetters, Bob Marley & Wailers, Carl Dawkins)

FAMILY ON HOLIDAY

Year	Catalogue	Title	Value
81	Fabidoo S81CUS 1140	Who's A Pretty Boy Then/You're As Cute As A Dead Gerbil (p/s)	15

FAMOUS ECCLES & MISS FREDA THING

Year	Catalogue	Title	Value
56	Parlophone R 4251	My September Love/COUNT JIM MORIARTY & GRAVELEY STEPHENS: You Gotta Go Oww! (with The Alberts)	10

(see also Spike Milligan)

FAMOUS IMPOSTORS

Year	Catalogue	Title	Value
85	COR COR 7	WOULD ANYTHING CHANGE (12" EP p/s)	10

FAMOUS JUG BAND

MINT VALUE £

FAMOUS JUG BAND
69	Liberty LBF 15224	The Only Friend I Own/A Leaf Must Fall	10
69	Liberty LBS 83263	SUNSHINE POSSIBILITIES (LP, blue labels)	100
70	Liberty LBS 83355	CHAMELEON (LP, textured sleeve, blue labels)	100

(see also Incredible String Band, C.O.B.)

FAMOUS MUSIC BAND
69	Philips 6006 111	Nine By Nine/Going In The Out (with John Dummer)	8

(see also John Dummer)

FAMOUS PLAYERS
80	Page 45 AH 1001	Who's Kissing You/Angel In Black (p/s)	70

FANATICS
89	Chapter 22 12 CHAP 38	SUBURBAN LOVE SONGS (12" EP)	18

(see also Ocean Colour Scene)

FAN-CLUB
78	M&S SJP 791B	Avenue/Night Caller (p/s, photocopied insert)	15

FANCY
73	Sticky STY 3	Starlord/Brother John	30
74	Antic K11514	Touch Me/I Don't Need Your Love	8
75	Arista ARISTA 3	She's Riding The Rock Machine Part 1/Part 2	8
76	Arista ARIST 32	Music Maker/Bluebird	8
73	Atlantic K 51502	WILD THING (LP)	20
75	Arista ARTY 102	SOMETHING TO REMEMBER (LP)	20

(see also Ray Fenwick, Judas Priest)

FANDANGO
73	York SYK 562	High Class Girl/Sha La La	12

(see Nic Simper's Fandango, under 'S')

COSEY FANNI TUTTI
83	Flowmotion	TIME TO TELL (cassette with booklet)	50

(see also Throbbing Gristle, Chris & Cosey)

FANS
79	Fried Egg EGG 3	Giving Me That Look In Your Eyes/Stay The Night/He'll Have To Go (p/s)	50
79	Albion ION 0004	True (dayglo inner, inc bonus 7" & lyric sheet)	20
80	Albion FAN 01	Cars And Explosions/Dangerous Goodbyes (p/s)	20
81	Fried Egg EGG 10	You Don't Live Here Anymore/Following You (p/s)	60

FANTASIA (1)
67	Stateside SS 2031	Gotta Get Away/She Needs My Love	15

FANTASIA (2)
88	Greenwood SRT8KL 1456	THIS OLD TOWN (LP)	50
89	Greenwood SRT9KL2225	PICTURES IN MY MIND (LP)	100

FANTASTIC BAGGYS
76	United Artists UP 36142	Summer Means Fun/JAN & DEAN: Surf City/Sidewalk Surfin'	10

(see also Jan & Dean)

FANTASTIC FOUR
68	Tamla Motown TMG 678	I Love You Madly/I Love You Madly (Instrumental)	22
68	T. Motown TML 11105	THE FANTASTIC FOUR (LP, mono)	60
69	T. Motown STML 11105	THE FANTASTIC FOUR (LP, stereo)	50

FANTASTIC PUZZLES
76	Right On 106	Come Back/Come Back Part 2	35

FANTASTIC SOMETHING
84	Cherry Red CHERRY 61	If She Doesn't Smile (It'll Rain)/The Thousand Guitars Of St. Dominiques (p/s)	12

FANTASTICS
68	MGM MGM 1434	Baby Make Your Own Sweet Music/Who Could Be Lovin' You	20
68	MGM MGM 1434DJ	Baby Make Your Own Sweet Music/ Who Could Be Lovin' You (DJ promo)	30
69	Deram DM 264	Face To Face With Heartache/This Must Be My Rainy Day	6
70	Deram DM 283	Waiting Round For Heartaches/Ask The Lonely	20
71	Deram DM 334	For Old Times Sake/Exodus Main Theme	6

(see also Velours)

FANTASY
73	Polydor 2058 405	Politely Insane/I Was Once Aware	40
73	Polydor 2383 246	PAINT A PICTURE (LP, gatefold sleeve, red label)	1000
21	Record Collector RCLP 033	PAINT A PICTURE (LP, gatefold, reissue, red vinyl)	20

FANTOMS
83	Ear To Ear GRIN 1	Hearts Of Stone (Break Hearts OF Glass)/Really Mystified (p/s)	10

BARRY FANTONI
66	Fontana TF 707	Little Man In A Little Box/Fat Man	35
67	Columbia DB 8238	Nothing Today/The Spanish Lady Tango	8

FAPARDOKLY
83	Psycho PSYCHO 5	FAPARDOKLY (LP, 300 only)	20

(see also Mu)

FARAWAY FOLK
70s	Tabitha TAB 3	Shadow Of A Pie/Folsom Prison Blues/Rent A Man/Soulful Shade Of Blue	12
70	RA EP 7001	INTRODUCING THE FARAWAY FOLK (EP)	26
70	RA LP 6006ST	LIVE AT THE BOLTON (LP)	30
70	RA LP 6012ST	TIME AND TIDE (LP)	30
74	RA LP 6019	ON THE RADIO (LP)	30
75	RA LP 6022	ONLY AUTHORISED EMPLOYEES TO BREAK BOTTLES (LP, with Harry H. Corbett)	22
75	RA LP 6029	SEASONAL MAN (LP, gatefold sleeve with insert)	200
80s	RA	BATTLE OF THE DRAGONS (LP)	15

(see also Harry H. Corbett)

FAR CRY

MINT VALUE £

FAR CRY
69	Vanguard SVRL 19041	THE FAR CRY (LP)	30

DON FARDON
67	Pye International 7N 25437	(The Lament Of The Cherokee) Indian Reservation/Dreamin' Room	10
69	Pye International 7N 25483	We Can Make It Together/Coming On Strong	25
69	Pye International 7N 25486	Good Lovin'/Ruby's Pictures On My Wall	8
69	Youngblood YB 1003	I'm Alive/Keep On Loving Me	40
69	Young Blood YB 1007	It's Been Nice Loving You/Let The Love Live	25
70	Young Blood YB 1010	Belfast Boy/Echoes Of The Cheers	20
70	Young Blood YB 1015	Indian Reservation/Hudson Bay	10
70	Young Blood SSYB 4	I'VE PAID MY DUES! (LP)	20
70	Young Blood SSYB 13	RELEASED (LP)	15

(see also Sorrows)

FAR EAST FAMILY BAND
75	Vertigo 6370 850	NIPPONJIN (LP)	40

DICK FARINA & ERIC VON SCHMIDT
63	Folklore F-LEUT/7	DICK FARINA & ERIC VON SCHMIDT (LP, featuring 'Blind Boy Grunt')	100

(see also Bob Dylan, Richard & Mimi Farina, Four For Fun)

RICHARD & MIMI FARINA
65	Fontana STFL 6060	CELEBRATIONS FOR A GREY DAY (LP)	30
65	Fontana STFL 6075	REFLECTIONS IN A CRYSTAL WIND (LP)	30

(see also Dick Farina & Eric Von Schmidt)

FARINAS
64	Victor Buckland Sound Studio	Bye Bye Johnny/All You Gotta Do/Twist And Shout (as James King & Farinas)	400
64	Fontana TF 493	You'd Better Stop/I Like It Like That	80

TAL FARLOW
57	Columbia 33CX 10029	THE INTERPRETATIONS OF (LP)	15

CHRIS FARLOWE (& THUNDERBIRDS)
62	Decca F 11536	Air Travel/Why Did You Break My Heart?	60
63	Columbia DB 7120	I Remember/Push Push (as Chris Farlowe & Thunderbirds)	40
64	Columbia DB 7237	Girl Trouble/Itty Bitty Pieces (as Chris Farlowe & Thunderbirds)	40
64	Columbia DB 7311	Just A Dream/What You Gonna Do? (as Chris Farlow & Thunderbirds)	40
64	Columbia DB 7379	Hey, Hey, Hey, Hey/Hound Dog (as Chris Farlowe & Thunderbirds)	30
65	Columbia DB 7614	Buzz With The Fuzz/You're The One (withdrawn, as Chris Farlow & Thunderbirds, demos more common £100)	200
65	Immediate IM 016	The Fool/Treat Her Good	15
66	Immediate IM 023	Think/Don't Just Look At Me	30
66	Immediate IM 035	Out Of Time/Baby Make It Soon (3.13 version, CBS pressing, matrix 1F//1)	7
66	Immediate IM 035	Out Of Time/Baby Make It Soon (3.28 version, Philips pressing, matrix 1F V2)	7
66	Columbia DB 7983	Just A Dream/Hey, Hey, Hey	15
66	Immediate IM 038	Ride On Baby/Headlines	12
67	Immediate IM 041	My Way Of Giving/You're So Good To Me	15
67	Immediate IM 049	Yesterday's Papers/Life Is Just Nothing	8
67	Immediate IM 056	Moanin'/What Have I Been Doin'?	8
67	Immediate IM 065	Handbags And Gladrags/Everyone Makes A Mistake	10
68	Immediate IM 066	The Last Goodbye/Paperman Fly In The Sky (B-side with Thunderbirds)	15
68	Immediate IM 071	Paint It Black/I Just Need Your Loving	10
69	Immediate IM 074	Dawn/April Was The Month	15
70	Polydor 2066 017	Black Sheep Of The Family/Fifty Years (as Chris Farlowe with The Hill)	6
70	Polydor 2066 046	Put Out The Light/Questions (as Chris Farlowe & Hill)	10
78	Beeb BEEB 022	Gangsters (as Chris Farlowe & Dave Greenslade)/DAVE GREENSLADE'S GANGSTERS: Sarah Gant Theme	6
65	Decca DFE 8665	CHRIS FARLOWE (EP)	100
65	Immediate IMEP 001	FARLOWE IN THE MIDNIGHT HOUR (EP)	50
66	Immediate IMEP 004	CHRIS FARLOWE HITS (EP)	40
66	Island IEP 709	STORMY MONDAY (EP)	120
66	Columbia SX 6034	CHRIS FARLOWE AND THE THUNDERBIRDS (LP, black/blue labels with "sold in the U.K..." text)	150
66	Music For Pleasure MFP 1186	STORMY MONDAY (LP, reissue of Chris Farlowe & Thunderbirds LP)	20
66	Immediate IMLP 005	14 THINGS TO THINK ABOUT (LP, lilac label)	75
66	Immediate IMLP 006	THE ART OF CHRIS FARLOWE (LP, mono, lilac label)	70
66	Immediate IMSP 006	THE ART OF CHRIS FARLOWE (LP, stereo, lilac label)	100
67	EMI Regal REG 2025	CHRIS FARLOWE (LP, export issue)	40
68	Immediate IMCP 010	THE BEST OF CHRIS FARLOWE VOLUME ONE (LP, lilac label)	30
69	Immediate IMLP 021	THE LAST GOODBYE (LP, pink label with "sold in U.K..." text)	100
70	Polydor 2425 029	FROM HERE TO MAMA ROSA (LP, as Chris Farlowe & Hill, gatefold sleeve, insert)	60

(see also Thunderbirds, Beazers, Little Joe Cook, Crane/Farlowe, Atomic Rooster, Colosseum, Dave Greenslade, Spectrum)

FARM
74	Spark SRL1105	Fat Judy/Gysy Mountain Woman	30

ART FARMER
54	Esquire 20-033	ART FARMER SEXTET — WORK OF ART (10" LP)	50
55	Esquire 32 042	CHARTS (LP)	30
55	Esquire 32-037	WILD PARTY (LP)	50
56	Esquire 32-072	TWO TRUMPETS (LP, with Donald Byrd)	50
56	Esquire 32-137	FARMERS MARKET (LP)	75
58	Contemporary LAC 12197	PORTRAIT OF ART FARMER (LP)	30
59	London SAH-T 6028	MODERN ART (LP)	35
60	London Jazz LTZ-T 15184	BRASS SHOUT (LP)	35
60	London Jazz LTZ-T 15198	THE AZTEC SUITE (LP)	35

			MINT VALUE £
60	Pye Jazz NJL 45	MEET THE JAZZTET (with Benny Golson)	35
61	Esquire 32 197	EARLY ART (LP)	40
61	Esquire 32-120	EARTHY (LP)	35
64	London HA-K/SH-K 8135	INTERACTION (LP, as Art Farmer Quartet featuring Jim Hall)	25
73	Mainstream MSL 1013	GENTLE EYES (LP, gatefold)	20
77	CTI CTI 7073	CRAWL SPACE (LP, gatefold)	15

(see also Clifford Brown, Benny Golson, Donald Byrd)

JULES FARMER
59	London HLP 8967	Love Me Now/Part Of Me (Is Still With You)	10

MYLENE FARMER
91	Polydor 873 738 7	Desenchantee (Edited Version)/Desenchantee (Chaos Mix) (Promo only)	20

FARMLIFE
82	Dining Out TUX 19	Susie's Party/Simple Men	6
83	Whaam! WHAAM 13	Big Country 1 & 2 (unreleased; Echantillan test pressings only)	40

GILES FARNABY'S DREAM BAND
73	Argo AFW 112	Newcastle Brown/29th Of May	12
73	Argo ZDA 158	GILES FARNABY'S DREAM BAND (LP)	60

(see also Druids)

FARNBOROUGH FIREWORK FACTORY
72	Decca F13290	Too Many People/She's Against The Law	15

(see also Mike Batt)

ROBERT FARNON ORCHESTRA
56	Decca F 10818	Westminister Waltz/Poodle Parade	6
63	Philips BF 1299	Charade/Gina Gina Don't You Cry	6
55	Decca LK 4119	CANADIAN IMPRESSIONS (LP)	20
56	Vogue Coral LVA 9005	GENTLEMEN MARRY BRUNETTES (LP, soundtrack)	30
60	Delyse ECB 3157/DS 6057	CAPTAIN HORATIO HORNBLOWER (LP, soundtrack, mono)	30
60	Delyse DS 6057	CAPTAIN HORATIO HORNBLOWER (LP, soundtrack, stereo)	30
68	Philips SBL 7867	SHALAKO (LP, soundtrack)	15

(see also Jack Saunders)

ROBERT FARNON & TONY COE
70	Chapter One CHS 804	POP MAKES PROGRESS (LP)	30

(see also Tony Coe)

FARON'S FLAMINGOS
63	Oriole CB 1834	Do You Love Me?/See If She Cares	25
63	Oriole CB 1867	Shake Sherry/Give Me Time	30
79	Raw RAW 28	Bring It On Home/C'mon Everybody	10

(see also Big Three, Mojos)

WAYNE FARO'S SCHMALTZ BAND
69	Deram DM 222	There's Still Time/Give It Time	40

FARQUAHAR
71	Elektra EK45713	Hanging On By A Thread/Start Living	6

GARY FARR (& THE T-BONES)
65	Columbia DB 7608	Give All She's Got/Don't Stop And Stare (as Gary Farr & T-Bones) (demo in p/s)	100
65	Columbia DB 7608	Give All She's Got/Don't Stop And Stare (as Gary Farr & T-Bones)	50
68	Marmalade 598 007	Everyday/Green (with Kevin Westlake)	25
69	Marmalade 598 017	Hey Daddy/The Vicar And The Pope	25
71	CBS 5430	Revolution Of The Seasons/Old Man Boulder	12
65	Columbia SEG 8414	DEM BONES, DEM BONES, DEM T-BONES (EP)	120
69	Marmalade 608 013	TAKE SOMETHING WITH YOU (LP)	300
71	CBS 64138	STRANGE FRUIT (LP, with Richard Thompson & Mighty Baby)	200
08	Sunbeam SBR2LP5051	TAKE SOMETHING WITH YOU (2-LP, reissue)	20

(see also T-Bones, Richard Thompson, Mighty Baby, Meic Stevens, Kevin Westlake & Gary Farr)

FARRAGO
79	ESP 9269	I Wouldn't Wanna Be Like You/If I Can't Have You (no p/s)	15

MARY ANN FARRAR & SATIN SOUL
76	Brunswick BR 38	Stoned Out Of My Mind/Living In The Footsteps Of Another Girl (DJ Copy)	30
76	Brunswick BR 38	Stoned Out Of My Mind/Living In The Footsteps Of Another Girl	20
76	Brunswick BRLS 3022	NEVER GONNA LEAVE YOU (LP)	30

BILLY FARRELL
58	Philips PB 828	Yeah Yeah/Someday (You'll Want Me To Want You)	22

DO & DENA FARRELL
57	HMV POP 427	Young Magic/New Love Tonight	15

MICK FARREN
78	Logo GO 321	Half Price Drinks/I Don't Want To Go This Way (thick card p/s, black and yellow on front)	6
70	Transatlantic TRA 212	MONA (THE CARNIVOROUS CIRCUS) (LP, lilac label with "t" logo)	150
78	Logo LOGO 2010	VAMPIRES STOLE MY LUNCH MONEY (LP, with lyric insert)	25
84	Psycho PSYCHO 20	MONA (THE CARNIVOROUS CIRCUS) (LP, reissue)	20

(see also Deviants, Twink)

FARRIERS
69	Broadside BRO 112	FARRIERS (LP)	20
76	Broadside BRO 119	KEMPION BRUMMAGEM BALLADS (LP, featuring Dick Brice)	50

FARTZ
82	Alt. Tentacles VIRUS 21	BECAUSE THIS FUCKIN' WORLD STINKS (EP)	12
82	Alt. Tentacles VIRUS 17	WORLD FULL OF HATE (12" EP with poster)	25

FASCINATIONS
67	Stateside SS 594	Girls Are Out To Get You/You'll Be Sorry	75
67	Stateside SS 594	Girls Are Out To Get You/You'll Be Sorry (DJ copy)	150
68	Sue WI 4049	Girls Are Out To Get You/You'll Be Sorry (reissue)	40
71	Mojo 2092 004	Girls Are Out To Get You/You'll Be Sorry (2nd reissue)	10

FASCINATORS (1)

MINT VALUE £

71	Mojo 2092 018	I'm So Lucky (He Loves Me)/Say It Isn't So	8

FASCINATORS (1)
58	Capitol CL 14942	Chapel Bells/I Wonder Who	300
59	Capitol CL 15062	Oh, Rose Marie/Fried Chicken And Macaroni	150

FASCINATORS (2)
81	Penthouse PENT 9	Blue Movies/Monochrome Moon (p/s)	70

FASHAWN
10	High Water HWM013	BOY MEETS WORLD (2-LP)	50

FASHION
81	Arista 12440	Move On/Mutant Dance Move (p/s)	10
79	Fashion FML001	PRODUCT PERFECT (LP)	15

FASHIONS
68	Stateside SS 2115	I.O.U. (A Lifetime Of Love)/When Love Slips Away	10
69	Evolution E 2444	I.O.U. (A Lifetime Of Love)/He Gives Me Love (La La La)	8

FAST
76	CBS SCBS 6236	Boys Will Be Boys/Wow Pow Bash Crash	6

FASTBACKS
89	Subway SUBWAY 26	Wrong Wrong Wrong/In America (p/s)	6

FAST BREEDERS
82	Breeder BMS 82001 S82 CUS 1570	How Could You/Strange Party	20

FAST BREEDERS & RADIO ACTORS
78	Nuke NUKE 235	Nuclear Waste/Digital Love (in p/s, with insert)	18
78	Nuke NUKE 235	Nuclear Waste/Digital Love	10

(see also Radio Actors)

FAST CARS
79	Streets Ahead SA 3	The Kids Just Wanna Dance/You're So Funny (1,000 only, p/s)	200
01	Detour DR 075	Everyday I Make Another Mistake/I'm All Right (p/s, pink vinyl, 100 only)	10

FAST EDDIE (1)
82	Well Suspect BLAM 001	My Babe/Help Me/Sweet Sensations (p/s)	8

FAST EDDIE (2)
88	Westside DJINT 04	Acid Thunder (Smooth Thunder)/AA Aacid/Fast Thunder/Tyree's Supercooper Mix (12")	25
88	Westside PROMO 18	My Melody/Halloween House (12") (with Slick Master Rick)	20
88	DJ International DJART 902	JACK TO THE SOUND (LP with free 12")	15

FAST LINE
70	Highwire HW 001	Look Into My Mind/A Nice Time To Die (p/s)	40

FAST SET
80	Axis AXIS 1	Junction One/Children Of The Revolution (p/s)	25

FAT
71	RCA LSA 3009	FAT (LP)	50

FATAL CHARM
79	Company CR 005	Paris/Glitterbit/Out Of My Head	8
87	Native 7N TV 20	Lucille/To Master A Plan (p/s)	6
89	Fatal 1	THIS STRANGE ATTRACTION (LP)	25

FATAL MICROBES
79	Small Wonder SMALL 20	Violence Grows/Beautiful Pictures/Cry Baby (p/s)	20

(see also Pete Fender)

FATAL MICROBES/POISON GIRLS
79	Small Wonder WEENY 3	FATAL MICROBES MEET THE POISON GIRLS (12" EP, with insert)	15

(see also Poison Girls)

FATBACK BAND
74	Polydor 2391 143	KEEP ON STEPPIN' (LP)	15
75	Polydor 2391 184	YUM YUM (LP)	15

FATES
85	Taboo HAG 1	FURIA (LP)	25

FATHEAD
83	Greensleeves GRED 118	Champion/Stop All The Fight (12")	20

FATHER THOMAS
70	Candidate 1	Look For The Sun/There's A Dream	70

FATHER JOHN MISTY
15	Bella Union BELLA 487V	I Loved You Honeybee/I've Never Been A Woman (heart-shaped red vinyl)	40
15	Bella Union BELLA 476VX	I LOVE YOU HONEYBEAR (2-LP, CD coloured vinyl and musical pop up sleeve)	50
15	Bella Union BELLA 476V	I LOVE YOU HONEYBEAR (LP, with CD, poster)	25
15	Bella Union BELLA 527V	LIVE AT ROUGH TRADE (LP)	18
17	Bella Union BELLA 628VX	PURE COMEDY (2-LP, aluminium/copper vinyl, poster, tarot card and 4 sleeve variations)	30

(see also Fleet Foxes)

FATHER'S ANGELS
68	MGM MGM 1459	Don't Knock It/Bok To Bach	250
68	MGM MGM 1459	Don't Knock It/Bok To Bach (DJ Copy)	300
75	Black Magic BM 103	Bok To Bach/Disco Trucking	6

FATHER'S BROWN
70	Decca F23059	Maybe/The Yellow Moon Is High	20

FAT LARRY'S BAND
82	WMOT VS 491	Act Like You Know/Get Down And Get Funky	20

FATMAN VERSUS JAH SHAKA
80	Live & Love LAP12	IN A DUB CONFERENCE (LP)	35

FAT MATTRESS
69	Polydor 56352	Naturally/Iridescent Butterfly	10
69	Polydor 56367	Magic Forest/Bright New Way	15

Eric FATTER

MINT VALUE £

70	Polydor 2058 053	Highway/Black Sheep Of The Family	15
69	Polydor 582/583 056	FAT MATTRESS (LP, open-out sleeve, red label)	50
70	Polydor 2383 025	FAT MATTRESS II (LP, red label)	50

(see also Jimi Hendrix Experience, Flowerpot Men, Juicy Lucy)

ERIC FATTER
69	Camel CA 20	Since You've Been Gone (actually Eric Fratter)/WINSTON HINES: Cool Down (B-side actually by Winston Hinds)	25

(see also Eric Fratter, Afrotones)

FAT TULIPS
90	Heaven HV 01	Where's Clare Grogan Now?/To Put It Bluntly (p/s)	10
90	Heaven HV 02	FOUR SONGS FOR SIMON EP	6
90	Heaven HV 04	FERENSWAY EP (hand-painted sleeve)	6
91	Marineville MARINE 1	Passionate Friend/Treason/Reward (p/s, 'The Tulip Explodes' artwork)	6
88	Sweet William BILLY 001	You Opened My Eyes/ROSEHIPS: Ask Johnny Dee (33rpm flexi, p/s w/insert)	15

ERNIE FAULKNER
63	Sway SW 003	Beautiful Girl/SAM DANIELS: Tell Me Baby (both with The Planets)	8

FAUST
72	Faust/Polydor 2001-299	It's A Bit Of A Pain/So Far	25
79	Recommended RR 2.5	It's A Bit Of A Pain/So Far (p/s, reissue)	8
96	Die Stadt 011	Right Between Yr Eyes (p/s, Uberschall Festival single, with Stereolab and Foetus)	20
90	Chemical Imbalance CI 08	Live In Hamburg (issued free with Chemical Imbalance magazine)	25
79	Recommended RR 1.5	EXTRACTS FROM FAUST PARTY 3: Extract 1/Extract 4 (EP)	12
80	Recommended RR 6.5	EXTRACTS FROM FAUST PARTY 3: Extract 2/Extract 6 (EP)	12
71	Polydor 2310 142	FAUST (LP, initial pressing on clear vinyl, with clear sleeve & clear insert)	150
71	Polydor 2310 142	FAUST (LP, insert)	70
72	Polydor 2310 196	SO FAR (LP, with 9 prints in wallet)	150
73	Virgin VC 501	THE FAUST TAPES (LP)	25
73	Virgin V 2004	FAUST IV (LP)	40
79	Recommended R.R. 1	FAUST (LP, reissue, clear vinyl, clear sleeve, insert)	30
79	Recommended R.R. 2	SO FAR (LP, reissue, with 10 insert prints, numbered, 600 only)	50
80	Recommended R.R. 6	THE FAUST TAPES (LP, plastic bag cover)	20
86	Recommended R.R. 125	MUNICH AND ELSEWHERE (LP)	20
88	ReR Megacorp Rer 36	THE LAST LP (LP, numbered)	20
10	ReR Megacorp VF2	THE FAUST TAPES (LP, reissue, 180 gm vinyl)	18

(see also Toni Conrad & Faust)

FAVOURITES
80	4 Play FOUR 002	S.O.S./Favourite Shoes (p/s)	80
80	4 Play FOUR 003	Angelica/Cold (p/s)	30

FAVOURITE SONS
65	Mercury MF 911	That Driving Beat/Walkin' Walkin' Walkin'	175

DAVE FAWCETT
81	DMF MK 1	My Car/Danger In The Night (no p/s)	30

WALLY FAWKES (& HIS TROGLODYTES)
58	Decca F 11002	The Pilot Fish And The Whale/Pale Blues	10
57	Decca DEF 6407	AND HIS TROGLODYTES (EP)	10
60	Decca DFE 6600	FLOOK DIGS JAZZ (EP)	10
61	Decca STO 136	A NIGHT AT THE SIX BELLS (EP)	10
58	Decca LF 312	FAWKES ON HOLIDAY (LP)	15

(see also Sandy Brown)

CHARLIE FAWN
79	WEA K 17835	Blue Skies/Dream World	7
79	WEA/Hansa K17430	Hothead Handshake Tremble/Playthings	7
80	Warner Bros K 17566	Always Something There To Remind Me/Poet For A Generation	8

BILL FAY
67	Deram DM 143	Some Good Advice/Screams In The Ears	60
70	Deram Nova SDN 12	BILL FAY (LP, stereo)	400
70	Deram Nova DN 12	BILL FAY (LP, mono)	500
71	Deram SML 1079	TIME OF THE LAST PERSECUTION (LP, red/white label)	1000
09	Deram Nova SDN 12	BILL FAY (LP, reissue, stereo)	25

FAY & THE BITTER SWEET
74	A Rover AR 02	You're A Pirate Lover/Message To You	6

ALMA FAYE
79	Flamingo FM 5	Don't Fall In Love/I Believed (DJ copy)	60
78	Flamingo FM 5	Don't Fall In Love/I Believed	50
79	Flamingo 12 FM 5	Don't Fall In Love/I Believed (12")	15

FRANCIS FAYE
61	Vogue V 9186	I Wish I Could Shimmy Like My Sister Kate/Night And Day	10
65	Stateside SL 10129	YOU GOTTA GO! GO! GO! (LP)	20

FAZE II
95	Ugly UGM 002	HOUSE OF LZ (12")	10

FAZED IDJUTS
99	U Star USR 002	Dust Of Life (12", single sided)	20
99	U Star USR 004	Dust Of Life - Joe Clasuusee Remixes (12")	10

FBD PROJECT
92	Bang In Tunes BT 001	F.B.D./Blasted (12" white label)	20
93	Bang In Tunes BT 002	Terminate/F-B-D Remix/Blasted (Remix) (12" white label)	40
93	Bang In Tunes BT 003	Breakin Up/The Core (12", black labels)	50
93	FBD Project FBD 03	Deep Dance EP (12", pink labels)	40
93	Bang In Tunes BT 004	Ruff To Da Smooth (The Remixes) (12")	35
94	Bang In Tunes BT 005	Journeys/Just Wanna Live (12")	35

F.B.I. (FOLK BLUES INC.)

MINT VALUE £

94	Bang In Tunes BIT 009	She's So (Revisited)/Ruffguide (12")	25
98	Bang In Tunes BITRP 001	The Core/Terminate (12")	40
16	Bang In Tunes BITRLP002	The Core - 2016 Remixes (2 x 12")	30

F.B.I. (FOLK BLUES INC.)
66	Eyemark EMS 1006	Don't Hide/When The Ship Comes In	25
73	A&M AMS 7050	I Wonder What She's Doing Tonight/Boogaloo Boo-Boo	10
76	Good Earth GD 6	F.B.I./The Time Is Right To Leave The City	25
77	Good Earth GDS 802	F.B.I. (LP)	60

FEAR FACTORY
95	Roadrunner RR 8856-1	DEMANUFACTURE (LP)	35

FEAR OF FLYING (1)
81	Fear Of Flying 001	Tired/This Thing	8

FEAR OF FLYING (2)
06	Young And Lost YALC 0011	Three's A Crowd/Forget-Me-Nots (p/s)	7

FEARN'S BRASS FOUNDRY
68	Decca F 12721	Don't Change It/John White	50
68	Decca F 12835	Now I Taste The Tears/Love, Sink And Drown	25

FEAR OF FALLING
83	Excellent XL 7	Like A Lion/You My Prodigal Son (p/s)	20

CHARLIE FEATHERS
76	Red Neck R 100	Tongue Tied Jill/Gone Gone Gone	10
76	Charley CEP 116	CHARLIE FEATHERS (EP)	10

CHARLIE FEATHERS/MAC CURTIS
74	Polydor 2310 293	ROCKABILLY KINGS (LP)	20

(see also Mac Curtis)

FEATURES (1)
77	Progress PR 01	Drab City/Job Satisfaction	50

FEATURES (2)
80	Double D DDEE 3	Go Now/Make Me Wanna	10
80	ASM HIT 06	She Makes Me Blue/Don't Let Them Know	20
81	AFM PET 01	Monday-Friday/Cue The Next Army	20

FEDERALMEN
70	London HLU 10303	Soul Serenade/Scorcher	8

FEDERALS (JAMAICA)
67	Island WI 3126	Penny For Your Song/I've Passed This Way Before	30
68	Island WI 3152	Shocking Love/By The River	25
69	High Note HS 024	Wailing Festival/Me And My Baby (B-side actually "By The River")	15
70	Camel CA 40	In This World/You Better Call On Me (B-side actually "Shocking Love")	100

FEDERALS (U.K.)
63	Parlophone R 4988	Brazil/In A Persian Market	15
63	Parlophone R 5013	Boot Hill/Keep On Dancing With Me	15
64	Parlophone R 5100	The Climb/Dance With A Dolly	15
64	Parlophone R 5139	Marlena/Please Believe Me	15
64	Parlophone R 5193	Twilight Time/Lost And Alone	15
65	Parlophone R 5320	Bucket Full Of Love/Leah	25

(see also Winston's Fumbs, Yes)

FEDS
85	FED rated NSFRED 1	Don't Take My Love Away/Louise	8

FEEDER
96	Echo ECS 13	TWO COLOURS: Pictures Of Rain/Chicken On A Bone (p/s, clear vinyl)	40
96	Echo ECSCD 13	TWO COLOURS: Pictures Of Rain/Chicken On A Bone (CD, 1,000 only)	40
96	Echo ECS 27	Stereo World/My Perfect Day (p/s)	10
97	Echo ECS 32	Tangerine/Rhubarb (die-cut p/s)	10
01	Echo	Turn/Bad Hair Day (6-12 white label promo competition prizes. 7" die-cut sleeve)	10
04	Echo ECS157A/B -1	Tumble and Fall/Victoria (12" white label promos auctioned for Warchild charity)	15
96	Echo ECHLP 9	SWIM (LP, inner)	40
97	Echo ECHLP 15	POLYTHENE (LP, vinyl re-issue of original CD album, with free High 7", 500 only)	120
97	Echo ECHLP 15	POLYTHENE (LP, vinyl re-issue of original CD album, without free 7")	80
99	Echo ECHLP 28	YESTERDAY WENT TOO SOON (LP, top opening sleeve, inner)	80
01	Echo ECHLP 34	ECHO PARK (LP, gatefold, inner)	75
02	Echo ECHLP 43	COMFORT IN SOUND (LP, white vinyl)	60
04	Echo ECHLP 52	PICTURE OF PERFECT YOUTH (3xLP)	40
05	Echo ECHLP 60	PUSHING THE SENSES (LP)	40
08	Echo ECHLP 79	SILENT CRY (LP)	30

FEELIES
79	Stiff (no cat. no.)	Fa Ce La/The Boy With Perpetual Nervousness/ Everybody's Got Something To Hide (Except Me And My Monkey) (flexidisc, promo only, free with Be Stiff fanzine issue 6, 5,000 only)	6
79	Rough Trade RT 24	Fa Ce La/Raised Eyebrows (p/s)	10
80	Stiff BUY 65	Everybody's Got Something To Hide/Original Love (p/s)	7
80	Stiff SEEZ 20	CRAZY RHYTHMS (LP)	40
86	Rough Trade ROUGH 104	THE GOOD EARTH (LP)	18
09	Domino REWIGLP 65	CRAZY RHYTHMS (LP, reissue, stickered sleeve)	15
09	Domino REWIGLP 66	THE GOOD EARTH (LP, reissue)	15

FEIST
12	Roadrunner 5439 19780 0	Black Tongue/MASTODON: A Commotion	8

FELDER'S ORIOLES
65	Piccadilly 7N 35247	Down Home Girl/Misty	40
65	Piccadilly 7N 35269	Sweet Tasting Wine/Turn On Your Lovelight	20
66	Piccadilly 7N 35311	I Know You Don't Love Me No More/Only Three Can Play	20

Victor FELDMAN BIG BAND/QUARTET

MINT VALUE £

| 66 | Piccadilly 7N 35332 | Back Street/Something You Got | 25 |

(see also V.I.P.s, Mike Patto)

VICTOR FELDMAN BIG BAND/QUARTET

56	Tempo A 142	Big Top/Cabaletto	15
57	Tempo A 154	Jackpot/You Are My Heart's Desire	15
62	Fontana 267233	A Taste Of Honey/Valerie	10
55	Tempo EXA 29	BIG BAND (EP)	50
57	Tempo EXA 57	VICTOR FELDMAN IN LONDON -- THE QUARTET VOLUME 1 (EP)	60
57	Tempo EXA 67	VICTOR FELDMAN IN LONDON VOLUME 2 (EP)	60
58	Tempo EXA 85	MUTUAL ADMIRATION (EP, with Dizzy Reece)	75
53	Esquire EP 43	MODERN JAZZ QUARTET (EP)	40
53	Esquire EP 54	MODERN JAZZ QUARTET (EP)	20
53	Esquire EP 64	MODERN JAZZ QUINTET/SEXTET (EP)	25
53	Esquire EP 84	MODERN JAZZ QUARTET/SEXTET (EP)	20
54	Esquire EP 104	MODERN JAZZ QUARTET (EP)	40
54	Esquire EP 114	VIC FELDMAN ENCORE (EP)	20
54	Esquire 20 - 046	MULTIPLE TALENTS (LP)	60
55	Esquire 20 - 064	EXPERIMENT IN TIME (LP)	60
55	Tempo LAP 5	VICTOR FELDMAN'S SEXTET (10" LP)	300
56	Tempo LAP 6	VICTOR FELDMAN MODERN JAZZ QUARTET (10" LP)	200
57	Tempo TAP 8	VICTOR FELDMAN IN LONDON VOL. 1 (LP)	150
57	Tempo TAP 12	VICTOR FELDMAN IN LONDON VOL. 2 (LP)	150
58	Tempo TAP 19	TRANSATLANTIC ALLIANCE (LP)	350
59	Contemporary LAC 12172	THE ARRIVAL OF VICTOR FELDMAN (LP)	20
61	Riversode RLP 366	MERRY OLDE SOUL (LP)	20
63	MGM C 8954	SOVIET JAZZ THEMES (LP)	15
64	Contemporary LAC 580	LATINSVILLE! (LP)	50
67	United Artists UAS 529006	PLAYS EVERYTHING IN SIGHT (LP)	15
82	Jasmine JASM 2023	IN LONDON VOL. 1 (LP, reissue)	15
82	Jasmine JASM 2023	IN LONDON VOL. 2 (LP, reissue)	15

(see also Dizzy Reece, Tubby Hayes)

VICTOR FELDMAN, TERRY GIBBS & LARRY BUNKER

| 60 | Top Rank 30/007 | VIBES TO THE POWER OF THREE (LP) | 20 |

FELICE BROTHERS

| 07 | Loose VJLP 171 | LIVE AT THE ARIZONA (LP) | 100 |

JOSE FELICIANO

| 74 | RCA RCA PB10094 | Golden Lady/Virgo | 60 |

FELIUS ANDROMEDA

| 67 | Decca F 12694 | Meditations/Cheadle Heath Delusions | 60 |
| 72 | Cactus CT 2 | After The Storm/Rainbow Chasing (as Andromeda) | 15 |

(see also Denis Couldry)

FELIX & HIS GUITAR

| 59 | London HLU 8875 | Chili Beans/Puerto Rican Riot | 8 |

LENNIE FELIX, BRIAN LEMON, KEITH INGHAM, RALPH SUTTON

| 75 | 77 77S 58 | PIANO SUMMIT (LP) | 20 |

JULIE FELIX

71	RAK 108	Snakeskin/Watching Waiting	40
72	RAK 14	Clothos Web/Windy Morning	25
65	Decca DFE 8613	SINGS BOB DYLAN & WOODY GUTHRIE (EP)	10
66	Fontana TE 17474	SONGS FROM THE FROST REPORT (EP)	10
64	Decca LK 4626	JULIE FELIX (LP)	20
65	Decca LK 4683	SINGS DYLAN AND GUTHRIE (LP)	20
65	Decca LK 4724	SECOND ALBUM (LP)	20
66	Decca LK 4820	THIRD ALBUM (LP)	20
66	Fontana TL 5386	CHANGES (LP, mono/stereo)	20
67	Fontana (S) TL 5437	FLOWERS (LP)	20
72	Rak SRKA 6752	CLOTHOS WEB (LP)	20

MIKE FELIX

| 66 | Pye 7N 17058 | You Belong To Me/Booga Dee | 25 |
| 67 | Decca F 12701 | Blueberry Hill/I Don't Think You Want Me Anymore | 8 |

(see also Migel 5)

RORY FELLOWES

| 68 | S n B 55-3877 | Nina/Endlessly Friendlessly Blue | 20 |

GRAHAM FELLOWS

79	EMI INT 598	Men Of Oats And Creosote/Rebecca (promo, in envelope p/s)	40
83	Toadstool AM 219	Through The Line/Sleeping Beauty (p/s)	6
85	Wicked Frog FROG 01	LOVE AT THE HACIENDA (LP)	50

(see also Jilted John)

FELT

79	Shanghai S79/CUS 321	Index/Break It (hand-made p/s, early copies with poem on rear sleeve 100 only, yellow labels)	300
79	Shanghai S79/CUS 321	Index/Break It (hand-made p/s, no poem on rear sleeve)	150
81	Cherry Red CHERRY 26	Something Sends Me To Sleep/Red Indians/Something Sends Me To Sleep (Version)/Red Indians (p/s)	40
82	Cherry Red CHERRY 45	My Face Is On Fire/Trails Of Colour Dissolve (p/s)	40
83	Cherry Red CHERRY 59	Penelope Tree/A Preacher In New England (p/s)	25
83	Cherry Red 12CHERRY 59	Penelope Tree/A Preacher In New England/Now Summer's Spread Its Wings Again (12")	25
84	Cherry Red CHERRY 78	Mexican Bandits/The World Is As Soft As Lace (p/s)	30
84	Cherry Red CHERRY 81	Sunlight Bathed The Golden Glow/Fortune (p/s)	25
84	Cherry Red 12CHERRY 81	Sunlight Bathed The Golden Glow/Fortune/Sunlight Strings (12", p/s)	20

Narvel FELTS

MINT VALUE £

Year	Label/Cat	Title	Value
85	Cherry Red 12CHERRY 89	Primitive Painters/Cathedral (12", p/s, with Liz Frazer)	15
86	Creation CRE 027	Ballad Of The Band/I Didn't Mean To Hurt You (p/s)	15
86	Creation CRE 027T	Ballad Of The Band/I Didn't Mean To Hurt You/Candles In A Church/Ferdinand (12")	15
86	Creation CRE 032	Rain Of Crystal Spires/I Will Die With My Head In Flames (p/s)	15
86	Creation CRE 032T	Rain Of Crystal Spires/Gather Up Your Wings And Fly/I Will Die With My Head In Flames/Sandman's On The Rise Again (12", p/s)	18
87	Creation CRE 048T	The Final Resting Of The Ark/Autumn/Fore Circle/There's No Such Thing As Victory/Buried Wild Blind (12", p/s)	12
88	Creation CRE 060	Space Blues/Tuesday's Secret (ltd. ed. die-cut company sleeve)	12
88	Creation CRE 060T	Space Blues/Be Still/Female Star/Tuesday's Secret (12")	25
89	el GPO F44	Get Out Of My Mirror (1-side flexi, in-store freebie)	12
82	Cherry Red MRED 25	CRUMBLING THE ANTISEPTIC BEAUTY (LP, 1st pressing, full photo, white label)	50
82	Cherry Red MRED 25	CRUMBLING THE ANTISEPTIC BEAUTY (LP, 2nd pressing, black rectangle on right side of photo, white label)	30
84	Cherry Red MRED 57	THE SPLENDOUR OF FEAR (LP)	40
84	Cherry Red BRED 63	THE STRANGE IDOLS PATTERN AND OTHER SHORT STORIES (LP)	50
84	Cherry Red MRED 25	CRUMBLING THE ANTISEPTIC BEAUTY (LP, reissue, black labels)	18
85	Cherry Red B-RED 65	IGNITE THE SEVEN CANNONS AND SET SAIL FOR THE SUN (LP, textured sleeve with lyric insert)	40
86	Creation CRELP 009	LET THE SNAKES CRINKLE THEIR HEADS TO DEATH (LP)	40
86	Creation CRELP 011	FOREVER BREATHES THE LONELY WORD (LP, with inner sleeve)	40
87	Creation CRELP 017	POEM OF THE RIVER (LP)	40
87	Creation CRE BRED 79	GOLD MINE TRASH (LP, with inner)	40
88	Creation CRELP 030	PICTORIAL JACKSON REVIEW (LP)	40
88	Creation CRELP 033	TRAIN ABOVE THE CITY (LP)	35
89	el ACME 24	ME AND A MONKEY ON THE MOON (LP)	40
90	Creation CRELP 069	BUBBLEGUM PERFUME (LP)	40
18	Cherry Red FLT180	CRUMBLING THE ANTISEPTIC BEAUTY (LP, reissue)	20
18	Cherry Red FLT181	THE SPLENDOUR OF FEAR (LP, reissue)	20
18	Cherry Red FLT182	THE STRANGE IDOLS PATTERN AND OTHER SHORT STORIES (LP, reissue)	20
18	Cherry Red FLT183	IGNITE THE SEVEN CANNONS AND SET SAIL FOR THE SUN (LP, reissue)	20
18	Cherry Red FLT184	THE SEVENTEETNTH CENTURY (LP, reissue)	20
18	Cherry Red FLT185	FOREVER BREATHES THE LONELY WORLD (LP, reissue)	20
18	Cherry Red FLT186	POEM OF THE RIVER (LP, reissue)	20
18	Cherry Red FLT187	PICTORIAL JACKSON REVIEW (LP, reissue)	20
18	Cherry Red FLT188	TRAIN ABOVE THE CITY (LP, reissue)	20
18	Cherry Red FLT189	ME AND A MONKEY ON THE MOON (LP, reissue)	20

(see also Denim, Versatile Newts, Maurice Deebank, Cocteau Twins, Go-Kart Mozart, Supermarket)

NARVEL FELTS
75	ABC 4062	Reconsider Me/Foggy Mountain Morning	6

FENCE
80	BFD BFD 2	Thinking That I Shouldn't/Thru With You/Hey Girl (p/s)	15

JAYMES FENDA & VULCANS
64	Parlophone R 5210	Mistletoe Love/The Only Girl	8

JAN FENDER
71	Prince Buster PB 5	Sea Of Love/PRINCE BUSTER: Heaven Help Us All	25
71	Fab FAB 164	Sweet P/CLIFF & ORGANIZERS: Mr Brown	40
71	Fab FAB 166	Holly Holy Version/Old Kentrone Version (as Jal Fender)	20

PETE FENDER
81	Xntrix 2002	FOUR FORMULAS (EP, in 8" silk-screened book p/s)	30

(see also Fatal Microbes, Omega Tribe)

FENDER BENDERS
79	Sticky SL 001	Big Green Thing/Hillman Hunter Paranoia (textured p/s, various colours)	6

FENDERMEN
60	Top Rank JAR 395	Mule Skinner Blues/Torture	12
60	Top Rank JAR 513	Don't You Just Know It/Beach Party	20

FENMEN
64	Decca F 11955	Rag Doll/Be My Girl	20
65	Decca F 12269	I've Got Everthing You Need Babe/Every Little Day Now	15
66	CBS 202075	California Dreamin'/Is This Your Way?	12
66	CBS 202236	Rejected/Girl Don't Bring Me Down	25

(see also Bern Elliott & Fenmen, Pretty Things)

DAVID FENTON
83	Razor RZS 106	Fresh Air/Buried In The Snow (p/s)	20

PETER FENTON
66	Fontana TF 748	Marble Breaks, Iron Bends/Small Town	20
67	Fontana TF 789	I Was Lord Kitcheners Valet/Walking In Circles	15

SHANE FENTON (& FENTONES)
61	Parlophone R 4827	I'm A Moody Guy/Five Foot Two, Eyes Of Blue	8
62	Parlophone R 4866	Walk Away/Fallen Leaves On The Ground	8
62	Parlophone R 4883	It's All Over Now/Why Little Girl	8
62	Parlophone R 4921	Cindy's Birthday/It's Gonna Take Magic	10
62	Parlophone R 4951	Too Young For Sad Memories/You're Telling Me	8
63	Parlophone R 4982	I Ain't Got Nobody/Hey Miss Ruby	8
63	Parlophone R 5020	A Fool's Paradise/You Need Love (solo)	8
63	Parlophone R 5047	Don't Do That/I'll Know (solo)	10
64	Parlophone R 5131	Hey, Lulu/I Do, Do You?	10
72	Fury FY 305	Eastern Seaboard/Blind Fool	8
77	EMI NUT 2696	SHANE FENTON & THE FENTONES (EP)	10
74	Contour 2870 409	GOOD ROCKIN' TONIGHT (LP)	15

(see also Fentones)

FENTONES

MINT VALUE £

FENTONES
62	Parlophone R 4899	The Mexican/Lover's Guitar	10
62	Parlophone R 4937	The Breeze And I/Just For Jerry	10

(see also Shane Fenton)

FENWAYS
65	Liberty LIB 66082	Walk/Whip And Jerk	25

RAY FENWICK
78	Mercury 6007 176	Queen Of The Night/I Wanna Boogie	6
71	Decca SKL 5090	KEEP AMERICA BEAUTIFUL, GET A HAIRCUT (LP, blue/silver label with small logo)	60

(see also Spencer Davis Group, After Tea, Fancy, Ian Gillan Band, Wizard's Convention, Murgatroyd Band, Marlon, Syndicats, South Coast Ska Kings, Rupert's People)

FENWYCK
68	ERA ERA 100	State Of Mind/Away	80

FENZYX
81	Ellie Jay EJSP 9655	Soldiers/Angels Of Mercy (p/s)	25

FERDIA
78	Polydor 2904 012	A SIGH FOR OLD TIMES (LP)	15

FERDINAND & DILL
70	Pama PM 805	Take Back Your Nicklet/Blueberry Hill	8

WINSTON FERGUS
78	Arawak ARK DD 001	Fly Natty Dread/Loving Pauper (12")	40
79	Burning Rockers BRD 016	Corner Girl/Corner Dub (12")	20
82	Burning Rockers BRD 037	Pay To Live/Earth In Dub (12")	40
82	Fergie Music FM 002	In Ting Sound/My Own Way Heart (12")	150
83	Burning Sounds BSD 060	Keep On Dancing/One Day Up (12")	20
85	John Dread JPD 002	I WILL SING (LP)	15

HELENA FERGUSON
67	London HLZ 10164	Where Is The Party?/My Terms	50

JESSIE LEE FERGUSON & OUTER LIMITS
69	Pye International 7N 25492	New Shoes/Puttin' It On, Puttin' It Off	8

JOHNNY FERGUSON
60	MGM MGM 1059	Angela Jones/Blue Serge And White Lace	10
61	MGM MGM 1119	No One Can Love You/The Valley Of Love	7

MAYNARD FERGUSON ORCHESTRA
58	Emarcy EJL 1270	JAM SESSION (LP)	15
58	Emarcy EJL 1275	AROUND THE HORN (LP)	20
58	Emarcy EJL 1287	DIMENSIONS (LP)	20
59	Columbia 33SX 1146	MESSAGE FROM NEWPORT (LP)	20
60	Mercury MMC 14250	THE BOY WITH LOTS OF BRASS (LP, also stereo CMS 18034)	20
60	Columbia 33SX 1210	MESSAGE FROM BIRDLAND (LP, also stereo SCX 3245)	15
60	Columbia 33SX 1270	JAZZ FOR DANCING (LP, also stereo SCX 3338)	20
61	Columbia 33SX 1301	NEWPORT SUITE (LP, also stereo SCX 3368)	20
62	Columbia 33SX 1439	MAYNARD 62 (LP)	20
66	Fontana TL 5274	BLUES ROAR (LP)	20
66	Fontana TL 5293	COLOR HIM WILD (LP)	20
67	Fontana TL 5310	SEXTET (LP)	20
68	Atlantic 2464008	FREAKY (LP)	20
69	CBS 63514	BALLAD STLYE OF MAYNARD FERGUSON (LP)	40
71	CBS 64432	ALIVE AND WELL IN LONDON (LP)	20
72	CBS 65027	M.F. HORN 2 (LP, gatefold)	15
73	CBS 65589	M.F. HORN 3 (LP)	20
73	CBS 65952	M.F. HORN 4 (LIVE AT JIMMYS) (LP)	20

ALEX FERGUSSON
92	Private Pressing AF 001	ALEX FERGUSSON (LP, white label, 500 copies, no sleeve)	30

(see also Alternative TV, Psychic TV)

FERKO STRING BAND
55	London HL 8140	Alabama Jubilee/Sing A Little Melody	25
55	London HLF 8183	Ma (She's Making Eyes At Me)/You Are My Sunshine	25
55	London HLF 8215	Happy Days Are Here Again/Deep In The Heart Of Texas	25
58	London HL 7052	Happy Days Are Here Again/Alabama Jubilee (export issue)	18
56	London RE-F 1041	PHILADELPHIA MUMMERS PARADE VOL. 1 (EP)	10
56	London RE-F 1052	PHILADELPHIA MUMMERS PARADE VOL. 2 (EP)	10
57	London HB-C 1064	THE FERKO STRING BAND VOL. 1 (10" LP)	15

FERMENA
71	Pama PM 839	Come What May/Version (B-side with Ranny)	8
73	Pama PM 879	Wonderful Dreams/Version	8

PHIL FERNANDO
58	Pye Nixa 7N 15142	Blonde Bombshell/Make Ready for Love	10
62	Palette PG 9029	(Come On And) Do The High Life/High Life Girl	10

ANDY FERNBACH
69	Liberty LBL/LBS 83233	IF YOU MISS YOUR CONNEXION (LP, blue label)	200

(see also Groundhogs)

MAJA FERNICK
72	Philips 6006 196	Give Me Your Love Again/Flowers In The City	20

PIERRE FEROLDI
94	Disco Magic DISK 001	Moving Now (Extended)/Moving Now (Italian Version) (12" featuring Linda Ray)	20

FERRANTE & TEICHER
60	London HLT 9164	Theme From The Apartment/Lonely Room	7

CHRISTIAN FERRAS
61	HMV ASD 427	MOZART VIOLIN CONCERTOS NO 4 & 6 (LP, stereo)	400

Diane FERRAZ & NICKY SCOTT

			MINT VALUE £
63	HMV ASD 531	FERRAS & BARBIZET : ENESCO & DEBUSSY SONATAS ETC (LP, Stereo with Pierre Barbizel)	800
64	HMV ASD 572	BERG: CONCERTO FOR VIOLIN AND ORCHESTRA (LP, stereo)	150

DIANE FERRAZ & NICKY SCOTT
| 66 | Columbia DB 7824 | Me And You/Don't Pretend | 8 |

(see also Nicky Scott, Ferris Wheel)

JOE FERRER & HIS DEVILS BOYS
| 61 | Oriole CB 1629 | Rockin' Crickets/Blue Guitar | 20 |

FERRET
| 74 | Deram DM 412 | Hudson Bay/Henry's Song | 7 |

EUGENE FERRIS
| 66 | Planet PLF 112 | There Was A Smile In Your Eyes/Soft Moonlight (without p/s) | 15 |
| 66 | Planet PLF 112 | There Was A Smile In Your Eyes/Soft Moonlight (with p/s) | 30 |

GEORGE FERRIS
| 71 | Ackee ACK 117 | With Every Dream/Diana | 20 |

(see also George Faith)

FERRIS WHEEL
67	Pye 7N 17387	I Can't Break The Habit/Number One Guy	30
68	Pye 7N 17538	Let It Be Me/You Look At Me	8
68	Pye 7N 17631	The Na Na Song/Three Cool Cats	8
69	Polydor 56366	Can't Stop Now/I Know You Well	6
67	Pye NPL 18203	CAN'T BREAK THE HABIT (LP)	100
70	Polydor 583 066	FERRIS WHEEL (LP, lyric insert, red label)	60

(see also Linda Lewis, West Five)

BRYAN FERRY
73	Island IDJ 1	These Foolish Things/Sympathy For The Devil/Baby I Don't Care/ Loving You Is Sweeter Than Ever (promo)	30
74	Island WIP 6196	The 'In' Crowd/Chance Meeting (in p/s)	8
75	Island WIP 6234	You Go To My Head/Re-Make, Re-Model (DJ copies in generic promo p/s)	20
78	Polydor PPSP 10	Hold On I'm Coming/Take Me To The River (12", unissued, promo only, numbered stamped p/s)	20
76	Island ILPS 9367	LET'S STICK TOGETHER (LP, original issue)	15
93	Virgin V2700	TAXI (LP, inner)	40
94	Virgin V2751	MAMOUNA (LP)	150
95	Virgin V 2791	MORE THAN THIS - THE BEST OF BRYAN FERRY AND ROXY MUSIC (2-LP)	100
99	Virgin 8482711	AS TIME GOES BY (LP)	200
02	Virgin LPVIR 167	FRANTIC (LP)	100
07	Virgin V3026	DYLANESQUE (LP, inner)	150
10	Virgin/Vinyl Factory VF 021	OLYMPIA (LP, gatefold)	150
14	BMG 538013701	AVONMORE (LP, with CD)	35

(see also Roxy Music)

CATHERINE FERRY
| 76 | Barclay BAR 42 | One, Two, Three/1, 2, 3 | 8 |

MANFREDO FEST
| 79 | Bluebird BRT 1 | Jungle Kitten (5.30)/Jungle Kitten (3.36)/Send In The Clowns (12") | 60 |
| 79 | Bluebird BRT 1 | Send In The Clowns/Jungle Kitten | 40 |

FESTIVAL (1)
| 72 | RCA 2275 | Today/Warm Me (demo only) | 90 |

(see also 10cc)

FESTIVAL (2)
| 78 | Nevis NEV 107 | Something In Your Smile/Let's Make Love | 60 |

FEVER
| 71 | Decca F23156 | The Moth And The Flame/It's So Peaceful | 10 |

FEVER TREE
68	MCA MU 1043	San Francisco Girls/Come With Me	10
68	Uni UNLS 102	FEVER TREE (LP)	100
68	MCA MUPS 347	ANOTHER TIME, ANOTHER PLACE (LP)	70

FEWS
| 15 | Speedy Wunderground SW012 | III (Part 1)/(Part 2) | 18 |

FFWD
| 94 | Inter Modo INTA001 | FFWD (2-LP, inners) | 35 |

(see also King Crimson, Orb)

FICKLE FINGER
| 69 | Page One POF 150 | Fickle Lizzie-Anne/Cellophane Mary Jane | 10 |

(see also Matchmakers, Mark Wirtz)

FICKLE PICKLE
70	Fontana TF 1069	Millionaire/Sam And Sadie	15
70	Philips 6006 038	Maybe I'm Amazed/Sitting On A Goldmine	10
72	B & C CB 178	California Calling/Doctor Octopus	12

EDDIE FICTION
| 79 | Absurd A2 | U.F.O. Part 1/U.F.O. Part 2 | 8 |

FIDD
| 69 | Polydor 56320 | Guai Guai (From the film 'Baby Love')/Happy Walk | 25 |

FI-DELS
72	Jay Boy BOY 69	Try A Little Harder/You Never Do Right	15
72	Jay Boy BOY 69	Try A Little Harder/You Never Do Right (DJ Copy)	30
76	DJM DJS 689	Try A Little Harder/KEYMAN STRINGS: Instrumental Version (DJ copy p/s £20)	30
13	Outta Sight OSV097	Try A Little Harder/You Never Do Right (My Baby) (reissue)	7

KEITH FIELD
| 68 | Polydor 56278 | The Day That War Broke Out/Stop Thief | 30 |

Alan FIELDING

MINT VALUE £

ALAN FIELDING
61	Decca F 11404	Scatter Brain/I've Got To Learn To Forget	7

FENELLA FIELDING
66	Columbia DB 8086	Big Bad Mouse/Later	7

JERRY FIELDING & HIS ORCHESTRA
54	London HL 8017	When I Grow Too Old To Dream/Button Up Your Overcoat	30
55	London HL 7001	Faintly Reminiscent/Blues Serenade (export issue)	12
55	London HL 7002	Pea-nut Vendor/Can't Help Lovin' Dat Man (export issue)	12
55	London HL 7003	Tea For Two/Here In My Arms (export issue)	15
55	London HL 7004	I'm In Love/Blue Prelude (export issue)	15
55	Brunswick 05399	The Gypsy In My Soul/The Glory Of Love	10

FIELD MICE
88	Sarah SARAH 012	Emma's House/When You Sleep/Fabulous Friend/The Last Letter (p/s, with poster)	50
88	Sarah SARAH 18	Sensitive/When Morning Comes To Town/Penguins (foldout p/s, with poster)	30
89	Caff CAFF 2	I Can See Myself Alone Forever/Everything About You (foldaround p/s in poly bag with insert)	30
90	Sarah SARAH 024	Autumn Store Pt. 1/If You Need Someone/World In Me (p/s)	25
90	Sarah SARAH 025	Autumn Store Pt. 2/Anyone Else Isn't You/Bleak (p/s)	25
91	Waaaaah BULL 40	Burning Word (1-sided flexi)	10
91	Sarah SARAH 44	September's Not So Far Away/Hello And Goodbye (p/s, with insert)	25
91	Sarah SARAH 57	Missing The Moon/A Wrong Turn And Raindrops/An Earlier Autumn (12", p/s)	20
90	Sarah SARAH 38	SO SAID KAY EP 10", p/s)	30
90	Sarah SARAH 402	SNOWBALL (10" LP)	30
90	Sarah SARAH 601	SKYWRITING (LP)	40
90	Sarah SARAH 606	COASTAL (LP)	50
91	Sarah SARAH 607	FOR KEEPS (LP)	45

(see also Northern Picture Library)

FIELD MUSIC
12	Memphis Industries	Heart/Rent (white vinyl)	8
05	Memphis Industries NI 043LP	FIELD MUSIC (LP)	18
07	Memphis industries NI 074LP	TONES OF MUSIC (LP)	25
10	Memphis Industries MI0149LP	FIELD MUSIC (MEASURE) (2-LP)	25
12	Memphis Industries MI0208LP	PLUMB (LP, purple vinyl)	15
16	Memphis Industries MIO 387LPX	COMMONTIME (2-LP orange vinyl)	20
16	Memphis Industries MIO 387LPX	COMMONTIME (2-LP green vinyl with signed poster)	30
16	Memphis Industries MIO 387LPX	COMMONTIME (2-LP green vinyl without signed poster)	20
18	Memphis Industries MIO 476LPX	OPEN HERE (LP, blue vinyl)	25

FIELD ROUTE
16	Box Bedroom Rebels BBR25	FIELD ROUTE EP (p/s, inserts, numbered, 200 copies)	10

BILLY FIELDS
59	Mercury AMT 1067	The Greatest Love In The World/No Other Love	7

ERNIE FIELDS & HIS ORCHESTRA
60	London HL 9100	Chattanooga Choo Choo/Workin' Out	10
60	London HL 9227	Raunchy/My Prayer	8
60	London RE 1260	SAXY (EP)	30
60	London HA 2263	IN THE MOOD (LP)	30

FIELDS OF THE NEPHILIM
84	Tower N1	BURNING THE FIELDS (12" EP, red/black p/s)	200
85	Tower N1/Jung. JUNG 28T	BURNING THE FIELDS (12" EP, green p/s with insert & band photo label)	40
85	Tower N1/Jung. JUNG 28T	BURNING THE FIELDS (12" EP, green & other coloured vinyl export issue)	40
86	Situation 2 SIT 42	Power/Secrets (7", white label promos only, stickered plain sleeve)	15
87	Situation 2 SIT 46	Preacher Man/Laura II (p/s, swith Beggars Banquet sticker)	35
87	Situation 2 SIT 46	Preacher Man/Laura II (p/s)	25
87	Situation 2 SIT 48T	Blue Water (1 track 12" promo)	20
87	Situation 2 SIT 48	Blue Water/In Every Dream Home A Heartache (p/s)	10
87	Situation 2 SIT 48T	Blue Water (Electrostatic)/In Every Dream Home A Heartache (live)/Blue Water (Hot Wire) (12", p/s, with poster)	15
89	Situation 2 SIT 57	Psychonaut/Celebrate (Second Seal) (blue/green p/s)	6
88	Situation 2 SITU 22	THE NEPHILIM (LP, gatefold sleeve, with inner)	18
88	Situation 2 SITU 22L	THE NEPHILIM (LP, 2 x 45rpm 12", gatefold sleeve, numbered)	20
90	Beggars Banquet BEGA 115	ELIZIUM (LP)	15
02	Jungle FREUD 063	FALLEN (LP)	15
12	Sacred Symphony SS LP 0666	CEREMONIES (2-LP)	40
12	Sacred Symphony SS CD 0666	CEREMONIES (2-LP red vinyl, 2-CD, DVD box set)	300

FIELDS (1)
69	Uni UNLS 104	FIELDS (LP)	100

FIELDS (2)
71	CBS 7555	A Friends Of Mine/Three Minstrels	15
71	CBS 69009	FIELDS (LP, with poster)	125
71	CBS 69009	FIELDS (LP, without poster)	50
16	Black Gold BG 008	FIELDS (LP, reissue)	18

(see also Rare Bird, Greenslade)

FIEND
84	Endangered EDR 1	STAND ALONE EP	18

FIESTAS

MINT VALUE £

FIESTAS
59	London HL 8870	So Fine/Last Night I Dreamed	40
59	London HL 8870	So Fine/Last Night I Dreamed (78)	20
71	Atlantic 2091 121	So Fine/Broken Heart	8

FIFE REIVERS
69	Columbia SCX 6371	FIFE REIVERS (LP)	15

15 16 17
76	Morpheus MOR 1022	If You Love Me Smile/Version	18
77	Morpheus DEB 06	Black Skin Boy/Version	25
78	DEB DEB 003	Emotion/Castro Black Speaks To Dennis Bovell	12
78	DEB DEB 012	Good Times/Black Skin Boys (12")	20
79	DEB DBR 101	Someone Special/Suddenly Happiness	12
79	DEB RIC 103	Baby Love/I'm Hurt	20
80	Cha Cha CHAD 24	I Need A Man/OVERNIGHT PLAYERS: Next Cut (12")	25
06	DEB DEB LP 101	MAGIC TOUCH (LP, issue of unreleased LP from 1978)	20

FIFTH AVENUE
65	Immediate IM 002	The Bells Of Rhymney/Just Like Anyone Would Do (in blue/white Immediate sleeve)	40
65	Immediate IM 002	The Bells Of Rhymney/Just Like Anyone Would Do (in black/white Immediate sleeve)	30

(see also Denny Gerrard, Warm Sounds)

FIFTH AVENUE BAND
69	Reprise RSPL 6369	FIFTH AVENUE BAND (LP)	35

FIFTH COLUMN
66	Columbia DB 8068	Benjamin Day/There's Nobody Here	50

(see also Gerry Rafferty)

5TH DIMENSION
67	Liberty LIB 12051	Go Where You Wanna Go/Too Poor To Die	35
67	Liberty LIB 12051	Go Where You Wanna Go/Too Poor To Die (DJ Copy)	45
67	Liberty LIB 15037	Paper Cup/Poor Side Of Town	20
67	Liberty LBF 15014	Up Up And Away/Pattern People	6
67	Liberty LIB 12056	Another Day, Another Heartache/Rosecrans Blvd	8
68	Liberty LBF 15052	Carpet Man/Magic Garden	15
68	Liberty LBF 15072	Stoned Soul Picnic/Sailboat Song	10
68	Liberty LBF 15081	Ticket To Ride/Orange Air	6
68	Liberty LBF 15130	California Soul/It'll Never Be The Same	12
69	Liberty LBF 15243	Sunshine Of Your Love/Working On A Groovy Thing	6
69	Liberty LBF 15308	Blowing Away/Skinny Man	6
70	Liberty LBF 15356	I'll Be Lovin' You Forever/Train Keep On Movin'	25
68	Liberty LBL/LBS 83098E	MAGIC GARDEN (LP)	15
67	Liberty LBL/LBS 83038	UP UP AND AWAY (LP)	15
68	Liberty LBL/LBS 83155E	STONED SOUL PICNIC (LP)	15

FIFTH ESTATE
67	Stateside SS 2034	Ding Dong The Witch Is Dead/Rub A Dub	10
67	Stateside SS 2068	Heigh Ho/It's Waiting There For You	10
68	Stateside SS 2105	Do Drop In/That's Love	7
69	Stateside SS 2125	Coney Island Sally/Tomorrow Is My Turn	10

5TH OF HEAVEN
88	Mix Out SRT8KL 1715	Without You (Baby I'm Lost)/Who You Gonna Love Tonight?	10
88	Mix Out 12 FOH 1	Just A Little More/(Surrender Mix) (12', p/s)	40
90	Mix Out 12 FOH 3	I Need Your Love/(Lurve Mix)/(Passion Mix) (12")	8

FIFTY FANTASTICS
79	South Circular SGS 108	God's Got Religion/STEPPES: The Beat Drill (white label)	15
80	Dining Out TUX 5	God's Got Religion/The Beat Drill (reissue, foldout p/s, hand made labels)	15

(see also Disco Zombies)

FIFTY FIVE DEGREES
79	No label or cat number	There's Gonna Be A Showdown/There's Gonna Be A Showdown (p/s)	20

FIFTY FOOT HOSE
69	Mercury SLML 4030	CAULDRON (LP)	200

53 BUS
83	Custom Cars 100MPH	Horizontal Dancing/Horizontal D.I.Y.	50

50 YEAR VOID
92	BLADE 1	Blade's Love Machine (1-sided 12", white label promo, 100 only)	30

(see also St. Etienne, Sarah Cracknell)

57TH PARALLEL
81	Rising sun RS 005	In This Light/Psalm Fifty Seven	20

FIGGY DUFF
80	Dingles DIN 326	FIGGY DUFF (LP)	25
85	Celtic CM 023	AFTER THE TEMPEST (LP, with insert)	30

FIGHT
93	Epic EPC 474547	WAR OF WORDS (LP, white vinyl)	60

(see also Judas Priest, Halford)

NESTOR FIGUERAS, DAVID TOOP & PAUL BURWELL
77	Bead Records BEAD 6	NESTOR FIGUERAS, DAVID TOOP & PAUL BURWELL (LP)	40

PAULINE FILBY
60s	Church Miss. Soc. LIV/SP/81	I'm Hungry/NADIA CATTOUSE: The Larder	8
68	Herald ELR 1081	MY WORLD BY PAULINE FILBY (EP)	20
69	Herald LLR 567	SHOW ME A RAINBOW (LP)	100

(see also Narnia, Accolade, Gordon Giltrap)

PHILIP JOHN FILBY
71	Dart ART2007	David McKenzie/Close My Eyes And Stick With Me	20

FILE UNDER POP
79	Rough Trade RT 011	Heathrow/Corrugate/Heathrow SLB (p/s)	6

(see also AK Process, AK 47)

FILM CAST
79	True Friends TF 001	Life In A Film Cast/Stations And Answers	8
80	True Friends TF 002	Admission (Yours)/Colour - Colour (as FILMCAST)	8
84	True Friends TF 004	The Distant Heart/World Of Light	25

FILTHY RICH
87	JM TR 102	She's 17/Love Ain't A Fool (p/s)	20

(see also Trident)

FILTHY SIX
10	Acid Jazz AJX228S	Get Carter/Knockout	8
12	Acid Jazz AJX290S	Girlfriend/Instrumental Version	6
10	Acid Jazz AJXLP229	THE FILTHY SIX (LP)	15
12	Acid Jazz AJXLP288	THE FOX (LP)	15

FINAL ACADEMY
83	Spectrum SPEC 005	Night Cafe/The Collector	40

FINAL CONFLICT
86	Futuresound FS 001	EP (EP)	10
86	Futuresound FS 002	THE TIME HAS ARRIVED (EP, with 22-page booklet)	10
89	Futuresound VFS 001	My England/Across The Room (stickered white sleeve)	20

FINAL PROGRAM
81	Program FINAL 001	PROTECT AND SURVIVE (EP)	40

FINAL TOUCH
70s	Myrrh MYR 1188	LOVE SONG (LP)	25

FINCH
78	Rockburgh ROC 103	GALLEONS OF PASSION (LP)	18

FINDERS KEEPERS (U.K.)
66	CBS 202249	Light/Power Of Love (withdrawn, promos may exist)	65
66	CBS 202249	Light/Come On Now	20
67	Fontana TF 892	Friday Kind Of Monday/On The Beach	40
68	Fontana TF 938	Sadie (The Cleaning Lady)/Without Her	20

(see also Trapeze, Glenn Hughes, News)

FINDERS KEEPERS (U.S.)
67	London HLH 10117	Lavender Blue/MICKEY DOLENZ: Don't Do It	12

JEM FINER
00s	no cat. no.	LONGPLAYER (LP, with book)	15

FINESSE
82	CBS A13 2169	Feel It/Inside Your Head (12")	15

FINGERS (1)
66	Polydor	I Go To Sleep/Oh!	10
66	Columbia DB 8026	I'll Take You Where The Music's Playing/My Way Of Thinking	20
67	Columbia DB 8112	All Kinds Of People/Circus With A Female Clown	45

(see also Crocheted Doughnut Ring, Legend)

FINGERS (2)
79	Ratched RAT 101	Marching Band/The Bandleader (Baz's Tune) (no p/s)	40
79	Ratchet RAT 102	Saints Alive/We're Alright	40

FINGERS INC.
87	Jack Trax 12 J TRAX 8	Distant Planet Club Mix/Distant Planet Dub Mix (12", stickered die-cut company sleeve)	45
88	Desire WANTX 6	Can You Feel It/My House (Acapella) (12", die-cut p/s)	30
88	Jack Trax JTX 8	Distant Planet (Remix, 4 Mixes) (12")	60
88	Jack Trax JTX 20	Can You Feel It (4 Mixes) (12", p/s)	25
89	Jack Trax JTX 2	Never No More Lonely/Music Takes Me Up/Distant Planet (Club Mix) (12")	30
88	Jack Trax FING 1	ANOTHER SIDE (2-LP, gatefold sleeve)	40

(see also Mr. Fingers, Larry Heard)

FINI TRIBE (101)
84	Finiflex FT 1001	CURLING & STRETCHING EP (12", p/s, original issue)	10
88	Finiflex FT 002	DESTIMONY EP (12", p/s)	10

FINK BROTHERS
85	Zarjazz JAZZ S2	Mutants In Mega-City One/Mutant Blues (shaped picture disc)	10
85	Zarjazz JAZZ2-12	Mutants In Mega-City One/Mutant Blues (12", p/s with poster)	12

(see also Madness)

LEE FINN & RHYTHM MEN
63	Starlite ST45 103	High Class Feelin'/Pour Me A Glass Of Wine	50

LIAM FINN
08	Transgressive TRANS 079	Second Chance/I'm Liam And This Is Eliza-Jane	8
08	Transgressive TRANS 080X	I'LL BE LIGHTNING (LP with CD-R)	25

FINN MACCUILL
76	Radio Edinburgh REL 451	FINN MACCUILL (LP)	150
77	Radio Edinburgh REL 460	SINK YE - SWIM YE (LP)	200

SIMON FINN
70	Mushroom 100 MR 2	PASS THE DISTANCE (LP, with lyric insert, white/brown labels)	500

LARRY FINNEGAN
62	HMV POP 1022	Dear One/Candy Lips	15
62	London HLU 9213	Pretty Suzy Sunshine/It's Walkin' Talkin' Time	20
65	Ember EMB S 207	The Other Ringo (A Tribute To Ringo Starr)/When My Love Passes By (p/s)	20
65	Ember EMB S 207	The Other Ringo (A Tribute To Ringo Starr)/When My Love Passes By	10

ALBERT FINNEY
77	Tamla Motown TMG 1084	Those Other Men/What Have They Done (To My Home Town)	7

Mike FINNIGAN

MINT VALUE £

MIKE FINNIGAN
78 CBS 6656   Just One Minute More/Blood Is Thicker Than Water 10
FINS
81 SRTS 81 CUS 1075   Voice Of America/Omega Man 25
FIRE
68 Decca F 12753   Father's Name Is Dad/Treacle Toffee World 500
68 Decca F 12856   Round The Gum Tree/Toothie Ruthie 70
70 Pye NSPL 18243   THE MAGIC SHOEMAKER (LP, blue/black labels with logo banner at top) 600
90 See For Miles SEE 794   THE MAGIC SHOEMAKER (LP, reissue) 20
97 Tenth Planet TP 029   UNDERGROUND AND OVERHEAD: THE ALTERNATE FIRE (LP, gatefold sleeve, numbered, 1,000 only) 18

(see also Strawbs, Paul Brett's Sage)

LUTAN FIRE AND BUSH CHEMIST
03 Conscious Sounds CD 1003   16 Years/King David's House (10") 10
FIREBALL
73 Spark SRL 1093   Bachonola/I Dunno 10
FIREBALLS
59 Top Rank JAR 218   Torquay/Cry Baby 15
60 Top Rank JAR 276   Bulldog/Nearly Sunrise 10
60 Top Rank JAR 354   Foot-Patter/Kissin' 10
60 Top Rank JAR 507   Vaquero (Cowboy)/Chief Whoopin'-Koff 7
61 Pye International 7N 25092   Quite A Party/Gunshot 6
62 Stateside SS 106   Rik-A-Tik/Yacky Doo 7
63 Stateside SS 151   Carioca/Find Me A Golden Street 7
68 Stateside SS 2106   Goin' Away/Groovy Motions 15
61 Top Rank 35/105   VAQUERO (LP) 25

(see also Jimmy Gilmer, Buddy Holly)

FIREBIRD (2)
79 Rat SRTS79/CUS576   Change/Nightride (in p/s) 150
79 Rat SRTS79/CUS576   Change/Nightride 40
FIREBRAND
85 What WR 71   Never Felt This Way Before/I'm Leaving (p/s) 50
FIRECLOWN
83 Fireclown FC 1001   INVASION EP (Magic/Poor Man/Invasion) (10", no p/s) 12
FIRE ENGINES
80 Codex Comms. CDX 01   Get Up And Use Me/Everything's Roses (p/s) 20
81 Pop:Aural POP 010   Candy Skin/Meat Whiplash (foldout p/s in poly bag) 15
81 Pop:Aural POP 013   Big Gold Dream/Sympathetic Anaesthetic (p/s) 6
81 Pop:Aural POP 01312   Big Gold Dream/Sympathetic Anaesthetic/New Thing In Cartons (12", non-gatefold p/s) 10
81 Accessory ACC 001   LUBRICATE YOUR LIVING ROOM (LP, in plastic bag) 30
92 Rev-Ola CREV 001LP   FOND (LP) 30
FIRE EXIT
79 Time Bomb Explosion 1   Timewall/Talkin' About Myself (p/s, stamped labels) 100
FIREFLIES
59 Top Rank JAR 198   You Were Mine/Stella Got A Fella 20
59 Top Rank JAR 198   You Were Mine/Stella Got A Fella (78) 20
60 London HLU 9057   I Can't Say Goodbye/What Did I Do Wrong 35
FIREFLY (1)
71 Decca F131192   My Friend/Younger Days 8
FIREFLY (2)
81 Excalibur EXC 506   Love (Is Gonna Be On Your Side)/Forget It 10
FIREFOX
96 Philly Blunt PB 006   Bonanza Kid/Buck Rogers (12") 20
FIRE HYDRANT MEN
85 MCHMLP 3   BACKS (LP) 20
FIRE KINGS
77 Terminal TM 107   Poor Man Cry/Version 8
FIREMAN
98 Hydra HYPRO 12 007   Rushes: Bison/Fluid/Appletree Cinnabar Amber (12" with massive fold-out poster) 100
98 Hydra HYPRO 12 007   Rushes: Bison/Fluid/Appletree Cinnabar Amber (12" without massive fold-out poster) ... 20
99 Hydra HYPRO 12 008   Fluid (12", p/s, promo only) 35
93 Parlophone FIRE 1   STRAWBERRIES OCEANS SHIPS FOREST (2-LP, clear vinyl, numbered white sleeve, with inners, promo only) 150
93 Parlophone PCSD 145   STRAWBERRIES OCEANS SHIPS FOREST (2-LP, clear vinyl, red sleeve, with inners) 150
98 Hydra 4970551   RUSHES (2-LP, inners) 200
08 One L. Indian TPLP 1003   ELECTRIC ARGUEMENTS (2-LP, CD, numbered) 50
08 One L. Indian TPLP1016   ELECTRIC ARGUEMENTS (2-LP, CD, un-numbered) 30
09 One L. Indian TPLPDE1016   ELECTRIC ARGUEMENTS (Box set, 2-LP, 2-CD, DVD in paper satchel) 200

(see also Paul McCartney, Youth, Killing Joke, Brilliant, Twin Freaks)

FIRE SESSION
70 Revolution REVR 009   Honey Don't/Maximum Serenade 25
70 Revolution REV 10   Souvenir/Bad Girl 25
70 Revolution REV 13   Sleeping Reggae/CAROLS: Everyday I Have To Cry Some 25
70 Revolution REV 14   Death Of The Ugly One/Big Feet 35
FIRESIGN THEATRE
72 CBS CQ 30737   FIRESIGN THEATRE (LP, quadrophonic) 15
FIRESTONE
71 Flash FL002   Turning Away From Me/Empty Pages 12
FIRESTONES
62 Decca F 11436   Party Twist (Medley) (Parts 1 & 2) 6

			MINT VALUE £
FIRING SQUAD (1)			
64	Parlophone R 5152	A Little Bit More/Bull Moose	50
FIRING SQUAD (2)			
80	Shattered SHAT 5	Big Red Car/Night Manoeuvres (p/s)	8
FIRING SQUAD (3)			
83	Instant IMR 002	A Piece Of The Night/Muscle Talk (no p/s)	30
FIRKIN THE FOX			
84	Woodworm WR 005	BEHIND BARS (LP)	25
FIRM (1)			
80	SRTS 80 CUS 806	Angry Young Man/Not Gonna Turn Back Anymore/Mainstream (stamped paper sleeve)	20
FIRST AID			
77	Decca TXS 117	NOSTRADAMUS (LP)	50
FIRST AID KIT			
08	Wichita WEBB201LP	DRUNKEN TREES EP (12" and CD, white vinyl)	10
09	Wichita WEBB206S	You're Not Coming Home Tonight/Tangerine	12
09	Wichita WEBB234S	Hard Believer/Waltz For Richard	10
11	Wichita WEBB319S	The Lion's Road/Marianne's Son	8
14	Columbia 88843066611	STAY GOLD (LP, CD gold vinyl)	20
FIRST CHOICE			
73	Pye International 7N 25613	This Is The House Where Love Died/One Step Away (unissued, demos may exist, this price for acetate)	400
74	Bell BLL 1376	The Player (Parts 1 & 2)	8
73	Bell BELLS 229	ARMED AND EXTREMELY DANGEROUS (LP)	18
76	Warner Bros. K 56266	SO LET US ENTERTAIN YOU (LP)	15
78	Salsoul SSLP 1503	DELUSIONS (LP)	15
79	Salsoul SSLP 1514	HOLD YOUR HORSES (LP)	15
93	Charly CPLP 8060	DELUSIONS (LP, reissue)	15
FIRST CLASS			
74	Sunny EON 102	Beach Baby/Surfer Queen	6
74	UK UKAL 1008	THE FIRST CLASS (LP)	18
76	UK UKAL 1022	S.S.T. (LP)	18

(see also White Plains, Edison Lighthouse, Brotherhood Of Man, Carter-Lewis & Southerners, Ivy League)

FIRST DOWN			
90	Cobden Capers FD1	Jaw Warfare/From Now On/Dedication	70
93	Ill Gotten Gains FD002	LET THE BATTLE BEGIN (EP)	25
94	Blitz Vinyl EFA61008	MAD DOGS AND ENGLISHMAN (EP)	12
94	Blitz Vinyl EFA61009	WORLD SERVICE (LP)	18
FIRST EDITION			
68	Reprise RS 20655	Just Dropped In (To See What Condition My Condition Was In)/Shadow In The Corner Of Your Mind	40
68	Reprise RS 20693	Charlie The Fer'de Lance/Look Around I'll Be There	8
68	Reprise RSLP 6276	THE FIRST EDITION (LP)	15

(see also Kenny Rogers)

FIRST GEAR			
64	Pye 7N 15703	A Certain Girl/Leave My Kitten Alone	200
65	Pye 7N 15763	The 'In' Crowd/Gotta Make Their Future Bright	70
FIRST IMPRESSION/GOOD EARTH			
68	Saga FID 2117	SWINGING LONDON (LP)	25

(see also Good Earth, Mungo Jerry)

FIRST IMPRESSIONS			
65	Pye 7N 15797	I'm Coming Home/Looking For Her	25

(see also Legends)

FIRST LIGHT			
82	Oval FLIGHT 22/12	Don't Be Mistaken/Horse With No Name (12" p/s)	8
FIRST NATIONAL NOTHING (FEATURING J MARKS)			
70	CBS 5120	Purple Song/I Got The Answer (purple vinyl)	8
FIRST OFFENCE			
88	Metal Other OTH 11	FIRST OFFENCE (LP, with insert)	30
88	Metal Other OTH 11	FIRST OFFENCE (LP, without insert)	25
1ST OFFENCE			
82	Chaos	NIGHT THE PUNKS TURNED UGLY EP (fold out sleeve)	15
1ST QUOTE			
96	Groove Yard GYARD 10	BUMP AND GRIND EP (12")	20
FIRST REFUSAL			
78	Rainbow RSL 015	FIRST REFUSAL EP (500 only)	40
FIRST STEPS			
80	English Rose ER I	The Beat Is Back/She Ain't In Love/Let's Go Cuboids (p/s, with insert)	30
81	English Rose ER III	Anywhere Else But Here/Airplay/I Got The News (p/s)	20
FIRST COLLABORATION			
72	Cavendish CAV 8	FIRST COLLABORATION (LP)	50
CLARE FISCHER			
62	Fontana 688124 ZL	FIRST TIME OUT (LP)	15
WILD MAN FISCHER			
69	Reprise RSLP 6332	AN EVENING WITH WILD MAN FISCHER (LP, gatefold sleeve)	60

(see also Frank Zappa)

FISCHERMAN'S FRIEND			
91	EG OP 51	Money (12", with "Orb Clubmix", 500 only)	12
FISCHERSPOONER			
01	International Deejay Gigolo Records GIGOLO 70	#1 (2-LP)	40
02	FS Studios FSMOSLP1	#1 (LP, remastered and re-sequenced)	35

F F & Z (FISHBAUGH FISHBAUGH & ZORN)

MINT VALUE £

05	FS Studios FSLPDJ 2	ODYSSEY (2-LP, picture disc)	45

F F & Z (FISHBAUGH FISHBAUGH & ZORN)
72	CBS 8163	Everybody Got Out Of Bed/Spaced On Happy	20
72	CBS 64783	FISHBAUGH, FISHBAUGH & ZORN (LP)	25

ARCHIE FISHER
68	Xtra XTRA 1070	ARCHIE FISHER (LP)	25
70	Decca SKL 5057	ORFEO (LP)	50
76	Topic 12TS 277	WILL YE GANG LOVE (LP)	20
82	Celtic Music CM 007	ARCHIE FISHER (LP, reissue)	20

(see also Barbara Dickson)

ARCHIE FISHER, BARBARA DICKSON & JOHN MACKINNON
69	Trailer LER 3002	THE FATE O' CHARLIE: SONGS OF THE JACOBITE REBELLIONS (LP, first pressing, white label)	60
69	Trailer LER 3002	THE FATE O' CHARLIE: SONGS OF THE JACOBITE REBELLIONS (LP, second pressing, red label)	30

CHIP FISHER
59	Parlophone R 4604	Poor Me/No One	15
59	RCA RCX 143	AT THE SUGAR BOWL (EP)	60

CILLA FISHER & ARTIE TREZISE
76	Trailer LER 2100	BALCANQUHAL (LP, yellow label)	15
79	Kettle KAC 1	FOR FOUL DAY AND FAIR (LP)	15

EDDIE FISHER
53	HMV 7M 101	I'm Yours/That's The Chance You Take	15
53	HMV 7M 115	Everything I Have Is Yours/You'll Never Know	10
53	HMV 7M 116	Trust In Me/Forgive Me	10
53	HMV 7M 117	Outside Of Heaven/Lady Of Spain	15
53	HMV 7M 125	Even Now/If It Were Up To Me	10
53	HMV 7M 126	Downhearted/Am I Wasting My Time On You	10
53	HMV 7M 133	I'm Walking Behind You (with Sally Sweetland)/Hold Me	12
53	HMV 7M 146	Just Another Polka/When I Was Young (Yes, Very Young)	8
53	HMV 7M 159	Wish You Were Here/A Fool Was I	10
53	HMV 7M 168	Many Times/With These Hands	10
54	HMV 7M 172	Oh My Papa/(I Never Missed You) Until You Said "Goodbye"	10
56	HMV POP 273	Cindy, Oh Cindy/Fanny	15

FAYE FISHER
65	Columbia DB 7575	Our Love/I Just Don't Know What To Say	7
65	Columbia DB 7732	Oh Heartache You're Bothering Me/It's You	7

MARY ANN FISHER
11	Jukebox Jab JBJ 1018	Put On My Shoes/Wild As You Can Be (reissue)	20
13	Outtasight RSV 031	Put On My Shoes/FAYE ADAMS: The Hammer	8

MATTHEW FISHER
73	RCA SF8380	JOURNEY'S END (LP)	18
74	RCA APL 1	I'LL BE THERE (LP)	15

(see also Procol Harum, Green Bullfrog)

RAY FISHER
72	Trailer LER 2038	THE BONNY BIRD (LP, red label)	25

TONI FISHER
60	Top Rank JAR 261	The Big Hurt/Memphis Belle	6
60	Top Rank JAR 341	How Deep Is The Ocean/Blue, Blue, Blue (as Miss Toni Fisher)	7

WILLIE FISHER
77	Jama JA 35	Put Your Lovin' On Me/Take Time To Know Her	30

FISHER BROTHERS
64	London HLN 9928	Big Round Wheel/By The Time You Read This Letter	10

FISH GOAT & SUFFURAH
93	Sound N Presuure SNP 001	Warm The Nation/Version (12")	20
94	Sound N Presuure SNP 003	Against The Tide/High Tide Shark Attack/School Of Fish Dub/Deep Sea Dubbing (12" as Fish and Goat at the Controls)	12

FISH TURNED HUMAN
79	Sequel PART 1	TURKEYS IN CHINA (EP)	15

FIST
80	Neat NEAT 04	Name Rank And Serial Number/You'll Never Get Me In One Of Those (p/s, with poster insert)	15
80	Neat NEAT 04	Name Rank And Serial Number/You'll Never Get Me In One Of Those (p/s)	8
80	MCA MCA 615	Name Rank And Serial Number/You'll Never Get Me (In One Of Those) (p/s, reissue, with poster insert)	30
80	MCA MCA 615	Name Rank And Serial Number/You'll Never Get Me (In One Of Those) (p/s, reissue, without poster insert)	20
80	MCA MCA 640	Forever Amber/Brain Damage (p/s)	12
81	MCA MCA 663	Collision Course/Law Of The Jungle (p/s)	100
81	MCA MCA 663	Collision Course/Law Of The Jungle	30
82	Neat NEAT 021	The Wanderer/Too Hot (p/s)	10
80	MCA MCF 3082	TURN THE HELL ON (LP)	15
82	Neat NEAT 1003	BACK WITH A VENGEANCE (LP, yellow vinyl)	30
82	Neat NEAT 1003	BACK WITH A VENGEANCE (LP)	15

JOHN FITCH & ASSOCIATES
71	Beacon BEA 117	Romantic Altitude/Stoned Out Of It	90

FITS
83	Corpus Christi ITS 9	Tears Of A Nation/Bravado/Breaking Point (p/s)	6
84	Trapper FIT 1	Action/Achilles Heel (p/s)	7
81	Beat The System FIT 1	YOU SAID WE'D NEVER MAKE IT (EP, wraparound p/s)	10
82	Rondelet ABOUT 6	YOU'RE NOTHING, YOU'RE NOWHERE (LP)	15

FITZ & COOLERS
68	Nu Beat NB 003	Cover Me/Darling	20

ELLA FITZGERALD
SINGLES
66	Stateside SS 569	These Boots Were Made For Walkin'/Stardust (DJ Copy)	50
66	Stateside SS 569	These Boots Were Made for Walkin'/Stardust	8
69	Reprise RS 20850	Get Ready/Open Your Window	30
69	Polydor 56767	Hey Jude/Sunshine Of Your Love	10
71	Reprise RS 23507	I Heard It Through The Grapevine/Days Of Wine & Roses	8

ALBUMS
53	Brunswick LA 8581	SOUVENIR ALBUM (10")	15
54	Brunswick LA 8648	ELLA SINGS GERSHWIN (10")	15
55	Brunswick LAT 8056	ELLA — SONGS IN A MELLOW MOOD	15
56	Brunswick LAT 8091	SWEET AND HOT	15
56	Brunswick LAT 8115	LULLABIES OF BIRDLAND	15
68	Polydor 583737	SUNSHINE OF YOUR LOVE (LP)	20

(see also Count Basie)

ELLA FITZGERALD & LOUIS ARMSTRONG
56	HMV CLP 1098	ELLA AND LOUIS (LP)	20

ELLA FITZGERALD/BILLIE HOLIDAY
58	Columbia Clef 33CX 10100	AT NEWPORT (LP)	15

G.F. FITZGERALD
70	Uni UNLS 115	MOUSEPROOF (LP, gatefold sleeve, with insert, yellow swirl label)	200

PATRIK FITZGERALD
77	Small Wonder SMALL 4	SAFETY PIN STUCK IN MY HEART (EP, with lyrics)	10
78	Small Wonder SMALL 6	Buy Me, Sell Me/The Little Dippers/Trendy/The Backstreet Boys (p/s)	8
79	Polydor 2059 091	All Sewn Up/Hammersmith Odeons (p/s)	8
79	Polydor 2059 135	Improve Myself/The Bingo Crowd/My New Family (p/s, as Patrik Fitzgerald)	8
78	Small Wonder WEENY ONE	THE PARANOID WARD/THE BEDROOM TAPES (12" EP)	10
79	Polydor 2383 533	GRUBBY STORIES (LP)	15
82	Red Flame EF8	GIFTS & TELEGRAMS (LP)	20

MAGGIE FITZGIBBON
59	Pye Int. 7N 25047	Kooka Burra/The Right Kind Of Man	7
68	Page One PDF 057	I'll Walk Alone/Girls Are Made Loving (p/s)	8

FITZROY (STERLING) & HARRY
70	Bullet BU 439	Reggae Sounds Are Boss/Goodbye My Love	30
70	Escort ERT 827	Pop A Top Train/Doing The Moonwalk	25

FIVE AMERICANS
66	Pye International 7N 25354	I See The Light/The Outcasts	25
66	Pye International 7N 25373	Evol — Not Love/Don't Blame Me	20
67	Stateside SS 2012	Western Union/Now That It's All Over	10
68	Stateside SS 2036	Sound Of Love/Sympathy	7

5 A.M. EVENT
66	Pye 7N 17154	Hungry/I Wash My Hands (In Muddy Water)	325

FIVE & A PENNY
68	Polydor 56282	You Don't Know Where Your Interest Lies/Mary Go Round	75
77	Polydor 56282	You Don't Know Where Your Interest Lies/Mary Go Round (2nd pressing injection moulded)	25

FIVE BLIND BOYS
64	Vocalion EPVP 1276	NEGRO SPIRITUALS (EP, 2 tracks by Spirits Of Memphis)	20
64	Vocalion EPVP 1282	FIVE BLIND BOYS (EP)	10

FIVE BLOBS
58	Philips PB 881	The Blob/Saturday Night In Tijuana	20

FIVE BY FIVE
68	Pye International 7N 25477	Fire/Hang Up	70

FIVE CARD STUD
67	Philips BF 1567	Beg Me/Once	15

FIVE CHESTERNUTS
58	Columbia DB 4165	Jean Dorothy/Teenage Love	200
58	Columbia DB 4165	Jean Dorothy/Teenage Love (78)	100

(see also Shadows, Pete Chester)

FIVE COUNTS
62	Oriole CBA 1769	Watermelon Walk/Spanish Nights	30

FIVE CRESTAS
66	Excel ES SP 288/289	How Sweet It Is (To Be Loved By You)/You Used To Love Me (private pressing)	100

FIVE DALLAS BOYS
58	Columbia DB 4231	Fatty Patty/Do You Wanna Jump Children?	7
59	Columbia DB 4313	Morning Papers/I'm Aware	7
60	Columbia SEG 8035	THE FIVE DALLAS BOYS (EP)	12

FIVE DAY RAIN
70	Private pressing	FIVE DAY RAIN (LP, no sleeve, 20-30 copies only)	2000
93	Private pressing	FIVE DAY RAIN (LP, re-pressing in signed, numbered sleeve, signed note in run-out groove & letter of authenticity, 25 only)	80

(see also Scots Of St. James, Hopscotch, One Way Ticket, Glencoe)

FIVE DAY WEEK STRAW PEOPLE
68	Saga FID 2123	FIVE DAY WEEK STRAW PEOPLE (LP, black/silver labels)	200

(see also Attack, Andromeda, John Du Cann)

FIVE DE MARCO SISTERS
55	Brunswick 05425	Dreamboat/Two Hearts, Two Kisses (Make One Love)	6

FIVE DU-TONES

MINT VALUE £

FIVE DU-TONES
63	Stateside SS 206	Shake A Tail Feather/Divorce Court	20

FIVE EMPREES
65	Stateside SS 470	Little Miss Sad/Hey Lover	20

FIVE FINGER DEATH PUNCH
09	Park/Spinefarm SPI360LP.272045	WAR IS THE ANSWER (2-LP, red vinyl)	20

FIVE FLEETS
58	Felsted AF 103	Oh What A Feeling/I Been Cryin'	100
58	Felsted AF 103	Oh What A Feeling/I Been Cryin' (78)	40

FIVE FLIGHTS UP
70	Bell BLL 1123	Do What You Wanna Do/Black Cat	6

FIVE GO DOWN TO THE SEA
83	Kabuki KAFIVE 5	KNOT A FISH (EP)	15

FIVE KEYS
54	Capitol CL 14184	Ling, Ting, Tong/I'm Alone	300
54	Capitol CL 14184	Ling, Ting, Tong/I'm Alone (78)	50
55	Capitol CL 14313	The Verdict/Make Me Um Pow Pow (triangular centre)	300
55	Capitol CL 14313	The Verdict/Make Me Um Pow Pow (78)	50
55	Capitol CL 14325	(Close Your Eyes) Take A Deep Breath/Doggone It, You Did It (tri centre)	300
55	Capitol CL 14325	(Close Your Eyes) Take A Deep Breath/Doggone It, You Did It (78)	40
56	Capitol CL 14545	Gee Whittakers!/'Cause You're My Lover	300
56	Capitol CL 14545	Gee Whittakers!/'Cause You're My Lover (78)	25
56	Capitol CL 14582	She's The Most/I Dreamt I Dwelt In Heaven	250
56	Capitol CL 14582	She's The Most/I Dreamt I Dwelt In Heaven (78)	25
56	Capitol CL 14639	That's Right/Out Of Sight, Out Of Mind	150
56	Capitol CL 14639	That's Right/Out Of Sight, Out Of Mind (78)	20
57	Capitol CL 14686	The Wisdom Of A Fool/Now Don't That Prove I Love You?	150
57	Capitol CL 14686	The Wisdom Of A Fool/Now Don't That Prove I Love You? (78)	25
57	Capitol CL 14736	Four Walls/Let There Be You	100
57	Capitol CL 14736	Four Walls/Let There Be You (78)	30
57	Capitol CL 14756	The Blues Don't Care/This I Promise You	150
57	Capitol CL 14756	The Blues Don't Care/This I Promise You (78)	40
58	Capitol CL 14829	From Me To You/Whippety Whirl	150
58	Capitol CL 14829	From Me To You/Whippety Whirl (78)	45
58	Capitol CL 14967	One Great Love/Really-O Truly-O	150
57	Capitol T 828	THE FIVE KEYS ON STAGE! (LP)	200

FIVE MILES OUT
73	Action ACT 4614	Super Sweet Girl Of Mine/Set Your Mind Free	25

FIVE NITES
64	Decca F 11963	With A Loving Kiss/Let's Try Again	15

FIVE OF DIAMONDS
65	Oak RGJ 150 FD	FIVE OF DIAMONDS (EP)	400

FIVE ROYALES
60	Ember EMB S 124	Dedicated To The One I Love/Miracle Of Love	150

FIVE SAPPHIRES
78	Rocket ROKN 539	Love Music/Where Did All The Good Times Go	7

FIVE SATINS
57	London HL 8501	To The Aisle/Wish I Had My Baby	450
57	London HL 8501	To The Aisle/Wish I Had My Baby (78)	40
59	Top Rank JAR 199	Wonderful Girl/Weeping Willow	30
59	Top Rank JAR 239	Shadows/Toni My Love	50
60	MGM MGM 1087	Your Memory/I Didn't Know	60

FIVE SMITH BROTHERS
54	Decca F 10403	A.B.C. Boogie/Veni-Vidi-Vici (with Dennis Wilson Quartet)	20
55	Decca F 10507	Paper Valentine/You're As Sweet Today (As Yesterday)	7
55	Decca F 10527	Don't Worry/I'm In Favour Of Friendship	7
55	Parlophone GEP 8667	UP NORTH WITH THE FIVE SMITH BROTHERS (EP)	10

FIVE STAIRSTEPS (& CUBIE)
68	Pye International 7N 25248	A Million To One/Something's Missing (with Cubie)	12
69	Buddah 201 026	Stay Close To Me/I Made A Mistake (with Cubie)	12
69	Buddah 201 070	We Must Be In Love/Little Young Lovers (with Cubie)	12
70	Buddah 201 083	Dear Prudence/O-o-h Child	15
70	Buddah 201 036	O-o-h Child/Who Do You Belong To?	8

(see also Stairsteps)

FIVE STEPS BEYOND
67	CBS 202490	Not So Young Today/Meanwhile Back In My Heart	25
95	Tenth Planet TP 019	FAINT HEARTS AND FAIR MAIDS (LP, 600 only)	20
96	Tenth Planet TP 021	SMILE (LP, with A4 booklet, 600 only)	20

FIVE THIRTY/5.30
87	Other 12 OTH 2	THE CATCHER IN THE RYE EP (12", p/s)	20

FIVE TOWNS
67	Direction 58-3115	It Isn't What You've Got/Advice	10

FIVE YEAR PLAN
87	Breaking Down Break 3	Hit The Bottle/Swallow Your Pride	20

FIVEPENNY PIECE
74	EMI 2187	Butterflies And Songbirds/Save Your Last Kiss For Me	6

FIVER
76	EMI 2401	When Love Walks Out The Door/I Don't Wanna Be Alone Tonight	6

FIVE'S COMPANY
MINT VALUE £

FIVE'S COMPANY
66	Pye 7N 17118	Sunday For Seven Days/The Big Kill	15
66	Pye 7N 17162	Some Girls/Big Deal	6
66	Pye 7N 17199	Session Man/Dejection	20
69	Saga FID 2151	THE BALLAD OF FRED THE PIXIE (LP)	20

(see also Brunning Hall Sunflower Blues Band)

5 SECONDS OF SUMMER
14	Capito l3797518	Amnesia/American Idiot (p/s)	50
15	Capitol 4746076	She's Kinda Hot/The Girl Who Cried Wolf (p/s, red vinyl)	30

THE 5, 6, 7, 8'S
04	Sweet Nothing 7SN028	Woo Hoo/Guitar Date (p/s)	15
04	Sweet Nothing 7SN029	I'm Blue/(I'm Sorry Mama) I'm A Wild One (p/s)	12
02	Sweet Nothing SNLP 035	TEENAGE MOJO WORKOUT (LP)	15

FIVE STAR GAS
79	Warp Records SRTS/79/CUS - 540WARP 001	Smokey Bubble Shoo Fly Pie/Sledge Hammer (500 only, no p/s)	20

5UU'S
88	RER Megacorp RER 33	ELEMENTS (LP)	25

FIXED PENALTY
92	FPT 001	Man Of Action/All Of Us (12")	18
92	FPT 002	To You/Bubble Up (12")	20
92	FPT 004	Party Rocker/I Only Hear What I Want To/A Few Words (12")	10

FIXER
78	Rainbow RSL 116	Bright And Rosy/Peaceful Atom Bomb (no p/s)	40

FIXIT
79	Ellie Jay SJSP9246	Eighteen Plus/April Fool	50

FIZZBOMBS
87	Narodnik NRK 003	Sign On The Line/The Lines That (p/s)	10

FIZZLER
79	Aerco AERS 105	Brill Plus (You Know Us)/Margy's Song (no p/s, 500 only)	10

FKA TWIGS
14	Young Turks YTLP 118X	LP 1 (LP, with free 7" and prints, gatefold)	40

FK9
81	ABS 001	Our Condition/These Children/All That Fall (p/s)	10
81	ABS SBS 2	Stranger At The Heart/Complete Surveillance (p/s)	10

ROBERTA FLACK
69	Atlantic 584 294	Compared To What/Hey, That's No Way To Say Goodbye	6
69	Atlantic 588 204	FIRST TAKE (LP, 1st pressing, orange/plum label)	40
71	Atlantic K 40097	CHAPTER TWO (LP)	20
72	Atlantic K 40297	QUIET FIRE (LP)	20
72	Atlantic K 40040	FIRST TAKE (LP, 2nd pressing, turquoise/orange label)	15
73	Atlantic K 50021	KILLING ME SOFTLY (LP, folding piano sleeve)	20
75	Atlantic K 50049	FEEL LIKE MAKIN' LOVE (LP)	15

(see also Donny Hathaway)

FLACK OFF
80	Sofa SEAT 003	FLACK OFF EP: COCKTAILS AT SIX	25

FLAG OF CONVENIENCE
82	Sire SIR 4057	Life On The Telephone/The Other Man's Sin (no p/s)	6

(see also Steve Diggle, Buzzcocks)

FLAIRS
57	Oriole CB 1392	Swing Pretty Mama/I'd Climb The Hills And Mountains	500
57	Oriole CB 1392	Swing Pretty Mama/I'd Climb The Hills And Mountains (78)	100

LES FLAMBEAUX
71	Mushroom 100 MR 13	LES FLAMBEAUX (LP, 2 different sleeve designs)	30

FLAME
70	Stateside SS 2183	See The Light/Get Your Mind Made Up	18
71	Stateside SSL 10312	THE FLAME (LP)	40

(see also Flames [South Africa], Beach Boys)

GEORGE FLAME
76	Seville 1014	You're Gone/Where Did Your Love Come From	8

FLAME 'N' KING & BOLD ONES
79	Grapevine GRP 123	Ho Happy Day/Ain't Nobody Jivin'	30

FLAMES (SOUTH AFRICA)
68	Flame FAN 101/1	Streamliner/Follow The Sun (p/s)	20
68	Page One FOR(S) 009	BURNING SOUL (LP)	50

(see also Beach Boys)

FLAMES (1)
64	Island WI 130	He's The Greatest/Someone Going To Bawl (both actually by the Maytals)	90
64	Island WI 136	Little Flea/Good Idea (both actually by the Maytals)	40
64	Island WI 138	When I Get Home/Neither Silver Nor Gold (both actually by the Maytals)	40
64	Island WI 139	Broadway Jungle/Beat Lied (both actually by the Maytals)	200
64	Blue Beat BB 205	Helena Darling/My Darling (both actually by Plamers)	20

(see also Maytals, Vikings)

FLAMES (2)
69	Nu Beat NB 028	You've Lost Your Date/Little Girl (B-side actually Stars by Cornel Campbell and Eternals)	70
73	Ackee ACK 528	Feeling Good/Zig Zag	10

(see also Alton Ellis & Flames, Righteous Flames, Larry Marshall, Winston Jarrett)

FLAMING EMERALDS
78	Grapevine GRP 104	Have Some Everybody/Have Some Everybody (Instrumental)	10

FLAMING GNOMES
09	Fruits De Mer Crustacean 05	Care Of Cell 44/Love Song With Flute (300 only, purple vinyl)	30

FLAMING STARS

MINT VALUE £

FLAMING STARS
95	Vinyl Japan PAD 23	HOSPITAL, HEAVEN OR HELL (EP)	10
95	Vinyl Japan PAD 30	MONEY TO BURN (EP)	10
96	Vinyl Japan PAD 31	DOWNHILL WITHOUT BRAKES (EP)	10
98	Vinyl Japan PAD 59	Sweet Smell Of Success/The Day The Earth Caught Fire (p/s, numbered, 2000 only)	6
00	Vinyl Japan PAD 71	You Don't Always Want What You Get/Saturday Night Special (p/s)	6
01	Vinyl Japan PAD 73	Some Things You Don't Forget/Only Tonight (p/s)	6
02	Vinyl Japan PAD 79	A Little Bit Like you/The Man Who Would Be King (p/s)	6
96	Vinyl Japan ASKLP 62	SONGS FROM THE BAR ROOM FLOOR (LP)	25
99	Vinyl Japan ASKLP 83	PATHWAY (LP)	20
00	Vinyl Japan ASKLP 121	A WALK ON THE WIRED SIDE (LP)	20
02	Vinyl Japan ASKLP 139	SUNSET & VOID (LP)	20
04	Vinyl Japan ASKLP 146	NAMED AND SHAMED (LP)	20

FLAMING LIPS
89	Glitterhouse EFA 40153	Drug Machine In Heaven/Strychnine/What's So Funny (About Peace, Love And Understanding) (p/s)	20
91	City Slang 04063-05	Unconsciously Screamin'/Ma, I Didn't Notice/Let Me Be It/Lucifer Rising (clear vinyl, hologram sleeve)	8
92	Warner Bros. PRO S 5452	Ballrooms Of Mars/MR BUNGLE: Sudden Death (promo, grey vinyl, no p/s)	15
94	Warner Bros. SAM 1431	She Don't Use Jelly/Translucent Egg/Turn It On (Bluegrass Version)/The Process (12" promo)	15
86	Enigma 2173-1	HEAR IT IS (LP with poster)	15
89	Enigma ENVLP523	TELEPATHIC SURGERY (LP)	20
03	Warner Bros. 9362481411	YOSHIMI BATTLES THE PINK ROBOTS (LP, inner sleeve, pink vinyl)	30
06	Warner Bros. WEA 9362 49966-1	AT WAR WITH THE MYSTICS (2-LP, one orange & one turquoise LP)	25
10	Warner Bros. 520857-1	EMBRYONIC (2-LP, blue/yellow vinyl)	20
10	Warner Bros. 523541-1	DOING THE DARK SIDE OF THE MOON (LP, green vinyl, CD, insert, 500 only)	20
13	Bella Union BELLAV 388	THE TERROR (2-LP, 7" and CD)	25

JOHNNY FLAMINGO
57	Vogue V 9089	My Teen-Age Girl/When I Lost You	100
57	Vogue V 9089	My Teen-Age Girl/When I Lost You (78)	30
58	Vogue V 9100	So Long/Make Me A Present Of You	75
58	Vogue V 9100	So Long/Make Me A Present Of You (78)	40

FLAMINGOS
57	London HLN 8373	Would I Be Crying?/Just For A Kick	600
57	London HLN 8373	Would I Be Crying?/Just For A Kick (78)	100
57	Brunswick 05696	The Ladder Of Love/Let's Make Up	500
57	Brunswick 05696	The Ladder Of Love/Let's Make Up (78)	80
59	Top Rank JAR 213	Love Walked In/Yours	50
60	Top Rank JAR 263	I Only Have Eyes For You/I Was Such A Fool	60
60	Top Rank JAR 367	Nobody Loves Me Like You/You, Me And The Sea	40
60	Top Rank JAR 519	Mio Amore/At Night	35
66	Philips BF 1483	Boogaloo Party/Nearness Of You	25
69	Philips BF 1786	Boogaloo Party/Nearness Of You (reissue, in p/s)	10
69	Philips BF 1786	Boogaloo Party/Nearness Of You (reissue)	8
70	Polydor 2066-007	Buffalo Soldier/Fontaineous Combustion	10
69	Philips SBL 7906	HITS NOW AND THEN (LP)	30

FLAMIN' GROOVIES
71	Kama Sutra 2013 031	Teenage Head/Evil-Hearted Ada	12
72	Kama Sutra 2013 042	Gonna Rock Tonite/Keep A-Knockin'/SHA NA NA: Rock'n'Roll Is Here To Stay/At The Hop/Duke Of Earl	8
72	United Artists UP 35392	Slow Death/Talahassie Lassie (in promo only p/s)	60
72	United Artists UP 35392	Slow Death/Talahassie Lassie	7
72	United Artists UP 35464	Married Woman/Get A Shot Of Rhythm And Blues	10
76	Sire 6198 086	Don't You Lie To Me/She Said Yeah/Shake Some Action (p/s)	7
76	Sire 6078 602	Shake Some Action/Teenage Confidential (p/s, 2 different versions of A-side)	6
76	United Artists REM 406	SLOW DEATH (EP)	10
71	Kama Sutra 2683 003	FLAMIN' GROOVIES (2-LP)	20
76	Sire 9103 251	SHAKE SOME ACTION (LP)	30
78	Sire 9103 333	THE FLAMIN' GROOVIES NOW! (LP)	20
86	Edsel ED 173	SUPERSNAZZ (LP, reissue)	18
88	Dojo DOJOLP 58	TEENAGE HEAD (LP, reissue)	15

(see also Mike Wilhelm)

FLAMING YOUTH
69	Fontana TF 1057	Guide Me Orion/From Now On (Immortal Invisible)	20
70	Fontana 6001 002	Every Man, Woman And Child/Drifting	18
70	Fontana 6001 003	From Now On/Space Child	18
69	Fontana STL 5533	ARK II (LP, with laminated multifold plastic window sleeve)	150
69	Fontana STL 5533	ARK II (LP, later sleeve pressing with unlaminated multifold plastic window sleeve)	60
69	Fontana STL 5533	ARK II (LP, gatefold sleeve, white front, black/silver labels)	50

(see also Genesis, Jackson Heights)

FLAMMA-SHERMAN
68	SNB 55-3488	No Need To Explain/Bassa Love	20
68	SNB 55-3769	Love Is In The Air/Super Day	18
69	SNB 55-4142	Move Me/Where Is He	18
69	SNB 55-4142	Move Me/Where Is He (DJ copy)	50

BUD FLANAGAN
69	Pye 7N 17854	Who Do You Think You're Kidding Mr. Hitler?/BERNARD BEDFORD CHORUS: It Ain't Gonna Rain No Mo'!	8

TOMMY FLANAGAN
59	Esquire 32-156	THE CATS (LP, with John Coltrane)	75

FLANAGAN BROTHERS
58	Vogue Coral Q 72342	Salton City/Early One Evening	20

TOMMY FLANDERS
69	Verve SVLP 6020	MOONSTONE (LP)	25

(see also Blues Project)

FLARES
61	London HLU 9441	Foot Stompin'/Hotcha Cha-Cha Brown	25
63	London HA-U 8034	FOOT STOMPIN' HITS (LP)	75

FLASH
72	Sovereign SOV 105	Small Beginnings/Morning Haze	7
73	Sovereign SOV 116	Watch Your Step/Lifetime	7
72	Sovereign SVNA 7251	FLASH (LP, laminated outer gatefold sleeve)	35
72	Sovereign SVNA 7255	FLASH IN THE CAN (LP, in unissued 'band in studio' proof sleeve)	25
72	Sovereign SVNA 7255	FLASH IN THE CAN (LP, gatefold sleeve)	20
73	Sovereign SVNA 7260	OUT OF OUR HANDS (LP, gatefold sleeve)	30

(see also Peter Banks, Yes)

FLASH & BOARD OF DIRECTORS
68	Bell BLL 1007	Busy Signal/Love Ain't Easy	10

FLASH CADILLAC & THE CONTINENTAL KIDS
75	Private Stock PVT 29	Hot Summer Girls/Time Will Tell	6
77	Private Stock PVT 92	See My Baby Jive/Brown Water (Apocalypse Blues)	6
75	Private Stock PVLP 1002	SONS OF THE BEACHES (LP)	15

FLASHBACK
82	Aaron FB 001	Angel/You Won't Change Me/Don't Mess With The Best (no p/s)	30

FLASH CATS
82	Lark LS 1	Tonight/I Want You/Gene Vincent Can't Be Dead (p/s)	7

FLASHPOINT
87	Private pressing FP 01	NO POINT OF REFERENCE (LP)	40

FLAT EARTH SOCIETY
83	Psycho PSYCHO 17	WALEECO (LP)	20

FLATMATES
86	Subway SUBWAY 6	I Could Be In Heaven/Tell Me Why/So In Love With You (foldaround p/s with insert in poly bag)	8
87	Subway SUBWAY 9	Happy All The Time/Thinking Of You (p/s)	8
87	Subway SUBWAY 14	You're Gonna Cry/Life Of Crime (p/s)	6
88	Subway SUBWAY 17	Shimmer/On My Mind (p/s)	6
88	Subway SUBWAY 17T	Shimmer/On My Mind/If Not For You/Bad (12", p/s, with 'flat sharing guide')	12
13	Optic Nerve OPT4 007	POTPOURRI (2-LP, pink vinyl)	20

(LESTER) FLATT & (EARL) SCRUGGS
67	Mercury MF 1007	Foggy Mountain Breakdown/My Cabin In Caroline	6

LINDA FLAVELL
66	Decca F 12312	And The Trouble With Me Is You/Over And Over	12

JACKIE FLAVELLE
72	York FYK 408	ADMISSION FREE (LP)	25

FLAVOR (1)
68	Direction 58-3597	Sally Had A Party/Shop Around	15

FLAVOR (2)
77	Tamla Motown STML 12066	IN GOOD TASTE (LP)	15

LOS FLECHAZOS
94	Detour Records DRO 13	Try It/You Drove Me Crazy (p/s, 100 red vinyl)	7

FLEE REKKERS
60	Triumph RGM 1008	Green Jeans/You Are My Sunshine (as Fabulous Flee-Rakkers)	25
60	Top Rank JAR 431	Green Jeans/You Are My Sunshine (reissue, as Fabulous Flea-Rakkers)	30
60	Pye 7N 15288	Sunday Date/Shiftless Sam	20
60	Pye 7N 15326	Blue Tango/Bitter Rice	10
61	Piccadilly 7N 35006	Lone Rider/Miller Like Wow	15
62	Piccadilly 7N 35048	Stage To Cimarron/Twistin' The Chestnuts	15
62	Piccadilly 7N 35081	Sunburst/Black Buffalo	15
63	Piccadilly 7N 35109	Fireball/Fandango	15
61	Pye NEP 24141	THE FABULOUS FLEE-REKKERS (EP)	40
91	C5 C5 564	JOE MEEK'S FABULOUS FLEE REKKERS (LP)	15

FLEETWOOD MAC
SINGLES
67	Blue Horizon 57-3051	I Believe My Time Ain't Long/Rambling Pony (as Peter Green's Fleetwood Mac, p/s)	100
67	Blue Horizon 57-3051	I Believe My Time Ain't Long/Rambling Pony (as Peter Green's Fleetwood Mac)	20
68	Blue Horizon 57-3138	Black Magic Woman/The Sun Is Shining	10
68	Blue Horizon 57-3139	Need Your Love So Bad/Stop Messin' Around	10
68	Blue Horizon 57-3145	Albatross/Jigsaw Puzzle Blues	6
69	Immediate IM 080	Man Of The World/EARL VINCE & VALIANTS: Somebody's Gonna Get Their Head Kicked In Tonight	10
69	Blue Horizon 57-3157	Need Your Love So Bad/Black Magic Woman (unissued)	0
69	Blue Horizon 57-3157	Black Magic Woman/No Place To Go (unissued)	0
69	Blue Horizon 57-3157	Need Your Love So Bad/No Place To Go	6
69	CBS 3051	I Believe My Time Ain't Long/Rambling Pony (reissue)	6
69	Reprise RS 27000	Oh Well (Parts 1 & 2)	6
70	Reprise RS 27007	The Green Manalishi (With The Two-Prong Crown)/World In Harmony (with p/s)	30
70	Reprise RS 27007	The Green Manalishi (With The Two-Prong Crown)/World In Harmony	8
72	Reprise K 14014	Spare Me A Little Of Your Love/Sunny Side Of Heaven	6

FLEETWOODS

MINT VALUE £

75	Reprise K 14403	Warm Ways/Blue Letter (with p/s)	6
76	Reprise K 14430	Rhiannon/Sugar Daddy (with p/s)	6

ALBUMS

68	Blue Horizon 7-63200	PETER GREEN'S FLEETWOOD MAC (mono, laminated front cover)	250
68	Blue Horizon 7-63200	PETER GREEN'S FLEETWOOD MAC (stereo, with stereo sticker, laminated front)	175
68	Blue Horizon 7-63205	MR. WONDERFUL (LP, mono, gatefold sleeve)	100
68	Blue Horizon (S)7-63205	MR. WONDERFUL (LP, stereo, gatefold sleeve)	75
69	Blue Horizon S 7-63215	THE PIOUS BIRD OF GOOD OMEN	40
69	Reprise RSLP 9000	THEN PLAY ON (gatefold sleeve, 'steamboat' label)	100
70	Reprise RSLP 9004	KILN HOUSE (gatefold sleeve, with insert)	80
70	Reprise RSLP 9004	KILN HOUSE (gatefold sleeve, without insert)	60
71	CBS Blue Horizon 63875	THE ORIGINAL FLEETWOOD MAC	30
72	Reprise K 44181	BARE TREES	20
77	Reprise K 54043	FLEETWOOD MAC (white vinyl with lyric sheet)	20
77	Warner Bros. K56244	RUMOURS (LP, with gatefold lyric insert)	35
77	Warner Bros K 56344	RUMOURS (white vinyl with lyric sheet)	40
79	Warner Bros. K66088	TUSK (2-LP, embossed sleeve, 4 inners)	20

(see also Peter Green, Buckingham-Nicks, Jeremy Spencer, Christine Perfect, Danny Kirwan, John Mayall, Otis Spann, Eddie Boyd, Duster Bennett, Chicken Shack, Shotgun Express, Bo Street Runners, Cheynes, Tramp, Brunning Hall Sunflower Blues Band)

FLEETWOODS

59	London HLU 8841	Come Softly To Me/I Care So Much	8
59	London HLU 4003	Come Softly To Me/I Care So Much (stereo export issue)	15
59	London HLU 8895	Graduation's Here/Oh Lord Let It Be Me	10
59	Top Rank JAR 202	Mr. Blue/You Mean Everything To Me	10
60	Top Rank JAR 294	Outside My Window/Magic Star (in p/s)	20
60	Top Rank JAR 294	Outside My Window/Magic Star	10
60	Top Rank JAR 383	Runaround/Truly Do	10
61	London HLG 9341	Tragedy/Little Miss Sad One	10
61	London HLG 9426	He's The Great Imposter/Poor Little Girl	10
62	Liberty LIB 62	They Tell Me It's Summer/Lovers By Night Strangers By Day	10
63	Liberty LIB 75	Goodnight My Love Pleasant Dreams/Jimmy Beware	10
64	Liberty LIB 93	Ruby Red Baby Blue/Lonesome Town	10
65	Liberty LIB 10191	Almost There/Before And After (Losing You)	10
60	Top Rank BUY 028	MR BLUE (LP, with 3 tracks by Little Bill & Bluenotes, Frantics and Bonnie Guitar)	20
61	London HA-G 2388	SOFTLY (LP, mono)	30
61	London SAH-G 6188	SOFTLY (LP, stereo)	40
61	London HA-G 2419	DEEP IN A DREAM (LP)	30

DEBBIE FLEMING

75	Bradleys BRAD 7519	Long Gone/All About You	6

GARFIELD FLEMING

19	Becket BKD 505	Don't Send Me Away/You Got Dat Right (12", reissue)	15
18	Cordial CORD 12001	GARFIELD FLEMING (LP)	15

HELEN FLEMING

66	Blue Beat BB 341	Eve's Ten Commandments/Don't Take Your Love Away	20

JOY FLEMING

75	Antic K 11518	A Bridge Of Love/Divorcee	10
76	Private Stock PVT 54	Are You Ready For Love/Alabama Standby	10

RAY FLEMING

63	MGM MGM 1196	I'm Glad I Have You/Humpty Dumpty	10

WADE FLEMONS

59	Top Rank JAR 206	Slow Motion/Walking By The River	12
60	Top Rank JAR 327	What's Happening?/Goodnight, It's Time To Go	12
60	Top Rank JAR 371	Easy Lovin'/Woops Now	15

FLESH

79	Dancing Industries DI 001	My Boy Lollipop/Flesh	7

FLESHEATERS

81	Initial IRC 007	A MINUTE TO PRAY, A SECOND TO DIE (LP)	18

FLESH VOLCANO

87	Some Bizzare SLUT 1	Slut/The Universal Cesspool/Bruisin' Chain (12", p/s)	10

(see also Marc Almond, Foetus)

AMELIA FLETCHER

91	Fierce FRIGHT 052	Can You Keep A Secret/Wrap My Arms Around Him (p/s)	20

(see also Heavenly, Talulah Gosh)

DARROW FLETCHER

66	London HLU 10024	The Pain Gets A Little Deeper/My Judgement Day	75
66	London HLU 10024	The Pain Gets A Little Deeper/My Judgement Day (DJ copy)	150

DON FLETCHER

66	Vocalion VP 9271	Two Wrongs Don't Make A Right/I'm So Glad	25

GUY FLETCHER

68	Pye 7N 17523	Keep On Loving Me/Loving Bird	10
69	Pye 7N 17765	Magic Woman/All Fall Down	6
71	Philips 6303013	GUY FLETCHER (LP, gatefold sleeve, black/silver labels)	25

LINDA FLETCHER

78	Ariola AHA 532	Hush/Fadin Away	6

FLEUR-DE-LYS

65	Immediate IM 020	Moondreams/Wait For Me	300
66	Immediate IM 032	Circles/So Come On	800
66	Polydor 56124	Mud In Your Eye/I've Been Trying	800
67	Polydor 56200	I Can See A Light/Prodigal Son	100
68	Polydor 56251	The Gong With The Luminous Nose/Hammer Head	300

FLEURITY

MINT VALUE £

| 68 | Atlantic 584 193 | Stop Crossing The Bridge/Brick By Brick (Stone By Stone) | 65 |
| 69 | Atlantic 584 243 | Liar/One Girl City | 200 |

(see also John Bromley, Terry Durham, Tony & Tandy, Sharon Tandy, Rupert's People, Shyster, Quotations, Chocolate Frog, Gordon Haskell, Waygood Ellis)

FLEURITY
| 94 | Aesthetic Death ADEP 001 | A DARKER SHADE OF EVIL EP (p/s) | 20 |
| 08 | Aesthetic Death ADLP 001 | MIN TID SKAL KOMME (2-LP, numbered sleeve, insert, 600 only) | 18 |

VIC FLICK SOUND
67	Rediffusion International RIM 1	Sexton Blake/West Of Winward	15
70	Chapter One CH 136	Hang On/Wonderful World	15
71	Chapter One CH 155	Quest For Love/Clarice	6
68	Rediffusion ZS5	WEST OF WINWARD (LP)	20

FLICK OF THE WRIST
| 81 | Do Nutt 0101 | Movietone/Ruth (no p/s) | 100 |

FLIES
66	Decca F 12533	I'm Not Your Stepping Stone/Talk To Me	175
67	Decca F 12594	House Of Love/It Had To Be You	80
68	RCA RCA 1757	The Magic Train/Gently As You Feel	75

(see also Bulldog Breed, T2)

FLIGHT 77
| 82 | Flight 77 | Looking For The Aliens/Stranger (p/s) | 25 |

MICK FLINN BAND
| 78 | EMI EMI 2805 | Doin' It Right/Do What You Wanna Do | 20 |

(see also Mixtures)

SHELBY FLINT
| 61 | Warner Bros WB 30 | Angel On My Shoulder/Somebody | 12 |
| 66 | London HLT 10068 | Cast Your Fate To The Wind/The Lilly | 20 |

FLINT (1)
| 78 | Rak YRAK275 | A Real Fine State Of Mind/Country Summer Days | 6 |

FLINT (2)
| 03 | Coolkills 980009-9 | ASTEROIDS (1-sided pink neon 10", p/s with inner) | 30 |

(see also The Prodigy)

FLINTSTONES
| 64 | HMV POP 1266 | Safari/Work Out | 20 |

BUNNY FLIP
| 72 | Pressure Beat PB 5510 | Shanky Dog (actually "Skanky Dog" by Winston Scotland)/JOE GIBBS & NOW GENERATION: Boney Dog | 10 |

(see also Winston Scotland, Peter Tosh)

FLIP & DATELINERS
| 64 | HMV POP 1359 | My Johnny Doesn't Come Around Anymore/Please Listen To Me | 60 |

(see also Vivienne Chering)

FLIPPER
| 81 | Alt. Tentacles VIRUS 8 | Ha Ha Ha/Love Canal (p/s, with insert) | 15 |
| 82 | Subterranean SUB UK1 | ALBUM GENERIC FLIPPER (LP) | 25 |

FLIRTATIONS
68	Deram DM 195	Someone Out There/How Can You Tell Me?	10
68	Deram DM 216	Nothing But A Heartache/Christmas Time Is Here Again	25
69	Deram DM 252	What's Good About Goodbye My Love?/Once I Had A Love	8
70	Deram DM 281	Keep On Searchin'/Moma I'm Coming Home	8
70	Deram DM 295	Can't Stop Loving You/Everybody Needs Somebody	8
71	Deram DM 329	Give Me Love/This Must Be The End Of The Line	8
72	Deram DM 351	Need Your Lovin'/I Wanna Be There	8
71	Polydor 2058 167	Little Darlin'/Take Me In Your Arms And Love Me	20
73	Mojo 2092 058	Why Didn't I Think Of That?/Oh Mia Bamba	6
72	Polydor 2058 249	Love A Little Longer/Hold On To Me Babe	8
74	Polydor 2058 495	Dirty Work/No Such Thing As A Miracle	6
75	RCA 2554	Mr. Universe/Somebody Cares For Me	7
98	London Traffic TRAF 1	Nothing But A Heartache (1-sided, reissue promo, 500 only)	10
69	Deram DML/SML 1046	SOUNDS LIKE THE FLIRTATIONS (LP)	40
72	Deram SPA 218	THE WORLD OF THE FLIRTATIONS (LP)	15
75	RCA SF8448	LOVE MAKES THE WORLD GO ROUND (LP)	15

(see also Gypsies)

FLO & EDDIE
| 72 | Reprise K 44201 | THE PHLORESCENT LEECH AND EDDIE (LP) | 15 |
| 73 | Reprise K 44234 | FLO AND EDDIE (LP) | 15 |

(see also Turtles, Frank Zappa/Mothers Of Invention)

FLOATING BRIDGE
| 69 | Liberty LBS 83271 | FLOATING BRIDGE (LP) | 100 |

FLOATING OPERA
| 74 | DJM DJS 321 | Keep On Streaking/Home Run | 20 |

FLOATING POINTS
11	Eglo EGLO 19	Danger/Miniature 27	10
11	Eglo EGLO 22	SHADOWS EP (2 x 12", 1st pressing, 180gram, gatefold)	30
13	Eglo EGLO 29	Wires (1-sided 12" with screen printed insert)	12
15	Pluto FPLP 01	ELAENIA (LP)	18
17	Pluto RE001LP	REFLECTIONS - MOJAVE DESERT (LP, with DVD)	18
19	Ninja Tune ZEN 259	CRUSH (LP)	18
20	Luaka Bop 6 80899 0097-1-3	PROMISES (LP, with London Symphony Orchestra and Pharoah Saunders)	20
21	Luaka Bop 6 80899 0097-1-3/0097	PROMISES (LP, reissue, blue marbled or yellow marbled vinyl with London Symphony Orchestra and Pharoah Saunders)	80

FLOCK

(see also Maalem Mahmoud Guinia)

MINT VALUE £

FLOCK
70	CBS 4932	Tired Of Waiting For You/Store Bought — Store Thought	15
69	CBS 63733	THE FLOCK (LP, orange label)	15
70	CBS 64055	DINOSAUR SWAMPS (LP, orange label, gatefold sleeve)	20

(see also Mahavishnu Orchestra)

THE FLOOD
84	Midnight Music DING 7	Cold Cold World/2 Shots Of Jealousy	10

FLORENCE AND THE MACHINE
08	Moshi Moshi MOMO15	Kiss With A Fist/Hospital Beds (p/s)	15
08	Moshi Moshi 171	Dog Days Are Over/You've Got The Love (p/s)	15
09	Moshi Moshi 2710003	Rabbit Heart (Raise It Up)/Are You Hurting The One You Love? (p/s)	15
09	Moshi Moshi 2718895	Drumming Song (Acoustic)/My Boy Builds A Coffin (Acoustic)	15
09	Moshi Moshi 2726062	You've Got The Love/You've Got The Love (Jamie XX Re-Write) (p/s)	20
10	Moshi Moshi 2736273	Dog Days Are Over/Dog Days Are Over (Optimo Mix)	15
10	Moshi Moshi 2744152	Cosmic Love/Cosmic Love (Isa Machine Mix)	15
11	Vinyl Factory VF-04X	Never Let Me Go/Never Let Me Go (Clams Casino Mix) (12" white vinyl, hand numbered, 500 only)	60
11	Vinyl Factory VF-04Y	Spectrum/Spectrum (Calvin Harris Mix)/Spectrum (Aluna George Mix)/Spectrum (Mary Jane Coles Mix (12" white vinyl hand numbered, 500 only)	50
11	Vinyl Factory VF 035	Shake It Out/Shake It Out (Weekend Remix) (12" white vinyl, hand numbered, 500 copies)	60
12	Universal/Talenthouse S76	Only If For A Night (1-sided, 100 only)	60
12	Vinyl Factory VF 038	No Light, No Light/No Light, No Light (DAS Mix) (12" white vinyl, hand numbered, 500 only)	70
12	Vinyl Factory VF 044	Never Let Me Go/Clams Casino Remix (12" p/s, white vinyl, numbered)	35
09	Island 2709106	LUNGS (LP)	20
11	Island 2784790	CEREMONIALS (2-LP)	20
15	Island GB-UM7-15-00288	HOW BIG, HOW BLUE, HOW BEAUTIFUL (LP as 6 x 7")	60
15	Island 602547244956	HOW BIG, HOW BLUE, HOW BEAUTIFUL (2-LP)	20

KEITHER FLORENCE
17	BK 001	Free (Instrumental Version)/Future (reissue)	10

FLORIBUNDA ROSE
67	Piccadilly 7N 35408	One Way Street/Linda Loves Linda	60

(see also Scrugg, John T. Kongos)

FLOWCHART
90s	Enraptured RAPT 4527	NO. 7 IN THE STRESS FREE SERIES: Gip Part One/Gip Part 2 (in box)	6

FLOWERPOT MEN
67	Deram DM 160	A Walk In The Sky/Am I Losing You?	8
68	Deram DM 183	A Man Without A Woman/You Can Never Be Wrong	8
68	Page One POF 065	Mighty Quinn/Voices From The Sky	10
69	Deram DM 248	In A Moment Of Madness/Young Birds Fly	10

(see also Ivy League, Friends, Carter-Lewis & Southerners, Edison Lighthouse, Fat Mattress, Gordon Haskell, Kestrels, One & One)

FLOWERS
79	Pop Aural POP 1	Confessions/(Life) After Dark	10

FLOWERS FOR AGATHA
85	Leeds Independent 12 LIL 3	THE FREEDOM CURSE EP (12" p/s)	12
85	Off Beat OB 10	Presentation/The Thickest Head (p/s)	20
86	Leeds Independent 12 LIL 8	YOUNG FOOLISH OLD AND STUPID EP (12" p/s)	15

FLOWERS & FROLICS
77	Free Reed FRR 016	BEES ON HORSEBACK (LP, featuring June Tabor & Bob Davenport)	35

FLOWERS IN THE DUSTBIN
84	All The Madmen MAD 7	FREAKS RUN WILD IN THE DISCO (12" EP)	20
85	Mortarhate MORT 16	Nails Of The Heart/All Fools Day/The Reason Why	12
86	Cold Harbour COLD 1002	Lick My Crazy Colours!/The Continuing Tragedy Of Mr. Smith/Stranger In A Strange Land	12

LLOYD FLOWERS & RECO'S RHYTHM GROUP
62	Blue Beat BB 88	I'm Going Home/Lover's Town	15

(LLOYD) FLOWERS & ALVIN (RANGLIN)
72	Explosion EX 2067	Howdy And Tenky/SHORTY PERRY: Sprinkle Some Water	7
72	Grape GR 3028	In De Pum Pum/MAYTONES: If Loving You Was Wrong	10
72	Bullet BU 512	Howdy And Tenky/SHORTY PERRY: Sprinkle Some Water	7
73	Duke DU 150	Rastaman Going Back Home/LITTLE YOUTH: Barble Dove Skank	6

PHIL FLOWER(S)
69	A&M AMS 766	Like A Rolling Stone/Keep On Sockin' It Children	20

FLOWER SERMON
92	Rough Trade 45REV 13	Sugar Lullaby (p/s with insert)	8

FLOWER SHOPPE
72	Polydor 2066 096	You've Come A Long Way/Kill The Monster	10

FLOWERS OF EVIL
82	Marching Men MAME 001	First Blood/Joy (p/s)	20

FLOWER TRAVELLING BAND
71	Atlantic 2091 128	Satori (Enlightment) (Parts 1 & 2)	20

BOBBY FLOYD
72	Pama PM 860	Sound Doctor/YOUNG DILLINGER: Doctor Skank	50

EDDIE FLOYD
66	Atlantic 584 041	Knock On Wood/Got To Make A Comeback	10
67	Stax 601 001	Raise Your Hand/I've Just Been Feeling Bad (dark blue label)	10
67	Stax 601 001	Raise Your Hand/I've Just Been Feeling Bad (light blue label)	8
67	London HL 10129	Set My Soul On Fire/Will I Be The One?	8
67	Speciality SPE 1001	Never Get Enough Of Your Love/Bye Bye Baby	20

FLUDD

MINT VALUE £

67	Stax 601 016	Things Get Better/Good Love, Bad Love	15
67	Stax 601 024	On A Saturday Night/Under My Nose	15
68	Stax 601 035	Big Bird/Holding On With Both Hands	30
68	Stax STAX 104	I've Never Found A Girl (To Love Me Like You Do)/I'm Just The Kind Of Fool	15
69	Stax STAX 108	Bring It On Home To Me/Sweet Things You Do	10
69	Stax STAX 116	I've Got To Have Your Love/Girl I Love You	10
69	Stax STAX 125	Don't Tell Your Mama/Consider Me	10
70	Stax STAX 153	My Girl/Laurie	7
72	Polydor 2025 098	Yum Yum Yum/I Want Some/Tears Of Joy	7
67	Stax 589 006	KNOCK ON WOOD (LP)	50
68	Stax (S)XATS 1003	I'VE NEVER FOUND A GIRL (LP)	30
69	Stax SXATS 1023	YOU'VE GOT TO HAVE EDDIE (LP)	30
70	Stax SXATS 1036	CALIFORNIA GIRL (LP)	20
74	Stax STX 1002	SOUL STREET (LP)	15
88	Stax SX 010	THE BEST OF EDDIE FLOYD (LP)	15

(see also Falcons, Primettes/Eddie Floyd)

FLUDD
| 75 | Private Stock PVT 30 | What An Animal/Boarding School | 6 |

FLUFF
| 70 | DJM DJS 215 | Make Believe/Love Machine | 12 |

FLUTTERS
| 70s | STEW 101 | Haunted Staircase/Something For The Children (p/s) | 10 |

FLUX OF PINK INDIANS
81	Crass 321984/2	NEU SMELL (EP, foldout poster sleeve)	12
83	Spiderleg SDL 8	STRIVE TO SURVIVE CAUSING THE LEAST SUFFERING POSSIBLE (LP, with booklet)	35
84	Spiderleg SDL 13	THE FUCKING CUNTS TREAT US LIKE PRICKS (2-LP)	20

(see also Epileptics, Licks)

FLY ON THE WALL
| 79 | Next Wave NEXT 1 | DEVON DUMB (EP, numbered, 1000 only) | 35 |

FLYING BRIX
| 80 | Modello MHMS 194 | BLACK COLOURS EP (p/s, with booket, 500 only) | 20 |

FLYING BURRITO BROTHERS
69	A&M AMS 756	The Train Song/Hot Burrito No. 1	6
69	A&M AML(S) 931	THE GILDED PALACE OF SIN (LP)	30
70	A&M AMLS 983	BURRITO DELUXE (LP)	18
71	A&M AMLS 64295	THE FLYING BURRITO BROTHERS (LP)	15

(see also Byrds, Gram Parsons, Gene Parsons, Stephen Stills & Manassas, Country Gazette, Skip Battin)

FLYING CIRCUS
| 71 | Harvest SHSP 4010 | PREPARED IN PEACE (LP, no EMI box on label) | 75 |

FLYING COLOURS
| 81 | No Records NO 1 | Abstract Art/Ape Notes (p/s) | 25 |

FLYING IS EASY
| 70 | High Key HK1 | Stone Cross/Magic Pastures | 50 |

FLYING LIZARDS
| 80 | Virgin V2150 | FLYING LIZARDS (LP) | 20 |
| 81 | Virgin V2190 | FOURTH WALL (LP) | 18 |

FLYING LOTUS
07	Warp WAP 228	Reset (12")	15
08	Warp WARPLP 165	LOS ANGELS (2-LP)	25
10	Warp WARPLP 195	COSMOGRAMMA (2-LP, plastic sleeves and grease proof sleeve, MP3 download)	20
12	Warp WARPLP230	UNTIL THE QUIET COMES (2-LP)	20
14	Warp WARPLP 256	YOU'RE DEAD (2-LP)	20
19	Warp WARPLP 291	FLAMAGRA (2-LP)	20

FLYING MACHINE
69	Pye 7N 17722	Smile A Little Smile For Me/Maybe We've Been Loving Too Long	7
69	Pye 7N 17722	Baby Make It Soon/Smile A Little Smile For Me	6
69	Pye 7N 17811	Send My Baby Home Again/Look At Me, Look At Me	7
70	Pye 7N 17914	Hanging On The Edge Of Sadness/Flying Machine	7
70	Pye 7N 45001	The Devil Has Possession Of Your Mind/Hey Little Girl	30
70	Pye 7N 45093	Yes I Understand/Pages Of Your Life	6
70	Pye NSPL 18328	DOWN TO EARTH WITH THE FLYING MACHINE (LP, blue/black label with logo-banner on top)	40

(see also Pinkertons, Pinkerton's Assorted Colours, Tony Newman)

FLYING SAUCER ATTACK
92	Heartbeat FSA 6	Soaring High/Standing Stone (p/s, 500 only, 1st few with autographed postcards)	25
92	Heartbeat FSA 6	Soaring High/Standing Stone (p/s, 500 only, with various different designs)	20
93	Heartbeat FSA 61	Wish/Oceans (p/s, 700 only)	20
94	Domino RUG 23	Land Beyond The Sun/Everywhere Was Everything (p/s, hand-painted rear sleeve, 500 only)	6
95	Planet PUNK 008	Beach Red Lullaby/Second Hour (p/s, 1,300 only)	6
96	Enraptured RAPT 4505	At Night/JESSAMINE: From Hereto And Now Otherwise (500 on clear vinyl)	12
96	Enraptured RAPT 4505	At Night/JESSAMINE: From Hereto And Now Otherwise (2500 on black vinyl)	8
98	Earworm WORMSC 1	Land Beyond The Sun (2 -Track Version)/Instrumental For Silence (green vinyl, 500 only)	6
93	Heartbeat FSA 62	FLYING SAUCER ATTACK (LP, 1st pressing, 1,000 only, black and white sleeve, hand numbered, booklet insert)	50
93	FSA FAS 62	FLYING SAUCER ATTACK (LP, 2nd pressing, 923 copies, coloured sleeve, insert)	25
93	FSA FAS 62	FLYING SAUCER ATTACK (LP, 3rd pressing, 1,000 only, blue vinyl, stamped white sleeve, photocopied insert)	25
94	Domino WIGLP 12	DISTANCE (LP)	15
94	Domino WIGLP 20	FURTHER (LP, gatefold sleeve, insert)	20
95	Domino WIGLP 22	CHORUS (LP, inert)	15

FLYING SAUCERS

MINT VALUE £

| 97 | Domino WIGLP 38 | NEW LANDS (LP) | 20 |
| 00 | FSA 64 | MIRROR (LP, clear vinyl) | 18 |

FLYING SAUCERS
76	Alaska ALA 2001	Fabulous/Fish On The Line	6
76	Alaska ALA 2003	Keep On Comming/Shadow Walk	6
76	Alaska ALA 2009	Oh Carol/I Need Your Love	6
76	Alaska ALA 2014	Texas Calls You Home/Pretty Baby (p/s)	8
78	Alaska ALA 2014	Texas Calls You Home/Pretty Baby	6
76	Nevis NEV LP 114	PLANET OF THE DRAPES (LP)	15
91	Rawking Music	THE ROCKING SANDY FORD (LP)	25

JOHNNY FLYNN
| 08 | Vertigo 1766662 | A LARUM (LP, pop up sleeve) | 80 |

PATTI FLYNN
| 82 | SRT S82CUS1431 | Soul Stuntman/Stuntman (500 only, no p/s) | 10 |

STEVE FLYNN
| 67 | Parlophone R 5625 | Mr Rainbow/Let's Live For Tomorrow | 50 |
| 68 | Parlophone R 5689 | Your Life And My Life/Come Tomorrow | 10 |

(see also Mark Wirtz)

FLYS
78	EMI EMI 2747	Love And A Molotov Cocktail/Can I Crash Here?/Civilisation (p/s)	20
78	EMI EMI 2795	Fun City/E.C. 4 (p/s)	10
78	EMI EMIY 2867	Waikiki Beach Refugees/We Don't Mind The Rave (p/s, yellow vinyl)	10
79	EMI EMI 2907	Beverley/Don't Moonlight On Me (p/s)	6
79	EMI EMI 2936	Name Dropping/Fly V Fly (p/s, some on green vinyl)	15
79	EMI EMI 2979	We Are The Lucky Ones/Living In The Sticks (p/s)	10
77	Zama ZA 10 EP	BUNCH OF FIVE (33rpm EP, die-cut sleeve)	50
80	Parlophone R 6063	FOUR FROM THE SQUARE (demo copies)	20
80	Parlophone R 6063	FOUR FROM THE SQUARE (EP, p/s)	10
78	EMI EMC 3249	WAIKIKI BEACH REFUGEES (LP)	15

FLYTE REACTION
| 91 | Woronzow W0014 | SONGS IN A CIRCLE (LP) | 20 |

FOALS
06	Try Harder	Try This On Your Piano/Look At My Furrows Of Worry (700 only, hand-numbered)	35
07	Transgressive TRANS 049	FOALS LIVE (12" promo, 1000 only p/s)	25
07	Transgressive TRANS 050	Hummer/Astronauts And All (p/s, 1000 only)	20
07	Transgressive TRANS 053	Mathletics/Big Big Love (1,500 only)	18
08	Transgressive TRANS 089.5	Super Inuit/HOLY FUCK: Balloons (die cut sleeve decorated by band, 250 only)	12
10	Warner Bros. WEA 471X	This Orient/Spanish Sahara (Chad Valley Remix)	6
10	Warner Bros. WEA 471	This Orient/This Orient (Starkey Remix)	6
08	Transgressive TRANS 071LP	ANTIDOTES (LP, insert, poster, stickered sleeve)	50
10	Warner Bros. 5051865913900	TOTAL LIFE FOREVER (LP)	35
13	Warner Bros. 825646522248	HOLY FIRE (LP)	20
13	Warner Bros. 825646521388	HOLY FIRE (Box set, marbled vinyl LP, CD, DVD, 7", numbered)	60

FOAMPLATE
| 16 | System SYSTM 012 | Lionize/696 (12") | 40 |

GREG FOAT GROUP
11	Jazzman JMANLP041	DARK IS THE SUN (LP, 1st pressing)	40
12	Jazzman JMANLP054	GIRL AND ROBOT WITH FLOWERS (LP)	20
15	Jazzman JMANLP041	DARK IS THE SUN (LP, repressing, purple and silver screen printed cover)	15

FOCAL POINT
| 68 | Deram DM 186 | Love You Forever/Sycamore Sid | 60 |

FO'C'SLE
| 72 | Tradition TSC 1 | FROM THE FOREST (LP, 100 copies only) | 25 |

FOCUS
71	Blue Horizon 2094 006	Hocus Pocus/Janis	15
72	Blue Horizon 2096 008	Tommy/Focus II	15
71	Polydor 2344 003	IN AND OUT OF FOCUS (LP, gatefold sleeve)	15
71	Blue Horizon 2096 2931	MOVING WAVES (LP, 1st pressing, white/blue labels, Matrixes: Side 1, 2931002 A etched (with 2431011 crossed out) A//1 V 420 1 1 2, Side 2 2931002 B etched (243101 stamped not crossed out) B//1 V 420 11 4, Blue Horizon logo on rear of E.J. Group sleeve)	25
76	Harvest SHSP 4068	SHIP OF MEMORIES (LP)	15
73	Polydor 2442 118	AT THE RAINBOW (multifold sleeve)	15

(see also Jan Akkerman, Brainbox, Robin Lent)

THE FOCUS GROUP
| 11 | Ghost Box GBX 002 | SKETCHES AND SPELLS (LP) | 30 |
| 13 | Ghost Box GBX 018 | ELEKTRIK KAROUSEL (LP) | 18 |

FOCUS THREE
| 67 | Columbia DB 8279 | 10,000 Years Behind My Mind/The Sunkeeper | 80 |

FOETUS UNDER GLASS
| 85 | Self Immolation. WOMB S201 | Spite Your Face/OKFM (p/s) | 15 |

(see also You've Got Foetus On Your Breath, Philip & His Foetus Vibrations, Scraping Foetus Off The Wheel)

FOGCITY
| 93 | Houseplant/Mighty Force HP1061/MF005 | FOGCITY EP (12", white label, 250 only) | 20 |

FOGCUTTERS
| 64 | Liberty LIB 55793 | Cry Cry Cry/You Say | 15 |

JOHN FOGERTY
| 75 | Fantasy FT 526 | JOHN FOGERTY (LP) | 15 |

(see also Creedence Clearwater Revival, Blue Ridge Rangers)

FOGG
74	EMI EMI 2182	Water In My Wine/Just Like Me	8
75	Warner Bros. K16622	Rock N Roll Star/You Got Something	6

FOGGY
72	York SYK 534	How Come The Sun/Take Your Time	10
73	York SYK 542	Kitty Starr/She's Far Away (p/s)	15
73	York SYK 542	Kitty Star/She's far Away (no p/s)	10
72	York FYK 411	SIMPLE GIFTS (LP, with insert, featuring Strawbs)	30
75	Canon CNN 5759	PATCHWORK (LP)	20

(see also Strawbs, Foggy Dew-O)

FOGGY DEW-O
68	Decca F 12776	Reflections/Grandfather's Clock	8
71	York SYK 503	Me And Bobby McGee/Feelin' Groovy	6
68	Decca LK/SKL 4940	THE FOGGY DEW-O (LP, blue/silver labels with large unboxed logo)	25
70	Decca LK/SKL 5035	BORN TO TAKE THE HIGHWAY (LP, blue/silver label with small boxed logo)	15

(see also Strawbs, Foggy)

FOGHAT
72	Bearsville K15501	What A Shame/Hole To Hide In	6
74	Bearsville K15511	Long Way To Go/Ride Ride Ride	6
72	Bearsville K45503	FOGHAT (LP)	40

(see also Black Cat Bones, Warren Philips & The Rockets)

FOKUS
95	Lucky Spin LRS 025	Trigger Happy (Original)/Trigger Happy (Voyager Remix) (12")	35
95	Lucky SPin LSR 025	Wired/Brave New World (12")	45
95	Dee Jay DJX 028	On Line (Original)/On Line Drum N Bass)/On Line (Trip Hop) (12")	40

ELLEN FOLEY (& CLASH)
81	Epic EPC A 9522	The Shuttered Palace/Beautiful Waste Of Time (p/s)	6
81	Epic EPC A 1160	Torchlight/Game Of A Man (p/s)	6
81	Epic SEPC 84809	SPIRIT OF ST. LOUIS (LP, with inner sleeve)	20

(see also Clash)

RED FOLEY
54	Brunswick 05321	Skinnie Minnie (Fishtail)/Thank You For Calling	8
55	Brunswick 05508	Croce Di Oro (Cross Of Gold) (with Betty Foley)/The Night Watch	8
55	Brunswick 05363	Hearts Of Stone/RED FOLEY & BETTY FOLEY: Never	18

(see also Roberta Lee)

RED FOLEY & ERNEST TUBB
55	Brunswick OE 9148	COUNTRY DOUBLE DATE (EP, with Minnie Pearl)	15

(see also Ernest Tubb)

SIMON FOLEY
77	Look LKLP 6324	TO STRIVE WITH PRINCES (LP, with booklet)	20

FOLKAL POINT
72	Midas MR 003	FOLKAL POINT (LP)	1500

FOLK DEVILS
84	Ganges RAY 1	Hank Turns Blue/Chewin' The Fat (with p/s)	15
84	Ganges RAY 1	Hank Turns Blue/Chewin' The Fat	8

CALVIN FOLKES
63	Rio R 5	Someone/Kentucky Home	10
63	Rio R 8	You'll Never Know/Is It Time?	10
64	Port-O-Jam PJ 4117	My Bonnie/What A Day	12
64	Port-O-Jam PJ 4118	Hello Everybody/IRVING SIX: King's Boogie	15

FOLKLANDERS
60s	Urban PB 001	TWO LITTLE FISHES (EP)	10

FOLKLORE
77	Tank BSS 210	ROOM FOR COMPANY (LP)	20

FOLK(S) BROTHERS
61	Blue Beat BB 30	Carolina/I Met A Man (original, blue label, as Folks Brothers)	18
60s	Fab BB 30	Carolina (as Folks Brothers)/ERIC 'HUMPTY DUMPTY' MORRIS: Humpty Dumpty	7
70s	Blue Beat BB 30	Carolina/I Met A Man (reissue, white label, as Folk Brothers)	6

FOLK SONG CLUB
65	white label (no cat. no.)	IMPERIAL COLLEGE (LP, private pressing)	100

FOLKUS
70	Thule SLP 102	ALIVE (LP)	100

ROY FONTAINE
86	Abstract ADT 9	One Is A Lonely Number (Vocal)/(Instrumental Version) (12" white label only)	40

CLAUDIA FONTAINE
81	JB JBD 033	Natural High/CORNER SHOT: Take Me To The Sky (12", clear, blue, red or black vinyl)	12
81	JB JBS 033	Natural High/CORNER SHOT: Take Me To The Sky	6
81	Decca FX13905	Natural High/GLEN SLOWLY: Let's Love (12", p/s)	12
82	JB JBS 043	Is It Always Gonna Be Like This (as Ray and Claudia)/RAYMOND SIMPSON: Paradise In Your Eyes	6
89	SC 001	I You Wanna Lover/(Instrumental)/(Dub Mix) (12" stamped white labels as Serious Chocolate featuring Claudia Fontaine)	20

EDDIE FONTAINE
55	HMV 7M 304	Rock Love/All My Love Belongs To You (with Neal Hefti & Excels)	150
55	HMV B 10852	Rock Love/All My Love Belongs To You (with Neal Hefti & Excels) (78)	20
56	Brunswick 05624	Cool It, Baby/Into Each Life Some Rain Must Fall	100
56	Brunswick 05624	Cool It, Baby/Into Each Life Some Rain Must Fall (78)	20
58	London HLM 8711	Nothin' Shakin' (But The Leaves On The Trees)/Don't Ya Know	50

FONTAINES
87	51st Parallel FONT 1	I Want Everything/Bernadette (p/s)	30

Arlene FONTANA

MINT VALUE £

ARLENE FONTANA
59	Pye International 7N 25010	I'm In Love/Easy	7

WAYNE FONTANA & THE MINDBENDERS
63	Fontana TF 404	Hello! Josephine/Road Runner	25
63	Fontana TF 418	For You, For You/Love Potion No.9	15
64	Fontana TF 436	Little Darlin'/Come Dance With Me	20
64	Fontana TF 451	Stop Look And Listen/Duke Of Earl	10
65	Fontana TF 535	The Game Of Love/Since You've Been Gone	6
65	Fontana TF 579	It's Just A Little Bit Too Late/Long Time Comin'	10
65	Fontana TF 611	She Needs Love/Like I Did	8
69	Fontana H 1022	Um, Um, Um, Um, Um, Um/The Game Of Love (p/s)	8
64	Fontana TE 17421	ROAD RUNNER (EP)	50
64	Fontana TE 17435	UM, UM, UM, UM, UM, UM (EP)	20
65	Fontana TE 17449	THE GAME OF LOVE (EP)	15
65	Fontana TE 17453	WALKING ON AIR (EP)	40
64	Fontana TL 5230	WAYNE FONTANA AND THE MINDBENDERS (LP)	60
65	Fontana TL 5257	ERIC, RICK, WAYNE, BOB — IT'S WAYNE FONTANA AND THE MINDBENDERS (LP)	65
67	Wing WL 1166	WAYNE FONTANA AND THE MINDBENDERS (LP, reissue)	15

(see also Wayne Fontana, Mindbenders)

WAYNE FONTANA
65	Fontana TF 642	It Was Easier To Hurt Her/You Made Me What I Am Today	10
66	Fontana TF 737	Goodbye Bluebird/The Sun's So Hot Today	6
66	Fontana TF 770	Pamela Pamela/Something Keeps Calling Me Back	6
67	Fontana TF 827	24 Sycamore/From A Boy To A Man	6
67	Fontana TF 866	The Impossible Years/In My World	12
67	Fontana TF 889	Gina/We All Love The Human Race	6
68	Fontana TF 911	Storybook Children/I Need To Love You	6
68	Fontana TF 933	The Words Of Bartholomew/Mind Excursion	6
68	Fontana TF 976	Never An Everyday Thing/Waiting For A Break In The Clouds	40
69	Fontana TF 1008	Dayton Ohio 1903/Say Goodbye To Yesterday	7
69	Fontana TF 1054	Charlie Cass/Linda (withdrawn issue)	25
69	Fontana TF 1054	We're Building A Love/Charlie Cass	10
69	Fontana TF 1027	Come On Home/Pamela Pamela (p/s)	10
70	Philips 6006 035	Give Me Just A Little More Time/I'm In Love (withdrawn)	150
70	Philips 6006 035	Give Me Just A Little More Time/I'm In Love (withdrawn) (DJ Copy)	100
73	Warner Bros K 16269	Together/One Man Woman	6
66	Fontana (S)TL 5351	WAYNE ONE (LP, black/silver labels)	25

(see also Mindbenders)

FONTANE SISTERS
54	London HL 8099	Happy Days And Lonely Nights/If I Didn't Have You	30
55	London HL 8113	Hearts Of Stone/Bless Your Heart	30
55	London HL 8126	Rock Love/You're Mine	30
55	London HLD 8177	Seventeen/If I Could Be With You	35
55	London HLD 8211	Rolling Stone/Daddy-O	30
56	London HLD 8225	Adorable/Playmates	20
56	London HLD 8265	Eddie My Love/Yum Yum	20
56	London HL 7009	Eddie My Love/Yum Yum (export issue)	20
56	London HLD 8289	I'm In Love Again/You Always Hurt The One You Love (gold lettering label)	25
56	London HLD 8289	I'm In Love Again/You Always Hurt The One You Love (later silver lettering label)	10
56	London HLD 8318	Voices (with narration by Pat Boone)/Willow Weep For Me (gold lettering label)	20
56	London HLD 8318	Voices (with narration by Pat Boone)/Willow Weep For Me (later silver lettering label)	10
56	London HLD 8343	Silver Bells/Nuttin' For Christmas	10
57	London HLD 8378	The Banana Boat Song/Lonesome Lover Blues (gold lettering)	10
57	London HLD 8488	Fool Around/Which Way To Your Heart?	8
58	London HLD 8621	Chanson D'Amour (Song Of Love)/Cocoanut Grove	8
59	London HLD 8861	Billy Boy/Chanson D'Amour	10
55	London RE-D 1029	FONTANE SISTERS NO. 1 (EP)	25
55	London RE-D 1037	FONTANE SISTERS NO. 2 (EP)	25
57	London HA-D 2053	THE FONTANES SING (LP)	50

(see also Pat Boone, Perry Como)

SAM FONTEYN
66	Parlophone R 5519	Lost In Space/BERNARD SHARPE: Jorrocks	10

BILLY FONTEYNE
63	Oriole CB 1917	Little Child/Look Before You Leap	15

FOO FIGHTERS

SINGLES
95	Roswell CL 753	This Is A Call/Winnebago (p/s)	10
95	Roswell 12CL 753	This Is A Call/Winnebago/Podunk (12", luminous vinyl)	20
95	Roswell CL 757	I'll Stick Around/How I Miss You (red vinyl, p/s)	12
95	Roswell 12CL 757	I'll Stick Around/How I Miss You (12" p/s)	15
95	Roswell CL 762	For All The Cows/Watershed (blue vinyl, p/s)	8
95	Roswell CL 768	Big Me/Floaty/Gas Chamber (white vinyl, p/s)	12
97	Roswell CL 788	Monkey Wrench/Up In Arms (red vinyl, p/s)	15
97	Roswell CL 792	Everlong/Drive Me Wild (blue vinyl, p/s)	80
97	Roswell CL 796	My Hero/Dear Lover (red vinyl, stickered poly sleeve, with insert)	30
00	RCA 74321 80926-7	Next Year/Big Me (live) (p/s)	6
02	RCA 74321 97315-7	All My Life/Sister Europe (numbered p/s)	12
03	RCA 74321 98955-7	Times Like These/Lack Of Illision (numbered p/s)	6
03	BMG 82876-52256-7	Low/Never Talking To You Again (Live Version) (numbered p/s, 3,000 only)	10

FOOL

MINT VALUE £

| 05 | RCA 82876 72279-7 | D.O.A./Razor (Acoustic) (p/s, yellow vinyl) | 6 |

ALBUMS

95	Roswell EST 2266	FOO FIGHTERS (LP)	70
97	Roswell EST 2295	THE COLOUR AND THE SHAPE (LP)	100
99	RCA 07863678921	THERE IS NOTHING LEFT TO LOSE (LP, stickered gatefold sleeve, with tattoo transfer)	60
02	RCA 74321973481	ONE BY ONE (LP, gatefold sleeve with inner)	40
05	BMG 82876680381	IN YOUR HONOUR (4-LP)	40
07	RCA 88697 22526 1	ECHOES, SILENCE, PATIENCE & GRACE (2-LP)	20
11	RCA 88697844931	WASTING LIGHT (LP, 2 x 12")	20
11	RCA 869798322 1	THE COLOUR AND THE SHAPE (2-LP, reissue, download card)	20
11	Roswell 88697983211RE1	FOO FIGHTERS (LP, reissue, download card)	15
14	RCA 88843 09008 18	SONIC HIGHWAYS (LP, various different sleeve designs)	18
15	RCA 88697983241RE1	THERE IS NOTHING LEFT TO LOOSE (LP, reissue)	18
15	RCA 8869798327RE1	IN YOUR HONOUR (2-LP, reissue)	18

(see also Nirvana, Probot)

FOOL

| 69 | Mercury MF 1111 | We Are One/Shining Light | 10 |
| 69 | Mercury SMCL 20138 | THE FOOL (LP, gatefold sleeve. black/silver labels) | 100 |

FOOLS DANCE

87	L. T. T. Slaughter LTS 22	They'll Never Know/Empty Hours (p/s)	10
87	L. T. T. Slaughter LTS 22T	They'll Never Know/The Collector/Empty Hours/The Ring (12", p/s)	15
85	Top Hole Turn TURN 19	FOOLS DANCE (mini-LP)	20

(see also Cure, Stranglers)

FOOT IN COLD WATER

73	Island WIP 6162	(Isn't Love Unkind) In My Life/Deep Freeze	7
74	Elektra K12164	I Know What You Need/Para – Dice	8
74	Elektra K 52011	OR ALL AROUND US (LP)	20

FOOT SOLDIER

| 93 | Blipton Factor Wreckords BLIP 002 | SO WHAT HAPPENS NOW EP (stamped white labels) | 18 |
| 93 | Blipton Factor Wreckords BLIP 004 | WE HAVE SUCH SIGHTS TO SHOW YOU EP (12" stamped white labels) | 35 |

CHUCK FOOTE

| 62 | London HLU 9495 | You're Running Out Of Kisses/Come On Back | 10 |

FOR CARNATION

| 00 | Domino WIGLP 77 | FOR CARNATION (LP, stickered sleeve) | 15 |

FORBES

| 77 | Power Exchange PX 253 | The Beatles/Sweet Kiss Of Fire | 7 |

BILL FORBES

58	Columbia DB 4232	My Cherie/God's Little Acre	6
59	Columbia DB 4269	Once More/Believe In Me	8
59	Columbia DB 4386	Too Young/It's Not The End Of The World	8
61	Columbia DB 4566	You're Sixteen, You're Beautiful/Backward Child	10
61	Columbia DB 4619	That's It, I Quit, I'm Moving On/Big City Boy	10

(see also Contrasts)

SMOKY FORBES

| 71 | Beacon BEA 176 | My Kind Of Music/Loves Goes | 6 |

FORBIDDEN

| 88 | Under One Flag FLAG 27 | FORBIDDEN EVIL (LP) | 15 |

FORCE/CASH CREW

| 88 | Vinyl Lab VL04T | Mission Impossible/Microphone Maniac (12") | 15 |

FORCE FIVE

64	United Artists UP 1051	Don't Make My Baby Blue/Shaking Postman	30
65	United Artists UP 1089	Yeah, I'm Waiting/I Don't Want To See You Again	35
65	United Artists UP 1102	Baby Don't Care/Come Down To Earth	35
65	United Artists UP 1118	I Want You Babe/Gee Too Tiger	50
66	United Artists UP 1141	Don't Know Which Way To Turn/Baby Let Your Hair Down	45

(see also Crocheted Doughnut Ring)

FORCE MAJOR

| 82 | Harbour City 14 | Put It In Your Pipe/Say What You Feel | 15 |

FORCE OF MUSIC

| 78 | Ballistic UAS 530190 | FREEDOM FIGHTERS DUB (LP) | 20 |

FORCE WEST

65	Decca F 12223	I Can't Give What I Haven't Got/Why Won't She Stay	12
66	Columbia DB 7908	Gotta Find Another Baby/Talkin' About Our Love	15
66	Columbia DB 7963	When The Sun Comes Out (Weatherman)/Gotta Tell Somebody	12
67	Columbia DB 8174	All The Children Sleep/Desolation	15
68	CBS 3632	I'll Walk In The Rain/What's It To Be?	8
68	CBS 3798	I'll Be Moving On/Like The Tide, Like The Ocean	8
69	CBS 4385	Sherry/Mister Blue	8

ALVIN FORD

| 75 | Torpedo TOR 45 | Tears On My Pillow (I Can't Take It Reggae)/Version | 8 |

DEAN FORD (& GAYLORDS)

64	Columbia DB 7264	Twenty Miles/What's The Matter With Me?	25
64	Columbia DB 7402	Mr Heartbreak's Here Instead/I Won't	25
65	Columbia DB 7610	The Name Game/That Lonely Feeling	25
76	EMI 2717	The Fever/You Are The One	6
75	EMI EMC 3079	DEAN FORD (LP)	15

(see also Gaylords, Marmalade, Junior Campbell)

Dee DEE FORD

MINT VALUE £

DEE DEE FORD
60   London HLU 9245   Good-Morning Blues/I Just Can't Believe 40

(see also Don Gardner & Dee Dee Ford)

DONETTE FORD
91   Jah Works JW 007   Rhythm Of Resistance/Dub Wilderness (10") 15

EDDIE/EDDY FORD
72   Pressure Beat PB 5512   You Wrong Fe Trouble Joshua/KENNETH POWER: Joshua Row Us Home 7

EMILE FORD (& THE CHECKMATES)
60   Pye 7N 15268   You'll Never Know What You're Missin' 'Til You Try/Still 8
63   Piccadilly 7N 35116   Hold Me Thrill Me Kiss Me/Doin' What You Do To Me (as Emile Ford and the Big Six) 10
59   Pye NEP 24119   EMILE (EP) 10
60   Pye NEP 24124   EMILE FORD HIT PARADE (EP) 12
60   Pye NEP 24133   EMILE FORD HIT PARADE VOL. 2 (EP) 12
60   Pye NPL 18049   NEW TRACKS WITH EMILE (LP) 20
61   Piccadilly NPL 38001   EMILE (LP) 30

(see also Original Checkmates, Checkmates)

'TENNESSEE' ERNIE FORD
54   Capitol CL 14005   Give Me Your Word/River Of No Return 15
54   Capitol CL 14006   Catfish Boogie/Kiss Me Big 25
56   Capitol CL 14500   Sixteen Tons/You Don't Have To Be A Baby To Cry 20
56   Capitol CL 14506   The Ballad Of Davy Crockett/Farewell 20
61   Capitol CL 15210   Little Red Rockin' Hood/I Gotta Have My Baby Back 20

(see also Dinning Sisters)

'TENNESSEE' ERNIE FORD & BETTY HUTTON
54   Capitol CL 14133   This Must Be The Place/The Honeymoon's Over (green label) 18

FRANKIE FORD
59   London HL 8850   Sea Cruise/Roberta (with Huey 'Piano' Smith & Clowns) (black triangular centre) 60
59   London HL 8850   Sea Cruise/Roberta (with Huey 'Piano' Smith & Clowns) (later silver-top triangular
                                  centre) 30
59   Top Rank JAR 186   Alimony/Can't Tell My Heart (What To Do) (with Huey 'Piano' Smith & Clowns) 12
60   Top Rank JAR 282   Cheatin' Woman/HUEY 'PIANO' SMITH & CLOWNS: Don't You Just Know Kokomo 20
60   Top Rank JAR 299   Time After Time/I Want To Be Your Man 10
60   London HLP 9222   If You've Got Troubles/You Talk Too Much 20
65   Sue WI 366   Sea Cruise/Roberta (with Huey 'Piano' Smith & Clowns) (reissue) 25
65   Sue WI 369   What's Going On?/Watchdog 40

(see also Huey Piano Smith)

JASON FORD & THE BULLDOGS
62   Piccadilly 7N 35193   Nobody Knows/Am I The One 10

JOHN FORD
73   UK UKR31   It's Alright Bill/Captain Of Your Ship 8

JON FORD
68   Philips BF 1690   Two's Company, Three's A Crowd/Place In Your Heart 7
69   Philips BF 1791   I Know It's Love/Look Before You Leap 6
69   Philips BF 1817   Ice Cream Man/This Was The Time 6
70   Philips BF 1833   Yesterday When I Was Young/Running Around 6
70   Philips 6006 030   You've Got Me Where You Want Me/You're All Alone Tonight 100
70   Philips 6006 030   You've Got Me Where You Want Me/You're All Alone Tonight (DJ Copy) 150

LITA FORD & OZZY OSBOURNE
89   Dreamland PA 49396   Close My Eyes Forever (Remix)/Under The Gun/Blueberry (12", picture disc) 20

(see also Ozzy Osbourne, Runaways)

MIKE FORD & THE CONSULS
63   Piccadilly 7N 35127   Jump Jeremiah/The Greenman 20

PERRY FORD (& SAPPHIRES)
59   Parlophone R 4573   Bye, Bye Baby, Goodbye/She Came As A Stranger 15
60   Parlophone R 4633   Crazy Over You/Garden Of Happiness 15
60   Parlophone R 4683   Don't Weep (Little Lady)/Little Grown-Up 15
62   Decca F 11497   Baby, Baby (Don't You Worry)/Prince Of Fools (with Sapphires & Blue Flames) 15

(see also Ivy League, Georgie Fame)

RICKY FORD (& TENNESSEANS)
63   Parlophone R 5018   Sweet And Tender Romance/Cheat Cheat 10
64   Parlophone R 5230   You Are My Love/Long Way From Home (with Tennesseans) 7

SIR TED FORD
77   Barak BAR 3   I Wanna Be Near You/Ridin' Too High 10
79   Ardent ADS 9001   Disco Music/I've Got A Goal 80

JOHN FORDE
77   EMI EMI 2656   Stardance/Flight Of The Jumping Bean (12", p/s, some on blue vinyl) 25
78   EMI EMI 2763   Atlantis/Atlantis (Instrumental) 30
79   Sidewalk 12 YSID 107   Woman/Stardance/Don't You Know Who Did It (12", p/s) 30
79   Sidewalk SID 107   Woman/Don't You Know Who Did It 20

FORD WORKERS ON STRIKE
78   WG 0001/S/78/CUS-182   FORD WORKERS ON STRIKE EP (with insert) 6

EDDIE 'BUSTER' FOREHAND
69   Action ACT 4519   Young Boy Blues/You Were Meant For Me 35

FOREHEADS IN A FISHTANK
80   Stuff Records FAB 4   She Loves You, Yeah/Baby Love (p/s) 8

FOREIGN BODIES
84   Alien 1   Take A Look/Love By Love (p/s) 25

FOREIGN LEGION
86   Rent-A-Racket RRR0001   TRENCHLINE (EP) 12
89   Schlawiner SO5   SURF CITY (EP, 350 copies only, black/green vinyl) 10

FOREIGN PRESS

MINT VALUE £

90	Venture VR/FL 100	WELCOME TO FORT ZINDERNEUF (LP)	15

FOREIGN PRESS
80	Streets Ahead SA 1	Downpour/Crossfire/Behind The Glass (1st pressing, gatefold sleeve)	15
80	Streets Ahead SA1	Downpour/Crossfire/Behind The Glass (2nd pressing, non-gatefold black and white or blue and white sleeve)	6

FORELAND
77	Flams	FORELAND (LP)	35

JOHN FOREMAN
66	Reality RY 1004	THE 'OUSES IN BETWEEN (LP)	15

FORERUNNERS
64	Solar SRP 100	Bony Maronie/Pride	60

FORERUNNERS
60s	Key KL 008	THE FORERUNNERS (LP)	18
60s	Key KL 004	RUNNING BACK (LP)	18

FOREST SWORDS
10	No Pain In Pop NPIP 013	Rattling Cage/Hjurt (p/s)	10

FOREST (1)
69	Harvest HAR 5007	Searching For Shadows/Mirror Of Life	20
69	Harvest SHVL 760	FOREST (LP, gatefold sleeve, no EMI logo on label)	400
70	Harvest SHVL 784	FULL CIRCLE (LP, gatefold sleeve, no EMI logo on label)	700
88	Zap! ZAP 3	FULL CIRCLE (LP, reissue)	25

FOREST (2)
76	Midland International MID 1	Do Ya (Do Ya Want My Love)/I'll Stay With You	8

SHARON FORESTER
73	Ashanti ASH 403	Silly Wasn't I?/NOW-GEN: Silly Wasn't I? — Version	25
74	Ashanti ASH 411	Put A Little Love Away/Words With No Meaning	15
74	Ashanti ASH 416	Don't Let Me Be Lonely Tonight/Which Craft Is Witchcraft?	20
75	Ashanti ASH 420	Silly Wasn't it/Funny	25
76	Vulcan VUL 1011	Here Comes The Sun/Next Time	20
74	Ashanti SHAN 105	SHARON (LP)	30

FOREVER AMBER
69	Advance (no cat. no.)	THE LOVE CYCLE (LP, private pressing, 99 copies only)	2500
07	10th Planet TP060	THE LOVE CYCLE (LP, reissue)	20

FOREVER MORE
70	RCA RCA 2024	Put Your Money On A Pony/Yours	6
70	RCA SF 8016	YOURS FOREVER MORE (LP, gatefold sleeve, orange label)	75
71	RCA LSA 3015	WORDS ON BLACK PLASTIC (LP, laminated front sleeve)	60

(see also Scots Of St. James, Hopscotch)

FOREVER PEOPLE
92	Sarah SARAH 54	Invisible/Sometimes (p/s, insert)	25

FORGEMASTERS
89	WARP WAP 1	Track With No Name/Shall We (12", p/s)	10

FORK IN THE ROAD
70	Ember EMB 311	I Can't Turn Around/Skeleton In My Closet (test pressing)	150
70	Ember EMB S 311	I Can't Turn Around/Skeleton In My Closet	100

FORMAT (1)
69	CBS 4600	Maxwell's Silver Hammer/Music Man	10

(see also Fourmost)

FORMATIONS
68	MGM MGM 1399	At The Top Of The Stairs/Magic Melody	120
68	MGM MGM 1399	At The Top Of The Stairs/Magic Melody (DJ Copy)	220

FORMERLY FAT HARRY
71	Harvest SHSP 4016	FORMERLY FAT HARRY (LP, with EMI logo on label)	100

(see also Country Joe and the Fish)

FORMINX
65	Vocalion V 9235	Jenka Beat/Geronimo Jenka	30

(see also Aphrodite's Child, Vangelis)

FORMIX
72	Tulip TP 001	What Would You Want Of Me/Shake	40

FORMULA
65	HMV POP 1438	Close To Me/If Ever	10

FORMULA 1
65	Warner Bros WB 155	I Just Can't Go To Sleep/Sure Know A Lot About Love	30

FORMULA TWO
72	CBS SCBS 8285	Easy Times/Girl Who Lives Next Door	6

ANDY FORRAY
68	Parlophone R 5715	Sarah Jane/Don't Care Anymore	10
68	Parlophone R 5729	The Proud One/Messin' Round With Me	15
68	Decca F 12723	Epitaph To You/Dream With Me	80
69	Fontana TF 999	Let The Sunshine In/Baby Is Coming	10

HELEN FORREST
56	Capitol CL 14594	Taking A Chance On Love/I Love You Much Too Much	10
56	Capitol LC 6834	VOICE OF THE NAME BANDS (10" LP)	15

JANE FORREST
56	Columbia SCM 5213	Sincerely Yours/A Girl Can't Say	10

FOR(R)ESTERS
65	Polydor 56038	Broken Hearted Clown/Lonely Boy	10
65	Polydor 56057	How Can I Tell Her/So Shy	10
66	Polydor 56104	Early Morning Hours/World Is Mine	8
66	Columbia DB 8040	Sometimes When You're Lonely/Today Or Tomorrow (as Forresters)	7
66	Columbia DB 8086	Mr. Smith/Ship On The Sea (as Forresters)	10

Bruce FORSYTH

MINT VALUE £

| 67 | Columbia DB 8176 | Comin' Home In The Evening/Sunshine's On Its Way (as Foresters) | 6 |

BRUCE FORSYTH
| 60 | Parlophone GEP 8807 | I'M IN CHARGE (EP) | 10 |
| 60 | Parlophone PMC 1132 | MR ENTERTAINMENT (LP, also stereo PCS 3031) | 15 |

FORTES MENTUM
68	Parlophone R 5684	Saga Of A Wrinkled Man/Mr. Partridge Passed Away Today	50
68	Parlophone R 5726	I Can't Go On Loving You/Humdiggle We Love You	15
69	Parlophone R 5768	Gotta Go/Marrakesh	15

(see also Angel Pavement, Pussy)

FORTUNATE PEOPLE
| 69 | Dukesbury DB 002 | Simple Skies/Stop | 90 |

JOHNNY FORTUNE
| 60s | Sonet SON 2139 | Soul Surfer/Dragster | 15 |

LANCE FORTUNE
60	Pye 7N 15240	Be Mine/Action (with Johnny Prendy, alias John Barry)	6
60	Pye 7N 15260	This Love I Have For You/All On My Own	8
60	Pye 7N 15297	I Wonder/Will You Still Be My Girl?	10
61	Pye 7N 15347	Who's Gonna Tell Me?/Love Is The Sweetest Thing	15

FORTUNES
63	Decca F 11718	Summertime Summertime/I Love Her Still (as Fortunes & Cliftones) (in p/s)	30
63	Decca F 11718	Summertime Summertime/I Love Her Still (as Fortunes & Cliftones)	15
64	Decca F 11809	Caroline/If You Don't Want Me Now	30
64	Decca F 11809	Caroline/If You Don't Want Me Now (later repressing with boxed Decca logo)	10
64	Decca F 11912	Come On Girl/I Like The Look Of You (curved logo)	15
64	Decca F 11985	Look Homeward Angel/I'll Have My Tears To Remind Me	15
66	Decca F 12321	This Golden Ring/Someone To Care	6
66	Decca F 12429	You Gave Me Somebody To Love/Silent Street	10
66	Decca F 12485	Is It Really Worth Your While?/Am I Losing My Touch	8
67	Decca F 12612	Our Love Has Gone/Truly Yours	6
67	United Artists UP 1188	The Idol/His Smile Was A Lie	10
68	United Artists UP 2218	Loving Cup/Hour At The Movies	6
68	United Artists UP 2239	Seasons In The Sun/Louise	6
69	United Artists UP 35027	Ballad Of The Alamo/Save A Little Dream	6
69	United Artists UP 35054	Lifetime Of Love/Sad Sad Sad (withdrawn, existence unconfirmed)	0
69	United Artists UP 35054	Books And Films/Sad Sad Sad	7
72	Capitol CL 15719	Baby By The Way/Long Way Home	6
72	Capitol CL 15732	Everything Is Out Of Season/Don't Sing To Me	6
72	Capitol CL 15739	Secret Love/I Can't Remember When The Sun Went In	8
65	Decca LK 4736	THE FORTUNES (LP, mono)	35
65	Decca SKL 4736	THE FORTUNES (LP, stereo)	60
72	Capitol ST 21891	THE FORTUNES (LP)	15

(see also Glen Dale)

45'S
| 79 | Chopper CHEAP 5 | Couldn't Believe A Word/Lonesome Lane (no p/s) | 7 |
| 81 | 45's Records ONE 45 | Secrets And Whispers/Driving/Little Honda (p/s) | 8 |

49 AMERICANS
| 80 | Choo Choo Train CHUG 2 | TOO YOUNG TO BE IDEAL (12" EP) | 10 |

FORUM
| 67 | London HLM 10120 | The River Is Wide/I Fall In Love (All Over Again) | 15 |

FORWARD INTENSE
| 92 | Harm HARM1 | Stated/Imply The Calm (12") | 50 |

SHIRLEY FORWOOD
| 57 | London HLD 8402 | Two Hearts (With An Arrow Between)/Juke Box Lovers | 20 |

FOSSIL
| 74 | Pennine PSS14 | Black Night/For Your Love/Smile On Me/Wishing Well | 75 |

BOBBY FOSTER
| 70 | Bread BR 1101 | Tell Me Why You Say Goodbye/YOUTH: I'll Make Him Believe In You | 8 |

FRANK FOSTER
| 60s | Esquire 32 033 | WAIL FRANK WAIL (LP) | 18 |

JACKIE FOSTER
| 63 | Sway SWAY 001 | Dry Up Your Tears/Try To Understand | 20 |
| 63 | Planetone RC 13 | Oh Leona/I Fell In Love | 15 |

JOHN FOSTER
| 66 | Island ILP 939 | JOHN FOSTER SINGS (LP) | 40 |

LARRY FOSTER & SOUL EXPLOSION
| 70 | Fab FAB 130 | Boom Biddy Boom/Next To Me (actually by Sugar Simone) | 10 |

(see also Sugar Simone)

LES FOSTER
| 69 | Wolf WM 02 | You And Your Love/Turning Point (actually by Delroy Dennis) | 12 |
| 70 | Torpedo TOR 7 | Run Like A Thief/Nobody's Fool | 80 |

LES FOSTER & ANSELL COLLINS
| 73 | Camel CA 102 | The Man In Your Life/Version | 8 |

(see also Sugar Simone, Lance Hannibal)

LESLIE FOSTER
| 69 | Jolly JY 022 | Muriel/Nowhere To Hide | 7 |

RONNIE FOSTER
| 95 | Blue Note 7243 8 30282 1 | TWO HEADED FREAP (LP, reissue) | 50 |

VINCENT FOSTER
| 69 | Escort ES 803 | Shine Eye Gal/Who Nest (B-side actually "Who Next" by Carl Bryan) | 100 |

FOTHERINGAY

MINT VALUE £

FOTHERINGAY			
70	Island WIP 6085	Peace In The End/Winter Winds	15
70	Island ILPS 9125	FOTHERINGAY (LP, pink label/'i' logo, gatefold sleeve)	150
70	Island ILPS 9125	FOTHERINGAY (LP, later issue, pink rim label/'palm tree' logo, gatefold sleeve)	30
86	Hannibal HNBL 4426	FOTHERINGAY (LP, reissue)	18

(see also Sandy Denny, Trevor Lucas, Eclection, Exception[s], Fairport Convention, Mick Greenwood)

FOTOSTAT			
79	Sour Grape SG 112	Fotostat/Fotostat II (p/s)	20
FOUL PLAY			
92	Oblivion OR 001	VOLUME 1 EP: The Alchemist/Ragatere/Ricochet/Feel The Vibe (12")	25
92	Oblivion OR 002	VOLUME 2 EP: Survival/Dubbing You/Ricochet (No Stopping The Remix)/Feel The Vibe (Again) (12")	25
93	Section 5 SECTION 04	Finest Illusion/Screwface (12" white label)	60
93	Section 5 SECTION 4	Finest Illusion/Screwface (12" printed labels)	50
93	Section 5 SECTION 4	Finest Illusion/Screwface (12", 2nd pressing, black labels, actually no labels at all!)	50
93	Moving Shadow SHAD 29	VOLUME III EP: Open Your Mind/Murder Most Foul/Survival (Remix)/ Dub in U (Remix) (12", p/s)	10
93	Moving Shadow SHAD 29R	VOLUME III REMIXES: Open Your Mind (Tango remix)/Open Your Mind (Foul Play remix)(10", p/s)	10
93	Moving Shadow SHAD 29R2	VOLUME III REMIXES PART 2: Open Your Mind (Nookie Remix)/Finest Illusion (Legal Mix)(10", p/s)	10
94	Moving Shadow SHAD 49R1	VOLUME 4 - Remixes Part 1 (10")	20
95	Moving Shadow ASHADOW 2 LP	SUSPECTED (LP as 2 x 12")	18
AL FOULCER			
81	Heart & Soul FOU A1	Video Man/Song For John	8

(see also Crystal Set)

FOUNDATIONS			
69	Pye 7N 17809	Born To Live, Born To Die/Why Did You Cry	10
69	Pye 7N 1784	Baby I Couldn'tSee/Penny Sir	10
70	Pye 7N 17904	Take A Girl Like You/I'm Gonna Be A Rich Man	10
70	Pye 7N 17956	I'm Gonna Be A Rich Man/Who Am I	10
71	MCA MCA 5075	Stoney Ground/I'll Give You Love	20
77	Summit SU 100	Where Were You When I Needed Your Love/Love Me Nice 'n Easy	6
78	Psycho P 2603	Closer To Loving You/Change My Life	250
68	Pye NEP 24297	IT'S ALL RIGHT (EP)	25
67	Pye NPL 18206	FROM THE FOUNDATIONS (LP)	25
68	Pye NPL 18227	ROCKING THE FOUNDATIONS (LP, mono)	20
68	Pye NSPL 18227	ROCKING THE FOUNDATIONS (LP, stereo)	25
69	Pye N(S)PL 18290	DIGGING THE FOUNDATIONS (LP, gatefold sleeve)	20

(see also Pluto, New Foundations, Clem Curtis)

FOUNDED			
82	Heroes ER 02	Looking For Love/Run To Hell	60
JAMES FOUNTAIN			
76	Cream CRM 5002	Seven Day Lover/Malnutrition	8
THE 4			
64	Decca F 11999	It's Alright/There's Nothing Like It	20
4 BY FOUR			
60s	Victor Buckland	Roll Over Beethoven/Till There Was You/You Better Move On/Chains	75
FOUR ACES (JAMAICA)			
65	Island WI 178	Hoochy-Koochy-Kai-Po/River Bank Coberly Again	25
65	Island WI 178	Hoochy-Koochy-Kai-Po/SKATALITES: Sucu Sucu (different B-side)	25
65	Island WI 179	Sweet Chariot/Peace And Love	18
65	Island WI 180	Little Girl/CLARENDONIANS: Day Will Come	20

(see also Desmond Dekker)

FOUR ACES (U.K.)			
60s	Anton/E.R.S. EAG 178/179	Why Do You/Fortune Teller (private pressing)	250
FOUR ACES (U.S.)			
54	Brunswick 05256	The Gang That Sang "Heart Of My Heart"/Heaven Can Wait	8
54	Brunswick 05308	Three Coins In The Fountain/Wedding Bells (Are Breaking Up This Gang Of Mine)	15
54	Brunswick 05322	It Shall Come To Pass/Dream	8
54	Brunswick 05355	Mister Sandman/(I'll Be With You) In Apple Blossom Time	15
55	Brunswick 05480	Love Is A Many Splendored Thing/Shine On Harvest Moon	15
53	Brunswick LA 8614	JUST SQUEEZE ME (10" LP)	15
FOURBEATS (1)			
63	Oxford University UTF 164	Do You Love Me/Mr Postman/Baby Its Me/They Say (p/s)	30
FOURBEATS (2)			
82	SRTS 82 CUS 1460	Back Door/If Pigs Could Fly	20
FOUR BELOW ZERO			
01	Expansion EXPAND 82	My Baby's Got E.S.P./CHARLES JOHNSON: Never Had A Love So Good (12")	20
16	Soul Jazz SJR391-7	E.S.P. Part 1/E.S.P. Part 2 (reissue)	20
4 DEGREES			
65	Oak RGJ 187	4 DEGREES (LP, 1-sided, no sleeve)	425
FOUR DOLLS			
57	Capitol CL 14778	Three On A Date/Proud Of You	10
58	Capitol CL 14845	Whoop-A-Lala/I'm Following You	10
FOUR DYNAMICS			
02	Grapevine 2002 122	Things That A Lady Ain't Supposed To Do/That's What Girls Are Made For	8
FOUR ESCORTS			
54	HMV 7M 277	Loop De Loop Mambo/Love Me	10

FOUR ESQUIRES

FOUR ESQUIRES
55	London HL 8152	The Sphinx Won't Tell/Three Things (A Man Must Do)	20
56	London HLA 8224	Adorable/Thunderbolt	10
57	London HL 8376	Look Homeward Angel/Santo Domingo (78) (unreleased on both 78 and 45)	0

FOUR EVERS
66	CBS 202549	A Lovely Way To Say Goodnight/The Girl I Wanna Bring Home	45

FOUR FOR FUN
63	Waverley ELP 113	FOUR FOR FUN (EP)	60

(see also Dick Farina, Carolyn Hester)

FOUR FULLER BROTHERS
69	MCA MU 1068	Groupie/Bitter Honey	10

FOUR GEES
67	President PT 160	Ethiopia/Rough Rider	20

(see also eddy Grant)

FOUR GIBSON GIRLS
58	Oriole CB 1447	No School Tomorrow/June, July And August	20
58	Oriole CB 1453	Safety Sue/VARIOUS ARTISTS: Safety Sue	15

FOUR GUNS
85	Gun 001	Sign Of The Crimes/Spirit Of The Thing (no'd p/s, 500 only)	20

FOUR GUYS
55	Vogue Coral Q 72054	Half Hearted Kisses/Mine	10

(see also Modernaires)

4 HERO
91	Reinforced RIVET 1203	IN ROUGH TERRITORY (LP, with free 12")	25
95	Reinforced LP 004	PARALLEL UNIVERSE (2-LP)	60
98	Reinforced/Talking Loud	TWO PAGES (LP as 4x12")	30
99	Talkin Loud 5860571	CREATING PATTERNS (3-LP)	40

4 HORSEMEN OF THE APOCALYPSE
93	Tone Def 013DJ	Drowning In Her/We Are The Future (12")	100

FOUR IDLE HANDS
90	Good Vibrations GOT 21	99 Streets/Friday Man	12

FOUR INSTANTS
66	Society SOC 1016	DISCOTHEQUE (LP)	60
69	Allied OPP 3013	DISCOTHEQUE (LP, reissue)	15

FOUR JACKS
58	Decca F 10984	Hey! Baby/The Prayer Of Love	15
58	Decca DFE 6460	HEY! BABY (EP)	50

FOUR JACKS & A JILL
68	RCA Victor RCA 1669	Master Jack/I Looked Back	7

FOUR JONES BOYS
56	Decca F 10717	Tutti Frutti/Are You Satisfied?	15

(see also Jones Boys, Annette Klooger)

FOUR JUST MEN
64	Parlophone R 5186	That's My Baby/Things Will Never Be The Same	80

(see also Just Four Men, Wimple Winch)

FOUR KENTS
68	RCA RCA 1705	The Moving Finger Writes/Searchin'	20

FOUR KESTRELS
61	Decca F 11333	Sound Off (Duckworth's Chant)/Can't Say That I Do	6

FOUR KINSMEN
67	Decca F 22671	It Looks Like The Daybreak/Forget About Him	15
67	Herald ELR 1080	WHEREVER HE GOES EP	15

(see also Kinsmen)

FOUR KNIGHTS
54	Capitol CL 14076	I Get So Lonely/Till Then	20
54	Capitol CL 14154	Easy Street/In The Chapel In The Moonlight	15
54	Capitol CL 14204	I Don't Wanna See You Cryin'/Saw Your Eyes	15
55	Capitol CL 14244	Honey Bunch/Write Me, Baby	15
55	Capitol CL 14290	Inside Out/Foolishly Yours	15
56	Capitol CL 14516	Guilty/You	15
59	Coral Q 72355	Foolish Tears/O' Falling Star	15
55	Capitol EAP1 506	THE FOUR KNIGHTS (EP)	15
53	Capitol LC 6604	SPOTLIGHT SONGS (10" LP)	20

FOUR LEAVED CLOVER
65	Oak RGJ 207	Alright Girl/Why	500

FOUR MACS
64	Parlophone R 5204	Come Back Silly Girl/Darlin'	8

(see also Sands Of Time)

FOUR MATADORS
66	Columbia DB 7806	A Man's Gotta Stand Tall/Fast Cars And Money	70

FOURMOST
63	Parlophone R 5056	Hello Little Girl/Just In Case	6
63	Parlophone R 5078	I'm In Love/Respectable	6
64	Parlophone R 5128	A Little Loving/Waiting For You	6
64	Parlophone R 5194	Baby I Need Your Loving/That's Only What They Say	6
65	Parlophone R 5304	Everything In The Garden/He Could Never	10
65	Parlophone R 5379	Girls Girls Girls/Why Do Fools Fall In Love?	8
66	Parlophone R 5491	Here, There And Everywhere/You've Changed	10
66	Parlophone R 5528	Auntie Maggie's Remedy/Turn The Lights Down	10
68	CBS 3814	Apples, Peaches, Pumpkin Pie/He Could Never	15

FOURMYULA

MINT VALUE £

69	CBS 4041	Rosetta/Just Like Before	50
69	CBS 4461	Easy Squeezy/Do I Love You?	20
72	Phoenix SNIX 126	Goodnight Sweet Dreams/Memphis	8
64	Parlophone GEP 8917	THE FOURMOST (EP)	35
64	Parlophone GEP 8892	THE FOURMOST SOUND (EP)	35
65	Parlophone PMC 1259	FIRST AND FOURMOST (LP)	100
75	Fourmost SOF 001	THE FOURMOST (LP)	15

(see also Format)

FOURMYULA
69	Columbia DB 8549	Honey Chile/Come With Me	20

FOUR OWLS
11	High Focus HFREP 001	NATURES GREATEST MYSTERY EP (12", 300 only)	50
14	High focus HFRLP 026	NATURES GREATEST MYSTERY (2-LP)	35

FOUR PALMS
58	Vogue V 9116	Jeanie, Joanie, Shirley, Toni/Consideration	600
58	Vogue V 9116	Jeanie, Joanie, Shirley, Toni/Consideration (78)	150

FOUR PENNIES (U.K.)
63	Philips BF 1296	Do You Want Me To/Miss Bad Daddy	10
64	Philips BF 1322	Juliet/Tell Me Girl (A- & B-sides supposedly flipped after original release)	20
65	Philips BF 1398	The Way Of Love/A Place Where No-One Goes	7
66	Philips BF 1469	Trouble Is My Middle Name/Way Out Love	7
66	Philips BF 1491	Keep The Freeway Open/Square Peg	8
66	Philips BF 1519	No Sad Songs For Me/Cats	10
66	Philips BL 7734	MIXED BAG (LP)	60

(see also Lionel Morton, Fritz Mike & Mo)

FOUR PENNIES (U.S.)
63	Stateside SS 198	My Block/Dry Your Eyes	40
63	Stateside SS 244	When The Boy's Happy (The Girl's Happy Too)/Hockaday Part 1	30

(see also Chiffons)

FOUR PLUGS
80	Disposable THROWAY ONE	Wrong Treatment/Biking Girl (p/s)	20

FOUR + ONE
65	Parlophone R 5221	Time Is On My Side/Don't Lie To Me	100

(see also In Crowd, Tomorrow, Keith West)

4 SAXOPHONES IN 12 TONES
56	Vogue V 2355	Fantastic/Frankly Speaking	7

FOUR SEASONS
SINGLES
62	Stateside SS 122	Sherry/I've Cried Before	7
63	Stateside SS 145	Big Girls Don't Cry/Connie-O	7
63	Stateside SS 169	Walk Like A Man/Lucky Ladybug	6
63	Stateside SS 194	Ain't That A Shame/Soon (I'll Be Home Again)	8
63	Stateside SS 216	Candy Girl/Marlena	10
63	Stateside SS 241	Santa Claus Is Coming To Town/Christmas Tears	15
64	Stateside SS 262	Peanuts/Silhouettes	15
64	Philips BF 1317	Dawn (Go Away)/No Surfin' Today	7
64	Philips BF 1334	Ronnie/Born To Wander	8
64	Stateside SS 315	Alone/Long Lonely Nights	10
64	Philips BF 1347	Rag Doll/Silence Is Golden	6
64	Stateside SS 343	Since I Don't Have You/Sincerely	15
65	Philips BF 1364	Save It For Me/Funny Face	8
65	Philips BF 1372	Big Man In Town/Little Angel	7
65	Philips BF 1395	Bye Bye Baby (Baby Goodbye)/Searching Wind	7
65	Philips BF 1411	Toy Soldier/Betrayed	8
65	Philips BF 1420	Girl Come Running/Cry Myself To Sleep	10
66	Philips BF 1493	Opus 17 (Don't Worry 'Bout Me)/Beggar's Parade	10
66	Philips BF 1511	I've Got You Under My Skin/Huggin' My Pillow	8
67	Philips BF 1538	Tell It To The Rain/Show Girl	10
67	Philips BF 1556	Beggin'/Dody (as the 4 Seasons)	15
67	Philips BF 1584	C'mon Marianne/Let's Ride Again	7
67	Philips BF 1600	Around And Around/WONDER WHO: Lonesome Road	15
67	Philips BF 1621	Watch The Flowers Grow/Raven	15
68	Philips BF 1651	Will You Love Me Tomorrow?/Silhouettes	15
68	Philips BF 1685	Saturday's Father/Goodbye Girl	15
69	Philips BF 1743	Electric Stories/Pity	15
69	Philips BF 1763	Rag Doll/Working My Way Back To You (p/s)	7
71	Warner Bros K 16107	Whatever You Say/Sleeping Man (withdrawn, 300 only) As Frankie Valli and the...	45
64	Stateside SE 1011	THE FOUR SEASONS SING (EP)	40

ALBUMS
63	Stateside SL 10033	SHERRY AND 11 OTHERS	30
63	Stateside SL 10042	AIN'T THAT A SHAME	40
63	Stateside SL 10051	THE FOUR SEASONS' GREETINGS	30
64	Philips BL 7611	BORN TO WANDER	20
64	Philips BL 7621	DAWN (GO AWAY) AND 11 OTHER GREAT SONGS	20
64	Philips BL 7643	RAG DOLL	18
65	Philips BL 7663	ENTERTAIN YOU	20
65	Philips (S)BL 7687	SING BIG HITS BY BURT BACHARACH ... HAL DAVID ... BOB DYLAN	20
65	Philips BL 7699	WORKING MY WAY BACK TO YOU	18
67	Philips (S)BL 7753	CHRISTMAS ALBUM	25

FOUR SIGHTS

MINT VALUE £

69	Philips (S)BL 7880	THE GENUINE IMITATION LIFE GAZETTE	25

(see also Beverly Hills Blues Band, Frankie Valli, Wonder Who)

FOUR SIGHTS
64	Columbia DB 7227	But I Can Tell/And I Cry	15

4-SKINS
81	Clockwork Fun CF 101	One Law For Them/Brave New World (p/s)	20
81	Secret SHH 125	Yesterday's Heroes/Justice/Get Out Of My Life (p/s)	10
82	Secret SHH 141	Lowlife/Bread Or Blood (p/s)	10
82	Secret SEC 4	THE GOOD, THE BAD AND THE 4-SKINS (LP, with photo inner)	25
83	Syndicate SYN 1	A FISTFUL OF ... 4-SKINS (LP)	18
89	Link LINK LP 090	LIVE AND LOUD!! (THE BRIDGEHOUSE TAPES) (LP)	18
84	Syndicate SYN LP 5	FROM CHAOS TO 1984 (LP)	20
01	Captain Oi! AHOY PD3	THE GOOD THE BAD AND THE 4-SKINS (LP, reissue, clear vinyl picture disc)	15

(see also Plastic Gangsters)

FOURSOME
76	Fanfare FR 6490	UPSIDE DOWN (LP)	40

FOUR SPICES
57	MGM MGM 944	Armen's Theme (Yesterday And You)/Fire Engine Boogie	100

FOUR SQUARES
64	Hollick & Taylor HT 1009	FOUR SQUARES (EP)	100

(see also Pink People)

FOURTEEN (14)
68	Olga OLE 002	Through My Door/Meet Mr. Edgar	20
68	Olga OLE 006	Umbrella/Drizzle (Rain)	20
68	Olga OLE 006	Umbrella/Drizzle (Rain) (Demo)	45
68	Olga S 051	Easy To Fool/Frosty Stars On A Window Pane	15

14 ICED BEARS
86	Frank COPPOLA 101	Inside/Blue Suit/Cut (hand-printed paper bag sleeve)	25
87	Frank CAPRA 202	Like A Dolphin/Balloon Song/Train Song/Lie To Choose (12", p/s)	10
88	Sarah SARAH 005	Come Get Me/Unhappy Days/Sure To See (poster p/s)	80
89	Thunderball 7TBL 2	Mother Sleep (7", unreleased, Mayking test pressings only)	25
90s	Thunderball Surfacer 002	Falling Backwards/World I Love/CROCODILE RIDE: Ex-Hipster/Satellite (Speed Mix) (numbered & stickered mailer, 1,000 only)	8
88	Thunderball TBLP 1	14 ICED BEARS (LP)	20
91	Borderline BORD 002	WONDER (LP)	15

FOUR TET
98	Output OPR 14	THIRTYSIXTWENTYFIVE EP (2 one-sided 12", p/s)	15
99	Output OPR 24	Glasshead/Calamine (Radio Mix) (12", p/s)	12
99	Output OPR 20	MISNOMER EP (12", p/s)	12
02	Domino RUG 139	I'm On Fire (Part 1)/I'm On Fire (Part 2) (p/s)	8
09	Text TEXT 006	Moth/Wolf Cub (12", black label, plain black sleeve with Burial)	15
11	Text TEXT 010	Ego/Mirror (12", with Thom Yorke and Burial, black labels on both sides)	18
11	Text TEXT 009	Pinnacles/DAPHNI: Ya Ya (12")	15
12	Text TEXT 013	Nova (1-sided 12", with Burial)	20
17	Text TEXT 045	SW9/SL/Planet (12")	12
99	Output OPR21	DIALOGUE (LP, inner)	30
01	Domino WIGLP94	PAUSE (LP, inner)	20
02	Domino WIGLP126	ROUNDS (2-LP, gatefold)	25
05	Domino WIGLP154	EVERYTHING ECSTATIC (2xLP, one sided etched, with bonus CD)	20
10	Domino WIGLP254	THERE IS LOVE IN YOU (2-LP)	25
13	Text TEXT 025	BEAUTIFUL REWIND (LP)	20
13	Four Tet FTC 001	COMPILATION ONE (LP, pink vinyl)	20
13	Domino REWIGLP88	ROUNDS (2-LP, reissue with live CD)	20
15	Text TEXT 036	MORNING/EVENING (LP)	20
17	Text TEXT 046	NEW ENERGY (2-LP)	25
20	Text TEXT 051	SIXTEEN OCEANS (2-LP)	20

(see also Fridge, Percussions, Thom Yorke)

4TH STREET ORCHESTRA
77	Rama RM 001	AH WHO SEH? GO-DEH! (LP)	70
77	Rama RM 002	AH FE WE DIS (LP)	75
77	Rama RM 004	(SCIENTIFIC) HIGHER RANKING DUB (LP)	200
77	Rama RMLP 005	YUH LEARN! (LP)	100

(see also Dennis Bovell, Matumbi)

FOURTH WORLD
95	B&W BWR 030	FOURTH WORLD (LP)	15

(see also Arto Moreira)

FOUR TONES
58	Decca F 11074	Voom Ba Voom/Rickshaw Boy	15

FOUR TOPHATTERS
55	London HLA 8163	Leave-a My Gal Alone/Go Baby Go	200
55	London HLA 8198	Forty Five Men In A Telephone Booth/Wild Rosie	200

FOUR TOPS
SINGLES
64	Stateside SS 336	Baby I Need Your Lovin'/Call On Me (DJ Copy)	70
64	Stateside SS 336	Baby I Need Your Lovin'/Call On Me	50
65	Stateside SS 371	Without The One You Love (Life's Not Worthwhile)/Love Has Gone (DJ Copy)	130
65	Stateside SS 371	Without The One You Love (Life's Not Worthwhile)/Love Has Gone	60
65	Tamla Motown TMG 507	Ask The Lonely/Where Did You Go? (DJ copy)	150
65	Tamla Motown TMG 507	Ask The Lonely/Where Did You Go?	90
65	Tamla Motown TMG 515	I Can't Help Myself/Sad Souvenirs (DJ copy)	150

FOUR TOPS

MINT VALUE £

Year	Label/Cat	Title	Value
65	Tamla Motown TMG 515	I Can't Help Myself/Sad Souvenirs	25
65	Tamla Motown TMG 528	It's The Same Old Song/Your Love Is Amazing (DJ copy)	100
65	Tamla Motown TMG 528	It's The Same Old Song/Your Love Is Amazing	25
65	Tamla Motown TMG 542	Something About You/Darling I Hum Our Song (DJ copy)	100
65	Tamla Motown TMG 542	Something About You/Darling I Hum Our Song	30
66	Tamla Motown TMG 553	Shake Me, Wake Me (When It's Over)/Just As Long As You Need Me (DJ copy)	100
66	Tamla Motown TMG 553	Shake Me, Wake Me (When It's Over)/Just As Long As You Need Me)	35
66	Tamla Motown TMG 568	Loving You Is Sweeter Than Ever/I Like Everything About You (DJ copy £100)	100
66	Tamla Motown TMG 568	Loving You Is Sweeter Than Ever/I Like Everything About You	30
66	Tamla Motown TMG 579	Reach Out, I'll Be There/Until You Love Someone (DJ copy)	100
66	Tamla Motown TMG 579	Reach Out, I'll Be There/Until You Love Someone (small print, later large print = £15)	18
67	Tamla Motown TMG 589	Standing In The Shadows Of Love/Since You've Been Gone (DJ copy)	100
67	Tamla Motown TMG 589	Standing In The Shadows Of Love/Since You've Been Gone (small print)	15
67	Tamla Motown TMG 589	Standing In The Shadows Of Love/Since You've Been Gone (later large print)	8
67	Tamla Motown TMG 601	Bernadette/I Got A Feeling (DJ copy)	100
67	Tamla Motown TMG 601	Bernadette/I Got A Feeling	15
67	Tamla Motown TMG 612	Seven Rooms Of Gloom/I'll Turn To Stone (DJ copy)	65
67	Tamla Motown TMG 612	Seven Rooms Of Gloom/I'll Turn To Stone	15
67	Tamla Motown TMG 623	You Keep Running Away/If You Don't Want My Love (DJ copy)	65
67	Tamla Motown TMG 623	You Keep Running Away/If You Don't Want My Love	12
67	Tamla Motown TMG 634	Walk Away Renee/Mame (DJ copy)	60
67	Tamla Motown TMG 634	Walk Away Renee/Mame	12
68	Tamla Motown TMG 647	If I Were A Carpenter/Your Love Is Wonderful (DJ copy)	60
68	Tamla Motown TMG 647	If I Were A Carpenter/Your Love Is Wonderful	12
68	Tamla Motown TMG 665	Yesterday's Dreams/For Once In My Life (DJ copy)	60
68	Tamla Motown TMG 665	Yesterday's Dreams/For Once In My Life	15
68	Tamla Motown TMG 675	I'm In A Different World/Remember When (DJ copy)	60
68	Tamla Motown TMG 675	I'm In A Different World/Remember When	15
69	Tamla Motown TMG 698	What Is A Man?/Don't Bring Back Memories (DJ copy)	70
69	Tamla Motown TMG 698	What Is A Man?/Don't Bring Back Memories	12
69	Tamla Motown TMG 710	Do What You Gotta Do/Can't Seem To Get You Out Of My Mind (DJ copy)	70
69	Tamla Motown TMG 710	Do What You Gotta Do/Can't Seem To Get You Out Of My Mind	18
70	Tamla Motown TMG 736	It's All In The Game/Love (Is The Answer) (DJ copy)	40
70	Tamla Motown TMG 736	It's All In The Game/Love (Is The Answer)	7
70	Tamla Motown TMG 752	Still Water (Love)/Still Water (Peace) (DJ copy)	40
70	Tamla Motown TMG 752	Still Water (Love)/Still Water (Peace)	7
71	Tamla Motown TMG 770	Just Seven Numbers (Can Straighten Out My Life)/I Wish I Were Your Mirror (DJ copy)	7
71	Tamla Motown TMG 770	Just Seven Numbers (Can Straighten Out My Life)/I Wish I Were Your Mirror	7
71	Tamla Motown TMG 785	Simple Game/You Stole My Love (DJ copy)	30
71	Tamla Motown TMG 785	Simple Game/You Stole My Love	7
72	Tamla Motown TMG 803	Bernadette/I Got A Feeling/It's The Same Old Song (DJ copy)	30
72	Tamla Motown TMG 829	I'll Turn To Stone/Love Feels Like Fire (DJ copy)	30
72	Tamla Motown TMG 829	I'll Turn To Stone/Love Feels Like Fire	10
74	Probe PRO 612	I Just Can't Get You Out Of My Mind/Am I My Brother's Keeper	15
75	Tamla Motown TMG 1011	Walk Away Renee/You Keep Running Away (reissue)	6
83	Tamla Motown TMG 1320	Medley/TEMPTATIONS: Papa Was A Rolling Stone	35
84	Calibre 124	Your Song/I'm Here Again (p/s, withdrawn)	100
84	Calibre 124	Your Song/I'm Here Again (withdrawn)	50

EPs

Year	Label/Cat	Title	Value
66	Tamla Motown TME 2012	THE FOUR TOPS (EP, flipback sleeve)	30
67	Tamla Motown TME 2018	FOUR TOP HITS	35

ALBUMS

Year	Label/Cat	Title	Value
65	Tamla Motown TML 11010	THE FOUR TOPS	80
66	Tamla Motown TML 11021	SECOND ALBUM (mono)	40
66	Tamla Motown STML 11021	SECOND ALBUM (stereo)	50
66	Tamla Motown TML 11037	FOUR TOPS ON TOP (mono)	35
66	Tamla Motown STML 11037	FOUR TOPS ON TOP (stereo)	45
67	Tamla Motown TML 11041	FOUR TOPS LIVE! (mono)	25
67	Tamla Motown (S)TML 11041	FOUR TOPS LIVE! (stereo)	30
67	Tamla Motown TML 11056	REACH OUT (mono)	25
67	Tamla Motown STML 11056	REACH OUT (stereo)	30
68	Tamla Motown STML 11061	FOUR TOPS GREATEST HITS (stereo)	25
68	Tamla Motown TML 11061	FOUR TOPS GREATEST HITS (mono)	20
69	Tamla Motown (S)TML 11087	YESTERDAY'S DREAMS (mono/stereo)	25
69	Tamla Motown TML 11113	FOUR TOPS NOW (mono)	25
69	Tamla Motown STML 11113	FOUR TOPS NOW (stereo)	20
70	Tamla Motown TML 11138	SOUL SPIN (mono)	25
70	Tamla Motown STML 11138	SOUL SPIN (stereo)	20
70	Tamla Motown STML 11149	STILL WATERS RUN DEEP	20
71	Tamla Motown STML 11173	CHANGING TIMES	20
72	Tamla Motown STML 11206	NATURE PLANNED IT	15
73	Probe SPB 1064	KEEPER OF THE CASTLE	15
73	Probe SPB 1077	SHAFT IN AFRICA (soundtrack, with Johnny Pate)	40
74	Probe SPBA 6233	MEETING OF THE MINDS	15
74	ABC ABCL 5035	SHAFT IN AFRICA (soundtrack, reissue)	15

(see also Supremes & Four Tops)

FOUR TUNES

MINT VALUE £

FOUR TUNES
55	London HL 8151	I Sold My Heart To A Junkman/The Greatest Feeling In The World	100
55	London HL 8151	I Sold My Heart To A Junkman/The Greatest Feeling In The World (78)	20
55	London HLJ 8164	Tired Of Waitin'/L'Amour, Toujours L'Amour (Love Everlasting)	50
55	London HLJ 8164	Tired Of Waitin'/L'Amour, Toujours L'Amour (Love Everlasting) (78)	20

FOURUM
78	Sirius SP 519	FOURUM (LP)	20
81	Guardian GRC 95	SINGING THE DALES (LP)	20

FOUR WINDS
58	London HLU 8556	Short Shorts/Five Minutes More	25

HARRY FOWLER
61	HMV POP 891	Buddies (with Mario Fabrizl)/Flower Flogger	8

KIM FOWLEY
66	Parlophone R 5521	Lights/Something New And Different	30
66	CBS 202243	They're Coming To Take Me Away Ha-Haaa!!/You Get More For Your Money On The Flip Side Of This Record Talking Blues	15
66	CBS 202338	Lights (The Blind Can See)/Something New And Different (reissue)	15
66	Island WI 278	The Trip/Beautiful People	20
72	Action ACT 4606	Born To Make You Cry/Thunder Road	7
77	Island WIP 278	The Trip/Beautiful People (p/s, reissue)	15
73	Capitol E-ST 11159	INTERNATIONAL HEROES (LP)	25

(see also Freaks Of Nature, Hollywood Argyles, Napoleon XIV, B. Bumble & Stingers)

(THE) FOX
68	CBS 3381	Mister Carpenter/Seek And You Find	300

FOX (1)
70	Fontana 6007 016	Second Hand Love/Butterfly	25
70	Fontana 6309 007	FOR FOX SAKE (LP, laminated sleeve, black/silver labels)	300
03	RPM RPM 254LP	FOR FOX SAKE (LP, gatefold, reissue)	15

FOX (2)
75	GTO GTLP 006	TAILS OF ILLUSION (LP, textured sleeve, lyric inner)	25
77	GTO GTLP 020	BLUE HOTEL (LP)	20

(see also Wooden Horse, Demick & Armstrong)

BOB FOX & STU LUCKLEY
78	Rubber RUB 028	NOWT SO GOOD'LL PASS (LP)	15

DON FOX
57	Decca F 10927	Be My Girl/You'll Never Go To Heaven	10
57	Decca F 10955	The Majesty Of Love/Party Time	10
58	Decca F 10983	Pretend You Don't See Her/Wasteland	10
58	Decca F 11057	She Was Only Seventeen/When You're A Long, Way From Home	10
60	Triumph RGM 1022	T'ain't What You Do/Out There	40
61	Oriole CB 1643	Don't Fool With Love/If You Go	10

PAUL FOX
90	Sound Business SB 1	Writing On The Wall/Version/LIBERATION TRIBE: African Mask (12")	40

(see also Tafari & Paul Fox)

UFFA FOX
60	Parlophone PMC 1112	UFFA SINGS (LP)	15

FOX IN SOCKS
81	Jest 001	Sound Patterns/Lonely House (p/s)	25

FOXX
71	MCA MUPS 419	REVOLT OF EMILY YOUNG (LP)	15

INEZ FOXX
63	Sue WI 301	Mockingbird/He's The One You Love (actually by Inez & Charlie Foxx)	25
64	Sue WI 304	Jaybirds/Broken-Hearted Fool (actually by Inez & Charlie Foxx)	25
64	Sue WI 314	Ask Me/Hi Diddle Diddle (actually by Inez & Charlie Foxx)	25
64	Sue WI 323	Hurt By Love/Confusion (actually by Inez & Charlie Foxx)	25
71	Pye International 7N 25546	You Shouldn't Have Set My Soul On Fire/Live For Today	10
73	Stax 2025 151	You Hurt Me For The Last Time/Watch The Dog (That Brings The Bone)	8

INEZ & CHARLIE FOXX
64	Sue WI 307	Competition/Here We Go Round The Mulberry Bush (as Charlie & Inez Foxx)	30
64	Sue WI 356	La De Da I Love You/Yankee Doodle Dandy	30
65	London HLC 9971	My Momma Told Me/I Feel Alright	10
65	London HLC 10009	Hummingbird/If I Need Anyone (Let It Be You)	12
66	Stateside SS 556	Come By Here/No Stranger To Love	30
67	Stateside SS 586	Tightrope/My Special Prayer	30
67	Stateside SS 586	Tightrope/My Special Prayer (DJ copy)	75
67	Direction 58-2712	I Ain't Goin' For That/Undecided	10
67	Direction 58-3192	(1, 2, 3, 4, 5, 6, 7) Count The Days/A Stranger I Don't Know	12
68	Direction 58-3816	Come On In/Baby Drop Your Dime	12
69	Direction 58-4042	Baby Give It To Me/You Fixed My Heartache	40
69	London HLC 10250	Mockingbird/Hummingbird (unissued)	0
69	United Artists UP 2269	Mockingbird/Hurt By Love	8
69	United Artists UP 35013	La De Da I Love You/Don't Do It No More	10
71	Pye International 7N 25561	Tightrope/Baby Take It All	10
83	Sue ENS 2	Mockingbird (EP)	15
64	Sue ILP 911	MOCKINGBIRD (LP)	100
65	London HA-C 8241	INEZ AND CHARLIE FOXX (LP, plum label)	70
65	London HA-C 8241	INEZ AND CHARLIE FOXX (LP, later black label)	40
68	Direction 8-63085	COME BY HERE (LP)	30
68	Direction 8-63281	GREATEST HITS (LP)	20
69	United Artists UA(S) 29275	MOCKINGBIRD (LP)	15

John FOXX

MINT VALUE £

JOHN FOXX
80	Virgin VS 338	No-One Driving (2.53 DJ Version)/Glimmer/This City/Mr. No (double pack, stickered gatefold p/s, matrix no. VS 338 A5DJ)	15
18	Electronic Sound ES 748	Underpass/Film One (p/s, red vinyl, reissue)	15
20	Electronic Sound ES 764	Howl/Last Time I Saw You (p/s)	8
80	Virgin V 2146	METAMATIC (LP)	20
81	Virgin V 2194	THE GARDEN (LP)	20
83	Virgin V 2233	THE GOLDEN SECTION (LP)	20
85	Virgin V 2355	IN MYSTERIOUS WAYS (LP)	15

(see also Ultravox)

FRABJOY & RUNCIBLE SPOON
69	Marmalade 598 019	I'm Beside Myself/Animal Song	30

(see also Godley & Creme, Doctor Father, Hotlegs, Mockingbirds, 10cc)

FRAGILE FRIENDS
83	KC KCT1	NOVELTY WEARS OFF (12" EP)	25
84	KC KC 001	Paper Doll/What I Call Beautiful	35

FRAGMENTS
80	Shattered SHAT 2	Some Other Guy/Intro Mental (p/s)	10

FRAME
66	RCA RCA 1556	My Feet Don't Fit In His Shoes/She	18
67	RCA RCA 1571	Doctor Doctor/I Can't Go On	65
70	Pye 7N 45213	Rockin' Machine/One More Time	10
74	Seven Sun SSUN 12	Billy The Dreamer/Rocking Machine	20

FRAMED
82	Thunderbay TBR 020A	Into My Life (1-sided)	60
82	Thunderbay TBR 021	Wonderland (1-sided)	60
82	Thunderbay TBR 021	Into My Life/Wonderland (test pressings)	50

(see also Girlschool, Sham 69)

FRAMES
79	Brain Booster BBC 2	False Accusations/69 (no p/s)	6

FRAN & ALAN
68	MGM MGM 1428	Such A Pity/Mrs Robinson	8

FRANCIS
67	Blue Beat BB 379	Warn The People (actually by Willie Francis)/SWINGERS: Simpleton (actually by Peter Tosh & Crackers)	75
72	Fab FAB 182	Rocking Machine/SOUL CLANS: Flying Rhythm	15
73	Fab FAB 251	Locks/Version	25

B. FRANCIS
65	Ska Beat JB 193	Judy Crowned/Who Crunch	15

BOBBY FRANCIS
67	JJ DB 1153	Chain Gang/Venus	175

(see also Winston Francis)

CLAIRE FRANCIS
66	Polydor 56079	I've Got My Own Thing Going/Here I Go Again	7
67	Polydor 56142	But I Don't Care/If You Don't Know	7

CONNIE FRANCIS
SINGLES
56	MGM SP 1169	My First Real Love (with Jaybirds)/Believe In Me (Crede Mi)	60
56	MGM MGM 932	My Sailor Boy/Everyone Needs Someone	30
57	MGM MGM 945	Little Blue Wren/I Never Had A Sweetheart	30
57	MGM MGM 962	Eighteen/Faded Orchid	30
60	MGM MGM 1070	Mama/Teddy (withdrawn; demos more common)	10
60	MGM MGM 1070	Mama/Teddy (withdrawn; demo copy)	10

CONNIE FRANCIS & MARVIN RAINWATER
58	MGM MGM 969	The Majesty Of Love/You My Darling You	35

(see also Marvin Rainwater)

(KING) JOE FRANCIS
65	Blue Beat BB 323	Wicked Woman/King Joe's Ska (as King Joe Francis)	15
65	Ska Beat JB 184	Waggling Tails/I Don't Want You No More	20
66	Ska Beat JB 262	Scarborough Ska/I Got A Scar (as Joe Francis & Ricky Logan & Snowballs)	20
66	Rio R 90	Have My Body (song actually "Have Mercy Baby")/Everybody's Got To Know (as King Joe Francis & Hijackers)	15
66	Rio R 94	Days Are Lonely/My Baby	25
67	Rainbow RAI 114	My Granny/Pull It Out (as J. Francis & Rico's Boys)	15

LEE FRANCIS (2)
78	Lonely I & I L 1	Be My Wife Little Girl/Loneliness	40
79	Lonely I & I L 2	A Lonely I & I/Paradise (12")	50
79	Lee & Roy L 3	Shadows Of My Youth/Deception Of Consciousness (12")	45
79	Lonely I & I L 4	Throwing Stones/No, You Don't Know (12")	80

NAT FRANCIS
66	Blue Beat BB 346	Mama Kiss Him Goodnight/Tra La La (with Prince Buster Junior & Sunsets)	20
66	Blue Beat BB 361	Just To Keep You (credited to B. Junior)/You Only Want My Money	18
67	Blue Beat BB 376	Seven Nights Of Love/Feeling Blue	20

PAT FRANCIS
77	Western Kingston WK 506	Rasta Protest/Part 2	8

RITCHIE FRANCIS
72	Pegasus PEG 11	SONGBIRD (LP, gatefold textured sleeve)	40

(see also Eyes Of Blue, Big Sleep)

RUDOLPH FRANCIS
79	Kim A 024	Time To Realise/Motherless Children (12")	125

Steve FRANCIS

MINT VALUE £

STEVE FRANCIS
| 64 | King KG 1012 | Watch Your Step/Lovey Dovey | 8 |

WILBERT FRANCIS & VIBRATORS
| 66 | Ska Beat JB 267 | Memories Of You/CHUCK JACQUES: Now That You're Gone | 25 |

(see also Little Willie, Vibrators [Jamaica])

WILLIE FRANCIS
69	Bullet BU 415	Motherless Children/I Am Not Afraid	90
71	Escort ERT 848	Burn Them/Poor Boy	10
71	Bullet BU 489	Willie's Rouster/Rouster Version	15
71	Pama PM 829	Oh What A Mini/Version	10
74	Magnet MA 38	Quick March/Africa Melody (actually by Charlie Organaire)	10

(see also Martin Riley)

WINSTON FRANCIS
69	Coxsone CS 7089	Reggae And Cry/FREEDOM SINGERS: Easy Come Easy Go (B-side actually by Righteous Flames)	150
69	Studio One SO 2086	Games People Play/GLADIATORS: The Kicks	125
69	Punch PH 5	Too Experienced/JACKIE MINTO: Mule Jerk (B-side actually by Jackie Mittoo)	20
69	Bamboo BAM 10	The Same Old Song/SOUND DIMENSION: Rattle On	60
70	Bamboo BAM 46	Turn Back The Hands Of Time/Soul Bowl	25
70	Bamboo BAM 48	California Dreaming/JACKIE MITTOO & SOUND DIMENSION: Soul Stew	30
72	Camel CA 99	Ten Times Sweeter Than You/Fat Boy	20
72	Rhino RNO 102	A Little Today A Little Tomorrow/Love Thy Neighbour	7
73	Fab FAB 271	Mr Fix It/Version	12
74	Ashanti ASH 415	California Dreaming/SOUND DIMENSION: Soul Food (reissue)	15
70	Bamboo BDLP 207	MR FIX IT (LP)	60
71	Bamboo BDLPS 216	CALIFORNIA DREAMING (LP)	80

(see also Bobby Francis, Jerry & Freedom Singers, Zimm & Dee Dee, Band Of Mercy & Salvation)

CLAUDE FRANCOIS
66	Fontana TF 725	In My Memory/Gone From My Mind	30
67	Fontana TF 799	Bench Number 3 Waterloo Station/Run To Daddy	80
78	EMI 2773	Bordeaux Rose/Magnolias (demo in p/s)	20
77	EMI EMC 3189	HIS HITS IN ENGLISH (LP)	30

JACKSON C. FRANK
78	B&C BCS 0012	Blues Run The Game/Milk & Honey	20
65	Columbia DB 7795	Blues Run The Game/Can't Get Away From My Love	100
65	Columbia 33SX 1788	JACKSON C. FRANK (LP)	400
78	B&C BCLP 4	AGAIN (LP, reissue of above LP)	40

FRANK & BARBARIANS
| 62 | Oriole CB 1758 | The Bouncer/Concerto In The Stars | 15 |

FRANKIE & CLASSICALS
| 67 | Philips BF 1586 | I Only Have Eyes For You/What Shall I Do? | 200 |

FRANKIE GOES TO HOLLYWOOD
SINGLES
83	ZTT 12 ZTAS 1	Relax (Original Mix)/Ferry Across The Mersey/Relax Bonus (Again) (12", ZTT sleeve or standard p/s, some copies play at 33rpm but list 45rpm)	10
83	ZTT 12 ZTAS 1 (matrix no.: 1A 2U)	Relax (Sex Mix [alias 8.20 "New York Mix"])/Ferry Across The Mersey Relax Bonus (Again) (12", p/s, 45rpm)	12
84	ZTT CTIS 105	The Power Of Love (Extended Version)/Trapped And Scrapped/Holier Than Thou (picture 'envelope' box)	8
84	ZTT XZTAS 3DJ	Two Tribes (Carnage)/Relax (U.S. Mix) (12", ZTT sleeve)	10
84	ZTT XZIP 1	Two Tribes (Hibakusha)/War (Hide Yourself)/Two Tribes/ One February Friday (12", ZTT sleeve)	15

(see also Spitfire Boys)

FRANKIE & JOHNNY
66	Decca F 22376	Never Gonna Leave You/I'll Hold You	400
66	Decca F 22376	Never Gonna Leave You/I'll Hold You (DJ Copy)	500
66	Parlophone R 5518	Climb Ev'ry Mountain/I Wanna Make You Understand	25
78	Inferno HEAT 8	I'll Hold You/Never Gonna Leave You (reissue)	10

(see also Maggie Bell)

FRANKIE & LARRY
| 60 | Capitol CL 15153 | Not Yet/A Fool For You | 12 |

FRANKIE AND THE NOCTURNES
| 71 | Dominoe DO 111 | Road To Destiny/Ballad Of Bowker Vale (no centre) | 6 |

FRANKIE & THE PHANTOMS
| 74 | RCA LPBO 5013 | Rock 'N' Roll Band/Jamburger | 6 |

FRANKIE & TIMEBREAKERS
| 68 | Philips BF 1696 | I'll Be Home/Is There Anybody | 7 |

ARETHA FRANKLIN
SINGLES
61	Fontana H 271	Love Is The Only Thing/Today I Sing The Blues (with Ray Bryant Combo)	15
61	Fontana H 343	Rock-A-Bye Your Baby With A Dixie Melody/Operation Heartbreak	10
65	CBS 201732	Can't You Just See Me/You Little Miss Raggedy Anne	20
67	CBS 202468	Cry Like A Baby/Swanee	6
67	CBS 3059	Take A Look/Lee Cross	6
67	Atlantic 584 084	I Never Loved A Man (The Way I Love You)/Do Right Woman – Do Right Man	8
67	Atlantic 584 115	Respect/Save Me	10
67	Atlantic 584 127	Baby I Love You/Going Down Slow	10
67	Atlantic 584 141	(You Make Me Feel Like) A Natural Woman/Never Let Me Go	8
67	Atlantic 584 157	(I Can't Get No) Satisfaction/Night Life (withdrawn B-side)	12
67	Atlantic 584 157	(I Can't Get No) Satisfaction/Chain Of Fools	8
67	Atlantic 584 157	Chain Of Fools/(I Can't Get No) Satisfaction	10

Rare Record Price Guide 2024

Carolyn FRANKLIN

MINT VALUE £

68	Atlantic 584 172	(Sweet Sweet Baby) Since You've Been Gone/Ain't No Way	10
68	Atlantic 584 186	Think/You Send Me	8
68	Atlantic 584 206	I Say A Little Prayer/See-Saw	10
69	Atlantic 584 239	Don't Let Me Lose This Dream/The House That Jack Built	25
69	Atlantic 584 252	The Weight/The Tracks Of My Tears	8
69	Atlantic 584 285	Share Your Love With Me/Pledging My Love/The Clock	8
69	Atlantic 584 306	Eleanor Rigby/It Ain't Fair	8
70	Atlantic 584 322	Call Me/Son Of A Preacher Man	8
70	Atlantic 2091 042	Border Song (Holy Moses)/You And Me (unissued)	0
70	Atlantic 2091 044	Oh No, Not My Baby/You And Me	40
71	Atlantic 2091 063	You're All I Need To Get By/The Border Song	6
71	Atlantic 2091 111	I Say A Little Prayer/(I Can't Get No) Satisfaction	6
71	Atlantic 2091 127	A Brand New Me/Spirit In The Dark	10
71	Atlantic 2091 168	Rock Steady/Oh Me, Oh My	10
72	Atlantic K 10154	Daydreaming / I've Been Loving You Too Long	8
72	Atlantic K 10224	Rock Steady/All The King's Horses	8

EPs

62	Fontana TE 467217	TODAY I SING THE BLUES	50

ALBUMS

61	Fontana TFL 5173	ARETHA	70
65	CBS (S)BPG 62566	YEAH!!! — IN PERSON	40
67	CBS (S)BPG 62744	SOUL SISTER	40
67	Atlantic 587/588 066	I NEVER LOVED A MAN	20
67	CBS (S)BPG 62969	TAKE IT LIKE YOU GIVE IT	20
67	CBS 63160	LEE CROSS	20
67	Atlantic 587/588 085	ARETHA ARRIVES	20
67	CBS 64536	GREATEST HITS	20
68	Atlantic 587/588 099	LADY SOUL	40
68	CBS 63269	TAKE A LOOK AT ARETHA FRANKLIN	20
68	Atlantic 587/588 114	ARETHA NOW	30
68	CBS 63064	GREATEST HITS VOL. 2	15
68	Atlantic 587/588 149	ARETHA IN PARIS — LIVE AT THE OLYMPIA	20
69	Atlantic 588 169	SOUL '69	20
72	Atlantic K40323	YOUNG GIFTED AND BLACK (LP)	25
73	Atlantic K40504	HEY NOW HEY (THE OTHER SIDE OF THE SKY) (LP, gatefold)	18
75	Atlantic K50191	YOU (LP)	20
76	Atlantic K56248	SPARKLE (LP)	20
77	Atlantic K50368	SWEET PASSION (LP)	15

CAROLYN FRANKLIN

69	RCA Victor RCA 1851	Boxer/I Don't Want To Lose You	8
70	RCA Victor RCA 2009	All I Want To Be Is Your Woman/You Really Didn't Mean It	6
69	RCA RD/SF 8035	BABY DYNAMITE! (LP)	30

ERMA FRANKLIN

67	London HLZ 10170	Piece Of My Heart/Big Boss Man	15
68	London HLZ 10201	Open Up Your Soul/I Just Ain't Ready For Love	10
68	London HLZ 10220	The Right To Cry/Don't Catch The Dog's Bone	10
69	Soul City SC 118	Don't Wait Too Long/Time After Time	25
69	MCA MU 1073	Gotta Find Me A Lover (24 Hours A Day)/Change My Thoughts From You	15
71	Jay Boy BOY 36	I Just Ain't Ready For Love/The Right To Cry	10
71	Jay Boy BOY 41	Piece Of My Heart/Big Boss Man (reissue)	10
70	MCA MUP MUPS 394	SOUL SISTER (LP)	25

MARIE FRANKLIN

68	MGM MGM 1455	You Ain't Changed/Don'tcha Bet No Money	10

GORDON FRANKS

60	Oriole CB 1541	Inn For Trouble/Twinkle Toes	6
62	Parlophone R 4910	Rag Trade Rag/Sid's Tune	6

JOHNNY FRANKS

55	Melodisc P 230	Tweedle Dee/Shake, Rattle And Roll (78)	25
58	Melodisc 1459	Good Old Country Music/Cheatin' On Me	7
58	Melodisc 1459	Good Old Country Music/Cheatin' On Me (78)	20

BONNIE (BLUE) FRANKSON

68	Jolly JY 014	Loving You/Shoo Be Do (both with Joe Nolan and his Band)	12
69	Jolly JY 021	London City/Dearest (both with Joe Nolan & Dynamic Heatwave)	12
69	Columbia Blue Beat DB 114	Dearest/London City	15
70	Ackee ACK 110	I'm So Glad/Lonely Road (both with Dotty)	8
73	Ackee ACK 512	Getting Things Together/Version	6

(see also Dotty & Bonnie)

FRANK XEROX AND THE COPYCATS

78	Arista ARIST 160	Judy In Disguise/Rock Show	10

FRANTIC ELEVATORS

79	TJM TJM 5	Voice In The Dark/Passion/Every Day I Die (p/s)	40
80	TJM TJM 6	Hunchback Of Notre Dame/See Nothing And Everything/Don't Judge Me (unreleased; demos only)	150
80	Eric's ERIC'S 6	You Know What You Told Me/Production Prevention (p/s)	50
81	Crackin' Up CRAK 1	Searching For The Only One/Hunchback Of Notre Dame (p/s)	20
82	No Waiting WAIT 1	Holding Back The Years/Pistols In My Brain (p/s)	20
87	TJM TJM 101	THE EARLY YEARS (mini-LP)	20
88	Receiver KNOB 2	THE EARLY YEARS (mini-LP, reissue with new sleeve & interview disc, as Mick Hucknall & Frantic Elevators)	15

FRANZ FERDINAND

MINT VALUE £

FRANZ FERDINAND
03	Domino RUG 164	Darts Of Pleasure/Shopping For Blood (p/s)	6
03	Domino RUG164T	Darts Of Pleasure/Van Tango/Shopping For Blood (12", p/s 500 only)	10
06	Domino 001	Swallow Smile/Take Me Out (Acoustic) (fan club release)	20
03	Chateau CHAT001	LIVE 2003 (LP, 10-track official bootleg/promo 500 copies)	15
04	Domino WIGLP 136	FRANZ FERDINAND (LP)	40
05	Domino WIGLP 161	YOU COULD HAVE IT SO MUCH BETTER (LP)	25
09	Domino WIGLP 205	TONIGHT: FRANZ FERDINAND (2-LP)	25
09	Domino WIG 205X	TONIGHT: FRANZ FERDINAND (6 x 7", 2 x CD & DVD box set)	20

(see also The Ampheta Meanies)

ANDY FRASER BAND
75	CBS 80731	THE ANDY FRASER BAND (LP)	20

(see also Free, Sharks)

ELIZABETH FRASER
00	Blancy Y Negro SAM 00346	Underwater (Charlie May Mix)/Underwater (Charlie May Instrumental) (12", stamped white label, 200 only)	150

(see also Cocteau Twins)

JOHN FRASER
59	Pye 7N 15212	Bye Bye, Baby, Goodbye/Golden Cage	7
58	Pye NEP 24068	PRESENTING JOHN FRASER (EP)	10

PHILLIP FRASER
78	White Rum/Red Stripe 102	Need To Be Loved/Loving Version	6

TERRY FRASER
69	Rude Boy RBH 001	Beng Beng Chitty/Soul Food	25

FRATELLIS
06	Island IS 924	THE FRATELLIS EP: Creeping Up The Backstairs/Stacie Anne/The Gutterati? (pink vinyl)	12
06	No Label	Cigarillo/Got Ma Nuts From A Hippy (Demo) (gig freebie, 500 only)	15

FRATERNITY BROTHERS
59	HMV POP 582	Passion Flower/A Nobody Like Me (B-side with Gil Fields)	6

FRATERNITY OF MAN
70	Stateside SS 2166	Don't Bogart Me/Wispy Paisley Skies	12

ERIC FRATTER
69	Trojan TR 655	Since You've Been Gone/AFROTONES: Things I Love	8

(see also Eric Fatter)

FRAYS
65	Decca F 12153	Keep Me Covered/Walk On	150
65	Decca F 12229	My Girl Sloopy/For Your Precious Love	50

(see also Mike Patto)

DEAN FRAZER
79	Cha Cha CHALP 006	PURE HORN (LP)	40

NORMA FRAZER
65	Ska Beat JB 223	Heartaches/Everybody Loves A Lover	200
67	Coxsone CS 7017	The First Cut Is The Deepest/BUMPS OAKLEY: Rag Doll	30
67	Studio One SO 2024	Come By Here/WAILERS: I Stand Predominate	250
68	Coxsone CS 7060	Respect/Time	250

(see also Sound Dimension, Righteous Homes, Viceroys, Tommy McCook, Soul Vendors)

PHILIP FRAZER
76	Student STU 1003	Blue Bird/Dub	8

CALVIN FRAZIER AND SAMSON PITTMAN
80	Flyright FLY LP 542	I'M IN THE HIGHWAY MAN (LP)	40

DALLAS FRAZIER
66	Capitol CL 15445	Elvira/That Ain't No Stuff	6
59	Capitol EAP 1035	DALLAS FRAZIER (EP)	10

FREAK POWER
94	4th & Broadway BRLP 606	DRIVE THRU BOOTY (2-LP)	35

FREAKS OF NATURE
66	Island WI 3017	People! Let's Freak Out/The Shadow Chasers	100

(see also Kim Fowley, Belfast Gypsies, Jackie McAuley)

FREAK SISTERS
92	Nucleus NUKE 003	Freak Boutique/We've Got To Live Together (12")	20

STAN FREBERG
54	Capitol CL 14187	Sh-Boom (Life Could Be A Dream) (with The Toads)/C'est Ci Bon	8
55	Capitol CL 14316	The Lone Psychiatrist/The Honey-Earthers (with Daws Butler)	8
56	Capitol CL 14509	The Yellow Rose Of Texas/Rock Around Stephen Foster	8
56	Capitol CL 14571	The Great Pretender/The Quest For Bridey Hammerschlaugen (B-side with June Foray)	8
56	Capitol CL 14608	Heartbreak Hotel/Rock Island Line	8

FRED BANANA COMBO
78	Warm AWMR 2004	No Destination Blues/Jerk Off All Nite Long (p/s)	7

FRED BLOGGS BAND
76	Firebrand DMO 12	Mr Sun/Seaside/Moonrock/The Tribe	8

JOHN FRED & HIS PLAYBOY BAND
67	Pye International 7N 25442	Judy In Disguise (With Glasses)/When The Lights Go Out	6
68	Pye International 7N 25453	Hey Hey Bunny/No Letter Today	20
68	Pye International 7N 25462	We Played Games/Lonely Are The Lonely	7
68	Pye International 7N 25470	Little Dum Dum/Tissue Paper	7
68	CBS 3167	Shirley/High Heel Sneakers	10
69	MCA MU 1088	Silly Sarah Carter/Back In The USSR	6
67	Pye Intl. NPL 28111	AGNES ENGLISH (LP)	20

FRED LOCKS
78	Tribesman TM 20	Love & Only Love/Stricker Ishion (12")	25
78	Revelations FRW 375	Love & Harmony/Joy & Harmony (featuring Brigadier Jerry) (p/s)	25

FREDDIE & THE DREAMERS

Year	Label & Cat#	Title	MINT VALUE £
78	Lloyd Coxsone LC 001	Voice Of The Poor/LEVI ROOTS: Poor Man's Story	25
81	Omega OM3	Redemption/Nice Up The Dance (12")	25
78	Form FORM 1091	LOVE & HARMONY (LP)	30
80	Rev 001 LP	NEBUCHADNEZZER KING OF BABYLON (FRED LOCKS MEETS CREATORS) (LP)	60
82	Regal RLP 002	LOVE AND ONLY LOVE (LP, with CREATION STEPPERS)	45
83	Vulcan VULA 502	BLACK STAR LINER (LP, inner with poster)	20

FREDDIE & THE DREAMERS

Year	Label & Cat#	Title	MINT VALUE £
65	Columbia DC 763	A Windmill In Old Amsterdam/A Love Like You (export issue)	8
66	Columbia DB 7929	Playboy/Some Day	10
66	Columbia DB 8033	Turn Around/Funny Over You	8
67	Columbia DB 8137	Hello, Hello/All I Ever Want Is You	8
67	Columbia DB 8200	Brown And Porter's (Meat Exporters) Lorry/Little Brown Eyes	8
68	Columbia DB 8496	Little Big Time/FREDDIE GARRITY: You Belong To Me	8
68	Columbia DB 8517	It's Great/Gaberdine Mac	8
69	Columbia DB 8606	Get Around Downtown Girl/What To Do	7
71	Philips 6006 098	Susan's Tuba/You Hurt Me Girl	7
63	Columbia SEG 8275	IF YOU GOTTA MAKE A FOOL OF SOMEBODY (EP)	10
63	Columbia SEG 8287	SONGS FROM THE FILM "WHAT A CRAZY WORLD" (EP)	10
64	Columbia SEG 8302	YOU WERE MADE FOR ME (EP)	12
64	Columbia SEG 8323	OVER YOU (EP)	12
64	Columbia SEG 8349	FREDDIE SINGS JUST FOR YOU (EP)	12
65	Columbia SEG 8403	READY, FREDDIE, GO! (EP)	12
65	Columbia SEG 8457	FREDDIE AND THE DREAMERS (EP)	15
67	EMI Regal	SEE YOU LATER ALLIGATOR (Export issue)	20
63	Columbia 33SX 1577	FREDDIE AND THE DREAMERS (LP)	15
64	Columbia 33SX 1663	YOU WERE MAD FOR ME (LP)	15
66	Columbia SX 6069	IN DISNEYLAND (LP, mono)	15
66	Columbia S(C)X 6069	IN DISNEYLAND (LP, stereo)	20
67	Columbia SX 6177	KING FREDDIE AND THE DREAMING KNIGHTS (LP)	20

(see also Freddie Garrity, Dreamers)

FREDDIE & THE DREAMERS/PETER & GORDON

Year	Label & Cat#	Title	MINT VALUE £
64	Columbia SEG 8337	JUST FOR YOU (EP, 2 tracks each)	15

(see also Peter & Gordon)

FREDDIE & FITZY

Year	Label & Cat#	Title	MINT VALUE £
60s	Dr Bird 1033	Do Good/SOUL BROTHERS: On The Town	40

(see also Clarendonians, Young Freddie, Freddie McGregor)

DOTTY FREDERICK

Year	Label & Cat#	Title	MINT VALUE £
59	Top Rank JAR 106	Ricky/Just Wait	40

TOMMY FREDERICK & HI-NOTES

Year	Label & Cat#	Title	MINT VALUE £
58	London HLU 8555	Prince Of Players/I'm Not Pretending	50
58	London HLU 8555	Prince Of Players/I'm Not Pretending (78)	20

BILL FREDERICKS

Year	Label & Cat#	Title	MINT VALUE £
76	Polydor 2058 946	Love With You/Someone Like You	15
77	Polydor 2058 895	Lovers/It's Just A Matter Of Time	30
78	Polydor 2059 035	Almost/Wind Of Change	75

DOLORES FREDERICKS

Year	Label & Cat#	Title	MINT VALUE £
56	Brunswick 05540	Cha Cha Joe/Whole Lotta Shakin' Goin' On	30

MARC FREDERICKS

Year	Label & Cat#	Title	MINT VALUE £
56	London HLD 8281	Mystic Midnight/Symphony To Anne	20

FREE (HOLLAND)

Year	Label & Cat#	Title	MINT VALUE £
69	Philips BF 1738	Soul Party/Down To The Bone	15
69	Philips BF 1754	Keep In Touch/Taking It Away	40

FREE (U.K.)

Year	Label & Cat#	Title	MINT VALUE £
69	Island WIP 6054	Broad Daylight/The Worm	60
69	Island WIP 6062	I'll Be Creepin'/Sugar For Mr Morrison	60
70	Island WIP 6082	All Right Now/Mouthful Of Grass (pink label)	8
73	Island WIP 6082	All Right Now/Mouthful Of Grass (reissue, pink rim, palm tree label)	8
76	Island WIP 6082	All Right Now/Mouthful Of Grass (reissue, orange palm tree label)	10
78	Island IEPJB 6	All Right Now/Wishing Well (jukebox copy, short version)	25
69	Island ILPS 9089	TONS OF SOBS (LP, gatefold sleeve, 1st pressing, pink label/ black & orange 'circle' logo)	300
69	Island ILPS 9089	TONS OF SOBS (LP, gatefold sleeve, 2nd pressing, pink label/black 'block' logo)	90
70	Island ILPS 9089	TONS OF SOBS (LP, gatefold sleeve, 3rd pressing, pink label/'i' logo)	35
71	Island ILPS 9089	TONS OF SOBS (LP, gatefold sleeve, 4th pressing, pink rim label/ 'palm tree' logo)	15
69	Island ILPS 9104	FREE (LP, gatefold sleeve, 1st pressing, pink label/'i' logo)	200
70	Island ILPS 9104	FREE (LP, gatefold sleeve, 2nd pressing, pink rim label/'palm tree' logo)	15
70	Island ILPS 9120	FIRE AND WATER (LP, 1st pressing, pink label/'i' logo)	120
70	Island ILPS 9120	FIRE AND WATER (LP, 2nd pressing, pink rim label/'palm tree' logo)	15
70	Island ILPS 9138	HIGHWAY (LP, pink rim, palm tree label)	20
71	Island ILPS 9160	LIVE (LP, in envelope sleeve with inner, pink rim, palm tree label)	40
72	Island ILPS 9192	FREE AT LAST (LP)	25
72	Island ILPS 9217	HEARTBREAKER (LP, lyric inner sleeve, pink rim, palm tree label)	20
74	Island ISLD 4	THE FREE STORY (2-LP, gatefold, with 4-page booklet, numbered)	25
09	Island 0600753181850	FIRE AND WATER (LP, 180 gram reissue with Island pink 'i' logo on label)	15
11	Music On Vinyl MOVLP 415	FREE (LP, reissue, single sleeve)	15

(see also Paul Kossoff, Rabbit, Kossoff Kirke Tetsu & Rabbit, Sharks, Andy Fraser Band, Black Cat Bones)

FREE WINDS

Year	Label & Cat#	Title	MINT VALUE £
66	Jon Hassell HAS 818/818	Blood Red River/Romping Roving Days/Till It's Time For You To Go/Abiline	100
66	MJB REV LP 397	FROM A NEW DIRECTION (10" LP)	200

FREE AGENTS

MINT VALUE £

FREE AGENTS
80	Groovy STP 1	FREE AGENTS (LP, 1000 only, hand-made sleeve)	20

(see also Pete Shelley)

ALAN FREED & HIS ROCK'N'ROLL BAND
57	Vogue Coral Q 72219	Teen Rock/Right Now, Right Now (with Alan Freed's Rock'n'Rollers)	100
57	Vogue Coral Q 72230	Rock'n'Roll Boogie/Teener's Canteen (with Alan Freed's Rock'n'Rollers)	100
56	Vogue Coral LVA 9033	ROCK'N'ROLL DANCE PARTY VOL. 1 (LP, featuring Modernaires)	60
57	Vogue Coral LVA 9066	ROCK'N'ROLL DANCE PARTY VOL. 2 (LP, with Jimmy Cavello)	60

(see also Jimmy Cavello)

FREE DESIGN
69	Project 3	HEAVEN/EARTH (LP)	30

BOB FREEDMAN ORCHESTRA
63	Island ILP 101	MUSIC TO STRIP BY (LP, with free G string)	40

J.A. FREEDMAN
69	Decca F12963	When You Walked Out Of My Life/Love's Got A Minf Of It's Own	25
69	Decca LK 5021	MY NAME IS J.A. FREEDMAN, I ALSO SING (LP)	40

FREEDOM
68	Mercury MF 1033	Where Will You Be Tonight/Trying To Get A Glimpse Of You (in p/s)	45
68	Mercury MF 1033	Where Will You Be Tonight/Trying To Get A Glimpse Of You	30
69	Plexium PXM 3	Escape While You Can/Kandy Kay	10
70	Probe PRO 504	Frustrated Woman/Man Made Laws	20
71	Vertigo 6059 051	Thanks/Miss Little Louise	30
70	Probe SPBA 6252	FREEDOM (LP, gatefold sleeve, pink label)	200
71	Vertigo 6360 049	THROUGH THE YEARS (LP, gatefold sleeve, small swirl label)	300
72	Vertigo 6360 072	FREEDOM IS MORE THAN A WORD (LP, die cut gatefold sleeve, small swirl label)	400
94	Tenth Planet TP 011	NEROSUBIANCO (LP, reissue, 500 only, booklet)	20

(see also Mick Abrahams, Procol Harum, Snafu)

FREEDOM GROUP
72	Randy's RAN 525	Sing A Song Of Freedom (actually by Max Romeo)/IMPACT ALLSTARS: Song Of Freedom (Version)	7

FREEDOM OF CHOICE
70	Wand	Doctor Tom/Rat Man	10

FREEDOM SINGERS (JAMAICA)
67	Studio One SO 2010	Have Faith/Work Crazy (B-side actually Dinah by Joe Higgs)	80
70	Bamboo BAM 21	Give Peace A Chance/SOUND DIMENSION: In Cold Blood	35

(see also Winston Francis, Leroy Sibbles)

FREEDOM SINGERS (U.K.)
70	New Beat NB 059	Election (with Live Stocks)/FLECE & LIVE SHOCKS: Tomorrow's World	10
71	New Beat NB 074	Your Testimony/Train Coming	8

FREED UNIT
99	Out-There OTT 06	MASONIC YOUTH (9" EP, triangular clear vinyl, 100 only)	50
01	Out-There OTT 09	SIX SIDED (7" EP, clear vinyl, 100 only)	25
98	Out-There OTTLP 04	FIELD REPORTS FROM OUT-THERE (LP, clear vinyl)	18
98	Enraptured RAPTLP 19	THINGS ARE LOOKING UP... (LP, orange vinyl)	15

FREEEZ
80	Pink Rhythm 12 PINKY 1	Keep In Touch/Keep In Touch (Edit) (12")	10
80	Pink Rhythm 12 PINKY 2	Stay/Hot Footing It (12")	100
80	Pink Rhythm EL PEE 1	SOUTHERN FREEEZ (LP)	50
80	Beggars Banquet BEGA 22	SOUTHERN FREEEZ (LP, reissue gatefold)	15
83	Beggars Banquet BEGA 48	GONNA GET YOU (LP)	15
84	Beggars Banquet BEGA 53	ANTI FREEEZ (LP)	15
85	Beggars Banquet BEGA 62	IDLE VICE (LP)	15

(see also Pink Rhythm, Gamer 3, Midi Rain)

FREE FERRY
69	CBS 4456	Mary, What Have You Become?/Friend	8
70	CBS 4647	Haverjack Drive/Flying	20

FREEFORM
95	Skam SKA 3	Fane/Recut/Rail/Siamese Telebox/The Brink/Many/Freeform Dub (12")	25
95	Skam SKA 4	FREE EP (12")	25

FREELANCE
83	Chav KMG S 83 CUS 1765	Writing On The Wall/Elinor/One More Time (die-cut cover)	40

ALAN FREEMAN AND THE TALMY STONE BAND
62	Decca F 11543	Madison Time/Madison Time	10

ART FREEMAN
66	Atlantic 584 053	Slippin' Around/Can't Get You Out Of My Mind	200

BOBBY FREEMAN
58	London HLJ 8644	Do You Want To Dance?/Big Fat Woman	30
58	London HLJ 8721	Betty Lou Got A New Pair Of Shoes/Starlight	40
59	London HLJ 8782	Shame On You Miss Johnson/Need Your Love	50
59	London HLJ 8898	Mary Ann Thomas/Love Me	40
60	London HLJ 9231	Sinbad/Ebb Tide (The Sea)	15
60	Parlophone R 4684	(I Do The) Shimmy Shimmy/You Don't Understand Me	20
64	Pye International 7N 25260	C'mon And Swim (Parts 1 & 2)	25
64	Pye International 7N 25280	S-W-I-M/That Little Old Heartbreaker Me	25
66	Pye International 7N 25347	The Duck/Cross My Heart	30
66	Pye International 7N 25347	The Duck/The Devil (2nd issue with different B-side)	10

BUD FREEMAN
66	Fontana TL 5370	BUD FREEMAN ESQ. (LP)	20
68	Fontana TL 5414	FREEMAN & CO (LP)	20

Carol FREEMAN

MINT VALUE £

CAROL FREEMAN
67   CBS 202579   The Rolling Sea/Leaving You Now 15

ERNIE FREEMAN
57   London HLP 8523   Raunchy/Puddin' 20
57   London HLP 7029   Dumplin's/Beautiful Weekend (export issue) 15
58   London HLP 8558   Dumplin's/Beautiful Weekend 15
58   London HLP 8660   Indian Love Call/Summer Serenade 10
60   London HLP 9041   Big River/Night Sounds 7
65   London HLP 9944   Raunchy '65/Jivin' Around 10
56   London RE-U 1059   ERNIE FREEMAN AND HIS RHYTHM GUITAR (EP) 30
59   London RE-P 1210   ERNIE FREEMAN VOL. 2 (EP) 30

GEORGE FREEMAN
71   Jay Boy BOY 54   I'm Like A Fish/Why Are You Doing This To Me 15

LOUISE FREEMAN
74   London HLM 10490   I Can Do It (If I Can See It)/How Could You Run Away 10

MARGARET FREEMAN
61   Starlite ST45 040   Forbidden Fruit/Mister Ting A Ling 15

PAUL FREEMAN
71   Punch PH 82   Don't Give Up/UPSETTERS: Give Up (Version) 15

RUSS FREEMAN & CHET BAKER QUARTET
60   Vogue EPV 1255   RUSS FREEMAN & CHET BAKER QUARTET (EP) 12
(see also Chet Baker)

FREE MOVEMENT
72   CBS 7768   The Harder I Try/Comin' Home 30

FREE 'N EASY (1)
68   Oak RGJ 628   FREE 'N EASY (LP, private pressing [Warren Coley W.C.P. 001]) 100

FREE 'N' EASY (2)
81   SRT/Clovis S81 CUS 1222 / BMC 003   FOUR EASY MOVES EP 30

FREE SAMPLE
79   Oblivion S/79/CUS 339   Hello My Friend/Something In Her Eyes 10

FREE SOULS
64   Blue Beat BB 264   I Want To Be Free/Angel 20

FREE SPIRIT
74   Chess 6145035   Love You As Long As I Can/As Long As I Can 10

FREESTYLE FELLOWSHIP
93   4th & Broadway BRLP 595   INNERCITY GRIOTS (LP) 50
93   4th & Broadway BRW 274   Hot Potato/Way Cool (p/s) 40

FREESTYLE ORCHESTRA
89   SBK 12SBKDJ 7011   Keep On Pumping It Up (12", promo only) 15

FREEWAY
79   Decca F 13824   I Love The Music/Sarah Girl (p/s) 8
79   Decca F 13843   That Was The Greatest Song/Lost In A Dream (p/s) 8
79   Decca TXS 131   FREEWAY (LP) 18
(see also Terry Melcher)

FREEWHEELERS
65   HMV POP 1406   Why Do You Treat Me Like A Fool?/Ad Lib Blues 8

FREEZE
79   A1.A.1.1.A.1   IN COLOUR (EP, p/s) 15
80   A1 A.1.1.S.1   Celebration/Cross-Over 8

ACE FREHLEY
78   Casablanca CAN 135   New York Groove/Snow Blind (p/s, blue vinyl with mask) 30
(see also Kiss)

DON FRENCH
59   London HLW 8884   Lonely Saturday Night/Goldilocks 40
59   London HLW 8989   Little Blonde Girl/I Look Into My Heart 100
59   London HLW 8989   Little Blonde Girl/I Look Into My Heart (78) 20

ROBERT FRENCH
85   Uptemp UTO 10   Something On My Mind/Help Yourself (12") 40

FRENCH IMPRESSIONISTS
82   Operation Twilight OPT 020   Santa Baby/THICK PIGEON: Jingle Bell Rock/MONKS IN THE SNOW: A Theme For This Special Evening (P/s, last track uncredited) 20
82   Operation Twilight 12OPT 20 Santa Baby/Jingle Bell Rock (12", p/s) 10
(see also Aztec Camera)

FRENCH REVOLUTION
69   Decca F 22898   Nine Till Five/Why? 70

FRENZ
70   Sugar SU 101   Mee Lei Moi/I Hear Music 12
71   Sugar ESS 103   It's A Secret/Dusty Shoes 10

FRENZY (1)
76   DJM DJS 633   Poser/Things You Do (To Me) 15

FRENZY (2)
81   Frenzy FRENZY 1   This Is The Last Time/Gypsy Dancer (no p/s) 50
81   Frenzy FRENZY 2   Blackburn Rovers/Up The Rovers 35
81   Frenzy FRENZY 3   Without You/Thanks For Nothing (no p/s) 50
84   Nervous NEP 002   Robot Riot/All Alone (p/s) 6
84   Nervous 12 NEP 002   Robot Riot/All Alone/Cry Or Die/Torment (12", p/s, 1st 500 on blue vinyl) 10
86   ABC EYE T7   I See Red/Whose Life (p/s) 10
86   I.D. NOSE 8   CLOCKWORK TOY (LP) 15
87   I.D. NOSE 19   SALLY'S PINK BEDROOM (LP) 15

FRESH

MINT VALUE £

FRESH
70	RCA RCA 2003	Stoned In Saigon/Just A Note	7
70	RCA SF 8122	FRESH OUT OF BORSTAL (LP)	20
71	RCA LSA 3027	FRESH TODAY (LP)	18

(see also Paul Korda, Brother Bung, Fruit Machine)

FRESH AIR
69	Pye 7N 17736	Running Wild/Stop, Look, Listen	200
71	Philips 6006 163	In The Sun/Too Many Reasons	7
72	Philips 6006 187	It Takes Too Long/Here Comes Summer	6
72	Columbia DB 8872	Bye Bye Jane/It's All Over	6

FRESH FLAVOUR
75	Buddah BDS 427	Without You Baby, I'm A Loser/Treat Here Like A Lady	7
75	Buddah BDS 427	Without You Baby, I'm A Loser/Treat Here Like A Lady (DJ Copy)	12

FRESH GROUND
70	Dortell DT1	Inside Out/Ways Of Man	80

FRESH MAGGOTS
71	RCA RCA 2150	Car Song/What Would You Do	40
71	RCA SF 8205	FRESH MAGGOTS (LP, orange label)	750

FRESH MEAT
73	Deram DMR 384	Never Mind The Money/Candy Eyes	7
73	Raft RA 18504	Hobo/If You Can't Live (You're Dead)	12

FRESH SKI & MO ROCK
88	Tuff GrooveTUFF003	Talking Pays/Pick Up On This (12")	100
91	Conscious CON003	THE LONG AWAITED PAROXYSM (EP)	20
11	Diggers With Gratitude DWG 010	THE COARSE SELECTORS (EP)	15

FRESH WINDOWS
67	Fontana TF 839	Fashion Conscious/Summer Sun Shines	200

FRESHIES
78	Razz RAZZXEP 1	BAISER (EP, with Chris Sievey solo tracks, 33rpm, no'd, handwritten labels)	40
79	Razz RAZZXEP 2	STRAIGHT IN AT NO. 2 (EP, handwritten labels with inserts, 1,000 only, numbered, green or orange p/s)	30
79	Razz RAZZ 3	THE MEN FROM BANANA ISLAND WHOSE STUPID IDEAS NEVER CAUGHT ON IN THE WESTERN WORLD AS WE KNOW IT (EP, black & white photocopied p/s or numbered blue p/s)	15
79	Razz RAZZ 5	We're Like You/CHRIS SIEVEY: Hey (p/s)	15
80	Absurd A9	Octopus/Sheet Music	10
80	Razz RAZZ 6	Yellow Spot/If It's News (p/s)	10
80	Razz RAZZ 7	No Money/Oh Girl (p/s)	10
80	Razz RAZZ 8	RED INDIAN MUSIC (EP, with Chris Sievey)	18
80	Razz RAZZ 11	I'm In Love With The Girl On The Virgin Manchester Megastore Checkout Desk/Singalong Version (p/s, with free lyric book)	15
80	Razz RAZZ 12	I'm In Love With The Girl On The Virgin Megastore Manchester Checkout Desk (Radio Version)/Singalong Version ('bleeped') (white label radio issue, 200 only)	15
80	Razz RAZZ 13	One To One/House Beautiful (unreleased)	0
81	MCA MCA 693	Wrap Up The Rockets And It's Gonna Get Better/Tell Her I'm Ill	10
81	CV CVS 1	If You Really Love ... Buy Me A Shirt/I Am A Walrus (p/s)	10
84	HANNA 1	Virgin Megastore/Wrap Up The Rockets/Buy Me A Shirt/Tell Her I'm Ill/Frank Talks To Chris (Conversation) (12", white label, stickered sleeve)	30
81	Razz CS-5	LONDON PLAYS (cassette, live & radio sessions, 1,000 only)	12
85	ETS 1	JOHNNY RADAR STORY (20-track, with bonus Frank Sidebottom 8-track: "Firm Favourites")	20

(see also Chris Sievey, Going Red?)

FRESHMEN
67	Pye 7N 17432	Papa Oom Mow Mow/Let's Dance	10
68	Pye 7N 17592	Go Granny Go (The Little Old Lady From Pasadena)/Look At The Sunshine	10
69	Pye 7N 17689	Just To See You Smile/Indian Lake	8
69	Pye 7N 17757	She Sang Hymns Out Of Tune/Mr. Beverly's Heavy Days	6
70	CBS 4842	Halfway To Where/Time Hasn't Changed Her	6
70	CBS 5168	Banquet For The World/Time Hasn't Changed Her	6
71	CBS 7241	One Bad Thing/Everywhere There Is Love	6
72	CBS 7694	Swanee River/Take The Time It Takes	8
68	Pye N(S)PL 18263	MOVIN' ON (LP)	100
70	CBS 64099	PEACE ON EARTH (LP)	40

STEPHEN FRETWELL
03	Tape Recordings TAPE 001	Something's Got To Give/Whenforever/Honey	20

FRIDA
82	Epic EPC A 2603	I Know There's Something Going On/Threnody (p/s)	10
82	Epic EPC A 2863	To Turn To Stone/I Got Something (p/s)	10
82	Epic EPC A 2863	To Turn To Stone/I Got Something (p/s, clear vinyl)	10
83	Epic EPC A 3435	Here We'll Stay/Strangers (p/s)	10
83	Epic EPC A 3983	Time/I Am A Seeker (p/s, with B.A. Robertson)	8
84	Epic EPC A 4717	Shine/That's Tough (p/s)	8
84	Epic EPC TA 4717	Shine (6.27 Version)/That's Tough (12", p/s)	12
84	Epic EPC A 4886	Heart Of The Country/Slowly (p/s)	15
84	Epic EPC TA 4886	Heart Of The Country/Slowly/I Know There's Something Going On (Extended) (12")	20

(see also Abba)

CAROL FRIDAY
65	Parlophone R 5297	Gone Tomorrow/Show Me The Way	10
65	Parlophone R 5369	Everybody I Know/Wasted Days	30
67	Parlophone R 5567	Big Sister/I Look Around Me	10

FRIDAY CLUB

			MINT VALUE £
85	2 Tone CHSTT28	Window Shopping/Window Shopping (instrumental) (p/s)	100
85	2 Tone CHSTT1228	Window Shopping (extended version)/Window Shopping (instrumental) 12" (p/s)	100

FRIDAY KNIGHTS
| 60 | Oriole CB 1579 | Poor Man's Roses/Don't Open That Door | 10 |

FRIDGE
97	Output OPR 06	CEEFAX (LP)	25
98	Output OPR 12	SEMAPHORE (2-LP)	25
99	Go Beat 547 1141	EPH (2-LP)	25
00	Text TEXT002LP	HAPPINESS (2-LP)	20

(see also Four Tet)

BRIAN JOSEPH FRIEL
| 74 | Dawn DNLS 3054 | BRIAN JOSEPH FRIEL (LP, gatefold sleeve with insert, pink 'sun' label) | 20 |

FRIEND & LOVER
| 68 | Verve VS 1515 | Reach Out Of The Darkness/Time Is On Your Side | 15 |

TERRY FRIEND & FRIENDS
| 77 | Tramp (no cat. no.) | COME THE DAY (LP, private pressing, 100 only) | 40 |

(see also Stonefield Tramp)

FRIENDLY FIRES
07	Moshi Moshi MOMO 11	Paris/Ex-Lover	10
08	XL XLS 387	Jump In The Pool (one-sided hand-numbered and stencilled sleeve, white labels, 250 only)	8
08	XL XLT 395	Paris (Aeroplane Remix)/Paris (Justus Kohncke Remix) (12", p/s)	15
10	XL XLT 486	Hold On (Instrumental)/HOLY GHOST: On Board/On Board (Instrumental) (12")	8
08	XL XLLP 383	FRIENDLY FIRES (LP)	25

FRIENDS (1)
| 68 | Deram DM 198 | Piccolo Man/Mythological Sunday | 30 |

(see also Flowerpot Men, Ivy League)

FRIENDS (2)
| 70 | United Artists UP 35146 | Futz/Costa Del Sol | 7 |

FRIENDS (3)
| 74 | Merlin HF 4 | FRIENDS (LP, white label test pressing, 1 copy only!) | 2000 |

(see also Ithaca, Alice Through The Looking Glass, Agincourt, Tomorrow Come Someday, BBC Radiophonic Workshop)

FRIENDS (4)
| 75 | Caroline C1511 | FRIENDS (LP, stickered with £1.49 price tag and quote from Jazz Forum) | 20 |

FRIENDS (5)
| 83 | Rock Shop RSR 002 | Night Walker/Wasted Time (no p/s) | 25 |

FRIENDS AGAIN
| 83 | Moonboot MOON 1 | Honey At The Core/Lucky Star (p/s) | 6 |

FRIENDS O' MINE
| 72 | Westwood WRS 021 | FRIENDS O' MINE (LP, 250 copies only) | 100 |

(see also Mark Kjeldsen)

FRIENDS OF DISTINCTION
| 69 | RCA 1838 | Grazing In The Grass/I Really Hope You Do | 12 |
| 69 | RCA SF 8032 | GRAZIN' (LP) | 20 |

FRIENDS OF ST. FRANCIS
| 74 | Charisma CB 229 | The Man Who Turned On The World/How Is The World Today | 6 |

FRIENDSHIP LEAGUE
| 75 | Luggage (no cat no) | FRIENDSHIP LEAGUE 5 TRACKS (plays at 33rpm) | 35 |

FRIGHTY
| 01 | Jah Tubbys JT 7009 | Call On Jah Name/OFFBEAT POSSE: Call On Dub | 25 |
| 03 | Jah Tubbys JT 10012 | Jah Jah Is Coming/Fright Jah Jah Is Coming Version/Dub Is Coming (10", with the Offbeat Posse) | 20 |

FRIJID PINK
70	Deram DM-R 288	The House Of The Rising Sun/Drivin' Blues	6
70	Deram DM 309	Sing A Song Of Freedom/End Of The Line	7
70	Deram DM 321	Heartbreak Hotel/Bye Bye Blues	8
71	Deram DM 332	Music For The People/Sloony	7
71	Deram DM 336	We're Gonna Be There (When Johnny Comes Marching Home)/Shortly Kline	8
71	Deram DM 347	Lost Son/I Love Her	8
70	Deram SML 1062	FRIJID PINK (LP)	100
70	Deram SML 1077	DEFROSTED (LP)	100

THOMAS FRIMPONG
84	Damfo Domino DDP 006	SASAKRROMA (LP)	40
85	Asona ASR 2010	AYE YI (LP)	100
86	Asona ASR 5010	ANASI SHUFFLE (LP)	50

(ROBERT) FRIPP & (BRIAN) ENO
73	Island HELP 16	NO PUSSYFOOTING (LP, gatefold sleeve, black label with pink 'i' logo)	40
75	Island HELP 22	EVENING STAR (LP, black label with pink 'i' logo)	30
77	Polydor 2343195	NO PUSSYFOOTING (LP, reissue)	15
86	Editions EG EGED 3	EVENING STAR (LP, reissue)	15
14	Discipline Global Mobile/Opal DGM LP 1	NO PUSSYFOOTING (LP, reissue, 200gm vinyl)	15
14	Discipline Global Mobile/Opal DGM LP 3	THE EQUATORIAL STARS (LP)	15

(see also Giles Giles & Fripp, King Crimson, Brian Eno, Roxy Music, Robert Fripp)

JACKIE FRISCO
| 63 | Decca F 11566 | You Can't Catch Me/Sugar Baby | 15 |
| 63 | Decca F 11692 | When You Ask About Love/He's So Near | 10 |

VONNIE FRITCHIE
| 55 | London HLU 8178 | Sugar Booger Avenue/There I Stood (To Throw Old Shoes And Rice) | 40 |

FRED FRITH

MINT VALUE £

FRED FRITH
74	Caroline C 1508	GUITAR SOLOS (LP)	30
76	Caroline C 1518	GUITAR SOLOS 2 (LP)	25

(see also Henry Cow)

FRITZ, MIKE & MO
65	Philips BF 1427	Somebody Stole The Sun/Let Me Hear Your Voice	10
65	Philips BF 1441	What Colour Is A Man?/So Now You're Gone	8

(see also Four Pennies)

FROCK
78	Frock Music FM 7848	SILKIE (LP, 250 only)	300

EDGAR FROESE
74	Virgin V 2016	AQUA (LP, gatefold)	15
75	Virgin V 2040	EPSILON IN MALAYSIAN PALE (LP beige "mirror" girl label)	15

(see also Tangerine Dream)

FROG
73	Jam JAM 39	Witch Hunt (Theme From Psychomania)/Living Dead (die-cut company sleeve)	150

(see also John Cameron)

FROG ISLAND SKIFFLE GROUP
57	77 Records EP 4	FROG ISLAND SKIFFLE GROUP (EP)	200

RAYMOND FROGGATT
68	Polydor 583 044	THE VOICE AND WRITING OF RAYMOND FROGGATT (LP, gatefold)	15
72	Bell BELLS 207	BLEACH (LP)	15
74	Reprise K 44257	ROGUES AND THIEVES (LP)	15

(see also Monopoly)

FROGMEN
61	Oriole CB 1617	Underwater/Mad Rush (withdrawn)	100

FROGMORTON
76	Philips 6308 261	AT LAST (LP, blue/silver labels)	25

FROM WEST TO EAST
72	Zella JHPS 128	FROM WEST TO EAST (LP)	20

FRONT
77	The Label TLR 005	System/Queen's Mafia (p/s)	8

DOM FRONTIERE & HIS ORCHESTRA
57	London HLU 8385	Jet Rink Ballad/Uno Mas	15

FRONT LINE
65	Atlantic AT 4057	I Don't Care/Got Love	40

FRONTLINE ORCHESTRA
81	Ice ICET 50	Don't Turn You Back On Me/No Entry (12")	40

FROST
69	Vanguard SVRL 19052	FROST MUSIC (LP)	18
69	Vanguard SVRL 19056	ROCK AND ROLL MUSIC (LP)	18

(see also Alice Cooper)

BERNIE FROST
74	Vertigo 6059 108	The House/What Do You Want To Hear Today	50

(see also Status Quo, Rossi & Frost, Boz Frost)

BOZ FROST
73	Vertigo 6059 089	Foreign Lady/Big White Seagull	25

(see also Status Quo, Rossi & Frost, Bernie Frost)

FROST LANE
71	Cutty Wren MM 1	FROST LANE (LP, actually various artists LP)	45

MAX FROST & TROOPERS
68	Capitol CL 15565	Shape Of Things To Come/Free Lovin'	30

(see also Millicent Martin)

FROZEN TEAR
69	Ra RA 5001	The Hunter/You Know What Has To Be (99 copies only)	450

FRUGAL SOUND
66	Pye 7N 17062	Norwegian Wood/Cruel To Be Kind	15
66	Pye 7N 17129	Just Outside The Door/I'm On Your Side	6
67	RCA Victor RCA 1556	Backstreet Girl/Reason To Believe	6

FRUIT EATING BEARS
78	DJM DJS 857	Door In My Face/Going Through The Motions (company sleeve)	45
78	Lightning GIL 509	Chevy Heavy/Fifties Cowboy (p/s)	40

FRUIT GUMS
70	Fab FAB 138	Sweet Pork/Crying All Night	6

FRUIT MACHINE
69	Spark SRL 1003	Follow Me/Cuddly Toy	80
69	Spark SRL 1027	I'm Alone Today/Sunshine Of Your Love (in title p/s)	200
69	Spark SRL 1027	I'm Alone Today/Sunshine Of Your Love	80

(see also Rare Bird)

FRUMPY
71	Philips 6003 133	Life Without Pain/Morning	20
71	Philips 6305 067	ALL WILL BE CHANGED (LP, black/silver labels)	120
72	Philips 6305 098	FRUMP 2 (LP, black & blue vinyl)	100

(see also Atlantis)

FRUUPP
74	Dawn DNS 1087	Prince Of Heaven/Jaunting Car	10
73	Dawn DNLS 3053	FUTURE LEGENDS (LP, gatefold sleeve)	150
74	Dawn DNLS 3058	SEVEN SECRETS (LP, with lyric insert)	150
74	Dawn DNLH 2	THE PRINCE OF HEAVEN'S EYES (LP, gatefold sleeve, with book)	150
74	Dawn DNLH 2	THE PRINCE OF HEAVEN'S EYES (LP, gatefold sleeve, without book)	100

Mark FRY

			MINT VALUE £
75	Dawn DNLS 3070	MODERN MASQUERADES (LP, gatefold sleeve, with lyric insert)	100

MARK FRY
06	Sunbeam SBRLPS 028	DREAMING WITH ALICE (LP, 180 gram vinyl reissue of original 1972 Italian pressing)	20

FUCHSIA
17	Fruits De Mer CRUSTACEAN 80	SONG (EP 2 x 7" black or grey vinyl)	10
71	Pegasus PEG 8	FUCHSIA (LP)	400
17	Fruits De Mer CRUSTACEAN 82	FUCHSIA II (200 only, 100 on magenta and 100 on green vinyl)	40
18	Fruits De Mer CRUSTACEAN 86	FUCHSIA (reissue, 2-LP gatefold, with DVD, poster)	50

FUCK BUTTONS
10	Rock Action ROCKACT 43	Colours Move (Shibuya Drunk Mix)/Mogwai Fear Satan (10", white vinyl p/s)	18
08	ATP ATPRLP 28	STREET HORRSING (2-LP)	25
09	ATP ATPRLP 35	TAROT SPORT (2-LP)	35
13	Epic Electronic ATPRLP 49	SLOW FOCUS (2-LP)	25

FUCKED UP
11	Fucked Up FU 010	The Other Shoe/The Truest Road (p/s, lyric sheet, original U.K. tour 7")	20

THE FUCKERS
97	Kalevala KALA 002	Sexy Roy Orbison/Sexy Roy Orbison (Version)	20

FUD (CHRISTIAN) & DEL
73	Duke DU 165	Beef Sticker/PRINCE HERON: Ten Commandments	6
73	Songbird SB 1086	Dr. Fud/FUD CHRISTIAN ALLSTARS: La-Fud-Del Skank	6

FUD CHRISTIAN ALLSTARS
71	Big Shot BI 571	Never Fall In Love (actually by Winston Heywood)/Never Fall In Love Version	8

(see also Linkers, Ansel Linkers)

FUDGE TUNNEL
91	Earache MOSH 36	HATE SONGS IN E MINOR (LP, with free hand-painted 7")	40
92	Earache MOSH 64	CREEP DIETS (LP, insert)	25
94	Earache MOSH 119LP	THE COMPLICATED FUTILITY OF IGNORANCE (LP)	30

FUGAZI
89	Dischord DIS 44	REPEATER (LP)	20
91	Dischord DIS 60V	STEADY DIET OF NOTHING (LP, inner)	25
93	Dischord DIS 60V	IN ON THE KILL TAKER (LP)	30
95	Dischord DIS 90V	RED MEDICINE (LP)	35
98	Dischord DIS 110V	END HITS (LP, gatefold)	25

FUGEES
96	Columbia 483549-1	THE SCORE (2-LP)	60

(see also Lauryn Hill)

FUGI
71	Blue Horizon 2096 005	Red Moon (Parts 1 & 2)	30

FUGITIVE
81	Private pressing FMR 050	Need My Freedom	20

FUGITIVES (JAMAICA)
67	Doctor Bird DB 1082	Musical Pressure/LESLIE BUTLER & FUGITIVES: Winchester Rocksteady	35
67	Doctor Bird 1097	Lecture/Canteloupe Rock	40

(see also Jo Jo Bennett & Fugitives, Two Kings, Jo Jo Bennett, Stranger Cole)

FUGITIVES (U.S.)
61	Vogue V 9176	Freeway/Fugitive	30

FUGS
68	Big T BIG 115	Crystal Liaison/When The Mode Of The Music Changes	15
68	Transatlantic TRA 180	TENDERNESS JUNCTION (LP, with poster)	55
68	Transatlantic TRA 180	TENDERNESS JUNCTION (LP, without poster)	25
68	Transatlantic TRA 181	IT CRAWLED INTO MY HAND, HONEST (LP)	40
69	Fontana (S)TL 5501	VIRGIN FUGS (LP)	30
69	Fontana (S)TL 5513	THE FUGS ... FIRST ALBUM (LP)	40
69	Fontana (S)TL 5524	FUGS II (LP)	35
69	Reprise RSLP 6359	THE BELLE OF AVENUE A (LP)	35
70	Reprise 6396	GOLDEN FILTH - LIVE AT THE FILLIMORE EAST (LP)	35

FULHAM FURIES
78	GM GMS 9050	These Boots Are Made For Walking/Under Pressure (no p/s)	35

(see also Lurkers)

BLIND BOY FULLER
57	Philips BBL 7512	BLIND BOY FULLER 1935-40 (LP)	25
68	Matchbox SDR 143	BLIND BOY FULLER ON DOWN VOLUME 1 (LP)	15
69	Matchbox SDR 168	BLIND BOY FULLER ON DOWN VOLUME 2 (LP)	15
60s	Flyright LP 105	CAROLINA BLUES (LP)	15

BOBBY FULLER FOUR
66	London HLU 10030	I Fought The Law/Little Annie Lou	30
66	London HLU 10041	Love's Made A Fool Of You/Don't You Ever Let Me Know	15
73	President PT 394	Another Sad And Lonely Night/Only When I Dream	10
67	President PTL 1003	MEMORIAL ALBUM (LP)	40

(see also Randy Fuller)

CURTIS FULLER/TOMMY FLANAGAN
58	Pye NPL28009	IT'S MAGIC (LP)	30

JERRY FULLER
62	Salvo SLO 1802	Lipstick And Rouge/Mother Goose At The Bandstand (99 copies only)	150

JESSE FULLER
65	Good Time Jazz GV 2426	San Francisco Bay Blues/New Midnight Special	10
67	Good Time Jazz GV 2427	Runnin' Wild/The Monkey And The Engineer	10
67	Fontana TF 821	Going Back To My Old Used To Be/Bye And Bye	10

Randy FULLER

MINT VALUE £

58	Good Time Jazz LAG 12159	JESSE FULLER (LP)	25
60	Good Time Jazz LAG 12279	LONE CAT (LP)	25
60	Topic 10T 59	WORKING ON THE RAILROAD (10" LP)	35
63	Good Time Jazz LAG 574	SAN FRANCISCO BAY BLUES (LP)	25
65	Stateside SL 10154	JESSE FULLER'S FAVOURITES (LP)	20
66	Fontana TL 5313	SESSION WITH JESSE FULLER (LP)	25
66	Topic 12T 134	MOVE ON DOWN THE LINE (LP)	35
60s	Vocalion VRLP 574	SAN FRANCISCO BAY BLUES (LP)	20
60s	Evolution Z 1004	LIVE IN LONDON (LP)	20

RANDY FULLER
67	President PT 111	It's Love, Come What May/The Things You Do	10

(see also Bobby Fuller Four)

FULL EXPERIENCE
12	Attack THB 7016	Young Gifted And Broke/Can't See You	10

FULL MOON (1)
79	SRTS/79/CUS 279	Stand Up/Fly Away (p/s)	35

FULL MOON (2)
87	Luna SRT 7K51283	The Eternal Now/Nemesis	25
89	Voices Of Wonder VOW11	FULL MOON (LP, insert)	25
92	Demi Monde DMLP 1031	EUPHORIA (LP)	20

LOWELL FULSON/FULSOM
65	Sue WI 375	Too Many Drivers/Key To Your Heart	40
66	Sue WI 4023	Talking Woman/Blues Around Midnight	40
66	Outasite 45-502	Stop And Think/Baby (with Leon Blue)	70
66	Polydor 56515	Black Nights/Little Angel	20
67	Fontana TF 795	Tramp/Pico	20
69	Fontana SFJL 920	SAN FRANCISCO BLUES (LP)	30
69	Polydor 2384 038	IN A HEAVY BAG (LP, as Lowell Fulsom)	20

MAURICE FULTON
00	Spectrum RAJLP 001	LIFE IS WATER FOR GERBADAISIES WHEN THEY ARE DANCING (2-LP)	40
01	Transfusion TFLP 001	WHY PUT ME THROUGH IT (2-LP)	20

FUMBLE (1)
73	Sovereign SOV 121	Alexandra Park (Palisades Park)/Mama I Can't Tell You	6

FUMBLE (2)
74	RCA 2479	Not Fade Away/After The Dance	6
76	Decca F 13671	Rock N Roll School/On The Raod To Fame	6
77	Decca F 13702	Carol Please Come Home/Giving The Best Years Away	6

FUMME
83	Sanity 12STY 008	Only You (Make It Right)/Only You (Make It Right - Instrumental)/Only You (Make It Right - Instrumental) (12")	70
83	Sanity STY 008	Only You (Make It Right)/(Only You (Make It Right) Instrumental	10

FUN AND GAMES
69	MCA MU 1083	We/Got To Say Goodbye	8

FUNBOY FIVE
80	Cool Cat Daddy-O PHUN 1	Life After Death/Compulsive Eater (foldover green, yellow, pink, blue and white p/s)	70

FUNERAL FOR A FRIEND
03	Infectious EW 269	Juneau/Getaway Plan (white vinyl, p/s)	15
03	Warner EW 274	She Drove Me To Daytime TV/Bullet Theory (blue vinyl, p/s)	15
03	Infectious INFEC 126S	Four Ways — This Year's Most Open Heartbreak/She Drove Me To Daytime Television//Kiss And Make Up (All Bets Are Off)/Escape Artists Never Die (2 x 7" red vinyl, gatefold p/s)	20
03	Infectious 2564609471	CASUALLY DRESSED AND DEEP IN CONVERSATON (2-LP)	20
05	Atlantic 5050467844	HOURS (2-LP)	50
08	Roadrunner RRCAR 7911-1	MEMORY AND HUMANITY (LP)	20

FUN FOUR
80	NMC NMC 010	Singing In The Showers/By Products/Elevator Crush (p/s)	100

(see also Orange Juice)

FUNGUS
73	Fungus FUN 1	PREMONITIONS (LP, private pressing)	200

(see also Secondhand)

FUNHOUSE
82	Ensign ENY 222	Out Of Control/This Could Be Hell (p/s)	6
82	Ensign ENYT 222	Out Of Control (Full Version)/This Could Be Hell (12", p/s)	10

(see also Another Pretty Face, DNV, Waterboys)

FUNKADELIC
70	Pye International 7N 25519	I Got A Thing, You Got A Thing, Everybody's Got A Thing/Fish, Chips & Sweat	10
71	Pye International 7N 25548	You & Your Folks, Me & Mine/Funky Dollar Bill	10
71	Janus 6146 001	Can You Get To That/Back In Our Minds	10
70	Pye Intl. NSPL 28137	FUNKADELIC (LP)	150
71	Pye Intl. NSPL 28144	FREE YOUR MIND AND YOUR ASS WILL FOLLOW (LP)	100
71	Janus 6310 201	MAGGOT BRAIN (LP)	100
75	20th Century W 215	LET'S TAKE IT TO THE STAGE (LP)	20
78	Warner Bros K 56299	HARDCORE JOLLIES (LP)	20
78	Warner Bros K 56539	ONE NATION UNDER A GROOVE (LP, with free 12" "One Nation Under A Groove")	30
06	Westbound SEW 002	MAGGOT BRAIN (LP, reissue)	15
17	Westbound SEW3 158	REWORKED BY DETROITERS (3-LP)	20

(see also Parliament, Parlet, Bootsy's Rubber Band, Dolby's Cube, P-Funk Allstars)

FUNKALOO
79	Rouge RMS 122	ROBOT DANCER (LP)	40

FUNK BAND INC.
76	Beeb 12	Get It Off/Part 2	10

FUNKEES

MINT VALUE £

FUNKEES
75	Contempo CS 2058	Tu Lay/Cool It Down	25
76	Black Magic BM 114	Abraka/Ole	10
74	Amba AM 001	POINT OF NO RETURN (LP)	200

FUNKGUS
76	Baal BDN 38032	Get It Together/Spill The Wine	8
76	Baal BAL 89002	II (LP)	25

FUNKMASTERS
84	Master Funk MF4	It's Over/(Versions) (12")	10

FUNKY BOTTOM CONGREGATION
69	Beacon BEA 122	Hare-Krishna/Things About Yourself	20

FUNKY BROWN & INNER CIRCLE
74	Rhino 128	I See You/Song Of The Swallow	10

FINBAR & EDDIE FUREY
68	Transatlantic TRA 168	FINBAR AND EDDIE FUREY (LP, laminated front sleeve, white/lilac labels)	15
72	Dawn DNLS 3037	THE DAWNING OF THE DAY (LP, with lyric insert, lilac label)	20

FUR FUR
80s	Daark Inc. D.I. 7	FUR FUR EP	12

(see also Karl Blake, Danielle Dax, Lemon Kittens, Gland Shrouds)

FURNITURE
80	Para 1	Shaking Story/Take A Walk Down Town (p/s)	30
80	Survival SUR 023	Dancing The Hard Bargain/Robert Nightmans Story	7
86	Stiff BUY 251	Brilliant Mind/To Gus	6
86	Stiff BUY 254	Love Your Shoes/Turnupspeed	7
90	Arista 12844	One Step Behind You/It Continues (p/s)	6
91	Survival SURT 53	Brilliant Mind (Extended)/Brilliant Mind (7" Version)/On A Bus With Peter Nero/Brilliant Strings (12", p/s)	12
83	Premonition PREM 4CA	WHEN THE BOOM WAS ON (Mini-LP)	20
86	Premonition PREM 6	THE LOVEMONGERS (LP)	20

FURRY DICE
80	White Line WHLS 001	Rudi Don't Take Your Love To Town/K.G.B. (p/s)	6

FURRY PHREAKS (FEATURING TERRA DEVA)
98	FSUK FSUKT3P	SOOTHE (2 x 12" promo)	10

TOMMY FURTADO
57	London HLA 8418	Sun Tan Sam/Isabella	40

FURY
77	Arista 150	Miss Demeanor/Stay On Your feet	6

BILLY FURY

78s
59	Decca F 11102	Maybe Tomorrow/Gonna Type A Letter	100
59	Decca F 11128	Margo/Don't Knock Upon My Door	150
59	Decca F 11158	Angel Face/Time Has Come	200
59	Decca F 11189	My Christmas Prayer/Last Kiss	250

SINGLES
59	Decca F 11102	Maybe Tomorrow/Gonna Type A Letter (triangular centre)	25
59	Decca F 11102	Maybe Tomorrow/Gonna Type A Letter (later pressing with round centre)	15
59	Decca F 11128	Margo/Don't Knock Upon My Door (triangular centre)	30
59	Decca F 11128	Margo/Don't Knock Upon My Door (later pressing with round centre)	20
59	Decca F 11158	Angel Face/Time Has Come (triangular centre)	30
59	Decca F 11158	Angel Face/Time Has Come (later pressing with round centre)	20
59	Decca F 11189	My Christmas Prayer/Last Kiss (triangular centre)	50
59	Decca F 11189	My Christmas Prayer/Last Kiss (later pressing with round centre)	25
60	Decca F 11200	Colette/Baby How I Cried (triangular centre)	40
60	Decca F 11200	Colette/Baby How I Cried (later pressing with round centre)	15
60	Decca F 11237	That's Love/You Don't Know (as Billy Fury & Four Jays)	20
60	Decca F 11267	Wondrous Place/Alright, Goodbye	20
60	Decca F 11311	A Thousand Stars/Push Push	12
61	Decca F 11334	Don't Worry/Talkin' In My Sleep (with Four Kestrels)	15
61	Decca F 11384	Jealousy/Open Your Arms	6
62	Decca F 11437	Letter Full Of Tears/Magic Eyes	15
62	Decca F 11458	Last Night Was Made For Love/King For Tonight	6
62	Decca F 11485	Once Upon A Dream/If I Lose You	6
62	Decca F 11508	Because Of Love/Running Around	6
63	Decca F 11582	Like I've Never Been Gone/What Do You Think You've Been Doing Of?	6
63	Decca F 11744	Somebody Else's Girl/Go Ahead And Ask Her	7
63	Decca F 11792	Do You Really Love Me Too?/What Am I Gonna Do?	7
64	Decca F 11888	I Will/Nothin' Shakin' (But The Leaves On The Trees) (some B-sides list "Nothin' Shakin'")	15
64	Decca F 11939	It's Only Make Believe/Baby What Do You Want Me To Do?	10
64	Decca F 40719	Hippy Hippy Shake/Glad All Over (export-only, with p/s)	80
64	Decca F 40719	Hippy Hippy Shake/Glad All Over (export-only)	50
65	Decca F 12048	I'm Lost Without You/You Better Believe It, Baby	10
65	Decca F 12178	In Thoughts Of You/Away From You	8
65	Decca F 12230	Run To My Lovin' Arms/Where Do You Run?	10
66	Decca F 12325	I'll Never Quite Get Over You/I Belong To The Wind	10
66	Decca F 12409	Don't Let A Little Pride Stand In Your Way/Didn't See The Real Thing Come Along	10
66	Decca F 12459	Give Me Your Word/She's So Far Out She's In	15
67	Parlophone R 5560	Hurtin' Is Loving/Things Are Changing	30
67	Parlophone R 5605	Loving You/I'll Go Along With It Now	20
67	Parlophone R 5634	Suzanne In The Mirror/It Just Don't Matter Now	40

FURYS

MINT VALUE £

67	Parlophone R 5658	Beyond The Shadow Of A Doubt/Baby Do You Love Me?	40
68	Parlophone R 5681	Silly Boy Blue/One Minute Woman	40
68	Parlophone R 5723	Phone Box/Any Morning Now	40
68	Parlophone R 5747	Lady/Certain Things	40
69	Parlophone R 5788	I Call For My Rose/Bye Bye	50
69	Parlophone R 5819	All The Way To The U.S.A./Do My Best For You	50
70	Parlophone R 5845	Why Are You Leaving?/Old Sweet Roll (Hi-De-Ho)	50
70	Parlophone R 5874	Paradise Alley/Well ... All Right	50
72	Fury FY 301	Will The Real Man Please Stand Up/At This Stage	40
74	Warner Bros WB 16402	I'll Be Your Sweetheart/Fascinating Candle Flame	30
76	NEMS NES 018	Halfway To Paradise/Turn My Back On You	10
82	Polydor POSP 528	Devil Or Angel/Don't Tell Me Lies ('microphone' p/s)	6
83	Polydor POSP 558	Let Me Go Lover/Your Words (same p/s as above but diff. A-side, 500 only)	20
83	Lyntone LYN 13078/BF 1	Devil Or Angel/Lost Without You (flexi free within memorial concert booklet)	20
83	Private pressing	BILLY FURY IN INTERVIEW WITH STUART COLEMAN (10", 500 white label copies only, 1st 200 numbered)	30
83	Private pressing	BILLY FURY IN INTERVIEW WITH STUART COLEMAN (10", 500 white label copies only, un-numbered)	20

EPs

59	Decca DFE 6597	MAYBE TOMORROW (triangular centre, orange/red p/s)	80
59	Decca DFE 6597	MAYBE TOMORROW (round centre, orange/red p/s)	60
59	Decca DFE 6597	MAYBE TOMORROW (round centre, yellow p/s)	100
61	Decca DFE 6694	BILLY FURY	45
62	Decca DFE 6699	BILLY FURY NO. 2	45
62	Decca DFE 6708	PLAY IT COOL	25
62	Decca DFE 6708	PLAY IT COOL (export issue, blue/green 'crouching' cover)	70
62	Decca DFE 8505	BILLY FURY HITS	20
63	Decca DFE 8525	BILLY FURY AND THE TORNADOS	30
63	Decca DFE 8558	AM I BLUE	50
65	Decca DFE 8641	BILLY FURY AND THE GAMBLERS	100

ALBUMS

60	Decca LF 1329	THE SOUND OF FURY (10")	200
60	Ace Of Clubs ACL 1047	BILLY FURY	30
61	Ace Of Clubs ACL 1083	HALFWAY TO PARADISE	30
63	Decca LK 4533	BILLY	40
63	Decca LK 4548	WE WANT BILLY! (with Tornados, mono)	40
63	Decca SKL 4548	WE WANT BILLY! (with Tornados, stereo)	45
65	Decca LK 4677	I'VE GOTTA HORSE (soundtrack)	40
81	Decca LFT 1329	THE SOUND OF FURY (10", reissue)	20

(see also Tornados, Gamblers)

FURYS

63	Stateside SS 182	Never More/Zing! Went The Strings Of My Heart	12
72	Jay Boy BOY 61	What Is Soul?/I Lost My Baby	8
72	Jay Boy BOY 68	I'm Satisfied With You/Just A Little Mixed Up	15
72	Jay Boy BOY 68	I'm Satisfied With You/Just A Little Mixed Up (DJ Copy)	30

FURY'S TORNADOES

74	Warner Bros K 16442	Telstar '74/I Would Give You Anything	8

(see also Billy Fury)

F.U.S.E.

93	Warp WAP38	Train Tracs (12", some white vinyl, p/s)	10

FUSION ORCHESTRA

73	EMI EMI 2056	When My Mama's Not At Home/Nuthouse Rock	8
73	EMI EMA 758	A SKELETON IN ARMOUR (LP, gatefold sleeve)	100

FUSION (1)

80	Telephone TEL 101	TILL I HEAR FROM YOU (LP, blue vinyl)	20

FUSION (2)

96	Ferox FER 021	GALAXY OF FUTURE VISIONS (12" EP)	10

FUSION FARM

71	SRT 71169	RUSH JOB (LP)	400

FUT

70	Beacon BEA 160	Have You Heard The Word/Futting Around	30

(see also Graham Bonnet, Bee Gees, Marbles, Maurice Gibb, Steve & Stevie; this record has NO Beatles involvement)

FUTURA 2000

83	Celluloid CYZ 104	The Escapades of Futura 2000/Instrumental Version (12", p/s, featuring The Clash)	15
83	Celluloid CYZ-7-104	The Escapades of Futura 2000/Instrumental Version (p/s, featuring The Clash)	15

(see also The Clash)

FUTURE BEAT ALLIANCE

96	Void VOID 002	Mode 2/Volatile Memory/Electric Blues/Deep Enuf (12")	20
97	Void VOID 006	Inside Out/Advance/Intruder (12")	15
99	Ferox FER 035	ABACO (12" EP)	10
97	Void VOID 009	HIDDEN EMOTION (LP as 2 x 12", white label only)	60

FUTURE BODIES

80	SGS 111	Terrorist/Science Of Romance (p/s, lyric insert, rubber stamped labels)	45

FUTURE DAZE

82	Polydor POSP 455	House On The Hill/Silent Room (p/s)	8

FUTURE OF THE LEFT

06	Too Pure PURE 206LP	CURSES! (LP)	30
09	4AD CAD2913	TRAVELS WITH MYSELF AND ANOTHER (LP)	25
12	Xtra Mile Recordings – XMR058LP	THE PLOT AGAINST COMMON SENSE (LP)	15

FUTURE PAST

MINT VALUE £

FUTURE PAST
91	B12 03	Our Paths Meet/Harmony Park/Your Hand In My Mind/Dance Intellect/TV People (12", black vinyl)	50

FUTURE SOUND OF HARDCORE
93	Dee Jay DJX 013	VOLUME 1 (12")	30
94	Dee Jay DJX 014	VOLUME 2 (12")	20
94	Dee Jay DJX 016A	Promised Land (Remix) (12" 1-sided)	50

FUTURE SOUND OF LONDON
91	Jumpin' & Pumpin' TOT 17	Papua New Guinea/Papua New Guinea (Andrew Weatherall Mix) (p/s)	6
91	Jumpin' & Pumpin' 12TOT 16	PULSE 3: Tingler/Owl/Bite The Bullet/Calcium	12
91	Jumpin' & Pumpin' 12TOT 17	Papua New Guinea (Dali Mix)/(Dumb Child Of Q Mix)/ (Qube Mix) (p/s)	12
92	Jumpin' & Pumpin' 12TOT 17R	Papua New Guinea (Andrew Weatherall Mix)/(Dub Mix)/(Journey To Pyramid)/(Monsoon Mix)/(Graham Massey Mix)/(Dumb Child Of Q Mix) (p/s)	15
94	Virgin promo 500	Slider/Snake Hips/You're Creeping Me Out/Herd Killing/Live In New York (2 x 12" p/s, promo only, 500 copies, FSOL under different names)	15
94	Virgin VST 1540P	Far Out Son Of Lung And The Ramblings Of A Madman/Snake Hips/Smokin' Japanese Babe/Amoeba (white vinyl, promo only)	20
95	Virgin SEMTEX DJ 1	Semtex (Part 1)/Semtex (Part 2)/We Have Explosive/Semtex (stamped sleeve, promo only, 500 copies)	15
92	Jumpin'/Pumpin' LPTOT 2	ACCELERATOR (LP)	20
94	Virgin V 2722	LIFEFORMS (2-LP, stickered gatefold sleeve with inner sleeves)	80
94	Virgin V 2755	ISDN (LP, embossed, fold-out black sleeve with insert)	50
94	Virgin VX 2755	ISDN (2-LP version)	50
96	Virgin V 2814	DEAD CITIES (2-LP, gatefold sleeve with inners)	40
15	LP TOT 59	ENVIROMENTS (LP, reissue)	20
19	Virgin 0602557787078	LIFEFORMS (2-LP, reissue)	20

(see also Amorphous Androgynous, Art Science Technology, Humanoid,

FUTUREHEADS
02	Project C'naut PCOS 001	Nul Book Standard — Park Inn/Robot/My Rules/Stupid And Shallow (p/s)	10
03	Private Pressing	Hounds Of Love (1-track white label: gig/fanclub 7")	8
04	Private Pressing	Meantime/Decent Days & Nights Remixes (1000, white label gig/fanclub 7")	6
04	679 579 L07T	FUTUREHEADS (2-LP)	30

FUTURES
74	Buddah BDS 477	You Better Be Certain/No One Could Compare (DJ Copy)	12
75	Buddah BDS 430	You Better Be Certain/No One Could Compare	8

FUZZ (1)
71	Mojo 2916 010	FUZZ (LP)	25

FUZZBIRD
95	Fuzzbird FR3	Can't Believe A Word/A Man Named Fly (p/s)	8

FUZZTONES
85	ABC S 006	She's Wicked/Epitaph For A Head (p/s)	6
86	ABC ABCS 011T	Bad News travels Fast/Green Slime/Strychnine/As Times Gone (12". p/s)	12
85	ABC LP 4	LYSERGIC EMANATIONS (LP)	15
91	Music Maniac MMLP 044	BRAINDROPS (LP)	20

FUZZY DUCK
71	MAM MAM 37	Double Time Woman/Just Look Around You	15
71	MAM MAM 51	Big Brass Band/One More Hour	15
90	Reflection MM50	Double Time Woman/One More Hour	8
71	MAM AS 1005	FUZZY DUCK (LP, laminated front sleeve, black/silver labels)	700
90	Reflection MM 05	FUZZY DUCK (LP, reissue with booklet & single "Double Time Woman"/ "One More Hour" [MMS 01])	25

(see also Andromeda, Greatest Show On Earth, Alvin Lee, Capability Brown, Cockney Rebel))

FX
79	Southern Rock SR 4501	THE SOUTH'S GONNA RISE AGAIN (EP, oversized 8" folding p/s)	200

HILTON FYLE BAND
87	Nadiya NADLP 1002	FRESH (LP)	60
88	Finesse FIN 401	SALUT AFRICA (LP)	30

FYNN MCCOOL
70	RCA RCA 1956	U.S. Thumbstyle/Diamond Lil	8
70	RCA SF 8112	FYNN McCOOL (LP, gatefold sleeve)	200

(see also Shakespears, Grapefruit, Sleepy)

G

TOMMY G & CHARMS
67	London HLB 10107	I Know What I Want/I Want You So Bad	40

WINSTON G (& WICKED)
65	Parlophone R 5266	Please Don't Say/Like A Baby	35
66	Parlophone R 5330	Until You Were Gone/That Way Too (as Winston G. & Wicked)	18
66	Decca F 12444	Cloud Nine/I'll Make You Cry Tomorrow	18
67	Decca F 12559	Mother Ferguson's Love Dust/Judge And Jury	75
67	Decca F 12623	Riding With The Milkman/Bye Bye Baby	20

B(ASIL) GABBIDON
61	Blue Beat BB 069-A	Warpaint Baby (miscredited to B. Cabbidon & Buster's Group)/ I Was Wrong (miscredited to Chuck & Dobbie with Buster's Group)	20
62	Blue Beat BB 111-A	Ivoree/Lover Man	15
62	Blue Beat BB 124	Independence Blues/For My Love (as B. Gabbidon)	20

Peter GABRIEL

MINT VALUE £

62	Blue Beat BB 129-A	Our Melody/Going Back To Ja (with Randy's All Stars)	20
62	Island WI 033	I Found My Baby (actually by Roy Braham)/No Fault Of Mine	30
63	Island WI 076	I Bet You Don't Know/3 x 7	30
63	Island WI 089	St. Louis Woman/Get On The Ball	40
63	Blue Beat BB 155-A	Eana Mena/Since You Are Gone (with Prince Buster All Stars)	20
63	Blue Beat BB 161	I'll Find Love (with Prince Buster All Stars)/ MELLOW LARKS: What You Gonna Do?	20
65	Blue Beat BB 288	Tick Tock (actually by Theo Beckford)/The Streets Of Glory (actually by Theo Beckford & Yvonne Harrison)	20

(see also Derrick Patsy & Basil, Mellow Larks, Derrick Morgan)

PETER GABRIEL

77	Charisma CB 302	Modern Love/Slowburn (no p/s, 'nude' picture label, withdrawn)	30
78	Charisma CB 319	D.I.Y. (Remix)/Mother Of Violence/Teddy Bear (no p/s, withdrawn)	20
15	Secret 7" S725	Sledgehammer (100 only, each with unique art sleeve)	50
92	Virgin PG 7	US (2-LP, inners)	30
16	Real World PGLPR5X	SO (2-LP, half-speed remaster, numbered)	40

(see also Genesis, Youssou 'Ndour & Peter Gabriel, Colin Scot, Charlie Drake)

RUSS GABRIEL

93	Ferox FER 002	PEACE EP (12", plain sleeve)	18
95	Input Neuron INMD(X)1	FUTURE FUNK VOL. 1 (12", double pack, p/s)	10
95	Input Neuron INMLP 004	VOLTAGE CONTROL (2-LP)	40

(see also Fusion, Too Funk)

RUSS GABRIEL & AFFIE YUSUF

94	Ferox FER 005	Sian's Tune/Deep Space (12")	18

GABRIEL & ANGELS

63	Stateside SS 150	That's Life (That's Tough)/Don't Wanna Twist No More	20

GABRIELLI BRASS

65	Polydor 56031	Angel Cake/Cat Walk	10
65	Polydor 56047	Ride Your Pony/Anyone Who Had A Heart	10
68	Polydor 56252	'Canterbury Tales' Theme/Working My Way Back To You	15

GABY & CABLES

72	Duke DU 129	Only Love Can Make You Smile/Only Love Version	15

(see also Gaby & Wilton)

GABY & WILTON

72	Camel CA 92	Only Love/CHARLEY ACE: The Ten Commandments Of Joshua	10

(see also Gaby & Cables)

PABLO GAD

77	Caribbean CBN 318	International Dread/International Dub	10
77	Caribbean CBM 320	Kunte Kinte/Jah Jah Say (with The Equators)	10
78	Burning Sounds BDS 009	Bloodsuckers/Jail House Pressure (12", red vinyl)	20
79	Burning Rockers BRD 007	Visions Of Pablo/Tru I De A Jail (12")	20
79	Burning Rockers BRD 008	Natty Loving/Trodding On Home (12")	20
79	Burning Rockers BRD 020	Riddle I Dis/Iration (12")	20
79	Burning Sounds BS 042	Blood Suckers/Blood Suckers Dub	6
79	Burning Sounds BSD 015	Throw Your Dreams/What Makes A Natty Dread Cry (12", red vinyl)	20
79	Burning Rockers BRD 014	Trafalgar Square/Chereene (12", red vinyl)	20
80	Burning Rockers BRD 043	Hard Time/Lighter Shade Of Black (12")	20
80	His Majesty HMD 010	Crisis Time/Saddest Mistake (12")	25
80	Burning Rockers BRD 044	Black Before Creation/Reggae Music (12")	15
80	Greensleeves GRED 33	Fly Away Home/Well Insane (12")	40
80	His Majesty HMD 012	Oh Jah/Little Young Girl (12")	35
80	FORM D001	Gun Fever/Fever Dub (12", red vinyl)	20
80	FORM D003	Nursery Rhyme/Bubbling Angelo (12", purple vinyl)	10
81	FORM D005	P.G. In Love/RANKING SIMEON: Ranking Love (12")	20
81	FORM D017	Beggarman's Child/Poor Man Versus Rich Man Dub (12")	10
86	Jah Shaka SHAKA 853	King Of Kings/Lord Of Lords (12")	15
96	Reggae On Top ROT 013	Sha Sha Mane/Dub (12")	10
80	Burning Sounds BS 1038	TRAFALGAR SQUARE (LP)	25
80	Federation Of Reggae FORM LP 1099	HARD TIMES (LP, red vinyl)	30

GADGETS

79	Final Solution FSLP 001	GADGETREE (LP, with insert, blue or beige picture on sleeve)	20
80	Final Solution FSLP 002	LOVE, CURIOSITY, FRECKLES & DOUBT (LP)	25
83	Glass GLALP 006	THE BLUE ALBUM (LP, with inner sleeve)	15

(see also The The, Matt Johnson, Colin Lloyd Tucker)

MEL GADSON

60	London HLX 9105	Comin' Down With Love/I'm Gettin' Sentimental Over You	20

GAFFA

77	Cleverly Bros CBM 002	NORMAL SERVICE WILL NEVER BE RESUMED EP (various hand-made p/s)	20
79	Gaffa ZZZZ S001	Hearts Of Stone/You Know I Love You (But I Don't Know How I Know) (various p/s)	15
79	Gaffa ZZZZ S002	ATTITUDE DANCING (LAND OF 1000 DUNCES)/LONG WEEKEND (four different p/s of 250 copies to go with pressing of 1000 records)	25
80	Gaffa ZZZZ 5003	Man With A Motive/Your Side/My Side	20
78	ZZZZ 001	NEITHER USE NOR ORNAMENT (LP)	15

GAGALACTYCA

90	Holyground HG 1135/Magic Mixture MM 3	GAGALACTYCA (LP, with booklet, actually by Lightyears Away & Thundermother, 425 only)	40

(see also David John & Mood)

MAJOR YURI GAGARIN

61	Britone MK 100	CONQUEST OF SPACE (EP)	20

GAGS

79	Look LKLP 6312	DEATH IN BUZZARD'S GULCH (LP)	30

LITTLE SAMMY GAHA
73 Decca FR 13436   Rock 'N' Roll Is Back Again/Come 'N' On Strong 10

DAVID GAHAN
03 Mute STUMM 216   PAPER MONSTERS (LP) 40
08 Mute STUMM 288   HOURGLASS (2-LP, gatefold with CD) 30

(see also Depeche Mode)

GAH-GA
85 Everbimes EVB 003   Give Your Love To Me/Transition (p/s) 40

BASIL GAIL
70 Bullet BU 454   I Wish/Black Is Black 8

SLIM GAILLARD (QUARTET/TRIO)
56 Parlophone GEP 8595   SLIM GAILLARD NO. 1 (EP) 15
56 Columbia Clef SEB 10046   MUSICAL AGGREGATIONS (EP) 15
60 London RED 1251   SLIM GAILLARD RIDES AGAIN (EP) 25

(see also Meade 'Lux' Lewis & Slim Gaillard)

DONNA GAINES
71 MCA MK 5060   Sally Go Round The Roses/So Said The Man 50

(see also Donna Summer)

PEGGY GAINES
98 Kent 6T 14   When The Boy That You Love/SAN FRANCISCO TKOS: Make Up Your Mind 25

GAINORS
58 London HLU 8734   The Secret/Gonna Rock Tonite 100
58 London HLU 8734   The Secret/Gonna Rock Tonite (78) 25

SERGE GAINSBOURG
79 Island ILPS 9581   AUX ARMES ET CAETERA (LP) 20

(see also Jane Birkin and Serge Gainsbourg)

GAK
94 Warp WAP 48   GAK EP (12") 60
94 Warp WAP 48CD   GAK (CD) 40

(see also Aphex Twin)

GALACTIC FEDERATION
66 Polydor BM 56093   The March Of The Sky People/Moon Shot 25

GALACTIC MUTHERLAND
20 UEG VALP008   A MUTHER'S PEARL (2-LP, purple vinyl, poster, 200 only) 40

GALACTIC SYMPOSIUM
80 Vague VOG 2   Money/In The Navy (gatefold p/s) 15

GALAHAD (1)
73 Bell BLL 1273   Rocket Summer/Elephant Stomp 30
72 Polydor 2058 215   Let's Dance/Jellyroll 10

GALAHAD (2)
87 Private pressing G 1001   Dreaming From The Inside/The Opiate (p/s, 500 only) 12

DIAMANDA GALAS
82 Y Y 18   LITANIES DU SATAN (LP) 40
86 Mute STUMM 27   THE DIVINE PUNISHMENT (LP) 20
86 Mute STUMM 33   SAINT OF THE PIT (LP) 18
88 Mute STUMM 46   YOU MUST BE CERTAIN OF THE DEVIL (LP) 20
91 Mute STUMM 83   PLAGUE MASS (2-LP) 60
92 Mute STUMM 103   THE SINGER (LP) 40
93 Mute STUMM 119   VENA CAVA (LP, inner) 40
94 Mute STUMM 127   THE SPORTING LIFE (LP, with John Paul Jones) 60

GALAXIE 500
90 Rough Trade RTD 199.006.7   Blue Thunder/Untitled (1-sided) 6
90 Caff CAFF 9   Rain/Don't Let Your Youth Go To Waste (p/s, with insert in bag) 40
89 Shimmy Disc Europe SDE 8908 LP   TODAY (LP) 25
89 Rough Trade ROUGH 146   ON FIRE (LP) 30
90 Rough Trade ROUGH 156   THIS IS OUR MUSIC (LP, with sticker and 3 postcards) 25
91 Rough Trade ROUGH 146L   ON FIRE (LP, reissue with shrinkwrapped CD single) 20
10 Domino REWIGLP69   TODAY (LP, reissue) 15

(see also Damon & Naomi, Luna)

GALAXIES
60 Capitol CL 15158   The Big Triangle/Until The Next Time 15

EDDIE GALE
69 Blue Note BST 84294   GHETTO MUSIC (LP) 15

ERICA GALE
81 Santic SAN 0019   Don't Draw The Line/SANTIC ALL STARS: I Need You (12") 10
81 Santic SAN 0020   Stranger In The Night/SANTIC ALLSTARS: Midnight Serenade (12") 40
82 Ital ITD 015   It's Allright/Moving Up (12") 30
82 Sanity STY 003   Tonight Tonight/Instrumental (12", as Erica) 20
82 Ital ITD 022   Where Are They Now/SANTIC ALL STARS: Quiet Place (12") 12
83 Cassia CAS 001   Ain't Gonna Loose My Head/Instrumental Version (12") 30

SANDRA GALE
63 Ember EMB S 162   Hello Heartbreak/If She's Right For You 10

SUNNY GALE
53 HMV 7M 147   Teardrops On My Pillow/Send My Baby Back To Me 8
54 HMV 7M 243   Goodnight, Well It's Time To Go/Close To Me 8
55 HMV 7M 344   C'est La Vie/Looking Glass 8
57 Brunswick 05659   Two Hearts (With An Arrow Between)/Maybe You'll Be There 8
57 Brunswick 05661   Come Go With Me/Please Go 8
58 Brunswick 05753   A Certain Smile/Just Friends 8

GALE BROTHERS

MINT VALUE £

61	London HLU 9322	Please Love Me Forever/Sunny	8

GALE BROTHERS
66	Parlophone R 5535	Every Day Of My Life/All Strung Out	6

GALENS
63	London HLH 9804	Baby I Do Love You/Love Bells	30

LIAM GALLAGHER
17	Warner Bros. 0190295793708	Wall Of Glass (1-sided 7", other side etched, die-cut sleeve, 500 only)	40
17	Warner Bros. 0190295768140	AS YOU WERE (LP, white vinyl, with 7" CD and book)	35

(see also Oasis, Beady Eye)

NOEL GALLAGHER'S HIGH FLYING BIRDS
11	Sour Mash JDNC 12	Aka...What a Life!/Let The Lord Shine A Light On Me	8
11	Sour Mash JDNC 11	If I Had A Gun/I'd Pick You Every Time	8
12	Sour Mash JDNC 14T	SONGS FROM THE GREAT WHITE NORTH EP (12", p/s numbered)	15
12	Sour Mash JDNC 11	Dream On/Shoot A Hole Into The Sun (12" p/s, numbered)	20
14	Sour Mash JDNC 19	In The Heat Of The Moment/Do The Damage (p/s, blue vinyl, mail-order only)	30
15	Sour Mash JDNC 20	Ballad Of The Mighty I/Revolution Song (p/s, pink glitter)	6
15	Sour Mash JDNC21TE	The Dying Of The Light (Demo) (10" 1-sided)	20
15	Sour Mash JDNC 21	The Dying Of The Light/The Girl With the X-Ray Eyes (Demo) (p/s, green vinyl)	6
15	Sour Mash JDNC 22	Lock All The Doors/Here's A Candle (For Your Birthday Cake) (p/s, yellow vinyl)	6
11	Sour Mash JDNCLP10	NOEL GALLAGHER'S HIGH FLYING BIRDS (LP)	15
14	Sour Mash JDNCLP18	CHASING YESTERDAY (LP, CD)	15
15	Sour Mash JDNC25T	WHERE THE CITY MEETS THE SKY - CHASING YESTERDAY - THE REMIXES (LP, 2 x 12")	15

(see also Oasis)

RORY GALLAGHER
71	Polydor 2814 004	It's You/Just The Smile/Sinner Boy (promo only)	50
75	Chrysalis CDJ 102	Souped Up Ford/I Take What I Want (p/s, promo only)	40
79	Chrysalis CHS 2281	Shadow Play/Brute Force And Ignorance/Souped-Up Ford (p/s)	6
79	Chrysalis CXP 2281	Shadow Play/Brute Force And Ignorance/Moonchild/Souped-Up Ford (10", p/s)	20
80	Chrysalis CHS 2453	Wayward Child/Keychain (p/s, as Rory Gallagher Live, clear vinyl)	20
82	Chrysalis CHS 2612	Big Guns/The Devil Made Me Do it (p/s, with free 'Jinx' LP patch)	20
71	Polydor 2383 044	RORY GALLAGHER (LP)	50
71	Polydor 2383 076	DEUCE (LP)	50
72	Polydor 2383 112	LIVE! IN EUROPE (LP, gatefold sleeve)	40
73	Polydor 2383 189	BLUEPRINT (LP)	50
73	Polydor 2383 230	TATTOO (LP)	50
74	Polydor 2659 031	IRISH TOUR '74 (2-LP)	35
75	Chrysalis CHR 1098	AGAINST THE GRAIN (LP)	18
76	Chrysalis CHR 1124	CALLING CARD (LP)	15
78	Chrysalis CHR 1170	PHOTO-FINISH (LP)	18
79	Chrysalis CHR 1235	TOP PRIORITY (LP)	20
80	Chrysalis CHR 1280	STAGE STRUCK (LP)	20
82	Chrysalis CHR 1359	JINX (LP)	20
87	Capo/Demon XFIEND 98	DEFENDER (LP, with bonus 7", "Seems To Me"/"No Peace For The Wicked")	20
90	Capo CAPO LP 14	FRESH EVIDENCE (LP)	18
92	Demon FIEND 719	EDGED IN BLUE (LP)	25
18	Universal RGBUND 001	RORY GALLAGHER (Box set, 15 LPs, remastered, 300 only, numbered)	200

(see also Taste, Killing Floor, Joe O'Donnell)

GALLAGHER-LYLE
67	Polydor BM 56170	Trees/In The Crowd	18
72	Capitol ST 21906	GALLAGHER AND LYLE (LP)	20
73	A&M AMLH 68148	WILLIE AND THE LAPDOG (LP, with booklet)	18

(see also James Galt, McGuinness Flint, Cups)

GALLAHADS
55	Capitol CL 14282	Ooh-Ah/Careless	15

RONNIE GALLANT
62	Warner Bros WB 61	In The Night/The Hole In The Wall	20

GALLANTS
64	Capitol CL 15366	Happy Beat/Rhino	10
65	Capitol CL 15408	Man From U.N.C.L.E. Theme/Vagabond	15

GALLERY (1)
72	Midas MFHR 046	THE WIND THAT SHAKES THE BARLEY (LP)	800
78	Look LK LP 6029	EACH DAY THROUGH (LP)	100

GALLERY (2)
82	Cobweb AP163/CWB814	EGYPTIAN THEORY (LP, with insert)	40

GALLEY
75	Guildhall GHS 10	HAIL SMILING MORN (LP, 50 only)	300

GALLIANO
91	Talkin Loud 848 493-1	IN PURSUIT OF THE 13TH NOTE (LP)	15
92	Talkin Loud 848 080-1	A JOYFUL NOISE UNTO THE CREATOR (LP)	25
94	Talkin Loud 522 452-1	THE PLOT THICKENS (2-LP)	30

GALLIARD
70	Deram DM 306	I Wrapped Her In Ribbons/The Hermit And The Knight	20
70	Deram Nova (S)DN 2	STRANGE PLEASURE (LP, red/silver labels)	300
70	Deram SML 1075	NEW DAWN (LP, white/red labels with small logo)	450

(see also Craig)

GALLIARDS
60	Topic STOP 101	Black And White/Bahnuah	7

BOB GALLION
59	MGM MGM 1028	Out Of A Honky Tonk/You Take The Table And I'll Take The Chairs	7
60	MGM MGM 1057	Froggy Went A Courtin'/Hey! Joe	7

VINCENT GALLO
01	Warp 7261-WARP01-7	Honey Bunny (Mono)/Honey Bunny (Stereo) (p/s)	15
01	Warp WAP 149	So Sad/So Sad (12", p/s)	18
01	Warp 7201 WAP01-7	Honey Bunny (Stereo)/Honey Bunny (Mono)	8
01	Warp WAPLP 87	WHEN (LP, 'book' cover)	200
02	Warp WAPLP 99	RECORDINGS OF MUSIC FOR FILMS (2-LP)	45

GALLON DRUNK
93	Clawfist XPIG 21	Known, Not Wanted/TINDERSTICKS: We Have All The Time In The World ('singles club' release, p/s, 1,400 only)	15
91	Clawfist HUNKA LP2	TONITE...THE SINGLES BAR (LP)	15
96	City Slang EFA04982-1	IN THE LONG STILL NIGHT (LP)	15

GALLOWS
07	Holy Roar HRR 006V	DEMO 2005 (white vinyl, 500 only)	40
07	Holy Roar HRR 006V	Just Because You Sleep Next To Me Doesn't Mean You're Safe/Abandon Ship/Will Someone Shoot That Fucking Snake/Swarm Over Death (white vinyl, 500 only)	12
07	Warner Bros. WEA425X	In The Belly Of A Shark/Sick Of Feeling Sick (live) (p/s, blue vinyl)	10
07	Thirty Days Of Night TDON 015	Sick Of Feeling Sick/If Credits What Matters I'll Take Credit/NOVEMBER COMING FIRE: Return Of The Black Dog/Bear Away (split 7", p/s, various coloured vinyl)	15
10	Thirty Days Of Night TDON015	Sick Of Feeling Sick/If Credits What Matters I'll Take Credit/NOVEMBER COMING FIRE: Return Of The Black Dog/Bear Away (brown vinyl, repressing, 500 only)	10
10	Thirty Days Of Night TDON015	Sick Of Feeling Sick/If Credits What Matters I'll Take Credit/NOVEMBER COMING FIRE: Return Of The Black Dog/Bear Away (repressing, white/blue vinyl, 20 only)	15
07	Warner Bros. 25646 9846 3	ORCHESTRA OF WOLVES (LP & CD, green vinyl)	30
09	Reprise 519232-1	GREY BRITAIN (LP, red/grey vinyl)	35

JAMES GALT
65	Pye 7N 15936	Comes The Dawn/My Own Way	12
65	Pye 7N 17021	With My Baby/A Most Unusual Feeling	75
65	Pye 7N 17021	With My Baby/A Most Unusual Feeling (DJ Copy)	100

(see also Gallagher-Lyle)

GAMBIT OF SHAME
82	Dead Hedgehog DHE 7009	No Bounds/18 Out Of 20 (p/s)	15

GAMBLER
72	Spaceward SRS24	TOMMY (LP)	100

GAMBLERS
63	Decca F 11780	You've Really Got A Hold On Me/Can I See You Tonight?	15
64	Decca F 11872	Nobody But Me (Kissin' Time)It's So Nice	15
65	Decca F 12060	Now I'm All Alone/Find Out What's Happening	30
66	Decca F 12399	Doctor Goldfoot (And His Bikini Machine)/It Seems So Long	20
67	Parlophone R 5557	Cry Me A River/Who Will Buy	30

(see also Billy Fury)

GAME
65	Pye 7N 15889	But I Do/Gotta Keep On Moving Baby	80
66	Decca F 12469	Gonna Get Me Someone/Gotta Wait	300
67	Parlophone R 5553	The Addicted Man/Help Me Mummy's Gone (withdrawn)	1000
67	Parlophone R 5553	The Addicted Man/Help Me Mummy's Gone (withdrawn) (demo copy)	700
67	Parlophone R 5569	It's Shocking What They Call Me/Help Me Mummy's Gone	500
97	Dig The Fuzz DIG 026	IT'S SHOCKING WHAT THEY CALL US (LP, gatefold, poster and free 7")	20

GAMER 3
91	Chemical CHEM 001	ACID FOR BLOOD EP (12")	30

(see also Freeez, Pink Rhythm)

GAMES
80	Games 001	Childsplay/First Law Of Games (p/s)	80
82	Open Eye OE 7	Dance This Way/Love Canal (p/s)	40

GAMMA
80	Elektra K12480	Something In The Air/Mayday	10

GAMMER
77	Pennine (EP) PSS 147	Market Place - Your Alone/San Diego (no p/s)	12

GAMMITT
73	Solar SL1	Queen Of Rock/We Dance	15

GANDALF THE GREY
80s	Heyoka	THE GREY WIZARD AM I (LP, reissue of U.S. LP)	25

RON GANDERTON
82	Centridge CENT 2	Giggle Amongst The Tears/Smothered In Love (p/s)	8

GANDOLF FOLK
73	Ra RA EP 7006	GANDOLF FOLK EP	12

LITTLE JIMMY GANDY
69	Roulette RO 510	Cool Thirteen/I'm Not Like The Others (Existence unconfirmed)	20

GANELIN TRIO
80	Leo LR 102	CATALOGUE, LIVE IN EAST GERMANY (LP)	15
83	Leo LR 112	NEW WINE...(LP)	30

GANG STARR
90	CBS 656377-7	Jazz Thing (Video Mix)/Jazz Thing (Movie MIx) (p/s)	10
89	Bellaphon BENNLP 1	NO MORE MISTER NICE GUY (LP, with free 12")	25
90	Cooltempo CTLP 21	STEP IN THE ARENA (LP)	35
92	Cooltempo CTLP 27	DAILY OPERATION (LP)	25
94	Chrysalis CTLP 38	HARD TO EARN (2-LP)	30
98	Noo Trybe 7243 8 59202 1 2	MOMENT OF TRUTH (3-LP)	40
99	EMI 7243 5 21189 15	FULL CLIP: A DECADE OF GANG STARR (4-LP)	50

GANG OF FOUR

MINT VALUE £

GANG OF FOUR
Year	Label	Title	Value
78	Fast Product FAST 5	DAMAGED GOODS (EP, 1st pressing, with b&w labels and 'dp delga press' credit some with sticker insert)	50
78	Fast Product FAST 5	DAMAGED GOODS (EP, 2nd pressing, with b&w labels, no 'dp delga press limited' credit, no sticker)	30
80	Fast Product FAST 5	DAMAGED GOODS (EP, reissue, red/yellow labels)	10
79	EMI 2956	At Home He's A Tourist/It's Her Factory (p/s)	6
80	Zonophpone Z1	Outside The Trains Don't Run On Time/He'd Send In The Army	6
86	Strange Fruit SFPS 008	PEEL SESSIONS (12")	12
79	EMI EMC 3313	ENTERTAINMENT! (LP, 1st pressing with 'crowd' image on b-side label, with inner sleeve)	60
79	EMI EMC 3313	ENTERTAINMENT! (LP, 2nd pressing without 'crowd' image on b-side label, with inner sleeve)	35
82	EMI EMC 3412	SONGS OF THE FREE (LP, with inner sleeve)	20
81	EMI EMC 3364	SOLID GOLD (LP, with insert)	20
83	EMI EMC 1652191	HARD (LP)	15
84	Mercury MERL 51	AT THE PALACE (LP)	15
19	Parlophone EMC 3313	ENTERTAINMENT! (LP, reissue, red vinyl)	25

GANGSTERS (1)
Year	Label	Title	Value
79	Stortbeat A45/B45	Harlow Town/Record Company	20
79	Stortbeat BEAT 3	Best Friend/Best Friend Dub (p/s)	10
79	Stortbeat BEAT 2	GANGSTERS (LP)	20

GANIM'S ASIA MINORS
Year	Label	Title	Value
58	London HLE 8637	Daddy Lolo/Halvah	12

ALAN GANLEY QUARTET
Year	Label	Title	Value
58	Pye Nixa NJE 1046	GONE GANLEY (EP)	100

ELMER GANTRY'S VELVET OPERA
Year	Label	Title	Value
67	Direction 58-3083	Flames/Salisbury Plain	20
68	Direction 58-3481	Mary Jane/Dreamy	20
69	Direction 58-3924	Volcano/A Quick 'B'	20
68	Direction 8-63300	ELMER GANTRY'S VELVET OPERA (LP, laminated front sleeve, yellow/black labels)	175

(see also Velvet Opera, Stretch, Strawbs, Hudson-Ford, Paul Brett's Sage)

GANTS
Year	Label	Title	Value
65	Liberty LIB 55829	Road Runner/My Baby Don't Care	35
67	Liberty LIB 55940	I Wonder/Greener Days	15

GARBAGE
Year	Label	Title	Value
95	Discordant CORD 001	Vow/Torn Apart (embossed metal 'G' logo sleeve, with insert, 3,000 pressed [934 issued], stickered, sealed)	20
95	Discordant CORD 001	Vow/Torn Apart (embossed metal 'G' logo sleeve, with insert, 3,000 pressed [934 issued], stickered, unsealed)	20
95	Discordant CORD 001	Vow/Torn Apart (plain black embossed 'G' logo sleeve, with insert in poly bag, 500 only, sealed)	12
95	Discordant CORD 001	Vow/Torn Apart (plain black embossed 'G' logo sleeve, with insert in poly bag, 500 only, unsealed)	12
95	Mushroom SX 1138	Subhuman/1 Crush (embossed rubber 'G' logo sleeve, with SX 1138 insert, some in white 'G' logo carrier bag, 3,000 only; with incorrect insert [S1138])	15
95	Mushroom S 1138	Subhuman/1 Crush (embossed card 'G' logo sleeve, with insert, 2,000 pressed [1,000 issued])	10
96	Mushroom SX 1271	Stupid Girl/Dog New Tricks (The Pal Mix) (10,000 only, stickered red 'Tak-Tile' cloth 'G' logo sleeve, with stickered shrinkwrap)	8
96	Mushroom SX 1271	Stupid Girl/Dog New Tricks (The Pal Mix) (10,000 only, stickered red 'Tak-Tile' cloth 'G' logo sleeve, without stickered shrinkwrap)	8
96	Mushroom SX 1271	Stupid Girl/Dog New Tricks (The Pal Mix) (10,000 only, stickered blue 'Tak-Tile' cloth 'G' logo sleeve, with stickered shrinkwrap)	8
96	Mushroom SX 1271	Stupid Girl/Dog New Tricks (The Pal Mix) (10,000 only, stickered blue 'Tak-Tile' cloth 'G' logo sleeve, without stickered shrinkwrap)	8
95	Mushroom L 31450	GARBAGE (LP) (as 2 x 45rpm 12", with inner sleeves)	20
95	Mushroom LX 31450	GARBAGE (LP) (as 6 x 7" singles in box set with 3 inserts [now import only], sealed)	20
95	Mushroom LX 31450	GARBAGE (LP) (as 6 x 7" singles in box set with 3 inserts [now import only], unsealed)	15
98	Mushroom MUSH29LP	VERSION 2.0 (LP)	40
99	Simply Vinyl SVLP 140	VERSION 2.0 (LP, 180 gram reissue)	40
01	Mushroom MUSH95LP	BEAUTIFUL GARBAGE (2-LP)	40

(see also Goodbye Mr. MacKenzie)

GARBO
Year	Label	Title	Value
82	Rarn RARN 201	Dancing Strange/Why Don't You Call Me?/Everyday Hallucinations (with p/s)	200
82	Rarn RARN 201	Dancing Strange/Why Don't You Call Me?/Everyday Hallucinations (without p/s)	50

GARBO'S CELLULOID HEROES
Year	Label	Title	Value
78	Big Bear BB 13	Only Death Is Fatal/Won't You Come to my Funeral (p/s)	10

JERRY GARCIA
Year	Label	Title	Value
71	Douglas DGL 69013	HOOTEROLL? (LP, with Howard Wales)	20
72	Warner Bros K 46139	GARCIA (LP)	15

(see also Grateful Dead, Diga Rhythm Band, Old & In The Way)

NUBYA GARCIA
Year	Label	Title	Value
18	Nyasha NYASHA0001	When We Are/Source/When We Are (K15 Remix)/Source (Maxwell Owin Remix) (12", p/s)	20
17	Jazz Refreshed JRF00012	NUBYAS 5IVE (LP	60

RUSS GARCIA ORCHESTRA
Year	Label	Title	Value
58	London HAU 2141	FANTASTICA! (LP)	15

GARDEN ODYSSEY (ENTERPRISE)
Year	Label	Title	Value
69	Deram DM 267	Sad And Lonely/Sky Pilot (8/M/1) (as Garden Odyssey Enterprise)	80
72	RCA RCA 2159	Joker/Have You Ever Been To Georgia (as Garden Odyssey)	70

(see also Graham Gouldman)

GARDEZ DARKX
Year	Label	Title	Value
78	New Bristol NBR 02	Freeze/Heartbeat (p/s)	6

Boris GARD(I)NER (& LOVE PEOPLE)

MINT VALUE £

79	Big Dwarf HURT 2	Bliss/Winter Scene	6

BORIS GARD(I)NER (& LOVE PEOPLE)

10	Jazzman JMANLP 036	EVERY NIGGER IS A STAR (LP, reissue)	40
69	High Note HS 010	Lucky Is The Boy/Bobby Sox To Stockings	100
69	Doctor Bird DB 1205	Elizabethan Reggae/Hooked On A Feeling	25
69	Duke DU 21	Never My Love/The Bold One	35
69	Duke 39	Elizabethan Reggae/BYRON LEE : Soul Serenade	15
70	Treasure Isle TI 7056	Hooked On A Feeling/MESSAGE: Turn Around Twice	12
70	Big Shot BI 537	Sweet Soul Special/Memories Of Love (with Love People)	30
70	Big Shot BI 538	Darkness/Watch This Music (B-side actually "Keep Out") (with Love People)	30
70	Big Shot BI 539	Hot Shot/Watch This Music (with Love People)	40
70	Dynamic DYN 404	Commanding Wife/Band Of Gold (as Boris Gardner & Happening)	20
70	Trojan TR 7753	Dynamic Pressure/Reggae Me Dis, Reggae Me Dat	7
70	Trojan TBL 121	REGGAE HAPPENING (LP)	20

PAUL GARDINER

81	Beggars Banquet BEG 61T	Stormtrooper In Drag/Night Talk (12", unreleased, white label promos only)	700
84	Numa NUM 1	Venus In Furs (Extended Mix)/No Sense/Venus In Furs (7" Mix) (12", p/s)	10

(see also Tubeway Army, Gary Numan)

REGINALD GARDINER

71	Decca F 5278	Trains/Trains (Continued)	6

AVA GARDNER

53	MGM SP 1005	Can't Help Lovin' Dat Man/Bill	10

DAVE GARDNER

58	Brunswick 05740	Hop Along Rock/All By Myself (B-side with Anita Kerr Singers)	30

DON GARDNER

02	Grapevine G2K-45-120	Cheatin Kind/Is This Really Love (reissue)	25

DON GARDNER & DEE DEE FORD

62	Stateside SS 114	I Need Your Loving/Tell Me	20
62	Stateside SS 130	Don't You Worry/I'm Coming Home To Stay	20
68	Soul City SC 101	Don't You Worry/I'm Coming Home To Stay (reissue)	10

(see also Baby Washington & Don Gardner, Dee Dee Ford)

JOHNNY GARFIELD

65	Pye 7N 15758	Stranger In Paradise/Anyone Can Lose A Heart	45

(see also Simon & Garfunkel, Tom & Jerry)

ART GARFUNKEL

74	CBS CQ 31474/Q 69281	ANGEL CLARE (LP, quadrophonic)	20

FRANK GARI

60	London HLU 9277	I Ain't Got A Girl/Utopia	10
61	London HL 9371	Lullaby Of Love/Tonight Is Our Last Night	7

JUDY GARLAND

53	MGM SP 1001	A Couple Of Swells/Medley: I Love A Piano/Snooky Ookums/When The Midnight Choo Choo Leaves (with Fred Astaire)	10
56	MGM SP 1157	Look For The Silver Lining/Who?	6
57	Capitol F17691	It's Lovely To Be Back In London (1-sided 7" given to audience at Gala Premiere of extended engagement at Dominion Theatre (p/s with insert)	10
63	Capitol CL 15291	I Could Go On Singing/Hello Bluebird	6
59	Capitol (S)T 1188	THE LETTER (LP, with paste-on letter intact)	25

RED GARLAND

56	Esquire 32 056	GROOVY! (LP)	50
57	Esquire 32 046	A GARLAND OF RED (LP)	50
60	Esquire 32-096	MANTECA (LP)	40
60	Esquire 32-099	ALL MORNING LONG (LP)	150
61	Esquire 32-116	RED IN BLUES VILLE (LP)	60
61	Esquire 32-126	AT THE PRELUDE (LP)	40
61	Esquire 32-136	SOUL JUNCTION (LP)	40
62	Esquire 32-146	ROJO (LP)	30
62	Esquire 32-166	HIGH PRESSURE (LP)	30

BILLY GARNER

00	BGPS 006	Brand New Girl/JACQUELINE JONES : Can't Stop The Show	15

KAY GARNER

64	Oriole CB 1951	I Still Get Jealous/Squeeze Me	10

REGGIE GARNER

76	Capitol CL 15874	Hot Line/Blessed Be The Name Of My Baby	10
76	Capitol CL 15874	Hot Line/Blessed Be The Name Of My Baby (DJ Copy)	15

COL GARNET

66	Page One POF 002	With A Girl Like You/Monday Monday	12

GALE GARNETT

64	RCA RCA 1418	We'll Sing In The Sunshine/Prism Song	10
65	RCA RCA 1451	I'll Cry Alone/Where Do You Go To Go Away?	60
65	RCA RCA 1451	I'll Cry Alone/Where Do You Go To Go Away? (DJ Copy)	100
65	RCA RD 7726	MY KIND OF FOLK SONGS (LP)	30
66	RCA RD 7750	LOVIN' PLACE (LP)	20

RACHELLE GARNIEZ

09	Third Man TMR 004	My House Of Peace (1-sided, 100 only, luminous vinyl)	70

CHRIS GARRETT AND SWEET POISON

75	Mandala MDS 59	Family Man/Cold N Rainy (p/s)	100

VERNON GARRETT

67	Stateside SS 2006	If I Could Turn Back The Hands Of Time/You And Me Together	40
67	Stateside SS 2006	If I Could Turn Back The Hands Of Time/You And Me Together (DJ copy)	80
67	Stateside SS 2026	Shine It On/Things Are Lookin' Better	50
67	Stateside SS 2026	Shine It On/Things Are Lookin' Better (DJ copy)	75

David GARRICK

			MINT VALUE £
68	Action ACT 4508	Shine It On/Things Are Lookin' Better (reissue)	30

DAVID GARRICK
67	Piccadilly NEP 34056	DAVID (EP)	30
66	Piccadilly NPL 38024	A BOY CALLED DAVID (LP, mono)	20
66	Piccadilly N(S)PL 38024	A BOY CALLED DAVID (LP, stereo)	25
67	Piccadilly N(S)PL 38035	DON'T GO OUT INTO THE RAIN, SUGAR (LP)	25
68	Pye NSPL 18223	LIVE! (LP, blue/black label)	30

MICHAEL GARRICK
63	Airborne NBP 002	CASE OF JAZZ (EP, with Shake Keane)	350
65	Argo EAF/ZFA 92	ANTHEM - MICHAEL GARRICK QUINTET (EP, mono/stereo with Shake Keane)	100
66	Argo EAF 115	BEFORE NIGHT/DAY (EP)	100
64	Airborne NMP 004	MOONSCAPE (LP)	3000
64	Argo ZDA 26/27	POETRY AND JAZZ IN CONCERT (2-LP, with Norma Winstone)	60
65	Argo DA 33	OCTOBER WOMAN (LP, mono, as Michael Garrick Quintet, with Joe Harriott)	300
65	Argo ZDA 33	OCTOBER WOMAN (LP, stereo, as Michael Garrick Quintet, with Joe Harriott)	350
65	Argo DA 36	PROMISES (LP, mono, as Michael Garrick Sextet, with Ian Carr)	250
65	Argo ZDA 36	PROMISES (LP, stereo, as Michael Garrick Sextet, with Ian Carr)	300
68	Argo DA 88	BLACK MARIGOLDS (LP, mono, as Michael Garrick Septet)	250
68	Argo ZDA 88	BLACK MARIGOLDS (LP, stereo, as Michael Garrick Septet)	300
68	Airborne NBP 0021	JAZZ PRAISES AT ST. PAULS (LP)	100
69	Argo ZPR 264/5	POETRY AND JAZZ IN CONCERT 250 (2-LP, as Michael Garrick Quintet)	80
69	Erase EO 254 S	JAZZ CANTATA (LP, 'Farnham Festival' release, music by Garrick words by John Smith)	300
70	Argo ZDA 135	HEART IS A LOTUS (LP, as Michael Garrick Sextet with Norma Winstone)	200
72	Argo ZDA 153	COLD MOUNTAIN (LP, as Michael Garrick Trio)	300
72	Argo ZDA 154	HOME STRETCH BLUES (LP, as Michael Garrick Band with Norma Winstone)	400
73	Impulse AS 49	ILLUMINATION (LP, as Michael Garrick Sextet)	200
74	Argo ZDA 163	TROPPO (LP)	200
81	Hep Records HEP2011	YOU'VE CHANGED (LP)	20
07	Trunk JBH 022 LP	MOONSCAPE (LP, reissue 500 only)	50
11	Trunk JBH 041 LP	RISING STARS (LP, with Shake Keane, 750 only)	20
13	Gearbox GB 1517	PRELUDE TO HEART IS A LOTUS (LP)	20

(see also Norma Winstone, Joe Harriott, Garrick's Fairground, Shake Keane)

GARRICK'S FAIRGROUND
71	Argo AFW 105	Epiphany/Blessed Are The Peacemakers	20
72	Argo ZAGF 1	MR. SMITH'S APOCALYPSE (LP)	70

(see also Michael Garrick)

FREDDIE GARRITY
68	Columbia DB 8348	Little Red Donkey/So Many Different Ways	7
74	Bus Stop BUS 1017	Hello Kids/It's Good For You	6
74	Bus Stop BUS 1022	The Chicken Song/Pooh Pooh Pooh	6
74	Bus Stop BUSLP 5002	LITTLE BIG TIME (LP)	15

(see also Freddie & Dreamers)

ROBIN GARSIDE & PAUL GOUGH
77	Northern Sound NSR 01	SEA SONGS (LP)	15

MORT GARSON
69	A & M AMLS 960	ELECTRIC HAIRPIECES (LP)	20

GARUDA
77	EMI EMC 3174	GARUDA (LP)	50

GUY GARVEY
15	Fiction 4758702	COURTING THE SQUALL (LP, lenticular sleeve)	25
15	Fiction 4758702	COURTING THE SQUALL (LP, signed)	30

REX GARVIN & MIGHTY CRAVERS
66	Atlantic 584 028	Sock It To 'Em J.B. (Parts 1 & 2)	25
67	Atlantic 584 097	I Gotta Go Now (Up On The Floor)/Believe It Or Not	25

SAM GARY
56	Esquire 32 017	SAM GARY SINGS (LP)	20

GARY & ARIELS
64	Fontana TF 476	Say You Love Me/Town Girl	15

(see also Garry Mills)

GARY & STU
72	Carnaby 6151 003	Sweet White Dove/Good Lady Fair	8
72	Carnaby 6302 012	HARLAN FARE (LP, white label with 'crab' logo)	100

(see also Koobas, March Hare)

GAS
80	Polydor POSP 192	It Shows In Your Face/Tomorrow (p/s)	15
81	Polydor POSP 264	Ignore Me/Do It, Don't Tell Me (p/s)	15
81	Polydor POSP 296	Treatment/That's It (p/s)	10
81	Polydor POSP 344	The Finger/Knock It Down (p/s)	18
82	Polydor POSP 411	Breathless/Heartache/Hostage (p/s)	7
81	Polydor POLE 1052	EMOTIONAL WARFARE (LP)	15
83	Good Vibrations GAS LP 1	FROM THE CRADLE TO THE GRAVE (LP)	15

GASKIN
81	Rondelet ROUND 7	I'm No Fool/Sweet Dream Maker (p/s)	25
82	Rondelet ROUND 21	Mony Mony/Queen Of Hams (p/s)	18
81	Rondelet ABOUT 4	END OF THE WORLD (LP, gatefold sleeve)	25
82	Rondelet ABOUT 8	NO WAY OUT (LP, with inner)	20

GASLIGHT
69	Jay Boy BOY 17	Move/And So To Sleep	18
70	SDE 32732	GASLIGHT (2-LP, private pressing, gatefold sleeve with inserts, 2nd disc by Gaslight Choir)	50

GASLIGHT ANTHEM

09	Side One Dummy SD 13287	Great Expectations/Miles Davis & The Cool (Acoustic) (p/s)	8
12	Mercury B0016941-01	HANDWRITTEN (LP, blue vinyl and free blue vinyl 7")	20

GAS MASK
71	Polydor 2383 068	THEIR FIRST ALBUM (LP)	20

GASOLIN
71	CBS 64685	GASOLIN (LP, gatefold sleeve, orange/black label)	50
72	CBS 65229	2 (LP, gatefold sleeve, orange/black label)	40
73	CBS 65798	3 (LP, orange label)	30
75	Epic SEPC 81436	WHAT A LEMON (LP, yellow/black label)	40

GASOLINE BAND
72	Cube HIFLY 9	GASOLINE BAND (LP, cube label)	200

GASP
79	Storm SR 028	Gaz's Boots/Jimmy The Fish (no p/s)	20

GASPAR NETSCHER ENSEMBLE
68	Pye 7N 17556	Get Out Of My Bed Darling/Until You're Here Beside Me	8

GASS COMPANY
68	President PT 170	Everybody Needs Love/Nightmare	60

(see also Wake)

GASS (1)
65	Parlophone R 5344	One Of These Days/I Don't Know Why	30
66	Parlophone R 5456	The New Breed/In The City	60
67	CBS 202647	Dream Baby (How Long Must I Dream?)/Jitterbug Sid	30
71	Polydor 2058 147	Something's Got To Change Your Ways/Mr Banana	10
70	Polydor 2383 022	JUJU (LP, featuring Peter Green)	150
70	Polydor 2383 022	JUJU (LP, featuring Peter Green, alternative sleeve, black/gold with Gass logo on front and drawing on rear, record has same matrix as other issue and red Polydor labels)	250
71	Polydor 2383 035	CATCH MY SOUL - THE ROCK-OTHELLO (LP, cast recording featuring Gass)	30

(see also Hummingbird, Humble Pie, Streetwalkers, Peter Green)

GASS (2)
97	Public Demand PPDT 28	Dark (2as1 & MJ Cole)/(Nocturnal Mix)/(Mascara Mix) (12")	30

GAS WORKS
73	Regal Zonophone RZ 3075	Standing Stiff/Keep On Rolling	6
73	Regal Zonophone RZ 3080	God's Great Spaceship/Cider With Rosie	6
73	Regal Zono. SRLZ 1036	GAS WORKS (LP)	25

SID GATELEY
74	Ra 5015	Dance To The Slosh/Beautiful Sunday (insert)	6
72	Ra 5009	The Farmers Wife/Worlds Fare Polka (with insert)	8

DAVID GATES
60	Top Rank JAR 504	The Happiest Man Alive/The Road That Leads To Love	30

(see also Bread)

PEARLY GATES
70	MCA MU 1109	Free/Carole's Epic Song	12
75	RCA PD 2605	Make It My Business/You're The One For Me	10

(see also Flirtations, Gypsies)

RAY GATES
66	Decca F 12502	It's Such A Shame/Have You Ever Had The Blues	40

GATES OF EDEN
66	Pye 7N 17195	Too Much On My Mind/I'm Warning You	25
67	Pye 7N 17252	In Your Love/Snoopy Versus The Red Baron	12
67	Pye 7N 17278	1 To 7/Hey Now	30

GATEWAY
18	Super Disco Edits SDE 32	Show Is Over Part 1/Part 2 (demo only, release cancelled)	25

GATHERERS
73	Duke DU 153	Words Of My Mouth/UPSETTERS: Version	110

GATOR CREEK
71	Mercury 6052 058	Danny's Song/Take A Look	15
71	Mercury 6338 035	GATOR CREEK (LP)	15

DICK GAUGHAN
72	Trailer LER 2072	NO MORE FOREVER (LP, red label)	25
76	Rubber RUB 019	FIVE HAND REEL (LP)	20
78	Topic 12TS384	GAUGHAN (LP, tan label)	15
81	Topic 12TS419	HANDFUL OF EARTH (LP)	15

GEORGES GAVARENTZ
69	Philips SBL 7898	THEY CAME TO ROB LAS VEGAS (LP, soundtrack)	40

JIMMY GAVIN
57	London HLU 8478	I Sit In My Window/Lonely Chair	80

JOHNNY GAVOTTE
60	Parlophone R 4631	It's Not Too Late/Can't Forget	10

ELAINE GAY
54	Parlophone MSP 6140	Love/Instantly	12

MAC GAYDEN
73	EMI EMA 760	McGAVOCK GAYDEN (LP)	50

(see also Area Code 615)

MARVIN GAYE
63	Oriole CBA 1803	Stubborn Kind Of Fellow/It Hurt Me Too	100
63	Oriole CBA 1803	Stubborn Kind Of Fellow/It Hurt Me Too (DJ Copy)	200
63	Oriole CBA 1846	Pride And Joy/One Of These Days	100
63	Oriole CBA 1846	Pride And Joy/One Of These Days (DJ Copy)	200
63	Stateside SS 243	Can I Get A Witness?/I'm Crazy 'Bout My Baby	90
63	Stateside SS 243	Can I Get A Witness?/I'm Crazy 'Bout My Baby (DJ Copy)	100

Marvin GAYE & TAMMI TERRELL

MINT VALUE £

64	Stateside SS 284	You're A Wonderful One/When I'm Alone I Cry	50
64	Stateside SS 284	You're A Wonderful One/When I'm Alone I Cry (DJ Copy)	100
64	Stateside SS 326	Try It Baby/If My Heart Could Sing	40
64	Stateside SS 326	Try It Baby/If My Heart Could Sing (DJ Copy)	70
64	Stateside SS 360	How Sweet It Is (To Be Loved By You)/Forever	30
64	Stateside SS 360	How Sweet It Is (To Be Loved By You)/Forever (DJ Copy)	90
65	Tamla Motown TMG 510	I'll Be Doggone/You've Been A Long Time Coming	40
65	Tamla Motown TMG 510	I'll Be Doggone/You've Been A Long Time Coming (DJ Copy)	120
65	Tamla Motown TMG 524	Pretty Little Baby/Now That You've Won Me	40
65	Tamla Motown TMG 524	Pretty Little Baby/Now That You've Won Me (DJ Copy)	90
65	Tamla Motown TMG 539	Ain't That Peculiar?/She's Got To Be Real	30
65	Tamla Motown TMG 539	Ain't That Peculiar?/She's Got To Be Real (DJ Copy)	90
66	Tamla Motown TMG 552	One More Heartache/When I Had Your Love	30
66	Tamla Motown TMG 552	One More Heartache/When I Had Your Love (DJ Copy)	80
66	Tamla Motown TMG 563	Take This Heart Of Mine/Need Your Lovin' (Want You Back)	35
66	Tamla Motown TMG 563	Take This Heart Of Mine/Need Your Lovin' (Want You Back) (DJ Copy)	80
66	Tamla Motown TMG 574	Little Darling (I Need You)/Hey Diddle Diddle	35
66	Tamla Motown TMG 574	Little Darlin' (I Need You)/Hey Diddle Diddle (DJ Copy)	120
67	Tamla Motown TMG 618	Your Unchanging Love/I'll Take Care Of You	20
67	Tamla Motown TMG 618	Your Unchanging Love/I'll Take Care Of You (DJ Copy)	50
68	Tamla Motown TMG 640	You/Change What You Can	20
68	Tamla Motown TMG 640	You/Change What You Can (DJ Copy)	40
68	Tamla Motown TMG 676	Chained/At Last (I Found A Love)	18
69	Tamla Motown TMG 686	I Heard It Through The Grapevine/Need Somebody	7
69	Tamla Motown TMG 686	I Heard It Through The Grapevine/Need Somebody (DJ Copy)	30
69	Tamla Motown TMG 705	Too Busy Thinking 'Bout My Baby/Wherever I Lay My Hat	7
69	Tamla Motown TMG 718	That's The Way Love Is/Gonna Keep On Tryin' Till I Win Your Love	8
70	Tamla Motown TMG 734	Abraham, Martin And John/How Can I Forget?	7
70	Tamla Motown TMG 734	Abraham, Martin And John/How Can I Forget? (DJ Copy)	30
71	Tamla Motown TMG 775	What's Going On?/God Is Love	8
71	Tamla Motown TMG 775	What's Going On/God Is Love (DJ Copy)	40
71	Tamla Motown TMG 796	Save The Children/Little Darling (I Need You)	8
72	Tamla Motown TMG 802	Mercy Mercy Me (The Ecology)/Sad Tomorrows	6
72	Tamla Motown TMG 817	Inner City Blues (Make Me Wanna Holler)/Wholly Holy	10
73	Tamla Motown TMG 846	Trouble Man/Don't Mess With Mister 'T'	12
73	Tamla Motown TMG 868	Let's Get It On/I Wish It Would Rain (DJ Copy)	40
74	Tamla Motown TMG 882	Come Get To This/Distant Lover	15
76	Tamla Motown TMG 1035	After The Dance Feel My Love Inside	7
76	Tamla Motown TMG 1026	I Want You/I Want You (Instrumental)	6
77	Tamla Motown TMG 1069	Got To Give It Up (Part 1)/(Part 2)	6
78	Tamla Motown 12TMG 1138	A Funky Space Reincarnation/Got To Give It Up (12", p/s)	10
79	Tamla Motown TMG 1168	Ego Tripping Out/(Instrumental) (p/s)	7
79	Tamla Motown 12TMG 1168	Ego Tripping Out/What's Going On/What's Happening Brother (12")	10
81	Tamla Motown 12TMG 1232	Heavy Love Affair/Far Cry (12")	10
86	Tamla Motown ZB 40757	Lonely Lover/The World Is Rated X (p/s)	25
94	Tamla Motoen TMG 1426	Lucky Lucky Me (Radio Edit)/(Pure Soul Mix) (p/s)	15
96	Chriskings 81156 DJ	This Love Starved Heart Of Mine/This Love Starved Heart Of Mine (promo, 500 only)	20
66	Tamla Motown TME 2016	MARVIN GAYE (EP)	60
67	Tamla Motown TME 2019	ORIGINALS FROM MARVIN GAYE (EP)	50
64	Stateside SL 10100	MARVIN GAYE (LP)	200
65	Tamla Motown TML 11004	HOW SWEET IT IS TO BE LOVED BY YOU (LP)	60
65	Tamla Motown TML 11015	HELLO BROADWAY (LP)	80
66	Tamla Motown TML 11022	A TRIBUTE TO THE GREAT NAT KING COLE (LP, mono)	65
66	Tamla Motown STML 11022	A TRIBUTE TO THE GREAT NAT KING COLE (LP, stereo)	80
66	Tamla Motown TML 11033	MOODS OF MARVIN GAYE (LP, mono)	50
66	Tamla Motown STML 11033	MOODS OF MARVIN GAYE (LP, stereo)	60
68	Tamla Motown TML 11065	MARVIN GAYE'S GREATEST HITS (LP, mono)	20
68	Tamla Motown STML 11065	MARVIN GAYE'S GREATEST HITS (LP, stereo)	20
69	Tamla Motown (S)TML 11091	IN THE GROOVE (LP, mono/stereo)	30
69	Tamla Motown (S)TML 1111	M.P.G. (LP, mono/stereo)	25
69	Tamla Motown TML 11123	MARVIN GAYE AND HIS GIRLS (LP, mono, with T. Terrell, M. Wells & K. Weston)	25
69	Tamla Motown STML 11123	MARVIN GAYE AND HIS GIRLS (LP, stereo, with T. Terrell, M. Wells & K. Weston)	22
70	Tamla Motown TML 11136	THAT'S THE WAY LOVE IS (LP, mono)	30
70	Tamla Motown STML 11136	THAT'S THE WAY LOVE IS (LP, stereo)	20
71	Tamla Motown STML 11190	WHAT'S GOING ON? (LP, textured sleeve A1/B1 matrixes, with lyric sheet)	40
73	Tamla Motown STMA 8013	LET'S GET IT ON (LP, gatefold)	30
73	Tamla Motoen STML 11225	TROUBLE MAN (LP, soundtrack)	20
74	Tamla Motown STMA 8018	MARVIN GAYE LIVE! (LP, gatefold)	15
76	Tamla Motown STML 12025	I WANT YOU (LP)	20
78	Tamla Motown TMSP 6008	HERE, MY DEAR (2-LP)	25
81	Tamla Motown STML 12149	IN OUR LIFETIME (LP)	15
82	CBS 85977	MIDNIGHT LOVE (LP, insert)	15

MARVIN GAYE & TAMMI TERRELL

67	Tamla Motown TMG 611	Ain't No Mountain High Enough/Give A Little Love	30
67	Tamla Motown TMG 611	Ain't No Mountain High Enough/Give A Little Love (DJ Copy)	80
67	Tamla Motown TMG 625	Your Precious Love/Hold Me Oh My Darling	25
67	Tamla Motown TMG 625	Your Precious Love/Hold Me Oh My Darling (DJ Copy)	50
67	Tamla Motown TMG 635	If I Could Build My Whole World Around You/If This World Were Mine	15

Marvin GAYE & MARY WELLS

MINT VALUE £

67	Tamla Motown TMG 635	If I Could Build My Whole World Around You/If This World Were Mine (DJ Copy)	30
68	Tamla Motown TMG 655	Ain't Nothin' Like The Real Thing/Little Ole Boy, Little Ole Girl	12
68	Tamla Motown TMG 655	Ain't Nothin' Like The Real Thing/Little Ole Boy, Little Ole Girl (DJ Copy)	30
68	Tamla Motown TMG 668	You're All I Need To Get By/Two Can Have A Party	8
69	Tamla Motown TMG 681	You Ain't Livin' Till You're Lovin'/Oh How I'd Miss You	12
69	Tamla Motown TMG 697	Good Lovin' Ain't Easy To Come By/Satisfied Feelin'	8
69	Tamla Motown TMG 715	The Onion Song/I Can't Believe You Love Me	6
69	Tamla Motown TMG 715	The Onion Song/I Can't Believe You Love Me (demo in p/s)	50
68	T. Motown TML 11062	UNITED (LP, mono)	40
68	T. Motown STML 11062	UNITED (LP, stereo)	45
68	T. Motown (S)TML 11084	YOU'RE ALL I NEED (LP, mono/stereo)	40
70	T. Motown TML 11132	EASY (LP, mono)	20
70	T. Motown STML 11132	EASY (LP, stereo)	18
70	T. Motown (S)TML 11153	GREATEST HITS (LP)	15

MARVIN GAYE & MARY WELLS

64	Stateside SS 316	Once Upon A Time/What's The Matter With You, Baby?	35
64	Stateside SS 316	Once Upon A Time/What's The Matter With You, Baby? (DJ Copy)	80
64	Stateside SL 10197	TOGETHER (LP)	75

MARVIN GAYE & KIM WESTON

64	Stateside SS 363	What Good Am I Without You?/I Want You Around	40
64	Stateside SS 363	What Good Am I Without You?/I Want You Around (DJ Copy)	80
67	Tamla Motown TMG 590	It Takes Two/It's Got To Be A Miracle (This Thing Called Love)	12
67	Tamla Motown TMG 590	It Takes Two/It's Got To Be A Miracle (This Thing Called Love) (DJ Copy)	70
67	T. Motown TML 11049	TAKE TWO (LP, mono)	40
67	T. Motown STML 11049	TAKE TWO (LP, stereo)	45

(see also Diana Ross, Tammi Terrell, Mary Wells, Kim Weston)

GAYLADS

64	R&B JB 159	There'll Come A Day/BILLY COOKE: Iron Bar	50
64	R&B JB 165	What Is Wrong With Me?/Whap Whap	60
66	Island WI 281	Goodbye Daddy/Your Eyes	30
66	Island WI 291	You Never Leave Him/Message To My Girl	35
66	Island WI 3002	Stop Making Love/They Call Her Dawn	40
66	Doctor Bird DB 1014	Lady With The Red Dress/Dinner For Two	25
66	Doctor Bird DB 1031	You Should Never Do That/WINSTON STEWART: I Don't Know Why I Love You	25
66	Rymska RA 104	You Should Never Do That/TECHNIQUES: So Many Times	35
67	Island WI 3022	Don't Say No/SONNY BURKE: You Rule My Heart	40
67	Island WI 3025	You No Good Girl/Yes Girl	35
67	Studio One SO 2002	Tears From My Eyes/Never Let Your Country Down	125
67	Studio One SO 2009	Won't You Come Home (actually DELROY WILSON)/PETER & HORTENSE : I've Been Lonely	70
67	Studio One SO 2013	I Am Going To Cool It (actually by Little Roy)/ MELODIANS: Let's Join Together	60
67	Studio One SO 2017	Love Me With All Your Heart/I Don't Care	45
67	Studio One SO 2021	IF You Knew/Festival Day	80
67	Rio R 125	Put On Your Style/SOUL BROTHERS: Soul Serenade	65
68	Blue Cat BS 110	Go Away/SOUL VENDORS: Julie On My Mind	50
68	Doctor Bird DB 1124	It's Hard To Confess/I Need Your Loving	40
68	Doctor Bird DB 1145	She Want It/Joy In The Morning	45
68	Fab FAB 62	Looking For A Girl/Aren't You The Guy	100
68	Hi Note HS 001	A B C Rocksteady/LESLIE BUTLER & COUNT OSSIE: Soul Drums	35
69	Trojan TR 688	You Had Your Chance/Wha' She Do Now	12
69	Upsetter US 323	The Same Things/I Wear My Slanders	40
70	Trojan TR 7703	There's A Fire/Last Time	8
70	Trojan TR 7738	That's What Love Will Do/This Time I Won't Hurt You	10
70	Trojan TR 7743	Young, Gifted And Black/BEVERLEY'S ALLSTARS: Moon Glow	15
70	Trojan TR 7763	Tell The Children The Truth/Something Is Wrong Somewhere	8
70	Trojan TR 7771	Soul Sister/BEVERLEY'S ALLSTARS: Version	15
70	Trojan TR 7782	It's All In The Game/BEVERLEY'S ALLSTARS: Version II	8
70	Trojan TR 7799	Fire And Rain/Cold And Lonely Night	10
71	Ackee AC 141	Accept My Apologies (actually by B.B. Seaton & Ken Boothe)/ My Version (actually by Conscious Minds)	10
71	Big BG 319	Can't Hide The Feeling/RUPIE EDWARDS ALLSTARS: Version	7
71	Camel CA 79	Seven In One Medley (Parts 1 & 2)	6
71	Summit SUM 8514	My Jamaican Girl/BEVERLEY'S ALLSTARS: Version	6
71	Bullet BU 462	My Love/Stranger Love	7
74	Dip DL 5009	You Made A Mistake/Shower Of Blessings	6
13	Summit THB 7024	Baby I'll Be Yours/Tribute To Prince Ruff	8
67	Coxsone CSL 8005	ROCKSTEADY (LP)	400
67	Coxsone CSL 8006	SUNSHINE IS GOLDEN (LP)	300
79	Ballistic UAG 30236	UNDERSTANDING (LP)	15

(see also Gaylords, Rockstones, Delano Stewart, Ken Boothe, B.B. Seaton, Brent Dowe, Dobby Dobson, Jackie Mittoo, Heptones, Clarendonians, Soul Vendors)

BONNIE GAYLE

75	Treble C CCC 008	Mellow Up Yourself/Version	20
76	Love LOV 0024	How Many Strong/CONSCIOUS MINDS: Version	50

VINLEY GAYLE

64	Black Swan WI 453	Go-Go/BABA BROOKS: Take Five	30

GAYLET(T)S

68	Island WI 3129	Silent River Runs Deep/You're Kind Of Man	45
68	Island WI 3141	I Like Your World/Lonely Feeling	25
68	Big Shot BI 502	If You Can't Be Good/Something About My Man	12

GAYLORDS (DOMINICA)

MINT VALUE £

69	Big Shot BI 516	Son-Of-A-Preacher-Man/That's How Strong My Love Is	18
70	London HLJ 10302	Son-Of-A-Preacher-Man/I Like Your World	7

(see also Judy Mowatt)

GAYLORDS (DOMINICA)
75	Cosmos C.S.P. 1001	I Man Suffering/Dread Lucks Version	200

GAYLORDS (JAMAICA)
66	Island WI 269	Chipmunk Ska/What Is Wrong? (both actually by Gaylads)	25

(see also Gaylads)

GAYLORDS (U.K.)
66	Columbia DB 7805	He's A Good Face But He's Down And Out/You Know It Too	15

(see also Dean Ford & Gaylords, Marmalade)

WILTON 'BOGEY' GAYNAIR QUARTET
61	Tempo EXA 103	BLUE BOGEY VOLUME ONE (EP)	60
59	Tempo TAP 25	BLUE BOGEY (LP)	500
83	Jasmine JASM 2016	BLUE BOGEY (LP, reissue)	20

GAYNOR (JUNIOR ENGLISH) & ERROL (DUNKLEY)
65	Blue Beat BB 286	My Queen/ROLAND ALPHONSO: Roland Plays Prince (B-side actually "Hanging The Beam" by Skatalites)	60

(see also Errol Dunkley)

GLORIA GAYNOR
78	Polydor 2066922	For The First Time In My Life/This Love Affair	20
75	MGM 2315 321	NEVER CAN SAY GOODBYE (LP)	15

MITZI GAYNOR
59	Top Rank JAR 258	Happy Anniversary/Play For Keeps	6
60	Top Rank JAR 289	I Don't Regret A Thing/The Touch Of Time	6
58	HMV 7EG 8460	MITZI (EP)	10

ROSEMARY GAYNOR
55	Columbia SCM 5196	Ain't That A Shame/A Happy Song	15

PAUL GAYTEN
57	London HL 8503	Yo, Yo, Walk/TUNE WEAVERS: Happy Happy Birthday Baby	80
59	London HLM 8998	The Hunch/Hot Cross Buns	50

GAYTONES (JAMAICA)
70	High Note HS 037	Target (actually "Musical Fight" by Crashers)/PATSY: Find Someone (song actually "True Love")	30
70	High Note HS 048	Ten To One/Another Version	12
71	High Note HS 055	Heart Of The Knights/One Toke Over The Line (B-side actually by Stranger & Gladdy)	15
71	Green Door GD 4016	Jamaican Hilite (Parts 1 & 2)	8
73	Smash SMA 2330	Blackman Kingdom Come/Swing And Dine (B-side actually by Melodians)	10
73	Action ACT 4610	Soul Makossa/Soul Makossa Part 2	12

(see also Righteous Flames, Max Romeo, Ethiopians, Jackie Brown, Jean & Gaytones, Huxbrown & Scotty, Charlie Ace, Delano Stewart, Teddy & Conquerors)

GAYTONES (U.S.)
73	Action ACT 4610	Soul Makossa/Soul Makossa (Version)	15

G BAND
76	Bell 1481	Tuna Biscuit/Don't Make Promises You Can't Keep	10

GBH
82	Clay CLAY 8	No Survivors/Self Destruct/Big Women (p/s)	8
82	Clay CLAY 11	Sick Boy/Slit Your Own Throat/Am I Dead Yet? (p/s)	8
82	Clay CLAY 16	Give Me Fire/Mantrap (p/s)	8
83	Clay CLAY 22	Catch 23/Hellhole (p/s)	8
84	Clay CLAY 36	Do What You Do/Four Men (p/s)	8
81	Clay PLATE 3	LEATHER, BRISTLES, STUDS AND ACNE (LP)	18
82	Clay CLAYLP 4	CITY BABY ATTACKED BY RATS (LP)	20

G-CLEFS
56	Columbia DB 3851	Ka-Ding Dong/Darla, My Darlin'	750
56	Columbia DB 3851	Ka-Ding Dong/Darla, My Darlin' (78 rpm)	35
62	London HLU 9530	A Girl Has To Know/(There Never Was A Dog Like) Dad	10
62	London HLU 9563	Make Up Your Mind/Call Me Away	15

GEDDES AXE
80	ACS ACS 1	Return Of The Gods/Wildfire/Aftermath (p/s, with insert)	20
81	Steel City AXE 1	Sharpen Your Wits/Rock 'N' Roll (p/s)	50

MICKEY GEE
77	Sonet SON 2124	Dr Livingstone/Jodi	6

RON GEESIN
65	RRG 319/320	RON GEESIN (EP, handmade p/s, 100 only)	100
67	Transatlantic (S)TRA 161	A RAISE OF EYEBROWS (LP)	50
72	KPM KPM 1102	ELECTROSOUND (LP, library issue, 1,000 only)	60
73	Ron Geesin RON 28	AS HE STANDS (LP)	30
75	KPM KPM 1154	ELECTROSOUND VOL. 2 (LP, library issue, 1,000 only)	60
75	Ron Geesin RON 31	PATRUNS (LP)	15
77	Ron Geesin RON 323	RIGHT THROUGH (LP)	18
77	KPM KPM 1201	ATMOSPHERES (LP, library issue, 1,000 only)	30
08	Glo Spot 1102	ELECTROSOUND (LP, reissue, different sleeve art, blue vinyl)	20

(see also Bridget St. John, Pink Floyd, Original Downtown Syncopators, Amory Kane)

RON GEESIN & ROGER WATERS
70	Harvest SHSP 4008	MUSIC FROM THE BODY (LP, soundtrack; green labels with Waters/Geesin photos)	50
87	Harvest SHSP 4008	MUSIC FROM THE BODY (LP, reissue, black label, barcode on rear of sleeve)	15

(see also Roger Waters, Pink Floyd)

AVIV GEFFEN
09	2006 Records 012 LP	AVIV GEFFEN (LP)	30

Max GELDRAY

MINT VALUE £

MAX GELDRAY
- 59 Parlophone GEP 8764   GOON WITH THE WIND (EP) 10

HERB GELLER QUARTET
- 56 London RE-U 1067   SENSATIONAL SAX OF HERB GELLER (EP) 15

HERB GELLER
- 75 Atlantic SD 1681   RHYME & REASON (LP) 25

GEM
- 81 SRTS 81 CUS 1147   Toast Of The Town/Change In The Air (p/s) 8

GEMAGE
- 80 Private pressing BGA 1   Story So Far/Bring Me Death (no p/s) 50

GEMINI (PORTUGAL)
- 78 Philips 6031 070   Dal-Li-Dou (Falling In Love)/Dal-Li-Dou 12

GEMINI (U.K.) (1)
- 65 Columbia DB 7238   Space Walk/Goodbye Joe (demos may credit the 'Original Tornados') 50

(see also Tornados)

GEMINI (U.K.) (2)
- 69 President PT 257   Never Say Die/Something Special 6

GEMINI (U.K.) (3)
- 81 Airship AP 345   COUNTER BALANCE (LP) 60

GEMINI (4)
- 97 Peacefrog PF 061   HIBERNATION EP (12") 70
- 97 NRK 003   REVOLUTION EP (12", p/s) 25
- 97 Peacefrog PF 065   ON THE NORTH STAR WITH GEMINI EP (12") 25
- 98 Cyclo CYC 005.6   TAKE YOUR TIME EP (12") 15
- 98 Classic CMG 81   IN MY HEAD EP (12") 35
- 97 Substance SUB 4844.1   IN NEUTRAL (2-LP) 30
- 97 Peacefrog PF 070   IN AND OUT OF FOG AND LIGHTS (2-LP) 50
- 99 Cyclo CYC 005.1   THE MUSIC HALL (LP as 2 x 12") 15
- 16 Anothertheday 004AD   IMAGINE-A-NATION (LP, reissue as 2 x 12") 20
- 17 Peacefrog PF 070   IN AND OUT OF FOG AND LIGHTS (2-LP, reissue) 20

GENE
- 94 Costermonger COST 1   For The Dead/Child's Body (p/s, 1,994 numbered copies only) 8
- 96 Costermonger GENE 1LP   OLYMPIAN (LP) 50
- 96 Polydor GENE 2LP   TO SEE THE LIGHTS (2-LP) 50
- 97 Polydor GENELP 3   DRAWN TO THE DEEP END (2-LP) 60
- 99 Polydor GENELP 4   REVELATIONS (LP, with booklet) 60

GENE & GARY
- 09 Kent 6T 26   Baby Without You/PARAMOUNT FOUR: Sorry Ain't The Word 20

GENE & DEBBE
- 67 London HLE 10165   Go With Me/Torch I Carry 6
- 68 London HLE 10179   Playboy/I'll Come Running 10
- 68 London HLE 10203   Lovin' Season/Love Will Give Us Wings 6

GENE & EUNICE
- 56 Vogue V 9062   I Gotta Go Home/Have You Changed Your Mind? 200
- 56 Vogue V 9062   I Gotta Go Home/Have You Changed Your Mind? (78) 40
- 57 Vogue V 9066   Move It Over, Baby/This Is My Story 150
- 57 Vogue V 9066   Move It Over, Baby/This Is My Story (78) 40
- 57 Vogue V 9071   Let's Get Together/I'm So In Love With You 150
- 57 Vogue V 9071   Let's Get Together/I'm So In Love With You (78) 30
- 57 Vogue V 9083   Doodle Doodle Doo/Don't Treat Me This Way 150
- 57 Vogue V 9083   Doodle Doodle Doo/Don't Treat Me This Way (78) 30
- 58 Vogue V 9106   I Mean Love/The Angels Gave You To Me 150
- 58 Vogue V 9106   I Mean Love/The Angels Gave You To Me (78) 30
- 58 Vogue V 9126   Strange World/The Vow 50

(The above 45s were originally issued with triangular centres, later issues with round centres are worth about half the values listed.)

- 58 Vogue V 9126   Strange World/The Vow (78) 30
- 59 Vogue V 9136   Bom Bom Lulu/Hi Diddle Diddle 100
- 59 Vogue V 9136   Bom Bom Lulu/Hi Diddle Diddle (78) 40
- 59 London HL 8956   Poco-Loco/Go-On Kokomo 50
- 59 London HL 8956   Poco-Loco/Go-On Kokomo (78) 40

GENE & GENTS
- 68 Pye 7N 17532   C'mon Everybody/Hound Dog 10

GENE LOVES JEZEBEL
- 82 Situation 2 SIT 18T   Shavin' My Neck/Sun & Insanity/Machismo/Glad To Be Alive (12", p/s) ... 15
- 82 Situation 2 SIT 20   Screaming (For Emaline)/So Young (Heave Hard, Heave Ho) (p/s) 8

GENERAL DOGGIE & TENOR SAW
- 88 Night Life Posse NP 001   Chill Out Chill Out/Cool Out Dub/To Love Somebody/To Love Ya This Dub (12") 10

(see also Tenor Saw)

GENERAL HAVOC
- 91 Chapati Heat BIRD 1   Moonshine/Vacuum Cleaner/Another Cup Of Tea Arch Deacon? 40

GENERAL JOHNSON
- 73 Invictus INV 531   Only Time Will Tell/Only Time Will Tell (Instrumental Version) 10
- 76 Arista 45   All In The Family/Ready Willing And Able 7

GENERAL LEVY
- 90 Musik Street MS 005   You Can't Hurry Love (with Junior Dunn)/JAZWAD: You Can't Hurry Dub (12", red or blue labels) 70
- 93 Ffrr/Fashion F214   Monkey Man (Fashion Radio Edit)/Mad Them (p/s) 20
- 93 Ffrr/Fashion FX 214   WICKEDER GENERAL EP (12", p/s) 25
- 92 Fashion FADLP 024   THE WICKEDER GENERAL (LP) 40

(see also M-Beat)

MIKEY GENERAL
85	Jagan Intl. J.I. 001	Bag A Respect/Yard A Yard (12")	35
85	Fashion FAD 043	Sound Doctor/Jump And Shout (12")	10

GENERAL T
88	Realistic RR09	Nah Tek De Coke/Version (12")	30

GENERATION
79	Grapevine GRP 131	Hold On/The Lonely Sea (reissue)	8

GENERATION GAP
69	Pye 7N 17845	She's Coming Home/Reach The Top	8
70	Pye 7N 17979	Any Old Time You're Lonely And Sad/Rainbows 'N' Sorrows	8

GENERATION X
77	GX 2	Perfect Hits 2: Rock On/No No No/Gimmie Some Truth/From The Heart (no p/s)	15
77	GX 1	Perfect Hits: Your Generation/Save My Life/Ready Steady Go (no p/s)	15
77	GX 101	Your Generation/Listen! (white label test pressing, official bootleg sold at gigs, no p/s)	100
77	Chrysalis CHS 2165	Your Generation/Day By Day (p/s, original copies with 'A' on label with band credits on front)	6
77	Chrysalis CHS 2165	Your Generation/Day By Day (sleeve only, unissued, featuring 'pre-peroxide' Billy Idol; 4 copies known to exist)	1000
77	Chrysalis CHS 2189	Wild Youth/Wild Dub (Version) (p/s, mispressing, plays "No No No", B-side matrix: CHS 2189 B/1)	40
79	Chrysalis CHS(A) 2261	King Rocker/Gimme Some Truth (pink vinyl, Tony James p/s)	10
79	Chrysalis CHS(B) 2261	King Rocker/Gimme Some Truth (red vinyl, Billy Idol p/s)	10
79	Chrysalis CHS(C) 2261	King Rocker/Gimme Some Truth (yellow vinyl, Mark Laff p/s)	10
79	Chrysalis CHS(D) 2261	King Rocker/Gimme Some Truth (orange vinyl, Bob Andrews p/s)	10
79	Chrysalis CHS 2261	King Rocker/Gimme Some Truth (black vinyl, Bob Andrews p/s)	10
79	Chrysalis CHS 2310	Valley Of The Dolls/Shakin' All Over (brownish vinyl, p/s)	6
79	Chrysalis CHS 2310	Valley Of The Dolls/Shakin' All Over (multi-coloured vinyl, p/s)	50
79	Chrysalis CHS 2330	Friday's Angels/Trying For Kicks/This Heat (p/s, black vinyl)	15
81	Chrysalis CHS 2488	Dancing With Myself/Untouchables/King Rocker/Rock On (as Gen X, p/s, on clear vinyl)	8
78	Chrysalis CHR 1169	GENERATION X (LP, with rare obi at bottom of sleeve)	40
78	Chrysalis CHR 1169	GENERATION X (LP)	25
79	Chrysalis CHR 1193	VALLEY OF THE DOLLS (LP, inner)	15

(see also Billy Idol, Sigue Sigue Sputnik, Empire, Westworld)

GENESIS (1)
SINGLES
68	Decca F 12735	The Silent Sun/That's Me	450
68	Decca F 12735	The Silent Sun/That's Me (promo copy)	500
68	Decca F 12775	A Winter's Tale/One Eyed Hound	600
68	Decca F 12775	A Winter's Tale/One Eyed Hound (promo copy, push out centre)	750
68	Decca F 12775	A Winter's Tale/One Eyed Hound (promo copy, solid centre)	950
68	London F12775	A Winter's Tale/One Eyed Hound (export promo single)	2000
69	Decca F 12949	Where The Sour Turns To Sweet/In Hiding	750
69	Decca F 12949	Where The Sour Turns To Sweet/In Hiding (promo copy)	600
70	Charisma GS 1/2	Looking For Someone/Visions Of Angels (promo only, push out centre)	900
70	Charisma GS 1/2	Looking For Someone/Visions Of Angels (promo only, solid centre)	1200
71	Charisma CB 152	The Knife (Parts 1 & 2) (in p/s, push out or solid)	600
71	Charisma CB 152	The Knife (Parts 1 & 2, push out or solid centre)	100
72	Charisma CB 181	Happy The Man/Seven Stones (promo copy, push out centre 'DJ Not For Sale' on both labels or A dise only)	150
72	Charisma CB 181	Happy The Man/Seven Stones (push out or solid centre, JOHN ANTHONY in capitals)	125
72	Charisma CB 181	Happy The Man/Seven Stones (p/s, solid or push out centre, with JOHN ANTHONY in capitals)	500
73	Charisma (no cat. no.)	Twilight Alehouse (1-sided flexidisc free with Zig Zag)	35
73	Charisma (no cat. no.)	Twilight Alehouse (1-sided flexidisc free with Zig Zag & later via fan club, without magazine)	20
73	Charisma (no cat. no.)	Twilight Alehouse (black vinyl, white label test pressings)	70
73	Charisma (no cat. no.)	Twilight Alehouse (1-sided flexidisc free via fan club, with letter, sticker, poster and Genesis "revolver")	80
74	Charisma CB 224	I Know What I Like (In Your Wardrobe)/Twilight Alehouse (push out or solid centre)	8
74	Charisma CB 224	I Know What I Like (In Your Wardrobe)/Twilight Alehouse (promos with press release)	100
74	Charisma CB 238	Counting Out Time/Counting Out Time (promo, push out centre)	50
74	Charisma CB 238	Counting Out Time/Counting Out Time (promo, solid centre)	85
74	Charisma CB 238	Counting Out Time/Riding The Scree	12
74	Charisma CB 238	Counting Out Time/Counting Out Time (solid centre)	85
75	Charisma CB 251	The Carpet Crawlers/The Waiting Room (Evil Jam)	25
75	Charisma CB 251	The Carpet Crawlers/The Waiting Room (Evil Jam) (promos copies)	65
76	Charisma CB 277	A Trick Of The Tail/Ripples (purple label)	8
76	Charisma CB 251	A Trick Of The Tale/Rippels (with Fuse Music Ltd or Copyright Control, push out or solid centre)	8
78	Charisma CB 309	Follow You, Follow Me/Ballad Of Big (p/s)	6
78	Charisma CB 315	Many Too Many/The Day The Light Went Out/Vancouver (p/s)	6
82	Charisma CB 393	Man On The Corner/Submarine (blue injection labels, large centre hole)	90
82	Charisma CB 93	Man On The Corner/Submarine (p/s, green injection labels, solid centre)	25
82	Lyntone LYN 11806	The Lady Lies (live) (green flexidisc free with Flexipop mag, issue 21)	12
83	Lyntone LYN 13143	Firth Of Fifth (live edit) (flexidisc, with numbered gatefold p/s)	18
83	Virgin TATAY 1	That's All/Taking It All Too Hard (uncut picture disc)	75
83	Charisma/Virgin TATA Y-1	That's All/Taking It All Too Hard (shaped picture disc)	15
84	Charisma/Virgin CB 300	Your Own Special Way/It's Yourself (blue label reissue, push out or solid centreno p/s)	25
84	Charisma/Virgin CB 356	Turn It On Again/Behind The Lines Part 2 (blue label reissue, no p/s)	6
84	Charisma CB 356	Turn It On Again/ Behind The Lines Part 2 (blue paper label reissue)	15
84	Charisma/Virgin CB 369	Misunderstanding/Evidence Of Autumn (blue label reissue, no p/s)	20

GENESIS (2)

MINT VALUE £

86	Charisma/Virgin GENS 3	Land Of Confusion/Feeing The Fire (mispressing, B-side plays Do The Neurotic)	10
87	Virgin CDEP 1	Tonight, Tonight, Tonight (Edit)/In The Glow Of The Night/ Invisible Touch (12" Remix)/Tonight, Tonight, Tonight (CD, gatefold p/s)	40
92	Virgin GENS 10	Invisible Touch (live)/Abacab (live) (no'd gatefold p/s)	8
98	Virgin SOLO2	Live Rehearsal: Mama (live)/Calling All Stations (live)/Invisible Touch (live)/ Follow You, Follow Me (live)/Turn It On Again (live) (CD 5-track promo)	50

ALBUMS

69	Decca LK 4990	FROM GENESIS TO REVELATION (mono, with 'mono' peephole, with red/pink lyric sheet, red/silver unboxed logo)	1500
69	Decca SKL 4990	FROM GENESIS TO REVELATION (stereo, with stereo 'peephole', with lyric sheet, unboxed logo)	500
70	Decca SKL 4990	FROM GENESIS TO REVELATION (stereo, with lyric sheet, blue/silver boxed logo)	100
70	Decca KSKC 4990	FROM GENESIS TO REVELATION (tape, boxed logo)	35
70	Charisma CAS 1020	TRESPASS (1st pressing, original pink scroll label & gatefold sleeve with lyric sheet, with bolder (p) 1970)	200
70	Charisma CAS 1020	TRESPASS (2nd pressing, original pink scroll label & gatefold sleeve with lyric sheet, with less bold (p) 1970 with more spaced text)	165
71	Charisma CAS 1052	NURSERY CRYME (LP, 1st pressing, textured sleeve, original pink scroll label, gatefold sleeve)	200
72	Charisma CAS 1058	FOXTROT (LP, gatefold sleeve, large 'Mad Hatter' logo and B&C credit on label)	35
72	Charisma CAS 1058	FOXTROT (LP, gatefold sleeve, 'Mad Hatter' logo and B&C credit on label, Michael Rutherford credited as Micheal Rutherford. Horizons listed as Horizon's)	30
72	Charisma CAS 1020	TRESPASS (LP, repressing, large 'Mad Hatter' label with 'Printed and made by the Bruin B.V - Zaandam/Holland' on label)	18
72	Charisma CAS 1052	NURSERY CRYME (LP, 1st reissue, large 'Mad Hatter' label, gatefold sleeve)	20
72	Charisma CAS 1052	NURSERY CRYME (LP, 1st reissue, large 'Mad Hatter' label, gatefold sleeve, mispressing plays 'Cabaret' OST)	60
73	Charisma CAS 1074	SELLING ENGLAND BY THE POUND (LP, dark green card insert, large 'Mad Hatter' logo)	25
73	Charisma CLASS 1	LIVE (LP, non laminated sleeve, large 'Mad Hatter' logo, with 'Charisma Live Giants - £1.99' sticker on front cover)	30
73	Charisma CLASS 1	LIVE (LP, non laminated sleeve, large 'Mad Hatter' logo)	25
74	Charisma CGS 101	THE LAMB LIES DOWN ON BROADWAY (2-LP, small 'Mad Hatter; label, original pressing with "Marketed by B&C..." label text on both LPs and "Printed and Made by Bruin B.V. Zaandam/Holland" credit on sleeve, some with Gold Chase contest insert)	100
74	Decca SKL 4990	IN THE BEGINNING (reissue of 1st LP, 'snake' sleeve with lyric insert)	20
74	Charima CAS 1052	NURSERY CRYME (LP, reissue, small 'Mad Hatter' label, gatefold sleeve)	15
75	Charisma CGS 102	GENESIS COLLECTION VOLUME ONE (2-LP, boxed set of Trespass & "Nursery Cryme" in original sleeves, with poster)	100
75	Charisma CGS 103	GENESIS COLLECTION VOLUME TWO (2-LP, boxed set of Foxtrot & "Selling England By The Pound", with poster)	100
75	Charisma CAs 1074	SELLING ENGLAND BY THE POUND (LP, insert, small 'Mad Hatter' logo)	18
75	Charisma CGS 101	THE LAMB LIES DOWN ON BROADWAY (2-LP, small 'Mad Hatter; label, Phonogram credits,"Printed and Made by Bruin B.V Zaandam/Holland" credit on sleeve)	25
76	Charisma CDS 4001	A TRICK OF THE TAIL (LP, textured gatefold sleeve, inner,sleeve printed by "Bruin BV or Robor Ltd")	15
76	Charisma CAS 1020	TRESPASS (LP, repressing, small 'Mad Hatter' label, pressed by PRS or Phonodisc)	15
80	Charisma CAS 1058	FOXTROT (LP, reissue, gatefold sleeve, blue label)	15
83	Charisma CHC 12	TRESPASS (LP, repressing, blue label, insert)	15
91	Virgin GENLP 3	WE CAN'T DANCE (2-LP, inners, gatefold sleeve)	25
91	Virgin Edits 1	WE CAN'T DANCE (CD, 6 track promo - tour edition marketed by Volkswagon)	50
91	Virgin GEN CD	WE CAN'T DANCE (CD & tape, housed in custom promo box With three hand numbered watercolours)	90
92	Virgin GEN LP 4	LIVE: THE WAY WE WALK (LP)	100
93	Virgin GENBOX1	LIVE: THE WAY WE WALK (2xCD in wooden box with certificate & badge (1000 only)	80
93	Virgin GEN LP 5	LIVE: THE WAY WE WALK VOLUME 2: THE LONGS (LP)	100
97	Virgin GENLP6	CALLING ALL STATIONS (2-LP fourth sided etched with band picture)	150
98	Virgin CDBOX6	GENESIS ARCHIVE 1967 – 1975 (4 CD Box Set)	40
97	EMI LPCENT 17	SELLING ENGLAND BY THE POUND (LP, reissue, EMI Centenary pressing, stickered sleeve)	40
98	Virgin VCDJBOX98	GENESIS ARCHIVE 1967 - 1975 The Interviews (2xCD promo, p/s)	30
99	Virgin VGP 000270	TURN IT ON AGAIN - THE HITS (CD, in store promo p/s - each song played for 1 min)	50
07	EMI CDBOX12	GENESIS 1976 - 1882 (2007 UK 12 disc set comprising of 6 Hybrid SA CD's)	70
07	EMI CDBOX13	GENESIS 1983 - 1998 (2007 UK 10 disc set comprising of 5 Hybrid SA CD's)	60
07	Charisma GENLPY 2	NURSERY CRYME (LP, remastered reissue, gatefold sleeve, 180gm vinyl)	35
07	Charisma 4790193	A TRICK OF THE TAIL (LP, reissue, gatefold, inner, 180gm)	18
08	Charisma GENPLY 3	FOXTROT (LP, reissue, gatefold sleeve)	18
08	Charisma GENLP 4	SELLING ENGLAND BY THE POUND (LP, reissue, 18ogm vinyl, insert)	20
08	Virgin LPBOX 14	1970 - 1975 (6-LP box set, inners & inserts)	175
13	Charisma GENLPY 1	TRESPASS (LP, repressing, half-speed master, gatefold sleeve, insert)	22
13	Back To Black 00600753454503	SELLING ENGLAND BY THE POUND (LP, picture disc)	35
13	Charisma GENLPY 5	THE LAMB LIES DOWN ON BROADWAY (LP, reissue, gatefold, 180gm vinyl)	25
15	Not Bad BADBOX001	FROM GENESIS TO REVELATION (3-LP, 3 x 7" box set)	60
15	Virgin LPBOX 13	1983 - 1998 (6-LP, pressed originally on 150gm vinyl, later repressed on 180gm vinyl)	100
18	Charisma 00602567489849	NURSERY CRYME (LP, reissue, half speed master)	20
21	Virgin 3542467	THE LAST DOMINO? (4-LP)	60

(see also Flaming Youth,, Peter Gabriel, Steve Hackett, Anthony Phillips, Quiet World)

GENESIS (2)

77	Pilgrim 438	ENJOY CHRISTMAS WITH GENESIS (LP)	15

GENEVA (1)

80	Valiant ROUND1	2.30/Geneva Street (p/s)	10

GENEVA (2)

88	SRT 8KS 1565	Out Of The Fire/Lady (p/s)	10

GENEVEVE

MINT VALUE £

GENEVEVE
66	CBS 202061	Once/Just A Whisper (in p/s)	25
66	CBS 202061	Once/Just A Whisper	15
66	CBS 202096	Nothing In The World/Summer Days	10
67	CBS 202524	That Can't Be Bad/I Love Him, I Need Him	10

GENGHIS KHAN (U.K.)
83	Genghis Khan GK 1	DOUBLE DEALIN' (If Heaven Is Hell/Highway Passion//Midnight Rendezvous Mean Streak) (EP, double pack)	80
83	Wabbit WAB 61/63	Love You/Lady Lady/Mongol Nation/Gone For A Drive (double pack)	40

GENITAL DEFORMITIES
89	Fair Dinkum FD 001	SHAG NAST OI! (LP)	15

GENIUS/GZA
95	Gaffe GEF 24813	LIQUID SWORDS (2-LP)	40
99	MCA MCA 2111969	BENEATH THE SURFACE (2-LP)	25

GENOCIDE
79	Safari SAP 2	IMAGES OF DELUSION (EP)	10

GENOCIDE EXIT
80	Slam SEM 016	Future Vibes/I'm Not Really Here/Dream Song/All I Want	50

GENTILES (JAMAICA)
70	High Note HS 046	Your Destiny/Lock Love Away (actually by Melodians)	10

(see also Melodians)

GENTILES (U.K.)
68	Pye 7N 17530	Goodbye Baby/Marlena	8

GENTLE DESPITE
90	Sarah SARAH 26	THE DARKEST BLUE EP (p/s, insert)	25
91	Sarah SARAH 45	Torment To Me/Bittersweet Kiss/Shadow Of A Girl (p/s, insert)	25

JOHNNY GENTLE
59	Philips PB 908	Wendy/Boys And Girls (Were Meant For Each Other)	7
59	Philips PB 945	Milk From The Coconut/I Like The Way	7
60	Philips PB 988	Darlin' Won't You Wait/This Friendly World	7
60	Philips PB 1069	After My Laughter Came Tears/Sonja	6
61	Philips PB 1142	Pick A Star/Darlin'	7
59	Philips BBE 12345	THE GENTLE TOUCH (EP)	25

(see also Darren Young)

GENTLE ONES
70	Solar SL 3	Roundabout/Time To Spare	25

TIM GENTLE & HIS GENTLEMEN
65	Oriole CB 1988	Without You/Someone's In The Kitchen With Dinah	8

GENTLE WAVES
99	Jeepster JPRLP 006	THE GREEN FIELDS OF FOREVERLAND... (LP)	20
00	Jeepster JPRLP 011	SWANSONG FOR YOU (LP)	50

(see also Belle & Sebastian, Isobel Campbell)

GENTLE GIANT
73	WWA WWP 1001	In A Glass House/An Inmate's Lullaby	30
74	WWA WWS 017	The Power And The Glory/Playing The Game	12
77	Chrysalis CHS 2160	I'm Turning Around/Just The Same (live)	6
70	Vertigo 6360 020	GENTLE GIANT (LP, 1st pressing, gatefold sleeve, large swirl label)	400
71	Vertigo 6360 020	GENTLE GIANT (LP, 2nd pressing, gatefold sleeve, small swirl label)	70
71	Vertigo 6360 041	ACQUIRING THE TASTE (LP, gatefold sleeve, small swirl label)	300
72	Vertigo 6360 070	THREE FRIENDS (LP, 1st pressing, no "made in England" under 1972 on top right hand side of label, gatefold sleeve, small swirl label)	200
72	Vertigo 6360 070	THREE FRIENDS (LP, 2nd pressing, "made in England" under 1972 on top right hand side of label, gatefold sleeve, small swirl label)	50
72	Vertigo 6360 080	OCTOPUS (LP, gatefold sleeve, small swirl label)	200
73	WWA WWA 002	IN A GLASS HOUSE (LP, silk-screen cover, with photo insert & lyric inner)	50
74	WWA WWA 010	THE POWER AND THE GLORY (LP, with insert, sleeve has 2 rounded corners)	40
74	Vertigo 6360041	ACQUIRING THE TASTE (LP, reissue, 'spaceship' label)	25
75	Vertigo 6360 020	GENTLE GIANT (LP, reissue, gatefold sleeve, spaceship label)	30
75	Vertigo 6360080	OCTOPUS (LP, reissue, 'spaceship' label)	30
75	Vertigo 6641 334	GIANT STEPS - (THE FIRST FIVE YEARS) 1970-1975 (2-LP, gatefold sleeve, spaceship label)	25
75	Chrysalis CHR 1093	FREE HAND (LP, lyric insert, green label)	15
77	Chrysalis CTY 1133	LIVE (PLAYING THE FOOL) (2-LP, with 12-page booklet)	20
77	Chrysalis CHR 1152	THE MISSING PIECE (LP, with inner sleeve)	15
78	Chrysalis CHR 1186	GIANT FOR A DAY (LP, with mask insert & lyric inner sleeve)	15
80	Chrysalis CHR 1285	CIVILIAN (LP, with lyric inner sleeve)	15
10	Tapestry TPT 255	ACQUIRING THE TASTE (LP, reissue)	15
12	Tapestry TPT 271	THREE FRIENDS (LP, reissue)	15

(see also Simon Dupree & Big Sound, Moles)

GENTLE INFLUENCE
69	Pye 7N 17666	Never Trust In Tomorrow/Easy To Love	15
69	Pye 7N 17743	Always Be A Part Of My Living/Captain Reale	22

GENTLE PEOPLE (1)
67	Columbia DB 8276	It's Too Late/Sea Of Heartbreak	12

GENTLE POWER OF SONG
67	Polydor 56211	Constant Penelope/A Court Garden Party, Circa 1580	8
67	Polydor 2310 285	CIRCUS (LP)	25

GENTLE RAIN
73	Polydor 2310 285	MOODY (LP)	200

BILL GENTLES
69	Gas GAS 104	Long Life/SCHOOL BOYS: O Tell Me	18

Errol GENTLES

MINT VALUE £

70	Pama PM 801	What A Woman/Sleepy Cat	40
70	Punch PH 54	Fight The Good Fight/Fight Beat	8
71	Escort ERT 853	Bachelor Boy/SCORPIONS: Colour Rites	8
72	Bullet BU 506	Pure In Heart/Clean Hands	6

(see also Bill Jentles, Bill Jenties)

ERROL GENTLES

| 79 | Attack TACK 11 | Tell Me Why/Far Far Away (12") | 20 |

GENTLE TOUCH

| 65 | London HLR 10175 | Among The First To Know/Merry Go Round | 7 |
| 83 | Tristar TRI3 | Dreams Of You/Dreams Of You (Instrumental) | 6 |

GENTRY

| 70 | Dolphin DO571 | Long Road/Sing Me A Sad Song/Attempt Contact (EP, Irish pressing) | 250 |
| 70 | Dolphin DOS 35 | Sing Me A Sad Song/Attempted Contact | 150 |

ART GENTRY

| 72 | Mojo 2092 048 | Breakthrough/Wonderful Dream | 15 |

BOBBIE GENTRY

67	Capitol (S)T 2830	ODE TO BILLIE JOE (LP)	15
68	Capitol ST2964	LOCAL GENTRY (LP)	15
68	Capitol (S)T 2842	THE DELTA SWEETE (LP)	15

GENTRY ICE

| 88 | Jack Trax JTX 15 | Do You Wanna Jack/Lost In The Sound (with Adonis) (12") | 20 |

GENTRYS

65	MGM MGM 1284	Keep On Dancing/Make Up Your Mind	20
66	MGM MGM 1296	Brown Paper Sack/Spread It On Thick	25
66	MGM MGM 1312	Everyday I Have To Cry/Don't Let It Be	15
68	Bell BLL 1012	I Can't Go Back To Denver/You Better Come Home	8

GENTS

| 81 | Posh POSH 001 | The Faker/The Pink Panther | 20 |
| 82 | Kosmic KOS 6886 | Schooldays/True Stories (p/s) | 8 |

GEOFFREY

| 78 | Music Bank BECK 694 | ABH (Who Wants To Listen To Punk Rock?)/Colt 45 Rock (p/s) | 15 |

GEORDIE

72	Regal Zonophone RZ 3067	Don't Do That/Francis Was A Rocker	8
72	EMI EMI 2031	Can You Do It/Red Eyed Lady	8
73	EMI EMC 3001	HOPE YOU LIKE IT (LP)	30
74	EMI EMA 764	DON'T BE FOOLED BY THE NAME (LP)	80
76	EMI EMC 3134	SAVE THE WORLD (LP)	40
83	Neat NEAT 1008	NO SWEAT (LP)	40

(see also Influence, AC/DC)

BARBARA GEORGE

| 62 | London HL 9513 | I Know (You Don't Love Me No More)/Love (Is Just A Chance You Take) | 25 |
| 64 | Sue WI 316 | Send For Me/Bless You | 50 |

EARL GEORGE

73	Count Shelly CS 025	Gonna Give Her All The Love/PRINCE JAZZBO: Wise Shepherd	15
76	Terminal TM 103	Love Depression/Love Is Something	8
76	Terminal TM 106	So Many Ways/Part 2	8
78	Burning Sounds BS 1015	ONE AND ONLY (LP)	20

(see also George Faith, George Ferris, Winston Reedy)

GEORGE GOLDEN

| 64 | R&B JB145 | Fire In My Feet/ One More Chance | 15 |
| 64 | R&B JB157 | Don't You Know/ Nancy Tell Me | 15 |

LLOYD GEORGE

| 62 | London HLP 9562 | Lucy Lee/Sing Real Loud | 60 |

GEORGE T

| 99 | Refried WOK1200/199 | UNDER ELEVATOR EP (12") | 20 |
| 00 | Under The Counter UTC 024 | SOME LUNAR PURSUITS EP (12") | 35 |

GEORGETTES

58	London HL 8548	Love Like A Fool/Oh Tonight	50
58	London HL 8548	Love Like A Fool/Oh Tonight (78)	30
60	Pye International 7N 25058	Down By The River/A Pair Of Eyes	10

GEORGIA SLIM/WALTER ROLAND

| 59 | Jazz Collector JEL 2 | THE MALE BLUES VOL. 1 (EP) | 10 |

GEORGIA TOM

| 60s | Riverside RLP 8803 | GEORGIA TOM AND FRIENDS (LP) | 20 |

(see also Paramount Allstars)

GEORGIE'S VARSITY 5

| 61 | Vogue Pop V 9189 | When My Sugar Walks Down The Street/Five Foot Two, Eyes Of Blue | 10 |

GERALDINE

| 71 | Beltona Sword SBE 128 | GERALDINE (LP) | 150 |

GERALDO 1969

| 69 | Morgan MRS 22 | QE2/Hello Again | 8 |

DANIEL GERARD

| 72 | CBS S8064 | From Japan To America/Rain | 12 |

WESLEY GERMS

| 72 | Upsetter US 390 | Whiplash/UPSETTERS: Whiplash Version | 25 |

GERONIMO BLACK

| 72 | Uni UNLS 127 | GERONIMO BLACK (LP) | 75 |

(see also Frank Zappa/Mothers Of Invention)

DENNY GERRARD

| 70 | Deram Nova DN 10 | SINISTER MORNING (LP, mono, with High Tide, Deram Nova on top right hand corner of sleeve with either Deram Nova or Decca Nova on label) | 300 |

GERRY & THE HOLOGRAMS

MINT VALUE £

70	Deram Nova SDN 10	SINISTER MORNING (LP, stereo, with High Tide, Deram Nova on top right hand corner of sleeve with either Deram Nova or Decca Nova on label)	150

(see also Warm Sounds, High Tide, Open Road, Fifth Avenue)

GERRY & THE HOLOGRAMS
79	Absurd ABSURD 4	Gerry And The Holograms/Increased Resistance (p/s)	30
79	Absurd ABSURD 5	The Emperor's New Music (unplayable record, glued into p/s)	30

GERRY & THE PACEMAKERS
64	Columbia DB 7268	Don't Let The Sun Catch You Crying/Show Me That You Care	6
64	Columbia DB 7353	It's Gonna Be Alright/It's Just Because	7
64	Columbia DB 7437	Ferry Cross The Mersey/You You You	6
65	Columbia DB 7504	I'll Be There/Baby, You're So Good To Me	6
65	Columbia DB 7738	Walk Hand In Hand/Dreams	6
66	Columbia DB 7835	La La La/Without You	8
66	Columbia DB 8044	Girl On A Swing/A Fool To Myself	8
74	DJM DJS 298	Remember (The Days Of Rock And Roll)/There's Still Time	10
63	Columbia SEG 8257	HOW DO YOU DO IT? (EP)	12
64	Columbia SEG 8295	YOU'LL NEVER WALK ALONE (EP, in misprinted sleeve listing "It's All Right" instead of "Jambalaya" on front)	25
64	Columbia SEG 8295	YOU'LL NEVER WALK ALONE (EP)	15
64	Columbia SEG 8311	I'M THE ONE (EP)	15
64	Columbia SEG 8346	DON'T LET THE SUN CATCH YOU CRYING (EP)	15
64	Columbia SEG 8367	IT'S GONNA BE ALRIGHT (EP)	20
65	Columbia SEG 8388	GERRY IN CALIFORNIA (EP)	30
65	Columbia SEG 8397	HITS FROM 'FERRY CROSS THE MERSEY' (EP)	30
65	Columbia SEG 8426	RIP IT UP (EP)	35
63	Columbia 33SX 1546	HOW DO YOU LIKE IT? (LP, mono)	20
63	Columbia 33SCX 1546	HOW DO YOU LIKE IT? (LP, stereo)	30
65	Columbia 33SX 1693	FERRY CROSS THE MERSEY (LP, soundtrack, with Cilla Black & Fourmost, mono)	25
65	Columbia 33SCX 1693	FERRY CROSS THE MERSEY (LP, soundtrack, with Cilla Black & Fourmost, stereo)	35
65	EMI Regal REG 2018	YOU'LL NEVER WALK ALONE (LP, export issue)	25

(see also Gerry Marsden)

GERVASE
68	Decca F12822	Pepper Grinder/Visions	20

GESCOM
94	Skam SKA 2	Dan One/Five/Cicada/Sciew Spo (12", card folder p/s)	35
95	Skam SKA 3	Snackwitch/Mag (12", bubblewrap sleeve with insert)	40
95	Skam SKA 3	Snackwitch/Mag (12", second issue, black sleeve)	20
95	Clear CLR 408	THE SOUNDS OF MACHINES OUR PARENTS USED (12", p/s)	40
96	Skam SKA 7	KEY NELL 1/2/3/4 (12", bubblewrap sleeve)	15
98	Skam SKA010 THAT	THAT (EP) (12", p/s 2 inserts)	15
98	Skam SKA010 THIS	THIS (EP) (12", p/s)	15
96	Warp WAP 88	Keynell/Keynell (12", p/s, remixes by Autechre)	10

(see also Autechre, Ad Vance Vs Gescom)

GESTURES
65	Stateside SS 379	Run Run Run/It Seems To Me	25

STAN GETZ (QUARTET/QUINTET)
62	HMV POP 1061	Disafinado/Jazz Theme From Dr. Kildare	6
64	Verve VS 520	The Girl From Ipanema (with JOAO GILBERTO)/Blowin' In The Wind	7
53	Esquire 20-007	STAN GETZ PLAYS (LP, 10")	25
54	Vogue LDE 089	AT STORYVILLE (LP, 10")	25
55	Vogue LDE 147	STAN GETZ QUARTET (LP, 10")	25
55	Columbia Clef 33CX 10000	AT THE SHRINE NO. 1 (LP, as Stan Getz Quintet)	25
55	Columbia Clef 33CX 10001	AT THE SHRINE NO. 2 (LP, as Stan Getz Quintet)	25
58	HMV CLP 1292	STAN GETZ/CHET BAKER (LP)	20
62	HMV CLP 1577	FOCUS (LP, also stereo CSD 1448)	20
63	Verve VLP 9013	JAZZ SAMBA (LP, with Charlie Byrd, mono)	20
63	Verve (S)VLP 9013	JAZZ SAMBA (LP, with Charlie Byrd, stereo)	20
63	Verve VLP 9024	BIG BAND BOSSA NOVA (LP)	20
63	Verve VLP 9038	JAZZ SAMBA ENCORE! (LP, with Luiz Bonfa, mono)	20
63	Verve (S)VLP 9038	JAZZ SAMBA ENCORE! (LP, with Luiz Bonfa, stereo)	20
64	Verve VLP 9065	GETZ-GILBERTO (LP)	25
65	MGM MGM-C 8001	MICKEY ONE (LP, soundtrack, mono, with booklet)	20
65	MGM MGM-C(S) 8001	MICKEY ONE (LP, soundtrack, stereo, with booklet)	25

(see also Dizzy Gillespie, Astrud Gilberto, Joao Gilberto, Johnny Smith)

GEZLIM
72	Helm 001	Dark Side Of Your Face (1-sided)	200

G-FORCE
80	Jet JET 183	Hot Gossip/Because Of Your Love (p/s)	20
80	Jet JET 194	You/Trust Your Lovin' (no p/s)	12
80	Jet JET 7005	White Knuckles/Rockin' And Rollin'/I Look At You (p/s)	15
80	Jet JETLP 229	G-FORCE (LP, with inner sleeve and patch)	20
80	Jet JETPD 229	G-FORCE (LP, picture disc)	18

(see also Gary Moore)

G.G. ALLSTARS
70	Explosion EX 2014	Barabus/This Kind Of Life	12
70	Explosion EX 2012	Champion/MAYTONES: Funny Man	25
70	Explosion EX 2023	Man From Carolina/Gold On Your Dress (B-side actually by Slickers)	10
70	Explosion EX 2024	African Melody/Serious Love (B-side actually by Maytones)	10
70	Explosion EX 2025	Ganja Plane/Deep River	12
70	Gas GAS 153	So Alive/Mercy Mr D.J.	8

G.G.F.H.

			MINT VALUE £
70	Escort ERT 835	African Melody/Man From Carolina	10
70	G.G. GG 4505	I Don't Like To Interfere/Version II	20
70	G.G. GG 4501	Music Keep On Playing (actually by Cornell Campbell)/ Music Keep On Playing Version	70
71	G.G. GG 4508	Cleanliness Version 2/MAYTONES: Cleanliness	7
71	G.G. GG 4510	Rocking On The G.G. Beat (actually by Maytones)/WINSTON WRIGHT: Rocking On The G.G. Beat Version II	15
71	G.G. GG 4511	Lonely Nights (actually by Eric Donaldson & West Indians)/MAYTONES: Let The Version Play	10
71	G.G. GG 4513	All One Nation (actually by Maytones)/VAL BENNETT: Judgement Warrant	8
71	G.G. GG 4526	Rod Of Righteousness (actually "Stretch Forth His Hand" by Jah Huntly)/ DENNIS ALCAPONE: King Of Kings (B-side actually "King Of Glory")	25
72	G.G. GG 4530	Donkey Face Version/MAYTONES: Donkey Face	8
72	Pama PM 846	I'm Feeling Lonely Version/MAYTONES: I'm Feeling Lonely	6
73	Bullet BU 528	People Get Funny Version/MAYTONES: People Get Funny	6
70	Trojan TBL 129	MAN FROM CAROLINA (LP)	70

(see also Paulette & Gee, Billy Dyce, Maytones, Charlie Ace, Monty Morris, Starlights, Lloyd & Carey, Gladdy & Stranger, Heptones, Shorty Perry, Barbara Jones)

G.G.F.H.
94	Peaceville CC8	Welcome To The Process/Too Much Punch/Dread (green vinyl, p/s)	15

G.G. RHYTHM SECTION
69	Blue Cat BS 165	T.N.T./MAYTONES: Botheration	35

AMOS GHERKIN QUARTET
70	Parlophone R 5872	Blakey And Me/Theme From An Unmade Silent Movie	8

GHETTO CHILDREN
73	CBS 1450	I Just Gotta Find Somebody To Love Me/Rat-A-Tat-Tat	10

GHETTO FUNK
00	G-Funk GFUNK 001	Doing My Thing (Light Side)/(Heavy Side) (12")	45

GHETTO PRIEST
03	On U Sound ON-ULP 1003	VULTURE CULTURE (LP)	15

GHETTO TEARS
84	Ghetto Tears GT 001	Ghetto Children/Ghetto Prayers (12" p/s)	80

WESS & DORI GHEZZI
74	Bradleys BRAD 7404	Let It Be Free/Turn Around	7
75	Bradleys BRAD 7515	Fallin'/Era	8

GHOST DANCE
86	Karbon KAR 604	The Grip Of Love/Where Spirits Fly (p/s)	8
88	Karbon KAR XL 303	GATHERING DUST (LP)	15

(see also Skeletal Family, All About Eve, Sisters Of Mercy)

GHOST (1)
69	Gemini GMS 007	When You're Dead/Indian Maid	50
70	Gemini GMS 014	I've Got To Get To Know You/For One Second	40
70	Gemini GME 1004	WHEN YOU'RE DEAD - ONE SECOND (LP, laminated front cover, with extra track, "I've Got To Get To Know Her")	750
70	Gemini GME 1004	WHEN YOU'RE DEAD - ONE SECOND (LP, laminated front cover, without extra track, "I've Got To Get To Know Her")	500
87	Bam Caruso KIRI 077	FOR ONE SECOND (LP, reissue of "When You're Dead" with extra track)	20

(see also Velvett Fogg, Shirley Kent, Virginia Tree, Wizzard)

GHOST (2)
10	Rise Above RISELP 124	OPVS EPONYMOVS (LP, 'Die Hard Edition', 300 only)	200

GHOSTFACE KILLAH
96	Razor Sharp EPC 485389 1	IRONMAN (2-LP)	50
00	Epic EPC 491955	SUPREME CLIENTELE (2-LP)	150
01	Epic EPC 501941 1	BULLETPROOF WALLETS (2-LP)	20
18	Daupe! DM SP 039	THE LOST TAPES (LP)	20
18	Daupe! DM SP 039	THE LOST TAPES (LP, gold vinyl)	20
18	Daupe! DM SP 039	THE LOST TAPES (LP, silver vinyl)	20
18	Daupe! DM SP 039	THE LOST TAPES (LP, white vinyl)	20
18	Daupe! DM SP 039	THE LOST TAPES (LP, yellow vinyl)	20
18	Daupe! DM SP 039	THE LOST TAPES (LP, glow in the dark vinyl)	30
18	Daupe! DM SP 039	THE LOST TAPES (LP, with obi strip, 40 copies)	250

GHOSTPOET
11	Brownswood BWOOD057LP	PEANUT BUTTER BLUES AND MELONCOLY JAM (LP, 1st pressing, 2014 reissue has different barcode)	30

GHOSTS
80	Arista ARIST 347	My Town/I'm Your Man (no p/s)	20

GHOSTS OF DANCE
82	Plastic Canvas PC001	Ghosts Of Dance/Walking Through Gardens (p/s)	20

BILL GIANT
61	MGM MGM 1135	Better Let Her Go/When I Grow Too Old To Dream	12

BILLY GIANT
65	Pye 25337	Leave My Girl Alone/Nice Girls	20

GIANT CRAB
68	Uni UN 509	Hot Line Conversation/E.S.P.	35

GIANT HAYSTACKS
83	BSB BSB 01	Baby I Need You/Baby I Need You (Instrumental) (p/s)	7

GIANTS
60s	Polydor LPHM 46426	IN GERMANY (LP, mono)	25
60s	Polydor SLPHM 237526	IN GERMANY (LP, stereo)	30

GIANT SIZE C
91	Afrocentric AFRO 1	Perspective/(Bedroom Mix)/(Rough Mix) (12")	150
93	Afrocentric AFRO 3	Hate (12")	15

GIANT SUNFLOWER

MINT VALUE £

GIANT SUNFLOWER
| 67 | CBS 2805 | February Sunshine/Big Apple | 20 |
| 67 | CBS 3033 | Mark Twain/What's So Good About Goodbye? | 10 |

BARRY GIBB
| 70 | Lyntone LYN 2375 | King Cathy/Summer Ends/I Can Bring Love | 100 |
| 70 | Polydor 2058 030 | I'll Kiss Your Memory/This Time | 8 |

(see also Bee Gees)

MAURICE GIBB
| 70 | Polydor 2058 013 | Railroad/I've Come Back | 8 |
| 84 | Audiotrax ATX 05 | Hold Her In Your Hand/Instrumental (gatefold sleeve) | 15 |

(see also Bee Gees, Fut)

ROBIN GIBB
69	Polydor 56337	Saved By The Bell/Mother And Jack	6
69	Polydor 56337	Saved By The Bell/Alexandria Good Time (withdrawn)	20
69	Polydor 56368	One Million Years/Weekend	8
70	Polydor 56371	August October/Give Me A Smile	7
69	Polydor 583 085	ROBIN'S REIGN (LP)	25

(see also Bee Gees)

DOUG GIBBONS
| 65 | Decca F 12122 | I Got My Tears To Remind Me/I Found Out | 6 |

STEVE GIBBONS (BAND)
71	Wizard WIZ 102	Alright Now/Lay Some Lovin' Down	10
76	Polydor 2058 745	Johnny Cool/Speed Kills	10
77	Polydor 2058 889	Tulane/Now You Know Me	7
71	Wizard SWZA 5501	SHORT STORIES (LP, gatefold sleeve, lyric insert, yellow vinyl)	100
71	Wizard SWZA 5501	SHORT STORIES (LP, gatefold sleeve, lyric insert, black vinyl)	30

(see also Uglys, Magic Christians, B,L&G)

CALY GIBBS
| 71 | Amalgamated AMG 870 | Seeing Is Believing/JOE GIBBS ALLSTARS: Ghost Capturer | 35 |

(see also Carlton Gibbs)

CARLTON GIBBS
| 70 | Amalgamated AMG 872 | Ghost Walk/Joy Stick | 45 |

GEORGIA GIBBS
55	Vogue Coral Q 72088	Ballin' The Jack/I Still Feel The Same About You	10
56	Vogue Coral Q 72182	If I Were A Bell/I'll Know	10
57	RCA RCA 1011	Sugar Candy/I'm Walking The Floor Over You	10
58	RCA RCA 1029	Great Balls Of Fire/I Miss You	45
58	Mercury 7MT 210	Arriverderci Roma/24 Hours A Day	10
58	Columbia DB 4201	The Hula Hoop Song/Keep In Touch	8
60	London HLP 9098	The Stroll That Stole My Heart/Seven Lonely Days	7
65	Stateside SS 423	Let Me Cry On Your Shoulder/Venice Blues	7
56	Mercury MPT 7500	SINGS THE OLDIES (10" LP)	15
57	Mercury MPT 7511	HER NIBS MISS GIBBS (10" LP)	15
57	Mercury MPL 6508	SWINGING WITH HER NIBS (LP)	15

JOE GIBBS (& DESTROYERS)
68	Amslgamated AMG 822	People Grudgeful (as Sir Joe)/Pan-Ya Machete (actually the Pioneers)	65
70	Amalgamated AMG 855	Nevada Joe (act. by Johnny Lover)/Straight To The Head (act. by Destroyers)	60
70	Amalgamated AMG 858	Franco Nero (actually by Count Machuki & Destroyers)/ Version Two (actually by Destroyers)	30
70	Amalgamated AMG 859	Rock The Clock/Version Two	50
70	Amalgamated AMG 860	Let It Be/Turn Back The Hands Of Time (both actually by Nicky Thomas)	25
70	Amalgamated AMG 861	La La/Reggae Fever (as Joe Gibbs All Stars)	40
70	Amalgamated AMG 865	Hijacked/Life Is Down In Denver	50
70	Amalgamated AMG 867	Movements/Caesar	160
70	Amalgamated AMG 869	Perfect Born Yah/Red Red Wine (as Jo Gibs All Stars)	65
70	Amalgamated AMG 868	Gift Of God (actually by Lizzy)/The Raper	15
70	Pressure Beat PR 5504	News Flash/Version Two	15
72	Pressure Beat DB5513	Money In My Pocket (actually by Dennis Brown)/Money Love	25
72	Pressure Beat PB 5514	Tipatone/Do It To Me (as Joe Gibbs All Stars)	15
73	Jackpot JP 811	Ration/Version (as Joe Gibbs All Stars)	8
04	Amalgamated TJSE 022	Movements/Caesar (reissue)	25
78	Lightning LIP 10	AFRICAN DUB ALMIGHTY (LP, with The Professionals)	20
78	Lightning LIP 11	AFRICAN DUB ALMIGHTY - CHAPTER TWO (LP)	15
78	Lightning LIP 12	AFRICAN DUB ALMIGHTY - CHAPTER THREE (LP)	15
88	Trojan TRLS 261	REGGAE TRAIN 1968 - 71 (LP)	15

(see also Lizzy, Reggae Boys, Bunny Flip, Destroyers, Dennis Brown, Caly Gibbs, Nicky Thomas)

MICHAEL GIBBS
70	Deram DML/SML 1063	MICHAEL GIBBS (LP)	50
71	Deram SML 1087	TANGLEWOOD '63 (LP)	50
72	Polydor 2683 011	JUST AHEAD (2-LP)	35
74	Polydor 2383 252	IN THE PUBLIC INTEREST (LP, with Gary Burton)	35
75	Bronze ILPS 9353	ONLY CHROME ... WATERFALL (LP)	15

(see also Neil Ardley, Gary Burton)

TERRY GIBBS SEXTET
| 56 | Vogue Coral LVA 9013 | TERRY (LP) | 20 |
| 56 | Vogue Coral LVA 9009 | JAZZTIME USA (LP, as Terry Gibbs Quartet & Sextet) | 20 |

(see also Terry Gibbs Big Band)

TERRY GIBBS BIG BAND
| 59 | Mercury CMS 18016 | LAUNCHING A NEW BAND (LP) | 15 |

NICK GIBLER
76	Chrysalis CHS 2104	Roxy Roller/Prophet's Tale	6

DON GIBSON
56	MGM SP 1177	Sweet Dreams/The Road Of Life Alone	125
58	RCA RCA 1056	Oh Lonesome Me/I Can't Stop Lovin' You	15
58	RCA RCA 1073	Blue Blue Day/Too Soon	12
58	RCA RCA 1098	Give Myself A Party/Look Who's Blue	20
59	RCA RCA 1110	A Stranger To Me/Who Cares?	10
59	RCA RCA 1150	Don't Tell Me Your Troubles/Heartbreak Avenue	18
59	RCA RCA 1158	Big Hearted Me/I'm Movin' On	15

(Originally issued with triangular centres; later round-centre copies are worth half these values.)

60	RCA RCA 1183	Just One Time/I May Never Get To Heaven	8
60	RCA RCA 1200	Far Far Away/A Legend In My Time	8
60	RCA RCA 1217	Sweet Dreams/The Same Street	8
61	RCA RCA 1243	Sea Of Heartbreak/I Think It's Best (To Forget Me)	8
62	RCA RCA 1272	Lonesome Number One/The Same Old Trouble	10
60	RCA RCX 1050	BLUE AND LONESOME (EP)	12
60	RCA RD 27158	THE GIBSON BOY (LP)	40

GINNY GIBSON
55	MGM SP 1121	Like Ma-a-d/Once There Was A Little Girl	15
58	MGM MGM 953	Whatever Lola Wants (Lola Gets)/If Anything Should Happen	15

JODY GIBSON & MULESKINNERS
59	Parlophone R 4579	Kissin' Time/Man On My Trail	15
60	Parlophone R 4645	If You Don't Know/So You Think You've Got Troubles	15

LORNE GIBSON TRIO
63	Decca F 11684	Some Do, Some Don't (Some Will, Some Won't)/Heaven's Above	7
66	Decca F12450	Roses From A Stranger/Jingle Jangle	20
69	RCA 1917	Eva Magdalena/A Thing Called Love	7

STEVE GIBSON & RED CAPS
57	HMV POP 417	Silhouettes/Flamingo	150
57	HMV POP 417	Silhouettes/Flamingo (78)	30

WAYNE GIBSON (& DYNAMIC SOUNDS)
63	Decca F 11713	Linda Lu/Beachcomber	20
64	Decca F 11800	Come On Let's Go/DYNAMIC SOUNDS : Pop The Whip	20
64	Pye 7N 15680	Kelly/See You Later Alligator	20
65	Pye 7N 15798	Portland Town/Please Baby Please	10
65	Parlophone R 5357	Ding Dong The Witch Is Dead/In The Night	8
65	Columbia DB 7683	One Little Smile/Baby, Baby, Baby Pity Me	30
66	Columbia DB 7911	Under My Thumb/It Always Happens (Icey) (solo)	60
66	Columbia DB 7911	Under My Thumb/It Always Happens (Icey) (solo) (DJ copy)	120
66	Columbia DB 7998	For No One/He's Got The Whole World In his Hands (solo)	10
72	Kingdom KV 8002	For No One/Come Around	10
74	Pye DDS 2001	Under My Thumb/The Game	10

GIBSONS
65	CBS 202015	Any Time That You're Lonely/Born To Be Free	7
66	CBS 202063	Come Summertime/Summer Affair	7
66	Deram DM 103	Two Kinds Of Lovers/Hey Girl	8
67	Deram DM 119	The Magic Book/You Know I Need Your Lovin'	12
67	Major Minor MM 524	Night And Day/City Life	25
67	Major Minor MM 538	Lazy Summer Day/She's Not Like Any Girl	25
67	Major Minor MM 547	Only When You're Lonely/Ode To A Dolls House	7

GIDEANS LEAGUE
72	Parlophone R 5933	Hey! Did You Know You've Got Your Face On Upside Down/You've Got A Mind Of Your Own	6

GIDIAN (& UNIVERSALS)
66	Columbia DB 7826	Try Me Out/There Isn't Anything	20
66	Columbia DB 7916	Fight For Your Love/See If She Cares	8
66	Columbia DB 8041	Feeling/Don't Be Sentimental (as Gidian & Universals)	10
70	UPC UPC 107	That's Love/We Are The Happiest	6

(see also Universals, Chris Lamb & Universals)

COLIN GIFFIN
69	CBS 4030	Changes In Our Time/When I Was So Young	40

GIFT (1)
81	Venus ORBIT 1	Crashing Down/It'll End In Tears (p/s)	20

GIFT (2)
88	Red Communications RED 001	You Don't Feel For Me/Torn Apart (p/s)	20

GIFTED CHILDREN
81	Whaam! WHAAM 001	Painting By Numbers/Lichtenstein Girl (p/s)	60

(see also Television Personalities)

GIGGETTY
78	Pye 7N 46136	Black Country Christmas/Motorway Mess	6
75	GE 100	DAWN TO DUSK IN THE BLACK COUNTRY (LP, with insert, credited to Giggetty and Jim Wm. Jones)	40
77	Bridge GE 101	TAMBOURINE (LP)	30
80	Bridge GE 103	BLACK COUNTRY TIME (LP, also listed as Revolver REV LP1)	30

GIGGLES
74	EMI 2212	Maria (The Enchildas Song)/Your Mother Wouldn't Like It	6
74	EMI 2246	Giggle Wiggle/For Just One Day	100
75	EMI EMI 2288	Glad To Be Alive/High School Girls	6
76	EMI EMI 2512	Just Another Saturday Night In The City/Bazooka (p/s)	6

GILBERTO GIL

MINT VALUE £

77	EMI EMI 2640	Reaching Out/Street Dancer	6

GILBERTO GIL
82	WEA K 79285 (T)	Palco/Samba De Los Angeles/Maracatu Atomico (12")	40
82	WEA K 79285	Palco/Samba De Los Angeles	20
71	Famous SFM 1001	GILBERTO GIL (LP)	40

GILBERT
67	CBS 3089	Disappear/You	15
68	CBS 3399	What Can I Do?/You	15
69	Major Minor MM 613	Mister Moody's Garden/I Wish I Could Cry	15

(see also Gilbert O'Sullivan)

BRUCE GILBERT
84	Mute STUMM 18	THS WAY (LP)	20
86	Mute STUMM 39	THE SHIVERING MAN (LP)	35
91	Mute STUMM 71	INSIDING (LP)	20
91	Mute STUMM 77	MUSIC FOR FRUIT (LP)	30

(see also Wire, Cupol, Dome, Gilbert & Lewis, Duet Emmo)

GEORGE GILBERT
74	Mime LPMS 7041	MEDWAY FLOWS SOFTLY (LP, with insert)	15

GILBERT & LEWIS
81	4AD AD 106	Ends With The Sea/Hung Up To Dry Whilst Building An Arch (p/s)	7
80	4AD CAD 16	3R4 (LP as B. C. Gilbert and G. Lewis)	30
82	Cherry Red BRED 27	MZUI (LP, PVC cover, insert sleeve)	25

(see also Wire, Dome, Cupol, Duet Emmo)

ASTRUD GILBERTO
65	Verve SVLP 9087	THE ASTRUD GILBERTO ALBUM (LP)	25
65	Verve VLP 9107	THE SHADOW OF YOUR SMILE (LP)	20
66	Verve (S)VLP 9163	A CERTAIN SMILE AND A CERTAIN SADNESS (LP)	20
67	Verve SVLP 9137	BEACH SAMBA (LP)	20
68	Verve 2317 021	WINDY (LP)	20
69	Verve (S)VLP 9242	I HAVEN'T GOT ANYTHING BETTER TO DO (LP)	20
70	Verve SVLP 9252	HOLIDAY (LP)	20
72	C.T.I. CTL 1	GILBERTO WITH TURRENTINE (LP, with Stanley Turrentine)	20

(see also Stan Getz, Stanley Turrentine)

JOAO GILBERTO
61	Parlophone PMC 1248	BOSSA-FINADO (LP)	15
62	Parlophone PMC 1247	THE LEADER OF THE REVOLUTION (LP)	20

(see also Stan Getz)

GILCHRIST
75	Route RT 03	Guardian In The Sky/Heading For The Grave	7

GILDED CAGE
69	Tepee TPR 1003	Long Long Road (For The Broken Heart)/Baby Grumpling	40

(see also She Trinity)

COSMO GILE
60	Top Rank JAR 410	Bambina D'Amsterdam/Tintarella Di Luna	6

GILES, GILES & FRIPP
68	Deram DM 188	One In A Million/Newly-Weds	100
68	Deram DM 210	Thursday Morning/Elephant Song	80
68	Deram DML 1022	THE CHEERFUL INSANITY OF GILES, GILES AND FRIPP (LP, mono)	150
68	Deram SML 1022	THE CHEERFUL INSANITY OF GILES, GILES AND FRIPP (LP, stereo)	150
70	Deram SPA 423	THE CHEERFUL INSANITY OF GILES, GILES AND FRIPP (LP, stereo reissue)	40
13	Cherry Red CRP 203	THE CHEERFUL INSANITY OF GILES, GILES AND FRIPP (LP, reissue)	15

(see also Brain, Trendsetters Ltd, League Of Gentlemen, King Crimson, Fripp & Eno, McDonald & Giles)

GILGAMESH
75	Caroline CA 2007	GILGAMESH (LP)	30

(see also Hugh Hopper, Colosseum, Whitesnake)

TERRY GILKYSON & EASY RIDERS
58	Philips JK 1007	Marianne/Goodbye Chaquita (jukebox issue)	18
60	Fontana TFE 17326	STROLLING BLUES (EP)	12
60	Fontana TFE 17327	LONESOME RIDER (EP)	10
61	London RER 1333	ROLLIN' (EP)	12
53	Brunswick LA 8618	GOLDEN MINUTES OF FOLK MUSIC (10" LP)	25
61	London HA-R 2301	ROLLIN' (LP, also stereo SAH-R 6111)	15
61	London HA-R 2323	REMEMBER THE ALAMO (LP, as Easyriders Including Terry Gilkyson)	15

JONATHAN GILL
73	Pye 7N 45206	I've Got To Please You/Isandulu Road	15

(IAN) GILLAN (BAND)
78	Island R 553-B	Twin Exhausted (live)/Smoke On The Water (live)/ILLUSION: Madonna Blue/Revolutionary (12", promo only, as Ian Gillan Band)	20
78	Island WIP 6423	Mad Elaine/Mercury High (as Ian Gillan Band, company sleeve)	8
79	Acrobat BAT 1212	She Tears Me Down/Puget Sound/Vengeance/Mr. Universe (12", stickered card sleeve, promo only)	20
81	Lyntone LYN 10599	Higher And Higher/Spanish Guitar (same tracks both sides, hard vinyl test pressing, handwritten white labels)	35
76	Polydor/Oyster 2490 136	CHILD IN TIME (LP, gatefold sleeve, as Ian Gillan Band)	15
77	Island ILPS 9511DJ	IAN GILLAN BAND SAMPLER (LP, 1-sided promo for "Scarabus", company sleeve)	20
77	Island ILPS 59511	SCARABUS (LP, as Ian Gillan Band)	15
78	Island ILPS 9545	LIVE AT THE BUDO-KAN (LP, unissued)	0
79	Acrobat ACRO 3	MR UNIVERSE (LP, inner)	15
80	Virgin V 2171	GLORY ROAD (LP, with bonus LP "For Gillan Fans Only" [VDJ 32], stickered, embossed sleeve & inner sleeves)	15
82	Virgin VP 2236	MAGIC (LP, picture disc)	15

Dana GILLESPIE
MINT VALUE £

81	Virgin V2196	FUTURE SHOCK (LP, gatefold sleeve, booklet)	15

(see also Episode Six, Deep Purple, Ray Fenwick, Split Knee Loons, John McCoy, Johnny Gustafson, Bernie Tormé, Thunderstick, Jerusalem, Quatermass, Colin Towns, White Spirit, Zzebra)

DANA GILLESPIE
65	Pye 7N 15872	Donna Donna/It's No Use Saying If	15
65	Pye 7N 15962	Thank You Boy/You're A Heartbreak Man	15
67	Pye 7N 17280	Pay You Back With Interest/Adam Can You Beat That	8
68	Decca F 12847	You Just Gotta Know My Mind/He Loves Me, He Loves Me Not	60
74	RCA RCA 2466	Andy Warhol/Dizzy Heights	8
69	Decca LK 5012	BOX OF SURPRISES (LP, mono)	100
69	Decca SLK 5012	BOX OF SURPRISES (LP, stereo)	150
73	RCA APL1 0354	WEREN'T BORN A MAN (LP, insert)	20
74	RCA APL1 0682	AIN'T GONNA PLAY NO SECOND FIDDLE (LP, gatefold sleeve)	15

(see also David Bowie)

DIZZY GILLESPIE & CHARLIE PARKER
61	Vogue LAE 12252	DIZ 'N BIRD IN CONCERT (LP)	15

(see also Charlie Parker)

DOBIE GILLIS
68	United Artists UP 2212	How Peculiar/I Wish I Was Harry	8

JIMMY GILMER & FIREBALLS
62	London HLD 9632	I'm Gonna Go Walkin'/Born To Be With You (as Chimmy Gilmer)	15
63	London HLD 9789	Sugar Shack/My Heart Is Free	8
64	London HLD 9827	Daisy Petal Pickin'/When My Tears Have Dried	8
64	London HLD 9872	Ain't Gonna Tell Nobody/Young Am I	8
64	London HLD 9898	Look At Me/I'll Send For You	7
64	London HA-D/SH-D 8150	SUGAR SHACK (LP)	30
65	Dot DLP 3577	BUDDY'S BUDDY - BUDDY HOLLY SONGS BY JIMMY GILMER (LP)	30

(see also Fireballs, Jim & Monica)

DAVID GILMOUR
78	Harvest HAR 5167	There's No Way Out Of Here/Deafinitely (no p/s)	7
84	Harvest 12HAR 5226	Blue Light (LP Version)/Cruise (12", p/s)	10
06	EMI EMIDJ 733	Take a Breath (1-sided clear vinyl promo)	100
06	EMI EM 717. 0946 384878 7 6	Arnold Layne (vocal by David Bowie)/Arnold Layne (vocal by Richard Wright)//Dark Globe (p/s)	20
78	Harvest SHVL 817	DAVID GILMOUR (LP, gatefold)	20
06	EMI 094635569513	ON AN ISLAND (LP, gatefold sleeve)	80
08	EMI 50999 2 35484 1 1	LIVE IN GDANSK (5-LP box set)	250

(see also Pink Floyd, Joker's Wild, Unicorn)

BILL GILONIS & TIM HODGKINSON
79	Woof WOOF 001	I DO I DO I DON'T I DON'T (EP, silkscreened sleeve)	12

JAMES GILREATH
63	Pye International 7N 25190	Little Band Of Gold/I'll Walk With You	10
63	Pye International 7N 25213	Lollipops, Lace And Lipstick/Mean Ole River	12

GORDON GILTRAP (BAND)
77	Electric WOT 11	Lucifer's Cage/The Echoing Green (demos only)	10
78	Electric WOT 19	Heartsong/The Deserter (demos only)	10
78	Electric WOT 29	Fear Of The Dark/Catwalks Blues/Inner Dream (12" picture disc)	8
95	Munchkin MRC 1	THE BROTHERHOOD SUITE (cassette, 300 only)	30
73	Philips 6006 344	No Way Of Knowing/I See A Road	15
68	Transatlantic TRA 175	GORDON GILTRAP (LP, lilac label with 't' logo)	50
69	Transatlantic TRA 202	PORTRAIT (LP)	45
71	MCA MKPS 2020	A TESTAMENT OF TIME (LP, red/pink 'dogbone' label)	40
73	Philips 6308 175	GILTRAP (LP, with lyric insert, blue/silver label)	20

(see also Accolade, Pauline Filby, Catherine Andrews)

GIMIK
78	Mik MR 1	Dancehall Queen/No More Magic	8
79	Mik MIK 003	Schools Out Forever/Jaqui	20

GIMMICKS
70	Decca Eclipse ECS-R 2054	BRAZILIAN SAMBA (LP)	30

W. GIMMICS
65	Polydor EPH 27 125	HOT RODS (EP, manufactured in Europe)	60

GIMMIX
79	Elektra K 12377	Too Much/Testing Testing 1 2 3	15

GIMPO
97	Kaleval KALA 003	Gimpo/Gimpo (version)	25

GINGER ALE
70	Famous FAM 102	In The Sand/Get Off My Life Woman	8

GINGER AND THE NUTS
81	Do Nutt 0100	Pig In The Freezer/Oil Wars (no p/s)	10

GINGERBREAD (1)
69	B&C CB 113	How Are You/Easy Girl	6

GINGERBREAD (2)
71	Pye 7N 45054	Pollution/Moody Trudy	8

GINGER HOBBY HORSE
70	Ra RALP 6004	GINGER HOBBY HORSE AND FRIENDS (LP)	40

GINGER JUG BAND
70s	GJB 001	GINGER JUG BAND (LP, private pressing)	25

GINGER SNAPS
65	RCA RCA 1483	The Sh Down Down Song/I've Got Faith In Him	20

GINGRINI

GINGRINI
73 Harry J. HJ 6647 — Zion 'Iah/Zion 'Iah (Version) 10

GINHOUSE
71 Charisma CAS 1031 — GINHOUSE (LP, gatefold sleeve) 200

(see also Kestrel. Mouse, Sammy)

GINNUNGAGAP
06 Aurora Borealis ABX 007 — REMEINDRE (LP, clear folder cover, white vinyl) 15

GINO & GINA
58 Mercury 7MT 230 — Pretty Baby/Love's A Carousel 20

ALLEN GINSBERG
60s Cape Goliard — Wales: A Visitation (single issued with book of same title) 15
65 Better Books (no cat. no.) — ALLEN GINSBERG READING AT BETTER BOOKS (LP) 20
65 Love Books Ltd. LB 0001 — ALLEN GINSBERG, LAURENCE FERLINGHETTI, GREGORY CORSO & ANDREI VOZNESENSKY READING AT THE ARCHITECTURAL ASSOCIATION (LP) 20
68 Transatlantic TRA 192 — GINSBERG'S THING (LP) 15

(see also Ginsbergs)

GINSBERGS
67 Saga Psyche PSY 3002 — THE GINSBERGS AT THE ICA (LP) 15

(see also Allen Ginsberg)

GINSENG SPARTA
83 Guardian GRC 210 — Forbidden Fruit/Lazy Hazy Day 25

GINTY
80 Wild Dog DOG 25 — I Am The Walrus/A Little Understanding/Say You Don't Mind 10

MARCELLO GIOMBINI
70 United Artists UP 35110 — Sabata - Main Title/Banjo Arrives 10

GIORGIO
66 Page One POF 003 — Full Stop/Believe Me 6
67 Page One POF 028 — How Much Longer Must I Wait/Bla Bla Diddly 12
69 MCA 5025 — Moody Trudy/Stop 20
71 Parlophone R 5935 — Son Of My Father/I'm Free Now 10
71 A&M AMS 822 — Underdog/Watch Yourself 6

(see also Giorgio Moroder, Giorgio & Marco's Men)

GIORGIO & MARCO'S MEN
66 Polydor 56101 — Run Run/Girl Without A Heart 7
68 Electratone EP 1003 — Baby I Need You/Maureen 70

GIPSY LOVE
72 BASF BAP 5026 — GIPSY LOVE (LP) 20

CHUCK GIRARD
75 Myrrh MYR 1025 — CHUCK GIRARD (LP) 15
70s Myrrh MYR 1065 — WRITTEN ON THE WIND (LP) 15
70s myrrh MYR 1089 — THE STAND (LP) 15

GIRL TALK (U.S.)
04 Apostles 12AP03 — STOP CLEVELAND HATE EP (12") 12

GIRL
80 Jet 176 — Hollywood Tease/My Number 8

(see also Def Leppard, Bernie Torme)

GIRL BAND
15 Rough Trade RTRADS 763 — Pears For Lunch (7", 1-side etched, numbered) 10
15 Rough Trade RTRADST 736 — THE EARLY YEARS (12", 500 only) 18
15 Rough Trade RTRADLP770 — HOLDING HANDS WITH JAMIE (LP, yellow vinyl with booklet, signed) 35
15 Rough Trade RTRADLP770 — HOLDING HANDS WITH JAMIE (LP, yellow vinyl with booklet, unsigned) 30

GIRL GUIDED MISSILES
79 Seandee CND 01 — Desperate Men/Fully Qualified Robot (p/s, 1000 only) 80

GIRL OF MY BEST FRIEND
89 Ambition AMB 003 — Warm Around You/Seasons (p/s) 8

GIRLFRIENDS
63 Colpix PX 712 — Jimmy Boy/For My Sake (DJ Copy) 125
63 Colpix PX 712 — Jimmy Boy/For My Sake 60

GIRLIE
69 Treasure Isle TI 7053 — Boss Cocky/LOVE SHOCKS: Musical True 100
69 Bullet BU 400 — Madame Straggae/LAUREL AITKEN: Stupid Married Man 20
69 Duke DU 42 — African Meeting (as Girlie & Junior)/JOSH: Higher And Higher 15
70 Joe JRS 7 — Small Change/Mind Your Business (as Girlie & Joe [Mansano]) 15
70 Ackee ACK 124 — Decimilization/Decimilization Version (as Girlie & Paul) 15

(see also Laurel Aitken & Girlie, Madame Dracula)

GIRLS
09 Fantasy Trashcan FANTASY 002 — Lust For Life/Life In San Francisco (p/s, 500 only) 7
09 Fantasy Trashcan FANTASY 004 — Hellhole Ratrace/Solitude (10" p/s) 10

GIRLS ALOUD
03 Polydor JUMP 2 — Jump (Almighty Vocal Mix)/Jump/Girls Allowed (Almighty Vocal Mix)/Jump (Almighty Dub Mix) (12" pink glitter promo) 20
03 Polydor NGA 2 — No Good Advice - Doublefunk Vocal Mix/Doublefunk Dub Mix/Dreadzone Vocal/Clean Version (12" promo, p/s) 12
05 Polydor 9874045 — Long Hot Summer/Long Hot Summer - Tony Lamezma Rides Again/Jump - Almighty Vocal Mix) (12", p/s) 15
04 Polydor WHATGA 3 — WHAT WILL THE NEIGHBOURS SAY? (LP, promo, pink vinyl) 20

GIRLS AT OUR BEST
80 Record Records RR 001 — Getting Nowhere Fast/Warm Girls (p/s) 15
81 Record Records RR 002 — Politics/It's Fashion (p/s) 10
81 Happy Birthday UR 4 — Go For Gold/I'm Beautiful Now (p/s) 10

GIRLSCHOOL
MINT VALUE £

81	Happy Birthday UR 6	Fast Boyfriends/This Train (p/s)	10
81	Happy Birthday RULP 1	PLEASURE (LP, with lyric insert, 1st 10,000 with free 'pleasure bag' with 2 postcards, sticker & stencil)	20

GIRLSCHOOL
79	City NIK 6	Take It All Away/It Could Be Better (p/s, red vinyl, pink p/s, b&w front photo)	7
79	Mulligan LUNS 723	Take It All Away/It Could Be Better (Irish version, no p/s, red vinyl)	8
88	GWR GWR14	Head Over Heals/Action (unissued)	10
81	Bronze BRON 534	HIT AND RUN (LP, red vinyl)	20

(see also Motorhead, Killjoys, Framed)

GIRLS IN SYNTHESIS
17	Blank/Own It BETBC008	SUBURBAN HELL EP (p/s)	40
18	Blank/Own It BETBC014	WE MIGHT NOT MAKE TOMORROW EP (p/s)	40
18	Blank/Own It BETBC015	FAN THE FLAMES EP (p/s, numbered)	40

GIRL TALK (U.K.)
84	Innervision IVST 4	Can The Rhythm (mixes) (12", p/s)	12

GIST
81	Rough Trade RT 58	This Is Love/Yanks (p/s)	8
81	Rough Trade RT 85	Love At First Sight/Light Aircraft (p/s)	7
83	Rough Trade RT 125	Fool For A Valentine/Fool For A Version (p/s)	7
83	Rough Trade ROUGH 25	EMBRACE THE HERD (LP)	15

GITS
89	Stig STIG 0019	Too Many People/Happy Song (p/s)	40

GITTE
64	Columbia DB 7440	The Heart That You Break (May Be Your Own)/Seems Just Like Old Times	10

JIMMY GIUFFRE
55	Capitol LC 6699	JIMMY GIUFFRE (10" LP)	20
57	London Jazz LTZK 15059	THE JIMMY GIUFFRE CLARINET (LP)	15
58	London Jazz LTZK 15130	JIMMY GIUFFRE (LP)	25
58	London Jazz LTZK 15137	TRAV'LIN' LIGHT (LP)	20

(see also Shelly Manne)

GIZMO
75	President PT 443	Just Like Velvet/Jesus Help Me Sleep	8

GLADDY (ANDERSON) & FOLLOWERS
69	Blue Cat BS 172	Judas/The World Come To An End	40

(see also Stranger & Glady)

GLADDY (ANDERSON) & STRANGER (COLE)
73	Pama PM 872	Dedicated To Illiteracy/G.G. ALLSTARS: Dub	8

(see also Gladstone Anderson, Stranger Cole, Stranger & Glady)

GLADE
72	Glade 1	Touching The Sky/Evil	80

GLADIATORS (1)
63	HMV POP 1134	Bleak House/Tovaritch	25

(see also Nero & Gladiators)

GLADIATORS (2)
68	Direction 58-3854	Girl Don't Make Me Wait/Can't Get Away From Heartbreak	18
69	Direction 58-4308	Waiting On The Shores Of Nowhere/I'll Always Love You	18
69	Direction 58-4507	As Long As I Live/Everything	10
69	Direction 58-4660	Twelfth Of Never/Lovin' My Baby Back Home	8

GLADIATORS (JAMAICA)
69	Studio One SO 2072	Hello Carol/RICHARD ACE: More Reggae	50
69	Studio One SO 2086	Kicks/Games People Play	45
69	Doctor Bird DB 1114	The Train Is Coming/Feeling So Fine	30
69	Bamboo BAM 7	Any Where/SOUND DIMENSION: Baby Face	30
70	Rock Steady Rev. REVR 12	Unusual Reggae/Andue	20
70	Duke DU 58	My Girl (actually by Glen Adams)/You Were To Be	25
72	Ackee ACK 149	Sonia/SOUND DIMENSION: Solas	30
77	Virgin VS 19312	Pocket Money/Money Version Disco Mix/Evil Doers/Disco Mix (12")	30
76	Virgin V2062	TRENCHTOWN MIX UP (LP, 1st pressing with white rim around labels)	60
76	Virgin V2062	TRENCHTOWN MIX UP (LP, 2nd pressing without white rim around labels)	40
78	Virgin Frontline FL 1002	PROVERBIAL REGGAE (LP)	30
78	Virgin Frontline FL 1035	NATURALITY (LP)	30
79	Virgin Frontline FL 1048	SWEET SO TILL (LP)	25
81	Virgin VX 1003	VITAL SELECTION (LP)	25
82	Nighthawk NIGHTHAWK	SYMBOL OF REALITY (LP)	20

GLADIOLAS
57	London HLO 8435	Little Darlin'/Sweetheart, Please Don't Go	100
57	London HLO 8435	Little Darlin'/Sweetheart, Please Don't Go (78 rpm)	25

(see also Maurice Williams & Zodiacs)

GLAM SLAM
91	Good Vibrations GOT 25	The Leader/Tell Him/Coz I Love You (fold out p/s)	30

GLASGOW
84	Neat NEAT 40	Stranded/Heat Of The Night (p/s)	15
84	Clydebank CLY 001	GLASGOW'S MILES BETTER (12" EP)	12

LUD GLASKIN
62	UPC 3428	To My Good Friend Jack Cotton, the 'Allo Twist (1-sided private pressing)	25

GLASS
82	Glass GLASS1	New Colours/Sweet Entropy (p/s)	22

GLASS MUSEUM
80	Fflang NAFF 1	Free Kings/Alternative Take	8

Philip GLASS

MINT VALUE £

PHILIP GLASS
76	Caroline CA 2010	MUSIC IN 12 (PARTS 1 & 2) (LP, 1st pressing in matt textured sleeve)	35
76	Caroline CA 2010	MUSIC IN 12 (PARTS 1 & 2) (LP, 2nd pressing in glossy sleeve)	20
77	Virgin V 2085	NORTH STAR (LP, 1st issue, with green "mirror" girl label)	15
78	Shandar SHAN 83515	SOLO MUSIC (LP)	15
79	CBS M4 38875	EINSTEIN ON THE BEACH (4-LP box set, with booklet)	40
82	CBS 73640	GLASSWORKS (LP)	15
83	Island ISTA 4	KOYAANISQATSI (LP, soundtrack)	25
85	CBS 13M39672	SATYAGRAHA (3-LP box set, booklet)	40
85	Nonsuch 979113-1	MISHIMA (LP)	15
86	CBS M342457	AKHNATEN (3-LP box set, booklet)	40
15	Music On Vinyl MOVCL015	HEROES SYMPHONY (LP, reissue, white vinyl)	35

GLASS ANIMALS
12	Kaya Kaya KKT001	LEAFLINGS EP (12", p/s)	60
13	Wolf Tone WOLFPROM01	Psylla/Black Mambo/Exxus/Woozy (10", p/s)	60
13	Wolf Tone WOLFTONE 1	Black Mambo/Exxus/Black Mambo (Zodiac Remix)/Exxus (Pattern Remix) (12", p/s, many signed)	70
14	Wolf Tone WOLFTONE 2	GOOEY (12", p/s)	60
15	Wolf Tone WOLFSTONERSD1	REMIXES EP (12", p/s)	40
19	Wolf Tone 7736623	ZABA STRIPPED (12", p/s)	20
14	Wolf Tone WOLFTONE001LP	ZABA (2-LP, 1st pressimg)	30
16	Wolf Tone WOLFTONE012LP	HOW TO BE A HUMAN BEING (2-LP)	30

GLASS HARP
72	MCA MUPS 431	GLASS HARP (LP)	25
72	MCA MUPS 449	SYNERGY (LP)	22

GLASS HOUSE
70	Invictus INV 506	Stealing Moments From Another Woman's Life/If It Ain't Love, It Don't Matter	8
71	Invictus INV 510	I Can't Be You/He's In My Life	8

GLASS MENAGERIE
68	Pye 7N 17518	She's A Rainbow/But That's When I Start To Love Her	12
68	Pye 7N 17568	You Didn't Have To Be So Nice/Let's All Run To The Sun	10
68	Pye 7N 17615	Frederick Jordan/I Said Goodbye To Me	240
69	Polydor 56318	Have You Forgotten Who You Are/Do You Ever Think?	10
69	Polydor 56341	Do My Thing Myself/Watching The World Pass By	25

(see also Paladin, Toe-Fat)

GLASS OPENING
68	Plexium P 1236	Silver Bells And Cockle Shells/Does It Really Matter	250

GLASS TORPEDOES
79	Teen Beat TBR 1	SOMEONE DIFFERENT EP	6

GLASVEGAS
04	Rebelstance J 21091979	I'm Gonna Get Stabbed/Ina Lvs Rab (CD-R, self release with lyric inner)	80
06	Waks WAKS 0035	Go Square Go/Legs 'N' Show (400 only, with lyric insert)	50
07	Sane Man SAN 001	Daddy's Gone/Flowers And Football Tops (p/s, 1,000 only, numbered)	20
08	Sane Man SAN 002	It's My Own Cheating Heart That Makes Me Cry/Be My Baby (2,000 only)	6
11	Columbia GOWOW23	Euphoria, Take My Hand/Georgia, Walk With Me	8
08	Columbia GOWOW012	GLASVEGAS (LP)	30

GLAXO BABIES
79	Heartbeat PULSE 5	Christine Keeler/Nova Bossanova (p/s)	10
79	Heartbeat PULSE 3	THIS IS YOUR LIFE (12" EP)	15
80	Cherry Red PULSE 8	Shake (The Foundations)/She Went To Pieces (Live 28-03-79)	7
80	Rough Trade Y6	LIMITED ENTERTAINMENT EP	6
80	Heartbeat HBM 3	PUT ME ON THE GUEST LIST (LP)	25
80	Heartbeat HB 2	NINE MONTHS TO THE DISCO (LP)	25

GLEN (BROWN) & LLOYD (ROBINSON)
66	Ska Beat JB 250	Live And Let Others Live/Too Late	45
67	Doctor Bird DB 1099	Feel Good Now/What You've Got (credited as Lloyd Glen)	45

GLENCOE
72	Epic EPC 8383	Look Me In The Eye/Telephonia	6
72	Epic EPC 65207	GLENCOE (LP)	25
73	Epic EPC 65717	SPIRIT OF GLENCOE (LP)	15

(see also Hopscotch, Five Day Rain, Greatest Show On Earth, Loving Awareness)

GLENDALES
79	Pennine PS 143	Morgan/Too Late To Change Your Mind/Toymaker (500 only, no p/s)	6

DARRELL GLENN
54	HMV 7MC 23	In The Chapel In The Moonlight/Once And Only Once (export issue)	8

GLIDE
95	Ochre OCH 001L	SPACE AGE FREAK OUT (LP)	20

(see also Echo & Bunnymen)

GLITTERHOUSE
68	Stateside SS 2129	Barbarella/BOB CREWE: An Angel Is Love	20
68	Stateside SS 2129	Barbarella/Love Drags Me Down (different B-side)	18

GLITTERS
60	Gala GSP 810	Red River Rock/PROMINEERS: Poison Ivy	8

GLOBAL COMMUNICATIONS
93	Evolution EVO 04	KEONGAKU EP (12", 4-track, plain sleeve)	25
94	Dedicated DEDLP 014L	76: 14 (2-LP, gatefold sleeve with bonus 12" [DEDLP 0145])	30
94	Dedicated DEDLP 014	76: 14 (2-LP, gatefold sleeve)	25
96	Dedicated DED 21LP	REMOTION - THE GLOBAL COMMUNICATIONS REMIX ALBUM (2-LP)	20
20	Evolution EVOR 11	TRANSMISSIONS (7-LP, box set)	150

(see also Mystic Institue, Link, Reload, Reload & E621, Chaos & Julia Set, Jedi Knights)

GLOBAL METHOD

GLOBAL METHOD
92 Not On Label GM1   VIBE TRIBE (EP) 110

GLOBAL VILLAGE TRUCKING COMPANY
76 Caroline C 1516   GLOBAL VILLAGE TRUCKING COMPANY (LP, with lyric insert, b/s & red label, twins logo) . 30

(see also Byzantium, Man)

GLOBE SHOW
69 Page One POF 128   Yes Or No/Gettin' On Back 30

(see also Chris Shakespeare Globe Show)

GLOBE TROTTERS
54 Parlophone CMSP 18   At Sundown/My Gal Sal (export issue) 10
54 Parlophone GEP 8528   SATURDAY NIGHT HOP (EP) 15

GLOBETROTTERS
70 RCA RCA 2017   Gravy/Cheer Me Up 10
71 RCA SF 8158   THE GLOBETROTTERS (LP) 15

GLOK
19 Bytes BYTES02LP   DISSIDENT (LP, green vinyl) 20
20 Bytes BYTES02LP   DISSIDENT REMIXED (2-LP, splatter vinyl) 30

(see also Ride)

GLOOMYS
68 Columbia DB 8391   Daybreak/Queen And King 15
71 DJM DJS 240   I'm A Bum/Let Me Dream 10

GLORIA
69 Columbia DB 8568   The Last Seven Days/Merry Dance 15

GLORIA MUNDI
78 RCA PB 5118   Glory To The World/Nothing To Say (p/s) 8
79 RCA PB 5169   YY?/Do You Believe (no p/s) 7
79 RCA PB 5193   Dangerous To Dream/Temporary Hell Part 2 (no p/s) 7
78 RCA PL2 5157   I INDIVIDUAL (LP, with inner sleeve) 15
79 RCA PL2 5244   THE WORD IS OUT (LP, with lyric inner) 15

GLORIANA
72 No label or cat no   MUSIC FOR A WHILE (LP, black labels) 200

GLORIAS ALLSTARS
70 Camel CA 48   Jumping Dick/News Room 25

GLORIES
67 CBS 2786   I Stand Accused (Of Loving You)/Wish They Could Write A Song 15
67 CBS 2786   I Stand Accused (Of Loving You)/Wish They Could Write A Song (DJ Copy) 20
67 Direction 58-3084   (I Love You Babe But) Give Me My Freedom/Security 20
68 Direction 58-3300   Sing Me A Love Song/Oh Baby That's Love 15
68 Direction 58-3646   My Sweet Sweet Baby/Stand By (I'm Comin' Home) 10

GLORY HUNTER
79 Rock Hard CPS 027   Thoughts Of Destiny/At The Crossroads (no p/s) 800

GLORY LANDERS
69 IBA SECC 1203   VOLUME 1 (LP) 15

GLOVE
83 Wonderland SHE 5   Punish Me With Kisses/The Tightrope (p/s) 8
83 Wonderland SHELP 2   BLUE SUNSHINE (LP, mispressing with double-printed sleeve) 20

(see also Cure, Siouxsie & Banshees)

ROGER GLOVER (& GUESTS)
74 Purple PUR 125   Love Is All/Old Blind Mole/Magician Moth 10
84 Polydor POSP 678   The Mask/So Remote (p/s, solo) 8
74 Purple TPSA 7514   THE BUTTERFLY BALL (AND THE GRASSHOPPER'S FEAST) (LP, g/fold sleeve) 15
84 Polydor POLD 5139   THE MASK (LP, solo, with insert) 15

(see also [Sheila Carter &] Episode [Six], Deep Purple, Elf, Eddie Hardin, Whitesnake, Rainbow, Glenn Hughes, John Lawton, Wizard's Convention, Marlon, Green Bullfrog, David Coverdale, Dio)

JEREMY GLUCK
86 Flicknife SHARP 037   I KNEW BUFFALO BILL (LP) 15

(see also Barracudas)

G MEN
82 Cro Magnon   G-MEN (EP, 1000 only) 20

GMT
91 Mausoleum BONE 12-83102   One By One (12", p/s) 10

GNAC
98 Earworm WORM 29   The Moustache/Armchair Thriller (p/s, black vinyl) 6

GNANK
99 Gnank GNANK 01   Gnank Gnank/Oi, Gnank (p/s) 8

GNASHER
74 Purple PUR 119   Medina Road/Easy Meat 10

GNIDROLOG
72 RCA SF 8261   IN SPITE OF HARRY'S TOE-NAIL (LP, gatefoldsleeve, orange label) 200
72 RCA SF 8322   LADY LAKE (LP, with lyric insert) 350
72 RCA SF 8322   LADY LAKE (LP, without lyric insert) 250

(see also Pork Dukes, Steeleye Span)

GNOMES OF ZURICH
66 Planet PLF 121   Please Mr Sun/I'm Coming Down With The Blues (with custom 'Planet' sleeve) 60
66 Planet PLF 121   Please Mr Sun/I'm Coming Down With The Blues (without custom 'Planet' sleeve) 30
67 CBS 202556   Hang On Baby/Blues For My Baby 30
67 CBS 2694   High Hopes/Pretender 30
67 RCA Victor RCA 1606   Second Fiddle/Publicity Girl 60

G-NOTES
58 Oriole CB 1456   Ronnie (How I Wish He'd Notice Me)/I Would 20

GOAT

MINT VALUE £

GOAT
12	Rocket LAUNCH 048	WORLD MUSIC (LP 1st pressing on orange vinyl, 300 only)	40

GOBBLEDEGOOKS
64	Decca F 12023	Now And Again/Where Have You Been	15

GOBBLINZ
79	Pinnacle P 8454	London/Women In Love (p/s)	80
79	Bacon SLICE 01	Love Me Too/All Of This And More (p/s)	80

GO-BETWEENS
80	Postcard 80-4	I Need Two Heads/Stop Before You Say It (brown label & brown co. sleeve)	25
80	Postcard 80-4	I Need Two Heads/Stop Before You Say It (b/w A side label, yellow/red B side label, cream co. sleeve)	35
82	Rough Trade RT 108	Hammer The Hammer/By Chance (p/s)	18
83	Rough Trade RT 144	Man O'Sand To Girl O'Sea/This Girl Black Girl (p/s)	15
83	Rough Trade RT 124	Cattle And Cane/Heaven Says (p/s)	18
84	Sire W9156	Bachelor Kisses/Rare Breed (p/s)	10
84	Sire W9156T	Bachelor Kisses/Rare Breed/Unkind And Unwise (Instrumental) (12", p/s)	15
84	Sire W9211	Part Company/Just A King In Mirrors (p/s)	10
84	Sire W9211T	Part Company/Just A King In Mirrors/Newton Told Me (12", p/s)	15
86	Beggars Banquet BEG 155	Spring Rain/The Life At Hand (p/s)	7
86	Situation 2 SIT 44T	ABLE LABEL SINGLES (12" EP, gatefold sleeve)	30
87	Beggars Banquet BEG 183D	Right Here/When People Are Dead/A Little Romance//Don't Call Me Gone/A Little Romance (live) (double pack)	8
88	Beggars Banquet BEG 218B	Streets On Your Town/Wait Until June (box set with 7", badge, photo and map)	10
05	Lo-Max 022V	WORLDS APART (12", p/s)	25
89	Strange Fruit SFPS 074	PEEL SESSIONS (12" EP)	20
82	Rough Trade ROUGH 45	SEND ME A LULLABY (LP, inner)	40
83	Rough Trade ROUGH 54	BEFORE HOLLYWOOD (LP)	40
84	Sire 925 197-1	SPRING HILL FAIR (LP)	30
86	Beggars Banquet BEGA 72	LIBERTY BELLE AND THE BLACK DIAMOND EXPRESS (LP, textured sleeve)	30
87	Beggars Banquet BEGA 81	TALLULAH (LP, inner)	30
88	Beggars Banquet BEGA 95	16 LOVERS LANE (LP, inner)	35
88	Beggars Banquet BBL 72	LIBERTY BELLE AND THE BLACK DIAMOND EXPRESS (LP, reissue, matt sleeve)	20
90	Beggars Banquet BEGA 104	1978 - 1990 (2-LP)	25
15	Domino REWIG89X	G STANDS FOR GO-BETWEENS VOLUME 1 (box set, 3-LP, 4, CD, booklet, print, insert, download card and book from Grant McLennan's library)	600
15	Domino REWIG90X	G STANDS FOR GO-BETWEENS VOLUME 1 (box set, 3-LP, 4, CD, booklet, songbook download card but no book from Grant McLennan's library)	500
19	Domino REWIG90X	G STANDS FOR GO-BETWEENS VOLUME 2 (box set, 5-LP, 4CD, booklet, songbook download card but no book from Grant McLennan's library)	200
19	Domino REWIG90X	G STANDS FOR GO-BETWEENS VOLUME 2 (box set, 5-LP, 4CD, booklet, songbook download card and book from Grant McLennan's library)	250

GOBLIN
79	EMI EMC 3222	SUSPIRIA (LP, soundtrack)	35

VIC GODARD (& SUBWAY SECT)
85	El Benelux EL 4T	Holiday Hymn/Nice On The Ice/Stop That Girl/Ice On The Volcano/ T.R.O.U.B.L.E. (12", p/s)	10
80	Oddball/MCA MCF 3070	WHAT'S THE MATTER BOY? (LP, with Subway Sect)	20
82	London SH 8549	SONGS FOR SALE (LP, with Subway Sect)	18
85	Rough Trade ROUGH 56	A RETROSPECTIVE (LP, inner sleeve, with Subway Sect)	20
85	MCA/El 01	HOLIDAY HYMN (LP, 10 test pressings only; abandoned issue of "T.R.O.U.B.L.E.")	40
86	Rough Trade ROUGH 86	T.R.O.U.B.L.E. (LP)	15
93	Postcard DUBH 936	END OF THE SURREY PEOPLE (LP)	15

(see also Subway Sect)

KEITH & DONNA GODCHAUX
75	Round RX 104	KEITH & DONNA GODCHAUX (LP)	18

(see also Grateful Dead)

GEOFF GODDARD
61	HMV POP 938	Girl Bride/For Eternity	50
62	HMV POP 1068	My Little Girl's Come Home/Try Once More	50
63	HMV POP 1160	Saturday Dance/Come Back To Me	40
63	HMV POP 1213	Sky Men/Walk With Me My Angel	80

GODFATHER DON
07	Diggers With Gratitude DWG 002	SLAVE OF NEW YORK (EP, 150 only)	180
09	Diggers With Gratitude DWG 005	BILLY BATHGATE (12", 20 only, green vinyl)	120
09	Diggers With Gratitude DWG 005	BILLY BATHGATE (12", 280 only, black vinyl)	30

GODFLESH
91	Earache MOSH 30 T	SLAVESTATE (12", p/s)	12
91	Earache MOSH 47	Slateman/Wound'91 (p/s)	6
91	Earache MOSH 56T	Cold World/Nihil/Nihil (Total Belief Mix)/Nihil (No Belief Mix) (12", p/s)	15
94	Earache MOSH 116	Merciless/Blind/Unworthy/Flowers (2 x 7", white vinyl, gatefold p/s)	15
88	Swordfish FLESH LP 1	GODFLESH (LP, textured sleeve, inner)	20
89	Earache MOSH 15	STREETCLEANER (LP)	15
92	Earache MOSH 32	PURE (LP, poster, insert)	20
94	Earache MOSH 85	SELFLESS (LP, insert)	20

HUGH GODFREY
67	Coxsone CS 7001	A Dey Pon Dem/SOUL BROTHERS: Take Ten	100
67	Studio One SO 2008	My Time/MARCIA GRIFFITHS: Hound Dog	80
67	Studio One SO 2015	Go Tell Him/MARCIA GRIFFITHS: After Laughter (b-side actually by Freddie McGregor)	80

(see also Soul Brothers)

Rare Record Price Guide 2024

Robert JOHN GODFREY

MINT VALUE £

ROBERT JOHN GODFREY
74 Charisma CAS 1084   FALL OF HYPERION (LP) 40

(see also Enid, Godfrey & Stewart, Don Bradshaw)

GODFREY & STEWART
88   The Enid ENID 11   THE SEED AND THE SOWER (LP) 15
80s The Stand HEARTLP   JOINED BY THE HEART (LP, fan club issue, 2,000 only) 20
80s The Stand HEARTC   JOINED BY THE HEART (LP, fan club issue) 12

(see also Robert John Godfrey, Enid)

GODIEGO
79   BBC RESL 66   Gandhara/The Birth Of The Odyssey/Monkey Magic 7

GODLEY & CREME
68   Blinkers 1215   Goodnight Blinkers/Hello Blinkers (die-cut sleeve) 300
79   Mercury SAMP 017   5 O'Clock/The Flood//Lost Weekend/Honolulu (double pack sampler, promo) 10

(see also Mockingbirds, Hotlegs, 10cc, Dave Berry, Frabjoy & Runcible Spoon, Cruisers, Whirlwinds, Doctor Father)

GOD MACHINE
91   Eve EVER 8T   PURITY: Home/The Blind Man/Purity (12", p/s) 20
92   Fiction FICSX 44   Desert Song/Prostitute/Commitment/Pictures Of A Bleeding Boy (12", p/s) 20
93   Fiction FICSX 47   Home/All My Colours/Train/Fever (12", p/s) 20
93   Fiction FIXH 23   SCENES FROM THE SECOND STOREY (2-LP) 150
94   Fiction FIXH 27   ONE LAST LAUGH IN A PLACE OF DYING (LP) 175

GODS
67   Polydor 56168   Come On Down To My Boat Baby/Garage Man 180
68   Columbia DB 8486   Baby's Rich/Somewhere In The Street 60
69   Columbia DB 8544   Hey! Bulldog/Real Love Guaranteed 40
69   Columbia DB 8572   Maria/Long Time, Sad Time, Bad Time 40
68   Columbia SX 6286   GENESIS (LP, mono, blue/black label with "sold in U.K..." text) 600
70   SCX 6286   GENESIS (LP, stereo, silver/black label) 350
70   Columbia SCX 6372   TO SAMUEL A SON (LP, black/silver labels with boxed logo) 600
76   Harvest SHSM 2011   GODS (LP) 30
15   Parlophone 0825646172375   GENESIS (LP, reissue, multicoloured vinyl) 15

(see also Uriah Heep, Shame, Toe-Fat, Birds Birds, Carmen, Jethro Tull)

GODS GIFT
79   Newmarket NEW 101   THESE DAYS EP 15

GOD SONS
72   Green Door GD 4024   Merry Up/Merry Up - Version 10

(see also Errol & U Roy, Carl Masters, Glen Brown)

GODSONS
71   Philips 6006155   All Dressed In White/We've Not Made It 15

(see also Orange Bicycle)

GODZ
67   Fontana STL 5500   CONTACT WITH THE GODZ (LP) 40
69   Fontana STL 5512   GODZ II (LP) 40

GOGMAGOG
85   F. For Thought YUMT 109   I Will Be There/Living In A Timewarp/It's Illegal, It's Immoral, It's Unhealthy But It's Fun (12", p/s & insert) 35

(see also Iron Maiden, Di'Anno, Def Leppard, Whitesnake, Gillan, White Spirit)

GO GO THUNDER
75   RCA RCA 2494   The Race/Mrs. Mann 20

GO-GO'S (U.K.)
64   Oriole CB 1982   I'm Gonna Spend My Christmas With A Dalek/Big Boss Man (in p/s) 60
64   Oriole CB 1982   I'm Gonna Spend My Christmas With A Dalek/Big Boss Man 40

GO-GO'S (U.S.)
80   Stiff BUY 78   We Got The Beat/How Much More (p/s) 10
81   I.R.S. PFP 1007   Our Lips Are Sealed/Surfing And Spying (p/s, pink vinyl) 6

(see also Jane Wiedlin)

GOING RED?
81   Razz CLEAN 1   Some Boys/Tune Kevin's Strings (p/s) 12
81   MCA MCA 673   Some Boys/Tune Kevin's Strings (reissue, p/s) 7

(see also Freshies, Chris Sievey, Jilted John)

HERBIE GOINS & NIGHT-TIMERS
66   Parlophone R 5478   No. 1 In Your Heart/Cruisin' 150
66   Parlophone R 5478   No. 1 In Your Heart/Cruisin' (DJ Copy) 200
66   Parlophone R 5533   The Incredible Miss Brown/Comin' Home To You 120
67   Parlophone PMC 7026   NUMBER ONE IN YOUR HEART (LP) 200

(see also Night-Timers, Alexis Korner's Blues Incorporated)

GO-KART MOZART
12   West Midlands GLUM 2   New World In The Morning/Gizmos Gadgets Unrock Electric Guitar Clock Tick Tock (100 only) 6
99   West Midlands Records BRUM 1 INSTANT WIGWAM AND IGLOO MIXTURE (LP, 1,000 only, with poster and small sealing sticker over opening) 40
04   West Midlands BRUM 4   ON THE HOT DOG STREETS (2-LP) 30

(see also Felt, Denim, Supermarket)

GOLANT PISTONS
78   Sawmills/Sonet SON 2165   I Can See Where I'm Going/Katy May (p/s) 6
79   Sawmills/Sonet SON 2184   Friday On My Mind/Break The Spell 7

DAVID GOLD
97   Fat Cat 10FAT 001   Respect City Police (10") 40

BARRY GOLDBERG (REUNION)
68   Pye International 7N 25465 Another Day/Capricorn Blues (as Barry Goldberg Reunion) 7
68   Pye Intl. NSPL 28116   BARRY GOLDBERG REUNION (LP) 20
69   Buddah 203 020   TWO JEWS BLUES (LP, with Mike Bloomfield) 15

GOLDEBRIARS

(see also Electric Flag, Mike Bloomfield)

GOLDEBRIARS
| 64 | Columbia DB 7384 | Sea Of Tears/I've Got To Love Somebody | 10 |

GOLDEN APPLES OF THE SUN
| 65 | Decca F 12194 | Monkey Time/Chocolate Rolls, Tea And Monopoly (unissued, test pressings only) | 100 |
| 65 | Immediate IM 010 | Monkey Time/Chocolate Rolls, Tea And Monopoly | 70 |

GOLDEN CRUSADERS
64	Columbia DB 7232	I'm In Love With You/Always On My Mind	10
64	Columbia DB 7357	Hey Good Lookin'/Come On, Come On	10
65	Columbia DB 7485	I Don't Care/That Broken Heart Is Mine	10

GOLDEN DAWN
| 88 | Sarah SARAH 009 | My Secret World/Spring-Heeled Jack/The Railway Track (p/s, with poster) | 45 |
| 89 | Sarah SARAH 017 | George Hamilton's Dead/The Sweetest Touch/Let's Build A Dyonsphere (p/s, with poster) | 25 |

GOLDEN EARRING(S)
68	Capitol CL 15552	I've Just Lost Somebody/The Truth About Arthur (as Golden Earrings)	25
68	Capitol CL 15567	Dong Dong Di Ki Di Gi Dong/Wake Up - Breakfast (as Golden Earrings)	20
69	Major Minor MM 601	Just A Little Peace In My Heart/Remember My Friend (as Golden Earrings)	20
69	Major Minor MM 633	It's Alright But It Could Be Better/Where Will I Be (as Golden Earrings)	12
70	Major Minor MM 679	Another Forty-Five Miles/I Can't Get Hold Of Her	25
70	Polydor BM 56514	That Day/Words I Need	20
70	Polydor 2001 073	Back Home/This Is The Time Of Year	8
73	Track 2094 116	Radar Love/Just Like Vince Taylor	6
69	Major Minor SMLP 65	EIGHT MILES HIGH (LP)	150
70	Polydor 2310049	GOLDEN EARRING (LP, gatefold sleeve)	70
71	Polydor 2310 135	SEVEN TEARS (LP)	30
72	Polydor 2310 210	TOGETHER (LP)	18
73	Track 2406 109	HEARING EARRING (LP, braille sleeve)	18
73	Track 2406 112	MOONTAN (LP, gatefold sleeve with insert)	18

GOLDEN FLEECE
| 67 | Decca F 12669 | Athens 6 a.m./Girl From Syracuse | 6 |

GOLDEN GATE STRINGS
| 65 | Columbia DB 7634 | Mr. Tambourine Man/With God On Our Side | 30 |

GOLDFRAPP
00	Mute P STUMM 188	FELT MOUNTAIN ALBUM SAMPLER (12" promo, p/s)	10
00	Mute STUMM 188	FELT MOUNTAIN (LP, with inner)	100
03	Mute STUMM 196	BLACK CHERRY (LP)	100
05	Mute STUMM 250	SUPERNATURE (LP, gatefold)	100
08	Mute STUMM 280	SEVENTH TREE (LP, with poster)	50
10	Mute STUMM 320	HEAD FIRST (LP, with CD insert)	30
13	Mute STUMM 356	TALES OF US (LP with CD)	15

GOLDIE
| 95 | FFRR 828 614-1 | TIMELESS (2-LP, gatefold) | 40 |

GOLDIE (AND THE GINGERBREADS)
65	Decca F 12070	Can't You Hear My Heartbeat/Little Boy	15
65	Decca F 12126	That's Why I Love You/The Skip	25
65	Decca F 12199	Sailor Boy/Please Please	15
66	Immediate IM 026	Going Back/Headlines (solo)	40
66	Fontana TF 693	I Do/Think About The Good Times (solo)	30

(see also Ten Wheel Drive)

JOHN GOLDING
| 74 | Cottage 101S | DISCARDED VERSE (LP, 2,000 only) | 20 |

GOLD IN THE SHADE
90	TSR TSCRT 4	Shining Through/Dance Mix (12")	50
91	TSR TSCRT 5/4	Over You/Shining Through (12")	60
91	TSR TSCRT 5/3	Over You/Mix 2/SPECIAL TOUCH: You're So Good (12")	50
92	DEEP 001	I Really Love You So/Mix 2/Mix 3/Mix 4 (12")	40

(see also Special Touch, Out Of The Shade)

GOLD LEAF
| 73 | Pembrook PEM 1 | After The Rain/The Sun (p/s) | 200 |
| 73 | Pembrook PEM 1 | After The Rain/The Sun (no p/s) | 50 |

GOLD MACHINE
| 80 | Auberge MH 29444 | Suspect/Twilight | 10 |

VIVIEN GOLDMAN
| 81 | Window WIN 1 | Launderette/Private Armies (gatefold p/s, with PiL) | 40 |
| 81 | Window 12WIN 1 | Launderette/Private Armies (12", different p/s, with PiL) | 30 |

(see also Public Image Ltd)

ANNA GOLDRICK
| 70s | Polydor 2384030 | IT'S HERSELF (LP) | 30 |

GOLDRUSH
| 73 | Decca F13380 | For A Few Dollars More/No More - No Less | 6 |

BOBBY GOLDSBORO
63	Stateside SS 193	The Runaround/The Letter	20
63	United Artists UP 1046	See The Funny Little Clown/Hello Loser	8
64	United Artists UP 1054	Whenever He Holds You/If She Was Mine	10
65	United Artists UP 1079	Little Things/I Just Can't Go On Pretending	15
65	United Artists UP 1091	Voodoo Woman/It Breaks My Heart	12
65	United Artists UP 1104	If You Wait For Love/If You've Got A Heart	10
66	United Artists UP 1120	Broomstick Cowboy/Ain't Got Time For Happy	10
66	United Artists UP 1128	It's Too Late/I'm Goin' Home	15

GOLDSMITH

MINT VALUE £

66	United Artists UP 1128	It's Too Late/I'm Goin' Home (DJ copy)	30
66	United Artists UP 1135	I Know You Better Than That/When Your Love Has Gone	7
66	United Artists UP 1146	Take Your Love/Longer Than Forever	25
67	United Artists UP 1156	It Hurts Me/Pity The Fool	10
67	United Artists UP 1166	No Fun At The Fair/Hold On	35
67	United Artists UP 1177	Too Many People/Goodbye To All You Women	200
67	United Artists UP 1177	Too Many People/Goodbye To All You Women (DJ copy)	250
68	United Artists UP 2223	Autumn Of My Life/She Chased Me	10
69	United Artists UP 2264	Love Arrester/Dissatisfied Man	15
69	United Artists UP 35034	Muddy Mississippi Line/Richer Man Than I	8
65	United Artists UEP 1006	LITTLE THINGS (EP)	45
66	United Artists UEP 1016	THE TALENTED BOBBY GOLDSBORO (EP)	45
65	United Artists ULP 1118	I CAN'T STOP LOVING YOU (LP)	35
66	United Artists (S)ULP 1135	IT'S TOO LATE (LP)	35
67	United Artists (S)ULP 1163	SOLID GOLDSBORO - GREATEST HITS (LP)	22
68	United Artists (S)ULP 1195	HONEY (LP, black label)	15
68	United Artists (S)ULP 1206	WORD PICTURES (LP)	20
69	United Artists UAS 29008	TODAY (LP)	18

GOLDSMITH
83	Bedlam BLM 001	Life Is Killing Me/Music Man (p/s)	50

GOL GAPPAS
86	él GPO 21	West 14/Roman (p/s)	12

GOLGOTHA
84	Golgotha GOTH 002	DANGEROUS GAMES (Dangerous Games/Old England's Green/Air/The Great Divide (EP, no p/s)	90
90	Communique CMGLP 003	UNMAKER OF WORLDS (EP, p/s)	15

GOLIARD
76	Broadside BRO 127	FORTUNE MY FOE (LP, with booklet)	18

GOLIATH
70	CBS 5312	Port And Lemon Lady/I Heard About A Friend	10
70	CBS 64229	GOLIATH (LP)	200

GOLINSKI BROTHERS
80	Badge BAD 6	Bloody/Toy	20

GOLLIWOGS
66	Vocalion VF 9266	Brown-Eyed Girl/You Better Be Careful	50
67	Vocalion VF 9283	Fragile Child/Fight Fire	50
72	Fantasy FAN 5996	GOLLIWOGS (LP, pressed in U.S. for U.K. distribution)	15

(see also Creedence Clearwater Revival)

GOLLUM & GARY D
97	UK 44 RMX 3	Black Arrows (Lord Of The Rings Mix)/Black Arrows (Poisoned Tip Mix)/Black Arrows (Original E.D.M. Mix) (12", p/s)	10

(see also DJ Gollum)

BENNY GOLSON
59	Esquire 32-125	GONE WITH GOLSON (LP)	35
60	Esquire 32-105	GROOVIN' WITH GOLSON (LP)	35

GOMEZ
98	Hut HUTDLP 49	BRING IT ON (2-LP)	40
99	Hut HUTDLP 54	LIQUID SKIN (2-LP, gatefold, inner)	60
02	Hut HUTDLP 72	IN OUR GUN (2-LP, gatefold)	40
04	Hut HUTDLP 84	SPLIT THE DIFFERENCE (LP)	40

GONDOLIERS
58	Starlite ST45 001	Fly, Seagull, Fly/God's Green Acres	6

GONG
71	Philips 6332 033	CONTINENTAL CIRCUS (LP, soundtrack)	20
71	Caroline C1520	CAMEMBERT ELECTRIQUE (LP, 'twin' label)	30
73	Virgin V 2002	RADIO GNOME INVISIBLE PART 1 - THE FLYING TEAPOT (LP, gatefold sleeve, 1st pressing original with black & white label design)	100
73	Virgin V 2002	RADIO GNOME INVISIBLE PART 1 - THE FLYING TEAPOT (LP, gatefold sleeve, 2nd pressing with colour girl and dragon label design)	40
73	Virgin V 2007	RADIO GNOME INVISIBLE PART 2 - ANGEL'S EGG (LP, 1st pressing, stickered gatefold sleeve, initially with b&w label; with booklet)	80
73	Virgin V 2007	RADIO GNOME INVISIBLE PART 2 - ANGEL'S EGG (LP, 1st pressing, gatefold sleeve, initially with b&w label; without booklet)	50
74	Virgin V 2007	RADIO GNOME INVISIBLE PART 2 - ANGEL'S EGG (LP, 2nd pressing, coloured "girl/dragon label")	20
74	Caroline C 1505	CAMEMBERT ELECTRIQUE (LP, unissued, released as Virgin VC 502 with 1505 matrix struck through and 502 added as well as a V in front of the C)	0
74	Virgin VC 502	CAMEMBERT ELECTRIQUE (LP)	35
74	Virgin V 2019	YOU (LP, 1st pressing, with lyric insert, coloured 'twin' label)	30
76	Virgin V 2046	SHAMAL (LP, gatefold)	25
76	Virgin V 2074	GAZEUSE (LP, green "mirror" girl label, with poster)	30
76	Virgin V 2074	GAZEUSE (LP, "two Virgins" round label, with poster)	20
77	Charly CRM 2000	LIVE FLOATING ANARCHY (LP, as Planet Gong)	18
77	Virgin VGD 3501	LIVE ETC. (2-LP, with cut-out cover & inner sleeves)	30
77	Affinity AFF 4	MAGICK BROTHER (LP, reissue)	25
78	Virgin V 2099	EXPRESSO II (LP)	20
78	Virgin V 2019	YOU (LP, repressing, with blue label)	20
82	Ottersongs	GONG LIVE A LYONS (cassette LP)	30
82	Charly C£ 30220	YOU (LP, reissue, different cover art)	20
84	Virgin OVED 14	RADIO GNOME INVISIBLE PART 1 - THE FLYING TEAPOT (LP, reissue)	20
84	Virgin OVED 15	ANGEL'S EGG (LP, reissue)	20
84	Virgin OVED 16	YOU (LP, reissue, green/red labels)	20

GONJASUFI

			MINT VALUE £
84	Virgin OVED 17	SHAMAL (LP, reissue)	15
84	Virgin OVED 18	GAZEUSE (LP, reissue)	15
89	Demi Monde DMLP 1018	THE MYSTERY AND THE HISTORY OF THE PLANET GONG (2-LP)	25
90	Ottersongs	HAUNTED CHATEAU (cassette LP)	25
09	Snapper 900501	ZERO TO INFINITY (2-LP)	40
09	G-Wave AAGWLPX001	2032 (2-LP, booklet, CD, poster, numbered)	70
09	G-Wave AAGWLPX001	2032 (2-LP, booklet, CD, poster, with A5 postcards, 200 only, numbered)	100
13	Celluloid CEL 7000	GONG EST MORT (2-LP, reissue)	20
14	Maddish SMALP1024	I SEE YOU (2-LP)	20

(see also Gilli Smyth & , Daevid Allen, Steve Hillage, Clearlight, Radio Actors, Sphynx, Tim Blake, Comus)

GONJASUFI
10	Warp WARPLP172	A SUFI AND A KILLER (2-LP)	30

GONKS
64	Decca F 11984	The Gonk Song/That's All Right, Mamma	30

(see also Twinkle)

PAUL GONSALVES
64	Vocalion LAE 587	BOOM JACKIE BOOM CHICK (LP)	1500
70	Deram SML 1064	HUMMINGBIRD (LP)	100
17	Spellbound SPELL 4004LP	BOOM JACKIE BOOM CHICK (LP, reissue)	20

(see also Tubby Hayes & Paul Gonsalves)

GONZALEZ
74	RAK 204	Hole In My Soul/Re-Souled	10
74	EMI EMC 3046	GONZALEZ (LP)	40
75	EMI EMC 3100	OUR ONLY WEAPON IS OUR MUSIC (LP)	18

BELLE GONZALEZ
72	Columbia DB 8852	Bottles/I Hate Sunday	10
65	Jupiter JEPOC 37	POETS SET IN JAZZ (EP, as Belle Gonzalez & Sextet)	18
66	Jupiter JEPOC 39	CONTEMPORARY POETS SET IN JAZZ (EP)	18
72	Columbia SCX 6484	BELLE (LP)	100

(see also Mark Wirtz)

JACK GOOD'S FAT NOISE
60	Decca F 11233	The Fat Washerwoman/The Fat Noise	10

ELMER GOODBODY
76	Charisma CB 279	Do Ya/Mad About You	8

GOODBYE MR. MACKENZIE
84	Scruples YTS 1	Death Of A Salesman/LINDY BERGMAN: Locked Inside Your Prison (no p/s, 500 only)	15
90	Parlophone PCS 7345	HAMMER AND TONGS (LP, unreleased, white label test pressings only)	30

(see also Garbage)o

GOOD EARTH
68	Saga FID 2112	IT'S HARD ROCK AND ALL THAT (LP)	40

(see also First Impression/Good Earth, Mungo Jerry, Ray Dorset)

ROBIN GOODFELLOW
74	Dawn DNS 1057	You Don't Know Me Now/Suddenly I'm Alive	7

GOOD GUYS
70	Duke DU 82	Death Rides/Destruction	20
70	Duke DU 83	Wreck It Up/Dynamic Groove	20
70	Duke DU 84	Happiness/Latissimo	20

(see also Byron Lee & Dragonaires)

PHILLIP GOODHAND-TAIT (& STORMSVILLE SHAKERS)
66	Parlophone R 5448	I'm Gonna Put Some Hurt On You/It's A Lie (with Stormsville Shakers)	20
66	Parlophone R 5498	No Problem/What More Do You Want (with Stormsville Shakers)	25
66	Parlophone R 5547	You Can't Take Love/J.C. Greaseburger (solo)	20
70	DJM DJLPS 411	REHEARSAL (LP)	15
71	DJM DJLPS 416	I THINK I'LL WRITE A SONG (LP, gatefold)	15
72	DJM DJLPS 425	SONGFALL (LP, gatefold)	20

(see also Circus, Larry Williams, Love Affair)

JOHNNY GOODISON
70	Deram DM 319	A Little Understanding/One Mistake	20

(see also Quotations, Johnny B. Great)

LEMME B GOOD
65	Mercury MF 874	I Can't Stop Myself/Mother May I	8

GOODLETTSVILLE FIVE
64	London HLW 9854	Eef/Bailey's Gone Eefing	12

JOHN GOODLUCK
74	Tradition TSR 015	SUFFOLK MIRACLE (LP, with insert)	20
75	Sweet Folk & Country SFA 047	SPEED THE PLOUGH: TRADITIONAL SONGS OF SUFFOLK (LP)	20

DAVE GOODMAN & FRIENDS
78	The Label TLR 008	Justifiable Homicide/Take Down Your Fences (p/s, 1st 15,000 on red vinyl)	8

GOOD MISSIONARIES
80	Unnormality NORM 002	DERANGED IN HASTINGS: Keep Going Backwards/Attitudes (hand made p/s)	15
80	Unnormality NORM 001	VIBING UP THE SENILE WORLD (The Good Missionary Part 1 [live]/The Good Missionary Part/Kif Kif's Free Freak Out [live]) (EP, 1,000 only)	15
79	Deptford Fun City DLP 04	FIRE FROM HEAVEN (LP)	20

(see also Mark Perry, Alternative TV)

GOOD RATS
69	London HLR 10237	The Hobo/The Truth Is Gone	15

GOOD SHIP LOLLIPOP
69	Ember EMB S 276	Maxwell's Silver Hammer/How Does It Feel (in p/s)	12
69	Ember EMB S 276	Maxwell's Silver Hammer/How Does It Feel	6

GOOD TIME LOSERS

MINT VALUE £

GOOD TIME LOSERS
67　Fontana TF 791　　　　　　　Trafalgar Square/Where Did My Heart Go 6
GOODTIMERS
62　Fontana H 360　　　　　　　It's Twistin' Time/Twisting Train 10
THE GOOD, 2 BAD & HUGLY
93　Ruff Kut! RUF T6　　　　　　THE RETURN OF THE DRUNKEN MASTER (12", p/s) 15
GOOD VIBRATIONS
70　Ember EMB S 270　　　　　 Call Me Lightning/Nantucket Ferry 6
ROD GOODWAY
90　Woronzow WOO 12　　　　ETHEREAL COUNTERBALANCE (LP) 18
RON GOODWIN CONCERT ORCHESTRA
53　Parlophone MSP 6035　　　Limelight/The Song From Moulin Rouge 18
53　Parlophone MSP 6044　　　The Melba Waltz (Dreamtime)/Shane 10
53　Parlophone MSP 6055　　　Tropical Mirage/The Man Between 12
54　Parlophone MSP 6064　　　Grand Waltz Of The Flowers And Dragonflies/The Lobster Quadrille 10
54　Parlophone MSP 6103　　　The Song Of The High Seas/Guadalcanal March 12
54　Parlophone MSP 6115　　　Cara Mia/Three Coins In The Fountain 12
54　Parlophone MSP 6136　　　Midnight Blue/On The Waterfront 12
55　Parlophone MSP 6159　　　Under The Linden Tree/Last Love 10
56　Parlophone MSP 6221　　　Concetta/Handyman 10
56　Parlophone 45 R-4235　　　War And Peace/The Christmas Tree 10
57　Parlophone R 4297　　　　Skiffling Strings (Swinging Sweetheart)/I'll Find You 8
57　Parlophone R 4349　　　　Swedish Polka/Lingering Lovers 10
58　Parlophone R 4391　　　　Colonel Bogey And The River Kwai March/Laughing Sailor 10
58　Parlophone R 4508　　　　Latin Lovers/Blue Grotto 8
58　Parlophone R 4608　　　　Lolita/All Strung Up 8
59　Parlophone R 4537　　　　The Whirlpool Theme/Herman's Theme From Whirlpool 8
60　Parlophone R 4632　　　　Tracey's Theme/My Girl 7
60　Parlophone R 4663　　　　Love Theme From Ben Hur/Theme From The Unforgiven 7
60　Parlophone R 4687　　　　Walkin' Down To Washington/Sunshine Cruise 7
61　Parlophone R 4821　　　　Murder She Says/Double Scotch 25
63　Parlophone R 5053　　　　Moonstrike/Midsummer Madness 12
64　Parlophone R 5146　　　　633 Squadron/Love Them From 633 Squadron 10
65　Parlophone R 5239　　　　The Fat Man/Colonel Schmendrick 8
65　Parlophone R 5394　　　　Theme From The Early Birds/Theme From The Alphabet Murders 8
69　United Artists UP 35040　　Battle Of Britain Theme/Luftwaffe March 8
54　Parlophone PMD 1014　　　FILM FAVOURITES (10" LP) 15
56　Parlophone PMD 1038　　　MUSIC TO SET YOU DREAMING (10" LP) 15
58　Parlophone PCS 3002　　　MUSIC FOR AN ARABIAN NIGHT (LP) 15
58　Parlophone PCS 3006　　　OUT OF THIS WORLD! (LP) 20
64　United Artists ULP 1071　　633 SQUADRON (LP, soundtrack) 20
65　Stateside SL 10136　　　　THOSE MAGNIFICENT MEN IN THEIR FLYING MACHINES (LP, soundtrack) 20
66　Polydor 582 004　　　　　　THE TRAP (LP, soundtrack) 40
68　Stateside (S)SL 10259　　　DECLINE AND FALL ... OF A BIRDWATCHER (LP, soundtrack) 125
69　Paramount SPFL 255　　　 MONTE CARLO OR BUST! (LP, soundtrack) 25

(see also 20th Century Fox Orchestra, Parlophone Pops Orchestra)

PETER GOODWRIGHT
75　MWS 002　　　　　　　　　When Christmas Comes To The Zoo (Part 1)/Part 2.. 6
GOOFERS
55　Vogue Coral Q 72051　　　 Hearts Of Stone/You're The One 50
55　Vogue Coral Q 72074　　　 Flip, Flop And Fly/My Babe 50
55　Vogue Coral Q 72094　　　 Goofy Drybones/Nare 30
56　Vogue Coral Q 72124　　　 Sick! Sick! Sick!/Twenty One 15
56　Vogue Coral Q 72171　　　 Tear Drop Motel/Tennessee Rock And Roll 25
57　Vogue Coral Q 72267　　　 Wow!/Push, Push, Push Cart 15
57　Vogue Coral Q 72289　　　 The Dipsy Doodle/Take This Heart 15
GOOM
72　Pye 7N 25587　　　　　　　Massai Part 1/Massai Part 2 15
DEREK GOOM
80　BBC RESL 84　　　　　　　Juliet Bravo/Madelena (p/s) 6
SAM GOPAL
69　Stable STA 5602　　　　　 Horse/Back Door Man (unissued, existence unconfirmed)... 0
69　Stable SLE 8001　　　　　 Escalator/Angry Faces/Cold Embrace/The Sky is Burning (LP sampler) 70
69　Stable SLE 8001　　　　　 ESCALATOR (LP, gatefold sleeve, black/silver label) 400
68　Stable SLE 8001　　　　　 ESCALATOR (LP, gatefold sleeve, label stating "DJ Copy not for resale) 400

(see also Hawkwind, Motorhead, Vamp, Isaac Guillory, Clark-Hutchinson, G. F. Fitzgerald)

PETE(R) GORDENO
61　Fontana H 319　　　　　　 Be My Girl/Haven't Got Time (as Pete Gordeno) 8
62　Parlophone R 4862　　　　I Got Eyes/You're Following Me 8
62　Parlophone R 4914　　　　Uptown/The Making Of A Man 8
62　Parlophone R 4931　　　　Down By The Riverside/The Boys Kept Hanging Around 7
65　Decca F 12088　　　　　　 Have You Looked Into Your Heart?/Don't Come To Me 6
ANITA GORDON
55　Brunswick 05456　　　　　 Lonesome Like Nobody Knows/His Hands 10
BARRY GORDON
56　MGM MGM 928　　　　　　I Can't Whistle/The Milkman's Polka 7
56　MGM MGM 935　　　　　　Rock Around Mother Goose/Nuttin' For Christmas 12
CHANCE GORDON
63　Pye 7N 15475　　　　　　　Instant Love/You Don't Want My Love 20

Chris GORDON

MINT VALUE £

CHRIS GORDON
68 Derpy ADMLP 390 IN THE EARLY MORNING RAIN (LP) 200

DEXTER GORDON
66 Fontana Jazz FJL 907 MASTER SWINGERS (LP, with Wardell Gray) 20
79 Blue Note BNS 40032 GO! (LP, reissue) 20
(see also Wardell Gray)

JOE GORDON (FOLK FOUR)
59 HMV POP 634 Dream Lover/Dance To Your Daddy 6

PHIL GORDON
55 Brunswick 05481 Get A Load Of That Crazy Walk/Strip Polka 10
56 Brunswick 05545 Down The Road Apiece/I'm Gonna Move To The Outskirts Of Town 50

ROBERT GORDON WITH LINK WRAY
77 Private Stock PVTS 127 Endless Sleep & The Fool/The Fool (12", B-side plays at 78rpm) 10
77 Private Stock PVLP 1027 ROBERT GORDON WITH LINK WRAY (LP) 15
(see also Link Wray)

RONNIE GORDON
63 R&B JB 127 Shake Some Time/Comin' Home 100

ROSCO(E) GORDON
60 Top Rank JAR 332 Just A Little Bit/Goin' Home (as Rosco Gordon) 25
63 Stateside SS 204 Just A Little Bit/What I Wouldn't Do 25
65 Vocalion V-P 9245 Keep On Doggin'/Bad Dream 30
65 Island WI 256 Surely I Love You/What You Do To Me 25
66 Island WI 272 No More Doggin'/Goin' Home 30

TONY GORDON
73 Grape GR 3056 Be True (actually by Alton Ellis)/Navajo Trail 35
(see also Alton Ellis)

VINCENT GORDON
69 Coxsone CS 7085 Soul Trombone/LARRY & ALVIN: Your Cheating Heart 300
69 Duke DU 37 Everybody Bawlin'/SILVERTONES: Come Look Here 40
69 Crab CRAB 16 Walking By/VICEROYS: Promises Promises 40
71 Fab FAB 5 Red Blood/CHOSEN FEW: Babylon (promo only, black label) 50
74 Big Shot BI 630 Come Go With Me/SKIN, FLESH & BONES: Dub Ali Dub 40
79 Attack TACK 10 Liquid Horns (as Vin Gordon & Corner Shots)/JUNIOR & CORNER SHOTS: Liquidator (12") 18
79 Third World TWDIS 17 Grass In The Sun/Split Second (12") 60
79 Third World TWDIS 18 Vin Cosmic/Enforcement (12") 20
70s Trojan TRO 9058 Liquid Horns/JUNIOR: Liquidator 10
75 DIP DLP 5001 MUSICAL BONES (LP, plain sleeve, white label with word 'upsetters' in red type) 300
(see also Don Drummond Junior)

TREV GORDON
66 Pye 7N 17168 Floating/Everyone Knows (possibly demo only) 15

GORDONS EIGHT
66 Airborne NBP 007 Bossa Caribbeanova/The Nit Wit 12

CHARLIE GORE
54 Parlophone CMSP 19 I'll Find Somebody/Heaven Sent You To Me (export issue) 25
54 Parlophone CMSP 26 Two Of A Kind/It's A Long Walk Back To Town (export issue) 20
54 Parlophone CMSP 30 I Didn't Know/Oh! Mis'rable Love (export issue) 20
(see also Hawkshaw Hawkins, Ruby Wright)

LESLEY GORE
63 Mercury AMT 1205 It's My Party/Danny 10
63 Mercury AMT 1210 Judy's Turn To Cry/Just Let Me Cry 10
63 Mercury AMT 1213 She's A Fool/The Old Crowd 12
64 Mercury MF 803 You Don't Own Me/Run Bobby Run 15
64 Mercury MF 810 That's The Way Boys Are/That's The Way The Ball Bounces 12
64 Mercury MF 821 I Don't Wanna Be A Loser/It's Gotta Be You 10
64 Mercury MF 829 Maybe I Know/Wonder Boy 12
64 Mercury MF 837 Hey Now/Sometimes I Wish I Were A Boy 10
65 Mercury MF 846 The Look Of Love/Little Girl Go Home 20
65 Mercury MF 862 Sunshine Lollipops And Rainbows/You've Come Back 15
65 Mercury MF 872 My Town, My Guy And Me/Girl In Love 15
65 Mercury MF 889 I Won't Love You Anymore (Sorry)/No Matter What You Do 15
66 Mercury MF 902 Young Love/I Just Don't Know If I Can 10
66 Mercury MF 963 California Nights/I'm Going Out (The Same Way I Came In) 10
66 Mercury MF 984 I'm Fallin' Down/Summer And Sandy 20
68 Mercury MF 1017 Magic Colours/It's A Happening World 10
64 Mercury 10017 MCE LESLEY GORE (EP) 35
63 Mercury MMC 14127 I'LL CRY IF I WANT TO (LP) 40
63 Mercury 20001 MCL SINGS OF MIXED-UP HEARTS (LP) 30
64 Mercury 20020 MCL BOYS BOYS BOYS (LP) 30
64 Mercury 20033 MCL GIRL TALK (LP) 30
65 Mercury 20071 MCL MY TOWN, MY GUY & ME (LP) 30
65 Mercury 20076 MCL ALL ABOUT LOVE (LP) 30

GORGONI, MARTIN & TAYLOR
71 Buddah 2011 102 Sweet Dream Woman/Got The Feeling Something Got Away 6
72 Buddah 2011-137 Toly Toly Guyluesha/I Can Make You Cry 7
72 Buddah 2318 067 GORGONI, MARTIN AND TAYLOR (LP) 15

GORILLA GRIP
78 Birnback KOM 019 King Of The Pipes/Birnback Island (500 only no p/s) 20
(see also DR Z)

GORILLAS
MINT VALUE £

GORILLAS
75	Chiswick NS 4	She's My Gal/Why Wait 'Til Tomorrow	15
78	Chiswick NS 8	Gatecrasher/Gorilla Got Me	15
78	Raw RAW 14	It's My Life/My Son's Alive	15
81	Chiswick CHIS 151	Move It/A Song For Rita	6
78	Raw RWLP 103	MESSAGE TO THE WORLD (LP, with insert)	20

(see also Hammersmith Gorillas, Jesse Hector)

GORILLAZ
00	Parlophone 10RDJ 6545	Tomorrow Comes Today/Rock The House/Latin Simone/12D3 (10", promo. p/s)	25
00	Parlophone 12R 6545	Tomorrow Comes Today/Rock The House/Latin Simone/12D3 (12", p/s)	20
01	7RDJ 6552	Clint Eastwood/Dracula (33 rpm dinked 7" - cartoon die-cut stickered sleeve)	10
02	Parlophone (no Cat no)	Tomorrow Comes Today/Tomorrow Dub (7" white label, stamped promo)	10
05	Parlophone R 6663	Feel Good Inc./68 State (picture disc in die-cut card sleeve)	30
06	Parlophone R 6685	Kids With Guns/El Manana (p/s, red vinyl, poster)	15
11	Parlophone P7300787	THE SINGLES COLLECTION 2001-2011 (8 x 7" box set)	30
01	Parlophone 724353113810	GORILLAZ (2-LP)	30
02	Parlophone 539 9821	LAIKA COME HOME (2-LP with comic)	40
05	Parlophone 07243 87383814	DEMON DAYS (2-LP)	150
05	Parlophone 07243 873838	DEMON DAYS INSTRUMENTALS (2-LP, promo die-cut stickered sleeve)	50
10	Parlophone 5099962616614	PLASTIC BEACH (2-LP)	30
11	Parlophone 5099909758810	THE FALL (LP, numbered)	30
11	Parlophone P730 0781	THE SINGLES COLLECTION 2001-2011 (2-LP)	40
17	Parlophone 9029585118	HUMANZ (2-LP, artbook version)	25
17	Parlophone 0190295818845	HUMANZ (LP as 14 x 12", coloured vinyl, hardback book, vinyl case)	200

(see also Blur, Damon Albarn)

GORKY'S ZYGOTIC MYNCI
93	Ankst ANKST/GZM 040	PATIO (10" EP)	15
94	Ankst ANKST 048	Merched Yn Neud Gwallt Eu Gilydd/Bocs Angelica/ When You Laugh At Your Own Garden In A Blazer (p/s)	10
94	Ankst ANKST 053	Game Of Eyes/Pentref Wrth Y Mor (p/s)	10
95	Ankst ANKST 058	Gewn Ni Gorffen/12 Impressionistic Soundscapes (clear vinyl, die-cut p/s, mail order only, 1,000 copies)	10
95	Ankst ANKST 056	LLANFFWROG (10" EP)	15
96	Ankst ANKST 068	AMBER GAMBLER EP (10", p/s)	12
98	Mercury ANKST GZM 5	Let's Get Together (In Our Minds)/Billy And The Sugarloaf Mountain/Hwiangerdd Mar (numbered p/s)	8
95	Ankst ANKST 059	BWYD TIME (LP, gatefold sleeve)	40
97	Fontana 534 769	BARAFUNDLE (LP)	60
98	Fontana 558 822-1	GORKY 5 (LP)	40
99	Mantra MNTPL 1015	SPANISH DANCE TROUPE (LP)	60
00	Mantra MNTLPM 1023	THE BLUE TREES (LP)	25
01	Mantra MNTLP 1025	HOW I LONG TO FEEL THAT SUMMER IN MY HEART (LP)	40

ROBERT GORL
83	Mute 12 MUTE 027	Mit Dir (Extended)/Beruhut Verfuhrt (Remixed) (12", p/s)	10

(see also D.A.F.)

JOHN GORMAN
77	DJM DJF 20491	GO MAN GORMAN (LP)	15

(see also Scaffold, Grimms)

EYDIE GORMÉ
54	Vogue Coral Q 2014	Frenesi/Climb Up The Wall	10
54	Vogue Coral Q 2027	Tea For Two/Sure	10
55	Vogue Coral Q 72092	Give A Fool A Chance/A Girl Can't Say	10
55	Vogue Coral Q 72103	Soldier Boy/What Is The Secret Of Your Success?	10
56	London HL 8227	Sincerely Yours/Come Home	15
62	CBS AAG 105	Yes, My Darling Daughter/Sonny Boy	6
63	CBS AAG 131	Blame It On The Bossa Nova/Guess I Should Have Loved Him More	7
63	CBS AAG 149	Don't Try To Fight It Baby/Theme From Light Fantastic	8
63	CBS AAG 163	I Want To Stay Here/Ain't Love (as STEVE & EYDIE)	6
63	CBS AAG 170	Everybody Go Home/The Message	8

(see also Steve Lawrence)

GORP
83	Beet Bop 1	THE WILD MEN OF GORP (LP)	15

FRANK GORSHIN
66	Pye International 7N 25402	The Riddler/Never Let Her Go (in p/s)	50
66	Pye International 7N 25402	The Riddler/Never Let Her Go	25

PETER GOSLING
70	Sonet SON 2010	Values/Peace	10

GOSPEL CLASSICS
68	Chess CRS 8080	More Love, That's What We Need/You Need Faith	100
68	Chess CRS 8080	More Love, That's What We Need/You Need Faith (DJ copy)	150

GOSPELFOLK
69	Emblem 7DR 324	PRODIGAL (LP)	150

GOSPEL GARDEN
68	Camp 602 006	Finders Keepers/Just A Tear	40

(see also Dimples, Amazing Blondel)

GOSPEL OAK
70	Uni UNS 527	Recollections Of Jessica/Brown Haired Girl	6
70	Uni UNLS 113	GOSPEL OAK (LP)	125

GOSPEL PEARLS
63	Liberty LBY 1191	THE GOSPEL PEARLS (LP)	25

Rachel GOSWELL

MINT VALUE £

RACHEL GOSWELL
04   4AD CAD 2414   WAVES ARE UNIVERSAL (LP) 25
(see also Slowdive)

GOTAN PROJECT
01   XL XLLP 148   LA REVANCHA DEL TANGO (2-LP, gatefold) 25

GOTHAM CITY WRECKERS
86   SRT 6KS 816   Counterfeit/Tube City 10

GOTHIC GIRLS
83   Backs NCH 007   Outrage/Devil (p/s) 10
84   Backs 12NCH 011   GLASS BABY EP (12", p/s) 15
84   Backs NCHM LP2   LILAC DREAMS EP (12", p/s) 10

GOTHIC HORIZON
70   Argo AFW 102   The Jason Lodge Poetry Book/Wilhelmina Before Sunrise 12
71   Argo AFW 104   Marjorie/Song 10
72   Argo AFW 107   If You Can Smile/Thoughts 8
72   Argo AFW 108   Girl With Guitar/Can't Bear To Think About You 8
71   Argo ZFB 26   THE JASON LODGE POETRY BOOK (LP) 100
72   Argo ZDA 150   TOMORROW IS ANOTHER DAY (LP) 150

GOTH TRAD
07   Deep Medi Musik MEDI 05   Cut End/Flags (12") 20
07   Skud SKUD 001   Back To Chill/Swamp/The Gate (12") 10
08   Skud SKUD 002   Far East Assassin/Far East Assassin (DJ Distance Remix) (12") 10

DALE GOULDER & LIZ DYER
70   Argo ZFB 10   JANUARY MAN (LP) 40
71   Argo ZFB 30   RAVEN & CROW (LP) 40

GRAHAM GOULDMAN
66   Decca F 12334   Stop! Stop! Stop! (Or Honey I'll Be Gone...)/Better To Have Loved And Lost 150
68   RCA Victor RCA 1667   Upstairs, Downstairs/Chestnut 40
69   Spark SRL 1026   Windmills Of Your Mind/Harvey's Theme (as Graham Gouldman Orchestra) 15
72   CBS 7739   Nowhere To Go/Growing Older 7
(see also 10cc, Whirlwinds, Mockingbirds, High Society, Frabjoy & Runcible Spoon, Manchester Mob, Garden Odyssey Enterprise, Friday Browne, Doctor Father)

GOVE
69   London HLE 10295   Sunday Morning Early/Death Letter Blues 12
72   UNI UNs547   Carry On (Till The Band Adjourns)/I've Been Thinking Of You Lately 8

DUSKO GOYKOVICH
67   Columbia SX 6260   SWINGING MACEDONIA (LP) 500
01   Cosmic CS14   BELGRADE BLUES (LP, reissue) 15

JOHN GRAAS SEPTET
54   London RE-P 1003   FRENCH HORN VOL. 1 (EP) 10

MICK GRABHAM
72   United Artists UAS 29341   MICK THE LAD (LP, laminated front cove sleeve) 20
(see also Plastic Penny, Cochise, Procol Harum)

GRACE
77   Zipp ZB 003   Old Stories/Rule Britannia (in p/s) 60
77   Zipp ZB 003   Old Stories/Rule Britannia (no p/s) 20
81   MCA MCA 667   Billy Boy/Ad Mad (p/s) 15

GRAME GRACE
76   RCA RCA 2633   Flambouyant Freak/Don't Hang Around Like That 6
75   RCA SF 8418   HAIL ME (LP, with insert) 15

CHARLIE GRACIE
57   Parlophone R 4290   Butterfly/Ninety-Nine Ways (initially gold lettering on label) 40
57   Parlophone R 4290   Butterfly/Ninety-Nine Ways (later pressing with silver lettering on label) 20
57   Parlophone R 4313   Fabulous/Just Lookin' (initially gold lettering on label) 40
57   Parlophone R 4313   Fabulous/Just Lookin' (later pressing with silver lettering on label) 15
57   London HL 8467   Wandering Eyes/I Love You So Much It Hurts (tri-centre) 12
57   London HLU 8521   Cool Baby/You Got A Heart Like A Rock (tri-centre) 20
58   London HLU 8596   Crazy Girl/Dressin' Up (tri-centre) 30
59   Coral Q 72362   Doodlebug/Hurry Up, Buttercup (tri-centre) 30
59   Coral Q 72362   Doodlebug/Hurry Up, Buttercup (78) 30
59   Coral Q 72373   Angel Of Love/I'm A Fool, That's Why (tri-centre) 15
59   Coral Q 72373   Angel Of Love/I'm A Fool, That's Why (later round centre) 10
59   Coral Q 72373   Angel Of Love/I'm A Fool, That's Why (78) 20
59   Coral Q 72381   Oh-Well-A/Because I Love You So 15
59   Coral Q 72381   Oh-Well-A/Because I Love You So (78) 25
60   Columbia DB 4477   The Race/I Looked For You 10
62   London HLU 9603   Pretty Baby/Night And Day, U.S.A. 20
65   Stateside SS 402   He'll Never Love You Like I Do/Keep My Love Next To Your Heart 75
65   Stateside SS 402   He'll Never Love You Like I Do/Keep My Love Next To Your Heart (DJ copy) 150
78   London HLU 10563   Fabulous/Makin' Whoopie/Wow...w (tri centre) 10
57   Parlophone GEP 8260   THE FABULOUS CHARLIE GRACIE (EP) 40
83   Rollercoaster ROLL 2005   LIVE AT THE STOCKHOLM GLOBE AUGUST 26 1957 (LP) 15

GRACIOUS!
68   Polydor 56333   Beautiful/What A Lovely Rain 35
70   Vertigo 6059 009   Once On A Windy Day/Fugue In D Minor 30
70   Vertigo 6360 002   GRACIOUS! (LP, gatefold sleeve, large swirl label) 500
72   Philips Intl. 6382 004   THIS IS ... GRACIOUS!! (LP, black/silver labels) 350
88   Beat Goes On BGO LP 26   GRACIOUS! (LP, reissue) 15

GRADUATE
79   Blue Hat 5 BHR   Mad One/Somebody Put Out The Fire 150

GRADUATES

MINT VALUE £

| 80 | Precision PAR 104 | Ever Met A Day/Shut Up (p/s, 1980 issue PAR 117 with no p/s = £3) | 6 |

(see also Tears For Fears)

GRADUATES
| 79 | Graduate GRAD 1 | If You Want It/Hey Young Girl (p/s) | 6 |

GRAFFIA
| 81 | Magic 102 | Stop It Stop/Cymer Di (die-cut company sleeve) | 10 |

GRAFITTI
| 76 | Beeb 19 | Dear Prudence/Come Together | 20 |

BILLY GRAHAM & ESCALATORS
| 67 | Atlantic 584 073 | Ooh Poo Pah Doo/East 24th Avenue | 15 |

BOB GRAHAM EXPERIENCE
| 78 | Anchor ANC 1055 | Blast Off (Percussion In Space)/Malfunction | 6 |

BOBBY/BOBBIE GRAHAM
| 65 | Fontana TF 521 | Skin Deep/Zoom Widge And Wag (as Bobbie Graham) | 25 |
| 66 | Fontana TF 667 | Teensville/Grotty Drums (as Bobby Graham) | 15 |

(see also Outlaws, Jimmy Page)

CHICK GRAHAM & COASTERS
| 64 | Decca F 11859 | Education/I Know | 12 |
| 64 | Decca F 11932 | A Little You/Dance Baby Dance | 12 |

DAV(E)Y GRAHAM
68	Decca F 12841	Both Sides Now/Tristano	12
62	Golden Guinea GGL 0224	THE GUITAR PLAYER (LP)	50
64	Decca LK 4649	FOLK, BLUES AND BEYOND (LP)	175
66	Decca LK 4780	MIDNIGHT MAN (LP)	100
68	Decca LK/SKL 4969	LARGE AS LIFE AND TWICE AS NATURAL (LP)	150
69	Decca LK/SKL 5011	HAT (LP)	100
70	Decca SKL 5056	HOLLY KALEIDOSCOPE (LP, as Davy Graham & Holly)	120
70	Decca LK 4649	FOLK, BLUES AND BEYOND (LP, 2nd issue, boxed Decca logo, laminated front cover)	100
70	President PTLS 1039	GODINGTON BOUNDARY (LP, with Holly)	150
76	Eron ERON 007	ALL THAT MOODY (LP, private pressing)	200

(see also Shirley Collins)

DAVY GRAHAM/THAMESIDERS
| 63 | Decca DFE 8538 | FROM A LONDON HOOTENANNY (EP, 2 tracks each) | 18 |

DAVY GRAHAM & ALEXIS KORNER
62	Topic TOP 70	3/4 A.D. (EP, first pressing in mauve sleeve with cream label)	90
62	Topic TOP 70	3/4 A.D. (EP, later pressings with lilac sleeve and blue label)	60
62	Topic TOP 70	3/4 A.D. (EP, later pressings with bronze sleeve and blue label)	30

(see also Alexis Korner)

ERNIE GRAHAM
| 78 | Stiff OFF 2 | Romeo And The Lonely Girl/Only Time Will Tell (p/s) | 7 |
| 71 | Liberty LBS 83485 | ERNIE GRAHAM (LP, textured sleeve, black label) | 250 |

(see also Clancy, Eire Apparent, Brinsley Schwarz, Help Yourself, Nick Lowe)

KENNY GRAHAM'S AFRO-CUBISTS
60	Starlite ST45 013	Bongo Chant/Beguine	10
57	Pye Jazz NJE 1053	PRESENTING KENNY GRAHAM PART 1 (EP)	20
57	Esquire EP 34	CARIBBEAN SUITE (EP)	20
57	Esquire EP 68	KENNY GRAHAM'S AFRO CUBISTS (EP)	20
57	Esquire EP 83	KENNY GRAHAM'S AFRO CUBISTS (EP)	25
56	MGM MGM-C 764	MOONDOG AND SUNCAT SUITES (LP, as Kenny Graham & His Satellites)	150
57	Nixa NJL 12	PRESENTING KENNY GRAHAM (LP)	120
57	Esquire 20-012	KENNY GRAHAM AFRO CUBISTS (LP)	90
57	Esquire 20-023	CARIBBEAN SUITE (LP)	120
10	Trunk JBH 036 LP	MOONDOG AND SUNCAT SUITES (LP, 800 only, as Kenny Graham And His Satellites)	20
10	Trunk JBH 036 LP	MOONDOG AND SUNCAT SUITES (LP, reissue, 500 only yellow vinyl, as Kenny Graham And His Satellites)	25

(see also Yolanda)

LEO GRAHAM
73	Upsetter US 399	News Flash/UPSETTERS: Flashing Echo	28
73	Summit SUM 8539	Three Blind Mice/UPSETTERS: Mice Skank	15
74	Fay Music FAY FM 101	Greedy Gal/Greedy Dub	10
75	Ethnic Fight EF 026	Big Tongue Buster/KING SCRATCH BAND: Bus-A-Dub	25
78	PM Records PMS DD 496	My Little Sandra/Dubbing Sandra (12")	35

(see also Bleechers)

LOU GRAHAM
| 58 | Coral Q 72322 | Wee Willie Brown/You Were Mean Baby | 400 |
| 58 | Coral Q 72322 | Wee Willie Brown/You Were Mean Baby (78) | 50 |

LYNDA GRAHAM
62	Philips 326 552BF	As Long As The River Flows/When I'm Sixteen	8
63	Philips BF 1249	Without Your Love/Wait And See	8
64	Philips BF 1308	You'd Better Believe It/That's The Last Thing I'd Do	10

GRAHAM CENTRAL STATION
| 74 | Warner Bros K 46206 | GRAHAM CENTRAL STATION (LP) | 15 |

(see also Sly & Family Stone)

RON GRAINER ORCHESTRA
62	Pye 7N 15411	Happy Joe/Old Ned	6
63	Decca F 11597	That Was The week That Was/Petit Louis	7
64	HMV POP 1366	Not So Much A Programme, More A Way Of Life/Ascot Gavotte	10
67	Pye 7N 17383	A Man In A Suitcase/Andorra (pink label, later blue)	12
67	RCA Victor RCA 1635	The Prisoner/Happening Sunday	75
69	RCA Victor RCA 1898	The Paul Temple Theme/The Jazz Age	10

Ross GRAINER

			MINT VALUE £
79	RK 1018	Tales Of The Unexpected/Paul Temple	7
79	RK 1021	Tales Of The Unexpected/Malice Aforethought (p/s)	7
60	Warner Bros WEP 6012	THEME MUSIC FROM "INSPECTOR MAIGRET" (EP)	10
79	Six Of One 6 OF 1	THE PRISONER ARRIVAL (EP, fan club issue)	30
69	RCA Intl. INTS 1020	THEMES LIKE... (LP)	15
78	RK LB 003	TALES OF THE UNEXPECTED (LP)	15

ROSS GRAINER
79	Music Factory MF102	Cardiff Roses/Wind And The Trees	12

COLIN GRAINGER & THE FRANK CORDELL ORCHESTRA
58	HMV POP 484	This I Know/Are You?	7
59	HMV POP 639	Love Only Me/Plain And Simple Girl	7

GLENDA GRAINGER
60s	Audio Fidelity AFSP 007	Mr. Kiss Kiss Bang Bang/Who	12

BILLY GRAMMER
58	London HLU 8752	Gotta Travel On/Chasing A Dream	10
59	Felsted AF 121	Bonaparte's Retreat/The Kissing Tree	7
59	Felsted GEP 1005	BILLY GRAMMER HITS (EP)	15
67	Monument LMO 5010	TRAVELIN' ON (LP)	15

GERRY GRANAHAN
58	London HL 8668	No Chemise, Please/Girl Of My Dreams	20
60	Top Rank JAR 262	It Hurts/RICHIE ROBIN: Strange Dream	15

GRANDADDY
98	Big Cat ABB5003507	A.M. 180/Here (p/s, stickered)	10
98	Big Cat – ABB 157 S	Everything Beautiful Is Far Away/For The Dishwasher (p/s)	7
98	Big Cat – ABB 161 S	Laughing Stock/G.P.C./12-PAK-599 (p/s)	8
98	Big Cat – ABB 162 S	Summer Here Kids/Levitz (Birdless)/My Small Love (p/s)	8
98	Big Cat ABB 152	UNDER THE WESTERN FREEWAY (LP, inner, stickered sleeve)	45
00	V2 VVR 1012231	SOPHTWARE SLUMP (LP, inner)	25
03	V2 VVR 1012251	SUMDAY (2-LP, with inner sleeves)	20
11	Mercury 00602527797038	SOPHTWARE SLUMP (2-LP, reissue)	50

GRAND FUNK RAILROAD
70	Capitol CL 15632	Heartbreaker/Please Don't Worry	8
71	Capitol CL 15668	Inside Looking Out/Paranoid (33rpm)	10
71	Capitol CL 15689	I Can Feel Him In The Morning/Are You Ready/Mean Mistreater (33rpm maxi-single)	12
76	EMI International INT 523	Can You Do It/1976	8
69	Capitol E-ST 307	ON TIME (LP)	50
70	Capitol E-ST 406	GRAND FUNK (LP)	40
70	Capitol E-ST 471	CLOSER THAN HOME (LP)	40
71	Capitol E-SW 764	SURVIVAL (LP)	25
72	Capitol E-AS 853	E PLURIBUS FUNK (LP, circular 'silver coin' sleeve)	50
73	Capitol E-AST 11099	PHOENIX (LP, gatefold sleeve)	18

GRANDISONS
63	RCA RCA 1339	All Right/True Romance	12

GRANDMASTER FLASH
99	Sequel NXTLP 305	BACK TO THE OLD SCHOOL (4-LP)	50

GRAND PRIX
80	RCA RCA 7	Thinking Of You/Feels Good (p/s)	15
83	Chrysalis PRIX 2	Shout/Keep On Believing (p/s, with patch)	8
83	Chrysalis PRIXX 2	Shout (12", p/s)	12

(see also McAuley Schenker Group, Praying Mantis, Stratus, Uriah Heep)

GRAND UNION
68	CBS 3956	Slowly But Surely/She Said	40

(see also Enough's Enough)

GERRI GRANGER
63	London HLX 9759	Just Tell Him Jane Said Hello/What's Wrong With Me	15

GRANNIE
71	SRT 71138	GRANNIE (LP, private pressing of 99 copies only, homemade sleeve)	2500
12	SRT 71138	GRANNIE (LP, reissue, hand-made sleeve, 750 only, insert, and signed numbered certificate)	100

GRANNY
73	DJM DJS. 291	Lady/Weirdie Deirdre's Dilemma	15

GRANNY'S INTENTIONS
67	Deram DM 158	The Story Of David/Sandy's On The Phone Again	25
68	Deram DM 184	Julie Don't Love Me Anymore/One Time Lovers	18
68	Deram DM 214	Never An Everyday Thing/Hilda The Bilda	25
70	Deram DM 293	Take Me Back/Maybe	20
70	Deram SML 1060	HONEST INJUN (LP, white/red label with small logo)	125

(see also Gary Moore)

AMY GRANT
82	Myrrh MYR 1124	AGE TO AGE (LP, with lyric insert)	15

CLINTON GRANT
75	Circle 5	I've Been Trying/Second Attempt	10

CY GRANT
62	Melodisc 45-1433	Heavy Weather/Lucky Oyster (tri centre)	10

DOMINIC GRANT
68	Mercury MF 1032	I've Been There/Don't Stop Girl	50

EARL GRANT
58	Brunswick 05762	The End/Hunky Dunky Doo	7
60	Brunswick 05824	House Of Bamboo/Two Loves Have I	10
62	Brunswick 05870	Swingin' Gently/Evening Rain	7

EDDY GRANT
75	Torpedo TOR 53	Nobody's Got Time (Part 1)/Nobody's Got Time (Part 2)	75
77	Ice GUY 2	Curfew/Jamaican Child (with GUY 2 sticker over ICE 2 catalogue number on both sides)	20
17	Torpedo TOR 53	Nobody's Got Time (Part 1)/Nobody's Got Time (Part 2) (reissue, 300 only)	20
75	Torpedo TOL 500	EDDY GRANT (LP)	200
92	Ice 920201	PAINTINGS OF THE SOUL (LP)	25

(see also Equals, Coach House Rhythm Section)

ERKEY GRANT & EARWIGS
63	Pye 7N 15521	I'm A Hog For You/I Can't Get Enough Of You	25

GOGI GRANT
55	London HLB 8192	Suddenly There's A Valley/Love Is	10
56	London HLB 8257	Who Are We/We Believe In Love	10
56	London HLB 8282	Wayward Wind/No More Than Forever	20
57	London HLB 8364	You're In Love/When The Tide Is High	10
58	London HLB 8550	The Golden Ladder/All Of Me	8

(see also Tony Martin)

JANIE GRANT
61	Pye International 7N 25093	Triangle/She's Going Steady With You	18
62	Pye International 7N 25148	That Greasy Kid Stuff/Trying To Forget You	18

JOHN GRANT
13	Bella Union BELLAV 395	STRONGROOM EP (12")	20
13	Bella Union BELLAV 433	GETS SCHOOLED (12")	10
15	Bella Union BELLA 514V	JOHN GRANT WITH ROYAL NORTHERN SINFONIA (12")	20
10	Bella Union BELLAV 235	QUEEN OF DENMARK (2-LP, gatefold, inners)	20
13	Bella Union BELLAV 377	PALE GREEN GHOSTS (2-LP, CD, green vinyl)	20
15	Bella Union BELLA 478V	WITH THE BBC PHILHARMONIC LIVE IN CONCERT (2-LP, silver vinyl)	50
15	Bella Union BELLA 505V	GREY TICKLES, BLACK PRESSURE (2-LP, lavender vinyl)	20

(see also Midlake)

JULIE GRANT
62	Pye 7N 15430	Somebody Tell Him/Ev'ry Letter You Write	10
62	Pye 7N 15447	So Many Ways/Unimportant Things	10
62	Pye 7N 15461	When You're Smiling/Lonely Sixteen	8
62	Pye 7N 15483	Up On The Roof/When You Ask About Love	6
63	Pye 7N 15508	Count On Me/Then, Only Then	7
63	Pye 7N 15526	That's How Heartaches Are Made/Cruel World	10
63	Pye 7N 15545	Don't Ever Let Me Down/Somebody Cares	10
63	Pye 7N 15590	Hello Love/It's Alright	12
64	Pye 7N 15684	Come To Me/Can't Get You Out Of My Mind	8
64	Pye 7N 15615	Every Day I Have To Cry/Watch What You Do With My Baby	10
64	Pye 7N 15652	You Are Nobody 'Til Somebody Loves You/I Only Care About You	8
65	Pye 7N 15756	Baby Baby (I Still Love You)/My World Is Empty Without You	10
65	Pye 7N 15812	Giving Up/Cause I Believe In You	8
65	Pye 7N 15884	Lonely Without You/As Long As I Know He's Mine	8
65	Pye 7N 15937	Stop/When The Lovin' Ends	15
62	Pye NEP 24171	THIS IS JULIE GRANT (EP)	25

LEE GRANT (& CAPITOLS)
66	Parlophone R 5531	Breaking Point/Don't Cry Baby (with Capitols)	20
70	Decca F 13029	A Little Love And Understanding/I Got To Get You Out Of My Mind (solo)	7

LITTLE BROTHER (GRANT)
70	Torpedo TOR 27	Baby Don't Let Me Down/Brother Strong Man (as Little Brother)	15
70	Torpedo TOR 28	Let's Do It Together/Hey Man, Why (as Little Brother Grant & Zapatta Schmidt)	35

(see also Equals)

NEVILLE GRANT
73	Attack ATT 8058	Baby Don't Get Hooked On Me/Happy Hippie	20
73	Downtown DT 509	Sick And Tired/PRINCE DJANGO: Hot Tip	80

NORMAN GRANT ORCHESTRA
61	Starlite ST45 060	Jive Medley/Speak Low	7

TOP GRANT
62	Island WI 034	Searching/David & Goliath	15
62	Island WI 052	Suzie/Jenny	15
63	Island WI 072	Riverbank Coberley (as Top-Grant)/Nancy	15
63	Island WI 074	Money Money Money/Have Mercy On Me	18
63	Island WI 077	War In Africa/The Birds	15

(see also Rhythm Aces)

GRAPE
92	Pencil Toast PENT 001	Baby In A Plastic Bag/Listen To Your Heart (p/s)	25

GRAPEFRUIT
68	RCA Victor RCA 1656	Dear Delilah/The Dead Boot	8
68	RCA Victor RCA 1677	Elevator/Yes	25
68	RCA Victor RCA 1716	C'mon Marianne/Ain't It Good	6
68	Stateside-Dunhill SS 8005	Someday Soon/Theme For Twiggy	7
69	Stateside-Dunhill SS 8011	Round Going Round/This Little Man	7
69	RCA Victor RCA 1855	Deep Water/Come Down To The Station	7
70	RCA Victor RCA 1907	Lady Godiva (Come Home)/Thunder And Lightning	6
71	Deram DM 243	Universal Party/Sha Sha	6
69	Stateside-Dunhill S(S)L 5008	AROUND GRAPEFRUIT (LP, black/white/red label with "sold in the U.K..." text)	100
69	RCA Victor SF 8030	DEEP WATER (LP)	80

(see also Tony Rivers & Castaways, Easybeats, Fynn McCool, Sleepy)

GRAPEVINE
68	Liberty LBF 15063	Things Ain't What They Used To Be Anymore/Ace In The Hole	8

GRAPHIC DESIGN

MINT VALUE £

GRAPHIC DESIGN
83 SRTS/83/CUS/1952 Lonely Life/Shock (p/s) 100

GRAPHITE
72 Beacon BEA 109 Gimme Your Number/Chestnut Loke (possibly promo only) 40

GRASS CUTTERS
72 Malbury MB 1 Inside A Dream/The Silence Is Over (p/s) 25

GRASSROOTS
66 RCA Victor RCA 1532 Where Were You When I Needed You/These Are Bad Times 10
67 Pye International 7N 25422 Let's Live For Today/Depressed Feeling 10
67 Pye International 7N 25431 Things I Should Have Said/Tip Of My Tongue 6
68 RCA Victor RCA 1737 Midnight Confessions/Who Will You Be Tomorrow 15
69 Stateside-Dunhill SS 8023 Who Will You Be Tomorrow/Midnight Confessions 8
69 Stateside-Dunhill SS 8029 I'd Wait A Million Years/Fly Me To Havana 12
69 Stateside-Dunhill SS 8033 Heaven Knows/Don't Remind Me 7
71 Probe PRO 515 Temptation Eyes/Keepin' Me Down 10
69 Stateside S(S)L 5005 GOLDEN GRASS (LP) 25
70 Stateside SSL 5012 LEAVING IT ALL BEHIND (LP) 25

(see also P.F. Sloan)

GRATEFUL DEAD
67 Warner Bros WB 7186 Born Cross-Eyed/Dark Star 50
70 Warner Bros WB 7410 Uncle John's Band/New Speedway Boogie 12
71 Warner Bros. Truckin'/Johnny B. Goode (unissued) 0
72 Warner Bros K 16167 One More Saturday Night (as Grateful Dead with Bobby Ace)/Bertha 7
73 Atlantic K 19201 Let Me Sing Your Blues Away/Here Comes Sunshine 7
74 United Artists UP 36030 U.S. Blues/Loose Lucy 6
77 Warner Bros SAM 79 Dark Star/Born Cross-Eyed (p/s, mail-order issue with Dark Star magazine) ... 40
79 Arista ARIST 236 Good Lovin'/Stagger Lee 6
87 Arista RIS 35 Touch Of Grey/My Brother Esau (grey vinyl, p/s) 6
67 Warner Bros. W 1689 THE GRATEFUL DEAD (LP, 1st pressing, mono, gold labels, front laminated flipback sleeves, mono) 100
68 Warner Bros. W 1689 THE GRATEFUL DEAD (2nd pressing, mono, orange labels, front laminated flipback sleeve) 80
68 Warner Bros. WS 1749 ANTHEM OF THE SUN (LP, 1st pressing, orange labels, front laminated flipback sleeve, stereo) 100
69 Warner Bros. WS 1790 AOXOMOXOA (LP, 1st pressing orange labels, front laminated flipback sleeve, original mix) 70
70 Warner Bros. WS 1830 LIVE/DEAD (2-LP, 1st pressing, orange labels) 60
70 Warner Bros. WS 1869 WORKINGMAN'S DEAD (LP, 1st pressing, orange labels) 50
70 Warner Bros. WS 1749 ANTHEM OF THE SUN (LP, 2nd pressing, green labels, front laminated flipback sleeve) ... 50
71 Warner Bros. WS 1893 AMERICAN BEAUTY (LP, 1st pressing, green labels, front laminated flipback sleeve) 45
71 Warner Bros. K 66009 GRATEFUL DEAD (SKULL AND ROSES) (2-LP, green labels) 45
71 Warner Bros. K66002 LIVE/DEAD (LP, 2nd pressing, green labels reissue) 35
72 Warner Bros. K 46049 WORKINGMAN'S DEAD (LP, 2nd pressing, green labels) 30
72 Warner Bros. K 46021 ANTHEM OF THE SUN (LP, 3rd pressing, green labels, matt sleeve) 30
72 Warner Bros. K 46027 AOXOMOXOA (LP, 2nd pressing, green labels, matt sleeve, original mix, reissue) 35
72 Warner Bros. K 46074 AMERICAN BEAUTY (LP, 2nd pressing, green labels, front laminated sleeve) 30
72 Polydor 2310 171 HISTORIC DEAD (LP) 25
72 Polydor 2310 172 VINTAGE DEAD (LP) 30
72 Warner Bros. K 66019 EUROPE '72 (3-LP, 1st pressing, green labels, triple fold-out sleeve, with 8 page booklet) . 35
73 Warner Bros. K 46021 ANTHEM OF THE SUN (LP, 4th pressing, 'Palm tree' labels, matt sleeve) 20
73 Warner Bros. K 46246 HISTORY OF GRATEFUL DEAD VOL. 1 (BEAR'S CHOICE) (LP) 20
73 Warner Bros. K 49301 WAKE OF THE FLOOD (LP, 1st pressing, matt sleeve 'picture' labels) 25
73 Warner Bros. K 46049 WORKINGMAN'S DEAD (LP, 3rd pressing, 'Palm tree' labels) 20
73 Warner Bros. K 66009 GRATEFUL DEAD (SKULL AND ROSES) (2-LP, 2nd pressing, 'Palm tree' labels) 25
73 Warner Bros. K 66002 LIVE/DEAD (2-LP, 3rd pressing, 'Palm tree' labels) 25
73 Warner Bros. K 46074 AMERICAN BEAUTY (LP, 3rd pressing, 'Palm tree' labels) 20
74 Warner Bros. K 66019 EUROPE '72 (3-LP, 2nd pressing, fold-out sleeve, 'Palm tree' labels) 25
74 Warner Bros. K 56024 SKELETONS FROM THE CLOSET: THE BEST OF GRATEFUL DEAD (LP, 1st pressing 'Palm tree' labels) 15
74 Warner Bros. K 59302 FROM THE MARS HOTEL (LP, 1st pressing, 'Picture' labels) 20
75 United Artists UA 29895 BLUES FOR ALLAH (LP, 1st pressing, laminated front sleeve, 'Picture' label) 20
76 United Artists UAD 60131/2 STEAL YOUR FACE (2-LP, 1st pressing, 'Picture labels' gatefold sleeve with bonus sampler LP For Dead Heads Only [FREE 2] in printed sleeve) 20
77 Arista 1016 TERRAPIN STATION (LP) 18
81 Arista DARTY 9 RECKONING (2-LP) 15
81 Warner Bros. K 46027 AOXOMOXOA (LP, 3rd pressing, cream labels, glossy sleeve) 15
81 Warner Bros. K 46049 WORKINGMAN'S DEAD (LP, 4th pressing, cream labels, glossy sleeve) 15
81 Warner Bros. K 46021X ANTHEM OF THE SUN (LP, 5th pressing, cream labels, glossy sleeve) 15
87 Edsel ED 221 THE GRATEFUL DEAD (LP, reissue of debut LP, glossy sleeve) 18

(see also Jerry Garcia, Mickey Hart, Kingfish, Robert Hunter, Keith & Donna Godchaux, Silver [U.S.], Diga Rhythm Band)

GRATIS
79 B.P.M. BPM 1 Downtown/Please Call My Number (1000 only, p/s) 40

GRATTITUDE
70 Moth NT 1 Dark Approaches/Sit Still (p/s) 100

GRAUZONE
81 EMI 3408 GRAUZONE (LP) 40

GRAVE
03 Century Media MORBID WAYS TO DIE (Numbered box set with 6 picture disc LPs and booklet) .. 60

GRAVEDIGGAZ
94 Gee Street GEEA 14 NIGGAMORTIS (LP, with inner sleeve) 20

NICK GRAVENITES
69	CBS 63818	MY LABORS (LP)	22

(see also Big Brother & Holding Company)

BILLY GRAVES
59	Felsted AF 119	The Shag (Is Totally Cool)/Uncertain (export issue)	25

CARL GRAVES
75	A&M AM 7151	Baby Hang Up The Phone/Walk Softly	6
76	A&M AMS 7235	My Whole World Ended (The Moment You Left Me)/Baby Don't Knock	6

TERESA GRAVES
69	RCA 1948	We're On Our Way/I Spent My Last Dream On You	10

GRAVY TRAIN
71	Vertigo 6059049	Alone In Georgia/Can Anybody Hear Me	30
73	Dawn DNS 1036	Strength Of A Dream/Tolpuddle Episode	8
74	Dawn DNS 1058	Starbright Starlight/Good Time Thing	8
75	Dawn DNS 1115	Climb Aboard The Gravy Train/Sanctuary	8
70	Vertigo 6360 023	GRAVY TRAIN (LP, gatefold sleeve, large swirl label)	400
71	Vertigo 6360 051	BALLAD OF A PEACEFUL MAN (LP, gatefold sleeve, small swirl label)	900
73	Dawn DNLS 3046	SECOND BIRTH (LP)	125
74	Dawn DNLH 1	STAIRCASE TO THE DAY (LP, gatefold sleeve, pink 'sun' label)	125

(see also Mandalaband)

BARRY GRAY (ORCHESTRA)
62	Lyntone LYN 249/250	Sabotage/Supercar Song/Supercar Twist (flexi, with p/s may exist)	30
62	Lyntone LYN 249/250	Sabotage/Supercar Song/Supercar Twist (flexi)	15
64	Melodisc MEL 1591	Fireball/Zero G (by Barry Gray & His Spacemakers; in p/s)	55
64	Melodisc MEL 1591	Fireball/Zero G (by Barry Gray & His Spacemakers)	20
65	Pye 7N 17016	Thunderbirds/Parker - Well Done (in p/s)	35
65	Pye 7N 17016	Thunderbirds/Parker - Well Done	15
67	Pye 7N 17391	Captain Scarlet/The Mysterons Theme (in p/s)	35
67	Pye 7N 17391	Captain Scarlet/The Mysterons Theme	15
68	Pye 7N 17625	Joe 90 - Title Theme/Joe 90 - Hijacked (in p/s)	50
68	Pye 7N 17625	Joe 90 - Title Theme/Joe 90 – Hijacked	25
62	Golden Guinea GGL 0106	SUPERCAR - FLIGHT OF FANCY (LP, with Edwin Astley)	50
67	United Artists ULP 1159	THUNDERBIRDS ARE GO! (LP, soundtrack, mono)	100
67	United Artists (S)ULP 1159	THUNDERBIRDS ARE GO! (LP, soundtrack, stereo)	120
87	Fanderson MAF 1	MUSIC FROM THE 21st CENTURY (7" mail order only mini-album, 33prm)	10
98	Fanderson FANSF6	SUPERCAR & FIREBALL XL5 (CD, mail order only)	30

(see also Century 21, Mary Jane with Barry Gray, Richard Harvey)

BARRY GRAY
04	Trunk JBH 010	UFO: THE ORIGINAL TELEVISION SERIES SOUNDTRACK (LP, 500 on clear vinyl)	60
04	Trunk JBH 010	UFO: THE ORIGINAL TELEVISION SERIES SOUNDTRACK (LP, 500 on black vinyl)	60
11	Trunk JBH 039	STAND BY FOR ADVERTS (LP, 500 only)	15

CHRIS GRAY
97	Music Is... MULP 01	A DEEPER LEVEL OF UNDERSTANDING (2-LP)	35

DAVID GRAY
93	Hut HUTLP 9	A CENTURY ENDS (LP, inner)	60

DOBIE GRAY
65	London HL 9953	The "In" Crowd/Be A Man	10
65	London HL 9953	The "In" Crowd/Be A Man (DJ Copy)	40
65	Pye International 7N 25307	See You At The Go Go/Walk With Love	25
65	Pye International 7N 25307	See You At The Go Go/Walk With Love (DJ Copy)	50
73	MCA MU 1221	Now That I'm Without You/Loving Arms	6
74	Sydna SYD 5028	Good Old Days/Never Ending Love	8
75	Black Magic BM 107	Out On The Floor/Be A Man	8
75	Black Magic BM 107	Out On The Floor/Be A Man (DJ Copy)	12

DOLORES GRAY
55	Brunswick 05382	Heat Wave/After You Get What You Want, You Don't Want It	15
55	Brunswick 05407	Rock Love/One	30
57	Capitol CL 14732	There'll Be Some Changes Made/Fool's Errand	7
57	Capitol T 897	WARM BRANDY (LP)	15

DORIAN GRAY
68	Parlophone R 5667	I've Got You On My Mind/Move On	12
68	Parlophone R 5732	Jingle Down A Hill/Get Goin' Baby	8

HERBIE GRAY
68	Giant GN 38	We're Staying Here/Life Ska	30

(see also Gene Rondo, Owen & Dandy, Tony Tribe)

JIMMIE GRAY
82	JKO 12JKO 100	The Kool People (Vocal)/The Kool People (Instrumental) (12")	40

JOHNNIE 'THE GASH' GRAY
58	Fontana H 123	Big Guitar/Tequila	10
58	Fontana H 134	Apache/Zach's Tune	10

LORRAINE GRAY
64	Fontana TF 435	Are You Getting Tired Of Your Little Toy?/ The Boy That I Want Doesn't Want Me	10
64	Fontana TF 484	The Little Girl That Cries/Talk To Him	6

MAUREEN GRAY
61	HMV POP 944	I Don't Want To Cry/Come On And Dance	10

OWEN GRAY
60	Starlite ST45 015	Far Love/Please Let Me Go	35
60	Starlite ST45 019	Jenny Lee/The Plea	40
60	Blue Beat BB 8	Cutest Little Woman/Running Around (with Ken Richards Band)	20
61	Blue Beat BB 43	Sinners Weep/Get Drunk (with Hersan & His City Slickers)	20

Owen GRAY

			MINT VALUE £
61	Starlite ST45 032	Mash It (Parts 1 & 2)	40
62	Starlite ST45 078	I Feel Good/Someone To Help Me	40
62	Starlite ST45 088	Let Me Go Free/In My Dreams	40
62	Blue Beat BB 75	Rockin' In My Feet/Nobody Else (with Jets)	20
62	Blue Beat BB 91	Millie Girl (with Buster's Group)/DERRICK MORGAN: Headache	25
62	Blue Beat BB 103	Lonely Days/No Good Woman (with Sonny Bradshaw Quartet)	18
62	Blue Beat BB 108	Keep It In Mind/Do You Want To Jump (with Les Dawson Combo)	18
62	Blue Beat BB 113	Best Twist/Grandma-Grandpa (B-side with Hersan & His City Slickers)	18
62	Blue Beat BB 127	Pretty Girl/Twist So Fine	18
62	Blue Beat BB 136	They Got To Move/I Love Her	18
62	Blue Beat BB 139	Tree In The Meadow/Lizebella (with Buster's Group)	18
62	Island WI 002	Patricia/Twist Baby	20
62	Island WI 020	Audrey/Dolly Baby (with Ernest Rauglin [sic] Orchestra)	20
62	Island WI 030	Midnight Trail/Time Will Tell	20
62	Island WI 048	I'm Still Waiting/Last Night	10
62	Chek TD 101	Come On Baby/My One Desire	15
62	Dice CC 3	On The Beach/Young Lover	30
63	Blue Beat BB 147	Big Mabel/Don't Come Knocking (with Edwards' Groupe)	15
63	Blue Beat BB 188	Call Me My Pet/Give Me Your Love	15
63	Blue Beat BB 201	Snow Falling/Oowee Baby (as Owen Gray & His Big Brother)	15
64	Blue Beat BB 217	Draw Me Nearer/Daddy's Girl	15
65	Blue Beat BB 290	Daddy's Gone/BUSTER'S ALLSTARS: Johnny Dark	85
65	Aladdin WI 603	Gonna Work Out Fine/Dolly Baby	20
65	Aladdin WI 607	Can I Get A Witness/Linda Lu	100
65	Island WI 252	Shook Shimmy And Shake/I'm Going Back	35
65	Island WI 258	You Don't Know Like I Do/Take Me Serious (with Sound System)	15
65	Venus VE 2	Too Many Heartaches/Baby It's True	10
66	Island WI 252	Shook, Shimmy And Shake/Gonna Work Out Fine	35
66	Island WI 267	Paradise/Bye Bye Love	10
66	Blue Beat BB 365	I'm Gonna Say So Long/The Days I'm Living	12
67	Island WIP 6000	Help Me/Incense	45
67	Collins Downbeat CR 003	Collins Greetings/Rock It Down (with Sir Collins & Band)	50
67	Collins Downbeat CR 004	I'm So Lonely (with Sir Collins & Band)/EL RECO, SIR COLLINS & J. SATCH: Shock Steady	90
68	Collins Downbeat CR 007	Am Satisfy (with Sir Collins & Band)/BOB STACKIE & SIR COLLINS & BAND: Sweet Music	150
68	Collins Downbeat CR 009	Grab It, Hold It, Feel It (with Bob Stackie)/DAN SIMMONS: Way Out Sound	65
68	Collins Downbeat CR 010	I'm Gonna Take You Back (with Bob Stackie)/GLEN ADAMS: King Sized	125
68	Coxsone CS 7047	Give Me A Little Sign/Ain't Nobody Home	300
68	Coxsone CS 7053	Give It To Me/Isn't It So	160
68	Blue Cat BS 123	These Foolish Things/This I Promise	100
69	Blue Cat BS 156	I Can't Stop Loving You/Tell Me Darling	30
68	Trojan TR 632	Lovey Dovey/Grooving	20
68	Revolution REV 001	Sitting In The Park/You've Got It	20
69	Fab FAB 90	Three Coins In The Fountain/Tennessee Waltz	15
69	Fab FAB 120	Understand My Love/Apollo 12	30
69	Fab FAB 96	Ay Ay Ay/Let It Be Me (with Rudies)	25
69	Fab FAB 126	Swing Low/Release Me	20
69	Trojan TR 650	I Can't Stop Loving You/Tell Me Darling	12
69	Trojan TR 670	Too Experienced/I Really Loved You Baby	12
69	Duke DU 12	Reggae Dance/I Know	40
69	Duke DU 33	Seven Lonely Days/He Don't Love You Like I Do	8
69	Downtown DT 423	Groovin'/HERBIE GRAY & RUDIES: These Memories	15
69	Camel CA 25	Girl What You Doing To Me/Woman A Grumble	25
69	Camel CA 34	Don't Take Your Love Away/Two Lovers	25
69	Camel CA 37	Every Beat Of My Heart/Don't Cry	20
70	Camel CA 50	Don't Sign The Paper/Packing Up Loneliness	20
70	Camel CA 51	Bring Back Your Love/Got To Come Back	20
70	Upfront UPF 3	Dream Lover/Mudda-Granma-Reggae (with Maximum Breed)	20
70	Bamboo BAM 47	I Can Feel It/I Don't Want (To Lose Your Love)	12
70	Crab CRAB 52	Just A Little Loving/DERRICK MORGAN: Take A Letter Maria	10
70	Pama PM 810	Sugar Dumpling/I Don't Know Why	8
70	Pama Supreme PS 299	I Am In Love Again/RANDY WILLIAMS: Version	6
70	Pama Supreme PS 302	Candida/When Will I Find My Way	6
70	Pama Supreme PS 310	You Gonna Miss Me/I Hear You Knocking	6
70	Supreme SUP 206	Surfin'/All The Love	6
70	Ackee ACK 102	No More/Don't Leave Me (both as Owen Gray & Omen)	15
71	Ackee ACK 123	Whispering Bells/CLANCY'S ALLSTARS: Whiplash (B-side actually "Jacket" by Dave Barker)	10
71	Camel CA 60	Groove Me/No Other One	20
71	Camel CA 73	Nothing Can Separate Us/Girl I Want You To Understand	35
71	Punch PH 87	Sincerely/Hold On I'm Coming	10
71	Pama Supreme PS 325	Summer Sand/Something To Remind Me	10
71	Pama Supreme PS 332	Greatest Hits (Parts 1 & 2)	10
72	Pama Supreme PS 351	Time/GRAHAM: Harlesden High Street	12
72	Pama Supreme PS 358	Hail The Man/I'll Follow You	6
72	Pama Supreme PS 360	Amazing Grace (with Graham Hawk)/SKETTO RICH: Don't Stay Out Late	6
78	Bushranger BAR 101	The Greatest Love Of All (with RANKING JAH SON)/TONY SEXTON & SUPERSTAR: Segregation (12")	30
76	Angen ANG 121	Blazing Fire/Version	6
76	Conflict CFT 1	Rizla/Rizla Version	10

			MINT VALUE £
61	Starlite STLP 5	OWEN GRAY SINGS (LP)	120
63	Melodisc MLP 12-153	CUPID (LP)	45
69	Trojan TTL 24	REGGAE WITH SOUL (LP)	30
77	Trojan TRLS 139	FIRE AND BULLETS (LP)	20
78	Trojan TRLS 150	DREAMS OF OWEN GRAY (LP)	25

(see also Laurel & Owen, Gray Brothers, Elki & Owen, Owen & Milie, Owen & Dandy, Dennis Lowe, Survivors, Denzil & Jennifer, Brother Dan, Glen Adam)

SHANE GRAY
68	Page One POF 102	Sing Out Loud/Come Back To My Heart Again	10

VERA GRAY
66	HMV CLP3531	LISTEN, MOVE & DANCE 4 (LP)	25

WARDELL GRAY
54	Brunswick LA 8646	THE CHASE (LP, with Dexter Gordon)	25

LARRY GRAYSON
72	York SYK 529	Shut That Door/Slack Alice	6
72	York MYK 602	WHAT A GAY DAY (LP)	15

MILTON GRAYSON
60	London HLU 9068	Forget You/The Puppet	8

RUDY GRAYZELL
54	London HL 8094	Looking At The Moon And Wishing On A Star/The Heart That Once Was Mine	200
54	London HL 8094	Looking At The Moon And Wishing On A Star/The Heart That Once Was Mine (78)	30

GRAZINA
62	HMV POP 1094	Lover Please Believe Me/So What	12
63	HMV POP 1149	Don't Be Shy/Another Like You	12
63	HMV POP 1212	Be My Baby/I Ain't Gonna Knock On Your Door	20
64	Giv-A-Disc LYN 568	Stay Awhile/Let Me Go Lover (with magazine)	10

(see also Lady Murray, Mr & Mrs Murray, Le Roys, Cliff Richard)

GREASE BAND
72	Harvest HAR 5052	Laughed At The Judge/All I Want To Do/Jesse James	6
71	Harvest SHVL 790	THE GREASE BAND (LP, textured sleeve first pressing)	60
72	Harvest SHVL 790	THE GREASE BAND (LP, second pressing with EMI boxed logo)	20
75	Goodear EAR 2902	AMAZING GREASE (LP)	15

(see also Joe Cocker, Wynder K. Frog, Made In Sheffield)

JOHNNY B. GREAT (& GOODMEN)
63	Decca F 11740	School Is In/She's A Much Better Lover Than You (with Goodmen)	10

(see also Quotations, Johnny Goodison)

GREAT ACES
72	Fab FAB 191	Gold And Silver/Liberty Rock	12
72	Fab FAB 200	Liberty Rock/Rock My Soul	25
72	Fab FAB 201	I Didn't Mean It/Boots And Shoes	20
72	Fab FAB 202	Baby Girl/Version	12
73	Fab FAB 203	Banana/My Sweet Lord	20

GREAT AWAKENING
69	London HLU 10284	Amazing Grace/Silver Waterfall	6

GREAT BRITISH HEROES (AKA GBH)
78	Lightning Records GIL 534	Eric Miller/Don't Give A Damn (unreleased, 1 known only)	1500

GREAT DELTAS
02	Funk 45 FUNK45.005	Stand Up And Be A Man/Tra La La (reissue)	6

GREATEST SHOW ON EARTH
70	Harvest HAR 5012	Real Cool World/Again And Again	20
70	Harvest HAR 5026	Tell The Story/Mountain Song	6
77	Harvest HAR 5129	Magic Touch Woman/Again And Again	8
70	Harvest SHVL 769	HORIZONS (LP, gatefold sleeve, no EMI on label)	150
70	Harvest SHVL 783	THE GOING'S EASY (LP, gatefold sleeve, no EMI logo on label)	150
75	Harvest SHSM 2004	THE GREATEST SHOW ON EARTH (LP)	15

(see also Ian Dury & Blockheads, Fuzzy Duck, Glencoe, Naturals)

GREAT EXPECTATIONS
72	Polydor 2058241	I'm So Glad I Gotcha/Time And Place	8
73	Polydor 2058348	Devils Gun/Bigger And Better	8
81	Phillips (no cat no)	Midnight Man/Pt. 2	15

GREAT METROPOLITAN STEAM BAND
69	MCA MNP/S 403	THE GREAT METROPLITAN STEAM BAND (LP)	25

GREAT SOCIETY
68	CBS 63476	CONSPICUOUS ONLY IN ITS ABSENCE (LP)	35

(see also Jefferson Airplane)

GREAT UNCLE FRED
67	Strike JH 324	I'm In Love With An Ex-Beauty Queen/Singalong Version	20

JOE GRECH
71	Electro ES 152	Marija L-Maltija/In-Nassab (export issue)	6

BUDDY GRECO
57	London HLR 8452	With All My Heart/Game Of Love (with B-G Skiffle Band)	10

(see also Johnny Desmond)

JULIETTE GRECO
58	Philips BBE 12219	TV SERIES (EP)	10

GREEDIES
80	Vertigo GREED 1	A Merry Jingle/A Merry Jangle (p/s)	6

(see also Professionals, Thin Lizzy, Sex Pistols)

ADAM GREEN
03	Rough Trade RTRADLP 107	FRIENDS OF MINE (LP, inner)	40
05	Rough Trade RTRADLP 194	GEMSTONES (LP)	25

Al GREEN(E)

MINT VALUE £

AL GREEN(E)
68	Stateside SS 2079	Back Up Train/Don't Leave Me (as Al Greene & Soul Mates)	25
68	Stateside SS 2079	Back Up Train/Don't Leave Me (as Al Greene & Soul Mates) (DJ copy)	40
69	Action ACT 4540	Don't Hurt Me No More/Get Yourself Together (by Al Greene)	20
70	London HLU 10300	You Say It/Gotta Find A New World	7
71	London HLU 10324	I Can't Get Next To You/Ride Sally Ride	7
71	Bell BLL 1188	Back Up Train/Don't Leave Me (as Al Green & Soul Mates, reissue)	12
77	London STO U 8685	I TRIED TO TELL MYSELF (EP)	10
71	London SHU 8424	AL GREEN GETS NEXT TO YOU (LP)	30
69	Action ACLP 6008	BACK UP TRAIN (LP)	60
72	London SHU 8430	LET'S STAY TOGETHER (LP)	30
72	London SHU 8443	I'M STILL IN LOVE WITH YOU (LP)	30
73	London SHU 8457	CALL ME (LP)	20
74	London SHU 8464	LIVIN' FOR YOU (LP)	20
74	London SHU 8479	EXPLORES YOUR MIND (LP)	20
75	London SHU 8481	GREATEST HITS (LP)	20
76	London SHU 8493	FULL OF FIRE (LP)	15
76	London SHU 8505	HAVE A GOOD TIME (LP)	20
86	Hi HI UK LP 401	GREEN IS BLUES (LP, reissue)	15
86	Hi HI UK LP 405	LET'S STAY TOGETHER (LP, reissue)	15
86	Hi HI UK LP 409	CALL ME (LP, reissue)	15

BARRY GREEN
71	Ember TBS 713	Together/Sexopolis	100
71	Decca F13171	I Wanna Join The Cavalry/When The Morning Returns (demo only)	15
72	Decca F 13282	Papa Do/Boomerang	8

BENNIE GREEN
61	Parlophone PMC 1180	HORNFUL OF SOUL (LP)	30

BRIAN GREEN
68	Fontana SFJL 912	BRIAN GREEN DISPLAY (LP)	40

CARL GREEN AND THE SCENE
79	Sirius SP 516	RECORD NOT FOUND EP	20
80	Benton Fun/Ginnis Bucka GRCGCS1	All The Tea In China/Business Aquaintance/Fish In The Sea (p/s, double sided insert)	100

GARLAND GREEN
69	MCA Soul Bag BAG 9	Jealous Kinda Fella/I Can't Believe You Quit Me	10
98	Kent 6T 16	Come Through Me/JUNIOR MCCANTS: Try Me For Your New Love	40
90	Kent KEND 097	THE SPRING SIDES (LP)	20

GRANT GREEN
65	Verve VLP 9111	HIS MAJESTY KING FUNK (LP)	25
93	Blue Note 89622	STREET FUNK AND JAZZ GROOVES (2-LP)	20

HUGHIE GREEN
61	Polydor Decca F11317	The Valley Of Peppermint Springs/The Puppet Song	6
66	Columbia DB 8085	Cuddle Up Baby/Clap Your Hands (B-side with Monica Rose)	7

IAN GREEN (REVELATION)
67	Polydor 56194	Last Pink Rose/Green Blues (solo)	30
69	CBS 3997	When You Love A Man/Santa Maria	6
69	CBS 4623	Revelation/Groover's Grave	6
70	CBS 63840	REVELATION (LP)	30

(see also Madeline Bell, Rosetta Hightower)

JIMMY GREEN
73	Duke DU 155	Suspicion/LLOYD'S ALL STARS: Suspicion - Version	10
73	Green Door GD 4062	I'll Be Standing By/LLOYD'S ALL STARS: I'll Be Standing By "Version"	15

(see also Jimmy London)

KATHE GREEN
69	Deram DM 279	If I Thought You'd Ever Change Your Mind/Primrose Hill	7
69	Deram SML 1039	RUN THE LENGTH OF YOUR WILDNESS (LP, white/red label)	35

KEITH GREEN
60s	Bird 118	NO COMPROMISE (LP)	30

LLOYD GREEN
75	Monument S MNT 81245	STEEL RIDES (LP)	20

PETER GREEN
71	Reprise RS 27012	Heavy Heart/No Way Out	25
72	Reprise K 14092	Heavy Heart/No Way Out (repressing)	20
72	Reprise K 14141	Beast Of Burden/Uganda Woman (with Nigel Watson)	25
78	PVK PV 16	Apostle/Tribal Dance	8
79	PVK PV 24	In The Skies/Proud Pinto (p/s)	8
81	PVK PV 103	Give Me Back My Freedom/Lost My Love	8
81	PVK PV 112	Promised Land/Bizzy Lizzy	8
82	Headline LIN 2	The Clown/Time For Me To Go	8
70	Reprise RSLP 9006	THE END OF THE GAME (LP, with Nigel Watson)	150
79	PVK PVLS 101	IN THE SKIES (LP, gatefold, green vinyl)	30
80	PVK PVLS 102	LITTLE DREAMER (LP, with inner sleeve)	15
81	PVK PET 1	WHATCHA GONNA DO? (LP)	20
82	Headline HED 1	WHITE SKY (LP)	20
83	Headline HED 2	KOLORS (LP)	20
85	Nightflight NTFL 2001	A CASE FOR THE BLUES/KATMANDU (LP)	20

(see also Fleetwood Mac, Peter B's, Shotgun Express, John Mayall & Bluesbreakers, Gass, Peter Bardens, Gass)

PHILIP GREEN & PINEWOOD STUDIO ORCHESTRA
60	Top Rank JAR 355	League Of Gentlemen March/"Golden Fleece" Theme	10

SALLY GREEN
62	Philips PB 1243	It Hurts Too Much To Laugh/When's He Gonna Kiss Me	15

TEDDY GREEN
63	Piccadilly 7N 35146	Gee What A Party/Dream Chaser	6

TOM GREEN
74	Action ACT 4621	Rock Springs Railroad Station/Endless Confusion	100

GREEN ANGELS
65	Parlophone R 5390	Rockin' Red Wing/Let It Happen	15
66	Parlophone R 5512	An Exile's Dream/Hanningan's Hooley	6

NORMAN GREENBAUM
70	Reprise RS 20846	Jubilee/Skyline	8
70	Reprise RS 20919	Canned Ham/Junior Cadillac	8
71	Reprise RS 21008	California Earthquake/Rhode Island Red	8
70	Reprise RSLP 6365	SPIRIT IN THE SKY (LP)	20
70	Page One POLS 017	WITH DR. WEST'S MEDICINE SHOW & JUNK BAND (LP)	22

(see also Dr. West's Medicine Show & Junk Band)

GREEN BEAN
69	Regal Zonophone RZ 3017	The Garden's Lovely/Sittin' In The Sunshine	7

GREENBEATS
67	Spin SP 2007	Pretty Woman/Thing	15

GREEN BULLFROG
72	MCA MKPS 2021	GREEN BULLFROG (LP, black/blue 'hexagon' label)	175

(see also Deep Purple, Roger Glover, Matthew Fisher)

GREEN DAY
94	Reprise W 0247	Longview/On The Wagon (p/s)	10
94	Reprise W 0247 T	Longview/Going To Pasalacqua (Infatuation)/FOD (Live)/ Christy Road (Live) (10", green vinyl, stickered PVC sleeve)	20
94	Reprise W 0257	Basket Case/Tired Of Waiting For You (Green vinyl, numbered p/s)	15
94	Reprise W 0269 T	Welcome To Paradise/Chump (Live)/Emenius Sleepus (green vinyl 12", stickered PVC sleeve)	15
95	Reprise W 0279 X	Basket Case/2,000 Light Years Away (Live) (numbered poster p/s, green vinyl)	12
95	Reprise W 0287X	Longview/Welcome To Paradise (live) (2nd issue with sticker sheet, p/s)	8
95	Reprise W 0327	Stuck With Me/When I Come Around (Live) (p/s)	10
98	Reprise W 0438	Redundant/The Grouch (live) (p/s)	10
94	Reprise 9362 45529 1	DOOKIE (LP, with crowd photo on back cover, green vinyl, numbered sticker)	50
95	Reprise 9362 46046 1	INSOMNIAC (LP, with inner)	50
97	Reprise 9362 46794 1	NIMROD (LP, with inner)	50
01	Reprise 48145	INTERNATIONAL SUPERHITS! (LP, insert, purple vinyl)	40
04	Reprise 9362-41777-1	AMERICAN IDIOT (2-LP)	35

CLAUDE 'FATS' GREENE & ORCHESTRA
66	Island WI 290	Fats Shake 'Em Up Parts 1 & 2 (actually with Al Thomas)	15

JEANIE GREENE
69	Atlantic 584 226	Sure As Sin/I've Been A Long Time Loving You	10

KELLIE GREENE
64	Stateside SS 303	Madrigal/Foggy Day	12

LAURA GREENE
79	Grapevine GRP 135	Can't Help Loving Dat Man/It's A Good Day For A Parade	7

(see also Diane Renay)

LORNE GREENE
64	RCA RCA 1428	Ringo/Bonanza	6
63	RCA RD 7566	YOUNG... AT HEART (LP)	15
65	RCA RD 7709	THE MAN (LP)	15

GREEN EYE
73	Whirl WH01	Sinister Jack/Run Run Run	25

GREENFIELD
71	Philips 6113002	Sweet America/Dorothys Daughter	15

GREENFIELD & COOK
72	Polydor 2121-105	Only Lies/You Return	8

GREENGAGE
74	Philips 6006393	Real Nice Time/SingSing a Song	8
78	RCA PB 5069	Rosie/River	8

GREEN GINGER THREE
65	Decca DFE 8623	FROM THE LAND OF GREEN GINGER (EP)	15

GREEN JELLY
93	Z 74321 15142-7	Three Little Pigs/Joey The Cowghod (p/s)	6

LEE GREENLEE
59	Top Rank JAR 226	Cherry, I'm In Love With You/Starlight	7

GREEN LINES
80	CMS MR 016X	A PIECE OF THE NIGHT (EP, folded p/s)	15

GREEN MAN
75	Private pressing	WHAT AILS THEE? (LP, 100 copies, Matrix Vem 107-A2/B2)	200
00	Slightly Discoloured FADE 01	WHAT AILS THEE? (LP, reissue)	18

GREEN PAJAMAS
89	Ubik Records BAKTUN 1	SUMMER OF LUST (LP, reissue)	15
99	Woronzow WOO 36 LP	SEVEN FATHOMS DOWN AND FALLING (LP)	20

GREEN RIVER
85	Homestead HMS 031	COME ON DOWN (EP, with insert)	20
88	Glitterhouse GR 0031	REHAB DOLL (LP)	20

(see also Mudhoney)

GREENSLADE
73	Warner Bros K 46207	GREENSLADE (LP, gatefold sleeve, green label)	25

Arthur GREENSLADE (& GEE MEN)

MINT VALUE £

73	Warner Bros K 46259	BEDSIDE MANNERS ARE EXTRA (LP, gatefold sleeve 'Burbank' label)	20
74	Warner Bros K 56055	SPYGLASS GUEST (LP, gatefold sleeve)	15
76	Warner Bros K 56306	CACTUS CHOIR (LP, lyric insert)	15
80	EMI EMSP 332	THE PENTATEUCH OF THE COSMOGONY (2-LP, with 47-page book, as Dave Greenslade)	40

(see also Wes Minster Five, Alan Price Set, Geno Washington & Ram Jam Band, Chris Farlowe, Colosseum, Samurai, Web, King Crimson, Stackridge)

ARTHUR GREENSLADE (& GEE MEN)

| 61 | Decca F 11363 | Rockin' Susannah/Eclipse (with Gee Men) | 10 |
| 66 | Columbia DB 7865 | Watermelon Man/Serenade To A Broken Jaw | 30 |

GREENTEA PENG

| 19 | Different DIF433EP | RISING (12", 1st pressing, green vinyl) | 80 |

GREEN TELESCOPE

| 86 | Imaginary MIRAGE 001 | Two By Two/Make Me Stay/Thinkin' About Toady (p/s, various designs) | 8 |

GREEN VELVET

| 95 | Open OPENP 017 | Flash (The Relief Remixes) (12") | 15 |

ELLIE GREENWICH

67	United Artists UP 1180	I Want You To Be My Baby/Goodnight, Goodnight	25
68	United Artists UP 2214	Sunshine After The Rain/A Long Time Comin'	12
70	Bell BLL 1105	I Don't Wanna Be Left Outside/Ain't That Peculiar	12
73	MGM 2006 306	Maybe I Know/Goodnight Baby/Baby I Love You	8
73	MGM 2315 243	LET IT BE WRITTEN, LET IT BE SUNG (LP)	30

(see also Popsicles, Raindrops [U.S.])

GREEN WILLOW

| 80 | Cotswold Music SFA 115 | COTSWOLD MUSIC (LP) | 30 |

GREEN WINDOWS

| 73 | Decca F 13427 | Twenty Years/Story Of A Man | 8 |

JONNY GREENWOOD

| 03 | Parlophone 5951471 | BODYSONG (LP) | 60 |

(see also Radiohead)

MICK GREENWOOD

| 71 | MCA MDKS 8003 | THE LIVING GAME (LP, gatefold sleeve, pink/orange 'dogbone' label) | 30 |
| 72 | MCA MKPS 2026 | TO FRIENDS (LP, black/blue 'hexagon' label) | 20 |

(see also Fotheringay)

NICHOLAS GREENWOOD

| 72 | Kingdom KVLP 9002 | COLD CUTS (LP) | 1000 |

(see also Crazy World Of Arthur Brown, Khan, Bryn Howarth)

STOCKER GREENWOOD & FRIENDS

| 79 | Changes | BILLY + NINE (LP) | 20 |

GINNY GREER

| 57 | Brunswick 05673 | Five Oranges, Four Apples/Kiss Me Hello (But Never Goodbye) | 6 |

GREGER

| 66 | Polydor 249 1103 | IN THE NIGHT (LP) | 25 |

BOBBY GREGG & FRIENDS

| 62 | Columbia DB 4825 | The Jam (Parts 1 & 2) | 15 |

JOEY GREGORASH

| 71 | Polydor 2121 032 | Jodie/The Key | 7 |

IA(I)N GREGORY

60	Pye 7N 15295	Time Will Tell/The Night You Told A Lie (as Ian Gregory)	30
61	Pye 7N 15397	Can't You Hear The Beat Of A Broken Heart/Because	25
62	Pye 7N 15435	Mr. Lovebug/Pocketful Of Dreams	35
63	Columbia DB 7085	Yellow Teddy Bear/How Many Times	12

JANE GREGORY

| 84 | D Sharp DSS 1004 | Do Not Go/After A Dream (p/s) | 150 |

JOHNNY GREGORY & HIS ORCHESTRA

62	Fontana TFE 17389	THE T.V. THRILLERS (EP)	10
72	Philips 6308 111	SPIES AND DOLLS (LP)	15
74	United Artists UAG 29546	A MAN FOR ALL SEASONS (LP)	25
74	United Artists QUAG 29546	A MAN FOR ALL SEASONS (LP, quadrophonic)	75

TONY GREGORY

66	Doctor Bird DB 1007	Baby Come On Home/Marie Elena	30
66	Doctor Bird DB 1016	Give Me One More Chance/I've Lost My Love	30
67	Island WI 3029	Get Out Of My Life/SOUL BROTHERS: Sugar Cane	40
67	Coxsone CS 7013	Only A Fool (Breaks His Own Heart)/Pure Soul	50
71	Horse HOSS 3	Bouncing All Over The World/Tell Me	10
67	Coxsone CSL 8011	TONY GREGORY SINGS (LP)	100

(see also Lloyd Charmers)

STAN GREIG'S JAZZ BAND

| 59 | Tempo EXA 90 | STAN GREIG'S JAZZ BAND (EP) | 25 |
| 80s | Calligraph CLGLP 004 | BLUES EVERY TIME (LP) | 20 |

GREMLINS

| 66 | Mercury MF 981 | The Coming Generation/That's What I Want | 20 |
| 67 | Mercury MF 1004 | You Gotta Believe It/I Can't Say | 20 |

JOEL GREY

54	MGM SPC 1	Last Night In The Back Porch/Two-Faced (export issue)	18
57	Capitol CL 14779	Everytime I Ask My Heart/Moonlight Swim	7
58	Capitol CL 14832	Be My Next/Shoppin' Around (demos is picture sleeves = £40)	20
61	London HLX 9442	Brigitte Bardot/BURT AND THE BACKBEATS: Felicidade	6

MAL GREY AND FLIGHT 56

| 75 | Arista 8 | Look Out For Love/Ballroom Queen | 10 |

RONNIE GREY & JETS

| 55 | Capitol CL 14329 | Run, Manny, Run/Sweet Baby | 20 |

Sarah GREY & ELLIE ELLIS

MINT VALUE £

SARAH GREY & ELLIE ELLIS
86 Greenwich Village GVR 231   YOU GAVE ME A SONG (LP, with insert) 15

GREY BROTHERS
68 Blue Cat BS 224   Always/Big Man 80

(see also Owen Gray)

GREYHOUND
71 Trojan TR 7820   Black And White/Sand In Your Shoes 6
71 Trojan TR 7834   Follow The Leader/Funky Jamaica 6
71 Trojan TR 7848   Moon River/I've Been Trying/Pressure Is Coming On (solid or push-out centre) 6
72 Trojan TRLS 27   BLACK AND WHITE (LP) 30

(see also Tillermen)

GREY PARADE
85 Plan B GREY 1   THE REASON (LP) 25

ANDREW GRIDLEY
83 ADG 001   Lost In Time/Reflections/Taking A Chance On Love/I'm A Fool In Love 10

GRIDS
80 Kings Head   NEW ANTHEMS (EP) 20

MERVA GRIER
83 Hawkeyes HD 053   Feeling Like A Million/HOPETON LINDO: We Are One (12") 25

ROOSEVELT GRIER
68 Action ACT 4515   People Make The World/Hard To Forget 15
69 Pama PM 774   Who's Got The Ball 15
69 Pama PM 784   C'mon Cupid/High Society Woman 20

GRANT GRIEVES
70 Injun 106   Four On The Floor/M1 Automatic 10

GRIFFIN
69 Bell BLL 1075   I Am The Noise In Your Head/Don't You Know 35
72 MGM 2006 088   What Happens In The Darkness/Calling You 10

(see also Heavy Jelly, Skip Bifferty, Every Which Way, Bell & Arc, Happy Magazine, Ginger Baker's Airforce)

JOHNNY GRIFFIN
62 Riverside RLP 420   THE KERRY DANCERS (LP) 80
69 Polydor 583734   THE MAN I LOVE (LP) 60
70 Youngblood SSYB 11   FOOT PATTING (LP) 50

JOHNNY GRIFFIN BIG SOUL BAND
61 Riverside REP 3203   THE BIG SOUL BAND (EP, with Clark Terry & Bobby Timmons) 10
61 Riverside RLP 12-3331   THE BIG SOUL BAND (LP, also stereo [RLP 9331] 20

(see also Eddie 'Lockjaw' Davis)

MERV GRIFFIN
61 London HLL 9339   The Charanga/Along Came Joe 10

SYLVIA GRIFFIN
88 Rocket BLAST 7   Love's A State Of Mind/Forgive The Girl (p/s, features George Harrison) 8
88 Rocket BLAST 712   Love's A State Of Mind/Forgive The Girl/Lonely Heart (12", p/s, features George Harrison) 12

ANDY GRIFFITH
55 Capitol CL 14263   Ko Ko Mo (I Love You So)/Make Yourself Comfortable 10
58 Capitol CL 14936   Midnight Special/She's Bad, Bad Business (with Dixie Seven) 8

JOE GRIFFITHS
69 Philips SBL 7902   OUT OF THE HEAD OF...(LP, black/silver labels) 20

MARCIA GRIFFITHS
66 Island WI 285   Funny/KING SPARROW: Beggars Have No Choice (B-side actually by Leonard Dillon & Wailers; some copies credit Marcia Griffiths on both sides) 120
67 Studio One SO 2008   Hound Dog (actually by Norma Fraser)/HUGH GODFREY: My Time 100
67 Studio One SO 2015   After Laughter/HUGH GODFREY: Go Tell Him 80
68 Coxsone CS 7035   Mojo Girl (actually by Nora Dean)/HAMLINS: Tell Me That You Love Me 200
68 Coxsone CS 7055   Feel Like Jumping/HORACE TAYLOR: Thundering Vibrations 75
68 Coxsone CS 7062   Hold Me Tight/BASIES: Home Sweet Home (B-side actually by Basses) 400
68 Studio One SO 2047   Words (as Marcia Griffiths & Jeff Dixon)/SHARKS: How Could I Live 150
68 Studio One SO 2059   Truly/SIMMS & ROBINSON: Drought 70
69 Gas GAS 111   Tell Me Now/STAN HOPE: The Weight 100
69 High Note HS 029   Talk (Parts 1 & 2) (correct title is actually "Toil") 15
69 Escort ES 808   Don't Let Me Down/REGGAEITES: Romper Room (B-side actually by Peter Tosh) 100
69 Trojan TR 693   Put A Little Love In Your Heart/J BOYS: Jay Fever 15
70 Harry J. HJ 6213   Put A Little Love In Your Heart/JAY BOYS: Bah Oop Ah 15
70 Harry J. HJ 6623   Band Of Gold/JAY BOYS: Cowboy (Version II) 25
70 Bamboo BAM 59   Shimmering Star/SOUND DIMENSION: Mun-Dun-Gu (B-side actually by Im & David) 100
75 Torpedo TOR 47   Survival/Version 40
70 Trojan TRLS 94   SWEET BITTER LOVE (LP) 50
74 Trojan TRLS 94   SWEET BITTER LOVE (LP, orange/white label) 30
78 Sky Note KYLP 17   STEPPIN' (LP) 20
79 Sky Note SKYLP 09   NATURALLY (LP) 25

(see also Bob & Marcia, Peter Touch/Tosh, Roy Richards, Soul Vendor, Bob Andy, Della Humphrey, Mr. Foundation, Bob Marley)

VICTOR GRIFFITHS
70 Punch PH 29   I Am Proud Of You/KING VICTOR ALL STARS: Version 20

FERRE GRIGNARD
68 Atlantic 584 158   Yellow You Yellow Me/La Si Do 7

GRIMES
10 No Pain In Pop – NPIP024   GEIDI PRIMES (LP) 75
11 Lo LCD 87   HALFAXA (LP) 20
12 4AD CAD3208   VISIONS (LP) 18
15 4AD CAD3535   ART ANGELS (LP) 20

Carol GRIMES (& DELIVERY)

MINT VALUE £

CAROL GRIMES (& DELIVERY)
70	B&C CB 129	Harry Lucky/Homemade Ruin (with Delivery)	12
74	Virgin VS 109	You're The Only One/Southern Boogie	7
76	Decca FR 13674	I Betcha Didn't Know THAT/Dynamite	6
70	Charisma CAS 1023	FOOLS MEETING (LP, with Delivery, gatefold sleeve)	250
74	Caroline CA 2001	WARM BLOOD (LP, black/white/red 'twins' labels)	25
75	Decca SKL-R 5268	CAROL GRIMES (LP, blue/silver labels)	20

(see also Uncle Dog, Babylon)

GRIMMS
73	Island ILPS 9248	ROCKIN' DUCK (LP, die cut 'duck' sleeve outside single sleeve, pink rim, palm tree logo)	20
76	DJM DJLPS 470	SLEEPERS (LP)	15

(see also Neil Innes, Liverpool Scene, Scaffold, Mike McGear, McGough & McGear, John Gorman, Zoot Money, Patto, Viv Stanshall, Andy Roberts, Bashers)

GRIM REAPER (1)
83	Ebony EBON 16	SEE YOU IN HELL (LP)	20
85	Ebony EBON 32	FEAR NO EVIL (LP)	20

GRIM REAPER (2)
94	No label or cat no	Free/Mighter Than Mighty/Go Chew/My Soul (12")	35

GRINDERMAN
07	Mute MUTE 370	Get It On (1-sided 7" other side etched, p/s)	15
07	Mute MUTE 373	No Pussy Blues (edit)/Chain Of Flowers (numbered, stickered p/s, poster)	8
07	Mute MUTE 381	(I Don't Need You To) Set Me Free (embossed p/s, one-sided etched disc)	8
07	Mute 12 MUTE 449	PALACES OF MONTEZUMA EP (12", splatter vinyl)	10
10	Mute 12 MUTE 441	Heathen Child/Star Charmer/Super Heathen Child (12", red vinyl, poster, first pressing with black sticker)	10
11	Mute 12 MUTE 666	EVIL EP (12", CD, die-cut sleeve, red glitter vinyl)	10
07	Mute STUMM 272	GRINDERMAN (LP)	35
11	Mute STUMM 299	GRINDERMAN 2 (LP & CD with poster and print)	25
11	Mute XCDSTUMM299	GRINDERMAN 2 RMX (2-LP & CD)	25

(see also Nick Cave)

GRINDERSWITCH
76	Capricorn 2089 030	Picking The Blues/The Best I Can	7

JANNY GRINE
70s	Sparrow BIRD 104	FREE INDEED (LP)	25

GRINGO
71	MCA MKS 5067	I'm Another Man/Soft Mud	6
71	MCA MKPS 2107	GRINGO (LP, red/pink 'dogbone' label)	80

(see also Caravan)

JOE GRINNE
69	Coxsone CS 7098	Mr Editor/How I Feel (both sides actually by Melodians)	250

GRIP
80	Mrs. Dixon MDR 3001	File It Under Maybe, Baby/Pavement Princess/Hole in The Wall (p/s)	25

GRIPPIN
72	Priory PR1	I See What You See/Times Over	80

GRISBY DYKE
69	Deram DM 232	The Adventures Of Miss Rosemary La Page/Mary Anne She	30

GRISSLE
74	Roach RC 3	Crazy Lady/She Goes	40

GRIZZARDS
98	Baban GRIZ 5	Grizzling/The Green Griz (p/s)	8

GROBBERT & DUFF
72	Sunlamp GRA 101	I Am I Think/The Man From Naz	100

DEWEY GROOM
62	Starlite ST45 085	Butane Blues/That's All I Want Out Of Life	20
63	Starlite ST45 095	You're Tearing My Heart Out Of Me/Walking Papers	10
63	Starlite ST45 105	Heartaches For Sale/Sometimes If I'm Lucky	8

GROOP (1)
68	CBS 3204	Woman You're Breaking Me/Mad Over You	30
78	CBS 3151	Lovin' Tree/Night Life	20

GROOP (2)
69	Bell BLL 1070	A Famous Myth/Tears And Joys	15
69	Bell BLL 1080	The Jet Song (When The Weekend's Over)/Nobody At All	18

GROOVE CHRONICLES
96	Old Dog NOOD 1	The Beginings Part 1/Part 2/Tidy Vibes (12")	15
97	DPR DPR 001	Angel Body/Natural (12" white label)	15
97	Groove Chronicles GC 001	Stone Cold/Hold On (12", white label)	35
97	Groove Chronicles GC 002	No Body (Chronicles Dub Flavour)/No Body (Wilkys Jazz House Pressure)/No Body Beats) (12")	12
98	Groove Chronicles GC 001e	Stone Cold/Hold On (12")	30
98	Groove Chronicles GC 003	Holiday Da Vybe (vocal)/Holiday Da Vybe (dub) (12")	12
98	Outlaw OUT 004	Your Sweetness/Sweet Dub (12")	12

GROOVE FARM
87	Raving Pop Blast RPBGF 1	SORE HEADS AND HAPPY HEARTS (EP, with insert & handwritten labels)	10
87	Raving Pop Blast RPBGF 2	ONLY THE MOST IGNORANT GUTLESS SHEEP-BRAINED POLTROON CAN DENY THEM NOW (EP)	12
88	Subway Organisation	Driving In Your New Car (Mini Mix)/Expanding Reindeer/I Can't Dance With You/Epistle To Duppy (12", white label promos only, with press release)	10

GROOVE TUNNEL
95	Detour DR 023	Rainy Day/How Do You Feel (p/s, white vinyl)	7

GROOVE (1)
69	Parlophone R 5783	The Wind/Play The Song	50

GROOVE (2)

MINT VALUE £

GROOVE (2)
80	Trendy WHIP 1	Heart Complaint/I Wanna Be Your Pygmy		15

GROOVE ARMADA
98	Tummy Touch TUCH 103	NORTHERN STAR (2-LP)		30
99	Pepper 0530331	VERTIGO (2-LP, inners)		40
00	Pepper 9230100	THE REMIXES (2-LP)		20
01	Pepper 9230491	GOODBYE COUNTRY (HELLO NIGHTCLUB) (3-LP)		50
02	Zomba 9230661	LOVEBOX (3-LP)		50
10	Music On Vinyl MOVLP223	WHITE LIGHT (LP)		80
10	Work It GABLP1	BLACK LIGHT (2-LP)		80

GROOVERIDER
97	Higher Ground 487219 1	THE PROTOTYPE YEARS (3-LP)		40
98	Higher Ground HIGH LP 6	MYSTERIES OF FUNK (4-LP)		30

GROOVERS
68	Amalgamated AMG 816	Having A Party/Day By Day		85
71	Camel CA 83	Put Me Down Easy/I Want To Go Back Home		15
71	Escort ERT 863	Bend Down Low/The Burning Feeling		20

(see also Lloyd & Groovers, Alva Lewis, Junior Byles, Dennis Walks)

WINSTON GROOV(E)Y
69	Grape GR 3005	Leaving Me Standing/Little Girl		20
69	Grape GR 3008	Merry X-mas/I Am Lonely		15
69	Nu Beat NB 041	Island In The Sun/Work It Up		15
69	Nu Beat NB 042	Josephine/Champagne And Wine		12
70	New Beat NB 053	Standing At The Corner/You Send Me		12
70	New Beat NB 055	Yellow Bird/For Your Love		12
70	New Beat NB 058	Here Is My Heart/Birds And Flowers		12
70	New Beat NB 066	Groovin'/Sugar Mama		12
70	New Beat NB 073	Tennessee Waltz/Old Man Trouble		10
70	Attack ATT 8018	I Can't Go On/Only You		10
70	Attack ATT 8019	You Can't Turn Your Back On Me/PAMA DICE: The Worm		20
70	Jackpot JP 708	Funky Chicken/CIMARRONS: Part 2 (B-side actually unknown instrumental)		25
70	Jackpot JP 709	Funny/CIMARRONS: Funny Version Two		10
70	Torpedo TOR 11	Please Don't Make Me Cry/Motion On The Ocean		20
70	Crab CRAB 63	I Like The Way/Tell Me Why		10
71	Crab CRAB 64	I've Got The Find A Way To Win Mary Back/Wanna Be There		10
71	Bullet BU 471	I Wanna Be Loved/Get Back Together		10
71	Pama PM 827	Don't Break My Heart/How Long Will This Go On		10
71	Pama Supreme PS 323	Free The People/Not Now		8
72	Pama Supreme PS 349	What You Gonna Do/Why Did You Leave		8
72	Pama Supreme PS 364	Sylvia's Mother/Here Is My Heart		8
73	Explosion EX 2086	Nose For Trouble/RHYTHM RULERS: Version		8
74	Explosion EX 2088	Please Don't Make Me Cry/So Easy		8
69	Pama PMP 2011	FREE THE PEOPLE (LP)		40
78	Trojan TRLS 155	THE GROOVEY COLLECTION (LP)		20

(see also King Horror, Upsetters)

PAUL GROOVY AND THE POP ART EXPERIENCE
87	Bite Back! – BB!012	Andy Watch Out!/Take Away The Pain (wrap-around p/s, sticker, lyric sheet)		30

GROSS CLUB
81	Caveman CMR 01	Second Chance/Look Away (sleeve is a paper insert glued on white inner sleeve)		100

G.G. GROSSETT
69	Crab CRAB 10	Run Girl Run/DENNIS WALKS: The Drifter		100
69	Crab CRAB 33	Greater Sounds/Live The Life I Love		50

STEFAN GROSSMAN
70	Big T BIG 133	Pretty Little Tune/Little Sally Walker		7
71	Big T BIG 140	'Joe Hill' - Themes		7
68	Fontana (S)TL 5463	AUNT MOLLY'S MURRAY FARM (LP)		25
69	Fontana STL 5485	THE GRAMERCY PARK SHEIK (LP)		20
70	Transatlantic TRA 217	YAZOO BASIN BOOGIE (LP)		15
71	Transatlantic TRA 246	THOSE PLEASANT DAYS (LP, with lyric insert)		15

(see also John Renbourn)

LUTHER GROSVENOR
71	Island WIP 6109	Here Comes The Queen/Heavy Day		6
72	Island WIP 6124	All The People/Waiting		6
71	Island ILPS 9168	UNDER OPEN SKIES (LP, gatefold sleeve pink rim palm tree logo)		50

(see also Hellions, Revolution, Art, Spooky Tooth, Mott The Hoople, Widowmaker)

CARL GROSZMANN
70	Decca F 13065	Thunderbird/Missouri Woman		6
75	Ring O' 2017 103	I've Had It/C'mon And Roll		15
77	Ring O' 2017 107	Face Of A Permanent Stranger/Your Own Affair (promo p/s)		15
77	Ring O' 2017 107	Face Of A Permanent Stranger/Your Own Affair (company sleeve)		10
75	Ring O' 2320 102	CARL GROSZMANN (LP, unreleased)		0

GROUND ATTACK
81	Ground Attack GAR 001	THE RED LION EP (Red Lion/Every Mother's Son) (gatefold p/s)		100
81	Ground Attack GAR 001	THE RED LION EP (Red Lion/Every Mother's Son) (later pressing with no p/s)		20

GROUND CONTROL
81	Sycamore SRS 001	Cover Girl/Lonely Guy		40

GROUNDHOGS
68	Liberty LBF 15174	You Don't Love Me/Still A Fool		30
69	Liberty LBF 15263	B.D.D./TONY McPHEE: Gasoline		35
70	Liberty LBF 15346	Eccentric Man/Status People		20

GROUP

MINT VALUE £

73	W. Wide Artists WWS 006	Sad Go Round/Over Blue	6
74	W. Wide Artists WWS 012	Plea Sing, Plea Sing/TONY McPHEE: Dog Me Bitch	6
76	United Artists UP 36095	Live A Little Lady/Boogie Withus	6
76	United Artists UP 36177	Pastoral Future/Live Right (as Tony McPhee & Groundhogs)	6
68	Liberty LBL 83199E	SCRATCHING THE SURFACE (LP, mono, blue label)	125
68	Liberty LBS 83199E	SCRATCHING THE SURFACE (LP, stereo, blue label)	75
69	Liberty LBS 83253	BLUES OBITUARY (LP, blue label)	100
70	Liberty LBS 83295	THANK CHRIST FOR THE BOMB (LP, gatefold sleeve, 1st pressing blue label)	150
71	Liberty LBG 83401	SPLIT (LP, gatefold sleeve, black label)	50
70	Liberty LBS 83295	THANK CHRIST FOR THE BOMB (LP, gatefold sleeve, 2nd pressing black label)	50
72	United Artists UAG 29347	WHO WILL SAVE THE WORLD... (LP, gatefold sleeve)	40
72	United Artists UAG 29419	HOGWASH (LP, tri-fold sleeve)	30
74	W. Wide Artists WWA 004	SOLID (LP, with lyric insert)	15
76	United Artists UAS 29917	CROSSCUT SAW (LP)	15
89	BGO BGOLP 67	THANK CHRIST FOR THE BOMB (LP, reissue, gatefold)	20

(see also Tony McPhee, Herbal Mixture, Home, Andy Fernbach, John Lee Hooker)

GROUP
72	Charisma CB 197	Bovver Boys/Piraeus Football Club/An Open Letter To George Best	6

(see also Neil Innes)

GROUP (FEATURING CECIL WASHINGTON)
98	Goldmine Soul Supply GS 209	I Don't Like To Lose/Can't Loose My Head (reissue)	15

GROUP B
67	Vocalion VF 9284	I Know Your Name Girl/I Never Really Knew	25

(see also Blue Cheer)

GROUP 1850
69	Philips SBL 7884	AGEMO'S TRIP TO MOTHER EARTH (LP, gatefold sleeve)	600

GROUP IMAGE
69	Stable SLE 8005	A MOUTH IN THE CLOUDS (LP)	90

GROUP ONE
58	HMV POP 463	She's Neat/Made For Each Other	30

GROUP SIX
59	Oriole CB 1488	Rock-A-Boogie/Rockin' The Blues	20

GROUP THERAPY
69	Philips BF 1744	River Deep Mountain High/Remember What You Said	6
69	Philips BF 1792	Can't Stop Lovin' You Baby/I Must Do	6
69	Philips SBL 7888	YOU'RE IN NEED OF GROUP THERAPY (LP)	20

GROUP TWO
68	Columbia DB 8374	It's Raining Outside/Western Man, Eastern Lady	7

GROUP X
63	Fontana 267 274 TF	There Are 8 Million Cossack Melodies - And This Is One Of Them/Teneriffe (in p/s)	15
63	Fontana 267 274 TF	There Are 8 Million Cossack Melodies - And This Is One Of Them/Teneriffe	10
63	Fontana TF 417	Roti Calliope/Cross Beat	10

GROUPER
07	Type TYPE 020V	WAY THEIR CREPT (LP, clear vinyl, 100 only)	50
07	Type TYPE 020V	WAY THEIR CREPT (LP)	20
08	Type TYPE 038V	DRAGGING A DEAD DEER UP A HILL (LP)	30

GROUP SOUNDS FOUR AND FIVE
21	Jazz In Britain JB 14 M LP	BLACK AND WHITE RAGA (LP)	20

GROUT
79	Urinating Vicar	DO IT YOURSELF (EP) (100 only, sound quality very poor)	400

GROW UP
79	Object Music OM 05	GROW UP (EP)	12
80	Object Music OM12	JOANNA (EP)	10
79	Object Music OBJ 5	THE BEST THING (LP)	20
81	UP Records GROWL 1	WITHOUT WINDS (LP)	15

GRUDGE
73	Black Label BL 002	When Christine Comes Around/I'm Gonna Smash Your Face In	50

GRUMBLEWEEDS
71	Phillips 78434	Never Before/Fiona McLaughlin	15
72	Phillips 6006208	String Of Beads (Good Old Leeds)/Simple Little Things	12
73	Decca F 13416	Trees/I Am A Grumbleweed	6
74	Decca F13513	(Hey Babe) Follow Me/Won't Say No Again	20
72	Philips 6308091	IN A TEKNIKOLOR DREAM (LP)	40

GRUNT FUTTOCK
72	Regal Zonophone RZ 3042	Rock 'N' Roll Christian/Free Sole	40

(see also Move, Roy Wood)

GRUNTRUCK
92	Roadrunner RR 9130 1	PUSH (LP)	60

DAVE GRUSIN
85	Arista GRP 5610	MOUNTAIN DANCE (LP, Nimbus Supercut, mail order only through Practical Hi Fi magazine)	40

GRUVY BEATS
70	Nu Beat NB 048	Share Your Popcorn/LAUREL AITKEN: Mr. Popcorn	15
70	Nu Beat NB 049	Blue Mink/LAUREL AITKEN: I've Got Your Love	20

GIGI GRYCE
60	Esquire 32-151	SAYIN' SOMETHIN' (LP)	100
60	Esquire 32-181	RAT RACE BLUES (LP)	100

GRYPHON
77	Harvest HAR 5125	Spring Song/Fall Of The Leaf	6
73	Transatlantic TRA 262	GRYPHON (LP, gatefold sleeve)	25

G.T.O.'s

MINT VALUE £

74	Transatlantic TRA 282	MIDNIGHT MUSHRUMPS (LP)	15
74	Transatlantic TRA 287	RED QUEEN TO GRYPHON THREE (LP)	15
75	Transatlantic TRA 302	RAINDANCE (LP)	15
77	Harvest SHSP 4063	TREASON (LP, with lyric inner sleeve)	20

(see also Richard Harvey, The Banned)

G.T.O.'S
67	Polydor 56721	She Rides With Me/Rudy Vadoo	75

(see also Joey & Continentals)

G.T.O.'S (GIRLS TOGETHER OUTRAGEOUSLY)
70	Straight STS 1059	PERMANENT DAMAGE (LP)	150

(see also Jeff Beck, Frank Zappa)

GTR
86	Arista GTR 1	When The Heart Rules The Mind/Reach Out (poster sleeve)	6

(see also Steve Hackett)

GUANA BATZ
84	Big Beat SW 89	You're So Fine/Rockin' In My Coffin/Jungle Rumble/Guana Rock (p/s)	6

GUARDIANS OF THE ANCIENT WISDOM
15	154 001	DESCEND THE STAIRWAY TO DARKNESS WITH... (2-LP, handmade sleeve, booklet and CD)	20

GUARDIANS OF THE RAINBOW
68	President PT 186	What Do You Do When You've Lost Your Love/Cry Alone	6

GUERNICA
87	Idol 12 ID 2	ORANGE AND RED EP (12")	150
88	Miss Pedestal MP 001	HUMMING OF THE ENGINE (12", p/s)	50

GUESS WHO
65	Pye International 7N 25305	Shakin' All Over/Till We Kissed	25
66	King KG 1044	His Girl/It's My Pride	25
67	Fontana TF 831	This Time Long Ago/There's No Getting Away From You	15
67	Fontana TF 861	Miss Felicity Grey/Flying On The Ground Is Wrong	10
70	RCA 1943	American Woman/No Sugar Tonight	6
69	RCA SF 8037	WHEATFIELD SOUL (LP)	15
70	RCA SF 8107	AMERICAN WOMAN (LP)	15

EARL GUEST
62	Columbia DB 4707	Honky Tonk Train Blues/Winkle Picker Stomp	6
64	Columbia DB 7212	Begin The Beguine/Foxy	20

GUEST & EDWARDS
72	Phillips 6006231	All Alone/Sing You A Picture	20

REG GUEST SYNDICATE
65	Mercury MF 927	Underworld/Guys, Guns, Dolls And Danger	125
66	Mercury 20089MCL	UNDERWORLD (LP)	40

GUGGENHEIM
72	Indigo GOLP 7001	GUGGENHEIM (LP, private pressing)	75

GUIDED BY VOICES
94	Domino RUG 11	CLOWN PRINCE OF THE MENTHOL TRAILER EP (p/s)	30
96	Fear & Loathing RCRPA 17	BRIGHTON ROCKS: Hot Freaks/Game Of Pricks (50 copies on blue vinyl with fanzine)	60
96	Fear & Loathing RCRPA 17	BRIGHTON ROCKS: Hot Freaks/Game Of Pricks (450 copies on black vinyl with fanzine)	40
96	Matador OLE 218-7	Cut Out Witch/Rhine Jive Click/Unleashed! The large Hearted Boy/(Some Drilling Implied (Live) (Picture disc)	10
99	Creation CRE 325	Teenage FBI/Flying Into Ashes/Tropical Robots (p/s)	20
99	Creation CRE 328	Hold On Hope/Perfect This Time (p/s, release cancelled)	200
11	Fire BLAZE 45188	DOUGHNUT FOR A SNOWMAN (p/s)	7
94	Matador OLE 084 1	BEE THOUSAND (LP, blue vinyl)	60
96	Matador OLE 161 1	UNDER THE BUSHES UNDER THE STARS (LP, with free 12")	40
97	Matafor OLE 241-1	MAG EARWHIG! (LP)	40
99	Creation CRELP 251	DO THE COLLAPSE (LP)	50
02	Matador OLE 547-1	UNIVERSAL TRUTHS AND CYCLES (LP, gatefold)	80

GUILLEMOTS
05	Fantastic Plastic FPS050	I SAW SUCH THINGS IN MY SLEEP EP (10", 300 only p/s)	15
05	Fantastic Plastic FPTEN055	Trains To Brazil/My Chosen One/Go Away (10", 1,000 only, p/s)	8
06	Polydor IC00309	THROUGH THE WINDOWPANE (2-LP, gatefold sleeve, inner sleeves & booklet)	25

ISAAC GUILLORY
74	Atlantic K 40521	ISAAC GUILLORY (LP)	18

(see also Shames)

GUILLOTEENS
65	Pye International 7N 25324	I Don't Believe/Hey You	60

GUILT EDGE
79	Fragile FRAG 001	Bye Bye/Wires (p/s)	15

MAALEM MAHMOUD GUINIA
15	Eglo EGBC001	MARHABA (12", p/s, with 20 page booklet, with Floating Points and James Holden)	30

BONNIE GUITAR
58	London HLD 8591	A Very Precious Love/Johnny Vagabond	15
59	Top Rank JAR 260	Candy Apple Red/Come To Me, I Love You	6
58	London HA-D 2122	MOONLIGHT AND SHADOWS (LP)	15

GUITAR CRUSHER WITH JIMMY SPURRILL
69	Blue Horizon 57-3149	Since My Baby Hit The Numbers/Hambone Blues	45

(see also Wild Jimmy Spurrill)

GUITAR RED
63	Pye International 7N 25219	Just You And I/Old Fashioned Love	35

GUITAR SHORTY
72	Flyright LP 500	CAROLINA SLIDE GUITAR (LP)	15

GUITAR GANGSTERS

MINT VALUE £

GUITAR GANGSTERS
89 Link LP 105   PROHIBITION (LP) 20

GULLIVER
70 Elektra 2101 011   Every Day's A Lovely Day/Angelina 6
70 Elektra 2410 006   GULLIVER (LP) 18

GULLIVER'S PEOPLE
66 Parlophone R 5435   Splendor In The Grass/Took This Land 20
66 Parlophone R 5464   Fi Fo Fum/Over The Hills 10
68 Parlophone R 5709   On A Day Like This/My Life 10
69 Columbia DB 8588   Somehow, Somewhere/I Found Love 10

GULLIVER'S TRAVELS
69 Instant INLP 003   GULLIVER'S TRAVELS (LP, withdrawn, front laminated sleeve, flipbacks) 200
(see also Mike D'Abo, Andrew Oldham)

GUMBAE CULTURE
85 Leyson LR 0105   Take It Easy/Ghetto Youth (12") 15

GUN
68 CBS 3764   Race With The Devil/3-4 In The Middle (different B-side) 10
69 CBS 4052   Drives You Mad/Rupert's Travels 7
69 CBS 4443   Hobo/Don't Look Back 7
69 CBS 4443   Hobo/Long Hair Wild Man (different B-side) 10
70 CBS 4952   Runnin' Wild/Drown Yourself In The River 6
69 CBS M63552   GUN (LP, mono, laminated front sleeve, orange label) 200
69 CBS 63552   GUN (LP, stereo, laminated front sleeve, orange label) 100
69 CBS 63683   GUNSIGHT (LP) 75
(see also Baker-Gurvitz Army, Parrish & Gurvitz, Rupert's People, Three Man Army, Knack)o

GUN CLUB
82 Animal/Chrysalis CHCAT 2635   The Fire Of Love/Walking With The Beast (p/s) 6
82 Beggars Banquet BEG 80   Ghost On The Highway/Sex Beat (p/s) 20
83 Animal/Chrysalis GUN 1   Death Party/House On Highland Avenue/The Lie (p/s) 12
83 Animal/Chrysalis GUN 12   Death Party/House On Highland Avenue/The Lie/Light Of The World/Come Back Jim (12", p/s) 10
88 Red Rhino RED 89   The Breaking Hands/Crabdance (p/s) 8
88 Red Rhino RED 89 12   The Breaking Hands/Crabdance/Nobody's City (12", p/s) 10
90 Fire BLAZE 47T   The Great Divide/Crabdance/St. John's Divine Part 2 (p/s) 12
81 Beggars Banquet BEGA 37   THE FIRE OF LOVE (LP) 35
82 Animal CHR 1398   MIAMI (LP) 35
83 ABC ABC LP 1   THE BIRTH THE DEATH THE GHOST (LP) 25
84 Animal CHR 1398   LAS VEGAS STORY (LP) 20
87 Red Rhino REDLP 84   MOTHER JUNO (LP) 25
85 Castle DOJOLP 8   TWO SIDES OF THE BEAST (LP) 15
90 Fire FIRELP 28   PASTORAL HIDE AND SEEK (LP) 15
08 Retro Delux RDBX 004   THE LIFE AND TIMES OF JEFFREY LEE PIERCE AND THE GUN CLUB (4-CD box set) 30
(see also Jeffrey Lee Pierce)

JON GUNN
67 Deram DM 133   I Just Made Up My Mind/Now It's My Turn 10
67 Deram DM 166   If You Wish It/I Don't Want To Get Hung Up On You Babe 10

JIM GUNNER
60 Decca F 11276   Hoolee Jump/Footloose (as Jim Gunner & Echoes) 15
61 Fontana H 313   Desperado/Baghdad (as Jim Gunner & His Sidekicks) 20

TONY GUNNER
62 London HLU 9492   Rough Road/You Gotta Get Home 20

SARAH OGAN GUNNING
67 Topic 12T 171   A GIRL OF CONSTANT SORROW (LP, mono, blue label) 20

GUNS FOR HIRE
80 Korova KOW 6   I'm Gonna Rough My Girlfriend's New Boyfriend Up/I'm Famous Now (p/s) 10
(see also Main T. Possee)

GUNSHIP
16 Horsie in The Hedge LLP HITH002LP   GUNSHIP (LP, picture disc) 70
17 Horsie in The Hedge LLP HITH003LP   GUNSHIP (2-LP) 25
18 Horsie in The Hedge LLP HITH008LPS DARK ALL DAY (2-LP) 30

GUNSHOT
94 Vinyl Solution STORM78L   Mind Of A Razor (10") 12
94 Vinyl Solution STEAM 92   SINGLES CONNECTION (LP, red vinyl) 15
17 Naked Ape NAR 017   INTERNATIONAL RESCUE (2-LP, reissue) 30

GUNSHY
87 Silverstar CMS 001   Where Are The Glory Boys/If You Leave Me (no p/s) 30

GUNSLINGER
84 Clyde CLY 001   Never A Dull Moment/Shake Some Action (no p/s) 20

GUNS N' ROSES
87 Geffen GEF 22   It's So Easy/Mr Brownstone (p/s) 10
87 Geffen GEF 22T   It's So Easy/Mr Brownstone/Shadow Of Your Love/Move To The City (12", p/s) 12
87 Geffen GEF 22TP   It's So Easy/Mr Brownstone/Shadow Of Your Love/ Move To The City (12", picture disc with stickered PVC sleeve) 40
87 Geffen GEF 30   Welcome To The Jungle/Whole Lotta Rosie (live) (red vinyl) 8
87 Geffen GEF 30T   Welcome To The Jungle/Whole Lotta Rosie (live)/It's So Easy (live)/Knockin' On Heaven's Door (live) (12", p/s) 20
87 Geffen GEF 30TW   Welcome To The Jungle/Whole Lotta Rosie (live)/It's So Easy (live)/Knockin' On Heaven's Door (live) (12", poster p/s) 10

Arthur GUNTER

MINT VALUE £

Year	Catalog	Description	Value
87	Geffen GEF 30P	Welcome To The Jungle/Whole Lotta Rosie (live)/It's So Easy (live)/Knockin' On Heaven's Door (live) (12", picture disc)	40
88	Geffen GEF 43TE	Sweet Child O' Mine/Out Ta Get Me/Rocket Queen (10", revolving p/s)	15
88	Geffen GEF 43TV	Sweet Child O' Mine/Out Ta Get Me/Rocket Queen (12", metallic p/s)	10
89	Geffen GEF 50P	Paradise City/I Used To Love Her (gun-shaped white picture disc in 'holster' sleeve)	15
89	Geffen GEF 50X	Paradise City/I Used To Love Her (p/s, slotted in holster p/s)	7
89	Geffen GEF 55W	Sweet Child O' Mine (Remix)/Out Ta Get Me (with tattoo)	10
89	Geffen GEF 55 X	Sweet Child O' Mine/Out Ta Get Me (Limited edition sticker pack)	10
89	Geffen GEF 55P	Sweet Child O' Mine/Out Ta Get Me/Rocket Queen (shaped pic disc & sticker)	12
89	Geffen GEF 55P	Sweet Child O' Mine/Out Ta Get Me/Rocket Queen (12" uncut shaped pic disc)	100
89	Geffen GEF 55T	Sweet Child O' Mine (Remix)/Move To The City/Whole Lotta Rosie (live)/ It's So Easy (live) (12", p/s)	10
89	Geffen GEF 60X	Nightrain/Reckless Life (live) (p/s, with patch)	7
93	Geffen GFS 70	Since I Don't Have You/You Can't Put Your Arms Around A Memory (p/s, orange vinyl)	6
08	Geffen 0602517906075	Chinese Democracy/Shackler's Revenge (p/s, promo)	10
87	Geffen 9240 148	APPETITE FOR DESTRUCTION (LP, withdrawn 'robot' sleeve, with stickers)	50
91	Geffen GEF 24415	USE YOUR ILLUSION I (2-LP)	50
91	Geffen GEF 24420	USE YOUR ILLUSION II (2-LP)	50
93	Geffen GEF24617	THE SPAGHETTI INCIDENT? (LP)	40
08	Geffen 0602517906136	CHINESE DEMOCRACY (2-LP)	50

ARTHUR GUNTER

Year	Catalog	Description	Value
72	Blue Horizon 2431 012	BLUES AFTER HOURS (LP)	75
70s	Contempo COLP 119	BLACK AND BLUES (LP)	25

HARDROCK GUNTER

Year	Catalog	Description	Value
55	Brunswick OE 9167	MOUNTAIN MUSIC (EP)	25

(see also Red Foley, Roberta Lee)

GURU

Year	Catalog	Description	Value
93	Cooltempo COOL 282	No Time To Play/Jazz Thing (p/s)	50
93	Chrysalis CTLP 34	JAZZMATAZZ VOL. 1 (LP)	80
95	Capitol 7243 8 34806 1 6	JAZZMATAZZ VOL. 2 (2-LP)	100
00	Virgin VUSLP 178	JAZZMATAZZ (STREETSOUL) (2-LP)	50
07	7 Grand VVR1046851	JAZZMATAZZ VOL 4: THE HIP HOP MESSENGER (2-LP)	80
18	Music On Vinyl MOVLP1111	JAZZMATAZZ VOL 1 (LP, reissue, blue vinyl)	30
18	Virgin 00600753820254	JAZZMATAZZ VOL 1 (3-LP, reissue, booklet)	50

GURU GURU

Year	Catalog	Description	Value
73	Atlantic K 50022	DON'T CALL US WE'LL CALL YOU (LP)	20
74	Atlantic K 50044	DANCE OF THE FLAMES (LP)	20

GURU GURU/ULI TREPTE

Year	Catalog	Description	Value
80s	United Dairies UDT 07	LIVE 72 & 73 (LP, 1 side each)	18

GURU JOSH

Year	Catalog	Description	Value
90	Deconstruction PT 44140	Freaky Dreamer (12")	15

GURUS

Year	Catalog	Description	Value
66	United Artists UP 1160	Blue Snow Night/Come Girl	30

GUS GUS

Year	Catalog	Description	Value
97	4AD DAD 7005	POLYDISTORTION (2-LP, inners)	50
99	4AD CAD 9006	THIS IS NORMAL (2-LP)	40
00	4AD CAD 2K02	GUS GUS VS T WORLD (2-LP)	30
02	Underwater H20 020 LP	ATTENTION (2-LP)	30

JOHNNY GUSTAFSON

Year	Catalog	Description	Value
65	Polydor 56022	Just To Be With You/Sweet Day	20
65	Polydor 56043	Take Me For A Little While/Make Me Your Number One	35

(see also Big Three, Merseybeats, Quotations, Hard Stuff, Johnny & John, Ian Gillan Band, G-Force)

CARL GUSTAV & 84'S

Year	Catalog	Description	Value
81	Convulsive CN 001	I Want To Kill Russians/Through Birds, Through Fire, But Not Through Glass (p/s)	10

ARLO GUTHRIE

Year	Catalog	Description	Value
67	Reprise RS 20644	Motorcycle Song/Now And Then	8
70	Reprise RS 20951	Valley To Pray/Gabriel's Mother's Hiway Ballad No. 16 Blues (demo-only)	7
67	Reprise RSLP 6267	ALICE'S RESTAURANT (LP, mono)	20
67	Reprise RLP 6267	ALICE'S RESTAURANT (LP, stereo)	20
68	Reprise RSLP 6269	ARLO (LP)	20
69	Reprise RSLP 6346	RUNNING DOWN THE ROAD (LP)	15
70	Reprise RSLP 6411	WASHINGTON COUNTY (LP)	15

GWEN GUTHRIE

Year	Catalog	Description	Value
82	Island WIP 6757	It Should Have Been You/God Don't Like Ugly (p/s)	6
86	4th & Broadway BRW 52	Seventh Heaven/Getting Hot (p/s or die-cut sleeve)	15
86	4th & Broadway BRW 1252	Seventh Heaven/It Should Have Been You/Getting Hot (12", p/s)	15

SHEILA GUTHRIE

Year	Catalog	Description	Value
63	Fontana TF 399	Mirror Mirror/It Doesn't Mean A Thing	8

WOODY GUTHRIE

Year	Catalog	Description	Value
55	Melodisc EPM7 84	HARD AIN'T IT HARD (EP)	20
55	Melodisc EPM7 85	WORRIED MAN BLUES (EP)	20
55	Melodisc EPM7 91	HEY LOLLY LOLLY (EP)	20
55	Melodisc MLP 12-106	MORE SONGS BY GUTHRIE (LP)	40
58	Topic 12T 31	BOUND FOR GLORY (LP)	35
64	RCA RD 7612	DUST BOWL BALLADS (LP)	25

GUTTERSNIPE ARMY

Year	Catalog	Description	Value
89	Link LUNK LP 076	NEVER DIE (LP)	50

GUTTERSNIPES

Year	Catalog	Description	Value
88	Razor GUTT 1	Addicted To Love/Love's Young Dream (p/s)	8

(see also Cocksparrer)

GUTTERSNYPES

MINT VALUE £

GUTTERSNYPES
94	Liberty Grooves LIB004	The Trials Of Life (Green vinyl radio edit) (12")	15
94	Liberty Grooves LIB005	The Trials Of Life (Blue, Red vinyl) (12")	10
94	Liberty Grooves LIB005	The Trials Of Life (White vinyl, promo version, limited edition, personalised by band) (12")	25
94	Liberty Grooves LIB006	The Trials Of Life (Clear vinyl, instrumentals) (12")	15

GUV'NERS
63	Piccadilly 7N 35117	Let's Make A Habit Of This/The Kissing Had To Stop	15

(see also Jess Conrad, Dickie Pride, Nelson Keene)

GUV'NORS
75	Cambrian CSP 740	Fly To The Sun/I'm With You To The End	10

BARRY GUY
76	Incus INCUS 22	STATEMENTS V-XI FOR DOUBLE BASS AND VIOLONE (LP)	50

(see also Derek Bailey Barry Guy & Paul Rutherford)

BUDDY GUY
65	Chess CRS 8004	Let Me Love You Baby/Ten Years Ago	20
68	Fontana TF 951	Mary Had A Little Lamb/Sweet Little Angel	18
72	Atlantic K 10195	Honey Dripper/Man Of Many Words	6
65	Chess CRE 6004	CRAZY MUSIC (EP)	40
68	Vanguard SVRL 19001	COMING AT YOU (LP)	40
68	Vanguard SVRL 19002	MAN AND HIS BLUES (LP)	40
68	Vanguard SVRL 19004	BLUES TODAY (LP)	40
69	Vanguard SVRL 19008	THIS IS BUDDY GUY! (LP)	40
69	Vanguard SVRL 79290	HOT AND COOL (LP)	40
69	Chess CRL(S) 4546	I LEFT MY BLUES IN SAN FRANCISCO (LP)	30
69	Python KM 2	FIRST TIME I MET THE BLUES (LP)	70
70	Harvest SHSP 4006	BUDDY AND THE JUNIORS (LP, with Junior Mance & Junior Wells)	65
70	Red Lightnin' RL 001	IN THE BEGINNING (LP)	15
72	Atlantic K 40240	PLAY THE BLUES (LP, with Junior Wells)	20
73	Vanguard VSD 79323	HOLD THAT PLANE (LP)	20

(see also Junior Wells, Eddie Boyd/Buddy Guy)

GUYS
69	Tepee TPR SP 1001	You Go Your Way/Little Girl	20

GEORGE GUZMAN
68	London SH 8384	INTRODUCING GEORGE GUZMAN (LP)	30

GWAR
91	Metal Blade ZORRO 37	AMERICA MUST BE DESTROYED (LP)	60

GWENNO
14	Peski PESK1030	Y DYFF OLAF (LP)	20
15	Heavenly HVNLP 118B	Y DYDD OLAF (LP, CD)	18

(see also Pipettes)

GWIGWIS BAND
67	77 AFRO/101	KWELA (LP)	100

GXFR
18	Daupe DM SP 018	DON'T GET SCARED NOW (LP, numbered on grey vinyl, 150 only)	200
16	Daupe DM SP 018	DON'T GET SCARED NOW (LP, numbered on black vinyl, 230 copies)	200
16	Daupe DM SP 018	DON'T GET SCARED NOW (LP, numbered with obi strip, 20 only)	250

KIKI GYAN
77	PVP ILPS 7777	AFRO REGGAE (LP)	40
12	Soundway SNDWLP047	24 HOURS IN A DISCO 1978-82 (LP)	20

(see also Osibisa, Kofi & Kiki)

GYGAFO
75	Look LK SP 6061	Broken Smiles/Wing	40
89	Holyground HG 1155	LEGEND OF THE KINGFISHER (LP, 160 copies only, posthumously designed semi-gatefold sleeve with insert)	60

GYMSLIPS
83	Abstract ABT 006	ROCKING WITH THE RENEES (LP, with insert)	20

GYNAECOLOGISTS
81	Teesbeat TB 2	The Red Pullover/The Offence (hand made p/s, 500 only)	12

(see also Basccax, Blitzkrieg Bop)

GYPP
79	Shy Talk AC 1065	YAAH EP: Marigoldz/Titania/Sister Darling (p/s)	20

(see also Martin Newell, Cleaners From Venus, Brotherhood Of Lizards)

GYPPO
79	United Artists UP36510	High Rise Love/Free Enterprise	100

GYPSIES
67	CBS 201785	Jerk It/Diamonds, Rubies, Gold And Fame	40

(see also Flirtations)

GYPSY QUEEN
72	Cactus CT1	Love Is In The Air/Everybody's Searching	10

GYPSY (1)
71	United Artists UP 35202	What Makes A Man A Man/I Want To Be Beside You	6
72	United Artists UP 35272	Changes Coming/Don't Cry On Me	6
71	United Artists UAG 29255	GYPSY (LP)	15
72	United Artists UAS 29420	BRENDA AND THE RATTLESNAKE (LP)	15

(see also Legay)

GYPSY (2)
84	Private Pressing	We Came To Be Free/Get It Right	50

HABIBIYYA

MINT VALUE £

HABIBIYYA
72 Island HELP 7   IF MAN BUT KNEW (LP, with inner sleeve, black/silver label, pink 'i' logo) 40
(see also Mighty Baby)

HABITS
66 Decca F 12348   Elbow Baby/Need You 40
(see also Charles Dickens, Nice, Brian Davison)

HACKENSACK
72 Island WIP 6149   Moving On/River Boat 12
71 Polydor 2383 263   UP THE HARD WAY (LP, with inner sleeve) 100
74 Zel UZ 003   HERE COMES THE JUDGE (LP, private pressing, as Hack & Sack) 125
(see also Megaton, Tiger [U.K.], Nicky Moore Band, Samson)

STEVE HACKETT
78 Charisma CB 312   How Can I?/Kim (with Ritchie Havens) 10
78 Charisma CB 318   Narnia (Remix)/Please Don't Touch 7
(see also Peter Banks, Genesis, GTR, Quiet World)

MARIKA HACKMAN
13 Dirty Hits DH0031   THAT IRON TASTE (LP, gatefold, blue vinyl, numbered) 30

VERNON HADDOCK'S JUBILEE LOVELIES
65 Columbia SX 6011   VERNON HADDOCK'S JUBILEE LOVELIES (LP) 125

IDA HAENDEL
58 HMV CLP 1021   IDA HAENDEL WITH GERALD MOORE AT THE PIANO (LP) 800
59 HMV CLP 1032   BRAHMS VIOLIN CONCERTO (LP) 250
60 HMV DLP 1190   TCHAIKOVSKY VIOLIN CONCERTO (LP) 450
77 HMV ASD 3352   A CLASSICAL RECITAL (LP) 150
80 EMI ASD 3785   BRAVISSIMA! (LP) 200

HAFFY'S WHISKY SOUR
71 Deram DM 345   Shot In The Head/Bye Bye Bluebird 10
(see also Easybeats, Paintbox)

HAFLER TRIO
84 Doublevision DVR 4   BANG! - AN OPEN LETTER (LP, with insert) 25
86 Charrm 3   THREE WAYS OF SAYING TWO - THE NETHERLANDS LECTURES (LP, stickered sleeve with booklet) 25
86 Touch T 05   THE SEA ORG (10", 'audio/visual' package with booklet) 20
(see also Cabaret Voltaire)

HAGALAZ RUNEDANCE
97 Elfenblut SAG III   When The Trees Were Silenced/A Tale Of Fate (Folkswang Awaits) (p/s, insert) 10

HAGAR THE WOMB
84 Abstract Sounds 12ABS 029 FUNNERY IN THE NUNNERY (12" EP) 15
84 Mortarhate MORT 2   WORD OF THE WOMB (12" EP) 15

HA HA HA
85 Hobby Horse SRTSKS 387 HA HA HA EP 10

HA HA MONO
82 SRTS 82 CUS 1481   Run For Miles/Snakes (p/s) 60

JOYCE HAHN
57 London HLA 8453   Gonna Find Me A Bluebird/I Saw You, I Saw You 10

PAUL HAIG
89 Circa YRT 25   Something Good (Extended Version)/Over You/Free To Go (Technology)/Something Good (Radio Edit) (12") 10
98 Syntactic NICE 49   Listen To Me (Looking/Irresponsible) (handmade p/s, with Billy McKenzie) 20
(see also Josef K, Rhythm Of Life, Juggernauts, Billy McKenzie)

ROBERT HAIGH
85 Laylah LAY 09   JULIET OF THE SPIRITS EP (12") 25
86 Laylah LAY 21   MUSIC FROM THE ANTE CHAMBER EP (12") 25
88 United Dairies UD 026 VALENTINE OUT OF SEASON (LP) 40
89 Le Rey LR 103   A WALTZ IN PLAIN C (CD) 50
(see also SEMA)

HAIM
13 Secret 7" S79   Better Off (100 only, each with unique art sleeve) 30

NORMAN HAINES (BAND)
70 Parlophone R 5871   Daffodil/Autumn Mobile (as Norman Haynes Band) 25
71 Parlophone SPSR 338   Den Of Iniquity/Everything You See (Mr. Armageddon) (promo only) 60
72 Parlophone R 5960   Give It To You Girl/Elaine (as Norman Haines) 20
71 Parlophone PCS 7130   DEN OF INIQUITY (LP, black/silver label with boxed logo) 1250
94 Shoestring BL001   DEN OF INIQUITY (LP, reissue) 30
14 Acid Nightmare ANM 011 DEN OF INIQUITY (LP, reissue, 400 only) 20
(see also Avalanche, Brumbeats, The Dog That Bit People, Locomotive)

HAIR (1)
69 Pye NSPL 18314   RAVE UP (LIVE FROM THE SHAFTESBURY THEATRE) (LP) 70
(see also Alex Harvey, Hairband)

HAIR (2)
70 Columbia SCX 6452   HAIRPIECE (LP, black/silver labels with boxed logo) 350

HAIRBAND
69 Bell BLL 1076   Big Louis/Travelling Song 18

HAIRPOWER

69	Bell SBLL 69	BAND ON THE WAGON (LP, blue/silver/black label with "sold in on the U.K..." text)	60

(see also Alex Harvey, Hair)

HAIRPOWER
70	CBS 4961	Royal International Love-in/Be There, Be Hair	10

HAIR & SKIN TRADING COMPANY
96	Aquese AQR 711	CROUCH END EP	6
94	Beggars Banquet BBQLP 141	OVER VALENCE (LP with free 12")	15

HAL
05	Heavenly HVN 147	Keep Love As Your Golden Rule/THE MAGIC NUMBERS: Animla Sola (Double A side tour single - 500 only p/s)	10

I. HALCIDEONS AND I. JARZIF
78	Greensleeves GRED 7	Rise Ethiopians/Signs Of The Messiah (12")	40

DENNIS HALE
55	Parlophone MSP 6153	The Butterscotch Mop/S'posin'	10

(see also Jack Parnell)

TERENCE HOLDERWAY HALE
60	Fontana H 285	Beauty And The Beast/My New Year's Eve	7

WILLIE 'BEAVER' HALE
80	T.K. S TKR 7587	Groove On/Party Times	6
01	Soul Brother 12-SBT-3	Groove On/Let The Good Times Roll (12" reissue)	18
80	T.K. S TKR 83392	BEAVER FEVER (LP)	15

TONY HALE AND ROGER PERKS
70	TET 135	A Lament For A Lost Soul/Plea For Public Support	8

BILL HALEY (& HIS COMETS)

78s
53	London L 1190	Crazy Man, Crazy/Whatcha Gonna Do (as Bill Haley with Haley's Comets) (gold label lettering)	30
53	London L 1216	Pat-A-Cake/Fractured (as Bill Haley with Haley's Comets, gold label)	30
54	London HL 1190	Crazy Man, Crazy/Whatcha Gonna Do (as Bill Haley with Haley's Comets) (reissue, silver label lettering)	20
54	London HL 1216	Pat-A-Cake/Fractured (reissue, silver label lettering, as Bill Haley with Haley's Comets)	20
56	Melodisc 1376	I'm Gonna Dry Ev'ry Tear With A Kiss/Why Do I Cry Over You	40
59	Brunswick 05788	I Got A Woman/Charmaine	20
59	Brunswick 05805	Shaky/Caldonia	20
59	Brunswick 05810	Joey's Song/Ooh! Look-A There, Ain't She Pretty	20

SINGLES
54	Brunswick 05317	(We're Gonna) Rock Around The Clock/Thirteen Women (gold lettering on label)	60
54	Brunswick 05317	(We're Gonna) Rock Around The Clock/Thirteen Women (silver lettering on label)	25
54	Brunswick 05338	Shake, Rattle And Roll/A.B.C. Boogie (gold lettering on label)	40
54	Brunswick 05338	Shake, Rattle And Roll/A.B.C. Boogie (silver lettering on label)	20
55	Brunswick 05373	Happy Baby/Dim, Dim The Lights (I Want Some Atmosphere) (gold lettering on label)	40
55	Brunswick 05373	Happy Baby/Dim, Dim The Lights (I Want Some Atmosphere) (silver lettering on label)	20
55	Brunswick 05405	Birth Of The Boogie/Mambo Rock (gold lettering on label)	40
55	Brunswick 05405	Birth Of The Boogie/Mambo Rock (silver lettering on label)	20
55	London HL 8142	Green Tree Boogie/Sundown Boogie (gold lettering on label)	150
55	London HL 8142	Green Tree Boogie/Sundown Boogie (silver lettering on label)	50
55	Brunswick 05453	Two Hound Dogs/Razzle Dazzle (gold lettering on label)	40
55	Brunswick 05453	Two Hound Dogs/Razzle Dazzle (silver lettering on label)	20
55	London HLF 8161	Farewell, So Long, Goodbye/I'll Be True (gold lettering on label)	100
55	London HLF 8161	Farewell, So Long, Goodbye/I'll Be True (silver lettering on label)	50
55	London HLF 8194	Ten Little Indians/Rocking Chair On The Moon (gold lettering on label)	100
55	London HLF 8194	Ten Little Indians/Rocking Chair On The Moon (silver lettering on label)	50
55	Brunswick 05509	Rock-A-Beatin' Boogie/Burn That Candle (gold lettering on label)	40
55	Brunswick 05509	Rock-A-Beatin' Boogie/Burn That Candle (silver lettering on label)	20
56	Brunswick 05530	See You Later, Alligator/The Paper Boy (On Main Street, USA) (gold lettering on label)	40
56	Brunswick 05530	See You Later, Alligator/The Paper Boy (On Main Street, USA) (silver lettering on label)	20
56	Brunswick 05565	The Saints Rock 'N' Roll/R-O-C-K	15
56	Brunswick 05582	Rockin' Through The Rye/Hot Dog Buddy Buddy	15
56	Brunswick 05615	Rip It Up/Teenager's Mother	15
56	Brunswick 05616	Rudy's Rock/Blue Comet Blues	15
57	Brunswick 05640	Don't Knock The Rock/Calling All Comets	15
57	Brunswick 05641	Hook, Line And Sinker/Goofin' Around	15
57	London HLF 8371	Rock The Joint/Yes Indeed! (gold label)	150
57	London HLF 8371	Rock The Joint/Yes Indeed! (silver label)	50
57	Brunswick 05658	Forty Cups Of Coffee/Choo Choo Ch'Boogie	15
57	Brunswick 05688	(You Hit The Wrong Note) Billy Goat/Rockin' Rollin' Rover	15
57	Brunswick 05719	Miss You/The Dipsy Doodle	15
58	Brunswick 05735	Mary, Mary Lou/It's A Sin	15
58	Brunswick 05742	Skinny Minnie/How Many	20
58	Brunswick 05752	Lean Jean/Don't Nobody Move	15
58	Brunswick 05766	Whoa Mabel!/Chiquita Linda	15
59	Brunswick 05788	I Got A Woman/Charmaine	15
59	Brunswick 05805	Shaky/Caldonia	15
59	Brunswick 05810	Joey's Song/Ooh! Look-A There, Ain't She Pretty	15

(The above 45s were originally issued with triangular centres; later round centres are worth two-thirds of these values.)

60	Brunswick 05818	Puerto Rican Peddler/Skokiaan	10
60	Warner Bros WB 6	Candy Kisses/Tamiami	10
61	London HLU 9471	Spanish Twist/My Kind Of Woman	10
63	Stateside SS 196	Tenor Man/Up Goes My Love	10
64	Warner Bros WB 133	Rock Around The Clock/Love Letters In The Sand	10

Year	Catalogue	Title	Value £
64	Brunswick 05910	Happy Baby/Birth Of The Boogie	15
64	Brunswick 05917	The Green Door/Yeah! She's Evil	15
68	Pye International 7N 25455	Crazy Man, Crazy/Dance With A Dolly (With A Hole In Her Stocking)	15

EXPORT SINGLES

Year	Catalogue	Title	Value £
54	Decca BM 05317	(We're Gonna) Rock Around The Clock/Thirteen Women	60
55	Decca BM 05405	Birth Of The Boogie/Mambo Rock	40
55	Decca BM 05509	Rock-A-Beatin' Boogie/Burn That Candle	40
56	Decca BM 05530	See You Later Alligator/The Paper Boy (On Main Street, USA)	40
56	Decca BM 31163	The Saints Rock 'N' Roll/R-O-C-K	30
56	Decca BM 31164	Rockin' Through The Rye/Hot Dog Buddy Buddy	30
56	Decca BM 31171	Rip It Up/Teenager's Mother	30
57	Decca BM 31174	Don't Knock The Rock/Choo Choo Ch'Boogie	30
68	Decca AD 1010	(We're Gonna) Rock Around The Clock/Shake, Rattle And Roll	12

EPs

Year	Catalogue	Title	Value £
55	Brunswick OE 9129	DIM, DIM THE LIGHTS (gold lettering label, 'stage' p/s, various colours)	40
55	Brunswick OE 9129	DIM, DIM THE LIGHTS (silver lettering label, 'stage' or 'cameo' p/s)	25
55	London REF 1031	ROCK AND ROLL	50
56	London REF 1049	LIVE IT UP PART 1	30
56	London REF 1050	LIVE IT UP PART 2	30
56	Brunswick OE 9214	ROCK AND ROLL WITH BILL HALEY	25
56	Brunswick OE 9250	ROCK AROUND THE CLOCK	20
56	Brunswick OE 9250	ROCK AROUND THE CLOCK (round centre, different sleeve, same design as "Bill Haley" [OE 9459])	35
56	London REF 1058	LIVE IT UP PART 3	35
56	Brunswick OE 9278	ROCK'N'ROLL STAGE SHOW PART 1	20
56	Brunswick OE 9279	ROCK'N'ROLL STAGE SHOW PART 2	20
56	Brunswick OE 9280	ROCK'N'ROLL STAGE SHOW PART 3	20
58	Brunswick OE 9349	ROCKIN' THE OLDIES PART 1	25
58	Brunswick OE 9350	ROCKIN' THE OLDIES PART 2	25
58	Brunswick OE 9351	ROCKIN' THE OLDIES PART 3	25

(Originally issued with triangular centres, later round-centre copies are worth two-thirds this value.)

Year	Catalogue	Title	Value £
59	Brunswick OE 9446	ROCKIN' AROUND THE WORLD	60
59	Brunswick OE 9459	BILL HALEY	50

(The above EPs were originally issued with triangular centres, later round-centre copies are worth half to two-thirds these values.)

Year	Catalogue	Title	Value £
60	Warners WEP 6001	BILL HALEY AND HIS COMETS	30
61	Warners WEP 6025	BILL HALEY'S JUKE BOX (mono)	30
61	Warners WSEP 6025	BILL HALEY'S JUKE BOX (stereo)	40
64	Warners WEP 6133	BILL HALEY VOLUME 1	30
64	Warners WEP 6136	BILL HALEY VOLUME 2	30

ALBUMS

Year	Catalogue	Title	Value £
55	London H-APB 1042	LIVE IT UP (10", gold lettering on label)	80
55	London H-APB 1042	LIVE IT UP (10", silver lettering on label)	25
56	Brunswick LAT 8117	ROCK AROUND THE CLOCK	30
56	Brunswick LAT 8139	ROCK AND ROLL STAGE SHOW	30
57	London HA-F 2037	ROCK THE JOINT	80
57	Brunswick LAT 8219	ROCKIN' THE OLDIES	60
57	Brunswick LAT 8268	ROCKIN' THE JOINT	60
59	Brunswick LAT 8295	BILL HALEY'S CHICKS (mono)	60
59	Brunswick STA 3011	BILL HALEY'S CHICKS (stereo)	70
60	Brunswick LAT 8326	STRICTLY INSTRUMENTAL	40
62	Columbia 33SX 1460	TWISTIN' KNIGHTS AT THE ROUNDTABLE (LIVE!)	30
65	Warner Bros W 1391	BILL HALEY'S JUKE BOX	20

(see also Kingsmen, Jodimars, Nick Nantos & His Fireballs)

HALF JAPANESE

Year	Catalogue	Title	Value £
81	Armageddon ABOX 1	1/2 GENTLEMEN NOT BEASTS (3-LP box set with poster, booklet & lyric insert)	50
81	Armageddon ARM 7	LOUD (LP)	15

(see also Jad Fair)

HALFBREED

Year	Catalogue	Title	Value £
75	United Artists UAG 29877	HALFBREED (LP, fold out sleeve)	20

HALFORD

Year	Catalogue	Title	Value £
00	Metal Is MISLP 001	RESURRECTION (LP)	100

(see also Judas Priest)

HALF PINT

Year	Catalogue	Title	Value £
85	Greensleeves GRED 178	Freedom Fighter/Hold On (12")	25

HAL HOPPERS

Year	Catalogue	Title	Value £
54	London HL 8107	More Love/Do Nothin' Blues	40
55	London HL 8129	Mother Of Pearl/Baby I've Had It	40

ADELAIDE HALL

Year	Catalogue	Title	Value £
60	Oriole CB 1556	Common Sense/Blue Bird On My Shoulder	10

AUDREY HALL AND DON EVANS

Year	Catalogue	Title	Value £
86	Trojan TRLS229	THE DYNAMIC DUO (LP)	20

BARBARA HALL

Year	Catalogue	Title	Value £
75	EMI INT 514	You Brought It On Yourself/Drop My Heart Off At The Door	10

BOB HALL & ALEXIS KORNER

Year	Catalogue	Title	Value £
78	Logo GO 331	Pinetop's Boogie Woogie/All I Got Is You	12

(see also Brunning Hall Sunflower Blues Band, Alexis Korner)

CAROLINE HALL

Year	Catalogue	Title	Value £
71	Decca F 13146	Hold My Hand/Put A Light In The Window	6

Derek HALL & MIKE COOPER

MINT VALUE £

DEREK HALL & MIKE COOPER
60s   Kennet KRS 766   OUT OF THE SHADES (EP) 35

DOLORES HALL
72   Jay Boy BOY 77   Good Lovin' Man/W-O-M-E-N 8

(see also Jackie Lee & Dolores Hall)

ERASMUS HALL
96   Westbound SEWD 112   YOUR LOVE IS MY DESIRE (LP, reissue) 40

GERRI HALL
66   Sue WI 4026   Who Can I Run To/I Lost A Key (unissued) 0
04   Grapevine 2000 143   Who Can I Run To/JADES: Lucky Fellow (reissue) 18

JIM HALL
59   Vogue LAE 12072   JAZZ GUITAR (LP) 50
64   Fontana FJL 121   THE WINNER! (LP, reissue of Jazz Guitar) 18

(see also Modest Jazz Trio)

JIMMY GRAY HALL
74   Epic EPC 2312   Be That Way/Possessed By The Moon 20

JUANITA HALL
62   Storyville SEP 382   STORYVILLE BLUES ANTHOLOGY VOL. 2 (EP) 10

LANI HALL
83   A&M AM 159   Never Say Never Again/MICHAEL LEGRAND: Un Chanson D'Amour (p/s) 8

LARRY HALL
60   Parlophone R 4625   Sandy/Lovin' Tree 15
62   Salvo SLO 1811   Ladder Of Love/The One You Left Behind (99 copies only) 20

RENE HALL'S ORCHESTRA
58   London HLU 8581   Twitchy/Flippin' 30

ROBIN HALL (& JIMMY MACGREGOR)
60   Collector JDS 3   Football Crazy/Rosin The Beau (with p/s) 10
60   Collector JDS 3   Football Crazy/Rosin The Beau 6
60   Decca F 11266   Football Crazy/Rosin The Beau (reissue, p/s) 7
66   Island PBM   A Little Bit Of Paper/Going Into Paper (promotional p/s, given away by British Paper and Board Maker's) 30

(see also Galliards)

RONNIE HALL
61   Piccadilly 7N 35001   The Code Of Love/Who Cares 7
61   Piccadilly 7N 35015   She's Mine/My Heart Is The Lover 7

ROY HALL
56   Brunswick 05531   See You Later, Alligator/Don't Stop Now (gold label lettering) 500
56   Brunswick 05531   See You Later, Alligator/Don't Stop Now (78) 50
56   Brunswick 05555   Blue Suede Shoes/Luscious 300
56   Brunswick 05627   Diggin' The Boogie/Three Alley Cats 500
56   Brunswick 05627   Diggin' The Boogie/Three Alley Cats (78) 50
70   Injun 105   One Monkey Don't Stop The Shop/Flood Of love 10

TONY HALL
77   Free Reed FRR 012   FIELDVOLE MUSIC (LP, with insert) 20

CHANCE HALLADAY
62   Vogue V 9203   John Henry/Thirteen Women 25

HALLELUJAH SKIFFLE GROUP
58   Oriole CB 1429   I Saw The Light/A Closer Walk With Thee (with Clinton Ford) 20

HALLIARD
67   Saga SOC 1058   IT'S THE IRISH IN ME (LP) 30
68   Broadside BRO 106   THE HALLIARD AND JON RAVEN (LP) 50

(see also Jon Raven, Nic Jones)

GERRY HALLOM
84   Fellside FE 036   A RUN A MINUTE (LP) 15

HALLUCINOGEN
94   Dragonfly BFLT 14   Alpha Centauri/LSD (12") 20
95   Tip TIP 004   Angelic Particles/Soothsayer (12", p/s) 12
95   Dragonfly BFLT 29   LSD (Live Mix)/(LS Doof Remix)/(Original Version) (12") 15
96   Twisted TWST 1   Deranger/Gamma Goblins (12") 15
95   Dragonfly BFLLP 15   TWISTED (2-LP, yellow vinyl or one green and one pink or black vinyl) 50
97   Twisted TWSLP1   THE LONE DERANGER (2-LP) 100

JOHNNY HALLYDAY
62   Philips BF 1238   Shake The Hand Of A Fool/Hold Back The Sun 10
63   Philips 373 012BF   Hey Little Girl/Caravan Of Lonely Men 10
65   Philips BF 1449   Pour Moi Tu Es La Seule/They Call Him A Man 10
62   Philips 432 813BE   ROCKING (EP) 100
66   Vogue VRE 5013   JOHNNY HALLYDAY (EP) 100
61   Philips BBL 7556   SINGS AMERICA'S ROCKIN' HITS (LP) 100

HALOES
83   Thor 1003 S   THE HALOES (LP, 200 only) 50

HALOS
61   London HLU 9424   Nag/Copycat 30

STUART HAMBLEN
54   HMV 7MC 20   This Ole House/When My Lord Picks Up The 'Phone (export issue) 25
55   HMV 7MC 30   Go On By/Just A Man (export issue) 10
56   HMV 7M 394   Hell Train/A Few Things To Remember 15

BILLY HAMBRIC
79   Grapevine GRP 139   She Said Goodbye/I Found True Love 12
12   Outta Sight RSV 012   Flaming Mamie/UPSETTERS: Jaywalking 7

CLAIRE HAMILL
72   Island WIP 6122   When I Was A Child/Alice In The Streets Of Darlington 6

HAMILTON

MINT VALUE £

HAMILTON
72	Island WIP 6133	Baseball Blues/Smile Your Blues Away	6
81	WEA K 18440	First Night In New York/Ultraviolet Light (B-side with Gary Numan) (p/s)	7
72	Island ILPS 9182	ONE HOUSE LEFT STANDING (LP, lyric inner sleeve)	40
73	Island ILPS 9225	OCTOBER (LP, gatefold sleeve, pink rim palm tree label)	20
74	Konk KONK 101	STAGE DOOR JOHNNIES (LP, gatefold sleeve, blue label)	15
75	Konk KONK 104	ABRACADABRA (LP, featuring Cafe Society, with lyric insert, blue label)	15

(see also Cafe Society, Gary Numan, Wishbone Ash)

HAMILTON
79	Muscle SJP 806/MUS 001	Jet Set Girl/Methodone And Coconuts (500 only, no p/s)	100

BILLY HAMILTON & STRANDSMEN
67	Philips BF 1622	Try To Remember/Don't You Believe It	7

(see also Strandsmen)

CHICO HAMILTON QUINTET
57	Decca DL 8614	SWEET SMELL OF SUCCESS (LP)	20
58	Vogue LAE 12045	CHICO HAMILTON QUINTET IN HIFI (LP)	20
64	HMV CLP 1807	MAN FROM TWO WORLDS (LP)	20

DAVE HAMILTON
12	Kent TOWN 144	Pisces Pace/BARRINO BROTHERS: The Bad Things You Said To Me	8

ED HAMILTON
70	Evolution E 3003	Emily's Eyes/All I Needed Was The Rain	8

EDWARD HAMILTON & ARABIANS
80	Grapevine GRP 134	Baby Don't You Weep/I'm Gonna Love You	20

GARY HAMILTON
67	Decca F 12697	Let The Music Play/Don't Ask	12
69	CBS 4674	Easy Rider/Hare Krishna	6

(see also Hamilton & [Hamilton] Movement)

GAVIN HAMILTON
67	King KG 1067	It Won't Be The Same/Turn The Key Softly	150

GEORGE HAMILTON IV
57	London HL 8361	A Rose And A Candy Bar/If You Don't Know (gold label print)	125
57	London HL 8361	A Rose And A Candy Bar/If You Don't Know (later silver label print)	30
63	RCA RCA 1353	Abilene/Oh So Many Years	6
59	HMV CLP 1263	SING ME A SAD SONG - A TRIBUTE TO HANK WILLIAMS (LP)	20

GUY HAMILTON
65	HMV POP 1418	A Lifetime Of Loneliness/Give The Game Away	15

(see also Neil Christian)

(KINGSIZE) HAMILTON & PLATTERMEN
66	Emerald MD 1048	Shake/I Got To Know	25

LITTLE JOHNNY HAMILTON
90	Horace's HRH 006	Oh How I Love You/ENTERTAINERS IV: Gettin' Back Into Circulation	10
99	Jay Boy 10	Keep On Moving/Oh How I Love You (DJ copy)	12

M. HAMILTON
67	Ska Beat JB 265	Something Gotta Ring/DENNIS LYNWARD & HIS GROUP: Jazz Session	35

MILTON HAMILTON
73	Explosion EX 2069	Long Long Road/Version	8
77	Wolf WM 005	Children Are You Ready/Part 2	8

ROY HAMILTON (1)
58	Fontana H 113	Don't Let Go/The Right To Love	25
58	Fontana H 143	Crazy Feelin'/In A Dream	15
59	Fontana H 180	Pledging My Love/My One And Only Love	15
59	Fontana H 193	I Need Your Loving/Somewhere Along The Way	15
61	Fontana H 298	You Can Have Her/Abide With Me	15
61	Fontana H 320	You're Gonna Need Magic/To The One I Love	15
63	MGM MGM 1210	Theme From "The VIPs"/The Sinner	15
64	MGM MGM 1251	There She Is/The Panic Is On	175
64	MGM MGM 1251	There She Is/The Panic Is On (DJ copy)	600
65	MGM MGM 1268	A Thousand Tears Ago/Sweet Violet	15
66	RCA RCA 1500	And I Love Her/Tore Up Over You	15
69	Deep Soul DS 9106	Dark End Of The Street/100 Years Ago	40
59	Fontana TFE 17160	WHY FIGHT THE FEELING (EP)	20
60	Fontana TFE 17163	THE MOOD MOVES (EP)	20
61	Fontana TFE 17170	COME OUT SWINGING (EP)	20
63	Columbia 33SX 1473	GREATEST HITS (LP)	40
64	MGM MGM-C 960	WARM SOUL (LP)	60

ROY HAMILTON (2)
83	HBS K CAP 1	Turn Up The Music/Instrumental Version (12", with Capiche)	20

RUSS HAMILTON
57	Oriole CB 1359	We Will Make Love/Rainbow	6
58	Oriole EP 7005	RUSS HAMILTON (EP)	10
58	Oriole MG 20031	WE WILL MAKE LOVE (LP)	20

SCOTT HAMILTON
65	Parlophone R5241	When Things Go Wrong/I Wonder	6
66	Parlophone R 5492	Good Day Sunshine/For No One	10

HAMILTON & MOVEMENT
65	Polydor BM 56026	Really Saying Something/I Won't See You Tonight	80
67	CBS 202573	I'm Not The Marrying Kind/My Love Belongs To You	40

(see also Gary Hamilton)

HAMLET
67	Decca F12571	She Won't See The Light/Go Play In Your Own Yard	20

HAMLETT

MINT VALUE £

HAMLETT
72	Pye 7N45171	Where'd The Day Go/Vampire Man	20

HAMLINS
67	Coxsone CS 7021	Trying To Keep A Good Man Down/SUMMERTAIRS: Oh My Darling (actually by Bob & Rita Marley)	90
67	Coxsone CS 7022	Soul And Inspiration/ETHIOPIANS: Let's Get Together	35
68	Coxsone CS 7048	Sentimental Reasons/SOUL VENDORS: Last Waltz	200
68	Blue Cat BS 115	Sugar And Spice/SOUL VENDORS: Mercy Mercy Mercy	200

(see also Minstrels)

JACK HAMMER
61	Oriole CB 1634	Young Only Once/Juliette	15
62	Oriole CB 1645	Kissin' Twist/Melancholy Boy	10
62	Oriole CB 1728	Crazy Twist/Twist Talk	10
62	Oriole CB 1753	Don't Let Baby Know/Number 2539	15
66	Polydor 56091	Thanks/Love Ladder	20
67	Polydor 56158	Joe Poor Loves Daphne Rich/Ode To A Discotheque	50
69	United Artists UP 35029	What Greater Love/The Mason Dixon Line	30
71	Youngblood B 1023	Swim/Colour Combination	40
63	Oriole PS 40020	HAMMER + BEAT = TWIST (LP)	80
66	Polydor 582001	BRAVE NEW WORLD (LP)	120

HAMMER (2)
85	Ebony EBON 29	CONTRACT WITH HELL (LP)	15

HAMMERHEAD
81	Linden Sounds LS 009	Time Will Tell/Lonely Man (p/s)	60

HAMMERS (JAMAICA)
70	Gas GAS 162	Hotter Than Scorcher/Someday Could See You	40

(see also Joan Ross)

HAMMERSMITH GORILLAS
74	Penny Farthing PEN 849	You Really Got Me/Leavin' 'Ome (p/s)	25
77	Raw RAW 2	You Really Got Me/Leavin' 'Ome (reissue, company sleeve)	15

(see also Gorillas, Helter Skelter, Jesse Hector)

PETER HAMMILL
75	Charisma CB 245	Birthday Special/Shingle Song	8
78	Charisma CB 339	The Polaroid (credited to Ricky Nadir)/The Old School Tie	10
78	Charisma PH 001	Crying Wolf/This Side Of The Looking Glass (promo only)	30
82	Naive NAV 3	Paradox Drive/Now More Than Ever (p/s)	6
83	Naive NAV 8	Film Noir/Seven Wonders	6
71	Charisma CAS 1037	FOOL'S MATE (LP, gatefold sleeve, pink 'scroll' label)	100
73	Charisma CAS 1067	CHAMELEON IN THE SHADOW OF THE NIGHT (LP, gatefold sleeve, large 'Mad Hatter' label)	40
73	Charisma CAS 1037	FOOL'S MATE (LP, reissue, 'Mad Hatter' label, gatefold)	40
74	Charisma CAS 1083	THE SILENT CORNER AND THE EMPTY STAGE (LP, gatefold sleeve., with lyric inner, large 'Mad Hatter' label)	20
74	Charisma CAS 1089	IN CAMERA (LP, with inner sleeve, small 'Mad Hatter' label)	20
75	Charisma CAS 1099	NADIR'S BIG CHANCE (LP, laminated sleeve, with inner sleeve small 'Mad Hatter' label)	15
77	Charisma CAS 1125	OVER (LP, with inner lyric sleeve, small 'Mad Hatter' label)	15
78	Charisma CAS 1137	THE FUTURE NOW (LP, with insert)	18
79	Charisma CAS 1146	PH7 (LP)	15
84	Foundry FOUND 1	THE MARGIN LIVE (LP, as Peter Hammill & K Group)	20

(see also Van Der Graaf Generator, Rikki Nadir, Colin Scot)

HAMMOND BROS.
74	London 10464	The Garbage Man/Soul Over Easy (featuring Maggie)	8

CLAY HAMMOND
72	Jay Boy BOY 78	Dance Little Girl/Twin Brother	6

JOHN HAMMOND
65	Fontana TF 560	Baby Won't You Tell Me/I Love The Life I Live	15
68	Atlantic 584 190	Brown Eyed Handsome Man/Crosscut Saw	18
64	Fontana TFL 6046	BIG CITY BLUES (LP)	60
65	Fontana TFL 6059	SO MANY ROADS (LP)	50
71	CBS 64365	SOURCE POINT (LP)	25
72	CBS 65051	I'M SATISFIED (LP)	25
72	Vanguard VSD 11/12	THE BEST OF JOHN HAMMOND - SOUTHERN FRIED (2-LP)	20

JOHNNY HAMMOND
93	Milestone MX 9062	GEARS (LP, reissue)	35
01	Soul Brother LP SBCS 9	GAMBLERS LIFE (LP, reissue)	18

CURLEY HAMNER & COOPER BROTHERS
59	Felsted SD 80061	Twistin' And Turnin'/King And Queen	10

BILLY HAMON
78	Bronze BRO 58	Butch Things/Amusement Arcade (p/s)	20

SUSAN HAMPSHIRE
65	Decca F 12185	When Love Is True/When The World Was Our Own	8

HEATH HAMPSTEAD
68	Polydor 56289	I Started A Joke/The Beginning Of The Ending	6

SLIDE HAMPTON & HIS BAND
62	London HA-K/SH-K 8008	JAZZ WITH A TWIST (LP)	18
62	London LZT-K 15245	LONDON JAZZ (LP, as Slide Hampton Octet)	18

HERBIE HANCOCK
63	Blue Note 45-1887	Blind Man, Blind Man (Parts 1 & 2)	10
70	Warner Bros WB 7358	Fat Mama/Wiggle-Waggle	15
74	CBS 2329	Chameleon/Vein Melter	6
75	CBS 3059	Palm Grease/Butterfly	6

66	MGM C(S) 78039	BLOW-UP (LP, soundtrack)	80
71	Warner Bros WS 1834	FAT ALBERT ROTUNDA (LP)	25
71	Warner Bros K 46077	MWANDISHI (LP)	25
72	Warner Bros K 46164	CROSSINGS (LP)	20
74	Warner Bros K 46039	FAT ALBERT ROTUNDA (LP, reissue)	15
74	CBS 60193	THRUST (LP)	20
74	CBS 80546	DEATH WISH (LP, soundtrack)	15
74	CBS 65582	SEXTANT (LP)	20
74	CBS 65928	HEADHUNTERS (LP)	20
75	DJM 22008	KAWAIDA (LP, with Don Cherry)	30
75	CBS 69185	MAN-CHILD (LP)	20
76	CBS 81591	SECRETS (LP)	20
77	Blue Note BNS 40020	MAIDEN VOYAGE (LP, reissue)	15
77	Blue Note BNS 40025	SPEAK LIKE A CHILD (LP, reissue)	15
78	CBS 82240	SUNLIGHT (LP)	20
79	CBS 83491	FEETS DON'T FAIL ME NOW (LP)	15
80	CBS 84237	MONSTER (LP)	15
80	CBS 84638	MR. HANDS (LP)	20
81	CBS 85144	MAGIC WINDOWS (LP)	20
82	CBS 32474	LITE ME UP (LP)	15
83	CBS 25540	FUTURE SHOCK (LP)	15
96	Premier 72438 5228018	BLOW-UP (LP, reissue, soundtrack)	15
97	Blue Note ST 46339	MAIDEN VOYAGE (LP, reissue)	15
01	Transparent HERBIE LP 1	FUTURE 2 FUTURE (2-LP)	20
07	Verve 0602517468344	RIVER: THE JONI LETTERS (2-LP)	20

(see also Headhunters, Kimiko Kasai)

OWEN HAND
61	Transatlantic TRA 127	SOMETHING NEW (LP)	100
66	Transatlantic TRA	I LOVED A LASS (LP)	80

JOHNNY HANDLE
61	Topic TOP 78	STOTTIN' DOON THE WAAL (EP)	10
75	Topic 12TS 270	THE COLLIER LAD (LP)	15

(see also Louise Killen & Johnny Handle, High Level Ranters)

HANDLEY FAMILY
73	GL 100	Wam Bam/Rum Dum And Baccy	8

HANDSLIPS
81	Victoria Park VICKY 1	Too Young To Date (But Not To Masturbate)/Art School Is For Wankers	6

HANDSOME BOY MODELLING SCHOOL
99	Tommy Boy TBV 1258	SO...HOWS YOUR GIRL? (2-LP)	60

HANDSOME BEASTS
81	Heavy Metal HEAVY 1	All Riot Now/Mark Of The Beast (p/s)	25
81	Heavy Metal HEAVY 2	Breaker/One In A Crowd/Crazy (wraparound p/s)	8
82	Heavy Metal HEAVY 11	Sweeties/You're One Your Own (p/s, with card sheet)	8
82	Heavy Metal HMRLP 2	BEASTIALITY (LP)	20

WAYNE HANDY
58	London HL 8547	Say Yeah/Could It Be (B-side with King Sisters)	200

PAUL HANFORD
60	Parlophone R 4680	Itsy Bitsy Teenie Weenie Little Polka Dot Bikini/Why Have You Changed Your Mind	10
60	Parlophone R 4694	If You Ain't Got Love/Ev'ry Little Girl	10
61	Parlophone R 4745	Everything/Cigarettes And Coffee Blues	10
61	Parlophone R 4813	Memphis Address/Flutter Flutter	10
62	Oriole CB 1779	Don't Be/Habit Of Loving You	10
63	Oriole CB 1830	Just When I Need You Most/Judy	10
63	Oriole CB 1866	The Minute You're Gone/High School Dance	10

HANG DAVID
90	Vacant HANG 01	HANG DAVID (12" EP, p/s)	18

HANGMAN'S BEAUTIFUL DAUGHTERS
87	Dreamworld DREAM 11	Love Is Blue/Popular Trend (p/s)	7

BOBBY HANNA
67	Decca F 12695	Blame It On Me/Goin' Where The Lovin' Is	7
68	Decca F 12783	Written On The Wind/Everybody Needs Love	10
68	Decca F 12833	To Wait For Love (Is To Waste Your Life Away)/Is It Wrong	6
69	Decca F 22917	Winter Love (E' L'Amore)/Time	6
70	Philips 6006 029	Better Men Than I/Look Into My Life	6

JOSH HANNA
65	Parlophone R 5285	When I Love You/Love Me, Love Me	6
66	Decca F 12532	Shut Your Mouth/Sweet To My Soul	20

PAUL HANNAH
94	Ferox FER 007	CONTROL EP (12", plain sleeve)	12

ROSS HANNAMAN
67	Columbia DB 8288	1969/Probably On A Thursday (with p/s)	50
67	Columbia DB 8288	1969/Probably On A Thursday	40
74	Bellwood BW1	A NIGHT AT FACTOTUM (LP, 100 only, as John and Rosalind)	20

MARTIN HANNETT
80	Factory FACT 14C	First Aspect Of The Same Thing/Second Aspect Of The Same Thing (flexi, most included first/second pressing of THE RETURN OF THE DURUTTI COLUMN LP)	25

(see also Durutti Column)

HANNIBAL
74	B&C HB 1	Winds Of Change/Winter	15
70	B&C CAS 1022	HANNIBAL (LP, gatefold sleeve)	200

Lance HANNIBAL

MINT VALUE £

(see also Wizzard)

LANCE HANNIBAL
69   Blue Cat BS 148   Read The News/RECO & RHYTHM ACES: Return Of The Bullet 45

(see also Sugar Simone, Les Foster)

JERRY HANSEN & RAMBLERS DANCE BAND
67   Decca WAP 24   DANCE WITH THE RAMBLERS (LP) 25

ANNETTE HANSHAW
65   VJM VEP 31   THAT'S ALL (EP) 10

HANSIE
79   Sonet SON 2195   Automobile/Tu Es Belle (p/s) 6

HANSON
73   Manticore K43507   NOW HEAR THIS (LP, gatefold sleeve) 20

HANSON & KARLSSON
67   Polydor 184 196   SWEDISH UNDERGROUND (LP) 15
69   Polydor 462 60   MONUMENT (LP) 60
69   Polydor 583 564   MAN AT THE MOON (LP) 60

(see also Bo Hansson)

BO HANSSON
72   Charisma CAS 1059   LORD OF THE RINGS (LP, insert, large 'Mad Hatter' label) 20
73   Charisma CAS 1073   MAGICIANS'S HAT (LP, large 'Mad Hatter' label) 15
76   Charisma CAS 1113   ATTIC THOUGHTS (LP, gatefold. 'Mad Hatter' label) 15

HAPPENINGS
66   Fontana TF 735   See You In September/He Thinks He's A Hero 10
66   Fontana TF 766   Go Away Little Girl/Tea Time 8
67   Pye International 7N 25501 My Mammy/I Believe In Nothing 7
67   Stateside SS 587   Goodnight My Love/Lillies By Monet... 8
67   Stateside SS 2013   I Got Rhythm/You're In A Bad Way 8
67   BT Puppy BTS 45532   Why Do Fools Fall In Love/When The Summer Is Through 7
68   BT Puppy BTS 45538   Music Music Music/When I Lock My Door 6
68   BT Puppy BTS 45540   Randy/Love Song Of Mummy And Dad 8
68   BT Puppy BTS 45543   Breaking Up Is Hard To Do/Anyway 6
67   Fontana TL 5383   BYE BYE, SO LONG, FAREWELL ... SEE YOU IN SEPTEMBER (LP) 35
67   BT Puppy BTLP 1003   PSYCLE (LP) 40
68   BT Puppy BTLPS 1004   GOLDEN HITS (LP) 20

HAPPY CATS
78   Grapevine 110   These Boots Are Made For Walkin'/Destroy That Boy 20

HAPPY CONFUSION
69   Penny Farthing PEN 706   Yes Sir/Hereditary Impediment 15

HAPPY FAMILY
82   4AD AD 204   Puritans/Innermost Thoughts/The Mistake (p/s) 15

(see also Josef K, Momus)

HAPPY MAGAZINE
68   Polydor 56233   Satisfied Street/Do Right Woman Do Right Man 20
69   Polydor 56307   Who Belongs To You (Ooby Dooby Doo)/Beautiful Land 10

(see also Griffin)

HAPPY MONDAYS
85   Factory FAC 129   FORTY FIVE EP : Delightful/This Feeling/Oasis (12" p/s) 12
86   Factory FAC 142   Freaky Dancing (Live)/The Egg (p/s) 8
87   Factory FACT 170   SQUIRREL & G-MAN TWENTY FOUR HOUR PARTY PEOPLE PLASTIC FACE CARNT SMILE
                                           (WHITE OUT) (LP, with "Desmond", 5,000 in plastic sleeve) 50
87   Factory FACT 170   SQUIRREL & G-MAN TWENTY FOUR HOUR PARTY PEOPLE PLASTIC FACE CARNT SMILE
                                           (WHITE OUT) (LP, with "Desmond") 30
88   Factory FACT 220   BUMMED (LP, embossed cover) 25
90   Factory FACT 320   PILLS 'N' THRILLS & BELLYACHES (LP, withdrawn 'sweet wrapper' sleeve) 50
90   Factory FACT 320   PILLS 'N' THRILLS & BELLYACHES (LP) 20
91   Factory FACT 322   LIVE (2-LP) 25
92   Factory FACT 420   ...YES PLEASE (LP, with inner and lyric insert) 35
07   Sequel SEQLP 012   UNCLE DYSFUNKTIONAL (LP) 35

(see also SWR, Black Grape)

HAPPY REFUGEES
82   Gymnasium REF no 1   Warehouse Sound/Enshrined In A Memory (p/s) 8
84   Gymnasium HREF 002   LAST CHANGE SALOON (LP) 15

HAPSHASH & THE COLOURED COAT
69   Liberty LBF 15188   Colinda/The Wall 25
67   Minit MLS 40001E   FEATURING THE HUMAN HOST AND THE HEAVY METAL KIDS (LP, with Art, red vinyl
                                           (MLL 40001) with insert) 200
67   Minit MLS 40001E   FEATURING THE HUMAN HOST AND THE HEAVY METAL KIDS (LP, with Art, later pressing
                                           on black vinyl) 60
69   Liberty LBL/LBS 83212R   THE WESTERN FLYER (LP, with Mike Batt, blue label) 100

(see also Tony McPhee, Warm Sounds, Marc Bolan/T. Rex, Art, Mike Batt)

HARBOUR FOLK
70   Polydor 583 080   WAXIE'S DARGLE (LP) 30

HARBOUR LITES
65   HMV POP 1426   Come Back Silly Girl/Revenge 8
65   HMV POP 1465   I Would Give All/They Call The Wind Maria 8
66   Fontana TF 682   Run For Your Life/Lonely Journey 8

HARDBACK
86   Streetwave 7 BOSS 3   The Champ/Bust The Champ 6

HARD CORPS
84   Hard Corps HC 01   Dirty/To Breathe (12", hand-written white labels, numbered) 20
84   Survival SUR 026   Dirty/Respirer (To Breathe) (white or printed labels, stickered plain black sleeve) 10

HARD-FI

MINT VALUE £

84	Survival SUR 12 026	Dirty/Respirer (To Breathe) (12", with sticker in plain black sleeve)	12
85	Immaculate 12 IMMAC 2	Je Suis Passée (Extended French Version)/(Extended Club Dub Mix) (12", p/s)	12
85	Polydor HARDA 1	Je Suis Passée (Hard Mix)/(French Mix)/(Dub Mix) (12", gatefold PVC sleeve, various colours, with poster)	20
85	Polydor HARD 1	Je Suis Passée/Instrumental Version (p/s)	8
85	Polydor HARD 2	To Breathe/Metal And Flesh (unreleased)	20
85	Polydor HARDX 2	To Breathe/Metal And Flesh/To Breathe (Instrumental) (12", unreleased)	25
90	Concrete P. CPPRODLP 011	METAL AND FLESH (LP, clear vinyl)	35

(see also Craze, Skunks, T.U.F.F.)

HARD-FI
| 05 | Necessary 5046786911 | STARS OF CCTV (2 x LP, HMV special with bonus Middle Eastern Holiday 7") | 60 |

HARDFLOOR
| 92 | Harthouse HARTUK 1 | HARDTRANCE ACPERIENCE EP (12", 4-track) | 10 |

HARD HORSE
| 71 | Dart ART 2001 | Let It Ride/Hang Old Freddy | 20 |
| 72 | Dart ART 2012 | (Get It) Up Down/So Long I'm Moving On | 30 |

(EDDIE) HARDIN & (PETE) YORK
69	Bell BLL 1064	Tomorrow Today/Candlelight (as Hardin-York)	30
69	Bell SBLL 125	TOMORROW TODAY (LP, gatefold sleeve, blue/silver/black label, with "Sold in the U.K..." text)	50
70	Bell SBLL 136	HARDIN & YORK (THE WORLD'S SMALLEST BIG BAND) (LP, gatefold)	50
71	Bell SBLL 141	FOR THE WORLD (LP, existence unconfirmed)	100
71	Decca SKL 5095	FOR THE WORLD (LP, reissue, blue/silver label with boxed logo)	15

(see also Eddie Hardin, Pete York, Spencer Davis Group)

EDDIE HARDIN
| 72 | Decca TXS 106 | HOME IS WHERE YOU FIND IT (LP, gatefold sleeve, green/silver label) | 25 |

(see also Hardin-York, Spencer Davis Group, Roger Glover, Wizards Convention)

RICHARD HARDIN
| 61 | HMV POP 887 | Jezebel/Temptation | 25 |

(see also Cresters, Mike Sagar & Cresters)

TIM HARDIN
66	Verve VS 1504	Hang On To A Dream/Reason To Believe	12
67	Verve VS 1511	Lady Came From Baltimore/Black Sheep Boy	10
68	Verve VS 1516	Don't Make Promises/Smugglin' Man	7
71	Verve 2009 006	If I Were A Carpenter/Hang On To A Dream	8
66	Verve (S)VLP 5018	TIM HARDIN 1 (LP)	40
67	Verve (S)VLP 6002	TIM HARDIN 2 (LP)	35
67	Atlantic 587/588 082	THIS IS TIM HARDIN (LP, plum label)	25
68	Verve (S)VLP 6010	LIVE IN CONCERT (LP)	30
69	Verve (S)VLP 6016	TIM HARDIN 4 (LP)	25
69	Verve (S)VLP 6019	THE BEST OF (LP)	20
69	CBS (S/M) 63571	SUITE FOR SUSAN MOORE AND DAMIAN (LP, gatefold sleeve, mono/stereo)	20
70	CBS 64335	BIRD ON A WIRE (LP)	15
72	CBS 65209	PAINTED HEAD (LP)	18
74	Verve 2683 048	TIM HARDIN 1/2 (2-LP, gatefold reissue)	20

(see also Eddie Hardin, Pete York, Spencer Davis Group)

MIKE HARDING
| 86 | Moonraker M 003 | BOMBERS MOON (LP) | 20 |

ROSEMARY HARDMAN (& BOB AXFORD)
69	Folk Heritage no cat. no.	QUEEN OF HEARTS (LP)	125
71	Trailer LER 2075	FIREBIRD (LP)	40
71	Trailer LER 3018	SECOND SEASON CAME (LP, by Rosemary Hardman & Bob Axford)	20
75	Alida Star Cottage	JERSEY BURGER (LP)	120

HARD MEAT
69	Island WIP 6066	Rain/Burning Up Years	15
70	Warner Bros WB 8010	Ballad Of Marmalade Emma And Teddy Grimes/Yesterday, Today, Tomorrow	8
70	Warner Bros WS 1852	HARD MEAT (LP, gatefold sleeve with photo insert)	150
70	Warner Bros WS 1879	THROUGH A WINDOW (LP, green label)	150

HARDNOISE
89	White HNX001	Untitled (different recording to Music Of Life version - 300 pressed) (12")	100
90	Music Of Life NOTE40	Untitled (12")	15
91	Music Of Life NOTE48	Serve Tea, Then Murder/Mice In The Presence Of The Lion (12")	15
12	Gibo GIB 001	Pure Destructive Power (12")	20
13	Gibo GIB 002	Pure Destructive Power (12", green vinyl, 50 pressed)	40
13	Gibo GIB 003	Untitled Sessions (12" EP, reissue)	25

HARD RAIN
| 88 | London LON 185 | Diamonds/Monkey House (p/s) | 12 |
| 88 | London LONX 185 | Diamonds/Monkey House/Diamonds (7" Version) (12", p/s) | 15 |

HARD ROAD
| 79 | Goodstuff LP 1002 | NO PROBLEM (LP, private pressing) | 15 |

HARD ROCK
| 83 | Inner Light DLT 103 | Feel No Way/Version (12") | 80 |

HARD SKIN
07	No Future OI 28	New Age/FUCKED UP: Toronto FC (250 copies with fold-out sleeve, 50 with hard cover)	15
96	Helen Of Oi H0031LP	HARD NUTS AND HARD CUNTS (LP, green vinyl)	15
13	JT Classics CLASS 003	ON THE BALLS (LP)	15
13	JT Classics CLASS 004	WHY DO BIRDS SUDDENLY APPEAR (LP)	15

HARD STUFF
| 72 | Purple PUR 103 | Jay Time/The Orchestrator | 30 |
| 73 | Purple PUR 116 | Inside Your Life/(It's) How Do You Do It! | 10 |

HARD TRAVELLIN'

MINT VALUE £

72	Purple TPSA 7505	BULLETPROOF (LP, gatefold sleeve)	70
73	Purple TPSA 7507	BOLEX DEMENTIA (LP, textured gatefold sleeve)	75

(see also Andromeda, Atomic Rooster, John Du Cann, Five Day Week Straw People, Johnny Gustafson, Bullet, Quatermass)

HARD TRAVELLIN'
71	Flams Ltd PR 1065	HARD TRAVELLIN' (LP, private pressing)	150

HARDWARE (1)
79	Narc NARC 001	Speed Unit/Wall To Wall/Walking/Fire (folded p/s)	8

HARDWARE (2)
85	Reset 7REST 7	Dance/Hey (p/s)	8
85	Reset 12REST 7	Dance/Hey (12", p/s)	15

HARDY
71	Ackee ACK 131	Glorious Morning/Hearing's Not Seeing	6

FRANCOISE HARDY
64	Pye 7N 15612	Catch A Falling Star/Only Friends	8
64	Pye 7N 15653	Tous Les Garcons Et Les Filles/L'Amour S'en Va	7
64	Pye 7N 15696	Pourtant Tu M'Aimes/Jaloux	7
64	Pye 7N 15740	Et Meme/Le Temps De L'Amour	8
65	Pye 7N 15802	All Over The World/Another Place	7
66	Vogue VRS 7001	Just Call And I'll Be There/You Just Have To Say The Word	7
66	Vogue VRS 7004	So Many Friends/However Much	10
66	Vogue VRS 7010	This Little Heart/The Rose	7
66	Vogue VRS 7011	La Maison Ou J'ai Grandi/Je Ne Suis La Pour Personne	7
66	Vogue VRS 7014	Autumn Rendezvous/It's My Heart	7
66	Vogue VRS 7020	Si C'est Ca/Je Serai La Pour Toi	7
66	Vogue VRS 7025	Voila/Qui Peut Dire	7
67	Vogue VRS 7026	On Se Quitte Toujours/Les Petits Garcons	8
68	United Artists UP 1208	Now You Want To Be Loved/Tell Him You're Mine	10
68	United Artists UP 2253	Will You Love Me Tomorrow/Loving You	10
69	United Artists UP 35011	Comment Te Dire Adieu/La Mer, Les Etoiles Et Le Vent	10
70	United Artists UP 35070	All Because Of You/Time Passing By	10
70	United Artists UP 35105	Soon Is Slipping Away/The Bells Of Avignon (mispelling on label)	50
64	Pye NEP 24188	C'EST FAB (EP)	10
64	Pye NEP 24192	FRANCOISE SINGS IN ENGLISH (EP)	10
64	Pye NEP 24193	C'EST FRANCOISE (EP)	10
65	Vogue VRE 5000	FRANCOISE (EP)	12
65	Vogue VRE 5001	FRANCOISE HARDY (EP)	12
65	Vogue VRE 5003	DIS LUI NON (EP)	12
66	Vogue VRE 5008	LE TEMPS DES SOUVENIRS (EP)	12
66	Vogue VRE 5012	CHANTE EN ALLEMAND (EP)	15
66	Vogue VRE 5015	L'AMITIE (EP)	15
66	Vogue VRE 5017	MON AMIE LA ROSE (EP)	15
67	Vogue VRE 5018	AUTUMN RENDEZVOUS (EP)	15
64	Pye NPL 18094	FRANCOISE HARDY (LP)	25
64	Pye NPL 18099	IN VOGUE (LP)	25
65	Vogue VRL 3000	FRANCOISE HARDY (LP)	25
66	Vogue VRL 3021	FRANCOISE HARDY (LP)	25
66	Vogue VRL 3023	LE MEILLEUR DE FRANCOISE HARDY (LP)	25
66	Vogue VRL 3025	SINGS IN ENGLISH (LP)	30
67	Vogue VRL 3028	FRANCOISE (LP)	25
67	Vogue VRL 3031	VOILA! FRANCOISE HARDY (LP)	25
68	United Artists SULP 1191	IL N'Y A PAS D'AMOUR HEUREUX (LP)	25
68	United Artists SULP 1207	EN ANGLAIS (LP)	25
70	United Artists UAS 29046	ONE-NINE-SEVEN-ZERO (LP)	40

LAVELL HARDY
68	Direction 58-3261	Don't Lose Your Groove/Women Of The World	20

COLIN HARE
70	Penny Farthing PEN 736	Grannie, Grannie/For Where Have You Been	20
71	Penny Farthing PEN 750	Underground Girl/Fighting For Peace	20
72	Warner Bros K 16203	Didn't I Tell You/Seek Not In The Wide World	20
71	Penny Farthing PELS 516	MARCH HARE (LP)	350

(see also Honeybus)

WINSTON HAREWOOD
71	Camel CA 64	I Will Never Fall In Love Again (actually by Winston Heywood)/LA-FUD-DIL ALL-STARS: La-Fud-Dil (actually "La-Fud-Del")	15

(see also Winston Heywood)

RON HARGRAVE
58	MGM MGM 956	Latch On/Only A Daydream	1000
58	MGM MGM 956	Latch On/Only A Daydream (78)	100

HARLAN COUNTY
70	Nashville 6076 002	Dr. Handy's Dandy Candy/Big Heat	8
70	Nashville 6336 002	HARLAN COUNTY (LP, red/black label)	25

HARLEM
77	DJM 10743	It Takes A Fool Like Me/There I Go	8

HARLEM SPEAKEASY
68	Polydor 56270	Aretha/Sight Of Pegasus	15

HARLESDEN MONKS
72	Pama Supreme PS 352	Time/Harlesden High Street	12
72	Pama Supreme PS 352	Rock Me Mister Ping Wing/Breakdown Rock	40

(see also Lloyd Charmers)

Steve HARLEY (& COCKNEY REBEL)

MINT VALUE £

STEVE HARLEY (& COCKNEY REBEL)
74   EMI EMI 2191   Psychomodo/Such A Dream (unreleased) 0
(see also Anderson Harley & Batt)

IAN G HARLING
80   P.TO. PT 209/EJSP 9280   Heavy Breathing/Black & White (no p/s) 15

HARLOW
79   Pepper UP 36452   Harry De Mazzio/Nothing To You 100

JEREMY HARMER
69   JH 001   IDIOSYNCRATICS & SWALLOW WINGS (LP, insert, 99 only) 300

LEE HARMER'S POPCORN
68   Page One POF 053   Love Is Coming/Hello Sunshine 20

HARMONIANS
70   Junior JR 112   Music Street/Version 15
70   Ackee ACK 107   Music Street/Group Of Girls 150
(see also Tony & Hippy Boys, Winston Shan)

HARMONIC 33
02   Alphabet Zoo AZEP 2002   EXTRAORDINARY PEOPLE (LP) 15
05   Warp WARPLP 127   MUSIC FOR FILM, TELEVISION AND RADIO VOLUME 1 (LP) 15

HARMONICA FATS
63   Stateside SS 184   Tore Up/I Get So Tired 50
68   Action ACT 4507   Tore Up/I Get So Tired (reissue) 25

HARMONISERS
69   Duke DU 32   Mother Hen/WINSTON SINCLAIR: Chastise Them 20

HARMONIZING FOUR
66   Rymska RA 102   Who Knows/Heart Of Stone (actually by Charms) 20
(see also Charms)

HARMONY BEACH
83   Surf King SK 1   HARMONY BEACH (EP, private pressing) 18

HARMONY GRASS
68   RCA RCA 1772   Move In A Little Bit Closer Baby/Happiness Is Toy Shaped 10
69   RCA RCA 1828   First Time Loving/What A Groovy Day 8
69   RCA RCA 1885   I Remember/Summer Dreaming 7
70   RCA RCA 1928   Mrs. Richie/Teach Me How (withdrawn) 10
70   RCA RCA 1932   Cecilia/Mrs. Richie 7
70   RCA RCA 2011   Stand On Your Own Two Feet/Sing In The Sunshine 7
70   RCA SF 8034   THIS IS US (LP) 40
(see also Capability Brown, Tony Rivers & Castaways)

HARMONY ROCKETS
95   Big Cat ABB90   PARALYZED MIND OF THE ARCHANGEL VOID (LP) 30
(see also Mercury Rev)

HARMONY & XTREME
92   Lucky Spin LSR 008   Treats/NRG Rush (12" white labels only) 60
93   Lucky Spin LSR 010   Love In My Heart/Journey Through Time (12") 40

JOE HARNELL
62   London HLR 9637   Fly Me To The Moon - Bossa Nova/Harlem Nocturne 6
78   MCA MCA 397   The Incredible Hulk Theme/Love Theme 15

BILLY HARNER
71   Kama Sutra 2013 029   What About The Music/Please Spare Me This Time 20
71   Kama Sutra 2013 029   What About The Music (instrumental)/Please Spare Me This Time (withdrawn) 1500

BENNY HARPER
06   Grapevine 2000 G2K 158   My Prayer/It's Love (reissue) 10

BUD HARPER
65   Vocalion VP 9252   Mr. Soul/Let Me Love You 60
65   Vocalion VP 9252   Mr. Soul/Let Me Love You (DJ copy) 100

CHARLIE HARPER AND CAPTAIN SENSIBLE
13   Time & Matter T&M 009   TOO MUCH REALITY EP (cream and purple splatter vinyl) 40
(see also U.K. Subs, Damned)

DON HARPER ORCHESTRA
68   Columbia DB 8519   World Of Sport March/England 88 15
73   Columbia DB 9023   World Of Sport/"Dr. Who" Theme (as Don Harper's Homo Electronicus) 25
74   Columbia SCX 6559   HOMO ELECTRONICUS (LP) 50
74   Impress IA 406   LIVE-NEUTRAL-EARTH (LP) 20
(see also Electricians)

JANICE HARPER
57   HMV POP 376   Bon Voyage/Tell Me That You Love Me Tonight 7
58   Capitol CL 14899   Devotion/In Time 10
59   Capitol CL 14977   I Was Hoping You'd Ask Me/I'm Making Love To You 6
59   Capitol T 1195   WITH FEELING (LP) 15

JESSIE HARPER
92   Kissing Spell KSLP 9203   GUITAR ABSOLUTION IN THE SHADE OF A MIDNIGHT SUN (LP, reissue of acetate-only album) ... 20
(see also Human Instinct)

JOE 'HARMONICA' HARPER
58   MGM MGM 983   Lazy Train/Her Lips Were Like Velvet 8

MIKE HARPER
70   Concord CON 026   You've Got Too Much Going For You/This Time 10
75   Tetreat RTS 264   I'm Crying /Goodbye 7

ROY HARPER
SINGLES
66   Strike JH 304   Take Me Into Your Eyes/Pretty Baby (in wraparound p/s) 100

Tim HARPER

MINT VALUE £

Year	Label/Cat#	Title	Value
66	Strike JH 304	Take Me Into Your Eyes/Pretty Baby	35
67	CBS 203001	Midspring Dithering/Zengem	20
68	CBS 3371	Life Goes By/Nobody's Got Any Money In The Summer	25
72	Harvest HAR 5059	Bank Of The Dead (Valerie's Song)/Little Lady (in p/s)	10
72	Harvest HAR 5059	Bank Of The Dead (Valerie's Song)/Little Lady	6
74	Harvest HAR 5080	(Don't You Think We're) Forever/Male Chauvinist Pig Blues	6
74	Harvest HAR 5089	Home (live)/Home (studio)	6
75	Harvest HAR 5096	When An Old Cricketer Leaves The Crease/Hallucinating Light (Acoustic Version) (p/s)	6
75	EMI PSR 407	Referendum/Another Day (live)/Tom Tiddler's Ground (live) (promo only)	8
77	Harvest HAR 5140	Sail Away/Cherishing The Lonesome (as Roy Harper's Black Sheep)	7
80	Harvest HAR 5203	Playing Games/First Thing In The Morning (p/s)	6
80	Harvest HAR 5207	Short And Sweet/Water Sports (live)/Unknown Soldier (live) (p/s)	6
83	Public PUBS 1002	I Still Care/Goodbye Ladybird (p/s)	6
88	Regal Zonophone HR 1	Laughing Inside/Laughing Inside (p/s, promo only; as Harry Rope)	10

ALBUMS : ORIGINAL LPS

Year	Label/Cat#	Title	Value
66	Strike JHL 105	SOPHISTICATED BEGGAR	500
67	CBS BPG 63184	COME OUT FIGHTING GHENGIS SMITH (mono, orange label)	100
67	CBS SBPG 63184	COME OUT FIGHTING GHENGIS SMITH (stereo, orange label)	120
69	Liberty LBL 83231	FOLKJOKEOPUS (mono, blue label)	125
69	Liberty LBS 83231	FOLKJOKEOPUS (stereo, blue label)	100
69	Harvest SHVL 766	FLAT, BAROQUE AND BERSERK (gatefold sleeve; first pressing with "H. Ash" label credit)	100
71	Harvest SHVL 789	STORMCOCK (gatefold sleeve with lyric insert, no EMI logo on label)	50
73	Harvest SHVL 808	LIFEMASK (foldout 'door' sleeve, with insert)	30
74	Harvest SHSP 4027	VALENTINE (1st pressing, with 'Made in GT. Britain' on bottom of label, initially with lyric booklet)	40
74	Harvest SHSP 4027	VALENTINE (1st pressing, with 'Made in GT. Britain' at bottom of label, without lyric booklet)	15
74	Harvest SHDW 405	FLASHES FROM THE ARCHIVES OF OBLIVION (2-LP, gatefold sleeve)	35
75	Harvest SHSP 4046	HQ (with lyric inner sleeve, EMI logo on label)	20
77	Harvest SHSP 4060	BULLINAMINGVASE (with inner sleeve & "Watford Gap"; some with 7" single, Referendum/"Another Day" (live)/"Tom Tiddler's Ground" [PSR 407])	20
77	Harvest SHSP 4060	BULLINAMINGVASE (2nd pressing with "Breakfast With You")	15
77	Harvest SHSP 4077	COMMERCIAL BREAK (unreleased; test pressing with proof sleeve)	300
78	Harvest	HARPER 1970-1975 (6-LP box set)	100
84	Hard Up PUB 5002	BORN IN CAPTIVITY (880 only)	30
92	Hard Up HU 2	BORN IN CAPTIVITY II (LIVE) (cassette)	15

ALBUMS : REISSUE ALBUMS

Year	Label/Cat#	Title	Value
71	Harvest SHVL 766	FLAT, BAROQUE AND BERSERK (gatefold sleeve; second pressing with "H. Ash" label credit and boxed EMI logo)	25
70	Young Blood SSYB 7	RETURN OF THE SOPHISTICATED BEGGAR (LP, with "Hup Hup Spiral" closed run-out groove, different sleeve)	20
71	Harvest SHVL 789	STORMCOCK (gatefold sleeve with lyric inner, with EMI logo on label)	20
73	Birth RAB 3	RETURN OF THE SOPHISTICATED BEGGAR (LP, 2nd reissue, with "Hup Hup Spiral" closed run-out groove, different sleeve)	15
74	Harvest SHSP 4027	VALENTINE (2nd pressing without 'Made in GT. Britain' at bottom of label, without lyric booklet)	15
75	Sunset SLS 50373	FOLKJOKEOPUS (LP)	15
77	Big Ben BBX 502	THE SOPHISTICATED BEGGAR (LP, different rear sleeve)	20
80	CBS (S) BPG 63184	COME OUT FIGHTING GHENGIS SMITH (LP, reissue)	15
86	Awareness AWL 1002	WORK OF HEART (LP, different sleeve with inner; 1st 1,000 with 2 x 7" "No One Gets Out Of Here Alive"/"Casualty (live) [PUBS 1001]" & "Still Care"/"Goodbye Ladybird" [PUBS2])	15
86	Awareness AWL 1002	WORK OF HEART (LP, different sleeve, 250 only on 'real time' quality tape)	15

(see also Rory Phare, Per Yarroh, Pink Floyd)

TIM HARPER

Year	Label/Cat#	Title	Value
95	Peacefrog PF 047	I Feel A Groove (12", plain sleeve)	18

TONI HARPER

Year	Label/Cat#	Title	Value
65	Vocalion VF 9239	Never Trust A Stranger/As Time Goes By	10

ROY HARPER & JIMMY PAGE

Year	Label/Cat#	Title	Value
85	Beggars Banquet BEGA 60	WHATEVER HAPPENED TO JUGULA? (LP)	15

HARPER'S BIZARRE

Year	Label/Cat#	Title	Value
67	Warner Bros WB 5890	59th Street Bridge Song (Feelin' Groovy)/Lost My Love Today	8
67	Warner Bros WB 7063	Anything Goes/Malibu U.	8
67	Warner Bros WB 7090	Chattanooga Choo Choo/Hey You In The Crowd	7
68	Warner Bros WB 7172	Cotton Candy Sandman's Coming)/Virginia City	6
68	Warner Bros WB 7223	Battle Of New Orleans/Green Apple Tree	7
69	Warner Bros WB 7238	I Love You, Alice B. Toklas!/Look To The Rainbow	6
67	Warner Bros W 1693	FEELIN' GROOVY (LP)	15
67	Warner Bros W 1716	ANYTHING GOES (LP)	20
68	Warner Bros W(S) 1739	THE SECRET LIFE OF HARPER'S BIZARRE (LP)	15

SLIM HARPO

Year	Label/Cat#	Title	Value
61	Pye International 7N 25098	Rainin' In My Heart/Don't Start Cryin' Now	25
63	Pye International 7N 25220	Don't Start Cryin' Now/Rainin' In My Heart	25
66	Stateside SS 491	Baby Scratch My Back/I'm Gonna Miss You (Like The Devil)	30
66	Stateside SS 527	Shake Your Hips/Midnight Blues	40
66	Stateside SS 557	I'm A King Bee/I Got Love If You Want It	50
67	Stateside SS 581	I'm Your Breadmaker Baby/Loving You (The Way I Do)	30
67	President PT 164	I'm Gonna Keep What I've Got/I've Got To Be With You Tonight	10
68	Liberty LBF 15176	Something Inside Me/PAPPA LIGHTFOOT: Wine Whisky And Women	30
68	President PT 187	Tip On In (Parts 1 & 2)	15

George HARRASSMENT & HOMOSEXUALS

MINT VALUE £

70	Blue Horizon 57-3175	Folsom Prison Blues/Mutual Friend	30
65	Stateside SL 10135	A LONG DRINK OF THE BLUES (LP, with Lightnin' Slim)	80
68	President PTL 1017	TIP ON IN (LP)	50
70	Blue Horizon 7-63854	HE KNEW THE BLUES (LP)	150
72	Blue Horizon 2431 013	TRIGGER FINGER (LP)	150
76	Flyright LP 520	BLUES HANGOVER (LP)	18
78	Sonet SNTF 769	HE KNEW THE BLUES (LP)	20
80	Flyright FLY 558	GOT LOVE IF YOU WANT IT (LP)	18

(see also Lightnin' Slim)

GEORGE HARRASSMENT & HOMOSEXUALS

| 80 | Black Noise 12 NO 6 | MASAI SLEEP WALKING (LP) | 35 |

(see also Homosexuals)

ROCQ-E HARRELL

| 89 | Nightmare MARES 113 | My Heart Keeps Beating Faster/Instrumental Version | 10 |

HARRIER

| 84 | Black Horse HARR 1T | OUT ON THE STREET EP (Out On The Street/Nickels And Dimes/Shine On) (12", p/s) | 15 |

DERRICK HARRIOT(T) (& CRYSTALITES)

62	Blue Beat BB 131	I Care/Have Faith In Me (as Derrick Harriott & Vagabonds)	15
63	Blue Beat BB 178	Be True/I Won't Cry	15
64	Island WI 157	What Can I Do (The Wedding)/Leona	15
65	Island WI 170	I Am Only Human (as Derak Harriott)/ROY PANTON: Good Man	30
65	Island WI 237	My Three Loves/The Jerk	40
65	Island WI 245	Together/Mama Didn't Lie	65
65	Ska Beat JB 199	Monkey Ska/Derrick!	50
66	Doctor Bird DB 1002	Jon Tom/AUDREY WILLIAMS: Solas Market	20
67	Island WI 3063	The Loser/Bless You	170
67	Island WI 3064	Happy Times/You My Everything	50
67	Island WI 3077	Walk The Streets/BOBBY ELLIS: Step Softly (B-side with Desmond Miles Seven)	80
67	Island WI 3089	Solomon/BOBBY ELLIS: The Emperor (B-side with Desmond Miles Seven)	75
68	Island WI 3135	Do I Worry?/BOBBY ELLIS & CRYSTALITES: Shuntin'	150
68	Island WI 3147	Born To Love You/IKE & CRYSTALITES: Alfred Hitchcock (existence unconfirmed)	40
68	Island WI 3153	Tang Tang Festival Song/CRYSTALITES: James Ray	125
69	Big Shot BI 505	Standing In/Bumble Bee	200
69	Big Shot BI 511	Another Lonely Night/Been So Long	100
70	Songbird SB 1013	Riding For A Fall/I'm Not Begging	130
70	Songbird SB 1014	Sitting On Top/You Were Meant For Me	160
70	Songbird SB 1022	Go Bye Bye/Laugh It Off	15
70	Songbird SB 1028	Message From A Black Man/(Version II)	15
70	Songbird SB 1029	Psychedelic Train (w/ Chosen Few)/Psychedelic Train (Pt. 2) (with Crystalites)	20
70	Songbird SB 1033	No Man Is An Island/CRYSTALITES: No Man Is An Island Part 2	10
70	Songbird SB 1042	Groovy Situation/CRYSTALITES: The Crystal Groove	10
70	Songbird SB 1043	Psychedelic Train Chapter Three/CRYSTALITES: Groovy Situation Version II	15
71	Songbird SB 1052	Candy/CRYSTALITES: Candy Version	7
71	Songbird SB 1055	Lollipop Girl/CRYSTALITES: Lollipop Version	15
71	Songbird SB 1063	Medley In 5 (Parts 1 & 2)	7
72	Songbird SB 1065	Have You Seen Her/CRYSTALITES: Have You Seen Her - Version	10
72	Songbird SB 1068	Over The River/River (Version)	10
72	Songbird SB 1071	Since I Lost My Baby/Baby (Version)	15
72	Songbird SB 1078	Being In Love/Love (Version)	10
72	Songbird SB 1084	Don't Rock The Boat/Rock (Version)	10
73	Attack ATT 8056	Brown Baby/CRYSTALITES: Brown Baby Version	20
73	Explosion EX 2071	Let Me Down Easy/Let Me Down Easy - Version	25
74	Harry J. HJ 6675	Some Guys Have All The Luck/Some Guys Have All The Luck - Version	10
65	Island ILP 928	THE BEST OF DERRICK HARRIOTT (LP)	175
67	Island ILP 955	DERRICK HARRIOTT'S ROCKSTEADY PARTY (LP, actually v/a LP)	500
68	Island ILP 983	THE BEST OF VOLUME TWO (LP, as Derrick Harriott & Crystalites)	250
69	Pama SECO 13	SINGS JAMAICA REGGAE (LP)	200
70	Trojan TTL 43	THE BEST OF DERRICK HARRIOTT (LP)	80
70	Trojan TTL 54	ROCKSTEADY PARTY (LP)	80
70	Trojan TBL 114	THE UNDERTAKER (LP, as Derrick Harriott & Crystalites)	75
70	Trojan TBL 141	PSYCHEDELIC TRAIN (LP, as Derrick Harriott & Crystalites)	90
75	Charmers LP 5	REGGAE DISCO ROCKERS (LP)	20
75	Trojan TRLS 116	GREATEST REGGAE HITS (LP)	20
81	Trojan TRTS 198	SONGS FOR MIDNIGHT LOVERS (LP)	15
95	Dr. Buster Dynamite DBD 108	FOR A FISTFUL OF JAMAICAN DOLLARS (LP, reissue of the Undertaker)	25

JOE HARRIOTT

56	Jazz Today JTE 106	WITH STRINGS (EP)	40
56	Pye Jazz NJE 1003	NO STRINGS (EP)	80
57	Columbia SEG 7665	JOE HARRIOTT QUARTET (EP)	100
59	Columbia SEG 7939	BLUE HARRIOTT (EP)	60
60	Melodisc EPM7 117	COOL JAZZ WITH JOE (EP)	75
61	Columbia SEG 8070	A GUY CALLED JOE (EP)	45
09	Gearbox GB 1503	BBC JAZZ FOR MODERNS (12" EP, p/s)	12
60	Jazzland JLP 49	FREE FORM (LP)	200
62	Columbia 33SX 1477	ABSTRACT (LP)	400
63	Columbia 33SX 1627	MOVEMENT (LP)	750
64	Columbia 33SX 1692	HIGH SPIRITS (LP)	750
67	Melodisc SLP 12150	SWINGS HIGH (LP)	200
66	Columbia SX/SCX 6025	INDO-JAZZ SUITE (LP, with John Mayer)	75

Joe HARRIOTT/DON RENDELL QUARTET

MINT VALUE £

Year	Label/Cat#	Title	Value
67	Columbia S(C) 6122	INDO-JAZZ FUSIONS (LP, with John Mayer)	50
68	Columbia S(C)X 6215	INDO-JAZZ FUSIONS II (LP, with John Mayer)	50
68	Columbia S(C)X 6249	PERSONAL PORTRAIT (LP)	100
69	Columbia SCX 6354	HUM-DONO (LP, with Amancio D'Silva)	1000
73	One Up OU 2011	MEMORIAL 1973 (LP)	50
89	Cadillac SGC/MLP 12-150	SWINGS HIGH (LP, reissue)	20
11	Gearbox GB 1506	PARTYING WITH JOE (LP)	20
11	Moonlighting MT 001	JOURNEY (LP)	15
14	Doxy DOK 230	FREE FORM (LP, reissue)	15
14	Doxy ACV 2040	ABSTRACT (LP, reissue, clear vinyl)	15
15	Vocalion VOCLP 3203	HUM-DONO (LP, reissue, with Amancio D'Silva)	15

(see also Tony Kinsey Trio & Joe Harriott, John Mayer, Michael Garrick)

JOE HARRIOTT/DON RENDELL QUARTET

Year	Label/Cat#	Title	Value
57	MGM MGM-EP 615	JAZZ BRITANNIA (EP, 2 tracks each)	60

(see also Don Rendell)

ANITA HARRIS

Year	Label/Cat#	Title	Value
61	Parlophone R 4830	I Haven't Got You/Mr One And Only	10
64	Vocalion V 9223	Lies/Don't Think About Love	6
65	Decca F 12082	Willingly/At Last Love	6
65	Pye 7N 15868	Trains And Boats And Planes/Upside Down	6
65	Pye 7N 15894	I Don't Know Anymore/When I Look At You	6
65	Pye 7N 15971	London Life/I Run To Hide	8
66	Pye 7N 17069	Something Must Be Done/Funny Kind Of Feeling	10
67	CBS 2991	The Playground/B.A.D. For Me	10
67	Pye NEP 24288	ANITA HARRIS (EP)	12
68	CBS EP 6401	DREAM A LITTLE DREAM OF ME (EP)	12
66	CBS BGP/SBPG 62894	SOMEBODY'S IN MY ORCHARD (LP)	15

(see also Brello Cabal)

ARTIE HARRIS & HIS BOYS

Year	Label/Cat#	Title	Value
63	Oriole CB 1816	Go Go Gaudeamus/Mexicana	8

BETTY HARRIS

Year	Label/Cat#	Title	Value
63	London HL 9796	Cry To Me/I'll Be A Liar	20
65	Stateside SS 475	What A Sad Feeling/I'm Evil Tonight	30
67	Stateside SS 2045	Nearer To You/12 Red Roses	20
69	Action ACT 4535	Ride Your Pony/Trouble With My Lover	60
80	Charly CTD 102	BETTY HARRIS EP	10
69	Action ACLP 6007	SOUL PERFECTION (LP)	100

(see also Betty Harris & Lee Dorsey)

BOBBY HARRIS

Year	Label/Cat#	Title	Value
73	London 10435	Sticky Sticky/Mr. Success	7

BRENDA JO HARRIS

Year	Label/Cat#	Title	Value
69	Roulette RO 503	I Can Remember/Play With Fire	7

CALVIN HARRIS

Year	Label/Cat#	Title	Value
08	Ministry Of Sound MINISTRY 065	I CREATED DISCO (2-LP)	50

EDDIE HARRIS

Year	Label/Cat#	Title	Value
69	Atlantic 584 218	Listen Here/Theme - In Search Of A Movie	10
69	Atlantic 584 232	It's Crazy/Live Right Now (unissued)	0
74	Atlantic K 10513	Is It In?/Funkarama	7
75	Atlantic K 10561	I Need Some Money/Don't Want Nobody	7

EMMYLOU HARRIS

Year	Label/Cat#	Title	Value
95	Gravevine GRALP 102	WRECKING BALL (LP)	50

GENE HARRIS & THE THREE SOUNDS

Year	Label/Cat#	Title	Value
96	Blue Note BN 724383533817	LIVE AT THE IT CLUB (LP)	18

JERRY HARRIS

Year	Label/Cat#	Title	Value
82	Prodeduce JAH 185	I'm So Glad/Natural Feelings/Natural Feeling Version (12")	10

JET HARRIS

Year	Label/Cat#	Title	Value
62	Decca F 11466	Besame Mucho/Chills And Fever	8
62	Decca F 11488	Main Title Theme (from The Man With The Golden Arm)/Some People	6
64	Decca F 11841	Big Bad Bass/Rifka	8
67	Fontana TF 849	My Lady/You Don't Live Twice	25
75	SRT SRT 75355	Theme For A Fallen Idol/This Sportin' Life (initial pressing)	10
75	SRT SRT 75355	Theme/This Sportin' Life (later pressing with shortened A-side title)	10
78	SRT SRT 77389	Guitar Man/Theme	10
62	Decca DFE 8502	JET HARRIS (EP)	25
78	Ellie Jay EJSP 8622	INSIDE JET HARRIS - THE LAST CONCERT (LP, 2,500 only)	20
70s	Q LPMM 1038	ANNIVERSARY ALBUM (LP)	20

(see also Shadows, Jet Harris & Tony Meehan, Keith Meehan, Peter Rawes)

JET HARRIS & TONY MEEHAN

Year	Label/Cat#	Title	Value
63	Decca F 11710	Applejack/The Tall Texan	6
63	Decca DFE 8528	JET AND TONY (EP)	12

(see also Shadows, Jet Harris, Tony Meehan, Vipers Skiffle Group)

JOHNNY HARRIS

Year	Label/Cat#	Title	Value
65	Mercury MF 942	Mynah Hop/Here Comes The Boot	15
69	Warner Bros WB 8000	Footprints On The Moon/Lulu's Theme	10
70	Warner Bros WB 8016	Fragment Of Fear/Stepping Stones	25
70	Warner Bros WS 3002	MOVEMENTS (LP, 1st pressing with orange labels)	50
72	Warner Bros K 46054	MOVEMENTS (LP, reissue)	25
73	Warner Bros K 46187	ALL TO BRING YOU MORNING (LP)	15

JUNE HARRIS
65	CBS 201774	Over And Over Again/Stand Back	12

LENNY HARRIS
84	Soul Stop 3008	Long After Tonight Is All Over/Impressions	10

MAX HARRIS
69	Pye 7N 17730	Theme From The Film 'Baby Love'/Roberts Theme From 'Baby Love'	6

OSCAR HARRIS
70	Upfront UPF 6	T.O.P/I Don't Wanna Listen	10

PAT HARRIS & BLACKJACKS
63	Pye 7N 15567	The Hippy Hippy Shake/You Gotta See Your Mama Ev'ry Night	25

(see also Blackjacks)

PHIL HARRIS
54	HMV 7M 199	I Know An Old Lady/Take Your Girlie To The Movies	8
54	HMV 7M 231	I Guess I'll Have To Change My Plan/The Persian Kitten	8
55	HMV 7M 289	I Wouldn't Touch You With A Ten-Foot Pole/There's A Lot More	8

RONNIE HARRIS (& CORONETS)
56	Columbia DB 3836	That's Right/A House With Love In It	10

(see also Coronets, Ruby Murray, Ray Burns)

ROY HARRIS
72	Topic 12TS 217	THE BITTER AND THE SWEET (LP, blue label)	15

SCOTT HARRIS
68	Morgan MR7S	Barry Johnson's Sad Eyes Inn/Morning Sun	30

SHAKEY JAKE HARRIS
69	Liberty LBS 83215	FURTHER ON UP THE ROAD (LP)	50
73	Polydor 2391 015	THE DEVIL'S HARMONICA (LP)	20

SUZANNE HARRIS
69	Polydor 56354	Sure That's What God Said/It's A Long Way From The Movies/Go Out And Multiply/Are You	15
70	R.F.S. Records RFS 8280	Here Come The Beautiful People/We're Using Up The World (p/s)	20

THURSTON HARRIS (& SHARPS)
57	Vogue V 9092	Little Bitty Pretty One/I Hope You Won't Hold It Against Me (with Sharps)	200
58	Vogue V 9098	Do What You Did/I'm Asking Forgiveness (as Thurston Harris & Sharps)	250
57	Vogue V 9092	Little Bitty Pretty One/I Hope You Won't Hold It Against Me (with Sharps) (78)	30
58	Vogue V 9098	Do What You Did/I'm Asking Forgiveness (as Thurston Harris & Sharps) (78)	20
58	Vogue V 9108	Be Baba Leba/I'm Out To Getcha	250
58	Vogue V 9108	Be Baba Leba/I'm Out To Getcha (78)	20
58	Vogue V 9122	Smokey Joe's/Only One Love Is Blessed	150
58	Vogue V 9122	Smokey Joe's/Only One Love Is Blessed (78)	20
58	Vogue V 9127	Tears From My Heart/Over Somebody Else's Shoulder	100
58	Vogue V 9127	Tears From My Heart/Over Somebody Else's Shoulder (78)	20
59	Vogue V 9139	Purple Stew (as Thurston Harris & Masters)/I Hear A Rhapsody	150
59	Vogue V 9139	Purple Stew (as Thurston Harris & Masters)/I Hear A Rhapsody (78)	20
59	Vogue V 9144	You Don't Know How Much I Love You/In The Bottom Of My Heart	100
59	Vogue V 9144	You Don't Know How Much I Love You/In The Bottom Of My Heart (78)	20
59	Vogue V 9146	Hey Little Girl/My Love Will Last	150
59	Vogue V 9146	Hey Little Girl/My Love Will Last (78)	30
59	Vogue V 9149	Runk Bunk/Bless Your Heart	150
59	Vogue V 9149	Runk Bunk/Bless Your Heart (78)	30
59	Vogue V 9151	Slip-Slop/Paradise Hill	200
59	Vogue V 9151	Slip-Slop/Paradise Hill (78)	40
66	Sue WI 4016	Little Bitty Pretty One/I Hope You Won't Hold It Against Me (reissue)	50

(see also Sharps)

WEE WILLIE HARRIS
57	Decca F 10970	Rockin' At The Two 'I's/Back To School Again	40
58	Decca F 10980	Love Bug Crawl/Rosie Lee	40
58	Decca F 11044	Got A Match/No Chemise, Please!	20
60	Decca F 11217	Wild One/Little Bitty Girl	20
63	HMV POP 1198	You Must Be Joking/Better To Have Loved	15
66	Parlophone R 5504	Someone's In The Kitchen With Diana/Walk With Peter And Paul (some A-sides list 'Dina')	10
66	Polydor 56140	Listen To The River Roll Along/Try Moving Baby (writing in black or white)	30
74	Decca F 13516	Together/Rock'n'Roll Jamboree	8
58	Decca DFE 6465	ROCKING WITH WEE WILLIE (EP)	150

WYNONIE 'MR BLUES' HARRIS
56	Vogue V 2127	Bloodshot Eyes/Lollipop Mama (triangular centre)	100
56	Vogue V 2127	Bloodshot Eyes/Lollipop Mama (round centre)	40
56	Vogue EPV 1103	WYNONIE 'MISTER BLUES' HARRIS (EP)	60
61	Blue Beat BBEP 301	BATTLE OF THE BLUES (EP)	80

WYNONIE HARRIS/EDDIE 'CLEANHEAD' VINSON
72	Polydor 2343 048	JUMP BLUES (LP)	15

(see also Tiny Bradshaw/Wynonie Harris, Eddie 'Cleanhead' Vinson)

HARRISON
84	Skipping Rope SKIP 1	There Is No Refrain/Simply This (p/s)	40

DANNY HARRISON
62	Starlite ST45 77	No One To Love Me/All The World is Lonely	6
62	Starlite ST45 91	Broken Love Affair/Have I Wasted My Life	6
63	Starlite ST45 108	Have You Ever Been Lonely/Mary Ann I'm Lonesome	6
65	Coral Q 72479	Speak Of The Devil/I'm A Rollin' Stone	15
62	Starlite STEP 23	INTRODUCING DANNY HARRISON (EP)	20

EARL HARRISON
67	London HL 10121	Humphrey Stomp/Can You Forgive Me	50

George HARRISON

MINT VALUE £

| 67 | London HL 10121 | Humphrey Stomp/Can You Forgive Me (DJ Copy) | 100 |

GEORGE HARRISON
SINGLES

Year	Label/Cat#	Title	Value
71	Apple R 5884	My Sweet Lord/What Is Life (in colour 'head' p/s)	12
71	Apple R5912	Bangla-Desh/Deep Blue (Demo copy)	70
71	Apple R 5912	Bangla-Desh/Deep Blue (with rare p/s [beware of new-looking counterfeits!])	80
73	Apple R 5988	Give Me Love (Give Me Peace On Earth)/Miss O'Dell (Demo copy)	70
74	Apple R 6001	Dark Horse/I Don't Care Anymore (unissued)	0
75	Apple R 6001	Dark Horse/Hari's On Tour (Express) (p/s)	10
75	Apple R 6007	You/World Of Stone (p/s)	8
76	Apple R 6012	This Guitar (Can't Keep From Crying)/Maya Love (no p/s)	35
76	Apple R 5884	My Sweet Lord/What Is Life (reissue, black & white 'gnome' p/s)	10
76	Dark Horse K 16856	This Song/Learning How To Love You (issued with U.S. p/s)	10
77	Dark Horse K 16896	True Love/Pure Smokey (no p/s)	6
77	Dark Horse K 16967	It's What You Value/Woman Don't You Cry For Me (no p/s)	15
79	Dark Horse K 17284	Love Comes To Everyone/Soft Hearted Hana	15
79	Dark Horse K 17423	Faster/Your Love Is Forever (with charity stickered plain white die-cut sleeve)	15
79	Dark Horse K 17423	Faster/Your Love Is Forever (picture disc, stickered PVC sleeve with insert)	30
81	Dark Horse K 17837DJ	Teardrops (Edited Version)/Save The World (DJ promo only, no p/s)	25
81	Dark Horse K 17837	Teardrops/Save The World (p/s)	10
82	Dark Horse 929 864-7	Wake Up My Love/Greece (p/s)	8
86	Ganga Publishing B.V.	Shanghai Surprise (with Vicki Brown) (unreleased, 1-sided promo only; no catalogue number, matrix: SHANGHAI 1)	500
87	Dark Horse W 8178B	Got My Mind Set On You/Lay His Head (box set with 2 postcards)	20
87	Dark Horse W 8178T	Got My Mind Set On You (Extended Version)/Got My Mind Set On You (Single Version)/Lay His Head (12", p/s with poster)	15
87	Dark Horse W 8178TP	Got My Mind Set On You (Extended Version)/Got My Mind Set On You (Single Version)/Lay His Head (12", picture disc)	20
88	Dark Horse W 8131B	When We Was Fab/Zig Zag (box set with fold-out poster & cut-out)	10
88	Dark Horse W 8131T	When We Was Fab (Unextended Version)/Zig Zag/That's The Way It Goes (Remix)/When We Was Fab (Reverse End) (12", p/s)	10
88	Dark Horse W 8131TP	When We Was Fab (Unextended Version)/Zig Zag/That's The Way It Goes (Remix)/When We Was Fab (Reverse End) (12", picture disc)	20
88	Dark Horse W 7913	This Is Love/Breath Away From Heaven (p/s)	8
88	Dark Horse W 7913T	This Is Love/Breath Away From Heaven/All Those Years Ago (12", p/s)	15
89	Dark Horse W 2696	Cheer Down/That's What It Takes (p/s)	8
89	Dark Horse W 2696T	Cheer Down/That's What It Takes/Crackerbox Palace (12", p/s)	15
20	Parlophone 8EOO604692M	My Sweet Lord/Isn't It A Pity (p/s)	8
88	Genesis SGH 777	SONGS BY GEORGE HARRISON (Limited Edition) (EP, 33rpm, issued with limited edition book Songs By George Harrison)	900
88	Genesis SGHCD 777	SONGS BY GEORGE HARRISON (CD EP, issued with limited edition book)	800
92	Genesis SGH 778	SONGS BY GEORGE HARRISON VOL. 2 (EP, with limited edition book Songs By George Harrison Vol. 2)	400
92	Genesis SGHCD 778	SONGS BY GEORGE HARRISON VOL. 2 (CD EP, with limited edition book)	600
03	Parlophone R 6601	Any Road/Marwa Blues (p/s)	7

ALBUMS

Year	Label/Cat#	Title	Value
68	Apple APCOR 1	WONDERWALL MUSIC (soundtrack; with insert, black inner sleeve, mono)	250
68	Apple SAPCOR 1	WONDERWALL MUSIC (soundtrack; with insert, black inner sleeve, stereo)	100
69	Zapple ZAPPLE 02	ELECTRONIC SOUND (with inner sleeve)	200
71	Apple STCH 639	ALL THINGS MUST PASS (3-LP box set with poster & lyric inner sleeves; initial batch in U.K. Box)	200
71	Apple STCH 639	ALL THINGS MUST PASS (3-LP box set with poster & lyric inner sleeves; later batch in U.S. box)	100
72	Apple STCX 3385	THE CONCERT FOR BANGLA DESH (3-LP box set, orange inside with BMI/ASCAP label credits, with booklet, featuring Bob Dylan)	75
73	Apple PAS 10006	LIVING IN THE MATERIAL WORLD (gatefold sleeve with inner)	18
74	Apple PAS 10008	DARK HORSE (LP, gatefold sleeve, inner sleeve, lyric insert)	30
75	Apple PAS 10009	EXTRA TEXTURE (LP with inner)	30
76	Dark Horse K56319	THIRTY THREE AND A THIRD (LP, gatefold with inner)	20
82	Dark Horse 923734-1	GONE TROPPO (LP, with inner)	20
87	Dark Horse 925643-1	CLOUD NINE (LP, with inner)	20
91	EPIC EPC 468835 1	THE CONCERT FOR BANGLA DESH (3-LP set in single sleeve)	25
92	Dark Horse 759926964-1	LIVE IN JAPAN (2xLP in single sleeve)	40
92	Apple SAPCOR 1	WONDERWALL MUSIC (reissue, gatefold sleeve with inner sleeve)	20
96	Zapple ZAPPLE 02	ELECTRONIC SOUND (reissue, with inner sleeve)	40
01	Parlophone 5304741	ALL THINGS MUST PASS (3-LP, reissue)	100
02	Dark Horse 5419691	BRAINWASHED (Gatefold LP with sticker on cover)	35
04	Apple/UMC 060253791387	THE APPLE YEARS (box set, 7-CD, DVD, booklet)	100
13	Universal 060253704439	EARLY TAKES VOL. 1 (LP, clear vinyl)	15
17	Apple STCH 639	ALL THINGS MUST PASS (3-LP reissue, poster)	50
17	Apple 0602557090277	THE VINYL COLLECTION (box set, 16 x LP, 2 x 12" picture discs)	250

(see also Beatles, Traveling Wilburys, Billy Connolly & Chris Tummings, Sylvia Griffin)

JAYE HARRISON

| 77 | Ember EMBS 351 | Value For Money/Instrumental Version | 8 |

MIKE HARRISON

75	Good Ear 611	We Can Work It Out/Maverick Woman Blues	8
71	Island ILPS 9170	MIKE HARRISON (LP, gatefold sleeve, pink rim, palm tree label)	40
72	Island ILPS 9209	SMOKESTACK LIGHTNING (LP, laminated sleeve, pink rim, palm tree label)	30
75	Good Ear EAR 7002	RAINBOW RIDER (LP)	20

(see also Art, Spirit, Spooky Tooth)

NEIL HARRISON
			MINT VALUE £
74	Decca F13520	Sad Eyes/Bicycle Driver	10

(see also Driftwood)

NOEL HARRISON
65	Decca F 12001	Trees/To Ramona	6
66	Decca F 12314	A Young Girl Of Sixteen/Tomorrow Is My Turn	6
66	Decca F 12345	It's All Over Now Baby Blue/Much As I Love You	6
67	Reprise RS 20615	Suzanne/Life Is A Dream	6
69	Reprise RS23395	Sparrow/California Weekend	10
69	Decca F12878	Young Girl (Of Sixteen)/She's A Woman	7
69	Decca F 12918	Love Minus Zero/No Limit/Just Can't Wait	6
57	HMV 7EG 8383	NOEL HARRISON (EP)	15
65	Decca DFE 8616	NOEL HARRISON (EP)	10
65	Decca DFE 8639	TO RAMONA (EP)	12
60	Philips BBL 7399	AT THE BLUE ANGEL (LP)	20
69	Reprise RSLP 6321	THE GREAT ELECTRIC EXPERIMENT IS OVER (LP)	15

REGGIE HARRISON
63	Cameo Parkway P 863	A Lonely Piano/HIPPIES: Memory Lane	20

VALERIE HARRISON
81	B&B BBD 135	Golden Touch/You're No Good (12")	15
81	B&B BBLP 1001	GOLDEN TOUCH (LP)	35

WILBERT HARRISON
59	Top Rank JAR 132	Kansas City/Listen My Darling	20
59	Top Rank JAR 132	Kansas City/Listen My Darling (78)	30
62	Island WI 031	I'm Broke/Off To School	20
65	Sue WI 363	Let's Stick Together/Kansas City Twist	40
70	London HL 10307	Let's Work Together/Stagger Lee	15
73	Action ACT 4613	Get It While You Can/Amen	8
70	London HA/SH 8415	LET'S WORK TOGETHER (LP)	40
85	Charly CRB 1102	LOVIN...PERATOR (LP)	15

YVONNE HARRISON
67	Caltone TONE 102	The Chase/Take My Hand	100
75	Camel CA 2003	Knotty Screw Face/UNDERGROUND PEOPLE: Face Dub	12

HARRIS SISTERS
55	Capitol CL 14232	Kissin' Bug/We've Been Walkin' All Night	20

KEVIN HARRISON
81	Cherry Red BRED 16	INSCRUTABLY OBVIOUS (LP)	40

DEBBIE/DEBORAH HARRY
93	Chrysalis TC-CHS 4900	I Can See Clearly/Standing In My Way (B-side with Joey Ramone)	7

(see also Wind In The Willows, Blondie, New York Blondes)

HARRY J. ALL STARS
69	Harry J TR 694	Spyrone/JOHN HOLT: Have Sympathy	40
69	Harry J. TR 675	Liquidator/GLEN & DAVE: La La Always Stay (green label)	8
70	Harry J. HJ 6601	The Big Three/Lavender (B-side actually "Lavender Blue" by Lloyd Robinson)	25
70	Harry J. HJ 6608	Reach For The Sky/Interrogator	12
70	Harry J. HJ 6621	Return Of The Liquidator (actually "Tons Of Gold" by Val Bennett)/All Day	30
72	Harry J. HJ 6641	Down Side Up/Down Side Up - Version	8
73	Blue Mountain BM 1028	U.F.O./Reggae With The Birds	12
70	Trojan TBL 104	THE LIQUIDATOR (LP)	35

(see also Jay Boys, Bob Andy, John Holt, Lizzy)

HARRY & RADCLIFFE
69	Camel CA 26	History/Just Be Alone	60
69	Punch PH 8	History/Just Be Alone	8

WARREN HARRY
76	Sonet SON-2088	I don't Care/Backwards Forwards	15
78	HAH 1/EJSP-8632	1965/Radio Show (500 only, no p/s)	30

HARSH REALITY
68	Philips PB 1710	Tobacco Ash Sunday/How Do You Feel	30
69	Philips PB 1769	Heaven And Hell/Praying For Reprieve	30
69	Philips (S)BL 7891	HEAVEN AND HELL (LP, gatefold sleeve, blue/silver labels)	500

(see also Matthews Southern Comfort)

CAJUN HART
69	Warner Bros WB 7258	Got To Find A Way/Lover's Prayer	700
69	Warner Bros WB 7258	Got To Find A Way/Lover's Prayer (DJ Copy)	800
06	Warner Bros WB 7258	Got To Find A Way/LINDA JONES: A Last Minute Miracle (A-label reissue)	20

DERRY HART & HARTBEATS
59	Decca F 11138	Come On Baby/Nowhere In This World	25

MICKEY HART
73	Warner Bros. K 46182	ROLLING THUNDER (LP)	15

(see also Grateful Dead, Diga Rhythm Band)

MIKE HART
70	Dandelion S 4781	Yawney Morning Song/Almost Liverpool 8	7
74	Deram DM 409	Son Son/Bad News Man	6
70	Dandelion 63756	MIKE HART BLEEDS (LP, black/red/silver labels)	50
72	Dandelion 2310 211	BASHER, CHALKY, PONGO AND ME (LP, as Mike Hart & Comrades)	50

(see also Clayton Squares, Liverpool Scene)

TIM HART
79	Chrysalis CHR 2335	Overseas/Hillman Avenger (p/s)	7

(see also Steeleye Span)

Tim HART & MADDY PRIOR

MINT VALUE £

TIM HART & MADDY PRIOR
68	Tepee TPRM 104	FOLK SONGS OF OLDE ENGLAND VOL. 1 (LP, gatefold sleeve)	100
69	Tepee TPRM 105	FOLK SONGS OF OLDE ENGLAND VOL. 2 (LP, gatefold sleeve)	100
69	Ad-Rhythm ARPS 3	FOLK SONGS OF OLDE ENGLAND VOL. 1 (LP, reissue)	25
69	Ad-Rhythm ARPS 4	FOLK SONGS OF OLDE ENGLAND VOL. 2 (LP, reissue)	25
71	B& C CAS 1035	SUMMER SOLSTICE (LP, gatefold sleeve)	30

(see also Steeleye Span, Maddy Prior)

CIARAN HARTE
80	Glass 003	Love Is Strange/Shimahero (p/s)	20

HARTLEPOOL FC
72	United Artists UP 35358	Who Put The Sugar In My Tea/Never Say Die	10

KEEF HARTLEY (BAND)
69	Deram DM 250	Leave It 'Till The Morning/Just To Cry	12
69	Deram DM 273	Waiting Around/Not Foolish, Not Wise	12
70	Deram DM 316	Roundabout (Parts 1 & 2)	12
73	Deram DM 380	Dance To The Music/You And Me	8
69	Deram DML 1037	HALFBREED (LP, mono, gatefold sleeve, 1st pressing has 'mono/stereo' holes on rear sleeve, white/red label)	100
69	Deram SML 1037	HALFBREED (LP, stereo, gatefold sleeve, 1st pressing has 'mono/stereo' holes on rear sleeve, white/red label)	80
69	Deram DML 1054	THE BATTLE OF N.W.6 (LP, mono, gatefold sleeve, 1st pressing with 'mono/stereo' holes on rear sleeve, white/red labels)	100
69	Deram SML 1054	THE BATTLE OF N.W.6 (LP, stereo, gatefold sleeve, 1st pressing with 'mono/stereo' holes on rear sleeve, white/red labels)	80
70	Deram SML 1071	THE TIME IS NEAR (LP, with booklet, white/red labels with small logo)	100
70	Deram SML 1071	THE TIME IS NEAR (LP, without booklet, white/red labels with small logo)	80
71	Deram SDL 2	OVERDOG (LP, gatefold sleeve, white/brown labels with small logo)	60
71	Deram SDL 4	LITTLE BIG BAND (LP, white/brown label, gatefold sleeve)	60
72	Deram SDL 9	SEVENTY SECOND BRAVE (LP, gatefold sleeve)	50
73	Deram SDL 13	LANCASHIRE HUSTLER (LP, gatefold sleeve, as Keeg Hartley)	40
74	Deram DPA 3011/2	THE BEST OF (2-LP, gatefold sleeve)	20

(see also Rory Storm & Hurricanes, Artwoods, John Mayall's Bluesbreakers, Miller Anderson, Dog Soldier, Henry Lowther, Wynder K. Frog)

TREVOR HARTLEY
79	Jah Child JC 002	Africa/Repatriation Version (12")	35
80	Matumbi MA 006	Selassi I/Skip Away (12", p/s)	30
80	Jungle Beat JB DC 808	Mama Say Son/Oppression (12")	80
86	Fu Manchu FU 001	It Must Be Love/Version (12")	10
79	Burning Rockers BR1011	INNOCENT LOVER (LP)	25

HARVEST
80	Secular Records SEC 001	Fashion Parade/Will You Be The One	70

HARVEST MINISTERS
92	Sarah SARAH 64	You Do My World The World Of Good/Petticoats (p/s, insert)	30
92	Sarah SARAH 68	Six O'Clock Is Rosary/The First Star (p/s, insert)	30
93	Sarah SARAH 84	If It Kills Me And It Will/Can Go It Alone (p/s, insert)	30
93	Sarah SARAH 616	LITTLE DARK MANSIONS (LP)	50

HARVESTERS
72	Westwood WRS 015	THE HARVESTERS (LP)	25

ALEX HARVEY (1) AKA THE SENSATIONAL ALEX HARVEY BAND
64	Polydor NH 52264	I Just Wanna Make Love To You/Let The Good Times Roll	60
64	Polydor NH 52907	Got My Mojo Working/I Ain't Worried Baby (as Alex Harvey & His Soul Band)	60
65	Polydor BM 56017	Ain't That Just Too Bad/My Kind Of Love (as Alex Harvey & His Soul Band)	60
65	Fontana TF 610	Agent 00 Soul/Go Away Baby	40
66	Fontana TF 764	Work Song/I Can Do Without Your Love	25
67	Decca F 12640	The Sunday Song/Horizon's	50
67	Decca F 12660	Maybe Some Day/Curtains For My Baby	60
69	Fontana TF 1063	Midnight Moses/Roman Wall Blues	70
72	Vertigo 6059 070	There's No Lights On The Christmas Tree Mother, (They're Burning Big Louie Tonight)/Harp	40
76	Mountain PSLP 183	Amos Moses/$25 For A Massage (promo only 12")	12
77	Mountain TOP 32	Mrs Blackhouse/Engine Room Boogie (p/s)	6
64	Polydor LPHM 46424	ALEX HARVEY AND HIS SOUL BAND (LP)	250
64	Polydor LPHM 46441	THE BLUES (LP)	200
69	Fontana (S)TL 5534	ROMAN WALL BLUES (LP)	400
73	Vertigo 6360 081	FRAMED (LP, as The Sensational Alex Harvey Band, gatefold sleeve, small swirl label)	200
72	Vertigo 6360 081	FRAMED (LP, as The Sensational Alex Harvey Band, gatefold sleeve, later spaceship label)	30
73	Vertigo 6360 103	NEXT (LP, as The Sensational Alex Harvey Band, spaceship label, 1st pressing, side 1 Matrix 1Y//1 1 6 3)	20
74	Vertigo 6360 112	THE IMPOSSIBLE DREAM (LP, gatefold sleeve, spaceship label)	15
75	Vertigo 9102 003	TOMORROW BELONGS TO ME (LP, gatefold sleeve, spaceship label)	15
77	K-Tel NE 984	ALEX HARVEY PRESENTS THE LOCH NESS MONSTER (LP, withdrawn, gatefold stickered sleeve, with 16-page 'descriptive diary')	50
78	Mountain TOPS 114	ROCK DRILL (with 'No Complaints Department'.)	35
78	Mountain TOPS 114	ROCK DRILL (Later copies with revised Track listing stickered on sleeve)	15
83	Power Supply AMP 2	THE SOLDIER ON THE WALL (LP, solo)	20

(see also Tear Gas, Hairband, Rock Workshop, Nazareth, Michael Schenker Group, Tandoori)

ALEX HARVEY (2)
71	Capitol E-ST 789	ALEX HARVEY (LP)	15

CARL HARVEY MEETS THE DUB MASTER
78	Cancer CANLP 003	ECSTACY OF MANKIND (LP)	40

JANCIS HARVEY
73	Pilgrim King KLPS 47	DISTANCE OF DOORS (LP)	45

Jane HARVEY

MINT VALUE £

73	Westwood WRS 029	WORDS YOU LEFT BEHIND (LP)	60
74	Westwood WRS 038	JANCIS HARVEY (LP)	60
75	Westwood WRS 054	TIME WAS NOW (LP)	60
76	Westwood WRS 107	A PORTRAIT OF JANCIS HARVEY (LP)	45
79	Westwood WRS 144	FROM THE DARKNESS CAME LIGHT (LP)	40

JANE HARVEY
60	Pye International 7N 25046	I'm Gonna Go Fishin'/Hundred Dreams From Now	6

LANCE HARVEY & KINGPINS
64	Pye 7N 15647	He's Telling You Lies/How Do You Fix A Broken Heart	10
64	Lyntone LYN 509	SINCE YOU WALKED OUT ON ME (Keele Rag flexidisc EP, with The Escorts)	15

MICK HARVEY
97	Mute STUMM 157	PINK ELEPHANTS (LP, inner)	25

(see also Nick Cave)

HARVEY (FUQUA) & MOONGLOWS
58	London HLM 8730	Ten Commandments Of Love/Mean Old Blues	300
58	London HLM 8730	Ten Commandments Of Love/Mean Old Blues (78)	50

(see also Moonglows, Etta & Harvey)

PETER HARVEY
62	Columbia DB 4873	Rainin' In My Heart/Please Don't Tell Joe	7

P.J. HARVEY
90	Private Pressing	P. J. Harvey (3-track demo, 'wooden' p/s includes pictures of P. J. and lyrics to Dress)	80
91	Too Pure PURE 5	Dress/Water (demo)/Dry (demo) (12")	20
92	Too Pure PURES 8	Sheela-Na-Gig/Joe (p/s, 400 only)	45
92	Too Pure PURE 8	Sheela-Na-Gig/Hair (demo)/Joe (demo) (12", p/s)	25
93	Island IS 538	50Ft Queenie/Reeling/Man-Size (Demo)	10
93	Island 12IS 538	50 Ft Queenie/Mansize (demo)/Hook (demo)/Reeling (12", p/s)	18
93	Island 12IS 569	Mansize/Wang Dang Doodle/Daddy (12", p/s)	20
95	Island IS 607	Down By the Water/Lying In The Sun/Somebody's Down Somebody's Name (p/s)	12
95	Island 12IS 614	C'Mon Billy/Darling Be There/Maniac (12", p/s)	15
95	Island IS 610	Send His Love To Me/Long Time Coming (Evening Session) (picture disc in 12" poster p/s)	15
95	Island CIDD J610	Send His Love To Me (Promo-only CD, exclusive 'rose dress' sleeve)	30
99	Island IS 730	The Wind/Rebecca/Nina In Ecstacy 2	15
00	Island IS 769	Good Fortune/66 Promises	30
01	Island IS 771	A Place Called Home/Kick It To The Ground (demo) (numbered)	25
01	Island IS 785	This Is Love/Angline (live) (p/s)	12
04	Island IS S869	You Come Through/Shame (p/s)	10
04	Island IS 861	The Letter/Bows And Arrows (p/s)	10
04	Island IS 873	Shame/Dance (p/s)	10
07	Island 1747513	When Under Ether/Wait (p/s)	10
07	Island 1753491	The Piano/Heaven (p/s)	10
08	Island 1764907	The Devil/Liverpool Tide (p/s)	10
11	Island 2768296	The Glorious Land/The Nightingale	10
11	Island 2762434	The Words That Maketh Murder/The Guns Called Me Back Again	15
17	Island 538287631	A Dog Called Money/I'll Be Waiting (tour 7")	30
92	Too Pure PURE(D) 10	DRY (LP, 1st 5,000 with bonus LP, "Demonstrations", inner sleeve and no'd sticker)	150
92	Too Pure PURE 10	DRY (LP with inner but without "Demonstrations")	100
92	Too Pure PUREDCD 10	DRY (CD, 1st 5,000 with additional "Demonstrations" LP tracks)	30
93	Island 5146961	RID OF ME (LP)	150
93	Island ILPM 2079	4 TRACK DEMOS (LP, with inner)	80
95	Island CIDZ 8035	TO BRING YOU MY LOVE & THE B-SIDES CD (2-CD)	40
95	Island ILPS 8035	TO BRING YOU MY LOVE (LP, 1st pressing, with inner and large photo on rear)	150
98	Island ILPS 8076	IS THIS DESIRE? (LP, with inner)	200
00	Island ILPS 8099	STORIES FROM THE CITY, STORIES FROM THE SEA (LP, with inner)	150
04	Island ILPS 8143	UH HUH HER (LP, with inner)	60
07	Island 1740335	WHITE CHALK (LP, inner)	40
10	Island 2758997	LET ENGLAND SHAKE (LP)	30
16	Island 4774545	THE HOPE SIX DEMOLITION PROJECT (LP)	20
19	Lakeshore LSINV223LP	ALL ABOUT EVE (LP)	15

(see also Automatic Dlamini, Grape, John Parish & Polly Jean Harvey)

RICHARD HARVEY
83	Anderburr HX 1010	Theme From Terrahawks (3.00)/Variations On The Theme (3.17) (p/.s)	10
83	Anderburr HX 21010	Theme From Terrahawks (4.50)/Variations On The Theme (7.25) (12", p/s with poster)	12
75	Transatlantic TRA 292	DIVISIONS ON A GROUND (LP)	15

(see also Gryphon, Barry Gray, The Banned)

TINA HARVEY
72	UK UK 2	Working My Way Back To You/Tina's Song	6
73	UK UK 24	Nowhere To Run/Tina's Second Song	25
76	UK UK 141	I'm Waiting For The Man/Baby, Let Me Follow You Down	15
73	UK UKAL 1002	TINA HARVEY (LP, bule/silver labels)	25

HARVEY BOYS
57	London HLA 8397	Nothing Is Too Good For You/Marina Girl	30

HARVEY & THE PHENOMENALS
04	Funk 45 FUNK45 018	Soul & Sunshine/What Can I Do (reissue)	20

HARVEY'S PEOPLE
69	Galliard GAL 4001	LOVING AND LIVING (LP)	15

CHRISTINE HARWOOD
06	Finders Keepers FKR45 002	Wooden Ships/Hear What I Have To Say (p/s)	10
70	Birth RAB 1	NICE TO MEET MISS CHRISTINE (LP, white 'rabbit' child' label)	200
06	Finders Keepers FKR005LP	NICE TO MEET MISS CHRISTINE (LP, reissue)	15

		MINT VALUE £

ELTON HARWOOD
85   Harwood HARD 01   Just Like Money/Instrumental (12", p/s) 60

HASH BROWN
02   Red Eye JAH 007   Reflections/Version 10

GORDON HASKELL
69   CBS 4509   Boat Trip/Time Only Knows 8
70   CBS 4795   Oo-La-Di-Doo-Da-Day/Born To Be Together 8
90   Wilderness WLD 700   Hambledon Hill/Mystical Illusion (p/s) 6
69   CBS 63741   SAILIN' MY BOAT (LP) 125
72   Atlantic K 40211   IT IS AND IT ISN'T (LP, with lyric insert) 40
73   RCA   SERVE AT ROOM TEMPERATURE (LP, unissued) 250

(see also Fleur-De-Lys, Cupid's Inspiration, Flowerpot Men, King Crimson)

JACK HASKELL (& HONEY-DREAMERS)
57   London HL 8426   Around The World/Away Out West 15

NAZIA HASSAN
80   HMV PEASD 12751   DISCO DEEWANE (LP) 40
82   HMV PEASD 2065   STAR (LP, with Zoheb Hassan) 15

JON HASSELL
81   Editions EG EGED 13   DREAM THEORY IN MALAYA (LP) 25
83   Editions EG EGED 31   AKA/DARBARI/JAVA- MAGIC REALISM (LP) 40
90   Land LAND 11   CITY: WORKS OF FICTION (LP) 15

JON HASSELL & BRIAN ENO
80   EG EGED 7   POSSIBLE MUSICS (LP) 35

(see also Roxy Music, Brian Eno, Fripp & Eno)

JOE HASSELVANDER
85   Pentagram DEVIL 3   LADY KILLER (LP) 15

HASSLES
67   United Artists UP 1199   You Got Me Hummin'/I'm Thinkin' 20

(see also Billy Joel)

HAT & TIE
66   President PT 105   Chance For Romance/California Jazz Club U.S.A. 15
67   President PT 122   Bread To Spend/Finding It Rough (demos credit A-side as "Bread") 150

(see also Patrick Campbell-Lyons, Nirvana [U.K.])

TONY HATCH ORCHESTRA
59   Top Rank JAR 107   Chick/Side Saddle 6
61   Pye International 7N 25085   Rocking Waltz/Devil's Herd 6
61   Pye 7N 15408   The Ghost Squad/What's All That About 7
62   Pye 7N 15434   Ben Casey Theme/Perry Mason Theme 7
62   Pye 7N 15460   Out Of This World Theme/Cyril's Tune (in p/s) 10
65   Pye 7N 15754   Crossroads Theme/The Marie Celeste (in p/s) 8
65   Pye 7N15972   Man Alive/Crosstown Commuter 8
65   Pye 7N 15930   Maori/Sugar And Spice 6
66   Pye 7N 17169   Crossroads Theme/Round Every Corner (in p/s) 10
67   Pye 7N 17263   Comedy Tonight/You're Lovely 10
67   Pye 7N 17298   Beautiful In The Rain/While The City Sleeps 6
69   Pye 7N 17814   Theme From Who-Dun-It/The Champions 30
69   Pye 7N 17864   The Doctors - Theme/Love Song 6
73   Pye 7N 45210   Memories Of Summer/Best In Football 6
78   EMI EMI 2780   Sweeney 2/Regan's Key 12
83   Tube TUBE 003   Airline/The HI-FA 6

(see also Jackie Trent)

GEORGE HATCHER BAND
77   United Artists UP 36233   Black Moon Rising/Find A New Lover (p/s) 7

(see also Budgie)

ROGER HATCHER
76   Mint CHEW 5   We Gonna Make It/High Blood Pressure 10

HATE
70   Famous SFMA 5752   HATE KILLS (LP, gatefold sleeve, orange labels) 125

BOBBY HATFIELD
68   Verve VS 570   Hang-Ups/Soul Cafe 10
68   Verve VS 576   Only You/The Wonder Of You 10
72   Warner Bros K 16251   Oo-Wee-Baby, I Love You/Rock'n'Roll Woman 12

(see also Righteous Brothers, Ringo Starr)

HATFIELD & THE NORTH
74   Virgin VS 116   Let's Eat (Real Soon)/Fitter Stoke Has A Bath 8
74   Virgin V 2008   HATFIELD AND THE NORTH (LP, gatefold sleeve, red 'twin' label) 50
76   Virgin V 2008   HATFIELD AND THE NORTH (LP, gatefold sleeve, repressing on "red mirror girl" label) 25
75   Virgin V 2030   THE ROTTER'S CLUB (LP, red Virgin inner, coloured 'twin' label) 30
79   Virgin VR 5   AFTERS (LP, withdrawn) 35

(see also Matching Mole, Egg, Khan, Camel, National Health, Caravan)

DONNY HATHAWAY
70   Atco 226 010   The Ghetto (Parts 1 & 2) 10
72   Atlantic K 10193   The Ghetto (Parts 1 & 2)/Little Ghetto Boy 8
73   Atlantic K 10354   Love Love Love/Someday We'll Be Free 10
71   Atco 2465 019   EVERYTHING IS EVERYTHING (LP) 40
71   Atlantic 2400 143   DONNY HATHAWAY (LP) 15
72   Atlantic K 40369   LIVE (LP) 15
73   Atlantic K 40487   EXTENSION OF A MAN (LP) 15

(see also Roberta Flack)

HAUSFRAUEN EXPERIMENT

MINT VALUE £

HAUSFRAUEN EXPERIMENT
10	Fruits De Mer Crustacean 12	Oscillations/Spirit Of The Age//Baby's On Fire/Sebastian (2x7", yellow/blue vinyl, foldover p/s)	30

ANNA VON HAUSSWOLF
14	Touch TONE45.6	KALLAN (LP, white label in white stickered sleeve)	50

HAVANA LETS GO
81	Polydor POSP 364	Spanish Cabaret/Continental Shelf (in p/s)	18
81	Polydor POSP 364	Spanish Cabaret/Continental Shelf (no p/s)	8

HAVANA 3AM
91	IRS EIRS 158	Reach The Rock/Hey Amigo (Tokyo Version) (p/s)	10
91	IRS EIRSA 1047	HAVANA 3AM (LP)	25

(see also Clash, The Good The Bad And The Queen)

ALAN HAVEN
62	Fontana 267253	My Mothers's Eyes/Lean Baby	10
63	Fontana TF 395	I Feel Pretty/Haven's Haunts	8
64	United Artists UP 1057	Theme From "A Jolly Bad Fellow"/Jee B'ees (with John Barry)	10
65	Fontana TF 542	Image/Romance On The North Sea	8
65	Fontana TF 590	The Knack/Satin Doll (with John Barry)	15
66	Fontana TF 658	Flamingo/Shangri-La	6
66	Fontana TF 754	Summer Samba/The Dachsund	6
67	Fontana TF 835	Image/Romance Of The North Sea (reissue)	8

JIM HAVEN
75	Penny Farthing PEN 868	Do It In Slow Motion/Do It In Slow Motion (Part 2)	10

RICHIE HAVENS
69	Verve VS 1519	Lady Madonna/Indian Rope Man	15
72	Polydor 2121098	What About Me/Fire And Rain	6
68	Verve (S)VLP 6005	SOMETHIN' ELSE AGAIN (LP)	20
68	Verve (S)VLP 6008	MIXED BAG (LP)	20
69	Verve (S)VLP 6014	1983 (LP)	20
69	Verve (S)VLP 6021	STONEHENGE (LP)	15
69	Transatlantic TRA 187	ELECTRIC HAVENS (LP)	15
69	Transatlantic TRA 199	THE RICHIE HAVENS RECORD (LP)	15

HAVENSTREET
76	Rissole KAB 1034	THE END OF THE LINE (LP, private pressing with booklet)	150

CYRIL HAVERMANS
73	MGM 2315 261	CYRIL (LP, gatefold sleeve, blue/gold 'lion' label)	25
74	MGM 2315 311	MIND WAVE (LP, blue/gold 'lion' label)	18

NICK HAWARD
83	Cradle Music CMINH1	Grey Day/Watching Through My Window (p/s)	30

HAMPTON HAWES
53	Esquire 20 079	HAMPTON HAWES (LP)	30
57	Contemporary LAC 12056	HAMPTON HAWES TRIO VOL. 1 (LP)	20
58	Contemporary LAC 12081	THIS IS HAMPTON HAWES VOL. 2 THE TRIO (LP)	30
56	Contemporary LAC 12091	EVERYBODY LIKES HAMPTON HAWES VOL. 3 - THE TRIO (LP)	40
62	Contemporary SCA 5028	FOR REAL! (LP)	40

PAT HAWES WITH DAVE CAREY'S RHYTHM
56	Tempo LAP 9	PAT HAWES (10" LP)	20

JACKSON HAWKE
76	CBS 5034	Into The Mystic/Fortune	6

TOMMY HAWKE
60	Top Rank JAR 348	Good Gravy (I'm In Love Again)/Umpteen Years (And A Million Tears)	12

HAWKEYES
57	Capitol CL 14764	Someone Someday/Who Is He?	20

BUDDY BOY HAWKINS/WILLIAM MOORE
50s	Heritage RE 102	BUDDY BOY HAWKINS/WILLIAM MOORE (EP)	60

(see also Blind Lemon Jefferson)

CAROL HAWKINS
73	Polydor 2058 387	Listen/All For One	8

COLEMAN HAWKINS
53	Capitol LC 6580	CLASSICS IN JAZZ (10" LP)	30
53	Capitol LC 6650	CAPITOL PRESENTS COLEMAN HAWKINS AND SONNY GREER (10" LP)	30
54	HMV DLP 1055	TEN COLEMAN HAWKINS' SPECIALS (10" LP)	30
58	London LTZ U 15117	THE HAWK FLIES HIGH (LP)	25
59	HMC CLP 1293	GENIUS OF COLEMAN HAWKINS (LP)	30
59	Felsted FJA 7005	THE HIGH AND MIGHTY HAWK (LP, also stereo SJA 2005)	35
61	Esquire 32-095	SOUL (LP)	35
61	Esquire 32-102	HAWK EYES (LP)	40
61	Moodsville MV 7	COLEMAN HAWKINS (LP)	25
62	Swingsville SVLP 2001	COLEMAN HAWKINS WITH THE RED GARLAND TRIO (LP)	20
62	Swingsville SVLP 2005	THE COLEMAN HAWKINS ALL STARS (LP)	20
62	Swingsville SVLP 2013	STASCH (LP)	20
63	HMV CLP 1630	DESAFINADO (LP, also stereo CSD 1484)	20
64	Verve VLP 9044	ALIVE! AT THE VILLAGE GATE (LP)	20
64	HMV CLP 1689	TODAY AND NOW (LP)	20
64	CBS BPG 62157	BACK IN BEAN'S BAG (LP, with Clark Terry)	15
64	Fontana FJL 102	SWING' (LP)	15
65	Fontana TL 5273	MEDITATION (LP)	15
66	Fontana SJL 131	CATTIN' (LP)	15

(see also Milt Jackson & Coleman Hawkins, Eddie 'Lockjaw' Davis, Sir Charles Thompson)

Coleman HAWKINS GROUP

MINT VALUE £

COLEMAN HAWKINS GROUP
58	London LTZC 15048	COLEMAN HAWKINS GROUP (LP)	18

(see also Coleman Hawkins)

COLEMAN HAWKINS & LESTER YOUNG
65	Stateside SL 10117	CLASSIC TENORS (LP)	20

DALE HAWKINS
57	London HL 8482	Susie-Q/Don't Treat Me That Way	500
57	London HL 8482	Susie-Q/Don't Treat Me That Way (78)	80
58	London HLM 8728	La-Do-Dada/Cross Ties	40
59	London HLM 8842	Yea-Yea (Class Cutter)/Lonely Nights	40
59	London HLM 9016	Liza Jane/Back To School Blues	40
60	London HLM 9060	Hot Dog/Our Turn	40
69	Bell SBLL 127	L.A., MEMPHIS AND TYLER, TEXAS (LP)	25
73	Checker 6467 301	OH! SUSIE Q (LP)	15

ERSKINE HAWKINS QUINTET
60	Brunswick LAT 8374	THE HAWK BLOWS AT MIDNIGHT (LP, also stereo STA 3042)	15

HAWKSHAW HAWKINS
54	Parlophone CMSP 1	Betty Lorraine/CHARLIE GORE & LOUIS INNIS: Mexican Joe (export issue)	30
63	London HL 9737	Lonesome 7-7203/Everything Has Changed	10
58	Parlophone GEP 8742	COUNTRY AND WESTERN (EP)	30
58	Vogue VE 170117	HAWKSHAW HAWKINS - COUNTRY AND WESTERN (EP)	30
64	London HA 8181	THE ALL NEW HAWKSHAW HAWKINS (LP)	20

(see also Charlie Gore, Louis Innis)

RONNIE HAWKINS (& HAWKS)
59	Columbia DB 4319	Forty Days (To Come Back Home)/One Of These Days	50
59	Columbia DB 4345	Mary Lou/Need Your Lovin' (Oh So Bad)	50
60	Columbia DB 4412	Southern Love (Whatcha-Gonna' Do)/Love Me Like You Can	20
60	Columbia DB 4442	Clara/Lonely Hours	30
63	Columbia DB 7036	Bo Diddley/Who Do You Love?	30
70	Roulette RO 512	Who Do You Love?/Bo Diddley	6
70	Atlantic 584 320	Down In The Alley/Matchbox	7
60	Columbia SEG 7983	ROCKIN' WITH RONNIE (EP, mono)	70
60	Columbia ESG 7792	ROCKIN' WITH RONNIE (EP, stereo)	100
60	Columbia SEG 7988	ROCKIN' WITH RONNIE (EP, mono)	70
60	Columbia ESG 7795	ROCKIN' WITH RONNIE (EP, stereo)	100
60	Columbia 33SX 1238	MR. DYNAMO (LP, mono)	70
60	Columbia SCX 3315	MR. DYNAMO (LP, stereo)	100
60	Columbia 33SX 1295	THE FOLK BALLADS OF RONNIE HAWKINS (LP, mono)	40
60	Columbia SCX 3358	THE FOLK BALLADS OF RONNIE HAWKINS (LP, stereo)	50
70	Roulette RCP 1003	ARKANSAS ROCK PILE (LP, with The Band)	20

(see also Band, Levon & Hawks)

SCREAMIN' JAY HAWKINS
58	Fontana H 107	I Put A Spell On You/Little Demon (78)	60
64	Columbia DB 7460	The Whammy/Strange	40
65	Sue WI 379	I Hear Voices/Just Don't Care	40
66	Sue WI 4008	I Put A Spell On You/Little Demon (unissued)	0
69	Direction 58-4097	I Put A Spell On You/Little Demon	20
80	Polydor POSP 183	I Put A Spell On You/Armpit 6 (with Keith Richards)	10
66	Planet PLL 1001	THE NIGHT AND DAY OF SCREAMIN' JAY HAWKINS (LP)	125
69	Direction (S) 8-63481	I PUT A SPELL ON YOU (LP, mono or stereo)	70
69	Mercury SMCL 20178	WHAT THAT IS (LP)	50

(see also Keith Richards)

H. HAWKLINE
12	Trash Aesthetics TA 1202	BLACK DOMINO BOX EP (12" with poster)	15
13	Turnstile TS 004	GHOULS EP (12")	10
10	Shape SHAPE 013	A CUP OF SALT (LP, numbered)	35
11	Shape SHAPE 017	THE STRANGE USES OF OX GALL (LP, numbered)	30
14	Heavenly HVNLPCC 108	SALT GALL BOX GHOULS (LP)	20

HAWKLORDS
78	Charisma HL 1	PSI Power/Death Trap (no p/s, promo only)	12
78	Charisma CB 323	PSI Power/Death Trap (no p/s)	8
79	Charisma CB 332	25 Years/(Only) The Dead Dreams Of A Cold War Kid (no p/s)	6
79	Charisma CB 332 12	25 Years/(Only) The Dead Dreams Of A Cold War Kid/PXR 5 (12", grey vinyl)	10
79	Charisma CB 332 12	25 Years/(Only) The Dead Dreams Of A Cold War Kid/PXR 5 (12", mispressed on black vinyl)	12
82	Flicknife FLS 209	Who's Gonna Win The War?/Time Of (p/s)	6
78	Charisma CDS 4014	25 YEARS ON (LP, with inner sleeve, sold with separate tour book)	20
78	Charisma CDS 4014	25 YEARS ON (LP, with inner sleeve)	15

(see also Hawkwind)

HAWKS (1)
69	Stateside SS 2147	The Grissle/SHEEP: Hide And Seek	12

HAWKS (2)
81	Five Believers FB 001	Words Of Hope/Sense Of Ending (p/s)	12

(see also Lilac Time, Stephen 'Tin Tin' Duffy)

ALAN HAWKSHAW
79	BBC RESL 64	Grange Hill/Stoned (credited to Deluxe)	20
72	Studio Two TWO 391	27 TOP TV THEMES AND COMMERCIALS (LP)	30
72	KPM 1080	FLUTE FOR MODERNS (with Alan Parker and Joe Hailer) (LP)	35

(see also Shadows, Bizarre)

Johnny HAWKSWORTH (ORCHESTRA)

MINT VALUE £

JOHNNY HAWKSWORTH (ORCHESTRA)
65	Pye 7N 15969	Lunar Walk/It's Murder (as Johnny Hawksworth Orchestra)	15
66	Columbia DB 8059	Goal/"Goal - World Cup 1966" Theme (as Sounds Of Johnny Hawksworth)	6
67	Columbia DB 8129	Wack Wack/On The Tiles	8
64	Columbia 33SX 1654	I'VE GROWN ACCUSTOMED TO MY BASS (LP)	50

(see also Johnny's Jazz)

HAWKSWORTH-VERRELL JAZZ GROUP
56	Decca FJ 10726	Ring Dem Bells/Always	6

HAWKWIND

SINGLES
70	Liberty LBF 15382	Hurry On Sundown/Mirror Of Illusion	400
72	United Artists UP 35381	Silver Machine/Seven By Seven ('machine' art p/s)	15
73	United Artists (WD 3637)	Sonic Attack (1-sided promo in cloth sleeve)	400
73	United Artists UP 35566	Urban Guerilla/Brainbox Pollution	15
73	United Artists USEP 1	HURRY ON HAWKWIND (EP)	50
74	United Artists UP 35715	The Psychedelic Warlords (Disappear In Smoke)/It's So Easy	10
75	United Artists UP 35808	Kings Of Speed/Motorhead (in p/s)	40
75	United Artists UP 35808	Kings Of Speed/Motorhead	10
76	Charisma CB 289	Kerb Crawler/Honky Dorky	10
77	Charisma CB 299	Back On The Streets/The Dream Of Isis (p/s)	8
77	Charisma CB 305	Quark, Strangeness & Charm/Forge Of Vulcan	8
78	United Artists UP 35381	Silver Machine/Seven By Seven (reissue, black-on-white p/s)	6
78	United Artists 12UP 35381	Silver Machine/Seven By Seven (12", silver p/s)	10
80	Bronze BRO 98	Shot Down In The Night/Urban Guerilla (1-sided gold vinyl flexidisc)	30
80	Bronze BRO 109	Who's Gonna Win The War?/Nuclear Toy (p/s, cream labels)	12
83	Liberty UPP 35381	Silver Machine/Seven By Seven (mispressed picture disc, plays Beatles' "Ask Me Why")	15
83	Flicknife FLS 214	Hawkwind And Co: Your Last Chance (p/s, sampler with Robert Calvert & Michael Moorcock)	6
85	Flicknife FLST 032	Needle Gun (extended)/Arioch (p/s)	8
86	Samurai HW 001	Silver Machine/Magnu (motorcycle-shaped picture disc)	15
90	Receiver REPLAY 3014	THE EARLY YEARS LIVE (12", p/s, blue vinyl)	15
93	4 Real 4R 1	SPIRIT OF THE AGE (SOLSTICE REMIXES) (12" EP)	12
93	4 Real 4R 2	DECIDE YOUR FUTURE (12" EP)	10
94	Emerg. Broadcast EBS 110	QUARK, STRANGENESS & CHARM (12" EP, clear vinyl, 200 only)	15

EPS : ORIGINAL ALBUMS
70	Liberty LBS 83348	HAWKWIND (LP, gatefold sleeve; blue label)	350
70	Liberty LBS 83348	HAWKWIND (LP, gatefold sleeve; black label)	60
71	United Artists UAG 29202	IN SEARCH OF SPACE (LP in foldout 'door' sleeve, with 'log book')	150
71	United Artists UAG 29202	IN SEARCH OF SPACE (LP in foldout 'door' sleeve, without 'log book')	75
72	United Artists UAG 29364	DOREMI-FASOL-LATIDO (LP, with inner sleeve, with poster)	200
72	United Artists UAG 29364	DOREMI-FASOL-LATIDO (LP, with inner sleeve, without poster)	150
73	Utd. Artists UAD 60037/8	SPACE RITUAL ALIVE (2-LP, foldout sleeve with inners)	100
74	United Artists UAG 29672	HALL OF THE MOUNTAIN GRILL (LP, with inner sleeve)	40
75	United Artists UAG 29766	WARRIOR ON THE EDGE OF TIME (LP, foldout pop-up sleeve with inner)	100
76	Charisma CDS 4004	ASTOUNDING SOUNDS. AMAZING MUSIC (LP)	20
76	United Artists UAK 29919	ROADHAWKS (LP, gatefold sleeve with poster & sticker)	20
76	Mushroom	THE XENON CODEX (LP, with inner, gatefold sleeve)	15
77	Charisma CDS 4008	QUARK STRANGENESS AND CHARM (LP, 'Mad Hatter' label)	40
79	Charisma CDS 4016	P.X.R.5 (LP, with family tree poster, with picture of incorrectly wired plug on rear)	30
79	Charisma CDS 4016	P.X.R.5 (LP, without family tree poster, but with uncensored wired plug on rear)	15
80	Bronze BRON 530	LEVITATION (LP, blue vinyl)	20
82	RCA Active RCALP 9004	CHURCH OF HAWKWIND (LP, with lyric booklet)	15
82	RCA Active RCALP 6055	CHOOSE YOUR MASQUES (LP)	18
84	Flicknife PSHARP 014	ZONES (LP, picture disc reissue)	18
84	Flicknife SHARP 022	STONHENGE: THIS IS HAWKWIND DO NOT PANIC (LP, with 12", gatefold sleeve or single sleeve with poster)	15
85	Demi Monde DM 002	BRING ME THE HEAD OF YURI GAGARIN (LP)	15
85	Flicknife SHARP 033	CHRONICLE OF THE BLACK SWORD (LP, with inner sleeve)	15
86	Hawkfan HWFB 2	HAWKFAN 12 (LP, with poster, sticker insert & carrier bag, 600 only)	70
86	Samurai SMR 046	APPROVED HISTORY OF HAWKWIND 1967-1982 (3-LP, pic discs & booklet)	45
87	Flicknife HWBOX 01	OFFICIAL PICTURE LOG BOOK (4-LP box set, [3 picture discs & interview disc] with badge & insert)	35
92	Essential ESSLP 181	ELECTRIC TEPEE (2-LP, 5,000 only, numbered)	35
94	Emergency Broadcast System EBS 111	THE BUSINESS TRIP (2-LP, clear vinyl, 1,500 only)	25
95	Emergency Broadcast System EBSLP 118	ALIEN 4 (2-LP, gatefold sleeve)	40
96	Emergency Broadcast System EBSLP 120	LOVE IN SPACE (2-LP, gatefold)	40
16	Cherry Red BRED 688	THE MACHINE STOPS (LP, with free 12")	25
17	Cherry Red BREDT700	INTO THE WOODS (2-LP)	20
17	Cherry Red BREDT721	AT THE ROUNDHOUSE (3-LP, poster)	35

ALBUMS : REISSUES
75	Sunset SLS 50374	HAWKWIND (LP, reissue)	15
77	United Artists UAG 29364	DOREMI-FASOL-LATIDO (LP, reissue, with poster and inner sleeve)	15
79	United Artists UAG 29766	WARRIOR ON THE EDGE OF TIME (LP, reissue)	20
80	Liberty LBR 1012	HAWKWIND (LP, reissue, 'Rock File' different p/s)	15
81	Liberty UAG 29766	WARRIOR ON THE EDGE OF TIME (LP, reissue)	15
81	Liberty LBG 29292	IN SEARCH OF SPACE (LP, reissue)	15
82	Charisma CDS 4008	QUARK STRANGENESS AND CHARM (LP, reissue, blue label)	15

Deane HAWLEY

Year	Label/Cat#	Title	Mint Value £
84	Liberty SLP 1972921	HAWKWIND (LP, reissue, picture disc, die-cut)	15
84	Liberty SLS 1972921	HAWKWIND (LP, reissue)	15
00	Simply Vinyl SVLP 266	IN SEARCH OF SPACE (2-LP, 180gm reissue)	20
11	Back On Black RCV010LP	HAWKWIND (2-LP, reissue, 180gm vinyl)	20
11	Back On Black RCV012LP	HALL OF THE MOUNTAIN GRILL (2-LP, reissue, black or yellow vinyl)	20
11	Back On Black RCV013LP	DOREMI-FASOL-LATIDO (2-LP, reissue)	20
11	Back On Black RCV017LP	SPACE RITUAL VOL 1. (2-LP, reissue, clear, green or black vinyl)	25
11	Back On Black RCV017LP	SPACE RITUAL VOL 2. (2-LP, reissue, green or yellow vinyl)	25
15	Let Them Eat Vinyl LETV307LP	WARRIOR ON THE EDGE OF TIME (LP, reissue, black or yellow vinyl)	15
15	Let Them Eat VInyl LETV 264LP	QUARK STRANGENESS AND CHARM (2-LP, reissue, clear vinyl)	20

(see also Hawklords, Robert Calvert, Michael Moorcock, Inner City Unit, Sphynx,, Tim Blake, Huw Lloyd Langton Group, Alan Davey, Motorhead, Dr. Technical & Machines, Magic Muscle, Opal Butterfly, Widowmaker, Adrian Shaw, Captain Jesus And The Sunray Team)

DEANE HAWLEY
61	Liberty LIB 55359	Pocketful Of Rainbows/That Dream Could Never Be	10

RICHARD HAWLEY
06	Mute 362	Born Under A Bad Sign/I'm Just Here To Get My Baby Out Of Jail (numbered p/s)	7
12	Parlophone RHSCBOX	THE SINGLE CLUB 1-IV (4 x 10" box set)	50
03	Setanta SETLP 110	LOWLEDGES (LP)	70
05	Mute STUMM 251	COLES CORNER (LP)	150
09	Mute STUMM 312	TRUELOVE'S GUTTER (2-LP, CD & signed print, 1000 only)	150
12	Parlophone 5099946369819	STANDING AT THE SKY'S EDGE (2-LP)	25
14	Setanta SETLP 088	LATE NIGHT FINAL (LP, reissue)	20
14	Setanta SETLP 153	RICHARD HAWLEY (LP, reissue)	20
18	Live Here Now 030	LIVE AT THE DEVIL'S ARSE (2-LP clear vinyl)	40
19	Setanta SETLP088	LATE NIGHT FINAL (LP, reissue, red or clear vinyl)	20
19	Setanta SETLP170	COLES CORNER (LP, reissue, red vinyl)	40
19	Setanta SETLP110	LOWLEDGES (LP, reissue)	20

(see also Longpigs)

GOLDIE HAWN
72	Reprise K 14211	Carey/I'll Be Your Baby Tonight	6

HAYDEN WOOD
69	NEMS 56 4499	House Beside The Mine/Lady Wants More	25
70	NEMS 4803	Sixty Years On/The Last One To Know	25
73	Jam JAM 46	I Don't Want To Lose You/Hand Me Down	6

HAYDOCK'S ROCKHOUSE
66	Columbia DB 8050	Cupid/She Thinks	70
67	Columbia DB 8135	Lovin' You/Mix A Fix	60

(see also Hollies)

BILL HAYES
53	MGM SP 1036	The Donkey Song/My Ever-Lovin'	15
55	London HL 8149	The Berry Tree/Blue Black Hair	25
56	London HLA 8220	Ballad Of Davy Crockett/Farewell	25
56	London HLA 8239	Kwela Kwela/The White Buffalo	20
56	London HLA 8300	Das Ist Musik/I Know An Old Lady	20
56	London HLA 8325	The Legend Of Wyatt Earp/That Do Make It Nice	15
57	London HL 8430	Wringle Wrangle/Westward Ho The Wagons	15
56	London RE-A 1051	GREAT PIONEERS OF THE WEST (EP)	15

ISAAC HAYES
74	Stax STXS 2004	Title Theme/Hung Up On My Baby (Instrumental)	8
69	Stax SXATS 1028	HOT BUTTERED SOUL (LP)	40
70	Stax SXATS 1032	THE ISAAC HAYES MOVEMENT (LP)	30
70	Stax 2465 016	BLUE HAYES (LP, with Presenting Isaac Hayes on labels)	25
71	Stax 2325 026	TO BE CONTINUED (LP)	30
71	Stax 2325 014	THE ISAAC HAYES MOVEMENT (LP, reissue)	15
72	Atlantic K 40327	IN THE BEGINNING (LP)	15
72	Stax 2628 004	BLACK MOSES (2-LP, cruciform sleeve)	50
73	Stax 2362 032	LIVE AT THE SAHARA TAHOE (2-LP)	25
74	Stax 2325 111	JOY (LP)	15
95	Virgin VPBLP24	BRANDED (LP)	30

LINDA HAYES
55	Parlophone MSP 6174	Please Have Mercy (with Platters)/Oochi Pachi (with Tony Williams)	300
55	Parlophone R 4038	Please Have Mercy (with Platters)/Oochi Pachi (with Tony Williams) (78)	50

(see also Platters)

PETER LIND HAYES
60	Brunswick 05821	Life Gets Tee-jus Don't It/Sing Me A Happy Song	8

(see also Peter & Mary)

TUBBY HAYES
56	Tempo A 148	Ode To Ernie/No, I Woodyn't	10
62	Fontana H 397	Sally/I Believe In You (as Tubby Hayes Quintet)	25
55	Tempo EXA 14	THE LITTLE GIANT (EP)	75
55	Tempo EXA 17	TUBBY HAYES AND HIS ORCHESTRA (EP)	30
55	Tempo EXA 27	THE SWINGING GIANT NO. 1 (EP, as Tubby Hayes Quartet)	50
56	Tempo EXA 28	THE SWINGING GIANT NO. 2 (EP, as Tubby Hayes Quartet)	50
56	Tempo EXA 36	MODERN JAZZ SCENE (EP, as Tubby Hayes & His Orchestra)	60
57	Tempo EXA 55	AFTER LIGHTS OUT (EP, as Tubby Hayes Quintet)	60
57	Tempo EXA 75	TUBBY HAYES AND THE JAZZ COURIERS (EP)	60
58	Tempo EXA 82	THE EIGHTH WONDER (EP, solo)	60
09	Trunk TTT005	VOODOO SESSION (EP, 1st pressing 666 copies only)	30

Tubby HAYES & CLEO LAINE

MINT VALUE £

10	Trunk TTT 005	VOODOO SESSION (EP, reissue, different label, no p/s)	10
57	Tempo TAP 6	AFTER LIGHTS OUT (LP, as Tubby Hayes Quintet)	600
57	Tempo TAP 15	JAZZ COURIERS (LP)	450
60	Tempo TAP 29	TUBBY'S GROOVE (LP, as Tubby Hayes Quartet)	450
61	Fontana TFL 5142	TUBBS (LP, also stereo STFL 562)	200
61	Ember EMB 3337	AN EVENING WITH MR. PERCUSSION (LP, with Tony Kinsey)	70
61	Fontana TFL 5183	TUBBS IN NEW YORK (LP, also stereo STFL 595)	120
63	Fontana 680 998 TL	DOWN IN THE VILLAGE (LP, mono)	350
63	Fontana 886 163TY	DOWN IN THE VILLAGE (LP, stereo)	250
64	Fontana (S)TL 5195	RETURN VISIT! (LP)	150
64	Fontana TL 5200	LATE SPOT AT SCOTT'S (LP)	250
66	Fontana (S)TL 5221	TUBBS' TOURS (LP, with Orchestra)	70
66	Fontana (S)TL 5410	100% PROOF (LP)	70
67	Wing WL 1162	TUBBS IN NEW YORK (LP, reissue)	20
69	Fontana SFJL 911	MEXICAN GREEN (LP)	100
71	Fontana 6309 002	THE TUBBY HAYES ORCHESTRA (LP)	30
72	Philips 6382 041	THIS IS JAZZ - 100% PROOF (LP)	20
81	Mole MOLE 2	MEXICAN GREEN (LP, reissue)	20
81	Mole MOLE 4	TUBBS' TOURS (LP, reissue)	20
82	Jasmine JASM 2015	AFTER LIGHTS OUT (LP, reissue)	20
90	CBS Masterpieces CBS 466363-1	TUBBY HAYES WITH CLARK TERRY THE NEW YORK SESSIONS (LP, reissue)	25
90	MMO 79	67 LIVE - FOR MEMBERS ONLY (LP)	20
09	Gearbox GB 1502	BBC JAZZ FOR MODERNS (LP)	30

(see also Jack Constanzo & Tubby Hayes, Jazz Couriers, London Jazz Quartet, Dave Lee, Ronnie Scott, Roy Castle)

TUBBY HAYES & CLEO LAINE
61	Fontana TFL 5151	PALLADIUM JAZZ DATE (LP, also stereo STFL 570)	20

(see also Cleo Laine)

TUBBY HAYES & PAUL GONSALVES ALLSTARS
67	Columbia SX 6003	JUST FRIENDS (LP)	300
60s	World Record Club T 631	CHANGE OF SETTING (LP)	120

(see also Paul Gonsalves)

LOU HAYLES
77	Myrrh MYR 1055	DON'T HIDE AWAY (LP)	22

ROY HAYNES QUARTET
62	HMV CLP 1628	OUT OF THE AFTERNOON (LP)	30

ROY HAYNES, PHINEAS NEWBORN, PAUL CHAMBERS TRIO
61	Esquire 32-103	WE THREE (LP)	30

STEVE HAYNES BAND
78	Black Bear BLA 2005	Back In My Arms Again/Walk On By (p/s)	20
78	Black Bear BLA 2008	Save Me Save Me/Strong Good Lovin' (p/s)	15

HAYSTACK
69	United Artists UP 35024	Letter To Josephine/Love You're Making A Fool Of Me	6
69	United Artists UP 35035	Tahiti Farewell/Pantomime People	6

HAYSTACKS BALBOA
70	Polydor	Spoiler/Bruce's Twist	25
70	Polydor 2489 002	HAYSTACKS BALBOA (LP)	100

CHARLES HAYWARD
87	Ink INK 31	SURVIVE THE GESTURE (LP)	20
17	Care In The Community CARE112LP	IMPROVISATIONS (LP, with Thurston Moore)	25

(see also This Heat, Camberwell Now)

JUSTIN HAYWARD
65	Pye 7N 17041	London Is Behind Me/Day Must Come	150
66	Parlophone R 5496	I Can't Face The World Without You/I'll Be Here Tomorrow	200
77	Deram DM 428	One Lonely Room/Songwriter (Part 2)	7
80	CBS 11-7731	The Eve Of The War/Horsell (12" picture disc)	15

(see also Wilde Three)

RICK HAYWARD
71	Blue Horizon 2431 006	RICK HAYWARD (LP)	200

(see also Accent, Christine Perfect)

SUSAN HAYWARD
62	Fontana 267224	You Bet I Would/I Won't Give My Lips To Anyone	6
56	MGM MGM-EP 555	I'LL CRY TOMORROW - SOUNDTRACK SELECTION (EP)	10

JOE HAYWOOD
65	Island WI 218	Warm And Tender Love/I Would If I Could	35

LEON HAYWOOD
66	Vocalion VL 9280	Ain't No Use/Hey, Hey, Hey	30
66	Vocalion VL 9280	Ain't No Use/Hey, Hey, Hey (DJ copy)	50
67	Vocalion VL 9288	Ever Since You Were Sweet Sixteen/Skate Awhile	30
69	MCA Soul Bag BAG 5	Mellow Moonlight/Tennessee Waltz	10
70	Capitol CL 15634	I Wanna Thank You/I Was Sent To Love You	15
75	20th Century BTC 2228	I Wanta Do Something Freaky To You/I Know What Love Is	6
78	Fantasy FTC 151	Baby Reconsider/Would I	20
67	Vocalion VAL 8064	SOUL CARGO (LP)	75
69	MCA MUPS 369	IT'S GOT TO BE MELLOW (LP)	20
73	Pye Intl. NSPL 28177	BACK TO STAY (LP)	25
75	20th Century BT 476	COME AND GET YOURSELF SOME (LP)	15

HAZARD
79	Rok ROK VII/VIII	Gotta Change My Life/CLERKS: No Good For Me	15

HAZE (1)

MINT VALUE £

HAZE (1)
74	Haze HAZE 00174	HAZE (LP, 100 only)	100

HAZE (2)
81	Mushroom MUSH 1	The Night/Dig Them Mushrooms	20
84	Gabadon GABL 001	C'EST LA VIE (LP)	25

EDDIE HAZEL
16	Be With BEWTH011LP	GAMES, DAMES AND GUITAR THANGS (LP, reissue)	40

HAZEL & JOLLY BOYS
67	Doctor Bird DB 1063	Stop Them/Deep Down	35

HAMMOND HAZLEWOOD
67	Pye 7N 17273	I Can Make The Rain Fall Up/The Hawkmoth And The Flame	12
69	Columbia DB 8579	Hey Love, Let Me In/Let The Sunshine In	10

LEE HAZLEWOOD
60	London HLW 9223	Words Mean Nothing/The Girl On Death Row (with Duane Eddy)	35
66	MGM MGM 1310	Sand/My Autumn's Done Come	10
67	MGM MGM 1348	My Baby Cried All Night Long/These Boots Are Made For Walkin'	12
67	Reprise RS 20613	Ode To Billie Joe/Charlie Bill Nelson	10
68	Reprise RS 20667	Rainbow Woman/I Am, You Are	10
72	RCA RCA 2185	Big Red Balloon/Down From Dover (with Nancy Sinatra)	10
73	Stateside SS 2225	Poet/Come Spend The Morning	10
66	MGM MGM-CS 8014	THE VERY SPECIAL WORLD OF LEE HAZLEWOOD (LP)	40
68	Reprise RSLP 6297	LOVE AND OTHER CRIMES (LP)	25
69	London HA-N/SH-N 8398	TROUBLE IS A LONESOME TOWN (LP)	40
69	Music For Pleasure MFP 1309	THE VERY SPECIAL WORLD OF LEE HAZLEWOOD (LP, reissue)	15
72	Reprise K 44161	REQUIEM FOR AN ALMOST LADY (LP)	50
74	Stateside SSL 10315	POET, FOOL OR BUM (LP)	40
02	City Slang 20194-1	FOR EVERY SOLUTION THERE IS A PROBLEM (LP)	30

(see also Nancy Sinatra & Lee Hazlewood, Duane Eddy)

OSTERWALK HAZY
72	Jam JAM 22	Oumbalo Oumbalo/Tai Weh	15

HAZZARD
81	Rammy EJSP9600	Snake In The Grass/Kicked To The Ground (p/s)	100

TONY HAZZARD
66	Columbia DB 7927	You'll Never Put Shackles On Me/Calling You Home	20
69	CBS 63608	TONY HARRARD SINGS (LP, orange label)	60
71	Bronze ILPS 9174	LOUDWATER HOUSE (LP, gatefold sleeve, lyric inner sleeve)	20
73	Bronze ILPS 9222	WAS THAT ALRIGHT THEN? (LP, gatefold sleeve, lyric inner sleeve)	20

MICHAEL HEAD & STRANDS
95	Megaphone Music MEGA 01	THE MAGICAL WORLD OF THE STRANDS (LP, gatefold sleeve)	60

(see also Pale Saints, Shack)

MURRAY HEAD
65	Columbia DB 7635	Alberta/He Was A Friend Of Mine	8
65	Columbia DB 7771	The Bells Of Rhymney/Don't Sing No Sad Songs For Me	10
67	Columbia DB 8102	Someday Soon/You Bore Me	8
67	Immediate IM 053	She Was Perfection/Secondhand Monday	70
69	MCA MK 5019	Superstar/John 1941 (p/s, with Trinidad Singers)	7
71	MCA MKS 5019	Superstar/John 1941 (p/s, reissue)	6
73	CBS 65503	NIGEL LIVED (LP, gatefold sleeve and booklet)	30
75	Island ILPS 9347	SAY IT AIN'T SO (LP, gatefold sleeve, blue rim palm tree label)	15

ROY HEAD (& TRAITS)
65	Pye International 7N 25340	Just A Little Bit/Treat Me Right	20
65	Vocalion VP 9248	Treat Her Right/So Long, My Love	20
66	Vocalion VP 9254	Apple Of My Eye/I Pass The Day	15
66	Vocalion VP 9269	My Babe/Pain	20
66	Vocalion VP 9274	Wigglin' And Gigglin'/Driving Wheel	20
66	London HLZ 10097	To Make A Big Man Cry/Don't Cry No More	15
70	Stateside SS 8050	Mama Mama/I'm Not A Fool Anymore	7
75	London HLD 10487	The Most Wanted Woman In Town/Gingers Breadman	8
66	Pye Intl. NEP 44053	JUST A LITTLE BIT OF ROY HEAD (EP)	50
70	Stateside SSL 5033	SAME PEOPLE (LP)	25

(see also Traits)

HEAD (1)
73	SRT 72254	GTF (LP)	150
75	Canon CNN 5970	RED DWARF (LP)	60

HEAD (2)
77	HEAD HSLP333333333C	BLACKPOOL COOL (LP)	60

HEAD (3)
79	Ellie Jay MB1	Nothing To Do In A Town Like Leatherhead/University '79	60
96	Headhunter HH 7 01	Gnu/Demonizer 48/48 (p/s, 1000 only)	15

HEADACHE
77	Lout 001	Can't Stand Still/No Reason For Your Call (p/s)	20

HEAD ARSE FUSION BAND
00	U-Star US 009	UNTITLED EP (12")	40

HEADBOYS
79	RSO 40	The Shape Of Things To Come/The Mood I'm In (p/s)	6

HEADCLEANERS
83	Xcentric Noise THIRD 1	THE INFECTION GROWS EP	70

HEADCOATS (THEE)
89	Hangman HANG 29 UP	HEADCOATS DOWN (LP)	18

HEADHUNTERS

MINT VALUE £

90	Hangman HANG 32 UP	THE KIDS ARE ALL SQUARE (LP)	18
91	Hangman HANG 40 UP	W.O.A.H. (LP)	18
01	Hangman HANG 54 UP	LIVE AT THE DIRTY WATER CLUB (LP)	18

(see also Milkshakes, Thee Headcoats)

HEADHUNTERS
76	Arista ARTY 116	SURVIVAL OF THE FITTEST (LP)	25
77	Arista SPART 1046	STRAIGHT FROM THE GATE (LP)	15

(see also Herbie Hancock)

HEADLESS CHICKENS
89	Hometown Atrocities 1	THE HOMETOWN ATROCITIES EP (wraparound p/s with 3 inserts, 'kylie')	100
89	Hometown Atrocities 1	THE HOMETOWN ATROCITIES EP (wraparound p/s, 'glossy')	40
89	Maelstrom Storm 1	THE HOMETOWN ATROCITIES EP (repress of above)	15

(see also Radiohead)

HEADLINERS (1)
59	Parlophone R 4593	The Bubble Car Song/Andy's Theme	7

HEADLINERS (2)
65	Decca F 12209	That's The Way I Must Go/Four Seasons	8
65	Decca F 12279	What Became Of Love/Even Though	7

HEAD MACHINE
70	Major Minor SMLP 79	ORGASM (LP, laminated front sleeve, 'Major Minor' on front sleeve beneath word 'Orgasm' red/white/black labels)	500

(see also Uriah Heep)

HEAD OF DAVID
89	Blast First WANT 001	WHITE ELEPHANT (LP, mail-order only)	15

HEADS
94	Rooster ROOSTER 1	Quad/Woke Up/Looking At You (p/s, 500 only, with "Rizla" papers)	45
94	Rooster ROOSTER 1	Quad/Woke Up/Looking At You (p/s, 500 only, without "Rizla" papers)	30
95	Headhunter HED 718	Television/Steamroller '95/Jellystoned Park (8.47 Edit) (p/s)	20
95	Rooster ROOSTER 2	Coogan's Bluff/J Walking/Theme (p/s 1000 only)	20
97	Butchers Hook HOOK 003	Dirty Water/MAGIC DIRT: Goofy Dumb (p/s, 1000 only)	10
98	Rocket LAUNCH 1	You Can Lean Back/LILLYDAMWHITE: Master F (p/s, 550 only, insert)	10
00	Rocket LAUNCH 008	Spilff Riff (Conga'd Out)/75 (All Of It) (p/s, 4 inserts, First press 100 yellow vinyl)	20
00	Rocket LAUNCH 008	Spilff Riff (Conga'd Out)/75 (All Of It) (p/s, 4 inserts, First press 400 black vinyl)	15
00	Rocket LAUNCH 008	Spilff Riff (Conga'd Out)/75 (All Of It) (p/s, 4 inserts, Second press, 300 purple vinyl)	10
95	Headhunter HUK 001	RELAXING WITH... (LP)	80
00	Sweet Nothing SNLP 007	EVERYBODY KNOWS WE GOT NOWHERE (2-LP)	35
02	Rocket LAUNCH 015	SESSIONS 02 (LP, limited edition of 100, blue vinyl with free 7", 10 inserts)	100
02	Rocket LAUNCH 015	SESSIONS 02 (LP, 900 copies, black vinyl)	35
02	Sweet Nothing SNLP 011	UNDER SIDED (2-LP)	30
03	Rocket LAUNCH 018	AT LAST (LP)	35
05	Invada INV 015	33 (LP, blue or black vinyl)	20
05	Invada INV 017	DEAD IN THE WATER (2-LP, pink marbled vinyl)	30
06	Rocket LAUNCH 26/INVLP 24	UNDER THE STRESS OF A HEADLONG DIVE (2-LP)	20
09	Rocket LAUNCH 033LP	COLLISIONS V.1 (LP, one side Heads one side WHITE HILLS, 150 orange vinyl with poster)	30
09	Rocket LAUNCH 033LP	COLLISIONS V.1 (LP, one side Heads one side WHITE HILLS, 150 orange vinyl without poster)	20

HEADS TOGETHER
74	SRT SRTM 73345	FUNKY STUFF (LP)	35

HEADS, HANDS & FEET
71	Island ILPS 9149	HEADS, HANDS AND FEET (LP, gatefold, pink rim palm tree label)	25
72	Island ILPS 9185	TRACKS (LP, gatefold, pink rim palm tree label)	22
73	Atlantic K40465	OLD SOLIDERS NEVER DIE (LP, gatefold sleeve, lyric insert)	15

(see also Tony Colton, Poet & One Man Band)

HEADSTONE
74	EMI EMA 766	BAD HABITS (LP, gatefold sleeve)	20
75	EMI EMC 3673	HEADSTONE (LP)	20

HEALEY SISTERS
64	HMV POP 1313	Give Me Back My Heart/After The Party	8

LARRY HEARD
94	Black Market BM1020LP	SCENERIES NOT SONGS, VOLUME ONE (LP)	75
98	Mecca MEC LP 002	ICE CASTLES (LP)	35

(see also Mr Fingers, Fingers Inc.)

HEART (1)
76	Arista Arista 86	Crazy On You/Soul Of The Sea	6
77	Arista ARISTA 140	Heartless/Here Song (withdrawn)	8
77	Arista SPART 1024	MAGAZINE (LP, withdrawn)	15
77	Arista SPART 1024	MAGAZINE (LP, picture disc)	15

HEARTBEAT
79	Chancery CH 42	Operator/Bounce Right Back (no p/s)	8

HEART BEATS
81	Nothing Shaking SHAD 1	Go/One Of The People (p/s, blue vinyl)	15

HEART BOUND
74	Decca F 13510	Baby Ruth/Sailor Man	8

HEARTBREAK ANGELS
81	MTI Angels 001	Shoot Me Down/Desperado (p/s)	8

HEARTBREAKERS
77	Track 2094 135	Chinese Rocks/Born To Lose (p/s)	10
77	Track 2094 135T	Chinese Rocks/Born To Lose (12", p/s)	15
77	Track 2094 137	One Track Mind/Can't Keep My Eyes On You (live)/Do You Love Me (p/s)	10
77	Track 2094 142	It's Not Enough/Let Go (p/s, withdrawn)	250

HEARTS (U.K.)

			MINT VALUE £
77	Track 2409 218	L.A.M.F. (LP)	35
79	Beggars Banquet BEGA 9	LIVE AT MAX'S KANSAS CITY (LP, with inner bag)	15
81	Jungle FREUD 1	D.T.K. - LIVE AT THE SPEAKEASY (LP, white or pink vinyl)	20
84	Jungle FREUD 4	L.A.M.F. REVISITED (LP, picture disc)	20
84	Jungle FREUD 4	L.A.M.F. REVISITED (white label with withdrawn test proof sleeve)	150
88	Jungle FREUDP 1	D.T.K. - LIVE AT THE SPEAKEASY (LP, reissue, picture disc)	18

(see also New York Dolls, Johnny Thunders)

HEARTS (U.K.)
64	Parlophone R 5147	Young Woman/Black Eyes	20

HEARTS (U.S.)
64	Stateside SS 268	Dear Abby/Dear Abby (Instrumental)	22

HEARTS & FLOWERS
67	Capitol CL 15492	Rock'N'Roll Gypsies/Road To Nowhere	12
68	Capitol CL 15549	She Sang Hymns Out Of Tune/Tin Angel	8

JOHN HEARTSMAN AND CIRCLES
09	Jazzman JMANLP 030	MUSIC OF MY HEART (2-LP)	25

HEARTS OF SOUL
70	Columbia DB 8670	Waterman/Fat Jack	20

HEAT EXCHANGE
79	EMI EMC 3306	ONE STEP AHEAD (LP)	15

(see also Brian Bennett)

HEATERS
70	Upsetter US 329	Melting Pot/UPSETTERS: Kinky Mood	30

JIMMY HEATH
60	Riverside RLP 333	REALLY BIG (LP)	20

TED HEATH ORCHESTRA
54	Decca F 10246	Skin Deep/Walking Shoes	12
58	Decca F 11000	Swingin' Shepherd Blues/Raunchy	6
58	Decca F 11003	Tequila/Little Serenade	6

(see also Joan Regan, Bobbie Britton, Johnston Brothers, Annette Klooger)

HEATHCLIFFE
68	Tangerine DP 0001	Holly Bush And Mistletoe/My World	8

HEATHER
65	King KG 1027	I'll Come Softly/No One In The Whole Wide World	7

HEATHMORE
69	Pye 7N 17734	Home Isn't Home Anymore/Blackmore Prison	6
73	Philips 6006 299	Reaching For The Moon/I Love You	6

HEATWAVE (1)
70	Penny Farthing PEN 738	Sister Simon (Funny Man)/Rastus Ravel	30

HEATWAVE (2)
75	Harp HSP 1055	One-Eyed Man/999	50
76	GTO GT 59	Ain't No Half Stepping/Special Offer	20

HEAVEN
72	CBS 7782	Hangin On/Funny Lines	25
71	CBS 66293	BRASS ROCK 1 (2-LP, ornate fold-out sleeve)	100

HEAVEN & EARTH
73	London SHO 8448	REFUGE (LP)	50

HEAVENLY
89	Sarah SARAH 30	I Fell In Love Last Night/Over And Over (p/s)	20
91	Sarah SARAH 41	Our Love Is Heavenly/Wrap My Arms Around Him (p/s, insert)	20
91	Sarah SARAH 51	So Little Deserve/I'm Not Scared Of You (p/s, insert)	15
93	Sarah SARAH 81	P.U.N.K. Girl/Hearts And Crosses (p/s, insert)	15
93	Sarah SARAH 82	Atta Girl/Dig Your Own Grave/So? (p/s, insert)	18
96	Wiiija WIJ 58	Space Manatee/You Tore Me Down/Art School (p/s)	10
91	Sarah SARAH 603	HEAVENLY VS SATAN (LP)	20
92	Sarah SARAH 610	LE JARDIN DE HEAVENLY (LP)	30
94	Sarah SARAH 623	THE DECLINE AND FALL OF HEAVENLY (LP)	35
96	Wiiija WIJLP 1053	OPERATION HEAVENLY (LP)	35

(see also Talulah Gosh, Amelia Fletcher)

HEAVEN 17
82	Virgin VS 483	Height Of The Fighting (He-La-Hu)/Honeymoon In New York (unissued, no p/s)	15

(see also B.E.F., Human League, Glenn Gregory & Claudia Brucken)

HEAVY COCHRAN
79	Psycho P 2619	I've Got A Little Prick/It's 12 Inches Long, But I Don't Use It As A Rule	6

(see also Lieutenant Pigeon)

HEAVY FEATHER
71	Penny Farthing 756	Beautiful And Black/Ceilings	10

HEAVY JEFF
74	Harry J HJ 6689	Black Pepper/Pepper Rock	12

HEAVY JELLY
69	Head HDS 4001	Time Out Chewn In/The Long Wait	20
69	Island WIP 6049	I Keep Singing The Same Old Song/Blue	30
70	Island HELP	HEAVY JELLY (LP, promo only)	250

(see also Jackie Lomax, Aynsley Dunbar Retaliation, Skip Bifferty, Griffin, Graham Bell, Arc)

HEAVY METAL KIDS
74	Atlantic K 50047	HEAVY METAL KIDS (LP, with poster)	15
77	Rak SRAK 523	KITSCH (LP)	15

(see also Kids)

HEAVY PETTIN'
82	Neat NEAT 17	Roll The Dice/Love Times Love (p/s)	10

HEAVY PUKE

MINT VALUE £

HEAVY PUKE
80 (No label or cat no) Spunk Bunny/Ozymandias (p/s, handwritten white labels) 30

HEAVYWEIGHT
91 One After D ODE3 The Way Of The Future (12") 45

HEAVYWEIGHTS
69 Spark SRL 1033 Utterly Funky/Shambala 30

BOBBY HEBB
66 Philips BF 1522 A Satisfied Mind/Love Love Love 40
67 Philips BF 1541 Love Me/Baby I'm Crazy 10
67 Philips BF 1570 I Love Everything About You/Some Kinda Magic 10
67 Philips BF 1610 Everything Is Coming Up Roses/Bound By Love 8
68 Philips BF 1702 You Want To Change Me/Dreamy 100
72 Philips 6051 023 Love Love Love/Sunny 10
72 Philips 6051 025 Some Kind Of Magic/Good Lovin' 6
66 Philips BL 7740 SUNNY (LP) 30

HEBREW CHILDREN & INNER CIRCLE
73 Ackee ACK 508 Dog And Bone/Version 6

DICK HECKSTALL-SMITH (QUINTET)
57 Pye Jazz NJE 1037 VERY SPECIAL OLD JAZZ (EP, as Dick Heckstall-Smith Quintet) 40
72 Bronze ILPS 9196 DUST IN THE AIR SUSPENDED MARKS THE PLACE ... WHERE A STORY ENDED (LP, gatefold sleeve with lyric inner sleeve) 50

(see also Graham Bond Organisation, John Mayall & Bluesbreakers, Alexis Korner, Colosseum, Rocket 88)

HECTOR
73 DJM DJS 289 Wired Up/Ain't Got Time 30
74 DJM DJS 303 Bye Bye Bad Days/Lady 30

JESSE HECTOR
99 No Hit NO HIT EP 1961 Fast Train To Memphis/My Bucket's Got A Hole In It/All By Myself/Nightmares (p/s) 6
98 Dig The Fuzz DIG 029 CRUSHED BUTLER : UNCRUSHED (10" LP gatefold) 20

(see also Crushed Butler, Hammersmith Gorillas, Gorillas, Helter Skelter)

HEDGEHOG AFFAIR
92 Purple Heart PH 002 RUSH TILL DAWN PRESENTS THE HEDGEHOG AFFAIR EP (12") 12
92 Basement BRSS 005 RUSH TILL DAWN PRESENTS THE HEDGEHOG AFFAIR PT. 2 EP (12") 12
92 Basement BRSS 010 RUSH TILL DAWN PRESENTS THE HEDGEHOG AFFAIR PT. 3 EP (12") 12
93 Sound Entity SENT 1203 RUSH TILL DAWN PRESENTS THE HEDGEHOG AFFAIR PT. 4 EP (12") 12
94 Sound Entity SENT 1206 RUSH TILL DAWN PRESENTS THE HEDGEHOG AFFAIR PT. 5 EP (12") 20

HEDGEHOG PIE
76 Rubber ADUB 8 Well I Know/Go With The Flow 6
71 Rubber RUB 004 HIS ROUND (LP, with Tony Capstick, first pressing with black label on side 1 and white label on side 2) 20
75 Rubber RUB 009 HEDGEHOG PIE (LP) 30
75 Rubber RUB 014 GREEN LADY (LP) 50
78 Rubber RUB 024 JUST ACT NORMAL (LP, with lyric insert) 20

(see also Dando Shaft)

HEDGEHOPPERS ANONYMOUS
65 Decca F 12298 Don't Push Me/Please Don't Hurt Your Heart For Me 6
66 Decca F 12400 Baby (You're My Everything)/Remember 10
66 Decca F 12479 Daytime/That's The Time 10
66 Decca F 12530 Stop Press/Little Memories 8

(see also Alan Avon & Toy Shop, Mick Tinsley)

HEDONE
84 Omgowa Power HEAD 001 Sensible/Everything's Going To Be Nice (no p/s) 50

HEERA
86 Arishma ARI 004 DIAMONDS FROM HEERA (LP) 20

HEFNER
97 Boogie Wonderland BWL020 A BETTER FRIEND EP (7" p/s with two inserts) 15
97 Boogie Wonderland BWL 023 Lee Remick/Schoolgirls Knees (p/s) 15
98 Sticky STICKY 23 A Hymn For The Alcohol/My Art College Days Are Over (p/s, 500 only) 15
98 Too Pure PURE 80S Pull Yourself Together/Christ 8
99 Too Pure PURE 98S I Took Her Love For Granted/A Belly Full Of Babies (7") 6
98 Too Pure PURE 83LP BREAKING GOD'S HEART (LP) 35
99 Too Pure PURE 92LP THE FIDELITY WARS (LP) 50
00 Too Pure PURE 99LP BOXING HEFNER (LP) 35
00 Too Pure PURE 106LP WE LOVE THE CITY (LP) 40
01 Too Pure PURE 105LP DEAD MEDIA (LP) 35

NEAL HEFTI & ORCHESTRA
66 CBS 201795 Girl Talk/Lonely Girl 7
66 RCA Victor RCA 1521 The Batman Theme/Batman Chase 30
54 Vogue/Coral LVC 10005 SWINGIN' ON A CORAL REEF (10" LP) 15
65 Warner Bros W 1599 HARLOW (LP, soundtrack) 15
65 United Artists (S)ULP 1098 HOW TO MURDER YOUR WIFE (LP, soundtrack) 15
67 London HA-D 8337 BAREFOOT IN THE PARK (LP, soundtrack) 15
68 Dot (S)LPD 514 THE ODD COUPLE (LP, soundtrack) 15

LUCILLE HEGAMIN
73 VJM VLP 50 BLUE FLAME (LP) 15

DONALD HEIGHT
66 London HLZ 10062 Talk Of The Grapevine/There'll Be No Tomorrow 130
66 London HLZ 10062 Talk Of The Grapevine/There'll Be No Tomorrow (DJ copy) 175
67 London HLZ 10116 Three Hundred & Sixty Five Days/I'm Willing To Wait 100
67 London HLZ 10116 Three Hundred & Sixty Five Days/I'm Willing To Wait (DJ copy) 140
71 Avco Embassy 6105 005 Dancin' To The Music Of Love/Rags To Riches To Rags 75

HEINZ (& WILD BOYS)

			MINT VALUE £
71	Jay Boy BOY 32	Talk Of The Grapevine/There'll Be No Tomorrow (reissue)	15
72	Jay Boy BOY 51	Three Hundred & Sixty Five Days/I'm Willing To Wait (reissue)	10
72	Jay Boy BOY 60	We Gotta Make Up/I Can't Get Enough	10

HEINZ (& WILD BOYS)

63	Decca F 11652	Dreams Do Come True/Been Invited To A Party	20
63	Decca F 11768	Country Boy/Long Tall Jack	6
64	Decca F 11831	You Were There/No Matter What They Say	10
64	Decca F 11920	Please Little Girl/For Loving Me This Way	20
64	Columbia DB 7374	Questions I Can't Answer/The Beating Of My Heart	20
65	Columbia DB 7482	Diggin' My Potatoes/She Ain't Comin' Back (with Wild Boys)	40
65	Columbia DB 7559	Don't Think Twice, It's All Right/Big Fat Spider	30
65	Columbia DB 7656	End Of The World/You Make Me Feel So Good	40
65	Columbia DB 7779	Heart Full Of Sorrow/Don't Worry Baby	40
66	Columbia DB 7942	Movin' In/I'm Not A Bad Guy	40
70s	Cargo CPS 010	Country Boy/Just Like Eddie	10
63	Decca DFE 8545	HEINZ (EP)	40
63	Decca DFE 8559	LIVE IT UP (EP)	30
64	Decca LK 4599	TRIBUTE TO EDDIE (LP)	50

(see also Tornados, Saints)

HEISENBERG

89	Uncertain HEI 5001	No More Dreams/Rain (p/s)	20

HELDEN

83	Zica 12 ZICA 01	Holding On/Once Upon A Time In The ... (12", p/s)	15

(see also Ultravox)

HELICOPTER

72	Maple Annie MA 102	I Belong To Yesterday/Lonely Tonight	25

(see also Galliard)

HELL

83	Deadly Weapons DWS 666	Save Us From Those Who Would Save Us/Death Squad	75

RICHARD HELL (& VOIDOIDS)

76	Stiff BUY 7	(I Could Live With You In) Another World/(I Belong To The) Blank Generation/You Gotta Lose (with p/s, numbered, 5,000 only with 4 point press-out centre)	30
76	Stiff BUY 7	(I Could Live With You In) Another World/(I Belong To The) Blank Generation/You Gotta Lose (repressing for THE STIFF BOX SET & numbered 001)	8
77	Sire 6078 608	Blank Generation/Liar's Beware/Who Says? (no p/s)	8
77	Sire 6078 608	Blank Generation/Liars Beware/Who Says? (12", p/s)	10
79	Radar ADA 30	The Kid With The Replaceable Head/I'm Your Man (p/s)	15
77	Sire 9103 327	BLANK GENERATION (LP, with inner sleeve)	40
77	Sire 9103 327	BLANK GENERATION (LP, without inner sleeve)	20
83	I.D. NOSE 2	DESTINY STREET (LP)	15

(see also Neon Boys)

HELLACOPTERS

01	Sweet Nothing 12SN007	HIGH ENERGY ROCK 'N' ROLL (mini-LP)	30
04	Sweet Nothing SNLP 040	STRIKES LIKE LIGHTNING (3 x 7" box set, cards, badge & pendant)	30

(see also Super$hit666)

HELLANBACH

80	Guardian GR/HC56	Out To Get You/Light Of The World/Let's Get This Show On The Road/Nobody's Fool	40
84	Neat NEAT 1006	NOW HEAR THIS (LP, with inner sleeve)	15
84	Neat NEAT 1019	THE BIG ... H (LP, with insert)	15

PETE HELLER'S BIG LOVE

98	Junior London CUT 001	Big Love/Atlanta (12")	40

HELLHAMMER

84	Noise N 008	APOCALYPTIC RAIDS (12" EP, 45/33rpm)	50
08	Century Media 9977392	DEMON ENTRAILS (3-LP, 180gm vinyl with booklet and poster)	80

DAVE HELLING

65	Stateside SS 409	It Ain't Me Babe/If You're Gonna Leave Me	10
66	Planet PLF 101	Christine/The Bells	50

HELLIONS

65	Piccadilly 7N 35213	Daydreaming Of You/Shades Of Blue	25
65	Piccadilly 7N 35232	Tomorrow Never Comes/Dream Child	25
65	Piccadilly 7N 35265	A Little Lovin'/Think It Over	25

(see also Revolution, Traffic, Roaring Sixties, Jim Capaldi, Dave Mason, Luther Grosvenor, Spooky Tooth)

HELLO

72	Bell BELL 1238	You Move Me/Ask Your Mama	15
72	Bell BELL 1265	C'mon/The Wench	10
73	Bell BELL 1333	Another School Day/C'mon Get Together (p/s)	10
76	Bell BELL 1479	Teenage Revolution/Keeps Us Off The Streets (demo copies only)	100
76	Bell BELLS 263	KEEP US OFF THE STREETS (LP)	15

HELLO PEOPLE

74	ABC 4034	Future Shock/Destiny	6

HELL PREACHERS INC.

69	Marble Arch MALS 1169	SUPREME PSYCHEDELIC UNDERGROUND (LP)	40

HELMET

92	Interscope 7567 92162-1	MEANTIME (LP, inner)	70

BOBBY HELMS

57	Brunswick 05711	Fraulein/(Got A) Heartsick Feeling	10
57	Brunswick 05721	My Special Angel/Standing At The End of My World	10
58	Brunswick 05730	No Other Baby/The Magic Song	15
58	Brunswick 05741	Love My Lady/Just A Little Lonesome	15
58	Brunswick 05748	Jacqueline/Living In The Shadow Of The Past	12
58	Brunswick 05754	Schoolboy Crush/Borrowed Dreams	15

Jimmy HELMS

			MINT VALUE £
58	Brunswick 05765	Jingle Bell Rock/Captain Santa Claus	10
59	Brunswick 05786	Miss Memory/New River Train	6
59	Brunswick 05801	Soon It Can Be Told/I Guess I'll Miss The Prom	6
59	Brunswick 05813	My Lucky Day/Hurry Baby	6
59	Brunswick 05813	My Lucky Day/Hurry Baby (78)	20
61	Brunswick 05852	Sad Eyed Baby/You're The One	8
60	Brunswick OE 9461	BOBBY HELMS (EP)	30
57	Brunswick LAT 8250	SINGS TO MY SPECIAL ANGEL (LP)	50

JIMMY HELMS
73	Capitol CL 15762	My Little Devil/Magnificent Sanctuary Band	6
73	Fly BUG 27	Gonna Make You An Offer You Can't Refuse/Words And Music	6
74	Pye 7N 45440	Ragtime Girl/Romeo & Juliet	60

HELP
71	MCA MWPS 4039	SECOND COMING (LP)	80

HELP YOURSELF
71	Liberty LBF 15459	Running Down Deep/Paper Leaves	20
72	United Artists UP 35255	Heaven Row/Brown Lady	15
72	United Artists UP35466	Mommy Won't Be Home For Christmas/Johnny B. Goode (demo in picture sleeve)	60
72	United Artists UP 35466	Mommy Won't Be Home For Christmas/Johnny B. Goode	40
71	Liberty LBS 83484	HELP YOURSELF (LP)	100
72	United Artists UAS 29287	STRANGE AFFAIR (LP, with inner sleeve)	100
72	United Artists UAS 29413	BEWARE OF THE SHADOW (LP)	75
73	United Artists UDG 4001 [UAS 29487/FREE 1]	THE RETURN OF KEN WHALEY/HAPPY DAYS (2-LP set in envelope sleeve with LPs in individual sleeves)	60
73	United Artists UAS 29487	THE RETURN OF KEN WHALEY (LP)	20

(see also Man, Deke Leonard, Tyla Gang, Wreckless Eric)

HELPLESS HUW
80	US US 002	Sid Vicious Was Innocent/Going Through The Motions/Baby We're Not In Love/When You're Weary (p/s in bag)	15

HELTER SKELTER (1)
69	Peach PO1	Between Dreams/Run	100

HELTER SKELTER (2)
77	Sticky STY 102	I Need You/Goodbye Baby	40

(see also Gorillas, Hammersmith Gorillas, Jesse Hector)

HEMLOCK
73	Deram DM 379	Mr Horizontal/Beggar Man	12
73	Deram SML 1102	HEMLOCK (LP, white/red label with small logo)	150

(see also Miller Anderson, Keef Hartley Band, Dog Soldier)

BILL HENDERSON
60	Top Rank JAR 412	Sweet Pumpkin/Joey, Joey, Joey	8

DORRIS HENDERSON
65	Columbia DB 7567	The Hangman/Leaves That Are Green	25
67	Fontana TF 811	Message To Pretty/Watch The Stars	25
65	Columbia SX 6001	THERE YOU GO (LP, with John Renbourn)	175
67	Fontana (S)TL 5385	WATCH THE STARS (LP, with John Renbourn)	175

(see also Eclection, John Renbourn)

FINIS HENDERSON
83	Motown TMGT 1304	Skip To My Lou/I'd Rather Be Gone/Vina Del Mar (12")	10

JOE HENDERSON
62	London HLU 9553	Snap Your Fingers/If You See Me Cry	12
63	London REU 1376	JOE HENDERSON (EP)	30

LORNA HENDERSON
60	Oriole CB 1549	Lollipops To Lipstick/Steady Eddie	25
60	Oriole CB 1590	A Thousand Stars/Murray, What's Your Hurry?	10

MARIAN HENDERSON
70	MCA MK 5046	Antique Annies Magic Lantern Show/Lady Of Carlisle	8

BOBBY HENDRICKS
58	London HL 8714	Itchy Twitchy Feeling/A Thousand Dreams	60
58	London HL 8714	Itchy Twitchy Feeling/A Thousand Dreams (78)	30
59	Top Rank JAR 193	Little John Green/Sincerely, Your Lover	20
61	Mercury AMT 1163	I'm Coming Home/Every Other Night	10
64	Sue WI 315	Itchy Twitchy Feeling/Thousand Dreams (reissue, as Bobby Henricks)	35

(see also Drifters)

HUGH HENDRICKS & UPSETTERS
70	Spinning Wheel SW 103	Land Of Kinks/O'NEIL HALL: This Man	60

JON HENDRICKS
56	Brunswick 05521	Four Brothers/Cloudburst (with Dave Lambert Singers)	8

(see also Dave Lambert)

JIMI HENDRIX (EXPERIENCE)

SINGLES
66	Polydor 56139	Hey Joe/Stone Free (1st pressing credited to Jimi Hendrix, Polydor printed in black type)	100
66	Polydor 56139	Hey Joe/Stone Free (1st pressing, variant credited to Jimi Hendrix, Polydor printed in white type)	40
66	Polydor 56139	Hey Joe/Stone Free (2nd pressing credited to Jimi Hendrix Experience)	20
67	Track 604 001	Purple Haze (1-sided promo, white label with black text)	450
67	Track 604 001	Purple Haze/51st Anniversary (white label)	20
67	Track 604 001	Purple Haze/51st Anniversary (black label)	15
67	Track 604 001	Purple Haze/51st Anniversary (black label, alternative mix, but no way of telling from either label or matrix number)	25
67	Track 604 004	The Wind Cries Mary/Highway Chile	12

Jimi HENDRIX (EXPERIENCE)

MINT VALUE £

67	Decca F22652	How Would You Feel?/You Won't Want Me (white label copies with stamped Decca logo and hand-written labels)	100
67	Track 604 007	The Burning Of The Midnight Lamp/The Stars That Play With Laughing Sam's Dice	15
67	Decca F 22652	How Would You Feel/You Don't Want Me (with Curtis Knight, test pressing, unreleased)	500
67	Track 604 009	How Would You Feel/You Don't Want Me (with Curtis Knight)	12
67	London HL 10160	Hush Now/Flashing (with Curtis Knight; demo)	50
67	London HL 10160	Hush Now/Flashing (with Curtis Knight)	10
68	Track 604 025	All Along The Watchtower/Long Hot Summer Night	12
69	Track 604 029	Crosstown Traffic/Gypsy Eyes	12
69	Track 604 033	Let Me Light Your Fire/The Burning Of The Midnight Lamp	10
70	London HLZ 10321	Ballad Of Jimi/Gloomy Monday (with Curtis Knight)	8
70	London HL 7126	Ballad Of Jimi/Gloomy Monday (with Curtis Knight, export issue)	30
70	Track 2095 001	Voodoo Chile/Hey Joe/All Along The Watchtower (p/s; later copies have white border on sleeve)	15
70	Track 2095 001	Voodoo Chile/Hey Joe/All Along The Watchtower (p/s; later copies with white border on sleeve)	8
70	Track 2095 001	Voodoo Chile/Hey Joe/All Along The Watchtower	6
71	RCA RCA 2033	No Such Animal (Parts 1 & 2) (initially in p/s, with Curtis Knight uncredited)	25
71	RCA RCA 2033	No Such Animal (Parts 1 & 2) (with Curtis Knight uncredited)	8
71	Track 2094 007	Angel/Night Bird Flying	10
71	Track 2094 010	Gypsy Eyes/Remember/Purple Haze/Stone Free (in p/s)	25
71	Track 2094 010	Gypsy Eyes/Remember/Purple Haze/Stone Free	8
72	Polydor 2001 277	Johnny B. Goode/Little Wing	6
73	Reprise K 14286	Hear My Train A-Comin/Rock Me Baby	10
73	Polydor/Sound For Industry SFI 1572	Red House/Spanish Castle Magic (1-sided flexidisc with Rolling Stone)	15
80	Polydor 260 8001	6 SINGLES PACK (6 plain sleeve singles [2141 275-280], open-out card p/s)	35
82	CBS CBS A 2749	Fire/Are You Experienced? (p/s)	8
82	CBS A 132749	Fire/Are You Experienced (12", p/s)	20
82	Polydor POSPX 401	All Along The Watchtower/Foxy Lady/Purple Haze/Manic Depression (12", p/s)	15
82	Polydor POSPX 608	Voodoo Chile (Slight Return)/Gypsy Eyes/Hey Joe/3rd Stone From The Sun (12", p/s)	15
84	Celluloid CART 332	Doriella Du Fontaine/(Instrumental Version) (12", p/s, as Lightnin' Rod/Jimi Hendrix)	12
88	Strange Fruit SFPS065	PEEL SESSIONS (12", p/s)	10
88	Polydor PZ 33	Purple Haze/51st Anniversary/All Along The Watchtower (12", p/s)	10
90	Polydor PO 71	Crosstown Traffic/Voodoo Chile (p/s)	7
90	Polydor PZ 71	Crosstown Traffic/Voodoo Chile/All Along The Watchtower (12", p/s)	15
10	Sony 886976 43587	Valleys Of Neptune/Cat Talkin To Me (p/s)	8
10	Sony 886976711187	Bleeding Heart/Peace In Mississippi (ps)	10
10	Sony MOVLP 225	Little Drummer Boy-Silent Night-Auld Lang Syne/Three Little Bears/Little Drummer Boy-Silent Night-Auld Lang Syne (10", p/s, green vinyl)	15
11	Celluloid CEL 166	Doriella Du Fontaine/(Instrumental Version) (12", p/s)	12
11	Experience Hendrix 88697 881517	Fire/Touch You (p/s, red vinyl)	10
11	Experience Hendrix 88765439527	Somewhere/Power Of Soul (p/s)	8
15	Experience Hendrix 88875073207	Purple Haze/Freedom (p/s)	6

ALBUMS : TRACK LPS

67	Track 612 001	ARE YOU EXPERIENCED (mono, laminated (front and back) sleeve)	700
67	Track 612 001	ARE YOU EXPERIENCED (mono, laminated front but matt rear sleeve)	350
67	Track 612 003	AXIS: BOLD AS LOVE (laminated gatefold sleeve, with gatefold insert mono)	750
67	Track 612 003	AXIS: BOLD AS LOVE (laminated gatefold sleeve, without gatefold insert, mono)	150
67	Track 613 003	AXIS: BOLD AS LOVE (laminated gatefold sleeve, with gatefold insert, stereo)	300
67	Track 613 003	AXIS: BOLD AS LOVE (laminated gatefold sleeve, without gatefold insert, stereo)	120
68	Track 612 004	SMASH HITS (mono)	100
68	Track 613 004	SMASH HITS (stereo)	40
68	Track 612004	SMASH HITS (LP, "Vanenti" credit for Hey Joe)	100
68	Track 612 008/009	ELECTRIC LADYLAND (2-LP, plain white non-gatefold sleeve, labels marked "Test Pressing", mono)	2000
68	Track 613 008/009	ELECTRIC LADYLAND (2-LP, laminated gatefold sleeve, stereo, blue text inside sleeve)	800
68	Track 613 008/009	ELECTRIC LADYLAND (2-LP, laminated gatefold sleeve, stereo, white text inside sleeve) ..	350
68	Track 613 010	ELECTRIC LADYLAND PART 1 (stereo only)	35
68	Track 613 017	ELECTRIC LADYLAND PART 2 (stereo only)	35
70	Track Super 2406 002	BAND OF GYPSYS (original 'puppet' sleeve, beware of 'fake' copies on eBay)	200
70	Track Super 2406 002	BAND OF GYPSYS (repressing, gatefold 'Isle Of Wight' sleeve)	50
70	Track Super 2406 002	BAND OF GYPSYS (2nd repressing, single sleeve)	20
70	Track 2407 010	BACKTRACK 10: ARE YOU EXPERIENCED? (budget reissue, mono, some state mono but play stereo)	20
70	Track 2407 010	BACKTRACK 10: ARE YOU EXPERIENCED? (budget reissue, stereo, but in Mono sleeve)	50
70	Track 2407 011	BACKTRACK 11: AXIS: BOLD AS LOVE (budget reissue, stereo)	20
71	Track 2856 002	ELECTRIC JIMI HENDRIX (mail-order only Record Club release)	800
71	Track 2408 101	THE CRY OF LOVE (gatefold sleeve)	30
71	Track 2408 101	THE CRY OF LOVE (red vinyl, factory custom pressing, 5 known copies. The LP was pressed to test dealer reaction to coloured vinyl with a view to marketing the Pink Fairies LP Never Never Land. Although the Cry Of Love is on both sides only side A has the correct (black) Track label with the other side having a red Polydor label stating 'The Very Best Of Bert Kaempfert'. It appears that initially these Hendrix LPs were sleeved in Never Never Land sleeves but over time they have been re-sleeved by owners in Hendrix Cry Of Love sleeves.)	3000
74	Track 603003	ARE YOU EXPERIENCED (LP, stereo with POLYDOR INT. GmbH on label, this is NOT the 1967 Stereo issue of ARE YOU EXPERIENCED)	40
88	Track/HMV C 881-16	ARE YOU EXPERIENCED (LP, box set, ltd. ed. of 2,500, no'd, with certificate)	30

ALBUMS : POLYDOR LPS

71	Polydor 2302 016	ISLE OF WIGHT	25
71	Polydor 2302 018	HENDRIX IN THE WEST (gatefold sleeve)	15
72	Polydor 2302 020	WAR HEROES	15
73	Polydor ACB 00219 Super	SMASH HITS (LP, Audio Club Of Great Britain issue)	20
73	Polydor 2657 012	ELECTRIC LADYLAND (2-LP, laminated gatefold sleeve, reissue)	60
73	Polydor 2310 271	ELECTRIC LADYLAND PART 1 (reissue)	20
73	Polydor 2310 272	ELECTRIC LADYLAND PART 2 (reissue)	20
74	Polydor 2310 301	LOOSE ENDS	15
75	Polydor 2310 398	CRASH LANDING	15
75	Polydor 2310 415	MIDNIGHT LIGHTNING	15
78	Polydor 2612 034	THE ESSENTIAL JIMI HENDRIX (2-LP, with bonus 1-sided 33rpm 7" Gloria [JIMI 1] in special bag)	40
79	St. Michael 2102/0102	JIMI HENDRIX (cat. no. also listed as Polydor 2891 139)	75
80	Polydor 2625 040	JIMI HENDRIX (13-LP box set [11 x LP + 1 x 2-LP])	75
80	Polydor POLS 1023	NINE TO THE UNIVERSE	15
84	Polydor SPDLP 3	ELECTRIC LADYLAND (2-LP, non-laminated gatefold sleeve, 2nd reissue)	40
90	Polydor 847 2311	CORNERSTONES: JIMI HENDRIX 1967-1970	15
83	Polydor PODV6	SINGLES ALBUM (2-LP, gatefold)	20
91	Polydor 847 234 1	ARE YOU EXPERIENCED? (LP, reissue with barcode on rear)	15
93	Polydor 847243	AXIS: BOLD AS LOVE (LP, reissue)	25

ALBUMS : OTHER LPS

68	London HA 8349	GET THAT FEELING (Mono, with Curtis Knight)	50
68	London SH 8369	GET THAT FEELING (Stereo, with Curtis Knight)	40
68	London HA 8369	STRANGE THINGS (Mono, with Curtis Knight)	50
68	London SH 8369	STRANGE THINGS (Stereo, with Curtis Knight)	40
71	Reprise K 40430	LIVE AT THE MONTEREY INTERNATIONAL POP FESTIVAL (shared with Otis Redding)	35
71	Reprise K 44159	RAINBOW BRIDGE (matt gatefold sleeve, 'steamboat' label, soundtrack)	20
73	Ember NR 5068	IN THE BEGINNING (textured gatefold sleeve)	15
74	Ember EMB 3428	LOOKING BACK WITH JIMI HENDRIX	15
75	DJM DJLMD 8011	FOR REAL (2-LP, gatefold sleeve)	25
89	Castle Comms. HBLP 100	LIVE AND UNRELEASED - THE RADIO SHOW (5-LP)	30
89	Castle CCSLP 212	RADIO ONE (2-LP, gatefold)	20

ALBUMS : CDS

84	Track 821 993 2	BAND OF GYPSYS	35
88	Polydor/HMV C88 LP 1-11	ARE YOU EXPERIENCED? (box set via HMV stores, 1,500 only)	25
89	Castle Comms. HBCD 100	LIVE AND UNRELEASED - THE RADIO SHOW (3-CD, box set)	30

(see also Eire Apparent, Jayne Mansfield, McGough & McGear, Fat Mattress, Curtis Knight, Billy Cox, Buddy Miles, Riot Squad)

MARGIE HENDRIX
66	Mercury MF 976	I Call You Lover But You Ain't Nothin' But A Tramp/The Question	25
67	Mercury MF 1001	Restless/On The Right Track	20

TONY HENDRIX
69	Pye Int. 7n 25485	The Grooviest Girl In The World/Majestic World	8

LARRY HENLEY
64	Hickory 45-1272	My Reasons For Living/Stickin' Up For My Baby	12

(see also Newbeats, Dean & Mark)

CHRISTIE HENNESSY
73	Westwood	CHRISTIE HENNESSY (LP)	35

HENNESSYS
69	Cambrian CLP 593	THE ROADS AND THE MILES (LP)	80
60s	Music Factory MF 106	KARDIFF AFTER DARK (LP)	90

ADRIAN HENRI
60s	Charivari	ADRIAN HENRI (LP)	45
60s	Argo PLP 1194	ADRIAN HENRI AND HUGO WILLIAMS (LP)	40

(see also Liverpool Scene, McGough & McGear)

BOB HENRY
65	Philips BF 1450	I Need Me Someone/Built Like A Man	18

(see also Robert Henry)

CLARENCE ('FROGMAN') HENRY
57	London HLN 8389	Ain't Got No Home/Troubles Troubles (as Clarence Henry) (gold lettering on label)	150
57	London HLN 8389	Ain't Got No Home/Troubles Troubles (as Clarence Henry) (silver lettering on label)	100
57	London HLN 8389	Ain't Got No Home/Troubles Troubles (as Clarence Henry) (78)	40
61	Pye International 7N 25078	But I Do/Just My Baby And Me	10
61	Pye International 7N 25089	You Always Hurt The One You Love/Little Suzy	7
61	Pye International 7N 25108	Lonely Street/Why Can't You	7
61	Pye International 7N 25115	Standing In The Need Of Love/On Bended Knees	10
62	Pye International 7N 25123	A Little Too Much/I Wish I Could Say The Same	12
62	Pye International 7N 25141	Dream Myself A Sweetheart/Lost Without You	12
62	Pye International 7N 25169	The Jealous Kind/Come On And Dance	15
64	London HLU 9936	Little Green Frog/Have You Ever Been Lonely?	30
66	London HLU 10025	Ain't Got No Home/Baby, Ain't That Love?	30
61	Pye Intl. NEP 44007	CLARENCE 'FROGMAN' HENRY HIT PARADE (EP)	30
61	Pye Intl. NPL 28017	YOU ALWAYS HURT THE ONE YOU LOVE (LP)	40

DANNY HENRY
81	Three Kings TK50	Sharon My Love/Version/African Gold (12")	40

MILTON HENRY
76	Cactus CT85	Gypsy Woman/Dub	25
85	Wackies LP 2450	WHO DO YOU THINK I AM? (LP)	40
87	Tachyon WR 2741	BABYLON LOOT (LP)	55

Pierre HENRY

MINT VALUE £

(see also Milton Morris)

PIERRE HENRY
66	Philips 4FE 8000	LE VOYAGE FROM THE TIBETAN BOOK OF THE DEAD (LP)	20
66	Philips 4FE 8504	VARIATIONS FOR A DOOR AND A SIGH (LP, UK record in French sleeve)	20
68	Philips 4FE 8004	MASS FOR THE PRESENT TIME (LP)	40

RICHARD HENRY
68	Regal Zonophone RZ 3014	Oh Girl/Lay Your Head Upon My Shoulder	6

ROBERT HENRY
66	Philips BF 1476	Walk Away Like A Winner/That's All I Want	70

(see also Bob Henry)

HENRY & LIZA
73	Dragon DRA 1004	Hole Under Cratches/TIVOLIS: Hole Under Cratches (Instrumental) (actually "Hole Under Crutches")	6

(see also Max Romeo)

HENRY & LOUIS
80s	2 Kings 2K7001	Jah Jah Never Fail/Dub Never Fail I	15

HENRY COW
73	Virgin V 2005	THE LEGEND (LP)	50
74	Virgin V 2011	UNREST (LP, gatefold sleeve, black/white 'twin' label)	30
75	Virgin V 2027	IN PRAISE OF LEARNING (LP)	30
76	Caroline CAD 3002	CONCERTS (LP)	30
79	Broadcast BC 1	WESTERN CULTURE (LP)	20
86	Broadcast BC 3	IN PRAISE OF LEARNING (LP, reissue)	15
12	ReR MegacorpRER VHC5 DLP	CONCERTS (2-LP, reissue)	40
17	ReR MegacorpRER VHC2	UNREST (LP, reissue)	18
17	ReR MegacorpRER VHC3	IN PRAISE OF LEARNING (LP, reissue)	15

(see also Slapp Happy, Art Bears, Fred Frith, Gong/Henry Cow/Global Trucking Company)

HENRY ESSENCE
79	Ellie Jay Records EJSP9392	Margarita/14 Year Old Lover (500 only, p/s)	150

HENRY III
67	Island WI 3078	Thank You Girl/Take Me Back	50
67	Island WI 3081	I'll Reach The End/Won't Go Away (B-side actually Lee's Special by Don Tony Lee)	60
67	RCA RCA 1568	So Much Love/Sitting In The Park	20
70	Dynamic DYN 402	Out Of Time/VICEROYS: Love For Everyone (both with Hubcap & Wheels)	15

(see also Uniques)

JUDY HENSKE
66	Reprise RS 20485	Road To Nowhere/Sing A Rainbow	15
65	Reprise RS 6203	DEATH DEFYING (LP)	30

JUDY HENSKE & JERRY YESTER
69	Straight STS 1052	FAREWELL ALDEBARAN (LP)	50

KEN HENSLEY
73	Bronze ILPS 9223	PROUD WORDS ON A DUSTY SHELF (LP, gatefold sleeve, lyric inner, Island credit on label)	60
75	Bronze ILPS 9307	EAGER TO PLEASE (LP, lyric inner, Island credit on label)	50
81	Bronze BRON 533	FREE SPIRIT (LP)	35

(see also Uriah Heep. Wasp)

ROBERT HENRY HENSLEY
68	Polydor 56295	You're Gonna See Me Cry/Montage	8

NICKY HENSON
63	Parlophone R 4976	Till I See You Cry/What Does It Mean?	20

DAVID HENTSCHEL
75	Ring O' 2017 101	Oh My My/Devil Woman	8

NAT HEPBURN
60s	Jump Up JU 516	River/Political Girl	6

HEPBURNS
87	Cherry Red 12CHERRY 98	GOALMOUTH INCIDENT (12" EP)	10
89	Let's Zine! (No Cat. No.)	Where You Belong/WALTONES: She Looks Right Through Me (Demo Version) (1-sided flexi, with Zine fanzine issue 10)	15
90	Magic MAGIC 01T	Electrified (From Countryside To City)/London Welshman/Dive (12", p/s)	25
88	Cherry Red BRED 83	THE MAGIC OF THE HEPBURNS (LP)	15

HEP STARS
66	Decca F 22446	Sunny Girl/No Response	45
67	Olga OLE 001	Wedding/Consolation	25
68	Olga OLE 013	Let It Be Me/Groovy Summertime (withdrawn, supposedly reissued 1969)	45
68	Olga OLE 014	Malaika/It's Nice To Be Back (in export p/s)	55
68	Olga OLE 014	Malaika/It's Nice To Be Back	25

(see also Abba)

HEPTONES
66	Rio R 104	Gunmen Coming To Town/TOMMY McCOOK & SUPERSONICS: Riverton City	100
67	Ska Beat JB 266	We've Got Love/I Am Lonely	180
67	Caltone TONE 105	Schoolgirls/Ain't That Bad?	60
67	Studio One SO 2005	A Change Is Gonna Come/Nobody Knows	150
67	Studio One SO 2014	Fat Girl/DELROY WILSON: Mother Word	30
67	Studio One SO 2021	If I Knew/Festival Day	50
67	Studio One SO 2026	Why Did You Leave?/GAYLADS: Don't Try To Reach Me	30
67	Studio One SO 2027	Why Must I?/SLIM SMITH: Try Again	65
67	Studio One SO 2031	Take Me (actually by The Soul Vendors)/DELROY WILSON: I'm Not A King	50
67	Studio One SO 2033	Only Sixteen/Baby	30
68	Studio One SO 2040	Tripe Girl/DELROY WILSON: Mr. D.J.	110
68	Studio One SO 2049	Cry, Baby, Cry/Mama	50
68	Studio One SO 2052	Dock Of The Bay/KING ROCKY (ELLIS): The Ruler	170

HERB & KAY

			MINT VALUE £
68	Studio One SO 2055	Party Time/Oil In Your Lamp	50
68	Coxsone CS 7052	Love Won't Come Easy/Gee Wee	100
68	Coxsone CS 7068	Equal Rights/Ting-A-Ling	60
68	Coxsone CS 7082	Soul Power/Love Me Always	125
69	Coxsone CS 7092	Sweet Talking/Ob-La-Di	70
69	Studio One SO 2083	I Shall Be Released/Love Me Always	50
69	Bamboo BAM 11	I Shall Be Released/Love Me Always (Power) (reissue)	30
70	Bamboo BAM 28	Young, Gifted and Black/SOUND DIMENSION: Joyland	30
70	Bamboo BAM 39	Young Generation/You Turned Away	45
70	Bamboo BAM 43	Message From A Blackman/SOUND DIMENSION: Jamaica Underground	30
70	Upsetter US 339	Hurry Up/Thanks We Get	30
70	Banana BA 311	Be A Man/U ROY: Shock Attack	20
71	Banana BA 325	Suspicious Minds/Haven't You Any Fight Left?	30
71	Banana BA 349	Freedom Line/SOUND DIMENSION: Version	20
72	Green Door GD 4020	Hypocrite/JOHNNY LOVER: Straight To The Head	12
72	Prince Buster PB 37	Our Day Will Come/PRINCE BUSTER: Protection	18
72	Ashanti ASH 411	I'm In The Mood For Love/TOMMY McCOOK & NOW GENERATION: Eight Years After	8
72	Duke DU 143	Save The Last Dance For Me/Be The One	8
72	Pama PM 843	You've Lost That Lovin' Feelin'/RUPIE EDWARDS ALLSTARS: Feeling Version	8
72	Pama Supreme PS 367	Save The Last Dance For Me/Save The Last Dance Version	7
72	Ackee ACK 407	I Miss You (Parts 1 & 2)	8
73	Ackee ACK 414	Let Me Hold Your Hand/Version	8
73	Downtown DT 515	Meaning Of Life/Version Of Life	20
73	Jaguar JAG 103	Drifting Away/BONGO LES: Zion Drum	18
73	Grape GR 3053	Old Time/G.G. ALLSTARS: Dub	8
73	Smash SMA 2328	Soul Sister/IMPACT ALLSTARS: Soul Sister (Version)	15
73	Count Shelley CS 017	Now I Know/AUGUSTUS PABLO: Version	15
74	Pama Supreme PS 390	Thanks We Get/Oppression (B-side by Delroy Butler)	25
75	Faith FA 012	Party Time/Version	8
76	Cancer CAN 003	Cool Rasta/Rasta Dub	12
76	Trojan Horse HOSS 124	Cool Rasta/Dreadlock	12
70s	Third World TWDIS 13	Losing You/Mount Zion (12")	15
67	Studio One SOL 9002	THE HEPTONES (LP)	300
68	Studio One SOL 9010	ON TOP (LP)	400
72	Trojan TBL 183	THE HEPTONES AND THEIR FRIENDS MEET THE NOW GENERATION (LP)	35
75	Island ILPS 9297	BOOK OF RULES (LP)	30
76	Island ILPS 9456	PARTY TIME (LP)	25
76	Island ILPS 9381	NIGHT FOOD (LP)	20
76	Trojan TRLS 128	COOL RASTA (LP)	15
78	Third World TDWD1	BETTER DAYS (LP)	20

(see also Soul Vendors, Ronald & Lloyd, Ed Nangle, Love Generation, Alton Ellis, Basil Daley, Ken Boothe, Jackie Mittoo)

HERB & KAY

54	Parlophone MSP 6127	This Ole House/Angels In The Sky	20
54	Parlophone CMSP 23	This Ole House/Angels In The Sky (export issue)	20
55	Parlophone CMSP 31	Coffee Blues/Juke Box Jig (export issue)	20

HERBAL MIXTURE

66	Columbia DB 8021	A Love That's Died/Tailor Made	250
66	Columbia DB 8083	Machines/Please Leave My Mind	350

(see also Tony McPhee, Groundhogs)

HERBALISER

95	Ninja Tune ZEN 18	REMEDIES (2-LP)	20
97	Ninja Tune ZEN 28	BLOW YOUR HEADPHONES (LP)	20
99	Ninja Tune ZEN 41	VERY MERCENARY (2-LP)	20

HERBIE & ROYALISTS

68	Saga FID 2121	SOUL OF THE MATTER (LP)	30

HERBIE'S PEOPLE

65	CBS 202005	Sweet And Tender Romance/You Thrill Me To Pieces	25
66	CBS 202058	One Little Smile/You Never Know	20
67	CBS 202584	Residential Area/Humming Bird	12

HERD

65	Parlophone R 5284	Goodbye Baby, Goodbye/Here Comes The Fool	50
65	Parlophone R 5353	She Was Really Saying Something/It's Been A Long Time Baby	50
66	Parlophone R 5413	So Much In Love/This Boy's Always Been True	60
67	Fontana TF 819	I Can Fly/Diary Of A Narcissist	15
67	Fontana TF 856	From The Underworld/Sweet William	7
67	Fontana TF 887	Paradise Lost/Come On - Believe Me (in p/s)	20
67	Fontana TF 887	Paradise Lost/Come On - Believe Me	7
68	Fontana TF 925	I Don't Want Our Loving To Die/Our Fairy Tale	6
68	Fontana TF 975	Sunshine Cottage/Miss Jones	8
69	Fontana TF 1011	The Game/Beauty Queen	10
71	B&C CB 154	You've Got Me Hangin' From Your Lovin' Tree/I Don't Wanna Go To Sleep Again	6
68	Fontana (S)TL 5458	PARADISE LOST (LP, flipback sleeve, black/silver labels)	80
72	Bumble GEMP 5001	NOSTALGIA (LP)	25

(see also Humble Pie, Judas Jump, Andy Bown, Preachers)

HERE & NOW

78	Deptford Fun City DLP 02	WHAT YOU SEE ... IS WHAT YOU ARE (LP, 1 side by Alternative TV)	15
83	Chick CHRL 003	FANTASY SHIFT (LP)	20

(see also Daevid Allen)

HERESY

85	Earache EAR 01	NEVER HEALED EP (Flexi)	20

HERESY/CONCRETE SOX

MINT VALUE £

89	In Your Face FACE 4	WHOSE GENERATION? EP (gatefold p/s)	10
88	In Your Face FACE 01	FACE UP TO IT! (LP)	15
89	In Your Face FACE 07	13 ROCKING ANTHEMS (LP)	15

HERESY/CONCRETE SOX
87 Manic Ears MOSH 2   HERESY/CONCRETE SOX (LP, inner, 1 side each) 15

HERETIC
84 Thunderbolt THBE 1004   BURNT AT THE STAKE EP (Water Of Vice/Keep On Telling Those Lies/Fever Of Love/Watch Me Grow (12", p/s) 25

HERITAGE
81 Rondelet ROUND 8   Strange Place To Be/Misunderstood (p/s) 20
82 Rondelet ABOUT 12   REMORSE CODE (LP, with lyric insert) 35
82 Plant Life PLR 040   LIVING BY THE AIR (LP) 15

HERMAN (CHIN-LOY)
71 Big Shot BI 573   El Fishy/HERMAN'S ALLSTARS: Nightmare (B-side actually "In The Spirit" by Lloyd Charmers) 15
71 Big Shot BI 577   Tar Baby (actually "Crazy Baby" by U. Roy Jr.)/TOMMY McCOOK: Archie 10
71 Big Shot BI 578   New Love/AUGUSTUS PABLO: The Mood 25
71 Big Shot BI 579   East Of The River Nile Version/AUGUSTO PABLO: East Of The River Nile 50
71 Duke DU 107   To The Fields/HERMAN'S VERSION MEN: Fields Version 40
71 Ackee ACK 133   Dunce Cap/AQUARIANS: Version Cap 10
71 Ackee ACK 140   Youth Man/AQUARIANS: Version 10
71 Explosion EX 2049   Love Brother/Uganda 6
71 Escort ERT 854   Love Brother/Love Brother Version (B-side actually by Tommy McCook) 7
71 Punch PH 55   Hold The Ghost/AQUARIUS SOUL BAND: Duppy Dance 15
71 Punch PH 58   Listen To The Beat/AQUARIANS: Sounds Only 7

(see also Jimbilin)

PRIEST HERMAN
64 Blue Beat BB 266   We Are Praying/BUSTER'S ALLSTARS: Dallas, Texas 60

WOODY HERMAN
54 London HL 8013   Wooftie/Moten Stomp (as Woody Herman & New Third Herd) 20
54 London HL 8031   Fancy Woman/Eight Babies To Mind (as Woody Herman's Woodchoppers) 20
54 Capitol CL 14183   Muskrat Ramble/Woodchopper's Mambo (Woody Herman & His Orchestra) 12
55 London HL 8122   Sorry 'Bout The Whole Darned Thing/Love's A Dog (with New Third Herd) 15
66 CBS 202522   Sidewinder/Greasy Sack Blues 30
69 Chess CRS 8095   Hush/Light My Fire 10

(see also David Rose Orchestra)

HERMAN'S HERMITS
65 Columbia DB 7546   Wonderful World/Dream On 6
66 Columbia DB 7861   You Won't Be Leaving/Listen People 7
66 Columbia DB 7947   This Door Swings Both Ways/For Love 6
66 Columbia DB 8012   No Milk Today/My Reservation's Been Confirmed 7
66 Columbia DB 8076   East-West/What Is Wrong, What Is Right? 8
67 Columbia DB 8235   Museum/Moonshine Man 6
68 Columbia DB 8327   I Can Take Or Leave Your Loving/Marcel's 6
69 Columbia DB 8563   My Sentimental Friend/My Lady 6
68 EMI SLES 15   No Milk Today/There's A Kind Of Hush (promo only, white label) 10
68 EMI SLES 16   London Look (promo only, white label) 8
69 Columbia DB 8626   Here Comes The Star/It's Alright Now 8
74 Buddah BDS 700   Train/Ride On The Water (withdrawn) 30
65 Columbia SEG 8380   HERMANIA (EP) 12
65 Columbia SEG 8440   MRS BROWN YOU'VE GOT A LOVELY DAUGHTER (EP) 10
65 Columbia SEG 8442   HERMAN'S HERMITS HITS (EP) 10
67 Columbia SEG 8520   DANDY (EP) 10
65 Columbia 33SX 1727   HERMAN'S HERMITS (LP) 20
66 Columbia SX 6084   BOTH SIDES OF HERMAN'S HERMITS (LP) 15
67 Columbia S(C)X 6174   THERE'S A KIND OF HUSH ALL OVER THE WORLD (LP) 15

(see also Peter Noone)

HERMITS
71 RCA 2135   She's A Lady (Say What You Want To Say)/Gold Mandela 15
72 RCA 2265   The Man/Effen Curly 50

HEROES
75 United Artists UP 36016   Growing Up/Losing You 8

TED HEROLD
60 Polydor NH 66817   I Don't Know Why/Moonlight 15

HERON
70 Dawn DNS 1015   Take Me Back Home/Minstrel And A King 15
71 Dawn DNX 2509   Bye And Bye/Through Time/Only A Hobo/I'm Ready To Leave (p/s) 25
71 Dawn DNLS 3010   HERON (LP, with insert, some with "this album was recorded live in a field" sticker) 250
72 Dawn DNLS 3025   TWICE AS NICE & HALF THE PRICE (2-LP, with postcard) 300
72 Dawn DNLS 3025   TWICE AS NICE & HALF THE PRICE (2-LP, without postcard) 150

(see also Mike Cooper)

DIANA HERON
79 Ethnic Fight DD4432   Be Thankful/Dub (12") 15
79 Ethnic Fight EF 088   Sweeter He Is/TIT COLLINS: Hey Boy 10

MIKE HERON('S REPUTATION)
71 Island ILPS 9146   SMILING MEN WITH BAD REPUTATIONS (LP, gatefold sleeve, pink rim, palm tree label) ... 40
75 Neighborhood 80637   MIKE HERON'S REPUTATION (LP) 20

(see also Incredible String Band)

BERNARD HERRMANN
69 Phase 4 Stereo PFS 4173   THE GREAT MOVIE THRILLERS (LP) 18

			MINT VALUE £
75	Phase 4 Stereo PFS 4309	THE FANTASY FILM WORLD OF BERNARD HERRMANN (LP)	30
76	Phase 4 Stereo PFS 4337	THE MYSTERIOUS FILM WORLD OF BERNARD HERRMANN (LP)	18

KRISTIN HERSH
94	4AD CAD 4002	HIPS & MAKERS (LP)	50
12	Music On Vinyl MOVLP489	HIPS & MAKERS (LP, reissue)	20

(see also Throwing Muses)

KIM HERTE
85	RMO 12-ZAM 1	Do You Wanna Danvce With Me/(Electro Mix) (12")	30

EVERIT HERTER
60	Capitol CL 15242	Don't Get Serious/Boys Were Made For Girls	10

PAT HERVEY & TIARAS & ART SNIDER
63	RCA 1332	Tears Of Misery/Brother, Can You Spare A Dime (as Pat Hervey)	7
67	President PT 110	Can't Get You Out Of My Mind/Givin' In	10

HERZFELD
93	Duophonic DS45 07	Two Mothers/Who The Scroungers Are (p/s, mail order only)	6

HESITATIONS
68	London HLR 10198	The Impossible Dream (The Quest)/Nobody Knows You When You're Down And Out	8
69	London HLR 10180	Born Free/Push A Little Bit Harder	20
68	London HA-R/SH-R 8360	THE NEW BORN FREE (LP)	30

CAROLYN HESTER
65	Dot DS 16751	Playboys And Playgirls/High Flyin' Bird	8
65	Dot DS 26751	What Does It Get You?/Now He's Gone	10
66	CBS (S)BPG 62033	CAROLYN HESTER (LP)	30
69	Pye Intl. NSPL 28121	THE CAROLYN HESTER COALITION (LP)	20

(see also Four For Fun)

HETHERINGTON
73	Mowest MW 3007	(It's Just A) Teenage Love Song/That Girl's Alright	6
73	Mowest MW 3007	(It's Just A) Teenage Love Song/That Girl's Alright (demo in p/s)	12

JOHN HETHERINGTON
70	RCA 1965	It's Only Me/Dreamboat Avenue	8

HEWETT SISTERS
59	HMV POP 567	Baby-O/Jerri-Lee (I Love Him So)	25

KEVIN HEWICK
82	Factory FAC 48	Ophelia's Drinking Song/Cathy Clown/He Holds You Tighter (p/s)	15

BEN HEWITT
59	Mercury AMT 1041	You Break Me Up/I Ain't Givin' Up Nothin'	50
59	Mercury AMT 1055	For Quite A While/Patricia June	35
59	Mercury AMT 1084	I Want A New Girl Now/My Search	50
60	Mercury ZEP 10035	BREAK IT UP WITH BEN HEWITT (EP)	200
84	Bear Family BFX 15150	THEY WOULD CALL ME ELVIS (LP, gatefold)	15
85	Bear Family BFX 15187	GOOD TIMES AND SOME MIGHTY FINE ROCK 'N' ROLL (LP, gatefold)	15

GARTH HEWITT
70s	Myrrh MYR 1051	LOVE SONGS FOR THE EARTH (LP)	30
78	Myrrh MYR 1078	I'M GRATEFUL (LP, insert)	30

RICHARD HEWSON ORCHESTRA
76	Splash CPLP 1002	LOVE IS (LP)	30

PETER HEWSON
83	Reset RES 2	Take My Hand/Her (p/s)	40
83	Reset REST 2	Take My Hand/Her (12", p/s)	60

HEX
93	Ninja Tune ZEN 05	SOUNDTRACK TO GLOBAL CHAOS (LP)	20
93	Ninja Tune ZEN 07	DIGITAL LOVE (LP)	20

EDDIE HEYWOOD
58	Mercury 7MT 131	Heywood's Bounce/Soft Summer Breeze	8
64	Stateside SS 264	Theme From The Film "The Prize"/Li'l Darlin'	6

(see also Hugo Winterhalter)

WINSTON HEYWOOD (& HOMBRES)
71	Dynamic DYN 424	Bam-Sa-Bo/Version	8
72	Dynamic DYN 441	Stop The War/Version	10
72	Dynamic DYN 457	Seek And You'll Find/Version	8
73	Attack ATT 8046	Da Doo Ron Ron/Version	8
76	Mango MAN 1013	Long Long Time/UPSETTERS: Long Time Dub	10

(see also Winston Harewood, Fud Christian All Stars)

HGB
81	Backshop BS 001	Chase The Night Away/Keep Off The Grass (p/s)	7

LENNIE HIBBERT & COUNT OSSIE BAND
69	Doctor Bird DB 1113	Pure Sole/PATSY: A Man Is Two Faced	200

(see also Sound Dimension)

AL HIBBLER
55	Brunswick 05420	Unchained Melody/Daybreak (gold label)	20
55	Brunswick 05420	Unchained Melody/Daybreak (silver label)	8
55	Brunswick 05454	They Say You're Laughing At Me/I Can't Put My Arms Around A Memory	10
55	London HL 8184	Now I Lay Me Down To Dream/Danny Boy	35

EDDIE HICKEY
59	Decca F 11153	Lady May/Cap And Gown	7
60	Decca F 11204	Who Could Be Bluer?/Plain Jane	10
60	Decca F 11241	Another Sleepless Night/Barbara	10

ERSEL HICKEY
59	Fontana H 198	You Threw A Dart/Don't Be Afraid Of Love	70
59	Fontana H 198	You Threw A Dart/Don't Be Afraid Of Love (78)	20

Dwayne HICKMAN

MINT VALUE £

DWAYNE HICKMAN
60 Capitol CL 15164 — I'm A Lover, Not A Fighter/I Pass Your House ... 10

HICKORY
68 Lyntone 1928 — Scottish Magic (Promo flexi for Tartan Ale, p/s) ... 20
69 CBS 3963 — Green Light/Key ... 30
(see also Equals)

HICKORY SIX
64 Oak RGJ 149 — Feelin Blue/Hello My Darling ... 80

COLIN HICKS (& CABIN BOYS)
57 Pye 7N 15114 — Wild Eyes And Tender Lips/Empty Arms Blues (with Cabin Boys) ... 15
57 Pye 7N 15125 — La Dee Dah/Wasteland ... 10
58 Pye 7N 15163 — Little Boy Blue/Jambalaya ... 10

DAN HICKS & HIS HOT LICKS
72 Blue Thumb ILPS 9204 — STRIKING IT RICH (LP) ... 18
(see also Charlatans (U.S.)

JIMMY HICKS
72 London HLU 10396 — I'm Mr. Big Stuff/Tell Her That I Love You ... 15

MARVA HICKS
78 Infinity 102 — Looking Over My Shoulder/Here I Go Again ... 15

HIDDEN CAMERAS
03 Rough Trade RTRADLP 077 — THE SMELL OF OUR OWN (LP, hand stencilled sleeve) ... 30

HIDDEN IDENTITY
94 Pure Rudeness HIDBBB1 — BLUNTED BUMPKIN BUSTERS (EP) ... 20
(see also Evil Ed)

HIDEAWAYS
69 Action ACT 4544 — Hide Out/Jolly Joe ... 25
71 Jay Boy BOY 29 — Hide Out/Jolly Joe (reissue) ... 8

HI-FI
84 Butt MGLS 003 — Louie Louie/Summertime ... 8
(see also Ian Matthews)

HI-FI FOUR
56 Parlophone MSP 6210 — Band Of Gold/Davy, You Upset My Life ... 70

HI FI (1)
78 Aura AUS 106 — Run Run/Sole Kitchen (p/s) ... 20

HI FI'S
63 Piccadilly 7N 35130 — Take Me Or Leave Me/I'm Struck ... 8
64 Pye 7N 15635 — Will Yer Won't Yer/She's The One ... 10
64 Pye 7N 15710 — I Keep Forgettin'/Why Can't I Stop Loving You? ... 35
65 Pye 7N 15788 — Baby's In Black/Kiss And Run ... 15
66 Alp 595 010 — It's Gonna Be Morning/I Wanna Hear You Say Yeah ... 70

JOE HIGGS
67 Coxsone CS 7004 — Neighbour Neighbour/MELODIANS: I Should Have Made It Up ... 200
67 Island WI 3026 — I Am The Song/Worry No More ... 80
68 Island WI 3131 — You Hurt My Soul/LYNN TAITT: Why Am I Treated So Bad? ... 100
70 Clandisc CLA 208 — Mademoiselle/DYNAMITES: Lion ... 30
71 Big BG 312 — Burning Fire/RUPIE EDWARDS ALL STARS: Version ... 15
71 New Beat NB 087 — Mother Radio/DAWN SHARON: Little Deeds ... 12
71 Supreme SUP 215 — Burning Fire/RUPIE EDWARDS ALL STARS: Push And Pull ... 12
72 Sioux SI 005 — The World Is Spinning Around/THE REACTION: Hallelujah ... 20
72 Sioux SI 014 — The Wave Of War/JUMBO STERLING: Shaft ... 25
72 Sioux SI 021 — Lay A Foundation/JACKIE ROWLAND: Lay A Foundation (Version) ... 15
75 Grounation GRO 2021 — More Slavery/Version ... 10
75 TorpedoTOR 41 — My Baby Still Love Me/Hard Time ... 30
76 Ethnic Fight EF 038 — Creation/AUGUSTUS PABLO & SUPER 8 CORPORATION: Creative Version ... 20
75 Grounation GROL 508 — LIFE OF CONTRADICTION (LP) ... 50
78 1 STOP STOP 1002 — UNITY IS POWER (LP) ... 25
(see also Higgs & Wilson, Bob Marley/Wailers, Soul Vendors)

(JOE) HIGGS & (ROY) WILSON
60 Blue Beat (B)B 3 — Manny Oh/When You Tell Me Baby (yellow label/blue writing [B3] or blue label/silver writing [BB 3]) (with Ken Richards & His Comets) ... 20
61 Starlite ST45 035 — Pretty Baby/I Long For The Day ... 20
61 Starlite ST45 036 — Lover's Song/It Is A Day ... 20
61 Starlite ST45 042 — Come On Home/The Robe ... 20
61 Starlite ST45 053 — Sha Ba Ba/Change Of Mind ... 20
62 Blue Beat BB 95 — How Can I Be Sure/Mighty Man ... 25
63 R&B JB 109 — Let Me Know/Bye And Bye ... 25
63 Blue Beat BB 190 — If You Want Pardon/BABA BROOKS BAND: Musical Communion ... 20
63 Island WI 081 — Last Saturday Morning/Praise The Lord ... 20
64 Rio R 29 — Love Is Not For Me/Gone Is Yesterday ... 15
65 Blue Beat BB 277 — Pain In My Heart/BUSTER ALL STARS: Going West ... 30
70 Clandisc CLA 218 — Don't Mind Me/GLEN AND ROY: Angel ... 8
(see also Clancy Eccles)

HIGH
69 CBS 4164 — Long Live The High/Beggar Man Dan ... 30

HIGH & MIGHTY
66 HMV POP 1548 — Tryin' To Stop Cryin'/Escape From Cuba ... 35

HIGH AUTHORITY
91 Optimisim OPT 12005 — I'm The Man (12") ... 10

HIGH BROOM
70 Island WI 6088 — Dancing In The Moonlight/Percy's On The Run ... 15

HIGHBURY MARCHERS

MINT VALUE £

73	Columbia DB 8969	Dancing In The Moonlight/Percy's On The Run (reissue)	7

(see also Leviathan, Jason Crest, Holy Mackerel)

HIGHBURY MARCHERS
72	Columbia DB 8930	The Official Arsenal March/Arsenal Boogie	8

HIGHER INTELLEGENCE AGENCY
93	Beyond HIA 1	SPEEDLEARN EP (12", p/s)	35
94	Beyond HIA 2	COLOUR REFORM (12" EP)	15
93	Beyond RBADLP 5	COLOURFORM (2-LP)	40
95	Beyond RBADLP 13	FREEFLOATER (2-LP)	40

HIGH FASHION
83	Capitol 1A 064-7122871	MAKE UP YOUR MIND (LP)	20
82	Capitol ST 12214	FEELIN LUCKY (LP)	20

HIGHGATE CHILDREN
62	Picadilly 7N 25065	The Battle Of Highgate Hill/Pity The Poor Pedestrian	6

HIGH KEYS
63	London HLK 9768	Que Sera Sera/Daddy, Ooh Long Legs	30

HIGH LEVEL RANTERS
68	Topic 12TS 186	NORTHUMBERLAND FOR EVER (LP, blue label, 2 different sleeves)	15
69	Leader/Trailer LER 2007	THE LADS OF NORTHUMBERLAND (LP)	18
77	Broadside BRO 128	ENGLISH SPORTING BALLADS (LP, 1-side Martin Wyndham-Read, 2,000 only)	25

HIGHLY LIKELY
74	BBC RESL 10	Whatever Happened To You? (Likely Lads Theme)/God Bless Everyone	10

(see also Mike Hugg, Rodney Bewes)

HIGH NUMBERS
64	Fontana TF 480	Zoot Suit/I'm The Face (textured labels with "Mono" on labels)	1500
80	Back Door DOOR 4	I'm The Face/Zoot Suit (reissue, picture sleeve, silver plastic labels)	20
92	Fontana TF 480	I'm The Face/Zoot Suit (reissue, smooth labels with "stereo" on labels, die-cut sleeve from Fontana Box)	20

(see also Who)

HIGH SHELF
70	Sprint SP 2	Suddenly You/Wendy	40

HIGH SOCIETY (1)
66	Fontana TF 771	People Passing By/Star Of Eastern Street	22

(see also Friday Browne, Graham Gouldman, Country Gentlemen, Manchester Mob)

HIGH SOCIETY (2)
70	CBS 4746	Only You Only You/Tell Me Now	15

HIGH STREET EAST
69	Rubber RUBBER ONE	Newcastle Brown/Everybody Knows (p/s)	70
69	Rubber RUBBER ONE	Newcastle Brown/Everybody Knows (no p/s)	45

HIGH TIDE (1)
69	Liberty LBS 83264	SEA SHANTIES (LP, gatefold sleeve, blue label)	250
70	Liberty LBS 83294	HIGH TIDE (LP, blue label)	175

(see also Hawkwind, Misunderstood, Denny Gerrard, Magic Muscle, Third Ear Band)

HIGH TIDE (2)
81	Sunday Morning (No Cat. No.)	Baby Dancing/Letter From A Coward (mail-order only)	8

DEAN HIGHTOWER
60	HMV CLP 1360	TWANGY - WITH A BEAT (LP)	50

DONNA HIGHTOWER
60	Capitol ST 1273	GEE BABY (LP)	15

ROSETTA HIGHTOWER
68	Toast TT 506	Pretty Red Balloons/How Can You Mistreat (The One You Love)?	30
68	Toast TT 509	I Can't Give Back The Love I Feel For You/Big Bird	100
69	CBS 4584	One Heart For Sale/What Do I Do?	10
70	CBS 4758	April Fools/I'll Hold Out My Hand	6
70	CBS 4988	Persuader/Come Together	10
71	CBS 7068	Go Pray For Tomorrow/Give Me Just A Little More Line	6
73	Philips 6006 291	The Walls Fell Down/Captain's Army	6
71	CBS 64201	HIGHTOWER (LP)	100
71	Rediffusion ZS 88	ROSETTA HIGHTOWER (LP)	30

(see also Orlons, Ian Green [Revelation])

HIGH TREASON
80	Burlington BURLS 001	Saturday Night Special/Waste My Love (p/s)	140
80	Burlington BURLS 001	Saturday Night Special/Waste My Love (no p/s)	80

HIGHWAY (1)
74	EMI EMC 3019	HIGHWAY (LP)	20
75	EMI EMA 770	SMOKING AT THE EDGE (LP, gatefold sleeve)	35

HIGHWAY (2)
88	Highway (no cat no)	Midnight Girl/Can't Let Go (p/s)	35

HIGH WINDOWS
68	CBS 3208	Maybe Someday/Your Eyes	10
68	CBS 3437	Anybody Need A Lover/El El Israel	10

HIGSONS
82	Two Tone CHSTT21	Tear The Whole Thing Down/Ylang Ylang (p/s, paper labels)	10
82	Two Tone CHSTT121	Tear The Whole Thing Down/Ylang Ylang (12", p/s)	12
83	Two Tone CHSTT24	Run Me Down/Put The Punk Back Into Funk (p/s, paper labels)	10
83	Two Tone CHSTT 1224	Run Me Down (extended)/Instrumental/Put The Punk Back Into Funk (1 & 2) (12", p/s)	15
82	Two Tone CHS TT 1	Tear The Whole Thing Down/Ylang Ylang (12" promo shared with Apollinaires)	35

(see also New York New York, Serious Drinking)

HIJACK
88	Music Of Life NOTE016	Style Wars (12")	15

HILARY HILARY

MINT VALUE £

88	Syndicate 655517 6	The Badman is Robbin'/Hold No Hostage/Doomsday (12" EP)	12
88	Music Of Life NOTE021	Hold No Hostage/Doomsday Of Rap (12")	15
89	Music Of Life NOTE016R	Style Wars Revenge (12")	12
91	Rhyme Syndicate 6555176	HORNS OF JERICHO (LP)	35
96	Reservoir RES 18	THE ORIGINAL HORNS OF JERICHO (LP)	80

HILARY HILARY

80	Modern STP 2	How Come You're So Dumb/Rich Kid Blues (p/s)	60

(see also Roger Taylor, Queen)

RAY HILDEBRAND

70s	Myrrh MST 6508	SPECIAL KIND OF MAN (LP)	20

DIANE HILDEBRANDE

69	Elektra EKSN 45055	Jan's Blues/Early Morning Blues And Greens	10
69	Elektra EKL 4031	EARLY MORNING BLUES AND GREENS (LP)	20

HI-LITERS

58	Mercury AMT 1011	Dance Me To Death/Cha Cha Rock	150
58	Mercury AMT 1011	Dance Me To Death/Cha Cha Rock (78)	35

HI LITES

65	London HL 9967	Hey Baby/Groovey	20

BENNY HILL

55	Decca F 10442	I Can't Tell A Waltz From A Tango/Teach Me Tonight	10
56	Columbia SCM 5238	Memories Are Made Of This/Who Done It? (as Benny Hill & Coronets)	10
65	Decca LK 4723	BENNY AT THE BBC (LP)	15

(see also Coronets)

BUNKER HILL & RAYMEN

62	Stateside SS 135	Hide & Go Seek Parts 1 & 2	25

DAVID HILL

57	Vogue V 9076	All Shook Up/Melody For Lovers (with Ray Ellis Orchestra, probably unreleased)	200
57	Vogue V 9076	All Shook Up/Melody For Lovers (78, with Ray Ellis Orchestra)	35
58	RCA RCA 1041	That's Love/Keep Me In Mind (with Joe Relsman's Orchestra & Chorus)	100
58	RCA RCA 1041	That's Love/Keep Me In Mind (78, with Joe Relsman's Orchestra & Chorus)	30

JEFF HILL BAND

77	Chiswick NS 16	I Want You To Dance With Me/Feel Like Loving You (p/s)	10
79	Baloon BLOW 1/SRTS/79/CUS-557	Something's Wrong With My Baby/Whatever She Wanted (p/s, 500 only)	60

JESSIE HILL

60	London HLU 9117	Ooh Poo Pah Doo Parts 1 & 2	25

LAURYN HILL

98	Columbia COL 489843 1	THE MISEDUCATION OF LAURYN HILL (2-LP)	50

(see also Fugees)

RONNI HILL

77	Creole CR 138	You Keep Me Hanging On/I Wouldn't Give You Up (as Roni Hill)	10

VINCE HILL

62	Pye 7N 17373	Not Any More/Just As Long (As You Belong To Me)	7
62	Piccadilly 7N 35043	The Rivers Run Dry/Not Any More	8
63	Piccadilly 7N 35108	A Day At The Seaside/Tricks Of The Trade	8
65	Columbia DB 7781	Take Me To Your Heart Again/Push Push	6
66	Columbia SEG 8509	FOUR SIDES OF VINCE HILL (EP)	10

(see also [Jackie &] Raindrops, Elmer Bernstein)

Z.Z. HILL

65	R&B MRB 5005	Someone To Love Me/Have Mercy Someone	30
69	Action ACT 4532	Make Me Yours/What Am I Living For?	100
71	Mojo 2092 019	Faithful And True/I Think I'd Do It	8
75	United Artists UP 35727	I Keep On Loving You/Whoever's Thrilling You	8
77	CBS 5553	Love Is So Good When You're Stealin' It/Need You By My Side	8
66	Sue IEP 711	GIMME GIMME (EP, 2 tracks each by Z.Z. Hill & Intentions; in p/s)	300
66	Sue IEP 711	GIMME GIMME (EP, 2 tracks each by Z.Z. Hill & Intentions)	100
69	Action ACLP 6004	WHOLE LOT OF SOUL (LP)	60
72	Mojo 2916 013	THE BRAND NEW Z.Z. HILL (LP)	20
75	Contempo CLP 515	THE BRAND NEW Z.Z. HILL (LP, reissue)	15
84	Kent KENT 018	DUES PAID IN FULL (LP, compilation)	20

(see also Intentions)

STEVE HILLAGE

77	Virgin VDJ 23	Leylines To Glassdome/GLEN PHILLIPS: Lies (p/s, gig freebie)	6
75	Virgin V 2031	FISH RISING (LP, lyric insert, coloured 'twin' label)	30
77	Virgin VGD 3501	LIVE HERALD (2-LP, with limited edition mail order lyric sheet in English, French or German)	30
78	Virgin V 2098	GREEN (LP, green vinyl, with insert)	15
79	Virgin VR1	RAINBOW DOME MUSIC (LP, clear vinyl, stickered sleeve)	15

(see also Gong, Khan, Arzachel, Clearlight, Radio Actors, System 7)

HILLER BROTHERS

60s	Honey Hit TB 124	Little Darlin'/Changin' My Mind (with p/s)	10
60s	Honey Hit TB 124	Little Darlin'/Changin' My Mind	6

JANE HILLERY

66	Columbia DB 7918	You've Got That Hold On Me/Take Me Away	40

(see also Magistrates)

MABLE HILLERY

69	Xtra XTRA 1063	IT'S SO HARD TO BE A NIGGER (LP)	50

CHRIS HILLS

72	Atlantic 2400208	EVERYTHING IS EVERYTHING (LP)	25

GILLIAN HILLS

65	Vogue VRS 7005	Tomorrow Is Another Day/Look At Them	10

HILLTOPPERS

MINT VALUE £

HILLTOPPERS
54	London HL 8026	From The Vine Came The Grape/Time Will Tell	15
54	London HL 8070	Poor Butterfly/Wrapped Up In A Dream	20
54	London HL 8081	Will You Remember?/The Old Cabaret	20
54	London HL 8092	If I Didn't Care/Bettina	20
55	London HL 8116	Time Waits For No One/You Try Somebody Else	20
55	London HLD 8168	The Kentuckian Song/I Must Be Dreaming	20
55	London HLD 8208	Searching/All I Need Is You	35
56	London HLD 8221	Only You (And You Alone)/(It Will Have To Do) Until The Real Thing Comes Along (gold label lettering)	30
56	London HLD 8221	Only You (And You Alone)/(It Will Have To Do) Until The Real Thing Comes Along (silver label lettering)	15
56	London HLD 8255	My Treasure/Last Word In Love	50
56	London HLD 8278	Do The Bop/When You're Alone	100
56	London HLD 8298	Tryin'/D-A-R-L-I-N'	30
56	London HLD 8333	So Tired/Faded Rose	30
57	London HLD 8381	Marianne/You're Wasting Your Time	15
57	London HLD 8441	I'm Serious/I Love My Girl	15
57	London HLD 8455	A Fallen Star/Footsteps	15
57	London HLD 8528	The Joker/Chicken, Chicken	40
58	London HLD 8603	You Sure Look Good To Me/Starry Eyes	20
60	London HLD 9038	Alone/The Prisoner's Song	10
55	London RE-P 1012	PRESENTING THE HILLTOPPERS	20
55	London RE-D 1030	THE HILLTOPPERS VOL. 2	20
57	London RE-D 1099	THE HILLTOPPERS VOL. 3	20
57	London HA-D 2029	THE TOWERING HILLTOPPERS	20
57	London HA-D 2071	TOPS IN POPS	20

(see also Sacca, Billy Vaughn)

NICKY HILTON
65	Decca F 12099	Give Us Your Blessing/Always In My Heart	6

RONNIE HILTON
55	HMV 7M 285	Prize Of Gold/A Blossom Fell	15
55	HMV 7M 303	Just Say You Love Her/My Loving Hands	10
56	HMV 7M 336	Bella Notte/He	6
67	HMV POP 1600	If I Were A Rich Man/Laughing Gnome (Bowie penned B-side)	40

(see also Alma Cogan)

HILTONAIRES
67	Coxsone CSL 8004	THE BEST OF THE HILTONAIRES (LP)	80

HIM & THE OTHERS
66	Parlophone R 5510	I Mean It/She's Got Eyes That Tell Lies	850

JUSTIN HINDS/HINES (& DOMINOES)
64	Ska Beat JB 176	King Samuel/River Jordan	25
65	Ska Beat JB 187	Mother Banner/DON DRUMMOND & HIS GROUP: Apanga	55
65	Island WI 171	Botheration/Satan (as Justin Hines & Dominoes)	30
65	Island WI 174	Jump Out Of The Frying Pan/Holy Dove (as Justin Hines & Dominoes)	30
65	Island WI 194	Rub Up, Push Up/The Ark	30
65	Island WI 232	Turn Them Back/TOMMY McCOOK: Rocket Ship	60
65	Island WI 236	Peace And Love/Skalarama (B-side actually by Lyn Taitt & Comets)	40
66	Doctor Bird DB 1048	The Higher The Monkey Climbs/Fight For Your Right	30
67	Island WI 3048	On A Saturday Night/Save A Bread	22
67	Treasure Isle TI 7002	Here I Stand/No Good Rudie	25
67	Treasure Isle TI 7005	Carry Go Bring Come/Fight Too Much	40
67	Treasure Isle TI 7014	On A Saturday Night/Save A Bread	20
67	Treasure Isle TI 7017	Once A Man/TOMMY McCOOK & SUPERSONICS: Persian Cat	25
68	Treasure Isle TI 7063	Botheration/VINCENT HINDS: Mouth Trombone	15
68	Treasure Isle TI 7068	Mighty Redeemer (Parts 1 & 2)	15
69	Trojan TR 652	You Should've Known Better/TOMMY McCOOK & SUPERSONICS: Third Figure	18
70	Duke Reid DR 2511	Say Me Say/I Want It	15
70	Duke DU 67	Drink Milk/Everywhere I Go (as Justin Hines & Dominoes)	18
72	Treasure Isle TI 7068	Mighty Redeemer/DUKE REID'S ALL STARS: Version	12
75	Pama PM 4001	Sinners Where You Going To Hide?/If It's Love You Need	8
12	Duke THB 7023	Sufferation 1969/Warm Up	30
76	Island ILPS 9416	JEZEBEL (LP)	30

(see also Lyn Taitt, Skatalites, Don Drummond)

NEVILLE HINDS
70	Duke Reid DR 2503	Sunday Gravy (as Neville Hines)/JOHN HOLT: Write Her A Letter	30
70	Camel CA 44	London Bridge/SCORCHERS: Things And Time (B-side act. by Wailing Souls)	20
70	Gas GAS 126	I Who Have Nothing/You Send Me	8
71	Explosion EX 2043	Delivered/Specially For You (B-side actually by Blake Boy)	10
72	Upsetter US 384	Blackman's Time/UPSETTERS: Version	25
73	Harry J HJ 6657	Musical Splendour/JOHN CROW GENERATION: Musical Drum & Bass	12

(see also Neville Irons & Byron Lee & The Dragonaires, Lloyd Robinson, Marvels, Alton Ellis)

RUPERT HINE
72	Purple PUR 105	Hamburgers/A Varlet Lad T'was Samuel Green (Historical Moments - Part 7)	6
76	Electric WOT 8	Snakes Don't Dance Fast/Hopi Smile	6
71	Purple TPSA 7502	PICK UP A BONE (LP, with David MacIver, textured gatefold sleeve)	50
73	Purple TPSA 7509	UNFINISHED PICTURE (LP, gatefold sleeve)	50

(see also Jon Pertwee, Quantum Jump)

FRAZER HINES
68	Major Minor MM 579	Who's Dr. Who?/Punch And Judy Man	70

Sonny HINES

MINT VALUE £

SONNY HINES
65 King KG 1009 — Anytime, Any Day, Anywhere/Nothing Like Your Love 25

HINGE
68 RCA RCA 1721 — The Village Postman/You'd Better Go Home 10

MICAH P HINSON
04 Sketchbook SKETCH XX3 — The Day Texas Sank To The Bottom Of The Sea/Can't Change A Thing/It's Hard To Look At You And Breathe At The Same Time (10") 10
04 Sketchbook SKETCH XX4 — Beneath The Rose/The Dreams Didn't Work Out Right 8
06 Sketchbook SKETCH XX6 — Jackeyed/Don't Leave Me Now! (Reprise) 8
06 Sketch 013LP — MICAH P HINSON AND THE OPERA CIRCUIT (LP) 40
06 Full Time Hobby FTH 056LP — MICAH P HINSON AND RED EMPIRE ORCHESTRA (LP) 35
10 Full Time Hobby FTH 093LP — MICAH P HINSON AND THE PIONEER SABOTEURS (2-LP) 25

JOE HINTON
64 Vocalion VP 9224 — Funny How Time Slips Away/You Gotta Have Love 30
66 Vocalion VP 9258 — Just A Kid Named Joe/Pledging My Love 10
66 Vocalion VA-P 8243 — FUNNY HOW TIME SLIPS AWAY (LP) 120

HI-NUMBERS
65 Decca F 12233 — Heart Of Stone/Dancing In The Street 60

HIPPIES
63 Cameo Parkway P 863 — Memory Lane/REGGIE HARRISON: A Lonely Piano 20

HIPPOLYTES
77 Top Deck TD 003 — Don;t Make The Promises/I Love Sue 7

HIPPY BOYS
69 Trojan TR 668 — Love/The Whole Family 25
69 Trojan TR 669 — Michael Row The Boat Ashore/Who Is Coming To Dinner 40
69 Bullet BU 412 — Hog In A Me Minte/Lorna Run 50
69 Bullet BU 413 — What's Your Excuse?/Tell Me Tell 60
69 Camel CA 29 — Cat Nip/Cooyah (both as Hippie Boys) 40
69 High Note HS 021 — Doctor No Go/Sailing (B-side actually "Faberge" by Baba Brooks & Band) 50
69 High Note HS 030 — Chicken Lickin'/BABA BROOKS: Old Man Flint 30
69 High Note HS 035 — Reggae Pressure/SOUL RHYTHMS: It Hurts 30
69 Unity UN 528 — Dreams To Remember/Peace Maker 70
70 High Note HS 038 — Piccadilly Hop/Nigeria 100
70 Duke DU 92 — Cloud Burst/LLOYD CHARMERS: Message From A Black Man 80
70 Explosion EX 2032 — Vengeance/Look-Ea-Py-Py 50
71 Big Shot 580 — Voodoo/LITTLE ROY: Hard Fighter 40
69 Big Shot BSLP 5005 — REGGAE WITH THE HIPPY BOYS (LP, actually on High Note label) 200
11 Sunspot LP 003 — REGGAE WITH THE HIPPY BOYS (LP reissue, 350 only, signed insert) 30

(see also Upsetters, Family Man, Danny Williams, Tony, Hippy Boys, Cynthia Richards, Pioneers)

HIPSTER IMAGE
65 Decca F 12137 — Can't Let Her Go/Make Her Mine 500
65 Lyntone LYN 951 — KEELE RAG RECORD (4 tracks but 2 by Hipster Image - All For You/A Little Piece Of Leather) 30
11 Decca F 12137 — Can't Let Her Go/Make Her Mine (reissue) 10

(see also Climax Chicago Blues Band)

HIPSTERS
88 Red Angel CNL 7/1062 — Black Chevrolet/She Can't Cut Me No More (p/s) 10

HI RHYTHM
76 London SHU 8506 — ON THE LOOSE (LP) 20

HIRSCHE NICHT AUFS SOFA
86 United Dairies UD 018 — MELCHIOR (LP, with Insert) 30

AL HIRT
63 RCA 1380 — Java/I Can't Get Started 6

HI-RYZE
93 General Production GPR(X) 15 — PROGRESS EP (12") 60

HI-SPOTS
58 Melodisc 1457 — Lend Me Your Comb/I Don't Hurt Anymore 22
58 Melodisc 1473 — Secretly/I Got 22

HIS WORD
87 Lyn 14747 — Loving In Degrees/Life + 1 = 3 60

ALFRED HITCHCOCK
58 London HA-P 2130 — MUSIC TO BE MURDERED BY (LP, music by Jeff Alexander Orchestra, mono) 20
58 London SH-P 6012 — MUSIC TO BE MURDERED BY (LP, music by Jeff Alexander Orchestra, stereo) 20
60 Wonderland LP 89 — ALFRED HITCHCOCK PRESENTS GHOST STORIES FOR YOUNG PEOPLE (LP, read by Peter Allen) 30

(see Jeff Alexander)

ROBYN HITCHCOCK (& THE EGYPTIANS)
81 Armageddon AS 008 — The Man Who Invented Himself/Dancing On God's Thumb (p/s, some with flexidisc "It's A Mystic Trip"/"Grooving On An Inner Plane" [4 SPURT 1]) 8
81 Armageddon AS 008 — The Man Who Invented Himself/Dancing On God's Thumb (p/s, some without flexidisc "It's A Mystic Trip"/"Grooving On An Inner Plane" [4 SPURT 1]) 6
82 Albion ION 103 — America/It Was The Night/How Do You Work This Thing? (p/s) 8
82 Midnight Music DING 2 — Eaten By Her Own Dinner/Listening To The Higsons/Dr. Sticky (p/s) 7
82 Midnight Music DONG 2 — Eaten By Her Own Dinner/Grooving On An Inner Plane/Messages Of The Dark The Abandoned Brain/Happy The Golden Prince (12", p/s) 10
83 Albion 12 ION 1036 — Nightride To Trinidad (Long Version)/Kingdom Of Love/Midnight Fish (12", p/s) 10
84 Bucketfull/Brains BOB 8 — Happy The Golden Prince (hard vinyl white label test pressing, 20 only) 30
81 Armageddon ARM 4 — BLACK SNAKE DIAMOND RÔLE (LP) 15

(see also Soft Boys)

HI-TONES
62 Island WI 029 — Going Steady/Darlin' Elaine 25

HIT PACK

MINT VALUE £

62	Wasp W 004	I'm In Love With You/Singing A Song	30
63	Island WI 086	Ten Virgins (actually by Angelic Brothers)/Too Young To Love (actually by Larry Marshall)	25
63	R&B JB 123	You Hold The Key/DON DRUMMOND: Rock Away	50

HIT PACK
65	Tamla Motown TMG 513	Never Say No To Your Baby/Let's Dance	150
65	Tamla Motown TMG 513	Never Say No To Your Baby/Let's Dance (DJ copy)	200

HIT PARADE (1)
84	JSH JSH 1	Forever/Stop (die-cut p/s)	10
84	JSH JSH 2	My Favourite Girl/It Rained On Monday Morning (die-cut p/s)	10
85	JSH JSH 3	The Sun Shines In Gerrards Cross/You Hurt Me Too (die-cut p/s)	10
85	JSH JSH 4	You Don't Love Me Then/Huevo's Mexicana (die-cut p/s with card)	10
86	JSH JSH 5	See You In Havana/Wipe Away The Tears (die-cut p/s)	10
87	JSH JSH 6	I Get So Sentimental/Sue (die-cut p/s)	10
90	Sarah SARAH 90	Autobiography/The Dispossessed/Now The Holiday's Over (p/s, insert)	40
91	Sarah SARAH 58	In Gunnersbury Park/Harvey (ps, insert)	20
91	Vinyl Japan ASKLP 5	MORE POP SONGS (LP)	18
94	Sarah SARAH 622	THE SOUND OF THE HIT PARADE (LP)	75

HIT PARADE (2)
82	Crass 221984/12	BAD NEWS (EP)	25
84	Crass 1984/2	PLASTIC CULTURE : Product of The Troubles/Media Son (12")	18
86	Crass No 9	NICK NACK PADDY WHACK (LP, with lyric inner)	25

HERMAN HITSON
90s	Special Agent 9003	You Are Too Much For The Human Heart/I Got That Will (reissue)	8
04	Goldmine G2K 149	You Can't Keep A Good Man Down/Ain't No Other Way (reissue)	8

HIT SQUAD
88	Eastern Bloc EASTERN 01	Wax On The Melt/SPM MC Tunes/Shure.4 (12", white label promo only, plain stickered sleeve)	30

(see also 808 State)

HITTERS
73	United Artists UP 35530	Hypocrite/The Version	22

(see also Brinsley Schwarz)

HIVES
01	Poptones MC5055LP	YOUR NEW FAVOURITE BAND (LP)	15
04	Polydor 9866988	TYRANNOSAURUS HIVES (LP, inner with free 7")	20

HMC
93	New Electronica ELEC 03P	Science Funktion (12", promo)	30

HOAX
80	Hologram HOAX 1	ONLY THE BLIND CAN SEE IN THE DARK (EP, 2000 only)	30
81	Hologram HOAX 3	SO WHAT (12" EP, p/s, blue vinyl, 2000 only)	15
81	Hologram HOAX 6	BLIND PANIC EP (p/s, 2000 only)	15
82	Hologram HOAX 4	QUIET IN THE SIXPENNY'S (p/s, 2000 only)	15

HOBBIES OF TODAY
79	Waxworks H.O.T. WAX 01	Metal Boys/Tightrope Walker (p/s)	30
85	Rune CAST 02/LYN 16721/2	In My Minds Eye/You (Company sleeve)	15
14	Waxworks H.O.T. WAX 00	HOBBIES OF TODAY (EP, deluxe edition in handmade sleeve with insert, photos and badge)	30

HOBBIT
72	Satril SAT 7	Only Friends/Everything's Turning Out Fine	10
71	Deroy 709	FIRST AND LAST (LP, private pressing, 99 only)	250

HOBBITS
68	Decca AD 1004	Daffodil Days (The Affection Song)/Sunny Day Girl (export issue)	20
68	MCA MU 1002	Daffodil Days (The Affection Song)/Sunny Day Girl	8
67	MCA MUP 301	DOWN TO MIDDLE EARTH (LP)	35

HOBBS
78	Big SOLD 4	Bop Around The Shop/(You've Got Me In A) Whirl Girl (gatefold p/s & insert)	6

CHRISTOPHER HOBBS/JOHN ADAMS/GAVIN BRYERS
75	Obscure OBS 2	ENSEMBLE PIECES (LP)	30

PAUL HOBBS
72	Deroy 759	HAVING SAID THAT (LP)	600

HOBBY HORSE
72	Bell BELL 1248	Summertime, Summertime/Sweet And Low	12

(see also Mary Hopkin)

HOBBY SHOP
68	Columbia DB 8395	Why Must It Be This Way?/Talk To Me	10

(see also Danny Storm)

LES HOBEAUX
57	HMV POP 377	Oh, Mary Don't You Weep/Toll The Bell Easy	12
57	HMV POP 403	Mama Don't Allow/Hey, Hey, Daddy Blues	12
58	HMV POP 444	Dynamo/Two Ships	15
57	HMV 7EG 8297	SOHO SKIFFLE (EP)	35

HOBNAIL
72	Bell Bell 1250	She's Just A Friend Of Mine/Boy Scout Jambouree	8

HOBO
76	United Artists UAS 29809	HOBO (LP)	15

HOBOKEN
73	Oak	HOBOKEN (LP, 6 copies only)	450

HOBOKIN
72	CBS 8002	Put The Blame On Easy/But Never Wine	7

GEORGE HOBSON
01	Grapevine 2000 G2K 109	Let It Be Real/A Place In Your Heart (reissue)	8

Trevor HOCKEY

MINT VALUE £

TREVOR HOCKEY
70s Beau Brummie TET 120ST — Happy 'Cos I'm Blue/BLUES PLAYERS: Keep Right On To The End Of The Road (p/s) 40

ARCHIE HODGE
01 Goldmine 2000 G2K 115 — I Really Want To See You Girl/If I Really Didn't Need You Woman (reissue) 10

CHRIS HODGE
72 Apple APPLE 43 — We're On Our Way/Supersoul (in p/s) 30
72 Apple APPLE 43 — We're On Our Way/Supersoul 20
74 RCA LPBO 5007 — Beautiful Love/Sweet Lady From The Sky 6

MARVA HODGE
70 Polydor 56792 — The Ghetto/Sometimes 8

CHARLES HODGES
69 Major Minor MM 654 — Try A Little Love/Someone To Love 20
(see also Outlaws, Cliff Bennett's Rebellion)

EDDIE HODGES
61 London HLA 9369 — I'm Gonna Knock On Your Door/Ain't Gonna Wash For A Week 10
62 London HLA 9505 — Bandit Of My Dreams/Mugmates 10
62 London HLA 9576 — (Girls, Girls, Girls) Made To Love/I Make Believe It's You 10
63 MGM MGM 1232 — Just A Kid In Love/Avalanche 10
65 Stateside SS 442 — New Orleans/Hard Times For Young Lovers 10
65 Stateside SS 469 — Love Minus Zero - No Limit/The Water Is Over My Head 10
62 London REA 1353 — EDDIE HODGES (EP) 30
(see also Hayley Mills & Eddie Hodges)

JOHNNY HODGES & HIS ORCHESTRA
52 Vogue LD 011 — JOHNNY HODGES (10" LP) 15

INGFRIED HOFFMAN
67 Polydor 583 015 — SOUL BOND (LP) 15

ANNIE HOGAN
85 Doublevision DVR 9 — PLAYS KICKABYE (12" EP) 15
(see also Marc Almond, Nick Cave, Soft Cell)

CLAIRE HOGAN
59 Top Rank JAR 161 — Sing A Smiling Song/I Wonder 10
(see also Teresa Brewer)

SILAS HOGAN
71 Blue Horizon 2431 008 — TROUBLE AT HOME (LP) 125
70s Flyright FLY 595 — I'M A FREE-HEARTED MAN (LP) 15

HOGARTH
68 Liberty LBF 15156 — Suzie's Getting Married/I've Been Dreaming 10

JAMES HOGG
72 Regal Zonophone RZ 3054 — Lovely Lady Rock/Happy Sad 15
72 Regal Zonophone RZ 3068 — California Blues/Everybody Smile 10
73 Regal Zonophone RZ 3078 — Gotta Be A Winner/Everybody Smile 10

SMOKEY HOGG
64 Realm RM 197 — I'M SO LONELY (LP) 25
72 Ember EMB 3405 — SINGS THE BLUES (LP) 20
70s Specialty SNTF 5018 — U BETTER WATCH THAT JIVE (LP) 15
(see also John Lee Hooker/Lightnin' Hopkins/Smokey Hogg)

HOGGS
80 Now PRR 2001 — See It Now/Time On The Line (p/s) 20

HOGIA R DOCIA
80 Recordia Sur SER 001 — Annwyl Ser/Ser 10

HOGS
69 Jay Boy BOY 5 — It's All Coming To Me Now/Motor Cycle Rider 15

SUZI JANE HOKUM
66 MGM MGM 1323 — Need All The Help I Can Get/Home 50

HOKUS POKE
72 Vertigo 6360 064 — EARTH HARMONY (LP, die-cut gatefold sleeve, small swirl label) 450

RON HOLDEN
60 London HLU 9116 — My Babe/Love You So 60

MARK HOLDER & THE POSITIVES
73 Atlantic K10280 — Whatever's Fair/Why Dear Lord 20

RAM HOLDER BROTHERS
66 Parlophone R 5471 — Just Across The River/Ram Blues 30
(see also Ram Jam Band, Ram John Holder)

RAM JOHN HOLDER
67 Columbia DB 8157 — I Need Somebody/She's Alright 12
67 Columbia DB 8262 — My Friend Jones/It Won't Be Long Before I Love You 40
68 Beacon BEA 108 — I Just Came To Get My Baby/Yes I Do 10
69 Upfront UPF 2 — Goodwill To All Mankind/BLACK VELVET: Goodwill Sermon 8
70 United Artists UP 35117 — Where Do The Dreams Go?/Miracle Happens Every Day 6
75 Fresh Air 6121 124 — Battering Ram/London Ghetto 6
63 Melodisc MLP 12-133 — RAM BLUES GOSPEL AND SOUL (LP) 60
69 Beacon BEAS 2 — BLACK LONDON BLUES (LP, white/black label with "Sold in U.K..." text) 70
70 Beacon BEAS 17 — BOOTLEG BLUES (LP, gatefold sleeve with lyric poster, white/black labels) 80
70 Beacon BEAS 17 — BOOTLEG BLUES (LP, gatefold sleeve without lyric poster, white/black labels) 30
(see also Ram Jam Band, Ram Holder Brothers, Geno Washington)

HOLE
91 City Slang EFA 04070-45 — Teenage Whore/Drown Soda (p/s, lilac, clear or green vinyl, 500 of each) 15
93 City Slang EFA 04916-45 — Beautiful Son/Old Age/20 Years In The Dakota (purple vinyl) 6
94 City Slang EFA 04936-7 — Miss World/Rock Star (Alternate Mix) (pink vinyl) 6
95 Geffen GFS P94 — Violet/Old Age (purple vinyl)//Violet/He Hit Me (And It Felt Like A Kiss) 7" double pack) ... 8

Billie HOLIDAY

MINT VALUE £

96	Mirromax 573 164-7	Gold Dust Woman/N.Y. LOOSE: Spit (gatefold p/s, 2 x 1-sided 7"s, with etched B-sides, 5,000 numbered)	6
91	City Slang SLANG 012	PRETTY ON THE INSIDE (LP, blue vinyl)	35
94	City Slang EFA 04935-1	LIVE THROUGH THIS (LP, 3000 on white vinyl)	100
94	City Slang EFA 04935-1	LIVE THROUGH THIS (LP, black vinyl)	40
98	Geffen GEF 25164	CELEBRITY SKIN (LP)	50
14	Music On Vinyl MOVLP 999	CELEBRITY SKIN (LP, orange vinyl repressing)	20

BILLIE HOLIDAY

59	MGM MGM 1033	Don't Worry About Me/Just One More Chance	6
54	Columbia 33S 1034	BILLIE HOLIDAY (10" LP)	30
54	Brunswick LA 8676	LOVER MAN (10" LP)	30
55	Philips BBR 8032	FAVOURITES (10" LP)	35
56	Columbia Clef 33C 9023	AT JAZZ AT THE PHILHARMONIC (10" LP)	20
56	Columbia Clef 33CX 10019	MUSIC FOR TORCHING (LP)	25
57	Columbia Clef 33CX 10064	VELVET MOOD (LP)	25
57	Columbia Clef 33CX 10076	SOLITUDE (LP)	20
57	Columbia Clef 33CX 10092	LADY SINGS THE BLUES (LP)	20
59	Columbia Clef 33CX 10145	SONGS FOR DISTINGUÉ LOVERS (LP)	20
66	Island ILP 929	LAST LIVE RECORDING (LP)	30

CHICO HOLIDAY

59	RCA RCA 1117	Young Ideas/Cuckoo Girl	30
61	Coral Q 72443	God, Country And My Baby/Fools (withdrawn)	30
59	RCA RCX 171	CHICO HOLIDAY (EP)	80

JIMMY HOLIDAY

63	Vocalion POP V 9206	How Can I Forget/Janet	30
64	London HLY 9868	I Lied/Alison	20
66	Liberty LIB 12040	Baby I Love You/You Won't Get Away	20
67	Liberty LIB 12048	Give Me Your Love/The Turning Point	20
67	Liberty LIB 12053	Everybody Needs Help/I'm Gonna Move To The City	20
68	Minit MLF 11008	Give Me Your Love/The Beauty Of A Girl In Love	15
69	Minit MLL/MLS 40010	SPREAD YOUR LOVE (LP)	60

JIMMY HOLIDAY & CLYDIE KING

67	Liberty LIB 12058	Ready, Willing And Able/We Got A Good Thing Goin'	30
67	Liberty LIB 12058	Ready, Willing And Able/We Got A Good Thing Goin' (DJ copy)	50
72	United Artists UP 35271	Ready, Willing And Able/JIMMY HOLIDAY: Give Me Your Love	8

HOLIDAYMAKERS

89	Woosh WOOSH 4	Cincinnati/Seventh Valley Girl (p/s)	10

HOLIDAYS

66	Polydor 56720	I'll Love You Forever/Makin' Up Time	100

(see also Edwin Starr)

BRIAN HOLLAND

74	Invictus INV 2553	I'm So Glad/I'm So Glad (Version)	10

EDDIE HOLLAND

62	Fontana H 387	Jamie/Take A Chance On Me	400
63	Oriole CBA 1808	If It's Love (It's All Right)/It's Not Too Late	500

LYNN HOLLAND

64	Ember EMB S 198	And The Angels Sing/I Can't Read Your Writing (For My Tears) (in p/s)	12
64	Ember EMB S 198	And The Angels Sing/I Can't Read Your Writing (For My Tears)	6
67	Polydor 56166	One Man In My Life/Wand'rin Boy	
67	Polydor 56187	Come And Love/May God Help You And Protect You	25
66	Polydor 56129	All The Love In The World/Loneliness	6
71	Pye 7N 45041	The Last Time/In A Railway Carriage	8
67	Polydor 236217	OH DARLING HOW I MISS YOU (LP)	25

(see also Holly)

MALCOLM HOLLAND

70	Fontana TF 1075	Dawning Of the Day/Wndy	10

TONY HOLLAND

63	HMV POP 1135	Sidewalk/Time Goes By	40

MICHAEL HOLLIDAY

56	Columbia SCM 5221	Sixteen Tons/The Rose Tattoo	10
56	Columbia SCM 5273	Hot Diggity (Dog Ziggity)/The Gal With The Yaller Shoes	10
56	Columbia DB 3813	The Runaway Train/Ten Thousand Miles	12

(see also Edna Savage)

SU(SAN) HOLLIDAY

64	Columbia DB 7363	Dark Despair/The Other Side (demos list A-side as "[Street Of] Dark Despair")	15
64	Columbia DB 7403	Any Day Now/Don't Come Knocking At My Door	15
65	Columbia DB 7616	Sometimes/Long Haired Boy	8
65	Columbia DB 7709	Nevertheless (I'm In Love With You)/Moonglow	8
66	Columbia SX 6067	I WANNA SAY HELLO (LP, as Su Holliday)	40

(see also Susan Singer)

TIM HOLLIER

70	Fontana TF 1080	In This Room/Love Song	6
71	Philips 6006 130	Circle Is Small/In A Corner Of My Life/Time Stood Still	6
68	United Artists (S)ULP 1211	MESSAGE TO A HARLEQUIN (LP, laminated front sleeve, blue/silver labels)	70
70	Fontana 6309 003	TIM HOLLIER (LP, laminated sleve, black/silver labels)	225
71	Philips 6308 044	SKY SAIL (LP, laminated sleeve, black/silver labels)	45

(see also Amory Kane)

HOLLIES

SINGLES

63	Parlophone R 5030	(Ain't That) Just Like Me/Hey, What's Wrong With Me	15

HOLLINGWORTH

			MINT VALUE £
63	Parlophone R 5052	Searchin'/Whole World Over	10
63	Parlophone R 5077	Stay/Now's The Time	8
64	Parlophone R 5104	Just One Look/Keep Off That Friend Of Mine	7
64	Parlophone R 5137	Here I Go Again/Baby That's All	7
64	Parlophone R 5178	We're Through/Come On Back	6
65	Parlophone R 5232	Yes I Will/Nobody	6
65	Parlophone R 5287	I'm Alive/You Know He Did	6
65	Parlophone R 5322	Look Through Any Window/So Lonely	7
65	Parlophone R 5392	If I Needed Someone/I've Got A Way Of My Own	10
66	Parlophone R 5409	I Can't Let Go/Running Through The Night	6
66	Parlophone R 5469	Bus Stop/Don't Run And Hide	7
66	United Artists UP 1152	After The Fox (with Peter Sellers)/BURT BACHARACH: The Fox-Trot	35
66	Parlophone R 5508	Stop! Stop! Stop!/It's You	8
67	Parlophone R 5562	On A Carousel/All The World Is Love	6
67	Parlophone R 5602	Carrie Anne/Signs That Will Never Change	6
67	Parlophone R 5637	King Midas In Reverse/Everything Is Sunshine	10
68	Parlophone R 5680	Jennifer Eccles/Open Up Your Eyes	6
68	Parlophone R 5733	Listen To Me/Do The Best You Can	7
69	Parlophone R 5765	Sorry Suzanne/Not That Way At All	7
69	Parlophone R 5806	He Ain't Heavy, He's My Brother/'Cos You Like To Love Me	6
72	Parlophone R 5939	Long Cool Woman (In A Black Dress)/Cable Car	6

EPs

64	Parlophone GEP 8909	THE HOLLIES	40
64	Parlophone GEP 8911	JUST ONE LOOK	35
64	Parlophone GEP 8915	HERE I GO AGAIN	35
64	Parlophone GEP 8927	WE'RE THROUGH	35
65	Parlophone GEP 8934	IN THE HOLLIES STYLE	50
65	Parlophone GEP 8942	I'M ALIVE	35
66	Parlophone GEP 8951	I CAN'T LET GO	50

ALBUMS

64	Parlophone PMC 1220	STAY WITH THE HOLLIES (mono)	100
64	Parlophone PCS 3054	STAY WITH THE HOLLIES (stereo, large 'stereo' on sleeve)	175
65	Parlophone PMC 1235	IN THE HOLLIES STYLE (mid-sized mono on front sleeve, "Sold in U.K..." text)	125
65	Parlophone PMC 1261	THE HOLLIES (small mono on front sleeve, "Sold in U.K..." text)	125
66	Parlophone PMC 7008	WOULD YOU BELIEVE? (mono, with "Sold in U.K..." text)	80
66	Parlophone PCS 7008	WOULD YOU BELIEVE? (stereo, "Sold in U.K..." text)	150
66	Parlophone PMC 7011	FOR CERTAIN BECAUSE (gatefold sleeve, mono, with "Sold in U.K..." text)	50
66	Parlophone PCS 7011	FOR CERTAIN BECAUSE (gatefold sleeve, stereo, with "Sold in U.K..." text)	80
67	Parlophone PMC 7022	EVOLUTION (mono, with "Sold in U.K..." text)	50
67	Parlophone PCS 7022	EVOLUTION (stereo, with "Sold in U.K..." text)	100
67	Parlophone PMC 7039	BUTTERFLY (mono, with "Sold in U.K..." text)	50
67	Parlophone PCS 7039	BUTTERFLY (stereo, with "sold in U.K..." text)	100
67	EMI Regal SREG 2024	THE HOLLIES (export compilation)	25
67	World Records ST 979	THE VINTAGE HOLLIES (stereo reissue of "In The Hollies Style")	35
68	World Records ST 1035	STAY WITH THE HOLLIES (record club reissue)	30
68	Parlophone PCS 7057	THE HOLLIES' GREATEST (stereo, with outtake version of Yes I Will)	15
69	Parlophone PMC 7078	THE HOLLIES SING DYLAN (mono, with "Sold in U.K..." text)	35
69	Parlophone PCS 7078	THE HOLLIES SING DYLAN (stereo, with "Sold in U.K..." text)	30
69	Parlophone PCS 7092	HOLLIES SING HOLLIES (gatefold sleeve)	20

(All Parlophone LPs listed above were originally issued with yellow/black labels; 1970s pressings with silver & black labels are worth £8)

70	Parlophone PCS 7116	CONFESSIONS OF THE MIND (with colour insert)	20
71	Parlophone PAS 10005	DISTANT LIGHT (gatefold sleeve)	18
72	Parlophone PCS 7148	THE HOLLIES' GREATEST HITS VOL. 2	15
72	Polydor 2383 144	ROMANY (gatefold sleeve)	15
74	Polydor 2383 262	HOLLIES (with lyric insert)	15
75	Polydor 2442 128	ANOTHER NIGHT (gatefold sleeve)	15
76	Polydor 2442 141	WRITE ON (with lyric inner)	15
76	Polydor 2383 421	RUSSIAN ROULETTE (with lyric inner)	15
78	Polydor 2383 474	A CRAZY STEAL (with lyric inner)	15
87	BGO BGOLP4	STAY WITH THE HOLLIES (LP, reissue)	15
87	BGO BGOLP8	IN THE HOLLIES STYLE (LP, reissue)	15
88	BGO BGOLP25	HOLLIES (LP, reissue)	15
88	BGO BGOLP9	FOR CERTAIN BECAUSE... (LP, reissue, gatefold)	15
88	BGO BGOLP24	WOULD YOU BELIEVE? (LP, reissue)	15
90	BGO BGOLP79	BUTTERFLY (LP, reissue)	15
90	BGO BGOLP80	EVOLUTION (LP, reissue)	15

(see also Allan Clarke, Graham Nash, Terry Sylvester, Haydock's Rockhouse, Peter Sellers & Sophia Loren)o

HOLLINGWORTH

71	Columbia DB 8808	Jump On My Wagon/This Town	18

MARK HOLLIS

03	Polydor 537 688-1	MARK HOLLIS (LP, reissue of 1997 CD-only album, 180gm pressing with inner)	100

(see also Talk Talk)

BRENDA HOLLOWAY

64	Stateside SS 307	Every Little Bit Hurts/Land Of A Thousand Boys	80
64	Stateside SS 307	Every Little Bit Hurts/Land Of A Thousand Boys (DJ Copy)	150
65	Tamla Motown TMG 508	When I'm Gone/I've Been Good To You	100
65	Tamla Motown TMG 508	When I'm Gone/I've Been Good To You (DJ copy)	200
65	Tamla Motown TMG 519	Operator/I'll Be Available	100
65	Tamla Motown TMG 519	Operator/I'll Be Available (DJ copy)	200

Laurie HOLLOWAY

MINT VALUE £

Year	Label/Cat#	Title	Value
66	Tamla Motown TMG 556	Together Till The End Of Time/Sad Song	150
66	Tamla Motown TMG 556	Together Till The End Of Time/Sad Song (DJ copy)	200
66	Tamla Motown TMG 581	Hurt A Little Everyday/Where Were You (demos credit Brenda Holiday)	100
66	Tamla Motown TMG 581	Hurt A Little Everyday/Where Were You (demos credit Brenda Holiday) (DJ copy)	125
67	Tamla Motown TMG 608	Just Look What You've Done/Starting The Hurt All Over Again	80
67	Tamla Motown TMG 608	Just Look What You've Done/Starting The Hurt All Over Again (DJ copy)	125
67	Tamla Motown TMG 622	You've Made Me So Very Happy/I've Got To Find It	45
69	Tamla Motown TMG 700	Just Look What You've Done/You've Made Me So Very Happy	18
68	T. Motown (S)TML 11083	THE ARTISTRY OF BRENDA HOLLOWAY (LP, mono/stereo)	150

LAURIE HOLLOWAY

79	Hobo HO 503	CUMULUS (LP)	100

LOLEATTA HOLLOWAY

71	United Artists UP 35273	Bring It On Up/Rainbow '71'	8
76	Salsoul SZ 2022	Dreamin'/Is It Just A Man's Way	8
96	Kent 6T 11	This Man's Arms/JOHN EDWARDS: Ain't That Good Enough	25
76	Salsoul SZS 5513	LOLEATTA (LP)	20

PATRICE HOLLOWAY

66	Capitol CL 15484	Love And Desire/Ecstasy	150
66	Capitol CL 15484	Love And Desire/Ecstasy (DJ Copy)	250

HOLLOW GROUND

80	Guardian GR/HG C57	FLYING HIGH EP (Flying High/Warlord/Rock On/Don't Chase The Dragon) (in p/s)	150
80	Guardian GR/HG C57	FLYING HIGH EP (Flying High/Warlord/Rock On/Don't Chase The Dragon)	45

BUDDY HOLLY

78s

Year	Label/Cat#	Title	Value
56	Brunswick 05581	Blue Days - Black Nights/Love Me	300
57	Vogue Coral Q 72293	Peggy Sue/Everyday	150
58	Coral Q 72288	Listen To Me/I'm Gonna Love You Too	25
58	Coral Q 72325	Rave On/Take Your Time	30
58	Coral Q 72333	Early In The Morning/Now We're One	35
58	Coral Q 72346	Heartbeat/Well ... All Right	50
59	Coral Q 72360	It Doesn't Matter Anymore/Raining In My Heart	30
59	Brunswick 05800	Rock Around With Ollie Vee/Midnight Shift	200
59	Coral Q 72376	Peggy Sue Got Married/Crying, Waiting, Hoping	200
60	Coral Q 72392	Heartbeat/Everyday	350

SINGLES

Year	Label/Cat#	Title	Value
56	Brunswick 05581	Blue Days - Black Nights/Love Me	800
57	Vogue Coral Q 72293	Peggy Sue/Everyday	50
58	Coral Q 72293	Peggy Sue/Everyday	20
58	Coral Q 72288	Listen To Me/I'm Gonna Love You Too	25
58	Coral Q 72325	Rave On/Take Your Time	25
58	Coral Q 72333	Early In The Morning/Now We're One	25
58	Coral Q 72346	Heartbeat/Well ... All Right	25
58	Coral Q 72360	It Doesn't Matter Anymore/Raining In My Heart	7
59	Brunswick 05800	Rock Around With Ollie Vee/Midnight Shift	40
59	Coral Q 72376	Peggy Sue Got Married/Crying, Waiting, Hoping	25

(The above 45s were originally issued with triangular centres; reissues with round centres are worth two-thirds these values.)

Year	Label/Cat#	Title	Value
60	Coral Q 72392	Heartbeat/Everyday	20
60	Coral Q 72397	True Love Ways/Moondreams	10
60	Coral Q 72411	Learning The Game/That Makes It Tough	10
61	Coral Q 72419	What To Do/That's What They Say	10
61	Coral Q 72432	Baby I Don't Care/Valley Of Tears	10
61	Coral Q 72445	Look At Me/Mailman, Bring Me No More Blues	15
62	Coral Q 72449	Listen To Me/Words Of Love	15
62	Coral Q 72455	Reminiscing/Wait Till The Sun Shines, Nellie	10
63	Coral Q 72459	Brown-Eyed Handsome Man/Slippin' And Slidin'	8
63	Coral Q 72463	Bo Diddley/It's Not My Fault	10
63	Coral Q 72466	Wishing/Because I Love You	10
63	Coral Q 72469	What To Do/Umm Oh Yeah	12
64	Coral Q 72472	You've Got Love/An Empty Cup (as Buddy Holly & The Crickets)	25
64	Coral Q 72475	Love's Made A Fool Of You/You're The One	20
66	Coral Q 72483	Maybe Baby/That's My Desire	40
68	Decca AD 1009	Rave On/Peggy Sue (p/s, export reissue)	40
69	MCA MU 1059	Love Is Strange/You're The One	10
84	MCA BHB 1	THAT'LL BE THE DAY (10 x 7" box set, comprising BH1-10 in p/s)	40

EPs

Year	Label/Cat#	Title	Value
58	Coral FEP 2002	LISTEN TO ME (brown cover, sleeve shows Holly without glasses; disc credits title as "Buddy Holly")	400
58	Coral FEP 2002	LISTEN TO ME (re-pressing, various shades of green/brown p/s, shows Holly with glasses; disc credits title as "Buddy Holly")	40
58	Coral FEP 2005	RAVE ON (various shades of green/brown p/s)	40
59	Coral FEP 2014	IT'S SO EASY	40
59	Coral FEP 2015	HEARTBEAT	40
59	Coral FEP 2032	BUDDY HOLLY	40
59	Brunswick OE 9456	BUDDY HOLLY NO. 1	60
59	Brunswick OE 9457	BUDDY HOLLY NO. 2	60

(The above EPs were originally issued with triangular centres; later pressings with round-centres are worth between half and two thirds of these values.)

60	Coral FEP 2044	THE LATE GREAT BUDDY HOLLY (tri centre)	50
60	Coral FEP 2044	THE LATE GREAT BUDDY HOLLY (round centre)	15

Stevie HOLLY

			MINT VALUE £
64	Coral FEP 2065	BUDDY - BY REQUEST	40
64	Coral FEP 2066	THAT TEX-MEX SOUND	50
64	Coral FEP 2067	WISHING	50
64	Coral FEP 2068	SHOWCASE VOLUME 1	40
64	Coral FEP 2069	SHOWCASE VOLUME 2	40
65	Coral FEP 2070	BUDDY HOLLY SINGS	40

ALBUMS

58	Vogue Coral LVA 9085	BUDDY HOLLY (Vogue-Coral labels & Coral sleeve)	100
58	Coral LVA 9085	BUDDY HOLLY	45
59	Coral LVA 9105	THE BUDDY HOLLY STORY ('High Fidelity Coral' logo on sleeve)	25
60s	Coral LVA 9105	THE BUDDY HOLLY STORY (reissue, different 'roll-neck sweater' sleeve with small 'Coral' logo)	40
60	Coral LVA 9127	THE BUDDY HOLLY STORY VOL. II	20
61	Ace Of Hearts AH 3	THAT'LL BE THE DAY	25
63	Coral LVA 9212	REMINISCING	25
64	Coral LVA 9222	SHOWCASE	25
65	Coral LVA 9227	HOLLY IN THE HILLS (with Bob Montgomery, withdrawn mispressing, sleeve & label list "Wishing", plays "Reminiscing"; matrix no's end with 1B both sides)	40
65	Coral LVA 9227	HOLLY IN THE HILLS (corrected edition, with Bob Montgomery, plays "Wishing", matrix numbers end with 1B on one side & 2B on other)	60
68	MCA MUP 320	WISHING (mono only, reissue of "Holly In The Hills")	18
69	MCA MUPS 371	GIANT	18

(Originally issued with yellow labels; later variations exist with various twin-toned designs.)

75	World Records SM 301/5	THE BUDDY HOLLY STORY (5-LP box set)	20
79	MCA Coral CDMSP 807	THE COMPLETE BUDDY HOLLY (6-LP box set with sepia-tinted book)	30

(see also Crickets, Fireballs)

STEVIE HOLLY
66	Planet PLF 107	A Strange World/Little Man	80

HOLLY (1)
65	Fontana TF 980	On With The Game/Paradise Lost	8

(see also Lynn Holland)

HOLLY (2)
79	Eric's ERIC'S 003	Yankee Rose/Treasure Island/Desperate Dan (p/s)	25
79	Eric's ERIC'S 007	Hobo Joe/Stars Of The Bars (p/s)	20

(see also Frankie Goes To Hollywood, Big In Japan)

HOLLY & JOEY
82	Virgin VS 478	I Got You Babe/HOLLY & THE ITALIANS: One More Dance (p/s)	12

(see also Ramones, Deborah Harry)

HOLLY & THE ITALIANS
81	Virgin VS 411	I Wanna Go Home/Fanzine (p/s)	15
81	Virgin VS 429	Just For Tonight/Baby Gets It All (p/s)	7
81	Virgin V 2186	THE RIGHT TO BE ITALIAN (LP, with lyric insert)	15

HOLLYRIDGE STRINGS
61	Capitol CL 15233	The Guns Of Navarone/Moon River	6
61	Capitol CL 15237	The Comancheros/A Thunder Of Drums	6

HOLLYWOOD ARGYLES
60	London HLU 9146	Alley Oop/Sho' Know A Lot About Love	10
60	Top Rank JAR 530	Gun Totin' Critter Called Jack/GARY PAXTON: Bug-Eye	20

(see also Kim Fowley, Skip & Flip, Gary Paxton)

HOLLYWOOD BRATS
79	Cherry Red CHERRY 6	Then He Kissed Me/Sick On You (p/s)	12
80	Cherry Red 12 CHERRY 6	Then He Kissed Me/Another School Day/Sick On You (12", p/s)	35
80	Cherry Red A RED 6	HOLLYWOOD BRATS (LP)	40

HOLLYWOOD FLAMES
57	London HL 7030	Buzz Buzz Buzz/Crazy (export issue)	50
58	London HL 8545	Buzz Buzz Buzz/Crazy	75
59	London HLW 8955	Much Too Much/In The Dark	75
59	London HLW 8955	Much Too Much/In The Dark (78)	25
60	London HLE 9071	If I Thought You Needed Me/Every Day Every Way	50

HOLLYWOOD FREEWAY
72	Deram DM 359	I've Been Moved/Cool Calamares	6
73	Pye 7N 45273	You're The Song (That I Can't Stop Singing)/This Feeling Called Love	8

(see also Tony Rivers)

HOLLYWOOD HURRICANES
64	Prima PR 1009	Beavershot/Have Love Will Travel	6

KENNY HOLLYWOOD
62	Decca F 11546	Magic Star/The Wonderful Story Of Love	25

HOLLYWOOD KILLERS
78	Rollerball ROLL 2	Goodbye Suicide/Tramp	50

(see also Jim Penfold & The Hollywood Killers)

HOLLYWOOD VINES
61	Capitol CL 15191	When Johnny Comes Slidin' Home/Cruisin'	12

MIKE HOLM
70	Major Minor MM 659	Mendocino/Cutey Girl	6

PETER HOLM
67	Major Minor MM504	This Is Not The Way/You Will Be Mine	15

BILL HOLMAN OCTET
54	Capitol KC 65000	Cousin Jack/Plain Folks	8

EDDIE HOLMAN
65	Cameo Parkway P 960	This Can't Be True/A Free Country	50
69	Action ACT 4549	I Love You/I Surrender	125

Carl HOLMES

MINT VALUE £

70	Stateside SS 2160	(Hey There) Lonely Girl/It's All In The Game	10
70	Stateside SS 2170	Since I Don't Have You/Don't Stop Now	8
77	Salsoul SZ 2026	This Will Be A Night To Remember/Time Will Tell	6
00	Grapevine G2K 45-138	Hold Me In Your Arms/MRS BAND: Diggin It	35
04	Grapevine 2000 G2K 150	She's Wanted (In Three States)/MRS BAND: Sunset On Ridge (reissue)	10
04	Grapevine 2000 G2K 160	Sweet Memories Are Haunting Me/Groovin' The Go Go (reissue)	10

CARL HOLMES
| 04 | Soul On 45 S 102 | Soul Dance Number 2/PARISIANS: Twinkle Litte Star | 15 |

CHRISTINE HOLMES
64	Mercury MF 813	This Is My Prayer/My Dream	10
64	Mercury MF 819	Play Me A Sad Song (Mr DJ)/Doesn't He Know	10
64	Mercury MF 831	Goodbye Boys Goodbye/Is It Love	10
65	Mercury MF 851	Many Things From Your Window/You'd Better Believe It	7
65	Mercury MF 887	Goin' Where The Lovin' Is/Where There's Some Smoke There's Fire	12

(see also Family Dogg)

DAVID HOLMES
| 97 | Go Beat GOB 6 | Don't Die Just Yet (Mogwai Mix)/Holiday Girl (Arab Strap Mix) (p/s, 500 only) | 6 |
| 02 | 13 Amp APM 001LP | COME GET IT I GOT IT (2xLP) | 40 |

(see also Mogwai)

ELDRIDGE HOLMES
| 68 | Pama PM 746 | Beverley/Wait For Me Baby | 18 |

IVAN HOLMES
| 67 | Columbia DB 8119 | The Light, The Love And The Life/Cocaine | 7 |

JAKE HOLMES
70	Ember EMB S 269	Saturday Night/Diner Song (p/s)	20
70	Polydor 583 579	JAKE HOLMES (LP)	30
70	Polydor 2425 036	SO CLOSE SO VERY FAR TO GO (LP)	22
72	CBS 64905	HOW MUCH TIME (LP)	20

LEROY HOLMES & ORCHESTRA
| 59 | MGM 1044 | Sweet Leilani/Alice Blue Gown | 6 |
| 59 | MGM 1058 | Theme From A Summer Place/Indiscreet | 6 |

RICHARD 'GROOVES' HOLMES
66	CBS 202240	Misty/Groove's Groove	7
67	Transatlantic PR 7435	SOUL MESSAGE (LP)	25
68	Transatlantic PR 7493	RICHARD 'GROOVES' HOLMES (LP)	20

HOLOCAUST (1)
80	Phoenix PSP 1	Heavy Metal Mania/Only As Young As You Feel (p/s)	20
80	Phoenix 12 PSP 1	Heavy Metal Mania/Love's Power/Only As Young As You Feel (12", p/s)	30
80	Phoenix 12 PSP 2	Smokin' Valves/Friend Or Foe (p/s)	10
80	Phoenix 12 PSP 2	Smokin' Valves/Friend Or Foe/Out My Book (12", p/s)	30
81	Phoenix PSP 3P	HOLOCAUST LIVE (EP)	25
82	Phoenix 12 PSP 4	Comin' Through/Don't Wanna Be A Loser/Good Thing Going (12", p/s)	30
81	Phoenix PSLP 1	THE NIGHTCOMERS (LP)	40
83	Phoenix PSPLP 4	LIVE (HOT CURRY AND WINE) (LP)	25
84	Phoenix PSPLP 5	NO MAN'S LAND (LP)	20

HOLOCAUST (2)
| 79 | Pile Driver HOL 201 | Slay That Dragon/Take Me To Your Lawyer/So Called Civilised Way (12", no p/s) | 1000 |

ERROL HOLT
76	Olympic MOR 1015	Those Who Have Eyes To See/Dub To See	35
77	Lior ROAR 111	Come Rock Me/Congo Dread (12")	50
78	Star Time EHLF 427	I Am Not A King (with PRINCE FAR I)/Version (12")	40
79	Hit Run HIT DD16	Yes Yes Yes/ROD TAYLOR: No One Can Tell I About Jah (12")	80
79	Hit Run HIT DD25	Sweet Reggae Music/PRINCE FAR I: Hairdressing Salon	90
70s	Dread DDLP 102	VISION OF AFRICA (LP)	50

JOHN HOLT
63	Island WI 041	I Cried A Tear/I'll Stay	30
68	Trojan TR 643	Tonight/Oh How It Hurts (B-side actually by Paragons)	25
69	Trojan TR 661	Ali Baba/I'm Your Man	75
69	Trojan TR 674	What You Gonna Do Now/Have You Ever Been To Heaven	12
69	Harry J TR 694	Have Sympathy/HARRY J ALLSTARS: Spyrone	40
69	Trojan TR 7702	Wooden Heart/All My Life	10
70	Duke Reid DR 2506	Come Out Of My Bed/WINSTON WRIGHT: Hide And Seek	18
70	Duke DU 73	Stealing, Stealing/WINSTON WRIGHT: Stealing, Stealing (Volume 2)	25
70	Duke DU 77	The Working Kind/Open Jaw	25
70	Jackpot JP 735	A Little Tear/JEFF BARNS: Get In The Groove	15
70	Bamboo BAM 44	A Love I Can Feel/JOHNNY LAST: Long Liver Man (B-side act. by Hugh Black)	25
70	Bamboo BAM 55	A Stranger In Love/WAILERS: Jailhouse (Good Rudy)	50
70	Bamboo BAM 62	Holly Holy/Do You Love Me?	20
70	Banana BA 314	Why Can't I Touch You/SOUND DIMENSION: Touching Version	15
70	Smash SMA 2303	My Heart Is Gone/PHIL PRATT ALL STARS: Version	12
70	Smash SMA 2305	I Had A Talk With My Woman/MAXINE: Life Is Not The Same Anymore	12
70	Supreme SUP 212	Share My Rest/AL BROWN: Allways	40
70	Unity UN 548	Sometimes/BUNNY LEE ALL STARS: Lash-La-Rue	30
70	Unity UN 549	Sea Cruise/LEE'S ALL STARS: Niney's Hop	12
70	Unity UN 552	Walking Along/LEE'S ALL STARS: Warefare	50
70	Unity UN 556	Give Her All The Love/BUSTY BROWN: Nobody But You	15
70	Success RE 903	Fat Girl, Sexy Girl/Man And Woman	30
71	Banana BA 340	O.K. Fred/Fancy Make-Up	15
71	Banana BA 345	Build Our Dreams/LEROY SIBBLES: Love In Our Nation	25
71	Treasure Isle TI 7061	Let's Build Our Dreams/TOMMY McCOOK & SUPERSONICS: Testify Version	25

Roosevelt HOLTS

			MINT VALUE £
71	Treasure Isle TI 7065	Sister Big Stuff/TOMMY McCOOK & SUPERSONICS: Black River	25
71	Treasure Isle TI 7066	Paragons Medley/TOMMY McCOOK & SUPERSONICS: Medley Version	15
71	Ashanti ASH 401	Again/MUDIES ALL STARS: Ten Steps To Soul Version	12
71	Camel CA 78	Linger A While/Version	7
71	Escort ERT 847	Knock On Your Door/URIEL ALDRIDGE: Set Me Free	6
71	Jackpot JP 772	Stick By Me/It's A Pleasure	8
71	Jackpot JP 774	It's A Jam In The Streets/A Man Needs A Woman	8
71	Jackpot JP 784	Anymore/Lost Love	6
71	Moodisc MU 3513	It May Sound Silly/MUDIE ALL STARS: Instrumental	6
71	Moodisc HM 105	It May Sound Silly/MUDE ALL STARS: Instrumental (reissue)	12
71	Punch PH 60	Strange Things/WINSTON WRIGHT: Want Money (B-side act. G.G. All Stars)	25
71	Smash SMA 2324	Mother And Father Love/AGGROVATORS: Mother Love Version	6
71	Prince Buster PB 26	All I Want From You/Version	12
72	Blue Beat BB 424	O.K. Fred/BIG YOUTH: Chi Chi Run	20
72	Prince Buster PB 40	Close To Me/Version	10
72	Prince Buster PB 41	Get Ready/Version	12
72	Prince Buster PB 42	Rain From The Skies/Version	12
72	Prince Buster PB 43	The First Time/Version	10
72	Prince Buster PB 49	For Your Love/Version	10
72	G.G. GG 4529	Keep It Up/A Love Like Yours	6
72	Fab FAB 188	A Little Happiness/DELROY WILSON: Diamond Rings	15
72	Jackpot JP 790	Don't You Know/Riding For A Fall	12
72	Jackpot JP 807	Looking Back/I'll Be There	10
72	Pama PM 845	I'll Always Love You/SLIM SMITH: 3 x 7 Rock And Roll	10
72	Pama PM 852	Pledging My Love/I Will Know What To Do	10
73	Fab FAB 224	Let's Go Dancing/Version	10
73	Fab FAB 244	Let's Go Dancing/Version (reissue)	10
73	Attack ATT 8045	Time And The River/Version	8
73	Smash SMA 2329	Don't Break Your Promise/I've Been Admiring You	12
73	Ackee ACK 513	Ecstacy/Version	10
83	Greensleeves GRED 120	Police In Helicopter/Youth Pon The Corner (12")	20
70	Bamboo BDLP 210	A LOVE I CAN FEEL (LP)	60
72	Melodisc MLP 12170	GREATEST HITS (LP)	40
72	Melodisc MLP 12180	OK FRED (LP)	45
70s	Melodisc MLP 12191	JOHN HOLT & FRIENDS (LP)	45
71	Trojan TRL(S) 37	STILL IN CHAINS (LP)	15
72	Trojan TBL 184	PLEDGING MY LOVE (LP)	15
73	Trojan TRLS 75	1000 VOLTS OF HOLT (LP)	20
74	Attack ATLP 1010	A LOVE I CAN FEEL (LP)	15
80	Lord Koos KLP 4	DON'T BREAK YOUR PROMISE (LP, colour or black and white cover)	40
83	Greensleeves GRED 120	POLICE IN HELICOPTER (LP)	25

(see also Jay & Joya, Neville Hinds, Jeff Barnes, Danny Simpson, Hugh Roy, U Roy Junior, Don Drummond, Interns)

ROOSEVELT HOLTS

68	Blue Horizon 7-63201	PRESENTING THE COUNTRY BLUES (LP)	85

HOLY FUCK

10	YTO48S	Red Lights/Dr Dr E	10

HOLY MACKEREL

72	CBS 8447	Rock-A-Bye/New Black Shoes	6
72	CBS 65297	HOLY MACKEREL (LP)	40
93	Tenth Planet TP 005	CLOSER TO HEAVEN (LP, numbered, 500 only)	20

(see also Jason Crest, High Broom)

HOLY MODAL ROUNDERS

68	Elektra EKL 4026	THE MORAY EELS EAT THE HOLY MODALS (LP, mono)	40
68	Elektra EKS 74026	THE MORAY EELS EAT THE HOLY MODALS (LP, stereo)	40
70	Transatlantic TRA 7451	HOLY MODAL ROUNDERS (LP)	40
70	Transatlantic TRA	HOLY MODAL ROUNDERS 2 (LP)	35

HOMBRES

67	Verve VS 1510	Let It Out (Let It All Hang Out)/Go Girl Go	15

HOME

72	CBS 7809	Fancy Lady, Hollywood Child/Shady Lady	6
72	(No Cat No)	You'll Get A Helping Hand At Barclays/Dreamer (p/s)	15
71	CBS 64356	PAUSE FOR A HOARSE HORSE (LP, gatefold sleeve)	40
72	CBS 64752	HOME (LP)	25
73	CBS 65550	THE ALCHEMIST (LP)	30

(see also Groundhogs, AC/DC, Wishbone Ash, Blue Rondos)

HOME AND ABROAD

89	SRT Z003/SRT9KS2194	Alison Please Don't Fall/Feel The Floor (p/s)	10

HOMERS KNODS

69	Pye 7N 17731	All She Said Was Goodbye/Mr Rainbow	20

HOME SERVICE

84	Coda NAT 001	THE MYSTERIES (LP)	15

HOMESICK JAMES

64	Sue WI 319	Crossroads/My Baby's Sweet	75
65	Sue WI 330	Set A Date/Can't Afford To Do It	50

HOMESICK JAMES/SNOOKY PRYOR

74	Caroline C 1502	HOMESICK JAMES AND SNOOKY PRYOR (LP)	20

HOMESTEAD

68	Road R3946	She/Will You Leave	15

HOMOSEXUALS

78	L'Orelei PF 151	Hearts In Exile/South South Africans (p/s, with insert)	15

		MINT VALUE £
79	Black Noise F12 No. 2	Divorce Proceedings/Mecho Madness (12", plain sleeve with sticker) 10
81	Black Noise BN 1	BIGGER THAN THE NUMBER YET MISSING THE DOT (EP, clear vinyl, fold-around hand-painted sleeve) 20
82	Black Noise BLACKNOISE 2	THE HOMOSEXUALS EP (12") 30
84	Recommended RR 18	THE HOMOSEXUALS RECORD (LP, with inserts) 20

(see also George Harrassment & Homosexuals, Ice La Bas, Amos & Sara, L-Voag, Sir Alick & Phraser)

MINAKO HONDA
87	Columbia DB 9153	Golden Days (English Version)/Crazy Nights (English Version) (p/s, features Brian May) ... 35

HONDELLS
64	Mercury MF 834	Little Honda/Hot Rod High 25
65	Mercury MF 925	Younger Girl/All American Girl 20
66	Mercury MF 967	Cheryl's Goin' Home/Show Me Girl 20

HONEST MEN
69	Tamla Motown TMG 706	Cherie/Baby 50
69	Tamla Motown TMG 706	Cherie/Baby (DJ Copy) 60

HONEY
87	Instant INST 5	More Wild Than Honey/More Scratch Than Honey/(Radio) More Wild Than Honey/Let's Call The Whole Thing Dub (12") 12

HONEY BEES
02	Fab-U-Lus FBU07014	Never In A Million Years/MELBA MOORE: The Magic Touch (reissue) 15

HONEYBOY
71	Trojan TR 7835	Jamaica/ITALS: Sea Wave 18
72	Banana BA 375	Homeward Bound/Peace In The Land 100
73	Sir Collins Music SCMW 004	Better Must Come/Lola (as Honeyboy Collins) 40
73	Cactus CT 16	Sweet Cherrie/Impossible Love 10
73	Count Shelly CS 030	Feeling High Version/Bush Ranger At His Workshop (with Tapper Zukie) 50
75	B & C BC 002	Darlin' Coming Home/SIR COLLINS: We A Come Dread 25
73	Count Shelly SSLP 101	THIS IS HONEY BOY (LP) 60
74	Cactus CTLP 201	IMPOSSIBLE LOVE (LP) 25

HONEYBUS
67	Deram DM 131	Delighted To See You/The Breaking Up Scene 12
67	Deram DM 152	Do I Figure In Your Life?/Throw My Love Away 12
68	Deram DM 207	Girl Of Independent Means/How Long 12
69	Deram DM 254	She Sold Blackpool Rock/Would You Believe 25
70	Deram DM 289	Story/The Right To Choose 7
72	Bell BLL 1205	She Is The Female To My Soul/For Where Have You Been 6
73	Warner Bros K 16250	For You/Little Lovely One 8
70	Deram DML/SML 1056	STORY (LP) 150
73	Warner Bros K 46248	RECITAL (LP, withdrawn, test pressings only) 300
79	See For Miles SEE 264	AT THEIR BEST (LP) 15

(see also Pete Dello, Colin Hare, Lace, Magic Valley, Red Herring)

HONEYCOMBAK
69	Carousel CAR 1	Sex Change Sadie/It's My Life 50

HONEYCOMBS
64	Pye 7N 15705	Is It Because/I'll Cry Tomorrow 8
64	Pye 7N 15736	Eyes/If You've Got To Pick A Baby 10
65	Pye 7N 15781	Don't Love You No More/I'll See You Tomorrow (withdrawn, promo only) 120
65	Pye 7N 15827	Something Better Beginning/I'll See You Tomorrow 10
65	Pye 7N 15890	That's The Way/Can't Get Through To You 6
65	Pye 7N 15979	This Year, Next Year/Not Sleeping Too Well Lately 10
66	Pye 7N 17089	Who Is Sylvia?/How Will I Know 15
66	Pye 7N 17138	It's So Hard/I Fell In Love 15
66	Pye 7N 17173	That Loving Feeling/Should A Man Cry 18
69	Pye 7N 17741	Have I The Right/Please Don't Pretend Again (stereo reissue) 6
65	Pye NEP 24230	THAT'S THE WAY (EP) 35
64	Pye NPL 18097	THE HONEYCOMBS (LP) 40
65	Pye NPL 18132	ALL SYSTEMS GO! (LP) 70

(see also Lemmings, Dennis D'Ell, Martin Murray)

HONEYCONE
70	Hot Wax HWX 103	While You're Out Looking For Sugar/The Feeling's Gone 8
71	Hot Wax HWX 105	Girls It Ain't Easy/Take Me With You 6
71	Hot Wax HWX 107	Want Ads/We Belong Together 10
72	Hot Wax HWX 111	One Monkey Don't Stop No Show/Stick Up 6
72	Hot Wax HWX 112	The Day I Found Myself/When Will It End 6
72	Hot Wax HWX 116	Sittin' On A Time Bomb/It's Better To Have Loved And Lost 10
71	Hot Wax SHW 5002	HONEYCONE (LP) 20
71	Hot Wax SHW 5004	SWEET REPLIES (LP) 20
72	Hot Wax SHW 5005	SOULFUL TAPESTRY (LP) 20
73	Hot Wax SHW 5010	LOVE, PEACE AND SOUL (LP) 20

HONEYCRACK
95	PPP 1	King Of Misery/5 Minutes (numbered p/s, 1500 only sold at gigs) 10
96	Epic 484230 0	PROZAIC (LP, with inner sleeve, white vinyl, 2000 only) 25
96	Epic 484230 1	PROZAIC (LP, with inner sleeve, black vinyl) 25

(see also Jellys, Wildhearts)

HONEYDEW
70	Argo AFW 101	Part Of This Game/To Make You Mine 20
70	Argo ZFB 15	HONEYDEW (LP) 150

HONEYDRIPPERS
84	Es Paranza SAM 220	Sea Of Love/Rockin' At Midnight (7" radio promo) 10

(see also Robert Plant)

HONEYEND

			MINT VALUE £
HONEYEND			
72	Spark SRL 1072	Heartbreaker/Beautiful Downtown	20
HONEYS			
63	Capitol CL 15299	Surfin' Down The Swanee River/Shoot The Curl	50
(see also American Spring, Beach Boys)			
HONEYTONES			
58	London HLX 8671	Don't Look Now, But.../I Know, I Know	60
58	London HLX 8671	Don't Look Now, But.../I Know, I Know (78)	35
HONEYTREE			
70s	Myrrh MYR 1039	EVERGREEN (LP)	20
HONG GANG			
72	Sioux SI 004	Reggae Mento/MONTEGO MELON: Swan Lake	12
73	Sioux SI 025	Smoking Wild/ROOSEVELT SINGERS: Heavy Reggae	12
(see also Bob Andy)			
HOOD			
92	Fluff HONEY 4	Sirens/Fault/Your Sixth Sense (p/s, 500 only)	12
93	Fluff HONEY 6	I Didn't Think You Were Going To Hit Me In The Face/In The Trap Of Doing/Choosing A Grimace (wraparound p/s, 500 only)	10
95	Orgasm ORGASM 08	A Harbour Of Thoughts/Disappointed/Uneven Conversation Should Point To Cause/Forced By The Reasoning Hand/John Clyde-Evans/Silo Crash (p/s)	7
96	Love Train PUBE 11	I've Forgotten How To Live/The Weather Side Of The Stone Mill Tower/Dimensions TBA	8
98	Rocket Racer ROCKET 04	The Year Of Occasional Lull/Fog Projections (1000 only, numbered, 20 with red artwork)	10
98	Happy Go Lucky HGL 12	Filmed Initiative/As Evening Changed The Day (different photo on each p/s)	12
98	555 Recordings 555 13	(The) Weight/Fallen Farmer/We Are Not Promote/Impossible Calm/Feel The Rush (Coming In From The Avant Garde)/I Know What To Squander/Mast-On-Hill/Collapsing Climate Soul (p/s)	6
00	Jonathan Whiskey 04	I Can't Find My Brittle Youth/Song Of The Sea/STEWARD: Silver Soda Pop/I'm A Woman Not Just A Toy/Flatter Me With Concern For Prejudice (envelope sleeve, 250 only)	20
94	Fluff ARC 01	CABLED LINEAR TRACTION (LP, 200 only)	50
98	Domino WIGLP 42	RUSTIC HOUSES FORLORN VALLEYS (LP)	30
99	Domino WIGLP 61	THE CYCLE OF DAYS AND REASONS (LP)	25
01	Domino WIGLP 102	COLD HOUSE (LP)	20
05	Domino WIGLP 148	OUTSIDE CLOSER (LP)	18
12	Domino REWIGLP85	COLD HOUSE (reissue, 2x12")	20
ROBBIN HOOD			
56	MGM SP 1178	The Rock-A-Bye Blues/Beautiful, Beautiful Love	15
HOODOO RHYTHM DEVILS			
78	Fantasy FTC 147	Gotta Lot Of Love In My Soul/MDR Of Love	15
HOOK			
68	Uni UN 507	In The Beginning/Show You The Way	10
MARCUS HOOK ROLL BAND			
72	Regal Zonophone RZ 3061	Natural Man/Boogalooing Is For Wooing	30
73	Regal zonophone RZ 3072	Louisina Lady/Ghoochie Coochie Har Kau	8
74	EMI 2119	Can't Stand The Heat/Moonshine Blues	20
EARL HOOKER			
69	Blue Horizon 57-3166	Boogie Don't Blot/Funky Blues	30
70	Blue Horizon 7-63850	SWEET BLACK ANGEL (LP)	120
70	Stateside SSL 10238	DON'T HAVE TO WORRY (LP)	60
(see also John Lee Hooker)			
JOHN LEE HOOKER			
78s			
52	Vogue V 2102	Hoogie Boogie/Whistlin' And Moanin' Blues	40
54	London HL 8037	Need Somebody/Too Much Boogie	40
SINGLES			
63	Stateside SS 203	Boom Boom/Frisco Blues	25
64	Stateside SS 297	Dimples/I'm Leaving	20
64	Stateside SS 341	I Love You Honey/Send Me Your Pillow	20
64	Pye International 7N 25255	High Priced Woman/Sugar Mama	20
64	Polydor NH 52930	Shake It Baby/Let's Make It Baby	20
65	Sue WI 361	I'm In The Mood/Boogie Chillun	40
66	Chess CRS 8039	Let's Go Out Tonight/In The Mood	20
66	Planet PLF 114	Mai Lee/Don't Be Messing With My Bread (with Groundhogs)	100
70	President PT 295	Dimples/Boom Boom	8
EPs			
60	Riverside REP 3202	WEDNESDAY EVENING	30
60	Riverside REP 3207	DEMOCRAT MAN	30
64	Stateside SE 1019	THE BLUES OF JOHN HOOKER	30
64	Stateside SE 1023	I'M JOHN LEE HOOKER	30
64	Ember EP 4561	THINKING BLUES	40
65	Pye Intl. NEP 44034	LOVE BLUES	35
65	Chess CRE 6000	DOWN AT THE LANDING	35
65	Atlantic AET 6010	JOHN LEE HOOKER	35
66	Chess CRE 6007	WALKING THE BOOGIE	30
66	Chess CRE 6014	THE JOURNEY	30
66	Chess CRE 6021	REAL FOLK BLUES VOL. 3	30
73	Impulse 9103	SERVES YOU RIGHT TO SUFFER	15
ALBUMS			
60	Advent LP 2801	JOHN LEE HOOKER AND HIS GUITAR	80
62	Riverside RLP 12-838	THE FOLK BLUES OF JOHN LEE HOOKER	45

John LEE HOOKER/LIGHTNIN' HOPKINS/SMOKEY HOGG

MINT VALUE £

62	Stateside SL 10014	THE FOLK LORE OF JOHN LEE HOOKER	70
63	London HA-K 8097	DON'T TURN ME FROM YOUR DOOR	80
64	Stateside SL 10053	THE BIG SOUL OF JOHN LEE HOOKER	80
64	Stateside SL 10074	I WANT TO SHOUT THE BLUES	60
64	Pye Intl. NPL 28042	HOUSE OF THE BLUES	60
64	Fontana 688 700 ZL	THE FOLK-BLUES OF HOOKER	45
65	Fontana FJL 119	BLUE!	70
65	Ember EMB 3356	SINGS THE BLUES	35
65	Riverside RLP 008	BURNING HELL	35
65	Chess CRL 4500	JOHN LEE HOOKER PLAYS AND SINGS THE BLUES	60
66	HMV CLP 5032	IT SERVES YOU RIGHT TO SUFFER (mono)	45
66	HMV CSD 3542	IT SERVES YOU RIGHT TO SUFFER (stereo)	60
66	Ember (ST)EMB 3371	DRIFTIN' THROUGH THE BLUES	25
67	Chess CRL 4527	THE REAL FOLK BLUES	40
67	HMV CLP/CSD 3612	LIVE AT THE CAFE A GO GO	40
67	Atlantic Special 590 003	DRIFTIN' BLUES	18
68	Joy JOY(S) 101	I'M JOHN LEE HOOKER	15
68	Joy JOY(S) 124	BURNIN'	15
68	Stateside (S)SL 10246	URBAN BLUES	40
69	Stateside (S)SL 10280	SIMPLY THE TRUTH	50
69	Joy JOYS 133	THE FOLKLORE OF JOHN LEE HOOKER	15
69	Joy JOYS 142	CONCERT AT NEWPORT	15
69	Joy JOYS 147	THE BIG SOUL OF JOHN LEE HOOKER	15
69	Storyville 673 005	YOU'RE LEAVIN' ME BABY	15
69	Joy JOYS 152	IN PERSON	15
70	Storyville 673 020	TUPELO BLUES	30
70	Stax SXATS 1025	THAT'S WHERE IT'S AT	20
71	Probe SPB 1016	IF YOU MISS 'IM . . . I GOT 'IM (with Earl Hooker)	30
71	Probe SPB 1034	ENDLESS BOOGIE	15
71	Stax 2362 017	THAT'S WHERE IT'S AT!	20
71	Xtra XTRA 1114	JOHN LEE HOOKER	40
71	United Artists UAS 29235	COAST TO COAST BLUES BAND	22
72	Probe SPB 1057	NEVER GET OUT OF THESE BLUES ALIVE	18
73	Green Bottle GN 4002	JOHNNY LEE	18
75	ABC ABCL 5059	FREE BEER AND CHICKEN	20
91	Silvertone ZL 75087	MR. LUCKY (LP)	30
95	Virgin VPBLP 22	CHILL OUT (LP)	100

(see also Canned Heat, Carlos Santana & Buddy Miles)

JOHN LEE HOOKER/LIGHTNIN' HOPKINS/SMOKEY HOGG

73	Specialty SNTF 5013	HOOKER HOPKINS HOGG (LP)	20

(see also Lightnin' Hopkins, Smokey Hogg)

STEVE HOOKER & HEAT

77	Takeaway TAKE 1/ EJR 577	If You Don't Do The Business/Rock & Roll Doctor/I'm Hooked/ Marionette (stamped white sleeve with insert)	8

HOOKFOOT

69	Page One POF 144	Way Of The Musician/Hookfoot	12
72	DJM DJS 272	Heart To Heart Talking/Red Man	8
72	DJM DJS 265	Sweet Sweet Funky Music/The Opener	8
73	DJM DJS 293	So You Want To Be A Rock And Roll Star/Mr. Money	8
71	DJM DJLPS 413	HOOKFOOT (LP, gatefold sleeve)	30
72	DJM DJLPS 422	GOOD TIMES A' COMIN' (LP, gatefold sleeve)	25
73	DJM DJLPS 428	COMMUNICATION (LP, gatefold sleeve)	20
75	DJM DJLMD 8013	HEADLINES (2XLP)	18

(see also Elton John, Loot, Caleb, Soul Agents)

MARSHALL HOOKS & CO.

71	Blue Horizon 2096 002	I Want The Same Thing Tomorrow/Hookin' It	20
71	Blue Horizon 2431 003	MARSHALL HOOKS & CO. (LP)	100

HOOKY

72	RCA Victor SF 8247	THE COLLECTED TALES OF HOOKY NO.1 (LP, gatefold sleeve)	20

TERRI HOOLEY

79	Fresh FRESH 4	Laugh At Me/Laugh At Me (Again) (p/s)	10

HOOTEN(ANNY) SINGERS

64	United Artists UP 1082	Gabrielle/Darling (most copies list artist as Hooten Singers)	35

(see also Abba, Hep Stars, Northern Lights)

BOB HOPE

58	London HLU 8593	Paris Holiday/Nothing In Common (with Bing Crosby)	10
60	Capitol EAP 1 20071	AIN'T WE GOT FUN (EP)	10
63	Brunswick LAT 8539	IN RUSSIA AND ONE OTHER PLACE (LP)	15

(see also Bing Crosby)

LYN(N) HOPE

57	Vogue V 9081	Blue Moon/Blues For Anna Bacca	20
57	Vogue V 9082	Eleven Till Two/Blues For Mary	20
60	Blue Beat BB 21	Shockin'/Blue And Sentimental	20
57	Vogue VE 170103	LYNN HOPE AND HIS TENOR SAX (EP)	40
60	Vogue VE 170146	LYNN HOPE AND HIS TENOR SAX (EP)	40

HOPE STREET

71	Parlophone R5982	Wait Until Tomorrow/Ladies At The Bottom Of the Garden	12

HOPE & KEEN

71	Excello XLO2	Crazy House/You Can Go My Way	12

HOPE BLISTERS

MINT VALUE £

HOPE BLISTERS
98	4AD CAD 8008	...SMILES OK (LP)	30

HOPETOWN (LEWIS) & GLENMORE (BROWN)
68	Fab FAB 43	Skinny Leg Girl/Live Like A King	90

MARY HOPKIN
68	Apple APPLE 2	Those Were The Days/Turn Turn Turn (First pressing)	10
68	Apple APPLE 2	Those Were The Days/Turn Turn Turn (later pressing crediting Mary Hopkins)	8
68	Apple APPLE 2	Those Were The Days/Turn Turn Turn (blank Apple label on A-side)	12
69	Apple APPLE 7	Lontana Dagli Occhi/Game (Europe-only, unreleased in U.K.)	0
69	Apple APPLE 9	Prince En Avignon/The Game (France-only, unreleased in U.K.)	0
69	Apple APPLE 10	Goodbye/Sparrow	6
69	Apple APPLE 16	Que Sera Sera/Fields Of St. Etienne (unreleased)	0
69	Cambrian CSP 703	Aderyn Llwyd/Y Blodyn Gwyn (p/s)	18
70	Cambrian CSP 712	Pleserau Serch/Tyrd Yn Ôl (p/s)	18
70	Apple APPLE 22	Temma Harbour/Lontano Dagli Occhi (black or green lettering on p/s)	6
70	Apple APPLE 26	Knock, Knock Who's There?/I'm Going To Fall In Love Again (p/s)	6
70	Apple APPLE 27	Que Sera Sera/Fields Of St. Etienne (unreleased in U.K., acetates only)	0
70	Apple APPLE 30	Think About Your Children/Heritage (p/s)	6
71	Apple APPLE 34	Let My Name Be Sorrow/Kew Gardens (p/s)	15
71	Apple APPLE 39	Water, Paper And Clay/Jefferson (p/s)	25
72	Regal Zonophone RZ 3070	Mary Had A Baby/Cherry Tree Carol	6
76	Good Earth GD 2	If You Love Me (I Won't Care): (some copies list "If You Love Me")/Tell Me Now	6
77	Good Earth GD 11	Wrap Me In Your Arms/Just A Dreamer (p/s)	10
68	Cambrian CEP 414	LLAIS SWYNOL MARY HOPKIN (EP)	15
69	Cambrian CEP 420	MARY AC EDWARD (EP, with Edward Morris Jones)	15
69	Apple APCOR 5	POST CARD (LP, laminated sleeve, with black or white inner sleeve, mono)	25
69	Apple SAPCOR 5	POST CARD (LP, laminated sleeve, with black or white inner sleeve, stereo)	20
71	Apple SAPCOR 21	EARTH SONG - OCEAN SONG (LP, gatefold sleeve, 'Apple' inner sleeve)	50
72	Apple SAPCOR 23	THOSE WERE THE DAYS (LP, with 'Apple' inner sleeve)	90
77	Decca SPA 546	THE WELSH WORLD OF MARY HOPKIN (LP)	30
89	Trax Modem 1045	SPIRIT (LP)	20
91	Apple SAPCOR 5	POST CARD (LP, reissue, gatefold sleeve with bonus 12" [SAPCOR 52])	30
92	Apple SAPCOR 21	EARTH SONG/OCEAN SONG (LP, reissue, gatefold sleeve with inner)	30

(see also Hobby Horse, Sundance, Oasis, Elfland Ensemble, Bob Johnson & Pete Knight, Roy Budd, Elmer Bernstein)

JOEL & LIGHTNIN' HOPKINS
60	Heritage H 1000	BLUES FROM EAST TEXAS (LP, 99 copies only)	120

(see also Lightnin' Hopkins)

LIGHTNIN' HOPKINS
61	Bluesville BVLP 1019	LIGHTNIN' HOPKINS (LP)	80
62	'77' LA 12/1	SAM LIGHTNIN' HOPKINS - THE ROOSTER CROWED IN ENGLAND (LP 99 copies only)	150
63	Stateside SL 10031	LIGHTNIN' STRIKES (LP)	90
63	Realm RM 128	LIGHTNIN' HOPKINS SINGS THE BLUES (LP)	35
63	Realm RM 171	DIRTY HOUSE BLUES (LP)	30
64	Stateside SL 10076	BLUES HOOT (LP, some tracks by Sonny Terry & Brownie McGhee)	60
65	Stateside SL 10110	HOOTIN' THE BLUES (LP)	60
65	Stateside SL 10155	DOWN HOME BLUES (LP)	60
65	Fontana AH 183	THE BLUES (LP)	40
65	FONTANA 688 007 ZL	PENITENTIARY BLUES (LP)	35
65	Fontana 688 301 ZL	LAST NIGHT BLUES (LP)	40
65	Fontana 688 801 ZL	BURNIN' IN L.A. (LP)	40
66	Fontana 688 803 ZL	BLUE BIRD BLUES (LP)	40
66	Fontana 688 807 ZL	BLUES PARTY (LP)	40
66	Ember EMB 3389	A TIME FOR BLUES (LP)	25
66	Ember EMB 3416	LIVE AT THE BIRD LOUNGE (LP)	25
67	Ember EMB 3423	I'VE BEEN BUKED AND SCORNED (LP)	25
66	Verve (S)VLP 5003	ROOTS OF HOPKINS (LP)	25
66	Verve (S)VLP 5014	LIGHTNIN' STRIKES (LP, reissue)	18
66	Saga ERO 8001	LIGHTNIN' HOPKINS (LP)	15
67	Xtra XTRA 5036	BLUES IN MY BOTTLE (LP)	18
68	Xtra XTRA 5044	GOT TO MOVE YOUR BABY (LP, reissue of Fontana 688 301 ZL)	20
68	Minit MLL/MLS 40006	EARTH BLUES (LP)	40
69	Liberty LBL 83254	KING OF DOWLING STREET (LP)	30
69	Joy JOY(S) 115	LIGHTNIN' STRIKES (LP, 2nd reissue)	15
69	Polydor 545 019	THAT'S MY STORY (LP)	25
70	Ace Of Hearts AH 183	THE BLUES (LP)	15
70	Poppy PYS 11000	LIGHTNIN'! VOLUME 1 (LP)	20
70	Poppy PYS 11002	LIGHTNIN'! VOLUME 2 (LP)	20
71	Liberty LBS 83293	THE CALIFORNIA MUDSLIDE (AND EARTHQUAKE) (LP)	30
71	Blue Horizon 2431 005	LET'S WORK AWHILE (LP)	120
71	Xtra XTRA 1127	THE ROOTS OF LIGHTNIN' HOPKINS (LP)	18
72	Carnival 2941 005	LONESOME LIGHTNIN' (LP)	18

(see also Sonny Terry & Brownie McGhee, Joel & Lightnin' Hopkins, Lightnin' Hopkins & John Lee Hooker, Big Joe Williams)

LIGHTNIN' HOPKINS & JOHN LEE HOOKER
69	Storyville 616 001	THERE'S GOOD ROCKIN' TONIGHT! (LP)	35
72	Storyville SLP 174	LIGHTNIN' HOPKINS AND JOHN LEE HOOKER (LP)	35

(see also John Lee Hooker/Lightnin' Hopkins/Smokey Hogg)

LINDA HOPKINS
61	Coral Q 72423	I Diddle Dum Dum/All In My Mind	20
62	Coral Q 72448	Mama's Doin' The Twist/My Mother's Eyes	20

Linda HOPKINS & JACKIE WILSON

MINT VALUE £

LINDA HOPKINS & JACKIE WILSON
63	Coral Q 72464	Shake A Hand/Say I Do	15
65	Coral Q 72480	Yes Indeed/When The Saints Go Marching In	15

(see also Jackie Wilson)

NICKY HOPKINS
66	CBS 202055	Mr Big/Jenni	18
67	Polydor 56175	Mister Pleasant/Nothing As Yet	18
68	MGM MGM 1419	Top Pops No. 1 (Medley)/(Part 2)	8
68	Fontana TF 906	High On A Hill/Trumpet Serenade (actually by Nigel Hopkins)	6
66	CBS (S)BPG 62679	THE REVOLUTIONARY PIANO OF NICKY HOPKINS (LP)	70
73	CBS 65416	THE TIN MAN WAS A DREAMER (LP, gatefold sleeve)	30

(see also Aquarian Age, Neil Christian & Crusaders, Cyril Davies R&B All-Stars, Poet & One Man Band, Quicksilver Messenger Service, Sweet Thursday)

WASH HOPKINS SINGERS
69	Action ACT 4546	He's Got Blessing/Rock In A Weary Land	20

HOPKIRK AND LEE
98	Rough Trade/For Us 001	Beneath The Apple Tree (7" 1,000 copies)	18

HUGH HOPPER
73	CBS 65466	1984 (LP)	40
76	Compendium FIDARDO 4	CRUEL BUT FAIR (LP)	20
77	Compendium FIDARDO 7	HOPPERTUNITY BOX (LP)	20
78	Ogun OG 527	ROGUE ELEMENT (LP, as Hopper, Dean, Gowen, Sheen - 'Soft Heap')	20
80	Red ROUGE 1	TWO RAINBOWS DAILY (LP, with Alan Gowen)	30

(see also Caravan, Elton Dean, Gilgamesh, Isotope, Matching Mole, Ninesense, Soft Machine)

HOPSCOTCH
69	United Artists UP 2231	Look At The Lights Go Up/Same Old Fat Man	140
69	United Artists UP 35022	Long Black Veil/Easy To Find	10

(see also Scots Of St. James, Five Day Rain, Forever More, Glencoe)o

HORACE & IMPERIALS
68	Nu Beat NB 012	Young Love/Days Like These	15

EDDIE HORAN
78	London HLU 10565	When I Fly With You/Turn My World Back Around	10

HORDEN RAIKES
73	Folk Heritage FHR 042	KING COTTON (LP)	15
72	Folk Heritage FHR 026	HORDEN RAIKES (LP)	20

HORIZON (1)
81	SRT SRTS 81432	Stage Struck/Remember The Bad Boys	10

HORIZON (2)
83	Orbit TRIP 4	Sunshine Reggae/Nightlife	6

(see also Mungo Jerry)

PAUL HORN
68	Liberty LBL 83084E	COSMIC CONSCIOUSNESS (LP)	30

LENA HORNE
65	United Artists UP 1101	The Sand And The Sea/It Had Better Be Tonight	25

HANK HORNSBY
57	MGM MGM 955	Pots And Pans/Cotton	6
58	MGM MGM 972	The Legend Of The Birds And Bees/Girls Girls Girls	6

HORNSEY AT WAR
79	War WAR 001	DEAD BEAT REVIVAL (EP, numbered p/s)	40

HORRORCOMIC
77	Lightning/B&C BVZ 0007	I'm All Hung Up On Pierrepoint/The Exorcist/Sex In The Afternoon (p/s)	40
78	Lightning GIL 512	I Don't Mind/England 77 (p/s)	90
79	B&C BCS 18	Jesus Crisis/Cut Your Throat (p/s)	400

HORRORS
06	Loog LOOG 015	Sheena Is A Parasite/Jack The Ripper (p/s, insert, 500 only)	80
06	Loog LOOG 016	Death At The Chapel/Crawdaddy Simone (p/s, 500 only with sticker)	12
06	Loog LOOG 18-7X	Count In Fives/A Knife In Their Eye (p/s, inner p/s, stickered PVC sleeve)	15
06	Loog LOOG 18-7	Count In Fives/Who Says (black sleeve, barcode sticker, with sticker inside)	18
07	Loog 1725544	Gloves/Kicking Kay (p/s)	10
07	Loog 1725539	Gloves/Death At The Chapel (p/s)	6
07	Loog 1735625	She Is The New Thing/Draw Japan (Dandi Wind Remix) p/s	6
07	Loog 1735628	She Is The New Thing/Sister Leonella (p/s)	6
09	XL XLS 417	Who Can Say/You Never Could Tell (p/s)	6
09	XL XLS 468	Whole New Way/Primary Colours (p/s)	8
13	XL XLBX 587	HIGHER (4 x 12", 2-CD, DVD box set)	50
07	Polydor 172 417-9	STRANGE HOUSE (LP, stickered gatefold sleeve, inner)	80
09	XL XLLP 418	PRIMARY COLOURS (2-LP, poster)	25
11	XL XLLP 539	SKYING (2-LP with 5 prints)	20

(see also Spider & The Flies)

FRANK HORROX
60	Embassy WEP 1038	JAZZ SESSION (EP, featuring Don Rendell)	20

HORSE
70	RCA Victor SF 8109	HORSE (LP, laminated sleeve)	400

(see also Saturnalia, Atomic Rooster)

HORSEBEACH
13	Box Bedroom BBR 5	HORSEBEACH EP (p/s, numbered, 125 copies)	20

HORSE MOUTH
75	Fight FT 010	Herb Vendor/DELROY BUTLER: Give Thanks	50

(see also Mad Roy, Silvertones)

HORSEPOWER
79	Square SQS 2	Outrageous/Highway Robbery	10

HORSLIPS

MINT VALUE £

76	DJM DJS 10754	Warm Sweet Breath Of Love/King Of Morning, Queen Of Day	6
73	Oats MOO 3	HAPPY TO MEET ... SORRY TO PART (LP, booklet octagonal sleeve)	45
73	Oats MOO 5	THE TAIN (LP, gatefold sleeve, lyric inner sleeve)	20
75	RCA Victor SF 8432	THE UNFORTUNATE CUP OF TEA (LP, orange label)	15

HORTENSE (ELLIS) & ALTON (ELLIS)
65	Island WI 230	Don't Gamble With Love/Something You Got (B-side actually by Alton Ellis & Flames)	40

(see also Hortense Ellis, Alton Ellis, Mr. Foundation)

HORTENSE (ELLIS) & DELROY (WILSON)
66	Rio R 119	We're Gonna Make It/SOUL BROTHERS: Ska Shuffle	35

(see also Hortense Ellis, Delroy Wilson)

HORTENSE (ELLIS) & JACKIE (OPEL)
64	R&B JB 138	Stand By Me/JACKIE OPEL: Solid Rock	50

(see also Hortense Ellis, Jackie Opel)

JOHNNY HORTON
59	Philips PB 932	The Battle Of New Orleans/All For The Love Of A Girl	7
59	Philips PB 951	Sal's Got A Sugar Lip/Johnny Reb	10
59	Philips PB 976	Take Me Like I Am/I'm Ready If You're Willing	10
60	Philips PB 995	Sink The Bismarck!/The Same Old Tale The Crow Told Me	10
60	Philips PB 1062	North To Alaska/The Mansion You Stole	7
61	Philips PB 1130	When It's Springtime In Alaska/Mr. Moonlight	8
61	Philips PB 1132	Sleepy Eyed John/They'll Never Take Her Love From Me	10
61	Philips PB 1170	Miss Marcy/Ole Slew Foot	10
62	Philips PB 1226	Words/Honky Tonk Man	10
63	CBS AAG 132	All Grown Up/I'm A One Woman Man	10
60	Mercury ZEP 10274	THE FANTASTIC JOHNNY HORTON (EP)	40
64	Mercury 10008 MCE	COUNTRY AND WESTERN ACES (EP)	20
60	Philips BBL 7464	THE SPECTACULAR JOHNNY HORTON (LP)	40
61	Philips BBL 7536	HONKY TONK MAN (LP)	40
63	London HA-U 8096	DONE ROVIN' (LP)	25

WALTER 'SHAKEY' HORTON
70	London HAK/SHK 8405	SOUTHERN COMFORT (LP, as Shakey Horton)	100
74	Xtra XTRA 1135	WALTER 'SHAKEY' HORTON WITH HOT COTTAGE (LP)	30
74	Sonet SNTF 677	BIG WALTER HORTON (LP, with Carey Bell)	25

JOHN HOSIER
70	Universal Editions LYN 2177	NEW SOUNDS IN CLASS (with St. Anne's Girls School)	30

LA/THE HOST
85	Quiet QU 1	The Big Sleep/Just Breaking Away (p/s)	8

HOT BUTTER
72	Pye Int. 7N.25598	Apache/Hot Butter	6

HOT CHIP
04	Moshi Moshi HOTCHIP7	Hittin Skittles/Back To The Future (300 only, hand-made sleeve)	10
06	EMI EM 682	Over And Over/The Girl In Me (p/s, orange vinyl)	12
07	EMI CHIPS 01	Rehab (AMY WINEHOUSE: Hot Chip Remix)/In The Morning (JUNIOR BOYS: Hot Chip Remix) (12")	12
09	Parlophone 50999 69399176	Transmission/JOY DIVISION: Transmission (demo)	12
12	Domino RUG 473T	Flutes/Flutes (instrumental) (12", 200 only)	15
12	Last Night On Earth LNOE009V	Flutes (Sasha Remix) (1-sided white vinyl 12", p/s)	100
12	Domino DNO 337	Look At Where We Are (Major Lazer Remix)/Look At Where We Are (Major Lazer v Junior Blender Remix) 7", large hole, die cut sleeve, 1000 only)	6
04	Moshi Moshi MOSHILP 06	COMING ON STRONG (LP, silkscreened cover, 500 only)	100
06	EMI 094634741811	THE WARNING (2-LP with free 7", Won't Wash/Bally)	80
06	EMI 094634741811	THE WARNING (2-LP)	70
08	EMI 5099952057717	MADE IN THE DARK (LP)	35
10	Vinyl Factory VF 012	ONE LIFE STAND (2-LP with free 7" Bubble/Do Not Wait, no'd gatefold sleeve)	50
10	Vinyl Factory VF012	ONE LIFE STAND (2-LP, 200gm, 250 only)	50
10	Moshi Moshi MOSHILP06	COMING ON STRONG (LP, reissue, different cover)	25
15	Domino WIGLP 313X	WHY MAKE SENSE? (LP, with free 12")	20
12	Domino WIGLP 293X	IN OUR HEADS (2-LP with 7")	25
15	Domino WIGLP 313	WHY MAKE SENSE? (LP)	15
17	Moshi Moshi MOSHILP06X	COMING ON STRONG (LP, reissue, different cover, yellow vinyl)	35

HOT CHOCOLATE (BAND)
69	Apple APPLE 18	Give Peace A Chance/Living Without Tomorrow (as Hot Chocolate Band)	80
73	Rak RAK 139	You'll Always Be A friend/Go Go Girl	15

(see also Errol Brown & Chosen Few, Tony Wilson)

HOT CITY
71	London HLU 10344	Leaving/I Believe In Life	15

HOT CLUB
82	RAK 346	The Dirt That She Walks On Is Sacred Ground To Me/Heat (p/s)	12
82	RAK 346	The Dirt That She Walks On Is Sacred Ground To Me/Heat (12", p/s)	10
82	RAK 361	It Ain't Me Girl/It Ain't Me Girl (Night Version) (p/s)	6

(see also Rich Kids, Spectres)

HOTFOOT GALE
78	Charly SYS 1044	Washin' Machine Boogie/Everybody's Feelin' Allright	6

HOT LEG
09	Barbeque Rock BRR0003V	RED LIGHT FEVER (LP, red)	25

(see also Darkness)

HOTLEGS
71	Philips 6006 140	Lady Sadie/The Loser	8
71	Philips 6308 047	THINKS: SCHOOL STINKS (LP, gatefold sleeve, black/silver label)	50

HOT NATURED

MINT VALUE £

71	Philips 6308 080	SONG (LP, gatefold sleeve, black/silver label)	60

(see also 10cc, Mindbenders, Godley & Creme, Tristar Airbus, Ramases)

HOT NATURED
13	Hot Creations HNLP 001	DIFFERENT SIDES OF THE SUN (3-LP)	30

HOT POTATO
73	PMTB 1	HOT POTATO (LP, private pressing)	200

HOT RAIN
90	Pine Tree TWIG 002	STAY TRUE (12", EP)	25

HOT RATS
09	No label or cat no	Damaged Goods/Fight For Your Right To Party (tour 7", 150-only, die-cut sleeve, signed)	12

(see also Supergrass)

HOT ROCKS
73	Bell Bell 1326	Chopper/Roly Poly	6

HOT ROCKS & JAH LOXLEY
80s	Gemini GSM 025	Jah Jah No Parcial/Badda Badda	20

HOT ROD
69	Joe's DU 41	The Judge/RON: Soul Of Soul Of Joel	20
73	President PT 397	I Want You (All Night Long)/Love Is All Right (Hey)	10

HOT ROD ALLSTARS
69	Duke DU 59	Lick A Pop/Treasure	50
70	Duke DU 65	Paint Your Wagon/Organ Man (Setters as artist on label)	150
70	Duke DU 66	Return Of The Bad Man/Caysoe Reggae	125
70	Trojan TR 7732	Strong Man/Sentimental	35
70	Trojan TR 7733	Virgin Soldier/Brixton Reggae Festival	50
70	Torpedo TOR 1	Pussy Got Nine Life/BOSS SOUNDS: Lick It Back	200
70	Torpedo TOR 5	Skinheads Don't Fear/Ten Commandments From The Devil	200
70	Torpedo TOR 10	Moonhop In London/Skinhead Moondust	300
70	Torpedo TOR 14	Control Your Doggy/Follow The Stars	75
70	Hot Rod HR 104	Skinhead Speaks His Mind/CARL LEVEY: Carnaby Street	200
70	Hot Rod HR 107	Strictly Invitation/PATSY & PEGGY: Dog Your Woman	100
70	Hot Rod HR 108	Beautiful World/Shocks Of A Drugs Man	100

(see also Setters, Betty Sinclair)

HOTRODS
65	Columbia DB 7693	I Don't Love You No More/Ain't Coming Back No More	50

HOT SPRINGS
66	Columbia DB 7821	It's All Right/All I Know About Love	20

HOT THUMBS O'RILEY
73	Charisma CAS 1071	HOT THUMBS O'RILEY (LP, gatefold sleeve, large 'Mad Hatter' label)	30

HOT-TODDYS
59	Pye International 7N 25020	Rockin' Crickets/Shakin' And Stompin'	30

(see also Rockin' Rebels)

HOT TUNA
70	RCA SF 8125	HOT TUNA (LP)	20

(see also Jefferson Airplane)

HOT VULTURES
77	Red Rag RRR 015	THE EAST STREET SHAKES (LP)	20
79	Plant Life PLR 018	UP THE LINE (LP)	20

(see also Ian (A) Anderson)

HOT WATER
78	Duff	Different Morning/Premium Bondage	8
79	Duff DWR 101	Get Lost!/Bird's Eye View (p/s)	7

HOUNDHEAD HENRY/FRANKIE JAXON
60	Jazz Collector JEL 10	THE MALE BLUES VOLUME 6 (EP)	18

HOUR GLASS
68	Liberty LBL83129/LBS 83129E	THE HOUR GLASS (LP)	40
74	United Artists USD 303/4	THE HOUR GLASS (2-LP)	25

(see also Allman Brothers)

HOUSE
72	Parlophone R 5962	Captain America/I Like It	7

HOUSE CREW
91	Production House PNT 029	Keep The Fire Burning/Get On Up (12")	12
91	Production House PNT 029R	Keep The Fires Burning (Remixes) (12")	20
92	Production House PNT 035	We Are Hardcore/Maniac (Hypermix) (12")	15
92	Production House PNT 035R	We Are Hardcore/Maniac (Remixes) (12")	15
93	Production House PNT 047	The Theme/Euphoria (12")	25
93	Production House PNT 047R	The Theme/Euphoria (Remixes) (12")	25
94	Production House PNT 060	Superhero (My Knight) (12")	15
94	Production House PNT 060R	Superhero (Remixes) (12")	15
94	Production House PNT 060RX	Superhero (Remixes II) (12")	15

HOUSEHOLD
67	United Artists UP 1190	I Guess I'll Learn How To Fly/Nothing You Can Do But Cry	6
68	United Artists UP 2210	Twenty First Summer/Winter's Coming On	6

HOUSEHOLD NAMES
81	Blue Chip BC 104	White Light/Much Too Young To Love	7

HOUSEMARTINS
85	Go! Discs GOD 7/GOD 9	Flag Day/Stand At Ease//Sheep/Drop Down Dead (shrinkwrapped double pack)	6
86	Go Discs! AGOLP 7	LONDON 0 HULL 4 (LP)	18
86	Go! Discs GODB 16	THE HOUSEMARTINS' CHRISTMAS BOX SET (4 singles in foldout sleeve, signed)	25

HOUSEMASTER BALDWIN

MINT VALUE £

07	Mercury 175 252-3	SOUP ('deluxe Fan Edition', in sealed/stickered tin: CD, DVD, T-shirt and mug)	60

(see also Beautiful South)

HOUSEMASTER BALDWIN
88	Koolkat KOOLT 21	DELTA HOUSE (12", p/s)	15
88	Koolkat KOOLT 22	DON'T LEAD ME (12", p/s)	15

HOUSE OF LORDS
69	B&C CB 112	In The Land Of Dreams/Ain't Gonna Wait Forever	25

HOUSE OF LOVE
87	Creation CRE 043T	Shine On/Love/Flow (12", p/s, 4,000 only)	20
87	Creation CRE 044T	Real Animal/Plastic/Nothing To Me (12", p/s, 4,000 only)	20
88	Creation CRE 057T	Destroy The Heart/Blind/Mr Jo (12", p/s)	10
92	Love 1	ROYAL ALBERT HALL EP (10" gig freebie, stickered)	25
88	Creation CRELP 034	HOUSE OF LOVE (LP, with free 7", "Shine On/Christine", matt sleeve)	20
88	Creation CRELP 034	HOUSE OF LOVE (LP, without 7")	15
89	Fontana 842 293-1	THE HOUSE OF LOVE (LP, stickered sleeve)	18
92	Fontana 512 549-1	BABE RAINBOW (LP)	30
93	Fontana 514 880-1	AUDIENCE WITH THE MIND (LP)	40

BOBBI HOUSTON
74	Action ACT 4622	I Want To Make It With You (Parts 1 & 2)	12

CISCO HOUSTON
60	Top Rank 30/028	THE CISCO SPECIAL (LP)	50
62	Fontana TFL 6007	CISCO SPECIAL! (LP)	25
62	Fontana TFL 6014	SINGS SONGS OF WOODY GUTHRIE (LP)	20
68	Fontana FJL 412	I AIN'T GOT NO HOME (LP)	15
69	Ember CW 135	CISCO HOUSTON AND WOODY GUTHRIE (LP)	15

CISSY HOUSTON
70	Pye International 7N 25557	I Just Don't Know What To Do With Myself/This Empty Place	45
70	Major Minor SMLP 80	PRESENTING CISSY HOUSTON (LP)	30

(see also Sweet Inspirations)

DAVID HOUSTON
55	London HL 8147	Blue Prelude/I'm Sorry I Made You Cry	30
63	Columbia DB 7159	Mountain Of Love/Poor Little Angeline	7
66	Columbia DB 7997	Almost Persuaded/We Got Love	7

DAVID HOUSTON & TAMMY WYNETTE
67	Columbia DB 8246	My Elusive Dreams/Marriage On The Rocks	8

SAM HOUSTON
65	Island WI 172	My Mother's Eyes/Danny Boy	12

THELMA HOUSTON
72	Tamla Motown TMG 799	I Want To Go Back There Again/Pick Of The Week	12
72	Mowest MW 3001	No One's Gonna Be A Fool Forever/What If	7
73	Mowest MW 3004	Black California/I'm Letting Go (withdrawn)	60
79	Tamla Motown TMG 1130	Saturday Night, Sunday Morning/I'm Not Strong Enough (To Love You Again) (demo only)	10
69	Stateside (S)SL 5010	SUNSHOWER (LP)	25
73	Mowest MWS 7003	THELMA HOUSTON (LP)	30

HOVERCRAFT
98	Blast First BFFP 160	EXPERIMENT BELOW (LP)	15

BEN HOWARD
11	Communication COMM009	Old Pine/Further Away/Follation Wood/Three Tree Down (2 x 7", p/s)	60
12	Island 3721238	THE BURGH ISLAND EP (12", 1-sided, download card, 1000 only)	70
12	Secret 7" S71	Black Flies (100 only, each with unique art sleeve)	80
11	Island 2782648	EVERY KINGDOM (LP, download card, pink rim palm tree logo)	15

BRIAN HOWARD & SILHOUETTES
62	Columbia DB 4914	Somebody Help Me/Young And Evil	25
63	Columbia DB 7067	The Worryin' Kind/Come To Me	25
64	Fontana TF 464	Back In The U.S.A./Hooked	20

JAN HOWARD
60	London HL 7088	The One You Slip Around With/I Wish I Could Fall In Love Again (export issue)	25

JOHN HOWARD
75	CBS 80173	KID IN A BIG WORLD (LP, with insert)	25

JOHNNY HOWARD BAND
62	Decca F 11423	Mind Reader/Spanish Gipsy Dance	8
64	Decca F 11925	Rinky Dink/Java	8
65	Decca LK 4735	THE EASY BEAT SOUND (LP)	15
67	Deram DML/SML 1001	THE VELVET TOUCH OF JOHNNY HOWARD (LP)	15

KEITH HOWARD
80	Rods HOT 2	LOOKING FOR YOU (LP, some sleeves contain Driver artwork inside sleeve)	35

(see also Victory)

LES HOWARD
53	HMV 7M 127	Love Evermore/I Lived When I Met You	10
53	HMV 7M 171	Rags To Riches/From Here To Eternity	10

NOAH HOWARD
69	Polydor Super 2383093	THE BLACK ARK (LP)	40

ROLAND S. HOWARD & LYDIA LUNCH
86	4AD BAD 210	Some Velvet Morning/I Fell In Love With A Ghost (12", p/s, with postcard)	12

(see also Lydia Lunch, Birthday Party)

ROWLAND S. HOWARD & NIKKI SUDDEN
87	Creation CRE 040T	Wedding Hotel/Hello Wolf/Girl Without A Name/Wedding Hotel (Original Mix) (12")	10

(see also Swell Maps, Last Bandits, Jeremy Gluck)

WAYNE HOWARD
			MINT VALUE £
70	Explosion EX 2042	All Kinds Of Everything/Cool And Easy (B-side actually by Lloyd Charmers)	7

HOWDY BOYS
80	Spectacle SP 1	Spectacle/Dancing In The Depression (p/s)	15

CATHERINE HOWE
71	Reflection HRS 11	Nothing More Than Strangers/It Comes With The Breezes	20
71	Reflection REFL 11	WHAT A BEAUTIFUL PLACE (LP, laminated front sleeve 'correction' sticker on rear sleeve)	1000
75	RCA Victor SF 8407	HARRY (LP)	18

STEVE HOWE
75	Atlantic K50151	BEGINNINGS (LP, gatefold sleeve)	15

(see also Yes)

HOWEEFEEL
75	Contempo CS2065	The Devil's On The Run/Just Can't Do Without Love	15

EDDIE HOWELL
76	Warner Bros K 16701	Man From Manhattan/Waiting In The Wings (features members of Queen)	6
77	Warner Bros K 16866	Sweet On You/Miss Amerika (features Gary Moore)	6

(see also Queen, Gary Moore, Brian May, Freddie Mercury)

EDDY HOWELL
69	Parlophone R5756	Easy Street/Judy's Good	45

FRANKIE HOWERD
54	Decca F 10420	(Don't Let The) Kiddy Geddin/Abracadabra	10
58	Columbia DB 4230	It's All Right With Me/Song And Dance Man	7
63	HMV CLP 1685	A FUNNY THING HAPPENED ON THE WAY TO THE FORUM (LP)	15

CHRIS HOWLAND
58	Columbia DB 4114	Mama (Ma, He's Making Eyes At Me)/Fraulein	7
59	Columbia DB 4194	Susie Darlin'/The Rain Falls On Ev'rybody	10

HOWLIN' WOLF
61	Pye International 7N 25101	Little Baby/Down In The Bottom	25
63	Pye International 7N 25192	Just Like I Treat You/I Ain't Superstitious	25
64	Pye International 7N 25244	Smokestack Lightnin'/Going Down Slow ('Slow' on B-side label)	25
64	Pye International 7N 25244	Smokestack Lightnin'/Going Down Slow ("South' on B-side label)	20
64	Pye International 7N 25269	Little Girl/Tail Dragger	22
64	Pye International 7N 25283	Love Me Darling/My Country Sugar Mama	22
65	Chess CRS 8010	Killing Floor/Louise	15
65	Chess CRS 8016	Ooh Baby/Tell Me What I've Done	15
69	Chess CRS 8097	Evil/Tail Dragger	15
56	London REU 1072	RHYTHM AND BLUES WITH HOWLIN' WOLF (EP)	200
63	Pye Intl. NEP 44015	SMOKESTACK LIGHTNIN' (EP)	40
64	Pye Intl. NEP 44032	TELL ME (EP)	30
66	Chess CRE 6017	REAL FOLK BLUES (EP)	30
64	Chess CRL 4006	MOANIN' IN THE MOONLIGHT (LP)	100
65	Chess CRL 4508	POOR BOY (LP)	45
66	Ember EMB 3370	BIG CITY BLUES (LP)	25
69	Chess CRLS 4543	THE HOWLIN' WOLF ALBUM (LP)	25
71	Syndicate Chapter SC 003	GOING BACK HOME (LP)	20
71	Chess 6310 108	MESSAGE TO THE YOUNG (LP)	22
71	Rolling Stones COC 49101	THE LONDON SESSIONS (LP)	20
71	Python PLP 13	HOWLIN' WOLF (LP)	60

(see also Hubert Sumlin)

HOWLIN' WOLF/JUNIOR PARKER/BOBBY BLAND
74	Polydor 2383 257	BLUES FOR MR. CRUMP (LP)	30

HOWLIN' WOLF, MUDDY WATERS & BO DIDDLEY
68	Chess CRL 4537	THE SUPER SUPER BLUES BAND (LP)	45

(see also Muddy Waters, Bo Diddley)

LINDA HOYLE
70	Vertigo 6059 018	Eli's Coming/United States Of Mind (as Linda Hoyle & Affinity)	40
71	Vertigo 6360 060	PIECES OF ME (LP, gatefold sleeve, small swirl label)	1000

(see also Affinity, Nucleus)

H.P. LOVECRAFT
67	Philips BF 1620	Wayfarin' Stranger/The Time Machine	7
68	Philips BF 1639	The White Ship (Parts 1 & 2) (unissued)	0
68	Philips BF 1639	The White Ship/I've Been Wrong Before	15
67	Philips (S)BL 7830	H.P. LOVECRAFT (LP)	80
68	Philips SBL 7872	H.P. LOVECRAFT II (LP, without watermark at start of each side)	50
68	Philips SBL 7872	H.P. LOVECRAFT II (LP, with watermark at start of each side)	20
72	Philips 6336 210	THIS IS H.P. LOVECRAFT (LP)	40
72	Philips 6336 213	H.P. LOVECRAFT VOL. 2 (LP)	25
88	Edsel DED 256	AT THE MOUNTAINS OF MADNESS (2-LP)	20

HQ SQUAD
89	Music Of Life NOTE33	Burial Proceedings In The Course Of Three Knights/Onslaught (12")	15

HRATCH
70	Decca F13007	Beautiful Bare Back Rider/Ain't It Tough	10
74	EMi 2170	You/Just In Case	6
77	DJM DJS 10765	Another Way Of Going Home/Life (promo only in p/s)	8

HT
66	Polydor 56127	You & Me/Love Can Wait	10

HTRK
07	Fire FIRELP 104	NOSTALGIA (LP, reissue)	15

H.T. SPLIFF

MINT VALUE £

H.T. SPLIFF
79 Septic SP 002   OUT OF THE EARTH'S WOMB (LP) 60

H2O
81 Spock PARA 2   Hollywood Dream/Children (with lyric insert) 6

FREDDIE HUBBARD
70 CTI 6001   RED CLAY (LP) 25
74 MSP/BASF BAP 5036   THE HUB OF HUBBARD (LP) 20

HUBCAP & WHEELS
70 Dynamic DYN 403   One Pound Weight/VICEROYS: Come Dance 20
(see also Byron Lee & Dragonaires)

WENDY HUBER
65 Philips BF 1446   Come Away Melinda/I Belong To The Wind 10

HUDDERSFIELD TRANSIT AUTHORITY
72 Polydor 2001284   Runaway/Bayou Farm 15
72 Polydor 2001344   A Different Drum/One Of The Old Time Greats 6

AL HUDSON
78 ABC 5151   Spread Love (slow start 3.25 version)/Spread Love (2.38 version) 30

HUDSON BROTHERS
75 Rocket PIG 18   Rendezvous/Medley: These Things We Do/Home And Four Others 6

JACK HUDSON
72 Folk Heritage FHR 041   SUMMER DAYS AND YOU (LP) 20

JOHNNY HUDSON & TEENBEATS
63 Decca F 11679   Charms/Makin' Up Is So Much Fun 10

KEITH HUDSON (& CHUCKLES)
69 Big Shot BI 528   Tambourine Man/Old Fashioned Way (both actually by Ken Boothe) 35
70 Smash SMA 2311   Don't Get Me Confused/D. SMITH: Ball of Confusion (B-side actually by Dennis
                                      Alcapone) 20
71 Smash SMA 2526   Light Of Day/I Thought You Knew 35
72 Spur SP 1   Darkest Night On A Wet Looking Road/Version 50
72 Duke DU 145   Satan Side (with Chuckles)/DON T. JUNIOR: Evil Spirit 40
72 Downtown DT 492   True True To My Heart/BIG YOUTH: Ace 90 Skank 22
73 Summit SUM 8541   Melody Maker/Uncover Me 30
75 Atra AT28   Lost All Sense Of Direction/Jah Jah 12
75 Mamba MAM 101   Wild Fire/Version 10
75 Faith FA 025   Blackbelt Jones/Version 20
77 Tunde TR 1000   I Wanna Be Where You Are/Still Water (12") 25
78 Greensleeves GRED 8   Bloody Eyes/Dub 25
78 Greensleeves GRED 8   Bloody Eyes/Dub (12") 25
79 Greensleeves GRED 26   Nuh Skin Up/Felt We Felt The Strain (12") 25
75 Magnet MGT 007   ENTER THE DRAGON (LP) 200
75 Mamba KH1   FLESH OF MY SKIN, BLOOD OF MY BLOOD (LP) 150
75 Mamba MAM 002   TORCH OF FREEDOM (LP) 50
75 Atra LP1001   TORCH OF FREEDOM (LP) 50
75 Atra ATLP 1002   PICK A DUB (LP) 100
76 Third World TWL 106   REBEL DUB (LP, produced by Keith Hudson) 100
76 Virgin V2056   TOO EXPENSIVE (LP) 25
77 BRAND BRD 001   BRAND (LP) 75
79 Greensleeves GREL 5   RASTA COMMUNICATION (LP) 25
88 Atra LP 1004   FLESH OF MY SKIN BLOOD OF MY BLOOD (LP, reissue) 30
94 Blood & Fire LP 003   PICK A DUB (LP, reissue) 30
01 Simply Vinyl SVLP 283   PICK A DUB (LP, reissue) 15
(see also Big Youth, Alton Ellis, Delroy Washington, Hugh Roy, Delroy Wilson)

KEITH HUDSON & I ROY
73 Randy's RAN 534   Silver Platter/Jean You Change Everything 30
(see also I Roy)

MIKE HUDSON
65 Columbia DB 7622   One Sided Love/I'll Wait Until Tomorrow 15

ROCK HUDSON
59 Brunswick 05816   Pillow Talk/Roly Poly 8

HUDSON-FORD
73 A&M AMS 7116   Floating In The Wind/Revelations 8
73 A&M AMLH 68208   NICKELODEON (LP, lyric insert, brown label) 15
77 Arnakata ARN 5001   REPERTOIRE (LP, for publishers' use) 20
(see also Strawbs, Monks, Elmer Gantry's Velvet Opera)

HUDSON PEOPLE
79 Ensign ENY 27   Trip To Your Mind/Part 2 25
78 Hithouse HIT 1   Trip To Your Mind/Power To The Hour (12") 60
79 Ensign ENY 2712   Trip To Your Mind/Power To The Hour (12", different mix) 40

HUDSONS
82 Streetwave STRA 13 2711   Show Me You Care (Extended)/Instrumental (12") 12
83 Epic A3373   Don't Try To Fight It/You Keep Me Up (promo only) 20
83 Epic TA 3373   Don't Try To Fight It (Vocal)/Instrumental/You Keep Me Up (12") 25

HUEYS
69 London HLU 10264   Coo-Coo Over You/You Ain't No Hippie 12

HUG
75 Polydor 2058 553   Keep Pushing On/City 6
75 Polydor 2383 230   NEON DREAM (LP) 20
(see also Mike Hugg)

MIKE HUGG
72 Polydor 2383 140   SOMEWHERE (LP, gatefold sleeve) 30

Bob HUGHES

			MINT VALUE £
73	Polydor 2383 213	STRESS AND STRAIN (LP)	30

(see also Manfred Mann, Hug, Highly Likely, Elton Dean)

BOB HUGHES
76	Puddlebrook 3SLP8	MY OLD MAN (LP, plain cover with pasted-on A4 information sheet)	200
78	Puddlebrook IRPH 16	THE KIDS ARE OK! (LP)	100

BOBBY HUGHES EXPERIENCE
99	Ultimate Diler UDRLP 008	FUSA RIOT (2xLP)	20

CAROL HUGHES
58	Columbia DB 4094	Lend Me Your Comb/First Date	15

DANNY HUGHES
69	Pye 7N 17750	Hi Ho Silver Lining/I Washed My Hands In Muddy Water	15

(see also Orange Machine)

FRED HUGHES
65	Fontana TF 583	Oo Wee Baby I Love You/Love Me Baby	30
76	Brunswick BR 37	Baby Boy/JOHNNY JONES & KING CASUALS: Purple Haze	10
76	DJM DJS 10717	Oo Wee Baby I Love You/My Cries Oh	6

GLENN HUGHES
77	Safari LONG 2	PLAY ME OUT (LP, with inner sleeve)	15

(see also Deep Purple, News, Finders Keepers, Trapeze, Roger Glover, Hughes-Thrall)

GUY HUGHES
79	Admiral AMC 01	The Last Admiral/Just Call Me (no p/s)	25

JIMMY HUGHES
63	London HL 9680	I'm Qualified/My Loving Time	30
64	Pye International 7N 25254	Steal Away/Lollipops, Lace And Lipstick	25
66	Sue WI 4006	Goodbye My Love/It Was Nice	50
66	Atlantic 584 017	Neighbour, Neighbour/It's A Good Thing	22
67	Atlantic 584 135	Hi-Heel Sneakers/Time Will Bring You Back	15
69	Stax STAX 117	Sweet Things You Do/Let 'Em Down Baby	8
69	Stax STAX 126	I'm Not Ashamed To Beg Or Plead/Chains Of Love	12
80	Charly CTD 103	JIMMY HUGHES EP	10
67	Atlantic 587 068	WHY NOT TONIGHT? (LP)	80
69	Stax SXATS 1010	SOMETHING SPECIAL (LP)	30

NIA HUGHES
70	Penny Farthing PEN 724	Turn On The Sun/The Wind	8

RHETTA HUGHES
11	Shotgun 107	Cry Myself To Sleep/Giving Up My Heartaches	10
69	Polydor 184 223	RELIGHT MY FIRE (LP)	80

HUGHES-THRALL
82	Epic EPC 25052	HUGHES-THRALL (LP, with inner sleeve)	15

(see also Glenn Hughes)

HUGO & LUIGI
57	Columbia DB 3978	Rockabilly Party/Shenandoah Rose	15
59	RCA RCA 1127	La Plume De Ma Tante/Honolulu Lu	6

ALAN HULL
70	Big T BIG 129	We Can Swing Together/Obadiah's Grave	10
73	Charisma CB 211	Just Another Sad Song/Waiting	6
75	Warner Brothers K16299	One More Bottle Of Wine/Squire	6
73	Charisma CAS 1069	PIPEDREAM (LP, gatefold sleeve, booklet, large 'Mad Hatter' label)	20
75	Warner Bros K56261	SQUIRE (LP, 'Burbank' label)	15

(see also Lindisfarne, Chosen Few)

HULLABALLOOS
64	Columbia DB 7392	I'm Gonna Love You Too/Why Do Fools Fall In Love	10
65	Columbia DB 7558	I'll Show You How To Love/Did You Ever	10
65	Columbia DB 7626	Don't Stop/I Won't Turn Away Now	10

(see also Bunch Of Fives)

GEORGE HULTGREEN
70	Warner Bros WB 8017	Say Hello/Before You Say Goodbye	6

HUMAN BEANS
67	Columbia DB 8230	Morning Dew (Take Me For A Walk)/It's A Wonder	50

(see also Love Sculpture)

HUMAN BEAST
70	Decca LK/SKL 5053	VOLUME ONE (LP)	1000
07	Sunbeam SBRLP 5044	VOLUME ONE (LP, reissue)	20

(see also Bread Love & Dreams)

HUMAN BEINGS
80	Airship AP 159	Amnesia/New Song/Mrs Marshall (p/s and sticker)	12

HUMAN BEINZ
67	Capitol CL 15529	Nobody But Me/Sueno	60
67	Capitol CL 15529	Nobody But Me/Sueno (DJ Copy)	100
68	Capitol CL 15542	Turn On Your Lovelight/It's Fun To Be Clean	25
77	Capitol CL 15529	Nobody But Me/Sueno (reissue)	12
86	Decal LIK 5	EVOLUTIONS (LP, reissue)	15

HUMAN CONDITION
81	THC 1	THE HUMAN CONDITION (Live at Collegiate Theatre 13th September 1981) (cassette, black inlay, white writing)	25
81	THC 1	THE HUMAN CONDITION (Live in Europe November 1981) (cassette, white inlay, black writing)	25

(see also Jah Wobble)

HUMAN INSTINCT
65	Mercury MF 951	Can't Stop Around/I Want To Be Loved By You My Friend	50
66	Mercury MF 972	The Rich Man/Illusions	70

HUMAN LEAGUE

			MINT VALUE £
67	Mercury MF 990	Go-Go/I Can't Live Without You	50
68	Deram DM 167	A Day In My Mind's Mind/Death Of The Seaside	140
68	Deram DM 177	Renaissance Fair/Pink Dawn	80

(see also Jessie Harper)

HUMAN LEAGUE
78	Fast Product FAST 4	Being Boiled/Circus Of Death (p/s, original issue with b&w picture labels)	20
79	Fast Product FAST 10	THE DIGNITY OF LABOUR (12" EP, with spoken-word flexidisc [F10x/VF 1])	30
80	Virgin SV 105	HOLIDAY '80 (EP, double pack, purple & blue labels, 10,000 only)	15
80	Virgin VS 351	Empire State Human/Introducing//Only After Dark/Toyota City (Long Version) (double pack, p/s, shrinkwrapped)	20
80	Virgin VS 351	Only After Dark/Toyota City (Long Version) (p/s)	6
81	Virgin SV 105-12	HOLIDAY '80 (12", 5-track EP, withdrawn)	80
79	Virgin VS 2133	REPRODUCTION (LP)	15
80	Virgin VS 2160	TRAVELOGUE (LP)	15
81	Virgin V 2192	DARE (LP, gatefold, inner)	20
90	Virgin V2624	ROMANTIC? (LP)	20
95	East West 4509 98750 1	OCTOPUS (LP)	60
11	Wall Of Sound WOS085DLP	CREDO (2-LP)	200
16	Virgin 571 111-5	A VERY BRITISH SYNTHESISER GROUP (3-LP)	60
18	Demon DEMREC 305	SECRETS (2-LP, reissue)	25
20	East West 0190295402341	OCTOPUS (LP, reissue)	15

(see also Heaven 17, Men, Respect)

HUMAN CABBAGES
81	Boys and Girls BAG TWO	The Witch/Air Raid Shelter/One More Fool (p/s)	40

HUMANOID
88	Westside WSR 7	Stakker Humanoid (Part 1)/Stakker Humanoid (Part 2) (p/s)	8
88	Westside Human 1989	GLOBAL (LP)	15
03	Rephlex CAT 130 LP	SESSIONS 84-88 (2-LP)	25

(see also Future Sound Of London, Art Science Technology)

HUMANTE & RABBIT IN THE MOON
95	Rising High RSN 106	East (The Remixes) (12")	15

HUMBLEBUMS
69	Big T BIG 122	Saturday Roundabout Sunday/Bed Of Mossy Green	6
69	Big T BIG 127	Coconut Tree/Her Father Didn't Like Me Anyway	6
70	Big T BIG 130	Shoeshine Boy/My Apartment	6
69	Transatlantic TRA 201	THE NEW HUMBLEBUMS (LP, lilac/white label with 't' logo)	20
70	Transatlantic TRA 218	OPEN UP THE DOOR (LP, laminated sleeve)	15
74	Transatlantic TRA 288	THE COMPLETE HUMBLEBUMS (3-LP, box set of above albums)	20

(see also Gerry Rafferty)

HUMBLE PIE
69	Immediate IM 082	Natural Born Bugie/Wrist Job	6
69	Immediate IM 082	Natural Born Bugie/Wrist Job (later pressing in p/s)	10
70	A&M AMS 807	Big Black Dog/Strange Days	7
71	A&M AMS 862	I Don't Need No Doctor/A Sonig For Jennie	7
72	A&M AMS 7003	Hot'n'Nasty/You're So Good For Me	7
73	A&M AMS 7052	Black Coffee/Say No More	7
73	A&M AMS 7070	Get Down To It/Honky Tonk Woman	7
73	A&M AMS 7090	Oh La De Da/Outcrowd	7
75	A&M AMS 7185	Rock'n'Roll Music/Scored Out	7
80	Jet JET 180	Fool For A Pretty Face/You Soppy Pratt (p/s)	7
69	Immediate IMSP 025	AS SAFE AS YESTERDAY IS (LP, lyric inner sleeve, pink label)	80
69	Immediate IMSP 027	TOWN AND COUNTRY (LP, lyric inner sleeve, pink label)	75
70	A&M AMLS 986	HUMBLE PIE (LP, textured gatefold sleeve, brown label)	75
71	A&M AMLS 2013	ROCK ON (LP)	25
71	A&M AMLH 63506	PERFORMANCE - ROCKIN' THE FILLMORE (2-LP)	25
72	A&M AMLS 64342	SMOKIN' (LP)	25
73	A&M AMLD 6004	EAT IT (2-LP, gatefold sleeve, booklet, brown label)	25
74	A&M AMLH 63611	THUNDERBOX (LP)	15
75	A&M AMLS 68282	STREET RATS (LP)	15
79	Jet LP231	ON TO VICTORY (LP)	20
80	Atco SD 38 131	GO FOR THE THROAT (LP)	20

(see also Steve Marriott, Small Faces, Herd, Natural Gas)

HUMBUG
70	CBS 4811	Groovin' With Mr Bloe/Marianna	20
70	CBS 5208	I Got A Feeling (Vocal)/I Got A Feeling (Instrumental)	20

HELEN HUMES
56	Vogue V 2048	Million Dollar Secret/If I Could Be With You One Hour Of The Day	10
61	Contemporary LAC 12245	HELEN HUMES AND THE BENNY CARTER ALL STARS (LP)	15

(see also Benny Carter, Jimmy Witherspoon/Helen Humes)

BOBBI HUMPHREY
17	Expansion EX7030	Baby Don't You Know/Baby Don't You Know (Instrumental) (reissue)	7
75	Blue Note UAG 20003	FANCY DANCER (LP)	25
98	Blue Note 7243 4 94706 1 3	BLUE BREAKBEATS (LP)	15
92	Blue Note B1 80503	THE BEST OF (LP)	18

DELLA HUMPHREY
69	Action ACT 4525	Don't Make The Good Girls Go Bad/Your Love Is All I Need	50
72	Fab FAB 183	Dreamland/Version	55

LES HUMPHRIES SINGERS
75	Antic K11519	She's Really Something Else/Mexico	8
76	Atlantic K11527	Indian War/Little Sparrow	8

HUMPY BONG

HUMPY BONG
70 Parlophone R 5859   Don't You Be Too Long/We're Alright 'Till Then 15
(see also Bee Gees, Jonathan Kelly, Morgan)

HUNGER
84 Psycho PSYCHO 14   STRICTLY FROM HUNGER (LP, reissue of U.S. LP) 15

HUNGRY TOUCH
88 Firehorse HT 188   Shake The System/She's Got The Hungry Touch/Riding High (12" p/s) 50

HUNGRY WOLF
70 Philips 6308 009   HUNGRY WOLF (LP, laminated sleeve, black/silver labels) 250
(see also Czar, Alan Parker, Ugly Custard)

GLORIA HUNNIFORD
69 Tangerine 0012   Are You Ready For Love/The Sound Of Love 6

PETER HUNNINGALE
86 Cosmic COSMIC 001   Untamed Love/Untamed Dub (12") 75
06 Peckings PS 0002   Mary Jane/Overcome 8

FRED HUNT TRIO
68 77 88LEU12/27   PEARLS ON VELVET (LP) 35

GERALDINE HUNT
69 Roulette RO 515   Never Never Leave Me/Push Sweep 10
75 EMI EMI 2275   You/It's All For You 6

MARSHA HUNT
69 Track 604 030   Walk On Gilded Splinters/Hot Rod Poppa 15
69 Track 604 034   Desdemona/Hippy Gumbo 20
70 Track 604 037   Keep The Customer Satisfied/Lonesome Holy Roller 10
73 Vertigo 6059 080   Beast Day/Somebody To Love (as Marsha Hunt's 22) 20
73 Vertigo 6059093   Medusa/Bop City (as Marsha Hunt's 22) 20
76 Electric WATT 1   C'est La Vie/Do You Really Believe In Voodoo 10
71 Track 2410 101   WOMAN CHILD (LP) 100

TOMMY HUNT
62 Top Rank JAR 605   The Door Is Open/I'm Wondering 20
68 Direction 58-3216   I Need A Woman Of My Own/Searchin' For My Baby Looking Everywhere 30
81 SRTS 81 CUS 1009   Crackin Up/Loving On The Losing Side/The Hungry Years/Sweetest Feelings (EP) 12
85 Kent TOWN 103   The Work Song/IVORYS: Please Stay 10
75 Spark SRLP 117   LIVE AT THE WIGAN CASINO (LP) 25
86 Kent KENT 059   YOUR MAN (LP) 30
(see also Ivorys)

WILLIE AMOS HUNT
67 Camp 602 003   Would You Believe/My Baby Wants To Dance 75

HUNT & TURNER
72 Village Thing VTS 11   MAGIC LANDSCAPE (LP) 60

CAROL HUNTER
73 Purple PUR 115   Look Out Cleveland/5/4 March 7
73 Purple TPS 3503   THE NEXT VOICE YOU HEAR (LP) 15

DANE HUNTER
65 Oriole CB 1985   The Evergreen Tree/Too Late 20
65 CBS 201777   Silly Little Girl/Cryin Sobbin Wailin 15
65 CBS 202004   Because You're Mine/Look The Other Way 15
16 Record Collector NORTHERN The Drifter (restored)/The Drifter (acetate version) (die-cut black sleeve) 10
    1

DANNY HUNTER (& GIANTS)
60 HMV POP 722   Make It Up/Little Girl (as Danny Hunter & Giants) 20
60 HMV POP 775   Who's Gonna Walk Ya Home?/Lonely And Blue 20
61 Fontana H 300   Lost Weekend/Age For Love 15

DAVE HUNTER
68 RCA RCA 1766   Love Me A Lifetime/She's A Heartbreaker 35
69 RCA RCA 1841   Don't Throw Your Love To The Wind/Hitchcock Railway 12

GREG HUNTER
66 Parlophone R 5483   Five O'Clock World/Away From Happiness 10

IAN HUNTER
76 CBS 4479   You Nearly Did Me In/Letter To Britannia From The Union Jack 15
77 CBS 5229   Justice Of The Peace/The Ballad Of Little Star (as Ian Hunter's Overnight Angels) 8
83 CBS TA 3541   All Of The Good Ones Are Taken/Death 'N' Glory Boys/Traitor (12", p/s) 10
(see also Mott The Hoople, At Last The 1958 Rock & Roll Show, Apex Rhythm & Blues All Stars, Mick Ronson, Roger Taylor)

IVORY JOE HUNTER
50 MGM MGM 271   I Almost Lost My Mind/S.P. Blues (78, with Orchestra) 20
56 London HLE 8261   A Tear Fell/I Need You By My Side 300
56 London HLE 8261   A Tear Fell/I Need You By My Side (78) 20
57 Columbia DB 3872   Since I Met You, Baby/You Can't Stop This Rockin' And Rollin' 250
57 Columbia DB 3872   Since I Met You, Baby/You Can't Stop This Rockin' And Rollin' (78) 20
57 London HLE 8486   Love's A Hurting Game/Empty Arms 150
57 London HLE 8486   Love's A Hurting Game/Empty Arms (78) 20
61 Capitol CL 15220   I'm Hooked/Because I Love You 30
61 Capitol CL 15226   You Better Believe It, Baby/May The Man Win 30

ROBERT HUNTER
74 Round RX 101   TALES OF THE GREAT RUM RUNNERS (LP) 15
80 Dark Star DSLP 8001   JACK O'ROSES (LP) 15
(see also Grateful Dead)

SUSAN HUNTER
55 Brunswick 05458   Not Yet/Was That The Right Thing To Do? 8

Tab HUNTER

MINT VALUE £

TAB HUNTER
57	London HLD 8380	Young Love/Red Sails In The Sunset (gold label)	15
57	London HLD 8410	Ninety-Nine Ways/I Don't Get Around Much Anymore	8
58	London HLD 8535	Don't Let It Get Around/I'm Alone Because I Love You	10
60	Warner Bros WB 8	(What Can I Give) My Only Love/(I'll Be With You) In Apple Blossom Time	6
60	Warner Bros WB 20	Waitin' For The Fall/Our Love	6
61	London HLD 9381	The Wild Side Of Life/My Devotion	7
62	London HLD 9559	Born To Lose/I Can't Stop Lovin' You	7
61	Warner Bros WSEP 2023	TAB HUNTER (EP, stereo)	15
60	Warner Bros WS 8008	TAB HUNTER (LP, stereo)	15
61	London HA-D 2401	YOUNG LOVE (LP, mono)	15
61	London SAH-G 6201	YOUNG LOVE (LP, stereo)	15

HUNTER MUSKETT
73	Bradleys BRAD 303	John Blair/Silver Coin (p/s)	6
70	Decca Nova SDN 20	EVERY TIME YOU MOVE (LP, blue/silver labels)	300
73	Bradleys BRADL 1003	HUNTER MUSKETT (LP, lyric inner sleeve)	35

HUNTERS (HOLLAND)
| 66 | RCA RCA 1541 | Russian Spy And I/Spring | 20 |

(see also Jan Akkerman, Brainbox)

HUNTERS (U.K.)
60	Fontana H 276	Teen Scene/Santa Monica Flyer	15
61	Fontana H 303	Golden Ear-rings/Tally Ho	15
61	Fontana H 323	The Storm/How's M'Chicks?	20
64	Fontana TF 514	Teen Scene/Someone Else's Baby	15
61	Fontana TFL 5140	TEEN SCENE: THE HUNTERS PLAY THE BIG HITS (LP, mono)	30
61	Fontana STFL 561	TEEN SCENE: THE HUNTERS PLAY THE BIG HITS (LP, stereo)	50
62	Fontana TFL 5175	HITS FROM THE HUNTERS (LP, mono)	50
62	Fontana STFL 572	HITS FROM THE HUNTERS (LP, stereo)	50

(see also Dave Sampson & Hunters, Maisie McDaniel)

HUNTING LODGE
| 85 | Sterile SER 04 | NOMAD SOULS (LP) | 20 |

HURDY GURDY
| 72 | CBS 64781 | HURDY GURDY (LP, gatefold sleeve) | 200 |

ARTHUR HURLEY & GOTTLIEB
| 73 | CBS 1779 | Sunshine Ship/Bobbys Song | 6 |

RED VINCENT HURLEY
| 76 | Pye 7N 45583 | When/Just A Little Love (p/s) | 7 |

HURRICANE STRINGS
| 63 | Columbia DB 7027 | Venus/In The Carrick | 15 |

HURRICANES
| 71 | Upsetter US 363 | Got To Be Mine/UPSETTERS: Version | 30 |

(see also Dave Barker)

MIKE HURST (& METHOD)
65	Philips BF 1389	The Last Time You'll Walk Out On Me/Something Told Me	6
65	Philips BF 1424	Show Me Around/I'm Running Away	7
71	Capitol CL 15681	Show Me The Way To Georgia/Over Again	6

(see also Springfields, Remo Four, Ashton Gardner & Dyke, Sundance)

MISSISSIPPI JOHN HURT
65	Vanguard SVRL 19005	THE IMMORTAL MISSISSIPPI JOHN HURT (LP)	35
66	Vanguard SVRL 19032	MISSISSIPPI JOHN HURT (LP)	35
67	Fontana TFL 6079	MISSISSIPPI JOHN HURT (LP)	35
71	Spokane SPL 1001	THE ORIGINAL 1928 RECORDINGS (LP)	50
73	Vanguard VSD 79327	LAST SESSIONS (LP)	20
72	Vanguard VSD 79220	TODAY (LP)	20

HURTS
10	Major MAJRE 017	Wonderful Life/(Mantronix Remix) (p/s, no'd)	15
10	Sony 88697741857	Better Than Love/Mother Nature (white label, p/s, 500 only)	12
10	Major MAJREC031	HAPPINESS (LP & CD)	40

(see also Daggers (2))

HUSH
| 68 | Fontana TF 944 | Elephant Rider/Grey | 500 |

HÜSKER DÜ
84	SST SST 025	Eight Miles High/Masochism World (live) (p/s)	12
86	Warner Bros W 8612	Sorry Somehow/All This I've Done For You//Celebrated Summer (Acoustic)/ Flexible Flyer (double pack in single sleeve)	8
86	Warner Bros W 8746T	Don't Want To Know If You're Lonely/All Work And No Play/ Helter Skelter (live) (12")	10
87	Warner Bros W 8456	Could You Be The One/Everytime	10
87	Warner Bros W 8456T	Could You Be The One/Everytime/Charity, Chastity, Prudence, Hope (12", p/s)	10
87	Warner Bros W 8276T	Ice Cold Ice/Gotta Lotta/Medley (12", p/s)	12
81	Alt. Tentacles VIRUS 25	LAND SPEED RECORD (LP)	18
82	Bespoke BES 03 LP	EVERYTHING FALLS APART (LP)	20
83	SST SST 020	METAL CIRCUS (LP)	30
84	SST SST 027	ZEN ARCADE (2-LP, gatefold)	40
86	Warner Bros WX40	CANDY APPLE GREY (LP)	20

(see also Bob Mould, Sugar)

HUS KINGPIN
17	Daupe! DM SP 026	COCAINE BEACH (LP, 125 copies)	100
17	Daupe! DM SP 026	COCAINE BEACH (LP, with obi strip 20 copies)	200
17	Daupe! DM SP 026	COCAINE BEACH (LP, yellow, white or blue vinyl 125 copies)	100

HUSKY
MINT VALUE £

HUSKY
75	Anchor ANC 1026	Give It Up/Silence Of Dreams	6
76	Anchor ANC 1030	Pretty Little Linda/Make It Turn Out Right	6

FERLIN HUSKY (& HIS HUSH PUPPIES)
57	Capitol CL 14753	A Fallen Star/Prize Possession	8
58	Capitol CL 14824	Wang Dang Doo/What'cha Doin' After School	20
58	Capitol CL 14883	Slow Down Brother/The Drunken Driver (& His Hush Puppies)	10
60	Capitol EAP2 1280	FERLIN'S FAVOURITES (EP)	10
58	Capitol T 880	BOULEVARD OF BROKEN DREAMS (LP)	15

(see also Simon Crum)

HUSSARS
82	Sunny EON 103	The Charge Of The Light Brigade/Your Country Needs You	30

NIPSEY HUSSLE
17	Omerta Inc. OMINC 013	CRENSHAW (2-LP, reissue 500 only, red and white vinyl, numbered)	100

JACQUES HUSTIN
74	EMI EMI 2143	Fleur De Liberté/Freedom For The Man	15

HUSTLERS
63	Philips BF 1275	Gimme What I Want/Not Much	7
64	Mercury MF 807	Be True To You/You Can't Sit Down	7
64	Mercury MF 817	Sick Of Giving/Easy To Find	20

WILLIE HUTCH
73	Tamla Motown TMG 862	Brother's Gonna Work It Out/I Choose You	20
78	ABC 4206	Love Runs Out/BOBBY HUTTON: Lend A Hand (DJ copy)	15
74	Tamla Motown TMG 1008	Love Power/Get Ready To Get Down	6
78	Whitfield K17318	Come On And Dance With Me/Easy Does It	30
73	Tamla Motown STMA 8003	THE MACK (LP, soundtrack)	35
73	Tamla Motown STML 11247	FULLY EXPOSED (LP)	25
74	Tamla Motown STML 11269	FOXY BROWN (LP, soundtrack)	40
74	Tamla Motown STML 11280	THE MARK OF THE BEAST (LP)	20
75	Tamla Motown STML 12015	ODE TO MY LADY (LP)	20
76	Tamla Motown STML 12023	CONCERT IN BLUES (LP)	15

ASHLEY HUTCHINGS
72	Island HELP 5	MORRIS ON (LP, actually by various folk artists)	20
76	Island HELP 24	RATTLEBONE (LP)	25
76	Harvest SHSM 2012	SON OF MORRIS ON (LP, actually by various folk artists)	18

(see also Albion Band, Fairport Convention, Steeleye Span)

HUTCH HUTCHINGS
77	Goodwood GM 12324	FEELS LIKE RAIN (LP)	35

SAM HUTCHINS
69	Bell BLL 1044	Dang Me/I'm Tired Of Pretending	12

DON HUTCHINSON
84	Pep 7001	What You Gonna Do/What You Gonna Do (Version) (dinked 7")	55

LEROY HUTSON
75	Warner Bros. K16536	All Because Of You/All Because Of You (Theme Instrumental)	30
74	Buddah BDLP 4013	THE MAN (LP)	20
75	Warner Bros K 56139	HUTSON (LP)	50
97	Deep Beats DEEP X 007	THE VERY BEST OF LEROY HUTSON (2-LP)	20
98	Deep Beats DEEP X 033	MORE WHERE THIS CAME FROM - THE BEST OF VOL. 2 (2-LP)	25
99	Sequel NEMLP 442	HUTSON II (LP, reissue)	20

J.B. HUTTO & HIS HAWKS
73	Delmark DS 617	HAWK SQUAT (LP)	30

BETTY HUTTON
54	Capitol LC 6639	CAPITOL PRESENTS BETTY HUTTON (10" LP)	15

(see also Hutton Sisters, Perry Como, 'Tennessee' Ernie Ford)

BOBBY HUTTON
78	ABC 4206	Lend A Hand/WILLIE HUTCH: Love Runs Out (DJ copy)	15

DANNY HUTTON
66	MGM MGM 1314	Funny How Love Can Be/Dreamin' Isn't Good For You	15

(see also Three Dog Night)

HUTTON SISTERS (BETTY & MARION)
55	Capitol CL 14250	Ko Ko Mo (I Love You So)/Heart Throb	25

(see also Betty Hutton)

ALDOUS HUXLEY
73	Lansdowne LSR003/4	SPEAKING PERSONALLY (2-LP)	40

HVL
15	Organic Analogue OA 002	AWAY FROM EVERYTHING WE KNOW EP (12", clear vinyl, 400 only)	12

HYACINTH GIRLS
88	Red RED 002	HAPPY NOW?	40

CHARLIE HYATT
65	Island IEP 707	RASS! (EP, as Bam & Charlie Hyatt)	30
66	Island ILP 932	KISS ME NECK (LP)	35

LEON HYATT
76	Nationwide NW 1014	40 Days And Nights/Third World Affairs	15

HYBRID KIDS
80	Cherry Red BRED 11	CLAWS (LP)	15

TANYA HYDE
79	Waldo's DS 008	Herr Wunderbar/Auf Der Anderen Seite (p/s)	15

HYGRADES
65	Columbia DB 7734	She Cared/We're Through	15

Brian HYLAND

MINT VALUE £

BRIAN HYLAND
60	London HLR 9161	Itsy Bitsy Teeny Weeny Yellow Polka Dot Bikini/Don't Dilly Dally, Sally (78)	100
60	London HLR 9113	Rosemary/Library Love Affair	20
60	London HLR 9203	Four Little Heels/That's How Much	6
61	London HLR 9262	Lop Sided, Over Loaded/I Gotta Go ('Cause I Love You)	6
61	HMV POP 915	Let Me Belong To You/Let It Die	8
61	HMV POP 955	The Night I Cried/I'll Never Stop Wanting You	8
63	HMV POP 1113	I May Not Live To See Tomorrow/It Ain't That Way At All	6
63	HMV POP 1143	If Mary's There/Remember Me	8
63	HMV POP 1169	Somewhere In The Night/I Wish Today Was Yesterday	8
63	HMV POP 1188	I'm Afraid To Go Home/Save Your Heart For Me	8
63	HMV POP 1237	Let Us Make Our Own Mistakes/Nothing Matters But You	8
64	Philips BF 1326	Here's To Our Love/Two Kinds Of Girls	10
65	Philips BF 1429	Stay Away From Her/I Can't Keep A Secret	10
65	Philips BF 1486	3,000 Miles/Sometimes They Do	10
66	Philips BF 1508	The Joker Went Wild/I Can Hear The Rain	20
66	Philips BF 1528	Run Run Look And See/Why Did You Do It	7
66	Philips BF 1555	Hung Up In Your Eyes/Why Mine	7
67	Philips BF 1569	Holiday For Clowns/Yesterday I Had A Girl	6
69	Dot 124	A Million To One/It Could All Begin Again (in You)	7
67	Philips BF 1601	Get The Message/Kinda Groovy	10
62	HMV 7EG 8780	SEALED WITH A KISS (EP)	
61	London HA-R 2289	THE BASHFUL BLONDE (LP)	80
62	HMV CLP 1553	LET ME BELONG TO YOU (LP)	30
63	HMV CLP 1759	COUNTRY MEETS FOLK (LP)	30
66	Philips BL 7762	THE JOKER WENT WILD (LP)	20
68	Fontana SFL 13008	HERE'S TO OUR LOVE (LP)	20

C. HYMAN
65	Ska Beat JB 200	The Ska Rhythm/The Ska Is Moving On	40

DICK HYMAN TRIO
56	MGM SP 1164	Theme From The Threepenny Opera/Baubles, Bangles And Beads	6
67	Command SCMD 105	BRAZILIAN IMPRESSIONS (LP)	15
69	Command SCMD 508	MOOG - THE ELECTRIC ECLECTICS OF DICK HYMAN (LP)	20
70	Command SCMD 946	THE AGE OF ELECTRONICUS (LP)	30

PHYLLIS HYMAN
75	Private Stock PVT 31	Leaving' The Good Life Behind/Leavin' The Good Life Behind (long version)	6
77	Buddah BDS 457	Loving You - Losing You/Loving You - Losing You (long version)	6
79	Arista ARIST 323	You Know How To Love Me/Give A Little More	15
79	Arista ARIST 323	You Know How To Love Me/Give A Little More (12", p/s)	10
77	Buddah BDLP 4046	PHYLLIS HYMAN (LP)	15
78	Buddah BDLP 4058	SING A SONG (LP)	40
79	Arista SPART 1114	YOU KNOW HOW TO LOVE ME (LP)	15
81	Artista SPART 1154	CAN'T WE FALL IN LOVE AGAIN (LP)	15

HYPA KONCEPT
91	No Label L8 001	Party People (Come Together) (3 Mixes) (12", hand written labels)	20
92	Club State CSR 12001	Love Addict (4 Mixes) (12", stamped white label)	40

HYPER ON EXPERIENCE
93	Moving Shadow SHADOW 30	DEAF IN THE FAMILY EP (12", white label stamped with cat. no. only as Hyper On exp.)	60
93	Moving Shadow SHADOW 30	DEAF IN THE FAMILY EP (12", p/s as Hyper-On Experience)	40
93	Moving Shadow SHADOW 40	THE FAMILY WE NEVER HAD EP (12", p/s, as Hyper-On Experience)	15
94	Moving Shadow SHADOW 40	THE FAMILY WE NEVER HAD (12" picture disc)	50

HYPER VYPER
88	SRTS SRT/DIY/NWOBHM	EASY LIVIN EP	15

HYSTERIA
84	Sculpture SCT4-1	BEHIND THE VEIL (12" EP, p/s)	20

I

I AM KLOOT
99	Ugly Man UGLY 16	Titanic/To You (7", 1,000 only in brown paper sleeve)	12
00	Ugly Man UGLY 17	Twist/ 86 TDs (red vinyl)	8
01	We Love You AMOUR 5	NATURAL HISTORY (LP)	40
03	Echo ECHLP 46A	I AM KLOOT (LP, gatefold, black sleeve and black vinyl)	60
03	Echo ECHLP 46A	I AM KLOOT (LP, gatefold, white sleeve and white vinyl)	40
05	Echo ECHLP 62	GODS AND MONSTERS (LP)	25
08	Pias 556 4763.010	PLAY MOOLAH ROUGE (LP)	35
10	Pias 556 A003 012	B (2-LP)	20
10	Pias PIASR 210 LP	SKY AT NIGHT (LP)	25
13	Pias PIASR330LP	LET IT ALL IN (LP)	15
14	Kudos Film & Television 4705187	FROM THERE TO HERE (LP)	15

(see also Johnny Dangerously)

Janis IAN

MINT VALUE £

JANIS IAN
67	Verve Folkways VS 1503	Society's Child (Baby I've Been Thinking)/Letter To Jon	20
68	Verve Folkways VS 1513	Sunflakes Fall, Snowrays Call/Insanity Comes Quietly To The Structured Mind	10
67	Verve Folkways (S)VLP 6001	JANIS IAN (LP)	30
67	Verve Forecast (S)VLP 6003	FOR ALL THE SEASONS OF YOUR MIND (LP)	30
68	Verve Forecast (S)VLP 6009	THE SECRET LIFE OF J. EDDY FINK (LP)	20
70	Verve Folkways SVLP 6023	WHO REALLY CARES? (LP)	25
71	Capitol E-ST 683	PRESENT COMPANY (LP)	20
77	CBS 31879	MIRACLE ROW (LP, gatefold)	15
85	CBS 60636	BETWEEN THE LINES (LP, Nimbus Supercut, mail order only through Practical Hi Fi magazine)	40

IAN (EDWARD) & ZODIACS
63	Oriole CB 1849	Beechwood 4-5789/You Can Think Again	35
65	Fontana TF 548	Just The Little Things/This Won't Happen To Me (as Ian Edward with Zodiacs)	30
66	Fontana TF 708	No Money, No Honey/Where Were You?	50
66	Fontana TF 753	Wade In The Water/Come On Along, Girl	60
65	Wing WL 1074	GEAR AGAIN - 12 HITS (LP)	25

(see also Koppykats, Wellington Wade)

IAN (MEESON) & BELINDA (GILLET)
89	Odeon ODO 112	Who Wants To Live Forever?/Who Wants To Live Forever? (Instrumental) (p/s, feat. Brian May, handful signed by Brian May for Blood Transfusion staff)	40

(see also Brian May)

IAN & SYLVIA
63	Fontana TF 426	Four Strong Winds/Long Lonesome Road	7
65	Fontana TFL 6053	EARLY MORNING RAIN (LP)	30

IAN AND THE MUSCLETONES
81	Muscletone MS 01	I Like It/Vampire State (p/s)	8

I BENJAHMAN
82	Lion Kingdom LK 002	Give Love A Try/Mind Blowing Dub/Version (12")	40
83	Lion Kingdom LKLP 01	INTRODUCING A FRACTION OF JAH ACTION (LP)	35

IBIBIO SOUND MACHINE
14	Soundway SNDWYLP057	IBIBIO SOUND MACHINE (LP)	15

IBM 7090 COMPUTER & DIGITAL TO SOUND TRANSCUDER
62	Brunswick STA 8523	MUSIC FOR MATHEMATICS (LP)	40

RAS IBUNA
77	Grove Music GM003	Diverse Doctrine/Version	35
78	Grove Music GMDM7	Pay Dem Dues/Diverse Doctrine (12", with Jah Woosh)	40
85	Studio Now SNT 01	Diverse Doctrine/Version/COOL BREEZE: Wi Nuh Want Nun A Dat (12")	12

ICARUS
69	Spark SRL 1012	The Devil Rides Out/You're In Life	175
72	Pye Int. NSPL 28161	THE MARVEL WORLD OF ICARUS (LP, laminated sleeve, blue/black labels)	200
12	Acme ADLP 1082	THE MARVEL WORLD OF ICARUS (LP, reissue)	15

(see also Soft Machine)

ICE (1)
67	Decca F 12680	Anniversary (Of Love)/So Many Times	80
68	Decca F 12749	Ice Man/Whisper Her Name (Maria Laine)	120

(see also Affinity)

ICE (2)
79	Storm SR 3307	SAGA OF THE ICE KING (LP, private pressing with booklet)	250
04	Kissing Spell KSLP9602	SAGA OF THE ICE KING (LP, repressing)	20

ICE BABIES
81	Groove Digger GOD 1	Genius Of Lies/Reason Not Rhyme	20

ICEBREAKERS
78	Virgin Frontline FL1010	PLANET MARS DUB (LP, as Icebreakers with the Diamonds)	20

ICE CREAM
74	Fontana 6007 039	Shout It Out/Hold Yourself Tight	25

ICE CUBE
90	4th & Broadway BRW 192	AmeriKKKa's Most Wanted/Once Upon A Time In The Projects (p/s)	20
91	4th & Broadway BRW 239	Steady Mobbin'/Us (p/s)	30
90	Island/Priority BRLP 551	AMERIKKA'S MOST WANTED (LP)	20
91	Island/Priority 510 656-1	DEATH CERTIFICATE (LP)	20
92	Island/Priority BRLP 592	THE PREDATOR (LP)	30
93	Priority 74321 16191-1	LETHAL INJECTION (LP)	30

ICE FACTORY
83	No Label	JERUSALEM EP	35

ICE NINE
83	Clockwork TIK 1	Another Love Affair/For Some Strange Reason (p/s)	10

ICEPICK
97	Backbone BR971AA	Phenomenal Criminal/Brixtonites Pt 1(12")	20
98	Backbone ICEEP1 BB002	ICEPICK (EP)	18

(see also Bodysnatchers)

ICE THE FALLING RAIN
83	Future FS 7	Lifes Illusion/Illusions (p/s)	20

ICI LA BAS
79	Black Noise NO 4	ICI LA BAS (12" EP, with booklet)	45

(see also Homosexuals)

ICON AD
82	Radical Change RC 3	DON'T FEED US SHIT!! (Fight For Peace/Face The Facts/What's Your Name (fold out p/s)	10
83	Radical Change RC 4	LET THE VUTURES FLY : Say No/Medals/For The Dead/Trident 1 And 2	10

ICONS OF FILTH
83	Corpus Christi CHRIST ITS 7	USED, ABUSED, UNAMUSED EP (fold-out p/s)	10

ICQ

			MINT VALUE £
84	Mortarhate MORT 10	BRAIN DEATH EP (p/s with insert)	10
85	Mortarhate MORT 18	THE FILTH AND THE FURY EP (Fold-out p/s)	10
97	BBP/Yellow Fever BBPV3/YF1	SHOW US YOU CARE EP (12 test pressings with red fold-out p/s and inserts)	25
97	BBP/Yellow Fever BBPV3/YF1	SHOW US YOU CARE EP (fold-out p/s, inserts)	6
84	Mortarhate MORT 5	ONWARD CHRISTIAN SOLDIERS (LP)	25

ICQ
82	Unsquare ICQ 1201	Final Approach/Loveland/One Finger Snap (12" white label)	25

IDEAL HUSBANDS
80	Discovery DIK 001	Town Planning/Out Of The Factory And Into The Wood (p/s)	50

IDEALS
61	Pye International 7N 25103	Knee Socks/Mary's Lamb	40

DAVID IDEMA
72	Buddah 2011 130	House On Holy Road/Dream Weaver	6

IDES OF MARCH (1)
66	London HLU 10058	You Wouldn't Listen/I'll Keep Searching (as I'des Of March)	15
68	London HLU 10183	Hole In My Soul/Girls Don't Grow On Trees	12
70	Warner Bros WB 7378	Vehicle/Lead Me Home, Gently	6
70	Warner Bros WB 7403	Superman/Home	6
70	Warner Bros WS 1863	VEHICLE (LP)	25

(see also Survivors)

IDES OF MARCH (2)
86	RS RSA 3	In Winters Land/Civilian (p/s)	8

IDIOT DANCERS
81	Retrospect HP 1001	Glances/Up And Down/Imagination (hand-stamped die cut sleeve)	15

IDJUT BOYS
94	U Star US 001	IDJUT BOY EP (12")	50
94	U Star US 003	PHANTOM SLASHER EP (12")	40
96	Noid NOID ONE	Girth Soup/Crouton Bonus/DJ HARVEY: Keep On Trying/Drums in 6 Twelve (12")	20
98	U Star USR 003	Turntable Turbulence/Staeb	8
98	Noid NOIDLP 001	NOID LONG PLAYER (LP, as 2x12")	30

IDJUT BOYS & LAJ
95	U Star US 004	NOT REGGAE (12")	30
95	U Star US 006	FOOLIN' (12")	30
95	U star US 007	BEARD LAW (EP)	15
96	U Star US 008	JAZ FOOK (12")	15
96	U Star US 010	WHOK TISH EP (12")	20
97	U Star USR 001	OUTHOUSE (12")	10
00	U Star USR 006	MORE OR LESS PART TWO (12")	10
17	U Star US 0000	U STAR EP (12")	12
00	U Star USRLP 001	MORE OR LESS (LP, as 3 x 12")	50

IDLE FLOWERS
84	Miles Ahead AHEAD 1	All I Want Is You/Fizz Music (p/s)	10

IDLE RACE
67	Liberty LBF 15026	The Imposters Of Life's Magazine/Sitting In My Tree	80
68	Liberty LBF 15054	The Skeleton And The Roundabout/Knocking Nails Into My House	30
68	Liberty LBF 15101	The End Of The Road/The Morning Sunshine	20
68	Liberty LBF 15129	I Like My Toys/The Birthday (unissued)	0
69	Liberty LBF 15218	Days Of Broken Arrows/Warm Red Carpet (B-side act. "Worn Red Carpet")	20
69	Liberty LBF 15242	Come With Me/Reminds Me Of You	25
71	Regal Zonophone RZ 3036	Dancing Flower/Bitter Green	12
68	Liberty LBL 83132	THE BIRTHDAY PARTY (LP, mono)	125
68	Liberty LBS 83132	THE BIRTHDAY PARTY (LP, stereo)	100
69	Liberty LBS 83221	THE IDLE RACE (LP)	150
71	Regal Zono. SLRZ 1017	TIME IS (LP)	200
73	Sunset SLS 50354	ON WITH THE SHOW (LP)	15
76	Sunset SLS 50381	THE BIRTHDAY PARTY (LP, reissue)	15
85	See For Miles SEE 60	LIGHT AT THE END OF THE ROAD (LP)	15

(see also Mike Sheridan &, Mike Sheridan's Lot, Lemon Tree, Move, E.L.O., Trevor Burton, Steve Gibbons Band, Wizzard)

IDLES
17	Bailey BALLEY 002	Divide & Conquer/Untitled (gold vinyl)	50
17	Bailey BALLEY 003	Well Done/Untitled (end vinyl)	25
17	Bailey BALLEY 004	Moter/Untitled (white vinyl)	25
17	Bailey BALLEY 001	BRUTALISM (LP)	20
18	Partisan PTKF2158-6	JOY AS AN ACT OF RESISTANCE (LP, pink vinyl)	20

IDLEWILD
97	Human Condition HC 0017	Queen Of The Troubled Teens/Faster/Self Healer (p/s, 1,000 only)	30
97	Fierce Panda NING 42	Chandelier/I Want To Be A Writer (p/s)	10
97	Deceptive BLUFF 057	Satan Polaroid/House Alone (die-cut p/s, numbered, 1,500 only)	8
98	Food FOODLP 28	HOPE IS IMPORTANT (LP)	35
00	Food FOODLP 32	100 BROKEN WINDOWS (LP)	30
02	Parlophone 5402431	THE REMOTE PART (LP, with inner sleeve)	30
09	Diverse DIV 020LP	POST ELECTRIC BLUES (LP)	25
16	Empty Words EWR 007	IDLEWILD LIVE (2-LP)	30

BILLY IDOL
93	Chrysalis CHR 6000	CYBERPUNK (LP, inner)	25

(see also Generation X)

IDOL DEATH
80	ID Records ID DISY 1234	Ignorance Is Bliss/Sticky Death	30

IDOL RICH

MINT VALUE £

IDOL RICH
84   Dork URIDOL 3   Blaze Of Love/Peso Trail 12

IDOLS (1)
65   Mercury MF 840   Don't Walk Away/You Don't Care 20
(see also Mike Sax & Idols)

IDOLS (2)
79   Ork NYC 2   You/Girl That I Love (p/s) 8
(see also New York Dolls)

I. E. M. (INCREDIBLE EXPANDING MINDFUCK)
96   Chromatic CHR 001   I.E.M. (LP) 30
03   Gates Of Dawn GOD 007   HAVE COME FOR YOUR CHILDREN (2-LP, no sleeve, 2 postcards, 90 only) 35
(see also Steven Wilson, Porcupine Tree, No-Man, Blackfield, Continuum (2))

IF
70   Island WIP 6083   Raise The Level Of Your Conscious Mind/I'm Reaching Out On All Sides 10
71   United Artists UP 35263   Far Beyond/Forgotten Roads 6
72   United Artists UP 35356   You In Your Small Corner/Waterfall 6
70   Island ILPS 9129   IF (LP, 1st pressing, pink label/'i' logo) 100
71   Island ILPS 9129   IF (LP, 2nd pressing, pink rim label/'palm tree' logo) 40
71   Island ILPS 9137   IF 2 (LP, pink label, pink rim label/'palm tree' logo) 50
71   United Artists UAG 29158   IF 3 (LP, gatefold sleeve) 50
72   United Artists UAG 29315   IF 4 (LP, gatefold sleeve with inner) 40
75   Gull GULP 1007   TEA-BREAK OVER - BACK ON YOUR 'EADS (LP) 15
74   Gull GULP 1004   NOT JUST ANOTHER BUNCH OF PRETTY FACES (LP, with inner sleeve) 15
(see also Ferris Wheel, Terry Smith)

TECWYN IFAN
76   Sain Sain 1071   DREF WEN (LP, with insert) 80

KRIS IFE
67   MGM MGM 1369   Hush/The Spectator 50
68   MGM MGM 1390   This Woman's Love/I Gotta Feeling 12
68   Music Factory CUB 3   Give And Take/Sands Of Time 20
68   Parlophone R 5741   Imagination/I'm Coming 'Round 20
69   Parlophone R 5770   Haven't We Had A Good Time?/Will I Ever Fall In Love Again? 10
73   Bumlade GE122   Wherever You Are/The Sun, The Sea, The Sand And The Wine 25
(see also Quiet Five, Judd)

I GAD
92   Nuff Tuff TUF 006   Brutality/ENHANCERS: Brutal Dub/Wicked Man/MANDINKA: Rootsman Corner/
               ENHANCERS: Wicked Dub (12") 50

IGANDA
79   021 Records OTO1   Slow Down/Mark Of Slavery (p/s) 50

'IGGINBOTTOM
69   Deram SML 1051   'IGGINBOTTOM'S WRENCH (LP, stereo) 350
69   Deram DML 1051   'IGGINBOTTOM'S WRENCH (LP, mono) 400
(see also Soft Machine)

IGNERANTS
79   Rundown ACE 008   Radio Interference/Wrong Place, Wrong Time (p/s) 30

IGUANA
72   Polydor 2383 108   IGUANA (LP, gatefold sleeve) 50

IGUANAS
65   RCA RCA 1484   This Is What I Was Made For/Don't Come Runnin' To Me 40

I HAICIDEONS & I JARZIF
78   Greensleeves GRED 7   Rise Ethiopians/Signs Of The Messiah (12") 40

I JAH MAN (LEVI)
76   Lucky LY 6016   Jah Heavy Load/Heavy Dub 80
76   Concrete Jungle CJ 750   Jah Heavy Load/Straight To Blackwax Locks 40
76   Concrete Jungle CJ 756   I Am Levi/Part 2 100
77   Ghetto Rocker PRE 1   Africa/Afrodub (handwritten labels) 40
78   Island WIP 6458   Heavy Load/I'm A Levi 20
80   Jahmani JMI 304   Moulding (as Ijahman)/HIS MAJESTERIANS: Jah Is Coming Again (12") 60
85   Jahmani JMI 501   Moulding/Jah Is Coming Again (12") 40
78   Island ILPS 9521   HAILE I HYMN (LP) 18

I-JOG & TRACKSUITS
79   Tracksuit JOG 1   Jah Jah Jah/Tao Tao Tao (p/s, as the TRACKSUITS) 6
80   Tyger TYG 1   Red Box/Worrying Man (p/s) 20

LEIAH IKAFA
79   Hobo HOS 002   Disco 2000/Together In Love 15
79   Hobo HOSD 002   Disco 2000/Together In Love (12" clear vinyl) 35

IKE (B) & CRYSTALITES
68   Island WI 3134   Illya Kuryakin/Anne Marie (B-side miscredited to Bobby Ellis & Crystalites) 60
68   Island WI 3151   Try A Little Merriness/Patricia (as Ike B & Crystalites) 20

IKETTES
62   London HLU 9508   I'm Blue/Find My Baby 25
65   Stateside SS 407   Peaches'N'Cream/The Biggest Players 40
65   Stateside SS 434   (He's Gonna Be) Fine Fine Fine/How Come 30
65   Sue WI 389   Prisoner In Love/Those Words 40
66   Polydor 56506   I'm So Thankful/Don't Feel Sorry For Me 20
66   Polydor 56516   (Never More) Lonely For You/Sally Go Round The Roses 20
66   London HLU 10081   What'cha Gonna Do?/Down, Down 80
67   Polydor 56533   I'm So Thankful/Don't Feel Sorry For Me (reissue) 8
73   Mojo 2092 063   Peaches'N'Cream/Sally Go Round The Roses 8
85   Kent 6T1   MARY LOVE: Hey Stoney Face/IKETTES: It's Been So Long/ETTA JAMES: Wallflower 20

ILANIT

			MINT VALUE £
65	Stateside SE 1033	FINE FINE FINE (EP)	175

(see also Ike & Tina Turner, P.P. Arnold)

ILANIT
77	Pye International 7N 25739	I'm No One (If You Leave Me)/I Can't Say I Love You (p/s)	10

I LIFE
64	R&B JB 140	Kiss You Gave Me/No More	18

ILLUSION
69	Dot DOT 122	Did You See Her Eyes?/Falling In Love	8
70	Dot DOT 137	Let's Make Each Other Happy/Beside You (unissued)	0
69	Dot (S)LPD 531	ILLUSION (LP)	25
70	Dot SLPD 537	TOGETHER (AS A WAY OF LIFE) (LP)	22
70	Paramount SPFL 264	IF IT'S SO (LP, originally planned for Dot SLPD 539)	15

ILLUSIONS
83	Zella ZEL LPS 405	ILLUSIONS (LP, 100 only, with insert)	50

ILLUSIVE DREAM
69	RCA Victor RCA 1791	Electric Garden/Back Again	30

(see also Christine Perfect)

ILLUSTRATION
69	Pye Int. NSPL 28140	ILLUSTRATION (LP)	25

SOLOMON ILORY
63	Blue Note 45-1899	Yabe E (Farewell) (Parts 1 & 2)	12

ERIK ILOTT, SHANTYMAN
73	Folk'sle Records FOR 7	SHIPSHAPE & BRISTOL FASHION (LP, card sleeve, pasted photo & booklet)	40

I LUV WIGHT
70	Philips 6006 043	Let The World Wash In/Mediaeval Masquerade (in p/s)	75
70	Philips 6006 043	Let The World Wash In/Mediaeval Masquerade	35

(see also Kaleidoscope, Fairfield Parlour)

IMAGE
65	Parlophone R 5281	Come To The Party/Never Let Me Go	50
65	Parlophone R 5352	Home Is Anywhere/I Hear Your Voice Again	50
66	Parlophone R 5442	I Can't Stop Myself/Let's Make The Scene	60

IMAGES
65	Polydor 56011	I Only Have Myself To Blame/Head Over Heels	30

IMAGINATION (1)
68	Status ST 001	Flying/The Magic Wand	50

IM & COUNT OSSIE
71	Banana CA 357	So Long Rastafari Calling/Give Me Back My Language & Culture	50

IM (CEDRIC BROOKS) & DAVID
70	Bamboo BAM 57	Candid Eye/SOUND DIMENSION: Federated Backdrop	40

IMITATIONS
71	Crystal CR 7013	Walking Up A One Way Street/One Way Street - Version	6

IMMEDIATE
05	Fierce Panda NING161	Never Seen/Say This (p/s)	7

IMMORTALS (1)
69	Amalgamated AMG 851	Bongo Jah/ANSELL COLLINS: My Last Waltz	40
77	Hawkeye HE 10	Why Keep A Good Man Down/Good Man	20

IMMORTALS (2)
86	MCA MCA 1057	No Turning Back/No Turning Back (The Chocks-Away Mix) (p/s)	25
86	MCA MCAT 1057	No Turning Back (Joy Stick Mix)/No Turning Back/No Turning Back (The Chocks-Away Mix) (12", p/s)	30

(see also Queen)

IMPAC
66	CBS 202402	Too Far Out/Rat Tat Ta Tat	80

IMPACT
83	Cyanide	PUNK CHRISTMAS EP	20

IMPACT ALL STARS
71	Bullet BU 483	Dandy Shandy Version 4/Go Back Version 3	12
71	Randy's RAN 519	Go Back Version 4/Version 3	15
71	Supreme SUP 223	Go Back/Version	15

(see also Randy's All Stars, Alton Ellis, Gregory Issacs, Errol Dunkley, C. Danovan, Heptones, Dennis Brown, Horace Andy)

IMPALAS
59	MGM MGM 1015	Sorry (I Ran All The Way Home)/Fool, Fool, Fool	15
59	MGM MGM 1015	Sorry (I Ran All The Way Home)/Fool, Fool, Fool (78)	25
59	MGM MGM 1031	Oh, What A Fool/Sandy Went Away	30
60	MGM MGM 1068	Peggy Darling/'Bye Everybody	30
59	MGM MGM-EP 696	SORRY (I RAN ALL THE WAY HOME) (EP)	400

IMPALERS
79	Decca F 13862	Gimme Some Lovin'/Wild About It	10

IMPERIAL POMPADOURS
80	Pompadour POMP 001	ERSATZ (LP, actually Inner City Unit with Robert Calvert & Barney Bubbles)	40

(see also Inner City Unit, Robert Calvert)

IMPERIALS (JAMAICA)
69	Bullet BU 417	Black Is Soul/Always With You	50

IMPERIALS (1)
72	Key KL 012	TIME TO GET IT TOGETHER (LP)	18
74	Key KL 025	FOLLOW THE MAN WITH THE MUSIC (LP)	15

IMPERIALS (2)
68	Nu Beat NB 012	Young Love/Days Like These	25

IMPERSONATORS
69	Big Shot BI 524	Make It Easy On Yourself/I've Tried Before	12

(see also Moffat Allstars)

IMPOSSIBLE DREAMERS

MINT VALUE £

IMPOSSIBLE DREAMERS
80	Merciful Release MR 1	Books Books Books/Not A Love Song/Waiting For The Girl/What Can You Do When You See Someone As Beautiful As You?	8

IMPOSSIBLE YEARS
85	Dreamworld DREAM 1	SCENES WE'D LIKE TO SEE (12" EP)	12

IMPOSTERS
69	Mercury MF 1080	Apache '69/Q Three	20

IMPRESSIONS
58	London HL 8697	For Your Precious Love/Sweet Was The Wine (as Jerry Butler & Impressions)	200
58	London HL 8697	For Your Precious Love/Sweet Was The Wine (78, as Jerry Butler & Impressions)	100
61	HMV POP 961	Gypsy Woman/As Long As You Love Me	50
63	HMV POP 1129	I'm The One Who Loves You/I Need Your Love	40
63	HMV POP 1226	It's Alright/You'll Want Me Back	25
64	HMV POP 1262	Talkin' About My Baby/Never Too Much Love	20
64	HMV POP 1295	I'm So Proud/I Made A Mistake	20
64	HMV POP 1317	Keep On Pushing/I Love You (Yeah)	20
64	HMV POP 1343	You Must Believe Me/See The Real Me	18
65	HMV POP 1408	People Get Ready/I've Been Trying	18
65	HMV POP 1429	Woman's Got Soul/Get Up And Move	18
65	HMV POP 1446	A Meeting Over Yonder/I Found That I've Lost	20
65	HMV POP 1472	I Need You/Never Could You Be	20
65	HMV POP 1492	Amen/Long Long Winter	12
66	HMV POP 1498	You've Been Cheatin'/Just One Kiss From You	40
66	HMV POP 1498	You've Been Cheatin'/Just One Kiss From You (DJ Copy)	100
66	HMV POP 1516	Since I Lost The One I Love/Falling In Love With You	15
66	HMV POP 1526	Too Slow/No One Else	15
66	HMV POP 1545	Can't Satisfy/This Must End	40
66	HMV POP 1545	Can't Satisfy/This Must End (DJ Copy)	100
67	HMV POP 1581	You Always Hurt Me/Little Girl	40
67	HMV POP 1581	You Always Hurt Me/Little Girl (DJ Copy)	100
68	Stateside SS 2083	We're A Winner/You've Got Me Runnin'	18
68	Buddah 201 021	Fool For You/I'm Loving Nothing	10
69	Stateside SS 2139	Can't Satisfy/You've Been Cheatin'	20
69	Buddah 201 062	Choice Of Colors/Mighty Mighty Spade And Whitey	15
70	Buddah 2011 030	Check Out Your Mind/Can't You See?	10
70	Buddah 2011 045	(Baby) Turn On To Me/Soulful Love	8
71	Buddah 2011 068	Ain't Got Time/I'm So Proud	8
71	Buddah 2011 087	Love Me/Do You Want Me To Win	8
71	Buddah 2011 099	Inner City Blues/Amen/Keep On Pushin'	6
72	Buddah 2011 124	Our Love Goes On And On/This Love's For Real	6
73	Probe PRO 584	People Get Ready/We're Rolling On	8
74	Buddah BDS 403	Finally Got Myself Together/I'll Always Be Here	8
76	ABC 4148	You've Been Cheating/Amen	6
65	HMV 7EG 8896	IT'S ALL RIGHT (EP)	100
66	HMV 7EG 8954	SOULFULLY (EP)	100
64	HMV CLP 1743	THE NEVER ENDING IMPRESSIONS (LP)	80
65	HMV CLP 1935	BIG SIXTEEN (LP, mono)	40
65	HMV CSD 1642	BIG SIXTEEN (LP, stereo)	50
66	HMV CLP/CSD 3548	RIDIN' HIGH (LP)	60
67	HMV CLP/CSD 3631	THE FABULOUS IMPRESSIONS (LP)	60
68	Stateside (S)SL 10239	WE'RE A WINNER (LP)	35
68	Joy JOYS 104	FOR YOUR PRECIOUS LOVE (LP, with Jerry Butler)	15
69	Buddah 203 012	THIS IS MY COUNTRY (LP)	30
69	Stateside (S)SL 10279	BIG SIXTEEN (VOL. 2) (LP)	30
70	Buddah 2359 003	THE YOUNG MOD'S FORGOTTEN STORY (LP)	30
70	Buddah 2359 009	AMEN (LP)	18
71	Buddah 2318 017	CHECK OUT YOUR MIND (LP)	20
72	Buddah 2318 059	TIMES HAVE CHANGED (LP)	18
73	Buddah BDLP 4003	FINALLY GOT MYSELF TOGETHER (LP)	15
75	ABC ABCL 5104	BIG SIXTEEN (LP, reissue)	15

(see also Curtis Mayfield, Jerry Butler)

IMPROVING SILENCE
77	Perky Pat CS LP 145/6	IMPROVING SILENCE EP (1,000, p/s with 8 page book insert)	40

IMPS
58	Parlophone R 4398	Dim Dumb Blonde/Let Me Lie	20

INADEQUATES
59	Capitol CL 15051	Pretty Face/Audie	25

INCANDESCENT LUMINAIRE
82	Clock House CHR 0501	Famous Names/The Warning	18

INCAS (1)
65	Lyntone LYN 765/6	KEELE RAG RECORD (EP, flexidisc, with 3 other bands)	30
66	Parlophone R 5551	One Night Stand/I'll Keep Holding On	60

INCAS (2)
75	Tank BSS 112	X CERTIFICATE (LP, private pressing)	50

ERROL INCE
65	Ember EMB 3360	DANCE TRINIDAD (LP, as Errol Ince and his Music Makers)	18

INCEE WINCEE SPIDER
88	Overspill SPILL1	Don't Know Anythin'/See My Love Shine (p/s)	30

INCH BY INCH
81	Blue Of London BOL 1	If It's Magic (We Don't Want It)/War's Not Inevitable (12". p/s)	30

INCOGNITO (2)

MINT VALUE £

INCOGNITO (2)
80	Ensign ENY 4412	Parisienne Girls/Summers Ended (12")	12
81	Ensign ENVY 504	JAZZ FUNK (LP)	20
91	Talkin Loud 848 546-1	INSIDE LIFE (LP)	15

INCREDIBLE BONGO BAND
73	MGM 2006 161	Bongo Rock/Bongolia	8
72	MGM 2315 255	BONGO ROCK (LP)	25
76	DJM DJS 20452	BONGO ROCK (LP, reissue)	15

INCREDIBLE CHERRY TREE BAND
76	Look LKLP 6037	INCREDIBLE CHERRY TREE BAND (LP)	30

INCREDIBLE HOG
73	Dart ART 2026	Lame/Tadpole	15
73	Dart 65372	VOLUME 1 (LP, laminated sleeve, pink/white/black label)	300
11	Rise Above Relics RARLP 009	VOLUME 1- 4 (LP, with 10")	25
11	Rise Above Relics RARLP 009	VOLUME 1- 4 (LP, with blue vinyl 10")	35
11	Rise Above Relics RARLP 009	VOLUME 1- 4 (LP, with 10" and 7" all on pink vinyl, 300 only)	35

INCREDIBLE KIDDA BAND
78	Psycho P 2608	Everybody Knows/No Nerve (in p/s)	100
78	Psycho P 2608	Everybody Knows/No Nerve (no p/s)	30
79	Carrere CAR 119	Fighting My Way Back/Saturday Night Fever (as KIDDA BAND)	130

INCREDIBLES
67	Stateside SS 2053	There's Nothing Else To Say/Heart And Soul	200
67	Stateside SS 2053	There's Nothing Else To Say/Heart And Soul (DJ copy)	300
74	Contempo CS 9008	There's Nothing Else To Say/Another Dirty Deal	20
13	Outta Sight OSV 089	There's Nothing Else To Say/AUDIO ART STRINGS: There's Nothing Else To Say (reissue)	7
74	Contempo CLP 212	HEART AND SOUL (LP)	25

INCREDIBLE STRING BAND
SINGLES
67	Elektra EKSN 45013	Way Back In The 1960s/Chinese White (white-label promo)	60
68	Elektra EKSN 45028	Painting Box/No Sleep Blues	15
69	Elektra EKSN 45074	Big Ted/All Writ Down	12
70	Elektra 2101 003	This Moment/Black Jack Davy	6

ALBUMS : ORIGINAL ALBUMS
66	Elektra EUK 254	THE INCREDIBLE STRING BAND (1st pressing, white label, green logo, black lettering)	225
67	Elektra EUK 257	THE 5000 SPIRITS OR THE LAYERS OF THE ONION (mono, orange label)	150
67	Elektra EUKS 7257	THE 5000 SPIRITS OR THE LAYERS OF THE ONION (LP, stereo, orange label, laminated sleeve)	150
68	Elektra EUKS 258	THE HANGMAN'S BEAUTIFUL DAUGHTER (mono, orange label, with lyric insert)	70
68	Elektra EUKS 7258	THE HANGMAN'S BEAUTIFUL DAUGHTER (stereo, orange label, with lyric insert)	80
68	Elektra EKL 4036/7	WEE TAM/THE BIG HUGE (2-LP, orange label, laminated gatefold sleeve, with insert; also stereo EKS 74036/7)	45
69	Elektra EKS 74057	CHANGING HORSES (red/white label, gatefold sleeve)	45
70	Elektra 2469 002	I LOOKED UP (red/white label)	50
70	Elektra 2665 001	U (2-LP, red/white label, gatefold sleeve, with foldover lyric insert)	35
70	Elektra 2665 001	U (2-LP, red label, gatefold sleeve, without foldover lyric insert)	25
70	Island ILPS 9140	BE GLAD FOR THE SONG HAS NO ENDING (pink rim label/'palm tree' logo)	18
71	Island ILPS 9172	LIQUID ACROBAT AS REGARDS THE AIR (gatefold sleeve, with inner, pink rim label/'palm tree' logo)	30
72	Island ILPS 9211	EARTHSPAN (with lyric inner sleeve, pink rim label/'palm tree' logo)	18
73	Island ILPS 9229	NO RUINOUS FEUD (with inner sleeve, pink rim label/'palm tree' logo)	15
74	Island ILPS 9270	HARD ROPE AND SILKEN TWINE (with inner sleeve, pink rim label/'palm tree' logo)	15
76	Island ISLD 9	SEASONS THEY CHANGE (2-LP, gatefold sleeve)	25

ALBUMS : REISSUE ALBUMS
66	Elektra EUK 254	THE INCREDIBLE STRING BAND (2nd pressing, orange label)	60

(All other 'butterfly' label re-issues £8-£10 each)

68	Elektra EKL 254	THE INCREDIBLE STRING BAND (3rd pressing, red label)	20
68	Elektra EKS 7257	THE 5000 SPIRITS OR THE LAYERS OF THE ONION (LP, stereo, red label)	150
68	Elektra EUK 257	THE 5000 SPIRITS OR THE LAYERS OF THE ONION (LP, mono, red label)	50
68	Elektra EKL 4036	WEE TAM (red label, also stereo EKS 74036)	15

(All other 'butterfly' label re-issues £8-£10 each)

68	Elektra EKL 4037	THE BIG HUGE (red label, also stereo EKS 74037)	15

(see also Robin Williamson, Mike Heron, Famous Jug Band, C.O.B., Shirley Collins)

IN CROWD (JAMAICA)
71	Spinning Wheel SW 105	Bush Jacket/Soul Face	25
78	Savannah SVN 12-1	Riding High/Version (12")	12
78	Cactus CT 111	Back A Yard/Yard (12")	18
78	Cactus CTLP 125	HIS MAJESTY IS COMING (LP)	25

IN CROWD (U.K.)
65	Parlophone R 5276	That's How Strong My Love Is/Things She Says	80
65	Parlophone R 5328	Stop! Wait A Minute/You're On Your Own	70
65	Parlophone R 5364	Why Must They Criticize?/I Don't Mind	60

(see also Tomorrow, Keith West, Steve Howe, Four + One)

INCROWD (U.K.)
69	Deram DM 272	Where In The World/I Can Make Love To You	15

INCUBUS
84	Guardian GRC 2165	TO THE DEVIL A DAUGHTER (LP)	18

PETER IND
61	Esquire 32 159	LOOKING OUT (LP)	120
68	Wave LP 3	IMPROVISATION (LP)	30
69	Wave LP 4	TIME FOR IMPROVISATION (LP)	30

INDECENT EXPOSURE

			MINT VALUE £
69	Wave LP 5	JAZZ AT THE RICHMOND FESTIVAL (LP, with Charlie Burchell, Bernie Cash & Derek Phillips)	30
70	Wave LP 20	COTRA-BACH (LP, with Bernard Cash)	30
74	Wave LP 29	NO KIDDING (LP, with Chas Burchell, Tox Drohar & Dave Cliff)	30

INDECENT EXPOSURE
| 84 | Index IS A1 | Riots (Single Version)/A Matter Of Time (no p/s) | 7 |

IN DEPTH PERCEPTION
| 93 | Lucky Spin GP 001 | Entropy/Rhizone (12") | 20 |

INDEX (1)
| 78 | Index INDY 001 | Jetlag/Total Bland (1st pressing, 500 only, push out centre, die cut stickered sleeve) | 30 |
| 78 | Index INDY 001 | Jetlag/Total Bland (2nd pressing, 500 only, solid centre, die cut sleeve) | 15 |

INDEX (2)
| 81 | Record Shack SHACK 128 | Starlight/Starlight (The Break) (12") | 40 |
| 81 | Record Shack SHACK 8 | Starlight/Starbright Instrumental Mix | 30 |

INDIAN SUMMER
| 71 | RCA Neon NE 3 | INDIAN SUMMER (LP, gatefold sleeve) | 250 |

(see also Badfinger)

INDIFFERENT DANCE CENTRE
| 81 | Recluse RECLUSE 1 | Flight & Pursuit/Release (p/s) | 25 |

INDO-BRITISH ENSEMBLE
| 69 | MFP 1307 | CURRIED JAZZ (LP) | 20 |

INDO JAZZMEN
| 68 | Saga FID 2145 | RAGAS AND REFLECTIONS (LP) | 15 |

INDUSTRIAL
| 92 | Kinetix KNT 007 | TIME TO ROCK EP (12") | 20 |

IN EMBRACE
82	Glass GLASS 019	THE INITIAL CARESS (12" EP)	15
82	Glass GLASS 024	Sun Brings Smiles/Play In Light (p/s)	8
83	Glass GLASS 030	Living Daylights/Blue Beach/Make (p/s)	6
82	Glass GLALP 001	PASSIONFRUIT PASTELS (LP)	18
83	Glass GLALP 004	TOO (LP)	15

INEPT
| 90 | Woodhouse | Experience/Roller Coaster (flexidisc) | 10 |

INERTIA (1)
| 80 | ERT 2 | DANCEBEAT ATTITUDE EP | 50 |

INEVITABLES
| 82 | Honk 1 | The Fourth Contender/The Puppeteer/Neutral News (p/s) | 25 |

INFANTES JUBILATE
| 68 | Music Factory CUB 5 | Exploding Galaxy/Take It Now | 60 |

INFA RIOT
81	Secret SHH 117	Kids Of The 80s/Still Out Of Order (p/s)	10
82	Secret SHH 133	The Winner/School's Out (p/s)	6
82	Secret SEC 7	STILL OUT OF ORDER (LP)	15
88	Link LINKLP 052	LIVE AND LOUD!! (LP)	15

(see also Infas)

INFAS
| 84 | Panache PAN 101 | Sound And Fury/Triffic Spiff Ya O.K. (p/s) | 8 |
| 84 | Panache PANLP 501 | SOUND AND FURY (LP) | 15 |

(see also Infa Riot)

INFERNAL BLUES MACHINE
| 76 | London SHU 8496 | ADIOS AMIGOS (LP) | 15 |

INFINITY PROJECT
89	Fabulous FABU 004	HYPERACTIVE (12" EP, sponged cover)	10
90	Fabulous FABU 005	UPHOLD THE LAW (12" EP)	10
95	Blue Room BRO005LP	MYSTICAL EXPERIENCES (2-LP)	35
95	TIP TIPLP 3	FEELING WEIRD (2-LP)	25

IN FLAMES
| 72 | Pama PM 842 | Rocket Man/I'm All Broke Up | 30 |

INFLUENCE
| 69 | Orange OAS 201 | I Want To Live/Driving Me Wild | 25 |

(see also John Miles, Geordie, Smokestack Crumble)

INFORMANTS
| 79 | Criminal SWAG 5 | My Radio/Grandpa (company sleeve) | 7 |

(see also Nirvana (U.K.))

INFORMATION
| 69 | Beacon BEA 121 | Orphan/Oh Strange Man | 30 |
| 70 | Evolution E 2461S | Lovely To See You/Face To The Sun | 20 |

INFRA RED HELICOPTERS
| 79 | 1979 | BRACKNELL (EP) | 25 |

RED INGLE
| 59 | Capitol EAP 20052 | CIGAREETS, WHUSKY AND WILD WILD WOMEN (EP) | 12 |

NICK INGMAN
| 75 | EMI EMI 2452 | American Pie/Brass Knuckles/Terminator | 10 |
| 75 | Studio Two TWOX 1045 | TERMINATOR (LP) | 40 |

JORGEN INGMANN
61	Fontana H 311	Cherokee/Anna	8
61	Fontana H 353	Hear My Song - Violetta/Pinetop's Boogie Woogie	6
62	Fontana 267 237 TF	Africa/Johnny's Tune	6
59	Pye Int. NPT 29000	GUITAR IN HI-FI (10" LP)	25

INGRAM
| 83 | Streetwave WAVE 3 | DJ's Delight/Smoothin Groovin (12") | 12 |

Luther INGRAM

MINT VALUE £

83	Streetwave WAVLP 001	WOULD YOU LIKE TO FLY (LP, with bonus 12")	40
83	Streetwave WAVLP 001	WOULD YOU LIKE TO FLY (LP, without bonus 12")	25

LUTHER INGRAM

70	Stax STAX 142	My Honey And Me/Puttin' Game Down	8
70	Stax STAX 148	Home Don't Seem Like A Home/Ain't That Lovin' You?	8
08	Kent Select CITY 007	Baby Don't You Weep/CHET POISON' IVY: Mata Hari	20
72	Koko KOS 2202	IF LOVING YOU IS WRONG I DON'T WANT TO BE RIGHT (LP, photo insert)	20

I 'N' I ONENESS MEETS UK PLAYERS

97	Jah Works JW 018S	Further/Further Into Dub (12")	20

INITIALS

64	London HLR 9860	School Day/Song Is Number One	18

AUTREY INMAN

63	Decca DFE 8571	AMERICAN COUNTRY JUBILEE NO. 1 (EP)	15

JOHN INMAN

75	DJM DJS 602	Are You Being Served, Sir?/We All Love Captain Ginger	6
75	DJM DJS 645	Teddy Bears Picnic/Sun Signs	6
75	DJM DJLPS 465	ARE YOU BEING SERVED SIR? (LP)	15

INMATE AND THE GENERAL

97	Groove Yard GYARD 15	OHMS EP (12")	30

INMATES

79	Soho SH 7	Dirty Water/Danger Zone (gatefold p/s)	8
79	Radar RAD 25	FIRST OFFENCE (LP)	15

INNER CIRCLE

74	Trojan TRO 9008	Duppy Gunman/None Shall Escape The Judgement	10
75	Trojan TR 7948	Road Block/Forward Jah Jah Children	10

INNER CIRCLE & FATMAN

00	Blood & Fire SVLP 293	HEAVY WEIGHT DUB KILLER DUB (2-LP)	20

INNER CITY BAND

78	Key KS 101	Happiness/Night At The Disco	25

INNER CITY EXPRESS

78	Ebony EYE 5	Fat On Funk/Sho' Dig Dancin' (12")	20

INNER CITY UNIT

79	Riddle RID 001/ICU 45	Solitary Ashtray/So Try As Id (Dub Version) (plain sleeve with colour insert)	8
79	Riddle RID 002	Paradise Beach/Amyl Nitrate (company die-cut sleeve)	8
81	Avatar AAA 113	Beer, Baccy, Bingo And Benidorm/In The Mood (Nude) (red vinyl, no p/s)	6
79	Riddle RID 002	PASS OUT (THE 360° PSYCHO DELERIA SOUND) (LP)	15

(see also Hawkwind, Sphynx, Radio Actors, Imperial Pompadours, Catherine Andrews, Big Amongst Sheep)

INNER LIFE

18	Salsoul SALSBMG12LP	INNER LIFE - THE STARS OF SALSOUL (2-LP)	20

INNER MIND

70	New Beat NB 067	Witchcraft Man/Night In Cairo	10
70	New Beat NB 069	Pum Pum Girl/Freedom	15
71	Bullet BU 465	Arawak Version/Cuffy Cuffy	10
71	Shades SHA 11	Dreams Of Yesterday/Never Over The Land	10
72	Shades SHA 12	Jesse James Hits Back/Let Me In	15

INNERSOULS

06	Funk 45 FUNK45 028	Just Take Your Time/Thoughts (reissue)	25

NEIL INNES

72	United Artists UP 35358	Slush/Rawlinson's End (different version from that on the Vivian Stanshall LP)	30
73	United Artists UP 35495	How Sweet To Be An Idiot/The Age Of Desperation	10
73	United Artists UP 35639	Momma B/Imoortal Invisible	7
74	United Artists UP 35676	Re-cycled Vinyl Blues/Fluff On The Needle	7
74	United Artists UP 35745	Lie Down And Be Counted/Bandwagon	7
75	United Artists UP 35772	What Noise Annoys An Oyster/Oo-Chuck-A-Mao-Mao	7
77	Arista ARISTA 106	Lady Mine/Crystal Balls	6
77	Arista ARISTA 123	Silver Jubilee (A Tribute)/Drama On A Saturday Night	6
78	Warner Bros K 17182	Protest Song/The Hard-To-Get	6
79	Polydor 2059 247	Kenny And Liza/Human Race	6
82	MMC MMC 100	Them/Rock Of Ages	6
82	MMC MMC 103	Mr. Eurovision/Ungawa	6
73	United Artists UAG 29287	HOW SWEET TO BE AN IDIOT (LP)	30
82	MMC MMC 001	OFF THE RECORD (2-LP)	30

(see also Grimms, Bonzo Dog [Doo Dah] Band, Rutles, World, Dirk & Stig, Group)

INN KEEPERS

71	Banana BA 328	Duppy Serenade/Sunshine Version (actually by Dennis Alcapone)	20

(see also WInston Matthews)

INNOCENCE

66	Kama Sutra KAS 203	There's Got To Be A Word!/I Don't Wanna Be Around You	8
66	Kama Sutra KAS 206	Mairzy Doats And Dozy Doats/Lifetime Of Lovin' You	8

INNOCENCE IN AFRICA

81	S/81/KUS 1205	Larger Than Life/Strangers Now (p/s)	25

INNOCENT BYSTANDERS

80	Rok ROK XVII/XVIII	Where Is Johnny?/DEBUTANTES: The Man In The Street (company sleeve)	6

INNOCENT VICARS

80	No Brain INV 001	She's Here/Antimatter (p/s, hand-stamped labels)	60

INNOCENTS (U.K.)

63	Columbia DB 7098	Stepping Stones/Grazina	15
63	Columbia DB 7173	A Fine, Fine Bird/Spanish Holiday	15
64	Columbia DB 7314	Stick With Me Baby/Not More Than Everything	10

(see also Mike Berry, Innocents & Leroys)

INNOCENTS (U.K.)
- 80   Kingdom KV 8010   One Way Love/Every Wednesday Night At Eight (p/s) 10

(see also Woodentops, Advertising, Secret Affair)

INNOCENTS (U.S.)
- 60   Top Rank JAR 508   Honest I Do/My Baby Hully Gullys 30
- 61   Top Rank JAR 541   Gee Whiz/Please Mr Sun 40

(see also Kathy Young)

INNOCENTS & LEROYS
- 64   Regal Zonophone RZ 502   HOT SIX: Don't Throw Your Love Away/My Girl Lollipop/I Love You Because/Not Fade Away/Tell Me When/I Believe (maxi-single, plain sleeve) 7

(see also Innocents [U.K.], Le-Roys)

INQUISITIVE PEOPLE
- 67   Decca F 12699   Big White Chief/Rhapsody Of Spring 10

INSANE
- 82   Insane INSANE 1   Why Die?/War And Violence (p/s) 15
- 82   Riot City RIOT 3   Politics/Dead And Gone/Last Day (p/s) 10
- 82   No Future OI 10   El Salvador/Nuclear War/Chinese Rock (p/s, with Rising Free Fanzine) 25

INSANE CLOWN POSSE
- 98   Island ISP 705   Hokus Pokus/Prom Queen (picture disc) 15

INSANE MACBETH
- 01   Insane 1203   True Heart (12") 10
- 00   Insane LP1   THE RETARDATION PROJECT (LP, 100 only) 100

(see also Kinetic Effect)

INSECT TRUST
- 69   Capitol E-(S)T 109   THE INSECT TRUST (LP) 80

INSERTS
- 80   Supermusic SUP 26   N.M.E/The Plague/Teenage Girls (with p/s) 35
- 80   Supermusic SUP 26   N.M.E/The Plague/Teenage Girls (without p/s) 25

INSEX
- 79   Dining Out TUX 3   Inner Sanction/Fractured (p/s) 12

INSIDE OV A COFFIN
- 98   Out-There OTT 1   Banking On Death (7", existence unconfirmed) 0

(see also Freed Unit)

INSIDERS
- 80   Satellite SATS 1002   Rollin' & Strollin'/She Had To Go (features Ray Dorset) 10

(see also Ray Dorset)

INSPIRAL CARPETS
- 80s   Own label   SONGS OF SHALLOW INTENSITY (p/s, demo) 20
- 80s   Own label   WAITING FOR OURS (p/s, demo) 20
- 80s   Own label   COW (p/s, demo) 20
- 88   Playtime AMUSE 2   Keep The Circle Around/Theme From Cow (p/s) 8
- 88   Playtime AMUSE 4   Butterfly/You Can't Take The Truth (unreleased, white label promos only) 10
- 88   Playtime AMUSE 4T   TRAIN SURFING (12" EP, unreleased, white label test pressings only) 10
- 88   Playtime AMUSE 2T   PLANE CRASH EP 20
- 87   Debris DEB 6   Garage Full Of Flowers/METRO TRINITY (flexi, 4000 pressed, free with Debris magazine) 10
- 92   Mute/Cow DUNG 19   REVENGE OF THE GOLDFISH (LP) 35
- 94   Mute/Cow LDUNG 25   DEVIL HOPPING (LP) 40
- 94   Mute/Cow LDUNG 25   DEVIL HOPPING (LP, with free red vinyl 10" EP) 60
- 95   Mute MOOTEL 3   THE SINGLES (2-LP, with free 7") 50
- 14   Cherry Red CRDUNG4   DUNG 4 (LP, 7", reissue) 30

INSPIRATION
- 73   Tavern STA 1004   Love Don't Grow On Trees/Dambusters March/Guitar Man/America 15

INSPIRATIONS (JAMAICA)
- 69   Camel CA 11   Down In The Park/Love Oh Love 80
- 69   Camel CA 21   Wonder Of Love/Cinderella 80
- 70   Amalgamated AMG 857   Take Back Your Duck/Nothing For Nothing 35
- 70   Amalgamated AMG 861   La La/Reggae Fever 35
- 70   Amalgamated AMG 862   The Train Is Coming/Man Oh Man 50
- 71   Upsetter US 355   Confusion/THE UPSETTERS: Confusion Version 40
- 70   Trojan TTL 27   REGGAE FEVER (LP) 50

(see also Untouchables, Niney)

INSPIRATIONS (U.S.)
- 67   Polydor 56730   Touch Me, Kiss Me, Hold Me/What Am I Gonna Do With You? 200

INSTANT AGONY
- 82   Half Man/Biscuit DUNK 1   Think Of England/Working Class Victim/News At Ten 10
- 83   Half Man/Biscuit DUNK 2   Fashion Parade/Anti Police/Dead End Kids 10

INSTANT AUTOMATONS
- 80   Deleted DEP 001   PETER PAINTS HIS FENCE EP (2x7", numbered, fold-out sleeve with inserts and stickers) .. 25

INSTANT FUNK
- 79   Salsoul SSLP 1511   I GOT MY MIND MADE UP (LP) 15

INSTITUTION
- 79   Industrial Accident SGS 112   Jane and John/Stephanie (500 only, hand stamped labels) 30

(see also Jazz Butcher)

INSYNC
- 92   Irdial Discs 27IRD INS 1   Storm/Warm (12") 50
- 93   Irdial Discs INS 2   UNTITLED EP (12", test pressings only) 150

INSYNC VS MYSTERON
- 95   Peacefrog PF 033   AUDIBLE ILLUSION EP (12", plain sleeve) 10
- 97   Fat Cat 12FAT 004   TALES FROM THE CRYPT (12", custom sleeve) 15

INTELLIGENT COMMUNICATION

MINT VALUE £

INTELLIGENT COMMUNICATION
91 Jumpin & Pumpin 12 TOT 15 PRINCIPLES OF MOTION (12" EP) 30
(see also Future Sound Of London)

INTENSE DEGREE
88 Strange Fruits SFPS 053 THE PEEL SESSIONS EP (12", p/s) 10
88 Earache MOSH 9 WAR IN MY HEAD (LP, with inner) 15

INTENSITY
73 Eden EDEN LP 68 TURN ABOUT INSIDE OUT PLASTIC COATED HUMANS (LP) 150

INTENSIVE CARE
87 Back To Back BTB 001 REBELS, ROCKETS AND RUBBERMEN (12", p/s) 12

INTENTIONS (U.S.)/Z.Z. HILL
66 Sue IEP 711 GIMME GIMME (EP, 2 tracks each by Intentions & Z.Z. Hill; 2 tracks mistakenly credited to Jackie Day on sleeve; in p/s) 300
66 Sue IEP 711 GIMME GIMME (EP, 2 tracks each by Intentions & Z.Z. Hill; 2 tracks mistakenly credited to Jackie Day on sleeve; no p/s) 100

INTERFACE
81 Blue Beat HIT 2358 Automaton/Electric Dreamland (p/s) 40

INTERGALACTIC TOURING BAND
77 Charisma CB 306 Love Station/Space Command 6

INTERNATIONAL CHRYSIS
94 PWL PWLT 303 Rebel Rebel (The Hole Mix)/Rebel Rebel (Extended Mix) (12", promo only) 15
(see also Dead Or Alive)

INTERNATIONAL PENPALS
03 Radical Wallpaper RADWAL 001 Day They Ate Ronald Reagan (p/s) 6

INTERNATIONAL SPARES
81 Spare KF 001 No Time At All/The Windmill 50

INTERNS (JAMAICA)
70 Jackpot JP 729 See You At Sunrise/LITTLE WONDER: Out Of Reach (B-side actually "Just Out Of Reach" by John Holt) 12
75 Attack ATT 8097 Nothing Is Impossible/HARDY BOYS: Black Out 20
79 Burning Rockers BR 1003 DETOUR (LP) 30
(see also Viceroys, Bob Marley & Wailers)

INTERNS (U.K.)
64 Philips BF 1320 Don't You Dare/Here There Everywhere 15
64 Philips BF 1345 Cry To Me/There's Love For You 15
66 Parlophone R 5479 Is It Really What You Want?/Just Like Me 50
67 Parlophone R 5586 Ray Of Sunshine/Please Say Something Nice 10
(see also Shadows)

INTERPOL
00 CHEM047CD fukd i.d #3 PDA/Precipitate/Roland/5 (CD, stickered card sleeve, 1,000 only) 80
02 Matador OLE 546-7 INTERPOL EP: PDA/Specialist 25
03 Matador OLE 582-7 Say Hello To The Angels/NYC (p/s) 6
07 Capitol/Parlophone CL 894 The Heinrich Maneuver/Concert Introduction (p/s) 6
07 Capitol/Parlophone CLS 894 The Heinrich Maneuver/Wrecking Ball (p/s) 8
02 Matador OLE 541 TURN ON THE BRIGHT LIGHTS (LP) 50
03 Black Sessions 1803 LIVE - BLACK SESSIONS (LP, red splatter vinyl) 30
04 Matador OLE 616-1 ANTICS (LP) 50
04 Matador (no. Cat. No) ANTICS (5 x 7" box set, only from Interpol Space Art Gallery, London) 40
05 Matador OLE 675 ANTICS - REMIXES (LP) 30
07 Capitol/Parlophone 0946 3 96248 1 OUR LOVE TO ADMIRE (2-LP) 50

INTERSTATE ROAD SHOW
69 President PT 249 Grindy Grind/All I Want To Do Is To Love You 8

INTESTINES
81 Alternative Capitalists AC51 Life In A Cardboard Box/New Recruit (p/s) 25

IN THE GYM
81 Taaga Records TAG 2 Playing The Fool/Don't Go Slow (no sleeve) 50

IN THE NURSERY
84 Paragon VIRTUE 5 Witness To A Scream/1984 (p/s) 15
85 New European BADVC 55 Sonority - A Strength (12" EP) 10
83 Paragon VIRTUE 2 WHEN CHERISHED DREAMS COME TRUE (mini-LP, silk-screened g/fold p/s) 25

IN THE WOODS...
96 Misanthropy OVL 69 White Rabbit/Mourning The Death Of Aase (p/s) 10
98 Misanthropy OVL 68 Let There Be More Light/Child Of Universal Tongue (p/s) 10
95 Misanthropy AMAZON 4 HEART OF THE AGES (LP, with booklet) 70
97 Misanthropy AMAZON 11 OMNIO (2-LP, gatefold sleeve, 1-sided etched disc) 50

INTIMATE OBSESSIONS
85 Third Mind TMLP 11 EREBUS TO HADES (LP) 15

INTIMATE STRANGERS
75 Alaska ALA 1005 Love Sounds/The Track 50

INTRA VEIN
79 Bum FP 001 Speed Of The City/Sick (printed PVC sleeve) 45
79 Bum FP 001 Speed Of The City/Sick (stamped plain sleeve) 35
(see also Veins)

INTRIGUE
82 Pressure PRESS D 1003 I Like It (Vocal)/I Like It (Instrumental) (12") 60
84 Project PR2 INT. UK Heaven Made/Ropes 6
84 Music Power MPR(T) 1 No Turning Back/Call Of The Heart (12") 25
86 Intrigue INT 12-001 One Touch/Touch Down (12") 15

INTRIGUES
69 London HL 10293 In A Moment/Scotchman Rock 10

INTRO

MINT VALUE £

INTRO
83   MCA MCA 794   Haunted Cocktails/Departure (p/s) 8

INTRODUCING DRAGONS
81   Zebra ZEBRA 3001   Via Media/Time Hangs (p/s) 20

INTROZE
82   Monarch MON 037   Doin' The Lambeth Walk/Kids In Uniform 50

INTRUDERS (1)
59   Top Rank JAR 158   Frankfurters And Sauerkraut/Creepin' 10

INTRUDERS (2)
66   London HL 10069   Up And Down The Ladder/United 40
69   Action ACT 4523   Slow Drag/So Glad I'm Yours 15
69   Ember EMB S 254   Cowboys To Girls/Turn Back The Hands Of Time 15
72   Ember EMB S 325   Cowboys To Girls/GOOD VIBRATIONS: Shake A Hand 7

IN2XS
81   XS IVE S81 CUS 1099   Cyberman/Amount To Nothing/In Khaki/Too Many 10

INVADERS (JAMAICA)
67   Columbia Bluebeat DB 105   Limbo Girl/Soul Of The Jungle 10
68   Columbia Bluebeat DB 109   Stop Teasing/Invaders At The Carnival 10
68   Studio One SO 2044   Soulful Music/SOUL VENDORS: Happy Organ 200
71   G.G. GG 4527   Got To Go Home/PAULETTE & GEE: How Long Will You Stay? 7

INVESTIGATORS
80   Inner City 104   Baby I'm Yours/I Want Your Love (12") 10

INVICTAS
64   United Artists UP 1013 Green Bow Tie/Touch Of Orchid 7

INVISIBLE MAN
92   Timeless DJ 005   On A Mission/Twisted/Intro (Think About It)/ The End (Drug Induced Psychosis
                             Mix)/Bonus Turbo Cut (12") 30
93   Timeless DJ 006   The Beginning/The End (12") 20
93   Timeless DJ 007   Skyliner/Power (12") 20
93   Timeless DJ 008   Skyliner (Remix)/MYSTERON: U Don't Know (12") 20
95   Timeless DJ 010   Skyliner (Top Buzz's 95 VIP Mix)/The Beginning (Innerspace Remix) (12") 10

INVITATIONS (JAMAICA)
71   Crab CRAB 66   Birmingham Cat/Now You're On Your Own 20

INVITATIONS (U.S.)
65   Stateside SS 453   Hallelujah/Written On The Wall 50
65   Stateside SS 478   What's Wrong With My Baby?/Why Did My Baby Turn Bad? 150
65   Stateside SS 478   What's Wrong With My Baby?/Why Did My Baby Turn Bad? (DJ copy) 300
70   Jay Boy BOY 24   How'd We Ever Get This Way?/Picking Up 35
72   Mojo 2092 055   What's Wrong With My Baby?/Why Did My Baby Turn Bad? (reissue) 8
74   Polydor 2066 366   Let's Love (And Find Together)/Love Has To Grow 10

INVOGUE
82   Street Life S 82 CUS 1474   EXPRESSIONS OF YOUTH EP 50

INXS
87   Mercury MERH 114   KICK (LP, gatefold) 15
94   Mercury 526 230-1   THE GREATEST HITS (2-LP) 40

IONA
78   Silver Scales   CUCKOO (LP) 35
70s   Celtic Music CM 001   IONA (LP) 35

I.O.W. CHEROKEES
66   69 69EP 001   I.O.W. CHEROKEES (EP, private pressing) 40

I.P.O.H
73   Pye 7N 45215   Caveman Billy/Doggy 8
75   CBS 3408   In Pursuit Of Happiness/Spearhead 7

IPSISSIMUS
69   Parlophone R 5774   Hold On/Lazy Woman 70

IPSO FACTO
84   IF IF 7 84   Noir Dior/Craving 15
84   IF IF 8 84   LIFE IS A CABARET - IS IT? (12" EP) 10

IQ
84   Jim White/IQ PROMO 101 Awake And Nervous/Through The Corridors (12", no p/s, 500 only) 30
84   IQFREEB 1   Hollow Afternoon (1-sided, Marquee gig freebie) 30
86   STAL Other Boxer 1   Nomzamo (Demo) (1-sided fan club single) 18
86   Sahara IQSD 1   It All Stops Here/Intelligence Quotient (shaped picture disc) 18
87   RLOG Another Boxer 1   Fascination/The Bold Grenadier Pt. 1 (fan club single) 18
88   RLOG One More Boxer 1 A Different Magic Roundabout (Honest!)/The Big Balls Of Bert Christ (fan club single) 12
85   STAL BOXER 1   NINE IN A POND IS HERE (2-LP, 1,000 copies only) 20

(see also Niadem's Ghost)

IQ PROCEDURE (ROOTS MANUVA)
94   Bluntly Speaking PHAT2 Run Tings/Can U Get With This/Big Up (12") 10

IQ ZERO
79   Object Music OM 9   (Everybody Kills) Insects/Electromotion/Quirky Pop Music (p/s) 20
80   Phony Gram SRTS/80/CUS 623   She's So Rare/Crazy Dolls 25
79   Logo GO 374   She's So Rare/Crazy Dolls (p/s) 15

IRATION STEPPAS
94   Iration Steppa BS 159 Scud Missile/High Rise Vibrations (12") 35
95   Iration Steppa IS 003 Kilimanjaro/High Altitude Mix/Summit Mix (10") 80
03   Tandori Space TS 012   Too Much War/Stop The War Dub/What's Wrong/What's Wrong Dub (10") 25

(see also Dubkasm)

IRATION STEPPAS & TENA STELIN
01   Tandori Space TSR 001 War Inna Babylon/Dub Version 20

David IRELAND

			MINT VALUE £
01	Tandori Space TSR 002	Jungle Jungle/Dub Version	20

(see also Tena Stelin)

DAVID IRELAND
| 73 | Sovereign SOV 120 | Shoot The Family Man/Coming Up Strong | 15 |

CLEMENT IRIE
| 88 | Blue Mountain BMD 039 | Follow Me/SENYA: Trying Woman (12") | 12 |

IRINI
| 95 | Here It Is HIILP 023 | DON'T MAKE ME WISH (LP) | 15 |

IRONBELLY
| 70 | Parlophone R5864 | Woha! Buck/Wild About My Loving | 10 |

IRON BUTTERFLY
68	Atco 2091 024	In-A-Gadda-Da-Vida/Termination (first pressing with Atco label and Polydor Records Limited type)	20
68	Atlantic 584 188	Possession/Unconscious Power	15
69	Atlantic 584 254	Soul Experience/In The Crowds	12
70	Atlantic 2091 024	In-A-Gadda-Da-Vida/Termination	12
68	Atco 2465 015	HEAVY (LP)	25
68	Atlantic 587/588 116	IN-A-GADDA-DA-VIDA (LP)	80
69	Atco 228 011	BALL (LP, gatefold sleeve)	25
70	Atlantic 2400 014	LIVE (LP)	18
71	Atlantic 2401 003	METAMORPHOSIS (LP)	50

(see also Ramatam, Captain Beyond)

IRON CROSS
| 72 | Spark SRL 1079 | Little Bit Of Soul/Sunshine | 6 |
| 74 | Spark 1112 | Everybody Rock On/All The Time | 20 |

IRON HORSE
| 71 | Bell BLL1148 | The Obeah Man/Magic Love | 20 |

IRON MAIDEN (1)
| 70 | Gemini GMS 006 | Falling/Ned Kelly | 45 |

IRON MAIDEN (2)
SINGLES
80	EMI EMI 5032	Running Free/Burning Ambition (p/s)	25
80	EMI EMI 5065	Sanctuary/Drifter (live)/I've Got The Fire (live) (uncensored p/s)	45
80	EMI EMI 5065	Sanctuary/Drifter (live)/I've Got The Fire (live) (censored p/s)	15
80	EMI EMI 5105	Women In Uniform/Invasion (p/s)	18
80	EMI 12EMI 5105	Women In Uniform/Phantom Of The Opera (live)/Invasion (12", p/s)	15
81	EMI EMI 5145	Twilight Zone/Wrathchild (p/s)	15
81	EMI EMI 5145	Twilight Zone/Wrathchild (p/s, clear vinyl)	25
81	EMI EMI 5145	Twilight Zone/Wrathchild (p/s, red vinyl)	30
81	EMI EMI 5145	Twilight Zone/Wrathchild (p/s, brown vinyl mispressing)	800
81	EMI TCEMI 5145	Twilight Zone/Wrathchild	8
81	EMI EMI 5184	Purgatory/Genghis Khan (p/s)	35
82	EMI EMI 5263	Run To The Hills/Total Eclipse (p/s)	6
82	EMI EMIP 5263	Run To The Hills/Total Eclipse (picture disc, mispressed, b-side picture both sides)	30
82	EMI EMI 5263	Run To The Hills/Total Eclipse (picture disc)	20
82	EMI EMI 5287	The Number Of The Beast/Remember Tomorrow (live) (p/s, red vinyl)	12
83	EMI EMI 5378	Flight Of Icarus/I've Got The Fire (p/s)	8
83	EMI 12EMIP 5378	Flight Of Icarus/I've Got The Fire (12", picture disc)	20
83	EMI EMIP 5397	The Trooper/Cross-Eyed Mary (soldier-shaped picture disc)	25
83	EMI EMIP 5397	The Trooper/Cross-Eyed Mary (uncut shaped picture disc)	800
84	EMI 12EMI 5489	2 Minutes To Midnight/Rainbow's Gold/Mission From 'Arry (12", picture disc)	15
84	EMI EMI 5502	Aces High/King Of Twilight (p/s)	8
84	EMI EMI 5502	Aces High/King Of Twilight (mispress, A side label on both sides)	10
84	EMI 12EMIP 5502	Aces High/King Of Twilight/The Number Of The Beast (live) (12", picture disc)	20
85	EMI EMI 5532	Running Free (live)/Sanctuary (live) (poster p/s)	7
85	EMI 12EMIP 5532	Running Free (live)/Sanctuary (live)/Murders In The Rue Morgue (live) (12", picture disc)	20
85	EMI EMI 5542	Run To The Hills (live)/Phantom Of The Opera (live) (with Xmas card)	8
85	EMI 12EMIP 5542	Run To The Hills (live)/Phantom Of The Opera (live)/Losfer Words (The Big 'Orra) (live) (12", picture disc)	20
86	EMI EMIP 5583	Wasted Years/Reach Out (computer-shaped picture disc)	20
86	EMI EMIP 5583	Wasted Years/Reach Out (uncut computer-shaped picture disc)	1000
86	EMI EMI 5589	Stranger In A Strange Land/That Girl (foldout poster p/s)	6
86	EMI 12EMIP 5589	Stranger In A Strange Land/That Girl/Juanita (12", picture disc)	18
88	EMI EMP 49	Can I Play With Madness/Black Bart Blues (shaped picture disc)	18
88	EMI EMP 49	Can I Play With Madness/Black Bart Blues (uncut shaped picture disc)	400
88	EMI EMP 64	The Evil That Men Do/Prowler '88 (uncut shaped picture disc)	200
88	EMI EMS 79	The Clairvoyant (live)/The Prisoner (live) (clear vinyl, poster p/s)	6
88	EMI EMP 79	The Clairvoyant (live)/The Prisoner (live) (shaped picture disc)	15
88	EMI EMP 79	The Clairvoyant (live)/The Prisoner (live) (uncut shaped picture disc)	200
89	EMI EMPD 117	Infinite Dreams (live)/Killers (live) (uncut shaped picture disc)	200
90	EMI EMS 171	Bring Your Daughter ... To The Slaughter/I'm A Mover (1-sided etched, p/s)	6
90	EMI 12EMP 171	Bring Your Daughter ... To The Slaughter/I'm A Mover (12", calendar pack)	10
90	EMI CDEM 171	Bring Your Daughter...To The Slaughter/I'm A Mover (UK pressed CD single)	100
92	EMI EMPD 240	From Here To Eternity/I Can't See My Feeling (uncut shaped picture disc)	150
92	EMI EMP 263	Fear Of The Dark (live)/Tailgunner (live) (poster p/s)	8
92	EMI EMPD 263	Fear Of The Dark (live)/Hooks In You (live) (uncut shaped picture disc)	150
92	EMI EMPD 263	Fear Of The Dark (live)/Hooks In You (live) (shaped picture disc, with mispressed B-side "Tailgunner" [live])	18
95	EMI 12EM 398	Man On The Edge/I Live My Way (12", picture disc, with poster, die-cut sleeve)	15

IRON MAIDEN (2)

MINT VALUE £

Year	Cat. No.	Title	Value
95	EMI CDMAN 2	Man On The Edge/The Edge Of Darkness/Sign Of The Cross (CD)	50
98	EMI EM 507	The Angel And The Gambler/Blood On The World's Hands (Live) (picture disc)	15
98	EMI 8860690	Futureal/ The Evil That Men Do(live)/ Man On The Edge(live)/ The Angel And The Gambler (video) (CD digi-pack Fan Club only issue with poster)	50
00	EMI EM 576	Out Of The Silent Planet/Aces High (live) (red vinyl, p/s insert)	6
02	EMI EM 612	Run To The Hills/Total Eclipse (live) (red vinyl, p/s)	6
03	EMI EM 627	Wildest Dreams/Pass The Jam (green vinyl, stickered p/s)	8
03	EMI EM 633	Rainmaker/Dance Of Death (Orchestral version) (blue vinyl, stickered p/s)	6
05	EMI EM 662	The Trooper (live)/Another Life (live) (p/s, poster, blue vinyl)	7
05	EMI 666A	The Number Of The Beast/The Number Of The Beast (live at Brixton) (red vinyl, p/s, poster)	7
06	EMI EM 714	Different World/Fear Of The Dark (Live 2006) (Picture disc, insert in stickered PVC sleeve)	8

SINGLES : PROMOS

Year	Cat. No.	Title	Value
80	EMI EMI 5032 DJ	Running Free (One-sided 7" DJ copy)	50
80	EMI EMI 5065	Sanctuary/Drifter (live)/I've Got The Fire (live) (DJ copy, censored p/s)	50
90	EMI EMDJ 153	Holy Smoke (1-sided 7" DJ copy, radio edit, censored)	50
90	EMI 12EMP 153	Holy Smoke/All In Your Mind/Kill Me Ce Soir (12", gold vinyl test pressing, promo only)	150
90	EMI EM 171	Bring Your Daughter ... To The Slaughter/I'm A Mover (Clear or white vinyl Test pressing for 12" picture disc)	100
90	EMI (no cat. no.)	NO PRAYER FOR THE DYING (CD, with interview , photos & bio, promo only)	100
92	EMI (no cat. No.)	FEAR OF THE DARK (CD, interview , EPK video, colour booklet, A4 poster in luminous flip top box)	150
95	EMI CDMAN 1	Man On The Edge (CD 1-track promo, slim jewel case)	12
96	EMI BEST 001	BEST OF THE BEAST (CD, Steve Harris interview disc, commercial CD, video, in 40cm x 30cm, flip-up 3D presentation box with 60-page book, 2 photographs, biography, promo only)	200
97	EMI CDINPROF 001	In Profile (CD, 31 track edit band history picture disc custom sleeve)	35
98	EMI CDONPROF 001	IN PROFILE (CD)	30
98	EMI HELLROM001	Maiden Hell promotional CD-Rom in full colour custom card sleeve	25
99	EMI EDHUNTER 666	ED HUNTER DEMO (CD-Rom, card p/s with booklet, press info and photo)	40
00	EMI no cat. no.	Tommy Vance Previews: The Wicker Man/Ghost Of The Navigator/ Brave New World/ Dream Of Mirrors/ The Nomad (CD-R with Thomas The Vance intros)	50
02	EMI RIOINTCD 001	ROCK IN RIO (Promo interview CD, with colour booklet)	50
02	EMI CDSP255	EDDIE'S ARCHIVE (CD, 8 track sampler in card sleeve)	50
04	BMG PUB049	Int Iron Maiden 10 track promo CD in custom sleeve	50

EPs

Year	Cat. No.	Title	Value
79	EMI EMCP 3400	THE SOUNDHOUSE TAPES (EP mispressing with labels on wrong sides, Matrix numbers ROK-1A SA LYN 7627-1T/ROK-1B EG SA LYN 7628-1T, p/s)	800
79	Rock Hard ROK 1	THE SOUNDHOUSE TAPES (EP, p/s; Matrix ROK-1A EG SA LYN 7627-1T/ ROK-1B EG SA LYN 7628-1T. counterfeits have slightly glossier sleeves. Any with different p/s and coloured vinyl are also counterfeit)	700
81	EMI 12EMI 5219	MAIDEN JAPAN EP (12" EP, p/s)	15

ALBUMS

Year	Cat. No.	Title	Value
80	EMI EMC 3330	IRON MAIDEN (LP, with poster)	40
80	EMI EMC 3330	IRON MAIDEN (LP, without poster)	25
81	EMI EMC 3357	KILLERS (LP)	30
82	EMI EMC 3400	NUMBER OF THE BEAST (LP, inner and Iron Maiden fan club flyer)	25
82	EMI EMCP 3400	THE NUMBER OF THE BEAST (LP, picture disc, with inner)	40
83	EMI EMA 800	PIECE OF MIND (LP, gatefold, black card inner)	25
84	EMI EJ 2402001	POWERSLAVE (LP, textured sleeve, inner)	25
84	EMI POWERP 1	POWERSLAVE (LP, picture disc)	40
85	EMI ES 24 0426 3	LIVE AFTER DEATH (2-LP, gatefold, inners & booklet)	30
86	EMI EMC 3512	SOMEWHERE IN TIME (LP, inner)	35
88	EMI EMD 1006	SEVENTH SON OF A SEVENTH SON (LP, inner)	30
88	EMI EMDP 1006	SEVENTH SON OF A SEVENTH SON (LP, picture disc, with banner)	35
90	EMI EMD 1017	NO PRAYER FOR THE DYING (LP, inner)	25
90	EMI EMPD 1017	NO PRAYER FOR THE DYING (LP, picture disc, die cut sleeve)	35
90	EMI (no cat. no.)	THE FIRST TEN YEARS - UP THE IRONS (10 x 12" double packs, box set available by mail order with tokens from records)	175
90	EMI (no cat. no.)	THE FIRST TEN YEARS - UP THE IRONS (10 x CD, box set available by mail order with tokens from CDs)	100
92	EMI EMD 1032	FEAR OF THE DARK (2-LP with merchandise leaflet)	100
93	EMI DON 1	LIVE AT DONINGTON (3-LP, numbered)	200
93	EMI EMD 1042	A REAL LIVE ONE (LP, gatefold sleeve with inner sleeve)	200
93	EMI EMD 1048	A REAL DEAD ONE (LP, gatefold sleeve and inner sleeve)	200
95	EMI 724383581917	THE X FACTOR (2-LP, clear vinyl, gatefold with poster)	200
96	EMI (no cat. No.)	THE STORY SO FAR PART 1 (5xCD box set, 1000 copies only)	300
96	EMI (no cat. No.)	THE STORY SO FAR PART 2 (5xCD box set, 1000 copies only)	300
96	EMI EMDX 1097	BEST OF THE BEAST (4-LP box set, with inners, book and bonus tracks)	350
97	EMI LPCENT 35	IRON MAIDEN (LP, reissue, EMI centenary, stickered sleeve)	30
97	EMI LPCENT 7	THE NUMBER OF THE BEAST (LP, reissue, 180gm vinyl)	35
98	EMI LPCENT 35	IRON MAIDEN (LP, reissue, 180gm vinyl)	30
98	EMI 4979990	EDDIE'S HEAD (13 CD boxset, plastic skull with flashing eyes)	175
98	EMI 4939151	VIRTUAL XI (2-LP gatefold, with inner sleeves)	250
00	EMI 526 6051	BRAVE NEW WORLD (2-LP, picture disc, gatefold, inner sleeves)	200
02	EMI 538 64316	ROCK IN RIO (3-LP, picture discs, trifold sleeve)	80
02	EMI 544 2772	EDDIE'S ARCHIVE (6-CD, tin box with insert, shot glass, pewter ring and Parchment. 1st issue blue lining)	100
02	EMI 544 2772	EDDIE'S ARCHIVE (6-CD, tin box with insert, shot glass, pewter ring and Parchment. 2nd issue red lining)	80

IRON VIRGIN

			MINT VALUE £
03	EMI 592 3401	DANCE OF DEATH (2-LP, picture disc, gatefold sleeve and inner sleeves)	125
05	EMI 336 4371	DEATH ON THE ROAD (2-LP, picture disc gatefold)	40
06	EMI 372 3211	A MATTER OF LIFE AND DEATH (2-LP, picture disc, gatefold, inner sleeves)	60
10	EMI 50999 64777016	THE FINAL FRONTIER (2-LP, picture disc)	80
12	EMI 50999 301587 1 9	EN VIVO! (2-LP, picture disc)	40
12	EMI 5099941648001	PICTURE DISC COLLECTION 1980 - 1988 (10-LP box set)	300
14	Parlophone 2564622290	THE COMPLETE ALBUMS COLLECTION 1980 - 1988 (box set, only contains Iron Maiden, Killers and The Number Of The Beast with space for 5 additional reissues. This price for original box that was manufactured too small to hold all the LPs)	70
14	Parlophone 2564622290	THE COMPLETE ALBUMS COLLECTION 1980 - 1988 (box set, only contains Iron Maiden, Killers and The Number Of The Beast with space for 5 additional reissues. This price for 'replacement' box that was manufactured the right size to hold all the LPs)	50
15	Parlophone 0825646089208	THE BOOK OF SOULS (3-LP)	50
17	Parlophone 0190295760878	THE BOOK OF SOULS: LIVE CHAPTER (3-LP)	35
17	Parlophone 0190295849498	THE COMPLETE ALBUMS COLLECTION 1990 - 2015 (Box set, only contains No Prayer For The Dying and Fear Of The Dark with additional space left for subsequent reissues)	30
20	Parlophone 0190295163037	NIGHTS OF THE DEAD, LEGACY OF THE BEAST: LIVE IN MEXICO CITY (3-LP, red, white and green vinyl)	30

(see also Bruce Dickinson, Di'Anno, Gogmagog, Samson, Urchin, Xero, Lionheart, Pat Travers, Stratus, Nicko McBrain, Money, White Spirit, McEnroe & Cash, Speed)

IRON VIRGIN
74	Deram DM 408	Jet/Midnight Hitcher	15
74	Deram DM 416	Rebels Rule/Ain't No Clown	25

NEVILLE IRONS
68	Blue Cat BS 104	Soul Glide/DYNAMICS: My Friends	45

(see also Neville Hinds)

IRRESTIBLE FORCE
92	Rising High RSNLP 5	FLYING HIGH (2-LP)	60
94	Rising High RSN LP 24	GLOBAL CHILLAGE (2-LP)	40
98	Ninja Tune ZEN 28	IT'S TOMORROW ALREADY (2-LP)	25

ANDY IRVINE
80	Tara 3002	RAINY SUNDAYS, WINDY DREAMS (LP, lyric insert)	15

ANDY IRVINE & PAUL BRADY
76	Mulligan LUN 008	ANDY IRVINE & PAUL BRADY (LP)	30

(see also Dr. Strangely Strange)

WELDON IRVINE
96	Hubbub HUB 12 LP	LIBERATED BROTHER (LP, reissue)	20
96	Hubbub HUB 13 LP	TIME CAPSULE (LP, reissue)	35

LONNIE IRVING
60	Melodisc MEL 1546	Pinball Machine/I Got Blues On My Mind	40

IRVING 6
70s	Port O Jam PJ4116	Ossie's Special/Trouble	20

(BIG) DEE IRWIN
64	Stateside SS 261	Donkey Walk/Someday You'll Understand Why	10
64	Colpix PX 11040	Heigh-ho/It's My Birthday	8
64	Colpix PX 11050	Personality/It's Only A Paper Moon	8
65	Stateside SS 450	You Satisfy My Needs/I Wanna Stay Right Here With You	125
65	Stateside SS 450	You Satisfy My Needs/I Wanna Stay Right Here With You (DJ copy)	200
68	Minit MLF 11013	I Can't Stand The Pain/My Hope To Die Girl (as Dee Irwin)	15

BIG DEE IRWIN & LITTLE EVA
63	Colpix PXE 301	SWINGING ON A STAR (EP)	20
70	Golden Guinea GSGL 10497	SWINGING ON A STAR (LP)	15

(see also Little Eva, Suzi & Big Dee Irwin)

DAVID ISAACS
66	Island WI 261	I'd Rather Be Lonely/See That Man	80
68	Trojan TR 616	Place In The Sun/UPSETTER ALL STARS: Handy-Cap	50
69	Upsetter US 302	Good Father/SLIM SMITH: What A Situation	40
69	Upsetter US 305	I've Got Memories/I'm Leaving	30
69	Upsetter US 311	He'll Have To Go/Since You're Gone	40
69	Upsetter US 319	Who To Tell/BUSTY BROWN: I Can't See Myself Cry	35
69	Punch PH 6	I Can't Take It Anymore/LLOYD DOUGLAS: Anyway	15
71	Punch PH 84	You'll Be Sorry/Knock Three Times	12
71	Bullet BU 459	Just Enough/ROY PATIN: Standing (B-side actually by Roy Panton)	35
71	Tropical AL 006	Love Has Join Us/MAX ROMEO: Cross Over The Bridge (correct title for A-side is 'Love Has Joined Us')	8
73	Upsetter US 400	Stranger On The Shore/DILLINGER: John Devour	70
73	Bread BR 1118	Just Enough/We Are Neighbours	30
79	Attack TACK 13	Just Like A Sea (with Jah Thomas)/WITTY'S ALL STARS: Just Like A Sea (Version) (12")	18

(see also Upsetters)

GREGORY ISAACS
70	Escort ERT 833	While There Is Life/HARRY YOUNG: Come On Over	15
70	Success RE 914	Too Late/KINGSTONIANS: You Can't Wine	25
70	Bullet BU 448	Set Back/SYDNEY'S ALLSTARS: Version II	30
71	Big Shot BI 584	Lonely Man/RUPIE EDWARDS ALL STARS: Lonely Man Version	12
73	Green Door GD 4054	Lonely Soldier/IMPACT ALL STARS: Version	12
74	Pyramid PYR 7012	Innocent People Cry/Version	8
74	Attack ATT 8066	Love Is Overdue Part 1/Love Is Overdue Part 2	8
74	Attack ATT 8081	Don't Go/Dubwise	10
74	Stop Points DL 0022	End Of The World/Gregory Shuffle	10
75	Black Wax WAX 9	Sunshine For Me/Version	12
75	Attack ATT 8095	Bad Da/Ad Dab	8
75	Attack ATT 8106	Fly Little Silver Bird/Dub	8

IKE ISAACS

MINT VALUE £

75	Camel CA 2008	Lonely Days/Version	8
75	Bullet BU 555	Lonely Days/Version	8
75	Torpedo TOR 34	Tomorrow's Sun (May Never Shine)/Way Of Life	20
75	Torpedo TOR 50	Help Up Get Over/All I Have Is Love	20
76	Morpheus MOR 1018	Extra Classic/Version	12
76	Third World TW 032	Look Before You Leap/K. SMILEY: Sata	20
76	Morpheus MOR 1016	Rasta Business/Version	15
76	Morpheus MOR 1017	Black Kill A Black/Version	15
77	Golden Age GAM 05	Mr. Cop/Mr. Cop Dub	15
77	Observer OBMM-1000	Soul On Fire/CHRISTINE: Saturday Night/TYRONE TAYLOR: Sufferation/ In Style (12")	40
77	GGs GG 040	The Border/Out Of Rome (12", with U BROWN)	15
78	Observer	Rock On/Murder Observer Style/DENNIS BROWN & DILLINGER: Jah Is Watching/ Hustling (12")	50
78	DEB DEB 004	Mr Know It All/OSSIE HIBBERT & REVOLUTIONARIES: War Of The Stars (12")	25
78	Hawkeye HE 008	John Public/LEGGO ALL STARS: Enemy No 1	8
78	Star PTP 1002	Lonely Days/U ROY: Nanny Skank (12")	15
79	Front Line FLS 12112	Soon Forward/Uncle Joe/Come Off Mi Toe (Feat. Prince Far I) (12")	15
79	Niagra NIADD 104	Going Down Town/Motherless Children (12")	20
80	Pre PRE 8	Poor And Clean/Tribute To Waddy	10
80	African Museum (no number)	If You See My Mary/Mary's Special (12", blue vinyl)	20
80	Solomonic SM 002	Sunday Morning/DENNIS BROWN: Running Around (12")	25
84	Fu Manchu PC 15484	No One But Me/Version (12", p/s)	15
85	African Museum AF 0050	G.P./Version (12")	25
86	Greensleeves GRED 230	Mind Ju Dis/Version (12")	18
88	Greensleeves GRED 221	Rumours/More Rumours (12")	30
88	Greensleeves GRED 225	Rough Neck/Version (12" with the Mighty Diamonds)	30
89	Jah Shaka SHAKA 874	Just Infatuation/Just Dub (12")	15
89	Greensleeves GRED 256	Report To Me/Report To Me (continued) (12")	30
75	Trojan TRLS 102	IN PERSON (LP)	15
76	Trojan TRLS 121	ALL I HAVE IS LOVE (LP)	20
78	Conflict COLP 2002	EXTRA CLASSIC (LP)	20
78	Burning Sounds BS1010	SLUM - GREGORY ISAACS IN DUB (LP)	30
78	DEB DEB LP 04	MR ISAACS (LP)	30
78	Virgin Front Line FL 1020	COOL RULER (LP)	18
79	Virgin Front Line FL 1044	SOON FORWARD (LP)	30
80	Shack BITE 200	EXTRA CLASSIC (LP, reissue)	20
82	Island 9721	NIGHT NURSE (LP, blue vinyl with poster)	20
83	Burning Sounds BS 1051	SLUM DUB (LP)	25
83	Pre PREX 1	THE LONELY LOVER (LP)	20

(see also Tony Brevett)

IKE ISAACS
68	Morgan MR 116P	I LIKE IKE (LP)	15

ISCA FAYRE
76	Candle CAN 761	THEN AROUND ME YOUNG AND OLD (LP)	15

ISH
79	TKS TKR 7540	Faster Than A Speeding Bullet/Don't Stop	6

JON ISHERWOOD
70	Decca LK/SKL 5051	A LAUGHING CRY (LP)	15

ISHMAEL UNITED
79	Kingsway 5NIL	Song Of The Last Generation/Crowd Trouble	20

ISHMAEL & ANDY
73	Myrrh MYR 1005	READY SALTED (LP)	20

ISLANDERS (1)
59	Top Rank JAR 215	The Enchanted Sea/Pollyanna	8
60	Top Rank JAR 305	Blue Train/Tornado	6

ISLANDERS (2)
65	Fontana TF 577	It Ain't Me Babe/Four Strong Winds	10

JIMMY ISLE
59	London HLS 8832	Diamond Ring/I've Been Waiting (78)	70
59	London HLS 8832	Diamond Ring/I've Been Waiting (tri centre)	20
60	Top Rank JAR 274	Billy Boy/Oh Judy	15

ISLEY BROTHERS
59	RCA RCA 1149	Shout (Parts 1 & 2) (tri centre)	30
59	RCA RCA 1149	Shout (Parts 1 & 2) (round centre)	25
59	RCA RCA 1149	Shout (Parts 1 & 2) (78)	200
60	RCA RCA 1172	Respectable/I'm Gonna Knock On Your Door	20
60	RCA RCA 1190	How Deep Is The Ocean/He's Got The Whole World In His Hands	20
60	RCA RCA 1213	Tell Me Who/Say You Love Me Too	20
62	Stateside SS 112	Twist And Shout/Spanish Twist	15
62	Stateside SS 132	Twistin' With Linda/You Better Come Home	15
63	Stateside SS 218	Nobody But Me/I'm Laughing To Keep From Crying	20
63	United Artists UP 1034	Tango/She's Gone	18
64	United Artists UP 1050	Shake It With Me Baby/Stagger Lee	20
64	Atlantic AT 4010	The Last Girl/Looking For A Love	45
66	Tamla Motown TMG 555	This Old Heart Of Mine (Is Weak For You)/There's No Love Left (1st press with narrow print on label)	20
66	Tamla Motown TMG 555	This Old Heart Of Mine (Is Weak For You)/There's No Love Left (2nd re-press - 1968 - with wider print)	10
66	Tamla Motown TMG 566	Take Some Time Out For Love/Who Could Ever Doubt My Love	35
66	Tamla Motown TMG 572	I Guess I'll Always Love You/I Hear A Symphony (1st pressing with "sold subject to" on	25

ISOLATION

MINT VALUE £

		centre piece)	
67	Tamla Motown TMG 606	Got To Have You Back/Just Ain't Enough Love	25
68	Tamla Motown TMG 652	Take Me In Your Arms (Rock Me A Little While)/Why When Love Is Gone	30
69	Tamla Motown TMG 683	I Guess I'll Always Love You/It's Out Of The Question	8
69	Tamla Motown TMG 693	Behind A Painted Smile/One Too Many Heartaches	7
69	Major Minor MM 621	It's Your Thing/Don't Give It Away	10
69	Tamla Motown TMG 708	Put Yourself In My Place/Little Miss Sweetness	7
69	Major Minor MM 631	I Turned You On/I Know Who You Been Socking It To	6
69	Tamla Motown TMG 719	Take Some Time Out For Love/Who Could Ever Doubt My Love (reissue)	7
70	Stateside SS 2162	Was It Good To You?/I Got To Get Myself Together	6
71	Stateside SS 2188	Warpath/I Got To Find Me One	6
71	Stateside SS 2193	Love The One You're With/He's Got Your Love	10
73	Tamla Motown TMG 877	Tell Me It's Just A Rumour, Baby/Save Me From This Misery	8
79	RCA PC 9411	Shout/Respectable/Tell Me Who (12", p/s)	10
64	RCA RCX 7149	THE ISLEY BROTHERS (EP)	80
60	RCA RD 27165	SHOUT (LP, mono)	60
60	RCA SF 7055	SHOUT (LP, stereo)	100
64	United Artists ULP 1064	THE FAMOUS ISLEY BROTHERS - TWISTING AND SHOUTING (LP)	80
66	Tamla Motown TML 11034	THIS OLD HEART OF MINE (IS WEAK FOR YOU) (LP, mono)	30
66	STML 11034	THIS OLD HEART OF MINE (IS WEAK FOR YOU) (LP, stereo)	35
68	T. Motown TML 11066	SOUL ON THE ROCKS (LP, mono)	30
68	T. Motown STML 11066	SOUL ON THE ROCKS (LP, stereo)	35
69	Major Minor SMLP 59	IT'S OUR THING (LP)	25
69	T. Motown TML 11112	BEHIND A PAINTED SMILE (LP, mono)	25
69	T. Motown (S)TML 11112	BEHIND A PAINTED SMILE (LP, stereo)	22
70	Stateside SSL 10300	THE BROTHERS: ISLEY (LP)	22
15	Sony 88875043972	THE RCA VICTOR AND T-NECK ALBUM MASTERS 1959-83 (box set, 23-CD, booklet)	40

ISOLATION
| 73 | Riverside HASLP 2083 | ISOLATION (LP, private pressing with insert) | 800 |

ISOTOPE
74	Gull GULP 1002	ISOTOPE (LP)	20
74	Gull GULP 1006	ILLUSION (LP)	20
75	Gull GULP 1017	DEEP END (LP, 1976 on both labels)	20

(see also Brian Auger, Hugh Hopper)

ISRAELITES
69	Downtown DT 413	Moma Moma/Melody For Two	25
69	Downtown DT 421	Games People Play/AUDREY: One Fine Day	25
69	Downtown DT 433	Seven Books/Chucka Beat	20
70	J-Dan JDN 4410	Can't Help From Crying/Can't Get Used To Losing You	8

(see also Music Doctors)

ISRAEL VIBRATION
78	Harvest HAR 184	The Same Song/Weep And Moan	15
79	Harvest 12 HAR 5189	Crisis/Crisis Dub (12", feat. Augustus Pablo)	30
79	Harvest SHSP 4099	THE SAME SONG (LP, black and red Harvest label)	25
88	RAS RAS 3037	STRENGTH OF MY LIFE (LP)	40
90	RAS RAS 3054	PRAISES (LP)	30
90	Greensleeves GREL 148	UNCONQUERED PEOPLE (LP, reissue)	15

HUGHIE ISSACHAAR
| 82 | House Of Asher HA2 | Don't Pretent You Love/Dub (12") | 15 |

HUGHY ISSACHAR
| 86 | Melody Muzik MM 001 | Mountain Rock/ORIGINAL ROCKERS: So Shall It Be (12") | 50 |

ITAL MICK
| 16 | System SYSTM 013 | Babylon Ways/Dub Ways/Kingly Character/Dub Character (12") | 18 |

ITALS (JAMAICA)
67	Giant GN 8	New Loving (with Soul Brothers)/I Told You Little Girl	40
67	Giant GN 12	Don't Throw It Away/Make Up Your Mind (both with Carib-Beats)	60
70	Big Shot BI-561	Put It On/Rasta Isies (as Hitals)	25
70	Big BG304	Everytime/Version	15
71	Big BG 325	Ba-Da-Doo-Ba-Dey/RUPIE EDWARDS ALL STARS: Version	10

(see also Alton Ellis, Honeyboy)

ITALS (U.K.)
| 71 | Black Swan BW 1404 | Dawn Patrol/Whiskey Bonga (DJ and Rhythm) | 12 |
| 71 | Black Swan BW 1407 | Judgement Rock (actually by Charlie Ace)/Night West | 12 |

ITHACA
| 73 | Merlin HF 6 | A GAME FOR ALL WHO KNOW (LP, with insert) | 1000 |
| 93 | Background HBG 01LP | A GAME FOR ALL WHO KNOW (LP, reissue) | 25 |

(see also Friends, Alice Through The Looking Glass, Agincourt, Tomorrow Come Someday, BBC Radiophonic Workshop)

IT'S A BEAUTIFUL DAY
69	CBS 4457	White Bird/Wasted Union Blues	8
70	CBS 4933	Soapstone Mountain/Do You Remember The Sun	15
69	CBS 63722	IT'S A BEAUTIFUL DAY (LP, gatefold sleeve)	35
70	CBS 64065	MARRYING MAIDEN (LP)	30
72	CBS 64314	CHOICE QUALITY STUFF - ANYTIME (LP, insert)	25

IT'S A TIGHTROPE
| 82 | TR 00112 | Soho/Loves Like That | 8 |

IT'S IMMATERIAL
80	Hit Machine HIT 001	Young Man (Seeks Interesting Job)/Doosha (A Success Story) (p/s)	6
81	Hit Machine IHM 002	Imitate The Worm/The Worm Turns (p/s)	10
86	Siren SIREN 15	Driving Away From Home/Trains, Boats, Planes (p/s)	6
84	Eternal JF 4	A Gigantic Raft In The Philippines/The Mermaid (p/s)	10

IVAN

IVAN
58	Coral Q 72341	Real Wild Child/Oh, You Beautiful Doll	200
58	Coral Q 72341	Real Wild Child/Oh, You Beautiful Doll (78)	50

(see also Jerry Allison, Crickets)

IVAN D. JUNIORS
63	Oriole CB 1874	Catch You If I Can/On My Mind	20

IVANS MEADS
65	Parlophone R 5342	A Little Sympathy/The Sins Of A Family	50
66	Parlophone R 5503	We'll Talk About It Tomorrow/The Bottle	40

BURL IVES
56	Brunswick 05510	Ballad Of Davy Crockett/Goober Peas	10

IVEYS
68	Apple APPLE 5	Maybe Tomorrow/And Her Daddy's A Millionaire	60
69	Apple APPLE 14	Dear Angie/No Escaping Your Love (unreleased; Europe & Japan only)	0
68	Apple SAPCOR 8	MAYBE TOMORROW (LP, unissued; Europe & Japan only)	0
92	Apple SAPCOR 8	MAYBE TOMORROW (LP, reissue, gatefold sleeve & bonus 12" [SAPCOR 82])	25

(see also Badfinger, Pleasure Garden)

IVOR & SHEILA
81	Eron 027	CHANGING TIMES (LP, with insert)	30

IVORIES
85	Kent TOWN 103	Please Stay/TOMMY HUNT: The Work Song	10

(see also Tommy Hunt)

JACKIE IVORY
66	Atlantic AT 4075	Hi-Heel Sneakers/Do It To Death	20
65	Atlantic ATL 5046	SOUL DISCOVERY (LP)	60
65	Atlantic ATL 5046	SOUL DISCOVERY (LP, 1966 reissue)	25

IVORY SUN
70	Jupiter	Another Yesterday/ Rainy Tomorrow/Black Gold	60

IVY
94	Sarah SARAH 91	Wish You Would/Nowhere To Mourn (p/s)	15
94	Sarah SARAH 92	Avenge/Sound The Deep Waters	15

IVY LEAGUE
64	Piccadilly 7N 35200	What More Do You Want?/Wait A Minute	10
65	Piccadilly 7N 35228	That's Why I'm Crying/A Girl Like You	6
66	Piccadilly 7N 35294	Running Round In Circles/Rain Rain Go Away	6
66	Piccadilly 7N 35326	Willow Tree/One Day	7
66	Piccadilly 7N 35348	My World Fell Down/When You're Young	8
67	Piccadilly 7N 35365	Four And Twenty Hours/Arrivederci Baby	10
67	Piccadilly 7N 35397	Suddenly Things/Tomorrow Is Another Day	10
67	Pye 7N 17386	Thank You For Loving Me/In The Not Too Distant Future	10
65	Piccadilly NEP 34038	FUNNY HOW LOVE CAN BE (EP)	15
65	Piccadilly NEP 34042	TOSSING AND TURNING (EP)	15
66	Piccadilly NEP 34048	OUR LOVE IS SLIPPING AWAY (EP)	20
65	Piccadilly NEP 34046	THE HOLLY AND THE IVY LEAGUE (EP)	10
65	Piccadilly NPL 38015	THIS IS THE IVY LEAGUE (LP)	30

(see also Carter-Lewis, White Plains, Edison Lighthouse, Flowerpot Men, Kestrels, One & One, Johnny Shadow, Perry Ford, First Class, Friends, Warm Sensations)

IVY THREE
60	London HLW 9178	Yogi/Was Judy There	15

DAFYDD IWAN
69	Welsh Teldisc WD 904	Croeso/Chwedeg Nain (p/s)	8

IWASACUBSCOUT
06	Fear And (No Cat. No.)	We Were Made To Love/That's Not A Crate, It's A Box Of Heaven Part Two (p/s)	6

IZZY POUND
69	Plexium PXM 9	Pumpkin Miny/Na Na Na Na	40

J

CLUE J. & HIS BLUES BLASTERS
60	Blue Beat BB 15	Easy Snappin'/Goin' Home (with vocal by Theophilus Beckford)	15
61	Blue Beat BB 37	Lovers' Jive/Wicked And Dreadful (actually with Neville Esson)	12
61	Blue Beat BB 60	Little Willie/Pine Juice	12

DAVID J. (& J. WALKERS)
81	4AD AD 112	Nothing/Armour (as David Jay & René Halkett) (p/s, with lyric sheet)	10
84	GLASS 12032	V For Vendetta: This Viscious Cabaret/V's Theme/Incidental/V's Theme (12" p/s)	15
83	Situation 2 SIT U 8	ETIQUETTE OF VIOLENCE (LP)	15
85	Glass GLALP 010	CROCODILE TEARS AND THE VELVET COSH (LP)	15
90	Beggars Banquet BEGA 112	SONGS FROM ANOTHER SEASON (LP)	15

(see also Bauhaus)

JABBERWOCK
77	MCA MCA 264	Sneakin' Snaky/Fortune Teller	15

JAB JAB MUSIC
81	Shades SH3	Loneliness Is Not Happiness/Sweet Socca Music	10

JABULA
75	Caroline CA 2004	JABULA (LP)	20
76	Caroline CA 2009	THUNDER INTO OUR HEARTS (LP)	15

JOY JACINTH

			MINT VALUE £
78	Jabula JBL 2003	AFRIKA AWAKE (LP)	18

JOY JACINTH
| 83 | Zebratone ZTD 93 | Baby Boy/Red Lights (12") | 15 |

JACK (BERNARD) & BEANSTALKS
| 69 | Supreme SUP 203 | Work It Up/Chatty Chatty | 18 |

(see also Kingstonians)

BILLY JACK (& CIMARONS)
70	Grape GR 3018	Let's Work Together/CORPORATION: Jam Monkey	15
70	Big Shot BI 558	Once A Man/Soul Mood (as Billy Jack & Cimarons)	7
70	Big Shot BI 559	Bet Your Life I Do/CANDY & CIMARONS: Ace Of Hearts	7

(see also Candy)

BOBBY JACK
| 59 | Top Rank JAR 190 | Tempting Me/Early Mornin' | 8 |

JACKAL (1)
| 74 | BASF BA 1009 | The Year Of The Tiger/Big Star | 10 |

JACKAL (2)
| 86 | Crim. Damage CRI 12-134 | Underneath The Arches/Thunder Machine (12", p/s) | 15 |

(see also Renegade Soundwave)

JACKIE (1)
| 78 | Fashion FAD 002 | It's Too Late Baby/Fashion On Fine Style (12") | 20 |

JACKIE (2)
| 80 | Cha Cha CHAD 28 | Who Can I Run To/OVERNIGHT PLAYERS: Dub Cuts (12", yellow vinyl) | 25 |

JACKIE & BRIDIE
68	Major Minor MM 562	Come Me Little Son/We Only Needed Time	6
64	Fontana TL 5212	HOLD BACK THE DAWN (LP)	25
70	Concord CONS 1002	FOLK WORLD OF JACKIE AND BRIDIE (LP)	15
71	Galliard GAL 4009	THE PERFECT ROUND (LP)	15

JACKIE & DOREEN
| 64 | Ska Beat JB 168 | Every Beat Of My Heart | 20 |
| 65 | Ska Beat JB 209 | The New Vow/Adorable You | 50 |

(see also Doreen Shaffer, Jackie Opel)

JACKIE (EDWARDS) & MILLIE (SMALL)
65	Island WI 253	This Is My Story/SOUND SYSTEM: Never Again	45
66	Island WI 265	My Desire/MILLIE: That's How Strong My Love Is	15
67	Island WIP 6012	In A Dream/Ooh Ooh	20
67	Island ILP 941	PLEDGING MY LOVE (LP, as Jackie Edwards & Millie Small)	60
68	Island ILP 963	THE BEST OF JACKIE AND MILLIE VOLUME TWO (LP)	60
70	Trojan TTL 52	THE BEST OF JACKIE AND MILLIE VOLUME TWO (LP, reissue)	20
70	Trojan TBL 155	JACKIE & MILLIE (LP)	40

(see also Wilfred & Millicent, Jackie Edwards, Millie)

JACKIE AND NICKY
| 74 | Bradleys BRAD 313 | Break Out In The Morning/Children Of Love | 15 |

(see also Jackie Lee (& Raindrops))

JACKIE & RAINDROPS
| 63 | Philips BF 1283 | Down Our Street/My Heart Is Your Heart | 8 |
| 64 | Philips BF 1328 | Come On Dream, Come On/Here I Go Again | 8 |

(see under Jackie Lee & Raindrops)

JACKIE & ROY
58	Vogue V 9101	You Smell So Good/Let's Take A Walk Around The Block	20
59	Vogue VE 1-70131	JACKIE AND ROY (EP)	30
58	Vogue VA 1-60111	JACKIE AND ROY (LP)	40

DAVID JACKMAN
| 96 | Speed Pig SP 001 | TEN CUT (10" clear vinyl, serrated edge, signed, no'd 80 only) | 50 |

JACKPOTS
| 69 | Sonet SON 2006 | Jack In The Box/Henbanes Sacrifice | 25 |

ALEXANDER JACKSON & TURNKEYS
| 65 | Sue WI 386 | The Whip/Tell It Like It Is (actually "Flea Pot"/"Sweetie Lester" by Lala Wilson) | 100 |

BOBBY JACKSON
| 10 | Jazzman JMANLP 035 | BOBBY JACKSON'S THE CAFE EXTRA-ORDINAIRE STORY (LP, reissue) | 20 |

CHRIS JACKSON
69	Soul City SC 112	I'll Never Forget You/Forever I'll Stay With You	50
70	444 Label	Since There's No Doubt/We Will Be Together (unissued, acetate only - 2 known copies)	800
70	Soul City 120	Since There's No Doubt/We Will Be Together (unissued)	0

CHUCK JACKSON
61	Top Rank JAR 564	I Don't Want To Cry/Just Once	40
62	Top Rank JAR 607	The Breaking Point/My Willow Tree	40
62	Stateside SS 102	Any Day Now/The Prophet	30
62	Stateside SS 127	I Keep Forgettin'/Who's Gonna Pick Up The Pieces	30
63	Stateside SS 171	Tell Him I'm Not Home/Getting Ready For The Heartbreak	25
64	Pye International 7N 25247	Beg Me/For All Time	25
64	Pye International 7N 25276	Any Day Now/The Prophet (reissue)	20
65	Pye International 7N 25287	Since I Don't Have You/Hand It Over	100
65	Pye International 7N 25287	Since I Don't Have You/Hand It Over (DJ Copy)	150
65	Pye International 7N 25301	I Need You/Chuck's Soul Brothers Twist	20
65	Pye International 7N 25321	If I Didn't Love You/Just A Little Bit Of Your Soul	25
66	Pye International 7N 25384	Chains Of Love/I Keep Forgettin'	100
66	Pye International 7N 25384	Chains Of Love/I Keep Forgettin' (DJ copy)	150
67	Pye International 7N 25439	Shame On Me/Candy	25
68	Tamla Motown TMG 651	Girls, Girls, Girls/(You Can't Let The Boy Overpower) The Man In You	30

Chuck JACKSON & MAXINE BROWN

MINT VALUE £

70	Tamla Motown TMG 729	Honey Come Back/What Am I Gonna Do Without You	20
73	Probe PRO 595	I Only Get The Feeling/Slowly But Surely	10
74	Probe PRO 617	I Can't Break Away/Just A Little Tear	10
75	All Platinum 6146 310	I've Got The Need/Beautiful Woman	15
75	Disco Demand DDS 116	These Chains Of Love/Any Day Now	8
85	Kent TOWN 104	Hand It Over/CANDY & KISSES: Mr Creator (withdrawn)	30
86	Kent 6T2	MELBA MOORE: Magic Touch/CHUCK JACKSON: Little By Little	20
80s	Inferno SIN 1	Chains Of Love/Good Things Come To Those Who Wait/Hand It Over/Any Day Now	20
92	Kent 8	What's With This Loneliness/Surf And Soul	20
66	Pye Intl. NPL 28082	TRIBUTE TO RHYTHM AND BLUES (LP)	60
68	T. Motown (S)TML 11071	CHUCK JACKSON ARRIVES! (LP, mono/stereo)	45
69	T. Motown TML 11117	GOIN' BACK TO CHUCK JACKSON (LP, mono)	50
69	T. Motown STML 11117	GOIN' BACK TO CHUCK JACKSON (LP, stereo)	50
72	Probe SPB 1084	THROUGH ALL TIMES (LP)	25
84	Kent 003	MR. EMOTION (LP)	15
87	Kent KENT 073	A POWERFUL SOUL (LP)	20

(see also Del[l]-Vikings)

CHUCK JACKSON & MAXINE BROWN

65	Pye International 7N 25308	Something You Got/Baby Take Me	20
65	Pye Intl. NPL 28091	SAYING SOMETHING (LP)	50

(see also Maxine Brown, Tammi Terrell)

DAVID JACKSON

82	Butt NOTT 5	THE LONG HELLO VOLUME 3 (LP)	20

(see also Van Der Graaf Generator)

DEON JACKSON

66	Atlantic AT 4070	Love Makes The World Go Round/You Said You Loved Me	45
66	Atlantic 584 012	Love Takes A Long Time Growing/Hush Little Baby	25
68	Atlantic 584 159	Ooh Baby/All On A Sunny Day	30
76	Contempo CS 9031	Love Makes The World Go Round/I Can't Go On	25

EARL JACKSON

76	ABC 410	Soul Self Satisfaction/Looking Thru' The Eyes Of Love (DJ Copy)	30
76	ABC ABC 4110	Soul Self Satisfaction/Looking Thru' The Eyes Of Love	20

GEORGE JACKSON

69	Capitol CL 15605	Find 'Em, Fool 'Em And Forget 'Em/My Desires Are Getting The Best Of Me	25
72	London HLU 10373	Aretha, Sing One For Me/I'm Gonna Wait	12
73	London HLU 10413	Let 'Em Know You Care/Patricia	12

GIDEON JACKSON

99	Conceive CON 001	Touch Me/Connexion (12", white labels)	40

GORDON JACKSON

69	Marmalade 598 010	Me And My Zoo/A Day At The Cottage	20
69	Marmalade 598 021	Song For Freedom/Sing To Me Woman	25
69	Marmalade 608 012	THINKING BACK (LP)	250
06	Sunbeam SBRLP5001	THINKING BACK (LP, reissue)	15

(see also Hellions, Jane Relf, Traffic)

HAROLD JACKSON & TORNADOES

58	Vogue V 9105	Move It On Down The Line Parts 1 & 2	100
58	Vogue V 9105	Move It On Down The Line Parts 1 & 2 (78)	40

JACKIE JACKSON

74	T. Motown STML 11249	JACKIE JACKSON (LP)	15

(see also Jacksons, Jackson 5)

JANET JACKSON

93	Virgin V 2720	JANET (2-LP, gatefold, inners)	80
97	Virgin V 2860	VELVET ROPE (2-LP, gatefold, inners)	100

JENNY JACKSON

69	Beacon BEA 110	Lean On Me/Please Come Home	10
69	Beacon BEA 136	Let's Go Somewhere/If I Didn't Love You	8

(see also Roots and Jenny Jackson)

JERRY JACKSON

63	London HLR 9689	Gypsy Eyes/Turn Back	40
66	Cameo Parkway P 100	It's Rough Out There/I'm Gonna Paint A Picture	175
66	Cameo Parkway P 100	It's Rough Out There/I'm Gonna Paint A Picture (DJ copy)	300

JIM JACKSON

66	RCA RCX 7182	R.C.A. VICTOR RACE SERIES VOL. 7 (EP)	10

JIMMY JACKSON('S ROCK 'N' ROLL SKIFFLE)

57	Columbia DB 3898	California Zephyr/I Shall Not Be Moved	20
57	Columbia DB 3937	Sittin' In The Balcony/Good Morning Blues	25
57	Columbia DB 3957	River Line/Lonely Road	15
58	Columbia DB 4085	Love-A Love-A Love A/Photographs (solo)	10
58	Columbia SEG 7750	ROCK 'N' SKIFFLE (EP)	60
58	Columbia SEG 7768	COUNTRY AND BLUES (EP)	60

J.J. JACKSON (& GREATEST LITTLE SOUL BAND IN THE LAND)

67	Polydor 56718	But It's Alright/Do The Boogaloo	20
67	Strike JH 329	Come See Me/Try Me	30
67	Warner Bros WB 2082	Sho Nuff (Got A Good Thing Going)/Here We Go Again	15
68	Warner Bros WB 2090	Down, But Not Out/Why Does It Take So Long?	15
68	Warner Bros WB 6029	Courage Ain't Strength/You Do It 'Cause You Wanna	15
69	Warner Bros WB 7276	Ain't Too Proud To Beg/But It's Alright	10
70	RCA RCA 1924	Bow Down To The Dollar/Indian Thing (as J.J.'s DILEMMA)	20
71	Mojo 2092 014	But It's Alright/Do The Boogaloo	10
67	Strike JLH 104	J.J. JACKSON WITH THE GREATEST LITTLE SOUL BAND (LP)	40

Levi JACKSON

MINT VALUE £

| 69 | MCA SKA 100 | GREATEST LITTLE SOUL BAND (LP) | 25 |
| 70 | RCA Victor SF 8093 | J.J. JACKSON'S DILEMMA (LP) | 30 |

(see also Greatest Little Soul Band)

LEVI JACKSON

| 71 | Columbia DB 8807 | This Beautiful Day/Don't You Be A Sinner | 100 |
| 71 | Columbia DB 8807 | This Beautiful Day/Don't You Be A Sinner (DJ copy) | 150 |

(see also Solomon King)

MICHAEL JACKSON
SINGLES

79	Epic 12EPC 7135	You Can't Win (Part 1)/You Can't Win (Part 2) (12")	10
79	Epic 12EPC 7763	Don't Stop 'Til You Get Enough/I Can't Help It (12")	15
82	Epic EPCA 11-2729	The Girl Is Mine (with Paul McCartney)/Can't Get Outta The Rain (picture disc)	30
83	Epic EPC 2906	GREATEST ORIGINAL HITS: Don't Stop 'Til You Get Enough/ She's Out Of My Life/Off The Wall/Rock With You (EP)	15
83	Motown TMG 986	Happy (Love Theme From 'Lady Sings The Blues')/We're Almost There (poster p/s)	8
83	Epic EPCA 3643	Thriller/JACKSONS: Things I Do For You (live) (poster p/s)	8
83	Epic TA 3643	Thriller (Album Version)/Thriller (Remix Short Version)/JACKSONS: Things I Do For You (live) (12", 'calendar' p/s)	50
83	Epic MJ 1 (1-9)	MICHAEL JACKSON'S 9 SINGLES PACK (9 x 7", p/s, each on red vinyl, in PVC foldout wallet)	40
87	Epic 650 202-0	I Just Can't Stop Loving You (with Siedah Garratt)/Baby Be Mine (poster p/s)	10
87	Epic 650 202-6	I Just Can't Stop Loving You (with Siedah Garratt)/Baby Be Mine (12", p/s with poster)	15
87	Epic 651 275-3	The Way You Make Me Feel (7" Mix)/(A Cappella)/(Dance Radio Edit)/ (Dub)/(Get Into The Groove -Put Either Side On The Turntable, Lower The Arm And See Which Your Needle Pix) (12", p/s double-groove)	12
88	Epic 651 389-9	Man In The Mirror (Single Mix)/Man In The Mirror (Instrumental) (Uncut 12", square-shaped picture disc)	250
88	Epic 651 388-9	Man In The Mirror (Single Mix)/Man In The Mirror (Instrumental) (square-shaped picture disc)	35
88	Epic 651 546-7	Dirty Diana/Dirty Diana (p/s, with 13" cardboard figure)	20
88	Epic 652 864-6	Dirty Diana/Dirty Diana (Instrumental)/Bad (Extended Dance Mix With False Fade) (12", with tour poster p/s)	15
88	Epic MJ 5	THE MICHAEL JACKSON BAD SOUVENIR SINGLES PACK (5 x 7" square picture discs in foldout PVC wallet, with lyric book)	45
88	Epic 652 844-9	Another Part Of Me/(Instrumental) (p/s, with Bad tour backstage pass)	25
88	Epic 652 844-0	Another Part Of Me/Another Part Of Me (Instrumental) (poster p/s)	8
88	Epic 653 026-0	Smooth Criminal/Smooth Criminal (Instrumental) (pack with 4 postcards)	20
88	Epic 653 170-6	Smooth Criminal (Extended Dance Mix)/ Smooth Criminal Extended (Dance Mix Dub Mix)/Smooth Criminal (A Cappella) (12" with "Moonwalker" advert calendar)	20
89	Epic 654 672-0	Leave Me Alone/Human Nature (pop-up p/s)	50
89	Epic 654 947-9	Liberian Girl (Edit)/Girlfriend (star mobile foldout card pack)	20
92	Epic EPC 658179-7	Who Is It/Rock With You (Masters At Work Remix) (limited edition, with free standing Jackson figure inserr)	12
92	Epic MJ 4 (658 281-1/4)	TOUR SOUVENIR PACK (CD, 4-picture disc, box set with booklet)	40
97	Epic 665 130 6	Smile/It It Scary (Deep Dish Dark And Scary Remix)/Is It Scary (Eddie's Rub-a-Dub Mix)/Is It Scary (Eddie's Love Mix)/Off The Wall (Junior Vasquez Remix) (12" p/s withdrawn. Beware of counterfeits with poor print quality on label, sleeve and especially the barcode)	200
03	Epic 674480-8	One More Chance (Album Version)/Billie Jean (album Version) (12" picture disc, numbered)	15
03	Epic XPR 3744	TWELVES (7 x 12" p/s in box with insert)	200

ALBUMS

78	Epic S EPC 83468	OFF THE WALL (LP, gatefold)	20
79	Epic EPC 83458/83468	OFF THE WALL (LP, gatefold sleeve, with 7" picture disc "You Can't Win (Parts 1)/(Part 2) [S EPC 7135], some with information sheet)	25
82	Epic EPC 85930	THRILLER (LP, gatefold, insert)	20
82	Epic EPC 11-85930	THRILLER (LP, picture disc in PVC sleeve)	30
83	MCA MCA 70000	E.T. - THE EXTRA TERRESTRIAL (LP, box set with booklet & poster, narration & "Someone In The Dark", with music by John Williams)	30
87	Epic 450 290-8	BAD GIFT PACK (pack, with note pad, highlighter pen & calendar)	15
87	Epic EPC 450290 1	BAD (LP, gatefold, insert)	20
87	Epic 450 290-0	BAD (LP, picture disc)	30
87	Epic 450 290-9	BAD (CD, picture disc, sealed in long PVC blister pack)	45
87	Epic 450 290-9	BAD (CD, picture disc, unsealed in long PVC blister pack)	25
91	Epic 465802 1	DANGEROUS (2-LP, inners)	25
95	Epic EPC 474709 1	HISTORY (3-LP, inners, 52-page booklet)	70
08	Sony 88697233441	THRILLER (2-LP 25th Anniversary special edition)	20
09	Sony 88697616541	THIS IS IT (4-LP box set with 36 page book, numbered)	45

PROMOS

82	Epic XPR 1242	Billie Jean/Rock With You/Burn This Disco Out/Off The Wall/Don't Stop Till You Get Enough/Shake Your Body (Down To The Ground)/Blame It On The Boogie/Thriller/Billie Jean (Disco Mix Club DJ 12", same tracks on both side, 1000 pressed most destroyed at request of Michael Jackson, 6 known copies)	400
92	Epic XPR 1814	Jam: (More Than Enuff Mix)/(Roger's Club Mix)/(E-Smoov Jazzy Jam)/ (Atlanta Techno Mix)/(Roger's Underground Mix)/(Silky 12")/(More Than Enuff Dub)/(Maurice's Jammin' Dub Mix)/(Roger's Club Dub)/(Atlanta Techno Dub)/(Roger's Slam Jam Mix)/(Silky Dub)/(A Capella Mix) (12", double pack, black & orange stickered white sleeve)	15
92	Epic XPR 1797	Who Is It (Patience Mix)/(Patience Beats)/(Most Patient Mix)/(HIS Mix)/ (The P-Man Dub) (12", company sleeve)	10
95	Epic XPR 2184	Scream: (Classic Club Mix)/(DM R&B Extended Mix)/(Def Radio Mix)/ (Naughty Main Mix)/(Naughty Main Mix No Rap)/(Dave 'Jam' Hall's Extended Urban Remix)/(Pressurised Dub Part 1)/(Pressurised Dub Part 2)/(Album Version)/(Single Edit No. 2)/(Naughty Pretty-Pella)/(Naughty A Capella) (12" double pack, red title sleeve)	20
95	Epic XPR 2266	DMC Megamix (15.40)/(11.18) (12", custom sleeve)	12
95	Epic XPR 2265	The Classic Remix Series: Wanna Be Startin' Something (Brothers In Rhythm Mix)/(Tommy D's Main Mix) (12", plain sleeve, sealed with title sticker)	10

Millie JACKSON

			MINT VALUE £
95	Epic XPR 2229	The Classic Remix Series: Rock With You (Frankie's Favorite Club Mix)/ (The Masters At Work Remix) (12", plain sleeve, sealed with title sticker)	12
96	Epic XPR 2207	Mj Club Megamix (MJ Mega Remix)/(MJ Urban Megamix) (12", blue & purple title sleeve)	15
96	Epic XPR 3030	They Don't Care About Us (The R&B Mixes): Track Masters Remix/ Dallas Austin Main Mix/Charles' Full Dirty Mix/LP Edit/Love To Infinity's Walk in The Park/Track Master's Instrumental (12" p/s)	10
97	Epic XPR 3159	HIStory (Tony Moran's HIStory Lesson)/(Tony Moran's HIStorical Dub) Is It Scary (Eddie's Love Mix)/(Eddie's Rub-A-Dub Mix)/(Eddie's Love Mix)/ (Radio Edit) (12", white embossed title p/s)	20
97	Epic XPR 3196	Is It Scary (Deep Dish Dark & Scary Remix)/(Deep Dish Double-O-Jazz Dub)/ (Deep Dish Dark & Scary Remix)/(Radio Edit) (12", black embossed title p/s)	35
04	Epic YPR 3829	Cheater (Demo)/One More Chance (R Kelly Remix) (12" p/s)	50

(see also Jackson 5, Paul McCartney, Jacksons)

MILLIE JACKSON

72	Mojo 2093 011	A Child Of God/You're The Joy Of My Life	10
72	Mojo 2093 015	Ask Me What You Want/I Just Can't Stand It	10
72	Mojo 2093 022	My Man, A Sweet Man/I Gotta Get Away (From My Own Self) (paper label)	6
76	Spring 2066 713	A House For Sale/There You Are	40
72	Mojo 2918 005	MILLIE JACKSON (LP)	20
74	Polydor 2391 147	CAUGHT UP (LP)	20
75	Polydor 2391 183	STILL CAUGHT UP (LP)	20
89	Jive HIP 77	BACK TO THE S..T (LP)	20

(see also Elton John)

MILT JACKSON

53	Vogue LDE 044	MILT JACKSON AND HIS NEW GROUP (10" LP)	20
55	Esquire 20-042	MILT JACKSON QUINTET (10" LP)	20
55	London Jazz LZ-C 14006	MILT JACKSON QUARTET (10" LP)	20

(see also Ray Charles, Modern Jazz Quartet, Stanley Turrentine, Miles Davis/Art Blakey, Coleman Hawkins)

PAPA CHARLIE JACKSON

60	Heritage R 100	PAPA CHARLIE JACKSON (EP) 99 only	80
60	Heritage HLP 1011	PAPA CHARLIE JACKSON (LP) 99 only	100

(see also Paramount Allstars, Blind Blake)

POOCH JACKSON

72	Sioux SI 013	You Just Gotta Get Ready/BROTHER DAN: Django's Valley	15
72	Sioux SI 017	King Of The Road/Circles/Mammy Blue	15
72	Sioux SI 016	Once Bitten (with Harry J. Allstars)/KING REGGAE: Slave Driver	15

(see also Circles)

PYTHON LEE JACKSON

70	Young Blood YB 1002	In A Broken Dream/Doing Fine (p/s)	6
72	Young Blood YB 3001	IN A BROKEN DREAM (LP, featuring Rod Stewart who is not credited on front or rear sleeve)	20

RALPH 'SOUL' JACKSON

69	Atlantic 584258	'Cause I Love You/Sunshine Of Your Love	30

SHIRLEY JACKSON

63	Decca F 11612	Don't Play Me A Love Song/You Gotta Love And Be Loved	7
63	Decca F 11661	The Boy Of The Year/I Miss You Most Of All	10
63	Decca F 11788	Broken Home/No Greater Love Than Mine	7

SHOVELVILLE K. JACKSON

60s	Melodisc MEL 1683	Be Careful Of Stones That You Throw/Kentucky Blues	12

SIMONE JACKSON

62	Piccadilly 7N 35087	Pop Pop Pop Pie/He Ain't Got No Time For Love	15
63	Piccadilly 7N 35124	Ain't Gonna Kiss Ya/Slow Motion	15
63	Piccadilly 7N 35149	Tell Me What To Do/Doing What You Know Is Wrong	12

STONEWALL JACKSON

59	Philips PB 941	Waterloo/Smoke Along The Track	7

TONY JACKSON (& VIBRATIONS)

64	Pye 7N 15685	Bye Bye Baby/Watch Your Step	25
64	Pye 7N 15745	This Little Girl Of Mine/You Beat Me To The Punch	40
65	Pye 7N 15766	Love Potion No. 9/Fortune Teller	50
65	Pye 7N 15876	Stage Door/That's What I Want (as Tony Jackson Group)	40
66	CBS 202039	You're My Number One/Let Me Know (as Tony Jackson Group)	40
66	CBS 202069	Never Leave Your Baby's Side/I'm The One She Really Thinks A Lot Of (solo)	40
66	CBS 202297	Follow Me/Walk Walk Walk Walk (solo)	60
66	CBS 202408	Anything Else You Want/Come On And Stop (solo)	40
91	Strange Things STZ 5005	JUST LIKE ME (LP)	15

(see also Searchers)

TOTLYN JACKSON

66	Airborne NBP 00010	Cha Cha In Bataseya/Little Boy	40

VIVIAN JACKSON & THE PROPHETS

78	Roots TS 100	72 Nation Bow/Ya Be Yoo	50
78	Nationwide PRO 001	CHANT DOWN BABYLON KINGDOM (LP)	120
78	Grove Music GMLP 4	BEWARE (LP)	40

(See also Yabby U.)

WALTER JACKSON

65	Columbia DB 7620	Welcome Home/Blowin' In The Wind	40
66	Columbia DB 7949	Tear For Tear/It's An Uphill Climb To The Bottom	75
66	Columbia DB 7949	Tear For Tear/It's An Uphill Climb To The Bottom (DJ copy)	125
66	Columbia DB 8054	A Corner In The Sun/Not You	30
67	Columbia DB 8254	Speak Her Name/They Don't Give Medals (To Yesterday's Heroes)	30
70	Atlantic 584 311	Any Way That You Want Me/Life Has Its Ups And Downs	10
73	Brunswick BR 5	Easy Evil/I Never Had It So Good	8

Wanda JACKSON

MINT VALUE £

WANDA JACKSON

Year	Label/Cat	Title	Value
59	Capitol CL 15033	You're The One For Me/A Date With Jerry	20
59	Capitol CL 15090	Reaching/I'd Rather Have You	20
60	Capitol CL 15147	Let's Have A Party/Cool Love	20
61	Capitol CL 15176	Mean Mean Man/Honey Bop	30
61	Capitol CL 15223	Right Or Wrong/Funnel Of Love	15
62	Capitol CL 15234	In The Middle Of A Heartache/I'd Be Ashamed	10
62	Capitol CL 15249	If I Cried Every Time You Hurt Me/Let My Love Walk In	10
58	Capitol EAP1 1041	WANDA JACKSON (EP)	75
62	Capitol EAP1 20353	A LITTLE BITTY TEAR (EP)	60
58	Capitol T 1041	WANDA JACKSON (LP)	150
60	Capitol T 1384	ROCKIN' WITH WANDA (LP)	120
61	Capitol T 1511	THERE'S A PARTY GOIN' ON (LP, mono)	80
61	Capitol (S)T 1511	THERE'S A PARTY GOIN' ON (LP, stereo)	100
61	Capitol T 1596	RIGHT OR WRONG (LP, mono)	50
61	Capitol (S)T 1596	RIGHT OR WRONG (LP, stereo)	60
62	Capitol T 1776	WONDERFUL WANDA (LP)	30
64	Capitol T 2030	TWO SIDES OF WANDA (LP, mono)	50
64	Capitol (S)T 2030	TWO SIDES OF WANDA (LP, stereo)	55
64	Capitol (S)T 2306	BLUES IN MY HEART (LP)	15
66	Capitol (S)T 2438	SINGS COUNTRY SONGS (LP, black label)	15
67	Capitol (S)T 2606	SALUTES THE COUNTRY MUSIC HALL OF FAME (LP, black label)	15
67	Capitol (S)T 2812	YOU'LL ALWAYS HAVE MY LOVE (LP)	15
69	Capitol (S)T 2976	CREAM OF THE CROP (LP, with Party Timers)	15

JACKSON BROTHERS

59	London HLX 8845	Tell Him No/Love Me	25

JACKSON 5

SINGLES

Year	Label/Cat	Title	Value
70	Tamla Motown TMG 738	ABC/The Young Folks (promo only p/s)	60
71	Tamla Motown TMG 769	Mama's Pearl/Darling Dear (promo only p/s)	60
71	Tamla Motown TMG 769	Mama's Pearl/Darling Dear	6
72	Tamla Motown TMG 833	Lookin' Through The Windows/Love Song (promo only p/s)	15
72	Tamla Motown TMG 837	THE CHRISTMAS EP: Santa Claus Is Coming To Town/ Someday At Christmas/Christmas Won't Be The Same This Year	12
73	Tamla Motown TMG 865	Skywriter/Ain't Nothin' Like The Real Thing (promo only p/s)	20
74	Lyntone LYN 2639	Talk And Sing Personally To Valentine Readers (33rpm flexidisc free with 'Valentine' magazine)	15
75	Rice Krispies (no cat. Nos.)	Sugar Daddy/Goin' Back To Indiana/Who's Loving You/Mama's Pearl/ ABC/The Love You Save (6 different Rice Krispies cut-out card discs, price is for each)	30
80	Motown SPTMG 2	THE MOTOWN 20TH ANNIVERSARY SINGLES BOX (15 x 7")	30

ALBUMS

Year	Label/Cat	Title	Value
70	Tamla Motown TML 11142	DIANA ROSS PRESENTS THE JACKSON 5 (flipback sleeve, mono)	30
70	Tamla Motown (S)TML 11142	DIANA ROSS PRESENTS THE JACKSON 5 (flipback sleeve, /stereo)	20
70	Tamla Motown TML 11156	ABC (flipback sleeve, mono, existence unconfirmed)	40
70	Tamla Motown STML 11156	ABC (flipback sleeve, stereo)	15
70	Tamla Motown STML 11168	THE JACKSON 5 CHRISTMAS ALBUM (flipback sleeve)	20
71	Tamla Motown STML 11174	THIRD ALBUM (original with flipback sleeve)	20
71	Tamla Motown STML 11188	MAYBE TOMORROW	20
72	Tamla Motown STML 11214	LOOKIN' THROUGH THE WINDOWS	20
73	Tamla Motown STML 11243	GET IT TOGETHER (with photo insert)	20
74	Tamla Motown STML 11275	DANCING MACHINE	15
75	Tamla Motown STML 11290	MOVING VIOLATIONS	15
77	Motown STMX 6006	MOTOWN SPECIAL - THE JACKSON 5	15
79	MFP MFP 50418	ZIP-A-DEE-DOO-DAH	15
81	Motown PR 84	JACKSON 5: HISTORY OF MOTOWN (4-LP box set, with 1 Michael Jackson LP)	30

(see also Michael Jackson, Jacksons)

JACKSON HEIGHTS

Year	Label/Cat	Title	Value
70	Charisma JH 1	Doubting Thomas/Insomnia	6
72	Vertigo 6059 068	Maureen/Long Time Dying	25
70	Charisma CAS 1018	KINGS PROGRESS (LP, pink 'scroll' label)	70
72	Vertigo 6360 067	5TH AVENUE BUS (LP, gatefold sleeve, swirl label)	250
72	Vertigo 6360 077	RAGAMUFFIN'S FOOL (LP, swirl label, with poster)	250
72	Vertigo 6360 077	RAGAMUFFIN'S FOOL (LP, swirl label, without poster)	80
73	Vertigo 6360 092	BUMP AND GRIND (LP, 'spaceship label')	60

(see also Nice)

JACKSONS

Year	Label/Cat	Title	Value
81	Epic EPC A 1294	Walk Right Now/Your Ways (picture disc)	15
84	Epic WA 4431	State Of Shock/Your Ways (7" picture disc)	15
79	Epic S XPR 1207	EPIC HITS FROM THE JACKSONS & MICHAEL JACKSON (LP, promo only)	20
84	Epic EPC 86203	VICTORY (LP, picture disc)	35
85	Epic SAI 7561	A TASTE OF VICTORY (LP, picture disc, promo only via Kelloggs offer)	60

(see also Jackson 5, Michael Jackson)

JACKSON SISTERS (1)

Year	Label/Cat	Title	Value
73	Mums SMUM 1591	(Why Can't We Be) More than Just Friends/Rockin' On My Porch	10
73	Mums SMUM 1829	I Believe In Miracles/Day In The Blue	50
74	Mums SMUM 2896	Boy, You're Dynamite/Shake Her Loose	8
87	Urban URB 4	I Believe In Miracles/Boy You're Dynamite	8
87	Urban URBX 4	I Believe In Miracles/Boy You're Dynamite (12", p/s)	20
87	Urban URBX 4	I Believe in Miracles/MACEO & THE MACS: Across The tracks/URBAN ALL STARS: It All	25

JACKSON & SMITH

MINT VALUE £

		Began In Africa (12" promo)	
JACKSON & SMITH			
65	Polydor 56051	Ain't That Loving You Baby/Every Day I Have The Blues	10
66	Polydor 56086	Party '66/And That's It	10
JACK THE LAD			
73	Charisma CB 206	One More Dance/Draught Genius (Polka) (p/s)	6
74	Charisma CAS 1085	IT'S JACK THE LAD (LP, small 'Mad Hatter' label)	15
74	Charisma CAS 1094	OLD STRAIGHT TRACK (LP, with lyric sheet, Charsima inner)	15
(see also Lindisfarne)			
JACKY			
68	Philips BF 1647	White Horses/Too Many Chiefs (Not Enough Indians)	10
68	Philips BF 1689	We're Off And Running/Well That's Loving You	6
69	Page One POF 122	Love Is Now/Never Will I Be	7
68	Philips SBL 7851	WHITE HORSES (LP)	35
(see also Jackie & Raindrops, Raindrops, Jackie Lee, Emma Rede, Vince Hill)			
DEBBIE JACOBS			
79	MCA MCF 3019	UNDERCOVER LOVER (LP)	15
DICK JACOBS (& HIS ORCHESTRA)			
57	Vogue Coral Q 72245	The Big Beat/The Tower Trot	15
57	Vogue Coral Q 72260	Rock-a-billy Gal/The Golden Strings	15
57	Vogue Coral LVA 9076	THE SKIFFLE SOUND (LP, as Dick Jacobs & His Skiffle Group)	30
59	Coral LVA 9102	THEMES FROM HORROR MOVIES (LP)	25
HANK JACOBS			
64	Sue WI 313	So Far Away/Monkey, Hips And Rice	40
83	Sue ENS 5	SO FAR AWAY EP: So Far Away/Out Of Sight/Hank's Groove/Summertime	10
JACQUELINE & BRIDIE			
64	Fontana TF 473	Roses/Roving Jack	6
64	Fontana TL 5212	HOLD BACK THE DAWN (LP)	20
(see also Jackie & Bridie)			
CHUCK JACQUES & LYNN TAITT & COMETS			
67	Ska Beat JB 264	Dial 609/VIBRATORS & TOMMY McCOOK & COMETS: Wait For Me	20
(see also Wilbert Francis & Vibrators)			
JADE			
70	DJM DJS 227	Alan's Song/Amongst Anemones	15
70	DJM DJLPS 407	FLY ON STRANGE WINGS (LP, gatefold sleeve)	200
JADE WARRIOR			
72	Vertigo 6059 069	The Demon Trucker/Snake	15
71	Vertigo 6360 033	JADE WARRIOR (LP, gatefold sleeve, swirl label)	200
71	Vertigo 6360 062	RELEASED (LP, multi-poster sleeve, small swirl label)	500
72	Vertigo 6360 079	LAST AUTUMN'S DREAM (LP, gatefold sleeve, swirl label)	175
74	Island ILPS 9290	FLOATING WORLD (LP, textured sleeve, pink rim palm tree label)	30
75	Island ILPS 9318	WAVES (LP, pink rim palm tree label)	20
76	Island ILPS 9393	KITES (LP)	18
79	Butt BUTT 001	REFLECTIONS (LP, lyric inner)	18
(see also July, Joe O'Donnell)			
JADIS			
84	Private pressing	BABOON ENQUIRIES EP	12
87	Private pressing DEM 1	G13/Out Of Reach	8
88	Private pressing DEM 2	Don't Keep Me Waiting/In The Dark	8
89	Private pressing	Lost For Words/This Changing Face	8
90	Back Beat 004-12	THE JADIS ALBUM (LP, numbered)	15
JAFFREY			
76	Tank	ALICE AT JAFFREY (LP)	100
CHRIS JAGGER			
73	GM GMS 3	Something New/Joy Of The Ride	6
73	GM GML 1003	CHRIS JAGGER (LP)	15
MICK JAGGER			
70	Decca F 13067	Memo From Turner/Natural Magic (in export p/s)	40
70	Decca F 13067	Memo From Turner/Natural Magic	15
70	United Artists UAS 29108	NED KELLY (LP, various artists soundtrack, only 1 Jagger track)	30
70	Warner Bros WS 2554	PERFORMANCE (LP, first pressing, orange label, soundtrack)	40
70	Warner Bros WS 2554	PERFORMANCE (LP, second pressing, green label, soundtrack)	30
93	Atlantic 7567 82436-1	WANDERING SPIRIT (LP)	50
01	Virgin 7243 8 11288 2 4	GODDESSINTHDOORWAY (2-LP)	50
(see also Rolling Stones)			
JAGS (1)			
61	Decca F 11397	The Hunch/Cry Wolf	8
JAGS (2)			
79	Island WIP 6501	Back Of My Hand/Double Vision (p/s)	6
80	Island WIP 6531	Woman's World/Dumb Blonde (p/s)	8
80	Island WIP 6587	Party Games/She's So Considerate (p/s)	10
80	Island WIP 6666	I Never Was A Beach Boy/Tune Into Heaven (p/s)	18
80	Island WIP 6683	The Sound Of G-O-O-D-B-Y-E/The Hurt (no p/s)	10
JAGUAR			
81	Heavy Metal HEAVY 10	Back Street Woman/Chasing The Dragon (p/s)	40
82	Neat NEAT 16	Axe Crazy/War Machine (p/s)	20
83	Neat NEAT 1007	POWER GAMES (LP, some on purple vinyl)	30
83	Neat NEAT 1007	POWER GAMES (LP, black vinyl)	18
84	Roadrunner RR 9851	THIS TIME (LP)	15

JAGUARS

MINT VALUE £

JAGUARS
63	Impression IMP 101	Opus To Spring/The Beat (1,000 only)	35
65	Contest RGJ 152	We'll Live On Happily/Now You Wonder Why	300

(see also Dave Mason)

JAGWA MA
12	Blue Rider BLUS001	Come Save Me/What Love	6

JAH BUNNY
77	Mainline ML2	Six And Seven Books/Version (actually by Reggae Scientist)	12
80	White Label	DUBBS INTERNATIONAL (LP)	40

JAH DAVE
85	Solid Groove SG 019	Informer/RANKING REUBEN: Taken Away (12")	40

JAH ELEMENT
86	Jah Element JE 001	Jah Alone/Summertime (12")	35

JAH FATTA & THE BLACK BROTHERS
79	Rite Sound RS DD 002	Free Rasta Free/BLACK BROTHER ALL STARS: Free Dub (12")	60

JAH FISH
72	Grape GR 3034	Vampire Rock/MOD STARS: El-Sisco Rock	20

JAH FRANKIE JONES
77	Third World TWS 916	SATTA & PRAISE JAH (LP)	45

JAH FREE
93	Jah Free	Lightning Clap/Lightning Dub/Jubilation/Jubilation Dub (12")	25

JAH GLEN
76	Love 0021	Jah Jah Bring Everything/RICHARD MCDONALD: Natty Lead The Way	25

(see also Glenmore Brown)

JAH GLOBE
84	Pyramid PAD 002	More People Are Walking/Keep It In Reality (12", with the Pyramid Posse)	25

JAH LARRY
79	Charmers LP 10	STAR LORD (LP)	20

JAH LION
83	Congo COS 2	Melody For Negus/Negus Dub	30
76	Island ILPS 9386	COLUMBIA COLLY (LP)	40
83	Kongo KLP 001	PRAISE JAH (LP)	100

(see also Jah Lloyd)

JAH LLOYD
73	Jaguar JAG 102	Channel One (with Douglas Boothe)/SOUL SYNDICATES: Channel Two	10
73	Jaguar JAG 104	Psalm Two/SOUL SYNDICATES: Channel Two	12
75	Treble C CCC 02	Once Bitten/CHARLEY ACE & INSWINGS: Real Red	8
76	Attack ATT 8121	World Class/World Class (Version)	6
74	DIP PL DL 1001	HERBS OF DUB...MORE HERBS (LP)	80
78	Virgin Frontline FL 1005	THE HUMBLE ONE (LP)	25
79	Virgin Frontline FL 1031	BLACK MOSES (LP)	15
79	His Majesty MH 1003	DREAD LION DUB (LP)	40
79	His Majesty MH 1004	REGGAE STICK (LP)	30

(see also Jah Lion)

JAH PALM
79	Soul & Fire SF 7	Cumbaya/Version (12")	30
85	Soul & Fire SF4	ALL CREATURE (LP)	60

JAH RUBY
77	Dynamic DYLP 3011	DREAD AFFAIR (LP)	25

JAH SHAKA
82	Jah Shaka 821	Revelation 18/Revelation Dub (12", red vinyl)	20
82	Jah Shaka 823	Jah Children (with Sister Pat)/SHAKA RIDIM SECTION : Jah Works (12")	35
82	Jah Shaka 828	Lion Youth/MAD PROFESSOR : Beyond The Realms (12")	20
82	Jah Shaka LP 824	THE COMMANDMENTS OF DUB (LP)	25
82	Rough Trade ROUGH 50	COMMANDMENTS OF DUB (LP)	18
83	Jah Shaka 833	REVELATION SONGS (LP)	15
84	Jah Shaka 841	COMMANDMENTS OF DUB PART 2 (LP)	15
84	Jah Shaka 845	KINGS MUSIC (VOCALS AND DUBS) (LP)	18
84	Jah Shaka 848	MESSAGE FROM AFRICA (LP)	15
84	Ariwa SALP 84	JAH SHAKA MEETS MAD PROFESSOR (LP)	20
85	Jah Shaka 847	COMMANDMENTS OF DUB PART 3 (LP)	15
85	Jah Shaka 849	JAH SHAKA MEETS PEPPER IN ADDIS ABABA STUDIOS (LP)	20
85	Jah Shaka 850	JAH SHAKA MEETS ASWAD (LP)	15
85	Jah Shaka 851	DUB ALMIGHTY - COMMANDMENTS OF DUB VOLUME 4 (LP)	15
85	Jah Shaka 856	JAH DUB CREATOR (LP)	15
86	Jah Shaka 860	DELIVERANCE - COMMANDMENTS OF DUB 6 (LP)	15
86	Jah Shaka 867	WARRIOR - COMMANDMENTS OF DUB 7 (LP)	15
88	Jah Shaka 777	MUSIC MESSAGE (LP)	15
89	Jah Shaka 887	DISCIPLES (LP)	20
89	Mango MPLM 1001	PRESENTS DUB MASTERS VOL. 1 (LP)	15
90	Jah Shaka SHAK 872	CORONATION DUB (LP)	20
91	Original OMLP 021	SENSI DUB VOLUME 5 (LP, with The Revolutionaries)	20
92	Jah Shaka SHAKA 924	DISCIPLES PART 2 - ADDIS ABABA (LP)	15
92	Jah Shaka SHAKA 923	NEW TESTAMENTS OF DUB PART 1 (LP)	15
93	Jah Shaka SHAKA 936	NEW TESTAMENTS OF DUB CHAPTER 2 (LP)	15

JAH SHAKA VS FATMAN
80	Live & Love LP 10	LIVE (LP)	30

JAH STITCH
77	Penguin PEN 16	Militant Man/Sugar Dandy	10
77	Third World TW 73	Black Harmony Killer/Natty on Top (12")	12

JAH THOMAS

MINT VALUE £

78	Aries PFUS 6000	Combination Three/Combine Version	8
75	Third World TWS 401	NO DREAD CAN'T DEAD (LP)	30
78	Cancer CANSLP 002	MY PRECIOUS LOCKS (LP)	25
78	Third World TWLP 701	WATCH YOUR STEP YOUTHMAN (LP)	20

JAH THOMAS
78	Greensleeves GRE 12	Stop Yu Loafin'/Bicycle Skank	10
78	Greensleeves GREL 3	STOP YU LOAFIN' (LP)	25
80	Daddy Kool DKLP 16	DANCE HALL STYLEE (LP)	25
83	Silver Camel SCLP 03	DANCE HALL CONNECTION (LP)	15

JAH WALTON
81	Music Force MFLP 02	TOUCH HERE WHERE SHE WANT IT MOST (LP)	80

JAH WARRIOR
96	Jah Warrior JW701	Babylon Shall Fall/Tumble Down Dub	20
96	Jah Warrior JW702	Dub From The Heart/Heartical Dub	8
96	Jah Warrior JWD 003	Judgement Day/Conquering Lion (12")	20
96	Jah Warrior JWD 004	Zulu/Equal Rights (12")	15
97	Jah Warrior JW 703	Hiding From Reality/Reality Dub	8
96	Jah Warrior JWLP 005	AFRICAN TRIBES DUB (LP)	15

JAH WOBBLE
79	Virgin VS 275	Dan Macarthur/Dan Macarthur (p/s)	7
83	Lago LAGO4	INVADERS OF THE HEART EP (12", p/s)	15
80	Virgin V 2158	THE LEGEND LIVES ON (LP)	18
91	Oval OVLP601	RISING ABOVE BEDLAM (LP)	20
94	Island ILSD 8044	HEAVEN & EARTH (2-LP)	30

(see also Bartok)

JAH WOBBLE, THE EDGE & HOLGER CZUKAY
83	Island IMA 1	SNAKE CHARMER (LP)	20

(see also Don Letts & Jah Wobble, Joolz, Public Image Ltd, The Edge, Orb, Can)

JAH WOBBLE, JAKI LIEBEZEIT, HOLGER CZUKAY
81	Island12WIP 6701	HOW MUCH ARE THEY? EP (12", p/s)	12

JAH WOOSH
74	Cactus CT 39	Judy Drownded/Crooked Skank	8
75	Lucky DL 5096	Don't Do That/That Dub	8
75	Lucky DL 5094	Rocking Blues/Version	7
75	Tropical AL 057	Iffie This Life/Iffie Version	10
76	Sunshot SS002	Religious Dread/Religious Dub	15
76	Sunshot SS005	Ital Feast/Dub Feast	12
76	Angen ANG 116	Set Up Yourself Dread/Version	10
76	Attack ATT 8124	I'm Alright/Version	18
76	Attack ATT 8129	Show I The Way/Show I The Way (Version)	12
77	Sunshot SS009	Whip Them Jah/Version	10
78	Grove Music GMDM 7	Pay Them Dues/Diverse Doctrine (with Ras Ibuna) (12")	20
78	Freedom Sounds FSD 001	Ales Skank/Different Style (12")	15
78	Attack ATT 8137	Marcus Say/Take Heed	8
79	Yard International YI 02	Jah Is The Ruler/Ruling Power/Jammys At The Control (12")	30
74	Cactus CTLP 103	JAH WOOSH (LP)	30
76	Student STULP 1003	CHALIS BLAZE (LP)	30
76	Trojan TRLS 133	DREADLOCKS AFFAIR (LP)	15
76	Black Wax WAX LP2	PSALMS OF WISDOM (LP)	100
76	Cactus CTLP 116	JAH JAH DEY DEY (LP)	25
77	K&B KBLP 002	LICK HIM WITH THE DUSTBIN (LP)	25
78	Trojan TRLS 157	RELIGIOUS DREAD (LP)	30
79	Creation Rebel CRBLP900	MARIJUANA WORLD TOUR (LP)	25
79	Dread & Dread 002	GATHERING ISRAEL (LP, multi-coloured vinyl)	35
90	Reggae Collectors RCLP 338	JAH WOOSH (LP, reissue)	15

JAH YOUTH
76	Caribbean CBN 307	Little Natty Dread/Little Natty Dread Version	6

JAHFA CULTURE & THE OFFBEAT POSSE
86	Jah Tubbys JT 017	Listen To We/Listen Mix (12")	175

JAHMA
97	Groove Yard GYARD 13	KEEP ON WALKING EP (12")	30

JAILHOUSE
72	Pye 7N 45172	Ya Hoo Hoo/Bad End	12

(see also Hamlett)

JAILHOUSE RECIPES
89	First Strike FS 01	ENERGY IN AN EMPTY TANK WORLD (LP)	15

JAKE & FAMILY JEWELS
70	Polydor 2425 027	JAKE AND THE FAMILY JEWELS (LP)	15

JAKLIN
69	Stable SLE 8003	JAKLIN (LP, laminated sleeve, black/silver labels)	400

JAKOB
78	SRTS 78 CUS 152	I Am A Child/Day By Day	25

JAKSZYK FRIPP AND COLLINS
11	Panegyric KCLP21	A SCARCITY OF MIRACLES (LP, gatefold)	30

(see also King Crimson)

(THE) JAM

SINGLES : ORIGINAL SINGLES
73	Fanfare	Taking My Love (From Me)/Blueberry Rock (acetate)	5000
73	Fanfare	Some Kinda Lovin'/Making My Way Back Home (acetate 6 copies only)	5000
75	Fanfare	When I Needed You/Please Don't Treat Me Bad/Taking My Love/Again (acetate)	5000

(the) JAM

MINT VALUE £

77	Polydor 2058 866	In The City/Takin' My Love (1st pressing, straight side opening p/s, plastic silver label)	8
78	Polydor 2059 054	David Watts/"A" Bomb In Wardour Street (1st pressing, double-A-sided 7"; A-side songwriter miscredited as "Ray Davis" without an "e")	15
78	Polydor POSP 8 (2059 068)	Down In The Tube Station At Midnight/So Sad About Us/The Night (7"; misprinted with erroneous B-side ref. to All Mod Cons)	15
80	Polydor POSPJ 113 2816 024	Going Underground/The Dreams Of Children p/s first 10,000 - with free live 7", Away From The Numbers/The Modern World/Down In The Tube Station At Midnight	8

SINGLES : REISSUES & RETROSPECTIVE SINGLES

89	Old Gold OG 9896	The Eton Rifles/Down In The Tube Station At Midnight (in p/s)	7
89	Old Gold OG 9897	Going Underground/Start! (in p/s)	7
89	Old Gold OG 9894	Town Called Malice/Absolute Beginners (in p/s)	7
92	Polydor PO 199	The Dreams Of Children/Away From The Numbers (live)	6
92	Polydor POCS 199	The Dreams Of Children/Away From The Numbers (live) (withdrawn)	6
97	Polydor 5715987	The Bitterest Pill (I Ever Had To Swallow)/The Butterfly Collector	20
02	Polydor 5876117	In The City/Takin' My Love (25th anniversary edition)	10
06	Polydor 9831170	THE SINGLES 1977-79 (9 x 7" box set)	80
06	Polydor 9831404	THE SINGLES 1980-82 (9 x 7" box set)	80
08	Genesis Publications (No Cat. No.)	FANFAREEP: In The City/Time For Truth/So Sad About Us/Sounds From The Street (12", 2000 only, this price with A Thousand Things book)	300
16	Secret S 732	Art School (1-sided, 100 only, numbered each with unique sleeve)	75

ALBUMS

77	Polydor 2383 447	IN THE CITY (LP)	25
77	Polydor 2383 475	THIS IS THE MODERN WORLD (LP)	25
78	Polydor POLD 5008	ALL MOD CONS (LP, inner)	25
79	Polydor POLD 5028	SETTING SONS (LP, embossed sleeve, sticker on rear, inner, insert)	20
80	Polydor POLD 5035	SOUND AFFECTS (LP)	20
80	Polydor 2683074	IN THE CITY/THIS IS THE MODERN WORLD (2-LP, gatefold)	20
82	Polydor POLD 5075	DIG THE NEW BREED (LP, die-cut cover)	15
82	Polydor POLD 5055	THE GIFT (LP, initial copies in pink/white striped paper bag)	40
82	Polydor POLD 5055	THE GIFT (LP)	20
83	Polydor SNAP 1/ SNAPL 45	SNAP! (2-LP, gatefold, with bonus 7" EP: Live! Wembley Arena 2 & 3.12.82 [SNAPL 45])	40
91	Polydor 8495541	GREATEST HITS (LP)	25
91	Receiver RRLP 141	LIVE AT THE ROXY (LP, unreleased, white label test pressings exist with printed proof sleeve shelved before release as the recording was actually only half a show from the 100 club 11/9/77)	500
92	Polydor 513 177-1	EXTRAS (2-LP, single sleeve with picture inners)	100
93	Polydor 519 667-1	LIVE JAM (2-LP, single sleeve with picture inners)	100
96	Polydor 531 493-1	THE JAM COLLECTION (2-LP, single sleeve, picture inners)	75
02	Simply Vinyl SVLP 108	ALL MOD CONS (LP, 180g vinyl, PVC sleeve, 2002)	18
02	Simply Vinyl SVLP 209	SETTING SONS (LP, 180g vinyl, PVC sleeve, 2002)	18
02	Polydor 5897811	THE SOUND OF THE JAM (2-LP)	80
12	Polydor/UMC 0602537185955	COPENHAGEN APRIL 1982 (LP)	100
14	Polydor/UMC 0602537946983	LIVE AT THE BRIGHTON CENTRE DECEMBER 1979 (2-LP)	150
15	Polydor/UMC 4747449	LIVE AT THE NEWCASTLE CITY HALL 28TH OCTOBER 1980 (2-LP)	125
16	Polydor/UMC 0602547930569	LIVE AT THE MUSIC MACHINE 2ND MARCH 1978 (2-LP)	35
16	Polydor/UMC 0602549726685	LIVE AT THE 100 CLUB 11TH SEPTEMBER 1977 (2-LP)	80
16	Polydor/UMC 5705857	ABOUT THE YOUNG IDEA - THE VERY BEST OF THE JAM (3-LP)	30
16	Polydor/UMC 0602547930620	LIVE AT READING UNIVERSITY 16TH FEBRUARY 1979 (2-LP)	70
17	Polydor/UMC 602557141092	LIVE AT THE HAMMERSMITH PALAIS 14TH DECEMBER 1981 (2-LP)	50
17	Polydor/UMC 0602557141122	LIVE AT THE WEMBLEY ARENA 2ND DECEMBER 1982 (2-LP)	60
19	Polydor/UMC SNAP 1/ 7752702	SNAP! (2-LP, with 7")	30

PROMOS

78	Polydor 2059 054DJ	David Watts/'A' Bomb In Wardour Street (p/s, with Ray Davies spelt as Davis in credits)	125
81	WEA SAM 144	4-Track white label EP featuring Little Boy Soldiers as well as tracks by the Beat, Bad Manners and the Clash)	200
82	Polydor POSP 400	Precious (1-sided 7", company sleeve)	50
82	Polydor DEN 1	Town Called Malice (Live at Hammersmith Palais 14.12.81)/ Precious (Extended Version) (12", white label promo)	30
82	Polydor PODJ 54	Beat Surrender (Censored)/Shopping (7", radio promo)	20
82	Polydor POSPX 540	Beat Surrender/Shopping/Move On Up/Stoned Out Of My Mind/War (12", white label promo)	15
83	Polydor LEE 1	Medley of Jam Songs to promote SNAP LP. 1-sided, plain white label)	60
83	Polydor SNAPL 45	LIVE! WEMBLEY ARENA (bonus Snap! EP, white label promo)	30
97	Polydor 2058 266/	In The City (1-sided 7", "20th anniversary party invite", co. sleeve; some copies with 'tax disc'-style card invite (ADMITS 1)	40
97	Polydor 2058 266/ ADMITS 1	In The City (1-sided 7", "20th anniversary party invite", co. sleeve; some copies with 'tax disc'-style card invite (ADMITS 1)	30

MISPRESSINGS

78	Polydor 2058 995	News Of The World/Aunties And Uncles (Impulsive Youths)/ Innocent Man (plays B-side on both sides)	40
78	Polydor POSP 8	Down In The Tube Station At Midnight/So Sad About Us/The Night (A-side plays John Travolta's "Sandy")	30
78	Polydor POSP 6	Sandy/Can't Let You Go (by John Travolta, B-side mispressed with "So Sad About Us")	30
79	Polydor POSP 69	When You're Young/Smithers-Jones (p/s, plays B-side both sides)	40
80	Polydor 2059 266	Start!/Liza Radley (A-side plays Village People's "Can't Stop The Music")	10

JAMAICA BAND

MINT VALUE £

82	Polydor POSP 400	Town Called Malice/Precious (7", both sides play "Precious")	30

FLEXIDISCS

80	Lyntone (no cat. no.)	When You're Young (live) (1-sided fan club flexi)	25
80	Lyntone LYN 9048	Boy About Town/Pop Art Poem (hard vinyl white label test pressing, same tracks both sides, without mailer, 1980)	60
80	Lyntone LYN 9048	Boy About Town/Pop Art Poem (hard vinyl white label test pressing, same tracks both sides, with mailer, 1980)	80
82	Lyntone (no cat. no.)	Tales From The Riverbank (re-recorded) (1-sided fan club flexi)	15

(see also Style Council, Paul Weller, Time U.K., Sharp)

JAMAICA BAND

73	Action ACT 4611	Sticky Fingers Part 1/Part 2	20

JAMAICA FATS

66	Blue Beat BB 368	Jacqueline/Please Come Home (actually by Al T. Joe & Celestials)	22

(see also Al T. Joe)

JAMAICA JUBILEE STOMPERS

67	Amusicon AMU 1002	Give Your Love To Me/I Cry To My Heart	15

JAMAICAN ACTIONS

68	Coxsone CS 7070	Catch The Quinella/JACKIE MITTOO: Songbird	100

JAMAICAN FOUNDATIONS

68	Coxsone CS 7036	Take It Cool/VICEROYS: Try Hard To Leave	200

JAMAICANS

66	Doctor Bird DB 1109	Cool Night/Ma And Pa	75
67	Trojan TR 007	Dedicated To You/The Things I Said To You	35
67	Treasure Isle TI 7007	Things You Say You Love/I've Got A Pain	35
67	Treasure Isle TI 7012	Baba Boom (Festival Song 1967) (actually by Baba Boom)/ TOMMY McCOOK & SUPERSONICS: Real Cool	25
67	Treasure Isle TI 7037	Peace And Love/Woman Gone Home	35
69	Escort ES 806	Early In The Morning/Mr. Lonely	15
70	Harry J. HJ 6604	Fire Parts 1 & 2	10
71	Dynamc DYN 410	Love Uprising/My Love For You	7
71	Dynamic DYN 417	Mary/CONSCIOUS MINDS: Soldier Boy	7
71	New Beat NB 084	Mary/CONSCIOUS MINDS: Soldier Boy	7
72	Dynamic DYN 442	Are You Sure/Are You Sure (Version)	8

(see also Norris Weir & Jamaicans, Tommy Cowan)

JAMAICAN SHADOWS

67	Coxsone CS 7005	HUGH GODFREY : Have Mercy/Blending Love	65
69	Upsetter US 320	Dirty Dozen (actually by Upsetters)/Crying Too Long	40

JAMAICA'S OWN VAGABONDS

64	Decca DFE 8588	BEHOLD (EP)	30
64	Decca LK 4617	SKA TIME (LP)	50
70	Decca Eclipse ECM 7028	SKA TIME (LP, reissue)	20

(see also Vagabonds, Jimmy James & Vagabonds)

AHMED JAMAL

59	London Jazz LTZ-M 15162	BUT NOT FOR ME : AHMED JAMAL AT THE PERSHING (LP)	18
59	London Jazz LTZ-M 15170	AHMED JAMAL (LP)	18
62	Pye Jazz NJL 38	ALHAMBRA (LP)	15
62	Pye Jazz NJL 47	ALL OF YOU (LP)	15
63	Pye Jazz NJL 52	POINCIANA (LP)	15

JAMES

84	Factory FAC 78	JIMONE EP: What's The World/Fire So Close/Folklore (p/s)	12
85	Factory FAC 119	Hymn From A Village/If Things Were Perfect (p/s)	15
85	Factory FAC 138	VILLAGE FIRE: What's The World/Fire So Close/Folklore/Hymn From A Village/If Things Were Perfect (12" EP)	12
86	Sire JIM 3T	Chain Mail/Uprising/Hup Springs (12", p/s)	15
86	Sire JIM 3	Chain Mail/Hup Springs (p/s)	6
86	Sire JIM 4	So Many Ways/Withdrawn (p/s)	25
86	Sire JIM 4T	So Many Ways/Just Hipper/Withdrawn (12", p/s)	15
88	Blanco Y Negro NEG 26	Yaho/Mosquito (p/s)	8
88	Blanco Y Negro NEG 26T	Yaho/Mosquito/Left Out Of Her Will/New Nature (12", p/s)	12
88	Blanco Y Negro NEG 31	What For/Island Swing (p/s)	10
88	Blanco Y Negro NEG 31T	What For (Climax Mix)/Island Swing/Not There (12", p/s)	10
88	Blanco Y Negro NEG 31C	What For (Climax Mix)/Island Swing/Not There (7", in video-style box)	8
89	Rough Trade RT 225	Sit Down/Sky Is Falling (p/s)	6
89	Rough Trade RTT 225	Sit Down/Goin' Away/Sky Is Falling (12", p/s, 1st 500 with postcard)	10
89	Rough Trade RT 245	Come Home/Promised Land (p/s)	6
89	Rough Trade RTT 245	Come Home (Long Version)/Come Home (7" Version)/Promised Land/Slow Right Down (Demo Version) (12", p/s)	10
90	Fontana JIMM 512	How Was It For You?/How Was It For You? (Different Mix)/Lazy/Undertaker (12", p/s, with stencil)	10
91	Fontana JIM 812	SIT DOWN (12" EP, recorded live at G-Mex)	10
90s	Lyntone	Weather Change (Demo Version) (flexidisc, with tour programme)	10
89	Rough Trade ONEMAN 1LP	ONE MAN CLAPPING (LP, with inner sleeve)	15
93	Fontana 5149431	LAID (LP, with mailing card insert)	45
93	Fontana 5149431	LAID (LP, without mailing card insert)	40
94	Fontana 5228271	WAH WAH (2-LP)	40
97	Fontana 534 3541	WHIPLASH (LP)	70
03	Simply Vinyl SVLP 158	LAID (2-LP, reissue)	25
12	Universal 2753129	THE GATHERING SOUND (12", 3-CD, DVD, memory stick, book, badges, stickers, signed art print, 500 only box set)	70

BARNABY JAMES

71	Decca F 13198	Feeling Alright/Gone Fishing	6

B.B. JAMES

MINT VALUE £

B.B. JAMES
70 Upsetter US 328 — Consider Me/Consider Me Version 20

BOB JAMES
76 CTI 6063 — THREE (LP, gatefold) 20

BRIAN JAMES (1)
68 Olga OLE 005 — Come Back Silly Girl/It Just Happened That Way 8

BRIAN JAMES (2)
79 BJ BJ 1 — Ain't That A Shame/LivingIn Sin/I Can Make You Cry (p/s) 10
82 Illegal ILS 0026 — Why? Why? Why?/When Did I Find A Girl Like You (p/s) 30
82 Illegal ILS 0026 — Why? Why? Why?/When Did I Find A Girl Like You (p/s, green vinyl) 10
(see also The Damned)

CALVIN JAMES
65 Columbia DB 7516 — Some Things You Never Get Used To/Remember 25

DANNY JAMES
72 Southern Sound BT 100 — Your Gravy Train/Devil Made Me Say That 7

DAVID JAMES
69 Crystal CR 7008 — Nothing Left To Lose/Go With The Times 25

DES JAMES
67 Fontana TF 847 — My Au Pair/City Street 40

DICK JAMES
56 Parlophone MSP 6199 — Robin Hood/The Ballad Of Davy Crockett 15
57 Parlophone R 4255 — The Garden Of Eden/I Accuse 10
57 Parlophone R 4375 — Skiffling Sing Song Medley 6
64 Parlophone R 5212 — Sing A Song Of Beatles With Dick James Medley (Parts 1 & 2) 12

ELMORE JAMES
64 Sue WI 335 — Dust My Blues/Happy Home (as Elmore James & Broom Dusters) 50
65 Sue WI 383 — It Hurts Me Too/Bleeding Heart 40
65 Sue WI 392 — Knocking At Your Door/Calling The Blues (B-side actually by Junior Wells & Earl Hooker) 120
66 Sue WI 4007 — I Need You/Mean Mistreating Mama 40
65 Sue ILP 918 — THE BEST OF ELMORE JAMES (LP) 80
65 Sue ILP 927 — THE ELMORE JAMES MEMORIAL ALBUM (LP) 80
68 Blue Horizon 7-63204 — TOUGH (LP, with 4 tracks by John Brim) 70
68 Bell MBLL/SBLL 104 — SOMETHING INSIDE OF ME (LP) 45
68 Ember EMB 3397 — THE LATE FANTASTICALLY GREAT ELMORE JAMES (LP) 25
70 United Artists UAS 29109 — THE LEGEND OF ELMORE JAMES (LP) 50
70 Blue Horizon 7-66230 — TO KNOW A MAN (2-LP) 75
73 Polydor 2383 200 — COTTON PATCH HOTFOOTS (LP, shared with Walter Horton) 20

ETTA JAMES
60 London HLM 9139 — All I Could Do Was Cry/Tough Mary 50
60 London HLM 9234 — My Dearest Darling/Girl Of My Dreams 30
61 Pye International 7N 25079 — At Last/I Just Want To Make Love To You 50
61 Pye International 7N 25080 — Trust In Me/Anything To Say You're Mine 20
61 Pye International 7N 25113 — Dream/Fool That I Am 20
62 Pye International 7N 25131 — Something's Got A Hold On Me/Waiting For Charlie To Come Home 40
62 Pye International 7N 25162 — Stop The Wedding/Street Of Tears 20
63 Pye International 7N 25205 — Pushover/I Can't Hold It In Any More 25
65 Sue WI 359 — Roll With Me Henry/Good Rockin' Daddy 60
67 Chess CRS 8052 — I Prefer You/I'm So Glad (I Found Love In You) 20
67 Chess CRS 8063 — Tell Mama/I'd Rather Go Blind 25
67 Chess CRS 8069 — Security/I'm Gonna Take What He's Got 15
68 Chess CRS 8076 — I Got You Babe/I Worship The Ground You Walk On 15
68 Chess CRS 8082 — You Got It/Fire 15
72 Chess 6145 016 — Tell Mama/I'd Rather Go Blind/I Found A Love 15
74 Chess 6145 033 — Out On The Streets Again/Come A Little Closer 10
78 Warner Brothers K 17173 — Piece Of My Heart/Lovesick Blues 8
85 Kent 6T1 — MARY LOVE: Hey Stoney Face/IKETTES: It's Been So Long/ETTA JAMES: Wallflower 20
65 Chess CRL 4502 — ETTA JAMES ROCKS THE HOUSE (LP) 75
67 Chess CRL 4524 — AT LAST (LP) 70
68 Ember EMB 3390 — THE SOUL OF ETTA JAMES (LP) 50
68 Chess CRL 4536 — TELL MAMA (LP) 40
73 Chess 6671 003 — PEACHES (2-LP) 25
(see also Etta & Harvey)

ETTA JAMES & SUGAR PIE DESANTO
65 Chess CRS 8025 — Do I Make Myself Clear/Somewhere Down The Line 30
(see also Sugar Pie DeSanto)

GARY JAMES
68 Polydor 56134 — Nicole/You're Gone 20
67 Polydor S6208 — Teddy Bear/In The Rain 15

GRAHAM JAMES
63 Columbia DB 7128 — You Could Have Fooled Me/Why Can't You See It My Way? 8

JANICE JAMES
09 Sonic Wax SW 004 — Set Your Sights (1-sided) 6

JASON JAMES
67 CBS 2705 — Miss Pilkington's Maid/Count Me Out 30

JERRY JAMES & BANDITS
64 Solar SRP 101 — Sweet Little Sixteen/Three Steps To Heaven 15

JESSE JAMES
54 Vocalion V 1037 — Southern Casey Jones/Lonesome Day Blues (78) 20
71 Mojo 2092 016 — Don't Nobody Want To Get Married/(Pt. 2) 7

JIMMY JAMES (& THE VAGABONDS)

MINT VALUE £

Year	Label/Cat#	Title	Value
00	Soul City 131	Love Is All Right (stereo mix)/Love Is All Right (mono mix)	8

JIMMY JAMES (& THE VAGABONDS)

Year	Label/Cat#	Title	Value
62	Dice CC 4	Bewildered And Blue/I Don't Want To Cry (solo)	20
63	R&B JB 112	Jump Children/Tell Me (solo)	25
64	Black Swan WI 437	Thinking Of You/Shirley (solo)	30
65	Columbia DB 7653	Shoo Be Doo You're Mine/We'll Never Stop Loving You	20
66	Ska Beat JB 242	Your Love/Someday (solo)	18
66	Piccadilly 7N 35298	I Feel Alright/I Wanna Be Your Everything (p/s)	75
66	Piccadilly 7N 35298	I Feel Alright/I Wanna Be Your Everything	30
66	Piccadilly 7N 35320	Hi Diddley Dee Dum Dum (It's A Good Good Feelin')/Come To Me Softly	20
66	Piccadilly 7N 35331	This Heart Of Mine/I Don't Wanna Cry (p/s)	100
66	Piccadilly 7N 35331	This Heart Of Mine/I Don't Wanna Cry	75
66	Piccadilly 7N 35349	Ain't Love Good, Ain't Love Proud/Don't Know What I'm Gonna Do	20
67	Piccadilly 7N 35360	I Can't Get Back Home To My Baby/Hungry For Love (solo)	12
67	Piccadilly 7N 35374	No Good To Cry/You Showed Me The Way	12
68	Pye 7N 17579	Red Red Wine/Who Could Be Loving You	10
71	Trojan TR 7806	Help Yourself/Why	25
72	Bamboo BAM 67	Riverboat Jenny/If I Wasn't Black	7
72	Stateside SS 2209	A Man Like Me/Survival	15
72	Stateside SS 2209	A Man Like Me/Survival (DJ copy)	35
75	Pye 7N 45472	Hey Girl/I Am Somebody	50
66	Piccadilly NEP 34053	JIMMY JAMES AND THE VAGABONDS (EP)	40
66	Piccadilly NPL 38027	THE NEW RELIGION (LP)	40
68	Pye N(S)PL 18231	OPEN UP YOUR SOUL (LP)	25

JIMMY JAMES & THE VAGABONDS/ALAN BOWN SET

Year	Label/Cat#	Title	Value
67	Pye N(S)PL 18156	LONDON SWINGS - LIVE AT THE MARQUEE CLUB (LP, 1 side each)	30

(see also Vagabonds, Jamaica's Own Vagabonds, Alan Bown Set)

JOHN JAMES

Year	Label/Cat#	Title	Value
70	Transatlantic TRA 219	MORNING BRINGS THE LIGHT (LP)	30
71	Transatlantic TRA 242	JOHN JAMES (LP)	20
76	Kicking Mule SNKF 128	DESCRIPTIVE GUITAR INSTRUMENTALS (LP)	15
78	Kicking Mule SNKF 136	LIVE IN CONCERT (LP)	18
84	Stoptime STOP 101	ACOUSTICA ECLECTICA (LP, signed)	35
84	Stoptime STOP 101	ACOUSTICA ECLECTICA (LP)	20

JONI JAMES

Year	Label/Cat#	Title	Value
53	MGM SP 1013	Why Don't You Believe Me?/Wishing Ring	10
60	MGM MGM-EP 728	THE SONGS OF HANK WILLIAMS (EP, mono)	10
60	MGM MGM-ES 3501	THE SONGS OF HANK WILLIAMS (EP, stereo)	10
54	MGM MGM-D 127	LET THERE BE LOVE (10" LP)	15

JOSE JAMES

Year	Label/Cat#	Title	Value
08	Brownsville BWOOD026LP	THE DREAMER (LP)	35

NICKY JAMES (MOVEMENT)

Year	Label/Cat#	Title	Value
63	Pye 7N 15560	My Colour Is Blue/Take Me Back	80
65	Columbia DB 7747	Stagger Lee/I'm Hurtin' Inside (as Nicky James Movement)	30
67	Philips BF 1566	I Need To Be Needed/So Glad We Made It	7
68	Philips BF 1635	Would You Believe/Silver Butterfly	18
68	Philips BF 1694	Lookin' Through Windows/Nobody But Me	7
69	Philips BF 1755	Time/Little Bit Of Paper	8
69	Philips BF 1804	Reaching For The Sun/No Life At All	7
72	Threshold TH 12	Why/Foreign Shore	6
73	Threshold TH 16	Black Dream/She Came To Me	6
73	Threshold TH 17	I Guess I've Always Loved You/My Style	8
71	Philips 6308 069	NICKY JAMES (LP, black/silver labels)	100
73	Threshold THS 10	EVERY HOME SHOULD HAVE ONE (LP, gatefold sleeve)	30
76	Threshold THS 19	THUNDERTHROAT (LP)	15

(see also Move)

OSCAR JAMES

Year	Label/Cat#	Title	Value
64	Carnival CV 7007	Louisa/Go 'Way	7

PHILIP JAMES & BLUES BUSTERS

Year	Label/Cat#	Title	Value
65	Island WI 219	Wide Awake In A Dream/MAYTALS: Tell Me The Reason	75

(see also Blues Busters)

RICKY JAMES

Year	Label/Cat#	Title	Value
57	HMV POP 306	Knee Deep in The Blues/Bluer Than Blue	20
57	HMV POP 334	Party Doll/Ninety-Nine Ways	20

ROGER JAMES FOUR

Year	Label/Cat#	Title	Value
65	Columbia DB 7556	Letter From Kathy/Leave Me Alone	10
66	Columbia DB 7813	Better Than Here/You're Gonna Come Home Cryin' (withdrawn)	70
66	Columbia DB 7829	Better Than Here/You're Gonna Come Home Cryin'	100

(see also Danny Storm)

ROGER JAMES

Year	Label/Cat#	Title	Value
71	NEMS 563719	If I Didn't Have You/I Know It's Love	20
72	Chapter 1 SCH 165	Gold/Something Wonderful	7
71	Chapter One CHS 807	RIDING FREE (LP, red/silver labels)	25

(see also Danny Storm, Prestons)

RUBY JAMES

Year	Label/Cat#	Title	Value
69	Fontana TF 1051	Gettin' Mighty Crowded/Don't Play That Song	20

SALLY JAMES

Year	Label/Cat#	Title	Value
74	Philips 6006 418	Isn't It Good/Wake Me When It's Over (p/s)	7

SKIP JAMES

Year	Label/Cat#	Title	Value
65	Vanguard VSD 79219	SKIP JAMES TODAY (LP)	40

Sonny JAMES

MINT VALUE £

67	Private PR3	1964-67 (LP, 99 copies only)	100
67	Vanguard SVRP 19001	SKIP JAMES TODAY (LP, reissue)	30
68	Vanguard VSD 79273	DEVIL GOT MY WOMAN (LP)	45
70	Spokane SPL 1003	THE ORIGINAL 1930/31 RECORDINGS (LP)	50
78	Vanguard VDP 20001	I'M SO GLAD (LP)	20
69	Storyville 670 185	THE GREATEST OF THE DELTA BLUES SINGERS (LP)	18

SONNY JAMES

56	Capitol CL 14635	The Cat Came Back/Hello Old Broken Heart	20
56	Capitol CL 14664	Twenty Feet Of Muddy Water/For Rent (One Empty Heart)	15
57	Capitol CL 14683	Young Love/You're The Reason I'm In Love	12
57	Capitol CL 14708	First Date, First Kiss, First Love/Speak To Me	15
57	Capitol CL 14742	Dear Love/Lovesick Blues	10
57	Capitol CL 14788	Love Conquered (Love Came, Love Saw)/A Mighty Lovable Man	10
57	Capitol CL 14814	Uh-Huh-Mm/Why Can't They Remember?	30
58	Capitol CL 14848	Kathaleen/Walk To The Dance	15
58	Capitol CL 14915	You Got That Touch/I Can See It In Your Eyes	6
59	Capitol CL 14991	Yo-Yo/Dream Big	10
60	London HL 9132	Jenny Lou/Passin' Through	10
57	Capitol EAP1 827	YOUNG LOVE (EP)	20
64	Capitol EAP1 20654	YOU'RE THE ONLY WORLD I KNOW (EP)	10
57	Capitol T 779	SOUTHERN GENTLEMAN (LP)	20
57	Capitol T 867	SONNY (LP)	20
63	London HA-D 8049	YOUNG LOVE (LP)	20

STU(ART) JAMES (& MOJOS)

65	Decca F 12231	Wait A Minute/Wonder If She Knows (as Stu James & Mojos)	12
76	Bradleys BRAD 7614	I'm In The Mood/Firefly (as Stuart James)	8

(see also Mojos)

SULLIVAN JAMES BAND

66	Parlophone R 5465	Goodbye Mr. Heartache/We're Gonna Make It	10

TOMMY JAMES & SHONDELLS

66	Roulette RK 7000	Hanky Panky/SHONDELLS: Thunderbolt	15
66	Pye International 7N 25398	It's Only Love/Ya! Ya!	10
67	Major Minor MM 511	I Think We're Alone Now/Gone Gone Gone	12
68	Major Minor MM 558	Wish It Were You/Get Out Now	8
68	Major Minor MM 567	Mony Mony/One, Two, Three And I Fell	7
68	Roulette RO 500	Do Something To Me/Somebody Cares	8
69	Roulette RO 502	Crimson And Clover/Some Kind Of Love	10
69	Roulette RO 507	Crystal Blue Persuasion/I'm Alive	12
69	Roulette RO 511	Ball Of Fire/Makin' Good Time	6
68	Major Minor MMLP/SMLP 27	SOMETHING SPECIAL (LP)	35
68	Roulette RRLP/SRLP 1	MONY MONY (LP)	30
68	Roulette RRLP/SRLP 2	CRIMSON AND CLOVER (LP)	40
69	Roulette RRLP/SRLP 3	CELLOPHANE SYMPHONY (LP)	20
72	Roulette 2432 002	THE BEST OF TOMMY JAMES & THE SHONDELLS (LP)	15

TONY JAMES

68	Jolly JY 002	Treat Me Right/Me Donkey's Dead	20

WINSTON JAMES

70	Hot Rod HR 106	Prison Sentence/JANET FERRON: Darling I Need You	45
70	Torpedo TOR 6	I May Never/Longest Day	80
70	Torpedo TOR 4	Gal You Think You Nice/White Silver Sands	100

BOBBY JAMES & DAVE (BARKER)

71	Smash SMA 2314	You Said It/AGGRO BAND: Hot Sauce	40

JAMES BOYS (1)

63	Direction 58-3721	The Mule (Instrumental)/The Horse (Vocal)	15

JAMES BROTHERS

68	Page One POF 077	I Forgot To Give You Love/The Truth About It	8
68	Page One POF 088	Does It Have To Be Me/You Don't Really Love Me	8
74	Penny Farthing PEN 857	Up Until Now/Pick A Bale Of Cotton	6

(see also Wheels)

JAMES GANG

70	Stateside SS 2158	Funk No. 48/Collage	15
70	Stateside SS 2173	Stop/Take A Look Around (withdrawn)	15
70	Probe PRO 502	Funk 49/Thanks	8
71	Probe PRO 533	Walk Away/Yadig?	8
70	Stateside SSL 10295	YER' ALBUM (LP)	20
70	Probe SPB 6253	RIDES AGAIN (LP)	18
71	Probe SPB 1038	THIRDS (LP)	15
71	Probe SPB 1045	LIVE IN CONCERT (LP, textured sleeve, flipback sleeve)	15
72	Probe SPB 1056	STRAIGHT SHOOTER (LP)	15

(see also Tommy Bolin)

BOBBY JAMESON

64	Decca F 12032	All I Want Is My Baby/Each And Every Day	40
64	London HL 9921	I Wanna Love You/I'm So Lonely	30
65	Brit WI 1001	Rum-Pum/Please Mr. Mailman	20
69	Joy JOYS 193	TOO MANY MORNINGS (LP)	100

STEPHEN JAMESON

73	Dawn DNLS 3044	STEPHEN JAMESON (LP)	15

JAMESON RAID

80	Blackbird BRAID 001	The Hypnotist/The Raid/Gettin' Hotter/Straight From The Butchers (p/s)	40

JAMIE JON & JERRY

MINT VALUE £

81	GBH GBH 1	Seven Days Of Splendour/It's A Crime/Catcher In The Rye (p/s, with lyric sheet, white sleeve)	50
81	GBH GBH 1	Seven Days Of Splendour/It's A Crime/Catcher In The Rye (p/s, with lyric sheet, later pressing with black sleeve)	30

JAMIE JON & JERRY
67	Decca F12642	You've Still Got A Place In My Heart/One Time Lover (All Time Fool)	6

JAMIES
58	Fontana H 153	Summertime Summertime/Searching For You	40
62	Columbia DB 4885	Summertime Summertime/Searching For You (reissue)	20

JAMIROQUAI
93	Acid Jazz JAZID 46	When You Gonna Learn/Too Young To Die	8
93	Acid Jazz JAZID 46T	When You Gonna Learn/Didgin' Out (12", p/s)	10
93	Sony 474069 1	EMERGENCY ON PLANET EARTH (2-LP)	50
94	Sony 477813 - 1	THE RETURN OF THE SPACE COWBOY (2-LP)	50
96	Sony 4839991	TRAVELLING WITHOUT MOVING (2-LP with bonus track Do You Know Where You're Coming From)	80
99	Sony S2 494517 1	SYNKRONIZED (2-LP)	80
00	Simply Vinyl SVLP 267	EMERGENCY ON PLANET EARTH (2-LP, reissue)	50
01	Sony 504069 1	A FUNK ODYSSEY (LP, numbered/un-numbered)	150
02	Simply Vinyl SVLP 365	THE RETURN OF THE SPACE COWBOY (2-LP, reissue)	50
05	Epic BL 96532	DYNAMITE (LP)	80
12	Art Vinyl AVLP14	A FUNK ODYSSEY (LP, reissue, with CD)	60
10	Mercury 2754292	ROCK DUST LIGHT STAR (2-LP)	30
17	Virgin/EMI V3178	AUTOMATON (2-LP)	30

JAMME
70	Stateside-Dunhill SSL 5024	JAMME (LP)	25

JOE JAMMER
73	Regal Zono. SRZA 8514	BAD NEWS (LP, gatefold sleeve, red/silver labels)	50

(see also Mitchell/Coe Mysteries)

JAM TODAY
81	Stroppy Cow SCJT 1	Stereotyping/Song About Myself (p/s, with insert)	50

JAN & ARNIE
58	London HL 8653	Jennie Lee/Gotta Getta Date	40
58	London HL 8653	Jennie Lee/Gotta Getta Date (78)	35

(see also Jan & Dean)

JAN & DEAN
59	London HLN 8936	Baby Talk/Jeanette, Get Your Hair Done	20
59	London HLN 8936	Baby Talk/Jeanette, Get Your Hair Done (78)	20
59	London HLU 8990	There's A Girl/My Heart Sings	25
59	London HLU 8990	There's A Girl/My Heart Sings (78)	40
60	London HLU 9063	Clementine/You're On My Mind	20
61	London HLH 9395	Heart And Soul/Midsummer Night's Dream	15
62	Liberty LIB 55397	A Sunday Kind Of Love/Poor Little Puppet	20
63	Liberty LIB 55531	Linda/When I Learn How To Cry	15
63	Liberty LIB 55580	Surf City/She's My Summer Girl	10
63	Liberty LIB 55613	Honolulu Lulu/Someday You'll Go Walkin' By	10
64	Liberty LIB 55641	Drag City/Schlock Rod Pt 1	15
64	Liberty LIB 55672	Dead Man's Curve/The New Girl In School	10
64	Liberty LIB 55704	The Little Old Lady From Pasadena/My Mighty GTO	10
64	Liberty LIB 55724	Ride The Wild Surf/The Anaheim, Azusa And Cucamonga Sewing Circle, Book Review And Timing Association	10
65	Liberty LIB 55727	Sidewalk Surfin'/When It's Over	10
65	Liberty LIB 55766	(Here They Come) From All Over The World/Freeway Flyer	12
65	Liberty LIB 55792	You Really Know How To Hurt A Guy/It's As Easy As 1, 2, 3	12
65	Liberty LIB 55833	I Found A Girl/It's A Shame To Say Goodbye	10
66	Liberty LIB 10225	Norwegian Wood/A Beginning From An End	20
66	Liberty LIB 55860	Batman/Bucket 'T'	25
66	Liberty LIB 10244	Popsicle/The Joker Is Wild	25
66	Liberty LIB 55923	The New Girl In School/School Day (Ring Ring Goes The Bell)	8
66	Liberty LIB 10252	Tennessee/Horace The Swinging School Bus Driver	12
67	CBS 202630	Yellow Balloon/A Taste Of Rain	25
65	Liberty LEP 2213	SURF 'N' DRAG HITS (EP)	30
66	Liberty LEP 2258	THE TITANIC TWOSOME (EP)	30
63	Liberty LBY 1163	SURF CITY AND OTHER SWINGING CITIES (LP)	30
64	Liberty LBY 1220	DEAD MAN'S CURVE/NEW GIRL IN SCHOOL (LP)	35
64	Liberty LBY 1229	RIDE THE WILD SURF (LP)	30
65	Liberty LBY 1279	GOLDEN HITS (LP)	30
65	Liberty LBY 1304	FOLK 'N' ROLL (LP)	30
66	Liberty LBY 1309	JAN AND DEAN MEET BATMAN (LP)	40
66	Liberty LBY 1339	FILET OF SOUL (A LIVE ONE) (LP)	25

(see also Legendary Masked Surfers, Fantastic Baggys, Jan & Arnie)

JAN & KELLY
63	Philips BE 12536	TIME FOR A LAUGH (EP)	10

JAN & KJELD
60	Ember EMB S 101	Banjo Boy/Don't Raise A Storm (in p/s)	10

BRUCE JANAWAY
78	Deep Range SRT/CUS/216	PURITANICAL ODES (LP, with insert)	300

JAN DUKES DE GREY
70	Decca Nova (S)DN 2	SORCERERS (LP)	350
71	Transatlantic TRA 234	MICE AND RATS IN THE LOFT (LP, gatefold sleeve, plastic inner/foam opening)	350

(see also Noy's Band)

JANE

MINT VALUE £

JANE
82	AM 106	It's A Fine Day (Jane)/It's A Fine Day (Lou) no p/s	15
83	Cherry Red CHERRY 65	It's A Fine Day/Of All/Leaves Were Falling (p/s)	7

MARY JANE WITH BARRY GRAY & SPACEMAKERS
63	Philips 326 587 BF	Robot Man/Just The Same As I Do (in p/s)	25
63	Philips 326 587 BF	Robot Man/Just The Same As I Do (no p/s)	15

(see also Barry Gray)

SARAH JANE
66	Pye 7N 17114	Listen People/The World Is Round	7

PETER JANES
67	CBS 203004	Emperors And Armies/Go Home Ulla (in p/s)	10
67	CBS 203004	Emperors And Armies/Go Home Ulla	6
68	CBS 3299	Do You Believe/For The Sake Of Time	20

BUSTER JANGLES' FLYING MATTRESS
72	RCA RCA 2112	Love Has Taken Over My Brain/The Little World I Knew	25

JANGLETTIES
81	Eskimo Vinyl	Happy All The Time/Backseat (p/s)	30

JANIE
61	Capitol CL 15180	You Better Not Do That/Only Girls Can Tell	12
70	President PT 309	Back On My Feet Again/Psycho	20

JANINE
81	Stiletto JAN 001	Crazy On You/Candy (p/s)	170

JOHNNY JANIS
58	London HLU 8650	The Better To Love You/Can This Be Love	6
60	Philips PB 1090	Gina/If The Good Lord's Willin'	6
58	HMV 7EG 8365	JOHNNY JANIS (EP)	30
66	London HA-U 8270	ONCE IN A BLUE MOON (LP)	20

BERT JANSCH
67	Big T BIG 102	Life Depends On Love/A Little Sweet Sunshine	12
73	Reprise K 14234	Oh My Father/The First Time Ever I Saw Your Face	7
74	Charisma CB 240	In The Bleak Midwinter/One For Jo	6
66	Transatlantic EP 145	NEEDLE OF DEATH (EP)	40
65	Transatlantic TRA 125	BERT JANSCH (LP)	80
65	Transatlantic TRA 132	IT DON'T BOTHER ME (LP)	50
66	Transatlantic TRA 143	JACK ORION (LP, 1st pressing with purple globe on top of labels)	70
66	Transatlantic TRA 143	JACK ORION (LP, 2nd pressing with purple and white globe around centre of labels)	40
67	Transatlantic TRA 157	NICOLA (LP)	50
69	Transatlantic TRA 179	BIRTHDAY BLUES (LP)	50
69	Vanguard VSD 79242	STEPPING STONES (LP)	40
69	Transatlantic TRASAM 10	THE BERT JANSCH SAMPLER (LP)	15
71	Transatlantic TRA 235	ROSEMARY LANE (LP)	40
72	Transatlantic TRASAM 27	BOX OF LOVE - THE BERT JANSCH SAMPLER VOL. 2 (LP)	20
73	Reprise K 44225	MOONSHINE (LP, with lyric insert)	25
74	Charisma CAS 1090	L.A. TURNAROUND (LP, with lyric insert)	35
75	Charisma CAS 1107	SANTA BARBARA HONEYMOON (LP)	15
77	Charisma CAS 1127	A RARE CONUNDRUM (LP, lyric inner)	15
79	Charisma CLASS 6	AVOCET (LP)	15
80	Kicking Mule SNKF 162	THIRTEEN DOWN (LP, as Bert Jansch Conundrum)	30
81	Logo LOGO 1035	HEARTBREAK (LP)	15
85	Konexion KOMA 788006	FROM THE OUTSIDE (LP, 500 only)	15
88	Demon TRANDEM1	BERT JANSCH (LP, reissue)	15

BERT JANSCH & JOHN RENBOURN
66	Transatlantic TRA 144	BERT AND JOHN (LP, 1st pressing, purple/white label with 'Transatlantic' logo on top)	75
66	Transatlantic TRA 144	BERT AND JOHN (LP, 2nd pressing, purple/white label with 'Transatlantic' logo on centre)	50
72	Transatlantic TRA 144	BERT & JOHN (LP, reissue with 'World globe' label)	15

(see also Conundrum, Pentangle, John Renbourn)

BERT JANSCH AND ROD CLEMENTS
88	Black Crow CRO 218	LEATHER LAUNDERETTE (LP)	40

JANUARY
69	CBS 4465	It Sings For Me/Julie	10

JAPAN
78	Ariola Hansa AHA 510	Don't Rain On My Parade/Stateline (solid or press-out centre, no p/s)	15
78	Ariola Hansa AHA 525	The Unconventional/Adolescent Sex (with p/s)	20
78	Ariola Hansa AHA 525	The Unconventional/Adolescent Sex	6
78	Ariola Hansa AHA 529	Sometimes I Feel So Low/Love Is Infectious (p/s, initial pressing on blue vinyl)	10
78	Ariola Hansa AHA 529	Sometimes I Feel So Low/Love Is Infectious (p/s)	8
79	Ariola Hansa AHA 540	Life In Tokyo (Short Version)/Life In Tokyo Pt 2 (p/s, red vinyl)	8
79	Ariola Hansa AHAD 540	Life In Tokyo (Long Version)/(Short Version) (12", p/s, red vinyl)	12
80	Ariola Hansa AHA 559	I Second That Emotion/Quiet Life (dull red vinyl, card p/s)	10
80	Ariola Hansa AHA 559	I Second That Emotion/Quiet Life (dull red vinyl, paper p/s)	6
80	Virgin VS 379	Gentlemen Take Polaroids/The Experience of Swimming (autographed by band, p/s)	75
80	Virgin VS 379	Gentlemen Take Polaroids/The Experience of Swimming/The Width Of A Room/Burning Bridges (double pack, gatefold p/s)	12
19	Electronic Sound ES 757	European Son/Suburban Berlin (p/s, red vinyl)	15
78	Ariola Hansa AHAL 8004	ADOLESCENT SEX (LP, 1st pressing, 'Damont' etched in run out groove, inner sleeve or lyric insert)	20
78	Ariola Hansa AHAL 8007	OBSCURE ALTERNATIVES (LP)	15
80	Virgin V 2180	GENTLEMEN TAKE POLAROIDS (LP)	20
80	Virgin V 2180	GENTLEMEN TAKE POLAROIDS (LP, with misprinted sleeve with sticker, Some Kind Of Fool listed instead of "Burning Bridges")	25

80	Ariola Hansa AHAL 8011	QUIET LIFE (LP, gatefold)	15
81	Virgin V 2209	TIN DRUM (LP)	15
84	Virgin VGD 3510	EXORCISING GHOSTS (LP)	15

(see also David Sylvian, Rain Tree Crow)

JARMAZ
84	Rash ITCH 1	Night City Life/Night City Life (Disco Remix) (p/s)	80

JARMELS
61	Top Rank JAR 560	She Loves To Dance/Little Lonely One	30
61	Top Rank JAR 580	A Little Bit Of Soap/The Way You Look Tonight	30

JEAN-MICHEL JARRE
85	Polydor POSPG 740	Zoolookologie (Remix)/Ethnicolor 2//Oxygene 4/Oxygene 6 (double pack)	8
97	Epic EPC 486984 1	OXYGENE 7-13 (LP)	18

MAURICE JARRE
65	Fontana (S)TL 5259	THE COLLECTOR (LP, soundtrack)	25
66	CBS (S)BPG 62843	IS PARIS BURNING? (LP, soundtrack)	18
67	RCA RD 7848	NIGHT OF THE GENERALS (LP, soundtrack)	30
67	RCA Victor RD/SF 7876	THE PROFESSIONALS (LP, soundtrack)	50
68	Dot (S)LPD 515	VILLA RIDES (LP, soundtrack)	15

ECCLETON JARRETT
86	CF CFD 010	Greedy Girl/Fling It Up (12")	40

KILLERMAN JARRETT
86	Trojan TROT 9086	War Ina South Africa/Dub/Bub 2 (12")	40

WAYNE JARRETT
79	Kingley Sounds REX 3	Anyone Who Had A Heart (with Tommy McCook)/WAYNE JARRETT/GLEN BROWN: Flute From South Side/Youth Man (12")	30
80	Greensleeves GRED 41	Saturday Night Jamboree (12")	20
81	Greensleeves GRED 61	Chip In/You Were On My Mind (12")	12
82	Echo ECHO 011	Satta Dread/Sadat (12")	35
97	Jah Shaka SHAKA 9772	Praises Unto HIM/JAH SHAKA: Dub Of Praise	10
82	Wackies W 191	BUBBLE UP (LP, blue label)	25
98	Wackies WR 191	BUBBLE UP (LP, reissue, black label)	15

(see also Winston Jarrett)

WINSTON JARRETT
74	Atra AR 21	No Time To Waste/Time Dub	30
77	Carib Gems CG 012	Sleepers/Sleepers Version (with the Righteous Flames)	20
78	Write Sounds WTS 1002	Spanish Town Road/Version	15
78	Ballistic UP 36416	War/Version (12")	15
80	Warrior WAR 144	Wise Man/I Shen Galore (12")	20
80	Kingley Sounds REX 3	Youth Man/Melodica (12")	18
80	Wambesi TWLP 1001	WISE MAN (LP)	25
84	VSLP 5008	ROCKING VIBRATION (LP)	15

(see also Righteous Flames)

MARIAN JARVIS
75	Chelsea 2005 038	A Penny For Your Thoughts/A Good Man To Wake Up To	30

STEVE JARVIS
74	Torpedo TOR 32	Every Step I Made/BABA BROOKS BAND: One Eyed Giant	20

JASARO PEOPLE
77	Timba T001	Suffering/Timba Version	200

JASMIN T
69	Tangerine DP 13	Some Other Guy/Evening (with p/s)	50
69	Tangerine DP 13	Some Other Guy/Evening	20

JASMINE MINKS
84	Creation CRE 004	Think/Work For Nothing (p/s)	10
84	Creation CRE 008	Where Traffic Goes/Mr. Magic (foldout p/s)	15
85	Creation CRE 018	What's Happening/Black & Blue (p/s)	6

JASON & THE SCORCHERS
10	Blue Rose BLULP 0508	HALCYON TIMES (2-LP, CD, features Ginger Wildheart)	30

JASON CREST
68	Philips BF 1633	Turquoise Tandem Cycle/Good Life (in export p/s)	175
68	Philips BF 1633	Turquoise Tandem Cycle/Good Life	60
68	Philips BF 1650	Juliano The Bull/Two By The Sea	40
68	Philips BF 1687	(Here We Go Round) The Lemon Tree/Patricia's Dream	60
69	Philips BF 1752	Waterloo Road/Education	40
69	Philips BF 1809	A Place In The Sun/Black Mass	200

(see also Holy Mackerel, High Broom)

JASON'S GENERATIONS
66	Polydor BM 56042	It's Up To You/Insurance Co.'s Are Very Unfair	80

JASPER
69	Spark SRLP 103	LIBERATION (LP, laminated front sleeve, blue/silver labels)	750

JEROME JASPER
82	NYC 1	I'll Do Anything/I'll Do Anything (Instrumental) (12" promo white label)	25
82	Rak 12RAK 354	I'll Do Anything For You/Treasure The Moment (12")	15

JAVAROO
80	Capitol CL 16131	Bring Out The Woman/Problem Child (demo only)	6
80	Capitol CL 16142	Breakin' In/Change It Up	10
80	Capitol 12CL 16142	Breakin' In/Change It Up/Bring Out The Woman (12")	50
80	Capitol CL 16168	Javaroo/The Buzz	20
80	Capitol E-ST 12052	OUT! (LP)	25

JAVELLS
77	Pye Disco Demand DDS 2003	Goodbye Nothin' To Say/Nothin' To Say	6

JAWBONE

MINT VALUE £

JAWBONE
70	Carnaby CNS 4007	How's Ya Pa?/Mister Custer	10
70	Carnaby CNS 4020	Way Down Down/Bulldog Goes West	10
72	B&C CB 190	Gotta Go/Automobile Blues	6
70	Carnaby CNLS 6004	JAWBONE (LP)	200

(see also Mirage, Portobello Explosion)

BOB JAXON (& HI-TONES)
55	London HL 8156	Ali Baba/Why Does A Woman Cry (as Bob Jaxon & Hi-Tones)	40
57	RCA RCA 1019	Beach Party/(Gotta Have Something In The) Bank Frank	80

FRANKIE JAXON/HOUNDHEAD HENRY
60	Jazz Collector JEL 10	THE MALE BLUES VOLUME 6 (EP)	10

JAY (BLACK)
64	Coral Q 72471	I Rise, I Fall/How Sweet It Is	35
67	United Artists UP 1174	What Will My Mary Say/Return To Me (as Jay Black)	10

(see also Jay & The Americans)

ABNER JAY
63	London HLN 9791	Cleo/Thresher	40

ERIC JAY
59	London HL 9004	The Little Drummer Boy/Blue Champagne Cha Cha	6

LAURIE JAY COMBO
62	Ember JBS 710	Shades Of Red/Nevada Sunsets	6
63	HMV POP 1234	Teenage Idol/Think Of Me (Demo copy)	60
63	HMV POP 1234	Teenage Idol/Think Of Me	75
64	HMV POP 1300	Love In My Heart/'Til You're Mine	6
64	HMV POP 1335	Maybe/Be Good To Me	6
65	Decca F 12083	A Song Called Soul/Just A Little Bit	25

(see also Nero & Gladiators)

LONNIE JAY & JAYNES
63	Stateside SS 197	Around And Around We Go/Somewhere	10

PATSY DEE JAY
77	Rama RMS 005	Peace Talking/EVE ORCHESTRA: Jumpers In Session	25

PETER JAY (& BLUE MEN)
60	Triumph RGM 1000	Just Too Late/Friendship (as Peter Jay & Blue Men)	40
60	Pye 7N 15290	Paradise Garden/Who's The Girl?	45

(see also Blue Men)

PETER JAY & JAYWALKERS
62	Decca F 11531	Can Can '62/Redskins	6
63	Decca F 11593	Totem Pole/Jaywalker	7
63	Decca F 11659	Poet And Peasant/Oo La La	10
63	Decca F 11757	Kansas City/The Parade Of Tin Soldiers	10
64	Decca F 11840	You Girl/If You Love Me	10
64	Piccadilly 7N 35199	Where Did Our Love Go/Caroline	10
64	Piccadilly 7N 35212	Tonight You're Gonna Fall In Love/Red Cabbage	10
65	Piccadilly 7N 35220	Parchman Farm/What's Easy For Two Is So Hard For One	20
65	Piccadilly 7N 35259	Before The Beginning/Solitaire	10

(see also Terry Reid, Miller, Big Boy Pete)

JAY (JOHN HOLT) & JOYA (LANDIS)
68	Trojan TR 633	I'll Be Lonely/SUPERSONICS: Second Fiddle	45

(see also John Holt, Joya Landis)

JAY & TECHNIQUES
67	Philips PB 1597	Apples, Peaches, Pumpkin Pie/Stronger Than Dirt	25
67	Philips PB 1618	Keep The Ball Rollin'/Here We Go Again	15
67	Mercury 6052 302	Apples, Peaches, Pumpkin Pie/Contact	7
68	Philips PB 1644	Strawberry Shortcake/Still (In Love With You)	12
68	Mercury MF 1034	Baby Make Your Own Sweet Music/Help Yourself To All My Lovin'	12
75	Polydor 2066 473	I Feel Love Comin' On/This World Of Mine	10
71	Mercury MCF 127360	Baby Make Your Own Sweet Music/Help Yourself To All My Lovin' (reissue)	6
67	Philips (S)BL 7824	APPLES, PEACHES, PUMPKIN PIE (LP)	30

JAY & THE AMERICANS
62	HMV POP 1009	She Cried/Dawning	40
63	United Artists UP 1002	This Is It/It's My Turn To Cry	8
63	United Artists UP 1018	What's The Use/Strangers Tomorrow	8
64	United Artists UP 1039	Come Dance With Me/Look Into My Eyes Maria	18
64	United Artists UP 1069	Come A Little Bit Closer/Goodbye Boys Goodbye	10
65	United Artists UP 1075	Let's Lock The Door (And Throw Away The Key)/I'll Remember You	10
65	United Artists UP 1088	Think Of The Good Times/If You Were Mine Girl	8
65	United Artists UP 1094	Cara Mia/When It's All Over	10
65	United Artists UP 1108	Some Enchanted Evening/Girl	8
66	United Artists UP 1119	Sunday And Me/Through This Doorway	12
66	United Artists UP 1129	Why Can't You Bring Me Home/Baby Stop Your Crying	20
66	United Artists UP 1132	Crying/I Don't Need A Friend	8
66	United Artists UP 1142	Livin' Above Your Head/She's The Girl (That's Messing Up My Mind)	30
66	United Artists UP 1162	(He's) Raining In My Sunshine/Reason For Living	7
67	United Artists UP 1178	You Ain't As Hip As All That Baby/Nature Boy	10
67	United Artists UP 1191	(We'll Meet In The) Yellow Forest/Got Hung Up Along The Way	60
68	United Artists UP 2211	French Provincial/Shanghai Noodle Factory	10
69	United Artists UP 2268	This Magic Moment/Since I Don't Have You	10
69	United Artists UP 35008	When You Dance/So Much In Love	10
69	United Artists UP 35026	Hushabye/No I Don't Know Her	6
70	United Artists UP 35074	Walkin' In The Rain/For The Love Of A Lady	10

JAYBIRDS

MINT VALUE £

65	United Artists UEP 1003	COME A LITTLE BIT CLOSER (EP)	40
66	United Artists UEP 1017	LIVING WITH JAY AND THE AMERICANS (EP)	40
66	United Artists (S)ULP 1117	JAY AND THE AMERICANS (LP)	50
66	United Artists (S)ULP 1128	SUNDAY AND ME (LP)	30
67	United Artists (S)ULP 1150	LIVIN' ABOVE YOUR HEAD (LP)	40
67	United Artists (S)ULP 1164	TRY SOME OF THIS (LP)	30

(see also Jay, Chapter Four)

JAYBIRDS
66	Sue WI 4013	Somebody Help Me/The Right Kind (without writer credits)	125
66	Sue WI 4013	Somebody Help Me/The Right Kind (with writer credits)	150

JAYBIRDS (U.K.)
64	Embassy WB 663	All Day And All Of The Night/Google Eye	6

(see also Ray Pilgrim & Beatmen)

JAY BOYS
69	Trojan TR 665	Splendour Splash/TREVOR SHIELD: Please	40
70	Harry J. HJ 6602	The Dog (Parts 1 & 2)	12
70	Harry J. HJ 6607	Jack The Ripper/Don't Let Me Down	80
70	Harry J. HJ 6609	Jay Moon Walk/Elcong	20
70	Harry J. HJ 6610	Je T'Aime/It Ain't Me Babe	15
70	Harry J. HJ 6617	Del Gago/Killer Version	50
70	Harry J. HJ 6618	Can't Get Next To You/(Part 2) (both actually by Charmers)	10
71	Harry J. HJ 6628	The Arcade Walk/The Arcade Walk Vers. II	12
72	Harry J. HJ 6644	African People/HARRY J. ALL STARS: African (Version)	15
72	Ashanti AHS 407	Rough Road/TREVOR SHIELD: Rough Road	18

(see also Roy Panton, Bob & Marcia, Cables)

JERRY JAYE
67	London HLU 10128	My Girl Josephine/Five Miles From Home	40

JAYE SISTERS
59	London HLT 9011	Sure Fire Love/G-3	60
59	London HLT 9011	Sure Fire Love/G-3 (78)	30

JAYHAWKS (1)
56	Parlophone R 4228	Stranded In The Jungle/My Only Darling	800
56	Parlophone R 4228	Stranded In The Jungle/My Only Darling (78)	100

JAYHAWKS (2)
92	Def American 512.986-1	HOLLYWOOD TOWN HALL (LP, with inner)	100
03	American B00000801	RAINY DAY MUSIC (2-LP)	30

JAYLADS
71	Punch PH 95	Royal Chord (actually by Melodians)/Version (actually "In The Spirit" by Lloyd Charmers)	18

(see also Melodians)

JAYNETTS
63	Stateside SS 227	Sally Go Round The Roses/Sally Go Round The Roses (Instrumental)	15

JAYS
63	Fontana TF 403	Shock A Boom/Across The Sea	10

JAYWALKERS
76	Cream CRM 5003	Can't Live Without You/Heartbroken Memories	10

JAZZ BUTCHER
83	Glass GLASS 027	Southern Mark Smith/Jazz Butcher Meets Count Dracula (p/s)	20
85	Glass GLASS 12041	Real Men/The Jazz Butcher V The Prime Minister/Southern Mark Smith (Original) (12")	20
86	Glass HMMM 001	Christmas With The Pygmies (p/s, promo freebie, given away at gigs)	10

(see also Institution)

JAZZ COMPOSERS ORCHESTRA
74	JCOA/Virgin JDA 3001	JAZZ COMPOSERS ORCHESTRA (2-LP, gatefold sleeve)	20

(see also Carla Bley, Mike Mantler, Larry Coryell)

JAZZ COURIERS
50s	(no cat. no.)	Top Spot Blues/Monk Was Here/Last Minute Blues (square flexi)	100
57	Tempo EXA 75	JAZZ COURIERS (EP)	60
59	Tempo EXA 87	JAZZ COURIERS (EP)	60
58	Tempo TAP 22	IN CONCERT (LP)	400
59	Tempo TAP 26	THE LAST WORD (LP)	350
60	London Jazz LTZ-L 15188	THE COURIERS OF JAZZ! (LP)	200
67	M. For Pleasure MFP 1072	IN CONCERT (LP)	15
80s	Jasmine JASM 2004	THE JAZZ COURIERS (LP, reissue)	20
80s	Jasmine JASM 2024	THE LAST WORD (LP, reissue)	15

(see also Tubby Hayes, Ronnie Scott)

JAZZ CRUSADERS
66	Fontana 688 149 ZL	THE THING (LP)	20
66	Fontana 688 117 ZL	LOOKIN' AHEAD (LP)	18

(see also Crusaders)

JAZZ DEFEKTORS
87	Factory FACT 205	THE JAZZ DEFEKTORS (LP)	15

JAZZ FIVE
61	Tempo TAP 32	THE FIVE OF US (LP)	400

(see also Vic Ash Quartet, Harry Klein Quartet)

JAZZ HIP TRIO
67	Major Minor MMLP 8	JAZZ IN RELIEF (LP)	125

JAZZ MAKERS
66	Ember FA 2023	SWINGIN' SOUNDS (LP)	20

JAZZ MODES
60	London Jazz LTZ-K 15191	THE MOST HAPPY FELLA (LP)	20

JAZZ ROCK EXPERIENCE

MINT VALUE £

JAZZ ROCK EXPERIENCE
70	Deram Nova SDN 19	JAZZ ROCK EXPERIENCE (LP)	100

J & B
66	Polydor 56095	Wow Wow Wow/There She Goes	50

(see also State Of Micky & Tommy)

THE JB
95	Back 2 Basics B2B12022	Back 2 Life (The Dedication) (Linarz Cru Remix)/(Original 12" Mix) (12", p/s)	30

J BLAST & 100% PROOF
92	Geek Street GEEK666JC001/ DJ D Zire	2 The Break Of Dawn (12")	10

J.B.'S
71	Mojo 2001 155	These Are The J.B.'s (Parts 1 & 2)	6
71	Mojo 2027 002	The Grunt (Parts 1 & 2)	6
72	Mojo 2093 007	Gimme Some More/The Rabbit Got The Gun	6
72	Mojo 2093 016	Hot Pants Road/Pass The Peas	6
72	Mojo 2093 021	Givin' Up Food For Funk (Parts 1 & 2)	6
72	Mojo 2918 004	PASS THE PEAS (LP)	20
72	Polydor 2391 034	FOOD FOR THOUGHT (LP)	20
74	Polydor 2391 087	DOING IT TO DEATH (LP)	20
75	Polydor 2391 194	HUSTLE WITH SPEED (LP)	20
76	Polydor 2391 204	GIVIN' UP FOOD FOR FUNK - THE BEST OF THE JB's (LP)	20

(see also Fred Wesley & JB's, James Brown, Bobby Byrd)

J.B'S ALLSTARS
85	2 Tone CHSTT29	The Alphabet Army/Al Arm (p/s)	40
85	2 Tone CHSTT1229	The Alphabet Army (extended mix)/The Alphabet Army (string mix)/The Alphabet Army/Al Arm (12" p/s)	40

JCB
80	Red Rat RR 401	I Wish I Was A Camera/Walk It Like You Talk It (p/s)	6

JC001/DJ D ZIRE
91	White JCDZ001	Favourite Breaks (12")	12

J.D. (THE ROC)
72	Sioux SI 008	Superbad/MONTEGO MELON: Lucky Dip	30

(see also Jeff Dixon)

CATHY JEAN & ROOMATES
61	Parlophone R 4764	Please Love Me Forever/Canadian Sunset	60

BOBBI JEAN
65	Mercury MF 921	Dry Your Tears/Pity The Man	10

JEAN & GAYTONES
71	Trojan TR 7817	I Shall Sing (actually by Judy Mowatt & Gaytones)/GAYTONES: Target	15

LANA JEAN
63	Pye International 7N 25214	It Hurts To Be Sixteen/Bad Boy	25

JEAN & STATESIDES
64	Columbia DB 7287	Putty In Your Hands/One Fine Day	40
64	Columbia DB 7439	You Won't Forget Me/Cold, Cold Winter	30
65	Columbia DB 7651	Mama Didn't Lie/Just Let Me Cry	30

JEAN-ETTES
59	Pye 7N 15185	May You Always/I Saw A Light	10

JEANNIE (& BIG GUYS)
63	Piccadilly 7N 35147	Don't Lie To Me/Boys (as Jeannie & Big Guys)	15
64	Piccadilly 7N 35164	I Want You/Sticks And Stones (as Jeannie & Big Guys)	15
65	Parlophone R 5243	I Love Him/With Any Other Girl	10

(see also Cindy Cole)

JEANNIE & REDHEADS
64	Decca F 11829	Animal Duds/ANDREW OLDHAM GROUP: Funky And Fleopatra	30

(see also Andrew Oldham Orchestra)

AUDREY JEANS
56	Decca F 10768	Ticky Ticky Tick (I'm Gonna Tell On You)/Will You, Willyum	10
56	Decca F 10788	It's Better In The Dark/The Bus Stop Song (A Paper Of Pins)	10
58	Decca F 11035	Send A Letter To Jeanette - Yet!/Bad Pianna Rag	7

JEDDAH
83	Death RIP 2001	Eleanor Rigby/Ghosts (Never Leave You Behind) (with poster, no p/s)	25

JEDI KNIGHTS
95	Clear CLR 406	MAY THE FUNK BE WITH YOU (12" EP, p/s)	12
95	Clear CLR 406X	MAY THE FUNK BE WITH YOU (12" EP, clear vinyl, embossed sleeve)	20

(see also Global Communications)

JEEP
80	Airport AIRP 001	Wild Rover/Lark In The Dark (over sized p/s)	8

JEEPS
66	Strike JH 308	He Saw Eesaw/The Music Goes Round	15
66	Strike JH 315	Ain't It A Great Big Laugh/I Put On My Shoes	15

JEFFERSON
68	Pye 7N 17634	Montage/Did You Hear A Heartbreak Last Night	15
69	Pye 7N 17706	The Colour Of My Love/Look No Further	8
69	Pye 7N 17810	Baby Take Me In Your Arms/I Fell Flat On My Face	8
69	Pye 7N 17855	Love And The World Loves You/I've Got To Tell Her	8
71	Pye 7N 45022	Spider/Can't Get You Out Of My Mind	30
75	Alaska ALA 1016	Workin' My Way Back To You/Baby You've Got Everything I Need	10
69	Pye NSPL 18316	THE COLOUR OF MY LOVE (LP)	15
73	Philips 6308 166	I LOVE YOU THIS MUCH (LP, blue/silver labels)	20

(see also Rockin' Berries, Sight & Sound)

JEFFERSON AIRPLANE

MINT VALUE £

JEFFERSON AIRPLANE
67	RCA Victor RCA 1594	Somebody To Love/She Has Funny Cars	15
67	RCA Victor RCA 1631	White Rabbit/Plastic Fantastic Lover	15
67	RCA Victor RCA 1647	Ballad Of You And Me and Pooneil/Two Heads	10
68	RCA Victor RCA 1711	Greasy Heart/Share A Little Joke (With The World)	12
68	RCA Victor RCA 1736	If You Feel Like China Breaking/Triad	10
70	RCA RCA 1933	Volunteers/We Can Be Together	6
70	RCA RCA 1964	Somebody To Love/White Rabbit	8
70	RCA RCA 1989	Mexico/Have You Seen The Saucers?	8
72	Grunt 65-0500	Pretty As You Feel/Wild Turkey	7
67	RCA Victor RD 7889	SURREALISTIC PILLOW (LP, black label, mono)	80
67	RCA Victor SF 7889	SURREALISTIC PILLOW (LP, black label, stereo)	50
68	RCA Victor RD 7926	AFTER BATHING AT BAXTERS (LP, black label, mono)	70
68	RCA Victor SF 7926	AFTER BATHING AT BAXTERS (LP, black label, stereo)	40
68	RCA Victor RD 7976	CROWN OF CREATION (LP, black label, mono)	70
68	RCA Victor SF 7976	CROWN OF CREATION (LP, black label, stereo)	30
69	RCA RD/SF 8019	BLESS ITS POINTED LITTLE HEAD (LP)	20
69	RCA Victor SF 7889	SURREALISTIC PILLOW (LP, repressing, orange label)	35
69	RCA Victor SF 7926	AFTER BATHING AT BAXTERS (LP, repressing, orange label)	25
69	RCA Victor SF 7976	CROWN OF CREATION (LP, repressing, orange label, 'SR Ltd' printing credit on sleeve)	40
70	RCA SF 8076	VOLUNTEERS (LP, gatefold sleeve)	20
71	Grunt FTR 1001	BARK (LP, bag cover with lyric sheet & brown inner sleeve)	15
71	RCA SF 8195	JEFFERSON AIRPLANE TAKES OFF (LP)	18
72	Grunt FTR 1007	LONG JOHN SILVER (LP, open-out box cover with inner lyric sleeve)	15

(see also Great Society, Paul Kantner, Hot Tuna)

ALAN JEFFERSON
15	Trunk JBH 056 LP	GALACTIC NIGHTMARE (2-LP)	20

BLIND LEMON JEFFERSON
50	Tempo R 38	Weary Dog Blues/Change My Luck Blues (78)	25
50	Tempo R 39	Lock Step Blues/Hangman's Blues (78)	25
51	Tempo R 46	Shuckin' Sugar Blues/Rabbit Foot Blues (78)	25
52	Tempo R 54	Gone Dead On You Blues/One Dime Blues (78)	25
53	Jazz Collector L 91	Shuckin' Sugar Blues/Rabbit Foot Blues (78)	20
53	Jazz Collector L 103	Jack O'Diamonds Blues/Clock House Blues (78)	20
54	Jazz Collector L 126	Gone Dead On You Blues/One Dime Blues (78)	20
50s	Poydras 99	BLIND LEMON JEFFERSON (10" LP)	50
53	London Jazz AL 3508	FOLK BLUES OF BLIND LEMON JEFFERSON (10" LP)	50
55	London Jazz AL 3546	PENITENTIARY BLUES (10" LP)	50
57	London Jazz AL 3564	SINGS THE BLUES (10" LP)	50
69	CBS 63738	THE IMMORTAL (LP)	20
70s	Roots Matchbox RL 301	BLIND LEMON JEFFERSON VOLUME 1 (LP)	20
70s	Roots Matchbox RL 306	BLIND LEMON JEFFERSON VOLUME 2 (LP)	18
70s	Roots Matchbox RL 331	BLIND LEMON JEFFERSON VOLUME 3 (LP)	18

(see also Paramount Allstars)

BLIND LEMON JEFFERSON/ED BELL
60	Jazz Collector JEL 13	THE MALE BLUES VOLUME 7 (EP)	10

BLIND LEMON JEFFERSON/BUDDY BOY HAWKINS
59	Jazz Collector JEL 8	THE MALE BLUES VOLUME 5 (EP)	10

BLIND LEMON JEFFERSON/LEADBELLY
61	Jazz Collector JEL 24	THE MALE BLUES VOLUME 8 (EP)	10

BLIND LEMON JEFFERSON & RAMBLING THOMAS
50s	Heritage HLP 1007	BLIND LEMON JEFFERSON AND RAMBLING THOMAS (LP, 99 only)	100

EDDIE JEFFERSON
67	Stateside SS 591	Some Other Time/When You Look In The Mirror	10

GEORGE PAUL JEFFERSON
68	Fontana TF 923	Looking For My Mind/Out Of Place	45

MARSHALL JEFFERSON
86	Affair TART 3	The House Music Anthem (12" EP)	10
88	FFRR FFRX 18	Open Our Eyes (Celestial Mix)/(Spiritual Mix)/(Marshall's Elevated Dub (12", p/s)	15

JE FRENCHIE
80	Guardian GFR 18	JE FRENCHIE EP	15

JEGA
96	Skam SKA 6	Phlax/Nortom Midgate/Bluette/Ionic/Evil Lee Kirtcele/Steel Drum/In With The In (12", custom sleeve)	45
97	Skam SKA 9	Card Hore/Oak Hanger/Nausicaa/Stainless Steel Drum/Star/Houdini (12", p/s)	10
98	Planet Mu ZIQ 001	TYPE XERO EP (12")	20
00	Planet Mu ZIQ 012	GEOMETRY (2-LP)	20

JEHST
99	Y n R Productions YNR 001	PREMONITIONS EP: (12", stickered (white die-cut sleeve, 1st pressing blue text)	50
99	Y n R YNR 1	PREMONITIONS (EP, 2nd pressing black text on label)	15
01	Lowlife LOW 12	THE HIGH PLAINS DRIFTER (EP, p/s)	40
01	Lowlife LOW 12 PRO	The Trilogy Remix (1-sided 12", 2 mixes 500 pressed)	30
02	Y n R YNR008	Alcoholic Author/Night Breed (12", p/s)	18
02	Lowlife LOW 18	The Return Of The Drifter/People Under The Weather (12", p/s, 3 mixes each)	12
13	Y n R YNR 055	Game Over (7")	7
14	Y n R YNR 062	Dolph Lundgren/Instrumental (gig-only 7" with STRANGE U)	20
17	Y n R BH71854-01	44th Floor/44th Floor (Instrumental) (100 only)	35
03	Lowlife LOW30	FALLING DOWN (LP)	50
05	High Plains REPHP 001	NUKE PROOF SUIT (LP)	30
11	YNR YNR 047LP	THE DRAGON OF AN ORDINARY FAMILY (LP, red & blue vinyl)	75

JELLIES

MINT VALUE £

12	YNR YNR 052	THE DRAGON OF AN ORDINARY FAMILY (LP, remixes 300 only)	15

JELLIES
81	Jelli 1	Jive Baby On A Saturday Night/Conversation (die-cut sleeve)	80
10	Trunk TTT 006	JIVE BABY ON A SATURDAY NIGHT (12" EP)	15

JELLY
72	Mother MOT9	I'll Meet You Half Way/Chicago Calling	40

JELLY BABIES
81	De Nada	DE NADA EP (hand-made p/s, white labels)	60

JELLY BEANS
64	Pye International 7N 25252	I Wanna Love Him So Bad/So Long	30
64	Red Bird RB 10011	The Kind Of Boy You Can't Forget/Baby Be Mine	30
75	Right On R 102	You Don't Mean Me No Good/I'm Hip To You	10

JELLYBREAD
69	Blue Horizon 57-3162	Chairman Mao's Boogaloo/No One Else	15
70	Blue Horizon 57-3169	Comment/Funky Wasp	15
70	Blue Horizon 57-3174	Rockin' Pneumonia And The Boogie-Woogie Flu/Readin' The Meters	15
70	Blue Horizon 57-3180	Old Man Hank/Faded Grace	15
71	Blue Horizon 2096 001	Creepin' And Crawlin'/The Loser/The Clergyman's Daughter	15
72	Blue Horizon 2096 006	Down Along The Cove/Sister Lucy	15
72	Liphook 1	JELLYBREAD (mini-LP)	325
69	Blue Horizon 7-63853	FIRST SLICE (LP)	100
71	Blue Horizon 2431 002	SIXTY-FIVE PARKWAY (LP, with lyric insert)	110
71	Blue Horizon 2431 002	SIXTY-FIVE PARKWAY (LP, without lyric insert)	70
72	Blue Horizon 2931 004	BACK TO THE BEGINNING AGAIN (LP, gatefold sleeve)	15

JELLYS
98	Mission Impossible MIRVL1	WELCOME TO OUR WORLD (LP, with inner sleeve, mail-order only)	18

(see also Honeycrack, Wildhearts)

JENA
88	Abacush AB 008	Reggae Vibes/Abacush (12")	150

DIANNE JENKINS
76	Crystal CR 7025	Tow-A-Way-Zone/Anniversary (as Diane Jenkins)	10

JOHNNY JENKINS
69	Atco 226 009	The Voodoo In You/Backside Blues	10
71	Atco 2400 033	TON-TON MACOUTE (LP)	25

LEROY JENKINS
76	JCOA/Virgin J 2005	FOR PLAYERS ONLY (LP)	15

BARBARA JENKYNS
67	Newbreed NB1	Shoult About It/Groovy Boy	50

JENNIFER (WARNES)
69	London HLU 10278	Let The Sun Shine In/Easy To Be Hard	7
70	London HLU 10312	Cajun Train/Old Folks (Les Vieux)	8

JENNIFERS
92	Nude NUD 2T	Just Got Back Today/Rocks And Boulders/Danny's Song/Tomorrow's Rain (12")	20
92	Nude NUD 2CD	Just Got Back Today/Rocks And Boulders/Danny's Song/Tomorrow's Rain (CD)	30

(see also Supergrass)

BILL JENNINGS
55	Parlophone MSP 6146	Stuffy/Solitude (as Bill Jennings-Leo Parker Quintet)	6
55	Parlophone MSP 6156	Soft Winds/What's New? (as Bill Jennings Quartet)	6

JENNORS
67	Coxsone CS 7024	Pressure And Slide (actually by Tennors)/SOUL BROTHERS: One Stop	40

(see also Tennors)

JENSEN AND THE GIANTS
83	SRT/KOFER/S83CUS1896	Ordinary Girl/Dancing On The Floor Of My Heart (p/s)	10

KRIS JENSEN
62	Fontana 267 241 TF	Torture/Let's Sit Down	15
63	Fontana 267 267 TF	Don't Take Her From Me/Claudette	15
64	Hickory 45-1224	Donna Donna/Big As I Can Dream	15
64	Hickory 45-1243	Lookin' For Love/In Time	15
64	Hickory 45-1256	Come Back To Me/You've Only Got Me To Lose	12
65	Hickory 45-1285	The Little Wind-Up Doll/Somebody's Smiling While I'm Crying	10
65	Hickory 45-1311	What Should I Do/That's A Whole Lotta Love	10

PAUL JENSEN & CAR THIEVES
78	Albatross TIT 3	Holiday In Spain/Always Arrive On Time (p/s)	6

JENSENS
68	Philips BF 1686	Deep Thinking/Marguerite	12

(see also Tempus Fugit)

BILL JENTIES
70	Smash SMA 2307	Stop Them (actually by Bill Gentles)/MAXINE: I Don't Care	12

(see also Bill Gentles/Bill Jentles)

BILL JENTLES
70	Pama PM 809	True True Train/JEFF BARNES: Give And Take	25
70	Pama PM 801	What A Woman/Sleepy Cat	40

(see also Bill Jenties)

JEREMIAH R
13	Organic Analogue OA 001	THE NEW WAY EP (12", white label, 400 only)	20

JEREMIAHS
85	No Label or catalogue number	Over The Stove/Wipe Away Your Tears/Never Come Back (printed insert and photo stuck on cover 25-50 copies only)	150
87	Abstract ABCT 112	DRIVING INTO THE SUN (12" EP)	45
87	Abstract ABS 053	DRIVING INTO THE SUN EP	25

JERICHO (JONES)

MINT VALUE £

JERICHO (JONES)
72	A&M AMS 883	Don't Let Me Down/Mona Mona	7
72	A&M AMS 7017	Hey Man/Champs	7
72	A&M AMS 7037	Mama's Gonna Take You Home/So Come On	7
71	A&M AMLH 68050	JUNKIES, MONKEYS & DONKEYS (LP, as Jericho Jones, gatefold, brown label)	200
72	A&M AMLS 68079	JERICHO (LP, beware of counterfeits with slightly thicker sleeves)	200

JERKS
78	Underground URA 1	Get Your Woofing Dog Off Me/Hold My Hand (p/s)	35
78	Lightning GIL 549	Cool/Jerkin' (p/s)	30
80	Laser LAS 25	Come Back Bogart (I Wish You Would)/Are You Strong Enough?/The Strangest Man Of All (p/s)	15
97	Overground OVER 65	JERK OFF (LP, 600 only pressed in U.K. for export to Japan)	20

JERMZ
78	One Way EFP 1	Power Cut/Me And My Baby (with p/s)	200
78	One Way EFP 1	Power Cut/Me And My Baby (without p/s)	80

JERONIMO
70	Major Minor MM695	Hey Ya/Na Na Hey Hey Kiss Him Goodbye	8

JERRY THE FERRET
78	Jerry The Ferret EGH 919	One Step Forward/I Think You're Lyin' (1000 only, no p/s)	50
80	Dead Horse	THE MUSIC GOES ON AND ON (EP)	20

JERRY & THE BLUEBELLS
75	Torpedo TOR 44	Girls/Girls Version	40

JERRY & FREEDOM SINGERS
70	Banana BA 308	It's All In The Game (duet Winston Francis)/ IM: The Way To My Heart (pseudonym for Cedric Brooks)	60

(see also Jerry Jones, Winston Francis)

JERRY O
67	London HLZ 10162	Karate Boo-ga-loo/The Pearl	12
71	Jay Boy BOY 53	Funky Boogaloo/Push Push	8
71	Jay Boy BOY 33	Karate Boo-ga-loo/The Pearl (reissue)	8
72	Jay Boy BOY 62	Dance What 'Cha Wanna/Afro-Twist Time	8

JERUSALEM (2)
72	Deram DM 358	Kamakazi Moth/Frustration	50
72	Deram SDL 6	JERUSALEM (LP, gatefold sleeve, white/brown label with large 'Deram' logo)	400
72	Deram SDL 6	JERUSALEM (LP, gatefold sleeve, later red/white label)	200

(see also Pussy, Ian Gillan)

JESS & JAMES
68	MGM MGM 1389	Move/What Was I Born For	25
68	MGM MGM 1420	Something For Nothing/I Let The Day Go By (with J.J. Band)	20
68	MGM MGM 1454	Thank You Show Biz/Motherless Child	10

STEVE JESSE
76	President PT 502	Shifting Sands/Post Hall Life	6

JESSUP
72	Beacon BEA 108	Little Friend/On The Run	15

JESTERS
62	R&L RL 15/16	Little Girl/Casa Pedro (blue and white labels)	30
73	Jam JAM 35	Fool For A Day/Can't Live Without You	15

JESUS & MARY CHAIN
84	Creation CRE 012	Upside Down/Vegetable Man (black & white wraparound p/s in poly bag with address on rear & name in red)	40
84	Creation CRE 012	Upside Down/Vegetable Man (red & white wraparound p/s in poly bag with address on rear & name in black)	40
84	Creation CRE 012	Upside Down/Vegetable Man (pink, blue or yellow wraparound p/s in poly bag; with small T-shirt offer insert)	25
84	Creation CRE 012	Upside Down/Vegetable Man (pink, blue or yellow wraparound p/s in poly bag; without small T-shirt offer insert)	12
85	Fierce FRIGHT 004	RIOT (EP, with 'LSD bar' & badge; 2 different sleeves)	40
85	Blanco Y Negro NEG 008	Never Understand/Suck (p/s)	6
85	Blanco Y Negro NEG 17	Just Like Honey/Head (p/s)	6
85	Blanco Y Negro NEG 17F	Just Like Honey/Head//Inside Me/Just Like Honey (Demo Oct 84) (double pack, gatefold p/s)	6
86	Creation CRE 012T	Upside Down/Vegetable Man/Upside Down (demo) (12" white label, no sleeve)	60
86	Blanco Y Negro NEG 19	SOME CANDY TALKING EP: Some Candy Talking/Psychocandy/Cut Dead/Psychocandy (acoustic)/You Trip Me Up/Some Candy (acoustic) (2x7" double pack)	6
89	Blanco Y Negro NEG 42/XB/Y/Z	Head On/Terminal Beach//Head On/Deviant Slice//Head On/I'm Glad I Never/Head On/In The Black (4 x 7" box set; each single sold separately)	12
91	Strange Fruit SFPMA210	PEEL SESSIONS (12")	15
94	Blanco Y Negro NEG 73	Come On/I'm In With The Out Crowd (orange vinyl, numbered limited edition)	6
85	Creation CRE(T) 1	LIVE (100 only, numbered, with press sheet)	100
85	Blanco Y Negro BYN 7	PSYCHOCANDY (LP, with inner)	25
87	Blanco Y Negro BYN 11	DARKLANDS (LP, with inner)	25
88	Blanco Y Negro BYN 15	BARBED WIRE KISSES (B-SIDES AND MORE) (LP)	15
89	Blanco Y Negro BYN 20W	AUTOMATIC (LP, gatefold sleeve, with insert)	20
92	Blanco Y Negro BYN 26	HONEY'S DEAD (LP)	30
94	Warner Bros. 4509-96717-4	STONED & DETHRONED (LP)	60
98	Creation CRELP 232	MUNKI (2-LP)	100
00	Strange Fruit SFRSLP092	THE COMPLETE PEEL SESSIONS (LP)	18
13	Demon CANDY 1	PSYCHOCANDY (LP, reissue, red splatter vinyl, poster)	25
13	Demon JAMCLPBOX 01	THE VINYL COLLECTION (11-LP box set)	80

(see also Acid Angels, Primal Scream, Meat Whiplash)

JESUS LIZARD
91	Touch & Go T&GLP #43	PURE (EP purple vinyl, numbered sticker on sleeve, 1500 only)	18

JET

MINT VALUE £

92	Own label	Gladiator (Marquee gig freebie)	8
93	Touch & Go TG 83	Puss/NIRVANA: Oh, The Guilt (p/s, blue vinyl, with poster)	25
93	Touch & Go TG 83	Puss/NIRVANA: Oh, The Guilt (p/s, blue vinyl, without poster)	12
90	Touch & Go T&GLP 54	HEAD (LP, red & white vinyl, numbered sticker on sleeve, 1500 only)	18
91	Touch & Go T&GLP 68	GOAT (LP, orange vinyl, numbered sticker on sleeve, 1000 only)	40
91	Touch & Go TG68P	GOAT (LP, picture disc)	18
92	Touch & Go TGLP 100	LIAR (LP, maroon vinyl, stickered no'd sleeve)	20
94	Touch & Go TG 131	DOWN (LP, with 4 postcards)	25

(see also Nirvana)

JET

75	CBS S CBS 3317	Nothing To Do With Us/Brian Damage	8
75	CBS S CBS 3143	My River/Quandary	8
75	CBS 80699	JET (LP, with lyric insert)	20

(see also Andy Ellison,John's Children, Nice, Radio Stars, Sparks)

JET (AUSTRALIA)

03	Elektra 7559-62956-1	GET BORN (2-LP, white vinyl, stickered, gatefold with inners)	30

JETHRO TULL

SINGLES

68	MGM MGM 1384	Sunshine Day/Aeroplane (miscredited to 'Jethro Toe'; counterfeits credit 'Jethro Tull')	600
68	Island WIP 6043	A Song For Jeffrey/One For John Gee	40
68	Island WIP 6048	Love Story/A Christmas Song (2 different pink label designs)	10
68	Island WIP 6048	Love Story/A Christmas Song (mispressing, B-side or both sides credited to Ian Henderson)	18
69	Island WIP 6056	Living In The Past/Driving Song (2 different pink labels)	15
69	Chrysalis WIP 6070	Sweet Dream/17 (push-out or large centre hole)	7
70	Chrysalis WIP 6077	The Witch's Promise/Teacher (in p/s)	20
70	Chrysalis WIP 6077	The Witch's Promise/Teacher	15
70	Chrysalis WIP 6081	Inside/Alive And Well And Living In	10
71	Chrysalis WIP 6098	Lick Your Fingers Clean/Up To Me (unissued)	0
74	Chrysalis CHS 2054	Bungle In The Jungle/Back Door Angels	6
77	Chrysalis CHS 2135	The Whistler/Strip Cartoon (in p/s)	25
77	Chrysalis CHS 2135	The Whistler/Strip Cartoon (no p/s)	8
78	Chrysalis CHS 2214	Moths/Life Is A Long Song (p/s)	10
78	Chrysalis CHS 2260	A Stitch In Time (3.30 Version)/Sweet Dream (p/s, white vinyl)	12
78	Chrysalis CHS 2260	A Stitch In Time (3.30 Version)/Sweet Dream (p/s, black vinyl)	8
78	Chrysalis CHS 2260	A Stitch In Time (4.20 Version)/Sweet Dream (p/s, white vinyl)	12
78	Chrysalis CHS 2260	A Stitch In Time (4.20 Version)/Sweet Dream (p/s, black vinyl)	8
79	Chrysalis CHS 2378	North Sea Oil/Elegy (p/s)	10
79	Chrysalis CHS 2394	Home/King Henry's Madrigal (Theme From Mainstream)/Warm Sporran (p/s)	12
79	Chrysalis CHS 2468	Working John, Working Joe/Flyingdale Flyer (p/s)	8
80	Chrysalis CHS 2619	Broadsword/Fallen On Hard Times (p/s)	6
84	Chrysalis TULLD 1	Lap Of Luxury/Astronomy//Automotive Engineering/Tundra (double pack, gatefold p/s)	10
84	Chrysalis TULL X 1	Lap Of Luxury/Astronomy/Automotive Engineering/Tundra (12", p/s)	10
86	Chrysalis TULL 2	Coronach (with David Palmer)/Jack Frost And The Hooded Crow (p/s)	7
86	Chrysalis TULLX 2	Coronach (with David Palmer)/Jack Frost And The Hooded Crow/ Living In The Past/Elegy (12", p/s)	40
87	Chrysalis TULLP 3	Steel Monkey/Down At The End Of Your Road (die-cut picture disc)	20
87	Chrysalis ZTULL 3	Steel Monkey/Down At The End Of Your Road/Too Many Too/I'm Your Gun (numbered edition of 3,000 with competition pack & badge)	15
87	Chrysalis TULLX 3	Steel Monkey/Down At The End Of Your Road/Too Many Too/I'm Your Gun (12", p/s)	10
88	Chrysalis TULLX 4	Said She Was A Dancer/Dogs In The Midwinter/The Waking Edge (p/s)	8
88	Chrysalis TULLCD 4	Said She Was A Dancer/Dogs In The Midwinter/Down At The End Of The Road/Too Many Too (CD, picture disc, limited issue)	25
89	Chrysalis TULL 5	Another Christmas Song (p/s)	10
89	Chrysalis TULLX5	Another Christmas Song/Intro-A Christmas Song/Cheap Day Return-Mother Goose/Outro-Locomotive Breath (12" p/s)	20

ALBUMS

68	Island ILP 985	THIS WAS (1st pressing, pink label/black & orange 'circle' logo, mono)	400
68	Island ILPS 9085	THIS WAS (1st pressing, pink label/black & orange 'circle' logo, stereo, laminated gatefold flipback sleeve, some issues as mono issues with stereo stickers)	250
69	Island ILPS 9103	STAND UP (1st pressing, gatefold sleeve pop-up inside, pink label/black & orange 'circle' logo)	225
70	Chrysalis ILPS 9123	BENEFIT (green Chrysalis or Island pink rim label)	100
70	Chrysalis ILPS 9123	BENEFIT (Island pink rim label 'palm tree' logo)	45
71	Island ILPS 9145	AQUALUNG (1st pressing, Matrixes ILPS 9145 A//1U and ILPS B//3U, Chrysalis labels with white 'i' at top of label, with textured E.J. Day Group gatefold sleeve with ILPS 9145 on top right hand corner, inner bag)	100
71	Island ILPS 9145	AQUALUNG (pink rim palm tree label, gatefold sleeve)	150
72	Chrysalis CHR 1003	THICK AS A BRICK (LP, 1st pressing with white 'i' at top of label, Matrixes: CHR1003 A-3U/CHR1003 B-2U, 'Porky' etched into dead wax side 1, 'Pecko' etched into dead wax side 2, textured sleeve with fold-out newspaper sleeve)	80
72	Chrysalis CJT 1	LIVING IN THE PAST (2-LP, with hard sleeve & booklet)	30
73	Chrysalis CHR 1040	A PASSION PLAY (gatefold sleeve with matt finish, with Linwell theatre booklet, Matrix CHR1040 A4U/B4, green label without small white "i", later presses have red wording on rim and A2U matrix)	45
78	Chrysalis CHR 1175	HEAVY HORSES (with insert)	15
84	Chrysalis CDLP 1461	UNDER WRAPS (picture disc)	15
88	Chrysalis Tbox1	20 YEARS OF JETHRO TULL (5-LP box set with 24-page booklet)	75
88	Chrysalis Tbox CD1	20 YEARS OF JETHRO TULL (3-CD box set with 24-page booklet)	50
89	Chrysalis CHRP 1708	ROCK ISLAND (Picture disc)	18
91	Chrysalis DCHR 1886	CATFISH RISING (Ltd edn. With 3-track 12" and lyric sheet inner sleeve)	20

JETLINERS

MINT VALUE £

| 93 | Chrysalis CDCHR 6004 | JETHRO TULL 25th ANNIVERSARY (4-CD cigar box set with 48-page booklet) | 55 |
| 95 | Chrysalis CHR 6109 | ROOTS TO BRANCHES (2-LP) | 80 |

ALBUMS : LP REPRESSINGS

68	Island ILP 985	THIS WAS (pink label/'i' logo, mono)	70
69	Island ILPS 9085	THIS WAS (pink label/black 'block' logo, 1st mix)	40
70	Island ILPS 9085	THIS WAS (pink label/'i' logo)	20
70	Chrysalis ILPS 9103	STAND UP (pop-up sleeve, pink label/black 'block' logo or pink label/'i' logo)	18
96	Chrysalis LP25AQUA1	AQUALUNG (2-LP, 25th anniversary edition)	50
97	EMI LPCENT 8	STAND UP (LP, reissue, EMI centenary, stickered sleeve)	30
97	EMI LPCENT 31	AS THICK AS A BRICK (LP, reissue, EMI centenary, stickered sleeve)	30
16	Chrysalis AQUA 1	AQUALUNG (LP, repressing, Steve Wilson mix, green vinyl, Sainsburys sticker)	20

PROMOS

76	Chrysalis CHS 3 PDJ	Ring Out/Solstice Bells/March, The Mad Scientist/Christmas Song/ Pan Dance (12")	25
79	Chrysalis CHS018-PDJ	Dark Ages (Special edited version) 12" promo	15
84	Chrysalis AS 1967	Under Wraps#1 (electric)/Under Wraps#2 (acoustic) (12" promo)	12
87	Chrysalis VAS 1039	Budapest (Special Radio Edit) (12" promo with illustrated sticker)	12
87	Chrysalis VAS 2796	Steel Monkey (12" promo)	12
87	Chrysalis VAS 2866	Farm On The Freeway (Special Rock Radio Edit) (12" promo)	15
88	Chrysalis VAS 1170	Part Of The Machine/Part Of The Machine (Edit) (12" promo with tour dates sticker)	18

(see also Mick Abrahams, Blodwyn Pig, Wild Turkey, The John Even Band)

JETLINERS
| 66 | Blue Beat BB 367 | Meditation (actually by Sugar & Dandy)/GIRL SATCHMO: Nature Of Love (actually with Jetliners) | 35 |

JETS (1)
| 73 | Cube BUG 35 | Yeah!/Rusty Corinthian Pillar | 15 |
| 78 | Soho SH 3 | Rockabilly Baby/James Dean | 7 |

JETS (2)
| 79 | Decca FR 13867 | Tearaway/Impossible | 100 |

JETS (3)
| 79 | Good Vibrations GV 1002 | Block 4/Iceburn (p/s) | 7 |

JET SET
| 62 | Delta DW 5001 | VC 10/Cruising 600 (some in p/s) | 15 |
| 64 | Parlophone R 5199 | You Got Me Hooked/True To You | 25 |

JETSET
84	Dance Network NET 1	BEST OF THE JETSET (EP)	10
85	Dance Network NET 3	APRIL, MAY, JUNE AND THE JETSET (12" EP)	12
85	Dance Network WORK 1	THERE GOES THE NEIGHBOURHOOD (LP, pink sleeve, poster)	20
86	Dance Network WORK 4	4 GO BANANAS (LP, with lyric insert)	20

JETSTREAMS
| 59 | Decca F 11149 | Bongo Rock/Tiger | 15 |

JETZ
| 78 | Pollen PBM 019 | Down By The River/Brother John/You Ain't Seen Nothing Yet/Easy Feeling | 25 |

JEVUTSHTA
| 78 | Zel-La JHSPS 226 | Fight Your Way Out/Stomp | 30 |

LEN JEWELL
| 09 | Soul City 144 | Betting On Love/All My Good Lovin' (reissue) | 10 |

JEWELLS (JAMAICA)
| 77 | Observer OB 005 | Black is The Highest Culture (Culture Version)/One Little Lick Version (12") | 45 |
| 77 | Observer OB 1101 | Jah I/LEROY SMART: Jah Is My Light/I-ROY: Wicked Eat Dirt (12") | 25 |

JEWELS
| 64 | Colpix PX 11034 | Opportunity/Gotta Find A Way | 30 |
| 65 | Colpix PX 11048 | But I Do/Smokey Joe | 18 |

JFK
| 92 | Fourth Dimension FDS24 | Sexodus/Temple Of Set (p/s, 500 only numbered) | 6 |

JIGSAW
68	Polydor 56241	I Need Your Love/I've Gotta Get Me Some Money (as Jig-Saw Band)	15
68	Music Factory CUB 4	Mister Job/Great Idea	15
68	Music Factory CUB 6	Let Me Go Home/Tumblin'	80
68	MGM MGM 1410	One Way Street/Then I Found You	100
70	Philips 6006 112	One Way Street/Coffucious Confusion	70
70	Fontana 6007 017	Lollipop And Goody Man/Seven Fishes	40
71	Philips 6006 131	Jesu Joy Of Man's Desiring/No Questions Asked	10
71	Philips 6006 182	Keeping My Head Above Water/It's Nice But It's Wrong	7
74	BASF BA 1002	I've Seen The Film I've Read The Book/Mention My Name	7
75	BASF BA 1013	Baby Don't Do It/Stand Next To Me	7
71	Philips 6308 033	LETHERSLADE FARM (LP)	80
72	Philips 6308 072	AURORA BOREALIS (LP)	50
73	BASF 29106-5	BROKEN HEARTED (LP, gatefold sleeve)	15

JILL & BOULEVARDS
| 62 | Columbia DB 4823 | And Now I Cry/Eugene | 25 |

JILL & Y'VERNS
| 60s | Oak RGJ 503 | My Soulful Dress/Anything He Wants Me To Do | 100 |

JILTED JOHN
78	Rabid TOSH 105	Jilted John/Going Steady (p/s)	15
78	EMI Intl. INS 3024	TRUE LOVE STORIES (LP, with board game insert)	25
78	EMI Intl. INS 3024	TRUE LOVE STORIES (LP)	15

(see also Going Red?)

JIM & JEAN
| 68 | Verve Folkways VLP 5017 | CHANGES (LP) | 40 |

JIM & JOE

MINT VALUE £

JIM & JOE
64 London HL 9831   Fireball Mail/Daisy Mae 20
(see also James Burton)

JIM & MONICA
64 Stateside SS 266   Slippin' And Slidin'/Sing Along Without Jim & Monica 20
(see also Jimmy Gilmer & Fireballs)

JIMBILIN
71 Bamboo BAM 68   Human Race/Let Love In (both actually by Herman Chin-Loy & Aquarians) 15
75 Ashanti ASH 421   Balaclava/Tacku 15

JOSE JIMINEZ
61 London HLR 9434   The Astronaut Part 1/Part 2 6

JIMMIE & NIGHT HOPPERS
59 London HLP 8830   Cruisin'/Night Hop 30
59 London HLP 8830   Cruisin'/Night Hop (78) 30

JIMMY AND THE DIMENSIONS
69 Youngblood YB 1008   Sugar Man/Slow Down 12
(see also Jimmy Powell & Red Alligator)

JIMMY J & CRU-L-T
94 Kniforce KF 027   Take Me Away (Slipmatt Remix)/FUTURE PRIMITIVE: Life Me Up (Slammin' Vinyl Remix)
                                          (12", p/s) 15

JIV-A-TONES
58 Felsted AF 101   Flirty Gertie/Fire Engine Baby 150
58 Felsted AF 101   Flirty Gertie/Fire Engine Baby (78) 50

JIVE FIVE
61 Parlophone R 4822   My True Story/When I Was Single 150
62 Stateside SS 133   What Time Is It?/Begging You Please 90
65 United Artists UP 1106   I'm A Happy Man/Kiss Kiss KIss 45

JIVERS (JAMAICA)
68 Trojan TR 604   Wear My Crown/Down On The Beach 30
(see also Brother Dan Allstars)

JIVERS (U.S.)
56 Vogue V 9060   Little Mama/Cherie 650
56 Vogue V 9060   Little Mama/Cherie (78) 150
57 Vogue V 9068   Ray Pearl/Dear Little One 600
57 Vogue V 9068   Ray Pearl/Dear Little One (78) 150

JIVING JUNIORS
60 Blue Beat BB 4   Lollipop Girl/Dearest Darling 30
60 Blue Beat BB 5   My Heart's Desire/I Love You 40
60 Starlite ST45 028   Lovers Line/Tu-Woo-Up-Tu-Woo 40
61 Starlite ST45 049   Slop & Mash/My Sweet Angel 40
61 Blue Beat BB 36   Over The River/Hip Rub (with Hersan & His City Slickers) 30
62 Island WI 003   Sugar Dandy/Valerie 25
62 Island WI 027   Andrea/Don't Leave Me 25
63 Island WI 129   Sugar Dandy/Valerie (reissue) 20
(see also Duke Reid)

J.J. ALLSTARS
68 Duke DU 3   One Dollar Of Music/CARL DAWKINS: I'll Make It Up 70
69 Trojan TR 691   Memphis Underground (Parts 1 & 2) 25
69 Doctor Bird DB 1308   Five miles High/CARL DAWKINS: Only Girl 50
70 Duke DU 94   Collecting Coins/Cabbage Leaf 15
70 Duke DU 95   This Land (actually by Carl Dawkins)/Land Version 12
70 Escort ES 821   Mango Tree/The Removers (both actually by Winston Wright & J.J. All Stars) 50
71 Big Shot BI 570   Perseverence Version/CARL DAWKINS: Perseverance 12
71 Explosion EX 2051   I Feel Good (Version 2)/CARL DAWKINS: I Feel Good 10
71 Duke DU 135   Soup/Soup (Version) (with Lloyd Young) 20
(see also Lloyd Young, Bleechers, Ethiopians)

J.J. BAND
71 CBS S 64396   THE J.J. BAND (LP) 25

JJ72
00 Lakota LAKLP 0017   JJ72 (LP) 20

JJ'S POWERHOUSE
83 Sillysybin COX 1657   Running For The Line/Blackrods (no p/s) 250

JME
15 Boy Better Know JME 051   INTEGRITY (LP, clear vinyl) 50
15 Boy Better Know JME 052   INTEGRITY - INSTRUMENTALS (LP, clear vinyl) 15

MARCY JO & EDDIE RAMBEAU
63 Stateside SS 235   Lover's Medley/When You Wore A Tulip 10
(see also Eddie Rambeau)

JOANIE, JOHNNY & HAL
60 Capitol CL 15126   When You Lose The One You Love/Miracles Are Always Happening 6

JOBELL (& ORCHESTRA DE SALSA)
77 Pye N25736   Never Gonna Let You Go/Disco Version 8

JOBRIATH
74 Elektra K 12156   Ooh La La/Gone Tomorrow (demo) 20
73 Elektra EKS 75070   JOBRIATH (LP) 20
74 Elektra K 42163   CREATURES OF THE STREET (LP) 20

JO'BURG HAWK
73 Charisma CAS 1064   JO'BURG HAWK (LP, gatefold sleeve, large 'Mad Hatter' label) 20

JOCELYNE JOCYA
69 CBS 4177   I Have Loved Me A Man/Time 60
69 CBS 4177   I Have Loved Me A Man/Time (DJ copy) 150

JODECI
MINT VALUE £

JODECI
92	MCA MCA 10534	FOREVER MY LADY (LP)	20
93	MCA MCA 11019	DIARY OF A MAD BAND (LP)	20
95	MCA MCA 11258	THE SHOW THE AFTER PARTY THE HOTEL (2-LP)	20

JODEY
79	Elliejay EJSP 9242	The Rocker/Front Man	150

JODIMARS
56	Capitol CL 14518	Well Now, Dig This/Let's All Rock Together	75
56	Capitol CL 14627	Rattle My Bones/Lotsa Love	75
56	Capitol CL 14641	Rattle Shakin' Daddy/Eat Your Heart Out Annie	75
56	Capitol CL 14642	Dance The Bop/Boom, Boom My Bayou Baby	75
56	Capitol CL 14663	Midnight/Clarabella	75
57	Capitol CL 14700	Cloud 99/Later	70
72	Specialty SPE 6608	WELL NOW DIG THIS (LP)	20

(see also Bill Haley & Comets)

JODY GRIND
69	Transatlantic TRA 210	ONE STEP ON (LP, gatefold sleeve, lilac label with 't' logo)	175
70	Transatlantic TRA 221	FAR CANAL (LP, white/lilac label with 't' logo)	175

(see also Vinegar Joe, Hummingbird, Heads, Hands & Feet)

JODY ST
81	Lips LIPS1	Fight Back/Granny Did It (private pressing)	150
81	Private Pressing	STREET (LP, private pressing)	125

AL T. JOE (& CELESTIALS)
62	Dice CC 9	Rise Jamaica/I'm On My Own	15
62	Blue Beat BB 126	You Cheated On Me/This Heart Of Mine (as Al T. Joe & Celestials)	15
63	Blue Beat BB 166	Goodbye Dreamboat/Please Forgive Me	15
63	Blue Beat BB 169	Fatso/Slow Boat	12
70	Duke DU 70	It's A Shame/Desertion	12
72	Duke DU 148	Vision/Young And Unlearned	15
72	Dynamic DYN 429	Oh What A Price/The Prisoners Song	15

(see also Jamaica Fats)

JOE & ANN
65	Black Swan WI 468	Gee Baby/Wherever You May Be	20

BILLY JOE & CHECKMATES
61	London HLU 9502	Percolator/Round & Round & Round & Round	8

JOE COOL (& THE KILLERS)
77	Ariola ARO 105	I Just Don't Care/My Way (p/s)	25

JOE CROW
82	Cherry Red CHERRY 48	Compulsion/Absent Friends	25

JOE & DELLA
65	Doctor Bird DB 1043	So Close/BABA BROOKS : Eight Games	20

JOE & EDDIE
59	Capitol CL 15038	Green Grass/And I Believed	7
65	Vocalion V-P 9250	Walkin' Down The Line/It Ain't Me Babe	10
65	Vocalion VAN 8046	WALKIN' DOWN THE LINE (LP)	30

JOE 9T & THUNDERBIRDS
79	Gemme JOE 9T/LYN 6526	Joe 9T Theme/THEY MUST BE RUSSIANS: Psycho Analysis (p/s, stamped white label)	15

(see also They Must Be Russians)

JOE 90
92	Full Effect FERT 112	Good Times/New Found Strength (12")	20

JOE PUBLIC (1)
79	Wavelength HURT 3	Herman's Back/Travelling With Raymond/Like It (p/s)	8

JOE PUBLIC (2)
85	Capital Class	Anti CND/Champagne Charlie	30

JOE (MANSANO) THE BOSS
70	Joe JRS 6	Son Of Al Capone/All My Enemies	30
70	Joe JRS 10	If Life Was A Thing/LLOYD KINGPIN: Daisy Bothering	120

(see also Joe's Allstars, Joe Mansano, Dice The Boss)

BILLY JOEL
72	Philips 6078 001	She's Got A Way/Everybody Loves You Now	8
74	Philips 6078 018	The Ballad Of Billy The Kid/If I Only Had The Words (To Tell You) (in p/s)	35
74	Philips 6078 018	The Ballad Of Billy The Kid/If I Only Had The Words (To Tell You)	25
79	CBS 7150	Honesty/Root Beer Rag (withdrawn)	20
72	Philips 6369 150	COLD SPRING HARBOR (LP)	15
73	Philips 6369 160	PIANO MAN (LP, withdrawn)	20
78	CBS H 82311	THE STRANGER (LP, half-speed master version)	20

(see also Hassles)

JOE MOD
79	Sonia AERS 7	Things Have Changed/Things Have Changed (Dub) (no p/s)	6

JOE'S ALLSTARS
69	Joe/Duke DU 24	Hey Jude/Musical Feet	75
69	Joe/Duke DU 28	Battle Cry Of Biafra/Funky Reggae Part 1	40
69	Joe/Duke DU 50	Brixton Cat/Solitude	50
70	Joe JRS 9	Tony B's Theme/JOE THE BOSS: Skinhead Revolt	180
72	Sioux SI 012	Tony B's Theme/RAY MARTELL: She Caught The Train	12
70	Trojan TBL 106	BRIXTON CAT (LP)	50

(see also Joe The Boss, Dice The Boss, King Horror, Pattie La Donne)

JOE SOAP
73	Polydor 2383 233	KEEP IT CLEAN (LP, laminated sleeve, correction sticker on rear)	150

JOE SOPE

MINT VALUE £

JOE SOPE
79 Redball RR 022   Gotta Be Something Else/Don't Understand 40

JOEY & GROUP
13 Blue Cat THB 7028   Soul Love/LORD COMIC: What A Situation 8

JOEY & CONTINENTALS
70 Polydor 56520   She Rides With Me/Rudy Vadoo 85
(see also G.T.O.'s)

JOEY & GENTLEMEN
64 Fontana TF 444   Like I Love You/I'll Never Let You Go 10
64 Fontana TF 485   Dummy Dum Song/Goodbye Little Girl 6

JOHANNE & JIMMY
64 Fontana TF 447   Everybody Knows/I Still Love you 8

JOHN
71 Capitol CL 15678   The Ten Lost Tribes Of Israel/Good Morning Old Man Time 10

ANDREW JOHN
71 CBS 7017   Streets Of London/Rick Rack 10
72 CBS 64835   THE MACHINE STOPS (LP) 20

BASIL JOHN
60s Planetone RC 12   Drink And Drive/MIKE ELLIOTT: J.K. Shuffle 10

CLIVE JOHN
75 United Artists UAS 29733 YOU ALWAYS KNOW WHERE YOU STAND WITH A BUZZARD (LP) 25
(see also Man)

COURTNEY JOHN
09 Peckings PTI 059   Lucky Man/LADY LEX: Don't Know Why 40

DAVID JOHN & MOOD
64 Vocalion V 9220   To Catch That Man/Pretty Thing 220
65 Parlophone R 5255   Bring It To Jerome/I Love To See You Strut 275
65 Parlophone R 5301   Diggin' For Gold/She's Fine 275
(see also Gagalactyca, Astral Navigations, Little Free Rock)

ELTON JOHN
SINGLES
68 Philips BF 1643   I've Been Loving You/Here's To The Next Time 250
69 Philips BF 1739   Lady Samantha/All Across The Havens 70
69 DJM DJS 205   It's Me That You Need/Just Like Strange Rain (in p/s) 100
69 DJM DJS 205   It's Me That You Need/Just Like Strange Rain 50
70 DJM DJS 217   Border Song/Bad Side Of The Moon 25
70 DJM DJS 222   Rock And Roll Madonna/Grey Seal 30
71 DJM DJS 244   Friends/Honey Roll 10
72 DJM DJX 501   Rocket Man/Holiday Inn/Goodbye (gatefold p/s) 10
72 DJM DJS 269   Honky Cat/Lady Samantha/It's Me That You Need 6
73 DJM DJ X502   Saturday Night's Alright For Fighting/Jack Rabbit/Whenever You're Ready (We'll Go Steady Again) (non-laminated p/s) 20
73 DJM DJX 502   Saturday Night's Alright For Fighting/Jack Rabbit/Whenever You're Ready (We'll Go Steady Again) (laminated p/s) 8
73 DJM DJS 290   Step Into Christmas/Ho! Ho! Ho! (Who'd Be A Turkey At Christmas) 8
75 DJM DJS 354   Philadelphia Freedom/I Saw Her Standing There (as Elton John Band; B-side featuring John Lennon with Muscle Shoals Horns) (p/s) 6
75 DJM DJS 610   Island Girl/Sugar On The Floor (p/s) 6
76 DJM DJS 10705   Benny And The Jets/Rock 'N' Roll Madonna 6
77 Rocket GOALD 1   The Goaldigger Song/Jimmy, Brian, Elton, Eric (mail-order, signed, 500 only, solid centre copies are counterfeits) 250
77 Rocket GOALD 1   The Goaldigger Song/Jimmy, Brian, Elton, Eric (mail-order, unsigned, 500 only, solid centre copies are counterfeits) 150
78 DJM DJS 10908   Candle In The Wind/I Feel Like A Bullet (In The Gun Of Robert Ford) (p/s, limited edition) 10
78 DJM EJ 12   THE ELTON JOHN SINGLES COLLECTION (12 x 7" box set [DJS 10901-12]) ... 50
78 DJM DJT 15000   FUNERAL FOR A FRIEND (12" EP) 10
79 Rocket XPRES 20   Mama Can't Buy You Love/Strangers (p/s; withdrawn, misspelt "Mamma") 350
79 Rocket XPRES 21   Victim Of Love/Strangers (p/s) 7
79 Rocket XPRES 2412   Johnny B. Goode/Thunder In The Night (12", p/s) 10
80 DJM DJS 10961   Harmony/Mona Lisas And Mad Hatters (glossy p/s) 8
80 Rocket XPRES 45   Dear God/Tactics (company sleeve) 40
80 Rocket ELTON 1   Dear God/Tactics//Steal Away Child/Love So Cold (double pack, p/s) 6
82 Rocket XPRPO 88   All Quiet On The Western Front/Where Have All The Good Times Gone (poster p/s) .. 10
83 Rocket XPRES 91   That's Why They Call It The Blues/Lord Choc Ice Goes Mental ('raised musical note' sleeve with shorter A-side title) 15
83 Rocket EJPIC 1   I'm Still Standing/Earn While You Learn (piano-shaped picture disc) 15
83 Rocket EJS 2/FREEJ 2   Kiss The Bride/Dreamboat//Ego/Song For Guy (double pack, p/s) 10
83 Rocket EJS 3/2   Cold As Christmas/Crystal//Don't Go Breaking My Heart/Snow Queen (double pack, gatefold p/s, 2nd 45 with Kiki Dee) 12
85 Rocket EJS 8   Act Of War (Part 1)/(Part 2) (with Millie Jackson, 'concertina pack' of video stills) 8
85 Rocket EJS 10/EJS 9   Wrap Her Up/Restless (live)//Nikita/The Man Who Never Died (double pack, stickered gatefold PVC wallet with 2 separate p/s's) 10
85 Rocket EJSP 10   Wrap Her Up/Restless (live) (with George Michael, oblong-shaped picture disc, with pictures on wrong sides) 25
85 Rocket EJS 1012/ELTON 1 Wrap Her Up (Extended Remix) (with George Michael)/Restless (live)/ Nikita/Cold As Christmas (12", double pack in stickered PVC sleeve) 10
86 Rocket EJSP 13   Slow Rivers (with Cliff Richard)/Billy & The Kids (picture disc) 30
86 Rocket EJS 13-12   Slow Rivers (with Cliff Richard)/Billy & The Kids/Lord Of The Flies (12", p/s) ... 12
88 Rocket EJS 1512   Candle In The Wind (live)/Sorry Seems To Be The Hardest Word (live)/ Your Song (live)/Don't Let The Sun Go Down On Me (live) (12", p/s) 12
88 Rocket EJSIP 16   I Don't Wanna Go On With You Like That/Rope Around A Fool/ (Radio 1 interview) (33rpm, poster sleeve) 10

JOHN LEE'S GROUNDHOGS

MINT VALUE £

88	Rocket EJS 1612	I Don't Wanna Go On With You Like That (Remix)/(7" Version)/ Rope Around A Fool (12", blue vinyl factory custom pressing, no p/s)	150
90	Rocket EJS 21	Club At The End Of The Street/Give Peace A Chance (p/s, withdrawn)	200
90	Rocket EJS 2112	Club At The End Of The Street/Give Peace A Chance (12", p/s, withdrawn)	500
97	Rocket EJSCD 41	Something About The Way You Look Tonight (Edited Version)/ I Know Why I'm In Love/ No Valentines/Something About The Way You Look Tonight (Album Version) (CD, card sleeve, unreleased)	40
97	Rocket EJSCX 41	Something About The Way You Look Tonight (Edited Version)/ I Know Why I'm In Love/ You Can Make History (Young Again)/Something About The Way You Look Tonight (Album Version) (CD, digipak, unreleased)	75
13	Secret 7" S78	Bennie And The Jets (100 only, each with unique art sleeve)	70

ALBUMS

69	DJM DJLP 403	EMPTY SKY (gatefold sleeve, mono)	150
69	DJM DJLPS 403	EMPTY SKY (gatefold sleeve, stereo, with 'stereo' sticker on sleeve)	30
70	Warlock Music WMM 101/2	WARLOCK MUSIC SAMPLER (untitled publishing sampler, 7 tracks by Elton, 4 by Linda Peters)	1000
70	DJM DJLPS 406	ELTON JOHN (textured gatefold sleeve)	35
70	DJM DJLPS 406	ELTON JOHN (later smooth gatefold sleeve)	20
70	DJM DJLPS 410	TUMBLEWEED CONNECTION (LP, with booklet)	35
71	DJM DJLPH 420	MADMAN ACROSS THE WATER (LP, gatefold)	35
72	DJM DJLPH 423	HONKY CHATEAU (LP, gatefold)	35
73	DJM DJLPD 1001	GOODBYE YELLOW BRICK ROAD (2-LP, tri-fold)	25
73	DJM DJLPH 427	DON'T SHOOT ME I'M ONLY THE PIANO PLAYER (LP, with booklet)	35
75	DJM DJLPX 1	CAPTAIN FANTASTIC AND THE BROWN DIRT COWBOY (LP, gatefold)	35
76	DJM DJE 29001	GOODBYE YELLOW BRICK ROAD (2-LP, yellow vinyl, triplefold sleeve)	60
78	DJM DJV 2300	CAPTAIN FANTASTIC AND THE BROWN DIRT COWBOY (picture disc)	40
78	DJM LSP 14512	ELTON JOHN (5-LP, box set)	40
90	Rocket 846 947 1	THE VERY BEST OF ELTON JOHN (2-LP)	20
91	Rocket 848 236-2	TO BE CONTINUED ... THE VERY BEST OF ELTON JOHN (4-CD, 12" x 8" box set with large colour booklet)	100
93	Happenstance HAPP 001	PLAYS THE SIRAN (private pressing, 50 only)	1000
93	Happenstance HAPP 002	THE FISHING TRIP (4-CD set, private pressing, 100 only, existence unconfirmed)	700
93	Rocket 518 478-1	DUETS (2-LP)	35
95	Mercury 526 185 1	MADE IN ENGLAND (LP)	100
95	Rocket 528 788 2	LOVE SONGS (2-LP)	80
97	Rocket ELTON 50	CELEBRATING ELTON JOHN'S 50TH BIRTHDAY (promo only)	50
99	Mercury ADV 1999/1	AIDA (with Sir Tim Rice) (box set with wallet, plinth stand, interview CD, booklet and calender cards, promo only)	50
99	Mercury ADV 1999/1	AIDA PRESS KIT (card box set with wallet, plinth stand, interview CD, booklet, calender cards, scented candle and broadcast CD-R, promo only)	50
05	Rocket 9872301	PEACHTREE ROAD (LP)	200
06	Mercury 1705730	THE CAPTAIN & THE KID (LP)	70
10	Mercury 2750475	THE UNION (2-LP, with Leon Russell)	25

(see also [Stu Brown &] Bluesology, Bread & Beer Band, Neil Sedaka, Kiki Dee, Aretha Franklin, Dionne Warwick Radio Heart, Argosy)

JOHN LEE'S GROUNDHOGS

66	Planet PLF 104	Over You Baby/I'll Never Fall In Love Again	100

(see also Groundhogs, Tony McPhee)

LITTLE WILLIE JOHN

56	Parlophone R 4209	Fever/Letter From My Darling	150
56	Parlophone R 4209	Fever/Letter From My Darling (78)	20
58	Parlophone R 4396	Uh, Uh, Baby/Dinner Date (With His Girl Friend)	50
58	Parlophone R 4432	Talk To Me, Talk To Me/Spasms	40
58	Parlophone R 4472	Let's Rock While The Rockin's Good/You're A Sweetheart	60
59	Parlophone R 4571	Leave My Kitten Alone/Let Nobody Love You	50
60	Parlophone R 4674	Heartbreak (It's Hurtin' Me)/Do You Love Me	30
60	Parlophone R 4699	Sleep/There's A Difference	30
61	Parlophone R 4728	Walk Slow/HANK BALLARD: The Hoochie Coochie Coo	40
11	Kent CITY 011	Home At Last/(I Need) Someone	8
59	Parlophone PMC 1163	SURE THINGS (LP)	175
64	London HA 8126	COME ON AND JOIN LITTLE WILLIE JOHN (LP)	70

MABLE JOHN

66	Atlantic 584 022	It's Catching/Your Good Thing (Is About To End)	15
67	Stax 601 010	Same Time Same Place/Bigger And Better (dark blue label)	15
67	Stax 601 010	Same Time Same Place/Bigger And Better (light blue label)	10
68	Stax 601 034	Able Mable/Don't Get Caught	15

MAVIS JOHN & JOANNE WILSON

81	Red Stripe SON 2222	How Can I Love Again?/JOANNE WILSON: Gotta Have You Back	15

MICHAEL JOHN

83	Loose LSE 48	Love Will Tear Us Apart/We're Together (p/s)	6

ROBERT JOHN (1)

68	CBS 3436	If You Don't Want My Love/Don't	15
68	A&M AMS 835	Raindrops Love And Sunshine/When The Party Is Over (DJ Copy)	100
68	A&M AMS 835	Raindrops Love And Sunshine/When The Party Is Over	50

ROBERT JOHN (2)

80	John 1	The Aliens Stalk The Wrecked Planet/The Aliens Stalk The Wrecked Planet (same track both sides, no p/s)	25

SAMMIE JOHN

67	Stateside SS 585	Little John/Boss Bag	20

JOHN & JOHNNY

63	Decca F 11719	I Want You To Be My Girl/It's You	6

JOHN & PAUL

65	London HLU 9997	People Say/I'm Walkin'	15

JOHNNIE & JOE

MINT VALUE £

JOHNNIE & JOE
58	London HLM 8682	Over The Mountain, Across The Sea/My Baby's Gone, On, On	150
58	London HLM 8682	Over The Mountain, Across The Sea/My Baby's Gone, On, On (78)	20

JOHNNY DANGEROUSLY
90	Village (no cat no)	Introducing Jane/Tear It Down/Subway Life (12" p/s)	20
89	Village (no cat no)	YOU, ME AND THE ALARM CLOCK (mini LP p/s with photo insert, 1,000 only)	35

(see also I Am Kloot)

JOHNNY G
78	Beggars Banquet BEG 7	The Hippys Graveyard/Miles And Miles (p/s)	6

JOHNNY & JAILBIRDS
79	Duke WIRP 001	Shang A-Lang A-Ding Dong/Slick Chick	8

LITTLE JOHNNY JONES
73	Pressure Beat PB 5515	More Dub/More Dub - Chapter Two	10

(see also Johnny Lover)

JOHNNY & THE ROCCOS
78	SRT SRTX/78/CUS 212	JOHNNY & THE ROCCOS (LP)	40

JOHNNY RONDO TRIO
78	Chiltern Sound RONDO 1	Las Bicicletas/Frog Dance (p/s, trio of Lol Coxhill, Chris Wood and Dave Holland)	10

(see also Lol Coxhill)

JOHNNY (OSBORNE) & ATTRACTIONS
67	Doctor Bird DB 1118	Young Wings Can Fly/DUDLEY WILLIAMSON: I'm Moving On	200
68	Doctor Bird DB 1117	Coming On The Scene/Anything You Want	400

JOHNNY (STEVENS) & THE BLUE BEATS
64	Blue Beat BB 229	Shame/Ball And Chain	15

JOHNNY & CHARLEY
65	Pye Int. 7N 25326	La Yenka/Baila La Yenka	7

JOHNNY & CHAZ & GUNNERS
61	Decca F 11365	Bobby/Out Of Luck	22

JOHNNY & THE COPYCATS
64	Norco AB 102	I'm A Hog For You Baby/I Can Never See You	60

(see also My Dear Watson)

JOHNNY & THE HURRICANES
59	London HL 8899	Crossfire/Lazy (triangular-centre)	20
59	London HL 8899	Crossfire/Lazy (later round centre)	10
59	London HL 8948	Red River Rock/Buckeye (triangular-centre)	10
59	London HL 8948	Red River Rock/Buckeye (later round centre)	6
59	London HL 9017	Reveille Rock/Time Bomb (triangular-centre)	10
59	London HL 9017	Reveille Rock/Time Bomb (later round centre)	6
59	London HL 9017	Reveille Rock/Time Bomb (78)	20
60	London HLI 9072	Beatnick Fly/Sand Storm	6
60	London HLI 9072	Beatnick Fly/Sand Storm (78)	40
60	London HLX 9134	Down Yonder/Sheba (78)	80
60	London HLX 9190	Rocking Goose/Revival (78)	100
60	London HL 7099	The Hep Canary/Catnip (export issue)	25
61	London HLX 9289	Ja-Da/Mr. Lonely	8
61	London HLX 9378	High Voltage/Old Smokie	8
62	London HLX 9491	Farewell, Farewell/Traffic Jam	10
62	London HLX 7116	You Are My Sunshine/Farewell, Farewell (export issue)	20
62	London HLX 9536	Salvation/Misirlou	8
62	London HLX 9617	Minnesota Fats/Come On Train	8
63	London HLX 9660	Whatever Happened To Baby Jane/Greens And Beans	8
64	Stateside SS 347	Money Honey/That's All	10
61	London REX 1284	ROCKING GOOSE (EP)	20
62	London REX 1347	JOHNNY AND THE HURRICANES (EP)	20
64	London REX 1414	JOHNNY AND THE HURRICANES VOL. 2 (EP)	25
60	London HA 2227	RED RIVER ROCK (LP, plum label)	25
60	London HA-I 2269	STORMSVILLE (LP)	25
61	London HA-X 2322	THE BIG SOUND OF JOHNNY AND THE HURRICANES (LP)	20

JOHNNY & JACK
54	HMV 7MC 21	Honey, I Need You/Goodnight, Well It's Time To Go (export issue)	20
59	RCA RCX 176	COUNTRY GUITAR VOL. 10 (EP)	10

JOHNNY & JOHN
66	Polydor 56087	Bumper To Bumper/Scrape My Boot	25

(see also Johnny Gustafson, Big Three)

JOHNNY & JUDY
59	Vogue Pop V 9128	Bother Me Baby/Who's To Say	500
59	Vogue Pop V 9128	Bother Me Baby/Who's To Say (78)	150

(see also John Walker)

JOHNNY & THE SELF ABUSERS
77	Chiswick NS 22	Saints And Sinners/Dead Vandals (p/s)	40

(see also Simple Minds)

JOHNNY & VIBRATONES
63	Warner Bros WB 107	Bird Stompin'/Movin' The Bird	12

JOHNNY F & KLM
92	Liberty Grooves LIB003	TAKIN' LIBERTIES VOL 1 (LP)	15

JOHNNY MOPED
76	Chiswick PROMO 3	BASICALLY, THE ORIGINAL JOHNNY MOPED TAPE (33rpm, no p/s)	20
77	Chiswick S 15	No-One/Incendiary Device (first pressing has laminate p/s)	20
78	Chiswick NS 27	Darling, Let's Have Another Baby/Something Else/It Really Digs (p/s)	6
78	Chiswick NS 41	Little Queenie/Hard Lovin' Man (p/s)	8

JOHNNY P
MINT VALUE £

78	Chiswick WIK 8	CYCLEDELIC (LP, with free single [PROMO 3])	30
90	Deltic DELTLP 6	THE SEARCH FOR XERXES (LP)	20

(see also Slime, Maxim's Trash)

JOHNNY P
88	Unity EE 07	Rude Boy/Talk About We (with Richie Davis)	35

JOHNNY'S BOYS
59	Decca F 11156	Sleep Walk/Ciao Ciao Bambina	10

JOHNNY'S JAZZ
56	Decca FJ 10663	R.J. Boogie/Get Happy (featuring Johnny Hawksworth)	6

BARRY JOHNS
58	HMV POP 472	Locked In The Arms Of Love/Are You Sincere	7

JOHN'S CHILDREN
66	Columbia DB 8030	The Love I Thought I'd Found/Strange Affair (very few in p/s)	500
66	Columbia DB 8030	The Love I Thought I'd Found/Strange Affair	300
67	Columbia DB 8124	Just What You Want - Just What You'll Get/But She's Mine	160
67	Track 604 003	Desdemona/Remember Thomas A'Beckett (in p/s)	150
67	Track 604 003	Desdemona/Remember Thomas A'Beckett	60
67	Track 604 005	Midsummer Night's Scene/Sara Crazy Child (withdrawn)	4000
67	Track 604 005	Come And Play With Me In The Garden/Sara Crazy Child (in p/s)	200
67	Track 604 005	Come And Play With Me In The Garden/Sara Crazy Child	90
67	Track 604 010	Go Go Girl/Jagged Time Lapse	80
82	Cherry Red BRED 31	ORGASM (LP, with inner)	20
87	Bam Caruso KIRI 095	MIDSUMMER NIGHT'S SCENE (LP)	30

(see also Marc Bolan, Andy Ellison, Radio Stars, Jook, Tyrannosaurus Rex)

GLYN JOHNS
65	Immediate IM 013	Mary Anne/Like Grains Of Yellow Sand	25

LYNDON JOHNS (& ISRAELITES)
69	Downtown DT 444	Don't Gamble With Love/Song Bird	40
69	Downtown DT 451	Oh Mama Oh Papa/Bring Back The Night (with The Israelites)	30

JOHN'S RADIO
82	Epidemic EPC 001	Song In My Head/Strange	20

AL JOHNSON & JEAN CARN
80	CBS 8545	I'm Back For More/You Are My Personal Angel	10

(see also Jean Carn)

ALEC JOHNSON
79	RFP RFP 001	Busman's Holiday/My Lady (no p/s)	12

(see also Nightwing)

ANTHONY JOHNSON
82	Rusty R 005	Dread Locks Fight/ANTHONY JOHNSON & RANKING TOYAN: Babyloving (12")	35
81	Greensleeves GRED 76	Let Go This One/BILLY BOYO: One Spliff A Day (12")	20
89	Unity UNI 7	Dance Hall Vibe/Version//TONTO IRIE: Wrap It UP MIx (12")	20
83	Rusty RILP 003	I'M READY (LP)	25
82	Midnight Rock MRLP 002	GUN SHOT (LP)	30

BETTY JOHNSON
56	London HLU 8307	I'll Wait/Please Tell Me Why	40
56	London HLU 8326	Honky Tonk Rock/Say It Isn't So, Joe	100
56	London HLU 8326	Honky Tonk Rock/Say It Isn't So, Joe (78)	30
57	London HLU 8365	I Dreamed/If It's Wrong To Love You	20
57	London HLU 8432	1492/Little White Lies	10
58	London HLE 8557	Little Blue Man/Song You Heard When You Fell In Love	10
58	London HLE 8678	Dream/How Much	15
58	London HLE 8701	There's Never Been A Night/Mr. Brown Is Out Of Town	25
58	London HLE 8725	Hoopa Hoola/One More Time	20
59	London HLE 8839	Does Your Heart Beat For Me?/You And Only You	20
59	London HLE 8839	Does Your Heart Beat For Me?/You And Only You (78)	20
59	London RE-E 1221	DREAM (EP)	75
59	London HA-E 2163	THE SONG YOU HEARD WHEN YOU FELL IN LOVE (LP)	40

BLIND WILLIE JOHNSON
58	Fontana TFE 17052	TREASURES OF NORTH AMERICAN NEGRO MUSIC NO. 2 (EP)	10
70	Xtra XTRA 1098	BLIND WILLIE JOHNSON (LP)	20

BOB JOHNSON & PETE KNIGHT
77	Chrysalis CHR 1137	THE KING OF ELFLAND'S DAUGHTER (LP, lyric insert, green label)	15

(see also Steeleye Span, Mary Hopkin)

BOBBY JOHNSON & ATOMS
67	Ember EMB S 245	Do It Again A Little Bit Slower/Tramp (in p/s)	20
67	Ember EMB S 245	Do It Again A Little Bit Slower/Tramp	10

BROWNIE JOHNSON
62	Longhorn BLH 0004	Best Dressed Beggar/Just Pretending (estimated that around 1000 pressed)	40

BUBBER JOHNSON
57	Parlophone R 4259	Confidential/Have A Little Faith In Me	35

BUDDY JOHNSON
59	Mercury ZEP 10009	BUDDY JOHNSON WAILS (EP, with Ella Johnson)	50
57	Mercury MPT 7515	ROCK AND ROLL (10" LP, with Ella Johnson)	150

CAREY JOHNSON
72	Banana BA 369	Correction Train/SOUL DEFENDERS: Version	25

DANIEL JOHNSON
65	Island WI 250	Come On My People/Brother Nathan	15

DEBRA JOHNSON
98	Kent 6T 19	To Get Love/DIPLOMATS: I Really Love You	30

Domino JOHNSON

MINT VALUE £

DOMINO JOHNSON
72	Green Door GD 4045	Summertime/SWANS: Grazing	25
73	Count Shelly	I've Seen The Light/BARRY CRUBER: This Yah Daughter	50

DOMINO JOHNSON & CHAMPIONS
70	Duke DU 89	You Broke My Heart/TONY & CHAMPIONS: Tell Me The Reason	12

GENERAL JOHNSON
76	Arista ARIST 45	All In The Family/Ready, Willing And Able	6
73	Invictus SVT 1008	GENERALLY SPEAKING (LP)	20

(see also Norman Johnson, Showmen, Chairmen Of The Board)

GINGER JOHNSON AND HIS AFRICAN MESSENGERS
67	Masquerade SM 02001	AFRICAN PARTY (LP)	125

HOWARD JOHNSON
71	Jay Boy BOY 47	The Slide/That Magic Touch Can Send You Flying	15

JIMMY JOHNSON
65	Sue WI 387	Don't Answer The Door Parts 1 & 2	35

J.J. JOHNSON
55	Vogue LDE 124	J.J. JOHNSON SEXTET (10" LP)	15
55	Vogue LDE 162	J.J. JOHNSON QUINTET (10" LP)	15
72	United Artists UAS 29451	ACROSS 110TH STREET (LP, soundtrack, with Bobby Womack)	20

(see also Sonny Stitt)

(JOHNNY JOHNSON &) THE BANDWAGON
68	Direction 58-3520	Baby Make Your Own Sweet Music/On The Day We Fall In Love (as Bandwagon)	7
68	Direction 58-3670	Breaking Down The Walls Of Heartache/Dancin' Master (as Bandwagon)	7
69	Direction 58-3923	You/You Blew Your Cool And Lost Your Fool	7
69	Direction 58-4180	Let's Hang On/I Ain't Lying (withdrawn)	12
69	Direction 58-4180	Let's Hang On/Don't Let It In	6
70	Bell BLL 128	(Blame It) On The Pony Express/Never Let Me Go	6
72	Stateside SS 2207	Honey Bee/I Don't Know Why	20
74	EMI EMI 2114	Strong Love, Proud Love/Fast Running Out Of World	25
69	Direction 8-63500	JOHNNY JOHNSON AND THE BANDWAGON (LP)	30
70	Bell SBLL 138	SOUL SURVIVOR (LP)	25

JUDI JOHNSON (& PERFECTIONS)
64	HMV POP 1371	My Baby's Face/Make The Most Of It (solo)	30
65	HMV POP 1399	How Many Times/A Way Out (as Judi Johnson & Perfections)	20

LARRY JOHNSON
70	Blue Horizon 7-63851	PRESENTING THE COUNTRY BLUES (LP)	150

LAURIE JOHNSON ORCHESTRA
56	HMV 7MC 47	Buttercup/Lullaby Of The Leaves (export issue)	10
57	HMV POP 404	The Moonraker/Call Of The Casbah	7
60	Pye 7N 15251	No Hiding Place/The Deputy	6
64	Pye 7N 15599	Dr Strangelove Theme/Nevada	6
64	Pye 7N 15715	Call Me Irresponsible/The Beauty Jungle	6
65	Pye 7N 15933	Latin Quarter/M1 (in p/s)	8
65	Pye 7N 15933	Latin Quarter/M1	6
65	Pye 7N 17015	The Avengers/Minor Bossa Nova (in p/s)	50
65	Pye 7N 17015	The Avengers/Minor Bossa Nova	30
69	MGM MGM 1457	There Is Another Song/Caesar Smith	25
71	Columbia DB 8826	The Jason King Theme/There Comes A Time	50
76	EMI EMI 2562	The New Avengers Theme/A Flavour Of The Avengers (in p/s)	10
76	EMI EMI 2562	The New Avengers Theme/A Flavour Of The Avengers	6
80	Unicorn Kachana MCPS 5	The Professionals Main Title/On Target/The New Avengers Main Title (p/s, by Laurie Johnson & London Studio Orchestra)	6
59	Pye Nixa NEP 24097	NO TREES IN THE STREET (LP)	10
63	Pye NPL 18088	THE NEW BIG SOUND OF THE LAURIE JOHNSON ORCHESTRA (LP)	15
65	Pye NPL 18103	THE BIG NEW SOUND STRIKES AGAIN (LP)	15
67	Marble Arch MAL 695	THE AVENGERS AND OTHER FAVOURITES (LP)	25
69	MGM C(S) 8104	THEMES AND ... (LP)	25
70	Columbia SCX 6412	LAURIE JOHNSON/LONDON JAZZ ORCHESTRA - SYNTHESIS (LP, with Joe Harriott, Tubby Hayes, Stan Tracey & Tony Coe)	60
80	Unicorn Kachana KPM 7009	MUSIC FROM THE AVENGERS, THE NEW AVENGERS AND THE PROFESSIONALS (LP, gatefold sleeve, with London Studio Orchestra)	20

LINTON KWESI JOHNSON
78	Virgin VX 1002	DREAD BEAT AN' BLOOD (LP, as Poet & The Roots)	25
79	Island ILPS 9566	FORCES OF VICTORY (LP, with inner sleeve)	15
80	Island ILPS 9605	BASS CULTURE (LP)	15
80	Island ILPS 9650	LKJ IN DUB (LP)	15

LONNIE JOHNSON
57	Parlophone GEP 8635	LONESOME ROAD (EP)	20
57	Parlophone GEP 8663	LONNIE'S BLUES (EP)	20
58	Parlophone GEP 8693	LONNIE'S BLUES NO. 2 (EP)	20
64	Storyville SLP 162	PORTRAITS IN BLUES VOL. 6 (LP)	20
64	Storyville 616 010	SEE SEE RIDER (LP, with Otis Spann)	40
60s	Xtra XTRA 1037	LONNIE JOHNSON (LP)	25

(see also Eddie Lang & Lonnie Johnson)

LORRAINE JOHNSON
78	EPIC S EPC 7089	FEED THE FLAME (LP)	25

LOU JOHNSON
63	London HLX 9805	Reach Out For Me/Magic Potion	50
63	London HLX 9805	Reach Out For Me/Magic Potion (DJ copy)	100
64	London HLX 9917	(There's) Always Something There To Remind Me/Wouldn't That Be Something	25
64	London HLX 9929	A Message To Martha (Kentucky Bluebird)/The Last One To Be Loved	15

Luther 'GEORGIA BOY SNAKE' JOHNSON

MINT VALUE £

65	London HLX 9965	Please Stop The Wedding/Park Avenue	20
65	London HLX 9994	A Time To Love, A Time To Cry/Unsatisfied	80
65	London HLX 9994	A Time To Love, A Time To Cry/Unsatisfied (DJ copy)	150
69	London HLX 10269	(There's) Always Something There To Remind Me/Message To Martha	10
12	Kent Select CITY 028	The Panic Is On/You Better Let Him Go	8
64	London REX 1438	THE MAGIC POTION OF LOU JOHNSON (EP)	150

LUTHER 'GEORGIA BOY SNAKE' JOHNSON
69	Transatlantic TRA 188	THE MUDDY WATERS BLUES BAND (LP, credits Muddy Waters on label)	30

MARV JOHNSON
59	London HLT 8856	Come To Me/Whisper (tri-centre)	100
59	London HLT 8856	Come To Me/Whisper	30
59	London HLT 9013	You Got What It Takes/Don't Leave Me (tri centre)	20
59	London HLT 9013	You Got What It Takes/Don't Leave Me	10
59	London HLT 9013	You Got What It Takes/Don't Leave Me (78)	20
60	London HLT 9109	I Love The Way You Love/Let Me Love You	20
60	London HL 7095	I Love The Way You Love/Let Me Love You (export issue)	20
60	London HLT 9165	Ain't Gonna Be That Way/All The Love I've Got	20
60	London HLT 9187	(You've Got To) Move Two Mountains/I Need You	20
61	London HLT 9265	Happy Days/Baby, Baby	20
61	London HLT 9311	Merry-Go-Round/Tell Me That You Love Me	30
65	Tamla Motown TMG 525	Why Do You Want To Let Me Go/I'm Not A Plaything	100
69	United Artists UP 35010	I Love The Way You Love/You Got What It Takes	6
68	Tamla Motown TMG 680	I'll Pick A Rose For My Rose/You Got The Love I Love	6
69	Tamla Motown TMG 713	I Miss You Baby (How I Miss You)/Bad Girl	10
70	Tamla Motown TMG 737	So Glad You Chose Me/I'm Not A Plaything	10
60	London HA-T 2271	MARVELLOUS MARV JOHNSON (LP)	150
69	T. Motown TML 11111	I'LL PICK A ROSE FOR MY ROSE (LP, mono)	30
69	T. Motown STML 11111	I'LL PICK A ROSE FOR MY ROSE (LP, stereo)	25

MATT JOHNSON
81	4AD CAD 113	BURNING BLUE SOUL (LP, original 'psychedelic eye' cover)	80

(see also Gadgets, The The)

MIRRIAM JOHNSON
61	London HLW 9337	Lonesome Road/Young And Innocent	15

NORMAN JOHNSON (& SHOWMEN)
69	Action ACT 4529	You're Everything/Our Love Will Grow	100
69	Action ACT 4545	Take It Baby/In Paradise	50
71	Action ACT 4601	You're Everything/Our Love Will Grow (reissue)	40

(see also General Johnson, Chairmen Of The Board, Showmen)

PETE JOHNSON
56	Vogue V 2007	J.J. Boogie/Yancey Special	35
56	Vogue V 2008	Swanee River Boogie/St. Louis Boogie	30
55	Vogue EPV 1039	PETE JOHNSON (EP)	30
59	Top Rank JKR 8009	ROLL 'EM BOY (EP)	25
55	London AL 3549	JUMPIN' WITH PETE JOHNSON (10" LP)	50
55	Vogue Coral LRA 10016	BOOGIE WOOGIE MOOD (LP)	30

(see also Joe Turner & Pete Johnson, Albert Ammons & Meade Lux Lewis)

PHILIP JOHNSON
82	Namedrop NR3	YOUTH IN MOURNING (LP, with 4 double sided A4 sheets)	20

PLAS JOHNSON (ORCHESTRA)
57	Capitol CL 14772	The Big Twist/Come Rain Or Come Shine	20
57	Capitol CL 14816	Swanee River Rock/You Send Me	20
58	Capitol CL 14836	Popcorn/Hoppin' Mad	20
58	Capitol CL 14903	Little Rockin' Deacon/Dinah	20
59	Capitol CL 14973	Robbins Nest Cha Cha/Plaz Jazz	10
57	London HB-U 1078	BOP ME DADDY (10" LP)	60

PROFESSOR JOHNSON & HIS GOSPEL SINGERS
51	Vocalion V 1013	Give Me That Old Time Religion/Where Shall I Be (78)	20
58	Brunswick OE 9352	PROFESSOR JOHNSON AND HIS GOSPEL SINGERS (EP)	20

RAY JOHNSON
57	Vogue V 9073	If You Don't Want Me Baby/Calypso Joe	40
58	Vogue V 9093	Calypso Blues/Are You There	40

ROBERT JOHNSON
62	Philips BBL 7539	ROBERT JOHNSON 1936-1937 (LP)	100
65	CBS BPG 62456	KING OF THE DELTA BLUES SINGERS (LP)	60
67	Kokomo K 1000	ROBERT JOHNSON (LP)	50
60s	Smokestack SS/LP 1	BLUES LEGEND 1936-1937 (LP)	40
70	CBS 64102	KING OF THE DELTA BLUES SINGERS VOL. 2 (LP)	30
85	Blue Diamond/CBS 22190	KING OF THE DELTA BLUES SINGERS VOLUMES 1 & 2 (2-LP)	20

ROY LEE JOHNSON
69	Action ACT 4518	So Anna Just Love Me/Boogaloo No. 3 (Red label)	40
69	Action ACT 4518	So Anna Just Love Me/Boogaloo No. 3 (Yellow label)	30

RUBY JOHNSON
67	Stax 601 020	If I Ever Needed Love (I Sure Do Need It Now)/Keep On Keeping On	30

SYL JOHNSON
73	London HL 10403	We Did It/Anyway The Wind Blows	15
73	London HL 10438	Back For A Taste Of Your Love/Wind Blow Her Back My Way	6
75	London HL 10476	Let Yourself Go/Please Don't Give Up On Me	6
74	London SHU 8469	BACK FOR A TASTE OF YOUR LOVE (LP)	20
74	London SHU 8477	DIAMOND IN THE ROUGH (LP)	30
75	London SHU 8494	TOTAL EXPLOSION (LP)	15

T J JOHNSON

MINT VALUE £

| 80 | Flyright FLY LP 569 | BRINGS OUT THE BLUES IN ME (LP) | 15 |
| 86 | Charly CRD 1125 | IS IT BECAUSE I'M BLACK (LP) | 15 |

(see also Lula Reed)

T J JOHNSON
| 83 | Switch DSW 003 | I Can Make It/Good For You (12") | 50 |

THEO JOHNSON
| 65 | Aladdin WI 604 | Masters Of War/The Water Is Wide | 15 |

TOMMY JOHNSON
| 60s | Saydisc SDM 224 | THE LEGACY OF TOMMY JOHNSON (LP) | 20 |

WILCO JOHNSONS SOLID SENDERS
78	Virgin VS 214	Walking On The Edge/Dr. Dupree	6
81	Fresh FRESH 31	Casting My Spell On You/Looked Out Of My Window	6
78	Virgin V 2105	SOLID SENDERS (LP, with free 'Live LP' stickered sleeve)	15
80	Fresh FRESH LP 4	ICE ON THE MOTORWAY (LP, with free 7", as Wilco Johnson)	15

(see also Dr. Feelgood)

BRUCE JOHNSTON COMBO
| 63 | London HL 9780 | Original Surfer Stomp/Pajama Party | 60 |

(see also Beach Boys, California Music, Fantastic Baggys, Sagittarius)

DANIEL JOHNSTON
92	Seminal Twang TWANG 13	Laurie/The Monster Inside Of Me/Whiz Kid/The Lennon Song (p/s)	10
93	Ay Carramba! EL BARTO 001	RESPECT (10" LP)	15
99	Pickled Egg EGG 6	Dream Scream/Funeral Girl	8
03	For Us FU 020	Mountain Top/Living It For The Moment	12
03	Sketchbook SKETCH XX2	Fish/Living It For The Moment	6
02	Pickled Egg EGG 22	REJECTED UNKNOWN (2-LP)	20
06	Coppertree CTR 007	FEAR YOURSELF (LP, 1000 only)	25

JOHNSTON BROTHERS
54	Decca F 10234	The Creep/Crystal Ball	10
54	Decca F 10286	Oh Baby Mine I Get So Lonely/My Love, My Life, My Own	10
54	Decca F 10302	The Bandit/KEYNOTES: A Dime And A Dollar	10
54	Decca F 10364	Sh-Boom (Life Could Be A Dream)/Crazy 'Bout Ya Baby	15
55	Decca F 10608	Hernando's Hideaway/Hey There	15
55	Decca F 10636	Join In And Sing Again Medley (both sides)	10
56	Decca F 10721	No Other Love/Flowers Mean Forgiveness	10
56	Decca F 10747	How Little We Know/The Street Musician	6
56	Decca F 10781	In The Middle Of The House (with Keynotes)/Stranded In The Jungle	10
56	Decca F 10814	Join In And Sing, No. 3 Medley (both sides)	10
56	Decca F 10828	Give Her My Love (When You Meet Her)/A Rose And A Candy Bar	10
57	Decca F 10860	Whatever Lola Wants (Lola Gets)/Heart	10
57	Decca F 10939	I Like Music - You Like Music/Seven Bar Blues	7
56	Decca DFE 6249	JOIN THE JOHNSTON BROTHERS (EP)	10

(see also Dennis Lotis, Vera Lynn, Joan Regan, Lita Roza, Suzi Miller, Ted Heath, Keynotes)

JOHNSTONS
68	Transatlantic TRA 169	THE JOHNSTONS (LP)	22
68	Transatlantic TRA 184	GIVE A DAMN (LP)	18
68	Transatlantic TRA 185	THE BARLEYCORN (LP)	18
70	Transatlantic TRA 211	BITTER GREEN (LP)	20
71	Transatlantic TRA 231	COLOURS OF THE DAWN (LP)	15

(see also Adrienne Johnston)

JOINER, ARKANSAS, JUNIOR HIGH SCHOOL BAND
| 60 | London HLG 9147 | Big Ben/National City | 7 |

JOINT PROJECT
| 92 | Soapbar SBR 001 | Total Feeling/Good Feeling (12") | 35 |
| 93 | Soapbar SBR 005 | Dark In Da Jungle/Fantasize (12") | 25 |

JO JO GUNNE (U.K.)
| 68 | Decca F 12807 | Every Story Has An End/Should Live Like That | 7 |
| 69 | Decca F 12906 | Beggin' You Baby/Bad Penny | 7 |

JO JO GUNNE (U.S.)
| 72 | Asylum AYM 501 | Run Run Run/Shake That Fat or Take It Easy as B-side (withdrawn) | 10 |

(see also Spirit)

JOKE SHOP
| 72 | Access ACC 01 | Lame Dog/Tell Her To Leave (p/s) | 15 |

JOKER (1)
| 84 | Lost Moment LM 018 | Back On The Road/Pusher (p/s) | 10 |

JOKER (2)
| 93 | Skanna 06 | The Joker/Roots (12") | 40 |

(see also Skanna)

JOKERS
| 62 | Salvo SLO 1806 | Blue Moonbeam/Dog Fight (99 only) | 35 |

JOKER'S WILD
| 66 | Regent Sound RSR 0031 | Don't Ask Me/Why Do Fools Fall In Love (handwritten labels, 50 only) | 500 |
| 66 | Regent Sound RSLP 007 | JOKER'S WILD: Why Do Fools Fall In Love/Walk Like A Man/Don't Ask Me/Big Girls Don't Cry/Beautiful Delilah (12", 1-sided, 50 copies only) | 1000 |

(see also Dave Gilmour, Pink Floyd)

JOHN JOLLIFFE
| 79 | Rocket XPRESS 9 | Follow The Wind/Dream Love | 6 |

JOLLIVER ARKANSAS
| 69 | Bell SBLL 119 | HOME (LP) | 30 |

(see also Leslie West, Mountain)

JOLLY BOYS
MINT VALUE £

JOLLY BOYS
70 Moodisc MU 3504   On The Water/MUDIES ALL STARS: Cash Register 15
JOLLY BROTHERS
78 Ballistic FORCE 2002   Conscious Man/PRODIGAL CREATOR: Life (actually dub to Lee Perry's Ne Jah Go Run)
                            (12") 18
81 Seven Leaves SL 008   Have A Litte Faith/Right Before My Eyes (12") 18
93 Roots RRLP 001   LEE PERRY PRESENTS THE JOLLY BROTHERS (LP) 20
JOLT
77 Polydor 2058 936   You're Cold/All I Can Do (p/s) 15
78 Polydor 2059 008   What'cha Gonna Do About It/Again And Again (die-cut p/s) 12
78 Polydor 2059 039   I Can't Wait/Route 66 (p/s) 12
79 Polydor 2229 215   Maybe Tonight/I'm In Tears/See Saw/Stop Look (p/s) 12
79 Polydor 2229 215DJ   Maybe Tonight/See Saw (promo only, no p/s) 12
78 Polydor 2383 504   THE JOLT (LP, flip-back sleeve) 30
JON
67 Parlophone R 5604   So Much For Mary/Polly Sunday (in p/s) 50
67 Parlophone R 5604   So Much For Mary/Polly Sunday 25
67 Columbia DB 8249   Is It Love/Sing Out 150
(see also Titus Groan, Still Life)
JON & ALUN
63 Decca LK 4547   RELAX YOUR MIND (LP, mono) 22
63 Decca SKL 4547   RELAX YOUR MIND (LP, stereo) 30
JON & DAVE
97 Earworm SS 1   Land Beyond The Sun/Instrumental For Silence (p/s, pale green vinyl, 500 copies only) 8
JON & JEANNIE
68 Beacon 3-105   Lover's Holiday/Something You Got 10
69 Beacon BEA 113   Don't Sign The Papers/We Got Lovin' 10
JON & ROBIN & IN-CROWD
67 Stateside SS 2027   Do It Again A Little Bit Slower/If I Need Someone It's You 15
JONAH
85 MW MW 7853   Tough/This Is Love (no p/s) 280
JOHNNY JONAS
75 Torpedo TOR 43   Happy Birthday/Birthday Dub 10
JONATHAN & CHARLES
69 Herald LLR 566   ANOTHER WEEK TO GO (LP) 30
JONCUNDO
72 Banana BA 366   I'd Like To Teach The World To Sing/Rope Of Sand 10
A JONES
04 Jah Tubbys JT 10020   Jah Bless I/MA-KAYA CREW: Iron Dub 25
AL JONES (1)
58 HMV POP 451   Mad, Mad, World/Lonely Traveller 200
58 HMV POP 451   Mad, Mad, World/Lonely Traveller(78) 20
AL JONES (2)
69 Parlophone PMC/PCS 7081 ALUN ASHWORTH JONES (LP, black/yellow label with "Sold in U.K..." text) 175
72 Village Thing VTS 19   JONESVILLE (LP) 175
ALAN JONES
82 Vada ABER 4134   MUSIC BY SECRETS EP 6
BARBARA JONES
72 Bullet BU 516   Sad Movies/SIR HARRY: Deejay Version 20
74 Count Shelley CS 045   Baby I'm Yours/Don't Turn Your Back On Me 8
74 Attack ATT 8077   Changing Partners/Part 2 8
75 Dip DL 5085   Where Do I Turn/G.G. ALL STARS: Version 8
76 Trojan TRLS 136   THE BEST OF BARBARA JONES (LP) 20
BEVERLEY JONES (& PRESTONS)
63 HMV POP 1109   The Boy I Saw With You/When It Comes To Love 10
63 HMV POP 1140   Why Do Lovers Break Each Other's Heart/I'm Just An In-Between 20
63 HMV POP 1201   Wait 'Til My Bobby Gets Home/A Boy Like You 15
64 Parlophone R 5189   Heatwave/Hear You Talking (with Prestons) 20
(see also Roger James)
B-LOU JONES & HIS JUPITERS
61 London HLU 9373   Anchors Aweigh (Parts 1 & 2) 10
BRENDA LEE JONES
75 UK USA 8   You're The Love Of My Life/Thread Your Needle (paper label) 8
(see also Dean & Jean)
CAROL JONES
60 Triumph RGM 1012   The Boy With The Eyes Of Blue/I Gave Him Back His Ring 125
CASEY JONES & THE ENGINEERS
63 Columbia DB 7083   One Way Ticket/I'm Gonna Love 35
CASEY JONES & THE GOVERNERS
64 Golden 12LP 106   DON'T HA HA (LP) 60
(see also Casey Jones & The Engineers)
CURTIS JONES
66 RCA RCX 7184   R.C.A. VICTOR RACE SERIES VOL. 9 (EP) 15
64 Decca LK 4587   CURTIS JONES IN LONDON (LP) 125
68 Blue Horizon 7-63207   NOW RESIDENT IN EUROPE (LP, mono) 80
68 Blue Horizon (S)-63207 NOW RESIDENT IN EUROPE (LP, stereo) 50
DATHAN JONES
05 Hayley 008   Contract On Love/Mysterious Desire (reissue) 8
DAVIE JONES & THE KING BEES
64 Vocalion V 9221   Liza Jane/Louie, Louie Go Home (Demo copy) 2000
64 Vocalion Pop V 9221   Liza Jane/Louie, Louie Go Home (beware of counterfeits without centres) 1500

Davy JONES

MINT VALUE £

78	Decca F 13807	Liza Jane/Louie, Louie Go Home (reissue)	25

(see also David Bowie, Davy Jones, Manish Boys, Calvin James)

DAVY JONES
65	Philips BF 1410	For Your Love/Love Bug	10

DAVY JONES (U.K.) (1)
65	Parlophone R 5250	You've Got A Habit Of Leaving/Baby Loves That Way (Demo)	900
65	Parlophone R 5315	You've Got A Habit Of Leaving/Baby Loves That Way	1000

(see also David Bowie)

DAVY JONES (U.K.) (2)
65	Colpix PX 784	What Are We Going To Do/This Bouquet	10
67	Pye 7N 17302	It Ain't Me Babe/Baby It's Me (in p/s)	12
67	Pye 7N 17302	It Ain't Me Babe/Baby It's Me	6
67	Pye 7N 17380	Theme For A New Love/Dream Girl (in p/s)	10
67	Pye 7N 17380	Theme For A New Love/Dream Girl	6
67	Pye International 7N 25422	Theme For A New Love/Dream Girl (reissue, withdrawn)	20
71	Bell BLL 1163	Rainy Jane/Welcome To My Love	6
83	J.J. 2001	I'll Love You Forever/When I Look Back On Christmas	12
67	Pye NPL 18178	DAVY JONES (LP)	20

(see also Davy Jones & Micky Dolenz, Monkees)

DAVY JONES (U.K.) & MICKY DOLENZ
71	Bell BLL 986	Do It In The Name Of Love/Lady Jane	12

(see also Monkees, Davey Jones)

DAVY JONES (U.K.) & THE LOWER THIRD/MANISH BOYS
79	EMI 2925	You've Got A Habit Of Leaving/Baby Loves That Way/MANISH BOYS: I Pity The Fool/Take My Tip (Demo copy, p/s)	20
79	EMI EMI 2925	You've Got A Habit Of Leaving/Baby Loves That Way/MANISH BOYS: I Pity The Fool/Take My Tip (p/s)	6
82	Charly CYM 1	You've Got A Habit Of Leaving/Baby Loves That Way/MANISH BOYS: I Pity The Fool/Take My Tip (10", p/s)	20

(see also David Bowie, Davie Jones & King Bees, Manish Boys, Calvin James)

DAVY JONES (U.S.)
60	Pye 7N 15254	Amapola/Mighty Man	10
61	Pye 7N 15318	Shenandoah/Scenery	10
61	Pye International 7N 25072	Model Girl/Scarlet Woman	10
61	Pye International 7N 25095	Bonnie Banks/Baby Baby	10
62	Piccadilly 7N 35038	Jezebel/Don't Come Crying To Me	40

(see also Thelonious Monk)

DILL JONES TRIO
61	Columbia DB 4635	St. David/The Preacher	6
56	Jazz Today JTE 104	PIANO MOODS VOL. 2 (EP)	25
56	Pye Jazz NJE 1024	PIANO MOODS VOL. 5 (EP)	25
57	Columbia SEG 7764	TOP OF THE POLL (EP)	10
60	Columbia 33SX 1336	JONES THE JAZZ (LP)	60
78	77 77SEU 12/45	UP JUMPED YOU WITH LOVE (LP)	20

DORIS JONES
76	Tomorrow LE 008	Stranded In The Wilderness/Stranded In The Wilderness (Instrumental) (promo only)	10

DOROTHY JONES
61	Philips PB 1169	Takin' That Long Walk Home/It's Unbearable	30

(see also Cookies)

GARY JONES
62	Piccadilly 7N 35084	It's Over/Little Miss Nose In The Air	8

GEORGE JONES
59	Mercury AMT 1036	White Lightning/Long Time To Forget	25
59	Mercury AMT 1058	Who Shot Sam/Into My Arms Again	15
59	Mercury AMT 1078	Big Harlan Taylor/Money To Burn	10
60	Mercury AMT 1100	Sparkling Brown Eyes/Accidentally On Purpose	10
61	Mercury AMT 1124	Candy Hearts/The Window Up Above	10
62	United Artists POP 1037	She Thinks I Still Care/Geronimo	10
63	United Artists UP 1015	I Saw Me/Not What I Had In Mind (as George Jones with Jones Boys)	10
64	United Artists UP 1044	Your Heart Turned Left (And I Was On The Right)/My Tears Are Overdue	10
65	United Artists UP 1080	The Race Is On/She's So Lonesome Again	15
59	Mercury ZEP 10036	GEORGE JONES (EP)	80
59	Melodisc EPM7 109	COUNTRY SONG HITS (EP)	40
64	Mercury 10009 MCE	C & W ACES (EP)	20
64	Ember EMB 4548	THE BEST OF AMERICAN COUNTRY MUSIC VOL. 4 (EP)	10
62	United Artists ULP 1007	THE NEW FAVOURITES OF GEORGE JONES (LP)	20
63	United Artists ULP 1014	MY FAVOURITES OF HANK WILLIAMS (LP)	20
63	Ember CW 101	THE CROWN PRINCE OF COUNTRY MUSIC (LP, original pressings have grey & orange label)	20

(see also Gene Pitney, Elvis Costello)

GEORGE JONES/JIMMIE SKINNER
59	Mercury ZEP 10012	COUNTRY AND WESTERN (EP, 2 tracks each)	10

JONES GIRLS
79	Philadelphia Intl. S PIR 7361	You Gonna Make Me Love Somebody Else/Who Can I Run To	6
82	Philadelphia Intl. PIR 12-2031	Nights Over Egypt/Love Don't Ever Say Goodbye (12")	20
79	Phil. Intl. PIR 83831	THE JONES GIRLS (LP)	15

GLORIA JONES
66	Capitol CL 15429	Heartbeat (Parts 1 & 2)	50
66	Stateside SS 555	Finders Keepers/Run One Flight Of Stairs	80
74	Tamla Motown TMG 910	Tin Can People/So Tired (Of The Way You're Treating Our Love Baby)	10

Grace JONES

MINT VALUE £

76	EMI EMI 2437	Get It On/Get It On (Version)	6
76	EMI EMI 2522	I Ain't Going Nowhere/Simplicity Blues	10
77	EMI 2570	Go Now (album version)/Drive Me Crazy (12" demos only)	65
77	EMI EMI 2570	Go Now/Drive Me Crazy	6
77	EMI EMI 2720	Bring On The Love (Why Can't We Be Friends Again)/Cry Baby	6
79	Inferno HEAT 6	Tainted Love/SANDY WYNNS: A Touch Of Venus (reissue)	15
14	Champion 5350752	Tainted Love/Come Go With Me (reissue)	15
74	Tamla Motown STML 11254	SHARE MY LOVE (LP)	25
76	EMI EMC 3159	VIXEN (LP, produced by Marc Bolan)	20

(see also Marc Bolan & Gloria Jones)

GRACE JONES

77	RCA 2058856	Sorry/That's The Trouble	15
80	Island 12WIP 6591	A Rolling Stone/Sinning (12")	12
80	Island 12WIP 6629	Private Life/She's Lost Control (Long Version) (12", p/s)	10
04	DPRO WL 12004	Clandestine Affair (Vocal)/(Instrumental)/We Know (12", clear with Tricky)	25
77	Island ILPS 9470	PORTFOLIO (LP)	15
78	Island ILPS 9525	FAME (LP)	15
80	Island ILPS 9592	WARM LEATHERETTE (LP, 1st pressing, blue labels)	18
81	Island ILPS 9624	NIGHTCLUBBING (LP, 1st pressing, gold 'picture' labels)	18
82	Island PILPS 9722	LIVING MY LIFE (LP, picture disc)	18
82	Island ILPS 9722	LIVING MY LIFE (LP, 1st pressing, blue labels, inner and 'video ad' insert)	15
85	Island GRACE 1	SLAVE TO THE RHYTHM (LP)	15
85	Island 207 572	ISLAND LIFE (LP)	20
10	Vinyl Factory VF 016	HURRICANE (2-LP, numbered)	150
11	Wall Of Sound WOS050DLPX	HURRICANE DUB (2-LP)	100
14	Island/Back To Black 0600753480540	NIGHTCLUBBING (2-LP reissue)	35
14	Island/Back To Black 535 142-8	ISLAND LIFE (LP, reissue)	25
16	Island 0600753660713	WARM LEATHERETTE (4-LP box set in 'leather finished' box)	50

GRANDPA JONES

57	Brunswick 05676	Eight More Miles To Louisville/Dark As A Dungeon	15
62	London HA-U/SH-U 8010	MAKES THE RAFTERS RING (LP)	20
64	London HA-U/SH-U 8119	YODELLING HITS (LP)	20

(see also Brown's Ferry Four)

HEATHER JONES

69	Cambrian CSP 704	Dodo Di/TBC	8
68	Welsh Teldisc TEP 872	CANEUON EP (p/s)	15
71	Newyddion Da ND 2	HEATHER EP (p/s, with Meic Stevens)	45
71	Sain SAIN 20	COLLI LAITH EP (p/s)	15
72	Sain SAIN 30	PAN DDAWR DYDD EP (p/s)	15
74	Sain SAIN 1008M	MAE'R OLYWYN YN TROI (LP)	50
76	Sain SAIN 1047M	JIAWL! (LP)	40

HUW JONES

69	Welsh Teldisc WD 912	Y ffoadur/Dewch I Ganu (La, La, La) (p/s)	6
69	Sain SAIN 1	Dwr/Fy Ngwlad Fy Hun	10
70	Sain SAIN 3	Paid Digalonni/Ffoi (p/s)	6

INDIGO JONES

70	Columbia DB 8744	Noel Highway/Prodigal Son	12

JACK JONES

58	Capitol CL 14969	Laffin' At Me/Deeply Devoted	10

JAKE JONES

71	MCA MVPS 432	JAKE JONES (LP)	25

JANET JONES

74	Midas MR 005	SING TO ME LADY (LP, red or yellow labels)	250
74	Midas MFHR 059	JANET JONES (LP, yellow label, released on Folk Heritage label)	250

JANIE JONES (& LASH)

65	HMV POP 1495	Witches Brew/Take-A My Tip	15
66	HMV POP 1514	Gunning For You/Go Go Away From Me	15
67	Columbia DB 8173	Tickle Me Tootsie Wootsies/High And Dry	15
68	Pye 7N 17550	Charlie Smith/Nobody's Perfect	12
68	Major Minor MM 577	The Girl's Song/I've Never Met A Boy Like You	12
70	President PT 309	Back On My Feet Again/Psycho	10
83	Big Beat NS 91	House Of The Ju-Ju Queen/Sex Machine (as Janie Jones & Lash, p/s)	20

(see also The Clash)

JERRY JONES

70	Banana BA 316	Still Waters (Love)/SOUND DIMENSION: Wig Wam	30
71	Bamboo BAM 65	Still Waters (Love)/BRENTFORD ALLSTARS: Wig Wam (reissue)	40
71	Bamboo BALPS 213	AT THE KINGSTON HOTEL, JAMAICA (LP)	65

JIMMY JONES

60	MGM MGM 1051	Handy Man/The Search Is Over	7
60	MGM MGM 1051	Handy Man/The Search Is Over (78)	40
60	MGM MGM 1078	Good Timin'/Too Long Will Be Too Late	7
60	MGM MGM 1078	Good Timin'/Too Long Will Be Too Late (78)	80
60	MGM MGM 1091	I Just Go For You/That's When I Cried	12
60	MGM MGM 1103	Ready For Love/For You	15
61	MGM MGM 1123	I Told You So/You Got It	15
61	MGM MGM 1133	Dear One/I Say Love	12
61	MGM MGM 1146	Mr Music Man/Holler Hey	15
62	MGM MGM 1168	You're Much Too Young/Nights Of Mexico	12

JO JONES TRIO

MINT VALUE £

65	Columbia DB 7592	Walkin'/Pardon Me	30
65	Cameo Parkway P 988	Don't You Just Know It	15
67	Stateside SS 2041	39-21-46/Personal Property	18
60	MGM MGM-EP 745	JIMMY HANDYMAN JONES (EP)	30
61	MGM MGM-EP 787	ORIGINAL HITS (EP)	30
60	MGM MGM-C 832	GOOD TIMIN' (LP)	50

JO JONES TRIO
59	Top Rank 25/039	JO JONES (LP)	18

JOE JONES
60	Columbia DB 4533	You Talk Too Much/I Love You Still	15

JOHN PAUL JONES
64	Pye 7N 15637	Baja/A Foggy Day In Vietnam (B-side by Andrew Oldham Orchestra, white label promo)	200
64	Pye 7N 15637	Baja/A Foggy Day In Vietnam (B-side actually by Andrew Oldham Orchestra)	150

(see also Led Zeppelin, Tony Meehan, Andrew Oldham Orchestra)

JOHNNY JONES & KING CASUALS
68	MCA MU 1031	Soul Poppin'/Blues For The Brothers	10
76	Cream CRM 5004	Purple Haze/Horsing Around	10
76	Brunswick BR 37	Purple Haze/FRED HUGHES: Baby Boy	10

JONAH JONES (QUARTET)
58	Capitol CL 14939	Night Train/Lots Of Luck Charley	7
62	Ember JBS 704	Down By The Riverside/Stars Fell On Alabama	7

JUSTIN JONES
61	London HLU 9463	Dance By Yourself/Love	150

KEN JONES (& HIS ROCK'N'ROLLERS)
60	Parlophone R 4628	Two Way Stretch/Paper Chase	8
61	Parlophone R 4763	Bluesville/On The Rebound	7
61	Parlophone R 4788	Joxville/Just Rollin'	6
58	Embassy WEP 1004	ROCK'N'ROLL TIME (EP, as Ken Jones & His Rock'n'Rollers)	12

KENNEY JONES
74	GM GMS 027	Ready Or Not/Woman Trouble	8

(see also Small Faces, Faces, Who)

LEATH JONES
81	All That DAT 1 EJSP 9772	Bad Boys/First Time (p/s)	20

LESLIE JONES
59	Pye NSEP 85004	FOUR FARNON FAVOURITES (EP, stereo)	10
59	Pye NSPL 83008/9	THE MUSIC OF ROBERT FARNON (2-LP)	20

LINDA JONES
67	Warner Bros WB 2070	Hypnotised/I Can't Stop Lovin' My Baby	60
72	London HLU 10368	For Your Precious Love/Don't Go	15
75	Warner Bros WB 16621	I Just Can't Live My Life/My Heart Will Understand	20
15	Soul Brother SB 701	I Just Can't Live My Life/My Heart Needs A Break	15

LLOYD JONES
70	Bullet BU 429	Rome/RHYTHM RULERS: Version	30

LOUIS JONES ROCK & ROLL BAND
50s	Vogue VE1 70111	ROCK AND ROLL (EP)	100

MAE JONES ENSEMBLE
54	Decca 45-F 10486	Tenderly He Watches/I Walked Into The Garden	7

MAGGIE JONES
70	VJM VLP 23	COLUMBIA RECORDINGS IN CHRONOLOGICAL ORDER VOL. 1 (LP)	15
70	VJM VLP 25	COLUMBIA RECORDINGS IN CHRONOLOGICAL ORDER VOL. 2 (LP)	15

NIC JONES
14	Topic STOP 2411	Canadee I-O/The Flandyke Shore (die-cut sleeve)	6
70	Trailer LER 2014	BALLADS AND SONGS (LP, white label)	60
70	Trailer LER 2014	BALLADS AND SONGS (LP, red label)	50
70	Trailer LER 2014	BALLADS AND SONGS (LP, later pressing with 'highway' label)	15
71	Trailer LER 2027	NIC JONES (LP, yellow label)	40
71	Trailer LER 2027	NIC JONES (LP, red label)	50
73	Trailer LER 2083	SONGS OF A CHANGING WORLD (LP, with Jon Raven & Tony Rose, red label with insert)	30
77	Trailer LER 2091	NOAH'S ARK TRAP (LP)	50
77	Trailer LER 2091	NOAH'S ARK TRAP (LP, reissue with Highway label)	15
78	Transatlantic LTRA 507	FROM THE DEVIL TO A STRANGER (LP)	60
80	Topic 12TS411	PENGUIN EGGS (LP)	50
09	Three Black Feathers TBFLP001	PENGUIN EGGS (LP, reissue, 200gm vinyl)	20
17	Topic 12TS 411	PENGUIN EGGS (LP, reissue white vinyl)	15

(see also Jon Raven, Halliard)

NIGEL MAZLYN JONES
76	Isle Of Light IOL 666/1	SHIP TO SHORE (LP)	50
78	Avada AVA 105	SENTINEL (LP, with inner sleeve, b/w picture label)	20
82	Isle Of Light IOL 0230	BREAKING COVER (LP)	20
91	Isle Of Light 1OL 0232LP	MAZLYN JONES (LP)	20

NORAH JONES
04	Blue Note 7243 5 3208813	COME AWAY WITH ME (LP)	25

PALMER JONES
68	Direction 58-3603	The Great Magic Of Love/Dancing Master	30

PATSY JONES
67	RCA 1600	Colours Of Love/There's A time And Place For Everything	7

PAUL JONES
66	HMV POP 1554	High Time/I Can't Hold On Much Longer	6
67	HMV POP 1576	I've Been A Bad Bad Boy/Sonny Boy Williamson	7

Poppa JONES

MINT VALUE £

67	HMV PSR 5307	Privilege (1-sided demo)	20
67	Columbia DB 8303	Sons And Lovers/Three Sisters	8
68	Columbia DB 8379	And The Sun Will Shine/The Dog Presides	25
68	Columbia DB 8417	When I Was Six Years Old/You Have No Idea	10
68	Columbia DB 8514	Aquarius/Pisces	6
69	Columbia DB 8567	It's Getting Better/Not Before Time	8
71	Vertigo 6059 053	Life After Death/The Mighty Ship	8
73	Philips 6006 282	Perfect Roadie/Mouth Organ	6
78	RSO RSO 003	Sheena Is A Punk Rocker/Pretty Vacant (p/s)	6
67	HMV 7EG 8975	PRIVILEGE (EP)	20
66	HMV CLP 3586	MY WAY (LP, mono)	25
66	HMV CSD 3586	MY WAY (LP, stereo)	30
67	HMV CLP 3602	LOVE ME, LOVE MY FRIENDS (LP, mono)	35
67	HMV CSD 3602	LOVE ME, LOVE MY FRIENDS (LP, stereo)	40
67	HMV CLP/CSD 3623	PRIVILEGE (LP, soundtrack, with George Bean Group & Mike Leander)	40
69	Columbia SX/SCX 6347	COME INTO MY MUSIC BOX (LP, mono/stereo)	20
71	Vertigo 6360 059	CRUCIFIX IN A HORSESHOE (LP, gatefold sleeve, swirl label)	150
70	President PTLS 1068	DRAKE'S DREAM (LP, soundtrack)	30

(see also Manfred Mann, Blues Band)

POPPA JONES

66	Parlophone R 5404	Birthday Cake Walk/The Street Parade	6

QUINCY JONES

62	Mercury AMT 1195	Soul Bossa Nova/On The Street Where You Live	10
72	A&M AMS 888	Ironside/Cast Your Fate To The Wind	15
72	Reprise K 14150	Money Runned	8
60	Mercury MMC 14038	THE BIRTH OF A BAND (LP, mono)	20
60	Mercury CMS 18026	THE BIRTH OF A BAND (LP, stereo)	25
65	Mercury 20047 MCL	GOLDEN BOY (LP)	15
65	Mercury 20063 SMCL	THE PAWNBROKER (LP, soundtrack)	30
66	Mercury 20072 (S)MCL	MIRAGE (LP, soundtrack)	25
66	Mercury 20078 (S)MCL	QUINCY'S GOT A BRAND NEW BAG (LP)	15
66	Fontana FJL 127	FAB! (LP)	15
67	Mercury SMWL 30003	TRAVELLIN' ON THE QUINCY JONES BANDWAGON (LP)	15
68	RCA Victor RD/SF 7931	IN COLD BLOOD (LP, soundtrack)	20
68	United Artists (S)ULP 1181	IN THE HEAT OF THE NIGHT (LP, soundtrack, with Ray Charles)	25
69	Uni UNLS 103	LOST MAN (LP, soundtrack)	25
69	Paramount SPFL 256	THE ITALIAN JOB (LP, soundtrack, with Matt Monro)	75
70	United Artists UAS 29128	THEY CALL ME MISTER TIBBS (LP, soundtrack)	60
72	WEA K 44168	THE HEIST (LP, soundtrack, with Little Richard)	15
72	Atlantic K 40371	HOW TO STEAL A DIAMOND IN FOUR UNEASY LESSONS (LP, soundtrack)	15
85	Nimbus/A&M AMLH 64285	SOUNDS AND STUFF LIKE THAT (LP, Nimbus Supercut, mail order only from Practical Hi Fi magazine)	40

(see also Annie Ross, Eddie Barclay & Quincy Jones, Diana Ross & Quincy Jones, John & Joan Shakespeare)

RICK JONES

72	Argo AFW106	Theme From The Aeronauts/Lovebug	10
73	Argo ZDA 156	HIYA MAYA (LP)	15

RICKIE LEE JONES

84	Warner Bros. K56628	RICKIE LEE JONES (LP, Nimbus Supercut, mail order only through Practical Hi-Fi magazine)	90

ROBIN JONES & HIS QUINTET

71	Apollo Sound APPS5012	DENGA (LP)	40
71	Apollo Sound APP S 5016	EL MAJA (LP, as Robin Jones Seven)	125
20	Jazz Room JAZZR 004	EL MAJA (reissue)	15

RONNIE JONES

64	Decca F 12012	Let's Pin A Rose On You/I Need Your Loving (B-side with Night Timers)	20
65	Decca F 12066	My Love/It's All Over	40
65	Decca F 12146	Anyone Who Knows What Love Is/Nobody But You	20
65	Parlophone R 5326	You're Lookin' Good/I'm So Clean (with Blue Jays)	40
67	CBS 2699	Little Bitty Pretty One/Put Your Tears Away	18
67	Polydor 56222	In My Love Mind/Mama Come On Home	15
68	CBS 3304	Without Love (There Is Nothing)/Little Bitty Pretty One	12

(see also Night-Timers)

SALENA JONES

66	Columbia DB 7818	A Walk In The Black Forest (Our Walk Of Love)/As Long As I Live	7
66	Columbia DB 7991	I Am Yours/I Only Know I Love You	7
67	Columbia DB 8212	When I Tell You (That I Love You)/Respect	8
67	Decca F 12708	I've Got The Blues/The Glory Of Love	25
70	CBS 4767	This Is Love/Everybodys Talkin'	6
71	CBS 7542	Baby Don't Ya Get Crazy/Fire And Rain	15
73	Indigo GOPOP	Live And Let Die/Some Other World (in p/s)	15
73	Indigo GOPOP	Live And Let Die/Some Other World	6
75	DJM DJS 381	In Love Like You And Me/Tell It Like It Is	6
69	CBS 63613	THE MOMENT OF TRUTH (LP)	35
70	CBS 63901	EVERYBODY'S TALKIN' ABOUT SALENA JONES (LP)	30
71	CBS 64435	PLATINUM (LP)	20
73	RCA Victor SF 8335	ALONE & TOGETHER (LP)	20
74	RCA LPL 1 5025	THIS'N'THAT (LP)	20

SALINA JONES

65	Polydor 56012	Longing/Too Late	7

Sam JONES

MINT VALUE £

SAM JONES
60	Riverside 12-324	SOUL SOCIETY (LP)	20

SAMANTHA JONES
65	United Artists UP 1072	It's All Because Of You/I Woke Up Crying	15
65	United Artists UP 1087	Don't Come Any Closer/Just Call And I'll Be There	15
65	United Artists UP 1105	Chained To A Memory/Just For Him	10
66	United Artists UP 1139	That Special Way/Somebody Else's Baby	10
67	United Artists UP 1185	Surrounded By A Ray Of Sunshine/How Do You Say Goodbye	80
67	United Artists UP 1185	Surrounded By A Ray Of Sunshine/How Do You Say Goodbye (DJ Copy)	150
67	United Artists UP 1200	Why Can't I Remember/Live For Life	8
68	United Artists UP 2248	Lonely Lonely Man/Doll On A Music Box	10
68	United Artists UP 2258	And Suddenly/Go Ahead And Love Me	50
69	Penny Farthing PEN 703	Today (Without You)/The Feelin' That I Get	10
69	Penny Farthing PEN 708	Do I Still Figure In Your Life?/I'm Sorry, But I Think I Love You	10
70	Penny Farthing PEN 734	My Way/Darling Be Home Soon	10
70	Penny Farthing PEN 746	Best Of Both Worlds/Guilty Of Loving You	10
74	Columbia DB 9031	I Believed It All/This I Find Is Beautiful	8
80	Ford SLE 19	Ford Leads The Way/Go Ahead And Love Me (p/s, Ford cars promo disc)	15
68	United Artists	CALL IT SAMANTHA (LP)	25
72	Contour 2870 303	MY WAY (LP)	15

(see also Vernons Girls, Krimson Kake)

SAMMY JONES
70	Gas GAS 123	You're My Girl/HONEYBOY MARTIN: Unchained Melody	10
72	Sioux SI 002	Mendicino/RUM RUNNERS: Sugar Brown	10
72	Sioux SI 003	Little Caesar/TWINKLE BROTHERS: Happy Song	10
72	Sioux SI 011	You're My Girl/HONEYBOY MARTIN: Unchained Melody	8

SANDIE JONES
72	Polydor 2058 223	Music Of Love/Ceol An Ghra	12

SOLOMON JONES
70	Bullet BU 452	Be Strong/Version	10
70	Pama PM 812	Here Comes The Night/RECO RODRIQUEZ: Jaded Ramble	18

SPIKE JONES
53	HMV 7M 121	Hot Lips/Hotter Than A Pistol (as Spike Jones & His Country Cousins)	10
53	HMV 7M 160	I Saw Mommy Kissing Santa Claus/Winter (as Spike Jones & His City Slickers)	10
54	HMV 7MC 3	Deep Purple/Dragnet (as Spike Jones & His City Slickers, export issue)	10
54	HMV 7MC 17	I Wanna Go Back To West Virginia/Little Bo-Beep Has Lost Her Jeep (as Spike Jones & His City Slickers, export issue)	10
55	HMV 7M 324	Secret Love/I'm In The Mood For Love (as Spike Jones & His City Slickers)	10

STAN JONES
58	Pye Disneyland DPL 39260	CREAKIN' LEATHER (LP)	15

STEVE JONES (1)
84	P Flight PFD01	I Need You (By My SIde)/FAT BOYS: The Challenge	90
84	P flight PFD 01	I Need You (By My SIde)/FAT BOYS: The Challenge (12")	150

STEVE JONES (2)
87	MCA MCF 3384	MERCY (LP)	15

(see also Sex Pistols, Professionals)

TAMIKO JONES
76	Contempo CX 15	Let It Flow/DORIS DUKE: Woman Of The Ghetto	15

THAD JONES
57	Esquire 32-065	OLIO (LP)	60
58	Esquire 32-080	AFTER HOURS (LP)	60
59	Pye Nixa NJL 13	MAD THAD (LP)	70

THELMA JONES
68	Sue WI 4047	Stronger/Never Leave Me	60
69	Soul City SC 110	The House That Jack Built/Give It To Me Straight	40
76	CBS 4711	Salty Tears/You're The Song	15

TOM JONES
64	Decca F 11966	Chills And Fever/Breathless	60
65	Columbia DB 7566	Little Lonely One/That's What We'll All Do	20
65	Columbia DB 7733	Lonely Joe/I Was A Fool	20
65	Decca F 12292	Thunderball/Key To My Heart	8
66	Decca F 12315	To Make A Big Man Cry/I'll Never Let You Go (export issue)	10
66	Decca F 12349	Stop Breaking My Heart/Never Give Away Love	10
66	Decca F 12461	This And That/City Girl	15
65	Columbia SEG 8464	TOM JONES (EP)	12
65	Decca DFE 8668	WHAT A PARTY (EP)	15
79	EMI1A 062 63224	DO YOU TAKE THIS MAN? (LP)	40

JONES TOWN MALE QUARTET/FRANKLIN LADIES TOWN TRIO
62	Son TD 104	We'll Never Say Goodbye/Living For J (split 45 rpm single)	25

U.K. JONES
69	Deram DM 231	Let Me Tell Ya/And The Rains Came Down	15
70	Ember EMB S 298	Take Me For What I Am/Love Is Here To Stay	6

(see also Mike Berry)

VIVIAN JONES
79	White Rum/Red Stripe 101 PROOF	Jah Music/Vibes (as V. Jones)	20
80s	Virgo Stomach VG 1003	Who's Gonna Get Caught/Horn Fingers (12", blue vinyl)	15
81	Cha Cha CHAD 37	One Of These Days/Dub (12")	40
85	Leo LEO 008	Physical/Energy (Instrumental)/Energy (Dub) (12")	200
86	Jah Shaka 859	Red Eye/Got A Light (12")	35

Winston JONES

MINT VALUE £

92	Imperial House IH 006	Ethiopian Eyes African Smile/African Love/African Dub (12")	15
87	Jah Shaka SHAKA 861	JAH WORKS (LP)	60
89	Ruff Cutt RCLP 001	BANK ROBBERY (LP)	120

WINSTON JONES
| 73 | Gayfeet GS 208 | You Make Me Cry/Version | 6 |

WIZZ JONES
69	United Artists (S)ULP 1209	WIZZ JONES (LP)	175
70	Village Thing VTS 4	LEGENDARY ME (LP)	100
72	CBS 64809	RIGHT NOW (LP)	100
74	Village Thing VTS 24	WHEN I LEAVE BERLIN (LP)	90
77	Plant Life PLR 009	MAGICAL FLIGHT (LP, with insert)	25

(see also Pete Stanley & Wizz Jones, Accolade)

JONES BOYS
57	Columbia DB 4046	Cool Baby/Rock-A-Hula Baby (Ukulele Lady)	15
58	Columbia DB 4217	The Day The Rains Came/Hideaway	10
59	Columbia DB 4278	Dream Girl/Straight As An Arrow	6

(see also Four Jones Boys)

JONES BROTHERS
| 69 | Pye Intl. 7N 25696 | Lucky Lady/Good Old Days | 75 |
| 02 | Grapevine 2000 G2K 123 | Good Old Days/Lucky Lady (reissue) | 10 |

JONESES
| 81 | Champagne FIZY 507 | Summer Groove/Summer Grove (12") | 40 |
| 81 | Champagne FIZY 507 | Summer Groove (Moving On)/Summer Groove Music/Summer Groove | 25 |

JONESY
73	Dawn DNS 1030	Ricochet/Every Day's The Same	20
72	Dawn DNLS 3042	NO ALTERNATIVE (LP, gatefold sleeve)	80
73	Dawn DNLS 3048	KEEPING UP (LP, with lyric insert, lilac label)	100
73	Dawn DNLS 3048	KEEPING UP (LP, without lyric insert, lilac label)	60
73	Dawn DNLS 3055	GROWING (LP, gatefold sleeve, with lyric insert, pink 'sun' label)	80
73	Dawn DNLS 3055	GROWING (LP, gatefold sleeve, without lyric insert, pink 'sun' label)	50

(see also Alan Bown, Ray Thomas)

JONID
| 80 | Prelude PLAY 001 | False Promises/Words (Without Motion) (p/s) | 10 |
| 81 | Ellie Jay EJSP 9741 | Kismet/The Association (p/s) | 12 |

JONIE D
| 89 | Positive Beat PBEP 001 | WHICH BASE (EP) | 15 |

JONJO
| 72 | Bumble GE 119 | Nine Years Old/Flash In The Pan | 80 |

KEN JONNART
| 69 | Mercury MF 1118 | From The Very First Time/There's A Place | 30 |

JONNIE & THE LUBES
| 79 | Attrix RB 05 | I Got Rabies/Terror In T/EXECUTIVES: Shy Little Girl/Never Go Home | 15 |

HARLEM JONNS RESHUFFLE
68	Fontana TF 970	You Are The One I Love/Good Lovin'	30
69	Fontana TF 1004	Everything Under The Sun/Let Love Come Between Us	20
69	Fontana (S)TL 5509	HARLEM JONNS RESHUFFLE (LP)	50

JONSI
| 10 | Parlophone 5099962617819 | GO (LP) | 20 |

(see also Sigur Ros)

JONSTON MCPHILBRY
| 66 | Fontana TF 663 | She's Gone/Woke Up At Eight | 75 |

JON THE POSTMAN
| 78 | Bent BIG BENT 2 | PUERILE (12" EP, stamped brown paper bag p/s, with inserts) | 20 |
| 78 | Bent BIG BENT 4 | PSYCHEDELIC ROCK'N'ROLL FIVE SKINNERS (12" EP, white label, foldover p/s in bag) | 20 |

JOOK
72	RCA RCA 2279	Alright With Me/Do What You Can	15
73	RCA RCA 2344	Shame/City And Suburban Blues	20
73	RCA RCA 2368	Oo-Oo-Rudi/Jook's On You	15
73	RCA RCA 2431	King Capp/Rumble	12
74	RCA RCA 5024	Bish Bash Bosh/Crazy Kids	18
78	Chiswick SW 30	Watch Your Step/La La Girl/Aggravation Place/Everything I Do (EP)	10

(see also John's Children, Sparks)

JANIS JOPLIN
69	CBS 3683	Turtle Blues/Piece Of My Heart (withdrawn)	30
71	CBS 7019	Me And Bobby McGee/Half Moon	7
71	CBS 7217	Cry Baby/Mercedes Benz	7
71	CBS 9136	Move Over/Cry Baby/Try/Piece Of My Heart (maxi-single)	10
72	CBS 8241	Down On Me/Bye Bye Baby	10
76	CBS 3960	Piece Of My Heart/Kozmic Blues (p/s)	10
69	CBS 63546	I GOT DEM OL' KOZMIC BLUES AGAIN, MAMA! (LP)	45
72	CBS 64792	JOPLIN IN CONCERT (2-LP)	20
71	CBS S 64188	PEARL (LP)	20
73	CBS CQ 30322/Q 64188	PEARL (LP, quadrophonic)	25
75	CBS 88115	JANIS (2-LP)	20
81	CBS S 64188	PEARL (LP, reissue)	15
82	CBS 85354	FAREWELL SONGS (LP)	15
99	Simply Vinyl SVLP 062	PEARL (LP, reissue, 180gm)	15
07	Columbia CS 9913	I GOT DEM OL' KOZMIC BLUES AGAIN, MAMA! (LP, reissue, 180gm)	20
07	Music On Vinyl MOVLP010	PEARL (LP, reissue, 180gm)	15
15	music On Vinyl MOVLP466	PEARL (LP, reissue, red vinyl, 300 numbered copies)	40

JORDAN BROTHERS

MINT VALUE £

(see also Big Brother & Holding Company)

JORDAN BROTHERS
59	London HLW 8908	Never, Never/Please Tell Me Now	30
59	London HLW 8908	Never, Never/Please Tell Me Now (78)	25
60	London HLW 9235	Things I Didn't Say/Polly Plays Her Kettle Drum	10
61	London HLW 9308	No Wings On My Angel/Living For The Day	10

CLIFFORD JORDAN
72	Polydor 2383206	CLIFFORD JORDAN IN THE WORLD (LP)	60

DANNY JORDAN
61	Mercury AMT 1159	Jeannie/Boom Ditty Boom	6

DICK JORDAN
60	Oriole CB 1534	Hallelujah, I Love Her So/Sandy	15
60	Oriole CB 1548	Little Christine/I'll Love You Forever	15
60	Oriole CB 1566	Garden Of Eden/Alive, Alive Oh!	6
60	Oriole CB 1591	Angel On My Shoulder/The Next Train Home	6
61	Piccadilly 7N 35035	Some Of These Days/I Want Her Back	75
62	Piccadilly 7N 35057	Fortune Teller/My Angel	6
63	Columbia DB 7016	Stop The Music/Dream Chaser	6
66	Parlophone R5475	Progress/Something's Going On In There	25

EARL JORDAN
72	Sovereign SVN 6501	JORDAN (LP, textured sleeve with flipbacks)	30

JACK JORDAN - HIS MUSIC
60	Parlophone R 4677	Golden Girl/Beauty And The Beach	7

LOUIS JORDAN (& HIS TYMPANY FIVE)
56	Melodisc 1349	Messy Bessy/I Seen What'cha Done (78)	20
60	Downbeat CHA 3	Ooo-Wee/I'll Die Happy	20
50s	Melodisc EPM7 66	LOUIS JORDAN (EP, as Louis Jordan Tympany Five, 3 different covers)	90
57	Mercury MPT 7521	SOMEBODY UP THERE DIGS ME (10" LP, with Tympany Five)	100
58	Mercury MPL 6541	MAN, WE'RE WAILIN' (LP, with Tympany Five)	60
64	HMV CLP 1809	HALLELUJAH, LOUIS JORDAN IS BACK (LP)	40

(see also Louis Armstrong)

LOUIS JORDAN & CHRIS BARBER'S BAND
63	Melodisc 45-1616	Is She Is Or Is She Ain't Your Baby/Fifty Cents	18

(see also Chris Barber)

RONNY JORDAN
92	Island ILPS 9988	THE ANTIDOTE (LP)	15
93	Island ILPSD 8009	THE QUIET REVOLUTION (2-LP)	20
94	Island IMA 8024	BAD BROTHERS (Mini-LP with D.J. Krush)	15
96	Island 524 212-1	LIGHT TO DARK (LP)	15
00	Blue Note 7243 5 20208 1 2	A BRIGHTER DAY (LP)	20

JORDANAIRES
57	Capitol CL 14687	Sugaree/Baby, Won't You Please Come Home?	40
57	Capitol CL 14773	Summer Vacation/Each Day	20
58	Capitol CL 14921	Little Miss Ruby/All I Need Is You	20
63	Capitol CL 15281	Don't Be Cruel/Don't Worry	20
62	Capitol T 1742	SPOTLIGHT ON THE JORDANAIRES (LP)	40

(see also Elvis Presley, Patsy Cline, Don Gibson, Marty Robbins)

JORGE
69	Aurora 7984	Everybody Wants To Be Loved/Tic Tac Toe	10

JOSEF K
79	Absolute ABS 1	Chance Meeting/Romance (p/s, 1,000 only)	45
80	Postcard 80-3	Radio Drill Time/Crazy To Exist (hand-coloured foldaround p/s, blue labels)	50
80	Postcard 80-3	Radio Drill Time/Crazy To Exist (2nd issue, brown sleeve & labels)	12
80	Postcard 80-3	Radio Drill Time/Crazy To Exist (cream/yellow sleeve & labels)	20
80	Postcard 80-5	It's Kinda Funny/Final Request (in poly bag, with picture insert)	35
80	Postcard 80-5	It's Kinda Funny/Final Request (2nd issue, brown label and brown company sleeve)	12
81	Postcard 81-4/TWI 023	Sorry For Laughing/Revelation (p/s)	20
81	Postcard 81-5	Chance Meeting/Pictures (die-cut sleeve, with postcard)	30
81	Postcard 81-5	Chance Meeting/Pictures (die-cut sleeve, without postcard)	12
81	Postcard 81-1	SORRY FOR LAUGHING (LP, unreleased, a few with proof sleeve)	400
81	Postcard 81-7	THE ONLY FUN IN TOWN (LP, with inner sleeve)	50
87	Supreme Intl. Edit. 87-6	YOUNG AND STUPID (LP, 'Endless Soul' on rear sleeve and labels)	15
12	Les Disques Du Crépuscule LTV 2549	SORRY FOR LAUGHING (LP, reissue, inner, with CD)	25
14	Les Disques Du Crépuscule TWI 052	THE ONLY FUN IN TOWN (2-LP, reissue with art print)	40

(see also Orange Juice, Paul Haig, Happy Family, Rhythm Of Life)

IRVING JOSEPH
60	London HLT 9027	I Left My Love/Lorena	8

KATHRYN JOSEPH
15	Hits The Fan (no cat no)	BONES YOU HAVE THROWN ME AND BLOOD I'VE SPILLED (LP, white vinyl, with 42-page booklet)	60

MARGIE JOSEPH
72	Stax 2025 052	Medicine Bend/Same Thing	10
73	Atlantic K10380	Ridin High/Come Lay Some Lovin On Me	6
75	Atlantic K10646	I Can't Move No Mountains/Just As Soon As The Feelings Over	20
72	Stax 2362 008	MAKES A NEW IMPRESSION (LP)	25
73	Atlantic K 40462	MARGIE JOSEPH (LP)	20
88	Stax SX 015	IN THE NAME OF LOVE (LP)	15

NERIOUS JOSEPH
85	Fashion FAD 042	You're My Special Lady/Danger Man (12")	20

JOSH
69	Duke DU 41	Judge/RON: Soul Of Joemel	15
70	Hot Rod HR 111	Leaving Everything/HOT ROD ALL STARS : Psychedelic Bird	45

(see also Girlie)

JOSH & HERBIE
60s	Kalypso AB 107	I'm Nobody's Child/How Can I Believe In You	6

JOSHUA
73	Key KL 014	JOSHUA (LP)	100

MARVA JOSIE
66	Polydor 56711	Crazy Stockings/I'll Get By	15

JOY & DAVID/DAVE
58	Parlophone R 4477	Whoopee!/My Oh My! (as Joy & David)	25
59	Decca F 11123	Rocking Away The Blues/If You Pass Me By (as Joy & David)	25
59	Decca F 11123	Rocking Away The Blues/If You Pass Me By (78, as Joy & David)	10
60	Triumph RGM 1002	Let's Go See Gran'ma/Believe Me (as Joy & Dave)	25
60	Decca F 11291	My Very Good Friend The Milkman/Doopey Darling (as Joy & Dave)	15
61	Parlophone R 4855	Joe's Been A-Gittin' There/They Tell Us Not To Love (as Joy & Dave)	20
61	Parlophone R 4855	Joe's Been A-Gittin' There/They Tell Us Not To Love (demo copies with alternate take of B-side)	30

MABEL JOY
75	Real RR 2004	MABEL JOY (LP)	25

JOY OF LIFE
85	New European BAD VC 62	ENJOY EP (12", p/s)	18
88	Cadre CR JOL67	HEAR THE CHILDREN (LP)	20

RODDIE JOY
65	Red Bird RB 10021	Come Back Baby/Love Hit Me With A Wallop	60

JOHNNY JOYCE
76	Freedom FLP 99003	JOYCE'S CHOICE MIXTURE (LP)	22

(see also Velvet Opera, Levee Breakers)

ROSALINE JOYCE
84	Hartone HAR 01	Are You Really Going/Version (12")	20
88	Jam Today 12 ROS 2	Falling In Love Again (12" Remix)/I Need All Your Loving/Falling In Love Again (Soulful Lovers Mix) (12")	30
88	Intrigue IGE 3T	This Time I Feel Love/Try (12")	20
89	Jam Today 12 ROS 1	No Questions No Answers (Yankee Style)/(Yankee Mix)/(London Mix)/(B-Boy Mix) (12")	25
89	Unyque UNQ111T	True 2 U/Try (Remix)/U Can Be (900 Remix) (12")	10
91	Unyque UNQ 14T	Waiting So Long (Nemesis Mix)/(Original Mix) (12")	20
87	Jam Today ROSLP 1	LOVERS SOUL (LP)	40

JOYCE'S ANGELS
67	Major Minor MM 526	Flowers For My Friends/Rodney Reginald Smithfield Harvey Jones	15

(see also Chris White)

JOY DE VIVRE
81	Crass CR & SS ENVY 1	Our Wedding (flexidisc, white vinyl, no p/s, with mailer)	300
81	Crass CR & SS ENVY 1	Our Wedding (flexidisc, white vinyl, no p/s, without mailer)	200

(see also Crass)

JOY DIVISION
SINGLES
78	Enigma PSS 139	AN IDEAL FOR LIVING (Warsaw/No Love Lost/Leaders Of Men/Failures) (EP, 1,000 only, foldout p/s; beware of counterfeits)	2000
78	Anonymous ANON 1	AN IDEAL FOR LIVING (Warsaw/No Love Lost/Leaders Of Men/Failures) (12" EP reissue, 1,200 only)	700
79	Factory FAC 13	Transmission/Novelty (1st pressing, 10,000 in textured p/s)	20
80	Factory FAC 23	Love Will Tear Us Apart/These Days/Love Will Tear Us Apart (p/s)	12
80	Factory FACUS T2	She's Lost Control/Atmosphere	15
80	Factory FAC23.12	Love Will Tear Us Apart/These Days/Love Will Tear Us Apart (12", laminated sleeve)	25
80	Factory FACUS 2/UK	Atmosphere/She's Lost Control (UK variant, 12", black vinyl)	30
80	Factory FACUS 2/UK	Atmosphere/She's Lost Control (UK variant, 12", red vinyl)	20
82	Factory FAC 13 12	Transmission/Novelty (12")	20
88	Factory FAC213	Atmosphere/The Only Mistake/Sound Of Music (12", p/s)	15
86	Strange Fruit SFPS 013	PEEL SESSIONS (12", p/s recorded 31/01/79)	12
87	Strange Fruit SFPS 033	PEEL SESSIONS (12" EP)	15
95	London YOJX 1	Love Will Tear Us Apart (Original Version)/Love Will Tear Us Apart (Radio Version)/Love Will Tear Us Apart (Arthur Baker Remix)/Atmosphere (12", stickered p/s)	10
11	Rhino FAC .33	Ceremony (Original Version)/In A Lonely Place (12" Version)//Ceremony (Heart & Soul Rehearsal Version)/In A Lonely Place (Unreleased Rehearsal Version) (12", 800 only)	25
10	Rhino 5186595937	SINGLES 1978-80 (10 x 7", art piece, 2 x CD-R, box set, 500 only)	200
14	Warner Bros. JDPM11	AN IDEAL FOR LIVING EP (reissue)	10

ALBUMS
79	Factory FACT 10	UNKNOWN PLEASURES (LP with inner sleeve, textured sleeve, 1st press turns a deep translucent red when held over a light)	150
79	Factory FACT 10	UNKNOWN PLEASURES (LP with inner sleeve, textured sleeve, 2nd non transluscent issue)	80
80	Factory FACT 25	CLOSER (LP, hard textured sleeve & inner, some 1st pressing turns a deep translucent red when held over a light)	100
80	Factory FACT 25	CLOSER (LP, hard textured sleeve & inner, 1st pressing, solid black vinyl)	50
81	Factory FACT 40	STILL (2-LP, hessian sleeve, card inners & white/blue ribbon)	150
81	Factory FAC 40	STILL (2-LP, gatefold)	40
85	Factory FACT 10c	UNKNOWN PLEASURES (reissue, cassette in box with insert)	30
85	Factory FACT 25c	CLOSER (reissue, cassette in box with insert)	30
85	Factory FACT 40c	STILL (reissue, cassette in box with insert)	30
88	Factory FACT 250	SUBSTANCE (LP)	40

Col JOYE & JOYBOYS

MINT VALUE £

90	Strange Fruit SFRLP 111	PEEL SESSIONS (LP, reissue of both EPs)	20
95	London 828624 1	PERMANENT (2-LP, insert)	50
01	Strange Fruit SFRSLP 094	THE COMPLETE BBC RECORDINGS (LP)	30
07	London 2564699291	JOY DIVISION: IN MEMORY (4xLP boxed set, 3000 only)	150
07	London 25646 40151	UNKNOWN PLEASURES (LP, remastered reissue on 180gm vinyl)	20
07	London 25645 4014 1	CLOSER (LP, remastered reissue on 180gm vinyl)	20
07	Ozit Morpheus OZIT 8797	MARTIN HANNETT'S PERSONAL MIXES (2-LP)	20

(see also New Order, Electronic, Other Two, Revenge, Bad Lieutenant, Monaco)

COL JOYE & JOYBOYS
59	Brunswick 05806	(Rockin' Rollin') Clementine/Bye Bye Baby Goodbye	20
60	Top Rank JAR 529	Be My Girl/Yes Sir, That's My Baby	10

JOYFUL SOUND
73	SRT SRT 73278	IT WILL BE WORTH IT ALL (LP)	300

JOYRIDE
69	RCA SF 8027	FRIEND SOUND (LP)	20

JOYRIDE GOODBYE
80	Joyride SRTS80/CUS 659	Goodbye/Something Special (no p/s)	30

JOY UNLIMITED
69	Page One POF 147	Daytime Night Time/Mister Pseudonym	30
69	Page One POF 160	Oh Darlin'/Feelin'	40
70	Page One POLS 028	TURBULENCE (LP)	80

J P SUNSHINE
95	Uncle Glitch Records UG 1	UNCLE GLITCH PRESENTS (LP, 500 only)	30

J.S.D. BAND
73	Cube BUG 29	Sarah Jane/Paddy Stacks (p/s)	6
74	Cube BUG 49	Hayes And Harlington Blues/Cuckoo	8
71	Regal Zono. SRLZ 1018	COUNTRY OF THE BLIND (LP, textured sleeve, first press with flipbacks)	90
71	Regal Zono. SRLZ 1018	COUNTRY OF THE BLIND (LP, textured sleeve, later press without flipbacks)	50
72	Cube HIFLY 11	J.S.D. BAND (LP)	15
73	Cube HIFLY 14	TRAVELLING DAYS (LP, fully laminated sleeve)	15

JUAN & JUNIOR
67	CBS 2949	The Chase/Nothing	6
68	CBS 3223	To Girls/Andurina	15

JUBILEE STOMPERS
70	Trojan TR 7725	Luciana/I Really Like It	6

JUDAS JUMP
70	Parlophone R 5828	Run For Your Life/Beer Drinking Woman	15
70	Parlophone R 5838	This Feelin' We Feel/Hangman's Playing	8
70	Parlophone R 5873	Beer Drinking Woman/I Have The Right	6
70	Parlophone PAS 10001	SCORCH (LP, gatefold sleeve, black/silver label with boxed logo)	80

(see also Herd, Amen Corner, Andy Bown)

JUDAS PRIEST
74	Gull GULS 6	Rocka-Rolla/Never Satisfied	30
76	Gull GULS 31	The Ripper/Island Of Domination	30
77	CBS S CBS 5222	Diamonds And Rust/Dissident Aggressor	7
79	Gull GULS 71	The Ripper/Victims Of Change	8
79	Gull GULS 7112	The Ripper/Never Satisfied/Victim Of Changes (12", p/s)	12
80	CBS TA 4298	United/Grinder (poster p/s)	12
83	Gull GULS 7612	Tyrant/Rocka-Rolla/Genocide (12", p/s, white vinyl)	15
86	CBS QTA 7144	Locked In (Extended)/Reckless/Desert Plains (live)/Freewheel Burning (live) (12", poster p/s)	10
91	Columbia 656589 0	A Touch Of Evil/Between The Hammer And The Anvil (shaped disc)	12
74	Gull GULP 1005	ROCKA ROLLA (LP, 1st pressing, 'bottle top' sleeve, with 'Thanks for the words Al!" credit on rear sleeve)	60
76	Gull GULP 1015	SAD WINGS OF DESTINY (LP)	25
76	Gull PGULP 1015	SAD WINGS OF DESTINY (LP, picture disc)	22
77	CBS 82008	SIN AFTER SIN (LP)	20
78	CBS 82430	STAINED CLASS (LP)	15
78	CBS 83135	KILLING MACHINE (LP, red vinyl)	20
79	CBS 83852	UNLEASHED IN THE EAST (LP, with free single "Rock Forever"/ Hell Bent For Leather/"Beyond The Realms Of Death" [SJP 1], and tour advertising flyer)	30
79	CBS 66357	BOX SET (3-LP, reissue of "Sin After Sin"/"Stained Class"/"Killing Machine")	25
80	CBS 84160	BRITISH STEEL (LP)	20
86	Shanghai PGLP 1026	JUDAS PRIEST (LP, picture disc)	20
88	CBS 461108	RAM IT DOWN (LP, with inner)	20
90	CBS 467290 1	PAINKILLER (LP)	35
93	CBS 473050	METAL WORKS (2xLP, gatefold sleeve)	40
98	SPV 0891 8542	98 LIVE MELTDOWN (2xLP)	40
04	Sony 5128933	METALOGY (4xCD, DVD, booklet, leather studded box set)	45
08	Sony 88697315572	NOSTRADAMUS (3-LP, 2-CD boxed set)	30
11	Sony 88697967872	COMPLETE ALBUMS COLLECTION (19 x CD box set. booklet)	50

(see also Trapeze, Fancy, Fight, Halford)

JUDD
70	Penny Farthing PEN 709	Snarlin' Mumma Lion/Stronger Than A Man	6
70	Penny Farthing PELS 504	JUDD (LP, die-cut sleeve, insert, red/black/yellow labels)	175

(see also Kris Ife)

F.C. JUDD
60	Castle EFX 1	ELECTRONIC SOUNDS AND MUSIC (EP)	50
60	Castle EFX 2	ELECTRONIC THEMES AND MUSIQUE CONCRETE (EP)	50
60	Castle EFX 3	RHYTHMIC ELECTRONIC MUSIC (EP)	50
60	Castle HMX 1	HAUNTED HOUSE, MYSTERY SOUNDS AND MUSIC (EP)	25

67	(No label or cat no)	ELECTRONIC SOUNDS AND EFFECTS (flexi, free with Practical Electronics)	15

PAA JUDE
92	Asona ARC 019	SEAMAN JOLLY (LP)	60

JUDGE HAPPINESS
85	Mynah SCS 8501	Hey Judge/Pig In Pink (very few with p/s)	25
85	Mynah SCS 8501	Hey Judge/Pig In Pink	10

(see also Mock Turtles)

TERRY JUDGE & THE BARRISTERS
63	Oriole CB 1896	Hey Look At Her/Kind Of Girl You Can't Forget	10
64	Oriole CB 1938	I Don't Care/Try To Forget	10
65	Fontana TF 599	Come With Me And Love Me/Waitin' For The Night To Come	10

JUG TRUST
70	Parlophone R5825	Goodbye Train/Cat And Mouse (demos are in p/s)	10

JUGGERNAUTS
84	Supreme Int. Editions 84-2	Come Throw Yourself/My First Million (p/s)	10

(see also Paul Haig)

JUICE CREW
08	Diggers With Gratitude DWG 004	THE JUICE CREW (EP, 75 only, red vinyl)	90
08	Diggers With Gratitude DWG 004	THE JUICE CREW (EP, 75 only, blue vinyl)	90
08	Diggers With Gratitude DWG 003	THE JUICE CREW (EP, 75 only, white vinyl)	90
08	Diggers With Gratitude DWG 002	THE JUICE CREW (EP, 125 only, black vinyl)	60

JUICY LUCY
70	Fontana TF 1068	Who Do You Love/Walking Down The Highway (unissued)	0
70	Vertigo V1/6059 001	Who Do You Love/Walking Down The Highway	10
70	Vertigo 6059 015	Pretty Woman/I'm A Thief	18
72	Polydor 2001 279	It Ain't Easy/Promised Land	7
69	Vertigo VO 2	JUICY LUCY (LP, first press with 'Philips' credit on large swirl label, gatefold sleeve)	200
69	Vertigo VO 2	JUICY LUCY (LP, later press without 'Philips' credit on large swirl label, gatefold sleeve)	70
70	Vertigo 6360 014	LIE BACK AND ENJOY IT (LP, large swirl label, gatefold poster sleeve)	200
71	Bronze ILPS 9157	GET A WHIFF OF THIS (LP, textured sleeve, Island credit on label)	30
72	Polydor 2310 160	PIECES (LP)	25

(see also Misunderstood, Van Der Graaf Generator, Ray Owen, Paul Williams' Big Roll Band)

TM JUKE
03	Try Thoughts TRULP 050	MAPS FROM THE WILDERNESS (2-LP)	70

JIMMY JUKEBOX
75	Sonet SON 2057	Motorboat/25 Hours A Day	40
77	Sonet SON 2057	Motorboat/25 Hours A Day (1977 re-issue with new Savage Pencil p/s sleeve but original 1975 records inside)	20

(see also Kim Fowley)

JULIAN (SCOTT)
59	Pye Nixa 7N 15236	Sue Saturday/Can't Wait	30
59	Pye Nixa N 15236	Sue Saturday/Can't Wait (78)	20

(see also Brian Bennett)

JULIAN (JUDY MOWATT) & CHOSEN FEW
71	High Note HS 054	Joy To The World/Joyful Version	12

JULIAN (JUDY MOWATT) & GAYTONES
72	High Note HS 059	She Kept On Talking/Version	20

JULIAN'S TREATMENT
70	Young Blood YB 1009	Phantom City/Alda, Dark Lady Of The Outer Worlds	25
70	Young Blood SYB 2/3	A TIME BEFORE THIS (2-LP, laminated gatefold sleeve, white/red labels)	400

(see also Julian Jay Savarin)

JULIET & GRACE
80	Atra 32 DA	What Can I Do/MILITANT BARRY: Lovers Styly (12". p/s)	20

(see also Militant Barry)

JULY
68	Major Minor MM 568	My Clown/Dandelion Seeds	200
68	Major Minor MM 580	Hello, Who's There?/The Way	80
68	Major Minor MMLP 29	JULY (LP, laminated front sleeve, red/white/black labels)	1000
87	Bam Caruso KIRI 097	DANDELION SEEDS (LP, reissue of above LP with extra tracks & different sleeve)	25
95	Essex 1011LP	JULY (LP, reissue with bonus 7": "Hello Who's There?"/"The Way" [p/s, 10117])	20

(see also Jade Warrior, Tom Newman)

ISSA JUMA
90	Discafrique AFRILP 008	SIGALAME 2 (LP)	60

JUMBLE LANE
71	Holyground HG 115	JUMBLE LANE (LP, 99 copies only)	600

JUMBO
72	CBS 7820	She Said/Wasting My Time	8
72	CBS S 8082	Promises/Sitting Thinking	12
72	Epic EPC S 8057	Round And Round/Sewing Circle	12

JUMP
80	Caveman CLUB 1	Shake Up/All In Vain (p/s)	25

JUMPBACKS
73	Maxi M3	Shake/Hello Stranger	30

JUMPIN' JACKS
58	HMV POP 440	My Girl, My Girl/Tried And Tested	25

JUMPLEADS
82	Ock OC 001	THE STAG MUST DIE (LP, with insert)	15

JUMP SQUAD

MINT VALUE £

JUMP SQUAD
81 101 UR 2   Lord Of The Dance/Debt (p/s) 20
(see also Embryo)

JUNCO PARTNERS
65 Columbia DB 7665   As Long As I Have You/Take This Hammer 70
79 Rigid JUNK 1028   Swinging Sixties Boys/Peepin' And Hidin' 6
81 Energy NRGX 4   Tall Windows (Extended)/Noizez In My Head (Extended) (12", stickered white label,
                                                       plain sleeve, promo only) 10
71 Philips 6308 032   JUNCO PARTNERS (LP, laminated sleeve, black/silver labels) 150

JUNCTION
87 New Youth NYJ 175   PANDORAS BOX EP 20

JUNCTION 32
75 Holyground HGS 119   JUNCTION 32 (LP, 100 copies only) 550

JUNCUNO
71 Banana BA 361   The End (as Joncuno)/HORACE ANDY: See A Man's Face 50
(see also Jon Cundo)

ROSANNE JUNE
56 London HLU 8352   The Charge Of The Light Brigade/Broken Windows 20
58 Oriole CB 1430   When A Woman Cries/The Great Chicago Fire 8

ROSEMARY JUNE
59 Pye International 7N 25005   I'll Be With You In Apple Blossom Time/Always A Bridesmaid 6

JUNE BRIDES
84 Pink PINKY 1   In The Rain/Sunday To Saturday (p/s) 10
84 Pink PINKY 2   Every Conversation/Disneyland (die-cut sleeve, with insert) 8
84 Pink PINKY 2   Every Conversation/Disneyland (die-cut sleeve) 7
85 Pink PINKY 5   THERE ARE EIGHT MILLION STORIES... (LP, insert) 15
(see also Phil Wilson)

JUNG COLLECTIVE
02 Nanny Tango NT 1   Injustice/Street Preacher (Plaid Mix) (clear vinyl, poly sleeve w/sticker insert) 20

CARL GUSTAV JUNG
63 Piccadilly FTF 38505   FACE TO FACE (LP) 20

JUNGLE BROTHERS
88 Gee St. GEEA 001   STRAIGHT OUT THE JUNGLE (LP, with free 12") 15

JOHNNY JUNGLE
93 Dee Jay DJX 005   REMIXES 1 (12") 20
93 Dee Jay DJX 006   REMIXES 2 (12") 15

JUNGLE WARRIOR
94 Strictly Underground STUR 38   No Surrender/New Style (12") 25
95 Strictly Underground STUR 47   Jungle Jesus (Pope John Paul Mix)/(Absolution Mix) (12") 35

JUNIOR (SIMPSON)
68 Giant GN 18   I'm Gonna Leave You Girl/I Love You I Love You 20
68 Giant GN 25   Come Cure Me/I Want Your Loving 25

JUNIOR B
92 Eastern Sher ES 001   Meditation/Black And White (12") 40

JUNIOR BROWN
78 Tempus TEMD 01   Jah Find Babylon Guilty (feat. Ranking Ruben)/Dub (12") 18
80 Jah Shaka SHAKA 829   Fly Me Away/Travelling Dub (12") 30
82 Jah Shaka SHAKA 822   Warrior/Right Fight (12") 15
92 Jah Shaka SHAKA 822   Warrior/Right Fight (12", reissue) 10

JUNIOR AND THE COOL NOTES
75 Torpedo TOR 36   Curley Locks/Version Locks 15

JUNIOR DELGADO
77 Deb TIC 1001   Tiction/Tiction Volume 2 18
78 Deb DEB 001   Tonight & Tune In/Armed Robbery (12") 20
78 Deb DEB 019   Trickster/CARLTON & HIS SHOES: Better Days (12") 35
79 Greensleeves GRED 15   Love Tickles Like Magic/PRINCE JAMMY & AGGROVATORS : Prince Jammy's Magic (12") . 20
79 Burning Sounds BRD 005   Raiders/Warrior (12") 20
79 DEB 026   Warrior (with Ras Bug)/DEB PLAYERS: Version (12") 30
80 Greensleeves GRED 39   Midnight Raver/365 days (12", blue vinyl) 15
80 Niagra NIADD 108   Fort Augustus/Escape Prisioners (12") 35
82 Incredible Jux 04   Trouble Part 1/Trouble Part 2 (12") 20
86 Incredible IM001   Poverty/Version (12") 30
87 Fashion FAD 040   Hot Stuff/It Takes Two To Tango (12") 15
88 Mango IS 368   Hanging Tree/Hey Good Looking (12") 20
89 Fashion FAD 066   Dub School/We A Blood (12") 25
79 Deb DEBLP 05   TASTE OF THE YOUNG HEART (LP) 40
79 Deb DEBLP 010   EFFORT (LP) 40
82 Incredible Jux HBLP 001   BUSHMAN REVOLUTION (LP) 40
86 Mango ILPS 9856   RAGAMUFFIN YEAR (LP) 15
86 Fashion FADLP 003   IT TAKES TWO TO TANGO (LP) 18

JUNIOR DISPROL
01 SFDB A027658   Fight Club/Junq Waffle 25

JUNIOR ENGLISH
79 Ethnic Fight ETH 1328   Keep On Trying/HORSEMOUTH: Herb Vendor (12") 20

JUNIOR GEE
86 Scorcher 1032   The Truth (12") 50

JUNIOR GEE & THE CAPITAL BOYS
84 Tai Wan 1948   Check Us Out/The Break (12") 15

Hugh ROY JUNIOR

MINT VALUE £

HUGH ROY JUNIOR
71	Big BG 329	Papcito/RUPIE EDWARDS: I'm Gonna Live Some Life	12
72	Duke DU 137	Live It Up/DENNIS BROWN: Baby Don't Do It	15
72	Ashanti ASH 405	King Of The Road/ROOSEVELT ALL STARS: Version	15
72	Jackpot JP 806	Two Ton Guletto/Version	20

(see also U Roy Junior)

JUNIOR KEITHING
80	Grand Masters GM 001	Jah Wrote Me A Letter/Letter Dub (12")	20

JUNIOR MCCANTS
98	Kent 6T 16	Try Me For Your New Love/GARLAND GREEN: Come Through Me	40

JUNIOR MURVIN
68	Doctor Bird DB 1112	Miss Cushie (as Junior Soul)/LYNN TAITT & JETS: Dr. Paul	250
68	Big Shot BI 503	Chattie Chattie/The Magic Touch	300
69	Big Shot BI 527	The Hustler/The Magic Touch	200
70	Gayfeet GS 205	Jennifer/Slipping	12
76	Island 12WIP 6539	Police & Thieves/JAH LION: Soldier & Police War/GLEN DACASTA: Magic Touch/THE UPSETTER: Grumblin' Dub (12", p/s)	12
76	Island WIP 6316	Police & Thieves/Grumblin Dub	8
77	Island IPR 2001	Tedious/Memories	30
77	Island 12WIP 2010	Upsetter Revue Feat. Junior Murvin: Dread Locks In Moonlight/Closer Together (12")	20
80	Black Ark ARK 007	Cross Over/I Am In Love (12")	25
82	Dread At The Controls DATCD 009	Bad Man Posse/Riddim Request To All Posse Smoker Posse (12")	18
86	Greensleeves GRED 199	Apartheid/Jack Slick (12")	15
77	Island ILPS 9499	POLICE AND THIEVES (LP)	35
82	Dread At The Controls DATC 007	BADMAN POSSE (LP)	30
84	Greensleeves GREL 70	MUGGERS IN THE STREET (LP)	20

JUNIOR REID
80	Negus Roots NERT 02	Sister Dawn/Dub Version (12")	20
81	Negus Roots NERT 09	IF I/Versions (12")	40
82	King Imperial KG 008	Jail House/We Got To Leave (12")	50
84	Greensleeves GRED 163	Boom Shack A Lack/Old Time Something (12")	15
85	Greensleeves GREL 78	BOOM SHACK A LACK (LP)	20

JUNIOR ROOTS
81	Black Roots BR 24	Natty Dread Time/BLACK TRAP: Into The Light (12")	15

JUNIOR ROSS AND THE SPEARS
76	K&B KB 5529	Judgement Time/Version	25

JUNIOR SENIOR
03	Mercury 0679201	D-D-DON'T STOP THE BEAT (LP)	30

TREVOR JUNIOR
84	Tonos TON 002	Ghetto Living/Have Faith In Jah (12")	50

JUNIOR TUCKER
81	Island WIP 6607	The Kick (Rock On)/COMPASS POINT ALL STARS: Peanut Butter	8

JUNIORS
64	Columbia DB 7339	There's A Pretty Girl/Pocket Size	55

JUNIOR'S EYES
69	Regal Zonophone RZ 3009	Mr. Golden Trumpet Player/Black Snake	30
69	Regal Zonophone RZ 3018	Woman Love/White Light Part 2 (withdrawn B-side)	30
69	Regal Zonophone RZ 3018	Woman Love/Circus Days	20
69	Regal Zonophone RZ 3023	Star Child/Sink Or Swim	20
69	Regal Zono. SLRZ 1008	BATTERSEA POWER STATION (LP, laminated front, flipbacks, "Sold in U.K..." label text)	200

(see also David Bowie, Tickle, Bunch Of Fives, Outsiders)

JUNIPER GREEN
71	Columbia DB 8809	Dreams In The Sky/Cascade Of Ice	20

JUNK SHOP RADIOS
91	Junk JUNK 001	Summer Rain/Missed Again (die-cut hand-stamped sleeve)	15

LENA JUNOFF
68	Olga OLE 8	Yesterday Has Gone/Good Kind Of Hurt	40

JUNO REACTOR
95	Blue Room BR009LP	BEYOND THE INFINITE (4-LP)	30
97	Blue Room Released BR042LP	BIBLE OF DREAMS (3-LP)	20
00	Electric M.E.L.T. ELM 8033LP	SHANGO (2-LP)	20

JUNO'S CLAW
79	MPA EMP 081	Barbara/The Master/Big City (EP, no p/s)	100

JUPITER
72	Parlophone R 5967	The Meteor Song/Life Is Getting Better Every Day	25

ERIC JUPP & HIS ORCHESTRA
53	Columbia SCM 5070	Jog Trot/Doina Voda	7
54	Columbia SCM 5081	Ooop De Ooh (Lazy Mambo)/Footsteps In The Fog	7
54	Columbia SCM 5140	They Were Doin' The Mambo/Skokiian (with Coronets)	7
56	Columbia DB 3817	Theme From 'East Of Eden'/When The Lilac Blooms Again	7
57	Columbia DB 4030	Bleep! Bleep!/Three-Two-One-Zero!	12
55	Columbia SEG 7589	ERIC JUPP AND HIS ORCHESTRA (EP)	10

(see also Coronets)

MICKEY JUPP
78	Stiff UPP1	My Typewriter/Nature's Radio (as Mickey Jupp with Legend, promo)	8
78	Stiff BUY 36	Old Rock N Roller/S.P.Y. (p/s)	6

(see also Rossi & Frost, Legend)

JURASSIC 5

MINT VALUE £

JURASSIC 5
98	Pan PAN 015 LP	JURASSIC FIVE (LP)	35

JUS BADD
87	Tuff Groove TUFF001	Freestyle/Proud (12")	50

JUST A HE HE
84	PRT JH 1	Lucky Day/Take Time (p/s)	8

JUST BROTHERS
80s	Soul City SC 127	Carlena/IVORIES: Please Stay (die-cut company sleeve)	8
01	Hayley HR 003	Honey/Carlena	8

JUST MEASURES
83	It's War Boy £5	FLAGELLATION (LP)	20

JUST THE JOB
80	KIK 2	Fears Of The Years/Street Feelings/London Lights (with p/s)	50
80	KIK 2	Fears Of The Years/Street Feelings/London Lights (without p/s)	30

JUST WATER
78	Stiff BUY 31	Singin In The Rain/Witness To The Crime (p/s)	7

SAMANTHA JUSTE
66	Go AJ 11402	No One Needs My Love Today/If Trees Could Talk	25

JUST FOUR MEN
64	Parlophone R 5186	That's My Baby/Things Will Never Be The Same (withdrawn, as Four Just Men)	80
64	Parlophone R 5208	That's My Baby/Things Will Never Be The Same	60
65	Parlophone R 5241	There's Not One Thing/Don't Come Any Closer	60

(see also Wimple Winch, Four Just Men, Pacific Drift)

JUST FRANK
79	Rok ROK III/IV	You/SPLIT SCREENS: Just Don't Try (die-cut company sleeve)	35

JIMMY JUSTICE
60	Pye 7N 15301	I Understand Just How You Feel/Bloodshot Eyes (as Jimmy Justice & Jury)	20
61	Pye 7N 15351	When Love Has Left You/The Teacher	15
61	Pye 7N 15376	A Little Bit Of Soap/Little Lonely One	15
62	Pye 7N 15443	Ain't That Funny/One (with p/s)	10
62	Pye 7N 15443	Ain't That Funny/One	6
62	Pye 7N 15457	Spanish Harlem/Write Me A Letter	6
62	Pye 7N 15469	Parade Of Broken Hearts/Dawning	7
63	Pye 7N 15502	The World Of Lonely People/I Wake Up Crying	7
63	Pye 7N 15509	Little Cracked Bell/Lighted Windows	7
63	Pye 7N 15528	The Guitar Player/Don't Let The Stars Get In Your Eyes	8
63	Pye 7N 15558	You're Gonna Need My Lovin'/Since You've Been Gone (with Exchequers)	8
63	Pye 7N 15601	Don't Say That Again/Green Leaves Of Summer	8
69	Decca F 12899	Running Out Of Time/There Goes My World	8
65	Pye 7N 15963	Only Heartbreak For Me/Everything In The Garden	10
68	RCA Victor RCA 1681	I'm Past Forgetting You/Walking Away With My Heart	25
63	Pye NEP 24159	HIT PARADE (EP)	12
62	Pye NPL 18080	TWO SIDES OF JIMMY JUSTICE (LP)	30
62	Pye NPL 18085	SMASH HITS (LP)	20

JUSTIFIED ANCIENTS OF MU MU (J.A.M.S)
87	KLF Comm. JAMS 23	All You Need Is Love (Original) (12", white label, 1-sided, 500 only)	50
87	KLF Comm. JAMS 23(s)	All You Need Is Love (Me Ru Con Mix)/(Ibo Version) (1,000 only, plain sleeve)	10
87	KLF Comm. JAMS 23T	All You Need Is Love/Ivum Naya/Rap, Rhyme And Scratch Yourself (12", 'James Anderton' p/s, 5,000 only)	15
87	KLF Comm. JAMS 24T	Whitney Joins The JAMs (120 bpm) (12", 1-sided, 'Scottish' issue, 500 only)	15
87	KLF Comm. JAMS 25T	1987 - The 45 Edits (12", p/s)	15
87	KLF Comm. JAMS 26T	BURN THE BEAT (12" EP, 5,000 for export only)	10
87	KLF Comm. JAMS 27	Down Town/118 BPM 27 (p/s)	8
87	KLF Comm. JAMS 27	Down Town (A-side Mix) (12", 1-sided, white label, 500 only)	12
87	KLF Comm. JAMS 27	Down Town (B-side Mix) (12", 1-sided, white label, 500 only)	12
87	KLF Comm. JAMS 27	Down Town (A-side Mix)/(B-side Mix) (12", white label)	12
87	KLF Comm. JAMS 27T	Down Town (118 bpm)/Down Town (12", JAMs label, generic sleeve)	10
87	KLF Comm. JAMS 27T	Down Town (118 bpm)/Down Town (12",mispressed 'album' label, generic sleeve)	15
90	KLF Comm.	It's Grim Up North (Original Vocal Mix) (1st pressing, 12", grey vinyl, 1-sided, 350 pressed but most sent back and destroyed due to error matrix in run-out groove. This one has "IT'S GRIM UP NORTH JA" and no cat no)	500
90	KLF Comm. JAMS 28T	It's Grim Up North (Original Vocal Mix) (2nd pressing, 12", grey vinyl, 1-sided, 350 only, "IT'S GRIM UP NORTH JAMS-28T JA" in run out groove)	100
87	KLF Comm. JAMS DS 1	Deep Shit (flexidisc, unreleased)	150
91	KLF Comm. JAMS 028R	It's Grim Up North (Original Vocal Mix) (12", black vinyl, 1-sided promo)	8
88	Fierce FRIGHT 34(T)	20 GREATEST HITS (12" EP; not actually by J.A.M.s!)	12
87	KLF Comm. JAMS LP 1	1987 (WHAT THE FUCK IS GOING ON?) (LP, withdrawn)	100
88	JAMS CLP 1	1987 (WHAT THE FUCK IS GOING ON?) (cassette LP)	30
88	KLF Comm. JAMS LP 2	WHO KILLED THE JAMS? (LP, stickered sleeve with insert)	20
89	KLF Comm. JAMS DLP 3	SHAG TIMES (2-LP)	50
89	KLF Comm. JAMS CD 3	SHAG TIMES (CD)	40

(see also KLF, Timelords, Disco 2000, Space, Orb, Bill Drummond)

JUSTIN CASE
80	Rok ROK XIX	TV/STRAIGHT UP: One Out All Out (die-cut company sleeve)	40

DAVE JUSTIN
67	Polydor 56221	Everybody's Gone Home/Lincoln Green	12
68	Polydor 56253	You Outside/Thinking Twice	12

JAY JUSTIN
68	Columbia DB 8439	I Sell Summertime/Time (withdrawn)	10

JUSTIN & KARLSSON
66	Piccadilly 7N 35295	Somewhere They Can't Find Me/What More Do You Want	40

JUSTINE

			MINT VALUE £
JUSTINE			
69	Dot DOT 121	Leave Me Be/Clown	10
69	Buffalo BFS 1001	Right Now/Place Where Sorrow Hides	30
70	Uni UNS 528	She Brings Back The Morning With Her/Back To Boulder	8
70	Uni UNLS 111	JUSTINE (LP)	90
JUSTIN'S TIMEPEICE			
68	Reverberation CKS 20001	Lonely Man/Bull Durham's Workout	40
JUSTINS			
71	Punch PH 65	Cholera/LLOYD ALL STARS: Black Bird	20
BILL JUSTIS & HIS ORCHESTRA			
57	London HLS 8517	Raunchy/The Midnight Man	20
58	London HLS 8614	College Man/The Stranger (B-side with Spinners)	25
63	Mercury AMT 1201	I'm Gonna Learn To Dance/Tamoure	10
69	Sun 6094 003	Raunchy/Flip, Flop And Bop	10
JUST LIKE THAT			
76	Tank BS 122	JUST LIKE THAT (LP)	20
JUST OTHERS			
74	Goodwill Records WS 1	AMALGAM (LP, 250 only)	1000
JUST PLAIN JONES			
71	CBS CBS 7480	Crazy, Crazy/Should Have Stayed With Mary	20
(see also Just Plain Smith, Esprit De Corps)			
JUST PLAIN SMITH			
69	Sunshine SUN 7702	February's Child/Don't Open Your Mind (with p/s)	135
69	Sunshine SUN 7702	February's Child/Don't Open Your Mind	60
(see also Just Plain Jones, Esprit De Corps)			
JUST US			
66	CBS 202068	I Can't Grow Peaches On A Cherry Tree/I Can Save You	7
JUST WILLIAM			
68	Spark SRL 1018	I Don't Care/Cherrywood Green	30
JUVENILES			
66	Pye International 7N 25349	Bo Diddley/Yes I Believe	100
JYL			
84	Thunderbolt THBL 036	JYL (LP)	50
JYNX			
64	Columbia DB 7304	How/Do What They Don't Say	75

K

CAROLINE K			
87	Earthly Delights EARTH 1	NOW WAIT FOR LAST YEAR (LP, 1,500 only)	15
JOHNNY K			
63	Fontana TF 408	Lemonade/Come Closer Melinda	12
MOSES K & PROPHETS			
65	Decca F 12244	I Went Out With My Baby Tonight/So Long	25
(see also Them)			
SIMON K			
69	B&C CB 111	You Know I Do/Bring Your Love Back	40
KABBALA			
82	Red Flame RF 1211	Ashewo Ara/Voltan Dance (12", black or red p/s)	60
83	Red Flame RFB 37	Yen-Nbo-Ose/Yo You Dance (p/s)	10
83	Red Flame RFB 37 12	Yen-Nbo-Ose/Yo You Dance (12", p/s)	20
88	INK 728	Ashewo Ara (Mix 88)/Voltan Dance (p/s)	12
88	INK 1228	Ashewo Ara (Mix 88)/Voltan Dance (12", p/s)	20
97	MAMA MAMT 015	ASHEWO ARA: Side Afro Funk/Side House (12", p/s)	15
KABUKI			
82	Kabaret Noir KAB 1	I Am A Horse/My Hair (p/s)	30
KADDO STRINGS			
80	Grapevine GRP 146	Nothing But Love/Crying Over You	15
(see also Duke Browner, Tartans)			
KADENZA			
82	PRT 12P 247	Let's Stay Together (Night Club Mix)/Let's Stay Together (Vocal 2)/(Instrumental Version) (12")	30
82	PRT 7P 247	Let's Stay Together (Night Club Mix)/Let's Stay Together (Vocal)	6
82	PRT 12P 261	Let's Do It/(Instrumental) (12")	40
82	PRT 12P 261	Let's Do It/(Instrumental)	20
KADETTES			
82	Blank GET 1	Fireball XL5/Mission Impossible	8
KAINE & ABEL			
66	Philips BF 1472	Then You Must Know My Love/Crying In The Rain	8
KAISER CHIEFS			
04	B-Unique BUN088-7	I Predict A Riot/Take My Temperature (150 signed 7" with p/s)	15
05	KAISERCRIBS001	KAISER CHIEFS: Another Number/THE CRIBS: Modern Way (Double 'A' Side sold at gigs during 2005 tour dates. 1000 copies)	10
05	No Label	You Can Have It All (1-sided Xmas 2005 single sent out to first 2000 website subscribers. Christmas card fold-out sleeve. B side with 'I predict Some Quiet' label	6
07	No Label	The Angry Mob/The Angry Mob (Paul Emmanuel Off The Streets Mix) (mail-order only, with poster, 1,000 only)	8

KAISERS

			MINT VALUE £
07	B-Unique BUN119-7	Ruby/Admire You (red vinyl, p/s)	6
05	B-Unique BUN093LP	EMPLOYMENT (LP)	40
07	B-Unique BUN122LP	YOURS TRULY, ANGRY MOB (2-LP)	30
08	B-Unique BUN144LP	OFF WITH THEIR HEADS (2-LP)	25
11	B-Unique GUM 003	THE FUTURE IS MEDIEVAL (2-LP, numbered)	80

KAISERS
94	No Hit Records NO HIT 14	IN STEP WITH THE KAISERS (LP)	15
93	No Hit NO HIT 012	SQUAREHEAD STOMP! (LP)	18

KAJANUS/PICKETT
72	Signport SGA 5001	HI HO SILVER (LP, sleeve with cut flap)	20

KAKKO
90	CBS 656023	What Kind Of Fool (mixes)/I Pledge You My Heart (12", p/s)	12
90	CBS 655 710 6	We Should Be Dancing (mixes) (12", p/s)	12
90	CBS 655 710 8	We Should Be Dancing (mixes) (12", p/s)	18

KALA
73	Bradleys BRADL 1002	KALA (LP)	15

(see also Quintessence)

KALANI BOB AND REMEGEL
95	Groove Yard GYARD 005	THE CHEESE AND PICKLE EP (12")	50
96	Groove Yard GYARD 008	CHEESE AND PICKLE EP 2 (12")	10

ALAN KALANI
59	Vogue V 9147	A Touch Of Pink/SURFERS: Mambo Jambo	20
59	Vogue V 9147	A Touch Of Pink/SURFERS: Mambo Jambo (78)	20

KALASANDRO!
60	Warner Bros WB 13	Chi Chi/Forbidden City	12

KALEIDOSCOPE (U.K.)
67	Fontana TF 863	Flight From Ashiya/Holidaymaker (in p/s)	100
67	Fontana TF 863	Flight From Ashiya/Holidaymaker	60
68	Fontana TF 895	A Dream For Julie/Please Excuse My Face	40
68	Fontana TF 964	Jenny Artichoke/Just How Much Are You	50
69	Fontana TF 1002	Do It Again For Jeffrey/Poem	50
69	Fontana TF 1048	Balloon/If You So Wish	110
69	Decca (No Cat. No.)	Black Fjord (1-sided)	130
67	Fontana (S)TL 5448	TANGERINE DREAM (LP, unlaminated sleeve, flipbacks, black/silver label)	1000
69	Fontana STL 5491	FAINTLY BLOWING (LP, laminated gatefold sleeve; without watermark on beginning of each side)	1000
69	Fontana STL 5491	FAINTLY BLOWING (LP, laminated gatefold sleeve; with watermark on beginning of each side)	400
87	5 Hours Back TOCK 005	TANGERINE DREAM (LP, stereo reissue)	20
87	5 Hours Back TOCK 006	FAINTLY BLOWING (LP, reissue, single sleeve)	20
03	Circle CPWL 104	PLEASE LISTEN TO THE PICTURES (2-LP, BBC sessions, split LP with Fairfield Parlour)	20

(see also Fairfield Parlour, I Luv Wight)

KALEIDOSCOPE (U.S.)
70	CBS 64005	BERNICE (LP, as American Kaleidoscope)	30

JOHNNY KALENDAR BAND
79	CJMO PX 109`	FOOLING YOURSELF EP (p/s)	50

(see also Def Leppard)

KALIN TWINS
59	Brunswick 05775	Oh! My Goodness/It's Only The Beginning	7
59	Brunswick 05797	Cool/When I Look In The Mirror	7
59	Brunswick 05803	Moody/Sweet Sugar Lips	8
59	Brunswick 05814	The Meaning Of The Blues/Why Don't You Believe Me?	8
60	Brunswick 05826	Chicken Thief/Loneliness	8
60	Brunswick 05844	Zing! Went The Strings Of My Heart/No Money Can Buy	10
61	Brunswick 05848	Momma Poppa/You Mean The World To Me	12
61	Brunswick 05862	One More Time/I'm Forever Blowing Bubbles	15
58	Brunswick OE 9383	WHEN (EP)	20
59	Brunswick OE 9449	THE KALIN TWINS (EP)	25

KITTY KALLEN
54	Brunswick 05261	Are You Looking For A Sweetheart/In The Chapel In The Moonlight	15
54	Brunswick 05287	Little Things Mean A Lot/I Don't Think You Love Me Anymore	20
54	Brunswick 05357	Heartless Heart/The Spirit Of Christmas	15
54	Brunswick 05359	I Want You All To Myself/(Don't Let The) Kiddy Geddin'	12

DICK KALLMAN
56	Brunswick 05608	Two Different Worlds/Love Me As Though There Were No Tomorrow	6
60	Vogue V 9162	Born To Be Loved/Just Squeeze Me But Don't Teeze Me	10
63	HMV CLP 1642	SPEAK SOFTLY (LP)	20

BOBBY KALPHAT
68	Nu Beat NB 007	Rhythm And Soul/BUNNY & RUDDY: True Romance	80
73	Tropical AL 049	Natty Rock/Natty Dub	15
74	Faith FA 008	Zion Hill/Dub Hill	20

BOBBY KALPHAT & PHIL PRATT
76	Terminal TERM 001	ZION HILL DUB (LP)	350
79	Phil Pratt SSLP 1007	THE WAR IS ON DUB STYLE (LP)	75

CAROL KALPHAT
78	Hit Run HIT DD 1	African Land (featuring Clint Eastwood)/DOCTOR PABLO AND THE CRYTUFF ALLSTARS -African Melody (12", title sleeve)	70

YUSSEF KAMAAL
16	Brownswood BWOOD0157LP	BLACK FOCUS (LP, white vinyl)	70
16	Brownswood	BLACK FOCUS (LP)	15

KAMARAS
MINT VALUE £

BWOOD0157LP

KAMARAS
69   CBS 4199   Let This Moment Pass Away/I Just Can't Break Away From This Lovin' 25

KAMIKAZE
05   No Cat or label number   Ghetto Kyote (Instrumental)/(Remix)/(Vocal Mix) (12" white labels) 30

KAMIKAZE PILOTS
83   Lowther 002   Dark Night Of The Soul/Red Indian Song 10
85   Lowther HCW 003   Sharon Signs To Cherry Red/It Goes Boing (p/s) 8

INI KAMOZE
84   Island IMA 7   INI KAMOZE (LP) 20

KANDAHAR
74   Sounds Superb 4M048-97401   LONG LIVE THE SLICED HAM (LP) 30

AMORY KANE
68   MCA MU 1036   Reflections Of Your Face/Four Ravens 15
70   CBS 5111   Him Or Me/Forever Waiting 10
70   UNI UNS 518   You Were On My Mind/All The Best Songs And Marches 6
68   MCA MUP(S) 348   MEMORIES OF TIME UNWOUND (LP, with insert) 50
70   CBS 63849   JUST TO BE THERE (LP) 40
(see also Ron Geesin)

DOUG KANE
80   Video VIDEO 2   ONE BETWEEN THE EYES (LP) 35
(see also Eyes (2))

EDEN KANE
60   Pye 7N 15284   Hot Chocolate Crazy/You Make Love So Well 35
62   Decca F 11460   I Don't Know Why/Music For Strings 6
62   Decca F 11504   House To Let/I Told You 7
63   Decca F 11568   Sounds Funny To Me/Someone Wants To Know 7
63   Fontana TF 398   Tomorrow Night/I Won't Believe You (some in p/s) 7
63   Fontana TF 413   Like I Love You/Come Back (with Earl Preston's TTs) 8
64   Fontana TF 462   Rain Rain Go Away/Guess Who It Is 6
64   Fontana TF 508   Hangin' Around/Gonna Do Something About You 7
65   Fontana TF 582   If You Want This Love/Have I Done Something Wrong 10
62   Decca DFE 6696   WELL I ASK YOU! (EP) 12
62   Decca DFE 8503   HITS (EP) 10
64   Decca DFE 8567   SIX GREAT NEW SWINGERS (EP) 15
64   Fontana TFE 17424   IT'S EDEN (EP) 15
62   Ace Of Clubs ACL 1133   EDEN KANE (LP) 25
64   Fontana TL 5211   IT'S EDEN (LP) 20
(see also Brothers Kane, Sarstedt Brothers)

HELEN KANE
55   MGM EP 549   THE BOOP BOOP A DOOP GIRL (EP) 15

JEFF KANE
69   Tangerine DP 0006   Pretty Young Lady/On My Darkest Day 35

JON KANE
69   Warner Bros WB 8003   Soulful Lady/In Ancient Times (Jerusalem) 10

LEE KANE
55   Capitol CL 14297   Ev'ry Day/How Would You Have Me? 8
55   Capitol CL 14328   Around And Around/Merci Beaucoup 8

MARIA KANE
65   Decca F 12184   Love Is Slipping Away/Love Is Strange 10

MILES KANE
10   Columbia 8869784487   Inhaler/Rainbow Woman (p/s, numbered, with poster) 12
11   Columbia 8597940117   Inhaler/Hey Bulldog (live) (p/s, blue vinyl, different cover) 6
11   Columbia 88697843567/ 88697843607 Come Closer/Come Closer (Steve Mason Remix)//Come Closer/Before Midnight (live) (2 x 7", edition of 500 with signed lyric sheet) 8
11   Columbia 88697888187   A Girl Like You/Our Man Flint (p/s, numbered) 6
12   Columbia 88691976881   First Of My Kind/Night Runner/Looking Out Of My Window/Colour Of The Trap (10") 12
11   Columbia 886978276414   COLOUR OF THE TRAP (LP, gatefold) 50
(see also Arctic Monkeys, Rascals (3))

STEPHANIE KANE
64   Oriole CB1908   It's Love/Think Of Me 25

KAN KAN
80   Kabaret Music TRAIN 1   Film Noir/The Watchmaker 20

KANO
03   Jahmektheworld JB 005   Vice Versa (Boys Love Girls)/JAMMER: Return To The Future (12" white label) 10
(Demon Of (East Co))

KANSAS
76   Epic SEPC 4932   Carry On Wayward Son/Questions Of My Childhood 6

KANSAS HOOK
70   UNI UNI 5515   Echo Park/Manhattan Woman 10
71   Decca F13117   Nervous Shaking/Mr. Universe 40

KANTATA
84   Oval OVLP 508   ASIKO (LP) 15
86   Asona ASR 3010   IT'S HIGH TIME NOW (LP) 20

PAUL KANTNER
71   RCA Victor SF 8163   BLOWS AGAINST THE EMPIRE (LP, gatefold sleeve with booklet, as Paul Kantner & Jefferson Starship) 20
71   Grunt FTR 1002   SUNFIGHTER (LP, gatefold sleeve with booklet & inner sleeve; as Paul Kantner, Grace Slick & Jefferson Starship) 15
(see also Jefferson Airplane/Starship)

Pandit KANWAR SAIN TRIKHA

MINT VALUE £

PANDIT KANWAR SAIN TRIKHA
71 Mushroom 100 MR 7 — THREE SITAR PIECES (LP) 45

KAPLAN
68 Philips BF 1636 — Do You Believe In Magic/I Like 18
68 Philips BF 1699 — I Love It/Trousers Down 20

KAPT. KOPTER & FABULOUS TWIRLY BIRDS
73 Epic EPC 65381 — KAPT. KOPTER & THE FABULOUS TWIRLY BIRDS (LP) 20
(see also Spirit)

JASMINE KARA
12 Acid Jazz AJX281S — Ain't No More Room/Ordinary Joe 20

LAKIS KARALIS
71 KAR 1 — SUPERMARKET 14 (LP, name, title track listing and liner notes written in Greek) 40

KAREEM
97 Exploding Plastic EXP8 — Never Give Up On Love/Restless Soul (Peaktime Radio Mix)/Hipster Mix 30

KENNY KAREN
61 Philips PB 1213 — Oh Susie Forgive Me/The Light In Your Window 15

KARIBS
70s Karibs KA1 — Aching Heart/Sugar Lips 8

KARINA
71 United Artists UP 35205 — Tomorrow I'm Coming Your Way/Something 15

BILLY KARLOFF (& EXTREMES)
78 Wanted CULT-45-001 — Crazy Paving/Back Street Billy (p/s) 10
(see also Tom Robinson Band, Stiff Little Fingers)

BORIS KARLOFF
60 Caedmon CAL 102/1 — HANS CHRISTIAN ANDERSEN (LP) 15
67 Brunswick LAT 8678 — AN EVENING WITH BORIS KARLOFF AND FRIENDS (LP) 30

KARMA SUTRA
87 Paradoxical PARODY 1 — DAYDREAMS OF A PRODUCTION LINE WORKER (LP, with booklet) 40

STEVE KARMEN BIG BAND
75 United Artists UP 35770 — Breakaway/Breakaway (Vocal Version) (featuring Jimmy Radcliffe) 10
(see also Jimmy Radcliffe)

KAROO
65 Oak RGJ 193 — Mamma's Out Of Town/Lonely Weekend 200

KARPET KETCHUP
85 Newspaper KK1 — Penny Drops/Deep Inside 15

KARRIER
84 Unit TRANS 101 — I'm Back/Dreaming (no p/s) 30
86 Status JEMS 101 — Poor Little Rich Girl/Endless Shadow 30
85 Unit TRALP 2001 — WAY BEYOND THE NIGHT (LP) 15

KASABIAN
03 BMG Paradise 02 — Processed Beats (10" 45 rpm screen print sleeve with elastic bands) 25
04 BMG Paradise 04 — Reason Is Treason (10" p/s 1,000 only) 18
04 BMG Paradise 06 — Club Foot (Jagz Kooner Mix) (12" with man-shaped hole sleeve) 20
04 BMG Paradise 09 — Club Foot/(Jagz Kooner Vocal Mix)/(Paradise Mix) (with poster p/s) 8
04 BMG Paradise 15 — L.S.F (Lost Souls Forever)/Club Foot (Live @ Cabinet War Rooms)/(Jagz Kooner Mix (Full Version) (10" poster p/s) 12
07 No label — Fast Fuse/Thick As Thieves (10" 200 only die-cut sleeve, stamped labels given away at Somerset House gig 2007) 35
11 Sony BMG 88697523092 — Days Are Forgotten/Pistols At Dawn (10") 12
04 BMG Paradise 18 — KASABIAN (LP, 2 x 10", embossed gatefold sleeve) 35
06 Paradise PARADISE 38 — EMPIRE (LP, 2x10") 18
09 Paradise PARADISE 59 — WEST RYDER PAUPER LUNATIC ASYLUM (LP, 2x10") 25
11 Paradise PARADISE 72 — VELOCIRAPTOR! (2-LP) 25

KIMIKO KASAI
18 Be With BEWITH028LP — BUTTERFLY (LP, reissue, with Herbie Hancock) 20
(see also Herbie Hancock)

MURRAY KASH
68 RCA 1767 — Sleeping Beauty/Everything's OK 6

AL KASHA
60 Coral Q72429 — Where Thete's A Will There's A Way/My Arms, My Lips, My Heart 6

KASHIF
83 Arista 205 347 — KASHIF (LP) 20

KASHMERE
02 Receptor RR 001 — RAW STYLES (EP) 12
04 Receptor RR 002 — RAW STYLES VOL 2 (EP) 12
06 Receptor RR 004 — Playing With Fire (12") 10
06 Receptor RR 005 — 20 MINUTES OF CHAOS (12", p/s) 20
04 Low Life LOW 35 LP — BACKHAND SLAP TALK/TECHNICAL ILLNESS (LP, with VERB T) 30
10 Boot BLP 003 — GALAKTUS: POWER COSMIC (LP, numbered) 30

EDWARD KA-SPEL
84 In Phaze HAZ 6 — DANCE CHINA DOLL (EP 12") 20
84 In Phaze PHA 6 — EYES CHINA DOLL (LP) 25

KASUALS
81 KAS 101 — Mr. O/A Girl I Know 8

KATATONIA
96 Misanthropy AMAZON 010 — Scarlet Heavens/PRIMORDIAL: To Enter Pagan MCMXCVI (10", p/s) 20
06 Peaceville VILELP 128 — THE GREAT COLD DISTANCE (LP, gatefold, red vinyl) 40

KATCH-22 (1)
66 Fontana TF 768 — Major Catastrophe/Hold Me 90
67 Fontana TF 874 — Makin' Up My Mind/While We're Friends 25
68 Fontana TF 930 — The World's Gettin' Smaller/Don't Bother 20

KATCH 22 (2)

MINT VALUE £

68	Fontana TF 984	Pumpkin Mini/100,000 Years	25
69	Fontana TF 1005	Out Of My Life/Baby Love	15
69	CBS 4644	It's The Sunshine/Mrs. Jones	20
68	Saga EROS 8047	IT'S SOFT ROCK & ALLSORTS (LP, with insert, Saga inner sleeve)	20

KATCH 22 (2)
| 84 | Mynah BBM 841 | Workshop Life/Visions Of Freedom | 12 |

KATCHIES
| 79 | Chart PSS 162 | Shambles/To Be A Musician | 20 |

KATE
68	CBS 3631	Strange Girl/I Don't Make A Sound	100
68	CBS 3815	Hold Me Now/Empty World	20
69	CBS 4123	Shout It/Sweet Little Thing	70

(see also Viv Prince, Pretty Things)

KATINA
| 72 | Cactus CT 4 | Don't Stick Stickers On My Paper Knickers/Version | 6 |
| 72 | Cactus CT 3 | Don't Stroke My Pussy/Don't Stroke My Pussy (Version) | 8 |

KATZ (1)
| 60s | Tetlow TET 118 | LIVE AT THE RUM RUNNER (EP) | 75 |

KATZ (2)
| 79 | SRTS/79/CUS/533 | Talkin' About You/I'm So Nasty (no p/s, 200 only) | 250 |

ARTHUR KAY'S ORIGINALS
| 80 | Red Admiral NYMPH 1 | Ska-Wars/Warska (p/s) | 8 |
| 80 | Red Admiral NYMPH 2 | Sooty Is A Rudie/Play My Record (p/s) | 10 |

BARBARA KAY
| 65 | Pye 7N 15774 | That's What Angels Are For/What's The Good Of Loving | 6 |
| 65 | Pye 7N 15914 | Yes I'm Ready/Someone Has To Cry | 20 |

JANET KAY
77	D Roy DR 007	I Do Love You/Lovely Dub	6
77	Stonehouse SH 003	Loving You/Version	8
82	Solid Groove SGL 103	CAPRICORN WOMAN (LP)	20

JANET K(AY)
| 78 | Bushays BFM 108 | Silhouette (with Rico)/PRINCE JAZEBO & RICO: Silhouette Gone Clear (12") | 20 |

JOHN KAY
| 72 | Probe SPB 1054 | FORGOTTEN SONGS AND UNSUNG HEROES (LP) | 15 |

(see also Steppenwolf)

SHIRLEY KAY
| 68 | Trojan TR 015 | Make Me Yours/We Have Happiness | 75 |

(see also Phyllis Dillon)

KAYAK
| 74 | Harvest SHSP 4033 | SEE SEE THE SUN (LP) | 20 |
| 74 | Harvest SHSP 4036 | KAYAK (LP) | 20 |

DAVE KAYE (& DYKONS)
64	Decca F 11866	A Fool Such As I/It's Nice Isn't It (as Davy Kaye)	35
65	Decca F 12073	In My Way/All The Stars In Heaven (as Dave Kaye)	25
69	Major Minor MM 641	Yesterday When I Was Young/Say You Love Me (as Dave Kaye & Dykons)	12

KATHIE KAY(E)
55	HMV 7M 335	Suddenly There's A Valley/Teddy Bear	8
56	HMV 7M 363	Jimmy Unknown/Dreams Can Tell A Lie	10
56	HMV POP 265	A House With Love In It/To Be Sure	7
57	HMV POP 352	We Will Make Love/Wind In The Willow	8

LINDA KAYE
| 66 | Columbia DB 7915 | I Can't Stop Thinking About You/When We Meet Again | 25 |

TONY KAYE & HEARTBEATS
| 67 | Pye International 7N 25412 | Hey, Hey Little Orphan Annie/Dream World | 8 |

KAYES
| 67 | Major Minor MM 515 | It's No Secret/Remember Me | 8 |

(see also Kaye Sisters)

KAYE SISTERS
58	Philips PB 806	Are You Ready, Freddy?/The Pansy	15
58	Philips PB 832	Stroll Me/Torero	10
59	Philips PB 892	Jerri-Lee (I Love Him So)/Deeply Devoted	10

(see also Three Kayes/Three Kaye Sisters, Kayes, Frankie Vaughan)

LAINIE KAZAN
| 69 | MGM MGM 1476 | Window Of My Mind/It's You | 30 |

KCF & SKELLA TON
| 91 | Kold Sweat KS112 | Taken To Heart/In Session (12") | 10 |

ERNIE K-DOE
61	London HLU 9330	Mother-In-Law/Wanted, $10,000.00 Reward	15
61	London HLU 9390	Te-Ta-Te-Ta-Ta/Real Man	20
65	Vocalion VP 9233	My Mother In Law (Is In My Hair Again)/Looking Into The Future	20
68	Action ACT 4502	Dancing Man/Later For Tomorrow	25
68	Action ACT 4512	Gotta Pack My Bags/How Sweet You Are	25

KEANE
00	Zoomorphic (No cat. no)	Call Me What You Like/Rubbernecking/Closer Now (CD, 500 only)	80
01	Zoomorphic ZOO12101	Wolf At The Door/Call Me What You Like/She Has No Time (CD, 500 only)	80
04	Island CID849	Somewhere Only We Know/Snowed Under (numbered, p/s)	6
05	Island KEANE2	The Sun Ain't Gonna Shine Anymore/Your Eyes Open (Fan club issue 1000 only p/s)	40
06	Island (no cat no)	Nothing In My Way (512MB memory stick, 1500 only, numbered in title sleeve)	20
06	Island 1723054	A Bad Dream (512MN memory stick, numbered in title sleeve)	20
06	Island KEANEBX1	Atlantic (single sided 7" in box)	15

Shake KEANE

MINT VALUE £

07	Island 1723058	A Bad Dream/She Sells Sanctuary (with fold-out sleeve, numbered)	12
08	Universal PSBOX1	Spiralling (1-sided 7" in box, 2,000 only, numbered)	20
04	Island ILPS 8145	HOPES AND FEARS (LP, 1000 only)	150
04	Island (no cat no)	HOPES AND FEARS (CD promo, 200 only)	30
04	Island (no cat no)	HOPES AND FEARS (DVD sampler, jewel case, promo)	30
05	Island	SINGLES BOX SET (1000 only, 5x7" from HOPES AND FEARS LP)	120
06	Island (no cat no)	THE VIDEOS (Fan club issue only)	50
06	Island ILPS 8167	UNDER THE IRON SEA (2-LP)	70
08	Island 1785966	PERFECT SYMMETRY (LP)	30

SHAKE KEANE

55	HMV 7MC 38	Akinla/Fire, Fire (export issue)	15
64	Airborne NBP 005	Calle Washington/Bossanova Trieste	10
62	Columbia SEG 8239	BOSSA NEGRA (EP)	40
62	Columbia SEG 8140	IN MY CONDITION (EP)	40
64	Airborne NBP 002	A CASE OF JAZZ (EP, as Shake Keane and Michael Garrick Quartette, 99 copies only)	350
65	Decca SKL 4720	SHAKE KEANE WITH THE KEATING SOUND (LP)	20
66	Ace Of Clubs ACL 1219	THAT'S THE NOISE (LP)	25
69	Phase 4 Stereo PFS 4154	DIG IT (LP, with Ivor Raymonde Orchestra)	40
70	Pama SECO 30	RISING STARS AT EVENING TIME (LP with Gordon Langford and Hastings Girl Choir)	30
91	KLJ LP 008	REAL KEEN REGGAE INTO JAZZ (LP)	15
11	Trunk JBH 041 LP	RISING STARS (LP, with Michael Garrick, 750 only)	20

(see also Marie Bryant, Michael Garrick)

JOHNNY KEATING ORCHESTRA

63	Picadilly 7N 35113	The Preacher/Whoop Up (with the Z men)	10
57	Oriole MG 20011	BRITISH JAZZ (LP)	60
58	London LTZ-15122	SWINGIN' SCOTS (LP)	25
64	Ace Of Clubs ACL 1160	SIXTEEN HITS FOR YOUR DANCE PARTY (LP)	20
64	Decca PFS 4038	SWING REVISITED (LP)	25
64	Decca PFS 4078	STRAIGHT AHEAD (LP)	30
72	Studio Two TWO 393	SPACE EXPERIENCE (LP)	15
72	Studio Two Q4 TWO 393	SPACE EXPERIENCE (LP, quadrophonic)	25
75	Studio Two TWOX 1044	SPACE EXPERIENCE 2 (LP)	15

PAUL KEELEY

08	Anjunadeep ANJDEE-023	A Sort Of Homecoming (Michael Cassette Mix)/(Radio Edit)/(Jaytech Saturday Mix) (12", p/s)	50

YVONNE KEELEY

74	EMI 2206	Tumbling Down/Loretta's Theme	7

KEEN

90	Scaredy Cat PUR 003	FELINE GROOVY EP (12")	30

JEFF KEEN

12	Trunk JBH 047 LP	NOISE ART (LP, 500 only silkscreened sleeves. 100 black sleeve/clear vinyl, 100 red sleeve/red and clear vinyl, 100 yellow sleeve/clear/red/yellow vinyl, 100 blue sleeve/clear/red/yellow and 100 blue vinyl and silver sleeve with clear/red/yellow/blue and silver vinyl)	40

JOHN KEEN

72	Track 2094 103	Old Fashioned Girl/That's The Way It Is	8
73	Track 2094 108	Let Us In/Keep On The Grass	8

(see also Speedy Keen, Thunderclap Newman)

SPEEDY KEEN

71	Track 2406 105	PREVIOUS CONVICTIONS (LP)	15

(see also John Keen, Thunderclap Newman)

MARION KEENE

56	HMV 7M 395	Fortune Teller/A Dangerous Age	7
57	HMV POP 375	In The Middle Of An Island/It's Not For Me To Say	6

NELSON KEENE

60	HMV POP 771	Image Of A Girl/Ocean Of Love	15
60	HMV POP 814	Keep Loving Me/Teenage Troubles	15
61	HMV POP 916	Miracles Are Happening To Me/Poor Little Rich Boy	15

(see also Guv'ners)

REX KEENE

56	Columbia DB 3831	Rebel In Town/Happy Texas Ranger	10

KEETH

77	SMR 018	SPEEDWAY EP	10

KEETY ROOTS

94	Black Legacy BL 003	African Blood/TENASTELIN: Spirit of	80

ACE KEFFORD STAND

69	Atlantic 584 260	For Your Love/Gravy Booby Jam (small centre hole)	50
69	Atlantic 584 260	For Your Love/Gravy Booby Jam (large centre hole)	40

(see also Move, Cozy Powell, Young Blood, Big Bertha, Bedlam, Carl Wayne)

KEITH

66	Mercury MF 940	Ain't Gonna Lie/It Started All Over Again	8
67	Mercury MF 955	98.6/The Teeny Bopper Song	10
67	Mercury MF 968	Tell Me To My Face/I Can't Go Wrong	10
67	Mercury MF 989	Daylight Savin' Time/Happy Walking Around	15
67	Mercury MF 1002	Sugar Man/Easy As Pie (in p/s)	12
67	Mercury MF 1002	Sugar Man/Easy As Pie	6
67	Mercury MCL 20103	98.6/AIN'T GONNA LIE (LP)	30

BRYAN KEITH

63	London HLU 9707	Sad Sad Song/Mean Woman	20

RON KEITH

76	A&M AMS 7217	Party Music/Gotta Go By What You Tell Me	90

KEITH (Stewart) & ENID (Cumberland)

MINT VALUE £

KEITH (STEWART) & ENID (CUMBERLAND)
60	Blue Beat BB 6	Worried Over You/Everything Will Be Alright	10
60	Blue Beat BB 11	Send Me/TRENTON SPENCE GROUP: People Will Say We're In Love	10
61	Starlite ST45 047	Never Leave My Throne/Only A Pity (as Keith & Enid with Caribs)	12
61	Starlite ST45 067	You're Gonna Break My Heart/What Have I Done	12
62	Blue Beat BB 125	When It's Spring/True Love (with Sonny Bradshaw Orchestra)	10
63	Dice CC 14	Sacred Vow/My Dreams	8
63	Dice CC 20	Just A Closer Walk/Don't Yield To Temptation	8
64	Black Swan WI 429	Lost My Love/I Cried	10
63	Island ILP 901	KEITH & ENID SING (LP)	50
70	Trojan TTL 37	KEITH & ENID SING (LP, reissue)	20

KEITH (POPPIN) & IMPACT ALL STARS
| 71 | Randy's RAN 515 | Down By The Riverside/IMPACT ALL STARS: Version Two | 6 |

KEITH (LYN) & KEN (LAZARUS)
| 65 | London HA-R/SH-R 8229 | YOU'LL LOVE JAMAICA (LP) | 40 |

KEITH (ROWE) & TEX (DIXON)
67	Island WI 3085	Tonight/LYN TAIT & JETS: You Have Caught Me	175
68	Island WI 3091	Stop That Train/BOBBY ELLIS: Feeling Peckish (with Desmond Miles Seven)	175
68	Island WI 3137	Hypnotizing Eyes/Lonely Man	150
70	Explosion EX 2008	Tighten Up Your Gird/Look To The Sky	50
03	Trojan TJGSE 009	Stop That Train/Leaving On That Train (reissue, die-cut Trojan sleeve)	20

KEITHY
| 77 | Xamayca XAD 002 | Struggling In A Babylon (with Imperial Hudson)/XAMAYCA BAND: Togetherness | 25 |

ROGER KELLAWAY
| 67 | Liberty LBS 583061E | SPIRIT FEEL (LP) | 25 |

JERRY KELLER
59	London HLR 8890	Here Comes Summer/Time Has A Way (triangular centre)	10
59	London HLR 8980	If I Had A Girl/Lovable	6
60	London HLR 9106	Now, Now, Now/Lonesome Lullaby	7
60	London HA-R 2261	HERE COMES JERRY KELLER (LP, mono)	35
60	London SAH-R 6083	HERE COMES JERRY KELLER (LP, stereo)	40

PAT KELL(E)Y
68	Giant GN 37	Little Boy Blue/You Are Not Mine (as Pat Kelley & Uniques)	80
68	Island WI 3121	Somebodies Baby (as Pat Kelly)/BEVERLY SIMMONS: Please Don't Leave Me	45
68	Island WI 3124	Twelfth Of Never/VAL BENNETT: Caledonia	50
69	Gas GAS 110	The Workman Song/Never Give Up (as Pat Kelly)	15
69	Gas GAS 115	How Long/Try To Remember (as Pat Kelly)	20
69	Gas GAS 124	Festival Time (Parts 1 & 2) (as Pat Kelley)	20
69	Gas GAS 125	If It Don't Work Out/I Am Coming Home (as Pat Kelly)	15
70	Gas GAS 144	Tammy/I Am Not Your Guy (as Pat Kelley)	15
70	Gas GAS 145	Striving For The Right/When A Boy Fall In Love (as Pat Kelley)	15
70	Gas GAS 157	I Just Don't Know What To Do With Myself/What's He Got That I Ain't Got (B-side actually titled 'Lorna') (as Pat Kelley)	8
70	Jackpot JP 734	I Just Don't Know What To Do With Myself/Lorna (as Pat Kelley)	8
71	Camel CA 65	Talk About Love (as Pat Kelley)/PHIL PRATT ALL STARS: Version	15
71	Gas GAS 171	Love/With All Your Heart (as Pat Kelley)	10
71	Punch PH 88	Soulful Love (as Pat Kelly)/HUGH ROY & PARAGONS: One For All	20
72	Pama Supreme PS 353	I'm Gonna Give Her All The Love I've Got (as Pat Kelley)/ MAYTONES: As Long As You Love Me	8
73	Pama Supreme PS 379	Twelfth Of Never (as Pat Kelley)/JERRY LEWIS: 5000 Watts	10
73	Pama Supreme PS 384	I Wish It Could Rain (as Pat Kelley)/PAT KELLY SINGERS: Hallelujah	10
75	Black Wax WAX 1	Sunshine/Sunshine Version	6
77	Rainbow Stepper RK 231	Carefree Girl/Version	8
69	Pama PMLP 12	PAT KELLEY SINGS (LP)	100
71	Pama PMP 2013	COOL BREEZING (LP)	60
77	Burning Rockers BR 007LP	SO PROUD (LP)	25
78	Burning Sounds BS1001	LONELY MAN (LP)	30
78	KG Imperial KGLP 001	TALK ABOUT LOVE (LP)	30

PETER KELLEY
| 69 | London HAK 8402 | PATH OF THE WAVE (LP) | 40 |
| 71 | Polydor 2310 119 | DEALIN' BLUES (LP) | 25 |

MURRAY KELLUM
| 64 | London HLU 9830 | Long Tall Texan/GLEN SUTTON: I Gotta Leave This Town | 15 |

KELLY
| 66 | RCA RCA 1507 | Be My Man/Here Comes My Baby | 6 |
| 69 | Deram DM 277 | Mary Mary/Reverend Richard Baily | 30 |

CHARLIE KELLY
| 68 | Island WI 3155 | So Nice Like Rice/STRANGER & GLADDY: Over Again | 25 |

CHRIS KELLY
| 71 | CBS 7331 | Red Bird/Sweet Albuquerque | 7 |

DAVE KELLY
| 69 | Mercury 20151 SMCL | KEEPS IT IN THE FAMILY (LP, laminated sleeve, black/silver labels) | 200 |
| 71 | Mercury 6310 001 | DAVE KELLY (LP, with Jo-Ann Kelly & Brunning-Hall Sunflower Band) | 250 |

(see also John Dummer Blues Band, Brunning-Hall Sunflower Blues Band)

DAVID WILLIAM KELLY
| 83 | Ethereal ETH 1 | Heart Of Hearts/Chemistry Of MInd (no p/s) | 50 |

FRANK KELLY & HUNTERS
62	Fontana 267 242 TF	Send Me The Pillow That You Dream On/'Cept Me	10
63	Fontana 267 261 TF	I Saw Linda Yesterday/Good And True	15
63	Fontana 267 277 TF	What Do You Wanna Do/She Loves Me So	12

Gene KELLY

MINT VALUE £

64	Fontana TF 454	Some Other Time/Why Baby Why	12

GENE KELLY
53	MGM SP 1012	Singin' In The Rain/All I Do Is Dream Of You	8
53	MGM SP 1015	'S Wonderful (with Georges Guetary)/I Got Rhythm (with Children's Choir)	7

JO-ANN KELLY
64	GW EP 1	BLUES AND GOSPEL (EP, live at the Bridge House Club)	150
66	Harlequin HAL 1/HW 349	NEW SOUNDS IN FOLK (LP, with other artists)	80
69	CBS 63841	JO-ANN KELLY (LP, laminated front sleeve)	200
76	Red Rag RRR 006	DO IT (LP, with Peter Emery)	35

(see also Chilli Willi & Red Hot Peppers, Dave Kelly, Tramp)

JO-ANN KELLY & TONY McPHEE
72	Sunset SLS 50209	THE SAME THING ON THEIR MINDS (LP)	30

(see also Tony McPhee, Dave Kelly)

JONATHAN KELLY
69	Parlophone R 5805	Denver/Son John	6
70	Parlophone R 5830	Make A Stranger Your Friend/Daddy Don't Take Me Down Fishing No More	8
70	Parlophone R 5851	Don't You Believe It?/Billy (Eric Clapton on guitar)	40
70	Parlophone PCS 7114	JONATHAN KELLY (LP, black/silver labels with boxed logo)	100
72	RCA SF 8262	TWICE AROUND THE HOUSES (LP, laminated cover)	20
73	RCA SF 8353	WAIT TILL THEY CHANGE THE BACKDROP (LP, gatefold sleeve)	20

(see also John Ledingham, Humpy Bong, Boomerang)

KEITH KELLY
60	Parlophone R 4640	(Must You Always) Tease Me/Ooh-La-La	25
60	Parlophone R 4676	Listen Little Girl/Uh-Huh	30
60	Parlophone R 4713	With You/You'll Break My Heart	20
61	Parlophone R 4797	Cold White And Beautiful/When You First Fall In Love	20
65	CBS 201794	Laurie/Save Your Love For Me	10

PAUL KELLY
65	Atlantic AT 4053	Chills And Fever/Only Your Love	45
67	Philips BF 1591	Sweet Sweet Lovin'/Cryin' For My Baby	25
72	Atlantic K 10272	Chills And Fever/Only Your Love (reissue)	10

PETE KELLY'S SOULUTION
68	Decca F 12755	Midnight Confessions/If Your Love Don't Swing	30
68	Decca F 22829	Midnight Confessions/BERNIE & BUZZ BAND: The House That Jack Built (export issue)	20

(see also Bernie & Buzz Band, Rhythm & Blues Inc.)

PETER D KELLY
74	DJM DJS 333	Rock To The Juke Box/Brotherhood Within (promo p/s)	10
74	DJM DJS 333	Rock To The Juke Box/Brotherhood Within	5

R. KELLY
93	Jive HIP 144	12 PLAY (2-LP)	20
95	Jive HIP 166	R KELLY (2-LP)	25
95	Jive 0517931	R. (3-LP)	30

SALLY KELLY
59	Decca F 11175	Little Cutie/Come Back To Me	12
60	Decca F 11238	He'll Have To Stay/Honey That's Alright	7

SEYMOUR KELLY
68	Columbia DB8445	Indian Scene/Worlds Apart	15

TABBY CAT KELLY
78	Arawak ARK DD005	Don't Call Us Immigrants/Version	25

WYNTON KELLY TRIO
60	Top Rank 35-107	KELLY GREAT (LP)	40
65	Verve VLP 9103	UNDILUTED (LP)	20

KELLY BROTHERS
67	Sue WI 4034	Falling In Love Again/Crying Days Are Over	150
68	President PT 143	You Put Your Touch On Me/Hanging In There	25
70	Blue Horizon 57-3177	That's What You Mean To Me/Comin' On In	30
68	President PTL 1019	SWEET SOUL (LP)	100

KELV
81	Axis Industries AXLP1	ATTACKING VESSELS (LP, 250 only, insert)	18

WAYNE KEMP
66	Atlantic 584 006	Watch That First Step/Little Home Wrecker	12

KEMPION
77	Broadside BRO 123	KEMPION (LP)	18
77	Sweet Folk & C. SFA 044	CAM YE O'ER FRAE FRANCE (LP)	15

BOB KEN
80	Square S2SP	Keep Me Warm This Winter/More Than Life	6

KEN & NEW ESTABLISHMENT
73	Fab FAB 264	Soul Mood/Golden Locks	35

KEN & STEPPING TONY
78	Rama RMD 005	Sticks Man Affair/ROCKA & DAVE & GIRL WONDER: Skip-A Dip (12")	30

JOHNNY KENDALL & HERALDS
64	RCA RCA 1416	St. James Infirmary/Little Girl	10

KENDALL SISTERS
58	London HLM 8622	Won't You Be My Baby/Yea, Yea	30
58	London HLM 8622	Won't You Be My Baby/Yea, Yea (78)	20

ANDY KENDRICK
94	Fence Beater FBKA 001	Another Night In The Ghetto/Re-Incarnation	15
94	Fence Beater FBKA 002	Zion/Zion Dub	12
94	Fence Beater FBKLP 001	ANOTHER NIGHT IN THE GHETTO (LP)	20

Linda KENDRICK

MINT VALUE £

LINDA KENDRICK
66	Polydor 56076	It's The Little Things/When Your Love Is Warm	30
66	Polydor 56076	It's The Little Things/When Your Love Is Warm (DJ copy)	50
69	Philips BF 1750	I Will See You There/Inside My Heart	8
69	Philips BF 1816	Hold On/Fa La La La La La Le	8
71	Philips 6006-078	Generation (Light Up The Sky)/Come With The Beautiful People	25
70	Philips SBL 7921	LINDA KENDRICK (LP)	15

NAT KENDRICK & SWANS
60	Top Rank JAR 351	(Do The) Mashed Potatoes Parts 1 & 2	30
60	Top Rank JAR 387	Dish Rag Parts 1 & 2	20

(see also James Brown)

LORETTA KENDRICK
01	Hayley HR004	Neither One Of Us/My Feelings Keep Getting In The Way	12

EDDIE KENDRICKS
72	Tamla Motown TMG 845	If You Let Me/Just Memories (DJ Copy)	45
72	Tamla Motown TMG 845	If You Let Me/Just Memories	20
74	Tamla Motown TMG 916	Girl You Need A Change Of Mind Part 1/Part 2	10
83	Tamla Motown TMG 985	Keep On Truckin (Part 1)/Keep On Truckin (Part 2) (reissue)	10
71	T. Motown STML 11186	ALL BY MYSELF (LP)	15
72	T. Motown STML 11213	PEOPLE...HOLD ON (LP)	30
73	T. Motown STML 11245	EDDIE KENDRICKS (LP)	15

KENICKIE
95	Slampt U.O. SLAMPT 1	CATSUIT CITY (EP)	12
97	EMI ADISC 002	AT THE CLUB (LP)	30

CALUM KENNEDY
62	Ember EMB 5167	The Celtic Chorus/Danny Boy	25

CHERYL KENNEDY
68	Columbia DB 8347	Love Is Blue/I Could Be Happy With You	6

JOHN F. KENNEDY
64	Stateside SL 10064	THE PRESIDENTIAL YEARS 1960-1963 (LP)	15

LOU KENNEDY
55	Columbia SCM 5198	Stars Shine In Your Eyes/The Kentuckian Song	10
56	Columbia SCM 5216	Whisper/Sincerely Yours	10

MIKE KENNEDY
69	Major Minor MM 614	I'll Never Forget/I'll Never Get You	6
69	Major Minor MM 629	Johnny Rebel/Golden Memories	6
72	Youngblood YB 1035	Louisiana/Look Up In The Sky	20

CHRIS KENNER
61	London HLU 9410	I Like It Like That Parts 1 & 2	35
65	Sue WI 351	Land Of 1,000 Dances/That's My Girl	35
66	Atlantic 587 008	LAND OF 1000 DANCES (LP)	40

KENNY (EVERETT) & (DAVE) CASH
65	Decca F 12283	Knees/The B Side	6

KENNY & DENY
65	Decca F 12138	Try To Forget Me/Little Surfer Girl	70

(see also Jimmy Page, Tony Rivers & The Castaways, Harmony Grass, Capability Brown)

KENNY & WRANGLERS
64	Parlophone R 5224	Somebody Help Me/Who Do You Think I Am?	25
65	Parlophone R 5275	Doobie Doo/Moonshine	25

(see also Kenny Bernard & Wranglers)

JERRI BO KENO
75	Phil Spector Intl. 2010 001	Here It Comes (And Here I Go)/I Don't Know Why	20

KENT
99	RCA 7432164593-7	747/Unprofessional (p/s)	30

AL KENT
67	Track 604 016	You Got To Pay The Price/Where Do I Go From Here	50
71	Mojo 2092 015	You Got To Pay The Price/Where Do I Go From Here (unissued)	0

CINDY KENT
73	York FYK 418	I AM YOUR SERVANT (LP)	125

DAVE KENT
88	SRT/RANA SRT 8KS 1795 RANA 001	Out Of My Mind/I Will Be A Stranger	10

ENOCH KENT
62	Topic TOP 81	SINGS THE BUTCHER BOY AND OTHER BALLADS (EP)	10

KLARK KENT
78	Kryptone KK 1	Don't Care/Office Girls/Thrills (p/s, black vinyl)	8
78	A&M AMS 7376	Don't Care/Office Girls/Thrills (p/s or die-cut sleeve, black vinyl)	20

(see also Police)

MARY KENT
69	CBS 4510	Lost Generation/Gentle Moments	10

PAUL KENT
71	B&C CB 165	Do You/Helpless Harry	6
70	RCA SF 8083	P.C. KENT (LP)	60
71	B&C CAS 1044	PAUL KENT (LP)	50

RICHARD KENT STYLE
66	Columbia DB 7964	No Matter What You Do/Go, Go Children	200
66	Columbia DB 8051	You Can't Put Me Down/All Good Things	150
67	Columbia DB 8182	Marching Off To War/I'm Out	120
68	MCA MU 1032	Love Will Shake The World Awake/Crocodile Tears	40
69	Mercury MF 1090	A Little Bit O' Soul/Don't Tell Lies	40

SHIRLEY KENT
80	Tadpole TAD 001	My Dad/Marianne	6
66	Keele University 103	THE MASTER SINGERS AND SHIRLEY KENT SING FOR CHAREC 67 (EP)	35

(see also Ghost, Virginia Tree)

SONIA KENT
66	Parlophone R 5401	This Is My Wonderful Day/Somebody Must Care	7

(see also Diamond Twins)

KENT (BROWN) & DIMPLE (HINDS)
63	Island WI 046	Day Is Done/Linger A While	20

KENT (BROWN) & JEANNIE WITH CITY SLICKERS
62	Blue Beat BB 98	Daddy/Hello Love	20

(see also Kent Brown & Rainbows)

RIK KENTON
76	EMI EMI 2413	The Libertine/Messin' Round	6

(see also Woody Kern, Roxy Music)

KEN-TONES
56	Parlophone MSP 6229	Get With It/In Port Afrique	12
57	Parlophone R 4257	I Saw Esau/Yaller, Yaller Gold	8

(see also Benny Lee)

KENTUCKY BOYS
55	HMV 7M 312	Don't Fetch It/A Little Fella Like Me	12

KENTUCKY COLONELS
74	United Artists UAS 29514	THE KENTUCKY COLONELS (LP)	18

(see also Byrds)

BILL KENWRIGHT (& RUNAWAYS)
67	Columbia DB 8239	I Want To Go Back There Again/Walk Through Dreams (with Runaways)	10
68	MGM MGM 1430	Giving Up/Love's Black And White (solo)	6
69	MGM MGM 1478	Baby I Could Be So Good At Loving You/A Boy And A Girl	6
69	Fontana TF 1065	Sugar Man/Epitaph (When Times Were Good)	6

PATRICK KERR
65	Decca F 12069	Magic Potion/It's No Trouble To Love You	30

RICHARD KERR
66	Decca F12478	Concrete Jungle/You Got Nothing To Loose	12
66	Decca F12538	Hard Lovin'/Auntie's Insurance Policy	15
67	Deram DM 138	Happy Birthday Blues/Mother's Blue-Eyed Angel	20
73	Warner Bros K 46206	FROM NOW UNTIL THEN (LP, laminated cover, foldout lyric insert)	15

JOHN KERRUISH
70	A&M AMS 604	Time To Wander/Today, Tonight And Tomorrow Morning	70

CHRIS KERRY
65	Mercury MF 957	Seven Deadly Sins/The Place	15
66	Mercury MF 985	Watermelon Man/I've Got My Pride	25

DOUG KERSHAW
69	Warner Bros WB 7304	Feed It To The Fish/You Fight Your Fight (I'll Fight Mine)	8
70	Warner Bros WB 7413	Orange Blossom Special/Swamp Rat	6

(see also Rusty & Doug)

KEN KESEY
83	Psycho PSYCHO 4	THE ACID TEST (LP, 300 only)	30

BARNEY KESSEL
54	Vogue LDE 085	BARNEY KESSEL (10" LP)	20
55	Contemporary LDC 153	BARNEY KESSEL VOLUME 2 (10" LP)	20
77	Phil Spector Intl. 2307 011	SLOW BURN (LP)	15

(see also Rick Nelson)

LARRY KESSLER
96	Lissey's LISS 5S	Radar Eyes/Godz Mix (p/s)	10

KESTREL
75	Cube HIFLY 19	KESTREL (LP)	800

(see also Spiders From Mars)

KESTRELS
59	Pye 7N 15234	There Comes A Time/In The Chapel In The Moonlight	10
60	Pye 7N 15248	I Can't Say Goodbye/We Were Wrong	8
61	Decca F 11391	All These Things/That's It	8
62	Piccadilly 7N 35056	Wolverton Mountain/Little Sacka Sugar	8
62	Piccadilly 7N 35079	Don't Want To Cry/Love Me With All Your Heart	8
63	Piccadilly 7N 35104	Walk Right In/Moving Up The King's Highway	10
63	Piccadilly 7N 35126	There's A Place/Little Star	10
63	Piccadilly 7N 35144	Love Me With All Your Heart/Lazy River	6
60s	Donegal MAU 500	THE KESTRELS (EP)	20
63	Piccadilly NPL 38009	SMASH HITS (LP)	30

(see also Ivy League, Flowerpot Men, White Plains)

JACK KETCH & CROWMEN
87	Hangmen HANG 19 UP	BRIMFULL OF HATE (LP)	35

KEYBOARD
75	Eyelett EYE 4	Will You Shut Up/Move On	20

EBONY KEYES
66	Piccadilly 7N 35358	Sitting In The Ring/If You Knew	100
67	Piccadilly 7N 35375	Cupid's House/If Our Love Should End	10
67	Piccadilly 7N 35390	Country Girl/How Many Times	10
67	Piccadilly 7N 35407	Don't/Sweet Mary (Sweeter Than A Rose)	12

KAROL KEYES
64	Fontana TF 517	You Beat Me To The Punch/No-One Can Take Your Place (in p/s)	30

Troy KEYES

MINT VALUE £

64	Fontana TF 517	You Beat Me To The Punch/No-One Can Take Your Place	20
66	Columbia DB 7899	A Fool In Love/The Good Love, The Bad Love	20
66	Columbia DB 8001	One In A Million/Don't Jump	75
67	Fontana TF 846	Can't You Hear The Music/The Sweetest Touch	12

(see also Volunteers)

TROY KEYES
68	Stateside SS 2087	Love Explosions/I'm Crying (Inside)	22
69	Stateside SS 2149	Love Explosions/I'm Crying (Inside) (reissue)	10

KEY LARGO
71	Blue Horizon 57-3178	Voodoo Rhythm/As The Years Go Passing By	20
70	Blue Horizon 7-63859	KEY LARGO (LP)	60

KEY MASSIVE
89	Hat Music HT 001	Oh Girl/Sweet Sensi (12")	25
97	Wild Bunch WBRTDJ8	Risingson/Instrumental/Single Mix/Neanderthal Mix/Darren Emerson Mix/Underdog Mix/Underdog Instrumental (2 x 12", clear vinyl promo)	18

KEYMEN
59	HMV POP 584	Gazackstahagen/Miss You	6
62	Columbia DB 4902	Five Weeks In A Balloon/Secretly	8
57	Vogue Coral LVA 9048	THE VOCAL SOUNDS OF THE KEYMEN (LP)	15

KEYNOTES
54	Decca F 10302	A Dime And A Dollar/JOHNSTON BROTHERS: Bandit	10
55	Decca F 10643	Relax-Ay-Voo/Steam Heat	10
56	Decca F 10745	Let's Go Steady/Chincherinchee	8

(see also Bobbie Britton, Johnston Brothers, Dave King, Suzi Miller)

KEYNOTES
63	Planetone 14	I'm In Love/In The Valley	15

BOBBY KEYS
75	Ring O' Records 2017 102	Gimmie The Key/Honky Tonk	7
72	Warner Bros K 46141	BOBBY KEYS (LP)	25

EBONY KEYS
71	Parlophone R 5909	Brother Joe/Under The Apple Tree	8

KEYS (1)
64	Oriole CB 1968	Sleep Sleep My Baby/Colour Slide	20
65	CBS 201804	Go Get Her/My Everything	10

KEYS (2)
80	A&M AMS 7511	Just A Camera/It Ain't So (p/s)	15
81	A&M AMS 8121	One Good Reason/Saturday To Sunday Morning (p/s)	10
81	A&M AMS 8142	I Don't Wanna Cry/Listening In (p/s)	15
81	A&M AMS 8236	Greasy Money/Run Run Run (p/s)	6
81	A&M AMLH 68526	THE KEYS ALBUM (LP)	15

KEYTONES
85	Keytone KEY 3	Good To Be Alive/Now's The Time	15

KEYWI
83	Virgin VS 623	Lets Get It Right/Dub Version/Short Version (12")	15

KGB
81	A Major KGB 001	The KGB/See Me (stamped die cut p/s)	8

K GROOVE
91	The White Label KG 1	The Future/On FB/10 To 10/BYS (12")	60

KHAN
72	Deram SDL-R 11	SPACE SHANTY (LP, gatefold, white/red label, small logo)	70
72	Deram SDL 11	SPACE SHANTY (LP, gatefold, white/red label, small logo, later stickered sleeve)	35

(see also Steve Hillage, Egg, Nick Greenwood, Arzachel, Hatfield & The North)

ASHISH KHAN
68	Liberty LBL 83083E	ASHISH KHAN (LP)	15

USTAD ALI AKBAR KHAN
69	HMV ASD 2367	MUSIC FROM INDIA NO. 5 (LP)	15
69	Transatlantic TRA 183	DHUN PALAS KAFI (LP)	20
71	Mushroom 100 MR 14	THE PEACEFUL MUSIC OF USTAD ALI AKBAR KHAN (LP)	35

(see also Ravi Shankar)

USTAD VILAYET KHAN
70	Transatlantic TRA 239	RAGA TILAKKAMOD (LP)	15

STEVE KHAN
85	Nimbus AN 3023	EVIDENCE (LP, Nimbus Supercut, mail order only from Practical Hi Fi Magazine)	25

KHANDARS
65	Blue Beat BB 332	Don't Dig A Hole For Me/BUSTER'S ALL STARS: Skara	60

KHANS
62	London HLU 9555	New Orleans, 2 AM/Blue Mist	18

KHARTOMB
83	Whaam! WHAAM 14	Swahili Lullaby/Teekon Warriors	6

KHEMISTRY
14	Expansion EX7001	Can You Feel My Love/Whatever It Takes (reissue)	6

KIASMOS
12	Erased Tapes ERATP044LP	THROWN (12", p/s)	30

KICK (1)
79	EMI 2962	ROUGH N SMOOTH EP	15

KICK (2)
84	Footwear FWR 01	Let's Get Back Together/A Shot In The Dark/Don't Ever Change (p/s)	10
86	Countdown VAIN 03	I Can't Let Go/Armchair Politician (p/s)	8

KICKER BOYS
89	Link LINKLP 071	KICKER BOYS (LP)	25

KICK PARTNERS

MINT VALUE £

KICK PARTNERS
83 RAW 1 Just My Imagination/Crazy World 6

KICKS
80 Carrere CAR 138 Get Off The Telephone/Big Boys Don't Cry (p/s) 30
81 Blue Chip BC 102 If Looks Could Kill/Don't She Look Fab 70

JOHNNY KIDD (& PIRATES)
59 HMV POP 615 Please Don't Touch/Growl 30
59 HMV POP 674 Feelin'/If You Were The Only Girl In The World (solo) 25
60 HMV POP 698 You Got What It Takes/Longin' Lips 18
60 HMV POP 753 Shakin' All Over/Yes Sir, That's My Baby 15
60 HMV POP 790 Restless/Magic Of Love 18
61 HMV POP 853 Linda Lu/Let's Talk About Us 20
61 HMV POP 919 Please Don't Bring Me Down/So What 20
62 HMV POP 978 Hurry On Back To Love/I Want That (with The Mike Sammes Singers) 25
62 HMV POP 1088 A Shot Of Rhythm And Blues/I Can Tell (blue or black label) 15
63 HMV POP 1173 I'll Never Get Over You/Then I Got Everything 6
63 HMV POP 1228 Hungry For Love/Ecstasy 8
64 HMV POP 1269 Always And Ever/Dr. Feelgood 10
64 HMV POP 1309 Jealous Girl/Shop Around 15
64 HMV POP 1353 Whole Lotta Woman/Your Cheatin' Heart 20
65 HMV POP 1397 The Birds And The Bees/Don't Make The Same Mistake As I Did 20
65 HMV POP 1424 Shakin' All Over '65/Gotta Travel On 40
65 HMV POP 1520 It's Got To Be You/I Hate To Get Up In The Morning (solo) 30
66 HMV POP 1559 Send For That Girl/The Fool 40
60s HMV JO 674 Feelin'/If You Were The Only Girl In The World (export issue, black label) 30
97 Cruisin' 50 CASB 005 Shakin' All Over/Please Don't Touch (78rpm, 300 only) 30
60 HMV 7EG 8628 SHAKIN' ALL OVER (EP) 30
64 HMV 7EG 8834 JOHNNY KIDD AND THE PIRATES (EP) 40

(see also Pirates)

KIDDA BAND
79 Carrere CAR 119 Fighting My Way Back/Saturday Night Fever 130

KID DYNAMITE
73 Pye 7N 45274 Call Me Sunshine Superman/Breaking The Ice 15

KID GUNGO
69 Escort ES 801 Hold The Pussy/KING CANNON: Wha Pen (B-side actually by Carl Bryan) 18

KID 'N' PLAY
88 Cooltempo COOLXR 175 2 Hype (12" promo) 20

KIDROCK
73 Youngblood YB 1058 Ice Cream Man/Dream Dream 35

KIDS
75 Atlantic K 50143 ANVIL CHORUS (LP, with inner, stickered sleeve) 25

(see also Heavy Metal Kids)

KIDS NEXT DOOR
65 London HLR 9993 Inky Dinky Spider/Goodbye Don't Cry 7

BRENDAN KIDULIS
80 Grey GR 001 Rusty Love/One FIrst Kiss 6

KIDZ
79 P 1099 I'll Get Caught/Prototype Pete (no p/s) 35

KIDZ NEXT DOOR
79 Warner Bros K 17492 What's It All About?/The Kidz Next Door (p/s) 50

PETE KIELY
79 Elephant TUN 1 Forgotten Song/Troubadour (gatefold p/s) 8

KIKROKOS
78 Polydor 2393 208 JUNGLE DJ AND DIRTY KATE (LP) 15

KILBURN & HIGH ROADS
74 Dawn DNS 1090 Rough Kids/Billy Bentley 10
75 Dawn DNS 1102 Crippled With Nerves/Huffety Puff 12
78 Warner Bros K 17225 Billy Bentley/Pam's Moods 8
75 Dawn DNLS 3065 HANDSOME (LP, pink 'sun' label) 40
78 Warner Bros. K56513 WOTABUNCH (LP) 15

(see also Ian Dury & Blockheads, 999, Nine Days Wonder, Davey Payne)

ROY KILDARE
64 Blue Beat BB 226 I Won't Leave/What About It 15

JUDY KILEEN
56 London HLU 8328 Just Walking In The Rain/A Heart Without A Sweetheart 35

MERLE KILGORE
54 London HL 8103 Seeing Double, Feeling Single/It Can't Rain All The Time 300
54 London HL 8103 Seeing Double, Feeling Single/It Can't Rain All The Time (78) 20
57 London HLP 8392 Ernie/Trying To Find (Someone Like You) 100
57 London HLP 8392 Ernie/Trying To Find (Someone Like You) (78) 29
60 Melodisc MEL 1545 Dear Mama/Jimmie Bring Sunshine 10
62 Mercury AMT 1193 42 In Chicago/A Girl Named Liz 15
65 London HA-B 8244 THERE'S GOLD IN THEM THAR HILLS (LP) 15

THEOLA KILGORE
67 Sue WI 4035 I'll Keep Trying/He's Coming Back To Me 40

KILLA INSTINCT
92 Music Of Life NOTE061 The Bambi Murders (12") 15
92 Music Of Life NOTE063 Den Of Thieves/Ununited Kingdom (12") 15
93 European Rhyme ERR02 WHISPERS OF HATRED (EP) 18
94 Move MOVE7013 1 ESCAPISM (EP) 10

KILLER

MINT VALUE £

96	Move MOVE7017 5	THE PENULTIMATE SACRIFICE (EP)	10

(see also Total Fiasco)

KILLER

77	Ariola ARL 5003	KILLER (LP)	35

(see also Joe Cool & The Killers)

KILLERHERTZ

91	Evasion EVA 1	The Enforcer/X.XS (12", p/s)	12
92	FX FXUKT 9	Distant Dream (X-Static Mix)/Love Byte (Apocalypse Mix)/Love Byte (Stronthium Mix)/Distant Dream (Flying Fader Mix) (12")	40

KILLERMETERS

79	Psycho P 2620	Why Should It Happen To Me/Cardiac Arrest (in p/s)	100
79	Psycho P 2620	Why Should It Happen To Me/Cardiac Arrest	30
80	Gem GEMS 22	Twisted Wheel/SX 225 (p/s, demo copies £50)	90
97	Detour DRLP 013	METRIC NOISE (2xLP, gatefold, 'sparkly' clear vinyl)	20

KILLERS (2)

03	Lizard King LIZARD007X	Mr Brightside/Smile Like You Mean It (white vinyl, 500 only p/s)	80
04	Lizard King LIZARD009X	Somebody Told Me/The Ballad Of Michael Valentine (pink vinyl, 2,000 only p/s and poster)	20
04	Lizard King LIZARD010X	Mr Brightside/Who Let You Go (red vinyl, p/s and poster)	25
04	Lizard King LIZARD012X	All These Things That I've Done/Andy, You're A Star (Radio 1 session) yellow vinyl, 2000 only, with poster)	10
04	Lizard King IND1ERR	Glamorous Indie Rock & Roll (1-sided promo, 400 only)	15
05	Lizard King LIZARD014X	Somebody Told Me (Mylo Remix)/Somebody Told Me (Glimmers Mix) (12")	12
05	Lizard King LIZARD015X	Smile Like You Mean It/Ruby, Don't Take Your Love To Town (Radio 1 Session) (p/s, red vinyl)	12
06	Vertigo 170 672-1	When You Were Young/Where The White Boys Dance (numbered p/s)	6
07	Vertigo 17245686	Read My Mind/Steve Bays Remix (numbered p/s)	8
09	Vertigo 2707364	The World We Live In (1-sided picture disc)	10
09	Vertigo 2714744	A Dustyard Fairytale/Forget About What I Said (picture disc)	15
04	Lizard King LIZARD011X	HOT FUSS (LP, blue vinyl)	125
05	Island B0005491-21	HOT FUSS (LP as 11 x 7" box set)	80
08	Island 602517902534	DAY & AGE (LP)	30
12	Island 602537118762	BATTLE BORN (2-LP, red and black vinyl, 200 only autographed for Wembley concert)	40
17	Island 00602557937572	WONDERFUL WONDERFUL (LP, pink vinyl)	30

KILLER WATT

87	Raglan RGS 312	DEATH (EP)	25

JOHN KILLIGREW

71	Penny Farthing PELS 513	JOHN KILLIGREW (LP, with Pete Dello, red/black/yellow labels)	175

(see also Pete Dello)

KILLING FLOOR

70	Penny Farthing PEN 745	Call For The Politicians/Acid Bean	20
69	Spark (S)RLP 102	KILLING FLOOR (LP, blue/silver labels)	500
70	Penny Farthing PELS 511	OUT OF URANUS (LP, gatefold sleeve, red/black/yellow label)	450
73	Spark Replay SRLM 2004	ORIGINAL KILLING FLOOR (LP, reissue)	30

(see also Rory Gallagher)

KILLING JOKE

79	Malicious Damage MD 410	Nervous System/Turn To Red/Are You Receiving (10" EP in bag, with picture & 4 cards)	35
79	Malicious Damage MD 410	Nervous System/Turn To Red/Are You Receiving (10" EP in bag, without picture & 4 cards)	10
80	Island WIP 6550	Turn To Red/Nervous System ('A' label)	15
80	Island 12 WIP 6550	Almost Red/Nervous System/Are You Receiving/Turn To Red (12", p/s)	10
80	Malicious Damage MD 540	Wardance/Psyche (p/s, with 'call up paper' insert)	15
80	Malicious Damage MD 540	Wardance/Psyche (Mispressed B-side plays 'unknown artist', p/s)	25
80	E.G. EGMX 1.00	Requiem/Change/Change/Requiem (12", stamped sleeve)	10
83	E.G. EGOXD 14	Me Or You/Feast Of Blaze/Wilful Days//Let's All Go (To The Fire Dances)/The Fall Of Because (live)/Dominator (Version) (12", sealed double pack)	15
84	E.G. DJ17	A New Day/Dance Day (DJ promo)	12
85	E.G. EGOY 20	Love Like Blood (Gestalt Mix)/Love Like Blood/Blue Feather (12", p/s)	10
85	E.G. EGOY 21	Kings And Queens (Knave Mix) (12", p/s)	10
85	E.G. EGOX 21	Kings And Queens (The Right Royal Mix)/The Madding Crowd/Kings And Queens (12", different withdrawn p/s)	10
90	ODIC1	Beautiful Dead (1-sided fan club flexi)	10
80	E.G. EGM5.45	KILLING JOKE (LP, gatefold)	30
81	E.G. EGMD 5.50	WHAT'S THIS FOR...! (LP)	30
82	E.G. EGMD 3	REVELATIONS (LP)	15
83	E.G. EGMD 5	FIRE DANCES (LP)	15
85	E.G. EGLP 61	NIGHT TIME (LP, inner)	20
86	EG EGLP 57	KILLING JOKE (LP, reissue, black and red EG labels, gatefold)	15
86	EG EGLP 58	WHAT'S THIS FOR...! (LP, reissue, black and red EG labels)	15
94	Butterfly BFLLP9	PANDEMONIUM (2-LP)	30
06	Let Them Eat Vinyl LETV005LP	HOSANNAS FROM THE BASEMENTS OF HELL (2-LP, gatefold blue vinyl)	30
08	Let Them Eat Vinyl LETV003LP	DEMOCRACY (2-LP gatefold, white vinyl, reissue)	25
08	Let Them Eat Vinyl LETV014LP	KILLING JOKE (2-LP, reissue, black and white vinyl, gatefold sleeve)	30
08	Let Them Eat Vinyl LETV015LP	WHAT'S THIS FOR...! (2-LP reissue, red and green vinyl, gatefold)	25

(see also Youth, Peyr, Brilliant, Firemen)

KILLJOYS (1)

77	Raw RAW 3	Johnny Won't Get To Heaven/Naive (p/s, 4 different label designs)	35
91	Dam. Goods FNARR LP10	NAIVE (LP, green vinyl)	20

(see also Girlschool)

KILLS

MINT VALUE £

KILLS
02	Domino RUG 144T	BLACK ROOSTER EP (10")	12
02	Rug RUG 152	Fuck The People (1-sided, stamped card sleeve, 500 only)	8
08	Domino RUG 282	Cheap And Cheerful/Kiss The Wrong Side	8
11	Domino RUG 425	Baby Says/Willow Weep For Me	10
12	Domino RUG 450	The Last Goodbye/One Silver Dollar (picture disc)	8
16	Domino RUG 759	Doing It To Death (1-sided, B-side etched)	15
03	Domino WIGLP 124	KEEP ON YOUR MEAN SIDE (LP, with fold-out insert)	25
05	Domino WIGLP 140	NO WOW (LP, with DVD)	30
08	Domino WIGLP 184	MIDNIGHT BOOM (LP)	15
11	Domino WIGLP 249	BLOOD PRESSURES (LP, gatefold, download card)	15
16	Domino WIGLP 289X	ASH & ICE (2-LP, pink and blue vinyl)	20

(see also Dead Weather)

KILOWATTS
68	JJ DB 1140	Bring It On Home/What A Wonderful World (with Doctor Bird label cat no)	30

(see also West Indians)

PAT KILROY
67	Elektra EKL 311	LIGHT OF DAY (LP)	80

KILTIES
56	Beltona BL 2666	Teach You To Rock/Giddy-Up-A Ding Dong	15

ANDY KIM
69	Dot DOT 125	Baby I Love You/Gee Girl	12

KIM & KINETICS
60s	Mortonsound 3032/3033	Without A Song/Stormy Monday	60
60s	Mortonsound 3036/3033	Wee Wee Hours/Stormy Monday	60

(see also Kim Davis)

WILLIAM E. KIMBER
68	Parlophone R 5735	Kilburn Towers/Goodbye (withdrawn)	8
69	Parlophone R 5796	Black Sheep Boy/And The Sun Began To Shine	6

(see also E William)

STEVIE KIMBLE
66	Decca F 12378	Some Things Take A Little Time/All The Time In The World (DJ Copy)	50
66	Decca F 12378	Some Things Take A Little Time/All The Time In The World	25

KINDNESS
70	RCA 1942	Light Of Love/Lindy Lou	7

KINESPHERE
76	Kinesphere KIN 5001	ALL AROUND YOU (LP)	100

KINETIC EFFECT
93	Insane 1201	Borderin' Insanity/Beyond The Parameters (12" green vinyl, 500 pressed)	30
93	Insane 1201	Borderin' Insanity/Beyond The Parameters (12")	18
97	Insane 1202	Man Bites Dog/The Effect Of Fear (12")	18
12	Insane 1001	A Physical Exorcise/The Catalyst (clear vinyl 10")	15

(see also 2 The Top and Insane Macbeth)

AL KING
68	Sue WI 4045	Think Twice Before You Speak/The Winner	40

ALBERT KING
67	Atlantic 584 099	Crosscut Saw/Down Don't Bother Me	20
67	Stax 601 015	Born Under A Bad Sign/Personal Manager	10
68	Stax 601 029	Cold Feet/You Sure Drive A Hard Bargain	10
68	Stax 601 042	(I Love) Lucy/You're Gonna Need Me	8
67	Polydor 2343 026	TRAVELLIN' TO CALIFORNIA (LP)	40
68	Stax (S)XATS 1002	LIVE WIRE - BLUES POWER (LP)	40
69	Atlantic 588 173	KING OF THE BLUES GUITAR (LP)	40
69	Stax SXATS 1017	KING DOES THE KING'S THINGS (LP)	35
69	Stax SXATS 1022	YEARS GONE BY (LP)	35
71	Stax 2363 003	LIVE WIRE - BLUES POWER (LP, reissue)	15
71	Stax 2325 042	LOVEJOY	35
73	Stax 2325 089	I'LL PLAY THE BLUES FOR YOU (LP)	20
74	Stax STX 1003	I WANNA GET FUNKY (LP)	20

(see also Steve Cropper & Albert King)

ALLAN KING
73	Duke DU 151	Africa Wants Us All/JOE GIBBS: Liberation (B-side actually by Joe Gibbs' All Stars)	6

ANNA KING
65	Philips BF 1402	If Somebody Told You/Baby, Baby, Baby (as Anna King & Bobby Byrd)	15
65	Philips BBE 12584	BACK TO SOUL (EP)	40
65	Philips (S)BL 7655	BACK TO SOUL (LP)	60

(see also Bobby Byrd)

ANTHONY KING
70s	Peer Intl.	ELECTRICAL BAZAAR - SYNTHESIZERS UNLIMITED (LP, library issue)	20

B.B. KING
62	HMV POP 1101	Tomorrow Night/Mother's Love	25
64	Ember EMB S 196	Rock Me Baby/I Can't Lose	25
65	Sue WI 358	The Letter/You Never Know	30
66	HMV POP 1568	Don't Answer The Door Parts 1 & 2	20
67	HMV POP 1580	Night Life/Waitin' On You	15
67	HMV POP 1594	I Don't Want You Cuttin' Your Hair/Think It Over	15
67	Polydor 56735	Jungle/Long Gone Baby	15
68	Stateside SS 2112	Paying The Cost To Be The Boss/Having My Say	10
68	Blue Horizon 57-3144	The Woman I Love/Blues For Me	20
69	Stateside SS 2141	Don't Waste My Time/Get Myself Somebody	6

Ben E. KING

MINT VALUE £

Year	Label/Cat#	Title	Value
69	Blue Horizon 57-3161	Everyday I Have The Blues/Five Long Years	20
70	Stateside SS 2161	The Thrill Is Gone/You're Mean	10
70	Stateside SS 2169	So Excited/Confessin' The Blues	7
71	Probe PRO 546	Ain't Nobody Home/Alexis' Boogie (with Alexis Korner)	10
65	HMV CLP 1870	LIVE AT THE REGAL (LP)	50
66	HMV CLP 3514	CONFESSIN' THE BLUES (LP)	30
67	HMV CLP 3608	BLUES IS KING (LP)	30
68	Stateside (S)SL 10238	BLUES ON TOP OF BLUES (LP)	30
67	Ember EMB 3379	THE R&B AND SOUL OF B.B. KING (LP)	30
68	Blue Horizon 7-63216	THE B.B. KING STORY CHAPTER 1 (LP)	50
69	Stateside (S)SL 10272	LUCILLE (LP)	40
69	Stateside SSL 10284	HIS BEST - THE ELECTRIC B.B. KING (LP)	20
69	Blue Horizon 7-63226	THE B.B. KING STORY CHAPTER 2 - BEALE STREET BLUES (LP)	75
70	Stateside SSL 10297	LIVE AND WELL (LP)	30
70	Stateside SSL 10299	COMPLETELY WELL (LP)	30
70	Probe SPBA 6255	INDIANOLA MISSISSIPPI SEEDS (LP)	30
71	Blue Horizon 2431 004	TAKE A SWING WITH ME (LP, mono)	100
71	Probe SPB 1032	LIVE IN COOK COUNTY JAIL (LP)	30

(see also U2)

BEN E. KING

Year	Label/Cat#	Title	Value
61	London HLK 9258	Spanish Harlem/First Taste Of Love	10
61	London HLK 9358	Stand By Me/On The Horizon	15
61	London HLK 9416	Amor, Amor/Souvenir Of Mexico	10
61	London HLK 9457	Here Comes The Night/Young Boy Blues	15
62	London HLK 9517	Ecstasy/Yes	10
62	London HLK 9544	Don't Play That Song (You Lied)/The Hermit Of Misty Mountain (later copies have Atlantic labels instead of London Atlantic, this price is for both pressings)	10
62	London HLK 9586	Too Bad/My Heart Cries For You	15
63	London HLK 9631	I'm Standing By/Walking In The Footsteps Of A Fool	15
63	London HLK 9691	How Can I Forget/Gloria, Gloria	15
63	London HLK 9778	I (Who Have Nothing)/The Beginning Of Time	10
63	London HLK 9819	I Could Have Danced All Night/Gypsy	10
64	London HLK 9840	Around The Corner/Groovin'	20
64	Atlantic AT 4007	It's All Over/Let The Water Run Down	22
65	Atlantic AT 4018	Seven Letters/River Of Tears	22
65	Atlantic AT 4025	The Record (Baby I Love You)/The Way You Shake It	20
65	Atlantic AT 4043	Cry No More/(There's) No Place To Hide	40
66	Atlantic AT 4065	Goodnight My Love, Pleasant Dreams/Tell Daddy	12
66	Atlantic AT 4065	Goodnight My Love, Pleasant Dreams/I Can't Break The News To Myself (demos with blank label on different B-side)	400
66	Atlantic 584 008	So Much Love/Don't Drive Me Away	15
66	Atlantic 584 046	I Swear By The Stars Above/Get In A Hurry	12
67	Atlantic 584 069	What Is Soul?/They Don't Give Medals To Yesterday's Heroes	12
67	Atlantic 584 090	Save The Last Dance For Me (as Ben E. King & Drifters)/Stand By Me	8
67	Atlantic 584 106	Tears, Tears, Tears/A Man Without A Dream	15
68	Atlantic 584 149	Seven Letters/Goodnight My Love	10
68	Atlantic 584 184	Don't Take Your Love From Me/Forgive This Fool	25
68	Atlantic 584 205	It's Amazing/Where's The Girl	12
69	Atlantic 584 238	'Till I Can't Take It Any More/It Ain't Fair	12
71	Atlantic 2091 100	It's Amazing/Tears, Tears, Tears	10
71	CBS 7397	White Moon/All Of Your Sorrows	6
72	CBS 7785	Take Me To The Pilot/I Guess It's Goodbye	6
75	Atlantic K 10565	Supernatural Thing (Parts 1 & 2)	10
75	Atlantic K 10618	Happiness Is Where You Find It/Drop My Heart Off	15
03	Atco 67855	I Can't Break The News Myself/BOBBY SHEEN: Something New To Do	15
63	London REK 1361	BEN E. KING (EP)	40
63	London REK 1386	I'M STANDING BY (EP)	40
64	Atlantic AET 6004	WHAT NOW MY LOVE (EP)	40
61	London HA-K 2395	SPANISH HARLEM (LP, mono)	50
61	London SAH-K 6195	SPANISH HARLEM (LP, stereo)	70
62	London HA-K 8012	DON'T PLAY THAT SONG! (LP)	50
63	London HA-K 8026	SONGS FOR SOULFUL LOVERS (LP, cover credits Sings For Soulful Lovers; mono)	50
63	London SH-K 8026	SONGS FOR SOULFUL LOVERS (LP, cover credits Sings For Soulful Lovers; stereo)	70
65	Atlantic ATL 5016	GREATEST HITS (LP, plum label)	40
65	Atlantic ATL 5024	SEVEN LETTERS (LP)	50
66	Atlantic 587/588 055	SONGS FOR SOULFUL LOVERS (LP, cover credits Sings For Soulful Lovers; reissue)	18
67	Atlantic 587 072	WHAT IS SOUL? (LP)	25
70	Crewe CRWS 203	ROUGH EDGES (LP)	15

(see also Drifters, Soul Clan)

BOB KING & THE COUNTRY KINGS

Year	Label/Cat#	Title	Value
59	Oriole CB 1497	My Petite Marie/Hey Honey	80
59	Oriole CB 1497	My Petite Marie/Hey Honey (78)	20

BRENTON KING

Year	Label/Cat#	Title	Value
73	Downtown DT 505	Why Do People Have To Cry/Version	6

BUZZY KING

Year	Label/Cat#	Title	Value
60	Top Rank JAR 278	Schoolboy Blues/Your Picture	20

CANNON BALL KING

Year	Label/Cat#	Title	Value
69	Camel CA 14	Danny Boy/Reggae Happiness	40
69	Gas GAS 133	Stagger Back/The Creeper	50
70s	Junior JR 103	Reggay Got Soul/Land Of Love (actually by Soul Cats)	15

Carl KING

(see also Carl Bryan, King Cannon, Cannon Ball & Johnny Melody)

CARL KING
66	CBS 202407	Out Of My Depth/Keep It Coming	25
67	CBS 202553	You And Me/Satin Doll	8

CAROLE KING
62	London HLU 9591	It Might As Well Rain Until September/Nobody's Perfect	7
66	London HLU 10036	Road To Nowhere/Some Of Your Lovin'	40

CLAUDE KING
61	Philips PB 1173	Big River Big Man/Sweet Loving	6
61	Philips PB 1199	The Comancheros/I Can't Get Over The Way You Got Over Me	6
62	CBS AAG 108	Wolverton Mountain/Little Bitty Heart	10
62	CBS AAG 119	Burning Of Atlanta/Don't That Moon Look Lonesome	6
65	CBS EP 6067	TIGER WOMAN (EP)	15
62	CBS BPG 62114	MEET CLAUDE KING (LP)	20

DANNY KING('S MAYFAIR SET)
64	Columbia DB 7276	Tossin' And Turnin'/Young Blood	35
65	Columbia DB 7456	Pretty Things/Outside Of My Room	40
65	Columbia DB 7792	Amen (My Teenage Prayer)/It's Such A Shame (as Danny King's Mayfair Set)	25

(see also Trevor Burton, Lemon Tree, Roy Wood)

DAVE KING
56	Decca F 10684	Memories Are Made Of This (& Keynotes)/I've Changed My Mind A 1000 Times	6
56	Decca F 10720	You Can't Be True To Two/A Little Bit Independent	6
56	Decca F 10741	The Birds And The Bees/Hot Chocolatta (with Keynotes)	6
57	Decca DFE 6385	DAVE KING (EP)	10
58	Decca DFE 6514	DAVE KING NO. 2 (EP)	10

DAVE KING REGGAE BAND
70	Attack ATT 8014	Hey Little Girl/Why Don't You Try Me	12

DEE KING
66	Piccadilly 7N 35316	Sally Go Round The Roses/It's So Fine	12

DENNIS KING
74	EMI 2247	Galloping Home/Within These Walls/Screen Scene	6
77	EMI EMI 2578	Regan's Theme From The Film 'Sweeney'/F.J.'s Tune	20
79	Columbia DB 9061	Dick Turpin/Belinda (as Denis King Orchestra)	6

(see also King Brothers)

DR. MARTIN LUTHER KING
68	Tamla Motown TML 11076	THE GREAT MARCH TO FREEDOM (LP)	60

EDDIE KING
65	Columbia DB 7572	Always At A Distance/If You Wish	8
65	Columbia DB 7654	I Wanna Love Her So Bad/If All You Need	10

FREDDY/FREDDIE KING
61	Parlophone R 4777	Hideaway/I Love The Woman	50
65	Sue WI 349	Driving Sideways/Hideaway	40
69	Atlantic 584 235	Play It Cool/Funky	15
69	Atlantic 588 186	FREDDIE IS A BLUES MASTER (LP)	45
69	Polydor 2343 009	KING OF R&B VOL. 2 (LP)	15
69	Python PLP-KM 5	FREDDY KING VOLUME 1 (LP, 99 copies only)	100
69	Python PLP-KM 7	FREDDY KING VOLUME 2 (LP, 99 copies only)	100
69	Python PLP-KM 11	FREDDY KING VOLUME 3 (LP, 99 copies only)	100

(Pre-1970 releases are usually credited to Freddy King, post-1970 releases to Freddie King.)

72	A&M AMLS 68113	TEXAS CANNONBALL (LP)	15
72	Black Bear 904	LIVE PERFORMANCES VOLUME 1 (LP)	15
72	Black Bear 905	LIVE PERFORMANCES VOLUME 2 (LP)	15

(see also Lula Reed & Freddy King)

HAMILTON KING
64	HMV POP 1289	Not Until/I Wanna Live	6
64	HMV POP 1356	Ain't It Time/Money, Money	12
65	HMV POP 1425	Bird Without Wings/Shoppin'	12

HANK KING
63	Starlite STEP 41	COUNTRY AND WESTERN (EP)	25
66	Starlite GRK 510	COUNTRY AND WESTERN (EP, reissue, around 999 pressed)	10

JAY W. KING
66	Stateside SS 505	I'm So Afraid/I Don't Have To Worry (Not Anymore)	15

MORGAN KING
93	OM Records 12OM006	I Am Free (12" promo)	10
93	OM Records 12OM006	I Am Free (12")	10
93	OM Records 12OM0006 T	I Am Free (8 Mixes) (2 x12")	40

P. KING
83	Red Bus RBUS 79	Hey Rosalyn/Lyin' Again	6

(see also Paul King)

P. RUFUS KING
73	Dawn DNS 1031	Look At Me Now/Nobody Knows	25

(see also Paul King, Mungo Jerry)

PAUL KING
72	Dawn DNS 1023	Whoa Buck/Zoe	7
72	Dawn DNLS 3035	BEEN IN THE PEN TOO LONG (LP, textured sleeve with lyric insert)	40

(see also Mungo Jerry, P. King, P. Rufus King, King Earl Boogie Band, D'Jurann Jurran, Jigilo Jug Band)

PEE WEE KING & HIS BAND
54	HMV 7MC 14	Bimbo/Changing Partners (export issue)	7

(see also Hank Snow)

PETER KING (1)
68	Crab CRAB 3	Reggae Limbo/DERRICK MORGAN: River To The Bank	20
75	Torpedo TOR 38	My Eyes Adore You/Version	8

PETER KING (2)
78	Miles Music MM 076	BROTHER BERNARD (LP, with Alan Skidmore)	20

PETER KING (3)
75	Orbitone OTLP 007	MILIKI SOUND (LP)	100
76	Orbitone OTLP 010	OMU LEWA (LP)	150
77	Orbitone OTLP 012	A SOULFUL PETER KING (LP)	20
93	Spindle LP 07	MILIKI SOUND (LP, reissue)	30
93	Spindle LP 08	OMO LEWA (LP, reissue)	35

PETER KING (4)
85	Fashion FAD 029	Step On The Gas/Ten Commandments Of An MC (12")	30
85	Fashion FAD 045	Bad Memory/Rewind/Jack It Up (12")	30

RAMONA KING
64	Warner Bros WB 125	It's In His Kiss/It Couldn't Happen To A Nicer Guy	25

RAY KING SOUL BAND
67	Piccadilly 7N 35394	Behold/Soon You'll Be Gone	20
68	Direction 8-63394	LIVE AT THE PLAYBOY CLUB (LP)	20

REG KING
71	United Artists UP 35204	Little Boy/10,000 Miles (as Reg King & B.B. Blunder)	25
71	United Artists UAG 29157	REG KING (LP)	120

(see also Action, Andy Leigh, B.B. Blunder, Mark Charig, Elton Dean, Mighty Baby)

ROBERT KING
82	Charisma PRE 23	Paper Heart/Theme For Love	10

(see also Scars)

SAMMY KING (& VOLTAIRS)
64	HMV POP 1285	What's The Secret/Great Balls Of Fire (as Sammy King & Voltairs)	10
64	HMV POP 1330	Rag Doll/We're Through	8
65	HMV POP 1384	Only You (And You Alone)/A Kiss, A Promise	10
66	HMV POP 1540	If You Can Find Someone To Love You/Past Caring (with Voltairs)	8

SID KING & FIVE STRINGS
56	Philips PB 589	Booger Red/Oobie-Doobie (78)	50

SOLOMON KING
67	Columbia DB 8306	She Wears My Ring/Try Try (withdrawn B-side)	10
70	Columbia DB 8676	Say A Prayer/This Beautiful Day	100
70	Columbia DB 8676	Say A Prayer/This Beautiful Day (demo copy)	150
72	Polydor 2058258	When You Gotta Go/Life Child	30

(see also Levi Jackson)

TEDDI KING
57	Vogue EPV 1204	STORYVILLE PRESENTS MISS TEDDI KING (EP)	12

(see also George Shearing)

TEDDY KING & BUSTER'S ALLSTARS
67	Fab FAB 27	Mexican Divorce/SOUL TOPS: Baby I Got News	35

TOBY KING
75	President PT 430	First Man To Die From The Blues/Country Bump	6

TONY KING (& HIPPY BOYS)
69	Trojan TR 667	Proud Mary/My Devotion (as Tony King & Hippy Boys)	20
70	Gas GAS 156	Daddy, Daddy Don't Cry/I Like It	12

(see also Maytals)

TRACY KING
86	DMD 002	Don't Stop/Love Again (12")	20

KING AND QUEEN
79	Decca F 13863	Reunited/Reunited (Dub)	40

KINGBEES
66	Tempo TPO 103	I'm A Kingbee/My Little Red Book (Irish-only, in p/s)	350
66	Tempo TPO 103	I'm A Kingbee/My Little Red Book (Irish-only)	250

KING BISCUIT BOY
70	Paramount SPFL 270	OFFICIAL MUSIC (LP)	18
71	Paramount SPFA 7001	GOODUNS (LP)	18

(see also Bobby Bland)

KING BROTHERS
57	Parlophone R 4288	Marianne/Little By Little	10
59	Parlophone R 4554	Hop, Skip And Jump/Civilization (Bongo, Bongo, Bongo)	10
57	Parlophone GEP 8638	HARMONY KINGS (EP)	12
57	Parlophone GEP 8651	SING AL JOLSON (EP)	10
58	Parlophone PMC 1060	THREE KINGS AND AN ACE (LP)	15
64	Oriole CB 1978	Real Live Girl/Every Time It Rains	8

(see also Jim Dale, Dennis King)

KING CANNON
69	Trojan TR 663	Soul Scorcher/GLEN & DAVE: Lucky Boy	60
69	Harry J TR 664	Soul Special/TREVOR SHIELD: Moon Is Playing Tricks On Me	60
69	Crab CRAB 6	Mellow Trumpet/VAL BENNETT: Reggae City	80
71	Hillcrest HCT 2	Reggay Got Soul/SOUL CATS: Land Of Love	18
71	Moodisc HME 109	Raw Deal (as King Cannon Allout; actually by Carl Bryan)/ MUDIE'S ALL STARS: Shirley's Hide Out	18

(see also Cannon Ball & Johnny Melody, Carl Bryan, Max Romeo, Lester Sterling, Kid Gungo, Erroll Dunkley)

KING CANNON (BALL)
68	Trojan TR 636	Thunderstorm/BURT WALTERS: Honey Love	65

KING CC
76	Concrete Jungle CJ 751	Rasta Poker/LUCKY ALL STARS: Babylon Fall Down	100

KING CHUBBY

MINT VALUE £

(see Prince Far I, King Cry Cry)

KING CHUBBY
70	Pama Supreme PS 297	What's The World Coming To/Live As One	15
70	Supreme PS 297	What's The World Coming To/Live As One (reissue)	10

(see also Junior Byles)

KING CRIMSON

SINGLES
69	Island WIP 6071	The Court Of The Crimson King (Parts 1 & 2)	40
70	Island WIP 6080	Cat Food/Groon (in p/s)	40
70	Island WIP 6080	Cat Food/Groon	10
74	Island WIP 6189	The Night Watch/The Great Deceiver	7
76	Island WIP 6274	21st Century Schizoid Man/Epitaph (in p/s)	30
76	Island WIP 6274	21st Century Schizoid Man/Epitaph	10

ALBUMS : ORIGINAL ALBUMS
69	Island ILPS 9111	IN THE COURT OF THE CRIMSON KING (LP, 1st pressing, Matrixes ILPS 9111 A 2 1 2 4/ ILPS 9111B//4 1 1 1or ILPS 9111 A//3 1 1 3/ILPS 9111 B//3 123 gatefold sleeve, 'Printed and made by E.J. Day, London.' sleeve credit , pink label/'i' logo)	600
70	Island ILPS 9111	IN THE COURT OF THE CRIMSON KING (LP, 2nd pressing, gatefold sleeve no printer credits, pink rim label/'palm tree' logo)	70
70	Island ILPS 9127	IN THE WAKE OF POSEIDON (LP, 1st pressing, textured gatefold sleeve made by E.J. Day, A1/B1 matrixes deep pink lightly texturured label with 'i' logo)	250
70	Island ILPS 9127	IN THE WAKE OF POSEIDON (LP, 2nd pressing, pink rim label/'palm tree' logo)	40
70	Island ILPS 9141	LIZARD (LP, 1st pressing with E. J. Day Co sleeves, Matrix ILPS9141 A-2U/B-2U, laminated gatefold sleeve, pink rim label/'palm tree' logo. Sleeve variation with title 'Lizard' inverted on spine)	200
70	Island ILPS 9141	LIZARD (LP, 1st pressing with E. J. Day Co sleeves, Matrix ILPS9141 A-2U/B-2U, laminated gatefold sleeve, pink rim label/'palm tree' logo)	100
70	Island ILPS 9141	LIZARD (LP, 2nd pressing with Robor sleeves, laminated gatefold sleeve, pink rim label/'palm tree' logo)	30
71	Island ILPS 9175	ISLANDS (LP, pink rim label/'palm tree' logo, with fold-out gatefold inner)	60
71	Island ILPS 9111	IN THE COURT OF THE CRIMSON KING (LP, 3rd pressing, pink rim palm tree label with rough finish, no printers credits, Matrixes: ILPS+9111+A2/ILPS+9111+B2, Basing Street London W11 address)	40
72	Island ILPS 9111	IN THE COURT OF THE CRIMSON KING (LP, 4th pressing, smooth labels, PRINTED IN ENGLAND by ROBOR LIMITED sleeve credit, Matrixes ILPS 9111 A-4U PD 2/ILPS 9111 B-4U HM 2)	30
72	Island HELP 6	EARTHBOUND (LP, 1st pressing, black/pink label, Matrixes: HELP 6A - 2U GM 1/HELP 6 B - 1U PR 1)	60
73	Island ILPS 9230	LARKS' TONGUES IN ASPIC (LP, 1st pressing in shrinkwrap with 'King Crimson' sticker, pink rim label/'palm tree' logo, with inner)	150
73	Island ILPS 9230	LARKS' TONGUES IN ASPIC (LP, 1st pressing, no shrinkwrap without 'King Crimson' sticker, pink rim label/'palm tree' logo, with inner)	60
74	Island ILPS 9275	STARLESS AND BIBLE BLACK (LP, textured gatefold sleeve printed by Robor, palm tree logo, matrixes: A/3U, B/3U, 'Garc' etched into dead wax side A, 'Sean & Ray' etched into dead wax side B, with inner)	60
74	Island ILPS 9308	RED (LP, pink rim label/'palm tree' logo, with inner sleeve)	45
75	Island ILPS 9316	U.S.A. (LP, pink rim label/'palm tree' logo, with inner)	35
76	Island ISLP 7	A YOUNG PERSON'S GUIDE (2-LP, gatefold sleeve, with booklet)	30
81	EG EGLP 49	DISCIPLINE (LP)	50
82	EG EGLP 51	BEAT (LP)	25
84	EG EGLP 55	THREE OF A PERFECT PAIR (LP)	15

ALBUMS : REISSUES
77	Polydor 2683-080	IN THE COURT OF THE CRIMSON KING/LARKS TONGUES IN ASPIC (2-LP)	20
77	Polydor 2302 059	LIZARD (LP, reissue, gatefold sleeve)	15
77	Polydor 2302 060	ISLANDS (LP, reissue)	15
77	Polydor 2343 092	EARTHBOUND (LP, reissue)	15
77	Polydor 2302 061	LARKS TONGUES IN ASPIC (LP, reissue)	15
77	Polydor 2302 065	STARLESS AND BIBLE BLACK (LP, reissue)	15
77	Polydor 2302 066	RED (LP, reissue)	15
87	EG EGLP 5	ISLANDS (LP, reissue)	15
87	EG EGLP 15	RED (LP, reissue)	15
89	EG EGLP 4	LIZARD (LP, reissue, gatefold sleeve)	15
91	EG EGLP 7	LARKS TONGUES IN ASPIC (LP, reissue)	15
09	Discipline Global Mobile KCCBX1	IN THE COURT OF THE CRIMSON KING (box set, reissue, 5-CD, DVD and booklet)	70
10	KCCBXLP1	IN THE COURT OF THE CRIMSON KING (3-LP box set)	50
11	Discipline Global Mobile DGM KCLP2	IN THE WAKE OF POSEIDON (LP, reissue, 200gm vinyl)	20
12	Discipline Global Mobile KCLP3	LIZARD (LP, reissue, 200gm vinyl)	15
13	Discipline Global Mobile/ Opal DGM KCLP5	LARKS TONGUES IN ASPIC (LP, reissue, 200gm vinyl)	15
13	Discipline Global Mobile/ Opal DGM KCLP7	RED (LP, reissue, 200gm vinyl)	15
13	Discipline Global Mobile KCCBX7	THE ROAD TO RED (boxed set, reissue, 21-CD, DVD, 2-blue ray, prints and booklet)	80
14	Discipline Global Mobile DGM KCLP4	ISLANDS (LP, reissue, 200gm vinyl)	18
14	Discipline Global Mobile KCCBX6	STARLESS (Boxed set, reissue, 23-CD, 2 DVD, 2 Blue ray, booklet)	90
15	Discipline Global Mobile/ Opal DGM KCLP6	STARLESS AND BIBLE BLACK (LP, reissue 200gm vinyl)	20
15	Discipline Global Mobile KCCBX13	THRAK BOX (LIVE AND STUDIO 1994-1997) (boxed set, reissue, 12-CD 2 DVD, 2 blue ray and booklet)	80

(see also Giles Giles & Fripp, Fripp & Eno, Gordon Haskell, Shame, McDonald & Giles, Emerson Lake & Palmer, Uriah Heep, Boz, Trendsetters Ltd., Pete Sinfield, Jakszyk, Fripp and Collins)

KING CRY CRY (PRINCE FAR I)
71	Banana BA 356	I Had A Talk/BURNING SPEAR: Zion Higher	35

(see also King C C)

KING CURTIS
62	London HLU 9547	Soul Twist/Twistin' Time (as King Curtis & Noble Knights)	20
64	Capitol CL 15346	Soul Serenade/More Soul	20
67	Atlantic 584 109	Good To Me/Hold On I'm Comin'	12
67	Atlantic 584 134	Memphis Soul Stew/Blue Nocturne	15
68	Speciality SPE 1000	Wiggle Wobble/Night Train	8
69	Atlantic 584 287	La Jeanne/Little Green Apples	10
70	Atco 2091 012	Teasin'/Soulin' (as King Curtis & Delaney Bramlett, Eric Clapton & Friends)	15
60	London RE-K 1307	HAVE TENOR SAX, WILL BLOW (EP)	40
60	London HA-K 2247	HAVE TENOR SAX, WILL BLOW (LP)	70
62	RCA RD 27252	ARTHUR MURRAY'S MUSIC FOR DANCING - THE TWIST (LP)	30
62	Esquire 32-161	THE NEW SCENE OF KING CURTIS (LP)	40
67	Atlantic 587 067	PLAYS THE GREAT MEMPHIS HITS (LP)	20
68	Ember SPE/LP 6600	SOUL SERENADE (LP)	20
68	Atlantic 587 093	KINGSIZE SOUL (LP, as King Curtis & Kingpins)	20
69	Atco 228 002	BEST OF KING CURTIS (LP)	15
68	Atlantic 587/588 115	SWEET SOUL (LP)	20
69	Atco 228 027	INSTANT GROOVE (LP)	20
71	Atlantic 2400159	LIVE AT FILLMORE WEST (LP, gatefold)	20

(see also Champion Jack Dupree, Eric Clapton)

KING CURTIS, OLIVER NELSON & JIMMY FORREST
63	Esquire 32-189	SOUL BATTLE (LP)	30

KING DIAMOND
89	Roadrunner RR 9461-1	CONSPIRACY (LP, inner)	15
89	Roadrunner RR 94616	CONSPIRACY (LP, picture disc)	20

KINGDOM
70	United Artists UP 35145	All I Need/Nothing Could Be Better	25

BOBBY KINGDOM/BLUE BEATS
61	Blue Beat BB 44	Honey Please/BLUE BEATS: That's My Girl	25
62	Blue Beat 45/BB/77	Spanish Town Twist/Brand New Automobile	12

KINGDOM COME (U.K.)
71	Polydor 2001 234	Eternal Messenger/I D Side To B Side The C Side	10
72	Polydor 2001 416	Spirit Of Joy/Come Alive	10
72	Polydor 2310 130	GALACTIC ZOO DOSSIER (LP, gatefold sleeve, with poster)	100
72	Polydor 2310 130	GALACTIC ZOO DOSSIER (LP, gatefold sleeve, without poster)	30
72	Polydor 2310 178	KINGDOM COME (LP)	30
73	Polydor 2310 254	JOURNEY (LP)	25

(see also Arcadium. Arthur Brown, Kiki Dee, Spirit Of John Morgan, Arcadium)

KING-EARL BOOGIE BAND
72	Dawn DNS 1024	Plastic Jesus/If The Lord Don't Get You	6
72	Dawn DNS 1028	Starlight/Goin' To Germany	6
72	Dawn DNLS 3040	TROUBLE AT MILL (LP, with poster)	30
72	Dawn DNLS 3040	TROUBLE AT MILL (LP, without poster)	20

(see also Mungo Jerry, Paul King)

KING EDWARDS ALL STARS
66	Rio R 077	North Coast/Kingston 11	150

(KING) EDWARDS GROUP
63	Island WI 040	Dear Hearts/Oh Mary (B-side actually by Ransford Barnett)	25
63	Island WI 047	Russian Roulette (actually by King Edwards All Stars)/You're Mine (actually by Douglas Brothers)	30
63	Island WI 082	He Gave You To Me/Kings Priests And Prophets (both actually by The Schoolboys)	20
63	Island WI 087	Hey Girl/Skies Are Grey (both actually by Ransford Barnett)	18

KING FIGHTER
60s	Jump Up JU 518	People Will Talk/Same Thing	8

KINGFISH
76	United Artists UAG 29922	KINGFISH (LP)	15
77	Jet UAG 30080	LIVE AND KICKIN' (LP, early copies with picture inner sleeve)	15

(see also Grateful Dead)

KING FLOYD
71	Atlantic 2091-051	Groove Me/What Our Love Needs	8
71	Atlantic 2466014	GROOVE ME (LP)	20

KING GENERAL
96	Conscious Sounds DNC EP 01	Gunman/Dub/Conscious Ites Cut 5/CULTURE FREEMAN: The Fittest/High Speed Dubbing/C23000 Dubbing (12")	30

KING GENERAL & BUSH CHEMISTS
96	Conscious Sounds DNC 006	MONEY RUN TINGS (LP, 1st pressing)	35

KING GEORGE
67	RCA RCA 1573	Drive On James/I'm Gonna Be Somebody Someday	30

KING GIZZARD AND THE LIZARD WIZARD
14	Heavenly HVN 281	Head On/Pill (1-sided 12" picture disc)	100
14	Heavenly HVN 296	Cellophane/The Wholly Ghost (3D p/s, comes with 3D glasses)	60
14	Heavenly 5414939920240	I'M IN YOUR MIND FUZZ (LP)	25
15	Heavenly HVNLP 114	QUARTERS! (LP)	20
15	Heavenly HVNLP 124	PAPER MACHE DREAM BALOON (LP)	25
16	Heavenly HVNLP 127	NONAGON INFINITY (LP)	20
17	Wizard 01	POLYGONWANALAND (LP, blue, pink, clear, red and green vinyl - 100 each)	25
17	Shake Appeal SA 1	POLYGONWANALAND (LP, smoke effect marbled vinyl)	25
17	Static Caravan VAN 327	POLYGONWANALAND (LP, limited edition of 20 numbered lathe cut copies)	60

KING HARVEST

			MINT VALUE £
17	Hyperloop HL 1	POLYGONWANALAND (LP, limited edition of 50 numbered lathe cut copies)	40
17	Phwoar And Peace BWR 039	POLYGONWANALAND (LP, limited edition of 300 copies on red/black vinyl)	20

KING HARVEST
| 73 | Pye Int. 7N 25605 | Dancing in The Moonlight/Marty And The Captain | 8 |
| 73 | Pye NSPL 28174 | DANCING IN THE MOONLIGHT (LP) | 15 |

KING HORROR
69	Joe/Duke DU 34	Dracula Prince Of Darkness/JOE'S ALL STARS: Honky	50
69	Grape GR 3003	Cutting Blade/Vampire	50
69	Grape GR 3006	The Hole/WINSTON GROOVY: Lover Come Back	30
69	Grape GR 3007	Lochness Monster/VISIONS: Zion I	60
69	Jackpot JP 713	Wood In The Fire/The Naked City	25
69	Jackpot JP 714	Police/PAMA DICE: Honky Tonk Popcorn	40
70	Nu Beat NB 051	Frankenstein/WINSTON GROOVY: I Can't Stand It	60
70	Reggae REG 3005	Slave Driver	20

(see also Laurel Aitken)

KING IWAH
| 72 | Upsetter US 382 | Give Me Power # 2/UPSETTERS: Public Enemy Number One | 30 |

KING KONG
85	Now Generation NG 013	Predominant/Version (12")	12
86	Greensleeves GRED 206	Paro Them Paro/BUBBLERS COMPUTER STARS : Paranoia (12")	30
87	Digikal DIG 006	Digital We Digital/FRANKIE PAUL: Rambo (12")	20

KING KOSS
| 69 | Polydor 56329 | Spinning Wheel/Louisiana | 8 |

KING KURT
82	Thin Sliced TSR 2	Zulu Beat/Rockin' Kurt (first pressing, orange vinyl with hand-painted sleeves by band members)	125
82	Thin Sliced TSR 2	Zulu Beat/Rockin' Kurt (second, green vinyl, 159 copies, with hand-painted sleeves by band members)	100
82	Thin Sliced TSR 2	Zulu Beat/Rockin' Kurt (second pressing, green vinyl, 1529 copies, sleeves not hand painted by band members)	40
82	Thin Sliced TSR 2	Zulu Beat/Rockin' Kurt (later pressings, yellow/gold/purple vinyl, different sleeves)	30
84	Stiff P BUY 206	Banana Banana/Bo Diddley Goes East (shaped picture disc)	8
85	Stiff P BUY 235	Slammers/Ape Hour (shaped picture disc)	6

KINGLY BAND
| 69 | Decca F 12926 | The Bitter And The Sweet/Standing At The Crossroads | 7 |
| 69 | Decca LK 5002 | ROCKSTEADY (LP) | 25 |

KING MIGUEL
| 73 | Bullet BU 524 | The Word Is Black/Town Talk | 10 |

KING OF LUXEMBOURG
| 86 | él GPO 14 | Valleri/Sketches Of Luxembourg (p/s) | 12 |

KINGPINS (U.K.)
| 65 | Oriole CB 1986 | Two Right Feet/That's The Way It Should Be | 35 |

KINGPINS (U.S.)
| 58 | London HLU 8658 | Ungaua Parts 1 & 2 | 15 |

KING ROCK & WILLOWS
| 67 | Caltone TONE 111 | You Are The One/ALVA LEWIS: Return Home | 130 |

KING ROCKY
| 68 | Studio One SO 2045 | The King Is Back/THREE TOPS: Vex Till Yuh Buss | 85 |

(see also Leroy & Rocky, Clancy Eccles, Heptones)

KINGS IV
| 59 | London HLT 8914 | Some Like It Hot/The World Goes On | 10 |

KINGS OF TOMORROW
| 01 | Defected DFECT 37X | FINALLY EP (2x12") | 20 |

KINGS COUNTY CARNIVAL
| 69 | United Artists UP 2267 | Don't Vote For Luke McCabe/The Proof Of The Pudding | 18 |

KING SCRATCH
| 70s | Ethnic ETH 16 | Spiritual Whip/Version | 18 |
| 70s | Ethnic ETH 30 | Mash Finger/Version | 20 |

(see also Lee Perry/Upsetters, Skatalites)

KINGSFOLK FOLK GROUP
| 67 | Outlet OUT 008 | Black Velvet Band/Love Is Teasin | 10 |

KING'S HENCHMEN
| 59 | Coral FEP 2025 | ALAN FREED PRESENTS VOL. 1 (EP) | 150 |

KINGSIGHTER
| 78 | Trojan TRLS 166 | THE ONE EYED GIANT (LP) | 15 |

KING SISTERS
57	Capitol CL 14711	While The Lights Are Low/In Hamburg (When The Nights Are Long)	10
58	Capitol CL 14865	Deep Purple/Unbelievable	6
57	Capitol T 808	ALOHA (LP)	15
60	Capitol ST 1333	BABY THEY'RE SINGING OUR SONG (LP)	15

PADDY KINGSLAND
| 74 | EMI 2110 | Spinball/Wobulator Rock | 6 |
| 74 | Studio 2 TWOX 1024 | SUPERCHARGED (LP) | 20 |

CHARLES KINGSLEY CREATION
| 65 | Columbia DB 7758 | Summer Without Sun/Still In Love With You | 70 |

EVELYN KINGSLEY & TOWERS
| 58 | Capitol CL 14944 | To Know Him Is To Love Him/FRANK PERRY & TOWERS: Let Me Be The One | 20 |

(see also Towers)

KINGSMEN (1)
| 58 | London HLE 8735 | Better Believe It/Week-End | 30 |
| 59 | London HLE 8812 | Conga Rock/The Cat Walk | 30 |

KINGSMEN (2)

MINT VALUE £

59	London REE 1211	THE KINGSMEN (EP)	100

(see also Bill Haley & Comets)

KINGSMEN (2)

63	Pye International 7N 25231	Louie Louie/Haunted Castle	30
64	Pye International 7N 25262	Little Latin Lupe Lu/David's Mood	15
64	Pye International 7N 25273	Death Of An Angel/Searching For Love	10
65	Pye International 7N 25292	The Jolly Green Giant/Long Green	8
65	Pye International 7N 25311	The Climb/Waiting	10
65	Pye International 7N 25322	Annie Fanny/Something's Got A Hold On Me	10
66	Pye International 7N 25366	Little Latin Lupe Lu/Louie Louie	15
66	Pye International 7N 25370	Killer Joe/Little Green Thing	10
67	Pye International 7N 25406	Daytime Shadows/Trouble	10
71	Wand WN 14	Louie Louie/If I Needed Someone	8
64	Pye Intl. NEP 44023	THE KINGSMEN (EP)	30
65	Pye Intl. NEP 44040	MOJO WORKOUT (EP)	35
66	Pye Intl. NEP 44063	FEVER (EP)	40
63	Pye Intl. NPL 28050	THE KINGSMEN IN PERSON (LP, live)	25
64	Pye Intl. NPL 28054	THE KINGSMEN VOLUME II (LP)	25
65	Pye Intl. NPL 28068	THE KINGSMEN ON CAMPUS (LP)	25
66	Pye Intl. NPL 28085	15 GREAT HITS (LP)	20

(see also Touch)

KINGS OF CONVENIENCE

01	Source SOURLP 019	QUIET IS THE NEW LOUD (LP)	40
01	Source SOURLP 040	VERSUS (LP, gatefold sleeve)	30
04	Source SOURLP 099	RIOT ON AN EMPTY STREET (LP)	50

KINGS OF LEON

03	Handmedown HMD 20	HOLY ROLLER NOVOCAINE EP: Molly's Chambers/California Waiting/Holy Roller Novocaine (10", clear red vinyl, numbered p/s, 1000 only)	10
03	Handmedown HMD 28	Molly's Chambers/Holy Roller Novocaine (10", limited issue, numbered p/s)	10
04	Handmedown HMD 43	The Bucket/Trani (Live) (numbered p/s)	10
05	Handmedown HMD 50	King Of The Rodeo/Soft (Live) (numbered p/s)	6
08	RCA 88697 36890 7	Sex On Fire/Beneath The Surface (p/s)	15
08	RCA 88697 4122 7	Use Somebody/Knocked Up (Lykke Li Vs Rodeo Remix) (p/s)	10
03	Handmedown HMD 26	YOUTH & YOUNG MANHOOD (LP, 2 x 10", p/s with picture inners)	35
04	Handmedown HMD 40	AHA SHAKE HEARTBREAK (2-LP, 10" clear vinyl, gatefold sleeve)	35
08	RCA 88697 32712 1	ONLY BY THE NIGHT (2-LP)	20
10	RCA 88697 78241 1	COME AROUND SUNDOWN (2-LP, gatefold, inners)	25

KING SOUNDS

78	Grove Music GMDM 5	Spend One Night In Babylon (feat. Trinity)/Keep Us Down In Poverty (feat. Jah Woosh) (12")	25
78	Grove Music GM 13	To The Other Man/Bad Water	10
79	Grove Music GMDM 11	They That Hate Us (wrongfully)/Ungrateful Brethren (12")	15
79	Grove Music GMDM 20	Kill Them Dead/Look Into Youself (12")	20
79	Grove GMLP 22	COME ZION SIDE HAPPINESS (LP)	15

KING SPARROW

58	Melodisc MEL 1447	Leading Calypsonians/BILLY MOORE: Love Is Everywhere	10
58	Melodisc MEL 1475	Familysize Cokes/Clara Honey Bunch	10
59	Melodisc MEL 1491	Goaty/I Confess	10

(see also Mighty)

KING SPORTY

70	Banana BA 321	Inspiration/Choice Of Music	20
70	Banana BA 322	Lover's Version (as Sporty & Wilson)/DUDLEY SIBLEY: Having A Party	22
70	Punch PH 44	For Our Desire/WINSTON WRIGHT: Version	15
71	Banana BA 323	D.J. Special/RICHARD & MAD: Creation Version	20
73	Green Door GD 4063	Yearful Of Sundays/Version	8
86	Dancefloor DFLP 3002	MEET ME AT THE DISCO (LP)	15

(see also Delroy Wilson)

KING STITT

69	Clandisc CLA 200	Who Yea/DYNAMITES: Mr Midnight	20
69	Clandisc CLA 202	Vigerton Two/On The Street	20
69	Clandisc CLA 203	On The Street/CYNTHIA RICHARDS: Foolish Fool	25
69	Clandisc CLA 206	The Ugly One/CLANCY ECCLES: Dance Beat	45
70	Clandisc CLA 207	Herbsman Shuffle (with Andy [Capp])/HIGGS & WILSON: Don't Mind Me	20
70	Clandisc CLA 223	King Of Kings/DYNAMITES: Reggaedelic	20
71	Clandisc CLA 235	Merry Rhythm/CLANCY ECCLES: John Crow Skank	15
71	Banana BA 332	Back Out Version/VEGETABLES: Holly Rhythm	25
71	Banana BA 334	Rhyming Time/Reality	30

(see also Kurass)

KINGSTON JOE

64	Blue Beat BB 253	Time Is On My Friend (actually by Lloyd Barnes)/Wear And Tear (B-side actually by Lascelles Perkins)	30

KINGSTON PETE & BUSTER'S ALL STARS

67	Blue Beat BB 403	Little Boy Blue/I'm A Lover Try Me (actually by Larry Marshall)	200

(see also Larry Marshall)

KINGSTON ALLSTARS

66	Dice CC 25	Happy Hunter/LITTLE NORMA: Ten Commandments Of Woman	125

KINGSTONIANS

67	Rio R 140	Winey Winey/I Don't Care	30
68	Coxsone CS 7066	Mother Miserable/I Make A Woman	300
68	Doctor Bird DB 1120	Put Down Your Fire/Girls Like Dirt	150
68	Doctor Bird DB 1123	Mummy And Daddy/False Witness	100

KINGSTON TRIO

                                                                                                                    MINT VALUE £

68	Doctor Bird DB 1126	Fun Galore/Crime Don't Pay	100
68	Trojan TR 627	Mix It Up/I'll Be Around	40
69	Big Shot BI 508	Sufferer/Kiss A Little Finger	75
69	Big Shot BI 526	Nice Nice/I'll Be Around	80
69	Crab CRAB 19	Hold Down/BARRY YORK: Who Will She Be	150
69	Bullet BU 409	I Am Just A Minstrel/Yesterday	25
69	Crab CRAB 43	The Clip/KEITH & TEX: Tighten Up Your Gird (white labels only)	300
69	Songbird SB 1011	The Clip/BRUCE ANTHONY: Little Miss Muffett	50
70	Songbird SB 1019	Singer Man/CRYSTALITES: Version	15
70	Songbird SB 1041	Rumble Rumble/CRYSTALITES: Version	35
70	Songbird SB 1045	Out There/CRYSTALITES: Out There Version II	35
70	Trojan TR 7708	I'll Need You Tomorrow/I'm Gonna Make It	10
70	Duke DU 88	You Can't Wine/RUPIE EDWARDS ALLSTARS: Bee Sting	20
72	Duke DU 126	Lion's Den/Version	15
70	Trojan TBL 113	SUFFERER (LP)	70

(see also Jack (Bernard) & Beanstalks, Gregory Isaacs, Jackie Bernard)

KINGSTON TRIO

58	Capitol CL 14951	Tom Dooley/Ruby Red	6
60	Capitol CL 15161	Everglades/This Mornin', This Evenin', So Soon	7

(see also John Stewart)

KING TRUMAN

89	Acid Jazz JAZID 9T	Like A Gun (Safe Sax Mix)/(Dub Version)/(Radio Edit) (12", p/s)	80

(see also Style Council, Paul Weller)

KING TUBBY

75	Grounation GROL 502	THE ROOTS OF DUB (LP)	35
75	Live & Love LALP 02	MEETS THE AGGROVATORS AT THE DUB STATION (LP)	100
76	Fay FMLP 307	SURROUNDED BY DREAD AT THE NATIONAL ARENA (LP)	80
76	Klik KLIP 9002	SHALOM DUB (LP)	45
77	Fay Music FMLP 304	KING TUBBY MEETS THE UPSETTER AT THE GRASS ROOTS OF DUB (LP, with Lee Perry)	60
78	Studio 16 WE 100	KING TUBBY MEETS THE UPSETTER AT THE GRASS ROOTS OF DUB (LP, reissue, with Lee Perry)	35
78	Studio 16 WE 102	SURROUNDED BY DREAD AT THE NATIONAL ARENA (LP, re-issue)	35
79	Star PTLP 1029	MAJESTIC DUB (LP)	25
81	Live & Love LAP 015	UPSETS THE UPSETTER (LP)	35
81	Vista Sounds VSLP 2006	KING AT THE CONTROL (LP)	50
94	Blood & Fire BAFLP 002	DUB GONE CRAZY (LP)	20
99	Blood & Fire SVLP 260	DUB LIKE DIRT (2-LP)	25

KING TUBBY & THE AGGROVATORS

82	Black Music BMLP 804	DUBBING IN THE BACKYARD (LP)	50

KING TUBBY, PRINCE JAMMY & SCIENTIST

81	K&G Imperial KGLP 002	FIRST, SECOND AND THIRD GENERATION OF DUB (LP)	60

KING TUBBY MEETS ROOTS RADICS

81	Copasetic COPLP 5002	DANGEROUS DUB (LP)	50

KING TUBBY & YABBY U

76	Prophets (No Cat No)	PROPHECY OF DUB (LP, green label in plain sleeve)	140

KINKS

SINGLES : PYE SINGLES

64	Pye 7N 15611	Long Tall Sally/I Took My Baby Home	120
64	Pye 7N 15611	Long Tall Sally/I Took My Baby Home (Demo copy)	150
64	Pye 7N 15636	You Still Want Me/You Do Something To Me	200
64	Pye 7N 15636	You Still Want Me/You Do Something To Me (Demo copy)	150
64	Pye 7N 15673	You Really Got Me/It's All Right	15
64	Pye 7N 15673	You Really Got Me/It's All Right (Demo copy)	150
64	Pye 7N 15714	All Day And All Of The Night/I Gotta Move	12
64	Pya 7N 15673	All Day And All Of The Night/I Gotta Move (Demo copy)	150
65	Pye 7N 15759	Tired Of Waiting For You/Come On Now	12
65	Pye 7N 15759	Tired Of Waiting For You/Come On Now (Demo copy)	100
65	Pye 7N 15813	Everybody's Gonna Be Happy/Who'll Be The Next In Line	10
65	Pye 7N 15854	Set Me Free/I Need You	8
65	Pye 7N 15919	See My Friend/Never Met A Girl Like You Before	8
65	Pye 7N 15981	Till The End Of The Day/Where Have All The Good Times Gone	10
66	Pye 7N 17064	Dedicated Follower Of Fashion/Sittin' On My Sofa	8
66	Pye 7N 17125	Sunny Afternoon/I'm Not Like Everybody Else	8
66	Pye 7N 17222	Dead End Street/Big Black Smoke (some labels list "Deadend")	8
67	Pye 7N 17321	Waterloo Sunset/Act Nice And Gentle	10
67	Pye 7N 17400	Autumn Almanac/Mr. Pleasant	10
68	Pye 7N 17468	Wonderboy/Polly	15
68	Pye 7N 17573	Days/She's Got Everything	15
69	Pye 7N 17724	Plastic Man/King Kong	15
69	Pye 7N 17776	Drivin'/Mindless Child Of Motherhood	35
69	Pye 7N 17812	Shangri-La/Last Of The Steam-Powered Trains (unissued, acetates only)	0
69	Pye 7N 17812	Shangri-La/This Man He Weeps Tonight	25
69	Pye 7N 17865	Victoria/Mr Churchill Says	15
70	Pye 7N 17961	Lola/Berkeley Mews	6
70	Pye 7N 45016	Apeman/Rats	8
71	Pye PMM 100	You Really Got Me/Set Me Free/Wonder Boy/Long Tall Shorty (maxi-single, no p/s)	10
71	Pye 7NX 8001	PERCY (33rpm 4-track maxi-single, p/s)	20
74	Pye 7N 45313	Where Have All The Good Times Gone/Lola (p/s)	20

KINKS

MINT VALUE £

SINGLES : EXPORT SINGLES

65	Pye 7N 15981	Till The End Of The Day/Where Have All The Good Times Gone (export p/s)	150
66	Pye 7N 17100	Well Respected Man/Milk Cow Blues	120
67	Pye 7N 17314	Mr. Pleasant/This Is Where I Belong	100
67	Pye 7N 17405	Autumn Almanac/David Watts	100
71	Pye 7N 8001	God's Children/Moments (in p/s)	60
71	Pye 7N 8001	God's Children/Moments	30

SINGLES : RCA SINGLES

72	RCA RCA 2211	Supersonic Rocket Ship/You Don't Know My Name	6
72	RCA RCA 2299	Celluloid Heroes/Hot Potatoes	8
73	RCA RCA 2387	Sitting In The Midday Sun/One Of The Survivors	8
73	RCA RCA 2418	Sweet Lady Genevieve/Sitting In My Hotel	8
74	RCA RCA 5015	Mirror Of Love/Cricket	12
74	RCA RCA 5042	Mirror Of Love/He's Evil	12
74	RCA RCA 2478	Holiday Romance/Shepherds Of The Nation	10
75	RCA RCA 2546	Ducks On The Wall/Rush Hour Blues	10
75	RCA RCA 2567	You Can't Stop The Music/Have Another Drink	10
76	RCA RCM 1	No More Looking Back/Jack The Idiot Dunce/The Hard Way (p/s)	12

SINGLES : ARISTA SINGLES

77	Arista ARIST 153	Father Christmas/Prince Of The Punks (p/s)	10
78	Arista ARIST 189	A Rock'n'Roll Fantasy/Artificial Light	8
78	Arista ARIST 210	Black Messiah/Misfits (p/s)	8
79	Arista ARIST 300	Moving Pictures/In A Space (p/s)	8
80	Arista ARIST 404	Lola (live)/Celluloid Heroes (live) (export only)	12
81	Arista ARIST 415	Better Things/Massive Reductions (p/s)	10
81	Arista ARIST 415/KINKS 1	Better Things/Massive Reductions//Lola (live)/David Watts (live) (double pack, gatefold p/s)	8
83	Arista ARIST 524	Don't Forget To Dance/Bernadette (p/s)	7

SINGLES : OTHER SINGLES

84	Music Week LONF119	How Are You/The Video (freebie with Music Week magazine)	7
86	London LON 119	How Are You/Killing Time (p/s)	12
88	London LON 165	The Road (7" Edit)/Art Lover (p/s)	8
89	London LON 239	Down All The Days (Til 1992)/You Really Got Me (live) (p/s)	6
90	London LON 250	How Do I Get Close/War Is Over (p/s)	6

EPs

64	Pye NEP 24200	KINKSIZE SESSION	30
64	Pye NEP 24203	KINKSIZE HITS	40
65	Pye NEP 24221	KWYET KINKS	45
66	Pye NEP 24258	DEDICATED KINKS	120
68	Pye NEP 24296	THE KINKS	275
75	Pye AMEP 1001	THE KINKS ('Yesteryear' export issue, red or blue vinyl)	22

ALBUMS : PYE ALBUMS

64	Pye NPL 18096	THE KINKS (mono)	175
64	Pye NSPL 83021	THE KINKS (stereo, export only)	250
65	Pye NSPL 18096	THE KINKS (stereo, export only, reissue)	275
65	Pye NPL 18112	KINDA KINKS	150
65	Pye NPL 18131	THE KINK KONTROVERSY	100
65	Pye NSPL 18131	THE KINK KONTROVERSY (reprocessed stereo with stickered catalogue number, export only)	300
66	Pye NPL 18149	FACE TO FACE (mono)	120
66	Pye NSPL 18149	FACE TO FACE (stereo, stickered sleeve "export only")	225
66	Pye NSLP 18149	FACE TO FACE (LP original issue)	100
67	Golden Guinea GGL 0357	THE KINKS (reissue, mono)	25
67	Golden Guinea GGGL 10357	THE KINKS (reissue, stereo)	30
67	Pye NPL 18191	LIVE AT KELVIN HALL (mono)	100
67	Pye N(S)PL 18191	LIVE AT KELVIN HALL (stereo)	150

(The Pye LPs listed above were originally issued with laminated flipback sleeves, pink labels & light blue labels.)

67	Pye NPL 18193	SOMETHING ELSE BY THE KINKS (mono)	200
67	Pye N(S)PL 18193	SOMETHING ELSE BY THE KINKS (stereo)	150
68	Pye N(S)PL 18233	THE KINKS ARE THE VILLAGE GREEN PRESERVATION SOCIETY (unissued, 12-track version, test pressings only)	1000
68	Pye NPL 18233	THE KINKS ARE THE VILLAGE GREEN PRESERVATION SOCIETY (15-track version, mono)	500
68	Pye N(S)PL 18233	THE KINKS ARE THE VILLAGE GREEN PRESERVATION SOCIETY (15-track version, stereo)	300
69	Pye NPL 18317	ARTHUR (mono, gatefold sleeve "Quiien Victoria" insert)	300
69	Pye N(S)PL 18317	ARTHUR (stereo, gatefold sleeve "Quiien Victoria" insert)	250
70	Pye NPL 18326	THE KINKS (2-LP, gatefold sleeve)	20
70	Pye NSPL 18359	THE KINKS PT 1 - LOLA VS POWERMAN & THE MONEY-GO-ROUND (gatefold sleeve)	150
71	Pye NSPL 18365	SOUNDTRACK FROM THE FILM 'PERCY' (soundtrack)	50
73	Pye 11PP 100	ALL THE GOOD TIMES (4-LP, box set)	80
83	PRT KINK 1	GREATEST HITS (with bonus 10" EP of unreleased material)	40

ALBUMS : OTHER ALBUMS

71	RCA SF 8243	MUSWELL HILLBILLIES (gatefold sleeve)	100
72	RCA DPS 2035	EVERYBODY'S IN SHOWBIZ, EVERYBODY'S A STAR (2-LP, gatefold sleeve)	25
73	RCA SF 8392	PRESERVATION ACT 1	40
74	RCA LPL2 5040	PRESERVATION ACT 2 (2-LP, gatefold sleeve)	35
75	RCA SF 8411	SOAP OPERA (gatefold sleeve)	35
75	RCA RS 1028	SCHOOLBOYS IN DISGRACE	40
76	RCA RS 1059	CELLULOID HEROES	20

77	Arista SPART 1002	SLEEPWALKER (LP, with photo inner sleeve)	25
78	Arista SPARTY 1055	MISFITS (LP, photo inner sleeve)	20
79	Arista SPART 1099	LOW BUDGET (LP, with photo inner sleeve)	20
80	Arista DARTY 6	ONE FOR THE ROAD (2-LP, gatefold)	30
81	Arista SPART 1171	GIVE THE PEOPLE WHAT THEY WANT (LP)	20
83	Arista 205 275	STATE OF CONFUSION (LP)	15
84	Arista 206 685	WORD OF MOUTH (LP)	15
86	London LONLP 27	THINK VISUAL (LP, inner)	15
89	London LONLP 49	LIVE: ON THE ROAD (LP)	15
89	London 828 165 1	UK JIVE (LP)	20
93	Sony 472489-1	PHOBIA (omits 2 tracks from CD)	35
94	Konk KNKLP 1	TO THE BONE (LP)	70
98	Earmark 42004	FACE TO FACE (LP, reissue)	18
01	Sanctuary SANTV 010	BBC SESSIONS 1964-1977 (3-LP)	80

ALBUMS : REISSUES

79	Pye NPL 18096	THE KINKS (LP, reissue, mono, grey labels)	15
79	Pye NPL 18131	KINDA KINKS (LP, reissue, grey labels)	15
79	Pye NPL1831	THE KINK KONTROVERSY (LP, reissue, grey labels)	15
79	Pye NPL 18131	FACE TO FACE (LP, reissue, grey labels)	15
79	Pye NSPL 18191	LIVE AT KELVIN HALL (LP, reissue, grey labels)	15
79	Pye NSPL 18193	SOMETHING ELSE BY THE KINKS (LP, reissue, stereo, grey labels)	15
79	Pye NSPL 18233	THE KINKS ARE THE VILLAGE GREEN PRESERVATION SOCIETY (LP, reissue, stereo, grey labels)	15
81	Precision NSPL 18191	LIVE AT KELVIN HALL (LP, reissue, blue/white labels)	15
82	Fame FA 3048	SLEEPWALKER (LP, reissue)	15
82	PRT 18096	THE KINKS (LP, reissue, green/red labels)	15
82	PRT NPL 18149	FACE TO FACE (LP, reissue, red/green labels)	15
82	Pye NSPL 18191	LIVE AT KELVIN HALL (LP, reissue, green/red labels)	15
82	PRT NSPL 18233	THE KINKS ARE THE VILLAGE GREEN PRESERVATION SOCIETY (LP, reissue, green/red labels)	15
85	PRT FBLP 8091	THE KINKS ARE THE VILLAGE GREEN PRESERVATION SOCIETY (LP, reissue, different cover)	20
87	PRT 6002	THE KINKS (LP, reissue, grey labels)	15
87	PRT PYL 6003	KINDA KINKS (LP, reissue, green/red labels)	15
87	PRT PYL 6004	THE KINK KONTROVERSY (LP, reissue, green/red labels)	15
87	Pye PYL 6005	FACE TO FACE (LP, reissue)	15
87	Pye PYL 6008	LIVE AT KELVIN HALL (LP, reissue, grey labels)	15
87	PRT PYL 6008	THE KINKS ARE THE VILLAGE GREEN PRESERVATION SOCIETY (LP, reissue)	15
87	PRT NSPL 18193	SOMETHING ELSE BY THE KINKS (LP, reissue, green/red labels)	15
97	Castle ORLP 005	THE KINKS ARE THE VILLAGE GREEN PRESERVATION SOCIETY (LP, reissue, free 7")	25
00	Castle ESMLP 482	THE KINKS (LP, reissue)	15
00	Castle ESLP 483	KINDA KINKS (LP, reissue)	15
00	Castle ESMLP 484	THE KINK KONTROVERSY (LP, reissue)	15
00	Castle ESMLP 485	FACE TO FACE (LP, reissue)	15
00	Castle CMHLP 875	SOMETHING ELSE BY THE KINKS (LP, reissue)	15
00	Castle CMHLP 001	ARTHUR (LP, reissue)	15
00	Castle CMHLP 012	LIVE AT KELVIN HALL (LP, reissue)	15
00	Castle ESMLP 890	THE KINKS PT 1 - LOLA VS POWERMAN & THE MONEY-GO-ROUND (LP, reissue)	15
00	Castle ESMLP 891	PERCY (LP, reissue)	15
11	UMC/Sanctuary 273220	THE KINKS ARE THE VILLAGE GREEN PRESERVATION SOCIETY (2-LP, reissue, marbled green vinyl, 1000 only)	60
12	UMC/Sanctuary 2732148	SOMETHING ELSE BY THE KINKS (2-LP, reissue, red vinyl, 500 only)	50
12	UMC/Sanctuary 2732277	ARTHUR (2-LP, reissue, white vinyl, 500 only)	40
16	Sanctuary/BMG KINKSBOX003	THE MONO COLLECTION (10-LP, box set)	350
12	UMC/Sanctuary 2783111	FACE TO FACE (2-LP, reissue, blue vinyl, 500 only)	40
18	BMG BMGAA 09 BOX	THE KINKS ARE THE VILLAGE GREEN PRESERVATION SOCIETY (3-LP, 5-CD, 3 x 7" reissue box set)	100
19	BMG BMGCAT 407 BOX	ARTHUR (3-CD, 3 x 7", box set reissue)	40

(see also Dave Davies, Maple Oak, Leapy Lee)

TONY KINSEY (QUARTET)

55	Decca F 10548	She's Funny That Way/Fascinatin' Rhythm	15
55	Decca F 10606	Close Your Eyes/Pierrot	15
55	Decca F 10648	Hey! There/Ballet	25
56	Decca F 10708	Stompin' At The Savoy/China Boy (with Dill Jones)	6
56	Decca F 10709	Moonglow/One O'Clock Jump	6
56	Decca FJ 10725	Starboard Bow/Body And Soul	6
56	Decca FJ 10760	Lullaby Of The Leaves/Isolation	12
56	Decca FJ 10773	In A Ditch/A Smooth One	8
57	Decca FJ 10851	Mean To Me/Supper Party	12
57	Decca F 10952	The Midgets/Blue Eyes	6
62	Ember JBS 707	Girl In Blue/Weber The Great	20
56	Decca DFE 6282	PRESENTING THE TONY KINSEY QUARTET NO. 1 (EP)	40
56	Decca DFE 6285	PRESENTING THE TONY KINSEY QUARTET NO. 2 (EP)	40
58	Decca DFE 6461	MY FAIR LADY (EP)	15
59	Parlophone SGE 2004	RED BIRD - JAZZ AND POETRY (EP, mono [GEP 8765]/stereo, with Christopher Logue)	15
59	Parlophone SGE 2008	FOURSOME (EP, stereo, also mono GEP 8895)	15
57	Decca LK 4186	INTRODUCING THE QUINTET (LP)	100
57	Decca LK 4207	JAZZ AT THE FLAMINGO (LP)	150
58	Decca LK 4274	TIME GENTLEMEN PLEASE (LP)	100

Tony KINSEY TRIO & JOE HARRIOTT

MINT VALUE £

61	Ember EMB 3337	AN EVENING WITH ... (LP)	70
63	Decca LK 4534	HOW TO SUCCEED IN BUSINESS WITHOUT REALLY TRYING (LP, with Gordon Beck)	50

TONY KINSEY TRIO & JOE HARRIOTT

54	Esquire EP 36	TONY KINSEY TRIO & JOE HARRIOTT (EP)	50
54	Esquire EP 52	TONY KINSEY TRIO & JOE HARRIOTT (EP)	50
54	Esquire EP 82	TONY KINSEY TRIO & JOE HARRIOTT (EP)	50

(see also Joe Harriott)

KINSMEN

68	Decca F 22724	Glasshouse Green, Splinter Red/It's Started To Rain Again	45
68	Decca F 22777	It's Good To See You/Always The Loser	10

(see also Four Kinsmen)

KIPPINGTON LODGE

67	Parlophone R 5645	Shy Boy/Lady On A Bicycle	40
68	Parlophone R 5677	Rumours/And She Cried	40
68	Parlophone R 5717	Tell Me A Story/Understand A Woman	40
68	Parlophone R 5750	Tomorrow Today/Turn Out The Light	40
69	Parlophone R 5776	In My Life/I Can See Her Face	90
78	EMI NUT 2894	KIPPINGTON LODGE (EP)	12

(see also Brinsley Schwarz, Nick Lowe)

KIRBY

76	Anchor ANC 1031	Love Letters/Flasher	12
78	Hot Wax WAX 1/ANCHO 1	Bottom Line/That's Some Dream	10
78	Hot Wax HW 2	COMPOSITION (LP)	75
94	Backtrack Archive HW 2	COMPOSITION (LP, reissue)	30

(see also Curved Air, Stretch)

KATHY KIRBY

60	Pye 7N 15313	Love Can Be/Crush Me	20
61	Pye 7N 15342	Danny/Now You're Crying	20
62	Decca F 11506	Big Man/Slowly	7
66	Decca F 12432	The Adam Adamant Theme/Will I Never Learn?	25
68	Columbia DB 8400	I Almost Called Your Name/Let The Music Start	8
68	Columbia DB 8521	Come Back Here With My Heart/Antonio	8
69	Columbia DB 8559	I'll Catch The Sun/Please Help Me I'm Falling	8
69	Columbia DB 8634	Is That All There Is?/Knowing When To Leave	8
70	Columbia DB 8682	Wheel Of Fortune/Lucky	8
70	Columbia DB 8721	My Way/Little Green Apples	8
71	Columbia DB 8795	So Here I Go/Yes - I've Got (A-side titled "Here I Go Again" on demos)	8
71	Decca F 13228	Bill/Can't Help Lovin' Dat Man	7
72	Columbia DB 8910	Do You Really Have A Heart/Dream On, Dreamer	8
73	Columbia DB 8965	Little Song For You/Here, There And Everywhere	8
73	Orange OAS 216	Singer With The Band/Hello Morning	60
76	President PT 455	My Prayer/Nobody Loves Me Like You Do	7
81	President PT 491	He/Nobody Loves Me Like You	7
63	Decca DFE 8547	KATHY KIRBY (EP)	10
65	Decca DFE 8596	KATHY KIRBY VOL. 2 (EP)	10
65	Decca DFE 8611	A SONG FOR EUROPE (EP)	10
67	Decca LK 4746	MAKE SOMEONE HAPPY (LP)	25
68	Columbia S(C)X 6259	MY THANKS TO YOU (LP)	40

LARRY KIRBY & ENCORES

59	Top Rank JAR 143	My Baby Don't Love Me/My Rose Of Kentucky	15

PAT KIRBY

56	Brunswick 05560	Happiness Is A Thing Called Joe/Don't Tell Me Not To	7
56	Brunswick 05575	What A Heavenly Night For Love/Greensleeves	7
57	Brunswick 05697	Tammy/Don't Keep Silent	7
58	Brunswick 05731	Sayonara/Please Be Gentle With Me	7

BASIL KIRCHIN (BAND)

59	Parlophone R 4527	Rock-A-Conga/Skin Tight (as Basil Kirchin Band)	6
71	Columbia SCX 6463	WORLD WITHIN WORLDS (LP)	800
74	Island HELP18	WORLD WITHIN WORLDS (not a reissue but second LP)	80
03	Trunk JBH 003 LP	QUANTUM LP, hand numbered, 500 only)	80
04	Trunk JBH 005 LP	CHARCOAL SKETCHES/STATES OF MIND (LP, 500 only)	60
05	Trunk JBH 012 LP	ABSTRACTIONS OF THE INDUSTRIAL NORTH (LP)	75
06	Trunk JBH 021 LP	PARTICLES (LP)	20
10	Trunk JBH 038 LP	PRIMITIVE LONDON (LP, 500 only)	18
19	Trunk JBH 080 LP	WORLDS WITHIN WORLDS PARTS 1 & 2 (LP, gold vinyl)	50
19	Trunk JBH 080 LP	WORLDS WITHIN WORLDS PARTS 1 & 2 (LP, black vinyl)	20

(see also Basil Kirchin, London Studio Group)

(IVOR & BASIL) KIRCHIN BAND

54	Parlophone MSP 6144	Mambo Macoco/Tangerine (as Kirchin Band)	10
55	Decca F 10434	Minor Mambo/Mother Goose Jumps (as Kirchin Band)	15
56	Parlophone R 4222	The Roller/St. Louis Blues (as Ivor & Basil Kirchin)	7
56	Parlophone R 4237	Rockin' & Rollin' Thru The Darktown Strutters' Ball/Ambush	20
57	Parlophone R 4266	Rock Around The World Medley (with Shani Wallis)	18
57	Parlophone R 4335	Teenage World/So Rare (as Kirchin Band & Bandits)	10
55	Psrlophone GEP 8556	THE BIGGEST LITTLE BAND IN THE WORLD (EP)	15
55	Decca DFE 6237	MEET THE KIRCHINS (EP)	15
55	Parlophone GEP 8531	KIRCHIN BANDBOX (EP)	15
56	Parlophone GEP 8569	THE IVOR AND BASIL KIRCHIN BAND (EP)	30

DEE KIRK

62	Salvo SLO 1809	I'll Cry/My Used To Be (99 copies only)	15

KEVIN KIRK

MINT VALUE £

KEVIN KIRK
62	Columbia DB 4909	Sweet/Don't Waste Your Tears On Him	6
62	Columbia DB 4863	Teenage Heartache/Midnight	7

RICHARD H. KIRK
86	Rough Trade RTT 199	Hypnotic/Martyrs Of Palestine (12", p/s)	15
81	Industrial IRC 34	DISPOSABLE HALF TRUTHS (cassette)	20
83	Doublevision DVR 2	TIME HIGH FICTION (2-LP)	30
86	Rough Trade RTM 189	UGLY SPIRIT (LP)	15
86	Rough Trade ROUGH 99	BLACK JESUS VOICE (LP)	15
94	Warp WARPLP 19	VIRTUAL STATE (2-LP)	25
95	Warp WARPLP 32	THE NUMBER OF MAGIC (2-LP)	30

(see also Cabaret Voltaire,, Cold Warrior, Chemical Agent,, Multiple Transmission, Papdoctrine, Robots and Humanoids, Sandoz, Electronic Eye, Sweet Exorcist)

(RAHSAAN) ROLAND KIRK
64	Mercury 10015 MCE	THE KIRK QUARTET MEETS THE BENNY GOLSON ORCHESTRA (EP)	10
65	Mercury 10016 MCE	ROLAND SPEAKS (EP, with Benny Golson Orchestra)	10
62	Esquire 32-164	KIRK'S WORK (LP, with Jack McDuff)	30
63	Mercury MMC 14126	WE FREE KINGS (LP)	30
64	Mercury MCL 20002	THE KIRK QUARTET MEETS THE BENNY GOLSON ORCHESTRA (LP)	30
64	Mercury MCL 20021	KIRK IN COPENHAGEN (LP)	20
64	Mercury SMWL 21020	GIFTS & MESSAGES (LP)	15
65	Mercury MCL 20045	DOMINO (LP)	20
65	Fontana FJL 114	HIP! (LP)	20
66	Mercury (S)LML 4005	I TALK WITH THE SPIRITS (LP)	15
66	Mercury (S)LML 4015	RIP, RIG AND PANIC (LP)	15
67	Mercury (S)LML 4019	SLIGHTLY LATIN (LP)	20
67	Verve 9193	NOW PLEASE DON'T YOU CRY BEAUTIFUL EDITH (LP)	18
68	Atlantic 588112	THE INFLATED TEAR (LP)	20
69	Atlantic 588 207	VOLUNTEERED SLAVERY (LP)	20
70	Atlantic 588178	LEFT & RIGHT (LP)	25

KIRKBYS
66	RCA RCA 1542	It's A Crime/I've Never Been So Much In Love	150

(see also 23rd Turnoff, Jimmy Campbell, Rockin' Horse, Merseybeats)

KEN KIRKHAM
56	Columbia SCM 5244	It's Almost Tomorrow/No Not Much	10
58	Columbia DB 4116	Now And For Always/Cathy	6
61	Decca F 11336	A Kiss In Time (Can Save A Broken Heart)/Never	6

JOHN KIRKPATRICK (& SUE HARRIS)
72	Trailer LER 2033	JUMP AT THE SUN (LP, with Sue Harris, first pressing with red/black label)	25
75	Trailer LER 2033	JUMP AT THE SUN (LP, with Sue Harris, repressing with yellow label)	15
76	Topic 12TS 295	AMONG THE MANY ATTRACTIONS AT THE SHOW WILL BE A REALLY HIGH-CLASS BAND (LP, with Sue Harris)	20

(see also Jon Raven)

JULIAN KIRSCH
69	Columbia DB 8541	Clever Little Man/The Adventures Of A Young Cuckoo	40

DANNY KIRWAN
75	DJM DJS 10783	Hot Summer's Day/Love Can Always Bring You Happiness (demo in p/s)	8
75	DJM DJS 10783	Hot Summer's Day/Love Can Always Bring You Happiness	6
75	DJM DJLPS 454	SECOND CHAPTER (LP, gatefold sleeve)	15

(see also Fleetwood Mac, Tramp)

KISS
SINGLES
75	Casablanca CBX 503	Nothin' To Lose/Love Theme From Kiss	25
75	Casablanca CBX 510	Rock And Roll All Nite/Anything For My Baby	25
76	Casablanca CBX 516	Shout It Out Loud/Sweet Pain	15
76	Casablanca CBX 519	Beth/God Of Thunder	18
77	Casablanca CAN 102	Hard Luck Woman/Calling Dr Love/Beth (in p/s)	35
77	Casablanca CAN 102	Hard Luck Woman/Calling Dr Love/Beth	10
77	Casablanca CAN 110	Then She Kissed Me/Hooligan/Flaming Youth	15
77	Casablanca CANL 110	Then She Kissed Me/Hooligan/Flaming Youth (12", company sleeve)	10
78	Casablanca CAN 117	Rocket Ride/Love Gun (live)	8
78	Casablanca CANL 117	Rocket Ride/Detroit Rock City (live)/Love Gun (live) (12", company sleeve)	12
78	Casablanca CAN 126	Rock And Roll All Nite/C'Mon And Love Me (in p/s)	25
78	Casablanca CAN 126	Rock And Roll All Nite/C'Mon And Love Me	8
79	Casablanca CAN 152	I Was Made For Lovin' You/Hard Times	8
79	Casablanca CANL 152	I Was Made For Lovin' You (extended)/Charisma (12", p/s)	10
79	Casablanca CAN 163	Sure Know Something/Dirty Livin' (no p/s)	6
80	Casablanca NB 1001	2000 Man/I Was Made For Lovin' You/Sure Know Something (p/s)	15
80	Casablanca NBL 1001	2000 Man/I Was Made For Lovin' You/Sure Know Something (12", co. sleeve)	12
80	Casablanca MER 19	Talk To Me/She's So European (p/s)	10
80	Casablanca KISS 1	What Makes The World Go 'Round/Naked City (p/s)	10
82	Casablanca KISS 3	Killer/I Love It Loud (pull-out tongue p/s)	12
82	Casablanca KISS 312	Killer/I Love It Loud/I Was Made For Lovin' You (12", p/s)	15
82	Casablanca KISS 4	Creatures Of The Night/Rock And Roll All Nite (live) (p/s, picture label)	10
82	Casablanca KISS 4	Creatures Of The Night/Rock And Roll All Nite (live) (p/s, silver label)	8
82	Casablanca KISS 412	Creatures Of The Night/War Machine/Rock And Roll All Nite (live) (12", p/s)	15
82	Casablanca KISSD 4	Creatures Of The Night/Rock And Roll All Nite (live) (12", double groove, autographs engraved on 1 side)	20
83	Vertigo KISSP 5	Lick It Up/Not For The Innocent (poster p/s)	6
83	Vertigo KPIC 5	Lick It Up/Not For The Innocent (tank-shaped picture disc)	20

KATIE KISSOON
MINT VALUE £

ALBUMS
75	Casablanca CBC 4003	KISS (blue 'Bogart' label) 25
75	Casablanca CBC 4004	DRESSED TO KILL (blue 'Bogart' label, embossed sleeve) 20
76	Casablanca CBC 4008	DESTROYER (blue 'Bogart' label with inner sleeve) 20
76	Casablanca CBC 4011/2	ALIVE! (2-LP, blue 'Bogart' label, gatefold sleeve with insert, sleeve also lists CBSP 401) ... 20
77	Casablanca CALH 2001	ROCK AND ROLL OVER ('lovegun' label, red vinyl) 40
77	Casablanca CAL 2006	KISS (reissue, 'lovegun' label, red vinyl) 40
77	Casablanca CAL 2007	HOTTER THAN HELL ('lovegun' label, red vinyl) 40
77	Casablanca CAL 2008	DRESSED TO KILL (reissue, 'lovegun' label, red vinyl) 40
77	Casablanca CAL 2009	DESTROYER (reissue, different sleeve, 'lovegun' label, red vinyl) 40
77	Casablanca CALD 5001	ALIVE! (2-LP, reissue, 'lovegun' label, red vinyl) 50
77	Casablanca CALH 2017	LOVE GUN ('lovegun' label, red vinyl with picture inner sleeve) 40
77	Casablanca CALD 5004	KISS ALIVE II (2-LP, 'lovegun' label, with colour booklet & transfer sheet) 25
77	Casablanca CALD 5004	KISS ALIVE II (2-LP, 'lovegun' label, red vinyl with colour booklet) 50
78	Casablanca CALD 5005	DOUBLE PLATINUM (2-LP, 'lovegun' label, silver foil embossed sleeve & insert; sleeve & insert pressed in U.S. with U.K. cat. no. sticker) 20
79	Casablanca CALH 2051	DYNASTY ('lovegun' label, black vinyl, colour inner sleeve & poster) 15
80	Mercury 6302 032	UNMASKED (with poster) 15
81	Casablanca 6302 163	(MUSIC FROM) THE ELDER (single sleeve or gatefold) 15
92	Mercury 848 037 1	REVENGE (LP) 35
98	Mercury PLP 31453 8137-2	PSYCHO CIRCUS (LP, promo only picture disc) 40

(see also Gene Simmons, Ace Frehley, Peter Criss, Paul Stanley)

KATIE KISSOON
| 69 | Columbia DB 8525 | Don't Let It Rain/Will I Never See The Sun .... 6 |
| 83 | Jive T37 | You're The One/You're The One (Instrumental) (12") .... 10 |

(see also Peanut, Marionettes, Rag Dolls [U.K.])

MAC KISSOON
| 60s | Boulevard (no cat. no.) | Wear It On Your Face/In A Dream .... 10 |

(see also Marionettes, Rag Dolls [U.K.])

KISS THE BLADE
85	Incision CUT 1-7	The Party's Begun/The Night Comes Down (p/s) 15
85	Incision CUT 1	The Party's Begun/The Night Comes Down/The Bridge (12", p/s) 25
86	Incision CUT 3	Young Soldier/The Love I Give (12" p/s) 40

KIT KATS
| 66 | London HLW 10075 | Won't Find Better Than Me/That's The Way .... 18 |

(see also New Hope)

KITCHENS
| 79 | Red Square RS 001 | DEATH OF ROCK AND ROLL EP .... 30 |

KITE
| 78 | Solent SS 050 | KITE (LP) .... 25 |

EARTHA KITT
54	HMV 7M 191	Under The Bridges Of Paris/Lovin' Spree 12
54	HMV 7M 198	Somebody Bad Stole De Wedding Bell/Sandy's Tune 8
54	HMV 7M 234	Santa Baby/Let's Do It (Let's Fall In Love) 15
56	HMV 7M 422	Honolulu Rock-A-Roll-A/Je Cherche Un Homme (I Want A Man) 20
56	MGM SP 1178	Diamonds Are A Girl's Best Friend/Good Little Girls 6
57	HMV POP 309	Just An Old-Fashioned Girl/If I Can't Take It With Me When I Go (gold label) 10
57	HMV POP 346	There Is No Cure For L'Amour/Hey Jacque 10
70	Spark SRL 1039	Hurdy Gurdy Man/Catch The Wind 20

KITTENS
| 64 | Decca F 12036 | Round About Way/Don't Stop Now .... 15 |

KIX
| 80 | Creole CR 205 | Fear Of Flying/Werewolf Walking (p/s) .... 6 |

MARK KJELDSEN
| 80 | Back Door DOOR 2 | Are You Ready/Somethings Happening .... 10 |

KLAATU
| 77 | Capitol E ST 11542 | KLAATU (LP, insert) .... 15 |

KLAN (1)
| 62 | Palette PG 9052 | Fifi The Fly/Already Mine .... 10 |

KLAN (2)
| 74 | Flux 301 | Hey Diddle Diddle/Lord .... 20 |

KLAXON 5
| 86 | él GPO 20 | Never Underestimate The Ignorance Of The Rich/Great Railway Journeys (p/s) .... 8 |

KLAXONS
06	Angular ARC 012	Gravity's Rainbow/The Bouncer (500, white label, numbered) 12
07	RINSELP1T	MYTHS OF THE NEAR FUTURE (LP, 1 side etched) 25
10	RINSELP2T	SURFING THE VOID (2-LP, 500 only, white vinyl) 20

SUSIE KLEE
| 66 | Polydor BM 56082 | Mr Zero/Punch And Judy Girl .... 15 |

KLEEER
| 81 | Atlantic K 60614 | I LOVE TO DANCE (LP) .... 15 |
| 84 | Atlantic 7801451 | INTIMATE CONNECTION (LP) .... 20 |

KLEENEX
| 79 | Rough Trade/Sunrise RT 9 | Ain't You/Hedi's Head (poster p/s) .... 15 |
| 79 | Rough Trade RT 014 | You/U (p/s) .... 10 |

(see also Liliput)

ALAN KLEIN
62	Oriole CB 1719	Striped Purple Shirt/You Gave Me The Blues 15
62	Oriole CB 1737	Three Coins In The Sewer/Danger Ahead 15
65	Parlophone R 5292	It Ain't Worth The Lonely Road Back/I've Cried So Many Tears 6

Harry KLEIN QUARTET

MINT VALUE £

69	Page One POF 119	Honey Pie/You Turned A Nightmare Into A Dream	8
70	Decca F 13033	Dinner's In The Ice Box/Here I Am, There You Are	7
64	Decca LK 4621	WELL, AT LEAST IT'S BRITISH (LP)	15

HARRY KLEIN QUARTET
56	Jazz Today JTE 105	BRASH BARITONE (EP)	30
56	Nixa NJE 1009	NEW SOUND (EP)	25
56	Nixa NJE 1022	HARRY KLEIN QUARTET (EP)	25
57	Columbia SEG 7647	BARITONE SAX (EP)	20

(see also Jazz Five)

KLEPTOMANIA
| 92 | Hypno-Genesis HG 001 | Amadeus (Martini Mix)/Amadeus (Stringi Wingi Mix)/Morf (Plastascene Mix)/Morf (Scratchi Waxi Mix) (12") | 70 |

DEAN KLEVATT
| 74 | Decca F 13495 | Don't Bury Molly/The Story Of His Life | 10 |

KLF
89	KLF Comms 004M	What Time is Love (Monster Attack Mix) (1-sided 12", 3 only)	300
89	KLF Comms. KLF 004T	What Time Is Love? (Trance Mix)/What Time Is Love? (Mix 2) (12", 'Pure Trance 1', original issue with black/green p/s)	12
89	KLF Comms. KLF 004R	What Time Is Love? ('89 Primal Remix)/What Time Is Love? (Techno Slam)/ What Time Is Love? (Trance Mix 1) (12", stickered p/s)	12
89	KLF Comms. KLF 006T	Love Trance/What Time Is Love (12", p/s, 3 copies known)	500
89	KLF Comms. KLF 008R	Last Train To Trancentral (Remixes 1 & 2) (12", p/s, 'Pure Trance 5', 2,000 pressed, some warped, price is for unwarped copy)	40
89	KLF Comms. KLF 010IR	Deep Shit Deep Shit Part 3 (the Illegal Remix)/Deep Shit Part 2/The Lovers' Side (unreleased 12", 6 copies only)	700
89	KLF PROMO 2	Kylie Said To Jason (Full Length)/Kylie Said Trance (12", promo & press sheet)	15
89	KLF Comms. KLF 010(S)	Kylie Said To Jason (Edit)/Kylie Said Trance (p/s)	8
89	KLF Comms. KLF 010T	Kylie Said To Jason (Full Length)/Kylie Said Trance (12", stickered p/s & pstr)	15
89	KLF Comms. KLF 010R	Kylie Said To Jason (Trance Kylie Express)/Kylie In A Trance/ Kylie Said Harder (12" remix, p/s, export issue)	15
89	KLF Comms. KLF 010RR	Kylie In A Trance/Kylie Said Mu (12", p/s, export edition, 500 only)	40
89	KLF Comms. KLF 010RR	Kylie In A Trance/Kylie Said Mu (12", p/s, export edition, 500 only, shrinkwrapped with KLF 010R)	70
89	KLF Comms. KLF 010CD	Kylie Said To Jason (Full Length)/Madrugada Eterna/Kylie Said Trance (CD)	40
90	KLF Comms. KLF 011T	Madrugada Eterna (Club Mix)/Madrugada Eterna (Edit)/Madrugada Eterna (Ambient House Mix) (12", 20 only, beware of counterfeits!)	150
90	KLF Comms. ETERNA 1	Madrugada Eterna (Club Mix) (12", 1-sided, white label, 6 pressed, beware of counterfeits!)	200
90	KLF Comms. KLF 004X	What Time Is Love? (Live At Trancentral)/Techno Gate Mix (12", p/s, mispressing, B-side actually plays "Wandafull Mix", matrix no.: KLF 004X-B)	25
90	KLF Comms. KLF 004P	What Time Is Love? (Live At Trancentral)/Wandafull Mix (12", w/l, 1,500 only)	10
90	KLF Comms. KLF 005R	3AM Eternal 'Single Edit'/Blue Danube Orbital Mix/Moody Boys Version/ 3PM Electro (12", original issue with stickered p/s)	10
91	KLF Comms. KLF 005S	3AM Eternal (Live At The S.S.L.) (Radio Freedom Edit) (white label, 500 only)	12
91	KLF Comms. CHOC ICE 2	Justified And Ancient (Stand By The J.A.M.s)/Justified And Ancient (Let Them Eat Ice Cream) (12", white label promo)	12
91	KLF Comms. CHOC ICE 3	Justified And Ancient (Anti-Acapella Version) (12", 1-sided, w/l, 200 only)	50
91	KLF Comms. LP PROMO 1	Make It Rain/No More Tears (12", promo only, 1,729 pressed)	20
91	KLF Comms. 92PROMO 2	America: What Time is January? (12", 1-sided, white label promo, 50 - 250 only)	100
91	KLF Comms. 3AM 1	3AM Eternal (feat. Extreme Noise Terror) (p/s, mail order only)	20
92	KLF Comms. KLF 5 TOTP	3AM Eternal (Xmas Top Of The Pops Version) (1-sided, with Extreme Noise Terror, mail-order only, with insert & mailing envelope; beware of bootlegs!)	30
92	KLF Comms. KLF 5 TOTP	3AM Eternal (Xmas Top Of The Pops Version) (1-sided, w/Extreme Noise Terror, mail-order only, without insert & mailing envelope; beware of bootlegs!)	8
92	KLF Comms. 92PROMO 3	What Time Is Love (Acid Mix) (12", 1-sided, w/l promo, perhaps 20 only)	300
92	KLF Comms. USA 4X/ CHOC ICE 2	Justified And Ancient/America: What Time Is Love? (12", 'longboat' picture disc, export edition, 4,000 only)	30
97	KLF Comms.	Fuck The Millennium (4-track CD, in white carrier bag Fuck The Millennium kit, with T-shirt, window sticker, certificate)	50
89	KLF Comms. JAMS LP 4	THE WHAT TIME IS LOVE STORY (LP)	30
89	KLF Comms. JAMS CD 4	THE WHAT TIME IS LOVE STORY (CD)	30
89	KLF Comms. JAMS LP 5	CHILL OUT (LP)	80
89	KLF Comms. JAMS CD 5	CHILL OUT (CD)	40
89	KLF Comms. JAMS LP 6	(TUNES FROM) THE WHITE ROOM (LP, 9-track white label, unreleased, promo only, beware of counterfeits!)	50
91	KLF Comm. JAMS LP 006	THE WHITE ROOM (LP)	40

(see also Angels One 5, Timelords, Disco 2000, Bill Drummond, Space, Orb)

TONY KLINGER & MICHAEL LYONS
| 72 | Deram SML 1095 | EXTREMES (LP, soundtrack) | 100 |

KLINGONS
| 80 | Kang KLING001 | Dr. Jekyl And Mr Hyde/The First Question (p/s) | 15 |

PETER KLINT (QUINTET)
| 66 | Mercury MF 997 | Walkin' Proud/Shake | 20 |
| 68 | Atlantic 584 208 | Hey Diddle Diddle/Just Holding On (solo) | 18 |

KLO
| 83 | International INTER 1 | Fun/Weirdo | 6 |

KLONES
| 80 | Red Hot RED 001 | Metal Man/Neon Age (stamped die-cut sleeve) | 8 |

ANNETTE KLOOGER
56	Decca F 10701	The Rock And Roll Waltz/Rock Around The Island (with Ted Heath Music)	15
56	Decca F 10733	The Magic Touch/We'll Love Again (with Four Jones Boys)	15
56	Decca F 10738	Why Do Fools Fall In Love?/Lovely One (with Four Jones Boys)	15
56	Decca F 10776	Mama, Teach Me To Dance/Mama, I Long For A Sweetheart (with Edmundo Ros Orchestra)	10

KLUBS

MINT VALUE £

57	Decca F 10844	The Wisdom Of A Fool/Tra La La	10

(see also Four Jones Boys, Ted Heath Orchestra)

KLUBS
68	Cam CAM 681	I Found The Sun/Ever Needed Someone	200

EARL KLUGH
85	Blue Note UAG 20009	LIVING INSIDE YOUR LOVE (LP, Nimbus Supercut, mail order only with Hi Fi Today magazine)	50

KMA PRODUCTIONS
96	Urban Beat URB 004	Cape Fear/Phantasy Trip (12", stamped white labels)	35
96	Urban Beat URB 004	Phantasy Trip/Cape Fear (12")	30
97	KMA Productions KMA001	BREAKING OUT EP (12")	25

KNACK (U.K.)
65	Decca F 12234	She Ain't No Good/Who'll Be The Next In Line	60
65	Decca F 12278	It's Love Baby (24 Hours A Day)/Time Time Time	50
66	Piccadilly 7N 35215	Did You Ever Have To Make Up Your Mind?/Red Hearts	15
66	Piccadilly 7N 35322	Stop! (Before You Get Me Going)/Younger Girl	15
66	Piccadilly 7N 35347	Save All My Love For Joey/Take Your Love	15
67	Piccadilly 7N 35367	(Man From The) Marriage Guidance And Advice Bureau/ Dolly Catch Her Man	15

(see also Gun, Sky)

BERNIE KNEE QUARTETTE
55	HMV 7M 306	Chocolate Whiskey And Vanilla Gin/Scrape Off De Bark	7

(see also Bernie Nee)

KNEES
74	United Artists UP 35773	Day Tripper/Slow Down	10

(see also Brinsley Schwarz)

KNICKERBOCKERS
66	London HLH 10013	Lies/The Coming Generation	20
66	London HLH 10035	One Track Mind/I Must Be Doing Something Right	20
66	London HLH 10061	High On Love/Stick With Me	30
66	London HLH 10093	Rumours, Gossip, Words Untrue/Love Is A Bird	18
67	London HLH 10102	Can You Help Me/Please Don't Love Him	18
66	London HA-H 8294	THE FABULOUS KNICKERBOCKERS (LP)	60

KNIFE
04	Rabid Records RABIDT 020	HEARTBEATS EP (12", p/s)	10
06	Brille BRILLP 103	SILENT SHOUT (2-LP)	35
06	Brille BRILLP 105	DEEP CUTS (2-LP, inners)	70
13	Brille BRILLP 117	SHAKING THE HABITUAL (3-LP, 2 booklets, 2 x CD)	20

KNIFE EDGE
80	No Hessle F001	Favourite Girl/Say You Will (p/s)	40

KNIFEWORLD
09	Believers Roast BRR002LP	BURIED ALONE: TALES OF CRUSHING DEFEAT (LP)	15
14	Inside Out IOMLP 402	THE UNRAVELLING (LP, with CD)	15

BAKER KNIGHT
66	Reprise RS 20465	Would You Believe It/Tomorrow's Good Time Girl	12

CURTIS KNIGHT (& ZEUS)
69	RCA RCA 1888	Fancy Meeting You Here/Love In	12
70	RCA RCA 1950	Down In The Village/No Point Of View	15
74	Dawn DNS 1049	Devil Made Me Do It/Oh Rainbow	7
74	Dawn DNS 1065	People Places And Things/Mysterious Lady	7
74	Dawn DNLS 3060	THE SECOND COMING (LP, laminated sleeve, lyric insert, pink 'sun' label)	100
74	Dawn DNLS 3060	THE SECOND COMING (LP, laminated sleeve, no lyric insert, pink 'sun' label)	45

(see also Jimi Hendrix, Blue Goose)

GLADYS KNIGHT (& PIPS)
SINGLES
64	Stateside SS 318	Giving Up/Maybe Maybe Baby	35
64	Stateside SS 352	Lovers Always Forgive/Another Love	35
65	Sue WI 394	Letter Full Of Tears/You Broke Your Promise	40
66	Tamla Motown TMG 576	Just Walk In My Shoes/Stepping Closer To Your Heart	60
66	Tamla Motown TMG 576	Just Walk In My Shoes/Stepping Closer To Your Heart (DJ copy)	150
67	Tamla Motown TMG 604	Take Me In Your Arms And Love Me/Do You Love Me Just A Little Honey	15
67	Tamla Motown TMG 619	Everybody Needs Love/Stepping Closer To Your Heart (demo-only B-side)	100
67	Tamla Motown TMG 619	Everybody Needs Love/Since I've Lost You	18
67	Tamla Motown TMG 629	I Heard It Through The Grapevine/It's Time To Go Now	25
68	Tamla Motown TMG 645	The End Of Our Road/Don't Let Her Take Your Love From Me	20
68	Tamla Motown TMG 660	It Should Have Been Me/You Don't Love Me No More	18
68	Tamla Motown TMG 674	I Wish It Would Rain/It's Summer	18
69	Tamla Motown TMG 714	The Nitty Gritty/Got Myself A Good Man	10
70	Tamla Motown TMG 728	Didn't You Know (You'd Have To Cry Sometime)/Keep An Eye	12
70	Tamla Motown TMG 756	Friendship Train/You Need Love Like I Do (Don't You)	10
71	Tamla Motown TMG 765	If I Were Your Woman/The Tracks Of My Tears	8
72	Tamla Motown TMG 805	Make Me The Woman That You Go Home To/I Don't Want To Do Wrong	15
72	Tamla Motown TMG 813	Just Walk In My Shoes/I'm Losing You	10
73	Ember EMB S 326	Every Beat Of My Heart/Room In Your Heart	6
73	Tamla Motown TMG 844	The Look Of Love/You're My Everything	6
73	Tamla Motown TMG 864	Take Me In Your Arms And Love Me/No One Could Love You More	200
74	Contempo CS 2021	Why Don't You Leave Me/Maybe Baby	6
75	Tamla Motown TMG 945	You've Lost That Loving Feeling/This Child Needs A Father	15
89	MCA MCASP 1339	Licence To Kill/MICHAEL KAMEN: Pain (p/s with postcards & lyric sheet)	6

Jason KNIGHT

MINT VALUE £

ALBUMS
67	T. Motown TML 11058	EVERYBODY NEEDS LOVE (mono)	35
67	T. Motown STML 11058	EVERYBODY NEEDS LOVE (stereo)	40
68	Bell MBLL 103	TASTIEST HITS	40
68	T. Motown TML 11080	FEELIN' BLUESY (mono)	30
68	T. Motown STML 11080	FEELIN' BLUESY (stereo)	35
69	T. Motown TML 11100	SILK 'N' SOUL (mono)	40
69	T. Motown STML 11100	SILK'N'SOUL (stereo)	35
69	T. Motown TML 11135	THE NITTY GRITTY (mono)	30
69	T. Motown (S)TML 11135	THE NITTY GRITTY (stereo)	22
70	T. Motown STML 11148	GREATEST HITS (original with flipback sleeve)	20
71	T. Motown STML 11187	IF I WERE YOUR WOMAN	20
74	T. Motown STML 1120	STANDING OVATION (LP)	20

(see also Pips, Dionne Warwick)

JASON KNIGHT
67	Pye 7N 17399	Love Is Getting Stronger/Standing In My Shoes	150
67	Pye 7N 17399	Love Is Getting Stronger/Standing In My Shoes (DJ copy)	250
73	Pye 7N 45287	Love Is Getting Stronger/Standing In My Shoes (reissue)	7

JEAN KNIGHT
71	Stax 2025 049	Mr Big Stuff/Why Do I Keep Living These Memories	8
72	Stax 2362 022	MR. BIG STUFF (LP)	20

MARIE KNIGHT
61	Fontana H 354	Nothing/Come Tomorrow	20
65	Stateside SS 419	Cry Me A River/Comes The Knight	20
85	Kent TOWN 102	That's No Way To Treat A Girl/JACK MONTGOMERY: Dearly Beloved	15

PETER KNIGHT & KNIGHT RIDERS
61	Pye 7N 15388	Lucky Stars/Double Trouble	7
62	Pye 7N 15472	Camel Train/Scarlett	7
64	Pye 7N 15687	Wonderful Day Like Today/It Isn't Enough	8

PETER KNIGHT ORCHESTRA/SINGERS
55	Parlophone MSP 6183	Twenty Minutes South (Medley) (both sides, as Peter Knight Singers)	6
67	Mercury SML 30023	SGT. PEPPER'S LONELY HEARTS CLUB BAND (LP)	15

ROBERT KNIGHT
62	London HLD 9496	Free Me/The Other Half Of Man	30
68	Monument MON 1008	Everlasting Love/Somebody's Baby	15
68	Monument MON 1016	Blessed Are The Lonely/It's Been Worth It All	8
68	Monument MON 1017	The Power Of Love/Love On A Mountain Top	35
68	Bell BLL 1029	Isn't It Lonely Together/We'd Better Stop	8

SONNY KNIGHT
57	London HLD 8362	Confidential/Jail Bird (gold label print)	200
57	London HLD 8362	Confidential/Jail Bird (silver label print)	60
57	London HLD 8362	Confidential/Jail Bird (78 rpm)	20
57	London HL 7016	Confidential/Jail Bird (export issue)	60
59	Vogue Pop V 9134	But Officer/Dear Wonderful God	150
59	Vogue Pop V 9134	But Officer/Dear Wonderful God (78)	40

TERRY KNIGHT & PACK
66	Cameo Parkway C 102	I (Who Have Nothing)/Numbers	60

(see also Grand Funk Railroad)

TONY KNIGHT
64	Decca F 11989	Did You Ever Hear The Sound?/I Feel So Blue (as Tony Knight & Live Wires)	40
65	Decca F 12109	How Sweet/Surfer Street (as Tony Knight's Chessmen)	35

KNIGHT BROTHERS
65	Chess CRS 8015	Sinking Low/Temptation 'Bout To Get Me	30
66	Chess CRS 8046	That'll Get It/She's A1	30

KNIGHTRIDER
87	Omega KS 1299	Shout Out Loud	30

KNIGHTS OF THE ROUND TABLE
68	Pama PM 734	Lament To Bobby Kennedy/If You Were My Girl	7

KNIGHTSBRIDGE STRINGS
60	Top Rank JAR 304	Tracey's Theme/Misty	7
61	Top Rank JAR 532	The Singer Not The Song/Anacleto's Theme	12

K9'S
79	Dog Breath WOOF 1	The K9 Hassle/Idi Amin/Sweeney Todd (1st issue in numbered blue p/s, with insert, 1000 only)	45
79	Dog Breath WOOF 1	The K9 Hassle/Idi Amin/Sweeney Todd (reissue, 500 only in stamped die cut sleeve)	15

KNOCKER JUNGLE
70	Ember EMB S 293	I Don't Know Why/Reality (p/s)	6
71	Ember NR 5052	KNOCKER JUNGLE (LP, gatefold sleeve)	75

KNOCKOUTS
60	Top Rank JAR 279	Riot In Room 3C/Darling Lorraine	25

KNOCK UP
82	Movie Music MM 002	Telling Lies/Need Your Love (no p/s)	30

MARK KNOPFLER
84	Vertigo DSDJ 7	Joy (from 'Comfort And Joy') (unissued, 1-sided promo only)	12
84	Vertigo DSTR 712	Joy (from 'Comfort And Joy')/Fistful Of Ice Cream (12", p/s)	12
84	Vertigo MARK ONE	Comfort And Joy (12", 1-sided promo)	25
02	Mercury 063292-1	THE RAGPICKERS DREAM (2-LP, numbered)	80
04	Mercury 9867262	SHANGRI-LA (2-LP)	45

(see also Dire Straits, Randy Newman)

KNOPOV'S POLITICAL PACKAGE
MINT VALUE £

KNOPOV'S POLITICAL PACKAGE
80 White label — Misadventure/You're In The Army Now 6

(see also Mission)

KENNY KNOTS
86 Unity UNO 18 — Watch How The People Dancing/ERROL BELLUT: A Weh Do She (12") 30
88 Unity UNO 22 — Ring Up My Number/MIKEY MURKA: We Try (12") 15
02 Honest Jon's HJP1 — Watch How The People Dancing/Watch How The People Dancing (Version)/Watch How The People Dancing (Dubplate)/MIKEY MURKA: We Try/We Try (Version) (12" reissue) ... 12
06 Jah Tubby's JT 10023 — Babylon Fall Down/Gully Bank Rock (10" with Bush Chemists) 25

KNOTT SISTERS
58 London HLX 8713 — Undivided Attention/SHADES with KNOTT SISTERS: Sun Glasses 40

KNOWLEDGE
78 A&M AMLH 68500 — HAIL DREAD (LP) 30
96 Tamoki Wambesi TWLP 1034 — STUMBLING BLOCK (LP) 50

SONNY KNOWLES
72 Rex R11077 — Do I Love You/I'm Just A Country Boy 7

BOBBY KNOX
70 Penny Farthing PEN 714 — Kissin Walkin/Down A Back Street 12

BUDDY KNOX
57 Columbia DB 3914 — Party Doll/My Baby's Gone (gold label print) 50
57 Columbia DB 3952 — Rock Your Little Baby To Sleep/Don't Make Me Cry (as Lieutenant Buddy Knox, gold label print) 50
57 Columbia DB 4014 — Hula Love/Devil Woman 25
58 Columbia DB 4077 — Swingin' Daddy/Whenever I'm Lonely 25
58 Columbia DB 4180 — Somebody Touched Me/C'mon Baby 20
59 Columbia DB 4302 — To Be With You/I Think I'm Gonna Kill Myself 15
61 London HLG 9268 — Lovey Dovey/I Got You 12
61 London HLG 9331 — Ling Ting Tong/The Kisses (They're All Mine) 12
61 London HLG 9472 — Three-Eyed Man/All By Myself 10
62 Liberty LIB 55411 — Chi-Hua-Hua/Open Your Loving Arms 10
62 Liberty LIB 55473 — She's Gone/Now There's Only Me 20
63 Liberty LIB 55592 — Shadaroom/Tomorrow Is Coming 10
64 Liberty LIB 55694 — All Time Loser/Good Loving 10
69 United Artists UP 35019 — God Knows I Love You/Night Runners 8
57 Columbia SEG 7732 — ROCK-A-BUDDY KNOX (EP) 50
62 Liberty LBY 1114 — GOLDEN HITS (LP) 20

KNUCKLEHEAD
93 Saucerman ART 01 — Red Eye, Dead Eye/Spirit Matter (p/s, hand-painted label, 150 copies only) 15

FRANKIE KNUCKLES
87 Portrait PARTY 1 — You Can't Hide From Yourself/Dub Mix (p/s) 8
89 FFRR FX 102 — Tears (Classic Vocal)/(Accapella)/(Classic Instrumental) (with Satoshi Tomiie, 12", die-cut p/s (12") 10
89 Radical Records TRAXT 3 — Your Love/Baby Wants To Ride (12", p/s) 25
89 Trax TRAX 3 — Your Love/Baby Wants To Ride (p/s) 30
11 Nocturnal Groove NCTGD 064V — Your Love (Director's Cut Signature Mix)/(Belocca And Soneec Vocal Club Nocturnal Groove) (12" p/s reissue) 30
91 Virgin America VUSLP 36 — BEYOND THE MIX (LP) 18

KNXWLEDGE
16 All City ACKWTLPX1 — WRAPTAYPES (2-LP, gatefold) 25

KOBALT 60
91 Music Of Life NOTE57 — Chaos From Order/Concrete Show (12") 15

KOCK
83 Hard ON 11 — One-Eyed Giant/Hickory Dickory Kock (p/s) 6

KODA
94 Lucky Spin STU 8 1 — Untitled (12" 1-sided white label) 20
94 Dee Jay DJX 019 — The Deep/Spacetek (12") 40

KODIAKS
69 Decca F 12942 — All Because You Wanna See Me Cry/Tell Me Rhonda 20

(SPIDER) JOHN KOERNER
63 Palette PG 9035 — Cool Ghoul/Sapphire 7
67 Elektra EKSN 45005 — Won't You Give Me Some Love/Don't Stop 25
69 Elektra EKSN 45063 — Friends And Lovers/Magazine Lady (with Willie Murphy) 10
66 Elektra EKL 267 — (LOTS MORE) BLUES RAGS AND HOLLERS (LP, with Dave Ray and Tony Glover, US sleeve but UK pressed record with golden Elektra "guitar player' logo) 45
65 Elektra EKL 290 — SPIDER BLUES (LP) 50
68 Elek. EKL 4041/EKS 74041 — RUNNING JUMPING STANDING STILL (LP, with Willie Murphy) 30

KOFFIE AND JAMES
69 Philips BF 1800 — You're My Everything/Different Shades 10

MOE KOFFMAN
58 London HLT 8633 — Little Pixie/Koko Mamey 8
58 London HLJ 8549 — Swingin' Shepherd Blues/Hambourg Bound 6
63 Palette PG 9035 — Cool Ghoul/Sapphire 6

KOFI
87 Ariwa ARI 73 — Didn't I/PROFESSOR DOPPLER: I'm A Dropout (12") 35
89 Ariwa ARI LP 042 — BLACK...WITH SUGAR (LP) 30
93 Ariwa ARILP 092 — WISHING WELL (LP) 30
94 Ariwa ARILP064 — FRIDAY'S CHILD (LP) 25

KOFI & KIKI
79 Bronze 12 BRO 70 — 24 Hours In A Disco/(Instrumental Version) (12") 15
79 Bronze BRO 70 — 24 Hours In A Disco/(Instrumental Version) 10

(see also Koki Gyan)

Leonid KOGAN

MINT VALUE £

LEONID KOGAN
58	Columbia 33CX 1562	PAGANINI VIOLIN CONCERTO NO. 1 IN D MAJOR (LP, mono)	150
60	Columbia SAX 2307	BRAHMS VIOLIN CONCERTO (LP, stereo)	1000
60	Columbia SAX 2329	LALO: SYMPHONIE ESPAGNOLE/TCHAIKOVSKY: SERENADE MELANCOLIQUE, LP, stereo, turquiose/silver label)	1500
60	Columbia SAX 2323	TCHAIKOVSKY: VIOLIN CONCERTO OP 35 & MEDITATION D MINOR OP 42 with Paris Conservatoire Orchestra, turquoise/silver label) LP, stereo)	1500
60	Columbia 33CX 1711	TCHAIKOVSKY: VIOLIN CONCERTO OP 35 & MEDITATION D MINOR OP 42 with Paris Conservatoire Orchestra, LP, blue label, mono)	50
60	Columbia SAX 2386	BEETHOVEN VIOLIN CONCERTO (LP, stereo, turquoise/silver label)	2000
64	Columbia SAX 2531	SONATAS FOR TWO VIOLINS (with ELISABTH GILELS) (LP, stereo, turquoise/silver label)	1500
64	Odeon SAX 2388	SONATAS FOR TWO VIOLINS (with ELISABTH GILELS) (LP, stereo export edition, black label)	500

KOKANE GUNS
82	SRTS 82 CUS 1644	Delta Woman/Crying Shame	12

KOKOMO
60	London HLU 9305	Asia Minor/Roy's Tune	7

KO KO TAYLOR
66	Chess CRS 8035	Wang Dang Doodle/Blues Heaven	35
66	Chess CRS 8035	Wang Dang Doodle/Blues Heaven (DJ copy)	60
72	Chess 6145 018	Violent Love/The Egg Or The Hen/Wang Dang Doodle	8

KOLETTES
64	Pye International 7N 25278	Who's That Guy?/Just How Much	50
73	Chess 6145 021	Who's That Guy?/Just How Much (reissue)	10

BONNIE KOLOC
72	London HLO 10377	Jazz Man/Got To Get What You Can	6
72	London HLO 10392	Burgundy Wine/We Are Ships	6
72	London SHO 8432	AFTER ALL THIS TIME (LP)	25
72	London SHO 8440	HOLD ON TO ME (LP)	20

MO KOLOURS
17	22a 018	AXUM (p/s, 300 only, with insert)	15

MO KOLOURS/R.O. MAMODE IV
14	22a 003	MO KOLOURS/R.O. MAMODE IV (12" split EP, stamped white labels)	15

JIMMIE KOMACK
54	Vogue Coral Q 2031	Cold Summer Blues/The Nic-Name Song	10
55	Vogue Coral Q 72061	Wabash 4-7473/An Old Beer Bottle	10
55	Vogue Coral Q 72087	Rock-A-Bye Your Baby With A Dixie Melody/This Is The Place	10

CHRISTOPHER KOMEDA
66	Polydor 580001	CUL DE SAC (soundtrack EP)	150
68	Dot (S)LPD 519	ROSEMARY'S BABY (LP, as Kryzstophe Komeda)	50

KOMYTEA
08	Anjunaseep ANJDEE 027	Professional Killers/My Personal Summer (12")	80

MANJEET KONDAL
86	Multitone MUT 1018	HOLLE HOLLE (LP)	30
88	Arishma ARI 1006	WICKED AND WILD (LP)	30
91	Nachural LNR 0206	SPECIAL BREW (LP)	40

KONGAS
74	Barclay 80524	AFRO ROCK (LP)	15

JOHN (T.) KONGOS
66	Piccadilly 7N 35241	I Love Mary/Goodtime Party Companion (as John T. Kongos)	10
69	Dawn DNS 1002	Flim Flam Pharisee/Blood	6
71	Fly BUG 8DJ	He's Gonna Step On You Again/Sometimes It's Not Enough (DJ copy in p/s)	10
69	Dawn DNLS 3002	CONFUSIONS ABOUT A GOLDFISH (LP, with sticker)	50
69	Dawn DNLS 3002	CONFUSIONS ABOUT A GOLDFISH (LP, without sticker)	40
71	Fly HIFLY 7	KONGOS (LP, gatefold sleeve, insert, Fly label)	20

(see also Scrugg, Floribunda Rose)

V. KONGS
63	Halagala HG 18	Tomorrow Will Soon Be Here/Pretty Little Girl	20

LEE KONITZ
56	London LTZK 15025	LEE KONITZ WITH WAYNE MARSH (LP)	20

KONK
82	Rough Trade RT 110T	KONK PARTY EP (12", p/s)	10
84	4th & Broadway BRW 7	Your Life/Dub	15
04	Soul Jazz SJR LP 90	THE SOUND OF KONK (2-LP)	20

KONKRETE CANTICLE
71	Arts Council Of Great Britain AC 1971	EXPERIMENTS IN DISINTEGRATING LANGUAGE (LP)	70

KONRADS
65	CBS 201812	Baby It's Too Late Now/I'm Over You	50

KONSTRUKTIVITS
83	Flowmotion FM 001	VOLUME 1 (cassette)	60
83	Flowmotion FM 002	A DISSEMBLY (LP)	35
83	Third Mind TMLP 02	PSYKO GENETIKA (LP)	35
84	Third Mind TMLP 05	BLACK DECEMBER (LP)	30
85	Sterile SR 10	GLENNASCAUL (LP)	15

(see also Whitehouse)

KOOBAS
65	Pye 7N 17012	Take Me For A Little While/Somewhere In The Night	50
66	Pye 7N 17087	You'd Better Make Up Your Mind/A Place I Know	60
66	Columbia DB 7988	Sweet Music/Face	60
67	Columbia DB 8103	Sally/Champagne And Caviar	35

KOOGA

MINT VALUE £

67	Columbia DB 8187	Gypsy Fred/City Girl	30
68	Columbia DB 8419	The First Cut Is The Deepest/Walking Out	55
69	Columbia S(C)X 6271	THE KOOBAS (LP, black/silver label, boxed logo, "Sold in U.K..." text)	1500
88	Bam Caruso KIRI 047	BARRICADES (LP)	18

(see also Kubas, Van Der Graaf Generator, Gary & Stu, Juicy Lucy, March Hare)

KOOGA
88	Kooga KO 001	Don't Break My Heart/Lay Down Your Love (p/s, private pressing)	8

(see also Skin)

KOOKS
05	Private Pressing	Slave To The Game (1-sided, stamped label, tour single, 500 only)	8
06	Virgin (no Cat no)	Naive (1-sided promo, hand-stamped label)	6
06	Virgin VS 1911	Naive/Tea & Biscuits (clear vinyl)	12
06	Virgin VS 1913	She Moves In Her Own Way/I Already Miss You	6
07	Virgin VSDJ1968	Pull Me In (1-sided promo)	8
09	Virgin VSDJ1908	Slave To The Game (1-sided, white label, gig-only single, 500 pressed)	10
06	Virgin VX 3016	INSIDE IN/INSIDE OUT (LP, with 'bonus' live LP)	70
08	Virgin V3043	KONK (LP)	30

KOOL
67	CBS 203003	Look At Me, Look At Me/Room At The Top	20
69	CBS 2865	Step Out Of Your Mind/Funny (What A Fool A Man Can Be)	80
69	MCA MU 1085	Lovin'/Baby's Out Of Reach	12

BO KOOL
81	Tania TAN 001S	(Money) No Love/Love Money (12", purple vinyl)	20

KOOL KEITH/PHAROE MONCH/AKINYELLE
95	Liberty Grooves	Freestyle Frenzy/Gotta Go Down (7")	45

KOOL & THE GANG
70	London HLZ 10308	Kool And The Gang/Raw Hamburgers	10
74	Polydor 2001 500	Jungle Boogie/North, East, South, West	7
71	Mojo 2347 001	LIVE AT P.J.'S (LP)	20
71	Mojo 2347 002	THE BEST OF KOOL AND THE GANG (LP)	15
72	Mojo 2347 003	LIVE AT THE SEX MACHINE (LP)	15
73	Mojo 2347 004	MUSIC IS THE MESSAGE (LP)	15
74	Polydor 2310299	WILD AND PEACEFUL (LP)	15
74	Poydor 2310 357	LIGHT OF WORLDS (LP)	18
75	Polydor 2310 416	SPIRIT OF THE BOOGIE (LP)	20
76	Polydor 2310 441	LOVE & UNDERSTANDING (LP)	18

AL KOOPER
65	Mercury MF 885	Parchman Farm/You're The Lovin' End (as Alan Kooper)	20
69	CBS 4011	You Never Know Who Your Friends Are/Soft Landing On The Moon	6
69	CBS 4160	Hey Western Union Man/I Stand Alone	8
72	CBS 8084	Monkey Time/Bended Knees (Please Don't Let Me Down)	10
69	CBS 63538	I STAND ALONE (LP, orange label)	30
69	CBS 63651	YOU NEVER KNOW WHO YOUR FRIENDS ARE (LP, orange label)	20
70	CBS 63797	KOOPER SESSION - WITH SHUGGIE OTIS (LP, orange label)	20
70	CBS 66252	EASY DOES IT (2-LP, orange label)	20
71	United Artists UAS 29210	THE LANDLORD (LP, soundtrack, with Staple Singers & Lorraine Ellison)	20
71	CBS 64340	NEW YORK CITY (YOU'RE A WOMAN) (LP, gatefold sleeve, orange label)	15
72	CBS 64208	A POSSIBLE PROJECTION OF THE FUTURE/CHILDHOOD'S END (LP, orange label)	15
73	CBS 65193	NAKED SONGS (LP)	15

(see also Blues Project, Blood Sweat & Tears, Shuggie Otis)

AL KOOPER, MIKE BLOOMFIELD & STEPHEN STILLS
68	CBS 3770	Season Of The Witch/Albert's Shuffle	12
68	CBS 63396	SUPER SESSION (LP)	20
73	CBS CQ 30991	SUPER SESSION (LP, quadrophonic)	25

(see also Mike Bloomfield & Al Kooper, Stephen Stills)

KOPPYKATS
68	Fontana SFT 13052/3	BEATLES' BEST (2-LP)	35

(see also Ian [Edward] & Zodiacs)

TAMARA KORAN WITH PERCEPTION
68	Domain D7	Veils Of Mourning Lace/Don't Throw Our Love Away (DJ copy)	400
68	Domain D7	Veils Of Mourning Lace/Don't Throw Our Love Away	350

TOMMY KÖRBERG
69	Sonet SON 2005	Dear Mrs. Jones/Bird You Must Fly	8

PAUL KORDA
66	Columbia DB 7994	Go On Home/Just Come Closer To Me	30
69	Parlophone R5778	Seagull (West Coast Oil Tragedy Of '68)/Night Of The Next Day (with p/s)	30
69	Parlophone R 5778	Seagull (West Coast Oil Tragedy Of '68)/Night Of The Next Day	15
71	MAM AS 1003	PASSING STRANGER (LP, gatefold sleeve)	75

(see also Tim Andrews & Paul Korda, Dada)

KOREA
84	Romac (No cat no)	I Don't Know/Deep In Your Heart (no p/s)	50

KORELESS
11	Pictures Music PICT 005	4D (12", stamped white labels)	20
13	Young Turks YT088	YUGEN (12")	20

KORN
95	Epic KORN 1	Blind/Fake/Sean Olson (10", p/s numbered)	18
96	Epic 6638450	No Place To Hide/Proud (white vinyl, 7,500 only)	15

ALEXIS KORNER (BLUES INCORPORATED)
58	Tempo A 166	I Ain't Gonna Worry No More/County Jail (as Alexis Korner Skiffle Group)	100
58	Tempo A 166	I Ain't Gonna Worry No More/County Jail (78)	50

Artie KORNFELD'S TREE

MINT VALUE £

63	Lyntone LYN 299	Blaydon Races/Up-Town (as Blues Incorporated With Alexis Korner, free with women's magazine Trio)	100
63	Parlophone R 5206	I Need Your Loving/Please Please Please (as Alexis Korner's Blues Inc.)	40
65	Parlophone R 5247	Little Baby/Roberta (as Alexis Korner's Blues Inc.)	40
65	King KG 1017	See See Rider/Blues A La King (as Alexis Korner's All Stars)	45
66	Fontana TF 706	River's Invitation/Everyday (I Have The Blues)	25
67	Fontana TF 817	Rosie/Rock Me	25
75	CBS 3520	Get Off My Cloud/Strange'n'Deranged	10
76	CBS 3877	Ain't That Peculiar/Tree Top Fever	8
58	Tempo EXA 76	BLUES FROM THE ROUNDHOUSE VOL. 1 (EP, as Alexis Korner Skiffle Group)	175
59	Tempo EXA 102	BLUES FROM THE ROUNDHOUSE VOL. 2 (EP, as Alexis Korner's Blues Inc.)	300
62	Topic TOP 70	3/4 A.D. (EP, with Davy Graham, first pressing in mauve sleeve with cream label)	90
62	Topic TOP 70	3/4 A.D. (EP, with Davy Graham, later pressing with lilac sleeve and blue label)	60
62	Topic TOP 70	3/4 A.D. (EP, with Davy Graham, later pressings with bronze sleeve and blue label)	30
57	'77' LP/2	BLUES FROM THE ROUNDHOUSE (10" LP, 99 only, as Alexis Korner Breakdown Group)	1000
62	Ace of Clubs ACL 1130	R&B FROM THE MARQUEE (LP, claret labels, with Long John Baldry)	120
64	Transatlantic TRA 117	RED HOT FROM ALEX (LP, with Herbie Goins)	150
64	Oriole PS 40058	AT THE CAVERN (LP, live, with Herbie Goins, laminated sleeve with flipbacks)	375
65	Ace of Clubs ACL 1187	ALEXIS KORNER'S BLUES INCORPORATED (LP)	100
65	Spot JW 551	SKY HIGH (LP, featuring Duffy Power)	400
67	Fontana TL 5381	I WONDER WHO (LP, mono)	150
67	Fontana (S)TL 5381	I WONDER WHO (LP, stereo)	200
67	Polydor Special 236 206	BLUES INCORPORATED (LP, 1st issue, listing 4 tracks on Side A on sleeve/label)	80
67	Polydor Special 236 206	BLUES INCORPORATED (LP, 2nd issue, listing 5 tracks on Side A on sleeve/label)	50
68	Liberty LBL/LBS 83147	A NEW GENERATION OF BLUES (LP)	75
69	Transatlantic TRASAM 7	ALEXIS KORNER'S ALL STAR BLUES INCORPORATED (LP, reissue of "Red Hot From Alex", different cover)	30
71	Rak SRAK 501	ALEXIS KORNER (LP, textured sleeve)	45
72	Rak SRAKSP 51	BOOTLEG HIM! (2-LP, with booklet)	55
73	Transatlantic TRA 269	ACCIDENTALLY BORN IN NEW ORLEANS (LP, as Snape)	35
75	CBS 69155	GET OFF MY CLOUD (LP)	25

(see also Cyril Davies, C.C.S., Bob Hall & Alexis Korner, Herbie Goins, Duffy Power, Long John Baldry, Rocket 88, Davy Graham, Beryl Bryden, Jimmy Cotton, Ken Colyer, Jack Bruce, Snape & Little Brother Montgomery)

ARTIE KORNFELD'S TREE
70	Probe SPB 1022	A TIME TO REMEMBER (LP)	20

KORPERAYSHUN
89	BPM BP12007	K Factor/Non Stop (12")	30

KOSMICHER LAUFER
13	Unknown Capability UCKL001V	THE SECRET MUSIC OF THE EAST GERMAN OLYMPIC PROGRAMME 1972-83 VOLUME ONE (LP, CD with postcards)	60
13	Unknown Capability UCKL001V	THE SECRET MUSIC OF THE EAST GERMAN OLYMPIC PROGRAMME 1972-83 VOLUME ONE (LP)	35
14	Unknown Capability UCKL002V	THE SECRET MUSIC OF THE EAST GERMAN OLYMPIC PROGRAMME 1972-83 VOLUME TWO (LP, red vinyl)	35
15	Unknown Capability UCKL003V	THE SECRET MUSIC OF THE EAST GERMAN OLYMPIC PROGRAMME 1972-83 VOLUME THREE (LP, yellow vinyl with CD)	40
18	Unknown Capability UCKL004V	THE SECRET MUSIC OF THE EAST GERMAN OLYMPIC PROGRAMME 1972-83 VOLUME FOUR (LP, blue vinyl, some with CD)	35

KOSMIK KOMMANDO
94	Rephlex CAT 007EP	Cat 007 (I)/Cat 007 (II)/Cat 007 (III)/Cat 007 (IV) (12", clear vinyl)	12
93	Rephlex MX 202	UNIVERSAL INDICATOR YELLOW EP (12")	18
01	Machine Codes CODE 1010	ANALOGUE ANDROID (LP, 100 only, signed insert)	50

(see also Aphex Twin)

LEE KOSMIN
78	Polydor 2059034	Ain't No Way/How Fine I Feel	20

DAVID KOSSOFF
61	Oriole CB 1597	I'm Shy Mary Ellen I'm Shy/When Father Papered The Parlour	6
60	Oriole EP 7053	I'M SHY MARY ELLEN (EP)	10
60	Oriole MG 20043	LARKIN SINGIN' (LP)	15

PAUL KOSSOFF
73	Island ILPS 9264	BACK STREET CRAWLER (LP, pink rim palm tree label)	15
77	DJM DJE 29002	KOSS (2-LP)	15

(see also Free, Kossoff Kirke Tetsu & Rabbit, Creepy John Thomas)

KOSSOFF, KIRKE, TETSU & RABBIT
71	Island ILPS 9188	KOSSOFF, KIRKE, TETSU AND RABBIT (LP, gatefold sleeve, pink rim palm tree label)	50

(see also Paul Kossoff, Rabbit, Free)

CHIM KOTHARI
66	Deram DM 108	Sitar'N'Spice/Indian Bat	12
66	Deram DML 1002	SOUND OF THE SITAR (LP)	40

KOUMBA
82	Greensleeves GRED 105	We Are Leggo/Billy (12")	10

JENNIFER KRAAL
69	NEMS 56-4200	The Men In My Life/Sinful Davey	8

KRACKER
73	Rolling Stones RS 19106	A Song For Polly/Medicated Goo	12
74	Rolling Stones COC 49102	KRACKER BRAND (LP, gatefold sleeve)	20

KRAFTWERK
SINGLES
74	Vertigo 6147 012	Autobahn/Kometenmelodie 1	15
75	Vertigo 6147 015	Comet Melody 2/Kristallo	30
76	Capitol CL 15853	Radio Activity/Antenna (in p/s)	15

KRAFTY KUTS

MINT VALUE £

76	Capitol CL 15853	Radio Activity/Antenna	12
77	Capitol CL 15917	Trans-Europe Express/Europe Endless	20
77	Capitol CL 104	Showroom Dummies/Europe Endless	12
77	Capitol CLX 104	Showroom Dummies/Europe Endless (12", 'train station' p/s)	18
78	Capitol CL 15981	The Robots (edited version)/Spacelab (demo copy, special die cut sleeve)	35
78	Capitol CL 15981	The Robots/Spacelab (foldout p/s)	15
78	Capitol CL 15981	The Robots (alternative mix)/Spacelab (foldout p/s)	30
78	Capitol CL 15998	Neon Lights/Trans-Europe Express/The Model	10
78	Capitol 12CL 15998	Neon Lights/Trans-Europe Express/The Model (12", luminous vinyl, dayglo sleeve)	30
78	Capitol 12CL 16098	Showroom Dummies/Spacelab/Europe Endless (12", reissue, 'red shirts' p/s)	15
81	EMI EMI 5175	Pocket Calculator/Dentaku (p/s)	8
81	EMI TCEMI 5175	Pocket Calculator/Numbers/Dentaku (cassette in cigarette'-pack style box)	35
81	EMI 12EMI 5175	Pocket Calculator/Numbers/Dentaku (12", p/s)	12
81	Vertigo VER 3	Kometenmelodie 2/Vom Himmel Hoch (p/s)	15
81	EMI 12EMI 5207	Computer Love/The Model (12", p/s, original issue)	12
82	EMI EMI 5272	Showroom Dummies/Numbers (p/s, some with mispressed B-side "The Model")	8
83	EMI EMI 5413	Tour De France/Tour De France (Instrumental) (p/s, red or yellow labels)	8
83	EMI TCEMI 5413	Tour De France/Tour De France (Short Version)/ Tour De France (2" Etape)	15
83	EMI 12EMI 5413	Tour De France (Long Version)/(7" Version)/(2" Etape) (12", p/s, red or yellow labels)	18
84	EMI EMI 5413	Tour De France (Kevorkian Remix)/Tour De France (Original 7" Version) (reissue, 'Breakdance' p/s)	7
84	EMI 12EMI 5413	Tour De France (Kevorkian Remix)/Tour De France (Different Extended Version)/Tour De France (Original 7" Version) (12", reissue, 'Breakdance' p/s)	18
84	EMI Golden 45's G45 16	Computer Love/The Model (p/s)	8
86	EMI EMI 5588	Musique Non-Stop/Musique Non-Stop (Different Version) (p/s)	10
86	EMI 12EMI 5588	Musique Non-Stop (6.15)/Musique Non-Stop (7" Version) (12", p/s)	15
87	EMI EMI 5602	The Telephone Call/Der Telefon Anruf (p/s)	15
87	EMI 12EMI 5602	The Telephone Call (Remix)/House Phone/Der Telefon Anruf (12", p/s)	20
91	EMI EM 201	Radioactivity (Francois Kevorkian Remix)/(William Orbit Mix) (p/s)	6
97	EMI KLANG BOX 101	KRAFTWERK (4 x 12" box set, including "Trans Europe Express", Numbers, "Musique Non Stop" & "Homecomputer"; with separate white or black T-shirt, promo only)	100
97	EMI KLANG BOX 101	KRAFTWERK (4 x 12" box set, including "Trans Europe Express", "Numbers", Musique Non Stop & "Homecomputer"; without T-shirt, promo only)	60

ALBUMS

72	Vertigo 6641 077	KRAFTWERK (2-LP, gatefold sleeve, small 'swirl')	400
72	Vertigo 6641 077	KRAFTWERK (2-LP gatefold sleeve, 'spacecraft' labels)	100
74	Vertigo 6360 616	RALF AND FLORIAN ('spacecraft' label, embossed sleeve)	150
74	Vertigo 6360 620	AUTOBAHN (embossed blue sleeve)	50
75	Vertigo 6360 629	EXCELLER 8 (some with stickered sleeve)	35
76	Capitol E-ST 11457	RADIO-ACTIVITY (with insert)	30
77	Capitol E-ST 11603	TRANS-EUROPE EXPRESS (LP, inner)	30
78	Capitol E-ST 11728	MAN MACHINE (LP, inner with round edges)	30
81	EMI EMC 3370	COMPUTER WORLD (LP, inner)	25
81	Vertigo 6449 066	ELEKTROKINETIK (LP)	25
81	Vertigo 6641077	KRAFTWERK (2-LP, reissue in single sleeve, spaceship labels)	50
83	EMI EMC 3407	TECHNOPOP (unissued, sleeves only)	0
83	Fame FA 4131031	RADIO-ACTIVITY (LP, reissue)	15
83	Fame 41 31511	TRANS-EUROPE EXPRESS (LP, reissue)	15
85	Fame FA4131181	MAN MACHINE (LP, reissue)	15
86	EMI EMD 100130	ELECTRIC CAFE (LP, gatefold)	25
91	EMI EM 1408	THE MIX (2-LP, with inner sleeves)	30
03	EMI 591 708 1	TOUR DE FRANCE SOUNDTRACKS (2-LP, single stickered sleeve with inners)	50
04	EMI KLANG BOX 001	THE CATALOGUE (8-CD, in card box, 1,000 only)	80
05	EMI 560 6111	MINIMUM - MAXIMUM (4-LP box set)	100
05	EMI 45855	MINIMUM - MAXIMUM (2-CD, DVD box set)	35

(see also Organisation, Electric Music, Karl Bartos)

KRAFTY KUTS
99	Southern Fried ECB17	Gimme The Funk (12")	10
99	Lacerba CERBAL 14	SLAM THE BREAKS ON (3-LP)	20

KRAKEN
80	Knave EJSP 9370	FANTASY REALITY (EP, no p/s)	50

BILLY J. KRAMER
67	Parlophone R 5552	Sorry/Going Going Gone	10
68	CBS 56-3396	1941/His Love Is Just A Lie	10
68	NEMS 56-3635	A World Without Love/Going Through It	8
69	MGM MGM 1474	The Colour Of My Love/I'm Running Away	10
73	Decca F 13426	A Fool Like You/I'll Keep You Satisfied	7
73	Decca F 13442	Darlin' Come To Me/Walking	7
74	BASF BA 1006	Stayin' Power/Blue Jean Queen	7
77	EMI EMI 2661	San Diego/Warm Summer Rain	6
78	EMI EMI 2740	Ships That Pass In The Night/Is There Anymore At Home Like You	6
79	Hobo HOS 010	Blue Christmas/Little Love (p/s, blue vinyl)	10
82	Runaway BJK 1	Rock It/Dum Dum	6

BILLY J. KRAMER & THE DAKOTAS
65	Parlophone R 5234	It's Gotta Last Forever/Don't You Do It No More	6
65	Parlophone R 5285	Trains And Boats And Planes/That's The Way I Feel	8
65	Parlophone R 5362	Neon City/I'll Be Doggone	10
66	Parlophone R 5408	We're Doing Fine/Forgive Me	10
66	Parlophone R 5482	You Make Me Feel Like Someone/Take My Hand	10
67	Reaction 591 014	Town Of Tuxley Toymakers/Chinese Girl	50

Wayne KRAMER

			MINT VALUE £
63	Parlophone GEP 8885	THE BILLY J. KRAMER HITS (EP)	10
63	Parlophone GEP 8895	I'LL KEEP YOU SATISFIED (EP)	12
64	Parlophone GEP 8907	LITTLE CHILDREN (EP)	15
64	Parlophone GEP 8921	FROM A WINDOW (EP)	15
65	Parlophone GEP 8928	BILLY J. PLAYS THE STATES (EP)	50
63	Parlophone PMC 1209	LISTEN (LP, mono)	25
65	Regal REG 1057	BILLY J (LP, export only)	30

(see also Dakotas)

WAYNE KRAMER
78	Stiffwick DEA/SUK 1	Ramblin' Rose/Get Some (numbered p/s)	8
79	Radar ADA 41	The Harder They Come/East Side Girl (p/s)	6

(see also MC5)

KRAVIN AS
91	Hangman HANG 39 UP	KRAVE ON! (LP)	15

KRAY CHERUBS
88	Fierce FRIGHT 014	No (p/s, 1-sided)	20
89	Snakeskin SS 002	Rot In Hell Mom/SAUCERMAN: Motor Drag (numbered black p/s, 300 only)	12
89	Snakeskin SS 002	Rot In Hell Mom/SAUCERMAN: Motor Drag (later reissue in purple p/s)	8
89	Forced Exposure FE 18	Teen Camel/I Hate My Job (p/s)	15

(see also Art Attacks, Savage Pencil)

BILL KRENZ & HIS RAGTIMERS
56	London HLU 8258	There'll Be No New Tunes On This Old Piano/Goofus	35

KREW KATS
61	HMV POP 840	Trambone/Peak Hour	15
61	HMV POP 894	Samovar/Jack's Good	25

(see also Shadows, Brian Bennett)

VEIRA KREW
85	VK 1000	Sexy Lady (Vocal)/(Instrumental)/Welcome To A Dream (12")	100

KRIMSON KAKE
69	Penny Farthing PEN 707	Feelin' Better/Waiter	30

(see also Samantha Jones, Vernons Girls)

KRIS
79	V-KRIS VKR 1	Okay/Trouble With The Law	30

DAVE KRISS
72	Deroy	EMIGRATING (2-LP)	40

KRISSI K
74	People PEO110	Stick Up/Who Do You Think You Are?	10

SONJA KRISTINA
68	Polydor 56299	Let The Sunshine In/Frank Mills	15
80	Chopper CHOP 101	St Tropez/Mr Skin (p/s)	10
80	Chopper CHOPE 5	SONJA KRISTINA (LP)	35

(see also Curved Air)

LEE KRISTOFFERSON
77	Thrust RUFF 1	Night Of The Werewolf/Dinner With Drac	7

DANNY KRIVIT
03	Strut STRUTLP 016	EDITS BY MR K (3 x 12")	40

KROKODIL
69	Liberty LBS 83306	KROKODIL (LP)	50
70	Liberty LBS 83417	SWAMP (LP)	50

KROME & TIME
92	Suburban B. SUBBASE 011	This Sound Is For The Underground/Manic Stampede (12", p/s)	25
92	Suburban B. SUBBASE 11R	This Sound Is For The Underground (E.5 Remix)/Manic Stampede (DJ Hype's Sandringham Road Mix) (12")	20
93	Suburban B. SUBBASE 26	The Slammer/Into The Night (12", p/s as DJ Krome & Mr Time)	20

KROMESTAR
06	Deep Medi Musik medi 01	Kalawanji/Surgery (12")	30
15	System SYSTM 006	Mere Sher/Flute Song (12")	30
18	System SYSTM 021	Davinchi Kode/Know Your Enemy (12")	10

KRONSTADT UPRISING
80s	Spider SDL 12	The Unknown Revolution (p/s)	10

KRS-ONE
93	Jive HIP 142	RETURN OF THE BOOM BAP (2-LP)	20
95	Jive HIP 165	KRS ONE (2-LP)	20

HARDY KRUGER
59	Top Rank TR 5005	Blind Date (I'm A Lonely Man)/PINEWOOD ORCHESTRA: Blind Date (p/s)	8

KRU POPS
82	Electric Bubble Gum EB 101	Yummy Yummy Yummy/Gimme One More Dance	40

KRUZA
79	Black Hole Records BHE 101	Movies in The Night/Sun In My Eyes/Someone's There/All Stood Up (p/s)	20

KRYPTIC MINDS
09	Swamp 81 SWAMP 001	One Of Us/Six Degrees (12", p/s)	20
10	Swamp 81 SWAMP LP 001	ONE OF US (LP as 3 x 12")	40
11	Black Box BLACKBOX012	CAN'T SLEEP (LP as 3 x 12")	30

KRYPTON TUNES
78	Black & Red FIRE 1	Behind Your Smile/Coming To See You (p/s)	12
78	Lightning GIL 546	Limited Vision/All In Jail	12
79	Secret SR 009	EXTENDED PLAY EP	8

KRYSIA (KOCJAN)
74	RCA LPL1 5052	KRYSIA (LP)	18

(see also Natural Acoustic Band, Fairport Convention)

KRYSTAL GENERATION

MINT VALUE £

KRYSTAL GENERATION
72 Mercury 6052 120 Wanted Dead Or Alive/Every Man Seems To Be For Himself 10

BOB KUBAN & INMEN
66 Stateside SS 488 The Cheater/Try Me Baby 60
66 Stateside SS 488 The Cheater/Try Me Baby (DJ copy) 110
66 Stateside SS 514 The Teaser/All I Want 20
68 Bell BLL 1027 The Cheater/Try Me Baby (reissue) 10

KUBAS
65 Columbia DB 7451 I Love Her/Magic Potion 60
(see also Koobas)

DAVE KUBINEC
69 Parlophone R5762 Schopi/The Lady Loves 20

KUF-LINX
58 London HLU 8583 So Tough/What'cha Gonna Do 80
58 London HLU 8583 So Tough/What'cha Gonna Do (78) 25

LENNY KUHR
69 Philips BF 1777 The Troubadour/Oh No Monsieur 10

KUKL
84 Crass 1984/1 THE EYE (LP, foldout sleeve) 20
85 Crass No. 4 HOLIDAYS IN EUROPE (LP, with inner sleeve) 20
(see also Sugarcubes)

KULA SHAKER
96 Columbia SHAKER 1LP K (LP, inner) 30
99 Columbia SHAKER 2LP PEASANTS, PIGS & ASTRONAUTS (LP, gatefold) 30
10 Strangefolk SFKS003LP PILGRIM'S PROGRESS (LP, 300 only with signed screenprinted cover) 80
10 Strangefolk SFK S003LP PILGRIM'S PROGRESS (LP) 40

KULT
69 CBS 4276 No Home Today/Mister Number One 300

CHARLIE KUNZ
54 Decca F 10419 Charlie Kunz Piano Medley, No. 114 10

KURASS
70 Escort ES 825 Stampede/KING STITT: You Were Meant For Me (B-side actually by Lee Perry) 40

KURSAAL FLYERS
77 CBS 5705 TV Dinners/Revolver (A label demo only) 12
77 CBS 5771 Television Generation/Revolver (p/s as Kursaals) 7

KUSTOM
82 Red Bus RBUS 71 Let The Girl Dance/Arrested 20

KUT
81 Half Kut HKR 001 Can't Sleep at Night/Faithful (no p/s) 35

FELA RANSOME KUTI (& AFRICA '70)
72 Regal Zonophone RZ 3052 Chop And Quench/Egbe Mi O (with Africa '70 & Ginger Baker) 10
72 Regal Zono. SLRZ 1023 FELI RANSOME-KUTI & THE AFRICA '70 WITH GINGER BAKER LIVE! (LP) 50
73 Regal Zono. SLR2 103Y AFRODISIAC (LP, red/silver labels with EMI boxed logo) 200
75 Decca/Aphrodisia DWAPS 2005 UPSIDE DOWN (LP) 25
75 Creole CRLP 501 SHAKARA (LP, with Africa '70) 40
77 Creole CRLP 509 EVERYTHING SCATTER (LP) 30
77 Creole CRLP 511 ZOMBIE (LP, with Africa '70) 40
78 Phase 4 Stereo PFS 4412 YELLOW FEVER (LP) 50
79 Creole CRLP 502 GENTLEMEN (LP) 20
81 Arista SPART 1167 BLACK PRESIDENT (LP) 30
82 Arista SPART 1177 ORIGINAL SUFFERHEAD (LP) 30
83 EMI EDP 1547203 FELA ANIKULAPO KUTI (2-LP) 25
97 Talkin Loud 547 035-1 BOX SET 1 (Box set, 6-LP, booklet, postcards) 80
(see also Ginger Baker)

BEN KWELLER
02 679 777201 SHA SHA (LP) 25

JIM KWESKIN JUG BAND
65 Fontana TFL 6036 JIM KWESKIN JUG BAND (LP) 20
67 Fontana (S)TFL 6080 SEE REVERSE SIDE FOR TITLE (LP) 18
68 Vanguard SVRL 19046 WHATEVER HAPPENED TO THOSE GOOD OLD DAYS AT CLUB 47 (LP) 18

KWICK
80 EMI America EA 117 Can't Help Myself/Serious Business 6
80 EMI America 12 EA 117 We Ought To Be Dancing/Can't Help Myself/Let This Moment Be Forever (12") 15
81 EMI America EA 133 Night Life/Here I Go Again (Another Weekend) 6
81 EMI America Night Life/Here I Go Again (Another Weekend)/Split Decision (12") 15

KYDD
75 Dart ASRT 2052 Voodoo Magic/You Need Love Love Love 8

(THE) KYDDS
69 NEMS 56-4095 The Sun Is A Laughing Child/Touch Of The Sun 15

CHARLES KYNARD
72 Mainstream MSL 1009 WOGA (LP) 30
73 Mainstream MSL 1017 YOUR MAMA DON'T DANCE (LP) 25
96 BGP BGPD 1056 REELIN' WITH THE FEELIN' (LP, reissue) 15
96 BGP BGPD 1057 WA-TU-WA-ZUI (BEAUTIFUL PEOPLE) (LP, reissue) 15

KYODS
70 President PT 289 Judas In Blue/Where Did I Go Wrong 6

KYTES
66 Pye 7N 17136 Blessed/Call Me Darling 15
66 Pye 7N 17179 Frosted Panes/I'll Give You Better Love 35

KYTTOCK KYND

MINT VALUE £

| 68 | Island WI 6027 | Running In The Water/The End Of The Day | 80 |

KYTTOCK KYND
| 70 | Dorian 4782 | KYTTOCK KYND (LP) | 40 |

KYUSS
94	Elektra EKR 192	Demon Cleaner/Freedom Run (live) (p/s, sky blue vinyl)	40
94	Elektra SAM 1371	SKY VALLEY PART 2 (1-sided 12" sampler, stated white labels, stickered die-cut sleeve)	40
95	Elektra 7559-61571-1	WELCOME TO SKY VALLEY (2-LP)	80

PATTI LA BELLE (& BLUE BELLES)
64	Sue WI 324	Down The Aisle/C'est La Vie	30
65	Cameo Parkway P 935	Danny Boy/I Believe	20
65	Atlantic AT 4055	All Or Nothing/You Forgot How To Love (as Patty La Belle & Her Belles)	30
66	Atlantic AT 4064	Over The Rainbow/Groovy Kind Of Love (as Patty La Belle & Her Belles)	15
66	Atlantic 584 007	Patti's Prayer/Family Man (as Patti La Belle & Her Belles)	12
67	Atlantic 584 072	Take Me For A Little While/I Don't Want To Go On Without You	12
66	Atlantic 587 001	OVER THE RAINBOW (LP)	50

(see also Blue-Belles)

LABRADFORD
95	Flying Nun FN 329	A STABLE REFERENCE (LP, reissue, numbered sleeve)	30
96	Blast First BFFP 136	LABRADFORD (LP, die-cut sleeve, 2 inserts)	30
97	Blast First BFFP 144	MI MEDIA NARANJA (LP)	40
99	Blast First BFFP 157	E LUXO SO (LP)	40
00	Blast First BFFP 167	FIXED :: CONTENT (LP)	20

LACE
| 68 | Columbia DB 8499 | People People/The Nun | 25 |
| 69 | Page One POF 135 | I'm A Gambler/Go Away | 10 |

(see also Universals, Pete Dello, Honeybus, Red Herring, Gary Walker & Rain)

DAVE LACEY & CORVETTES
| 65 | Philips BF 1419 | That's What They All Say/I've Had Enough | 10 |

LACKEY & SWEENEY
| 73 | Village Thing VTS 23 | JUNK STORE SONGS FOR SALE (LP, inner) | 50 |

LACK OF KNOWLEDGE
81	LOK LOK 1	The Uninvited/Ritual (with A4 photocopied inserts)	30
83	Crass Records 121984/6	GREY (EP)	20
85	Chainsaw TEXT 7	SENTINEL (EP)	10
84	Corpus Christi CHRIST 15	SIRENS ARE BACK (LP)	20

JUNIOR LACY
| 77 | Aries ARI 003 | You Will See Jah Light/Jah Love Version (12") | 35 |

STEVE LACY
57	Esquire 32 143	SOPRANO TODAY (LP)	50
72	Emanem 301	SOLO (LP)	25
73	Emanem 304	THE CRUST (LP)	35

STEVE LACY & DEREK BAILEY
| 76 | Incus 26 | COMPANY 4 (LP) | 25 |

(see also Derek Bailey)

LADDERS
| 83 | Statik TAK 2 | Gotta See Jane/Krugerrands (p/s) | 6 |
| 83 | Statik TAK 2-12 | Gotta See Jane/Krugerrands (12", p/s) | 10 |

LADD'S BLACK ACES
| 56 | London AL 3556 | LADD'S BLACK ACES (10" LP) | 15 |

LA-DE-DA BAND
| 69 | Parlophone R 5810 | Come Together/Here Is Love | 18 |

LADIES
| 80s | Music Of Life MOLIS 6 | Turned On To You/I Knew That Love (12") | 15 |

TOMMY LADNIER
| 54 | London AL 3524 | BLUES AND STOMPS VOLUME ONE - TOMMY LADNIER (10" LP) | 20 |
| 55 | London AL 3548 | PLAYS THE BLUES WITH MA RAINEY & EDMONIA HENDERSON (10" LP) | 20 |

(see also Ma Rainey)

PATTIE LA DONNE
| 69 | Joe/Duke DU 23 | Friends And Lovers/JOE'S ALLSTARS: Hot Line | 12 |

LADY GAGA
| 08 | Interscope LGDANCEUP1 | JUST DANCE - THE REMIXES (LP, promo, pink vinyl) | 45 |

LADY JANE
| 84 | Schizoid SCHIZ 01 | For You Tonight/Out For The Count/Whisky And Leather (private pressing) | 60 |

LADY JANE & VERITY
| 59 | Pye International 7N 25036 | The Slow Look/Cry Baby | 8 |

LADY JUNE
| 74 | Caroline C 1509 | LADY JUNE'S LINGUISTIC LEPROSY (LP, with perforated lyric sheet) | 35 |

(see also Kevin Ayers, Eno)

LADY LEE
64	Decca F 11961	I'm Into Something Good/When Love Comes Along	12
65	Decca F 12147	99 Times Out Of 100/I Can Feel It	8
65	Columbia DB 7121	My Whole World (Seems To Be Tumbling Down)/Girl	10

LADY PENELOPE
97	Emitta EMT 100	Devotion To Love/Up & Down/Deeper Part 2 (12:")	18

(see also Abstrac & Lady Penelope)

LADYBIRDS
64	Columbia DB 7197	Lady Bird/I Don't Care Any More	10
64	Columbia DB 7250	The White Cliffs Of Dover/It's Not The Same Without A Boy	10
64	Columbia DB 7351	Memories/Try A Little Love	10
65	Columbia DB 7523	I Wanna Fly/O.K. Fred	10
70	Decca F13014	Love As High As A Mountain/Stand Up And Be Counted	12

(see also Sharades, Russ Loader, Marion Davies, De Laine Sisters)

LADYHAWKE
12	Modular MODVL 151	Black White And Blue/(Big Pink Remix) (250 only)	6
08	Modular MODVL 104	LADYHAWKE (LP, gatefold, booklet)	40

LADY LEX
04	Peckings PT 1013	Love Doctor/NATIJAH: Open My Gate	15
06	Peckings PT 1005	God Bless The Child/RICHIE DAVIES: It's True	6
09	Peckings PTI 059	COURTNEY JOHN: Lucky Man/LADY LEX: Don't Know Why	40

LADYTRON
01	Invicta Hi Fi LIQ 014	604 (2-LP, white vinyl)	40
02	Telstar TELP 3296	LIGHT & MAGIC (LP)	70
11	Nettwork 0 6700 30924 2 5	GRAVITY THE SEDUCER (LP, black vinyl)	60
11	Nettwork 0 6700 30924 2 5	GRAVITY THE SEDUCER (LP, clear vinyl)	70
12	Nettwork 0 6700 30946 1 0	WITCHING HOUR (LP, reissue, red vinyl)	30

LAFAYETTE AFRO ROCK BAND
99	Strut STRUTLP 003	DARKEST LIGHT - THE BEST OF (2-LP)	40

LAFAYETTES
62	RCA RCA 1299	Life's Too Short/Nobody But You	10
62	RCA RCA 1308	Caravan Of Lonely Men/I Still Do	10

JACK LA FORGE
65	Stateside SS 444	Our Crazy Affair/Bossa Bossa Nova (withdrawn)	25

L.A. GUNS
88	Vertigo VERH 55	L.A. GUNS (LP)	20

FRANCIS LAI
67	Brunswick LAT/STA 8689	I'LL NEVER FORGET WHAT'S 'ISNAME (LP, soundtrack)	50
69	United Artists SULP 1231	HANNIBAL BROOKS (LP)	30
69	Philips SBL 7876	MAYERLING (LP)	20
70	United Artists UAS 29137	RIDER IN THE RAIN (LP)	25

LAIBACH
84	L.A.Y.L.A.H. LAY 002	Boji/Sila/Brat Moj (12", p/s)	12
84	East West 12 EWS 3	Panarama/Decree (12", p/s)	10
85	Cherry Red 12CHERRY 91	Die Liebe/Die Liebe Ist Grösste Kraft, Die Alles Schafft (12", p/s)	10
86	Cherry Red BRED 67	NOVA AKROPOLA (LP)	15
86	Side Effects SER 08	OCCUPIED EUROPE TOUR '85 (LP)	15
94	Mute STUMM 121	NATO (LP)	50
96	Mute STUMM 136	JESUS CHRIST SUPERSTARS (LP)	60
03	Mute STUMM 223	WAT (2-LP)	60

LAIKA
94	Too Pure PURE 42	SILVER APPLES ON THE MOON (LP)	30
97	Too Pure PURE 62	SOUNDS OF THE SATELLITES (2-LP)	30
00	Too Pure PURE 89	GOOD LOOKING BLUES (2-LP)	30

CLEO LAINE
54	Parlophone MSP 6107	I Got Rhythm/I Know You're Mine (with Johnny Dankworth Orchestra)	10
55	Parlophone MSP 6147	Ain't Misbehavin'/I Got It Bad, And That Ain't Good (with Johnny Dankworth Orchestra)	10
60	Fontana H 269	Let's Slip Away/Thieving Boy	10
61	Fontana H 326	You'll Answer To Me/I Only Have Eyes For You	6
71	Philips 6006 077	Model City's Programme/Night Owl	50
57	Pye Nixa Jazz NJE 1026	THE APRIL AGE (EP, as Cleo Laine & Dave Lee Quintet)	20
57	Esquire EP 102	CLEO LAINE (EP, as Cleo Laine & Keith Christie Quintet)	20
57	Esquire EP 122	CLEO LAINE (EP, as Cleo Laine & Keith Christie Quintet)	20
55	Esquire 15-007	CLEO LAINE (10" LP)	40
58	Pye Nixa NPT 19024	CLEO'S CHOICE (10" LP)	40
58	MGM MGM-C 765	SHE'S THE TOPS (LP)	25
62	Fontana 680 992 TL	ALL ABOUT ME (LP, also stereo 886 159 TY)	15
64	Fontana (S)TL 5209	SHAKESPEARE AND ALL THAT JAZZ (LP)	15
66	Fontana (S)TL 5316	WOMAN TALK (LP)	15
68	Fontana STL 5483	SOLILOQUY (LP)	15

(see also Johnny Dankworth, Tubby Hayes & Cleo Laine, Dudley Moore)

DENNY LAINE
67	Deram DM 122	Say You Don't Mind/Ask The People	15
68	Deram DM 171	Too Much In Love/Catherine's Wheel	30
69	Deram DM 227	Say You Don't Mind/Ask The People (reissue)	10
73	Wizard WIZ 104	Find A Way Somehow/Move Me To Another Place	15
77	EMI 2588	Moondreams/Heartbeat	6
77	Palladin PAL 5014	Caroline/Blues	6
86	Preseident PT 555	Land Of Peace/If I Tried	6
73	Wizard SW2 2001	AHH...LAINE (LP, yellow labels)	20

(see also Paul McCartney/Wings, Balls, Trevor Burton, Magic Christians, Ginger Baker's Airforce, BL&G)

LINDA LAINE (& SINNERS)
64	Columbia DB 7204	Doncha Know, Doncha Know, Doncha Know/Ain't That Fun	20

Scott LAINE
MINT VALUE £
64	Columbia DB 7370	Low Grades And High Fever/After Today	20
65	Columbia DB 7549	Don't Do It Baby/All I Want To Do Is Run	20

(see also Sinners)

SCOTT LAINE
63	Windsor WB 114	Tearaway Johnnie/John Silver	40

DENZIL LAING
71	Songbird SB 1054	Medicine Stick/CRYSTALITES: Short Cut	15

(see also Soul Vendors, Dennis Alcapone)

LAKE
76	CBS 5015	Do I Love You/Key To The Rhyme	6

ALAN LAKE
70	Ember EMB S 278	Good Times/Got To Have Tenderness (p/s)	15

BONNIE LAKE & HER BEAUX
56	Brunswick 05622	Thirteen Black Cats/The Miracle Of Love	20

(see also Jack Pleis)

LAKELANDERS
60s		THE LAKELANDERS IN CONCERT (LP, hand-typed labels)	80

JOYCE LALOR
66	Airbourne NBP 006	Carribean Child/Evening Time (with the Fabulous Frats Quintet)	30

LEE LAMAR & HIS ORCHESTRA
57	London HLB 8508	Teenage Pedal Pushers/Sophia	75

GENE LAMARR
72	Injun 112	You Don't Love Me Anymore/Crazy Little House On The Hill	15

LAMB
96	Fontana PY 281	LAMB (2-LP, inner)	30
99	Mercury 558 821-1	FEAR OF FOURS (2-LP)	30
01	Mercury 586 4351	WHAT SOUND (2-LP)	60
03	Mercury 986 591-7	BETWEEN DARKNESS AND WONDER (LP)	25

CHRIS LAMB & UNIVERSALS
65	Decca F 12176	Mysterious Land/If You Ask Me	15

(see also Universals, Gidian)

KEVIN LAMB
70	Concord CON 23	Who Is The Hero?/The Road To Antibes	6
72	Birth RAB 4	WHO IS THE HERO? (LP, white label with 'rabbit' child logo)	40

LAMBCHOP
10	City Slang SLANG 0680056	TOUR BOX (8-CD, 2-DVD in canvas box, 1000 only sold on 2010 tour)	90

JEANNIE LAMBE
67	CBS 202636	Miss Disc/Montano Blues (with Gordon Beck Orchestra)	25
67	CBS 2731	Day After Day After Day/City At Night	20
67	CBS 3000	This Is My Love/Where Have All The Endings Gone (as Jeanne Lam)	8

DAVE LAMBERT, JON HENDRICKS & ANNIE ROSS
60	Philips BBL 7368	DAVE LAMBERT, JON HENDRICKS & ANNIE ROSS (LP, stereo SBBL 562)	15

(see also Jon Hendricks, Annie Ross)

TREVOR LAMBERT
72	Duke DU 132	Bald Head Teacher (act. by Max Romeo)/HEADMASTERS: Bald Head Version	10

LAMBERT & NUTTYCOMBE
70	A&M AMLS 997	AT HOME (LP)	60

LAMBRETTAS
79	Rocket XPRES 23	Go Steady/Listen Listen/Cortinas (p/s)	15
80	Rocket XPRES 25	Poison Ivy/Runaround (with '2-Stroke' die-cut sleeve & label)	20
80	Rocket XPRES 25	Poison Ivy/Runaround (with ROCKET die-cut sleeve & label)	12
80	Rocket XPRES 36	Page 3/Steppin' Out (Of Line) (withdrawn; one copy known to exist with p/s)	1000
81	Rocket XPRES 52	Anything You Want/Ambience (Rocket die-cut sleeve)	6
81	Rocket XPRES 62	Decent Town/Da-a-a-ance (p/s)	6
81	Rocket XPRES 6212	Decent Town/Da-a-a-ance/Total Strangers/Young Girls (12", p/s)	12
82	Rocket XPRES 74	Somebody To Love/Nobody's Watching Me (p/s)	8
82	Rocket XPRES 74	Somebody To Love/Nobody's Watching Me (p/s, mispressing, crediting Leap Before You Look on label & sleeve)	8
80	Rocket TRAIN 10	BEAT BOYS IN THE JET AGE (LP, with inner)	15

LAME DUCK
73	Perth PR 001	Sitting Still/Hold Out Your Hand	25

LAMELLA
80	Direct DO B1	When Julie Dances/Wasting Your Time (no p/s, 500 only)	50

TONI LAMOND
68	Philips BF 1722	Silent Voices/They Don't Give Medals (To Yesterday's Heroes)	15

DUNCAN LAMONT
68	Morgan MRSAM 2	THIS GUY (LP)	15

LA MORTGAGE
79	Metro 0501/EJSP 9289	Fallin/The Shady Lane (p/s)	30

LAMPLIGHTERS
55	Parlophone DP 416	Salty Dog/Ride Jockey Ride (78, export issue)	40

(see also Thurston Harris)

LAMP SISTERS
68	Sue WI 4048	A Woman With The Blues/I Thought It Was All Over	40

LANA SISTERS
58	Fontana H 148	Ring-A My Phone/Chimes Of Arcady	25
59	Fontana H 176	Buzzin'/Cry, Cry, Baby	25
59	Fontana H 190	Mister Dee-Jay/Tell Him No	25
59	Fontana H 221	(Seven Little Girls) Sitting In The Back Seat (with Al Saxon)/ Sitting On The Sidewalk	20
60	Fontana H 235	My Mother's Eyes/You've Got What It Takes	12
60	Fontana H 252	Someone Loves You, Joe/Tinatarella Di Luna	10

Cynthia LANAGAN

MINT VALUE £

60	Fontana H 283	Two-some/Down South	10

(see also Al Saxon, Dusty Springfield, Chantelles)

CYNTHIA LANAGAN
54	Columbia SCMC 2	Body And Soul/I Can't Believe You're In Love With Me (export issue)	10
57	Parlophone R 4316	Jamie Boy/Silent Lips (as Cynthia Lanigan)	7
57	Parlophone R 4383	I'm Available/(Don't Stop, Don't Stop) Tell Me More	10

LANCASHIRE FAYRE
80	Folk Heritage FHR 113	LANCASHIRE FAYRE (LP)	20

STEVE LANCASTER
67	Polydor 56215	San Francisco Street/Miguel Fernando San Sebastian Brown	15

LANCASTRIANS
64	Pye 7N 15732	We'll Sing In The Sunshine/Was She Tall	20
65	Pye 7N 15791	Let's Lock The Door (And Throw Away The Key)/If You're Goin' To Leave Me	7
65	Pye 7N 15846	There'll Be No More Goodbyes/Never Gonna Come On Home	7
65	Pye 7N 15927	Lonely Man/I Can't Stand The Pain	7
66	Pye 7N 17043	The World Keeps Going Round/Not The Same Anymore	40

MAJOR LANCE
63	Columbia DB 7099	The Monkey Time/Mama Didn't Know	35
63	Columbia DB 7099	The Monkey Time/Mama Didn't Know (DJ copy)	60
63	Columbia DB 7168	Hey Little Girl/Crying In The Rain	25
64	Columbia DB 7205	Um, Um, Um, Um, Um, Um/Sweet Music	30
64	Columbia DB 7271	The Matador/Gonna Get Married	40
64	Columbia DB 7365	Rhythm/Please Don't Say No More	40
65	Columbia DB 7463	I'm So Lost/Sometimes I Wonder	35
65	Columbia DB 7527	Come See/You Belong To Me, My Love	40
65	Columbia DB 7609	Pride And Joy/I'm The One	60
65	Columbia DB 7688	Too Hot To Hold/Dark And Lonely	80
65	Columbia DB 7787	Everybody Loves A Good Time/I Just Can't Help It	30
65	Columbia DB 7787	Everybody Loves A Good Time/I Just Can't Help It (DJ Copy)	75
66	Columbia DB 7967	Investigate/Little Young Lover	100
66	Columbia DB 7967	Investigate/Little Young Lover (DJ copy)	200
67	Columbia DB 8122	Ain't No Soul (Left In These Ole Shoes)/You'll Want Me Back	100
67	Columbia DB 8122	Ain't No Soul (Left In These Ole Shoes)/You'll Want Me Back (DJ copy)	175
69	Atlantic 584 277	Follow The Leader/Since You've Been Gone	15
69	Atlantic 584 302	Sweeter As The Days Go By/Shadows Of A Memory	20
69	Soul City SC 114	The Beat/You'll Want Me Back	25
70	Buddah 2011 046	Gypsy Woman/Stay Away From Me	15
72	Stax 2025 124	I Wanna Make Up/That's The Story Of My Life	15
72	Epic EPC 8404	Um, Um, Um, Um, Um, Um/Sweet Music (reissue)	6
73	Contempo C 1	The Right Track/Um, Um, Um, Um, Um, Um	6
73	Contempo C 9	Ain't No Soul (Left In These Ole Shoes)/Investigate	8
73	Contempo C 26	Dark And Lonely/My Girl	20
73	Warner Bros K 16334	Sweeter/Wild & Free	8
74	Warner Bros K 16385	Without A Doubt/Open The Door To Your Heart	15
74	Contempo CS 2017	Gimme Little Sign/How Can You Say Goodbye	25
74	Contempo CS 9015	The Right Track/Ain't No Soul (Left In These Ole Shoes)	6
75	Contempo CS 2045	Don't You Know I Love You (Parts 1 & 2)	20
75	Pye 7N 45487	You're Everything I Need (Parts 1 & 2)	15
76	Pye International 7N 25705	Nothing Can Stop Me/Follow The Leader	10
64	Columbia SEG 8318	UM UM UM UM UM UM (EP)	100
65	Columbia 33SX 1728	THE RHYTHM OF MAJOR LANCE (LP)	150
73	Contempo COLP 1001	GREATEST HITS LIVE AT THE TORCH (LP, sitting under a tree is first pressing)	50

HICK LANCELOT & SEVEN KNIGHTS
66	RCA RCA 1502	Say Girl/Live Like A Lion	15

LANCERS
54	London HL 8027	Stop Chasin' Me Baby/Peggy O'Neil	15
54	London HL 8079	So High, So Low, So Wide/It's You, It's You I Love	15
54	Vogue Coral Q 2038	Mister Sandman/The Little White Light	15
55	Vogue Coral Q 72062	Timberjack/C-r-a-z-y Music	20
55	Vogue Coral Q 72081	Get Out Of The Car (as Lancers & Georgie Auld)/Close Your Eyes	20
55	Vogue Coral Q 72100	Jo-Ann/The Bonnie Banks Of Loch Lomon'	10
56	Vogue Coral Q 72128	Alphabet Rock/Rock Around The Island	40
56	Vogue Coral Q 72157	Little Fool/A Man Is As Good As His Word	8
57	Vogue Coral Q 72282	Charm Bracelet/And It Don't Feel Bad	6
58	Coral Q 72300	The Stroll/Don't Go Near The Water	6
55	London REP 1027	PRESENTING THE LANCERS (EP)	20
54	London H-APB 1029	OH SWEET MAMA (10" LP)	25
61	London HA-P 2307	CONCERT IN CONTRASTS (LP)	15

BILLY LAND
62	Oriole CB 1750	I Go Walking/You're Too Much	10

HAROLD LAND
58	Contemporary LAC 12178	HAROLD IN THE LAND OF JAZZ (LP)	15

LAND OF BARBARA
93	Loble L02	Alcohol/Phosphorus For The Mutiny (p/s)	8

BOB LANDER & SPOTNICKS
62	Oriole CB 1784	Midnight Special/My Old Kentucky Home	15

(see also Spotnicks)

BILL & BRETT LANDIS
59	Parlophone R 4516	Since You've Gone/Bright Eyes	15
59	Parlophone R 4551	By You, By You/Forgive Me	10

Jerry LANDIS

MINT VALUE £

59	Parlophone R 4570	Baby Talk/Love Me True	15

JERRY LANDIS
62	Oriole CB 1930	Carlos Dominquez/He Was My Brother	40

(see also Paul Simon)

JOYA LANDIS
68	Trojan TR 620	Kansas City/Out The Light	20
68	Trojan TR 622	Angel Of The Morning/ALTON PHILLIPS: Love Letters	40
69	Trojan TR 641	Moonlight Lover/I Love You True	45

(see also Jay & Joya, Hugh Roy)

LANDLORD
90	Debut DEBTX 3084	I Like It (12")	10

HOAGY LANDS
67	Stateside SS 2030	The Next In Line/Please Don't Talk About Me When I'm Gone	250
67	Stateside SS 2030	The Next In Line/Please Don't Talk About Me When I'm Gone (DJ copy)	400
68	Stateside SS 2085	I'm Yours/Only You	20
72	Action ACT 4605	Why Didn't You Let Me Know/Do You Know What Life Is All About	35
75	UK USA 13	Friends And Lovers Don't Go Together/True Love At Last	30
75	UK USA 14	The Next In Line/I'm Yours	10

NEIL LANDSTRUMM
95	Mosquito MSQ 02	PASCAL EP (12", custom sleeve)	20

(see also Blue Arsed Fly)

ANITA LANE
93	Mute STUMM 81	DIRTY PEARL (LP)	35

DES(MOND) LANE
56	Decca F 10821	Penny-Whistle Rock/Penny-Whistle Polka	8
57	Decca F 10847	Rock Mister Piper/Plymouth Rock	10
59	Top Rank JAR 203	Moonbird/The Clanger March (as Des Lane Orchestra, with John Barry)	6

(see also Cyril Stapleton, John Barry)

GARY LANE & GARRISONS
61	Fontana H 338	Start Walking Boy/How Wrong Can You Be	15
62	Fontana 267221 TF	I'm A Lucky Boy/A Love Like You	10

LOIS LANE
67	RCA RCA 1570	One Little Voice/Sing To Me	6
68	Mercury MF 1042	Punky's Dilemma/Lazy Summer Day	6
69	Mercury MF 1115	Lovin' Time/Winds Of Heaven	6
68	Mercury SMCL 20125	LOIS LANE (LP)	20

(see also Caravelles)

MICKEY LEE LANE
64	Stateside SS 354	Shaggy Dog/Oo Oo	20
65	Stateside SS 456	Hey Sah-Lo-Ney/Of Yesterday	75
65	Stateside SS 456	Hey Sah-Lo-Ney/Of Yesterday (DJ copy)	150

PENNY LANE
68	Columbia DB 8377	Loving Or Losing You/Deep Down Inside	10
68	CBS 3718	The Boy Who Never Grew Up/I'm Going Back	8
70	CBS 4749	Bouzouki/Make Up Or Break Up	10
72	CBS 7916	Legend In Your Own Time/Driving Me Out Of My Mind	10
70	CBS 4905	Heartbreak House/He's Got A Hold Of My Heart	6
70	CBS 5311	Rock Me In The Cradle (Of Your Loving Arms)/I'm Free	10

RONNIE LANE & SLIM CHANCE
73	GM GMS 011	How Come/Tell Everyone/Done This One Before (p/s)	8
74	Island WIP 6216	What Went Down (That Night With You)/Lovely	7
75	Island WIP 6229	Brother Can You Spare A Dime/Ain't No Lady (p/s)	7
76	Island WIP 6258	Don't Try And Change My Mind/Well, well, Hello (The Party)	7
77	Polydor 2058 944	Street In The City/Annie (with Pete Townshend)	6
79	Gem GEMS 12	Kuschty Rye/You're So Right (p/s)	8
74	GML 1013	ANYMORE FOR ANYMORE (LP)	30
75	Island ILPS 9321	RONNIE LANE AND SLIM CHANCE (LP, gatefold)	30
75	Island ILPS 9366	ONE FOR THE ROAD (LP)	20
76	Atlantic K 50308	MAHONEY'S LAST STAND (LP, with Ron Wood, soundtrack)	15
80	Gem GEMLP 107	SEE ME (LP, with insert)	15

(see also Small Faces, Faces, Pete Townshend & Ronnie Lane)

ROSEMARY LANE
60	Philips PB 1041	Down By The River/My First Love Letter	8

SUZI LANE
79	Elektra K12390T	Harmony/Givin It Up (12")	10

TONY LANE & DELTONES
64	Sabre SA-45-5	It's Great/Now She's Mine	30

PATTIE LANE
68	Polydor 56260	Paper Dreams/My Four Walls	40

LANE BROTHERS
60	London HLR 9150	Mimi/Two Dozen And A Half	10

MARK LANEGAN
99	Beggars Banquet BBQLP215	I'LL TAKE CARE OF YOU (LP)	70
03	Beggars Banquet BBQ 373TT	HERE COMES THAT WEIRD CHILL (10" LP, as Mark Lanegan Band)	60
04	Beggars Banquet BBQLP 237	BUBBLEGUM (LP, as Mark Lanegan Band)	70

(see also Screaming Trees, Soulsavers, Isobel Campbell & Mark Lanegan)

LANE SISTERS
61	Columbia DB 4671	Peek A Boo Moon/Birmingham Rag	10

DON LANG (& HIS "FRANTIC" FIVE)
56	HMV 7M 354	Four Brothers/I Want You To Be My Baby (solo)	30

Eddie LANG & LONNIE JOHNSON

MINT VALUE £

56	HMV 7M 381	Rock Around The Island/Jumpin' To Conclusions (solo)	30
56	HMV 7M 416	Rock And Roll Blues/Stop The World I Wanna Get Off (solo)	30
56	HMV POP 260	Sweet Sue - Just You/Lazy Latin (solo)	20
57	HMV POP 289	Rock Around The Cookhouse/Rock Mister Piper	30
57	HMV POP 335	Rock-A-Billy/Come Go With Me (B-side with Skifflers)	30
57	HMV POP 350	School Day (Ring! Ring! Goes The Bell)/Six-Five Special	30
57	HMV POP 382	White Silver Sands/Again 'N' Again 'N' Again	15
57	HMV POP 414	Red Planet Rock/Texas Tambourine	25
58	HMV POP 434	Ramshackle Daddy/6-5 Hand Jive	25
58	HMV POP 465	Tequila/Junior Hand Jive	25
58	HMV POP 488	Witch Doctor/Cool Baby Cool	10
58	HMV POP 510	Hey Daddy!/The Bird On My Head	10
58	HMV POP 547	Queen Of The Hop/La-Do-Da-Da (solo)	15
59	HMV POP 585	Wiggle Wiggle/(You Were Only) Teasin' (solo)	15
59	HMV POP 623	Percy Green/Phineas McCoy (solo)	15
59	HMV POP 649	A Hoot An' A Holler/See You Friday	8
59	HMV POP 682	Reveille Rock/Frankie And Johnny	15
60	HMV POP 714	Sink The Bismarck!/They Call Him Cliff (solo)	30
60	HMV POP 805	Time Machine/Don't Open That Door	15
62	Decca F 11483	Wicked Women/Play Money (as Don Lang & Boulder Rollers)	10
57	HMV 7EG 8208	ROCK 'N' ROLL (EP)	100
57	HMV DLP 1151	SKIFFLE SPECIAL (LP, 10", by Don Lang & His Skiffle Group)	120
58	HMV DLP 1179	INTRODUCING THE HAND JIVE (LP, 10")	150
62	Ace Of Clubs ACL 1111	TWENTY TOP-TWENTY TWISTS (LP)	20

(see also Gordon Langhorn)

EDDIE LANG & LONNIE JOHNSON

67	Parlophone PMC 7019	BLUE GUITARS (LP)	20
70	Parlophone PMC 7106	BLUE GUITARS VOLUME 2 (LP)	20

(see also Blind Willie Dunn's Gin Bottle Four)

STEVIE LANGE

81	RCA RCA 152	Remember My Name/I Don't Want To Know (1st issue, p/s)	8
81	RCA LIM 1	Remember My Name/I Don't Want To Know (2nd issue, p/s)	6

GORDON LANGHORN

55	Decca F 10591	Give A Fool A Chance/Don't Stay Away Too Long	15

(see also Don Lang, Cyril Stapleton)

MARY LANGLEY

67	CBS 2862	Stay In My World/Summer Love	12
67	CBS 3032	It Always Rains On Sunday/All My Life Is You	6

(see also Perpetual Langley, Langleys)

PERPETUAL LANGLEY

66	Planet PLF 110	We Wanna Stay Home/So Sad	40
66	Planet PLF 115	Surrender/Two By Two	150

(see also Mary Langley, Langleys)

LANGLEYS

65	Fontana TF 544	Green Island/You Know I Love You	6

(see also Hawkwind, Widowmaker)

(HUW) LLOYD LANGTON (GROUP)

83	Flicknife SHARP 015	OUTSIDE THE LAW (LP, 1,000 with bonus 7": "Working Time"/ I See You [FREE 001], as Huw Lloyd Langton)	15

(see also Hawkwind, Widowmaker)

PHIL LANGTON TRIO

60s	Holyground	PHIL LANGTON TRIO (LP)	18

LANGUAGE FROM MEMORY

81	Squad SQA 001	Fortune/The Coat (1st pressing, p/s)	10
81	Towerbell TOW 15	Fortune/The Coat (p/s)	6

SNOOKY LANSON

56	London HLD 8223	It's Almost Tomorrow/Why Don't You Write	100
56	London HLD 8236	Stop (Let Me Off The Bus)/Last Minute Love	200
56	London HLD 8249	Seven Days/Tippity Top	200
56	London HL 7005	Seven Days/Tippity Top (export issue)	80

(see also Teresa Brewer)

JENNIFER LARA

79	Hit Run HIT DD 14	Jah Will Lead Us Home/RANKING PURPLE: Ah Fi We Jah (12")	60

LARAAJI

80	Editions EG EGAMB 003	AMBIENT 3 - DAY OF RADIANCE (LP)	15
10	Universal Sound USLP 30	CELESTRAL VIBRATION (LP, reissue)	15
13	All Saints WAST 037LP	ESSENCE/UNIVERSAL (LP, reissue, clear vinyl)	18

LARD

90	Alternative Tentacles VIRUS 84	LAST TEMPTATION OF REID (LP, with free 12")	15

TOBI LARK

06	Kent Select CITY 001	True True Love/LITTLE ANN: Sweep It Out In The Shed (reissue)	10
08	Kent TOWN 116	Challnge My Love/O.C. TOLBERT: You Got Me Turned Around (reissue)	10

PHILIP LARKIN

58	Mervell Press	LESS DECEIVED (LP, 100 only, numbered)	125
68	Listen	LESS DECEIVED (LP)	40
75	Argo PLP 1202	HIGH WINDOWS (LP)	25

LARKS

86	Exalation 12 LARX 2	All Or Nothing Girl/Whatever You Say/Teachers: Parents/Heartless (12", p/s)	12

LARKS (1)

64	Pye International 7N 25284	The Jerk/Forget Me	50

LARKS (2)

			MINT VALUE £
64	Pye International 7N 25284	The Jerk/Forget Me (DJ copy)	80

LARKS (2)
87	Exaltation 12LARX 3	PAIN IN THE NECK EP (12", p/s)	20
87	Exaltation LARX 3	Pain In The Neck/I Am A Clean Boy	20

LARO
60	Kalypso XX 21	Jamaican Referendum Calypso/Wrong Impressions Of A Soldier	8

WINSTON LARO
70	Downtown DT 461	Goodnight My Love/BOYSIE: I Don't Want To Be Hurt	12

JULIUS LA ROSA
55	London HL 8154	Mobile/Pass It On	15
55	London HLA 8170	Domani/Mama Rosa	15
55	London HLA 8193	Suddenly There's A Valley/Everytime I Kiss Carrie	15
56	HMV 7M 384	Lipstick And Candy And Rubber-Sole Shoe/Winter In New England	7
56	London HLA 8272	No Other Love/Rosanne	15
57	London HA-A 2031	JULIUS LA ROSA (LP)	20

LARRY'S ALL STARS
71	Ackee ACK 125	In The Fields/Teardrops Got The Feeling	15
71	Ackee ACK 130	Pre-Fight/The Prayer	20

(see also Larry Lawrence, Delroy Wilson, Hugh Roy, Sensations)

LARRY (MARSHALL) & ALVIN
68	Studio One SO 2065	Nanny Goat/Smell You Crep	30
68	Studio One SO 2067	Can't You Understand/Hush Up	70
69	Studio One SO 2080	Lonely Room (No One To Give Me Love)/You Mean To Me	45
69	Coxsone CS 7081	Love Got Me/BOB ANDY: Lady With The Bright Light (both sides actually by Glen [Brown] & Dave [Barker])	150
70	Bamboo BAM 22	Girl Of My Dream/SOUND DIMENTION: Give It Away	60

(see also Larry Marshall, Sound Dimension, Vincent Gordon)

LARRY & JOHNNY
65	Outasite 45 501	Beatle Time Parts 1 & 2 (99 copies only)	150

(see also Larry Williams & Johnny 'Guitar' Watson)

LARRY & LINDA
70	Beacon BEA 146	Most Peculiar Girl/Magnificent Opupouring	10

LARRY & TOMMY
68	Polydor 56741	You've Gotta Bend A Little/Yo-Yo (A side written and produced by John Cale)	35

KIM LARSEN & JUNGLE DREAMS
82	CBS A 2232	Rock 'N' Roll City/Time Bomb	20

JACK LARSON
61	Top Rank JAR 573	I Love The Way She Laughs/The Hammer Bell Song	8

LAS
14	System SYSTM 004	FIREPUSHER EP (12" with GANTZ)	20
14	System SYSTM 007	Backyard/Tic (12")	30
17	System SYSTM 016	Crowded/Recsystem (12")	20

LA'S
87	Go! Discs GOLAR 112	Way Out/Knock Me Down/Endless/Liberty Ship (Demo)/Freedom Song (Demo) (12", blue & silver stickered p/s listing 5 tracks)	10
88	Go! Discs LASEP 2	There She Goes/Way Out/Who Knows/Come In Come Out (EP, blue p/s, 5,000 only)	12
88	Go! Discs GOLAS 2	There She Goes/Come In Come Out (red p/s)	15
89	Go! Discs GOLAS 3	Timeless Melody/Clean Prophet (p/s, unissued; 10 test pressings only)	60
89	Go! Discs LASEP 3	Timeless Melody (10", unissued)	0
89	Go! Discs LASDJ 212	Timeless Melody/Clean Prophet/Knock Me Down/Over (12", promo, 500 only)	15
90	Go! Discs GOLAB 5	There She Goes/Freedom Song (numbered box set with badge & 3 stickers)	10
91	Go! Discs GOLAS 6	Feelin'/Doledrum (p/s)	6
91	Go! Discs GOLAB 6	Feelin'/IOU (Alternate Version)/Feelin' (Alternate Version)/Doledrum (numbered box set with badge & 3 stickers)	10
91	Go! Discs 828 202-1	THE LA'S (LP)	50
99	Viper VLP 002	LOST LA's 1984-1986 BREAKLOOSE (LP)	20
01	Viper VLP 008	LOST LA's 1986-1987: CALLIN' ALL (LP)	20
17	Viper VIPERLP 124	1987 (LP)	20

(see also Cast)

BONGO LES (CHEN) & BUNNY (HERMAN)
72	Attack ATT 8041	Feel Nice (Version)/WINSTON SCOTLAND: Quick And Slick	20

(see also Bongo Herman)

DENISE LASALLE
71	Janus 6310206	TRAPPED BY A THING CALLED LOVE (LP)	25
72	Westbound 6309 102	DOIN' IT RIGHT (LP)	20

EMMANUEL LASKEY
07	Hayley 013	(Put Your Name) In The Hall Of Fame/A Different Kind Of Different	8

LAST BANDITS
89	Solid ROK 722	The Angels Are Calling/The Dalkey Rake (p/s)	10

(see also Swell Maps, Nikki Sudden)

LAST CHANT
81	Chicken Jazz JAZZ 4	Run Of The Dove/Strength Alone/Tradition (p/s)	8

(see also Waterboys)

LAST EXIT
75	Wudwink WUD 01	Whispering Voices/Evensong (no p/s, push-out centre)	60
79	Wudwink WUD 01	Whispering Voices/Evensong (reissue, solid centre)	30
75	Wudwink WUD.C.101	FIRST FROM LAST EXIT (cassette only, pink card insert, sold at gigs, only 3 copies known to exist)	500

(see also Newcastle Big Band, Police, Sting)

LAST FLIGHT
81	Heavy Metal HEAVY 5	Dance To The Music/I'm Ready (p/s)	8

LAST MAN IN EUROPE

MINT VALUE £

LAST MAN IN EUROPE
85 Cocteau CO 22 — A Certain Bridge/TV Addict (p/s) 18

LAST POETS
72 Douglas DGL 69012 — THIS IS MADNESS (LP) 30

LAST RESORT (1)
78 Red Meat RMRS 01 — Having Fun?/F.U.2 (die-cut printed paper sleeve) 30

LAST RESORT (2)
82 Last Resort LR 1 — SKINHEAD ANTHEMS (LP, red vinyl) 30
82 Last Resort LR 1 — SKINHEAD ANTHEMS (LP, white vinyl) 30
82 Last Resort LR 1 — SKINHEAD ANTHEMS (LP, blue vinyl) 30
82 Last Resort LR 1 — SKINHEAD ANTHEMS (LP, black vinyl) 40

LAST RITES
83 Flicknife FLS 219 — We Don't Care/Step Down (p/s) 20
84 Essential 004 — FASCISM MEANS WAR (No Right To Take/Convicted Without Trial/Protest And Survive/The Dreams Of Many) (EP, gatefold p/s) 25
84 Essential 001 — THIS IS THE REACTION (LP) 30

LAST ROUGH CAUSE
85 LRC 001 — THE VIOLENT FEW (EP, with lyric sheet) 40

LAST STAND
81 Silly Symbol SJP 825 — Just A Number/Caviare (p/s) 40

LAST STRAW
78 Solent SS 049 — Oh Lady/Fly By Night (p/s) 50

LAST WORD
74 Polydor 2066 429 — Keep On Bumping Before You Run Out Of Gas/Funky And Some 8

LAST WORDS
79 Rough Trade RT 022 — Animal World/No Music In The World Today (p/s) 10
79 Remand REMAND 2 — Todays Kidz/There's Something Wrong (p/s) 6
80 Armageddon AS 02 — Top Secret/Walk Away (p/s) 8
81 Armageddon ARM 2 — THE LAST WORDS (LP) 15

LAST LAUGH
85 Hmmm! HA 1 — GLEE SWITCH EP 25

LAST SHADOW PUPPETS
08 Domino RUG 288 — The Age Of The Understatement/Two Hearts In Two Weeks 6
08 Domino RUG 301X — Standing Next To Me/Sequels 8
08 Domino RUG 309X — My Mistakes Were Made For You/Seperate And Ever Deadly (Live From New Theatre Oxford) 8
08 Domino RUG 309 — My Mistakes Were Made For You/Paris Summer (Live) 8
08 Domino WIGLP 208 — AGE OF THE UNDERSTATEMENT (LP, insert) 20
(see also Arctic Monkeys)

BILL LASWELL
84 Rough Trade ROUGH 51 — BASELINES (LP) 15
88 Venture VE12 — HEAR NO EVIL (LP) 25
(see also Material)

LATE ARRIVALS
67 Highlight HL1 — No One Cares/Voices Above 25

LATE OF THE PIER
07 Wow 02 — Space And The Woods/Heartbeat, Flicker, Line (7", 500 only) 10
08 EMI 228 0331 — FANTASY BLACK CHANNEL (LP, inner, stickered sleeve) 60

LATE ROAD LUNATICS
86 Star Dust SD 001 — THE LATE ROAD LUNATICS EP 10

LATE SHOW
78 Decca F 13777 — Drop Dead/Ain't Gonna Stamp On His Face (p/s) 15
78 Decca F13788 — I Like It/I Wrote A Book 6
79 Decca F 13835 — Chains/Screws On You (p/s) 7

YUSEF LATEEF
58 Esquire 32-069 — THE SOUNDS OF YUSEF (LP) 150
58 Columbia Clef 33CX 10124 — BEFORE DAWN (LP) 50
59 Esquire 32-139 — CRY! TENDER (LP) 60
64 Realm RM 228 — FABRIC OF JAZZ (LP) 25
64 Transatlantic PR 7319 — EASTERN SOUNDS (LP) 30
67 HMV CSD 3615 — THE GOLDEN FLUTE (LP) 20
72 Atlantic K 40359 — GENTLE GIANT (LP) 20
73 Prestige PR 24007 — YUSEF LATEEF (LP) 15
74 Atlantic K 50041 — PART OF THE SEARCH (LP) 15
76 Impulse IMPL 8013 — CLUB DATE (LP) 15

LATIMORE
73 President PTLS 1058 — S.T. (LP) 15
74 President PTLS 1062 — MORE MORE MORE (LP) 15

LATIN BREED
02 Funk 45 FUNK45 007 — I Turn You On/Hard To Handle (reissue) 7

MARCEL LATOUR
69 United Artists UP 350058 — Women In Love/Kes 8

GENE LATTER
66 Decca F 12364 — Just A Minute Or Two/Dream Lover 30
66 Decca F 12397 — Mother's Little Helper/Please Come Back To Me Again 25
67 CBS 202483 — Something Inside Me Died/Don't Go 8
67 CBS 202655 — Always/A Woman Called Sorrow 8
67 CBS 2843 — A Little Piece Of Leather/Funny Face Girl 40
67 CBS 2843 — A Little Piece Of Leather/Funny Face Girl (DJ copy) 60
67 CBS 2986 — With A Child's Heart/Ways 10
68 Direction 58-3245 — A Tribute To Otis/Bring Your Love Home 10

Stanley LAUDAN

			MINT VALUE £
68	Spark SRL 1015	My Life Ain't Easy/Angie (as Gene Latter & Detours)	6
69	Spark SRL 1022	Sign On The Dotted Line/I Love You	10
69	Spark SRL 1031	The Old Iron Bell/Holding A Dream	170
69	Parlophone R 5800	Help Me Judy, Help Me/On The Highway	7
69	Parlophone R 5815	Tiger Bay/We Can Make Out	10
70	Parlophone R 5853	Someday You'll Need My Love/Come On Home	6
71	Parlophone R 5896	Catch My Soul/Happiness	10
71	Parlophone R 5913	Sing A Song Of Freedom/Too Busy Thinking About My Baby	10

(see also Detours)

STANLEY LAUDAN
58	Oriole CB 1434	Two Guitars/Blue Shawl	8

THE LAUGHING APPLE
81	Autonomy AUT 001	HA HA HEE HEE (EP)	15
81	Autonomy AUT 002	Participate!/Wouldn't You? (foldover p/s)	15
82	Essential ESS 001	Precious Feeling/Celebration (p/s)	15

(see also Biff Bang Pow!, Revolving Paint Dream)

LAUGHING GAS
70	RCA RCA 2006	All Shapes And Sizes/Opus No. 1	6

LAUGHING GASS
79	Wessex WEX 264	New Tart/Bandito (p/s, numbered)	12

LAUGHING MOTHERS
85	Motherkare MUM 1	Tunnel/Cats Cradle (p/s)	20

LAUREL (AITKEN) & OWEN (GRAY)
62	Blue Beat BB 149	She's Going To Napoli/Have Mercy Mr Percy	15

(see also Laurel Aitken, Owen Gray)

LAURELS
68	RCA Victor RCA 1741	Sunshine Thursday/Threepence A Tune	15
69	RCA Victor RCA 1836	Making It Groovy/Rainmaker	40
70	Pye 7N 17980	Shame Shame/Make Believe	10
71	Pye 45034	The Devil's Well/Underground	60

ROD LAUREN
59	RCA RCA 1165	If I Had A Girl/No Wonder	10

LAURENT
71	Pye 7N 25566	Sing Sing Barbara/Le Temple Bleu	8

JOHN LAURENZ
55	London HL 8138	Goodbye, Stranger, Goodbye/Red Roses	20

LAURI
78	Thelopian THEO1	If We Can't Have It Neither Can They/Reconciling Trades (p/s)	6

MISS LAVELL
65	Vocalion VP 9236	Everybody's Got Somebody/The Best Part Of Me	25

JUNE LAVERICK
60	Oriole CB 1537	Stop/JOHNNY WEBB: Concertino	6

(see also Johnny Webb)

ROGER LA VERN & MICRONS
63	Decca F 11791	Christmas Stocking/Reindeer Ride	25

(see also Tornados)

BETTY LAVETTE
67	Stateside SS 2015	I Feel Good All Over/Only Your Love Can Save Me	60
67	Stateside SS 2015	I Feel Good All Over/Only Your Love Can Save Me (DJ copy)	75
68	Pama PM 748	Only Your Love Can Save Me/I Feel Good All Over (reissue)	60
70	Polydor 56786	He Made A Woman Out Of Me/Nearer To You	10
72	Mojo 2092 030	Let Me Down Easy/I Feel Good All Over/What I Don't Know Won't Hurt Me	10
73	Atlantic K 10299	Your Turn To Cry/Soul Tambourine	10
78	Atlantic K 11198	Doin' The Best That I Can Parts 1 & 2	6
82	Tamla Motown TMG 1265	I Can't Stop/Either Way We Lose	8

LAW AND AUDER
95	Sub + Bleep BLEEP 12 002	Gimme (The Weed) (Mix 1)/(Mix 2)/Cant Tekkie (12")	25
95	Sub + Bleep BLEEP 12 003	Sunshine/Lively Body (12")	20
95	G-Fource 951	Feel It/Acid Jungle (12", white label)	80
95	G-Fource 952	Who Gose/Untitled (12", white label)	35
95	G-Fource 953	Too Right/Untitled (12", white label)	40
95	Slamming Wreck SLAM 003	It's Alright/Bust The New Jam (12", stamped white labels)	15

PETER LAW
67	Major Minor MM 522	Lingering On/Memories Of You	6

LAW (THE)
79	Smile SR011	Be My Girl/Dead City Kicks/I Just Want Your Body (500 pressed)	50

GASPAR LAWAL
80	Cap	AJOMASE (LP)	20

AZIE LAWRENCE
59	Mezzotone ME 7001/7002	West Indians In England/Jump Up	12
59	Mezzotone ME 7004	Love In Every Land/No Dice	8
60	Starlite ST45 022	West Indians In England/Jump Up (with Carib Serenaders)	15
61	Starlite ST45 041	No Dice/Love In Every Land	10
61	Melodisc M 1563	Jamaica Blues/Come Rumble & Tumble With Me	8
61	Melodisc M 1572	You Didn't Want To Know/I Want To Be In Love	8
61	Blue Beat BB 71	So Far Apart/Palms Of Victory (with Melobeats)	12
64	Blue Beat BB 222	Pempelem/Lovers Understand	400

DIANE LAWRENCE
67	Doctor Bird DB 1075	I Won't Hang Around Like A Hound Dog/Read It Over	35
68	Jolly JY 005	Treat Me Nice/I've Been Loving You	12

Earl LAWRENCE

MINT VALUE £

EARL LAWRENCE
85 Ariwa ARI 44 — Dancing On A Bassline/Dancing On A Bassline (Version) (12") 80

GENE LAWRENCE
67 Jump Up JU 505 — Longest Day Meringue/Bachelor Boy 10
67 Jump Up JU 510 — Meringue Triniana/Devil Woman 10

LARRY LAWRENCE (JAMAICA)
63 Island WI 091 — Garden Of Eden/DERRICK MORGAN: Sendin' This Message 15

(see also Larry's Allstars, McBean Scott & Champions)

LARRY LAWRENCE (U.S.)
59 Pye International 7N 25042 — Goofin' Off/Bongo Boogie (as Larry Lawrence & Band Of Gold) 10
60 Ember EMB S 106 — Squad Car Theme/Jug-A-Roo (with Beatniks, in art p/s) 15
60 Ember EMB S 106 — Squad Car Theme/Jug-A-Roo (with Beatniks) 10

LEE LAWRENCE (& CORONETS)
55 Columbia SCM 5201 — Suddenly There's A Valley/Mi Muchacha (Little Girl) 10
57 Columbia DB 3855 — Rock 'n' Roll Opera/Don't Nobody Move 40

STEVE LAWRENCE
53 Parlophone MSP 6038 — Say It Isn't True/This Night (Madalena) (as Steve & Bernie Lawrence) 10
54 Parlophone MSP 6080 — Remember Me (You Taught Me To Love)/Too Little Time 10
54 Parlophone MSP 6106 — You Can't Hold A Memory In Your Arms/King For A Day 10

TERRY LAWRENCE
71 Pye Int. 7N 25558 — Medicine Man/Let Me Be Free 7

VALERIE ANN LAWRENCE
65 Decca F 12273 — My Love Loves Me/12A Heartache Square 7

VICKI LAWRENCE
73 Stateside SS 2210 — The Night The Lights Went Out In Georgia/Dime A Dance 7

ZACK LAWRENCE
73 Pemini Organisation — ASSASSIN EP (with p/s) 70
73 Pemini Organisation — ASSASSIN EP (without p/s) 30

LAWRENCE AND COMFORTABLE SOCIETY
86 LCA LCS 1 — Sleeper/Heartache (hand-made sleeve) 150

BILLY (M.) LAWRIE
69 Polydor 56363 — Roll Over Beethoven/Come Back Joanna (as Billy M. Lawrie) 25
73 RCA RCA 2439 — Rock And Roller/Shalee Shala 6
73 RCA SF 8395 — SHIP IMAGINATION (LP, die-cut gatefold sleeve) 25

ELOISE LAWS
00s Inferno HEAT 15 — Love Factory/JUST BROTHERS : Sliced Tomatoes (reissue) 10
13 Outta Sight OSV 104 — Love Factory/JUST BROTHERS : Sliced Tomatoes (reissue) 8

JOHN LAWSON
79 SRTX 79 CUS 617 FMR 024 — 1 X 6 (LP) 25

JULIET LAWSON
72 Sovereign SOV 111 — Only A Week Away/Weeds In The Yard 7
72 Sovereign SVNA 7257 — BOO (LP, textured gatefold sleeve) 200

(see also Trees)

SHIRLEY LAWSON
68 Soul City SC 108 — The Star/One More Chance 200

LAWSON-HAGGART ROCKIN' BAND
59 Brunswick OE 9451 — BOPPING AT THE HOP (EP) 15
59 Brunswick STA 3010 — BOPPING AT THE HOP (LP) 30

LOU LAWTON
67 Ember EMB S 232 — Doin' The Philly Dog/I Am Searching 30
68 Speciality SPE 1005 — I'm Just A Fool/Wrapped In A Dream 30

LAXTON & OLIVER
69 Blue Cat BS 168 — Wickeder/Stay In My Arms 20

GRAHAM LAYDEN
72 Penny Farthing PEN 792 — Tiny Lover/All You Lovers 10

OSSIE LAYNE
65 R&B MRB 5006 — Come Back/Never Answer That 'Phone 35

EDDIE LAYTON
59 Mercury AMT 1064 — Duck Walk/Doodles 10

PAUL LAYTON
68 Paradox PAR 45901 — Mister Mister/Sing Sadman Sing (p/s) 25

KEN LAZ(A)RUS (& CREW)
65 Island WI 220 — Funny (as Ken Lazrus & Byron Lee Orchestra)/ BYRON LEE ORCHESTRA: Walk Like A Dragon 15
71 Explosion EX 2056 — Girl/TOMORROW'S CHILDREN: Sister Big Stuff 8
72 Explosion EX 2064 — Hail The Man/Where Do I Go 7
72 London HLH 10379 — Hail The Man/Where I Go 6
70 London HA-J 8412 — REGGAE SCORCHER (LP, unissued) 0
70 London ZGJ 107 — REGGAE - GREATEST HITS VOL. 1 (LP) 20

PETER LAZONBY
96 Brainiak BRAINK 40R — Wavespeech (12") 30

LAZY FOUR
79 SGS SGS 110 — Callow Capital/I Won't Shed A Tear 15

LAZY LATINS
67 Morgan MR 110 P — LAZY LATIN (LP) 15

LAZY SMOKE
80s Heyoka — CORRIDOR OF FACES (LP, reissue of U.S. LP) 15

LCD SOUNDSYSTEM
02 Output OPR DFA 002 — Losing My Edge/Beat Connection (12", p/s) 10
04 DFA DFAEM17 — Daft Punk Is Playing At My House/Jump In The Fire (p/s) 10
07 EMI 0094639493470 — All My Friends (John Cale Version)/All My Friends (Album Version) 10

LE TIGRE

			MINT VALUE £
07	EMI 0094639645374	All My Friends (Franz Ferdinand Version)/All My Friends (Edit)	10
07	EMI 0094638505877	North American Scum/Hippie Priest Burn-Out (with free poster)	10
10	Parlophone 5099963244571	Drunk Girls/WOODEN SHJIPS: Drunk Girls (Version)	6
05	DFA DFAEMIDJ 2138LP	LCD SOUNDSYSTEM (2-LP promo, die-cut sleeve)	35
05	DFA DFAEMI2138LP	LCD SOUNDSYSTEM (2-LP)	30
07	EMI DFAEMI 2163lp	45:33 (2 x 12")	15
07	EMI 0946 3 85114 1 0	SOUND OF SILVER (2-LP, inners, poster)	30
10	DFA DFA 22502	THIS IS HAPPENING (2-LP)	25
14	DFA DFA2362LP	THE LONG GOODBYE – LCD LIVE AT MADISON SQUARE GARDEN (5-LP box set)	150

LE TIGRE
99	Wiiija WIJ 107	HOT TOPIC EP (p/s)	10
99	Wiiija WIJ LP 1108	LE TIGRE (LP)	35

BARBARA LEA
56	London HB-U 1058	A WOMAN IN LOVE (10" LP)	20
56	Esquire 32/043	NOBODY ELSE BUT ME (LP)	20
57	Esquire 32/063	IN LOVE (LP)	20

JIMMY LEA
85	Trojan KANE 001	Citizen Kane/Poland (p/s)	15

(see also Slade)

LEADBELLY (HUDDIE LEDBETTER)

EPs
56	Melodisc EPM7 63	THE MUSIC OF HUDDIE LEDBETTER	10
58	Melodisc EPM7 77	LEADBELLY	10
58	Melodisc EPM7 82	SEE SEE RIDER	10
59	Melodisc EPM7 87	PARTY PLAYS AND SONGS	10
59	RCA RCX 146	ROCK ISLAND LINE	10
61	Capitol EAP1 1821	HUDDIE LEDBETTER'S BEST NO. 1	10
61	Capitol EAP4 1821	HUDDIE LEDBETTER'S BEST NO. 2	10
61	Capitol EAP1 20111	LEADBELLY	10
61	Storyville SEP 337	LEADBELLY	10
62	Storyville SEP 387	STORYVILLE BLUES ANTHOLOGY VOL. 7	15

ALBUMS
53	Capitol LC 6597	LEADBELLY SINGS CLASSICS IN JAZZ (10")	40
57	Melodisc MLP 511	LEADBELLY VOL. 1 (10", green & silver labels)	30
57	Melodisc MLP 512	LEADBELLY VOL. 2 (10", green & silver labels)	30
58	Melodisc MLP 515	LEADBELLY VOL. 3 (10", green & silver labels)	30
58	Melodisc MLP 517	PLAYS PARTY SONGS (10", green & silver labels)	30
58	Melodisc MLP 12-107	THE SAGA OF LEADBELLY (green & silver or blue & black labels)	20
59	Melodisc MLP 12-113	LEADBELLY'S LAST SESSIONS VOLUME 2 PART 1	20
59	Melodisc MLP 12-114	LEADBELLY'S LAST SESSIONS VOLUME 2 PART 2	20
62	Storyville SLP 124	A DEMON OF A MAN - BLUES ANTHOLOGY	20
63	Storyville SLP 139	LEADBELLY 2 - T.B. BLUES	20
63	Capitol T 1821	HIS GUITAR, HIS VOICE, HIS PIANO: HUDDIE LEDBETTER'S BEST	15
63	RCA Victor RD 7567	GOOD MORNING BLUES	20
65	Verve (S)VLP 5002	TAKE THIS HAMMER	20
66	Elektra EKL 301/2	THE LIBRARY OF CONGRESS RECORDINGS (3-LP)	30
67	Verve (S)VLP 5011	KEEP YOUR HANDS OFF HER	15
69	Xtra XTRA 1046	LEADBELLY SINGS FOLK SONGS	18
69	Xtra XTRA 1126	SHOUT ON	15

LEADBELLY & BLIND LEMON JEFFERSON
61	Jazz Collector JEL 124	THE MALE BLUES VOLUME 8 (EP)	10

(see also Blind Lemon Jefferson)

LEADERBEATS
60	Top Rank JAR 405	Dance, Dance, Dance/Washington Square	12

LEADERS (JAMAICA)
68	Amalgamated AMG 804	Tit For Tat (actually by Lynn Taitt & Jets)/MARVETTS: You Take Too Long	35

(see also Pioneers, Stranger Cole)

LEADERS (U.K.)
65	Fontana TF 602	Night People/Love Will Find A Way	10

LEADING FIGURES
67	Deram DML/SML 1006	OSCILLATION 67! (LP)	65
67	Ace Of Clubs ACL 1225/SCL 1225	SOUND AND MOVEMENT (LP, mono/stereo)	65

(see also Jon Lord, Deep Purple)

LEAF HOUND
05	Rise Above 7/68	Freelance Fiend/Too Many Rock N Roll Times	40
71	Decca SKL-R 5094	GROWERS OF MUSHROOM (LP)	2500

(see also Brunning Sunflower Blues Band, Black Cat Bones, Atomic Rooster, Cactus)

LEAF DOG
14	High Focus HFRFP003	FROM A SCARECROW'S PERSPECTIVE (2-LP)	35

LEAGUE
67	President PT 167	Nothing On/Hey Conductor	25

LEAGUE OF GENTLEMEN (1)
65	Columbia DB 7666	Each Little Falling Tear/And I Do Now	70
66	Planet PLF 109	How Can You Tell/How Do They Know (with Planet company sleeve)	100

LEAGUE OF GENTLEMEN (2)
80	EG/Virgin EGEDS 1	Heptaparaparshinokh/ROBERT FRIPP: Marriagemuzic	6
81	EG EGED 9	THE LEAGUE OF GENTLEMEN (LP)	25

(see also Giles Giles & Fripp, Brain)

LEAGUE OF NATIONS

MINT VALUE £

LEAGUE OF NATIONS
84 Glaze GZLP 102 — MUSIC FOR THE NEW DEPRESSION (LP) 50

LEAH
73 GM GMS 10 — Arise Sir Henry/Uptight Basil 7

(see also Pete Dello, Red Herring)

JOE LEAHY
65 Capitol CL 15417 — Life/Pink Powder Puff 8

BOB LEAPER
65 Pye 7N 15700 — High Wire (Theme From 'Danger Man')/The Lost World 40
64 Decca LK 4639 — BIG BAND, BEATLE SONGS (LP) 20

LEAPERS CREEPERS SLEEPERS
66 Island WI 275 — Precious Words/Ba Boo 30

KEVIN 'KING' LEAR
67 Polydor 56203 — Count Me Out/Pretty Woman 15
68 Page One POF 087 — Power Of Love/Mr. Pearly 20
68 Page One POF 109 — Cry Me A River/Shoe Shine Sam 20
69 Page One POF 132 — The Snake/Man In The Funnies 15

LEARGO
79 Motor City DNS 87903 — The Artist/Played Out Angel (p/s) 40

TIMOTHY LEARY MEETS THE GRID
90 Evolution EVO 1 — Origins Of Dance (Electronic Future Mix)/(Hi-Tec Pagan Mix) (12") 10

(see also the Grid)

LEATHERCOATED MINDS
67 Fontana (S)TL 5412 — A TRIP DOWN THE SUNSET STRIP (LP) 80

(see also J.J. Cale)

LEATHERFACE
90 Roughneck HYPE 1 — Razor Blades And Asprin/Colorado Joe, Leningrad Vlad/Post War Product Of A Fat Man's Wallet 15
91 Roughneck HYPE 14 — I Want The Moon/You Are My Sunshine/Dreaming 10
92 Clawfist XPIG 15 — Hops And Barley/Discipline/A Public House/Not Superstitious/James Whale (split release with Wat Tyler 2 x 7") 10
90 Meantime COXEP 3 — BEERPIG (EP, with insert) 30
90 Roughneck HYPE 6T — SMOKEY JOE (12" EP) 10
91 Roughneck HYPE 9T — NOT SUPERSTITIOUS (12" EP) 15
92 Roughneck HYPE 17T — COMPACT AND BIJOU (10" EP) 10
93 Roughneck HYPE 22T — DO THE RIGHT THING (12", pls) 15
89 Meantime COX 017 — CHERRY KNOWLE (LP) 20
90 Roughneck NECKLP 1 — FILL YOUR BOOTS (LP, with insert) 30
91 Roughneck NECKLP 5 — MUSH (LP, inner) 50
93 Roughneck NECK 11LPS — MINX (LP, with bonus 7" Can't Help Falling In Love/Dreaming (HYPE 24) 40
93 Roughneck NECKLP 11 — MINX (LP) 30

(see also Frankie Stubbs)

LEATHERHEAD
74 Philips 6006 371 — Gimme Your Money Please/Epitaph (die-cut 'Leatherhead' sleeve) 20

LEATHER NUN
79 Industrial IR 0006 — SLOW DEATH (EP) 20
84 Criminal Damage CRI MLP 113 — SLOW DEATH (Reissue, mini LP) 25

LEA VALLEY SKIFFLE GROUP
58 Esquire EP 163 — LEA VALLEY SKIFFLE GROUP (EP) 40

LEAVES
66 Fontana TF 713 — Hey Joe/Funny Little World 40

OTIS LEAVILL(E)
71 Atlantic 2091 160 — There's Nothing Better/I'm So Jealous 8

CATE LE BON
07 Recordiau Reandomonium 70300h — No One Can Drag Me Down/Disappear (p/s, 500 only) 20
08 Pesky Peski 009 — Edrych Yn Llygaid Ceffyl Benthyg EP (10" white vinyl) 25
12 Ovni/Turnstile OVNI 012/796.A032.133 — CYRK II (12" EP with download) 30
14 Turnstile TS005S1 — He's Leaving/Solitude (die-cut p/s, tour 7") 20
12 Ovni / Turnstile OVNI010LP/796.A028.010 — CYRK (LP, with inner) 20
13 Turnstile TS005S1 — MUG MUSEUM (LP, pink vinyl with insert and CD) 25
16 Turnstile//Caroline TS022LP — CRAB DAY (LP, with inner and download) 20
19 Mexican Summer MEX 250 — REWARD (LP, splatter vinyl, limited linked sleeve with inner and insert) 20
22 Mexican Summer MEX 315 — POMPEII (LP, pink/white marbled vinyl with inner. Mail order only) 45
22 Mexican Summer MEX 315 — POMPEII (LP, clear vinyl, Rough Trade exclusive) 30

LECUONDA CUBAN BOYS
55 Columbia 33S 1075 — BENEATH THE CUBAN MOON (10" LP) 15

JOHN LEDINGHAM
68 Pye 7N 17488 — Love Is A Toy/Thank You Mrs. Gilbert 6

(see also Jonathan Kelly)

CHRIS LEDOUX
79 Westwood WRS 143 — RODEO'S SINGING BRONC RIDER (LP) 60

LED ZEPPELIN
SINGLES
69 Atlantic 584 268 — Good Times, Bad Times (unissued, 1-sided EMIdisc and LDC acetates only) 2000
69 Atlantic 584 269 — Communication Breakdown/Good Times, Bad Times (unissued, promo only) 700
69 Atlantic/Emidisc — Whole Lotta Love (Edit)/Whole Lotta Love (Edit) (Acetate) 2000
69 Atlantic 584 309 — Whole Lotta Love (Edit)/Livin' Lovin' Maid (She's A Woman) (withdrawn, large centre hole, clean label or "5th Dec 1969" stamp on label) 600

LED ZEPPELIN

MINT VALUE £

69	Atlantic 584 309	Whole Lotta Love (Edit)/Livin' Lovin' Maid (She's A Woman) (withdrawn, solid centre with small centre hole, 1 copy known)	1500
69	Atlantic 584 309	Whole Lotta Love (Edit)/Living Loving Maid (She's A Woman) (withdrawn, large centre hole, mispressing with Living Loving Maid labels on both sides)	600
70	Emidisc	Immigrant Song (unissued one sided acetate, scheduled to be released as Atlantic 2091 043 on 27th November 1970)	3000
73	Trident	D'Yer Mak'er (Unissued one sided acetate)	1200
73	Atlantic K 10296	D'Yer Mak'er/Over The Hills And Far Away (unreleased, promo only)	350
75	Swan Song DC 1	Trampled Underfoot/Black Country Woman (white label test pressing)	350
75	Swan Song DC 1	Trampled Underfoot/Black Country Woman (Red label test pressing)	500
75	Swan Song SSK 19403	Trampled underfoot/Black Country Woman (withdrawn first pressing)	150
75	Swan Song DC 1	Trampled Underfoot/Black Country Woman (Limited edition dealer incentive promo, die-cut title sleeve)	25
75	Swan Song SSK 19403	Trampled Underfoot/Black Country Woman (push mispressed cat. no.)	150
79	Swan Song SSK 19421	Wearing And Tearing/Darlene (cancelled Knebworth 45, existence unconfirmed)	0
90	Atlantic LZ 3	Stairway To Heaven/Whole Lotta Love (white label test pressing)	350
90	Atlantic LZ 2	Stairway To Heaven/Immigrant Song/Whole Lotta Love/Good Times Bad Times (10", p/s, promo only)	40
90	Atlantic LZ 2	Stairway To Heaven/Immigrant Song/Whole Lotta Love/Good Times Bad Times (10", test pressing, white labels)	350
90	Atlantic CD LZ 1	Stairway To Heaven/Immigrant Song/Whole Lotta Love/Good Times Bad Times (CD, promo only, in Zeppelin-design long box)	30
90	Atlantic LZ 3	Stairway To Heaven/Whole Lotta Love (with East West Records internal memo, 150 copies only, promo)	175
90	Atlantic LZ 3 LC	Stairway To Heaven/Whole Lotta Love (jukebox single, push-out centre)	30
97	Atlantic AT 0013 LC	Whole Lotta Love/Whole Lotta Love (jukebox promo)	25
97	Atlantic AT 0031LC	Whole Lotta Love (Edit)/Whole Lotta Love (Edit) (jukebox issue, with pushout centre)	15
03	Warner Vision PR 03945	What Is And What Should Never Be/In My Time Of Dying/Rock And Roll (DVD, promo sampler)	25
18	Atlantic R 7566332	Rock And Roll (Sunset Sound Mix)/Friends (Olympic Studio Mix) RSD, yellow vinyl	20

ALBUMS

69	Atlantic 588 171	LED ZEPPELIN (LP, 1st pressing, red/maroon label, turquoise sleeve lettering, "Superhype" publishing credit)	3000
69	Atlantic 588 171	LED ZEPPELIN (LP, 2nd pressing, red/maroon label, orange sleeve lettering, "Superhype" publishing credit)	300
69	Atlantic 588 171	LED ZEPPELIN (LP, 2nd pressing, red/maroon label, orange sleeve lettering, "Warner Bros" publishing credit)	300
69	Atlantic 588 198	LED ZEPPELIN II (LP, 1st pressing, red/maroon label, with "Living Loving Wreck" miscredit, light brown gatefold sleeve with blue-green edge)	500
69	Atlantic 588 198	LED ZEPPELIN II (LP, 1st pressing, red/maroon label, with "The Lemon Song" credit, light brown gatefold sleeve with blue-green edge)	200
70	Atlantic 588 198	LED ZEPPELIN II (LP, light brown sleeve, 2nd pressing, credits "Killing Floor" instead of "The Lemon Song" on label)	40
70	Atlantic Deluxe 2401 002	LED ZEPPELIN III (LP, 1st pressing, red/maroon label, gatefold rotating-wheel sleeve, 'Do What Thou Wilt' in run-off side 1, "Produced by Jimmy Page" and "Executive Producer Peter Grant" on top of label. Catalogue number "2401002" on label)	400
70	Atlantic Deluxe 2401 002	LED ZEPPELIN III (LP, 2nd pressing, red/maroon label, gatefold rotating-wheel sleeve, no Peter Grant Credit. Catalogue number 2401 002 on label)	200
70	Atlantic K50002	LED ZEPPELIN III (LP, reissue, gatefold, green/orange labels)	25
71	Atlantic Deluxe 2401 012	LED ZEPPELIN IV (FOUR SYMBOLS) (1st pressing, 1st labels, LP, gatefold sleeve, red/maroon label with 2 'stickers' covering Peter Grant credit and also revised publishing details to "Kinney Music Ltd/Superhype Music Inc."	500
71	Atlantic Deluxe 2401 012	LED ZEPPELIN IV (FOUR SYMBOLS) (1st Pressing, 1st labels, LP, gatefold sleeve, red/maroon label with Peter Grant credit, 'Led Zeppelin' at bottom, "Pecko Duck" etched onto run out groove on side 1 and "Porky" on side 2. Matrix numbers A//3 and B//3)	400
71	Atlantic Deluxe 2401 012	LED ZEPPELIN IV (FOUR SYMBOLS) (1st pressing, 2nd labels, LP, gatefold sleeve, red/maroon label without Peter Grant credit, 'Led Zeppelin' at top, 'Atlantic Recording' credit in central white band, full 'Kinney Music Ltd/Superhype Music Inc' credit. 'Misty Mountain Hop' spelt as 'Misty Mountain Top'.)	100
71	Atlantic Deluxe 2401 012	LED ZEPPELIN IV (FOUR SYMBOLS) (1st pressing, 3rd labels, with 'Misty Mountain Top' corrected to 'Misty Mountain Hop')	65
71	Atlantic Deluxe 2401 012	LED ZEPPELIN IV (FOUR SYMBOLS) (1st pressing, 4th labels, stickered sleeve, some corrected pressings with a sticker on the sleeve that has the Atlantic logo, K50008, audio information and record label credits)	75
72	Atlantic K50008	LED ZEPPELIN IV (FOUR SYMBOLS) (2nd pressing, first green/orange labels, no four symbols, 'Misty Mountain Top' spelling error, matrix 2401012/K 50008 in run-out grooves)	75
72	Atlantic K50008	LED ZEPPELIN IV (FOUR SYMBOLS) (2nd pressing mispressing on 'Asylum' label)	150
72	Atlantic K40037	LED ZEPPELIN II (LP, first reissue on green/orange label)	25
72	Atlantic K40031	LED ZEPPELIN (LP, repressing)	25
73	Atlantic K 50014	HOUSES OF THE HOLY (LP, original pressing, unlaminated sleeve with 'obi' around the sleeve, textured inner sleeve with thumb notch, matrix A2/B2)	150
73	Atlantic K50014	HOUSES OF THE HOLY (LP, original pressing, unlaminated sleeve without 'Obi')	40
75	Swan Song SSK 89400	PHYSICAL GRAFFITI (2-LP, First pressing MATRIXES: SSK89400 A1/B5/C1/D1 (There are some with A1/B4/C1/D1). (Sleeve must have "Swan Song/484 Kings Road, London SW10", inner wraparound on thick card with a matt finish and a spine at the bottom, inner sleeves on thick card, labels have "Made in UK" at 9 "o" clock and NO Warners logo at 3 "o" clock. die-cut sleeve, inner sleeve, folded insert)	100
76	Swan Song SSK 59402	PRESENCE (LP, shrinkwrapped gatefold sleeve with 'Led Zeppelin Presence' sticker)	50
76	Swan Song SSK59402	PRESENCE (LP, shrinkwrapped gatefold sleeve without 'Led Zeppelin Presence' sticker)	30
76	Swan Song SSK 89402	THE SONG REMAINS THE SAME (2-LP, textured gatefold sleeve with booklet)	35
78	Atlantic K 50008	LED ZEPPELIN IV (FOUR SYMBOLS) (LP, purple vinyl testpressing or mispressing of lilac vinyl reissue)	250
78	Atlantic K 50008	LED ZEPPELIN IV (FOUR SYMBOLS) (LP, lilac vinyl reissue)	50
79	Swan Song SSK 59410 A-F	IN THROUGH THE OUT DOOR (LP, 6 different covers with inner sleeves; set labelled 'A' to 'F', each in individual paper outer; available separately with paper outer £25 each)	100
82	Swansong A0051	CODA (LP, embossed gatefold sleeve, inner)	40
88	Atlantic K 50008/C 88 1-4	FOUR SYMBOLS (LP, HMV 'Classic Collection' box set, with booklet, numbered)	25
88	Atlantic 250008/C 88 1-4	FOUR SYMBOLS (CD, HMV 'Classic Collection' box set, with booklet, numbered)	30

Alvin LEE

MINT VALUE £

90	Atlantic ZEP 1	REMASTERS (3-LP, triple gatefold sleeve)	40
90	Atlantic 7567 82144-1	LED ZEPPELIN (5-LP, box set)	60
97	Atlantic 7567 83061-1	BBC SESSIONS (4-LP, box set, book and print)	150
99	Atlantic 7567 83268-1	EARLY DAYS - THE BEST OF LED ZEPPELIN VOLUME 1 (LP)	40
00	Atlantic 7567 83278-1	LATTER DAYS - THE BEST OF LED ZEPPELIN VOLUME 2 (LP)	35
08	Rhino/Atlantic/Swan Song 8122799489	SOUNDTRACK FROM 'THE SONG REMAINS THE SAME' (4-LP. 180gm expanded edition)	75
08	Rhino/Atlantic/Swan Song 8122799489	SOUNDTRACK FROM 'THE SONG REMAINS THE SAME' (4-LP 180 gm expanded edition, white vinyl, 200 only)	600
08	Rhino/Atlantic/Swan Song 8122799513	MOTHERSHIP (4-LP, 180gm vinyl)	70
14	Atlantic 8122796435	LED ZEPPELIN III (box set reissue, 2-CD, 2-LP, download, 30,000 with art print)	80

(see also Jimmy Page, Robert Plant, John Paul Jones, Dansette Damage, Listen, Family Dogg, Ian Whitcomb, P.J. Proby, Lord Sutch, Yardbirds, Coverdale Page, Page & Plant)

ALVIN LEE

74	Chrysalis CHS 2020	The World Is Changing/Riffin' (with Myron Le Fevre)	6
73	Chrysalis CHR 1054	ON THE ROAD TO FREEDOM (LP, with Myron Le Fevre)	20

(see also Ten Years After)

LEE & CLARENDONIANS
72	Green Door GD 4038	Night Owl/Night Owl Version	15

LEE (PERRY) & JIMMY (RILEY)
75	Dip DL 5075	Rasta Train/Yagga Yagga	25

LEE (PERRY) & JUNIOR (BYLES)
75	Dip DL 5060	Dreader Locks/Militant Rock	20

LEE & PAUL
59	Philips PB 912	The Chick/Valentina, My Valentina	7

ARTHUR LEE
72	A&M AMLS 64356	VINDICATOR (LP)	35

(see also Love)

BENNY LEE (& KEN-TONES)
56	Parlophone R 4245	Rock 'N' Rollin' Santa Claus/Life Was Made For Livin' (with Ken-Tones)	10

(see also Ken-Tones)

BRENDA LEE

78s
58	Brunswick 05755	Ring-A-My-Phone/Little Jonah (Rock On Your Little Steel Guitar)	50
59	Brunswick 05780	Bill Bailey, Won't You Please Come Home/Hummin' The Blues Over You	40
60	Brunswick 05819	Sweet Nuthin's/Weep No More My Baby	80

SINGLES
56	Brunswick 05628	I'm Gonna Lasso Santa Claus/Christy Christmas (triangular centre)	75
57	Brunswick 05685	Dynamite/Love You Til I Die (with Anita Kerr Singers, triangular centre)	60
57	Brunswick 05720	Ain't That Love/One Teenager To Another (w/ Anita Kerr Singers, tri-centre)	60
58	Brunswick 05755	Ring-A-My-Phone/Little Jonah (Rock On Your Little Steel Guitar) (tri-centre)	60
58	Decca BM 31186	Fairyland/One Step At A Time (export issue, triangular centre)	40
66	Brunswick 05957	Too Little Time/Time And Time Again	20
66	Brunswick 05963	Ain't Gonna Cry No More/It Takes One To Know One	10
66	Brunswick 05967	Coming On Strong/You Keep Coming Back To Me	10
67	Brunswick 05976	Where's The Melody?/Born To Be By Your Side	15

EPs
59	Brunswick OE 9462	ROCK THE BOP (green p/s & tri-centre)	35
59	Brunswick OE 9462	ROCK THE BOP (blue p/s & round centre)	15

BUNNY LEE ALLSTARS
69	Unity UN 541	Daydream/Joy Ride	40
69	Unity UN 543	Ivan Itler The Conqueror/The Spice	70
70	Camel CA39	Three Stooge/Isle Of Love	25
70	Pama PM 803	Annie Pama/Mr Magoo	25
70	Unity UN 543	Ivan Itler The Conqueror/The Spice	75
71	Smash SMA 2304	Stanley (Parts 1 & 2) (as Bunnie Lee Allstars)	15
78	Jamaica Sound JS 013	SUPER DUB DISCO STYLE (LP, with the Aggrovators)	50

(see also Lloyd Charmers, Sonny Binns & Rudies, Copy Cats, John Holt, Lloyd & Doreen, Delroy Wilson)

BYRON LEE & DRAGONAIR(E)S
60	Blue Beat B 2	Dumplin's/Kissin' Gal (vocal: Buddy Davidson) (white label, blue print)	20
60	Blue Beat BB 2	Dumplin's/Kissin' Gal (vocal: Buddy Davidson) (2nd pressing, blue label, silver print)	15
61	Blue Beat BB 28	Mash! Mr. Lee/Help Me Forget (vocal: Keith Lyn)	20
61	Starlite ST45 045	Joy Ride/Over The Rainbow	15
64	Parlophone R 5124	River Bank/Musical Communion	20
64	Parlophone R 5125	Sour Apples/Hanging Up My Heart	20
64	Parlophone R 5140	Sammy Dead/Say Bye Bye (both actually by Eric Morris with Byron Lee)	20
64	Parlophone R 5177	Beautiful Garden/Too Late	20
64	Parlophone R 5182	Come Back/Jamaica Ska	20
64	MGM MGM 1256	Night Train From Jamaica/Ska Dee Wah (with Danny Davis)	20
66	Doctor Bird DB 1003	Sloopy/Gold Finger	20
67	Pyramid PYR 6015	Sloopy/Gold Finger (reissue)	10
68	Trojan TR 624	Soul Limbo/The Whistling Song	8
68	Trojan TR 631	Mr Walker/Sunset Jump Up	8
70	Trojan TR 7731	Squeeze Up (Parts 1 & 2)	20
70	Trojan TR 7736	Birth Control/Love At First Sight	10
70	Trojan TR 7747	Bond In Bliss/Musical Scorcher	15
70	Duke DU 39	Elizabethan Reggae/Soul Serenade	10
70	Duke DU 91	Cashbox/WINSTON WRIGHT: Strolling Thru' The Park	6
71	Dynamic DYN 405	Hitching A Ride/Hitching A Ride Version	8

LITTLE MR. LEE & CHEROKEES

MINT VALUE £

71	Duke DU 69	The Law Part 1/The Law Part 2	12
71	Duke DUN 110	One Bad Apple/Poop-A-Poom	10
71	Dynamic DYN 409	My Sweet Lord/Shock Attack	7
71	Dynamic DYN 414	Way Back Home/Version	7
72	Dynamic DYN 435	Make It Reggae/DENNIS ALCAPONE: Go Johnny Go	15
73	Dragon DRA 1008	In The Mood/Black On	7
65	Atlantic AET 6014	SKA TIME (EP, as Byron Lee Ska Kings)	35
64	Island ILP 905	CARIBBEAN JOY RIDE (LP)	35
66	Atlantic 587018	JUMP UP (LP)	35
69	Trojan TTL 5	ROCKSTEADY EXPLOSION (LP)	40
69	Major Minor SMLP 53	BYRON LEE & THE DRAGONAIRES (LP)	20
70	Trojan TRLS 18	REGGAE WITH BYRON LEE (LP)	20
71	Trojan TRL 28	REGGAE SPLASH DOWN (LP)	25

(see also Mighty Avengers, Ken Lazarus, Hopeton Lewis, Danny Davis Orchestra, Good Guys, Neville Hinds, Hubcaps & Wheels, Mighty Sparrow, Blues Busters)

LITTLE MR. LEE & CHEROKEES
66	Vocalion VP 9268	Young Lover/I Don't Want To Go	40

CHRISTOPHER LEE
74	Studio Two TWOA Q4 5001	HAMMER PRESENTS DRACULA (LP, gatefold sleeve, quadrophonic)	15

CURTIS LEE
60	Top Rank JAR 317	With All My Heart (I Love You)/Pure Love	60
61	London HLX 9313	Pledge Of Love/Then I'll Know	25
61	London HLX 9397	Pretty Little Angel Eyes/Gee How I Wish You Were Here	20
61	London HLX 9445	Under The Moon Of Love/Beverly Jean	20
62	London HLX 9533	A Night At Daddy Gee's/Just Another Fool	20
67	CBS 2717	Get My Bag/Everybody's Going Wild (as Curtis Lee & K.C.P.s)	40
67	CBS 2717	Get My Bag/Everybody's Going Wild (as Curtis Lee & K.C.P.s) (DJ copy)	80
72	Stateside SS 2208	Under The Moon Of Love/Beverly Jean (reissue)	6

DAVE LEE SOUND
74	Sea Cruise SCDL 100	DAVE LEE SOUND EP	20
73	Southern Sound 401	PLAY ROCK N ROLL REQUESTS (LP, white labels)	30
73	Southern Sound SSLP 204	LIVE AT THE STARDUST (LP)	20
75	Throstle Nest TN 001	CARRY ON (LP)	20

DAVE LEE (& STAGGERLEES)
63	Decca F 11600	Take Four/Five To Four On	10
63	Oriole CB 1864	Dance Dance Dance/Love Me (as Dave Lee & Staggerlees)	10
63	Oriole CB 1907	Sweet & Lovely/Forever And Always (as Dave Lee & Staggerlees)	10
66	Fontana TF 723	Adam Adamant/Georgie's Theme (as Dave Lee & His Orchestra)	15

DAVE LEE
66	Colpix PXL 550	OUR MAN CRICHTON (LP, with Tubby Hayes)	80

(see also Tubby Hayes)

DAVID H. LEE
65	Pye 7N 15809	Heaven With No Angel	8
69	Morgan MR 1	Johnny's Eyes/You're The Only One	7

DEBBIE LEE
64	Decca F 11931	For Every Man There's A Woman/Can't You See	8

DEREK LEE
66	Parlophone R 5468	Girl/You've Done Something To My Heart	10

DICK LEE
53	Columbia SCM 5066	All I Want Is A Chance/The Show Is Ended	10
53	Columbia SCM 5078	I Thought You Might Be Lonely/Happy Bells	10
54	Columbia SCM 5094	The Book/(Stay In My Arms)Cinderella	12

DICKIE/DICKEY LEE
62	Mercury AMT 1190	Patches/More Or Less	12
62	Mercury AMT 1196	I Saw Linda Yesterday/The Girl I Can't Forget	12
62	Mercury AMT 1200	Don't Wanna Think About Paula/Just A Friend	10
65	Stateside SS 433	Laurie (Strange Things Happen)/Party Doll (as Dickey Lee)	7
65	Stateside SS 464	The Girl From Peyton Place/A Girl I Used To Know (as Dickey Lee)	7

DINAH LEE
65	Aladdin WI 606	I'll Forgive You Then Forget You/Nitty Gritty	35
65	Brit 1005	I Can't Believe What You Say/Pushin' A Good Thing Too Far (unissued)	0
65	Aladdin WI 608	I Can't Believe What You Say/Pushin' A Good Thing Too Far	40

DON (TONY) LEE
68	Big Shot BI 504	It's Reggae Time (as Don Tony Lee)/ERROL DUNKLEY: The Clamp Is On	50
68	Doctor Bird DB 1106	Lee's Special (as Don Tony Lee)/LLOYD & GROOVERS: My Heart And Soul	40
68	Island WI 3160	It's Reggae Time (as D. Tony Lee)/ERROL DUNKLEY: The Clamp Is On	45
69	Unity UN 519	Peyton Place/Red Gal In The Ring (as Don Tony Lee)	20
70	Gas 163	Work Out/Too Long (as Donald Lee)	35

(FREDDIE) 'FINGERS' LEE (& UPPER HAND)
65	Fontana TF 619	The Friendly Undertaker/Little Bit More (as 'Fingers' Lee)	25
66	Fontana TF 655	I'm Gonna Buy Me A Dog/I Can't Drive (as 'Fingers' Lee)	40
66	Columbia DB 8002	Bossy Boss/Don't Run Away (as Fingers Lee & Upper Hand)	40
77	Beeb 020	Down On the Farm/My Bucket's Got A Hole In It	8

(see also At Last The 1958 Rock & Roll Show)

GEORGE LEE (& MUSIC DOCTORS)
69	Downtown DT 443	Talking Boss/Jungle Fever (solo)	45
70	J-Dan JDN 4407	Johnny Dollar/Tough Of Poison (with Music Doctors)	25

(see also Desmond Riley)

HUBERT LEE
73	Downtown DT 498	Something On Your Mind/IMPACT ALL STARS: Mind Version	8

Jackie LEE (U.K.) (Female)

MINT VALUE £

| 74 | Ackee ACK 524 | Tonight Will You Still Love Me/IMPACT ALL STARS: Version | 6 |

JACKIE LEE (U.K.) (FEMALE)
55	Decca F 10550	I Was Wrong/For As Long As I Live	12
65	Decca F 12068	I Cry Alone/Cause I Love Him	12
65	Columbia DB 7685	Lonely Clown/Love Is Gone	12
66	Columbia DB 7860	I Know, Know, Know I'll Never Love/So Love Me	10
66	Columbia DB 8052	The Town I Live In/You Too	12
67	Decca F 12663	Born To Lose/Saying Goodbye	10
69	Pye 7N 17829	Love Is a Gamble/Something Borrowed, Something Blue	10
70	Pye 7N 45003	Rupert/Going To The Circus	6

(see also Jacky, Jackie Lee & Raindrops, Emma Rede)

JACKIE LEE & RAINDROPS (U.K.) (FEMALE)
62	Oriole CB 1702	I Was The Last One To Know/There's No One In The Whole World	10
62	Oriole CB 1727	There Goes The Lucky One/I Built My Whole World Around You	10
62	Oriole CB 1757	Party Lights/Midnight	15
63	Oriole CB 1800	The End Of The World/Goodbye Is Such A Lonely Word	12
63	Philips BF 1283	Down Our Street/My Heart Is Your Heart (as Jackie & Raindrops)	10
64	Philips BF 1328	Here I Go Again/Come On Dream Come On (as Jackie & Raindrops)	10
72	ICI Pharmaceuticals Division ICI 1	Space Age Lullaby/Sleep (p/s)	15

(see also Jacky, Jackie Lee [U.K.], Raindrops [U.K.], Emma Rede, Boeing Duveen and the Beautiful Soup)

JACKIE LEE (U.S.) (MALE)
60	Top Rank JAR 286	Rancho/Like Sunset	10
65	Fontana TF 646	The Duck/Let Your Conscience Be Your Guide	40
66	Jay Boy BOY 28	Would You Believe/You're Everything	10
68	London HLM 10233	The Duck/Dancing In The Street	15
70	Jay Boy BOY 26	Do The Temptation Walk/The Shotgun And The Duck	10
72	Jay Boy BOY 66	Oh! My Darlin'/Don't Be Ashamed	15
72	Jay Boy BOY 66	Oh! My Darlin'/Don't Be Ashamed (DJ copy)	30
72	Jay Boy BOY 76	African Boo-Ga-Loo/Bring It Home	8
85	Kent TOWN 107	Darkest Days/EDDIE BISHOP: Call Me	25
67	London HA-M 8336	THE DUCK (LP)	50

(see also Bob & Earl, Earl Nelson, Jackie Lee & Delores Hall)

JACKIE LEE & DELORES HALL
| 69 | B&C CB 105 | Whether It's Right Or Wrong/Baby I'm Satisfied | 10 |
| 72 | Jay Boy BOY 52 | Whether It's Right Or Wrong/Baby I'm Satisfied (reissue) | 6 |

(see also Jackie Lee [U.S.], Delores Hall)

JAMIE LEE & ATLANTICS
| 63 | Decca F 11571 | In The Night/Little Girl In Blue | 45 |

JIMMY LEE
| 61 | Starlite ST45 059 | All My Life/Chicago Jump | 30 |

JOHNNIE LEE
59	Pye 7N 15201	Echo/It's-A Me, It's-A Me, It's-A Me My Love	8
59	Pye 7N 15233	I'm Finally Free/I Fell (with The King's Men)	8
60	Fontana H 257	They're Wrong/Cindy Lou	8
60	Fontana H 280	Poetry In Motion/Let It Come True	10
61	Fontana H 306	Lonely Joe/Nobody	8

JULIA LEE (& HER BOYFRIENDS)
| 51 | Capitol LC 6535 | PARTY TIME (10" LP, 2 different sleeves) | 50 |

LAURA LEE (U.K.)
60	Triumph RGM 1030	Tell Tommy I Miss Him/I'm Sending Back Your Roses	50
62	Decca F 11513	Too Young To Be In Love/Brand New Heartbeat	15
68	Columbia DB 8495	Love In Every Room/Master Jack	12
71	Columbia DB 8770	Someone To Love Me/Look Left-Look Right	8

LAURA LEE (U.S.)
67	Chess CRS 8062	Dirty Man/It's Mighty Hard	7
68	Chess CRS 8070	As Long As I Got You/A Man With Some Backbone	10
72	Tamla Motown TMG 831	To Win Your Heart/So Will I	60
72	Tamla Motown TMG 831	To Win Your Heart/So Will I (DJ copy)	150
72	Hot Wax HWX 115	Rip Off/Two Lovely Pillows	6
73	Hot Wax HWX 118	Wedlock Is A Padlock/Since I Fell For You	6
73	Hot Wax HWX 119	You've Got The Love To Save Me/Crumbs Off The Table	12
71	Hot Wax SHW 5006	WOMEN'S LOVE RIGHTS (LP)	15
73	Hot Wax SHW 5009	TWO SIDES OF LAURA LEE (LP)	15

LEAPY LEE
| 66 | Decca F 12369 | King Of The Whole Wide World/Shake Hands (featuring the Kinks) | 50 |
| 68 | MCA MUIPS 354 | LITTLE ARROWS (LP) | 15 |

LOCKS LEE
| 75 | Atra ATRA 28 | What Can I Do/Dreader Version | 8 |

MANDY LEE
| 69 | Dandelion S 4494 | Bottle Up And Go (Parts 1 & 2) | 6 |

MICHELLE LEE
| 68 | CBS 3350 | L. David Sloan/Everybody Loves My Baby | 6 |

MICKEY LEE
| 73 | Smash SMA 2332 | Hello My Little Queen/AUGUSTUS PABLO: African Queen | 10 |

NICKIE LEE
| 69 | Deep Soul DS 9103 | And Black Is Beautiful/Faith Within | 25 |

NORMA LEE
| 67 | CBM CBM 002 | Hurt/Rollin' On | 6 |

Peggy LEE

MINT VALUE £

PEGGY LEE
SINGLES
65   Capitol CL 15394   Bewitched/Sneakin' Up On You 12
(see also Bing Crosby, George Shearing)
ROBERT LEE
87   Josiah KJ 008   Easy Norman/MICHAEL MARTIN ALLSTARS: Version (12") 40
ROBERTA LEE
52   Brunswick 04876   The Little White Cloud That Cried/Tell Me Why (78, with Grady Martin) 8
54   HMV 7M 261   True Love And Tender Care/When The Organ Played At Twilight 10
55   Brunswick 05388   Ridin' To Tennessee/I'll Be There If Ever You Want Me 10
(see also Red Foley, Hardrock Gunter)
ROBIN LEE
62   Reprise R 20068   Gambling Man/An Angel With A Broken Wing 12
ROY LEE
61   Decca F 11406   Two Initials/Honey Lies 6
RUDY LEE & STEPPER
89   Wau! Mr. Modo MOWLP 003   TEAM WORKS PRESENTS (LP) 25
VINNY LEE & RIDERS
61   HMV POP 856   Mule Train/Gambler's Guitar 15
WARREN LEE
69   Pama PM 762   Underdog Backstreet/Come Put My Life In Order 20
WILMA LEE & STONEY COOPER
64   Hickory 45-1257   Big John's Wife/Pirate King 7
BRAD LEEDS
60   Pye International 7N 25050 A Teenage Love Is Born/I'm Walking Behind You 6
PHIL LEEDS
66   London HLR 10044   Would You Believe It?/FRANK GALLOP: The Ballad Of Irving 8
LEEDS UNITED FOOTBALL CLUB
72   Chapter 1 SCH 168   Leeds United/Leeds, Leeds, Leeds 6
MARK LEEMAN FIVE
65   Columbia DB 7452   Portland Town/Gotta Get Myself Together 50
65   Columbia DB 7648   Blow My Blues Away/On The Horizon 60
66   Columbia DB 7812   Forbidden Fruit/Goin' To Bluesville 40
66   Columbia DB 7955   Follow Me/Gather Up The Pieces 40
64   No label or cat no   RHYTHM AND BLUES PLUS (LP, private pressing) 500
(see also Cheynes)
THOMAS LEER
78   Oblique ER 101   Private Plane/International (folded photocopied p/s, hand-stamped labels) 60
78   Company/Oblique OBCO 1   Private Plane/International (reissue, printed p/s) 20
82   Cherry Red 12CHERRY 52   All About You/Saving Grace (12", p/s) 12
82   Cherry Red ERED 26   CONTRADICTIONS EP (12", double pack) 15
18   Electronic Sound ES 746   Splash Momentum/ROBERT RENTAL: The Waltz Of The Fatman (p/s) 8
79   Industrial IR 0007   THE BRIDGE (LP, with Robert Rental) 40
(see also Act, Robert Rental)
JOHN LEES
74   Polydor 2058 513   Best Of My Love/You Can't Get It 15
73   Harvest SHVL 811   A MAJOR FANCY (LP, released as SHSM 2018) 20
(see also Barclay James Harvest)
RAYMOND LEFEVRE & HIS ORCHESTRA
68   Major Minor MM 559   Soul Coaxing (Ame Caline)/When A Man Loves A Woman 8
LEFT BANKE
66   Philips BF 1517   Walk Away Renee/I Haven't Got The Nerve 8
67   Philips BF 1540   Pretty Ballerina/Lazy Day 8
67   Philips BF 1575   Ivy Ivy/And Suddenly 8
67   Philips BF 1614   Desiree/I've Got Something On My Mind 7
87   Bam Caruso OPRA 023   Walk Away Renee/Ivy Ivy (DJ/jukebox issue) 6
67   Philips (S)BL 7773   WALK AWAY RENEE/PRETTY BALLERINA (LP) 50
LEFTFIELD
90   Outer Rhythm FOOT 3   Not Forgotten (12") 15
92   Hard Hands HAND 002R   Song Of Life (Remixes)/Release The Horns (12") 10
92   Hard Hands HAND 002T   Song Of Life/Dub Of Life/Fanfare Of Life (12") 10
95   Hard Hands HANDLP 2   LEFTISM (2-LP, gatefold sleeve) 30
95   Hard Hands HANDLP 2T   LEFTISM (3-LP, gatefold sleeve) 40
99   Hard Hands HANDLP 4   RHYTHM AND STEALTH (2-LP) 20
99   Hard Hands HANDLP 4T   RHYTHM AND STEALTH (5 x 10" box set, limited edition) 25
00   Simply Vinyl SVLP 194   LEFTISM (2-LP reissue) 20
(see also Curve)
LEFT HAND DRIVE
77   Bankrupt Records BECK 611 Jailbait/Motorway Crow (1,000 only, no p/s) 50
79   Bankrupt BAN 012   Who Said Rock & Roll Is Dead/I Know Where I Am (p/s) 10
LEFT-HANDED MARRIAGE
67   Private pressing   ON THE RIGHT SIDE OF THE LEFT-HANDED MARRIAGE (LP) 500
96   Tenth Planet TP 022   ON THE RIGHT SIDE OF THE LEFT-HANDED MARRIAGE (LP, reissue, gatefold sleeve) 25
(see also Queen)
LEFT SIDE
69   Columbia DB 8575   Welcome To My House/This Little Village 6
LEGAL AID
81   Earshot ERA 1   That's Life/Limbo 15
LEGATO
85   Adelphi ADE T002   Buttercup/Butterdub (12") 45

MINT VALUE £

LEGAY
69	Fontana TF 904	No-One/The Fantastic Story Of The Steam Driven Banana	175

(see also Gypsy)

LEGEND!
83	Creation CRE 001/Lyntone LYN 12903	'73 In '83/You (Chunka Chunka) Were Glamorous (foldaround p/s in poly bag, with 33rpm flexidisc "I Wonder Why! (live)" by The Pastels/"Wouldn't You? By Laughing Apple)	15
84	Creation CRE 010	The Legend Destroys The Blues/Arrogant Bastards (foldaround p/s in poly bag)	6

TOBI LEGEND
78	RK RK 1004	Time Will Pass You By/DEAN PARRISH: I'm On My Way/JIMMY RADCLIFFE: Long After Tonight Is All Over (with p/s)	10
78	RK RK 1004	Time Will Pass You By/DEAN PARRISH: I'm On My Way/JIMMY RADCLIFFE: Long After Tonight Is All Over	6

LEGEND (1)
69	Bell BLL 1048	National Gas/Wouldn't You	20
69	Bell BLL 1082	Georgia George Part 1/July	15
70	Vertigo 6059 021	Life/Late Last Night	20
71	Vertigo 6059 036	Don't You Know/Someday	15
69	Bell MBLL/SBLL 115	LEGEND (LP, blue/silver labels with "Sold in U.K..." text)	175
71	Vertigo 6360 019	LEGEND ('RED BOOT') (LP, gatefold sleeve, large swirl label)	300
72	Vertigo 6360 063	MOONSHINE (LP, gatefold sleeve, small swirl label)	400

(see also Procol Harum, Mickey Jupp)

LEGEND (2)
81	Legend LEG 1	Hideaway/Heaven Sent (p/s)	70

LEGEND (3)
82	Workshop WR 3478	FRONTLINE EP (Frontline/Sabre & Chatila/ Stormers Of Heaven/Open The Skies (12")	25
81	Workshop WR 2007	LEGEND (LP)	90
82	Workshop WR 3477	DEATH IN THE NURSERY (LP, with insert)	20

LEGENDARY FLOBS
79	Flobs FLO 1	Dead Popes/You're In Danger (p/s)	25

LEGENDARY HEARTS
88	Surfin' Pict	IN A WORLD LIKE THIS (12" EP)	30

LEGENDARY LONNIE
81	Nervous NER 002	Constipation Shake/Devil's Guitar (p/s)	6

LEGENDARY MASKED SURFERS
73	United Artists UP 35542	Gonna Hustle You/Summertime, Summertime	18

(see also Beach Boys, Jan & Dean)

LEGENDARY PINK DOTS
81	Mirrordot MD 01	ONLY DREAMING (cassette, all different hand-made covers)	100
81	Mirrordot MD02/03	CHEMICAL PLAYSCHOOL 1/2 (double cassette, 24 copies all different handmade covers)	120
81	Cassetteking CK04	DOTS ON THE EYE (cassette)	45
82	Flowmotion FMC 09	PREMONITION (cassette, around 60 copies)	45
82	Mirrordot MD/03/II	CHEMICAL PLAYSCHOOL 2 EDITION 2 (cassette, 9 copies, different handmade copies)	120
82	Mirrordot MD 02-03	CHEMICAL PLAYSCHOOL 3/4 (double cassette, 120 copies, different covers)	75
82	Mirrordot MD 04	KLEINE KRIEG (cassette, 120 copies, individual hand-made covers)	80
82	In Phaze 4	BRIGHTER NOW (cassette, 300 copies, different mixes on some tracks)	45
82	In Phaze IPNER 1	BRIGHTER NOW (LP)	25
83	Third Mind TMT 08	BASILISK (cassette, 1000 copies)	30
83	In Phaze PHA 2	CURSE (LP, 2500 copies)	20
84	In Phaze PHA	THE TOWER (LP, 2500 copies)	20

LEGENDS
65	Pye 7N 15904	I've Found Her/Something's Gonna Happen	20
67	Parlophone R 5581	Tomorrow's Gonna Be Another Day/Nobody Laughs Anymore	40
67	Parlophone R 5613	Under The Sky/Twenty-Four Hours A Day	20

(see also First Impressions)

B. LEGGS
71	Green Door GD 4004	Drums Of Passion/Love And Emotion (Version)	18

(see also Morgan's All Stars, Righteous Flames)

LEGION
84	Off Beat S LEG 003	Yesterday/Anticks (p/s)	15

LEGION OF PARASITES
84	Fight Back FIGHT 2	UNDESIRABLE GUESTS (12" EP)	15
85	Thrash THRASH 1	THE PRISON OF LIFE! (LP)	15
87	Stud STUDLP 3	DAWN TO DUST (LP)	15

LEGO FEET
91	Skam SKA 001	LEGO FEET (LP, in black die-cut sleeve like a 12")	175
12	Skam SKA 001	LEGO FEET (2-LP, reissue)	25

MICHEL LEGRAND
73	Tamla Motown TMG 848	Love Theme From "Lady Sings The Blues"/Any Happy Home (demo in p/s)	10
64	Mercury SML 30020	VIOLENT VIOLINS (LP)	18
66	Philips (S)BL 7792	THE YOUNG GIRLS OF ROCHEFORT (LP, soundtrack)	25
68	United Artists SULP 1218	THE THOMAS CROWN AFFAIR (LP, soundtrack)	35
70	Sunset SLS 50519	THE THOMAS CROWN AFFAIR (LP, reissue)	20
70	United Artists UAS 29284	THE HAPPY ENDING (LP, soundtrack)	20

LE GRIFFE
83	Bullet BOL 1	Fast Bikes/Where Are You? (p/s)	8
83	Bullet BOLT 1	Fast Bikes/Where Are You?/The Actor (12", p/s)	15
84	Bullet BOL 7	You're Killing Me (p/s)	8
84	Bullet BOLT 7	You're Killing Me/E.T.A. (12", p/s)	15
84	Bullet BULP 2	BREAKING STRAIN (mini-LP)	20

LEGS

MINT VALUE £

LEGS
74	Warner Bros K 16257	So Many Faces/You Bet You Have	15

(see also Curved Air, Stretch)

LEIBER-STOLLER ORCHESTRA
| 62 | HMV 1050 | Cafe Expresso/Blue Baion | 25 |

LEIBSTANDARTE SS MB
81	Come Organisation WDC 881015	TRIUMPH OF THE WILL (LP, 500 only)	100
81	Come Organisation WDC 881018	WELTANSCHAUUNG (LP)	100
82	Come Organisation WDC 883023	MENSES (cassette)	70

ANDREW LEIGH
| 70 | Polydor 2343 034 | MAGICIAN (LP) | 75 |

(see also Reg King, Spooky Tooth)

ROBERTA LEIGH
| 58 | HMV EH 8339 | THE ADVENTURES OF TWIZZLE (EP) | 15 |

BERNIE LEIGHTON
| 63 | Pye International 7N 25177 | Lawrence Of Arabia Theme/The Wonderful World We Live In (in p/s) | 8 |

LEISURE ADDICTS
| 80 | Addictive ADIC 1 | Subway Suicide/Prefab 13 (no p/s) | 20 |

LEISURE RESEARCH
| 84 | Innocent INNOC 1 | Discontent/Reasons (p/s) | 20 |

(see also Tools)

LEITMOTIV
| 83 | Paragon VIRTUE 3 | CARESS AND CURSE EP (12") | 15 |
| 84 | Pax PAX 17 | Silent Run/(Living In A) Tin | 10 |

LELU/LU'S
| 86 | Possum POST 001 | Africa/Fragile Thigs/Blipverts (12", p/s) | 15 |
| 86 | Possum POST 001 | Africa/Fragile Thigs/Blipverts (p/s) | 12 |

LE MAT
| 82 | Whaam 008 | Waltz For A Fool/Every Dream | 10 |

GARY LEMEL
| 67 | London HLM 7124 | Beautiful People/Take Me With You (export issue) | 20 |

JOHN LE MESURIER
| 76 | Reprise K54080 | WHAT IS GOING TO BECOME OF US ALL (LP) | 20 |

LEMMINGS
| 65 | Pye 7N 15837 | Out Of My Mind/My Little Girl | 20 |
| 65 | Pye 7N 15899 | You Can't Blame Me For Trying/Bring Your Heart With You | 20 |

(see also Honeycombs, Martin Murray)

LEMMY & UPSETTERS WITH MICK GREEN
| 90 | Sunnyside STYLE 777 | Blue Suede Shoes/Paradise (p/s) | 7 |

(see also Motorhead, Rockin' Vickers)

LEMON D
92	Planet Earth PEDJ 01	DJ ON WAX (12" EP)	60
93	Planet Earth PDJ 02	PURSUIT OF A VISION (12" EP)	60
93	Planet Earth PDJ 03	TOXIC RHYTHMS (12" EP)	10
93	Planet Earth PDJ 05	THE REMIXES? (12" EP)	10
95	Conqueror OC 7	I Feel It/Don't Make Me Wait/Bad Man (12")	10
95	Conqueror OC 9	VOL II (12" EP)	15
95	Metalheadz METH 014	Urban Style Music/This Is LA (12")	15

LEMON DIPS
| 69 | De Wolfe DW/LP 3114 | WHO'S GONNA BUY? (10" LP, library issue) | 75 |

LEMONHEADS
| 90 | Atlantic 82137 | LOVEY (LP) | 15 |
| 93 | Atlantic 82537 | COME ON FEEL (LP) | 30 |

LEMON INTERRUPT
| 93 | Junior Boys Own JBO 12002 | Eclipse/Bigmouth (12") | 15 |
| 93 | Junior Boys Own JBO 712 | Dirty/Minneapolis/Minneapolis (Airwaves) (12") | 15 |

(see also Underworld)

LEMON JELLY
01	Soft Rock SOFTROCK 001	Soft/Rock (blue vinyl, denim sleeve with condom, 1000 only)	40
01	Soft Rock SOFTROCK 001	Soft/Rock (2nd pressing, black vinyl, brown sleeve)	12
02	XL IFXLT 147P	Space Walk/Return To Patagonia (10", leather title sleeve, 3000 only)	10
03	X IFXLS 156	Nice Weather For Ducks (Radio Edit)/Soft (p/s)	7
03	Rolled Oats RO 01	Rolled/Oats (gold vinyl, hessian sleeve, 1200 only)	15
98	Impotent Fury IF 001	THE BATH EP: In The Bath/Nervous Tension/A Tune For Jack (10", 1000 only, stickered cardboard sleeve, 1st 250 hand-printed p/s)	80
98	Impotent Fury IF 001	THE BATH EP: In The Bath/Nervous Tension/A Tune For Jack (10", 1000 only, stickered)	30
99	Impotent Fury IF 002	THE YELLOW EP: His Majesty King Raam/The Staunton Lick/Homage To Patagonia (10", 1000 only, stickered cardboard sleeve, 1st 240 in hand-printed p/s)	70
99	Impotent Fury IF 002	THE YELLOW EP: His Majesty King Raam/The Staunton Lick/Homage To Patagonia (10", 1000 only, stickered cardboard sleeve)	20
00	Impotent Fury IF 003	THE MIDNIGHT EP: Kneel Before Your God/Page One/Come (10", 1000 only, stickered cardboard sleeve, 1st 350 in hand-printed p/s)	80
00	Impotent Fury IF 003	THE MIDNIGHT EP: Kneel Before Your God/Page One/Come (10", 1000 only, stickered cardboard sleeve)	20
00	XL IXXLLP 139	KY (2-LP gatefold sleeve with insert)	100
02	XL IFXLLP 160	LOST HORIZONS (2-LP, gatefold sleeve, with booklet, 'Lemon Jelly' sticker on front)	100
05	XL IFXLLP182	'64 - '95 (4 x 10" box set)	100

LEMON KITTENS
| 79 | Step Forward SF 10 | SPOONFED AND WRITHING (EP) | 25 |

LEMON LINE

MINT VALUE £

81	United Dairies UD 07	CAKE BEAST (12" EP, with inner sleeve & insert) 25
80	United Dairies UD 02	WE BUY A HAMMER FOR DADDY (LP, with inner sheet) 35
83	Illuminated JAMS 131	THE BIG DENTIST (LP) 35

(see also Danielle Dax, Shock Headed Peters, Underneath, Gland Shrouds, Karl Blake, Fur Fur)

LEMON LINE
67	Decca F 12688	For Your Precious Love/You Made Me See The Light 15

LEMON MEN
69	Polydor 56365	I've Seen You Cut Lemons/Lemon Strip/Lemon Walk 15

LEMON PIPERS
68	Pye International 7N 25444	Green Tambourine/No Help From Me 7
68	Pye International 7N 25454	Rice Is Nice/Blueberry Blue 10
68	Pye International 7N 25464	Jelly Jungle (Of Orange Marmalade)/Shoeshine Boy 6
68	Pye Intl. NPL 28112	GREEN TAMBOURINE (LP) 30
68	Pye Intl. NSPL 28118	JUNGLE MARMALADE (LP) 20

(see also Ram Jam)

LEMON PIPERS/1910 FRUITGUM CO.
68	Pye Intl. NEP 44091	PRESENTING ... (EP, 1 side each) 15

(see also 1910 Fruitgum Co.)

LEMONS
81	Race RB 004	My Favourite Band/English Summer (p/s) 20

LEMON TREE
68	Parlophone R 5671	I Can Touch A Rainbow/William Chalker's Time Machine 50
68	Parlophone R 5739	It's So Nice To Come Home/Come On Girl 40

(see also Idle Race, Uglys, Danny King's Mayfair Set, Balls)

LEN & HIS SEXTET
63	Melotone ME 100	Blowin' The Top/Don't Stop 25

LEN & HONEYSUCKERS
66	Rio R 75	One More River/Emergency Ward 10

FREDDIE LENNON
66	Piccadilly 7N 35290	That's My Life (My Love And My Home)/The Next Time You Feel Important 40

(see also Loving Kind)

JIMMY LENNON & ATLANTICS
64	Decca F 11825	Louisiana Mama/I Learned To Yodel 35

JOHN LENNON/PLASTIC ONO BAND
SINGLES
69	Apple APPLE 13	Give Peace A Chance/Remember Love (p/s, as Plastic Ono Band; with Parlophone catalogue number, dark green label, only second pressings have R5795 added to catalogue number) 18
69	Apple APPLE 13	Give Peace A Chance/Remember Love (p/s, as Plastic Ono Band, first press with "sold in UK..." label text) 40
69	Apple APPLES 1001	Cold Turkey/Don't Worry Kyoko (Mummy's Only Looking For A Hand In The Snow) (p/s, as Plastic Ono Band) 15
69	Apple APPLES 1002	You Know My Name (Look Up The Number)/What's The New Mary Jane? (as Plastic Ono Band, unreleased; vinyl test pressings only with typed Apple 'Custom Recording' labels & hand written catalogue number) 3000
70	Apple APPLES 1003	Instant Karma!/Who Has Seen The Wind? (p/s, as Lennon/Ono with Plastic Ono Band) ... 12
71	Apple R 5892	Power To The People/YOKO ONO & PLASTIC ONO BAND: Open Your Box (p/s, full apple label both sides or full/half apple label) 15
72	Apple R 5970	Happy Xmas (War Is Over) (as John & Yoko/Plastic Ono Band with Harlem Community Choir)/YOKO ONO & PLASTIC ONO BAND: Listen, The Snow Is Falling (p/s green vinyl) ... 15
72	Apple R 5953	Woman Is The Nigger Of The World/Sisters O Sisters (unreleased, test pressings only). 2500
73	Apple R 5994	Mind Games/Meat City (demo copy) 30
73	Apple R 5994	Mind Games/Meat City (p/s) 7
74	EMI PSR 369	Interview With John Lennon By Bob Mercer And Message To The Salesmen/Whatever Gets You Thru' The Night (promo only) 500
74	Apple R5998	Whatever Gets You Thru The Night/Beef Jerky (demo copy) 40
74	Apple R5998	Whatever Gets You Thru The Night/Beef Jerky 7
75	Apple R 6005	Stand By Me/Move Over Ms. L (demo copy) 45
75	Apple R 6003	9 Dream (Edited Version)/What You Got (demo only) 80
75	Apple R 6009	Imagine/Working Class Hero (demo copy) 30
75	Apple R 6009	Imagine/Working Class Hero (p/s) 12
80	WEA Geffen K 79186	(Just Like) Starting Over/ YOKO ONO : Kiss Kiss Kiss (Green vinyl, promo) 500
81	WEA K 79207	Watching The Wheels/YOKO ONO: I'm Your Angel (Pink vinyl "in house" promo) 500
84	Polydor PODJ 700	Nobody Told Me (1-sided white label promo) 60
84	Polydor POSP 712	Every Man Has A Woman Who Loves Him/SEAN ONO LENNON: It's Alright (p/s, with poster) 10
84	Polydor PODJ 701	Borrowed Time (Edited Version)/YOKO ONO: Your Hands (promo only) 25
88	Parlophone RP 6199	Imagine/Jealous Guy (picture disc) 15
88	Parlophone 12R 6199	Imagine/Jealous Guy/Happy Xmas (War Is Over) (12" p/s) 18

ALBUMS
68	Apple APCOR 2	UNFINISHED MUSIC NO. 1: TWO VIRGINS (with Yoko Ono, mono; black inner, no track listing, with "Merrie In England..." blurb on front sleeve) 3000
68	Apple SAPCOR 2/Track 613 012	UNFINISHED MUSIC NO. 1: TWO VIRGINS (with Yoko Ono, stereo; black inner, with track listing & "Merrie In England..." blurb on back sleeve & Track Records logo on label, dark green label, "Sold in U.K..." "Mfd in UK" label text) 700
69	Zapple ZAPPLE 01	UNFINISHED MUSIC NO. 2: LIFE WITH THE LIONS (with Yoko Ono, with inner sleeve, dark green label, "Sold in U.K..." "Mfd in UK" label text) 250
69	Apple SAPCOR 11	WEDDING ALBUM (with Yoko Ono; gatefold sleeve in box set, includes wedding certificate glued to inside box lid, press booklet, poster, white 'Bagism' bag, passport photographs, postcard & picture of wedding cake) 800
69	Apple CORE 2001	LIVE PEACE IN TORONTO 1969 (as Plastic Ono Band, with stapled calendar, sealed, 1st pressing with rough surface label and Apple publishing credit on side 2, dark green label with "Sold in U.K..." text) 200
69	Apple CORE 2001	LIVE PEACE IN TORONTO 1969 (as Plastic Ono Band, with stapled calendar, unsealed) 20

John LENNON & BLEECHERS (JAMAICA)

MINT VALUE £

Year	Label/Cat#	Title	Value
70	Apple PCS 7124	JOHN LENNON : PLASTIC ONO BAND (LP, with inner)	60
72	Apple PAS 10004	IMAGINE (LP, with inner sleeve, poster & postcard, 1st pressing with laminated sleeve/'sniped' spine edges)	80
72	Apple PAS 10004	IMAGINE (LP, with inner sleeve, without poster & postcard)	30
72	Apple Q4PAS 10004	IMAGINE (LP, quadrophonic, with inner sleeve, poster & postcard)	150
72	Apple PCSP 716	SOMETIME IN NEW YORK CITY (2-LP, gatefold, inner sleeve & postcard)	45
72	Apple PCSP 716	SOMETIME IN NEW YORK CITY (2-LP, gatefold, inner sleeve & without postcard)	20
73	Apple PCS 7165	MIND GAMES (LP, inner, 1U/1U matrix)	20
75	Apple PCS 7169	ROCK 'N' ROLL (LP)	25
74	Apple PCTC 253	WALLS AND BRIDGES (LP, gatefold, with booklet and inner sleeve)	25
75	Apple PCS 7173	SHAVED FISH (LP, lyric inner)	30
81	Parlophone JLB 8	THE JOHN LENNON BOX (9-LP set, with insert)	100
84	Polydor POLH P5	MILK AND HONEY (picture disc, original pressing, thin vinyl, 2,000 only)	40
84	Polydor POLH P5	MILK AND HONEY (picture disc, 2nd pressing, thicker vinyl, 1,000 only)	50
86	Parlophone PCS 7301	LIVE IN NEW YORK CITY (LP, with inner)	15
86	Parlophone PCS 7308	MENLOVE AVENUE (LP, with inner)	20
88	Parlophone PCSP 722	IMAGINE : JOHN LENNON (2xLP with inner)	20
90	Parlophone CDS 79 5220	LENNON (4 x CD set)	70
97	Parlophone 8 21954 2	LENNON LEGEND (2-LP with inner)	150
97	EMI LPCENT 9	ROCK 'N' ROLL (LP, reissue, EMI Centenary, stickered sleeve)	40
97	EMI LPCENT 27	IMAGINE (LP, reissue, EMI centenary, stickered sleeve)	40
98	Parlophone 8306142	ANTHOLOGY (4-CDR, jewel cases with Abbey Road studio inlays, incorrect track listing and missing "Grow Old With Me" from CD4, promo only)	80
99	Capitol 497 6391	WONSAPONEATIME (2-LP with inner)	50
99	Apple PCTC 253	WALLS AND BRIDGES (LP, reissue, inner & booklet)	30

(see also Beatles, Yoko Ono, Bill Elliott/Elastic Oz Band, Elephant's Memory, Musketeer Gripweed, Elton John)

JOHN LENNON & BLEECHERS (JAMAICA)

70	Punch PH 23	Ram You Hard/UPSETTERS: Soul Stew	100

(see also Bleechers, Lee Graham)

LENNON SISTERS

56	Vogue Coral Q 72176	Graduation Day/Toy Tiger	8
57	Vogue Coral Q 72259	Young And In Love/Teenage Waltz	8
57	Vogue Coral Q 72285	Shake Me I Rattle/Pocohontas	8
61	London HLD 9417	Sad Movies/I Don't Know Why	15

ANNIE LENNOX

04	Simply Vinyl SVLP 081	DIVA (LP, reissue)	25
09	Sony 88697368051	THE ANNIE LENNOX COLLECTION (2-LP, inners)	80

MIKE LENNOX

68	Decca F 12736	Images Of You/Words I Like	7

LENNY AND THE LAWBREAKERS

79	Rip Off RIP 11	Me And Bobby McGee/Suzy D (die cut p/s)	50

J.B. LENOIR (& AFRICAN HUNCH RHYTHM)

65	Sue WI 339	I Sing Um The Way I Feel/I Feel So Good (with His African Hunch Rhythm)	50
65	Bootleg 503	Man Watch Your Woman/Mama Talk To Your Daughter (99 copies only)	60
66	Blue Horizon 45-1004	Mojo Boogie/I Don't Care What Nobody Say (99 copies only)	150
68	Python PLP 25	J.B. LENOIR (LP, 99 copies only)	75
70	Polydor 2482 014	CRUSADE (LP)	40
75	Rarity LP 2	J.B. LENOIR (LP)	25
70s	CBS 62593	ALABAMA BLUES (LP)	40

ROBIN LENT

71	Nepentha 6347 002	SCARECROW'S JOURNEY (LP, gatefold sleeve, with Focus)	175

(see also Focus, Jan Akkerman)

VAN LENTON

65	Immediate IM 008	Gotta Get Away/You Don't Care	80

LEON (SILVERA) & OWEN (GRAY)

62	Blue Beat BB 117	Murder (with Drumbago All Stars)/ROY PANTON: Forty Four	15

(see also Owen & Leon, Owen & Millie)

CHRIS LEON

72	Dynamic DYN 450	(Last Night) I Didn't Get To Sleep At All/DYNAMITES: Instrumental Version	8

DEKE LEONARD

73	United Artists UAG 29463	ICEBERG (LP, gatefold sleeve)	15
74	United Artists UAG 29544	KAMIKAZE (LP, gatefold sleeve)	15

(see also Man, Marty Wilde, Help Yourself, Pete Brown's Piblokto, Gary Pickford-Hopkins & Friends)

LEONARD FAMILY

72	Beacon BEA 186	Once You Understand/It Won't Happen Again	6

ANN LEONARDO

57	Capitol CL 14723	Straws In The Wind/Travelling Stranger	15
57	Capitol CL 14755	Lottery/One And Only	10

LEONIE & JOE NOLAN BAND

68	Jolly JY 015	Move And Groove/Don't Let Me Do It	8

LE ORME

73	Charisma CAS 1072	FELONA AND SORONA (LP, gatefold sleeve, large 'Mad Hatter' label)	60

(see under 'O')

LEO'S SUNSHIPP

80	Grapevine RED 3	Give Me The Sunshine/I'm Back For More	35
80	Grapevine REDC 3	Give Me The Sunshine/I'm Back For More (12")	20
86	Expansion EXAPND 03	Give Me The Sunshine/I'm Back For More (Mini-Trio)/I'm Back For More (Vocal)/Give Me The Sunshine (Mini-Trio) (12", reissue)	15
18	Dynamite Cuts DYNAM7013 14	Give Me The Sunshine/I'm Back For More/Get Down People/Madame Butterfly (reissue, 2 x 7", p/s)	8
96	Expansion EXLPM 2	WE NEED EACH OTHER (LP, reissue)	30

MINT VALUE £

LEPRECHAUN
81	Excalibur EXC 508	Loc It Up/Party Freaks	10
81	Excalibur EXC 508	Loc It Up/Party Freaks (12")	15

LE RITZ
77	Breaker BS 2001	Punker/What A Sucker (p/s)	15

MIKE LEROY
64	Columbia DB 7316	Five Hundred Miles/The Big City	6
70	CBS 4998	With A Little Love (Just A Little Love)/All I Need Is You	8

LEROY & ROCKY (ELLIS)
68	Studio One SO 2042	Love Me Girl/WRIGGLERS: Reel Up	80

(see also King Rocky, Leroy Sibbles, Alva Lewis)

LE ROYS
64	HMV POP 1274	Gotta Lotta Love (Ciribiribin)/Don't Cry Baby	10
64	HMV POP 1312	Chills/Lost Out On Love	15
64	HMV POP 1368	I Come Smiling On Through/California GL 903	10

(see also Mike Sarne, Simon Scott, John Leyton, Mike Berry, Grazina, Billie Davis, Billy Boyle, Don Spencer)

LES & SILKIE
70	Torpedo TOR 13	I Don't Want To Tell You/DENZIL DENNIS: Come On In	30

LES KITTIES
81	Camille CAM 1	What's That?/Little Claw (500 only, no p/s)	15

BILL LE SAGE
64	World Records T/ST 346	PRESENTING THE BILL LESAGE/RONNIE ROSS QUARTET (LP, stereo sticker on front)	40

(see also Ronnie Ross)

LES CHANSONETTES
03	Shrine SRG 105	Don't Let Him Hurt You/Deeper (reissue)	10

LORNE LESLEY
59	Parlophone R 4581	So High, So Low/I Don't Know	30

DESMOND LESLIE
05	Trunk JBH 014 LP	MUSIC OF THE FUTURE (LP)	25

JOHN & CHRIS LESLIE
76	Cottage COT 901	THE SHIP OF TIME (LP)	15

MICHAEL LESLIE
65	Pye 7N 15835	Momma Didn't Know/I Don't Wanna Know	6
65	Pye 7N 15908	Penny Arcade/Bye Bye Baby	12
65	Pye 7N 15959	Make Up Or Break Up/She Can't See Me	25

LES ROCKETS
77	Decca FR 13752	Space Rock/Let's Be Sad (Please note demos, state Let's Be Sade)	40
77	Decca FR 13752	Space Rock (extended)/Don't Be Sad (12")	20

LESTER & DENWOOD
73	Atlantic K10381	America (What Have You Done)/Song For Joanne	10

HEDDY LESTER
77	Sonet SON 2013	The World Keeps Turning/Never Saw Him Laughing (p/s)	6

KETTY LESTER
62	London HLN 9527	Love Letters/I'm A Fool To Want You	7
62	London HLN 9574	But Not For Me/Moscow Nights	6
62	London HLN 9608	You Can't Lie To A Liar/River Of Salt	7
62	London HLN 9635	This Land Is Your Land/Love Belongs To Everyone	6
63	London HLN 9698	A Warm Summer Day/I'll Never Stop Loving You	7
64	RCA Victor RCA 1394	Some Things Are Better Left Unsaid/The House Is Haunted	60
64	RCA Victor RCA 1394	Some Things Are Better Left Unsaid/The House Is Haunted (DJ copy)	100
64	RCA Victor RCA 1403	Roses Grow With Thorns/Please Don't Cry Anymore	40
64	RCA Victor RCA 1421	I Trust You Baby/Theme From "The Luck Of Ginger Coffey"	15
65	RCA Victor RCA 1460	Looking For A Better World/Pretty Eyes	7
65	Capitol CL 15427	West Coast/I'll Be Looking Back	30
66	Capitol CL 15447	When A Man Loves A Woman/We'll Be Together Again	8
62	London RE-N 1348	KETTY LESTER (EP)	40
63	London HA-N 2455	LOVE LETTERS (LP)	60
64	RCA Victor RD 7669	THE SOUL OF ME (LP)	40
65	RCA Victor RD 7712	WHERE IS LOVE (LP)	40
67	Stateside S(S)L 10196	WHEN A MAN LOVES A WOMAN (LP)	80

LAZY LESTER
64	Stateside SS 277	I'm A Lover Not A Fighter/Sugar Coated Love	40
71	Blue Horizon 2431 007	MADE UP MY MIND (LP)	150
77	Flyright FLYLP 526	THEY CALL ME LAZY (LP)	15
79	Flyright FLYLP 544	POOR BOY BLUES (LP)	15

LESTER AND THE BREW
81	PL EP 001	A BAD DAY AT THE CITY (EP)	25

LETHAL
94	White BAD 1	Portrait Of A Young Man As An Artist (12")	15

JOE LETHAL
78	Lethal CI 200526	Don't Come Back/You Ain't Free (no p/s)	35

LETIMOV
85	Reconciliation RECONCILE 2	To The Suffering/The Gift Of Life (p/s)	15

LET'S WRESTLE
09	Stolen SR666	IN THE COURT OF THE WRESTLING LETS (LP, silkscreen sleeve, 300 only)	25

LETS GET DRESSED
83	Predetent LGP 003	Love Another Way/Before You Take Everything (p/s)	7

LETTERMEN (1)
61	Capitol CL 15222	The Way You Look Tonight/That's My Desire	7
62	Capitol CL 15248	Come Back Silly Girl/Song For Young Love	6

LETTERMEN (2)

MINT VALUE £

LETTERMEN (2)
74	Stag SG 10175	FIRST CLASS (LP, private pressing)	90

LETTERS
79	Heartbeat PULSE 9	Nobody Loves Me/Don't Want You Back (p/s)	90

DON LETTS & JAH WOBBLE
79	Virgin VS 239	Steel Leg: Stratetime & The Wide Man/Electric Dread: Haile Unlikely (p/s)	10
79	Virgin VS 239-12	Steel Leg: Stratetime & The Wide Man/Electric Dread: Haile Unlikely (12", p/s)	12

(see also Jah Wobble)

JANE LEUNG
70	Jane (No cat on)	Heaven Help Up All/Now You're Gone (no p/s)	30

LARRY LEVAN
00	Strut STRUT LP 006	LARRY LEVAN LIVE AT THE PARADISE GARAGE (3-LP, compilation)	60

LEVEE BREAKERS
65	Parlophone R 5291	Babe I'm Leaving You/Wild About My Loving	25

(see also Beverley, Johnny Joyce)

LEVEE CAMP MOAN
69	County Recording Service COUN LP 133	LEVEE CAMP MOAN (LP, private pressing)	750
69	County Recording Srvice COUN LP 158	PEACOCK FARM (LP, private pressing)	750

LEVEL 42
79	Elite DAZZ 4	Sandstorm/Journey To The Powerline (Remix) (12", white label test pressing, no p/s)	75
80	Elite DAZZ 5	Love Meeting Love/Instrumental Love (7", unreleased)	0
80	Elite DAZZ 5	Love Meeting Love/Instrumental Love (12", company die-cut stickered sleeve)	25
91	Polydor 511 635-2	THE COMPLETE LEVEL 42 (9-CD box set)	40

LEVELLERS
91	On The Fiddle OTF EP 1	Police On My Back/Where The Hell Are We Going To Love?/Travelogue (4am Mix) (12", fan club issue, p/s)	15
92	On The Fiddle OTF LP 2	LIVE 1992 (LP, fan club issue, 2,000 only)	18

GERRY LEVENE (& AVENGERS)
64	Decca F 11815	It's Driving Me Wild (solo)/Dr. Feelgood	40

ANNABEL LEVENTON
69	Morgan MR 20	Easy To Be Hard/My Dear Friend	8

LEVERS
79	Bead Records BEAD 10	LEVERS (LP)	25

CARL LEV(E)Y & CIMARRONS
70	Hot Rod HR 100	Walk The Hot Street/PEGGY & CIMARRONS: You Say You Don't Love Me	35
70	Hot Rod HR 101	Remember Easter Monday/PEGGY & JIMMY: Pum Pum Lover	20

(see also Hot Rod Allstars, Rita Alston, Peggy)

FRANKIE LEVI
86	Firm (no cat no)	Steady Rock/KEVIN GAD: Bloodlines Connections (12")	150

LEVIATHAN
68	Elektra EKSN 45052	Remember The Times/Second Production	45
69	Elektra EKSN 45057	The War Machine/Time	30
69	Elektra EKSN 45052/45057	(WAY IN) THE FOUR FACES OF LEVIATHAN (Remember The Times/Second Production/The War Machine/Time) (2 x 7" press pack, A4 folder sleeve, some overprinted with 'Harrods' logo, with bio & photo, promo, some commercial)	250
69	Elektra EKSN 45075	Flames/Just Forget Tomorrow	30
69	Elektra EKS 74046	LEVIATHAN (2-LP, unissued, acetates only, 1 copy known)	2000
12	Record Collector RCLP004	UNLEASHED (2-LP, 1 side etched, gatefold)	50

(see also High Broom)

HANK LEVINE ORCHESTRA
61	HMV POP 947	Image (Parts 1 & 2)	10
65	HMV POP 1390	Image (Parts 1 & 2) (reissue)	6

LEVITICUS
94	Philly Blunt PB 001	Burial (Lovers Rock Mix)/(Mademoiselle Mix) (12")	30

LEVITTS
69	ESP Disk/Fontana STL 5518	WE ARE THE LEVITTS (LP)	25

LEVON & HAWKS
65	Atlantic AT 4054	The Stones I Throw/He Don't Love You	70

(see also Band)

BARRINGTON LEVY
79	JB JBD 009	Call You On The Phone/RANKING TOYAN: London Girl (12")	10
79	Bushays BFM 128	Sister Debby/Blacksin Dub (12", with Jah Thomas)	20
70s	Burning Vibrations BVD 003	A Ya We Deh/Give Thanks And Praise (12", with Trinity)	25
79	Burning Rockers BRD 033	Shine Eye Gal/Dub version (12". Jah Thomas toasts on A-side but is uncredited)	12
79	Burning Sounds BRD 029	Hunting Man (feat. Jah Thomas)/Hunting Dub (12")	25
79	Greensleeves GRED 27	Lose Respect (feat. Trinity)/ROMAN STEWART & TRINITY: Since You're Gone (12")	15
80	Greensleeves GRED 28	Englishman/SCORCHER & ROOTS RADICS BAND: The Daughter Them Ire (12")	20
80	Greensleeves GRED 35	Mary Long Tongue/Look Youthman (12")	20
80	Greensleeves GRED 40	Crucifixion/Eventide Fire A Disaster (red vinyl 12")	18
80	Cha Cha CHAD 22	Warm and Sunny Day/GENERAL SAINT - DJ cut (12")	50
80	His Majesty HMD 004	Shaolin Temple/Version (12")	20
80	Strong Like Sampson SLSD8	Wicked Intention/ROD TAYLOR (12")	40
80	Lovelinch LL 03	Skylarking/HORTENSE ELLIS - You Done Me Wrong (12")	25
82	Greensleeves GRED 80	Tomorrow Is Another Day/PAPA TULLO: Delaware (12")	20
80	Strong Like Sampson SLSD 017	She Rob And Gorn/PAPPA TULLO: Cat Called Francella (12")	15
82	Oak Sounds OSD 008	Open Book/Open version (12")	20
84	Greensleeves GRED 136	Prison Oval Rock (master mix)/Prison Oval Rock (dub plate mix) (12")	15
84	Greensleeves GRED 145	Pon Your Toe/Girl I Love You (12")	18
85	MGR MGR 4	Get Up Stand Up/Do The Dance (12")	10

Ben LEVY

MINT VALUE £

85	Time TR009	Here I Come/Trouble A Come/Run Come Dub/Rub A Dub (12")	18
87	Live & Learn LLD014	Juggling Soldier/Version (12")	20
87	Time I TR 026	Living Dangerously/Version	8
87	Time I 7TR 0200	Struggler/Version	8
79	Greensleeves GREL 9	ENGLISHMAN (LP)	30
79	Burning Sounds BS 1039	SHINE EYE GAL (LP)	30
80	JB JBLP 01	DOH RAY ME (LP)	60
80	Jah Guidance JA CC 14	ROBIN HOOD (LP)	40
82	Trojan TRLS 209	POOR MAN STYLE (LP)	15
83	GG's GG 0032	BARRINGTON LEVY'S LIFE STYLE (LP)	40
83	Burning Sounds BS 1050	HUNTER MAN (LP)	20
85	Time Records TRLP 003	HERE I COME (LP)	30

BEN LEVY

66	Ska Beat JB 245	Doreen/Never Knew Love	20
66	Ska Beat JB 255	I'll Make You Glad/Keep Smiling	20

JONA LEWIE

74	Sonet SON 2048	Piggy Back Sue/Papa Don't Go	6
78	Stiff BUY 37	Halleluja Europe/Police Trap (Unreleased, test pressings only)	50
80	Stiff BUY 85-5	Big Shot - Momentarily/I'll Get By In Pittsburg (5" single)	6
79	Stiff SEEZ 8	ON THE OTHER HAND THERE'S A FIST (LP, yellow vinyl)	15
78	Stiff SEEZ 8	ON THE OTHER HAND THERE'S A FIST (LP, picture disc)	15

(see also Brett Marvin & Thunderbolts)

CARL LEWIN

71	Bullet BU 456	Knock Three Times/SIDNEY ALL STARS: The Whealing Mouse	12
71	Punch PH 98	Nobody Told Me/WING: Don't Play That Song Again (version)	12

ALVA (REGGIE) LEWIS

67	Caltone TONE 111	Return Home/KING ROCK & WILLOWS: You Are The One	100
67	Island WI 3080	I'm Indebted/GROOVERS: You've Got To Cry	50
68	Blue Cat BS 125	She Is leaving/UNIQUES: Girls Like Dirt	80
68	Jolly HY 009	Hang My Head And Cry/COOL CATS: Hold Your Love	100
72	Upsetter US 391	Natty Natty (as Reggie Lewis)/UPSETTERS: Version	20

(see also Reggae Boys, Webber Sisters, Lester Sterling, Cool Cats)

LEWIS & CLARKE EXPEDITION

67	RCA 1633	Blue Revelations/I Feel Good (I Feel Bad)	20

ANDY LEWIS & PAUL WELLER

97	Acid Jazz AJX 193P	Are You Trying To Be Lonely?/Tell Me Once Again You Love Me (7" promo, A-label in Acid Jazz sleeve, 50 copies only)	40

(see also Paul Weller)

BARBARA LEWIS

63	London HLK 9724	Hello Stranger/Think A Little Sugar	25
63	London HLK 9724	Hello Stranger/Think A Little Sugar (DJ Copy)	60
63	London HLK 9779	Straighten Up Your Heart/If You Love Her	25
64	London HLK 9832	Snap Your Fingers/Puppy Love	25
64	Atlantic AT 4013	Pushin' A Good Thing Too Far/Come Home	40
65	Atlantic AT 4031	Baby I'm Yours/Hello I Say Love	20
65	Atlantic AT 4041	Make Me Your Baby/Love To Be Loved	20
66	Atlantic AT 4068	Don't Forget About Me/It's Magic	20
66	Atlantic 584 037	Make Me Belong To You/Girls Need Loving Care	20
67	Atlantic 584 061	Baby What Do You Want Me To Do/I Remember The Feeling	60
68	Atlantic 584 153	Hello Stranger/Baby I'm Yours (reissue)	8
68	Atlantic 584 174	Sho Nuff (It's Got To Be Your Love)/Thankful For What I Got	20
71	Atlantic 2091 143	Someday We're Gonna Love Again/Baby I'm Yours	15
72	Atlantic K 10128	Someday We're Gonne Love Again/Baby I'm Yours (reissue)	10
65	Atlantic AET 6015	SNAP YOUR FINGERS (EP)	70
66	Atlantic ATL 5042	BABY I'M YOURS (LP)	40
66	Atlantic 587 002	IT'S MAGIC (LP, mono)	50
66	Atlantic 588 002	IT'S MAGIC (LP, stereo)	60
70	Stax SXATS 1035	THE MANY GROOVES OF BARBARA LEWIS (LP)	50

BOBBY LEWIS

61	Parlophone R 4794	Tossin' And Turnin'/Oh Yes, I Love You	20
61	Parlophone R 4831	One Track Mind/Are You Ready	25
62	Stateside SS 126	I'm Tossin' And Turnin' Again/Nothin' But The Blues	25

CAPPY LEWIS

61	Vogue V 9184	Bullfight/OLYMPICS: Little Pedro	20

(see also Olympics)

DAVE LEWIS (1)

66	Pye Intl. NEP 44057	GIVIN' GAS (EP)	40
64	Pye Intl. NPL 28021	LITTLE GREEN THING (LP)	30

DAVE LEWIS (2)

76	Polydor 2383 420	FROM TIME TO TIME (LP, with lyric sheet)	18

DAVID LEWIS

70	AX 1	SONGS OF DAVID LEWIS (LP, private pressing, paste-on sleeve)	400

(see also Andwella['s Dream], David Baxter)

FURRY LEWIS

69	Blue Horizon 7-63228	PRESENTING THE COUNTRY BLUES (LP)	80
70	Matchbox SDR 190	IN MEMPHIS (LP)	30
71	Xtra XTRA 1116	FURRY LEWIS (LP)	20
71	Spokane SPL 1004	THE EARLY YEARS 1927-1929 (LP)	30

(see also John Estes)

Gary LEWIS & PLAYBOYS

MINT VALUE £

GARY LEWIS & PLAYBOYS
65	Liberty LIB 10187	This Diamond Ring/Tijuana Wedding	10
65	Liberty LIB 55778	Count Me In/Little Miss Go-Go	10
65	Liberty LIB 55809	Save Your Heart For Me/Without A Word Of Warning	10
65	Liberty LIB 55818	Everybody Loves A Clown/Time Stands Still	7
66	Liberty LIB 55846	She's Just My Style/I Won't Make That Mistake Again	20
66	Liberty LIB 55898	My Heart's Symphony/Tina	20
66	Liberty LIB 55914	(You Don't Have To) Paint Me A Picture/Looking For The Stars	10
67	Liberty LBF 15025	Jill/Needles And Pins	10
65	Liberty LBY 1259	THIS DIAMOND RING (LP)	30
66	Liberty LBY 1322	JUST OUR STYLE (LP)	25

GEORGE LEWIS/FREDDIE KOHLMAN
53	Brunswick LA 8627	NEW ORLEANS JAZZ CONCERT (10" LP)	15

HOPETON LEWIS
67	Island WI 3054	Rock Steady/Cool Collie	150
67	Island WI 3055	Finder's Keepers/ROLAND ALPHONSO: Shanty Town Curfew	100
67	Island WI 3056	Let Me Come On Home/Hardships Of Life (with Merritone All Stars)	75
67	Island WI 3057	Run Down/Pick Yourself Up	150
67	Island WI 3059	Let The Little Girl Dance/This Music Got Soul	125
67	Island WI 3068	Rock A Shacka/I Don't Want Trouble	125
68	Island WI 3076	Everybody Rocking/Stars Shining So Bright	125
68	Fab FAB 43	Skinny Leg Girl/Live Like A King (as Hopetown Lewis & Glenmore Brown)	90
70	Duke Reid DR 2505	Boom Shaka Lacka/TOMMY McCOOK QUINTET: Dynamite	25
70	Duke Reid DR 2516	Testify/TOMMY McCOOK: Super Soul	25
71	Duke DU 112	Grooving Out Of Life (with Byron Lee & Dragonaires) (actually titled Grooving Out On Life)/BYRON LEE & DRAGONAIRES: Fire Fire	15
71	Treasure Isle TI 7060	To The Other Man/TOMMY McCOOK: Stampede	15
72	Treasure Isle TI 7071	Judgement Day (actually by Hopeton Lewis & Dennis Alcapone)/ EARL LINDO: Version Day	15
72	Attack ATT 8035	Starting All Over Again/DYNAMITES: Instrumental Version	10
72	Dynamic DYN 436	Come Together/Going Back To My Hometown	10
72	Dynamic DYN 447	Good Together/Version	10
73	Dragon DRA 1001	City Of New Orleans/The Wind Cries Mary	10
73	Dragon DRA 1011	Groovin' Out On Life/God Bless Whoever Sent You	10
12	Duke Reid THB 7015	Live It Up/JOHN HOLT WITH TOMMY McCOOK AND THE SUPERSONICS: Ali Baba/Dub	18
67	Island ILP 957	TAKE IT EASY: ROCKSTEADY WITH HOPETON LEWIS (LP)	200
71	Trojan TRL 36	GROOVING OUT ON LIFE (LP)	30

(see also Glenmore Brown & Hopeton Lewis)

HUGH X. LEWIS
66	London HLR 10032	Looking In The Future/Too Late	10

JEFFREY LEWIS
01	Rough Trade RTRADES 20	The Chelsea Hotel Oral Sex Song (1-sided promo, stamped label, with comic)	10

JENNIFER LEWIS & ANGELA STRANGE
65	Columbia DB 7662	Bring It To Me/You Know	10
66	Columbia DB 7814	I've Heard It All Before/Bad Storm Coming	12

JERRY LEWIS
53	Capitol LC 6591	CAPITOL PRESENTS JERRY LEWIS (10" LP)	20
57	Brunswick LAT 8173	JUST SINGS (LP)	15
58	Brunswick LAT 8222	MORE JERRY LEWIS (LP)	15

(see also Dean Martin)

JERRY LEWIS (JAMAICA)
72	Pama PM 862	The Godfather/ALTON ELLIS: Some Day	20
73	Explosion EX 2077	Rhythm Pleasure/AGGROVATORS: Doctor Seaton	20

(see also I Roy)

JERRY LEE LEWIS

78s
57	London HLS 8529	Great Balls Of Fire/Mean Woman Blues	20
58	London HLS 8559	You Win Again/I'm Feelin' Sorry	30
58	London HLS 8592	Breathless/Down The Line	20
58	London HLS 8700	Break-Up/I'll Make It All Up To You	35
59	London HLS 8780	High School Confidential/Fools Like Me	50
59	London HLS 8840	Lovin' Up A Storm/Big Blon' Baby	50
59	London HLS 8941	Let's Talk About Us/The Ballad Of Billy Joe	60
59	London HLS 8993	Little Queenie/I Could Never Be Ashamed Of You	100
96	Cruisin' The 50s CASB 002	Wild One/Old Black Joe (numbered, 300 only)	35

SINGLES
57	London HLS 8457	Whole Lotta Shakin' Goin' On/It'll Be Me	30
57	London HLS 8529	Great Balls Of Fire/Mean Woman Blues	20
58	London HLS 8559	You Win Again/I'm Feelin' Sorry	25
58	London HLS 8592	Breathless/Down The Line	20
58	London HLS 8700	Break-Up/I'll Make It All Up To You	20
59	London HLS 8780	High School Confidential/Fools Like Me	20
59	London HLS 8840	Lovin' Up A Storm/Big Blon' Baby	20
59	London HLS 8941	Let's Talk About Us/The Ballad Of Billy Joe (no triangular centre)	20
59	London HLS 8993	Little Queenie/I Could Never Be Ashamed Of You (no triangular centre)	20

(Originally issued with triangular centres; round-centre pressings are worth two-thirds of these values.)

60	London HLS 9083	I'll Sail My Ship Alone/It Hurt Me So	15
60	London HLS 9131	Baby, Baby, Bye Bye/Old Black Joe	20
60	London HLS 9202	John Henry/Hang Up My Rock And Roll Shoes	20
61	London HLS 9335	What'd I Say?/Livin' Lovin' Wreck	10

Jimmy LEWIS

MINT VALUE £

61	London HLS 9414	It Won't Happen With Me/Cold Cold Heart	8
61	London HLS 9446	As Long As I Live/When I Get Paid	8
62	London HLS 9526	I've Been Twistin'/Ramblin' Rose	8
62	London HLS 9584	Sweet Little Sixteen/How's My Ex Treating You	12
63	London HLS 9688	Good Golly Miss Molly/I Can't Trust Me (In Your Arms Anymore)	10
63	London HLS 9722	Teenage Letter/Seasons Of My Heart (B-side with Linda Gail Lewis)	10
63	Mercury AMT 1216	Hit The Road Jack/Pen And Paper	10
64	Philips BF 1324	I'm On Fire/Bread And Butter Man	10
64	London HLS 9867	Lewis Boogie/Bonnie B	20
65	Philips BF 1371	Hi-Heel Sneakers/You Went Back On Your Word	7
65	Philips BF 1407	Baby Hold Me Close/I Believe In You	8
65	Philips BF 1425	Rockin' Pneumonia And The Boogie Woogie Flu/This Must Be The Place	10
65	London HLS 9980	Carry Me Back To Old Virginia/I Know What It Means	10
66	Philips BF 1521	Memphis Beat/If I Had It All To Do Over	10
67	Philips BF 1594	It's A Hang-Up Baby/Holdin' On	8
67	Philips BF 1615	Turn On Your Love Light/Shotgun Man	10

SINGLES : EXPORT SINGLES

58	London HL 7050	High School Confidential/Fools Like Me	20
62	London HL 7117	Save The Last Dance For Me/Hello Josephine	30
63	London HL 7120	Good Golly Miss Molly/I Can't Trust Me (In Your Arms Anymore)	20
63	London HL 7123	In The Mood/I'm Feelin' Sorry	40

EPs

58	London RE-S 1140	JERRY LEE LEWIS - NO. 1 (with triangular centre)	40
58	London RE-S 1140	JERRY LEE LEWIS - NO. 1	20
59	London RE-S 1186	JERRY LEE LEWIS - NO. 2 (with triangular centre)	40
59	London RE-S 1186	JERRY LEE LEWIS - NO. 2	25
59	London RE-S 1187	JERRY LEE LEWIS - NO. 3 (with triangular centre)	40
59	London RE-S 1187	JERRY LEE LEWIS - NO. 3	25
61	London RE-S 1296	JERRY LEE LEWIS - NO. 4	30
62	London RE-S 1336	JERRY LEE LEWIS - NO. 5	30
63	London RE-S 1351	JERRY LEE LEWIS - NO. 6	30
63	London RE-S 1378	FOUR MORE FROM JERRY LEE LEWIS	30
66	Philips BE 12599	COUNTRY STYLE	30

ALBUMS

59	London HA-S 2138	JERRY LEE LEWIS	100
62	London HA-S 2440	JERRY LEE'S GREATEST	50
64	Philips (S)BL 7622	GOLDEN HITS	20
65	Philips (S)BL 7646	LIVE AT THE STAR CLUB, HAMBURG (with Nashville Teens)	25
65	Philips BL 7650	THE GREATEST LIVE SHOW ON EARTH	15
65	Philips BL 7668	THE RETURN OF ROCK	15
65	London HA-S 8251	WHOLE LOTTA SHAKIN' GOIN' ON	50
67	London HA-S 8323	BREATHLESS	30

(see also Nashville Teens)

JIMMY LEWIS

68	Minit MLF 11002	The Girls From Texas/Let Me Know	20

JOHN LEWIS

60	London Jazz LTZ-K 15186	IMPROVISED MEDITATIONS AND EXCURSIONS (LP)	15
61	London Jazz LTZ-K 15218	THE GOLDEN STRIKER (LP, also stereo SAH-K 6152)	15

(see also Modern Jazz Quartet)

JOHN LEWIS AND SACHA DISTEL

59	UK Oriole MG20036	AFTERNOON IN PARIS (LP)	25

LEW LEWIS (REFORMER)

76	Stiff BUY 5	Caravan Man/Boogie On The Street (p/s, with Dr. Feelgood, 1st pressing with push-out centre)	8
78	Lew Lewis LEW 1	Lucky Seven/Night Talk (500 only, plain white sleeve, handwritten-style white label)	20
78	Stiff LEW 1	Lucky Seven/Night Talk (handwritten-style green label)	10

(see also Oil City Sheiks, Dr. Feelgood, Eddie & the Hot Rods)

LINDA LEWIS

67	Polydor 56173	You Turned My Bitter Into Sweet/Do You Believe In Love	150
71	Reprise K 14096	We Can Win/Hampstead Way	6
72	Reprise K 14209	Old Smokey/It's The Frame	6
75	Arista ARIST 17	It's In His Kiss/Walk About (p/s)	6
73	Raft RA 18502	Rock A Doodle Doo/Reach For The Truth	6
71	Reprise K 44130	SAY NO MORE (LP)	25
72	Reprise K 44208	LARK (LP, textured gatefold sleeve)	20
75	Artista ARTY 109	NOT A LITTLE GIRL ANYMORE (LP)	15
77	Arista SPARTY 1003	WOMAN OVERBOARD (LP)	15
73	Raft RA 48501	FATHOMS DEEP (LP, die-cut sleeve with inner)	18
79	Ariola ARL 5033	HACIENDA VIEW (LP)	15
83	Epic EPC 25478	A TEAR AND A SMILE (LP)	20
95	Turpin TPN 3	SECOND NATURE (LP)	15
96	Turpin TPN 5	WHATEVER (2-LP)	25

(see also Ferris Wheel)

LOUISE LEWIS

79	Inferno HEAT 120	Wee Oo I'll Let It Be You Babe/Instrumental Version (unissued and unconfirmed, this price for test pressings may exist)	100

MARGARET LEWIS

62	Starlite ST45 081	Sometin's Wrong Baby/John De Lee	30

Meade 'LUX' LEWIS

MINT VALUE £

MEADE 'LUX' LEWIS
55	Vogue EPV 1065	MEADE 'LUX' LEWIS (EP)	15
56	Melodisc EPM7 107	BOOGIE WOOGIE AND BLUES (EP)	15

(see also Albert Ammons, [Big] Joe Turner)

MEADE 'LUX' LEWIS & SLIM GAILLARD
56	Columbia Clef 33C 9021	JAZZ AT THE PHILHARMONIC (10" LP)	20

(see also Slim Gaillard)

MIA LEWIS
65	Decca F 12117	Wish I Didn't Love Him/This Is The End	10
65	Decca F 12240	It's Goodbye Now/The Luckiest Girl	8
66	Parlophone R 5526	Nothing Lasts Forever/(Baby) I'm Feeling Good	15
67	Parlophone R 5585	No Time For Lovin'/Onion	6
67	Parlophone R 5617	Woman's Love/You Won't Get Away	6

MICHAEL LEWIS
73	United Artists UP 35569	Theatre Of Blood Theme/Edwina's Theme	15

NIGEL LEWIS
86	Media Burn MB10	WHAT I FEEL NOW (LP)	25

NORMA LEWIS
81	Challenge LOVER 1	This Feelings Killing Me/The Girl's A Fool/(Instrumental) (12")	30
82	Jive JIVE T 11	This Feelings Killing Me/The Girl's A Fool/T.B.C. Magic Bullet (features Atmosfear uncredited) (12")	18
82	Jive JIVE 11	This Feelings Killing Me/T.B.C. Magic Bullet (features Atmosfear uncredited)	8

(see also Atmosfear)

PATTI LEWIS
56	Columbia DB 3825	Earthbound/Happiness Street (Corner Sunshine Square)	10
57	Columbia DB 3923	Your Wild Heart/A Poor Man's Roses (Or A Rich Man's Gold)	8
57	Columbia DB 3967	Pull Down De Shade/Speak For Yourself John	8
55	Philips BBE 12028	PATTI LEWIS (EP)	10

PHILLIPPA LEWIS
65	Decca F 12152	Just Like In The Movies/Get Along Without You	10

RAMSEY LEWIS (TRIO)
65	Chess CRS 8020	The 'In' Crowd/Since I Fell For You (as Ramsey Lewis Trio)	15
65	Chess CRS 8024	Hang On Sloopy/Movin' Easy (as Ramsey Lewis Trio)	8
66	Chess CRS 8029	A Hard Day's Night/'Tout A Doubt (as Ramsey Lewis Trio)	8
66	Chess CRS 8031	Hi-Heel Sneakers (Parts 1 & 2) (as Ramsey Lewis Trio)	10
66	Chess CRS 8041	Wade In The Water/Ain't That Peculiar (as Ramsey Lewis Trio)	60
66	Chess CRS 8041	Wade In The Water/Ain't That Peculiar (as Ramsey Lewis Trio) (DJ copy)	200
66	Chess CRS 8044	Uptight (Everything's Alright)/Money In The Pocket	10
67	Chess CRS 8051	Day Tripper/Hurt So Bad	20
67	Chess CRS 8055	1-2-3/Down By The Riverside	8
67	Chess CRS 8058	Function At The Junction/Hey Mrs. Jones	10
67	Chess CRS 8060	Saturday Night After The Movies/China Gate	8
67	Chess CRS 8061	Girl Talk/Dancing In The Street	8
67	Chess CRS 8064	Soul Man/Struttin' Lightly	10
69	Chess CRS 8096	Cry Baby Cry/Wade In The Water	20
69	Chess CRS 8096	Cry Baby Cry/Wade In The Water (DJ copy)	45
70	Chess CRS 8104	Julia/Do What You Wanna	10
72	Chess 6145 004	Wade In The Water/Ain't That Peculiar (paper label)	15
72	Chess 6145 013	The 'In' Crowd/Soul Man	6
72	CBS 8280	Slipping Into Darkness/Collage	8
66	Chess CRE 6019	A HARD DAY'S NIGHT (EP, as Ramsey Lewis Trio)	30
65	Pye Jazz NJL 55	AT THE BOHEMIAN CAVERNS (LP)	20
65	Chess CRL 4511	THE 'IN' CROWD (LP)	25
65	Chess CRL 4518	CHOICE! THE BEST OF RAMSEY LEWIS (LP)	25
66	Chess CRL 4520	HANG ON RAMSEY! (LP)	20
66	Chess CRL 4522	WADE IN THE WATER (LP)	40
67	Chess CRL 4528	GOIN' LATIN (LP)	25
67	Chess CRL 4531	THE MOVIE ALBUM (LP)	20
68	Chess CRL(S) 4533	DANCIN' IN THE STREET (LP)	25
68	Chess CRLS 4535	UP POPS RAMSEY LEWIS (LP)	25
68	Chess CRLS 4539	MAIDEN VOYAGE (LP)	25
69	Chess CRLS 4545	MOTHER NATURE'S SON (LP)	30
68	Fontana SFJL 962	DOWN TO EARTH (LP)	20
72	Chess 6310 106	BACK TO THE ROOTS (LP)	15
72	Chess 6310 114	THE BEST OF RAMSEY LEWIS (LP)	15
72	Chess 6310 124	TOBACCO ROAD (LP)	15
73	CBS 65307	FUNKY SERENITY (LP)	20
73	CBS CQ 31196	UPENDO NI PAMOJA (LP, quadrophonic)	15
74	CBS S80677	SUN GODDESS (LP)	30
76	CBS 81406	SALONGO (LP)	18

(see also Young-Holt Unlimited)

RICHARD LEWIS & HIS BAND
60	Downbeat CHA 1	Hey, Little Girl/Hey, Little Boy	40

SHIRLEY LEWIS
83	High Energy	Loves Warming Up/Dub Mix (12")	15

SMILEY LEWIS
53	London L 1189	Big Mamou/Play Girl (78, some copies miscredited to Smiley Davis)	100
56	London HLU 8312	One Night/Ain't Gonna Do It	800
56	London HLU 8312	One Night/Ain't Gonna Do It (78)	100
56	London HLU 8337	Down Yonder We Go Ballin'/Don't Be That Way (Please Listen To Me)	800

Stevie LEWIS

MINT VALUE £

56	London HLU 8337	Down Yonder We Go Ballin'/Don't Be That Way (Please Listen To Me) (78)	100
57	London HLP 8367	Shame, Shame, Shame/No, No (gold lettering)	500
57	London HLP 8367	Shame, Shame, Shame/No, No (silver lettering)	400
57	London HLP 8367	Shame, Shame, Shame/No, No (78)	70
70	Liberty LBF 15337	I Hear You Knocking/Play Girl	10
70	Liberty LBS 83308	SHAME, SHAME, SHAME (LP)	25
78	United Artists UAS 30167	I HEAR YOU KNOCKING (LP)	15

STEVIE LEWIS

65	Mercury MF 871	Take Me For A Little While/My Whole World Seems To Be Tumbling Down	22
65	Polydor 56003	Heard It All Before/Wild	7

TAMALA LEWIS

79	Destiny DS 1010	You Won't Say Nothing/If You Can Stand Me	8
79	Destiny DS 1010	You Won't Say Nothing/If You Can Stand Me (DJ copy)	15

TINA LEWIS

83	Inferno BURN 5	Back Street/The Way You've Been Acting Lately	12

TINY LEWIS

60	Parlophone R 4617	Too Much Rockin'/I Get Weak	150

VIC LEWIS

68	NEMS 56-3893	Goodnight/Julia (as Vic Lewis, his Orchestra and singers)	10
69	NEMS 56 3712	Sunshine Superman/Mellow Yellow	8
69	NEMS 56-4057	Blackbird/I Will	20
55	Decca LF 1216	PROGRESSIVE JAZZ (10" LP)	30
62	HMV CLP 1641	PLAY BOSSA NOVA HOME AND AWAY (LP, features Tubby Hayes)	50
70	Ember CJS 807	AT THE BEAULIEU FESTIVAL (LP)	25
60s	Ember SE 8018	BIG BAND EXPLOSION (LP)	30
70s	DJM SPECB 103	MY LIFE MY WAY (LP)	15

LEWIS SISTERS

65	Tamla Motown TMG 536	You Need Me/Moonlight On The Beach (DJ Copy)	150
65	Tamla Motown TMG 536	You Need Me/Moonlight On The Beach	120

DAVE LEWRY

72	Westwood WRS 019	ALL I WANT TO DO IS PLAY GUITAR (LP)	35

MONIQUE LEYRAC

68	CBS 3309	Time Time/Love Is Blue	7

LEYTON BUZZARDS

78	Small Wonder SMALL 7	19 And Mad/Villain/Youthanasia (p/s)	8
79	Chrysalis CHR 1213	JELLIED EELS TO RECORD DEALS (LP, as Buzzards)	15

JOHN LEYTON

60	Top Rank JAR 426	Tell Laura I Love Her/Goodbye To Teenage Love	30
60	HMV POP 798	The Girl On The Floor Above/Terry Brown's In Love With Mary Dee	50
61	Top Rank JAR 585	Wild Wind/You Took My Love For Granted	6
62	HMV POP 992	Lone Rider/Heart Of Stone	10
62	HMV POP 1014	Lonely City/It Would Be Easy	10
62	HMV POP 1054	Down The River Nile/I Think I'm Falling In Love	7
62	HMV POP 1076	Lonely Johnny/Keep On Loving You	8
63	HMV POP 1122	Cupboard Love/Land Of Love	6
63	HMV POP 1175	I'll Cut Your Tail Off/The Great Escape	7
63	HMV POP 1204	On Lover's Hill/Lovers Lane	8
63	HMV POP 1230	I Guess You Are Always On My Mind/Beautiful Dreamer	8
64	HMV POP 1264	Make Love To Me/Missing You (as John Leyton & Le Roys)	12
64	HMV POP 1338	Don't Let Her Go Away/I Want A Love I Can See	12
64	HMV POP 1374	All I Want Is You/Every Day Is A Holiday (with Grazina Frame & Mike Sarne)	15
73	York SYK 551	Dancing In The Graveyard/Riversong	15
74	York YR 210	Rock 'N' Roll/Highway Song	15
62	Top Rank JKP 3016	JOHN LEYTON (EP)	30
62	HMV 7EG 8747	HIT PARADE (EP)	20
64	HMV 7EG 8843	BEAUTIFUL DREAMER (EP)	20
64	HMV 7EG 8854	TELL LAURA I LOVE HER (EP)	25
61	HMV CLP 1497	THE TWO SIDES OF JOHN LEYTON (LP)	30
62	HMV CLP 1664	ALWAYS YOURS (LP, with Charles Blackwell's Orchestra)	40

(see also Le Roys)

LFB

78	Family FAM 1	Certain Politicians/Dreamteller (p/s)	7

L.F.O.

90	Warp/Outer WAP5R	LFO Remix/Mentok 1/Quijard (12")	10
90	Warp WAP 5	L.F.O. (The Leeds Warehouse Mix)/L.F.O. (Track 4)/Probe (The Cuba Edit) (12", p/s)	20
91	Warp WAP 14	We Are Back/Nurture (12")	10
92	Warp WAP 17	What Is House (LFO Remix)/Push/Tan Ta Ra (Moby Remix) (12")	10
91	Warp WARPLP3	FREQUENCIES (LP)	35
96	Warp WARPLP39	ADVANCE (2-LP)	30
03	Warp WARPLP110	SHEATH (LP)	15

LG & LOPEZ

01	Sit Tight STR001	Life Long/Tempered Waters/Storming (EP)	10
02	Sit Tight STR002	Rocket Fuel/City Breaks	10
06	Sit Tight STRLP 03	SMOKE RINGS (LP)	15

LIAISON

82	Catweazle CR 001	Play It With A Passion/Caught In A ... (grey p/s)	35
82	Catweazle CR 001	Play It With A Passion/Caught In A ... (yellow p/s)	10
84	Liaison LSN 0020	Only Heaven Knows/Ease The Pain Away	100

LIAISONS DANGEREUSES

82	Mute 023	Los Ninos Del Parque/Mystere Dans Le Broulard (p/s)	7

LIAR

MINT VALUE £

LIAR
79	Bearsville K 55524	SET THE WORLD ON FIRE (LP, picture disc)	15

LIARS
14	Mute 12MUTE 511	Mess On A Mission/Blah Vets/Mess On A Mission (Black Bananas Freezer Jam Remix)/Mess On A Mission (Silent Servant Remix) (12" clear vinyl with embedded coloured strings)	25
04	Mute STUMM 225	THEY WERE WRONG SO WE DROWNED (LP, gatefold, white vinyl, booklet)	20
05	Mute STUMM 246	DRUM'S NOT DEAD (LP with DVD)	25
07	Mute STUMM 287	LIARS (LP, white vinyl, inner)	15
13	Mute STUMM 343	WIXIW (LP & CD, all dipped in wax, 355 copies)	50
14	Mute (No Cat. No.)	MESS (LP, clear vinyl, vacuum sealed with coloured string)	35

SVEN LIBAEK
06	Trunk JBH 020 LP	INNER SPACE: THE LOST FILM MUSIC OF SVEN LIBAEK (LP, 500 only)	30

LIBERACE COUGHS UP BLOOD
81	Vital VTL 0002	Messerschmidt/Too Many Places/NIK TOWNEND: Gunslinger (p/s)	15

LIBERATION SUITE
75	Myrrh MYR 1027	LIBERATION SUITE (LP)	20

LIBERATORS
65	Stateside SS 424	It Hurts So Much/You Look So Fine	15

(see also Pinkerton's Assorted Colours)

EVE LIBERTINE & CRASS
84	Crass 1984/4	ACTS OF LOVE (LP, with book)	15

(see also Crass)

LIBERTINES
02	Rough Trade RTRADES 054	What A Waster/I Get Along (p/s, 2000 only)	25
02	Rough Trade RTRADES 064	Up The Bracket/Boys In The Band (p/s)	10
03	Rough Trade RTRADES 074	Time For Heroes/The 7 Deadly Sins (demo version) (p/s)	12
03	Rough Trade RTRADS 119	Don't Look Back Into The Sun/Death On The Stairs (blue vinyl, fold-out poster sleeve in PVC slipcase, 3000 only)	20
04	Rough Trade RTRADS 163	Can't Stand Me Now/The Tide That Left Never Came Back/(I've Got) Sweets (p/s)	8
04	Rough Trade RTRADS 215	What Became Of The Likely Lads?/(Reworked)/Boys In The Band (Live at Brixton Sat 6/3/04) (Free LP poster p/s)	8
16	Virgin/EMI (no cat no)	Don't Look Back To The Sun (Live)/What A Waster (Live) (p/s, 250 only)	12
16	Virgin/EMI (no cat no)	LIVE FROM NOTTINGHAM 2015: Can't Stand Me Now/Time For Heroes (p/s, 250 only)	12
02	Rough Trade RTRADELP 065	UP THE BRACKET (LP)	50
04	Rough Trade RTRADELPX166	THE LIBERTINES (LP, gatefold 3000 only)	40
04	Rough Trade RTRADELP166	THE LIBERTINES (White label test pressing, 10 only)	100
07	Rough Trade RTRADLP 421	TIME FOR HEROES - THE BEST OF THE LIBERTINES (LP, red vinyl)	50
15	Virgin/EMI 4746281	ANTHEMS FOR DOOMED YOUTH (LP)	15
15	Virgin/EMI 4746283	ANTHEMS FOR DOOMED YOUTH (LP, 2-CD boxed set, 4000 only)	25

(see also Babyshambles, Wolfman)

LIBERTY
80s	Mortarhate MORT 19	Our Voices Tomorrow's Hope	12
80s	Mortarhate MORT 25	THE PEOPLE WHO CARE ARE ANGRY (LP)	25

LIBERTY BELLES
71	Jay Boy BOY 40	Shing-A-Ling Time/Just Try Me	10

LIBIDO 1
73	Mooncrest MOON 2	Hold On To Your Fire/Weren't Born A Man	20

LIBRA LIBRA
86	Champion CHAMP 26	I Like It/Celebreties Like It (p/s)	8

LICKS
79	Stortbeat BEAT 8	1970S EP	15

(see also Epileptics, Flux Of Pink Indians)

GARETH LIDDIARD
10	ATP ATPRLP41	STRANGE TOURIST (2-LP)	80

JAMIE LIDELL
97	Mosquito MSQ 08	FREEKIN' THE FRAME (12" EP)	10

LIDJ INCORPORATED
89	Youth Sound YSR 001	Black Liberation/Version 1/Version 2/Version 3 (12", white labels only)	40
90	Youth Sound YSR 002	Line Up/Version/Ole Pan Sound/Version (12")	30
90	Youth Sound YSR 003T	General Peniteniary/Version/G.P. (12")	30
90	Youth Sound YOLP 002	DUB LIBERATION - LIDJ INCORPORATED MEETS SOUND IRATION (LP)	25
95	Eastern Sher ES 001	BLACK LIBERATION (LP)	25

BUNNY LIE LIE
81	Greensleeves GRED 52	Babylonian/WAYNE WADE: Poor And Humble (12")	20

LIES ALL LIES
86	SRT 6KS 802 LA	Still Night Air/Armchair Holiday (p/s)	8

LIEUTENANT PIGEON
73	Decca SKL 5154	MOULDY OLD MUSIC (LP)	20
73	Decca SKL 5174	PIGEON PIE (LP)	20
74	Decca SKL 5196	PIGEON PARTY (LP)	25

(see also Shel Naylor, Stavely Makepeace, Heavy Cochran)

LIFE
69	Polydor 56778	Hands Of The Clock/Ain't I Told You Before	22
72	Philips 6006247	Hold On (I'll Find You)/Love Nest	30
73	Philips 6006 280	Cats Eyes/Death In The Family (paper label)	20
73	Philips 6006 280	Cats Eyes/Death In The Family (moulded label)	10
74	Polydor 2058 500	Woman/Bless My Soul	6
74	Polydor 2383 295	LIFE AFTER DEATH (LP)	60

LIFE AFTER LIFE
85	Timetrack SRTSKL 453	LIFE AFTER LIFE (LP, private pressing)	120

LIFE 'N' SOUL

MINT VALUE £

LIFE 'N' SOUL
67 Decca F 12659 Ode To Billy Joe/Peacefully Asleep 25
68 Decca F 12851 Here Comes Yesterday Again/Dear Paul 15

LIFE OF RILEY
74 Enisgn 11 Turn The Pages Over/I Love My Life (p/s) 10

LIFE STUDIES
83 Occasion OCC 001 Girl On Fire/Inside Out/Citizen Of Love 20

LIFE SUPPORT
79 Slug SLUG 1 Leader Deceiver/Confusion (p/s, white labels) 25

LIFE WITHOUT BUILDINGS
00 Tugboat TUGS 016 The Leanover/New Town (p/s) 10
00 Tugboat TUGS 019 Is Is & The IRS/Let's Get Out (p/s) 8
00 Tugboat TUGLP 023 ANY OTHER CITY (LP) 30

LIFESTYLE
77 MCA MCA 308 Katrina/Love Can Make You Cry 20

LIFETIME
70 Polydor 2066 050 One Word/Two Worlds 20

(see also Tony Williams [Lifetime], Jack Bruce, John McLaughlin)

LIFETONES
83 Tone Of Life LTM 001 FOR A REASON (LP) 100

LIFT TO EXPERIENCE
01 Bella Union BELLAV 23 THE TEXAS JERUSALEM CROSSROADS (2-LP) 50

JOE LIGES
63 Blue Beat BB 172 Spit In The Sky/Tell Me What (both actually by Delroy Wilson) 25

(see also Delroy Wilson)

(THE) LIGHT
96 AAA Recordings TRIP 002 Dusk (12") 15

LIGHT BEARER
11 Eyes Of Sound EOSLP 035 LAPSUS (2-LP, 'wings' cover, inserts, 200 only) 30

BEN LIGHT
56 HMV 7M 350 Bring Me A Bluebird/You 10

ENOCH LIGHT
65 Pye Command PCLS 873 DISCOTHEQUE (LP) 20
69 Studio Two TWO 312 SPACED OUT (LP) 20
70 Project 3 PERMISSIVE POLYPHONICS (LP) 20

LIGHT FANTASTIC
73 MAM R 105 Love Is Everywhere/Gone Are The Days 10
73 MAM 112 Alley Oop/Peace And Love To The World 8
73 RCA RCA 2331 Jeanie/You Don't Care 20
74 Blue Jean BJS 701 Take Me, Shake Me/Don't Let Go 8
75 Blue Jean BJS 704 We Are The Song/Raining 6

J.J. LIGHT
69 Liberty LBF 15228 Heya/On The Road Now 10

LIGHT OF THE WORLD
80 Ensign ENVY 14 ROUND TRIP (LP) 18
82 EMI EMC 3410 CHECK US OUT (LP) 20

LIGHT YEARS
87 Amanda AM 7006 No Matter Where I Go/You Won't Break Me Down 8

GORDON LIGHTFOOT
62 Decca F 11527 (Remember Me) I'm The One/Daisy-Doo (as Gord Lightfoot) 20
63 Fontana 267 275TF Negotiations/It's Too Late, He Wins (as Gordie Lightfoot) 10
63 Fontana TF 405 The Day Before Yesterday/Take Care Of Yourself (as Gordie Lightfoot) 6

PAPA (GEORGE) LIGHTFOOT
69 Liberty LBF 15176 Wine Whiskey And Woman/SLIM HARPO: Something Inside Me 25
60s Jan & Dil JR 451 MORE DOWN HOME BLUES (EP) 35
71 Liberty LBS 83353 NATCHEZ TRACE (LP, as Papa George Lightfoot) 30

TERRY LIGHTFOOT'S (NEW ORLEANS) JAZZMEN
61 Columbia 33SX 1290 TRAD PARADE (LP, with New Orleans Jazzmen, also stereo SCX 3354) 15
61 Columbia 33SX 1353 WORLD OF TRAD (LP) 15
62 Columbia 33SX 1449 LIGHTFOOT AT LANSDOWNE (LP) 15

LIGHTHOUSE
69 RCA RCA 1884 Eight Miles High/If There Ever Was A Time 7
70 RCA RCA 1982 The Chant (Nam Myo-Ho Renge' Kyo)/Could You Be Concerned 10
71 Vertigo 6073 150 Hats Off (To The Strangers)/Sing Sing Sing 12
72 Philips 6073 152 One Fine Morning/Little Kind Words 12
72 Philips 6073 153 Take It Slow/Sweet Lullaby 20
70 RCA SF 8103 SUITE FEELING (LP) 15
71 Vertigo 6342 010 ONE FINE MORNING (LP, gatefold sleeve, swirl label) 150
71 Vertigo 6342 011 THOUGHTS OF MOVIN' ON (LP, gatefold sleeve, swirl label) 100

LIGHTNIN' SLIM
72 Blue Horizon 2096 013 Just A Little Bit/You're Old Enough To Understand/Mind Your Own Business 30
65 Stateside SL 10135 A LONG DRINK OF BLUES (LP, with Slim Harpo) 80
69 Python PLP 8 THE DOWNHOME BLUES PART 1 (LP, 99 copies only) 60
70 Blue Horizon 7-63863 ROOSTER BLUES (LP) 85
72 Blue Horizon 2931 005 LONDON GUMBO (LP) 150
78 Flyright FLYLP 533 TRIP TO CHICAGO (LP) 18
79 Flyright FLYLP 583 THE FEATURE SIDES 1954 (LP) 15
80 Flyright FLYLP 612 WE GOTTA ROCK TONIGHT (LP) 18

(see also Slim Harpo)

LIGHTNING LEON

MINT VALUE £

LIGHTNING LEON
60s	Jan & Dil JR 450	DOWN HOME BLUES - SIXTIES STYLE (EP)	35

LIGHTNING RAIDERS
80	Arista ARIST 341	Psychedelik Musik ('adult' version)/Views (p/s)	18
80	Arista ARIST 341DJ	Psychedelik Musik ('censored' version)/Views (promo only, no p/s)	35
81	Revenge REVS 200	Criminal World/Citizens (p/s)	10
81	Revenge RSS 39	Sweet Revenge/Rowdies/Addiction/Soul Rescue (12", promo only)	45

(see also Pink Fairies, Professionals)

LIGOTAGE
84	Picasso PIKM005	FORGIVE AND FORGET (LP, lyric insert)	15

LIJADU SISTERS
78	Afrodisia DWPS 2046	SUNSHINE (LP)	50
12	Soul Jazz SJR LP 246	AFRO-BEAT SOUL SISTERS (2-LP)	40

LIKE
10	Geffen 2740655	He's Not A Boy/Why When Love Is Gone	15

LIKE A SONG
73	De Wolfe DW/LP 3273	LIKE A SONG (LP, library issue)	18

LIKE ICE LIKE FIRE
86	Maiden Country LILF 01	Executioners Song/Dark Rosaline	12

LIL LOUIS
89	Rough TOUGH 4	Frequency (Remix) (12", 3,000 copies)	15
89	Ffrr FX 115	French Kiss/Wargames (12")	12

LILAC TIME
88	Swordfish LILAC 1	Return To Yesterday/Trumpets From Montparnasse (no p/s)	8
88	Swordfish 12 LILAC 1	Return To Yesterday/Railway Bazaar/Trumpets From Montparnasse/Reunion Ball (12", p/s)	12
90	Caff CAFF 12	Madresfield/Bird On The Wire (p/s, with insert)	25
88	Swordfish SWF LP 6	THE LILAC TIME (LP, original issue)	15

(see also Hawks, Stephen Duffy)

LILIPUT
80	Rough Trade RT 047	Spilt/Die Matrosen (p/s)	12
81	Rough Trade RT 062	Eisiger Wind/When The Cat's Away Then The Mice Will Play	15
82	Rough Trade ROUGH 43	LILIPUT (LP)	20

(see also Kleenex)

LILLIAN AXE
92	Music For Nations MFN 131	POETIC JUSTICE (LP)	40
93	Music For Nations MFN 151	PSYCHOSCHITZOPHRENIA (LP)	80

BEATRICE LILLIE
56	Brunswick OE 9091	PRESENTING (EP)	12
61	Decca DFE 6697	WHAT'S NEW WITH BEA LILLIE? (EP)	10

LILLY AK & YOUTH
84	Intrigue 12 84 1/2	Take Me Now/(Remix) (12")	15

LILYS
96	Ché CHE 51	Returns Every Morning/Touch The Water (white vinyl, p/s, 500 only)	6
96	Ché CHE 65	A Nanny In Manhattan/More Than Is Deserved (coffee-coloured vinyl, p/s, 500 only)	6

LIMELIGHT (1)
75	United Artists UP 35779	I Should Have Known Better/Tell Me Why	12

(see also Brinsley Schwarz)

LIMELIGHT (2)
80	Future Earth FER 006	Metal Man/Hold Me Touch Me (p/s)	12
82	Future Earth FER 010	Ashes To Ashes/Knife In Your Back (p/s, with insert)	12
82	Future Earth FER 010	Ashes To Ashes/Knife In Your Back (p/s, some with insert)	10
80	Future Earth FER 008	LIMELIGHT (LP)	22
81	Avatar AALP 5005	LIMITED LIMELIGHT (LP, with bonus single)	20
81	Avatar AALP 5005	LIMITED LIMELIGHT (LP)	15

LIMEYS
66	Decca F 12382	Cara-Lin/Feel So Blue	30

LIMIT (1)
78	Private Stock PVT 156	Please Please Me/My World At Night (company sleeve)	45

LIMIT (2)
81	Survival 002	Shockwaves/Ok Go (p/s)	15
81	Survival SUR 004	Taki It/Do It (p/s)	15

LIMMIE
78	Psycho P 2604	Saturday Night's The Night/Party	50
14	Super Disco Edits CATS DE6	Saturday Night's The Night/Can't Turn You Loose (reissue, as Limmie Funk Ltd)	40

LIMPS/NO SUPPORT
79	Matchbox Classics MC 1	OPPOSITE SIDES EP (Split 7" with 2 tracks by Limps and 2 tracks by No Support, p/s)	20
79	Matchbox Classics MC 2	ANOTHER MATCHBOX CLASSIC? (Split EP, 2 tracks by Limps and 2 by No Support, with folded p/s)	40
79	Matchbox Classics MC 2	ANOTHER MATCHBOX CLASSIC? (Split EP, 2 tracks by Limps and 2 by No Support, without folded p/s, just die-cut stamped sleeve)	15

PETER LINCOLN
67	Major Minor MM 520	In The Day Of My Youth/My Monkey Is A Junkie	30

(see also Peter Sarstedt, Sarstedt Brothers, Brothers Kane)

PHILAMORE LINCOLN
68	NEMS 56-3711	Running By The River/Rainy Day	70
70	CBS 5007	The County Jail Band/You're The One	40

LINCOLN TURNPIKE
71	Polydor 2058109	Green On The Other Side Of The Mountain/You Can Call Everybody Your Friend	8

LINCOLNS
66	Parlophone R 5418	Mister Loneliness/Only Love Will Break Your Heart	6

BOB LIND
66	Fontana TF 670	Elusive Butterfly/Cheryl's Goin' Home	6
66	Fontana (S)TL 5340	DON'T BE CONCERNED (LP)	20
66	Verve F'ways (S)VLP 5015	THE ELUSIVE BOB LIND (LP)	15

LINDA AND THE DARK
80	Crash Point	Horror Movies/I Don't Want To See You Out With Somebody Else (p/s)	20

DADDY LINDBERG
67	Columbia DB 8138	Shirl/Wade In The Shade	120

(see also Crocheted Doughnut Ring)

ANITA LINDBLOM
62	Fontana 267223 TF	Uptown/Mr Big Wheel	10

LINDISFARNE
70	Charisma CB 137	Clear White Light Part II/Knackers Yard Blues	15
71	Charisma CB 153	Lady Eleanor/Nothing But The Marvellous Is Beautiful (with p/s)	6
70	Charisma CAS 1025	NICELY OUT OF TUNE (LP, pink 'scroll' label)	35
71	Charisma CAS 1050	FOG ON THE TYNE (LP, gatefold textured sleeve, pink 'scroll' label)	25
72	Charisma CAS 1057	DINGLY DELL (LP, with inner sleeve & poster)	15

(see also Alan Hull, Jack The Lad, Chosen Few, Radiator)

WILLIE LINDO
76	Klik KLP 9019	FAR AND DISTANT (LP)	15
78	Black Wax WAX 21	Midnight/After Midnight	25

JIMMY LINDSAY AND THE BEANS
70	Q 2203	Peace To You Brother/Tribute To Jimi Hendrix	15

JIMMY LINDSAY
77	Black Swan BS 8	Easy/FABIAN: Prophecy (12")	30
77	Tribesman TM 008	Easy/FABIAN: Prophecy (12")	30
78	Music Hive MH002	Ain't No Sunshine/EXODUS : Take Six/DIMBALA : And Ting (12")	30
82	Music Hive MH004	Turn Out The Lights/Dole Queue (12")	30
80	Gem GEMLP 110	CHILDREN OF RASTAFARI (LP)	15

MARK LINDSAY
69	CBS 4699	Arizona/Man From Houston	10
70	CBS 5055	Silver Bird/So Hard To Leave You	8
70	CBS 5219	And The Grass Won't Pay No Mind/Funny How Little Men Care	8
71	CBS 5408	Problem Child/Bookends	8
71	CBS 7330	Been Too Long On The Road/All I Really See Is You	8
71	CBS 7551	Are You Old Enough/Don't You Know	8
71	CBS 7690	Something Big/Pretty Pretty	8

(see also Paul Revere & Raiders)

TERRY LINDSEY
69	President PT 232	It's Over/One Day Up, Next Day Down	15

BJORN J. SON LINDT
83	Sonet SON 2254	Cloud Pump/From Here To Eternity (p/s)	12

DAVID LINDUP ORCHESTRA
66	Columbia DB 7979	Informer Theme/Blue Mountain	10
66	Polydor 56106	Survival Theme/New Forest	20
70	Aristocrat AR 1021	WHEN THE SAINTS GO (LP)	20

LINDYS
60	Decca F 11253	The Train Of Love/You Know How Things Get Around	15
60	Decca F 11272	Boy With The Eyes Of Blue/Someone Else's Roses	15

LINES
78	Linear SJP 782	White Night/Barbican (p/s)	12
79	Illegal ILS 0011	White Night/Barbican (p/s, reissue)	7
79	Red RS 001	On The Air/Not Through Windows/Dance For A Drop Of Blood	8
80	Red Linear RL 007	Nerve Pylon/Over The Brow (screen-printed p/s)	8
80	Red Linear RL12 005	COOL SNAP EP (12")	12
81	Red RS 010	Transit/Part II (p/s)	7
83	Red ROUGE 3	ULTRAMARINE (LP)	15

BUZZY LINHART
69	Philips SBL 7885	BUZZY (LP, laminated gatefold sleeve, black/silver labels)	40
71	Kama Sutra 2319011	THE TIME TO LIVE IS NOW (LP, textured gatefold sleeve, yellow/red labels)	25
71	Buddah 2318028	MUSIC (LP)	15

LINK
92	Evolution EVO 05	THE FIRST LINK EP (12", plain sleeve)	35
95	Warp WAP 59	ANTACID EP (12", p/s)	15
95	Warp WAP 59R	ANTACID REMIXES EP (12", p/s as Link & E621)	10

(see also Reload, Global Communications, Mystic Institute)

LINKERS
71	Big Shot BI 567	Bongo Man/FUD CHRISTIAN ALLSTARS: Creation Version	20

(see also Links)

ANSEL LINKERS & FUD CHRISTIAN ALL STARS
73	Summit SUM 8540	Memories By The Score/FUD CHRISTIAN ALL STARS: Scorer	7

(see also Links)

LINKS
72	Tropical AL 0010	Sing A Song Of Freedom/TROPICAL ALL STARS: Love Rhythm (A-side actually by Linkers)	6

LINN COUNTY
68	Mercury SMCL 20142	PROUD FLESH SOOTHSEER (LP)	25
69	Mercury SMCL 20165	FEVER SHOT (LP)	20
70	Philips SBL 7923	TILL THE BREAK OF DAWN (LP)	18

ELMO LINN
63	Starlite ST45 101	Another Man's Arms/Sam Houston	18

Joe LINTHECOME

MINT VALUE £

JOE LINTHECOME
50s Poydras 87 — Pretty Mama Blues/Hummingbird Blues 15

LIONHEART
85 Epic A 5001 — Die For Love/Dangerous Games (p/s) 7
84 Epic EPC26214 — HOT TONIGHT (LP) 15
(see also Iron Maiden, Wildfire)

LIONROCK
92 M.E.R.C. 002 — Roots'n'Culture (Part One)/Lionrock (12", original issue) 10
92 De Construction 74321124381 — Lionrock - The Remixes: (Most Excellent Mix)/(Roots 'n' Culture)/(A Trumpet Jamboree In Edinburgh)/(A Dubtastic Jamboree In Edinburgh) (12") 10
93 Distort & Cavort — Dub Plate No. 1 (12") 10
98 Concrete HARD 3112 — Rude Boy Rock/Best Foot Forward/Push Button Cocktail (p/s) 8

LIONS
69 Polydor 56757 — Twisted Nerve/My Friend The Blackbird 30

LIONS (JAMAICA)
77 Truth & Right L 001 — Natty Congo I/Version 150

LIONS OF JUDAH
69 Fontana TF 1016 — Our Love's A Growin' Thing/Katja 20

LION TAMERS
68 Polydor 56283 — Speak Your Mind/Light 50

LION YOUTH
78 Virgo Stomach VG 104 — Rat Cut A Bottle/Rub A Dub (12", black or purple vinyl) 30
79 Virgo Stomach VG 013 — Three Million On The Dole/Three Million Posse On Employed In A Dub (12") 15
83 Music Hawk MH 04 — I Don't Like It/Government Dub (12") 15
81 Virgo Stomach VGLP 001 — LOVE COMES AND GOES (LP) 25

LIP MOVES
79 Tichonderoga HP 1 — Guest/What Is (p/s with insert, stickered white labels, signed) 40
79 Tichonderoga HP 1 — Guest/What Is (p/s with insert, stickered white labels) 30

THE LIPS
78 GTO GT 219 — Say Hello To My Girl/Be Cool From School (no p/s) 8

PEGGY LIPTON
70 CBS 4779 — Lu/Let Me Pass By 15

LIQUID
95 XL XLT 28 — Sweet Harmony/Phog/Sweet Harmony (Remix)/Feel 3 (12") 15
95 XL XLLP 113 — CULTURE (2-LP) 20

LIQUID CRYSTAL
91 Bizarre BIZZ 2 — Inner Sense/Dischord (12") 25
92 Bizarre BIZZ 3 — The Power Within/Let It Go/Inner Sense ('92 remix) (12") 25
92 Bizarre BIZZ 3R T — The Power Within (Remix)/Radiate/Inner Sense (Original) (12", p/s) 25
92 Ruff On Wax ROWT 1 — CHROMATIC EP (12", stickered plain sleeve) 70
92 Ruff On Wax ROWTR 1 — CHROMATIC 2 EP: (12", stickered plain sleeve) 60

LIQUID LIQUID
97 Mo Wax MWLP 078 — Cavern (Remix)/Lock Groove (Live)/New Walk (U.N.K.L.E) (12", promo only) 15
97 Mo Wax MW 078LP — LIQUID LIQUID (2-LP) 30
08 Domino REWIGLP 34 — SLIP IN AND OUT OF PHENOMENON (LP, 12", CD) 20
97 Mo Wax MW 078LP — LIQUID LIQUID (2-LP) 20

LIQUID SMOKE
75 Pye Int. 7N 25677 — Dance Dance Dance/Where Is Our Love 8
70 Avco Embassy 646 6003 — LIQUID SMOKE (LP) 50

LIQUID STONE
81 Liquid Stone LIQ 001 — Here Comes The Weekend/Because Of You (no p/s, hand stickered labels) 350

LIQUORICE (1)
78 Perno PER 1 — It's Gonna Turn You On/This Is The B-Side 10

LIQUORICE (2)
95 4AD CAD 5008 — LISTENING CAP (LP) 15

DAVID LISBON
61 Philips PB 1136 — Deer Stalker/Almost Grown Up 7
61 Philips PB 1163 — Joy Ride/Swiss Miss 6
61 Philips BBE 12469 — LIKE LISBON (EP) 10

LISSEN
78 Madrigal MDG 101 — PRECIS EP (p/s) 8

LISTEN
65 CBS 202456 — You'd Better Run/Everybody's Gonna Say 300
(see also Robert Plant, Led Zeppelin)

LIT
99 RCA 74321 678591 — A PLACE IN THE SUN (LP) 50

SHIRLEY LITES
83 West End WEND 1 — Heat You Up, Melt You Down/(Melt Down Mix) 10
83 West End WEND 121 — Heat You Up, Melt You Down/(Melt Down Mix) (12") 12

LITMUS
09 Rise Above RISELP 125 — AURORA (2-LP, 1 side etched) 20

LITTER
69 Probe CLPS 4504 — EMERGE (LP) 75

LITTLE ANNIE
92 On U Sound ON UP LP 60 — SHORT AND SWEET (LP) 20
(see also Annie Anxiety)

'BIG' TINY LITTLE
57 Vogue Coral Q 72263 — School Day/That's The Only Way To Live 40
57 Vogue Coral Q 72263 — School Day/That's The Only Way To Live (78) 20
60 Coral FEP 2058 — HONKY TONK PIANO VOL. 1 (EP) 10
60 Coral FEP 2059 — HONKY TONK PIANO VOL. 2 (EP) 10

SHARON LITTLE
81	One Love (no number)	Don't Mash Up Creation/Version (12")	150
81	One Love	Don't Mash Up Creation/Version	100
10	Jah Shaka SHAKA 108	Mash Up Creation/YOUNG WARRIOR: Creation Dub (12", 1st reissue, blue ink on white label)	30
13	Jah Shaka SHAKA 108	Don't Mash Up Creation/YOUNG WARRIOR: Creation Dub (12", 2nd reissue, black ink)	20

LITTLE SIMZ
17	Age 101 Music AGE1011X	STILLNESS IN WONDERLAND (2-LP, signed)	80
17	Age 101 Music AGE1011X	STILLNESS IN WONDERLAND (2-LP, unsigned)	60

LITTLE ANGELS
87	Little Angels LAN 001	LITTLE ANGELS '87 (12" EP)	30
87	Powerstation AMP 14	TOO POSH TO MOSH (mini-LP)	18

LITTLE ANN
98	Kent TOWN 111	What Should I Do/O.C. TALBOT: I'm Shooting High (I Reach For The Sky)	15
99	Kent TOWN 112	Who Are You Trying To Fool/I Got To Have You	20
09	Kent CITY 010	Lean Lanky Daddy/DAVID HAMILTON ORCHESTRA: Who Are You Trying To Fool (reissue)	10
16	Deep Soul DEEP SOUL 02	Deep Shadows/TURN AROUNDS: Stay Away	7

LITTLE ANTHONY & IMPERIALS
58	London HLH 8704	Tears On My Pillow/Two People In The World	40
58	London HLH 8704	Tears On My Pillow/Two People In The World (78)	30
59	London HL 8848	So Much/Oh Yeah	50
59	London HL 8848	So Much/Oh Yeah (78)	40
59	Top Rank JAR 256	Shimmy, Shimmy, Ko-Ko Bop/I'm Still In Love With You	25
60	Top Rank JAR 366	My Empty Room/Bayou, Bayou, Baby	15
64	United Artists UP 1065	I'm On The Outside Looking In/Please Go	15
64	United Artists UP 1073	Goin' Out Of My Head/Make It Easy On Yourself	15
65	United Artists UP 1083	Hurt So Bad/Reputation	25
65	United Artists UP 1098	Take Me Back/Our Song	20
65	United Artists UP 1112	I Miss You/Get Out Of My Life	15
66	United Artists UP 1126	Hurt/Never Again	40
66	United Artists UP 1137	Better Use Your Head/The Wonder Of It All	80
66	United Artists UP 1137	Better Use Your Head/The Wonder Of It All (DJ copy)	150
66	United Artists UP 1151	Gonna Fix You Good (Every Time You're Bad)/You Better Take It Easy Baby	75
68	United Artists UP 2260	Let The Sunshine In/The Gentle Rain (as Anthony)	10
69	United Artists UP 35017	Anthem/Goodbye Goodtimes (as Anthony & Imperials)	7
72	United Artists UP 35345	Gonna Fix You Good (Every Time You're Bad)/You Better Take It Easy Baby (reissue)	10
76	United Artists UP 36118	Better Use Your Head/Gonna Fix You Good (Every Time You're Bad)	10
65	United Artists UEP 1004	LITTLE ANTHONY AND THE IMPERIALS (EP)	100
76	United Artists REM 405	Goin' Out Of My Head/I'm On The Outside Looking In/Hurt So Bad/ Gonna Fix You Good (Every Time You're Bad) (EP)	10
64	United Artists ULP 1089	I'M ON THE OUTSIDE LOOKING IN (LP)	100
66	United Artists ULP 1100	GOIN' OUT OF MY HEAD (LP)	80

LITTLE ARCHIE
68	Atlantic 584 209	I Need You/I Am A Carpet	40

LITTLE AXE
94	Wired WIRED 17	THE WOLF THAT HOUSE BUILT (2-LP)	25
96	Wired WIRED 133	SLOW FUSE (2-LP)	35

LITTLE BEAVER
72	President PTLS 1060	JOEY (LP)	25
75	President PTLS 1063	PARTY DOWN (LP)	100

LITTLE BEVERLEY
68	Pama PM 731	What A Guy/You're Mine	8

(see also Beverley Simmons)

LITTLE BIG HORN
70	Polydor 2058042	Another Man's Song/Just A Game	40

LITTLE BILL & BLUE NOTES
59	Top Rank JAR 176	I Love An Angel/Bye, Bye Baby	25
59	Top Rank JAR 176	I Love An Angel/Bye, Bye Baby (78)	25

(see also Blue Notes)

LITTLE BOOTS
08	50 Bones 4BONES	Meddle/Meddle (Toddla T & Ross Orton Mix) (green vinyl with tattoo set, 500 only)	35

LITTLE BOY BLUE
69	Jackpot JP 701	Dark End Of The Street/MR VERSATILE: Apple Blossoms	25

LITTLE CLARKIE & THE OFFBEAT POSSE
86	Jah Tubbys JT 015	Selector Him Good/COLONEL MITE: Bless The Selector/JAH TUBBY: Select The Rhythm (12")	80
86	Jah Tubbys JT 20	Live Stock Party/Bounty Hunter (12")	50
87	Y&D YDD 0107	Bubble-N-Rock/Cowboy Stylee (12")	50
88	Y&D YDD 0134	Can't Come A Dance And Stand Up/Never Give You Up (12")	30

LITTLE DARLING
65	Blue Beat BB 325	No One/BUSTER'S ALL STARS: Congo Revolution	150

LITTLE DARLINGS
65	Fontana TF 539	Little Bit O' Soul/Easy To Cry	100

LITTLE DES
70	J-Dan JDN 4400	Somebody's Baby/Spy Man	7

LITTLE DIPPERS
60	Pye International 7N 25051	Forever/Two By Four	10
61	London HLG 9269	Lonely/I Wonder, I Wonder, I Wonder	15

LITTLE EVA
62	London HLU 9633	Keep Your Hands Off My Baby/Where Do I Go	8

LITTLE FEAT

MINT VALUE £

63	Colpix PX 11013	The Trouble With Boys/What I Gotta Do (To Make You Jealous)	12
63	Colpix PX 11019	Please Hurt Me/Let's Start The Party Again	12
64	Colpix PX 11035	Run To Her/Making With The Magilla	15
65	Stateside SS 477	Stand By Me/That's My Man	20
63	London HA-U 8036	L-L-L-L-LOCO-MOTION (LP, original with plum label & laminated sleeve)	30

(see also Big Dee Irwin & Little Eva)

LITTLE FEAT
72	Warner Bros. K 46072	LITTLE FEAT (LP)	15
72	Warner Bros. K 46156	SAILIN' SHOES (LP, gatefold)	15
75	Warner Bros. K 66038	THE LAST RECORD ALBUM (LP)	15
77	Warner Bros. K 56349	TIME LOVES A HERO (LP)	15
86	Nimbus 80027	FEATS DON'T FAIL ME NOW (LP, reissue, Nimbus Supercut, mail order only through Practical Hi Fi magazine)	70

LITTLE FISH
| 72 | Plant Life PLR 011 | HERTFORDSHIRE FOLK SONGS (EP, with insert) | 50 |

LITTLE FOLK
| 71 | Studio Republic CR 1001 | LEAVE THEM A FLOWER (LP) | 18 |

LITTLE FRANKIE (& COUNTRY GENTLEMEN)
65	Columbia DB 7490	The Kind Of Boy You Can't Forget/I'm Not Gonna Do It	20
65	Columbia DB 7578	Make-A-Love/Love Is Just A Game (with Country Gentlemen)	40
65	Columbia DB 7681	It Doesn't Matter Anymore/Happy, That's Me	20

(see also Chimes featuring Denise)

LITTLE FREDDY (MCGREGOR)
| 70 | Unity UN 551 | Why Did My Little Girl Cry/PETER AUSTIN: Change Partners | 10 |

(see also Freddie McGregor)

LITTLE FREE ROCK
| 69 | Transatlantic TRA 208 | LITTLE FREE ROCK (LP, laminated sleeve, white/lilac labels, 't' logo) | 175 |

(see also David John & Mood)

LITTLE GEORGE
| 64 | Rio R 45 | Mary Anne/EDWARDS ALLSTARS: Blue Night | 20 |

LITTLE GRANT
| 70 | Torpedo TOR 27 | Baby Don't Let Me Down/Brother Strong Man | 30 |

(see also Equals, Pyramids, Eddy Grant)

LITTLE GRANTS & EDDIE (GRANT)
| 67 | President PT 159 | Rudy's Dead/Everything's Alright | 20 |
| 67 | President PT 172 | Rock Steady '67/Bingo | 20 |

(see also Equals, Pyramids, Eddy Grant)

LITTLE HANK
66	London HLU 10090	Mr. Bang Bang Man/Don't You Know (withdrawn)	150
66	London HLU 10090	Mr. Bang Bang Man/Don't You Know (withdrawn) (DJ copy)	150
70	Monument MON 1045	Mr. Bang Bang Man/Don't You Know (reissue)	15
01	Grapevine 2000 108	Try To Understand/Mr Bang Bang Man (reissue)	8

LITTLE HOWIE
| 85 | Look To Afrika LTAF 03 | Original Love Me/EARL ANTHONY Sensi Man Rock (12") | 100 |

LITTLE JOE BLUE
| 78 | Flyright FLY LP 534 | DON'T TAX ME IN (LP) | 20 |

LITTLE JOE (JAMAICA)
| 70 | Torpedo TOR 15 | Bad Blood/Maxi-Mini War | 40 |

(see also Sexy Girls)

LITTLE JOE (& THRILLERS)
| 60 | Fontana H 281 | Stay (as Little Joe & Thrillers)/Cherry | 25 |
| 63 | Reprise R 20142 | Peanuts/No No I Can't Stop | 20 |

LITTLE JOEY & FLIPS
| 62 | Pye International 7N 25152 | Bongo Stomp/Lost Love | 12 |

LITTLE JOHN
67	Pama PM 702	Let's Get Married/Around The World	20
70	Unity UN 561	No Love/A Little Tear (both sides actually by John Holt)	15
84	Greensleeves GRELD 139	Form A Line/YELLOWMAN: Rub & Go Down (12")	15
84	Music Hawk MH15	Walk Away/Version (12")	20
84	Vista VSLP 4061	UNITE (LP)	20

(see also John Holt)

ALAN LITTLEJOHN BAND
| 62 | Oriole CB 1734 | Out Of The Blue/There Ain't No Sweet Man Worth The Salt Of My Tears | 15 |

LITTLE JOHN & BILLY BOYO
82	Greensleeves GRED 86	Bushmaster Connection/BILY BOYO: Little Girl (12")	18
82	Greensleeves GRED 92	Janet Sinclair/Agony Column Dub (12")	25
82	Rusty International RI 003	What You Want To Be/PROFESSOR & ROOTS RADICS: Combination (12")	20

LITTLE JOHN ANTHONY
| 60 | Ember EMB 3302 | TEENAGE DANCE PARTY (LP) | 20 |

LITTLE JOHNNY & THREE TEENAGERS
| 58 | Decca F 10990 | Baby Lover/Rickety Rackety Rendezvous | 20 |

LITTLE KIRK
| 70s | Ruddys RM 004 | Ghetto People Broke/Version (12") | 45 |
| 70s | Ruddys RM 001 | Weed Them Out/Version (12") | 50 |

LITTLE LULU
| 72 | FAB FAB 21 | Love & Obey/AL CAMPBELL & FREDDIE MCGREGOR: Free Man | 200 |

LITTLE LUMAN
| 64 | Rio R 44 | Hurry Harry/R. ALPHONSE: Hucklebuck (B-side actually by Roland Alphonso) | 15 |

LITTLE LUTHER
| 64 | Pye International 7N 25266 | Eenie Meenie Minie Moe/Twirl | 70 |

LITTLE MACK & BOSS SOUNDS

MINT VALUE £

LITTLE MACK & BOSS SOUNDS
66	Atlantic 584 031	In The Midnight Hour/You Can't Love Me (In The Midnight Hour)	25

MARIE LITTLE
71	Argo ZFB 19	FACTORY GIRL (LP)	150
73	Trailer LER 2084	MARIE LITTLE (LP, red or yellow label)	50

LITTLE MILTON
65	Pye International 7N 25289	Blind Man/Blues In The Night	15
65	Chess CRS 8013	We're Gonna Make It/Can't Hold Back The Tears	20
65	Chess CRS 8013	We're Gonna Make It/Can't Hold Back The Tears (demo copy)	35
65	Chess CRS 8018	Who's Cheating Who?/Ain't No Big Deal On You	20
66	Sue WI 4021	Early In The Morning/Bless Your Heart (actually by Roy Milton)	40
69	Chess CRS 8087	Grits Ain't Groceries/I Can't Quit You Baby	25
69	Chess CRS 8100	Let's Get Together/I'll Always Love You	15
72	Stax 2025 095	That's What Love Will Make You Do/I'm Living Off The Love You Give	8
74	Stax STXS 2003	Behind Closed Doors/Bet You I Win	8
75	Stax STA 100	If That Ain't A Reason/Mr. Mailman	6
69	Chess CRLS 4552	GRITS AIN'T GROCERIES (LP)	80
72	Chess 6310 120	GOLDEN DECADE (LP)	15
74	Stax STX 1013	BLUES 'N' SOUL (LP)	25

LITTLE NELL
75	A&M AMS 7351	Do The Swim/Stilettos And Lipstick/Tropical Isle (red vinyl, p/s)	8

LITTLE RICHARD
78s
57	London HLO 8446	Lucille/Send Me Some Lovin' (as Little Richard & His Band)	20
57	London HLO 8470	Jenny, Jenny/Miss Ann (as Little Richard & His Band)	20
58	London HLU 8560	Good Golly Miss Molly/Hey-Hey-Hey-Hey	25
58	London HLO 8647	Ooh! My Soul/True, Fine Mama	30
59	London HLU 8831	By The Light Of The Silvery Moon/Early One Morning	30
59	London HLU 8868	Kansas City/She Knows How To Rock	50
60	London HLU 9065	Baby/I Got It	90

SINGLES
56	London HLO 8336	Rip It Up/Ready Teddy (gold label print)	150
56	London HLO 8336	Rip It Up/Ready Teddy (later pressing with silver label print)	30
50s	London HLO 8336	Rip It Up/Ready Teddy (repressing, silver-top label, round centre)	25
57	London HLO 8366	Long Tall Sally/Tutti Frutti (gold label print)	125
57	London HLO 8366	Long Tall Sally/Tutti Frutti (later silver label print)	40
50s	London HLO 8366	Long Tall Sally/Tutti Frutti (repressing, silver-top label, round centre)	20
57	London HLO 8382	The Girl Can't Help It/She's Got It (gold label print)	125
57	London HLO 8382	The Girl Can't Help It/She's Got It (later silver label print)	30
50s	London HLO 8382	The Girl Can't Help It/She's Got It (repressing, silver-top label, round centre)	20
57	London HLO 8446	Lucille/Send Me Some Lovin' (as Little Richard & His Band)	30
57	London HLO 8470	Jenny, Jenny/Miss Ann (as Little Richard & His Band)	30
57	London HLO 8509	Keep A Knockin'/Can't Believe You Wanna Leave	30
58	London HLU 8560	Good Golly Miss Molly/Hey-Hey-Hey-Hey	30
58	London HLO 8647	Ooh! My Soul/True, Fine Mama	15
58	London HLU 8770	Baby Face/I'll Never Let You Go	8
59	London HLU 8831	By The Light Of The Silvery Moon/Early One Morning	8
59	London HLU 8868	Kansas City/She Knows How To Rock	10

(The above 45s were originally issued with triangular centres; later round-centres are worth around half to two-thirds these values.)

60	London HLU 9065	Baby/I Got It	15
61	Mercury AMT 1165	Joy Joy Joy (Down In My Heart)/He's Not Just A Soldier	8
62	Mercury AMT 1189	He Got What He Wanted (But He Lost What He Had)/ Why Don't You Change Your Ways?	8
63	London HLK 9708	Crying In The Chapel/Hole In The Wall	8
63	London HLK 9756	Travelin' Shoes/It Is No Secret	8
64	London HL 9896	Bama Lama Bama Loo/Annie's Back	10
64	Fontana TF 519	Blueberry Hill/Cherry Red	10
64	Stateside SS 340	Whole Lotta Shakin' Goin' On/Goodnight Irene	10
64	Mercury MF 841	Joy, Joy, Joy (Down In My Heart)/Peace In The Valley	10
66	Fontana TF 652	I Don't Know What You've Got But It's Got Me (Parts 1 & 2)	30
66	Stateside SS 508	Holy Mackeral/Baby, Don'tcha Want A Man Like Me?	20
66	Sue WI 4001	Without Love/Dance What You Wanna	40
66	Sue WI 4015	It Ain't Watcha Do (It's The Way How You Do It)/Crossover	40
66	Columbia DB 7974	Poor Dog/Well	25
66	Columbia DB 8058	I Need Love/The Commandments Of Love	20
67	Columbia DB 8116	Get Down With It/Rose Mary	25
67	Columbia DB 8240	A Little Bit Of Something/Money	50
67	Columbia DB 8240	A Little Bit Of Something/Money (DJ copy)	75
67	Columbia DB 8263	I Don't Want To Discuss It/Hurry Sundown	50
67	Columbia DB 8263	I Don't Want To Discuss It/Hurry Sundown (DJ copy)	85
68	MCA MU 1006	Try Some Of Mine/She's Together	10
68	London HLU 10194	Good Golly Miss Molly/Lucille	10
68	President PT 201	Whole Lotta Shakin' Goin' On/Lawdy Miss Clawdy	10
69	Action ACT 4528	Baby What Do You Want Me To Do (Parts 1 & 2)	10
70	Reprise RS 20907	Dew Drop In/Freedom Blues	10
71	Reprise K 14124	Green Power/Dancing In The Street	10

SINGLES : EXPORT SINGLES
57	London HL 7022	Jenny, Jenny/Miss Ann (as Little Richard & His Band)	30
58	London HL 7049	Ooh! My Soul/True, Fine Mama	15

LITTLE ROOSTERS

MINT VALUE £

58	London HL 7056	Baby Face/I'll Never Let You Go	15
59	London HL 7074	She Knows How To Rock/Early One Morning	20
59	London HL 7079	By The Light Of The Silvery Moon/Kansas City	20
59	London HL 7085	Whole Lotta Shakin' Goin' On/All Around The World	40
68	Decca AD 1006	She's Together/Try Some Of Mine	25

EPs

57	London RE-O 1071	LITTLE RICHARD AND HIS BAND VOL. 1 (gold tri-centre)	40
57	London RE-O 1071	LITTLE RICHARD AND HIS BAND VOL. 1 (later silver label)	30
57	London RE-O 1074	LITTLE RICHARD AND HIS BAND VOL. 2 (later silver label)	40
57	London RE-O 1074	LITTLE RICHARD AND HIS BAND VOL. 2 (gold tri-centre, later silver)	20
57	London RE-O 1103	LITTLE RICHARD AND HIS BAND VOL. 3	25
57	London RE-O 1106	LITTLE RICHARD AND HIS BAND VOL. 4	25
59	London RE-U 1208	LITTLE RICHARD AND HIS BAND VOL. 5	25
60	London RE-U 1234	LITTLE RICHARD AND HIS BAND VOL. 6	30
60	London RE-U 1235	LITTLE RICHARD AND HIS BAND VOL. 7	35

(The above EPs were originally issued with triangular centres; later round-centre pressings are worth between half to two thirds of these listed values.)

63	London REK 1400	HE'S BACK	40
64	Vocalion VEP 170155	MEMPHIS SLIM AND LITTLE RICHARD	80
66	Stateside SE 1042	DO YOU FEEL IT	60

ALBUMS

89	Ace ABOXLP 1	THE SPECIALITY SESSIONS (8-LP box set, booklet)	35
57	London HA-O 2055	HERE'S LITTLE RICHARD (flipback, rear sleeve in gloss red)	100
57	London HA-O 2055	HERE'S LITTLE RICHARD (flipback)	50
57	London HA-O 2055	HERE'S LITTLE RICHARD (small flipback sleeve)	55
57	London HA-O 2055	HERE'S LITTLE RICHARD (non-flipback sleeve)	35
58	London HA-U 2126	LITTLE RICHARD VOL. 2 (flipback sleeve)	75
58	London HA-U 2126	LITTLE RICHARD VOL. 2 (non-flipback sleeve)	40
59	RCA Camden CDN 125	LITTLE RICHARD (8 tracks only; others by Buck Ram Orchestra, picture of Richard in "frame" on sleeve, brown wooden effect is first pressing)	25
59	London HA-U 2193	THE FABULOUS LITTLE RICHARD (flipback sleeve)	75
59	London HA-U 2193	THE FABULOUS LITTLE RICHARD (non-flipback sleeve)	40
60	Top Rank 25/025	PRAY ALONG WITH LITTLE RICHARD VOL. 1: A CLOSER WALK WITH THEE (plain white sleeve, mail-order only)	40
60	Top Rank 25/026	PRAY ALONG WITH LITTLE RICHARD VOL. 2: I'M QUITTING SHOW BUSINESS (plain white sleeve, mail-order only)	80
64	Stateside SL 10204	SINGS GOSPEL	25
64	Coral LVA 9220	COMING HOME	25
65	Mercury MCL 20036	IT'S REAL	15
65	Fontana TL 5235	IS BACK!	25
67	Columbia SX/SCX 6136	THE EXPLOSIVE LITTLE RICHARD	40
68	Fontana SFL 13010	KING OF THE GOSPEL SINGERS	15
70	Reprise RSLP 6406	THE RILL THING	15

(see also Canned Heat, Sister Rosetta Tharpe, Buck Ram's Ramrocks)

LITTLE ROOSTERS

79	Pye 7P 152	She Cat Sister Floozie/Roostering With Intent (p/s)	6
80	Ami AIS 101	That's How Strong My Love Is/Suspicious (p/s)	6
80	Ami AIS 107	I Need A Witness/The Age Of Reason (p/s)	6

(see also Cocksparrer, Alison Moyet)

LITTLE ROY

69	Crab CRAB 39	Without My Love (actually by Roy & Joy)/WINSTON SAMUELS: Here I Come Again	35
70	Bullet BU 445	Keep Trying/Version (actually by the Matadors)	20
70	Bullet BU 445	Keep Trying/THE MATADORS: Version II	15
70	Camel CA 43	Scrooge/In The Days Of Old	20
70	Camel CA 52	Fight Them/Dreadlock	20
70	Camel CA 46	You Run Come/THE LITTLE ROYS: Skank King (actually "Skank Me" by Little Roy)	20
71	Escort ERT 850	Yester-Me Yester-You Yesterday/MATADOR ALL-STARS: Yes Sir	10
71	Punch PH 75	Hard Fighter/COUNT OSSIE: Back To Africa Version	12
81	Copasetic COP 5001	COLUMBUS SHIP (LP)	40

LITTLE ROYS

69	Camel CA 36	Bongonyah/CREATIONS: Dad Name (B-side actually "Bad Name")	25
70	Camel CA 42	Gold Digger (actually by Wailing Soul)/MATADORS: The Mine	25
70	Camel CA 57	Selassie Want Us Back/ROY AND JOY: Make It With You	25

(see also Little Roy, Hippy Boys)

LITTLE SAL WITH DANDY & SUPERBOYS

68	Giant GN 19	I'm In The Mood/I'm A Lover	30

(see also Dandy & Superboys, Superboys)

LITTLE SISTER

70	Atlantic 2091001	You're The One (Part 2)/(Part 1)	8
71	Atlantic 2091053	Somebody's Watching You/Stanga	6
72	Atlantic K 10194	You're The One/Stanga/Someone's Watching You	8

LITTLE SISTERS

63	MGM MGM 1192	Goin' To Boston/Where Does It Lead	7

LITTLE SONNY

71	Stax 2363 005	NEW KING OF THE BLUES HARMONICA (LP)	20

LITTLE SUZIE

61	Warner Bros WB 35	Young Love/The Boy I Left Behind	12

LITTLE TONY

75	RCA 2638	Shakin' All Over/Together	6

LITTLE TONY & HIS BROTHERS

MINT VALUE £

LITTLE TONY & HIS BROTHERS
59	Durium DC 16639	Who's That Knockin'/The Beat	25
59	Durium DC 16657	Four An' Twenty Thousand Kisses/Bella Marie	20
59	Decca F 11164	I Can't Help It/Arrivederci Baby	10
59	Decca F 11169	The Hippy Hippy Shake/Hey Little Girl	10
59	Decca F 11190	Too Good/Foxy Little Mama	8
60	Decca F 21218	I Love You/The Magic Of Love	8
60	Decca F 21223	Princess/I Love You	8
60	Decca F 21247	Teddy Girl/Kiss Me, Kiss Me	10
61	Durium DC 16657	Bella Marie/Four An' Twenty Thousand Kisses	8
66	Durium DRS 54008	Let Her Go/What Did I Do	7
67	Durium DRS 54012	Long Is The Lonely Night/People Talk To Me About You (as Little Tony)	7
58	Durium U 20058	PRESENTING LITTLE TONY AND HIS BROTHERS (EP)	20

LITTLE WALTER
60	London HLM 9175	My Babe/Blue Midnight	70
64	Pye International 7N 25263	My Babe/You Better Watch Yourself	20
56	London RE-U 1061	LITTLE WALTER AND HIS JUKES (EP)	200
64	Pye Intl. NPL 28043	LITTLE WALTER (LP)	70
67	Chess CRL 4529	SUPER BLUES (LP, with Bo Diddley & Muddy Waters)	45
68	Marble Arch MAL 815	LITTLE WALTER (LP, reissue)	15
69	Python PLP-KM 20	LITTLE WALTER AND HIS DUKES (LP, 99 copies only)	55

LITTLE WILBUR (& PLEASERS)
57	Vogue V 9091	Plaything/I Don't Care	500
57	Vogue V 9091	Plaything/I Don't Care (78)	100
58	Vogue V 9097	Heart To Heart/Alone In The Night (solo)	600
58	Vogue V 9097	Heart To Heart/Alone In The Night (solo) (78)	150

(see also Wilbur Whitfield)

LITTLE WILLIE (FRANCIS)
63	Blue Beat BB 151	Settle Down/I'm Ashamed	12

(see also Wilbert Francis & Vibrators)

LITTLE WINSTON
79	Crazy Lane SP 001	Time And Time Again/Come Back Baby (no p/s)	20

LIVELY ONES
63	London HA 8082	SURF DRUMS (LP)	70
63	London HA 8107	SURF RIDER (LP, mono)	70
63	London SH 8107	SURF RIDER (LP, stereo)	85

LIVELY SET
65	Pye 7N 15880	Don't Call My Name/What Kind Of Love	6
66	Capitol CL 15472	Let The Trumpets Sound/The Green Years	6

LIVERPOOL ECHO
73	Spark	LIVERPOOL ECHO (LP)	20

(see also Mandrake Paddle Steamers)

LIVERPOOL EXPRESS
76	Warner Brothers K 56281	TRACKS (LP)	15

LIVERPOOL F.C.
65	Seddon SED 100	EE AYE ADDIO: SEVENTY YEARS WAITING (LP)	20

LIVERPOOL FISHERMEN
71	Mushroom 150 MR 9	SWALLOW THE ANCHOR (LP)	50

LIVERPOOL SCENE
68	RCA RCA 1762	Son Son/Baby	6
69	RCA RCA 1816	The Woo-Woo/Love Is	6
67	CBS BPG 63045	THE INCREDIBLE NEW LIVERPOOL SCENE (LP)	40
68	RCA SF 7995	THE AMAZING ADVENTURES OF THE LIVERPOOL SCENE (LP)	18
68	RCA SF 7995	THE AMAZING ADVENTURES OF THE LIVERPOOL SCENE (LP, unlaminated cover)	18
69	RCA SF 8057	BREAD ON THE NIGHT (LP)	18
70	RCA SF 8100	ST. ADRIAN AND CO. BROADWAY & 3RD (LP)	18
70	RCA SF 8134	HEIRLOON (LP)	18

(see also Clayton Squares, Adrian Henri, Brian Patten, Mike Hart, Andy Roberts, Grimms)

LIVERPOOL SPINNERS
61	Topic TOP 69	SONGS SPUN IN LIVERPOOL (EP)	10

(see also Spinners [U.K.])

LIVES OF ANGELS
86	Fire FIRE LP 2	ELEVATOR TO EDEN (LP)	45

RICKY LIVID & TONE DEAFS
64	Parlophone R 5136	Tomorrow/Nuts And Bolts	8

(see also Bill Oddie)

LIVING DAYLIGHTS (1)
67	Philips BF 1561	Let's Live For Today/I'm Real (B-side actually titled "It's Real")	30
79	E.S.R. S/79/CUS 523	HEARTSTOP EP (Personality Changes/Outdoor Girl/Don't Fit/Let Me Know (33 rpm, die-cut p/s, also listed as ESR 3)	45
67	Philips BF 1613	Always With Him/Baila Maria	50

(see also Greatest Show On Earth, Naturals)

LIVING DAYLIGHTS (2)
79	E.S.R. S/79/CUS 523	HEARTSTOP EP (Personality Changes/Outdoor Girl/Don't Fit/Let Me Know (33 rpm, die-cut p/s, also listed as ESR 3)	200

LIVING FORCE
84	Chapter 1 SCH 161	Ride Ride Ride/Some People	20

LIVING INTENTS
81	Powerful Pierre PPP 01	(All The) Nice Boys/Genine/Said It's So (p/s)	20

CARLTON LIVINGSTONE
84	Greensleeves GRED 144	100 Weights Of Collie Weed/Soundman Clash (12")	12

Dandy LIVINGSTONE

MINT VALUE £

DANDY LIVINGSTONE
72	Horse HOSS 16	Suzanne Beware Of The Devil/Right On Brother	6
79	More Cuts RIC 109	Instant Music/Living In Sus	15
70s	Night Owl NOR 5002	Calling Africa/Yee Fre Afrikafo Nde	25
80	Mint Music MMD2	Fever/Righteous Man (12")	200
81	Trojan TMX 4008	RUDY, A MESSAGE TO YOU (EP, p/s)	15
72	Trojan TRLS 45	DANDY LIVINGSTONE (LP)	25

(see also RD Livingstone, Dandy)

J C LIVINGSTONE
73	Penny Farthing Pen 808	Let's Spend The Summer Together/Viva La Eva	6
73	Penny Farthing Pen 824	Momma Was A Steamroller Lady/OO La La Me	15

R D LIVINGSTONE
76	B&C CB 291	Roots Man/Mo' Roots	10

LIVIN STONES
65	Oak	I Can't Hold Out/The Music Played On (acetate only)	50

LIZA & JET SET
65	Parlophone R 5248	How Can I Know?/Dancing Yet	15

(see also Liza Strike)

LIZZARD
76	Attack ATT 8130	Fight Down/Jah Jah Bless I	10
76	Black Wax WAX 14	Satta I/I And Eye (p/s as Lizard)	25
76	Trojan TRLS 138	SATTA (LP)	40

LIZZIE & DELROY WILSON
71	Jackpot JP 771	Double Attack/AGGRAVATORS: The Sniper	20

(see also Lizzy)

LIZZY
70	Harry J HJ 6625	More Heartaches/HARRY J ALL STARS: Version	30
70	Pressure Beat PB 5508	Ten Feet Tall (actually "Wear You From The Ball"/JOE GIBBS & DESTROYERS: Chapter (actually "Harmony Hall" by Mr Nigel)	15
73	Duke DU 161	Love Is A Treasure/FREDDIE McKAY: Love Is A Treasure	20

LIZZY & DENNIS (ALCAPONE)
70	Ackee ACK 114	Happy Go Lucky Girl/BOBBY & DAVE: Sammy	20

LIZZY & PARAGONS
71	Ackee ACK 118	On The Beach/DAVE BARKER: Maria	30

LJ IV
69	CBS 63512	AN ELIZABETHAN SONGBOOK (LP)	125

(see also London Jazz Four)

LLAN
66	CBS 202405	Realise/Anytime	40

(see also Vogues)

A.L. LLOYD
62	Topic TOP 71	A.L. LLOYD EWAN MACCOLL (EP)	12
57	Topic T7	A.L. LLOYD EWAN MACCOLL (10" LP with insert)	30
57	Topic T8	THE BLACK BALL LINE (8" EP, insert, with Ewan MaCColl)	25
60	Topic 12T 51	OUTBACK BALLADS (LP, blue label)	40
64	Topic 12T 103	ENGLISH AND SCOTTISH FOLK BALLADS (LP, with Ewan MacColl, with blue label & booklet)	30
64	Topic 12T 103	ENGLISH AND SCOTTISH FOLK BALLADS (LP, with Ewan MacColl)	20
65	Topic 12T 135	BIRD IN THE BUSH (LP, with Anne Briggs & Frankie Armstrong, blue label)	60
66	Topic 12T 118	FIRST PERSON (LP, blue label)	30
67	Topic 12T 174	LEVIATHAN! (LP, blue label with booklet)	35

(see also Frankie Armstrong, Anne Briggs)

A.L. LLOYD & MARTYN WYNDHAM-READ
71	Topic 12TS 203	THE GREAT AUSTRALIAN LEGEND (LP, blue label with booklet)	65

(see also Ewan MacColl, Peggy Seeger, Martin Wyndham-Read)

LLOYD ALEXANDER REAL ESTATE
67	President PT 157	Whatcha Gonna Do/Gonna Live Again	100

LLOYD & BARBARA
73	Grape GR 3045	Dear Lonely Hearts/LLOYD BANTAM: I Tried To Love You	6

LLOYD & CAREY WITH G.G. ALL STARS
72	Attack ATT 8029	Scorpion/MAYTONES: Hands And Feet	10

(see also Carey & Lloyd, Pat Satchmo)

LLOYD & CLAUDETTE
70	Big Shot BI 546	Queen Of The World/PROPHETS: Top Of The World	80

LLOYD (ROBINSON) & DEVON (RUSSELL)
69	Punch PH 14	Love Is The Key/VIRTUES: High Tide	30
69	Blue Cat BS 151	Out Of The Fire/Can't Understand (B-side actually by Austin Faithful)	100

(see also Cobbs, Derrick Morgan)

LLOYD & DOREEN
71	Jackpot JP 762	Midnight/BUNNY LEE'S ALL STARS: Midnight - Version	7

(see also Lloyd Clarke/Doreen Shaeffer)

LLOYD (ROBINSON) & GLEN (BROWN)
67	Coxsone CS 7011	That Girl/You Got Me Wrong	200
67	Doctor Bird DB 1058	Jezebel/TOMMY McCOOK & SUPERSONICS: Jam Session	50
67	Doctor Bird DB 1071	Keep On Pushing/BOBBY AITKEN & CARIBBEATS: You Won't Regret (B-side actually by Lloyd & Glen)	60
67	Doctor Bird DB 1099	Feel Good Now/What You've Got	40
68	Doctor Bird DB 1105	Successful Man/I'll Give You Love	60

LLOYD (JACKSON) & GROOVERS
67	Caltone TONE 108	Do It To Me Baby/DIPLOMATS: Meet Me At The Corner	50
68	Caltone TONE 109	My Heart My Soul/DIPLOMATS with TOMMY McCOOK & SUPERSONICS: Going Along	60

LLOYD & JOHNNY

MINT VALUE £

68	Caltone TONE 112	Listen To The Music/DIPLOMATS: Strong Man ... 60

(see also Groovers, Don Lett)

LLOYD & JOHNNY
68	Island WI 3158	My Argument (actually by Lloyd Terrell)/JOHNNY MELODY: Foey Man (actually by George Dekker) ... 300

(see also Lloyd Terrell)

LLOYD & KEN
72	Punch PH 110	Have I Sinned/Version ... 10

(see also Lloyd Charmers/Ken Boothe)

LLOYD & LARRY
71	New Beat NB 080	Monkey Spanner/LLOYD & LARRY'S ALL STARS: Version ... 22

LLOYD & THE PROPHETS
70	Big Shot BI 553	Bush Beat/PATRICK & PROPHETS: Please Come Come ... 50
70	Big Shot BI 556	Jaco/Soul Reggae ... 40

(see also Prophets [Jamaica], Patrick & Lloyd)

ANDY LLOYD
78	Ariola/Hansa AHA 519	Back To School/It's Up To You ... 12

CAROL LLOYD
83	Philly World PWSL 104	Come See About Me/I Just Want To Love You (12") ... 10
83	Philly World PWLP 1004	LOVE CAROL (LP) ... 50

CHARLES LLOYD (QUARTET)
67	Atlantic 584 125	Sombrero Sam (Parts 1 & 2) ... 6
66	Atlantic 588025	DREAMWEAVER (LP) ... 20
67	Atlantic 587/588 077	LOVE-IN (LP) ... 20
68	Atlantic 587/588 101	JOURNEY WITHIN (LP) ... 20
68	Atlantic 588 108	IN EUROPE (LP) ... 15
70	MCA MUPS 421	MOON MAN (LP) ... 15
71	Atlantic 2400 108	IN THE SOVIET UNION (LP) ... 20

LLOYD, DICE & THE BARRISTER
70	Joe JRS 14	Appeal Of Pama Dice/BOSS ALL STARS: Young And Strong Version 2 ... 20

LLOYD, DICE & HIS MUM
70	Joe JRS 5	Trial Of Pama Dice/NYAH SHUFFLE: Jughead Returns Version 1 ... 25
72	Sioux SI 022	Trial Of Pama Dice/Lonely Man (reissue) ... 15

FRED LLOYD
65	Polydor BM 56055	Girl From Chelsea/You Kissed Him ... 8

IAN LLOYD
74	Kama Sutra KSS 702	Another Love/THE STORIES: Love Is In Motion ... 6

JIMMY LLOYD
58	Philips PB 795	The Prince Of Players/Ever Since I Met Lucy ... 10
58	Philips PB 827	Witch Doctor/For Your Love ... 8
58	Philips PB 871	The End/Street In The Rain ... 6
59	Philips PB 909	I Kneel At Your Throne/Sapphire ... 10
59	Philips PB 978	That's Why I Dream/Take A Giant Step ... 10
60	Philips PB 1010	Teenage Sonata/Falling ... 10
60	Philips PB 1055	I Double Dare You/Just For A Thrill ... 8
61	Philips PB 1120	Pony Time/Three Handed Woman ... 10
59	Philips BBE 12186	FOCUS ON JIMMY LLOYD (EP) ... 12
62	Philips BBE 12509	YOU ARE MY SUNSHINE (EP) ... 12

LLOYD & JOY
71	Explosion EX 2047	Back To Africa (actually by Alton Ellis)/Born To Lose ... 20

LLOYD (CAMPBELL) THE MATADOR
72	Sioux SI 010	The Train/EXODUS: Julia Sees Me ... 50

RUE LLOYD
72	Green Door GD 4033	Loving You/Version ... 15
72	Green Door GD 4036	Cheer Up/Version ... 10

(see also Joe White)

TREVOR LLOYD
70	Explosion EX 2018	Chinee Brush/DICE & CUMMIE: Real Colley ... 60
70	Explosion EX 2019	Give Me Back Your Love/Hold Me ... 20

LLOYDIE & LOWBITES
73	Harry J HJ 6660	Pussy Cat/Skanky Pussy ... 10
71	Lowbite LOW 001	CENSORED! (LP, green/silver label) ... 40

(see also Lloyd Tyrell/Charmers)

LLOYD'S ALLSTARS
69	Doctor Bird DB 1178	Love Kiss Blue/UNIQUES: Secretly ... 80

(see also Justins, U Roy Junior, Jimmy Green, Victors)

ELERI LLWYD
72	Cambrian CSP 730	Mae Bywyd Yn Galed/Breuddwyn (p/s) ... 8
77	Sain 1073	AM HEDDIW MAE NGHAN (LP) ... 25

LLYGOD FFYRNIG
78	Pwdwr PWDWR 1	N.C.B./Sais/Cariad Y Bus Stop (p/s, white rubber stamped labels) ... 100
78	Pwdwr PWDWR 1	N.C.B./Sais/Cariad Y Bus Stop (p/s, printed green labels) ... 150

DICKIE LOADER
61	Palette PG 9015	Heatwave/Happiness ... 30

RUSS LOADER
65	Columbia DB 7522	When Your Heart Is Broken/That Girl Of Mine (with Breakaways Orchestra) ... 10
65	Columbia DB 7643	Just Lies/Mona Lisa ... 8
65	Columbia DB 7696	Count The Stars/Triyng Too Hard (with Ladybirds) ... 10
66	Columbia DB 7839	Too Soon/Just A Little Step To Heaven ... 10

(see also Mark Wirtz)

LOBO

MINT VALUE £

LOBO
71	Phillips 6073 802	She Didn't Do Magic/I'm The Only One	6

EDU LOBO
71	A&M AMLS63035	SERGIO MENDES PRESENTS (LP)	20

LOCAL HEROES
80	Junior Records	Blast The Pop!/Tomorrow (p/s)	50

LOCKETS
63	Pye International 7N 25282	Don't Cha Know/Little Boy	40

LOCKJAW
77	Raw RAW 8	Radio Call Sign/The Young Ones (p/s)	20
78	Raw RAW 19	Journalist Jive/I'm A Virgin/A Doonga Doonga (p/s, beware of counterfeits)	100

(see also the Cure)

GERRY LOCKRAN
69	Decca F 12873	Hey Jude/This Train	6
69	Decca F 12919	Standing On Your Own/You're Not There	20
67	Planet PLL 1002	HOLD ON, I'M COMING (LP)	150
68	Waverley ZLP 2091	BLUES VENDETTA (LP)	60
69	Spark SRLP 104	THE ESSENTIAL GERRY LOCKRAN (LP)	50
72	Polydor 2383 122	WUN (LP)	60
76	Decca SKL-R 5257	RAGS TO GLADRAGS (LP)	40
80	BML 2536	ACROSS THE TRACKS (LP)	15

ANNA LOCKWOOD
70	Tangent TGS 104	THE GLASS WORLD OF ANNA LOCKWOOD (LP)	40

MALCOLM LOCKYER ORCHESTRA
61	HMV POP 929	The Pursuers T.V. Theme/Stranger Than Fiction	10
65	Columbia DB 7552	The Intelligence Men/Brighton Run	20
65	Columbia DB 7663	The Eccentric Dr. Who/Daleks And Thals	60

LOCOMOTIVE
67	Direction 58-3814	Rudy A Message To You/Broken Heart	25
68	Parlophone R 5718	Rudi's In Love/Never Set Me Free	20
69	Parlophone R 5758	Mr. Armageddon/There's Got To Be A Way (in promos p/s)	30
69	Parlophone R 5758	Mr. Armageddan/There's Got To Be A Way	15
69	Parlophone R 5801	I'm Never Gonna Let You Go/You Must Be Joking	20
70	Parlophone R 5835	Movin' Down The Line/Roll Over Mary	10
71	Parlophone R 5915	Rudi's In Love/You Must Be Joking	20
69	Parlophone PCS 7093	WE ARE EVERYTHING YOU SEE (LP, laminated front sleeve)	1000
88	Zap! ZAP 5	WE ARE EVERYTHING YOU SEE (LP, reissue)	20

(see also Norman Haines Band, Dog That Bit People, Steam-Shovel)

LOCOMOTIVE GT
74	Epic EPC 80229	LOCOMOTIVE GT (LP)	15

LOEFAH
04	Big Apple BAM 006	Jungle Infiltrator/Jazz Lick/Indian Dub/Life Dub (12")	60
05	DMZ DMZ 006	Root/The Goat Stare (12")	40
05	Tectonic TEC 003	28g/Fearless (12")	15
06	DMZ DMZ 009	Mud/Rufage (12")	50
06	Six Six Six 001	Voodoo/Voodoo (Omen Mix)	25
06	Tectonic TEC 008	System/DIGITAL MYSTIKZ: Molten (10")	30

LOFT
84	Creation CRE 009	Why Does The Rain/Like (foldaround p/s in poly bag)	15
85	Creation CRE 015	Up The Hill And Down The Slope/Lonely Street (foldaround p/s in poly bag)	10
06	Static Caravan VAN 116	Model Village/Rickety Frame (p/s)	6

(see also Weather Prophets, Wishing Stones)

CRIPPLE CLARENCE LOFTON
59	Vogue EPV 1209	CRIPPLE CLARENCE LOFTON (EP)	50
54	London AL 3531	A LOST RECORDING DATE (10" LP)	50
55	Vogue LDE 122	JAZZ IMMORTALS NO. 1 (10" LP)	50

LOFTUS ROADRUNNERS
77	QPR QPR 1	Queens Park Rangers/Drive Me Down To QPR	10

LORA LOGIC
81	Rough Trade RT 087	Wonderful Offer/Stereo (p/s)	6
81	Rough Trade Rt087	Wonderful Offer/Stereo/Rather Than Repeat (12", p/s)	15
82	Rough Trade ROUGH 28	PEDIGREE CHARM (LP)	20

(see also Essential Logic)

LOGIC (1)
83	Okey Doke LOGIC 03	Pied Piper/Backstabber	20
83	Okey DokeLOGIG 01 OD 3	Hi Ho Hi Ho/Never Break My Love	40

LOGIC (2)
90	Planet Pacific PPAC1	The Warning (Eco-Planet Mix)/(Copy Mix) (p/s)	7
00	HoneyBeat HBEZ 005	Blues For You (Mixes)(12")	8

LOGIC CONTROL MCS
90	Conscious CONN2	High Pursuit/Gangster Trip (12")	12

LOG 10
83	Sonic SR 77	In The Dark/Dark Step Dub (p/s, with insert)	25
84	Sonic SR 78	You're Not There/Freefall (die-cut sleeve)	20

L.O.K.
79	Fetish FET 001	Fun House/Starlet Love/Tell Me (p/s)	7

LOL
73	Columbia DB 9009	Naughty Nola/Bumbler	60

(see also 10cc)

LOLITA

MINT VALUE £

LOLITA
60 Polydor NH 66818   Sailor (Your Home Is The Sea)/La Luna (Quanda La Luna) 10

LOLLIPOP SHOP
85 Big Beat WIK36   JUST COLOUR (LP) 15

LOLLIPOPS
71 Atlantic 2091 114   Nothing's Gonna Stop Our Love/I Believe In Love 10

LAURIE LOMAN
54 London HL 8101   Whither Thou Goest/I Was The Last One To Know (gold triangular centre) 50

ALAN LOMAX (& RAMBLERS)
56 Decca F 10787   Dirty Old Town/Hard Case (as Alan Lomax & Ramblers) 10
57 Nixa Jazz NJL 11   MURDERER'S HOME (LP) 15
58 HMV CLP 1192   GREAT AMERICAN BALLADS (LP, with Alexis Korner & Guy Carawan) 30

LOMAX ALLIANCE
67 CBS 2729   Try As You May/See The People 50

(see also Jackie Lomax)

JACKIE LOMAX
68 CBS 2554   Genuine Imitation Life/One Minute Woman 20
68 Apple APPLE 3   Sour Milk Sea/The Eagle Laughs At You 35
69 Apple APPLE 11   New Day/I Fall Inside Your Eyes 15
70 Apple APPLE 23   How The Web Was Woven/Thumbin' A Ride (in p/s) 30
70 Apple APPLE 23   How The Web Was Woven/Thumbin' A Ride 15
69 Apple APCOR 6   IS THIS WHAT YOU WANT (LP, with inner sleeve, mono) 200
69 Apple (S)APCOR 6   IS THIS WHAT YOU WANT (LP, with inner sleeve, stereo, 'McNeill Press', on sleeve) 150
91 Apple SAPCOR 6   IS THIS WHAT YOU WANT (LP, reissue, gatefold sleeve with bonus 12" [SAPCOR 62]) 40

(see also Lomax Alliance, Undertakers, Takers, Heavy Jelly, Badger)

AL LOMBARDY & HIS ORCHESTRA
54 London HL 8076   The Blues/The Boogie 40
55 London HL 8127   In A Little Spanish Town/Flying Home 20

LONDON
78 MCA MCF 2823   ANIMAL GAMES (LP) 15

JIMMY LONDON
71 Randy's RAN 514   Shake A Hand/CARL MURPHY: Lick I Pipe 6
71 Randy's RAN 517   Bridge Over Troubled Waters/RANDY'S ALLSTARS: War 20
71 Randy's RAN 520   A Little Love/IMPACT ALLSTARS: Version 8
75 Black Wax WAX 4   Am I That Easy To Forget/100 Years Of Dub 8
72 Trojan TRL 39   BRIDGE OVER TROUBLED WATERS (LP) 30
78 Burning Sounds BS 1016   WELCOME TO MY WORLD (LP) 18
79 Jama JALP 003   JIMMY IN LONDON (LP) 35
80 JB JBLP 03   CHILDREN CRYING IN THE GHETTO (LP) 15

(see also Jimmy Green, The Inspirations)

JOE LONDON
59 London HLW 9008   Lonesome Whistle/It Might Have Been 15

JULIE LONDON
SINGLES
56 London HLU 8240   Cry Me A River/S'Wonderful (gold label print) 80
56 London HLU 8240   Cry Me A River/S'Wonderful (later silver label print) 20
56 London HLU 8279   Baby, Baby All The Time/Shadow Woman (gold label print) 40
57 London HLU 8394   The Meaning Of The Blues/Now! Baby, Now! (gold label print) 30
57 London HLU 8394   The Meaning Of The Blues/Now! Baby, Now! (later silver label print) 15
57 London HLU 8414   The Boy On A Dolphin/Tall Boy 10
58 London HLU 8602   Saddle The Wind/It Had To Be You 10
58 London HLU 8657   My Strange Affair/It's Easy 10

EPs
57 London RE-U 1076   JULIE SINGS FILM SONGS (gold label print) 20
57 London RE-N 1092   LONDON'S GIRL FRIENDS VOL. 1 20
58 London RE-U 1151   MAKE LOVE TO ME - PART ONE 10
58 London RE-U 1152   MAKE LOVE TO ME - PART TWO 10
58 London RE-U 1153   MAKE LOVE TO ME - PART THREE 10
59 London RE-U 1180   JULIE - PART ONE 10
59 London RE-U 1181   JULIE - PART TWO 10
59 London RE-U 1182   JULIE - PART THREE 10
63 Liberty LEP 2103   DESAFINADO 10
66 Liberty LEP 2260   ALL THROUGH THE NIGHT 10

ALBUMS
56 London HA-U 2005   JULIE IS HER NAME 30
57 London HA-U 2038   CALENDAR GIRL 30
58 London HA-U 2083   MAKE LOVE TO ME 30
58 London HA-U 2091   ABOUT THE BLUES 30
58 London HA-U 2112   JULIE 30
59 London HA-U 2171   LONDON BY NIGHT 25
59 London HA-U 2186   JULIE IS HER NAME VOL. 2 (also stereo SAH-U 6042) 30
60 London HA-W 2225   SWING ME AN OLD SONG 20
60 London HA-W 2229   YOUR NUMBER PLEASE 25
60 London HA-G 2280   JULIE AT HOME (mono) 18
60 London SAH-G 6097   JULIE AT HOME (stereo) 20
61 London HA-G 2299   AROUND MIDNIGHT 20
61 London HA-G 2353   SEND FOR ME (mono) 18
61 London SAH-G 6154   SEND FOR ME (stereo) 20
62 London HA-G 2405   WHATEVER JULIE WANTS (mono) 18

LAURIE LONDON

			MINT VALUE £
62	London SAH-G 6205	WHATEVER JULIE WANTS (stereo)	20
63	Liberty (S)LBY 1113	LOVE ON THE ROCKS	20
63	Liberty (S)LBY 1136	SINGS LATIN IN A SATIN MOOD	15
66	Liberty (S)LBY 1300	ALL THROUGH THE NIGHT	15
67	Liberty (S)LBY 1334	FOR THE NIGHT PEOPLE	15
67	Liberty (S)LBY 1364	NICE GIRLS DON'T STAY FOR BREAKFAST	15
69	Liberty LBL/LBS 83183E	YUMMY, YUMMY, YUMMY	15

LAURIE LONDON
57	Parlophone R 4359	He's Got The Whole World In His Hands/The Cradle Rock	8
58	Parlophone R 4426	I Gotta Robe/Casey Jones	6
58	Parlophone R 4499	Up Above My Head/Three O'Clock	7
59	Parlophone R 4557	Pretty-Eyed Baby (with Gitte)/Boom-Ladda-Boom-Boom	8
60	Parlophone R 4662	Banjo Boy/Hear Them Bells	7
61	Parlophone R 4747	Todays Teardrops/Darling Sue	8
57	Parlophone GEP 8664	LAURIE LONDON (EP)	10
58	Parlophone GEP 8689	LITTLE LAURIE LONDON No. 2 (EP)	20

MARK LONDON
65	Pye 7N 15825	Stranger In The World/Moanin'	15

MICHAEL LONDON
62	HMV POP 1026	Miracles Sometimes Happen/Stranger On The Shore (with Acker Bilk)	8

PETER LONDON
65	Pye 7N 15957	Bless You/Baby I Like The Look Of You	50

(see also Peter Cook)

LONDONAIRES
66	Decca F12379	Dearest Emma/Bugles A Go-Go	15

LONDON & BRIDGES
66	CBS 202056	It Just Ain't Right/Leave Her Alone	40

LONDON FUNK ALLSTARS
96	Ninja Tune ZEN 24	FLESH EATING DISCO ZOMBIES VERSUS THE BIONIC HOOKERS FROM MARS (3xLP)	30

LONDON HOSPITAL
60s	Private Pressing WAD 9-1	LONDON HOSPITAL CHRISTMAS FACTOR (EP)	60

LONDON JAZZ CHAMBER GROUP
72	Ember CJS 823	ADAM'S RIB SUITE (LP)	20

(see also Ken Moule's London Jazz Chamber Group, Ken Moule Seven)

LONDON JAZZ COMPOSERS ORCHESTRA
70s	Incus 7	ODE (LP, with insert)	50

LONDON JAZZ FOUR
66	Polydor 56092	Norwegian Wood/I Feel Fine	25
67	Polydor 56214	It Strikes A Chord/Song For Hilary	30
67	Polydor 582 005	TAKE A NEW LOOK AT THE BEATLES (LP)	60

(see also London Jazz Quartet, LJ IV)

LONDON JAZZ QUARTET
60	Tempo TAP 28	LONDON JAZZ QUARTET (LP, with Tubby Hayes & Tony Crombie)	350
60s	Ember EMB 3306	LONDON JAZZ QUARTET (LP)	150

(see also London Jazz Four, Tubby Hayes, Tony Crombie)

LONDON POPS ORCHESTRA
68	Pye 7N 17630	Eleanor Rigby/If I Only Had Time	6

LONDON POSSE
88	Justice JT003	Money Mad (12")	50
87	Big Life BLR2T	London Posse/My Beatbox Reggae Style (12")	12
93	Bullet BULT 2	How's Life In London?/Shut The Fuck Up/How I Make Papes (12")	12
96	Bullet BULT 5	Style (12")	20
90	Mango MLPS1066	GANGSTER CHRONICLE (LP)	15

(see also Rodney P)

LONDON PX
80	New Puritan NP 1	Orders/Eviction (p/s)	25
82	Terrapyn SYD 1	Arnold Layne/Indian Summer (1-sided flexidisc)	12

LONDON STRING CHORALE
72	Polydor 2058 280	Galloping Home/Vicky	6

LONDON STUDIO GROUP
66	De Wolfe DW/LP 2974	THE WILD ONE (10" LP, tricolour label)	60

(see also Ivor & Basil Kirchen Band)

LONDON UNDERGROUND
81	Situation Two SIT 9	Train Of Though/All Too Many (p/s)	6
83	On-U Sound LP 22	AT HOME WITH THE LONDON UNDERGROUND (LP)	20

LONDON WAITS
66	Immediate IM 030	Softly Softly/Serenadio	30

LONDON ZOO
80	Gramaphone STB 80	Who's Driving This Car?/You And Your Great Ideas (stamped white labels, no p/s)	6

LONE ARCHER
74	Strand ST11	I'll Come To You/Glass Web	15

LONE PIGEON
01	Sketchbook SKETCH 001	CONCUBINE RICE (LP)	25
10	Domino REWIGCD77X	TIME CAPSULE (7-CD box set)	35

(see also Beta Band)

LONE RANGER
79	Island WIPDJ 6517	Barnabus Collins/Dub Part 2	8
82	Greensleeves GRED 85	Johnny Make You Bad So/TAXI GANG: Outside Right (12")	12
80	GG's GG 021	BARNABAS COLLINS (LP)	20
81	Black Joy DHLP 002	ROSEMARIE (LP)	18

LONE WOLF (1)

MINT VALUE £

LONE WOLF (1)
80	Wolf Music LW 001	Cash For Candy/Pipedream Mary (p/s)	150
82	Guardian GRC 144	Leave Me Behind/High Class Hooker	20
84	Neat NEAT 44-12	Nobody's Move/Town To Town/Leave Me Behind (12")	20

LONE WOLF (2)
81	Kai KR 02	Fighting For Sommerlund/Vonotar The Traitor (p/s)	15

LONELADY
06	Filthy Home FHV 0101	Army/Intuition	8
07	Too Pure PURE 211 S	Early The Haste Comes/Joy	8

LONELY HEARTS
84	Tenacity TROIA	FM Fantasy/Young Girl (p/s)	10

LONERS
67	Stone ST 1	Visions Of You/Falling	100

LONESOME DRIFTER
70	Injun 104	Eager Boy/Teardrop Valley	10

JOHNNY LONESOME
61	HMV POP 837	Marie Marie/Doctor Heartache	20

LONESOME STONE
73	Reflection RL 306	LONESOME STONE (LP, stage production recording)	18

(see also Sheep)

LONESOME SUNDOWN
71	Blue Horizon 7-63864	LONESOME LONELY BLUES (LP)	100
77	Flyright LP 529	BOUGHT ME A TICKET (LP)	18
83	Flyright LP 587	LONESOME WHISTLER (LP)	18

LONESOME TONE
81	Stiff BUY DJ 111	Mum Dad Love Hate And Elvis/Ghost Town (promo only)	20

LONESOME TRAVELLERS
70	Tradition TSR 004	THE LONESOME TRAVELLERS (LP)	25
70s	Nebula NEB 100	THE LOST CHILDREN (LP)	15

LONG & SHORT
64	Decca F 11964	The Letter/Love Is A Funny Thing	35
64	Decca F 12043	Choc Ice/Here Comes The Fool	40

LONG BLONDES
04	Thee Sheffield SPC 005	New Idols/Long Blonde (p/s pink vinyl, playing card & newsletter insert)	20
04	Angular Recording ARC 007	Giddy Stratospheres/Polly/Darts (p/s, 500 only, blue vinyl)	15

FITZROY D. LONG & BUSTER ALL STARS
68	Fab FAB 32	Get A New Girl/BUSTER'S ALL STARS: Come And Do It With Me	50

(see also Larry Marshall)

LONG HELLO
73	Private pressing	THE LONG HELLO (LP, mail-order only, numbered white sleeve)	20

(see also Van Der Graaf Generator)

SHORTY LONG
65	Tamla Motown TMG 512	Out To Get You/It's A Crying Shame	125
65	Tamla Motown TMG 512	Out To Get You/It's A Crying Shame (DJ copy)	200
66	Tamla Motown TMG 573	Function At The Junction/Call On Me	45
66	Tamla Motown TMG 573	Function At The Junction/Call On Me (DJ copy)	60
67	Tamla Motown TMG 600	Chantilly Lace/Your Love Is Amazing	20
68	Tamla Motown TMG 644	Night Fo' Last (Vocal)/Night Fo' Last (Instrumental)	25
68	Tamla Motown TMG 663	Here Comes The Judge/Sing What You Wanna	18
68	T. Motown (S)TML 11086	HERE COMES THE JUDGE (LP, mono/stereo)	45
70	T. Motown STML 11144	THE PRIME OF SHORTY LONG (LP)	35

(see also Art Mooney)

LONG TALL SHORTY
79	Warner Bros K 17491	By Your Love/1970's Boy (p/s, withdrawn)	80
81	Dr Creation LYN 9904	If I Was You/That's What I Want (flexidisc)	12
81	Ramkup CAC 007	Win Or Lose/Ain't Done Wrong (p/s)	50
85	Diamond DIA 002	On The Streets Again/I Fought The Law/Promises (p/s, with poster)	25
85	Diamond DIA 002	On The Streets Again/I Fought The Law/Promises (p/s, without poster)	12
86	Diamond DIA 005	What's Going On/Steppin' Stone/Win Or Lose/England (p/s)	15
88	001	ROCKIN' AT THE SAVOY (LP, official bootleg, with poster)	25
88	001	ROCKIN' AT THE SAVOY (LP, official bootleg, without poster)	20

(see also Case, Rage)

LONGBOATMEN
66	Polydor 56115	Take Her Any Time/Only In Her Home Town	500

LONGDANCER
73	Rocket PIG 1	If It Was So Simple/Silent Emotions (p/s)	15
74	Rocket PIG 11	Puppet Man/Cold Love	15
77	Rocket PIGL 6	TRAILER FOR A GOOD LIFE (LP, die cut gatefold sleeve)	15

CLAUDINE LONGET
67	A&M AMS 708	Good Day Sunshine/The Look Of Love	8
67	A&M AML 903	CLAUDINE (LP)	20

LONGPIGS
96	Mother MUM 9602	THE SUN IS OFTEN OUT (LP)	100

(see also Richard Hawley)

LONGPORT BUZZ
78	Buzz 13	CANTERBURY POP EP (White labels, most handwritten)	30
80	Criminal Records SWAG 14	Fun/Who Is He (different sleeve to Canterbury Pop version, with sticker)	25

LOOK BACK IN ANGER
81	L.B.A. LBA 1	Caprice/Mannequin (oversized card sleeve)	25
84	Criminal Damage CRI MLP 118	CAPRICE (mini-LP)	15

LOOKING GLASS (1)

		MINT VALUE £
LOOKING GLASS (1)		
72 Philips BF 1837	Can You Believe/Freedom In Our Time	8
72 Epic 65041	LOOKING GLASS (LP)	20
LOOKING GLASS (2)		
87 Dreamworld DREAM 012	Mirror Man/Through The Looking Glass For Tea (p/s)	8
LOOP		
86 Head HEAD 5	16 Dreams/Head On/Burning World (12", p/s)	18
87 Head HEAD 7L	Spinning Parts 1 & 2 (juke box centre, plain black die-cut sleeve)	15
87 Head HEAD 7	Spinning/Deep Hit/I'll Take You There (12", p/s)	20
88 Situation 2 LCHAP 27	Collision (Edit)/Crawling Heart (juke box centre, die-cut sleeve)	7
88 Chapter 22 12 CHAP 27	COLLISION EP (12")	10
88 Chapter 22 12 CHAP 32	BLACK SUN EP (12")	10
88 Chapter 22 CAT 065	Torched (flexidisc, with The Catalogue magazine no. 65)	12
88 CHEREE Cheree 1	TELESCOPES: Forever Close Your Eyes/LOOP: Soundhead (33rpm flexi, 1,000 only)	10
89 Situation 2 SIT 64	Arc Lite (Sonar)/Arc Lite (Radiated) (juke box centre, die-cut sleeve)	8
89 Situation 2 SIT 64T	ARC LITE EP (12", p/s)	10
87 Head HEAD LP 1	HEAVEN'S END (LP, with inner sleeve)	25
87 Head HEAD LP 2	WORLD IN YOUR EYES (LP)	20
88 Chapter 22 CHAPLLP 34	FADE OUT (LP, 2 x 45rpm 12", gold stickered gatefold sleeve, signed)	40
88 Chapter 22 CHAPLLP 34	FADE OUT (LP, 2 x 45rpm 12", gold stickered gatefold sleeve)	30
88 Chapter 22 CHAPL 44	ETERNAL - SINGLES (LP)	15
90 Situation 2 SITU 27	A GILDED ETERNITY (2-LP with free 7")	40
90 Situation 2 SITU 27	A GILDED ETERNITY (2-LP, without free 7")	30
91 Reactor REACTORLP 3	WOLF FLOW - JOHN PEEL SESSIONS 1987-90 (2-LP, contains merchandise sheet)	20
91 Reactor REACTOR LP1	HEAVEN'S END (LP, reissue)	20
92 Reactor REACTOR LP5	DUAL (LP, blue vinyl)	30
92 Reactor REACTOR LP4	FADE OUT (LP, reissue, grey vinyl)	15
14 Reactor REACTOR 04 LP	A GILDED ETERNITY (2 x 12", 7", reissue)	20
LOOP OF SOUND		
95 SECRET 007	VOL 1. (12")	25
LOOPFLESH		
91 Clawfist XPIG 07	Like Rats/FLESHLOOP: Straight To Your Heart (foldover p/s in poly bag, actually by Loop and Godflesh)	10
LOOSE ENDS (1)		
66 Decca F 12437	Send The People Away/I Ain't Gonna Eat My Heart Out Anymore	40
66 Decca F 12476	Taxman/That's It	150
LOOSE ENDS (2)		
82 Virgin VS 497-12	In The Sky/Only A Day Away/In The Sky (Instrumental) (12", p/s, as Loose End)	15
LOOSE FITTINGS		
69 Amber AM 01	Sightings Of Emily/It's Down To Us	50
LOOSE RAIL		
68 Denby DB 002	Leave Me/A Place To Die (p/s)	100
72 Homewatch HW 1	Silence In The Sky/Magic Well (p/s)	75
LOOSE SHOES		
81 Applause CLAP 2	Put The Blame On Me/Nobody's Clown	8
LOOSE TALK		
82 Jet JET 7025	Dan Dare/Home Planet (p/s)	8
LOOSE TAPESTRIES		
12 Sony 88691969131	THE LUXURY COMEDY TAPES (2-LP, gatefold)	60
LOOSE TIE		
73 M&M 331	Tie The Knot/Look Here You	12
LOOT		
66 Page One POF 013	Baby Come Closer/Baby	15
67 Page One POF 026	I've Just Gotta Love You/You Need Someone To Love	20
67 CBS 2938	Whenever You're Ready/I Got What You Want	18
68 Page One POF 095	She's A Winner/Radio City (withdrawn B-side)	30
68 Page One POF 095	She's A Winner/Save Me	22
68 CBS 3131	Don't Turn Around/You Are My Sunshine Girl	25
69 Page One POF 115	Try To Keep It A Secret/Radio City	40
(see also Soul Agents, Hookfoot)		
LINDA LOPEZ MAMBO ORCHESTRA		
55 Parlophone MSP 6179	Limehouse Blues Mambo/Nursery Mambo	7
TRINI LOPEZ		
63 London HL 9808	Jeanie Marie/Love Me Tonight	6
07 Kent TOWN 142	Sinner Not A Saint/JOHNNY COPELAND: No Puppy Love	8
65 Stateside SE 1013	SINNER NOT A SAINT (EP)	30
DENISE LOR		
54 Parlophone MSP 6120	If I Give My Heart To You/Hallo Darling	10
55 Parlophone MSP 6148	Every Day Of My Life/And One To Grow On	12
KENNY LORAN		
59 Capitol CL 15081	Mama's Little Baby/Magic Star	30
L'ORANGE MECHANIK		
86 Art Pop POP 44	Symphony/Intermezzo (Sprechstimme)/Scherzo (p/s)	15
(see also Times)		
JON LORD		
76 Purple PUR 131	Bourée/Aria	7
82 Harvest HAR 5220	Bach Onto This/Going Home (p/s)	6
84 Safari SAFE60	The Country Diary Of An Edwardian Lady (main theme)/Love Theme	8
71 Purple TPSA 7501	GEMINI SUITE (LP, textured gatefold sleeve)	70
74 Purple TPSA 7513	WINDOWS (LP, gatefold sleeve)	20

	76	Purple TPSA 7516	SARABANDE (LP, die-cut sleeve)	15

(see also Artwoods, Deep Purple, [Paice] Ashton & Lord, Wizard's Convention, Episode Six, Leading Figures, Whitesnake, Cozy Powell)

TONY LORD
	66	Planet PLF 102	World's Champion/It Makes Me Sad	40

JERRY LORDAN
	59	Parlophone R 4588	I'll Stay Single/Can We Kiss	8
	60	Parlophone R 4627	Who Could Be Bluer?/Do I Worry?	10
	60	Parlophone R 4653	Sing Like An Angel/Ev'ry Time	12
	60	Parlophone R 4695	Ring, Write Or Call/I've Still Got You	12
	61	Parlophone R 4748	You Came A Long Way From St. Louis/Let's Try Again	15
	62	Parlophone R 4903	One Good Solid 24 Carat Reason/Second Hand Dress	20
	70	CBS 5057	The Old Man And The Sea/Harlequin Melodies	30
	61	Parlophone PMC 1133	ALL MY OWN WORK (LP, mono)	70
	61	Parlophone PCS 3014	ALL MY OWN WORK (LP, stereo)	100

(see also Lee & Jay Elvin)

LORD BEGINNER
	60s	Melodisc CAL 1	Victory Test Match - Calypso/Sergeant Brown (reissue)	10

(see also Lord Kitchener)

LORD BRISCO(E)
	64	Rio R42	Fabulous Eyes/What You See	20
	64	Black Swan WI 447	Spiritual Mambo/BABA BROOKS: Fly Right	20
	64	Black Swan WI 450	My Love Has Come/BABA BROOKS: Sweet Eileen	25
	64	Black Swan WI 454	Trojan/I Am The Least	20
	64	Island WI 131	Praise For I/Tell You The Story	35
	65	Island WI 187	Jonah (The Master)/Mr. Cleveland	15

LORD BRYNNER & SHEIKS
	66	Island WI 266	Congo War/Teach Me To Ska	40

(see also Roland Alphonso)

LORD BUCKLEY
	62	Fontana 688 010ZL	IN CONCERT (LP)	20
	67	Fontana TL 5396	BLOWING HIS MIND (AND YOURS, TOO) (LP)	20

LORD CHARLES & HIS BAND
	70s	Sound Of Jamaica JA 1	Jamaican Bits And Pieces/JA Island Soul	8

LORD COMIC
	70	Bamboo BAM 66	Rhythm Rebellion/ROY RICHARDS: Reggae Children	50
	70	Pressure Beat PR 5507	Jack Of My Trade/CYNTHIA RICHARDS: United We Stand	70

(see also Sir Lord Comic)

LORD CREATOR
	62	Island WI 001	Independant [sic] Jamaica Calypso/Remember (B-side is actually Remember Your Mother And Father)	20
	63	Kalypso XX 24	Peeping Tom/Second Hand Piano	25
	64	Port-O-Jam PJ 4005	Rhythm Of the Blues/Simple Things	12
	64	Port-O-Jam PJ 4119	Jamaica's Anniversary/Mother's Love	22
	64	National Calypso NC 2001	Drive With Care/Sweet Jamaica	20
	65	Blue Beat BB 292	Evening News/Good For Creator	45
	65	Black Swan WI 463	Wicked Lady/MAYTALS: My Little Ruby	25
	66	Doctor Bird DB 1029	Obeah Wedding/BERTRAM ENNIS COMBO: Part Two	10
	67	Jump Up JU 503	Jamaica Jump Up/Laziest Man	25
	67	Jump Up JU 524	Big Bamboo/Marjorie And Harry	25
	76	Island WIP 6344	Big Pussy Sally/UPSETTERS: Big Pussy Dub	6

(see also Creator, Kentrick Patrick, Fabulous Flames)

LORD CRISTO
	67	Jump Up JU 515	Dumb Boy And The Parrot/General Hospital	35
	67	Jump Up JU 517	Election War Zone/Bad Luck Man	35

LORD KITCHENER
	59	Melodisc MEL 1498	Black Puddin'/Piccadilly Folk	7
	59	Melodisc MEL 1538	If You're Brown/Come Back In The Morning	7
	60	Melodisc MEL 1577	Jamaica Turkey/Edna What You Want	7
	63	Melodisc CAL 2	Kitch/Rebound Wife	6
	63	Melodisc CAL 3	Muriel And The Bug/Nora And The Yankee	6
	63	Melodisc CAL 4	Kitch Take It Easy/Redhead	6
	63	Melodisc CAL 5	Drink A Rum/Your Wife	15
	63	Melodisc CAL 6	Too Late Kitch/Saxophone Number Two	6
	63	Melodisc CAL 7	Wife And Mother/Mango Tree	6
	64	Melodisc CAL 10	Kitch Mambo Calypso/Ghana	6
	64	Melodisc CAL 11	Life Begins At Forty/Short Skirts	6
	64	Melodisc CAL 12	Romeo/Kitch Calypso Medley	6
	64	Melodisc CAL 14	Federation/Alfonso In Town	6
	64	Melodisc CAL 19	Black Puddin'/Piccadilly Folk	6
	64	Melodisc CAL 21	Come Back In The Morning/If You're Brown	6
	64	Melodisc CAL 22	Jamaica Turkey/Edna What You Want	6
	64	Melodisc CAL 23	Carnival/More Rice	6
	60s	Jump Up JU 504	Love In The Cemetery/Jamaica Woman	15
	60s	Jump Up JU 506	Road On Carnival Day/Neighbour, Neighbour	15
	64	Jump Up JU 511	Dr. Kitch/Come Back Home Meh Boy	15
	65	Jump Up JU 530	Kitch You So Sweet/Ain't That Fun	15
	65	Aladdin WI 612	Dr. Kitch/Come Back Home Meh Boy (reissue)	15
	71	Duke DU 115	Dr. Kitch/Love In The Cemetary	10
	55	Melodisc MLP 500	KITCH - KING OF CALYPSO (10" LP)	25
	57	Melodisc MLP 510	KING OF CALYPSO VOL. 2 (10" LP)	25

LORD KITCHENER/FITZROY COLEMAN BAND

MINT VALUE £

60s	Melodisc 12-129	CALYPSOS TOO HOT TO HANDLE (LP)	30
60s	Melodisc 12-130	CALYPSOS TOO HOT TO HANDLE VOL. 2 (LP)	30
60s	Melodisc 12-199	CALYPSOS TOO HOT TO HANDLE (LP, reissue with extra tracks)	30
60s	Melodisc 12-200	CALYPSOS TOO HOT TO HANDLE VOL. 2 (LP, reissue with extra tracks)	30

(see also Lord Beginner)

LORD KITCHENER/FITZROY COLEMAN BAND
56	no label	City And United 1956/The Manchester Football Double (78)	60

LORD LARGE (FEATURING DEAN PARRISH)
06	Acid Jazz AJX 185S	Left Right & Centre/Sun In The Sands (7", co. sleeve)	6

LORD LEBBY
58	Kalypso RL 101	Dr Kinsey Report/Ethiopia	15
58	Kalypso XX 05	Sweet Jamaica/Mama Want No Rice No Peas)	10
60	Starlite ST45 018	Caldonia/One Kiss For My Baby	150

LORD MELODY
58	Melodisc MEL 1440	The Devil/No, No	6
58	Melodisc MEL 1449	Robbery/Men Company	8
58	Melodisc MEL 1474	Do Able/Happy Holiday	6
59	Melodisc MEL 1491	I Confess/MIGHTY SPARROW: Goaty	8
59	Melodisc MEL 1503	Tom Dooley/Jealous Woman	6
59	Melodisc MEL 1504	Romeo/Knock On Any Door	6

LORD NELSON
63	Stateside SS 189	I Got An Itch/Problems On My Mind	12
64	Stateside SS 281	It's Delinquency/Proud West Indian	15
68	Direction 58-3909	Michael/No Hot Summer	10
64	Stateside SE 1024	PROUD WEST INDIAN (EP)	30

LORD POWER
69	Coxsone CS 7079	Temptation/AL & VIBRATORS: Change Everything	80

LORD RIGBY
60s	Kalypso XX 29	The Milkman/Old Veterans	6
64	National Calypso NC 1001	Carnival Jamaica/Music Teacher	20

LORD ROCKINGHAM'S XI
58	Decca F 11024	The Squelch/Fried Onions	10
59	Decca F 11104	Wee Tom/Lady Rockingham, I Presume?	6
59	Decca F 11139	Ra-Ra Rockingham/Farewell To Rockingham	8
62	Decca F 11426	Newcastle Twist/Rockingham Band Twist	8
58	Decca DFE 6555	OH BOY! (EP)	25
68	Columbia S(C)X 6291	THE RETURN OF LORD ROCKINGHAM'S XI (LP, mono/stereo)	25

(see also Robinson Crew)

LORD ROSE
60s	Kalypso XX 25	Independent Jamaica/Twistin' Uncle	40

LORDS
67	Columbia DB 8121	Don't Mince Matters/No One Knows	140
68	Columbia DB 8367	Gloryland/Gypsy Boy	18

LORDS OF RAP
92	Mad Dog MADDOG001	STIX 'N' STONES (EP)	15

LORDS OF THE UNDERGROUND
94	Pendulum 7243 8 30710 1 2	KEEPERS OF THE FUNK (2-LP)	35

LORD SASSAFROST
82	Star Light SDLP 911	HORSE MAN CONNECTION (LP)	20

LORD SITAR
68	Columbia SX/SCX 6256	LORD SITAR (LP)	40

LORD SPOON
70	Escort ERT 839	Woman A Love In The Night Time/World On A Wheel	15

LORD TANAMO
60	Kalypso XX 20	Blues Have Got Me Down/Sweet Dreaming	20
64	Rio R 21	I Had A Dream/OSBOURNE GRAHAM: Be There	12
64	Ska Beat JB 177	Night Food Ska/My Business	60
65	Ska Beat JB 217	Mattie Rag/BABA BROOKS BAND: Mattie Rag	25
65	Ska Beat JB 224	I'm In The Mood For Ska/You Never Know	150
66	Ska Beat JB 243	Mother's Love/Downtown Gal	30
60s	Caribou CRC 3	I Love You Truly/If You Were Only Mine	150
70	Bamboo BAM 45	Rainy Night In Georgia/KEN PACKER: When You're Gone	30
71	Banana BA 319	Keep On Moving/JACKIE MITTOO: Totaly [sic] Together	125

LORELEI
74	CBS 2048	S.T.O.P. (Stop)/I'll Never Let You Down	15

SOPHIA LOREN
58	Philips PB 857	Love Song From "Houseboat"/Bing! Bang! Bong!	6

(see also Peter Sellers & Sophia Loren)

LORENZO
69	Harry J HE 6687	Saturday Vocal Night/Intro	10
69	Beacon BEA 134	I Ain't Afraid/Beggar	12

(see also Laurel Aitken)

GARY & JOHN LORRAINE
65	Pye 7N 15836	I'm Not To Blame/Alone Again	10

MYRNA LORRIE
55	London HLU 8187	Underway/I'm Your Man, I'm Your Gal (B-side with Buddy DeVal)	25
56	London HLU 8294	Life's Changing Scene/Listen To My Heartstrings	25

LORRIES
79	Redball RR 016	The Night/Steal You Anyway/Pushover/Idiot Dances (p/s)	6

DICK LORY
56	London HLD 8348	Cool It Baby/Ball Room Baby	400
56	London HLD 8348	Cool It Baby/Ball Room Baby (78)	50
61	London HLG 9284	My Last Date/Broken Hearted	30
62	Liberty LIB 55415	Handsome Guy/The Pain Is Here	10
63	Liberty LIB 55529	Welcome Home Again/I Got Over You	10

LOS DOURADOS
70	EMI Regal/Starline SRS 5018	INTRODUCING LOS DOURADOS (LP)	15

JOE LOSS (& HIS ORCHESTRA)
66	HMV POP 1500	Thunderbirds Theme/"The Avengers" Theme	15
66	HMV POP 1517	The England World Cup March/Auld Lang Syne (March)	10

LOST
94	Tenth Planet TP 009	LOST IN ACTION (LP, with free 7")	20

LOST CHERREES
83	Riot RIOT 3	NO FIGHTING NO WAR (EP)	10
85	Mortarhate MORT 12	UNWANTED CHILDREN (12" EP, with inner)	10
84	Fight Back FIGHT 6	ALL PART OF GROWING UP (LP, with lyric inner)	15

LOST DOG
71	Phoenix SNIX 143	Latch Key Child/One More Time	60

LOST FAMOUS
82	Silent SR6703	Anywhere Else/A Warning	30

LOST HORIZONS
17	Bella Union BELLA700RT	OJALA (2-LP, die-cut sleeve, sky blue and silver vinyl, Rough Trade version, with CD)	20

LOST JOCKEY
82	Operation Twilight OPT 11	Professor Slack/Rise And Fall/Animal/Behaviour And Crude Din (10" p/s)	10

LOT 39 (STRANGERS)
60s	Eyemark EMS 1004	I'll Get Over You/I Still Love You	12

LOTHAR & THE HAND PEOPLE
69	Capitol CL 15610	Sdrawkcab (Backwards)/Today Is Only Yesterday's Tomorrow	20
69	Capitol E-ST 247	SPACE HYMN (LP)	80

DENNIS LOTIS
54	Decca F 10287	Such A Night/Cuddle Me (with Ted Heath Music & Johnston Brothers)	12
54	Decca F 10392	Honey Love/Manhattan Mambo (with Ted Heath Music)	12
55	Decca F 10469	Face Of An Angel, Heart Of A Devil/The Golden Ring	7
55	Decca F 10471	Chain Reaction/Go, Go, Go (with Ted Heath Music)	7
67	Polydor 56225	Together/Spellbound	10
68	Polydor 56266	Funny One/One Man's Life	10
68	Polydor 56298	Celebration/Why Do They Have To Fall In Love	10
68	Polydor 56346	One Woman Man/The Finger Points At you	10

(see also Johnstone Brothers)

PETER LOTIS
60	Ember EMB S 110	Doo-Dah/You're Singing Our Love Song To Somebody Else (with p/s)	6

LOTUS CRUISE
83	Armbury ARM 603	Billy's Got A Gun/Tonight	50

BONNIE LOU
53	Parlophone MSP 6021	Seven Lonely Days/Dancin' With Someone	50
53	Parlophone MSP 6036	Hand-Me-Down Heart/Scrap Of Paper	50
53	Parlophone MSP 6048	Tennessee Wig Walk/Just Out Of Reach	50
53	Parlophone MSP 6051	Pa-Paya Mama/Since You Said Goodbye	40
54	Parlophone MSP 6072	The Texas Polka/No Heart At All	30
54	Parlophone MSP 6095	Don't Stop Kissing Me Goodnight/The Welcome Mat	30
54	Parlophone MSP 6108	No One/Huckleberry Pie	30
54	Parlophone MSP 6117	Blue Tennessee Rain/Wait For Me, Darling	30
54	Parlophone MSP 6132	Two Step - Side Step/Please Don't Laugh When I Cry	30
55	Parlophone MSP 6151	Tennessee Mambo/Train Whistle Blues	40
55	Parlophone MSP 6157	Tweedle Dee/The Finger Of Suspicion Points At You	40
55	Parlophone MSP 6173	Drop Me A Line/Old Faithful And True Love	25
55	Parlophone MSP 6178	The Barnyard Hop/Tell The World	20
55	Parlophone MSP 6188	Dancin' In My Socks/Daddy-O	40
56	Parlophone MSP 6223	Darlin' Why/Miss The Love (That I've Been Dreaming Of)	20
56	Parlophone MSP 6234	Bo Weevil (A Country Song)/Chaperon	20
56	Parlophone MSP 6253	Lonesome Lover/Little Miss Bobby Sox	25
56	Parlophone R 4215	No Rock 'N' Roll Tonight/One Track Love	25
57	Parlophone R 4350	Teenage Wedding/Runnin' Away	25
58	Parlophone DP 545	I'm Available/Waiting In Vain (export issue)	20

BONNIE LOU & RUSTY YORK
58	Parlophone R 4409	Let The School Bell Ring Ding-A-Ling/La Dee Dah	80
58	Parlophone R 4409	Let The School Bell Ring Ding-A-Ling/La Dee Dah (78)	30

BUBBA LOU & THE HIGHBALLS
81	Stiff BUY 114	Love All Over The Place/Over You (Unissued)	25
81	Silent SSH3	Love All Over The Place/Over You	10

LOU & KEVIN
78	Bushays BFM 103	Reunited/Reunited Stepping Out (12")	10

(see also Rusty York)

LOUD E
08	Ambassador's Reception ABR 001	Robotlove/Au Paradise/Jungleman Life (12")	18
08	Ambassador's Reception ABR 003	Y.O.Y./Deli Disco/Afrika Afrika (12")	12

LOUDER ANIMAL GROUP
80	Ears Pop POP 701	Pip Pop/Six Magnificent Cathedrals (p/s)	10

John D. LOUDERMILK

MINT VALUE £

80	Ears Pop POP 702F	The Fossil Record (1-sided flexi on cardboard with 2 posters & inserts in poly bag)	12

JOHN D. LOUDERMILK

62	RCA RD 27248/SF 5123	THE LANGUAGE OF LOVE (LP)	20

(see also Johnny Dee)

(THE) LOUDWATER TERN

68	Morgan MR 6S	Senorita/I'll Be Where You Are (some demos credit Damon J Hardy and Polly Perkins)	40

LISA LOUGHEED

87	Ariola 111 713	Run With Us (Remix)/Ain't No Planes	20

JOE HILL LOUIS

65	Bootleg 502	Heartache Baby/I Feel Like A Million (99 copies only)	40
67	Advent LP 2803	MEMPHIS BLUES AND BREAKDOWNS (LP)	70
74	Polydor 2383 214	BLUE IN THE MORNING (LP)	30

LOUISIANA RED

64	Columbia DB 7270	Keep Your Hands Off My Woman/Don't Cry	40
64	Sue WI 337	I Done Woke Up/I Had A Feeling	40
64	Columbia 33SX 1612	LOWDOWN BACK PORCH BLUES (LP)	45
72	Atlantic K 40436	SINGS THE BLUES (LP)	20
72	Carnival 2941 002	THE SEVENTH SON (LP)	20

LOUNGE SOCIETY

20	Speedy Wunderground SW034	Generation Game Part 1/Part 2 (die-cut p/s)	15

LOUVIN BROTHERS

59	Capitol CL 14989	Knoxville Girl/I Wish It Had Been A Dream	20
59	Capitol CL 15078	You're Learning/My Curly Headed Baby	10
56	Capitol EAP1 769	TRAGIC SONGS OF LIFE (EP)	10
58	Capitol EAP1 910	IRA AND CHARLIE (EP)	10
59	Capitol EAP1 1106	COUNTRY LOVE BALLADS (EP)	10
84	Stetson HAT 3043	TRAGIC SONGS OF LIFE (LP, reissue)	25

LOVABLES

68	Stateside SS 2108	You're The Cause Of It/Beautiful Idea	25

ALAN LOVE AND MERLIN

74	CBS 3452	Too Too Much/Gettin' Involved	6

ARNIE LOVE AND THE LOVELESS

12	Soul Spectrum SLSP008	We Had Enough/Invisible Wind (reissue)	35

C.P. LOVE

02	Grapevine 2000 G2K 127	Trick Bag/Plenty Of Room For More (reissue)	10

CHRISTOPHER LOVE

69	London HLU 10263	The Curse Goes On/You May Be The Next	18

DARLENE LOVE

63	London HLU 9725	(Today I Met) The Boy I'm Gonna Marry/Playing For Keeps	40
63	London HLU 9765	Wait 'Til My Bobby Gets Home/Take It From Me	40
63	London HLU 9815	A Fine Fine Boy/Marshmallow World	50
69	London HLU 10244	Wait 'Til My Bobby Gets Home/(Today I Met) The Boy I'm Gonna Marry	15
74	Warner Bros K 19011	Christmas (Baby Please Come Home)/Wait Till My Bobby Comes Home (blue vinyl)	20
77	Phil Spector Intl. 2010 019	Lord If You're A Woman/Johnny Baby Please Come Home	20
77	Phil Spector Intl. 2010 019	Lord If You're A Woman/Johnny Baby Please Come Home (12", some copies 1-sided)	15
90	Warner Brothers W 9535	Mr Fix-It/K.D. LANG with TAKE SIX: Ridin' The Rails (with p/s)	20
90	Warner Brothers W 9535	Mr Fix-It/K.D. LANG with TAKE SIX: Ridin' The Rails	20
64	London RE-U 1411	WAIT TILL MY BOBBY GETS HOME (EP)	250

(see also Bob B. Soxx & Blue Jeans, Crystals, Phil Spector, Blossoms, Allisons [U.S.], Date With Soul, Cinders)

GARFIELD LOVE & JIMMY SPRUILL

69	Blue Horizon 57-3150	Next Time You See Me/Part Time Love	35

GEOFF LOVE ORCHESTRA

61	Columbia DB 4627	Coronation Street Theme/Sophia	7
74	EMI EMI 2105	Match Of The Day/Bless This House	6

(see also Mandingo)

MARY LOVE

65	King KG 1024	You Turned My Bitter Into Sweet/I'm In Your Hands	250
67	Stateside SS 2009	Lay This Burden Down/Think It Over Baby	75
67	Stateside SS 2009	Lay This Burden Down/Think It Over Baby (DJ copy)	125
68	Stateside SS 2135	The Hurt Is Just Beginning/If You Change Your Mind	15
82	Kent TOWN 501	You Turned My Bitter Into Sweet/SWEETHEARTS: This Couldn't Be Me (green vinyl)	10
85	Kent 6T1	Hey Stoney Face/IKETTES: It's Been So Long/ETTA JAMES: Wallflower	20

MIKE LOVE

83	Creole CR 61	Jingle Bell Rock/Let's Party (p/s)	8

(see also Beach Boys)

NANA LOVE

77	Golden Age GAM 01	When The Heart Decides/Give Me The Chance	80
78	Nestor NES 01	Chains Of Love/Sahara	50
78	Nestor NES 0201	DISCO DOCUMENTARY - FULL OF FUNK (LP)	200
14	BBE BBE250ALP	DISCO DOCUMENTARY - FULL OF FUNK (2-LP, CD, reissue)	20

PRESTON LOVE

00s	Beat Goes Public BGPS 009	Cissy Popcorn/BRENDA GEORGE: I Can't Stand It	8

RONNIE LOVE

61	London HLD 9272	Chills And Fever/Pledging My Love	50
78	Grapevine GRP 108	Let's Make Love/Nothing To It	8

SYLVIA LOVE

79	RCA PC 5168	Extraterrestrial Lover/(Instrumental) (12")	15

WILLIE LOVE/WILLIE NIX

66	Highway 51 H 700	THE TWO WILLIES FROM MEMPHIS (LP, 99 copies only)	75

LOVE (1)

LOVE (1)
SINGLES

Year	Label/Cat	Title	Value £
66	London HLZ 10053	My Little Red Book/Hey Joe	60
66	London HLZ 10073	7 And 7 Is/No. Fourteen	60
67	Elektra EKSN 45010	She Comes In Colours/Orange Skies	30
67	Elektra EKSN 45016	Softly To Me/The Castle	30
68	Elektra EKSN 45024	Alone Again Or/Bummer In The Summer	30
68	Elektra EKSN 45026	The Daily Planet/Andmoreagain	60
68	Elektra EKSN 45038	Your Mind And We Belong Together/Laughing Stock	45
70	Elektra EKSN 45086	I'm With You/Robert Montgomery	15
70	Harvest HAR 5014	Stand Out/Doggone	15
70	Harvest HAR 5030	The Everlasting First/Keep On Shining	15
70	Elektra 2101 019	Alone Again Or/Bummer In The Summer (reissue, red label)	10
73	Elektra K 12213	Alone Again Or/Andmoreagain	6
75	RSO 2090 151	Time Is Like A River/You Said You Would	6
76	ElektraK 12231	Alone Again Or/The Castle (mispressing, A side plays And More)	10
10	Elektra EK 45605	7 And 7 Is/No. Fourteen (reissue, 750 only, large centre)	8

ALBUMS : ORIGINAL ALBUMS

Year	Label/Cat	Title	Value £
67	Elek. EKL 4001/EKS 74001	LOVE (LP, 1st pressing, gold labels, in U.S. sleeve)	150
66	Elek. EKL 4001/EKS 74001	LOVE (LP, 2nd pressing, orange labels in U.S. sleeve or fully laminated UK sleeve)	75
67	Elek. EKL 4005/EKS 74005	DA CAPO (LP, 1st pressing, mono/stereo, orange label with 'Manufactured in England by Elektra Records (U.K.) Ltd' at the bottom of labels in U.S. sleeves)	120
67	Elek. EKL 4005/EKS 74005	DA CAPO (LP, 2nd pressing with 'Manufactured in Gt Britain' and 'Polydor Records Ltd' at the bottom of labels in either US or fully laminated UK sleeves)	120
68	Elektra EKL 4013	FOREVER CHANGES (LP, 1st pressing, orange labels, laminated sleeve, mono)	200
68	Elektra EKS 74013	FOREVER CHANGES (LP, 1st pressing, orange labels, laminated sleeve, stereo)	150
69	Elektra EKS 74013	FOREVER CHANGES (LP, 2nd pressing, lighter orange label with silver lettering, stereo, laminated sleeve)	70
70	Elektra EKS 74013	FOREVER CHANGES (LP, 3rd pressing, red labels, laminated sleeve, stereo)	70
71	Elektra K 42015	FOREVER CHANGES (LP, 4th pressing, 'butterfly' labels, matt sleeve, band picture on rear)	35
76	Elektra K 42015	FOREVER CHANGES (LP, 5th pressing, butterfly labels, matt sleeve, Arthur Lee picture on rear)	30
69	Elektra EKL 4049	FOUR SAIL (LP, orange label, mono, existence unconfirmed)	70
69	Elektra EKS 74049	FOUR SAIL (LP, orange label, stereo)	70
70	Harvest SHDW 3/4	OUT HERE (2-LP, gatefold sleeve)	50
71	Harvest SHVL 787	FALSE START (LP, gatefold sleeve)	70
71	Elektra 2469 009	LOVE REVISITED (LP, gatefold sleeve)	18
73	Elektra K 32002	LOVE MASTERS (LP)	18
74	RSO 2394 145	REEL TO REAL (LP)	20

ALBUMS : REISSUES

Year	Label/Cat	Title	Value £
71	Elektra EKS 74005	DA CAPO (LP, 'butterfly' label)	18
72	Elektra K 42011	DA CAPO (LP, 'butterfly' label)	15
72	Elektra K 42068	LOVE (LP, 'butterfly' label)	25
72	Elektra K 42030	FOUR SAIL (LP, 'butterfly' label)	15
81	Elektra K 42011	DA CAPO (LP, reissue)	15
87	Edsel ED 218	LOVE (LP, reissue)	15
87	Elektra 7559 60656-1	DA CAPO (LP, reissue)	15
88	Big Beat WIKA 69	OUT THERE (LP)	15
13	Music On Vinyl MOVLP677	LOVE (LP, reissue)	15
15	Elektra 8122797215	FOREVER CHANGES (LP, reissue)	15
16	Music On Vinyl MOVLP1002	DA CAPO (LP, reissue, gold vinyl, 500 only)	15

(see also Arthur Lee)

LOVE (2)

Year	Label/Cat	Title	Value £
90	Fierce FRIGHT 036	Welsh Girl (1-sided, p/s in bag, hand-finished labels, mail-order only)	20

LOVE AFFAIR

Year	Label/Cat	Title	Value £
67	Decca F 12558	She Smiled Sweetly/Satisfaction Guaranteed	70
67	CBS 3125	Everlasting Love/Gone Are The Songs Of Yesterday	6
68	CBS 3366	Rainbow Valley/Someone Like Me (in p/s, says 'Someone Like Us' on p/s)	20
68	CBS 3366	Rainbow Valley/Someone Like Us	8
68	CBS 3674	A Day Without Love/I'm Happy	6
69	CBS 3994	One Road/Let Me Know	8
69	CBS 4300	Bringing On Back The Good Times/Another Day	8
69	CBS 4631	Baby I Know/Accept Me For What I Am	10
70	CBS 4780	Lincoln County/Sea Of Tranquility	10
70	Pye 7N 45218	Let Me Dance/Love's Looking Out At You	8
71	Parlophone R 5887	Wake Me I Am Dreaming/That's My Home	12
71	Parlophone R 5918	Help (Get Me Some Help)/Long Way Home	12
72	CBS 5017	Speak Of Peace Speak Of Joy/Brings My Whole Life Tumbling Down	10
77	Creole CR 146	Private Lives/Let A Little Love Come In	7
68	CBS 63416	THE EVERLASTING LOVE AFFAIR (LP, mono/stereo)	40
70	CBS 64109	NEW DAY (LP)	40

(see also Ellis, Steve Ellis, Elastic Band, Widowmaker, Morgan, Phillip Goodhand-Tait, English Rose, Rainbow Ffolly)

LOVE AMBASSADEUX

Year	Label/Cat	Title	Value £
85	Rumpo 12002	Black Mischief/Driftwood/Oyster Syndrome (12")	10

LOVE & UNITY

Year	Label/Cat	Title	Value £
79	Studio 16 WE 0014	Can't Let You Go/Dub Version (12")	30
80	Studio 16 WE 001	Put It On/(feat Ranking Bogart)/Dub	35
80	Studio 16 WE N1	Just Don't Care/Cut From The Master Tape (12")	25
80	Studio 16 WEA 347	I Adore You/CAPTAIN DESMOND : Lover In Dance (12")	25

LOVE AND WAR

MINT VALUE £

LOVE AND WAR
80s SRT SRT9KS 2323 — Touch Of Class (p/s) 100

LOVE CHILDREN
69 Deram DM 268 — Easy Squeezy/Every Little Step 15
70 Deram DM 303 — Paper Chase/My Turkey Snuffed It 20

LOVE COMMITTEE
76 Ariola AA 105 — Can't Win For Losing/Love Wins Every Time 10

LOVE CONNECTION
77 Strong Like Sampson SLS01 — It's My House/Fall In Love (12") 20

LOVECUT D.B.
91 Suburbs Of Hell SOH 009EP — Heartspin/Heartspin (Dripping Clock Mix)/(Marisco Disco Mix)/(Porn Cable Mix) (12") ... 10
92 Suburbs Of Hell SOH 011EP — JOURNEY TO THE CENTRE OF LOVE EP (12") 10
(see also Sarah Cracknell, St. Etienne)

LOVE DIMENSION
79 Black Bear BLA 2010 — You Stepped Into My Life/The Game 15

LOVE GENERATION (JAMAICA)
73 Grape GR 3046 — Money Raper/HEPTONES: The Magnificent Heptones 3 In One ... 12
73 Grape GR 3041 — Warrika Hill/Battlefield (Third And Fourth Generation) 12

LOVE GENERATION (U.S.)
67 Liberty LBF 15018 — She Touched Me/The Love In Me 10
68 Liberty LBL/LBS 83121E — LOVE GENERATION (LP) 25

JOY LOVEJOY
72 Chess 6145 010 — In Orbit/Uh! Hum (paper label/moulded label) 30

LOVEJOYS
80s Solid Groove SG 016 — Stranger/Let Me Rock You (12") 20

LOVELACE GREEN
69 Concord CON 003 — Sister George/Pauper Millionaire 20

LOVELITES
78 Grapevine GRP 107 — Get It Off My Conscience/Oh, What A Day 10

LOVELY BODIES
81 Shark Hits LB 1 — Swelter In The Shelter/Come On Too Strong (p/s) 30

LOVE PARADE
90 Turntable Friend TURN 03 — GUILT CHEST (EP) 25

JOHNNY LOVER
70 Amalgamated AMG 871 — Pumpkin Eater/Version 20
70 Amalgamated AMG 873 — Two Edged Sword/Version 35
(see also Little Johnny Jones, Heptones)

LOVERS
58 Vogue Pop V 9111 — Let's Elope/I Wanna Be Loved 500
58 Vogue Pop V 9111 — Let's Elope/I Wanna Be Loved (78) 150

LOVERS DUB
80 Venture — CUT 7 (LP) (actually by Eargasm) 40
(see also Tradition)

LOVE SCULPTURE
68 Parlophone R 5664 — River To Another Day/Brand New Woman 20
68 Parlophone R 5731 — Wang-Dang-Doodle/The Stumble 20
69 Parlophone R 5807 — Seagull/Farandole 15
70 Parlophone R 5831 — In The Land Of The Few/People People 20
68 Parlophone PMC 7059 — BLUES HELPING (LP, 1st pressing, yellow/black label, mono) 80
68 Parlophone PCS 7059 — BLUES HELPING (LP, 1st pressing, yellow/black label, stereo) 50
69 Parlophone PCS 7090 — FORMS AND FEELINGS (LP, 1st pressing, yellow/black label) 100
70 Parlophone PCS 7059 — BLUES HELPING (LP, 2nd pressing, silver/black label) 25
70 Parlophone PCS 7090 — FORMS AND FEELINGS (LP, 2nd pressing, silver/black label) 25
(see also Human Beans)

EDDIE LOVETTE
69 Big Shot BI 519 — You're My Girl/Let Them Say 15
70 London HLJ 10311 — Too Experienced/Little Blue Bird 10
70 London HA-J 8413 — TOO EXPERIENCED (LP, unissued) 0

LENE LOVICH
76 Polydor 2058 812 — I Saw Mommy Kissing Santa Claus/The Christmas Song (Merry Christmas To You)/Happy Christmas (p/s) 40
78 Stiff BUYJ 32 — I Think We're Alone Now (Japanese)/Lucky Number (mail-order promo only) ... 25
78 Stiff BUY 32 PLUG — I Think We're Alone Now/Lucky Number ("plug" copy on label. p/s) 10
78 Stiff BUY 35 — Home/Lucky Number (unreleased, test pressings only) 100
79 Stiff BUY 46 DJ — Say When (1-sided promo, black vinyl) 7

LOVIN'
67 Page One POF 035 — Keep On Believing/I'm In Command 35
67 Page One POF 041 — All You've Got/Do It Again 75
(see also Nerve)

LOVIN' SPOONFUL
65 Pye International 7N 25327 — Do You Believe In Magic?/On The Road Again 12
66 Pye International 7N 25344 — You Didn't Have To Be So Nice/My Gal 15
66 Kama Sutra KAS 200 — Summer In The City/Bald Headed Lena 8
66 Kama Sutra KAS 201 — Rain On The Roof/Warm Baby 7
67 Kama Sutra KAS 204 — Nashville Cats/Full Measure 7
67 Kama Sutra KAS 207 — Darling Be Home Soon/Darlin' Companion 12
67 Kama Sutra KAS 208 — Six O'Clock/The Finale 10
67 Kama Sutra KAS 210 — She Is Still A Mystery/Only Pretty, What A Pity 8
67 Kama Sutra KAS 211 — Money/Close Your Eyes 8
68 Kama Sutra KAS 213 — Never Going Back/Forever 12

LOVING AWARENESS

MINT VALUE £

66	Kama Sutra KEP 300	DID YOU EVER HAVE TO MAKE UP YOUR MIND (EP)	20
66	Kama Sutra KEP 301	JUG BAND MUSIC (EP)	20
66	Kama Sutra KEP 302	SUMMER IN THE CITY (EP)	20
67	Kama Sutra KEP 303	DAY BLUES (EP)	20
67	Kama Sutra KEP 304	NASHVILLE CATS (EP)	25
67	Kama Sutra KEP 305	LOVIN' YOU (EP)	30
67	Kama Sutra KEP 306	SOMETHING IN THE NIGHT (EP)	35
65	Pye Intl. NPL 28069	DO YOU BELIEVE IN MAGIC? (LP)	25
66	Pye Intl. NPL 28078	DAYDREAM (LP)	35
67	Kama Sutra KLP 401	HUMS OF THE LOVIN' SPOONFUL (LP)	20
67	Kama Sutra KLP 402	YOU'RE A BIG BOY NOW (LP, soundtrack)	18
68	Kama Sutra KLP 404	EVERYTHING PLAYING (LP)	15
68	Kama Sutra K(S)LP 405	THE BEST OF THE LOVIN' SPOONFUL VOL. 2 (LP)	15
69	Kama Sutra 602 009	REVELATION: REVOLUTION '69 (LP)	15

(see also John Sebastian, Mugwumps, Zalman Yanovsky, Even Dozen Jug Band)

LOVING AWARENESS
76	More Love ML 001	LOVING AWARENESS (LP, gatefold sleeve with 2 posters)	15

(see also Glencoe, Skip Bifferty, Ian Dury)

LOVING KIND
66	Piccadilly 7N 35299	Accidental Love/Nothing Can Change This Love	15
66	Piccadilly 7N 35318	I Love The Things You Do/Treat Me Nice	18
66	Piccadilly 7N 35342	Ain't That Peculiar/With Rhyme And Reason	25

(see also Freddie Lennon)

LOW
96	Vernon Yard YARD 24	Over The Ocean/Violence	10
96	Vernon Yard YARD 22	FINALLY... (EP)	20
98	Tugboat TUGS 001	Joan Of Arc/Long Long Long	6
98	Rough Trade RTRADELP 061	TRUST (2-LP)	30
99	Tugboat TUGLP 007	SECRET NAME (2-LP)	35
01	Tugboat TUGLP 027	THINGS WE LOST IN THE FIRE (2-LP, 4th side etched with lyrics)	25

BRUCE LOW
56	HMV JO 464	Just Walking In The Rain/Cindy Oh Cindy (export issue)	20

LOW NUMBERS
79	Warner Brothers K 17493	Keep In Touch/Nine All Out (p/s)	25

LOW PROFILE
80	Ellie Jay EJSP 9434	Hangin' Around/Substitute (p/s)	50

LOWBITES
70	Black Swan BW 1403	I Got It/I Got It (Version)	6
80	Black Joy DH 800	Can I Go With You?/BOBBY DODSON & TRINITY: Having My Baby (12")	15

DENNIS LOWE
70	Downtown DT 465	What's Your Name/MUSIC DOCTORS: Mr Locabe	20
70	Downtown DT 468	Stand Up For The Sound/OWEN & DENNIS: Old Man Trouble	20

EARL LOWE
75	Tafari WL 708	Jah Can Count On I/Bongo Nyah (12")	70

JEZ LOWE
80	Fellside FE 034	JEZ LOWE (LP, textured sleeve, light green label, large 'Rams Horn' logo)	15
83	Fellside FE 034	THE OLD DURHAM ROAD (LP)	15
85	Fellside FE 049	GALLOWAYS (LP, with lyric insert)	15

JIM LOWE
55	London HLD 8171	Close The Door/Nueva Laredo (gold label print)	40
56	London HLD 8276	Blue Suede Shoes/Maybellene (silver label print)	100
56	London HLD 8276	Blue Suede Shoes/Maybellene (silver label print) (78)	20
56	London HLD 8288	Love Is The $64,000 Dollar Question/Rene La Rue (gold label print)	80
56	London HLD 8317	The Green Door/The Little Man In Chinatown (as Jim Lowe & High Fives, gold label print)	50
56	London HLD 8317	The Green Door/The Little Man In Chinatown (as Jim Lowe & High Fives, later silver print label)	25
57	London HLD 8368	I Feel The Beat/By You, By You, By You (gold label print)	50
57	London HLD 8368	I Feel The Beat/By You, By You, By You (later silver print label)	30
57	London HLD 8431	Four Walls/Talkin' To The Blues	25
58	London HLD 8538	Roc-A-Chicka/The Bright Light (with Billy Vaughan's Orchestra)	125
60	London HLD 9043	He'll Have To Go/(This Life Is Just A) Dress Rehearsal	6
58	London HA-D 2108	SONGS THEY SING BEHIND THE GREEN DOOR (LP)	30
59	London HA-D 2146	WICKED WOMEN (LP)	20

(see also John Barry Seven)

NICK LOWE
76	Stiff BUY 1	So It Goes/Heart Of The City (promo, 'plug' copy)	40
76	Stiff BUY 1	So It Goes/Heart Of The City, (push-out centre)	15
77	Stiff LAST 1-12	Bowi EP (Born A Woman//Marie Provost/Endless Sleep, 12" promo, 50 only)	100
77	Stiff BUY 21	Halfway To Paradise/I Don't Want The Night To End	6

MUNDELL LOWE QUARTET
56	London American LTZ U 15020	MUNDELL LOWE QUARTET (LP)	30

LOWER LEVELS
81	Pushover 1	Get It/So Bloody Lazy (p/s)	20

LOWLIFE
89	LOLIF DEMO 1	THE DEMOS (LP, white label test pressings only, hand-written white sleeve)	60

LOW/PIANO MAGIC/TRANSIENT WAVES
98	Rocket Girl RGIRL 4	Sleep At The Bottom/TRANSIENT WAVES: Green Acres (p/s)	6

LOWRELL
79	AVI AVISL 108	Mellow Mellow Right On (Four Mixes) (12")	10

Philip LOWRIE

MINT VALUE £

79	AVI AVIS 108	Mellow Mellow Right On/You're Playing Dirty	7
80	AVI AVLP 504	LOWRELL (LP)	20

PHILIP LOWRIE
63 Ember EMB S 179   I Might Have Known (Before)/I Might Have Known (After) 10

ART LOWRY
54 Columbia SCMC 1   The Curse Of An Aching Heart/Heart Of My Heart (export issue) 10

HENRY LOWTHER BAND
70 Deram SML 1070   CHILD SONG (LP) 175
(see also Manfred Mann, John Mayall & Bluesbreakers, Keef Hartley Band, Ricotti & Albuquerque)

MARK LOYD
65 Parlophone R 5277   I Keep Thinking About You/Will It Be The Same 10
65 Parlophone R 5332   Everybody Tries/She Said No 60
66 Parlophone R 5423   When Evening Falls/When I'm Gonna Find Her 400
66 Parlophone R 5423   When Evening Falls/When I'm Gonna Find Her (DJ copy) 500

L7
92 London/Slash 828 307-1   BRICKS ARE HEAVY (LP, green marbled vinyl with poster) 40

LTG EXCHANGE
76 Atlantic K10824   Huddle/You'll Never Learn (About Love) 8

JEREMY LUBBOCK
58 Parlophone R 4421   Lemon Twist/Tonight 10
58 Parlophone GEP 8745   JUST FOR THE FUN OF IT (EP) 10

LUCA C & BRIGANTE
12 Southern Fried ECB 346   Flash Of Light (Original Mix)/(Tales Of Us And Minds Against Mix)/(Solomon Mix) (12", featuring Roisin Murphy) 35

LUCAS (& MIKE COTTON SOUND)
66 Polydor 56114   I Saw Pity In The Face Of A Friend/Dance Children Dance (solo) 20
67 Pye 7N 17313   Step Out Of Line/Ain't Love Good, Ain't Love Proud 50
68 MGM MGM 1398   Soul Serenade/We Got A Thing Going Baby 45
68 MGM MGM 1427   Jack And The Beanstalk/Mother-In-Law 30
(see also Mike Cotton Sound, Artwoods)

BUDDY LUCAS BAND
60 Pye International 7N 25045   I Want To Know/Deacon John 20

LUCAS AND THE DYNAMOS
91 SRTS 91 S2904   Rock And Roll Is Good For The Soul/Blood Shot/My Gal/Baby Baby 15

TREVOR LUCAS
66 Reality RE 505   Waltzing Matilda/It's On 20
66 Reality RY 1002   OVERLANDER (LP) 275
(see also Eclection, Fotheringay, Fairport Convention, Bronco, Sandy Denny)

JON LUCIEN
74 RCA ALP1-0493   MINDS EYE (LP) 30

LUCIENNE
80 Pan 101   Caribbean/This Boy (p/s) 8

LUCIFER (1)
71 Lucifer L 001   Don't Care/Hypnosis 15
72 Lucifer L 003/004   Fuck You/Bad 8
72 Lucifer L 005/006   Prick/Want It 8
72 Lucifer L 005/006/L 003/004   Prick/Want It/Fuck You/Bad (double pack, black box set) 40
73 Lucifer L007   Mr Jack/Mr Jack 50
72 Lucifer LLP 1   BIG GUN (LP, private pressing, with poster/inserts, sold via Oz mag) 125
72 Lucifer LLP 1   BIG GUN (LP, private pressing, without poster/inserts, sold via Oz mag) 80
72 Lucifer LLP 2   EXIT (LP, private pressing, with poster, sold via Oz magazine) 150
72 Lucifer LLP 2   EXIT (LP, private pressing, without poster, sold via Oz magazine) 70

LUCIFER'S FRIEND
71 Philips 6003 092   Ride The Sky/Horla 15
71 Philips 6305 068   LUCIFER'S FRIEND (LP) 250
(see also John Lawton, Uriah Heep)

THE LUCK OF EDEN HALL
11 Fruits De Mer Winkle 03   She Comes In Colours/Never My Love/Chrysalide/The Ottoman Girl (folded p/s, green vinyl, insert) 20

LUCY SHOW
84 Piggy Bank BANK 999   Electric Dreams/History Part 1 (p/s) 7
85 A&M AMY 261   Ephemeral/White Space (12", p/s) 20

TOM LUCY
82 Bridgehouse BHS 15   Paris, France/Man Found Dead In Graveyard (no p/s) 6
(see also Wasted Youth)

LUCY (1)
69 Major Minor MM667   Georgie/With Him 8

LUCY (2)
77 Lightning BCS 008   Really Got Me Goin'/Oy (export only p/s) 15
77 Lightning BCS 008   Really Got Me Goin'/Oy (no p/s) 10
78 Lightning GIL 516   Never Never/Feel So Good (with export p/s) 100
78 Lightning GIL 516   Never Never/Feel So Good (without export p/s) 30
(see also Def Leppard)

LUCY PEARL
00 Pookie 7243 8 49393 1 1   LUCY PEARL (2-LP) 30

LUDDITES
83 Xcentric Noise SECOND 1   STRENGTH OF YOUR CRY (EP, black foldout p/s) 15
83 Xcentric Noise SECOND 1   STRENGTH OF YOUR CRY (EP, pink foldout p/s) 10

LUDLOWS
61 Pye NEP 24252   THE SEA AROUND US (EP) 20
66 Pye NPL 18150   THE WIND AND THE SEA (LP) 18

LUDUS

MINT VALUE £

(see also Jim McCann)

LUDUS
81	New Hormones ORG 8	My Cherry Is In Sherry/Anatomy Is Not Destiny (p/s)	7
81	New Hormones ORG 12	Mother's Hour/Patient (p/s, with poster)	8
81	New Hormones ORG 16	THE SEDUCTION (2 x 12" EP, each in p/s; whole package in poly bag)	12
82	New Hormones ORG 20	DANGER CAME SMILING (LP, insert)	18

LUKE & BLAKE
66	CBS 202467	Just You/Wandering Man	8

ROBIN LUKE
58	London HLD 8676	Susie Darlin'/Living's Loving You	10
58	London HLD 8771	Chicka Chicka Honey/My Girl	30
58	London HLD 8771	Chicka Chicka Honey/My Girl (78)	20
59	London RED 1222	ROBIN LUKE (EP)	50

LUKIE D
89	Uptempo TEMP 030	Rough Neck A Town/Love Will Find A Way (12")	75
89	Original Sounds OS 1003 LP	GOLDEN RULE (LP)	30

LULU (& LUVVERS)
64	Decca F 11884	Shout/Forget Me Baby (as Lulu & Luvers)	6
64	Decca F 11965	Can't Hear You No More/I Am In Love	20
64	Decca F 12017	Here Comes The Night/That's Really Some Good	15
65	Decca F 12128	Satisfied/Surprise Surprise (as Lulu & Luvers)	18
65	Decca F 12169	Leave A Little Love/He Don't Want Your Love Anymore	6
65	Decca F 12214	Try To Understand/Not In This Whole World	8
65	Decca F 12254	Tell Me Like It Is/Stop Fooling Around	20
66	Decca F 12326	Call Me/After You	7
66	Decca F 12491	What A Wonderful Feeling/Tossin' And Turnin'	12
67	Columbia DB 8169	The Boat That I Row/Dreary Days And Nights	8
67	Columbia DB 8221	Let's Pretend/To Sir With Love	10
67	Columbia DB 8295	Love Loves To Love/You And I	12
68	Columbia DB 8425	Boy/Sad Memories	6
69	Atco 226 008	Oh Me, Oh My (I'm A Fool For You Baby)/Sweep Around Your Own Backyard	6
71	Atco 2091049	Move To My Rhythm/Got To Believe In Love	8
65	Decca DFE 8597	LULU (EP)	35
65	Decca LK 4719	SOMETHING TO SHOUT ABOUT (LP)	50
67	Ace Of Clubs ACL 1232	LULU! (LP)	20
67	Fontana (S)TL 5446	TO SIR, WITH LOVE (LP, soundtrack, with Ron Grainer & Mindbenders)	35
67	Columbia S(C)X 6201	LOVE LOVES TO LOVE LULU (LP, John Paul Jones arrangements)	30
69	Columbia S(C)X 6365	LULU'S ALBUM (LP)	25
69	Atco 228 031	NEW ROUTES (LP)	15
70	Atco 2400017	MELODY FAIR (LP)	15

(see also Luvvers)

LULU BELLE & SCOTTY
65	London HA-B 8277	SWEETHEART STILL (LP)	15

BOB LUMAN
60	Warner Bros WB 12	Dreamy Doll/Buttercup	15
62	Warner Bros WB 60	Louisiana Man/Rocks Of Reno (unissued)	0
64	Hickory 45-1238	The File/Bigger Men Than I	10
61	Warner Bros WEP 6046	LET'S THINK ABOUT LIVIN' (EP, mono)	15
61	Warner Bros WSEP 2046	LET'S THINK ABOUT LIVIN' (EP, stereo)	25
62	Warner Bros WEP 6055	LET'S THINK ABOUT LIVIN' NO. 2 (EP, mono)	15
62	Warner Bros WSEP 2055	LET'S THINK ABOUT LIVIN' NO. 2 (EP, stereo)	20
62	Warner Bros WEP 6102	LET'S THINK ABOUT LIVIN' NO. 3 (EP, mono)	15
62	Warner Bros WSEP 2102	LET'S THINK ABOUT LIVIN' NO. 3 (EP, stereo)	20
60	Warner Bros WM 4025	LET'S THINK ABOUT LIVIN' (LP, mono)	20
60	Warner Bros WS 8025	LET'S THINK ABOUT LIVIN' (LP, stereo)	25

(see also Sue Thompson & Bob Luman)

RUFUS LUMLEY
66	Stateside SS 516	I'm Standing/Let's Hide Away (Me And You)	200
66	Stateside SS 516	I'm Standing/Let's Hide Away (Me And You) (DJ copy)	400
78	EMI International INT 556	I'm Standing/Let's Hide Away (Me And You) (reissue)	15

LUNA
95	Beggars Banquet BBQLP 178	PENTHOUSE (LP)	20
97	Beggars Banquet BBQLP 194	PUP TENT (LP)	20
99	Beggars Banquet BBQLP 209	THE DAY OF OUR NIGHTS (LP, white vinyl)	20

(see also Galaxie 500)

LUNA C
93	Knifeforce KF 001	THE LUNA C PROJECT EP (12")	40
93	Knifeforce KF 002	LUNA C PROJECT 2 - MISSION OF MADNESS (12")	40
93	Knifeforce KF 012	Death Of A Psychopath/Bass Drum Jungle Music (12")	10
94	Knifeforce KF 025	Piano Progression (Double Whopper Mix)/Onward (Extra Pepperami Mix) (12")	10

LUNAR TWO
60s	Spot JWS 551	Get It Take It/Don't Ever Leave Me	20

LUNATIC FRINGE
82	Resurrection	Keep In Touch	8
84	COR 1	CRINGE WITH THE FRINGE (EP)	15

LYDIA LUNCH
91	UFO UFOPF 1	Spooky (mono)/Spooky (stereo) (no p/s, promo only)	6
93	Clawfist X-PIG 19	Unearthly Delights/Busted (p/s)	8
80	Celluoid CEL 2 6561	QUEEN OF SIAM (LP)	25
82	Situation 2 SITU 6	13.13 (LP, with inner sleeve)	20

Art LUND

			MINT VALUE £
84	Doublevision DVR 5	IN LIMBO (LP, red vinyl with inner sleeve)	20
86	Widowspeak SWP 01/07	THE INTIMATE DIARIES OF THE SEXUALLY INSANE (cassette, box set with book, signed)	25
87	Widowspeak WSP 8	HYSTERIE (2-LP, with inners and poster)	20

(see also Eight-Eyed Spy, Roland S. Howard, No Trend)

ART LUND
65	United Artists UP 1100	Branded/Gonna Have A Little Talk	6
57	Vogue Coral LVA 9056	THIS IS ART (LP)	20

BRAD LUNDY
73	Pyramid PYR 7006	I Could Never Have Another (After Loving You)/It Ain't Always What You Do	12

TED LUNE
60	Philips PB 1068	Mr Custer/Time Machine	6

(see also Michael Medwin 8 Army Game Cast)

LUNG LEG
97	Versuvius POMPLP 007	MAID TO MINX (LP)	15

LARRY LUREX
73	EMI EMI 2030	I Can Hear Music/Goin' Back (demo)	400
73	EMI EMI 2030	I Can Hear Music/Goin' Back (press-out centre; beware of solid-centered counterfeits)	350

(see also Queen)

LURKERS
77	Beggars Banquet BEG 1	Free Admission Single: Shadow/Love Story (p/s, black vinyl)	15
77	Beggars Banquet BEG 1	Free Admission Single: Shadow/Love Story (p/s, reissue, red, blue or white vinyl)	12
77	Beggars Banquet BEG 2	Freak Show/Mass Media Believer (p/s)	10
78	Beggars Banquet BEG 6	Ain't Got A Clue/Ooh Ooh I Love You (p/s, 15,000 with gold flexidisc, 'Chaos Brothers Fulham Fallout Firty Free' [BEG 61/2])	6
78	Beggars Banquet BEGA 2	FULHAM FALLOUT (LP, gatefold sleeve, some with picture disc flexi 'Chaos Brothers Fulham Fallout Fifty Free' [BEG 6 ½] & stickered sleeve)	20

(see also Fulham Furies, Rowdies)

LUSH
89	4AD JAD 911	SCAR (mini-LP)	15
90	4AD CAD 0017	GALA (LP)	30
92	4AD CAD D 2002	SPOOKY (LP as 2x10")	30
94	4AD CAD 2002	SPOOKY (LP)	35
94	4AD CAD 4011	SPLIT (LP)	50
96	4AD CAD 6004	LOVELIFE (LP, clear vinyl)	40
16	4AD LUSH BOX 2	ORIGAMI (5-LP box set)	80

DON LUSHER BAND
55	Decca F 10560	Rock 'n' Roll/On With The Don	20
56	Decca F 10740	Fast And Furious/Let's Do It	8
67	CBS 62883	FROM LUSHER WITH LOVE (LP)	15

LUSTMØRD
81	Sterile SR 3	LUSTMØRD (LP, 1st pressing, white cover with 2 postcards)	60
81	Sterile SR 3	LUSTMØRD (LP, 2nd pressing, grey cover)	35
86	Side Effects SER 07	PARADISE DISOWNED (LP)	20

NELLIE LUTCHER (& HER RHYTHM)
54	Brunswick 05352	Blues In The Night/Breezin' Along With The Breeze	10
55	Brunswick 05437	It's Been Said/Please Come Back	7
55	Brunswick 05497	Whose Honey Are You?/If I Didn't Love You Like I Do	8
60	Capitol CL 15106	My Mother's Eyes/The Heart Of A Clown	6
60	Capitol EAP 20066	REAL GONE (EP)	15
56	Philips BBE 12045	NELLIE LUTCHER (EP)	15
51	Capitol LC 6506	REAL GONE! (10" LP)	30
57	London HA-U 2036	OUR NEW NELLIE (LP)	25

LUTHER & LITTLE EVA
57	Parlophone R 4292	Love Is Strange/Ain't Got No Home	400
57	Parlophone R 4292	Love Is Strange/Ain't Got No Home (78)	100

LUV BUG
86	Roxy!-Ritz TEASE 2	You Can Count On Me/You Can't Have It (p/s)	7

LUV MACHINE
71	Polydor 2058 080	Witches Wand/In The Early Hours	30
71	Polydor 2460 102	LUV MACHINE (LP)	300
06	Rise Above Relics RARLP 001	TURNS YOU ON (2-LP)	20

LUVVERS
66	Parlophone R 5459	The House On The Hill/Most Unlovely	70

(see also Lulu)

MICK LUVZIT
66	Decca F 12421	Long Time Between Lovers/Though I Still Love You	10

LUXURY
91	Spare Beat SBRR 001	LUXURY EP 1 (12")	15
92	Spare Beat SBRR 003	The Silencer/You And Me (12")	15

LUXURY ITEM
77	GTF! NIIM 1	Trade/Brenda Cries Her Eyes Out (p/s)	6

L-VOAG
79	Sesame Songs MOVE 1	MOVE (EP, p/s with handmade labels & insert)	30
81	Axis No. 9	THE WAY OUT (LP, with booklet & poster)	40

(see also Homosexuals)

LYADRIVE
84	Bridge BR 003	Anytime/White Dress (no p/s)	30

LYDS
96	Dig The Fuzz DIG 014	Fly Away With Me/Seperations (p/s)	15

ARTHUR LYMAN GROUP
61	Vogue V 9183	Yellow Bird/Havah Magila	6

Frankie LYMON (& TEENAGERS)

MINT VALUE £

59	Vogue VA 160142	TABOO VOL. 1 (LP, mono)	15
59	Vogue SAV 8002	TABOO VOL. 1 (LP, stereo)	18
61	Vogue VA 160174	TABOO VOL. 2 (LP, also stereo SAV 8003)	15

FRANKIE LYMON (& TEENAGERS)

56	Columbia SCM 5265	Why Do Fools Fall In Love?/Please Be Mine (as Teenagers featuring Frankie Lymon)	60
56	Columbia SCM 5285	I Want You To Be My Girl/I'm Not A Know It All	50
56	Columbia DB 3819	Who Can Explain?/I Promise To Remember	50
56	Columbia DB 3858	Share/The A.B.C.'s Of Love	50
57	Columbia DB 3878	I'm Not A Juvenile Delinquent/Baby, Baby	30
57	Columbia DB 3910	Teenage Love/Paper Castles	40
57	Columbia DB 3942	Miracle In The Rain/Out In The Cold Again	40
57	Columbia DB 3983	Goody Goody/Creation Of Love	20
57	Columbia DB 4028	My Girl/So Goes My Love	25
58	Columbia DB 4073	Thumb Thumb/Footsteps (solo)	30
58	Columbia DB 4134	Mama Don't Allow It/Portable On My Shoulder (solo)	20
59	Columbia DB 4245	Melinda/The Only Way To Love (solo)	20
59	Columbia DB 4295	Up Jumped A Rabbit/No Matter What You've Done (solo)	25
60	Columbia DB 4499	Little Bitty Pretty One/Creation Of Love (solo)	25
66	King KG 1042	Why Do Fools Fall In Love?/I'm Not A Juvenile Delinquent	6
57	Columbia SEG 7662	TEENAGE ROCK (EP)	30
57	Columbia SEG 7694	THE TEENAGERS FEATURING FRANKIE LYMON (EP)	35
57	Columbia SEG 7734	FRANKIE LYMON AND THE TEENAGERS (EP)	30
58	Columbia 33S 1127	FRANKIE LYMON IN LONDON (10" LP, solo)	50
58	Columbia 33S 1134	ROCKIN' WITH FRANKIE LYMON (10" LP, solo)	300

LEWIS LYMON & TEENCHORDS

| 58 | Oriole 45-CB 1419 | Too Young/Your Last Chance | 400 |
| 58 | Oriole CB 1419 | Too Young/Your Last Chance (78) | 75 |

DERMOTT LYNCH

68	Blue Cat BS 101	Hot Shot/I've Got Your Number	100
68	Blue Cat BS 122	I Got Everything/Echo	200
68	Doctor Bird DB 1115	Adults Only/Cool It	50

(see also Trevor, Carl Dawkins, Joe White)

E D LYNCH

| 66 | Fontana TF688 | Sad Songs/Shoe Of True Love | 15 |

KENNY LYNCH

60	HMV POP 751	Mountain Of Love/Why Do You Treat Me This Way?	10
60	HMV POP 786	Slowcoach/You Make Love So Well	8
61	HMV POP 841	So/Love Me	6
61	HMV POP 900	The Story Behind My Tears/Steady Kind	6
61	HMV POP 985	There's Never Been A Girl/Doll Face	6
62	HMV POP 1005	It Would Take A Miracle/Strolling Blues	6
62	HMV POP 1057	Puff/Happy That's Me	15
62	HMV POP 1090	Up On The Roof/Jump On Your Broomstick	10
63	HMV POP 1136	Misery/Shut The Door	10
63	HMV POP 1165	You Can Never Stop Me Loving You/Crazy Crazes	6
64	HMV POP 1280	Stand By Me/Baby It's True	7
64	HMV POP 1321	That's What Little Girls Are Made For/What Am I To You?	6
64	HMV POP 1367	My Own Two Feet/So Much To Love You For	40
65	HMV POP 1430	I'll Stay By You/For Loving You Baby	7
65	HMV POP 1476	Nothing But The Real Thing/Don't Ask Me To Stop Loving You	6
65	HMV POP 1496	Get Out Of My Way/One Look At You	10
66	HMV POP 1534	The World I Used To Know/Come On Come On	7
67	HMV POP 1577	I Just Wanna Love You/It's Too Late	15
67	HMV POP 1604	Movin' Away/Could I Count On You	150
68	Columbia DB 8329	Mister Moonlight/The Other Side Of Dreamland	15
68	Columbia DB 8498	Along Comes Love/Sweet Situation	15
69	Columbia DB 8599	The Drifter/Did I Stay Too Long?	30
70	Columbia DB 8703	In Old Kentucky/Loving You Is Sweeter Than Ever	8
63	HMV 7EG 8820	HEY GIRL (EP)	12
64	HMV 7EG 8855	KENNY LYNCH (EP)	15
65	HMV 7EG 8881	WHAT AM I TO YOU (EP)	12
63	HMV CLP 1635	UP ON THE ROOF (LP, mono)	45
63	HMV CSD 1489	UP ON THE ROOF (LP, stereo)	50

LEE LYNCH (& BLUE ANGELS)

66	Decca F 12375	You Won't See Me/You Know There's Me (as Lee Lynch & Blue Angels)	10
69	Ember EMB S 262	Stay Awhile/Bad Time To Stop Loving Me (p/s)	10
70	Ember EMB S 271	Sweet Woman/Can't Take My Eyes Off You (p/s)	10
70	Ember EMB S 282	Joe Poor Loves Daphne Elizabeth Rich/It's Love (p/s)	10
67	Pye 7N 17363	I'll Hold You In My Heart/Looking Through My Teardrops	10

LYNCH MOB

| 90 | Elektra EKT 81 | WICKED SENSATION (LP) | 30 |
| 92 | Elektra7559 61322 1 | LYNCH MOB (LP) | 40 |

LINDA LYNDELL

| 68 | Stax 601 041 | Bring Your Love Back To Me/Here I Am | 75 |

ANDREA LYNN

| 83 | Sanity STY 007 | Feel Your Love (Mix 1)/(Mix 2)/(Mix 3) (12" stamped white labels) | 50 |

BARBARA LYNN

64	London HLW 9918	Oh! Baby (We Got A Good Thing Goin')/Unfair	40
65	Immediate IM 011	You Can't Buy My Love/That's What A Friend Will Do	45
66	London HLU 10094	You Left The Water Running/Until I'm Free	35

Bobbi LYNN

MINT VALUE £

67	Sue WI 4028	Letter To Mommy And Daddy/Second Fiddle Girl	50
67	Sue WI 4038	You'll Lose A Good Thing/Lonely Heartaches	55
71	Atlantic 2091 133	Take Your Love And Run/(Until Then) I'll Suffer	25
75	Oval OVAL 1006	Letter To Mommy And Daddy/You'll Lose A Good Thing	10
67	Sue ILP 949	THE BARBARA LYNN STORY (LP)	200
76	Oval OVLM 5002	HERE IS (LP)	20

BOBBI LYNN
68	Stateside SS 2088	Earthquake/Opportunity Street	50
68	Stateside SS 2088	Earthquake/Opportunity Street (DJ copy)	75
71	Bell BLL 1168	Earthquake/Opportunity Street (reissue)	10

CHERYL LYNN
78	CBS S CBS 83145	CHERYL LYNN (LP)	15

JESSE LYNN DEAN
79	Creole CR 176	Do It/My Boyfriend's Back In Town (p/s)	20

(see also the Wasps)

DONNA LYNN
64	Capitol CL 15359	Silly Girl/There Goes The Boy I Love With Mary	6

KARI LYNN
61	Oriole CB 1632	Yo Yo/Summer Day	15
61	Oriole CB 1644	You've Got To See Mamma Every Night/Lonesome And Sorry	15

PATTI LYNN
62	Fontana H 370	I See It All Now/Someone Else's Valentine	15
62	Fontana H 391	Johnny Angel/Tonight You Belong To Me	15
62	Fontana 267 247 TF	Tell Me Telstar/Big Big Love	20
62	Fontana TFE 17392	PATTI (EP)	40

TAM(M)I LYNN
66	Atlantic AT 4071	I'm Gonna Run Away From You/The Boy Next Door	70
66	Atlantic AT 4071	I'm Gonna Run Away From You/The Boy Next Door (DJ Copy)	100
71	Mojo 2092 001	I'm Gonna Run Away From You/The Boy Next Door (reissue)	10
71	Mojo 2092 012	That's Understanding/Never No More	6
75	Contempo CS 9026	I'm Gonna Run Away From You/The Boy Next Door (2nd reissue)	8
71	Mojo 2916 007	LOVE IS HERE AND NOW YOU'RE GONE (LP)	30

VERA LYNN
52	Decca F 9927	Auf Wiederseh'n, Sweetheart/From The Time You Say Goodbye	10
54	Decca F 10372	My Son, My Son/Our Heaven On Earth (with Frank Weir & His Saxophone)	15

(see also Johnstone Brothers, Frank Weir & His Orchestra)

GLORIA LYNNE
64	London HLY 9846	I Wish You Love/Through A Long And Sleeping Night	8
64	London HLY 9888	I Should Care/Indian Love Call	8
69	Fontana TF 1017	Problem Child/I've Got To Be Someone	6
59	Top Rank JKP 2024	MEET GLORIA LYNNE (EP, with Wild Bill Davis)	20
60	Top Rank BUY 031	LONELY AND SENTIMENTAL (LP)	25
64	London HA-Y 8112	AT THE LAS VEGAS THUNDERBIRD (LP, with Herman Foster Trio)	15
65	Fontana TL 5215	INTIMATE MOMENTS (LP)	15
72	Mojo 2916 016	HAPPY AND IN LOVE (LP)	25

SUE LYNNE
68	RCA Victor RCA 1724	Reach For The Moon/All Alone	10
69	RCA Victor RCA 1822	You/Don't Pity Me	300
69	RCA Victor RCA 1822	You/Don't Pity Me (DJ copy)	400
69	RCA Victor RCA 1874	Baby Baby Baby/You Lose Again	7

PHIL LYNOTT
80	Vertigo PHIL 1	SOLO IN SOHO (LP, picture disc, die-cut sleeve)	15

(see also Thin Lizzy, Gary Moore & Phil Lynott, John Sykes, Rockers)

JACKIE LYNTON
61	Piccadilly 7N 35012	Over The Rainbow/High In The Sky	6
62	Piccadilly 7N 35055	Don't Take Away Your Love/Wishful Thinking	8
62	Piccadilly 7N 35064	All Of Me/I'd Steal	7
63	Piccadilly 7N 35107	I Believe/The Girl In The Wood	7
63	Piccadilly 7N 35140	Jeannie With The Light Brown Hair/Teddy Bear's Picnic	7
63	Piccadilly 7N 35156	I'm Talkin' About You/Lawdy Miss Clawdy	6
65	Decca F 12052	Three Blind Mice/Corrina Corrine	6
67	Columbia DB 8097	He'll Have To Go/Only You	10
67	Columbia DB 8180	Decision/Sporting Life	10
67	Columbia DB 8224	Answer Me/I Never Loved A Girl Like You	25
79	Thumb TR003	Dan (The Hedgehog Song)/Farting With The Famous	8
74	WWA WWA 012	THE JACKIE LYNTON ALBUM (LP)	15

(see also Savoy Brown Blues Band)

LYNX
78	ST Products SRTS/78/CUS 112	See The Light/C.I.A. (no p/s, 500 only)	250

LYNYRD SKYNYRD
76	MCA MCA 251	Free Bird/Sweet Home Alabama/Double Trouble (p/s)	8
76	MCA MCA 275	Free Bird (Edit)/Gimme Three Steps (p/s)	8
74	MCA MCG 3502	PRONOUNCED LEH-NERD SKIN-NERD (LP, gatefold sleeve)	20
74	MCA MCF 2547	SECOND HELPING (LP)	20
77	MCA MCG 3525	STREET SURVIVORS (LP, gatefold sleeve with tour dates on inner sleeve)	15

BARBARA LYON
55	Columbia SCM 5186	I Love To Dance With You/Yes You Are	10
55	Columbia SCM 5207	Whisper/Where You Are	10
56	Columbia SCM 5232	Band Of Gold/Such A Day	10

Richard LYON

MINT VALUE £

56	Columbia SCM 5276	Puppy Love/The Birds And The Bees	8
56	Columbia DB 3826	It's Better In The Dark/A Heart Without A Sweetheart	6
56	Columbia DB 3865	Falling In Love/Letter To A Soldier	15
60	Triumph RGM 1027	My Charlie/Tell Me	40
56	Columbia SEG 7640	MY FOUR FRIENDS (EP)	15

RICHARD LYON
59	Fontana H 206	All My Own/Private Eye	22

SUE LYON
62	MGM 1159	Lolita Ya Ya/LEROY HOLMES : Main Theme From Lolita	10

(See also Leroy Holmes)

LYONS & MALONE
69	Jay Boy BOY 9	Doctor Gentle/She's Alright	60

LYRICS
67	Coxsone CS 7003	A Get It/KEN PARKER: How Strong	75
68	Coxsone CS 7067	Music Like Dirt/TONETTES: I Give It To You	150
70	Randy's RAN 504	Give Thanks And Praises/TOMMY McCOOK: Get Ready	15
71	Randy's RAN 511	Give Thanks/RANDY'S ALL STARS: Give - Version	15

(see also Randy's All Stars, Viceroys, Jackie Mittoo, Fred Locks)

LARS LYSTEDT SEXTET
64	Realm REP 4004	LARS LYSTEDT SEXTET (EP)	10

JIMMY LYTELL
59	London HL 8873	Hot Cargo/A Blues Serenade	10

JOHNNY LYTLE
68	Minit MLF 11006	Gonna Get That Boat (Parts 1 & 2)	15

HUMPHREY LYTTELTON (& HIS BAND)
SINGLES
51	Saturn EGX 105	When The Saints Go Marching In/Careless Love (78, picture disc)	60
53	Parlophone MSP 6001	Out Of The Gallion/The Old Grey Mare	10
53	Parlophone MSP 6034	Shake It And Break It/Jail Break	10
54	Parlophone MSP 6076	East Coast Trot/Breeze	10
56	Tempo A 10	When The Saints Go Marching In/Careless Love	8
57	Parlophone R 4333	Early Call (Bermondsey Bounce)/Creole Serenade	10
58	Parlophone CMSP 41	Bad Penny Blues/Baby Doll (export issue)	20
59	Parlophone R 4519	Saturday Jump/The Bear Steps Out	8

EPs
55	Tempo EXA 1	HUMPHREY LYTTELTON & HIS BAND (EP)	10

ALBUMS : LPS
53	Parlophone PMD 1006	JAZZ CONCERT (10" LP)	30
54	Parlophone PMC 1012	HUMPH AT THE CONWAY (LP)	30
55	Parlophone PMD 1032	JAZZ AT THE ROYAL FESTIVAL HALL (10" LP)	20
56	Parlophone PMD 1035	JAZZ SESSION WITH HUMPH (10" LP)	15
56	Parlophone PMD 1044	HUMPH SWINGS OUT (10" LP)	25
57	Parlophone PMD 1049	HERE'S HUMPH (10" LP)	15
58	Parlophone PMD 1052	KATH MEETS HUMPH (10" LP, with Kathy Stobart)	20
58	Parlophone PMC 1070	HUMPH IN PERSPECTIVE (LP)	20
58	Decca LK 4276	I PLAY AS I PLEASE (LP)	20
59	Parlophone PMC 1110	TRIPLE EXPOSURE (LP)	70
54	Esquire 32-007	HUMPHREY LYTTELTON AND HIS BAND (LP)	20
60	Columbia 33SX 1239	BLUES IN THE NIGHT (LP)	20
60	Columbia 33SX 1305	HUMPH PLAYS STANDARDS (LP)	20
60	Columbia 33SX 1364	HUMPH MEETS CAB (LP)	30
61	Columbia 33SX 3382	HUMPH RETURNS TO THE CONWAY (LP)	18
62	Columbia 33SX 1484	LATE NIGHT FINAL (LP)	18

(see also Shirley Abicair, George Brown, Helen Shapiro, Radiohead)

M

MABEL
78	Sonet SON 2147	Boom Boom/FBI On The Nail (p/s)	6

MOMS MABLEY
69	Mercury MF 1127	Abraham, Martin And John/Sunny	12
71	Mercury 6052 109	That's Pops/I Surrender Dear	6

WILLIE MABON
64	Sue WI 320	Got To Have Some/Why Did It Happen To Me	50
65	Sue WI 331	Just Got Some/That's No Big Thing	50
65	Sue WI 382	I'm The Fixer/Some More	50

MABRAK
78	Different GET A101	DRUM TALK (mixed by King Tubby) (LP, cover laminated front and back)	150

DEBBIE MAC
80	Active ACT 1	Hots For You/Words (promo only)	8

SPENCER MAC
70	Penny Farthing PEN 723	Blues Up In Down Town/Ka Ka Kabya Mow Mow	100
70	Penny Farthing PEN 742	Commuter/Better By You - Better By Me	60

MACABRE
87	Vinyl Solution SOL 18	GRIM REALITY (LP, with insert)	18

Glo MACARI

			MINT VALUE £
89	Vinyl Solution SOL 020	GLOOM (LP)	15

GLO MACARI
| 65 | Piccadilly 7N 35218 | He Knows I Love Him Too Much/I've Lost You | 15 |
| 71 | Columbia DB 8821 | Looking For Love/People Like You | 15 |

NEIL MACARTHUR
69	Deram DM 225	She's Not There/World Of Glass	25
69	Deram DM 262	Don't Try To Explain/Without Her	15
69	Deram DM 275	It's Not Easy/12.29	15

(see also Colin Blunstone, Zombies)

MACARTHUR PARK
| 70 | Columbia DB 8683 | Taffeta Rose/Sammy | 12 |
| 71 | Philips 6006 086 | Lottie Lottie/Love Is Coming | 6 |

(see also Shadows)

MACATTACK
| 86 | Baad! Records 12HIP1AZ | ART OF DRUMS (12" EP) | 15 |

DAVID MACBETH
| 59 | Pye Nixa 7N 15231 | Mr. Blue/Here's A Heart | 7 |
| 62 | Piccadilly 7N 35072 | Have I Told You Lately That I Love You/A Brother Like You | 6 |

MACC LADS
86	Hectic House HHS 1	EH UP! MACC LADS (EP)	8
85	FM Revolver FMLP 56	BEER AND SEX AND CHIPS'N'GRAVY (LP, white vinyl)	15
88	FM Revolver WKFMLP 115	LIVE AT LEEDS (LP, blue vinyl)	15

MACCABEES
06	Fiction 170 404-3	Preciosu Time (Lamacq Live Session)/X-Ray (Filthy Dukes Society Remix (picture disc)	10
06	Fierce Panda NIN 180	Latchmere/Bicycles (p/s)	8
06	Promise PROM 001	X-Ray/Lego	15
06	Fiction 170 708-6	First Love/Just Like The Rain/Diamond Solitare	8
08	Fiction 174 653-4	Toothpaste/Kisses/Mary (Live At The Roundhouse) (picture disc)	30
09	Fiction 2710467	CAN YOU GIVE IT (box set 2 x 7" with CD)	20
12	Fiction 2791611	Pelican/World Asleep	8
12	Fiction 2796568	Feel To Follow/Feel To Follow (Casually Here Mix)	8
15	Secret 7" S724	Go (100 only, each with unique art sleeve)	40
09	Fiction 2703065	WALL OF ARMS (LP)	25
15	Fiction COLOUR LP 1	COLOUR IT IN (LP, numbered, black and white cover)	80
15	Fiction COLOUR LP 2	COLOUR IT IN (LP, colour cover)	80
12	Fiction 2787390	GIVEN TO THE WILD (2-LP)	75
15	Fiction MACC4001	MARKS TO PROVE IT (LP)	25
17	Fiction MACCBOX 1	THE COMPLETE COLLECTION (4-LP box set, with 12" and DVD)	100

EWAN MACCOLL
58	Topic 10T 26	BARRACK ROOM BALLADS (10" LP)	20
58	Topic 10T 36	BOLD SPORTSMEN ALL (10" LP, with A.L. Lloyd)	20
58	Topic 10T 50	STILL I LOVE HIM (10" LP with booklet, with Isla Cameron)	20
60	Topic 12T 41	STREETS OF SONG (LP, with Dominic Behan, with booklet and original blue label)	15
62	Topic 12T 79	THE JACOBITE REBELLIONS (LP, with original blue label)	15
64	Topic 12T 103	ENGLISH AND SCOTTISH FOLK BALLADS (LP, with A.L. Lloyd, initial pressing with blue label & booklet)	15
64	Topic 12T 103	ENGLISH AND SCOTTISH FOLK BALLADS (LP, with A.L. Lloyd)	15
67	Topic 12T 130	BUNDOOK BALLADS (LP, originally with blue label)	15
67	Argo ZFB 12	SOLO FLIGHT (LP; reissued 1972)	15
67	Xtra 1052	BLOW BOYS BLOW - SONGS OF THE SEA (LP, with A.L. Lloyd)	15
68	Argo (Z)DA 85	THE WANTON MUSE (LP, with booklet)	15

(see also A.L. Lloyd)

EWAN MACCOLL & PEGGY SEEGER (& CHARLES PARKER)
57	Topic 10T 13	SHUTTLE AND CAGE (10" LP)	20
61	Topic 12T 16	CHORUS FROM THE GALLOWS (LP, original pressing with blue label, insert)	15
64	Topic 12T 104	STEAM WHISTLE BALLADS (LP, blue label)	15
64	Topic 12T 104	STEAM WHISTLE BALLADS (LP, later reissue with booklet)	15
65	Argo RG 474	THE BALLAD OF JOHN AXON (LP, by Ewan MacColl & Charles Parker)	18
67	Topic 12T 147	THE MANCHESTER ANGEL (LP, original pressing with blue label)	18
67	Argo DA 140	THE BIG HEWER - A RADIO BALLAD BY EWAN MacCOLL, PEGGY SEEGER, CHARLES PARKER (LP, documentary with music)	20
67	Argo (Z)DA 66	LONG HARVEST 1 (LP)	15
67	Argo (Z)DA 67	LONG HARVEST 2 (LP)	15
67	Argo (Z)DA 68	LONG HARVEST 3 (LP)	15
67	Argo (Z)DA 69	LONG HARVEST 4 (LP)	15
67	Argo RG 502	SINGING THE FISHING (LP, with Charles Parker)	25
67	Argo DA 142	SINGING THE FISHING (LP, reissue, with Charles Parker)	18
60s	XTRA 1054	SCOTS BALLADS (LP)	20
60s	Folkways FW 8958	SONGS OF ROBERT BURNS (LP)	30
70	Argo DA 133	THE TRAVELLING PEOPLE (LP, with Charles Parker)	15
71	Argo DA 136	ON THE EDGE (LP)	15

(see also Peggy Seeger, A.L. Lloyd, Isla Cameron)

KIRSTY MACCOLL
79	Stiff BUY 47	They Don't Know/Motor On (yellow label, 'plug copy' promo, p/s)	15
79	Stiff BUY 47	They Don't Know/Motor On (yellow label, push-out centre p/s)	7
79	Stiff BUY 57	You Caught Me Out/Boys (with Boomtown Rats, unreleased, demos only)	50
81	Polydor POSP 225	Keep Your Hands Off My Baby/I Don't Need You (p/s)	7
81	Polydor POSP 368	You Still Believe In Me/Queen Of The High Teas (p/s)	15
83	Stiff BUY DJ 190	Terry/Quietly Alone (Pink promo. "A" label)	15
84	Stiff BUY 216	A New England/Patrick (British flag p/s)	10

Galt MaCDERMOT

MINT VALUE £

85	Polydor SEPLP 95825 791	KIRSTY MACCOLL (LP)	15

(see also Drug Addix)

GALT MACDERMOT
73	Decca SKLR 5164	TWO GENTLEMEN OF VERONA (LP)	30

GAVIN MACDONALD
72	Regal Zono. SLRZ 1027	LINES (LP, red/silver label)	25

(see also Country Joe & Fish)

RALPH MACDONALD
76	T.K. XL 14030	SOUND OF A DRUM (LP)	15

MACEO & ALL THE KING'S MEN
72	Pye International 7N 25571	Got To Get 'Cha/Thank You For Letting Me Be Myself Again (Part 1)	18
72	Mojo 2916 017	FUNKY MUSIC MACHINE (LP)	30
75	Contempo CRM 114	FUNKY MUSIC MACHINE (LP, reissue)	15

(see also Maceo & The Macks, James Brown, Maceo Parker)

BIG MACEO
62	RCA RCX 203	KINGS OF THE BLUES (EP)	10

MACEO & THE MACKS
87	Urban URB 1	Cross The Tracks (We Better Go Back)/Soul Power (printed die-cut sleeve)	15
87	Urban URBX 1	Cross The Tracks (We Better Go Back) (Extended Version)/Party Part 1/ Soul Power (12", printed die-cut sleeve)	15
74	Polydor 2391 122	US (LP)	30

(see also Maceo & All The King's Men, James Brown)

TEO MACERO
57	Esquire 32-113	TEO (LP)	30

MACEYS WINDOW
72	Parlophone R 5893	It's Getting Harder/Pray For Sister Sunshine	60

CIARAN MAC GOWAN
80	Good Vibrations MAC 1	Little Susi/London Trip (p/s)	6

SHANE MACGOWAN & THE POPES
97	ZTT MACG003P	MORE SONGS ABOUT DRINKING AND THINKING (10" EP, p/s)	15

(see also Pogues, Nick Cave & Shane MacGowan)

MACH HOMMY
17	Daupe! DM SP 022	DOLLAR MENU (12", p/s, 200 copies)	150
17	Daupe! DM SP 022	DOLLAR MENU (12", p/s, green vinyl, 100 copies)	150
17	Daupe! DM SP 022	DOLLAR MENU (12", p/s, grey vinyl, 100 copies)	150
17	Daupe! DM SP 022	DOLLAR MENU (12", p/s, with obi strip, 20 copies)	200

MACHINE MEN
71	AXE 1	Counting Time/Young Blood	15

MACHINE (1)
67	Granta GR 7STD	Stupidity/Please Stay (private pressing)	40

MACHINE (2)
69	Polydor 56760	Spooky's Day Off/Nobody Wants You	18

(see also Swinging Soul Machine)

MACHINE (3)
78	Plastic SRTS/78/CUS/198	Bored With The City/Brown Eyed Girl (100 only, no p/s)	275

MACHINES
78	Wax EAR 1	True Life/Everything's Technical/You Better Hear/Evening Radio (stamped p/s, white labels)	150
96	Gecko 5	True Life/Everything's Technical/You Better Hear/Evening Radio (reissue, pink or orange vinyl)	8

MACHO
78	EMI 2882	I'm A Man/Cose There's Music In The Air	6

ALURA MACK
50s	Poydras 84	Everybody's Man Is Mine/Monkey Blues	8

CHRIS MACK
97	Confetti CO EP 010	RYDIM 4 YA EP (12" as Chris Mac)	25
97	Confetti CODB 03	Plenty More/Get It (Come) (Remix) (12")	30
98	Suspect SUS 001	Every Day/Every Day (12", no artist name on labels)	20
98	First Class FC 002	KA-BOOM EP (12")	35
98	Main Ingredient MAIN 011	Feel Good/Alright/Alright Mix (12")	30

FREDDIE MACK'S EXTRAVEGANZA IN SOUND
73	Contempo C31	People - Part 1 (Vocal)/PArt 2 (Instrumental)	10

FREDDY MACK
67	Rayrik TPMLP 143	LIVE AT TOFT CLUB FOLKSTONE (LP, as Freddy Mack Show, 99 copies only)	300

JOHNNY MACK
70	Columbia Blue Beat DB 116	Reggae All Night Long/A Million Marvellous Feelings	12

LONNIE MACK
63	Stateside SS 207	Memphis/Down In The Dumps	25
63	Stateside SS 226	Wham!/Susie-Q	25
64	Stateside SS 312	Lonnie On The Move/Say Something Nice To Me	18
65	Stateside SS 393	Sa-Ba-Hoola/Chickin' Pickin'	20
67	President PT 127	Where There's A Will/Baby What's Wrong?	7
67	President PT 142	Save Your Money/Snow On The Mountain	7
68	President PT 198	Soul Express/I Found A Love	10
69	Elektra EKSN 45044	Memphis/Why (Edited Version)	10
69	Elektra EKSN 45060	Save Your Money/In The Band	8
71	Elektra EK 45715	Lay It Down/She Even Woke Me Up To Say Goodbye	6
67	President PTL 1004	THE WHAM OF THAT MEMPHIS MAN (LP)	30
69	Elektra EKL 4040	GLAD I'M IN THE BAND (LP, orange label, also stereo EKS 74040)	30
69	Elektra EKS 74050	WHATEVER'S RIGHT (LP, orange label)	30

MACK SISTERS

			MINT VALUE £

MACK SISTERS
56 London HLU 8331 — Long Range Love/Stop What You're Doing ... 60

WARNER MACK
58 Brunswick 05728 — Roc-A-Chicka/Since I Lost You (with Anita Kerr Quartet) ... 200
58 Brunswick 05728 — Roc-A-Chicka/Since I Lost You (with Anita Kerr Quartet) (78) ... 50
58 Decca — Roc-A-Chicka/Since I Lost You (export issue, with Anita Kerr Quartet) ... 60

ANDY MACKAY
75 Island WIP 6243 — Wild Weekend/Walking The Whippet (in promo p/s) ... 6
(see also Roxy Music, Rock Follies)

DUNCAN MACKAY
80 Edge EDGE 5 — Visa/Gin Sing ... 10
80 Edge EDGE 5 — Visa/Gin Sing (12") ... 150
81 Edge EDGE 14 — Sirius II Mark II/In The Pink (no p/s) ... 20
80 Edge HOG 3 — VISA (LP) ... 15

MAHNA MACKAY
69 Parlophone R 5808 — Mah Na Mah Na/Daydream ... 6

RABBIT MACKAY
68 MCA MU 1041 — Hard Time Woman/Candy ... 8
68 MCA MUPS 351 — BUG CLOTH (LP) ... 15

GISELE MACKENZIE
55 HMV 7M 318 — Hard To Get/Boston Fancy ... 8

MACKENZIE JET COMBO
70 Torpedo TOR 18 — Milkman's Theme/Capadulah Recipe ... 30

JUDY MACKENZIE
70 Key KL 005 — JUDY (LP) ... 22
71 Key KL 009 — PEACE AND LOVE AND FREEDOM (LP, with poster) ... 22

MACKENZIES
86 Ron Johnson ZRON 9 — New Breed/Dog's Breakfast (p/s) ... 6

KEN MACKINTOSH (& HIS ORCHESTRA)
57 HMV POP 327 — Almost Paradise/Rock Man Rock ... 15
57 HMV POP 358 — Poni Tail/Keep It Movin' ... 10
57 HMV POP 396 — Marching Along To The Blues/Six-Five Blues ... 8
57 HMV POP 426 — Raunchy/Mojo ... 10
58 HMV POP 441 — The Stroll/The Swingin' Shepherd Blues ... 8
56 HMV 7EG 8170 — TEENAGER'S SPECIAL (EP) ... 15
55 HMV DLP 1093 — KEN MACKINTOSH (10" LP) ... 15
58 HMV DLP 1178 — ONE NIGHT STAND (10" LP) ... 15

PETE MACLAINE & CLAN
63 Decca F 11699 — Yes I Do/U.S. Mail ... 10

DOUGIE MACLEAN
88 Dunkeld DUN 008 — REAL ESTATE (LP) ... 20

JOHN MACLEOD SOUND
67 Spectrum SP 12 — Russian Roulette/West Wind ... 6
60s Transatlantic TRASP 12 — Russian Roulette/West Wind ... 6

JOHN MACLEOD'S FIRST XI
66 Fontana TF 696 — Don't Shoot The Ref/Tomato Crisps ... 7

ANGUS MACLISE
87 Fierce FRIGHT 010 — Trance (1-sided, with 'Dopechoc' & badge) ... 10

PATRICK MACNEE & HONOR BLACKMAN
64 Decca F 11843 — Kinky Boots/Let's Keep It Friendly ... 35
(see also Honor Blackman)

MADELINE MACNEIL
69 Skyline DD 103 — PATCHWORK (LP) ... 30

JOSH MACRAE
60 Top Rank JAR 290 — Talkin' Army Blues/Talkin' Guitar Blues ... 6
60 Pye NEP 24131 — WALKIN', TALKIN', SINGIN' (EP) ... 10
60 Top Rank JKP 2061 — JOSH MACRAE (EP) ... 10

MADAME DRACULA
73 Sunbeam SB 004 — Big Ten/Version ... 50
(see also Girlie)

JOHNNY MADARA
57 HMV POP 389 — Be My Girl/Lovesick ... 10

OSIBERT MADDO
84 Sunsplash SNS 003 — King In The Ring/PAPA SAN: Ghetto Life (12") ... 100

MAD DOG (1)
74 Chappell LPC 1053 — POP SOUNDS (LP, library edition) ... 40

MAD DOG (2)
85 Brainy CUTN 1 — Sheriff/You're A Beautiful Sight (p/s) ... 50
86 Stud STUDLP1 — MAD DOG (LP) ... 40

JOHNNY MADDOX (& HIS ORCHESTRA)
55 London MSD 1503/1504 — Nickelodeon Tango/Solitude (unissued, demos only) ... 30
55 London HL 8134 — The Crazy Otto - Medley/Humoresque ... 15
55 London HLD 8203 — Do, Do, Do/When You Wore A Tulip (And I Wore A Big Red Rose) ... 15
56 London HLD 8277 — Hop Scotch Boogie/Hands Off ... 25
56 London HLD 8347 — Heart And Soul/Dixieland Band ... 20
58 London HLD 8540 — Yellow Dog Blues/Sugar Train ... 15
59 London HLD 8826 — The Hurdy Gurdy Song/Old Fashioned Love ... 10
55 London RE-P 1020 — PRESENTING JOHNNY MADDOX AND THE RHYTHMASTERS (EP) ... 12
55 London RE-P 1040 — PRESENTING JOHNNY MADDOX AND THE RHYTHMASTERS NO. 2 (EP) ... 12
58 London RE-D 1150 — HONKY TONK JAZZ (EP) ... 10

Rose MADDOX

MINT VALUE £

ROSE MADDOX
59	Capitol CL 15023	Gambler's Love/What Makes Me Hang Around 10

MADE IN BRITAIN
91	White MIB001	Break The Crunch/Mellow Infection (12") 50

MADE IN ENGLAND (1)
81	Gargoyle GARG 1	Dance Of The Warriors/The Quest (p/s) 50

MADE IN ENGLAND (2)
86	Red Bus RBUS 2208	Prospects/Stay Sharp (A-side with Ray Dorset, p/s) 6

(see also Ray Dorset)

MADE IN SHEFFIELD
67	Fontana TF 871	Amelia Jane/Right Satisfied 30

(see also Joe Cocker, Grease Band, Chris Stainton)

MADE IN SWEDEN
69	Sonet SLP 71	MADE IN SWEDEN (LP) 40
69	Sonet SLP 2504	SNAKES IN A HOLE (LP) 30
70	Sonet SLP 2506	LIVE AT THE GOLDEN CIRCLE (LP) 30
70	Sonet SLP 2512	MADE IN ENGLAND (LP) 35
71	Sonet SNTF 621	MAD RIVER (LP) 45

MAD HATTERS
76	Epic EPC 4151	The Humphrey Song/Loving You Ain't Easy 6
76	Epic EPC 460	Love Potion No. 9/Loser 8

MAD JOCKS & ENGLISHMEN
80	Wild Dog DOGLP 18	TONGUE IN CHEEK (LP) 18
80s	Wild Dog DOGLP 50	THUD & BLUNDER (LP) 18

MAD LADS (JAMAICA)
69	Coxsone CS 7099	Losing You/WINSTON JARRETT: Peck Up A Pagan 180

MAD LADS (U.S.)
65	Atlantic AT 4051	Don't Have To Shop Around/Tear Maker 18
66	Atlantic AT 4083	I Want Someone/Nothing Can Break Through 18
66	Atlantic 584 038	Sugar Sugar/Get Out Of My Life Woman 25

MADLIB
03	Blue Note 7243 5 36447 1 0	SHADES OF BLUE (2-LP) 35
14	Blue Note 0602537781997	SHADES OF BLUE (2-LP, reissue, 180gm) 25
19	Keep Cool 190759349212BT	BANDANA (LP, with Freddie Gibbs, variant cover by Tom J Newall, 250 only, signed) 60

(see also Madvillain)

MADNESS
SINGLES
79	2-Tone TT 3	The Prince/Madness (paper label, company sleeve) 20
79	2-Tone TT 3	The Prince/Madness (later blue plastic label, company sleeve) 100
79	Stiff BUY IT 56	One Step Beyond/Mistakes/Nutty Theme (12", p/s) 15
79	Stiff MAD 1	Don't Quote Me On That/Swan Lake (12", promo only, 500 copies) 50
80	Stiff BUY 84	Baggy Trousers/The Business (p/s, blue labels instead of green, Mike Barson not credited as songwriter) 75
81	Stiff BUY IT 112	Grey Day/Baggy Trousers/Take It Or Leave It/Un Paso Adelante (12", p/s, white or yellow labels) 20
81	Stiff BUY 112	Grey Day/Memories (p/s, rare edition with legs instead of feet on label) 15
82	Stiff GRAB 1	THE MADNESS PACK (6 x 7" in clear plastic folder) 20
85	Zarjazz JAZZF 7	Uncle Sam/Please Don't Go ('flag bag' edition) 20
85	Zarjazz JAZZF 7	Uncle Sam/Please Don't Go/Insanity Over Christmas (picture disc) 18
86	Zarjazz JAZZ B9-12	(Waiting For) The Ghost-Train/Maybe In Another Life/Seven Year Scratch (12", p/s with 8-page booklet) 10
86	Zarjazz JAZZS 9	(Waiting For) The Ghost Train/Maybe In Another Life (square picture disc) 45
86	Strange Fruit SFPS 0007	THE PEEL SESSIONS (12" p/s, brown label) 10
86	Zarjazz JAZZY 8	Sweetest Girl/Jenny (A Portrait Of) (picture disc, stickered PVC sleeve) 18
87	Virgin VS 876	Our House/Walking With Mr. Wheeze 15
88	Virgin VSX 1054	I Pronounce You/4BF/Patience/11th Hour (as The Madness, box with badge, 2 cards & sticker) 8
88	Virgin VS 1078	What's That/Be Good Boy (p/s) 8
88	Virgin VST 1078	What's That/Be Good Boy/Flashings (12", p/s) 10
88	Virgin VSJ 1078	What's That/Flashings ('Jig' disc, 1st of 2 interlocking shaped picture discs) 30
88	Virgin VSS 1078	What's That/Be Good Boy 'Saw' disc, 2nd of 2 interlocking shaped picture discs) 30
89	2-Tone TTP1	THE SPECIALS: Rudi, A Message To You/Ghost Town//SELECTER: On My Radio/ MADNESS: One Step Beyond (promo, 40 only) 200
92	Go! Discs GOD 93	The Harder They Come/Tomorrow's Just Another Day/Take It Or Leave It (p/s, blue labels) 8
99	Virgin VSLH 1737	Love Struck/We Are Love (Jukebox issue) 10
99	Virgin VSLH 1740	Johnny The Horse/I Was The One (Jukebox issue) 12
05	V2 VVR55033247	Shame And Scandal/Shame And Scandal (Dub Mix) p/s, 2500 only) 6

ALBUMS
79	Stiff SEEZ 17	ONE STEP BEYOND (LP, first pressing, sleeve lists 'Bed & Breakfast' not 'Bed & Breakfast Man') 20
80	Stiff SEEZ 29	ABSOLUTELY (LP, first pressing with slightly different front cover image) 15
82	M.I.S. (no cat. no)	THIRTY MINUTES OF CULTURE (fan club cassette) 25
84	Stiff PSEEZ 53	KEEP MOVING (LP, picture disc, U.S. running order) 15
85	Zarjazz JZLP1	MAD NOT MAD (LP, withdrawn edition, alternative sleeve omitting gold on front) 75
86	M.I.S. (no cat. no)	SONGS FROM AROUND THE PLONET (fan club cassette, live compilation) 35
90	Virgin VVIP 107	IT'S MADNESS (LP, 1000 copies) 70
90	Virgin TPAK 8	ONE STEP BEYOND/ABSOLUTELEY/RISE & FALL (3-CD box set, picture discs) 50
92	Virgin V2692	DIVINE MADNESS (2-LP, gatefold) 25
92	Virgin MDV 2692	DIVINE (Mini disc) 20
92	Go! Discs 828 367-1	MADSTOCK (LP, with picture inner sleeve) 20

MADONNA

MINT VALUE £

94	Simply Vinyl SVLP 309	DIVINE (LP, reissue)	15
99	Virgin MADBOX 2	THE LOT (6-CD box set of first 6 studio albums)	40
09	Lucky Seven 003SE	THE LIBERTY OF NORTON FOLGATE (LP, 3-CD box set including poster, membership card, rule book, letter & badge)	50
09	Lucky Seven LUCKY7003LP	THE LIBERTY OF NORTON FOLGATE (LP)	25
10	Size 12 SIZE 1001	ONE STEP BEYOND (LP, reissue as 2 x 10")	25

FLEXIDISCS

81	Lyntone LYN 10208	Take It or Leave It (free with Take It Or Leave It magazine)	10
81	Lyn. LYN 10353/EVENT 2	Event - The Madness (with Event magazine)	10
82	Lyntone LYN 11546	My Girl (Ballad) (hard vinyl test pressing of Flexipop free flexi)	200
82	Lyntone LYN 10719	Carols On 45 (fan club disc)	10
84	Lyntone LYN 15280/1	Insanity Over Christmas/Visit To Castle Dracstein (fan club disc)	10
85	Lyntone LYN 16981	Merry Christmas: Samantha (live)/Mad Not Mad (live)	10
85	Lyntone LYN 16676	From Us ... To You (Mad Not Mad tour disc, with tour programme)	18
86	Lyntone LYN 18201	Last Christmas With Madness:Ghost Train (The Demo)/The Final Goodbye (fan club disc)	20

(see also Argonauts, Fink Brothers)

MADONNA

SINGLES : SIRE SINGLES

82	Sire W 9899	Everybody/Everybody (Dub Version) (WEA sleeve, no p/s)	175
82	Sire W 9899T	Everybody/Everybody (Dub Version) (12", WEA sleeve, no p/s)	125
83	Sire W 9522	Lucky Star (Edit)/I Know It ('sunglasses' p/s with no Jellybean credit on label)	1000
83	Sire W 9522T	Lucky Star (Full Length Version)/I Know It (12", 'sunglasses' p/s;	50
83	Sire W 9522TV	Lucky Star (U.S Remix)/I Know It (12", stickered plain white die-cut sleeve)	35
83	Sire W 9405	Holiday (Edit)/Think Of Me ('train' p/s)	6
84	Sire W 9522T	Lucky Star (Full Length Version)/I Know It (12" reissue, stickered 'TV screen' p/s)	10
84	Sire W 9522T	Lucky Star (Full Length Version)/I Know It (12" reissue, stickered 'TV screen' p/s, with poster)	30
84	Sire W 9260F	Borderline (Edit)/Physical Attraction//Holiday (Edit)/Think Of Me ('map' p/s, double pack with European p/s, copies of "Holiday", shrinkwrapped & stickered: beware of counterfeits with less than Mint picture sleeves)	100
84	Sire W 9210T	Like A Virgin (U.S. Dance Remix)/Stay (12", p/s, with poster & sticker)	35
85	Sire W 9083T	Material Girl (Jellybean Dance Mix)/Pretender (12", with poster p/s)	35
85	Sire WA6323	Crazy For You/Sammy Hagar "I'll Fall In Love Again" (7" Madonna shaped picture Disc in stickered PVC sleeve. No p/s.)	50
85	Sire WA6323	Crazy For You/Sammy Hagar "I'll Fall In Love Again" (Uncut 7" Picture disc on 10" vinyl in PVC sleeve. No p/s)	800
85	Sire W 8934P	Into The Groove/Shoo-Be-Doo (heart-shaped picture disc with 2 stickers)	40
85	Sire W 8934P	Into The Groove/Shoo-Be-Doo (12" uncut heart-shaped picture disc, very few copies)	1000
85	Sire W 8934P	Into The Groove/Everybody/Shoo-Be-Doo (12", p/s, with poster)	25
85	Sire W 9405T	Holiday (Full Length Version 6.08)/Think Of Me (12", 'cross earring' p/s reissue)	15
85	Sire W 9405P	Holiday (Full Length Version 6.08)/Think Of Me (12", picture disc)	30
85	Sire W 8881P	Angel (Edit)/Burning Up (shaped pic disc, with cardboard plinth)	45
85	Sire W 8881P	Angel (Edit)/Burning Up (shaped pic disc)	35
85	SireW8881P	Angel (Edit)/Burning Up (Uncut 7" pic disc on 12" vinyl in PVC sleeve, no p/s)	1000
85	Sire A6585	Gambler/Black 'n' Blue:Nature Of The Beach (7" p/s)	7
85	Sire QA6585	Gambler/Black 'n' Blue:Nature Of The Beach (7" foldout poster p/s)	30
85	Sire TA6585	Gambler (Extended Dance Mix)/(Instrumental Remix) Black 'n' Blue: Nature Of The Beach (12" p/s)	20
85	Sire W 8848TF	Dress You Up (12" Formal Mix)/(Casual Instrumental)/I Know It (12", foldout p/s with Virgin Tour Video Advert on back)	35
85	Sire W 8848P	Dress You Up/I Know It ('Xmas tree star'-shaped picture disc)	35
85	Sire W 8848P	Dress You Up (Uncut 7" picture disc on 12" vinyl, no p/s)	750
86	Sire W 9560P	Borderline/Physical Attraction (Madonna-shaped picture disc in pvc sleeve no p/s)	50
86	Sire W 9560P	Borderline/Physical Attraction (Uncut 7" picture disc on 12" vinyl,pvc sleeve no p/s)	1000
86	Sire W 8717T(W)	Live To Tell (LP Version)/(Edit)/(Instrumental) (12", p/s, with poster)	20
86	Sire W8636T	Papa Don't Preach(Extended Version)/(LP Vesion) Ain't No Big Deal (12" with poster in stickered p/s)	20
86	Sire W 8636T(W)	Papa Don't Preach (Extended Version)/Papa Don't Preach (LP Version)/ Ain't No Big Deal (12", p/s, initially with free poster)	15
86	Sire W 8636TP	Papa Don't Preach (Extended Remix)/Ain't No Big Deal (LP Version)/ Papa Don't Preach (LP version) (12", picture disc	20
86	Sire W 8550TP	True Blue (Extended Dance Version)/Holiday (Full Length Version) (12" picture disc)	20
87	Sire W 8378TP	La Isla Bonita (Extended Remix)/(Extended Instrumental) (12", picture disc)	20
87	Sire W 8341TX	Who's That Girl (Extended Version)/Who's That Girl (Dub Mix)/ White Heat (12" Remix) (12", p/s)	20
87	Sire W 8341TP	Who's That Girl (Extended Version)/White Heat (12", picture disc; beware of original decaying PVC sleeves)	40
87	Sire W 8224	Causing A Commotion (Silver Screen Single Mix)/Jimmy Jimmy (withdrawn p/s, with sticker stating 'Free personality poster W 8224W', most destroyed when withdrawn in favour of 'badge' insert, no poster))	100
87	Sire W 8224	Causing A Commotion (Silver Screen Single Mix)/Jimmy Jimmy (p/s, with badge shrinkwrapped to p/s)	60
87	Sire W 8224TP	Causing A Commotion (Silver Screen Mix)/Causing A Commotion (Movie House Mix)/Jimmy Jimmy (Fade) (12", picture disc)	15
87	Sire W 8115TW	The Look Of Love/Love Don't Live Here Anymore/I Know It (12", p/s & poster)	15
87	Sire W 8115TP	The Look Of Love/Love Don't Live Here Anymore/I Know It (12", picture disc)	20
89	Sire 925 681-2	Papa Don't Preach (7" Version)/(12" Version)/Pretender (Video)(5" CD-Video p/s)	40
89	Sire W 7539TX	Like A Prayer (12" Dance Mix)/(Churchapella Mix)/(7"Remix Edit) (12", p/s)	10
89	Sire W 7539TP	Like A Prayer (12" Extended Remix)/(12" Club Version)/ Act Of Contrition (12", picture disc)	15
89	Sire W 7539CD	Like A Prayer/(12" Extended Remix)/(12" Club Version)/Act Of Contrition (3" Gatefold CD)	12
89	Sire W 2948X	Express Yourself (7" Remix)/The Look Of Love (LP) (poster p/s)	25

MADONNA

MINT VALUE £

Year	Catalog	Description	Value
89	Sire W 2948C	Express Yourself (7" Remix)/The Look Of Love (LP) ('jeans zipper' p/s)	40
89	Sire W 2948TP	Express Yourself/(Non-Stop Express Mix)/(Stop + Go Dubs) (12", 'nude' picture disc)	15
89	Sire W 2883TP	Cherish (Extended Version)/(7" Version)/Supernatural (12")	10
89	Sire W 2668TW	Dear Jessie/Till Death Do Us Part/Holiday (12" Version) (12", poster p/s)	12
89	Sire W 2268CDX	Dear Jessie/Till Death Do Us Part/Holiday (12" Version) (CD, picture disc)	125
89	Sire 925 681-2	Papa Don't Preach (7" Version)/(12" Version)/Pretender (LP Version)/ Papa Don't Preach (CD Video)	35
90	Sire W 9851TW	Vogue (12" Version)/Keep It Together (12" Remix) (12", p/s, with 'Face of the 80s' poster)	15
90	Sire W 9851TX	Vogue (12" Version)/Vogue (Strike-A-Pose Dub) (12", p/s, with 'X-rated' 30" x 20" poster)	20
90	Sire W 9851TP	Vogue (12" Version)/Keep It Together (12" Remix) (12", picture disc)	20
90	Sire W 9789TP	Hanky Panky (Bare Bottom 12" Mix)/(Bare Bones Single Mix)/More (LP Version) (12", picture disc with gatefold insert & foldout poster)	20
91	Sire W 0008P	Crazy For You (Remix)/Keep It Together (Single Remix) (shaped picture disc with plinth & insert)	15
91	Sire W0024TW	Rescue (Titanic Mix)/(Houseboat Mix)/(Titanic Mix) (12" with free poster, p/s)	10
91	Sire W 0037TP	Holiday/True Blue (12", clear vinyl picture disc with insert in PVC sleeve)	15

SINGLES : MAVERICK SINGLES

Year	Catalog	Description	Value
92	Maverick W 0138TP	Erotica (Album Version 5.12)/Erotica (Instrumental 5.12)/Erotica (Radio Edit 4.31) (12", picture disc with gold insert, withdrawn, 138 only)	2500
92	Maverick W 0138TW	Erotica (Album Version 5.12)/Erotica (Instrumental 5.12)/Erotica (Radio Edit 4.31) (12", Free Poster, p/s)	10
92	Maverick W 0146TP	Deeper And Deeper (Shep's Classic 12")/(Shep's Deep Makeover Mix)/ (Shep's Deep Beats)/David's Klub Mix)/David's Deep Mix)/(Shep's Deeper Dub) (12", picture disc)	15
93	Maverick W0154TW	Bad Girl (Edit)/Erotica (William Orbit 12")/Erotica (William Orbit Dub)/ Erotica (Madonna's In My Jeep Mix) (12", Free Poster, p/s)	30
93	Maverick W0168T	Fever (Hot Sweat 12")/(Extended 12")/(Shep's Remedy Dub)/(Murk Boys Miami Mix)/(Murk Boys Deep South Mix)/(Oscar G's Dope Dub) (12" stickered, p/s)	10
95	Warner Bros W0285TX	Bedtime Story (Junior's Sound Factory Mix)/(Junior's Sound Factory Dub/ (Orbital Mix)/Junior's Wet Dream Mix) (12" Glitter Holographic Sleeve)	15

SINGLES : OTHER SINGLES

Year	Catalog	Description	Value
92	Reciever RRSPT 1007	Shine A Light/On The Ground/Little Boy (12", picture disc)	15

ALBUMS

Year	Catalog	Description	Value
85	Sire WX 20P	LIKE A VIRGIN (LP, picture disc in die-cut sleeve)	50
86	Sire WX 54	TRUE BLUE (LP, with tour poster)	15
87	Sire WX 76	YOU CAN DANCE (LP, with poster & gold 'obi')	15
90	Sire 7599 264932	ROYAL BOX (box set with "Immaculate Collection" CD in satin digipak, video, poster & postcards)	75
90	Sire 7599-26440 1	THE IMMACULATE COLLECTION (2-LP)	25
92	Sire WX49	EROTICA (Dirty Version) (2-LP, gatefold, stickered)	25
92	Sire WX49	EROTICA (Clean Version) (2-LP, gatefold, stickered)	25
94	Sire 9362 45767 1	BEDTIME STORIES (LP)	35
95	Sire 9362 46100-1	SOMETHING TO REMEMBER (LP)	40
04	Sire 9362 46847-1	RAY OF LIGHT (Reissue, 2-LP with inner sleeve 180 gram deluxe vinyl, stickered)	20
06	Sire 9362 494601	CONFESSIONS ON A DANCE FLOOR (2-LP, gatefold, pink vinyl)	50
12	Interscope 0602527977515	MDNA (2-LP, 180gm vinyl)	80
15	Interscope 0602547211699	REBEL HEART (2-LP, 200gm vinyl)	35
16	Sire 8122 797358	TRUE BLUE (LP, blue vinyl, 'Sainsbury's' sticker)	60
16	Sire 8122 79731-7	LIKE A PRAYER (LP, red vinyl, 'Sainsburys' sticker)	60
17	Warner Bros. 8122-79735-9	LIKE A VIRGIN (LP, clear vinyl, 'Sainsburys' sticker)	60
17	Maverick/Sire/Warner Bros. 9362-46847-1	RAY OF LIGHT (2-LP, blue vinyl, 'Sainsburys' sticker)	60
18	Maverick/Sire/Warner Bros. 8122-79735-6	EROTICA (2-LP, reissue, white vinyl, 'Sainsburys' sticker)	60

PROMOS

Year	Catalog	Description	Value
85	Sire SAM 251	Into The Groove (Edit) Holiday (Edit) (12" white label, die-cut sleeve, stickered)	100
87	Sire SAM 412	Spotlight (Dub)/Holiday (Dub)/Over And Over (Dub)/Into The Groove (Dub) 12" white label, die-cut WEA sleeve, no p/s)	50
89	Sire SAM 641	Keep It Together (12" Remix)/(Dub)/(Extended Remix)/(12" Mix)/ (Bonus Beats)/(Instrumental) (12")	15
90	Sire SAM 659	Vogue (12" Version)/Vogue (Strike A Pose Dub) (12")	15
90	Sire SAM 738	Justify My Love (Remix) (One-sided 12" die-cut sleeve, p/s)	15
91	Sire SAM 800	Holiday (Edit) (CD)	50
92	Sire SAM 1103	Erotica (Album Version) (12")	25
92	Sire SAM 1118	Deeper And Deeper (Edit)/Shep's Deep Makeover Mix)/Shep's Classic 12") David's Klub Mix)/David's Love Dub)/David's Deeper Dub) 12" white label no p/s	25
93	Sire SAM 1131	Fever (Hot Sweat 12" Mix)/(Shep's Remedy Dub)/(Dub One)/(Dub Two)/(Bugged Out Bonzai Mix)/(Peggy's Nightclub Mix)/(Radio Edit)/(Murk Boys Miami Mix)/(Murk Boys Deep South Mix)/(Album Version)/(Oscar G's Dope Dub)/(Back To The Dub One)/(Back To The Dub Two) (2x12")	50
95	Warner Bros SAM 1653	Human Nature: The Remixes/(Mixes) (12", stickered title sleeve)	15
95	Warner Bros SAM 1526	Bedtime Story (Junior's Sound Factory Mix)/(Junior's Sound Factory Dub)/ (Orbital Mix)/Junior's Wet Dream Mix)	15
96	Sire SAM 1880	Love Don't Live Here Anymore (Mark!s It's A Girl Dub)/(Mark!s It's A Boy Dub)/(Mark!s Full On Vocal) (12")	25
96	Warner Bros SAM 1982	Don't Cry For Me Argentina (Miami Mix)/(Mixes) (12", title sleeve)	10
98	Warner Bros 3331000037	Drowned World/Substitute For Love (BT & Sasha's Bucklodge Ashram Remix)/ Sky Fits Heaven (Sasha Remix)/Substitute For Love (Victor Calderone Remix Edit) (12")	20
98	Sire SAM 3173	Frozen (Extended Club Mix)/(Stereo MC's Mix)/(Meltdown Mix - Long Version) (12" no p/s)	10
98	Warner Bros SAM 3247	Ray Of Light (Sasha's Ultra Violet Mix)/(William Orbit's Liquid Mix) (12")	15
98	Warner Bros SAM 3248	Ray Of Light (Calderone Club Mix)/(Album Version) (12" no p/s)	15
98	Warner Bros SAM 3268	Ray Of Light (Sasha's Twilo Mix)/(Victor Calderone Drum Mix) (12")	15

MADONNA & MISSY (ELLIOTT)

			MINT VALUE £
98	Warner Bros SAM 3269	Ray Of Light (Sasha's Strip Down Mix)/(Orbit's Ultra Violet Mix) (12")	15
98	Maverick W0444 LC	Ray Of Light/Has To Be (jukebox promo)	15
98	Maverick W 0453 LC	Drowned World/Substitute For Love//Sky Fits Heaven (promo only)	8
99	Maverick W 495 LC	Beautiful Stranger/Calderone Radio Mix) (Juke box promo)	10
00	Maverick W 519 LC	American Pie (Album Version)/(Richard 'Humpty' Vission Radio Mix) (jukebox promo	10
00	Warner Bros PRO 6584	Music (mixes) (12" doublepack, title-stickered sleeve)	15
01	Warner Bros MADZ 01	What It Feels Like For A Girl (Perfecto Mix)/(Above & Beyond Remix) (12" stickered white label, A4 press release, die-cut sleeve no p/s)	25
01	Warner Bros SAM 00586	GHV2 (CD, 10" x 10" gatefold p/s)	50
02	Warner Bros SAM 00721	Die Another Day (Dirty Vegas Main Mix)/(Mixes) (12" double pack, stickered title sleeve)	15
03	Warner Bros SAM 00824	Hollywood (Oakenfold 12" Full Remix)/(Jacques Lu Cont Thin White Duck Mix) /Album Version/(Deepsky Home Sweet Home Vocal Remix) (12")	10
06	Warnere Bros. PRO 15953	Get Together (Tiefschwarz Remix)/(James Holden Remix) (12" 'mirrorball' p/s)	80

PROMOS : ALBUM PROMO

89	Sire MER 0120	LIKE A PRAYER (Box set in 10" x 7" x 1" box, includes CD, sealed cassette, press Release, badge, slides Rolling Stone re-print, 2 photos)	200

MADONNA & MISSY (ELLIOTT)

03	Maverick RRCG 0301	Into The Hollywood Groove/Hollywood (Jack Lu Cont's Thin White Dick Mix) (GAP in-store promo)	25

MAD PROFESSOR

82	Ariwa ARILP 001	DUB ME CRAZY (LP)	20
82	Ariwa ARILP 002	BEYOND THE REALMS OF DUB (LP)	20
83	Ariwa ARILP 005	THE AFRICAN CONNECTION - DUB ME CRAZY PART 3 (LP)	25
83	Ariwa ARILP 011	ESCAPE TO THE ASYLUM OF DUB (LP)	20
85	Ariwa ARILP 025	CARIBBEAN TASTE OF TECHNOLOGY GONE CRAZY (LP)	20
86	Ariwa ARILP 030	SCHIZOPHRENIC DUB ME CRAZY VOL. 6 (LP)	15
85	Ariwa ARILP 021	DUB ME CRAZY - VOLUME 5 (LP)	15
93	Ariwa ARILP 095	BLACK LIBERATION DUB (LP)	15
94	Ariwa ARILP 057	PSYCHEDELIC DUB DUB - DUB ME CRAZY PART 10 (LP)	15
09	Ariwa AROLP 001LP	DUB ME CRAZY (LP, reissue)	15

MAD PROFESSOR & JAH SHAKA

96	Ariwa AEILP 116	NEW DECADE OF DUB (LP)	25

MAD RAGGA JON

91	Boogie Times MRJ 001	Rydim Come Forward (Mix 1)/(Mix 2)/(Mix 3) (12" white label)	10
92	Mad House M/HSE 001	Original Bad Boy/So Good (12")	15
93	Mad House HTP07	Fall Down On Me/The Power (12")	15

MADRIGAL

71	Decca F13110	Blue Eyes In Paradise/Wendy	20
72	Sovereign SOV 1071	Time Of The Season/Tapestry	20
73	Madrigal MAD 100	BENEATH THE GREENWOOD TREE (LP, private pressing)	60

MAD RIVER

69	Capitol (S)T 2985	MAD RIVER (LP)	125
85	Edsel ED 140	MAD RIVER (LP, reissue)	15

MAD SEASON

95	Columbia 478 5071	ABOVE (LP, with free 1-sided etched 12")	80

MADVILLAIN

04	PIAS PIASX 040	MADVILLAINY (2-LP)	40

(see also Madlib, Cookin Soul)

JOHNNY MAESTRO

61	HMV POP 875	What A Surprise/The Warning Voice	25
61	HMV POP 909	Mr. Happiness/Test Of Love	25
64	United Artists UP 1004	Before I Love Her/Fifty Million Heartbeats	25
71	Buddah 2011 061	Rain Came/Never Knew This Kind Of Hurt Before	10

(see also Crests, Brooklyn Bridge)

MAGAZINE

78	Virgin VS 200	Shot By Both Sides/My Mind Ain't So Open (card p/s)	15
78	Virgin VS 200	Shot By Both Sides/My Mind Ain't So Open (paper p/s)	8
78	Virgin VS 237	Give Me Everything/I Love You You Big Dummy	6
78	Virgin V2100	REAL LIFE (LP, original blue labels)	30
78	Virgin V2100	REAL LIFE (LP, reissue, green/red labels)	15
79	Virgin V2121	SECONDHAND DAYLIGHT (LP, gatefold)	30
80	Virgin V2156	THE CORRECT USE OF SOAP (LP)	25
80	Virgin V2184	PLAY (LP)	20
81	Virgin V2200	MAGIC, MURDER AND THE WEATHER (LP)	20
82	Virgin VM 1	AFTER THE FACT (LP)	20
11	Wire Sound WIRED 22	NO THYSELF (LP)	15

(see also Buzzcocks)

MAGENTA

78	Cottage COT 821	CANTERBURY MOON (LP, with insert)	40
80	Little Stan LSP 811	RECOLLECTIONS (2-LP, gatefold sleeve with insert)	35
81	Little Stan LSP 831	WOT'S NEXT THEN (LP, with insert)	25

MAGGIE

68	Columbia DB 8389	L. David Sloane/Too Young To Get Married	6

MAGIC CARPET

72	Mushroom 200 MR 20	MAGIC CARPET (LP, white/brown labels)	300
95	Magic Carpet MC 1001 LP	MAGIC CARPET (LP, reissue)	25

(see also Clem Alford)

MAGIC CHRISTIANS

69	Major Minor MM 673	If You Want It/Nuts	12
69	Major Minor MM 673	Come And Get It/Nuts (2nd pressing with correct title)	20

MAGIC DISCO MACHINE

MINT VALUE £

| 70 | Major Minor SMLP 71 | THE MAGIC CHRISTIANS (LP) .... 40 |

(see also Trevor Burton, Gary Wright, Denny Laine, Steve Gibbons)

MAGIC DISCO MACHINE
| 75 | Tamla Motown TMG 1004 | Control Tower/Scratchin .... 8 |
| 75 | Motown TML 11289 | DISC-O-TECH (LP) .... 18 |

MAGIC LANTERNS
66	CBS 202094	Excuse Me Baby/Greedy Girl 7
66	CBS 202250	Rumplestiltskin/I Stumbled 40
67	CBS 202459	Knight In Rusty Armour/Simple Things 10
67	CBS 202637	Auntie Grizelda/Time Will Tell (If I'm A Loser) 10
67	CBS 2750	We'll Meet Again/What Else Can It Be But Love? 10
68	Camp 602 007	Shame Shame/Baby I Gotta Go Now 10
69	Camp 602 009	Melt All Your Troubles Away/Bossa Nova 1940 - Hello You Lovers 10
70	Polydor 2038 058	One Night Stand/Frisco Annie 6
67	CBS (S)BPG 62935	LIT UP WITH THE MAGIC LANTERNS (LP) 40

MAGIC MIXTURE
| 68 | Saga STFID 2125 | THIS IS MAGIC MIXTURE (LP, black/silver labels) .... 150 |

MAGIC MUSCLE
88	Five Hours Back TOCK 009	THE PIPE, THE ROAR, THE GRID (LP, with booklet) 18
89	One Big Guitar OBGLP 9005	100 MILES BELOW (LP) 15
91	Woronzow WOO 17	GULP! (LP) 20

(see also Keith Christmas, Hawkwind, High Tide, Twink)

MAGIC MUSHROOM BAND
86	Pagan PM 003	THE POLITICS OF ECSTASY (LP, 100 with A1 poster) 50
86	Pagan PM 003	THE POLITICS OF ECSTASY (LP, 500 with A3 insert) 25
87	Aftermath AFT 3	BOMSHAMKAR (LP) 15
91	Fungus FUN 005	SPACED OUT (LP, foldout sleeve with A4 booklet) 15

MAGIC NIGHT
| 74 | Pye International 7N 25643 | Baby You Belong To Me/Lost And Lonely Boy .... 8 |
| 75 | Pye 7N 25698 | If You And I Had Never Met/(version) .... 10 |

MAGIC NOTES
| 60 | Blue Beat BB 9 | Album Of Memory/Why Did You Leave Me .... 12 |
| 61 | Blue Beat BB 51 | Rosabel/I'm Not Worthy .... 12 |

MAGIC SAM
69	Python PEN 701	Twenty One Days In Jail/Easy Baby (99 copies only) 45
69	Rooster 707	MEAN MISTREATER (EP) 20
70	Blue Horizon 7-63223	MAGIC SAM: 1937-1969 (LP) 100
70	Delmark DS 615	WEST SIDE SOUL (LP, blue label) 30
71	Delmark DS 620	BLACK MAGIC (LP, blue label) 35

MAGIC VALLEY
| 69 | Penny Farthing PEN 701 | Taking The Heart Out Of Love/Uptight Basil .... 10 |

(see also Pete Dello, Honeybus)

MAGICIAN
| 79 | Hobo HOS 008 | House Of The Purple Mist (Part 1)/(Part 2) .... 40 |
| 79 | Hobo HO 501 | MAGICIAN (LP) .... 40 |

MAGICIANS
66	Decca F 12374	The Liars/Poggy Goes Pop 6
67	Decca F 12602	The Tarzan March/What A Day For A Metamorphosis 10
68	MCA MU 1046	Painting On Wood/Slow Motion 40

MAGISTRATES
68	MGM MGM 1437	After The Fox/Tear Down The Walls (with Jean Hillary) 15
68	MGM MGM 1425	Here Comes The Judge/Girl 10
68	MGM MGM 1437	After The Fox/Tear Down The Walls (with Jean Hillary) 12

(see also Jane Hillery)

MAGITS
| 79 | Outer H. SRTS/79/CUS/401 | Fragmented/Disconnected/Disjointed/Detached (p/s, with 3 page magazine insert) ...... 140 |
| 79 | Outer H. SRTS/79/CUS/401 | Fragmented/Disconnected/Disjointed/Detached (p/s, without magazine) .... 100 |

(see also Rudimentary Peni)

MAGMA
74	A&M AMS 7119	Mekanik Machine/Mekanik Machine (Version) 20
70	Philips 6359 051/2	MAGMA (2-LP) 70
71	Philips 6397 031	1001 CENTIGRADE (LP) 40
74	A&M AMLH 64397	MEKANIK DESTRUCTIW KOMMANDOH (LP, gatefold sleeve, lyric insert) 40
74	A&M AMLH 68260	KOHN TARKOSZ (LP) 20

MAGNA CARTA
69	Fontana TF 1060	Romeo Jack/7 O'Clock Man 20
69	Mercury MF 1096	Mid-Winter/Spinning Wheels Of Time 20
70	Vertigo 6059 013	Airport Song/Elizabethan 10
71	Vertigo 6059 043	Time For The Leaving/Wayfarin' 8
72	Vertigo 6059 073	All My Life/Falkland Green 12
73	Vertigo 6059 092	Give Me Luv/Song Of Evening 10
69	Mercury MCL 20166 S	MAGNA CARTA (LP, laminated sleeve, black/silver labels) 200
70	Vertigo 6360 003	SEASONS (LP, 1st pressing, gatefold sleeve, large swirl label, "Vertigo" at base of label) . 120
70	Vertigo 6360 003	SEASONS (LP, 2nd pressing, gatefold sleeve, small swirl label, "Vertigo" beneath swirl above centre hole) 50
71	Vertigo 6360 040	SONGS FROM WASTIES ORCHARD (LP, multifold sleeve, large swirl label) 150
72	Vertigo 6360 068	IN CONCERT (LP, gatefold sleeve, small swirl label) 18
73	Vertigo 6360 093	LORD OF THE AGES (LP, 1st pressing, side 1 matrix, 1 (crossed out 2) Y//1 1 1 1, gatefold sleeve, lyric insert, spaceship label) 15
74	Vertigo 6360 003	SEASONS (LP, 3rd pressing, 'spaceship label') 15

MAGNET

MINT VALUE £

MAGNET
69	CBS 4472	Let Me Stay/Mr Guy Fawkes	30
70	CBS 4844	Something To Remember Me By/Everything	6

MAGNETIC FORCE
97	Time 2 Flex TTFLEX 01	REFLECTIONS EP (12")	20

MAGNETICS
00	Grapevine 2000 G2K 104	The Look On Your Face/You Were Made For Love (with Johnny McKinney)	10
02	Grapevine 2000 G2K 119	I'll Keep Holding On/Jackie Baby	10
02	Grapevine 2000 G2K 130	When I'm With My Baby/Count The Days	10

MAGNETS
79	Hurricane FIRE 1	Who's The Fool (Me Or You)/Best (with insert, round white cut-out sheet)	25

MAGNIFICENT
88	Link LINKLP 027	HIT AND RUN (LP)	20

MAGNIFICENT MEN
66	Capitol CL 15462	Peace Of Mind/All Your Lovin's Gone To My Head	30
68	Capitol CL 15530	Sweet Soul Medley Parts 1 & 2	10
68	Capitol CL 15570	Save The Country/So Much Love Waiting	6

MAGNIFICENT MERCURY BROTHERS
74	Transatlantic BIG 532	New Girl In School/What About Us	8
74	Transatlantic BIG 536	Why Do Fools Fall In Love/(I'm Not A) Juvenile Delinquent	8

(see also Decameron)

MAGNOG
90s	Enraptured RAPT 4508	Mist Waves Riding The Hills/Moving Ahead Again/Ghost States (p/s)	6

MAGNUM
75	CBS S CBS 2959	Sweets For My Sweet/Movin' On (no p/s)	45
78	Jet SJET 116	Kingdom Of Madness/In The Beginning	7
81	Jet JET 7007	Black Nights (possibly promo only)	12
86	Polydor POSPP 833	Midnight (Remix)/Back Street Kid/Kingdom Of Madness (live)/Midnight (You Won't Be Sleeping)(12", picture disc)	15
78	Jet JETLP 210	KINGDOM OF MADNESS (LP, original 'king' sleeve)	25
83	FM WKFMPD 111	THE ELEVENTH HOUR (LP, picture disc)	25
85	FM WKFM LP 34	ON A STORYTELLER'S NIGHT (LP, with bonus single)	20
85	FM WKFMG/CLP34	ON A STORYTELLER'S NIGHT (LP, clear vinyl)	20
85	FM WKFM G/C LP 34	ON A STORYTELLER'S NIGHT (LP, gold or clear vinyl, with poster)	15
85	FM WKFM PD 34	ON A STORYTELLER'S NIGHT (LP, picture disc)	18
86	Polydor POLD 5198	VIGILANTE (LP, with inner)	15
87	FM Revolver WKFMHP 106	MIRADOR (LP, blue vinyl, gatefold sleeve, poster and blue vinyl 12" (12HP106)	18
88	FM Revolver WKFMPD 119T	MAGNUM II (LP, reissue, picture disc)	15
90	FM Revolver WKFMBX 145	FOUNDATION (6-LP box set)	45
92	Music For Nations MFN 143	SLEEPWALKING (LP)	80

MAGOO
95	Noisebox NBX 013	MUDSHARK EP: Tom, Lou And Me/Elsie's Skinny Arms/Hop Your Mouth (orange vinyl, numbered p/s, 500 only)	10
98	Fierce Panda NING 47	Black Sabbath/MOGWAI: Sweet Leaf (p/s)	7

MAGPIES
68	Doctor Bird DB 1129	Lulu/Must I Be Lonely	18
68	Doctor Bird DB 1132	Blue Boy/I Guess I'm Crazy	18

MAG SPIES/MAGAZINE SPIES/MAGSPIES
79	Dance Fools Dance GLITCH 1	LIFEBLOOD (12" EP, 2 tracks by Mag Spies/2 by Obtainers)	400

(see also The Cure)

ALEX MAGUIRE
87	Incus INCUS 52	LIVE AT OSCARS (LP)	35

LEO MAGUIRE
62	Parlophone R 4917	Small World/Crying For The Moon	7

MAGUS
80	Northern Sound NSR 200	BREEZIN' AWAY (LP, private pressing)	50

(see also Blue Epitaph)

TAJ MAHAL
68	Direction 58-3547	Everybody's Got To Change Sometime/Statesboro Blues	12
69	Direction 58-4044	Ee Zee Rider/You Don't Miss Your Water	12
70	Direction 58-4586	Give Your Woman What She Wants/Further On Down The Road	8
71	CBS 7413	Diving Duck Blues/Fishin' Blues	10
67	Direction 8-63279	TAJ MAHAL (LP)	30
69	Direction 8-63397	THE NATCH'L BLUES (LP)	30
69	Direction 8-66226	GIANT STEP/DE OLE FOLKS AT HOME (2-LP)	25

MAHAVISHNU ORCHESTRA
75	CBS 3007	Can't Stand Your Funk/Eternity's Breath Part 1	6
72	CBS 64717	THE INNER MOUNTING FLAME (LP, with insert)	15
74	CBS CQ 31996	BIRDS OF FIRE (LP, quadrophonic)	20

(see also John McLaughlin)

SKIP MAHONEY & CASUALS
80	Underworld UND 1	Janice/Don't Stop Me Now	10
76	Contempo CLP 539	LAND OF LOVE (LP)	20

MAIL
71	Parlophone R 5916	Omnibus/Life Goes On	25

MAIN
96	Beggars Banquet HERTZ 16LP	Hz (2-LP)	25

MAIN ATTRACTION
72	Pye 7N45186	Oh Girl/Telephone Line	10

MAIN ATTRACTIONS

MAIN ATTRACTIONS
77 Solid Sound SS 001   Love/Doug's Love (with Augustus Pablo) 20

MAIN INGREDIENT
77 Power Exchange PX 265   Everything Man/Reggae Disco 6
71 RCA LSA 3020   TASTEFUL SOUL (LP) 15

MAINFRAME (1)
83 MC Squared MC 004   Radio (Will Bring Me Home)/The Message/The Room (Part 2) (p/s) 15
83 MC Squared MC 005   TALK TO ME EP 15
83 MC Squared MC 007   TENANTS OF THE LATTICE WORK (LP) 20

MAINFRAME (2)
84 YYY 001   INTO TROUBLE WITH THE NOISE OF ART (12", 7-track EP) 10

MAINHORSE
71 Polydor 2383 049   MAINHORSE (LP) 45

MIKE MAINIERI
69 Solid State USS 7006   INSIGHT (LP) 30

MAINLAND
79 Christy ACML 0200   EXPOSURE (LP) 15

MAINLINER
03 Remorse LP 01   MELLOW OUT (LP, red vinyl) 15
(see also Acid Mothers Temple)

JULIE MAIRS & CHRIS STOWELL
77 Cottage COT 211   SOFT SEA BLUE (LP) 25

MAJAMOOD
66 Doc. Bird/W.I.R.L. DB 1052 Two Hundred Million Red Ants/Faces Amassed 30

MAJESTERIANS
81 Daddy Kool DKR 125   So Many Times/Flute On Fire (12") 30

MAJESTIC CHOIR AND SOUL STIRRERS
69 Chess CRS 8101   Why Am I Treated So Bad/We Can All Walk A Little Prouder 15

MAJESTICS (1)
73 Cube BUG 34   Living It All Again/She Troubles My Mind 25

MAJESTICS (2)
03 Funk 45 FUNK45 010   Funky Chic/Coming On (reissue) 8

MAJOR
78 North Star NS 104   MAJOR EP 50

MAJOR ACCIDENT
82 M. Melodies MAME 1001   Warboots/Terrorist Gang (unissued, test pressings only) 40
83 Step Forward SF 23   Mr. Nobody/That's You (p/s) 12
83 Flicknife FLS 016   Fight To Win/Free Man (p/s) 15
83 Flicknife FLS 023   Leaders Of Tomorrow/Dayo/Breakaway (p/s) 12
84 Flicknife FLS 026   Respectable/Man On The Wall (p/s) 12
83 Step Forward SFLP 9   MASSACRED MELODIES (LP) 30
84 Syndicate SYNLP 9   TORTURED TUNES LIVE (LP) 25
85 Flicknife SHARP 027   PNEUMATIC PNEUROSIS (LP) 25
(see also Accident)

MAJOR B LASER
80 Charly CYS 1064   Next To You/Rock On Bolan (p/s) 8

MAJORETTES
63 Lyntone LYN 982   White Levi's (flexidisc) 15

MAJOR FORCE
94 Mo' Wax MW 082LP   Return Of The Original Artform/(Mixes) (5 x 12" box set) 25

MAJORINE
69 Pyramid 6069   Loving Shrine/I Live 20

MAJORITY
65 Decca F 12186   Pretty Little Girl/I Don't Wanna Be Hurt No More 20
65 Decca F 12271   A Little Bit Of Sunlight/Shut 'Em Down In London Town 25
66 Decca F 12313   We Kiss In A Shadow/Ring The Bells 15
66 Decca F 12453   Simplified/One Third 100
66 Decca F 12504   To Make Me A Man/Tears Won't Help 15
67 Decca F 12573   I Hear A Rhapsody/Wait By The Fire 20
67 Decca F 12638   Running Away With My Baby/Let The Joybells Ring 20
68 Decca F 12727   All Our Christmases/People 25

MAJORS (1)
62 London HLP 9602   A Wonderful Dream/Time Will Tell 20
62 London HLP 9627   She's A Troublemaker/A Little Bit Now 20
63 London HLP 9693   What In The World/Tra La La 20
64 Liberty LBF 66009   Ooh Wee Baby/I'll Be There 30
63 London RE-P 1258   MEET THE MAJORS (EP) 50
63 London HA-P 8068   MEET THE MAJORS (LP) 80

MAJORS (2)
77 Magnet MAG 79   It Only Happens/One Sided Love Affair 20

MAJOR SURGERY
77 Next 104   NEXT CUT (LP) 40

MAJOR TOM
76 Satril SAT 113   Spaceman Boy/Spaceman Boy (Instrumental) 25

MAKADOPOLOUS
60 Palette PG 9205   Never On Sunday/Yasou (p/s) 8

CARMEN MAKI
69 CBS 4298   (Sometime I Feel Like) A Lonely Baby/Anata Ga Hoshii 10

MAKIN' TIME
85 Countdown VAIN 1   Here Is My Number/Nothing Else (p/s) 8

MAKKA BEES

			MINT VALUE £
86	Countdown VAIN 5	Pump It Up/Walk A Thin Line (p/s)	8
85	Countdown DOWN 1	RHYTHM 'N' SOUL (LP)	15
86	Ready To Eat READY 1	NO LUMPS OF FAT OR GRISTLE GUARANTEED (LP)	18
87	Re-Elect/President ELECT 1	TIME, TROUBLE AND MONEY (LP)	18

(see also Charlatans)

MAKKA BEES
| 77 | Congo CO 1 | Nation Fiddler/Fire | 20 |

MAL & PRIMITIVES
| 65 | Pye 7N 15915 | Every Minute Of Every Day/Pretty Little Face | 80 |

(see also Primitives, Mal Ryder & Spirits)

MALA
05	DMZ DMZ 003	Da Wrath Souljahz Vip Mix/LOEFAH: Twisup Vip (12")	25
06	DMZ DMZ 010	Left Leg Out/Vlue Notez (12")	20
07	DMZ DMZ 011	Bury Da Bwoy/Hunter (12")	25
07	DMZ DMZ 012	Lean Forward/Learn (12")	30

MALARIA!
| 82 | Jungle JUNG 3 | NEW YORK PASSAGE (12" EP) | 20 |
| 19 | Electronic Sound ES 753 | Your Turn To Run/GUDRUN GUT: Boys Keep Swinging (p/s) | 15 |

CARL MALCOLM
| 75 | Black Wax WAX 7 | Miss Wire Waist/SKIN, FLESH & BONES: Wire Dub | 8 |
| 77 | Grove Music GMDM 1 | Repatriation (feat. Ranking Trevor)/Take A Tip From Me (feat. Ranking Trevor) (12") | 40 |

CARLOS MALCOLM & AFRO CARIBS
| 65 | Island WI 173 | Bonanza Ska/Papa Luiga | 20 |

HUGH MALCOLM
| 68 | Amalgamated AMG 827 | Good Time Rock/LYNN TAITT & JETS: Sleepy Ludy | 50 |
| 68 | Amalgamated AMG 829 | Mortgage/CANNONBALL BRYAN TRIO: Man About Town | 50 |

MALIBU
| 78 | Cleverly Bros CBSP 1000 100 | Skateboarding/Billy | 20 |

MALLARD
| 77 | Virgin VS 168 | Harvest/Green Coyote | 7 |
| 76 | Virgin V 2045 | MALLARD (LP) | 15 |

(see also Captain Beefheart & His Magic Band)

MALLET
| 80 | Rox ROX 014 | C C Rider/Route 66 | 25 |

STEPHEN MALLINDER
| 82 | Fetish FM 2010 | POW-WOW (LP) | 30 |

(see also Cabaret Voltaire)

SIW MALMKVIST
59	Oriole CB 1486	Sermonette/The Preacher	20
61	Parlophone R 4765	Wedding Cake/Red Roses And Little White Lies	6
68	Atlantic 584 229	The Man Who Took The Valise Off The Floor Of Grand Central Station/Sadie The Cleaning Lady	6

MALO
| 72 | Warner Bros. K16155 | Suavecito/Nena | 10 |

CINDY MALONE
| 61 | RCA RCA 1254 | Weird Beard/Young Marriage | 8 |

WIL MALONE
| 70 | Fontana STL 5541 | WIL MALONE (LP) | 1500 |
| 10 | Morgan Bluetown BT 5005 | WIL MALONE (LP, reissue, 750 only with signed certificate) | 35 |

(see also Barnaby Rudge, Motherlight, Wilson Malone Voiceband)

WILSON MALONE VOICEBAND
| 68 | Morgan MR 112P | FUNNY SAD MUSIC (LP) | 50 |

(see also Motherlight, Wil Malone)

MALPRACTICE
| 80 | SRTS/80/CUS 762 | It's OK/Wish You Would/Don't Take It Out | 100 |

RICHARD MALTBY
| 61 | Columbia DB 4606 | The Rat Race/Walkie Talkie | 8 |

MAMA LAPATO
| 82 | Bead Records BEAD 20 | MAMA LAPATO (LP) | 20 |

MAMA LION
| 72 | Philips 6078002 | Ain't Too Proud To Beg/Mr. Invitation | 6 |
| 72 | Philips 6369 153 | PRESERVE WILDLIFE (LP) | 20 |

MAMAS & PAPAS
66	RCA Victor RCA 1503	California Dreamin'/Somebody Groovy	8
66	RCA Victor RCA 1533	I Saw Her Again/Even If I Could	6
67	RCA Victor RCA 1564	Words Of Love/I Can't Wait	7
67	RCA Victor RCA 1613	Creeque Alley/No Salt On Her Tail	6
67	RCA Victor RCA 1630	Straight Shooter/12.30/Young Girls Are Coming To The Canyon	6
67	RCA Victor RCA 1649	Glad To Be Unhappy/Hey Girl	7
68	RCA Victor RCA 1710	Safe In My Garden/Too Late	7
68	RCA Victor RCA 1726	Dream A Little Dream Of Me/Midnight Voyage (as Mama Cass with the Mamas & Papas)	6
68	RCA Victor RCA 1744	For The Love Of Ivy/Strange Young Girls	8
66	RCA Victor RD 7803	IF YOU CAN BELIEVE YOUR EYES AND EARS (LP)	20
66	RCA Victor RD/SF 7834	CASS, JOHN, MICHELLE, DENNY (LP)	20
67	RCA Victor RD/SF 7880	DELIVER (LP)	20
68	RCA Victor RD/SF 7960	THE PAPAS AND THE MAMAS (LP)	20
68	Stateside (S)SL 5002	THE MAMAS AND THE PAPAS GOLDEN ERA VOL. 2 (LP)	15
70	Probe SPB 1013/14	A GATHERING OF FLOWERS (2-LP)	20
71	Probe SPB 1048	PEOPLE LIKE US (LP)	15
78	St. Michael MO 101225	CALIFORNIA DREAMIN' (LP, exclusive to Marks & Spencer)	15

MAMA'S BOYS

(see also Mama Cass [Elliot], John Phillips, Michelle Phillips, Scott McKenzie, Barry McGuire, Mugwumps, Big Three [U.S], Spanky & Our Gang)

MAMA'S BOYS
83	Spartan 12SP 6	Too Little Of You To Love/Freedom Fighters (12", p/s, with free "Official Bootleg" LP)	10

MAMA'S PRIDE
75	Atlantic K 10709	Blue Mist/Missouri Skyline	6

MAMMATH
84	Neat NEAT 42	Rock Me/Rough 'N' Ready (p/s)	7

MAMMOTH
89	Jive MOTHX 4	All The Days/Fatman/Bet You Wish (12", picture disc, PVC sleeve, withdrawn)	20

(see also John McCoy, Gillan, Samson, Tiger, Nicky Moore Band, Hackensack)

BATTI MAMZELLE
74	Fly 17	I SEE THE LIGHT (LP)	20

MAN
69	Pye 7N 17684	Sudden Life/Love	35
71	Liberty LBF 15448	Daughter Of The Fireplace/Country Girl	18
74	United Artists UP 35643	Don't Go Away (possibly unissued)	15
74	United Artists UP 35703	Taking The Easy Way Out Again/California Silks And Satins	6
69	Pye N(S)PL 18275	REVELATION (LP, mono, original pressing with sky blue label with black at top)	100
69	Pye N(S)PL 18275	REVELATION (LP, stereo, original pressing with sky blue label with black at top)	80
69	Dawn DNLS 3003	2 OZS OF PLASTIC WITH A HOLE IN THE MIDDLE (LP, orange label, gatefold sleeve)	50
69	Dawn DNLS 3003	2 OZ'S OF PLASTIC WITH A HOLE IN THE MIDDLE (LP, later pressings with lilac then pink 'sun' labels, gatefold sleeve)	20
70	Liberty LBG 83464	MAN (LP, gatefold textured sleeve)	40
72	United Artists UAS 29236	DO YOU LIKE IT HERE NOW (ARE YOU SETTLING IN ALRIGHT?) (LP)	40
72	United Artists USP 100	LIVE AT THE PADGET ROOMS, PENARTH (LP)	30
72	United Artists UAG 29287	BE GOOD TO YOURSELF AT LEAST ONCE A DAY (LP, fold out 'map' in gatefold sleeve with 'family tree' inner)	45
73	United Artists UDX 205/6	CHRISTMAS AT THE PATTI (LP, 2 x 10", with other artists)	22
73	Utd Artists UAD 60053/4	BACK INTO THE FUTURE (2-LP, gatefold sleeve, some stickered)	20
74	United Artists UAG 29631	RHINOS WINOS AND LUNATICS (LP, laminated gatefold)	15
74	United Artists UAG 29675	SLOW MOTION (LP, lyric inner sleeve)	15
75	United Artists UAG 29872	MAXIMUM DARKNESS (LP, gatefold sleeve, with poster)	15
77	MCA MCF 2815	ALL'S WELL THAT ENDS WELL (LP, initial batch with History Of Man booklet)	20

(see also Bystanders, Eyes Of Blue, Ancient Grease, Big Sleep, Clive John, Alkatraz, Help Yourself, Deke Leonard, Neutrons, Gary Pickford-Hopkins & Friends, Wild Turkey, Martin Ace)

T. MAN & T. BONES
72	Sioux SI 007	True Born African (actually by Winston Jarrett & Righteous Flames)/JAYBOYS:Tropical Chief	70

MAN UPSTAIRS
82	Clock House CH 0502	Summa/The Gospel According To Mark (p/s)	15
85	Sideline SIDE 1	Sad In My Heart/Country Boy (p/s)	15
85	Sideline 1SIDE12	CONSUMERS EP (12", p/s)	40

(STEPHEN STILLS') MANASSAS
72	Atlantic K 60021	MANASSAS (2-LP, with 2 inner sleeves & lyric poster)	25
73	Atlantic K 40440	DOWN THE ROAD (LP, with inner sleeve)	20

(see also Stephen Stills, Crosby Stills & Nash, Flying Burrito Brothers)

MANASSEH
77	Genesis 12	MANASSEH (LP, with insert)	20

JUNIOR MANCE
60	HMV CLP 1342	JUNIOR (LP)	25
71	Atlantic 2400 028	WITH A LOTTA HELP FROM MY FRIENDS (LP)	20

STEVE MANCHA/J.J. BARNES
69	Stax SXATS 1012	RARE STAMPS (LP)	60

(see also J.J. Barnes)

MANCHESTER CITY F.C.
72	RCA 2200	Boys In Blue/Funky City	6

MANCHESTER MEKON
79	Newmarket NEW 102	No Forgetting/Have A Go-Go/Jonathan Livingstone Seafood (hand-painted p/s with insert, 1,000 only)	25

MICKY MANCHESTER
75	Rainbow RBW 2001	Have You Seen Your Daughter, Mrs Jones?/Chamberlain Said	10

MANCHESTER MOB
67	Parlophone R 5552	Bony Maronie At The Hop/Afro Asian	40

(see also Graham Gouldman, High Society, 10cc, Friday Browne)

MANCHESTER UNITED FOOTBALL SQUAD
79	RCA MAN 1	Onward Sexton's Soldiers/Come On You Reds (red vinyl)	7

(see also Status Quo)

MANCHESTERS
66	Ember	TRIBUTE TO THE BEATLES (LP)	20

MANCHESTER'S PLAYBOYS
66	Fontana TF 745	I Feel So Good/I Close My Eyes	150

MANCINI & FOX
72	Polydor 2066 170	Light Song/The Colours Are Still There	8

HENRY MANCINI & HIS ORCHESTRA
59	RCA RCA 1134	Peter Gunn Theme/The Brothers Go To Mother's	10
62	RCA RCA 1285	Experiment In Terror/Tooty Twist	10
62	RCA RCA 1312	Man Of The World Theme/Fluter's Ball	6
57	Brunswick LAT 8162	ROCK, PRETTY BABY (LP, soundtrack, with Rod McKuen)	80

DAVID MANCUSO
99	Nuphonic NUX 136	DAVID MANCUSO PRESENTS THE LOFT (4 x 12")	100
00	Nuphonic NUX 154	DAVID MANCUSO PRESENTS THE LOFT VOL. 2 (4 x 12")	100

MANDALABAND

MINT VALUE £

MANDALABAND
75	Chrysalis CHR 1095	MANDALABAND (LP)	20
78	Chrysalis CHR 1181	THE EYE OF WENDOR: PROPHECIES (LP, with booklet)	20

MANDARIN KRAZE
70	Carnaby CNS 4008	How Long Does It Take/Magazine Cottage	25

HARVEY MANDEL
74	Janus 6146 024	Uno Ino/Shangrenade	6
68	Philips SBL 7873	CRISTO REDENTOR (LP)	45
69	Philips SBL 7904	RIGHTEOUS (LP)	20
70	Philips SBL 7915	GAMES GUITARS PLAY (LP)	15
71	Dawn DNLS 3015	BABY BATTER (LP)	40
71	Philips 6336 009	CRISTO REDENTOR (LP, reissue)	15
72	London SH-O 8426	GET OFF IN CHICAGO (LP)	15
72	Janus 6310 210	THE SNAKE (LP)	15

(see also Canned Heat, Dewey Terry)

RICHARD MANDEL
69	London HL 10256	Loneliness/Young And Warm And Wonderful	12

DAVE MANDELL & STEVE WILSON
72	Wilfa WIL 50	NUCLEAR POWER STATION (LP)	50

MANDIBLE RUMPUS
79	Mayhem HEM 1	Whats My Line/Shadows And Passions (p/s)	12

MANDINGO
73	EMI EMI 2014	Medicine Man/Black Rite	15
73	EMI 2062	Fever Pitch/The Cheetah	10
73	Studio Two TWO 400	PRIMEVAL RHYTHM OF LIFE (LP)	40
73	Studio Two Q4TWO 400	PRIMEVAL RHYTHM OF LIFE (LP, quadrophonic)	40
73	EMI EMC 3010	SACRIFICE (LP)	20
75	EMI EMC 3038	MANDINGO 3: STORY OF SURVIVAL (LP)	30
77	EMI EMC 3217	SAVAGE RITE (LP)	25

(see also Geoff Love)

MANDRAGORA
89	SAB 01	OVER THE MOON (LP, 1st pressing with white label/cream sleeve)	50
89	Babbleon Bab 1	OVER THE MOON (LP, 2nd pressing with blue label/yellow/blue/white/cream sleeve)	30
91	Resonance 33-9133	HEAD FIRST (LP)	20
93	Mystic Stones RUNE 13	EARTHDANCE (LP)	15
95	Mystic Stones RUNE 14	TEMPLE BALL (LP)	15

MANDRAKE
60	Philips PB 1093	Mandrake/The Witch's Twist	10
61	Philips BF 1153	Thank Goodness It's Friday/Queen Of Sheba	7

MANDRAKE MEMORIAL
69	RCA SF 8028	MEDIUM (LP)	125
70	RCA/Poppy PYS 11003	PUZZLE (LP)	140

MANDRAKE PADDLE STEAMERS
69	Parlophone R 5780	Strange Walking Man/Steam	130
88	Bam Caruso NRIC 033	Strange Walking Man/Steam (reissue, gatefold p/s)	12

(see also Liverpool Echo)

MANDRILL
72	Polydor 2391 030	MANDRILL IS (LP, gatefold)	40
73	Polydor 2391 061	COMPOSITE TRUTH (LP)	20
73	Polydor 2391 092	JUST OUTSIDE OF TOWN (LP)	15
73	United Artists UAS 29783	SOLID (LP)	15
75	United Artists UAS 29920	BEAST FROM THE EAST (LP)	20
75	Polydor 2391 188	THE BEST OF (LP)	15
77	Arista SPART 1035	WE ARE ONE (LP)	15
78	Arista ARTY 162	NEW WORLDS (LP)	25

M&S BAND
05	Funk 45 FUNK45 023	Egg Roll (1-sided)	10

MANEATERS
82	Editions EG EGO 8	Nine To Five/SUZI PINNS: Jerusalem (withdrawn 'Adam & Toyah' p/s)	100

(see also Adam & The Ants)

MAN FRIDAY & JIVE JUNIOR
83	Malaco MAL 011	Picking Up Sounds/Picking Up Sounds (Radio Mix) (p/s, features John Deacon)	20
83	Malaco MAL 1211	Picking Up Sounds (Extended)/Picking Up Sounds (Radio Mix) (12", p/s, features John Deacon)	35

(see also Queen)

MAN FROM DELMONTE
87	Ugly Man UGLY 3	Drive Drive Drive (22 And Still In Love With You)/Sun Serious (p/s)	25
87	Ugly Man UGLY 5	Water In My Eyes/Bored By You (p/s)	12
87	Ugly Man UGLY 5T	Water In My Eyes/Bored By You/The Country (12", p/s)	18
88	Ugly Man UGLY 7	(Will Nobody Save) Louise/Good Things In Life (p/s)	10
88	Ugly Man UGLY 7T	(Will Nobody Save) Louise/Good Things In Life/Like A Millionaire (12", p/s)	25
89	Bop Cassettes BIP 502	WAITING FOR ANN (12" EP)	15

RAY MANG
96	Noid NOID 099	NUMBER ONE EP (12")	20
08	Mangled REG 008	Angel/Cerela Lover (12")	15

MANGO GREEN
70	Ackee ACK 109	Birds Of A Feather/Run Down	15

MANHATTANS
65	Sue WI 384	I Wanna Be (Your Everything)/Searchin' For My Baby	50
66	Carnival CAR 100	Baby I Need You/Teach Me (The Philly Dog)	20

MANHATTEN BROTHERS

MINT VALUE £

66	Carnival CAR 101	That New Girl/Can I	20
74	CBS 2117	Soul Train/I'm Not A Run Around	6
73	London SHB 8449	A MILLION TO ONE (LP)	30

MANHATTEN BROTHERS
65	Columbia 33SX 1704	EMERGENT VOICES (LP)	40

MANIAC
85	Rentaracket RKT 1	KILLING FOR PLEASURE EP (p/s, with booklet)	6

MANIACS
77	United Artists UP 36327	Chelsea 1977/Ain't No Legend (p/s)	20
77	United Artists UP 36327	Chelsea 1977/Ain't No Legend (p/s, green labels, demo versions different mixes)	30

(see also Rings, Physicals)

MANIAX
66	White Label WLR 101/102	Out Of Reach/The Devil's Home	20

MANIC JABS
81	Waldo's MS 009	Autophagus/The Injuns Are Comin'/Thing Wild (p/s)	10

MANIC STREET PREACHERS

SINGLES
88	SBS SBS 002	Suicide Alley/Tennessee (I Get Low) (hand-made p/s with press-cuttings glued to plain card cover)	1000
88	SBS SBS 002	Suicide Alley/Tennessee (I Get Low) (blue p/s, 200 only)	600
88	SBS SBS 002	Suicide Alley/Tennessee (I Get Low) (no p/s, 100 only)	300
90	Hopelessly Devoted 1	UK Channel Boredom/LAURENS: I Don't Know What The Trouble Is (p/s flexidisc, free with Hopelessly Devoted fanzine; later repressed)	35
90	Hopelessly Devoted 1	UK Channel Boredom/LAURENS: I Don't Know What The Trouble Is (p/s flexidisc, without Hopelessly Devoted fanzine; later repressed)	45
90	Damaged Goods YUBB 4	NEW ART RIOT EP: New Art Riot/Strip It Down/Last Exit On Yesterday/Teenage 20/20 (12", white label, 100 copies, plain sleeves rubber stamped with "Made In Wales")	35
90	Damaged Goods YUBB 4	NEW ART RIOT EP: New Art Riot/Strip It Down/Last Exit On Yesterday/Teenage 20/20 (12" EP, p/s, 1st 1,000 black & white label)	20
90	Damaged Goods YUBB 4	NEW ART RIOT EP: New Art Riot/Strip It Down/Last Exit On Yesterday/Teenage 20/20 (12" EP, p/s, 2nd 1,000 on black-on-yellow labels)	15
90	Damaged Goods YUBB 4	NEW ART RIOT EP: New Art Riot/Strip It Down/Last Exit On Yesterday/Teenage 20/20 (12" EP, p/s, later pressing on red, orange & silver & green labels)	10
91	Damaged Goods YUBB 004P	NEW ART RIOT EP: New Art Riot/Strip It Down/Last Exit On Yesterday/Teenage 20/20 (12" EP, p/s, reissue on pink vinyl)	25
91	Heavenly HVN 812	Motown Junk/Sorrow 16/We Her Majesty's Prisoners (12", withdrawn p/s)	35
91	Heavenly HVN 8CD	Motown Junk/Sorrow 16/We Her Majesty's Prisoners (CD, withdrawn sleeve)	125
91	Heavenly HVN 10	You Love Us/Spectators Of Suicide (p/s)	15
91	Heavenly HVN 1012	You Love Us/Spectators Of Suicide/Starlover/Strip It Down (live) (12", p/s)	20
91	Columbia 6573377	Stay Beautiful/R.P. McMurphy (p/s)	8
91	Columbia 657337 6	Stay Beautiful/R.P. McMurphy/Soul Contamination (12", p/s)	15
91	Columbia 657337 8	Stay Beautiful/R.P. McMurphy/Soul Contamination (12", stickered poster p/s)	30
91	Columbia 6575827	Love's Sweet/Repeat (p/s)	8
91	Columbia 657582 6	Repeat (U.K.)/Love's Sweet Exile/Democracy Coma (12", p/s)	12
91	Columbia 657582 8	Repeat/Democracy Coma/Love's Sweet Exile/Stay Beautiful (live) (12", gatefold, stickered p/s)	15
91	Caff CAFF 15	FEMININE IS BEAUTIFUL: Repeat After Me/New Art Riot (p/s, 500 only)	250
92	Columbia 6577247	You Love Us/A Vision Of Dead Desire (p/s)	6
92	Columbia 657724 6	You Love Us/A Vision Of Dead Desire/It's So Easy (live) (12" gatefold p/s)	10
92	Columbia 657873 7	Slash'N'Burn/Motown Junk (p/s)	6
92	Columbia 657873 6	Slash'N'Burn/Motown Junk/Ain't Goin' Down (12", with print, stickered p/s)	12
92	Columbia 658083 7	Motorcycle Emptiness/Bored Out Of My Mind	6
92	Columbia 658083 6	Motorcycle Emptiness/Bored Out Of My Mind/Under My Wheels (12")	15
92	Columbia 658083 6	Motorcycle Emptiness/Bored Out Of My Mind/Under My Wheels (12", picture disc, stickered PVC sleeve)	25
92	Columbia 658382 7	Theme From MASH EP (Suicide Is Painless)/FATIMA MANSIONS: Everything I Do (I Do It For You) (p/s)	6
92	Columbia 658382 6	Theme From MASH EP (Suicide Is Painless)/FATIMA MANSIONS/ Everything I Do (I Do It For You)/Sleeping With The NME (12", p/s)	12
92	Columbia 6587967	Little Baby Nothing/Never Want Again/Suicide Alley (p/s)	12
93	Columbia 6594776	La Tristesse Durera (Scream To A Sigh)/Parick Bateman/Repeat (Live)/Tennessee (12", with 20 x 30 inch poster)	20
93	Columbia 6597277	Roses In The Hospital/Us Against You/Donkeys (p/s, red vinyl)	12
93	Columbia 6597276	Roses In The Hospital (OG Psychoval Mix/51 Funk Salute Mix)/Filet-O-Gang Mix/(ECG Mix)/(Original Version) (12")	12
93	Columbia 6593376	From Despair To Where/Hibernation/Spectators Of Suicide (Heavenly) (12")	12
94	Columbia 5500707	Life Becoming A Landslide/Comfort Comes (p/s, pink vinyl)	12
94	Columbia 6600706	Life Becoming A Landslide/Comfort Comes/Are Mothers Saints (12" with poster)	18
94	Epic 6604470	P.CP./Faster/Sculpture Of Man (10")	20
94	Epic 6604477	Faster/P.C.P. (p/s)	6
94	Epic 6608950	She Is Suffering/Love Torn Us Under/The Drowners/Stay With Me (10")	20
98	Epics MSP 12	If You Tolerate This Your Children Will Be Next (Massive Attack Remix)/(Massive Attack Instrumental Remix)/(Class Reunion Of Of The Sunset Marquise Mix) (12")	15
01	Epic 6708177	Found That Soul/The Masses Against The Classes(Love) (p/s)	6
07	Columbia 8697075597	Underdogs (1-sided, p/s)	20
07	Columbia 88697159347	Indian Summer/You Know It's Going To Hurt (p/s)	8
10	Columbia 88697769677	(It's Not War)Just The End Of Love/I Know The Numbers (p/s)	10
10	Columbia 88697821177	Some Kind Of Nothingness/Time Ain't Nothing (p/s)	10
11	Heavenly HVN 8	Motown Junk/Sorrow 16 (reissue, 1000 only, p/s)	20
11	Columbia 88697854657	Postcards From A Young Man/The Passing Show (p/s)	12
11	Columbia 88697946246	NATIONAL TREASURES - THE COMPLETE SINGLES (box set, 38 x CD, DVD and 3 x 7" singles)	300
11	SEAT UMPC 014	ON TRACK WITH SEAT (12")	200

MANICURED NOISE

			MINT VALUE £
14	Phantasy Sound PH 36	Europa Geht Durch Mich (Erol Alkan's Mesmerise Eins Rework)/(Erol Alkan's Mesmerise Eins Rework) (12")	25
16	Sony/Columbia 8875188501	A Design For Life/Dead Trees And Traffic Islands/A Design For Life (Stelath Sonic Orchestra Remix)/Mr Carbohydrate (12")	10
17	Columbia 88985188501	Your Love Alone Is Not Enough (Demo)/(Demo)/(Demo) (12")	10
18	Columbia 19075800927	International Blue/Holding Patterns	12
18	Secret S 741	No Surface All Feeling (1-sided, unique p/s)	300

ALBUMS

92	Epic 471060 1	GENERATION TERRORISTS (2-LP)	60
92	Columbia 471060 0	GENERATION TERRORISTS (2-LP, picture discs, inner sleeves, 5,000 only)	40
93	Columbia 474064 1	GOLD AGAINST THE SOUL (LP, inner sleeve)	100
94	Epic 477421 0	THE HOLY BIBLE (LP, picture disc)	70
96	Epic 483930	EVERYTHING MUST GO (LP)	70
98	Epic 4917031	THIS IS MY TRUTH TELL ME YOURS (LP)	80
01	Epic 501880	KNOW YOUR ENEMY (LP, inner)	50
02	Epic 5095511	FOREVER DELAYED - THE GREATEST HITS (2-LP)	50
03	Sony 5123861	LIPSTICK TRACES (3 x LP, 1,000 only with tactile sleeve)	350
04	Sony 519995 1	LIFEBLOOD (2-LP, with booklet)	175
07	Columbia 88697 07563 1	SEND AWAY THE TIGERS (LP)	50
09	Columbia 88697520581	JOURNAL FOR PLAGUE LOVERS (LP)	60
10	Columbia 88697778601	POSTCARDS FROM A YOUNG MAN (LP)	40
10	Music On Vinyl MOVLP 129	KNOW YOUR ENEMY (LP, reissue)	50
10	Music On Vinyl MOVLP 221	FOREVER DELAYED - THE GREATEST HITS (2-LP, repressing)	80
11	Columbia QMAGMANIACS	NATIONAL TREASURES - THE SELECTED SINGLES (LP, exclusive to Q magazine)	80
11	Music On Vinyl MOVLP 261	THIS IS MY TRUTH TELL ME YOURS (LP, reissue)	60
12	Music On Vinyl MOVLP 194	EVERYTHING MUST GO (LP, reissue)	60
12	Columbia 88725471251	GENERATION TERRORISTS (2-LP, reissue, adds Theme From MASH)	40
13	Columbia 888834745291	REWIND THE FILM (LP)	35
14	Columbia 88843049621	FUTUROLOGY (LP)	35
14	Columbia 88875036002	THE HOLY BIBLE 20 (LP, reissue, with 2 x CD, misprint with 4st 7lb listed as last track on side 1)	100
14	Columbia 88875036002	THE HOLY BIBLE 20 (LP, reissue, with 2 x CD)	50
15	Columbia 88875140661	THE HOLY BIBLE 20 (LP, reissue, US mix, picture disc)	30
16	Columbia 88985317831	EVERYTHING MUST GO (2-LP, reissue)	50
16	Columbia 88985317831	EVERYTHING MUST GO (LP, reissue, blue vinyl)	50
16	Columbia 88875036002	EVERYTHING MUST GO (LP, 2 x Cd, 2 x DVD reissue)	40
17	Sony 88985435081	THIS IS MY TRUTH TELL ME YOURS (LP, reissue)	35
18	Sony 19075895241	THIS IS MY TRUTH TELL ME YOURS (2-LP, reissue, misprint without band name and title)	60
18	Sony 190758909911	THIS IS MY TRUTH TELL ME YOURS (2-LP)	40
18	Columbia 19075809891	RESISTANCE IS FUTILE (LP)	25
18	Columbia 19075809891	RESISTANCE IS FUTILE (LP, white or red vinyl)	20
21	Columbia 19439895431	THE ULTRA VIVID LAMENT (LP)	20
21	Columbia 19439906001	THE ULTRA VIVID LAMENT (LP, alternative artwork HMV exclusive)	30
21	Columbia 19439895461	THE ULTRA VIVID LAMENT (LP, picture disc)	20

PROMOS

90	Damaged Goods YUBB 4	NEW ART RIOT EP (12", white label, 100 copies with press kit)	300
91	Heavenly HVN 10P	You Love Us (Radio Edit) (promo-only, some with stickered p/s, 1-sided white label, 500 only)	25
93	Columbia/Damont XPS 272	Symphony Of Tourette (1-sided, white label, no p/s)	80
93	Columbia XPR 1966	Roses In The Hospital (OG Psychoval Mix(51 Funk Salute Mix)/Filet-O-Gang Mix)/(ECG Mix)/(Original Version) (12	40
94	Columbia	DONE AND DUSTED (12", Chemical Brothers Remixes)	15
96	Columbia XPR 3043	A Design For Life (Stealth Sonic Orchestra Remix)/(Instrumental) (12")	25
96	Epic 0166307000	A Design For Life/Bright Eyes (Live Version) (white label jukebox copy)	10
96	Epic 6634680	Everything Must Go/Raindrops keep Falling On My Head (Live) (Jukebox copy)	10
96	Columbia XPR 3081	Kevin Carter (Stealth Sonic Orchestra Remix) (12", white label, 1-sided, stickered card sleeve, 30 only)	20
96	Columbia XPR 3094	Australia (Lionrock Remix) (12", white label, 1-sided, stickered card sleeve, 20 only)	30
96	Epic 6640440	Australia/A Design For lLife (Live) (jukebox copy)	10
97	Columbia MANIC 1-6CD	SIX SINGLES FROM GENERATION TERRORISTS (6-CD box set)	90
98	Epic 6663457	If You Tolerate This Your Children Will Be Next (white label, jukebox copy)	10
98	Epic 66867	The Everlasting/The Everlasting (white label, jukebox copy)	10
98	Epic 6666865	The Everlasting (Deadly Avenger Remixes)/Psalm 315/Psalm 215 Instrumental/69th St Mix/69th St Instrumental (12")	25
99	Epic XPR 3307	You Stole The Sun From My Heart (David Holmes Mixes) (12")	20
99	Epic XPR 3320	Tsunami (Cornelius Remix)/(Electron Ray Tube Mix by Stereolab) (12", p/s, sealed with sticker, promo only)	22
09	Columbia MSP 02	COOKING- CLEANING - FLOWER ARRANGING: JOURNAL FOR PLAGUE LOVERS (2 x 12", white labels)	100

(see also James Dean Bradfield, Nicky Wire)

MANICURED NOISE

80	Pre PRE 006	Faith/Free Time (p/s)	6

(see also Weatherman & Friends)

MANISH BOYS

65	Parlophone R 5250	I Pity The Fool/Take My Tip	1000
65	Parlophone R 5250	I Pity The Fool/Take My Tip (Demo copy)	500

(see also David Bowie)

MANISH BOYS/DAVY JONES & LOWER THIRD

79	EMI 2925	I Pity The Fool/Take My Tip/DAVY JONES You've Got A Habit Of Leaving/Baby Loves That Way (Demo copy p/s)	20
79	EMI EMI 2925	I Pity The Fool/Take My Tip/DAVY JONES & LOWER THIRD: You've Got A Habit Of	10

MANITOBA (1)

MINT VALUE £

82	Charly CYM 1	Leaving/Baby Loves That Way (p/s) / I Pity The Fool/Take My Tip/DAVY JONES & LOWER THIRD: You've Got A Habit Of Leaving/Baby Loves That Way (10", p/s, reissue)	7

(see also David Bowie, Davy Jones, Davie Jones & King Bees)

MANITOBA (1)
71	RCA 2055	Come On Down To My Boat/Dead End Street	10

MANITOBA (2)
01	Leaf BAY 16V	STOP BREAKING MY HEART (LP)	20
03	Leaf BAY 26V	UP IN FLAMES (LP)	20
03	Leaf BAY 26VX	UP IN FLAMES (LP, clear vinyl)	20

(see also Caribou)

MANIX
91	Reinforced RIVET 1209	Manic Minds (12", die-cut p/s)	12
92	Reinforced RIVET 1221	Rainbow People (12")	15
94	Reinforced RIVET 1275	Intelligent Hoodlums EP (2x12")	12

EARLE MANKEY
78	Bronze BRO 53	Mau Mau/Crazy	15

MANKIND
78	Pinnacle PIN 71-12	Dr. Who/Time Traveller (12", p/s, blue vinyl)	10
78	Motor Records MTR 001/12	Dr. Who/Time Traveller (12", p/s, blue vinyl, p/s)	12

SYDNEY MANKIND
82	Musical Ambassador MAPD 001	The Truth/EDI FITZROY: Chant It To The Rhythm (12")	40

ABEL MANN
70	Trend TNY 51	The Sun In The Morning/It's So Easy	7

BARRY MANN
61	HMV POP 911	Who Put The Bomp (In The Bomp Bomp)/Love True Love	25
61	HMV POP 949	Little Miss U.S.A./Find Another Fool	20
62	HMV POP 1084	Hey Baby I'm Dancin'/Like I Don't Love You	15
63	HMV POP 1108	Bless You/Teenage Has Been	15
64	Colpix PX 776	Talk To Me Baby/Amy	15
66	Capitol CL 15463	Angelica/Looking At Tomorrow	15
68	Capitol CL 15538	The Young Electric Psychedelic Hippy Flippy Folk And Funky Philosophic Turned On Groovy 12 String Band/Take Your Love	10
63	HMV CLP 1559	WHO PUT THE BOMP IN THE BOMP BOMP BOMP? (LP)	125
72	CBS 64805	LAY IT ALL OUT (LP, gatefold)	15

CARL MANN
59	London HLS 8935	Mona Lisa/Foolish One	50
59	London HLS 9006	Pretend/Rockin' Love	35
59	London HLS 9006	Pretend/Rockin' Love (78)	30
60	London HLS 9170	South Of The Border/I'm Comin' Home	25
60	London HA-S 2277	LIKE MANN - CARL MANN SINGS (LP)	250

GARY MANN ORCHESTRA
73	Penny Farthing PEN 820	The Original 'Big Match' Theme/Newscoop (The Original 'Grandstand' Theme)	12

GLORIA MANN
56	Brunswick 05569	Why Do Fools Fall In Love/Partners For Life	20
56	Brunswick 05610	It Happened Again/My Secret Sin	10

HERBIE MANN
66	Atlantic 584 058	Love Theme (From 'Is Paris Burning')/Happy Brass	7
66	Atlantic 584 052	Philly Dog/DAVE PIKE: Sunny	10
68	A&M AMS 719	Unchain My Heart/Glory Of Love	10
67	Atlantic 584112	The Beat Goes On/Free For All	10
69	Atlantic 584 297	Memphis Underground/New Orleans	10
72	Atlantic K 10179	Philly Dog/Memphis Underground/It's A Funky Thing (Right On) Part 1	6
75	Atlantic K 10580	Hijack/Orient Express	15
75	Atlantic SAM 26	Hijack (Disco Cut)/Bertha Boogie Part 1 (12", "Disco Special Cut" on label)	60
58	Fontana TFL 5013	SALUTE TO THE FLUTE (LP)	15
60	Top Rank 25/015	FLUTE FOR ETERNITY (10" LP, with Buddy Collette)	20
63	London HA-K/SH-K 8043	RIGHT NOW (LP)	20
64	Atlantic ATL 5008	HERBIE MANN AT NEWPORT (LP)	15
65	Atlantic ATL/SAL 5035	THE ROAR OF THE GREASE PAINT (LP)	20
66	CBS (S)BPG 62585	LATIN MANN (LP)	20
66	Atlantic ATL/SAL 5038	STANDING OVATION AT NEWPORT (LP)	15
66	Atlantic 587/588 003	MONDAY NIGHT AT THE VILLAGE GATE (LP)	15
66	Atlantic 587/588 028	NIRVANA (LP, with Bill Evans)	15

LORIE MANN
59	Top Rank JAR 116	A Penny A Kiss, A Penny A Hug/Dream Lover	6
59	Top Rank JAR 148	Just Keep It Up/You Made Me Care	8
59	Top Rank JAR 237	So Many Ways/I Wonder	7
61	Pye Int. 7N 25069	Happy Feet/The Busker	6

MANFRED MANN
63	HMV POP 1189	Why Should We Not/Brother Jack	30
63	HMV POP 1225	Cock-A-Hoop/Now You're Needing Me	20
64	HMV POP 1252	5-4-3-2-1/Without You	7
64	HMV POP 1282	Hubble Bubble (Toil And Trouble)/I'm Your Kingpin	8
64	HMV POP 1346	Sha La La/John Hardy	6
65	HMV POP 1413	Oh No Not My Baby/What Am I Doing Wrong	6
65	HMV POP 1466	If You Gotta Go, Go Now/Stay Around	6
66	HMV POP 1541	You Gave Me Somebody To Love/Poison Ivy	12
65	HMV 7TEA 2124	There's No Living Without Your Loving/Tired Of Trying, Bored With Lying, Scared Of Dying (demo-only EP sampler)	30

MANFRED MANN & MIKE HUG(G)

MINT VALUE £

Year	Catalogue	Title	Value
66	Fontana TF 730	Just Like A Woman/I Wanna Be Rich	6
67	Fontana TF 812	Ha! Ha! Said The Clown/Feeling So Good (in p/s)	8
67	Fontana TF 828	Sweet Pea/One Way	10
67	Fontana TF 862	So Long, Dad/Funniest Gig	7
68	Fontana TF 908	Up The Junction/Sleepy Hollow (in p/s)	18
69	Fontana TF 1013	Ragamuffin Man/A 'B' Side	8
64	HMV 7EG 8848	MANFRED MANN'S COCK-A-HOOP WITH 54321 (EP)	25
65	HMV 7EG 8876	GROOVIN' WITH MANFRED MANN (EP)	20
65	HMV 7EG 8908	THE ONE IN THE MIDDLE (EP)	10
65	HMV 7EG 8922	NO LIVING WITHOUT LOVING (EP)	18
66	HMV 7EG 8942	MACHINES (EP)	25
66	HMV 7EG 8949	INSTRUMENTAL ASYLUM (EP, with Jack Bruce)	25
66	HMV 7EG 8962	AS WAS (EP)	25
66	Fontana TE 17483	INSTRUMENTAL ASSASSINATION (EP)	12
64	HMV CLP 1731	THE FIVE FACES OF MANFRED MANN (LP)	60
64	Odeon PCLP 1731	THE FIVE FACES OF MANFRED MANN (LP, export issue gold/red odeon sticker on cover)	90
65	HMV CLP 1911	MANN MADE (LP, mono)	30
65	HMV CSD 1628	MANN MADE (LP, stereo)	40
66	HMV CLP 3559	MANN MADE HITS (LP)	35
66	Fontana TL 5377	AS IS (LP, 'alcove' cover, mono)	20
66	Fontana (S)TL 5377	AS IS (LP, 'alcove' cover, stereo)	30
66	Fontana (S)TL 5377	AS IS (LP, 'locomotive' cover, mono/stereo)	60
67	HMV CLP 3594	SOUL OF MANN (LP, mono)	50
67	HMV CSD 3594	SOUL OF MANN (LP, stereo)	70
68	Fontana (S)TL 5460	UP THE JUNCTION - ORIGINAL SOUNDTRACK RECORDING (LP)	50
68	Fontana SFL 13003	WHAT A MANN (LP)	20
68	Fontana TL 5470	MIGHTY GARVEY! (LP, mono)	25
68	Fontana (S)TL 5470	MIGHTY GARVEY! (LP, stereo)	15
70	Fontana 6852 005	UP THE JUNCTION - ORIGINAL SOUNDTRACK RECORDING (LP, reissue)	25

(see also Paul Jones, Blues Band, Mike Hugg, Henry Lowther, Mike D'Abo, McGuinness Flint, Jack Bruce, Coulson & Dean, Lyn Dobson, Paddy Klaus & Gibson)

MANFRED MANN & MIKE HUG(G)

Year	Catalogue	Title	Value
71	Ski SKI 1	Ski 'Full-Of-Fitness' Theme/Baby Jane (in p/s)	15
71	Ski SKI 1	Ski 'Full-Of-Fitness' Theme/Baby Jane	7
71	Michelin MIC+01	The Michelin Theme (Go Radial, Go Michelin) (1-sided, gatefold p/s)	15

MANFRED MANN'S CHAPTER III

Year	Catalogue	Title	Value
70	Vertigo 6059 012	Happy Being Me/Devil Woman	10
69	Vertigo VO 3	MANFRED MANN CHAPTER III (LP, 1st pressing, "Manfred Mann Chapter Three" and VO 3 847 902 VTY" in large type on B side, gatefold sleeve, large swirl label)	175
70	Vertigo VO 3	MANFRED MANN CHAPTER III (LP, 2nd pressing, "Manfred Mann Chapter Three" and VO 3 847 902 VTY" in smaller type on B side, gatefold sleeve, large swirl label)	125
70	Vertigo VO 3 847 902 VTY	MANFRED MANN CHAPTER III (LP, 3rd pressing, without 'A Philips Record Product' text, gatefold sleeve, large swirl label)	80
70	Vertigo 6360 012	MANFRED MANN CHAPTER III VOL. 2 (LP, gatefold sleeve, large swirl label)	175

MANFRED MANN'S EARTH BAND

Year	Catalogue	Title	Value
71	Philips 6006 122	Living Without You/Tribute (as Manfred Mann)	6
71	Philips 6006 159	Mrs Henry/Prayer (as Manfred Mann)	6
72	Philips 6006 251	Meat/Glorified Magnified (as Earth Band)	6
73	Vertigo 6059 078	Get Your Rocks Off/Sadjoy (as Earth Band)	7
71	Philips 6308 062	STEPPING SIDEWAYS (LP, unissued)	0
72	Philips 6308 086	MANFRED MANN'S EARTH BAND (LP, black/silver labels)	40
72	Philips 6308 125	GLORIFIED MAGNIFIED (LP, gatefold sleeve, 1st pressing, black/silver labels)	50
72	Philips 6308 086	GLORIFIED MAGNIFIED (LP, gatefold sleeve, 2nd pressing, blue/silver labels)	20
73	Vertigo 6360 087	MESSIN' (LP, die cut gatefold sleeve, 'spaceship' label)	25
73	Bronze ILPS 9265	SOLAR FIRE (LP, gatefold sleeve, lyric inner sleeve, Island label credit)	20
74	Bronze ILPS 9306	THE GOOD EARTH (LP, lyric inner sleeve with uncut corner, Island label credit)	20
75	Bronze ILPS 9337	NIGHTINGALES AND BOMBERS (LP, 1st pressing with Island matrix numbers ILPS 9337 A-2U/B-2U, "MELYS I.B.C" etched into dead wax)	20

(see also Australian Playboys, Trifle, AC/DC, Thin Lizzy, Alan Parsons Project, Jeff Wayne)

ROBERTO MANN ORCHESTRA

Year	Catalogue	Title	Value
68	Decca F13904	Love Theme From Witchfinder General/Both Sides Now	30
69	Deram DM 249	Theme From The Film "Baby Love" (Guai Guai)/Serenade To Summertime	6

SHADOW MANN

Year	Catalogue	Title	Value
69	Roulette RO 504	Come Live With Me/One By One	12

SHELLY MANNE

Year	Catalogue	Title	Value
68	Atlantic 584 180	Daktari/Out On A Limb	12
54	Vogue LDE 072	SHELLY MANNE AND HIS MEN VOL. 1 (10" LP)	15
55	Contemporary LDC 143	SHELLY MANNE VOL. 2 (10" LP, with Andre Previn & Leroy Vinegar)	15
56	Contemporary LDC 190	SHELLY MANNE, SHORTY ROGERS AND JIMMY GIUFFRE - THE THREE (10" LP)	15
56	Contemporary LDC 192	SHELLY MANNE AND RUSS FREEMAN (LP)	15
56	Contemporary LAC 12075	SHELLY MANNE AND HIS FRIENDS (LP, with Andre Previn & Leroy Vinegar)	15
62	Contemporary LAC12315	CHECKMATE (LP)	15

(see also Gerry Mulligan & Shelly Manne, Shorty Rogers & His Orchestra)

MANNIN FOLK

Year	Catalogue	Title	Value
76	Kelly MAN 2	KING OF THE SEA (LP)	35
70s	Kelly KEP 1	MANNIN FOLK SING (LP)	20

BERNARD MANNING

Year	Catalogue	Title	Value
72	Decca SKL 5030	SINGS 16 FAVOURITE SONGS (LP)	15

LINDA MANNING

Year	Catalogue	Title	Value
66	King KG 1039	Buy Me Something Pretty, Joey/Downtown Lonely Girl Blues	7

MARC MANNING
                                                                                                MINT VALUE £

MARC MANNING
13 Box Bedroom BBR 8   AMBIENCE 1 (p/s, with CD, numbered, 150 copies) 12

MARTY MANNING & CHEETAHS
67 CBS 2721   Tarzan March/Sunny 10

EDDIE MANNION
60 HMV POP 804   Just Driftin'/Quiet Girl 50

CAROL MANNS
79 SRTS 79 CUS 425   You Me And The Boogie/Seagulls 20

MAN ON THE MOON
69 Philips 88457 DE   MAN ON THE MOON (EP, spoken word, 2-part tri-foldout p/s with insert, 'historic
                                   souvenir' available via News Of The World newspaper) 10

WINGY MANONE ORCHESTRA
57 Brunswick 05655   Party Doll/Real Gone 20

MAN...OR ASTROMAN
94 One Louder LOUDER 4   YOUR WEIGHT ON THE MOON (10 LP", pink, silver or luminous vinyl) 15
95 Clawfist XPIG 28   WELCOME TO THE SONIC SPACE AGE EP (p/s) 10
95 One Louder LOUDER 8   INTRAVENOUS TELEVISION CONTINUUM (LP) 15
96 One Louder LOUDER 12   EXPERIMENTAL ZERO (LP, yellow vinyl, with poster) 15

MANOWAR
87 Atlantic B 9463   Blow Your Speakers/Violence And Bloodshed (p/s) 10
87 Atlantic BT 9463   Blow Your Speakers/Violence And Bloodshed (12", embossed p/s, with poster) 25
87 Atlantic BT 9463   Blow Your Speakers/Violence And Bloodshed (12", embossed p/s, without poster) 15
83 Music For Nations MFN 6   INTO GLORY RIDE (LP, with inner) 25
84 Music For Nations MFN 19   HAIL TO ENGLAND (LP, inner) 30
84 10 Records 206 639   SIGN OF THE HAMMER (LP) 15
87 Atco 790 563   FIGHTING THE WORLD (LP) 20
07 SPV 85601   GODS OF WAR (3-LP) 20
(see also Orson Welles)

MAN PARRISH
82 Polydor POLD 5101   MAN PARRISH (LP) 15

JOE MANSANO
69 Blue Cat BS 150   Life On Reggae Planet/RECO & RHYTHM ACES: Z.Z. Beat 50
72 Sioux SI 022   The Trial Of Pama Dice/JACKIE ROWLAND: Lonely Man 20
(see also Joe The Boss, Joe's Allstars, Dice The Boss)

TONY MANSELL
54 Parlophone MSP 6130   The High And The Mighty/Hold My Hand (with Johnny Dankworth Orchestra) 8
56 Parlophone MSP 6222   Zambesi (Sweet African)/11th Hour Melody (with Johnny Dankworth Orchestra) 8
(see also Johnny Dankworth)

JAYNE MANSFIELD
67 London HL 10147   As The Clouds Drift By/Suey (with Jimi Hendrix, demos more common, £35) 50
62 World Record Club TP 262   JAYNE MANSFIELD IN LAS VEGAS (LP) 60
(see also Jimi Hendrix)

KEITH MANSFIELD ORCHESTRA
68 CBS 3895   Beautiful/Soul Thing 20
72 2066 170   Beautiful/The Colours Are Still There 8
68 CBS 63426   ALL YOU NEED IS KEITH MANSFIELD (LP) 40
70 CBS 70073   LOOT (LP, soundtrack, with Steve Ellis) 40
79 Amphonic AMPS 123   NIGHT BIRD (LP) 125

MANSFIELD ORGANISATION
67 President PT131   Daddy Russian Stoned/Ol' Nick 20

CHARLES MANSON
80 Come Org. WDC 883008   LIE (cassette) 50
86 Fierce FRIGHT 006   Rise/Sick City (p/s, 1 side etched, handwritten labels) 20
88 Fierce FRIGHT 012   It's Comin' Down Fast (Helter Skelter) (p/s, 1 side etched, hand-made labels) 20
86 Fierce FRIGHT 001   LOVE AND TERROR CULT (LP) 30

EDDY MANSON
55 HMV 7M 325   Oh! No!/The Lovers 8

JEANE MANSON
79 CBS S CBS 7222   I've Already Seen It In Your Eyes/J'ai Deja Vu Ca Dans Tes Yeux 15

MARILYN MANSON
03 Universal 9807728   Mobscene/Paranoiac (poster p/s) 10
12 FRY 509   No Reflection (Edit)/No Reflection (Album Version) (white vinyl, p/s) 10
98 Simply Vinyl SVLP 055   ANTICHRIST SUPERSTAR (2-LP, 180 gm vinyl, gatefold sleeve) 250
98 Simply Vinyl SVLP 195   MECHANICAL ANIMALS (2-LP, 180 gm vinyl) 150
99 Interscope ADV 490 394-2   MECHANICAL ANIMALS (CD, promo, numbered, card sleeve, with comic, PVC slipcase) ... 45
99 Simply Vinyl SVLP 121   PORTRAIT ON AN AMERICAN FAMILY (2-LP) 200
00 Nothing 490 790 1   HOLY WOOD (2-LP) 200
01 Simply Vinyl SVLP 208   SMELLS LIKE CHILDREN (LP, 180 gm vinyl) 200
04 Interscope 9864285   LEST WE FORGET - THE BEST OF (2-LP) 150
12 Cooking Vinyl COOKLP 554   BORN VILLAIN (2-LP) 40

MANSUN
95 Sci Fi Hi Fi MANSON 1   Take It Easy Chicken/Take It Easy Chicken (as Manson, same track both sides, die-cut
                                   sleeve, 500 only; promos with "Manson Promo" on label £30) 15
99 Fan club MANSUN 001   Taxloss/Everyone Must Win (live) (fanclub-only release) 18
97 Parlophone CPCS 7387   ATTACK OF THE GREY LANTERN (LP, gatefold sleeve, with inners and poster) 60
98 EMI 749672314   SIX (2-LP, gatefold, inners) 60
00 Parlophone 724352778218   LITTLE KIX (2-LP) 40

JOHN MANTELL
65 CBS 201783   Remember Child/I'll See You Around 10

MIKE MANTLER
75 Watt WATT 3   133/4 (LP, with Carla Bley; with insert) 20

Bob MANTON

(see also Carla Bley, Jazz Composers Orchestra)

MINT VALUE £

BOB MANTON
81 Mainstreet MS 101   No Trees In Brixton Prison/Brixton Walkabout (p/s) 8

(see also Purple Hearts)
MANUELLA
65 Decca F 22275   The Nitty Gritty/Two Shadows 150

MANYANA
80 Modello AVR 1938   LIVE CARROTS (LP, cat. no MHR 101 on sleeve) 15

PHIL MANZANERA (& 801)
76 Island ILPS 9444   801 LIVE (LP) 15

(see also Roxy Music, Quiet Sun)
RAY MANZAREK
74 Mercury SRM 1703   THE WHOLE THING STARTED WITH ROCK'N'ROLL (LP) 15

(see also Doors, Philip Glass)
MAP OF AFRICA
05 Whatever We Want WEWW 004 Black Skin Blue Eyed Boys (12") 30

THOMAS MAPFUMO
86 Earthworks EMW 5506   GWINDINGWI RINE SHUMBA (LP, insert) 50

MAPLEOAK
70 Decca F 13008   Son Of A Gun/Hurt Me So Much 20
71 Decca SKL 5085   MAPLEOAK (LP, blue/silver label, boxed logo) 300

LUCILLE MAPP
57 Columbia DB 3916   Mangos/On Treasure Island 10
57 Columbia DB 4040   I'm Available/Lovin' Ya, Lovin' Ya, Lovin' Ya 8
59 Columbia DB 4261   Chinchilla/Follow Me 15

TOMMY MARA
55 MGM SP 1128   Pledging My Love/Honey Bunch 10
58 Felsted AF 109   Where The Blues Of The Night/What Makes You So Lonely 10
58 Felsted GEP 1003   PRESENTING TOMMY MARA (EP) 12

MARABAR CAVES
85 Tiki MBAR 1   Sally's Place Crew/Seeds That Never Grew 10

MARATHONS
61 Pye International 7N 25088 Peanut Butter/Down In New Orleans 20
61 Vogue V 9185   Peanut Butter/Talkin' Trash 25

MARAUDERS
63 Decca F 11695   That's What I Want/Hey What D'ya Say 15
63 Decca F 11748   Always On My Mind/Heart Full Of Tears 15
64 Decca F 11836   Lucille/Little Egypt 15
65 Fontana TF 609   Baby I Wanna Be Loved/Somebody Told My Girl 20

(see also Danny Davis)
MARBLE STAIRCASE
83 Whaam! WHAAM 11   Still Dreaming/Dark Ages (p/s) 12

MARBLES
69 Polydor 56310   The Walls Fell Down/Love You 7
70 Polydor 56378   Breaking Up Is Hard To Do/I Can't See Nobody 6

(see also Graham Bonnet, Fut)
MARBOO
76 EMI 2424   What About Love?/I Remember Sunday Morning 12

MARC & MAMBAS
82 Some Bizzare BZS 512   Fun City/Sleaze (Take It, Shake It)/Taking It And Shaking It (12", p/s, fan club issue, mail-order only) 20
82 Some Bizzare BZS 15   Big Louise/Empty Eyes (unreleased, artwork only) 0
82 Some Bizzare BZS 1512   Big Louise/Empty Eyes/The Dirt Behind The Neon (Sleaze Revisited) (12", unreleased, artwork only) 0
84 Gutterhearts GH 1   BITE BLACK AND BLUES - RAOUL & THE RUINED LIVE (LP, fan club issue) ... 15

(see also Soft Cell, Marc Almond)
LYDIA MARCELLE
66 Sue WI 4025   Another Kind Of Fellow/I've Never Been Hurt Like This Before 80

MUZZY MARCELLINO
56 London HLU 8355   Mary Lou/MR. FORD & MR. GOON-BONES: Ain't She Sweet 25

MARCELS
61 Pye International 7N 25073 Blue Moon/Goodbye To Love 8
61 Pye International 7N 25083 Summertime/Teeter Totter Love 12
61 Pye International 7N 25105 You Are My Sunshine/Find Another Fool 15
61 Pye International 7N 25114 Heartaches/My Love For You 15
62 Pye International 7N 25124 My Melancholy Baby/Really Need Your Love 15
63 Pye International 7N 25201 I Wanna Be The Leader/Give Me Back Your Love 30
61 Pye Intl. NPL 28016   BLUE MOON (LP) 50

(see also Tommy Regan)
GLORIA MARCH
58 London HLB 8568   Baby Of Mine/Nippon Wishing Well 25

HAL MARCH
58 London HLD 8534   Hear Me Good/One Dozen Roses 25

JO MARCH
58 London HLR 8696   Dormi, Dormi, Dormi (Sleep, Sleep, Sleep)/Fare Thee Well, Oh Honey 8

(LITTLE) PEGGY MARCH
63 RCA RCA 1338   I Will Follow Him/Wind Up Doll (as Little Peggy March) 10
63 RCA RCA 1350   My Teenage Castle/I Wish I Were A Princess (as Little Peggy March) 10
63 RCA RCA 1362   Hello Heartache, Goodbye Love/Boy Crazy (as Little Peggy March) 10
64 RCA RCA 1426   Watch What You Do With My Baby/Can't Stop (Peggy March) 10

Bobby MARCHAN

MINT VALUE £

65	RCA RCA 1472	Let Her Go/Your Girl	10
68	RCA RCA 1687	If You Loved Me/Thinking Through My Tears	30
68	RCA RCA 1687	If You Loved Me/Thinking Through My Tears (DJ copy)	60
68	RCA RCA 1752	I've Been Here Before/Time And Time Again	7
69	RCA RCA 1809	What Am I Going To Do Without You/Lilac Skies	7

BOBBY MARCHAN
68	Atlantic 584 155	Get Down With It/Half A Mind	12
69	Action ACT 4533	Ain't No Reason For Girls To Be Lonely Parts 1 & 2	20

(see also Huey 'Piano' Smith & Clowns)

MARCH HARE
68	Chapter One CH 101	Cry My Heart/With My Eyes Closed	20
69	Deram DM 258	I Could Make It There With You/Have We Got News For You	30

(see also Gary & Stu, Koobas)

MARCHING GIRLS
81	Pop:Aural POP 011	True Love/First In Line (p/s)	45

MARCH VIOLETS
82	Merciful Release MR 013	Religious As Hell/Fodder/Children On Stun/Bon Bon Babies (p/s)	30
83	Merciful Release MR 017	Grooving In Green/Stream (p/s)	8

MARCIA & JEFF
68	Studio One SO 2047	Words/SHARKS: How Could I Live	150

MARCO
74	Torpedo 31	Do Me Bump/Bump On	15
75	Torpedo TOR 33	I'm Coming Home/I'm Coming Home Again	50

MARCUS
76	United Artists UAS 30000	MARCUS (LP)	15

MARCY JO
63	Stateside SS 235	Lover's Medley : The More I See You/When I Fall In Love/When You Wore A Tulip	8

(see also Eddie Rambeau)

JANIE MARDEN
55	Decca F 10600	Soldier Boy/Hard To Get	10
55	Decca F 10605	I'll Come When You Call/Thank You For The Waltz (with Frank Weir & His Saxophone)	8
55	Decca F 10673	You Are My Love/A Teen Age Prayer	8
56	Decca F 10765	Allegheny Moon/Magic Melody	8
63	Piccadilly 7N 35128	Make The Night A Little Longer/Walk Alone	10
65	Decca F 12101	They Long To Be Close To You/This Empty Place	15
65	Decca F 12155	You Really Didn't Mean It/Only The One You Love	10

MARDEN HILL
86	él GPO 18	Curtain/Let's Make Shane & MacKenzie (p/s)	10
87	él GPO 30	Robe/Hangman (p/s)	8
88	El ACME 13	CADAQUEZ (LP)	20

MARDI GRAS
71	Bell BLL 1270	Girl I've Got News For You/If I Can't Have You	10

ARIF MARDIN
68	Atlantic 584201	Lullaby From "Rosemary's Baby"/The Blue Bull	6
69	Atlantic 584 295	Glass Onion/How Can I Be Sure	8
73	Atlantic K10309	Theme From Brother Sun, Sister Moon/Yester Year	10

ERNIE MARESCA
62	London HLU 9531	Shout Shout Knock Yourself (Out) /Crying Like A Baby Over You	20
62	London HLU 9579	Mary Jane/Down On The Beach	30
63	London HLU 9720	Love Express/Lorelei	22
64	London HLU 9834	Rovin' Kind/Please Be Fair	15
65	London HLU 10008	It's Their World/I Can't Dance	10
66	Stateside SS 560	Rockin' Boulevard Street/Am I Better Off Than Them	25

MARGAH MAN
93	Margah MMTB1	Funky Bumpkin (12")	15

MARGARET AND ANGLE
72	Zella JHLPS 128	KNOCK GOD UP (LP)	75

MARGO
69	Deram DM 274	The Spark That Lights The Flame/Left Over Love	20

MARGO & MARVETTES
64	Parlophone R 5154	Say You Will/Cherry Pie	18
64	Parlophone R 5227	Copper Kettle/So Fine	15
67	Piccadilly 7N 35387	Seven Letters/That's How Love Goes	15
67	Pye 7N 17423	When Love Slips Away/I'll Be Home (When You Call)	50
67	Pye 7N 17423	When Love Slips Away/I'll Be Home (When You Call) (DJ copy)	75

(see also Liza Dulittle)

MARGUERITA
64	Black Swan WI 431	Woman Come/ERIC MORRIS: Number One	30

VERA MARIA
69	NEMS 56-4043	Martha My Dear/Goodbye Yesterday	10

MARIANNE
68	Columbia DB 8420	As For Marionettes/You Know My Name	18
68	Columbia DB 8456	You Had Better Change Your Evil Ways/Like A See Saw	25

MARIANNE & MIKE
64	Vocalion V 9218	As He Once Was Mine/MARIANNE: Go On	8
64	Vocalion V 9225	You're The Only One/One Good Turn Deserves Another	8

(see also Friday Brown. These records do not feature Mick Jagger or Marianne Faithfull)

CHARLIE MARIANO
56	London LTZN15031	CHARLIE MARIANO QUARTET (LP)	70

A.C. MARIAS

MINT VALUE £

A.C. MARIAS
81 Dome DOM 451   Drop/So (black die cut distressed sleeve) 15

ANNE MARIE
65 Fontana TF 523   Runaround/There Must Be A Reason 10

MARIE CELESTE
71 Private pressing   AND THEN PERHAPS (LP) 400

TEENA MARIE
81 Tamla Motown 12TMG 1251   Portuguese Love/The Ballad Of Cradle Rob And Me (12") 10
79 Motown STML 12109   WILD AND PEACEFUL (LP) 15

MARIETTA
82 Polydor POSP 305   You're Only Lonely/Making Up My Mind (p/s, with Rick Parfitt, Gary Twigg, Kevin Godley
                                     and Cliff Richard) 12
82 Polydor POSP 483   Do You Wanna Dance/Only In Your Eyes (p/s, with Rick Parfitt, Gary Twigg, Kevin Godley
                                     and Cliff Richard) 12
(see also Status Quo)

MARILLION
82 EMI 12 EMIP 5351   Market Square Heroes/Three Boats Down From The Candy/Grendel (12", picture disc,
                                     3,000 only) 25
83 EMI 12 EMIP 5362   He Knows, You Know/Charting The Single/He Knows, You Know (Full Length Version) (12",
                                     picture disc, unreleased) 0
83 EMI EMIP 5393   Garden Party/Margaret (live) ('jester'-shaped picture disc) 35
83 EMI 12 EMIS 5393   Garden Party (Extended Version)/Charting The Single (live)/ Margaret (Extended Live
                                     Version) (12", p/s with poster) 10
84 EMI 12 MARIL 2   Assassing (Full Length Version)/Cinderella Search (Full Length Version) (12", p/s) 15
88 EMI MARLIP 9   Freaks (live)/Kayleigh (live) (Uncut 'jester'-shaped picture disc) 50
83 EMI EMC 3429   SCRIPT FOR A JESTER'S TEAR (LP, gatefold) 20
84 EMI EMCP 3429   SCRIPT FOR A JESTER'S TEAR (LP, picture disc) 20
84 EMI EG 2603201   REEL TO REEL (LP) 15
85 EMI JESTP 1   REAL TO REEL (LP, picture disc) 25
84 EMI EMC 2400851   FUGAZI (LP) 20
84 EMI MRLP 1   FUGAZI (LP, picture disc) 25
85 EMI EJ 2403401   MISPLACED CHILDHOOD (LP) 15
85 EMI MRLP 2   MISPLACED CHILDHOOD (LP, picture disc) 15
87 EMI EMD 1002   CLUTCHING AT STRAWS (LP) 20
88 EMI MARL 1   THE THIEVING MAGPIE (2-LP) 20
89 EMI 064 7 92877 1   SEASONS END (LP, gatefold) 20
91 EMI EMD 1022   HOLIDAYS IN EDEN (LP) 40
94 EMI 7243 8 280321 8   BRAVE (2-LP, gatefold) 175
95 EMI EMD 1079   AFRAID OF SUNLIGHT (LP, inner) 100
97 EMI LPCENT 25   MISPLACED CHILDHOOD (LP, reissue, EMI 100 Centenary, stickered sleeve) 100
04 Chocolate Frog FRC 015   CURTAIN CALL (A LIVE ARCHIVE 1983 - 1988) (6-CD box set) 150
06 Intact Records IntactLP 01   MARBLES (2-LP, marbled vinyl, numbered) 150
09 Intact Records IntactLP 02   HAPPINESS IS THE ROAD VOLUME 1 (LP as 2 x 12") 40
09 Intact Records IntactLP 03   HAPPINESS IS THE ROAD VOLUME 2 (LP as 2 x 12") 45
12 Madfish SMALP982   MARILLION.COM (2-LP, reissue) 20
12 Madfish SMALP991   ANORAKNOPHOBIA (2-LP, reissue) 20
13 Madfish SMALP996   RADIATION 2013 (2-LP, reissue, blue vinyl, 180gm) 20
17 Parlophone 0190295865511   MISPLACED CHILDHOOD (box set, remaster, 4-LP) 100
(see also Chemical Alice)

MARINA & THE DIAMONDS
09 Neon Gold GOLD 004   CROWN JEWELS (EP, 200 only) 30
09 679 Recordings 679L168   Mogwli's Road/Space And The Woods (200 only, in envelope, numbered and signed) 40
10 679 Recordings 679L173X   I Am Not A Robot/I Am Not A Robot (Clock Opera Remix) (p/s, signed edition) 15
10 679 Recordings 679L17OX   Hollywood/Hollywood (Gonzales Remix) (signed edition) 15

MARINE GIRLS
82 In Phaze COD 2   On My Mind/The Lure Of The Rockpools (p/s, with insert) 15
80 private release   A DAY BY THE SEA (cassette, 50 copies only) 50
81 In Phaze Tapes 002   BEACH PARTY (cassette, with photocopied drawings, game & handmade sleeve) 40
81 Whaam!/In Phaze COD 1   BEACH PARTY (LP, black & white sleeve & labels, with 2 inserts) 25
83 Cherry Red BRED 44   LAZY WAYS (LP, textured sleeve) 20
(see also Tracey Thorn, Everything But The Girl, Jane)

MARINERS
55 London HLA 8201   I Love You Fair Dinkum/(At The) Steamboat River Ball 10

MARINO MARINI QUARTET
59 Durium DLU 96034   COME PRIMA (10" LP) 15

MARION (FINLAND)
73 Columbia DB 8987   Tom Tom Tom/My Son John 15

MARIONETTES (1)
65 Decca F 12056   Whirlpool Of Love/Nobody But You 10
65 Parlophone R 5300   Was It Me?/Under The Boardwalk 10
65 Parlophone R 5356   Raining It's Pouring/Pick Up Your Feet (withdrawn) 12
66 Parlophone R 5416   Like A Man/Tonight It's Going To Storm 25
(see also Rag Dolls [U.K.], Katie Kissoon, Mac Kissoon)

MARIONETTES (2)
90 Maze Music DSMBC   AVE DEMENTIA (LP) 20

MARK & JOHN
64 Decca F 12044   Walk Right Back/Karen 6

JON MARK
65 Brunswick 5952   Paris Bells/Little Town Girl 12
69 Philips BF 1772   All Neat In Black Stockings/Run To Me 10
(see also Johnny Almond Music Machine, John Mayall, Mark-Almond)

Louisa MARK

MINT VALUE £

LOUISA MARK
75	Safari SF 1105	Caught You In A Lie/Caught Dubbing	20
75	Safari SF 1109	All My Loving/Sitting By The Wayside	10
77	Trojan TRO 9005	Keep It Like It Is/TROJANS: Fatty Bum Bum Gone To Jail	15
78	Bushays BFM 100	Even Though You're Gone/Gone Clear (12")	30
79	Bushays BFM 107	Six Street Six/Instrumental (12")	12
79	Robot RRS 2	Six Street Six/Version	8
81	Bushays BFM LP 101	BREAKOUT (LP)	40

MARK-ALMOND
71	Harvest HAR 5044	The City/The Ghetto	12
71	Harvest SHSP 4011	MARK-ALMOND (LP, no EMI logo on label)	25
73	Harvest SHVL 809	RISING (LP, EMI logo on label)	20

(see also Johnny Almond Music Machine, Jon Mark, John Mayall)

MARKETTS
62	Liberty LIB 55401	Surfer's Stomp/Start (as Mar-kets)	15
62	Liberty LIB 55443	Balboa Blue/Stompede	15
64	Warner Bros WB 120	Out Of Limits/Bella Delana	25
64	Warner Bros WB 130	Vanishing Point/Borealis	20
66	Warner Bros WB 5696	The Batman Theme/Richie's Theme (with p/s)	40
66	Warner Bros WB 5696	The Batman Theme/Richie's Theme	20
67	Warner Bros WB 5847	Tarzan's March/Stirrin' Up Some Soul	40
67	Warner Bros WB 5847	Tarzan's March/Stirrin' Up Some Soul (DJ copy)	50
63	Warner Bros WM 8140	THE MARKETTS TAKE TO WHEELS (LP)	50
64	Warner Bros WM 8147	OUT OF LIMITS (LP)	40
66	Warner Bros W 1642	BATMAN (LP)	50

MAR-KEYS
61	London HLK 9399	Last Night/Night Before	20
61	London HLK 9449	Morning After/Diana	15
62	London HLK 9510	Foxy/One Degree North	15
66	Atlantic AT 4079	Philly Dog/Honey Pot	15
67	Atlantic 584 074	Last Night/Night Before	8
62	London HA-K 8011	DO THE POP-EYE (LP)	50
66	Atlantic 587/588 024	THE GREAT MEMPHIS SOUND (LP)	20
68	Atlantic 587/588 135	MELLOW JELLY (LP)	20
69	Stax SXATS 1021	DAMNIFIKNOW! (LP)	25
69	Stax 2363 008	DAMNIFIKNOW! (LP, reissue)	15

(see also Booker T. & M.G.'s)

MARK FIVE
64	Fontana TF 513	Baby What's Wrong/Tango	65

(see also Nazareth)

MARK FOUR
64	Mercury MF 815	Rock Around The Clock/Slow Down	30
64	Mercury MF 825	Try It Baby/Crazy Country Hop	65
65	Decca F 12204	Hurt Me If You Will/I'm Leaving	70
66	Fontana TF 664	Work All Day (Sleep All Night)/Going Down Fast	100
85	Bam-Caruso OPRA 037	LIVE AT THE BEAT SCENE CLUB (EP, promo, 500 only)	12

(see also Creation)

PIGMEAT MARKHAM
68	Chess CRS 8077	Here Comes The Judge/The Trial	12
68	Chess CRS 8085	Sock It To 'Em Judge/The Hip Judge	15

MARK II
60	Columbia DB 4549	Night Theme/Confusion	10

MARKSMEN
63	Parlophone R 5075	Smersh/Orbit Three	20

(see also Mark Rogers & Marksmen, Houston Wells & Murksmen)

MARLEY MARL
87	MCA 1135	He Cuts So Fresh/FINESSE & SYNQUIS: Bass Game (p/s, moulded silver label)	40
87	MCA 1135	He Cuts So Fresh/FINESSE & SYNQUIS: Bass Game (p/s, paper label)	50

MIKE MARLAN
73	Bronze ILPS 9221	FAIR WARNING (LP, gatefold sleeve, label with Island credit)	20

BOB MARLEY/WAILERS
SINGLES

63	Island WI 088	Judge Not/Do You Still Love Me (as Robert Marley)	300
63	Island WI 128	ERNEST RANGLIN: Exodus/R. MARLEY: One Cup Of Coffee	300
65	Island WI 188	It Hurts To Be Alone/Mr. Talkative	90
65	Island WI 206	Play Boy/Your Love	100
65	Island WI 211	Hoot Nanny Hoot (actually by Peter Tosh & Wailers)/ BOB MARLEY: Do You Remember (actually with Wailers)	160
65	Island WI 212	Hooligan/Maga Dog (B-side actually by Peter Tosh & Wailers)	70
65	Island WI 215	Shame And Scandal (as Peter Touch [Tosh] & Wailers)/The Jerk	100
65	Island WI 216	Donna/Don't Ever Leave Me	60
65	Island WI 254	What's New Pussycat/Where Will I Find	70
65	Ska Beat JB 186	Simmer Down/I Don't Need Your Love	60
65	Ska Beat JB 211	Lonesome Feelings/There She Goes	70
65	Ska Beat JB 226	I Made A Mistake/SOUL BROTHERS: Train To Skaville	200
66	Ska Beat JB 228	Love And Affection/Teenager In Love	70
66	Ska Beat JB 230	And I Love Her/Do It Right	70
66	Ska Beat JB 249	Lonesome Tracks/Zimmerman	80
66	Island WI 260	Jumbie Jamboree/SKATALITES: Independent Anniversary Ska (I Should Have Known Better)	100

Bob MARLEY/WAILERS

MINT VALUE £

66	Island WI 268	Put It On/Love Won't Be Mine	50
66	Island WI 3001	He Who Feels It Knows It/Sunday Morning	90
66	Island WI 3009	Let Him Go (Rude Boy Get Bail)/Sinner Man (B-side matrix: WI-3009B+)	70
66	Island WI 3009	Let Him Go (Rude Boy Get Bail)/The Masher (actually by Beverley's All Stars or Soul Brothers) (B-side matrix: WI-3009 B+2)	70
66	Rio R 116	Dancing Shoes/Don't Look Back	45
66	Doctor Bird DB 1013	Rude Boy/ROLANDO AL & SOUL BROTHERS: Ringo's Theme (This Boy)	90
66	Doctor Bird DB 1021	Good Good Rudie (Jailhouse)/CITY SLICKERS: Oceans II	75
66	Doctor Bird DB 1039	Rasta Put It On/ROLAND AL & SOUL BROTHERS: Ska With Ringo	150
67	Island WI 3035	Baby I Need You (credited to Ken Boothe)/KEN BOOTHE: I Don't Want To See You Cry	100
67	Island WI 3042	I Am The Toughest (by Peter Touch [Tosh] & Wailers)/ MARCIA GRIFFITHS: No Faith	70
67	Island WI 3043	Bend Down Low/Freedom Time	80
67	Coxsone CS 7021	Oh My Darling/HAMLINS: Trying To Keep A Good Man Down	90
67	Doctor Bird DB 1091	Nice Time/Hypocrite	65
67	Studio One SO 2010	Have Faith In The Lord (with Heavenly Sisters; actually by Peter Austin)/ JOE HIGGS: Dinah	70
67	Studio One SO 2024	I Stand Predominate/NORMA FRAZER: Come By Here	250
68	Fab FAB 34	Pound Get A Blow/Funeral (white label only)	150
68	Fab FAB 36	Thank You Lord/Mellow Mood (white label only)	170
68	Fab FAB 37	Nice Time/Hypocrites (white label only)	80
68	Fab FAB 41	Burial/Bus Them Shut (existence unconfirmed)	0
68	Trojan TR 617	Stir It Up/This Train	45
70	Bamboo BAM 55	Jailhouse (Good Rudy)/JOHN HOLT: A Stranger In Love	50

(Credited to Wailers unless stated.)

70	Trojan TR 7759	Soul Shake Down Party/BEVERLY'S ALLSTARS: Version	30
70	Escort ERT 842	Run For Cover/To The Rescue	70
70	Unity UN 562	Duppy Conqueror/UPSETTERS: Duppy Conqueror (Version)	40
70	Jackpot JP 730	Mr Chatterbox (as Interns)/DOREEN SHAEFFER: Walk Thru' This World	35
70	Upsetter US 340	My Cup (solo)/LEE PERRY & WAILERS: Son Of Thunder	35
70	Upsetter US 348	Doppy Conqueror (song actually titled "Duppy Conqueror" but plays Runaway Child by Dave Barker)/UPSETTERS: Justice	20
70	Upsetter US 349	UPSETTERS: Upsetting Station (actually plays "Dig Your Grave" by Bob Marley & Wailers/ UPSETTERS: Justice (Instrumental)	40
71	Upsetter US 354	Mr. Brown/UPSETTERS: Dracula	50
71	Upsetter US 356	Kaya/UPSETTERS: Version	45
71	Upsetter US 357	Small Axe/All In One	35
71	Upsetter US 368	Picture On The Wall (as Rass Dawkins & Wailers)/UPSETTERS: Version	45
71	Upsetter US 369	More Axe (as Bob Marley)/UPSETTERS: Axe Man	30
71	Upsetter US 371	Dreamland (as Wailers)/UPSETTERS: Version	35
71	Upsetter US 372	More Axe (as Bob Marley, different version)/UPSETTERS: Axe Man	30
71	Bullet BU 464	Soultown/Let The Sun Shine On Me	40
71	Bullet BU 493	Lick Samba/Samba	40
71	Punch PH 69	Small Axe/DAVE BARKER: What A Confusion	65
71	Punch PH 77	Down Presser (as Wailers)/JUNIOR BYLES: Got The Tip	40
71	Summit SUM 8526	Stop The Train/Caution (as Wailers)	35
71	Green Door GD 4005	Trench Town Rock/Grooving Kingston 12	25
71	Green Door GD 4022	Lively Yourself Up/TOMMY McCOOK: Lively	25
72	Green Door GD 4025	Guava Jelly/Redder Than Red	20
72	Upsetter US 392	Keep On Moving/African Herbsman	35
72	CBS 8114	Reggae On Broadway/Oh Lord, I Got To Get There (as Wailers)	25
73	Blue Mountain BM 1021	Baby Baby We've Got A Date/Stop That Train	15
73	Punch PH 101	Screw Face/Face Man	25
73	Punch PH 102	Lively Up Yourself/TOMMY McCOOK: Version	20
73	Supreme SUP 216	I Like It Like This (as Bob Marley)/BUNNY GALE: Am Sorry	60
73	Island WIP 6164	Concrete Jungle/Reincarnated Soul	10
73	Island WIP 6167	Get Up, Stand Up/Slave Driver (as Wailers)	10
73	Island IDJ 2	I Shot The Sheriff/Pass It On/Duppy Conqueror (promo only)	30
74	Trojan TR 7911	Soul Shake Down Party/Caution	8
74	Trojan TR 7926	Mr Brown/Version	10
76	Island WIP 6478	Stir It Up/Rat Race (withdrawn, demos only)	15
77	Island WIP 6390	Exodus/Exodus (dub)	8
77	Island WIP 6402 1DJ	Promotional Advert For "Exodus" (handwritten label, same track both sides, with Marley commentary)	30
78	Island WIP 6440	Satisfy My Soul/Smile Jamaica (p/s)	8
80	Island/Tuff Gong WIP 6641	Three Little Birds/Every Need Got An Ego To Feed (A label demo in die cut Tuff Gong sleeve)	10
84	Daddy Kool DK 12101	Rainbow Country (Vocal)/Rainbow Country (Dub)/PABLO & UPSETTERS: Lama Lava (12", p/s)	20
84	Daddy Kool DK 12102	Natural Mystic/Natural Mystic Rhythm (12", p/s)	20
84	Island 12ISPX 169	One Love/One Love (Dub Version) (p/s)	7
80s	Island 12 BMRM 1	Get Up Stand Up/Get Up Stand Up (live) ('Rasta' p/s, promo only)	8
99	Columbia XPR 2533	Turn Your Lights Down Low (with Lauryn Hill)/(original version) (die-cut p/s, promo only)	8
03	Trojan/Sanctuary TJITV005	LEE PERRY: Disco Devil/BOB MARLEY & WU CHU: Keep On Moving (12" reissue)	40

ALBUMS

71	Upsetter/Trojan TBL 126	SOUL REBELS (LP)	100
71	Trojan TBL 126	SOUL REBELS (reissue)	65
71	Trojan TTL 66A/B	SOUL REVOLUTION (LP, white label, test pressing only)	125
72	Island ILPS 9241	CATCH A FIRE (original 'pink rim' label, 'zippo lighter' sleeve)	250
73	Island ILPS 9256	BURNIN' (original label, gatefold sleeve with photos on innner)	20
73	Trojan TRLS 62	AFRICAN HERBSMAN (original issue with "12 Neasden Lane" address and rough orange/white paper labels)	60

Rita MARLEY

MINT VALUE £

73	BBC TS 133425/6	POP SPECTACULAR IN CONCERT (LP, in buff sleeve with printed sheets)	300
73	Black Power PW2	WAILERS (LP, no title, no sleeve, pink label)	50
74	Trojan TRLS 89	RASTA REVOLUTION (reissue of TBL 126 with 2 extra tracks)	25
75	Island ISS 3	BOB MARLEY & THE WAILERS RADIO SAMPLER (with photos & press release, promo only)	40
75	Island ISS 3	BOB MARLEY & THE WAILERS RADIO SAMPLER (promo only)	20
77	Island ILPS 9498	EXODUS (LP, embossed sleeve)	15
77	BBC	ROCK GOES TO COLLEGE IN CONCERT (LP, re-issue of BBC TS 133425/6)	80
79	Island ILPS 9542	SURVIVAL (LP)	15
83	Island PILPS 97690	CONFRONTATION (picture disc)	25
83	Trojan TRLS 62	AFRICAN HERBSMAN (LP, reissue)	20
84	Island BMSP 100	THE BOX SET (All 9 Island albums in presentation box - 10,000 only)	125
84	Island PBMW 1	LEGEND - THE BEST OF BOB MARLEY (picture disc)	15
87	Receiver RRPL 106	SOUL REBELS (LP, reissue)	20

(see also Peter Tosh, Rita Marley, Ernest Ranglin, Interns, Skatalites, Rass Dawkins & Wailers, Family Man, Norma Frazer)

RITA MARLEY

65	Island WI-226	One More Chance (as Rita and Soulettes)/SKALITES: Dick Tracey	80
67	Rio R 108	Pied Piper/It's Alright	90
67	Island WI 3052	Come To Me/SOUL BOYS: Blood Pressure	150

(see also Soulettes, Soul Brothers)

LAURA MARLING

07	Way Out West WOW 003	LONDON TOWN EP (500 only)	60
07	Virgin VS 1956	MY MANIC AND I EP (with separate promotional booklet)	50
07	Virgin VS 1956	MY MANIC AND I EP (signed with booklet)	35
07	Virgin VS 1956	MY MANIC AND I EP (unsigned with booklet)	15
08	Virgin VS 1964	Ghosts/Man Sings About Romance	12
08	Virgin VS 1973	Cross Your Fingers/I'm A Fly	10
08	Virgin VS 1979	Night Terror/Alpha Shallows	20
09	Virgin VS 2004	Goodbye England (Covered In Snow) (1-sided)	12
10	Third Man TMR 044	Blues Run The Game/The Needle And The Damage Done (US pressing but 100 shipped over and sold in UK, 3 colour vinyl, signed)	120
11	Virgin – 5099967838073	Sophia/Rest In Bed (demo)	12
13	Universal/Talenthouse	The Beast (1-sided, Secret Seven, 100 only, each with unique art sleeve)	100
08	Virgin V 3040	ALAS I CANNOT SWIM (LP, with bonus DVD)	70
10	Diverse DIV 028LP	I SPEAK BECAUSE I CAN (LP, gatefold)	18
11	Virgin CDVX 3091	A CREATURE I DON'T KNOW (Box set, picture disc LP, CD, DVD, postcard, slide viewer and booklet)	40

MICKI MARLO

| 55 | Capitol CL 14271 | Prize Of Gold/Foolish Notion | 15 |
| 57 | London HL 8481 | That's Right/What You've Done To Me (B-side with Paul Anka) | 25 |

(see also Paul Anka)

MARLON

| 74 | Purple PUR 120 | Let's Go To The Disco/Broken Man | 7 |

(see also Roger Glover, Ray Fenwick)

ROBERT MARLOW

83	Reset 12REST 1	Pictures Of Dorian Grey/The Tale Of Dorian Grey (12", p/s)	10
83	Reset 12REST 3	I Just Want To Dance/No Heart (12", p/s)	10
84	Reset 12REST 4	Claudette/This Happy World (12", p/s)	10
85	Reset 7REST 6	Calling All Destroyers/In Retrospect (p/s)	10
85	Reset 12REST 6	Calling All Destroyers/In Retrosepct (12", p/s, existence unconfirmed)	0

(see also Vince Clarke, Erasure)

MARION MARLOWE

| 56 | London HLA 8306 | The Hands Of Time/Ring, Phone, Ring (withdrawn) | 100 |
| 56 | London HLA 8306 | The Hands Of Time/Ring, Phone, Ring (78) | 50 |

MARMALADE

66	CBS 202340	It's All Leading Up To Saturday Night/Wait A Minute Baby	20
67	CBS 202643	Can't Stop Now/There Ain't No Use In Hangin' On	25
67	CBS 2948	I See The Rain/Laughing Man	25
67	CBS 3088	Man In A Shop/Cry (The Shoob Doroorie Song)	15
68	CBS 3412	Lovin' Things/Hey Joe	6
68	CBS 3708	Wait For Me Mary-Anne/Mess Around	12
69	CBS 4287	Baby Make It Soon/Time Is On My Side	6
69	CBS 4615	Butterfly/I Shall Be Released	6
70	Decca F13035	Rainbow/The Ballad Of Cherry Flavar	6
72	Decca F13297	Radancer/Sarah/Just One Woman	6
76	Target TGT 105	Falling Apart At The Seams/Fly Fly Fly	6
68	CBS 63414	THERE'S A LOT OF IT ABOUT (LP)	25
70	CBS PR 36	THE BEST OF THE MARMALADE (LP)	15
70	Decca LK 5047	REFLECTIONS OF MARMALADE (LP, mono)	30
70	Decca SKL 5047	REFLECTIONS OF THE MARMALADE (LP, stereo)	15
71	Decca SKL 5211	SONGS (LP)	20
99	Tenth Planet TP 044	KALEIDOSCOPE (LP)	15

(see also Dean Ford [& Gaylords], Gaylords, Junior Campbell, Chris McClure Section)

LORENZO MARQUES

| 82 | Siren S82 CUS 1321 | Wardrobes/Lorenzo Marques | 10 |

MARQUIS DE SADE

| 81 | Xpose XP-02 | Somewhere Up In The Mountain/Black Angel (p/s with insert) | 200 |

MARQUIS OF KENSINGTON

| 67 | Immediate IM 052 | Changing Of The Guard/Reverse Thrust | 30 |

HANK MARR

| 60 | Blue Beat BB 26 | Tonk Game/Hob-Nobbin | 15 |

Randy MARR

MINT VALUE £

RANDY MARR
70 Warner Bros WB 6115   I Wonder Who's Kissing Her Now/1941 6
MARRAKESH
73 Bell 1325   The Prodigal Son Returns/Let Me Down Easy 8
73 Bell 1315   I Don't Wanna Say Goodnight/Stone 7
MARRATXI
79 Clubland SJP 901   Rock With Me/Swedish Lady 150
RICARDO MARRERO
06 Jazzman JM 056   Babalonia (Yu Qui You Version)/Babalonia (Don Version) 6
09 Jazzman JMANLP 027   A TASTE (LP, reissue as Ricardo Marrero And The Group) 45
MARRIAGE
71 Decca F13178   Ever Find Yourself Running/She Follows The Band 6
STEVE MARRIOTT
63 Decca F 11619   Give Her My Regards/Imaginary Love 200
76 A&M AMS 7230   Star In My Life/Midnight Rollin'. 8
85 Aura AUS 145   Wha'cha Gonna Do About It/All Shook Up 8
76 A&M AMLH 64572   MARRIOTT (LP) 25
(see also Small Faces, Humble Pie, Spectrum, Pollcats)
MARS
86 Windowspeak WSP 10   78 (LP) 20
JOHNNY MARS
72 Polydor 2460 168   BLUES FROM MARS (LP) 15
BERYL MARSDEN
63 Decca F 11707   I Know (You Don't Love Me No More)/I Only Care About You 15
64 Decca F 11819   When The Lovelight Starts Shining Through His Eyes/ Love Is Going To Happen To Me 20
65 Columbia DB 7718   Who You Gonna Hurt?/Gonna Make Him My Baby 35
65 Columbia DB 7797   Music Talk/Break-A-Way 35
66 Columbia DB 7888   What's She Got/Let's Go Somewhere 35
(see also Shotgun Express, She Trinity)
GERRY MARSDEN
67 CBS 2784   Please Let Them Be/I'm Not Blue 10
67 CBS 2946   Gilbert Green/What Makes Me Love You 15
68 CBS 3575   Liverpool/Charlie Girl (as Gerry Marsden & Derek Nimmo) 10
68 NEMS 56-3831   In The Year Of April/Every Day 10
69 NEMS 56-4229   Every Little Minute/In Days Of Old 6
71 Decca F 13172   I've Got My Ukelele/What A Day 6
76 DJM DJS 10708   My Home Town/Lovely Lady (p/s) 10
74 DJM DJS 314   They Don't Make Them Like That Any More/Can't You Hear The Song 6
76 DJM DJS 10708   My Home Town/Lovely Lady 6
(see also Gerry & Pacemakers)
LYNNE MARSDEN
84 Derelict DRL1   Cocktails For Two/Firefly 10
BRENDA MARSH
68 Mercury MF 1044   Cross Town Bus/Close 7
PETER MARSH
81 Polydor POSP 210   You Say You Wanna Love Me/I Won't Let You Go 15
STEVIE MARSH
59 Decca F 11181   If You Were The Only Boy In The World/Leave Me Alone 6
60 Decca F 11209   You Don't Have To Tell Me (I Know)/Wish 6
60 Decca F 11244   A Girl In Love/Over And Done With 6
62 Ember EMB S 139   I Shouldn't Be Kissing You/Time And Time Again 8
WARNE MARSH
57 London LTZ-P 15080   JAZZ OF TWO CITIES (LP) 30
WAYNE MARSH
70 Wave LP 6   RELEASE RECORD SEND TAPE (LP) 35
75 Wave LP 10   JAZZ FROM THE EAST VILLAGE (LP) 30
CHUCK MARSHALL & TWIST STARS
62 Brunswick STA 3062   TWIST TO SONGS EVERYBODY KNOWS (LP) 15
GARY MARSHALL
61 Parlophone R 4758   One Twitchy Baby/Ev'ry Chance I Get 12
60 Parlophone R 4636   Oh You Beautiful Doll/Large As Life 6
JOY MARSHALL
64 Decca F 11863   When You Hold Me Tight /Rain On Snow 12
65 Decca F12189   Heartache Hurry On By/He's For Me 40
65 Decca F 12222   My Love Come Home/When A Girl Really Loves You 12
66 Decca F 12422   The More I See You/Taste Of Honey 20
68 Toast 512   And I'll Find You/I'm So Glad You're Back 15
65 Decca LK 4678   WHO SAYS THEY DON'T WRITE GOOD SONGS ANY MORE? (LP) 35
LARRY MARSHALL
67 Blue Beat BB 374   Move Your Feet/Find A New Baby 70
67 Blue Beat BB 380   Suspicion/Broken Heart 175
67 Doctor Bird DB 1008   Snake In The Grass/ROLAND ALPHONSO: V.C. 10 125
68 Caltone TONE 126   No One To Give Me Love/PHIL PRATT: Safe Travel 175
70 Bamboo BAM 22   Girl Of My Dreams/SOUND DIMENSON: Give It Away 30
70 Bamboo BAM 52   Man From Galilee/Give It Away (as Larry Marshall & Enid Cumberland) 30
70 Bamboo BAM 61   Let's Make It Up/BURNING SPEAR: Free 35
70 Banana BA 300   Stay A Little Longer/MAYTALS: He'll Provide 20
71 Banana BA 364   Maga Dog/OSSIE ROBINSON: Economical Heatwave 25
73 Pama PM 873   True Believer/FLAMES: Water Your Garden 15
75 Ocean OC 004   Can't You Understand/KING TUBBY : Locks Of Dub 18

Owen MARSHALL

MINT VALUE £

75	Black & White CP 4326	I Admire You/KING TUBBY: Watergate Rock	10
79	Yard International YI 103	Birdsong/She's Gone (12")	15
86	Java LM001LP	I ADMIRE YOU (LP, reissue, blue or black labels)	40
95	Original OMLP 029	THROW MI CORN (LP)	30

(see also Larry & Alvin, Irving Brown, Fitzroy D. Long, Kingston Pete & Buster's Allstars, Max Romeo, Jackie Mittoo)

OWEN MARSHALL
12	Jazzman JMANLP 048	THE NAKED TRUTH (LP, with free 7", reissue)	30

WAYNE MARSHALL
85	Jah Tubbys JT 013	Give Me The Mix/Mike In My Hand (12", with the Offbeat Posse)	75

WILLIE MARSHALL
70	Torpedo TOR 20	Loosen Up Strong Man/Strong Man	40

MARSHMELLOW HIGHWAY
68	London HLR 10204	I Don't Wanna Live This Way/Loving You Makes Everything Alright	18

MARSHMALLOW WAY
69	United Artists UP 35031	C'mon Kitty Kitty/Michigan Mints	8

MARSUPILAMI
70	Transatlantic TRA 213	MARSUPILAMI (LP, white/lilac label, 't' logo)	200
71	Transatlantic TRA 230	ARENA (LP, white/lilac label, 't' logo)	200

LENA MARTELL
67	Pye 7N 17276	The Pop Group Song/Reflections	10

PIERA MARTELL
74	CBS S CBS 2293	My Ship Of Love/Mein Ruf Nach Dir	12

RAY MARTELL
70	Joe JRS 3	She Caught The Train/PAMA DICE: Tea House From Emperor Rosko	100
70	Attack ATT 8015	Loving Lover/Cora	6
70	Doctor Bird DB 1503	This Little Light/Lover	6
70	Trojan TR 7787	This Little Light/Lover	6
72	Sioux SI 012	She Caught The Train/JOE'S ALLSTARS: Tony B.'s Theme	12
73	Rays RA 1	Working For My Love/King Fuzz - Downtown Rock	12
73	Rays RA 2	Lover/Dub	8
73	Rays RA 3	I Wish You Luck/Version	8
73	Rays RA 4	Angelina/Angelina Part 2	8
77	Rays RA 077	Falling In Love/Everlasting Love	8

MARTELLS
66	Decca F 12463	Time To Say Goodnight/The Cherry Song	40

MARTHA (REEVES) & VANDELLAS
63	Oriole CBA 1814	I'll Have To Let Him Go/My Baby Won't Come Back	450
63	Oriole CBA 1819	Come And Get These Memories/Jealous Lover	275
63	Stateside SS 228	Heatwave/A Love Like Yours (Don't Come Knockin' Every Day)	50
63	Stateside SS 228	Heatwave/A Love Like Yours (Don't Come Knockin' Every Day) (DJ copy)	150
64	Stateside SS 250	Quicksand/Darling, I Hum Our Song	55
64	Stateside SS 250	Quicksand/Darling, I Hum Our Song (DJ copy)	125
64	Stateside SS 272	Live Wire/Old Love (Let's Try It Again)	60
64	Stateside SS 272	Live Wire/Old Love (Let's Try It Again) (DJ copy)	100
64	Stateside SS 305	In My Lonely Room/A Tear For The Girl	80
64	Stateside SS 305	In My Lonely Room/A Tear For The Girl (DJ copy)	150
64	Stateside SS 345	Dancing In The Street/There He Is (At My Door)	20
64	Stateside SS 345	Dancing In The Street/There He Is (At My Door) (DJ copy)	125
65	Stateside SS 383	Wild One/Dancing Slow	50
65	Stateside SS 383	Wild One/Dancing Slow (DJ copy)	200
65	Tamla Motown TMG 502	Nowhere To Run/Motoring	25
65	Tamla Motown TMG 502	Nowhere To Run/Motoring (DJ copy)	120
65	Tamla Motown TMG 530	You've Been In Love Too Long/Love (Makes Me Do Foolish Things)	35
65	Tamla Motown TMG 530	You've Been In Love Too Long/Love (Makes Me Do Foolish Things) (DJ copy)	100
66	Tamla Motown TMG 549	My Baby Loves Me/Never Leave Your Baby's Side	40
66	Tamla Motown TMG 549	My Baby Loves Me/Never Leave Your Baby's Side (DJ copy)	120
66	Tamla Motown TMG 567	What Am I Going To Do Without Your Love/Go Ahead And Laugh	35
66	Tamla Motown TMG 567	What Am I Going To Do Without Your Love/Go Ahead And Laugh (DJ copy)	100
66	Tamla Motown TMG 582	I'm Ready For Love/He Doesn't Love Her Anymore	20
66	Tamla Motown TMG 582	I'm Ready For Love/He Doesn't Love Her Anymore (DJ copy)	50
67	Tamla Motown TMG 599	Jimmy Mack/Third Finger, Left Hand	12
67	Tamla Motown TMG 621	Love Bug Leave My Heart Alone/One Way Out	35
67	Tamla Motown TMG 621	Love Bug Leave My Heart Alone/One Way Out (DJ copy)	75
68	Tamla Motown TMG 636	Honey Chile/Show Me The Way	18
68	Tamla Motown TMG 657	I Promise To Wait, My Love/Forget Me Not	18
68	Tamla Motown TMG 669	I Can't Dance To That Music You're Playing/I Tried	25
69	Tamla Motown TMG 684	Dancing In The Street/Quicksand	7
69	Tamla Motown TMG 694	Nowhere To Run/Live Wire	7
71	Tamla Motown TMG 762	Forget Me Not/I Gotta Let You Go	7
71	Tamla Motown TMG 794	Bless You/Hope I Don't Get My Heart Broke	7
72	Tamla Motown TMG 599	Jimmy Mack/Third Finger, Left Hand (reissue)	6
73	Tamla Motown TMG 843	No One There/(I've Given You) The Best Years Of My Life	125
73	Tamla Motown TMG 843	No One There/(I've Given You) The Best Years Of My Life (DJ Copy)	200
65	Tamla Motown TME 2009	MARTHA AND THE VANDELLAS (EP)	120
66	Tamla Motown TME 2017	HITTIN' (EP)	150
63	Oriole PS 40052	COME AND GET THESE MEMORIES (LP)	400
65	Tamla Motown TML 11005	HEATWAVE (LP)	60
65	Tamla Motown TML 11013	DANCE PARTY (LP)	70
67	Tamla Motown TML 11040	GREATEST HITS (LP, original with flipback sleeve, mono)	25
67	Tamla Motown (S)TML	GREATEST HITS (LP, original with flipback sleeve, stereo)	30

MARTIAN SCHOOLGIRLS

MINT VALUE £

67	Tamla Motown (S)TML 11040	GREATEST HITS (LP, re-pressing non-flipback sleeve)	15
67	Tamla Motown TML 11051	WATCH OUT! (LP, mono)	50
67	Tamla Motown STML 11051	WATCH OUT! (LP, stereo)	50
68	Tamla Motown TML 11078	RIDIN' HIGH (LP, mono)	30
68	Tamla Motown STML 11078	RIDIN' HIGH (LP, stereo)	35
69	Tamla Motown (S)TML 11099	DANCING IN THE STREET (LP, mono/stereo)	25
70	Tamla Motown TML 11134	SUGAR N' SPICE (LP, mono)	35
70	Tamla Motown STML 11134	SUGAR N' SPICE (LP, stereo)	25
70	Tamla Motown STML 11166	NATURAL RESOURCES (LP)	25
72	Tamla Motown STML 11204	BLACK MAGIC (LP)	30

MARTIAN SCHOOLGIRLS
79	Red Planet RPR 1	Life In The 1980's/Lonely Nights (p/s)	10

MARTIN
68	Coxsone CS 7056	I Second That Emotion (actually by Martin Riley)/ROY TOMLINSON: I Stand For I	150

ALAN MARTIN
63	Rio R 3	The Party/Indeed	8
63	Rio R 6	You Came Late/Dreaming	8
63	Rio R 9	Secretly/Fame And Fortune	8
63	Rio R 10	Mother Brother/Tell Me	8
65	Rio R 66	Must Know I Love You/VIC BROWN'S COMBO: Rio Special	12
65	Rio R 67	Sweet Rosemarie/HONEYSUCKERS: Banjo Man	8
65	Rio R 68	Why Must I Cry/Shirley I Love You	12
65	Rio R 74	Since I Married Dorothy/You Promised Me	8
65	Venus VE 1	Cry Myself To Shame/Baby Don't Go	10
66	Rio R 94	Days Are Lonely/My Baby	15
66	Rio R 96	Rome Wasn't Built In A Day/I'm Hurt	15

MARTIN & DERRICK
61	Blue Beat BB 48	Times Are Going/I Love You Baby (with Cavaliers Combo)	15
62	Island WI 024	Come On/MONTY & CYCLONES: Organisation	20

(see also Derrick Morgan)

MARTIN & FINLEY
73	Tamla Motown TMG 867	It's Another Sunday/Best Friends (withdrawn, demo only)	350

BOBBI MARTIN
65	Coral Q 72478	I Can't Stop Thinking About You/Million Thanks To You	6

CHRIS MARTIN
59	HMV POP 664	Lonely Street/Swing A Little Lover	10
60	HMV POP 692	Point Of No Return/I Don't Regret A Thing	6

DAVE MARTIN
64	Port-O-Jam PJ 4112	Let Them Fight/OSSIE IRVING SIX: Why I Love You	18
64	Port-O-Jam PJ 4115	All My Dreams/Take Your Belongings	18

DEAN MARTIN
SINGLES
54	Capitol CL 14123	Hey Brother, Pour The Wine/I'd Cry Like A Baby (green label)	15
54	Capitol CL 14123	Hey Brother, Pour The Wine/I'd Cry Like A Baby (purple label)	10
54	Capitol CL 14138	Sway/Pretty As A Picture	40

(Originally issued with triangular centres; round-centre reissues are worth around half these values.)

56	Capitol CL 14523	Memories Are Made Of This/Change Of Heart	12
59	Capitol CL 15015	Rio Bravo/My Rifle, My Pony And Me	10

(see also Jerry Lewis, Frank Sinatra)

DEREK MARTIN
64	Sue WI 308	Daddy Rolling Stone/Don't Put Me Down Like This (credited as Derak Martin)	100
65	Columbia DB 7694	You Better Go/You Know	40
68	Stax 601 039	Soul Power/Sly Girl	30

DON MARTIN & DANDY (& SUPERBOYS)
67	Giant GN 6	Got A Feelin'/CONNECTIONS: At The Junction	25
68	Giant GN 24	Keep On Fighting/Rock Steady Boogie (with Superboys)	25

(see also Dandy & Superboys)

GEORGE MARTIN & HIS ORCHESTRA
64	Parlophone R 5135	I Saw Her Standing There/All My Loving	12
64	Parlophone R 5166	And I Love Her/Ringo's Theme (This Boy)	12
65	Parlophone R 5222	All Quiet On The Mersey Front/Out Of The Picture	15
65	Parlophone R 5256	I Feel Fine/The Niagara Theme	10
65	Parlophone R 5375	Yesterday/Another Girl	15
66	United Artists UP 1154	By George! - It's The David Frost Theme/Double Scotch	15
66	United Artists UP 1165	Love In The Open Air/Theme From "The Family Way"	20
67	United Artists UP 1194	Theme One/Elephants And Castles	20
72	United Artists UP 35423	Pulp - Theme/Pulp - Love Theme	10
65	Parlophone GEP 8930	MUSIC FROM "A HARD DAY'S NIGHT" (EP)	35
64	Parlophone PMC 1227	OFF THE BEATLE TRACK (LP, mono)	18
64	Parlophone PCS 3057	OFF THE BEATLE TRACK (LP, stereo)	20
65	Parlophone TA-PMC 1227	OFF THE BEATLE TRACK (reel-to-reel, mono only)	12
65	Columbia SX 1775	PLAYS HELP! (LP, mono)	20
65	Studio Two TWO 102	PLAYS HELP! (LP, stereo)	20
66	United Artists (S)ULP 1157	INSTRUMENTALLY SALUTES THE BEATLES GIRLS (LP)	30
66	Studio Two TWO 141	AND I LOVE HER (LP)	20
67	Decca LK 4847	THE FAMILY WAY (LP, mono, soundtrack)	70
67	Decca SKL 4847	THE FAMILY WAY (LP, stereo, soundtrack)	90

Grady MARTIN & THE SLEWFOOT FIVE

			MINT VALUE £
68	United Artists (S)ULP 1196	BRITISH MAID (LP)	25
70	Sunset SLS 50182	BY GEORGE! (LP)	20
73	United Artists UAS 29475	LIVE AND LET DIE (LP, soundtrack, gatefold sleeve)	25
74	Polydor Super 2383 304	BEATLES TO BOND AND BACH (LP)	15
78	St. Michael IMP 105	BEATLES TO BOND AND BACH (LP, exclusive to Marks & Spencer)	20

(see also Beatles, Ray Cathode)

GRADY MARTIN & THE SLEWFOOT FIVE
56	Brunswick 05535	Nashville/Don't Take Your Love From Me	15

HONEYBOY MARTIN
67	Caltone TONE 103	Dreader Than Dread (and the Voices)/DANDY: In The Mood	50
70	Gas GAS 123	Unchained Melody/SAMMY JONES: You're My Girl	10
72	Sioux SI 011	Unchained Melody/SAMMY JONES: You're My Girl (reissue)	8
72	Harry J HJ 6643	Have You Ever Seen The Rain/Spanish Harlem	7

(see also Lynn Tait & Jets)

JACKI MARTIN
64	Fontana TF 487	Will You/Till He Tells Me	12

JANIS MARTIN
60	Palette PG 9000	Here Today And Gone Tomorrow Love/Hard Times Ahead	25
80	RCA PE 9494	JANIS MARTIN (EP)	10
80	RCA PL 43153	THE COMPLETE RCA JANIS MARTIN (2-LP)	25

JEAN MARTIN
63	Decca F 11751	Ain't Gonna Kiss Ya/Three Times Three Is Love	10
64	Decca F 11897	Save The Last Dance For Me/Will You Still Love Me Tomorrow	10

JERRY MARTIN
63	London HLU 9692	Shake-A Take-A/Exchange Student	15

KERRY MARTIN
58	Parlophone R 4449	Stroll Me/Cold Hands, Warm Heart	12

LUCIA MARTIN
62	Parlophone R 4915	Big Jim/Star From Heaven	12

MARK MARTIN
67	Page One POF 020	Extraordinary Girl/Love Could Be Like Hell	6

MILES MARTIN FOLK GROUP
71	Amber	MILES MARTIN FOLK GROUP (LP, private pressing)	70

MILLICENT MARTIN
63	Parlophone R5033	Get Lost My Love/Gravy Waltz	15
63	Parlophone R 4998	That Was The Week That Was/Gotta Lotta Lovin' (with David Frost)	7
64	Parlophone R 5120	Suspicion/Nothing But The Best	6
59	Columbia 33SX 1145	MILLICENT (LP)	150
64	Philips BL 7591	MR & MRS (LP)	15

(see also David Frost)

PATRICK D. MARTIN
80	Deram DM 433	Lucy 'Lectric/I Like Electric Motors/Mutant (p/s)	10

PAUL MARTIN
67	Sue WI 4041	Snake In The Grass/I've Got A New Love	70

RAY MARTIN (& HIS) CONCERT ORCHESTRA
53	Columbia SCM 5001	Blue Tango/Belle Of The Ball	8
53	Columbia SCM 5002	The Marching Strings/The Waltzing Cat	8
53	Columbia SCM 5063	Swedish Rhapsody/Hi-Lili Hi-Lo	10
56	Columbia SCM 5264	The Carousel Waltz/Port Au Prince	7

(see also Ray Burns)

REMY MARTIN
82	Cartridge CRD 14	I Want You/I Want You (Dub) (12")	60

RICKY MARTIN & TYME MACHINE
68	Olga OLE 4	Something Else/Blue Suede Shoes	15

RODGE MARTIN
67	Polydor 56725	When She Touches Me/Lovin' Machine	10

RON MARTIN & JUBILEE STOMPERS
68	Doctor Bird DB 1151	Give Your Love To Me/I Cry My Heart	20

RUPIE MARTIN('S ALLSTARS)
69	Ackee ACK 101	The Arena/Naturally	60
70	Torpedo TOR 24	Last Flight/Super Lotus	30
70	Torpedo TOR 26	Musical Container (Parts 1 & 2)	100
70	Punch PH 43	Death In The Arena (actually by Rupie Martin All Stars)/ MAN COMETH: Julia Caesar (actually by Charlie Ace)	30

SETH MARTIN
68	Page One POF 073	Another Day Goes By/Look At Me	15

SHANE MARTIN
68	CBS 2894	You're So Young/I Need You	275
68	CBS 2894	You're So Young/I Need You (DJ copy)	350

TONY MARTIN
53	HMV 7M 105	Tenement Symphony (both sides)	7
56	HMV 7M 414	Walk Hand In Hand/Flamenco Love	8
56	HMV 7MC 41	Walk Hand In Hand/Flamenco Love (export issue)	8
65	Stateside SS 394	Talkin' To Your Picture/Our Rhapsody	120
65	Tamla Motown TMG 537	The Bigger Your Heart Is (The Harder You'll Fall)/The Two Of Us	220
65	Tamla Motown TMG 537	The Bigger Your Heart Is (The Harder You'll Fall)/The Two Of Us (DJ copy)	300

(see also Gogi Grant)

TRADE MARTIN
63	London HL 9662	Hula Hula Dancin' Doll/Something In The Wind	15

VINCE MARTIN
56	London HL 8340	Cindy Oh Cindy/Only If You Praise The Lord	8

MARTIN & THE BROWNSHIRTS

			MINT VALUE £
59	HMV POP 594	Old Grey Goose (Aunt Rhodie)/Goodnight, Irene	8

(see also Tarriers)

MARTIN & THE BROWNSHIRTS
78	Lightning GIL 507	Taxi Driver/Boring	40

WINK MARTINDALE
59	London HLD 8962	Deck Of Cards/Now You Know How It Feels (tri centre)	10
63	London RED 1370	DECK OF CARDS (EP)	12
60	London HA-D 2240	WINK MARTINDALE (LP)	20

MARTIN ISLAND
83	Contraband CON 1	Don't Give It Up/Part 2 (p/s)	200

AL MARTINO
54	Capitol CL 14128	Wanted/There'll Be No Teardrops Tonight (Green label, tri centre)	10
54	Capitol CL 14148	On And On (In Love With You)/Give Me Something To Go With The Wine (Green label, tri centre)	10
54	Capitol CL 14163	The Story Of Tina/Destiny (No One Can Change) (Green label, tri centre)	15
54	Capitol CL 14163	The Story Of Tina/Destiny (No One Can Change) (Purple label, tri centre)	10
55	Capitol CL 14343	The Man From Laramie/To Please My Lady	15

(Originally issued with triangular centres; round-centre reissues are worth around half these values.)
67	Capitol 15516	More Than The Eye Can See/Red Is Red	20
61	Capitol EAP 1.20153	TO PLEASE MY LADY (EP)	10

MARTINS
65	Studio 66 KEP 113/4	MARTINS EP (no p/s)	50

MARTIN'S MAGIC SOUNDS
67	Deram DM 141	Mon Amour, Mon Amour/Midem Melody	6

JOHN MARTYN
71	Island WIP 6116	May You Never/Just Now	20
77	Island WIP 6385	Over The Hill/Head And Heart	6
78	Island WIP 6414	Dancing/Dealer (Version)	6
78	Island WIP	Dancing/Dealer (Version) (promo)	8
80	Island WIP 6547	Johnny Too Bad/Johnny Too Bad (Version)	6
81	Island IPR 2046	Johnny Too Bad (Extended Dub Version)/Big Muff (Extended Mix) (12", promo)	10
82	WEA K 259987-7	Gun Money (US Remix)/Hiss On the Tape (live)	6
86	Island CID 265	Classic John Martyn: Angeline/Tight Connection To My Heart (Has Anybody Seen My Love)/May You Never/Solid Air/Glistening Glyndebourne (CD, foldout sleeve)	15
67	Island ILP 952	LONDON CONVERSATION (LP, 1st pressing, with black & orange 'circle' logo)	350
68	Island ILP 991	THE TUMBLER (LP, 1st pressing, with black 'circle' logo, mono)	250
68	Island ILPS 9091	THE TUMBLER (LP, 1st pressing, with black 'circle' logo, stereo)	60
69	Island ILP 952	LONDON CONVERSATION (LP, 2nd pressing, pink label, white 'i' logo)	70
69	Island ILP 952	LONDON CONVERSATION (LP, 3rd pressing, 'pink rim' label, 'palm tree' logo)	40
70	Island ILPS 9091	THE TUMBLER (LP, 2nd pressing, 'pink rim' label, 'palm tree' logo, fully laminated sleeve)	40
71	Island ILPS 9167	BLESS THE WEATHER (LP, 'pink rim' label, 'palm tree' logo)	80
73	Island ILPS 9226	SOLID AIR (LP, gatefold sleeve with lyric sheet 'pink rim' label, 'palm tree' logo)	100
73	Island ILPS 9253	INSIDE OUT (LP, gatefold sleeve with inner, 'pink rim' label, 'palm tree' logo)	30
74	Island ILPS 9296	SUNDAY'S CHILD (LP, with lyric inner sleeve, 'palm tree' label)	30
75	Island ILPS 9343	LIVE AT LEEDS (LP, mail-order, 10,000 only, numbered & some signed)	30
77	Island ILPS 9492	ONE WORLD (LP, inner)	20

JOHN & BEVERLEY MARTYN
70	Island WIP 6076	John The Baptist/The Ocean	12
70	Island ILPS 9113	STORMBRINGER (LP, 1st pressing, pink label with 'i' logo)	100
70	Island ILPS 9113	STORMBRINGER (LP, 2nd pressing, 'pink rim' label, 'palm tree' logo)	15
70	Island ILPS 9133	THE ROAD TO RUIN (LP, 'pink rim' label, 'palm tree' logo)	25

(see also Beverley)

KID MARTYN
62	77 77LA 12/20	IN NEW ORLEANS WITH KID SHEIK'S BAND (LP)	15

MARVELETTES
61	Fontana H 355	Please Mr Postman/So Long Baby	55
62	Fontana H 386	Twistin' Postman/I Want A Guy	70
62	Oriole CBA 1764	Beechwood 4-5789/Someday Someway	155
63	Oriole CBA 1817	Locking Up My Heart/Forever	400
64	Stateside SS 251	As Long As I Know He's Mine/Little Girl Blue (DJ copy)	90
64	Stateside SS 251	As Long As I Know He's Mine/Little Girl Blue	60
64	Stateside SS 273	He's A Good Guy (Yes He Is)/Goddess Of Love (DJ copy)	100
64	Stateside SS 273	He's A Good Guy (Yes He Is)/Goddess Of Love	60
64	Stateside SS 334	You're My Remedy/A Little Bit Of Sympathy, A Little Bit Of Love (DJ copy)	100
64	Stateside SS 334	You're My Remedy/A Little Bit Of Sympathy, A Little Bit Of Love	45
65	Stateside SS 369	Too Many Fish In The Sea/Need For Love (DJ copy)	125
65	Stateside SS 369	Too Many Fish In The Sea/Need For Love	40
65	Tamla Motown TMG 518	I'll Keep Holding On/No Time For Tears (DJ copy)	400
65	Tamla Motown TMG 518	I'll Keep Holding On/No Time For Tears	120
65	Tamla Motown TMG 535	Danger Heartbreak Dead Ahead/Your Cheating Ways (DJ copy)	200
65	Tamla Motown TMG 535	Danger Heartbreak Dead Ahead/Your Cheating Ways	100
66	Tamla Motown TMG 546	Don't Mess With Bill/Anything You Wanna Do (DJ copy)	85
66	Tamla Motown TMG 546	Don't Mess With Bill/Anything You Wanna Do	50
66	Tamla Motown TMG 562	You're The One/Paper Boy (DJ copy)	75
66	Tamla Motown TMG 562	You're The One/Paper Boy	45
67	Tamla Motown TMG 594	The Hunter Gets Captured By The Game/I Think I Can Change You (DJ copy)	60
67	Tamla Motown TMG 594	The Hunter Gets Captured By The Game/I Think I Can Change You	30
67	Tamla Motown TMG 609	When You're Young And In Love/The Day You Take One, You Have To Take The Other	15
68	Tamla Motown TMG 639	My Baby Must Be A Magician/I Need Someone	22

MARVELLOUS CAIN

MINT VALUE £

68	Tamla Motown TMG 659	Here I Am Baby/Keep Off, No Trespassing	25
69	Tamla Motown TMG 701	Reachin' For Something I Can't Have/Destination Anywhere	15
73	Tamla Motown TMG 860	Reachin' For Something I Can't Have/Here I Am Baby (DJ copy, plays "My Baby Must Be A Magician")	100
73	Tamla Motown TMG 860	Reachin' For Something I Can't Have/Here I Am Baby	10
75	Tamla Motown TMG 1000	Finders Keepers, Losers Weepers/KIM WESTON: Do Like I Do	100
65	Tamla Motown TME 2003	THE MARVELETTES (EP)	110
65	Tamla Motown TML 11008	THE MARVELLOUS MARVELETTES (LP)	250
67	Tamla Motown TML 11052	THE MARVELETTES (LP, mono)	50
67	Tamla Motown STML 11052	THE MARVELETTES (LP, stereo)	55
69	Tamla Motown (S)TML 11090	SOPHISTICATED SOUL (LP, mono/stereo)	40
70	Tamla Motown STML 11145	IN FULL BLOOM (LP)	30
71	Tamla Motown STML 11177	THE RETURN OF THE MARVELETTES (LP, unissued)	0
75	Tamla Motown STML 11258	THE BEST OF THE MARVELETTES (LP)	40

MARVELLOUS CAIN
95	Suburban Base SUBBASELP3	GUN TALK (2-LP)	20

MARVELOWS
65	HMV POP 1433	I Do/My Heart	30
65	HMV POP 1433	I Do/My Heart (DJ Copy)	40

MARVELS (JAMAICA)
62	Dice CC 8	Come To The Wedding/Angelo	10
63	Blue Beat BB 191	Sonia/The More We Are Together	12
64	Blue Beat BB 221	Millie/Saturday	20
70	Pama PM 813	Love One Another/Falling Rain	8
70	Pama PM 817	Don't Let Him Take Your Love From Me/A Little Smile	10
70	Gas GAS 138	Sail Away/Fight A Broke	15
70	Gas GAS 139	Someday We'll Be Together/MOHAWKS: The Rhythm	20
71	Pama PM 819	Oh Lord Why Lord/NEVILLE HINDS: Love Letter	8
71	Pama Supreme PS 338	Rocksteady/ Be My Baby	30

MARVELS (U.K.)
68	Columbia DB 8341	Keep On Searching/Heartache	120

MARVELS FIVE
65	HMV POP 1423	Bye Bye Baby Bunting/In Front Of Her House	7
65	HMV POP 1452	Don't Play That Song/(You Lied) I Forgive	15

MARVETTE
68	Amalgamated AMG 804	Tit For Tat (actually by Lyn Taitt & Jets)/You Take So Long To Know	50
68	Sacred Sound SS 001	We Are Not Divided/He Is So Real To Me	8
68	Sacred Sound SS 002	We Shall Have A Grand Time/Let The Power Fall On Me	8
68	Sacred Sound SS 003	I Was Once Lost In Sin/What A Wonderful Thing	8
68	Tabernacle TS 1001	I Want A Revival/Tell It	15
68	Tabernacle TS 1003	Sweet Jesus/When I Look Back	7
60s	Coxsone TLP 1002	IT'S REVIVAL TIME (LP)	60

MARVIN & FARRAR
73	EMI EMI 2044	Music Makes My Day/Skin Deep (with Olivia Newton-John)	10
75	EMI EMI 2335	Small And Lonely Light/Galadriel (Spirit Of Starlight)	7
73	EMI EMA 755	HANK MARVIN AND JOHN FARRAR (LP, with Olivia Newton-John on recorder)	20

(see also Shadows, Hank Marvin, Marvin Welch & Farrar)

MARVIN & JOHNNY
57	Vogue V 9074	Yak Yak/Pretty Eyes	300
57	Vogue V 9074	Yak Yak/Pretty Eyes (78)	75
58	Vogue V 9099	Smack, Smack/You're In My Heart	300
58	Vogue V 9099	Smack, Smack/You're In My Heart (78)	75
65	Black Swan WI 467	Cherry Pie/Ain't That Right	20

BRETT MARVIN & THUNDERBOLTS
70	Sonet SNTF 616	BRETT MARVIN AND THE THUNDERBOLTS (LP)	15
71	Sonet SNTF 619	12 INCHES OF BRETT MARVIN & THE THUNDERBOLTS (LP)	20

(see also Jona Lewie)

HANK (B.) MARVIN
68	Columbia DB 8326	London's Not Too Far/SHADOWS: Running Out Of World	15
69	Columbia DB 8552	Goodnight Dick/Wahine	8
69	Columbia DB 8601	Sacha/Sunday For Seven Days	8
69	Columbia DB 8628	Midnight Cowboy/SHADOWS: Slaughter On Tenth Avenue	12
70	Columbia DB 8693	Break Another Dawn/Would You Believe It? (demo-only, unissued B-side)	100
70	Columbia DB 8693	Break Another Dawn/Morning Star	10
69	Columbia SCX 6352	HANK MARVIN (LP, blue/black label, mono)	35
69	Columbia SCX 6352	HANK MARVIN (LP, blue/black label, stereo)	30

(see also Shadows, Marvin & Farrar, Marvin Welch & Farrar, Bruce Welch, Cliff Richard, Spaghetti Junction, Jean-Michel Jarre)

JOEL MARVIN
70	Explosion EX 2028	Too Late/Each Day (both actually by Gregory Isaacs)	15

(see also Gregory Isaacs)

MARVIN, WELCH & FARRAR
72	Regal Zono. Q4SRZA 8504	SECOND OPINION (LP, quadrophonic)	25

(see also Shadows, Marvin & Farrar, Bruce Welch [& Hank Marvin])

GROUCHO MARX
72	A&M AMS 7057	Show Me A Rose/Lydia The Tattooed Lady	7

(see also Jerry Colonna & Groucho Marx)

MARY JANE GIRLS
83	Tamla Motown TMGT 1309	All Night Long/Musical Love (12")	18

MARZ

MINT VALUE £

MARZ
80   Frozen Owl SRR 0023   Lady Of The Night/On The Road To Freedom/Daydreamer (p/s, with badge) 90

MARZIPAN
70   Trend 6099 007   My Kind Of Music/Sweet Water Mary 10

MASAI (1)
74   Contempo CS 2007   Across The Track (We Better Go Back) (Parts 1 & 2) 30

MASAI (2)
82   Turbo TURB 01   Stranger To Myself/Lightning (p/s) 8

MASCARA
79   Ensign ENVY 9   SEE YOU IN LA (LP) 40

MASCOTS
63   Pye International 7N 25189   Hey Little Angel/Once Upon A Love 20

HUGH MASEKELA
68   Uni UN 504   Grazing In The Grass/Bajabula Bonke 10
69   Uni UN 510   I Haven't Slept/Where Has All The Grass Gone? 6
68   Uni UNL(S) 101   ALIVE AND WELL AT THE WHISKEY (LP) 20
69   Fontana SFL 13056   HUGH MASEKELA (LP) 20
71   Rare Earth SRE 3002   HUGH MASEKELA AND THE UNION OF SOUTH AFRICA (LP) 25
72   Blue Thumb ICD 3   HOME IS WHERE THE MUSIC IS (LP) 30

MASHMAKAN
70   CBS S 5170   As The Years Go By/Days When We Are Free 15
74   Youngblood YB1063   Dance A Little Step/One Night Stand 6

MASKED PHANTOM
66   Parlophone R 5437   These Clogs Are Made For Walking/Fried Scampi 7

MASKMAN & AGENTS
69   Direction 58-4059   One Eye Open/Y'awll 10

JIMMIE LEE MASLON
74   Southern Sound SSR 501   Long Gone Daddy/Down The Line/Don't Mean Maybe Baby 15

MASON
74   Antic K 11505   Follow Me/Peacefully 8
73   Dawn DNLS 3050   MASON (LP, export issue, do finished copies exist?) 20

BARBARA MASON
65   London HL 9977   Yes, I'm Ready/Keep Him 40
65   London HL 9977   Yes, I'm Ready/Keep Him (DJ copy) 75
68   Direction 58-3382   Oh How It Hurts/Ain't Got Nobody 50
69   Action ACT 4542   Slipping Away/Half A Love 25
72   Buddah 2011 133   Bed And Board/Yes It's You 10
73   Buddah 2011 154   Give Me Your Love/You Can Be With The One You Don't Love 7
75   Buddah BDS 425   From His Woman To You/When You Wake Up In Georgia 6
69   Action ACLP 6002   OH HOW IT HURTS (LP) 75
75   Buddah BDLP 4027   TRANSITION (LP) 20
75   Buddah BDLP 4032   LOVE'S THE THING (LP) 20
84   Other End OEBM1   TIED UP (LP) 20

BARRY MASON
66   Decca F 12401   Misty Morning Eyes/Take Your Time 10
66   Deram DM 104   Over The Hills And Far Away/A Collection Of Recollections 45
67   MGM MGM 1356   Rowbottom Square/American Girl 12
69   Decca F 12895   I'm In Love With You, Pom Pom/Mister D.J. Play Me A Sad Song 7
70   MCA MK 5034   When You Do What You're Doing/Oh Baby 6
70   MCA MKS 5054   High Time/You Put Your Tears Away/Monte Carlo 6

(see also Sounds Of Les & Barry)

BILL MASON BAND
79   Kingsway KMS 903   Out On The Streets/Mr. G (p/s) 15

DAVE MASON
68   Island WIP 6032   Just For You/Little Woman 12
70   Harvest SHTC 251   ALONE TOGETHER (LP, gatefold sleeve with 'gimmick' die cut, ' Gramophone Co' on label rim, no EMI logo, both matrix numbers end in -1 as well as crossed out matrix numbers SHVL 778 A-1/B-1) 45
72   Blue Thumb ILPS 9203   HEAD KEEPER (LP) 15

(see also Hellions, Revolution, Traffic, Fox, Jaguars)

DAVE MASON & CASS ELLIOT
71   Probe PRO 513   Something To Make You Happy/Next To You (as Mason & Cass, special sleeve) 6
71   Probe SPBA 6259   DAVE MASON AND CASS ELLIOT (LP, gatefold sleeve, pink label) 15

(see also Dave Mason, Mama Cass [Elliot])

GLEN MASON
56   Parlophone MSP 6240   Hot Diggity (Dog Ziggity Boom)/Baby Girl Of Mine 10
56   Parlophone R 4203   Love, Love, Love/Glendora 8
56   Parlophone R 4244   The Green Door/Why Must You Go, Go, Go 10
57   Parlophone R 4271   Don't Forbid Me/Amore 6
57   Parlophone R 4291   Round And Round/Walking And Whistling 6
57   Parlophone R 4334   Crying My Heart Out For You/Why Don't They Understand 6
58   Parlophone R 4415   I May Never Pass This Way Again/A Moment Ago 7
58   Parlophone R 4451   I Know Where I'm Going/Autumn Souvenir 6
58   Parlophone R 4485   The End/Fall In Love 6
59   Parlophone R 4562   The Battle Of New Orleans/I Don't Know 6
60   Parlophone R 4626   You Got What It Takes/If There's Someone 8
60   Parlophone R 4723   That's What I Want!/I Like It When It Rains 6
61   Parlophone R 4834   Don't Move/Shadrack 6
62   Parlophone R 4900   St. Louis Blues/That's Life 6

HARVEY MASON
77   Arista ARIST 12188   Till You Take My Love/What's Going On (12") 10

JAMES MASON
96	Mighty Fine MFR 002	I Want Your Love/Nightgruv (12")	60
00	Soul Brother 12SBT1	I Want Your Love/Nightgruv/I Want Your Love (Blacksmith Edit)	15
17	Dynamite Cuts DYNAM7001/7002	Sweet Power Your Embrace/Free/I've Got Me Eyes On You/Slick City (2 x 7", p/s)	15
93	Sureshot SURE1LP	RHYTHM OF LIFE (LP, reissue)	30
99	Soul Brother LP SBC53	RHYTHM OF LIFE (LP, reissue)	40

MARLIN MASON
56	Vogue Coral Q 72168	Don't Throw My Love Away/The Mystery Of Love	10

SPENCER MASON
67	Parlophone R 5555	Flugel In Carnaby Street/Albuferia	10

MASONICS
91	Hangman HANG 43 UP	MASONICS (LP)	20

(see also Milkshakes)

MASQUERADERS
68	Bell BLL 1032	I Ain't Got To Love Nobody Else/I Got It	10
70	Now! NOW 1001	Love Peace And Understanding/Tell Me You Love Me	10
05	Grapevine 2000 G2K 157	That's The Same Thing/How Big Is Big (reissue)	8
11	Outta Sight OSV 044	That's The Same Thing/Talk About A Woman (reissue)	8

(see also Lester Tipton)

MASS
80	4AD AD 14	You And I/Cabbage (with poster insert in die-cut sleeve)	25
80	4AD AD 14	You And I/Cabbage (in die-cut sleeve)	12
81	4AD CAD 107	LABOUR OF LOVE (LP, with inner sleeve)	15

(see also Models, Rema-Rema, Wolfgang Press)

MASSIEL
68	Philips BF 1667	La La La/He Gives Me Love (La La La)	7

MASSIVE ATTACK
88	Massive Attack MASS 001	Any Love/Any Love (Bonus)Any Love (Instrumental)/Any Love (Acapella) (12", stickered plain black die-cut sleeve)	15
91	Wild Bunch WBRT 2	Unfinished Sympathy/Instrumental (12", p/s, as MASSIVE)	15
91	Wild Bunch WBRR 2	Unfinished Sympathy (Nellee Hooper 12" Mix)/ (Nellee Hooper Instrumental Mix)/(Original) (12", p/s)	15
91	Wild Bunch WBRR 3	Safe From Harm (7" Version)/(Original)/(Perfecto Mix) (12", p/s)	10
91	Wild Bunch WBRR 3	Safe From Harm (Perfecto Mix)/(Just A Dub)/(Instrumental) (12")	10
92	Wild Bunch WBRT 4	MASSIVE ATTACK EP (Hymn Of The Big Wheel (Nellee Hooper Mix)/Home Of The Whale/Be Thankful (Paul Oakenfold MIx)/Any Love (Larry Heard Mix) (12")	10
95	Wild Bunch WBRT 7	Karmacoma: (Portishead Experience)/(The Napoli Trip)/U.N.K.L.E. Situation)/(Blacksmith Daydreaming) (12")	10
98	Wild Bunch WBRT 9	Teardrop: (LP Version)/Euro Zero Zero/Tear Drop (Scream Team Remix)/Teardrop (Mad Professor Remix) (12")	15
98	Wild Bunch WBRLH 9	Teardrop/Euro Zero Zero (jukebox issue)	15
98	Circa MASBOX 2	SINGLES 90/98 (11 x 12" singles in numbered heat sensitive box)	80
02	Melankolic SADT 15	I Against I/I Against I (Inst.) (12", 300 only)	15
04	Virgin VSADJ 1886	DANNY THE DOG (10" sampler)	10
06	Virgin VSTDJ 1915	False Flags/United Snakes (12" promo)	10
09	Vinyl Factory VF 006	SPLITTING THE ATOM EP (12", numbered p/s. 180 gram vinyl, 1000 only)	35
11	Vinyl Factory	Four Walls/Paradise Circus (12" as Massive Attack V Burial, silk-screened glitter sleeve, 1000 only)	125
11	Vinyl Factory VF 020	ATLAS AIR EP (12", numbered)	40
14	Secret 7" S719	Karmacoma (100, only, each with unique art sleeve)	45
16	Vinyl Factory VF 250	Dear Friend/Dear Friend (Version) (12" blue vinyl)	40
16	Virgin VST 2129	RITUAL SPIRIT EP (12" numbered, grey vinyl, 300 copies, 4 different sleeves)	100
16	Virgin VST 2142	The Spoils/Come Near Me (12", lavender vinyl)	10
91	Wild Bunch WBRLP1	BLUE LINES (LP, as Massive)	70
94	Wild Bunch WBRLP2	PROTECTION (LP)	80
96	Wild Bunch WBRLP3	NO PROTECTION (LP)	50
98	Wild Bunch WBRLP4	MEZZANINE (2-LP)	80
03	Virgin V2967	100th WINDOW (3-LP, gatefold)	80
06	Virgin V3017	COLLECTED (3-LP, gatefold)	75
10	Vinyl Factory VF013	HELIGOLAND (2-LP, CD and booklet deluxe edition)	125

MASSIVE DREAD
79	His Majesty HM 1001	MASSIVE DREAD (LP)	30
83	Upfront UPF 10	IT'S MASSIVE (LP)	30

MASTERFLEET
73	Sussex LPSX 5	HIGH ON THE SEA (LP)	25

MASTERMINDS
65	Immediate IM 005	She Belongs To Me/Taken My Love	40

(see also Badfinger)

MASTERPLAN
78	Satril SAT 136	Love Crazy (Theme From 'Carry On Emmanuel')/Since I've Been Away From My Love (p/s)	10

CARL MASTERS
72	Big Shot BI 604	Va Va Voom/GOD SONS: Rebel	15

(see also Max Romeo, Dennis Alcapone)

SAMMY MASTERS
60	Warner Bros WB 10	Rockin' Red Wing/Lonely Weekend	25
60	Warner Bros WB 10	Rockin' Red Wing/Lonely Weekend (78)	100
65	London HLR 9949	I Fought The Law (And The Law Won)/Big Man Cried	15

VALERIE MASTERS
58	Fontana H 132	Sharing/The Secret Of Happiness	6
58	Fontana H 145	(Well-a, Well-a) Ding-Dong/Merci Beaucoup	6

MASTERSAFE

MINT VALUE £

59	Fontana H 175	Dreams End At Dawn/Wonder	6
59	Fontana H 195	Jack O' Diamonds/Say When	6
59	Fontana H 224	If There Are Stars In My Eyes/Just Squeeze Me	6
60	Fontana H 238	Oh, Gee/No One Understands	6
60	Fontana H 253	Banjo Boy/Cow Cow Boogie	6
60	Fontana H 268	Sweeter As The Day Goes By/Fools Fall In Love	6
61	Fontana H 293	Too Late For Tears/I Got Rhythm	8
62	Fontana H 367	African Waltz/All Night Long	7
63	HMV POP 1125	The End Of The World/Sometime Kind Of Love	10
64	Columbia DB 7426	Christmas Calling/He Didn't Fool Me	50
65	Polydor 56056	It's Up To You/Next Train Out	30
66	Polydor 56135	Don't Ever Go/Say Hello	75

MASTERSAFE
92	Formation FORM 12014	ASPERATIONS EP (12")	20

MASTER'S APPRENTICES
71	Regal Zonophone RZ 3031	I'm Your Satisfier/Because I Love You	35
71	Regal Zono. SLRZ 1016	MASTER'S APPRENTICES (LP, red/silver labels with no EMI logo)	300
71	Regal Zono. SLRZ 1022	A TOAST TO PANAMA RED (LP, red/silver label with EMI logo)	250

MASTERS AT WORK
96	Talkin' Loud 578795-1	NUYORICAN SOUL (6-LP box set)	30

MASTERS OF REALITY
88	Def American DEFA 1	The Candy Song/The Blue Garden	10
88	Def American 838 474-1	THE MASTERS OF REALITY (LP)	20

MASTERS OF THE MONOTONAL GROOVE
94	3 Beat 3BTT32	VOL V (12")	35

MASTERSTROKE
80s	DTS DTS 043	Prisoner Of Love/Burning Heart (no p/s)	75

MASTERSWITCH
78	Epic S EPC 6259	Action Replay/Mass Media Meditation (no p/s)	25

MASTODON
11	Warner Bros./Reprise 527517-7	Just Got Paid/ZZ TOP: Just Got Paid (yellow vinyl, jukebox centre)	6
12	Roadrunner 5439 19780 0	A Commotion/FEIST: Black Tongue	8

SUE MASUMA
83	Dreams DR11/S83 CUS 1903	Pain & Pleasure/Fallout Shelter (p/s)	12

MATADOR
71	Big Shot BI 594	Nyah Festival (actually "What Am I Living For" by Derrick Morgan)/Brixton Serenade	12

MATADORS
69	Crab CRAB 27	Death A Come (actually by Lloyd Robinson)/The Sword (actually "Zylon" by Lloyd Tyrell [Charmers])	80
70	Camel CA 45	Dark Of The Sun (actually by Jackie Mittoo)/Dreader Than Dread	30
71	Green Door GD 4017	I'm Sorry (actually by Tony Brevett)/JOE WHITE: I'm Sorry Version	20

(see also Emotions, Little Roys, Ethiopians)

MATATA (AIR-FIESTA)
72	President PT 380	Wanna Do My Thing/Wild River	20
73	President PT 406	I Feel Funky/I Want You	20
74	President PT 417	Return To You/Something In Mind (as Matata)	20
75	President PT 438	Good Good Understanding/Gimme Some Lovin' (as Matata)	20
72	President PTLS 1052	MATATA: AIR FIESTA (LP)	60
75	President PTLS 1057	INDEPENDENCE (LP)	80

MATAYO
75	RAK RAK 222	Matayo/I Like Rock 'N' Roll	20

MATCHBOX (1)
69	Polydor 56327	Run Much Faster/Every Little Thing She Does	150

MATCHBOX (2)
71	Rak 113	Don't Shut Me Out/Rod	15

MATCHBOX (3)
78	Raw	Rock Rollin' Boogie/Troublesome Bay (p/s)	15
81	Dawn DNS 1104	Rock 'N' Roll Bank/Born To R 'N' R	12

(see also Cyclone)

MATCHING MOLE
72	CBS 8101	O Caroline/Signed Curtain	22
72	CBS 64850	MATCHING MOLE (LP, slightly textured sleeve, orange label)	80
72	CBS 65260	MATCHING MOLE'S LITTLE RED RECORD (LP, orange label with red inner sleeve)	80
79	CBS 32105	MATCHING MOLE (LP, reissue)	20

(see also Robert Wyatt, Soft Machine, Caravan, Hatfield & The North)

MATCHMAKERS
71	Chapter One	BUBBLEGUM A GO GO (LP)	25

(see also Mark Wirtz, Philwit & Pegasus, Fickle Finger)

MATERIAL
81	Red RS 12.006	TEMPORARY MUSIC (12", EP. p/s)	20
81	Red RS 12.008	TEMPORARY MUSIC 2 (12", EP. p/s)	20
82	Red RS 012	Ciquri/Detached (p/s)	8
81	Celluloid ILPS 59693	MEMORY SERVES (LP)	15
86	Jungle FREUD 11	SECRET LIFE (2-LP)	20
89	Virgin V 2596	SEVEN SOULS (LP)	15
94	Axiom 518 351 1	HALLUCINATION ENGINE (LP, with booklet)	40
12	Music On Vinyl MOVLP541	HALLUCINATION ENGINE (LP, reissue)	30

(see also Bill Laswell)

MATHEMATIQUES MODERNES
81	Celluloid 12WIP 6743	Disco Rough (Long Version)/Jungle Hurt (12")	30

		MINT VALUE £
81 Celluloid ILPS 9690	LES VISITEURS DU SOIR (LP)	30

MATHETAI
77 Cavs CAV 017	KNOWING (LP)	50

JODI MATHIS
75 Capitol CL 15827	Mama/Don't You Care Anymore	10
75 Capitol CL 15827	Mama/Don't You Care Anymore (DJ Copy)	20

JOHNNY MATHIS
57 Philips JK 1029	The Twelfth Of Never/Chances Are (jukebox issue)	10
84 CBS A4889	Love Never Felt So Good/One Love (p/s)	40

MATIC 16
82 Music Hive (No cat. No)	Jahovah/Ten Man (12")	50
82 Regent RGTDS 1001	No Money Today/Matic Rock (12")	40

MATRIX RISE
92 Mutant 12 MUTATE 6	D.O.Y.L.E. Factor/Reality (12")	25
92 Mutant 12 MUTATE 8	Moments Of Pleasure/The Preacher (12")	40

AL MATTHEWS
75 CBS 3429	Fool/Don't Run From My Love	8
78 Electric Co 23	Run To You/People Are People	15

CARL MATTHEWS
88 ICR ICR 25	OLD & NEW (cassette)	35
80 M 601	AKSU (cassette)	70
81 Mirage	FREEWHEEL TO FREEDOM (cassette, either black or bespoke Mirage sleeve and details on cassette)	40
81 Mirage	INTERVENTION '87 (cassette)	40
82 Mirage M606	EASTWEST (cassette)	40
83 Mirage M609	IRIDESCENCE (cassette)	50
84 Mirage M 412	CALL FOR WORLD SAVIOURS (Cassette)	40
89 Electronical Dreams 010	LAST WORD FROM MOTHERSHIP (cassette)	40

IAN MATTHEWS
71 Vertigo 6059041	Hearts/Little Knows	12
73 Elektra K 12111	These Days/Same Old Man	7
71 Vertigo 6360 034	IF YOU SAW THRO' MY EYES (LP, 1st pressing textured gatefold sleeve, large swirl label)	150
71 Vertigo 6360 034	IF YOU SAW THRO' MY EYES (LP, 2nd LP textured gatefold sleeve, small swirl label)	40
72 Vertigo 6360 056	TIGERS WILL SURVIVE (LP, textured gatefold sleeve, small swirl label)	150
73 Elektra K 42144	VALLEY HI (LP, textured gatefold sleeve, 'butterfly' label)	30
74 Elektra K 42160	SOME DAYS YOU EAT THE BEAR, SOME DAYS THE BEAR EATS YOU (LP)	20
74 Mooncrest CREST 18	JOURNEYS FROM GOSPEL OAK (LP)	20
76 CBS 81316	GO FOR BROKE (LP)	18

(see also Pyramid, Fairport Convention, Matthews Southern Comfort, Plainsong, Hi-Fi)

JOE MATTHEWS
68 Sue WI 4046	Sorry Ain't Good Enough/You Better Mend Your Ways	90
98 Wigan Casino 202	She's My Beauty Queen/JACKIE BEAVERS: I Need My Baby (p/s, reissue)	8

MILT MATTHEWS
75 London HLF 10479	All These Changes/When Kids Rule The World	8

RANDY MATTHEWS
70s Myrrh MXX 1035	NOW DO YOU UNDERSTAND (LP, gatefold sleeve)	25

TOBIN MATTHEWS
63 Warner Brothers WB 117	Can't Stop Talking About You/When You Came Along	6

WINSTON MATTHEWS
71 Banana BA 329	Sun Is Shining/INN KEEPERS: My Friend (B-side actually "The Pressure Is On" by Purpleites)	18

MATTHEWS SOUTHERN COMFORT
70 Uni UNS 513	Colorado Springs Eternal/The Struggle	12
70 Uni UNS 521	Ballad Of Obray Ramsey/Parting	7
70 Uni UNLS 108	MATTHEWS SOUTHERN COMFORT (LP, gatefold, lyric insert, yellow swirl label)	40
70 Uni UNLS 112	SECOND SPRING (LP, textured sleeve, lyric insert, yellow swirl label)	30
70 Uni MKPS 2015	LATER THAT SAME YEAR... (LP, red/pink 'dogbone' label)	20

(see also Ian Matthews, Marc Ellington, Southern Comfort)

MATTHIAS
74 Decca F13545	Deep Down Under/I Hear A Song	12

MATUMBI
73 G.G. GG 4540	Brother Louie Parts 1 & 2	10
77 Matumbi Music MA004	Music In The Air/Guide Us (12")	40
78 Matumbi Music MR 86	After Tonight/Take It From Me (12")	30
78 EMI SHSP 4090	SEVEN SEALS (LP, red/black label with inner, some on green vinyl)	20
80 Extinguish MR 007	DUB PLANET ORBIT 1 (LP)	200

DENNIS MATUMBI
77 More Cut MCT 001	Raindrops/Eye Water	25
77 Rama CJ6N	Blood Ah Go Run/Blood Dem	30
78 Serious Business SBD004	Blood Ah Go Run/Blood Dem	30
78 Serious Business SBD004	Rolling Down The River/Choose Me	40

HARVEY MATUSOW'S JEWS HARP BAND
69 Head HDS 4004	Afghan Red/Wet Socks	8
69 Head HDLS 6001	WAR BETWEEN THE FATS & THE THINS (LP)	40

MA2
95 Formation FORM 12267	Rollers Music/Hearing Is Believing (12")	20

MAUDS
67 Mercury MF 1000	Hold On/C'mon And Move	10
67 Philips BL 7791	HEY, LOOK ME OVER (LP)	25

Susan MAUGHAN

MINT VALUE £

SUSAN MAUGHAN
61	Philips BF 1216	Mama Do The Twist/Blue Night In Yokohama	15
62	Philips BF 1236	Baby Doll Twist/Some Of These Days	15
62	Philips 326 533BF	I've Got To Learn To Forget/I Didn't Mean What I Said	15
63	Philips 326 562BF	Hand A Handkerchief To Helen/I'm A Lonely One Too	6
63	Philips 326 586BF	She's New To You/Don't Get Carried Away	6
63	Philips BF 1266	The Verdict Is Guilty/Bachelor Girl	7
64	Philips BF 1301	Hey Lover/Stop Your Foolin'	7
64	Philips BF 1336	Kiss Me Sailor/Call On Me	8
64	Philips BF 1363	Little Things Mean A Lot/That Other Place	12
64	Philips BF 1382	Make Him Mine/South American Joe	7
65	Philips BF 1399	You Can Never Get Away From You/Don't Be Afraid	8
65	Philips BF 1417	When She Walks Away/Come Along Down And See	8
65	Philips BF 1445	Poor Boy/Your Girl	8
66	Philips BF 1495	Come And Get Me/Don't Love Him Too Much	8
66	Philips BF 1518	Where The Bullets Fly/I'll Never Stop Loving You	10
67	Philips BF 1564	Don't Go Home (My Little Darlin')/Somebody To Love	10
68	Philips PF 1679	I Remember Loving You/Why Don't You Say You Love Me	10
68	Philips BF 1713	Cable Car For Two/Off My Mind	10
69	Philips BF 1824	We Really Go Together/I'll Never Forget You	10
62	Philips BBE 12525	HI, I'M SUSAN MAUGHAN AND I SING (EP)	15
63	Philips BBE 12549	FOUR BEAUX AND A BELLE (EP)	15
62	Philips 433 621 BE	EFFERVESCENT MISS MAUGHAN (EP)	15
63	Philips 433 641 BE	MORE OF MAUGHAN (EP)	15
63	Philips 632 300 BL	I WANNA BE BOBBY'S GIRL BUT ... (LP)	25
64	Philips BL 7577	SWINGIN' SUSAN (LP)	20
65	Philips BL 7637	SENTIMENTAL SUSAN (LP)	20

MAU-MAUS
82	Pax PAX 6	SOCIETY'S REJECTS (EP, black or blue sleeve)	15
82	Pax PAX 8	No Concern/Clampdown/Why Do We Suffer (p/s)	15
83	Pax/Paragon PAX 12	FACTS OF WAR (EP)	15
85	Rebellion REBEL 701	TEAR DOWN THE WALLS (EP)	15
85	Rebellion REBEL 1202	NOWHERE TO RUN (12" EP)	15
83	Pax PAX 16	LIVE AT THE MARPLES (LP)	20
84	Pax PAX 20	RUNNING WITH THE PACK (LP)	25
85	Rebellion REBLP01	FEAR NO EVIL (LP)	15

MAUREENY WISHFULL
68	Moonshine WO 2388	THE MAUREENY WISHFULL ALBUM (LP, 300 copies, beware of counterfeits)	100

(see also Jimmy Page, Big Jim Sullivan, John Williams, Brothers William)

MAURICE & MAC
68	Chess CRS 8074	You Left The Water Running/You're The One	12
68	Chess CRS 8081	Why Don't You Try Me/Lean On Me	12

(see also Radiants)

JOHN MAUS
06	Upset The Rhythm UTR 003	SONGS (LP, pink vinyl)	40
08	Upset The Rhythm UTR 015V	LOVE IS REAL (LP, clear or white vinyl)	50
11	Upset The Rhythm UTR 003	SONGS (LP, reissue)	25
11	Upset The Rhythm UTR 015V	LOVE IS REAL (LP, reissue, pink vinyl)	40
11	Upset The Rhythm UTR 049	WE MUST BECOME THE PITILESS CENSORS OF OURSELVES (LP, blue vinyl with CD, 100 only)	30
11	Upset The Rhythm UTR 049	WE MUST BECOME THE PITILESS CENSORS OF OURSELVES (LP, clear vinyl with CD)	20

MAVE & DAVE
80	Red Stripe SON 2215	Do Ypu Really Want My Love/You Are Delicious	60

MAWAMBA DUB
78	Warrior DRLP 1001	MAWANDA DUB (LP)	70

(see also Dennis Bovell, Alton Ellis)

MAX
74	Caroline C1506	MAX (LP, black Virgin inner, black/red 'Twin' label, artist is Max Handley)	20

MAX & GREGORY
73	Ackee ACK 525	My Jamaican Collie/Push It Down, Rub It Up	7

(see also Max Romeo)

MAX HEADROOM & CARPARKS
80	Parlophone R 6034	Don't Panic/Rhythm And Bluebeat (p/s)	6
82	Bandwagon B001	Soldier (no p/s)	20

PAT MAX AND THE SPECIALISTS
68	Pye 7N 17470	Too Much/Girl From New Orleans	12

SMILEY MAXEDON & HIS OKAW VALLEY BOYS
54	Columbia SCMC 3	Crazy To Care/In The Window Of My Heart (export issue)	15

JOE S. MAXEY
73	Action ACT 4607	Sign Of The Crab/May The Best Man Win (actually plays Packers' "Hole In The Wall"/"Go Ahead On")	20

MAXI
73	Decca F 13394	Do I Dream/Here Today And Gone Tomorrow	6

MAXIE (ROMEO) & GLEN
71	G.G. GG 4520	Jordan River (actually by Max Romeo & Glen Adams)/ GLEN ADAMS:Version Two	12

(see also Max Romeo, Ethiopians)

MAXIE, SCIENTIST AND BARNABAS
81	Silver Camel SCLP 001	THREE THE HARD WAY (LP)	80

MAXIMILIAN
61	London HLX 9356	The Snake/The Wanderer	35

MAXIMO PARK

MINT VALUE £

MAXIMO PARK
03	Billingham Records	Graffiti/Going Missing (red vinyl, 500 only, p/s)	35
04	Warp 7WAP 183	The Coast Is Always Changing/The Night I Lost My Head (500 only, p/s)	15
05	Warp 7WAP 190	Going Missing (1-sided 7" other side etched)	6
05	Warp WARPLP 130	A CERTAIN TRIGGER (LP, inner)	25
07	Warp WARPLP 130	OUR EARTHLY PLEASURES (LP)	30

MAXIM'S TRASH
| 79 | Gimp GIMP 1 | Disco Girls/Blu Shoes (plastic p/s & inner, hand-stamped white labels, tracks actually recorded in 1975) | 40 |

(see also Captain Sensible, Johnny Moped)

MAXIMUM BAND
| 68 | Fab FAB 51 | Cupid/Hold Me Tight | 20 |

MAXIMUM JOY
81	Y 11	Stretch/Silent Street (p/s)	20
81	Y Y 11	Stretch/Silent Street (12", p/s)	20
82	Y Y 15	White And Green Place/Building Bridges (12", p/s)	20
82	Y 26	In The Air/Simmer Till Done (p/s)	10
82	Y 12 Y 26	In The Air (Extended)/Simmer Till Done (p/s)	15
83	Garage GAR 1	Why Can't We Live Together/Man Of Tribes (p/s)	8
83	Garage GAR 112	Why Can't We Live Together (Remix)/Man Of Tribes (Remix) (p/s)	12
82	Y 28	STATION MXJY (LP)	35

ERNEST MAXIN
| 59 | Top Rank JAR 267 | On The Beach/Take A Giant Step | 6 |
| 60 | Top Rank JAR 335 | Conspiracy Of Hearts/No Orchids For My Lady | 6 |

BRIAN MAXINE
| 72 | EMI Starline SRS 5140 | BRIAN MAXINE SINGS (LP) | 40 |
| 75 | Columbia SCX 6575 | RIBBON OF STAINLESS STEEL (LP) | 30 |

(see also Fairport Convention)

MAXINE (1)
| 70 | Smash SMA 2301 | My Boy Lollipop/Everybody Needs Love | 10 |

MAXINE (2)
| 97 | 0181 12 0181 R1 | Crazy (Sky Joose Remix)/Crazy (DHSS Remix) (12, white label) | 20 |
| 97 | 12 0181 R2 | Fade Away (Vocal)/Fade Away (Instrumental) (12", white label) | 40 |

MAXWELL
96	Columbia 483699 1	MAXWELL'S URBAN HANG SUITE (2-LP)	80
98	Columbia 489420-1	EMBRYA (2-LP)	30
01	Columbia 497454-1	NOW (LP)	30
09	Columbia 88697518521	BLACKSUMMER'S NIGHT (LP, CD)	50

HOLLY MAXWELL
| 69 | Buddah 201 056 | Suffer/No-One Else | 10 |

BRIAN MAY
83	EMI EMI 5436	Starfleet (Single Version)/Son Of Starfleet (p/s)	15
91	Parlophone RDJ 6304	Driven By You (Edited Version)/(Pollarded Version)/(Special Version)/(Proper Version) (promo only, no stars on p/s)	70
92	Parlophone CDRS 6320	Too Much Love Will Kill You (Album Version)/I'm Scared (Single Version)/Too Much Love Will Kill You (Guitar Version)/Driven By You (New Version) (CD, red circular gatefold card p/s)	18
92	Parlophone RDJ 6289	Back To The Light (Radio Version)/Nothin' But Blue (Guitar Version) (promo only, p/s)	50
93	Parlophone 0 7777 80400 19	BACK TO THE LIGHT (LP, textured sleeve)	30
98	EMI 4949731	ANOTHER WORLD (LP, picture disc, with inner sleeve)	100

(see also Queen, MC Spy-D & 'Friends', Eddie Howell, Holly Johnson, D-Rok, Ian & Belinda, Cozy Powell, Black Sabbath)

MARY MAY
| 63 | Fontana 267266TF | Our Day Will Come/But I Know Now | 8 |
| 64 | Fontana TF 440 | Anyone Who Had A Heart/They Say It's Wonderful | 10 |

JOHN MAYALL (& BLUESBREAKERS)

SINGLES
64	Decca F 11900	Crawling Up A Hill/Mr. James (as John Mayall & Blues Breakers)	75
65	Decca F 12120	Crocodile Walk/Blues City Shakedown	45
65	Immediate IM 012	I'm Your Witchdoctor/Telephone Blues	60
66	Purdah 45-3502	Lonely Years/Bernard Jenkins (as John Mayall & Eric Clapton, 500 copies only)	450
66	Decca F 12490	Parchman Farm (solo)/Key To Love (B-side with Bluesbreakers)	30
66	Decca F 12506	Looking Back/So Many Roads (as John Mayall's Bluesbreakers & Peter Green)	18
67	Decca F 12545	Sitting In The Rain/Out Of Reach (as John Mayall's Bluesbreakers)	15
67	Decca F 12588	Curly/Rubber Duck (as Bluesbreakers)	12
67	Decca F 12621	Double Trouble/It Hurts Me Too (as John Mayall's Bluesbreakers)	20
67	Immediate IM 051	I'm Your Witchdoctor/Telephone Blues (reissue, as John Mayall with Eric Clapton)	30
67	Decca F 12684	Suspicions (Parts 1 & 2) (as John Mayall's Bluesbreakers)	15
68	Decca F 12732	Picture On The Wall/Jenny (as John Mayall)	12
68	Decca F 12792	No Reply/She's Too Young (as John Mayall's Bluesbreakers)	12
68	Decca F 12846	The Bear/2401	10
69	Polydor 56544	Don't Waste My Time/Don't Pick A Flower	12
70	Polydor 2066 021	Thinking Of My Woman/Plan Your Revolution	12
76	Decca F12120	Crocodile Walk/Blues City Shakedown (reissue, with boxed Decca logo, uninverted label matrix numbers, double A side)	15

EPs
| 67 | Decca DFE-R 8673 | THE BLUESBREAKERS WITH PAUL BUTTERFIELD (EP) | 60 |

ALBUMS
65	Decca LK 4680	PLAYS JOHN MAYALL - LIVE AT KLOOKS KLEEK!	120
66	Decca LK 4804	BLUES BREAKERS WITH ERIC CLAPTON (original label, mono, "Beano" cover)	150
67	Decca LK/SKL 4853	A HARD ROAD (as John Mayall & Bluesbreakers)	50

MAYBERRY MOVEMENT

MINT VALUE £

67	Decca LK 4890	CRUSADE (Mono, as John Mayall & Bluesbreakers)	50
67	Decca SKL 4890	CRUSADE (Stereo, as John Mayall & Bluesbreakers)	30
67	Ace of Clubs ACL/SCL 1243	THE BLUES ALONE (LP, "A Hard Road" on back cover)	30
68	Decca LK/SKL 4918	THE DIARY OF A BAND VOL. 1	30
68	Decca LK/SKL 4919	THE DIARY OF A BAND VOL. 2	30
68	Decca LK/SKL 4945	BARE WIRES (gatefold sleeve, as John Mayall & Blues Breakers)	40
68	Decca LK/SKL 4972	BLUES FROM LAUREL CANYON (LP, unboxed logo, gatefold sleeve)	40

(The Decca LPs listed above were originally issued with unboxed Decca label logos.)

69	Decca LK/SKL 5010	LOOKING BACK (gatefold sleeve)	25
69	Polydor 583 571	THE TURNING POINT	20
69	Decca SKL 4804	BLUES BREAKERS WITH ERIC CLAPTON (reissue, original label, stereo)	40
70s	Decca LK 4804	BLUES BREAKERS WITH ERIC CLAPTON (reissue, boxed logo, mono)	20
71	Decca SKL 4804	BLUES BREAKERS WITH ERIC CLAPTON (reissue, boxed logo, stereo)	15
70	Polydor 583 580	EMPTY ROOMS (with lyric insert)	15
70	Polydor 2425 020	U.S.A. UNION	20
71	Polydor 2657 005	BACK TO THE ROOTS (2-LP)	30
71	Polydor 2425 085	MEMORIES	15
71	Polydor 2483 016	BEYOND THE TURNING POINT	15
71	Decca SKL 5086	THRU THE YEARS	25
72	Polydor 2425 103	JAZZ-BLUES FUSION	15
73	Polydor 2391 047	MOVING ON	15
73	Polydor 2482 111	TEN YEARS ARE GONE	15
74	Polydor 2391 141	THE LATEST EDITION	15

(see also Paul Butterfield, Eric Clapton, Jack Bruce, Peter Green, McGuinness Flint, Johnny Almond Music Machine, Alan Skidmore, Mick Taylor, Dick Heckstall-Smith, Keef Hartley, Paul Williams, Ray Warleigh, Colosseum, Henry Lowther, Jon Mark, Aynsley Dun

MAYBERRY MOVEMENT

06	Kent 6T 21	I See Him Making Love To You/THE DEVONNES: Doin' The Gittin' Up	20

MAY BLITZ

70	Vertigo 6360 007	MAY BLITZ (LP, gatefold sleeve, large swirl label)	400
71	Vertigo 6360 037	THE 2ND OF MAY (LP, gatefold sleeve, swirl label)	450

(see also Jeff Beck, Boxer, Sounds Inc.)

MAYDAY

80	Reddingtons R.R. DAN 2	Day After Day/Love In The Spaceage (p/s)	20

JOHN MAYER (GROUP)

66	Columbia DB 8237	Acka Raga (as John Mayer's I-J-7)/Gana (as John Mayer & Joe Harriott Quintet)	30
68	National Petrol W 1	Music For People Who Go Your Own Way Themes 1 & 2 (p/s, with Frank Cordell)	10
66	Columbia S(C)X 6025	INDO-JAZZ SUITE (LP, with Joe Harriott)	75
67	Columbia SX 6122	INDO-JAZZ FUSIONS (LP, with Joe Harriott)	50
67	Columbia S(C)X 6215	INDO-JAZZ FUSIONS II (LP, with Joe Harriott)	50
69	Sonet SNTF 603	ETUDES (LP, as John Mayer Indo-Jazz Fusions)	15
71	Columbia SCX 6462	RADHA KRISHNA (LP)	20

(see also Joe Harriott & John Mayer, Radha Krishna)

NATHANIEL MAYER & FABULOUS TWILIGHTS

62	HMV POP 1041	Village Of Love/I Want A Woman	50

CURTIS MAYFIELD

70	Buddah 2011 055	(Don't Worry) If There's A Hell Below We're All Going To Go (Edit)/ The Makings Of You	8
71	Buddah 2011 080	Move On Up/Give It Up/Beautiful Brother Of Mine (maxi-single)	10
71	Buddah 2011 101	We Got To Have Peace/People Get Ready	6
72	Buddah 2011 119	Keep On Keepin' On/Stone Junkie	6
72	Buddah 2011 141	Freddie's Dead (Theme From "Superfly")/Underground	6
72	Buddah 2011 156	Superfly/Give Me Your Love (Love Song)	8
73	Buddah 2011 187	Back To The World (edit)/The Other Side Of Town	6
74	Buddah BDS 402	Kung Fu/Right On For The Darkness	6
74	Buddah BDS 410	Move On Up/Give It Up	8
75	Buddah BDS 426	Mother's Son/Love Me Right In The Pocket	6
71	Buddah 2318 015	CURTIS (LP, 1st pressing, black and silver labels, gatefold sleeve)	50
71	Buddah 2659 004	CURTIS/LIVE (2-LP)	20
72	Buddah 2318 045	ROOTS (LP, gatefold sleeve)	30
72	Buddah 2318 065	SUPERFLY (LP, soundtrack, gatefold sleeve)	20
73	Buddah 2318 085	BACK TO THE WORLD (LP, gatefold sleeve)	20
73	Buddah 2318 091	CURTIS IN CHICAGO (LP, TV soundtrack, gatefold sleeve, with Impressions, Jerry Butler, Gene Chandler & Leroy Hutson)	15
74	Buddah BDLH 5001	SWEET EXORCIST (LP)	30
74	Buddah BDLH 5005	CURTIS (LP, 2nd pressing, pink rim 'Buddah' label, 1974 on labels, gatefold)	30
74	Buddah BDLP 4010	CLAUDINE (LP, soundtrack, with Gladys Knight)	15
75	Buddah BDLP 4033	THERE'S NO PLACE LIKE AMERICA TODAY (LP)	20
76	Buddah BDLP 4042	GIVE, GET TAKE AND HAVE (LP)	15

(see also Impressions)

PERCY MAYFIELD

63	HMV POP 1185	The River's Invitation/Baby Please	10
76	Speciality SON 5007	Please Send Me Someone To Love/The River's Invitation	6
67	HMV CLP/CSD 3572	MY JUG AND I (LP)	40

MAYFIELD'S MULE

69	Parlophone R 5817	Double Dealing Woman/(Drinking My) Moonshine (in p/s)	30
69	Parlophone R 5817	Double Dealing Woman/(Drinking My) Moonshine	15
70	Parlophone R 5843	I See A River/"Queen" Of Rock'n'Roll	15
70	Parlophone R 5858	We Go Rollin'/My Way Of Living	10

(see also Elastic Band, Sweet, Amen Corner, Andy Scott)

MAYFLY

73	Bumble GE 121	It's Elusive/Orphan Girl	10

JUDY MAYHAN
71	Atlantic 2466006	MOMENTS (LP)	15

MAYHEM
82	Riot City RIOT 13	GENTLE MURDER EP	10
83	Riot City RIOT 24	PULLING PUPPETS STRINGS EP	15
85	Vigilante VIG 1	Bloodrush/Addictive Risk (p/s, lyric insert)	10
85	Vigilante VIG 1T	Bloodrush/Addictive Risk/I Defy (12", p/s)	15
96	Black Metal BMR 002	Freezing Moon/Carnage (12", picture disc)	20
97	Misanthropy HH 666	Ancient Skin/Necrolust (CD single in printed PVC sleeve, hand numbered insert, gig freebie, 500 only, beware of bootleg 7" singles)	40
97	Misanthropy AMAZON 012	WOLF'S LAIR ABYSS (LP)	40
97	Misanthropy AMAZON CPD 012	WOLF'S LAIR ABYSS (LP, picture disc)	50

(TOOTS &) THE MAYTALS
63	Blue Beat BB 176	Hallelujah/Helping Ages Past	20
64	Blue Beat BB 215	He Is Real/Domino	20
64	Blue Beat BB 220	Pain In My Belly/BUSTER'S ALL STARS: City Riot	100
64	Blue Beat BB 231	Dog War/RECO & CREATORS: I'll Be Home	70
64	Blue Beat BB 245	Little Slea (song actually "Little Flea")/Don't Talk (song actually Pain In My Belly) (both sides miscredited as V. Maytals)	25
64	Blue Beat BB 254	Sweet Love/PRINCE BUSTER: Wings Of A Dove	35
64	Blue Beat BB 255	Judgement Day/Goodbye Jane	20
64	Blue Beat BB 270	You've Got Me Spinning/Lovely Walking	40
64	R&B JB 130	Hurry Up/Love Divine	20
64	R&B JB 141	Another Chance/FRANKIE ANDERSON: Always On A Sunday	20
64	R&B JB 153	Give Me Your Love/He Will Provide	20
64	R&B JB 164	Hello Honey/ROLAND ALPHONSO: Crime Wave	50
64	R&B JB 174	Christmas Feelings/Let's Kiss	25
65	Blue Beat BB 281	Looking Down The Street/PRINCE BUSTER: Blues Market	50
65	Blue Beat BB 299	Light Of The World/Lovely Walking	30
65	Blue Beat BB 306	Ska War (song actually "Treating Me Bad")/SKATALITES: Perhaps	90
65	Ska Beat JB 202	Let's Jump/Joy And Jean	25
65	Island WI 200	Never You Change/What's On Your Mind	25
65	Island WI 213	My New Name/It's No Use	35
65	Black Swan WI 464	John James/THEO BECKFORD: Sailing On	25
66	Doctor Bird DB 1019	If You Act This Way/SIR LORD COMIC & HIS COWBOYS: Ska-ing West	45
66	Doctor Bird DB 1038	Bam Bam/So Mad In Love (with Byron Lee and the Dragoniares)	40
68	Pyramid PYR 6030	54-46, That's My Number/ROLAND ALPHONSO: Dreamland	30
68	Pyramid PYR 6043	Struggle/ROLAND ALPHONSO: Stream Of Life	50
68	Pyramid PYR 6048	Just Tell Me/Reborn	80
68	Pyramid PYR 6050	Bim Today, Bam Tomorrow/Hold On	25
68	Pyramid PYR 6052	We Shall Overcome/DESMOND DEKKER & ACES: Fu Manchu	125
68	Pyramid PYR 6055	Schooldays/Big Man	35
68	Pyramid PYR 6056	Ben Johnson Day (actually by Derrick Morgan and George Dekkar)/MAYTALS: Ain't Got No Tip	125
68	Pyramid PYR 6057	Do The Reggay/BEVERLEY'S ALLSTARS: Motoring	55
68	Pyramid PYR 6064	Scare Him/In My Heart	20
69	Pyramid PYR 6066	Don't Trouble Trouble/BEVERLEY'S ALLSTARS: Double Action	110
69	Pyramid PYR 6070	Aldina/Hold On	45
69	Pyramid PYR 6073	Pressure Drop/BEVERLEY'S ALLSTARS: Express	30
69	Pyramid PYR 6074	Sweet And Dandy/Oh Yeah	20
69	Trojan TR 7709	Pressure Drop/BEVERLEY'S ALLSTARS: Smoke Screen	25
69	Nu Beat NB 031	My Testimony/JOHNSON BOYS: One Dollar Of Soul (actually by Ethiopians)	35
69	Trojan TR 7711	Monkey Man/Night And Day	30
70	Trojan TR 7726	Sweet And Dandy/54-46, That's My Number	16
70	Trojan TR 7741	Bla Bla Bla/Reborn	15
70	Trojan TR 7757	Water Melon/She's My Scorcher	18
70	Trojan TR 7786	Doctor Lester/Sun, Moon And Star	15
70	Summit SUM 8510	Peeping Tom/BEVERLEY'S ALLSTARS: Version	15
71	Trojan TR 7808	54-46 Was My Number/BEVERLEY'S ALLSTARS: 54-46 Instrumental	25
71	Trojan TR 7849	Johnny Cool Man/BEVERLEY's ALLSTARS: Version	10
71	Summit SUM 8513	Monkey Girl/BEVERLEY'S ALLSTARS: Version	20
71	Summit SUM 8520	One Eye Enos/BEVERLEY'S ALLSTARS: Enos Version	10
71	Summit SUM 8527	It's You/BEVERLEY'S ALLSTARS: Version	10
71	Summit SUM 8529	Walk With Love/BEVERLEY'S ALLSTARS: Version	10
71	Summit SUM 8533	Never You Change/BEVERLEY'S ALLSTARS: Version	10
72	Attack ATT 8042	It Was Written Down/Sweet And Dandy	10
72	Summit SUM 8536	Thy Kingdom Come/BEVERLEY'S ALLSTARS: Version	10
72	Summit SUM 8537	It Must Be True Love/BEVERLEY'S ALLSTARS: Version	10
72	Blue Mountain BM 1020	Christmas Song/I Can't Believe	10
72	Dynamic DYN 438	Redemption Song	10
72	Trojan TR 7865	Louie Louie/Pressure Drop '72	30
73	Dragon DRA 1007	Sit Right Down/Screwface Underground/Pomps & Pride (as Toots & Maytals)	8
73	Dragon DRA 1013	Country Road/Funky Kingston (as Toots & Maytals)	40
73	Dragon DRA 1016	In The Dark/Sailing On (as Toots & Maytals)	7
74	Dragon DRA 1021	Fever/It Was Written Down	7
74	Dragon DRA 1024	Time Tough/Time Tough Version	7
74	Dragon DRA 1026	Sailing On/If You Act This Way (as Toots & Maytals)	7
76	Island WIP 6269	Reggae Got Soul/Dog War (p/s)	8
80	Island 1EP 11 DJ	Pressure Drop (1-sided promo)	20

MAYTONES

MINT VALUE £

80	Island 1EP 11	Pressure Drop/54 46 Was My Number/Stick It Up Mister/Time Tough EP	12
11	Beverlys THB 7008	Do The Boogaloo/Bim Today Bam Tomorrow	15
13	Island WI 3162	Monkey Man/She's My Scorcher	8
64	Ska Beat JBL 1113	PRESENTING THE MAYTALS (NEVER GROW OLD) (LP)	1000
66	Doctor Bird DLM 5005	THE SENSATIONAL MAYTALS (LP)	300
70	Trojan TBL 107	MONKEY MAN (LP, laminated front cover)	60
73	Trojan TRLS 65	FROM THE ROOTS (LP)	35
73	Dragon DRLS 5002	FUNKY KINGSTON (LP)	40
74	Dragon DRLS 5004	IN THE DARK (LP)	25
74	Prince Buster PB 11	ORIGINAL GOLDEN OLDIES VOLUME 3 (LP)	20
77	State ETAT16	TOOTS PRESENTS THE MAYTALS (LP)	15
85	Island IRG 1	REGGAE GREATS (LP)	15

(see also Vikings, Flames, Philip James & Blues Busters, Don Drummond, Stranger, Lord Creator, Larry Marshall, Derrick Morgan, Brentwood Road Allstars, Roland Alphonso, Charmers)

MAYTONES

68	Blue Cat BS 149	Billy Goat/Call You Up	100
69	Blue Cat BS 152	Loving Reggae/Musical Beat	75
69	Blue Cat BS 166	Copper Girl/Love	80
69	Blue Cat BS 173	We Nah Tek You Lick/Dig Away De Money	80
69	Camel CA 27	Sentimental Reason/Lover Girl	30
69	Songbird SB 1009	I've Been Loving You/Memphis Reggae	10
70	Punch PH 35	Serious Love/CHARLIE ACE: Musical Combination	10
70	Explosion EX 2012	Funny Man/G.G. ALLSTARS: Champion	20
70	Explosion EX 2013	Sentimental Reason/Lover Girl	7
70	Explosion EX 2014	Barrabus/G.G. ALLSTARS: Barrabus Part 2 (B-side actually "This Kind Of Life")	60
70	Explosion EX 2027	Cecelia (actually by Keeling Beckford)/Chariot Without Horse (B-side actually "Willie My Darling")	10
70	Explosion EX 2033	Another Festival/Happy Time	10
70	Bullet BU 446	I Don't Like To Interfere/Preaching Love	8
70	Camel CA 47	Black And White/GLORIA'S ALLSTARS: Jumbo Jet	15
70	Camel CA 49	Since You Left/GLORIA'S ALL STARS: Bird Wing	20
71	Duke DU 116	Babylon A Fall/TONY KING: Version Buggy	18
71	Camel CA 61	Judas (actually by Gladstone Anderson & Followers)/Mi Nah Tek	15
71	Camel CA 63	Cleanliness/Sister Hold On	20
71	G.G. GG 4508	Cleanliness/G.G. ALL STARS: Cleanliness Version 2	10
71	G.G. GG 4511	Let The Version Play/Lonely Nights	10
71	G.G. GG 4522	Black And White/TREVOR BROWN: Mr. Brown	10
71	G.G. GG 4525	Bongo Man Rise/ROY & BIM: Remember	10
72	G.G. GG 4530	Donkey Face/G.G. ALL STARS: Donkey Face - Version	10
72	G.G. GG 4531	As Long As You Love Me (Side One)/As Long As You Love Me (Side Two)	10
72	Attack ATT 8029	Hands And Feet/LLOYD & CAREY: Scorpion	10
72	Grape GR 3028	If Loving You Was Wrong/FLOWERS & ALVIN: In De Pum Pum	10
72	Pama PM 846	I'm Feeling Lonely/G.G. ALLSTARS: Version	10
72	Explosion EX 2076	Brown Girl/SHORTY PERRY: Half-Way-Tree Rock	10
73	Pama PM 871	All Over The World People Are Changing/Changing World (Dubwise)	8
73	Bullet BU 528	People Get Funny/G.G. ALL STARS: Version	7
77	GG's GG 021	Money Trouble (with I Roy)/GG'S ALL STARS: Dub Part Two (12")	25
82	Burning Sounds BS 1052	BEST OF (LP)	15

(see also Vern & Alvin, Vern & Son, Roland Alphonso, G.G. Rhythm Section, Cynthia Richards, Max Romeo, Charlie Ace, Dennis Alcapone)

MAZE (U.K.)

| 66 | Reaction 591 009 | Hello Stranger/Telephone | 100 |
| 67 | MGM MGM 1368 | Catari Catari/Easy Street | 40 |

(see also M.I. Five, Deep Purple, Paice, Ashton & Lord)

MAZE (FEATURING FRANKIE BEVERLY)

77	Capitol CAPS 1039	MAZE FEATURING FRANKIE BEVERLY (LP)	20
78	Capitol E ST 11710	GOLDEN TIME OF DAY (LP)	15
79	Capitol E ST 11912	INSPIRATION (LP)	15
80	Capitol EST 12087	JOY AND PAIN (LP)	15
81	Capitol EST SP22	LIVE IN NEW ORLEANS (2-LP)	20

(See also Frank Beverly)

ANA MAZZOTTI

| 99 | Treasure Trove LPR 184 | NINGUEM VAI ME SEGURAR (LP, reissue) | 40 |

MAZZY STAR

93	Rough Trade Singles Club 45 rev 19	Five String Serenade/Under My Car (p/s)	15
94	Capitol 10CL720	Fade Into You/Five String Serenade/Under My Car/Bells Ring (Acoustic) (10" p/s, numbered)	100
13	Rhymes RHYMES 0045RT	Seasons Of Your Day/Sparrow (300 only)	10
96	Capitol CL 781	FLOWERS IN DECEMBER (EP, blue vinyl)	25
90	Rough Trade ROUGH 158	SHE HANGS BRIGHTLY (LP)	100
93	Capitol EST2206	SO TONIGHT THAT I MIGHT SEE (LP)	150
96	Capitol 8272241	AMONG MY SWAN (LP)	150
13	Rhymes RHYMES 004	SEASONS OF YOUR DAY (2-LP, transparent purple vinyl)	40
17	Capitol 00602557537574	SO TONIGHT THAT I MIGHT SEE (LP, reissue)	40

M.B.C. BAND AND CHICHIRI QUEENS

| 73 | Ng Omo MBC 002 | Angwazi Kawiri-Kawiri | 20 |
| 74 | Ng Omo MWLP 1 | KOKOLIKO KU MALAWI (LP) | 50 |

M-BEAT

| 94 | Renk 12RENKT 42 | Incredible (Original Mix)/(Booyaka Mix)/(Instrumental Version) (12", featuring General Levy) | 18 |
| 94 | Renk RENK LP1 | ALBUM (LP) | 20 |

M.B.P. MIX

MINT VALUE £

94	Renk RENK LP2	WICKED ALBUM (LP)	18

M.B.P. MIX
69	Major Minor MM66	Light My Fire/There's A Baby	30

MBT
85	MBT MBT 1	You Know Too Much/(Extended Version) (12")	100

MC FYRE
88	DTI MAC 3	It's My Rhythm/Kold Rockin' The Crowd (12")	40

MC GROOVE
89	Sing A Song SASM2	The Groove/Drop The Pressure (12")	12

MC SOLAAR
94	Talkin Loud 523 979-1	PROSE COMBAT (2-LP)	150

MC X
92	Pound Sterling POUND T002	F**K AmMeriKKAA (Version 1)/F**K AmMERIKKAA (Version 2) (12")	50

MCALMONT AND BUTLER
95	Hut HUTLP 32	THE SOUND OF...MCALMONT AND BUTLER (LP, inner)	30

(see also Bernard Butler, Suede)

WINSTON MCANUFF
79	Third World	I Love Jah/FREDDIE McGREGOR : Massachusetts (12")	30

JACKIE MCAULEY
71	Dawn DNS 1011	Turning Green/It's Alright	8
72	Dawn DNS 1020	Rocking Shoes/One Fine Day	7
71	Dawn DNLS 3023	JACKIE McAULEY (LP, gatefold sleeve)	150

(see also Them, Belfast Gypsies, Trader Horne, Freaks Of Nature)

MCAULEY SCHENKER GROUP
90	EMI EMPD 127	Anytime/What We Need/Anytime (Edit) (uncut picture disc)	30

(see also Group, Grand Prix)

GERRY MCAVOY
79	Bridgehouse BHS 004	Street Talk/Many Rivers To Cross (p/s)	10

JOHNNY MCBEE
63	Airborne NBP 0001	Nothing But Love/Rose-A-Lee	80

CECIL MCBEE
79	Inner City IC3023	MUSIC FROM THE SOURCE (LP)	15

NICKO MCBRAIN
91	EMI NICKO 1	Rhythm Of The Beast/Beehive Boogie (p/s)	8
91	EMI NICKOPD 1	Rhythm Of The Beast/McBrain Damage Interview (shaped picture disc with insert & plinth)	15

(see also Iron Maiden, Streetwalkers, Pat Travers)

FRANKIE MCBRIDE
67	Emerald MD 1081	Five Little Fingers/Do You Mind If You Leave Me Sleeping	6

DAN MCCAFFERTY
75	Mountain TOP 1	Out Of Time/Cinnamon Girl	6
75	Mountain DAN 1	Stay With Me Baby/Out Of Time/Watcha Gonna Do About It (p/s)	7
79	Mountain TOP 47 DJ	Watcha Gonna Do About It/(7.30 maxi version)/Boots Of Spanish Leather (12" promo)	10

(see also Nazareth, Sensational Alex Harvey Band, Mitchell/Coe Mysteries, Roger Glover)

JERRY MCCAIN
69	Python 02	Homogenised Love/728 Texas (99 copies only)	50

CASH MCCALL
63	Ember EMB S 173	Anytime/From The Very First Rose	10
65	Ember EMB S 204	Many Are The Words (I've Left Unspoken)/Buenos Noches	12
67	Chess CRS 8056	It's Wonderful (To Be In Love)/Let's Try It Over	20

DARRELL MCCALL
61	Capitol CL 15196	My Kind Of Lovin'/Beyond Imagination	8
63	Philips 304 002 BF	Dear One/I've Been Known	10
63	Philips BF 1259	Hud/No Place To Hide	7

TOUSSAINT MCCALL
67	Pye International 7N 25420	Nothing Takes The Place Of You/Shimmy	30

DAVID MCCALLUM
66	Capitol CL 15439	Communication/My Carousel	12
66	Capitol (S)T 2432	MUSIC ... A PART OF ME (LP)	25
66	Capitol (S)T 2498	MUSIC ... A BIT MORE OF ME (LP)	15

MCCALMANS
70	CBS 564145	TURN AGAIN (LP)	35
73	One Up OU 2161	McCALMANS' FOLK (LP)	15

JIM MCCANN
72	Polydor 2489 053	McCANNED! (LP)	40

(see also Ludlows)

LES MCCANN (LTD)
67	Mercury MF 973	All/Bucket O'Grease	15
69	Atlantic 584 284	With These Hands/Burnin' Coal	15

DON MCCARLOS
80	Negus Roots NERT 003	I Don't Care/I Love Jah (12")	45

MCCARTHY
86	Wall Of Salmon MAC 001	In Purgatory/The Comrade Era/Something Wrong Somewhere (foldover p/s in poly bag, white labels)	25
86	Pink PINKY 12	Red Sleeping Beauty/From The Damned (stickered p/s)	8
87	September SEPT 1	The Well Of Loneliness/Antiamericancretin/Unfortunately (p/s)	6
88	September SEPTT 4	This Nelson Rockefeller (p/s)	10

(see also Stereolab)

KEITH MCCARTHY
67	Coxsone CS 7014	Everybody Rude Now/BASES: Beware	25

Lyn & GRAHAM McCARTHY

MINT VALUE £

LYN & GRAHAM MCCARTHY
65	Columbia DB 7584	Seven Doves/Out After Ale	6
66	Columbia DB 7921	I Can't Help But Wonder/There's Got To Be Love	6
66	Columbia DB 8087	The Turkey's Trial/Bitter Withy	6
68	Columbia DB 8422	I Think It's Going To Rain/Once I Was	7

MARY MCCARTHY
67	CBS 2832	The Folk I Love/You Know He Did	100
67	CBS 2987	Happy Days And Lonely Night/Easy Kind Of Love	70

CECIL MCCARTNEY
68	Columbia DB 8474	Hey Aleuthia I Want You/Liquid Blue	25
69	Columbia DB 8595	Orange And Green/Cloudy	15
68	Columbia S(C)X 6283	OM (LP, first pressing with blue/black label with "Sold in UK..." text)	150
68	Columbia S(C)X 6283	OM (LP, second pressing with black/silver label, boxed logo)	40

LINDA MCCARTNEY
98	Parlophone 4979101	WILD PRAIRIE (LP)	80

(see also Suzy & The Red Stripes)

PAUL MCCARTNEY/WINGS
SINGLES
71	Apple R 5889	Another Day/Oh Woman, Oh Why	12
71	Apple R 5914	The Back Seat Of My Car/Heart Of The Country (as Paul & Linda McCartney)	12
72	Apple R 5932	Love Is Strange/I Am Your Singer (unreleased)	1500
72	Apple R 5936	Give Ireland Back To The Irish/(Version) (as Wings, yellow 'Wings' die-cut sl.)	12
72	Apple R 5949	Mary Had A Little Lamb/Little Woman Love (p/s)	10
72	Apple R 5973	Hi Hi Hi/C Moon	6
73	Apple R 5985	My Love/The Mess (as McCartney's Wings, demos and early retail copies shipped in a plain red sleeve)	20
73	Apple R 5987	Live And Let Die/I Lie Around	6
73	Apple R 5993	Helen Wheels/Country Dreamer	6
74	Apple R 5996	Jet/Let Me Roll It	6
74	Apple R 5997	Band On The Run/Zoo Gang	10
74	Apple R 5999	Juniors Farm/Sally G	8
75	Capitol R 6006	Listen To What The Man Said/Love In Song (p/s)	7
75	Capitol R 6008	Letting Go/You Gave Me The Answer	8
75	Capitol R 6010	Venus And Mars; Rock Show/Magneto And Titanium Man	8
78	Parlophone R 6018	Mull Of Kintyre/Girls School (yellow juke box 'Best selling British single ever' p/s)	60
78	Parlophone R 6020	I've Had Enough/Deliver Your Children (p/s, as Wings)	10
80	Parlophone 12R 6039	Temporary Secretary/Secret Friend (12", p/s)	35
82	Parlophone R 6054	Ebony And Ivory/Rainclouds (unreleased sepia-toned 'studio photo' p/s; beware of clever counterfeits)	50
82	Epic A 11-2729	The Girl Is Mine (with Michael Jackson)/MICHAEL JACKSON: Can't Get Outta The Rain (picture disc)	30
84	Parlophone 12RP 6080	No More Lonely Nights (Extended Version)/Silly Love Songs/ No More Lonely Nights (Ballad) (12", picture disc)	20
84	Parlophone RP 6086	We All Stand Together/We All Stand Together (Humming Version) (with Frog Chorus, shaped picture disc, in printed PVC sleeve)	18
85	Parlophone RP 6118	Spies Like Us/My Carnival (shaped picture disc)	15
85	Parlophone 12RP 6118	Spies Like Us (Party Mix)/Spies Like Us (Alternative Mix)/Spies Like Us (DJ Version)/My Carnival (Party Mix) (12", picture disc)	20
86	Parlophone 10R 6133	Press/It's Not True/Press (Video Edit) (10", circular foldout p/s)	12
86	Parlophone R 6133	Press (video edit)/It's Not True (p/s)	10
86	Parlophone R 6148/ R 6018	Only Love Remains/Tough On A Tightrope//Mull Of Kintyre/Girls' School (p/s, stickered double pack in PVC sleeve, no p/s on R 6018)	8
87	A&M FREE 21	Long Tall Sally (live)/I Saw Her Standing There (live) (p/s, free with "The Prince's Trust 10th Anniversary Birthday Party" LP [AMA 3906])	6
89	Parlophone 12RS 6235	Figure Of Eight/Ou Est Le Soliel? (12" etched vinyl)	25
89	Parlophone RX 6223	This One/The Long And Winding Road (p/s, envelope pack with 6 postcards)	12
89	Parlophone R 6238	Party Party (1 side etched, p/s)	10
97	Parlophone RP 6472	The World Tonight/Used To Be Bad (Picture disc)	6
01	Parlophone R 6567	From A Lover To A Friend/Riding Into Jaipur (p/s)	6
04	Parlophone R6649	Tropic Island Hum/We All Stand Together (p/s, yellow vinyl)	6
05	Parlophone R 6673	Fine Line/Growing Up Falling Down (p/s, plus art print)	6
05	Parlophone R 6678	Jenny Wren/Summer Of '59 (red vinyl, p/s)	7
05	GRA2010	Really Love You/Lalula (1-side etched, McCartney remixes by TWIN FREAKS 2,500 only)	20
07	HearMusic 88072306219	Ever Present Past/House Of Wax (live) (p/s)	6
13	MPL/Universal	Maybe I'm Amazed - Short Version (mono)/Album Version (mono)//Maybe I'm Amazed - Short Version (stereo)/Album Version (stereo) (12" die cut sleeve)	15
15	No label or cat no	Sweet Thrash/Sweet Thrash (12, hand-written labels, RSD secret release, 100 only, plain die-cut sleeve)	500

ALBUMS
70	Apple PCS 7102	McCARTNEY (LP, gatefold sleeve)	50
70	Apple TA 7102	McCARTNEY (reel-to-reel tape, jewel case, mono)	120
70	Apple TD-PCS 7102	McCARTNEY (reel-to-reel tape, jewel case, stereo)	50
70	Parlophone PPCS 7102	McCARTNEY (LP, export edition, black/silver label, 'Parlophone' and 'EMI' boxed logos)	200
71	Apple PAS 10003	RAM (LP, laminated gatefold sleeve)	40
71	Apple PCS 7142	WILD LIFE (LP, sleeve with 'sniped' spine edges, yellow inner)	60
73	Apple PCTC 251	RED ROSE SPEEDWAY (LP, laminated gatefold sleeve, with booklet)	100
73	Apple PCTC 251	RED ROSE SPEEDWAY (LP, gatefold sleeve, without booklet)	70
73	Apple PAS 10007	BAND ON THE RUN (LP, with lyric inner sleeve & poster)	50
73	Apple PAS 10007	BAND ON THE RUN (LP, export edition, Apple logo on textured label above catalogue number, circle indent on label, etched not stamped matrix ZYEX-929-3/ZYEX-930-3, 'BLAIR' etched onto dead wax)	60

Paul MCCARTNEY/WINGS

MINT VALUE £

Year	Label/Cat No	Title	Value
75	Capitol PCTC 254	VENUS AND MARS (LP, gatefold sleeve, inner sleeve, 2 posters & stickers)	50
76	MPL PCSP 720	WINGS OVER AMERICA (3-LP, with poster)	35
79	Parlophone PCTC 257	BACK TO THE EGG (LP, with inner)	30
80	Parlophone PCTC 258	MCCARTNEY II (LP, with inner)	20
80	Parlophone CHAT 1	MCCARTNEY INTERVIEW (LP)	30
84	Fame FA 413100-1	McCARTNEY (LP, gatefold sleeve)	15
84	Nimbus PAS 10007	BAND ON THE RUN (LP, with 'Nimbus' sticker)	300
87	Fame FA 3191	RED ROSE SPEEDWAY (LP, gatefold sleeve)	20
89	Parlophone PCSDX 106	FLOWERS IN THE DIRT (LP, World Tour pack with outer folder, 'Part' 7" single, poster, family tree, sticker, postcards & tour itinary)	50
90	Parlophone PCST 7286	TRIPPING THE LIVE FANTASTIC (3-LP in slip sleeve with inners and 12" x 12" booklet)	40
91	EMI PAUL 1	LIVERPOOL ORATORIO (2-LP, box set with booklet)	20

(With Carl Davis and others. McCartney does not play on this record which is his first classical composition in collaboration with Carl Davis)

Year	Label/Cat No	Title	Value
93	Parlophone PCSD 125	OFF THE GROUND (LP, gatefold)	100
93	Parlophone PCSD 147	PAUL IS LIVE (2 x LP)	120
97	Parlophone PCSD 171	FLAMING PIE (LP, gatefold)	100
99	Parlophone 5223511	RUN DEVIL RUN (LP, gatefold)	100
99	Parlophone 5232291	RUN DEVIL RUN (8 x 7", box set with booklet)	70
99	EMI Classics 5568971	WORKING CLASSICAL (2 x LP, gatefold)	40
99	Parlophone 4991761	BAND ON THE RUN (2 x LP, gatefold, 25th Anniversary)	30
01	Parlophone 5355101	DRIVING RAIN (2 x LP)	100
01	Parlophone 5328501	WINGSPAN (4 x LP, gatefold)	120
05	Parlophone 3383452	CHAOS AND CREATION IN THE BACKYARD (LP, gatefold with 4 art prints)	80
12	Universal 088072335981	KISSES ON THE BOTTOM (LP)	20
12	MPL HRM 33451-01	RAM (2-LP reissue)	20

PROMOS : PROMO SINGLES

Year	Label/Cat No	Title	Value
71	Apple R 5889	Another Day/Oh Woman, Oh Why (demo)	70
71	Apple R 5914	The Back Seat Of My Car/Heart Of The Country (demo)	50
73	Apple R5993	Helen Wheels/Country Dreamer (demo)	40
74	EMI R 5997	Band On The Run (Edited Version)/(Full Version) (demo)	150
74	Apple R 5999	Junior's Farm (Edited Version)/Junior's Farm (Full Version) (demo)	100
75	Apple R 5999	Sally G/Junior's Farm (reversed sides, demo)	150
75	Capitol R 6010	Venus And Mars; Rock Show/Magneto And Titanium Man (demo)	30
76	Parlophone R 6015	Let 'Em In (Edited Version)/Let 'Em In (Full Version) (demo)	55
76	Parlophone R 6014	Silly Love Songs (Edited Version)/Silly Love Songs (Full Version) (demo)	50
77	MPL Publishing MPL 1	We've Moved! (music publishing sampler with excerpts by Wings, Peggy Lee, Gene Vincent, Frank Sinatra, etc.; with press pack and insert)	350
77	MPL Publishing MPL 1	We've Moved! (music publishing sampler with excerpts by Wings, Peggy Lee, Gene Vincent, Frank Sinatra, etc.; without press pack and insert)	250
77	Capitol R 6018	Mull Of Kintyre (Edited Version)/Girls' School (Edited Version) (demo)	50
78	Parlophone R 6019	With A Little Luck (Edited Version)/Backwards Traveller-Cuff Link (demo)	40
80	Parlophone R 6037DJ	Waterfalls (3.22) (edit)/Check My Machine (demo)	40
80	Parlophone R 6039A	Temporary Secretary (1-sided demo, no p/s)	80
84	Parlophone 12RDJ 6080T	No More Lonely Nights (Mole Mix) (12", 1-sided, plain white numbered sleeve with plain white inner sleeve & insert, 250 only; beware of counterfeits with scratched [not stamped] matrix)	250
84	Parlophone 12R(DJ) 6080	No More Lonely Nights (Extended Version)/Silly Love Songs/No More Lonely Nights (Ballad) (12", promo, blue 'Give My Regards To Broad Street' label, black die-cut sleeve)	50
85	Parlophone RDJ 6118	Spies Like Us (DJ Version 3.46)/My Carnival (demo, white printed die-cut sleeve)	35
88	Parlophone PMBOX 11-19	ALL THE BEST! ('Special Edition') (9 x 7" box set, in black die-cut sleeves, with signed 7" print; with genuine signatures)	200
88	Parlophone PMBOX 11-19	ALL THE BEST! ('Special Edition') (9 x 7" box set, in black die-cut sleeves, with signed 7" print)	75
89	Parl. 12R LOVE 6223	This One (Lovejoy's Remix) (12", 1-sided, plain label, black die-cut sleeve)	35
89	Parlophone GOOD 1	Good Sign (6.51)/Good Sign (Groove Mix) (7.22) (12", black die-cut sleeve)	45
89	Parlophone RDJ 6235	Figure Of Eight (Edited Version 3.59)/Ou Est Le Soleil? (Edited Version 3.57) (demo, standard p/s)	30
89	Parlophone RDJ 6238	Party (Remix By Bruce Forest)/Party (different remix) (12", some listed as 'Party Party', with insert)	40
89	Parlophone RDJ 6238	Party (Remix By Bruce Forest)/Party (different remix) (12")	30
89	Parlophone R 6213	My Brave Face/Flying To My Home (promo in retro Parlophone sleeve)	50
90	Parlophone 12 SOL 1	Où Est Le Soleil? (Tub Dub Mix)/Où Est Le Soleil? (Instrumental Mix) (12", black die-cut stickered sleeve, with insert)	40
90	Parlophone 12 SOL 1	Où Est Le Soleil? (Tub Dub Mix)/Où Est Le Soleil? (Instrumental Mix) (12", black die-cut stickered sleeve, some without insert)	20
90	Parlophone R 6271	Birthday Boy/Good Day Sunshine (promo in repro Parlophone sleeve)	30
90	Parlophone R 6278	All My Trials/C Moon (promo in repro Parlophone sleeve)	20
93	Parlophone CDRDJ 6338	C'mon People (Radio Edit)/C'mon People (CD)	30
93	Parlophone CDRS 6347	Biker Like An Icon/Things We Said Today/Mean Woman Blues/ Midnight Special (CD, unissued)	0
93	Parlophone CDRDJ 6347	Biker Like An Icon/Things We Said Today/Mean Woman Blues/ Midnight Special (CD, no inlay, jewel case with large sticker; beware of counterfeits with thicker blurred label print & smaller sticker on case)	70
93	Parlophone 12 DELIVDJ 1	Deliverance/Deliverance (Dub Mix) (12", green label, plain black die-cut sleeve)	20
99	Parlophone RDR03	Run Devil Run/Blue Jean Bop (mock 50's Parlophone label/sleeve)	30
00	Hydra FREE 02	Free Now (as Liverpool Sound Collage, 1-sided, p/s)	25
01	WINDJ 002	Silly Love Songs (Loop Da Loop Mix)/Coming Up (Linus Loves Mix) (12" 50 copies)	150
03	Parlophone TEMPSEC 01	Temporary Secretary (Re-edited by Audioslave) (12", 1-sided)	20

PROMOS : PROMO ALBUMS

Year	Label/Cat No	Title	Value
79	Parlophone PCTCP 257	BACK TO THE EGG (LP, as Wings, MPL in-house picture disc; die-cut sleeve, matrix numbers YEX 987-2 & YEX 988-4 or -1; beware of counterfeits)	950
79	Parlophone PCTC 257	BACK TO THE EGG (LP, box set with badge, booklet, sticker, postcard & 5 cigarette cards;	300

Caroline McCAUSLAND

MINT VALUE £

79	Capitol (no cat. no.)	with or without T-shirt; beware of counterfeits with blurred printing).................... MPL PRESENTS (6-LP, box set, hand-numbered, 25 only)	700

(see also Beatles, Country Hams, Percy 'Thrills' Thrillington, Fireman, Mike McGear, Suzy & The Red Stripes, George Martin, Spirit Of Play, Ferry Aid, Michael Jackson, Twin Freaks)

CAROLINE MCCAUSLAND
60s	Happy Face MMLP 1022	SONGS FOR GALA (LP)	40

DAVE MCCLAREN
71	Big BG 323	Love Is What I Bring (actually by Dave Barker & Uniques)/ RUPIE EDWARDS ALL STARS: Love Version (with U Roy Junior)	18

DELBERT MCCLINTON
62	Decca F 11541	Hully Gully/Baby Heartbreak	12

CHRIS MCCLURE (SECTION)
66	Decca F 12346	The Dying Swan/The Land Of The Golden Tree	10
68	Polydor 56227	Hazy People/I'm Just A Country Boy	15
68	Polydor 56259	Answer To Everything/Meditation	7
69	RCA RCA 1849	Our Song Of Love/Weather Vane	7
69	CBS 7646	You're Only Passing Time/Sing Our Song (as Chris McClure Section)	8

(see also Marmalade)

BRIAN MCCOLLOM FOLK GROUP
66	Pye 7N 17198	This Dusty Road/Henry Joy McCraken	6

TOMMY MCCOOK (& SUPERSONICS)
63	Island WI 102	Adam's Apple/MAYTALS: Every Time (B-side actually by Tonettes)	30
63	Island WI 118	Below Zero/LEE PERRY: Never Get Weary	40
63	Island WI 124	Junior Jive/HORACE SEATON: Power	25
64	R&B JB 139	Sampson/ROY & ANNETTE: My Arms Are Waiting	50
64	R&B JB 163	Bridge View/NAOMI & CO: What Can I Do (B-side actually by Naomi & Clive) .	45
64	Port-O-Jam PJ 4001	Exodus (& His Group)/LEE PERRY: Help The Weak	60
64	Port-O-Jam PJ 4003	Jam Rock/LEE PERRY: Band Minded People	40
64	Port-O-Jam PJ 4010	Road Bloack/LEE PERRY: Chatty Chatty Woman	70
64	Black Swan WI 422	Two For One/LASCELLES PERKINS: I Don't Know	25
65	Island WI 232	Rocket Ship/JUSTIN HINDS & DOMINOES: Turn Them Back	60
66	Rio R 100	Jerk Time (with Supersonics)/UNIQUES: The Journey	70
66	Rio R 101	Out Of Space (with Supersonics)/UNIQUES: Do Me Good	100
66	Rio R 103	Ska Jam/Smooth Sailing (with Supersonics)	100
66	Rio R 104	Riverton City/HEPTONES: Gunmen Coming To Town	100
66	Doctor Bird DB 1028	More Love/SILVERTONES: True Confession	80
66	Doctor Bird DB 1032	Naked City (with Supersonics)/NORMA FRASER: Heartaches	45
66	Doctor Bird DB 1047	Spanish Eyes (with Lynn Taitt)/STRANGER & HORTENSE: Loving Wine	30
66	Doctor Bird DB 1051	A Little Bit Of Heaven (& His Band)/LLOYD WILLIAMS: Sad World	30
66	Doctor Bird DB 1053	Indian Love Call (with Supersonics)/OWEN & LEON: How Would You Feel	25
66	Doctor Bird DB 1056	Danger Man (with Supersonics)/ERIC MORRIS: If I Didn't Love You	40
66	Doctor Bird DB 1061	What Now/Don't Stay Away	70
67	Doctor Bird DB 1058	Jam Session (with Supersonics)/LLOYD & GLEN: Jezebel	50
67	Island WI 3047	One Two Three Kick/TREASURE ISLE BOYS: What A Fool (B-side actually by Silvertones) ..	50
67	Island WI 3049	Saboo (with Supersonics)/MOVING BROTHERS: Darling I Love You	40
67	Treasure Isle TI 7017	Persian Cat/JUSTIN HINDS: Once A Man	20
67	Treasure Isle TI 7018	Saboo (with Supersonics)/MOVING BROTHERS: Darling I Love You (reissue) .	25
67	Treasure Isle TI 7020	Shadow Of Your Smile/SILVERTONES: Cool Down	60
68	Treasure Isle TI 7027	Soul For Sale/SILVERTONES: In The Midnight Hour	25
68	Treasure Isle TI 7032	Venus/Music Is My Occupation (with Supersonics)	30
68	Treasure Isle TI 7039	Our Man Flint (with Supersonics)/SILVERTONES: Old Man River	150
68	Treasure Isle TI 7042	Moving (with Supersonics)/SILVERTONES: Slow And Easy	80
68	Doctor Bird DB 1135	Mad Mad World/Wonderful World (with Lloyd Williams)	30
68	Unity UN 501	Last Flight To Reggie (Reggae) City (with Stranger Cole)/Watch Dem Go	80
69	Trojan TR 642	Breaking Up/Party Time (with Supersonics) (both actually by Alton Ellis)	40
69	Trojan TR 652	Third Figure/You Should've Known Better	25
69	Trojan TR 657	When The Saints Go Marching In/SOUL OFROUS: Ease Me Up Officer (B-side actually by Righteous Flames)	40
69	Trojan TR 671	Moonshot/PHYLLIS DILLON: Get On The Right Shot	60
69	Trojan TR 686	Tribute To Rameses/PHYLLIS DILLION: Lipstick On Your Collar	25
69	Trojan TR 7706	Black Coffee (with Supersonics)/VIC TAYLOR: Heartaches	20
69	Unity UN 506	The Avengers/LAUREL AITKEN: Donkey Man	30
69	Unity UN 534	Dream Boat/Tommy's Dream	25
69	Unity UN 535	Peanut Vendor/100,000 Tons Of Rock	40
70	Duke DU 76	The Rooster (with Supersonics) (actually by Jeff Barnes)/ PHYLLIS DILLON: Walk Through This World	10
70	Duke DU 77	Open Jaw (with Supersonics)/JOHN HOLT: The Working Kind	25
70	Duke DU 78	Key To The City (with Supersonics)/DOROTHY REID: Give It To Me	10
71	Treasure Isle TI 7058	My Best Dress/PHYLISS DILLON: One Life To Live	20
71	Treasure Isle TI 7061	Testify Version/JOHN HOLT: Let's Build Our Dreams	25
71	Treasure Isle TI 7065	Black River/JOHN HOLT: Sister Big Stuff	25
71	Treasure Isle TI 7066	Paragon's Medley Version/JOHN HOLT: Paragon's Medley	18
71	Treasure Isle TI 7070	Midnight Confession Version/PHYLLIS DILLON: Midnight Confession	30
71	Big Shot BI 585	Psalm Nine To Keep In Mind (with Observers)/Psalm Nine (Version)	20
71	Spinning Wheel SW 109	Crying Everynight (with Supersonics) (actually by Stranger Cole)/ HERMAN MARQUIS: Tom's Version	50
71	Spinning Wheel SW 110	Stupid Doctor (with Supersonics)/ROB WALKER: Grooving In Style (B-side actually by Ken Parker)	125
73	Technique TE 927	Rub It Down/Rub It Down (Version) (as Tommy McCook Stars)	6
73	G.G. GG 4539	Bad Cow Skank (with Bobby Ellis)/ GLADSTONE ANDERSON: Drummer Roach	8
75	Vulcan VUL 1002	Kojak/Cannon (with Aggrovators)	12

Tommy McCOOK & GLEN BROWN

MINT VALUE £

79	Grove Music GMDM 26	Sensimena/TONY TUFF: You Wrong (12")	20
13	Trojan THB 7025	Michelle/The Lesson	7
70	Trojan TBL 111	GREATER JAMAICA (MOONWALK REGGAE) (LP, actually by various artists)	60
74	Attack ATLP 1007	TOMMY McCOOK (LP)	35
75	Trojan HRLP 706	COOKIN' (LP)	30
77	Third World TWS 920	HOT LAVA (LP)	30
77	Justice JUS LP 07	INSTRUMENTAL (LP)	45

(see also Denis Alcapone, Dave Barker, Dennis Brown, Shenley Duffas, Dennis & Lizzy, Dobby Dobson, Dynamics, Alton Ellis, Ethiopians, Eagles, Emotions, Herman, Heptones, Jamaicans, Hopeton Lewis, Lloyd & Glen, Lloyd & Groovers, Bob Marley, Maytals, Melodians, Mellodites, Millions, Paragons, Hugh Roy, Karl Walker Allstars)

TOMMY MCCOOK & GLEN BROWN
76	Groundation GROL 10	HORNY DUB (LP, white label)	300

TOMMY MCCOOK & BOBBY ELLIS
77	Grove Music GM 006	Blazing/No Water	40
75	Grove Music GMLP 002	BLAZING HORNS (LP)	80

JASON MCCORD
65	Pye 7N 15925	It Was A Very Good Year/Song Of The Pine Tree	35

MCCORMICK BROTHERS
63	Polydor NH 66986	Red Hen Boogie/Blue Grass Express	50
66	Hickory LPE 1509	AUTHENTIC BLUEGRASS HITS (EP)	22

GEORGE MCCORMICK
55	MGM SPC 6	Don't Fix Up The Doghouse/Gold Wedding Band (export issue)	18

CHARLIE MCCOY
75	Monument MNT 5103	Stone Fox Chase/Honestly I Love You	6

CLYDE MCCOY
57	Mercury MEP 9513	DANCING TO THE BLUES (EP)	15

JOE MCCOY
59	Collector JDL 81	One In A Hundred/One More Greasing	30

VIOLA MCCOY
50s	Ristic LP 27	VIOLA McCOY 1923-1927 (10" LP)	40

N MCCOY & ALBIANS
78	K&K K001	The People/Talk To The People (12")	70

(see also Albians)

MCCOYS
65	Immediate IM 001	Hang On Sloopy/I Can't Explain It	8
65	Immediate IM 021	Fever/Sorrow	12
66	Immediate IM 028	Don't Worry Mother, Your Son's Heart Is Pure/Ko-Ko	10
66	Immediate IM 029	Up And Down/If You Tell A Lie	10
66	Immediate IM 034	Runaway/Come On Let's Go	10
66	Immediate IM 037	(You Make Me Feel) So Good/Every Day I Have To Cry	10
67	Immediate IM 046	I Got To Go Back/Dynamite	15
67	London HLZ 10154	Say These Magic Words/I Wonder If She Remembers Me	25
68	Mercury MF 1067	Jesse Brady/Resurrection	8
66	Immediate IMEP 002	HITS VOL. 1 (EP)	40
66	Immediate IMEP 003	HITS VOL. 2 (EP)	40
65	Immediate IMLP 001	HANG ON SLOOPY (LP)	55
68	Mercury (S)MCL 20128	THE INFINITE McCOYS (LP)	40
71	Joy JOYS 196	HANG ON SLOOPY (LP, reissue)	15

(see also Rick Derringer)

JIMMY MCCRACKLIN
58	London HLM 8598	The Walk/I'm To Blame (as Jimmy McCracklin & His Band)	50
58	London HL 7035	The Walk/I'm To Blame (export issue, as Jimmy McCracklin & His Band)	15
62	Top Rank JAR 617	Just Got To Know/The Drag	25
65	R&B MRB 5001	I Got Eyes For You/I'm Gonna Tell Your Mother	25
66	Outasite 45 120	Christmas Time (Parts 1 & 2) (99 copies only)	40
65	Liberty LIB 66094	Every Night, Every Day/Can't Raise Me	10
66	Liberty LIB 66129	Think/Steppin' Up In Class	10
68	Minit MLF 11003	How Do You Like Your Love/Get Together	10
68	Minit MLF 11009	Pretty Little Sweet Thing/A And I	10
65	Vocalion VEP 170160	JIMMY McCRACKLIN (EP)	100
68	Minit MLL/MLS 40003	A PIECE OF JIMMY McCRACKLIN (LP)	40

GWEN MCCRAE
74	President PT 416	It's Worth The Hurt/90% Of Me Is You	10
82	Atlantic FLAM 1	Keep The Fire Burning/Funky Sensation	10
82	Atlantic FLAM 1T	Keep The Fire Burning/Funky Sensation (12")	20

DANNY MCCULLOCH
69	Capitol CL 15607	Blackbird/Time Of Man	8
70	Pye Intl./Festival 7N 25514	Colour Of The Sunset/Smokeless Zone	8
69	Capitol E-(S)T 174	WINGS OF A MAN (LP, black/silver label with boxed logo)	40

(see also Animals)

IAN MCCULLOCH
64	Decca F11855	Come On Home/Down By The River	50

ED MCCURDY
66	Bounty BY 6017	BLOOD BOOZE N BONES (LP)	20
60s	Elektra ELK 110	WHEN DALLIANCE WAS IN FLOWER AND MAIDENS LOST THEIR HEADS (LP, with insert)	40
60s	Elektra ELK 140	WHEN DALLIANCE WAS IN FLOWER VOL 2 (LP)	40

GEORGE MCCURN
63	London HLH 9705	I'm Just A Country Boy/In My Little Corner Of The World	10

LUKE MCDANIEL
55	Parlophone CMSP 29	The Automobile Song/I Can't Steal Another's Bride (export issue)	40

MAISIE McDANIEL

MINT VALUE £

MAISIE MCDANIEL
63	Fontana TE 17397	MEET MAISIE McDANIEL! (EP, with The Hunters)	10
63	Fontana TE 17398	COUNTRY STYLE (EP, with The Hunters)	12

(see also Hunters)

EUGENE MCDANIELS
71	Atlantic 2465 022	OUTLAW (LP)	30
71	Atlantic 2400 163	HEADLESS HEROES OF THE APOCALYPSE (LP, US sleeve with sticker over US cat no. UK pressed record)	80
02	Warner Bros. 756793113-1	HEADLESS HEROES OF THE APOCALYPSE (LP, reissue)	20

GENE MCDANIELS
61	London HLG 9319	A Hundred Pounds Of Clay/Take A Chance On Love	10
61	London HLG 9396	A Tear/She's Come Back	15
61	London HLG 9448	Tower Of Strength/Secret	10
62	Liberty LIB 55405	Chip Chip/Another Tear Falls	10
62	Liberty LIB 55480	Point Of No Return/Warmer Than A Whisper	15
63	Liberty LIB 55510	Spanish Lace/Somebody's Waiting	6
63	Liberty LIB 55541	The Puzzle/Cry Baby Cry	6
63	Liberty LIB 55597	It's A Lonely Town/False Friends	30
63	Liberty LIB 10130	Anyone Else/New Love In Old Mexico	8
64	Liberty LIB 55723	In Times Like These/Make Me A Present Of You	15
65	Liberty LIB 55752	(There Goes The) Forgotten Man	45
65	Liberty LIB 55805	Walk With A Winner/A Miracle	100
65	Liberty LIB 55805	Walk With A Winner/A Miracle (DJ copy)	250
61	London REG 1298	GENE McDANIELS (EP)	40
62	Liberty LEP 2054	A CHANGE OF MOOD (EP)	40
61	London HA-G 2384	A HUNDRED POUNDS OF CLAY (LP, mono)	60
61	London SAH-G 6184	A HUNDRED POUNDS OF CLAY (LP, stereo)	80
62	Liberty LBY 1003	... SOMETIMES I'M HAPPY (LP)	40
62	Liberty LBY 1021	TOWER OF STRENGTH (LP)	40
63	Liberty (S)LBY 1128	SPANISH LACE (LP)	40
63	Liberty LBY 1179	THE WONDERFUL WORLD OF GENE McDANIELS (LP)	40
68	Sunset SLS 50017E	FACTS OF LIFE (LP)	15

BILL MCDAVID
61	Starlite ST45 63	Kiss Me For Christmas/Little Shepherd Boy	8

CHAS MCDEVITT (SKIFFLE GROUP)
57	Oriole CB 1352	Freight Train (with Nancy Whiskey)/The Cotton Song	15
57	Oriole CB 1357	It Takes A Worried Man/The House Of The Rising Sun	10
57	Oriole CB 1371	Green Back Dollar (with Nancy Whiskey)/I'm Satisfied	10
57	Oriole CB 1386	Face In The Rain (with Nancy Whiskey)/Sporting Life (with Tony Kohn)	10
57	Oriole CB 1395	Sing, Sing, Sing/My Old Man	10
58	Oriole CB 1403	Johnny-O (with Nancy Whiskey)/Bad Man Stack-O-Lee	10
58	Oriole CB 1405	Across The Bridge (with Shirley Douglas)/Deep Down	10
58	Oriole CB 1457	Real Love (with Shirley Douglas)/Juke-Box Jumble	15
59	Oriole CB 1511	Teenage Letter (with Shirley Douglas)/SHIRLEY DOUGLAS: Sad Little Girl	10
60	Top Rank JAR 338	Dream Talk/Forever (with Shirley Douglas)	10
57	Oriole EP 7002	CHAS AND NANCY (EP, with Nancy Whiskey)	20
57	Oriole MG 10018	THE INTOXICATING MISS WHISKEY (10" LP, with Nancy Whiskey)	30
65	Columbia 33SX 1738	SIXTEEN BIG FOLK HITS (LP, with Shirley Douglas)	15

(see also Nancy Whiskey, Coffee Bar Skifflers)

(COUNTRY) JOE MCDONALD
71	Vanguard 6076 252	Hold On It's Coming Parts 1 & 2	6
71	Vanguard 6359 004	TONIGHT I'M SINGING JUST FOR YOU (LP)	15
71	Sonet SNTF 622	QUIET DAYS IN CLICHY (LP, soundtrack)	15
71	Vanguard VSD 79314	HOLD ON - IT'S COMING (LP)	15
71	Vanguard VSD 79315	WAR WAR WAR (LP)	15

(see also Country Joe & The Fish)

LARRY MCDONALD & DENZIL LAING
71	Clandisc CLA 228	Name Of The Game/FABULOUS FLAMES: Holly Version	10

RITCHIE MCDONALD
79	Warrior WAR 137	Hard Road/WIRE LINDO: African Sound (12")	80
72	Duke DU 141	Boat To Progress/Boat To Progress - Version (with Glen Brown)	20

RORY MCDONALD
71	Philips 6006 117	Your Love Is Indescribably Delicious/If I Had A Mind To	30

SHELAGH MCDONALD
70	B&C CAS 1019	THE SHELAGH McDONALD ALBUM (LP, textured sleeve)	200
71	B&C CAS 1043	STAR GAZER (LP, with inner sleeve)	200

(see also Keith Christmas)

SKEETS MCDONALD
56	Capitol CL 14566	Fallen Angel/It'll Take Me A Long, Long Time	8
59	Capitol EAP1 1040	GOING STEADY WITH THE BLUES (EP)	40

TESFA MCDONALD
72	Dynamic DYN 455	Life Is The Highest/Recarnate (Re-Incarnate) (actually by Bobby Ellis and Tommy McCook)	30

MCDONALD & GILES
70	Island ILPS 9126	McDONALD AND GILES (LP, 1st pressing, pink label, with 'i' logo)	200
73	Island ILPS 9126	McDONALD AND GILES (LP, 2nd pressing, 'pink rim' label, 'palm tree' logo)	40
77	Polydor 2302 070	McDONALD AND GILES (LP, repressing)	25

(see also King Crimson; Giles, Giles & Fripp)

(MISSISSIPPI) FRED MCDOWELL
66	Bounty BY 6022	MY HOME IS IN THE DELTA (LP)	45

Fred & ANNIE MAE McDOWELL

MINT VALUE £

66	Fontana 688 806 ZL	MISSISSIPPI DELTA BLUES (LP)	40
69	CBS 63735	LONG WAY FROM HOME (LP)	30
69	Polydor 236 278	GOING DOWN SOUTH (LP)	30
70	Capitol E-ST 409	I DO NOT PLAY NO ROCK & ROLL (LP)	25
70	Transatlantic TRA 194	LONDON 1 (LP)	18
71	Transatlantic TRA 203	LONDON 2 (LP)	18
71	Revival RVS 1001	EIGHT YEARS RAMBLIN' (LP, with Johnny Woods)	18
74	Xtra XTRA 1136	MISSISSIPPI FRED McDOWELL 1904-1972 (LP)	15

FRED & ANNIE MAE McDOWELL
| 64 | Polydor 236 570 | GOING DOWN SOUTH (LP) | 18 |

BROTHER JACK MCDUFF
64	Stateside SS 275	Sanctified Samba/Whistle While You Work	10
64	Stateside SS 302	Rock Candy/Real Good 'Un	12
64	Stateside SS 328	Carpetbaggers (Main Theme)/The Pink Panther (Theme)	10
66	Atlantic 584 036	Down In The Valley/A Change Is Gonna Come	10
64	Stateside SL 10060	BROTHER JACK McDUFF LIVE! (LP)	20
64	Stateside SL 10101	THE DYNAMIC JACK McDUFF (LP, as Brother Jack McDuff Quartet)	20
65	Stateside SL 10121	BROTHER JACK McDUFF QUARTET LIVE! AT THE JAZZ WORKSHOP (LP)	20
65	Stateside SL 10142	PRELUDE (LP)	20
66	Stateside SL 10165	THE CONCERT McDUFF (LP)	18
66	Atlantic 587 030	A CHANGE IS GONNA COME (LP)	20
67	Transatlantic PR 7404	SILK AND SOUL (LP)	15
67	Transatlantic PR 7476	WALK ON BY (LP)	15
68	Transatlantic PR 7286	AT THE JAZZ WORKSHOP (LP)	15
68	Transatlantic ATRA 5056	DYNAMIC JACK McDUFF (LP)	15

(see also Roland Kirk, Kenny Burrell, Jimmy Witherspoon)

JOHNNY MCEVOY
67	Pye 17375	Funny Man/Was It You	6
73	Hawk HALPX 112	JOHNNY McEVOY (LP)	15
74	Hawk HALPX 117	SOUNDS LIKE JOHNNY McEVOY (LP)	20

(see also Rambler)

BOB MCFADDEN & DOR
| 59 | Coral Q 72378 | The Mummy/The Beat Generation (tri centre) | 20 |
| 59 | Coral Q 72378 | The Mummy/The Beat Generation (round centre) | 10 |

(see also Rod McKuen)

MC5
69	Elektra EKSN 45056	Kick Out The Jams/Motor City Is Burning	50
69	Elektra EKSN 45067	Ramblin' Rose/Borderline	35
69	Elektra EKL 4042	KICK OUT THE JAMS (LP, orange label, gatefold sleeve, mono)	200
69	Elektra EKS 74042	KICK OUT THE JAMS (LP, orange label, gatefold sleeve, stereo)	100
70	Atlantic 2400 016	BACK IN THE U.S.A. (LP)	100
71	Atlantic 2400 135	HIGH TIME (LP)	80
77	Atlantic K50346	BACK IN THE USA (LP, reissue)	25
77	Elektra K42027	KICK OUT THE JAMS (LP, reissue with 'Brothers & Sisters' edit)	30

(see also Wayne Kramer, Destroy All Monsters)

MIKE MCGEAR
72	Island WIP 6131	Woman/Kill	15
74	Warner Bros K 16446	Leave It/Sweet Baby (p/s)	12
74	Warner Bros K 16446	Leave It/Sweet Baby	8
75	Warner Bros K 16520	Sea Breezes/Givin' Grease A Ride	8
75	Warner Bros K 16573	Dance The Do/Norton	10
75	Warner Bros K 16658	Simply Love You/What Do We Really Know (in p/s)	15
75	Warner Bros K 16658	Simply Love You/What Do We Really Know	8
76	EMI EMI 2485	Doing Nothing All Day/A To Z	6
80	Carrere CAR 144	All The Whales In The Ocean/I Juz Want What You Got Money! (in p/s)	30
80	Carrere CAR 144	All The Whales In The Ocean/I Juz Want What You Got - Money!	15
81	Conn SRTS/81/CUS 1112	No Lardidar/God Save The Gracious Queen (in p/s)	55
81	Conn SRTS/81/CUS 1112	No Lardidar/God Save The Gracious Queen	35
72	Island ILPS 9191	WOMAN (LP, gatefold, pink rim palm tree label)	50
74	Warner Bros K 56051	McGEAR (LP, gatefold sleeve with folded lyric insert)	25
74	Warner Bros KMG 1	McGEAR'S LIMITED EDITION (7-track white label sampler & press kit)	45
80s	Centre Labs	McGEAR (LP, 6-track reissue, 500 only, numbered & signed)	60

(see also Grimms, Scaffold, McGough & McGear, Paul McCartney)

FRANCINE MCGEE
| 77 | RCA PC 0216 | Feelin Good (Disco Mix)/Delerium (Disco Mix) (12") | 20 |
| 78 | RCA PB 9216 | Feelin Good/Delerium | 20 |

LARRY MCGEE REVOLUTION
| 05 | Liquorice Soul LSD 010T | The Burg (Nick Faber Edit)/(Original Version)/(Fat Camp Re-edit)/(Bonus Beats) (12", reissue) | 20 |
| 18 | Dynamite Cuts DYNAM7003 | The Burg/Happy Bicentennial USA (reissue, p/s) | 7 |

BROWNIE MCGHEE
| 63 | Columbia SEG 8226 | BLUES ON PARADE NO. 1 (EP) | 20 |
| 60s | Xtra 1021 | BROWNIE McGHEE (LP) | 20 |

BROWNIE MCGHEE & DAVE LEE
| 57 | Pye Jazz NJE 1060 | THE BLUEST (EP) | 22 |

(see also Sonny Terry & Brownie McGhee)

DONNA MCGHEE
78	Anchor ANC 1061	Do As I Do/Mr Blindman	25
78	Anchor ANCT 1061	Do As I Do/Mr Blindman (12")	35
78	Anchor ANCL 2027	MAKE IT LAST FOREVER (LP)	100

Howard McGHEE

MINT VALUE £

HOWARD McGHEE
61	Parlophone PMC 1811	DUSTY BLUE (LP, black/gold label)	70
61	Fontana FJL906	THE SHARP EDGE (LP)	40

(see also Scaffold, Adrian Henri, Mike McGear, Jimi Hendrix, Grimms)

(ROGER) McGOUGH & (MIKE) McGEAR
68	Parlophone PMC/PCS 7047	McGOUGH AND McGEAR (LP, with phasing on "So Much"; black/yellow label with "Sold in U.K...." text)	275
89	Parlophone PCS 7332	McGOUGH AND McGEAR (LP, stereo reissue with inner sleeve, without phasing on "So Much")	15

ROGER McGOUGH & BRIAN PATTEN
75	Argo ZPL 1190	READ THEIR OWN VERSE - BRITISH POETS OF OUR TIME (LP)	25

MAUREEN McGOVERN
73	Pye Intl. 7N 25603	The Morning After/Midnight Storm (p/s)	8

CHRIS McGREGOR('S BROTHERHOOD OF BREATH)
68	Polydor 184 137	VERY URGENT (LP, as Chris McGregor Group)	80
68	Polydor 583 072	UP TO EARTH (LP, unreleased, test pressings only)	150
71	RCA Neon NE 2	CHRIS McGREGOR'S BROTHERHOOD OF BREATH (LP, gatefold sleeve)	70
72	RCA SF 8260	BROTHERHOOD (LP, gatefold sleeve, as Chris McGregor's Brotherhood Of Breath)	70
74	Ogun OG 100	LIVE, WILLISAU (LP)	25
77	Ogun OG 521	IN HIS OWN TIME (LP)	25
78	Ogun OG 524	PROCESSION (LP)	25

(see also Brotherhood Of Breath, Tunji)

FREDDIE McGREGOR
73	Fab FAB 261	Wise Words/NEW ESTABLISHMENT: Version	35
75	Sol Fa SA 02	Get Involved/BAILEY'S ALL STARS: Part 2	30
79	Observer OBS 903	Run Come Rally (12")	60
81	Yashemabeth YM01	Wine Of Violence/Once A Man (12")	15
81	JB JBD 030	Leave Yah/20 Miles Blackstar Liner/U BROWN: Step It Up (12", blue/yellow vinyl)	40
83	Intense INT 007	Jumping Jack/Pretty Woman (12")	12
84	Real Authentic Sound RAS 7008	Across The Border/Version (12")	30
96	Blacker Dread BDTL 05	Mr. Pressure Man/CLIVE HYLTON: Babylon Keep On Knocking (12")	35
79	Jackal JALP 7000	FREDDY McGREGOR (LP)	30

(see also Soul Brothers, Young Freddie)

JIMMY McGRIFF
64	Sue WI 303	All About My Girl/M.G. Blues	40
64	Sue WI 310	Last Minute (Parts 1 & 2)	40
64	Sue WI 317	I've Got A Woman (Parts 1 & 2)	40
64	Sue WI 333	'Round Midnight/Lonely Avenue	40
66	United Artists UP 1170	See See Rider/Hallelujah	20
70	United Artists UP 35025	The Worm/What's That	30
64	Sue ILP 907	I'VE GOT A WOMAN (LP)	100
64	Sue ILP 908	GOSPEL TIME (LP)	100
65	London HA-C 8247	BLUES FOR MISTER JIMMY (LP)	60
66	London HA-C 8242	AT THE APOLLO (LP)	75
66	United Artists (S)ULP 1158	A BAG FULL OF SOUL (LP)	30
68	United Artists (S)ULP 1270	THE BIG BAND (LP)	25
72	Groove Merchant GM 503	GROOVE GREASE (LP)	20
74	People PLEO 14	FLY DUDE (LP)	15
74	People PLEO 19	LET'S STAY TOGETHER (LP)	15
74	People PLEO 23	IF YOU'RE READY COME GO WITH ME (LP)	15

BILL McGUFFIE (TRIO)
53	Parlophone MSP 6040	Concerto For Boogie/Begin The Beguine (as Bill McGuffie Trio)	7
67	Philips BF 1550	Fugue For Thought (from the film 'Dalek Invasion Earth 2150AD')/ Fair's Fair	25
55	Philips BBR 8054	JAZZ WITH McGUFFIE (LP)	15
55	Philips BBR 8087	McGUFFIE MAGIC (LP)	20
56	Philips BBL 7072	MORE JAZZ WITH McGUFFIE (LP)	20
58	Philips BBL 7261	CONTINENTAL TOUR (LP)	20

ROGER McGUINN
74	CBS 2649	Peace On You/Without You	6
77	CBS 5231	American Girl/Russian Hill	6

(see also Byrds)

McGUINNESS FLINT
70	Capitol EA-ST 22625	McGUINNESS FLINT (LP, gatefold sleeve)	20
71	Capitol ST 22794	HAPPY BIRTHDAY, RUTHY BABY (LP)	15

(see also Manfred Mann, Blues Band, John Mayall, Coulson Dean McGuinness Flint, Gallagher & Lyle, Paladin)

BARRY McGUIRE
66	RCA Victor RCA 1525	Cloudy Summer Afternoon/You've Got To Hide Your Love Away (B-side with Mamas & Papas)	15
65	RCA Victor RD 7751	SINGS EVE OF DESTRUCTION (LP)	30
76	Sparrow BIRD 105	C'MON ALONG (LP)	15

(see also Mamas & Papas)

McGUIRE SISTERS
54	Vogue Coral Q 2028	Lonesome Polecat/Muskrat Ramble	15
55	Vogue Coral Q 72050	Sincerely/No More	10
55	Vogue Coral Q 72052	Melody Of Love/Open Up Your Heart	10
55	Vogue Coral Q 72082	Something's Gotta Give/It May Sound Silly	10
55	Vogue Coral Q 72108	Christmas Alphabet/He	10
56	Vogue Coral Q 72117	Young And Foolish/Doesn't Anybody Love Me?	10
56	Vogue Coral Q 72145	Missing/Be Good To Me (Baby, Baby)	10
56	Vogue Coral Q 72161	Delilah Jones/Picnic	10

MCIB
MINT VALUE £

56	Vogue Coral Q 72188	Weary Blues/In The Alps	10
56	Vogue Coral Q 72201	My Baby's Got Such Lovin' Ways/Endless	10
56	Vogue Coral Q 72209	Tip Toe Through The Tulips With Me/Do You Remember When?	10
56	Vogue Coral Q 72216	Goodnight My Love, Pleasant Dreams/Mommy	10
57	Vogue Coral Q 72238	Heart/Sometimes I'm Happy	10
57	Vogue Coral Q 72249	Kid Stuff/Without Him	10
57	Vogue Coral Q 72265	Rock Bottom/Beginning To Miss You	10
57	Vogue Coral Q 72272	He's Got Time/Interlude	10
57	Vogue Coral Q 72296	Forgive Me/Kiss Them For Me	10
58	Coral Q 72305	Sugartime/Banana Split	6
58	Coral Q 72334	Volare/Do You Love Me Like You Kiss Me?	6
59	Coral Q 72356	May You Always/Achoo-Cha-Cha	6
59	Coral Q 72370	Peace/Summer Dreams	8
59	Coral Q 72379	Red River Valley/Compromise	6
61	Coral Q 72435	Will There Be Space A The Spaceship/Tears On My Pillow	6
56	Vogue Coral LVA 9024	DO YOU REMEMBER WHEN? (LP)	20
57	Vogue Coral LVA 9072	CHILDREN'S HOLIDAY (LP)	20
58	Coral LVA 9073	TEENAGE PARTY (LP)	20

MCIB
88	Unyque UNQ 1	Word/Men From The Boys/Money/Like This (12")	15

KEN MCINTIRE
60	Esquire 32-133	LOOKING AHEAD (LP, with Eric Dolphy)	60

DAVID MCIVOR
69	Warner Bros WB8002	Closing My Eyes/Love That Burns	30

MCKAY
03	Go! Beat GOBX 57	Take Me Over/Thinking Of You (D.R.U.N.K. Remix/Thinking Of You (12", p/s)	25
03	Go! Beat TAKE 7	Take Me Over/(Mafia & Fluxy Remix)	70
03	Go! Beat 065 631 1	MCKAY (LP)	25

FREDDIE MCKAY
71	Banana BA 348	Picture On The Wall/SOUND DIMENSION: Version	25
71	Banana BA 353	Sweet You, Sour You/High School Dance	20
71	Banana BA 358	High School Dance/SOUND DIMENSION: High School Version	20
71	Moodisc HM 110	Old Joe/Too Much Fire	15
72	Banana BA 370	Drunken Sailor/SOUND DIMENSION: Version	60
73	Bullet BU 525	Go On This Way/SANTIC ALL STARS: Santic Dub	20
73	Dragon DRA 1012	Our Rendezvous/Black Beauty	15
73	Atra ATRA 003	I'm A Freeman/SWEET HARMONY: Santic Special	25
73	Grape GR 3060	Our Rendezvous/SOUL DYAMITES: Version	12
78	Art & Craft ACD 004	A Love Like Mine/Version (12")	12
81	Greensleeves GRED 46	Another Weekend/EARL SIXTEEN: Live Together (12")	30
82	Greensleeves GRED 84	Roots Man Skanking/TOYAN: Version (12")	12
82	Live & Love LLDIS 2014	In Times Of Trouble/Version (12")	30
71	Banana BALPS 01	PICTURE ON THE WALL (LP)	65
73	Attack ATLP 1013	PICTURE ON THE WALL (LP, reissue)	40
78	GG GG 009	BEST OF (LP)	40
79	Plant PLAN 10003	CREATION (LP)	40
85	Move MVLP 6	TRIBAL INNA YARD (LP)	80

(see also Lizzy)

SCOTT MCKAY
67	Columbia DB 8147	I Can't Make Your Way/Take A Giant Step	40

SCOTTY MCKAY
64	London HLU 9885	Cold Cold Heart/What You Wanna	10

TONY MCKAY
66	Polydor BM 56513	Nobody's Perfect/Detroit	8

LONETTE MCKEE
75	Sussex SXX 4	Save It (Don't Give It Away)/Do It To Me	15

VAL MCKENNA
65	Piccadilly 7N 35237	Baby Do It/I Believe In Love	15
65	Piccadilly 7N 35256	Mixed Up Shook Up Girl/Now That You've Made Up Your Mind	25
66	Piccadilly 7N 35286	I Can't Believe What You Say/Don't Hesitate	15
69	Spark SRL 1005	House For Sale/I'll Be Satisfied	10
69	Spark SRL 1023	It's All In My Imagination/Sweet Sweet Lovin'	7
70	Spark SRL 1038	Love Feeling/It's All In My Imagination (silver label)	25

MCKENNA MENDELSON MAINLINE
69	Liberty LBF 15235	You Better Watch Out/She's Alright	6
69	Liberty LBF 15276	Don't Give Me No Goose For Christmas/Beltmaker	6
69	Liberty LBS 83251	STINK (LP)	50

CANDY MCKENZIE
10	Trojan THB 7003	Breakfast In Bed/Ice Cream	25
11	Upsetter TBL 210	LEE PERRY PRESENTS (LP)	55

MERLENE MCKENZIE
68	Double D DD 106	Left Me For Another/BOBBY AITKEN & CARIBBEATS: Cell Block Eleven	20

SCOTT MCKENZIE
67	Capitol CL 15509	Look In Your Eyes/All I Want Is You	20
67	CBS 3009	Like An Old-Time Movie/What's The Difference Chapter II	7
68	CBS 3393	Holy Man/What's The Difference (Chapter 3)	6
67	CBS (S)BPG 63157	THE VOICE OF SCOTT McKENZIE (LP)	20
70	A&M AMLS 999	STAINED GLASS MORNING (LP)	18

(see also Mamas & Papas)

TOMMY McKENZIE

			MINT VALUE £
TOMMY MCKENZIE			
68	Pama PM 720	Fiddlesticks/Please Stay	35
71	Pama Supreme PS 327	Eastern Promise/Fiddlesticks (as Tommy McKenzie Orchestra)	10
MCKENZIE, DOUG & BOB			
82	Mercury HOSER 1	Take Off/Elron McKenzie (p/s)	20
(see also Rush)			
MCKENZIE & GARDINER			
83	Sound Of London TSOLL 501	From Time/From Time (Version) (12")	80
83	Sound Of London TSOL 501	From Time/(Special Instrumental Remix)	30
LESLIE MCKEOWN			
79	Ego Trip EGOS 7	Shall I Do It (One More Number One)/Do It All Again (p/s)	7
79	Ego Trip EGO 001	ALL WASHED UP (LP, gatefold, with poster)	20
MCKINLEYS			
64	Columbia DB 7230	Someone Cares For Me/A Million Miles Away	20
64	Columbia DB 7310	When He Comes Along/Then I'll Know It's Love	10
64	Parlophone R 5211	Sweet And Tender Romance/That Lonely Feeling	12
65	Columbia DB 7583	Give Him My Love/Once More	15
ROD MCKUEN			
57	London HLU 8390	Happy Is A Boy Named Me/Jaydee	15
(see also Bob McFadden & Dor, Mike Redway, Mike Sarne, Henri Mancini)			
HAL MCKUSICK SEXTET/QUINTET			
57	Vogue Coral Q 72258	Kelly And Me (as Sextet)/When I Fall In Love (as Quintet)	6
TOMMY MCLAIN			
66	London HL 10065	Sweet Dreams/I Need You So	10
66	London HL 10091	Think It Over/I Can't Take No More	8
(MAHAVISHNU) JOHN MCLAUGHLIN			
69	Marmalade 608 007	EXTRAPOLATION (LP)	200
70	Polydor 02343 012	EXTRAPOLATION (LP, reissue)	25
71	Douglas DGL 65075	DEVOTION (LP, gatefold sleeve)	20
71	Douglas DGL 69014	MY GOAL'S BEYOND (LP, as Mahavishnu John McLaughlin, gatefold sleeve)	15
74	CBS Q 69037	LOVE, DEVOTION, SURRENDER (LP, quadrophonic issue)	15
JACKIE MCLEAN QUINTET			
55	Esquire 32-041	LIGHTS OUT (LP)	150
56	Esquire 32-111	JACKIE'S PALS (LP)	50
(see also Lifetime, Tony Williams [Lifetime], Mahavishnu Orchestra, John Surman, Santana)			
NANA MCLEAN			
71	Banana BA 355	A Little Love/SOUND DIMENSION: Heavy Beat	50
PHIL MCLEAN			
61	Top Rank JAR 597	Small Sad Sam/Chicken	6
CRAIG MCLEARIE			
79	Wealden WS 187	WARP FACTOR (LP)	125
GERALD MCLEASH			
71	G.G. GG 4516	False Reaper/G.G. ALL STARS: Reaping Version	25
LARIS MCLENNON			
67	CBM 04	Confusion/Turn Me Loose	15
ENOS MCLEOD			
68	Blue Cat BS 135	You Can Never Get Away/ENOS & SHEILA: La La La Bamba	200
83	Stewmac SB 003	BY THE LOOK IN YOUR EYES (LP)	50
96	Pressure Sounds PSLP 008	THE GENIUS OF ENOS (LP)	20
(see also Enos & Sheila)			
SEAN MCLEOD			
69	Aurora 4594	Living Without You/Love Songs From Another Planet	30
VINCENT MCLEOD			
69	Jackpot JP 711	Too Late/SIR COLLINS: Late Night	12
OSCAR MCLOLLIE & HIS HONEYJUMPERS			
55	London HL 8130	Take Your Shoes Off, Pop/Love Me Tonight	250
55	London HL 8130	Take Your Shoes Off, Pop/Love Me Tonight (78)	40
EDDIE MCLOYD			
75	Brunswick BR 27	Once You Fall In Love/Baby Get Down	10
BOBBY MCLURE			
66	Chess CRS 8048	Peak Of Love/You Got Me Baby	45
66	Chess CRS 8048	Peak Of Love/You Got Me Baby (DJ copy)	75
75	Island USA 006	You Bring Out The Love In Me/SURVIVAL KIT: Daybreak	20
(see also Fontella Bass)			
MCLUSKY			
02	Too Pure PURE124S	TO HELL WITH GOOD INTENTIONS (7" EP)	10
02	Too Pure PURE 117LP	MCLUSKY DO DALLAS (LP)	40
02	Too Pure PURE 117LP	MCLUSKY DO DALLAS (LP, orange or white vinyl)	50
03	Too Pure PURE 132LP	MY PAIN AND SADNESS IS MORE SAD AND PAINFUL THAN YOURS (LP, vinyl reissue of CD release)	30
04	Too Pure PURE 154LP	THE DIFFERENCE BETWEEN YOU AND ME IS THAT I'M NOT ON FIRE (LP, with poster)	35
MCLYNNS			
70	CBS 63836	OLD MARKET ST. (LP)	50
ROSS MCMANUS			
64	HMV POP 1279	Patsy Girl/I'm The Greatest	10
66	HMV POP 1543	Stop Your Playing Around/Girlie Girlie	10
67	Decca F 12618	Can't Take My Eyes Off Of You/If I Were A Rich Man	6
72	Rediffusion ZS 122	THE LEAVING OF LIVERPOOL (LP)	15
(see also Day Costello)			
MC MELLO			
89	Republic LICT007	Bizzie Rhymin'/Comin' Correct/Wize (EP)	12

92	Funki Dreds PA6640	Gone Crazy/Talk Dem Way/Firm Stance (EP)	20
94	Natural Response MELLO 1	I Hear Voices/Live At Portland (promo only)	18
90	Republic 4353ILE	THOUGHTS RELEASED (LP)	15

MARGARET McMILLEN
65	Decca F 12272	You Can't Be True Dear/The Love Of My Man	6

JAMES VINCENT McMORROW
11	Believe BLVDIG 07	We Don't Eat/Higher Love (500 only, hand numbered)	8

IAN McNABB
91	Way Cool WAY 147	Great Dreams Of Heaven/That's Why I Believe	8

BARBARA McNAIR
66	Tamla Motown TMG 544	You're Gonna Love My Baby/The Touch Of Time (DJ copy)	400
66	Tamla Motown TMG 544	You're Gonna Love My Baby/The Touch Of Time	350
13	Tamla Motown 424 542 0	It Happens Every Time/DAVID RUFFIN: I Can't Be Hurt Anymore	6
59	Coral FEP 2021	FRONT ROW CENTRE VOL. 1 (EP)	40
64	Warner Bros WEP 6129	I ENJOY BEING A GIRL (EP)	40

(see also Billy Williams & Barbara McNair)

HAROLD McNAIR
68	RCA Victor RCA 1742	The Hipster/Indecision	80
65	Island ILP 926	AFFECTIONATE FINK (LP, with Ornette Coleman's Sidemen)	500
68	RCA SF 7969	HAROLD McNAIR (LP, 1st pressing, black RCA red dot label)	300
68	RCA SF 7969	HAROLD McNAIR (LP, 2nd pressing, orange label)	150
70	RCA Intl. INTS 1096	FLUTE AND NUT (LP)	50
70	B&C CAS 1016	THE FENCE (LP, gatefold with pink envelope containing balloon)	80
70	B&C CAS 1016	THE FENCE (LP, gatefold with pink envelope without balloon)	40
72	B&C CAS 1045	HAROLD McNAIR (LP)	70

(see also Ginger Baker's Airforce)

CHARLIE McNAIR'S JAZZ BAND
60	Waverly SLP 504	Big House Blues/Fish Man	6

BIG JAY McNEELY
59	Top Rank JAR 169	There Is Something On Your Mind/...Back...Shack...Track ('vocal: Little Sonny')	40
65	Sue WI 373	There Is Something On Your Mind/...Back...Shack...Track ('vocal: Little Sonny') (reissue)	20
64	Warner Bros WM 8143	BIG JAY'S PARTY (LP)	30

AARON McNEIL
73	Action ACT 4619	Soul Of A Black Man/Reap What You Sow	12

DAVID McNEIL
68	President PT 212	Don't Let Your Chance Go By/Space Plane	40

LLOYD McNEIL QUARTET
10	Universal Sound USLP 31	ASHA (LP, reissue)	20
11	Universal Sounds USLP39	WASHINGTON SUITE (LP, reissue)	25

PAUL McNEILL
66	Decca LK 4803	TRADITIONALLY AT THE TROUBADOUR (LP)	40

PAUL McNEILL & LINDA PETERS
68	MGM MGM 1408	You Ain't Goin' Nowhere/I'll Show You How To Sing	6

(see also Linda Peters, Richard & Linda Thompson)

RONNIE McNEIR
75	London HLA 10494	Wendy Is Gone/Give Me A Sign	10
75	Tamla Motown STML 2036	RONNIE McNEIR (LP)	30
76	Motown STML 12041	LOVES COMIN DOWN (LP)	15

McPEAKE FAMILY/FOLK GROUP
60s	Topic	IRISH TRADITIONAL FOLK SONGS AND MUSIC (LP, blue label)	30
60s	Topic 12T 87	THE McPEAKE FAMILY (LP)	20
64	Fontana TL 5214	IRISH FOLK! (LP, as McPeake Family)	20
65	Fontana TL 5358	AT HOME WITH THE McPEAKES (LP)	20
67	Fontana TL 5433	PLEASANT AND DELIGHTFUL (LP, as McPeake Family)	20
69	Evolution 7 1002	WELCOME HOME (LP, as McPeake Folk Group)	40

CLYDE McPHATTER

SINGLES
56	London HLE 8250	Seven Days/I'm Not Worthy Of You	400
56	London HLE 8250	Seven Days/I'm Not Worthy Of You (78)	30
56	London HL 7006	Seven Days/I'm Not Worthy Of You (export issue)	125
56	London HLE 8293	Treasure Of Love/When You're Sincere (gold label lettering)	150
56	London HLE 8293	Treasure Of Love/When You're Sincere (silver label lettering)	60
57	London HLE 8462	Just To Hold My Hand/No Matter What (triangular centre)	150
57	London HLE 8462	Just To Hold My Hand/No Matter What (78)	20
57	London HLE 8476	Long Lonely Nights/Heartaches (triangular centre)	100
57	London HLE 8476	Long Lonely Nights/Heartaches (triangular centre) (78)	20
57	London HLE 8525	Rock And Cry/You'll Be There (triangular centre)	90
57	London HLE 8525	Rock And Cry/You'll Be There (later round centre)	40
57	London HLE 8525	Rock And Cry/You'll Be There (78)	20
58	London HLE 8707	Come What May/Let Me Know (triangular centre)	60
58	London HLE 8707	Come What May/Let Me Know (78)	25
58	London HLE 8755	A Lover's Question/I Can't Stand Up Alone (triangular centre)	30
58	London HLE 8755	A Lover's Question/I Can't Stand Up Alone (78)	20
59	MGM MGM 1014	I Told Myself A Lie/(I'm Afraid) The Masquerade Is Over	20
59	London HLE 8878	Lovey Dovey/My Island Of Dreams (triangular centre)	30
59	London HLE 8878	Lovey Dovey/My Island Of Dreams (78)	25
59	London HLE 8906	Since You've Been Gone/Try Try Baby (triangular centre)	40
59	London HLE 8906	Since You've Been Gone/Try Try Baby (78)	30
59	MGM MGM 1040	Twice As Nice/Where Did I Make My Mistake	18
59	London HLE 9000	You Went Back On Your Word/There You Go	40

Tony (T.S.) McPHEE

MINT VALUE £

59	London HLE 9000	You Went Back On Your Word/There You Go (78)	40
59	MGM MGM 1048	Bless You/Let's Try Again	18
60	London HLE 9079	Just Give Me A Ring/Don't Dog Me	45
60	MGM MGM 1061	Think Me A Kiss/When The Right Time Comes Along	18
60	Mercury AMT 1108	I Ain't Givin' Up Nothin' (If I Can't Get Something)/Ta Ta	15
60	Mercury AMT 1120	You're For Me/I Just Want To Love You	18
61	Mercury AMT 1136	Tomorrow Is A-Comin'/I'll Love You Till The Cows Come Home	40
62	Mercury AMT 1174	Lover Please/Let's Forget About The Past	20
62	Mercury AMT 1181	Little Bitty Pretty One/Next To Me	20
66	Stateside SS 487	Everybody's Somebody's Fool/I Belong To You	18
66	Stateside SS 567	A Shot Of Rhythm And Blues/I'm Not Going To Work Today	30
67	Stateside SS 592	Lavender Lace/Sweet And Innocent	20
68	Deram DM 202	Only A Fool/Thank You Love	25
69	Deram DM 223	Baby I Could Be So Good At Loving You/Baby You've Got It	25
69	Pama PM 775	A Shot Of Rhythm And Blues/I'm Not Going To Work Today (reissue)	12
69	B&C CB 106	Denver/Tell Me	12

EPs

59	London RE-E 1202	CLYDE McPHATTER	250
60	London RE-E 1240	CLYDE MCPHATTER NO. 2 (unissued)	0
59	MGM MGM-EP 705	TWICE AS NICE	60
60	MGM MGM-EP 739	THIS IS NOT GOODBYE	60

ALBUMS

63	Mercury MMC 14120	LOVER PLEASE	100
64	Atlantic ATL 5001	THE BEST OF CLYDE McPHATTER	90
71	MCA MUPS 418	WELCOME HOME	20
73	Atlantic K 30033	A TRIBUTE TO CLYDE McPHATTER	20

(see also Drifters, Jackie Wilson, Dominoes, Billy Ward & Dominoes, Jackie Wilson/Clyde McPhatter)

TONY (T.S.) McPHEE

66	Purdah 45-3501	Someone To Love Me/Ain't Gonna Cry No Mo' (as T.S. McPhee)	200
83	TS 001	Time Of Action/Born To Be With You (sold at gigs)	10
68	Liberty LBL/LBS 83190	ME AND THE DEVIL (LP)	60
71	Sunset SLS 50209	THE SAME THING ON THEIR MINDS (LP, with Jo-Ann Kelly)	30
73	World Wide Artists WWA 1	THE TWO SIDES OF TONY (T.S.) McPHEE (LP, with insert)	25

(see also Groundhogs, Champion Jack Dupree, Jo-Ann Kelly, John Dummer Blues Band, Hapshash & Coloured Coat, Herbal Mixture)

CHARLES MCPHERSON
65	Stateside SL 10151	BEBOP REVISITED (LP)	15

GILLIAN MCPHERSON
71	RCA Victor SF 8220	POETS AND PAINTERS AND PERFORMERS OF THE BLUES (LP)	80

HERB MCQUAY
75	Bell 1398	Runnin' Away From You/Storm Clouds	18

KEVIN MCQUINN
62	Top Rank JAR 598	Every Step Of The Way/Keep Me On Your Mind	10

RON MCQUINN
77	Decca F13693	Look At Love Bleed/Banshee	20

CARMEN MCRAE
57	Brunswick 05652	Whatever Lola Wants (Lola Gets)/Ooh (What 'Cha Doin' To Me) (with Dave Lambert Quartet)	10
57	London RE-N 1094	LONDON'S GIRL FRIENDS (EP)	15
56	Brunswick LAT 8133	TORCHY (LP)	15

(see also Sammy Davis Jnr.)

IAN MCSHANE
62	Columbia DB 4932	Harry Brown/The Tinker	6

MC SPY-D & 'FRIENDS'
95	Parlophone 12RDJ 6404	The Amazing Spider-Man (Solution Mix)/(Solution Chilled Mix)/(B&J White Trouser Mix) (12", no p/s, promo only)	25

(see also Brian May)

BLIND WILLIE MCTELL
66	Transatlantic PR 1040	LAST SESSION (LP)	35
67	Storyville 670 816	BLIND WILLIE McTELL 1940 (LP)	22
60s	Roots RL 324	BLIND WILLIE McTELL 1929-1935 (LP)	20
73	Atlantic K 40400	ATLANTA TWELVE STRING GUITAR (LP)	18

RALPH MCTELL
69	Big T BIG 125	Summer Comes Along/Girl On A Bicycle	8
70	Big T BIG 131	Kew Gardens/Father Forgive Them	8
70	Big T BIG 134	Spiral Staircase/Terminus	8
68	Transatlantic TRA 165	8 FRAMES A SECOND (LP, white/lilac label with 't' logo)	35
69	Transatlantic TRA 177	SPIRAL STAIRCASE (LP, laminated sleeve, with insert)	25
69	Transatlantic TRA 209	MY SIDE OF YOUR WINDOW (LP, textured sleeve)	20
70	Transatlantic TRA 227	REVISITED (LP)	20

MCTELLS
87	Frank TRUFFAUT 303	Jesse Man Rae/If Only/Rotten/M.T.B. (p/s in bag)	10

RAY MCVAY SOUND
65	Pye 7N 15777	Raunchy/Revenge (Promo copies have "Macvay" spelling)	45
65	Pye 7N 15816	Kinda Kinky/Kinkdom Come	50
66	Parlophone R 5460	Genesis/House Of Clowns (as Ray MacVay Band)	10
69	Mercury MF 1221	Destination Moon/Mexican Scavenger	10
71	Philips 6006 083	They Call Me Mr. Tibbs (as Ray McVay & Orchestra)	25

CARL MCVOY
58	London HLU 8617	Tootsie/You Are My Sunshine	200
58	London HLU 8617	Tootsie/You Are My Sunshine (78)	40

David McWILLIAMS

MINT VALUE £

DAVID MCWILLIAMS
66	CBS 202348	God And My Country/Blue Eyes	10
67	Major Minor MM 533	Harlem Lady/The Days Of Pearly Spencer (some copies later 'flipped')	15
68	Major Minor MM 561	This Side Of Heaven/Mister Satisfied..	8
69	Major Minor MM 592	The Stranger/Follow Me..	10
69	Major Minor MM 616	Oh Mama Are You My Friend?/I Love Susie In The Summer...................................	8
71	Parlophone R 5886	Days Of Pearly Spencer/Harlem Lady (reissue)	6
67	Major Minor MMLP 2	SINGING SONGS BY DAVID McWILLIAMS (LP, laminated sleeve, also stereo SMLP 2)	15
67	Major Minor MMLP 10	DAVID McWILLIAMS VOL. 2 (LP, laminated front cover, also stereo SMLP 10).............	15
68	Major Minor MMLP 11	VOLUME III (LP, also stereo SMLP 11)	15
69	Major Minor MCP 5026	THE DAYS OF DAVID McWILLIAMS (LP)	15
72	Dawn DNLS 3039	LORD OFFALY (LP, textured gatefold sleeve)	20
73	Dawn DNLS 3047	THE BEGGAR AND THE PRIEST (LP)	20
74	Dawn DNLS 3059	LIVING'S JUST A STATE OF MIND (LP)	18

M.D.C.
83	Crass 121984/5	MULTI DEATH CORPORATION (EP)	12

VAUGHN MEADER
63	MGM MGM 1239	No Hiding Place/The Elephant Song	6

MEADOW SWEET
73	Sunday SUN 1	Behind You/Dreams In Colour	40

MEAN MACHINE
76	Chrysalis CHS 2089	Boogie To The Drummer/Running With The Rat Pack	10

(see also Brian Bennett)

ME & THEM
64	Pye 7N 15596	Feels So Good/I Think I'm Gonna Kill Myself..	18
64	Pye 7N 15631	Everything I Do Is Wrong/Show You Mean It Too	15
64	Pye 7N 15683	Get Away/Tell Me Why	15

MEANIES
79	Vendetta VD 002	Waiting For You/It's True (p/s)	100

MEANSTREAK
81	Meanstreak MS1	(Time I) Played It Right/You Took The Fire/I Know (p/s)	50

MEAN STREET
77	Vortex/NEMS NES 115	Bunch Of Stiffs/WASPS: Can't Wait 'Til '78 (p/s)	18

MEAN STREET DEALERS
79	Graduate GRAD 5	Japanese Motorbikes/Tight Skirts (p/s)	20
79	Mean St. Dealers MSD 001	BENT NEEDLES (LP)	25
79	Graduate GRADLP 1	BENT NEEDLES (LP, reissue)	18

(see also Tea & Sympathy)

MEANWHILE BACK IN COMMUNIST RUSSIA...
00	Jitter JTR 1SP	No Cigar/Morning After Pill (p/s, 300 only)	7

MEASLES
65	Columbia DB 7531	Casting My Spell/Bye Birdie Fly	40
65	Columbia DB 7673	Night People/Dog Rough Dan	25
66	Columbia DB 7875	Kicks/No Baby At All	35
66	Columbia DB 8029	Walkin' In/Looking For Love	25

MEAT LOAF
75	Ode ODS 66304	Clap Your Hands, Stamp Your Feet/Stand By Me (withdrawn)..............................	25
79	Epic S EPC 12-7018	Bat Out Of Hell/Heaven Can Wait (12", p/s, red vinyl)	10
82	Epic EPC 11 82419	BAT OUT OF HELL (LP, picture disc)	15

(see also Stoney & Meat Loaf, Rocky Horror Show)

MEAT WHIPLASH
85	Creation CRE 020	Don't Slip Up/Here It Comes (foldaround p/s in poly bag; 1st pressing has photo of band by fence)	20
85	Creation CRE 020	Don't Slip Up/Here It Comes (foldaround p/s in poly bag; 2nd pressing has photo of band in field)	8

(see also Jesus & Mary Chain)

MECANO
82	CBS A 3140	The Uninvited Guest/London (p/s)	20

MECHANICAL HEARTS
91	Mechanartz 017	Precious Time/Pay The Driver	60

MEDDY EVILS
65	Pye 7N 15941	Find Somebody To Love/A Place Called Love	125
66	Pye 7N 17091	It's All For You/Ma's Place	160

(see also Stu James and the Mojos, the Quik)

MEDIA (1)
79	Takeaway TA 001	TV Kids/Don't Sit Back/Just For You/Rose And Crown (500 only, p/s)	100

MEDIATORS
69	Coxsone CS 7101	Darling, There I Stand/PRINCE CHARLIE: Hit And Run	100
70	Supreme SUP 210	When You Go To A Party (actually by Mediators)/ RUPIE EDWARDS ALLSTARS: Stop The Party	15

(see also Meditators)

MEDICINE HEAD
69	Dandelion S 4661	His Guiding Hand/This Love Of Old	20
70	Dandelion S 5075	Coast To Coast/All For Tomorrow	12
71	Dandelion DAN 7003	(And The) Pictures In The Sky/Natural Sight (also listed as K 19002) (in p/s)	10
72	Dandelion 2001 276	Kum On/On The Land	6
72	Dandelion 2001 325	Only To Do What Is True/Sittin' In The Sun	6
72	Dandelion 2001 383	How Does It Feel/Morning Light	6
69	Dandelion 63757	NEW BOTTLES, OLD MEDICINE (LP)	60
71	Dandelion DAN 8005	HEAVY ON THE DRUM (LP, gatefold sleeve, 1st pressing with lyric insert with DAN 8005 on sleeve, label and matrix)	125

MEDITATIONS (1)

			MINT VALUE £
71	Dandelion DAN 8005	HEAVY ON THE DRUM (LP, gatefold sleeve, later pressing listed as K 49005; without lyric insert)	50
71	Dandelion 2310 166	DARK SIDE OF THE MOON (LP, with insert)	35
73	Polydor 2310 248	ONE & ONE IS ONE (LP, fold-out sleeve)	15
74	Polydor 2383 272	THRU' A FIVE (LP)	15

(see also Ashton Gardner & Dyke, British Lions)

MEDITATIONS (1)
68	Liberty LBF 15045	Transcendental Meditation/Beautiful Experience	7

MEDITATIONS (2)
78	Island IPR 2022	Life Is Not Easy/Much Smarter (12")	25
70s	GG's GG 097	Justice/Version (12")	25
80	JB JBD21	Vanity Lover/Part 2 (12")	15
81	Kingdom KV 8020 12	Stranger In Love/Unity (12")	15
77	United Artists UAS30178	MESSAGE FROM THE MEDITATIONS (LP)	20
78	Third World TWS 929	WAKE UP! (LP)	25
79	Tad's TRDLP 101579	GUIDANCE (LP)	25
83	Greensleeves GREL52	NO MORE FRIEND (LP)	15

MEDITATORS
69	Bullet BU 403	Duba Duba/CECIL NICKY THOMAS: Running Alone	20
69	Success RE 901	Look Who Bust A Style/RUPIE EDWARDS ALL STARS: Look Who Bust A Style	35
70	Big BG 302	When You Go To A Party/Good Morning Mother Cuba	20
71	Big BG 305	Music Alone Shall Live/RUPIE EDWARDS AND ALL STARS: Music Alone - Version	20
73	Pyramid PYR 7010	Great Messiah/Nana Nana	12
73	Smash SMA 2331	Things Not Easy/BONGO HERMAN & BINGY BUNNY: Ration	10

(see also Busty Brown, Pat Satchmo)

MEDIUM
68	CBS 3404	Edward Never Lies/Colours Of The Rainbow	40

MEDIUM MEDIUM
80	APT SAP-01	Them Or Me/Freeze (p/s)	7
81	Cherry Red CHEER 18	Hungry, So Angry/Nadsat Dream (p/s)	7
81	Cherry Red BRED 19	THE GLITTERHOUSE (LP)	15

MEDIUM WAVE
69	Ember EMB 5265	Walk In The Sunshine/Looking Towards The Sky (p/s)	15

BILL MEDLEY
68	MGM MGM 1418	I Can't Make It Alone/One Day Girl	6
68	MGM MGM 1432	Brown Eyed Woman/Let The Good Times Roll	6
69	MGM MGM-C(S) 8091	BILL MEDLEY 100% (LP)	20

(see also Righteous Brothers, Garnet Mimms)

JOE MEDLIN
59	Mercury AMT 1032	I Kneel At Your Throne/Out Of Sight, Out Of Mind	25

MICHAEL MEDWIN
58	HMV POP 490	The Army Game/What Do We Do In The Army? (with Bernard Bresslaw, Alfie Bass & Leslie Fyson)	6

KEITH MEEHAN
69	Marmalade 598 016	Darkness Of My Life/TONY MEEHAN: Hooker Street	30

TONY MEEHAN
64	Decca F 11801	Song Of Mexico/Kings Go Fifth	8

(see also Shadows, Jet Harris & Tony Meehan, Keith Meehan, John Paul Jones)

JOE MEEK ORCHESTRA
63	Decca F 11796	The Kennedy March/The Theme Of Freedom	30

(see also Blue Men)

CARL MEEKS
88	Redman Intl. RED LP 12	WEH DEM FAH (LP)	22
89	Greensleeves GREL 132	JACKMANDORA (LP)	20

MEET JESUS MUSIC
72	Echo ECH 002	MEET JESUS MUSIC (LP)	20

MEGA CITY 2
92	Hear Dis HDR 001	London To Essex In 3 Hours/Darker Side Of Evil (12")	20
93	Extra Terrestrial ETR 002	Nightwalker/Atmospheric Disturbance (12")	40
93	Extra Terrestrial VERYDARK001	DEMONS BY DAYLIGHT EP (12")	30

MEGADETH
87	Capitol CL 476	Wake Up Dead/Black Friday (live) (p/s)	10
87	Capitol CLP 476	Wake Up Dead/Black Friday (live) (skull-shaped picture disc with insert)	18
87	Capitol 12CL 476	Wake Up Dead/Black Friday (live)/Devil's Island (live)/Wake Up Dead/Black Friday (live) (12", p/s, allegedly shrink-wrapped with 7" picture disc)	25
87	Capitol 12CL 476	Wake Up Dead/Black Friday (live)/Devil's Island (live)/Wake Up Dead/Black Friday (live) (12", p/s)	15
87	Capitol 12CL 476	Wake Up Dead/Black Friday (Tommy Vance Show)/Devil's Island (Tommy Vance Show) (12", stickered p/s, with 'Deth' certificate)	15
88	Capitol CL 480	Anarchy In The U.K./Liar (p/s)	10
88	Capitol CLP 480	Anarchy In The U.K./Liar (U.K.-shaped picture disc)	15
88	Capitol CL 489	Mary Jane/Hook In Mouth	6
90	SBK SBKPD 4	No More Mr. Nice Guy/DEAD ON: "Different Breed" (chair-shaped pic disc)	15
90	SBK 12 SBKP 4	No More Mr. Nice Guy/DEAD ON: "Different Breed"/DANGEROUS TOYS: Demon Bell [The Ballad Of Horace Pinker] (12", poster p/s)	10
91	Capitol CLS 604	Hangar 18 (MJ 12 Edit)/The Conjuring (live) (p/s, shrinkwrapped with patch)	15
91	Capitol CLPD 604	Hangar 18 (MJ 12 Edit)/The Conjuring (live) (Vic-shaped picture disc)	20
92	Capitol 12CLS 662	Symphony Of Destruction/Breakpoint/Go To Hell (12", p/s, clear vinyl with giant autographed poster)	20
92	Capitol CLP 669	Skin O' My Teeth (LP Version)/Holy Wars... The Punishment Due (The General Schwarzkopf Mix) (poster p/s, board game)	6

MEGATON (1)

MINT VALUE £

92	Capitol CLP 669	Skin O' My Teeth (LP Version)/Holy Wars... The Punishment Due (The General Schwarzkopf Mix)/High Speed Dirt (live)/The Passes (Mustaine Remarks On Game) (10" bronze Megadeth box with passes & game rules)	20
92	Capitol CL 669	Symphony Of Destruction/Skin O' My Teeth (yellow vinyl, p/s)	12
94	Capitol CL 730	Train Of Consequences/Crown Of Worms (clear vinyl with sticker)	6
88	M. For Nations MFN 46P	KILLING IS MY BUSINESS ... AND BUSINESS IS GOOD (LP, picture disc with insert)	20
88	Capitol ESTP 2022	PEACE SELLS ... BUT WHO'S BUYING? (LP, picture disc with insert)	20
88	Capitol ESTP 2053	SO FAR, SO GOOD ... SO WHAT (LP, picture disc with insert)	30
90	Capitol EST 2132	RUST IN PEACE (LP)	40
90	Capitol ESTPD 2132	RUST IN PEACE (LP, picture disc, die cut sleeve)	30
94	Capitol ESTPD 2244	YOUTHANASIA (LP, picture disc)	50
94	Capitol ESTPD 2244	YOUTHANASIA (LP, gatefold sleeve, blue vinyl, 1000 only)	150
97	Capitol EST 2297	CRYPTIC WRITINGS (LP, gatefold)	200
07	EMI 50995 13187 28	WARCHEST ('ammo' box set with 4 CD's, DVD and booklet)	35

MEGATON (1)

71	Deram DM-R 331	Out Of Your Own Little World/Niagara	30
71	Deram SML-R 1086	MEGATON (LP, white/red label with small logo)	1000

MEGATON (2)

81	Hot Metal HMM 69	Aluminium Lady/Diehard (p/s)	80

MEGATONS (JAMAICA)

70	Downtown DT 464	Take It Easy/Funk The Beat	15
70	Downtown DT 469	Militant Man/MUSIC DOCTORS: Reggae Jeggae Version	20

(see also Revelation)

MEGATONS (U.S.)

65	Sue WI 325	Shimmy Shimmy Walk (Parts 1 & 2)	40

(see also Billy Lee Riley)

MEGATRONS

59	Top Rank JAR 146	Velvet Waters/The Merry Piper	6
59	Top Rank JAR 236	Tootie Flootie/Whispering Winds	6

GEORGE MEGGIE

72	Bullet BU 504	Hard To Believe/MAX ROMEO: Softie	7
72	Punch PH 112	People Like People/MAX ROMEO: Softie	7

MEKONS

78	Fast Products FAST 1	Never Been In A Riot/32 Weeks/Heart And Soul	50
78	Fast Products FAST 7	Where Were You?/I'll Have To Dance Then (On My Own) (p/s)	10
82	CNT CNT 1	This Sporting Life (6.12)/Frustration (6.21)/(mystery live track) (12", p/s)	10
82	CNT CNT 008	This Sporting Life/Fight The Cuts (p/s)	10
79	Virgin V2143	THE QUALITY OF MERCY IS NOT STRNEN (LP)	25
82	CNT CNT 009	THE MEKONS STORY (LP)	20
85	Sin 001	FEAR AND WHISKEY (LP)	20
91	Blast First BFFP 80	THE CURSE OF THE MEKONS (LP)	15

(see also Batfish Boys, Ut)

MEL & DAVE

70	Upsetter US 330	Spinning Wheel/Version	40

MEL & TIM

70	Concord CON 004	Backfield In Motion/Do Right Baby (pink label design)	6
70	Concord CON 004	Backfield In Motion/Do Right Baby (multi design)	6
70	Concord CON 004	Backfield In Motion/Do Right Baby (egg design)	6
73	Stax 2025 125	Starting All Over Again/It Hurts To Want You So Bad	8
73	Stax 2025 171	What's Your Name/Free For All	8
73	Stax 2325 090	STARTING ALL OVER AGAIN (LP)	25

MELANCHOLY MAN

91	Warriors Dance WAFT 22	Precaution/Caution/Extra Precaution (12")	18

MELANIE

68	Buddah 2011 033	Alexander Beetle/Christopher Robin/Animal Crackers (p/s)	6
69	Buddah 201 063	Tuning My Guitar/Beautiful People (withdrawn, demos may exist)	10

TERRY MELCHER

68	Rex R 11039	Indian Lake/Be My Girl	8
74	Reprise K 54016	TERRY MELCHER (LP)	20

(see also Terry Day, The Rip Chords, Freeway)

GIL MELLE (QUINTET)

55	Vogue LDE 141	GIL MELLE QUINTET (10" LP)	15

SUSAN MELLEN

75	MAM MAMAS 1014	THE MELLEN BIRD (LP, with insert)	30

MELLODIES

64	R&B JB 179	Vacation/TOMMY McCOOK: Music Is My Occupation	50

MELLO & MELLOTONES

72	Summit SUM 8538	Haile Selasie/Old Man River	10

(see also Mellotones)

MELL(O)TONES

68	Amalgamated AMG 812	Fat Girl In Red/VERSATILES: Trust The Book	35
68	Amalgamated AMG 817	Feel Good (actually maybe by Bleechers)/Soulful Mood (actually by Tommy McCook & Supersonics)	30
68	Doctor Bird DB 1136	None Such/VAL BENNETT: Popeye On The Shore	50
68	Trojan TR 612	Uncle Charlie/What A Botheration	45
68	Pyramid PYR 6060	Let's Join Together/BEVERLEY'S ALLSTARS: I Don't Know	50
69	Camel CA 18	Facts Of Life/TERMITES: I'll Be Waiting	35
70	Escort ERT 844	Work It/SOUL MAN: Good Lover	15

(see also Sexy Girls)

MELLOW CANDLE

68	SNB 55-3645	Feeling High/Tea With The Sun	100

MELLOW CATS with Count Ossie & Warrickas

MINT VALUE £

72	Deram DM 357	Dan The Wing/Silversong (with promotional p/s)	500
72	Deram DM 357	Dan The Wing/Silversong	80
72	Deram SDL 7	SWADDLING SONGS (LP)	2000
11	Rise Above Relics RARLP007	SWADDLING SONGS PLUS (Box set, 2-LP, white vinyl, 2 x 7" booklet)	70

(see also Alison O'Donnell)

MELLOW CATS WITH COUNT OSSIE & WARRICKAS
61	Blue Beat BB 68	Rock A Man Soul/MONTO & CYCLONES: Lazy Lou (B-side actually by Monty [Alexander] & Cyclones)	25

(see also Melo Cats)

MELLOW FRUITFULNESS
67	Columbia S(C)X 6242	MEDITATION (LP, mono/stereo)	15

MELLOW LARKS
60	Blue Beat BB 16	Time To Pray (Alleluia)/Love You Baby	20
61	Blue Beat BB 38	No More Wedding/Lite Of My Life	20

(see also Basil Gabbidon)

MELLOW ROSE
80	Studio 16 WE 0018	Too Much Heaven/Strike (12", with Vin Gordon)	25
80	Studio 16 WE 348	Imitation Love/SGT. PEPPER: Dub A Rub Ina Imitation Way (12")	25

MELLOW SOUNDS
70	Axe AXE 1	Turn It Down/A Night Of Fear	50

GEORGE MELLY (& MICK MULLIGAN BAND)
51	Tempo A 96	Rock Island Line/Send Me To The 'Lectric Chair (78, as The George Melly Trio)	10
61	Columbia SEG 8093	THE PSYCHOLOGICAL SIGNIFICANCE OF ANIMAL SYMBOLISM IN AMERICAN NEGRO FOLK MUSIC AND ALL THAT JAZZ (EP)	10

(see also Mick Mulligan Band)

MELO CATS
61	Blue Beat BB 54	Another Moses/ROLAND ALPHONSO & ALLEY CATS: Hully Gully Rock	20

(see also Mellow Cats)

MELODIANS
66	Island WI 3014	Lay It On/Meet Me	40
67	Coxsone CS 7004	I Should Have Made It Up/JOE HIGGS: Neighbour Neighbour	150
67	Treasure Isle TI 7006	You Don't Need Me/I Will Get Along	30
67	Treasure Isle TI 7022	You Have Caught Me/I Know Just How She Feels	50
67	Treasure Isle TI 7023	Last Train To Expo. '67/TOMMY McCOOK & SUPERSONICS: Expo	35
68	Treasure Isle TI 7028	Come On, Little Girl/TOMMY McCOOK & SUPERSONICS: Got Your Soul	30
68	Doctor Bird DB 1125	Little Nut Tree/You Are My Only Love	25
68	Doctor Bird DB 1139	Swing And Dine/I Could Be King	25
68	Masters Time MT 004	Let's Join Hands Together/My Last Word	60
68	Fab FAB 61	Sweet Rose/It Comes And Goes	30
69	Gas GAS 108	Ring Of Gold/You've Got It	40
69	Gas GAS 116	Personally Speaking/LLOYD ROBINSON: Trouble Trouble	20
69	Crab CRAB 15	When There Is You/UNIQUES: My Woman's Love	80
69	Trojan TR 660	Everybody Bawlin'/TOMMY McCOOK: Kilowatt	25
69	Trojan TR 695	Sweet Sensation/It's My Delight	12
70	Trojan TR 7720	A Day Seems So Long/BEVERLEY'S ALLSTARS: Project	12
70	Trojan TR 7764	Say Darling Say/Come Rock It To Me	12
70	High Note HS 044	Love Is A Good Thing/No Nola	12
70	Summit SUM 8505	Walking In The Rain/Rivers Of Babylon	12
70	Summit SUM 8508	Rivers Of Babylon/BEVERLEY'S ALL STARS: Babylon Version	12
71	Duke DU 128	The Sensational Melodians (Parts 1 & 2)	12
71	Summit SUM 8512	It Took A Miracle/BEVERLEY'S ALLSTARS: Miraculous Version	15
71	Summit SUM 8522	Come Ethiopians, Come/BEVERLEY'S ALL STARS: Version Two	12
71	Summit SUM 8532	My Love, My Life/My Love, My Life - Version	12
72	Summit SUM 8534	The Time Has Come/BEVERLEY'S ALL STARS: McIntosh (B-side actually "No Sins At All" by Melodians)	12
72	Bullet BU 496	Tropical Land/HUGH ROY & SLIM SMITH: Love I Bring	12
72	Duke DU 130	The Mighty Melodians (Adapted) (Parts 1 & 2)	8
72	Attack ATT 8025	This Beautiful Land/MELODIOUS RHYTHMS: Version	8
72	Attack ATT 8031	Without You (What Would I Do)/DYNAMITES: Instrumental	6
72	Punch PH 111	Round And Round/UPSETTERS: Round Version	15
73	Randy's RAN 530	Passion Love/Love Makes The World Go Round	10
75	Torpedo TOR 46	I'll Take You To Where The Music's Playing/It's All In The Family	20
78	Sky Note SKYLP18	PRE MEDITATION (LP)	30

(see also Gentiles, Tony Brevett, Brent Dowe, Jaylads, Gaylads, Joe Grinne)

MELODY
11	Soul People SWSP 15	Love Makes A Woman/Selfish One	6

BOBBY MELODY
69	Duke DU 20	The Break (actually by Winston Francis)/BAND OF MERCY AND SALVATION: Suffering Stink	200
79	Hit Run HIT DD5	Anger & Strife (ft. Jah Lion)/JAH LION: Johnnie Walker (12")	30
82	Negus Roots NERT012	True True Loving/I'm Gonna Keep On Trying (12")	20

JOHNNY MELODY
68	Pyramid PYR 6041	You Treating Me Bad/ROLAND ALPHONSO: Peace And Love	40
67	Pyramid PYR 6023	Govern Your Mouth (actually by George Dekker)/ROLAND ALPHONSO: Peace And Love	30

(see also Lloyd & Johnny Melody under 'L', Lloyd Terrell)

RICKY MELODY
88	Wolrd Enterprise WED 61	What An Act/Version (12")	80

MELODY ENCHANTERS
63	Island WI 049	Enchanter's Ball/I'll Be True	20
63	R&B JB 117	Gone Gone/Blueberry Hill	18

MELODY FAIR

MINT VALUE £

MELODY FAIR
68 Decca F 12801   Something Happened To Me/Sittin', Watchin', Waitin' 6

KANSAS CITY MELROSE/CASINO SIMPSON
72 Chicago Piano 12-001   KANSAS CITY MELROSE/CASINO SIMPSON (LP) 15

MONIQUE MELSEN
71 Decca F 23170   The Love Beat/Pomme Pomme Pomme 12

JOE MELSON
61 Polydor NH 66959   Oh Yeah!/What's The Use I Still Love You 30
61 Polydor NH 66961   Hey Mister Cupid/No One Really Cares.. 25

MELTATIONS
87 Meltations MEL 701   32 Sweet Teeth/I'll Take It As A Compliment (p/s) 80

MELTING BEAR
85 Beggars Banquet BEG 144   It Makes No Difference/Nature's Way/Sea Song (unreleased, test pressings only) 15

MELTON CONSTABLE
72 SIS Studio 101   MELTON CONSTABLE (LP) 150

KATIE MELUA
04 Dramatico DRAMLP 001   CALL OFF THE SEARCH (LP) 100
06 Dramatico DRAMLP 002   PIECE BY PIECE (LP, 180gm, numbered) 150
08 Dramatico DRAMLP 003   PICTURES (LP) 100
09 Dramatico DRAMLP 007   LIVE AT THE O2 ARENA (2-LP, 180gm) 80
10 Dramatico DRAMLP 016   THE HOUSE (LP, with CD) 60
12 Dramatico DRAMLP 020   SECRET SYMPHONY (LP, with CD) 50

HAROLD MELVIN & BLUE NOTES
73 Philadelphia Int. SPIR 1879   The Love I Lost (Part 1)/The Love I Lost (Part 2) 6
75 Route RT 06   Get Out (And Let Me Cry)/You May Not Love Me 8
79 Source SRC 102   Prayin/Your Love Is Taking Me On A Journey 15
79 Source 12 SRC 102   Prayin/Your Love Is Taking Me On A Journey (12") 10
86 Source SOURCE 2   Prayin (1986 Remix)/(Instrumental Remix) (p/s) 10
73 CBS 65350   HAROLD MELVIN & THE BLUES NOTES (LP) 15
73 CBS Q 65859   BLACK AND BLUE (LP, quadrophonic) 15
75 Philadelphia Int. PI SPIR 80399 TO BE TRUE (LP) 15
75 Philadelphia Int. PIR 69293   WAKE UP EVERYODY (LP, with free 7" EP) 20
75 Philadelphia Int. PIR 69293   WAKE UP EVERYODY (LP) 15

(see also Teddy Pendergrass)

MELVINS
90 Tupelo TUPEP 10   Sweet Young Thing Ain't Sweet No More/STEEL POLE BATH TUB: I Dreamed I Dream (12", p/s, green vinyl, 600 only) 20
89 Tupelo TUPL 7   OZMA (LP) 25
91 Tupelo TUP LP 26   BULLHEAD (LP) 25

MELVIN'S MARAUDERS
79 Birdsnest BN118   Buzz Buzz A Diddle It/Three Months To Kill 10

MEMBERS
78 Stiff/One Off OFF 3   Solitary Confinement/Rat Up A Drainpipe (p/s) 15
79 Virgin VS 242   The Sound Of The Suburbs/Handling The Big Jets (clear vinyl, window p/s) 6
83 Albion ION1050   Working Girl/The Family (square coloured vinyl, p/s) 8

MEMBRANES
80 Vinyl Drip VD 005   Fashionable Junkies/Almost China (flexi in p/s) 10

MEMO
74 Decca F13539   Kick A Tin Can/Attilah 8

MEMORIES
74 Rex R 11091   Lay It On Me/Did Ya Get It 20

MEMOS
59 Parlophone R 4616   The Biddy Leg/My Type Of Girl 60

MEMPHIS BEND
73 United Artists UP 35571   Louisiana Hoedown/Right String Baby But The Wrong Yo Yo 10
76 United Artists UP 36132   Ubangi Stomp/Tennessee... 8

MEMPHIS HORNS
71 Atlantic 2091 080   Woolly Bully/I Can't Turn You Loose 10
77 RCA PB 0836   Get Up And Dance/Don't Abuse It 6
71 Mojo 2466 010   THE MEMPHIS HORNS (LP) 25

MEMPHIS JUG BAND
55 HMV 7EG 8073   MEMPHIS JUG BAND (EP, withdrawn) 30

MEMPHIS MINNIE
64 Heritage H 103   MEMPHIS MINNIE (EP)... 75
69 Limited Edition (no cat. no.)   MEMPHIS MINNIE 1934-1936 (LP) 40
69 Limited Edition (no cat. no.)   MEMPHIS MINNIE 1934-1941 (LP) 40
69 Sunflower ET 1400   MEMPHIS MINNIE 1941-1949 (LP, 99 copies only) 50

MEMPHIS SLIM
60 Collector JDN 102   Pinetop's Blues/How Long 25
62 Storyville A 45055   Big City Girl/El Capitan (p/s) 15
61 Collector JEN 5   GOING TO KANSAS CITY (EP) 30
62 Storyville SEP 385   STORYVILLE BLUES ANTHOLOGY VOL. 5 - BOOGIE WOOGIE AND THE BLUES (EP) 22
63 Vocalion VEP 170155   MEMPHIS SLIM AND LITTLE RICHARD (EP) 80
63 Summit LSE 2041   WORLD'S FOREMOST BLUES SINGERS (EP) 12
61 Collector JGN 1004   MEMPHIS SLIM U.S.A. (LP) 45
61 Collector JGN 1005   MEMPHIS SLIM U.S.A. (VOL. 2) (LP) 45
62 Bluesville BV 1018   JUST BLUES (LP) 30
62 Storyville SLP 118   MEMPHIS SLIM (LP) 22
62 Storyville SLP 138   THIS IS A GOOD TIME TO WRITE A SONG (LP) 22
62 Fontana 688 302 ZL   NO STRAIN (LP) 25

MEMPHIS THREE

			MINT VALUE £
63	United Artists ULP 1042	BROKEN SOUL BLUES (LP)	30
64	Storyville SLP 118	TRAVELLIN' WITH THE BLUES (LP)	22
64	Xtra XTRA 1008	MEMPHIS SLIM (LP)	18
64	Fontana 688 701	ALONE WITH MY FRIENDS (LP)	30
65	Fontana TL 5254	CLAP YOUR HANDS (LP)	25
65	Melodisc MLPS 12-149	FATTENIN' FROGS FOR SNAKES (LP)	25
66	Fontana 688 315 ZL	FRISCO BAY BLUES (LP)	30
67	Polydor 623 211	PINETOP'S BLUES (LP)	18
68	Polydor 623 263	BLUESINGLY YOURS (LP, with Mickey Baker)	18
68	Xtra XTRA 5060	ALL KINDS OF BLUES (LP)	15
69	Xtra XTRA 1085	CHICAGO BLUES (LP)	15
72	Barclay 920 214	BLUE MEMPHIS (LP, with Peter Green)	75

(see also Washboard Sam, Ivory Joe Hunter, Otis Spann)

MEMPHIS THREE
68	Page One POF 070	Wild Thing/She's A Yum Yum	7

MEN
79	Virgin VS 269	I Don't Depend On You/Cruel (p/s)	25
79	Virgin VS 269-12	I Don't Depend On You/Cruel (12", p/s)	30

(see also Human League, Heaven 17)

MENACE
77	Illegal IL 004	Screwed Up/Insane Society (p/s)	15
77	Illegal IL 004	Screwed Up/Insane Society (12", p/s)	20
77	Small Wonder SMALL 5	G.L.C./I'm Civilized (p/s)	20
78	Illegal IL 008	I Need Nothing/Electrocutioner (p/s)	15
79	Small Wonder SMALL 16	Final Vinyl: Last Year's Youth/Carry No Banners (p/s)	10
82	Fresh FRESH 14	The Young Ones/Tomorrow's World/Live For Today (p/s)	15
86	Razor RAZ 18	GLC - RIP (LP)	25

(see also Aces, Vermilion & Aces)

MENACE
01	Plastica DPFT 004	Reap What You Sow (12")	15

MENACE MAKES 3
92	Danse City DC 1203	Pure Hysteria (Give Me A Mother Mix)/Do You Feel What I'm Feeling? (Matrix Rise Remix)(12")	50

CARLOS MENDES
72	Pye International 7N 25581	Shadows/Glow-Worm	8

MENDES PREY
83	MP AM 076	On To The Borderline/Runnin' For You (p/s)	20
86	Wag WAG 2	Wonderland/Can You Believe It (p/s)	25
86	Wag 12 WAG 2	Wonderland/Can You Believe It (12", p/s)	25

E.T. MENSAH & HIS TEMPO'S BAND
58	Decca WAL 1001	A SATURDAY NIGHT (10" LP)	20
58	Decca WAL 1002	MORE MENSAH (10" LP)	20
59	Decca WAPS 27	MENSAH's AFRICAN RHYTHMS (LP)	35

MENTAL
79	Kamikaze Pig RAM 1	God For A Day/18/Kill The Bill/Off The Rails (600 only, p/s)	80

MENTAL CUBE
90	Debut DEBTX 3104	Chile Of The Bass Generation/Q/Drop Module (12", p/s)	15

MIKE MERCADO
67	Parlophone 5589	Hey Mister Monk It's Page Nine/Popcorn	15

MARY MAE MERCER
65	Decca DFE 8599	MARY MAE MERCER (EP)	50

SANDY MERCER
79	H&L 6105091	Now That You're In (What Cha Gonna Do About It)/Work Your Body (Work That Body)	8

MICKEY MERCIAN
84	Unity Sound UN 029	Ride The Rhythm/Go Anywhere (12")	25

FREDDIE MERCURY
84	CBS WA 4735	Love Kills/GEORGIO MORODER: Rotwang's Party (picture disc)	30
85	CBS DA 6019	I Was Born To Love You/Stop All The Fighting//Love Kills (Extended)/Stop All The Fighting (Extended) (double pack)	15
85	CBS WA 6413	Made In Heaven (Remix)/She Blows Hot And Cold (shaped picture disc)	30
85	CBS WA 6413	Made In Heaven (Remix)/She Blows Hot And Cold (uncut shaped picture disc)	500
85	CBS A 6725	Love Me Like There's No Tomorrow/Let's Turn It On (p/s)	30
85	CBS TA 6725	Love Me Like There's No Tomorrow (Extended Version)/Let's Turn It On (Extended Version) (12", p/s)	25
85	CBS DTA 6725	Love Me Like There's No Tomorrow (Extended Version)/Let's Turn It On (Extended Version)//Living On My Own (Extended 6.38)/My Love Is Dangerous (Extended 6.25) (12" double pack, shrinkwrapped with sticker)	50
85	CBS TA 6725	Love Me Like There's No Tomorrow (Extended Version)/Let's Turn It On (Extended Version) (12", promo, white card sleeve, with sticker)	50
87	Parlophone RP 6151	The Great Pretender/Exercises In Free Love (Mercury Vocal) (shaped picture disc)	30
87	Parlophone RP 6151	The Great Pretender/Exercises In Free Love (Mercury Vocal) (shaped picture disc, with unfolded or folded plinth)	60
87	Parlophone RP 6151	The Great Pretender/Exercises In Free Love (Mercury Vocal) (shaped picture disc, with unfolded or folded plinth)	40
87	Parlophone RP 6151	The Great Pretender/Exercises In Free Love (Mercury Vocal) (uncut shaped picture disc)	350
87	Parlophone 10R 6151	The Great Pretender (Extended Version)//(7" Version)/Exercises In Free Love (7" Version) (10", 1-sided, printed white label, plain black die-cut sleeve, promo only)	25
87	Polydor POSP 887	Barcelona/Exercises In Free Love (Caballé Vocal) (with Montserrat Caballé, with gatefold p/s)	6
87	Polydor POSPP 887	Barcelona (7" Version)/Exercises In Free Love (Caballé Vocal) (7" Version)/ Barcelona (Extended Version) (12", picture disc)	30
87	Polydor POCD 887	Barcelona/Exercises In Free Love (Version 2) (Caballé Vocal)/ Barcelona (Extended) (CD, 300

MERCURY REV

MINT VALUE £

87	Polydor PO 23 DJ	autographed card p/s, promo only)	
		The Golden Boy (with Montserrat Caballé) (radio edit) (1-sided DJ sampler, p/s, with sticker)	100
88	Polydor POSPX 23	The Golden Boy/The Fallen Priest/The Golden Boy (Instrumental) (12", p/s)	20
88	Polydor PZCD234	The Golden Boy/The Fallen Priest/The Golden Boy (Instrumental) (CD)	35
88	Polydor PO 29	How Can I Go On/Overture Piccante (with Montserrat Caballe) (p/s)	15
88	Polydor POSX 29	How Can I Go On/Overture Piccante (with Montserrat Caballe) (picture disc)	45
89	Polydor PZ 29	How Can I Go On/Guide Me Home/Overture Piccante (12", p/s)	25
89	Polydor PZCD 29	How Can I Go On/Guide Me Home/Overture Piccante (CD, picture disc)	35
88	Polydor CD 3 125 211	The Golden Boy/La Japanese/Barcelona (CD promo, unreleased p/s, jewel case)	100
89	Polydor 0805 548-2	Ensueno/Barcelona (Edit 4.24)/Exercises In Free Love/Barcelona (Extended Version 7.02)/Barcelona (Video) (CD Video)	40
89	Polydor 0805 580-2	The Fallen Priest/The Golden Boy (Album Version)/The Golden Boy (Instrumental Version)/The Golden Boy (Video) (CD Video)	40
92	Polydor PO 234	How Can I Go On/The Golden Boy (yellow p/s)	7
92	Parlophone R 6331	In My Defence/Love Kills (Wolf Euro Mix) (p/s)	6
06	Parlophone KILLS 001	Love Kills (Glimmer Mix)/(Pixel 82 Mix)/I Was Born To Love You (George Demure Mix) (12" promo)	15
06	Parlophone KILLS 003	Living On My Own (mixes) (12" promo)	15
92	Parlophone 077778099918	THE FREDDIE MERCURY ALBUM (LP)	50
94	Parlophone 7234 8 2814 10	FREDDIE MERCURY REMIXES (LP, unreleased)	150
97	EMI LPCENT 10	THE FREDDIE MERCURY ALBUM (LP, reissue, EMI Centenary, stickered sleeve)	40
00	Parlophone FMRARE001	THE SOLO COLLECTION (10 CD & 2 DVD box set)	80

(see also Queen, Larry Lurex, Eddie Howell, Billy Squier)

MERCURY REV

91	Mint Film MINT 5	Car Wash Hair/Coney Island Cyclone (4 track demo) (200 copies only, p/s)	15
93	Beggars Banquet BBQ 5 T	The Hum Is Coming From Her (as Mercury Theremin Sextet)/So There (as Mercury Rev Orchestra with Robert Creely) (10", p/s)	8
91	Mint Film MINTLP 4	YERSELF IS STEAM (LP, blue or pink vinyl)	30
92	Beggars Banquet BBQLP 125	YERSELF IS STEAM (LP, reissue with bonus LP 'Lego My Ego')	40
92	Beggars Banquet BBQLP 135	LEGO MY EGO (LP)	20
93	Beggars Banquet BBQLP 140	BOCES (LP, clear red vinyl)	40
93	Beggars Banquet BBQLP 140	BOCES (LP)	30
95	Beggars Banquet BBQLP 176	SEE YOU ON THE OTHER SIDE (LP)	50
95	Beggars Banquet BBQLP176P	SEE YOU ON THE OTHER SIDE (LP, picture disc)	30
98	V2 VVR 1002771	DESERTERS SONGS (LP)	50
01	V2 175218	ALL IS DREAM (LP)	40
05	Virgin VVR1029231	THE SECRET MIGRATION (LP)	30

(see also Harmony Rockets)

MERCY

69	London HLZ 10273	Love (Can Make You Happy)/Fireball	20

MERCYFUL FATE

83	Music For Nations MFN 10	MELISSA (LP, inner)	15
84	Music For Nations MFN 28	DON'T BREAK THE OATH (LP, inner)	15

MIKEY MERICAN

85	Hands & Hearts HHDD 007	Family Affair/Family Dub (12")	20
86	Unity UN 024	Control The Dance/Version/Automatic/Version (12")	20
86	Unity UN 029	Ride The Rhythm/Version/Go Anywhere/Version (12")	20
86	Regal RG 001	Rub A Dub Party/Money Lover (12", as Mikey Merica)	15

TRUMAN MERIT

93	Spurt 3	ALIEN BOOGIE (LP and free 7")	18

LOTTIE MERLE

72	Flyright 001	Howling In The Moonlight/Catfish	10

MERLIN Q

69	Pye 7N 17828	The Secret/Love's Beautiful	25

RAY MERRELL

60	Ember EMB S 113	Why Did You Leave Me?/Teenage Love (p/s)	10
60s	Aral PS 115	Battle Of Waterloo/Not Any More (p/s)	10
70	Jay Boy BOY 22	Tears Of Joy/Searchin' (withdrawn) (Beware of bootlegs!)	200
70	Jay Boy BOY 22	Tears Of Joy/Searchin' (withdrawn) (Beware of bootlegs!) (DJ copy)	350

TONY MERRICK

66	Columbia DB 7913	Lady Jane/Michelle	10
66	Columbia DB 7995	Wake Up/It's For You	6

BOB MERRILL

58	Columbia DB 4086	Nairobi/Jump When I Say Frog	15

BUDDY MERRILL

66	Vocalion VN 9261	Sweet September/Sherk	12

HELEN MERRILL

58	Mercury MMB 12000	THE NEARNESS OF YOU (LP, features Bill Evans)	40

MERRITTS

70	Hot Rod HR 113	I Don't Want To (Part 1)/HOT ROD ALL STARS: Version	30

MERRY MAKER

76	Western Kingston WK 505	Untouchable Special/Straight To Music City Head	20

MERRYMEN

66	Doctor Bird DB 1004	Big Bamboo/Island Woman	15
69	Trojan TR 7707	Little Drummer Boy/Mary's Boy Child	10
71	Duke DU 113	Big Bamboo/King Ja-Ja (both sides actually with Emille Straker)	12
68	Island ILP 984	CARIBBEAN TREASURE CHEST (LP)	30

(see also Soul Brothers)

JASON MERRYWEATHER

69	Crystal CR 001	My Summer Love/Abigail	10

MERSEYBEATS

MINT VALUE £

(see also Ricky Valance)

MERSEYBEATS
63	Fontana TF 412	It's Love That Really Counts/The Fortune Teller	12
64	Fontana TF 459	Don't Turn Around/Really Mystified	6
64	Fontana TF 504	Last Night/See Me Back	10
65	Fontana TF 568	Don't Let It Happen To Us/It Would Take A Long Long Time	10
65	Fontana TF 607	I Love You, Yes I Do/Good Good Lovin'	8
65	Fontana TF 645	I Stand Accused/All My Life	10
69	Fontana TF 1025	I Think Of You/Wishin' And Hopin' (p/s)	10
81	Tudor CHEM 001	This Is Merseybeat (both sides) (p/s)	6
64	Fontana TE 17422	ON STAGE (EP)	25
64	Fontana TE 17423	I THINK OF YOU (EP)	30
64	Fontana TE 17432	THE MERSEYBEATS (EP)	30
64	Fontana TL 5210	THE MERSEYBEATS (LP)	60
69	Wing WL 1163	THE MERSEYBEATS (LP)	15

(see also Merseys, Rockin' Horse, Tony Crane, Kirkbys, Quotations, Johnny Gustavson)

MERSEYBOYS
64	Ace Of Clubs ACL 1169	15 GREAT SONGS BY JOHN, PAUL AND GEORGE (LP)	20

MERSEYS
66	Fontana TF 694	Sorrow/Some Other Day	6
66	Fontana TF 732	So Sad About Us/Love Will Continue	15
66	Fontana TF 776	Rhythm Of Love/Is It Love?	10
67	Fontana TF 845	The Cat/Change Of Heart	25
68	Fontana TF 916	Penny In My Pocket/I Hope You're Happy	10
68	Fontana TF 955	Lovely Loretta/Dreaming	15

(see also Merseybeats, Crackers)

WIM MERTENS
87	Factory FACT 190c	EDUCES ME (cassette, in bespoke box with insert)	200

MERTON PARKAS
79	Beggars Banquet BEG 22	You Need Wheels/I Don't Want To Know You (coloured p/s with patch)	10
79	Beggars Banquet BEG 22	You Need Wheels/I Don't Want To Know You (coloured p/s)	7
79	Beggars Banquet BEG 22	You Need Wheels/I Don't Want To Know You (reissue, with silver moulded label, black & white p/s)	7
79	Beggars Banquet BEG 25	Plastic Smile/The Man With The Disguise (p/s)	6
79	Beggars Banquet BEG 30	Give It To Me Now/Gi's It (p/s)	7
80	Beggars Banquet BEG 43	Put Me In The Picture/In The Midnight Hour (p/s)	7
83	Well Suspect BLAM 002	Flat 19/Band Of Gold (p/s)	10
79	Beggars Banquet BEGA 11	FACE IN THE CROWD (LP)	18

(see also Style Council)

MESCALINE UNITED
92	R&S RS 92019	We Have Arrived (Aphex Twin QQT Reconstruction Mix)/We Have Arrived (Aphex Twin TTQ Reconstruction Mix) (limited issue 12", also known as "PCP Remixed" plain paper sleeve)	70

MESS
82	Reasonable MEP 1	Tried And Tested/I'm Falling	12

MESSAGE (1)
70	Doctor Bird DB 1503	Rum-Bum-A-Loo/Drummer Boy	125
72	Reggae REG 3004	Wrestling/Tricia	60

(see also Boris Gardner)

MESSAGE (2)
75	Decca SKL-R 5213	MESSAGE (LP, blue/silver label)	25

MESSAGE (3)
81	Is It Original...? ISIT1	Empty Promise/War Of The Music	100

RICKY MESSENGER & SEMI PROFESSIONALS
80s	Kim 019	Now Is The Time For Jah/Mr. Richman (12")	20

MESSENGERS
64	Columbia DB 7344	I'm Stealin' Back/This Little Light Of Mine	10
65	Columbia DB 7495	When Did You Leave Heaven/More Pretty Girls Than One	8

MESSENGERS (JAMAICA)
73	Attack ATT 8057	Crowded City/Thula Thula	25
73	Bread BR 1116	Cherry Baby/B.B. SEATON: Summertime	10
73	Mirto MIR 100	Is It Because I'm Black/Just Like A Shelter (actually by Ken Boothe and Lloyd Charmers)	18

MESSENGERS OF THE CROSS
69	Emblem JDR 21	MESSENGERS OF THE CROSS (LP)	20

METABOLIST
79	Drömm DRO 1	Drömm/Slaves/Eulam's Beat (p/s, rough screen-printed & folded p/s)	20
79	Drömm DRO 1	Drömm/Slaves/Eulam's Beat (p/s, smooth printed & stapled p/s)	10
80	Drömm DRO 3	Identity/Tizhoznam (p/s)	15
79	Drömm NCN	GOATMANAUT (cassette)	50
80	Drömm DRO 2	HANSTEN KLORK (LP)	20
81	Cassetteking CK2	STAGMANAUT! (cassette)	50

METAL BOYS
79	Rough Trade RT 016	Sweet Marilyn/Fugue For A Darkening Island (p/s)	8

(see also Metal Urbain)

METAL HEADS
92	Synthetic SYNTH 003	TERMINATOR (12", p/s)	20

METALLICA

SINGLES
84	Music For Nations 12 KUT 105	Jump In The Fire/Seek And Destroy (live)/Phantom Lord (live) (12", p/s, initial pressing with beige labels)	25
84	Music For Nations 12 KUT	Jump In The Fire/Seek And Destroy (live)/Phantom Lord (live) (12", p/s, later pressing	20

Rare Record Price Guide 2024   824

METALLICA

MINT VALUE £

Year	Label/Cat#	Description	Value
		105 with red/yellow labels)	
84	Music For Nations CV12 KUT 105	Jump In The Fire/Seek And Destroy (live)/Phantom Lord (live) (12", red vinyl, p/s)	25
84	Music For Nations 12 KUT 112	Creeping Death/Am I Evil?/Blitzkrieg (12", p/s, initial pressing with beige label)	20
84	Music For Nations 12 KUT 112	Creeping Death/Am I Evil?/Blitzkrieg (12", p/s, later pressing with red/yellow labels)	18
84	Music For Nations CV12 KUT 112	Creeping Death/Am I Evil?/Blitzkrieg (12", p/s, blue vinyl, red/yellow or 'Special Anniversary Edition' labels)	35
84	Music For Nations GV12 KUT 112	Creeping Death/Am I Evil?/Blitzkrieg (12", no p/s, 'Anniversary Gold Edition', gold vinyl, 3000 only; mispressing with 1 side gold, 1 side black vinyl)	80
84	Music For Nations GV12 KUT 112	Creeping Death/Am I Evil?/Blitzkrieg (12", no p/s, 'Anniversary Gold Edition', gold vinyl, 3000 only)	70
84	Music For Nations P12 KUT 112	Creeping Death/Am I Evil?/Blitzkrieg (12", picture disc, initially without barcode)	30
84	Music For Nations CD12 KUT 112	Creeping Death/Am I Evil?/Blitzkrieg Jump In The Fire/ Seek And Destroy (live)/Phantom Lord (live) (CD)	60
86	Music For Nations 12 KUT 105XP	Jump In The Fire/Seek And Destroy (live)/Phantom Lord (live) (12", repressing, stickered sleeve with sew-on patch)	80
86	Music For Nations PKUT 105	Jump In The Fire/Phantom Lord (live) (shaped picture disc, initial pressing without barcode)	25
86	Music For Nations PKUT 105	Jump In The Fire/Phantom Lord (live) (shaped picture disc, later pressing with barcode)	20
86	Music For Nations PKUT 105	Jump In The Fire/Phantom Lord (live) (uncut picture disc)	150
87	Vertigo METAL 112	$5.98 EP - GARAGE DAYS RE-REVISITED: Helpless/Crash Course In Brain Surgery/The Small Hours/Last Caress - Green Hell (medley) (12" p/s, later copies add "The Wait")	35
88	Vertigo METAL 212	Harvester Of Sorrow/Breadfan/The Prince (12", p/s, some with 'skull' label)	18
89	Vertigo METAL 312	Jump In The Fire/Seek And Destroy/Phantom Lord (live) (12", p/s, reissue)	10
89	Vertigo METAL 412	Creeping Death/Am I Evil? (12", p/s, reissue)	10
89	Vertigo 842-219-2	Creeping Death/Am I Evil?/Blitzkrieg/Jump In The Fire/Seek And Destroy (live)/Phantom Lord (live) (CD)	50
89	Vertigo METAP 5	One/Seek And Destroy (live) (card p/s, some stickered, with rolled poster)	15
89	Vertigo METPD 510	One/Seek And Destroy (live) (10", picture disc with card)	30
89	Vertigo METAL 5	One/Seek And Destroy (live) (silver/black labels, paper p/s)	10
89	Vertigo METAL 512	One (Demo Version)/For Whom The Bell Tolls (live)/Welcome Home (Sanitarium) (live) (12", p/s initial pressing with white labels)	12
89	Vertigo METAL 512	One (Demo Version)/For Whom The Bell Tolls (live)/Welcome Home (Sanitarium) (live) (12", p/s later pressing with yellow labels)	10
89	Vertigo METAL 512	One (Demo Version)/For Whom The Bell Tolls (live)/Welcome Home (Sanitarium) (live) (12", p/s mis-labelled as "Seek and Destroy" [live])	10
89	Vertigo METG 512	One (Demo Version)/For Whom The Bell Tolls (live)/Welcome Home (Sanitarium) (live) (gatefold p/s, with booklet, mispressed with B-side label on both sides)	20
90	Vertigo 875 487 1	THE GOOD, THE BAD AND THE LIVE - THE 6 1/2 YEARS ANNIVERSARY COLLECTION (6 x 12", with live 4-track EP [METAL 612])	80
91	Vertigo METAL 7	Enter Sandman/Stone Cold Crazy (p/s)	8
91	Vertigo METAL 7	Enter Sandman/Stone Cold Crazy (picture disc in p/s, stickered)	15
91	Vertigo METBX 712	Enter Sandman/Stone Cold Crazy/Enter Sandman (Demo) (12", box with 4 photo prints)	30
91	Vertigo METCD 7	Enter Sandman/Stone Cold Crazy/Enter Sandman (Demo) (CD, picture disc in box with room for 3 more CDs)	30
92	Vertigo METAL 10	Nothing Else Matters/Enter Sandman (live) (p/s, black & white label)	10
93	Vertigo METAL 11	Sad But True/Nothing Else Matters (p/s, stickered, no labels)	6
93	Vertigo METAL 1112	Sad But True/Nothing Else Matters (Elevator Version)/Creeping Death (live)/Sad But True (Demo) (12" picture disc with insert)	20
96	Vertigo METJB 12	Until It Sleeps/Until It Sleeps (jukebox issue, no p/s)	10
97	Vertigo METJB 13	Hero Of The Day/Hero Of The Day (jukebox issue, no p/s)	8
97	Vertigo METJB 15	The Memory Remains/For Whom The Bell Tolls (Haven't Heard It Yet Remix) (Jukebox issue no p/s)	18
03	Columbia GABBA 1	53rd & 3rd/Outsider (by GREEN DAY)/I Wanna Be Sedated (by OFFSPRING) (blue vinyl, stickered p/s withdrawn single)	400
03	Vertigo 9865411	St. Anger/We're A Happy Family	6
90s	Vertigo METJB 19	Whiskey In The Jar/Turn The Page (Jukebox issue no p/s)	20
10	Vertigo 00602527391100	Frantic (UNKLE Remix)/BLACK SABBATH: Paranoid (Alternative Vocal Version) (12", 1000 only)	20

ALBUMS

Year	Label/Cat#	Description	Value
83	Music For Nations MFN 7	KILL 'EM ALL (LP, 1st issue with beige labels)	50
83	Music For Nations MFN 7	KILL 'EM ALL (LP, later pressing with red/yellow labels)	30
84	M. For Nations MFNCD 7	KILL 'EM ALL (CD)	30
84	Music For Nations MFN 27	RIDE THE LIGHTNING (LP, with inner sleeve, initial pressing with beige labels & without barcode)	40
86	Music For Nations MFN 60	MASTER OF PUPPETS (LP, with inner sleeve & insert)	40
86	Music For Nations MFN 60	MASTER OF PUPPETS (LP, mispressing, Side 1 label on both sides)	30
86	Music For Nations MFN 60P	MASTER OF PUPPETS (LP, picture disc, initially without barcode)	25
86	Music For Nations MFN 60P	MASTER OF PUPPETS (LP, picture disc, with barcode)	25
86	M. For Nations MFNCD 60	MASTER OF PUPPETS (CD)	30
86	Music For Nations MFN 27P	RIDE THE LIGHTNING (LP, picture disc, initial pressing with no barcode)	30
86	Music For Nations MFN 27P	RIDE THE LIGHTNING (LP, picture disc, with barcode)	20
86	Music For Nations MFN 7P	KILL 'EM ALL (LP reissue, picture disc, lacking picture on 1 side, initially lacking barcode)	25
86	Music For Nations MFN 7P	KILL 'EM ALL (LP reissue, picture disc, with picture on 1 side and barcode)	22
87	Music For Nations MFN 7DM	KILL 'EM ALL (2-LP, 'direct metal mastered' reissue, gatefold sleeve)	35
87	Music For Nations MFN 60DM	MASTER OF PUPPETS (2-LP, 'direct metal mastered' reissue, gatefold sleeve with poster)	30
87	Music For Nations MFN 27DM	RIDE THE LIGHTNING (2-LP, 'direct metal mastered' reissue, gatefold sleeve with insert)	30
88	Vertigo VERH 61	...AND JUSTICE FOR ALL (2-LP)	40
89	Vertigo 838-140-1	RIDE THE LIGHTNING (LP, reissue, mispressing, Side 1 lists Master Of Puppets tracks)	20
91	Vertigo 510 022-1	METALLICA (2-LP)	70

METAL MIRROR

MINT VALUE £

91	Vertigo MECAN 1/510-022-0	THE METALLICAN (CD, gold disc in metal 'paint can' with video & T-shirt; 35,000 only)	100
93	Vertigo 518-725-0	LIVE SHIT, BINGE & PURGE (3-CD box set with 3 videos & 72-page book)	80
96	Elektra 532618	LOAD (2-LP, gatefold)	80
97	Elektra 536209	RELOAD (2-LP, gatefold, stickered sleeve with inners)	50
98	Vertigo 538 351-1	GARAGE INC. (3-LP, gatefold, inners)	80
08	Vertigo 00602517737310	DEATH MAGNETIC (Box set, 5x12")	40
08	Vertigo 00602517800502	DEATH MAGNETIC (LP, coffin-shaped box set, CD, DVD, T-shirt, guitar picks, flag, poster and credit card)	75
08	Universal 0600753085271	KILL 'EM ALL (2-LP, reissue, gatefold with obi)	20
08	Universal 0600753085240	RIDE THE LIGHTNING (2-LP, reissue, gatefold with obi)	25
08	Universal 0600753101162	MASTER OF PUPPETS (2-LP, reissue, gatefold with obi)	25

PROMOS

88	Vertigo METDJ 2	Harvester Of Sorrow/Harvester Of Sorrow (unique p/s)	60
88	Vertigo MET CD 100	THE WHIPLASH SAMPLER (CD)	70
89	Vertigo METDJ 5	One/One (Edit) (unique blue cover, plus insert)	100
89	Vertigo METDJ 512	One (Demo Version)/For Whom The Bell Tolls (live)/Welcome Home (Sanitarium) (live) (12", unissued, promo-only p/s)	70
91	Vertigo METAL 7	Enter Sandman/Stone Cold Crazy (jukebox promo)	10
91	Vertigo METDJ 7	Enter Sandman (Radio Edit)/Stone Cold Crazy (p/s B-side actually silent)	15
91	Vertigo METDJ8	The Unforgiven (edit)/Killing Time (p/s)	25
96	Mercury MM CJ-1	MANDATORY METALLICA (CD, 7-track sampler)	30
96	Vertigo MET INT 1	LOAD - THE INTERVIEW (CD, with cue booklet)	50
97	Vertigo MMCJ-2	MANDATORY METALLICA 2 (2-CD, 17-track sampler)	35
03	Vertigo FRANTICDJ 1	Frantic (12" promo)	15

METAL MIRROR

80	M&M MM 001	Rock 'N Roll Ain't Never Gonna Leave Us/English Booze (in p/s)	80
80	M&M MM 001	Rock 'N Roll Ain't Never Gonna Leave Us/English Booze	50

METAL URBAIN

77	Rough Trade RT 001	Paris Maquis/Cle De Contact (p/s)	18
78	Radar ADA 20	Hysterie Connective/Pas Poubelle	12

METAPHORCE

95	Ill Gotten Gains FDN004	Recipes For Disaster/Behind Enemy Lines (12")	10

METEORS (1)

64	Polydor NH 52263	Get A Load Of This/Ruby Ann	10

METEORS (2)

79	EMI EMI 2987	It's Only You/Blitzkreig (p/s)	8

METEORS (3)

81	Ace SWT 65	METEOR MADNESS (10" EP, white label test pressings only, custom p/s)	250
81	Ace SW 65	METEOR MADNESS (EP, on blue vinyl)	25
81	Ace SW 65	METEOR MADNESS (EP)	15
81	Lost Souls LOST 101	The Crazed/Attack Of The Zorch Men (p/s)	12
81	Chiswick CHIS 147	Radioactive Kid/Graveyard Stomp (p/s)	12
81	Ace NS 74	Radioactive Kid/Graveyard Stomp (p/s, reissue, black vinyl)	8
81	Ace NS 74	Radioactive Kid/Graveyard Stomp (p/s, reissue, some clear or blue vinyl)	10
82	I.D. EYE 1	Johnny Remember Me/Fear Of The Dark/Wreckin' Crew (p/s)	8
82	WXYZ ABCD 5	Mutant Rock/The Hills Have Eyes (p/s)	10
84	Mad Pig PORK 1	I'm Just A Dog/Electro Rock (p/s)	6
85	Mad Pig PORK 2	Fire, Fire/Little Red Riding Hood (p/s)	10
85	Mad Pig PORK 2T	Fire, Fire/Little Red Riding Hood/Stampede (King Ray Bat Scalator In The Dark Mix) (12", p/s)	10
85	Mad Pig PORK 3	Bad Moon Rising/Rhythm Of The Bell (p/s)	10
86	I.D. EYET 10	MUTANT ROCK (12" EP, green or blue vinyl)	12
86	Anagram ANA 31	Surf City/The Edge (p/s)	10
86	Anagram 12ANA 31	Surf City (Has Beens From Outer Space Mix)/The Edge/Johnny's Here (12", p/s)	15
87	Anagram ANA 35	Go Buddy Go/You Crack Me Up (p/s)	7
81	Ace MAD 1	THE METEORS MEET SCREAMIN' LORD SUTCH (mini-LP, 1 side each, 1,000 only, stickered cartoon print on plain card sleeve)	100
81	Lost Soul LOSTLP 3001	IN HEAVEN (LP)	20
86	Big Beat WIKA 47	TEENAGERS FROM OUTER SPACE (LP)	18
86	Anagram GRAM 27	SEWERTIME BLUES (LP)	15
88	Anagram GRAM 37	MUTANT MONKEY AND AND THE SURFERS FROM ZORCH (LP)	20

(see also Tall Boys, Clapham South Escalators, [Screamin'] Lord Sutch, Deadbeats)

METERS

69	Stateside SS 2140	Sophisticated Cissy/Sehorn's Farm	12
70	Direction 58-4751	Look-Ka-Py-Py/This Is My Last Affair	12
74	Island IDJ 3	Ride Your Pony/Look-Ka-Py-Py (DJ album sampler)	25
74	Reprise K 14367	People Say/Africa	6
75	Reprise K 14405	Fire On The Bayou/They All Ask'd For You	6
72	Reprise K 44242	CABBAGE ALLEY (LP)	20
74	Reprise K 54027	REJUVENATION (LP)	20
74	Island ILPS 9250	CISSY STRUT (LP)	30
75	Reprise K 54044	FIRE ON THE BAYOU (LP)	15
76	Reprise K 54076	BEST OF THE METERS (LP)	15
76	Reprise K 54078	TRICK BAG (LP)	18

METGUMBNERBONE

83	Aeon (No Cat. No.)	COPS OF MATTER (cassette)	40
83	Amission REV 13:15	LIGELIAHORN (LP, 500 only, with insert)	100
84	Private cassette	FOR THE RAVEN (cassette)	40

METHOD ACTORS

80	Armageddon AS 6	The Method/Can't Act (p/s)	7

METHOD MAN

		MINT VALUE £
81 Armageddon AS 11	Round World/Eye (p/s)	7

METHOD MAN
94 Def Jam 523 839-1	TICAL (LP)	25

(see also Wu Tang Clan)

METHODS
70 DJM DJS 225	Chasing The Sun/And That Is Life	15

METRO
84 CSA SPCSA 12008	The Girl Is Mine (with Yellowman)/AL CAMPBELL: Bad Boy (12")	25

PETER METRO
82 Greensleeves GRED 97	Warn Them Teach Them (with Squiddly Ranking)/Carribean Connection (12")	10

METRO TRINITY
87 Cafeteria CAFF 1	DIE YOUNG EP (12")	60

METRO AREA
02 Source SOURLP 070	METRO AREA (LP as 2 x 12")	25

METRO GLIDER
80 Racket RKT 1	Do It Right/Consequences	20

METROPAK
80 Metropak PAK 001	You're A Rebel/OK Let's Go/Run Run Run (numbered p/s)	6

METROPHASE
79 Neo London MS 01	In Black/Neo Beauty/Cold Rebellion (photocopied p/s with lyric insert)	12
79 Neo London MS 02	New Age/Frames Of Life (foldout p/s, stamped white labels)	25
81 Fresh FRESH 6	In Black/Neo Beauty/Cold Rebellion (reissue, better quality p/s with insert)	6

(see also Swell Maps)

METROPOLIS
82 Gargoyle GRGL 4	See No Reason/Russian Romance (no p/s)	20

METROPOLITAN POLICE BAND
66 Columbia DB 8095	Thunderbirds March/P.C. ALEXANDER MORGAN: Sussex By The Sea	8

METROTONE
98 Earworm WORM 21	THE LESS YOU HAVE THE MORE YOU ARE (LP, test pressings only)	25

PAUL METSERS
81 Highway SHY 7014	CAUTION TO THE WIND (LP)	18

MEW
02 Epic 672854 7	Am I Wry? No/Like Paper Cuts	10

MEXICANO
77 Pioneer PIOLP !	MOVE UP STARSKY (LP)	15

MEXICANS
68 Pye 7N 17613	Alexander Higginbottom/Julie	12
68 Pye 7N 17657	Without Your Love	12

MEXICO RED
88 Hummingbird	Eternal Flame/Follow Me To Heaven (p/s, insert)	80

ANTHONY MEYNELL
82 Hi-Lo LO 01	HITS FROM 3000 YEARS AGO (LP, purple sleeve)	15

(see also Squire)

LEE MEZA
67 Stateside SS 589	If It Happens/One Good Thing Leads To Another	30

M-G-M SINGING STRINGS
66 MGM 1307	Lara's Theme From "Dr Zhivago"/The Old And The New	6

M-G-M STUDIO ORCHESTRA
55 MGM SP 1144	Rock Around The Clock/"Blackboard Jungle" Love Theme	25

MIAMI
75 Jay Boy JSL 5	THE PARTY FREAKS (LP)	15
76 Jay Boy JSL 11	NOTORIOUS MIAMI (LP)	15

MIAOW
85 Venus VENUS 1	Belle Vue/Fate (p/s)	6
86 Venus VENUST 1	Belle Vue/Fate/Grocer's Devil Daughter (12", p/s)	10
87 Factory FAC 189	Break The Code/Stolen Ears (p/s)	10

MICHA
65 Pye 7N 15982	Protest Singer/Serpent	8

GEORGE MICHAEL
87 Epic EPC 460000 1	FAITH (LP, inner & insert)	20
90 Epic 467295 1	LISTEN WITHOUT PREJUDICE (LP)	20
96 Virgin V2802	OLDER (LP)	500
14 Aegean/Virgin 379244-6	SYMPHONICA (2-LP)	500

(see also Wham!, High, Elton John, Queen)

RAS MICHAEL & THE SONS OF NEGUS
75 Grounation GRD 2037	None A Jah Children/Glory Dawn	25
74 Trojan TRLS 118	NYAHBINGHI (LP)	20
75 Trojan TRSL 113	DADAWAH (PEACE & LOVE) (LP, credited to DADAWAH)	45
75 Vulcan VUL 005	RASTAFARI (LP)	25
75 Grounation GROL 505	RASTAFARI (LP)	25
76 Trojan TRLS 203	TRIBUTE TO THE EMPEROR RASTAFORI (LP, with Jazzbo Abubaka)	20
76 Dynamic DYLP 3004	FREEDOM SOUNDS (LP, as The Sons Of Negus)	20
91 Greensleeves GREL 158	KIBIR AM LAKE (LP)	18

MICHAEL SCHENKER GROUP
82 Chysalis PCHR 1393	ASSAULT ATTACK (LP, picture disc)	18
83 Chysalis CHRP 1441	BUILT TO DESTROY (LP, picture disc, U.S. remixes)	18

(see also McAuley Schenker Group, Scorpions, UFO, Cozy Powell, Graham Bonnet, Alex Harvey Band)

CODY MICHAELS
79 Grapevine GRP 121	7 Days - 52 Weeks/VIRTUE ORCHESTRA: Don't Look Back (Instrumental)	8

MARILYN MICHAELS

MINT VALUE £

MARILYN MICHAELS
60 RCA RCA 1208   Tell Tommy I Miss Him/Everyone Was There But You 10

MICHIGAN RAG
72 Blue Horizon 2096 009   Don't Run Away/She's Looking Good 20

MICHIGANS
63 Vogue V 9207   Intermission Riff/Tea For Two 15

MICKEY & LUDELLA
95 Vinyl Japan ASKLP 52   BEDLAM A GO GO (LP) 30
(see also Milkshakes, Billy Childish, Del Monas, Thee Headcoatees)

MICKEY (BAKER) & KITTY (NOBLE)
60 London HLE 9054   Buttercup/My Reverie 35

MICKEY (BAKER) & SYLVIA
57 HMV POP 331   Love Is Strange/I'm Going Home 100
57 HMV POP 331   Love Is Strange/I'm Going Home (78) 30
58 RCA RCA 1064   Rock And Stroll Room/Bewildered 50
58 RCA RCA 1064   Rock And Stroll Room/Bewildered (78) 30
60 RCA RCA 1206   Sweeter As The Day Goes By/Mommy Out De Light 15
65 RCA Victor RCA 1487   Love Is Strange/Dearest 15
65 RCA Camden CDN 5133   LOVE IS STRANGE (LP) 200
(see also Mickey Baker, Sylvia [Robbins])

MICKEY FINN (1)
64 Blue Beat BB 203   Tom Hark/Please Love Me (as 'Mickey Finn & the Blue Men') 25
64 Oriole CB 1927   Pills/Hush Your Mouth (as 'Mickey Finn & the Blue Men') 80
64 Oriole CB 1940   Reelin' & A'Rockin'/I Still Want You (as 'Mickey Finn') 50
65 Columbia DB 7510   The Sporting Life/Night Comes Down (as 'The Mickey Finn') 100
66 Polydor 56719   I Do Love You/If I Had You Baby (as 'The Mickey Finn') 100
67 Direction 58-3086   Garden Of My Mind/Time To Start Loving You (as 'The Mickey Finn') 200
95 Noiseburger 3   Ain't Necessarily So/God Bless The Child (foldaround p/s in poly bag, 1,000 only, 1st 500 signed) 8

MICKEY FINN (2)
93 Dee Jay DJX 011   D Pressed/Reality (12") 15

BOBBY "BOBCATS" MICKLEBURGH
55 Esquire EP 40   MICKLEBURGH'S BOBCATS (EP) 10
56 Esquire EP 73   MICKLEBURGH'S BOBCATS (EP) 10

MICRODISNEY
82 Kabuki KAMD 2   Hello Rascals/The Helicopter Of The Holy Ghost (p/s) 6
88 Virgin V2505   39 MINUTES (LP) 18
84 Rough Trade ROUGH 75   EVERYBODY IS FANTASTIC (LP) 15
84 Rough Trade RTM 155   WE HATE YOU SOUTH AFRICAN BASTARDS (LP) 20
85 Rough Trade ROUGH 85   THE CLOCK COMES DOWN THE STAIRS (LP) 15

MICRON
88 White SG045   Eastenders Rap (12") 15
(see Rebel MC)

STEPHAN MICUS
76 Caroline C 1517   ARCHAIC CONCERTS (LP) 25

MIDAS MOULD
72 Columbia DB 8868   Information Emily/Love Sweet Love 15

MIDAS (1)
70 Solar SL003   I've Seen A New Life/Visit The Sun 40

MIDAS (2)
83 Small Run SRR 0008   Can't Stop Loving You/Power In The Sky (p/s with insert) 200

MIDAS (3)
77 Quest PPS 009   Pladda Island/Evensong (no p/s) 6

MIDDLE OF THE ROAD
72 RCA SF 8305   THE BEST OF (LP) 15

MAX MIDDLETON & ROBERT AWWAI
79 Harvest SHSP 4103   ANOTHER SLEEPER (LP) 18

TONY MIDDLETON
65 London HLR 9983   My Little Red Book (as Burt Bacharach Orchestra with Tony Middleton)/BURT BACHARACH ORCHESTRA: What's New Pussycat 30
66 Polydor BM 56704   To The Ends Of The Earth/Don't Ever Leave Me 450
66 Polydor BM 56704   To The Ends Of The Earth/Don't Ever Leave Me (DJ copy) 500
78 Grapevine GRP 115   Paris Blues/Out Of This World 10
(see also Willows, Burt Bacharach)

MIDI RAIN
94 Vinyl Solution STEAM 56   ONE (2-LP) 30
(see also John Rocca, Freeez, Pink Rhythm, Gamer 3)

MIDLAKE
05 Bella Union BELLAV85   Balloon Maker/Mornings Will Be Kind 6
06 Bella Union BELLAV 128   Head Home/Roscoe 8
10 Is It Balearic? IIBR 002   Roscoe (Beyond The Wizard Sleeve Re:animation) (12", B-side contains 5 silent tracks) 15
08 Bella Union BELLAV 117   THE TRIALS OF VAN OCCUPANTHER (LP) 50
10 Bella Union BELLACD224SP   THE COURAGE OF OTHERS (2-LP) 25
10 Bella Union CD02245P   THE COURAGE OF OTHERS (Box set, 2-LP, DVD, CD & 32 page booklet) 50
(see also John Grant)

MIDNIGHT
78 Ariola ATTA 514DJ   Don't Bother To Knock/Keep Walking By (DJ Copy, p/s) 80
78 Ariola ATTA 514   Don't Bother To Knock/Keep Walking By (p/s) 75
79 Magnet MAG 148   Love's Gonna Hit You Like A Bullet/Minute To Midnight (as Midnite) 20

THE MIDNIGHT
17 155694   ENDLESS SUMMER LP 40

MIDNIGHT CRUISER

MINT VALUE £

MIDNIGHT CRUISER
77   It IT 2   Rich Bitch/Striker (p/s) 10

MIDNIGHT RAGS
80   Ace ACE 005   Public Enemy/Alcatraz/Mamma Said (p/s) 8
80   Velvet Moon VM 1   The Cars That Ate New York/Oscar Automobile (p/s, withdrawn) 8
(see also Paul Roland, Weird Strings)

MIDNIGHT SHIFT
66   Decca F 12487   Saturday Jump/Living Fast 30

MIDNIGHT SUN
71   MCA MKPS 2019   MIDNIGHT SUN (LP, red/pink 'dogbone' label) 60
72   MCA MKPS 2024   WALKING CIRCLES (LP, black/blue hexagon label) 60

MIDNIGHTERS
55   Parlophone DP 422   Annie Had A Baby/THUNDERBIRDS: Pledging My Love (78, export issue) 10
(see also Hank Ballard)

MIDNIGHTS
66   Ember EMB S 220   (Won'tcha) Show Me Around/Only Two Can Play 18
63   MEP 101/MN 1/EAG-EP-134   MIDNIGHTS (EP, private pressing) 130

M.I. FIVE
66   Parlophone R 5486   You'll Never Stop Me Loving You/Only Time Will Tell 150
(see also Deep Purple)

MI5 (1)
80   Public PUB 002   Alright On The Night/Television Screen Heroes/Don't Make Waves (p/s) 7

MI5 (2)
95   Lucky Spin LSR 021   I Can't Understand/Experience (12") 30

MIGHT OF COINCIDENCE
72   Entropia BM 0001   WHY COULDN'T PEOPLE WAIT (LP) 100

MIGHTY ABIJANS
80   No 1 Rock   Untamed(vocal & DJ Cut)/Dubwise (12") 35

MIGHTY AVENGERS (JAMAICA)
66   Rymska RA 101   Scatter Shot (actually by Byron Lee & Dragonaires)/BYRON LEE: Like You Do (B-side
                                                           actually "No One" by Techniques) 30

MIGHTY AVENGERS (U.K.)
64   Decca F 11891   Hide Your Pride/Hey Senorita 18
64   Decca F 11962   So Much In Love/Sometime They Say 25
65   Decca F 12085   Blue Turns To Grey/I'm Lost Without You 25
65   Decca F 12198   (Walkin' Thru The) Sleepy City/Sir Edward And Lady Jane 35
(see also Andrew Oldham)

MIGHTY BABY
71   Blue Horizon 2096 003   Devil's Whisper/Virgin Spring 80
69   Head HDLS 6002   MIGHTY BABY (LP, gatefold sleeve, yellow label) 400
71   Blue Horizon 2931 001   A JUG OF LOVE (LP, with lyric insert) 650
71   Blue Horizon 2931 001   A JUG OF LOVE (LP) 400
84   Psycho PSYCHO 31   EGYPTIAN TOMB (LP, reissue of "Mighty Baby" in different sleeve) 30
(see also Action, Robin Scott, Habibiyya, Keith Christmas, Gary Farr, Stone's Masonry, Andy Roberts)

THEE MIGHTY CAESARS
86   Empire LWC 604   Ten Bears Of The Comanches/Baby What's Wrong (p/s) 15
86   Media Burn MB 5   Little By Little/The Swag/What You've Got/Cyclonic (12", p/s) 25
88   Swag SWG 001   She's Just Fifteen Years Old/The Swag (flexi in p/s with Pandora's Box fanzine) 18
95   Toe Rag RAG 1A   Billy B Childish/Dolli Bambi (Free single as FRAT SHACK, p/s) 8
16   Empire L WC 604   Ten Bears Of The Comanches/Baby What's Wrong? (lathe cut 7", 20 copies only) 30
85   Milkshakes NER - 0   S.T. (LP) 40
86   Milkshakes APOLL - 0   THEE CAESARS OF TRASH (LP) 20
86   Milkshakes PLAT - 0   ACROPOLIS NOW (LP) 35
86   Big Beat WIK45   BEWARE OF THE IDES OF MARCH (LP) 30
87   Hangman HANG 3 UP   DON'T GIVE ANY DINNER TO HENRY CHINASKI (LP) 50
87   Hangman HANG 7 UP   PUNK ROCK SHOWCASE (LP) 60
88   Crypt LP 014   ENGLISH PUNK ROCK EXPLOSION (LP) 15
87   Big Beat WIK 60   LIVE IN ROME (LP) 20
87   Ambassador AMBAS 2   WISE BLOOD (LP, colour sleeve) 30
89   Hangman HANG 26 UP   WISE BLOOD (LP, reissue, black and silver sleeve) 20
(see also Milkshakes, Prisoners, Billy Childish, Thee Headcoats)

MIGHTY DIAMONDS
75   Black Wax WAX13   I Need A Roof/Joe Joe Dub 15
75   Virgin VS 137   Have Mercy/Them Never Love Poor Marcus 12
75   Locks LOX 10   Back Weh (You No Mafia)/Mafia Dub 8
77   JAMA JAMA 014   Hey Girl/JUNIOR BYLES & I ROY: Fade Away (12") 20
79   Virgin Frontline FLS 122 12 Bodyguard/One Brother Short (12", p/s) 10
80   Greensleeves GRED 45   Gates Of Zion/SLY AND ROBBIE - Zion In Dub (12", green vinyl) 40
76   Virgin V 2052   RIGHT TIME (LP) 20
77   Virgin V 2078   ICE ON FIRE (LP) 15
79   Virgin Frontline FLD 6001   DEEPER ROOTS (LP, with bonus dub LP) 25
80   Mobiliser SRE 31   LEADER OF THE BLACK COUNTRY (LP) 20
(see also Diamonds)

MIGHTY DOUGLAS
60s   Jump Up JU 501   Laziest Man/Dance Me Lover 8
60s   Jump Up JU 508   Teacher Teacher/Split Me In Two 8
60s   Jump Up JU 509   Ugliness/My Wicked Boy Child 8

MIGHTY 'EM
73   Decca FR 13446   Jekyll And Hyde/What A Way To Go 35

MIGHTY ETHNICZ

			MINT VALUE £
MIGHTY ETHNICZ			
88	Good Times EB20	Freestyle/B Style (12")	30
MIGHTY FLEA & MICKEY BAKER			
72	Polydor 2058 328	Bloodshot Eyes/Charley Stone	6
73	Polydor 2460 185	LET THE GOOD TIMES ROLL (LP)	22
MIGHTY FLYERS			
74	Myrrh MYR 1016	LOW FLYING ANGELS (LP, with insert)	20
(see also Mick Abrahams)			
MIGHTY HARD			
70	Pye 7N 17878	Save The Life Of My Child/House Of The Rising Sun	30
MIGHTY MAYTONES			
76	Mango MAN 1010	Madness/Madness Version	6
78	GG's GG 029	Searching In Disco (with Trinity)/Madness In Disco (with U Brown) (12")	20
76	Burning Sounds BS 1002	MADNESS (LP)	25
78	Burning Sounds BS 1022	BOAT TO ZION (LP)	25
(see also Maytones)			
MIGHTY MEN			
62	Salvo SLO 1804	No Way Out/You Too Much (99 copies only)	30
MIGHTY MICRO			
79	Warner Bros. K18134	Replaced By A Micro Chip/Everything With Chips (no p/s)	20
MIGHTY MIGHTY			
86	Girlie GAY 1	Everybody Knows The Monkey/You're On My Mind (foldover p/s, poly bag)	10
87	Sha La La Ba Ba Ba Ba Ba 001	Throwaway (Throwaway Version)/CLOUDS: Jenny Nowhere (p/s, flexi)	10
87	Sha La La Ba Ba Ba Ba Ba 001	Throwaway (Throwaway Version)/CLOUDS: Jenny Nowhere (p/s, flexi, with Baby Honey Fanzine 1)	20
MIGHTY MO			
72	Columbia DB 8851	Ape Call/Heavy Bear	10
MIGHTY POWER			
67	Jump Up JU 513	You're Wasting Your Time/Smart Barbarian	8
MIGHTY SAM			
66	Stateside SS 534	Sweet Dreams/Good Humor Man	15
66	Stateside SS 544	Fannie Mae/Badmouthin'	15
68	Stateside SS 2076	When She Touches Me/Just Like Old Times	15
70	Soul City SC 115	Papa True Love/I Need A Lot Of Lovin'	25
70	Soul City SCM 004	MIGHTY SOUL (LP)	85
MIGHTY 7			
84	EMI 12PUSH 1	Push The Button (To The Beat)/Call Me (12")	100
84	EMI PUSH 1	Push The Button (To The Beat)/Call Me	40
MIGHTY SPARROW			
60	Kalypso XX 22	Mr. Herbert/Simpson	6
64	Jump Up JU 523	Village Ram/Pull Pistle Gang	10
68	NEMS 56-3558	Mr. Walker/Carnival In '68	6
69	Fab FAB 116	Mr. Walker/Jane	6
70	Fab FAB 147	I Don't Wanna Lose You/The Truth	6
60	Kalypso XXEP 1	THIS IS SPARROW (EP)	10
60	Kalypso XXEP 2	MAN, DIG THIS SPARROW (EP)	10
60	Kalypso XXEP 3	A PARTY WITH SPARROW (EP)	10
61	Kalypso XXEP 4	THIS IS THE SPARROW AGAIN (EP)	10
61	Kalypso XXEP 5	GREETINGS FROM SPARROW (EP)	10
62	Kalypso XXEP 6	SPARROW THE CONQUEROR (EP)	10
63	Island ILP 902	THE SLAVE (LP)	30
66	RCA RD 7516	SPARROW COME BACK (LP)	15
68	Melodisc MLPWI 12-146	CALYPSO CARNIVAL (LP)	25
68	Melodisc MLPWI 12-148	MR WALKER (LP)	30
72	Trojan TRL49	HOTTER THAN EVER (LP)	15
(see also King, Lord Melody)			
MIGHTY VIKINGS			
67	Island WI 3060	Do Re Mi/The Sound Of Music	35
67	Island WI 3074	Rockitty Fockitty/Give Me Back My Gal (both actually with Sammy Ismay)	35
MIGHTY RYEDERS			
18	Dynamite Cuts DYNAM7004/7005	Evil Vibrations/The Mighty Ryeders/Lovely/Everybody Groove (reissue, 2 x 7", p/s)	20
18	Dynamite Cuts DYNAM7006	Star Children/Help Us Spread The Message (reissue, p/s)	6
MIGIL FIVE			
64	Pye 7N 15645	Near You/Don't Wanna Go On Shaking	6
64	Pye 7N 15677	Boys And Girls/I Saw Your Picture	6
65	Pye 7N 15757	Just Behind The Rainbow/Seven Lonely Days	7
65	Pye 7N 15874	One Hundred Years/I'm In Love Again	8
67	Columbia DB 8196	Together/Superstition	20
68	Jay Boy BOY 4	If I Had My Way/Somebody's Stolen The Moon	6
64	Pye NEP 24191	MEET THE MIGIL FIVE (EP)	15
64	Pye NPL 18093	MOCKING BIRD HILL (LP)	30
(see also Migil Four, Mike Felix)			
MIGIL FOUR			
63	Pye 7N 15572	Maybe/Can't I?	7
(see also Migil Five)			
MIKA			
06	Casablanca MIKA 7001	Relax (Take It Easy)/Billy Brown (die-cut p/s with printed inner sleeve, 500 only)	12
MIKE & MODIFIERS			
62	Oriole CB 1775	I Found Myself A Brand New Baby/It's Too Bad	800

MIKE STUART SPAN

MINT VALUE £

MIKE STUART SPAN
66	Columbia DB 8066	Come On Over To Our Place/Still Nights	100
67	Columbia DB 8206	Dear/Invitation	80
68	Jewel JL 01	Children Of Tomorrow/Concerto Of Thoughts	500
68	Fontana TF 959	You Can Understand Me/Baubles And Bangles	25
93	117 CPAT 1171	EXPANSIONS: Second Production/Rescue Me/Remember The Times/World In My Head (EP)	15
95	Tenth Planet TP 014	TIMESPAN (LP, gatefold sleeve, numbered, 1,000 copies only)	25

(see also Leviathan, High Defenders, Tony's Defenders, High Broom)

MIKE & RICH
96	Rephlex CAT 027LP	EXPERT KNOB TWIDDLERS (2-LP)	40

(see also Aphex Twin, Caustic Window, Polygon Window, Q-Chastic, Kosmic Kommando, Tuss, U-Ziq)

MIKEY B
95	Vision VSN 004	So Wrong/So Much Love (12")	30

MIKI
69	RCA RCA 1782	Dear Auntie Mary/A Piece Of Heaven	7
69	RCA RCA 1844	Knight In White Armour/It's Easy To Say	8

(see also Miki Anthony)

BOBBY MILANO
55	Capitol CL 14252	A King Or A Slave/If You Cared	10
55	Capitol CL 14309	If Tears Could Bring You Back/Make Me A Present Of You	10

AMOS MILBURN
57	Vogue V 9064	Every Day Of The Week/Girl Of My Dreams (triangular centre)	150
57	Vogue V 9064	Every Day Of The Week/Girl Of My Dreams (round centre)	40
57	Vogue V 9069	Rum And Coca Cola/Soft Pillow (triangular centre)	150
57	Vogue V 9069	Rum And Coca Cola/Soft Pillow (triangular centre) (78)	85
57	Vogue V 9080	Thinking Of You Baby/If I Could Be With You (One Hour Tonight) (triangular centre)	150
57	Vogue V 9080	Thinking Of You Baby/If I Could Be With You (One Hour Tonight) (78)	35
60	Vogue V 9163	One Scotch, One Bourbon, One Beer/Bad, Bad Whiskey	100
57	Vogue VE 1-70102	ROCK AND ROLL (EP)	250

AMOS MILBURN JNR
63	London HLU 9795	Gloria/Look At Me Fool	20

MILDRED AND THE MICE
09	Third Man TMR 003	I Like My Mice (Dead)/Spider Bite (100 only, luminous vinyl)	40

PERCY MILEM
66	Stateside SS 566	Crying Baby, Baby, Baby/Call On Me	100
66	Stateside SS 566	Crying Baby, Baby, Baby/Call On Me (DJ copy)	150

ARTHUR MILES
90	Ffrr 148	Trippin On Your Love/Helping Hand	12

BUDDY MILES (EXPRESS)
68	Mercury MF 1065	Train (Parts 1 & 2)	10
69	Mercury 20137 SMCL	EXPRESSWAY TO YOUR SKULL (LP)	20
69	Mercury 20163 SMCL	ELECTRIC CHURCH (LP)	20
70	Mercury 6338 016	THEM CHANGES (LP)	15
71	Mercury 6338 028	WE GOT TO LIVE TOGETHER (LP)	15

(see also Electric Flag, Jimi Hendrix, Carlos Santana & Buddy Miles)

DICK & SUE MILES
79	Sweet Folk & Country SFA 106	THE DUNMOW FLITCH (LP)	18

GARRY MILES
60	London HLG 9155	Look For A Star/Afraid Of Love	10
60	London REG 1264	LOOK FOR A STAR (EP)	25

JOHN MILES
70	Orange OAS 508	Why Don't You Love Me?/If I Could See Through	20
73	Orange OAS 213	One Minute Every Hour/Hollywood Queen (DJ Copy)	60
73	Orange OAS 213	One Minute Every Hour/Hollywood Queen	70
78	Decca FR 13757	No Hard Feelings/Nice Man Jack	6
79	Decca FR 13827	Can't Keep A Good Man Down/Sweet Lorraine	6

(see also Influence)

LENNY MILES
61	Top Rank JAR 546	Don't Believe Him Donna/Invisible	30

LIZZIE MILES
56	HMV 7EG 8178	THE BLUES THEY SANG (EP, 1 side by Billy Young, both with Jelly Roll Morton)	20

ROBERT MILES
96	Deconstruction 74321429741	DREAMLAND (2-LP, stickered sleeve)	75

MILITAIRES
66	Airborne 0009	I Need You/Maybe	15

MILITANT BARRY
79	Manic PFU 1805	Pistol Boy/Pistol Version/Green Valley (no p/s)	8
79	Manic PFU 1105	Pistol Boy/Pistol Version/Green Valley (12")	12
77	Conflict COND 2000	Idi Amin Disco/Blood Up/Free Black People (12", die-cut p/s)	15
78	Conflict COND 2003	Ambition/Can't Stop Me (12")	15
79	Vista Sounds STLP 1012	GREEN VALLEY (LP)	30

(see also Juliet & Grace)

MILK & COOKIES
75	Island WIP.6222	Little Lost And Innocent/Good Friends (as Milk 'n' Cookies)	12

MILK FROM CHELTENHAM
83	Its War Boys £3	TRIPTYCH OF POISONERS (LP, silkscreened sleeve red or blue vinyl)	50

MILKSHAKES
82	Havasong BILK-O	Please Don't Tell My Baby/It's You (p/s)	25

MILK TEETH

			MINT VALUE £
83	Upright UP 6	Soldiers Of Love/Shimmy Shimmy (p/s)	12
84	Big Beat NS 94	Brand New Cadillac/Commanche/Jezebel/Jaguar And Thunderbird (p/s)	12
84	Big Beat SW 105	Ambassadors Of Love/No More/Gringles And Groyles Again/ Remarkable (p/s)	12
86	Empire UXF 228	Let Me Love You/She Tells Me She Loves Me (p/s)	15
83	Big Beat NED 4	14 RHYTHM AND BEAT GREATS (LP, red, lilac and blue sleeves)	20
83	Upright UPLP 1	AFTER SCHOOL SESSION (LP, laminated sleeve)	20
84	Milkshake GARB-O	THEE KNIGHTS OF TRASH (LP)	30
84	Milkshake HARP-O	NOTHING CAN STOP THESE MEN (LP)	20
84	Big Beat WIK 22	SHOWCASE (LP)	25
85	Big Beat WIK 30	THEY CAME, THEY SAW, THEY CONQUERED (LP)	20
86	Media Burn MB 6	THE 107 TAPES (2-LP)	25
86	Milkshake MILK-O	TALKING 'BOUT MILKSHAKES (LP, with poster)	40
86	Milkshake MILK-O	TALKING 'BOUT MILKSHAKES (LP, without poster)	25
87	Hangman HANG 11 UP	LIVE FROM CHATHAM (LP)	18
87	Hangman HANG 1 UP	REVENGE - TRASH FROM THE VAULT (THE LEGENDARY MISSING 9th ALBUM) (LP)	25
92	Vinyl Japan ASKLP 10	STILL TALKING 'BOUT (LP)	25
05	Damaged Goods DAMGOOD 249LP	IN GERMANY (LP)	15

(see also Prisoners/Milkshakes, Pop Rivits, Len Bright Combo, Billy Childish, Thee Headcoats, Mickey & Ludella, Masonics)

MILK TEETH
74	Bead Records BEAD 1	A TOUCH OF THE SUN (LP)	150

MILLENIUM
84	Guardian GRC 2163	MILLENIUM (LP)	20

MILLER
65	Oak RGJ 190	Baby I've Got News For You/The Girl With The Castle	300
65	Columbia DB 7235	Baby I Got News For You/The Girl With The Castle	400

(see also Big Boy Pete, Peter Jay & Jaywalkers, Pete Miller, News)

BETTY MILLER
59	Top Rank JAR 115	Pearly Gates/Old Time Religion	6
59	Top Rank JAR 127	Jack O' Diamonds/(It Took) One Kiss	8

BOB MILLER & MILLERMEN
57	Columbia DB 4017	The Scamp/The Sack Line (as Bob Miller Music)	6
59	Fontana H 181	Dig This!/The Poacher	10
60	Fontana H 284	Night Theme/Last Date	10
61	Parlophone R 4779	Trouble Shooter/Hootin'	10
61	Parlophone R 4854	The "Oliver" Twist/That's It	7
65	Mercury MF 947	Uptown And Downtown/Carnaby Street Parade	10
65	Polydor 56005	6-5 Special/Dick Van Dyke Theme	10
66	Columbia DB 7877	Get Smart/Bony's Blues (as Bob Miller & His Millermen)	8
72	Spiral DIT 3	Doin' The Slosh/Sloshing Around	8

BOBBIE MILLER
65	Decca F 12064	What A Guy/You Went Away	40
65	Decca F 12252	Every Beat Of My Heart/Tomorrow	15
66	Decca F 12354	Everywhere I Go/IAN STEWART & RAILROADERS: Stu-Ball	80

(see also Mongrels, Rolling Stones)

BRANKO MILLER
68	CBS 3955	Candy/Today Is Better Than Yesterday (Branko Miler on demos)	8

CHUCK MILLER
56	Capitol CL 14543	Rogue River Valley/No Baby Like You	15
57	Mercury 7MT 153	The Auctioneer/Me Head's In De Barrel	20
58	Mercury 7MT 215	Down The Road A-Piece/Mad About Her Blues	100
60	Mercury ZEP 10058	GOING GOING GONE (EP)	50

COUNT PRINCE (MILLER)
70	Downtown DT 460	I'm Gonna Keep On Trying/Girl I Need You (as Count Prince)	12

(see also Jimmy James & The Vagabonds)

FRANKIE MILLER
59	Melodisc MEL 1519	True Blue/Black Land Farmer	15
59	Melodisc MEL 1529	Poppin' Johnnie/Family Man	15
60	Melodisc MEL 1552	Rain, Rain/Baby Rocked Her Dolly	15
62	Top Rank JKP 3013	COUNTRY MUSIC (EP)	20
64	Ember CW 107	THE TRUE COUNTRY STYLE OF FRANKIE MILLER (LP)	20

GARY MILLER
64	Pye 7N 15698	Aqua Marina/Stingray	12
57	Nixa NPL 18008	MEET MISTER MILLER (LP)	15

GLEN MILLER
67	Doctor Bird DB 1089	Where Is The Love/Funky Broadway	400
68	Doctor Bird DB 1128	Rocksteady Party(A-side with Booker T & MGs)/Book Of Memories	50

JACOB MILLER
75	Sound Tracs SK5	Dock Of The Bay/Version	8
76	Neville King NK 02	Tired Fe Lick Weed In A Bush/Chillum In A Gully	12
78	Hawkeye HD 009	Each One Teach One/Matthews Lane Dub/TETRACK: Let's Get It Together/Black Arts Dub (12")	40
82	Greensleeves GREL 166	WHO SAY JAH NO DREAD (LP)	15

JAMES MILLER
70	Trojan TR 7804	You Got To Me/2001	12

JIMMY MILLER & (NEW) BARBECUES
57	Columbia DB 4006	Sizzlin' Hot/Free Wheelin' Baby (as Jimmy Miller & Barbecues)	60
58	Columbia DB 4081	Jelly Baby/Cry, Baby, Cry (as Jimmy Miller & New Barbecues)	60
58	Columbia DB 4081	Jelly Baby/Cry, Baby, Cry (as Jimmy Miller & New Barbecues) (78)	30

(see also Station Skiffle Group)

JODY MILLER
64	Capitol CL 15356	The Fever/In My Room	15
65	Capitol CL 15404	Silver Threads And Golden Needles/Melody For Robin	6
65	Capitol CL 15415	Home Of The Brave/This Is The Life	15
65	Capitol T 2416	HOME OF THE BRAVE (LP, mono)	20
65	Capitol (S) T 2416	HOME OF THE BRAVE (LP, stereo)	25
66	Capitol T 2446	JODY MILLER SINGS THE GREAT HITS OF BUCK OWENS (LP, mono)	20
66	Capitol (S) T 2446	JODY MILLER SINGS THE GREAT HITS OF BUCK OWENS (LP, stereo)	25

KENNY MILLER
65	Stateside SS 405	Restless/Take My Tip	150

MITCH MILLER
60	Philips PB 1146	The Guns Of Navarone/Alouette March	6
62	CBS AAG 118	The Longest Day (Vocal Version)/The Longest Day (Instrumental Version)	6
63	CBS AAG 158	The Great Escape March/It's A Darn Good Thing	7

MR MILLER
69	Jackpot JP 707	Feel It/LYN BECKFORD: Kiss Me Quick (actually by Keeling Beckford)	120

NED MILLER
63	Capitol CL 15301	Go On Back You Fool/Dark Moon	8
63	London HL 9728	Just Before Dawn/Mona Lisa	7
63	London HL 9766	Another Fool Like Me/Magic Moon	6
64	London HL 9838	Sunday Morning Tears/Big Love	7
64	London HL 9873	Invisible Tears/Old Restless Ocean	7
64	London HL 9937	Do What You Do Do Well/Dusty Guitar	6
63	Capitol EAP1 20492	NED MILLER (EP)	15
63	London RE 1382	NED MILLER (EP)	15
63	London HA 8272	FROM A JACK TO A KING (LP)	25

PAULETTE MILLER
79	Burning Rockers PR 157	Woman In Love/In Love Dub (12")	20

PETE MILLER
97	Tenth Planet TP 030	SUMMERLAND (LP, numbered, 1000 only)	15

(see also Miller, Big Boy Pete)

RUSS MILLER
57	HMV POP 391	I Sit In My Window/Wait For Me, My Love	50

STEPHEN MILLER & LOL COXHILL
73	Caroline C 1503	COXHILL MILLER (LP, black/white/red 'Twin' label)	25
74	Caroline C 1507	THE STORY SO FAR ... OH REALLY? (LP)	30

(see also Lol Coxhill)

STEVE MILLER BAND
68	Capitol CL 15539	Sittin' In Circles/Roll With It	15
68	Capitol CL 15564	Living In The U.S.A./Quicksilver Girl	15
69	Capitol CL 15604	My Dark Hour/Song For Our Ancestors	15
69	Capitol CL 15618	Little Girl/Don't Let Nobody Turn You Around	7
70	Capitol CL 15656	Going To The Country/Never Kill Another Man	6
68	Capitol (S)T 2920	CHILDREN OF THE FUTURE (LP, 'rainbow rim' label)	50
69	Capitol (S)T 2984	SAILOR (LP, 'rainbow rim' label)	40
69	Capitol E-ST 184	BRAVE NEW WORLD (LP, mono)	60
70	Capitol E-ST 184	BRAVE NEW WORLD (LP, stereo)	40
70	Capitol E-ST 331	YOUR SAVING GRACE (LP)	20
77	Mercury 9286 455	BOOK OF DREAMS (LP)	15

(see also Boz Scaggs)

SUZI MILLER
54	Decca F 10389	Happy Days And Lonely Nights/Tell Me, Tell Me (with Johnston Brothers)	20
54	Decca F 10423	Two Step, Side Step (with Johnston Brothers)/ Hang My Heart On A Christmas Tree (with Keynotes)	10
55	Decca F 10475	Tweedlee Dee (with Johnston Brothers)/That's All I Want From You	15
55	Decca F 10512	Dance With Me Henry (Wallflower) (with Johnston Brothers)/ Butterfingers (with Marilyn Sisters)	15
55	Decca F 10593	The Banjo's Back In Town/Go On By	10
56	Decca F 10677	Ay-Ay-Senores/Reckless	10
56	Decca F 10722	Get Up! Get Up! (You Sleepy Head)/The Key To My Heart	7

(see also Johnston Brothers)

STEVE MILLER TRIO
86	Matchless MR 09	MILLERS TALE (LP)	25

MILLER'S THUMB
76	Tradition TSC 3	SITTING ON THE RIGHT SIDE (LP, 100 copies only)	20

MILLIE (SMALL)
63	Fontana TF 425	Don't You Know/Until You're Mine	10
64	Fontana TF 449	My Boy Lollipop/Something's Gotta Be Done	6
64	Fontana TF 479	Sweet William/Oh Henry	7
64	Fontana TF 502	I Love The Way You Love/Bring It On Home To Me	8
64	Cadbury's BNVT 01F	The Bournvita Song/Three Nights A Week (p/s)	25
65	Fontana TF 515	I've Fallen In Love With A Snowman/What Am I Living For	10
65	Fontana TF 529	See You Later Alligator/Chilly Kisses	12
65	Fontana TF 591	My Street/It's Too Late	10
65	Fontana TF 617	Bloodshot Eyes/Tongue Tied	18
65	Brit WI 1002	My Street/A Mixed Up, Fickle, Moody, Self-Centred, Spoiled Kind Of Boy	15
66	Fontana TF 740	Killer Joe/Carry Go Bring Come (as Millie Small)	8
67	Fontana TF 796	Chicken Feed/Wings Of A Dove (as Millie Small)	8
67	Island WIP 6021	You Better Forget/I Am In Love	10
68	Fontana TF 948	When I Dance With You/Hey Mr. Love	10

Spike MILLIGAN

MINT VALUE £

69	Decca F 12948	Readin' Writin' Arithmetic/I Want You Never To Stop	12
70	Pyramid PYR 6080	My Love And I/Tell Me About Yourself	10
70	Trojan TR 7744	Enoch Power/Mayfair	25
70	President PT 306	We're All In A Zoo/Piccaninny Man	15
70	Trojan TR 7801	Honey Hush/Sunday Morning	10
61	Blue Beat BBEP 302	MILLIE (EP, with Little Roy & Owen Gray; with sleeve)	140
61	Blue Beat BBEP 302	MILLIE (EP, with Little Roy & Owen Gray; without sleeve)	20
64	Fontana TE 17425	MY BOY LOLLIPOP (EP)	50
66	Island IEP 705	MILLIE AND HER BOYFRIENDS (EP)	40
64	Fontana TL 5220	MORE MILLIE (LP, mono)	40
64	Fontana (S)TL 5220	MORE MILLIE (LP, stereo)	50
65	Fontana TL 5276	MILLIE SINGS FATS DOMINO (LP)	60
67	Island ILP 953	THE BEST OF MILLIE SMALL (LP)	50
69	Trojan TTL 17	MILLIE AND HER BOYFRIENDS (LP)	20
69	Trojan TTL 49	THE BEST OF MILLIE SMALL (LP, reissue)	15
70	Trojan TBL 108	TIME WILL TELL (LP)	20

(see also Jackie & Millie, Roy & Millie, Owen & Millie)

SPIKE MILLIGAN

58	Parlophone R 4406	Wish I Knew/Will I Find My Love Today?	12
61	Parlophone R 4839	I'm Walking Out With A Mountain/The Sewers Of The Strand	8
62	Parlophone R 4891	Wormwood Scrubs Tango/Postman's Knock	8
69	Parlophone R 5771	The Q.5 Piano Tune/Ning, Nang, Nong	10
61	Parlophone PMC 1148	MILLIGAN PRESERVED (LP, mono)	15
61	Parlophone PCS 18	MILLIGAN PRESERVED (LP, stereo)	20

(see also Famous Eccles)

MARY MILLINGTON

| 99 | Trunk/Bonk B 01 | COME PLAY ME (EP) | 60 |

SIR EUGENE MILLINGTON-DRAKE

| 65 | Decca LK 4659 | MIXED GRILL (LP) | 60 |

JEB MILLION

| 86 | WEA YZ 82 | Speed Up My Heartbeat/Who Sent You (p/s) | 6 |
| 86 | WEA YZ 82T | Speed Up My Heartbeat (Extended Mix)/Speed Up My Heartbeat/ Who Sent You (12", p/s) | 12 |

MILLIONAIRES (IRELAND)

| 66 | Decca F 12468 | Wishing Well/Chatterbox | 100 |

MILLIONAIRES (U.S.)

| 67 | Mercury 6052301 | Never For Me/If I Had You Babe (paper labels) | 35 |
| 67 | Mercury 6052301 | Never For Me/If I Had You Babe (plastic labels) | 15 |

MILLIONS

| 73 | Duke DU 154 | Murmuring/TOMMY McCOOK & BOBBY ELLIS: Murmuring - Version | 10 |
| 73 | Downtown DT 516 | Love Of Jah Jah Children/Jah Jah Version | 30 |

BARBARA MILLS

65	Hickory 45-1323	Queen Of Fools/Make It Last, Take Your Time	400
65	Hickory 45-1323	Queen Of Fools/Make It Last, Take Your Time (DJ copy)	500
65	Hickory 45-1392	Try/Let's Make A Memory	15
75	London HLE 10491	Queen Of Fools/Make It Last, Take Your Time (reissue)	10
79	Inferno HEAT 9	Queen Of Fools/Make It Last, Take Your Time (reissue)	8

BETTY LOU MILLS

| 60s | Shal SHAL 1 | Where Is My Star/Rock Him | 30 |
| 60 | Pilgrim JLPS 101 | EVERYWHERE I LOOK (LP) | 25 |

GARRY MILLS

59	Top Rank JAR 119	Hey Baby (You're Pretty)/You Alone	20
59	Top Rank JAR 219	Seven Little Girls Sitting In The Back Seat/The Night You Became 17	8
59	Oriole CB 1529	Living Lord/Big Story Breaking	10
59	Oriole CB 1530	I Am The Great I Am/Rhythm In Religion	10
60	Top Rank JAR 301	Running Bear/Teen Angel	7
60	Top Rank JAR 336	Look For A Star/Footsteps	7
60	Top Rank JAR 393	Comin' Down With Love/I'm Gonna Find Out	12
60	Top Rank JAR 500	Top Teen Baby/Don't Cheat Me Again (in p/s)	10
60	Top Rank JAR 500	Top Teen Baby/Don't Cheat Me Again	6
61	Top Rank JAR 542	Who's Gonna Take You Home Tonight?/Christina	7
61	Decca F 11358	I'll Step Down/Your Way Is My Way	10
61	Decca F 11383	Bless You/Footprints In The Sand	15
61	Decca F 11415	Treasure Island/Sad Little Girl	15
62	Decca F 11471	Never Believed In Love/Save A Dream For Me	15

(see also Gary & Ariels)

HAYLEY MILLS

| 61 | Decca F 21396 | Let's Get Together/Cobbler Cobbler | 6 |
| 62 | Decca LK 4426 | LET'S GET TOGETHER (LP) | 15 |

HAYLEY MILLS & EDDIE HODGES

| 63 | HMV POP 1179 | Flitterin'/Beautiful Beulah | 7 |

(see also Eddie Hodges)

JEFF MILLS

| 61 | Ember EMB S 133 | Daddy's Home/TIMMY REYNOLDS: Lullaby Of Love | 70 |

RUDY MILLS

67	Island WI 3092	A Long Story/BOBBY ELLIS: Now We Know (actually. with Desmond Miles Seven)	40
68	Island WI 3136	I'm Trapped/BOBBY ELLIS & CRYSTALLITES: Dollar A Head	55
69	Big Shot BI 509	John Jones/A Place Called Happiness	70
69	Explosion EX 2007	Lemi Li/Goody Goody	20
69	Crab CRAB 20	Tears On My Pillow/I'm Trapped	20

Stephanie MILLS

MINT VALUE £

| 69 | Crab CRAB 24 | A Heavy Load/Wholesale Love | 60 |
| 69 | Pama SECO 12 | REGGAE HITS (LP) | 150 |

STEPHANIE MILLS
74	Paramount PARA 3050	I Knew It Was Love/The Passion And The Pain	6
76	Tamla Motown TMG 1020	This Empty Place/I See You For The First Time (unissued)	50
76	Tamla Motown STML 12017	FOR THE FIRST TIME (LP)	20

MILLS BROTHERS
54	Brunswick 05325	How Blue?/Why Do I Keep Lovin' You?	7
55	Brunswick 05439	Smack Dab In The Middle/Opus One	7
55	Brunswick 05488	That's All I Ask Of You/Suddenly There's A Valley	7
55	Brunswick 05487	Mi Muchacha (Little Girl)/Gum Drop	10
56	Brunswick 05606	That's Right/Don't Get Caught	8
58	London HLD 8553	Get A Job/I Found A Million Dollar Baby	15
60	London HLD 9169	I Got You/Highways Are Happy Ways	8

(see also Louis Armstrong)

MILLWALL F.C.
| 72 | Decca F1 3350 | Millwall/The Ballad Of Harry Cripps | 8 |

RONNIE MILSAP
66	Pye International 7N 25392	Ain't No Soul (Left In These Old Shoes)/Another Branch From The Same Old Tree	60
66	Pye International 7N 25392	Ain't No Soul (Left In These Old Shoes)/Another Branch From The Same Old Tree (DJ copy)	100
69	Pye International 7N 25490	Denver/Nothing Is As Good As It Used To Be	6
72	Wand WN 26	Ain't No Soul (Left In These Old Shoes)/Another Branch From The Same Old Tree (reissue)	10

RONNIE MILSAP/ROSCOE ROBINSON
| 66 | Pye Intl. NEP 44078 | SOUL SENSATIONS (EP) | 50 |

NATHAN MILSTEIN
62	Columbia SAX 2518	VIVALDI: FOUR CONCERTI (LP, stereo, turquoise/silver label)	500
63	Columbia SAX 2563	MUSIC OF OLD RUSSIA (LP, stereo, red label)	450
65	Columbia SAX 5254	MOZART VIOLIN CONCERTOS (LP, stereo, red label)	100
66	Columbia SAX 5275	PROKOFIEV: THE TWO CONCERTOS FOR VIOLIN & ORCHESTRA (LP, stereo, red label)	350
66	Columbia SAX 5285	BACH: TWO VIOLIN CONCERTOS/VIVALDI: TWO VIOLIN CONCERTOS (LP, Stereo)	400

JOHNNY MILTON & CONDORS
| 64 | Decca F 11862 | A Girl Named Sue/Somethin' Else (as Johnny Milton & Condors) | 8 |
| 64 | Fontana TF 488 | Cry Baby/Hurt | 6 |

(see also Symbols)

REGINALD MILTON & THE SOUL JETS
| 06 | Funk 45 FUNK45 030 | Clap Your Hands/Jickle Jeek Beat (reissue) | 10 |

TED MILTON
| 79 | Echt! ECHT! ONE | Confessions Of An Aeroplane Farter/I Don't Want To Go Poo Poo! (7" in 12" p/s) | 50 |

MILVA
63	Oriole CB 1899	I Can't Believe You're Leaving Me/Loneliness Of Autumn	8
64	Oriole CB 1952	I'll Set My Love To Music/Come Sempre	8
67	Major Minor MM 510	Love Is A Feeling/Seasons Of Love	6

MILWAUKEE COASTERS
| 68 | Pama PMLP 2 | WEST COAST ROCK'N'ROLL 1968 (LP) | 15 |

ILHAN MIMAROGLU
| 69 | Turnabout TV34177S | ELECTRONIC MUSIC III (LP) | 20 |

GARNET MIMMS (& ENCHANTERS)
63	United Artists UP 1033	Cry Baby/Don't Change Your Heart (with Enchanters)	25
63	United Artists UP 1038	Baby Don't You Weep/For Your Precious Love (with Enchanters)	20
64	United Artists UP 1048	Tell Me Baby/Anytime You Want Me (with Enchanters)	25
65	United Artists UP 1090	It Was Easier To Hurt Her/So Close	30
66	United Artists UP 1130	I'll Take Good Care Of You/Looking For You	100
66	United Artists UP 1130	I'll Take Good Care Of You/Looking For You (DJ copy)	200
66	United Artists UP 1147	It's Been Such A Long Way Home/Thinkin'	20
66	United Artists UP 1153	My Baby/It Won't Hurt Half As Much	25
66	United Artists UP 1172	All About Love/The Truth Hurts	20
67	United Artists UP 1181	Roll With The Punches/Only Your Love	25
67	United Artists UP 1186	As Long As I Have You/Yesterday	200
68	Verve VS 569	I Can Hear My Baby Crying/Stop And Think It Over	20
68	Verve VS 569	I Can Hear My Baby Crying/BILL MEDLEY: That Lucky Old Sun (mispress)	10
68	Verve VS 574	We Can Find That Love/Can You Top This	35
76	United Artists REM 403	REMEMBER GARNET MIMMS (EP)	10
63	United Artists ULP 1067	CRY BABY AND 11 OTHER HITS (LP, with Enchanters)	125
66	United Artists (S)ULP 1145	WARM AND SOULFUL (LP)	70
67	United Artists (S)ULP 1174	LIVE (LP, as Garnet Mimms & Senate)	60

MINA
| 60 | Oriole CB 1600 | This World We Live In/Please Don't Leave Me | 60 |
| 61 | Oriole EP 7050 | IL CIELO IN UNA STANZA (EP) | 80 |

MIND OVER MATTER
| 70 | Haflex HF 01 | Sunrise/Enter The Dragon | 40 |

MINDBENDERS
66	Fontana TF 697	Can't Live With You, Can't Live Without You/One Fine Day	8
66	Fontana TF 731	Ashes To Ashes/You Don't Know About Love	7
66	Fontana TF 780	I Want Her, She Wants Me/The Morning After	18
67	Fontana TF 806	We'll Talk About It Tomorrow/Far Across Town	10
67	Fontana TF 869	The Letter/My New Day And Age	10
67	Fontana TF 877	Schoolgirl/Coming Back	40
68	Fontana TF 910	Blessed Are The Lonely/Yellow Brick Road	20

MINDSEYE

MINT VALUE £

68	Fontana TF 961	Uncle Joe, The Ice Cream Man/The Man Who Loved Trees	15
69	Fontana H 1026	A Groovy Kind Of Love/Ashes To Ashes (p/s)	6
66	Fontana TL 5324	THE MINDBENDERS (LP, mono)	45
66	Fontana (S)TL 5324	THE MINDBENDERS (LP, stereo)	55
67	Fontana (S)TL 5403	WITH WOMAN IN MIND (LP)	60

(see also Wayne Fontana & Mindbenders, Hotlegs, Lulu)

MINDSEYE
82	Man 1	No One Else/Don't Stop/Risk (no p/s)	15

SAL MINEO
57	Philips JK 1024	Start Movin' (In My Direction)/Love Affair (jukebox issue)	20
58	Fontana H 118	Little Pigeon/Cuttin' In	20
58	Fontana H 135	Seven Steps To Love/A Couple Of Crazy Kids	10
58	Fontana TFL 5004	SAL (LP)	30

SEXTON MING
88	Hangman HANG-1-UP	OLD HORSE OF THE NATION (LP)	15
90	Hangman HANG 36 UP	BIRDS WITH TEETH (LP)	15
98	Hangman's Daughter HANG 018UP	6 MORE MILES TO THE GRAVEYARD (LP)	18

(see also Billy Childish etc.etc. etc.)

SEXTON MING (& HIS DIAMOND GUSSETS)
96	D. Goods DAMGOOD 71	I'm In Love With Danny Edwards/Break His Spirit/Son Of Tractor Nits (p/s)	8

CHARLES/CHARLIE MINGUS
56	Vogue LDE 178	CHARLIE MINGUS PRESENTS JAZZ WORKSHOP VOL. 2 (10" LP)	40
59	Parlophone PMC 1092	EAST COASTING (LP)	40
59	Philips BBL 7352	MINGUS AH HUM (LP)	80
60	Atlantic 587 166	REINCARNATION OF A LOVEBIRD (LP)	40
60	London Jazz LTZ-K 15194	BLUES AND ROOTS (LP, also stereo SAH-K 6087)	50
62	Atlantic SD 8005	CHARLES MINGUS PRESENTS CHARLES MINGUS (LP, U.K. issue of U.S. LP)	30
62	United Artists ULP 1004	JAZZ PORTRAITS (LP)	25
62	London HA-K/SH-K 8007	OH YEAH (LP, by Charlie Mingus & Jazz Group)	40
63	RCA RD/SF 7514	TIJUANA MOODS (LP)	30
63	Vocalion LAE 543	CHAZZ (LP)	40
64	HMV CLP 1694	THE BLACK SAINT AND THE SINNER LADY (LP)	40
65	United Artists ULP 1068	TOWN HALL CONCERT (LP)	30
65	Vocalion LAEF/SEAF 591	CHARLIE MINGUS QUINTET WITH MAX ROACH (LP)	30
65	HMV CLP 1742	MINGUS, MINGUS, MINGUS (LP, also stereo CSD 1545)	35
65	HMV CLP 1796	MINGUS PLAYS PIANO (LP)	30
65	Atlantic ATL/SAL 5019	TONIGHT AT NOON (LP)	30
66	Realm RM 211	JAZZ COMPOSERS WORKSHOP (NO. 1) (LP)	30
66	CBS (S)BPG 62261	MINGUS DYNASTY (LP)	30
68	Atlantic 587131	PITHECANTTHROPUS ERECTUS (LP)	30

MINI DRESSES
14	Box Bedroom Rebels BBR12	MINI DRESSES EP (p/s, insert, numbered)	15

MINIM
67	Polydor 582 011	WRAPPED IN A UNION JACK (LP)	30

MINIMAL MAN
93	Guerrila GRRR 54	MINIMAL MAN EP (12")	15
01	Vinyl Classics VC 02	Treatment Fee (Remixes) (12")	20

MINISTRY
92	Sire W 0096	Jesus Built My Hotrod/T.V. Song (p/s)	15
83	Arista 205 306	WORK FOR LOVE (LP)	15
89	Sire 926 004 1	THE MIND IS A TERRIBLE THING TO TASTE (LP)	15
92	Sire WX 481	ΚΕΦΑΛΗΞΘ (10" LP, limited edition)	25

MINISTRY OF SOUND
66	Decca F 12449	White Collar Worker/Back Seat Driver	40

MINNY POPS
81	Factory FAC 31	MINNY POPS EP: Dolphin Spurt/Goddess	10
82	Factory FAC 57	Secret Story/Island	15

KYLIE MINOGUE
SINGLES
89	PWL PWLT 35R	Hand On Your Heart (Heartache Mix)/Hand On Your Heart (Dub mix) Just Wanna Love You (12", with stickered p/s)	30
89	PWL PWLT 42R	Wouldn't Change A Thing (Espagna Mix)/Wouldn't Change A Thing (7" Mix)/It's No Secret (Extended) (12", stickered p/s)	20
91	PWL PWLP 72	What Do I Have To Do (New Mix)/What Do I Have To Do (Instrumental) (stickered p/s, with postcards)	15
91	PWL PWLT 72R	What Do I Have To Do (Between The Sheets Mix) (12", withdrawn, no p/s)	100
91	PWL PWL P81	Shocked (DNA 7" Mix)/Shocked (Harding & Curnow 7" Mix) (picture disc)	15
91	PWL PWLT204R	Word Is Out (Summer Breeze Remix) (1-sided 12" Limited Edition with etched Kylie autograph on other side, p/s)	20
97	DeCon. 7432 1517257	Some Kind Of Bliss/Love Takes Over Me (numbered limited edition 7", die-cut p/s)	30

ALBUMS
88	PWL HFD 4	KYLIE (DAT)	150
90	PWL HFL 18	RHYTHM OF LOVE (LP, gold leaf sleeve, 100 only)	80
98	30DeCon. 74321 58715 1	MIXES (3xLP, inner sleeves, pink silhouette Kylie outer p/s)	20
10	Parlophone 6429051	APHRODITE (LP)	60
12	Parlophone PO15 8611	THE ABBEY ROAD SESSIONS (2-LP, CD, inners and booklet)	60
15	Parlophone 0825640048	KYLIE CHRISTMAS (LP, white vinyl)	100
15	PWL KYLIE 1 X	KYLIE (LP, reissue,, picture disc, 2-CD and DVD)	80
15	PWL KYLIE 3 X	RHYTHM OF LOVE (LP, reissue, picture disc, 2-CD and DVD)	100

MINOR CLASSICS

MINT VALUE £

15	PWL KYLIE 2 X	ENJOY YOURSELF (LP, reissue, picture disc, 2-CD and DVD)	60
15	PWL KYLIE 4 X	LET'S GET TO IT (LP, reissue, picture disc, 2-CD and DVD)	200
17	Parlophone 0190295846428	FEVER (LP, white vinyl, 'Sainsburys' sticker)	50
18	Parlophone 0190295680855	LIGHT YEARS (2-LP, blue vinyl, 'Sainsburys' sticker)	40

PROMOS

94	DeConstruction KM 100	KYLIE MINOGUE (CD, promo, gatefold sl. in lilac slipcase with silver lettering)	50
88	PWL (no cat. no.)	Made In Heaven (3:26) PWL 1-track in-house promo cassette, custom PWL logo inlay typled/stickered, 1 only)	30
90	PWL PWLT 56R	Better The Devil You Know (KC Cohen 'US' Remix) (1-sided 12" promo, withdrawn, die-cut sleeve, 50 only)	30
91	PWL PWLT 72R	What Do I Have To Do (Between The Sheets Mix) (1-sided 12" promo, withdrawn die-cut sleeve)	30
91	PWL ZR-A1	Keep On Pumpin' It (12" white label issued under pseudonym of 'Angel K', includes Angelic Remix' & 'Astral Flight Mix', handwritten/stamped labels, Some with 'I Guess I Like It' titles. Die-cut sleeve)	30
91	PWL (no cat. no.)	I Guess I Like It Like That (12" 1-sided white label issued under pseudonym of 'Angel K', includes 'Extended/Album Version', 200 only)	20
91	PWL ANGEL-2	Do You Dare (12" white label issued under pseudonym of 'Angel K', includes NRG Mix' & 'New Rave Mix', handwritten labels, die cut sleeve, 100 only)	20
92	PWL PWLT 227	Finer Feelings (Brothers In Rhythm 12" Mix)/Closer (Pleasure Mix) ('Black Diamond' limited promo 12", black diamond label, die cut sleeve)	10
92	PWL PWLT 257	Celebration (Have A Party Mix)/Let's Get To It (Album Version) ('Black Diamond' limited promo 12", Christmas "leaving PWL" promo p/s, black Diamond label)	25
94	DeCon. 21 227477 JB	Confide In Me (Radio Mix)/(Truth Mix) (7" jukebox issue, no p/s)	10
94	DeCon. 21 246577 JB	Put Yourself In My Place (Radio Mix)/(All Star Mix) (7" jukebox issue, no p/s)	15
94	DeCon. 21 293617 JB	Where Is The Feeling? (BIR Bish Bosh Mix Edit)/(BIR Dolphin Mix) (7" jukebox issue, no p/s)	10
95	DeConstruction FEEL2	Where Is The Feeling? (BIR Dolphin Mix)/(Morales Club Mix) (12", die-cut sleeve, limited quantities)	30
95	DeConstruction FEEL3	Where Is The Feeling? (Da Klubb Feelin' Mix)/(Aphroheadz Powerlite Mix)/(Three Rad Vid Clash Mix) (12", promo, no p/s, 200 only)	25
95	Deconstruction TIME1	Time Will Pass You By (Paul Masterson's 'Wand Silver Screen Remix') (1-sided 12" White Label, handwritten labels, unreleased mix, withdrawn, 20 only)	40
97	DeConstruction DID2	Did It Again (Trouser Enthusiasts' Goddess of Contortion Mix)/(Razor N Go Mix) (12" promo, custom Deconstruction death cut sleeve, limited to 500 only)	20
97	DeCon. 21 535707 JB	Did It Again (Radio Edit)/Tears (7" jukebox issue, no p/s)	20
98	DeCon. 21 570137 JB	Breathe (Radio Edit)/(Tee's Radio Edit) (7" jukebox issue, no p/s)	20
98	DeConstruction TOOFAR 1	Too Far (Brothers In Rhythm Mix)/(Junior Vasquez Remix) (12", promo, no p/s)	25
98	Arthrob ART021TJ	GBI (Sharp Boys Deee-Liteful Dub)/(Album Version)/(Kylie-Pella) (with Towa Tei) (UK promo 12" part 1, custom Arthrob sleeve)	15
98	Arthrob ART021TJX	GBI (Rekut/DJ Krust Mix)/(Ebony Boogie Down Mix)/Bold Line (not Kylie) (with Towa Tei) (UK promo 12" part 2, custom Arthrob sleeve)	15
00	Parlophone BUTTERFLO1A	Butterfly (Sandstorm Dub) (12" 1-sided DJ white label, butterfly logo stamped die cut paper sleeve)	40
00	Parlophone 12MIND 1	Spinning Around (Messy Boyz Remix) (12" 1-sided promo featuring unreleased mix, die cut sleeve, Handwritten label, withdrawn, 10 only)	40
00	Parlophone SHARP DJ 1	Spinning Around (Sharp Vocal Mix)/Spinning Around (Sharp Double Dub) (12" Pink Promo DJ Vinyl, die-cut sleeve, 100 only)	40
00	Parlophone 12RDJ 6551	Please Stay (Metro Mix)/Please Stay (7th District Club Flava Mix)/ Please Stay (7th District Club Dub) (12" promo, p/s, with inner sleeve)	20
01	Parlophone RLH6562	Can't Get You Out Of My Head/Boy (7" jukebox issue, no p/s) NOTE: Clear 7" jukebox pressings carrying this 'RLH6562' catalogue number with 'Can't Get Blue Monday out Of my Head' as the B-side are unofficial bootlegs)	7
01	Parlophone 12RDJY 6562	Can't Get Out Of My Head (Superchumbo Todo Mamado Mix)/ Can't Get Out Of My Head (Superchumbo Leadhead Dub)/(Superchumbo Voltapella Mix) (12" promo issued under the pseudonym of 'Special K', die-cut sleeve)	7
04	Parlophone RDJ6633	Red Blooded Woman (Promo 1-sided clear 7" vinyl featuring otherwise unreleased 'Play Paul Radio Edit', 50 only)	30
04	Parlophone (no cat. no)	Chocolate (Violanti's Remix) (1-sided 12" white label, unreleased remix, Withdrawn, hand-written label)	30
00	Parlophone LIGHTX 001	LIGHT YEARS (LP Promo, unique blue outer 'Kylie' logo sleeve, inner picture sleeve, does not include 'Kids' or 'Password', 100 only)	30
00	Parlophone LIGHTX 002	LIGHT YEARS (LP Promo, unique blue outer 'Kylie' logo sleeve, inner picture sleeve, includes 'Kids' but not 'Password', 100 only)	30
00	BMG HITS1	HITS+ (CD promo, original withdrawn artwork, card slip case, withdrawn at Kylie's request when she disliked the picture used, most copies incinerated, less than 5 copies exist)	40

MINOR CLASSICS

82	Chiswick DICE 4	Sign Language/This Side Of Paradise	50

MINORBOPS

58	Vogue V 9110	Need You Tonight/Want You For My Own	800
58	Vogue V 9110	Need You Tonight/Want You For My Own (78)	250

MINOR THREAT

83	Discord DISCHORD 10	OUT OF STEP EP (12", reissue, red print, insert)	20
85	Discord DISCHORD 15	Salad Days/Stumped Good Guys (p/s)	18

MINSTRELS

67	Studio One SO 2036	People Get Ready/HAMLINS: Everyone's Got To Be There	200
68	Studio One SO 2050	Miss Highty Tighty/WESTMORELITES: Let Me Be Yours Until Tomorrow	90

MINT JULEPS

87	Stiff BUY DJ 264	Docklands/Under Pressure (12" test pressing of last Stiff single for 20 years)	30

MINT (1)

69	Tangerine 014	Luv/Simone	20
73	Pye 7N.45299	I'll Meet You Halfway/Three Score And Ten	6
73	President PT 393	Dog Eats Dog/All Night Lover	6

MINT (2)

79	Black Vinyl HT/SPS 1595	Marlene/Mediterranean Nights (no p/s)	6

Derek MINTER

MINT VALUE £

DEREK MINTER			
60	Sound Stories EP 304	STARS OF SPEED (EP)	10
MINTS			
57	London HLP 8423	Night Air/KEN COPELAND: Pledge Of Love	100
MINUCCI			
56	Vogue Coral LVA 9015	GINA LOLLO BRIGIDA PRESENTS MUSIC OF GINO BY MINUCCI (LP, photo of Gina on cover)	15
MINUTE MEN			
61	Capitol CL 15206	Yankee Diddle/Blue Pearl	6
MINUTEMEN			
83	SST SST 002	PARANOID TIME (8-track EP)	18
85	Homestead REFLEX-L	TOUR SPIEL (EP, live 4-track)	10
MIRACLE MILE			
86	Miracle MIR 001	Bless This Ship/Breaking Down The Barriers (p/s)	35
(SMOKEY ROBINSON &) MIRACLES			
61	London HL9276	Shop Around/Who's Lovin' You (DJ Copy)	100
61	London HL 9276	Shop Around/Who's Lovin' You	60
61	London HL 9366	Ain't It Baby/The Only One I Love (DJ Copy)	200
61	London HL 9366	Ain't It Baby/The Only One I Love	100
62	Fontana H 384	What's So Good About Goodbye/I've Been So Good To You	200
63	Oriole CBA 1795	You've Really Got A Hold On Me/Happy Landing	120
(Credited to The Miracles.)			
63	Oriole CBA 1863	Mickey's Monkey/Whatever Makes You Happy	80
64	Stateside SS 263	I Gotta Dance To Keep From Crying/Such Is Love, Such Is Life (DJ Copy)	100
64	Stateside SS 263	I Gotta Dance To Keep From Crying/Such Is Love, Such Is Life	55
64	Stateside SS 282	The Man In You/Heartbreak Road (DJ Copy)	70
64	Stateside SS 282	The Man In You/Heartbreak Road	40
64	Stateside SS 324	I Like It Like That/You're So Fine And Sweet (DJ Copy)	70
64	Stateside SS 324	I Like It Like That/You're So Fine And Sweet	45
64	Stateside SS 353	That's What Love Is Made Of/Would I Love You (DJ Copy)	80
64	Stateside SS 353	That's What Love Is Made Of/Would I Love You	35
65	Stateside SS 377	Come On Do The Jerk/Baby Don't You Go (DJ Copy)	60
65	Stateside SS 377	Come On Do The Jerk/Baby Don't You Go	45
65	Tamla Motown TMG 503	Oo Baby Baby/That's All Good (DJ Copy)	140
65	Tamla Motown TMG 503	Ooo Baby Baby/All That's Good	40
65	Tamla Motown TMG 522	The Tracks Of My Tears/Fork In The Road (DJ Copy)	100
65	Tamla Motown TMG 522	The Tracks Of My Tears/A Fork In The Road	45
65	Tamla Motown TMG 540	My Girl Has Gone/Since You Won My Heart (DJ Copy)	100
65	Tamla Motown TMG 540	My Girl Has Gone/Since You Won My Heart	40
66	Tamla Motown TMG 547	Going To A Go-Go/Choosey Beggar (DJ Copy)	200
66	Tamla Motown TMG 547	Going To A Go-Go/Choosey Beggar	25
66	Tamla Motown TMG 569	Who Lotta Shakin' In My Heart/Oh Be My Love (DJ Copy)	80
66	Tamla Motown TMG 569	Whole Lotta Shakin' In My Heart/Oh Be My Love	45
66	Tamla Motown TMG 584	(Come Round Here) I'm The One You Need/Save Me (DJ Copy)	80
66	Tamla Motown TMG 584	(Come 'Round Here) I'm The One You Need/Save Me	25
(All of the singles listed above are credited to The Miracles.)			
67	Tamla Motown TMG 598	The Love I Saw In You Was Just A Mirage/Swept For You Baby (DJ Copy)	80
67	Tamla Motown TMG 598	The Love I Saw In You Was Just A Mirage/Swept For You Baby	25
67	Tamla Motown TMG 614	More Love/Swept For You Baby (DJ Copy, mislabelled, B-side plays Come Spy With Me)	80
67	Tamla Motown TMG 614	More Love/Swept For You Baby (mislabelled, B-side plays Come Spy With Me)	25
67	Tamla Motown TMG 614	More Love/Come Spy With Me	80
67	Tamla Motown TMG 631	I Second That Emotion/You Must Be Love (DJ Copy)	70
67	Tamla Motown TMG 631	I Second That Emotion/You Must Be Love	12
68	Tamla Motown TMG 648	If You Can Want/When The Words From Your Heart Get Caught Up In Your Throat (DJ Copy)	40
68	Tamla Motown TMG 648	If You Can Want/When The Words From Your Heart Get Caught Up In Your Throat	15
68	Tamla Motown TMG 661	Yester-Love/Much Better Of (DJ Copy)	40
68	Tamla Motown TMG 661	Yester-Love/Much Better Off	15
68	Tamla Motown TMG 673	Special Occasion/Give Her Up (DJ Copy)	40
68	Tamla Motown TMG 673	Special Occasion/Give Her Up	15
69	Tamla Motown TMG 687	Baby, Baby Don't Cry/Your Mother's Only Daughter (DJ Copy)	40
69	Tamla Motown TMG 687	Baby, Baby Don't Cry/Your Mother's Only Daughter	15
69	Tamla Motown TMG 696	The Tracks Of My Tears/Come On Do The Jerk (DJ Copy)	40
69	Tamla Motown TMG 696	The Tracks Of My Tears/Come On Do The Jerk	7
70	Tamla Motown TMG 745	The Tears Of A Clown/You Must Be Love (DJ Copy)	40
70	Tamla Motown TMG 745	The Tears Of A Clown/You Must Be Love (with withdrawn B-side)	40
70	Tamla Motown TMG 745	The Tears Of A Clown/Who's Gonna Take The Blame	6
71	Tamla Motown TMG 761	(Come Round Here) I'm The One You Need/We Can Make It We Can (DJ Copy)	35
71	Tamla Motown TMG 761	(Come Round Here) I'm The One You Need/We Can Make It, We Can	6
71	Tamla Motown TMG 774	I Don't Blame You At All/That Girl (DJ Copy)	35
71	Tamla Motown TMG 774	I Don't Blame You At All/That Girl	6
72	Tamla Motown TMG 811	My Girl Has Gone/Crazy Bout The La La La (DJ Copy)	30
72	Tamla Motown TMG 811	My Girl Has Gone/Crazy 'Bout The La-La-La	6
73	Tamla Motown TMG 853	Going To A Go-Go/Whole Lotta Shakin' In My Heart/Yester-Love (DJ Copy)	25
73	Tamla Motown TMG 853	Going To A Go-Go/Whole Lotta Shakin' In My Heart/Yester-Love	6
74	Tamla Motown TMG 891	Don't Let It End (Til You Let It Begin)/I Wanna Be With You	6
76	Tamla Motown TMG 1023	Nightlife/The Miracle Workers: Overture (as The Miracles)	6
87	Motown ZB 41147 D	Just To See Her/Te Queiro Como Si No Hubiera Um Manana//Being With You/ What's In Your Life For Me? (solo, double pack)	6
61	London RE 1295	SHOP AROUND (EP, as The Miracles)	200

MIRAGE

MINT VALUE £

63	Oriole PS 40044	HI! WE'RE THE MIRACLES (LP)	250
64	Stateside SL 10099	THE FABULOUS MIRACLES (LP)	140
65	Tamla Motown TML 11003	I LIKE IT LIKE THAT (LP)	80
66	Tamla Motown TML 11024	GOIN' TO A GO-GO (LP, as Smokey Robinson & The Miracles, mono)	45
66	Tamla Motown TML 11024	GOIN' TO A GO-GO (LP, as Smokey Robinson & The Miracles, stereo)	55
66	Tamla Motown TML 11031	THE MIRACLES FROM THE BEGINNING (LP, mono)	50
66	Tamla Motown STML 11031	THE MIRACLES FROM THE BEGINNING (LP, stereo)	50
67	Tamla Motown TML 11044	AWAY WE A-GO-GO (LP, mono)	50
67	Tamla Motown STML 11044	AWAY WE A-GO-GO (LP, stereo)	65
68	Tamla Motown TML 11067	MAKE IT HAPPEN (LP, mono)	30
68	Tamla Motown STML 11067	MAKE IT HAPPEN (LP, stereo)	35
68	Tamla Motown (S)TML 11072	GREATEST HITS (LP, mono/stereo)	20
69	Tamla Motown (S)TML 11089	SPECIAL OCCASION (LP, mono/stereo)	25
69	Tamla Motown (S)TML 11107	SMOKEY ROBINSON & THE MIRACLES LIVE! (LP, mono/stereo)	25
70	Tamla Motown (S)TML 11129	TIME OUT FOR SMOKEY ROBINSON & THE MIRACLES (LP)	18
70	Tamla Motown STML 11151	FOUR IN BLUE (LP)	25
70	Tamla Motown STML 11163	WHAT LOVE HAS JOINED TOGETHER (LP, unissued)	0
70	Tamla Motown STML 11172	SMOKEY ROBINSON & THE MIRACLES (LP)	15
71	Tamla Motown STML 11172	POCKETFUL OF MIRACLES (LP)	20
73	Tama Motown STMA 8010	RENAISSANCE (LP, gatefold as The Miracles)	15

MIRAGE

65	CBS 201772	It's In Her Kiss/What Ye Gonna Do 'Bout It	20
65	CBS 202007	Go Away/Just A Face	20
66	Philips BF 1534	Tomorrow Never Knows/You Can't Be Serious	50
67	Philips BF 1554	Hold On/Can You Hear Me	50
67	Philips BF 1571	The Wedding Of Ramona Blair/Lazy Man	80
68	Page One POF 078	Mystery Lady/Chicago Cottage	12
68	Page One POF 111	Carolyn/World Goes On Around You	12

(see also Yellow Payges, Caleb, Jawbone, Spencer Davis Group, Portobello Explosion)

MIRETTES

69	MCA Soul Bag BAG 8	Whirlpool/Ain't You Trying To Cross Over	8
72	Jay Boy BOY 65	Now That I've Found You Baby/He's Alright With Me	8
69	MCA MUP(S) 344	IN THE MIDNIGHT HOUR (LP)	20

(see also Ikettes)

MIRK

79	Mother Earth MUM 1205	MODDANS BOWER (LP)	80
82	Spring Thyme SPR 1009	TAK A DRAM AFOR YE GO (LP)	25

MIRKWOOD

71	Flams Ltd PR 1067	MIRKWOOD (LP)	1000
93	Tenth Planet TP 003	MIRKWOOD (LP, reissue, numbered with insert, 500 only)	30

MIRO

90	Sacret Heart SH 30008	GREETINGS FROM GOLBORNE ROAD EP (hand-made and signed p/s)	20

STEVE MIRO & EYES

78	Object Music OM 03	Up And About/Smiling In Reverse (p/s)	6
80	Object Music OBF 008	RUDE INTRUSIONS (LP)	15
81	Object Music OBJ 015	SECOND SENTENCE (LP)	15
84	Glaze GZLP101	TRILEMNA (LP)	15

(see also Eyes, Noyes Bros)

MIRROR

68	Philips BF 1666	Gingerbread Man/Faster Than Light	60

MIRRORS

78	Lightning GIL 503	Cure For Cancer/Nice Vice (p/s)	15
79	Lightning GIL 540	Dark Glasses/999 (p/s)	25

MISBELIEVED ONES

71	Croft CR 1	Suddenly It Rains/Doctor Death	70

MISA NEGRA

98	People PEOPLE 008	Spiritual Vibes (Aeronaut Dub)/(Original Reprise)/(Afro Boogie House Mix) (12")	30

MISBELIEVERS

71	Plumett PL01	High In The Sky/Devil You	35

MI 7

91	Chill TUV 20	Rockin Down The House/Rockin Down The House (Chop Mix) (12")	20

MISFITS (U.K.)

66	A.S.C.C. PRI 101	You Won't See Me/Hanging Around (Aberdeen Students Charities Campaign)	10

(see also Complex)

MISFITS (U.S.)

80	Plan 9/Cherry Red PLP 9	BEWARE (12" EP)	250

MISHKA

99	Creation CRELP 244	MISHKA (LP)	40

MISSES MISTY

79	Freedom Sounds FSD 018	Mellow Mellow Ride On/FREEDOM FIGHTER BAND: Ladies Night (12")	70

MISSING

94	3rd Party 3RD 11	Flex & Relax/Back To Consciousness (12")	15

MISSING SCIENTISTS

80	Rough Trade RT 057	Big City, Bright Lights/Discotheque X (p/s)	20

(see also Television Personalities, Slaughter)

MISSION

86	Mercury MYSG 1	Stay With Me/Blood Brother (autographed, gatefold p/s)	8

MISSION BELLES

			MINT VALUE £
87	Mercury MYTHP3	Severina/Tomorrow Never Knows (poster p/s)	7
87	Phonogram MYTHB 2	IV: Wasteland/Shelter From The Storm (Live)/Serpent's Kiss (Live)/1969 (Live) (doublepack, in box, with insert and photo's)	12
80s	Flexi FLEX 1	Crazy (1-track flexidisc)	12
01	Playground PGND 001	Evangeline/Anyone But You//Melt/Swoon (Reprise) (doublepack, pink & blue vinyl, gatefold p/s)	8
02	Playground PGND003	Shine Like The Stars/Never Let Me Down/Spider And The Fly (In The Ointment)/ Never (2 x 7" on green and white vinyl, gatefold p/s)	8
95	Equator SMEELP 001	NEVERLAND (2-LP)	40
96	Equator SMEELP 002	BLUE (LP)	40

(see also Sisters Of Mercy, Dead Or Alive, Pauline Murray, Artery, Red Lorry Yellow Lorry, Expelaires, Knopov's Political Package)

MISSION BELLES
65	Decca F 12154	Sincerely/When A Girl Really Loves You	10

MISSISSIPPI
70	Fox FOX 1	Mr. Union Railway Man/Main Street	100

MISS JANE
68	Pama PM 704	Bad Mind People/My Heart Is Aching (B-side act. "Witch Doctor" by Coolers)	55

MISS KATE
79	TJM TJM 10	Ebony Eyes/I Love You	20

MISSPENT YOUTH (1)
79	Sequel PART III	FOREVER EP (p/s)	30

MISSPENT YOUTH (2)
79	Big Bear BB20	Betcha Won't Dance/Birmingham Boys (p/s)	20

MISS X (JOYCE BLAIR)
63	Ember EMB S 175	Christine/S-E-X	10

MISTAKEN IDENTITY
85	RAM 17CHP 7010	The Answer/The Answer (Club Version) (12")	25

MISTAKES
81	Twist And Shout TN5	Radiation/16 Pins (insert p/s)	15

MR. MOST
69	Downtown DT 408	Push Wood/Reggae Train	12

MISTER VERSATILE
69	Jackpot JP 701	Apple Blossom/LITTLE BOY BLUE: Dark End Of The Street (act. by Pat Kelly)	20
69	Jackpot JP 702	Devil's Disciples/ERROL DUNKLEY: Having A Party	8

(see also Lester Sterling)

MISTY IN ROOTS
78	People Unite SJP 781	Six One Penny/Six One Penny Version	18
78	People Unite SJP 789	Oh Wicked Man/Version	15
79	People Unite PU 001	See Them A Come/How Long Jah (12", p/s)	25
80	People Unite PU 002	Rich Man/Salvation (12", p/s)	18
80	People Unite PU 004	Zapatta/Viva Zapatta	10
81	People Unite PU 006	Wandering Wanderer/Cry Out For Peace (12")	20
81	People Unite PU 003	Peace And Love/Ball Out (12")	15
83	People Unite PU 103S	Poor And Needy/Follow Fashion	8
83	People Unite PU 103	Poor And Needy/Follow Fashion (12")	25
86	People Unite PU 007	Own Them Control Them/Own Them Control Them (Version)	15
88	People Unite PUM 3	Together/Together In Dub (12")	12
79	People Unite PU 003	LIVE AT THE COUNTER EUROVISION '79 (LP)	30
82	People Unite PU 101 ALB	WISE AND FOOLISH (LP, inner)	25
83	People Unite PU 102	EARTH (LP)	25
85	People Unite PU 105	MUSI-O-TUNYA (LP)	25

MISTY MEADOWS
70	Rhone RH 002	Visions/We See The Sun	150

MISTY (1)
70	Parlophone R5852	Hot Cinnamon/Cascades	80

MISTY (2)
77	Cottage COT 511	MISTY (LP)	18

MISUNDERSTOOD
66	Fontana TF 777	I Can Take You To The Sun/Who Do You Love	80
69	Fontana TF 998	Children Of The Sun/I Unseen (small centre hole)	70
69	Fontana TF 998	Children Of The Sun/I Unseen (large centre hole)	50
69	Fontana TF 1028	You're Tuff Enough/Little Red Rooster (as Misunderstood featuring Glenn "Fernando" Campbell, in p/s)	60
69	Fontana TF 1028	You're Tuff Enough/Little Red Rooster (as Misunderstood featuring Glenn "Fernando" Campbell)	35
69	Fontana TF 1041	Never Had A Girl (Like You Before)/Golden Glass (as Misunderstood featuring Glenn "Fernando" Campbell)	45
81	Cherry Red CHERRY 22	Children Of The Sun/Who Do You Love/I'll Take You To The Sun (p/s)	7
82	Cherry Red B RED 32	BEFORE THE DREAM FADED (LP, with inner)	25

BLUE MITCHELL
73	Mainstream MSL 1015	THE LAST TANGO = BLUES (LP)	18

CHAD MITCHELL
62	London HLR 9509	Lizzie Borden/Super Skier	7

DENNY MITCHELL SOUNDSATIONS
64	Decca F 11848	I've Been Crying/For Your Love	25

(see also Preachers, Moon's Train)

GROVER MITCHELL
68	London HLU 10221	Turned On/Blue Over You	18
76	Vanguard VS 5003	What Hurts/Super Hero	50

Guy MITCHELL

MINT VALUE £

GUY MITCHELL
SINGLES : SINGLES & EPS

Year	Label/Cat #	Title	Value
53	Columbia SCM 5018	Feet Up (Pat Him On The Po-Po)/Jenny Kissed Me	15
53	Columbia SCM 5022	Cause I Love Ya, That's A-Why/Train Of Love (both with Mindy Carson)	15
53	Columbia SCM 5032	She Wears Red Feathers/Why Should I Go Home?	15
53	Columbia SCM 5037	Pretty Little Black-Eyed Susie/MITCH MILLER HORNS: Horn Belt Boogie	20
56	Philips JK 1001	Singing The Blues/Crazy With Love (jukebox issue)	12
57	Philips JK 1005	Knee Deep In The Blues/Take Me Back Baby (jukebox issue)	12
57	Philips JK 1015	Rock-A-Billy/Got A Feeling (jukebox issue)	12
57	Philips JK 1023	Sweet Stuff/In The Middle Of A Dark, Dark Night (jukebox issue)	10
57	Philips JK 1027	Call Rosie On The Phone/Cure For The Blues (jukebox issue)	10
58	Philips PB 766	C'mon Let's Go/The Unbeliever	8
58	Philips PB 798	Wond'rin' And Worryin'/If Ya Don't Like It, Don't Knock It	6
58	Philips PB 830	Hangin' Around/Honey Brown Eyes	10
58	Philips PB 858	Let It Shine, Let It Shine/Butterfly Doll	10
58	Philips PB 885	My Heart Cries For You (2nd Version)/Till We're Engaged	7
59	Philips PB 915	Alias Jesse James/Pride O' Dixie	7
59	Philips PB 964	Heartaches By The Number/Two (with triangular centre)	12
63	Pye International 7N 25179	Go, Tiger, Go/If You Ever Go Away (unreleased)	0
66	CBS 202238	Singing The Blues/Rock-A-Billy	8
54	Columbia SEG 7513	PRETTY LITTLE BLACK EYED SUSIE (EP, plain sleeve)	10
55	Columbia SEG 7598	JENNY KISSED ME (plain sleeve)	10

JONI MITCHELL

Year	Label/Cat #	Title	Value
68	Reprise RS 20694	Night In The City/I Had A King	15
69	Reprise RS 23402	Chelsea Morning/Both Sides Now	12
72	Asylum AYM 511	You Turn Me On, I'm A Radio/Urge For Going	8
83	Geffen DA 3122	Chinese Cafe/Ladies Man (double pack, with bonus interview 7")	8
68	Reprise RSLP 6293	JONI MITCHELL (LP, gatefold sleeve, 'steamboat' label)	50
69	Reprise RSLP 6341	CLOUDS (LP, textured single sleeve, 'steamboat' label)	45
69	Reprise RSLP 6341	CLOUDS (LP, 2nd pressing, stickered U.S. gatefold sleeve, 'steamboat' label)	15
70	Reprise RSLP 6376	LADIES OF THE CANYON (LP, gatefold sleeve, 'steamboat' label)	30
71	Reprise K 44128	BLUE (LP, gatefold sleeve, with blue inner sleeve)	35
71	Reprise K 44128	BLUE (LP, gatefold sleeve)	25
73	Asylum SYLA 8753	FOR THE ROSES (LP, gatefold sleeve)	15
74	Asylum SYLA 8756	COURT AND SPARK (LP, gatefold sleeve)	20
75	Asylum SYLA 8763	THE HISSING OF SUMMER LAWNS (LP)	25
75	Asylum SYSP 902	MILES OF AISLES (2-LP, gatefold sleeve with inner flap)	20
79	Asylum K 53091	MINGUS (LP, triple gatefold sleeve)	15
70s	Asylum K 53053	HEJIRA (LP, gatefold sleeve)	15
82	Asylum/Nimbus K 53018	THE HISSING OF SUMMER LAWNS (LP, audiophile pressing, mail order issue)	60

MCKINLEY 'SOUL' MITCHELL

Year	Label/Cat #	Title	Value
68	President PT 125	The Town I Live In/No Love Like Your Love	10
68	President PTL 1005	McKINLEY 'SOUL' MITCHELL (LP)	40

PHILIP MITCHELL

Year	Label/Cat #	Title	Value
71	Jay Boy BOY 37	I'm Gonna Build California From All Over The World/ The World Needs More People Like You	30
71	Jay Boy BOY 37	I'm Gonna Build California From All Over The World/ The World Needs More People Like You (DJ copy)	50
72	Jay Boy BOY 57	Free For All/Flower Child	10
72	Jay Boy BOY 57	Free For All/Flower Child (DJ copy)	10
74	London HLU 10444	Ain't No Love In My Life/Turning Over The Ground	40

RED MITCHELL

Year	Label/Cat #	Title	Value
56	London LTZ N15041	RED MITCHELL (LP)	80
62	London LZ-N1 4017	HAPPY MINORS (10" LP)	40
61	Vogue LAE 12286	REJOICE! (LP)	35
63	London SH-K 8027	HEAR YE!! HEAR YE!! (LP)	20

RONNIE MITCHELL

Year	Label/Cat #	Title	Value
60	London HLU 9220	How Many Times/The Only Love	8

SINX MITCHELL

Year	Label/Cat #	Title	Value
64	Hickory 45-1248	This Weird Sensation/Love Is All I'm Asking For	20

(see also Crickets, Earl Sinks)

VALERIE MITCHELL

Year	Label/Cat #	Title	Value
65	Oak RGJ 160	There Goes My Heart Again/If I Didn't Love You (p/s)	60
65	HMV POP 1422	Bitter Tears/Forbidden	6
65	HMV POP 1462	There Goes My Heart Again/If I Didn't Love You	6
65	HMV POP 1490	Go My Way/Green Eyes	8
66	HMV POP 1509	Play With Me/Never Let It Be Said	10
66	HMV POP 1529	You Can Go/The Windmill Girls	8
67	Columbia DB 8186	Love Can Be The Sweetest Thing/I'm Sorry	6
67	Columbia DB 8265	Sunshine/You Belong To Me	6

WILLIE MITCHELL

Year	Label/Cat #	Title	Value
64	London HLU 9926	20-75/Secret Home	20
64	London HLU 9926	20-75/Secret Home (DJ Copy)	40
65	London HLU 10004	Everything Is Gonna Be Alright/That Driving Beat (Boxed logo)	15
65	London HLU 10004	Everything Is Gonna Be Alright/That Driving Beat	20
65	London HLU 10004	Everything Is Gonna Be Alright/That Driving Beat (DJ copy)	50
66	London HLU 10039	Bad Eye/Sugar T.	10
66	London HLU 10085	Mercy/Sticks And Stones	10
68	London HLU 10186	Soul Serenade/Buster Browne	10
68	London HLU 10215	Prayer Meetin'/Rum Daddy	8

MITCHELL/COE MYSTERIES

MINT VALUE £

68	London HLU 10224	Up Hard/Beale Street Mood	10
70	London HLU 10313	Robbin's Nest/Six To Go	8
73	London HLU 10407	Last Tango In Paris/Six To Go	6
74	London HLU 10545	The Champion (2 parts) (DJ copy)	30
80	Cream CS 104	That Driving Beat/Mercy/Everything Is Gonna Be Alright	15
67	London HA-U 8319	THE HIT SOUND OF WILLIE MITCHELL (LP)	30
68	London HA-U/SH-U 8365	SOUL SERENADE (LP)	20
68	London HA-U/SH-U 8368	LIVE (LP)	20
69	London HA-U/SH-U 8372	SOLID SOUL (LP)	20
70	London HA-U/SH-U 8388	ON TOP (LP)	20
70	London HA-U/SH-U 8408	SOUL BAG (LP)	20

MITCHELL/COE MYSTERIES
80	RCA PL 25297	EXILED (LP, with inner sleeve, with gatefold sleeve)	15

(see also Colin Blunstone, Lesley Duncan, Dan McCafferty, Francis Rossi & Berni Frost, Ray Russell, Joe Jammer, Complex, Monsoon)

ROBERT MITCHUM
55	Brunswick OE 9197	RACHEL AND THE STRANGER (EP)	10
67	Monument LMO 5011	THAT MAN (LP)	20

MITHRANDIR
82	New Leaf SVC 570	Dreamers Of Fortune/After Tomorrow (p/s)	50
82	New Leaf SVC 01	MAGICK EP (p/s)	75

JACKIE MITTOO
66	Island WI 293	Killer Diller (as Jackie Mitto & Soul Brothers)/PATRICK HYTTON: Oh Lady	150
67	Rio R 114	Home Made/ETHIOPIANS: I'm Gonna Take Over Now	75
67	Rio R 123	Got My Buglaoo/ETHIOPIANS: What To Do	225
67	Coxsone CS 7002	Somebody Help Me/GAYLADS & SOUL VENDORS: The Sound Of Silence	125
67	Coxsone CS 7009	Ba Ba Boom/SLIM SMITH & FREEDOM SINGERS: Mercy Mercy	125
67	Coxsone CS 7019	Ram Jam/SUMMERTAIRES: You're Gonna Leave	40
67	Coxsone CS 7026	Something Stupid/LYRICS: Money Lover	50
68	Coxsone CS 7040	Norwegian Wood/GAYLADS: Most Peculiar Man	60
68	Coxsone CS 7042	Sure Shot/OCTAVES: The Bottle	200
68	Coxsone CS 7046	Man Pon Spot/BOP & BELTONES: Not For A Moment	50
68	Coxsone CS 7050	Napoleon Solo/CANNON BALL BRYAN: You're My Everything	100
68	Coxsone CS 7070	Songbird/JAMAICAN ACTIONS: Catch The Quinella	100
68	Coxsone CS 7075	Mission Impossible/HEPTONES: Giddy Up (B-side actually by Actions)	80
68	Studio One SO 2043	Put It One/SOUL VENDORS: Chinese Chicken	30
68	Studio One SO 2056	Race Track/BASES: I Don't Mind	40
69	Studio One SO 2082	Hi-Jack/TREVOR CLARKE: Sufferer	40
69	Doctor Bird DB 1177	Dark Of The Sun/MATADOR ALL STARS: Bridge View	60
69	Bamboo BAM 6	Our Thing (with Sound Dimension)/C. MARSHALL: Tra La La Sweet '69	60
69	Bamboo BAM 15	Clean Up/Spring Time (as Jackie Mittoo & Sound Dimension)	40
70	Bamboo BAM 17	Dark Of The Moon/Moon Walk (as Jackie Mittoo & Sound Dimension)	40
70	Bamboo BAM 20	Gold Dust/SUPERTONES: Real Gone Loser	40
70	Bamboo BAM 31	Can I Change My Mind/BRENTFORD ALLSTARS: Early Duckling	40
70	Bamboo BAM 38	Baby Why/ETHIOPIANS: You'll Want To Come Back	40
70	Bamboo BAM 51	Dancing Groove/BLACK & GEORGE: Peanut Butter	50
70	Banana BA 315	Holly Holy/LARRY MARSHALL: I've Got To Make It	20
71	Banana BA 320	Peenie Wallie/ROY RICHARDS: Can't Go On	20
72	London HLU 10357	Wishbone/Soul Bird (as Jackie Mittoo - The Reggae Beat)	7
79	Justice DIS 001	Disco Jack/Disco Dub (12")	35
80	Rite Sound RTA 06	Mystic World/Version (12")	20
81	Black Roots BR20	These Eyes/Wall Street/Killer Thriller (12", p/s)	30
67	Coxsone CSL 8009	IN LONDON (LP)	150
68	Coxsone CSL 8014	EVENING TIME (LP, with Soul Vendors)	150
69	Coxsone CSL 8020	KEEP ON DANCING (LP)	150
70	Bamboo BDLP 209	NOW (LP)	80
72	London SHU 8436	WISHBONE (LP)	25
78	Third World TWS 931	IN COLD BLOOD (LP)	40
79	Third World TWS 501	KEYBOARD KING (LP)	35
10	Universal Sound USLP 8	THE KEYBOARD KING AT STUDIO ONE (2-LP)	20

(see also Lord Tanamo, Jamaican Actions, Matadors, Jackie Opel, Soul Vendors, Winston Francis, Donna & Freedom Singers, Skatalites)

MIX BLOOD
80	Creole CR 201	Last Train To Skaville/Move And Move (p/s)	10

MIXED BAG
69	Decca F 12880	Potiphar (with Ramases III Orchestra)/Million Dollar Bash	6
69	Decca F 12907	Round And Round/Have You Ever Been In Love	6

MIXED FEELINGS
73	Scotty SCO 2	Make Me Jump/Stop	20

MIXMAN
90	Citizen Kane 12KANE 2	Bright Child (Manmix)/Bright Child (Dancemix) (12", p/s)	15
94	Blakamix BLKM012	Carriacou Cargo EP (12")	15

MIXRACE & PRO-TON-ISOSPACE
94	Stronghold STRONG 3	The Endless Skies (Hyper-On-Experience Remix)/True Jungle (Brown & Dangerman Remix)/The Endless Skies/True Jungle (12")	20

MIXTURE
65	Fontana TF 640	One By One/Monkey Jazz	10
69	Parlophone R 5755	Sad Old Song/Never Trust In Tomorrow	7

MIXTURES
71	Polydor 205813	Never Be Untrue/She's Gone Away	20

BILLY MIZE
60	Top rank JAR 391	Little Coco Palm/The Windward Isle	7

Hank MIZELL

MINT VALUE £

HANK MIZELL
76 Charly CEP 115 — HANK MIZELL (EP) 10
VIC MIZZY, HIS ORCHESTRA & CHORUS
65 RCA RCA 1440 — Addams Family Main Theme/Kentucky James Main Theme 20
M.J.6
60 Decca F 11212 — Tracy's Theme/Private Eye 6
MO2VATION
93 No Noise NNDJ 008 — Lowdown & Funky/That Ruff Track (with L Double, 12") 15
93 Pure Noise DASH 3 — THE RHYTHM RIDE EP (12") 10
MO2VATION & APEX
92 Hypno Genesis HG 002 — ANIMATION EP (12") 25
MOB (1)
68 Mercury MF 1026 — Disappear/I Wish You Would Leave Me Alone 15
71 Polydor 2001 127 — I Dig Everything About You/Love's Got A Hold On Me 20
71 Polydor 2001 169 — Give It To Me/I'd Like To See More Of You 10
74 UK USA 4 — Give It To Me/I'd LIke To See More Of You 8
75 Private Stock PVT 32 — I Can't Stop This Love Song/Hot Music 8
71 Polydor 2344 001 — MOB (LP) 15
MOB (2)
80 Kalida AKB 1/2 — Send Me To Coventry/Mobbed (p/s) 8
MOB (3)
80 All The Madmen MAD 1 — Youth/Crying Again (p/s) 40
80 All The Madmen MAD 002 — Witch Hunt/Shuffling Souls/What's Going On (EP, handwritten white labels with sticker & foldout, stapled, gatefold p/s) 12
82 Crass 321984/7 — No Doves Fly Here/I Hear You Laughing (foldout p/s) 12
83 All The Madmen MAD 6 — The Mirror Breaks/Stay (screen-printed p/s, with lyric insert) 10
83 Cause For Concern CFC 2 — LIVE AT THE LMC (LP, with the APOSTLES) 30
83 All The Madmen MAD 4 — LET THE TRIBE INCREASE (LP, with lyric poster) 25
86 All The Madmen MAD 13 — CRYING AGAIN (EP) 30
80s All/Madmen MADPACK 1 — MAD PACK 1 (3 x 7" in 12" pack) 25
HANK MOBLEY
56 Esquire 32-029 — MOBLEY'S MESSAGE (LP) 150
59 Columbia 33SX 1160 — MONDAY NIGHT AT BIRDLAND (LP, with Billy Root, Chris Fuller & Lee Morgan) 60
JOHN MOBLEY
62 Stateside SS 136 — Tunnel Of Love/Work Out 15
MOBSTER
80 Ensign ENY 41 — The Mobster Shuffle/Simmer Down (p/s) 6
MOBY
93 Equator ATLASLP 001 — THE STORY SO FAR (LP) 25
93 Equator ATLASLP 002 — AMBIENT (LP) 40
95 Mute STUMM 130 — EVERYTHING IS WRONG (LP) 30
96 Mute STUMM 150 — ANIMAL RIGHTS (LP) 40
97 Mute STUMM 168 — I LIKE TO SCORE (LP) 25
99 Mute STUMM 172 — PLAY (2-LP, inner, 500 only) 100
02 Mute STUMM 202 — 18 (2-LP, gatefold) 80
05 Mute STUMM 240 — HOTEL (LP) 35
05 Little Idiot MOB2VINIOT03OVXX — HOTEL : AMBIENT (LP) 20
08 Mute STUMM 275 — LAST NIGHT (2-LP) 30
09 Little Idiot IDIOT 001T — LITTLE IDIOT (2-LP) 30
11 Little Idiot IDIOT 010LP — DESTROYED (2-LP, CD) 35
13 Little Idiot IDIOT 110 — PLAY (2-LP, gatefold, reissue, 500 only, all signed by Moby) 80
13 Little Idiot IDIOT 111 — 18 (2-LP, gatefold, reissue, 500 only, all signed by Moby) 80
16 Mute STUMM 130 — EVERYTHING IS WRONG (LP, reissue) 15
16 Mute STUMM 150 — ANIMAL RIGHTS (LP, reissue) 18
MOBY DICK
82 Ebony EBON 5 — Nothing To Fear/Can't Have My Body Tonight 20
MOBY GRAPE
67 CBS 2953 — Omaha/Hey Grandma 20
68 CBS 3555 — Can't Be So Bad/Murder In My Heart For The Judge 15
69 CBS 3945 — Trucking Man/Ooh Mama Ooh 8
67 CBS (S)BPG 63090 — MOBY GRAPE (LP) 60
68 CBS 63271 — WOW (LP, mono & stereo) 40
69 CBS 63430 — 69 (LP, mono & stereo) 40
69 CBS 63698 — TRULY FINE CITIZEN (LP, stereo) 40
69 CBS 63698 — TRULY FINE CITIZEN (LP, mono) 60
71 Reprise K 44152 — 20 GRANITE CREEK (LP) 15
74 CBS 64743 — GREAT GRAPE (LP) 15
MOCCA-SIN & THE TP'S
78 Alaska ALA 2013 — Cherokee Dance/The Raindance 10
MOCEDADES
73 Bell BELL 1303 — Touch The Wind/Eres Tu 6
MOCKINGBIRDS
65 Columbia DB 7480 — That's How It's Gonna Stay/I Never Should Have Kissed You 50
65 Columbia DB 7565 — I Can Feel We're Parting/The Flight Of The Mockingbird 50
65 Immediate IM 015 — You Stole My Love/Skit Skat 150
66 Decca F 12434 — One By One/Lovingly Yours 60
66 Decca F 12510 — How To Find A Lover/My Story 50

(see also 10cc, Graham Gouldman, Whirlwinds, Doctor Father, Hotlegs, Godley & Greme)

M.O.D.

MINT VALUE £

M.O.D.
79 Vertigo 6059 233 — M.O.D./M.O.D. (2) (p/s, allegedly mispressed on 2-Tone label) 30
79 Vertigo 6059 233 — M.O.D./M.O.D. (2) (p/s) 7
(see also David Essex)

MODE
66 Private pressing — THE MODE (EP, white labels, no p/s) 400

MODEL 500
89 Kool Kat KOOL T 507 — The Chase (Express Mix)/(Neutral Mix)/(Mayday Mix) (12", p/s) 15
90 Kool Kat KOOLT 601 — Ocean To Ocean (Juan's Magic Mix)/Info World/Wanderer (12", p/s) 10
(see also Rhythim Is Rhythim)

MODEL MANIA
79 Boob MM1 A/MM 1AA — No Pride Slow Suicide/Epic Cowboy (250 with handmade stamped label) 100
79 Boob MM1 A/MM 1AA — No Pride Slow Suicide/Epic Cowboy (750 with black labels) 75
(see also Power Farm)

MODEL WORKERS
81 Make It Yourself 007BOND — Cry/My Winter Of Discontent/ (p/s, yellow, pink and blue variants) 50

MODELS
77 Step Forward SF 3 — Freeze/Man Of The Year (p/s, 1st pressing with The Models and The Freeze on labels) 20
77 Step Forward SF-3 — Freeze/Man Of The Year (p/s, 2nd pressing with Models and Freeze on labels) 15
(see also Adam & The Ants, Mass, Rema Rema, Wolfgang Press)

MODE-M
96 Void VOID 001 — Space Based/Cohesion (12") 30
97 Void VOID 005 — INNER WORLD EP (2 x 12") 20

MODERATES
81 Hyped BMRB 53 — Emile/For What It's Worth (not released in p/s) 10
80 Open Eye OEEP 1001 — FETISHES (12" EP) 15

MODERN ART
84 Color Disc COLORS 1 — Dreams To Live/Beautiful Truth (p/s) 25
86 Color Disc COLORS 5 — Penny Valentine/One Way Ticket (1-sided, clear vinyl flexidisc, 1,000 only) 12
87 Color Disc COLOR 3 — STEREOLAND (LP, hand-stencilled with insert, 300 only) 60
94 Acme 8007 LP — ALL ABOARD THE MIND TRAIN (LP, 500 only, numbered) 18

MODERN ENGLISH
79 Limp LMP 2 — Drowning Man/Silent World (p/s) 30
80 4AD AD 6 — Swans On Glass/Incident (p/s) 15
80 4AD AD 15 — Gathering Dust/Tranquility Of A Summer Moment (p/s) 15
81 4AD CAD 105 — MESH AND LACE (LP) 20
(see also This Mortal Coil)

MODERN EON
80 Modern Eon EON 001 — PIECES (EP) 20
81 Dinsales 2 — Euthenics/Choreography/Waiting For The Cavalry/The Real Hymn (12", white label LP sampler) 20

MODERN FOLK QUARTET (M.F.Q.)
64 Warner Bros WB 147 — The Love Of A Clown/If You All Think 25
66 RCA RCA 1514 — Night Time Girl/Lifetime (as M.F.Q.) 30
63 Warner Bros WM/WS 8135 — THE MODERN FOLK QUARTET (LP) 20
85 Off Beat WIK 55 — MOONLIGHT SERENADE (LP) 15

MODERN JAZZ QUARTET (M.J.Q.)
55 Esquire 20-069 — MODERN JAZZ QUARTET (10" LP) 20
55 Esquire 20-038 — MODERN JAZZ QUARTET VOL. 2 (10" LP) 20
55 Esquire 20-090 — THE CLASSICAL PERFORMANCES OF... (10" LP) 20
56 Esquire 320024 — MJQ IN HI FI (LP) 20
57 London Jazz LTZK 15022 — FONTESSA (LP, also stereo SAH-K 6031) 20
58 London Jazz LTZK 15085 — AT THE MUSIC INN (LP) 20
58 London Jazz LTZ 15136 — MODERN JAZZ QUARTET (LP) 20
59 London Jazz LTZ-K 15140 — PLAYS ONE NEVER KNOWS (LP, also stereo SAH-K 6029) 20
59 London Jazz LTZK 15181 — ODDS AGAINST TOMORROW (LP) 20
59 Columbia Clef 33CX 11028 — MODERN JAZZ QUARTET & OSCAR PETERSON AT THE OPERA HOUSE (LP) 20
60 London Jazz LTZ-K 15193 — PYRAMID (LP, also stereo SAH-K 6086) 20
61 London Jazz LTZ-K 15207 — THIRD STREAM MUSIC (LP, with Beaux Arts String Quartet & Jimmy Giuffre Three) 20
63 London HA-K/SH-K 8016 — LONELY WOMAN (LP) 15
68 Apple APCOR 4 — UNDER THE JASMINE TREE (LP, mono) 50
68 Apple SAPCOR 4 — UNDER THE JASMINE TREE (LP, stereo) 35
69 Apple SAPCOR 10 — SPACE (LP, gatefold sleeve, dark green label, black inner) 40
73 Apple SAPCOR 10 — SPACE (LP, later pressing, light green label, single sleeve, white 'Apple' inner) 50
93 Apple SAPCOR 4 — UNDER THE JASMINE TREE (LP, reissue, gatefold sleeve with inner) 20
93 Apple SAPCOR 10 — SPACE (LP, reissue) 20
(see also John Lewis, Milt Jackson, Sonny Rollins)

MODERN JAZZ SEXTET
56 Columbia Clef 33CX 10048 — MODERN JAZZ SEXTET (LP) 20

MODERNAIRES (U.K.)
80 Illuminated JAMS 3 — WAY OF LIVING (LP) 15

MODEST JAZZ TRIO
60 Vogue LAE 12278 — GOOD FRIDAY BLUES (LP) 25
(see also Jim Hall)

MODEST MOUSE
00 Matador OLE 464-1 — NIGHT ON THE SUN (12" EP, p/s) 15
00 Matador OLE 4501 — MOON AND ANTARCTICA (2-LP) 30

MO-DETTES
79 Mode/Rough Trade MODE 1 — White Mice/Masochistic Opposite (pink [card or paper] or white p/s) 6
80 Deram DET-R-1/MODE 11/2 — Paint It Black/Bitta Truth (with free flexidisc "Twist And Shout" & insert, black & white or blue & white p/s) 6

MODIFIES

MINT VALUE £

	81	Human HUM 10	White Mice/Kray Twins (live) (p/s) ... 7
	80	Deram SML 1120	THE STORY SO FAR (LP, with insert & free colour sticker) ... 20

MODIFIES
	70	Punch PH 45	Bye Bye Happyness/Sufferation We Must Bear ... 12

MODS (1)
	64	RCA RCA 1399	Something On My Mind/You're Making Me Blue ... 25

MODS (2)
	80	Bootlegged Records 007	LOST TOUCH (LP; sold only in Portobello Market, London) ... 25

MODULATIONS
	74	Buddah BDS 406	I Can't Fight Your Love/Your Love Has Locked Me Up (DJ Copy) ... 30
	74	Buddah BDS 406	I Can't Fight Your Love/Your Love Has Locked Me Up ... 15

PETER MOESSER'S MUSIC
	70	Stateside SS 2182	Hello/Bye Bye (withdrawn) ... 7

MOFFAT ALL STARS
	70	Jackpot JP 719	Riot/IMPERSONATORS: Girls And Boys ... 200

LENROY MOFFATT
	74	Atra AR 20	What It Takes/I Love You Darling ... 45

MOGODONS
	82	Total Demoralisation MOG 1	ZUVEMBE EP (p/s) ... 10

MOGUL THRASH
	70	RCA RCA 2030	Sleeping In The Kitchen/St. Peter ... 15
	71	RCA SF 8156	MOGUL THRASH (LP) ... 150

(see also Colosseum, Eclection, King Crimson)

MOGWAI
	96	Rock Action RAR 01	Tuner/Lower (p/s, 500 only) ... 70
	96	Ché CHE 59	4 TRACK 3 BAND TOUR EP (with Urusei Yatsura & Backwater, p/s, 50 only) ... 40
	96	Ché CHE 61	Angels Vs Aliens/DWEEB: Buzzsong (p/s, 1st 500 on green vinyl) ... 12
	96	Ché CHE 61	Angels Vs Aliens/DWEEB: Buzzsong (p/s) ... 6
	96	Love Train PUBE 014	Summer/Ithica 27/9 (p/s, 1,500 only, inserts) ... 20
	97	Wurlitzer Jukebox WJ 22	New Paths To Helicon (Parts 1 & 2) (foldover p/s in polythene bag, 2 inserts, 1,000 only) .. 15
	97	Flotsam/Jetsam SHAG13.04	Stereo Dee/PH FAMILY: Club Beatroot Part 4 (p/s, 400 only) ... 15
	97	Chemikal CHEM 015	4 SATIN EP ... 15
	98	Chemikal Underground CHEM 026	NO EDUCATION = NO FUTURE (FUCK THE CURFEW) EP (12") ... 12
	99	Chemikal CHEM 036	EP (12") ... 15
	01	Rock Action ROCKACT 10	My Father My King (1-sided 12") ... 15
	06	PIAS PIAS X066T	TRAVEL IS DANGEROUS EP (12") ... 10
	11	Rock Action ROCKACT 54	Mexican Grand Prix/Slight Domestic (white vinyl) ... 10
	13	Rock Action ROCKACT 73	LES REVENANTS EP (10") ... 18
	97	Chemikal CHEM 818LP	YOUNG TEAM (2-LP, gatefold) ... 125
	98	Eye Q EYEUKLP 019	KICKING A DEAD PIG (2-LP, with poster) ... 50
	99	Chemikal Underground CMEM 033	COME ON DIE YOUNG (2-LP) ... 50
	01	Southpaw PAWLP1	ROCK ACTION (LP) ... 30
	03	Pias PIASX 035LP	HAPPY SONGS FOR HAPPY PEOPLE (LP, silvered sleeve) ... 35
	05	Pias PIAS051LP	GOVERNMENT COMMISSIONS : BBC SESSIONS 1996-2003 (2-LP) ... 25
	06	Chemikal Underground CHEM 106	YOUNG TEAM (4-LP reissue) ... 100
	06	Pias PIAS X067DLP	ZIDANE (2-LP) ... 35
	07	Pias PIAS X062DLP	MR BEAST (2-LP, one sided etched) ... 30
	10	Rock Action ROCKACT 48	SPECIAL MOVES (3-LP, CD, DVD and signed poster) ... 50
	14	Rock Action ROCKACT80	RAVE TAPES (Box set, LP, 12", 7" & CD, 3 art prints & download card) ... 30
	14	Rock Action ROCKACT80LP	RAVE TAPES (LP, with free 7") ... 18
	16	Rock Action ROCKACTION102LPX	ATOMIC (2-LP, orange vinyl) ... 25

(see also Magoo, Fuck Buttons)

ESSRA MOHAWK
	75	Mooncrest CREST 24	ESSRA MOHAWK (LP, with insert) ... 15
	77	Private Stock PVLP 1016	ESSRA (LP) ... 15

MOHAWKS
	68	Pama PM 309	The Clock/Version ... 35
	68	Pama PM 719	The Champ/Sound Of The Witchdoctors (blue label) ... 30
	68	Pama PM 719	The Champ/Sound Of The Witchdoctors (purple label) ... 20
	68	Pama PM 739	Baby Hold On (Parts 1 & 2) ... 20
	68	Pama PM 751	Sweet Soul Music/Hip Jigger ... 20
	68	Pama PM 757	Mony Mony/Pepsi ... 70
	69	Pama PM 758	Ride Your Pony/Western Promise ... 25
	69	Pama PM 798	Skinhead Shuffle/RICO: Red Cow ... 40
	70	Supreme SUP 205	Wicked Lady/For Our Liberty ... 15
	70	Pama PM 796	Landscape/Number 1 ... 25
	70	Supreme SUP 204	Let It Be/Looking Back ... 15
	70	Supreme SUP 205	For Our Liberty/Wicked Lady ... 10
	70	Supreme SUP 207	Give Me Some/(Instrumental) ... 50
	70	Supreme SUP 208	Funky Funky/Funky Funky (instrumental) ... 12
	72	Supreme PS 362	Storm/And I Love Her ... 40
	73	Supreme PS 376	The Champ/Cherry Pink ... 40
	70s	Star PTP 1011	Whiter Shade Of Pale/My One Desire ... 15
	86	Pama PM (T) 1	The Champ/Landscape (12", p/s) ... 12
	68	Pama PMLP 5	THE CHAMP (LP) ... 200

(see also Sid & Joe & Mohawks)

Louis MOHOLO

MINT VALUE £

LOUIS MOHOLO
78 Ogun OG 520   SPIRITS REJOICE (LP) 80

MOIST
95 Chrysalis 12CHSS 5019   SILVER (12" EP, clear vinyl) 10

MOJAVE 3
95 4AD CAD 5013   ASK ME TOMORROW (LP) 150
98 4AD CAD 8018   OUT OF TUNE (LP) 150
00 4AD CAD 2K05   EXCUSES FOR TRAVELLERS (LP) 150
03 4AD CAD 2309 LP   SPOON & RAFTER (LP) 75
06 4AD CAD 2604   PUZZLES LIKE YOU (LP) 75
17 Sonic Cathedral SCRO73LP   ASK ME TOMORROW (LP, reissue, green vinyl, 500 only) 25
(see also Slowdive)

MOJO HANNAH
72 Kingdom KV 8004   St. Jeremy/You'll Be Alright 25
73 Kingdom KVL 9001   SIX DAYS ON THE ROAD (LP, orange label) 35

MOJO MEN
65 Pye International 7N 25296   Dance With Me/Loneliest Boy In Town 30
66 Reprise RS 20486   Hanky Panky/She's My Baby 30
67 Reprise RS 20539   Sit Down I Think I Love You/Don't Leave Me Crying Like Before 20
67 Reprise RS 20580   Me About You/When You're In Love 15

MOJOS
63 Decca F 11732   They Say/Forever 15
64 Decca F 11853   Everything's Alright/Give Your Lovin' To Me 6
64 Decca F 11918   Why Not Tonight/Don't Do It Any More 7
64 Decca F 11959   Seven Daffodils/Nothin' At All 10
65 Decca F 12127   Comin' On To Cry/That's The Way It Goes 15
67 Decca F 12557   Goodbye Dolly Gray/I Just Can't Let Her Go 25
68 Liberty LBF 15097   Until My Baby Comes Home/Seven Park Avenue 60
64 Decca DFE 8591   THE MOJOS (EP) 70
(see also Stu James & Mojos, Faron's Flamingos)

MOLDY PEACHES
01 Rough Trade RTRADES 016   Who's Got The Crack?/NYC's Like A Graveyard (p/s) 10
01 Rough Trade RTRADELP 014   THE MOLDY PEACHES (LP) 80

MOLES
68 Parlophone R 5743   We Are The Moles (Parts 1 & 2) 30

MOLOKO
95 Echo ECHLP 7   DO YOU LIKE MY TIGHT SWEATER (2-LP) 40
98 Echo ECHLP 21   I AM NOT A DOCTOR (2-LP, triple gatefold) 80
00 Echo ECHLP 31   THINGS TO MAKE AND DO (2-LP) 80
03 Echo ECHLP 44   STATUES (LP) 125

MO-L-RANA
73 Polydor 2121-158   So Mt Daddy Says/Alone 6

MOMENT
85 Diamond DIA 004   In This Town/Just Once 6
80s Tenth Floor   Poor Mr. Diamond (Parts 1 & 2) 10
89 Big Stuff   Ready To Fall (promo only) 8
86 Rave RAVE UP 1   THE WORK GETS DONE (LP, coloured vinyl) 15

MOMENT OF TRUTH
77 Salsoul SZS 5509   MOMENT OF TRUTH (LP) 15

MOMENTS (1)
63 London HLN 9656   Walk Right In/Walk Right In (Instrumental) 12

MOMENTS (2)
76 All Platinum 6146313   Nine Times/When The Morning Comes 8
76 All Platinum SOUL 001   Nine Times (Disco Version)/THE RIMSHOTS: Do What You Feel (Disco Version) (12") 50
73 London SHU 8471   THE BEST OF THE MOMENTS (LP) 15

MOMUS
86 él GPO 9T   Nicky/Don't Leave/See A Friend In Tears (12") 15
87 Creation CRE 037 T   Murderers, The Hope Of Women (12", p/s) 12
86 el ACME 2   CIRCUS MAXIMUS (LP) 15
88 Creation CRELP 036   TENDER PERVERT (LP, with free 7") 15
90 Creation CRELP 052   DON'T STOP THE NIGHT (LP) 15
91 Creation CRELP 097   HIPPOPOTAMOMUS (LP, with "Michelin Man" track & Michelin Man style inlay, withdrawn) 15
(see also Happy Family)

MONACO (1)
78 Firebird/Pinnacle PIN 64   Earthy/God Only Knows 8

STEPHEN MONAHAN
67 London HLR 10145   City Of Windsor/Lost People 12

MONARCHS
64 London HLU 9862   Look Homeward Angel/What's Made You Change Your Mind 30

GRACHAN MONCUR III
74 JCOA/Virgin J2003   ECHOES OF PRAYER (LP) 25

JULIE MONDAY
66 London HLU 10080   Come Share The Good Times With Me/Time Is Running Out For Me 8

MONDO KANE
86 Lisson DOLEQ 2   New York Afternoon (mixes)/Manhattan Morning (12", p/s) 10
(see also Georgie Fame)

MONEY (1)
69 Major Minor MM 571   Welcome Me Love/Breaking Her Heart 8
69 Major Minor MM 620   Come Laughing Home/Power Of The Rainbow 8

MONEY (2)

MINT VALUE £

MONEY (2)
79	Gull GULL 64	Aren't We All Searching/Where Have All The Dancers Gone	8
80	Hobo HOS 011	FAST WORLD (EP, p/s)	80
79	Gull GULP 1031	FIRST INVESTMENT (LP)	18

MONEY JANGLE
72	President PT 362	Home/Away Away	20

MONEY PIT
97	Bluepose	Smile It's Sugar/Strange And Silent Staircase (P/S)	10

ZOOT MONEY('S BIG ROLL BAND)
64	Decca F 11954	The Uncle Willie/Zoot's Suit (solo)	50
65	Columbia DB 7518	Good/Bring It Home To Me	40
65	Columbia DB 7600	Please Stay/You Know You'll Cry	35
65	Columbia DB 7697	Something Is Worrying Me/Stubborn Kind Of Fellow	30
65	Columbia DB 7768	The Many Faces Of Love/Jump Back (as Paul Williams & Zoot Money Band)	30
66	Columbia DB 7876	Let's Run For Cover/Self-Discipline	30
66	Columbia DB 7975	Big Time Operator/Zoot's Sermon	20
66	Columbia DB 8090	The Star Of The Show (The La La Song)/The Mound Moves	35
67	Columbia DB 8172	Nick Knack/I Really Learnt How To Cry	15
70	Polydor 2058 020	No One But You/Prisoner	8
80	Magic Moon/MPL MACH 3	Your Feet's Too Big/Ain't Nothin' Shakin' But The Bacon (solo)	12
80	Magic Moon/MPL MACH 6	The Two Of Us/Ain't Nothin' Shakin' But The Bacon (solo)	30
66	Columbia SEG 8519	BIG TIME OPERATOR (EP)	200
66	Columbia S(C)X 6075	ZOOT! - LIVE AT KLOOK'S KLEEK (LP, mono)	100
66	Columbia S(C)X 6075	ZOOT! - LIVE AT KLOOK'S KLEEK (LP, stereo)	120
65	Columbia 33SX 1734	IT SHOULD'VE BEEN ME (LP)	150
68	Direction 8-63231	TRANSITION (LP)	100
70	Polydor 2482 019	ZOOT MONEY (LP)	80

(see also Paul Williams & Big Roll Band, Dantalian's Chariot, Eric Burdon & Animals, Grimms, Centipede, Ellis, Johnny Almond Music Machine)

MONGOLFIER BROS
84	Incurable	I Know/Things That Go Bump	20

MONGREL
73	Polydor 2383 182	GET YOUR TEETH INTO THIS (LP)	25

(see also Wizzard)

MONGRELS
64	Decca F 12003	I Long To Hear/Everywhere	30
65	Decca F 12086	My Love For You/Stewball	30

(see also Bobbie Miller)

MONITORS (1)
69	T. Motown TML 11108	GREETINGS WE'RE THE MONITORS (LP, mono)	100
69	T. Motown STML 11108	GREETINGS WE'RE THE MONITORS (LP, stereo)	90

MONK BOUGHT LUNCH
91	Own Label	Love And Hate/Paint It White/The Sailor's Tilted Hat (p/s)	40

THELONIOUS MONK
56	Vogue EPV 1115	THELONIOUS MONK (EP)	10
55	Esquire 20-039	THELONIOUS MONK QUINTET (10" LP)	45
55	Esquire 20-049	THELONIOUS MONK (10" LP)	45
56	Esquire 20-075	THELONIOUS MONK PLAYS (10" LP)	45
57	London LTZU 15097	BRILLIANT CORNERS (LP)	50
60	Esquire 32-109	THELONIOUS MONK QUINTETS (LP)	50
61	Esquire 32-115	WORK! (LP, with Art Blakey & Sonny Rollins)	60
61	Esquire 32-119	MONK'S MOODS (LP)	60
61	Riverside RLP 12-201	MONK PLAYS ELLINGTON (LP)	50
61	Philips BBL 1510	THELONIOUS MONK VOL. 1 (LP)	50
61	Riverside RLP 12-226	BRILLIANT CORNERS (LP)	80
61	Riverside RLP 12-262	MONK IN ACTION (LP)	40
62	Riverside RLP 12-300	AT THE TOWN HALL (LP, also stereo RLP 1138)	40
62	Riverside RLP 12-323	AT THE BLACK HAWK (LP, also stereo RLP 1171)	40
62	Philips BBL 1511	THELONIOUS MONK VOL. 2 (LP)	40
62	Riverside RLP 12-242	MONK'S MUSIC (LP)	80
63	CBS (S)BPG 62135	MONK'S DREAM (LP)	50
63	Riverside RLP 12-235	THELONIOUS HIMSELF (LP)	50
63	Riverside JLP (9)46	THELONIOUS MONK AND JOHN COLTRANE (LP)	50
64	Riverside RLP 002	IN EUROPE (VOL. 1)	35
64	CBS (S)BPG 62173	CRISS-CROSS (LP)	35
64	Blue Note (B)BLP 1510	THE GENIUS OF MODERN MUSIC (VOL. 1) (LP)	25
64	Blue Note (B)BLP 1511	THE GENIUS OF MODERN MUSIC (VOL. 2) (LP)	25
64	Riverside RLP 279	MISTERIOSO (LP)	25
64	CBS (S)BPG 62248	BIG BAND AND QUARTET IN CONCERT (LP)	25
65	CBS (S)BPG 62391	IT'S MONK'S TIME (LP)	25
65	Riverside RLP 305	FIVE BY MONK BY FIVE (LP)	25
65	Riverside RLP 003	IN EUROPE (VOL. 2) (LP)	20
65	CBS (S)BPG 62497	MONK (LP)	20
65	Riverside RLP 312	ALONE IN SAN FRANCISCO (LP)	20
65	Fontana FJL 113	WAY OUT! (LP)	20
65	Realm RM 52223	NICA'S TEMPO (LP, with Gigi Gryce)	20
65	CBS (S)BPG 62549	SOLO (LP)	20
65	Stateside SL 10252	THE GOLDEN MONK (LP)	20
67	Transatlantic PR7169	WORK (LP)	20
69	CBS 63609	MONKS BLUES (LP)	15

(see also John Coltrane, Sonny Rollins, Art Blakey, Miles Davis)

MONKEES

MINT VALUE £

MONKEES
66	RCA Victor RCA 1560	I'm A Believer/(I'm Not Your) Stepping Stone	6
67	RCA Victor RCA 1580	A Little Bit Me, A Little Bit You/The Girl I Knew Somewhere	6
67	RCA Victor RCA 1604	Alternate Title/Forget That Girl	6
67	RCA Victor RCA 1620	Pleasant Valley Sunday/Words	7
67	RCA Victor RCA 1645	Daydream Believer/Goin' Down	7
68	RCA Victor RCA 1673	Valleri/Tapioca Tundra	6
68	RCA Victor RCA 1706	D.W. Washburn/It's Nice To Be With You	8
69	RCA RCA 1802	Teardrop City/Man Without A Dream	10
69	RCA RCA 1824	Someday Man/Listen To The Band	10
69	RCA RCA 1862	Daddy's Song/The Porpoise Song	12
69	RCA RCA 1887	Mommy And Daddy/Good Clean Fun	12
70	RCA RCA 1958	Oh My My/Love You Better	12
74	Bell BLL 1354	Monkees Theme/I'm A Believer	6
67	RCA Victor RD 7844	The MONKEES (LP, mono)	15
67	RCA Victor RD 7868	MORE OF THE MONKEES (LP, mono)	18
67	RCA Victor SF 7868	MORE OF THE MONKEES (LP, stereo)	20
67	RCA Victor RD 7886	HEADQUARTERS (LP, mono)	20
67	RCA Victor SF 7886	HEADQUARTERS (LP, stereo)	20
67	RCA Victor RD 7886	HEADQUARTERS (LP, with different 'beard' photo on back, mono)	25
67	RCA Victor SF 7886	HEADQUARTERS (LP, with different 'beard' photo on back, stereo)	30
67	RCA Victor RD/SF 7912	PISCES, AQUARIUS, CAPRICORN AND JONES LTD. (LP)	22
68	RCA Victor RD/SF 7948	THE BIRDS, THE BEES & THE MONKEES (LP)	22

(The above albums were originally issued with black labels; later orange label copies are worth the same value.)

69	RCA RD 8016	INSTANT REPLAY (LP, mono)	30
69	RCA SF 8016	INSTANT REPLAY (LP, stereo)	25
69	RCA RD 8051	HEAD (LP, soundtrack, mono)	90
69	RCA SF 8051	HEAD (LP, soundtrack, stereo)	60
79	Arista MONK-1 1/2	MONKEEMANIA (LP)	20
89	Circus BOY 1	IDOLISED, PLASTICISED, PSYCHOANYLYSED, STERILISED (LP, spoken-word convention issue, white vinyl)	15
89	Circus BOY 1	IDOLISED, PLASTICISED, PSYCHOANYLYSED, STERILISED (LP, spoken-word convention issue, picture disc)	18

(see also Micky Dolenz, Davy Jones, Michael Nesmith, Tommy Boyce & Bobby Hart)

BOB MONKHOUSE
68	CBS 3958	I Remember Natalie/In My Dream World	7
69	CBS 4607	Another Time, Another Place, Another World/When I Found You	7

MONKS (1)
74	Rex R11 095	Roller Coaster Rock N Roll/It's A Crying Shame	10

MONKS (2)
79	EMI 2999	Johnny B Rotten/Drugs In My Pocket	6

MONOCHROME SET
79	Rough Trade RT 005	Alphaville/He's Frank (p/s)	10
79	Rough Trade RT 019	Eine Symphonie Des Grauens/Lester Leaps In (1st 1,000 with labels on wrong side with explanatory insert, p/s)	12
79	Rough Trade RT 019	Eine Symphonie Des Grauens/Lester Leaps In (p/s)	10
79	Rough Trade RT 028	The Monochrome Set/Mr Bizarro	10
79	Disquo Bleu BL 1	He's Frank (Slight Return)/Silicon Carne/Fallout (all cuts live) (no p/s)	8
82	Cherry Red CHERRY 51	Cast A Long Shadow/The Bridge	6
83	Cherry Red CHERRY 60	Jet Set Junta/Love Goes Down The Drain/Noise (Eine Kleine Symphonie)	6
80	Dindisc DID 4	STRANGE BOUTIQUE (LP)	25
80	DinDisc DID 8	LOVE ZOMBIES (LP, with lithograph)	20
82	Cherry Red BRED 34	ELIGIBLE BACHELORS (LP)	15
83	Cherry Red MRED 47	VOLUME CONTRAST BRILLIANCE (LP)	15

(see also Art Attacks, BID)

MONOCONICS
80	One Zone 001	Such A Shame (About You)/Exit Stage Left/Sensible Breakdown (p/s)	6

MONOGRAMS
59	Parlophone R 4515	Juke Box Cha Cha/The Greatest Mistake Of My Life	8

MONOLITH (1)
78	None	(I'm Not Your) Stepping Stone/Guns Of Time (no p/s)	60

MONOLITH (2)
10	Rephlex CAT 210EP	VOLUME 1 (12" EP)	30
15	Central Processing Unit 00010001	FLEKTRO (12" EP, as MNLTH)	30
16	Organic Analogue OA04	LASER 80 (12" EP, as MNLTH)	30

MONOPOLY
67	Polydor 56164	House Of Lords/Magic Carpet	20
67	Polydor 56188	We're All Going To The Seaside/It Isn't Easy	6
70	Pye 7N 17940	We Belong Together/Gone Tomorrow	25

(see also Raymond Froggatt)

MONOS
79	RCA PB 5178	Ericafire/Louie	6
79	RCA PB 5206	U.F.O./Teenage Confessions	6

MONOTONES (U.K.)
64	Pye 7N 15608	What Would I Do/Is It Right	10
64	Pye 7N 15640	It's Great/Anymore	10
65	Pye 7N 15761	No Waiting/Like A Lover Should	10
65	Pye 7N 15814	Something's Hurting Me/A Girl Like That	10

MONOTONES (U.S.)
58	London HLM 8625	Book Of Love/You Never Loved Me	40

MATT MONRO

MINT VALUE £

58	London HLM 8625	Book Of Love/You Never Loved Me (78)	20

MATT MONRO

56	Decca F 10816	Ev'rybody Falls In Love With Someone/Out Of Sight, Out Of Mind	10
57	Decca F 10845	The Garden Of Eden/Love Me Do	10
57	Decca F 10870	My House Is Your House/The Bean Song	10
61	Ember EMB S 120	The Ghost Of Your Past/Quite Suddenly	15
69	capitol CL 15603	On Days Like These/On A Clear Day (You Can See Forever)	25
70	Capitol CL 15643	We''re Gonna Change The World/You're Closer To Me	7
63	Parlophone GEP 8889	SINGS THE THEME FROM THE FILM 'FROM RUSSIA FROM LOVE' (EP)	10
57	Decca LF 1276	BLUE AND SENTIMENTAL (10" LP)	20

(see also John Barry)

BARRY MONROE

66	Polydor 56088	World Of Broken Hearts/Never Again	6

BILL MONROE (& HIS BLUE GRASS BOYS)

56	Brunswick 05567	New John Henry Blues/Put My Little Shoes Away	15

MARILYN MONROE

54	HMV 7M 232	The River Of No Return/I'm Gonna File My Claim	60
59	London HLT 8862	I Wanna Be Loved By You/I'm Thru' With Love	35
78	United Artists UP 36484	I Wanna Be Loved By You/Running Wild/I'm Thru With Love (gatefold p/s)	6
55	HMV 7EG 8090	THERE'S NO BUSINESS LIKE SHOW BUSINESS - SOUNDTRACK EXCERPTS (EP, company sleeve)	25
59	London RET 1231	SOME LIKE IT HOT (EP, soundtrack; first pressing with triangular centre)	80
59	London RET 1231	SOME LIKE IT HOT (EP, soundtrack; later round centre)	20
60	Philips BBE 12414	LET'S MAKE LOVE - FILM SOUNDTRACK (EP, with Yves Montand & Frankie Vaughan; mono)	30
60	Philips SBBE 9031	LET'S MAKE LOVE - FILM SOUNDTRACK (EP, with Yves Montand & Frankie Vaughan; stereo)	40
53	MGM MGM-D 116	GENTLEMEN PREFER BLONDES (10" LP, soundtrack with other artists)	75
59	London HA-T 2176	SOME LIKE IT HOT (LP, soundtrack with other artists, mono)	50
59	London SAH-T 6040	SOME LIKE IT HOT (LP, soundtrack with other artists, stereo)	60
60	Philips BBL 7414	LET'S MAKE LOVE (LP, soundtrack, with Yves Montand & Frankie Vaughan; mono)	40
60	Philips SBBL 592	LET'S MAKE LOVE (LP, soundtrack, with Yves Montand & Frankie Vaughan; stereo)	40
63	Stateside S(S)L 10048	MARILYN (LP, soundtrack, mono)	30
63	Stateside S(S)L 10048	MARILYN (LP, soundtrack, stereo)	40

(see also Frankie Vaughan)

VAUGHN MONROE (& HIS ORCHESTRA)

53	HMV 7M 144	Less Than Tomorrow (But More Than Yesterday)/Ruby	10
54	HMV 7M 247	They Were Doin' The Mambo/Mister Sandman	10
56	HMV 7M 332	Black Denim Trousers And Motorcycle Boots/All By Myself	20
57	HMV POP 354	Wringle Wrangle/Westward Ho The Wagons!	7
59	RCA RCA 1124	The Battle Of New Orleans/Hercules	8

MONSOON (1)

71	Trojan TR 7831	Hot Honolulu Night/Come Back Jane	6
72	Blue Mountain BM 1006	Night Of The Fly/Caroline The Wine Was Good	40

MONSOON (2)

81	Indipop IND 1	Ever So Lonely/Sunset Over The Ganges/The Mirror Of Your Mind/Shout! (Till You're Heard) (in plastic sleeve with insert)	8

(see also Complex)

MONSTER MAGNET

93	A&M 580 280-7	Twin Earth/Nod Scene (live) (stickered p/s, sticker, insert)	10
93	A&M 580 281-1	Twin Earth/Nod Scene (live)/Medicine (live) (12" 1-sided etched sick, p/s)	10
93	A&M AMYDK 291	Twin Earth/Nod Scene (live)/Medicine (live) (12" promo)	10
95	A&M AMDJ 7	Negasonic Teenage Warhead/Eclipse This (12", promo, stickered die-cut black sleeve)	10
95	A&M AMDJ 10	Dopes To Infinity/I'm Five Years Ahead Of My Time (12" promo)	10
95	A&M 540 315-1	DOPES TO INFINITY (2-LP)	80
98	A&M 540 908-1	POWERTRIP (2-LP)	100

MONTANAS

65	Piccadilly 7N 35262	All That Is Mine Can Be Yours/How Can I Tell	12
66	Pye 7N 17183	That's When Happiness Began/Goodbye Little Girl	50
67	Pye 7N 17282	Ciao Baby/Anyone There	10
67	Pye 7N 17338	Take My Hand/Top Hat	10
67	Pye 7N 17394	You've Got To Be Loved/Difference Of Opinion	20
68	Pye 7N 17499	A Step In The Right Direction/Someday (You'll Be Breaking My Heart Again)	12
68	Pye 7N 17597	You're Making A Big Mistake/Run To Me	10
69	Pye 7N 17697	Roundabout/Mystery	15
69	Pye 7N 17729	Ciao Baby/Someday (You'll Be Breaking My Heart Again)	6
70	MCA MK 5036	Let's Get A Little Sentimental/Hey Diddle Diddle	8
71	MAM R45	No Smoke Without Fire/Seaport	15
71	MAM MAMR62	Suzanne/Your Love Is Growing	15

(see also Trapeze)

MONTANA SEXTET

83	Virgin VS 600	Who Needs Enemies With A Friend Like You/Friendly Vibes (12")	15

MONTCLAIRS

74	Contempo CS 2008	Make Up For Lost Time/How Can One Man Live	8
75	Contempo CS 2036	Hung Up On Your Love/I Need You More Than Ever	30
01	Grapevine 114	Hey You Don't Fight It/Never Ending Love	45
74	Contempo CLP 503	DREAMING OF A SEASON (LP)	15

LOU MONTE

54	HMV 7M 176	A Baby Cried/One Moment More	7
54	HMV 7M 190	Darktown Strutters' Ball/I Know How You Feel	7
54	HMV 7M 249	Chain Reaction/Vera's Veranda	7

		MINT VALUE £
VINNIE MONTE		
59	London HL 8947	Summer Spree/I'll Walk You Home ... 10
63	Stateside SS 156	Joanie Don't Be Angry/Take Good Care Of Her ... 18
MONTEGO MELON		
68	Sioux SI 004	Swan Lake/HONG GANG: Reggae Mento ... 15
HUGO MONTENEGRO ORCHESTRA		
62	Oriole CB 1765	Palm Canyon Drive/Dark Eyes ... 7
63	Oriole CB 1792	Get Off The Moon/Sherry ... 20
65	RCA 1462	Darlin' Jill/Candy's Theme ... 6
68	RCA Victor RCA 1771	Hang 'Em High/Tomorrow's Love ... 8
65	RCA Victor RD 7758	THE MAN FROM U.N.C.L.E. (LP, soundtrack) ... 40
66	RCA Victor RD 7832	MORE MUSIC FROM THE MAN FROM U.N.C.L.E. (LP, soundtrack) ... 45
67	RCA Victor RD/SF 7877	HURRY SUNDOWN (LP, soundtrack) ... 20
69	RCA SF 8053	MOOG POWER (LP) ... 20
69	Stateside S(S)L 10267	LADY IN CEMENT (LP, soundtrack) ... 40
70	Pye Intl. NSPL 28136	DAWN OF DYLAN (LP) ... 15
BOBBY MONTEZ		
60	Vogue V 9165	Holiday In Havana/Jungle Stars ... 8
CHRIS MONTEZ		
62	London HLU 9650	Some Kinda Fun/Tell Me (It's All Over) ... 6
63	London HLU 9764	My Baby Loves To Dance/In An English Towne ... 7
66	Pye International 7N 25348	Call Me/Go 'Head On ... 15
66	Pye International 7N 25381	There Will Never Be Another You/You Can Hurt The One You Love ... 7
73	CBS 1291	Come on, Let's Go/Somebody Loves You ... 6
63	London REU 1392	LET'S DANCE (EP) ... 40
66	Pye Intl. NEP 44071	THE MORE I SEE YOU (EP) ... 10
66	Pye Intl. NEP 44080	CHRIS MONTEZ (EP) ... 10
63	London HA-U 8079	LET'S DANCE AND HAVE SOME KINDA FUN!!! (LP) ... 30
JACK MONTGOMERY		
85	Kent TOWN 102	Dearly Beloved/MARIE KNIGHT: That's No Way To Treat A Girl ... 15
80s	Soul City 124	Dearly Beloved/Do You Believe It ... 15
LITTLE BROTHER MONTGOMERY		
61	Columbia DB 4595	Pinetop's Boogie Woogie/Cow Cow Blues ... 25
61	Columbia 33SX 1289	LITTLE BROTHER MONTGOMERY (LP, with Alexis Korner) ... 70
62	77' 77LA 12/21	LITTLE BROTHER MONTGOMERY/SUNNYLAND SLIM (LP) ... 30
65	Decca LK 4664	LITTLE BROTHER MONTGOMERY (LP) ... 30
66	Xtra XTRA 1018	LITTLE BROTHER MONTGOMERY (LP) ... 20
71	Xtra XTRA 1115	FARRO ST. JIVE (LP) ... 20
71	Saydisc SDR 213	LITTLE BROTHER MONTGOMERY 1930-1969 (LP) ... 20
72	Saydisc SDM 223	HOME AGAIN (LP) ... 20
MARIAN MONTGOMERY		
67	Reaction 591 018	Love Makes Two People Sing/Monday Thru Saturday ... 25
72	Polydor 2383 159	MARIAN IN THE MORNING (LP) ... 20
ROY MONTGOMERY		
97	Enraptured RAPT 4510	Trajectory One/Trajectory Two (p/s, 27 in handmade p/s) ... 15
97	Enraptured RAPT 4510	Trajectory One/Trajectory Two (p/s, 280 clear vinyl) ... 8
STUART MONTGOMERY		
69	Private pressing	CERTAIN SEA WORDS (LP, with insert) ... 15
WES MONTGOMERY		
60	Riverside RLP 12-320	THE INCREDIBLE JAZZ GUITAR OF WES MONTGOMERY (LP, mono) ... 15
60	Riverside RLP 12-320	THE INCREDIBLE JAZZ GUITAR OF WES MONTGOMERY (LP, stereo) ... 20
MONTY, DERRICK & PATSY		
65	Blue Beat BB 280	Stir The Pot/Mercy ... 50
(see also Monty Morris, Derrick Morgan)		
MONTY (MORRIS) & ROY		
61	Blue Beat BB 61	In And Out The Window/Tra La La Boogie (with Dumbago's Orchestra) ... 12
61	Blue Beat BB 63	Sweetie Pie/ROLAND ALPHONSO'S GROUP: Green Door ... 18
(see also Monty Morris)		
MONTY PYTHON('S FLYING CIRCUS)		
72	Charisma CB 192	Spam Song/The Concert (as Monty Python's Flying Circus, p/s) ... 6
74	NME/Charisma SFI 1259	Monty Python's Tiny Black Round Thing (D.P. Gumby Presents "Election '74"/ The Lumberjack Song) (live flexidisc free with NME) ... 10
79	Warner Bros K 17495	Always Look On The Bright Side Of Life/Brian (p/s) ... 15
80	Charisma CB 374	I Like Chinese/I Bet You They Won't Play This Song On The Radio/Finland (p/s) ... 15
88	Warner Bros W 7653	Always Look On The Bright Side Of Life/Brian (p/s, reissue) ... 10
76	Charisma MP 001	PYTHON ON SONG (EP, double pack [CBS 268/PY 2]) ... 10
70	BBC REB 73M	MONTY PYTHON'S FLYING CIRCUS (LP, mono, mustard label) ... 18
70	Charisma CAS 1049	ANOTHER MONTY PYTHON RECORD (LP, inner sleeve, 3 inserts, 'scroll' label) ... 20
73	Charisma CAS 1063	MONTY PYTHON'S PREVIOUS RECORD (LP, with free flexidisc in p/s, Teach Yourself Heath & inner sleeve) ... 15
73	Charisma CAS 1080	MATCHING TIE AND HANDKERCHIEF (LP, parallel grooves on side 2, die-cut sleeve, 2 inserts) ... 15
(see also John Cleese, Rutles)		
MONUMENT		
71	Beacon BEAS 15	THE FIRST MONUMENT (LP) ... 60
(see also Zior)		
MONUMENTAL		
81	Impact IMP 001	Boy On The Run/Free (p/s) ... 10
MONUMENTUM		
95	Misanthropy AMAZON 007	IN ABSENTIA CHRISTI (LP) ... 50

MOOCHE
MINT VALUE £

MOOCHE
69	Pye 7N 17735	Hot Smoke And Sasafrass/Seen Through A Light	20

MOOD MOSAIC
66	Columbia DB 7801	A Touch Of Velvet, A Sting Of Brass/Bond Street P.M.	35
66	Columbia DB 7801	A Touch Of Velvet, A Sting Of Brass/Bond Street P.M.(DJ Copy)	50
67	Columbia DB 8149	Chinese Chequers/The Real Mr. Smith	25
68	Parlophone R 5716	The Yellow Spotted Capricorn/ELMER HOCKETT'S HURDY GURDY: Fantastic Fair	15
69	Columbia DB 8618	A Touch Of Velvet, A Sting Of Brass/Bond Street P.M. (reissue)	15
67	Columbia SX 6153	MOOD MOSAIC (LP, mono)	35
67	Studio Two TWO 160	MOOD MOSAIC (LP, stereo)	25

(see also Mark Wirtz Orchestra & Chorus, Keith West)

MOOD OF HAMILTON
67	Columbia DB 8304	Why Can't There Be More Love?/King's Message	25

MOOD REACTION
69	Gas 136	Too Much Loving/Roaring Twenties	20
70	Gas GAS 143	Change Of Heart/Run Away Man	20
70	Pama PSP 1007	LIVE AT THE CUMBERLAND (LP)	40

MOOD SIX
82	EMI EMI 5336	She's Too Far/Venus (unreleased; white label copies exist with p/s)	30
85	Psycho PSYCHO 4001	PLASTIC FLOWERS (12" EP)	10

MOODS
63	Starlite ST45 098	Duckwalk/Easy Going	22

MOODY
73	Polydor 2310 285	THE GENTLE RAIN (LP)	200

AMEIL MOODY
69	Blue Cat BS 143	Mullo Reggae/Lifeline (as Amiel Moodie)	250
69	Blue Cat BS 164	Ratchet Knife/Bend The Tree	750

MOODY BLUES
64	Decca F 11971	Steal Your Heart Away/Loose Your Money (But Don't Loose Your Mind) (as Moodyblues)	45
64	Decca F 12022	Go Now!/It's Easy Child	6
65	Decca F 12095	I Don't Want To Go On Without You/Time Is On My Side	7
65	Decca F 12166	From The Bottom Of My Heart (I Love You)/And My Baby's Gone	7
65	Decca F 12266	Everyday/You Don't (All The Time)	10
66	Decca F 12498	Boulevard De La Madelaine/This Is My House (But Nobody Calls)	12
67	Decca F 12543	Life's Not Life/He Can't Win (withdrawn)	60
67	Decca F 12607	Fly Me High/Really Haven't Got The Time	30
67	Decca F 12670	Love And Beauty/Leave This Man Alone	20
68	Deram DM 196	Voices In The Sky/Doctor Livingstone, I Presume	10
68	Deram DM 213	Ride My See-Saw/A Simple Game	8
69	Deram DM 247	Never Comes The Day/So Deep Within You	7
69	Threshold TH 1	Watching And Waiting/Out And In	8
83	Threshold TH 30	Blue Wind/Going Nowhere (p/s, with free T-shirt)	6
65	Decca DFE 8622	THE MOODY BLUES (EP, original label)	30
65	Decca DFE 8622	THE MOODY BLUES (EP, reissue with boxed Decca logo)	10
65	Decca LK 4711	THE MAGNIFICENT MOODIES (LP, unboxed red/silver Decca label logo)	100
65	Decca LK 4711	THE MAGNIFICENT MOODIES (LP, boxed red/silver Decca label logo)	20
67	Deram DML 707	DAYS OF FUTURE PASSED (LP, originally with white band on sleeve & 'DSS' labels, mono)	30
67	Deram SML 707	DAYS OF FUTURE PASSED (LP, originally with white band on sleeve & 'DSS' labels, stereo)	15
68	Deram DML 711	IN SEARCH OF THE LOST CHORD (LP, gatefold sleeve, mono, 'DSS' label)	40
69	Deram DML 1035	ON THE THRESHOLD OF A DREAM (LP, gatefold sleeve with stapled booklet, mono. Label is white/brown with large logo)	30
69	Deram SML 1035	ON THE THRESHOLD OF A DREAM (LP, gatefold sleeve with stapled booklet, stereo)	20
69	Threshold THM 1	TO OUR CHILDREN'S CHILDREN'S CHILDREN (LP, gatefold, with insert, white/pink label, mono)	40
69	Threshold THS 1	TO OUR CHILDREN'S CHILDREN'S CHILDREN (LP, gatefold, with insert, white/lilac label, stereo)	20
70	Threshold THS 3	A QUESTION OF BALANCE (1st pressing, Matrixes 10009P-1W/10010P-1W, 'flap' gatefold sleeve with lyric sheet)	25
71	Threshold THS 5	EVERY GOOD BOY DESERVES A FAVOUR (LP, gatefold, lyric insert, white/blue label)	18
72	Threshold THS 7	SEVENTH SOJOURN (LP, gatefold sleeve, lyric insert, white/blue label)	18

(see also Justin Hayward, Denny Laine, Gerry Levene & Avengers)

GEORGE MOODY
65	Fontana TF 631	Bring A Little Sunshine (To My Heart)/Santa The Swagman	6

JAMES MOODY
55	Esquire 20-071	MOODY HI FI (10" LP)	20

MOOG MACHINE
69	CBS 63807	SWITCHED ON ROCK (LP)	20

(THE) MOOG
92	Delirious DELIS 2	Rush Hour/Jungle Muffin/Live Forever/Hopelessly Volatile/Subtone (12")	30
92	Delirious DELIS 4	THE MOOG REMIX EP: Jungle Muffin (Micky Finn Remix)/Rush Hour (Rotor Remix)/Live Forever (Mercy Remix)/Going Crazy (Justice Remix) (12")	12

MOOM
95	Delerium DELEC LP 035	TOOT (LP)	15

MOON
68	Liberty LBF 15076	Someday Girl/Mothers And Fathers	25
70	Liberty LBF 15333	Pirate/Not To Know	10
68	Liberty LBL/LBS 83146	WITHOUT EARTH (LP)	80

(see also Beach Boys)

Keith MOON

MINT VALUE £

KEITH MOON
75	Polydor 2058 584	Don't Worry Baby/Together	20
75	Polydor 2442 134	TWO SIDES OF THE MOON (LP)	30

LARRY MOON
63	Ember EMB 171	Tia Juana Ball/Bouquet Of Roses	20

PERRY MOON
63	Sway SW 002	Nine Five Baby/PLANTES: Water Front	10

TERRY MOON
63	Planetone RC 11	Moon Man/MIKE ELLIOT: This Love Of Mine	10

MOON BOYS
69	Amalgamated AMG 846	Apollo 11/PIONEERS: Love Love Everyday	150

(see also Hippy Boys)

MOONCHILD
75	Look LKSP 5010	Hourglass/War Orphan (Brother Of The Day)	20

MOONDOG
54	London REP 1010	ON THE STREETS OF NEW YORK (EP)	30
59	Esquire 32-055	MOONDOG (LP)	200
69	CBS 63906	MOONDOG (LP, gatefold sleeve)	50
04	Honest Jons HJRLP 18	THE VIKING OF SIXTH AVENUE (2-LP)	20
09	Honest Jons HJRLP 107	THE STORY OF MOONDOG (LP, reissue)	15

MOONDOGS (1)
78	Lyntone LT 002	Heads I Win/Two's A Crowd (p/s)	40

MOONDOGS (2)
79	Good Vibrations GOT 10	She's Nineteen/Ya Don't Do Ya (foldout p/s)	20
80	Real ARE 13	Who's Gonna Tell Mary/Overcaring Parents (p/s)	15
81	Real ARE 14	Talking In The Canteen/Make Her Love Me (p/s, with neckerchief)	35
81	Real ARE 14	Talking In The Canteen/Make Her Love Me/You Said (p/s)	15
81	Real ARE 16	Imposter/Baby Snatcher (p/s)	15

ART MOONEY (& HIS ORCHESTRA)
53	MGM SP 1037	I Played The Fool/I Just Couldn't Take It, Baby (with Cathy Ryan)	10
53	MGM SP 1045	Baby Don't Do It/Believe In Me (with Cathy Ryan)	10
54	MGM SP 1088	Oh Boy What Joy We Had/Silhouette D'Amour	8
55	MGM SP 1134	No Regrets/Honey Babe	8
55	MGM SP 1145	Give Me A Band And My Baby/The Girl I Left Behind Me	8
56	MGM SP 1166	Memories Of You/I'm Looking Over	8
57	MGM MGM 923	Rebel Without A Cause Theme/"East Of Eden" Theme	15
57	MGM MGM 943	Giant/There's Never Been Anyone Else But You	15
57	MGM MGM 951	Rock And Roll Tumbleweed/Is There A Teenager In The House (with Ocie Smith)	22

(see also Ocie Smith, Shorty Long, Cloverleafs, Cathy Ryan)

MOONGLOWS
57	London HLN 8374	I Knew From The Start/Over And Over Again	700
57	London HLN 8374	I Knew From The Start/Over And Over Again (78)	70

(see also Harvey & Moonglows, Etta & Harvey)

MOONI
73	Polydor 2058-367	Wine Ridden Talks/Nightmare	10

(see also Mott The Hoople)

MOONKYTE
71	Mother SMOT 1	COUNT ME OUT (LP, with insert, cover has a die-cut spire)	600

MOONLIGHTERS (1)
63	Island WI 043	Going Out/Hold My Hands	20

MOONLIGHTERS (2)
65	Columbia DB 7602	Come On Home/It's Too Late	10
66	Columbia DB 7910	We'll See It Through/Too Late To Come Home	10

MOONPIE
74	Philips 6006380	Going away Today/The Race Keeps Moving On	10

MOONQUAKE
73	London HL 10446	Remember/This Winter	8

MOON ROCKS & PRINCE JAZZBO
78	Bushay's BFM 101	Unite Jah People/Have No Fear (12")	40

MOONSHADOW
76	Maxi M003	Chase Me/Fight Hard	15

MICKY MOONSHINE
74	Decca F 13555	Baby Blue/Name It You Got It	20
74	Decca F 13555	Baby Blue/Name It You Got It (DJ copy)	40

MOONSHINE (1)
70	KJ Roberts ZDR56312	Susannah/Garden Of Men	60

MOONSHINE (2)
76	Moo Records MOO 1	MOONSHINE EP (EP)	70

MOONSHINERS
67	Page One POLS 004	HOLD UP (LP)	22

MOONSTOMP
89	Link LINK LP 086	THEY NEVER SEE (LP)	20

MOONSTONES
65	Parlophone R 5331	Heaven Fell Last Night/Little Roses	6
66	Parlophone R 5497	Violets Of Dawn/Power Of Decision	6
67	Mercury MF 1011	How Many Times/Louisville	6

MOON'S TRAIN
67	MGM MGM 1333	Deed I Do/It's In My Mind	40
98	Tenth Planet TP 037	MOON'S TRAIN (LP)	15

(see also Denny Mitchell, Preachers)

MOONTREKKERS

MINT VALUE £

MOONTREKKERS
61	Parlophone R 4814	Night Of The Vampire/Melodie D'Amour	30
62	Parlophone R 4888	There's Something At The Bottom Of The Well/Hatashiai	30
63	Decca F 11714	Moondust/The Bogey Man	20

MICHAEL MOORCOCK('S DEEP FIX)
82	Flicknife EJS P9831	Brothel In Rosenstrasse/Time Centre (numbered, 500 only, with autographed lyric sheet)	30
75	United Artists UAG 29732	NEW WORLD'S FAIR (LP, with inner sleeve)	40

(see also Hawkwind)

ALICE MOORE
50s	Poydras MC 66	Prison Blues/My Man Blues	22

ANTHONY MOORE
71	Polydor 2310 062	PIECES FROM THE CLOUDLAND BALLROOM (LP)	60
72	Polydor 2310 079	SECRETS OF THE BLUE BAG (LP)	40
76	Virgin V 2057	OUT (LP, unissued)	0

BARBARA MOORE
67	CBS (S) BPG 62839	A LITTLE MOORE BARBARA (LP)	40

BOBBY MOORE (& RHYTHM ACES)
66	Chess CRS 8033	Searching For My Love/Hey Mr D.J.	25
75	Pye International 7N 25691	Call Me Your Anything Man/Call Me Your Anything Man (Disco Version) (solo)	6
66	Chess CRL 4521	SEARCHIN' FOR MY LOVE (LP)	75

BUTCH MOORE
64	Piccadilly 7N 35170	Foolin Time/Too Soon To Know	10
64	Pye 7N 15727	Down Came The Rain/Bye Bye Till Then	8
64	Piccadilly 7N 35182	I Missed You/Touch Me	12
65	Pye 7N 15832	Walking The Streets In The Rain/I Stand Still	10
65	Pye 7N 15910	Our Love WIll Go On/Words	8
67	Pye 7N 17368	Till Then My Love/The Incredible Miss Brown	7

CHRISTY MOORE
69	Mercury 20170 SMCL	PADDY ON THE ROAD (LP)	400
72	Trailer LER 3035	PROSPEROUS (LP)	15
75	Polydor 2383 344	WHATEVER TICKLES YOUR FANCY (LP)	25
76	Polydor 2383 426	CHRISTY MOORE (LP)	25
70s	WEA WX 286	VOYAGE (LP)	15

CURLEY MOORE & THE COOL ONES
71	Pye 25570	Funky Yeah/Shelly's Rubber Band	35

DOROTHY MOORE
76	Contempo CLP 535	MISTY BLUE (LP)	15

DUDLEY MOORE (TRIO)
61	Parlophone R 4772	Strictly For The Birds (solo)/Duddly Dell (B-side as Dudley Moore Trio)	10
68	Decca F 12850	30 Is A Dangerous Age, Cynthia/The Real Stuff	10
69	Decca F 12882	Keep It Up/Gently (as Dudley Moore Trio)	25
66	Decca LK 4788	GENUINE DUD (LP, as Dudley Moore Trio)	20
68	Decca SKL 4923	BEDAZZLED (LP, stereo, soundtrack)	100
69	Decca LK/SKL 4976	THE DUDLEY MOORE TRIO (LP)	30

(see also Peter Cook & Dudley Moore, Cleo Laine)

G T MOORE
74	B&C CB 236	I'm Still Waiting/Judgement Day	8

GARY MOORE
78	MCA MCA 386	Back On The Streets/Track Nine (in p/s)	30
83	Virgin VS 564	Falling In Love With You/(Instrumental) (p/s, with comic)	6
73	CBS 65527	GRINDING STONE (LP, as Gary Moore Band)	20
78	MCA MCF 2853	BACK ON THE STREETS (LP, with inner sleeve)	18
81	Jet JETLP 245	LIVE AT THE MARQUEE (LP, withdrawn test pressing, white sleeve with Jet Info sticker)	100
82	Virgin V 2245	CORRIDORS OF POWER (LP, with free live EP [VDJ 34])	20
84	EMI OVED 206	VICTIMS OF THE FUTURE (LP, with inner & poster)	20
86	10 DIXP 16	RUN FOR COVER (LP, picture disc, die-cut sleeve)	30
87	10 DIXG 56	WILD FRONTIER (2-LP, gatefold sleeve)	20

(see also Granny's Intentions, Dr. Strangely Strange, Skid Row, Thin Lizzy, Gary Moore & Phil Lynott, Eddie Howell, G-Force, Cozy Powell, Jack Bruce, National Head)

GARY MOORE & PHIL LYNOTT
85	10 TENS 49	Out In The Fields/Military Man (2 1-sided interlocking shaped picture-disc set, stickered gatefold PVC sleeve)	15
85	10 TENC 49-12	Military Man (12", 1-sided, B-side etched with signatures, promo only)	12

JACKIE MOORE
74	Atlantic K40544	SWEET CHARLIE BABE (LP)	20
76	RCA RS 1033	MAKE ME FEEL LIKE A WOMAN (LP)	20
79	CBS 83786	I'M ON MY WAY (LP)	15

JACQUELINE MOORE
65	Decca F 12165	Queen Of The House/What's Going On Here	7

JERRY MOORE
69	Fontana STL 5502	LIFE IS A CONSTANT JOURNEY HOME (LP)	40

JOHNNY MOORE (2)
02	Grapevine 2000 G2K 147	Yesterday Today And Tomorrow/Come Fly With Me	8
03	Beecool 101	Can't Live Without Your Love/DOTTIE PEARSON: Hello Baby (promo only)	8

JOHNNY MOORE (1)
67	Caltone TONE 101	Sound And Soul/ROY SHIRLEY: Get On The Ball	60
69	Doctor Bird DB 1180	Big Big Boss/CARL CANNONBALL BRYON: Reggae This Reggae	100

(see also Cannonball & Johnny Melody, Alton Ellis)

MATTHEW MOORE
66	Capitol CL 15467	A Face In The Crowd/St. James Infirmary	6

MERRILL E. MOORE

MINT VALUE £

MERRILL E. MOORE
55	Capitol CL 14369	Five Foot Two, Eyes Of Blue/Hard Top Race (as Merrill Moore)	200
55	Capitol CL 14369	Five Foot Two, Eyes Of Blue/Hard Top Race (as Merrill Moore) (78)	20
56	Capitol F 3397	King Porter Stomp/Rock Island Line (export only)	150
68	Ember EMB S 253	Down The Road A-Piece/Buttermilk Baby	15
69	B&C CB 100	Sweet Mama Tree Top Tall/Little Green Apples	8
70	Bulldog BD 20	House Of Blue Lights/Red Light	8
67	Ember EMB 3392	BELLYFUL OF BLUE-THUNDER (LP)	40

NICKY MOORE BAND
81	Street Tunes STS 006	Year Of The Lie	10

(see also Tiger, Samson, Hackensack, Mammoth)

OSCAR MOORE TRIO
55	London H-APB 1035	KENYA (10" LP)	20

ROGER MOORE
65	CBS 202014	Where Does Love Go/Tomorrow After Tomorrow (in p/s)	20
65	CBS 202014	Where Does Love Go/Tomorrow After Tomorrow	10

SCOTTY MOORE
64	Columbia 33SX 1680	THE GUITAR THAT CHANGED THE WORLD! (LP)	60

(see also Elvis Presley)

SHELLEY MOORE (& MOORE SESSIONEERS)
58	Starlite ST45 002	You've Tied Me Up/Gone On The Guy	7
58	Starlite ST45 003	Where Is The Bluebird?/Everything Is Gonna Be All Right	7

SYLVIA MOORE
70	Sunshine SUN 3	JUNGLE MAGIC (LP)	40

THURSTON MOORE & DON FLEMING
97	Via Satellite V.SAT 6	Telstar/E.A.R.: Sputnik	8

TIM MOORE
75	Mooncrest Moon 41	A Fool Like You/Aviation Man	12

MELBA MOORE
78	Buddah BDS 464	Standing Right Here/Living Free	8
86	Kent 6T 2	Magic Touch/CHUCK JACKSON: Little By Little	30
87	Horace's 001	Magic Touch/TOMMY HUNT: The Pretty Part Of You	20
03	Kent TOWN 119	DEAN PARISH: Broken Bottles And Sticks/MELBA MOORE: Magic Touch	8

ALAN MOORHOUSE ORCHESTRA
66	Pye 7N 17073	(The Ballad Of) The Green Berets/London Bridge	6
68	Page One POF 104	Stop Press/Chloe	7
70	Columbia DB 8674	Haunting Me/Soul Bossa	6

BIG MOOSE (WALKER)
68	Python PKM 1	Puppy Howl Blues/Rambling Woman (pressed with reversed labels)	35

MOOSE (1)
70	Escort ERT 840	Engine No. 9/KUKASS: Do It	30

MOOSE (2)
92	Hut HUTLP 5	XYZ (LP, without free 7")	15
92	Hut HUTLP 5	XYZ (LP, with free 7")	20
94	PIAS BIAS 260	HONEY BEE (LP, with free 7")	25

MOPEDS
68	Col. Blue Beat DB 108	Whiskey And Soda/Do It	7

(see also Cindy Starr & Mopeds)

MOQUETTES
64	Columbia DB 7315	Right String, But The Wrong Yo-Yo/You Came Along	50

SANTOS MORADOS
68	Island WIP 6034	Tonopah/Anytime	6

JOHN MORALES
09	BBE BBE 129CLP	THE M&M MIXES (3-LP)	20

NONO MORALES & HIS ORCHESTRA
54	HMV 7MC 5	Istanbul (Not Constantinople)/Am I Blue (export single)	6

MORAL SUPPORT
79	Round RSR 001	Just Where It's At Tonight/Sin	20

MIKE MORAN
70s	Alba TAR 053	PENNY WHISTLES OF ROBERT LOUIS STEVENSON (LP)	20

MOYA MORAY
62	Piccadilly 7N 35023	My Heart Will Make A Fool Of Me/You're Running Out Of Kisses	12

MORBID ANGEL
89	Earache MOSH 11	ALTARS OF MADNESS (LP, pink splattered vinyl, stickered sleeve)	30
89	Earache MOSH 11P	ALTARS OF MADNESS (LP, picture disc)	30
91	Earache MOSH 31	BLESSED ARE THE SICK (LP)	20
91	Earache MOSH 31	BLESSED ARE THE SICK (LP on 6 x 7" in box with 4 page insert)	40
91	Earache MOSH 48	ABOMINATIONS OF DESOLATION (LP)	25
94	Earache MOSH 112	LAIBACH REMIXES EP (God Of Emptiness/Sworn To The Black/Sworn To The Black [Laibach Remix]/God Of Emptiness [Laibach Remix]) (12", p/s)	30
95	Earache MOSH 134 LP	DOMINATION (LP)	20

MORE
80	Atlantic K 11561	We Are The Band/Atomic Rock (with p/s)	6
82	Atlantic K 11744	Trickster/Hey Joe (p/s)	15

MANDY MORE
72	Philips 6006 199	Come With Me To Jesus/Alone In My Yellow	25
73	Philips 6006 277	San Francisco 5AM/Coffee Cups	25
73	Philips 6006 343	Every Mother's Child/Blue Seasons	25
75	Fresh Air 6121 119	Rose Coloured Window/If I Smiled On Saturday	25
72	Philips 6308109	BUT THAT IS ME (LP)	250

MORE MONEY SYSTEM

MINT VALUE £

MORE MONEY SYSTEM
69 Leeds Permanent Building Society LPB 001   Do Your Own Thing/Call It Anything (p/s) 10

AIRTO MOREIRA AND THE GODS OF JAZZ
93 B&W BW 051   KILLER BEES (LP, in box with prints) 50

(see also Fourth World)

MORGAN
73 RCA SF 8321   NOVA SOLIS (LP, with insert) 40

(see also Mott The Hoople, Love Affair, Humpy Bong)

AL MORGAN
58 London HLU 8741   Jealous Heart/Foolish Tears 12

MORGAN AND THE MARK 7
66 Polydor BM 56283   I'm Gonna Turn My Life Around/Undercover Man 35

MORGAN BROTHERS
59 MGM MGM 1026   Kissin' On The Red Light/Milk From The Coconut 6

CARLTON B MORGAN
82 CNT 0666   DEVILS MUSIC (LP) 15

DAVID/DAVY MORGAN
65 Columbia DB 7624   Tomorrow I'll Be Gone/Ain't Got Much More To See (as Davy Morgan) 45
68 Parlophone R 5692   True To Life/Dawning (as David Morgan) 25

(see also Wishful Thinking)

DERRICK MORGAN
60 Blue Beat BB 7   Fat Man/I'm Gonna Leave You 30
60 Blue Beat BB 12   Don't Cry/I Pray For You (as Derrick Morgan & Ebonies) 25
60 Blue Beat BB 18   Lover Boy/Oh My! 25
61 Blue Beat BB 31   Now We Know/Nights Are Lonely (with Trenton Spence Orchestra) 25
61 Blue Beat BB 35   Leave Earth/Wigger Wee Shuffle (with Clue J. & His Blues Busters) 25
61 Blue Beat BB 62   Shake A Leg/Golden Rule (as Derrick & Drumbago All Stars) 25
62 Blue Beat BB 76   Sunday, Monday/Be Still 25
62 Blue Beat BB 82   Don't You Know Little Girl (actually by Derrick & Basil)/ B. GABBIDON: Hully Gully Miss Molly 25
62 Blue Beat BB 85   Come On Over/Come Back My Darling (with Buster's Group) 25
62 Blue Beat BB 91   Headache/OWEN GRAY: Millie Girl 25
62 Blue Beat BB 94   Meekly Wait/Day In And Day Out (both sides with Yvonne [Sterling]) 20
62 Blue Beat BB 100   In My Heart/BELL'S GROUP: Kingston 13 30
62 Blue Beat BB 110   Are You Going To Marry Me?/Troubles (as Derrick Morgan & Patsy) 25
62 Blue Beat BB 130   Should Be Ashamed/Marjorie (with Buster's Group) 20
62 Blue Beat BB 141   Joybells (with Duke Reid Group)/Going Down To Canaan (with Denzil Dennis) 20
62 Island WI 004   Travel On/Teach Me Baby 35
62 Island WI 006   The Hop/Tell It To Me 35
62 Island WI 011   Forward March/Please Don't Talk About Me (B-side actually with Eric Morris) 25
62 Island WI 013   Cherry Home/See And Blind 35
63 Blue Beat BB 148   Jezebell/Burnette 25
63 Blue Beat BB 177   Patricia My Dear/The Girl I Left Behind 25
63 Blue Beat BB 187   Tears On My Pillow/You Should Have Known 25
63 Blue Beat BB 196   Telephone/Life Is Tough (B-side actually "Tough Man Tough") 35
63 Island WI 037   Dorothy/Leave Her Alone 25
63 Island WI 051   Blazing Fire/DERRICK & PATSY: I'm In A Jam 25
63 Island WI 053   No Raise, No Praise/Loving Baby 25
63 Island WI 080   Angel With Blue Eyes/Corner Stone 25
63 Rio R 1   Blazing Fire/Edmarine 20
64 Black Swan WI 402   Street Girl/Edmarine 25
64 Black Swan WI 425   Cherry Pie (actually by Frederick Hibbert)/BOB WALLS: Beware 20
64 Blue Beat BB 233   Let Them Talk/Sleeping 30
64 Blue Beat BB 239   Miss Lulu/DERRICK & PALOY: She's So Young (B-side act. by Derrick & Patsy) 20
64 Blue Beat BB 261   The Soldier Man/BUSTER'S ALL STARS: Jet 707 100
64 Blue Beat BB 268   Katy Katy/Call On Me 18
65 Blue Beat BB 276   Weep No More/I Want A Girl 18
65 Blue Beat BB 283   Johnny Grave/BUSTER'S ALL STARS: Yeah Yeah 30
65 Blue Beat BB 311   Throw Them Away/Baby Face 25
65 Blue Beat BB 329   Sweeter Than Honey/You Never Know (with Prince Buster) 25
65 Ska Beat JB 185   Heart Of Stone/Let Me Go (with Baba Brooks Group) 25
65 Ska Beat JB 218   Don't Call Me Daddy/BABA BROOK'S BAND: Girl's Town Ska 30
65 Island WI 193   Two Of A Kind/I Want A Lover (both actually with Naomi) 30
65 Island WI 225   Starvation/I Am A Blackhead Again 30
66 Island WI 277   It's Alright/I Need Someone (both sides actually with Blenders) 35
66 Island WI 289   Ameletia (actually by Frank Cosmo)/Don't You Worry (B-side with Patsy Todd) 20
66 Island WI 3010   Gather Together Now (Jamaican Independence Song)/Soft Hand (actually "So Hard") (both sides actually with Blenders) 25
66 Rio R 122   Cool Off Rudies/Take It Easy 25
67 Island WI 3079   Someone (actually by Derrick & Pauline Morgan)/Do You Love Me (with Pauline) 18
67 Pyramid PYR 6010   Tougher Than Tough/ROLAND ALPHONSO: Song For My Father 25
67 Pyramid PYR 6013   Greedy Gal/SOUL BROTHERS: Marcus Junior 30
67 Pyramid PYR 6014   Court Dismiss/FREDERICK McCLEAN: Fine Fine Fine 35
67 Pyramid PYR 6019   Judge Dread In Court/Last Chance 30
67 Pyramid PYR 6021   Kill Me Dead/Don't Be A Fool 25
67 Pyramid PYR 6024   No Dice/I Mean It 25
67 Pyramid PYR 6025   Do The Beng Beng/Revenge 45
68 Island WI 3094   Conquering Ruler/LLOYD & DEVON: Red Rum Ball 100
68 Island WI 3101   Gimme Back/VICEROYS: Send Requests 60

Freddy MORGAN

MINT VALUE £

Year	Label/Number	Title	Value
68	Island WI 3159	Hold You Jack/One Morning In May	40
68	Pyramid PYR 6029	I Am The Ruler/I Mean It	40
68	Pyramid PYR 6039	Woman A Grumble/Don't Be A Fool	25
68	Pyramid PYR 6040	Want More/ROLAND ALPHONSO: Goodnight My Love	25
68	Pyramid PYR 6045	Try Me/I'm Leaving (B-side with Pauline)	25
68	Pyramid PYR 6046	King For Tonight (with Pauline)/Last Chance	20
68	Pyramid PYR 6053	Me Naw Give Up/BEVERLEY'S ALLSTARS: Dreadnaught	50
68	JJ PYR 6061	What's Your Grouse/BEVERLEY'S ALLSTARS: Sly Mongoose	30
68	JJ PYR 6063	Johnny Pram Pram/Don't Say (B-side with Pauline Morgan	85
68	Amalgamated AMG 824	I Want To Go Home/JACKIE ROBINSON: Let The Little Girl Dance	40
68	Crab CRAB 3	River To The Bank/PETER KING: Reggae Limbo	20
68	Trojan TR 626	Fat Man/VAL BENNETT: South Parkway Rock	45
68	Nu Beat NB 016	I Love You/JUNIOR SMITH: Searching	25
68	Big Shot BI 506	Shower Of Rain/VAL BENNETT: It Might As Well Be Spring	20
69	Crab CRAB 8	Seven Letters/TARTANS: Lonely Heartaches (B-side act. by Clarendonians)	20
69	Crab CRAB 11	My First Taste Of Love/TARTANS: Dance All Night	20
69	Crab CRAB 18	Don't Play That Song/How Can I Forget You?	20
69	Crab CRAB 23	Send Me Some Loving/Come What May	20
69	Crab CRAB 22	Mek It Tan Deah/Gimme Back	20
69	Crab CRAB 28	Hard Time/ROY RICHARDS: Death Rides A Horse	50
69	Crab CRAB 30	Man Pon Spot/What A Thing	25
69	Crab CRAB 32	Moon Hop/Harris Wheel	40
69	Jackpot JP 700	Seven Letters/Too Bad	10
69	Unity UN 507	Belly Woman/PAULETT & LOVERS: Please Stay	35
69	Unity UN 540	Derrick - Top The Pop/GLEN ADAMS: Capone's Revenge	22
70	Unity UN 546	Return Of Jack Slade/Fat Man	20
70	Unity UN 569	The Conqueror/Bedweight (as Derrick)	50
70	Crab CRAB 44	A Night At The Hop/Telephone	30
70	Crab CRAB 51	I Wish I Was An Apple/The Story	10
70	Crab CRAB 52	Take A Letter Maria/OWEN GRAY: Just A Little Loving	10
70	Crab CRAB 57	My Dickie (as The Commentator)/THE KURAAS: Brixton Hop	45
70	Crab CRAB 58	I Can't Stand It No Longer/Beyond The Wall	10
70	Crab CRAB 59	Endlessly/Who's Making Love	10
70	Crab CRAB 62	Hurt/Julia	10
70	Pama PM 822	Love Bug/My Dickie	10
71	Bullet BU 467	Nobody's Business/Standing By	10
71	Camel CA 84	I Am Just A Sufferer/We Want To Know	10
71	Crab CRAB 67	Searching So Long/MORGAN'S ALL STARS: Drums Of Passion	10
72	Grape GR 3032	Send A Little Rain/DERRICK MORGAN ALL STARS: A Little Rain (Version)	10
72	Jackpot JP 793	Let Them Talk/Bringing In the Guns	12
72	Jackpot JP 794	Won't Be This Way/Ain't No Love	12
72	Jackpot JP 797	Me Naw Run/All Night Long	15
72	Jackpot JP 802	Festival 10/Festival 10 - Version	7
72	Punch PH 107	Forward March/Plenty Of One	7
72	Buster PB 60	Tears On My Pillow/KEITH REID: Worried Over You (actually by Keith & Enid)	7
73	Attack ATT 8048	Derrick's Big Eleven/My Ding A Ling	7
63	Island ILP 903	FORWARD MARCH (LP)	250
69	Doctor Bird DLMB 5014	BEST OF DERRICK MORGAN (LP)	150
69	Island ILP 990	DERRICK MORGAN AND HIS FRIENDS (LP)	150
69	Pama ECO 10	DERRICK MORGAN IN LONDON (LP)	100
69	Pama PSP 1006	MOON HOP (LP)	100
69	Trojan TTL 5	SEVEN LETTERS (LP)	60
70	Trojan TTL 38	FORWARD MARCH (LP, reissue)	30
74	Magnet MGT 004	IN THE MOOD (LP)	90

(see also Roland Alphonso; Frank Cosmo; Copy Cats, Derrick & Lloyd; Derrick, Morris & Patsy; Derrick & Patsy; Derrick & Naomi; Derrick & Paulette; Derrick & Pauline; Morgan's All Stars; Martin & Derrick; Larry Lawrence; Matador, Jackie Robinson)

FREDDY MORGAN

Year	Label/Number	Title	Value
59	London HL 7077	Side Saddle/64 Rue Blondell (export issue)	8

GEORGE MORGAN

Year	Label/Number	Title	Value
57	Philips BBE 12149	COUNTRY AND WESTERN SPECTACULAR (EP)	20
68	London HAB 8353	COUNTRY HITS BY CANDLELIGHT (LP)	22

MORGAN JAMES DUO

Year	Label/Number	Title	Value
64	Philips BF 1462	Sweet Pussycat/Bye Bye Brown Eyes	7
64	Philips BF 1325	Sometimes I'm Happy/It Ain't Necessarily So	7
67	Philips BF 1630	If It Comes To That/Tell Me Where Our Love Went Wrong	7
68	Philips BF 1707	Let's Ride/After The Storm	25
66	Fontana SFL 13071	AT THE BAR OF MUSIC (LP)	30
66	Philips BL 7702	SHHHH...TALENT STRIKES AGAIN (LP)	20

JANE MORGAN (& TROUBADORS)

Year	Label/Number	Title	Value
55	London HL 8148	Why - Oh Why/The Heart You Break (May Be Your Own)	15
57	London HLR 8395	From The First Hello To The Last Goodbye/ Come Home, Come Home, Come Home	20
57	London HLR 8436	Around The World/It's Not For Me To Say	10
57	London HLR 8468	Fascination (with Troubadors)/Why Don't They Leave Us Alone	10
58	London HLR 8539	I'm New At The Game Of Romance/It's Been A Long Long Time (with Troubadors)	10
58	London HLR 8611	I've Got Bells On My Heart/Only One Love	15
58	London HLR 8649	Enchanted Island/Once More, My Love, Once More	10
58	London HL 7064	The Day The Rains Came/I May Never Pass This Way Again (export issue)	10
67	Columbia DB 7645	Maybe/Walking The Streets In The Rain	15
67	HMV POP 1608	This Is My World Without You/Somebody, Someplace	10

Jaye P. MORGAN

			MINT VALUE £
57	London HA-R 2086	FASCINATION (LP)	15
58	London HA-R 2110	ALL THE WAY (LP, with Troubadors)	15
58	London HA-R 2133	SOMETHING OLD, SOMETHING NEW, SOMETHING BORROWED, SOMETHING BLUE (LP)	15
61	London HA-R 2371	JANE MORGAN TIME (LP)	15

(see also Troubadors, Roger Williams)

JAYE P. MORGAN
55	HMV 7M 327	The Longest Walk/Swanee	15
56	HMV 7M 348	If You Don't Want My Love/Pepper Hot Baby	25
56	HMV 7M 365	Not One Goodbye/My Bewildered Heart	10
56	Brunswick 05519	Have You Ever Been Lonely?/Baby Don't Do It	10
57	RCA RCA 1014	You, You Romeo/Graduation Ring	8
60	MGM MGM 1093	I Walk The Line/Wondering Where You Are	6
62	MGM MGM 1182	Heartache Named Johnny/He Thinks I Still Care	6
62	MGM MGM 1190	Brotherhood Of Man/Nobody's Sweetheart	6
54	London RE-P 1013	JAYE P. SINGS (EP)	12
59	MGM MGM-C 793	SLOW AND EASY (LP)	15

JOHN MORGAN
72	Carnaby 6302 010	KALEIDOSCOPE (LP, white label with red 'crab' logo)	100
70s	SWP 1007	LIVE AT DURRANT HOUSE (LP, private pressing)	100

(see also Spirit Of John Morgan)

LEE MORGAN
61	Columbia 33SX 1399	THE BIRDLAND STORY VOL. 1 (LP)	20
62	Stateside SL 10016	EXPOOBIDENT (LP)	30

MACE MORGAN THUNDERBIRDS
63	Starlite STEP 36	SHAKE AND SWING (EP)	60

MARIA MORGAN
75	President PT 440	Touch Me Baby/Reaching Out For Your Love	7

MARY MORGAN
56	Parlophone MSP 6204	Jimmy Unknown/You Are My Love	10
56	Parlophone R 4227	From The Candy Store On The Corner/No-One Was There But You	10
57	Parlophone R 4348	A Call To Arms/One For Sorrow, Two For Joy	6

P.C. ALEXANDER MORGAN
66	Columbia DB 8095	Sussex By The Sea/METROPOLITAN POLICE BAND: Thunderbirds March	8

SAMMY MORGAN
70	Bullet BU 455	Get Out Of This Land/SYDNEY ALL STARS: Landmark	10

TONY MORGAN
69	Beacon BEA 115	Racial Segregation/Racial Segregation (instrumental)	15
72	Beacon BEA 188	Black Skin Blue Eyed Boys/Why Build A Mountain	15
78	Ice GUY 11	Black Skin Blue Eyed Boys/Why Build A Mountain (reissue)	10

MORGAN TWINS
58	RCA RCA 1083	T.V. Hop/Let's Get Going	60
58	RCA RCA 1083	T.V. Hop/Let's Get Going (78)	20

MORGAN'S ALL STARS
71	Camel CA 76	I Love You The Most (actually by Lloyd Clarke)/I Love You The Most - Version	25

(see also B. Leggs, Derrick Morgan, Marvels)

TIM MORGON
72	MCA MU 1173	Take A Look Around/For All We Know	6

(RON PAUL) MORIN & (LUKE P.) WILSON
72	Sovereign SVNA 7252	PEACEFUL COMPANY (LP)	20

JOHNNY MORISETTE
62	Stateside SS 107	Meet Me At The Twistin' Place/Any Time Any Day Any Where	15

ALANIS MORISSETTE
95	Maverick 9362 45901	JAGGED LITTLE PILL (LP, German pressing but imported into U.K.)	50
12	Maverick 8122797168	JAGGED LITTLE PILL (LP, reissue)	15

MORNIN
69	CBS 4883	Cheatin' On You/Let Me Love You	20

MORNING
70	Liberty LBS 83463	MORNING (LP)	40
72	United Artists UAS 29537	STRUCK LIKE SILVER (LP)	20

MORNING AFTER
71	Sky SKYLP 71014	BLUE BLOOD (LP)	300

MORNING GLORY
71	Chapter 1 CHS 148	Green On The Other Side Of The Mountain/Monday Street	7
73	Island ILPS 9237	MORNING GLORY (LP, gatefold, pink rim palm tree label)	30

(see also John Surman)

MOROCCAN COCO
83	SR 001	Steam Radio/One Day (p/s)	35

GIORGIO MORODER
66	Page One POF 003	Full Stop/Believe Me	15
67	Page One POF 028	How Much Longer Must I Wait/Bla Bla Diddley	15
79	Casablanca CANL 244	Chase/Love's Theme (12")	12
80	Polydor POSP 134	Night Drive/The Apartment	7
90s	Cause-N-Effect	I Wanna Rock You (Thee Maddcat Mix)/(Thee DrumDrum Mix) (12", no p/s)	15

(see also Giorgio)

ENNIO MORRICONE ORCHESTRA
67	RCA Victor RCA 1596	A Fistful Of Dollars/The Man With No Name	6
67	RCA Victor RCA 1634	For A Few Dollars More/La Resi Dei Conti	6
69	RCA RCA 1892	Once Upon A Time In The West (Jill's Theme)/Finale	6
67	RCA Victor RD/SF 7875	A FISTFUL OF DOLLARS (LP, soundtrack)	30
68	RCA Victor RD 7994	A FISTFUL OF DOLLARS/FOR A FEW DOLLARS MORE/THE GOOD, THE BAD AND THE UGLY	15

Byron MORRIS AND UNITY

MINT VALUE £

		(LP, soundtrack)	
68	United Artists (S)ULP 1197	THE GOOD, THE BAD AND THE UGLY (LP, soundtrack)	15
69	United Artists UAS 29005	A PROFESSIONAL GUN (LP, soundtrack)	25
70	CBS 70067	LOVE CIRCLE (LP, soundtrack)	50
70	MCA MKPS 2013	TWO MULES FOR SISTER SARA (LP, soundtrack)	30
72	United Artists UAS 29345	A FISTFUL OF DYNAMITE (LP, soundtrack)	40

BYRON MORRIS AND UNITY
01	Universal Sound USLP 17	BLOW THRU YOUR MIND (LP, reissue)	30

CHRIS MORRIS
83	Tivoli TIV 4	Cross My Palm/Somethings So Right (p/s)	8

ERIC MORRIS
61	Starlite ST45 052	Search The World/Buster's Shack	40
61	Blue Beat BB 53	Humpty Dumpty/Corn Bread And Butter (as Eric 'Humpty Dumpty' Morris & Drumbago All Stars; [B-side actually by Drumbago All Stars])	20
62	Blue Beat BB 74	My Forty-Five/I've Tried Everybody (as Eric 'Humpty Dumpty' Morris & Drumbago All Stars)	30
62	Blue Beat BB 81	Sinners Repent And Pray/Now And Forever More (B-side act. by Alton Ellis)	20
62	Blue Beat BB 83	Money Can't Buy Life (with Buster's Group)/A. ELLIS: True Love	25
62	Blue Beat BB 105	Pack Up Your Troubles/Oh What A Smile Can Do (with D. Cosmo & Drumbago's All Stars)	20
62	Blue Beat BB 115	G.I. Lady/Going To The River	20
62	Blue Beat BB 128	Over The Hills/Lazy Woman (with Buster's Group)	20
62	Blue Beat BB 137	Miss Peggy's Grandmother/BUSTER'S GROUP: Megaton	25
62	Blue Beat BB 140	Seven Long Years/For Your Love	20
63	Blue Beat BB 153	Lonely Blue Boy/PRINCE BUSTER: Oh We	22
63	Blue Beat BB 184	Sweet Love/BUSTER, DEREK, ERIC: Country Girl	15
64	Blue Beat BB 218	Love Can Break A Man/Worried People	20
64	Blue Beat BB 273	Stitch In Time/For Ever	20
64	Black Swan WI 412	Sampson/BABA BROOKS: Jelly Beans	30
64	Black Swan WI 414	Solomon Grundie/BABA BROOKS: Key To The City	40
64	Black Swan WI 433	Supper In The Gutter/Words Of My Mouth	20
64	Black Swan WI 439	River Come Down/Seek And You'll Find	20
64	Black Swan WI 445	Home Sweet Home/LESTER STERLING: '64 Special	25
64	Island WI 142	Penny-Reel/DUKE REID'S GROUP: Darling When (B-side act. Dotty & Bonnie)	35
64	Island WI 147	Mama No Fret/FRANKIE ANDERSON: Santa Lucia (B-side w/Roland Alphonso)	20
64	Island WI 150	Drop Your Sword/Catch A Fire (B-side actually by Roland Alphonso)	25
64	Island WI 151	What A Man Doeth/DUKE REID'S GROUP: Rude Boy (B-side actually by Baba Brooks)	25
64	Port-O-Jam PJ 4006	Oh My Dear/Lena Belle	25
64	Rio R 39	Little District/True And Just	25
64	Rio R 48	Live As A Man/Man Will Rule	25
65	Rio R 72	By The Sea/I Wasn't Around	25
65	Island WI 177	Drop Your Sword/Catch A Fire	25
65	Island WI 183	Love Can Make A Mansion (actually "Love Can Break A Man")/ Ungodly People	15
65	Island WI 185	Suddenly/Many Long Years	25
65	Island WI 199	Fast Mouth/The Harder They Come	18
65	Island WI 234	Children Of Today/BABA BROOKS: Greenfield Ska	25
65	Blue Beat BB 298	Those Teardrops/DON DRUMMOND: Ska Town	50
66	Blue Beat BB 349	I'm The Greatest/BUSTER'S ALL STARS: Picket Line	60
60s	Fab BB 30	Humpty Dumpty (as Eric 'Humpty Dumpty' Morris & Buster All Stars)/ FOLKS BROTHERS: Carolina	7
13	Island WI 3163	Terrible Mistake/Festival Time	30

(see also Monty Morris, Byron Lee & Dragonaires, Cool Sticky, Tommy McCook, Zoot Simms, Marguerita, Cool Cats)

HELMSLEY MORRIS
67	Caltone TONE 104	Love Is Strange/DON D. JUNIOR: Sir Pratt Special	90
68	Pama PM 720	Stay Loose Mama/You Think I'm A Fool (as Hainsley Morris)	35

LIBBY MORRIS
56	Parlophone R 4225	When Liberace Winked At Me/None Of That Now	6
66	RCA RD 7789	AD-LIBBY (LP)	15

MILTON MORRIS
69	Upsetter US 318	No Bread And Butter/UPSETTERS: Soulful I	12

(see also Milton Henry)

MONTY MORRIS
67	Doctor Bird DB 1067	Play It Cool/BABA BROOKS' BAND: Open The Door	70
67	Doctor Bird DB 1081	Put On Your Best Dress/BABA BROOKS' BAND: Faberge	150
68	Doctor Bird DB 1162	Last Laugh/You Really Got A Hold On Me	150
68	Pama PM 721	Say What You're Saying/Tears In Your Eyes	40
68	Nu Beat NB 011	Simple Simon/BUNNY & RUDDY: On The Town	75
69	Doctor Bird DB 1176	Same Face/A Little Bit Of This (miscredited to Tennors)	60
69	Big Shot BI 513	Deportation/Say I'm Back	100
69	Camel CA 12	Can't Get No Peace/UPSETTERS: For A Few Dollars More	70
69	Camel CA 28	No More Teardrops/Love Me Or Leave Me (as Monty Morris & Maples)	50
70	Unity UN 557	Do It My Way/Where In The World (Are You Going)	12
70	Explosion EX 2016	Higher Than The Highest Mountain/G.G. ALL STARS: Musical Shot	25
73	Ackee ACK 527	I'm Ready To Go/TOMMY McCOOK: Flower Pot	15
10	Duke THB 7004	Deep In My Soul/TOMMY McCOOK: Reggae To Jeggae	30

(see also Eric Morris, Monty, Derrick & Patsy, Monty & Roy, Alton Ellis)

NAGGO MORRIS
79	Hit Run DD 111	Jah Will Explain/DOCTOR PABLO: Wicked Feel It (12")	25
82	S & G SG 12	A True You Na No/Going Places (12")	50
82	S & G SG 23	False Rasta/Two Time Girl (12")	70
82	Black Roots BR0036A	A True Them No Know/Version/Africa/Version (12")	30

Richie MORRIS

MINT VALUE £

RICHIE MORRIS
73 Satril SAT 11   Zimbabwa/Seasons Change 8

ROGER MORRIS
72 Regal Zono. SRZA 8509   FIRST ALBUM (LP, textured gatefold sleeve, red/silver label) 500

RUSSELL MORRIS
69 Decca F 22964   The Real Thing (Parts I & II)/It's Only A Matter Of Time 80

VICTOR MORRIS
68 Amalgamated AMG 813   Now I'm Alone/Rise And Fall 20

MORRIS & MINORS
80 Round MOR 1   STATE THE OBVIOUS (EP, p/s in poly bag) 10

MORRIS & MITCH
57 Decca F 10900   Cumberland Gap/I'm Not A Juvenile Delinquent 10
57 Decca F 10929   What Is A Skiffler?/The Tommy Rot Story 6
58 Decca F 11086   Highway Patrol/Bird Dog 6
68 Trend TRE 1010   The Magical Musherishi Tourists/Mister D.J. Man 15
58 Decca DFE 6486   SIX FIVE NOTHING SPECIAL (EP) 15

MORRIS FAMILY & GOSPEL JUBILEERS
60 Top Rank JAR 322   Wake Up Jonah/He Never Complained 7

CURLEY JIM MORRISON
61 Starlite ST45 065   Air Force Blues/Didn't I Tell You 50

DOROTHY MORRISON
69 Elektra EKSN 45070   All God's Children Got Soul/Put A Little Love In Your Heart 12
70 Elektra K 42095   BRAND NEW DAY (LP) 18

PROFESSOR MORRISON'S LOLLIPOP
68 London HLU 10228   You Got The Love/Gypsy Lady 6
69 London HLU 10254   Oo-Poo-Pah Susie/You Take It 6

VAN MORRISON
67 London HLZ 10150   Brown-Eyed Girl/Goodbye Baby (Baby Goodbye) 50
70 Warner Brothers WB 7383 Come Running/Crazy Love 10
70 Warner Brothers WB 7434 Domino/Sweet Jannie 20
70 Warner Brothers WB 7434 Domino/Sweet Jannie (DJ Copy) 35
70 President PT 328   Brown-Eyed Girl/Goodbye Baby (Baby Goodbye) (reissue) 15
72 Warner Brothers K 16210 Jackie Wilson Said/You've Got The Power 10
74 London HLM 10453   Brown-Eyed Girl/Goodbye Baby (Baby Goodbye) (2nd reissue) 15
74 Warner Brothers K 16392 Caldonia/What's Up, Crazy Pup 10
77 Warner Brothers K 16939 The Eternal Kansas City/Joyous Sound (p/s) 8
77 Warner Brothers K 16986 Joyous Sound/Mechanical Bliss 6
68 London HA-Z 8346   BLOWIN' YOUR MIND (LP) 175
69 Warner Brothers WS 1768 ASTRAL WEEKS (LP, laminated front sleeve, flipbacks, orange label) 250
71 Warner Brothers WS 1768 ASTRAL WEEKS (LP, green label) 50
70 Warner Brothers WS 1835 MOONDANCE (LP, orange label) 175
70 Warner Brothers WS 1835 MOONDANCE (LP, green label) 20
71 Warner Brothers WS 1884 HIS BAND AND STREET CHOIR (LP, green label) 35
71 President PTLS 1045   THE BEST OF VAN MORRISON (LP) 15
71 Warner Brothers K 46114 TUPELO HONEY (LP, gatefold sleeve, green label) 30
72 Warner Brothers K 46172 SAINT DOMINIC'S PREVIEW (LP, with folded insert, green label) 35
73 Warner Brothers K 46024 ASTRAL WEEKS (LP, reissue, 'Burbank' label) 25
73 Warner Brothers K 46040 MOONDANCE (LP, reissue, 'Burbank' label) 15
73 Warner Brothers K 46066 HIS BAND AND STREET CHOIR (LP, reissue, 'Burbank' label) 15
73 Warner Brothers K 46242 HARD NOSE THE HIGHWAY (LP, gatefold sleeve, 'Burbank' label) 15
74 London HSM 5008   T.B. SHEETS (LP, laminated front cover) 15
74 Warner Brothers K 86007 IT'S TOO LATE TO STOP NOW (2-LP, gatefold sleeve, 'Burbank' label) 15
74 Warner Brothers K 56068 VEEDON FLEECE (LP, 'Burbank' label) 20
77 Bang 6467 625   THIS IS WHERE I CAME IN (LP) 15
84 Mercury MERH 54   A SENSE OF WONDER (LP, white label test pressings with "Crazy Jane On God") 25
84 Mercury MERH 54   A SENSE OF WONDER (LP, credits but doesn't play "Crazy Jane On God") 15
87 Mercury MERH 110   POETIC CHAMPIONS COMPOSE (LP) 20
91 Polydor 849 026 1   HYMNS TO THE SILENCE (2-LP) 80
93 Polydor 519219   TOO LONG IN EXILE (2-LP) 60
95 Verve 529 136-1   HOW LONG HAS THIS BEEN GOING ON (LP, with Georgie Fame and Friends) 45
95 Exile 527307   DAYS LIKE THIS (LP) 80
97 Exile 5371011   HEALING GAME (LP) 80
99 Simply Vinyl SVLP 253   BACK ON TOP (LP) 200
02 Polydor 589177-1   DOWN THE ROAD (2-LP) 100
05 Exile 9871428   MAGIC TIME (LP) 60

(see also Them)

MORRISSEY
SINGLES
88 HMV POP 1618   Suedehead/I Know Very Well How I Got My Name 6
88 HMV 12 POP 1618   Suedehead/I Know Very Well How I Got My Name/Hairdresser On Fire (12", 1st pressings in brown p/s) 20
88 HMV POP 1619   Everyday Is Like Sunday/Disappointed (p/s) 7
88 HMV 12 POP 1619   Everyday Is Like Sunday/Sister I'm A Poet/Disappointed/ Will Never Marry (12", p/s) 10
89 HMV 12 POP 1620   The Last Of The Famous International Playboys/Lucky Lisp/Michaels Bones (12") 10
89 HMV 12 POP 1621   Interesting Drug/Such A Little Thing Makes Such A Big Difference/ Sweet And Tender Hooligan (live) (12", p/s) 10
89 HMV 12 POPS 1621   Interesting Drug/Such A Little Thing Makes Such A Big Difference (12", p/s, 1 side etched) 12
90 HMV POP 1622   Ouija Board, Ouija Board/Yes, I Am Blind (p/s) 6
90 HMV POP 1623   November Spawned A Monster/He Knows I'd Love To See Him (p/s) 6

MORRISSEY

MINT VALUE £

Year	Catalogue	Title	Value
90	HMV 12 POP 1623	November Spawned A Monster/Girl Least Likely To/ He Knows I'd Love To See Him (12", p/s)	10
90	HMV POP 1624	Piccadilly Palare/Get Off The Stage (p/s)	8
90	HMV 12 POP 1624	Piccadilly Palare/At Amber/Get Off The Stage (12, p/s)	10
91	HMV 12 POP 1625	Our Frank/Journalists Who Lie/Tony The Pony (12", p/s)	12
91	HMV POP 1626	Sing Your Life/That's Entertainment (p/s)	6
91	HMV POP 1627	Pregnant For The Last Time/Skin Storm (p/s)	8
91	HMV 12 POP 1627	Pregnant For The Last Time/Skin Storm/Cosmic Dancer (live)/ Disappointed (live) (12", p/s)	15
92	Parlophone R6243	You're The One For Me, Fatty/Pashernate Love	7
92	Parlophone 12POP 1630	You're The One For Me, Fatty/Pashernate Friend/There Speaks A True Friend (12")	10
92	HMV 12POP 1629	We Hate It When Our Friends Become Successful/Suedehead/I've Changed My Plea To Guilty/Pregnant For The Last Time (12", p/s)	12
92	HMV CDPOP 1629	We Hate It When Our Friends Become Successful/Suedehead/I've Changed My Plea To Guilty/Alsatian Cousin (12", p/s)	10
92	EMI CDMOZBX 1	THE SINGLES COLLECTION 1986-1992 (13 x CD singles set hinged black/purple box with numbered insert)	90
92	Parlophone POP 1631	Certain People I Know/Jack The Ripper	8
92	Parlophone POP 1631	Certain People I Know/You've Had Her/Jack The Ripper (12")	10
94	Parlophone R 6372	The More You Ignore Me, The Closer I Get/Used To Be A Sweet Boy (poster, no'd p/s)	7
94	Parlophone 12R6372	The More You Ignore Me, The Closer I Get/Used To Be A Sweet Boy/I'd Love To (poster, numbered p/s)	10
94	Parlophone RDJ 6372	The More You Ignore, Me The Closer I Get/Used To Be A Sweet Boy (yellow p/s)	12
94	Parlophone R6383	Hold On To Your Friends/Moonriver (numbered p/s)	8
94	Parlophone 12 R6383	Hold Onto Your Friends/Moonriver (12", gatefold sleeve)	25
95	Parlophone R 6400	Boxers/Have-A-Go Merchant (p/s)	8
95	Parlophone 12R 6400	Boxers/Have-A-Go Merchant/Whatever Happens. I Love You (12")	12
95	RCA 74321332947	Boy Racer/London (Live Version) (p/s)	10
95	Parlophone R6243	Sunny/Black-Eyed Susan	10
95	RCA Victor LC 0316	Dagenham Dave/Nobody Loves Us (p/s)	15
97	Island IS 667	Alma Matters/Heir Apparent (p/s)	25
97	Parlophone 12 IS 667	Alma Maters/Heir Apparent/I Can Have Both (12")	25
97	Island IS 671	Roy's Keen/Lost (p/s)	25
97	Island 12 IS 671	Roy's Keen/Lost/The Edges Are No Longer Paralle (12")	45
97	Island IS 686	Satan Rejected My Soul/Now I Am A Was (p/s)	25
97	Island 12IS 686	Satan Rejected My Soul/Now I Am A Was/This Is Not Your Country (12")	60
00	EMI EMI 8872932	SINGLES 88-91 (10 x CDs, card sleeves)	40
01	EMI EMI 8797452	SINGLES 91-95 (9 X CDs, card sleeves, in box)	40
04	Attack ATKI002	Irish Blood, English Heart/It's Hard To Walk Tall When You're Small	6
04	Attack ATKSE008	Let Me Kiss You/Don't Make Fun Of Daddy's Voice	6
04	Attack ATKSE 011	I Have Forgiven Jesus/No One Can Hold A Candle To You	7
06	Attack ATKSE021	First Of The Gang To Die/My Life Is A Succession Of People Saying Goodbye	8
06	Attack ATKTW 020	First Of The Gang To Die (12" 4-track EP)	20
06	Attack ATKTW 019	Irish Blood, English Heart (12" 4-track EP)	20
06	Attack ATKTW025	I Just Want To See The Boy Happy/Sweetie-Pie/I Want The One I Can't Have/ Speedway/Late Night, Maudlin Street (12" picture disc, 1,000 only)	10
06	Attack ATKSE021	In The Future When All's Well/Christian Dior	7
09	Decca F20006/Polydor 4781539	I'm Throwing My Arms Around Paris/Death Of A Disco Dancer ('naked' band inner)	8
10	Major Minor MM 721	Everyday Is Like Sunday/Everyday Is Like Sunday (live) (die-cut sleeve)	6
10	Major Minor MM 721	Everyday Is Like Sunday/Trash (live) (p/s with 2 inserts)	10

ALBUMS

Year	Catalogue	Title	Value
88	HMV CSD 3787	VIVA HATE (LP)	40
90	HMV CLP 3788	BONA DRAG (LP)	40
91	EMI CSD 3789	KILL UNCLE (LP, gatefold)	40
92	HMV CSD 3790	YOUR ARSENAL (LP)	50
93	HMV CSD 3791	BEETHOVEN WAS DEAF (LP)	60
94	Parlophone/EMI PCSD 148	VAUXHALL AND I (LP, gatefold)	100
95	RCA Victor 74321299531	SOUTHPAW GRAMMAR (LP, with limited edition booklet)	150
95	RCA 29953 1	SOUTHPAW GRAMMAR (LP)	100
95	Parlophone PCS 7374	BONA DRAG (LP, reissue)	20
95	Parlophone PCS 7375	KILL UNCLE (LP, reissue)	20
95	Parlophone PCS 7376	VIVA HATE (LP, reissue)	20
97	Island ILPS 8059	MALADJUSTED (LP)	40
97	EMI EMC 2771	SUEDEHEAD: THE BEST OF MORRISSEY (2-LP, gatefold)	50
97	Parlophone PCSD 163	WORLD OF MORRISSEY (LP, classic yellow/black Parlophone label)	50
04	Attack ATKLP 001	YOU ARE THE QUARRY (LP, 5,000 only)	150
06	Attack ATKLP 016	RINGLEADER OF THE TORMENTORS (LP, gatefold)	100
08	Decca SKL 6003	GREATEST HITS (2-LP, inners, download card)	70
09	Polydor/Decca SKL6014/ 4781581	YEARS OF REFUSAL (LP)	50
10	Major Minor SMLP70	BONA DRAG (2-LP, 20th aniversary edition, inners, poster)	20
21	Major Minor SMLP 70	BONA DRAG (2-LP, reissue, teal coloured vinyl, obi)	30

PROMOS

Year	Catalogue	Title	Value
88	Factory FA 244+	I Know Very Well How I Got My Note Wrong (7" promo, as Vincent Gerrard and Stephen Patrick, 1,000 only)	50
88	Factory FACD 244+	I Know Very Well How I Got My Note Wrong (CD promo, as Vincent Gerrard and Stephen Patrick, 1,000 only)	40
88	HMV 12POP DJ 1618	Suedehead/I Know Very Well How I Got My Name/Hairdresser On Fire (12" promo)	25
88	HMV 12 POP DJ 1619	Everyday Is Like A Sunday (12", promo, 1-sided)	20
89	Parlophone POP 1620	The Last Of The Famous International Playboys/Lucky Lisp (test pressing with different version of Lucky Lisp to official release - matrixes A-1U-1-1/B-1U-1-1)	200

MORRISSEY & SIOUXSIE

MINT VALUE £

89	HMV 12POP DJ 1620	The Last Of The Famous International Playboys/Lucky Lisp/Michaels Bones (12" promo)	20
89	EMI SPM 29	Interesting Drug/Such A Little Thing Makes Such A Big Difference (12" die cut red sleeve, promo)	15
89	EMI SPM 29	Interesting Drug/etched B side (12", die cut black sleeve, promo)	60
89	Parlophone 12POPDJ 1622	Ouija Board, Ouija Board/Yes, I Am Blind/East West (12" A label promo)	30
90	HMV POPDJ1623	November The Second (12" promo, white label 'Dance Mix' destroyed on order of Morrissey, 1 known copy)	2000
90	Parlophone 12POPDJ 1623	November Spawned A Monster/He Knows I'd Love To See Him/ Girl Least Likely To (12" promo)	30
90	HMV POPDJ 1624	Piccadilly Palare/Get Off The Stage (promo, in die-cut HMV sleeve)	35
91	Parlophone POPDJ1625	Our Frank/Journalists Who Lie (red 'A' label promo in die-cut retro sleeve)	200
91	HMV POP DJ 1626	Sing Your Life/That's Entertainment (promo, die-cut HMV sleeve)	35
91	HMV POP DJ 1627	Pregnant For The Last Time/Skin Storm (promo)	50
91	HMV POPDJ1628	My Love Life/I've Changed My Plea To Guilty ('A' label promo in die cut sleeve)	80
92	HMV POP DJ 1630	You're The One For Me, Fatty/You're The One For Me, Fatty (10", A-side plays at 45rpm, B-side at 78rpm, die-cut sleeve)	40
92	HMV POP DJ 1629	We Hate It When Our Friends Become Successful/We Hate It When Our Friends Become Sucessful (10", A-side plays at 45rpm, B-side at 78rpm, die-cut sleeve)	40
92	HMV POPDJ 1631	Certain People I Know/Jack The Ripper (die-cut 'Moz' p/s, 300 only)	175
93	Parlophone POPDJ1632	Jack The Ripper/Sister I'm A Poet (promo in p/s)	25
93	HMV POPDJ 1632	Jack The Ripper/Sister I'm A Poet (p/s)	12
94	Parlophone RDJ 6372	The More You Ignore Me The Closer I Get/Used to Be A Sweet Boy ('photographer' sleeve)	50
94	Parlophone CDRDJ 6372	The More You Ignore, Me The Closer I Get (CD, with "45rpm" logo on disc, withdrawn)	45
94	Parlophone R 6383	Hold Onto Your Friends/Moonriver (promo in different p/s, 150 only)	100
95	Parlophone RDJ 6400	Have-A-Go Merchant/Whatever Happens, I Love You (p/s)	25
95	Parlophone/EMI RDJ 6400	Have-A-Go Merchant/Whatever Happens, I Love You p/s, promo for unreleased single)	75
95	RCA SOLO 1	OUTSIDE TOUR SAMPLER (CD promo features Boy Racer)	60
04	Sanctuary (No Cat. No)	YOU ARE THE QUARRY (CD-R interview promo)	35
11	Stateside SS 2242	Glamorous Glue (2011 remaster)/VINCE EAGER: The World's Loneliest Man (Retro A label 'Stateside' promo in die-cut 'Stateside' sleeve, 150 only)	250

(see also Smiths, Durutti Column)

MORRISSEY & SIOUXSIE

94	Parlphone R 6365	Interlude/Interlude (Extended)	8
94	Parlophone 12R 6365	Interlude/Interlude (Extended)/Interlude (Instrumental) (12")	15

DICK MORRISSEY

61	77' LEU 12/8	HAVE YOU HEARD? (LP)	350
61	Fontana TFL 5149	IT'S MORRISSEY MAN! (LP)	400
67	Mercury 20093	HERE AND NOW AND SOUNDING GOOD (LP)	300
67	Mercury 20077MCL	STORM WARNING (LP)	350

(see also If)

BUDDY MORROW & HIS ORCHESTRA

53	HMV 7M 145	Heap Big Beat/I Can't Get Started	6
53	HMV 7M 151	I Can't Get Started/Heap Big Beat (reissue)	6
53	HMV 7M 162	Dragnet/Your Mouth's Got A Hole In It	8
54	HMV 7M 216	Knock On Wood (with Shaye Cogan)/All Night Long	10
60	RCA RCA 1167	Staccato's Theme/Scraunchy	6
60	RCA RCX 174	IMPACT (EP)	10

ELLA MAE MORSE

55	Capitol CL 14223	Bring Back My Baby To Me/Lovey Dovey	50
55	Capitol CL 14303	Smack Dab In The Middle/Yes, Yes I Do	50
55	Capitol CL 14332	Livin', Livin', Livin'/Heart Full Of Hope	50
55	Capitol CL 14341	Razzle-Dazzle/Ain't That A Shame (with Big Dave & His Music)	100
55	Capitol CL 14341	Razzle-Dazzle/Ain't That A Shame (with Big Dave & His Music) (78)	25
55	Capitol CL 14362	Seventeen/Piddily Patter Song (with Big Dave & His Music)	100
55	Capitol CL 14362	Seventeen/Piddily Patter Song (with Big Dave & His Music) (78)	25
55	Capitol CL 14376	Birmin'ham/An Occasional Man	40

(The 45s listed above were originally issued with triangular centres; later round-centres issues are worth around half to two-thirds of these values.)

56	Capitol CL 14508	When Boy Kiss Girl (It's Love)/Sing-Ing-Ing-Ing	30
56	Capitol CL 14572	Rock And Roll Wedding/Down In Mexico	40
56	Capitol CL 14572	Rock And Roll Wedding/Down In Mexico (78)	20
57	Capitol CL 14726	What Good'll It Do Me/Mister Money Maker	20
57	Capitol CL 14760	I'm Gone/Sway Me	20
55	Capitol EAP1 513	BARRELHOUSE BOOGIE AND THE BLUES (EP)	15
54	Capitol LC 6687	BARRELHOUSE BOOGIE AND THE BLUES (10" LP)	20

(see also 'Tennessee' Ernie Ford)

ELLA MAE MORSE & FREDDIE SLACK

67	Ember SPE 6605	ROCKIN' BREW (LP)	25

MORTA SKULD

93	Peaceville CC 4	Sacrificial Rite/VITAL REMAINS: Amulet Of The Conquering (clear vinyl, p/s)	15
93	Deaf DEAF 11	DYING REMAINS (LP)	25
94	Deaf DEAF 15	HUMANITY FADES (LP)	20

MORTICIANS

87	Tin Soldier TIN 1	FREAK OUT WITH THE MORTICIANS (LP)	20

MORTIMER

67	Philips BF 1664	Dedicated Music Man/To Understand Someone	10

AZIE MORTIMER

60	London HLX 9213	Lips/Wrapped Up In A Dream	100

MIKE MORTON CONGREGATION

70	Plexium PXM 19	Burning Bridges/You Gotta Be Mine	15

Lionel MORTON

MINT VALUE £

LIONEL MORTON
67	Philips BF 1578	What To Do With Laurie/I'll Just	7
67	Philips BF 1607	First Love Never Dies/Try Not To Cry	7
69	RCA RCA 1875	Waterloo Road/Floral Street	7
72	Cube BUG 24	What A Woman Does/Listen To The Music	6
75	Beeb 011	Don't Let Life Get You Down/Play Away	7

(see also Four Pennies)

MANDY MORTON (BAND)
79	Banshee BANS 791	Song For Me (Music Prince)/Little Inbetween (with Spriguns)	15
80	Polydor 2382 101	Ghost Of Christmas Past/Black Nights (p/s)	6
78	Banshee BAN 1011	MAGIC LADY (LP, with lyric insert, 1,000 only)	350
78	Banshee BAN 1011	MAGIC LADY (LP, with lyric insert, blue vinyl, 20 only)	600
80	Polydor 2382 101	SEA OF STORMS (LP, solo, with insert)	70
83	Banshee	VALLEY OF LIGHT (LP, private pressing)	100

MORWELLS
75	Sir Jessus JES 4	Come On Little Girl/Version '75	15
79	Attack TACK 5	Kingston Twelve Tuffie/PRINCE JAMMY: Jammin' For Survival (12")	12
79	Greensleeves GRED 17	Thief A Dub (12")	40
77	Burning Sounds BS 1006	CRAB RACE (LP)	50
79	Bushays BFMLP 100	COOL RUNNING (LP)	35
80	Trojan TRLS 193	A1 DUB (LP)	35

MOSAIC
71	Parlophone R5928	Blue Bird/Bird Of Fire	15

MOSAICS
66	Columbia DB 7990	Let's Go Drag Racing/Now That You're Here	35

HARRY MOSCO
80	Samba SA003	Step On/Sexy Dancer (12")	20

ADRIAN MOSELY
68	Redcar RC001	Silent Night/Ellusive Face	60

JOSHUA MOSES
78	More Cut MCT 6001	Africa Is Our Land/Home (12", die-cut p/s)	70

LEE MOSES
07	Castle CMFDV1522	TIME AND PLACE (2-LP, reissue)	100

PABLO MOSES
75	Treble C CCC 01	I Man A Grasshopper/Grasshopper (Part 2)	20
75	Treble C CCC 09	Blood Money/Version	20
76	Lizzard 001	We Should Be In Angola/Dubbing In Angola	25
76	Klik KL 625	Give I Fe I Name/Version	8
80	Island 12WIP	Dubbing Is A Must/Revolutionary Step (12")	25
82	Island 10WIP 6781	Proverbs Extractions/Music Is My Desire (10")	35
77	Klik KLP 9026	REVOLUTIONARY DREAM (LP)	60
78	Different GETL 104	REVOLUTIONARY DREAM (LP)	20

MOSFETS
82	Sub SUB 1	The Great War/Power Games (p/s)	60

MOSIAH
79	Big SOLD 6	Rumours Of War/Channel Dub	35

MOSKOW (1)
78	Moskow SRS 2103	Man From U.N.C.L.E./White Black (p/s)	8

MOSKOW (2)
82	Rygel RY6	Heat House/Robot (p/s)	30

MOSQUITOS
83	Discovery DIX 003	How Could They Know/Somethin Outa Nothin (p/s)	7

MOSS
06	Rise Above RISE7/085 5	MOSS: Maimed & Slaughtered/THE PLAGUE OF GENTLEMEN: Rainbow Demon (test pressings only)	100
08	Rise Above RISELP 108	SUB TEMPULUM (2-LP)	25

BILL MOSS
69	Pama PM 765	Sock It To 'Em Soul Brother (Parts 1 & 2)	15
70	Pama PM 796	Number One/MOHAWKS: Lanscape	20

BUDDY MOSS
60s	Kokomo K 1003	GEORGIA BLUES VOLUME 2 (LP)	50

JENNY MOSS
63	Columbia DB 7061	Hobbies/Big Boys	40

STIRLING MOSS
60	HMV 7EG 8583	MOTOR RACING WITH STERLING MOSS (EP)	10
61	Redemption RLP 5004	THE STIRLING MOSS STORY (LP)	15

TEDDY MOSS/JOSH WHITE
62	Jazz Collector JEL 5	THE MALE BLUES (EP)	10

GERRY MORRIS
72	York SYK 525	Come On Home/Nothing To Declare	20
73	York SYK 557	Sunlove/Only The Beginning	30
73	York FYK 415	ONLY THE BEGINNING (LP)	150

MOST
79	SRT SRTS/CUS/570	Carefree/In And Out (1,000 only stamped lyric insert)	60

ABE MOST OCTET
55	London RE-P 1028	PRESENTING THE ABE MOST OCTET (EP)	20

MOST DOMINANT
93	Kold Sweat KSEP210	PUSHED TO DA LIMIT (EP)	15

MICKIE MOST (& GEAR)
63	Decca F 11664	Mr. Porter/Yes Indeed I Do	30
63	Columbia DB 7117	The Feminine Look/Shame On You Boy	15

MOST BROTHERS

MINT VALUE £

63	Columbia DB 7180	Sea Cruise/It's A Little Bit Hot	15
64	Columbia DB 7245	Money Honey/That's Alright (as Mickey Most & Gear)	20

(see also Most Brothers)

MOST BROTHERS
57	Decca F 10968	Whistle Bait/I'm Comin' Home	20
58	Decca F 10998	Whole Lotta Woman/Teen Angel	20
58	Decca F 11040	Don't Go Home/Dottie	20

(see also Mickie Most, Alex Murray)

MOTHER BRAINTREE
17	Super Disco Edits SDE 26	Sailing/Let Me Stay Beside You	10

MOTHER EARTH
69	Mercury MF 1081	I Did My Part/Goodnight Melda Grebe The Telephone Company Has Cut Us Off	8
68	Mercury SMCL 20143	LIVING WITH THE ANIMALS (LP)	25

MOTHER FREEDOM BAND
77	All Platinum 6146326	Beautiful Summer Day/Flick Of the Wrist	20

MOTHER LIZA
83	Vista VSLP 2005	MOTHER LIZA MEETS PAPA TOLLO (TULLO) (LP)	15

MOTHER NATURE (1)
71	B & C CB 166	Orange Days And Purple Nights/Where Did She Go	12
72	Kingdom KV8003	Once There Was A Time/Clear Blue Sky	10

MOTHER NATURE (2)
84	Ariwa ARILP 017	A BREATH OF FRESH AIR (LP)	15

MOTHER NATURES CHILDREN
77	President PT468	Money Back Ride/Rollin Down	10

MOTHER YOD
97	Prescription DRUG 1	MOTHER YOD (LP, 99 copies only)	25

MOTHERLIGHT
69	Morgan Bluetown BT 5003	BOBAK, JONS, MALONE (LP)	600
88	Morgan Blue Town BT5008	BOBAK, JOHNS, MALONE (LP, reissue)	35

(see also Will Malone [Voice Band], Orange Bicycle)

MOTHERLODE
69	Buddah 201 064	When I Die/Hard Life	6
69	Buddah 2318 043	WHEN I DIE (LP)	15

MOTHER LOVE BONE
90	Polypro 843 191	APPLE (LP)	80

MOTHER'S RUIN
81	Spectra SPC 1	Streetfighters/Leaving You (in p/s)	55
81	Spectra SPC 1	Streetfighters/Leaving You	40
82	Spectra SPC 6	Street Lights/Turn A Corner (p/s)	20
82	Spectra SPC 7	Say It's Not True/It's Illogical (p/s)	35

MOTHER'S SONS
70	J-Dan JDN 4415	I Want To Tell The World/Underground Man	6

MOTHMEN
79	Absurd ABSURD 6	Does It Matter Irene?/Please Let Go (p/s)	6
81	Do It DUN 12	Show Me Your House And Car/People People (p/s, deleted after 1 day)	8
81	Do It DUNIT 12	Show Me Your House And Car/People People (12", p/s, deleted after 1 day)	10
80s	On-U-Sound LP 2	PAY ATTENTION (LP)	15

(see also Alberto Y Lost Trios Paranoias)

MOTHS
69	Deroy	MOTHS (LP, private pressing in plain white sleeve)	500

MOTIFFE
72	Deroy 777	MOTIFFE (LP, private pressing in hand-illustrated white sleeve, 99 only)	1500

MOTIFS
82	MM1	Shadow Of Fear/On The Inside	50

MOTION
79	DD Records DDLP04	MOTION (LP)	40

(see also Aswad)

MOTION PICTURES
80	STAT 100	Twisted Avenues/Unknown Quantity	8

MOTIONS
66	Pye International 7N 25390	Stop Your Crying/Every Step I Take	25

MOTIVATION
68	Direction 58-3248	Come On Down/Little Man	35

MOTIVES
80	Romantic RR 0001	King Of The Dub/Lies And Stories	15

FRANK MOTLEY & KING HERBERT
99	Jazzman JM 002	Ya Ya/Ooga Boogaloo (as Frank Motley & The Bridge Crossing)	10
98	Jazzman JMANLP 001	CANADA'S MESSAGE TO THE METERS (THE BEST OF...) (LP)	20

MOTLEY CREW (1)
68	MJB BEV 429	MOTLEY CREW (EP, hand made sleeve)	25

MOTLEY CREW (2)
80	Cherrys CHERRYS 1	City Girl/Don't Start Me Talkin	8

MÖTLEY CRÜE
84	Elektra E 9756T	Looks That Kill/Piece Of The Action/Live Wire (12", p/s with free tattoo)	15
84	Elektra E 9756TP	Looks That Kill/Piece Of The Action/Live Wire (12", picture disc)	20
84	Elektra E 9732T	Too Young To Fall In Love/Take Me To The Top (12", p/s, with poster)	15
86	Elektra EKR 16TP	Smokin' In The Boys' Room/Use It Or Lose It (mask-shaped pic disc & sticker)	15
86	Elektra EKR 33P	Smokin' In The Boys' Room/Home Sweet Home (2 different interlocking mask-shaped picture disc set)	20
86	Elektra EKR 33T	Smokin' In The Boys' Room/Home Sweet Home/Shout At The Devil (12", p/s with poster)	20

MOTORCYCLE RIDE

MINT VALUE £

87	Elektra EKR 59V	Girls, Girls, Girls/Sumthin' For Nuthin' ('X-rated' stickered p/s, 3,000 only)	10
88	Elektra EKR 65TB	You're All I Need/Wild Side/Home Sweet Home/Looks That Kill (12", box set with poster, tour pass & patch)	10
83	Elektra 9602 89-1	SHOUT AT THE DEVIL (LP, with bonus 12" picture disc & poster)	20

MOTORCYCLE RIDE
93	Fierce FRIGHT 060	Union City Blue/Atomic (p/s)	12

(see also Ride, Andy Bell)

MOTORDAMN
07	DJB66613	Over The Top (MotorDamn)/Ballroom Blitz (The Damned with Lemmy)	10

(see also Damned, Motorhead)

MOTÖRHEAD
SINGLES : SINGLES AND EPS

76	Stiff BUY 9	Leaving Here/White Line Fever (Unreleased, but included in Stiff box set of first 10 singles and some also sold via mail order)	50
77	Stiff BUY 9	Leaving Here/White Line Fever (mispressing, A side plays Neat Neat Neat by THE DAMNED)	100
77	Chiswick S 13	Motörhead/City Kids (p/s)	20
77	Chiswick S 13A	Motörhead/City Kids (12", p/s)	20
78	Bronze BRO 60	Louie Louie/Tear Ya Down (p/s)	8
79	Bronze BRO 67	Overkill/Too Late, Too Late (p/s, with 'Overkill' badge)	10
79	Bronze 12 BRO 67	Overkill/Too Late, Too Late (12", p/s)	10
79	Bronze BRO 78	No Class/Like A Nightmare (3 different sleeves)	50
79	Bronze BRO 85	Bomber/Over The Top (p/s, on blue vinyl)	10
79	Big Beat NS 13	Motörhead/City Kids (p/s, black, pink, blue, orange or white vinyl)	7
80	Big Beat NSP 13	Motörhead/City Kids (p/s, blue & white picture disc)	15
80	Bronze BRO 92 DJ	Leaving Here (live)/Stone Dead Forever (live) (2-track promo for Golden Years EP)	40
80	Bronze BRO 106	Ace Of Spades/Dirty Love (p/s)	10
80	Bronze BROX 106	Ace Of Spades/Dirty Love (12", 'Xmas' sleeve)	10
82	Bronze BRO 146	Iron Fist/Remember Me I'm Gone (p/s, blue vinyl)	12
82	Bronze BRO 146	Iron Fist/Remember Me I'm Gone (p/s, red vinyl)	6
82	Bronze BRO 151	Stand By Your Man/No Class/Masterplan (p/s, as Lemmy & Wendy O. Williams)	8
83	Bronze BRO 167	Shine/Hoochie Coochie Man (live) (p/s)	7
83	Bronze BROX 167/BROX 92	Shine/Hoochie Coochie Man (live)/Don't Need Religion (live)/THE GOLDEN YEARS (12", p/s, stickered, shrinkwrapped double pack)	18
83	Lyntone LYN 4383	In Their Own Words/BRONZ: Taken By Storm (flexi free with Kerrang! mag)	10
84	Bronze BROP 185	Killed By Death/Under The Knife (logo skull-shaped picture disc)	20
84	Bronze BROX 185	Killed By Death (Full Length Version)/Under The Knife/Under The Knife (12", stickered p/s, with poster)	15
84	Bronze BROP 185	Killed By Death/Under The Knife (logo skull-shaped picture disc, mispressing, A side plays Banana Banana and B side plays Bo Diddley Goes East by KING KURT)	100
88	GWR GWR 15	Ace Of Spades/Dogs/Traitor (sold at concerts & through fan club, no p/s)	20
90	Epic 656578 0	The One To Sing The Blues/Dead Man's Hand (shaped picture disc)	15
80	Big Beat SWT 61	BEER DRINKERS EP (12", p/s, blue vinyl)	10
80	Big Beat SWT 61	BEER DRINKERS EP (12", p/s, pink or orange vinyl)	15
80	Big Beat SWT 61	BEER DRINKERS EP (12", p/s, brown vinyl)	40
81	Bronze BROX 116	ST. VALENTINES DAY MASSACRE (10" EP, with Girlschool)	15

ALBUMS

77	Chiswick WIK 2	MOTÖRHEAD (LP, black and silver sleeve with inner, 600 only)	750
77	Chiswick WIK 2	MOTÖRHEAD (LP, black & white laminated sleeve with inner)	50
77	Chiswick CWK 3008	MOTÖRHEAD (LP, white vinyl)	30
78	United Artists LBR 1004	ON PAROLE (LP)	25
79	Bronze BRON 515	OVERKILL (LP, green vinyl)	30
79	Bronze BRON 523	BOMBER (LP, 3 different shades of blue vinyl)	35
80	Bronze BRON 531	ACE OF SPADES (LP)	30
80	Bronze BRONG 531	ACE OF SPADES (LP, gold vinyl, stickered sleeve)	80
80	Big Beat WIK 2	MOTÖRHEAD (LP, reissue, red or clear vinyl with inner sleeve)	15
81	Bronze BRONG 535	NO SLEEP 'TIL HAMMERSMITH (LP, gold vinyl, stickered sleeve)	40
82	Bronze BRNA 539	IRON FIST (LP)	20
84	Bronze/Pro MOTOR 1	NO REMORSE (2-LP, leather sleeve with inners)	25
86	GWR GWRLP 1	ORGASMATRON (LP, picture disc)	20
90	Castle TFOLP 024	BOMBER/ACE OF SPADES (2-LP, reissue)	20
91	Epic 467481-0	1916 (LP, picture disc, stickered PVC sleeve)	20
91	Epic 467481 9	1916 (CD, 'tour' picture disc shrinkwrapped with booklet, stickered case)	30
92	Receiver RRLP 005	JAILBAIT (2-LP)	30
93	Castle CTVLP 125	ALL THE ACES (2-LP, gatefold)	40
93	Castle/Bronze CTVCD 125	ALL THE ACES (CD, numbered promo, in box with metal skull, 10 only)	200
00	Metal-Is MISL 002	THE BEST OF...(3-LP, numbered with insert & bonus exclusive live EP)	45
10	Back To Black 5326582	ACE OF SPADES (LP, picture disc, reissue, with download card)	15
10	Motorhead Music UDR – UDR 0005 LP	THE WORLD IS YOURS (LP, gatefold, silver vinyl, 1000 only)	50
10	Motorhead Music UDR – UDR 0005 LP	THE WORLD IS YOURS (LP, gatefold)	20

(see also Lemmy & Upsetters, Hawkwind, Girlschool, Wild Horses, Young & Moody, Rocking Vickers, Blue Goose, Motordamn, Persian Risk)

MOTORWAY
79	Neat NEAT 01	All I Wanna Be Is Your Romeo/It's Easy When You're Alone	10

MOTOWN SOUNDS
79	Tamla Motown TMG 1143	Space Dance/Bad Mouthin	10
79	Motown 12TMG 1143	Space Dance/Bad Mouthin' (12")	20
79	Motown STML 12105	SPACE DANCE (LP)	15

MOTT THE HOOPLE
69	Island WIP 6072	Rock And Roll Queen/Road To Birmingham	25

Ken MOULE'S LONDON JAZZ CHAMBER GROUP

MINT VALUE £

71	Island WIP 6105	Midnight Lady/The Debt (in p/s)	18
71	Island WIP 6105	Midnight Lady/The Debt	6
71	Island WIP 6112	Downtown/Home	10
69	Island ILPS 9108	MOTT THE HOOPLE (LP, gatefold sleeve, pink label with white 'i' logo; with "Backsliding Fearlessly" in correct order)	100
69	Island ILPS 9108	MOTT THE HOOPLE (LP, pink label; mispress with 5 alternate mixes & Road To Birmingham in place of "Backsliding Fearlessly" or one alternative mix with "Road To Birmingham", and "Rock And Roll Queen" correctly credited. This price for each copy)	90
70	Island ILPS 9119	MAD SHADOWS (LP, pink label with pink 'i' logo, gatefold sleeve)	50
71	Island ILPS 9144	WILD LIFE (LP, gatefold, pink rim palm tree label)	50
71	Island ILPS 9178	BRAIN CAPERS (LP, pink rim palm tree label & inner sleeve, with mask)	100
71	Island ILPS 9178	BRAIN CAPERS (LP, pink rim palm tree label & inner sleeve, without mask)	40
72	CBS 65184	ALL THE YOUNG DUDES (LP, with inner sleeve)	40
72	Island ILPS 9215	ROCK AND ROLL QUEEN (LP, pink rim palm tree label)	25
73	CBS 69038	MOTT (LP, die-cut gatefold sleeve with plastic flap, inner sleeve, orange label, stickered)	40
74	CBS 69062	THE HOOPLE (LP, with insert)	40
80	Island IRSP 8	TWO MILES FROM HEAVEN (LP, early copies listing "Moving On" on rear sleeve)	20
80	Island IRSP 8	TWO MILES FROM HEAVEN (LP)	15

(see also Ian Hunter, At Last The 1958 Rock & Roll Show, Morgan, Mick Ronson, British Lions, Luther Grosvenor, Charlie Woolfe)

KEN MOULE'S LONDON JAZZ CHAMBER GROUP
70	Ember EMB S 275	Mae West/Zsa Zsa Gabor (in p/s)	15
69	Ember CJS 823	ADAM'S RIB SUITE (LP)	70

(see also London Jazz Chamber Group, Ken Moule Seven)

KEN MOULE SEVEN
54	Decca LK 4087	MODERN JAZZ AT THE FESTIVAL HALL (LP, also features Don Rendell and Tony Crombie Orchestra)	50
57	Decca LK 4192	KEN MOULE ARRANGES FOR (LP)	25
58	Decca LK 4261	JAZZ AT TOAD HALL (LP)	30

(see also London Jazz Chamber Group)

MOULIN ROUGE
81	Teesbeat TB3	Easy/Holding Out (p/s)	8

MATTIE MOULTRIE
67	CBS 202547	That's How Strong My Love Is/The Saddest Story Ever Told	20
67	CBS 202547	That's How Strong My Love Is/The Saddest Story Ever Told (DJ Copy)	40

MOUND CITY BLUE BLOWERS
60	Collector JEL 1	BLUES BLOWING JAZZ VOL. 1 (EP)	10

MOUNT KIMBIE
11	Hotflush CNL 003	CARBONATED EP (2 x 12")	15
13	Hotflush HF 021	MAYBES EP (12")	12
13	Beat/Warp WAP 251J	You Took Your Time (Oneman Remix) (12")	30

MOUNT RUSHMORE
68	Dot DOT 115	Stone Free/She's No Good To Me	10

MOUNTAIN
70	Bell BLL 1112	Mississippi Queen/The Laird	15
70	Bell BLL 1125	Sittin' On A Rainbow/To My Friend	20
71	Island WIP 6119	Roll Over Beethoven/Crossroader	8
70	Bell SBLL 133	MOUNTAIN CLIMBING! (LP)	25
71	Island ILPS 9148	NANTUCKET SLEIGHRIDE (LP, 'pink rim palm tree' label)	20
71	Island ILPS 9179	FLOWERS OF EVIL (LP, 'pink rim palm tree' label)	15

(see also West Bruce & Laing, Leslie West, Jolliver Arkansas)

MOUNTAIN ASH
75	Witches Bane LKLP 6036	THE HERMIT (LP, private pressing with insert)	200

MOUNTAIN MEN
65	Eos CE 717	Too Many People/Without You	250

VALERIE MOUNTAIN
62	Pye 7N 15450	Some People/Yes You Did	7
62	Pye NEP 24158	SOME PEOPLE - SOUNDTRACK (EP, some tracks by Eagles)	12

(see also Eagles)

MOURNING AFTER
94	Detour DR 017	Doin' Me In/Out For The Count (p/s, 100 blue vinyl)	6

MOURNING PHASE
71	Eden	MOURNING PHASE (LP, private pressing)	200
91	Eden EDEN 1	EDEN (LP, reissue of "Mourning Phase")	20

MOUSE
73	Sovereign SOV 122	We Can Make It/It's Happening To Me And You	20
74	Sovereign SOV 127	All The Fallen Teen Angels/Just Came Back	12
73	Sovereign SVNA 7262	LADY KILLER (LP, gatefold sleeve)	300

(see also Ginhouse, Ray Russell Quartet, Running Man)

MOUSE & TRAPS
68	President PT 174	L.O.V.E. Love/Beg Borrow And Steal	40
68	President PT 210	Sometimes You Just Can't Win/Crying Inside	20

MOUSE ON MARS
94	Too Pure PURE 36	VULVALAND (LP, with free 12")	20
97	Too Pure PURE 70	AUTODITACKER (LP)	20
95	Too Pure PURE 48	LAORA TAHITI (LP)	20
99	Domino WIGLP 70	NIUN NIGGUNG (LP)	20

MOUSETRAP
71	Aurora AU 4324	Susie/Greenfields	35

MOUTH
81	Recreationa SPORT 3	Ooh Ah Yeah/Ooh	8

MOUTH TO MOUTH

			MINT VALUE £
82	Y Y20	Who's Hot/Catch A Cab	8

MOUTH TO MOUTH
79	Mouth To Mouth MT 1	Gallery Of Dolls/Life In The Subbterrain (hand stamped labels, no p/s)	200

MOVE
66	Deram DM 109	Night Of Fear/Disturbance	8
67	Deram DM 117	I Can Hear The Grass Grow/Wave The Flag And Stop The Train	10
67	Regal Zonophone RZ 3001	Flowers In The Rain/(Here We Go Round) The Lemon Tree	7
67	Regal Zonophone	Cherry Blossom Clinic/Vote For Me (unissued)	0
68	Regal Zonophone RZ 3005	Fire Brigade/Walk Upon The Water	7
68	Regal Zonophone RZ 3012	Wild Tiger Woman/Omnibus	12
69	Regal Zonophone RZ 3015	Blackberry Way/Something	7
69	Regal Zonophone RZ 3021	Curly/This Time Tomorrow	7
70	Regal Zonophone RZ 3026	Brontosaurus/Lightnin' Never Strikes Twice	7
71	Harvest HAR 5036	Ella James/No Time (unissued)	0
68	Regal Zono. TRZ 2001	SOMETHING ELSE FROM THE MOVE (EP, 33rpm)	75
68	Regal Zono. LRZ 1002	THE MOVE (LP, mono, red/silver labels with "Sold in the U.K..." text)	150
68	Regal Zono. SLRZ 1002	THE MOVE (LP, stereo, red/silver labels with "Sold in the U.K..." text)	100
70	Regal Zono. SLRZ 1012	SHAZAM (LP, many with pressing flaw on track "Don't Make My Baby Blue" that makes record skip on this track, red/silver label)	150
70	Fly HIFLY 1	LOOKING ON (LP, white label, 'Fly' logo)	40
71	Harvest SHSP 4013	MESSAGE FROM THE COUNTRY (LP, with EMI logo on label)	80
74	Harvest SHSP 4035	CALIFORNIA MAN (LP)	20

(see also Roy Wood, ELO, Idle Race, Trevor Burton, Nicky James Movement, Ace Kefford Stand, Grunt Futtock, Rick Price, Uglys, Charlie Wayne)

MOVEMENT (1)
68	Pye 7N 17443	Tell Her/Something You've Got	120
68	Target 7N 17443	Something You've Got/Tell Her (Irish issue)	120
68	Big T BIG 112	Head For The Sun/Mister Mann	180

MOVEMENT (2)
80	Ballistic TRIF 2	No Man Is An Island/JAMDOWN PLAYERS: Levi's Choice (dubwise)/Togetherness/Deviate/Consolidate/Progression (12")	30

MOVERS (1)
65	Ska Beat JB 191	Jo-Anne/DON DRUMMOND: Don De Lion	45

MOVERS (2)
68	Capitol CL 15562	Birmingham/Leave Me Loose	25

MOVERS (3)
60s	Junior Records Ltd JR 109	Rock Rock/Reggay Rock	200

MOVIES (2)
80	Gem GEMS 20	Love Is A Sacrifice/Fat Girl	6

MOVIE STARS
82	Lansater LG10	No Time To Kill/Heroes (no p/s)	30

MOVIETONE
94	Planet PUNK 003	She Smiled Mandarine Like/Orange Zero (p/s)	6
95	Planet PUNK 010	MOVIETONE (LP)	30
97	Domino WIGLP 36	DAY AND NIGHT (LP)	30
00	Domino WIGLP 79	THE BLOSSOM FILLED STREETS (LP)	30
03	Domino WIGLP 131	THE SAND AND THE STARS (LP)	20

MOVING BROTHERS
67	Island WI 3049	Darling I Love You/TOMMY McCOOK & SUPERSONICS: Saboo	40
67	Treasure Isle TI 7018	Darling I Love You/TOMMY McCOOK & SUPERSONICS: Saboo (reissue)	25

MOVING ENGLAND
80	English ER 001	Moving Back/Stretching Back (Part 3)	30

MOVING FINGER
68	Mercury MF 1051	Jeremy The Lamp/Pain Of My Misfortune	50
69	Mercury MF 1077	Higher And Higher/Shake And Fingerpop	70
73	Decca F 13406	So Many People/We're Just As Happy As We Are	8

(see also Anglians)

MOVING VIOLATION
74	Atlantic 10516	Spinnin' Top/Wild Goose Chase	10

JUDY MOWATT
71	Trojan GPW 33	The Gardener/Vesion (white label only)	35
73	Gayfeet GS 207	Emergency Call/Emergency Call - Version	8
75	Torpedo 52	Too Good For Me/Cry To Me	10
78	Grove Music GM 8	Black Woman/JOY TULLOCH: Black Beauty	10
80	Grove Music IPR 2041	Black Woman (feat. Joy Tulloch)/My My People (12")	25

(see also Jean & Gaytones, Gaylettes)

IRVIN MOWREY
79	Initial IRS 001	The Queen Of Maybe/Fat City	6

MOWREY JNR. & WATSON
76	Riverdale RRL 1000	BUSKER (LP, with insert)	30

MR. BLOE
70	DJM DJS 216	Groovin' With Mr. Bloe/Sinful	6
70	DJM DJLPS 036	GROOVIN' WITH MR. BLOE (LP)	18

(see also Harry Pitch)

MR BROOKS
74	EMI 2168	The Family Theme/Easy Going	10

MR. BUNGLE
91	London 828 276-1	MR BUNGLE (LP, picture disc)	40

MR. B WACKA
97	Humboldt County BOLDT6	Traffic Jam/Bus Stop (12")	60

MR. CALYPSON
71	Jump Up JU 40	Mohammed Ali/SAMSON DE LARK: Undemocratic Rhodesia	6

MR. CEE

MINT VALUE £

MR. CEE
87 Asona ASR 7010 — NYE WONKO (LP) 20

MR CHIPPS
77 Spiral SPF 7014 — The Way I Am/Lady Elaine (no p/s) 30

MR CLEAN & SOUL INC
09 Jazzman JSERATO 001 — What's Going On?/Serato Conrol Tone (die-cut sleeve) 10

MR. CONCEPT
85 Cordelia ERICAT 009 — NOVEMBER (LP) 30

MR. DYNAMITE
67 Sue WI 4027 — Sh'mon/DYNAMITE ORCHESTRA: Sh'mon (Part Two) 300

MR. FINGERS
89 Jack Trax JTX 32 — LOVE AND JUSTICE (12") 20
88 Jack Trax 12 J TRAX 10 — SLAM DANCE EP (12") 50
90 FFRR F181 — What About This Love/Dub Version (die-cut sleeve) 20
92 MCA MCS 18313 — Closer/U.S.S.R (p/s) 6
89 Jack Trax FING 2 — AMMNESIA (2-LP) 80
92 MCA MCA 10571 — INTRODUCTION (LP with free 12") 40
94 Black Market BMI 022 LP — BACK TO LOVE (LP) 35
95 Black Market BMI 024 LP — CLASSIC FINGERS (2-LP) 30
18 Alleviated ML 9017 — CEREBAL HEMISPHERES (3-LP) 20
(see also Larry Heard, Fingers Inc.)

MR. FLOOD'S PARTY
71 Ember EMB S 312 — Compared To What/Unbreakable Toy 20
71 Ember EMB S 312 — Compared To What/Unbreakable Toy (DJ copy) 40
75 Bulldog BD 6 — Compared To What/Unbreakable Toy (reissue) 10
(see also Mike Corbett & Jay Hirsch)

MR. FORD & MR. GOON-BONES
56 London HLU 8355 — Ain't She Sweet/MUZZY MARCELLINO: Mary Lou 25
(see also Mr. Goon-Bones & Cavaliers)

MR FOUNDATION
67 Studio One SO 2001 — See Them A Come/KEN PARKER: Have A Good Time 70
67 Studio One SO 2003 — All Rudies In Jail (actually by Zoot Sims)/HORTENSE & ALTON Easy Squeeze 90
68 Studio One SO 2061 — Timo Oh/DUDLEY SIBLEY & PETER AUSTIN: Hole In Your Soul 125
68 Studio One SO 2069 — Reggae Rumble/MARCIA GRIFFITHS : You Keep Me On The Move 180
69 Supreme SUP 201 — Time To Pray (actually by Lloyd Robinson)/Young Budd (by Leonard Dillon) 20
(see also Busty & Cool, Simms & Robinson, Sound Dimension)

MR. FOX
70 Big T BIG 135 — Little Woman/Join Us In Our Game 8
70 Transatlantic TRA 226 — MR FOX (LP) 75
71 Transatlantic TRA 236 — THE GIPSY (LP, gatefold sleeve, plaatic inner with foam opening) 125
75 Transatlantic TRA 303 — THE COMPLETE MR FOX (2-LP, reissue of "Mr Fox" & "The Gypsy") 20
(see also Bob Pegg, Bob & Carol Pegg)

MR. MO'S MESSENGERS
67 Columbia DB 8133 — Feelin' Good/The Handyman 15

MISTER MOST
69 Downtown DT 409 — Reggae Train/Pushwood 30

MR. PINK/MR. BLONDE
96 Resevoir BP1 — Payin' The Price/Death Before Dishonour (12") 15
97 Resevoir BP2 — Jamaica Crime Wave (12") 12

MR. REJECT
71 Private pressing — MR. REJECT (LP) 40

MR. SCRUFF
99 Ninja Tune ZEN 42 — KEEP IT UNREAL (2xLP, gatefold) 25
99 Ninja Tune ZEN 42 — KEEP IT UNREAL (2xLP, gatefold, purple sleeve) 30
99 Ninja Tune ZEN 65 — TROUSER JAZZ (2xLP, gatefold) 25

MR STONE
79 Strictly Pre PRE 1 — Jah Jah Higher Than I/Unbeliever (12") 60

MR. TWISTER & TORNADOS
63 Starlite ST45 099 — Big Twist (Parts 1 & 2) 15

MR. THING X MICALL PARKNSUN
17 White 157067E2/A — THE RAW EP (12", p/s, 100 only) 25
18 Village Live TVI 019 — FINISH WHAT WE STARTED (LP, with obi strip) 30

MTUME
78 Epic EPC 84629 — IN SEARCH OF THE RAINBOW SEEKERS (LP) 20
83 Epic EPC 25399 — JUICY FRUIT (LP) 20

MU
74 United Artists UAG 29709 — LEMURIAN MUSIC (LP) 35

MU5
72 Crystal CR 7015 — Mrs Watson/Rain Dance 50

MUCKY DUCK
70 Deram DM314 — Jefferson/Psycho's On The Run 15

MUD
67 CBS 203002 — Flower Power/You're My Mother (in p/s) 50
67 CBS 203002 — Flower Power/You're My Mother 35
68 CBS 3355 — Up The Airy Mountain/Latter Days 30
69 Philips BF 1775 — Shangri-La/House On The Hill 20
70 Philips 6006 022 — Jumping Jehoshaphat/Won't Let It Go 20
(see also Dum)

MUDHONEY
88 Glitterhouse GR 0034 — SUPERFUZZ BIGMUFF (12" EP) 18

MUD HUTTERS

MINT VALUE £

89	Blast First BFFP 46	Halloween/SONIC YOUTH: Touch Me I'm Sick (12", with tour/gig flyer)	10
95	Reprise 9362 458401	MY BROTHER THE COW (LP, with 6-track EP, [PRO S 7492])	20

(see also Sonic Youth, Greenriver)

MUD HUTTERS

79	Defensive SRTS/79/CUS 263	INFORMATION EP (paper wrap p/s)	50
79	Defensive SRTS/79/CUS 496	THE DECLARATION EP (paper wrap p/s)	30
80	Defensive PACT 1	FACTORY FARMING (LP)	30

MUDIE'S ALL STARS

70	Moodisc HM 3503	Wha Who Wha - Version/G.G. RUSSELL: Wha Who Wha	20

(see also I Roy, Eternals, King Cannon, John Holt, Niney, Jolly Boys, Jo Jo Bennett)

MUDLARKS

58	Columbia DB 4064	Mutual Admiration Society/A New Love	7
58	Columbia DB 4099	Lollipop/Young Dove's Calling	7
58	Columbia DB 4133	Book Of Love/Yea, Yea	7
59	Columbia DB 4250	Abdul The Bulbul Amer Cha Cha/The Love Game	6
59	Columbia DB 4331	Waterloo/Mary	6
60	Columbia DB 4513	(You've Got To) Move Two Mountains/You're Free To Go	6
62	Columbia DB 4788	Them Twistin' Bones/Coney Island Washboard	7
62	Columbia DB 4861	Mañana Pasado Mañana/March Of The Broken Hearts	6
63	Decca F 11601	The Little Cracked Bell Of San Raquel/La De Da	6
64	Fontana TF 495	Walk Around/Here's Another Day	8
58	Columbia SEG 7854	THE MUDLARKS! (EP)	20

DOMENICO MODUGNO

58	Oriole ICB 5000	Volare (Nel Blu Difinto Di Blu)/Nisciuno Po' Sape	8

MUFF

71	Mother MOT 7	Hurdy Gurdy/Why Did You Leave Me	15

MUFFIN

72	Dart ART 2018	Smokey Blues Away/Acapulco Gold	6

MUGGINS BLIGHT

79	Look LK/EP 6455	Mr Somebody/They Go Up! They Go Down!/Malcolm Where's the Talcum? (p/s)	25

MUGWUMPS

64	Warner Bros WB 144	I'll Remember Tonight/I Don't Wanna Know	12
67	Warner Bros W 1697	THE MUGWUMPS - AN HISTORICAL RECORDING (LP)	35
70	Valiant VS 134	THE MUGWUMPS - AN HISTORICAL RECORDING (LP, reissue)	18

(see also Mamas & Papas, Mama Cass Elliot, Lovin' Spoonful, Zalman Yanovsky)

IDRIS MUHAMMAD

77	Kudu KUDU 935	Could Heaven Ever Be Like This/Turn This Mutha Out	7
74	Kudu KU 17	POWER OF SOUL (LP)	50
77	Kudo KU 34	TURN THIS MUTHA OUT (LP)	30
78	Fantasy FT 552	YOU AIN'T NO FRIEND OF MINE (LP)	20
78	Kudu KU 38	BOOGIE TO THE TOP (LP)	20
79	Fantasy FT 562	FOXHUNTIN' (LP)	15

BOBBY MUIR & BLUEBEATS

60	Blue Beat BB 20	Baby What You Done Me Wrong/Go Pretty Baby Go (as Blue Beats)	12
61	Blue Beat BB 44	Honey Please/That's My Girl (as Bobby Kingdom & Blue Beats)	25
62	Blue Beat BB 77	Brand New Automobile/Spanish Town Twist (as Bobby Kingdom & Blue Beats)	12

JAMIE MUIR & DEREK BAILEY

81	Incus INCUS 41	DART DRUG (LP)	50

(see also Derek Bailey)

LINDSAY MUIR'S UNTAMED

66	Planet PLF 113	Daddy Long Legs/Trust Yourself A Little Bit (initial release with plain white white sleeve)	250
66	Planet PLF 113	Daddy Long Legs/Trust Yourself A Little Bit (with Planet company sleeve)	240

(see also Untamed)

MULCAYS

55	London HLF 8188	Harbour Lights/Dipsy Doodle	20
54	London REP 1016	MERRY CHRISTMAS (EP)	12

MULDOONS

65	Decca F 12164	I'm Lost Without You/Come Back Now Baby	30

MULESKINNERS

65	Fontana TF 527	Back Door Man/Need Your Lovin'	200
65	Keepoint KEE-EP-7104	MULESKINNERS (EP, private pressing, no p/s)	750

(see also Small Faces, Faces)

ARTHUR MULLARD

67	Masquerade MP 2003	ARTHUR MULLARD OF LONDON (LP)	30

MOON MULLICAN

56	Parlophone MSP 6254	Seven Nights To Rock/Honolulu Rock-A Roll-A (with Boyd Bennett & His Rockets)	300
56	Parlophone R 4195	Seven Nights To Rock/Honolulu Rock-A Roll-A (with Boyd Bennett & His Rockets) (78)	50
59	Parlophone GEP 8794	COUNTRY ROUND UP (EP)	60
50s	Parlophone CGEP 13	MOON MULLICAN (EP, export issue)	40
50s	Parlophone CGEP 15	PIANO BREAKDOWN (EP, export issue, company sleeve)	20

(see also Boyd Bennett & His Rockets)

GERRY MULLIGAN

53	Capitol LC 6621	THE GERRY MULLIGAN TENTETTE - ROCKER (10" LP)	15
53	Vogue LDE 029	THE GERRY MULLIGAN QUARTET VOL. 1 (10" LP)	15
53	Vogue LDE 030	THE GERRY MULLIGAN QUARTET VOL. 2 (10" LP)	15
53	Vogue LDE 031	THE GERRY MULLIGAN QUARTET VOL. 3 (10" LP)	15
54	Vogue LDE 075	THE GERRY MULLIGAN QUARTET (10" LP)	15
54	Vogue LDE 083	THE GERRY MULLIGAN QUARTET VOL. 4 (10" LP)	15
54	Esquire 20-032	GERRY MULLIGAN ALLSTARS - MULLIGAN'S TOO (10" LP)	20

MICK MULLIGAN'S JAZZ BAND

MINT VALUE £

55	Vogue LDE 156	GERRY MULLIGAN QUARTET WITH LEE KONITZ (10" LP)	20
56	Esquire 32-014	GERRY MULLIGAN ALLSTARS (LP)	20
56	Vogue LAE 12006	THE GERRY MULLIGAN QUARTET (LP)	20
56	Vogue LAE 12015	THE GERRY MULLIGAN QUARTET - PARIS JAZZ FAIR 1954 (LP)	20
56	Emarcy EJL 101	PRESENTING THE GERRY MULLIGAN SEXTET (LP)	25
57	Emarcy EJL 1259	MAINSTREAM OF JAZZ (LP, by Gerry Mulligan Sextet)	25
58	Columbia Clef 33CX 10113	GERRY MULLIGAN AND PAUL DESMOND QUARTET (LP)	25
58	HMV CLP 1204	PHIL SUNKEL'S "JAZZ CONCERTO GROSSO" (LP, with Bob Brookmeyer)	25
59	Philips SBBL 552	WHAT IS THERE TO SAY? (LP, stereo)	25
59	Vogue SEA 5006	GERRY MULLIGAN SONGBOOK (LP, stereo)	25
59	Vogue SEA 5007	REUNION WITH CHET BAKER (LP, stereo, as Gerry Mulligan Quartet)	25
59	London Jazz LTZT 15161	I WANT TO LIVE (LP, with Shelly Manne)	20
60	HMV CLP 1373	GERRY MULLIGAN MEETS BEN WEBSTER (LP)	20
61	HMV CLP 1432	THE CONCERT JAZZ BAND (LP, also stereo CSD 1351)	20
61	Vocalion LAE 12268	THE GENIUS OF GERRY MULLIGAN (LP)	20
62	HMV CLP 1465	GERRY MULLIGAN MEETS JOHNNY HODGES (LP, also stereo CSD 1372)	20
62	HMV CLP 1488	AT THE VILLAGE VANGUARD (LP, also stereo CSD 1396)	20
62	Riverside RLP 12-247	MULLIGAN MEETS MONK (LP, with Thelonious Monk)	20
62	HMV CLP 1549	A CONCERT IN JAZZ (LP, also stereo CSD 1432)	20
62	HMV CLP 1585	ON TOUR (LP, with Zoot Sims)	20
63	Philips BL 7597	NIGHT LIGHTS (LP)	25

(see also Gerry Mulligan, Chet Baker, Shelly Manne, Annie Ross)

MICK MULLIGAN'S JAZZ BAND

57	Tempo TAP 14	JAZZ AT THE RAILWAY ARMS (LP, with George Melly)	50
59	Pye Jazz NJL 21	MEET MICK MULLIGAN (LP)	20
59	Parlophone PMC 1103	THE SAINTS MEET THE SINNERS (LP, with George Melly & Saints Jazz Band)	6

(see also George Melly)

TED MULRY

71	Polydor 2058106	Fallin In Love Again/Louisa	6

MULTIPLE TRANSMISSION

95	Alphaphone ALPHA 002	Earthloop/Low Load/Antichrist (12")	25

(see also Cabaret Voltaire, Richard H. Kirk)

MULTI STORY

83	Loco LOCO 1010	Cutting Close/Star Traveller (no p/s)	10

MUM

02	Fat Cat FATLP 18	FINALLY WE ARE NO ONE (2 x 10")	50
07	Fat Cat FATLP46	GO GO SMEAR THE POISON IVY (LP, with bonus 7")	18

GENE MUMFORD

58	Philips PB 862	More Than You Know/Please Give Me One More Chance	8

MUMFORD & SONS

08	Chess Club CC 006	LEND ME YOUR EYES EP (10", p/s)	175
08	Chess Club CC 009	LOVE YOUR GROUND EP (10", p/s)	150
09	Gentlemen Of The Road/Island 2728222,	Winter Winds/Hold On To What You Believe (p/s, cream coloured vinyl)	20
09	Chess Club CC 015	The Cave/My Heart Told My Head (Winter Winds) (1-sided 10", gatefold p/s, 300 only, signed)	100
09	Chess Club CC 015	The Cave/My Heart Told My Head (Winter Winds) (1-sided 10", gatefold p/s, 300 only, unsigned)	50
09	Island 2720975	Little Lion Man/To Darkness (p/s)	8
10	Universal 27424111	Roll Away Your Stone/White Blank Page (live) (p/s, green vinyl)	12
12	Gentlemen Of The Road/Island 3716215	I Will Wait/I Will Wait (live) (p/s, no'd, 500 only)	18
12	Gentlemen Of The Road/Island 3723020	Lover Of The Light/Thistle & Weeds (live) (p/s, 1000 only, no'd)	15
13	Gentlemen Of The Road/Island 3732348	Whispers In The Dark/Whispers In The Dark (live) (p/s, no'd 1000 only)	6
10	Chess Club WEDDING 1	FIRST DANCE EP (tour 10" as The Wedding Band)	80
09	V2 VVR 723601	SIGH NO MORE (LP)	15
12	Gentlemen Of The Road 3710659	BABEL (LP, gatefold)	15

MUMMIES

89	Hangman HANG 47 UP	FUCKS C.D.S. ITS...(LP)	20

MUMMY CALLS

83	MC 12	Mary I Swear/Unicorn Jones (p/s)	10

MUNDANES

79	Groucho	Groucho Party/Groucho Party (faux 2-Tone sleeve, insert)	8

HUGH MUNDELL

78	Greensleeves GRE9	Let's All Unite/Unity Dub	15
79	Warrior WAR 131	Stop Them Jah/Push Dawta Push (12")	30
80	J&F 002	Jah Fire Will Be Burning/King Of Israel (12")	30
81	Greensleeves GRED 54	Can't Pop No Style/JUNIOR REID: Know Myself (12")	50
80	Mun Rock MMLP 001	TIME AND PLACE (LP)	25
80	Live And Love LAP 13	JAH FIRE (LP, with Lacksley Castell and Augustus Pablo)	60
82	Greensleeves GREL 36	MUNDELL (LP)	20
86	Greensleeves GREL 94	AFRICA MUST BE FREE BY 1983 (LP, reissue)	30
88	Atra 1007	ARISE (LP)	35

(see also Ray Dorset, Good Earth, King Earl Boogie Band, Horizon, Made In England, Jigilo Jug Band, P. King, Paul King, P. Rufus King,, Good Earth)

MUNGO JERRY

70	Pye 7N 2502	In The Summertime/Mighty Man (jukebox issue)	8
71	Dawn DNX 2510	Lady Rose/Have A Whiff On Me/Milk Cow Blues/Little Louis (p/s, withdrawn)	12
85	Orbit TRIP 4	Sunshine Reggae/Nightlife (reissue of Horizon 45; as Mungo Jerry & Horizon)	6
70	Dwn DNLS 3008	MUNGO JERRY (LP, gatefold sleeve, with 3-D glasses)	40

Ray MUNNINGS

			MINT VALUE £
71	Dawn DNLS 3028	YOU DON'T HAVE TO BE IN THE ARMY (LP, gatefold sleeve, with lyric insert)	15
71	Dawn DNLS 3020	ELECTRONICALLY TESTED (LP, gatefold sleeve)	20
72	Dawn DNLS 3041	BOOT POWER (LP, with 'Dennis The Menace' or 'gun' gatefold sleeve)	15

(see also Ray Dorset, Good Earth, King Earl Boogie Band, Horizon, Made In England, Jigilo Jug Band, P. King, Paul King, P. Rufus King,, Good Earth)

RAY MUNNINGS
79	Tammi TAM 102	It Could Happen To You/Let's Boogie	20
79	Tammi TAM 103	Funky Nassau/Jump In The Water	20
79	Tammi TAM 103	Funky Nassau/Jump In The Water (12")	50

CAROLINE MUNRO
67	Columbia DB 8189	Tar And Cement/The Sporting Life	20

(see also Gary Numan)

SHEILA MUNRO
79	Munrover SM 1	Summertime/Vehicle/You Made Me So Very Happy (promo only)	25

ADRIAN MUNSEY
79	Virgin VS 266	C'Est Sheep (Part 1)/C'Est Sheep (Part 2) (p/s)	6

(see also Sparks)

STEPHAN MUNSON & FRIENDS
82	Rhythmic RMNS 2	And David Cried/And Dem Bahnhoff (fold-out photocopied p/s)	8

MURCOF
02	Leaf BAY 23	MARTES (2-LP)	25
05	Leaf BAY 47 V	REMEMBRANZA (2-LP)	20

MURDER INC.
80	MIL MIL 1	SOUNDS SO FALSE (EP)	8

(see also Business)

MURDER THE DISTURBED
79	Small Wonder SMALL 17	Walking Corpses The Ultimate System/Small Seventeen (p/s)	8

BILLY MURE (ORCHESTRA)
61	London HAR 2400	TOUGH STRINGS (LP)	20

(see also Supersonics)

MURGATROYD BAND
71	Decca F 12809	Magpie (Theme From The TV Series)/Twice A Week (p/s)	40
71	Decca F 13256	Magpie (Theme From The TV Series)/Twice A Week (without p/s)	15
71	Decca F 13256	Magpie (Theme From The TV Series)/Twice A Week (with p/s)	25

(see also Spencer Davis Group, Ray Fenwick)

MURMAIDS
63	Stateside SS 247	Popsicles And Icicles/Comedy And Tragedy	20

MURMURS OF URMA
97	Dolly 001	Coloured Rice/Magic Shop/Vacuum Cleaner/Cloudwatch HQ (P/S)	12
99	Dolly 002	Banoffe Boy Writing To A Friend/Super Vacillation Day Snails Into Fast Food (p/s)	8

ARTHUR MURPHY
59	Parlophone R 4523	Sixteen Candles/Molly Malone	10

BRIAN MURPHY
78	Pye 7N 46086	Jogging/THe Great Gnome Robbery	7

KEITH MURPHY & THE DAZE
68	Polydor 56542	Slightly Reminiscent Of Her/Dirty Old Sam	40

LYLE MURPHY
58	Contemporary LAC 12785	GONE WITH THE WOODWINDS (LP)	20

MARK MURPHY
57	Brunswick 05701	Goodbye Baby Blues/The Right Kind Of Woman	6
63	Riverside RIF 106908	Fly Me To The Moon/Why Don't You Do Right	40
64	Fontana TF 489	And Now You've Gone/Midnight Train	20
65	Fontana TF 572	High On Windy Hill/Broken Heart	15
67	Fontana TF 803	(Ain't That) Just Like A Woman/Do You Wonder If I Love You	25
57	Brunswick LAT 8172	MEET MARK MURPHY (LP)	20
60	Capitol (S)T 5011	HIT PARADE (LP)	20
64	Fontana (S)TL 5217	MARK TIME! (LP)	20
66	Immediate IMLP/IMSP 004	WHO CAN I TURN TO (LP)	40
69	Phoenix PMS 1001	THIS MUST BE EARTH (LP)	100
71	Riverside RLP 395	RAH (LP)	30

NOEL MURPHY
67	Fontana TL 5450	NYA-A-A-H! (LP)	15
73	Village Thing VTS 25	MURF (LP)	15

PETER MURPHY
86	Beggars Banquet BEGA 69	SHOULD THE WORLD FAIL TO FALL APART (LP, gatefold)	20
88	Beggars Banquet BEGA 92	LOVE HYSTERIA (LP)	20
89	Beggars Banquet BEGA 107	DEEP (LP)	40
92	Beggars Banquet BEGA 123	HOLY SMOKE (LP)	40
19	Live Here Now LHN065LP	LIVE IN LONDON (3-LP, red vinyl)	35
21	Beggars Arkive BBQ2209LPX	PETER MURPHY (7-LP box set)	150

(see also Bauhaus)

ROISIN MURPHY
05	Echo ECSY 158	SEQUINS EP 1 (12")	10
05	Echo ECHLP 63	RUBY BLUE (2-LP, with booklet)	50
07	EMI 507 0911	OVERPOWERED (2-LP, promo version on pink/orange vinyl)	100
14	Vinyl Factory VF 104	MI SENTI (2 x 12", gatefold white vinyl, signed)	80
14	Vinyl Factory VF 104	MI SENTI (2 x 12", gatefold white vinyl, unsigned)	50

(see also Moloko)

ROSE MURPHY
52	Oriole/Mercury MG 10024	SONGS BY ROSE MURPHY (10" LP)	20

MURPHY FEDERATION

MURPHY FEDERATION
81	London Madras LM 1/2	The Fed Up Skank/Slipping Past On The Inside (handmade p/s, cut up wallpaper with artwork on each side stapled together, paper inner sleeve)	70

ALEX MURRAY
60	Decca F 11203	Teen Angel/Paper Doll	6
60	Decca F 11225	All On My Own/String Along	7
61	Decca F 11345	When You Walked Out/Send For Me	7

(see also Most Brothers)

DAVID MURRAY
78	Cadillac SGC 1007	CONCEPTUAL SAXOPHONE (LP)	20
79	Cadillac SGC 1008/9	THE LONDON CONCERT (2-LP)	20

LADY MURRAY
66	Clan 597 002	Mister Abercrombie Taught Me/In My Imagination	30

(see also Grazina, Mr & Mrs Murray)

MARTIN MURRAY
66	Pye 7N 17070	I Know What I Want/Goodbye Baby	10

MICKEY MURRAY
67	Polydor 56738	Shout Bama Lama/Lonely Room	10

MISTER MURRAY
65	Fontana TF 623	Down Came The Rain/Whatever Happened To Music?	8
66	Fontana TF 674	I Drink To Your Memory/I Was A Good Song	6

(see also Mitch Murray Clan, Mr & Mrs Murray)

MITCH MURRAY CLAN
66	Clan 597 001	Skyliner/Cherokee	15

MR & MRS MURRAY
68	CBS 3633	You're Outa Your Mind/A Little Bit Of You	6

(see also Mitch Murray Clan, Lady Murray, Grazina, Mister Murray)

RUBY MURRAY
55	Columbia SCM 5162	Softly, Softly/What Could Be More Beautiful	30
55	Columbia SCM 5169	If Anyone Finds This, I Love You (with Anne Warren)/Before We Know It	10
58	Columbia 33S 1135	ENDEARING YOUNG CHARMS (10" LP)	15

(see also Norman Wisdom & Ruby Murray, Ray Burns, Ronnie Harris, Diana Decker)

MURRYS MONKEY
65	Pye &N 15800	Gipsy/I'll Be There	10

JOHN MURTAUGH
70	Polydor 2482 015	BLUES CURRENT (LP)	20

MUSCLE SHOALS HORNS
76	Bang SHOT 001	BORN TO GET DOWN (LP)	20
76	Atlantic K 50283	THE CREAM OF MUSCLE SHOALS (LP)	20

MUSE
SINGLES
99	Mushroom MUSH 50S	Uno/Agitated (p/s, clear vinyl)	40
99	Mushroom MUSH 58S	Cave/Cave (Instrumental Remix) (clear vinyl, p/s)	40
99	Mushroom MUSH 66S	Muscle Museum/Escape (p/s)	15
99	Mushroom MUSH 66S	Muscle Museum/Minimum (clear vinyl, autographed p/s, 1000 only)	80
99	Mushroom MUSH 68S	Sunburn/(Live Acoustic Version) (stickered p/s, clear vinyl)	18
00	Mushroom MUSH 72S	Unintended/Sober (p/s, clear vinyl)	18
00	Mushroom MUSH 84S	Muscle Museum/Sober (The Saint Remix) (p/s)	12
01	Mushroom MUSH 89S	Plug In Baby/Nature 1 (p/s)	20
01	Mushroom MUSH 92S	New Born/Shrinking Universe (p/s, limited issue)	18
01	Mushroom MUSH 96S	Bliss/Hyper Chondriac Music (p/s)	15
01	Mushroom MUSH 96S	Bliss/The Gallery (p/s)	15
01	Mushroom MUSH 97S	Hyper Music/Feeling Good (numbered p/s)	18
01	Mushroom MUSH 104S	Dead Star/In Your World (p/s)	15
03	East West EW 272	Time Is Running Out/The Groove (clear vinyl, p/s)	15
03	East West EW 278	Hysteria/Eternally Missed (clear vinyl, p/s)	15
04	East West EW 285	Sing For Absolution/Fury (p/s, clear vinyl)	15
04	Atlantic ATUK 003	Butterflies And Hurricanes/Butterflies And Hurricanes (Glastonbury 2004) (p/s, clear vinyl)	12
06	Warner Brothers HEL 3003	Starlight/Supermassive Black Hole (Remix) (picture disc, stickered)	15
06	A & E HEL 3004	Knights of Cydonia/Assassion (picture disc, stickered)	18
07	Warner Brothers HEL3005	Invincible/Glorious (picture disc, stickered)	18
07	Warner Brothers HEL3005	Invincible/Glorious (in static shield bag, this price for unopened)	30
07	Warner Brothers HEL3005	Invincible/Glorious (in static shield bag, this price for opened)	15

EPs
98	Dangerous DREX CDEP 103	MUSE EP (CD, 999 copies, numbered sticker)	300
98	Dangerous DREX CDEP 104	MUSCLE MUSEUM EP: Sober/Uno/Unintended/Instant Messenger/Muscle Museum # 2/Muscle Museum (CD, 999 copies, numbered sticker)	175

ALBUMS : ORIGINAL ALBUMS
00	Mushroom MUSH 59LP	SHOWBIZ (2-LP, clear vinyl, gatefold sleeve, with inners, numbered)	150
01	Mushroom MUSH 93LP	ORIGIN OF SYMMETRY (2-LP, gatefold sleeve, with lyric inner sleeves, 1500 only)	100
03	East West 5046 68587-1	ABSOLUTION (2-LP, gatefold sleeve)	40
09	Warner Bros. 825646869664	THE RESISTANCE (2-LP)	30
09	Warner Bros. 825646869664	THE RESISTANCE (Box set, CD, DVD, USB stick)	50
12	Warner Bros. 825646568772	THE 2ND LAW (2-LP)	20
12	Warner Bros. 2564656876	THE 2ND LAW (Box set, 2-LP, DVD, CD, book, print and heat sensitive sleeve)	50
15	Warner Bros. 0825646121212	DRONES (2-LP, red vinyl, CD, DVD)	35

ALBUMS : ALBUMS - REISSUES
15	Warner Bros.	SHOWBIZ (2-LP, reissue)	20

MUSHROOM

MINT VALUE £

15	Warner Bros. 0825646912223	ORIGIN OF SYMMETRY (2-LP, reissue)	20
15	Warner Bros. 0825646909452	ABSOLUTION (2-LP, reissue)	20
15	Warner Bros. 0825646909445	THE RESISTANCE (2-LP, reissue)	20
15	Warner Bros. 0825646865475	BLACK HOLES AND REVELATIONS (LP)	18
	Warner Bros. 0825646350919		

MUSHROOM
73	Hawk HASP 320	Devil Among The Tailors/Sun Ni Dhuibir/King Of Ireland's Daughter	25
74	Hawk HASP 340	Kings And Queens/Met A Friend	25
73	Hawk HALPX 116	EARLY ONE MORNING (LP, with poster inner)	700
73	Hawk HALPX 116	EARLY ONE MORNING (LP, without poster inner)	450

(see also Joe O'Donnell)

THE MUSIC
01	Fierce Panda NING 107	Take The Long Road And Walk It/The Walls Get Smaller (p/s, 1,000 only)	8
01	Fierce Panda NINGT 107	Take The Long Road And Walk It/The Walls Get Smaller (12", p/s, 250 only)	18
02	Hut HUTDLP 76	THE MUSIC (2-LP)	50
04	Virgin 724386437310	WELCOME TO THE NORTH (2-LP)	25
08	Polydor 1771689	STRENGTH IN NUMBERS (LP)	30

MUSIC BOX (2)
69	VOY	FUN PALACE (LP)	1500

MUSIC BOX (1)
72	Westwood MRS 013	SONGS OF SUNSHINE (LP)	150

MUSIC DOCTORS
69	Downtown DT 447	Music Doctor (Parts 1 & 2)	20
71	Downtown DT480	The Pliers/Pliers (Version)	18
70	J-Dan JDN 4402	Electric Shock/KING DENNIS: Black Robin	20
70	J-Dan JDN 4403	Bush Doctor/Lick Your Stick	20
70	J-Dan JDN 4411	The Wild Bunch/ISRAELITES: Born To Be Strong	40
70	J-Dan JDN 4414	In The Summertime/Foundation Track	15
70	J-Dan JDN 4417	Discretion Version/Doctor Dan, Boy Friday And Friend	15
70	Trojan TBL 117	REGGAE IN THE SUMMERTIME (LP)	30

(see also Dennis Lowe, Desmond Riley, Megatons, Prince Of Darkness, Gene Rondo)

MUSIC EMPORIUM
83	Psycho PSYCHO 11	MUSIC EMPORIUM (LP)	15

MUSIC EXPLOSION
67	Stateside SS 2028	A Little Bit O' Soul/I See The Light	25
67	Stateside SS 2054	Sunshine Games/Can't Stop Now	20
67	Philips BF 1547	Little Black Egg/Stay By My Side	10
69	London HLP 10272	A Little Bit O' Soul/Everybody	10
67	London HA-P/SH-P 8352	A LITTLE BIT O' SOUL (LP)	50

MUSIC MACHINE
67	Pye International 7N 25407	Talk Talk/Come On In	50
67	Pye International 7N 25414	The People In Me/Masculine Intuition	60

MUSIC MOTOR
70	Deram DM 282	Happy/Where Am I Going?	15

MUSIC SPECIALISTS
70	London HLJ 10309	Dynamic Pressure/Flip	7

MUSIC STAND
69	Fresh FR 003	Sunbird/Dreamland	20

MUSIC THROUGH SIX
68	Domain D3	Riff Raff/ROY DOCKER: Mellow Moonlight	30

(see also Jason Sims & Music Through Six)

MUSIC UK
82	Fairview FMR 061	Jose/Unemployment/House With A Red Gate	30

MUSIC WARRIORS
72	Sir Collins SCMW 734	Some Day/Untitled (white labels only)	80

MUSICA ELETTRONICA VIVA
69	Polydor 583 769	MUSICA ELETTRONICA VIVA (LP)	100

MUSICAL DOCTORS
69	Downtown DT 447	Musical Doctor Chaper 1/Musical Doctor Chapter 2	20

MUSICIANS
66	King KG 1055	Jaunty Joe/The Chelsea Set	7

JIM MUSICMAN
90	Bosh JIM 101	I Can't Help Myself/I Can't Help Myself (12", purple vinyl)	80

MUSICOLOGY
91	B12 B1201	Musicology (12")	40
91	B12 B1201	Musicology (12", clear vinyl)	60
92	B12 B1204	Outlook (12", green vinyl, 300 only)	40
92	B12 B1206	Hall Of Mirrors (12")	15
92	B12 B1206	Hall Of Mirrors (12" Ltd, yellow vinyl)	40

MUSIQUE CONCRET
81	United Dairies UD 010	BRINGING UP BABY (LP, blue vinyl, 100 only)	120
81	United Dairies UD 010	BRINGING UP BABY (LP, black vinyl, 400 only)	100
87	United Dairies UDT 10	BRINGING UP BABY (cassette)	40

MUSKETEER GRIPWEED & THIRD TROOP
66	United Artists UP 1196	How I Won The War/Aftermath	175
66	United Artists UP 1196	How I Won The War/Aftermath (demo copy)	100

(see also John Lennon)

MUSKETEERS
- 69 Philips BF 1773 — Fight/Magnifico 6

MUSKYTEERS
- 69 Upsetter US 309 — Endlessly/Kiddy-O 45

(see also Silvertones (Jamaica))

MUSLIMGAUZE
- 83 Hessian 1 — Hammer And Sickle/Fear Of Gadaffi/Nettle Cloth/Baize Tents 25
- 84 Limited Editions LIMITED 1 — HUNTING OUT WITH AN AERIAL EYE (12" 45rpm EP) 25
- 83 Product Kinematograph PKR-1 — KABUL (LP, die cut 12" sleeve, some with Facsimile fanzine) 60
- 84 Recloose LOOSE 008 — BUDDHIST ON FIRE (LP, some with free Triptych EP and inserts) 60
- 85 Limited Editions LIMITED 2 — BLINDED HORSES (LP) 40
- 86 Limited Editions LIMITED 3 — FLAJELATA (LP) 40
- 86 Limited Editions LIMITED 4 — HAJJ (LP) 40
- 87 Limited Editions LIMITED 5 — JAZIRAT-UL-ARAB (LP) 40
- 87 Limited Editions LIMITED 6 — ABU NIDAL (LP) 40
- 88 Limited Editions LIMITED 7 — THE RAPE OF PALESTINE (LP) 40

(see also Eg Oblique Graph)

CHARLIE MUSSELWHITE BLUES BAND
- 69 Vanguard SVRL 19012 — STONE BLUES (LP) 22

MUSTANG
- 67 Parlophone R 5579 — Why/Here, There And Everywhere 25

MUSTARD
- 74 EMI EMI 2165 — Good Time Comin'/I Saw I Heard 25

MUS-TWANGS
- 61 Mercury AMT 1140 — Roch Lomond/Marie 12

MUTANTS
- 77 Rox ROX 002 — Boss Man/Back Yard Boys (p/s) 15
- 78 Rox ROX 005 — School Teacher/Hard Time/Lady (p/s, red vinyl) 10

MUTATION
- 13 (No label or Cat. No.) — I: THE FRANKENSTEIN EFFECT/II: ERROR 500 (2-LP black.red splatter vinyl) 40

(see also Ginger Wildheart, Wildhearts)

MUTE DRIVERS
- 80s Mute Drivers MD 001 — MUTE DRIVERS (LP, with insert in handmade painted sleeve, 300 only) 15

(see also Anonymes)

MUTT 'N' JEFF
- 66 Decca F 12335 — Don't Nag Me Ma/Strolling The Blues 12

MVP'S
- 71 Buddah BDS 469 — Turnin' My Heartbeat Up/Every Man For Herself 35

M.W.A.B.
- 83 M.W.A.B. Records — Angus Young/Is Michael Bum An Apple? 15

MWANAMKE MWFICA
- 82 African Woman AWLP 101 — AFRICAN WOMAN ABROAD (LP) 100

MX-80 SOUND
- 77 Island ILPS 9520 — HARD ATTACK (LP, insert) 30

MY BLOODY VALENTINE
- 86 Fever FEV 5X — No Place To Go/Moonlight (p/s) 60
- 86 Fever FEV 5 — GEEK! (12" EP) 40
- 86 Kaleid. Sound KS 101 — THE NEW RECORD BY MY BLOODY VALENTINE (12" EP) 50
- 87 Lazy LAZY 04 — Sunny Sundae Smile/Paint A Rainbow (p/s) 30
- 87 Lazy LAZY 04T — Sunny Sundae Smile/Paint A Rainbow/Kiss The Eclipse/ Sylvie's Head (12", p/s) 40
- 87 Lazy LAZY 07 — Strawberry Wine/Never Say Goodbye/Can I Touch You (12", p/s) 50
- 88 Creation CRE 055 — You Made Me Realise/Slow (die-cut company sleeve) 35
- 88 Creation CRE 055T — You Made Me Realise/Slow/Thorn/Cigarette/Drive It All Over Me (12", p/s) 50
- 88 Creation CRE 061 — Feed Me With Your Kiss/Emptiness Inside (plays "I Believe") (die-cut company sleeve) 25
- 88 Creation CRE 061T — Feed Me With Your Kiss/I Believe/Emptiness Inside/I Need No Trust (12", p/s) 35
- 89 Creation CRE 085 — To Here Knows When/Swallow (p/s) 15
- 89 Creation CRE 085T — Tremolo/To Here Knows When (12", p/s) 30
- 89 Lyntone CAT 067 — Sugar/PACIFIC: December, With The Day (square flexidisc free with The Catalogue magazine, issue 67) 15
- 90 Creation CRE 073 — Soon/Glider (p/s) 15
- 90 Creation CRE 073T — GLIDER EP (12", p/s) 30
- 90 Creation CRE 073X — GLIDER EP (12", remixed by Andy Weatherall, stickered die-cut sleeve) 25
- 87 Lazy LAZY 08 — ECSTACY (mini-LP, 3,000 only) 50
- 88 Creation CRELP 040 — ISN'T ANYTHING (LP, first pressing with black label, 3,000 copies with bonus 7", "Instrumental"/"Instrumental" [CRE FRE 4, no p/s] & stickered sleeve) 100
- 88 Creation CRELP 040 — ISN'T ANYTHING (LP, 2nd pressing, brown label, without bonus 7") 60
- 89 Lazy LAZY 12 — ECSTACY & WINE (LP, compilation of LAZY 07 & LAZY 08) 30
- 91 Creation CRELP 060 — LOVELESS (LP, inner) 150
- 98 Creation CRELP 040 — ISN'T ANYTHING (LP, reissue, has new Creation address on rear: 109 Regents Park Road, London NW1 8UR) 25
- 11 Lazy LAZY 12 — ECSTASY AND WINE (LP, reissue) 20
- 13 MBV mbvlp01 — M.B.V (LP, gatefold with CD) 25
- 18 MBV mbvlp02 — ISN'T ANYTHING (LP, alternative mix, white sleeve) 35

(see also Primal Scream, Collapsed Lung, Snowpony, Dinosaur Jr.)

MY CAPTAINS
- 81 4AD AD 103 — Fall/Converse/History/Nothing (p/s) 15

MY CHEMICAL ROMANCE
- 03 20:20 TWENTY 7s 003 — Honey, This Mirror Isn't Big Enough For The Two Of Us/This Is The Best Day Ever (p/s) 50
- 04 20:20 TWENTY 7S 004 — Headfirst For Halos/Our Lady Of Sorrows (Live) (p/s) 45
- 04 Reprise W 661 — Thank You For The Venom/Jack The Ripper (Live) (red vinyl, p/s) 40

MY DEAR WATSON

			MINT VALUE £
05	Reprise W 666	I'm Not Okay (I Promise)/Bury Me In Black (Demo) (red vinyl, p/s)	7
06	Reprise 116796-1	THE BLACK PARADE (2-LP box set)	35

MY DEAR WATSON
68	Parlophone R 5687	Elusive Face/The Shame Just Drained	30
68	Parlophone R 5737	Make This Day Last/Stop, Stop, I'll Be There	30
70	DJM DJS 224	Have You Seen Your Saviour/White Line Road	10

(see also Johnny & Copycats)

MY DYING BRIDE
90	Private pressing	Towards The Sinister EP (4 track demo cassette)	40
92	Peaceville VILE 27	Symphonaire Infernus Et Spera Empyrium Act 1/ Symphonaire Infernus Et Spera Empyrium Act 2 (12", p/s)	25
93	Peaceville VILE 44T	I Am The Bloody Earth/Transcending (Into The Exquisite) (12", p/s)	20
93	Peaceville VILE 37T	The Thrash Of Naked Limbs/Le Cerf Malade/Gather Me Up Forever (12", p/s)	25
93	Unbridled Voyage (No Cat. No)	Unreleased Bitterness: The Bitterness And The Bereavement (1-sided flexidisc, fold-out p/s in poly sleeve, 1150 only)	20
94	Peaceville CC5	Sexuality Of Bereavement/Crown Of Sympathy (Remix) (p/s)	25
94	Peaceville VILE 45	THE STORIES EP (box set, 1000 only)	75
92	Peaceville VILE 30	AS THE FLOWER WITHERS (LP, gatefold sleeve, with poster)	40
93	Peaceville VILE 39	TURN LOOSE THE SWANS (2-LP)	50
95	Peaceville VILE 50	THE ANGEL AND THE DARK RIVER (LP)	40
96	Peaceville VILE 65	LIKE GODS OF THE SUN (LP)	40
98	Peaceville VILE 74	37.488% (LP)	40

TIM MYCROFT
71	Parlophone R5919	Shadra/Bournemouth Rock	15

AMINA CLAUDINE MYERS
80	Leo LR 100	SONG FOR MOTHER E (LP)	20
80	Leo LR 103	AMINA CLAUDINE MYERS SALUTES BESSIE SMITH (LP)	45

ROWLAND MYERS
75	MSE MSE 2SSP/P	Give Them A Hand/Pandemonium	30
74	Deroy DER 1063	JUST FOR THE RECORD (LP, private pressing, also listed as Music Sound Enterprise MSE 1)	120

STEVE MYERS
86	Pressure P HAVE 7	Cinderella/Shake Me	60

MY FRIENDS AND I
69	Marroo MR 001	Susan/Wake The Dead	40

MY KIND OF PEOPLE
70	CBS 555133	Somebodys Coming/Nobody Knows Why The Butterfly Died	25

BILLY MYLES
57	HMV POP 423	The Joker (That's What They Call Me)/Honey Bee	50

MEG MYLES
56	Capitol CL 14555	Sing On, Baby/Will You Shed A Tear For Me?	7

MY LIFE STORY
86	Think Tank CHAPTER 1	HOME SWEET ZOO: Boring Dream/Sliding Bookcase (gatefold p/s, 500 only)	30

MY LORDE SHERIFFE'S COMPLAINTE
79	Frog FROG 1	MY LORDE SHERIFFE'S COMPLAINTE (LP, private pressing)	15

MYND MUZIC
94	Poor Person Prod.	IMAGINE THIS (LP, handmade sleeve, 500 only)	20

MYRON
98	Island 12 MYRON 1	We Can Get Down (Groove Chronicles Remix) (1-sided 12")	25

MYRTELLES
63	Oriole CB 1805	Don't Wanna Cry Again/Just Let Me Cry	40

(see also Sue & Sunshine, Sue & Sunny, Stockingtops)

MYSTERIES
64	Decca F 11919	Give Me Rhythm And Blues/Teardrops	30

MYSTERIOUS FOOTSTEPS
80	Yest YET 1	White Dread/Like They Do In The Movies	10

WILLIAM MYSTERIOUS
82	Mezzanine MEZ 1	Security Of Noise/Alright (p/s, with Fay Fife & Revettes)	10

(see also Rezillos, Revillos)

MYSTERY GIRLS
79	Strange HAM 1	SOUNDS LIKE THE MYSTERY GIRLS EP	20
81	Strange HAM 002	I'm A Believer/Modern Mystery Pop/Walking Backwards (p/s)	10

MYSTERY GUESTS
80	Boys Own/Heater Volume BO 1	Wurlitzer Junction/The Merry Shark You Are (handmade stickered white labels)	10
81	Boys Own BO 3	The Sparrow That Ate New York/The Nude (p/s)	10

MYSTERY JETS (1)
78	Raw RAW 21	The Sun Story/A Song For Gene	7

MYSTERY JETS (2)
03	679 679L156	Two Doors Down/Somewhere In My Heart	12
08	No label or cat. no.	TWENTY ONE (LP, 300 copies only, numbered)	50
08	No label or cat. no.	POWERCUT SERENADES EP (300 only, numbered)	20
10	Rough Trade RTRADLP 551	SEROTONIN (LP with free 7")	25
15	Transgressive TRANS 159	LIVE AT THE ROYAL FESTIVAL HALL (2-LP, gold vinyl)	35

MYSTERY MAKER
77	Caves UHC 3	MYSTERY MAKER (LP, private pressing with booklet)	120

MYSTERY BLONDE
87	Freshman 7KS1236	Stay With Me/Game Of Life (p/s)	20

MYSTIC EMP
80	His Majesty HMD 006	Reality/JAH THOMAS: Throw Away Vanity/MYSTIC EMP & JAH THOMAS: Reality Dub (12")	20

MYSTIC EYES

MINT VALUE £

MYSTIC EYES
79	Greensleeves GRED 11	Perilous Times (with Trinity)/REVOLUTIONARIES: Roots Man Version (12")	30
79	Warrior WAR 135	Elaine/MIKEY DREAD: Schoolgirls (12")	40
78	Burning Sounds BS 1033	MYSTERIOUS (LP)	45

MYSTIC HARMONY
82	SS LLSMD 015	That Feeling/SS BAND: Sweet Feeling (12")	12
83	Clouds CLSD 001	Night Over Egypt/SS BAND: Night Out In London	200
84	Clouds CLSD 008	Living In The Country/Independent Lady (12")	20

MYSTIC INSTITUTE
92	Evolution EVO 06	CYBERDON EP (12")	18

(see also Global Communications, Reload, Link)

MYSTIC MATT & THE ANTHILL MOB
99	Love Peace & Unity LOVE 05	A SHOCK 2 DA SYSTEM EP (12", p/s)	25

(see also Anthill Mob)

MYSTIC MERLIN
80	Capitol EST 12047	MYSTIC MERLIN (LP)	15

MYSTIC MOODS
73	Warner Bros K 16265	Cosmic Sea/Awakening	7
74	Warner Bros K 46250	AWAKENING (LP)	15

MYSTIC NUMBER NATIONAL BANK
69	Probe SPB 1001	THE MYSTIC NUMBER NATIONAL BANK (LP)	25

MYSTIC RADICS
81	Water Mount WMT 1	Nation Wide/Dub Version (12")	250

MYSTIC TOUCH
81	Champagne FIZZ 505	Get Yourself Together/Pary People	15

MYSTICS
59	HMV POP 646	Hushabye/Adam And Eve	30
59	Top Rank JAR 243	Don't Take The Stars/So Tenderly	30

MYSTIC SLOT
93	Black Cock BCOK 007	No Way Back/Disco Adventure (12", beware of US pressed bootlegs)	45

MYSTREATED
94	Twist TWIST 15	SHE'S GONE (EP)	6
95	Twist TWIST 18	LIVE AT THE BBC (EP)	6
96	Hangman's Daughter KETCH 7 UP	Never Question Why/Take A Look In The Mirror (p/s, 500 only)	8
97	Detour DR 054	(What's In) Your Mind Today/I'll Be There (p/s)	10
92	Hangman TWISTBIG 4	10 BOSS CUTS (LP)	20
94	Twist TWISTBIG 4	LOOKING RIGHT THROUGH (LP)	15
95	Twist TWISTBIG 7	EVERY QUESTIONING WHY (LP)	15

MYTHRA
79	Guardian GRMA 16	DEATH & DESTINY: Death And Destiny/Killer/Overload/UFO (EP, no p/s)	12
80	Streetbeat LAMP 2	Death Or Destiny/Killer/U.F.O. (with p/s)	90
80	Streetbeat LAMP 2	Death Or Destiny/Killer/U.F.O.	10
80	Streetbeat 12 LAMP 2	Death Or Destiny/Killer/Overlord/U.F.O. (12", with p/s)	125
80	Streetbeat 12 LAMP 2	Death Or Destiny/Killer/Overlord/U.F.O. (12")	20

M ZONE & DJ GOLLUM
97	UK44 UK44 EP3	Harmony (Get Me)/Harmony (12")	12

(see also DJ Gollum)

N

NABAY
80	Grapevine GRP 143	Believe It Or Not/Believe It Or Not (Instrumental)	30

ESTEE NACK & SADHU GOLD
18	Daupe! DM SP 053	SURFINONGOLD.WAV (LP, splatter vinyl, 100 copies)	100
20	Daupe! DM SP 053	SURFINONGOLD.WAV (LP, red vinyl, 100 copies)	40
20	Daupe! DM SP 053	SURFINONGOLD.WAV (LP, green vinyl, 100 copies)	50
20	Daupe! DM SP 053	SURFINONGOLD.WAV (LP, with obi strip, 20 copies)	100

RICKY NADIR
75	Charisma CB 345	Birthday Special/Shingle Song	10
79	Charisma CB 339	The Polaroid/PETER HAMMILL: The Old School Tie	10

(see also Peter Hammill)

MARISSA NADLER
06	My Kung Fu MYKUNGFU 016	Diamond Heart/Leather Made Shoes	6

NADRIAN
71	Dolphin DO 514	Something Passing By/You Can't Lose Out	250

NAFFI
79	Absurd ABSURD 8	Slice 1/Slice 2 (as Naafi Sandwich)	25
81	Naffi Productions RUM 5	D'ya Hear Me/Freedie's Fever (dub)/The Hutch (dub)	20
82	Ark DOVE 1	YUM YUM YUM YA (LP)	25
85	Situation Two DOVE 2	NAFFI-LOCKSMAN (LP, as Naffi Locksman)	50

NAIL
98	Remote REM 009	BROTHERS AND SISTERS (12", EP, die-cut sleeve)	18

NAIROBI SISTERS
76	Jamatel JAL 07	Promised Land/Version	35

NAKED CITY

MINT VALUE £

NAKED CITY
90 Earache MOSH 28 TORTURE GARDEN EP (12") 20

NAKED LUNCH
81 Ramkup CAC 003 Rabies/Slipping Again (p/s) 15
84 Plezure PLZS 841 You Tie Me Down/Laugh Your Mind Away 10

NAKED TRUTH
70 Deram DM 287 Two Little Rooms/Rag Doll Boy 7

NAME
80 Din Disc DIN 14 Forget Art, Let's Dance/Misfits (p/s) 10
87 China WOK 15 Jesus And The Devil/The Great Depression (p/s) 8

NAMES
80 Factory FAC 29 Nightshift/I Wish I Could Speak Your Language (p/s) 12

KOICHI NAMIKI, KATSUHIRO HAYASHI & SHIGERU OHWADA
15 Data Discs DAT 004 SUPER HANG ON (LP, die cut sleeve, Obi) 35

ZBIGNIEW NAMYSLOWSKI MODERN JAZZ QUARTET
64 Decca LK/SKL 4644 LOLA (LP) 200

NANCY BOYS
82 Rola RO12 I Like I Like I Like/Do You Wanna Touch 12

NANETTE
70 Columbia DB 8659 Flying Machine/You're Wasting Your Time 35
70 Columbia DB 8673 Every Night When I Cry Myself To Sleep/Jamie 10
70 Columbia DB 8733 Let Me Be The One/To Be Loved 10
71 Columbia DB 8751 Everybody's Singing Right Now/Could I Forget 10
70 Columbia SCX 6398 NANETTE (LP) 30

ED NANGLE
68 Blue Cat BS 120 Good Girl/ENFORCERS: Musical Fever 225
68 Coxsone CS 7038 Whipping The Prince (actually by Ed Nangle & Alton Ellis & Soul Vendors)/HEPTONES: If You Knew 100

NICK NANTOS & HIS FIREBALLERS
63 Summit LSE 2042 GUITARS ON FIRE (EP) 15
64 Summit ATL 4114 GUITARS ON FIRE (LP) 15
(see also Bill Haley & Comets)

NAOMI
70 Gayfeet GS 207 You're Not My Kind/GAYTONES: You're Not My Kind (Version II) 20
70 High Note HS 047 Natural Woman/GAYTONES: Natural Woman - Version 20
(see also Derrick Morgan, Tommy McCook)

NAPALM DEATH
87 Strange Fruit SFPS 049 THE PEEL SESSIONS (12", p/s) 15
89 Rise Above RISE 001 NAPALM DEATH EP (poster p/s, sold at gigs) 25
89 Earache 7MOSH 14 Mentally Murdered/Cause And effect (stickered p/s) 10
89 Earache MOSH 014 MENTALLY MURDERED EP (Rise Above/The Missing Link/Mentally Murdered Walls Of Confinement/Cause And Effect/No Mental Effort) (12", p/s) 20
90 Earache 7MOSH 24L Suffer The Children/The Kill/Scum/Extremity Retained/Life? (stickered p/s, sticker sheet) 10
90 Earache MOSH 024 Suffer The Children/Siege Of Power/Harmony Corruption (12", p/s) 10
91 Earache 7MOSH 46 Mass Appeal Madness/Pride Assassin (p/s) 10
91 Earache MOSH 046 Mass Appeal Madness/Pride Assassin/Unchallenged Hate/Social Sterility (12", p/s) 10
92 Earache MOSH 65 THE WORLD KEEPS TURNING EP (12", p/s) 12
93 Earache 7MOSH 92 Nazi Punks Fuck Off/Aryanisms/Nazi Punks Fuck Off (Live)/Contemptuous (Xtreem Mix) (p/s) 20
95 Earache MOSH 146 GREED KILLING EP (Greed Killing/My Own Worst Enemy/Self Betrayal/Finer Truths White Lies/Antibody/All Links Severed/Plague Rages [Live]) (10", p/s) 15
96 Earache 7 MOSH 168 Food Chains/Upward And Uninterested (demo version)/COALESCE: A Safe Place/Harvest Of Maturity) (p/s, insert, purple vinyl) 15
96 Earache 7 MOSH 168 Food Chains/Upward And Uninterested (demo version)/COALESCE: A Safe Place/Harvest Of Maturity) (p/s, insert) 10
87 Earache MOSH 3 SCUM (LP, lyric insert, black/orange, black/green, black red or black/yellow cover) 20
88 Earache MOSH 8 FROM ENSLAVEMENT TO OBLITERATION (LP, gatefold sleeve, free 7" EP The Curse [7MOSH 8]) 35
90 Earache MOSH 19/19L HARMONY CORRUPTION (2-LP, with inserts) 30
90 Earache MOSH 19P HARMONY CORRUPTION (LP, picture disc) 20
91 Earache MOSH 3 SCUM (LP, reissue, white and black swirl vinyl, black and gold sleeve, 2000 only) 18
92 Earache MOSH 53 UTOPIA BANISHED (LP, free 7" EP [MOSH 53L]) 25
02 Feto SLAVE001LP ORDER OF THE LEECH (LP, purple vinyl) 20
06 Earache MOSH 003PD SCUM (LP, 2nd reissue, picture disc, stickered PVC sleeve, 1500 only) 15

MARTY NAPOLEON
55 London EZ-NI9001 NAPOLEON SINGS AND SWINGS (EP) 15

NAPOLEON XIV
66 Warner Bros WB 5831 They're Coming To Take Me Away Ha-Haa!/ !Aah-Ah Yawa Em Ekat Ot Gnimoc Er'Yeht 7
66 Warner Bros WB 5853 I'm In Love With My Little Red Tricycle/Doin' The Napoleon 15
66 Warner Bros W 1661 THEY'RE COMING TO TAKE ME AWAY HA-HA-A! (LP) 40
(see also Jerry Samuels, Kim Fowley)

RAYMOND NAPTALI AND ROY RANKING
81 KG Imperial KG 006 New Cross Fire/Brixton Incident (12", blue vinyl) 25

NAPTHALI
91 Black Legacy BLLP 001 MENTAL SLAVERY SHOWCASE (LP) 60

NINO NARDINI
02 Jazzman JM 019 Tropicola/ANTHONY KING: Filigree Funk 15
02 Jazzman JM 024 Afro-Beat/Poltergeist 12

PETER NARDINI
80s Kettle KS 701 I Think You're Great/Ma Maw's A Mod (in p/s) 15
80s Kettle KS 701 I Think You're Great/Ma Maw's A Mod 8

NARNIA

NARNIA
74	Myrrh MYR 1007	NARNIA - ASLAN IS NOT A TAME LION (LP)	80

(see also After The Fire, Pauline Filby)

NAS
13	Secret 7" S712	The Don (100 only, each with unique art sleeve)	40
94	Columbia COL 475959-1	ILLMATIC (LP)	25
96	Columbia 484196 1	IT WAS WRITTEN (LP)	30
99	Columbia COL 4953120	NASTRADAMUS (LP)	30
99	Columbia COL 489419-1	I AM (LP)	25

BILLY NASH
61	Philips PB 1181	Sunset/Nobody Loves Me Like You (as Billy Nash Combo)	7
63	Philips 370 406 BF	The Madison Step/Madison Rhythm (as Billy Nash Rock Band)	7

GRAHAM NASH
71	Atlantic 2091 096	Chicago/Simple Man	6
71	Atlantic 2091 135	Military Madness/I Used To Be A King	6
71	Atlantic 2401 011	SONGS FOR BEGINNERS (LP)	20

(see also Hollies, Crosby Stills Nash & Young)

JOHNNY NASH
57	HMV POP 402	Ladder Of Love/I'll Walk Alone	10
58	HMV POP 435	Won't You Let Me Share My Love With You?/A Very Special Love	10
58	HMV POP 475	It's Easy To Say/My Pledge To You	10
58	HMV POP 553	Almost In Your Arms/Midnight Moonlight	7
59	HMV POP 597	Walk With Faith In Your Heart/Roots Of Heaven	7
59	HMV POP 620	As Time Goes By/Voice Of Love	7
59	HMV POP 651	And The Angels Sing/Baby, Baby, Baby	7
59	HMV POP 673	Take A Giant Step/Imagination	6
60	HMV POP 746	A Place In The Sun/Goodbye	6
60	HMV POP 822	Somebody/Kisses	6
62	Warner Bros WB 65	Don't Take Away Your Love/Moment Of Weakness	20
62	Warner Bros WB 76	Ol' Man River/My Dear Little Sweetheart	30
63	Warner Bros WB 93	Cigareets, Whiskey And Wild, Wild Women/I'm Moving On	15
64	Pye International 7N 25250	Love Ain't Nothin'/Talk To Me	60
65	Chess CRS 8005	Strange Feelin'/Rainin' In My Heart	25
66	Pye International 7N 25353	Let's Move And Groove (Together)/Understanding	20
66	Pye International 7N 25363	One More Time/Tryin' To Find Her	20
68	Regal Zono. RZ 3010	Hold Me Tight/Let's Move And Groove Together	10
68	Major Minor MM 586	You've Got Soul/Don't Cry	7
68	Major Minor MM 603	Cupid/People In Love	10
69	MGM MGM 1480	(I'm So) Glad You're My Baby/Stormy	35
71	MAM MAM R 9	Falling In And Out Of Love/People In Love	7
64	RCA Victor RCX 7163	PRESENTING JOHNNY NASH (EP)	100
59	HMV CLP 1251	JOHNNY NASH (LP)	40
59	HMV CLP 1299	QUIET HOUR WITH JOHNNY NASH (LP)	25
60	HMV CLP 1325	I GOT RHYTHM (LP, mono)	30
60	HMV CSD 1288	I GOT RHYTHM (LP, stereo)	30
62	Encore ENC 2005	LET'S GET LOST (LP)	15
69	Major Minor MMLP/SMLP 47	YOU GOT SOUL (LP)	15
69	Major Minor MMLP/SMLP 56	SOUL FOLK (LP)	15
69	Major Minor MMLP/SMLP 63	PRINCE OF PEACE (LP)	15

KATE NASH
07	Moshi Moshi MOMO 4	Caroline's A Victim/Birds	6
06	Fiction 1755804	MADE OF BRICKS (LP, pink vinyl)	50

TONY NASH
70	Hot Rod HR 110	Keep On Trying/WINSTON JAMES: Just Can't Do Without Your Love	40

NASHVILLE FIVE
62	Decca F 11427	Stand Up And Say That/Like Nashville	7
62	Decca F 11484	Some Other Love/Brainwave	7
62	Decca DFE 6706	LIKE NASHVILLE (EP)	40

NASHVILLE TEENS
64	Decca F 11930	Tobacco Road/I Like It Like That	8
64	Decca F 12000	Google Eye (some misspelled "Goggle Eye" on label)/T.N.T.	8
65	Decca F 12089	Find My Way Back Home/Devil-In-Law	10
65	Decca F 12143	This Little Bird/Whatcha Gonna Do?	8
65	Decca F 12255	I Know How It Feels To Be Loved/Soon Forgotten	10
66	Decca F 12316	The Hard Way/Upside Down	15
66	Decca F 12458	Forbidden Fruit/Revived 45 Time	25
66	Decca F 12542	That's My Woman/Words	18
67	Decca F 12580	I'm Coming Home/Searching	10
67	Decca F 12657	The Biggest Night Of Her Life/Last Minute	10
68	Decca F 12754	All Along The Watchtower/Sun-Dog	15
69	Major Minor MM 599	The Lament Of The Cherokee Reservation Indian/Looking For You	18
69	Decca F 12929	Tobacco Road/All Along The Watchtower	6
71	Parlophone R 5925	Ella James/Tennessee Woman	20
72	Parlophone R 5961	You Shouldn't Have Been So Nice/Tell The People (unissued)	0
73	Enterprise ENT S101	Lawdy Miss Clawdy/Let It Rock/Rocking On The Railroad/Break Up	7
65	Decca DFE 8600	THE NASHVILLE TEENS (EP)	50
75	New World NW 6002	THE NASHVILLE TEENS (LP)	40

NASTY FACTS

MINT VALUE £

(see also Arizona Swamp Company, Jerry Lee Lewis, Carl Perkins)

NASTY FACTS
81	5th Column FC 2	Drive My Car/Gotta Get To You/Crazy 'Bout you (p/s)	60

NASTY HABITS
91	NHS NHS 001	Make Some Noise/Street Knowledge (12")	25
92	NHS NHS 003	Let's Go/No Dominator (12")	25
92	Reinforced RIVET 1233	As Nasty As I Wanna Be (12")	25
92	Reinforced RIVET 1233R	As Nasty As I Wanna Be (Remixes) (12")	25

NASTY MEDIA
78	Lightning GIL 542	SPIKED COPY EP (p/s)	40

NATCHBAND
78	Far In FARS 01	Cadillac (Made In USA)/Being From The Sky (p/s)	6

BARRY NATHAN TRIO
80	EMAL BNT 1	MORNING SONGRISE (LP)	50

NATIONAL
05	Beggars Banquet BBQ 385	Abel/Warm Singing Whores (p/s)	10
07	Beggars Banquet BBQ 405	Mistaken For Strangers/Blank Slate (p/s)	8
07	Beggars Banquet BBQ 407	Apartment Story/Mansion On The Hill (live) (yellow vinyl)	15
07	Beggars Banquet BBQ 408 CDP	EXTRAS EP (tour CD, 1000 only)	30
10	4AD AD3X50	Terrible Love/You Were A Kindness (purple vinyl, p/s)	12
17	Beggars Banquet (No Cat. No.)	England (Live)/BELLE & SEBASTIAN: The State I Am In (12" p/s, splatter vinyl, booklet)	60
03	Brassland HWY 003	SAD SONGS FOR DIRTY LOVERS (LP)	40
05	Beggars Banquet BBQLP 241	ALLIGATOR (LP)	20
07	Beggars Banquet BBQLP 252	BOXER (LP, inner)	20
10	4AD CAD 3X03X	HIGH VIOLET (2-LP, violet vinyl)	30
13	4AD CAD 3315	TROUBLE WILL FIND ME (2-LP, clear vinyl, card inserts box set)	40
15	4AD TAD 3504	A LOT OF SORROW (9-LP box set, clear vinyl)	150
17	4AD 4AD0020LPE	SLEEP WELL BEAST (2-LP, blue vinyl, 7" blue flexi and poster)	30

NATIONAL ART HATE WEEK
09	No Cat no	God Save Marcel Duchamp/Silent Revolt (p/s, mail order only, 350 copies, numbered)	15

NATIONAL-ELLS
67	Parlophone R 5609	Mr. Moon/Dance, Dance	7

NATIONAL HEAD BAND
71	Warner Bros K 46094	ALBERT 1 (LP)	50

(see also Caravan, Gary Moore, Toe-Fat, Uriah Heep)

NATIONAL HEALTH
78	Affinity AFF 6	NATIONAL HEALTH (LP)	30
78	Charly CRL 5010	OF QUEUES AND CURES (LP)	25

(see also Hatfield & The North)

NATIONAL PINION POLE
66	Planet PLF 111	Make Your Mark Little Man/I Was The One You Came In With (in Planet sleeve)	80
66	Planet PLF 111	Make Your Mark Little Man/I Was The One You Came In With	45

NATIONAL FLAG
75	Private Pressing	THANK YOU AND GOODNIGHT (LP, insert, 100 only)	400

NATIVES
84	Fearless FEAR 2	Here Is The News/Love In A Day	20

NATO
81	DV DVR 1	Gangland/Tied Down (p/s)	50

NAT RUS & RANKING GLAD
77	Nat Rus	Mash It/Come From Africa/Africa (12")	40

NATUAH
06	Peckings PT 1031	LittleGirl Jah See/Peckings Special	6

NATURAL ACOUSTIC BAND
72	RCA SF 8272	LEARNING TO LIVE (LP, textured gatefold sleeve)	35
72	RCA SF 8314	BRANCHING IN (LP, with lyric insert)	25

(see also Krysia)

NATURAL BRIDGE BUNCH
69	Atlantic 584 231	Pig Snoots (Parts 1 & 2)	7

CLIVE NATURAL
77	WIRL WIRL 1	Marridge Rekka/No Money (12")	50

NATURAL FOUR
75	Curtom 16583	Love's So Wonderful/What's Happening Here	15
75	Curtom K 56142	HEAVEN RIGHT HERE ON EARTH (LP)	40
76	Custom K56224	NIGHTCHASER (LP)	15
95	Charlie CPLP 8127	NATURAL FOUR (LP, reissue)	18

NATURAL GAS
76	Private Stock PVLP 1007	NATURAL GAS (LP, gatefold sleeve with inner sleeve)	15

(see also Badfinger, Blue Goose, Humble Pie, Uriah Heep, Quiver)

NATURAL HI
81	KBK KBSK 001T	Fame (Got You On My Mind)/Fame (Hi-Re-Mix) (12")	70

NATURAL IMPULSE
08	Soul Junction SJ 502	She Went Away/Time Was Right	10

THE NATURAL ITES AND THE REALISTICS
83	CSA 12CSA 501	Picture On My Wall/Jah Works Mama (12")	18
84	Realistic RR 03	Black Roses/Gwan Do It (12")	50
85	CSA CSLP 18	PICTURE ON THE WALL (LP)	25

NATURAL MAGIC
75	Oyster OYR 102	Strawberry Fields Forever/Isolated Lady	10

(see also Roger Glover, Eddie Hardin)

NATURAL MYSTIC

MINT VALUE £

NATURAL MYSTIC
- 81 Ethnic Fight ETH 1326 — NATURAL LOVE (LP) 35
- 85 Starlight SDLP 914 — GROOVE ROCKING (LP) 45

NATURAL MYSTIQUE
- 82 Dune 2AA — Generals/In This Time (p/s) 60

NATURAL ROOTS
- 82 Fasim FS106 — Know Yourself/Ain't Got No Money (12") 20

NATURAL VIBES
- 83 Suffering & Faith SWEET 1 — Sweet Sensation/Version (12") 30
- 82 Starlight Records SDLP 907 — LIFE HARD IN A YARD (LP) 40

NATURALITY
- 69 Ackee ACK 101 — The Arena/Natural 50

NATURALLY
- 79 Bushays BFM 111 — I'll Get By/All I Have Is Written In Your Eyes (12") 15

NATURALS (U.K.) (1)
- 64 Parlophone R 5116 — Daisy Chain/That Girl 12
- 64 Parlophone R 5165 — I Should Have Known Better/Didn' I? 10
- 64 Parlophone R 5202 — It Was You/Look At Me Now 15
- 65 Parlophone R 5257 — Blue Roses/Shame On You 15

(see also Greatest Show On Earth)

NATURALS (U.K.) (2)
- 80 Refined RR2 — STRANGE DAYS (EP, 500 only) 30
- 81 Just For The Records — Six Girls & Alice (fold-out cover) 15
- 82 Logo GO 414 — Six Girls & Alice (fold-out cover, reissue) 8

NATURALS (U.S.)
- 55 MGM SP 1123 — The Finger Of Suspicion Points At You/You Forgot To Remember 12
- 57 MGM MGM 939 — The Buccaneers/The Ballad Of Sir Lancelot 8

(see also Debbie Reynolds)

NAUGHTY THOUGHTS
- 82 Maestro MR 004 — All Of Nothing/Weekdays (foldover p/s, some with press release inserts) 30

FATS NAVARRO
- 56 London LZ-C 14015 — MEMORIAL (LP) 20

NAVY BLUE
- 82 AP 572 — THE PUSSERS (EP) 15

JERRY NAYLOR
- 61 Top Rank JAR 591 — Stop Your Crying/You're Thirteen 25
- 67 Stateside SS 2029 — Sweet Violets/Temptation Leads Me 6

SHEL NAYLOR
- 63 Decca F 11776 — How Deep Is The Ocean/La Bamba 20
- 64 Decca F 11856 — One Fine Day/It's Gonna Happen Soon 200

(see also Lieutenant Pigeon, Stavely Makepeace)

NAZARETH
- 72 Pegasus PGS 2 — Dear John/Friends 25
- 72 Pegasus PGS 2 — Dear John/Friends (2nd issue, PEG label, B-side lists 'Occasional Failure') 30
- 72 Pegasus BCP 3 — Dear John/Witchdoctor Woman/Morning Dew (unreleased, promo only, stamped white labels and insert) 75
- 72 Pegasus PGS 4 — Morning Dew/Spinning Top (PEG label) 20
- 72 Pegasus PGS 5 — If You See My Baby/Hard Living (PEG label) 20
- 72 Pegasus BCP 8 — Fool About You/Woke Up This Morning/Morning Dew (unreleased, promo only, handwritten white labels) 75
- 73 Mooncrest MOON 1 — Broken Down Angel/Witchdoctor Woman (promo, custom sleeve) 15
- 73 Mooncrest MOON 9 — Bad Bad Boy/Hard Living/Spinning Top (initial copies in p/s) 10
- 75 Mooncrest MOON 47 — My White Bicycle/My White Bicycle (A label promo only) 15
- 76 Mountain TOP 14 (DJ) — You're The Violin (edit)/Loretta (promo only edit with different label layout) 10
- 76 Mountain PSLP191 — I Don't Want To Go On Without You/Waiting For The Man (12" promo) 18
- 78 Mountain TOP 37 — Place In Your Heart/Kentucky Fried Blues (mispressing, B-side plays Bee Gees track, company sleeve) 20
- 79 Mountain NAZ 4 — Whatever You Want Babe/Telegram Parts 1, 2 & 3 (p/s, purple vinyl) 10
- 80 NEMS BSD 1 — NAZARETH LIVE (2 x 7", gatefold) 7
- 71 Pegasus PEG 10 — NAZARETH (LP, 1st issue, Pegasus picture label, with promo booklet, textured matt sleeve) 200
- 71 Pegasus PEG 10 — NAZARETH (LP, 1st issue, Pegasus picture label, without promo booklet, textured matt sleeve) 150
- 72 Pegasus PEG 10 — NAZARETH (LP, 2nd issue, PEG label/glossy sleeve) 50
- 72 Pegasus PEG 14 — EXERCISES (LP, Peg label, gatefold sleeve) 100
- 73 Mooncrest CREST 1 — RAZAMANAZ (LP, gatefold sleeve, initial copies with inner and stickered sleeve) 75
- 73 Mooncrest CREST 4 — LOUD 'N' PROUD (LP, gatefold sleeve) 70
- 74 Mooncrest CREST 10 — NAZARETH (LP, reissue) 15
- 75 Mountain TOPS 103 — EXERCISES (LP, reissue) 15
- 74 Mooncrest CREST 15 — RAMPANT (LP, embossed sleeve, inner sleeve, dollar sticker insert) 75
- 75 Mountain TOPS 104 — RAZAMANAZ (LP, reissue) 15
- 75 Mooncrest CREST 27 — HAIR OF THE DOG (LP, with inner) 70
- 76 Mountain TOPS 109 — CLOSE ENOUGH FOR ROCK 'N' ROLL (LP) 40
- 76 Mountain TOPS 113 — PLAY 'N' THE GAME (LP, with inner sleeve) 30
- 77 Mountain TOPS 115 — EXPECT NO MERCY (LP, with inner sleeve) 20
- 79 Mountain TOPS 123 — NO MEAN CITY (LP, with inner sleeve) 15
- 80 Mountain TOPS 126 — MALICE IN WONDERLAND (LP, inner sleeve) 15
- 81 NEMS NELD 102 — SNAZ (2-LP, gatefold sleeve, inner) 20
- 85 Sahara SAH 130 — SOUND ELIXIR (LP, Marimba label, withdrawn) 20
- 85 Sahara SAH 137 — 20 GREATEST HITS (LP, withdrawn) 20
- 85 Sahara SAH 131 — LOUD 'N' PROUD (LP, reissue) 15

NAZIS AGAINST FASCISM

92	Mausoleum 3670010.1	NO JIVE (LP, insert)	15
01	Receiver RRLT 009Z	BACK TO THE TRENCHES: LIVE 72-84 (3-LP, gatefold sleeve, booklet)	25

(see also Dan McCafferty, Mark Five, Sensational Alex Harvey Band, Tandoori Cassette, Billy Rankin)

NAZIS AGAINST FASCISM
79	Truth TRUTH 1	Sid Did It (Intelligible)/Sid Did It (Radio Version) (p/s, 2 different issues)	12

(see also Vibrators)

NAZZ
68	Screen Gems SGC 219001	Open My Eyes/Hello It's Me	25
69	Screen Gems SGC 219002	Hello It's Me/Crowded	15
69	Screen Gems SGC 219003	Not Wrong Long/Under The Ice	10
69	Screen Gems SGC 221001	NAZZ (LP)	65

(see also Todd Rundgren)

'N BETWEENS
66	Columbia DB 8080	You Better Run/Evil Witchman (demos credit In-Be-Tweens)	400

(see also Slade, Vendors)

CHRIS NEAL
71	Fly BUG 15	Blame It All On Eve/All The Time In The World (p/s)	6

JOHNNY NEAL & STARLINERS
65	Pye 7N 15838	And I Will Love You/Walk Baby Walk	80
70	Parlophone R 5870	Put Your Hand In The Hand/Now	7

(see also Storyteller)

TOMMY NEAL
68	Vocalion VL 9290	Goin' To A Happening/Tee Ta	75
68	Vocalion VL 9290	Goin' To A Happening/Tee Ta (DJ copy)	150
11	Outta Sight OSV 16	Goin' To A Happening/TONY HESTOR: Spaceland (reissue)	8

NEARLY NORMAL
80	Insurrection Now! INA 1	Bedtime/Die Baby Die!(hand-made p/s)	60

NEAT
80s	Neatbeat LYN 6269	Hormones In Action/Take Your Chances (p/s)	50

NEAT CHANGE
68	Decca F 12809	I Lied To Auntie May/Sandman (in foldout p/s)	120
68	Decca F 12809	I Lied To Auntie May/Sandman	60

(see also Peter Banks, English Rose)

NEBULA
03	Sweet Nothing SNLP 026	ATOMIC RITUAL (LP)	30

NEBULA II
92	Reinforced RIVET 1232R	X-Plore H-Core/Peace Maker (Remixes) (12")	15

NECESSARIES
81	Sire SRK 3573	BIG SKY (LP)	40
82	Sire SRK 3574	EVENT HORIZON (LP)	40

(see also Arthur Russell)

NECROMANDUS
90	Reflection MM 09	QUICKSAND DREAM (LP, 500 only)	18

NEDS ATOMIC DUSTBIN
91	Furtive 4681121	GOD FODDER (LP)	18
92	Sony Soho Square 4726331	ARE YOU NORMAL? (LP)	25
95	Sony Soho Square 478330 1	BRAINBLOODVOLUME (LP)	35

BERNIE NEE
58	Philips PB 794	Lend Me Your Comb/Medal Of Honour	10

(see also Bernie Knee)

NEED
80	SKITZ 1	Let Them Eat Valium/Seduction (p/s)	30

NEEDLES (1)
80	Ellie Jay EJSP 9340	Gotta Know You/Jayneski (no p/s)	100

LOUIS NEEFS
69	Columbia DB 8561	Jennifer Jennings/I Love You	25

ELGIN NEELY
65	Vogue V 9240	Four Walls/I Could Be	12

SEYOUM NEFTA
81	Mink	BURNING AN ILLUSION (LP)	30

NEGATIVE FX
84	Fundamental HOLY 7	NEGATIVE FX (LP)	25

NEGATIVES
78	Look LK/SP 6478	Stakeout (50 copies with p/s)	200
78	Look LK/SP 6478	Stakeout (no p/s)	40
80	Aardvark STEAL 1	Electric Waltz/Money Talks (p/s)	10
81	Aardvark STEAL 3	Scene Of The Crime (p/s)	8

NEGATIVES IN COLOUR
82	NEG 1	Caught In Possession/Everyman	18

NEGAZIONE
85	Children Of The Revolution GURT 7	MUCCHIO SELVAGGIO (split LP with DECLINO)	75

NEGRIL (1)
75	Torpedo TOR 51	I Shot The Sheriff/Negril	20
75	Klik KLP 9005	NEGRIL (LP)	30

NEGRIL (2)
80	Tuff Rank TRA 903	Alone Some Time/Dub Ten Thousand (12")	120

NEGRO
80	Negro NEG 1	Unite/DJ A HUMBLE I: Unite Tonight	150

NEGUS DAWTAS
78	Natty Congo NATTY 001	I Speak The Truth/Hail Rastafari (Actually by Ranking Reuben)	20

NEGUS ROOTS MEETS THE MAD PROFESSOR

MINT VALUE £

NEGUS ROOTS MEETS THE MAD PROFESSOR
83	Negus Roots NERLP 009	DUB ROCKERS VOLUME 2 (LP)	80

(see also Lackley Castell)

CHRISTOPHER NEIL
72	RAK SRKA 6753	WHERE I BELONG (LP)	25

EARL NEIL
78	Studio 16 We 401	Rough And Tough/PRINE JAZZBO: Suffer Must Live (12")	30

FRED NEIL
69	Elektra EKSN 45036	Candy Man/The Water Is Wide	8
69	Capitol CL 15616	Everybody's Talkin'/Badi-Da	12
67	Elektra EKS 7293	BLEECKER & MACDOUGAL (LP)	60
70	Capitol E-ST 657	OTHER SIDE OF THIS LIFE (LP)	35

NEKTAR
73	United Artists NEK 1	What Ya Gonna Do?/Day In The Life Of A Preacher Pt. One (Edit) (p/s)	15
74	United Artists UP 35706	Fidgety Queen/Little Boy	10
75	United Artists UP 35853	Astral Man/Nelly The Elephant	10
73	United Artists UAD 60041/2	SOUNDS LIKE THIS (2-LP)	40
74	United Artists UAS 29499	A TAB IN THE OCEAN (LP, gatefold sleeve)	35
74	United Artists UAG 29545	REMEMBER THE FUTURE (LP, gatefold)	35
74	United Artists UAG 29680	DOWN TO EARTH (LP, gatefold sleeve)	30
76	Decca SKL-R 5250	RECYCLED (LP)	15

(see also Robert Calvert)

NELLIE
69	Gas GAS 126	I Who Have Nothing/You Send Me	60

BILL NELSON('S RED NOISE)
71	Smile LAF 2182/HG 116	NORTHERN DREAM (LP, 250 only, numbered, in foldover gatefold sleeve with booklet)	70
71	Smile LAF 2182/HG 116	NORTHERN DREAM (LP, 250 second pressing unnumbered, (reissues on the Butt label, £15)	30
78	Harvest SHSP 4095	SOUND ON SOUND (LP)	15
85	Cocteau JEAN 1	PERMANENT FLAME SINGLES BOX (box set of 5 singles)	10
85	Cocteau JEAN 2	TRIAL BY INTIMACY (THE BOOK OF SPLENDOURS) (4-LP, box set, with book & postcards, initial copies misspelt as "The Book Splendours")	20
11	Esoteric COCDBOX 1002	THE PRACTICE OF EVERYDAY LIFE (8-CD box set)	40

(see also A - Austr, Astral Navigations, Gagalactyca, Be-Bop Deluxe)

CLARE NELSON
59	MGM MGM 1025	The Valley Of Love/You Are My Sunshine	8

EARL NELSON
59	London HLW 8950	No Time To Cry/Come On	30

OLIVER NELSON
60	Esquire 32-148	SCREAMIN THE BLUES (LP, as the Oliver Nelson Sextet)	50
61	His Masters Voice CSD 1422	THE BLUES AND THE ABSTRACT TRUTH (LP)	40
61	Esquire 32 168	STRAIGHT AHEAD (LP, with Eric Dolphy)	50
62	Esquire 32 188	MAIN STEM (LP, with Joe Newman)	25
63	Verve VLP 9053	FULL NELSON (LP)	15
66	His Masters Voice CSD 3570	OLIVER NELSON PLAYS MICHELLE (LP)	15
68	HMV CLP 1868	MORE BLUES AND THE ABSTRACT TRUTH (LP)	18

OZZIE & HARRIET NELSON
59	London HA-P 2145	OZZIE AND HARRIET NELSON (LP)	30

PETER NELSON
65	Piccadilly 7N 35278	Donna/I Want To Be Wanted	8
66	Piccadilly 7N 35314	Don't Make Promises (You Can't Keep)/No Need To Cry	7
72	Peacock PEA502	Good Scotch Whiskey/I Am A Ship	20

RICK(Y) NELSON
78s
57	HMV POP 355	I'm Walkin'/A Teenager's Romance	40
57	HMV POP 390	You're My One And Only Love/BARNEY KESSEL: Honey Rock	40
57	London HLP 8499	Be-Bop Baby/Have I Told You Lately That I Love You	20
58	London HLP 8542	Stood Up/Waitin' In School	20
58	London HLP 8594	Believe What You Say/My Bucket's Got A Hole In It	20
58	London HLP 8732	Someday/I Got A Feeling	20
58	London HLP 8738	Lonesome Town/My Babe	20
59	London HLP 8817	It's Late/Never Be Anyone Else But You	20
59	London HLP 8927	Just A Little Too Much/Sweeter Than You	25
60	London HLP 9021	I Wanna Be Loved/Mighty Good	60
60	London HLP 9121	Young Emotions/Right By My Side	30
60	London HLP 9188	Yes, Sir, That's My Baby/I'm Not Afraid	60

SINGLES
57	HMV POP 355	I'm Walkin'/A Teenager's Romance (gold label lettering)	150
57	HMV POP 355	I'm Walkin'/A Teenager's Romance (silver label lettering)	40
57	HMV POP 390	You're My One And Only Love/BARNEY KESSEL: Honey Rock	50
57	London HLP 8499	Be-Bop Baby/Have I Told You Lately That I Love You	20
58	London HLP 8542	Stood Up/Waitin' In School	20
58	London HLP 8594	Believe What You Say/My Bucket's Got A Hole In It	20
58	London HLP 8738	Lonesome Town/My Babe	8
59	London HLP 8817	It's Late/Never Be Anyone Else But You (all black or silver-top label)	8
59	London HLP 8894	Just A Little Too Much/Sweeter Than You (unreleased)	0
59	London HLP 8927	Just A Little Too Much/Sweeter Than You	10

(The 45s listed above were originally issued with triangular centres; later round-centre copies are worth half to two-thirds these values.)

59	London HL 7081	Just A Little Too Much/Sweeter Than You (export issue)	10
60	London HLP 9021	I Wanna Be Loved/Mighty Good	10

Sandy NELSON

MINT VALUE £

61	London HLP 9260	You Are The Only One/Milk Cow Blues	20
61	London HLP 9260	You Are The One And Only/Milk Cow Blues (with different label credit)	15
61	London HLP 9440	Everlovin'/A Wonder Like You	6

(The 45s listed above are credited to Ricky Nelson)

62	London HLP 9524	Young World/Summertime	10
62	London HLP 9583	Teen Age Idol/I've Got My Eyes On You (And I Like What I See)	10
65	Brunswick 05939	Come Out Dancin'/Yesterday's Love	10
66	Brunswick 05964	Louisiana Man/You Just Can't Quit (as Ricky Nelson)	10
66	Liberty LIB 12033	I Need You/Wonder Like You	10

EPs

58	London RE-P 1141	RICKY PART 1	20
58	London RE-P 1142	RICKY PART 2	20
58	London RE-P 1143	RICKY PART 3	20
58	London RE-P 1144	RICKY PART 4	20
59	London RE-P 1168	RICKY NELSON PART 1	20
59	London RE-P 1169	RICKY NELSON PART 2	20
59	London RE-P 1170	RICKY NELSON PART 3	20
59	London RE-P 1200	RICKY SINGS AGAIN PART 1	20
59	London RE-P 1201	RICKY SINGS AGAIN PART 2	20
60	London RE-P 1238	I GOT A FEELING	20
60	London RE-P 1249	RICKY SINGS SPIRITUALS	20
61	London RE-P 1300	RICKY NELSON PART 4	20

(The EPs listed above are credited to Ricky Nelson)

62	London RE-P 1339	IT'S A YOUNG WORLD	20
63	London RE-P 1362	IT'S UP TO YOU	30
63	Brunswick OE 9502	ONE BOY TOO LATE	30
64	Liberty LEP 4001	SINGS FOR YOU	60
64	Liberty LEP 4019	THAT'S ALL	60
65	Liberty LEP 4028	I'M IN LOVE AGAIN	60
65	Brunswick OE 9512	HAPPY GUY	30

ALBUMS : LPS

57	London HA-P 2080	RICKY	40
58	London HA-P 2119	RICKY NELSON	40
59	London HA-P 2159	RICKY SINGS AGAIN	30
59	London HA-P 2206	SONGS BY RICKY	30
60	London HA-P 2290	MORE SONGS BY RICKY (gatefold sleeve, mono)	25
60	London SAH-P 6102	MORE SONGS BY RICKY (gatefold sleeve, stereo)	30
61	London HA-P 2379	RICK IS 21 (mono)	25
61	London SAH-P 6179	RICK IS 21 (stereo)	25

(Credited to Ricky Nelson)

62	London HA-P 2445	ALBUM SEVEN (mono)	25
62	London SAH-P 6236	ALBUM SEVEN (stereo)	25
63	London HA-P 8066	IT'S UP TO YOU	25
63	Brunswick LAT 8545	FOR YOUR SWEET LOVE (mono)	25
63	Brunswick STA 8545	FOR YOUR SWEET LOVE (stereo)	30
64	Brunswick LAT 8562	RICKY SINGS "FOR YOU" (mono)	25
64	Brunswick STA 8562	RICKY SINGS "FOR YOU" (stereo)	40
64	Liberty LBY 3027	MILLION SELLERS	20
64	Brunswick LAT/STA 8581	THE VERY THOUGHT OF YOU	20
64	Brunswick LAT/STA 8596	SPOTLIGHT ON RICK	20
65	Brunswick LAT 8615	BEST ALWAYS	20
65	Brunswick LAT/STA 8630	LOVE AND KISSES	20
66	Brunswick LAT/STA 8657	BRIGHT LIGHTS, COUNTRY MUSIC	20
67	Brunswick LAT/STA 8680	COUNTRY FEVER	20

SANDY NELSON

59	London HLP 9015	Drum Party/The Big Noise From Winnetka (tri centre)	12
59	London HLP 9015	Drum Party/The Big Noise From Winnetka (78)	25
60	London HLP 9214	I'm Walkin'/Bouncy (as Sandy Nelson & His Combo)	10
61	London HLP 9377	Get With It/Big Noise From The Jungle	10
62	London HLP 9521	Drums Are My Beat/My Girl Josephine	7
62	London HLP 9558	Drummin' Up A Storm/Drum Stomp	8
62	London HLP 9612	...And Then There Were Drums/Live It Up	7
63	London HLP 9717	Ooh Poo Pah Doo/Feel So Good	8
64	Liberty LIB 66060	Teen Beat '65/Kitty's Theme	7
66	Liberty LIB 12062	Hey Joe/Come On Let's Go	7
60	Top Rank JKP 2060	RUSHING FOR PERCUSSION (EP, 2 tracks by Preston Epps)	20
62	London REP 1337	LET THERE BE DRUMS (EP)	10
63	London REP 1371	IN THE MOOD (EP)	10
65	Liberty LEP 4033	SANDY NELSON PLAYS (EP)	15
60	London HA-P 2260	TEEN BEAT (LP, mono)	25
60	London SAH-P 6082	TEEN BEAT (LP, stereo)	25
61	London HA-P 2425	LET THERE BE DRUMS (LP, mono)	20
61	London SAH-P 6221	LET THERE BE DRUMS (LP, stereo)	25
62	London HA-P 2446	DRUMS ARE MY BEAT! (LP, mono)	20
62	London SAH-P 6237	DRUMS ARE MY BEAT! (LP, stereo)	25
62	London HA-P 8009	DRUMMIN' UP A STORM (LP, mono)	20
62	London SH-P 8009	DRUMMIN' UP A STORM (LP, stereo)	25
63	London HA-P/SH-P 8029	COMPELLING PERCUSSION (LP)	20
63	London HA-P/SH-P 8051	TEENAGE HOUSE PARTY (LP)	20

Terry NELSON (& FIREBALLS)

MINT VALUE £

65	Liberty LBY 3007	SANDY NELSON PLAYS (LP)	20
65	Liberty LBY 3035	LIVE IN LAS VEGAS (LP)	20
66	Liberty LBY 3061	DRUMS A GO-GO (LP)	20
66	Liberty (S)LBY 3080	SUPERDRUMS (LP)	20

(see also Preston Epps)

TERRY NELSON (& FIREBALLS)

65	Dice CC 22	I'll Stand By You/Love On A Saturday Night	10
65	Dice CC 23	Run Run Baby/Bonita (as Terry Nelson & Fireballs)	12
65	Dice CC 25	Bulldog Push/Pretty Little Girl (as Terry Nelson & Fireballs)	12
65	Dice CC 27	Tomorrow Will Soon Be Here/My Blue Eyed Baby	8
65	Blue Beat BB 326	Help/PRINCE BUSTER: Johnny Dollar	25
66	Halagala HG 11	Take These Chains From My Heart/Let-Kiss	6
69	Rude Boy RBH 002	Woman Whine And Grine/Dem CIty GIrls (actually the FIRE-BALLS)	20

WILLIE NELSON

66	RCA Victor RD 7749	COUNTRY WILLIE (LP)	15
66	Liberty (S)LBY 1240	AND THEN I WROTE (LP)	15
69	RCA RD 7997	TEXAS IN MY SOUL (LP)	15

NELSON TRIO (U.S.)

60	London HLL 9019	All In Good Time/The Town Crier	15

NEMESIS

89	Intrigue IGE 5T	Heartbreaker/After The Storm (12")	20
89	Intrigue IGE 5T	After The Storm/Oh Baby Now/Heartbreaker/Give Me An Intro (12")	15
89	Intrigue IGE 7T	The Way Love Is/(Instrumental Version) (12")	30
90	Intrigue IGE 8T	I Need You So Bad/SHADES OF BLACK: Just A Little Bit (12")	15
91	Intigue IGE18T	CLASSIC CUTS 1 (12" EP)	12

NEMO

71	Parlophone R 5927	The Sun Has Got His Hat On/Bernie's Song	6

NEO MAYA

67	Pye 7N 17371	I Won't Hurt You/U.F.O.	75

(see also Episode Six)

CHIITRA NEOGY

68	Morgan Bluetown MI003L	THE PERFUMED GARDEN (LP)	30
68	Gemini GMX 5030	THE PERFUMED GARDEN (LP, reissue)	25

NEON BOYS

90	Overground OVER 11	TIME (12" EP, 20 test pressings only)	20
91	Overground OVER 19	That's All I Know (Right Now)/Love Comes In Spurts/High Heeled Wheels/Don't Die/Time (last 2 tracks credited to Richard Hell & Voidoids [Part III]) (12" p/s, 2,000 only, clear vinyl)	8

(see also Richard Hell, Television)

NEON DIOR

80	Diskatron DTRON 1	Kid At Heart/It's In Her Kiss (p/s)	10

NEON HEARTS

77	Neon Hearts NEON 1	Venus Eccentric/Regulations (8" p/s)	40
78	Satril SAT 133	Answers/Armchair Thriller (p/s)	15
79	Satril SAT 139	Popular Music/Pretty As A Picture (p/s)	8
79	Satril SATL 4012	POPULAR MUSIC (LP)	15

NEON (1)

78	Sensible FAB 3	Anytime Anyplace Anywhere/Bottles/I'm Only Little	10

NEON (2)

80	3D 3D1	Making Waves/Me I See In You (p/s)	20
80	Carrere 201	Communication Without Sound/Remote Control	12

NEON BARBS

81	Ligical Step	Break Your Chains/Adjust To Red (p/s)	8

NEON TETRA

82	Deeda DD 01	Tightrope/Night Boat To Amsterdam	20

NEPTUNE'S EMPIRE

71	Polymax PXX 01	NEPTUNE'S EMPIRE (LP)	200

NERO & GLADIATORS

61	Decca F 11329	Entry Of The Gladiators/Boots	15
61	Decca F 11367	In The Hall Of The Mountain King/The Trek To Rome	15
61	Decca F 11413	Czardas/That's A Long Time Ago	20

(see also Laurie Jay, Gladiators, Screaming Lord Sutch & Savages, State Of Mickey & Tommy)

PETER NERO

69	CBS 4277	Soulful Strut/For Once In My Life	8
69	CBS 4464	Theme From Picasso Summer/Be In	6

PAUL NERO (SOUNDS)

68	Liberty LBL 83100	NERO'S SOUL PARTY (LP)	25

NERVE (1)

67	Page One POF 019	No. 10 Downing Street/Georgie's March	12
68	Page One POF 055	Magic Spectacles/Come The Day	20
68	Page One POF 081	It Is/Mystery Lady	18
68	Page One POF 097	Piece By Piece/Satisfying Kind	15

(see also Lovin')

NERVE (2)

95	Straw B001	Submarine/Seeds From The Electric Garden (p/s)	6

NERVES (1)

78	Lightning GIL 520	TV Adverts/Sex Education (p/s)	35

NERVES (2)

81	Good Vibrations BIG 3	NOTRE DEMO (LP, official bootleg, foldover sleeve with booklet)	20

NERVES (3)

94	Inflammable Material BURN	Bits/SUBSTANDARD: Rostock (p/s)	7

NERVE SENTA

NERVE SENTA
81	Tense Raven FRM 041	You Turn Me On/Secret Admirer	25

NERVOUS CHOIR
89	Cathexis CRN 5407	O'David/Tonight We Start On Witches/Alsatians/Introducing (p/s, with inserts)	7

NERVOUS GERMANS
82	Rondelet ROUND 3000	These Boots Are Made For Walking/Watch Out	6

(see also Razar, Soho Jets)

NERVOUS NORVUS
56	London HLD 8338	Ape Call/Wild Dog Of Kentucky (gold label print)	50
56	London HLD 8338	Ape Call/Wild Dog Of Kentucky (silver label print)	20
57	London HLD 8383	Dig/Bullfrog Hop (gold label print)	60
57	London HLD 8383	Dig/Bullfrog Hop (silver label print)	30
62	Salvo SLO 1812	Does A Chinese Chicken Have A Pigtail/ROD BARTON: Dear Old San Francisco	20
85	Big Beat NED 12	NERVOUS NORVUS (mini-LP)	15

NERVOUS WRECKS
72	No label or cat. no	NERVE ENDING (LP)	300

JIM NESBIT
65	Vocalion V 9241	Tiger In My Tank/I Can't Stand This Living Alone	25

SAM NESBIT
75	Right On 103	Keep On Hustling Baby/Instrumental Version	6

MICHAEL NESMITH (& FIRST/SECOND NATIONAL BAND)
70	RCA SF 8136	MAGNETIC SOUTH (LP, with First National Band)	25
71	RCA SF 8209	NEVADA FIGHTER (LP, with First National Band)	25
72	RCA SF 8276	TANTAMOUNT TO TREASON VOLUME ONE (LP, with Second National Band)	20
73	RCA APL1 0164	PRETTY MUCH YOUR STANDARD RANCH STASH (LP, solo)	15
75	Island ILPS 9428	THE PRISON (LP, boxed with book, unreleased in U.K.)	0
76	RCA RS 1064	THE BEST OF MICHAEL NESMITH (LP)	15

(see also Monkees, Wichita Train Whistle)

NESSIE
81	SRTS 81 CUS 1092	Can I See Her Tomorrow/Tell Her	10

NEU!
73	United Artists UP 35485	Super/Neuschnee (p/s)	25
73	United Artists UP 35485	Super/Neuschnee	20
75	United Artists UP 35874	Isi/After Eight	20
72	United Artists UAS 29396	NEU (LP, laminated cover)	100
73	United Artists UAS 29500	NEU II (LP, gatefold sleeve)	100
75	United Artists UAS 29782	NEU '75 (LP, gatefold sleeve)	80
82	Cherry Red BRED 37	BLACK FOREST GATEAU (LP, compilation)	30
10	Gronland LPGRONI	NEU (LP, gatefold, reissue, white vinyl)	18
10	Gronland LPGRONII	NEU 2 (LP, gatefold, reissue, white vinyl)	18
10	Gronland LPGRONIII	NEU '75 (LP, reissue)	18
10	Gronland LPGRONIV	NEU! '86 (LP, yellow vinyl)	15
10	Gronland LPGRONV5065001040981	NEU! (4-LP box set with 12", inserts)	100

(see also Kraftwerk, La Dusseldorf)

NEU ELEKTRIKK
79	Synthethesia SGS 107	Lust Of Berlin/Distractions (p/s, stamped white labels)	20
80	Synthethesia SYN 1	COVER GIRL EP	10

NEUROSIS
04	Neurot NR 033	THE EYE OF EVERY STORM (LP, gatefold, inner, poster, grey marbled vinyl)	30
07	Neurot NR 050	GIVEN TO THE RISING (LP, gatefold, inner, black/white splattered vinyl)	20

NEUTRAL MILK HOTEL
95	Fire BLAZE 79	Everything Is/Snow Song Part 1	20
98	Blue Rose BRRC 10237	Holland, 1945/Engine (picture disc, numbered fold-out poster in polythene bag)	30

NEUTRONS
74	United Artists UAG 29652	BLACK HOLE STAR (LP, with inner sleeve)	25
75	United Artists UAG 29726	TALES FROM THE BLUE COCOONS (LP, laminated gatefold sleeve)	20

(see also Clive John, Gentle Giant, Man)

AARON NEVILLE
67	Stateside SS 584	Tell It Like It Is/Why Worry	20
67	Stateside SS 584	Tell It Like It Is/Why Worry (DJ Copy)	40
91	A&M AMY 835	Voodoo/Close Your Eyes/Hercules (12")	15
67	Liberty LBY 3089	LIKE IT 'TIS (LP)	50
86	Charly CRB 1111	MAKE ME STRONG (LP)	15

NEW AGE
82	Dining Out TUX 18	LIVIN FOR NOW (12" EP, p/s)	15
82	Dining Out TUX 25	ALL THE MONKEYS AREN'T IN THE ZOO, MARYLOO (LP)	20

NEW AGE STEPPERS
80	On-U Sound ONU 1	Fade Away/LONDON UNDERGROUND: Learn A Language (p/s)	15
81	Statik 6	My Love/Love Forever	6
81	Statik 612	My Love/Love Forever (12")	20
80	On-U Sound ONULP 1	NEW AGE STEPPERS (LP)	30
81	Statik/On U Sound STATLP 2	ACTION BATTLEFIELD (LP)	30
82	On-U Sound ONULP 21	FOUNDATION STEPPERS (LP)	30

NEWBAN
11	BBE BBE223ALP	NEWBAN & NEWBAN 2 (2-LP, reissue)	20

NEWBEATS
64	Hickory 45-1269	Bread And Butter/Tough Little Buggy (pink or black/blue label)	7
64	Hickory 45-1282	Everything's Alright/Pink Dally Rue	10

NEW BLOCKADERS

MINT VALUE £

65	Hickory 45-1290	Break Away/Hey O Daddy O	10
65	Hickory 45-1305	The Birds Are For The Bees/Better Watch Your Step	8
65	Hickory 45-1320	I Can't Hear You No More/Little Child	15
65	Hickory 45-1332	Run Baby Run/Mean Woolly Willie	30
65	Hickory 45-1332	Run Baby Run/Mean Woolly Willie (DJ copy)	70
66	Hickory 45-1366	Shake Hands (And Come Out Crying)/Too Sweet To Be Forgotten	20
66	Hickory 45-1387	Crying My Heart Out/Short Of Love	40
66	Hickory 45-1387	Crying My Heart Out/Short Of Love (DJ copy)	70
66	Hickory 45-1422	My Yesterday Love/Patent On Love	10
71	London HLE 10341	Run Baby Run (Back Into My Arms)/Am I Not My Brother's Keeper	6
65	Hickory LPE 1503	NEWBEATS (EP)	30
65	Hickory LPE 1506	AIN'T THAT LOVIN' YOU BABY (EP)	30
66	Hickory LPE 1510	OH! GIRLS GIRLS (EP)	30
65	Hickory LPM 120	BREAD AND BUTTER (LP)	35
72	London SHE 8428	RUN BABY RUN (LP)	15

(see also Dean & Mark, Larry Henley)

NEW BLOCKADERS
| 82 | Private Pressing | CHANGEZ LES BLOCKEURS (LP, 100 only, white label A4 sheet as cover) | 300 |
| 91 | Hypnagogia GOG 01 | SYMPHONIE IN X MAJOR (LP, 500 only, numbered) | 20 |

NEWBOY
| 73 | Count Shelly CS007 | Sweet Talk/J ENGLISH: One And Only | 20 |

NEW BREED
| 65 | Decca F 12295 | Friends And Lovers Forever/Unto Us | 75 |

MICKEY NEWBURY
| 72 | Elektra K 12047 | An American Trilogy/San Francisco Mabel Joy | 6 |

NEWBY
| 65 | Pye 7N 15986 | I Can't Grow Peaches On A Cherry Tree/The Children Sleep | 7 |

NEWBY & JOHNSON
| 70 | Mercury 6052 027 | I Want To Give You My Everything/Sweet Happiness | 25 |

NEWCASTLE BIG BAND
| 72 | Impulse ISS NBB 106 | NEWCASTLE BIG BAND (LP, white labels, 2,000 only) | 150 |

(see also Last Exit, Police, Sting, Radio Actors)

NEW CENSATION
| 75 | DJM DJS 10371 | First Round Knockout/Everybody's Got A Story | 8 |

NEWCLEUS
| 84 | Sunnyview SVLP 6600 | JAM ON REVENGE (LP) | 18 |

NEW COLONY SIX
66	London HLZ 10033	I Confess/Dawn Is Breaking	75
66	Stateside SS 522	At The River's Edge/I Lie Awake	50
68	Mercury MF 1030	I Will Always Think About You/Hold Me With Your Eyes	12
69	Mercury MF 1086	Things I'd Like To Say/Come And Give Your Love To Me	10

NEWCOMERS
| 72 | Stax 2025 063 | Pin The Tail On The Donkey/Mannish Boy | 8 |
| 75 | Stax STXS 2023 | Keep An Eye On Your Close Friends/(Instrumental Version) | 10 |

NEW CULTURE
| 72 | Priory PRY 002 | Seek Out The Sun/Strange | 100 |

NEW CUOREY
| 73 | Taurus TR 101 | Vietnam/The Girl I Had | 25 |

NEW DAWN
| 69 | private pressing | MAINLINE (LP) | 80 |

NEW DEAL STRING BAND
| 69 | Argo ZDA 104 | DOWN IN THE WILLOW (LP, with insert) | 30 |

NEW DECADE
| 92 | Out Of Romford ROCC 002 | Get The Message/ABC Remix (12", stamped white labels) | 10 |

NEW DEPARTURES QUARTET
| 60s | Transatlantic TRA 134 | THE NEW DEPARTURES QUARTET (LP, with Stan Tracey) | 40 |

(see also Stan Tracey)

MARTIN NEWELL
| 80 | Off Street OSR 001 | Young Jobless/Sylvie In Toytown (p/s) | 30 |
| 80 | Liberty BP 392 | Young Jobless/Sylvie In Toytown (p/s reissue) | 8 |

(see also Gypp, Cleaners From Venus)

DENNIS NEWEY
61	Philips PB 1134	Checkpoint/Title Unknown	10
61	Philips PB 1198	Border Patrol/Yes Yes	10
62	Philips 326 588 BF	The Nightriders/The Pied Piper	10

NEW FACES
65	Pye 7N 15842	So Small/Blue Mist	10
65	Pye 7N 15931	Never Gonna Love Again/You'll Be Too Late	8
66	Pye 7N 17029	Like A Man/Shake Up The Party (Myra)	15
67	Pye 7N 17335	Lace Covered Window/The Life That I Lead	10
68	Decca F 12746	We Can Get There By Candlelight/The Yellow Road	8
68	Decca F 12862	Someday/Biscuit Coloured Overcoat	7
69	Decca F 12933	Carnival Day/Grandfather Dugan	7
69	Decca F 12968	There Is An Island In The Sun/Happy The Heart That I Own	7
74	Ember MBS 334	Where Would I Find Another You/Lullaby	6

NEW FORESTERS
| 65 | Lyntone LYN 932/933 | Travel/LIZARDS: My Love Goes On (Sheffield Students Rag record) | 30 |

NEW FORMULA
| 67 | Piccadilly 7N 35381 | Do It Again A Little Bit Slower/I'm On The Outside Looking In | 18 |
| 67 | Piccadilly 7N 35401 | I Want To Go Back There Again/Can't You See That She Loves Me | 18 |

NEW FOUNDATIONS

MINT VALUE £

68	Pye 7N 17552	My Baby's Coming Home/Burning In The Background Of My Mind	20
69	Pye 7N 17818	Stay Indoors/Hare Krishna (in export p/s)	40
69	Pye 7N 17818	Stay Indoors/Hare Krishna	25

NEW FOUNDATIONS
75	Pye 45533	I Need Your Love/Something For My Baby	8

(see also Foundations)

NEW GENERATION (1)
69	Spark SRL 1000	Sadie And Her Magic Mister Garland/Digger	15
69	Spark SRL 1007	Smokey Blues Away/She's A Soldier Boy	10
70	Spark SRL 1019	Police Is Here/Mister C.	15

NEW GENERATION (2)
80	Fight FT DD 4454	Long And Winding Road/BLACK STALLIONS: New Experience (12")	50

NEW HEARTS
77	CBS 5800	Just Another Teenage Anthem/Blood On The Knife (p/s)	10
78	CBS 6381	Plain Jane/My Young Teacher (p/s)	10

(see also Secret Affair)

NEW HERITAGE
73	Westwood WRS 028	ALL MANNER OF THINGS (LP)	50

NEW HOPE
69	London HL 10296	Won't Find Better Than Me/They Call It Love	18

(see also Kit Kats)

NEW HORIZON
73	Decca F13463	Hullabaloo/Believe In Yourself	10

NEW INSPIRATION
67	Major Minor MM 539	You Made A Fool of Me/M.T.	25
73	Penny Farthing PEN 803	Medicine Man/Is It Really That Hard To Understand	10

NEW JACK PIMPS
94	Steppaz STEP 001	Water Jelly (Amen Lick)/Water Jelly (Copter Lick) (12")	25

NEW JAZZ GROUP
56	Tempo EXA 39	MODERN JAZZ SCENE (EP)	50

NEW JAZZ ORCHESTRA
65	Decca LK 4690	WESTERN REUNION LONDON 1965 (LP, mono)	80
65	Decca SKL 4690	WESTERN REUNION LONDON 1965 (LP, stereo)	150
69	Verve SVLP 9236	DEJEUNER SUR L'HERBE (LP)	250

(see also Neil Ardley, Nucleus)

NEW JERSEY CONNECTION
82	Nitelife LIFE 1	Love Don't Come Easy/Love Don't Come Easy (Instrumental)	10
82	Nitelife LIFE 1	Love Don't Come Easy/Love Don't Come Easy (Instrumental) (12")	16

NEW JERSEY KINGS
92	Acid Jazz JAZIDLP 33	PARTY TO THE BUS STOP (LP)	15
95	Acid Jazz JAZID123LP	STRATOSPHERE BREAKDOWN (LP)	15

(see also James Taylor Quartet)

NEW JUMP BAND
68	Domain D 1	The Only Kind Of Girl/Seven Kinds Of Sweet Lovin'	25

NEW KINGDOM
93	Gee Street 518 362 1	HEAVY LOAD (LP)	40

NEW LEAF
80	LEAF 101	Warning Take Warning/Roots Rock Reggae (no p/s)	30

ANTHONY NEWLEY
59	Decca DFE 6566	IDLE ON PARADE (EP)	10
60	Decca DFE 6629	TONY'S HITS (EP)	10
60	Decca DFE 6655	MORE HITS FROM TONY (EP)	12

ANDY NEWMAN
72	Track 2406 103	RAINBOW (LP, gatefold sleeve, black/silver label)	25

(see also Thunderclap Newman)

BRAD NEWMAN
62	Fontana H 357	Somebody To Love/This Time It's Love	15
62	Fontana H 369	Get A Move On/Here And Now And Evermore	10
62	Fontana 267 220TF	Stay By Me/Candy Lips	10
62	Fontana 267 243TF	Point Of No Return/Now I've Lost You	10
63	Fontana 267 273TF	I'll Find You Another Baby/No Man Should Ever Be Alone	10
64	Piccadilly 7N 35174	Please Don't Cry/Every Hour Of Living	8

CARLTON NEWMAN
85	Roots Pool RP 003	Front Line/EDI FITZROY: Pressure	30

COLIN NEWMAN
80	Beggars Banquet BEG 48	B/Classic Remains/Alone On Piano (p/s)	6
81	Beggars Banquet BEG 52	Inventory/This Picture (p/s)	6
82	4AD AD 209	We Means We Starts/Not To (p/s)	10
80	Beggars Banquet BEGA 20	A-Z (LP, inner)	30
81	4AD CAD 108	PROVISIONALLY ENTITLED THE SINGING FISH (LP)	20
82	4AD CAD 201	NOT TO (LP)	20

(see also Wire)

DEL NEWMAN SOUND
67	Columbia SCX 6181	FLOWER GARDEN (LP)	20

JIMMY (C.) NEWMAN
57	London HLD 8460	A Fallen Star/I Can't Go On This Way	30
59	MGM MGM 1009	What'cha Gonna Do/So Soon	15
59	MGM MGM 1037	Grin And Bear It/The Ballad Of Baby Doe	10
60	MGM MGM 1085	A Lovely Work Of Art/What About Me	8
61	MGM MGM 1112	Now That You're Gone/Wanting You With Me Tonight	8

			MINT VALUE £
59	MGM MGM-EP 706	GRIN AND BEAR IT - COUNTRY AND WESTERN STYLE (EP)	30

MARK NEWMAN
69	Lestar 712	MARK NEWMAN (EP)	30

NANETTE NEWMAN
77	B&C BCS 0004	Fun Food Factory/Morris (The Studio Mouse)	6

PAUL NEWMAN
66	Mercury MF 969	Ain't You Got A Heart/Tears On My Pillow	50

RANDY NEWMAN
68	Reprise R(S)LP 6286	RANDY NEWMAN CREATES SOMETHING NEW UNDER THE SUN (LP)	15
70	Reprise RSLP 6373	12 SONGS (LP)	15
85	Warner Bros. K56404	LITTLE CRIMINALS (LP, Hi Fi News, Nimbus supercut)	70

(see also Harry Nilsson, Tom Petty & Heartbreakers)

TOM NEWMAN
75	Virgin VS120	Sad Sing/Ali's Got A Broken Bone	8
75	Virgin VS133	Sleep/Darling Corey	6
75	Virgin V 2022	FINE OLD TOM (LP, features Mike Oldfield)	20
75	Virgin V 2042	LIVE AT THE ARGONAUT (LP, unreleased, test pressings only)	80
77	Decca TXS 123	FAERIE SYMPHONY (LP, gatefold sleeve)	30
88	Oceandisc	OZYMANDIAS (LP, unissued, 20 test pressings only in proof sleeve)	30

(see also Jade Warrior, July, Mike Oldfield)

TONY NEWMAN
68	Decca F 12795	Soul Thing/Let The Good Times Roll	30
70	Decca F 13041	Soul Thing/Let The Good Times Roll (reissue)	10

(see also Sounds Incorporated, Flying Machine, Pinkerton['s Assorted Colours], May Blitz, Three Man Army)

THE NEW MASTERSOUNDS
00	Blow It Hard BIH 017	One Note Brown/Burnt Black	20
01	Deep Funk DFLP 001	KEB DARGE PRESENTS (LP)	40

NEW MATH
79	Reliable Gum 002	Die Trying/Angela (original issue, p/s)	20
79	CBS 7916	Die Trying/Angela (p/s, reissue)	8

NEWMENS
72	Parlophone R5941	Start My Life Again/A Million Tears	10

NEW MODEL
83	Mr. Clean MERC 001	Chilean Warning/The World Thru Our Eyes/Totalitarian Terror (p/s, in 7" x 10" folder)	10
83	Mr. Clean MERC 001	Chilean Warning/The World Thru Our Eyes/Totalitarian Terror (p/s)	6

NEW MODEL ARMY
83	Shout QS 002/QF 001	Bittersweet/Betcha/Tension (p/s, with flexi "Fashion"/"The Cause")	15
93	Epic 473562 1	THE LOVE OF HOPELESS CAUSES (LP)	40

NEW MODEL SOLDIER
81	Bunny Rabbit BUN 001	DANCE THE DEATH OF A THOUSAND CUTS EP	200

NEW MONITORS
72	Buddah 2011 118	Fence Around Your Heart/Have You Seen Her	30

PETER NEWNHAM
77	B & C BCS 011	Rudi/Outside My Window (100 only)	150

NEW ORDER (1)
81	Come Org WDC 883011	BRADFORD RED LIGHT DISTRICT (cassette)	50
81	Come Org. CARA12	BRADFORD RED LIGHT DISTRICT (LP)	110

(see also Come)

NEW ORDER (2)

SINGLES
81	Factory FAC 33	Ceremony/In A Lonely Place (embossed metallic p/s)	15
81	Factory FAC 33T	Ceremony/In A Lonely Place (12", British racing green, with bronze type)	20
81	Factory FAC 33T	Ceremony/In A Lonely Place (12", later forest green with gold type)	12
81	Factory FAC 3312	Ceremony (Re-recording)/In A Lonely Place (Extended) (12", cream & blue p/s)	12
81	Factory FAC 53	Procession/Everything's Gone Green (9 different coloured sleeves : black, brown, red, orange, yellow, green, aquamarine, blue and purple on a grey background)	10
81	Factory Benelux FBNL 8	Everything's Gone Green/Mesh/Cries & Whispers (12", yellow sleeve)	20
82	Factory FAC 51B	Rocking Carol/Ode To Joy (flexidisc, given away at Hacienda, 4,000 only)	30
82	Factory FAC 63	Temptation/Hurt (p/s)	10
82	Factory FAC 63	Temptation/Hurt (12", p/s)	20
83	Factory FAC 7312	Blue Monday/The Beach (12", first pressing, die-cut sleeve, silver insert)	30
83	Factory FAC 7312	Blue Monday/The Beach (12", second pressing, die-cut sleeve, black insert)	12
83	Factory FAC 93	Confusion/Confused Beats/Confusion (Instrumental)/Confusion (Rough Mix) (12", p/s, embossed sleeve)	10
85	Factory FAC 123	The Perfect Kiss/The Kiss Of Death (p/s)	10
85	Factory FAC 123	The Perfect Kiss/The Kiss Of Death/Perfect Pit (12", embossed silver p/s, black/blue inner)	10
85	Factory FAC 123	The Perfect Kiss/The Kiss Of Death/Perfect Pit (12", embossed silver p/s, pink)	15
85	Factory FAC 133	Sub Culture/Dub Culture (12", die cut sleeve)	12
85	Factory FAC 133	Sub-Culture/Dub Vulture (p/s)	10
86	Factory FAC 163-7	Bizarre Love Triangle/Bizarre Dub Triangle (7", p/s)	12
86	Factory FAC 163	Bizarre Love Triangle/Bizarre Dub Triangle (12", p/s)	10
86	Strange Fruit SFPS001	PEEL SESSIONS (12")	15
87	Strange Fruit SFPS039	PEEL SESSIONS 1981 (12")	12
88	Factory FAC 223	Fine Time/Don't Do It/Fine Line (12", p/s)	10
88	Factory FAC 73R	Blue Monday 1988/Beach Buggy (12")	12
88	Factory FACDV 73R	Blue Monday 1988 (12 Inch)/Blue Monday 1988 (7 Inch)/Beach Buggy/Blue Monday 1988 (CD Video)	50
88	Factory FACDV 183	True Faith (Remix 12 Inch)/Evil Dust/True Faith (7 Inch) (CD Video)/True Faith (CD Video)	40
89	Factory FAC 273	Run 2/Run 2 (Extended Version)/MTO/MTO (Minus Mix) (12", p/s)	10

NEW ORLEANS BOOTBLACKS

			MINT VALUE £
09	Rhino FAC 63	Temptation/Hurt (p/s, reissue)	6
11	Rhino FAC 33	Ceremony (Original Version)/In A Lonely Place (12" Version)//Ceremony (Heart & Soul Rehearsal Version)/In A Lonely Place (Unreleased Rehearsal Version) (12")	25
16	Mute MUTE 553	People On The High Line (Richard X Video Mix)/(Claptone Radio Edit) (uncut picture disc)	100

SINGLES : PROMOS
83	Factory FAC 93	Confusion (Edit)/Confusion (Edit) (p/s, DJ promo only)	20
84	Factory FAC 103	Thieves Like Us (Edit)/Lonesome Tonight (Edit) (p/s, DJ promo only)	15
85	Factory FAC 123	Perfect Kiss/Kiss Of Death (7" promo)	12
88	Factory FAC 223	Fine Time/Don't Do It/Fine Line (12" promo, pink p/s)	25
88	Factory FAC 73RD	Blue Monday 1988/Blue Monday (DJ-only mix) (12", p/s, DJ promo only)	10
89	Factory FAC 263DJ	Round & Round (Ben Grosse Mix)/(12" Mix)/(Detroit Mix) (12", p/s, DJ only)	12
89	Factory FAC 273/7	Run 2 (Edit)/MTO (Edit) (DJ promo only, 500 pressed)	20

ALBUMS
81	Factory FACT 50	MOVEMENT (LP, blue cardboard sleeve)	40
83	Factory FACT 75	POWER CORRUPTION & LIES (LP, 1st pressing, die cut sleeve, A1/B1 Matrix numbers	40
83	Factory FACT 75	POWER CORRUPTION & LIES (LP, repressing, A2/B2 Matrixes)	20
85	Factory FACT 100	LOW-LIFE (LP, onion paper outer sleeve)	40
86	Factory FACT 150SP	BROTHERHOOD (LP, limited metallic sleeve)	40
86	Factory FACT 150	BROTHERHOOD (LP)	20
87	Factory FACT 200	THE GATEFOLD SUBSTANCE (LP, numbered gatefold sleeve, 1,000 only)	100
87	Factory FACT 200	SUBSTANCE (LP, 1st pressing, embossed sleeve, 2 inners)	40
87	Factory FACT 200	SUBSTANCE (LP, non-embossed sleeve, 2 inners)	30
87	Factory FACT 200c	SUBSTANCE (cassette, 200 only in box set with insert)	20
89	Factory FACT 275	TECHNIQUE (LP, inner)	20
90	Strange Fruit SFRLP 110	PEEL SESSIONS (LP)	15
93	London 8284131	REPUBLIC (LP)	40
94	London 8285801	(THE BEST OF) NEW ORDER (2-LP, with inner sleeve)	50
95	London 8286571	(THE REST OF) NEW ORDER (2-LP)	35
01	London 8573896211	GET READY (LP)	40
05	London 2564622021	WAITING FOR THE SIREN'S CALL (2-LP)	30
13	Rhino 2564662715	LOST SIRENS (LP, CD)	15
13	London 2564 68879-7	MOVEMENT (LP, reissue, clear vinyl)	40
15	Mute BXSTUMM 390	MUSIC COMPLETE (8 x 12", coloured vinyl, boxed set, signed)	100
15	Mute BXSTUMM 390	MUSIC COMPLETE (8 x 12", coloured vinyl, boxed set, unsigned)	60
17	Live Here Now LHN018LP	NOMC15 (3-LP, clear vinyl)	40

(see also Joy Division, Electronic, Other Two, Revenge, Monaco, Bad Lieutenant)

NEW ORLEANS BOOTBLACKS
54	Columbia SCM 5090	Flat Foot/Mad Dog	8

NEW OVERLANDERS
69	RCA 1861	Thought Back/These Are Not My People	6
70	RCA 1953	Unchained Melody/Memories	6

NEW RACE
83	Statik STAT LP 16	THE FIRST & THE LAST (LP)	25

NEW RECRUITS
82	Dischord DIS 1	Over The Pillow/The Aufrau Principle/All In An Hour (no p/s)	20

NEW RELIGION
72	Bamboo BAM 70	In The Beautiful Caribbean/Black Is Black	175
73	Ackee ACK 526	Walk Away Renee/What's It All About	8

NEWS FROM BABEL
84	Recommended RE 6116	NEWS FROM BABEL - WORK RESUMED ON THE TOWER (LP, hand-screened sleeve)	30
86	Re RE 1 14	LETTERS HOME (LP)	25

NEWS (1)
66	Decca F 12356	The Entertainer/I Count The Tears	18
66	Decca F 12477	This Is The Moment (from the TV series "Adam Adamant")/Ya Ya Da Da	12

(see also Patto, Glenn Hughes, Finders Keepers, Miller, Big Boy Pete)

NEWS (2)
78	GENTS WIB 001	Get Out Of My Bed/Tearing Away (1st pressing without 'Gents' name or sticker)	8

NEW SEEKERS
71	Coca-Cola CPZ 2593	Buy The World/Ivor Raymand's Orchestra - It's The Real Thing	10

NEW SETTLERS
74	York YR 218	She Didn't Forget Her Shoes/Lifelight	12

NEWSFLASH
89	Newsflash NF 002	Touch Me/Finding Out The Hard Way/White Beat (12" p/s)	40
90	Newsflash 001	Nobodies Home/Mundane Me And You (p/s)	50

JOANNA NEWSOM
05	Drag City DC 303	YS (2-LP, gatefold, booklet)	20

BOBBY NEWSOME
72	Mojo 2093 018	Jody Come And Get Your Shoes/Post Office	10

WAYNE NEWTON
73	Chelsea 2005 001	May The Road Rise To Meet You/While We're Still Young	6

OLIVIA NEWTON-JOHN
66	Decca F 12396	Till You Say You'll Be Mine/For Ever	350
71	Pye International 7N 25543	If Not For You/The Biggest Clown	6
80	Jet JET 10-185	Xanadu/Fool Country (10" pink vinyl, die-cut p/s, with ELO)	12
78	EMI EMAP 789	TOTALLY HOT (LP, picture disc)	20

(see also Toomorrow, Marvin & Farrar)

NEWTOWN NEUROTICS
79	No Wonder A 45	Hypocrite/You Said No (no p/s, with insert & sticker)	80
79	No Wonder A 45	Hypocrite/You Said No	20

NEW TRENDS

			MINT VALUE £
80	No Wonder NOW 4	When The Oil Runs Out/Oh No (p/s)	40
82	CNT 4/No Wonder NOW 56	Kick Out The Tories!/Mindless Violence! (p/s)	15
82	CNT CNT 010	Licensing Hours/No Sanctuary (p/s)	18
83	Razor RZS 107	Blitzkrieg Bop/Hypocrite (New Version)/I Remember You (p/s)	12
84	No Wonder NOW 6T	Suzi/Fools (p/s)	12
83	Razor RAZ 6	BEGGARS CAN BE CHOOSERS (LP)	25

NEW TRENDS
| 67 | Columbia SX 6245 | THE NEW TRENDS (LP) | 20 |

NEW VICTORY BAND
| 78 | Topic 12TS 382 | ONE MORE DANCE AND THEN (LP) | 15 |

NEW WALK
| 83 | Web WEB 22 | Pressure Point/Shape Of Things To Come (p/s) | 12 |

NEW WANDERERS
| 79 | Grapevine GRP 144 | This Man In Love/Adam And Eve | 15 |
| 79 | Grapevine GRP 144 | This Man In Love/Adam And Eve (DJ Copy) | 30 |

NEW WORLD
| 83 | Slipped Discs HD 106 | I Talk To My Car (Some copies have New crossed out) | 60 |

NEW YORK NEW YORK
83	Urchin NY 2001	Roger Wilson Said/Too Drunk To Drive (p/s)	8
85	Beach Culture 2 BC	I WANNA BE LIKE YOU (12" EP)	15
85	Izuma IZUMA LP 1	NEW YORK NEW YORK (LP)	18

(see also Higsons. Terry Edwards, Serious Drinking)

NEW YORK DOLLS
73	Mercury 6052 402	Jet Boy/Vietnamese Baby	20
74	Mercury 6052 615	Stranded In The Jungle/Who Are The Mystery Girls	10
77	Mercury 6160 008	Jet Boy/Babylon/Who Are The Mystery Girls	10
73	Mercury 6338 270	NEW YORK DOLLS (LP, laminated front and black sleeve)	60
74	Mercury 6338 498	TOO MUCH TOO SOON (LP)	40
77	Mercury 9286.996/7	NEW YORK DOLLS (LP)	20

(see also Johnny Thunders, Heartbreakers, Idols)

NEW YORK PUBLIC LIBRARY
66	Columbia DB 7948	I Ain't Gonna Eat Out My Heart Anymore/Rejected	25
68	MCA MU 1025	Gotta Get Away/Time Wastin'	15
68	MCA MU 1045	Love Me Two Times/Which Way To Go	10
72	B & C CB 176	Whei Ling Ty Luu/Boozy Queen	8

NEW YORK ROCK ENSEMBLE
| 71 | CBS 5292 | Running Down The Highway/Law And Order | 15 |

NEW YORK PORT AUTHORITY
| 77 | Invictus S INV 81951 | THREE THOUSAND MILES FROM HOME (LP) | 15 |

NEXT BAND
| 78 | Gannet SRTS/79/CUS 159 | FOUR BY THREE EP (p/s) | 60 |

(see also Red Alert (3))

NEXUS 21
89	Blue Chip BLUE C34T	(Still) Life Keeps Moving (12")	10
89	Blue Chip BLUE C34R	(Still) Life Keeps Moving Remix (12")	10
90	Network NWKT 15	PROGRESSIVE LOGIC EP (12", p/s)	35
91	Network NWKT 35	I Know We Can Make It (12", white label)	10
89	Blue Chip BLUE TEC. 2	THE RHYTHM OF LIFE (LP)	15

(see also Altern 8)

NIADEM'S GHOST
| 86 | Hibination HIDE 001 | IN SHELTERED WINDS (LP) | 25 |

(see also IQ)

NIANATTY
| 81 | S&G SG 13 | One Love Stylee/DESMOND RHYTHM SECTION: One Love (12") | 60 |

NERMIN NIAZI
| 84 | Sirrocco LPMDY 001 | DISCO SE AAGAY (LP) | 100 |

NICE
67	Immediate IM 059	The Thoughts Of Emerlist Davjack/Angel Of Death	15
68	Immediate IM 068	America/The Diamond Hard Blue Apples Of The Moon (pink label, in p/s)	20
68	Immediate IM 068	America/The Diamond Hard Blue Apples Of The Moon (pink label)	10
68	Immediate IM 072	Brandenburger/Happy Freuds	10
69	Immediate AS 4	She Belongs To Me/She Belongs To Me ('single sampler', promo)	20
70	Charisma CB 132	Country Pie/One Of Those People	6
70s	Immediate IM 068	America/The Diamond Hard Blue Apples Of The Moon (white label, reissue in p/s)	6
67	Immediate AS 2	ALBUM SAMPLER - THE THOUGHTS OF EMERLIST DAVJACK (1-sided LP, promo only)	60
67	Immediate IMLP 016	THE THOUGHTS OF EMERLIST DAVJACK (LP, mono)	70
67	Immediate IMSP 016	THE THOUGHTS OF EMERLIST DAVJACK (LP, stereo)	50
68	Immediate IMSP 020	ARS LONGA VITA BREVIS (LP, laminated front, flipbacks, pink label, "Sold in U.K..." text)	40
69	Immediate IMSP 026	THE NICE (LP, gatefold sleeve)	30
70	Charisma CAS 1014	FIVE BRIDGES (LP, pink label, gatefold sleeve)	20
71	Charisma CAS 1030	ELEGY (LP, gatefold sleeve pink 'scroll' label)	20
72	Charisma CS1	AUTUMN '67 AND SPRING '68 (LP)	30

(see also Keith Emerson, Emerson Lake & Palmer, Jackson Heights, Habits, Brian Davison, Refugee, Attack, Jet, P.P. Arnold)

NICK NICELY
80	Voxette VOX 1001	D.C.T. Dreams/Treeline (p/s, reissue copies £4)	20
81	EMI EMI 5256	Hilly Fields (1892)/49 Cigars (p/s)	15
12	Fruits De Mer Crustacean 27	Hilly Fields (1982)/Hilly Fields (The Mourning) (p/s, 300 on dark red and 300 on grey vinyl)	8
04	Tenth Planet TP 059	PSYCHOTROPIA (LP, 1000 copies only)	20

Albert NICHOLAS

MINT VALUE £

ALBERT NICHOLAS
56 Tempo A 129 — How Long Blues (with Al Fairweather)/Rose Room (with Lise West) ... 10

PAUL NICHOLAS
70 Polydor 56374 — Freedom City/Run Shaker Life (with p/s) ... 100
70 Polydor 56374 — Freedom City/Run Shaker Life ... 70
71 Polydor 2058 086 — The World Is Beautiful/Lamplighter ... 45

(see also Oscar, Paul Dean)

BILLY NICHOLLS
68 Immediate IM 063 — Would You Believe/Daytime Girl (features Small Faces) ... 70
73 Track 2094 109 — Forever's No Time At All/This Song Is Green (with Pete Townshend) ... 20
74 GM GMS 018 — White Lightning/Daytime Girl ... 20
68 Immediate IMCP 009 — WOULD YOU BELIEVE (LP, withdrawn) ... 5000
74 GM GML 1011 — LOVE SONGS (LP) ... 80
98 Tenth Planet TP 042 — WOULD YOU BELIEVE (LP, reissue, with insert) ... 45
99 South West SELP 003 — SNAPSHOT (LP) ... 25
07 Castle CMQLP 1523 — WOULD YOU BELIEVE (2-LP, reissue, black or green vinyl) ... 40

PENNY NICHOLS
68 Pye int 7N 2451 — Look Around Rock/Farina ... 35

ROSEMARY NICHOLS
70 Gemini GMS 013 — Once Upon A Time/Baby ... 10

HAL NICHOLSON
76 Concrete Jungle CJ 755 — Blackman In A Babylon/Part 2 ... 15

LEA NICHOLSON
72 Trailer LER 3010 — HORSEMUSIC (LP) ... 20
72 Transatlantic TRA 254 — GOD BLESS THE UNEMPLOYED (LP, with Stan Ellison) ... 18

ROGER NICHOLSON
72 Trailer LER 3034 — NONESUCH FOR DULCIMER (LP, red label) ... 20

VIVIAN NICHOLSON
79 SRTS 79414 — Spend Spend Spend/You're Number One ... 50

NICKELSON
72 Decca F13328 — Sitting On A Fence/Oh How Much ... 8

NICKY AND THE DOTS
78 Small Wonder SMALL 12 — Never Been So Stuck/Linoleum Walk (p/s) ... 15

NICO
65 Immediate IM 003 — I'm Not Sayin'/The Last Mile (early copies in blue/white "immediate" sleeves) ... 90
65 Immediate IM 003 — I'm Not Sayin'/The Last Mile (in standard black/white "immediate" sleeves) ... 80
81 Flicknife FLS 206 — Vegas/Saeta (p/s) ... 8
82 Immediate IMS 003 — I'm Not Saying/The Last Mile (p/s, reissue) ... 25
83 Aura AUS 137 — Heroes/One More Chance (p/s) ... 20
88 Strange Fruit SFPS 064 — PEEL SESSIONS (12", p/s) ... 15
10 Elektra 8122797856 — Frozen Warnings/No One Is There (die-cut sleeve, 750 only) ... 8
18 Immediate IM003 — I'm Not Saying/The Last Mile (p/s, reissue, white vinyl) ... 15
68 Elektra EKL 4029 — THE MARBLE INDEX (LP, orange label, mono) ... 100
68 Elektra EKS 74029 — THE MARBLE INDEX (LP, orange label, stereo) ... 80
71 Reprise RSLP 6424 — DESERT SHORE (LP, with John Cale) ... 60
71 Reprise K 44102 — DESERT SHORE (LP, with John Cale, 2nd pressing) ... 30
71 MGM Select 2353 025 — CHELSEA GIRL (LP) ... 50
74 Island ILPS 9211 — THE END (LP) ... 40
81 Aura AUL 715 — DRAMA OF EXILE (LP, colour cover) ... 19
85 Island ILPS 9211 — THE END (LP, reissue, blue label) ... 18
86 Polydor 2353 025 — CHELSEA GIRL (LP, reissue) ... 15
86 Dojo DOJOLP 27 — BEHIND THE IRON CURTAIN (2-LP) ... 20

(see also John Cale, Velvet Underground, Ayers Cale Nico & Eno)

NICODEMUS
81 Cha Cha CHAD 44 — Gunman Connection/It Have To Ram (12") ... 30
81 Greensleeves GRED 75 — BONE CONNECTION/LEROY SMART: All My Love (12") ... 15
82 Cha Cha CHALP 011 — GUNMAN CONNECTION (LP) ... 40
82 Black Joy DHLP 2003 — DANCE HALL STYLE (LP) ... 50

JIMMY NICOL (& SHUBDUBS)
64 Pye 7N 15623 — Humpty Dumpty/Night Train ... 25
64 Pye 7N 15666 — Husky/Don't Come Back (solo) ... 18
64 Pye 7N 15699 — Baby Please Don't Go/Shub Dubbery (possibly unissued) ... 20

(see also Sound Of Jimmy Nicol, Georgie Fame)

NICOLETTE
89 Shut Up & Dance SUAD 14 — Waking Up (12") ... 10
92 Shut Up & Dance SUAD 004 — NOW IS EARLY (LP) ... 20

WATT NICOLL
71 Xtra XTRA 1122 — NICE TO BE NICE (LP, laminated front cover) ... 15

NICRA
77 Ogun OG 010 — LISTEN/HEAR (LP) ... 18

(see also Keith Tippett)

NIDDY GRIDDY BAND
68 Pye 7N 17461 — Dinny Girgy/Summertime ... 6

LENNIE NIEHAUS OCTET
62 Contemporary LAC 1222 — ZOUNDS! (LP) ... 40

NIEMEN
72 CBS 564896 — STRANGE IS THIS WORLD (LP, orange/black label) ... 25

STEVE NIEVE
80 Comb 1 — OUTLINE ON A HAIRDO (EP) ... 20

NIGGER KOJAK
83	Nigger Kojak NKLP 002	ROCK JACK KOJAK (LP)	15

NIGGY HOI!
80s	Deli K1Z	Theme From Niggy Hoi!/Titanium Kedi (p/s)	8

NIGHT DOCTOR
81	Race Records RB DIS 001	Romancin'/Menelik (12")	35
81	Race RB 001	Just Enough/Hit And Miss Affair	10

NIGHTAIR
76	SRTY 79 CUS 410	NIGHTAIR (LP)	15

NIGHTBIRDS
59	Oriole CB 1490	Cat On A Hot Tin Roof/The Square	12

NIGHTBLOOMS
90	Fierce FRIGHT 041	Crystal Eyes/Never Dream At All (p/s)	10

NIGHTCHILL
13	Kent CITY 031	I Don't Play Games/ROMEO & JULIET : You Got What It Takes (reissue)	8

NIGHTCRAWLERS
67	London HLR 10109	The Little Black Egg/You're Running Wild	60

NIGHTIME FLYER (1)
69	Pye 7N 17739	Talk To Me/Spinning Wheel	6
69	Pye 7N 17798	Don't Push Me Baby/Thru' Loving You	7
71	Pye 7N 45046	Love On Borrowed Time/It's A Hurtin' Thing	6

NIGHTIME FLYER (2)
81	Red Eye EYE 2	Out With A Vengeance/Heavy Metal Rules (p/s)	20
03	Phoenix NWOBHM 7007	Out With A Vengeance/Heavy Metal Rules (yellow vinyl reissue, numbered, 250 copies, 7.5 inch sleeve)	10

MAXINE NIGHTINGALE
69	Pye 7N 17739	Talk To Me/Spinning Wheel	10
69	Pye 7N 17798	Don't Push Me Baby/Thru Loving You	6
71	Pye 7N 45046	Love On Borrowed Time/It's That Hurtin Thing	6

TUNDE NIGHTINGALE & HIS HIGHLIFE BOYS
68	Melodisc MLPAS 12-142	THE BIRDS THAT SINGS ALL THE NIGHT (LP)	15

NIGHTINGALES
81	Rough Trade/Vindaloo RT 075/UGH 4	Idiot Strength/Seconds	8
82	Cherry Red BRED 39	PIGS ON PURPOSE (LP)	15
84	Vindaloo VILP 1	1983-4 JUST THE JOB (LP)	15

NIGHTMARE
79	PVK PV 30	Great Balls Of Fire/Witch Woman (p/s)	10
83	PVK PV 119	I Wanna Be Shot/Ruth Ellis (P/S)	6

NIGHTMARES IN WAX
79	Inevitable INEV 0002	BIRTH OF A NATION (EP, with wraparound p/s)	20
84	KY KY 9	Black Leather/Shangri-La (12", 'horror' p/s)	18
85	KY KY 9 1/2	Black Leather/Shangri-La/Girls Song (12", different p/s, 3,000 only)	20

(see also Dead Or Alive)

NIGHTMARES ON WAX
91	Warp WARPLP 4	A WORD OF SCIENCE (THE 1st & FINAL CHAPTER) (LP)	20
95	Warp WARPLP 36	SMOKERS DELIGHT (2-LP, gatefold, inners)	40
99	Warp WARPLP 61	CARBOOT SOUL (2-LP, gatefold, inners)	30
02	Warp WARPLP 95	MIND ELEVATION (2-LP, gatefold, inners)	20
06	Warp WARPLP 133	IN A SPACE OUTTA SOUND (2-LP)	35
08	Warp WARPLP 159	THOUGHT SO (2-LP, gatefold, inners)	20
13	Warp WARPLP 241	FEELIN GOOD (2-LP)	20

NIGHT MOVES
83	GC GCT 2	Transdance (New York Disco Mix)/Transdance (UK Disco Mix)/Nightdrive (12")	30
84	GC/MCA GCT 1001	Transdance (Robot Rock) (UK Club Mix)/You Can Take My Love/Beat This/Nightdrive (12", p/s)	20

NIGHT PILOTS
79	Christy CML 0107	Dancing With Myself/Open Top Sports Car	10

NIGHTRIDER
79	Wessex WEX 272	DIGITAL TECHNIQUES EP: Gruesome Girls/Stay Clean/Happy Day (p/s)	35

NIGHTRIDERS (1)
66	Polydor BM 56066	Love Me Right Now/Your Friend (withdrawn)	120
66	Polydor BM 56066	Love Me Right Now/Your Friend (promo copy)	85
66	Polydor BM 56116	It's Only The Dog/Your Friend	100
79	Stardust STR 1001	I Saw Her With Another Guy/London Town (picture insert)	25

(see also Mike Sheridan & Nightriders, Mike Sheridan's Lot, Idle Race)

NIGHTRIDERS (2)
79	Stardust STR 1001	I Saw Her With Another Guy/London Town (picture insert)	25

NIGHT RUN
81	RUN 001	Forever/Crime Of Passion (no ps)	80

NIGHTSHIFT (1)
65	Piccadilly 7N 35243	Corrine Corrina/Lavender Tree	15
65	Piccadilly 7N 35264	That's My Story/Stormy Monday Blues	18

NIGHTSHIFT (2)
79	Zoom Zum 9	Jet Set/Bad Dreams (p/s)	6

NIGHT-TIMERS
65	Parlophone R 5355	The Music Played On/Yield Not To Temptation (featuring Herbie Goins)	70

(see also Herbie Goins & Night-Timers, Ronnie Jones)

NIGHTWING
80	Ovation OVS 1209	Barrel Of Pain/Nightwing (p/s)	10
84	Gull GULS 75	Treading Water/Call Your Name (p/s)	6

NIGHTWISH

			MINT VALUE £
84	Gull GULS 7512	Treading Water/Call Your Name/Barrel Of Pain (12", red vinyl, p/s)	10
84	Gull GULS 77	Night Of Mystery/Dressed To Kill (p/s)	10
84	Gull GULS 7712	Night Of Mystery/Dressed To Kill (12", p/s)	12
83	Gull PGULP 1038	STAND UP AND BE COUNTED (LP, picture disc)	15

(see also Alec Johnson Band, Nutz)

NIGHTWISH

04	Back On Black BOBV 003 DPD	ANGELS FALL FIRST (2-LP picture discs, stickered bag)	20
04	Back On Black BOBV 004 DPD	OCEANBORN (2-LP picture discs, stickered bag)	20
04	Back On Black BOBV 006 DPD	WISHMASTER (2-LP picture discs, stickered bag)	20
04	Back On Black BOBV 007 DPD	OVER THE HILLS AND FAR AWAY (2-LP picture discs, stickered bag)	20
04	Back On Black BOBV 008 DPD	CENTURY CHILD (2-LP picture discs, stickered bag)	20
05	Back On Black BOBV 035 DPD	ONCE (2-LP picture discs, stickered bag)	20

NIGHTWRITERS

88	Jack Trax JTX 19	Let The Music Use You (Club Mix)/(Radio Mix)/(Dub Mix) (12")	20

NIHILIST SPASM BAND

85	United Dairies UD 016	1X - X = X (LP)	20

BILL NILES

67	Decca F 12661	Pashionella Grundy/Bric-A-Bric Man	15

WILLY NILLY

84	Ad Hoc AH 1	On The Spur Of The Moment/Half A Job (p/s, with 'time-table' insert)	45

(see also Randy Newman, Ringo Starr, Cher)

(HARRY) NILSSON

69	RCA RCA 1864	Maybe/The Puppy Song	6
72	RCA RCA 2266	You're Breaking My Heart/Spaceman (possibly withdrawn, Demo stamped copy)	12
68	RCA Victor RD/SF 7928	PANDEMONIUM SHADOW SHOW (LP, mono)	25
68	RCA Victor RD/SF 7928	PANDEMONIUM SHADOW SHOW (LP, stereo)	20
68	RCA RD/SF 7973	AERIAL BALLET (LP, mono)	25
68	RCA RD/SF 7973	AERIAL BALLET (LP, stereo)	20
69	RCA SF 8010	SKIDOO (LP, soundtrack)	20
69	RCA SF 8046	HARRY (LP)	20
74	Rapple/RCA APL1-0220	SON OF DRACULA (LP, soundtrack, with Ringo Starr, fold-out sleeve)	15
80	RCA 6302 022	FLASH HARRY (LP, first pressing, those with 'barcode' are repressings)	30

NIMBO

71	Pye 7N 450097	Maisie Jones/Forget Her	8
72	Pye 7N 45174	When The Swallows Fly/Noticeingly By	15

LEONARD NIMOY

68	Dot (S)LPD 511	MR. SPOCK PRESENTS MUSIC FROM OUTER SPACE (LP)	25
72	Rediffusion ZS 156	MUSIC FROM OUTER SPACE (LP, reissue of DOT (S) LPD 511)	20

NINA

69	CBS 4681	Do You Know How Christmas Trees Are Grown?/The More Things Change	12

NINE BELOW ZERO

80	M&L ML 1	NINE BELOW ZERO EP	10

NINE DAYS WONDER

71	Harvest SHSP 4014	NINE DAYS WONDER (LP, textured sleeve, EMI logo on label)	100

(see also Gnidralog)

NINE INCH NAILS

90	Island 12IS 482	Down On It (Skin)/Terrible Lie (Sympathetic Mix)/Down On It (Shred)/Down On It (Singe)/Terrible Lie (Empathetic Mix)/Down On It (Demo) (12", numbered limited edition)	20
91	Island 10ISP 484	Head Like A Hole (Slate)/Head Like A Hole (Copper) (10", poster p/s)	8
91	Island 12IS 484	Head Like A Hole (Slate)/Head Like A Hole (Copper)/Head Like A Hole (Opal) (12", ps)	10
91	Island ISDJ 484	Head Like A Hole (Radio Edit) (promo, stickered p/s, same track both sides)	20
91	Island ISDJ 508	Sin (Radio Edit)/(same) (promo only, stickered p/s)	12
91	Island 9IS 508	Sin (Long)/Sin (Dub)/Get Down Make Love (9", p/s)	10
92	Island IS 552DJ	Wish (Radio Edit) (1-sided, stickered plain sleeve, promo only)	12
92	Island IS 552	Physical (You're So)/Suck	15
94	Island 9IS 592	March Of The Pigs/A Violent Fluid/All The Pigs, All Lined Up/Underneath The Skin (9",numbered p/s)	12
94	Island 12IS 596	Closer (Deviation)/Closer (Further Away)/Closer (6.26)/Closer (Precursor)/Closer (Internal) (12", p/s)	10
94	Island 12ISX 596	Closer to God/March Of The Fuckheads/Heresy (Blind)/Memorabilia (12", p/s)	10
91	Island ILPS 9973	PRETTY HATE MACHINE (LP)	20
92	Interscope ILPM 8004	BROKEN (1-sided 6 track mini LP with free 7" 'Physical'/'Suck')	30
92	Island ILPM 8005	FIXED (remix mini LP)	20
94	Island ILPSD 8012	THE DOWNWARD SPIRAL (double LP, gatefold sleeve, insert)	70
99	Island ILPST 8091	THE FRAGILE (3-LP, inners booklet, white stickered sleeve)	125
17	Nothing B002568201	THE FRAGILE (3-LP reissue, stickers sleeve)	35

999

77	Labritain LAB 999	I'm Alive/Quite Disappointing (p/s)	20
77	United Artists UP 36299	Nasty Nasty/No Pity (p/s, green vinyl)	15
77	United Artists FREE 7	Nasty Nasty/No Pity (78rpm promo, 50 copies only)	400
78	United Artists 12FREE10	Waiting/Action (12", p/s, given away free with mail order copies of SEPARATES LP)	10
80	Polydor POSP 99	Trouble/Made A Fool Of You (p/s)	7
81	Albion ION 1011	Obsessed/Change/Lie, Lie, Lie (live) (p/s, with laminated sleeve, shrinkwrapped with patch)	6
81	Albion ION 1017	Li'l Red Riding Hood/Waiting For Your Number To Be Called/I Ain't Gonna Tell Ya (live) (p/s, with stencil; shrinkwrapped)	6

Sadie NINE

MINT VALUE £

82	Albion ION 1033	Wild Sun/Scandal In The City (p/s)	7
83	Albion ION 155	13th Floor Madness/Night Shift (p/s)	12
78	United Artists UAG 30199	999 (LP, with inner sleeve)	25
78	United Artists UAG 30209	SEPARATES (LP, with inner sleeve)	18
80	United Artists POLS 1013	BIGGEST PRIZE IN SPORT (LP)	15
80	United Artists UA SOS 999	THE 999 SINGLES ALBUM (LP)	15
90	Link LINK LP 125	CELLBLOCK TAPES (LP)	15

(see also Kilburn & High Roads)

SADIE NINE
81	Precious AVE 3	If You Take A Morning From My Life/Kiss Me Not Him	6

9.30 FLY
72	Ember NR 5062	9.30 FLY (LP, textured gatefold sleeve)	250

NINESENSE
76	Ogun OG 900	OH! FOR THE EDGE (LP)	30
77	Ogun OG 910	HAPPY DAZE (LP)	30

(see also Elton Dean, Julie Tippetts, Keith Tippett, Mark Charig, Harold Beckett, Alan Skidmore)

1984 (1)
69	Big T BIG 117	This Little Boy/Rosalyn	12
69	Big T BIG 120	Got To Have Your Love/Here We Are	8
71	Decca F23159	Little Girl/Laramee	12

1984 (2)
79	LaVista	Music Press/She's A Razor (stamped plain die cut sleeve)	60

1919
82	Red Rhino RED 22	Repulsion/Tear Down These Walls (p/s)	6
82	Red Rhino RED 22	Repulsion/Tear Down These Walls (white hand-written labels, 500 only)	25
83	Abstract 12 ABS 017	Cry Wolf/Dream/Storm (12", p/s)	18
83	Red Rhino REDLP 25	MACHINE (LP, inner)	35

1910 FRUITGUM CO.
68	Pye International 7N 25458	May I Take A Giant Step (Into Your Heart)/(Poor Old) Mr. Jensen	6
68	Pye Intl. 7N 25468	1,2,3, Red Light/Sticky Sticky	6
68	Pye Int. 7N.25478	Pop Goes The Weasel/The Year 2001	7
68	Pye Intl. N(S)PL 28115	SIMON SAYS (LP)	15
69	Buddah 203 014	GOODY GOODY GUMDROPS (LP)	15
70	Buddah 2359 006	HARD RIDE (LP)	20

1910 FRUITGUM CO./LEMON PIPERS
68	Pye Intl. NEP 44091	PRESENTING... (EP, 1 side each)	10

1991
13	Astro Dynamics ADLP 01	1991 (LP, blue vinyl, clear plastic sleeve)	20

90 DEGREES
76	Vertigo 6059 155	Little Wing/Slave Trade	15
79	Virgin VS 311	No Doctor/Fantasy Woman (p/s)	8
76	Vertigo 6060 139	90 DEGREES INCLUSIVE (LP)	20

NINEY (& DESTROYERS/OBSERVERS)
70	Amalgamated AMG 856	Niney Special/Danger Zone	40
70	Pressure Beat PR 5501	Honey No Money (with SLIM SMITH)/INSPIRATIONS: This Message To You	45
71	Big BG 317	You Must Believe Me/You Must Believe Version	15
71	Big Shot BI 568	Blood And Fire/Mud And Water	20
71	Big Shot BI 586	Message To The Ungodly/Message To The Ungodly - Version	15
71	Supreme SUP 214	You Must Believe Me/RUPIE EDWARDS ALLSTARS: Funk The Funk	12
71	Gas GAS 171	Blood And Fire/ROLAND ALPHONSO: 33 66	25
72	Big Shot BI 609	Beg In The Gutter/Beg In The Gutter Version	8
72	Big Shot BI 610	Everyday Music (by the Observers)/Observing The Avenue	10
72	Bullet BU 503	Aily And Ailaloo (& Max)/Version	8
88	Trojan TRLS 263	BLOOD & FIRE (LP)	15
05	Auralux LUXXLP 009	SUFFERATION (2-LP)	25
12	Kingston KSLP039	SING IT WICKED STYLE (LP)	15

(see also Niney's All Stars, Observers)

NINEY'S ALL STARS
70	Unity UN 563	Skankee/Skankee - Version	10

(see also Niney, Observers)

NING
71	Decca F 23114	Machine/More Ning	30

NINO & EBBTIDES
61	Top Rank JAR 572	Those Oldies But Goodies/Don't Run Away	25

9TH CREATION
75	Pye 12138	FALLING IN LOVE (LP)	20

NIPPLE ERECTORS
78	Soho SH 1/2	King Of The Bop/Nervous Wreck (with glossy p/s)	40
78	Soho SH 1/2	King Of The Bop/Nervous Wreck (later matt p/s)	20

(see also Nips, Pogues)

NIPS
78	Soho SH 4	All The Time In The World/Private Eyes (foldover p/s)	40
80	Soho SH 9	Gabrielle/Vengeance	30
80	Soho SH 9	Gabrielle/Vengeance (tour copy with 'licensed to cool' stamp)	30
80	Chiswick CHIS 119	Gabrielle/Vengeance (reissue, p/s)	15
81	Test Pressing TP 5	Happy Song/Nobody To Love (p/s)	50
80	Soho HOHO 1	ONLY AT THE END OF THE BEGINNING (LP, with insert, white labels)	35
87	Soho WIKM 66	BOPS, BABES, BOOZE & BOVVER (LP)	20

(see also Nipple Erectors, Pogues)

NIRVANA (U.K.)

MINT VALUE £

NIRVANA (U.K.)

67	Island WIP 6016	Tiny Goddess/I Believe In Magic	30
67	Island WIP 6020	Pentecost Hotel/Feelin' Shattered	25
68	Island WIP 6029	Rainbow Chaser/Flashbulb	25
68	Island WIP 6038	Girl In The Park/C Side In Ocho Rios	25
68	Island WIP 6045	All Of Us (The Touchables)/Trapeze	15
69	Island WIP 6052	Wings Of Love/Requiem To John Coltrane	25
69	Island WIP 6057	Oh! What A Performance/Darling Darlene	30
70	Pye International 7N 25525	The World Is Cold Without You/Christopher Lucifer	20
71	Vertigo 6059 035	The Saddest Day Of My Life/(I Wanna Go) Home	25
71	Philips 6006 127	Pentecost Hotel/Lazy Day Drift	12
72	Philips 6006 166	Stadium/Please Believe Me	12
76	Bradleys BRAD 7602	Two Of A Kind/Before Midnight	6
76	Island WIP 6180	Rainbow Chaser/Tiny Goddess (p/s)	10
81	Zilch ZILCH 8	The Picture Of Dorian Gray/No It Isn't	6
88	Bam Caruso OPRA 45	Black Flower/WIMPLE WINCH: Save My Soul (jukebox issue, die-cut sleeve)	12
67	Island ILP 959	THE STORY OF SIMON SIMOPATH (LP, mono, pink label, black/orange circle logo)	300
67	Island ILPS 9059	THE STORY OF SIMON SIMOPATH (LP, stereo, pink label, black/orange circle logo)	400
68	Island ILPS 9087	ALL OF US (LP, pink label, black/orange circle logo)	250
70	Pye Intl. NSPL 28232	DEDICATED TO MARKOS III (LP)	250
71	Vertigo 6360 031	LOCAL ANAESTHETIC (LP, gatefold sleeve, swirl label)	300
72	Philips 6308 089	SONGS OF LOVE AND PRAISE (LP)	150
87	Bam-Caruso KIRI 061	BLACK FLOWER (LP)	20

(see also Patrick Campbell-Lyons, Ray Singer, Pica, Hat & Tie, Informants)

NIRVANA (U.S.)

SINGLES

89	Tupelo TUP EP8	Blew/Love Buzz/Been A Son/Stain (12", p/s)	40
89	Tupelo TUP CD8	Blew/Love Buzz/Been A Son/Stain (CD)	30
90	Tupelo TUP 25	Sliver/Dive (gatefold p/s, green vinyl only, 2,000 pressed)	25
91	Tupelo TUP EP25	Sliver/Dive/About A Girl (live)/Dive (12", p/s)	15
91	Tupelo TUP EP25	Sliver/Dive/About A Girl (live)/Dive (12", repressing, blue vinyl, p/s)	20
91	Geffen DGCT 5	Smells Like Teen Spirit (Edit)/Even In His Youth/Even In His Youth (12", p/s)	15
91	Geffen DGCS 5	Smells Like Teen Spirit/Drain You (p/s)	10
91	Geffen DGCTP 5	Smells Like Teen Spirit (Edit)/Drain You (LP Version)/Aneurysm (12", picture disc, die-cut p/s)	15
92	Geffen DGCS 7	Come As You Are/Endless Nameless (silver labels)	20
92	Geffen DGCTP 7	Come As You Are/Endless Nameless/School (Live)	35
92	Geffen DGCTP 7	Come As You Are/Endless, Nameless/School (live) (12", picture disc, die-cut p/s)	20
92	Geffen DGCS 9	Lithium/Been A Son (live)	7
92	Geffen DGCTP 9	Lithium/Been A Son (live)/Curmudgeon (12", picture disc, die-cut p/s)	20
92	Geffen GFS 34	In Bloom/Sliver (live)/Polly (live) (p/s)	15
92	Geffen DGCTP 34	In Bloom/Sliver (live)/Polly (live) (12", picture disc, die-cut p/s)	20
93	Touch & Go TG 83	Oh, The Guilt/JESUS LIZARD: Puss (p/s, blue vinyl, with poster)	40
93	Touch & Go TG 83	Oh, The Guilt/JESUS LIZARD: Puss (p/s, blue vinyl, without poster)	15
93	Geffen GFS 54	Heart Shaped Box/Marigold	6
93	Geffen GFST 54	Heart Shaped Box/Milk It/Marigold (12" p/s)	15
93	Geffen GF 566	All Apologies/Rape Me/MV	6
93	Geffen GFST 66	All Apologies/Rape Me/MV (12", p/s with 2 art prints)	12
94	Geffen (no cat. no.)	Penny Royal Tea (Scott Litt Mix)/Where Did You Sleep Last Night (live) (unreleased, 10 test pressings only)	600
94	Geffen NIRPRO (no cat. no.)	Penny Royal Tea (Scott Litt Mix) (CD, 1-track, no inlay, promo only)	600
95	Geffen GED 24901	SINGLES (6 x CD box set)	25
11	DGC B0015411-01	HOARMOANING (12", brown vinyl)	25

ALBUMS

89	Tupelo TUP LP 6	BLEACH (LP, 300 on white vinyl)	175
89	Tupelo TUP LP 6	BLEACH (LP, 2,000 on green vinyl)	50
89	Tupelo TUP LP 6	BLEACH (LP, black vinyl)	30
89	Tupelo TUPLP 6	BLEACH (LP, mispressing with A side labels on both sides)	25
91	Geffen DGC 24425	NEVERMIND (LP, with inner sleeve)	45
92	Geffen GEF 24504	INCESTICIDE (LP, inner)	15
93	Geffen GEF 24536	IN UTERO (LP, inner)	40
94	Geffen GED 24727	UNPLUGGED IN NEW YORK (LP, white vinyl with inner sleeve)	35
96	Geffen GEF 25105	FROM THE MUDDY BANKS OF THE WISHKAH (2-LP)	25
98	Simply Vinyl SVLP 0048	IN UTERO (LP)	20
98	Simply Vinyl SVLP 053	UNPLUGGED IN NEW YORK (LP, reissue)	40
02	Sub Pop 9878700341	BLEACH (LP, reissue, 13 tracks, white marbled vinyl)	20
02	Sub Pop 9878400341	BLEACH (LP, reissue, 11 tracks, white vinyl)	15
09	DGC B0013538-01	LIVE AT READING (2-LP)	20
09	Simply Vinyl SVLP 0038	NEVERMIND (LP, reissue)	15
11	Geffen/Back To Black 602527779041	NEVERMIND (4 x LP, gatefold sleeve)	50
11	Geffen/Back To Black 602527779041	NEVERMIND (4 x picture disc, gatefold sleeve)	80

(see also Foo Fighters, Probot)

NISHI STREAK

90	Wink WR 001	1999/Hypnotise (p/s)	40
90	Wink WR 001	1999/Hypnotise (12")	80
91	Wink WR 002	In Love With You/Hypnotise (12")	40

NITE-LITERS

72	RCA SF 8282	INSTRUMENTAL DIRECTIONS (LP)	20

NITE PEOPLE

MINT VALUE £

NITE PEOPLE
66	Fontana TF 747	Sweet Tasting Wine/Nobody But You	25
67	Fontana TF 808	Trying To Find Another Man/Stay As Sweet As You Are	20
67	Fontana TF 885	Summertime Blues/In The Springtime	60
68	Fontana TF 919	Morning Sun/Where You There	50
69	Page One POF 149	Love, Love, Love/Hot Smoke And Sassafras (with insert)	25
69	Page One POF 149	Love, Love, Love/Hot Smoke And Sassafras	15
69	Page One POF 159	Is This A Dream/Cream Tea	25
70	Page One POF 174	Season Of The Rain/P.M.	20
69	Page One POLS 025	P.M. (LP)	600

(see also Banana Bunch)

NITE ROCKERS
58	RCA RCA 1079	Nite Rock (Lonely Train)/Oh! Baby	50
58	RCA RCA 1079	Nite Rock (Lonely Train)/Oh! Baby (78)	30

NITESHADES
65	CBS 201763	Be My Guest/I Must Reveal	18
65	CBS 201817	Fell So Fast/I'm Not Gonna Worry	12

NITE WATCH
80	Channel CH 1	Baby Come Back (Home)/Get Down ('Cause I Love Your Body) (no p/s)	6

NITS
79	CBS 8049	Tutti Raqazzi/Harrow Accident	8

NITTY GRITTY
85	Greensleeves GRED 187	Hog In A Minty/Run Down The World	12
86	Greensleeves GRED 195	Man In A House/Version/False Alarm/Version (12")	15
86	Greensleeves GREL 93	TURBO CHARGED (LP)	18

NITTY GRITTY DIRT BAND
67	Liberty LIB 55948	Buy Me For The Rain/Candy Man	10
68	Liberty LBF 15099	Collegiana/End Of Your Line	10
69	Liberty LBF 15275	Some of Shelly's Blues/Yukon Railway	6
70	Liberty LBF 15358	Rave On/The Cure	6
68	Liberty LBL/LBS 83122	PURE DIRT (LP)	30
69	Liberty LBL/LBS 83286	DEAD AND ALIVE (LP)	25
71	Liberty LBG 83345	UNCLE CHARLIE AND HIS DOG TEDDY (LP, gatefold sleeve)	20
72	United Artists UAS 29284	ALL THE GOOD TIMES (LP)	15

(see also Kaleidescope, Chris Darlow)

JACK NITZSCHE
63	Reprise R 20202	The Lonely Surfer/Song For A Summer Night	30
63	Reprise R 20337	Night Walker/Green Grass Of Texas	15
78	MCA MCA 366	Hard Workin' Man (featuring Captain Beefheart)/Coke Machine	15
74	Warner Bros K 41211	ST GILES CRIPPLEGATE (LP)	20

(see also Date With Soul, Mick Jagger, Captain Beefheart, Randy Newman, Crazy Horse)

NIX
82	Electric Bubblegum EB 102	Requiem For Mr. Spock/Hoots Mon (no p/s)	40

NIX-NOMADS
64	HMV POP 1354	You're Nobody (Till Somebody Loves You)/She'll Be Sweeter Than You (demos miscredited to Nix-Nomands)	60

MEL NIXON
72	Parlophone R5958	Pillars Of Straw/Ev'ry Little Beat Of Your Heart	6
75	Alaska ALA 26	Every Beat Of Your Heart/ASTRA NOVA ORCHESTRA: Soul Sleeper	6

NKENGAS
73	Orbitone OT 005	DESTRUCTION (LP)	100
73	Orbitone OT 006	NKENGAS IN LONDON (LP)	30

KWAME NKRUMAH
74	Elegance BB 1011	THE VOICE OF KWAME NKUMAH OF AFRICA (LP)	60

NMONIC
00	YNR YNR002	REQUIEM (EP)	20

NO DEPOSIT
79	None	NO RETURN (LP, die cut white sleeve, hand stamped, hand numbered, lyric insert)	100

NO SUPPORT/LIMPS
79	Matchbox Classics MC 1	OPPOSITE SIDES EP (Split 7" with 2 tracks by Limps and 2 tracks by No Support, p/s)	20
79	Matchbox Classics MC 2	ANOTHER MATCHBOX CLASSIC? (Split EP, 2 tracks by Limps and 2 by No Support, with folded p/s)	40
79	Matchbox Classics MC 2	ANOTHER MATCHBOX CLASSIC? (Split EP, 2 tracks by Limps and 2 by No Support, without folded p/s, just die-cut stamped sleeve)	15

NO WORRIES
95	Groove Yard GYARD 004	MADE IN THE SHADE EP (12")	10

NOAH HOUSE OF DREAD
82	On U Sound DP6	Murder/Stand Firm (10" p/s)	40
82	On U Sound ON UP LP 20	HEART (LP)	40
86	Noah HEART 2	HEART 2 (LP)	18

RAB NOAKES
78	Ring O' 2017 115	Waiting Here For You/Restless (in p/s)	18
78	Ring O' 2017 115	Waiting Here For You/Restless	12
78	Ring O' 2017 117	I Won't Let You Down/Long After Dark (unreleased)	0
70	Decca SKL 5061	DO YOU SEE THE LIGHTS (LP)	40
72	A&M AMLS 68219	RAB NOAKES (LP, with Stealers Wheel)	25
75	Warner Bros. K56114	NEVER TOO LATE (LP)	15

NOBELMEN
59	Top Rank JAR 155	Thunder Wagon/Dragon Walk	20

IKE NOBLE
87	Timeless TRPL 100	IKE NOBLE (LP)	18

Keith NOBLE & RADO KLOSE

			MINT VALUE £
KEITH NOBLE & RADO KLOSE			
70	Eden EDEN LP 14	MR COMPROMISE (LP,, private pressing, handmade sleeve, white labels)	750
PATSY ANN NOBLE			
61	HMV POP 980	Good Looking Boy/The Guy Who Can Mend A Broken Heart	25
63	Columbia DB 4956	Don't You Ever Change Your Mind/Sour Grapes	15
63	Columbia DB 7008	Heartbreak Avenue/I'm Nobody's Baby	15
63	Columbia DB 7060	I Was Only Foolin' Myself/Ordinary Love	10
63	Columbia DB 7088	Accidents Will Happen/He Tells Me With His Eyes	15
63	Columbia DB 7148	It's Better To Cry Today/Don't Tell Him I Told You	10
64	Columbia DB 7258	I Did Nothing Wrong/Better Late Than Never	10
64	Columbia DB 7318	Private Property/Crack In The Door	10
64	Columbia DB 7386	Tied Up With Mary/Green Eyed People	10
65	Columbia DB 7472	Then You Can Tell Me Goodbye/If You Wanna Be More Than Friends	10
65	Polydor BM 56054	He Who Rides A Tiger/City Of Night	30
(see also Trisha Noble)			
TRISHA NOBLE			
67	MGM MGM 1371	Live For Life/The New Is Rarely Patchka	20
(see also Patsy Ann Noble)			
WOODROW NOBLE			
79	Baby Mother HIT DD10	Reggae A The Best (Feat. Prince Hammer)/Strike The Hammer Wild (12")	30
NOBLE KIND			
86	TNK 001	Back In The Race/Where's Christopher?	15
CLIFF NOBLES (& CO.)			
68	Direction 8-63477	THE HORSE (LP)	25
NO CHOICE			
83	Riot City RIOT 20	SADIST DREAM (EP)	10
NO COVER			
82	Guardian GRC 136	200 Voices/Seen Too Much (some with p/s)	200
NOCTURNAL EMISSIONS			
81	Sterile ION 2	FRUITING BODY (LP)	50
84	Sterile SR 6	NO SACRIFICE (12", p/s, 2,000 only)	12
84	CFC LP 2	CHAOS - LIVE AT THE RITZY (LP)	20
84	Illuminated JAMS LP 33	VIRAL SHEDDING (LP)	20
84	Sterile EMISS 001	TISSUE OF LIES (LP, 1st batch numbered, some with 2 inserts)	75
84	Sterile EMISS 001	TISSUE OF LIES (LP, later pressing in blue sleeve)	30
84	Sterile SR 4	DROWNING IN A SEA OF BLISS (LP)	50
84	Sterile SR 5	BEFEHLSNOTSTAND (LP)	25
85	Sterile SR 7	SONGS OF LOVE AND REVOLUTION (LP)	15
86	Sterile SR 9	SHAKE THOSE CHAINS, RATTLE THOSE CAGES (LP)	15
87	Earthly Delights EARTH 02	THE WORLD IS MY WOMB (LP)	20
88	Earhtly Delights EARTH 04	SPIRITFLESH (LP)	20
89	Earthly Delights EARTH 03	STONEFACE (LP)	15
89	Earthly Delights EARTH 05	BEYOND LOGIC (LP, 250 signed)	25
89	Earthly Delights EARTH 05	BEYOND LOGIC (LP)	18
90	Earthly Delights EARTH 06	MOUTH OF THE BABES (LP)	30
93	Earthly Delights EARTH 08	THE QUICKENING (LP, 250 signed)	25
93	Earthly Delights EARTH 08	THE QUICKENING (LP)	18
(see also Caroline K)			
NOCTURNES (1)			
55	MGM SP 1120	Whodat? (Buck Dance)/Hey Punchinello	10
55	MGM SP 1148	Birmin'ham/Toodle-oo Igaloo	10
NOCTURNES (2)			
64	Solar SRP 102	Trioka/Rawhide	15
NOCTURNES (3)			
67	Columbia DB 8158	Wish You Would Show Me Your Mind/I Do, I Do	10
67	Columbia DB 8219	Why (Am I Treated So Bad?)/Save The Last Dance For Me	10
68	Columbia DB 8332	A New Man/Suddenly Free	10
68	Columbia DB 8453	Carpet Man/Look At Me	15
68	Columbia DB 8493	Montage/Fairground Man	40
68	Columbia S(C)X 6223	THE NOCTURNES (LP)	30
68	Columbia S(C)X 6315	WANTED LIVE (LP)	30
(see also Lyn Paul)			
NOCTURNS			
64	Decca F 12002	Carryin' On/Three Cool Cats	10
NOCTURNUS			
92	Earache MOSH 55	THRESHOLDS (LP)	20
PROFESSOR ERNEST NODE & HIS MUG & JUG BAND			
67	Columbia DB 8100	The Egg Plant That Ate Chicago/I'm In The Doghouse	7
NODENS ICTUS			
87	(No cat no)	THE GROVE OF SELVES (Cassette LP)	50
(see also Ozric Tentacles)			
DICK NOEL			
56	London HLH 8295	(The Same Thing Happens With) The Birds And The Bees/Birth Of The Blues	20
(see also Nick Nobel)			
NOEL & THE FIREBALLS			
70	Pama PM 807	Confussion (sic)/We Got To Have Loving	15
70	Pama PM 808	Can't Turn You Loose/Skinny Legs	18
NO ENTRY BAND			
78	Kube KA 1	COLD AND LONELY LIVES EP (p/s)	10

NO EXIT
80 Slug SLIMY 1   Casablancan Night/Anything You Say (p/s) 8

NO FAITH
81 No Faith NF 001   Double Trouble/Only The Good Die Young (p/s, private pressing)................. 120

JACKY NOGUEZ
60 Pye Int. 7N.25063   Never On Sunday/Chanson Du Jan Gadeiro 6

NOHUMANEYE
82 Rhodium SRS 801   Wet Your Lips/The Owners Loose A Package (p/s) 8

NOIR
71 Dawn DNLS 3029   WE HAD TO LET YOU HAVE IT (LP, with insert) 150

NOISE
79 Rok ROK IX/X   Criminal/BLUE MOVIES: Mary Jane 15

NOISE ANNOYS
80 Adult Entertainment ADD 1   Tomorrow/BATTERY BOYS: Cheap Local Talent (p/s, stamped white labels) 20

NOISE FACTORY
92 3rd Party 3RD#01   MY MIND EP (12") 20
92 3rd Party 3RD#02   THE FIRE EP (12") 75
92 3rd Party 3RD#03   ALIENATION EP (12") 25
92 3rd Party 3RD#04   THE CAPSULE EP (12") 50
93 3rd Party 3RD#05   YEAR OF THE LADIES EP (12") 18
93 Ibiza IR 026   Can You Feel The Rush/Run Come Follow Me (12") 30
93 3rd Party 3RD#07   A NEW SOMETHING EP (12") 25

NOISE TOYS
79 Anti Pop AP 1   Pocket Money/ARTHUR 2 STROKE: The Wundersea World Of Jacques Cousteau (p/s) 7

NOIZ BOIZ
81 Caveman CMR 03   Noiz Boiz/Flashback (p/s) 30

NO KIDDING
74 Wave   NO KIDDING (LP) 15

NO KNOWN CURE
83 Frooty FM 001   Subway/Borderline (stamped white die cut sleeves) 12

DENNIS NOLAN
90 Blakamix BLKM 003   Pillow Talk/Killer Thriller (12") 15

JOE NOLAN & HIS BAND
69 Jolly JY 013   Cool It With Reggae/Reggae With Me 150
69 Jolly JY 016   Confidential/Poison Reggae 40

(see also Bonnie Frankson)

TERRY NOLAND
58 Coral Q 72311   Oh Baby! Look At Me/Puppy Love 80
58 Coral Q 72311   Oh Baby! Look At Me/Puppy Love (78) 25

PIERRE NOLES
63 Oriole CB 1791   Jacqueline/Marilyn 7

NAZ NOMAD & NIGHTMARES
84 Big Beat WIK 21   GIVE DADDY THE KNIFE CINDY (LP, purple vinyl) 20

(see also Damned)

NOMADS (1)
65 Grampian NAN 1008   I'm Coming Home/Hey Little Girl 70

NOMADS (2)
70 Pye 7N 17906   The Singer Sang His Song/Lovin' Him 6

NOMADS (3)
83 Mundane MM 003   The Other Way/One Way Street (no p/s) 6

NO-MAN
90s Hidden Art HA4   Colours/Colours Remodelled (7", promo, fold-out cover, 8 page press sheet) 30
90 Probe Plus PP27T   COLOURS (EP) (12") 35
91 One Little Indian 57TP12   DAYS IN THE TREES EP (12") 20
92 One Little Indian 63TP12   OCEAN SONG EP (12") 20
93 One Little Indian 83TP12   ONLY BABY EP (12") 20
93 Hidden Arts   SPEAK 1988-1989 (cassette) 60
91 One Little Indian TPLP 47M   LOVESIGHS - AN ENTERTAINMENT (LP) 20
93 One Little Indian TPLP 057   LOVEBLOWS & LOVECRIES - A CONFESSION (LP) 50
94 One Little Indian TPLP 067   FLOWERMOUTH (2-LP) 70
06 Tonefloat TF 24   ((SPEAK)) (LP, 12" blue vinyl, 500 only) 30
06 Tonefloat TF 24   ((SPEAK)) (LP) 15
06 Tonefloat TF 26   RETURNING JESUS - THE COMPLETE SESSIONS (3-LP, purple vinyl) 60
06 Tonefloat TF 26   RETURNING JESUS - THE COMPLETE SESSIONS (3-LP) 40
08 Tonefloat TF 48   SCHOOLYARD GHOSTS (2-LP, 7" marbled vinyl) 30
08 Tonefloat TF 48   SCHOOLYARD GHOSTS (2-LP) 20
12 Burning Shed BSHED 1201T   LOVE AND ENDINGS (2-LP, 300 only) 70
15 Kscope KSCOPE 864   SCHOOLYARD GHOSTS (2-LP, reissue) 20
19 Caroline Int. CAROL 020LP   LOVE YOU TO BITS (LP, blue vinyl) 40

(see also Porcupine Tree, Japan, Blackfield, Steven Wilson, Continuum (2))

NO MAN IS AN ISLAND
89 Plastic Head   The Girl From Missouri/Forest Almost Burning/Night Sky Sweet Earth/The Ballet Beast (uncedited) (12") 60

(see also No-Man, Porcupine Tree, Japan)

BILLY NOMATES
20 Invada INV024LP   BILLY NOMATES (LP, red vinyl, 150 copies) 40
20 Invada INV024LP   BILLY NOMATES (LP, gold vinyl, 200 copies) 30

NOMEANSNO
89 Alternative Tentacles VIRUS 77   WRONG (LP, insert) 15
93 Alternative Tentacles VIRUS   WHY DO THEY CALL ME MR. HAPPY (LP) 40

KLAUS NOMI
81	RCA RCALP 6026	KLAUS NOMI (LP)	15
82	RCA PL 70229	SIMPLE MAN (LP)	15

NON
80	Mute MUTE 7	I Can't Look Straight/SMEGMA: Flash Cards (p/s, with 2 centre holes)	20
81	Mute MUTE 015	NON EP (Rise/Out Out Out/Romance Fatal Dentro Deun Auto) (12", p/s)	15
00	Mute MUTE 250	Solitude/Receive The Flame (p/s, two centre holes, A-side plays at 45 rpm, B-side has closed grooves and plays at any speed, 700 copies only)	10
87	Mute STUMM 32	BLOOD AND FLAME (LP)	20

(see also Boyd Rice)

NO NAMES
65	Polydor NH 59080	All Because Of You/She Is Mine	40

NONE SO BLIND
83	Beat Trouser PANT 01	The Virus/My Favourite Eyes	6

NOOKIE
92	Absolute 2 ABS 005DJ	THE LOVE IS EP (12", p/s)	10
92	Reflective REFLECT 003	ACCOUSTIC ASSAULT SQUAD EP (12")	40
93	Reinforced RIVET 1239	RETURN OF NOOKIE EP (12", p/s)	25
94	Reinforced RIVET 1255	Give A Little Love/Give A Little Love (Manix Mix)/Livin' Inside A Dream/T-Three (12")	15
94	Reinforced RIVET 1268	Only You/Celebrate Life (12")	10
95	Reinforced RIVET LP 05	THE SOUND OF MUSIC (2xLP)	40

NOONDAY UNDERGROUND
03	Setana SET 120	I'll Walk Right On (Paul Weller on vocals)/The Light Brigade (Cut Copy Remix)	6
00	Guided Missile GUIDE 45LP	SELF ASSEMBLY (LP)	15

PETER NOONE
71	RAK 114	Oh You Pretty Thing/Together Forever (first pressing with incorrect song title)	15
71	RAK 114	Oh You Pretty Things/Together Forever (second pressing with correct song title)	10
71	RAK 121	Walnut Whirl/Right On Mother	15
72	RAK 129	Shoo Be Doo Ah/Because You're There	6
72	RAK 136	Should I/Each And Every Minute	6
76	Bus Stop BUS 1034	We Don't Need The Money/Love Don't Change	7
77	Bus Stop BUS 1057	Goodbye Sam Hello Samantha/Can I Put My Song In Your Heart	7

NO OTHER NAME
79	Daylight LD 500	DEATH INTO LIFE (LP, with insert)	25

NO QUARTER
83	Reel REEL 1	Survivors/Time And Space/Racing For Home (12", foldout p/s)	40
83	Bonzo Bear	BIRDS OF PREY EP (12")	30

NORA/BUNNY
72	Tropical AL 0015	Butterfly/TROPICAL ALL STARS: Fly Version	8

NORBITON SURFERS
80	Hut S/80/CUS 700	Ivor The Engine/My Ego Dies (DIY p/s)	30

KEN NORDINE
57	London RE-D 1091	KEN NORDINE READS (EP, with Billy Vaughn Orchestra)	10
59	London Jazz EZ-D 19040	WORD JAZZ (EP)	15
67	Philips BL 7785	COLOURS (LP)	70

(see also Billy Vaughn & His Orchestra)

NORFOLK & JOY
79	Dara MPA 031	SCOTSOUNDS (LP)	30

NO RIGHT TURN
83	Chelful CHL 001	NO (LP)	25

NORMA & TONY
69	(No Cat. No.)	YOU ARE ALWAYS WELCOME AT OUR HOUSE (LP, private pressing, 100 only)	80

NORMAL
78	Mute MUTE 001	Warm Leatherette/T.V.O.D (p/s)	15
11	Mute MUTE 001	Warm Leatherette/T.V.O.D (p/s, reissue, white vinyl, 500 only)	7

(see also Robert Rental)

NORMAL DAY
81	BRS 007 ND1	Somebody Said/Angelina, Angelina (no p/s)	20

NORMAN CONQUEST
67	MGM MGM 1376	Two People/Upside Down	120

(see also Factory, Peter & Wolves, John Pantry)

NORMAN & HOOLIGANS
77	President PT 461	I'm A Punk/Re-Entry	20

NORMAN & INVADERS
64	United Artists UP 1031	Stacey/Our Wedding Day	12
64	United Artists UP 1058	Our Wedding Day/Stacey (reissue)	6
65	United Artists UP 1077	Night Train To Surbiton/Likely Lads	12

LARRY NORMAN
81	Solid Rock CS 103A	I Feel Like Dying/Alwyn Wall - Hold On	12
76	Solid Rock ROCKY 1	IN ANOTHER LAND (LP, gatefold sleeve)	15

MONTY NORMAN
55	HMV 7M 349	The Shifting, Whispering Sands/Bonnie Blue Gal	8
57	HMV POP 281	The Garden Of Eden/Priscilla	8
63	United Artists UEP 1010	EXCERPTS FROM DR.NO - FILM SOUNDTRACK (EP)	20
63	United Artists ULP 1097	DOCTOR NO (LP, soundtrack, mono)	50
63	United Artists (S)ULP 1097	DOCTOR NO (LP, soundtrack, stereo)	100

OLIVER NORMAN
67	Polydor 56176	Down In The Basement/Drowning In My Own Despair	150
68	Polydor 56247	People People/You'll Find It Will Come	6

NORMIL HAWAIIANS
- 80 Dining Out TUX 13   The Beat Goes On/Ventilation (p/s) 8
- 81 Illuminated ILL 7   Still Obedient/Should You Forget? (p/s) 8
- 81 Red Rhino RED 8   GALA FAILED (12" EP, p/s) 10
- 82 Illuminated JAMS 23   MORE WEALTH THAN MONEY (2-LP) 30
- 84 Illuminated JAMS 28   WHAT'S GOING ON? (LP) 30

ROY NORTH
- 63 Oak RGJ 107   Blues In Three/Blues In Five 50

TOM NORTHCOTT
- 68 Warner Bros WB 7160   1941/Other Times 12

NORTHERN LIGHT
- 75 CBS 3370   Minnesota/Minnesota (DJ Version) 25

NORTHERN LIGHTS (1)
- 66 United Artists UP 1123   No Time/Time To Move Along 50
- 66 United Artists UP 1161   Through Darkness, Light/Baby Those Are The Rules 50

(see also Hooten[anny] Singers, Abba)

NORTHERN LIGHTS (2)
- 79 MPA SMP 077   Bad Girl/Exodus (no p/s) 25

NORTHERN PICTURE LIBRARY
- 93 Vinyl Japan TASK 6   Love Song For The Dead Che/The Way That Stars Die (12", p/s) 18
- 94 Vinyl Japan TASK 25   BLUE DISSOLVE EP (12", p/s) 18
- 94 Sarah SARAH 94   Paris/Norfolk Windmills (p/s, insert) 35
- 94 Sarah SARAH 95   Last September's Farewell Kiss/Signs (p/s, insert) 35
- 93 Vinyl Japan ASKLP 23   ALASKA (LP) 50

(see also the Field Mice)

NORTHERN JAZZ ORCHESTRA
- 79 SRTY 79 CUS 410   THAT'S THE ONE (LP) 15

NORTHSIDE
- 91 Factory FACT 310   CHICKEN RHYHMS (LP) 25

NORTH STARS
- 65 Fontana TF 581   For My True Love/Nothing But The Best 10
- 66 Fontana TF 726   She's So Far Out She's In/Eeenie Meenie Minee Mo 30

N.W. 10
- 79 Low Brow LBW1   TAKE-AWAYS EP (p/s) 8

NORTHWIND
- 71 Regal Zono. SLRZ 1020   SISTER, BROTHER, LOVER (LP) 350

(see also Elastic Band)

NOSEBLEEDS
- 77 Rabid TOSH 12   Ain't Bin To No Music School/Fascist Pigs (p/s) 30

(see also Durutti Column, Ed Banger, Blue Orchids)

NO SECURITY
- 89 Peaceville VILE 11   BURY THE DEBT NOT THE DEAD (split LP with DOOM) 18

NO SMOKE
- 89 Warriors Beat WAFT 11   Koro Koro/Black Is Black/Koro Koro (Dub Dance)/(Dub Dance II) (12") 15
- 90 Warriors Dance WAFT 17   International Smoke Signals (Dancin Mix)/(Chantin Mix)/Ra Ra...East Of Eden (Addis Mix)/(Original Version) (12") 20

NO SPORTS
- 90 Unicorn PHZA-6   Stay Rude Say Rebel/Tour De France/Love Song/Girl (Tango) (12", p/s) ... 12
- 87 Unicorn PHZ 49   KING SKA (LP) 15

NOSTROMO
- 79 Bronze BRO 80   Alien/Around The World In 60 Seconds ('Alien' p/s) 7
- 79 Bronze BRO 12BRO80   Alien/Around The World In 60 Seconds (12", 'Alien' p/s) 15

NO SWEAT (1)
- 79 Rip Off RIP 4   Start All Over Again/You Should Be So Lucky (p/s) 30

(see also Clive Culbertson)

NO SWEAT (2)
- 78 Eel Pie EPS 002   Work On Her/Gimme Some Action 6

NOTATIONS (U.K.)
- 72 Chapter One SCH 174   Need Your Love/Just Nothing Left To Give 25

NOTATIONS (U.S.)
- 76 Curtom K 56211   NOTATIONS (LP) 30

FREDDIE NOTES & RUDIES
- 69 Downtown DT 427   I Don't Wanna Lose That Girl/Train From Vietnam 20
- 69 Grape GR 3010   Guns Of Navarone/Yester-Me, Yester-You 50
- 69 Grape GR 3011   Babylon/Girl I've Got A Date 20
- 69 Trojan TR 7713   Shanghai/Rome Wasn't Built In A Day 15
- 70 Bullet BU 421   The Feeling Is Fine/Girl You're Killing Me 12
- 70 Trojan TMX 531   Rocco/The Bull (white labels only) 150
- 70 Trojan TR 7724   Rocco/Don't Tell Your Mama 60
- 70 Trojan TR 7734   Down On The Farm/Easy Street 30
- 70 Trojan TR 7791   Montego Bay/RUDIES: Blue Mountain 10
- 70 Trojan TR 7810   Walk A Mile In My Shoes/JOHNNY ARTHEY ORCHESTRA: Reggae Rouser 6
- 70 Duke DU 63   The Bull/River Ben Come Up 75
- 70 Duke DU 68   Chicken Inn/Chicken Scratch 15
- 70 B&C CB 125   It Came Out The Sky/Well Oh Well (p/s) 6
- 70 Trojan TBL 109   UNITY (LP) 25
- 70 Trojan TBL 152   MONTEGO BAY (LP) 20

NOTHINGS
- 65 CBS 201779   At Times Like This/Love So Sweet 15

NOTSENSIBLES
- 79 Redball RR 02   (I'm In Love With) Margaret Thatcher/Little Boxes/Gary Bushell's Band Of The Week (p/ 30

NOTTINGHAM JAZZ ORCHESTRA

MINT VALUE £

80	Bent SMALL BENT 5	Death To Disco/Coronation Street Hustle/Lying On The Sofa (p/s)	25
80	Snotty Snail NELCOL 2	(I'm In Love With) Margaret Thatcher/Little Boxes/Gary Bushell's Band Of The Week (p/s, reissue)	12
80	Snotty Snail NELCOL 3	I Thought You Were Dead/I Make A Balls Of Everything I Do/Teenage Revolution (p/s)	12
81	Snotty Snail NELCOL 6	I Am The Bishop/The Telephone Rings Again (p/s)	10
80	Bent BIGBENT 6	INSTANT CLASSICS (LP)	50
80	Snotty Snail SSLP 1	INSTANT CLASSICS (LP, reissue)	30

NOTTINGHAM JAZZ ORCHESTRA
71	Swift SP 55	FESITVAL SUITE (LP)	50

NOTTS ALLIANCE
72	Tradition TSR 011	THE CHEERFUL 'ORN (LP, with Roy Harris)	15

NOUVELLE VAGUE
95	Peacefrog PFG 051	NOUVELLE VAGUE (LP, inner)	35
06	Peacefrog PFG 079	BANDE A PART (LP, poster)	20

HEATHER NOVA
93	Big Life BFL LP2	GLOW STARS (LP)	80

NOVA LOCAL
69	MCA MUPS 377	NOVA 1 (LP)	40

PAUL NOVA
82	Exhibit 1 EX 001	Julie Ann/Video Age	60
83	Exhibit 1 EX 002	Famous Boys/Home Sweet Home	60
85	Exhibit 1 EX 004	FANTASY AND FEELING EP	60
84	Exhibit 1 EX 003	TREES WITHOUT LEAVES (LP)	300

NOVAK
97	Enraptured WORM 2	Silver Seas/Schmaltz (p/s in outer hand-sewn cloth sleeve with embroidered "Hand-knitted by Novak" label, 200 only, each different)	15
97	Enraptured WORM 2	Silver Seas/Schmaltz (p/s, 800 only)	8
97	Kitty Kitty CHOOSY 007	Rapunzel/Almost Chinook (hand crayoned p/s, 1,000 only)	8

NOVAS (1)
63	RCA RCA 1360	Push A Little Harder/Oh, Gee Baby!	30

NOVAS (2)
65	London HLU 9940	The Crusher/Take 7	35

NOVEAU RICHE
81	Long Vehicle CND 1	Modern Disease/Soul Boy (no p/s)	50

KAREN NOVOTNY X
10	Great Pop Supplement GPS 66	UNTITLED EP (300 only)	10

NOW (1)
69	NEMS 56-4125	Marcia/The Hands On My Clock Stand Still	35
73	President PT 401	I Wanna Be Free/People Are Standing	12

NOW (2)
77	Ultimate ULT 401	Development Corporations/Why (p/s)	20
77	Ultimate ULT 401	Development Corporations/Why (p/s, blue vinyl)	40
79	Raw RAW 31	Into The 80s/Nine O'Clock (no p/s, 800 only)	200

NO WAY
78	Our Own IS/NW/1035	Breaking Point/TV Pox/30 Seconds (p/s)	200

NOW GENERATION
73	Green Door GD 4055	Alone Again, Naturally/MIND-BODY-SOUL: My Part (Version)	8
73	Pyramid PYR 7007	Baby Don't Do It/You'll Never Know	8
74	Trojan TRLS 78	FOR THE GOOD TIMES (LP)	25

(see also I Roy, B.B. Seaton, Audley Rollins)

NOYES BROTHERS
80	Object Music OBJ 009/010	SHEEP FROM GOATS (2-LP)	25

(see also Steve Miro & Eyes, Spherical Objects)

NOY'S BAND
74	Dawn 1075	Love Potion Number 9/Eldorado	10

(see also Jan Dukes De Grey)

NOYS OF US
60s	KPS KPS 502	He's Alright Jill/What Can I Do	30

NQB
72	Epic S EPC 2151	Long Long Weekend/Free The People	6

N.R.B.Q. (NEW RHYTHM & BLUES QUINTET)
69	CBS 63653	N.R.B.Q. (LP)	20

(see also Carl Perkins)

N.S.U.
69	Stable SLE 8002	TURN ON OR TURN ME DOWN (LP)	200

PETE NU
80	No label or cat no	Moroccan Reggae/Dub Version (no p/s, handwritten white labels)	10

GUITAR NUBBITT
64	Bootleg 501	Georgia Chain Gang/Hard Road (99 copies only)	45
60s	XX MIN 705	GUITAR NUBBITT (EP)	20

NUCLEAR ASSAULT
88	Under One Flag 12 FLAG 107	GOOD TIMES, BAD TIMES (12" EP)	10
88	Under One Flag FLAG 21P	SURVIVE (LP, picture disc)	15
88	Under One Flag FLAG 21	SURVIVE (LP)	20
89	Under One Flag FLAG 35	HANDLE WITH CARE (LP)	20

NUCLEAR SOCKETTS
81	Subversive SUB 001	HONOUR BEFORE GLORY (EP, folded p/s, 33rpm)	25
81	Subversive SUB 002	Play Loud/Shadow On The Map	25
82	None	Riot Squad (magazine flexi-disc with fold out picture insert)	20

(ian CARR'S) NUCLEUS

MINT VALUE £

(IAN CARR'S) NUCLEUS

70	Vertigo 6360 008	ELASTIC ROCK (LP, die cut gatefold sleeve, large swirl label) 200
70	Vertigo 6360 008	ELASTIC ROCK (LP, die cut gatefold sleeve, later 'spaceship' label) 60
71	Vertigo 6360 027	WE'LL TALK ABOUT IT LATER (LP, die cut gatefold sleeve, large swirl label).............. 200
71	Vertigo 6360 027	WE'LL TALK ABOUT IT LATER (LP, die cut gatefold sleeve, 'spaceship' label) 60
71	Vertigo 6360 039	SOLAR PLEXUS (LP, as Ian Carr's Nucleus, 1st pressing, gatefold sleeve, large swirl label) 250
72	Vertigo 6360 076	BELLADONNA (LP, as Ian Carr, 1st pressing, Matrix side 1, 6360076 1Y//1 1 1 3 Side 2, 6360076 2Y//1 1 1 3, gatefold sleeve, swirl label) 250
73	Vertigo 6360 039	SOLAR PLEXUS (LP, as Ian Carr's Nucleus, 2nd pressing, gatefold sleeve, small swirl label) 100
74	Vertigo 6360 076	BELLADONNA (LP, as Ian Carr, 2nd pressing, Matrix side 1, 6360076 1Y//1 1 1 4 Side 2, 6360076 2Y//1 1 1 5, gatefold sleeve, swirl label) 100
73	Vertigo 6360 091	LABYRINTH (LP, 'spaceship' label, any with swirl are Italian pressings!) 60
73	Vertigo 6360 100	ROOTS (LP, 'spaceship' label) 150
74	Vertigo 6360 110	UNDER THE SUN (LP, 'spaceship' label) 70
75	Vertigo 6360 076	BELLADONNA (LP, as Ian Carr, gatefold sleeve, 'spaceship' label) 60
75	Vertigo 6360 119	SNAKE HIPS ETCETERA (LP, laminated sleeve, 'spaceship' label) 50
75	Vertigo 6360 124	ALLEY CAT (LP, 'spaceship' label) 100
76	Vertigo 6360 039	SOLAR PLEXUS (LP, as Ian Carr's Nucleus, 3rd pressing gatefold sleeve, 'spaceship' label) . 30
76	Vertigo 9286 019	DIRECT HITS (LP, 'spaceship' label) 40
77	Capitol EST 11771	IN FLAGRANTI DELICTO (LP) 40
79	Capitol E-ST 11916	OUT OF THE LONG DARK (LP) 30
89	BGO LP 47	ELASTIC ROCK (LP, reissue) 15
14	Timeless TIME 733	SOLAR PLEXUS (LP, reissue) 18
14	Gearbox GB 1529	LIVE 1970 (2-LP) 20
21	Be With BEWITH102LP	ROOTS (LP, reissue) 20

(see also Don Rendell & Ian Carr Quintet, Neil Ardley, Centipede, Michael Garrick, New Jazz Orchestra, Linda Hoyle)

TED NUGENT (& AMBOY DUKES)

74	Discreet K 19200	Sweet Revenge/Ain't It The Truth (as Ted Nugent & Amboy Dukes) 8
75	Discreet K 59203	CALL OF THE WILD (LP) 15

(see also [American] Amboy Dukes)

NUGGETS

55	Capitol CL 14216	Quirl Up In My Arms/So Help Me, I Love You 12
55	Capitol CL 14267	Shtiggy Boom/Anxious Heart 12

GARY NUMAN

SINGLES

79	Beggars Banquet BEG 23	Cars/Asylum (p/s, orange plastic labels) 6
79	Beggars Banquet BEG 23	Cars/Asylum (p/s, 'mispressed' on dark red vinyl) 10
79	Beggars Banquet BEG 29	Complex/Bombers (live) (p/s, 'mispressed' on dark red vinyl) 18
80	Beggars Banquet BEG 35	We Are Glass/Trois Gymnopedies (First Movement) (p/s, custom factory pressings on green and yellow vinyl) 500
80	Beggars Banquet BEG 35	We Are Glass/Trois Gymnopedies (1st Movement) (p/s, 'mispressed' on dark red vinyl)... 12
80	Beggars Banquet BEG 46	I Die, You Die/Down In The Park (Piano Version) (p/s, dark red vinyl 'mispress') 8
80	Beggars Banquet BEG 46	I Die, You Die/Down In The Park (Piano Version) (p/s, mispressing, plays Remember I Was Vapour & "On Broadway" [SAM 126]) 22
81	Beggars Banquet BEG 62	She's Got Claws/I Sing Rain (p/s, mispressing, plays Dollar's Hand Held In Black And White) 60
82	Beggars Banquet BEG 77	We Take Mystery (To Bed)/The Image Is (mispressed sleeve, no writing) 35
83	Beggars Banquet BEG 95P	Warriors/My Car Slides (Uncut, aeroplane-shaped picture disc) 400
84	Beggars Banquet TUB 1	This Is My Life (unissued promo for "THE PLAN LP", 300 white label test pressings only) 100
85	Numa NUP 9	Your Fascination/We Need It (mispressed picture disc with pictures on the wrong side)... 18
85	Numa NU PROMO 1002	WHITE NOISE (12" 4-track sampler Beserker/We Are Glass/Cars/Are "Friends" Electric?) 30
85	Numa NUM 7	THE LIVE EP (12", p/s, custom factory pressing on multicoloured vinyl) 200
85	Numa NUM 13	Miracles (Extended)/The Fear (Extended) (12" mispressed sleeve: no red writing) 30
86	Numa NUMX 16	This Is Love/Survival/Call Out The Dogs (Extended)/No Shelter/This Ship Comes Apart (12", p/s, stickered double pack, shrinkwrapped) 10
86	Numa NUP 17	I Can't Stop/Faces (Uncut, aeroplane-shaped picture disc) 100
86	Numa NUM 17 DJ	I Can't Stop (Special Club Mix) (12" 1-sided DJ promo) 10
87	Beggars Banquet BEG 199T	Cars Extended E Reg Model/Are Friends Electric?/Cars (E Reg Model)/Cars (Motorway Mix) (12" yellow/green/silver labels, export copies p/s) 25
88	I.R.S. ILSPD 1004	America/Respect (live) (mispressed picture disc, 'Gary' picture both sides) 45
91	I.R.S. NUMAN 1	Heart/Icehouse (p/s, black vinyl) 6
92	Numa NU 24DJ	Machine & Soul/Machine & Soul (fan club issue, white label, mail-order only) 8
93	Beggars Banquet BEG 264T	Cars (Multivalve)/Cars (Endurance Model)/Cars (Top Gear Model) (12", black vinyl, promo only) 12
93	Beggars Banquet BEG 264	Cars ('93 Sprint)/Cars (Top Gear) (poster p/s) 6
93	Beggars Banquet BEG 246L	Cars ('93 Sprint)/Cars (Endurance (Uncut McLaren F1-shaped picture disc) 175
93	Beggars Banquet	Cars ('93 Sprint)/(Multivalve)/(Classic)/(Endurance)/(Top Gear)/(Motorway Mix)/ ('E' Reg Version) (CD, withdrawn, Extended 'E' Reg Model replaces Motorway Mix) 30
93	Beggars Banquet BEG 264CD	Cars '93 Sprint)/(Multivalve)/(Classic)/(Endurance)/(Top Gear)/(Motorway Mix)/'E' Reg Model) (CD, Autosports Awards issue, 300 only) 40
94	Numa NUM 26	A Question Of Faith (12", withdrawn, black labels with blue print) 25
94	Numa NU 26	A Question Of Faith/Whisper Of Truth (fan club issue, white label, mail-order only) 25
96	The Record Label SPIND 6	Radio (with N.R.G.)/Radio (extended mix) (CD, withdrawn) 150
17	Electronic Sound 107481	My Name Is Ruin (Meat Beat Manifesto Poison Remix) Part One/Part Two (p/s) 20

ALBUMS

80	Beggars Banquet BEGA 19	TELEKON (LP, dark red vinyl 'mispressing', with stickered sleeve.; with bonus single SAM 126 "Remember I Was Vapour [live]"/"On Broadway" [Live]) 20
80	Beggars Banquet BEGA 19	TELEKON (LP, dark red vinyl 'mispressing', with stickered sleeve) 15
84	B. Banquet BEGA 55P	THE PLAN (LP, picture disc) 15

NUMBER NINE BREAD STREET

MINT VALUE £

84	Numa NUP 4	BESERKER (Uncut picture disc)	375
84	Numa NUMA 1001	BESERKER (LP, mispressing, plays Imagination's GOLD on side 2)	80
86	Numa NUMAP 1003	THE FURY (LP, mispress picture disc, "Your Fascination" 12" photo on A-side with lyric insert)	25
86	Numa GNFCDA 1	IMAGES 1 & 2 (2-LP, fan club issue with photo inserts, mail-order only, initial signed copies)	20
87	Numa GNFCDA 2	IMAGES 3 & 4 (2-LP, fan club issue with photo inserts, mail-order only, initial signed copies)	20
87	Numa GNFCDA 3	IMAGES 5 & 6 (2-LP, fan club issue with photo inserts, mail-order only, initial signed copies)	20
87	Numa GNF CDA 4	IMAGES 7 & 8 (2-LP, fan club issue with photo inserts, mail-order only, initial signed copies)	20
89	Numa GNF CDA 5	IMAGES 9 & 10 (2-LP, fan club issue with photo inserts, mail-order only, initial signed copies)	20
88	Beggars Banquet BBL 47	WARRIORS (LP, 'Lowdown' reissue, white lettering on sleeve)	35
94	Numa NUMA 1010	DREAM CORROSION (3-LP, autographed gatefold sleeve; copies bought at HMV with signed 10" x 8" photo)	20
94	Numa NUMA 1011	SACRIFICE (LP, with lyric sheet, stickered sleeve & bonus single: The Seed Of A Lie [5.26]/"The Seed Of A Lie [7.07]")	40
96	Polygram TV 531 149-2	PREMIER HITS (CD, mispressing, plays Mark Knogfler's Golden Heart)	40
98	Eagle EAGBX025	THE NUMA YEARS (5-CD set of Beserker, The Fury, Strange Charm, Machine and Soul Sacrifice..)	40
03	Jagged Halo JHLP 5	HYBRID (2-LP, numbered gatefold sleeve)	30
06	Mortal Records LP001	JAGGED (1,000 only, white vinyl, first 250 copies hand signed, numbered and sold via offical Gary Numan website)	45
06	Mortal Records LP001	JAGGED (LP, 1,000 only, white vinyl)	25
08	OTB LP1	PURE (LP, 300 pressed in purple/red/clear vinyl (100 of each). Final 2 tracks pressed on separate yellow vinyl 7)	35
08	OTB LP2	EXILE (LP, 300 copies, turquoise/white/orange vinyl (100 of each)	30
08	VIN 180 LP 001	THE PLEASURE PRINCIPLE (LP, reissue)	15
10	Vinyl 180 VIN180LP027	1978/79 (4-LP box set, 500 copies comprising of Tubeway Army/Replicas/The Pleasure Principle and The Plan only for those who had bought earlier reissues of Replicas and The Pleasure Principle)	90
11	Vinyl 180 VIN180LP038	1980/81 (5-LP box set, Telekon 2-LPs, and Living Ornaments 3-LPs))	60
11	Vinyl 180 VIN180LP037	TELEKON (2-LP reissue in gatefold sleeve)	25
12	Let Them Eat Vinyl LETV044LP	EXILE (2-LP, grey vinyl)	80
13	Mortal MORTAL LP 14	SPLINTER (2-LP, first issue with limited edition 12" x 12" signed print sold via official Gary Numan website)	30
15	Beggars Banquet BBQLP 10	THE PLEASURE PRINCIPLE (LP, reissue, grey vinyl, 600 copies, gig only)	40
15	Beggars Banquet BBQLP 19	TELEKON (LP, reissue, red vinyl, 600 copies, gig only)	45
21	Ear Music 0216425EMX	EXILE (LP, reissue, obi, silver vinyl)	50

(see also Tubeway Army, Paul Gardiner, Dramatis, Claire Hamill, Radio Heart, Nicky Robson, Paper Toys, Caroline Munro, Generator, Bauhaus, Bill Sharpe, Sharpe & Numan, Battles)

NUMBER NINE BREAD STREET

| 67 | Holy Ground HG 112/1109 | NUMBER NINE BREAD STREET (LP, 250 copies only) | 400 |

NUMBERS

79	Blasto SRTS 79/CUS/358	ROCK STARS (EP, with insert)	50
80s	Homegrown HG 701	Here Today/Put 'Em All To Shame/Another Day/Tear You Down (photocopied or green & white sleeve; with poster)	10
80s	Homegrown HG 701	Here Today/Put 'Em All To Shame/Another Day/Tear You Down (photocopied or green & white sleeve; without poster)	10

NUMSKULLZ

96	High Noon NUM003	Enough Of That (12")	12
98	Hombre MEX003	Signs Of The End/The Difference (12")	10
98	Hombre MEX005	THE UNEXPECTED (EP)	10
00	Hombre MEX 018	AD INFINITUM (LP)	15

NU NOTES

| 63 | HMV POP 1232 | Hall Of Mirrors/Fury | 20 |
| 64 | HMV POP 1311 | Kathy/Sunset | 20 |

(see also Russ Sainty & Nu Notes)

NUNS

| 81 | Butt FUN 2 | Wild/Suicide Child (p/s) | 15 |
| 81 | Butt ALSO 001 | THE NUNS (LP) | 15 |

NURON

| 93 | Likemind LM 02 | Likemind 02 (12", 2 tracks by Nuron and 2 by Fugue) (12") | 60 |

(see also Stasis)

NURSE WITH WOUND

83	L.A.Y.L.A.H. LAY 3	GYLLENSKÖLD, GEIJERSTAM AND I AT RYDBERG'S (12" EP)	40
84	L.A.Y.L.A.H. LAY 7	BRAINED BY FALLING MASONRY (12" EP)	12
86	Torso 33016	SPIRAL INSANA (12" EP)	12
87	Crystal/Wisewound WW 01	Crank/TERMITE QUEEN: Wisecrack (numbered plain black sleeve with printed band, 500 only)	20
88	Yangki 002	FAITH'S FAVOURITES EP: Swamp Rat (with Current 93)/Ballad Of The Pale Girl (12", laminated p/s)	30
88	Idle Hole MIRROR 003	Cooloorta Moon/Great Empty Space (12", p/s)	20
90	Harbinger 001	The Burial Of The Stoned Sardine/CURRENT 93: No Hiding From The Blackbird	15
90	United Dairies UD 031	SORESUCKER EP: I Am The Poison/Journey Through Cheese (12", p/s, 2,000 only)	20
90	Shock SX 004	Sinister Senile: Human Human Human/Psychedelic Underground (45/33rpm, 1,000 only)	25
92	Clawfist 12	Steel Dream March Of The Metal Men/The Dadda's Intoxication ('singles club' release, 33rpm, foldover p/s in poly bag, 1,400 only)	15
93	Clawfist 20	CRUMB DUCK (10" EP, shared with Stereolab, 37 with handmade p/s (Gain/Sadier only)	100
93	Clawfist 20	CRUMB DUCK (10" EP, shared with Stereolab, 1450 regular without handmade p/s)	20

NU-SOUND EXPRESS LTD.

MINT VALUE £

Year	Label/Cat.	Title	Value
93	World Serpent WS 7003	Alien (1-sided, company sleeve 1,000 only)	25
95	WN 001	ALICE THE GOON (1-sided 12", p/s, 500 only)	75
04	United Durtro – UNITED DURTRO/JNANA 1974	HAVING FUN WITH THE PRINCE OF DARKNESS (7", p/s, insert, signed by Stapleton, also 'stamped' with image of Stapleton, UK edition of 40 copies)	70
79	United Dairies UD 01	CHANCE MEETING ON A DISSECTING TABLE OF A SEWING MACHINE AND AN UMBRELLA (LP, 500 only, originals have hand-painted numbers; beware of bootlegs with printed numbers)	200
80	United Dairies UD 03	TO THE QUIET MEN FROM A TINY GIRL (LP, numbered, 500 only, originals have hand-painted numbers; beware of bootlegs with printed numbers)	150
80	United Dairies UD 04	MERZBILD SCHWET (LP, numbered, 500 only, originals have hand-painted numbers; beware of bootlegs with printed numbers)	150
81	United Dairies UD 08	INSECT AND INDIVIDUAL SILENCED (LP, 500 only)	80
83	Mi Mort MI MORT iii	GYLLENSKÖLD, GEIJERSTAM & FRIENDS, LIVE AT BAR MALDOROR (LP, some with insert)	40
83	Third Mind TMR 03	OSTRANENIE 1913 (LP, 3,000 only)	60
85	L.A.Y.L.A.H. LAY 15	THE SYLVIE AND BABS HI-FI COMPANION (LP, gatefold sleeve)	25
85	United Dairies UD 110	DRUNK WITH THE OLD MAN OF THE MOUNTAINS (LP)	25
85	United Dairies UD 012	HOMOTOPY TO MARIE (LP, 5,000 only)	35
86	United Dairies UD 019	AUTOMATING VOL. 1 (LP, 3,000 only)	30
86	United Dairies UD 020	A MISSING SENSE (LP, 1 side only; other side by Organum; 2,000 only)	30
87	United Dairies UD 025	DRUNK WITH THE OLD MAN OF THE MOUNTAINS (LP, reissue, handmade custom sleeve, with insert, signed, 100 only)	150
88	United Dairies UD 027	ALAS THE MADONNA DOES NOT FUNCTION (mini-LP, 45/33rpm, 3,000 only)	25
88	Idle Hole MIRROR ONE	SOLILOQUY FOR LILITH (3-LP box set, 1,000 only)	80
88	Idle Hole MIRROR 1C	SOLILOQUY FOR LILITH PTS 5/6 (LP, with insert)	25
89	Idle Hole MIRROR TWO	PRESENTS THE SISTERS OF PATAPHYSICS (LP, 1,000 only)	25
89	United Dairies UD 030	AUTOMATING VOL. II (LP)	20
89	United Dairies UD 032	A SUCKED ORANGE (LP, with full colour insert)	35
89	United Dairies UD 032	A SUCKED ORANGE (LP)	30
89	Yangki 003	LUMBS SISTER (LP)	30
90	United Dairies UD 134	PSILOTRIPITAKA (3-LP [UD 01, 03 & 04], with bonus LP "Registered Nurse" [UD 00], 1,000 only, in leather bag)	400
90	United Dairies UD 134	PSILOTRIPITAKA (3-LP [UD 01, 03 & 04], with bonus LP "Registered Nurse" [UD 00], 1,000 only)	150
90	United Dairies UD 134CD	PSILOTRIPITAKA (3-CD [UD 01, 03 & 04], with bonus CD "Registered Nurse" [UD 00CD], 1,000 only, 30 in 'leather bondage bag')	400
90	United Dairies UD 134CD	PSILOTRIPITAKA (3-CD [UD 01, 03 & 04], with bonus CD "Registered Nurse" [UD 00CD], 1,000 only))	60
90	L.A.Y.L.A.H. LAY 30	BRAINED/GYLLENSKÖLD (LP, withdrawn)	35
90	United Dairies UD 01	CHANCE MEETING ON A DISSECTING TABLE OF A SEWING MACHINE AND AN UMBRELLA (LP, reissue)	50
90	United Dairies UD 04	MERZBILD SCHWET (LP, reissue)	40
91	United Dairies UD 038	CREAKINESS (LP, with Spasm)	20
91	United Dairies UD 09	THE 150 MURDEROUS PASSIONS (LP)	30
91	United Dairies UD 09CD	THE 150 MURDEROUS PASSIONS (CD, sealed in black plastic, 500 only)	30
93	United Dairies UD 059	CRUMB DUCK (LP, shared with Stereolab, reissue of Clawfist EP, 50 copies on pink vinyl)	50
93	United Dairies UD 059	CRUMB DUCK (LP, shared with Stereolab, reissue of Clawfist EP, 500 on fluorescent yellow vinyl)	25
94	United Dairies UD 043	SECOND PIRATE SESSION - ROCK'N'ROLL STATION - SPECIAL EDITION (LP, red vinyl, 500 only)	40
99	United Dairies UD 056	AN AWKWARD PAUSE (2-LP, translucent grey vinyl, 500 only, 1 side not available on CD)	40
00	United Dairies UD 081	ALICE THE GOON (1-sided reissue, 800 copies)	50
02	United Durtro UD 102	MAN WITH THE WOMAN FACE (LP, ltd. edition clear vinyl, poly sleeve, 2 inserts)	15
03	United Dairies UD 110	DRUNK WITH THE OLD MAN OF THE MOUNTAINS (LP, reissue)	25
00s	United Dairies UDX 092	SOLILOQUY FOR LILITH (3-CD box set)	30
07	United Dairies UD 08.C	INSECT AND INDIVIDUAL SILENCED (CD, 120 copies numbered with "insect")	90
09	United Dirter DPROMOCD 72	THE SURVEILLANCE LOUNGE/THE MEMORY SURFACE (3-CD)	30
09	United Dirter DPROMDLP71	CHANCE MEETING ON A DISSECTING TABLE OF A SEWING MACHINE AND AN UMBRELLA (2-LP, reissue, box set, T-shirt, badge, numbered, 250 only)	60
09	United Dirter DPROMDLP71	CHANCE MEETING ON A DISSECTING TABLE OF A SEWING MACHINE AND AN UMBRELLA (2-LP, reissue)	35
16	Dirtier DPROMBX119	SOLILOQUY FOR LILITH (4-LP box set reissue)	50

(see also Current 93, Organum/New Blockaders, Diana Rogerson, Sol Invictus, Steven Stapleton & David Tibet, Tibet & Stapleton, Whitehouse)

NU-SOUND EXPRESS LTD.

72	Pye Int'l 7N 25580	One More Time Y'all/A Rose For A Lady	20

NUTHIN' FANCY

80	Dynamic Cat DC 1001	Looking For A Good Time/Too Much Rock'n'Roll (p/s)	250

(see also Terraplane, Thunder)

NU TORNADOS

58	London HLU 8756	Philadelphia U .S.A./Magic Record	10

NUTRONS

60s	Melodisc M 1593	The Very Best Things/Stop For The Music	15

NUTSHELL

77	Myrrh MYR 1056	FLYAWAY (LP, inner)	18
75	Myrrh MYR 1029	IN YOUR EYES (LP, lyric inner sleeve)	20

MAY'F NUTTER

66	Vocalion VL 9282	Head Shrinker/Don't Know What To Do	15
73	London HLL 10414	I Don't Care/Hitch Hike Nightmare	6

NUTTY SQUIRRELS

59	Pye Int. 7N.25044	Uh! Oh! (Pts. 1 & 2)	7

NUTZ

75	A&M AMLS 68306	NUTZ TOO (LP)	15

(see also Rage, Nightwing)

NUYORICAN SOUL

			MINT VALUE £
NUYORICAN SOUL			
97	Talkin Loud 534 451-1	NUYORICAN SOUL (2-LP)	30
96	Talkin Loud 578 795-1	NUYORICAN SOUL (6 x 12" box set)	40
NYAH FEARTIES			
86	Nya DOPLP 001	A TASTY HEIDFUL (LP)	25
NYAH SHUFFLE			
70	Grape GR 3021	Sting Ray/Paradise	60
70	Grape GR 3019	Boot Lace/Honey Won't You Stay?	35
NYAM NYAM			
81	Vital VTL 004	When We Can't Make Laughter Stay/Knowledge (Chapter II)	10
ADOMAKO NYAMEKYE			
82	YEB YEB 002	ANO PLAN (LP)	40
83	YEB OLB 506	KA NEA MAYE (LP)	60
JUDY NYLON			
82	On-U-Sound LP 16	PAL JUDY (LP)	40
(see also John Cale, Snatch)			
NYLONS			
82	Attic NYLON 1	A Million Ways/Up On The Roof (p/s)	8
MICHAEL NYMAN			
76	Obscure OBS 6	DECAY MUSIC (LP)	40
82	Piano SHEET 1	UNTITLED (LP)	40
89	VRL VEBN55	THE NYMAN GREENAWAY SOUNDTRACKS (4-LP box set, booklet)	40
NYMONIC			
00	Y N R YNR02	REQIEM (EP)	18
LAURA NYRO			
67	Verve Forecast VS 1502	Wedding Bell Blues/Stoney End	15
68	CBS 3604	Eli's Coming/Sweet Blindness	8
68	CBS 4031	Once It Was Alright Now (Farmer Joe)/Woman's Blues	7
69	CBS 4719	Time And Love/The Man Who Sends Me Home	7
68	CBS 63346	ELI AND THE THIRTEENTH CONFESSION (LP, gatefold sleeve, orange label)	40
69	CBS 63510	NEW YORK TENDABERRY (LP, orange label)	20
69	Verve Forecast SVLP 6022	THE FIRST SONGS (LP)	15
70	CBS 64157	CHRISTMAS AND THE BEADS OF SWEAT (LP, orange label)	15
71	CBS S 64770	GONNA TAKE A MIRACLE (LP, with Labelle)	20

O

OAK			
71	Topic 12TS 212	WELCOME TO OUR FAIR (LP)	55
(see also Peta Webb)			
OAK TREE			
70	President PT 316	The Sun It Always Shone/My Baby Don't Cry	6
OAKENSHIELD			
82	Acorn OAK 001	ACROSS THE NARROW SEAS (LP)	18
85	Acorn OAK 002	AGAINST THE GRAIN (LP, with insert)	18
OASIS			
SINGLES			
94	Creation CRE 176	Supersonic/Take Me Away (p/s)	18
94	Creation CRE 176T	Supersonic/Take Me Away/I Will Believe (Live) (12", p/s)	15
94	Creation CRE 182T	Shakermaker/D'Yer Wanna Be A Spaceman?/Alive (8 Track Demo) (12", p/s)	25
94	Creation CRE 182	Shakermaker/D'Yer Wanna Be A Spaceman (p/s)	18
94	Creation CRE 185	Live Forever/Up In The Sky (Acoustic) (jukebox issue, large centre hole)	20
94	Creation CRE 185	Live Forever/Up In The Sky (Acoustic) (numbered foldover p/s in stickered poly bag)	15
94	Creation CRE 185T	Live Forever/Up In The Sky (Acoustic)/Cloudburst (12", p/s)	15
94	Creation CRE 190	Cigarettes & Alcohol/I Am The Walrus (live at Glasgow Cathouse June '94) (p/s, numbered)	12
94	Creation CRE 190T	Cigarettes & Alcohol/I Am The Walrus (live at Glasgow Cathouse June '94)/Fade Away (12", p/s)	15
94	Creation CRE 195T	Whatever/(It's Good) To Be Free/Slide Away (12". p/s)	20
94	Creation CRE 195	Whatever/(It's Good) To Be Free (no'd foldover p/s in stickered poly bag)	18
95	Creation CRE 204T	Some Might Say/Talk Tonight/Acquiesce (12", p/s)	20
95	Creation CRE 212T	Roll With It/It's Better People/Rockin' Chair (12", p/s)	15
95	Creation CRE 215	Wonderwall/Round Are Way (wraparound p/s)	15
95	Creation CRE 215T	Wonderwall/Round Are Way/The Swamp Song (12", p/s)	15
96	Creation CRE 221T	Don't Look Back In Anger/Step Out/Underneath The Sky (12", p/s)	30
96	Creation CRE 221	Don't Look Back In Anger/Step Out (p/s, with poly outer)	10
97	Creation CRE 256T	D'You Know What I Mean?/Heroes/Angel Child (Demo) (12", p/s)	15
97	Creation CRE 278T	Stand By Me/I Got The Fever/My Sister Lover (12", p/s)	18
97	Creation CRE 278	Stand By Me/I Got The Fever (gatefold p/s)	7
97	Creation CRE 282T	All Around The World/The Fame/Flashbax (12", p/s)	30
00	Creation RKID 001T	Go Let It Out/Let's All Make Believe/(As Long As They've Got) Cigarettes In Hell (12", p/s)	18
00	Big Brother RKID 003T	Who Feels Love/One Way Road/Helter Skelter (12", p/s)	15
00	Big Brother RKID 004T	Sunday Morning Call/Carry Us All/Full On (12", p/s)	15
02	Big Brother RKID 24T	Stop Crying Your Heart Out/Thank You For The Good Times/Shout It Out Loud (12", p/s)	15

OASIS

MINT VALUE £

Year	Label/Cat	Description	Value
02	Big Brother RKID 23	The Hindu Times/Just Getting Older (p/s, limited edition)	6
02	Big Brother RKID 23T	The Hindu Times/Just Getting Older/Idler's Dream (12", p/s)	15
02	Big Brother RKID 26	Little By Little/She Is Love	8
02	Big Brother RKID 26T	Little By Little/She Is Love/My Generation (12", p/s)	15
03	Big Brother RKID 27	Songbird/(You've Got) The Heart Of A Star	8
03	Big Brother RKID 27T	Songbird/(You've Got) The Heart Of A Star/Columbia (Live) (12", p/s)	20
05	Big Brother RKID 31	The Importance Of Being Idle/Pass Me Down The WIne	6
06	Big Brother RKID 37	Stop The Clocks EP (2 x 7", stickers, numbered)	12
14	Big Brother RKID 70BOXX	Whatever/(It's Good) To Be Free/Side Away (12", p/s, reissue, mail-order or given away by band website with copies of Definitely Maybe boxed set)	20
14	Big Brother RKID74T	Acquiesce (1-sided 12" sold by HMV shops)	15

ALBUMS

Year	Label/Cat	Description	Value
94	Creation CRELP 169	DEFINITELY MAYBE (2-LP, gatefold sleeve)	150
95	Creation CRELP 189	(WHAT'S THE STORY) MORNING GLORY? (2-LP, multifold sleeve, black inners, postcard)	150
97	Creation (no cat. no.)	BE HERE NOW (LP, mail-order 12" box set, with The Making Of Be Here Now booklet, 1,000 only)	200
97	Creation (no cat. no.)	BE HERE NOW (CD, mail-order 12" box set, with The Making Of Be Here Now booklet, 1,000 only)	50
97	Creation CRELP 219	BE HERE NOW (2-LP, gatefold)	100
98	Creation CRELP 241	THE MASTERPLAN (3-LP)	100
00	Big Brother RKID LP005	FAMILIAR TO MILLIONS (3-LP)	100
00	Big Brother RKID LP002	STANDING ON THE SHOULDER OF GIANTS	50
02	Big Brother RKID LP25	HEATHEN CHEMISTRY (LP, booklet)	60
05	Big Brother RKID LP30X	DON'T BELIEVE THE TRUTH (LP, numbered art print)	50
06	Big Brother RKID LP36	STOP THE CLOCKS (3-LP box-set)	150
08	Big Brother RKIDBOX 51	DIG OUT YOUR SOUL (LP as 4 x 12", CD, DVD boxed set)	50
09	Big Brother RKIDBOX 58	LP BOX SET (8-LP, numbered, 1,500 only)	400

ALBUMS : ALBUMS: REISSUES

Year	Label/Cat	Description	Value
09	Big Brother RKIDLP006X	DEFINITELY MAYBE (2-LP, reissue)	20
09	Big Brother RKIDLP007X	(WHAT'S THE STORY) MORNING GLORY? (2-LP, reissue)	30
09	Big Brother RKIDLP008X	BE HERE NOW (2-LP, reissue)	25
09	Big Brother RKIDLP009X	THE MASTERPLAN (2-LP, reissue)	40
09	Big Brother RKIDLP002X	STANDING ON THE SHOULDER OF GIANTS (LP, reissue)	25
09	Big Brother RKIDLP25X	HEATHEN CHEMISTRY (2-LP, reissue)	30
14	Big Brother	DEFINITELY MAYBE (Box set, 3-CD, 2-LP, 7" and booklet)	150
16	Our Kid RKIDLP85BOX	BE HERE NOW (Box set, 4-CD, LP, 12" and 7")	200

PROMOS : PROMOS: SINGLES

Year	Label/Cat	Description	Value
93	Creation CTP 8	Columbia (Demo) (12", 1-sided, white label, 510 pressed)	200
94	Creation CRE 176TP	Supersonic/Take Me Away/I Will Believe (Live) (12", company sleeve)	40
94	Creation CRE 182TP	Shakermaker/D'Yer Wanna Be A Spaceman?/Alive (8 Track Demo) (12")	60
94	Creation CRE 185TP	Live Forever/Up In The Sky (Acoustic)/Cloudburst (12")	70
94	Creation CTP 190TP	I Am The Walrus (Live At Glasgow Cathouse June '94) (12", 250 only, co. sl.)	250
94	Creation CTP 190CL	Cigarettes & Alcohol (12", 1-sided)	75
94	Creation CTP 190CL	Cigarettes & Alcohol/I Am The Walrus (live Glasgow Cathouse June '94)/ Fade Away (12", 300 only)	75
94	Creation CRE 195TP	Whatever (12", 1-sided, 560 only)	75
94	Creation CTP 195	(It's Good) To Be Free (12", 1-sided, 360 only)	50
94	Creation CREDM 001	DEFINITELY MAYBE (4 x 7" box set, in silver cigarette-pack-shaped plastic box, with booklet & interview CD)	40
95	Creation CCD 169	Slide Away (CD, 1-track Brits Awards issue, 1,000 only; beware of counterfeits)	30
95	Creation CCD 204	Some Might Say (CD, 1-track, 350 only)	60
95	Creation CREMG 001	(WHAT'S THE STORY) MORNING GLORY? (4 x 7" box set, in gold cigarette-pack-shaped plastic box, with booklet & interview CD)	60
95	Creation CTP 204	Acquiesce (12", 1-sided, 570 only)	80
95	Creation CCD 204P	Acquiesce (CD, 1-track, 300 only)	60
95	Creation CTP 212	Roll With It (12", 1-sided)	40
95	Creation CTP 215	Round Are Way (12", 1-sided, 843 only)	60
96	Creation CTP 221X	Cum On Feel The Noize/Champagne Supernova (Lynchmob Beats Mix) (12", 1,203 pressed, plain die-cut sleeve; beware of counterfeits)	40
96	Creation CCD 221	Cum On Feel The Noize (CD, pic. disc, 1-track, with football motif, no inlay, 500 only)	60
97	Creation CTP 256	D'You Know What I Mean?/Heroes (12")	30
97	Creation CTP 278	Stand By Me/I Got The Fever (12")	35
97	Creation CTP 282	All Around The World/Street Fighting Man (12", black die-cut sleeve)	25
97	Creation (no cat. no.)	VOX BOX (9-CD, wooden guitar-amp-shaped box set in outer box, with booklets from "Silver" & "Gold" CD box sets; contains commerical issues of "Supersonic" through to "Don't Look Back In Anger"; in house giveaway only)	500
98	Creation CRELP 241P	THE MASTERPLAN SAMPLER (Acquiesce/Underneath The Sky/I Am The Walrus/The Masterplan) (12" sampler)	35
00	Creation CTP 327	Go Let It Out (12", 1-track, 1-sided, p/s)	25
00	Big Brother FITB 001	Fuckin' In The Bushes (12", 1-sided, white label)	40
00	Big Brother RKID 004TP	Sunday Morning Call (12", 1-sided, flipback laminated p/s)	25
00	Big Brother RKID 03TP	Who Feels Love? (12", 1-sided, laminated p/s)	30
01	Own label OASIS 10	10 YEARS OF NOISE & CONFUSION (Columbia/Rock & Roll Star (Live)/ Acquiesce/Fuckin' In The Bushes) (10", promo-only, custom labels, die-cut sleeve, 200 only, with press release)	35
01	Own label OASIS 10	10 YEARS OF NOISE & CONFUSION (Columbia/Rock & Roll Star (Live)/ Acquiesce/Fuckin' In The Bushes) (10", promo-only, custom labels, die-cut sleeve, 200 only, without press release)	30
02	Big Brother RKID23TP	The Hindu Times (Spike Mix) (12", promo-only, custom logo sleeve, 250 only)	25
02	Big Brother RKID24TP	Stop Crying Your Heart Out (Spike Mix) (12", custom sleeve, 250 only)	20
02	Big Brother RKID25TPX	Hung In A Bad Place (12", 1-track, 1-sided, custom mauve/pink or brown sleeve)	30

OBERON

			MINT VALUE £
02	Big Brother RKID26TPX	My Generation (12" 1-sided promo with Union Jack Sleeve. 800 only)	35
02	Big Brother RKID27TP	Columbia (Live)/(You've Got) The Heart Of A Star (12", custom sleeve)	30
02	Big Brother (No cat. no)	Songbird (Demo) (CD-R promo, 25 only)	200
05	Big Brother RKID28TPX	Can You See It Now? I Can See It Now (12" 1-sided white label promo 50 only)	200
05	Big Brother RKID29TP	Lyla (12" 1-sided promo. 770 only)	25
05	Big Brother RKID31TP	Turn Up The Sun (12" 1-sided promo in card sleeve and inner sleeve. 1,120 only)	35
05	Big Brother RKID32TP	Mucky Fingers (12" 1-sided promo in double p/s. 950 copies)	30
05	Big Brother RKID1 NIL	Meaning Of Soul (CD-R promo)	150
05	Big Brother (No cat. no)	Cast No Shadow (UNKLE Beachhead Mix) (CD-R promo)	30
06	Big Brother RKIDSCD35TP	Champagne Supernova (Lynchmob Beats Mix) (12", promo-only)	20
06	Big Brother RKIDSCD35P	Champagne Supernova (Lynchmob Beats Mix) (CD-R, promo-only)	200
06	Big Brother RKIDSCD37P1	Acquiesce	10
06	Big Brother RKIDSCD37P2	The Masterplan	10
07	Big Brother RKIDSCD39TP	Lord Don't Slow Me Down (12", promo-only)	40
07	Big Brother RKIDSCD39P	Lord Don't Slow Me Down (CD-R, promo)	40
14	Big Brother RKID72T	Columbia (1-sided 12", reissue sold at HMV shops)	15
14	Big Brother RKID73BOXX	Cum On Feel The Noize/Champagne Supernova (Lynchmob Beats Mix) (12" reissue)	15
14	Big Brother RKID70BOX	Supersonic (Live At Glasgow Tramshead)/Cigarettes And Alcohol (Live at Manchester Academy) (p/s, part of box set, this price for alone)	10
14	Big Brother RKID73BOX	Hello (Demo)/She's Electric (Demo) (part of box set, but this price alone)	15

PROMOS : PROMOS: ALBUMS

94	Creation CRECD 169P	DEFINITELY MAYBE (CD)	50
95	Creation CRECD 189P	(WHAT'S THE STORY) MORNING GLORY? (CD, with "Step Out", black card p/s, withdrawn, beware of counterfeits)	45
95	Creation CRECD 189P	(WHAT'S THE STORY) MORNING GLORY? (CD, without "Step Out", black card p/s)	30
95	Creation C-CRE 189P	(WHAT'S THE STORY) MORNING GLORY? (cassette, with "Step Out", card p/s, withdrawn)	25
97	Creation CCD 219	BE HERE NOW (CD, black card sleeve, in custom picture sleeve)	30
98		THE MASTERPLAN (CD, slimline case, p/s)	35
98	Creation CRELX 241	THE MASTERPLAN (mail-order 7 x 10" single box set)	175

(see also Beady Eye. Liam Gallagher,Noel Gallagher And HIgh Flying Birds)

OBERON
71	Acorn OBE LPS 1	A MIDSUMMER NIGHT'S DREAM (LP, private pressing)	1000

OBITUARY
89	Roadracer RO 9489	SLOWLY WE ROT (LP)	18
90	Roadracer RO 9370	CAUSE OF DEATH (LP)	15

HUGH O'BRIAN
58	HMV POP 539	Legend Of Wyatt Earp/Down In The Meadow	7
58	Oriole CB 1480	I'm Looking For A Girl/Ain't Got A Nickel	6
58	HMV DLP 1189	TV'S WYATT EARP SINGS (10" LP)	15

DERMOT O'BRIEN
66	Envoy ENV 016	The Merry Plough Boy(Off To Dublin In The Green)/Come Down the Mountain Katie Daly	8

JIMMY O'BRYANT
60	Heritage RE-101	FAMOUS ORIGINAL WASHBOARD BAND, VOL. 1 (99 copies only) (EP)	20
60	Heritage RE-106	FAMOUS ORIGINAL WASHBOARD BAND, VOL. 2 (99 copies only) (EP)	20

OBSCURE BY DEGREES
81	Ka KA 10	I'm Dying/A Woman Like You (p/s)	40

OBSERVERS ALL STARS & KING TUBBY
75	Attack ATLP 017	DUBBING WITH THE OBSERVER (LP)	50

OBSERVERS (1)
71	Big Shot BI 575	Brimstone And Fire/Lightning And Thunder	20
71	Big Shot BI 588	Keep Pushing/Hot Tip	10
72	Big Shot BI 610	Everyday Music/NINEY: Observing The Av	10

(see also Niney)

OBSERVERS (2)
80	ST ST2	This Age/Suicide (p/s)	8

OBSESSION
82	Wilde Bros SRTS 82 CUS 1344	Clockwork Man/Hava Naglia	50

OBTAINERS
79	Dance Fools Dance (No cat. no.)	Yeh Yeh Yeh/Pussy Wussy/MAG-SPYS: Lifeblood/Bombs (stickered plain sleeve, 100 only)	400

(see also Cure)

OBX
81	Cara CARA 002	Sailplane/Breakdown And Cry	20

OCCASIONALLY DAVID
79	Oven Ready OD 77901	TWIST AND SHOUT (EP)	20
80	Oven Ready OD 1/98002	I Can't Get Used To Losing You (So I'm Coming Back)/Will You Miss Me Tonight? (foldout p/s)	20

OCCASIONAL WORD ENSEMBLE
69	Dandelion 63753	THE YEAR OF THE GREAT LEAP SIDEWAYS (LP)	50

OCCULT CHEMISTRY
80	Bikini Girl (no. cat. no.)	Water Earth Fire Air (Rough Version) (5" clear flexidisc in stamped envelope with Bikini Girl magazine)	15
81	Dining Out TUX 4	Water Earth Fire Air/Fire Air Water Earth (handmade p/s)	15

(see also Twilight Zonerz)

OCCULT PUNK BAND
78	Gaslight GAS 001	Happy With My Life/Black Mass (no p/s, 200 only)	15

OCEAN COLOUR SCENE
90	!Phffft WAVE 1P	One Of These Days/Talk On (p/s, promo only)	15
90	!Phffft WAVE 1	One Of These Days/Talk On (12", p/s, promo only)	20
90	!Phffft FIT 001	Sway/Talk On (p/s)	6

Frank OCEAN

MINT VALUE £

90	!Phffft FITX 001	Sway (Extended)/Lullaby/Sway (7" Version)/One Of These Days (12", p/s)	10
91	!Phffft FIT 002	Yesterday Today/Another Girl's Name/Fly Me (p/s, promos with sticker £5)	7
91	!Phffft FITX 002	Yesterday Today/Another Girl's Name/Fly Me/No One Says (12", p/s)	10
95	MCA OCS 1	You've Got It Bad/You've Got It Bad (p/s, promo only)	20
96	MCA OCS 2	You've Got It Bad (Full Length Demo Version)/Mona Lisa Eyes (feat, Jimmy Miller) (p/s, mail-order only)	8
96	MCA MCSJB 40077	The Circle/Day Tripper (jukebox centre)	12
96	MCA MCSJB 86946	The Day We Caught The Train/You've Got It Bad (jukebox centre)	12
96	MCA MCS 40021	The Riverboat Song/So Bad (p/s)	20
92	Fontana 512 2692	OCEAN COLOUR SCENE (LP)	50
96	MCA MCA 60008	MOSELEY SHOALS (2-LP, inners, stickered sleeve)	100
97	MCA MCD 60034	B-SIDES, SEASIDES AND FREE RIDES (2-LP, with lyric booklet)	80
97	MCA MCA 60048	MARCHIN' ALREADY (2-LP, with booklet)	80
99	Island 546 671-1	ONE FROM THE MODERN (2-LP)	80
01	Island 548 686-1	MECHANICAL WONDER (LP)	50
03	Sanctuary SANLP 160	NORTH ATLANTIC DRIFT (LP)	50
05	Sanctuary SANLP 332	A HYPERACTIVE WORKOUT FOR THE FLYING SQUAD (LP)	50
07	Moseley Shoals SANLP 332	ON THE LEYLINE (LP)	30
15	Moseley Shoals OCSV3	LIVE AT THE BRIDGEWATER HALL (2-LP)	50
17	Moseley Shoals OCSV4RSD	LIVE AT THE HYDRO (LP, picture disc)	25

(see also Boys, Fanatics, Echo Base)

FRANK OCEAN

16	88395801421 9	BOYS DON'T CRY (book/magazine in foil wrapper, 2-track CD Mitsubishi Sony and Easy, 500 only)	150

HUMPHREY OCEAN

78	Stiff BUY 29	Whoops A Daisy/Davy Crockett (p/s, blue, black, red, green, white and clear vinyl pressed, p/s)	7

OCEAN (1)

71	Kama Sutra 2013027	No Other Woman/Deep Enough For Me	6

OCEAN (2)

89	Baseline BASL 005	You Are (To Be Mine)/Midnight Traveller (12")	40

OCEANLAB

09	Anjunabeats ANJ-124	ON A GOOD DAY (12", p/s)	80

(see also Above & Beyond)

OCEANS

80	Record Shack SHACK 129	Bad Guy, Good Guy/Synth Good Guy (12" white label)	40
82	Record Shack SHACK 129	Pacific Dreams/Pacific Dreams (Instrumental) (12", white label, stickered or stamped label)	150

OCEAN WISDOM

15	High Focus HFRT 1002	SPLITTIN' THE RACKET EP (12", p/s)	35
17	High Focus HFRLP 048	CHAOS '93 (LP, gold vinyl)	25
18	High Focus HFRLP 068	WIZVILLE (LP)	20

PHIL OCHS

66	Elektra EKSN 45002	I Ain't Marching Any More/That Was The President	15
68	A&M AMS 716	Outside Of A Small Circle Of Friends/Miranda	8
65	Elektra EKL 269	ALL THE NEWS THAT'S FIT TO SING (LP, 'guitar player' label, UK record in US sleeve)	30
65	Elektra EKL 287	I AIN'T MARCHIN' ANYMORE (LP)	30
66	Elektra EKL 310	PHIL OCHS IN CONCERT (LP, gold label)	30
67	A&M AML(S) 913	PLEASURES OF THE HARBOR (LP)	25
68	A&M AMLS 919	TAPE FROM CALIFORNIA (LP)	25
69	A&M AMLS 934	REHEARSALS FOR RETIREMENT (LP)	25
70	A&M AMLS 973	GREATEST HITS (LP)	18

DES O'CONNOR

62	Piccadilly 7N 35023	Thin Chow Min/Twist Drive	6

OCTAGON MAN

95	Electron TRONLP5X	THE EXCITING WORLD OF... (3 LP)	20

JOHNNY OCTOBER

59	Capitol CL 15070	Growin' Prettier/Young And In Love	15
60	Capitol CL 15121	So Mean/There'll Always Be A Feeling	15

OCTODRED

95	Acid Fever MDMA 9501	BIG FOOT EP (12")	40
95	Acid Fever MDMA 9502	DOUBLE DIPPED EP (12")	15
96	Acid Fever MDMA 9601	TECHNOLOGICAL ILLUSIONS VOL. 1 EP (12")	30
96	Acid Fever MDMA 9603	TECHNOLOGICAL ILLUSIONS VOL. 2 EP (12")	25
96	Acid Fever MDMA 9606	UNTITLED EP (12")	40
96	Acid Fever MDMA 9608	PSYCHIK MONK EP (12")	30

OCTOPUS

69	Penny Farthing PEN 705	Laugh At The Poor Man/Girl Friend	20
70	Penny Farthing PEN 716	The River/Thief	20
73	Mooncrest MOON 7	Hey Na Na/Future Feelings	6
70	Penny Farthing PELS 508	RESTLESS NIGHT (LP, gatefold sleeve, red/black label)	700
96	Essex ESSEX 1013LP	RESTLESS NIGHT (LP, reissue, gatefold sleeve)	20

(see also Cortinas)

MARTIN O'CUTHBERT

78	SRTS/78/CUS-114 Esoteric EEE 1	B.E.M.S (Bug Eyed Monsters)/Fragments Of A Possessed Ego (1st pressing, 1000 copies, push-out centre, folded b/w sleeve with SRTS cat no)	20
78	SRTS/78/CUS-114 Esoteric EEE 1	B.E.M.S (Bug Eyed Monsters)/Fragments Of A Possessed Ego (2nd pressing, 1000 copies, push-out centre, folded b/w sleeve with EEE1 cat no)	10
78	Esoteric EE 2	Serene Machines/Space Shall Weave Our Destiny	8
83	Martoc 001	FOR ALIEN EARS (LP)	30

Ray O'DANIEL

MINT VALUE £

RAY O'DANIEL
62 Longhorn BLH 0001   What Goes Up Always Comes Down/You're The Only Love For Me 8

ANITA O'DAY
56 HMV POP 245   You're The Top/Honeysuckle Rose 12
56 HMV CLP 1085   ANITA (LP) 15
56 Columbia Clef 33C 9020   ANITA O'DAY COLLATES (10" LP) 15
57 Columbia Clef 33CX 10068   AN EVENING WITH ANITA O'DAY (LP) 15
58 Columbia Clef 33CX 10125   ANITA SINGS THE MOST (LP) 15

PAT O'DAY
55 MGM SP 1129   Earth Angel (Will You Be Mine?)/A Rusty Old Halo 25
55 MGM SP 1142   Soldier Boy/Annie Oakley 15
60 Pye International 7N 25048 I'll Build A Stairway To Your Paradise/No One Understands 6

ODD BAND
82 Gyro GY 010   Xmas On The Dole/Christmas Dub 10

ODD
84 OK OK 007   Last Time I Saw You/Look Into My Eyes (p/s) 15

BILL ODDIE
66 Parlophone R 5433   I Can't Get Through/Because She Is My Love 15
(see also Ricky Livid)

ODDS
80 Double R RED 001   Saturday Night/Not Another Love Song (p/s) 15
81 JSO EAT 1   Yesterday Man/So You Think (p/s) 25
81 JSO EAT 7   Dread In My Bed/Spare Rib (with press release) 10

ODDSOCKS
75 Sweet Folk & C. SFA 030   MEN OF THE MOMENT (LP) 20
(see also Bevis Frond)

ODDWORX
98 Sessions SES 002   BODY LANGUAGE EP (12") 20

ANN ODELL
73 DJM DJS 10280   Swing Song/Everything's Fine Sunshine 6
73 DJM DJLPS 434   A LITTLE TASTE (LP, gatefold) 30
(see also Chopyn, Blue Mink, CMU)

MAC ODELL
54 Parlophone CMSP 25   The Stone Was Rolled Away/Heaven-Bound Gospel Train (export issue) 8

RONNIE O'DELL & HIS ORCHESTRA
57 London HLD 8439   Melody Of Napoli/Struttin' Down Jane Street 10

ODEONS
80 Ellie Jay EJSP 9480   Maybe Today/5.30 Anthem (p/s) 25

ODIN'S PEOPLE
67 Major Minor MM 501   From A Distance/I Need You 10
67 Major Minor MM 505   Tommy Jones/I Need Your Hand In Mine 10

JOE ODOM
69 Capitol CL 15600   Big Love/It's In Your Power 15

AL O'DONNELL
72 Trailer LER 2073   AL O'DONNELL (LP, red label) 20

ALISON O' DONNELL
08 Fruits De Mer CRUSTACIAN 03   Day Is Done/Frozen Warnings (p/s. coloured vinyl 300 only) 25
(see also Mellow Candle)

JOE O'DONNELL
77 Polydor 2383 465   GAODHAL'S VISION (LP) 22
(see also East of Eden, Mushroom, Rory Gallagher, Jade Warrior)

ROCK O'DOODLE
73 Decca F 13450   Queen Of Rock & Roll/Woman 10
(see also Patrick Campbell-Lyons)

ODYSSEY (U.K.)
66 Strike JH 312   How Long Is Time/Beware 35
(see also Sons Of Fred)

ODYSSEY (U.S.)
73 Mowest MWS 7002   ODYSSEY (LP) 75

OEDIPUS COMPLEX
69 Phillips BF 1771   Up Down Round & Round/Empty Highways 40

OF MONTREAL
01 Jonathon Whisky 16   Inside A Room Full Of Treasures, A Black Pygmi Horse's Head Pops Up Like A Periscope/LATE B.P. HELIUM: Song For Marie/Alright Yeah (P/s, 250 only) 10
03 Track & Field LANE 18   Jennifer Louise/There Is Nothing Wrong With Hating Rock Critics (p/s) 8
02 Track & Field HEAT 10 LP   ALDHILS ARBORETURN (LP) 20

OFFENBACH
74 Surrey Int. SIT 5003   Judy In Disguise (With Glasses)/No Letter Today 6

OFFICERS & GENTLEMEN
84 Gap GAP 001   That's Life And Love/Noise (no p/s) 50

OFFICIAL SECRETS
81 Round RR1   Fooling My Heart/Paradise Time (p/s) 40

OFFSIDE
70 Pye Intl. 25534   Match Of The Day/Small Deal (p/s) 15

OFFSPRING (1)
72 RCA Victor 2198   Windfall/She Lives In A Big House 25

OFFSPRING (2)
84 Offspring Records OP001/SRT4K5169   One More Night/Nota Sad Song (this is how it is typed on B-side label) 30

OFO
74 Decca F13496 — Let's Go Where The Action Is/The Book 10

OFO THE BLACK COMPANY
72 London FL12261 — Allah Wakbarr/Beautiful Daddy 75

JAMES O'GWYNN
59 Mercury AMT 1052 — How Can I Think Of Tomorrow/Were You Ever A Stranger 10

JOHN O'HARA
72 Spark SRL 1075 — Hand Me Down Man/I Am The Candidate For Love 12

O'HARA'S PLAYBOYS
66 Fontana TF 763 — Start All Over/I've Been Wondering 6
67 Fontana TF 793 — Spicks And Specks/One Fine Lady 8
67 Fontana TF 872 — Ballad Of The Soon Departed/Tell Me Why 50
67 Fontana TF 893 — Island In The Sun/Harry 6
68 Fontana TF 924 — In The Shelter Of My Heart/Goodnight Mr. Nightfall 6
68 Fontana TF 974 — I Started A Joke/Show Me 10
68 Fontana (S)TL 5461 — GET READY (LP) 50

OHIO EXPRESS
68 Pye Intl. 7N 25469 — Down At Lulu's/She's Not Coming Home 6
69 Pye Intl. NSPL 28117 — OHIO EXPRESS (LP) 20
69 Buddah 203 015 — CHEWY CHEWY (LP) 15

(see also Joey Vine)

OHIO KNOX
71 Reprise RSLP 6435 — OHIO KNOX (LP, gatefold sleeve) 20

(see also Fifth Avenue Band)

OHIO PLAYERS
69 Capitol CL 15587 — Here Today And Gone Tomorrow/Bad Bargain 10
73 Westbound 6146 100 — Funky Worm/Paint Me 8
74 Mercury 6338 497 — SKIN TIGHT (LP) 18
74 Mercury 9100 009 — FIRE (LP) 18
75 DJM DJSLM 2015 — FIRST IMPRESSIONS (LP) 15
75 Mercury 9100 014 — HONEY (LP) 15
89 Westbound SEW 014 — PLEASURE (LP, reissue) 20
89 Westbound SEW 004 — PAIN (LP, reissue) 18

BOB OHIRI
77 Ashiko 001 — UHURU AIYE (LP) 300

OHM
79 OHM 001 — Kanon/Airship To Bali (no p/s) 8
79 OHM 003 — Whale Song/Ohm Sweet Ohn (no p/s, as Overhead Music) 7

OHR MUSIK
97 Prescription DRUG 2 — OHR MUSIK (LP, 99 copies only) 50

(see also Spiral Sky)

OH SEES
17 Castle Face CF-99 — Dead Medic/A Few Days Of Reflection (12", blue vinyl) 20
16 Castle Face CF-080 — A WEIRD EXITS (2-LP, green vinyl) 30
16 Castle Face CF-085 — AN ODD ENTRANCES (2-LP, green vinyl and yellow flexi) 25
17 Castle Face CF-093 — ORC (2-LP, bone coloured vinyl) 30

OI POLLOI
86 EDR 5 — RESIST THE ATOMIC MESSAGE (EP) 10
88 Words Of Warning WOW 5 — OUTRAGE (EP) 10
89 Words Of Warning WOW 17 — OMNICIDE (EP) 12
87 Oi! OIR 011 — UNITE AND WIN (LP, with lyric sheet) 15

OIL CITY SHEIKS
79 United Artists UP 36514 — Don't Take But A Few Minutes/Blues Jam (p/s) 7

(see also Dr. Feelgood, Lew Lewis)

O'JAYS
65 Liberty LIB 66102 — Lipstick Traces/Think It Over Baby 50
65 Liberty LIB 66102 — Lipstick Traces/Think It Over Baby (DJ copy) 90
66 Liberty LIB 66197 — Stand In For Love/Friday Night 30
67 Stateside SS 2073 — I'll Be Sweeter Tomorrow/I Dig Your Act 60
67 Stateside SS 2073 — I'll Be Sweeter Tomorrow/I Dig Your Act (DJ copy) 100
68 Bell BLL 1020 — Look Over Your Shoulder/I'm So Glad I Found You 30
68 Bell BLL 1020 — Look Over Your Shoulder/I'm So Glad I Found You (DJ copy) 50
68 Bell BLL 1033 — The Choice/Going Going Gone 15
70 Now! NOW 1002 — Don't You Know A True Love/That's Alright 8
72 United Artists UP 35277 — Working On Your Case/Hold On 15
73 CBS 1181 — Love Train/Who Am I? 6
73 Mojo 2092 052 — I Dig Your Act/I'll Be Sweeter Tomorrow (reissue) 8
74 Philadelphia PIR 2186 — For The Love Of Money/People Keep Telling Me 6
72 Philadelphia Intl. PIR 65299 — BACK STABBERS (LP) 18
73 EPIC EPC 65469 — IN PHILADELPHIA (LP) 15

O'KAYSIONS
68 Stateside SS 2126 — Girl Watcher/Deal Me In 25
68 Stateside SS 2126 — Girl Watcher/Deal Me In (DJ copy) 50

JOHNNY O'KEEFE (& DEE JAYS)
58 Coral Q 72330 — Shake Baby Shake/Real Wild Child (as Johnny O'Keefe & Dee Jays) 150
58 Coral Q 72330 — Shake Baby Shake/Real Wild Child (as Johnny O'Keefe & Dee Jays) (78) 60
60s Zodiac ZR 0016 — Sing/Tell The Blues So Long 10

(ROGER) EARL OKIN
67 Parlophone R 5644 — Yellow Petals/I Can't Face The Animals (as Roger Earl Okin) 6
69 CBS 4495 — Stop And You'll Become Aware/You're Not There At All (as Earl Okin) 22

OLA (& JANGLERS)

			MINT VALUE £
OLA (& JANGLERS)			
67	Decca F 12646	I Can Wait/Eeny Meeny Miney Moe	15
68	Big T BIG 108	What A Way To Die/That's Why I Cry (solo)	15
69	Sonet SON 2004	Let's Dance/Bird, Bird	10
BABATUNDE OLATUNJI			
73	Paramount PARA 3038	Soul Makossa (Parts 1 & 2)	10
73	Paramount SPFL 289	SOUL MAKOSSA (LP)	15
O.L.D.			
88	Earache MOSH 7	OLD LADY DRIVERS (LP)	40
91	Earache MOSH 41	LO FLUX TUBE (LP)	35
OLD SCHOOL TIE			
80	Modelló MHMS 195	Gambler/Oscar (p/s)	10
OLDEST PROFESSION			
72	Midas Private Pressing	THE OLDEST PROFESSION (LP)	150
MIKE OLDFIELD			
SINGLES			
74	Virgin VS 101	Mike Oldfield's Single ("Tubular Bells" Theme)/ Froggy Went A-Courtin' (in p/s)	10
85	Virgin VSD 836	Pictures In The Dark/Legend/Moonlight Shadow/Rite Of Man (double pack in PVC gatefold stickered sleeve)	8
86	Virgin VSS 863	Shine (with Jon Anderson)/The Path (uncut picture disc)	200
ALBUMS			
73	Virgin V 2001	TUBULAR BELLS (LP, gloss laminate sleeve with "130 Notting Hill Gate" address, White/black 'Twin' label)	40
74	Virgin QV 2001	TUBULAR BELLS (LP, quadrophonic, with model plane noise at the end of side 2, stickered sleeve)	20
74	Virgin V2013	HERGEST RIDGE (LP, A-1U/B-1U matrixes, poor pressing and many returned, most other "girl/dragon" pressings £5)	15
75	Virgin QVQS 2043	OMMADAWN (LP, quadrophonic, stickered sleeve)	18
75	Virgin VD 2502	V (2-LP, compilation, includes long version of 'Don Alfonso')	20
76	Virgin QV 2043	OMMADAWN (LP, different quadrophonic mix, stickered sleeve)	18
76	Virgin VBOX 1	BOXED (4-LP box set, with booklet)	20
78	Virgin VDT 101	INCANTATIONS (2-LP, some with 7" red vinyl of Julie Covington, & poster)	30
78	Virgin VP 2001	TUBULAR BELLS (LP, picture disc, die-cut sleeve, stereo remix of 1976 Boxed quadrophonic mix; with or without model plane noise)	15
79	Virgin V 2141	PLATINUM (LP, with inner sleeve & "Sally"; matrix reads "V 2141 B1" or B2, 30,000 copies, withdrawn)	20
79	Tellydisc TELLY 4	IMPRESSIONS (LP, mail-order only)	20
84	Virgin V 2328	THE KILLING FIELDS (LP, with 20 page film booklet)	15
97	Virgin LPCENT 18	TUBULAR BELLS (LP, coloured Dean label, audiophile pressing)	20
01	Simply Vinyl SVLP 322	OMMADAWN (LP, Audiophile pressing on 180g vinyl, with 2 stickers)	15
PROMOS			
74	Virgin VS 112	Hergest Ridge (1-sided white label)	100
75	Virgin VDJ 1	Extract from The Orchestral Tubular Bells/Extract from The Orchestral Tubular Bells	40
75	Virgin VS 117	Don Alfonso ('A' label)	15
75	Virgin VDJ 9	An Extract From Ommadawn Part 1/An Extract From Ommadawn Part 2 (On Horseback) (12")	50
77	Virgin VS 167	The William Tell Overture/Argiers (blue Virgin 'A' label)	8
79	Virgin VSDJ 317	Blue Peter (1-sided)	20
85	Virgin SWALLOW 1	Etude/Moonlight Shadow/Portsmouth/In Dulci Jubilo (p/s, promo-only for "The Complete Mike Oldfield")	30
87	Virgin CDEP 6	Islands/When The Night's On Fire/The Wind Chimes(Part One)/ Islands (Extended Version) (white gatefold stickered card p/s)	20
92	WEA SAM 1094	OLDFIELD V THE ORB: Sentinel (Total Overhaul/Sentinel Nobel Prize Mix/ Sentinel Orbular Bells/Sentinel 7" Mix (12")	15
92	WEA SAM 1150	SENTINEL RESTRUCTURE MIXES: Satoshi Tomii Interpretation/ Global Lust Mix/ TranceMix/Tubular Beats (12", title stickered red sleeve)	15
92	WEA SAM 1470	A SHOT OF MOONSHINE: Jungle Mix (Featuring Rankin' Sean & Peter Lee)/ A Shot Of Moonshine (Jungle Instrumental)/A Shot of Moonshine (Solution Hoedown Mix) (12", lists artist as MOT2)	12
92	WEA YZ 708CDDJ	Tattoo (stickered p/s)	12
76	Virgin QVQS 2043	OMMADAWN (LP, unreleased different quadrophonic mix, promo stickered sleeve)	30
76	Virgin V BOX 1	COLLABORATIONS (LP, green/yellow label in stamped white sleeve)	20
79	(no cat. no.)	THE SPACE MOVIE (4 x 1-sided acetates of unreleased LP containing music from soundtrack to the 'Space Movie' video; includes Orchestral Hergest Ridge, Orchestral Tubular Bells, Incantations, Ommadawn and Portsmouth, some extracts otherwise released)	400
92	WEA WX 2002	TUBULAR BELLS 2 (LP, stickered sleeve)	15
94	WEA SAM 1477	THE SONGS OF DISTANT EARTH (CD in film can, with 2 inserts)	100

(see also Sallyangie, David Bedford, Kevin Ayers & Whole World, Pekka, Lea Nicholson, Tom Newman)

OLD GOLD			
70	Trend TNT 56	It's Goodbye/Teachers Of Electricity	30
ANDREW OLDHAM (ORCHESTRA)			
64	Decca F 11878	365 Rolling Stones/Oh I Do Like To See Me On The 'B' Side	30
64	Decca F 11987	We Don't All Wear D'Same Size Boots/Right Of Way	30
64	Ace Of Clubs ACL 1180	16 HIP HITS (LP)	40
64	Decca LK 4636	LIONEL BART'S MAGGIE MAY (LP)	40
66	Decca LK/SKL 4796	THE ROLLING STONES SONGBOOK (LP)	100

(see also Aranbee Pop Symphony, Rolling Stones, Cleo, Bo & Peep, Jeannie & Her Redheads, Gulliver's Travels, Mighty Avengers, John Paul Jones)

WILL OLDHAM			
97	Domino WIGLP 39	JOYA (LP, insert)	15
00	Domino WIGLP 74	GUARAPERO (LOST BLUES 2) (2-LP)	20

(see also Bonnie 'Prince' Billy, Palace Brothers)

OL DIRTY BASTARD

MINT VALUE £

OL DIRTY BASTARD
99 Elektra 7559624141 N***A PLEASE (2-LP) 40

(see also Wu Tang Clan)

OLD SKOOL FLAVA
97 HMB OFF 397P VOLUME 3 (12") 30

TONY O'LEARY AND THE CAPITOL
71 Dolphin DOS61 She Meant Everything/Whole World Shaking 6

JOHNNY OLENN & HIS BAND
57 London HLU 8388 I Ain't Gonna Cry No More/My Idea Of Love 250
57 London HLU 8388 I Ain't Gonna Cry No More/My Idea Of Love (78) 60
59 Mercury AMT 1050 Born Reckless/You Lovable You (as Johnny Olenn & Blockbusters) 150

O-LEVEL
78 Psycho PSYCHO 2 East Sheen/Pseudo Punk ('map' p/s) 175
78 Psycho PSYCHO 2 East Sheen/Pseudo Punk ('schoolboy' p/s) 150
78 Psycho PSYCHO 1 East Sheen/Pseudo Punk ('collage' p/s) 175
78 Kings Road KR 002 THE MALCOLM EP (photocopied wraparound p/s) 150
78 Kings Road KR 002 THE MALCOLM EP (printed p/s) 40

(see also Teenage Filmstars, Times, Television Personalities)

OLIVE BRANCH
68 Wren WRE 1044 WREN (EP) 15

JOHNNY OLIVER
56 MGM SP 1165 Chain Gang/These Hands 25
60 Mercury AMT 1095 What A Kiss Won't Do/That's All I'm Living For 12

OLIVER (1)
70 Crewe CRW 1 Jean/Good Morning Starshine (Arrangement) (p/s) 6

OLIVER (2)
74 Olive OL 1 STANDING STONE (LP, private pressing, withdrawn blue sleeve) 1000
74 Olive OL 1 STANDING STONE (LP, private pressing, withdrawn, later green sleeve) 800
92 Tenth Planet TP 001 STANDING STONE (LP, reissue, numbered, 500 only) 30

OLLIE & NIGHTINGALES
69 Stax STAX 109 You're Leaving Me/Showered With Love 12

NIGEL OLSSONS DRUM ORCHESTRA & CHORUS
71 DJM DJS 239 Natures Way/Natures Way 10
72 DJM DJS 266 Alabama/Sunshine Looks Like Rain 10
71 DJM DJLP 5 NIGEL OLSSON'S DRUM ORCHESTRA AND CHORUS (LP, with poster) 25

(see also Elton John, Hookfoot, Plastic Penny)

OLYMPICS
58 HMV POP 528 Western Movies/Well! 12
58 HMV POP 564 (I Wanna) Dance With The Teacher/Everybody Needs Love 20
59 Columbia DB 4346 Private Eye/(Baby) Hully Gully 25
60 Vogue Pop V 9174 I Wish I Could Shimmy Like My Sister Kate/Workin' Hard 15
61 Vogue Pop V 9181 Dance With A Dolly/Dodge City 25
61 Vogue Pop V 9184 Little Pedro/CAPPY LEWIS: Bullfight 20
62 Vogue Pop V 9196 The Twist/Everybody Likes To Cha Cha Cha 15
62 Vogue Pop V 9198 The Stomp/Mash Them 'Taters 20
62 Vogue Pop V 9204 Baby It's Hot/The Scotch 25
64 Sue WI 348 The Bounce/Fireworks 40
65 Warner Bros WB 157 Good Lovin'/Olympic Shuffle 15
66 Fontana TF 678 We Go Together (Pretty Baby)/Secret Agents 20
66 Fontana TF 778 Baby, Do The Philly Dog/Western Movies 20
69 Action ACT 4539 Baby, Do The Philly Dog/Mine Exclusively 20
70 Action ACT 4556 I'll Do A Little Bit More/Same Old Thing 40
71 Jay Boy BOY 27 Hully Gully/Big Boy Pete 10
72 Jay Boy BOY 56 Baby, Do The Philly Dog/Secret Agents 12
72 Jay Boy BOY 74 I'll Do A Little Bit More/Same Old Thing (reissue) 10
61 Vocalion VAH 8059 DANCE BY THE LIGHT OF THE MOON (LP) 100
67 London HA-M 8327 SOMETHING OLD, SOMETHING NEW (LP, unissued) 0
67 Fontana TL 5407 SOMETHING OLD, SOMETHING NEW (LP) 60
72 Jay Boy JSX 2008 THE OLYMPICS (LP) 20

(see also Cappy Lewis)

OMEGA RED STAR
69 Decca LK/SKL 4974 OMEGA RED STAR (LP, unboxed Decca on label) 250

OMEGA TRIBE
82 Crass 221984/10 ANGRY SONGS (EP) 15
84 Corpus Christi CHRIST ITS12 It's A Hard Life/Young John 6
83 Corpus Christi CHRIST O5 NO LOVE LOST (LP, inner) 30
00 Rugger Bugger SEEP 018LP MAKE TEA NOT WAR (LP, printed inner sleeve) 15

(see also Pete Fender)

OMEGA (1)
75 Decca SKL-R 5219 HALL OF FLOATERS IN THE SKY (LP) 20
76 Decca SKL-R 5243 TIME ROBBER (LP) 20

OMEGA (2)
85 Rock Machine MACH 1 THE PROPHET (LP) 35

OMEN
69 Ackee ACK 102 Don't Leave Me Never/No More 20

OMEN SEARCHER
82 OCS 001 Too Much/Teacher Of Sin (p/s) 50
82 OCS 002 Teacher Of Sin/Too Much (p/s) 50

OMENKA BROTHERS
77 Ashiko MR CROOKED CHIAUOTU (LP) 35

OMERTA

MINT VALUE £

OMERTA
05	Northern Ambition NAM 007	Everyone Is Frozen/Learn To Love The System (p/s)	70
05	Northern Ambition NAM 008	One Chance/Synchronise Your Smiles (p/s)	50
06	Northern Ambition NAM 0011	One More Minute/Follow Me Down (p/s)	40

(see also Slow Readers Club)

OMNI TRIO
93	Moving Shadow SHADOW 32	MYSTIC STEPPERS VOL 2 (12" EP)	15
93	Moving Shadow SHADOW 36	RENEGADE SNARES VOL 3 (EP)	25
95	Moving Shadow ASHADOWLP 1	THE DEEPEST CUT VOL. 1 (2-LP)	30
96	Moving Shadow ASHADOWLP 6	HAUNTED SCIENCE (2-LP)	30
99	Moving Shadow ASHADOW 20LP	BYTE SIZED LIFE (4-LP)	25
01	Moving Shadow ASHADOW 25 LP	EVEN ANGELS CAST SHADOWS (2-LP)	25

OMNIA OPERA
93	Delerium DELEC LP 011	OMNIA OPERA (LP)	30
97	Delerium DELECLP 044	RED SHIFT (LP)	20

ON A FRIDAY
86	OAF (no cat no)	ON A FRIDAY (11-track demo cassette)	300
88	(No label or cat no)	Happy Song/To Be A Brilliant Light/Sinking Ship (cassette)	250
90	(No label or cat no)	THE GREAT SHINDIG (Cassette, 15 tracks, as SHINDIG)	250
91	(No label or cat no)	What Is That You Say?/Stop Whispering (Demo)/Give It Up (Cassette, 3 known different cover inlays)	250
91	(No label or cat no)	I Can't (Demo)/Nothing Touches Me/Thinking About You (EP Version)/Phillipa Chicken/You (Demo) (Cassette, known as "Manic hedgehog" demos)	250

(see also Radiohead)

ONDIOLINE BAND
66	London HL 10022	Last Bicycle To Brussels/Lovers Of Cologne	6

ONE
69	Fontana STL 5539	ONE (LP, gatefold sleeve, black/silver label)	300

ONE & ONE
64	Decca F 11948	I'll Give You Lovin'/It's Me	15

(see also Ivy League, Flowerpot Men)

ONE EYED JACKS (1)
65	Ember EMBS 206	For Us There'll Be No Tomorrow/Soul Chart	8

ONE EYED JACKS (2)
78	Pennine PSS 154	TAKE AWAY (LP, in "One Eyed Jacks" brown paper carrier bag)	25
78	Pennine PSS 154	TAKE AWAY (LP)	20

ONE GANG LOGIC
79	Stark 1	Alienate/Queue Here/Repeat Action/Who Killed Sex (numbered p/s)	15

ONE HIT WONDERS
72	CBS 7760	Hey Hey Jump Now/Goodbye	18

101'ERS
76	Chiswick (N)S 3	Keys To Your Heart/5 Star Rock & Rock Petrol (with p/s)	50
76	Chiswick (N)S 3	Keys To Your Heart/5 Star Rock & Rock Petrol	10
79	Big Beat NS 3	Keys To Your Heart/5 Star Rock & Rock Petrol (reissue, with p/s)	20
79	Big Beat NS 3	Keys To Your Heart/5 Star Rock & Rock Petrol	15
80	Big Beat NS 63	Sweet Revenge/Rabies (From The Dogs Of Love) (p/s)	15
81	Andalucia AND 101	ELGIN AVENUE BREAKDOWN (LP, gatefold flip back sleeve with booklet)	40
81	Andalucia AND 101	ELGIN AVENUE BREAKDOWN (LP, without booklet)	25
05	Andalucia 0825646170035	ELGIN AVENUE BREAKDOWN REVISITED (2-LP, red vinyl)	30

(see also Clash, Alvaro, Aquila)

100% PROOF
80	Smile SR 929	NEW WAY OF LIVIN' (EP)	25
81	Myrrh MYR 1207	100% PROOF (LP, with insert)	50

100% PURE POISON
74	EMI Untl. 501	You Keep Coming Back/(And When I Said) I Love You	20
18	Dynamite Cuts DYNAM7011 12	Windy C/Puppet On A Chain/No More City. No More Country/Holes In My Shoes (reissue, 2 x 7", p/s)	10
77	EMI Intl. INS 3001	COMING RIGHT AT YOU (LP)	150

ONE IN A MILLION
67	CBS 202513	Use Your Imagination/Hold On	250
67	MGM MGM 1370	Fredereek Hernando/Double Sight	1000

(see also Thunderclap Newman)

ONE MILLION FUZZTONE GUITARS
82	Monsters In Orbit TVEYE 3	Heaven/Annuese (foldover p/s, at least 2 different designs)	6

1 SYNTAX
84	Proteus PRT 101	Negatives/Feel No Touch (p/s)	25

ONE BLOOD
81	One Blood NKRLP 001	IN LOVE (LP)	18
82	One Blood NKRLP 002	SUPER SHOWCASE (LP)	15

ONE CUT
98	Hombre MEX 006	CUT COMMANDER (12" EP, Banksy artwork)	400
00	Hombre MEX 016	UNDERGROUND TERROR TACTICS (12" EP Banksy artwork)	300
00	Hombre MEX 029	MR X/RHYTHM GEOMETRY (12" EP, Banksy artwork)	400
00	Hombre MEX 024	GRAND THEFT AUTO (2-LP, Banksy artwork)	200

ONE HAND CLAPPING
MINT VALUE £

ONE HAND CLAPPING
79	Curve Of The Earth COTE 001	The Rich Get Rich/Running Down Creek (poster p/s)	7

MATTY O'NEIL
54	London L 1037	Don't Sell Daddy Any More Whiskey/Little Rusty (gold label, tri-centre)	30
54	London L 1037	Don't Sell Daddy Any More Whiskey/Little Rusty (silver label, tri-centre)	15
54	London L 1037	Don't Sell Daddy Any More Whiskey/Little Rusty (silver top, round centre)	10

ONE LOVE
77	Lightning TRO 9025	The Slave Trade/Roots	25

ONE TAKES
80	No Choice NC 001	Accident/Street Kid/Backdoor Dump/Eviction Orders (p/s)	20

1,000 MEXICANS
83	Whaam! WHAAM 12	The Art Of Love/News For You (p/s, 1,500 only)	6

1,000 VIOLINS
85	Dreamworld DREAM 2	Halcyon Days/I Remember When Everybody Used To Ride Bikes ... Now We All Drive Cars (12", p/s, 1,000 only)	20
86	Dreamworld DREAM 8	Please Don't Sandblast My House/Time I Broke Down (p/s, 2,000 only)	12
86	Dreamworld DREAM 8T	Please Don't Sandblast My House/You Ungrateful Bastard/Though It Poured The Next Day, I Never Noticed The Rain (12", p/s)	12
87	Dreamworld DREAM 14	Locked Out Of The Love-In (p/s)	15
87	Report REPX 1	If I Were A Bullet (Then For Sure I'd Find A Way To Your Heart)/Poet (p/s)	8
89	Immaculate IMMAC 9	If Only Words (Would Let Me Conquer You)/Orange Sunshine Ride	6
89	Immaculate 12 IMMAC 9	If Only Words (Would Let Me Conquer You)/Orange Sunshine Ride/I Left My Mind In San Francisco (12", p/s)	20
88	Immaculate IMMACLP 1	HEY MAN, THAT'S BEAUTIFUL (LP)	20
00	Vinyl Japan ASKLP 119	LIKE ONE THOUSAND VIOLINS (LP)	20

(see also Page Boys)

ONE TIME SYNCOPATED CODPIECE
71	Jon Hassell HASLP 1195	ONCE MORE WITH FEELING (LP, insert)	100

ONE TWO & THREE
65	Decca F 12093	Black Pearl/Bahama Lullaby	15
65	Decca LK 4682	BLACK PEARLS AND GREEN DIAMONDS (LP)	200

ONE WAY SYSTEM
82	Lightbeat WAY 1	Stab The Judge/Riot Torn City/Me And You (p/s)	12
83	Anagram ANA 5	Jerusalem/Jackie Was A Junkie (p/s)	10
83	Anagram ANA 9	Cum On Feel The Noise/Breakin' In (p/s)	6
83	Anagram GRAM 003	ALL SYSTEMS GO (LP, with lyric inner)	15
83	Anagram GRAM 008	WRITING ON THE WALL (LP, with lyric inner)	15

ONE WAY TICKET
78	President PTLS 1069	TIME IS RIGHT (LP)	200

(see also Five Day Rain)

ONLOOKERS
82	Demon D 1012	You And I/Understand/Julia (p/s)	18

ONLY ONES
77	Vengeance VEN 001	Lovers Of Today/Peter And The Pets (p/s)	12
77	Vengeance VEN 001	Lovers Of Today/Peter And The Pets (12", with 7" x 7" sticker)	12
78	CBS S CBS 6228	Another Girl, Another Planet/Special View (p/s, paper labels)	60
78	CBS S CBS 6228	Another Girl, Another Planet/Special View (p/s, injection moulded labels)	40
78	CBS S CBS 6576	Another Girl, Another Planet/As My Wife Says	10
78	CBS S CBS 12-6576	Another Girl, Another Planet/As My Wife Says (12", p/s)	20
79	CBS S CBS 7086	You've Got To Pay/This Ain't All (It's Made Out To Be) (p/s)	6
79	CBS S CBS 12-7285	Out There In The Night/Lovers Of Today/Peter And The Pets (12", p/s, blue vinyl, 2 slight sleeve variations)	10
79	CBS S CBS 7963	Trouble In The World/Your Chosen Life (withdrawn 'group' black & red p/s)	350
78	CBS 82830	THE ONLY ONES (LP, orange label, with insert)	30
79	CBS 83451	EVEN SERPENTS SHINE (LP, gold embossed sleeve, orange label)	20
80	CBS 84089	BABY'S GOT A GUN (LP, with insert, orange label)	20
89	Strange Fruit SFRLP 102	PEEL SESSIONS ALBUM (LP)	15
07	Pure Pleasure PPAN 82830	THE ONLY ONES (LP, reissue 180gm vinyl)	15

(see also England's Glory)

SEIGEN ONO
88	Venture VE10	CHINESE GREEN TABLE (LP)	15
88	Venture VE 51	COMMES DES GARCONS VOLUME 1 (LP)	40
89	Venture VE 52	COMMES DES GARCONS VOLUME 2 (LP)	40

YOKO ONO
71	Apple APPLE 38	Mrs. Lennon/Midsummer New York	20
72	Apple APPLE 41	Mind Train/Listen, The Snow Is Falling (p/s)	25
73	Apple APPLE 47	Death Of Samantha/Yang Yang	20
73	Apple APPLE 48	Run Run Run/Men Men Men	20
70	Apple SAPCOR 17	YOKO ONO/PLASTIC ONO BAND (LP, with inner sleeve)	60
71	Apple SAPTU 101/2	FLY (2-LP, laminated gatefold, inner sleeves, poster & postcard)	100
73	Apple SAPDO 1001	APPROXIMATELY INFINITE UNIVERSE (2-LP, with lyric inner sleeves)	40
73	Apple SAPCOR 26	FEELING THE SPACE (LP)	40

(see also John Lennon, Bill Elliott & Elastic Oz Band)

ON 1 CREW
93	Bump BUST 3	LET EM AVE IT EP (12")	40
93	Bump BUST 4	SINISTER BY DESIGN EP (12")	30

ONSLAUGHT (1)
83	Complete Control TROL 1	First Strike/State Control/No More (p/s)	12
85	Children Of The Revolution GURT 2	POWER FROM HELL (LP, with inner)	20

ONSLAUGHT (2)

MINT VALUE £

ONSLAUGHT (2)
85	69 Records SRTSK 5375	My Generation/Angel Of Mercy	15

ON THE CARDS
84	OTC 001	This Is My Home Town/All In Vain	18

ON THE WATERFRONT
86	Wizz	The Kids Are Allright/Never Surrender/Far From The Madding Crowd/Mrs. Harrington (12", p/s)	60

ONYX
68	Pye 7N 17477	You've Gotta Be With Me/It's All Put On	30
68	Pye 7N 17622	My Son John/Step By Step	30
69	Pye 7N 17768	Tamaris Khan/So Sad Inside	70
69	CBS 4635	Time Off/Movin' In	20
71	Parlophone R 5888	Air/Our House	12
71	Parlophone R 5906	The Next Stop Is Mine/What's That You Say	12

OO BANG JIGGLY JANG
71	President PT 356	Hanging Tree/1000 Leagues	15

OPAL
85	One Big Guitar OBG 002T	Northern Line/Empty Bottles/Soul Giver (12")	15
87	Rough Trade RTT 129	Fell From The Sun/Freight Train/Grains Of Sand (12")	15
87	Rough Trade ROUGH 116	HAPPY NIGHTMARE BABY (LP)	30
89	Rough Trade ROUGH 128	EARLY RECORDINGS (LP)	30

(see also Mazzy Star)

OPAL BUTTERFLY
68	CBS 3576	Beautiful Beige/Speak Up	60
69	CBS 3921	Mary Anne With The Shakey Hand/My Gration Or?	75
70	Polydor 2058 041	You're A Groupie Girl/Gigging Song	75

(see also Hawkwind, Motorhead, Mott The Hoople)

JACKIE OPEL
63	Jump Up JU 512	TV In Jamaica/Worrell's Captaincy	25
64	Black Swan WI 421	You're No Good/King Liges	40
64	R&B JB 138	Stand By Me (as Jackie Opel & Hortense Ellis)/Solid Rock	50
65	King KG 1011	Cry Me A River/Eternal Love	30
64	R&B JB 160	Pity The Fool/The Day Will Come	50
65	Island WI 203	Wipe Those Tears/Don't Take Your Love	30
65	Island WI 209	Go Whey/Shelter The Storm	250
65	Island WI 227	Old Rockin' Chair/SKATALITES: Song Of Love (B-side is actually "Ska In Vienna Woods")	250
65	Ska Beat JB 190	Done With A Friend/More Wood In The Fire	40
65	Ska Beat JB 227	The Lord Is With/A Little More (beware of counterfeits)	150
66	Island WI 264	A Love To Share/ROLAND ALPHONSO: Devoted To You	25
66	Rio R 117	I Am What I Am/JACKIE MITTOO & SKATALITES: Devil's Bug	60
66	Rio R120	I Don't Want Her/SOUL BOYS: Rudie Get Wise	60

(see also Jackie & Doreen, Doreen & Jackie, Hortense & Jackie)

OPEN
03	Loog 9813076	NEVER ENOUGH EP (1,000 only, p/s)	12
04	Loog 9817238	Close My Eyes/The View (mail order only 12" p/s)	12

OPEN BOOK
87	HAG 002	Pension Day/I'm Incomplete	8

OPEN CASKET
73	Royal RY1	Turning To The Sun/She Can Leave Now	30

OPEN HOUSE
72	Nest NRS 102A	Mr Sparky/My Song	40

OPEN MIND
69	Philips BF 1805	Magic Potion/Cast A Spell (Demo copy)	500
69	Philips BF 1790	Horses And Chariots/Before My Time	100
69	Philips BF 1805	Magic Potion/Cast A Spell	600
69	Philips SBL 7893	OPEN MIND (LP, laminated sleeve, black/silver label)	1000
86	Antar ANTAR 2	OPEN MIND (LP, reissue)	20

(see also Drag Set)

OPEN ROAD
72	Greenwich GSS 102	Swamp Fever/Lost And Found	12
71	Greenwich GSLP 1001	WINDY DAZE (LP, gatefold sleeve)	60

(see also Warm Sounds, Denny Gerrard, Donovan)

OPERA
79	Bead records BEAD 13	OPERA (LP)	25

OPETH
01	Music For Nations MFSN 264	BLACKWATER PARK (2-LP)	35
02	Peaceville DLPVILE 78	STILL LIFE (2-LP, 1000 only)	40
03	Music For Nations MFSN 297	DAMNATION (LP)	45
10	Peaceville VILLELP 78	STILL LIFE (2-LP, reissue, 2000 only)	30

OPPRESSED
83	Oppressed OPPO 1	Work Together/Victims (p/s)	20
83	Firm NICK 1	NEVER SAY DIE (EP)	18
84	Oppressed OPLP 1	OI! OI! MUSIC (LP)	20
85	Skinhead CREW 1	FATAL BLOW (LP)	20
88	OIR 12	DEAD AND BURIED (LP)	15

(see also Rude Boys (2))

OPTIMISTS
81	Armageddon AS 018	Mull Of Kintyre/The Plumbers Song (p/s)	18

OPUS
70	Columbia DB 8675	Baby, Come On/Angela Grey	15

ORA

MINT VALUE £

ORA
69	Tangerine OPLOP 0025	ORA (LP)	350

(see also Byzantium, Movies)

ORAL
82	Conquest Quest 6	SEX (LP)	20

ORAL EXCITERS
79	Three Elms TE 001	It's A Holiday/Tonight (p/s, 500 only)	60

DAPHNE ORAM
10	Sound And Music SB 01	Look At Life/Manchester: Single Cymbals Bit Study/Belbury Poly: Monsoon (1-sided in screen printed plastic sleeve, insert)	12
62	HMV 7EG8762	LISTEN, MOVE AND DANCE 3 - ELECTRONIC SOUND PATTERNS (EP)	30
20	Electronic Sound ES 772	ELECTRONIC SOUND PATTERNS (EP, turquoise vinyl)	8
62	HMV CLP 3531	LISTEN MOVE AND DANCE 1-3 (LP)	40
72	HMS CLP 3762	LISTEN MOVE AND DANCE 1-3 (LP, reissue)	30
10	Young Americans YOUNGAM 001	ORAMICS (4-LP)	30
11	Young Americans YOUNGAM 003	THE ORAM TAPES VOLUME ONE (4-LP)	35
13	Young Americans YOUNGAM 001	ORAMICS (4-LP, repressing, clear vinyl)	40
14	Ecstatic ELP 005	SOUND HOUSES (LP)	15
19	Young Americans YOUNGAM 001	ORAMICS (4-LP, repressing, clear vinyl, '2019 Edition' sticker on front)	30

O RANG
94	Echo ECSY 6	SPOOR (12", p/s)	12
94	Echo ECHLP 2	HEARD OF INSTINCT (LP)	70
97	Echo ECHLP 10	FIELDS AND WAVES (LP)	80

ORANGE ALABASTER MUSHROOM
98	Earworm WORM 36	The Slug/Ethel Tripped A Mean Gloss (p/s, with sticker)	8

ORANGE BICYCLE
67	Columbia DB 8259	Hyacinth Threads/Amy Peate	35
67	Columbia DB 8311	Laura's Garden/Lavender Girl	25
68	Columbia DB 8352	Early Pearly Morning/Go With Goldie	20
68	Columbia DB 8413	Jenskadajka/Nicely	18
68	Columbia DB 8483	Sing This All Together/Trip On An Orange Bicycle	25
69	Parlophone R 5789	Tonight I'll Be Staying Here With You/Last Cloud Home	15
69	Parlophone R 5811	Carry That Weight/You Never Give Me Your Money/Want To B Side	18
70	Parlophone R 5827	Take Me To The Pilot/It's Not My World	20
70	Parlophone R 5854	Jelly On The Bread/Make It Rain	20
71	Regal Zonophone RZ 3029	Goodbye Stranger/Country Comforts	15
70	Parlophone PCS 7108	ORANGE BICYCLE (LP, laminated front sleeve, black/silver label)	250
88	Morgan Bluetown MBT 5003	LET'S TAKE A TRIP ON AN ORANGE BICYCLE (LP)	15
11	Morgan Bluetown BT 5007	ORANGE BICYCLE (LP, reissue, 500 only, orange vinyl, with numbered certificate)	20

(see also Motherlight)

ORANGE BLOSSOM
74	Westwood WRS 038	KEEP ON PUSHING (LP)	30

ORANGE DISASTER
80s	Neuter OD 1	Something's Got To Give/Out Of The Room/Hiding From Frank	20

(see also Varicose Veins)

ORANGE GOBLIN
04	Rise Above RISE7/051	Some You Win, Some You Lose/White Night Cyanide (p/s)	6
00	The Music Cartel TMC 036LP	THE BIG BLACK (LP)	20
04	Rise Above RISELP 46	THIEVING FROM THE HOUSE OF GOD (LP, orange vinyl, 1000 only)	25
07	Mayan MYNLP 058	HEALING THROUGH FIRE (LP)	18
12	Back On Black BOBV 289LP	A EULOGY FOR THE DAMNED (LP, gatefold, merchandise insert, clear vinyl)	20

ORANGE JUICE
80	Postcard 80-1	Falling And Laughing/Moscow Olympics/Moscow (foldover p/s in poly bag, with postcard; and with flexidisc "Felicity (live)" [I Wish I Was A Postcard 1], 963 only)	400
80	Postcard 80-1	Falling And Laughing/Moscow Olympics/Moscow (foldover p/s in poly bag, without postcard and without flexidisc)	100
80	I Wish I Was A Postcard 1	Felicity (live) (freebie flexidisc, also given away with fanzines)	15
80	Postcard 80-2	Blue Boy/Lovesick (hand-coloured p/s in poly bag, blue labels)	60
80	Postcard 80-2	Blue Boy/Love Sick (b/w and yellow labels/cream company sleeve)	18
80	Postcard 80-2	Blue Boy/Love Sick (3rd issue, brown labels in brown company sleeve)	15
80	Postcard 80-6	Simply Thrilled Honey/Breakfast Time (p/s, with picture insert in poly bag)	65
80	Postcard 80-6	Simply Thrilled Honey/Breakfast Time (2nd issue, brown labels in brown company sleeve)	10
80	Postcard 80-6	Simply Thrilled Honey/Breakfast Time (3rd issue, darker labels in brown company sleeve, A & B labels reversed to correct previous errors)	10
81	Postcard 81-2	Poor Old Soul/Poor Old Soul Pt. 2 (die-cut co. sleeve, with postcard)	30
81	Postcard 81-2	Poor Old Soul/Poor Old Soul Pt. 2 (die-cut co. sleeve, without postcard)	10
82	Polydor OJ 1	A Million Pleading Faces/Breakfast Time (12" promo in title sleeve)	15
83	Polydor POSPD 547	Rip It Up/Snake Charmer/Love Sick (live)/A Sad Lament (2 x 7" with poster p/s)	6
83	Polydor POSP 547	Rip It Up/Snake Charmer (p/s, with free The Felicity Flexi Session cassette)	6
83	Polydor OJ 4	Flesh Of My Flesh/Lord John White And The Bottleneck Train	6
84	Polydor OJ 5/JUICE 1	Bridge/Out For The Count (stickered p/s, with free flexidisc Poor Old Soul [live])	6
84	Polydor OJ 6/OJC 6	What Presence?!/A Place In My Heart (Dub) (p/s, with free cassette The Felicity Flexi Session: The Formative Years)	6
82	Polydor POLS 1057	YOU CAN'T HIDE YOUR LOVE FOREVER (LP, inner)	25
82	Polydor POLS 1076	RIP IT UP (LP)	25
84	Polydor 8237961	THE ORANGE JUICE (LP)	15
92	Postcard DUBH 922	OSTRICH CHURCHYARD (LP, 1,000 with inner sleeve, bonus 10" "Irritation Disc" [922TEN])	40

ORANGE MACHINE

			MINT VALUE £
93	Postcard DUBH 932	THE HEATHER'S ON FIRE (LP)	60
10	Domino REWIGCD38X	...COALS TO NEWCASTLE (7-CD box set)	30

(see also Edwyn Collins, Paul Quinn & Edwyn Collins, Fun Four, Josef K)

ORANGE MACHINE
68	Pye 7N 17559	Three Jolly Little Dwarfs/Real Life Permanent Dream	200
69	Pye 7N 17680	You Can All Join In/Dr. Crippen's Waiting Room	175

(see also Danny Hughes)

ORANGE PEEL
71	Reflection HRS 5	I Got No Time/Searching For A Place To Hide	25

ORANGE SEAWEED
68	Pye 7N 17515	Stay Awhile/Pictures In The Sky	70

(see also Fadin' Colours)

ORB

SINGLES
89	Wau! Mr Modo MWS 010T	KISS (12" EP, 949 only, die-cut company sleeve)	15
90	Wau! Mr Modo MWS 017T	A Huge Ever Growing Pulsating Brain That Rules From The Centre Of The Ultraworld: Loving You (Orbital Mix)/(Bucket And Spade Mix)/Why Is 6 Scared of 7? (12" p/s, B-side matrix states 'MWS 016T')	15
90	Big Life BLR 270T	A Huge Ever-Growing Pulsating Brain That Rules From The Centre Of The Ultraworld : Loving You (edited)/(Bucket And Spade Mix)/(Why Is 6 Scared of 7?) (12" p/s, 8,000 only, B-side matrix 'MWS 016T')	10
92	Big Life BLRT 75	Blue Room Part 1/Blue Room Part 2 (12", p/s)	15
20	Electronic Sound ES 763	Hawk Kings/Golden Clouds (p/s)	12

ALBUMS
91	Big Life BLRDLP 5	THE ORB'S ADVENTURES BEYOND THE UNDERWORLD (2-LP, with inner sleeve, 'classical pressing' sticker on sleeve)	40
91	Big Life BLRLP 14	THE ORB AUBREY MIXES: THE ULTRAWORLD EXCURSIONS (LP, with inner sleeve, deleted on day of release)	25
93	Island ILPSQ 8022	LIVE 93 (4-LP)	30
94	Island ORBLP 1 5240131	POMME FRITZ (LP)	30
95	Island ILPSD 8037	ORBUS TERRARUM (2-LP)	40
92	Big Life BLRLA 18	U.F.ORB (2-LP, 12" and 2 art prints in unopened blue plastic cover)	40
92	Big Life BLRLA 18	U.F.ORB (2-LP, 12" and 2 art prints in opened blue plastic cover)	25
99	Island CID 8100	CYDONIA (2-LP)	40
04	Simply Vinyl S160026	BICYCLES AND TRICYCLES (LP)	18
10	Sony 88697760441	METALLIC SPHERES (2-LP)	20
16	Wau! Mr Modo/Island 0600753592861	THE ORB'S ADVENTURES BEYOND THE UNDERWORLD (4-LP, gatefold sleeve, reissue)	70

PROMOS
90	Wau! Mr Modo MWS 017T	A Huge Ever-Growing Pulsating Remix/From One Ear To Another/Why Is 6 Scared Of 7? (12", white label, 100 only)	20
90	Wau! Mr Modo MWS 017R	A Huge Ever-Growing Pulsating Brain That Rules From The Centre Of The Ultraworld (Orbital Dance Mix)/(Orbital Radio Mix)/(Aubrey Mix Mk II) (12", stamped white label, 1,000 only)	15
90	Big Life ORB PROMO 2	Little Fluffy Clouds (Dance Mk 1)/Into The Fourth Dimension/Little Fluffy Clouds (Ambient Mk 1) (12")	10
91	Big Life ORB PICTURE 3	Perpetual Dawn: Ultrabass II (12", 1-sided picture disc, mispressing, plays "Towers Of Dub (Ambient)", 400 pressed but 300 allegedly destroyed)	15

(see also System 7, KLF, Jah Wobble, Apollo XI, Space)

ORBIDÖIG
81	Situation 2 SIT 15	Nocturnal Operation/Down Periscope (p/s)	25

(see also Sensational Creed)

ROY ORBISON

SINGLES
60	London HLU 9149	Only The Lonely (Know How I Feel)/Here Comes That Song Again	6
60	London HLU 9149	Only The Lonely (Know How I Feel)/Here Comes That Song Again (78)	400
60	London HLU 9207	Blue Angel/Today's Teardrops	10
61	London HLU 9307	I'm Hurtin'/I Can't Stop Loving You	10
61	London HLU 7108	I'm Hurtin'/I Can't Stop Loving You (export issue)	15
61	London HLU 9342	Runnin' Scared/Love Hurts	7
64	Ember EMB S 197	Rock House/You're My Baby	20
64	Ember EMB S 200	This Kind Of Love/I Never Knew (in p/s)	20
64	Ember EMB S 200	This Kind Of Love/I Never Knew	8
65	Ember EMB S 209	Sweet And Easy To Love/You're Gonna Cry (in p/s)	15
65	London HLU 9978	(Say) You're My Girl/Sleepy Hollow	6
65	London HLU 9986	Ride Away/Wondering	7
67	London HLU 10113	So Good/Memories	7
67	London HLU 10143	Cry Softly Lonely One/Pistolero	7
67	London HLU 10159	She/Here Comes The Rain Baby	7
68	London HLU 10176	Born To Be Loved By You/Shy Away	10
68	London HLU 10206	Walk On/Flowers	6
68	London HLU 10222	Heartache/Sugar Man	7
69	London HLU 10261	My Friend/Southbound Jerico Parkway	7
69	London HLU 10285	Penny Arcade/Tennessee Owns My Soul	8
69	London HLU 10294	Break My Mind (by Roy Orbison & Art Movement)/How Do You Start Over	8
70	London HLU 10310	So Young/If I Had A Woman Like You	8
71	London HLU 10339	(Love Me Like You Did It) Last Night/Close Again	10
72	London HLU 10358	God Love You/Changes	10
72	London HLU 10388	Memphis Tennessee/I Can Read Between The Lines	10

EPs
57	London RE-S 1089	HILLBILLY ROCK (orange p/s, mauve/silver label, triangular centre)	150

			MINT VALUE £
57	London RE-S 1089	HILLBILLY ROCK (orange p/s, mauve/silver label, round centre)	100
60	London RE-U 1274	ONLY THE LONELY	25
63	London RE-S 1089	HILLBILLY ROCK (re-pressing, yellow p/s, silver-top, round centre)	80
63	London RE-U 1354	ROY ORBISON	20
	(Later pressings are on London Monument label as were later pressings of RE-U 1274 and RE-U 1354)		
63	London RE-U 1373	IN DREAMS	10
64	Ember EP 4546	SWEET AND EASY TO LOVE	40
64	Ember EP 4563	TRYIN' TO GET TO YOU	40
64	London RE-U 1435	IT'S OVER	10
64	London RE-U 1437	OH PRETTY WOMAN	10
65	London RE-U 1439	ROY ORBISON'S STAGE SHOW HITS	15
65	Ember EP 4570	DEVIL DOLL	40
65	London RE-U 1440	LOVE HURTS	15

ALBUMS : LONDON LPS

61	London HA-U 2342	LONELY AND BLUE	20
62	London HA-U 2437	CRYIN' (mono)	20
62	London SAH-U 6229	CRYIN' (stereo)	25
63	London HA-U 8108	IN DREAMS (mono)	15
63	London SH-U 8108	IN DREAMS (stereo)	25
64	London HA-U 8207	OH, PRETTY WOMAN	15
65	London HA-U 8252	THERE IS ONLY ONE ROY ORBISON (mono)	15
65	London SH-U 8252	THERE IS ONLY ONE ROY ORBISON (stereo)	20
66	London HA-U 8279	THE ORBISON WAY (mono)	15
66	London SH-U 8279	THE ORBISON WAY (stereo)	20
66	London HA-U 8297	THE CLASSIC ROY ORBISON (mono)	15
	(The London LPs listed above were originally issued with plum labels [mono] or blue labels [stereo]. Later copies were re-pressed with black labels [mono] or plum labels [stereo] with a boxed London logo)		
66	London HA-U 8297	THE CLASSIC ROY ORBISON (black label mono)	15
66	London SH-U 8297	THE CLASSIC ROY ORBISON (blue label stereo)	15
67	London HA-U 8318	SINGS DON GIBSON (black label mono)	15
67	London SH-U 8318	SINGS DON GIBSON (blue label stereo)	15
68	London HA-U/SH-U 8357	CRY SOFTLY, LONELY ONE	15
70	London HA-U 8406	THE BIG "O" (mono)	15

ALBUMS : OTHER ALBUMS

64	Ember NR 5013	THE EXCITING SOUNDS OF ROY ORBISON (original copies list 'Great Newport Street' address on cover; reissued 1972)	25
64	Ember NR 5013	THE EXCITING SOUNDS OF ROY ORBISON (reissued 1972)	15
65	Ember FA 2005	ROY ORBISON AND OTHERS (with 4 tracks by Orbison)	15

(see also Traveling Wilburys)

ORBIT FIVE

68	Decca F 12799	I Wanna Go To Heaven/Walking (in p/s)	25
68	Decca F 12799	I Wanna Go To Heaven/Walking	15

ORBITAL
SINGLES

89	Oh Zone ZONE 1	Chime/Deeper (12", p/s)	20

ALBUMS

91	FFRR 828248-1	ORBITAL (2-LP)	50
93	Internal TRULP 2	ORBITAL 2 (2-LP)	50
94	Internal TRULP 5	SNIVILISATION (2-LP, gatefold sleeve, poster)	50
96	Internal TRULP 10	IN SIDES (3-LP)	100
99	FFRR 556 076-1	THE MIDDLE OF NOWHERE (2-LP)	60
02	FFRR 092746190	WORK 1989-2002 (2-LP)	50
03	EMI 7243 5 93784 11	OCTANE (LP, soundtrack)	20
04	Orbital Music Orbital V001	BLUE ALBUM (2-LP)	50
12	ACP ACPV1203	WONKY (2-LP)	20
15	Vinyl Collector 0825646128747	ORBITAL (2-LP, 1st album, reissue 180gm)	30
15	Warner Bros. TRULP 2-1	ORBITAL (2-LP, 2nd album, reissue 180gm)	35

ORCA

92	Micro Genetic 001	9 Lives/Shining Bright (12")	20
92	Lucky Spin LSR-ORC 1	DANCES WITH DOLPHINS EP NO. 1 (12", stickered, black die-cut sleeve)	40
92	Lucky Spin LSR 002	My Brothers/The Power (12")	10
93	Lucky Spin LRS 006	DANCES WITH DOLPHINS EP NO. 2 (12")	25
93	Lucky Spin LSR 011	4AM/Pure Bliss/Jungle Vibes/Pure Bliss (Remix) (100 on red vinyl)	40
93	Lucky Spin LSR 011	4AM/Pure Bliss/Jungle Vibes/Pure Bliss (Remix) (black vinyl)	30
93	Lucky Spin ORCA 6	BACK TO THE JUNGLE EP (12")	20
94	Lucky Spin STU 06	4AM (Remix 1)/4AM (Remix 2) (12")	20
94	Lucky Spin LSR 016	Intalect/Tranquility To Earth (12")	100
95	Lucky Spin LSR 023	My Eyes/Liar (12")	30
95	Lucky Spin LSR 026	Intalect (Remix)/Sample And Hold (12")	18

ORCHESTRA BAOBAB

89	World Circuit WCB 014	PIRATES CHOICE - LEGENDARY 1982 SESSION (LP)	50

ORCHESTRA DEL ORO

62	Pye Int 7N.25143	Main Theme From Lolita/Lolita Ya Ya (in PS)	8

ORCHESTRAL MANOEUVRES IN THE DARK (O.M.D.)

79	Factory FAC 6	Electricity/Almost (black 'braille' p/s)	100
80	Din Disc DIN 15-10	Messages (Extended)/Waiting For The Man/Taking Sides Again (10", p/s)	6
80	Din Disc DIN 22	Enola Gay (Extended)/Annex (p/s)	6
84	Virgin VSS 660	Locomotion/Her Body In My Soul (uncut train-shaped picture disc)	35

ORCHIDS (1)

MINT VALUE £

85	Virgin VSY 766-14	So In Love (Extended)/Concrete Hands (Extended)/Maria Gallant (12" picture disc)	15
85	Virgin VS 766	So In Love/Concrete Hands//Maria Gallante/White Trash (live) (double pack, stickered gatefold p/s)	6
10	100% BNL002T	If You Want It/Alone (p/s, yellow vinyl)	10
10	100% BNL003T	Sister Marie Says/History Of Modern (Parts III and IV) (p/s, lilac vinyl)	10
13	100%100RSD27	THE FUTURE WILL BE SILENT (10", p/s)	30
15	Pledge Music WN2PICDISC	DAZZLE SHIPS AT THE MUSEUM OF LIVERPOOL (12", picture disc)	30
17	100%100T65	Isotope/Skin (12", p/s)	20
17	100% 100T67	The Punishment Of Luxury (Extended)/Lampe Licht/The Punishment Of Luxury (12", p/s)	18
19	Virgin 0602577481901	Electricity/Almost (Vince Clarke Remix) (reissue, p/s, clear vinyl)	10
80	Din Disc DID 2	ORCHESTRAL MANOEUVRES IN THE DARK (LP, 12" x 12" grid sleeve, black, blue or grey outer sleeves with orange, pink or red inner)	25
80	Din Disc DID 6	ORGANISATION (LP, stickered sleeve, with insert & 7": "Introducing Radios"/ Distance Fades Between Us"/"Progress"/"Once When I Was Six" [DEP 2])	15
91	Virgin V 2648	SUGAR TAX (LP, mispressing with extra track "All She Wants Is Everything" instead of "Neon Lights")	15
84	Virgin V 2310	JUNK CULTURE (LP, stickered sleeve, with free 7": "[Angels Keep Turning] The Wheels Of The Universe" [JUNK 1])	15
93	Virgin V2715	LIBERATOR (LP)	40
96	Virgin V2807	UNIVERSAL (LP)	80
10	100% BNLP001LP	HISTORY OF MODERN (2-LP, CD)	50
13	100% 100LP26	ENGLISH ELECTRIC (LP, with CD)	50
14	OTB OMD 1	LIVE (2-LP, blue or white vinyl, 100 only of each)	75
16	Live Here Now LHN004LP	ORCHESTRAL MANOEUVRES IN THE DARK/ARCHITECTURE AND MORALITY/DAZZLE SHIPS (3-LP, reissue, 1000 only)	50
17	100% 100LP66	THE PUNISHMENT OF LUXURY (LP)	20
17	100%100LP66Y	THE PUNISHMENT OF LUXURY (LP, yellow vinyl)	25
18	100% 100LP7C	HISTORY OF MODERN (2-LP, reissue, orange vinyl)	40

ORCHIDS (1)

63	Decca F 11743	Gonna Make Him Mine/Stay At Home	25
63	Decca F 11785	Love Hit Me/Don't Make Me Mad	20
64	Decca F 11861	I've Got That Feeling/Larry	25

(see also Exceptions)

ORCHIDS (2)

88	Sarah SARAH 002	I've Got A Habit/Give Me Some Peppermint Freedom/Apologies (foldover p/s with poster, 1,000 only)	100
88	Sarah SARAH 011	UNDERNEATH THE WINDOW, UNDERNEATH THE SINK EP (p/s)	20
88	Sha La La BaBaBaBaBa 5	From This Day/SEA URCHINS: Summertime (flexi, 2,500 only, 1,000 in p/s)	15
89	Sarah SARAH 023	WHAT WILL WE DO NEXT? EP (p/s)	20
90	Sarah SARAH 029	Something For The Longing/Farewell Dear Bonnie/On A Sunday (p/s, with inserts)	15
90	Caff CAFF 11	An Ill Wind That Blows/All Those Things (p/s, with insert)	20
91	Sarah SARAH 042	PENETRATION EP (12", p/s with insert)	18
92	Sarah SARAH 66	Thaumaturgy/I Was Just Dreaming/Between Sleeping And Waking (p/s, insert)	15
91	Sarah SARAH 605	UNHOLY SOUL (LP)	35
94	Sarah SARAH 617	STRIVING FOR THE LAZY PERFECTION (LP)	50
95	Sarah SARAH 401	LYCEUM (10" mini-LP)	25
95	Sarah SARAH 611 LP	EPICUREAN: A SOUNDTRACK (2-LP)	40

ORDINARY PEOPLE

97	Social Circles SC 001	Keep Your Love/Milton Blues/Bonus Beatz (12")	50
97	Social Circles JKSC 001	Baby You Make My Heart Sing/I Need/I'll Take You There (12")	80
98	Social Circles JKSC 002	Baby You Make My Heart Sing/I'll Take You There (12", reissue)	60
98	Social Circles JKSC 003	I'M MISSING EP (12", featuring Jude Mansi)	20

ORE

82	Bandit BR 003	Your Time Will Come/Yellow River (p/s)	100

ORGAN

06	Too Pure PURE 195LP	GRAB THAT GUN (LP, reissue of 2004 LP)	75

CHARLES ORGANAIRE

64	Blue Beat BB 241	The Red Sea/You May Not Believe (as Big Charlie)	18
64	R&B JB 149	Little Village/It Happens On A Holiday	35
64	Rio R 28	Little Village/It Happens On A Holiday (reissue)	20

ORGANIC STNTHETIC

97	Bang In Tunes BIT 012	Organic/Transmissions (12")	15

ORGANISATION

70	RCA SF 8111	TONE FLOAT (LP)	400

(see also Kraftwerk)

ORGANISERS

66	Pye 7N 17022	Lonesome Road/The Organiser	75

ORGANUM

94	Aeroplane AR 15	Gloria (1-sided, numbered p/s, 113 only)	50
95	Aeroplane AR 16	Lysis (1-sided, 72 only)	50
95	Aeroplane AR 17	Kanroku (1-sided 12", black outer sleeve, illustrated, stamped, signed and no'd inner sleeve, 111 only)	60
95	Aeroplane AR 19	Rotor (1-sided, signed, no'd, 83 only, p/s)	60
95	Aeroplane AR 20	Arc (1-sided, signed, no'd, 85 only, p/s)	50
96	Aeroplane AR 23	Shovels (1-sided, signed, no'd, 91 only, p/s)	50
96	Aeroplane AR 24	Raw (1-sided, signed, no'd, 83 only, p/s)	50
88	United Dairies UN 023	SUBMISSION (LP, 1000 only)	40
94	Aeroplane AR 14	SPHYX (LP, black picture label, 546 only)	20
94	Aeroplane AR 14	SPHYX (LP, blue picture label, 509 only, reissue)	20

(see also David Jackman)

ORGANUM/NEW BLOCKADERS

MINT VALUE £

ORGANUM/NEW BLOCKADERS
84	Aeroplane AR 7	Pulp Parts 1 & 2 (gatefold p/s, 279 only)	60
85	Laylah/Antirecords LAY 19	IN EXTREMIS (LP)	20
88	Laylah LAY 012	TOWER OF SILENCE (LP)	20

(see also Current 93, Nurse With Wound, Eddie Prevost Band, David Jackman, New Blockaders)

ORIGINAL CASTE
69	Bell BLL 1079	One Tin Soldier/Live For Tomorrow	6

ORIGINAL CHECKMATES
62	Pye 7N 15428	Hot Toddy/Tuxedo Junction	10
62	Pye 7N 15442	Begin The Beguine (Stomp)/Begin The Beguine	15
63	Decca F 11688	Union Pacific/The Spy	30

(see also Checkmates)

ORIGINAL DOWNTOWN SYNCOPATORS
63	J.R.T. Davies DAVLP 301/2	THE ORIGINAL DOWNTOWN SYNCOPATORS (10" LP, white labels only)	20

(see also Ron Geesin)

ORIGINAL DYAKS
67	Columbia DB 8234	Got To Get A Good Thing Going/Would You Love Me Too	10

ORIGINAL NEW ORLEANS RHYTHM KINGS
54	Columbia SCM 5113	Golden Leaf Strut/She's Crying For Me	10

ORIGINAL ROCKERS
93	Different Drummer LP GOO 1	ROCKERS TO ROCKERS (LP)	15

ORIGINAL SIN
84	Sin S1N	The Shadow/Salvation (12", p/s, private pressing)	25

ORIGINALS (1)
62	Top Rank JAR 600	Gimme A Little Kiss, Will Ya, Huh/At Times Like This	35

ORIGINALS (2)
67	Tamla Motown TMG 592	Goodnight Irene/Need Your Lovin', Want You Back	80
67	Tamla Motown TMG 592	Goodnight Irene/Need Your Lovin', Want You Back (DJ copy)	150
70	Tamla Motown TMG 733	Baby I'm For Real/The Moment Of Truth	18
72	Tamla Motown TMG 822	God Bless Whoever Sent You/I Like Your Style/Baby I'm For Real	8
69	Tamla Motown TMG 702	Green Grow The Lilacs/You're The One	20
76	Tamla Motown TMG 1066	Six Million Dollar Man/Mother Nature's Best (unreleased)	0
69	Tamla Motown TML 11116	GREEN GROW THE LILACS (LP, mono)	60
69	Tamla Motow STML 11116	GREEN GROW THE LILACS (LP, stereo)	55

ORIGINAL TORNADOS
75	SRT SRTS 75350	Telstar/Red Rocket	10

(see also Tornados)

ORIGINATION
92	Rudeboy RUDE 001	Break Down/Bass/R.E.S.P.E.C.T. (12")	15
92	Rudeboy RUDE 002	Breakdown (Remix)/Breakdown (Original Edit)/ Breaking Out The B-Line/Gimme Ya Luv (12")	12
93	Rudeboy RUDE 005	Sunrise/Sunrise (Ruff Mix)/Make Ya Wanna Do Right/Out Of This World (12")	10
93	Rudeboy RUDE 006	Music Takes Control/Signal To Noise/Music Takes Control (Remix) (12")	10
94	Rudeboy RUDE 007	Shine on '94/Shine On (Unreleased '92 Remix)/ Shine On '94 (Dub Version)/Shine On (Original '92 Mix) (12")	30

ORIGINELLS 4
64	Columbia DB 7259	My Girl/Kathy (as Origenells)	20
64	Columbia DB 7388	Nights/I Can Make You Mine	18

ORIGIN UNKNOWN
92	Ram RAMM 002	Untitled (6.03)/Untitled (5.01)/Untitled (5.22)/Untitled (6.12) (12", stamped white labels, promo only, not released)	20
93	Ram RAMM 004	The Touch/Valley Of The Shadows (12")	10
93	Ram RAMM 004R	The Touch (Part 2)/Valley Of The Shadows (Long Dark Remix) (12")	10
95	Ram RAMM 014	Truly One/Mission Control (12")	12
90s	Ram RAMM 002	EASTERN PROMISE EP (12", stamped white label, 4 untitled tracks, promo only)	120
96	Ram RAMM 16	Valley Of The Shadows (original Mix)/Valley Of The Shadows (Awake '96 Remix) (12")	10

ORION (1)
84	Lost Moment LM 02	Insane In Another World/Storm (p/s)	15

ORION (2)
87	Gypsy GYP 001	JACK ORION (LP)	30

ORIOR
79	Crystal Groove 7E 2	Elevation/Tutankhamen/Quiet Sky (wraparound p/s, insert)	35

ORKIDEA
99	Steel Fish Blue SFB 001	Unity (12", white label)	45
05	Sential SE 002	BEAUTIFUL EP (12", p/s)	60

TONY ORLANDO
61	Fontana H 308	Halfway To Paradise/Lonely Tomorrows	20
61	Fontana H 330	Bless You/Am I The Guy	10
61	Fontana H 350	Happy Times (Are Here To Stay)/Lonely Am I	10
62	Fontana H 366	Talkin' About You/My Baby's A Stranger	10
62	Columbia DB 4871	Chills/At The Edge Of Tears	20
63	Columbia DB 4954	Beautiful Dreamer/The Loneliest	25
63	Columbia DB 4991	Shirley/Joanie	8
64	Columbia DB 7288	Tell Me What Can I Do/She Doesn't Know It	10
63	Columbia SEG 8238	BLESS YOU (EP)	40
63	Fontana TFL 5167	BLESS YOU (LP, mono)	50
63	Fontana STFL 582	BLESS YOU (LP, stereo)	60

ORLANDO (1)
69	NEMS 56-4159	Am I The Same Guy/Poor Little Me	100

ORLONS

MINT VALUE £

ORLONS
62	Columbia DB 4865	The Wah Watusi/Holiday Hill	35
62	Cameo Parkway C 231	Don't Hang Up/The Conservative	25
63	Cameo Parkway C 243	South Street/Them Terrible Boots	20
63	Cameo Parkway C 257	Not Me/My Best Friend	15
63	Cameo Parkway C 273	Crossfire/It's No Big Thing	15
63	Cameo Parkway C 287	Bon Doo Wah/Don't Throw Your Love Away	20
63	Cameo Parkway C 295	Shimmy Shimmy/Everything Nice	15
64	Cameo Parkway C 319	Rules Of Love/Heartbreak Hotel	15
64	Cameo Parkway C 332	Knock Knock (Who's There)/Goin' Places	15
66	Planet PLF 117	Spinnin' Top/Anyone Who Had A Heart	150
72	Mojo 2092 029	Spinnin' Top/Anyone Who Had A Heart (reissue)	15
62	Cameo Parkway C 1033	ALL THE HITS (LP)	60
63	Cameo Parkway C 1061	BIGGEST HITS (LP)	60
78	London HA-U 8504	CAMEO PARKWAY SESSIONS (LP)	30

(see also Rosetta Hightower)

OROONIES
91	Demi Monde DMLP 1027	OF HOOF AND HORN (LP)	18

JIM O'ROURKE
99	Domino WIGLP 62	EUREKA (LP)	40
01	Domino WIGLP 104	INSIGNIFICANCE (LP)	30
03	Three Poplars 3P08	SCEND (LP, reissue, clear vinyl)	20

ORPHAN (1)
80	Orphan Records ORP-1	Little Mother/I Don't Want To Go (To Work Tomorrow), stamped inner sleeve and insert p/s	20

ORPHAN (2)
85	Swoop RTLS 013	Nervous/Little England (p/s)	15

ORPHEUS
66	Red Bird RB 10-041	My Life/Music Minus Orpheus	40
68	MGM MGM 1413	I've Never Seen Love Like This/Lesley's World	12
68	MGM MGM C(S) 8072	ORPHEUS (LP)	25

RIZ ORTOLANI
71	United Artists UP 35278	The Hunting Party/CAROL CARMICHAEL: Where's Poppa?	8

BETH ORTON
96	Heavenly HVN 56	I Wish I Never Saw The Sunshine (p/s, 1-sided limited edition, 500 only)	20
96	Heavenly HVNLP 17	TRAILER PARK (LP, 100 copies only)	100
99	Heavenly HVNLP 22	CENTRAL RESERVATION (2-LP, gatefold sleeve, 1000 copies only)	100
02	Heavenly HVNLP 37	DAYBREAKER (LP)	40
12	Anti 7118-1	SUGARING SEASON (LP & CD)	15

(see also Spill)

PAUL ORWELL
14	Heavy Soul ROR 059	Tell Me Tell Me/Little Reason (250 only, all signed)	70
15	Heavy Soul ROR 064	You're Nothing Special/Like I Did Before (p/s, 250 only)	25
16	Heavy Soul ROR 068	Attack/Let You Go (p/s, 200 only)	15
16	Heavy Soul ROR 075	Don't Do As I Do Do As I Say/Pleasure Pill (300 only, die cut sleeve)	15
16	Heavy Soul ROR 079	Too Young To Die (1-sided, p/s, 50 only in different coloured sleeves blue, yellow, green, pink and white)	30
17	Heavy Soul ROR	Needles And Sins (1-sided white flexidisc)	40
15	Heavy Soul ROR 065	BLOWING YOUR MIND AWAY	45

EILEEN OSBORNE
75	Seagull SG1	SINGING SHORES (LP)	15

MIKE OSBORNE
71	Turtle TUR 300	OUTBACK (LP)	60
73	Cadillac SGC 1002	ORIGINAL (LP, as Mike Osborne & Stan Tracey)	20
75	Ogun OG 300	BORDER CROSSING (LP)	15
76	Ogun OG 700	ALL NIGHT LONG (LP)	20
77	Ogun OG 210	TANDEM - LIVE AT BRACKNELL FESTIVAL (LP, with Stan Tracey)	18
77	Ogun OG 810	MARCEL'S MUSE (LP)	25

(see also Stan Tracey)

OZZY OSBOURNE
80	Jet JET 197	Crazy Train/You Looking At Me Looking At You (p/s)	6
80	Jet JET 7003	Mr. Crowley (live)/You Said It All (live) (p/s)	8
80	Jet JET 12003	Mr. Crowley (live)/You Said It All (live)/Suicide Solution (live) (12", p/s)	10
80	Jet JETP 12003	Mr. Crowley (live)/You Said It All (live)/Suicide Solution (live) (12", picture disc)	15
82	Jet JET 7030	Symptom Of The Universe/N.I.B. (p/s)	6
82	Jet JETP 7030	Symptom Of The Universe/N.I.B. (picture disc)	10
83	Epic TA 3915	Bark At The Moon/One Up The B-Side (12", p/s, silver vinyl)	15
83	Epic WA 3915	Bark At The Moon/One Up The B-Side (12", picture disc, unreleased)	0
84	Epic WA 4452	So Tired/Bark At The Moon (live)/Waiting For Darkness/Suicide Solution/Paranoid (live) (12", p/s, gold vinyl)	12
86	Epic A 6859	Shot In The Dark/Rock'n'Roll Rebel (p/s, with autographed signature card)	40
86	Epic QA 6859	Shot In The Dark/Rock'n'Roll Rebel (poster p/s)	8
88	Epic 653 063-9	Miracle Man/Crazy Babies (head-shaped picture disc)	25
88	Epic 652875 6	BACK TO OZ (12" EP, p/s, with poster)	15
90	Epic 465941 1	JUST SAY OZZY (12" EP, p/s)	12
91	Epic 657 4406	No More Tears (extended version)/S.I.N./Party With The Animals (12" pic. disc)	12
93	Epic 659 3406	Changes/Changes (extended version)/No More Tears (live)/ Desire (12" picture disc, with insert)	15
96	Epic 663570 6	I Just Want You/Aimee/Voodoo Dancer (12", one side etched)	20
81	Jet LP 234	BLIZZARD OF OZ (LP, with poster)	40
81	Jet LP 234	BLIZZARD OF OZ (LP, without poster)	20

OSBORNE BROTHERS

MINT VALUE £

81	Jet LP 237	DIARY OF A MADMAN (LP)	20
82	Jet JETDP 401	TALK OF THE DEVIL (2-LP)	20
83	Epic EPC 25739	BARK AT THE MOON (LP, 1st pressing with blue lettering)	20
86	Epic EPC 26404	THE ULTIMATE SIN (LP)	15
86	Epic EPC 11-26404	THE ULTIMATE SIN (LP, picture disc)	20
87	Epic EPC 450475 1	RANDY RHOADS TRIBUTE (2-LP)	20
88	Epic EPC 462581 1	NO REST FOR THE WICKED (LP)	20
93	Epic 4737961	LIVE & LOUD (2-LP)	80

(see also Black Sabbath, Lita Ford & Ozzy Osbourne)

OSBORNE BROTHERS

62	MGM MGM 1184	The Banjo Boys/Poor Old Cora	6

JOHNNY OSBOURNE (& SENSATIONS)

70	Big Shot BI 549	See And Blind (solo)/THE TECHNIQUES: Scar Face	30
72	Techniques TE 916	See And Blind/TECHNIQUES ALL STARS: Rema Skank	30
75	Torpedo TOR 37	Put Away Your Gun/Version Gun	60
80	Jammys JM 002	Long Long Life/HIGH MUNDELL: Walk With Jah (12")	25
80	Cha Cha CHAD 27	Kiss Somebody/Version (12")	35
80	Black Joy DH 810	Purify Your Heart/Politician (blue vinyl)	40
80	Greensleeves GRED 34	Fally Ranking/Trench Town School (12")	40
80	Unity UN 003	Original Rewind/LEROY SMART: Back Off (12")	15
81	Greensleeves GRED 50	Back Off (with PAPA TULLO).Dub (12")	35
81	Cha Cha CHAD 31	Nightfall/Dub Fall (12")	20
81	Greensleeves GRED 60	Trying To Turn Me On/Turn On Dub (12")	15
81	Simba LION 1	13 Dead (Nothing Said)/Black Lion Band Murder (12")	25
81	Simba SIM 002	Don't Bite The Hand (with ASWAD)/Dub (10")	25
82	Oak Sounds OSD 006	Yo Yo/ECHO MINOTT : Man In Love (12")	15
82	Greensleeves GRE 884	Never Stop Fighting/ROOTS RADICS: Never Stop Dub	20
86	Greensleeves GRED 208	Dub Plate Playing/COCOA TEA: Cocoa Tea Medley (12")	40
89	Live & Love LLD 119	Chain Grabber/Watch Them A Watch (12", with PAPPA SAN)	18
98	Riz RIZ 012	Rise Up/RIZ ALL STARS: Version	10
70	Trojan TTL29	COME BACK DARLING (LP)	40
73	Big Shot BILP 103	READY OR NOT (LP)	100
80	Greensleeves GREL 12	FALLY LOVER (LP, red vinyl)	30
80	Jammy's JAM 1000	FOLLY RANKING (LP, orange vinyl)	50
81	Cha Cha CHALP 010	IN NAH DISCO STYLE (LP)	50
81	Black Joy DHLP 2001	WARRIOR (LP)	35
82	Arrival ALP 002	YO YO (LP)	15
82	Greensleeves GREL 38	NEVER STOP FIGHTING (LP)	30
84	Selection SELP 01	REALITY (LP)	25

BOB OSBURN

64	London HLD 9869	Bound To Happen/Think Of Me	15

OSCAR BICYCLE

68	CBS 3237	On A Quiet Night/The Room Revolves Around Me	60

OSCAR (1)

66	Reaction 591 003	Club Of Lights/Waking Up	60
66	Reaction 591 006	Join My Gang/Days Gone By	40
67	Reaction 591 012	Over The Wall We Go/Every Day Of My Life	40
67	Reaction 591 016	Holiday/Give Her All She Wants	30
68	Polydor 56257	Open Up The Skies/Wild Ones	30

(see also Paul Dean, Paul Nicholas)

OSCAR (2)

74	Buk BULP 2001	OSCAR (LP)	15

OSCILLATORS

79	Warren Records WAR-SEP-465	Leonard Cheshire/Fast Breeder Reactor (fold-out p/s, with or without 'group' drawing, 1000 only)	60
80	Yawn SRTS/80/CUS693	Marilyn Brown/E-Boat (fold out p/s)	20

PETER OSGOOD

70	Penny Farthing PEN 715	Chelsea/Stamford Bridge	10

OSHAMA

82	Smokey SMJD 007	Highway/Come The Time (12")	70

OSIBISA

71	Smoke SS 1001	Black Ant/Kotoko	20
71	MCA MDKS 8001	OSIBISA (LP, gatefold, purple/red 'dogbone' label)	50
71	MCA MDKS 8005	WOYAYA (LP, gatefold, black/blue/white hexagon label)	35
72	MCA MDKS 8007	HEADS (LP, gatefold, black/blue/white label)	20
73	Warner Bros. WB 56022	HAPPY CHILDREN (LP)	15
73	Buddah 2318 087	SUPER FLY T.N.T. (LP, soundtrack)	15
74	MCA MCG 3508	OSIBISA (LP, reissue, rainbow label)	15
74	MCA MCG 3506	WOYAWA (LP, reissue, rainbow label)	15
74	Warner Bros. K 56048	OSIBIROCK (LP)	15
75	Bronze ILPS 9355	WELCOME HOME (LP)	30
76	Bronze ILPS 9411	OJAH AWAKE (LP)	15
77	Bronze BRSP 3	BLACK MAGIC NIGHT (2-LP)	20
80	Calibre CAB LP 1002	MYSTIC ENERGY (LP)	15
82	Magnet MAGL 5053	UNLEASHED (2-LP)	25
84	Premier CBR 1035	LIVE AT THE MARQUEE (LP)	15

(see also Del Richardson, Sundae Times, Bessa Simons, Kiki Gyan, Spartacus R)

OSMOSIS

70	RCA VICTOR LPS 4369	OSMOSIS (LP)	20

OSMOND BROTHERS

MINT VALUE £

OSMOND BROTHERS
63	MGM MGM 1208	Be My Little Baby Bumble Bee/I Wouldn't Know	15
63	MGM MGM 1245	Travels Of Jamie McPheeters/Aura Lee	12
63	MGM MGM-C 1011	NEW SOUND OF THE BROTHERS (LP)	30

OSSIE & SWEET BOYS
| 67 | Polydor 56167 | Nothing Takes The Place Of You/Brixton Boo-Ga-Loo | 15 |

OSSIE & UPSETTERS
| 66 | Doctor Bird DB 1018 | Turn Me On/True Love | 40 |

(see also Upsetters)

AL OSTER
| 60s | Dominion LP 1321 | ECHO OF THE YUKON (LP) | 20 |

OSU
| 83 | Shaka XAKA 2 | Light Up My Fire/Merry Go Round (p/s) | 80 |

GILBERT O'SULLIVAN
| 71 | Columbia DB 8779 | I Wish I Could Cry/Mr Moody's Garden | 8 |

(see also Gilbert)

PETER O'SULLIVAN
| 76 | Charisma CAS 1160 | PETER O'SULLIVAN TALKS TURF (LP) | 15 |

OSUNLADE
08	Strictly Rhythm SR12653	MOMMAS GROOVE (THE REMIXES) (12" p/s)	40
13	Yoruba YSD 56	Dionne/What Gets You High? (p/s, 250 only)	70
17	BBE/Yoruba BBE380ALP	PYROGRAPHY (3-LP. reissue with booklet)	35

RAMON OTANO
| 64 | Jump Up/Island JU 250 | Fiesta En La Joya/Mambo Trinidad | 10 |

OTHER BROTHERS
| 69 | Pama PM 785 | Let's Get Together/Little Girl | 25 |

OTHER SIDE
| 87 | Casual Sax SRT 8KS 1432 | Is It Any Wonder/Let's Be Perfect (p/s) | 40 |

OTHER TWO (1)
64	Decca F 11911	I Wanna Be With You/Grumbling Guitar	12
65	RCA RCA 1465	Don't You Wanna Love Me Baby/Hold Back The Light Of Dawn	10
66	RCA RCA 1531	I'll Never Let You Go/Hot At Night	12

OTHER TWO (2)
| 93 | London 520028.1 | THE OTHER TWO AND YOU (LP) | 50 |

(see also Joy Division, New Order, Bad Lieutenant)

OTHERS (1)
| 64 | Fontana TF 501 | Oh Yeah/I'm Taking Her Home | 60 |

(see also Sands, Sundragon)

JOHNNY OTIS SHOW
58	Capitol CL 14817	Bye Bye Baby (as Johnny Otis Show with Marie Adams)/Good Golly	15
58	Capitol CL 14837	The Light Still Shines In My Window/All I Want Is Your Love (with Marie Adams)	25
58	Capitol CL 14854	Well, Well, Well, Well!/You Just Kissed Me Goodbye (with Mel Williams)	25
58	Capitol CL 14875	Ring-A-Ling/The Johnny Otis Hand Jive	25
58	Capitol CL 14875	Ring-A-Ling/The Johnny Otis Hand Jive (78)	20
58	Capitol CL 14941	Crazy Country Hop/Willie Did The Cha Cha	25
59	Capitol CL 15008	You/My Dear (as Johnny Otis Show with Mel Williams)	18
59	Capitol CL 15018	Castin' My Spell/Telephone Baby (as Johnny Otis Show with Marci Lee)	25
59	Capitol CL 15057	Three Girls Named Molly Doin' The Hully Gully/I'll Do The Same Thing For You	20
60	Capitol CL 15112	Mumblin' Mosie/Hey Baby, Don't You Know?	15
64	Ember EMB S 192	Hand Jive One More Time/Baby I Got News For You	10
69	Sonet SON 608	Country Girl/Signifyin' Monkey	6
72	Epic EPC 7896	The Watts Breakaway/You Can Depend On Me	8
72	Epic EPC 8071	The Watts Breakaway/Willie And The Hand Jive	8
59	Capitol EAP1 1134	THE JOHNNY OTIS SHOW (EP)	25
65	Vocalion VEP 170162	JOHNNY OTIS (EP)	50
58	Capitol T 940	THE JOHNNY OTIS SHOW (LP)	100
69	Sonet SNTF 613	COLD SHOT (LP)	15
72	Ember SPE 6604	FORMIDABLE (LP)	15

(see also Marie Adams)

SHUGGIE OTIS
| 70 | CBS 63996 | HERE COMES SHUGGIE OTIS (LP) | 35 |

(see also Al Kooper & Shuggie Otis)

NOIT OTNI & PITS
| 79 | Automotive AERS 107 | A Heart Can Only Be Broken Once/Moving Target (in p/s) | 35 |
| 79 | Automotive AERS 107 | A Heart Can Only Be Broken Once/Moving Target | 25 |

FRAN O TOOLE
| 74 | Emerald MD 1179 | Clap Your Hands And Stamp Your Feet/Drift Away | 10 |

JOHN OTWAY
72	County COUN 215	Gypsy/Misty Mountain (private pressing, County Recording Service, Bracknell on label, with duplicated lyric sheet)	25
76	Viking YRS CF 01	Louisa On A Horse/Beware Of The Flowers (private pressing)	15
79	Polydor 2059 105	Frightened And Scared (instrumental)/Are You On My Side? (p/s, only 3 copies pressed!)	50
86	'Warner Bros' OTWEAY 1	The New Jerusalem/The Tyger (private pressing)	20

JOHN OTWAY & WILD WILLY BARRETT
73	Track 2094 111	Murder Man/If I Did	8
77	Polydor 2058 916	Racing Cars (Jet Spotter Of The Track)/Running From The Law	10
77	Polydor 2058 951	Really Free/Beware Of The Flowers (Cos I'm Sure They're Going To Get You Yeh) (p/s)	6
82	Stiff Indie STIN 1	Headbutts/Live Version Headbutts (p/s)	7
82	Empire HAM 5T	12 STITCH EP (12" EP in polythene bag with jay-card)	15

77	Extracted EXLP 1	JOHN OTWAY AND WILD WILLY BARRETT (LP, handmade stickered sleeve)	20
77	White label OBL 1	OTWAY AND BARRETT LIVE AT THE ROUNDHOUSE (private pressing LP, freebie, handwritten labels, plain sleeve, 250 numbered copies only)	35

(see also Wild Willy Barrett)

OUCH
92	Cavell CVLL 1	I Need You More/Carina	7

OUR PLASTIC DREAM
67	Go AJ 11411	A Little Bit Of Shangrila/Encapsulated Marigold	200

OUT
79	Rabid TOSH 113	Who Is Innocent/Linda's Just A Statue (p/s)	7

OUT OF THE SHADE
05	Roc Solid Records RSR 1	What You Want/What You Want (Version) (12")	100

(see also Gold In The Shade)

OUTCASTS
78	It IT 4	Frustration/Don't Want To Be No Adult/You're A Disease (p/s)	30
78	Good Vibrations GOT 3	Just Another Teenage Rebel/Love Is For Sops (poster p/s, various colours; 'band' p/s)	50
78	Good Vibrations GOT 3	Just Another Teenage Rebel/Love Is For Sops (poster p/s, various colours; 'type' p/s)	50
79	Good Vibrations GOT 17	Self Conscious Over You/Love You For Never (p/s)	15
81	GBH GBH 001	Magnum Force/Gangland Warfare (p/s)	20
79	Good Vibrations BIG 1	SELF CONSCIOUS OVER YOU (LP)	25
82	Abstract ABT 004	BLOOD & THUNDER (LP)	20

OUT DARE
94	Gash T5	OUT DARE EP (12", white label, with press sheet)	150

OUTER LIMITS (1)
67	Elephant LUR 100	When The Work Is Thru'/5 MAN CARGO: What A Wonderful Feeling (Leeds Students Charity Rag record)	55
67	Deram DM 125	Just One Me Chance/Help Me Please	80
68	Immediate IM 067	Great Train Robbery/Sweet Freedom (demo only)	70
68	Instant IN 001	Great Train Robbery/Sweet Freedom	80

(see also Christie, Acid Gallery)

OUTER LIMITS (2)
71	Decca F 13176	The Dark Side Of The Moon/Black Boots	15
74	Snow/Deroy 1049	(I'm Not) Your Stepping Stone/Great Balls Of Fire	500

OUTLAW BLUES BAND
69	Stateside SSL 10290	BREAKING IN (LP)	30

OUTLAW POSSE
91	Outlaw OP1	Sonz Of The Devil (12")	15

OUTLAWS
61	HMV POP 844	Swingin' Low/Spring Is Near	15
61	HMV POP 877	Ambush/Indian Brave	15
61	HMV POP 927	Valley Of The Sioux/Crazy Drums	20
62	HMV POP 990	Ku-pow!/Last Stage West	20
62	HMV POP 1074	Sioux Serenade/Fort Knox	20
63	HMV POP 1124	The Return Of The Outlaws/Texan Spiritual	20
63	HMV POP 1195	That Set The Wild West Free/Hobo	20
63	HMV POP 1241	Law And Order/Do-Da-Day	20
64	HMV POP 1277	Keep-A-Knockin'/Shake With Me	40
61	HMV CLP 1489	DREAM OF THE WEST (LP, mauve label, gold print)	80
61	HMV CLP 1489	DREAM OF THE WEST (LP, later black label)	60

(see also Mike Berry, Bobbie Graham, Chaps, Rally Rounders, Houston Wells [& Marksmen])

OUT OF DARKNESS
70	Key KL 006	OUT OF DARKNESS (LP, laminated front sleeve)	200

OUT OF ORDER (1)
81	Daviton SPEP 120	OUT OF CONTROL (EP, export copy, 500 only)	40

OUT OF ORDER (2)
93	P19J20	Dark Sheep/Right Guard/Tears (12", white label)	60
93	XYZ 123	Stung/Emotions (12", white label)	60

OUTPATIENTS
80	KIK 1	Life On Earth/Home Is Where The Heart Is (with p/s)	50
80	KIK 1	Life On Earth/Home Is Where The Heart Is (without p/s)	30

OUTRAGEOUS
92	Kinetix KX2	THE TECHKORE EP (12")	20

OUTRIDERS
74	Dart ART 2049	The Telegram Song/Love You More Than Any Other	8

OUTSIDERS (U.K.)
78	Xciting Plastic	Vital Hours/Take Up (unissued)	0

(see also Second Layer, Sound)

OUTSIDERS (U.K. 1)
65	Decca F 12213	Keep On Doing It/Songs We Sang Last Summer	35

(see also Bunch Of Fives, Junior's Eyes, Tickle)

OUTSIDERS (U.K. 2)
77	Raw Edge RER 002	ONE TO INFINITY (EP)	50
77	Raw Edge RER 001	CALLING ON YOUTH (LP, laminated sleeve)	60
78	Raw Edge RER 003	CLOSE UP (LP, with insert)	50

OUTSIDERS (U.S.)
66	Capitol CL 15435	Time Won't Let Me/Was It Really Real?	35
66	Capitol CL 15435	Time Won't Let Me/Was It Really Real? (DJ copy)	50
66	Capitol CL 15450	Girl In Love/What Makes You So Bad, You Weren't Brought Up That Way	15
66	Capitol CL 15468	Respectable/Lost In My World	20
66	Capitol CL 15480	Help Me Girl/You Gotta Look	10
67	Capitol CL 15495	I'll Give You Time/I'm Not Tryin' To Hurt You	20

OUTSKIRTS OF INFINITY

MINT VALUE £

OUTSKIRTS OF INFINITY
87 Woronzow WOO 7 — LORD OF THE DARK SKIES (LP) ... 15

OUT TO LUNCH
76 Transatlantic BIG 547 — Jeepers Creepers/Everythings Nice ... 6

OVALTINEES
83 BAA 021 — BRITISH JUSTICE EP (p/s) ... 80

OVARY LODGE
73 RCA SF 8372 — OVARY LODGE (LP) ... 100
76 Ogun OG 600 — OVARY LODGE (LP) ... 30
(see also Keith Tippett)

OVATIONZ
81 Dread At The Controls DCD 005 — Forever Love/Forever Dub (12") ... 15

OVERCOMERS
68 Bamboo BAM 64 — Stop And Let Me Tell You/Take Courage Soul (unissued: white labels only) ... 50

OVERDRIVE
81 Boring Grantham BGR 1 — ON THE RUN (EP) ... 80

OVERKILL
80 Killer EJSP 9357 — Elemental/On My Own ... 75

OVERLANDERS
63 Pye 7N 15544 — Summer Skies And Golden Sands/Call Of The Wild ... 12
63 Pye 7N 15568 — Movin'/Rainbow ... 7
66 Pye NEP 24245 — MICHELLE (EP) ... 25
66 Pye NPL 18138 — MICHELLE (LP, laminated front sleeve with flipbacks) ... 35
(see also Cuppa T)

OVERLOAD
80 MCA MCA 618 — Into Overload/Follow The Lines (p/s) ... 10
81 MCA MCA 656 — Who Are You/Drift Away ... 10

OVERLORD
78 Airebeat ABT 3 — Lucy/Guardsman/Johnny (p/s) ... 30

RUNE OVERMAN
63 Decca F 11605 — Big Bass Boogie/Madison Piano ... 10

OVERNIGHT PLAYERS
80 Cha Cha CHALP 008 — BABYLON DESTRUCTION (LP, black, orange, yellow or red vinyl) ... 80

OVERTAKERS
68 Amalgamated AMG 803 — That's The Way You Like It/The Big Take-Over ... 50
68 Amalgamated AMG 809 — Girl You Ruff/KEITH BLAKE: Woo Oh Oh ... 50

BILL OWEN
81 Look LK/SP 6681 — Compo Has Gone And Lost His Wellies/Friends (p/s) ... 6

OWEN (GRAY) & DANDY (LIVINGSTONE)
69 Downtown DT 428 — Lovey Dovey/HERBIE GRAY & RUDIES: Kitty Wait ... 8

OWEN (SILVERA) & LEON
64 Island WI 146 — Nextdoor Neighbour/ROLAND ALPHONSO: Feeling Fine ... 35
64 Island WI 163 — My Love For You/How Many Times ... 25
64 Island WI 165 — Running Around/SKATALITES: Around The World ... 35
65 Island WI 170 — I Want My Cock/BABA BROOKS & DON DRUMMOND: Dr Decker ... 50
65 Ska Beat JB 189 — Woman/BABA BROOKS with DON DRUMMOND: Doctor Decker ... 30
(see also Leon & Owen, Tommy McCook)

OWEN (GRAY) & MILLIE
62 Blue Beat BB 96 — Sit And Cry/Do You Know (with City Slickers Orchestra) ... 10
62 Island WI 014 — Sugar Plum/OWEN GRAY: Jezebel ... 15
(see also Owen Gray, Millie, Owen & Leon, Leon & Owen)

RAY OWEN('S MOON)
69 Fontana TF 1045 — Tonight I'll Be Staying Here With You/Down, Don't Bother Me (solo) ... 6
71 Polydor 2058 095 — Hey Sweety/Free Man (as Ray Owen's Moon) ... 7
71 Polydor 2066-119 — Try My Love/Talk To Me ... 25
71 Polydor 2325 061 — RAY OWEN'S MOON (LP, textured sleeve) ... 80
(see also Juicy Lucy)

REG OWEN & HIS ORCHESTRA
59 Pye International 7N 25009 — Manhattan Spiritual/Ritual Blues ... 6
60 Palette PG 9004 — Obsession/Sunday Morn ... 10
56 Parlophone PMD 1045 — SWING ME HIGH (10" LP) ... 20

BUCK OWENS (& BUCKAROOS)
59 Capitol CL 15009 — Everlasting Love/Second Fiddle ... 10
60 Capitol CL 15123 — Above And Beyond/Til These Dreams Come True ... 7
60 Capitol CL 15162 — Excuse Me (I Think I've Got A Heartache)/I've Got A Right To Know ... 7
62 Longhorn BLH 0006 — Down On The Corner Of Love/Right After The Dance (estimated that 1000 pressed) ... 7
63 Capitol EAP1 1550 — FOOLIN' AROUND (EP) ... 10
65 Capitol EAP1 20602 — ACT NATURALLY (EP) ... 10

DONNIE OWENS
58 London HLU 8747 — Need You/If I'm Wrong ... 25
59 London HLW 8897 — Ask Me Anything/Between Midnight And Dawn (unissued) ... 0

JAMIE OWENS
73 Light LS 7012 — LAUGHTER IN YOUR SOUL (LP) ... 15

ROBERT OWENS
93 U Star US 002 — Was I Here Before (Farley Mix)/(Route One Mix)/(Classic Mix)/Tell Me (Live Mix) (12") ... 10

OWL
68 United Artists UP 2240 — Run To The Sun/Shades Of Blue And Green Water Flies ... 20

O.W.L.
70s Shebazz SHE 002 — Shady Tree/4TH STREET ORCHESTRA: Sun Hot ... 8

TONY OXLEY (QUARTET)

			MINT VALUE £
69	CBS 52664	THE BAPTISED TRAVELLER (LP)	125
70	CBS 64071	4 COMPOSITIONS FOR SEXTET (LP, with Derek Bailey)	125
71	RCA SF 8215	ICHNOS (LP)	100
70s	Incus INCUS 8	TONY OXLEY (LP, with Derek Bailey, et al.)	100
70s	Incus INCUS 18	FEBRUARY PAPERS (LP)	40
80s	Bead BEAD 25	THE GLIDER & THE GRINDER (LP)	30

(see also Derek Bailey, Howard Riley)

TONY OXLEY, WOLFGANG FUCHS, PHILIPP WACHSMANN & HUGH METCALFE

87	Bead Records BEAD 25	THE GLIDER AND THE GRINDER (LP)	20

TONY OXLEY ALAN DAVIE DUO

74	ADMW 005	THE TONY OXLEY ALAN DAVIE DUO (LP)	60

OXYM

80	Cargo CRS 003	Music Power/Mind Key (p/s)	40

OYSTER BAND

86	Cooking Vinyl FRY 001	Hal-an-Tow/Ashes To Ashes (p/s)	6
89	Cooking Vinyl FRYX 012	Love Vigilantes/Polish Plain/I Fought The Law (Live)/Between The Wars (Live) (10", pink vinyl, poster sleeve)	10
82	Pukka YOP 01	ENGLISH ROCK 'N' ROLL, 1800-1850 (LP)	30
85	Pukka YOP 04	LIE BACK AND THINK OF ENGLAND (LP)	30
85	Pukka YOP 07	LIBERTY HALL (LP)	30

OYSTER CEILIDH BAND

80	Dingles DIN 309	JACK'S ALIVE (LP)	20

OZARKS

63	Vocalion V 9210	Who Stole My Bird Dog/Any Waltz	30

OZO

76	DJM DJS 628	Listen To The Buddah/Kites	6
77	DJM DJT 10764	Anambra (Edited Version)/Anambra (12")	40
82	Sphinx SPS 1201	Anambra River (Tranquil Rivers From The Floating Crystal City Of Budatan Shire Of Western Heaven)/Skintight (No Room To Move Up) (12")	15
76	DJM DJF 20488	LISTEN TO THE BUDDHA (LP)	40
78	DJM DJF 20517	MUSEUM OF MANKIND (LP)	18

OZOMATLI

98	Almo ALM LP61	OZOMATLI (LP)	40

OZRIC TENTACLES

91	Dovetail DOVEST 3	Sploosh!/Live Throbbe (12" P/s)	10
89	Demi-Monde DMLP 1017	PUNGENT EFFULGENT (LP)	20
90	Dovetail Records DOVE LP1	ERPLAND (2-LP)	30
91	Dovetail DOVE LP 3	STRANGETUDE (LP)	20
92	Black Adder OZT 01	MUCK KICKER (LP)	20
93	Dovetail DOVELP6	JURASSIC SHIFT (LP)	20
94	Dovetail DOVE LP7	ARBORESCENE (2-LP)	30
98	Snapper SMALP 410	CURIOUS CORN (LP)	40

(see also Oroonies)

P

AUGUSTUS PABLO

71	Big Shot BI 578	The Mood/HERMAN CHIN-LOY: New Love	40
71	Big Shot BI 579	East Of The River Nile/HERMAN CHIN-LOY: East Of River Nile Version (B-side actually by Aquarians)	45
71	Creole CR 1004	405 (actually "The Mood" by Tommy McCook)/Duck It Up (actually "Confidential Version" by Charmers)	25
71	Ackee ACK 134	Still Yet/AQUARIANS: Version	20
71	Ackee ACK 138	Snowball And Pudding/AQUARIANS: Version	25
71	Duke DU 122	Reggae In The Fields/TOMMY McCOOK: Love Brother	50
73	Randy's RAN 536	Bedroom Mazurka (as Augustus Pablo & Fay)/Melodica Version	30
73	Atra ATRA 011	Lover's Mood/Lover's Rock	25
74	Tropical AL 025	Too Late/Dub Organiser	15
74	Tropical AL 035	Tales Of Pablo/BOOTHE STARS: Tales Dub	18
74	Sydna DL1276	Pablo's Mercy/Version	20
75	Fay Music FM 603	Fort Augustus Rock/Augustus In Kingston	25
75	Island WIP 6226	King Tubby Meets The Rockers Uptown/Baby I Love You So	25
75	Island 12 WIP 6226	King Tubby Meets The Rockers Uptown/JACOB MILLER: Baby I Love You So (12")	30
75	Treble C CCC06	Liberation/Dubbing Pablo	15
75	Treble C CCC014	Don Drummond/Thunderbolt Lady	15
77	Hawkeye HE 005	East Of The River Nile/East Africa	15
77	EJI 011	No Entry/BIG YOUTH: Strictly Rockers (12")	40
78	Rough Trade RT 002	Pablo Meets Mr. Bassie/Mr. Bassie Special (with Rockers All Stars) (with colour sticker)	10
79	Rockers APD 5	Power Of The Trinity/West Abyssinia Dub (12")	30
79	Rockers APD 6	Twin Seal/Dub/NORRIS REID: Entrance To Jah World (12")	25
79	Rockers AP 1223	Crucial Burial/ROCKERS ALL STARS: Pope Paul Feel It/Sound Of Redemption - Scientist In Dub (12")	30
79	Rockers AB1	Israel In Harmony/HUGH MUNDELL: Feeling Alright/Dub (12")	35
79	Dub Vendor DVD 002	Oregan Style/Classical Illusion (12")	20
80	Greensleeves GRED 29	Presents El Rockers Chapters I - IV (12")	20
80	Rockers APD 7	Hot Milk/Dub/Robin Bay Step/Dub (12")	25

PACESETTERS

			MINT VALUE £
74	Tropical TROPS 101	THIS IS AUGUSTO PABLO (LP)	60
75	Trojan TRLS 115	ITAL DUB (LP, original issue with "12 Neasden Lane" address on sleeve and rough orange/white paper labels)	35
75	Nationwide NW 03	THRILLER (LP)	35
78	Greensleeves GREL 98	AFRICA MUST BE FREE BY 83 DUB (LP)	20
79	Greensleeves GREL 8	ORIGINAL ROCKERS (LP)	25
79	Atra ATRALP 1003	LEGENDS (LP)	20
80	Echo STLP 1002	THRILLER (LP, reissue)	20
86	Greensleeves GREL 90	RISING SUN (LP)	18
86	Trojan TRLS 115	ITAL DUB (LP, reissue, blue/white label)	15
89	Yard RLP 001	KING TUBBYS MEETS THE ROCKERS UPTOWN (LP, reissue)	25
91	Greensleeves GREL 145	ROCKERS INTERNATIONAL (LP)	25
92	Greensleeves GREL 168	ROCKERS INTERNATIONAL II (LP)	15

(see also Mickey Lee, I Roy)

PACESETTERS
70	Saga BC 101	Cool Coffee/Israelites	12
70	Escort ERT 829	Bits And Pieces/Nimrod Leap	20
74	Saga SAGA 8154	REGGAE MEETS POP (LP)	25

PACIFIC DRIFT
70	Deram DM 304	Water Woman/Yes You Do	20
70	Deram Nova DN 13	FEELIN' FREE (LP, mono, blue/silver labels)	250
70	Deram Nova SDN 13	FEELIN' FREE (LP, stereo, red/silver labels)	175

(see also Wimple Winch, Just Four Men)

PACIFIC EARDRUM
78	Charisma CAS 1136	BEYOND PANIC (LP)	20

PACIFIC GAS & ELECTRIC (P.G. & E.)
70	CBS 5039	Are You Ready?/Staggolee	6
69	B&C CAS 1003	GET IT ON (LP)	75
69	CBS 63822	PACIFIC GAS & ELECTRIC (LP, orange label)	30
70	CBS 64026	ARE YOU READY (LP, orange label)	30
71	CBS 64295	HARD BURN (LP, orange label)	30

PACIFIC SOUND
71	M&M FMSS 10012	Tribute To Jimi/Thick Fog	30

PACK (1)
65	Columbia DB 7702	Do You Believe In Magic?/Things Bring Me Down	40

PACK (2)
79	SS PAK 1	Brave New Soldiers/Heathen (p/s, 2,500 only)	20
79	Rough Trade RT 025	King Of Kings/Number 12 (p/s)	12
80	SS SS 1N2/SS 2N1	KIRK BRANDON AND THE PACK OF LIES (EP, with printed inner sleeve)	12

(see also Theatre Of Hate, Spear Of Destiny, Senate)

PACKABEATS
61	Parlophone R 4729	Gypsy Beat/Big Man	15
62	Pye 7N 15480	Evening In Paris/The Traitors	20
63	Pye 7N 15549	Dream Lover/Packabeat	20

PACKERS
66	Pye International 7N 25343	Hole In The Wall/Go 'Head On	20
69	Soul City SC 111	Hole In The Wall/Go 'Head On (reissue)	15
70	Soul City SCM 003	HOLE IN THE WALL (LP)	25

PAC-KEYS
68	Speciality SPE 1003	Stone Fox/Diggin'	20

PAD ANTHONY
86	Live & Love LLDIS 0027	Dangerous System/Version (12")	20
86	Witty MUMD 2	Turn Me Loose/Version (12")	20
87	Jammys JAM 7	Gotta Be Strong/Version//You Gonna Be Late/Version (12")	25

BERNARD PADDEN
83	Dancing Sideways DS6X6	Mass Movement/Career Advice (p/s)	15

PADDY, KLAUS & GIBSON
65	Pye 7N 15906	I Wanna Know/I Tried	20
66	Pye 7N 17060	No Good Without You Baby/Rejected	50
66	Pye 7N 17112	Teresa/Quick Before They Catch Us	40

(see also Manfred Mann, Big Three, Rory Storm & Hurricanes, Kingsize Taylor)

BETTY PADGETT
76	Dynamic DYN 125	My Eyes Adore You/Love Forever	30

PAGAN BEAU
82	RVNIC Records AMO 24	Odd Man Out/Natures Daughter (p/s)	15

PAGAN BO
78	Planet ICLP 01	TRADITIONAL BARD AND THE FUTURE INEVITABLE (LP)	175

BILLY PAGE
65	London HLU 10006	It's Pop/American Girl	12

CHRIS PAGE
66	Cameo Parkway CP 751	Wait And See/Mine Mine Mine	12

CLEO PAGE
79	JSP 4502	I Love To Eat It - Hamburger/Goodie Train	15
79	JSP JSP 1003	LEAVING MISSISSIPPI (LP)	15

HOT LIPS PAGE & HIS ORCHESTRA
55	Parlophone MSP 6172	Ain't Nothing Wrong With That Boy/The Cadillac Song	20

JIMMY PAGE
65	Fontana TF 533	She Just Satisfies/Keep Moving (promo sticker on label)	750
65	Fontana TF 533	She Just Satisfies/Keep Moving	650
88	Geffen GEF 41	Wasting My Time/Writes Of Winter (p/s, withdrawn)	8

PAGE ONE & THE OBSERVERS

MINT VALUE £

91	Fontana TF 533	She Just Satisifies/Keep Moving (reissue as part of Fontana box set)	15
12	Jimmypage.com JPRLP0002	LUCIFER RISING (AND OTHER SOUNDTRACKS) (LP, 93 signed)	100
12	Jimmypage.com JPRLP0002	LUCIFER RISING (AND OTHER SOUNDTRACKS) (LP, 418 copies, these unsigned)	60

(see also Led Zeppelin, Page & Plant, Firm, Yardbirds, Paul, Carter-Lewis & Southerners, Neil Christian & Crusaders, Bobby Graham, Robert Plant, Honeydrippers, Brian Auger, Cartoone, Maureeny Wishfull, Coverdale-Page)

PAGE ONE & THE OBSERVERS
76	Carib Gems CGLP 004	OBSERVATION OF LIFE DUB (LP)	60

PATTI PAGE
ALBUMS
54	Mercury MG 25101	FOLK SONG FAVOURITES (10")	20
55	Mercury MG 25197	PATTI'S SONGS (10")	20
56	Mercury MPT 7510	CHRISTMAS WITH PATTI PAGE (10")	20
57	Mercury MPT 7531	I'M GETTING SENTIMENTAL OVER YOU (10")	20

PAGE BOYS (U.K.)
83	Whaam! WHAAM 10	You're My Kind Of Girl/In Love With You (p/s, 1,000 only)	20

(see also 1,000 Violins)

PAGEBOYS (U.S.)
65	London HLU 9948	When I Meet A Girl Like You/I Have Love	10

PAGE FIVE
66	Parlophone R 5426	Let Sleeping Dogs Lie/I Know All About Her	35

LARRY PAGE (ORCHESTRA)
57	Columbia DB 3965	Cool Shake/Start Movin' (In My Direction)	25
58	Columbia DB 4012	That'll Be The Day/Please Don't Blame Me	20
58	Columbia DB 4080	Under Control/This Is My Life	20
59	Saga SAG 45-2902	Big Blon' Baby/I Vibrate	25
60	Saga SAG 45-2903	How'm I Doing, Hey Hey/Throw All Your Lovin' My Way	10
60	Saga SAG 45-2904	Little Old Fashioned You/Marylin	7
66	Pye 7N 17105	The Life And Soul Of The Party/You Can Be Wrong About Boys	6
69	Page One POF 125	Wichita Lineman/Scarboro Fair	6
65	Decca LK 4692	KINKY MUSIC (LP, as Larry Page Orchestra)	50
68	Page One POL(S) 002	EXECUTIVE SUITE (LP, as Larry Page Orchestra)	20

PAGE & PLANT
95	Fontana PPCDJ 3	Kashmir (CD promo, withdrawn)	30
98	Mercury ADV 1998	Walking Into Clarksdale (CD promo, card sleeve)	40
94	Fontana PP ID 1	NO QUARTER UNLEDDED (CD, radio-promo only, with 'question' booklet)	50
94	Fontana 526 3621	NO QUARTER UNLEDDED (2-LP, gatefold, inners)	75
98	Mercury ADV 982	TBA (CD, advance promo for WALKING INTO CLARKSDALE)	30
98	Mercury PPTIC 1	WALKING INTO CLARKSDALE AN INTERVIEW (CD radio promo)	30
98	Mercury 558 025 1	WALKING INTO CLARKSDALE (LP)	100

(see also Jimmy Page, Robert Plant)

PAGE TEN
65	Decca F 12248	Boutique/Colour Talk	18

(see also Niney)

CARLOS PAIAO
81	EMI EMI 5174	Playback (English)/Playback (Portuguese)	7

PAICE, ASHTON & LORD
77	Polydor/Oyster 2391 269	MALICE IN WONDERLAND (LP, with inner sleeve)	15

(see also Deep Purple, Jon Lord, Ashton & Lord, Ashton Gardner & Dyke, Elf)

MARTY PAICH
57	London LZ-U 14040	MARTY PAICH QUARTET (LP, with Art Pepper)	45

HAL PAIGE & WHALERS
60	Melodisc MEL 1553	Going Back To My Home Town/After Hours Blues	40

JOEY PAIGE
65	Fontana TF 554	Cause I'm In Love With You/Yeah Yeah Yeah	20

ROSALIND PAIGE
55	London HL 8120	When The Saints Go Marching In/Nobody's Sweetheart Now	30
57	MGM MGM 937	Love, Oh Careless Love/That Funny Melody	10

PAIN KILLER
91	Earache MOSH 45	GUTS OF A VIRGIN (LP)	20

PAIN FAMINE
86	A.V. AVS 1	Starvision/Vanity Fayre	7
86	A.V. AVS2	Liquid Light/Sunset Lullaby	7
86	A.V. AVS 3	The State Of Art/Sunset Lullaby	7

PAINS OF BEING PURE AT HEART
08	Atomic Beat ABR 003	Kurt Cobain's Cardigan/PARALLELOGRAMS: 1 2 3 Go/Pop The Bubbles (p/s)	45
09	Fortuna Pop! FPOP 84	Young Adult Friction/Ramona (p/s)	6
09	Fortuna Pop! FPOP83LP	THE PAINS OF BEING PURE AT HEART (LP)	15
09	Fortuna Pop! FPOP83LP	THE PAINS OF BEING PURE AT HEART (LP, white/black splatter vinyl)	20
11	Fortuna Pop! PIASR 500 LP	BELONG (LP, blue vinyl)	15

PAINTBOX
70	Young Blood YB 1013	Get Ready For Love/Can I Get To Know You	10
71	Young Blood YB 1029	Get Ready For Love/Can I Get To Know You (reissue)	6

(see also Easybeats, Haffy's Whiskey Sour)

PAINTED SHIP
67	Mercury MF 988	Frustration/I Told Those Little White Lies	130

PAISLEYS
83	Psycho PSYCHO 7	COSMIC MIND AT PLAY (LP, reissue)	20

PALACE BROTHERS
93	Big Cat ABB 51 S	Ohio Riverboat Song/Drinking Woman (p/s)	8
94	Domino RUG 21T	AN ARROW THROUGH THE BITCH (12" EP, p/s)	15

PALACE OF LIGHT

MINT VALUE £

95	Domino RUG 35T	The Mountain/Gulf Shores/(End Of) Travelling/West Palm Beach (12", stickered p/s as Palace)	18
93	Big Cat ABB 50	THERE IS NO ONE WHAT WILL TAKE CARE OF YOU (LP)	15
94	Domino WIG 14	PALACE BROTHERS (LP)	15
95	Domino WIGLP 21X	VIVA LAST BLUES (LP with 7" (RUG 39) stickered sleeve, as Palace Music)	40
95	Domino WIGLP 21	VIVA LAST BLUES (LP, as Palace Music, without 7")	25
96	Domino WIGLP 24	ARISE THEREFORE (LP)	20
98	Domino WIGLP 33	LOST BLUES AND OTHER SONGS (2-LP, gatefold, poster)	25

(see also Bonnie 'Prince' Billy, Will Oldham)

PALACE OF LIGHT
86	Bam Caruso OPRA 035	Safer/Bitter Seal	10

PALADIN
72	Bronze BRO 3	Sweet Sweet Music/Get On Together	10
71	Bronze ILPS 9150	PALADIN (LP, textured sleeve, Island credit on label)	75
72	Bronze ILPS 9190	CHARGE (LP, gatefold sleeve, Island credit on label)	75

(see also Arthur Brown, Glass Menagerie, McGuinness Flint)

PALE FOUNTAINS
82	Operation Twilight OPT 09	(There's Always) Something On My Mind/Just A Girl (p/s)	25
84	Virgin V 2274	PACIFIC STREET (LP)	20
85	Virgin V 2333	FROM ACROSS THE KITCHEN TABLE (LP, with inner sleeve)	20

(see also Shack, Michael Head & Strands)

PALE SAINTS
89	4AD BAD 910	BARGING IN THE PRESENCE OF GOD (12", p/s)	10
90	4AD BAD 0015	HALF-LIFE (12" EP, p/s)	10
91	4AD BAD 109	FLESH BALOON (12" EP, p/s)	10
91	4AD AD 1009	Kinky Love/Hair Shoes (demo) (p/s)	10
92	4AD BAD 2008	THROWING BACK THE APPLE (12" EP p/s)	10
94	4AD BAD 4013	FINE FRIENDS (12" EP, p/s)	10
90	4AD CAD 0002	THE COMFORTS OF MADNESS (LP, with 3 postcards)	35
90	4AD CAD 0002	THE COMFORTS OF MADNESS (LP, without postcards)	25
92	4AD CAD 2004	IN RIBBONS (LP, with free 7" "A Thousand Stars Burst Open"/A Revelation [RIB 1])	35
92	4AD CAD 2004	IN RIBBONS (LP, with no free 7")	25
94	4AD CAD 4014	SLOW BUILDINGS (LP)	40

TOM PALEY
76	Kicking Mule SNKF 119	HARD LUCK PAPA (LP)	18

(see also Peggy Seeger)

PALEY BROTHERS
78	Sire SRE 4005	Come On Let's Go/Magic Power (p/s, credited as Paley Brothers & Ramones on sleeve)	12
78	Sire 6078 613	Ecstacy/Rendezvous/Hide N' Seek/Come Out And Play (12", p/s)	12

(see also Ramones)

PALI GAP
82	Sinister SYN 001	Under The Sun/The Knives Are Out (p/s, with insert)	20

MORTY PALITZ & ACES
59	London HLJ 8778	The Grocer's Cha Cha Cha/Eso Es El Amor (This Is Love)	8

PALLAS
82	Granite Wax GWS 1	Arrive Alive/Stranger (On The Edge Of Time) (two different p/s, with insert)	50
82	Granite Wax GWS 1	Arrive Alive/Stranger (On The Edge Of Time) (two different p/s, without insert)	40
83	Cool King 12CK010	Paris Is Burning/The Hammer Falls/Stranger At The Edge Of Time (12", p/s)	12
84	EMI Harvest PLSP1	Eyes In The Night (Arrive Alive)/East West/Crown Of Thorns (12", p/s)	10
84	EMI Harvest 12PLS2	Shock Treatment/March On Atlantis/Heart Attack (12", p/s)	10
78	Sue-i-cide PAL/101	THE PALLAS EP (stamped plain die-cut sleeve)	50
85	Harvest 12PLS3D	THE KNIGHT MOVES EP (12" + free 7" Mad Machine / Stitch In Time, sealed in plastic sleeve)	15
83	Cool King CKLP002	ARRIVE ALIVE (LP)	15
84	Harvest SHSP2400 121	THE SENTINAL (LP, gatefold sleeve, with poster and sticker)	18
86	Harvest SHVL 850	THE WEDGE (LP + inner sleeve)	15

PALMA VIOLETS
12	Rough Trade RTRAD 5655	Best Of Friends/Last Of The Summer Wine (50 copies with sticker, purple vinyl, signed)	10
13	Rough Trade TRADS 702	Invasion Of The Tribbles (1-sided other side etched, 2 badges in fold-out sleeve)	35
13	Rough Trade RTRADELP700	180 (LP)	15

EARL PALMER & HIS TEN PIECE ROCKIN' BAND
58	Capitol EAP1 1026	SWINGIN' DRUMS (EP)	10

EDDIE PALMER
57	Decca F 10873	The Sky/The Twilight Theme	8

JERRY PALMER
66	London 10026	Walking The Dog/Don't Leave Me Baby	25

MICHAEL PALMER
84	Tonos 001	Modelling Girl/Soca Rumble (12")	20
84	Greensleeves GRED 144	I'm Still Dancing/ROBERT FRENCH: No War (12")	50
84	Greensleeves GREL 155	Done With It/Can't Take The Fuss (12")	15
84	Simba SM 08	Me Nah Run/JACKIE PARRIS: When Your Are Young (12", with Aswad)	25
84	Tonos TONLP 001	STAR PERFORMER (LP)	25

MICHAEL PALMER AND JIM BROWN
83	Greensleeves GRED 131	Ghetto Dance/JAH THOMAS & ROOTS RADICS: Ghetto Dub (12")	25

RICK PALMER
59	London HLL 8900	You Threw A Heart/My Greatest Wish (unreleased)	0

ROY PALMER & STATE STREET RAMBLERS
54	London AL 3518	A CHICAGO SKIFFLE SESSION (10" LP)	30

TONY PALMER
77	Eji E00009	Jah Shall Conquer/Commissioner (instrumental) (12")	20

TRISTAN PALMER/PALMA
81	Orbit ORB 801	Caly Man/Ungrateful Girl (12")	20
81	Greensleeves GRED 66	Entertainment/JAH THOMAS & TOYAN: Jah Guide (12")	15
81	Art & Craft ACS 011	Fussing And Fighting (with Ranking Joe)/Version (12")	20
82	Greensleeves GRED 93	Joker Smoker/PAPA BRUCE: Loafter Smoker (12")	25
83	Greensleeves GRED 126	No Shot No Fire/BARRY BROWN: Jukes And Watches (12")	20
83	Trojan TROT 9068	Settle Down Girl/Version (12")	15
82	Vista STLP 1017	TOUCH ME TAKE ME (LP)	15
82	Greensleeves GREL 43	JOKER SMOKER (LP)	20
83	Trojan TRLS 215	SETTLE DOWN GIRL (LP)	20

VIC PALMER COMBO
73	Ra RA EP 7009	ON HOLIDAY! (EP, p/s)	15

PALMETTO KINGS
60	Starlite ST45 021	Ten Rum Bottles/Home Cookin' Mama	15

CHARLIE PALMIERI
68	Atlantic 588157	LATIN BUGALU (LP)	40

PAN
93	Big Cat ABB 49	HANGIN' OUT FOR JUNE (LP)	15

PANACHE
83	Mach 1 MAGIC 004	I Wanna Dance/Crazy For Your Love (with Ray Dorset)	7

(see also Ray Dorset)

PANAMA FRANCIS BLUES BAND
64	Stateside SL 10070	TOUGH TALK!! (LP)	35

PANAMA LIMITED (JUG BAND)
69	Harvest HAR 5010	Lady Of Shallot/Future Blues	30
70	Harvest HAR 5022	Round And Round/Rotting Wooden In A White Collar's Grave	30
69	Harvest SHVL 753	PANAMA LIMITED JUG BAND (LP, laminated gatefold sleeve, "Sold in U.K..." text on 5 lines", no EMI on label)	250
70	Harvest SHVL 753	PANAMA LIMITED JUG BAND (LP, laminated gatefold sleeve, 2nd pressing, no "Sold in U.K..." no EMI on label)	60
70	Harvest SHVL 779	INDIAN SUMMER (LP, as Panama Limited, gatefold sleeve, no EMI on label)	450
08	Timeless TIME 713	INDIAN SUMMER (LP, reissue)	18

(see also Ian (A) Anderson)

ALPHONSO PANCHO
79	Attack TACK 3	Love Is A Pleasure/Never Give Up In A Babylon	20

(see also Pancho Alphonso)

GENE PANCHO
68	Giant GN 21	I Like Sweet Music/Seven Days (with Sandy & Superboys)	40

(see also Gene Rondo)

PANDA PEEPLE
73	Decca F13458	Melody World/Rhythm N Blues (promo only)	6

PANDEMONIUM
67	CBS 202462	Season Of The Witch/Today I'm Happy	60
67	CBS 2664	No Presents For Me/The Sun Shines From His Eyes	300
68	CBS 3451	Chocolate Buster Dan/Fly With Me Forever	70

PANDIT PRAN NATH
79	Transatlantic TRA 193	EARTH GROOVE (LP)	40

PANDORAS
67	Liberty LIB 55954	(I Could Write A Book) About My Baby/New Day	18

PANHANDLE
72	Decca SKL 5105	PANHANDLE (LP, laminated cover, blue/silver label with boxed logo)	30

(see also Chris Spedding)

PANIC IN THE YEAR ZERO
81	Vada ABER 4128	Liberty Caps/Sometimes I Don't Know	20

PANIK
77	Rainy City SHOT 1	IT WON'T SELL (EP)	15

PAN PIPERS
69	Pye 7N 17699	Stop/Money Or Love	125

PANS PEOPLE
74	Epic SEPC 2606	You Can Really Rock N Roll Me/The Singer Not The Song	8

PAN SONIC
95	Blast First VBFFP 118	VAKIO (2-LP, reissue)	25
97	Blast First BFFP 132	KULMA (LP, 2 x 12")	20
00	Blast First BFFP 166	AALTOPIIRI (2-LP, print)	20
04	Blast First BFFP 180BX	KESTO (4-CD box set)	30
10	Blast First Petite PTYT 043	HAINIO KEIJI - IN THE STUDIO (2-LP)	20

PANT
79	Redball RR019X	Mother Fo/Modern/No Possessions/Mummy Told You	25

GARY PANTER & JAY COTTON
90	Blast First FU 7	ONE HELL SOUNDWICH (LP, picture disc)	20

JAN PANTER
65	Oriole CB 1938	My Two Arms Minus You Equals Tears/Does My Heart Show	25
65	CBS 201810	Let It Be Now/Stand By And Cry	20
66	Pye 7N 17097	Scratch My Back/Put Yourself In My Place	250
69	President PT 241	Si Si Senor/Stella In Lights	10

PANTERA
90	Atco 7567-91372-1	COWBOYS FROM HELL (LP)	40
92	Atco 756791758-1	VULGAR DISPLAY OF POWER (LP)	60
93	East West 92302	FAR BEYOND DRIVEN (2-LP, gatefold)	60
96	East West 7559-61908-1	GREAT SOUTHERN TRENDKILL (LP)	50

PANTHER BURNS

MINT VALUE £

PANTHER BURNS
81	Rough Trade RT 077	Train Kept A Rollin'/Red Headed Woman (p/s)	10
81	Rough Trade ROUGH 32	BEHIND THE MAGNOLIA CURTAIN (LP, inner)	25

(see also Alex Chilton)

ROY PANTON
63	Blue Beat BB 182	Mighty Ruler/Run Old Man	30
64	Blue Beat BB 219	Good From The Bad/Hell Gate	30
64	Rio R 19	Cherita/Seek And You Shall Find	20
64	Rio R 33	You Don't Know Me/KING EDWARD'S ALLSTARS: Doctor No	40
64	Island WI 137	Goodbye Peggy Darling (actually "Goodbye Peggy" by Stranger Cole)/ BABA BROOKS: Portrait Of My Love	25
70	Harry J HJ 6624	The Same Old Life/JAYBOYS: Life Version	8

(see also Roy & Annette, Roy & Millie, Roy & Paulette, Roy & Yvonne, Roy & Duke Allstars, Roy & Patsy, Derrick Harriot, Leon & Owen, Charmers, Roy Patin)

JOHN PANTRY
72	Philips 6006 250	Net Of Concern/Words	10
79	Kingsway KMS 902	Nothing Is Impossible/Jesus On The Airwaves	8
72	Philips 6308 129	JOHN PANTRY (LP)	40
73	Philips 6308 138	LONG WHITE TRAIL (LP)	20
80	Kingsway KMR 323	TO STRANGERS AND FRIENDS (LP)	15
99	Tenth Planet TP 040	THE UPSIDE DOWN WORLD OF JOHN PANTRY (LP, limited edition, 1,000 only)	30

(see also Factory, Peter & Wolves, Norman Conquest, Sounds Around)

PANZA DIVISION
82	Panza Traz PTO1	We Will Rock The World/Standing On The Outside (p/s)	12

PAPA CHARJAN
82	CF CF 006	DJ Pumping/COURTNEY BARKELY: I Am Alright (12")	20

PAPA DOO RUN RUN
75	RCA RCA 2620	Be True To Your School/Disney Girls	8

PAPA MICHIGAN & GENERAL SMILEY
81	Tuff Gong IPR 2035	One Love Jam Down/FREDDIE MCGREGOR: Joggin' (12")	10

PAPA TULLO
81	Negus Roots NERT 006	Church And State/Righteous Rock (12")	15
82	Negus Roots NERLP 004	TULLO AT HOME (LP)	40

PAPADOCTRINE
95	Alphaphone ALPHA 001	Flesh Hunter/Hybrid Energy/Dreamreader (12")	15

(see also Cabaret Voltaire, Richard H. Kirk)

NIKKI PAPAS
59	Parlophone R 4590	49 State Rock/Try Again	40
60	Parlophone R 4652	By The River/Don't Leave Me Alone	10

PAPER BAGS
79	Retread TREAD 1	Joss Bay/Drat! (p/s)	7

PAPER BLITZ TISSUE
67	RCA Victor RCA 1652	Boy Meets Girl/Grey Man	500

(see also Cupid's Inspiration)

PAPER BUBBLE
70	Deram DML 1059	SCENERY (LP, white/red label, Mono)	350
70	Deram SML 1059	SCENERY (LP, white/red label, Stereo)	200

(see also Dave Cousins)

PAPER DOLLS
68	Pye 7N 17547	My Life Is In Your Hands/There's Nobody I'd Sooner Love	8
68	Pye 7N 17655	Someday/Any Old Time You're Lonely And Sad	7
70	RCA RCA 1919	My Boyfriend's Back/Mister Good Time Friday	7
70	RCA RCA 2007	Remember December/Same Old Story	7
68	Pye N(S)PL 18226	PAPER DOLLS HOUSE (LP)	60

PAPER DRAGON
69	Bell BLL 1054	April Fool/Get Something Going	12

PAPER TISSUE
72	Dresden DR2	Wild Fire/Visions In The NIght	50

PAPERHOUSE
91	Mystic Stones RUNE LP 11	SPONGY COMESTIBLES (LP)	20

PARADE
67	A&M AMS 701	Sunshine Girl/This Old Melody	18
67	A&M AMS 720	Radio Song/I Can See Love	15

VANESSA PARADIS
87	Polydor POSPG 902	Joe Le Taxi/Varvara Pavlovna (poster p/s)	6

PARADISE HAMMER
70	Polydor 2058048	She Is Love/You Got Me In	25
71	Polydor 2058084	1+1=2/To Live	15

PARADISE LOST
90	Peaceville VILE 17	LOST PARADISE (LP)	15
91	Peaceville VILE26L	GOTHIC (LP, gatefold, red vinyl)	25
91	Peaceville VILE26L	GOTHIC (LP, gatefold)	18
92	Music For Nations MFN 135	SHADES OF GOD (LP)	20
93	Music For Nations MFN 152	ICON (2-LP)	25
95	Music For Nations MFN 184	DRACONIAN TIMES (2-LP)	35
97	Music For Nations MFN 222	LOST (2-LP)	25

PARADISE SQUARE
74	None	NEVER THOUGHT I'D SEE THE DAY (LP, 100 only, hand-drawn covers)	800

PARADISE (1)
77	Clubland SJP 775	One Of These Days/You're The One I Need (no p/s, 500 only)	15

PARADISE (2)
80	Ebony EB 701	PARADISE (LP)	125
82	Ebony EB 702	WORLD'S MIDNIGHT (LP)	100
83	Priority PLP 1	LOVE IS THE ANSWER (LP)	100

PARADONS
60	Top Rank JAR 514	Diamonds And Pearls/I Want Love	60

PARADOX VOYEUR
80	Brigade BRIG 001	Deceit/E.D./Choosy (p/s)	15

PARADOX (1)
68	Polydor 56275	The Wednesday Theme/Ring The Changes	125

(see also David Walker)

PARAFFIN JACK FLASH LTD
68	Pye NSPL 18252	MOVERS AND GROOVERS (LP)	18

PARAGONS
66	Doctor Bird DB 1060	Happy-Go-Lucky Girl/Love Brings Pain	45
67	Island WI 3045	On The Beach/CAROL & TOMMY McCOOK: Sweet And Gentle (B-side actually by Tommy McCook & Supersonics)	40
67	Island WI 3067	Talking Love/If I Were You	40
67	Island WI 3093	So Depressed/We Were Meant To Be	80
67	Treasure Isle TI 7009	Only A Smile/The Tide Is High	25
67	Treasure Isle TI 7011	Mercy, Mercy, Mercy/Riding On A High And Windy Day	25
67	Treasure Isle TI 7013	The Same Song/TOMMY McCOOK & SUPERSONICS: Soul Serenade	30
67	Treasure Isle TI 7025	Wear You To The Ball/You Mean The World To Me	40
68	Treasure Isle TI 7034	Silver Bird/My Best Girl	25
68	Island WI 3138	Memories By The Score/The Number One For Me	30
69	Studio One SO 2081	Have You Ever Been In Love/Change Your Style	50
69	Duke DU 7	Left With A Broken Heart/I've Got To Get Away	80
69	Crab 13	Take Your Hand From My Neck/Equality And Justice (actually by VICEROYS)	40
77	Wildflower WF 523	Do The Best Thing/Best Thing	15
80	Virgin VS 389	The Tide Is High/U ROY: Tide Is High	15
12	Treasure Isle THB 7020	Joy In My Soul/THE TECHNIQUES: Travelling Man	15
67	Treasure Isle DLM 5010	ON THE BEACH (LP)	250
81	Starlight Records SLDLP 909	NOW (LP)	20
81	Island ILPS 9631	THE PARAGONS (LP)	15
74	Horse HRLP 703	THE PARAGONS WITH ROSALYN SWEAT (LP)	40
92	Trojan TRLS 299	MY BEST GIRL WEARS MY CROWN (ROCK STEADY 1966-1968)	18

(see also John Holt, Lester Sterling)

PARALEX
80	Reddingtons R.R. DAN 4	White Lightning/Travelling Man/Black Widow, (12", p/s, green vinyl)	50

PARALLELOGRAMS
08	Atomic Beat ABR 003	1 2 3 Go/Pop The Bubbles/PAINS OF BEING PURE AT HEART: Kurt Cobain's Cardigan (p/s)	45

PARAMEDIC SQUAD
81	Gargoyle GRGL 2	Movement In Time/For You/Thinking Psychedelia (p/s)	25

PARAMETER
70	Deroy	GALACTIC RAMBLE (LP, 450 only, 4 page inner)	300

NORRIE PARAMOR & HIS ORCHESTRA
53	Columbia SCM 5051	April In Portugal/The Song From Moulin Rouge	8
54	Columbia SCM 5126	Johnny Guitar/Paramambo	8
54	Columbia SCM 5136	The High And The Mighty/Rip Van Twinkle	8
56	Columbia SCM 5251	Theme From Threepenny Opera/Poor John	7
56	Columbia DB 3815	Autumn Concerto/Lullaby Of Birdland	6
60	Columbia DB 4419	Summer Place (Theme)/Half Pint	6
62	Columbia DB 4789	Theme From Z Cars/Them From Ballad Of A Soldier	6
64	Columbia DB 7114	Dream Of Tomorrow/Laramie	7
65	Columbia DB 7446	Dance Of The Warriors/Dragon Dance	6
68	Columbia DB 8430	Soul Coaxing/Autumn In London Town	7
70	Polydor 56375	Randall And Hopkirk (Deceased)/A Summer Palace	65

(see also Harry Gold)

PARAMORE
06	Fueled By Ramen ATUK 037	Emergency/O'Star (poster sleeve)	20
07	Fueled By Ramen ATUK 0279	Misery Business/My Hero (Electronic Mix) (Clear vinyl, poster sleeve)	10
07	Fueled By Ramen AT 0279X	Misery Business (Album Version)/Sunday Bloody Sunday (Bonus Version)	6
07	Fueled by Ramen AT 0284	Hallelujah (Album Version)/Decoy (Bonus Version) (gatefold p/s, poster)	10
07	Fueled By Ramen AT 0284X	Hallelujah (Album Version) (1-sided etched disc, poster sleeve)	6
07	Fueled By Ramen AT 0295	Crush Crush Crush (Album Version)/Misery Business (Live) (stickered p/s, sheet of stickers)	6
07	Fueled By Ramen AT 0295X	Crush Crush Crush (Album Version)/For A Pessimist I'm Pretty Optimistic (Live) (blue vinyl, printed PVC sleeve, insert)	10

PARAMOUNT ALL-STARS
50	Tempo R 20	Hometown Skiffle (Parts 1 & 2) (78)	20

(see also Blind Blake, Georgia Tom, Papa Charlie Jackson, Blind Lemon Jefferson, Charlie Spand)

PARAMOUNT FOUR
09	Kent 6T 26	Sorry Ain't The Word/GENE & GARY: Baby Without You	20

PARAMOUNTS
63	Parlophone R 5093	Poison Ivy/I Feel Good All Over	12
64	Parlophone R 5107	Little Bitty Pretty One/A Certain Girl	20
64	Parlophone R 5155	I'm The One Who Loves You/It Won't Be Long	25
64	Parlophone R 5187	Bad Blood/Do I	25
65	Parlophone R 5272	Blue Ribbons/Cuttin' In	20
65	Parlophone R 5351	You Never Had It So Good/Don't Ya Like My Love	50

PARANOIA

MINT VALUE £

64	Parlophone GEP 8908	THE PARAMOUNTS (EP)	300

(see also Procol Harum)

PARANOIA
84	Rot ASS 8	Dead Man's Dreams/Man In Black (p/s)	10
84	Rot ASS 11	SHATTERED GLASS (LP)	25

PARANOID LONDON
12	Paranoid London PDON 003	EATING GLUE EP (12", with Mutado Pintado)	30
12	Paranoid London PDON 004	PARIS DUB 1 EP (12" with Paris Brightledge)	20
13	Paranoid London PDON 005	TRANSMISSION 5 EP (12")	10
13	Paranoid London PDON 006	Paris Dub 2/Demo (12")	10

PARANOIDS
79	Hurricane FIRE 4	Anticipation/TV Heroes (p/s)	8
79	Hurricane FIRE 8	Stupid Guy/Road To Ruin (p/s)	10
80	Hurricane FIRE 14	The Love Job/Theme From Gravity's Rainbow (p/s)	10

PARCHMENT
73	Pye 7N 45214	Where Can I Find You/Working Man	8
72	Pye NSPL 18388	LIGHT UP THE FIRE (LP, textured sleeve with poster insert)	20
73	Pye NSPL 18409	HOLLYWOOD SUNSET (LP, gatefold)	15
75	Myrrh MYR 1028	SHAMBLEJAM (LP)	18
77	Pilgrim GRAPEVINE 106	REHEARSAL FOR A REUNION (LP)	15

WALTER PARDON
75	Leader LED 2063	A PROPER SORT (LP)	20

PAULA PARFITT
69	Beacon BEA 135	I'm Gonna Give You Back Your Ring/Love Is Wonderful (Beware of bootlegs! - originals have anti-slip grips around the label)	150
70	Up Front UPF4	Peace Of Mind/Baby You Give Me A Good Song To Sing	10

TINY PARHAM
50s	Audubon AAC	TINY PARHAM (10" LP)	25

PARIS
72	Avalanche AV 67312	I've Lost The Way/Long Time	8

BOBBY PARIS
68	Polydor 56747	Per So Nal Ly/Tragedy	80
69	Polydor 56762	Let The Sun Shine In/You	25
77	London HLU 10553	Night Owl/YVONNE BAKER: You Didn't Say A Word	10
79	Capitol CL 16067	I Walked Away/H.B. BARNUM: Heartbreaker	15
12	Outtasight OSV-070	Night Owl/Tears On My Pillow	6

PARIS CONNECTION
73	Explosion EX 2085	That Lady/Sonia	30

MICA PARIS
91	4th & Broadway 12BRWDJ207	A STAND FOR LOVE EP (12" promo p/s. Mispress, plays Prince's vocal version of 'A Stand For Love')	125

PRISCILLA PARIS
74	Rak RAK 184	I Love How You Love Me/Over You	10

(see also Paris Sisters)

PARIS SISTERS
61	Top Rank JAR 588	I Love How You Love Me/I'll Be Crying Tomorrow	50
64	MGM MGM 1240	Dream Lover/Lonely Girl	50

(see also Date With Soul, Priscilla Paris)

PARIS AND THE ATMOSPHERES
79	SRTS/79/CUS-281	Atmosphere/Deborah And Me (p/s)	10

JOHN PARISH & POLLY JEAN HARVEY
96	Island IS 648	That Was My Veil/Losing Ground (p/s)	12
09	Island 1796343	Black Hearted Love/Within A Month (p/s)	6
96	Island ILPS 8051	DANCE HALL AT LOUSE POINT (LP)	60
09	Island 1797426	A WOMAN A MAN WALKED BY (LP)	25

PARISH HALL
70	Liberty LBS 83374	PARISH HALL (LP)	200

SIMON PARK
74	EMI EMC 3059	SOMETHING IN THE AIR (LP)	20

PARKE
71	Folk Heritage FHR 018S	PARKE (LP)	350
72	Folk Heritage FHR 028	JOY HEALTH LOVE AND PEACE (LP)	200

ALAN PARKER
78	BEEB BBED 024	Angels/Santa Monica Bound	6
70	Aristocrat AR 1022	GUITAR FANTASY (LP)	20
73	MCA MUPS 471	BAND OF ANGELS (LP)	20

(see also Hungry Wolf, Ugly Custard)

BENNY PARKER & DYNAMICS
64	Decca F 11944	Boys And Girls/You'll Be On Your Way	45

BILLY PARKER
63	Decca F 11668	Thanks A Lot/Out Of Your Heart	7

BOBBY PARKER
61	London HLU 9393	Watch Your Step/Steal Your Heart Away	60
64	Sue WI 340	Watch Your Step/Steal Your Heart Away (reissue)	55
69	Blue Horizon 57-3151	It's Hard But It's Fair/I Couldn't Quit My Baby	45

BONNIE PARKER & ACME ATTRACTIONS
81	Orchid OR 1	Eve Of Destruction/It's OK	10

CHARLIE PARKER
ALBUMS
52	Vogue LDE 004	CHARLIE PARKER VOLUME ONE (10")	75

David PARKER

MINT VALUE £

53	Vogue LDE 016	CHARLIE PARKER VOLUME TWO (10")	75
56	Vogue LAE 12002	CHARLIE PARKER MEMORIAL ALBUM (gatefold sleeve w/ 2 inserts)	25
55	Melodisc MLP 12-105	BIRD AT ST. NICK'S	30
55	Columbia Clef 33CX 10004	CHARLIE PARKER BIG BAND	40
56	Columbia Clef 33C 9026	BIRD AND DIZ (10", with Dizzy Gillespie)	40
57	Columbia Clef 33CX 10081	APRIL IN PARIS (as Charlie Parker With Strings)	35
57	Columbia Clef 33CX 10090	CHARLIE PARKER PLAYS COLE PORTER	25
58	Columbia Clef 33CX 10117	CHARLIE PARKER JAZZ PERENNIAL	15
58	London Jazz LTZ-C 15104	THE IMMORTAL CHARLIE PARKER VOL. 1	15
58	London Jazz LTZ-C 15105	THE IMMORTAL CHARLIE PARKER VOL. 2	15
58	London Jazz LTZ-C 15106	THE IMMORTAL CHARLIE PARKER VOL. 3	15
58	London Jazz LTZ-C 15107	THE IMMORTAL CHARLIE PARKER VOL. 4	15
58	Mercury MPL 12-105	BIRD AT NICK'S	15
60	Collector JGN 1002	CHARLIE PARKER IN SWEDEN	30

(see also Dizzy Gillespie & Charlie Parker, Sir Charles Thompson)

DAVID PARKER
| 71 | Polydor 2460 101 | DAVID PARKER (LP) | 50 |

(see also Andwella's Dream)

DEAN PARKER & REDCAPS
| 62 | Decca F 11555 | Stormy Evening/Blue Eyes And Golden Hair | 45 |

DYON PARKER
| 69 | Marble Arch MAL 787 | OUT ON THE HIGHWAY (LP) | 20 |

EDDIE PARKER
| 55 | Columbia SCM 5211 | Far Away From Everybody/Bella Notte | 8 |
| 56 | Columbia DB 3804 | Love Me As Though There Were No Tomorrow/Rich In Love | 8 |

EDDIE PARKER (U.S.)
| 79 | Grapevine GRP 119 | Love You Baby (Parts 1 & 2) (in p/s) | 10 |
| 79 | Grapevine GRP 119 | Love You Baby (Parts 1 & 2) (in p/s) (DJ copy) | 20 |

EULA PARKER
| 58 | Oriole CB 1411 | Silhouettes/Hedgehopper | 20 |

(see also Frank Weir)

EVAN PARKER
75	Incus INCUS 19	SAXOPHONE SOLOS (LP)	40
78	Incus INCUS 27	MONOCEROS (LP)	30
80	Incus INCUS 39	SIX OF ONE (LP)	30
86	Incus INCUS 49	THE SNAKE DECIDES (LP)	50
89	Cadillac (no cat no)	COLLECTED SOLOS (4 x LP and cassette hand numbered to 200)	175

EVAN PARKER, DEREK BAILEY, HAN BENNINK
| 70 | Incus INCUS 1 | THE TOPOGRAPHY OF THE LUNGS (LP) | 150 |
| 77 | Incus INCUS 1 | THE TOPOGRAPHY OF THE LUNGS (LP, reissue) | 40 |

EVAN PARKER, BARRY GUY & PAUL LYTTON
| 83 | Incus INCUS 42 | TRACKS (LP) | 40 |

EVAN PARKER & GEORGE LEWIS
| 80 | Incus INCUS 35 | FROM SAXOPHONE & TROMBONE (LP) | 40 |

EVAN PARKER, GEORGE LEWIS, BARRY GUY & PAUL LYTTON
| 83 | Incus INCUS 45 | HOOK, DRIFT & SHUFFLE (LP) | 50 |

EVAN PARKER & PAUL LYTTON
| 72 | Incus INCUS 5 | COLLECTIVE CALLS (URBAN) (TWO MICROPHONES) (LP) | 40 |
| 75 | Incus INCUS 14 | AT THE UNITY THEATRE (LP) | 40 |

(see also Derek Bailey & Evan Parker, Derek Bailey Evan Parker & Han Bennink)

FESS PARKER
| 57 | Oriole CB 1378 | Wringle Wrangle/Ballad Of John Colter | 10 |

GRAHAM PARKER
| 80 | Stiff BUY 72 | Stupefaction/Paralysed (p/s) | 10 |

JIMMY PARKER
| 62 | Top Rank JAR 608 | We Gonna/No Word From Betty | 10 |

(LITTLE) JUNIOR PARKER
61	Vogue V 9179	Stand By Me/I'll Forget About You (as Little Junior Parker)	30
62	Vogue V 9193	Mary Jo/Annie Get Your Yo-Yo (as Little Junior Parker)	30
66	Vocalion VP 9256	These Kind Of Blues (Parts 1 & 2)	40
66	Vocalion VP 9256	These Kind Of Blues (Parts 1 & 2) (DJ copy)	60
66	Vocalion VP 9275	Goodbye Little Girl/Walking The Floor Over You	30
67	Mercury SMCL 20097	LIKE IT IS (LP)	50
72	Groove Merchant GM 502	BLUE SHADOWS FALLING (LP)	15
73	Groove Merchant GM 2205	GOOD THINGS DON'T HAPPEN EVERY DAY (LP, with Jimmy McGriff)	15
73	Vogue LDM 30163	MEMORIAL (LP)	15
73	People PLEO 4	YOU DON'T HAVE TO BE BLACK TO LOVE THE BLUES (LP)	20

KEN PARKER
67	Island WI 3082	How Could I/SONNY BURKE: Choo Choo Train	60
67	Studio One SO 2001	Have A Good Time/MR FOUNDATION: See Them A Come	50
68	Island WI 3096	Down Low/Sad Mood	50
68	Island WI 3105	Lonely Man/ERROL DUNKLEY: I Am Going Home	100
68	Giant GN 34	Change Is Gonna Come/VAL BENNETT: Jumping With Val	175
69	Bamboo BAM 1	My Whole World Is Falling Down/The Chokin' Kind	30
69	Amalgamated AMG 847	It's Alright/COBBS: One One	100
69	Amalgamated AMG 853	Only Yesterday/COBBS: Joe Gibbs Mood	40
70	Duke DU 79	I Can't Hide/TOMMY McCOOK: Kansas City	35
70	Unity UN 553	When You Were Mine/CLAREDONIANS: The Angels (song actually "The Angels Listened In")	15
71	Duke Reid DR 2504	Sugar Pantie (as Ken Parker & Tommy McCook; actually by Andy Capp)/ TOMMY	15

Larry PARKER

MINT VALUE £

71	Duke Reid DR 2521	McCOOK: All Afire	15
71	Big BG 332	Jimmy Brown/Version	15
72	Jackpot JP 805	Ain't Misbehaving/Genuine Love	12
72	Pama PM 844	Guilty/AGGROVATORS: Guilty (Version)	10
		Shake It Loose/TOMMY McCOOK: Shake It Loose - Version (actually titled "Help Me Make It Through The Night")	10
72	Treasure Isle TI 7073	Help Me Make It Through The Night/TOMMY McCOOK & ALLSTARS (Version)	10
73	Dragon DRA 1003	Will The Circle Be Unbroken/DYNAMITES: Instrumental	10
73	Dragon DRA 1015	Say Wonderful Things/It's True	10
74	Attack ATT 8063	Kiss An Angel/TOMMY McCOOK: Inez	10
74	Attack ATT 8073	Count Your Blessings/Count Your Blessings (Version)	6
72	Melodisc SMLP 12-190	KEEP YOUR EYES ON JESUS (LP)	85
74	Trojan TRLS 80	JIMMY BROWN (LP)	25
75	Pisces PS 5002	A TOUCH OF INSPIRATION (LP)	40

(see also Lyrics)

LARRY PARKER
80	Brightheath BRH 1	Perfect Dreams/Light	20

LEWIS PARKER
95	White JED1	B BOY ANTICS (EP, different recording to Bite It! version - first batch with a black and white sticker, later batch has coloured sticker)	70
96	Bite It! BITEDJ10	B BOY ANTICS (EP)	45
96	Bite It! BITE11	Rise/Visions Of Splendour/Sea Freestyle (12")	25
95	White LEWIS1	Wonderwall (7", 100 only)	30
98	Melankolic SADTDJ3	Shadows Of Autumn/101 Pianos (12")	10
00	M'lic LEWISTDJ1LC03098	THE OPTIONS (EP)	25
01	White SADTDJ13	It's All Happening Now/Schemes/What The Ancients Say (remixes) (EP, 50 copies only)	20
03	Dusty Vinyl DV1JEDI	Mr Parker's Siesta/Blood (12")	18
13	King Underground KU/WODV008	Fragments Of Glass (10" that came with a small number of THE PUZZLE: EPISODE 2)	15
98	Melankolic SADT4	MASQUERADES AND SILHOUETTES (LP)	75
02	Melankolic LPSAD14	IT'S ALL HAPPENING NOW (LP)	70
06	Dusty Vinyl DVJEDI008	MASQUERADES AND SILHOUETTES INSTRUMENTALS (LP, 200 only with unreleased track)	75
10	Project Moon Circle PMC 065	INTERNATIONAL SUMMERS (LP, with John Robinson)	25
13	King Underground KU/WODV007	THE PUZZLE EPISODE 2 - THE GLASS CEILING (LP)	45

MACEO PARKER
90	Verve 843 751-1	ROOTS REVISITED (LP)	30

(see also Maceo & The Macks, Maceo & All The Kings Men)

RAYMOND PARKER
66	Sue WI 4024	Ring Around The Roses/She's Coming Home	50

ROBERT PARKER
66	Island WI 286	Barefootin'/Let's Go Baby (Where The Action Is)	30
66	Island WI 3008	Happy Feet/The Scratch	20
74	Island USA 001	Get Ta Steppin'/Get Right On Down	8
74	Contemporaries CS 9010	Barefootin'/I Caught You In A Lie	15
66	Island ILP 942	BAREFOOTIN' (LP)	80

(see also Huey 'Piano' Smith & Clowns)

SONNY PARKER
56	Vogue V 2392	My Soul's On Fire/Disgusted Blues	300
56	Vogue V 2392	My Soul's On Fire/Disgusted Blues (78)	50

(see also Lionel Hampton)

WILLIE PARKER
67	President PT 171	You Got Your Finger In My Eye/I Live The Life I Love	10

WINFIELD PARKER
72	Mojo 2093 019	Stop Her On Sight/I'm On My Way	8

PARKING LOT
69	Parlophone R 5779	Carpet Man/World Spinning Sadly	45

PARKINGSON'S LAW
72	RCA RCA 2291	Daughter Of Thunder And Lightning/I Need Your Loving And I Can't Let Go	8

JIMMY PARKINSON
56	Columbia SCM 5236	The Great Pretender/Hand In Hand	30
56	Columbia SCM 5267	Walk Hand In Hand/Cry Baby	10
56	Columbia DB 3808	Gina/A Lover's Quarrel	8
56	Columbia DB 3833	In The Middle Of The House/You To Me	8
57	Columbia DB 3876	But You/Together (You And I)	6
57	Columbia DB 3912	Round And Round/Whatever Lola Wants (Lola Gets)	6
57	Columbia 33S 1109	SOLO (10" LP)	20

MICALL PARKNSUN
17	Boot BEP 013	PRACTISING TAG TEAM MOVES EP (12", p/s)	12

BERNICE PARKS
55	Coral Q 72056	Lovin' Machine/Only Love Me	15

LLOYD PARKS
70	Harry J. HJ 6603	Feel A Little Better/I'll Be Your Man	60
71	Upsetter US 379	Mighty Cloud Of Joy/UPSETTERS: Version	25
72	Randy's RAN 524	Stars/Stars - Version	20
74	Fab FAB 273	Schooldays/Version	15
75	Cactus CT 75	Mafia/Mafia Version (Dub)	25
74	Attack – ATLP 1009	OFFICIALLY (LP)	40
75	Trojan Records TRLS 109	GIRL IN THE MORNING (LP)	25

Sonny PARKS

MINT VALUE £

76	Trojan TRLS 126	LOVING YOU (LP)	40

(see also L. Sparks)

SONNY PARKS
63	Warner Bros WB 100	New Boy In Town/Us Kids Have Got To Make Up Our Minds	10

VAN DYKE PARKS
66	MGM MGM 1301	Number Nine/Do What You Wanta	12
69	Warner Bros W(S) 1727	SONG CYCLE (LP)	35
75	Warner Bros. K56161	CLANG OF THE YANKEE REAPER (LP)	15
86	Edsel ED 210	DISCOVER AMERICA (LP. reissue)	15
13	Bella Union BELLAV 396	SONGS CYCLED (2-LP, CD)	20

PARLET
79	Casablanca CAL 2052	INVASION OF THE BOOTY SNATCHERS (LP)	15

(see also Parliament)

PARLIAMENT
71	Invictus INV 513	The Silent Boatman/Livin' The Life	10
72	Invictus INV 522	Come In Out Of The Rain/Little Ole Country Boy	15
75	Casablanca CBX 505	Up On The Down Stroke/Presence Of A Brain	8
71	Invictus SVT 1004	OSMIUM (LP)	100
74	Casablanca NBLP 7002	UP FOR THE DOWN STROKE (LP)	50
75	Casablanca CBC 4009	MOTHERSHIP CONNECTION (LP)	40
75	Casablanca CAL 2012	CHOCOLATE CITY (LP)	40
77	Casablanca CALD 5002	PARLIAMENT LIVE (2-LP)	30
77	Casablanca CALH 2021	FUNKENTELECHY VS THE PLACEBO SYNDROME (LP, with booklet and poster, some on red vinyl)	35
90	Demon HDH LP 008	RHENIUM (LP)	20
99	Sequel NEMLP 997	OSMIUM (LP, reissue)	15

(see also Parliaments, Funkadelic, Parlet, Bootsy's Rubber Band, P-Funk Allstars)

PARLIAMENTS
67	Track 604 013	I Wanna Testify/I Can Feel The Ice Melting	30
69	Track 604 032	I Wanna Testify/I Can Feel The Ice Melting (reissue)	20

(see also Parliament, Funkadelic)

PARLOPHONE POPS ORCHESTRA
56	Parlophone R 4250	Giddy Up A Ding Dong/(We're Gonna) Rock Around The Clock	15

(see also Ron Goodwin)

PARLOUR
10	Parlour PARLOUR NO2	NO 2 (12", p/s)	35
13	Parlour PARLOUR NO3	NO 3 (12", p/s)	35

PARLOUR BAND
72	Deram SDL 10	IS A FRIEND? (LP, laminated gatefold sleeve, white/red label)	500

CHRIS PARMENTER ORCHESTRA
66	Polydor 56107	Cul De Sac/Donkey	20

JACK PARNELL (ORCHESTRA)
53	Parlophone MSP 6009	Waltzing The Blues/Catherine Wheel (as Jack Parnell Band)	10
53	Parlophone MSP 6031	Night Train/Hawk Talks (as Jack Parnell & His Music Makers)	10
53	Parlophone MSP 6046	Cotton Tail/April In Paris	10
53	Parlophone MSP 6054	Dragnet/Fuller Bounce (as Jack Parnell & His Music Makers)	12
54	Parlophone MSP 6066	Route 66/The Creep	12
54	Parlophone MSP 6078	Skin Deep/Devil's Eyes (B-side with Dennis Hale)	20
54	Parlophone MSP 6094	Knock Out/Blowin' Wild (B-side with Dennis Hale)	12
54	Parlophone MSP 6102	The Bandit (with Dennis Hale)/Annie's Blues (with Annie Ross)	18
54	Parlophone MSP 6138	Sky Blue Shirt And Rainbow Tie/Trip To Mars	10
58	Parlophone R 4500	Topsy/Cha Cha Rock	8
59	HMV POP 630	Kansas City/The Golden Striker	10
60	Philips PB 1005	77 Sunset Strip/Teen Ride	8
64	Decca F 11958	The Kiss/The Hidden Truth	10
55	Parlophone GEP 8532	JACK PARNELL AND HIS ORCHESTRA (EP)	10
55	Parlophone GEP 8564	PARNELL ON PARADE (EP)	10
58	Parlophone GEP 8707	KICK OFF! (EP)	10
52	Decca LF 1065	THE JACK PARNELL QUARTET (10" LP)	25
58	Parlophone PMD 1053	TRIP TO MARS (10" LP)	80

(see also Dennis Hale)

PAROT
73	Royal Blue RB 001	Wake Up/I've Dreamed Of The Sun (p/s)	25

CATHERINE PARR
65	Decca F 12210	You Belong To Me/He's My Guy	12

JACKIE PARRIS AND BIG YOUTH
79	Book Of Psalms BP 001	Let Him Try/Really Together (12")	15

BRIAN PARRISH
69	United Artists UP 35049	In Good Time (Love Chant)/I Wanna Go To Sleep	10

DEAN PARRISH
66	Stateside SS 531	Tell Her/Fall On Me	80
66	Stateside SS 531	Tell Her/Fall On Me (DJ copy)	125
66	Stateside SS 550	Turn On Your Lovelight/Determination	150
66	Stateside SS 550	Turn On Your Lovelight/Determination (DJ copy)	200
67	Stateside SS 580	Skate (Parts 1 & 2)	60
67	Stateside SS 580	Skate (Parts 1 & 2) (DJ copy)	100
75	UK USA 2	I'm On My Way/Watch Out	10
75	UK USA 2	I'm On My Way/Watch Out (DJ copy)	15
03	Kent TOWN 119	Broken Bottles And Sticks/MELBA MOORE: Magic Touch	8

PARRISH & GURVITZ

MINT VALUE £

PARRISH & GURVITZ
71   Regal Zono. SRZA 8506   PARRISH & GURVITZ (LP, textured gatefold sleeve) 35
(see also Baker Gurvitz Army, Three Man Army)

GAYLORD PARRY
67   CBS 2685   I'm On The Way Up/I'm Coming Home 10

SAM PARRY
73   Argo ZDA 155   IF SADNESS COULD SING (LP) 400

PARSON & SMITH
72   Polydor 2058229   The Letter/When It Rains 30

ALAN PARSONS PROJECT
77   Arista AL 7002   I ROBOT (LP) 15
(see also Andrew Powell & Philharmonic Orchestra)

BILL PARSONS & HIS ORCHESTRA
59   London HL 8798   The All American Boy/Rubber Dolly 12

GENE PARSONS
74   Warner Bros K 46257   KINDLING (LP) 18
(see also Byrds, Flying Burrito Brothers)

GRAM PARSONS
73   Reprise K 14245   The New Soft Shoe/She 8
73   Reprise K 44228   GP (LP, gatefold sleeve) 40
74   Reprise K 54018   GRIEVOUS ANGEL (LP, with Emmylou Harris) 40
76   A&M AMLH 65478   SLEEPLESS NIGHTS (LP, with Flying Burrito Brothers & Emmylou Harris) 35
82   Sundown SDLP 003   GRAM PARSONS AND THE FALLEN ANGELS (LP, featuring Emmylou Harris) 15
(see also Byrds, Flying Burrito Brothers)

PARTICULAR PEOPLE
68   Big T BIG 105   Boys Cry/What's The Matter With Juliet 6

PARTISANS (1)
82   No Future OI 2   Police Story/Killing Machine (p/s, with lyric insert) 15
82   No Future OI 12   17 Years Of Hell/The Power And The Greed/Bastards In Blue (p/s) 15
83   Cloak & Dagger PART 1   Blind Ambition/Come Clean (p/s) 15
83   No Future PUNK 4   PARTISANS (LP) 22
84   Cloak & Dagger PARTLP 1   THE TIME WAS RIGHT (LP, with inner) 40

PARTISANS (2)
88   Hotwire HWS 863   Open Your Eyes/Partisan (p/s) 8
(see also Blades)

PARTNERS IN CRIME
84   Epic A 4803   Hold On/She's Got Eyes For You (p/s) 6
85   Epic A 5040   Miracles/What You Gonna Do? (p/s) 6
85   Epic A 6170   Hollywood Dreams/She's Got Eyes For You (p/s) 7
85   Epic TX 6170   Hollywood Dreams (Extended)/She's Got Eyes For You (12", p/s) 10
(see also Status Quo)

PART ONE
82   Paraworm   FUNERAL PARADE (EP) 12

DON PARTRIDGE
69   Columbia DB 8617   Going To Germany/Ask Me Why 6
68   Columbia S(C)X 6280   DON PARTRIDGE (LP) 15
(see also Accolades)

PARTY DAY
83   Party Day FX 301   Row The Boat Ashore/Poison (p/s, insert) 15
84   Party Day FX 302   The Spider/Flies (p/s) 8
85   Rouska COME 1T   Glasshouse/My Heroine/Let Us Shine/Smile (12", p/s) 20
85   Party Day FXLP 401   GLASSHOUSE (LP) 30
86   Party Day PDLP 501   SIMPLICITY (LP) 30

PASADENA ROOF ORCHESTRA
78   CBS CBS 12-637   Pennies From Heaven/Back In Your Own Back Yard/Pennies From Heaven (10" p/s, 2nd side plays at 78 rpm) 15

PASHA
69   Liberty LBF 15199   Someone Shot The Lollipop Man/Pussy Willow Dragon 120
(see also Searchers)

JOE PASS
60s   Fontana 688 137 ZL   CATCH ME (LP) 20

PASSAGE
78   Object Music OMO 2   Love Song/The Competition/Slit Machine/New Kind Of Love (p/s) 10
79   Object OM 8   Taking My Time/Clock Paradox/Sixteen Hours/Time Delay (p/s) 6
(see also Contact)

PASSENGERS (1)
79   No label or cat. no   Something About You (I Don't Like)/Two Lovers (1st press, hand-written labels) 15
79   Blue Inc INC 8   Something About You (I Don't Like)/Two Lovers (2nd press, no p/s) 10
79   Epic EPC 7967   Two Lovers/Love Fades (no p/s) 6

PASSENGERS (2)
95   Island IS 625   Miss Sarajevo/One (live) (7", with poster in 12" card in PVC p/s) 10
96   Island OST 3   Your Blue Room (CD, 1-track promo, card sleeve, export issue) 30
95   Island OST 2   ORIGINAL SOUNDCHAT 1 (2-CD, music & interview disc, fold-out digipaks, with cue sheet, promo only) 60
95   Island ILPS8043   ORIGINAL SOUNDTRACKS (LP) 100
(see also U2, Brian Eno)

PASSION BLADES
83   Caprice CAP 1   Living In A Lighthouse/Dub Version (no p/s) 8

PASSION POLKA
82   Kinetic KR 01   Obsessions/Juliet (no p/s) 40

PASSION PIT
09	Frenchkiss 88697438861	MANNERS (LP)	40
12	Columbia 88725 41651 1	GOSSAMER (2-LP, with CD)	40

PASSIONS (1)
58	Capitol CL 14874	My Aching Heart/Jackie Brown	75

PASSIONS (2)
59	Top Rank JAR 224	Just To Be With You/Oh Melancholy Me	60
60	Top Rank JAR 313	I Only Want You/This Is My Love	70

PASSIONS (3)
79	Soho SH5	Needles And Pills/Body And Soul	10

PAST AND PRESENT
79	Rook CUS 423	FIRST TIME OUT (LP, private pressing)	30

PAST SEVEN DAYS
86	4AD AD 102	Raindance/So Many Others/Nothing (p/s)	15

PASTEL
21	Spirit Of Spike Island	DEEPER THAN HOLY (12", pink or orange neon vinyl, p/s)	40

PASTELS
82	Whaam! WHAAM 005	Songs For Children: Heavens Above!/Tea Time Tales (p/s)	80
83	Rough Trade RT 137	I Wonder Why/Supposed To Understand (p/s)	40
84	Creation CRE 005	Something Going On/Stay With Me Till Morning (foldaround p/s in poly bag)	35
84	Creation CRE 011T	A Million Tears/Baby Honey/Surprise Me (12", p/s)	15
85	Creation CRE 023T	I'm Alright With You/Couldn't Care Less/What It's Worth (12", p/s)	10
85	Villa 21 VILLA 3	Heavens Above!/Tea Time Tales/I Wonder Why (live)/Tea Time Tales (live) (p/s)	25
87	Glass 050	Crawl Babies/Empty House	6
87	Glass 053	Comin' Through/Sit On It Mother (p/s)	6
90	Overground OVER 06	Heavens Above!/Tea Time Tales/Something Going On (demo)/ Until Morning Comes (demo) (p/s; 200 clear vinyl)	10
90	Overground OVER 06	Heavens Above!/Tea Time Tales/Something Going On (demo)/Until Morning Comes (demo) (p/s; 157 green vinyl)	10
91	Paperhouse PAPER 008	Speeding Motorcycle/Speedway Star (p/s)	7
93	Paperhouse PAPER 023	Thank You For Being You/Kitted Out (p/s)	8
95	Domino RUG 36T	Worlds Of Possibility/Photogram/Love, It's Getting Better/Ever Far (12", p/s)	15
13	Domino RUG 520	Check My Heart/Illuminum Song (p/s)	10
87	Glass GLAL P021	UP FOR A BIT WITH THE PASTELS (LP, with inner)	20
88	Creation CRELP 031	SUCK ON (LP)	20
89	Chapter 22 CHAPLP 43	SITTIN' PRETTY (LP)	20
93	Paperhouse PAPLP 008	TRUCKROAD OF TROUBLE (2-LP)	40
94	Domino WIGLP 17	MOBILE SAFARI (LP, with free 7")	45
98	Domino WIGLP46	ILLUMINATI (2-LP)	40
97	Domino WIGLP 34	ILLUMINATION (LP)	50
03	Geographic GEOG18LP	LAST GREAT WILDERNESS (LP)	35
09	Geographic GEOG37LP	TWO SUNSETS (LP, with Tenniscoats)	20
13	Domino WIGLP 185	SLOW SUMMITS (LP)	15

(see also Buba & Shop Assistants, Jad Fair, Vaselines)

PASTEL SIX
63	London HLU 9651	The Cinnamon Cinder/Bandido	20

PASTORAL SYMPHONY
68	President PT 202	Love Machine/Spread A Little Love Around	20

PAT
71	Gas GAS 158	Teach Me (actually "Words Of Temptation" by Earl Lawrence)/RHYTHM RULERS: Sea Breeze (actually by Im & David)	30

PAT & MARIE
66	Ska Beat JB 234	I Try Not To Tell You/PAT RHODEN: Don't Blame It On Me	15
66	Ska Beat JB 235	You're Really Leaving/PAT RHODEN: Broken Heart	15

(see also Pat Rhoden)

PAT & ROXIE
65	Caribou CRC 2	Sing To Me/Things I Used To Do	10

PATCHES
72	Warner Bros K 16201	Living In America/Quicksand	8

PATCHWORK (1)
72	Decca FR 13346	Laughing Sam (On The Phone)/Afrodisiac	40

PATCHWORK (2)
78	Wasps WSP 1	JOhanne Of The Zuider Zee (Far Canal)/Nothing Wrong With Women (no p/s)	6

JOHNNY PATE ORCHESTRA
58	Parlophone 4437	I'm Stepping Out Of The Picture/Muskeeta	12
73	Probe SPB 1077	SHAFT IN AFRICA (LP, soundtrack, with Four Tops)	40
74	ABC ABCL 5035	SHAFT IN AFRICA (LP, soundtrack, reissue)	15

PAMELA PATERSON
72	Polydor 2001 278	Finally (Theme From 'Gumshoe')/OLYMPIC STUDIO CONCERT ORCHESTRA: Music From 'Gumshoe' (p/s)	20

PATHETIX
78	No Records NO 001	Aleister Crowley/Don't Touch My Machine/Snuffed It (p/s, with insert)	35
79	TJM TJM 9	Love In Decay/Nil Carborundum/What Do You Expect? (with p/s)	200
79	TJM TJM 9	Love In Decay/Nil Carborundum/What Do You Expect? (without p/s)	40

PATHFINDERS (1)
64	Decca F 12038	I Love You Caroline/Something I Can Always Do	18

PATHFINDERS (2)
64	Hayton SP 138/139	What Do You Do/What'd I Say (private pressing)	20

PATHFINDERS (3)
65	Parlophone R 5372	Don't You Believe It/Castle Of Love	20

(see also [White] Trash, Poets)

PATHWAY TO YOUR MIND

MINT VALUE £

PATHWAY TO YOUR MIND
68	Major Minor SMLP 19	PREPARING THE MIND AND BODY FOR MEDITATION (LP, spoken word)	25

PATIENCE & PRUDENCE
56	London HLU 8321	Tonight You Belong To Me/A Smile And A Ribbon (Gold label)	30
56	London HLU 8321	Tonight You Belong To Me/A Smile And A Ribbon (Silver label)	15
57	London HLU 8369	Gonna Get Along Without Ya Now/The Money Tree (Gold label)	30
57	London HLU 8369	Gonna Get Along Without Ya Now/The Money Tree (Silver label)	15
57	London HL 7017	Gonna Get Along Without Ya Now/The Money Tree (export issue)	20
57	London HLU 8425	Dreamer's Bay/We Can't Sing Rhythm And Blues	15
57	London HLU 8493	You Tattletale/Very Nice Is Bali Bali	15
58	London HLU 8773	Tom Thumb's Tune/Golly Oh Gee	8
57	London REU 1087	A SMILE AND A SONG (EP)	40

SALLY PATIENCE
84	Disc DEL 1	The Triangle Man/Buried In My Boots (p/s)	35

LEON PATILLO
70s	Maranatha MM 0049	DANCE CHILDREN, DANCE (LP)	18
70s	Myrrh MYR 1136	LIVE EXPERIENCE (LP)	18

SANDY & CAROLINE PATON
60	Topic TOP 57	HUSH LITTLE BABY (EP)	10

(see also Beat Brothers, Tony Sheridan & Beat Brothers)

BOBBY PATRICK BIG SIX
64	Decca F 11898	Shake It Easy Baby/Wildwood Days	40
64	Decca F 12030	Monkey Time/Sweet Talk Me Baby	30
64	Decca DFE 8570	TEENBEAT 3 (FROM STAR CLUB, HAMBURG) (EP)	120

DAN PATRICK
67	Stateside SS 2004	Tiger Lee/Call Of The Wild	10

KENTRICK PATRICK
63	Island WI 066	Man To Man/ROLAND ALFONSO: Blockade (B-side actually "Hit And Run")	40
63	Island WI 079	Don't Stay Out Late/Forever And Ever	30
63	Island WI 104	The End Of The World/Little Princess	35
63	Island WI 119	Golden Love/Beyond	40
64	Island WI 132	Take Me To The Party/I'm Sorry	25
64	Island WI 140	I Am Wasting Time/RANDY'S GROUP: Royal Charley	120

(see also Lord Creator, Pridigal Creator. Fitz Vaughan Bryan's Orchestra)

PATRICK & LLOYD
70	Big Shot BI 550	Return Of The Pollock/PROPHETS: Concorde	30

(see also Lloyd & Prophets)

PATRIOTS
66	Fontana TF 650	Prophet/I'll Be There	20

PATRON OF THE ARTS
66	Page One POF 012	The True Patron Of The Arts/Eleanor Rigby (USA release credits it as Queen City Show Band)	50

PATSY
68	Doctor Bird DB 1113	A Man Is Two Faced/LENNIE HIBBERT & COUNT OSSIE: Pure Soul	200
68	Doctor Bird DB 1122	Little Flea/The Retreat Song	60
68	High Note HS012	We Were Lovers/DELANO STEWART : Give Me A Chance	75

(see also Patsy Todd, Derrick & Patsy, Stranger & Patsy, Emotions)

PATSY & PEGGY
70	Hot Rod HR 107	Dog Your Woman/Strictly Invitation	100

BRIAN PATTEN
70	Caedmon TC 1300	BRIAN PATTEN (LP)	20
76	Tangent TGS 116	VANISHING TRICK (LP)	20

(see also Liverpool Scene, Roger McGough & Brian Patten)

DEE PATTEN
92	Hard Hands HAND 003 T	WHO'S THE BAD MAN EP (12")	30

PATTERN PEOPLE
68	MGM MGM 1429	Love Is A Lover Loving To Be Loved/Take A Walk In The Sunshine	20

PATTERNS
80	Heater Volume Records HVR 002	No Violent Pacing/Bishop In The Fridge	10

PATTERNS IN PERU
86	Vernon YZ 60	This Is The Night/Playing Games	25
86	Vernon YZ60T	This Is The Night (Extended)/Playing Games/This Is The Night (12" p/s)	40

BOBBY PATTERSON (& MUSTANGS)
68	Pama PM 735	Broadway Ain't Funky No More/I Met My Match (with Mustangs)	15
68	Pama PM 743	The Good Ol' Days/Don't Be So Mean	20
68	Pama PM 754	Busy Busy Bee/Sweet Taste Of Love (with Mustangs)	20
69	Pama PM 763	T.C.B. Or T.Y.A./What A Wonderful Night For Love (with Mustangs)	20
69	Pama PM 773	My Thing Is Your Thing/Keep It In The Family	20
72	Action ACT 4604	I'm In Love With You/Married Lady	90
77	Contempo 2115	I Got To Get Over/If He Hadn't Slipped And Got Caught	20
72	Mojo 2092 037	How Do You Spell Love/She Don't Have To See You	10

KELLEE PATTERSON
76	Mint CHEW 10	I'm Gonna Love You Just A Little More Baby/You Are So Beautiful	60
95	Hubbub HUBLP03	KELLEE (LP, reissue)	40

MARY-ANNE PATTERSON
70	Joy JOYS 162	ME (LP)	300

OTTILIE PATTERSON
55	Decca F 10472	I Hate A Man Like You/Reckless Blues (with Chris Barber's Jazz Band)	10
55	Decca F 10621	Weeping Willow Blues/Nobody Knows You When You're Down And Out	10
57	Pye 7N 15109	Kay-Cee Rider/I Love You Baby	10

Robert PATTERSON SINGERS

MINT VALUE £

58	Pye Jazz 7NJ 2015	Jailhouse Blues/Beale Street Blues	10
58	Pye Jazz 7NJ 2025	Trombone Cholly/Lawdy, Lawdy Blues	10
61	Columbia DB 4760	Blueberry Hill/I'm Crazy 'Bout My Baby	10
62	Columbia DB 4834	I Hate Myself/Come On Baby	12
63	Columbia DB 7140	Jealous Heart/Won't Be Long	10
63	Columbia DB 7208	Baby Please Don't Go/I Feel So Good (with Sonny Boy Williamson)	50
65	Columbia DB 7332	Tell Me Where Is Fancy/Oh Me What Eyes	10
69	Marmalade 598 016	Spring Song/Sound Of The Door As It Closes	25
69	Marmalade 598 020	Bitterness Of Death/Spring Song	25
56	Decca DFE 6303	BLUES (EP)	12
56	Pye Jazz Today NJE 1023	THAT PATTERSON GIRL VOL. 2 (EP)	10
60	Columbia SEG 7998	SWINGS THE IRISH (EP)	10
59	Pye NPL 18028	OTTILIE'S IRISH NIGHT (LP)	15
69	Marmalade 608 011	3000 YEARS WITH OTTILIE (LP)	125
69	Polydor 2384 031	SPRING SONG (LP)	35

(see also Chris Barber)

ROBERT PATTERSON SINGERS
60s	United Artists UAS 29003	THE SOUL OF GOSPEL (LP)	25
65	Fontana 688 516 ZL	I'M SAVED (LP)	18

PATTERSONS
70	CBS 5083	I Can Fly/An Cailin Deas	15
69	CBS M 63532	AGAIN (LP, mono)	18
69	CBS 63522	AGAIN (LP, stereo)	15

PATTERSON'S PEOPLE
66	Mercury MF 913	Shake Hands With The Devil/Deadly Nightshade	40

PATTIE
69	Columbia DB 8542	Gravitation/Let The Music Start	12

PATTI & PATETTES
75	Dart ART 2053	Bill/It's My Party	8
76	United Artists UP 36077	Summer Heartbreak/Too Much	12

HUBERT PATTISON
67	Fontana TF 859	My Home's In My Pocket/Saturday Morning Bride	10

LITTLE JOHN PATTISON
64	Giv-A-Disc LYN 510	Needles And Pins/All My Loving (flexidisc with Giv-A-Disc booklet)	10

(MIKE) PATTO
66	Columbia DB 8091	Can't Stop Talking About My Baby/Love (as Mike Patto)	100
74	Goodear EAR 106	Sitting In The Park/Get Up And Dig It (as Mike Patto)	10
70	Vertigo 6360 016	PATTO (LP, textured gatefold sleeve, large swirl label)	400
71	Vertigo 6360 032	HOLD YOUR FIRE (LP, 3-flap gatefold, small swirl label)	600
72	Island ILPS 9210	ROLL 'EM SMOKE 'EM PUT ANOTHER LINE OUT (LP, pink rim/palm tree label)	100

(see also Bo Street Runners, Breakaways, Boxer, News, Chicago Line, Timebox, Felder's Orioles, Steve York, Centipede, Grimms, Spooky Tooth, V.I.P.s)

ALEXANDER PATTON
66	Capitol CL 15461	A Lil Lovin' Sometimes/No More Dreams	250
66	Capitol CL 15461	A Lil Lovin' Sometimes/No More Dreams (DJ copy)	350

CHARLIE PATTON
50s	Heritage REU 4	CHARLIE PATTON (EP, 99 only)	60

JOHN PATTON
64	Blue Note 45-1889	I'll Never Be Free/Along Came John	8

PATTY & EMBLEMS
64	Stateside SS 322	Mixed Up Shook Up Girl/Ordinary Guy	50
64	Stateside SS 322	Mixed Up Shook Up Girl/Ordinary Guy (DJ copy)	100

PATTY FLABBIE'S COUGHED ENGINE
69	Stateside SS 2136	Billy's Got A Goat/Tin Can Eater	6

PAUL
65	Polydor BM 56045	Will You Follow Me/Head Death	80

(see also Jimmy Page)

ANDREW PAUL
85	Fashion FAD 038	Hustle Them A Hustle/Bad Boys (12")	25
85	Y&D YDD 0126	Under Me Sensima/Can't Take It No Longer (12", with the Offbeat Posse)	30
87	Digikal DIG 004	Too Stush/Gunshot A Flow (12", p/s)	30

BILLY PAUL
73	Epic EPC 65456	EBONY WOMAN (LP)	15
74	Phil. Intl. PIR 65861	WAR OF THE GODS (LP, gatefold sleeve)	15

BUNNY PAUL
54	Columbia SCM 5102	New Love/You'll Never Leave My Side	10
54	Columbia SCM 5112	Such A Night/I'm Gonna Have Some Fun	20
54	Columbia SCM 5131	Lovey Dovey/Answer The Call	20
54	Columbia SCM 5151	You Came A Long Way From St. Louis/You Are Always In My Heart	12
55	Capitol CL 14279	Please Have Mercy (On A Fool)/These Are The Things We'll Share	12
55	Capitol CL 14304	Leave My Heart Alone/Two Castanets	12
55	Capitol CL 14368	Song Of The Dreamer/For The Very First Time	10

CHRIS PAUL
87	CBL 1	City Nights/City NIghts (12")	15
93	Kikman KIK 009	DANCE THE DESTINY EP (12")	70

DARLENE PAUL
64	Capitol CL 15344	Act Like Nothing Happened/Little Bit Of Heaven	30

DEREK PAUL
73	Youngblood YB 1006	Drugtaker/Riverboat	8

DON PAUL
68	RCA 1666	Wise/Ways Of The World	12

Eugene PAUL

MINT VALUE £

EUGENE PAUL
70	Pama Supreme PS 303	Don't Let The Tears Fall/Another Saturday Night	6
70	Pama Supreme PS 305	I Found A Man In My Bed/So Many Things	6
71	Pama Supreme PS 317	Farewell My Darling/Whole Lot Of Woman	6
71	Pama Supreme PS 329	Somebody's Changing My Sweet Baby's Mind/Hard Minded Neighbour	6
72	Pama PM 838	Beautiful Sunday/Take Care Son	6
72	Pama Supreme PS 357	I'll Take You There/Beautiful Baby	6
73	Pama Supreme PS 382	Power To All Our Friends/RANNY WILLIAMS ALLSTARS: Wicked And Dreadful	7

EUGENE PAUL & PILOTS
70	Torpedo TOR 17	Sugar Dumpling/I May Dwell	40

FRANKIE PAUL
85	Greensleeves GRED 189	Fools Fighting/Fighting Dub (12")	12
85	Tonos TON 007	Shining Star/If I Am Wrong (12")	30

JAI PAUL
12	XL XLD 5574	Jasmine (Demo)/Jasmine (Demo) Instrumental (12", p/s, 100 only, numbered)	80

JASON PAUL
69	Pye 7N 17710	Shine A Little Light Into My Room/Paradise Pudding	20

(see also Svensk)

JOHN E. PAUL
67	Decca F 12685	Prince Of Players/I Wanna Know (DJ copy with curved Decca logo inverted matrix)	200
67	Decca F 12685	Prince Of Players/I Wanna Know (Boxed Decca logo, inverted matrix)	100
67	Decca F 12685	Prince Of Players/I Wanna Know (Matrix number 41387 correct way up)	20

LES PAUL (& MARY FORD)
54	Capitol CL 14185	Mandolino/Whither Thou Goest	8
55	Capitol CL 14212	Mister Sandman/That's What I Like	15
55	Capitol CL 14233	Someday Sweetheart/Song In Blue	8
55	Capitol CL 14300	No Letter Today/Genuine Love	8
55	Capitol CL 14342	Goodbye My Love/Hummingbird	8
56	Capitol CL 14502	Alabamy Bound/Texas Lady	8

LYN PAUL
74	Polydor 2058 472	Sail The Summer Winds/Lay Me Down (with John Barry)	7
75	Polydor 2383 340	GIVE ME LOVE (LP)	15

(see also Nocturnes)

SHELLEY PAUL
69	Jay Boy BOY 10	Clowns Are Coming In/Take Me To Your Heart	6

PAULA & JETLINERS
66	Rainbow RAI 102	The Great Pretender/The Legend Of The Man From U.N.C.L.E.	15
66	Rainbow RAI 105	I Know Someday/Something On My Mind (B-side with Carols)	8

PAUL & LINDA
69	Page One POF 140	You're Taking My Bag/When I Hear Your Name	10

PAUL & PAULA
63	Philips 304 016 BF	Young Lovers/Ba-hey-be	6
63	Philips BF 1256	First Quarrel/School Is Thru	7
63	Philips BF 1269	Something Old, Something New/Flipped Over You	7
63	Philips BF 1281	First Day Back At School/A Perfect Pair	7
64	Philips BF 1380	No Other Baby/Too Dark To See	7
63	Philips BBE 12639	YOUNG LOVERS (EP)	20
63	Philips 652 026BL	SING FOR YOUNG LOVERS (LP)	25
63	Philips BL 7573	WE GO TOGETHER (LP)	25
63	Philips BL 7587	HOLIDAY FOR TEENS (LP)	25

PAUL AND RITCHIE & CRYING SHAMES
66	Decca F 12483	September In The Rain/Come On Back (more common demos are worth, £80)	120

(see also Cryin' Shames, Gary Walker & Rain)

PAULETTE (WILLIAMS)
68	Major Minor MM 565	One Love In My Heart/Must We Say Goodbye	6
73	Summit SUM 8543	Every Day Is The Same Kind Of Thing/ SHORTY PERRY: The Sweat Of Your Brow	6

(see also Paulette & Gee)

PAULETTE & DELROY
63	Island WI 120	Little Lover/Lovin' Baby	30

(see also Paulette, Paulette & Gee)

PAULETTE & GEE
70	G.G. GG 4506	Hold On Tight/G.G. ALL STARS: Tight Version	8

(see also Paulette, Sister, Winston Wright)

PAULETTE SISTERS
55	Capitol CL 14294	Dream Boat/Leave My Honey Be	12
55	Capitol CL 14310	Ring-A-Dang-A-Doo/Lonely One	12
55	Capitol CL 14347	You Win Again/Mama, El Baion	12

PAULINE (& BROWN SUGAR)
80	Studio WE 706	I Am So Proud/NATTY LOCKS: Studio 16 Workshop (12")	25
80	Isis 1	Lion, Me And My Dread/Revelation Side (12")	40

(see also Brown Sugar)

PAUL'S DISCIPLES
65	Decca F 12081	See That My Grave Is Kept Clean/Sixteen Tons	35

PAUL'S TROUBLES
67	Ember EMB S 233	You'll Find Out/You've Got Something	25

PAUPERS
68	Verve Forecast VS 1514	Think I Care/White Song	15
69	Verve Forecast VS 1520	Southdown Road/Numbers	15
68	Verve Forecast (S)VLP 6017	ELLIS ISLAND (LP, mono/stereo)	30

(see also Lighthouse)

PAVEMENT (1)

MINT VALUE £

PAVEMENT (1)
| 69 | Crystal CRY 3000 | PAVEMENT (LP) | 40 |

PAVEMENT (2)
92	Big Cat ABB 35S	Trigger Cut/Sue Me Jack/So Stark (You're A Skyscraper) (p/s)	6
94	Big Cat ABB 55S	Cut Your Hair/Camera/Stare (p/s)	6
94	Big Cat UK ABB 55T	Cut Your Hair/Camera/Stare (uncredited track) (12")	10
94	Big Cat ABB 70T	Gold Soundz/Kneeling Bus/Strings Of Nashville/Exit Theory (12")	6
95	Big Cat ABB 77S	Range Life/Raft Coolin By Sound (p/s)	10
95	Big Cat ABB 91S	Father To A Sister Of Thought/Kris Kraft/Mussle Rock Is A Horse In Transition (p/s)	6
96	Big Cat ABB 110 S	Give It A Day/Gangsters & Pranksters/Saganaw/I Love Perth (p/s)	12
91	Big Cat ABB 34	SLANTED AND ENCHANTED (LP, with lyric sheet)	30
93	Big Cat ABB 40	WESTING (BY MUSKET AND SEXTANT) (LP)	45
94	Big Cat ABB 56L	CROOKED RAIN CROOKED RAIN (LP, with inner sleeve, some with free 7": "Haunt You Down"/"Jam Kids")	50
95	Big Cat LC 5661	WOWEE ZOWEE (2-LP, 3-sided, 1 side etched gatefold cover)	50
97	Domino WIGLP 31	BRIGHTEN THE CORNERS (LP)	50
99	Domino WIGLP 66	TERROR TWILIGHT (LP)	50
10	Domino WIGLP 250	QUARENTINE THE PAST (2-LP)	20

(see also Stephen Malkmus)

RITA PAVONE
63	RCA 1354	Il Ballo Del Mattone Part 1/Part 2	6
64	RCA RCA 1415	Remember Me/Just Once More	6
66	RCA RCA 1553	Heart/The Man Who Makes The Music	10
66	RCA RCA 1561	You Only You/Before You Go	7
64	RCA RD 7657	RITA PAVONE (mono)	20
64	RCA SF 7657	RITA PAVONE (stereo)	20

PAX EXTERNAL
| 71 | Decca F 13167 | A Second Chance Mr. Jones/You See Him As Your Brother | 6 |

GARY PAXTON
| 62 | Liberty LIB 55485 | Stop Twistin' Baby/Alley Oop Was A Two Dab Man | 15 |

(see also Skip & Flip)

TOM PAXTON
66	Elektra EKSN 45001	The Last Thing On My Mind/Goin' To The Zoo	20
67	Elektra EPK 802	TOM PAXTON (EP)	20
66	Elektra EKL 298/EKS 7298	AIN'T THAT NEWS (LP, U.K. pressing in U.S. sleeve)	20

DAVEY PAYNE & MEDIUM WAVE
| 69 | Ember EMB S 265 | Walk In The Sunshine/Looking Towards The Sky (p/s) | 30 |

DAVEY PAYNE
| 79 | Stiff HORN 1 | Saxophone Man/Foggy Day (p/s) | 7 |

(see also Kilburn & The High Roads, Ian Dury & The Blockheads)

FREDA PAYNE
62	HMV POP 1091	He Who Laughs Last (Desafinado)/Slightly Out Of Tune	15
71	Invictus INV 518	You've Got To Love Somebody/Mama's Gone	6
72	Invictus INV 520	You Brought Me Joy/Suddenly It's Yesterday	6
73	Invictus INV 533	Band Of Gold/The Easiest Way To Fall (reissue, withdrawn)	30
70	Invictus SVT 1001	BAND OF GOLD (LP)	20
71	Invictus SVT 1005	CONTACT (LP)	20

JACKIE PAYNE
| 77 | Barak 4 | I Found Myself/Instrumental | 15 |

JOHN PAYNTER
| 70 | Universal Editions LYN 2351 | HEAR AND NOW (EP) | 50 |

LOLA PAYOLA
| 81 | Epic EPC 1499 | Schoolgirl Song/I Got Married To A Man From Space (p/s) | 25 |

LAWRENCE PAYTON
| 74 | ABC 4021 | Tell Me You Love Me/Instrumental (DJ Copy) | 40 |
| 74 | ABC 4021 | Tell Me You Love Me/Instrumental | 25 |

(see also the Four Tops)

PAZ
79	Magnus 2	PAZ AT CHICHESTER (LP)	25
82	Spotlite SPH 518	PAZ ARE BACK (LP)	100
83	Spotlite SPJ 507	KANDEEN LOVE SONG (LP)	40
83	Coda CODA 18	LOOK INSIDE (LP)	15

(see also Lol Coxhill)

P BROTHERS
| 01 | White (Heavy Bronx) PBHB 01 | HEAVY BRONX EXPERIENCE VOL. 1 (EP) | 30 |
| 01 | White (Heavy Bronx) PBHB 002 | HEAVY BRONX EXPERIENCE VOL. 2 (EP) | 15 |

PC LTD
| 69 | Fontana TF 1032 | Sunny Was A Fool/Here We Come | 6 |

DAVE PEABODY
| 73 | Village Thing VTS 22 | PEABODY HOTEL (LP, with insert) | 50 |

PEACE
12	Deadly People	Follow Baby/Li'l Echo (picture disc, 500 only, 20 signed by band)	20
12	Deadly People 88725473021	DELICIOUS EP (12" p/s, white vinyl, 300 only)	80
13	Columbia 8883706487	California Daze (1-sided RSD picture disc)	8
13	Sony 88765473021	IN LOVE (LP, with red 12", booklet signed by band)	50
14	Columbia 88875001541	HAPPY PEOPLE (2-LP, yellow/blue vinyl)	35

DAVE PEACE QUARTET
| 69 | Saga FID 2155 | GOOD MORNING MR. BLUES (LP) | 15 |

(see also Birmingham)

PEACEMAKERS

MINT VALUE £

PEACEMAKERS
65	Herald ELR 1070	PEACEMAKERS EP	15
65	Herald ELR 1079	PEACEMAKERS EP (repressing)	15
66	Cathedral CL 755	PEACEMAKERS (LP)	50

PEACH PALF
97	Mighty Force MF 005	Hardbody/Off You Girl (12")	20

PEACHES
02	Kitty Yo XLLP 163	TEACHES OF PEACHES (LP as 5x12")	50
03	Kitty Yo XLLP 171	FATHERFUCKER (2-LP, pink vinyl)	35
06	XL XLLP 201	IMPEACH MY BUSH (LP, pink vinyl)	35
09	XL XLLP 415	I FEEL CREAM (2-LP, inners)	30
11	XL Recordings XLLP 163	TEACHES OF PEACHES (2-LP, reissue, pink vinyl)	20

PEACHES & HERB
67	CBS 202509	Let's Fall In Love/We're In This Thing Together	30
67	CBS 202509	Let's Fall In Love/We're In This Thing Together (DJ copy)	40
67	CBS 2711	Close Your Eyes/I Will Watch Over You	8
67	CBS 2866	For Your Love/I Need Your Love So Desperately	25
67	CBS 2866	For Your Love/I Need Your Love So Desperately (DJ copy)	40
67	Direction 58-3096	Love Is Strange/Two Little Kids	10
68	Direction 58-3415	Let It Be Me/I Need Your Love So Desperately	10
68	Direction 58-3548	United/Thank You	8
68	Direction 58-3829	Let's Make A Promise/Me And You	10
69	Direction 58-4085	When He Touches Me/Thank You	7
70	Direction 58-4909	Satisfy My Hunger/It's Just A Game, Love	8
70	Direction 58-5249	Soothe Me With Your Love/We're So Much In Love	8
71	CBS 5249	Soothe Me With Your Love/We're So Much In Love (reissue)	6
77	Epic EPC 4903	Soothe Me With Your Love/Satisy My Hunger (coloured vinyl)	6

PEACOCK
71	Famous FAM 109	Sun Was In Your Eyes/Just A Lonely Man	20

ANNETTE PEACOCK
72	RCA SF 8255	I'M THE ONE (LP)	50
79	Aura AUL 707	THE PERFECT RELEASE (LP)	20

ANNETTE PEACOCK & PAUL BLEY
73	Freedom 2383 105	DUAL UNITY (LP)	50

(see also Paul Bley, Bley-Peacock Synthesiser Show, Annette Peacock)

ROGER PEACOCK
65	Columbia DB7764	Everybody's Talking About My Baby/Times Have Changed	20

TREVOR PEACOCK
61	Decca F 11414	I Didn't Figure On Him To Come Back/Can I Walk You Home	22

PEAK FOLK
76	Folk Heritage FHR 082	THE PEAK FOLK (LP)	40

PEANUT
65	Pye 7N 15901	Thank Goodness For The Rain/I'm Not Sad	10
65	Pye 7N 15963	Home Of The Brave/I Wanna Hear It Again	30
66	Columbia DB 8032	I'm Waiting For The Day/Someone's Gonna Be Sorry	22
67	Columbia DB 8104	I Didn't Love Him Anyway/Come Tomorrow	20

(see also Katie Kissoon, Ragdolls U.K.)

PEANUT BUTTER CONSPIRACY
67	CBS 2981	It's A Happening Thing/Twice Is Life	15
68	CBS 3543	Turn On A Friend/Captain Sandwich	10
69	London HLH 10290	Back In L.A./Have A Little Faith	10
68	CBS 63277	THE GREAT CONSPIRACY (LP)	40

PEANUTS
71	Philips 6006087	Goldendays/Headin Straight For You	10

BOB PEARCE BLUES BAND
74	Westwood WRS 040	LET'S GET DRUNK AGAIN (LP)	18

(see also Brother Bung)

MARY PEARCE
92	Baseline BASL 010T	Love Away/Over (12")	20
92	Intrigue IGE 29T	Don't Worry/(Midnite Remix)/Over (12")	15

PEARL JAM
92	Epic 657 572-7	Alive/Once (white/red vinyl p/s)	10
92	Epic 657 572-6	Alive/Once/Wash (12", poster p/s)	10
92	Epic 657 857-8	Even Flow/Dirty Frank/Oceans (12", white vinyl, p/s)	15
92	Epic 658 258-7	Jeremy/Alive (live) (white vinyl, p/s)	10
92	Epic 658 258-6	Jeremy/Alive (live)/Footsteps (12", picture disc, with card insert)	25
92	Epic 658 258-2	Jeremy/Yellow Ledbetter/Alive (live) (CD, picture disc)	15
93	Epic 660 020-6	Daughter/Blood (Live)/Yellow Ledbetter (Live) (12", ltd. ed. poster sleeve)	15
93	Epic 659 795-6	Go/Alone/Elderly Woman Behind The Counter In A Small Town (Acoustic) (12", with free cassette [plays 'Animal' (Live)])	12
99	Epic 6674797	Last Kiss/Soldier Of Love (red vinyl, p/s)	35
00	Epic 669 374 7	Nothing As It seems/Insignificance (blue vinyl, p/s)	12
00	Epic 669628 7	Light Years/Soon Forget (live) (clear sleeve, insert, numbered)	10
91	Epic 468884	TEN (LP)	80
92	Epic 468 884-0	TEN (LP, printed plastic sleeve, insert, picture disc)	40
93	Epic 4745491	VS (LP, gatefold)	60
94	Epic 477861-1	VITALOGY (LP, embossed gatefold sleeve, booklet)	45
96	Epic 484448-1	NO CODE (LP, multi fold gatefold sleeve, inners, 9 photo cards)	70
98	Epic 489365-1	YIELD (LP, die-cut sleeve, inner sleeve)	50
98	Epic 429859-1	LIVE ON TWO LEGS (2-LP, stickered gatefold sleeve with inner sleeves)	80

PEARLS BEFORE SWINE

MINT VALUE £

| 00 | Sony E263665 | BINAURAL (2 x LP, 3-part fold out sleeve with booklet) | 50 |
| 02 | Epic 510000-1 | RIOT ACT (2-LP, gatefold sleeve, inner sleeves) | 80 |

(see also Temple Of The Dog, Mad Season)

PEARLS BEFORE SWINE
68	Fontana STL 5503	BALAKLAVA (LP)	45
68	Fontana STL 5505	ONE NATION UNDERGROUND (LP)	40
69	Reprise RSLP 6364	THESE THINGS TOO (LP)	20
70	Reprise RSLP 6405	THE USE OF ASHES (LP)	30
71	Reprise RSLP 6442	CITY OF GOLD (LP)	20
71	Reprise RSLP 6467	BEAUTIFUL LIES YOU COULD LIVE (LP)	15

PEARLS (1)
| 72 | Bell 1372 | Wizard Of Love/Playing Around | 6 |
| 74 | Bell 1394 | Doctor Love/Pass It On | 6 |

(see also Bud Ashton)

PEARLS (2)
| 75 | Private Stock PVT39 | The Cheater/I'm Gonna Steal Your Heart Away | 8 |

BUSTER PEARSON BAND
| 73 | Action ACT 4612 | Big Funky/Pretty Woman | 15 |
| 75 | K&B 5516 | Take It Easy/Instrumental | 6 |

DUKE PEARSON
| 68 | Polydor 583 723 | ANGEL EYES (LP) | 100 |

JOHNNY PEARSON
62	Oriole CB 1721	Doh La La/Johnny's Tune	7
62	Parlophone R 4977	Theme From The L-Shaped Room Part 1/Part 2	7
66	Columbia DB 7851	Rat Catcher's Theme/Weaver's Green Theme	20
73	BBC RESL 6	Spy Trap/Playgirl (with Quator)	10
70	Aristocrat AR 103	SOUNDS EXTRAVAGANZA (LP)	20

(see also John Barry Seven)

JOSH T PEARSON
| 06 | Bella Union BELLA SPECIAL 1 | I'm So Lonesome I Could Cry/DIRTY THREE: Doris (split 7" white marbled vinyl) | 12 |

KEITH PEARSON'S RIGHT HAND BAND
| 76 | Eron ER 014 | KEITH PEARSON'S RIGHT HAND BAND (LP) | 20 |

RONNIE PEARSON
| 58 | HMV POP 489 | Flippin' Over You/Teen-Age Fancy | 700 |
| 58 | HMV POP 489 | Flippin' Over You/Teen-Age Fancy (78) | 150 |

PEAS & BEANS OF CONSCIOUSNESS
| 92 | Tribe SAM 16 | Stomper (1-sided 12", 200 only) | 50 |

PEASANTS (1)
| 65 | Columbia DB 7642 | Got Some Lovin' For You Baby/Let's Get Together | 160 |

PEASANTS (2)
| 81 | Homestead HRSS 009 | Here She Comes/I Care For You/When I Close My Eyes/I Can Help | 250 |

PEBBLE
| 74 | Great Western DMHP 005 | A GIFT WITH LOVE (LP) | 30 |

PEBBLES & BAMM BAMM / FLINTSTONES
| 65 | Pye Int. 7N.25232 | Daddy (mono)/The World Is Full Of Joys (For Girls And Boys) | 7 |

PEBBLES (1)
68	Major Minor MM 574	40 Miles Inside Your Heart/Get Around	15
69	Decca F 22944	Incredible George/Playing Chess	15
70	Deram DM 305	Stand Up And Be Counted/May In The Morning	8
71	Parlophone R 5900	Goodnight Ma/Sadness Of A Summer's Afternoon	8
71	Parlophone R 5921	First Time Loving/Party	8

PEBBLES (2)
| 77 | Arakwak AR01 | Positive Vibrations/Cosmic Idrens | 20 |

PEDDLERS
64	Philips BF 1375	Let The Sunshine In/True Girl	8
65	Philips BF 1404	Whatever Happened To The Good Times/Song For The Blues	6
65	Philips BF 1455	Over The Rainbow/You Must Be Having Me On	6
66	Philips BF 1506	Adam's Apple/Anybody's Fool	6
66	Philips BF 1530	I've Got To Hold On/Gassin'	8
67	Philips BF 1557	What'll I Do/Delicious Lady	8
67	CBS 2947	Irresistable You/Murray's Mood	8
67	CBS 3055	You're The Reason I'm Living/Nine Miles High	8
68	CBS 3333	Handel With Care/Horse's Collar	8
68	CBS 3734	Comin' Home Baby/Empty Club Blues	25
68	CBS 4050	That's Life/Wasting My Time	8
69	CBS 4449	Birth/Steel Mill	8
69	CBS 4720	Girlie/P.S I Love You	6
70	Phillips 6006034	Tell The World We're Not In/Rainy Day In London	20
73	Philips 6006 283	Sing Me An Old Song/It's So Easy	30
74	EMI 2106	Is There Anyone Out There/Just A Thought Ago	8
66	Philips BE 12954	SWINGING SCENE (EP)	15
67	Philips (S)BL 7768	LIVE AT THE PICKWICK (LP, flipback sleeve)	15
67	CBS (S)BPG 63183	FREEWHEELERS (LP)	15
68	CBS 63411	THREE IN A CELL (LP)	15
68	Fontana SFL 13016	THE FANTASTIC PEDDLERS (LP)	15
68	CBS 63682	BIRTHDAY (LP)	15
70	Philips 6308 028	THREE FOR ALL (LP, flip top 'matchbox' cover)	15
71	Philips 6386 066	GEORGIA ON MY MIND (LP)	15
72	Philips 6308 102	SUITE LONDON (LP)	40

PEDESTRIANS

MINT VALUE £

PEDESTRIANS
| 81 | Metropolis MET 1 | Communter Fantasy/1984 | 8 |

MIKE PEDICIN QUINTET
| 62 | HMV POP 1001 | When Cats Come Twistin' In/Gotta Twist | 15 |

BOBBY PEDRICK
| 58 | London HLX 8740 | White Bucks And Saddle Shoes/Stranded | 25 |

ANN PEEBLES
71	London HLU 10328	I Pity The Fool/Heartaches, Heartaches	8
71	London HLU 10346	Slipped, Tripped And Fell In Love/99 lbs	12
72	London SHU 8434	STRAIGHT FROM THE HEART (LP)	20
74	London SHU 8468	I CAN'T STAND THE RAIN (LP)	30
76	London SHU 8490	TELLIN' IT (LP)	18

PEECH BOYS
| 82 | TMT TMTT 7001 | Don't Make Me Wait (Original)/(Alternative)/(Special)/(Acapella) (12") | 12 |
| 83 | Island ILPS 9761 | LIFE IS SOMETHING SPECIAL (LP) | 40 |

PAUL PEEK
| 61 | Pye International 7N 25102 | Brother In Law/Through The Teenage Years | 20 |
| 66 | CBS 202073 | Pin The Tail On The Donkey/Rockin' Pneumonia | 12 |

(see also Gene Vincent & Blue Caps)

DAVID PEEL (& LOWER EAST SIDE)
68	Elektra EKL 4032	HAVE A MARIJUANA (LP, red label, mono)	40
68	Elektra EKS 74032	HAVE A MARIJUANA (LP, red label, stereo)	25
70	Elektra 2401 001	AMERICAN REVOLUTION (LP)	20

PEELERS
| 72 | Polydor Folk Mill 2460 165 | BANISHED MISFORTUNE (LP) | 150 |

PEELS
| 66 | Stateside SS 513 | Juanita Banana/Fun | 8 |
| 66 | Audio Fidelity AFSP 527 | Scrooey Mooey/Time Marches On | 30 |

PEENUTS
| 67 | Ember EMB S 242 | The Theme For "The Monkees"/The World's Been Good To Me Tonight (in p/s) | 20 |
| 67 | Ember EMB S 242 | The Theme For "The Monkees"/The World's Been Good To Me Tonight | 10 |

PEEPERS
| 72 | Bumble GE102 | Ayeo/A Heavy Drinking Ego Shrinking | 20 |

PEEPS
65	Philips BF 1421	Now Is The Time/Got Plenty Of Love	15
65	Philips BF 1443	What Can I Say?/Don't Talk About Love	15
66	Philips BF 1478	Gotta Get A Move On/I Told You Before	60
66	Philips BF 1509	Tra La La/Loser Wins	10

(see also Martin Cure & Peeps, Sabres, Rainbows)

PEEP SHOW
| 67 | Polydor 56196 | Your Servant, Stephen/Mazy | 90 |
| 68 | Polydor 52226 | Esprit De Corps/Mino In A Mix Up | 15 |

BEV PEGG (AND FRIENDS)
| 75 | Beaujangle DB 0006 | AWAY FROM THE SAND (LP, 50 copies only) | 200 |

(see also Bev Pegg, Dave Cartwright, Brindley Brae)

BEV PEGG (& HIS GOIN' NOWHERE BAND)
| 78 | Beaujangle DB 0007 | NOSTALGIA IS A THING OF THE PAST (LP, private pressing, with booklet, 50 only; as Bev Pegg & His Goin' Nowhere Band) | 150 |
| 80 | Beaujangle DB 0008 | THE FOUNDRY DITTY AND THE INDUSTRIAL AIR (LP, private pressing, 500 only, 150 destroyed so only 350 out there...) | 45 |

(see also David Cartwright, Brindley Brae)

BOB PEGG
| 74 | Transatlantic TRA 280 | THE SHIPBUILDER (LP, with Nick Strutt, credited to Bob Pegg) | 18 |
| 75 | Transatlantic TRA 299 | ANCIENT MAPS (LP, with lyric insert) | 20 |

BOB & CAROL PEGG
| 71 | Trailer LER 3016 | HE CAME FROM THE MOUNTAIN (LP, red label, as Carole Pegg) | 35 |
| 72 | Galliard GAL 4017 | AND NOW IT IS SO EARLY - THE SONGS OF SYDNEY CARTER (LP) | 25 |

(see also Carol Pegg, Carolanne Pegg, Mr. Fox)

BOB PEGG & NICK STRUTT
| 73 | Transatlantic TRA 265 | BOB PEGG & NICK STRUTT (LP) | 25 |

CAROL(ANNE) PEGG
| 73 | Transatlantic TRA 226 | CAROLANNE PEGG (LP, gatefold sleeve) | 80 |

(see also Bob & Carol Pegg)

PEGGY
| 70 | Trojan TR 7752 | All Kinds Of Everything Part 1/CARL LEVEY: Instrumental Version | 6 |
| 70 | Hot Rod HR 103 | I Shall Follow The Star/CARL LEVEY: Gifted At The Top | 20 |

PEGGY & JIMMY
| 70 | Hot Rod HR 101 | Pum Pum Lover/CARL LEVY: Remember Easter Monday | 8 |

PEGGY'S LEG
| 73 | Bunch BAN 2001 | GRINILLA (LP, with insert) | 400 |

(see also Skid Row, Jimi Slevin)

PEKKA
| 75 | Virgin V 2036 | B THE MAGPIE (LP as Pekka Pohjolo) | 20 |
| 77 | Virgin V 2084 | THE MATHEMATICIANS AIR DISPLAY (LP, features Mike Oldfield) | 15 |

PEKO AND NAKA
| 77 | The Label TLR 002 | Ageso Na Omae/Yamete (p/s) | 10 |

DAVE PELL OCTET
54	London RE-P 1008	IRVING BERLIN GALLERY VOL. 1 (EP)	10
55	London RE-P 1018	RODGERS AND HART (EP)	10
54	London H-APB 1034	RODGERS AND HART GALLERY (10" LP)	15

Lana PELLAY

MINT VALUE £

LANA PELLAY
86   Sublime LIMET 101 — Pistol In My Pocket/Dirty Harry Version (12", p/s) 12

PELOTON
00   Chemikal Underground CHEM 040 — THE GREAT EASTERN (LP) 20

JACK PENATE
06   Young Turks YT 001 — Second Minute Or Hour/Got My Favourite... (die-cut p/s with colour numbered Polaroid photo initialled by artist, PVC bag, 1,000 only) 8

PENCILS
83   Next 705 — Pictures Of Paris/Steal Your Love 8

TRACY PENDARVIS
60   London HLS 9059 — A Thousand Guitars/Is It Too Late 30
60   London HLS 9213 — Is It Me/South Bound Line 25

MIKE PENDER
86   Sierra FED 23 — It's Over/Brothers And Sisters (p/s) 6
(see also The Searchers)

PENDLEFOLK
70   Folk Heritage FHR 007 — PENDLEFOLK (LP) 18

PENELOPES FRIEND
87   MTG MTG 1 — THE GAP EP (12") 40

PENETRATION
77   Virgin VS 192 — Don't Dictate/Money Talks (p/s, blue label) 15
78   Virgin VS 213 — Firing Squad/Never (p/s) 8
78   Virgin V 2109 — MOVING TARGETS (LP, 15,000 on luminous vinyl) 20
78   Virgin V 2109 — MOVING TARGETS (LP, black vinyl) 15
79   Virgin V2131 — COMING UP FOR AIR (LP) 15

PENETRATIONS
80   Kik KIK 5 — Coming To You/Cheap Thrills 100

JIM PENFOLD & THE HOLLYWOOD KILLERS
76   Rollerball ROLL 1 — Hot Hazy Days/Unknown Person (no p/s) 15
(see also Hollywood Killers)

BOB PENFOLD
78   A C Wall ACW 01 — Free/Mother Natures Child 12

EDWARD PENFOLD
16   Stolen Body SBR 012 — CAULKHEAD (LP, 1st pressing, 100 only in hand-made hessian sleeve) 20

PENGUINS
55   London HL 8114 — Earth Angel/Hey Senorita (gold label print, triangular centre) 1500
55   London HL 8114 — Earth Angel/Hey Senorita (large centre hole, export issue) 350
55   London HL 8114 — Earth Angel/Hey Senorita (78) 60

BOBBY PENN
10   Kent Select City 019 — Without Your Love/LARRY BANKS: Ooh It Hurts Me 8

DAWN PENN
66   Rio R 113 — Long Days Short Night/Are You There (label lists 'Dawn Tenn') 125
67   Studio One SO 2030 — You Don't Love Me/SOUL VENDORS: Portobello Road 70
68   Island WI 3097 — I'll Never Let You Go/MARK BROWN: Brown Low Special 50
94   Big Beat 9417 14255-1 — NO NO NO (2-LP) 30
(see also Max Romeo, Viceroys)

TONY PENN
62   Starlite ST45 083 — That's What I Like/I Won't Cry Anymore 30

LEONARD PENNARIO
54   Capitol CL 14173 — Midnight On The Cliffs/Dream Rhapsody (with Les Baxter Orchestra) 10
(see also Les Baxter)

PENNSYLVANIA SIXPENCE
67   Pye 7N 17326 — Love Of The Common People/Midweek Excursion 8

PENNY
61   Piccadilly 7N 35009 — Who Does He Think He Is/Sparks 8
62   Piccadilly 7N 35045 — Shall I Take My Heart And Go/What'd I Do? 8

PENNY CANDLES
89   Red Eye RED 04 — THE TAJ MAHAL EP (12" p/s) 20

GEORGE A. PENNY
68   Trojan TR 625 — Win Your Love/VAL BENNETT: All In The Game 60

HANK PENNY
56   Parlophone MSP 6202 — Bloodshot Eyes/Wham! Bam! Thank You Ma'am 100

PENNY PEEPS
68   Liberty LBF 15053 — Little Man With A Stick/Model Village 300
68   Liberty LBF 15114 — I See The Morning/Curly, The Knight Of The Road 40

PENNY WAGER
72   Folk Heritage FHR 0256 — LIGHT OF OTHER DAYS (LP) 75

PENNY AND THE PROFESSIONALS
83   Big Boy BB2-7 — Move Over Darling/Hollywood All Night (no p/s) 10

PENNY ARCADE
70   Pye 7N.17943 — The Two Of Us/Don't Need You Anymore 20

PENNYLANDERS
72   Ra RAEP 7005 — SONGS OF LOOE 15

PENNYWORTH
69   CBS 4573 — Malena Malena/Who Are You? 12

CHARLES PENROSE
57   Columbia SEG 7743 — THE ADVENTURE OF THE LAUGHING POLICEMAN (EP) 10

PENTAD
65   Parlophone R 5288 — Silver Dagger/Nothing But Love 25
65   Parlophone R 5368 — Don't Throw It All Away/Too Many Ways 20

PENTAGONS

MINT VALUE £

66	Parlophone R 5424	Something Other People Call Love/It Better Be Me	25

PENTAGONS
61	London HLU 9333	To Be Loved Forever/Down At The Beach	100

PENTAGRAM
87	Napalm FLAME 006	DAY OF RECKONING (LP)	45
93	Peaceville VILE 38	RELENTLESS (LP, reissue of US self-titled debut)	50
93	Peaceville VILE 40	DAY OF RECKONING (LP, reissue)	50
94	Peaceville VILE 42	BE FOREWARNED (2-LP, insert)	80

PENTANGLE
68	Big T BIG 109	Travellin' Song/Mirage (in title die-cut sleeve)	15
68	Big T BIG 109	Travellin' Song/Mirage	6
69	Big T BIG 124	Once I Had A Sweetheart/I Saw An Angel	20
70	Big T BIG 128	Light Flight/Cold Mountain	6
73	Big T BIG 567	Light Flight/Market Song/The Time Has Come	6
68	Transatlantic TRA 162	THE PENTANGLE (LP, laminated sleeve, 1st pressing with no 'A Shel Talmy Production' beneath band name)	100
68	Transatlantico TRA 162	THE PENTANGLE (LP, 2nd pressing, with 'A shel Talmy Production' beneath band name on labels)	50
68	Transatlantic TRA 178	SWEET CHILD (2-LP, gatefold, 1st pressing, internal flipback sleeve)	80
68	Transatlantic TRA 178	SWEET CHILD (2-LP, gatefold, 2nd pressing with no internal flapjack sleeve and MacNeil Press Limited printer credit)	50
69	Transatlantic TRA 205	BASKET OF LIGHT (LP, gatefold sleeve)	60
70	Transatlantic TRA 228	CRUEL SISTER (LP, gatefold sleeve)	40
71	Transatlantic TRA 240	REFLECTION (LP, gatefold sleeve with inner sleeve)	35
72	Reprise K 44197	SOLOMON'S SEAL (LP, with lyric insert)	70
72	Transatlantic TRASAM 23	HISTORY BOOK (LP)	20
73	Transatlantic TRASAM 29	PENTANGLING (LP)	20
85	Spindrift SPIN 111	OPEN THE DOOR (LP)	25

(see also Bert Jansch, John Renbourn, Duffy's Nucleus)

PENTHOUSE
71	Penny Farthing PEN 765	40 Days Of Rain/I'm Nobody's Fool	12

PENWYKE
70	Cannon CN 11	Time To Let Go/No One Cares (p/s)	20

PENYA
17	On The Corner OTCLP003	SUPER LIMINAL (LP)	15

PEOPLE BAND
70	Transatlantic TRA 214	THE PEOPLE BAND (LP, with Charlie Watts)	100

(see also Charlie Watts, Battered Ornaments)

PEOPLE (1)
69	Capitol CL 15553	I Love You/Somebody Tell Me My Name	22
69	Capitol CL 15599	Ulla/Turnin' Me In	22
70	RCA RCA 2028	I Am (The Preacher)/September's Son	10
71	Deram DM 346	In Ancient Times/Glastonbury	45
70	Paramount SPFL 261	THERE ARE PEOPLE AND THERE ARE PEOPLE (LP)	25

PEOPLE (2)
81	Race RB 003	Musical Man/Sons & Daughters	10

PEOPLE'S STAR
76	Emerge EMLP 001	FESTAC EXPLOSION - THE PEOPLE STAR IN LONDON (LP)	25

PEPPELKADE 14
88	Top Shelf CAV 031	TIME FLIES EP (12")	40

PEPPER
68	Pye 7N 17569	We'll Make It Together/(Look Out) I'm On The Way Down	10

ART PEPPER
54	Vogue LDE 067	ART PEPPER QUARTET (10" LP)	200
57	London HLZ V 14038	ART PEPPER QUARTET (10" LP)	100
60	Contemporary LAC 12229	MODERN JAZZ CLASSICS (LP, as Art Pepper Eleven)	25

(see also Chet Baker)

JIM PEPPER
71	Atlantic 2400 149	PEPPER'S POW WOW (LP)	25

KEN PEPPER
61	Top Rank JAR 535	Just A Little At A Time/I Get The Blues When It Rains	7

RED PEPPER
73	Phoenix SN1X 145	I'm Gonna Sit Right Down And Write Myself A Letter/I See A Land	20

DANNY PEPPERMINT (& JUMPING JACKS)
61	London HLL 9478	The Peppermint Twist/Somebody Else Is Taking My Place (with Jumping Jacks)	8
62	London HLL 9516	One More Time/La Dee Dah	10
62	London HLL 9614	Maybe Tomorrow (But Not Today)/Passing Parade	12
62	London HA-L 2438	TWIST WITH DANNY PEPPERMINT (LP)	30

PEPPERMINT CIRCUS
67	Olga OLE 007	All The King's Horses/It Didn't Take Long	10
68	Polydor 56288	I Won't Be There/Keeping My Head Above Water	6
69	Polydor 56312	Please Be Patient/Take My Love	6
70	A&M AMS 765	One Thing Could Lead To Another/It's So Easy	6

PEPPERMINT RAINBOW
68	MCA MU 1034	Walking In Different Circles/Pink Lemonade	12
69	MCA MU 1076	Will You Be Staying After Sunday/And I'll Be There	20
69	MCA MU 1091	Don't Wake Up In The Morning, Michael/Rosemary	10

PEPPERMINT TROLLEY COMPANY
68	Dot DOT 110	Baby You Come Rolling 'Cross My Mind/Nine O'Clock Business Man	10

PEPPI
63	Decca F 11638	Can You Waddle/I Never Danced Before	10

			MINT VALUE £
64	Fontana TF 446	So Used To Loving You/Don't Trust My Friend	8
65	Decca F 12055	The Skip/Do The Skip	8

ARMANDO PERAZA
68	Fontana STL 5525	WILD THING (LP)	25

PERCELLS
63	HMV POP 1154	What Are Boys Made Of?/Cheek To Cheek	20

PEREGRINE
72	Westwood WRS 016	SONGS OF MINE (LP)	150

RAY PEREIRA
70	Baf BAF 5	Don't Mess With Cupid/CATS: Falling In Love	8
70	Baf BAF 6	On Broadway/Hey Chick	30

PERERIN
80	Gwerin SYWM 215	HAUL AR YR EIRA (LP, with insert)	180
81	SYWM 230	TEITHGAN (LP)	120

PERE UBU
79	Chrysalis CHS 2372	The Fabulous Sequel (Have Shoes Will Walk)/Humour Me (live)/ The Book Is On The Table (p/s)	8
80	Rough Trade RT 049	Final Solution/My Dark Ages (p/s)	8
81	Rough Trade RT 066	Not Happy/Lonesome Cowboy Dave (p/s)	8
78	Radar RDR 1	DATAPANIK IN THE YEAR ZERO (12" EP)	18
17	Fire BLAZE 228	30 Seconds Over Tokyo/Heart Of Darkness (p/s, reissue)	10
78	Blank BLANK 001	THE MODERN DANCE (LP)	40
78	Chrysalis CHR 1207	DUB HOUSING (LP)	30
79	Rough Trade ROUGHUS 20	NEW PICNIC TIME (LP)	20
80	Rough Trade ROUGH 14	THE ART OF WALKING (LP, original with "Miles" & "Arabia")	18
81	Rough Trade ROUGH 22	THE MODERN DANCE (LP, reissue)	20
81	Rough Trade ROUGH 23	390° OF SIMULATED STEREO - UBU LIVE: VOLUME 1 (LP)	15
85	Rough Trade ROUGHUS 14	DUB HOUSING (LP, reissue)	15
85	Rough Trade ROUGH 83	TERMINAL TOWER (LP, gatefold sleeve)	15
88	Fontana SFLP 5	THE TENEMENT YEAR (LP)	15
88	Fontana SFLP 3	THE MODERN DANCE (LP, reissue, 1000 only)	15
15	Fire FIRELP 406	ELITISM FOR THE PEOPLE (2-LP, 12" with poster)	60
16	Fire FIRELP 422	ARCHITECTURE OF LANGUAGE 1979 - 1982 (4-LP box set)	50
17	Fire FIRELP 469	DRIVE, HE SAID 1994 - 2002 (4-LP box set, poster, download card)	45

(see also David Thomas)

CHRISTINE PERFECT
69	Blue Horizon 57-3165	When You Say/No Road Is The Right Road	35
70	Blue Horizon 57-3172	I'm Too Far Gone (To Turn Around)/Close To Me	35
70	Blue Horizon 7-63860	CHRISTINE PERFECT (LP)	200
82	CBS 32198	CHRISTINE PERFECT (LP, reissue)	15

(see also Fleetwood Mac, Illusive Dream, Chicken Shack, Rick Hayward)

PERFECT DISASTER
87	Glass GLALP 027	PERFECT DISASTER (LP)	30

PERFECT END
81	Hellfire HELL 1	Sweet Dreams/Natural Causes/Puppets	15

PERFECT PEOPLE
69	MCA MU 1079	House In The Country/Polyanna	15

PERFECTION
70	Stem ST 001	Ride High/Magic Meadow (p/s)	80

PERFECTORS
80	Active ACT 4	YT50295ID/Tiny Radios (p/s)	100

PERFORMANCE (1)
73	Polydor 2058 324	Funny Little Things/Rejoice	6

PERFORMANCE (2)
86	Clay CLAY 47	Wish I Was Free Again/Free Again	8

PERFORMERS
69	Action ACT 4552	I Can't Stop You/L.A. Stomp	25

PERFORMING FERRET BAND
80	Dead Hippy DHR3	Brow Beaton/Hoo-Shar/Disco One (EP, p/s)	20
81	Pig PIG 1	PERFORMING FERRET BAND (LP)	35

EMILIO PERICOLI
62	Warner Brothers WB 69	Al Di La/GINA PAOLI: Sassi	6

PERIDOTS
81	Optional Goods OG 1	Open Season/Calm (p/s)	20

PERISHERS
68	Fontana TF 965	How Does It Feel/Bye Bye Baby	40

(see also Seftones)

CARL PERKINS
78s
56	London HLU 8271	Blue Suede Shoes/Honey Don't	30
57	London HLS 8408	Matchbox/Your True Love	40
57	London HLS 8527	Glad All Over/Forever Yours	50
58	London HLS 8608	Lend Me Your Comb/That's Right	60
59	Philips PB 983	I Don't See Me In Your Eyes Anymore/One Ticket To Loneliness	70

SINGLES
56	London HLU 8271	Blue Suede Shoes/Honey Don't	175
57	London HLS 8408	Matchbox/Your True Love	175
57	London HLS8527	Glad All Over/Forever Yours	70
58	London HLS 8608	Lend Me Your Comb/That's Right	70
59	Philips PB 983	I Don't See Me In Your Eyes Anymore/One Ticket To Loneliness	20

George PERKINS

			MINT VALUE £
61	Philips PB 1179	Anyway The Wind Blows/The Unhappy Girls	15
64	Brunswick 05905	Help Me Find My Baby/I Wouldn't Have You	15
64	Brunswick 05909	Big Bad Blues/Lonely Heart (with Nashville Teens)	15
64	Brunswick 05923	The Monkey Shine/Let My Baby Be	15
67	Stateside SS 599	A Country Boy's Dream/If I Could Come Back	15
68	London HLP 7125	A Country Boy's Dream/Shine Shine Shine (export issue)	15
68	Spark SRL 1009	Lake County, Cotton Country/It's You	10
68	London HLS 10192	Blue Suede Shoes/Matchbox	10
69	CBS 3932	Restless/11.23	10
70	CBS 4991	All Mama's Children/Step Aside (with N.R.B.Q.)	6

ALBUMS

59	London HA-S 2202	THE DANCE ALBUM OF CARL PERKINS (plum label, flipback sleeve)	150
59	London HA-S 2202	THE DANCE ALBUM OF CARL PERKINS (plum label, non-flipback sleeve)	50
66	Ember NR 5038	SUNSTROKE (shared with Jerry Lee Lewis)	20
66	CBS Realm 52305	WHOLE LOTTA CARL PERKINS (original pressing with boxed square logo)	50
66	CBS Realm 52305	WHOLE LOTTA CARL PERKINS	25
68	CBS 63309	KING OF ROCK	15
68	London HA-P/SH-P 8366	COUNTRY BOY'S DREAM	20
82	Sun BOX 101	THE SUN YEARS (3-LP, box set with booklet)	20

(see also N.R.B.Q.)

GEORGE PERKINS

78	Hit And Run 5003	Keep On Trying/What The Deal Is	6

JOE PERKINS

63	London HLU 9794	Little Eeefin Annie/Encle Eeef	6
72	Mojo 2092 047	Wrapped Up In Your Love/Looking For A Woman	8

LASCELLES PERKINS

61	Blue Beat BB 41	Creation/Lonely Robin	20
63	Island WI 038	Tango Lips (with Yvonne)/DENNIS SINDREY: Rub Up (B-side actually plays "Jamaica's Song")	25
64	R&B JB 175	I Am So Grateful/When I Survey	20
70	Escort ES 814	Please Stay/MATADORS: Voyage From The Moon	35
71	Banana BA 317	Tell It All Brothers/SOUND DIMENSION: Polkadots	15

(see also Tommy McCook)

POLLY PERKINS

63	Decca F 11583	I Reckon You (as Polly Perkins & Bill)/The Girls Are At It Again	20
63	Oriole CB 1869	Sweet As Honey/I've Gotta Tell You	20
63	Oriole CB 1929	Young Lover/You Too Can Be A Beatle	20
63	Oriole CB 1979	Faling In Love Again/I Went By Your House Today	20
73	Chapter One CMS 1018	LIBERATED WOMAN (LP)	25

(see also Academy)

TONY PERKINS

58	RCA RCA 1018	Moonlight Swim/First Romance	12

KATIE PERKS

83	Plastichead PLAS 001	Small/Cold Stone (p/s)	8

PERMANENTS

63	London HLU 9803	Oh Dear, What Can The Matter Be/Let Me Be Baby	12

JEAN-JACQUES PERREY

72	Vanguard VAN 1005	Gossipo Perpetuo/Moog Indigo	10
73	Vanguard VAN 1008	Minuet Of The Robots/Porcupine Rock	10
71	Vanguard VSD 6525	KALEIDOSCOPIC VIBRATIONS - SPOTLIGHT ON THE MOOG (LP, 'kaleidoscope' sleeve, with Gershon Kingsley)	18
72	Vanguard VSD 6549	MOOG INDIGO (LP, title sleeve)	25
73	Vanguard VSD 79222	THE IN SOUND FROM WAY OUT! (LP, green/black 'starburst' sleeve, with Gershon Kingsley)	20
73	Vanguard VSD 79286	THE AMAZING NEW ELECTRONIC POP SOUND OF... (LP)	15

PAT PERRIN

68	Island WI 3115	Over You/LLOYD TERRELL: Lost Without You	25

PERRI'S

59	Oriole CB 1481	Jerri-Lee/Ballad Of A Happy Heart	15

BARBARA PERRY

70	Pama PM 795	Say You Need Me/Unloved	15
10	Kent CITY 015	A Man Is A Mean Thing/GLADYS BRUCE: I've Got A Feeling For You Baby	7

BRENDAN PERRY

99	4AD CAD 9015	EYE OF THE HUNTER (LP, inner)	100

JEFF PERRY

76	Arista ARIST 51	Love Don't Come No Stronger/I've Got To See You Right Away	40

LEE 'SCRATCH' PERRY (& UPSETTERS)

63	R&B JB 102	Prince In The Back/Don't Copy	50
63	R&B JB 104	Old For New/Prince And Duke	50
63	R&B JB 106	Mad Head/Man And Wife	50
63	R&B JB 135	Royalty/Can't Be Wrong	50
64	R&B PJ 40001	Help The Weak/TOMMY McCOOK: Exodus (promo copies only)	120
63	Island WI 118	Never Get Weary/TOMMY McCOOK: Below Zero	40
64	Port-O-Jam PJ 4001	Help The Weak/TOMMY McCOOK: Exodus	60
64	Port-O-Jam PJ 4003	Bad Minded People/TOMMY McCOOK & HIS GROUP: Jam Rock	60
64	Port-O-Jam PJ 4010	Chatty Chatty Woman/TOMMY McCOOK & HIS GROUP: Road Block	70
65	Island WI 210	Please Don't Go/Bye, St. Peter (both sides with Soulettes)	40
65	Island WI 223	Country Girl/Strange Country (as Upsetters; both act. by Ossie & Upsetters)	30
65	Ska Beat JB 201	Roast Duck/Hand To Hand, Man To Man	60
65	Ska Beat JB 203	Trail And Crosses/Jon Tom	50

Mal PERRY

			MINT VALUE £
65	Ska Beat JB 212	Wishes Of The Wicked/Hold Down	60
65	Ska Beat JB 215	Open Up/ROLAND ALPHONSO: Twin Double	50
66	Ska Beat JB 251	The Woodman/Give Me Justice	60
66	Island WI 259	Just Keep It Up/ROLAND ALPHONSO: James Bond	350
66	Island WI 292	Doctor Dick (as King Perry)/SOUL BROTHERS: Magic Star	40
66	Island WI 298	Rub And Squeeze (as King Perry & Soulettes)/SOUL BROTHERS: Here Comes The Minx	40
67	Doctor Bird DB 1073	Run For Cover/Something You've Got (as Lee 'King' Perry & Sensations)	45
67	Doctor Bird DB 1098	Whop Whop Man/Wind-Up Doll (with Dynamites)	50
68	Amalgamated AMG 808	The Upsetter/Thank You Baby	50
68	Doctor Bird DB 1146	People Funny Boy/BURT WALTERS: Blowing In The Wind	35
68	Trojan TR 629	Sentence (as Danny & Lee)/LEE PERRY: You Crummy	40
68	Trojan TR 644	Uncle Desmond/Bronco (with Upsetters)	25
69	Upsetter US 303	People Funny Fi True/UPSETTERS: Ten To Twelve	50
69	Upsetter US 324	Yakety Yak/Tackio (with Upsetters)	35
70	Upsetter US 325	Kill Them All/Soul Walk (with Upsetters)	35
71	Bullet BU 461	All Combine Pts 1&2 (as Lee Perry & Upsetters)	25
72	Upsetter US 385	French Connection (with Upsetters)/UPSETTERS: Version	20
72	Upsetter US 389	Back Biter (with Dennis Alcapone)/UPSETTERS: Version	25
73	Upsetter US 397	Jungle Lion/Freakout Skank	200
73	Upsetter US 398	Cow Thief Skank (actually by Lee Perry & Charlie Ace)/Seven And Three Quarters Skank	45
73	Bread BR 1111	Station Underground News/CARLTON & SHOES: Better Days	100
73	Downtown DT 513	Bucky Skank/Lucky Skank	70
73	Jackpot JP 812	Justice To The People/UPSETTERS: Version	65
74	Dip DL 5037	Dub A Pum Pum (with Silvertones)/Version	10
74	Dip DL 5060	Dreader Locks (& Junior Byles)/Militant Rock	20
76	Island WIP 6370	Dreadlocks In Moonlight/Cut Throat	6
79	Black Art BH 001	Reggae Music (actually by Hugo Blackwood)/DOC ALIMANTADO: Rastaman Train (12")	40
03	Trojan/Sanctuary TJITV005	Disco Devil/BOB MARLEY & WU CHU: Keep On Moving (12" reissue)	40
71	Trojan Records TBL 166	AFRICA'S BLOOD (LP, orange/white labels)	100
71	Trojan TBL 167	BATTLE AXE (LP)	60
73	RHINO 8002	CLOAK & DAGGER (LP, as Scratch The Upsetter)	85
75	Cactus CTLP 112	REVOLUTION DUB (LP)	150
75	DIP DLPD 6002	KUNG FU MEETS THE DRAGON (LP, as The Mighty Upsetter)	150
79	Island ILPS 9583	SCRATCH ON THE WIRE (LP)	18
79	Jet Star PTLP 1023	THE BEST OF (LP)	30
80	Black Ark Intl. BALP 4001	BLACK ARK VOLUME 2 (LP)	35
83	Seven Leaves SLLP5	MEGATON DUB 2 (LP)	20
83	Pama PTLP 1026	BEST OF LEE PERRY & THE UPSETTERS VOL. 2 (LP)	50
83	Seven Leaves SLLP3	HEART OF THE ARK (LP)	35
85	Trojan PERRY 1	UPSETTER BOX SET (3-LP)	40
88	Trojan TRLS 254	GIVE ME POWER (LP, as Lee Perry & Friends)	15
89	Trojan PERRY 2	OPEN THE GATE (3-LP as Lee Perry & Friends)	60
90	Anachron TSLP 9006	REVOLUTION DUB (LP, reissue)	35
95	Trojan Records TBL 166	AFRICA'S BLOOD (LP, reissue, blue/white labels)	18
95	Justice League JJLP5000	KUNG FU MEETS THE DRAGON (LP, reissue, various coloured vinyl)	20
98	Pressure Sounds PSLP19	PRODUCED & DIRECTED BY UPSETTER (2-LP)	20
99	Pressure Sounds PSLP32	DIVINE MADNESS DEFINITELY (LP)	25
05	Trojan TJBX 244	I AM THE UPSETTER (8 x 7" box set)	35
11	Honest Jons HJRLP 109	THE RETURN OF PIPECOCK JACKXON (LP, reissue)	15

(see also Upsetters, Defenders, Roland Alphonso, Bob Marley/Wailers, King Scratch, Punchers, Roy Shirley, Pioneers, Desmond Dekker)

MAL PERRY

58	Fontana H 133	That's When Your Heartaches Begin/Make Me A Miracle	7
58	Fontana H 149	Too Young To Love/Who Are They To Say	7
58	Fontana H 157	Things I Didn't Say/The Girl Next Door	8

MARK PERRY

80	NB NB 7	You Cry Your Tears/Music Death? (with Dennis Burns, p/s in poly bag)	7
80	Deptford Fun City DFC 12	Whole World's Down On Me/I Live - He Dies (p/s)	7
80	Deptford Fun City DLP 06	SNAPPY TURNS (LP)	25

(see also Alternative TV)

SHORT(L)Y PERRY

72	Attack ATT 8043	Musical Goat/WINSTON GRENNON & J. JACKSON: Stinging Dub	8
72	Explosion EX 2067	Sprinkle Some Water/FLOWERS & ALVIN: Howdy And Tenky	7
72	Bullet BU 512	Sprinkle Some Water/FLOWERS & ALVIN: Howdy And Tenky	7
73	Bullet BU 529	Yama Skank/U ROY JUNIOR: Doctor Run Come Quick	10
73	Downtown DT 517	Dedicated To Illiteracy/G.G. ALL STARS: Illiteracy Dub	8
73	Grape GR 3052	Abusing And Assaulting (by Flowers & Alvin)/Food Control	7
73	Green Door GD 4243	President Mash Up The Resident/President Mash Up The Resident Part Two	12

(see also Shorty, Cornell Campbell, Maytones, Paulette Williams)

STEVE PERRY

60	HMV POP 745	Step By Step/Because They're Young	15
62	Decca F 11462	Ginny Come Lately/Two Of A Kind	10
62	Decca F 11526	Young And In Love/Let It Come True	6
63	Decca F 11656	Find Me A Girl/My Dad	6
64	Decca F 11895	Crooked Little Man/Day Dreams	6

PERRY SISTERS

59	Brunswick 05802	Fabian/Willie Boy	25

PERSIAN FLOWERS

84	Fourth Dimension FDS 02	Somebody Else's Sin/Summer Of Love (1000 only, p/s)	7

(see also Wasted Youth)

PERSIAN RISK

PERSIAN RISK
81	SRT SRTS/81/CUS/1146	Calling For You/Chasing The Dragon (p/s)	140
83	Neat NEAT 24	Ridin' High/Hurt You (p/s)	25
84	Zebra 12RA3	Too Different/Sky's Falling Down/Dark Tower (12", p/s)	10
86	Metal Masters METALLP 2	RISE UP (LP)	18

(see also Motorhead)

PERSIANS
69	Pama PM 772	I Only Have Eyes For You/The Sun Gotta Shine In Your Heart	12
72	Capitol CL 15726	Baby Come Back Home/I Want To Go Home	8

PERSIMMON'S PECULIAR SHADES
68	Major Minor MM 554	Watchmaker/Coplington	40

PERSONALITIES
65	Dice CC 30	I Remember/Suffering	15
65	Ska Beat JB 222	Hey Little Girl/Teardrops	30
66	Blue Beat BB 354	Push It Down/BUSTER'S ALL STARS: Blues Market	50

PERSONS UNKNOWN
81	Po 1	Addiction/Addiction (p/s)	25

PERSPICO ACUMINE (HOLDINGS)
86	él ACME 4	A PERFECT ACTION (LP)	20

PERSUADERS
70	Nazarene ZR 1970	THE END IS NOT YET (LP)	35

PERSUADERS!
93	Detour DR 001	Finished Forever/In The Night (p/s, 300 only)	20
94	Detour DR 011	Waiting For The Nowhere Express/Girl/The Paperchase (p/s, 100 on red vinyl)	8

PERSUADERS (U.S.)
72	Atlantic K 40370	THE THIN LINE BETWEEN LOVE AND HATE (LP)	20
73	Atlantic K 40476	THE PERSUADERS (LP)	15

PERSUASIONS
65	Columbia DB 7560	I'll Go Crazy/Try Me	30
65	Columbia DB 7700	Big Brother/Deep Down Love	30
66	Columbia DB 7859	La, La, La, La, La/Opportunity	30

PERSUASIONS (U.S.)
69	Minit MLF 11017	Party In The Woods/It's Better To Have Loved And Lost	20
73	MCA MUS 1222	Good Old Acappella/You Must Believe Me	7
70	Straight STS 1062	A CAPPELLA (LP)	40
72	Island ILPS 9201	STREET CORNER SYMPHONY (LP)	20

MORRIS PERT
75	Chantry ABM 21	LUMINOS/CHROMOSPHERE/4 JAPANESE VERSES (LP)	40
80	Chantry CHT 001	LUMINOS/CHROMOSPHERE/4 JAPANESE VERSES (LP, reissue)	30
82	Chantry CHT 007	BOOK OF LOVE/FRAGMENTI I/ULTIMATE DECAY (LP)	30

JON PERTWEE
72	Purple PUR 111	Who Is The Doctor/Pure Mystery	20
85	Safari DOCTOR 1	Who Is The Doctor/Doctor Blood Donor (p/s)	6
62	Phillips BBL 7558	SONGS FOR VULGAR BOATMEN (LP)	20
80	Decca CROW 1	WORZEL GUMMIDGE SINGS (LP)	15

(see also Rupert Hine, Derek Roy, BBC Radiophonic Workshop)o

PERUVIAN HIPSTERS
88	Hip HIP 001	Tony Hadley/It Doesn't Happen Everyday (p/s)	35

PESHAY
95	Good Looking GLR 011	Piano Tune/Vocal Tune (12")	60
93	Reinforced RIVET 1248	PROTÉGÉ EP (12")	20

PESKY GEE!
69	Pye 7N 17708	Where Is My Mind/A Place Of Heart Break	50
69	Pye N(S)PL 18293	EXCLAMATION MARK (LP, textured sleeve)	250

(see also Black Widow, Agony Bag)

PEST
03	Ninja Tune ZEN 74	NECESSARY MEASURES (2-LP)	20

PETALS
63	Decca F 11650	Let's Do The Tamoure/Look At Me	8

PETARDS
69	Liberty LBF 15206	Misty Island/Tartarex	60

PETER
70	Sonet SON 2012	Peace/Values	15

PETER & ALEX
70	Carnaby 4018	/Sunny/Sonny Boy/Big Beat On The Loose	7

PETER & GORDON
66	Columbia DB 7951	Don't Pity Me/To Show I Love You	6
66	Columbia DB 8003	Lady Godiva/Morning's Calling	7
66	Columbia DB 8075	Knight In Rusty Armour/The Flower Lady	8
67	Columbia DB 8159	Sunday For Tea/Start Trying Someone Else	8
67	Columbia DB 8198	The Jokers/Red, Cream And Velvet	10
68	Columbia DB 8398	I Feel Like Going Out/The Quest For The Holy Grail	20
68	Columbia DB 8451	You've Had Better Times/Sipping My Wine	10
69	Columbia DB 8585	I Can Remember (Not Too Long Ago)/Hard Time, Rainy Day	10
64	Columbia SEG 8348	NOBODY I KNOW (EP)	15
64	Columbia 33SX 1630	PETER AND GORDON (LP, mono)	20
64	Columbia SCX 3518	PETER AND GORDON (LP, stereo)	25
64	Columbia 33SX 1660	IN TOUCH WITH PETER AND GORDON (LP, mono)	25
64	Columbia SCN 3532	IN TOUCH WITH PETER AND GORDON (LP, stereo)	25
65	Columbia 33SX 1761	HURTIN 'N' LOVIN' (LP, mono)	25

PETER & HEADLINES

MINT VALUE £

65	Columbia SCX 3565	HURTIN 'N' LOVIN' (LP, stereo)	30
66	Columbia SX 6045	PETER AND GORDON (LP, mono)	25
66	Columbia SCX 6045	PETER AND GORDON (LP, stereo)	30
66	Columbia SX 6097	SOMEWHERE... (LP, mono)	25
66	Columbia SCX 6097	SOMEWHERE... (LP, stereo)	30
65	Columbia SCXC 25	I GO TO PIECES (LP, export issue)	20
66	Columbia SCXC 29	WOMAN (LP, export issue)	20
66	Columbia SCXC 33	LADY GODIVA (LP, export issue)	25

(see also Gordon Waller)

PETER & HEADLINES
| 64 | Decca F 11980 | Don't Cry Little Girl/It Was Love | 15 |
| 64 | Decca F 12035 | Tears And Kisses/I've Got My Reasons | 15 |

(see also Count Downe & Zeros)

PETER & MARY
| 54 | Columbia SCMC 6 | Crazy Mix Up Song/What Shall We Do With The Lonesome Lover (export issue) | 6 |

(see also Peter Lind Hayes)

PETER & PAUL
| 66 | Blue Beat BB 364 | Hosana/Schoolgirl | 20 |

PETER & PERSUADERS
| 65 | Oak RGJ 197 | The Wanderer/Wine Glass Rock/Oh My Soul/Cross My Heart (EP) | 50 |

PETER & TEST TUBE BABIES
81	No Future OI 4	Banned From The Pubs/Moped Lads/Peacehaven Wild Lads (p/s)	18
82	No Future OI 15	Run Like Hell/Up Yer Bum (p/s)	8
83	Trapper EARS 1	Zombie Creeping Flesh/No Invitation/Smash And Grab (p/s)	6
83	Trapper EARS 2	The Jinx/Trapper Ain't Got A Bird (p/s)	6
82	No Future Punk 3	PISSED AND PROUD (LP, green vinyl)	25
83	Trapper THIN 1	MATING SOUNDS OF SOUTH AMERICAN FROGS (LP, with lyric inner)	20
85	Hairy Pie HP 1	THE LOUD BLARING PUNK ROCK LP (LP)	15
87	Dojo LP 49	SOBERPHOBIA (LP)	15

PETER & WOLVES
67	MGM MGM 1352	Little Girl Lost And Found/Is Me	35
68	MGM MGM 1374	Lanternlight/Break Up-Break Down	30
68	MGM MGM 1397	Julie/Birthday	20
68	MGM MGM 1452	Woman On My Mind/Old & The New	35
70	UPC UPC 104	Something In The Way She Moves/The Lady And Me	10

(see also Factory, Norman Conquest, John Pantry, Sounds Around)

PETER B'S
| 66 | Columbia DB 7862 | If You Wanna Be Happy/Jodrell Blues | 100 |

(see also Tony Colton, Peter Bardens, Peter Green, Cheynes, Shotgun Express)

PETER, PAUL & MARY
| 63 | Warner Bros WB 95 | Puff/Pretty Mary | 6 |

(see also Mary Travers)

PETER'S FACES
64	Piccadilly 7N 35178	Why Did You Bring Him To The Dance/She's In Love	10
64	Piccadilly 7N 35196	Try A Little Love My Friend/I Don't Care	10
64	Piccadilly 7N 35205	Just Like Romeo And Juliet/Wait	25
65	Piccadilly 7N 35225	De-Boom-Lay-Boom/Suzie Q	10

(see also Flowerpot Men, White Plains)

GORDON PETERS
| 61 | Embassy 45 WB 482 | Take Five/Take Good Care Of My Baby | 10 |

JANICE PETERS & PLAYBOYS
| 58 | Columbia DB 4222 | This Little Girl's Gone Rockin'/Kiss Cha Cha | 30 |
| 59 | Columbia DB 4276 | A Girl Likes/You're The One | 30 |

JO PETERS
| 61 | Pye 7N 15350 | I Love The Long Light Evenings/I May Be Wrong | 6 |
| 62 | Pye 7N 15413 | When Opportunity Knocks/Never Cheat Your Sweetheart | 7 |

JOHNNY PETERS
| 65 | Decca F 12172 | When You Ask About Love/People Say | 25 |

LENNIE PETERS
| 63 | Oriole CB 1887 | And My Heart Cried/For A Lifetime | 7 |
| 64 | Oriole CB 1956 | Let The Tears Begin/Love Me, Love Me (Love Me, Love Me) | 7 |

LINDA PETERS
| 70 | Warlock Music WMM 101/2 | WARLOCK MUSIC SAMPLER (LP, sampler, 7 tracks by Elton John) | 1000 |

(see also Paul McNeill & Linda Peters, Richard & Linda Thompson)

MARK PETERS & SILHOUETTES
63	Oriole CB 1836	Fragile (Handle With Care)/Janie	30
64	Oriole CB 1909	Cindy's Gonna Cry/Show Her	30
64	Piccadilly 7N 35207	Don't Cry For Me/I Told You So	15

PETER'S PRIVATE ARMY
| 83 | Spartan SP 9 | The Gaol Song (Hip Fol The Day)/Bounce Back | 7 |

SCOTT PETERS
61	Pye 7N 15343	Kookie Talk/Game Of Love	7
61	Pye 7N 15363	Bobbie Allen/It's The Natural Thing To Do	6
61	Columbia DB 8244	Go Tell The World/More And More	6

WENDY PETERS
| 68 | Saga OPP 1 | Morning Dew/I Don't Understand | 18 |

JENNY PETERS
| 79 | Redball RR008 | JENNY PETERS (EP) | 12 |

CLIVE PETERSEN
| 61 | Columbia DB 4687 | For Every Boy/If No One Tells You | 15 |

PAUL PETERSEN

MINT VALUE £

PAUL PETERSEN
62	Pye International 7N 25153	Keep Your Love Locked/Be Everything To Anyone You Love	7
62	Pye International 7N 25163	Lollipops And Roses/Please Mr Sun	10
63	Pye International 7N 25173	My Dad/Little Boy Sad	10
63	Pye International 7N 25196	Amy/Goody Goody	8
68	Tamla Motown TMG 670	A Little Bit For Sandy/Your Love's Got Me Burnin' Alive	35

PAUL PETERSEN & SHELLEY FABARES
62	Pye International 7N 25133	She Can't Find Her Keys/Very Unlikely	10

(see also Shelley Fabares)

BOBBY PETERSON (QUINTET)
59	Top Rank JAR 232	The Hunch/Love You Pretty Baby (as Bobby Peterson Quintet)	15
64	Sue WI 342	Rockin' Charlie (Parts 1 & 2) (solo)	30
65	Sue WI 346	Piano Rock/One Day (solo)	30

RAY PETERSON
59	RCA RCA 1131	The Wonder Of You/I'm Gone	8
59	RCA RCA 1154	Shirley Purley/Come And Get It	15
60	RCA RCA 1175	Answer Me/Goodnight My Love, Pleasant Dreams	15
60	RCA RCA 1195	Tell Laura I Love Her/Wedding Day	12
60	London HLX 9246	Corrine, Corrina/Be My Girl	15
61	London HLX 9332	Sweet Little Kathy/You Didn't Care	10
61	London HLX 9379	Missing You/You Thrill Me	10
62	London HLX 9489	I Could Have Loved You So Well/Why Don't You Write Me	15
62	London HLX 9569	You Didn't Care/You Know Me Much Too Well	8
63	London HLX 9746	Without Love/Give Us Your Blessing	8
65	MGM MGM 1288	I'm Only Human/One Lonesome Rose	7
61	London REX 1293	CORRINE CORRINA (EP)	30

PETER, SUE & MARC & PFURI, GORPS & KNIRL
79	EMI EMI 2940	Second Hand Company/Troedler & Co.	6

PET HATE
83	FM 12VHF 2	Roll Away The Stone/Caught/Playing With My Heart (12", p/s)	12

(see also Silverwing)

PETITES
60	Philips PB 1035	Get Your Daddy's Car Tonight/Sun Showers	10

PETR & PAVEL
68	Page One POF 112	Laska/Wencelas Square	6

PETS
58	London HL 8652	Cha-Hua-Hua/Cha-Kow-Ski	15
59	Pye International 7N 25004	(You Wandered) Beyond The Sea/Wow-ee!!!	10

PET SHOP BOYS
SINGLES
84	Epic A 4292	West End Girls/Pet Shop Boys (p/s)	20
84	Epic TA 4292	West End Girls (Extended)/Pet Shop Boys (12", p/s)	30
85	Parlophone R 6097	Opportunities (Let's Make Lots of Money)/In The Night (matrix: A-3-1-2) (1st mix, white p/s)	12
85	Parlophone 12R 6097	Opportunities (Let's Make Lots of Money) (Dance Mix)/In The Night (Extended) (12", white p/s)	20
85	Parlophone 12RA 6097	Opportunities (Let's Make Lots of Money) (Version Latina)/(Dub For Money Remix)/In The Night (Extended Mix) (12", large picture labels, die-cut sleeve)	40
85	Parlophone 12R 6097	Opportunities (Let's Make Lots of Money) (Dance Mix)/ In The Night (Extended) (12", p/s, mispressing, B-side plays "Opportunities [Dub For Money] Remix")	30
85	Parlophone 12R 6097	Opportunities (Let's Make Lots of Money) (Dance Mix)/ In The Night (Extended) (12", p/s, 2nd mispressing, A-side plays "Opportunities [Version Latina]")	30
85	Parlophone 10R 6115	West End Girls (Untitled Mix)/A Man Could Get Arrested (4.09 Mix)/ West End Girls (7" Mix) (10", round foldout p/s; sealed with sticker)	60
86	Parlophone 12RA 6115	West End Girls (Shep Pettibone Mastermix)/West End Dub/A Man Could Get Arrested (4.09 Mix) (12", black/blue/red p/s, standard labels)	10
86	Parlophone 12RA 6115	West End Girls (Shep Pettibone Mastermix)/West End Dub/A Man Could Get Arrested (4.09 Mix) (12", same as above with 6" yellow circle on sleeve)	10
86	Parlophone 12RA 6115	West End Girls (Shep Pettibone Mastermix)/West End Dub/A Man Could Get Arrested (4.09 Mix) (12", stickered black/blue/red p/s with 6" die-cut hole & 6" yellow picture labels)	10
86	Parlophone 10R 6116	Love Comes Quickly (Dance Mix)/That's My Impression (Disco Mix) (10", PVC sleeve with poster)	100
86	Parlophone 12R 6116	Love Comes Quickly (Dance Mix)/That's My Impression (Disco Mix) (12", large picture labels, die-cut white sleeve)	10
86	Parlophone RD 6140	Suburbia/Paninaro/Love Comes Quickly (Shep Pettibone Remix)/Jack The Lad/Suburbia Part Two (double pack, gatefold p/s)	6
88	Parlophone CDR 6177	Heart (Disco Mix)/I Get Excited (You Get Excited Too)/Heart (Dance Mix)	8
93	Parlophone R 6348	Can You Forgive Her? (7" Version)/Hey Headmaster (red or blue vinyl, factory custom pressing, p/s)	600
97	Parlophone Fan Club	It Doesn't Often Snow At Christmas (CD, fan club issue, in sealed silver bubble wrap)	125
10	Parlophone R6810	Love Life/A Powerful Friend (Jukebox centre, blue parlophone sleeve, 1000 only)	12
12	Parlophone R6879	Leaving/Leaving (Demo) (signed p/s)	20
12	Parlophone 12R 6879	Leaving (Lost Her Remix)/(Happy Sad Remix)/(Happy Hour Remix) (12" signed p/s)	20

ALBUMS
86	Parlophone PCS 7303	PLEASE (LP, inner)	18
87	Parlophone PCSDX 104	ACTUALLY (LP, with U.S. import "Always On My Mind" 12", stickered sleeve)	18
88	Parlophone PCSX 7325	INTROSPECTIVE (LP, 3 x clear vinyl 12" factory custom pressing, with wraparound paper strip, 10 copies only)	1500
88	Parlophone PCSX 7325	INTROSPECTIVE (LP, 3 x black vinyl 12", with picture labels & wraparound paper obi strip)	35
91	Parlophone PMTV3	DISCOGRAPHY (2-LP)	50
93	Parlophone PCSD 143	VERY (LP)	40

Year	Label/Cat#	Description	Value £
96	Parlophone PCSD 170	BILINGUAL (LP)	50
00	Parlophone 724352185719	NIGHTLIFE (LP)	35
02	Parlophone 0 724358146	DISCO 3 (3-LP)	25
03	Parlophone 5938241	POPART - THE HITS (3-LP)	50
09	Vinyl Factory VF 003	YES (11 x 12" in smoked perspex box with gold-plated 'tick' on cover, with art print, signed and numbered by both band members, 300 only)	1000
13	Vinyl Factory VF 090	ELECTRIC (Box set 5 x 12", coloured vinyl in acrylic box, 12 page booklet))	800
16	X2 008 VL1	SUPER (LP)	20

PROMOS

Year	Label/Cat#	Description	Value £
84	Epic A4292	West End Girls/Pet Shop Boys (p/s, 'A' label promo)	30
85	Parlophone R 12R 6097	Opportunities (Let's Make Lots of Money)/In The Night (12", "photocopy" sl.)	30
86	Parlophone R 6116	Love Comes Quickly (1-sided, p/s)	40
86	Parlophone 12R 6129	Opportunities (Let's Make Lots of Money) (7.18 Shep Pettibone Mastermix)/Opportunities (4.27 Reprise)/Opportunities (6.44 Original Dance Mix)/Was That What It Was (12", autographed black die-cut sleeve, with press release)	35
86	Parlophone 12R 6129	Opportunities (Let's Make Lots of Money) (7.18 Shep Pettibone Mastermix)/Opportunities (4.27 Reprise)/Opportunities (6.44 Original Dance Mix)/Was That What It Was (12", autographed black die-cut sleeve, without press release)	35
88	Parlophone 12RDJ 6198	Left To My Own Devices (The Disco Mix)/Left To My Own Devices/ The Sound Of The Atom Splitting (12", unique title sleeve)	12
89	Parlophone CDPCSD 113	BEHAVIOUR (CD, commercial issue, different inlay, in white monogrammed pouch, with full-album cassette & chronology)	50
91	Parlophone MFB 1	Music For Boys (12", 3 untitled mixes, hand-stamped white label)	25
91	Parlophone 12MFBX 1	Music For Boys (12", 2 untitled mixes, white label)	12
92	Parlophone CDRX 6332	Go West (7" Version)/West End Girls (Sacha Mix)/Forever/Go West (Extended Dance Mix) (cassette, title sleeve)	150
93	Parlophone 12RXDJ 6348	Can You Forgive Her? (MK Remix)/(MK Bicycle Dub)/I Want To Wake Up (Johnny Marr 1993 Remix)/(Johnny Marr Groove Mix) (12")	10
93	Abbey Road	COMPILED EP (CD-R, Abbey Road title sleeve; autographed by The Boys, 20 only)	800
94	Parlophone 12RDJ 6386	Yesterday When I Was Mad (Jam & Spoon Mix)/(Junior Vasquez Factory Dub)/(Junior Vasquez Fabulous Dub)/(Junior Vasquez Body Dub)/(Coconut 12" Mix)/(RAF Zone Mix)/(RAF Dub Zone)/Euroboy/Some Speculation (12", double pack unique p/s)	15
96	Parlophone 12RDJD 6431	Before (Classic Paradise Mix)/(Afrodisiac Mix)/(Hedboys Mix)/ (Dub)/(Extended Mix) (2 x 12", blue 'penis' p/s)	25
96	Parlophone 12RJD 6431	Before (Underground Mix)/(Bonus Dub)/(Underground Instrumental)/(Bonus Beats) (12", red 'penis' p/s)	25
97	Parlophone 12 BARDJ 2	The Truck Driver & His Mate/Before (Love To Infinity Classic Paradise Mix) (12", 'two knobs' p/s, 150 copies)	150
97	Parlophone 12RDJ 6460	A Red Letter Day (Trouser Enthusiasts Autoerotic Decapitation Mix)/(Trouser Enthusiasts Congo Dongo Dubstramental) (12")	10
97	Parlophone 12BOYDJ 101	The Boy Who Couldn't Keep His Clothes On (Main Vocal)/(INT... Club Mix)/(Banji Girlfriend Beats)/(On Stage At Twilo)/(Radio Edit) (12", die-cut sleeve)	60
99	Parlophone (no cat. no.)	NIGHTLIFE (10" x 10" box in PVC slip case, contains interview CD, music CD, book, EPK & 3 photographs)	50
01	10th Planet/PSBP/RUG	FIVE TITLES FROM CLOSER TO HEAVEN: Positive Role Model/Friendly Fire/ Shameless/ K-Hole/For All Of Us (CD-R, title sleeve, all sung by Neil Tennant)	150
93	Parlophone DF 118	RELENTLESS (3 x 12", on pink/yellow/blue vinyl)	60
96	Parlophone BILING 1	BILINGUAL (A4 yellow box set, including "A Taste Of Bilingual" CD: (Discoteca/Electricity/A Red Letter Day/It Always Comes As A Surprise/Se A Vida E) (with 2 photos & inset in transparent PVC box)	50
96	Parlophone PSBCDDJ 1	BILINGUAL (A4 pale blue launch party promo box set including "A Taste Of Bilingual" CD [Before/Se A Vida É], & album cassette, unique inlay)	200
01	Really Useful Group	CLOSER TO HEAVEN (CD-R, title sleeve; 19 tracks, all sung by Neil Tennant)	250
07	Parlophone DISCO004	DISCO 4 ALBUM SAMPLER (12" 4-tracks)	20
07	Parlophone (no cat. No.)	DISCO FOUR (Promo CD-R, 5-track album sampler and press sheet, 30 copies)	40
06	Parlophone FUNDA001	Fundamentalism Part 1 (12", promo)	15
06	Parlophone FUNDA002	Fundamentalism Part 2 (12", promo)	15
06	Parlophone PSB002	Psychological (1-sided 12" promo no Pet Shop Boys credit on label)	20
06	Parlophone REMIXES01	Psychological (Ewan Pearson Mixes) (12" promo)	25
06	Parlophone STUPID002	I'm With Stupid Remixes 1 (12" promo)	15
06	Parlophone STUPID001	I'm With Stupid Remixes 2 (12" promo)	15
06	Parlophone STUPID003	I'm With Stupid Remixes 3 (12" promo)	15
06	Parlophone PRIVATE001	In Private (Tomcraft Mixes) (12" promo)	20

(see also Eighth Wonder, Dusty Springfield, Electronic, Ian Wright)

PEPPER POT

Year	Label/Cat#	Description	Value £
73	Jumbo JB 034	Lift Up Your Shirt/Ride The Pony	12

MARY PETTI

Year	Label/Cat#	Description	Value £
61	RCA RCA 1239	Hey! Lawdy Lawdy/Gee, But It Hurts	40

PETTICOATS

Year	Label/Cat#	Description	Value £
80	Bla Bla Bla 01	Normal/Allergy/I'm Free (with insert)	20

FRANK PETTY TRIO

Year	Label/Cat#	Description	Value £
53	MGM SP 1010	St. Louis Blues (Boogie Woogie)/Somebody Stole My Girl	20
53	MGM SP 1033	Side By Side/Who's Sorry Now	7
53	MGM SP 1038	Sugar/Sioux City Sue	7
53	MGM SP 1053	Sweet Jenny Lee/Yes Sir That's My Baby	6
54	MGM SP 1092	Loch Lomond/Pino Pantaloni	6
54	MGM SP 1112	Mr Pogo/Sunday	6

NORMAN PETTY TRIO

Year	Label/Cat#	Description	Value £
54	HMV 7M 274	Mood Indigo/Petty's Little Polka	10

TOM PETTY (& HEARTBREAKERS)

Year	Label/Cat#	Description	Value £
77	Shelter ISA 5014	TOM PETTY AND THE HEARTBREAKERS (LP)	20
76	Shelter 1DJ 24A	OFFICIAL LIVE BOOTLEG (LP, with Heartbreakers, 1-sided 5-track, promo only)	20
78	Shelter ISA 5017	YOU'RE GONNA GET IT! (LP)	20
79	MCA MCF 3044	DAMN THE TORPEDOS (LP)	20
89	MCA Records MCG 6024	FULL MOON FEVER (LP)	25

John PFEIFFER

			MINT VALUE £
96	MCS 10864	GREATEST HITS (2-LP)	80
94	Warner Bros. 9362 45759-1	WILDFLOWERS (2-LP)	200
99	Warner Bros. 9362-47294-1	ECHO (2-LP)	100

(see also Randy Newman, Traveling Wilburys, k.d. lang & Roy Orbison)

JOHN PFEIFFER
| 68 | RCA VICS 1371 | ELECTRONOMUSIC - 9 IMAGES (LP) | 15 |

PFM
| 95 | Good Looking GLR 012 | One & Only/Dreams (12") | 20 |
| 95 | Good Looking GLR 012 | The Western Tune/Hypnotizing (12") | 35 |

P.F.M.
73	Manticore K 43502	PHOTOS OF GHOSTS (LP, laminated gatefold sleeve)	25
74	Manticore K 53502	THE WORLD BECAME THE WORLD (LP, die-cut sleeve with inner)	20
74	Manticore K 53506	COOK (LP)	15

P45
| 80 | Jet 190 | Right Direction/B.I.N.Y.C. | 15 |

PHANTOM
| 78 | Cool Ghoul COOL 1 | Lazy Fascist/Power Dub | 7 |

(see also Tom Robinson, Blazing Sons)

PHANTOM BAND
| 71 | Polydor 2058-176 | Loop-Di-Love/Funkin' About | 30 |
| 72 | Polydor 2058-290 | Silhouettes/Drummitt | 15 |

PHANTOM CHORDS
| 92 | Camden Town GNAR 003 | Town Without Pity/She's A Bad Motorcycle (p/s, 2,000 only) | 8 |

(see also Damned)

PHANTOM SLASHER
| 01 | Noid NOIDLP 003 | PUDDLE AND SPOUT (LP, as 2 x 12") | 20 |

PHANTOMS
| 61 | Palette PG 9014 | Phantom Guitar/Cachina | 20 |
| 60s | Arc ARC | GREAT GUITAR HITS (LP) | 20 |

PHARAOHS
| 58 | Decca DFE 6522 | THE PHARAOHS (EP) | 500 |

PHARCYDE
92	East West 7567-92222-1	BIZARRE RIDE II THE PHARCYDE (LP, European edition, 2-LP set is USA)	30
95	Go! Beat 828 736-1	LABCABINCALIFORNIA (2-LP, red and blue vinyl, free 12")	25
00	Four Music FOR 3003 1	BIZARRE RIDE II THE PHARCYDE (2-LP, reissue)	20

RORY PHARE
| 88 | Parlophone RP 1 | Laughing Inside/Laughing Inside (actually by Roy Harper; p/s, promo only) | 7 |

(see also Roy Harper)

PHASE 4
66	Decca F 12327	What Do You Say About That/Think I'll Sit Down And Cry (1st issue)	25
66	Fab FAB 1	What Do You Say About That/I'm Gonna Sit Down And Cry (2nd issue)	20
67	Fab FAB 6	Man Am I Worried?/Listen To The Blues	50

PHASE 5
| 70 | Polydor 2058 063 | Star Trek/Enterprise | 30 |

PHASE 3
| 71 | Mushroom SMR 5 | Walkin' Free/Bill Bailey | 10 |

PHATES
| 79 | Personal Propaganda PROP 4MODACOM | Cool Jerk/Tears Of A Dog (hand-made labels and p/s, 500 only) | 20 |

PHEETUS
| 78 | Ric Rac RRS 002 | Nomads/Blind Man (no p/s, 200 only) | 35 |

JAMES PHELPS
| 72 | Paramount PARA 3019 | Check Yourself/My Lover's Prayer | 12 |

PHENOMENA
| 85 | Bronze BRO 193 | Dance With The Devil/Hell On Wings (p/s) | 7 |
| 85 | Bronze BROX 193 | Dance With The Devil (Midnight Mix)/Hell On Wings (12", p/s with poster) | 10 |

(see also Trapeze, Whitesnake, Cozy Powell, Black Sabbath, Thin Lizzy, Budgie, A-Ha)

PHENOMYNA
| 94 | Applied Rhythmic Technology ART 6 | ART 5.1 EP (12") | 25 |
| 95 | Applied Rhythmic Telecnology ART 7.1 | ART 5.2 EP (12") | 25 |

PHEON BEAR
| 73 | Pye 7N 45232 | War Against War/87th Precinct | 25 |

PHILADELPHIA FLYERS
| 74 | GM Records GMS 026 | Run And Hide (Part 1)/Run And Hide (Part 2) | 6 |

PHIL & FLINTSTONES
| 64 | Bedrock PR 5371 | Love Potion No. 9/Honey Don't (private pressing) | 80 |

PHI LIFE CYPHER
98	Compressed Knowledge CK001	Baddest Man/Da Shinn/Rap 'N' Bullshit/Forever (12")	20
02	Jazz Fudge JFR 030	THE CHOSEN FEW EP (with Taskforce)	25
00	Jazz Fudge JFR 022	MILLENNIAL METAPHORS (2-LP)	25

PHILIP & HIS FOETUS VIBRATIONS
| 82 | Self Immol. WOMB KX 07 | Tell Me, What Is The Bane Of Your Life/Mother I've Killed The Cat (p/s) | 25 |

(see also You've Got Foetus On Your Breath, Foetus Äœber Frisco, Foetus Under Glass, Scraping Foetus Off The Wheel)

LOUIS PHILIPPE
86	él GPO 15	Like Nobody Do/Twangy Twangy (p/s)	6
87	él GPO 23	You Mary You/With And Without You (p/s)	6
87	él GPO 23T	YOU MARY YOU (12" EP, p/s)	12
87	él GPO 31	Anthony Bay/What If A Day (p/s)	6
88	él GPO 40	Guess i'm Dumb/Smash Hit Wonder/Cantilena (p/s)	7

Brendan PHILIPS

MINT VALUE £

88	él ACME 15	IVORY TOWER (LP)	20
86	él ACME 23	AN APPOINTMENT WITH VENUS (LP)	30
89	él ACME 36	YURI GAGARIN (LP)	20

BRENDAN PHILIPS
| 66 | Mercury MF 896 | Is It Worth A Try/When She's Kissing Me | 25 |

NOEL PHILIPS
| 71 | CBS 7036 | Eternal Loner/Snowman | 10 |
| 71 | CBS 7415 | If You Could Believe In Me/Such Is The Meaning Of Your Love | 10 |

TONY PHILIPS & THE HAYSEEDS
| 66 | CBS 202337 | Shropshire Lad/Situation Vacant | 12 |

PHILL MOST CHILL
06	Diggers With Gratitude DWG 001	BE INTELLIGENT (EP, 100 only)	300
11	Diggers With Gratitude DWG 008	ALL CUTS RECORDED RAW (LP)	35
11	Diggers With Gratitude DWG 008	ALL CUTS RECORDED RAW (LP, 25 copies only, alternative pressing, white stickered cover)	350
11	Diggers With Gratitude DWG 008	ALL CUTS RECORDED RAW (LP, coloured vinyl, alternative pressing EP and 7")	100

ANTHONY PHILLIPS
| 79 | Arista SPART 1085/AFLP 1 | SIDES (LP, 1st 500 copies sealed with free LP "Private Parts & Pieces") | 20 |

(see also Genesis)

BARRE PHILLIPS
| 69 | Music Man SMLS 601 | UNACCOMPANIED BARRE (LP) | 100 |

CONFREY PHILLIPS (TRIO)
| 57 | Decca F 10866 | Shotgun Rock 'n' Roll/Hokey-Kokey Rock 'n' Roll (as Confrey Phillips Trio) | 20 |

(LITTLE) ESTHER (PHILLIPS)
62	Stateside SS 140	Release Me/Don't Feel Rained On	25
63	Ember EMB S 174	Am I That Easy To Forget/I Really Don't Want To Know (as Little Esther Phillips)	15
65	Sue WI 395	The Chains/Feel Like I Wanna Cry (as Esther Phillips)	40
65	Atlantic AT 4028	And I Love Him/Shangri-La	18
65	Atlantic AT 4048	Let Me Know When It's Over/I Saw Me	15
66	Atlantic AT 4077	I Could Have Told You/Just Say Goodbye	80
66	Atlantic AT 4077	I Could Have Told You/Just Say Goodbye (DJ Copy)	100
66	Ember EMBS 221	Release Me/Be Honest With Me (as Little Esther Phillips)	12
66	Atlantic 584 013	When A Woman Loves A Man/Ups And Downs	15
67	Atlantic 584 062	Somebody Else Is Taking My Place/When Love Comes To The Human Race	10
67	Atlantic 584 103	And I Love Him/Shangri-La (reissue)	8
67	Atlantic 584 126	I'm Sorry/Cheater Man	15
69	Roulette RO 505	Too Late To Worry, Too Blue To Cry/I'm In The Mood For Love (Moody's Mood For Love)	8
69	Roulette RO 508	Tonight I'll Be Staying Here With You/Sweet Dreams	6
72	Atlantic K 10168	Catch Me I'm Falling/Release Me	18
72	Kudu KUS 4000	Home Is Where The Hatred Is/Til My Back Ain't Got No Bone	20
73	Kudu KUS 4002	I've Never Found A Man/Cherry Red	15
63	Ember CW 103	REFLECTIONS OF GREAT COUNTRY AND WESTERN STANDARDS (LP)	50
65	Atlantic ATL 5030	AND I LOVE HIM (LP)	50
67	Atlantic 587/588 010	ESTHER PHILLIPS SINGS (LP)	30
72	Kudu KUL 2	FROM A WHISPER TO A SCREAM (LP)	25
73	Kudu KUL 6	ALONE AGAIN, NATURALLY (LP)	18
75	Kudu KUL 12	PERFORMANCE (LP)	15

FLIP PHILLIPS
| 56 | Columbia/Clef 33C 9003 | FLIP PHILLIPS QUARTET (10" LP) | 15 |

GLENN PHILLIPS
| 75 | Caroline C 1519 | LOST AT SEA (LP) | 20 |

GREGORY PHILLIPS
63	Pye 7N 15546	Angie/Please Believe Me	12
64	Pye 7N 15593	Everybody Knows/Closer To Me (with Remo Four)	8
64	Pye 7N 15633	Don't Bother Me/Make Sure That You're Mine	8
65	Immediate IM 004	Down In The Boondocks/That's The One	30

(see also Remo Four)

JOHN PHILLIPS
| 70 | Stateside SS 8046 | Mississippi/April Anne | 6 |
| 70 | Stateside-Dunhill SSL 5027 | JOHN PHILLIPS: THE WOLFKING OF L.A. (LP) | 35 |

(see also Mamas & Papas)

LESLIE PHILLIPS
59	Parlophone R 4610	The Navy Lark/The Disc	7
62	Parlophone R 4912	Jolly Old Spring/I Must Resist Temptation	6
69	Columbia DB 8562	The Man Most Likely To/Marigold	6

MICHELLE PHILLIPS
76	A&M AMS 7250	No Love Today/Aloha Louie	7
77	A&M AMS 7340	Victim Of Romance/Lady Of Fantasy	15
77	A&M AMLS 64651	VICTIM OF ROMANCE (LP)	30

(see also Mamas & Papas)

NOEL PHILLIPS
| 80 | Jammys JM001 | Youth Man/Living In The Ghetto (12") | 25 |

PHIL PHILLIPS & TWILIGHTS
59	Mercury AMT 1059	Sea Of Love/Juella	35
60	Mercury AMT 1072	Take This Heart/Verdi Mae	30
60	Mercury AMT 1093	Your True Love Once More/What Will I Tell My Heart	30
61	Mercury AMT 1139	I Love To Love You/No One Else But You	30

Shawn PHILLIPS

MINT VALUE £

SHAWN PHILLIPS
65	Columbia DB 7611	Hey Nelly Nelly/Solitude	12
65	Columbia DB 7699	Doesn't Anybody Know My Name?/Nobody Listens	12
65	Columbia DB 7789	Little Tin Soldier/London Town	8
66	Columbia DB 7956	Summer Came/Storm	8
67	Parlophone R 5606	Stargazer/Woman Mine	80
70	A&M AMS 819	Christmas Song/Lovely Lady	6
65	Columbia 33SX 1748	I'M A LONER (LP)	120
66	Columbia S(C)X 6006	SHAWN (LP)	250
70	A&M AMLS 978	CONTRIBUTION (LP)	18
71	A&M AMLS 2006	SECOND CONTRIBUTION (LP, with insert)	18
72	A&M AMLS 64324	COLLABORATION (LP)	18

SID PHILLIPS BAND
| 56 | HMV POP 269 | Farewell Blues (Rock 'N' Roll Style)/It Goes Like This | 6 |

STU PHILLIPS
58	London HL 8673	The Champlain And St. Lawrence Line/The Priest Who Slept 100 Years	10
60	Pye International 7N 25062	Strangers When We Meet/BOB MERSEY ORCHESTRA: Song Of India	6
59	Pye Intl. NEP 44001	STU PHILLIPS (EP)	12

TEDDY PHILLIPS & HIS ORCHESTRA
54	Parlophone CMSP 4	Down Boy/Meet "Miss Pippin" (export issue)	12
54	Parlophone CMSP 12	The Old Red Barn/JIMMY BLUE CREW: The Old Shoe Cobbler (export issue)	8
54	Parlophone CMSP 28	Life Is Like A Slice Of Cake/One-Sided Love Affair (export issue)	12

TOM PHILLIPS/GAVIN BRYERS/FRED ORTON
| 78 | Obscure OBS 9 | IRMA - AN OPERA (LP) | 20 |

WARREN PHILLIPS & THE ROCKETS
| 69 | Decca (S)PA 43 | THE WORLD OF ROCK 'N' ROLL (LP) | 15 |

(see also Foghat)

WOOLF PHILLIPS & HIS ORCHESTRA
| 54 | Decca F 10416 | Count Your Blessings Instead Of Sheep/Your Heart, My Heart (B-side with Dennis Morley - Vocal) | 6 |

PHILLY DOG
| 74 | Penny Farthing PEN 581 | You Got The Gun/Hijack | 10 |

PHILOSOPHERS
| 69 | Pye 7N 17740 | The Lovedene Girls/I Believe Forever | 25 |

VINCE PHILPOTT & DRAGS
| 64 | Decca F 11997 | The Cramp/Eenie Meenie Miny Mo | 15 |

PHILWIT & PEGASUS
70	Chapter One CHR 130	And She Came - Final Thought/Pauper's Son	8
70	Chapter One CHR 131	And I Try/Pauper's Son	8
70	Chapter One CHR 137	The Elephant Song/Pseudo Phoney Mixed Up Croney	40
70	Chapter One CHSR 805	PHILWIT AND PEGASUS (LP)	40

(see also Mark Wirtz)

PAT PHOENIX
| 62 | HMV POP 1030 | The Rovers Chorus/Coronation Street Monologue | 12 |

PHOENIX (2)
| 81 | Rising PR 433032 | PHOENIX RISING EP (Lonely Attack/The Minstrel/Understanding/Phoenix Rising 'Av An 'Am) (12" EP) | 35 |

PHOENIX (3)
00	Source 7243 8 488531 1	UNITED (LP)	40
04	Source SOUR LP 095	ALPHABETICAL (LP)	35
09	V2 VVR703394	WOLFGANG AMEDUES PHOENIX (LP, white vinyl)	20

PHONADS
| 81 | SRT S81 CUS 1024 | Talk To Me/You And Me (plain stickered sleeve) | 50 |

PHOTEK
95	Photek PTK 04	Water Margin/Fusion (12")	20
95	Photex PTK 05	Seven Samurai/Complex (12")	18
95	Photek PTK 06	U.F.O./Rings Around Saturn (12", p/s)	20
96	Op ART OP 1	T-Raenon/(Version)/Kanei (12")	20
97	Science QEDT2	Ni-Ten-Ichi-Ryu/The Fifth Column (12")	20
97	Science QEDT2	MODUS OPERANDI (3-LP)	40
98	Virgin QEDLP2	FORM AND FUNCTION (3-LP)	40
00	Science QEDLP6	SOLARIS (2-LP)	20

PHOTOGRAPHED BY LIGHTNING
| 86 | Fierce FRIGHT 008 | Sleep's Terminator/Winter Trees (foldaround p/s, hand-coloured labels) | 30 |

PHOTOGRAPHS
| 79 | Do Not Bend AERS 106 | Second Best/Seas/Here I Go Again (no p/s) | 20 |

PHUTURE PHANTASY
| 88 | Low Fat Vinyl LFV 1 | SLAM (12") | 15 |

PHUTURE PRIMITIVE
| 93 | Knifeforce KF 006 | Full Metal Jacket/Twinkle (12") | 30 |
| 94 | Knifeforce KF 026 | Lift Me Up/Infect Me (12") | 15 |

PHYSICALS
| 79 | Big Beat NS 58 | Be Like Me/Pain In Love (p/s) | 6 |

(see also Maniacs)

PHYSICS HOUSE BAND
| 13 | Blood and Biscuits BSCTS024LP | Horizons/Rapture (12") | 45 |

PAUL PIACENTINI
| 85 | Acting School Again ASA 01 | OUT OF MY BOX (mini-LP) | 40 |

PIANO MAGIC
| 96 | i IRE 1071 | Wrong French/Non-Fiction/General Electric With Fairylights (12", p/s) | 10 |

PIANO RED

MINT VALUE £

97	i IRE 2031	Wintersport/Cross Country/Angel Pie/Magic Tree/Magnetic North (12", p/s) 10
97	Wurlitzer Jukebox WJ 26	For Engineers A/For Engineers AA (p/s) 7
98	Lissy's LISS 32	Music For Rolex/MATMOS: The Soldering Social (p/s) 6
98	Debut DEBT 001SP	French Mittens/Icebreaker: Melody For Nato (p/s) 8
98	Bad Jazz BEBOP 9	Music For Annahbird/Music For Wasps/Me At 19 (p/s) 8
98	Piao! PIAO! 12	The Fun Of The Century/The Sharpest Knife In The Drawer/Industrial Cutie/I Am The Sub-Librarian (12", p/s)... 12
00	Morr MUSIC 008	Panic Amigo - Piano Magic Remixed (12" EP) 10

PIANO RED
| 53 | HMV 7M 108 | Rockin' With Red/Red's Boogie .... 100 |
| 64 | RCA RCX 7138 | RHYTHM AND BLUES VOL. 2 (EP) .... 15 |

(see also Dr. Feelgood [U.S.])

PICA
| 70 | Polydor 2058 056 | Take The Barriers Down/Insurance Man .... 10 |
| 71 | Philips 6006 129 | Rainbow Chaser/Ad Lib .... 100 |

(see also Nirvana [UK])

PICADILLY LINE
67	CBS 2785	At The Third Stroke/How Could You Say You're Leaving Me 30
67	CBS 2958	Emily Small (The Huge World Thereof)/Gone Gone Gone 25
68	CBS 3595	Yellow Rainbow/Evenings With Corrina 30
68	CBS 3595	Yellow Rainbow/I Know, She Believes (reissue with different B-side) 25
68	CBS 3743	Evenings With Corrina/My Best Friend 20
67	CBS (S)BPG 63129	THE HUGE WORLD OF EMILY SMALL (LP, laminated front sleeve) 350
67	CBS (S)BPG 63129	THE HUGE WORLD OF EMILY SMALL (LP, laminated front sleeve, promo insert) 400

(see also Edwards Hand)

PIC & BILL
67	Page One POF 024	All I Want Is You/It's Not You 10
67	Page One POF 037	This Is It/Nobody But My Baby 10
68	Page One POF 052	Sad World Without You/Just A Tear 10

PIERO PICCIONI
| 67 | Fontana TF 898 | Main Theme From 'The Tenth Victim'/Part 2 (mono) .... 12 |

PICK A POW
| 93 | Sunjam SR 0014 | Time Hard/RICK WAYNE: Our Younger Years (12") .... 40 |
| 94 | Sunjam SR 0015 | Wicked People/Only You (12") .... 25 |

BUSTER PICKENS
| 60s | Heritage HLP 1008 | TEXAS PIANO (LP, 99 only) .... 60 |

J.B. PICKERS
| 71 | London HLU 10334 | Super Soul Sounds/KIM & DAVE: Nobody Knows .... 15 |

BOBBY (BORIS) PICKETT & CRYPT-KICKERS
62	London HLU 9597	Monster Mash/Monsters' Mash Party 10
73	London HLU 10436	Me And My Mummy/Monster Holiday 7
73	London ZGU 133	MONSTER MASH (LP) 20

DAN PICKETT
| 60s | XX MIN 710 | DAN PICKETT (EP) .... 15 |

KENNY PICKETT
| 80 | F Beat PRO 2 | Got A Gun/Same .... 15 |

(see also The Creation)

NICK PICKETT
| 72 | Warner Bros K 14156 | America/Lady Luck .... 6 |
| 72 | Reprise K 44172 | SILVERSLEEVES (LP) .... 30 |

(see also John Dummer Blues Band)

WILSON PICKETT
63	Liberty LIB 10115	It's Too Late/I'm Gonna Love You 30
65	Atlantic AT 4036	In The Midnight Hour/I'm Not Tired 20
65	MGM MGM 1286	Let Me Be Your Boy/My Heart Belongs To You 50
65	MGM MGM 1286	Let Me Be Your Boy/My Heart Belongs To You (DJ copy) 100
65	Atlantic AT 4052	Don't Fight It/It's All Over 12
66	Atlantic AT 4072	634-5789/That's A Man's Way 12
66	Atlantic 584 023	99 And A Half (Won't Do)/Danger Zone 12
66	Atlantic 584 039	Land Of 1000 Dances/You're So Fine 10
66	Atlantic 584 066	Mustang Sally/Three Time Loser 10
67	Atlantic 584 101	Everybody Needs Somebody To Love/Nothing You Can Do 10
67	Atlantic 584 107	New Orleans/Soul Dance III.. 10
67	London HLU 10146	Billy The Kid/I Don't Want No Part-Time Love (with Falcons) 10
67	Atlantic 584 130	Funky Broadway/I'm Sorry About That 10
67	Atlantic 584 142	Stag-O-Lee/I'm In Love 10
68	Atlantic 584 150	In The Midnight Hour/Danger Zone 7
68	Atlantic 584 173	That Kind Of Love/I've Come A Long Way 8
68	Atlantic 584 223	She's Looking Good/We've Got To Have Love 10
69	Atlantic 584 236	Hey Jude/Night Owl 8
69	Atlantic 584 261	Mini-Skirt Minnie/Back In Your Arms 10
70	Atlantic 584 313	You Keep Me Hangin' On/Now You See Me, Now You Don't 8
71	Atlantic 2091 124	Don't Knock My Love (Parts 1 & 2) 6
65	Atlantic ATL 5037	IN THE MIDNIGHT HOUR (LP) 50
66	Atlantic 587/588 029	THE EXCITING WILSON PICKETT (LP) 30
66	Atlantic 587 032	IN THE MIDNIGHT HOUR (LP, reissue) 25
67	Atlantic 587/588 057	THE WICKED PICKETT (LP) 30
67	Atlantic 587/588 080	THE SOUND OF WILSON PICKETT (LP) 30
68	Atlantic 587/588 092	THE BEST OF WILSON PICKETT (LP) 20
68	Atlantic 587/588 107	I'M IN LOVE (LP) 20

Gary PICKFORD-HOPKINS & FRIENDS

MINT VALUE £

68	Atlantic 587/588 111	MIDNIGHT MOVER (LP)	20
69	Atlantic 588 170	HEY JUDE (LP)	20
70	Atlantic 2465 002	RIGHT ON (LP)	20
70	Joy JOYS 181	IF YOU NEED ME (LP)	20
71	Atlantic 2400 026	ENGINE NO. 9 - IN PHILADELPHIA (LP)	20

(see also Falcons)

GARY PICKFORD-HOPKINS & FRIENDS

83	Spartan SP 143	Why? (The Song)/Why? (The Story) (p/s)	8
83	Spartan SP 143T	Why? (The Song)/Why? (The Story) (12") (p/s)	10

(see also Deke Leonard, Man, Alan Ross, Big Sleep, Eyes Of Blue, Wild Turkey)

PICKWICKS

64	Decca F 11901	Apple Blossom Time/I Don't Wanna Tell You Again	18
64	Decca F 11957	You're Old Enough/Hello Lady	15
65	Warner Bros WB 151	Little By Little/I Took My Baby Home	100

PICNIC BOYS

82	Challet BEAN 001	White Hotel/Dawn Patrol (p/s)	20

PICTURE BOOK

84	Crystal 2	Laughing In My Hand/Reflex Action (with insert)	70

PICTURE FRAME SEDUCTION

84	SOSO 33	I'm Good Enough For Me/Sabotage The Classes/Fur Queue	40
87	PFS 2	Try With A Little Help From My Friends/And Entertainment USA	40
85	Rot PFS 1	HAND OF THE RIDER (LP)	40

PICTURE POSTCARD

70	Polydor 2058 106	Give A Little Love To Someone/Another Day Another Dollar	8

PICTURES LIKE THIS

83	TW HIT 112	A Night's Vendetta/Defeat (p/s)	251

RANDY PIE AND FAMILY

72	Atlantic K10248	Queen Of Dreams/Train Goe On	10

PIED PIPERS (1)

54	Parlophone CMSP 21	Kissin' Drive Rock/Please Understand (export issue)	15

PIED PIPERS (2)

66	Columbia DB 7883	Ragamuffin/Fat Marie	30

JEFFREY LEE PIERCE

85	Statik STATLP 25	WILDWEED (LP, with free 7" PROMO 2)	20
85	Statik STATLP 25	WILDWEED (LP)	15

(see also Gun Club)

WEBB PIERCE

50s	Decca BM 311368	We'll Find A Way/Any Old Time (export issue)	30
55	Decca BM 31172	Teen Age Boogie/I'm Really Glad You Hurt Me (export)	150
56	Brunswick 05630	Teenage Boogie/Any Old Time	150
57	Brunswick 05682	Bye, Bye Love/Honky Tonk Song	40
59	Brunswick 05809	I Ain't Never/Shanghaied	20
60	Brunswick 05820	No Love Have I/Whirlpool Of Love	10
60	Brunswick 05842	Drifting Texas Sand/All I Need Is You	10
56	Brunswick OE 9253	WEBB PIERCE PT. 1 (EP)	10
56	Brunswick OE 9254	WEBB PIERCE PT. 2 (EP)	10
56	Brunswick OE 9255	WEBB PIERCE PT. 3 (EP)	10
62	Ember EMB 4520	COUNTRY AND WESTERN FAVOURITES VOL. 1 (EP)	10
59	Parlophone GEP 8792	COUNTRY ROUND UP (EP)	20
55	Brunswick LA 8716	THE WONDERING BOY (10" LP)	30
60	Brunswick LAT 8324	WEBB! (LP)	15
65	Brunswick LAT 8540	HIDEAWAY HEART (LP)	15
65	Brunswick LAT 8551	CROSS COUNTRY (LP)	15

(see also Red Sovine & Webb Pierce)

PIERCES

07	Lizard King 102X	Sticks And Stones/Turn On Billie	15
11	Polydor 2770932	YOU AND I (LP, insert)	45

PIG

91	Concrete CPRODLP 017	PRAISE THE LARD (LP)	70
17	Armalyte Industries ARMVNL 044	WRECKED (2-LP, reissue)	40

CLIVE PIG & THE HOPEFUL CHINAMEN

79	Pinnacle PIN 21	Happy Birthday Sweet Sixteen/Our Movement (p/s)	10

(see also Trixie's Big Red Motorbike)

MARTIN PIG

83	Rough Trade RT 092	Lovely Rita/Somebody Loves You	15

PIGEON DETECTIVES

06	Dance To The Radio DTTR 08	I'm Not Sorry/I'm Always Right (p/s)	8

PIGEON FLYERS

68	Columbia DB 8449	The Heaven We Shared Together/Keep On Sayin'	8

PIG RIDER

74	Deroy	BLOODY TURKEY SANDWICHES (LP, 6 acetates only)	200
75	Deroy	HETEROPHONIES (LP, acetate only)	200

PIGS

77	Bristol Recorder NBR 01	Youthenasia/They Say/Psychopath/National Front (p/s)	10

PIGSTY HILL LIGHT ORCHESTRA

71	Village Thing VTS 8	PIGGERY JOKERY (LP)	20

DAVE PIKE

66	Atlantic 584 052	Sunny/HERBIE MANN: Philly Dog	15
66	Atlantic 588 005	JAZZ FOR THE JET SET (LP)	25

RAY PILGRIM (& BEATMEN)
60	Oriole CB 1557	Baby Doll/Gambler's Guitar (solo)	15
61	Oriole CB 1616	Little Miss Makebelieve/Granada (solo)	8
62	Oriole CB 1710	Red Red Roses/There's Always Me (solo)	10

(see also Bud Ashton, Jaybirds, Typhoons)

PILGRIM FATHERS
69	Tangerine 009	Love And The World Will Love/Come A Day	7

TONY PILLEY
79	Barclay Towers BT2	Off The Hook/Mummy & Daddy (p/s, with poster)	15
79	Barclay Towers BT2	Off The Hook/Mummy & Daddy (p/s, without poster)	8

PILTDOWN MEN
60	Capitol CL 15149	McDonald's Cave/Brontosaurus Stomp	7
61	Capitol CL 15175	Piltdown Rides Again/Bubbles In The Tar	7
61	Capitol CL 15186	Goodnight Mrs Flintstone/The Great Imposter	8
61	Capitol CL 15211	Gargantua/Fossil Rock	12
62	Capitol CL 15245	A Pretty Girl Is Like A Melody/Big Lizzard	20
61	Capitol EAP1 20155	GOODNIGHT MRS. FLINTSTONE (EP)	25

SIR HUBERT PIMM
55	London HL 8155	Goodnight And Cheerio/Honky Tonk Train Blues	50
55	London RE-U 1032	PIMM'S PARTY (EP, with Ellen Sutton)	20

(see also Duke & Duchess)

PINCHERS
86	Blue Trac BTRP 001	CAN'T TAKE THE PRESSURE (LP)	40

MICHAEL PINDER
76	Threshold TH 23	Carry On/I only Want To Be With You	25

PINEAPPLE CHUNKS
65	Mercury MF 922	Drive My Car/Dream About	15

PINEAPPLE THIEF
00	Obtuse OBT 001	Sherbert Gods/Perpetual Flying Objects (wraparound p/s in poly bag)	25

PINEWOOD STUDIO ORCHESTRA
59	Top Rank JAR 112	Sapphire/Tiger Bay	6
62	Parlophone R 4906	The Waltz Of The Toreadors/Picture Parade	6

PINEWOOD TOM/TOM TALL
59	Jazz Collector JEL 5	THE MALE BLUES VOLUME 4 (EP)	18

'PING PING' & AL VERLANE
60	Oriole CB 1589	Sucu Sucu/Maria Della Montagna	8

PINK AND BLACK
85	Illuminated ILL4912	Sometimes I Wish (Dramadance U.S.A. Mix)/Sometimes I Wish (Radio)/Miss Fortune (12", p/s)	12

PINK ELEPHANT
72	Pye 7N 45143	Down In The Valley/I'm Living In This World Just For You	15

PINK FAIRIES
71	Polydor 2058 089	The Snake/Do It	25
72	Polydor 2059 302	Well Well Well/Hold On	25
76	Stiff BUY 2	Between The Lines/Spoiling For A Fight (promo 'plug' copy)	15
76	Stiff BUY 2	Between The Lines/Spoiling For A Fight (p/s)	10
71	Polydor 2383 045	NEVERNEVERLAND (LP, printed PVC outer & gatefold card inner, in yellow bag with photos & notes)	250
71	Polydor 2383 045	NEVERNEVERLAND (LP, printed PVC outer & gatefold card inner, pink vinyl & "pink plastic" in text on rear sleeve, around 100 pressed)	500
71	Polydor 2383 045	NEVERNEVERLAND (LP, black vinyl, standard sleeve)	50
72	Polydor 2383 132	WHAT A BUNCH OF SWEETIES (LP)	30
73	Polydor 2383 212	KINGS OF OBLIVION (LP, with poster)	50
75	Polydor 2384 071	FLASHBACK (LP)	18
87	Demon FIEND 105	KILL EM AND EAT EM (LP)	15

(see also Twink, Larry Wallis, Deviants, Lightning Raiders, Shagrat)

PINK FLOYD
SINGLES
67	Columbia DB 8156	Arnold Layne/Candy And A Currant Bun (solid centre)	100
67	Columbia DB 8156	Arnold Layne/Candy And A Currant Bun (push-out centre)	90
67	Columbia DB 8214	See Emily Play/Scarecrow (solid centre)	80
67	Columbia DB 8214	See Emily Play/Scarecrow (push-out centre)	65
67	Columbia DB 8310	Apples And Oranges/Paint Box (solid or push-out centre)	150
68	Columbia DB 8401	It Would Be So Nice/Julia Dream (solid centre)	150
68	Columbia DB 8401	It Would Be So Nice/Julia Dream (push-out centre)	100
68	Columbia DB 8511	Point Me At The Sky/Careful With That Axe Eugene (push-out centre)	100
79	Harvest HAR 5194	Another Brick In The Wall (Part 2)/One Of My Turns (initial pressing, plain B-side label without 'window' picture)	8
81	Harvest HAR 5217	Money (Edit)/Let There Be More Light (unreleased, die-cut sleeve)	0
81	Harvest 12HAR 5217	Money (Full Length)/Let There Be More Light (12", unreleased)	0
82	Harvest HAR 5222	When The Tigers Broke Free/Bring The Boys Back Home (gatefold p/s)	10
82	Harvest HAR 5222	When The Tigers Broke Free/Bring The Boys Back Home (standard p/s)	8
83	Harvest HAR 5224	Not Now John/The Hero's Return Parts 1 and 2 (p/s)	7
87	EMI EMDJ 26	Learning To Fly (Edited Version)/One Slip (Edited Version)/Terminal Frost (no p/s, mispressing without "One Slip", 50 on black vinyl)	20
87	EMI EMDJ 26	Learning To Fly (Edited Version)/One Slip (Edited Version)/Terminal Frost (no p/s, mispressing without "One Slip", 1,000 only on pink vinyl)	15
87	EMI EMP 34	On The Turning Away (Album)/Run Like Hell (Live Version) (p/s, pink vinyl, 1000 only)	10
87	EMI 12EMP 34	On The Turning Away (Album)/Run Like Hell (Live Version)/On The Turning Away (Live Version) (12", poster p/s)	12
87	EMI 12EMP 34	On The Turning Away (Album)/Run Like Hell (Live Version)/On The Turning Away (Live Version)	12

PINK FLOYD

			MINT VALUE £
88	EMI EMG 52	One Slip/Terminal Frost (pink vinyl, gatefold p/s with ticket application)	12
88	EMI 12EMP 52	One Slip/Terminal Frost/The Dogs Of War (live) (12", poster p/s)	10
94	EMI EM 309	Take It Back (Edit)/Astronomy Domine (live) (jukebox issue, black vinyl)	8
94	EMI EM 309	Take It Back (Edit) /Astronomy Domine (Live) (p/s)	7
94	EMI EM 309	Take It Back (Edit)/Astronomy Domine (live) (red vinyl, p/s)	10
94	EMI EM 342	High Hopes (Radio Edit)/Keep Talking (Radio Edit) (clear vinyl, poster p/s)	12
94	EMI 12EM 342	High Hopes (Album Version)/Keep Talking (Album Version)/One Of These Days (live) (12", 1-sided, laser-etched blue vinyl, p/s in outer gtefold p/s with 7 postcards)	40
13	Columbia DB 8214	See Emily Play/Scarecrow (p/s, reissue, pink vinyl, poster)	15
15	Parlophone 08256460186511	PINKFLOYD 1965 - THEIR FIRST RECORDINGS (2 x 7", 1050 only)	100

ALBUMS

67	Columbia SX 6157	THE PIPER AT THE GATES OF DAWN (LP, 1st pressing, mono, blue/black labels, with "Sold in U.K..."and "Gramophone Co" text, first known matrixes XAX 3419 - 2 G1/XAX 3420 - 1 G1, flipback laminated sleeve, grey back, Ernest J. Day printing credit)	800
67	Columbia SCX 6157	THE PIPER AT THE GATES OF DAWN (LP, 1st pressing, stereo, blue/black labels, with "Sold in the U.K..." and "Gramophone Co." text, first known matrixes YAX 3419 - 1G1/ YAX 3420 - 1-G1, flipback laminated sleeve, grey back, Ernest J. Day printing credit)	600
	(Second pressings have "File Under Pop" on the right of the flipback; first pressings do not have this. Second pressing worth half to a third less)		
69	Columbia SX 6157	THE PIPER AT THE GATES OF DAWN (2nd pressing, mono, black/silver labels with "sold in UK..." text, 1 EMI box, flipback laminated sleeve, grey back, Ernest J. Day printing credit)	500
68	Columbia SX 6258	A SAUCERFUL OF SECRETS (LP, 1st pressing, mono, blue/black label, "Sold in U.K..." text, front laminated flipback sleeve.Gilmour spelt 'Gilmore' on label and sleeve, some early labels misspell first track as 'Let There Me More Light' and all songs are credited to Magdalene Music. Other early labels spell song titles correctly but all songs are still credited to Magdalene Music.Earliest matrixes XAX 3633-1 G1/XAX 3634-1 G1)	600
68	Columbia SCX 6258	A SAUCERFUL OF SECRETS (LP, 1st pressing, stereo, blue/black label, "Sold in U.K..." text, front laminated flipback sleeve. Gilmour spelt 'Gilmore' on label and sleeve, early label credit all songs to Magdalene Music. Earliest matrixes YAX 3633-1 G1/YAX 3634-1 R1)	400
69	Columbia SCX 6157	THE PIPER AT THE GATES OF DAWN (3rd stereo pressing, black/silver labels without "Sold in the UK" but with "Gramophone Co." text, 1 EMI box, flipback laminated sleeve, grey back, Ernest J. Day printing credit)	125
69	Columbia SCX 6346	SOUNDTRACK FROM THE FILM 'MORE' (LP, 1st pressing, laminated flipback sleeve, 'couple facing west' photo on green-tinted rear sleeve, with black/silver label, boxed logo and "Sold in UK..." text)	100
69	Harvest SHDW 1/2	UMMAGUMMA (2-LP, 1st pressing, without EMI logo, laminated gatefold sleeve with 'London' spelt as 'Londen' with Ernest J Day & Co' printing credit)	100
69	Harvest SHDW 1/2	UMMAGUMMA (2-LP, 2nd pressing with EMI logo and 'The Gramophone Co Ltd' label text, laminated gatefold sleeve)	40
69	Harvest SHDW 1/2	UMMAGUMMA (2-LP, 3rd pressing, with EMI logo and 'EMI Records' label text, laminated gatefold sleeve)	30
69	Columbia SCX 6157	THE PIPER AT THE GATES OF DAWN (2nd stereo pressing, black/silver labels with "Sold in the UK" and "Gramophone Co." text, 1 EMI box, flipback laminated sleeve, grey back, Ernest J. Day printing credit)	150
69	Columbia SX 6258	A SAUCERFUL OF SECRETS (LP, 2nd pressing, mono, silver/black label, one EMI box at bottom of label. "Made in GT Britain. Sold in U.K..." text around bottom edge of label, front laminated flipback sleeve. Gilmour spelt 'Gilmore' on label and sleeve)	200
70	Columbia SCX 6258	A SAUCERFUL OF SECRETS (LP, 2nd pressing, stereo, silver/black label, one EMI box at bottom of label. "Made in GT Britain. Sold in U.K..." text around bottom edge of label, front laminated flipback sleeve. Gilmour spelt 'Gilmore' on label and sleeve)	150
70	Columbia SCX 6258	A SAUCERFUL OF SECRETS (LP, 3rd pressing, stereo, silver/black label, one EMI box at bottom of label. "Made in GT Britain" text around bottom edge of label but no "Sold in U.K...". Front laminated flipback sleeve. Gilmour spelt 'Gilmore' on label and sleeve)	100
69	Columbia SCX 6346	SOUNDTRACK FROM THE FILM 'MORE' (LP, laminated non-flipback sleeve, 'couple facing west' photo on black-tinted rear sleeve)	80
70s	Columbia SCX 6346	SOUNDTRACK FROM THE FILM 'MORE' (LP, laminated non-flipback sleeve, 'couple facing east' photo on black-tinted rear sleeve)	70
70	MGM 2315 002	ZABRISKIE POINT (LP, soundtrack, with Jerry Garcia/Kaleidoscope, et al.)	30
70	Harvest SHVL 781	ATOM HEART MOTHER (LP, 1st pressing, gatefold sleeve, no EMI logo)	150
	(First pressing Harvest LPs of UMMAGUMMA and ATOM HEART MOTHER have "The Gramophone..." text on label rim and "Harvest" on the left side of the label; second pressings have "The Gramophone..." text with a boxed EMI logo above "Harvest")		
71	Columbia SCX 6167	THE PIPER AT THE GATES OF DAWN (4th pressing, stereo, black/silver labels without "Sold in the UK..." text, 2 EMI boxes, "EMI records Ltd" text, Non-flipback laminated sleeve, white back, Garrod & Lofthouse printing credit)	100
71	Harvest SHVL 795	MEDDLE (LP, textured inside/outside gatefold sleeve, 'The Gramophone Co Ltd' label text and 'Patent No 1224339' on rear of sleeve)	100
71	Harvest SHVL 795	ATOM HEART MOTHER (LP, 2nd pressing with EMI logo, 'The Gramophone Co' label text, gatefold sleeve, matrixes SHVL 781 A-4 RD 2/SHVL 781 B-3 AO 1)	50
71	Harvest SHVL 795	MEDDLE (LP, textured outside gatefold sleeve, with 'The Gramophone Co Ltd' label text but no 'Patent no' on sleeve)	40
71	Columbia SCX 6258	A SAUCERFUL OF SECRETS (LP, 4th pressing, stereo, silver/black label, two EMI boxes at top and bottom of label. "Made in Gt Britain" text around the bottom edge of label but no "Sold in U.K..." Front laminated flipback sleeve. Gilmour spelt 'Gilmore' on label and sleeve) with 2 EMI box logos)	80
71	Starline SRS 5071	RELICS (LP, white textured sleeve)	15
72	Harvest SHSP 4020	OBSCURED BY CLOUDS (LP, rounded sleeve, EMI logo on label)	75
73	Harvest SHVL 804	THE DARK SIDE OF THE MOON (LP, first pressing, solid light blue triangle label, black inner, 2 posters & 2 stickers, gatefold sleeve, only one side opening)	1000
73	Harvest SHVL 804	THE DARK SIDE OF THE MOON (LP, blue & black label, gatefold sleeve with black inner, 2 posters & 2 stickers, with stickered sleeve)	60
73	Harvest SHVL 804	THE DARK SIDE OF THE MOON (LP, blue & black label, gatefold sleeve with black inner, 2 posters & 2 stickers, without stickered sleeve)	35
73	Harvest Q4 SHVL 804	THE DARK SIDE OF THE MOON (LP, quadrophonic, gatefold sleeve, no inserts)	40
73	Columbia SCX 6258	A SAUCERFUL OF SECRETS (LP, 5th pressing, stereo, silver/black label, two EMI boxes at top and bottom of label. "EMI Records Ltd" replaces "Gramophone Company" in label rim text. Front laminated non-flipback sleeve. Gilmour spelt 'Gilmore' on label and sleeve)	60
70s	Harvest SHVL 804	THE DARK SIDE OF THE MOON (LP, repressing, blue & silver label, gatefold sleeve with black inner, 2 posters & 2 stickers)	35
74	Harvest SHVL 781	ATOM HEART MOTHER (LP, 3rd pressing with EMI logo, 'EMI Records Ltd' label text,	40

PINK FLOYD

MINT VALUE £

Year	Catalogue	Description	Value
73	Harvest Q4 SHVL 781	ATOM HEART MOTHER (LP, quadrophonic, gatefold sleeve, with 'quadrophonic' logo on front sleeve)	40
73	Harvest Q4 SHVL 781	ATOM HEART MOTHER (LP, quadrophonic, gatefold sleeve, without 'quadrophonic' logo on front sleeve, logo is inside)	50
73	Harvest SHDW 403	A NICE PAIR (2-LP, gatefold sleeve, with 2 inner sleeves; early copies with 'Mr Phang' dentist cover)	40
73	Harvest SHDW 403	A NICE PAIR (2-LP, gatefold sleeve, with 2 inner sleeves, later pressing with 'Monk' cover)	35
75	Harvest SHVL 814	WISH YOU WERE HERE (LP, with inner sleeve, postcard & black cellophane wraparound with sticker, sealed)	500
75	Harvest SHVL 814	WISH YOU WERE HERE (LP, with inner sleeve, postcard & black cellophane wraparound with sticker, unsealed)	50
76	Harvest Q4 SHVL 814	WISH YOU WERE HERE (LP, quadrophonic, with inner sleeve)	75
77	Harvest SHVL 815	ANIMALS (LP, 1st pressing, picture labels, non-barcode gatefold sleeve printed by 'Garrod & Lofthouse', with card inner with rounded edges, large thumb notch at top and catalogue number on bottom right of inner, Matrix numbers: SHVL 815 A-2U/B-2U)	100
77	Harvest SHVL 815	ANIMALS (LP, contract pressing, no EMI stamper at 3 0 clock)	150
77	Harvest SHVL 815	ANIMALS (LP, gatefold, later pressings, gloss or matt sleeve, inner)	30
78	Harvest SHVLP 804	DARK SIDE OF THE MOON (LP, reissue, picture disc, 1000 only)	75
78	Columbia SCX 6157	THE PIPER AT THE GATES DAWN (LP, 5th stereo pressing, black/silver labels without "Sold in UK..." text, 2 EMI boxes, "EMI Records Ltd" text. Non-flipback laminated sleeve, white back, Garrod & Lofthouse printing credit)	50
79	Harvest SHDW 4111/4112	THE WALL (2-LP, First press, MATRIXES: SHSP 4111 A-2U/B-3U/SHSP 4112 A-1U/B-5U: TML-M/TML-X/TML-M/TML-M stamped into dead wax. Creamy coloured sleeve, bricks do not align right to bottom of sleeve, inner surface of sleeve is heavyweight card and creamy in colour, 8th brick states "produced by David Gilmour" then "written by Roger Waters". 9th brick "words and music Roger Waters except "Young Lust", "Comfortably Numb"" etc. Inner sleeve has rounded edges and thumb notch along top edge. "SHDW 4111/1" in bottom right corner. Gatefold sleeve with 'static' transparent "title" sticker)	80
79	Harvest SHDW 4111/4112	THE WALL (2-LP, later pressings, lighter inner card browner in colour. Inside gatefold on right hand side 9th brick "Bob Ezrin, Roger Waters", 10th brick: no text, then Pink Floyd, names of the band. Square inner sleeve - usually - with OC-15863411/SHSP4111/2 catalogue numbers. Gatefold sleeve)	20
79	Harvest PF 11	THE FIRST XI (11-LP set, original sleeves, plus exclusive "Dark Side Of The Moon" & "Wish You Were Here" picture discs, 1,000 only)	200
83	Columbia SCX 6258	A SAUCERFUL OF SECRETS (LP, 6th pressing, stereo, tan label)	30
83	Fame FA 3065	THE PIPER AT THE GATES OF DAWN (7th stereo pressing, yellow or tan labels, non-laminated, non-flipback sleeve)	25
83	Harvest SHPF 1983	THE FINAL CUT (LP, gatefold sleeve with title sticker)	25
84	Columbia SCX 6157	THE PIPER AT THE GATES OF DAWN (6th stereo pressing, tan labels, non-flipback laminated sleeve, white back, Garrod & Lofthouse printing credit)	35
84	Harvest SHVL 814	WISH YOU WERE HERE (LP, audiophile edition, Nimbus supercut sold through Hi-Fi Today magazine	800
85	Harvest SHVL 804	DARK SIDE OF THE MOON (LP, reissue, gatefold sleeve, 2 posters and stickers 'barcode' on sleeve)	20
85	Harvest SHVL 815	ANIMALS (LP, repressing, 'barcode' on sleeve)	15
86	Fame 3163	A SAUCERFUL OF SECRETS (LP, 7th pressing, stereo, yellow Fame label)	25
86	Harvest SHVL 795	MEDDLE (LP, repressing, black label)	25
87	EMI EMD 1003	A MOMENTARY LAPSE OF REASON (LP, gatefold sleeve with inner)	25
87	EMI EMD 1003	A MOMENTARY LAPSE OF REASON (LP, gatefold sleeve with inner, 2 posters, 'guaranteed' concert ticket application and stickered sleeve)	50
88	EMI EQ 5009	DELICATE SOUND OF THUNDER (2-LP, gatefold, 2 inners)	35
91	Fame 3163	A SAUCERFUL OF SECRETS (LP, 8th pressing, beige, tan label)	20
92	EMI CDS 7805572	SHINE ON (9-CD box set, with book and postcards)	90
94	EMI EMD 1055	THE DIVISION BELL (LP, gatefold sleeve, with inner)	75
95	EMI EMD 578	PULSE (4-LP box set in slipcase with hardback book)	300
97	EMI 859 857-1	THE PIPER AT THE GATES OF DAWN (LP, reissue, mono, gatefold sleeve with inner and 'art', inser)	65
97	EMI LPCENT 11	THE DARK SIDE OF THE MOON (LP, reissue, EMI 100 Centenary, stickered sleeve)	30
97	EMI EMD 1115	WISH YOU WERE HERE (LP, reissue, 'magnifying glass' cover)	25
97	EMI SIGMA 630	'97 VINYL COLLECTION (7-LP set, die-cut box, includes "The Piper At The Gates Of Dawn" [EMD 1110], "The Wall" [EMD 1111], "Atom Heart Mother" [EMD 1112], "Relics" [EMD 1113], "The Dark Side Of The Moon" [EMD 1114], "Wish You Were Here" [EMD 1115], each in	150
97	EMI EMD 1133	RELICS (LP, gatefold with poster)	40
01	EMI 724353611118	ECHOES (4-LP box set)	100
03	EMI 5821361	DARK SIDE OF THE MOON (LP, gatefold sleeve, 30th anniversary edition)	25
11	EMI 029 8801	WISH YOU WERE HERE (LP, reissue, poster and postcard)	18

ALBUMS : EXPORT LPS

Year	Catalogue	Description	Value
67	Odeon PSCX 6157	THE PIPER AT THE GATES OF DAWN (LP, stereo, UK sleeve with gold 'Odeon' sticker over Columbia logo on rear, 'The Gramophone Co Ltd' label text on rim and 'Made in Gt. Britain' on black/silver label)	2000
68	Odeon PSCX 6258	A SAUCERFUL OF SECRETS (LP, Stereo, UK sleeve with gold 'Odeon' sticker over 'Columbia logo on rear of sleeve, black/silver Odeon label)	1000
69	Odeon PSCX 6346	MORE (LP, UK sleeve with gold 'Odeon' sticker over Columbia logo on rear of sleeve, black/silver Odeon label)	800

PROMOS

Year	Catalogue	Description	Value
67	Columbia DB 8156	Arnold Layne/Candy And A Currant Bun (demo copy in promo-only p/s, push-out centre)	1500
67	Columbia DB 8156	Arnold Layne/Candy And A Currant Bun (demo copy without p/s, push-out centre)	500
67	Columbia DB 8214	See Emily Play/Scarecrow (demo copy in promo-only p/s, push-out centre)	1500
67	Columbia DB 8214	See Emily Play/Scarecrow (demo copy without p/s, push-out centre)	500
67	Columbia DB 8310	Apples And Oranges/Paintbox (demo copy in promo-only p/s, push-out centre)	1500
67	Columbia DB 8310	Apples And Oranges/Paintbox (demo copy without p/s, push-out centre)	500
68	Columbia DB 8401	It Would Be So Nice (1-sided demo, push-out centre)	1000
68	Columbia DB 8511	Point Me To The Sky/Careful With That Axe Eugene (demo, with newsletter, push-out	900

PINK INDUSTRY

MINT VALUE £

		centre)	
68	Columbia DB 8511	Point Me To The Sky/Careful With That Axe, Eugene (demo, with postcard, push-out centre)	800
69	Emidisc no cat. no.	The Narrow Way (acetate, different version, 1 copy only)	2000
81	Harvest HAR 5217	Money (1-sided pink vinyl promo in p/s, 200 only)	100
81	Harvest HAR 5217	Money (Edited Version) (1-sided, pink vinyl, 200 only)	40
81	Harvest HAR 5217	Money (Edited Version) (1-sided, pink vinyl, mispressing with "Let There Be More Light" label on B-side)	50
81	Harvest SHVL 822	A COLLECTION OF GREAT DANCE SONGS (LP)	20
83	Harvest HARDJ 5224	Not Now John/The Hero's Return (I & II)	30
87	EMI EMDJ 34	On The Turning Away (edit)/On The Turning Away (album) (stickered p/s)	10
88	EMI 12PF 1	Delicate Sound Of Thunder Sampler: Another Brick In The Wall Part 2/ One Of These Days/Run Like Hell (12", black & pink sleeve)	20
88	EMI PSLP 1026	Pink Floyd In Europe '88: Money/Shine On/Another Brick In The Wall Part 2/ One Slip/ On The Turning Away/Learning To Fly (12", with "Another Brick...Part 1" miscredit on rear p/s)	20

(see also Syd Barrett, Roger Waters, David Gilmour, Rick Wright, Nick Mason, Joker's Wild, Ron Geesin)

PINK INDUSTRY

82	Zulu ZULU 1	Is This The End?/47/Don't Let Go/Final Cry (12", p/s)	10
85	Zulu ZULU RA 8	What I Wouldn't Give/Bound By Silence (p/s)	15
87	Cathexis CRL 16	Don't Let Go/Ticket To Heaven/Empty Beach (Remix) (12", p/s)	15
83	Zulu ZULU 2	LOW TECHNOLOGY (LP)	15
83	Zulu ZULU 4	WHO TOLD YOU - YOU WERE NAKED (LP)	15
85	Zulu ZULU 7	NEW BEGINNINGS (LP)	25
88	Cathexis CRL 18	PINK INDUSTRY (LP)	25

(see also Pink Military, Big In Japan)

PINK MILITARY

80	Eric's ERIC'S 005	Did You See Her/Everyday (p/s)	7
80	Virgin/Eric's ERIC'S 004	DO ANIMALS BELIEVE IN GOD? (LP)	15

(see also Pink Industry, Big In Japan)

PINK PEOPLE

64	Philips BF 1355	Psychologically Unsound/Cow Catcher	50
64	Philips BF 1356	Indian Hate Call/I Dreamt I Dwelt In Marble Halls	20

(see also Four Squares)

PINK RHYTHM

85	Beggars Banquet BEG 126	Melodies Of Love/Walking In The Rain (p/s)	20
85	Beggars Banquet BEG 126T	Memories Of Love/Walking In The Rain (12", p/s)	20
85	Beggars Banquet BEG 136T	Can't Get Enough Of Your Love/Can't Get Enough Of Your Dub (12", p/s)	15
85	Beggars Banquet BEG 149	India/More And More (p/s)	8
85	Beggars Banquet BEG 149T	India/Trust Me/More And More/India (Instrumental) (12", p/s)	15

(see also Freeez, Gamer 3, Midi Rain)

PINKERTON'S ('ASSORTED' COLOURS)

65	Decca F 12307	Mirror Mirror/She Don't Care (as Pinkerton's 'Assort' Colours)	8
66	Decca F 12377	Don't Stop Loving Me Baby/Will Ya? (as Pinkerton's 'Assorted' Colours)	15
66	Decca F 12493	Magic Rocking Horse/It Ain't Right (as Pinkerton's Colours)	35
67	Pye 7N 17327	Mum And Dad/On A Street Car (as Pinkerton's Colours)	18
67	Pye 7N 17414	There's Nobody I'd Sooner Love/Look At Me (as Pinkerton's)	40
68	Pye 7N 17574	Kentucky Woman/Behind The Mirror (as Pinkerton's)	18

(see also Flying Machine, Liberators, Tony Newman)

FAYETTE PINKNEY

79	Chopper CHOP E 3	ONE DEGREE (LP)	15

PINKOES

79	Popular POP1	INTO THE RED (EP)	12

PINKY (& FELLAS)

65	Polydor BM 56009	All Cried Out/Back Where I Belong	10

PINKY & PERKY

63	Columbia 33SX 1550	PINKY & PERKY'S MELODYMASTER (LP)	20

PINNACLE

74	Stag HP 125	ASSASSIN (LP, laminated sleeve, black/silver label)	150

DELROY PINNOCK

81	SG 5	Babylon Walls/MIKEY RANKS : I Want To Be	70

GERALDO PINO

05	Soundway SNDWLP005	AFRO SOCO SOUL LIVE (LP, reissue, 1000 only)	20
05	Soundway SNDWLP006	LET'S HAVE A PARTY (LP, reissue, 1000 only)	20

BOB PINODO

78	Bonzark INLS 6128	THE SHOW MASTER (LP)	30

PINPOINT

79	Albion CEL 8	Richmond/Love Substiture (p/s)	80
80	Albion ION 102	Waking Up To Morning/Floods And Trickles (fold-out poster p/s, lyric insert and die-cut Albion sleeve)	10
80	Albion ALB103	THIRD STATE (LP, with free 12")	20

PIO BO

93	Nucleus NUKE 010	The Best Time To Go Swimming: Disco Swim/Funky Swim (12")	50

PIONEERS

66	Rio R 102	Good Nannie/Doreen Girl	40
66	Rio R 106	Too Late/Give Up	50
68	Blue Cat BS 100	Shake It Up/Goodies Are The Greatest	120
68	Blue Cat BS 103	Give It To Me/LEADERS: Someday Someway	120
68	Blue Cat BS 105	Whip Them/Some Having A Bawl	60
68	Blue Cat BS 139	Reggae Beat/Miss Eve	280
68	Caltone TONE 119	I Love No Other Girl/MILTON BOOTHE: I Used To Be A Fool	140
68	Amalgamated AMG 811	Give Me Little Loving/This Is Soul (B-side actually by Lyn Tait & Jets)	25

PIPES OF PAN (1)

MINT VALUE £

68	Amalgamated AMG 814	Long Shot/Dip And Fall Back	30
68	Amalgamated AMG 821	Jackpot/CREATORS: Kimble (B-side actually by Lee Perry)	30
68	Amalgamated AMG 823	No Dope Me Pony/LORD SALMONS: Great - Great In '68	45
68	Amalgamated AMG 826	Tickle Me For Days/VERSATILES: The Time Has Come	85
68	Amalgamated AMG 828	Catch The Beat/SIR GIBB'S ALLSTARS: Jana (B-side actually Immortals' "Jane Anne")	40
68	Amalgamated AMG 830	Sweet Dreams/DAN D JR: Caterpillar Rock	40
68	Pyramid PYR 6062	Easy Come, Easy Go/BEVERLEY'S ALLSTARS: Only A Smile (B-side actually by Lyn Tait & Jets) (some copies on JJ label)	55
69	JJ PYR 6065	Pee Pee Cluck Cluck/BEVERLEY'S ALLSTARS: Exclusively	125
69	Amalgamated AMG 833	Don't You Know/Me Naw Go A Believe	120
69	Amalgamated AMG 835	Mama Look Deh/BLENDERS: Decimal Currency	40
69	Amalgamated AMG 840	Who The Cap Fits/I'm Moving On	60
69	Amalgamated AMG 850	Alli Button/HIPPY BOYS: Death Rides	170
69	Trojan TR 672	Long Shot Kick The Bucket/RICO: Jumping The Gun	25
69	Trojan TR 685	Black Bud/Too Late	25
69	Trojan TR 698	Poor Rameses/BEVERLEY'S ALLSTARS: In Orbit (some in Hot Shot sleeve)	30
70	Trojan TR 7781	Money Day/BEVERLEY ALL STARS: Ska Ba Do	20
70	Trojan TR 7795	I Need Your Sweet Inspiration/Everything Nice	15
71	Summit SUM 8511	Starvation/BEVERLEY'S ALLSTARS: Version	20
72	Summit SUM 8535	Story Book Children/SIDNEY, GEORGE AND JACKIE: Gorgeous, Marvellous	15
74	Trojan TR 7923	Honey Bee/Hot Blooded Man	15
76	Mercury 6198061	Feel The Rhythm Of You and I/Version	8
77	Mercury 6007147	My Good Friend James/Secrets Of You	150
78	Trojan 9043	Riot In A Notting Hill/Ahuma	12
78	Ice GUY 14	My Good Friend James/Secrets Of You (reissue)	150
11	Doctor Bird THB 7007	Easy Come Easy Go/DERRICK MORGAN AND DESMOND DEKKER: Mercy Mercy	40
13	Trojan THB 7026	Mettle/BEVERLY ALL STARS: Hook, Line And Sinker	25
68	Amalgam. AMGLP 2003	GREETINGS FROM THE PIONEERS (LP)	150
70	Trojan TBL 103	LONGSHOT (LP)	45
70	Trojan TBL 139	BATTLE OF THE GIANTS (LP)	35
71	Trojan TRL 24	YEAH! (LP)	15
74	Trojan TRLS 64	FREEDOM FEELING (LP)	15
74	Trojan TRLS 98	I'M GONNA KNOCK ON YOUR DOOR (LP)	18
76	Mercury 9286172	FEEL THE RHYTHM (LP)	35
78	Trojan TRLS 156	PUSHER MAN (LP)	25
79	Trojan TRLS 172	GREATEST HITS (LP)	30

(see also Sir Gibbs, Rebels [Jamaica], Jackey Robinson, Moonboys, Sidney George & Jackie)

PIPES OF PAN (1)

67	Page One POF 038	Monday Morning Rain/Monday Morning Rain (Instrumental Mix)	20

PIPES OF PAN (2)

71	Rolling Stones COC 49100	BRIAN JONES PLAYS WITH THE PIPES OF PAN AT JOUJOUKA (LP, gatefold sleeve with foldout insert; front cover with misprinted title)	100
71	Rolling Stones COC 49100	BRIAN JONES PRESENTS THE PIPES OF PAN AT JOUJOUKA (LP, gatefold sleeve with foldout insert; "Presents" sticker on misprinted cover)	90
71	Rolling Stones COC 49100	BRIAN JONES PRESENTS THE PIPES OF PAN AT JOUJOUKA (LP, gatefold sleeve with foldout insert; corrected title on front cover)	80

(see also Rolling Stones)

PIPETTES

05	Unpopular UNPOP 6	I Like A Boy In Uniform/It Hurts To See You Dance So Well (hand-numbered p/s, insert, 500 only)	25
05	Transgressive TRANS 005	ABC/Judy/Simon Says (white vinyl, p/s, 500 only)	10
05	Total Gaylord TGR 008	Judy/It Hurts To See You Dance So Well/KFC (pink vinyl)	7
06	Memphis Industries MI 071S1	Pull Shapes/Guess Who Ran Off With The Milkman (white vinyl, p/s)	6
06	Memphis Industries MIO 71S1	COLLECTORS BOX (4 x 7", coloured vinyl, HMV exclusive)	25
06	Memphis Industries MII041111	WE ARE THE PIPETTES (LP)	25

(see also Gwenno)

PIPP

70	Decca F 23030	Otaki/Which Way Did She Go	12

PIPS

61	Top Rank JAR 574	Every Beat Of My Heart/Room In Your Heart	45

(see also Gladys Knight & Pips)

PIRATES

64	HMV POP 1250	My Babe/Casting My Spell	40
66	Polydor BM 56712	Shades Of Blue/Can't Understand	30
77	Warner Bros K 17002	Sweet Love On My Mind/You Don't Own Me/Don't Munchen It (p/s)	15
78	Warner Bros K 17113	All In It Together/Dr. Feelgood (p/s)	10

(see also Johnny Kidd & Pirates, [Billy J. Kramer &] Dakotas)

PISCES

71	Trailer LER 2025	PISCES (LP)	30

JAY JAY PISTOLET

08	Chess Club CC0001	We Are Free/Holly (p/s)	12

PISTONS

81	Humdrum ZIT 1	Solitary Reality/Hyper Active (p/s and insert)	70

HARRY PITCH

68	MOR MR 101P	HARMONICA JEWEL BOX (LP)	20

(see also Mr. Bloe)

PITCHSHIFTER

92	Earache MOSH 66	SUBMIT EP (12")	10

Gene PITNEY

MINT VALUE £

GENE PITNEY
SINGLES

Year	Label/Cat	Title	£
61	London HL 9270	(I Wanna) Love My Life Away/I Laughed So Hard I Cried	12
61	HMV POP 933	Every Breath I Take/Mr Moon, Mr Cupid & I	30
61	United Artists POP 952	Town Without Pity/Air Mail Special	10
62	United Artists POP 1018	The Man Who Shot Liberty Valance/Take It Like A Man	10
63	United Artists UP 1021	Mecca/Teardrop By Teardrop	8
64	United Artists UP 1045	That Girl Belongs To Yesterday/Who Needs It?	7
64	United Artists UP 1055	I'm Gonna Find Myself A Girl/Lips Are Redder On You	10
64	United Artists UP 1063	It Hurts To Be In Love/Hawaii	7
64	Stateside SS 358	I'm Gonna Be Strong/Aladdin's Lamp	6
67	Stateside SS 597	(In The) Cold Light Of Day/Flower Girl	8
67	Stateside SS 2060	Something's Gotten Hold Of My Heart/Building Up My Dream World (withdrawn)	20
68	Stateside SS 2131	Yours Until Tomorrow/She's A Heartbreaker	15
68	Stateside SS 2131	Yours Until Tomorrow/She's A Heartbreaker (DJ copy)	30
69	Stateside SS 2142	Maria Elena/The French Horn	6
71	Pye International 7N 25564	Run Run Road Runner/Rain Maker	10
75	Bronze BRO 63	Train Of Thought/I'll Still Be In Love With You (A label demo)	7

EPs

Year	Label/Cat	Title	£
63	HMV 7EG 8832	TOWN WITHOUT PITY	20
64	United Artists UEP 1001	TWENTY FOUR HOURS FROM TULSA	10
64	United Artists UEP 1002	THAT GIRL BELONGS TO YESTERDAY	10
65	Stateside SE 1032	GENE ITALIANO	10
66	Stateside SE 1036	GENE PITNEY SINGS JUST FOR YOU	10

ALBUMS : LPS

Year	Label/Cat	Title	£
62	HMV CLP 1566	THE MANY SIDES OF GENE PITNEY	30
63	United Artists ULP 1028	ONLY LOVE CAN BREAK A HEART (mono)	20
63	United Artists (S)ULP 1028	ONLY LOVE CAN BREAK A HEART (stereo)	30
63	United Artists ULP 1043	GENE PITNEY SINGS JUST FOR YOU	20
64	United Artists ULP 1061	BLUE GENE	20
64	United Artists ULP 1064	GENE PITNEY MEETS THE FAIR YOUNG LADIES OF FOLKLAND	20
64	United Artists ULP 1073	GENE PITNEY'S BIG SIXTEEN	15
65	Stateside SL 10120	I'M GONNA BE STRONG	15
65	Stateside SL 10132	GENE PITNEY'S MORE BIG SIXTEEN (VOL. 2)	15
65	Stateside SL 10147	GEORGE JONES AND GENE PITNEY (with George Jones)	15
65	Stateside SL 10148	LOOKING THRU THE EYES OF LOVE	15
65	Stateside SL 10156	SINGS THE GREAT SONGS OF OUR TIME	15
66	Stateside SL 10173	IT'S COUNTRY TIME AGAIN (with George Jones)	15

(see also Marc Almond & Gene Pitney, George Jones)

TERRY PITTS JAZZ BAND

Year	Label/Cat	Title	£
61	Oriole CB 1621	A Drop Of The Hard Stuff/Show Me The Way To Go Home	6

PIXIES

Year	Label/Cat	Title	£
88	4AD BAD 805	GIGANTIC EP (12", p/s)	12
89	4AD BAD 909	HERE COMES YOUR MAN EP (12", p/s)	15
89	4AD AD 904	Monkey Gone To Heaven/Manta Ray (p/s)	10
89	4AD BAD 904	MONKEY GONE TO HEAVEN EP (12", p/s)	12
89	4AD PIX ONE	DOOLITTLE SAMPLER: Debaser/Wave Of Mutilation/I Bleed/Gouge Away (12", 1-sided, title sleeve, promo only)	15
89	4AD PIX 2	Into The White/Wave Of Mutilation (U.K. Surf) (12", 1-sided, promo only)	10
90	4AD BAD 009	VELOURIA EP (12", p/s)	15
90	4AD AD 0014	Dig For Fire/Velvety (p/s)	8
90	4AD BAD 0014	DIG FOR FIRE EP (12", p/s)	15
90	4AD PIX 3	EXTRACTS FROM BOSSANOVA: Allison/Rock Music/Down To The Well/The Happening (12", 1-sided, promo only)	15
91	4AD BAD 1008	PLANET OF SOUND EP (12", p/s)	10
91	4AD PIX 4	EXTRACTS FROM TROMPE LE MONDE: U-Mass/Letter To Memphis/Subbacultcha (10", same track both sides, promo only)	15
87	4AD MAD 709	COME ON PILGRIM (mini-LP)	25
88	4AD CAD 803	SURFER ROSA (LP, with inner)	50
89	4AD CAD 905	DOOLITTLE (LP, with lyric booklet & postcard, in carrier bag)	50
89	4AD CAD 905	DOOLITTLE (LP, with lyric booklet & postcard)	40
90	4AD CAD 0010	BOSSANOVA (LP, with booklet, inner)	40
91	4AD CAD 1014	TROMPE LE MONDE (LP)	45
97	4AD DADD 7011	DEATH TO THE PIXIES (4-10" LP, box set)	100
02	Cooking Vinyl COOK 234	PIXIES - THE PURPLE TAPE (LP, inner, purple, green or orange vinyl)	45
11	4AD CAD 2406	WAVE OF MUTILATION: THE BEST OF (2-LP, orange vinyl)	20
14	Pixies PM006DLPR	INDIE CINDY (2x12", free 7" and download card)	18

(see also Breeders, Frank Black)

PIXIES THREE

Year	Label/Cat	Title	£
63	Mercury AMT 1214	Birthday Party/Our Love	25

PLACEBO

Year	Label/Cat	Title	£
95	Fierce Panda NING 13	Bruise Pristine/SOUP: M.E.L.T.D.O.W.N. (foldover p/s, 1500 only)	35
96	Deceptive BLUFF 024	Come Home/Drowning By Numbers (p/s)	12
96	Elevator BLUFF 001	36 degrees/Dark globe (p/s)	10
96	Hut FLOOR 3	Teenage Angst/Hug Bubble/Been Smoking Too Long (part 1 0f 2, p/s)	6
96	Hut FLOOR 4	Nancy Boy (Sex Mix)/Slackerbitch (p/s)	6
97	Hut FLOOR 5	Bruise Pristine/(One Punch Remix) (p/s)	10
98	Elevator FLOORLH 6	Pure Morning/Leeloo (jukebox issue)	8
98	Elevator FLOORLH 7	You Don't Care About Us/20th Century Boy (jukebox issue)	12

PLAGUE (1)

MINT VALUE £

99	Hut FLOOR TP 10	Without You I'm Nothing (with David Bowie) (UNKLE Remix)/(Flexirol Mix)/(Brothers In Rhythm Club Mix) (12" promo, 500 only, stickered die-cut sleeve)	15
03	Virgin 7432547480743	Special Needs/English Summer Rain (p/s)	10
04	Virgin 724381618776	Twenty Years/Detox 5	10
96	Hut LPFLOORY 2	PLACEBO (LP, gatefold, inner)	100
98	Elevator FLOORLP 8	WITHOUT YOU I'M NOTHING (LP, gatefold)	100
00	Elevator FLOORLP 13	BLACK MARKET MUSIC (LP, gatefold)	60
03	Elevator FLOORLP 17	SLEEPING WITH GHOSTS (LP, triple gatefold sleeve)	60
10	Elevator FLOORLP 17	COVERS (LP, reissue, 1000 only)	100
04	Elevator FLOORLP 23	ONCE MORE WITH FEELING (2-LP)	80
06	Elevator LPFLOOR 26	MEDS (LP, gatefold)	50
09	Dreambrother BATTLE01BS	BATTLE FOR THE SUN (2-LP, 2-DVD box set)	40

PLAGUE (1)

68	Decca F 12730	Looking For The Sun/Here Today, Gone Tomorrow	250
11	Decca F 12730	Looking For The Sun/Here Today, Gone Tomorrow (reissue)	8

PLAGUE (2)

79	Psycho P2615	In Love/Wimpey Bar Song (silk screened fold-out cover)	50
79	Psycho P 2615	In Love/Wimpey Bar Song (2nd pressing, printed sleeve, pink vinyl)	25
80	Evolution EV 4	Out With Me All Night/Er/Don't Want To Be Like Jimmy	50

PLAID

92	GPR GENP(X) 7	Scoobs In Columbia (remixes) (12", custom sleeve)	30
94	Clear CLR 409	ANDROID (12" EP, p/s, clear vinyl)	20
94	Clear CLR 409	ANDROID (12" EP, p/s, black vinyl)	15
95	Rumble RUMBLE 01	MIND OVER RHYTHM MEET THE MEN FROM PLAID (3 x 10" in p/s)	15
92	Black Dog Prods. LP 1	MBUKI MVUKI (LP)	80
97	Warp WARPLP54	NOT FOR THREES (2-LP)	25
99	Warp WARPLP63	REST PROOF CLOCKWORK (2-LP, gatefold)	40
00	Warp WARPLP74	TRAINER (3-LP, with poster)	30
01	Warp WARPLP84	DOUBLE FIGURE (2-LP)	30
03	Warp WARPLP114	SPOKES (LP)	20

(see also Black Dog)

PLAINSONG

72	Elektra K 12976	Even The Guiding Light/Yoko Man/Call The Tune	7
72	Elektra K 42120	IN SEARCH OF AMELIA EARHART (LP, gatefold sleeve with lyric insert)	25
73	Elektra K 42136	PLAINSONG II (LP, white label, promo only)	120

(see also Andy Roberts, Ian Matthews)

PLAN B

06	679 679L134	WHO NEEDS ACTION WHEN YOU GOT WORDS (2-LP)	50
10	679 5051865899303	THE DEFAMATION OF STRICKLAND BANKS (2-LP)	150

PLANET EARTH

78	Pye NSPL 18556	PLANET EARTH (LP)	25

PLANET GONG

77	Affinity AF 5101	Opium For The People/Poet For Sale (p/s)	8
78	Charly CYX 202	Opium For The People/Stoned Innocent Frankenstein (10", p/s)	18
78	Charly CRM 2000	FLOATING ANARCHY - LIVE 1977 (LP)	18

(see also Daevid Allen, Gong)

PLANETARY ASSAULT SYSTEMS

97	Peacefrog PF 063	ELECTRIC FUNK MACHINE (2-LP)	20
97	Peacefrog PF 079	THE DRONE SECTOR (2-LP)	20

PLANET P PROJECT

83	Geffen A3205	Why Me/Only You And Me (p/s)	6
85	MCA MCSP311	PINK WORLD (2LP, gatefold sleeve)	18

(see also Tony Carey, Rainbow)

PLANETS (1)

60	Palette PG 9008	Like Party/Ippy Yippy Beatnik (only this value if in p/s)	25
60	Palette PG 9008	Like Party/Ippy Yippy Beatnik (no p/s)	10

PLANETS (2)

60	HMV POP 818	Chunky/Screwball	20
61	HMV POP 832	Jam Roll/Delaney's Theme	25
61	HMV POP 895	Jungle Street/The Grasshopper	25

PLANETS (3)

73	Bullet BU 528	People Get Funny/DOCBIRD ALL STARS : Funny Version	15

ROBERT PLANT

67	CBS 202656	Our Song/Laughin' Cryin' Laughin' ('A' label demo)	300
67	CBS 202656	Our Song/Laughin', Cryin', Laughin'	350
67	CBS 202858	Long Time Coming/I've Got A Secret ('A' label demo)	250
67	CBS 202858	Long Time Coming/I've Got A Secret	300
82	Swan Song SSK 19429T	Burning Down One Side/Far Post (12", p/s)	10
82	Swan Song SAM154	PICTURES AT ELEVEN (LP, promo interview disc with cue sheet)	20
82	Es Paranza SAM 169	THE PRINCIPLE OF MOVEMENTS (LP, promo interview disc with cue sheet)	20
88	Es Paranza PR 2244	NON STOP GO! (LP, two disc set interview promo for NOW AND ZEN album)	15
90	Es Paranza WX 339X	MANIC NIRVANA (LP, gatefold, numbered, picture inner bag)	18
93	Fontana 514 867-1	FATE OF NATIONS (LP, inner)	100
02	Mercury 063094-1	DREAMLAND (2-LP, numbered)	100
05	Sanctuary SANLP 256	MIGHTY REARRANGER (LP)	100
10	Decca/Universal 2748338	BAND OF JOY (2-LP, second side of 2nd LP etched)	25

(see also Led Zeppelin, Listen, Jimmy Page, Robert Plant & The Strange Sensation, Page & Plant, Honeydrippers)

PLASMATICS

80	Stiff BUY 76	Butcher Baby/Tight Black Pants (black vinyl, p/s)	8
80	Stiff SEEZ 24	NEW HOPE FOR THE WRETCHED (LP, splatter vinyl)	20

PLASTIC BERTRAND

MINT VALUE £

PLASTIC BERTRAND
78 Sire 9103258   AN 1 (LP, gatefold) 20

PLASTIC GANGSTERS
83 Secret SHH 144   Plastic Gangster/Sretsgnag Citsalp (7", 12", no p/s on 12" stamped p/s on 7", unissued, 10 DJ copies only) 250
11 Secret SHH 144   Plastic Gangster (I Could Be So Good For You)/Sretsgnag Citsalp (reissue, on red, white or blue vinyl) 7

(see also 4 Skins)

PLASTIC PENNY
68 Page One POF 062   Nobody Knows It/Just Happy To Be With You 10
68 Page One POF 079   Your Way To Tell Me Go/Baby You're Not To Blame 20
69 Page One POF 107   Hound Dog/Currency 20
69 Page One POF 146   She Does/Genevieve 20
68 Page One POL(S) 005   TWO SIDES OF THE PENNY (LP, laminated front sleeve, flipbacks) 100
69 Page One POLS 014   CURRENCY (LP, laminated front sleeve, flipbacks) 150
70 Page One POLS 611   HEADS YOU WIN, TAILS I LOSE (LP) 75

(see also Universals, Circles, Mick Grabham)

PLASTIC PEOPLE
79 Rising Son RS1   Demolition/XTRAVERTS: Police State (multi coloured vinyl) 60

PLASTIC SANDWICHES
81 Ellie Jay EJSP 9746   Bayonets And Colours/Parties At War (p/s is two separate 7" pieces of paper) 20

PLASTICLAND
84 Bam Caruso KIRI 034   PLASTICLAND (LP) 15

PLASTICS
79 Rough Trade RT 030   Robot/Copy 8

PLASTIKMAN
94 Nova Mute L NO MU 37   MUSIK (2-LP, with bonus 1-sided etched 12") 20
95 Nova Mute NOMU22LP   SHEET ONE (2-LP) 20
98 Nova Mute NOMU 65LP   CONSUMED (LP as 3 x 12") 50
03 Nova Mute NOMULP 100LP   CLOSER (3-LP) 80
11 M_nus MINUS 100 Analog   ARKIVES 1993 - 2010 (Box set, 6 x 12") 100

PLATFORM SIX
65 Piccadilly 7N 35255   Money Will Not Mean A Thing/Girl Down Town 70

EDDIE PLATT
58 Columbia DB 4101   Tequila/Pop Corn 25

PLATTERS

78s
59 Mercury AMT 1039   Enchanted/The Sound And The Fury 20
59 Mercury AMT 1053   Remember When/Love Of A Lifetime (featuring Tony Williams) 30
60 Mercury AMT 1081   Harbour Lights/(By The) Sleepy Lagoon 40

SINGLES
56 Mercury MT 117   The Great Pretender/Only You (And You Alone) (export issue) 40
58 Mercury 7MT 197   Helpless/Indiff'rent 30
58 Mercury 7MT 205   Don't Let Go/Are You Sincere? 30
58 Mercury 7MT 214   Twilight Time/Out Of My Mind 10
58 Mercury 7MT 227   You're Making A Mistake (featuring Tony Williams)/My Old Flame 20
58 Mercury AMT 1001   I Wish/It's Raining Outside 18
59 Mercury AMT 1039   Enchanted/The Sound And The Fury 6
59 Mercury AMT 1053   Remember When/Love Of A Lifetime (featuring Tony Williams) 10
59 Mercury AMT 1066   My Blue Heaven/Wish It Were Me 6
60 Mercury AMT 1081   Harbour Lights/(By The) Sleepy Lagoon 7
61 Mercury AMT 1128   If I Didn't Care/True Lover 7
62 Ember JBS 701   Only You/Tell The World 80
66 Stateside SS 511   I Love You 1000 Times/Hear No Evil, Speak No Evil, See No Evil 25
66 Stateside SS 568   I'll Be Home/(You've Got) The Magic Touch 12
67 Stateside SS 2007   With This Ring/If I Had A Love 25
67 Stateside SS 2042   Washed Ashore (On A Lonely Island In The Sea)/What Name Shall I Give You My Love 25
67 Stateside SS 2042   Washed Ashore (On A Lonely Island In The Sea)/What Name Shall I Give You My Love (DJ copy) 60
67 Stateside SS 2067   Sweet Sweet Lovin'/Sonata 20
67 Stateside SS 2067   Sweet Sweet Lovin'/Sonata (DJ copy) 60
69 Stateside SS 2150   With This Ring/If I Had A Love (reissue) 8
71 Pye Intl. 7N 25559   Sweet Sweet Lovin'/Going Back To Detroit 15
71 Pye Intl. 7N 25569   With This Ring/I Washed Ashore (On A Lonely Island In The Sea) 8
87 Kent 6T3   SAMMY AMBROSE: Welcome To Dreamsville/PLATTERS: Not My Girl 25

EPs
56 Mercury MEP 9504   THE FABULOUS PLATTERS 10
57 Mercury MEP 9514   THE FABULOUS PLATTERS VOL. II 10
57 Mercury MEP 9524   THE FABULOUS PLATTERS VOL. III 12
58 Mercury MEP 9526   THE FLYING PLATTERS VOL. I 15
58 Mercury MEP 9528   THE FLYING PLATTERS VOL. II 15
58 Mercury MEP 9537   THE PLATTERS 15
59 Mercury ZEP 10000   PICK OF THE PLATTERS NO. 1 10
59 Mercury ZEP 10008   PICK OF THE PLATTERS NO. 2 10
59 Mercury ZEP 10025   PICK OF THE PLATTERS NO. 3 10
59 Mercury ZEP 10031   PICK OF THE PLATTERS NO. 4 10
59 Mercury ZEP 10042   PICK OF THE PLATTERS NO. 5 10
60 Mercury ZEP 10056   PICK OF THE PLATTERS NO. 6 10
60 Mercury ZEP 10070   PICK OF THE PLATTERS NO. 7 10
61 Mercury ZEP 10112   HARBOUR LIGHTS 10

PLAY

MINT VALUE £

62	Mercury ZEP 10126	THE PLATTERS ON A PLATTER	15

ALBUMS : LPS

57	Mercury MPL 6504	THE PLATTERS	35
57	Mercury MPL 6511	THE PLATTERS VOL. 2	30
58	Mercury MPL 6528	THE FLYING PLATTERS	30
58	Parlophone PMD 1058	THE PLATTERS (10")	200
59	Mercury MMC 14009	AROUND THE WORLD WITH THE FLYING PLATTERS	15
59	Mercury MMC 14010	THE PLATTERS ON PARADE	15
59	Mercury MMC 14014	REMEMBER WHEN?	15
60	Mercury MMC 14045	REFLECTIONS	15
61	Mercury MMC 14072	LIFE IS JUST A BOWL OF CHERRIES	15
67	Stateside S(S)L 10208	GOING BACK TO DETROIT	15

(see also Buck Ram's Ramrocks, Linda Hayes)

PLAY

82	Survival SUR 12 008	CHASING THE SUN EP (12", p/s)	10
84	Survival SUR 12 022	IN MY MIND EP (12", p/s)	10
85	Survival SUR B1	RED MOVIES (LP)	20

PLAY BOYS (JAMAICA)

71	Tropical AL 007	Change Change/TROPICAL ALL STARS: Version 2	8

PLAYBOYS (U.S.)

58	London HLU 8681	Over The Weekend/Double Talk	40

PLAYBOYS (U.S.)

69	Capitol CL 15621	Let's Get Back To Rock And Roll/Homemade Cookin'	6

(see also Rad Bryan)

PLAY DEAD

81	Fresh FRESH 29	Poison Takes A Hold/Introduction (p/s)	7
81	Fresh FRESH 38	T.V. Eye/Final Epitaph (p/s)	7

PLAYERS

63	Oriole CB 1861	Mockingbird/Bizet As It May	25

PLAYGIRLS (JAMAICA)

65	Black Swan WI 456	Looks Are Deceiving/BABA BROOKS: Dreadnaught	65

PLAYGIRLS (U.S.)

59	RCA RCA 1133	Hey Sport/Young Love Swings The World	15

PLAYGROUND

67	MGM MGM 1351	At The Zoo/Yellow Balloon	20
69	NEMS 56-4019	I Could Be So Good/The Girl Behind The Smile	10
69	NEMS 56-4442	Things I Do For You/Lazy Days	10

PLAYGROUP

82	On U Sound BRED 28	EPIC SOUND BATTLES CHAPTER ONE (LP)	10

PLAYING AT TRAINS

87	Idea IDT 001	A World Without Love/Just Around The Mountain/Playing At Trains/A Japanese Intervention (12", p/s)	85
89	Octopus OCT 5	Walk On Water/Where The Buffalo Roam (p/s)	200

(see also Waving At Trains)

PLAYMATES

57	Columbia DB 3941	Pretty Woman/Barefoot Girl	10
57	Columbia DB 4033	Island Girl/Darling, It's Wonderful	10
58	Columbia DB 4084	Jo-Ann/You Can't Stop Me From Dreaming	10
58	Columbia DB 4127	Let's Be Lovers/Give Me Another Chance	10
58	Columbia DB 4224	Beep Beep/Your Love	10
60	Columbia DB 4551	Wait For Me/Eyes Of An Angel	7
58	Columbia SEG 7864	AT PLAY WITH THE PLAYMATES (EP)	10
59	Columbia SEG 7949	PARTY PLAYMATES NO. 1 (EP)	10
59	Columbia SEG 7966	PARTY PLAYMATES NO. 2 (EP)	10

PLAYMATES (IRELAND)

70	Emerald MD 1150	Don't Fight It/Jodi	10

PLAYN JANE

84	A&M JAYN13	FRIDAY THE 13TH (LIVE AT THE MARQUEE) (LP)	15

PLAYTHINGS

70	Pye 7N 45212	Stop What You're Doing To Me/Sad (light blue label)	6
70	Pye 7N 45212	Stop What You're Doing To Me/Sad Songs	10

BOBBY PLEASE

57	London HLB 8507	Your Driver's Licence, Please/Heartache Street (unissued, 2x 1-sided demos - price is for BOTH demos together)	100
57	London HLB 8507	Your Driver's Licence, Please/Heartache Street (78)	40

PLEASERS

77	Solid Gold SGR 104	You Know What I'm Thinking Girl/Hello Little Girl	8
77	Arista ARIST 152	You Keep Tellin' Lies/I'm In Love/Who Are You (p/s, blue label)	10
78	Arista ARIST 180	The Kids Are Alright/Stay With Me (p/s)	12

PLEASURE BEACH

90s	Acid Jazz AJX 124S	Rollercoaster/Smells Like Teen Spirit (p/s)	6

PLEASURE CELL

86	(No label) ANG 1	New Age/Common Ground	25

PLEASURE CREW

87	Factory FAC 169	So Good/So Good (white labels only)	7

PLEASURE FAIR

68	Uni UN 500	Morning Glory Blues/Fade Out Fade In	12
67	Uni UNL(S) 100	PLEASURE FAIR (LP)	25

(see also Bread)

PLEASURE GARDEN

MINT VALUE £

PLEASURE GARDEN
- 68 Sound For Industry SFI 31H/32H Permissive Paradise/EMPEROR ROSKO & JONATHAN KING: Young London (flexidisc, art sleeve with small booklet) 100

(see also Iveys)

PLEASURES
- 65 Sue WI 357 Music City/If I Had A Little Money 45

PLEBS
- 64 Decca F 12006 Bad Blood/Babe I'm Gonna Leave You 80
- 60s Oak THE PLEBS (LP, 1-sided, private pressing) 1000

PLEIADIANS
- 95 Symbiosis SYB009 Pleiadians/Baording Pass To Balangan (12") 18
- 97 Dragonfly BFLL 24 IDENTIFIED FLYING OBJECT (2-LP) 50

PLEXUS
- 78 Look LKLP 6175 PLEXUS (LP) 65
- 79 Hill & Dale HD004 LIFE UP THE CREEK (LP) 55

PLINTH
- 13 Clay Pipe 08 MUSIC FOR SMALLS LIGHTHOUSE (LP, numbered, 500 only) 15
- 14 Kit (No cat no) WINTERSONGS (LP, lino cut sleeve, vinyl repressing, 200 only) 15

PLONE
- 99 Warp WARPLP64 FOR BEGINNER PIANO (LP) 20

PLUGS
- 79 Cathedral CATH 1 Too Late/UFO/Sally (gatefold p/s) 20
- 80 Pop 1 CRACKIN' UP EP 12
- 81 Plugpop GRGL 782 Indoor Shopping Centre/High Society 10

JEAN PLUM
- 76 London HLU 10514 Look At The Boy/Back At You 10

JON PLUM
- 69 SNB 55-3971 Alice/Sunshine 20
- 69 SNB 55-4317 You Keep Changing Your Mind/An Apple Falls 15

PLUM & YOUTH
- 80s Checkmount CHK 1 I Got You Babe/Got To Be Moving On (p/s, withdrawn) 15

(see also Cozy Powell, Rainbow, Big Bertha)

PLUMMERS
- 64 Blue Beat BB 260 Johnny/Little Stars (actually by Plamers) 22

PLUMMET AIRLINES
- 76 Stiff BUY 8 Silver Shirt/This Is The World (p/s, push-out centre) 8

PLUNDER
- 08 Lolarox ROX 1 Hellion Castle/I Spy On Love (hand-folded, p/s, booklet, 200 only) 6

PLUS
- 70 Probe SPB 1009 SEVEN DEADLY SINS (LP, laminated front sleeve, flipbacks) 120

PLUTO
- 71 Dawn DNS 1017 Rag A Bone Joe/Stealing My Thunder 20
- 72 Dawn DNS 1026 I Really Want It/Something That You Loved 30
- 71 Dawn DNLS 3030 PLUTO (LP, laminated sleeve, lilac label) 250
- 89 See For Miles SEE 265 PLUTO...PLUS (LP, reissue) 25

(see also Dry Ice, Foundations)

PLUTOS PEOPLE
- 78 Jay Lee JL 6 Little Lady/It's Up To You (no p/s) 15

PNEUMONIA (1)
- 68 Oak RGJ 625 I Can See Your Face 500

PNEUMONIA (2)
- 79 Plastic PLAS 001 Exhibition/Coming Attack/U.K. DECAY: U.K. Decay/Carcrash (folded p/s) 25

P'O
- 83 Court COURT 1 WHILST CLIMBING THIEVES VIE FOR ATTENTION (LP) 50

(see also Wire, Cupol, Dome, Gilbert & Lewis, Bruce Gilbert, A.C. Marias)

POCKETS
- 77 CBS 5780 Come Go With Me/Pt. 2 8

POEME ELECTRONIQUE
- 82 Carrere CAR 228 The Echoes Fade/V.O.I.C.E. (p/s) 200

POEMSO
- 81 Polka DOT 1 ACHIEVING UNITY (EP, initially with booklet) 10

(see also Strawberry Switchblade)

POET & ONE MAN BAND
- 69 Verve Forecast SVLP 6012 THE POET AND THE ONE MAN BAND (LP, laminated front sleeve, flipbacks) 100

(see also Tony Colton, Nicky Hopkins, Heads Hands & Feet)

POETS
- 64 Decca F 11995 Now We're Thru/There Are Some 20
- 65 Decca F 12074 That's The Way It's Got To Be/I'll Cry With The Moon 200
- 65 Decca F 12195 I Am So Blue/I Love Her Still 60
- 65 Immediate IM 006 Call Again/Some Things I Can't Forget 100
- 66 Immediate IM 024 Baby Don't You Do It/I'll Come Home 100
- 67 Decca F 12569 Wooden Spoon/In Your Tower 450
- 71 Strike Cola SC 1 Heyla Hola/Fun Buggy 50
- 88 Bam Caruso OPRA 088 I Love Her Still/GHOST: Time Is My Enemy (company sleeve, promo only) 12

(see also Pathfinders, [White] Trash, Blue)

POETS (IRELAND)
- 68 Pye 7N 17668 Locked In A Room/Alone Am I 240
- 68 Target 7N 17668 Locked In A Room/Alone Am I (Irish issue, different label) 240

POGUE MAHONE
- 84 Pogue Mahone PM 1 Dark Streets Of London/The Band Played Waltzing Mathilda 10
- 84 Pogue Mahone PM 1 Dark Streets Of London/The Band Played Waltzing Mathilda (white label tour copy with 50

POGUES

MINT VALUE £

'harp' stamp, 237 only)..

(see also Pogues)
POGUES
84	Stiff BUY DJ 212	The Irish Rover/DUBLINERS: Rare Old Mountain Dew (promo, dirty verse taken out for airplay)..	15
84	Stiff BUY 207	Dark Streets Of London/The Band Played Waltzing Mathilda (reissue of Pogue Mahone)	10
84	Stiff BUY 212	Boys From The County Hell/Repeal Of The Licensing Laws (green-tinted p/s)...........	10
84	Stiff BUY 212	Boys From The County Hell/Repeal Of The Licensing Laws (A-label promos in blue-tinted p/s)...	15
84	Stiff BUY 207/BUY 212	Dark Streets Of London/The Band Played Waltzing Mathilda//Boys From The County Hell/Repeal Of The Licensing Laws (shrinkwrapped double pack)...........................	20
85	Stiff BUY220	A Pair Of Brown Eyes/Whiskey You're The Devil (sealed and stickered with free copy of Boys From The County Hell 7")..	30
85	Stiff DBUY 220	A Pair Of Brown Eyes/Whiskey You're The Devil (picture disc).............................	15
85	Stiff BUYIT 220	A Pair Of Brown Eyes/Whiskey You're The Devil/Muirshin Durkin (12", p/s)..........	15
85	Stiff BUY 212/BUY 220	Boys From The County Hell/Repeal Of The Licensing Laws//A Pair Of Brown Eyes/ Whiskey You're The Devil (shrinkwrapped double pack)......................................	15
85	Stiff BUY 224	Sally MacLennane/Wild Rover (wraparound poster p/s, green vinyl).......................	10
85	Stiff BUY 224	Sally MacLennane/Wild Rover (wraparound poster p/s)..	7
85	Stiff BUY 224	Sally MacLennane/Wild Rover (standard p/s)..	6
85	Stiff BUYIT 229	Dirty Old Town/A Pistol For Paddy Garcia/The Parting Glass (12", with poster & stickered p/s)...	20
85	Stiff BUYIT 229	Dirty Old Town/A Pistol For Paddy Garcia/The Parting Glass (12", without poster & stickered p/s)..	15
85	Stiff MAIL 3	Dirty Old Town (live)/Sally MacLennane (live)/(interview) (12", mail-order)............	12
87	Stiff/Hell BLOOD 1	The Good, The Bad & The Ugly/Rake At The Gates Of Hell (unreleased)................	0
87	Stiff/Hell BLOODY 1	The Good, The Bad & The Ugly/Rake At The Gates Of Hell (12", unreleased)..........	0
85	Stiff SEEZ 58	RUM SODOMY & THE LASH (LP)..	15

(see also Pogue Mahone, Nips, Nipple Erectors, Radiators From Space, Shane MacGowan & the Popes)

POINDEXTER BROTHERS
66	Verve VS 550	(Git Your) Backfield In Motion/(Grandma) Give That Girl Some Slack...................	20

POINT
80	Pendulum PT 001	My Mind/Mr. Benson..	8
81	Pendulum PT 002	Metropolis/After Seven..	8

POINT BLANK
96	Phono PHONO 8	A Game Of Two Halves/Rog (12")...	25

POINT BLANK MCS
92	Kold Sweat KS120	Planting Semtex/Revenge Of The Ghetto Child (12")...	12

POINTED STICKS
79	Stiff BUY 59	Out Of Luck/What Do You Want Me To Do/Somebody's Mom ("Plug Copy on label, p/s)	10
79	Stiff BUY 59	Out Of Luck/What Do You Want Me To Do/Somebody's Mom (p/s)........................	9
79	Stiff BUY 59	Out Of Luck/What Do You Want Me To Do/Somebody's Mom (12", p/s).................	10

POINTS PROVEN
92	Payday PD002	Pass The Mic/Noisy Music Part 2/Funky Rhymes, Funky Style (EP).......................	12

POISON GIRLS
79	Small Wonder WEENY 4	HEX (12" EP, with lyric insert)..	18
80	Crass 421984/9	HEX (12", reissue)..	10
80	Crass/Xntrix 421984/1	Persons Unknown/CRASS: Bloody Revolutions (folded 21" x 14" poster p/s).........	20
81	Crass 421984/10	Pretty Polly/Bully Boys (live) (square red or clear flexidisc free with In The City fanzine, with magazine)...	10
80	Crass 421984/2	CHAPPAQUIDICK (LP, thin stapled gatefold sleeve with free flexidisc "Statement" [421984/7])...	30
81	XENTRIX XN2003	TOTAL EXPOSURE (LP, clear or black vinyl with outer poly bag)..........................	20
81	XENTRIX XN2006	WHERE'S THE PLEASURE? (LP, lyric insert)...	20
84	XENTRIX RM 101	7 YEAR SCRATCH (2-LP)...	20
85	XENTRIX XN 2208	SONGS OF PRAISE (LP)..	15

(see also Crass, Fatal Microbes/Poison Girls)

POISON IDEA
89	In Your Face FACE 06	IAN MACKAYE (EP)...	15
91	Vinyl Solution VS 29	Plastic Bomb/We Got The Beat/Harder They Come/Lawdy Miss Clawdy (double pack, p/ s)...	8
91	Vinyl Solution VS325	Punish Me/Mario The Cop (p/s, purple vinyl)..	8
93	Dirtier Promotions 7DPROMS 11	Feel The Darkness (Remix)/Feel The Darkness (Remix) (foldover p/s in poly bag, same track both sides free with Fear & Loathing fanzine)...	8
90	Vinyl Solution SOL 025	FEEL THE DARNESS (LP, inner)...	15
92	Vinyl Solution SOL 033	BLANK BLACKOUT VACANT (LP, inner, poster and free 7" [FART 4]).................	20

POISONED ELECTRIC HEAD
89	Dead Fly ACAD 002	Cap Of Flies/Trickeroo (p/s)...	10

POISON IVY
64	Granta GR 7EP 1011	CLINGING MEMORIES (EP)..	100

POLECATS
81	Nervous NER 001	Rockabilly Guy/Chicken Shack (p/s)...	6

POLES
88	Warm WARM 1	Letters To Send/Grow Old..	8

ROLO POLEY
69	Jackpot JP 704	Zapatoo The Tiger/Music House (both sides actually by Lester Sterling)................	45

POLICE
77	Illegal IL 001	Fall Out/Nothing Achieving (black & white p/s, red & black label, various designs)........	25
78	A&M AMS 7348	Roxanne/Peanuts (2.52) ('telephone' p/s, typed matrix no., 'All Rights ...' on top half of label)...	15
78	A&M AMS 7348	Roxanne/Peanuts (12", 'telephone' p/s)...	15
78	A&M AMS 7381	Can't Stand Losing You/Dead End Job (glossy p/s, original issue, label credited to 'Police', blue vinyl)..	10

POLIPHONY

MINT VALUE £

78	A&M AMS 7381	Can't Stand Losing You/Dead End Job (glossy p/s, original issue, label credited to 'Police', mid-blue vinyl)	7
79	A&M AMS 7348	Roxanne/Peanuts (3.54) (reissue, 'group' p/s, handwritten matrix number, blue vinyl)	6
79	A&M AMS 7348	Roxanne/Peanuts (2.52) (reissue, 'group' p/s, typed matrix number, blue)	6
79	A&M AMSP 7348	Roxanne/Peanuts (12", reissue, 'group' p/s)	10
79	A&M AMS 7381	Can't Stand Losing You/Dead End Job (reissue, label credited to 'The Police'; dark blue or light blue vinyl)	10
79	A&M AMS 7381	Can't Stand Losing You/Dead End Job (p/s, reissue, red, yellow, green or white vinyl)	10
79	A&M AMS 7381	Can't Stand Losing You/Dead End Job (p/s, misspressed B-side, plays "No Time This Time")	20
79	AMSP 7474	Message In A Bottle (Test pressing of unreleased 12")	700
79	Illegal IL 001	Fall Out/Nothing Achieving (reissue, various label designs, purple/blue p/s)	15
79	Illegal IL 001	Fall Out/Nothing Achieving (reissue, various label designs, black & orange p/s)	30
80	A&M AMPP 6001	POLICE PACK (6 x 7" printed foldout PVC pack [AMS 7348, 7381, 7402, 7474 & 7494] & "The Bed's Too Big Without You"/"Truth Hits Everybody" [AMPP 6001/E]; on blue vinyl with 6 inserts)	25
80	A&M SAMP 5	SIX-TRACK RADIO SAMPLER (custom p/s, promo radio sampler)	15
80	A&M AMS 7564	Don't Stand So Close To Me/Friends (poster p/s)	7
81	A&M AMS 8194	Spirits (In The Material World)/Low Life (poster p/s, with badge)	8
83	A&M AM 117/AM 01	Every Breath You Take/Murder By Numbers//Truth Hits Everybody/ Man In A Suitcase (double pack, gatefold p/s)	30
95	A&M 581 036 7	Can't Stand Losing You (live in Boston)/Roxanne (Live In Boston) (Police badge picture disc)	15
78	A&M AMLH 68502	OUTLANDOS D'AMOUR (LP, blue vinyl)	25
79	A&M AMLH 64792	REGGATTA DE BLANC (LP)	15
80	A&M AMLH 64831	ZENYATTA MONDATTA (LP)	15
81	A&M AMLK 63730	GHOST IN THE MACHINE (LP)	15
83	A&M AMLX 63735	SYNCHRONICITY (LP)	15

(see also Sting, Radio Actors, Zoot Money's Big Roll Band, Last Exit, Newcastle Big Band, Eberhard Schoener)

POLIPHONY
73	Zella JHLPS 136	POLIPHONY (LP, private pressing)	150

POLITICIANS (1)
72	Hot Wax HWX 114	Love Machine/Free Your Mind	15
72	Hot Wax SHW 5007	THE POLITICIANS FEATURING MCKINLEY JACKSON (LP)	80

POLITICIANS (2)
79	Political PEP 1	EP: Street Signs/Time Is Tight/Go Away/Fly With Me (p/s, 500 only)	150

FRANK POLK
65	Capitol CL 15389	Trying To Keep Up With The Joneses/Welcome Home, Baby	60
65	Capitol CL 15389	Trying To Keep Up With The Joneses/Welcome Home, Baby (DJ copy)	125

RAY POLLARD
65	United Artists UP 1111	The Drifter/Let Him Go (And Let Me Love You)	500
65	United Artists UP 1111	The Drifter/Let Him Go (And Let Me Love You) (DJ Copy)	600
66	United Artists UP 1133	It's A Sad Thing/All The Things You Are	100
66	United Artists UP 1133	It's A Sad Thing/All The Things You Are (DJ Copy)	200

(see also Wanderers)

POLLCATS
90	Community Charge AXT 1	Poll Tax Blues/Poll Tax Blues (same track both sides, p/s)	10

(see also Steve Marriott)

POLYGON WINDOW
93	Warp WARP 33	QUOTH (12" EP, clear vinyl)	18
92	Warp WARP LP 7	SURFING ON SINE WAVES (2-LP)	45
92	Warp WARP LP 7LTD	SURFING ON SINE WAVES (LP, clear vinyl)	75

(see also Aphex Twin)

POLYPHEMUS
93	BB 212	Masses Of Tiny Dots/Fire Breathing Annabella (p/s)	10
95	Acme AC 8010LP	SCRAPBOOK OF MADNESS (LP, reissue with insert, 500 only)	18
95	Acme AC 8016LP	STONEHOUSE (LP, gatefold sleeve, 700 only)	18

POLYPHONIC SPREE
02	679 679LO14	ORCHESTRAL: Light And Day/Soldier Girl (p/s, 500 only)	12
02	Good Records 679L011TLP	BEGINNING STAGES OF (2-LP)	40

POMPHEY
72	Green Door GD 4029	Jamaica Skank/JOHNNY MOORE: Bing Comes To Town	10

PONI-TAILS
58	HMV POP 516	Born Too Late/Come On Joey, Dance With Me (as Pony-Tails)	8
58	HMV POP 558	Close Friends/Seven Minutes In Heaven	10
59	HMV POP 596	Early To Bed/Father Time	12
59	HMV POP 644	Moody/Oom Pah Polka	15
59	HMV POP 663	I'll Be Seeing You/I'll Keep Tryin'	15
58	HMV 7EG 8427	THE PONI-TAILS (EP)	100

JEAN-LUC PONTY
69	Liberty LBL/LBS 83262	ELECTRIC CONNECTION (LP)	20
70	Liberty LBL/LBS 83375	KING KONG (LP)	20

(see also Frank Zappa)

PONY
73	Pye 7N 25663	It's Gonna Be So Easy/Til I Met You	25

POOGY
74	EMI EMI 2136	She Looked Me In The Eye (I Gave Her My Life)/Morris And His Turtle	8

POOH
72	CBS 7930	I'll Close The Door Behind Me/The Suitcase	20

POOH STICKS
88	Fierce FRIGHT 011	On Tape (p/s, 1-sided, etched)	40
88	Fierce FRIGHT 011	On Tape (p/s, 1-sided, with unetched B-side)	35

Brian POOLE

MINT VALUE £

88	Fierce FRIGHT 021	1-2-3 Red Light (p/s, 1-sided)	20
88	Fierce FRIGHT 023	Heartbreak (1-sided, etched B-side, hand-coloured promo p/s, with insert)	40
88	Fierce FRIGHT 021-025	FIERCE BOX SET (5 x 1-sided etched discs, hand-coloured labels, with insert)	50
88	Fierce FRIGHT 028	HEROES AND VILLAINS (LP, with inner)	18
89	Fierce FRIGHT 034	Dying For It (p/s, sold at U.L.U. gig, 300 only, signed)	25
89	Fierce FRIGHT 034	Dying For It (p/s, sold at U.L.U. gig, 300 only, unsigned)	15
89	Fierce FRIGHT 034	Dying For It (1-sided, different p/s to above)	15
89	Woosh WOOSH 007/6	Hard On Love (yellow flexi with Pooh Sticks fanzine)//GROOVE FARM: Heaven Is Blue/ESMERALDA'S KITE: Vampire girl (red flexi) (with Woosh fanzine 3)	12
92	Fierce/BMG FRIGHT 42	Million Seller (1-sided)	6
89	53rd & 3rd AGAMC 5	ORGASM (LP, pink vinyl with insert for export)	25
89	Fierce FRIGHT 025	THE POOH STICKS (mini-LP, with inner, black & white sleeve, 1-sided, side 2 etched)	20
89	Fierce FRIGHT 035	TRADE MARK OF QUALITY (LP, mail-order only, plain stickered sleeve with insert, numbered)	18

(see also Dumb Angels)

BRIAN POOLE

66	Decca F 12402	Hey Girl/Please Be Mine	10
66	CBS 202349	Everything I Touch Turns To Tears/I Need Her Tonight	22
67	CBS 202661	That Reminds Me Baby/Tomorrow Never Comes	6
67	CBS 3005	Just How Loud/The Other Side Of The Sky	20
75	Pinnacle P 8407	Satisfied/Red Leather (with Carousel)	6
83	Outlook OUT 100K	Do You Love Me/Twist And Shout/Time And Tide (with Tramline)	6

(see also Brian Poole & Tremeloes)

BRIAN POOLE & TREMELOES

62	Decca F 11455	Twist Little Sister/Lost Love (some with 'Trimiloes' on label)	15
62	Decca F 11515	That Ain't Right/Blue	12
63	Decca F 11567	A Very Good Year For Girls/Meet Me Where We Used Meet	10
63	Decca F 11616	Keep On Dancing/Run Back Home	10
63	Decca F 11694	Twist And Shout/We Know	6
63	Decca F 11771	I Can Dance/Are You Loving Me At All	6
64	Decca F 11823	Candy Man/I Wish I Could Dance	6
64	Decca F 11951	Twelve Steps To Love/Don't Cry	7
65	Decca F 12124	After A While/You Know	10
65	Decca F 12197	I Want Candy/Love Me Baby	10
65	Decca F 12274	Good Lovin'/Could It Be You	10
64	Decca DFE 8566	BRIAN POOLE AND THE TREMELOES (EP)	15
65	Decca DFE 8610	BRIAN POOLE AND THE TREMELOES (EP)	20
63	Ace of Clubs ACL 1146	BIG BIG HITS OF '62 (LP)	15
63	Decca LK 4550	TWIST AND SHOUT WITH BRIAN POOLE AND THE TREMELOES (LP)	25
65	Decca LK 4685	IT'S ABOUT TIME (LP)	30

(see also Brian Poole, Tremeloes)

LOU & LAURA POOLE

72	Jay Boy BOY 63	Only You And I Know/Look At Me	15

POOR SOULS

65	Decca F 12183	When My Baby Cries/My Baby She's Not There	25
66	Alp ALP 595 004	Love Me/Please Don't Change Your Mind	50

POOR THINGS

66	CBS 202431	We Trust In A Better Way Of Life/Danny Boy	50

POORBOYS

82	Ace SW 81	MOVE BABY MOVE EP (p/s)	8

GROOVY JOE POOVEY

70	Injun 100	Ten Long Fingers On The 88 Keys/Thrill Of Love	15
71	Injun 101	Move Around/BILL REEDER: Till I Waltz Again With You	15
81	President PR 497	Lightning From The Sky/You Are My Sunshine	10

IGGY POP

77	RCA PB 9093	China Girl/Baby	15
77	RCA PB 9160	Success/The Passenger	15
78	RCA PB 9213	I Got A Right/Sixteen (some in b/w picture sleeve)	10
78	Radar ADA 4	Kill City (with James Williamson/I Got Nothin'	8
79	Arista ARIST 255	I'm Bored/African Man	10
73	CBS 65586	RAW POWER (LP, with inner, orange label, as Iggy & Stooges)	100
78	Radar RAD 2	KILL CITY (LP, as Iggy Pop & James Williamson)	20
77	RCA PL12275	THE IDIOT (LP, 1st pressing, orange labels)	40
77	RCA PL12488	LUST FOR LIFE (LP, 1st pressing, orange labels)	50
77	RCA PL 12796	TV EYE - 1977 LIVE (LP)	15
79	Arista SPART 1092	NEW VALUES (LP)	25
80	Arista SPART 1117	SOLDIER (LP, insert)	25
81	Arista SPART 1158	PARTY (LP)	15
81	RCA Int. INTS 5172	THE IDIOT (LP, reissue, green labels)	30
81	RCA Int. INTS 5214	LUST FOR LIFE (LP, reissue, green labels)	30
82	Chrysalis CHR 1399	ZOMBIE BIRDHOUSE (LP)	15
84	RCA NL82488	LUST FOR LIFE (LP, reissue, black labels)	30
87	Revenge MIG 2W	I GOT A RIGHT (LP, picture disc)	18
88	A&M AMA 5145	BLAH BLAH BLAH (LP)	18
90	Virgin America VUSLP 19	BRICK BY BRICK (LP)	20
93	Virgin VUSLP 64	AMERICAN CAESAR (2-LP)	60
96	Virgin VUSLP 102	NAUGHTY LITTLE DOGGIE (LP)	50
96	Virgin VUSLP 115	NUDE & RUDE: THE BEST OF IGGY POP (2-LP)	100
97	EMI LPCENT 40	LUST FOR LIFE (LP, reissue)	35

(see also Stooges)

POP WILL EAT ITSELF

POP WILL EAT ITSELF
86	Desperate SRT 1	THE POPPIES SAY GRRrrr! (EP in stamped brown paper bag, stamped white labels)	40

POPCORNS
63	Columbia DB 4968	Zero Zero/Chinese Twist	15

TIM POPE
84	Fiction FICS 21	I Want To Be A Tree/The Double Crossing Of Two Faced Fred (p/s)	15
84	Fiction FICSX 21	I Want To Be A Tree/(Elephant) Song/The Double Crossing Of Two Faced Fred (12", p/s)	25

(see also Cure)

POP GROUP
79	Radar ADA 29	She Is Beyond Good And Evil/3.38 (p/s)	10
79	Radar ADAT 1229	She Is Beyond Good And Evil/3.38 (12", p/s)	25
79	Rough Trade RT 023	We Are All Prostitutes/Amnesty International Report On British Army Torture Of Irish Prisoners (p/s)	18
80	Rough Trade RT 039/ Y Y1	Where There's A Will There's A Way/SLITS: In The Beginning There Was Rhythm (p/s)	18
79	Radar RAD 20	Y (LP, with foldout colour poster)	70
80	Rough Trade ROUGH 9	FOR HOW MUCH LONGER DO WE TOLERATE MASS MURDER? (LP, with 4 black-and-white posters)	50
80	Y/Rough Trade ROUGH 12	WE ARE TIME (LP, plain black sleeve)	20
96	Radar SCAN LP14	Y (LP, reissue)	30

(see also Slits, Mark Stewart)

ANDRE POPP
74	Polydor 2383 278	MY MOVIE DREAMS (LP)	15

FRANK POPP ENSEMBLE
01	Blow Up BU026	Hip Teens Don't Wear Blue Jeans/The Catwalk	30

POPPIES
66	Columbia DB 7879	Lullaby Of Love/I Wonder Why	30

KEITH POPPIN
73	Randy's RAN 531	Kick The Bucket/I'm A Man Of My Word	6
75	Sunshot SS001	Envious/Fed Up	15
76	Sunshot SS004	Who Are You/Dub Heavier Than Lead	8
76	Sunshot SS006	It's Too Late/Part 2	8
76	Sunshot SS012	Someday Girl/Version	8
76	Mango 1002	Time Slipping Away/King Tubby's Time	12
79	JB Music JBD 006	Hold Not Thy Peace/Birdie (12")	50

POPPY FAMILY
69	Decca F 22976	Which Way You Going Billy/Endless Sleep	8
70	Decca F13092	That's Where It Went Wrong/Shadows On The Wall	10
71	Decca F 13132	I Was Wondering/Where Evil Grows	6

POPPYHEADS
88	Sha La La Ba Ba Ba Ba 4	POSTCARD FOR FLOSSY (EP, 1-sided flexidisc, p/s in poly bag)	10
88	Sarah SARAH 006	Cremation Town/Pictures You Weave/Dreamboat (foldaround p/s with large poster in poly bag)	50

POP RIVETS
79	M.T. Sounds HEP 001	BACK FROM NOWHERE (EP, no p/s)	30
79	M.T. Sounds HEP 002	BACK FROM NOWHERE (EP, split single with SULPHATE, no p/s)	30
79	Hypocrite JIM 1	FUN IN THE U.K. (EP, no p/s, double pack)	30
02	(No label) HAD 1	Kray Twins/BUFFS: All My Feelings Denied (no p/s, 450 free with Chatham's Burning fanzine)	25
02	(No label) HAD 01	Kray Twins/BUFFS: All MY Feelings Denied (no p/s, without Chatham's Burning fanzine)	10
79	Hypocrite HIP 007	THE POP RIVETS GREATEST HITS (LP, silk-screened sleeve, 50 only)	150
79	Hypocrite HIP 007	THE POP RIVETS GREATEST HITS (LP, title sleeve with Pop Rivets printed repeatedly across whole sleeve, stamped white labels, 50 only)	150
79	Hypocrite HIP 007	THE POP RIVETS GREATEST HITS (LP, printed sleeve, stamped white labels)	50
79	Hypocrite HIP-O	EMPTY SOUNDS FROM ANARCHY RANCH (LP, coloured back, stamped labels)	25
80	Hypocrite HIP 007	THE POP RIVETS GREATEST HITS (LP, screen printed sleeve, insert, 50 only)	150
89	Hangman HANG 27 UP	ORIGINAL FIRST ALBUM!!! (LP)	20
90	Hangman HANG 35 UP	LIVE IN GERMANY '79 (LP)	15
90s	Damaged Goods DAMGOOD 142	CHATHAM'S BURNING (LP, brown vinyl)	20

(see also Milkshakes)

POP ROCK
97	Acid UKN 010	PURPLE JELLY EP (2 x 12")	60

POPSICLES
65	Vocalion VH 9223	I Don't Want To Be Your Baby Anymore/Baby I Miss You	50

(see also Ellie Greenwich, Raindrops)

POP TOPS
69	Major MInor MM 594	That Woman/The Man I m Today (Adagio Cardinal)	10
72	A&M AMS 7001	Suzanne Suzanne/Oh Lord Why Lord	15

POPULAR 5
68	Minit MLF 11011	I'm A Lovemaker/Little Bitty Pretty One	15

POPULAR MECHANICS
87	Ark DOVE 5	INSECT CULTURE (LP)	50

POP WORKSHOP
68	Page One POF 091	Fairyland/When My Little Girl Is Happy	30
69	Page One POF 129	Punch And Judy Man/Love Is A One Way Highway	10

PORCUPINE TREE
SINGLES : SINGLES AND EPS
90	Private (No Cat. No.)	LOVE, DEATH AND MUSSOLINI (EP, 10 copies, plain black cassette with 3 page booklet)	400
92	Delerium DELEC EP 010	VOYAGE 34 (12" EP)	50
92	Delerium DELEC EP 007	VOYAGE 34 (Astralasia Remix) (12" EP)	25
92	Delerium DELECD EP 010	VOYAGE 34 (CD EP, first 100 with blue not green artwork)	60

PORK DUKES

MINT VALUE £

Year	Catalogue	Title	Value
94	Delerium DELEC EP 032	Stars Die/Moonloop (12", p/s)	15
96	Delerium DELEC EP 049	WAITING (EP 12")	25
98	Chromatic CHR 003	METANOIA (EP, 2 x 10", 1,000 only)	60
99	K-Scope/Snapper SMAS 103	Piano Lessons/Oceans Have No Memory (p/s, 1,000 copies)	18
99	K-Scope/Snapper SMAS 107	Stranger By The Minute/Hallogallo (p/s, 1,000 only)	18
99	K-Scope/Snapper SMAS 110	Pure Narcotic/Nine Cats - Acoustic (p/s)	15
00	K-Scope/Snapper SMAS 120	Shesmovedon/Novak (p/s, 1000 only)	12
00	K-Scope/Snapper SMAS 7111	4 Chords That Made A Million/Orchidia (p/s, 1,000 only)	15
01	Delerium (No Cat. No.)	TRANSMISSION IV - MOONLOOP EP (Free to Transmission Subscribers, 500 only)	80
16	Kscope KSCOPE 936	NIL RECURRING (12" EP reissue clear vinyl)	10

ALBUMS : ORIGINAL ALBUMS

Year	Catalogue	Title	Value
89	Delerium DELC 0002	TARQUIN'S SEAWEED FARM (cassette, 1st issue, around 50 only)	300
91	Delerium DELC 0002	TARQUIN'S SEAWEED FARM (cassette, 2nd issue, silver print, with A4 booklet, red/black text, 300 only)	100
91	Delerium DELC 0002	TARQUIN'S SEAWEED FARM (cassette, silver print, with photocopied A5 booklet, label on Side 1, 200 only)	50
91	Delerium DELC 0003	THE NOSTALGIA FACTORY (cassette, silver print, with A4 booklet, red/black text, 200 only)	200
91	Delerium DELC 0003	THE NOSTALGIA FACTORY (cassette, with photocopied A5 booklet, label on Side 1, 200 only)	60
92	Delerium DELEC 008	ON THE SUNDAY OF LIFE (2-LP, gatefold sleeve, 1,000 only)	100
93	Delerium DELEC 020	UP THE DOWNSTAIR (LP)	120
94	Magic Gnome MG 4299325	YELLOW HEDGROW DREAMSCAPE (CD, 2,500 only)	100
95	Delerium DELECLP 028	THE SKY MOVES SIDEWAYS (LP, 2,000 on blue vinyl with poster)	100
95	Delerium DELECLP 028	THE SKY MOVES SIDEWAYS (LP, black vinyl with poster)	120
96	Delerium DELECLP 045	SIGNIFY (double LP, gatefold sleeve)	100
97	Chromatic CHR 002	SPIRAL CIRCUS (LP, 500 only)	150
01	K-Scope SMACD840	RECORDINGS (CD, numbered slipcase, 20,000 only)	50
03	Lava 7567 931781	IN ABSENTIA (2-LP)	100
05	Gates Of Dawn GOD 009	DEADWING (2-LP, black vinyl with poster)	70
06	Delerium DELECLP 999	MOONLOOP (LP, 500 black vinyl in screen printed blue vinyl bag)	35
06	Delerium DELECLP 999	MOONLOOP (LP, 99 clear vinyl in screen printed blue vinyl bag)	70
06	Delerium DELECLP 999	MOONLOOP (LP, 500 white vinyl in screen printed blue vinyl bag)	40
06	Gates Of Dawn GOD 011	STUPID DREAM (2-LP, black/grey 'marbled' vinyl)	70
07	Tonefloat TF 40	FEAR OF A BLANK PLANET (2-LP, gatefold)	80
07	Tonefloat TF 40	FEAR OF A BLANK PLANET (2-LP, 1000 only special edition with poster, booklet and slipcase)	150
08	Tonefloat TF 46	WE LOST THE SKYLINE (LP, orange marbled vinyl)	80
08	Tonefloat TF 46	WE LOST THE SKYLINE (LP, black vinyl)	50
09	Tonefloat TF 82	THE INCIDENT (2-LP, with booklet in PVC slipcase, 2000 only)	100
09	Tonefloat TF 82	THE INCIDENT (2-LP, standard issue)	40
16	Kscope KSCOPE 894	THE DELERIUM YEARS 1994-1997 (Box set, 9-LP, booklet)	100
17	Kscope KSCOPE 893	THE DELERIUM YEARS 1991-1993 (Box set, 9-LP, booklet)	100

ALBUMS : ALBUM REISSUES

Year	Catalogue	Title	Value
08	Kscope KSCOPE 801	ON THE SUNDAY OF LIFE (2-LP, reissue, orange vinyl)	35
08	Kscope KSCOPE 801	ON THE SUNDAY OF LIFE (2-LP, reissue, black vinyl)	25
08	Kscope KSCOPE 802	UP THE DOWNSTAIR (2-LP, reissue, red vinyl)	25
08	Kscope KSCOPE 802	UP THE DOWNSTAIR (2-LP, reissue, black vinyl)	30
10	Tonefloat TF 102	IN ABSENTIA (2-LP, reissue coloured vinyl, 1500 only)	100
10	Tonefloat TF 102	IN ABSENTIA (2-LP, reissue black vinyl)	40
10	Kscope KSCOPE 803	VOYAGE 34 (2-LP, white vinyl, 2000 only)	40
11	Kscope KSCOPE 805	SIGNIFY (2-LP, reissue)	30
11	Kscope KSCOPE 813	RECORDINGS (2-LP, gatefold, reissue)	20
12	Kscope KSCOPE 834	COMA DIVINE (3-LP box set, reissue)	35
12	Kscope KSCOPE 825	THE SKY MOVES SIDEWAYS (2-LP, reissue)	25
13	Kscope KSCOPE 845	STUPID DREAM (2-LP, reissue)	20
15	Tonefloat TF 40	FEAR OF A BLANK PLANET (2-LP, reissue, black inner sleeves)	20

ALBUMS : PROMOS

Year	Catalogue	Title	Value
93	Delerium DELEC PROMO CD 1	RADIO ACTIVE (CD, promo, 500 only)	40
94	Delerium DELEC PROMO CASS 5	SPIRAL CIRCUS (cassette give away free with Transmission newsletter)	175
97	None	PORCUPINE TREE DEMO (cassette-only, promo)	100
97	Delerium DELEC PROMO CASS 10	INSIGNIFICANCE (promo cassette, demos and out-takes from SIGNIFY)	60

(see also No Man, Steven Wilson, Blackfield, Continuum (2))

PORK DUKES

Year	Catalogue	Title	Value
77	Wood WOOD 9	Bend And Flush/Throbbing Gristle (p/s)	10
77	Wood BRANCH 9	Making Bacon/Tight Pussy (12", p/s, yellow vinyl)	12
78	Wood Standard WOOD 56	Telephone Masturbator/Melody Makers (p/s)	10
94	Damaged Goods FNARR8	THE FILTHY NASTY PORK DUKES EP	6
78	Wood PORK 001	THE PORK DUKES (LP, pink vinyl with warning sticker & postcard)	25
80	Wood PORK 002	PIG OUT OF HELL (LP)	25

PORNO CASSETTES

Year	Catalogue	Title	Value
82	Heresy Records DOC 1	You're Face, A Fucking Disgrace/Dead End Yobs	150

PORNO FOR PYROS

Year	Catalogue	Title	Value
93	Warner Bros. 9362 45228-1	PORNO FOR PYROS (LP)	50

DAVID PORTER

Year	Catalogue	Title	Value
70	Stax STAX 155	One Part - Two Parts/Can't I See You When I Want To	8
70	Stax SXATS 1034	GRITTY, GROOVY AND GETTIN' IT (LP)	15

Nolan PORTER

MINT VALUE £

71	Stax STX 1030	VICTIM OF THE JOKE (LP)	35
71	Stax 2362 006	INTO A REAL THING (LP)	15

NOLAN PORTER
72	Probe PRO 580	If I Could Only Be Sure/Work It Out In The Morning	100
72	Probe PRO 580	If I Could Only Be Sure/Work It Out In The Morning (DJ copy)	175
72	Probe SPB 1067	NOLAN (LP)	25

ROBIE PORTER
66	MGM 1306	Here In My Arms/I've Often Wondered	6
66	MGM 1313	Either Way I Lose/That's The Way Love Goes	20

PORTER CUNNINGHAM
72	Folk Heritage FHR 027	OBSERVATIONS (LP)	100

PORTION CONTROL
82	In Phaze POR CON 006	Surface And Be Seen/Spinola (Blotch)/Terror Leads To Better Days/Simple As ABC/Monstrous Bulk/He Is A Barbarian (12", p/s, with plastic outer sleeve)	40
83	Illuminated ILL 2612	Raise The Pulse/Collapse/Bite My Head	8
83	Illuminated ILL 2612	Raise The Pulse/Collapse/Bite My Head (12", p/s)	10
85	Rhythmic/Havoc 12RMICX 7	The Great Divide (Julian Mendelsohn Remix)/Divided/Bolt It Down (12", p/s)	12
81	In Phaze PORCON 002	DINING ON THE FLESH (cassette box set with free flexi 7")	70
81	In Phaze PORCON 002	GAINING MOMENTUM (cassette)	40
82	In Phaze CP 007	I STAGGERED MENTALLY (LP)	50
82	In Phase NCN	WITH MIXED EMOTION (cassette)	40
82	Third Mind TMT 07	SHOT IN THE BELLY (cassette)	40
83	In Phaze EZ 2	HIT THE PULSE (mini-LP, 45/33rpm)	18
84	Illuminated JAMS 44	STEP FORWARD (LP)	12
85	In Phaze PHA 5	SIMULATE SENSUAL (LP, clear vinyl, PVC sleeve with insert)	20

PORTISHEAD
94	Go! Beat GODX 116	Sour Times/Sour Sour Times/Lot More/Sheared Times (12")	20
94	Go! Beat GODX 114	Numb/Numbed In Moscow/Revenge Of The Number/Earth - Linger Remix/A Tribute To Monk & Canatella (12")	20
94	Go! Beat GODX 120	Glory Box/Toy Box/Scorn/Sheared Box (12", p/s)	20
97	Go! Beat 571 597-1	All Mine/Cowboys/Cowboys (Instrumental) (12", p/s)	15
11	XL XLT 557	Chase The Tear/Doldrums Reimagine (12", signed)	30
94	Go Beat! 828 522	DUMMY (LP, 1st pressing, with incorrect sample credits on inner sleeve)	120
94	Go! Beat 828 522-1	DUMMY (LP, 2nd pressing, with correct sample credits on inner sleeve)	80
97	Go! Beat PORT LP PRO	PORTISHEAD (2-LP, numbered promo)	70
97	Go! Beat 314 539189-1	PORTISHEAD (2-LP)	50
97	Go! Beat 539189-1	PORTISHEAD (LP, gloss sleeve)	60
98	Go! Beat 559 424-1	ROSELAND NYC LIVE (2-LP, with poster)	50
99	Simply Vinyl SVLP 115	PORTISHEAD (2-LP, reissue)	40
00	Simply Vinyl SVLP 162	DUMMY (LP, reissue)	35
08	Island 1766390	THIRD (2-LP, etched 12", print, with USB stick, numbered)	60

(see also Jimi Entley Sound, Beak>, Beth Gibbon and Rustin Man)

PORTOBELLO EXPLOSION
69	Carnaby CNS 4001	We Can Fly/Hot Smoke And Sasafrass (label credits Portebello Explosion)	30

(see also Mirage, Jawbone, Spencer Davis Group)

PORTRAIT
71	Pye 7N 45043	Tokaido Lines/Cuddle Me Closer	6

PORTRAIT OF DAN TRACY
94	Direct Lite 726	Silly Girl/I Know Where Syd Barrett Lives/Remember Bridget Riley A Picture Of Dorian Grey (p/s)	10

PORTSMOUTH SINFONIA
73	Transatlantic TRA 275	PLAY THE POPULAR CLASSICS (LP)	40
74	Transatlantic TRA 285	HALLELUJAH (LP)	25
79	Philips 9109 231	20 CLASSIC ROCK CLASSICS (LP)	30

PORTWAY PEDLARS
84	Greenwich Village GVR 229	IN GREENWOOD SHADES (LP)	15

SANDY POSEY
66	MGM MGM 1321	Born A Woman/Caution To The Wind	7
66	MGM MGM 1330	Single Girl/Blue Is My Best Colour	7
67	MGM MGM 1335	What A Woman In Love Won't Do/Shattered	8
67	MGM MGM 1342	I Take It Back/The Boy I Love	8
67	MGM MGM 1364	Are You Never Coming Home/I Can Show You How To Live	8
67	MGM MGM-C(S) 8035	BORN A WOMAN (LP)	30
67	MGM MGM-C(S) 8042	SINGLE GIRL (LP)	25
68	MGM MGM-C(S) 8051	SANDY POSEY (LP)	25
68	MGM MGM-C 8060	THE BEST OF SANDY POSEY (LP, original with blue label)	20
68	MGM MGM-C(S) 8073	LOOKING AT YOU (LP)	25

POSH
81	Marathon RUN 1	Letter To Linda/Racey Tracey (p/s)	10

POSITIVE SIGNALS
80	Yob YOB 001	Media Man/Only For A Day/STRAND: Here Today Gone Tomorrow/Changing World (split EP, p/s)	15

POSSESSED (1)
07	Rise Above Relics RARLP 002	EXPLORATION (LP, black vinyl and black vinyl 7")	40
07	Rise Above Relics RARLP 002	EXPLORATION (LP, purple vinyl and purple vinyl 7")	35
07	Rise Above Relics RARLP 002	EXPLORATION (LP, clear vinyl and clear vinyl 7", 100 only)	50

POSSESSED (2)
86	Under One Flag FLAG 3	BEYOND THE GATES (LP)	15
87	Under One Flag M FLAG 16	THE EYES OF HORROR EP (12", p/s)	15

HOWIE POST & SWIFTIES
63	Fontana TF 421	Tom Swift/The Elephant	10

POST MORTEM
MINT VALUE £

POST MORTEM
83	Regime FM 006	BETER OFF DEAD (EP)	25

ADRIENNE POSTER/POSTA
63	Oriole CB 1890	Only Fifteen/There's Nothing You Can Do About That	40
63	Decca F 11797	Only Fifteen/There's Nothing You Can Do About That (reissue)	20
64	Decca F 11864	Shang A Doo Lang/When A Girl Really Loves You	40
65	Decca F 12079	He Doesn't Love Me/The Way You Do The Things You Do	25
65	Decca F 12181	The Winds That Blow/Back Street Girl	25
66	Decca F 12329	Something Beautiful/So Glad You're Mine	35
66	Decca F 12455	They Long To Be Close To You/How Can I Hurt You (as Adrienne Posta)	20
73	DJM DJS 286	Dog Song/Express Yourself	12

POSTHUMAN
12	Balkan BV 10	THE BENZ EP (12")	10
16	I Love Acid ILA 013	I LOVE ACID 013 (12", hand-stamped and numbered, 303 only)	15
16	Balkan BV 20	IT'S A HOUSE THING EP (12")	20
17	Balkan BV 21	Hoogland/Atari Queen (12")	12
10	Balkan BV 07P	SYN EMERGENCE (2 x 12" different picture discs, with CD)	20

POTATOES
66	Fontana TF 756	The Bend/Bend Ahead	7

POTENTIAL BAD BOY
93	Limited E Edition CW010	WORK THE BOX EP (12")	30
95	Redskin/Third Eye TE001	Guns Out (Remix)/Murder Jumppan Sound/In Between The Beats/Unknown (12" with Bad Vibes)	40
06	Sublogic/Ninety-Two Retro SLVR 001/9T2RX	Everyday Child (1-sided 12", 100 only, stamped and hand-numbered labels)	40

POTENTIAL THREAT
82	Out Of Town HOOT 7	WHAT'S SO GREAT BRITAIN! (EP, 1st pressing, red sleeve with insert)	30
80	XX MIN 709	WHAT'S SO GREAT BRITAIN! (EP, 2nd pressing, blue sleeve with insert)	20
84	Children Of The Revolution COR 6	Brainwashed/Turn A Blind Eye/A Cry For Help/Conflict (p/s)	15
86	Mortarhate MORT 24	DEMAND AN ALTERNATIVE (LP)	30

KEITH POTGER
69	Mercury MF 1073	The World Would Never Turn Again/Santa Marie (in p/s)	8
69	Mercury MF 1073	The World Would Never Turn Again/Santa Marie	6

(see also Seekers, Judith Durham)

POTION
81	Slapps & Sticks SAS 6	Catch The Feeling (Showstopper)/Showstopper (Instrumental) (12")	50
81	UK Champagne FUNK 5	Catch The Feeling/Showstopper	10
81	UK Champagne FUNKY 5	Catch The Feeling/Showstopper (12")	25

POT LIQUOR
72	Janus 6146 011	Cheer/Chatanooga	8
70	Dawn DNLS 3016	FIRST TASTE (LP, withdrawn)	90
72	Janus 6310 202	LEVEE BLUES (LP)	30

PHIL POTTER
76	Genesis GEN 10	MY SONG IS LOVE UNKNOWN (LP)	20
79	Dove DOVE 61	THE RESTORER (LP)	15

POTTERS
72	Trent JT 100	We'll Be With You/Theme For A Team	20

POTTING SHEDS
90	Mad Cat BSE 002	Second Best/Shape Out	15
92	Mad Cat BSE 005	GOLDFISH MEMORY EP (12")	15

POUND OF FLESH
75	Creole CR 106	Funky March/Part 2	10

ALLEN POUND'S GET RICH
66	Parlophone R 5532	Searchin' In The Wilderness/Hey You (rare stock copy)	1000
66	Parlophone R 5532	Searchin' In The Wilderness/Hey You (more common demo)	600
16	record Collector POUND ONE	Searchin' In The Wilderness/Hey You (p/s, reissue)	12

POUNDS X BUCKWILD
20	Daupe! DM SP 055	TRAFFICANTE (LP, 200 copies)	40
20	Daupe! DM SP 055	TRAFFICANTE (LP, green vinyl, 100 copies)	40
20	Daupe! DM SP 055	TRAFFICANTE (LP, splatter vinyl, 100 copies)	50
20	Daupe! DM SP 055	TRAFFICANTE (LP, silver vinyl, 100 copies)	40
20	Daupe! DM SP 055	TRAFFICANTE (LP, with obi strip, 20 copies)	100

FRANCK POURCEL
59	HMV POP 622	Only You/Rainy Night In Paris	8

BUD POWELL (TRIO)
55	Vogue EPV 1030	BUD POWELL TRIO (EP)	15
55	Vogue EPV 1033	BUD POWELL'S MODERNISTS (EP)	15
55	Vogue EPV 1036	BUD POWELL TRIO (EP)	15
55	Columbia Clef SEB 10013	BUD POWELL (EP)	15
57	Columbia Clef SEB 10074	GENIUS OF BUD POWELL (EP)	15
58	Columbia Clef SEB 10094	GENIUS OF BUD POWELL NO. 2 (EP)	15
52	Vogue LDE 010	THE BUD POWELL TRIO (10" LP)	20
54	Vogue LDE 053	JAZZ AT THE MASSEY HALL VOL. 2 (10" LP)	20
56	Columbia Clef 33C 9016	BUD POWELL TRIO (10" LP)	25
57	Columbia Clef 33CX 10069	JAZZ ORIGINAL (LP)	30
58	Columbia Clef 33CX 10123	BLUES FOR BUD (LP)	30
59	HMV CLP 1294	THE LONELY ONE (LP)	30
63	Vogue LAE 558	THE BUD POWELL TRIO (LP)	15
63	Columbia 33SX 1575	THE BUD POWELL TRIO FEATURING MAX ROACH (LP)	25

Cozy POWELL

MINT VALUE £

64	Fontana FJL 903	HOT HOUSE (LP)	25
68	Fontana SFJL 901	BLUES FOR BOUFFEMONT (LP)	25

COZY POWELL
73	Rak RAK 164	Dance With The Devil/And Then There Was Skin (export copy, European diff p/s)	10
73	Rak 4C 006 94962	Dance With The Devil/And Then There Was Skin (export issue, p/s, RAK 164 in run out groove, blue or yellow vinyl)	20
73	Rak 4C 006 94962	Dance With The Devil/And Then There Was Skin (export issue, p/s, RAK 164 in run out groove)	10

(see also Rainbow, Young Blood, Big Bertha, Ace Kefford Stand, Bedlam, Phenomena, Black Sabbath, Jeff Beck, Whitesnake, Michael Schenker Group, Donovan, Gary Moore, Young & Moody, Brian May, Chick Churchill, Graham Bonnet, Emerson Lake & Powell, Jack Bruce, Plum & Youth, Suzi Quatro)

JANE POWELL
54	Capitol LC 6665	THREE SAILORS AND A GIRL (10" LP)	20
57	HMV CLP 1131	JANE POWELL (LP)	20

(see also Marilyn Monroe)

JIMMY POWELL (& DIMENSIONS)
62	Decca F 11447	Sugar Babe (Parts 1 & 2) (solo)	15
62	Decca F 11544	Tom Hark/Dance Her By Me (solo)	10
63	Decca F 11570	Remember Them/Everyone But You (solo)	8
64	Pye 7N 15663	That's Alright/I'm Looking For A Woman	60
64	Pye 7N 15735	Sugar Babe/I've Been Watching You (as Jimmy Powell & 5 Dimensions)	20
66	Strike JH 309	I Can Go Down/Love Me Right	15
67	Decca F 12664	Unexpected Mirrors/Time Mends Broken Hearts (with Dimensions)	10
68	Decca F 12751	I Just Can't Get Over You/Real Cool (with Dimensions)	20
68	Decca F 12793	Sugar Baby (Parts 1 & 2)	10

JUDITH POWELL
67	RCA RCA 1569	Greener Days/No Goodbyes	6

KEITH POWELL (& VALETS)
63	Columbia DB 7116	The Answer Is No!/Come On And Join The Party (with Valets)	15
64	Columbia DB 7229	Tore Up/You Better Let Him Go (with Valets)	25
64	Columbia DB 7366	I Should Know Better (But I Don't)/Too Much Monkey Business (with Valets)	35
65	Piccadilly 7N 35235	People Get Ready/Paradise	15
65	Piccadilly 7N 35249	Come Home Baby/Beyond The Hill	15
66	Piccadilly 7N 35275	Goodbye Girl/It Was Easier To Hurt Her	15
66	Piccadilly 7N 35300	Victory/Some People Only	15
66	Piccadilly 7N 35353	It Keeps Rainin'/Song of The Moon	20

(see also Move, Carl Wayne & Vikings)

KEITH (POWELL) & BILLIE (DAVIES)
66	Piccadilly 7N 35288	When You Move, You Lose/Tastes Sour, Don't It? (as Keith & Billie)	15
66	Piccadilly 7N 35321	You Don't Know Like I Know/Two Little People	15
66	Piccadilly 7N 35340	Swingin' Tight/That's Really Some Good	15

(see also Keith Powell, Billie Davis)

MARILYN POWELL
64	Fontana TF 448	All My Loving/After The Party	7
65	Fontana TF 526	Please Go Away/Where Did I Go Wrong	40

POWER
82	Malaco MAL1	Groovin'/Instrumental	8

POWER CUT/CASH CREW
88	Vinyl Lab VL 004T	Mission Impossible/Microphone Maniac (12")	15

DUFFY POWER
59	Fontana H 194	Dream Lover/That's My Little Suzie	30
59	Fontana H 214	Kissin' Time/Ain't She Sweet	15
59	Fontana H 230	Starry-Eyed/Prettier Than You	15
60	Fontana H 279	Whole Lotta Shakin' Goin' On/If I Can Dream	30
61	Fontana H 302	I've Got Nobody/When We're Walking Close	20
61	Fontana H 344	No Other Love/What Now	20
63	Parlophone R 4992	It Ain't Necessarily So/If I Get Lucky Someday	20
63	Parlophone R 5024	I Saw Her Standing There (with Graham Bond Quartet)/Farewell Baby	50
63	Parlophone R 5059	Hey Girl/Woman Made Trouble	40
64	Parlophone R 5111	Parchman Farm/Tired, Broke And Busted (with Paramounts)	40
64	Parlophone R 5169	Where Am I?/I Don't Care	40
67	Parlophone R 5631	Davy O'Brien (Leave That Baby Alone)/July Tree	30
70	CBS 5176	Hell Hound/Hummingbird	15
71	Epic EPC 7139	Hummingbird/Hell Hound (reissue)	6
71	Transatlantic TRA 229	INNOVATIONS (LP)	60
73	GSF GS 502	DUFFY POWER (LP)	20
73	Spark SRLM 2005	DUFFY POWER (LP)	20
76	Buk BULP 2010	POWERHOUSE (LP, revised reissue of GSF GS 502)	15

(see also Alexis Korner, John McLaughlin, Jack Bruce, Graham Bond, Duffy's Nucleus)

POWER CUT CREW
88	PowerCut PC001	Power Cut 1/African Beats (12")	15

POWER FARM
83	Boob MM2	Which Way USA/Glass (p/s)	10

POWER GLOVE
14	Invada IVD132LP	FAR CRY 3 BLOOD DRAGON (2-LP, pink vinyl)	60

POWERHOUSE
66	Decca F 12471	Chain Gang/Can You Hear Me?	20
66	Decca F 12507	Raindrops/La Bamba	10

POWERLINE
81	Elite DAZZ 9	Step One/POWERLINE: Watching You (12")	80
81	Elite DAZZ 7	Journey (6.54)/Double Journey (13.05) (12", stickered die cut sleeve)	25

POWERMAD

MINT VALUE £

83	PLR PLR 1-7	Watching You (Vocal)/Watching You (Instrumental)	30
83	PLR 1-12	Watching You (Vocal)/Watching You (Instrumental) (12")	80
83	PLR 2-7	You The Girl (Vocal)/You The Girl (Instrumental)	30
83	PLR 2-12	You The Girl (Vocal)/You The Girl (Instrumental) (12")	75

POWERMAD
89	Reprise 925 937-1	ABSOLUTE POWER (LP)	30

POWERPACK
66	CBS 202335	It Hurts Me So/What You Gonna Do	50
67	CBS 202551	I'll Be Anything For You/The Lost Summer	20
69	Polydor 56319	Hannibal Brooks/Juliet Simkins	8
70	Polydor 2001 077	Oh Calcutta/Soul Searchin'	20
69	Polydor 583 057	SOUL CURE (LP)	60

(see also Procol Harum, Emperor Rosko & Power Pack)

POWERPILL
92	ffrreedom TAB 110	Pac-Man (Original Edit)/Pac-Man (Mickey Finn's Yum Yum Edit)	25
92	ffrreedom TABX 110	PAC MAN EP: Powerpill Mix/Ghost Mix/Choci's Hi Score Mix/Mickey Finn's Yum Yum Mix (12", limited edition yellow vinyl)	30
92	ffrreedom TABX 110	PAC MAN EP: Powerpill Mix/Ghost Mix/Choci's Hi Score Mix/Mickey Finn's Yum Yum Mix (12")	20

(see also Aphex Twin)

JETT POWERS
70	Liberty LBS 83320	CALIFORNIA LICENCE (LP)	40

(see also P.J. Proby)

JOEY POWERS
63	Stateside SS 236	Midnight Mary/Where Do You Want The World Delivered	10

POWERS OF BLUE
67	CBS 62953	FLIP OUT! (LP)	20

MIK POYNTER
96	Ugly FF 001	FAT FILTERS VOL. 1 (12")	45
96	Ugly FF 002	FAT FILTERS VOL. 2 (12")	40

P.P. & PRIMES
96	Nice (no cat. no.)	Understanding/STEVIE'S BUZZ (i.e. Buzzcocks): Autumn Stone (promo only)	25

(see also Primal Scream, P.P. Arnold)

PEREZ 'PREZ' PRADO & HIS ORCHESTRA
55	HMV 7M 295	Cherry Pink And Apple Blossom White/Maria Elena	10
58	RCA RCA 1082	Guaglione/Paris	10
58	RCA RD 27102	DILO (LP)	15
60	RCA RD 27046	LATIN SATIN (LP)	15
64	Parlophone PMC 1226	A CAT IN LATIN (LP)	15
74	Contour 2870 385	NOW (LP)	15

PRAG VEC
78	Spec SP 001	Wolf/Cigarettes/Existential/Bits! (p/s)	12
79	Spec SP 002	Expert/The Follower! (p/s)	10
81	Spec RESPECT 1	NO COWBOYS (LP, with insert)	22

(see also Foetus etc.)

PRAISE
76	No Seven 001	BLESSED QUIETNESS (LP)	40

PRAISE SPACE ELECTRIC
91	Pop God PGTT 005	PRAISE SPACE ELECTRIC (LP)	15
94	Delerium DELEC LP 015	LEAVING DEMONS (LP)	20

PRAM
93	Too Pure PURE 17	IRON LUNG EP (12", red vinyl)	10
92	Howl WAIL 001	GASH (LP)	20
93	Too Pure PURE 26	THE STARS ARE SO BIG THE EARTH IS SO SMALL…STAY AS YOU ARE (LP, lyric inner)	40
95	Too Pure PURE 46	SARGASSO SEA (LP, lyric inner)	40
98	Domino WIGLP 49	NORTH POLE RADIO STATION (LP)	30
00	Domino WIGLP 80	THE MUSEUM OF IMAGINARY ANIMALS (LP, lyric inner)	40
01	Too Pure PURE 41	HELIUM (LP)	35
03	Domino WIGLP 120	DARK ISLAND (LP)	35

PRAMS (1)
81	Product/Ltd. Edition TAKE 2/4	Me/Modern Men/TV PRODUCT: Nowhere's Safe/Jumping Off Walls (foldout p/s)	30

PRAMS (2)
85	Classic Quotes CLASS 1	Black Sheep/Classic Quotes (p/s)	6

PRATS
80	Rough Trade RT 042	1990's POP EP (p/s)	10

ANDY PRATT
73	Epic SEPC 1846	Give It All To Music/Deer Song	8
69	Polydor 2489 003	RECORDS ARE LIKE LIFE (LP)	25

GRAHAM & EILEEN PRATT
77	Cottage Records COT 811	CLEAR AIR OF THE DAY (LP)	20
80	Dingle's DIN 308	TO FRIEND & FOE (LP)	20
81	Dingle's DIN	BANDSTAND (LP)	18
85	Plant Life PLR 068	HEIROGLYPHICS (LP, insert)	15

PHIL PRATT
69	Jolly JY 008	Sweet Song For My Baby/THRILLERS: I'm Restless	550
76	Student STU LP 1004	THE BEST DUB ALBUM IN THE WORLD (LP)	150
78	Burning Sounds BS 1019	STAR WARS DUB (LP)	100

(see also Charlie Ace, Larry Marshall, Don Drummond)

PHIL PRATT ALL STARS
70	Jackpot JP 748	Cut Throat/KEN BOOTHE: You Left The Water Running	30

71	Punch PH 94	Winey Winey (actually "Kingstonians Medley" by Kingstonians)/There Is A Place (actually by Barrington Spence)	30

(see also Dennis Alcapone, Horace Andy, Dennis Brown, Ken Boothe, Erroll Dunkley, John Holt, Delroy Wilson)

PATTY PRAVO
74	RCA 2483	Crazy Idea/Don't Be Sad	20

PRAYING MANTIS
79	Ripper/Harvest HAR 5201	THE SOUNDHOUSE TAPES PART 2: Captured City/Johnny Cool (p/s)	75
79	Ripper/Harvest 12HAR 5201	THE SOUNDHOUSE TAPES PART 2 (12")	15
80	Gem GEMS 36	Praying Mantis/High Roller (p/s, with transfer)	20
80	Gem GEMS 36	Praying Mantis/High Roller (p/s)	18
81	Arista ARIST 397	All Day And All Of The Night/Beads Of Ebony (p/s)	12
81	Arista ARIST 478	Cheated/Thirty Pieces Of Silver/Flirting With Suicide/Panic In The Streets (2x7", gatefold sleeve)	8
82	Jet JET 7026	Tell Me The Nightmare's Wrong/A Question Of Time/Turn The Tables (p/s)	20
81	Arista SPART 1153	TIME TELLS NO LIES (LP, with inner sleeve)	25

(see also Stratus, Grand Prix, Uriah Heep)

PREACHERS
65	Columbia DB 7680	Hole In My Soul/Too Old In The Head	100

(see also Herd, Denny Mitchel & Soundsations, Moon's Train)

PRECIOUS LITTLE
80	Rock On ROR 2	Give It To Me Now/Clean Living Boy (p/s)	20

PRECISIONS
67	Track 604 014	If This Is Love (I'd Rather Be Lonely)/You'll Soon Be Gone	40
79	Grapevine GRP 129	Such Misery/A Lovers Plea	10

PREDATOR (1)
78	Bust! SOL 2	Punk Man/Paperboy Song (with insert)	60

PREDATOR (2)
85	CTM C 001	Don't Stop/Shotdown (in p/s)	80
85	CTM C 001	Don't Stop/Shotdown	30

PREDATORS
83	Ears And Eyes EER 012	SOCIAL DECAY (LP)	40

PREDATUR
82	Quicksilver QUICK 5	Take A Walk/Seen You Here (p/s)	75

PREFAB SPROUT
82	Candle CANDLE 1	Lions In My Own Garden (Exit Someone)/Radio Love	25
85	Kitchenware KWLP 3	STEVE MCQUEEN (LP, inner)	18
92	Columbia 4718861	THE BEST OF PREFAB SPROUT: A LIFE OF SURPRISES (LP)	18

PREFECTS (1)
79	Rough Trade TR 040	Going Through The Motions/Things In General (no p/s)	20
87	Strange Fruit SFPS 025	PEEL SESSIONS (12")	12

PREFECTS (2)
82	Variety BBY 402	Love Is All Around/I Saw The Night	6

PREFUSE 73
03	Warp WARPLP 105	ONE WORD EXTINGUISHER (2-LP)	30
03	Warp WARPLP 164	EXTINGUISHED: OUTTAKES (LP)	20

PREGNANT INSOMNIA
67	Direction 58-3132	Wallpaper/You Intrigue Me	50

PRELUDE (1)
72	Crotchet CME 18A/B	PRELUDE (LP, private pressing)	70
73	Dawn DNLS 3052	HOW LONG IS FOREVER (LP, textured gatefold sleeve)	20

PRELUDE (2)
72	Decca F13292	Edge Of The Sea/Looking For Indians	10

PRELUDE (3)
83	Black Crow CROS 1	Freedom/Prelude	10

PREMIERS (U.K.)
64	Silver Phoenix 1002	Tears, Tears/Bye Bye Johnny	45

PREMIERS (U.S.)
64	Warner Bros WB 134	Farmer John/Duffy's Blues	15
64	Warner Bros W 1565	FARMER JOHN "LIVE" (LP)	60

PREMO & HOPETON
67	Rio R 139	Your Safekeep/Loving And Kind	40
68	Pama PM 753	Peace On Earth/SCHOOL BOYS: Love Is A Message (as Premo & Joesph)	300

YVONNE PRENOSILOVA
65	Pye 7N 15751	When My Baby Cries/Come On Home	35

PRESENCE(1)
79	SRTS.79/CUS 296	No Reason/I Care For You (no p/s)	20

PRESENCE (2)
76	NC SLCW 1031	PRESENCE (LP)	35

PRESIDENTS (1)
64	Decca F 11826	Candy Man/Let The Sunshine In	50

ELVIS PRESLEY
78S : HMV 78S
56	HMV POP 182	Heartbreak Hotel/I Was The One	20
56	HMV POP 213	Blue Suede Shoes/Tutti Frutti	25
56	HMV POP 235	I Want You, I Need You, I Love You/My Baby Left Me	25
56	HMV POP 253	Love Me Tender/Anyway You Want Me (That's How I Will Be)	20
56	HMV POP 272	Blue Moon/I Don't Care If The Sun Don't Shine	30
57	HMV POP 295	Mystery Train/Love Me	40
57	HMV POP 305	Rip It Up/Baby, Let's Play House	40
57	HMV POP 330	Too Much/Playing For Keeps	30

Elvis PRESLEY

			MINT VALUE £
57	HMV POP 378	Paralyzed/When My Blue Moon Turns To Gold Again	30
57	HMV POP 408	Tryin' To Get To You/Lawdy, Miss Clawdy	40
58	HMV POP 428	I'm Left, You're Right, She's Gone/How Do You Think I Feel?	40

78S : RCA 78S

57	RCA RCA 1025	Santa Bring My Baby Back (To Me)/Santa Claus Is Back In Town	25
58	RCA RCA 1043	Don't/I Beg Of You	25
58	RCA RCA 1058	Wear My Ring Around Your Neck/Doncha' Think It's Time	30
58	RCA RCA 1070	Hard Headed Woman/Don't Ask Me Why	30
58	RCA RCA 1081	King Creole/Dixieland Rock	30
58	RCA RCA 1088	All Shook Up/Heartbreak Hotel	100
58	RCA RCA 1095	Hound Dog/Blue Suede Shoes	100
59	RCA RCA 1100	One Night/I Got Stung	60
59	RCA RCA 1113	(Now And Then There's) A Fool Such As I/I Need Your Love Tonight	60
59	RCA RCA 1136	A Big Hunk O' Love/My Wish Came True	100
60	RCA RCA 1187	Stuck On You/Fame And Fortune	500
60	RCA RCA 1194	A Mess Of Blues/The Girl Of My Best Friend	750

SINGLES : HMV 45S : PURPLE LABEL/SILVER PRINT

56	HMV 7M 385	Heartbreak Hotel/I Was The One	175
56	HMV 7M 405	Blue Suede Shoes/Tutti Frutti	250
56	HMV 7M 424	I Want You, I Need You, I Love You/My Baby Left Me	150
56	HMV POP 249	Hound Dog/Don't Be Cruel	100
56	HMV POP 253	Love Me Tender/Anyway You Want Me (That's How I Will Be)	100
56	HMV POP 272	Blue Moon/I Don't Care If The Sun Don't Shine	100
57	HMV POP 295	Mystery Train/Love Me	150
57	HMV POP 305	Rip It Up/Baby, Let's Play House	150
57	HMV POP 330	Too Much/Playing For Keeps	150
57	HMV POP 359	All Shook Up/That's When Your Heartaches Begin ('removable/replaceable' centre)	125
57	HMV POP 359	All Shook Up/That's When Your Heartaches Begin (solid centre)	50
57	HMV POP 378	Paralyzed/When My Blue Moon Turns To Gold Again	50
57	HMV POP 408	Tryin' To Get To You/Lawdy, Miss Clawdy	50
58	HMV POP 428	I'm Left, You're Right, She's Gone/How Do You Think I Feel?	50

SINGLES : HMV 45S: PURPLE LABEL/GOLD PRINT

56	HMV 7M 385	Heartbreak Hotel/I Was The One ('removable/replaceable' centre)	300
56	HMV 7M 385	Heartbreak Hotel/I Was The One (solid centre)	200
56	HMV 7M 405	Blue Suede Shoes/Tutti Frutti	300
56	HMV 7M 424	I Want You, I Need You, I Love You/My Baby Left Me ('removable/replaceable' centre)	300
56	HMV 7M 424	I Want You, I Need You, I Love You/My Baby Left Me ('solid centre)	200
56	HMV POP 249	Hound Dog/Don't Be Cruel	150
56	HMV POP 253	Love Me Tender/Anyway You Want Me (That's How I Will Be)	150
56	HMV POP 272	Blue Moon/I Don't Care If The Sun Don't Shine ('removable/replaceable' centre)	200
56	HMV POP 272	Blue Moon/I Don't Care If The Sun Don't Shine (solid centre)	150
57	HMV POP 295	Mystery Train/Love Me ('removable/replaceable' centre)	350
57	HMV POP 295	Mystery Train/Love Me (solid centre)	200
57	HMV 7MC 42	Mystery Train/I Forgot To Remember To Forget (U.K. issue of export single, gold label print only, smooth edge to labels)	300
57	HMV POP 305	Rip It Up/Baby, Let's Play House ('removable/replaceable' centre)	300
57	HMV POP 305	Rip It Up/Baby, Let's Play House (solid centre)	200
57	HMV POP 330	Too Much/Playing For Keeps	120
57	HMV POP 359	All Shook Up/That's When Your Heartaches Begin (push-out centre)	150
57	HMV POP 359	All Shook Up/That's When Your Heartaches Begin (solid centre)	100
57	HMV POP 378	Paralyzed/When My Blue Moon Turns To Gold Again	100

SINGLES : ORIGINAL RCA 45S: BLACK LABELS

57	RCA RCA 1013	(Let Me Be Your) Teddy Bear/Loving You	20
57	RCA RCA 1020	Party/Got A Lot O' Livin' To Do	20
57	RCA RCA 1025	Santa Bring My Baby Back (To Me)/Santa Claus Is Back In Town	20
58	RCA RCA 1028	Jailhouse Rock/Treat Me Nice	15
58	RCA RCA 1043	Don't/I Beg Of You	15
58	RCA RCA 1058	Wear My Ring Around Your Neck/Doncha' Think It's Time	15
58	RCA RCA 1070	Hard Headed Woman/Don't Ask Me Why	15
58	RCA RCA 1081	King Creole/Dixieland Rock	15
58	RCA RCA 1088	All Shook Up/Heartbreak Hotel	50
58	RCA RCA 1095	Hound Dog/Blue Suede Shoes	50
59	RCA RCA 1100	One Night/I Got Stung	15
59	RCA RCA 1113	(Now And Then There's) A Fool Such As I/I Need Your Love Tonight	15
59	RCA RCA 1136	A Big Hunk O' Love/My Wish Came True	15

SINGLES : ORIGINAL RCA VICTOR 45S: BLACK LABELS

62	RCA Victor RCA 1303	She's Not You/Just Tell Her Jim Said Hello	6
62	RCA Victor RCA 1320	Return To Sender/Where Do You Come From	6
63	RCA Victor RCA 1337	One Broken Heart For Sale/They Remind Me Too Much Of You	8
63	RCA Victor RCA 1374	Bossa Nova Baby/Witchcraft	6
62	RCA Victor RCA 1375	Kiss Me Quick/Something Blue	6
64	RCA Victor RCA 1390	Viva Las Vegas/What'd I Say	8
64	RCA Victor RCA 1404	Kissin' Cousins/It Hurts Me	6
64	RCA Victor RCA 1411	Such A Night/Never Ending	7
64	RCA Victor RCA 1422	Ain't That Loving You Baby/Ask Me	6
64	RCA Victor RCA 1430	Blue Christmas/White Christmas	8
65	RCA Victor RCA 1443	Do The Clam/You'll Be Gone	7
66	RCA Victor RCA 1509	Frankie And Johnny/Please Don't Stop Loving Me	15

Elvis PRESLEY

MINT VALUE £

Page	Catalogue	Title	Value
66	RCA Victor RCA 1526	Love Letters/Come What May	7
66	RCA Victor RCA 1545	All That I Am/Spinout	10
66	RCA Victor RCA 1557	If Every Day Was Like Christmas/How Would You Like To Be?	8
67	RCA Victor RCA 1565	Indescribably Blue/Fools Fall In Love	20
67	RCA Victor RCA 1593	The Love Machine/You Gotta Stop	15
67	RCA Victor RCA 1616	Long-Legged Girl (With The Short Dress On)/That's Someone You Never Forget	20
67	RCA Victor RCA 1628	Judy/There's Always Me	40
67	RCA Victor RCA 1642	Big Boss Man/You Don't Know Me	20
68	RCA Victor RCA 1663	Guitar Man/Hi-Heel Sneakers	10
68	RCA Victor RCA 1688	U.S. Male/Stay Away	15
68	RCA Victor RCA 1714	Your Time Hasn't Come Yet Baby/Let Yourself Go	15
68	RCA Victor RCA 1747	You'll Never Walk Alone/We Call On Him	30
68	RCA Victor RCA 1768	A Little Less Conversation/Almost In Love	25

SINGLES : ORIGINAL RCA VICTOR ORANGE LABEL 45S

Page	Catalogue	Title	Value
69	RCA Victor RCA 1795	If I Can Dream/Memories	10
69	RCA Victor RCA 1831	In The Ghetto/Any Day Now	6
69	RCA Victor RCA 1869	Clean Up Your Own Backyard/The Fair's Moving On	6
69	RCA Victor RCA 1900	Suspicious Minds/You'll Think Of Me (p/s)	10
70	RCA Victor RCA 1916	Don't Cry Daddy/Rubberneckin' (p/s)	15
70	RCA Victor RCA 1949	Kentucky Rain/My Little Friend (p/s)	10
70	RCA Victor RCA 1999	I've Lost You/The Next Step Is Love	6
71	RCA Victor RCA 2060	There Goes My Everything/I Really Don't Want To Know (p/s)	10
71	RCA Victor RCA 2084	Rags To Riches/Where Did They Go, Lord (p/s)	10
71	RCA Victor RCA 2125	I'm Leavin'/Heart Of Rome	6
71	RCA Victor RCA 2158	I Just Can't Help Believin'/How The Web Was Woven	6
72	RCA Victor RCA 2188	Until It's Time For You To Go/We Can Make The Morning (p/s)	10
72	RCA Victor RCA 2229	American Trilogy/The First Time Ever I Saw Your Face	10
72	RCA Victor RCA 2267	Burning Love/It's A Matter Of Time	8
72	RCA Victor RCA 2304	Always On My Mind/Separate Ways	7
73	RCA Victor RCA 2359	Polk Salad Annie/See See Rider	7
73	RCA Victor RCA 2393	Fool/Steamroller Blues	7
73	RCA Victor RCA 2435	Raised On Rock/For Ol' Times Sake	7
74	RCA Victor APBO 0196	Take Good Care Of Her/I've Got A Thing About You Baby (solid centre; most copies are U.S. imports with large centre hole in U.S. p/s)	200
74	RCA Victor APBO 0280	If You Talk In Your Sleep/Help Me	10
74	RCA Victor PB 10074	Promised Land/It's Midnight And I Miss You (2nd pressing with correct B-side title)	15
76	RCA Victor RCA 2674	Hurt/For The Heart	10

SINGLES : OTHER RCA 45S

Page	Catalogue	Title	Value
83	RCA RCAP 1028	Jailhouse Rock/The Elvis Medley (with "Hound Dog" credit on B-side) (reissue, picture disc)	15
83	RCA RCAP 369	I Can Help/If Every Day Was Like Christmas/The Lady Loves Me (10", picture disc in clear plastic sleeve)	15
84	RCA RCA 405	Green Green Grass Of Home/Release Me (And Let Me Love Again)/ Solitaire (p/s, with poster)	20
84	RCA RCAT 459	The Last Farewell/It's Easy for You (10", p/s)	10
87	RCA ARONT 1	Bossa Nova Baby/Ain't That Loving You Baby (12", p/s)	15
87	RCA ARONT 2	Love Me Tender/If I Can Dream (12", p/s)	10
88	RCA PB 49177	Are You Lonesome Tonight/Reconsider Baby (12", p/s)	10
88	RCA PB 49473	Mean Woman Blues/I Beg Of Of You (p/s)	10
88	RCA PT 49474	Mean Woman Blues/I Beg Of Of You (12", p/s)	20
88	RCA PT 49546	Stuck On You/Any Way You Want Me (12", p/s)	10
88	RCA PB 49943	Always On My Mind/Tomorrow Night (p/s)	10
88	RCA PT 49944	Always On My Mind/Tomorrow Night (12", p/s)	10
90	RCA TCB 1	(Now And Then There's) A Fool Such As I (Take 3)/Danny (promo only)	12
04	BMG 82876 619211	That's All Right/Blue Moon Of Kentucky (10", brown die-cut sleeve, with 'Sun' labels)	15

SINGLES : OTHER SINGLES AND FLEXIDISCS

Page	Catalogue	Title	Value
57	Weekend Mail (no cat. no.)	THE TRUTH ABOUT ME (1-sided 6" 78 rpm, mail-order only, in mailer)	40
57	Weekend Mail (no cat. no.)	THE TRUTH ABOUT ME (1-sided 6" 78 rpm, mail-order only, not in mailer)	25
77	RCA Victor 2694-2709	GOLD 16 SERIES (16 x p/s 7" in foldout cardboard carrier)	30
79	RCA LB 1	The Wonder Of You/Noel Edmonds Introduces Record Year (Lever Brothers premium)	20

SINGLES : RCA VICTOR 45S: BLACK LABEL REISSUES

Page	Catalogue	Title	Value
64	RCA Victor RCA 1020	Party/Got A Lot O' Livin' To Do	10
64	RCA Victor RCA 1025	Santa Bring My Baby Back (To Me)/Santa Claus Is Back In Town	15
64	RCA Victor RCA 1028	Jailhouse Rock/Treat Me Nice	15
64	RCA Victor RCA 1043	Don't/I Beg Of You	15
64	RCA Victor RCA 1058	Wear My Ring Around Your Neck/Doncha' Think It's Time	10
64	RCA Victor RCA 1070	Hard Headed Woman/Don't Ask Me Why	15
64	RCA Victor RCA 1081	King Creole/Dixieland Rock	15
64	RCA Victor RCA 1088	All Shook Up/Heartbreak Hotel	15
64	RCA Victor RCA 1095	Hound Dog/Blue Suede Shoes	15
64	RCA Victor RCA 1100	One Night/I Got Stung	10
64	RCA Victor RCA 1113	(Now And Then There's) A Fool Such As I/I Need Your Love Tonight	10
64	RCA Victor RCA 1136	A Big Hunk O' Love/My Wish Came True	10
64	RCA Victor RCA 1187	Stuck On You/Fame And Fortune	10
64	RCA Victor RCA 1194	A Mess Of Blues/The Girl Of My Best Friend	8
64	RCA Victor RCA 1207	It's Now Or Never (O Sole Mio)/Make Me Know It	15
64	RCA Victor RCA 1216	Are You Lonesome Tonight?/I Gotta Know	15
64	RCA Victor RCA 1226	Wooden Heart/Tonight Is So Right For Love	8
64	RCA Victor RCA 1227	Surrender (Torna A Surriento)/Lonely Man	8

Elvis PRESLEY

Year	Cat. No.	Title	Mint Value £
64	RCA Victor RCA 1244	Wild In The Country/I Feel So Bad	8
64	RCA Victor RCA 1258	(Marie's The Name) His Latest Flame/Little Sister	6
64	RCA Victor RCA 1270	Rock-A-Hula Baby/Can't Help Falling In Love	7

SINGLES : RCA VICTOR 45S: ORANGE LABEL REISSUES

Year	Cat. No.	Title	Mint Value £
69	RCA Victor RCA 1088	All Shook Up/Heartbreak Hotel	15
69	RCA Victor RCA 1095	Hound Dog/Blue Suede Shoes	15
69	RCA Victor RCA 1207	It's Now Or Never (O Sole Mio)/Make Me Know It	15
69	RCA Victor RCA 1216	Are You Lonesome Tonight?/I Gotta Know	15
69	RCA Victor RCA 1226	Wooden Heart/Tonight Is So Right For Love	30
69	RCA Victor RCA 1688	U.S. Male/Stay Away	100
71	RCA MAXI 2104	Heartbreak Hotel/Hound Dog/Don't Be Cruel ('Maximillion' sleeve)	10
71	RCA MAXI 2153	Jailhouse Rock/Are You Lonesome Tonight?/(Let Me Be Your)Teddy Bear/ Steadfast, Loyal And True ('Maximillion' sleeve)	10
75	RCA MAXI 2601	Blue Moon/You're A Heartbreaker/I'm Left, You're Right, She's Gone ('Maximillion' sleeve)	20

SINGLES : RETROSPECTIVE RCA BLUE LABEL 45S

Year	Cat. No.	Title	Mint Value £
81	RCA RCA 43	Guitar Man/Faded Love (with matt U.K. p/s [cat. no. RCA 43])	50
82	RCA RCA 196	Are You Lonesome Tonight? (Laughing Version)/From A Jack To A King (p/s)	6

SINGLES : SINGLES BOX SET

Year	Cat. No.	Title	Mint Value £
77	RCA (no cat. no.)	PRESLEY GOLD - 16 NUMBER ONES (16 x 7", each in p/s, black box set)	40

EXPORT SINGLES : HMV EXPORT 45S

Year	Cat. No.	Title	Mint Value £
57	HMV 7MC 42	Mystery Train/I Forgot To Remember To Forget (gold label print, serrated edge to labels)	300
57	HMV 7MC 45	I Want You, I Need You, I Love You/My Baby Left Me (gold label print)	200
57	HMV 7MC 50	Hound Dog/Don't Be Cruel (gold label print)	150
57	HMV JO 465	Love Me Tender/Anyway You Want Me (That's How I'll Be) (gold label print)	150
57	HMV JO 466	Too Much/Playing For Keeps (gold label print)	200
57	HMV JO 473	All Shook Up/That's When Your Heartaches Begin (gold label print)	150

EPS : EP BOXED SETS

Year	Cat. No.	Title	Mint Value £
82	RCA EP 1	THE EP COLLECTION (11-EP box set, reissues, with booklet)	35
83	RCA EP 2	THE EP COLLECTION VOL. 2 (11-EP box set, reissues, with booklet)	50

EPS : HMV EPS

Year	Cat. No.	Title	Mint Value £
57	HMV 7EG 8199	LOVE ME TENDER (soundtrack, round centre)	70
57	HMV 7EG 8199	LOVE ME TENDER (soundtrack, removeable centre)	100
57	HMV 7EG 8256	GOOD ROCKIN' TONIGHT (round centre only)	200

EPS : ORIGINAL RCA EPS : ROUND CENTRES

Year	Cat. No.	Title	Mint Value £
60	RCA RCX 190	SUCH A NIGHT	25
62	RCA RCX 211	FOLLOW THAT DREAM (soundtrack)	10
62	RCA RCX 211	FOLLOW THAT DREAM (mispressing, 2nd side features Jim Reeves)	100
62	RCA RCX 7106	KID GALAHAD (soundtrack)	10
64	RCA Victor RCX 7141	LOVE IN LAS VEGAS (soundtrack)	20
64	RCA Victor RCX 7142	ELVIS FOR YOU VOL. 1	50
64	RCA Victor RCX 7143	ELVIS FOR YOU VOL. 2	50
64	RCA Victor RCX 135	ELVIS IN TENDER MOOD	20
65	RCA Victor RCX 7173	TICKLE ME (soundtrack)	35
65	RCA Victor RCX 7174	TICKLE ME VOL. 2 (soundtrack)	35
67	RCA Victor RCX 7187	EASY COME, EASY GO (soundtrack)	40

EPS : RCA EPS : ROUND CENTRE REPRESSINGS

Year	Cat. No.	Title	Mint Value £
60s	RCA RCX 101	PEACE IN THE VALLEY	20
60s	RCA RCX 104	ELVIS PRESLEY	15
60s	RCA RCX 106	JAILHOUSE ROCK (soundtrack)	15
60s	RCA RCX 117	KING CREOLE VOL. 1 (soundtrack)	15
60s	RCA RCX 118	KING CREOLE VOL. 2 (soundtrack)	10
60s	RCA RCX 121	ELVIS SINGS CHRISTMAS SONGS (gatefold p/s)	60
60s	RCA RCX 131	ELVIS SAILS (interview record)	25
60s	RCA RCX 135	ELVIS IN TENDER MOOD	20
60s	RCA RCX 1045	A TOUCH OF GOLD	25
60s	RCA RCX 175	STRICTLY ELVIS	20
60s	RCA RCX 1048	A TOUCH OF GOLD VOL. 2	35

EPS : RCA EPS: TRIANGULAR CENTRES

Year	Cat. No.	Title	Mint Value £
57	RCA RCX 101	PEACE IN THE VALLEY	30
57	RCA RCX 104	ELVIS PRESLEY	40
58	RCA RCX 106	JAILHOUSE ROCK (soundtrack)	40
58	RCA RCX 117	KING CREOLE VOL. 1 (soundtrack, black label, cream or white rear p/s)	30
58	RCA RCX 118	KING CREOLE VOL. 2 (soundtrack, cream or white rear sleeve)	30
58	RCA RCX 121	ELVIS SINGS CHRISTMAS SONGS (1st issue, single sleeve)	60
58	RCA RCX 131	ELVIS SAILS (interview record, sleeve laminated front & back)	40
59	RCA RCX 135	ELVIS IN TENDER MOOD (with red print on rear sleeve)	40

(Originally issued with laminated front and back sleeves; later copies with front-only laminate are worth three quarters of these values.)

Year	Cat. No.	Title	Mint Value £
59	RCA RCX 1045	A TOUCH OF GOLD (laminated front sleeve only)	50
59	RCA RCX 175	STRICTLY ELVIS	40
60	RCA RCX 1048	A TOUCH OF GOLD VOL. 2	80

EPS : RCA VICTOR EPS: BLACK LABEL RE-PRESSINGS

Year	Cat. No.	Title	Mint Value £
64	RCA Victor RCX 101	PEACE IN THE VALLEY	15
64	RCA Victor RCX 104	ELVIS PRESLEY	15
64	RCA Victor RCX 106	JAILHOUSE ROCK (soundtrack)	15
64	RCA Victor RCX 117	KING CREOLE VOL. 1 (soundtrack)	15

Elvis PRESLEY

MINT VALUE £

64	RCA Victor RCX 118	KING CREOLE VOL. 2 (soundtrack)	15
64	RCA Victor RCX 121	ELVIS SINGS CHRISTMAS SONGS (single p/s)	30
64	RCA Victor RCX 131	ELVIS SAILS (interview record)	25
64	RCA Victor RCX 1045	A TOUCH OF GOLD	15
64	RCA Victor RCX 175	STRICTLY ELVIS	15
64	RCA Victor RCX 1048	A TOUCH OF GOLD VOL. 2	25
64	RCA Victor RCX 190	SUCH A NIGHT	10
64	RCA Victor RCX 211	FOLLOW THAT DREAM (soundtrack)	10
64	RCA Victor RCX 7106	KID GALAHAD (soundtrack)	10

EPS : RCA VICTOR EPS: ORANGE LABEL RE-PRESSINGS

69	RCA Victor RCX 101	PEACE IN THE VALLEY (push-out centre)	10
69	RCA Victor RCX 104	ELVIS PRESLEY (push-out centre)	12
69	RCA Victor RCX 106	JAILHOUSE ROCK (soundtrack, solid centre)	10
69	RCA Victor RCX 117	KING CREOLE VOL. 1 (soundtrack, push-out centre)	15
69	RCA Victor RCX 118	KING CREOLE VOL. 2 (soundtrack, push-out centre)	15
69	RCA Victor RCX 131	ELVIS SAILS (interview record, push-out or solid centre)	10
69	RCA Victor RCX 135	ELVIS IN TENDER MOOD (push-out or solid centre, with different take of "Lover Doll")	10
69	RCA Victor RCX 1045	A TOUCH OF GOLD (push-out centre)	15
69	RCA Victor RCX 1045	A TOUCH OF GOLD (solid centre)	10
69	RCA Victor RCX 175	STRICTLY ELVIS (push-out or solid centre)	10
69	RCA Victor RCX 1048	A TOUCH OF GOLD VOL. 2 (push-out centre)	15
69	RCA Victor RCX 1048	A TOUCH OF GOLD VOL. 2 (solid centre)	10
69	RCA Victor RCX 190	SUCH A NIGHT (push-out centre)	10

ALBUMS : CDS

84	RCA PD 89061/2/3	THE LEGEND (3-CD, gold box set, with booklet, numbered, 5,000 only)	40
84	RCA PD 89061/2/3	THE LEGEND (3-CD, silver box set, 5,000 only, with booklet, numbered)	40

ALBUMS : LPS: 'LARGE' ORANGE RCA VICTOR STEREO RE-PRESSINGS

72	RCA Victor SF 8232	ELVIS FOR EVERYONE ('blue shirt'/'TV Special' sleeve)	40

ALBUMS : LPS: 'SMALL' ORANGE RCA VICTOR MONO RE-PRESSINGS

69	RCA Victor RD 27052	ELVIS' CHRISTMAS ALBUM	40
69	RCA Victor RD 27088	KING CREOLE (soundtrack)	30
69	RCA Victor RD 27120	ELVIS	30
69	RCA Victor RD 27128	A DATE WITH ELVIS	30
69	RCA Victor RD 27159	ELVIS' GOLDEN RECORDS VOL. 2	30
69	RCA Victor RD 27171	ELVIS IS BACK! (gatefold sleeve)	30
69	RCA Victor RD 27192	G.I. BLUES (soundtrack)	30
69	RCA Victor RD 27211	HIS HAND IN MINE	15
69	RCA Victor RD 27224	SOMETHING FOR EVERYBODY	30
69	RCA Victor RD 27238	BLUE HAWAII (soundtrack)	30
69	RCA Victor RD 7528	ROCK 'N' ROLL NO. 2	30
69	RCA Victor RD 7630	ELVIS' GOLDEN RECORDS VOL. 3	30
69	RCA Victor RD 7723	FLAMING STAR AND SUMMER KISSES (soundtrack, orange label)	300
69	RCA Victor RD 7810	PARADISE, HAWAIIAN STYLE (soundtrack)	20
69	RCA Victor RD 7867	HOW GREAT THOU ART	20
69	RCA Victor RD 7917	CLAMBAKE (soundtrack)	30
69	RCA Victor RD 7924	ELVIS' GOLD RECORDS VOLUME 4	15
69	RCA Victor RD 7957	SPEEDWAY (soundtrack, with Nancy Sinatra)	20

ALBUMS : LPS: BLACK/RED SPOT RCA VICTOR RE-PRESSINGS

64	RCA Victor RD 7528	ROCK 'N' ROLL NO. 2 (reissue of HMV LP, mono)	18
64	RCA Victor SF 7528	ROCK 'N' ROLL NO. 2 (reissue of HMV LP, stereo)	25

ALBUMS : LPS: BLACK/SILVER SPOT RCA VICTOR RE-PRESSINGS

64	RCA Victor RC 24001	LOVING YOU (10" LP, mono only)	60
64	RCA Victor RD 27052	ELVIS' CHRISTMAS ALBUM (laminated front & back covers, no pictures on back cover, mono only)	60
64	RCA Victor RD 7528	ROCK 'N' ROLL NO. 2 (reissue of HMV LP, mono)	18
64	RCA Victor SF 7528	ROCK 'N' ROLL NO. 2 (reissue of HMV LP, stereo)	25
64	RCA Victor RD 27088	KING CREOLE (soundtrack, mono only)	30
64	RCA Victor RD 27120	ELVIS (mono only)	35
64	RCA Victor RD 27128	A DATE WITH ELVIS (mono only)	20
64	RCA Victor RD 27159	ELVIS' GOLDEN RECORDS VOL. 2 (mono only)	15
64	RCA Victor RD 27171	ELVIS IS BACK! (gatefold sleeve, mono)	30
64	RCA Victor SF 5060	ELVIS IS BACK! (gatefold sleeve, stereo)	40
64	RCA Victor RD 27192	G.I. BLUES (soundtrack, mono)	15
64	RCA Victor SF 5078	G.I. BLUES (soundtrack, stereo)	30
64	RCA Victor RD 27211	HIS HAND IN MINE (mono)	25
64	RCA Victor SF 5094	HIS HAND IN MINE (stereo)	30
64	RCA Victor RD 27224	SOMETHING FOR EVERYBODY (mono)	18
64	RCA Victor SF 5106	SOMETHING FOR EVERYBODY (stereo)	30
64	RCA Victor RD 27238	BLUE HAWAII (soundtrack, mono)	18
64	RCA Victor SF 5115	BLUE HAWAII (soundtrack, stereo)	25
64	RCA Victor RD 27265	POT LUCK (mono)	15
64	RCA Victor SF 5135	POT LUCK (stereo)	30

ALBUMS : LPS: GREEN RCA INTERNATIONAL ISSUES

72	RCA Intl. INTS 1414	BURNING LOVE AND HITS FROM HIS MOVIES (U.K. disc in U.K. sleeve)	30

ALBUMS : LPS: HMV ISSUES

56	HMV CLP 1093	ROCK 'N' ROLL	500
57	HMV CLP 1105	ROCK 'N' ROLL NO. 2	700

Elvis PRESLEY

MINT VALUE £

57	HMV DLP 1159	THE BEST OF ELVIS (10")	200

ALBUMS : LPS: ORIGINAL BLACK/RED SPOT RCA VICTOR ISSUES

64	RCA Victor RD 7630	ELVIS' GOLDEN RECORDS VOL. 3 (mono)	20
64	RCA Victor SF 7630	ELVIS' GOLDEN RECORDS VOL. 3 (stereo)	30
64	RCA Victor RD 7645	KISSIN' COUSINS (soundtrack, mono)	18
64	RCA Victor SF 7645	KISSIN' COUSINS (soundtrack, stereo)	30
64	RCA Victor RD 7678	ROUSTABOUT (soundtrack, mono)	15
64	RCA Victor SF 7678	ROUSTABOUT (soundtrack, stereo)	25
65	RCA Victor RD 7714	GIRL HAPPY (soundtrack, mono)	20
65	RCA Victor SF 7714	GIRL HAPPY (soundtrack, stereo)	30
65	RCA Victor RD 7723	FLAMING STAR AND SUMMER KISSES (soundtrack, mono only, black label)	50
65	RCA Victor RD/SF 7752	ELVIS FOR EVERYONE (mono, 'orange shirt' sleeve)	35
65	RCA Victor SF 7752	ELVIS FOR EVERYONE (stereo, 'orange shirt' sleeve)	45
65	RCA Victor RD 7767	HAREM HOLIDAY (soundtrack, mono)	20
65	RCA Victor SF 7767	HAREM HOLIDAY (soundtrack, stereo)	25
66	RCA Victor RD 7793	FRANKIE AND JOHNNY (soundtrack, mono)	20
66	RCA Victor SF 7793	FRANKIE AND JOHNNY (soundtrack, stereo)	30
66	RCA Victor RD 7810	PARADISE, HAWAIIAN STYLE (soundtrack, mono)	20
66	RCA Victor SF 7810	PARADISE, HAWAIIAN STYLE (soundtrack, stereo)	30
66	RCA Victor RD 7820	CALIFORNIA HOLIDAY (soundtrack, mono)	20
66	RCA Victor SF 7820	CALIFORNIA HOLIDAY (soundtrack, stereo)	30
67	RCA Victor RD 7867	HOW GREAT THOU ART (mono)	25
67	RCA Victor SF 7867	HOW GREAT THOU ART (stereo)	35
67	RCA Victor RD 7892	DOUBLE TROUBLE (soundtrack, mono)	15
67	RCA Victor SF 7892	DOUBLE TROUBLE (soundtrack, stereo)	20
68	RCA Victor RD 7917	CLAMBAKE (soundtrack, black/red dot labels, mono)	20
68	RCA Victor SF 7917	CLAMBAKE (soundtrack, black/red dot labels, stereo)	25
68	RCA Victor RD 7924	ELVIS' GOLD RECORDS VOLUME 4 (with "Never Ending" listed on sleeve instead of "Love Letters"; mono)	30
68	RCA Victor SF 7924	ELVIS' GOLD RECORDS VOLUME 4 (with "Never Ending" listed on sleeve instead of "Love Letters"; stereo)	30
68	RCA Victor RD 7924	ELVIS' GOLD RECORDS VOLUME 4 (corrected sleeve, mono)	25
68	RCA Victor SF 7924	ELVIS' GOLD RECORDS VOLUME 4 (corrected sleeve, stereo)	25
68	RCA Victor RD 7957	SPEEDWAY (soundtrack, with Nancy Sinatra, mono)	30
68	RCA Victor SF 7957	SPEEDWAY (soundtrack, with Nancy Sinatra, stereo)	25

ALBUMS : LPS: ORIGINAL BLACK/SILVER SPOT RCA ISSUES

57	RCA RC 24001	LOVING YOU (10", soundtrack)	75
57	RCA RD 27052	ELVIS' CHRISTMAS ALBUM (laminated front & back covers with 4 pictures on back cover)	100
58	RCA RD 27088	KING CREOLE (soundtrack)	40
59	RCA RD 27120	ELVIS	75
59	RCA RD 27128	A DATE WITH ELVIS	60
60	RCA RD 27159	ELVIS' GOLDEN RECORDS VOL. 2	30
60	RCA RD 27171	ELVIS IS BACK! (gatefold sleeve, mono)	40
60	RCA SF 5060	ELVIS IS BACK! (gatefold sleeve, stereo)	60
60	RCA RD 27192	G.I. BLUES (soundtrack, mono)	18
60	RCA SF 5078	G.I. BLUES (soundtrack, stereo)	25
61	RCA RD 27211	HIS HAND IN MINE (mono)	25
61	RCA SF 5094	HIS HAND IN MINE (stereo)	45
61	RCA RD 27224	SOMETHING FOR EVERYBODY (mono)	20
61	RCA SF 5106	SOMETHING FOR EVERYBODY (stereo)	35
61	RCA RD 27238	BLUE HAWAII (soundtrack, mono)	15
61	RCA SF 5115	BLUE HAWAII (soundtrack, stereo)	20
62	RCA RD 27765	POT LUCK (mono)	20
62	RCA SF 5135	POT LUCK (stereo)	30

ALBUMS : LPS: ORIGINAL BLACK/SILVER SPOT RCA VICTOR ISSUES

63	RCA Victor RD 7534	GIRLS! GIRLS! GIRLS! (soundtrack, mono)	15
63	RCA Victor SF 7534	GIRLS! GIRLS! GIRLS! (soundtrack, stereo)	35
63	RCA Victor RD 7565	IT HAPPENED AT THE WORLD'S FAIR (soundtrack, mono)	18
63	RCA Victor SF 7565	IT HAPPENED AT THE WORLD'S FAIR (soundtrack, stereo)	35
63	RCA Victor RD 7609	FUN IN ACAPULCO (soundtrack, mono)	20
63	RCA Victor SF 7609	FUN IN ACAPULCO (soundtrack, stereo)	35

ALBUMS : LPS: ORIGINAL ORANGE RCA VICTOR ISSUES

69	RCA Victor RD 8011	ELVIS ("TV Special" Soundtrack)	15
69	RCA Victor RD 8029	FROM ELVIS IN MEMPHIS (mono)	15
70	RCA Victor SF 8080/1	FROM MEMPHIS TO VEGAS - FROM VEGAS TO MEMPHIS (2-LP, with 2 x 10" x 8" photos, glossy cover)	30
70	RCA Victor SF 8080/1	FROM MEMPHIS TO VEGAS - FROM VEGAS TO MEMPHIS (2-LP, with 2 x 10" x 8" photos, matt cover)	25
70	RCA SF 8128	ON STAGE, FEBRUARY 1970 (with 30" x 20" colour poster; glossy cover)	15
71	RCA LPM 6402	THE OTHER SIDES - WORLDWIDE 50 GOLD AWARD HITS VOL. 2 (4-LP, box with material patch & colour portrait)	30
71	RCA Victor SF 8162	THAT'S THE WAY IT IS (glossy cover)	15
71	RCA Victor SF 8172	I'M 10,000 YEARS OLD - ELVIS COUNTRY (with colour print, glossy cover)	15
71	RCA Victor SF 8221	ELVIS SINGS THE WONDERFUL WORLD OF CHRISTMAS	15
72	RCA Victor SF 8266	ELVIS NOW	15
72	RCA Victor SF 8275	HE TOUCHED ME	15
73	RCA Victor SF 8378	ELVIS (with "Fool" sticker, must be UK disc and UK cover!)	40
73	RCA DPS 2040	ALOHA FROM HAWAII VIA SATELLITE (2-LP)	20
73	RCA APL1 0388	RAISED ON ROCK/FOR OL' TIMES SAKE (U.K. disc in U.K. sleeve)	150

Reg PRESLEY

MINT VALUE £

Year	Cat. No.	Title	Value
74	RCA APL1 0475	GOOD TIMES (back cover credits "Loving Arms" or "Lovin' Arms")	18
74	RCA APL1 0606	ELVIS AS RECORDED ON STAGE IN MEMPHIS	15
74	RCA LPL1 7527	HITS OF THE 70s	15
75	RCA APL1 0873	PROMISED LAND	15
75	RCA APM1 0818	HAVING FUN WITH ELVIS ON STAGE	20
75	RCA RS 1011	TODAY	18
76	RCA RS 1060	FROM ELVIS PRESLEY BOULEVARD, MEMPHIS, TENNESSEE	15
77	RCA PL 12274	WELCOME TO MY WORLD	15
80	RCA CPL8 3699	ELVIS ARON PRESLEY (8-LP, box set)	50
84	RCA PL 85172	A GOLDEN CELEBRATION (6-LP box set with inserts)	30

ALBUMS : LPS: SILVER SPOT/'RED SEAL' RCA ISSUES

Year	Cat. No.	Title	Value
58	RCA RB 16069	ELVIS' GOLDEN RECORDS (maroon 'silver spot' label, gatefold sleeve with stapled-in 4-page photo booklet)	100
60	RCA RB 16069	ELVIS' GOLDEN RECORDS ('Red Seal'/'silver spot' label, gatefold sleeve with stapled-in 2-page photo booklet)	30
63	RCA RB 16069	ELVIS' GOLDEN RECORDS ('Red Seal'/'black spot' label, no booklet, gatefold sleeve)	20
67	RCA RB 16069	ELVIS' GOLDEN RECORDS ('Red Seal'/'black spot' label, no booklet, single sleeve)	18

ALBUMS : OTHER LPS

Year	Cat. No.	Title	Value
71	Camden CDS 1088	YOU'LL NEVER WALK ALONE (LP, withdrawn)	150
78	St. Michael IMP 113	ELVIS (exclusive to Marks & Spencer)	60
78	St. Michael IMPD 204	THE WONDERFUL WORLD OF ELVIS PRESLEY (2-LP, via Marks & Spencer)	30
79	Hammer HMR 6002	THE KING SPEAKS (green sleeve)	30
84	Imperial Records DR 1124	AMERICAN TRILOGY (3-LP, box set)	25
85	Sunday 1	ELVIS: THE GOLDEN ALBUM (LP, available via Sunday Times magazine)	20
86	RCA AREP 1	ACUFF-ROSE PRESENTS ELVIS (promo-only, 300 copies)	150

ALBUMS : CASTLE REISSUES

Year	Cat. No.	Title	Value
00	Castle Music/BMG ELVIS 102	THAT'S THE WAY IT IS (5-LP)	45
99	Castle Music/BMG ELVIS 100P	ARTIST OF THE CENTURY (box set, 5 x picture disc LPs & booklet, numbered)	40
99	Castle Music/BMG ELVIS 100	ARTIST OF THE CENTUY (5-LP box set & booklet, numbered)	40
99	Castle Music/BMG ELVIS 100R	ARTIST OF THE CENTURY (box set, 5-LP red vinyl & booklet, numbered)	50
99	Castle Music/BMG ELVIS 100X	ARTIST OF THE CENTURY (box set, 5-LP, blue vinyl & booklet, numbered, HMV exclusive)	50
99	Castle Music/BMG ELVIS 101X	THE SUN SINGLES COLLECTION (6 x 7" box set, yellow vinyl, numbered HMV exclusive)	35
99	Castle Music/BMG ELVIS 101	THE SUN SINGLES COLLECTION (6 x 7" box set with poster, numbered)	35
00	Castle Music/BMG ELVIS 103	THE UK NO. 1 SINGLES COLLECTION (17 x 7" box set with booklet)	50
00	Castle Music/BMG ELVIS 103X	THE UK NO. 1 SINGLES COLLECTION (17 x 7" box set with booklet, coloured vinyl)	75
00	Castle Music/BMG ELVIS 104X	PEACE IN THE VALLEY (5-LP box set, with bonus 10" EP)	40
00	Castle Music/BMG ELVIS 104	PEACE IN THE VALLEY (5-LP box set)	30
01	Castle Music/BMG ELVIS 105	THE INTERNATIONAL EP COLLECTION (11 x 7" EP box set with insert)	30
01	Castle Music/BMG ELVIS 106	G.I. BLUES (LP, with bonus EP)	15
01	Castle Music/BMG ELVIS 108	LIVE IN LAS VEGAS (5-LP box set)	60
01	Castle Music/BMG ELVIS 107	BLUE HAWAII (LP, with bonus EP)	15
02	Castle Music/BMG ELVIS 111	JAILHOUSE ROCK (LP, with bonus EP)	15
02	Castle Music/BMG ELVIS 112	KING CREOLE (LP, with bonus EP)	15
02	Castle Music/BMG ELVIS 113	TICKLE ME (LP, with bonus EP)	25
02	Castle Music/BMG ELVIS 110	LOVING YOU (LP, with bonus EP)	15

(see also Jordanaires, Scotty Moore, Bill Black's Combo)

REG PRESLEY

Year	Cat. No.	Title	Value
69	Page One POF 131	Lucinda Lee/Wichita Lineman	8

(see also Troggs, Suzi Quatro)

PRESSGANG

Year	Cat. No.	Title	Value
89	Vox Pop VOX 022	ROGUES (LP)	15

RAY PRESSLEY

Year	Cat. No.	Title	Value
62	Longhorn BLH 0002	Living, Learning, Trying To Forget/Half A Love (estimated that around 1000 pressed)	15

PRESSURE

Year	Cat. No.	Title	Value
82	SRT/Macca SPLIFF 1/S82CUS 1394	Fool To Yourself/Dub To Yourself (no p/s)	8

PRESSURE GROUP

Year	Cat. No.	Title	Value
87	Poltroon POL 001	ONLY GOD IS PERFECT (EP, 300 only)	60

PRESSURE POINT

Year	Cat. No.	Title	Value
82	Pressure Point PP 001	Big Deal/Straight To The Point (p/s)	15

PRESSURE 28

Year	Cat. No.	Title	Value
82	Helen Of Oi! HOO 01	Get Ready/Up Yours	8

PRESSURE STOPS

Year	Cat. No.	Title	Value
80	Airplay PLAY 1	Crash Wanderer/Shirts	12

PRESTIGE BLUES SWINGERS

Year	Cat. No.	Title	Value
59	Esquire 32-082	BLUES GROOVE (Tiny Grimes & Coleman Hawkins as Prestige Blues Swingers) (LP)	20
60	Esquire 32-110	OUTSKIRTS OF TOWN (LP)	20

BILLY PRESTON

Year	Cat. No.	Title	Value
66	Sue WI 4012	Billy's Bag/Don't Let The Sun Catch You Cryin'	25
66	Capitol CL 15458	In The Midnight Hour/Advice	40
66	Capitol CL 15458	In The Midnight Hour/Advice (DJ copy)	50
66	Capitol CL 15471	Sunny/Let The Music Play	15
68	Soul City SC 107	Greazee Part 1/Part 2	10
69	President PT 263	Billy's Bag/Don't Let The Sun Catch You Crying (reissue)	10
69	President PT 263	Billy's Bag/Goldfinger (different B-side)	15

Earl PRESTON

MINT VALUE £

69	Apple APPLE 12	That's The Way God Planned It/What About You (p/s)	10
69	Apple APPLE 19	Everything's Alright/I Want To Thank You	20
70	Apple APPLE 21	All That I've Got/As I Get Older (some in p/s)	25
70	Apple APPLE 21	All That I've Got/As I Get Older (some in p/s)	8
70	Soul City SC 107	Greazee (Parts 1 & 2)	20
70	Soul City SC 107	Greazee (Parts 1 & 2) (DJ Copy)	100
67	Capitol (S)T 2532	WILDEST ORGAN IN TOWN (LP)	25
67	Sue ILP 935	THE MOST EXCITING ORGAN EVER (LP)	60
69	President PTLS 1034	APPLE OF THEIR EYE (LP)	20
69	Apple SAPCOR 9	THAT'S THE WAY GOD PLANNED IT (LP)	40
70	Apple SAPCOR 14	ENCOURAGING WORDS (LP)	70
70	Soul City SCM 002	GREAZEE SOUL (LP)	30
70	Joy JOYS 174	GOSPEL IN MY SOUL (LP)	20
91	Apple SAPCOR 9	THAT'S THE WAY GOD PLANNED IT (LP, gatefold sleeve, with bonus 12" [SAPCOR 92])	30
93	Apple SAPCOR 14	ENCOURAGING WORDS (LP, gatefold sleeve with bonus 12" [SAPCOR 142])	30

(see also Beatles)

EARL PRESTON

63	Fontana TF 406	I Know Something/Watch Your Step (as Earl Preston & T.T.'s)	20
64	Fontana TF 481	Raindrops/That's For Sure (as Earl Preston & Realms)	20

(see also Realm)

JOHNNY PRESTON

60	Mercury AMT 1079	Running Bear/My Heart Knows (78)	40
60	Mercury AMT 1092	Cradle Of Love/City Of Tears (some in p/s)	20
60	Mercury AMT 1092	Cradle Of Love/City Of Tears (no p/s)	6
60	Mercury AMT 1104	Feel So Fine/I'm Starting To Go Steady	10
60	Mercury AMT 1114	Charming Billy/Up In The Air	12
61	Mercury AMT 1129	Leave My Kitten Alone/Do What You Did	20
61	Mercury AMT 1145	Big Chief Heartbreak/Madre De Dios (Mother Of God)	20
61	Mercury AMT 1164	New Baby For Christmas/Rock And Roll Guitar	25
61	Mercury AMT 1167	Free Me/Kissing Tree	25
60	Mercury ZEP 10078	RUNNING BEAR (EP)	35
60	Mercury ZEP 10098	RING TAIL TOOTER (EP)	35
61	Mercury ZEP 10116	TOKEN OF LOVE (EP)	45
60	Mercury MMC 14051	JOHNNY PRESTON - RUNNING BEAR (LP)	80

MIKE PRESTON

58	Decca F 11053	A House, A Car And A Wedding Ring/My Lucky Love	6
58	Decca F 11087	Why, Why, Why/Whispering Grass	6
59	Decca F 11120	Dirty Old Town/In Surabaya	8
60	Decca F 11255	I'd Do Anything/Where Is Love?	6
60	Decca F 11287	Togetherness/Farewell My Love	6
66	Emerald MD1028	Our Love Will Go On/Forgive Me	10
60	Decca DFE 6635	FOUR SONGS BY RAY NOBLE (EP)	10
61	Decca DFE 6679	MARRY ME (EP)	12

PRETENDERS

94	WEA 4509-95822-1	LAST OF THE INDEPENDENTS (LP)	50

(see also Jimmy Edwards)

PRETTY BOY FLOYD & GEMS

79	Rip Off RIP OFF 1	Spread The Word Around/Hold Tight (p/s)	15
79	Rip Off RIP 10	Sharon/The Instigator (p/s)	20

PRETTY THINGS

64	Fontana TF 469	Rosalyn/Big Boss Man	15
64	Fontana TF 503	Don't Bring Me Down/We'll Be Together	12
65	Fontana TF 537	Honey I Need/I Can Never Say	12
65	Fontana TF 585	Cry To Me/Get A Buzz	20
65	Fontana TF 647	Midnight To Six Man/Can't Stand The Pain	22
66	Fontana TF 688	Come See Me/£.s.d.	35
66	Fontana TF 722	A House In The Country/Me Needing You	25
66	Fontana TF 773	Progress/Buzz The Jerk	30
67	Fontana TF 829	Children/My Time	20
67	Columbia DB 8300	Defecting Grey/Mr. Evasion	100
68	Columbia DB 8353	Talkin' About The Good Times/Walking Through My Dreams	80
68	Columbia DB 8494	Private Sorrow/Balloon Burning	40
69	Fontana TF 1024	Rosalyn/Don't Bring Me Down (p/s)	15
70	Harvest HAR 5016	The Good Mr. Square/Blue Serge Blues	12
70	Harvest HAR 5031	October 26/Cold Stone	10
71	Harvest HAR 5037	Stone-Hearted Mama/Summertime/Circus Mind	10
12	Fruits De Mer Crustacean 29	Honey I Need (live)/I Can Never Say (Demo) (p/s, 500 dark red translucent, 500 white and 200 black vinyl)	8
64	Fontana TE 17434	THE PRETTY THINGS (EP)	60
65	Fontana TE 17442	RAININ' IN MY HEART (EP)	70
66	Fontana TE 17472	ON FILM (EP)	150
12	Fruits De Mer Crustacean 31	S.F. SORROW LIVE IN LONDON EP (gatefold p/s, poster, white, black or maroon vinyl)	10
65	Fontana TL 5239	THE PRETTY THINGS (LP)	150
65	Fontana TL 5280	GET THE PICTURE (LP)	200
67	Wing WL 1164	BEST OF THE PRETTY THINGS (LP)	35
67	Fontana (S)TL 5425	EMOTIONS (LP, mono/stereo)	150
67	Wing WL 1167	THE PRETTY THINGS (LP, reissue)	40
68	Columbia SX 6306	S.F. SORROW (LP, gatefold sleeve, blue/black label, mono)	700
68	Columbia SCX 6306	S.F. SORROW (LP, gatefold sleeve, blue/black label, stereo)	400
70	Columbia SCX 6306	S.F. SORROW (LP, gatefold sleeve; silver/black label re-pressing, stereo)	50

Eddie PREVOST BAND

MINT VALUE £

70	Harvest SHVL 774	PARACHUTE (LP, gatefold sleeve)	125
70	Fontana Special SFL 13140	EMOTIONS (LP, reissue)	20
72	Warner Bros K 46190	FREEWAY MADNESS (LP, gatefold sleeve)	18
74	Swan Song SSK 59400	SILK TORPEDO (LP, gatefold sleeve with insert)	15
75	Harvest SHDW 406	S.F. SORROW/PARACHUTE (2-LP)	40
78	Butt Nott DO1	ELECTRIC BANANA THE SEVEN TIES (LP)	15
77	Harvest SHSM 2022	SINGLES A'S & B'S (LP)	20
89	Edsel XED236	S.F. SORROW (LP, reissue, gatefold)	20

(see also Electric Banana, Twink, Viv Prince, Sunshine, Fenmen, Kate)

EDDIE PREVOST BAND

78	Matchless MR 1	LIVE VOLUME 1 (LP)	30
78	Matchless MR 2	LIVE VOLUME 2 (LP)	20
77	Spotlite SPJ 505	NOW HERE THIS THEN... (LP)	20
85	Matchless MR 7	CONTINUUM (LP)	15

(see also Amm, Organum)

JOEL PREVOST

78	CBS SCBS 6300	Somewhere Sometime/Il Y Aura Toujours Des Violons	10

ALAN PRICE (SET)

65	Decca F 12217	Any Day Now (My Wild Beautiful Baby)/Never Be Sick On Sunday	12
66	Decca F 12367	I Put A Spell On You/Iechyd-Da	7
66	Decca F 12518	Willow Weep For Me/Yours Until Tomorrow	6
67	Decca F 12691	Shame/Don't Do That Again	8
68	Decca F 12774	When I Was A Cowboy/Tappy Turquoise (export issue)	20
69	Deram DM 263	Trimdon Grange Explosion/Falling In Love Again	6
70	Decca F 13017	Sunshine And Rain (The Name Of The Game)/ Is There Anybody Out There? (solo)	6
67	Decca DFE 8677	THE AMAZING ALAN PRICE (EP)	30
66	Decca LK 4839	THE PRICE TO PLAY (LP, laminate front cover, flipbacks)	30
67	Decca LK/SKL 4907	A PRICE ON HIS HEAD (LP, laminated front cover)	25

(see also Animals, Paul Williams Set, Johnny Almond Music Machine, Dave Greenslade)

KENNY PRICE

66	Stateside SS 554	Walking On New Grass/Wasting My Time	6

LLOYD PRICE

57	London HL 8438	Just Because/Why (triangular centre)	150
57	London HL 8438	Just Because/Why (round centre)	80
57	London HL 8438	Just Because/Why (78)	20
59	HMV POP 580	Stagger Lee/You Need Love	15
59	HMV POP 580	Stagger Lee/You Need Love (78)	25
59	HMV POP 598	Where Were You (On Our Wedding Day)?/Is It Really Love?	12
59	HMV POP 598	Where Were You (On Our Wedding Day)?/Is It Really Love? (78)	25
59	HMV POP 626	Personality/Have You Ever Had The Blues?	10
59	HMV POP 626	Personality/Have You Ever Had The Blues? (78)	25
59	HMV POP 650	I'm Gonna Get Married/Three Little Pigs	10
59	HMV POP 650	I'm Gonna Get Married/Three Little Pigs (78)	60
59	HMV POP 672	Won't 'Cha Come Home/Come Into My Heart	10
60	HMV POP 712	Lady Luck/Never Let Me Go	15
60	HMV POP 712	Lady Luck/Never Let Me Go (78)	30
60	HMV POP 741	For Love/No If's - No And's	10
60	HMV POP 772	Question/If I Look A Little Blue (as Lloyd Price Orchestra)	10
60	HMV POP 772	Question/If I Look A Little Blue (as Lloyd Price Orchestra) (78)	40
60	HMV POP 799	Just Call Me (And I'll Understand)/Who Coulda' Told You (They Lied)	10
61	HMV POP 826	Know What You're Doin'/That's Why Tears Come And Go (as Lloyd Price Orchestra)	10
61	HMV POP 926	Boo Hoo/I Made You Cry	10
62	HMV POP 983	Be A Leader/'Nother Fairy Tale	10
62	HMV POP 1100	Under Your Spell, Again/Happy Birthday Mama	10
63	Liberty LIB 10127	Misty/Cry On	10
72	President PT 321	Ready For Betty/Beat In Trinidad	10
73	GSF GSZ 5	Love Music/Just For Baby	10
73	GSF GSZ 11	Trying To Slip Away/They Get Down	10
59	HMV 7EG 8538	THE EXCITING LLOYD PRICE (EP, mono)	50
59	HMV GES 5784	THE EXCITING LLOYD PRICE (EP, stereo)	70
59	HMV CLP 1285	THE EXCITING LLOYD PRICE (LP)	60
59	HMV CLP 1314	MR. PERSONALITY (LP)	60
60	London HA-U 2213	LLOYD PRICE (LP)	60
60	HMV CLP 1361	MR. PERSONALITY SINGS THE BLUES (LP)	50
60	HMV CLP 1393	THE FANTASTIC LLOYD PRICE (LP, mono)	40
60	HMV CSD 1323	THE FANTASTIC LLOYD PRICE (LP, stereo)	50
62	HMV CLP 1519	COOKIN' (LP, mono)	25
62	HMV CSD 1413	COOKIN' (LP, stereo)	30
63	Encore ENC 2004	PRICE SINGS THE MILLION DOLLAR SELLERS (LP)	15
69	Major Minor SMLP 57	LLOYD PRICE NOW (LP)	20

RAY PRICE

57	Philips BBE 12137	RAY PRICE (EP)	25

(see also Cherry Wainer)

(ROCKIN') RED PRICE

56	Decca F 10822	Rocky Mountain Gal/Rock O' The North (as Red Price & His Rockin' Rhythm)	15
57	Woodbine	Woodbine Rock (78, with picture on label, promo only)	40
57	Woodbine	Woodbine Rock (78, without picture on label, promo only)	15
58	Pye 7N 15169	Weekend/The Sneeze	20
58	Pye 7N 15169	Weekend/The Sneeze (78)	25
60	Pye 7N 15262	Wow!/My Baby's Door	10

Red PRICE & BLUE BEATS

MINT VALUE £

61	Parlophone R 4789	Theme From "Danger Man"/Blackjack (as Red Price Combo)	30

RED PRICE & BLUE BEATS

64	Blue Beat BB 209	Blue Beats Over (The White Cliffs Of Dover)/Kiss The Baby (When You Grow Too Old To Dream)	10

RICK PRICE

70	Gemini GMS 012	Davey Has No Dad/Bitter Sweet	10
71	Gemini GMS 017	Top Ten Record/Beautiful Sally	10
71	Gemini GME 1017	TALKING TO THE FLOWERS (LP, laminated front sleeve)	50

(see also Move, Sheridan-Price, Sight & Sound)

RIKKI PRICE

58	Fontana H 162	Tom Dooley/(It Looks Like Rain In) Cherry Blossom Lane	6
59	Fontana H 171	Honey, Honey/The Very Thought Of You	8
59	Fontana H 217	Mr. Blue/Man On My Trail	6
62	Fontana H 371	You're For Real/When You Pass By	6
58	Fontana TFE 17100	RIKKI PRICE (EP)	20

(see also Sheridan-Price)

SAMMY PRICE

63	Storyville A 45 068	Boogieing With Big Sid/133 Street Boogie (with p/s)	30
63	Storyville A 45 068	Boogieing With Big Sid/133 Street Boogie	20
57	Columbia SEG 7679	ORIGINAL SAMMY BLUES (EP)	20
58	Vogue EPV 1146	SAMMY PRICE (EP)	60
58	Vogue EPV 1151	SAMMY PRICE'S BLUESICIANS (EP)	60
58	Vogue LAE 12027	SWINGIN' PARIS STYLE (LP)	40
62	London Jazz LTZ-R 15240	THE BLUES AIN'T NOTHIN' (LP, mono)	30
62	London Jazz SAH-R 6254	THE BLUES AIN'T NOTHIN' (LP, stereo)	40

(see also SIster Rosetta Tharpe)

VINCENT PRICE

77	EMI EMI 2659	The Monster Mash/The Bard's Own Recipe	10
59	Columbia 33SX 1141	VINCENT PRICE (LP)	45

PRIDE

85	Pride P.R.T. 001	What's Love/No Emotion (p/s)	25

DICKIE PRIDE

59	Columbia DB 4283	Slippin' 'N' Slidin'/Don't Make Me Love You	40
59	Columbia DB 4296	Fabulous Cure/Midnight Oil	30
59	Columbia DB 4340	Frantic/Primrose Lane	20
60	Columbia DB 4403	Betty, Betty (Go Steady With Me)/No John	20
60	Columbia DB 4451	You're Singin' Our Love Song To Somebody Else/Bye Bye Blackbird	10
59	Columbia SEG 7937	SHEIK OF SHAKE (EP)	250
61	Columbia 33SX 1307	PRIDE WITHOUT PREJUDICE (LP, mono)	60
61	Columbia SCX 3369	PRIDE WITHOUT PREJUDICE (LP, stereo)	70

(see also Guvners)

LOU PRIDE

06	Jazzman JMAN 048	SUEMI SESSIONS (Box set, 3 x 7")	10

LOUIS PRIMA (& HIS ORCHESTRA)

56	Capitol CL 14669	5 Months, 2 Weeks, 2 Days/Banana Split For My Baby	20
58	Capitol CL 14821	Buona Sera/Beep! Beep!	15
60	London HLD 9230	Ol' Man Moses (with Sam Butera's Witnesses)/Wonderland By Night	10
64	Prima PR 1001	Fee Fie Foo Part 1/Fee Fie Foo Part 2	6
59	Capitol EAP1 1132	STRICTLY PRIMA (EP)	10
58	Capitol T 908	THE WILDEST SHOW AT TAHOE (LP)	20
57	Capitol T 755	THE WILDEST (LP)	30
58	Capitol T 836	THE CALL OF THE WILDEST (LP)	20

(see also Sam Butera's Witnesses)

LOUIS PRIMA & KEELY SMITH

54	Columbia SCM 5092	Take A Little Walk Around The Block/LOUIS PRIMA: Oh! Cumari	6
59	Capitol T 1160	HEY BOY! HEY GIRL! (LP)	25

(see also Keely Smith)

PRIMAL SCREAM

85	Creation CRE 017	All Fall Down/It Happens (foldaround p/s in poly bag)	25
86	Creation CRE 026	Crystal Crescent/Velocity Girl (p/s)	18
86	Creation CRE 026T	Crystal Crescent/Velocity Girl/Spirea X (12", p/s)	15
87	Elevation ACID 5	Imperial/Star Fruit Surf Rider (p/s)	8
87	Elevation ACID 5T	Imperial/Star Fruit Surf Rider/So Sad About Us/Imperial (demo) (12", in poster p/s with 'special price' sticker)	10
92	Creation CRE 117T	DIXIE NARCO EP (12")	10
87	Elevation ELV 2	SONIC FLOWER GROOVE (LP)	20
89	Creation CRELP 054	PRIMAL SCREAM (LP, with bonus 45 "Split Wide Open 1"/ Lone Star Girl 1 [CREFRE 6, no p/s])	20
91	Creation CRELP 076	SCREAMADELICA (2-LP)	80
94	Creation CRELP 146	GIVE OUT BUT DON'T GIVE UP (2-LP, inners)	50
97	Creation CRELP 224P	ECHO DEK (LP, promo, die-cut sleeve)	25
97	Creation CREL 7224	ECHO DEK (5 x 7", box set)	30
98	Creation CRELP 178	VANISHING POINT (2-LP, gatefold)	75
99	Sony/Creation 88697811063	SCREAMADELICA (2-LP, reissue, red vinyl, numbered)	35
00	Creation CRELP 239	EXTERMINATOR (EXTMNTR) (2-LP)	60
02	Columbia 508923	EVIL HEAT (2-LP)	50
03	Columbia 5136031	DIRTY HITS (3-LP)	40
06	Columbia 82876831651	RIOT CITY BLUES (2-LP)	40
08	B-Unique BUN 142 LP	BEAUTIFUL FUTURE (Box set, LP, poster, booklet)	60
12	Sony 88697867991	SCREAMADELICA (2-LP reissue with free 12")	30

(see also Jesus & Mary Chain, Revolving Paint Dream, P.P. & Primes, Death In Vegas)

PRIMARY

MINT VALUE £

PRIMARY
83 Goldfish 002 — Radio Silence/Responding (p/s) 7

PRIMARY SOURCE
93 Reinforced RIVET 1234 — Smile/The Och/Lovin You/Mic Check (12") 45

PRIME-MATES
69 Action ACT 4530 — Hot Tamales (Versions 1 & 2) 30

PRIME MOVERS
89 Cyanide CND 001 — SINS OF THE FOURFATHERS (LP) 25

PRIME RHYME MASTERS
91 Kold Sweat KS115 — You Need Discipline/To Kill A Mockingbird (12") 15

PRIMETTES
68 Ember EMBS 3398 — LOOKING BACK WITH THE PRIMETTES AND EDDIE FLOYD (LP, 1 side each) 40
73 Windmill WMD 192 — THE ROOTS OF DIANA ROSS AND EDDIE FLOYD (LP, reissue) 15

(see also Supremes, Eddie Floyd)

PRIMITIVE MAN
71 Decca F13188 — Animal Love/Major Barmy From The Army 30

PRIMITIVES
86 Head HEAD 010 — Thru The Flowers/Across My Shoulder/Lazy/She Don't Need You (12", unreleased, white label test pressings only) 30
86 Lazy LAZY 01 — Thru The Flowers/Across My Shoulder/She Don't Need You/Lazy (12", p/s) 10
87 Lazy LAZY 05 — Ocean Blue/Shadow (2,000 only, given away free at London Astoria gig) 6

PRIMITIVES (1)
64 Pye 7N 15721 — Help Me/Let Them Tell 220
65 Pye 7N 15755 — You Said/How Do You Feel 250

(see also Mal & Primitives)

PRIMITIVES (2)
91 RCA PL 75086 — GALORE (LP) 20

PRIMROSE
69 NEMS 56-4129 — Just For You/Nine Till Five 25

PRIMROSE CIRCUS
70 President PT 314 — P.S. Call Me Lulu/In My Mind 10

PRIMUS
90 Caroline CAROLLP 10 — FRIZZLE FRY (LP) 40
91 Interscope 7567916591 — SAILING THE SEAS OF CHEESE (LP) 25

PRINCE

SINGLES

Year	Label	Title	Price
79	Warner Bros K 17537	I Wanna Be Your Lover/Just As Long As We're Together	10
79	Warner Bros K 17537T	I Wanna Be Your Lover/Just As Long As We're Together (12", company sleeve)	35
80	Warner Bros K 17590	Sexy Dancer/Bambi (die-cut company sleeve)	30
80	Warner Bros K 17590T	Sexy Dancer (Remix)/Bambi (12", die-cut company sleeve)	100
81	Warner Bros K 17768	Do It All Night/Head (die-cut company sleeve)	25
81	Warner Bros K 17768T	Do It All Night/Head (12", die-cut company sleeve)	60
81	Warner Bros K 17819	Gotta Stop (Messin' About)/Uptown (p/s)	60
81	Warner Bros K 17819	Gotta Stop (Messin' About)/I Wanna Be Your Lover (p/s)	60
81	Warner Bros LV 47	Gotta Stop (Messin' About)/Uptown/Head (12", stickered p/s)	60
81	Warner Bros LV 47	Gotta Stop (Messin' About)/I Wanna Be Your Lover/Head (12", stickered, colour p/s)	60
81	Warner Bros K 17866	Controversy/When You Were Mine (p/s)	20
81	Warner Bros K 17866T	Controversy/When You Were Mine (12", p/s)	30
82	Warner Bros K 17922	Let's Work/Ronnie, Talk To Russia (p/s)	40
82	Warner Bros K 17922T	Let's Work (Extended)/Ronnie, Talk To Russia (12", p/s)	40
83	Warner Bros W 9896	1999/How Come U Don't Call Me Anymore (paper labels, p/s, with free cassette mini-album in card p/s: "1999 (Edit)"/"Uptown"/"Controvesy"/"Dirty Minds"/"Sexuality")	40
83	Warner Bros W 9896	1999/How Come U Don't Call Me Anymore (paper labels, p/s)	8
83	Warner Bros W 9688	Little Red Corvette/Lady Cab Driver (p/s)	10
83	Warner Bros W 9688T	Little Red Corvette (Full Length Version)/Automatic/International Lover (12", stickered p/s, with poster insert)	40
83	Warner Bros W 9688T	Little Red Corvette (Full Length Version)/Automatic/International Lover (12", stickered p/s)	12
83	Warner Bros W 9688T	Little Red Corvette (Full Length Version)/Automatic/International Lover (12", 'negative image' p/s)	20
83	Warner Bros W 9436	Little Red Corvette/Horny Toad (poster calendar p/s)	55
83	Warner Bros W 9436	Little Red Corvette/Horny Toad (standard p/s)	40
83	Warner Bros W 9436T	Little Red Corvette (Full Length Version)/Horny Toad/D.M.S.R. (12", p/s)	15
83	Warner Bros W 9436T	Little Red Corvette (Full Length Version)/Horny Toad/D.M.S.R. (12", p/s, with spiral-bound calendar)	85
83	Warner Bros W 9436T	Little Red Corvette (Full Length Version)/Horny Toad/D.M.S.R. (12", p/s, with poster)	75
84	Warner Bros W 9286T	When Doves Cry/17 Days/1999/D.M.S.R. (12", stickered shrinkwrapped double pack)	20
84	Warner Bros W 9174P	Purple Rain/God (motorbike-shaped picture disc)	100
84	Warner Bros W 9174T	Purple Rain/God (instrumental)/God (12", p/s, initial pressing with poster)	15
84	Warner Bros W 9121TE	I Would Die 4 U (U.S. Remix)/Another Lonely Christmas (U.S. Remix) (12", p/s)	20
85	Paisley Park W 9052P	Paisley Park/She's Always In My Hair (shaped picture disc)	50
85	Paisley Park W 9052T	Paisley Park/She's Always In My Hair/Paisley Park (Remix) (12", mispressing with repeated 2nd track "She's Always In My Hair")	25
86	Paisley Park W 8751P	Kiss/Love Or Money (shaped picture disc with plinth)	30
86	Paisley Park W 8751T	Kiss (Extended)/Love Or Money (12", p/s, with poster)	15
86	Paisley Park W 8711TE	Mountains (Ext.)/Alexa De Paris (Extended) (10", white vinyl in PVC sleeve)	20
86	Paisley Park W 8711T	Mountains (Extended 9.56)/Alexa De Paris (12", p/s, with poster)	20
86	Paisley Park W 8586F	Girls And Boys (Edit)/Under The Cherry Moon//She's Always In My Hair/ 17 Days (double pack, gatefold p/s)	15
86	Paisley Park W 8586P	Girls And Boys (Edit)/Under The Cherry Moon (shaped picture disc)	40
86	Paisley Park W 8586T	Girls And Boys/Under The Cherry Moon/Erotic City (12", p/s, with poster advertising London gigs)	18

PRINCE ALLAH/ALLABA

MINT VALUE £

86	Paisley Park W 8521W	Anotherloverholenyohead/I Wanna Be Your Lover (paper or plastic labels, poster p/s) 12
86	Paisley Park W 8521T	Anotherloverholenyohead (Extended)/I Wanna Be Your Lover (12", p/s) 10
87	Paisley Park W 8334W	If I Was Your Girlfriend/Shockadelica (poster p/s) 8
87	Paisley Park W 8334E	If I Was Your Girlfriend/Shockadelica (peach vinyl, PVC cover, with postcards & stickers) . 15
87	Paisley Park W 8288TP	I Could Never Take The Place Of Your Man/Hot Thing (Remixed Edit) / Hot Thing (Extended) (12", picture disc) 15
88	Paisley Park 921 074-0	I Wish U Heaven (Parts 1/2/3)/CAMILLE: Scarlet Pussy (Edit) (12", blue or purple vinyl) 1000

ALBUMS

79	Warner Bros. K56772	PRINCE (LP, inner) 50
80	Warner Bros. K 56862	DIRTY MIND (LP) 40
81	Warner Bros. K 56950	CONTROVERSY (LP) 40
83	Warner Bros. 923 809-1	1999 (LP, original issue, single disc) 20
83	Warner Bros. 92 3720-1	1999 (2-LP) 20
84	Warner Bros. 925 110-1	PURPLE RAIN - MUSIC FROM THE MOTION PICTURE (LP, purple vinyl with poster) 80
84	Warner Bros. 925110-1	PURPLE RAIN - MUSIC FROM THE MOTION PICTURE (LP, with poster) 20
86	Paisley Park 925 395-1	PARADE (LP, gatefold) 20
86	Paisley Park WX 39P	PARADE - MUSIC FROM "UNDER THE CHERRY MOON" (LP, pic. disc, die-cut sleeve) 200
87	Paisley Park WX 88	SIGN O THE TIMES (2-LP, inners) 40
88	Paisley Park 925 720	LOVESEXY (LP, inner) 25
89	Warner Bros. 925 936-1	BATMAN (MOTION PICTURE SOUNDTRACK) (LP, inner) 20
91	Paisley Park 7599 25379-1	DIAMONDS AND PEARLS (2-LP, inners) 25
92	Warner Bros. 9362-45037-1	LOVE SYMBOL (2-LP) 100
94	Warners 936245793-1	BLACK ALBUM (LP, title sticker) 35
94	Warner Bros. 9362 45700-1	COME (LP) 50
95	NPG 6103-1	EXODUS (LP, as NPG) 15
95	Warner Bros. 9362-45999-1	THE GOLD EXPERIENCE (2-LP) 50
98	NPG BCT 9871	CRYSTAL BALL (4-CD, import only, as ß) 40
99	Arista 07822 14624 1	RAVE UN2 THE JOY FANTASTIC (2-LP) 40

PROMOS

81	Warner Bros SAM 172	Dance Music Sex Romance/Dance Music Sex Romance (12", p/s, promo only) 100
84	Warner Bros	Purple Rain (promo only p/s, purple vinyl) 60
84	Warner Bros SAM 230	I Would Die 4 U/I would Die 4 U 30
91	Warner Brothers SAM 888	Gett Off (Urge Single Edit) (1-sided promo) 15
92	Paisley Park W 0113	Thunder (DJ Edit) (1-sided promo only white label, stickered company sleeve) 15
95	NPG 61225	Get Wild (Money Maker Radio Mix) (CD, as NPG, radio programmer's picture disc) 45
95	NPG 61047	Get Wild/Beautiful Girl (no p/s, as NPG) 6
96	NPG 60667	Lovesign/MARGIE COX: Standing At The altar (no p/s, as ß) 10
96	NPG 60600	Lovesign (Radio Edit Mix)/(1-800 New Funk Version)/(The Storyboard Video Mix) (12", as ß, most with title sticker) 35
96	NPG 60605	Lovesign (Radio Edit Mix)/(1-800 New Funk Version)/(The Storyboard Video Mix) (CD, as ß) 30
04	Urban CK92560LP	MUSICOLOGY (2-LP, promo) 50

PRINCE ALLAH/ALLABA

75	Cactus CT79	Born A Fighter/TRADITION ALL STARS: Born A Fighter (Dub) (as Prince Allaba) 40
78	Freedom Sounds FSD 020	Bucket Bottom/FULL WOOD: Stop And Think Me Over (12") 20
92	Xamayca Music XA002	Jah Give I Love/Jerusalem (12") 40
02	Guiding Star GS 010	Their Reward/Version 18
04	Stars TJITW018	Daniel/TAPPA ZUKIE: Blackman (12") 15
96	Blood & Fire BAFLP 014	ONLY LOVE AN CONQUER 1976-1979 (LP) 40

(see also Rasalla, Keith Blake, The Leaders)

PRINCE BROTHERS

77	Carib Gems CG 010	Ram Jam/REVOLUTIONARIES: Version To Jam 6

PRINCE BUSTER (& ALL STARS)

61	Starlite ST45 052	Buster's Shack (as Buster's Group)/ERIC MORRIS: Search The World 30
62	Blue Beat BB 101	My Sound That Goes Around/They Got To Go (with Torchlighters) 22
62	Blue Beat BB 116	Independence Song (with Bluebeats)/RICO & BLUEBEATS: August 1962 25
62	Blue Beat BB 133	Time Longer Than Rope/Fake King (with Voice Of The People) 25
62	Blue Beat BB 138	One Hand Washes The Other/Cowboy Comes To Town 30
63	Blue Beat BB 150	Run Man Run/Danny, Dane And Lorraine 25
63	Blue Beat BB 169	Praise Without Raise/Three Against One (unreleased, white labels only) 100
63	Blue Beat BB 158	Open Up, Bartender/Enjoy It (B-side actually "Enjoy Yourself") 35
63	Blue Beat BB 162	Money/SCHOOL BOYS: Little Boy Blue 40
63	Blue Beat BB 163	King, Duke, Sir/I See Them In My Sight 30
63	Blue Beat BB 167	The Ten Commandments (with All Stars)/Buster's Welcome 20
63	Blue Beat BB 170	Madness/PRINCE BUSTER ALL STARS: Toothache 40
63	Blue Beat BB 173	Burning Creation/PRINCE BUSTER ALL STARS: Boop 30
63	Blue Beat BB 180	Three More Rivers To Cross/RAYMOND HARPER & PRINCE BUSTER ALL STARS: African Blood 30
63	Blue Beat BB 186	Fowl Thief/Remember Me 60
63	Blue Beat BB 189	Watch It Blackhead/Hello My Dear 35
63	Blue Beat BB 192	Rollin' Stone (with Charmers)/RICO & HIS BLUES BAND: This Day 30
63	Blue Beat BB 197	Window Shopping/Sodom And Gomorrah 35
63	Blue Beat BB 199	Spider And Fly/Three Blind Mice 30
63	Blue Beat BB 200	Wash All Your Troubles Away/RICO & BLUE BEATS: Soul Of Africa 20
63	Dice CC 6	They Got To Come/These Are The Times (with Voice Of The People) 15
63	Dice CC 11	Blackhead Chinaman/You Ask (I Had A Girl) 18
63	Dice CC 18	World Peace/The Lion Roars (as Prince Buster & Hazel) 15
64	Stateside SS 335	30 Pieces Of Silver/Everybody Ska 25
64	Blue Beat BB 210	Wash All Your Troubles Away/RICO & BLUE BEATS: Soul Of Africa (p/s reissue) 90

PRINCE BUSTER (& ALL STARS)

MINT VALUE £

Year	Label & Cat. No.	Title	Value £
64	Blue Beat BB 211	Bluebeat Spirit/Beggars Are No Choosers	35
64	Blue Beat BB 216	You're Mine/Tongue Will Tell	35
64	Blue Beat BB 225	Three Blind Mice/I Know	35
64	Blue Beat BB 232	Sheep On Top (song actually titled "She Pon Top")/Midnight	45
64	Blue Beat BB 234	She Loves You/Healing	70
64	Blue Beat BB 243	Jealous/Buster's Ska	35
64	Blue Beat BB 248	Thirty Pieces Of Silver/The National Dance	35
64	Blue Beat BB 254	Wings Of A Dove/MAYTALLS: Sweet Love	35
64	Blue Beat BB 262	Old Lady/Dayo Ska	40
64	Blue Beat BB 271	No Knowledge In College/In The Middle Of The Night	45
64	Blue Beat BB 274	I May Never Love You Again/Hey Little Girl	35
65	Blue Beat BB 278	Blood Pressure/Islam	250
65	Blue Beat BB 281	Blues Market/MAYTALS: Looking Down The Street	50
65	Blue Beat BB 282	Big Fight/Red Dress	45
65	Blue Beat BB 293	Agua Fumar/Long Winter (with Charmers)	40
65	Blue Beat BB 302	Ling Ting Tong/Walk Along	100
65	Blue Beat BB 307	Bonanza/Wonderful Life	35
65	Blue Beat BB 309	Here Comes The Bride (with Patsy Todd, as Jamaica's Greatest)/ BUSTER'S ALLSTARS: Burkes' Law	40
65	Blue Beat BB 313	Everybody Yeah Yeah (as Jamaica's Greatest)/ BUSTER'S ALLSTARS: Gun The Man Down	50
65	Blue Beat BB 314	Float Like A Butterfly/Haunted Room	50
65	Blue Beat BB 316	Sugar Pop/Feel Up (as Prince & Jamaica's Greatest)	40
65	Blue Beat BB 317	Come Home/I Thank You (as Jamaica's Greatest)	45
65	Blue Beat BB 321	My Girl/BUSTER'S ALL STARS: The Fugitive	60
65	Blue Beat BB 324	Al Capone/One Step Beyond (as Prince Buster's Allstars) (blue label)	15
65	Blue Beat BB 324	Al Capone/One Step Beyond (as Prince Buster's Allstars) (other label colours)	15
65	Blue Beat BB 328	Ambition/BUSTER'S ALL STARS: Ryging	40
65	Blue Beat BB 330	Rum And Coca Cola/I Love Her	100
65	Blue Beat BB 334	The Ten Commandments/BUSTER'S ALL STARS: Sting Like A Bee (reissue)	15
65	Blue Beat BB 335	Respect/BUSTER'S ALL STARS: Virginia (B-side actually Dance Jamaica by Val Bennett & Prince Buster's All Stars)	55
66	Blue Beat BB 338	Big Fight (Prince Buster Versus Duke Reid)/Adios, Senorita	40
66	Blue Beat BB 339	Under Arrest (But Officer)/PRINCE BUSTER'S ALLSTARS: Say Boss Man	40
66	Blue Beat BB 343	Prince Of Peace/Don't Throw Stones	130
66	Blue Beat BB 352	Day Of Light (song actually "Dayo")/It's Too Late	25
66	Blue Beat BB 355	Sunshine With My Girl/Girl Answer Your Name	120
66	Blue Beat BB 357	I Won't Let You Cry/Hard Man Fe Dead	80
66	Blue Beat BB 359	The Prophet (actually "Feel The Spirit" with Slim Smith)/ BUSTER'S ALL STARS: Lion Of Judah	125
66	Blue Beat BB 362	To Be Loved/BUSTER'S ALLSTARS: Set Me Free	30
66	Rainbow RAI 107	Your Turn (Sad Song)/If You Leave Me (with Allstars)	40
67	Blue Beat BB 370	Shanty Town (Get Scanty)/BUSTER'S ALL STARS: Duppy	45
67	Blue Beat BB 373	Knock On Wood/And I Love Her	65
67	Blue Beat BB 377	Dark End Of The Street/Love Oh Love	45
67	Blue Beat BB 378	Drunkard's Psalm (Wise Man)/7 Wonders Of The World (as Prince Buster All Stars)	175
67	Blue Beat BB 382	Sit And Wonder (with His All Stars)/ROLAND ALFONSO: Sunrise In Kingston	60
67	Blue Beat BB 383	Sharing You/You'll Be Lonely On The Blue Train (as Prince Buster's Allstars; A-side actually by Prince Buster, B-side actually by Rico's Band)	30
67	Blue Beat BB 384	Take It Easy/Why Must I Cry (2nd issue, B-side actually by Hopeton Lewis)	30
67	Blue Beat BB 387	Judge Dread (Judge Four Hundred Years)/FITZROY CAMPBELL & PRINCE BUSTER ALL STARS: Waiting For My Rude Girl	20
67	Blue Beat BB 388	Dance Cleopatra/All In My Mind	120
67	Blue Beat BB 390	Soul Serenade/Too Hot	60
67	Blue Beat BB 391	Land Of Imagination/The Appeal (B-side actually "The Barrister Appeal")	35
67	Blue Beat BB 393	Johnny Dollar/Rude Boys Rude	50
67	Blue Beat BB 395	This Gun's For Hire/Yes, Daddy	45
67	Blue Beat BB 397	Quit Place/Rude Boys Rude	60
67	Blue Beat BB 400	All In My Mind/Judge Dread Dance (The Pardon)	30
67	Blue Beat BB 402	Vagabond/PRINCE BUSTER ALLSTARS: Come Get Me	30
67	Philips BF 1552	The Ten Commandments/Don't Make Me Cry	20
67	Fab FAB 10	Shakin' Up Orange Street/Black Girl (with Allstars)	45
67	Fab FAB 11	Johnny Cool (Parts 1 & 2) (with Allstars)	50
67	Fab FAB 16	Bye Bye Baby/Human (with Allstars)	30
67	Fab FAB 25	Train To Girls Town/Give Love A Try (with Allstars)	40
67	Fab FAB 26	Going To The River (as Prince Buster & Allstars)/ PRINCE BUSTER'S ALLSTARS: Julie On My Mind	30
68	Fab FAB 31	Kings Of Old (My Ancestors)/Sweet Inspiration (with Allstars)	65
68	Fab FAB 35	Try A Little Tenderness/All My Loving (with Allstars)	600
68	Fab FAB 36	The Glory Of Love/Another Sad Nite	30
68	Fab FAB 37	This Is A Hold Up/Julie On My Mind (with Allstars)	40
68	Fab FAB 38	Free Love (with Allstars)/DALTONS: All Over The World	50
68	Fab FAB 40	Rough Rider (with Allstars)/PRINCE BUSTER: 127 Orange Street (B-side actually by Prince Buster Allstars)	30
68	Fab FAB 41	Shepperd Beng Beng (with Teddy King)/TENNORS: Ride Your Donkey	30
68	Fab FAB 47	Going To Ethiopia (as Prince Buster & Allstars)/ PRINCE BUSTER ALLSTARS: Shakin' Up Orange Street	35
68	Fab FAB 49	Glory Of Love/WAILERS: Mellow Mood (possibly white labels only)	100
68	Fab FAB 56	Intensified Dirt/Don't You Know I Love You So (with Allstars)	85
68	Fab FAB 57	Green Green Grass Of Home (as Prince Buster's Allstars; actually by Prince Buster & Allstars)/SOUL MAKERS: Girls Like You	25
68	Fab FAB 58	We Shall Overcome/Keep The Faith (as Prince Buster's Allstars; actually by Prince Buster & Allstars)	30

PRINCE CHARLIE

MINT VALUE £

68	Fab FAB 64	Cool, Stroker/It's You I Love (B-side actually by Little Roy)	40
68	Fab FAB 80	Hypocrite/New Dance (B-side actually by Little Roy)	120
68	Fab FAB 81	Wine And Grine/The Scorcher (with Allstars)	110
69	Unity UN 522	30 Pieces Of Silver/Everybody Ska (reissue)	20
69	Fab FAB 82	Dr. Rodney (Black Power)/Taxation	120
69	Fab FAB 92	Pharaoh House Crash/Ob-La-Di, Ob-La-Da	30
69	Fab FAB 93	Ob-La-Di, Ob-La-Da/Wreck A Pum Pum	15
69	Fab FAB 94	Hey Jude/Django Fever	50
69	Fab FAB 102	Black Soul/CALEDONIANS: Oh Baby (B-side actually by Claredonians)	45
69	Fab FAB 108	Whine And Grind/The Scorcher (with Allstars) (reissue)	20
69	Fab FAB 118	Bull Buck/ROLAND ALPHONSO: One Heart	25
69	Fab FAB 119	Let Her Go/Tie The Donkey's Tail	15
69	Fab FAB 122	Stand Up/Happy Reggae (with Allstars)	20
70	Fab FAB 127	Young Gifted And Black/PRINCE BUSTER'S ALLSTARS: The Rebel	20
70	Fab FAB 131	That's All/The Preachin (B-side actually titled "The Preacher")	50
70	Fab FAB 132	Ganja Plant/Creation	25
70	Fab FAB 140	Hit Me Back/Give Peace A Chance	30
70	Fab FAB 150	Big Five/Musical College	15
70	Prince Buster PB 1	Big Five/Musical College (reissue)	8
70	Prince Buster PB 2	Rat Trap/Black Organ (B-side with Allstars but actually by Ansell Collins & Prince Buster's Allstars)	15
71	Fab FAB 162	Baby Version (with Jan Fender)/Holly	15
71	Fab FAB 176	Police Trim Rasta (with Allstars)/Smooth (B-side actually by Ansell Collins & Prince Buster Allstars)	20
71	Prince Buster PB 4	Fishey/More Fishey	7
71	Prince Buster PB 7	I Wish Your Picture Was You/PRINCE BUSTER ALLSTARS: It Mash Up - Version (B-side actually by Dennis Alcapone)	12
71	Prince Buster PB 8	Sons Of Zion (actually by Dennis Alcapone)/ANSELL COLLINS: Short Circuit	12
71	Prince Buster PB 9	My Happiness/Human (with Allstars)	7
71	Prince Buster PB10	Still/Version	10
72	Prince Buster PB 14	Big Sister Stuff/Satta Massagana (with Allstars) (white label)	20
72	Prince Buster PB 15	Protection/Cool Operator (with Allstars)	12
72	Prince Buster PB 16	I Stand Accused/My Heart is Gone (with Allstars)	10
72	Prince Buster PB 19	4 And 1 Medley/Drums Drums (as Prince Buster & Allstars, B-side actually by Prince Buster Allstars)	10
72	Prince Buster PB20	They Got To Come/Time Longer Than Rope	20
72	Prince Buster PB24	Giant/Science	25
72	Prince Buster PB 32	Still/Sister Big Stuff (with Allstars)	7
72	Prince Buster PB 36	South Of The Border/South Of The Border (Version) (with Allstars)	7
72	Fab FAB 36	South Of The Border/South Of The Border (Version) (with Allstars)	7
72	Prince Buster PB 47	Baldhead Pum Pum/Giver Her (with Allstars)	7
79	Blue Beat DDBB 324	Al Capone/One Step Beyond (12", p/s)	12
79	Blue Beat DDBB 334	THREE OF THE BEST (12" EP, p/s)	10
79	Blue Beat DDPB 1	Big Five/FOLK BROTHERS: Carolina/ PRINCE BUSTER: Shaking Up Orange Street (12", p/s)	10
63	Blue Beat BBLP 802	I FEEL THE SPIRIT (LP)	150
65	Blue Beat BBLP 805	SKA-LIP-SOUL (LP, with His All Stars)	150
65	Blue Beat BBLP 806	IT'S BURKE'S LAW - JAMAICA SKA EXPLOSION! (LP, as Prince Buster All Stars; 2 different sleeves, laminated plain and unlaminated 'explosion')	300
67	Blue Beat BBLP 807	WHAT A HARD MAN FE DEAD - PRINCE BUSTER SINGS FOR THE PEOPLE (LP, with Baba Brooks)	300
67	Blue Beat BBLP 808	ON TOUR (LP)	150
67	Blue Beat BBLP 809	JUDGE DREAD (LP)	125
67	Blue Beat BBLP 820	SHE WAS A ROUGH RIDER (LP)	100
68	Fab BBLP 820	SHE WAS A ROUGH RIDER (LP, reissue on Fab label)	50
68	Fab BBLP 821	WRECK A PUM PUM (LP)	60
69	Fab BBLP 822	THE OUTLAW (LP, title listed as "Queen Of The Outlaws" on disc)	120
70	Fab MS 1	FABULOUS GREATEST HITS (LP, original issue with 'West Brothers Printers' credit on rear of sleeve)	40
70	Fab MS 2	I FEEL THE SPIRIT (LP, copies in blue ink sleeve are worth £100)	60
70	Fab MS 6	TUTTI FRUTTI (LP)	65
72	Melodisc MLP 12-156	SISTER BIG STUFF (LP)	50
72	Melodisc MLP 12-157	BIG FIVE (LP)	35
73	Prince Buster PB 9	ORIGINAL GOLDEN OLDIES VOLUME 1 (LP)	20
78	Fab MS 7	THE MESSAGE DUB WISE (LP)	150
80	Fab MS1	FABULOUS GREATEST HITS (LP, reissue)	15

(see also Buster's Allstars, Buster's Group, Dennis Alcapone, Jim Dakota, Hortense Ellis, Heptones, Eric Morris, Schoolboys, Protegue, Vietnam All Stars)

PRINCE CHARLIE

69	Coxsone CS 7101	Hit And Run/MEDIATORS: Darling, There I Stand	100

PRINCE FAR I

76	Morpheus MOR 19	Zion Call/Version	20
77	Lightning TRO 9000	Under Heavy Manners/Version	15
78	Virgin Front Line FLS 112	No More War/Version	10
82	On-U Sound DP 1	Virgin/Danger (10")	20
83	Pre PRE 11-12	83 Struggle (with ASHANTIE ROY)/KONGO ASHANTIE ROY/Weeping Waiing (12")	35
75	Carib Gems CGLP 1002	PSALMS FOR I (LP)	45
78	Virgin Front Line FL 1013	MESSAGE FROM THE KING (LP)	35
78	Virgin Front Line FL 1021	LONG LIFE (LP)	20
79	Trojan TRLS 175	FREE FROM SIN (LP)	20
79	Virgin Front Line FLX 4002	CRY TUFF DUB ENCOUNTER PART 2 (LP)	50

PRINCE HAMMER

MINT VALUE £

79	Hit Run APLP 9006	DUB TO AFRICA (LP, as Prince Far I & The Arabs)	65
79	Trojan Records TRLS 175	FREE FROM SIN (LP)	15
80	Daddy Kool DKLP 15	CRY TUFF DUB ENCOUNTER CHAPTER III (LP, as Prince Far I & the Arabs)	60
80	Trojan TRLS 205	CRY TUFF DUB ENCOUNTER CHAPTER IV (LP)	25
80	Trojan TRLS 190	JAMAICAN HEROES (LP)	30
80	Pre PRE XF 3	SHOWCASE IN A SUITCASE (LP)	50
80	Pre PRE X 7	LIVITY (LP)	35
81	Trojan TRLS 204	VOICE OF THUNDER (LP)	20
84	Kingdom KVL 9016	UMKHONTO WE SIZWE (LP)	15
95	Trojan TRLS 175	FREE FROM SIN (LP)	18

(see also Arabs, Prince Cry Cry, King CC)

PRINCE HAMMER
77	Baby Mother HIT DD 11	Them Must Fall/Ball Of Fire (12")	55
78	Hit Run HIT DP 15	Ten Thousand Lions/North London Thing (Carry The Swing) (12")	60
83	Saab (No catalogue number)	Warika Hill/Africa Dance Hall (12")	60
78	Virgin Frontline FL1004	BIBLE (LP)	25
79	Hit Run APLP 9007	WORLD WAR DUB PART 1 (LP)	120
79	Miss Pat Walker PW1	ROOTS ME ROOTS (LP)	60

(see also Gen Brown)

PRINCE HAROLD
66	Mercury MF 952	Forget About Me/Baby You've Got Me	15

PRINCE HERON
79	Jah Lion JBDC 806	Wip The Wicked Man/Kingston Rock (12", with Jah Brokie)	15

PRINCE JAMMY
79	Trojan TRLS 174	KAMIKAZI DUB (LP)	35
82	Greensleeves GREL 29	DESTROYS THE INVADERS (LP)	25
83	CSA Records – CSLP 10	OSBOURNE IN DUB (LP)	25
86	Greensleeves Records GREL 92	COMPUTERISED DUB (LP)	25
96	Trojan TRLS 174	KAMAKAZI DUB (LP, reissue)	15

(see also Crucial Bunny, Johnny Osborne)

PRINCE JAZZBO
73	Count Shelley CS 025	Wise Shepherd (with Linval Carthy)/ EARL GEORGE: Gonna Give Her All The Love I've Got	12
74	Cactus CT 31	Concubine Donkey/Part 2	12
74	Count Shelley CS 057	Step Forward Youth/Black Is Power	8
73	Grape GR 3047	Free From Chains/LLOYD & PATSY: Papa Do It Sweet	18
73	Techniques TE 921	Mr. Harry Skank/GLEN BROWN: Telavid Drums	25
74	Ackee ACK 532	Kick Boy Face/Version	10
74	Dip DL 5036	Penny Reel/Good Things	12
75	ABI AB 001	Bag A Wolf/Version	8
75	Jamatel JAL 04	Freedom/Free Dub	15
76	Attack ATT 8122	The Wormer/The Great Pablo	10
76	Third World TW 040	Stealing/Version	12
77	Ujama UJA 0012	Learn Some More/I Am Roots/JOHNNY KOOL: Obidah/JA TONY: Run Bag-A-Wire (12")	45
76	Third World TWLP 109	KICK BOY FACE (LP)	40
76	Black Wax WAXLP 1	NATTY PASSING THRU' (LP)	150

(see also Earl George)

PRINCE JAZZBO & I ROY
78	Live & Love LAP 003	STEP FORWARD YOUTH (LP)	25

PRINCE LASHA ENSEMBLE
66	CBS SBPG 62409	INSIGHT (LP)	30

PRINCE OF DARKNESS
69	Downtown DT 441	Burial Of Long Shot/MUSIC DOCTORS: Burial Of Long Shot	25
69	Downtown DT 448	Meeting Over Yonder/MUSIC DOCTORS: Ghost Rider	125
71	Downtown DT 467	Sound Of Today/MUSIC DOCTORS: Red Red Wine Version	50

PRINCE PATO EXPEDITION
76	Beacon BEAS 18	FIREBIRD (LP)	60

PRINCE & PRINCESS
65	Aladdin WI 609	Ready Steady Go/Take Me Serious	25

PRINCE SISTERS
55	Decca 45-F1050	A Rusty Old Halo/Love Love Beautiful Love	8

PRINCE TALLIS & THE CHALLIS
72	Upsetter US 383	Who Feels It/THE UPSETTERS: He Who Feels It (Chapter 2)	25

VIV PRINCE
66	Columbia DB 7960	Light Of The Charge Brigade/Minuet For Ringo	30

(see also Pretty Things, Bunch Of Fives, Kate, Vamp, Chicago Line)

PRINCE WILLIAMS
74	TKA ZA/B	Rasta Train/Good Old Days	22

PRINCESS
86	Supreme SU 1	PRINCESS (LP, with poster)	15

PRINCESS BALOU
81	PB YYS 11	Making Love To You/Making Love To You (Part II) (p/s)	200

PRINCESS & SWINEHERD
68	Oak RGJ 633	PRINCESS AND THE SWINEHERD (LP, plain black sleeve)	100

PRINCESS TINYMEAT
84	Rough Trade RTT 160	Sloblands/The Fairest Of Them All (12", some with sticker)	15
87	Rough Trade ROUGH 108	HERSTORY (LP)	20

(see also Iaso Virgin Prunes, Daniel Figgis)

PRINCIPAL EDWARDS MAGIC THEATRE
69	Dandelion S 4405	Ballad Of The Big Girl Now/Lament For The Earth	10

John PRINE

MINT VALUE £

73	Deram DM 398	Weekdaze/Whizzmore Kid	15
69	Dandelion 63752	SOUNDTRACK (LP, gatefold sleeve)	60
71	Dandelion DAN 8002	THE ASMOTO RUNNING BAND (LP, gatefold sleeve)	40
74	Deram SML 1108	ROUND ONE (LP, white/red label with small logo)	35

JOHN PRINE
| 72 | Atlantic K40357 | JOHN PRINE (LP) | 25 |

MADDY PRIOR
78	Chrysalis CHS 2232	Baggy Pants/Woman In The Wings	6
80	EMI EMI 5903	Wake Up England/Paradise (p/s, as Maddy Prior Band)	6
82	Plant Life PLRS 001	Face To Face/Half Listening (p/s, as Maddy Prior Band)	6
83	RCA/Spindrift RCA 379	Deep In The Darkest Night/Western Movies (p/s)	6
85	Making Waves SURF 108	Stookie/Incidental Music From Stookie (p/s)	6
85	Making Waves SURF 109	Deep In The Darkest Night/Western Movies (p/s, reissue)	6

(see also Steeleye Span, Tim Hart & Maddy Prior)

PRIORITY
| 79 | Brimstone BRS 1 | Visions Of Miranda Grey/Escape (p/s) | 30 |

PRIORY PARK
| 78 | Wild Dog DOGLP 16 | TRY FOR THE SUN (LP) | 40 |

PRISONERS
83	Big Beat NS 90	Hurricane/Tomorrow (She Said) (p/s)	12
86	Countdown VAIN 4	Whenever I'm Gone/Promised Land (p/s)	7
86	Countdown 12 VAIN 4	Whenever I'm Gone/Promised Land/Gravedigger (12" p/s)	8
97	Deceptive BLUFF 043	Shine On Me/Judgement Song (p/s)	7
84	Big Beat SW 98	ELECTRIC FIT (EP)	18
82	Own Up OWN UP U2	A TASTE OF PINK (LP)	30
83	Big Beat WIK 19	THE WISERMISERDEMELZA (LP)	20
85	Own Up OWN UP U2	A TASTE OF PINK (LP, reissue in pink sleeve on pink vinyl)	35
85	Own Up OWN UP U3	THE LAST FOURFATHERS (LP)	50
86	Countdown DOWN 2	IN FROM THE COLD (LP)	20
89	Hangman HANG 23 UP	RARE AND UNISSUED (LP)	35
91	Cyanide CND 2	RARE AND UNISSUED (LP, reissue)	20

(see also James Taylor Quartet)

PRISONERS/MILKSHAKES
| 86 | Empire MIC 001 | THE LAST NIGHT AT THE MIC CLUB (LP, live, 1 side each) | 18 |
| 86 | Media Burn MB 17 | THEE MILKSHAKES VS. THE PRISONERS (LP, live, 1 side each) | 18 |

(see also Milkshakes)

MARK PRITCHARD
| 09 | Ho Hum HOHUM 003 | ?/The Hologram (10") | 30 |
| 10 | Deep Medi Muisc MEDI 25 | Elephant Dub/Heavy As Stone (12") | 25 |

PRIVATE COLLECTION
| 82 | Galaxy GAL 003 | It's Hopeless/Private Collection | 10 |

PRIVATE DICKS
| 79 | Heartbeat PULSE 6 | She Said So/Private Dicks (p/s) | 20 |

PRIVATE EYE
| 83 | Spider SPY 001 | Water Under The Bridge/I Cry For You (no p/s) | 35 |

PRIVATE FLIGHT
| 89 | SRT SRT9KS2092 | Winter In Springtime/Nobody's Fool (p/s) | 12 |

PRIVATE FUNK-SHUN
| 86 | Private Funk-Shun KMJ 1 | All That I Wanted Was You/Fantasy (12") | 125 |

PRIVATE I'S
79	Cruise CR 001	Love Won't Let Me Wait/I'll Be Around	20
80	Cruise CR 003	Folk Song/Transgression Dub And Professor In Action	12
81	Top Notch TND 002	Do I worry/Worrier Style	12

PRIVATE LIFE
| 72 | Realm RM 3 | Put Her Down/Chasing Dragons | 400 |

PRIVATE PARTY
| 87 | IMW 1201 | Puppet Capers/Tennants Super Mix (12") | 10 |

PRIVATE SECTOR
| 78 | TJM TJM 8 | Just Just (Wanna) Stay Free/Things Get Worse (p/s) | 20 |

PRIVATE VIEW
| 84 | New 7NL 100 | Fashion Changeling/Walls (p/s) | 25 |

PRIVATES
| 82 | Dune DUNE 1 | Ashamed To Be White/Takes Your Breath Away (p/s) | 7 |

PROBOT
| 04 | Southern Lord SUNN 30LP | PROBOT (2-LP) | 60 |

(see also Foo Fighters, Nirvana)

P.J. PROBY
62	Liberty LIB 55367	Try To Forget Her/There Stands The One	10
65	Liberty LIB 10206	Let The Water Run Down/I Don't Want To Hear It Anymore	10
65	Liberty LIB 10215	That Means A Lot/My Prayer	10
66	Liberty LIB 10236	To Make A Big Man Cry/Wicked Woman	10
66	Fab FAB 2	You've Got Me Cryin'/I Need Love (in die-cut p/s)	20
66	Fab FAB 2	You've Got Me Cryin'/I Need Love	7
66	Liberty LIB 10250	I Can't Make It Alone/Sweet Summer Wine	12
67	Liberty LIB 55936	Nicki Hoeky/Good Things Are Coming My Way	15
67	Liberty LIB 55974	You Can't Come Home Again/Work With Me Annie	15
67	Liberty LIB 55974	You Can't Come Home Again/Work With Me Annie (DJ Copy)	30
68	Liberty LBF 15046	It's Your Day Today/I Apologise Baby	10
68	Liberty LBF 15046	It's Your Day Today/I Apologise Baby (DJ Copy)	30
68	Liberty LBF 15085	What's Wrong With My World/Why Baby Why	7

PROCESSION

MINT VALUE £

68	Liberty LBF 15152	The Day That Lorraine Came Down/Mery Hoppkins Never Had Days Like These (B-side features Led Zeppelin)	40
69	Liberty LBF 15245	Hanging From Your Loving Tree/Empty Bottles	15
70	Liberty LBF 15280	Today I Killed A Man/It's Too Good To Last	10
70	Liberty LBF 15386	It's Goodbye/Gift Of Love	10
70s	Rooster ROO 101	You've Got It All (with Polly Brown)/Starting All Over Again	20
72	Columbia DB 8874	We'll Meet Again/Clown Shoes	10
73	Ember EMB S 328	Put Your Head On My Shoulder/Momma Married A Preacher	7
74	Seven Sun SSUN 13	The Champ (Parts 1 & 2)	8
64	Liberty LEP 2192	P. J. PROBY (EP)	15
65	Liberty LEP 2229	SOMEWHERE (EP)	15
65	Liberty LEP 2239	CHRISTMAS WITH P. J. (EP)	15
66	Liberty LEP 2251	P. J.'s HITS (EP)	15
67	Liberty LEP 2267	PROBY AGAIN (EP)	20
65	Liberty LBY 1235	I AM P. J. PROBY (LP)	15
65	Liberty LBY 1264	P. J. PROBY (LP)	15
66	Liberty LBY 1291	P. J. PROBY IN TOWN (LP)	20
67	Liberty LBY 1361	ENIGMA (LP)	15
67	Liberty LBL/LBS 83045	PHENOMENON (LP)	15
68	Liberty LBL/LBS 83087	BELIEVE IT OR NOT (LP)	15
69	Liberty LBS 83219E	THREE WEEK HERO (LP, featuring Led Zeppelin on "Jim's Blues")	45

(see also Jett Powers, Marc Almond)

PROCESSION

68	Mercury MF 1053	Every American Citizen/Essentially Susan (p/s)	10
68	Mercury MF 1070	One Day In Every Week/Wigwam City	10
69	Mercury SMCL 20132	PROCESSION (LP)	30

PROCOL HARUM

67	Regal Zonophone RZ 3003	Homburg/Good Captain Clack	6
68	Regal Zonophone RZ 3007	Quite Rightly So/In The Wee Small Hours Of Sixpence	8
69	Regal Zonophone RZ 3019	A Salty Dog/Long Gone Geek	10
72	Chrysalis CHS 2003	Conquistador/Luskus Delph (PS)	6
67	Regal Zono. LRZ 1001	PROCOL HARUM (LP, laminated front sleeve, flipbacks, blue/silver label)	200
68	Regal Zono. LRZ 1004	SHINE ON BRIGHTLY (LP, mono), laminated front sleeve, blue/silver label)	200
67	Regal Zono. SLRZ 1004	SHINE ON BRIGHTLY (LP, stereo), laminated front sleeve, red/silver label)	125
69	Regal Zono. SLRZ 1009	A SALTY DOG (LP, laminated sleeve, red/silver label)	150
70	Regal Zono. SLRZ 1014	HOME (LP, with lyric sheet)	150
71	Chrysalis ILPS 9158	BROKEN BARRICADES (LP, gatefold sleeve, first pressing with a small white "i" at the top of the label)	50
71	Chrysalis ILPS 9158	BROKEN BARRICADES (LP, gatefold sleeve)	25
72	Fly TOOFA 7/8	A WHITER SHADE OF PALE/A SALTY DOG (2-LP, reissue)	20
73	Chrysalis CHR 1037	GRAND HOTEL (LP, gatefold sleeve, booklet, green label)	30
74	Chrysalis CHR 1058	EXOTIC BIRDS AND FRUIT (LP)	25
91	BMG PL 90589	THE PRODIGAL STRANGER (LP)	25

(see also Paramounts, Legend, Matthew Fisher, Robin Trower, Matthew Ellis, Freedom, Mick Grabham, Power Pack)

JUDD PROCTOR

61	Parlophone R 4769	Rio Grande/Plainsman	10
61	Parlophone R 4809	Palamino/Nola	10
61	Parlophone R 4841	Speakeasy/Clearway	10
62	Parlophone R 4885	The Turk/Mad	12
62	Parlophone R 4920	Backfire/It's Bluesy	12
64	Parlophone R 5126	Better Late/Boots	15
68	Morgan MR 103P	GUITARS GALORE (LP)	40
70s	Gemini GMX 5004	GUITARS GALORE (LP, reissue)	25

see also Ray Ellington

MIKE PROCTOR

67	Columbia DB 8254	Mr. Commuter/Sunday, Sunday, Sunday	225

PRODIGAL

82	D Records D7	Prodigal Son/Bye Bye Baby	12

PRODIGY

91	XL XLT 17	WHAT EVIL LURKS EP (What Evil Lurks/We Gonna Rock/Android/ Everybody In The Place) (12", company sleeve)	40
91	XL XLS 21	Charly/Charly (Original Mix)	10
91	XL XLT 21	Charly (Alley Cat Mix)/Pandemonium/Your Love/Charly (Original Mix) (12", p/s)	18
91	XL XLS 26	Everybody In The Place (Fairground Edit)/G-Force (Energy Flow)	15
92	XL XLS 30	Fire (Edit)/Jericho (Original Version)	12
92	XL XLT 30	Fire (Burning Version)/(Sunrise Version)/(Original Version)/(Genaside II Remix) (12", p/s)	18
92	XL XLS 35	Out Of Space/Ruff In The Jungle Bizness (Uplifting Vibes Remix)	18
92	XL XLT 35	Out Of Space (Original Mix)/(Techno Underworld Remix)/Ruff In The Jungle Bizness (Uplifting Vibes Remix)/Music Reach 1,2,3,4 (Live) (12", p/s)	20
93	XL XLS 39	Wind It Up (Rewound)/We Are The Ruffest	12
93	XL EB 1	EARTHBOUND 1 : One Love (original Mix)/Full Throttle (original Mix) (12")	60
95	XL SC 1	SCIENIDE (12", white label, 500 hand-stamped promos only)	60
95	XL XLT 58	Poison (95 EQ)/Rat Poison/Scienide/Poison (Enviromental Science Dub Mix) (12")	10
96	XL XLS 70 LC	Firestarter (Edit)/Molotov Bitch (Jukebox centre)	8
96	XL XLS 70	Firestarter (Instrumental)/(Empirion Mix)/Molotov Bitch (12", p/s)	20
96	XL XLS 80 LC	Breathe (Edit)/The Trick (jukebox centre)	8
97	XL XLT 90	Smack My Bitch Up (LP Version)/No Man Army/Smack My Bitch Up (DJ Hype Remix)/Mindfields (Headrock Dub)	18
98	XL XLT90DJ	Smack My Bitch Up/(DJ Hype Remix)/No Man Army/Minefields (Headrock Dub) (12" promo)	15

PRODUCERS

MINT VALUE £

04	XL XLXV1501	What Evil Lurks/We Gonna Rock/Android/Everybody In The Place (12", reissue)	12
05	XL XLT 213	Spitfire (05 Version)Spitfire (Future Funk Squad's "Dogfight" Remix/Spitfire (Nightbreed Remix) (12" stickered p/s, with 2 stickers, 2000 only)	25
05	XL XLS 213 CDE	Spitfire (05 Version)/Spitfire (Nightbreed Remix)/Spitfire (Future Funk Squad's "Dogfight" Remix) (CD stickered digipak 500 only)	30
09	Tame Me To The Hospital HOSP06	Invaders Must Die (Liam H Reamped Version)/Thunder (Doorely Remix) (p/s, green vinyl)	6
12	XL XLT590	THE ADDED FAT EP (12" EP)	10
15	Ram RAM 229	The Day Is My Enemy (Bad Company UK Remix) (1-sided, 12" p/s)	10
15	Take Me To The Hospital HOSPLP013	Ibiza/Instrumental (featuring Sleaford Mods) (p/s)	8
15	Take Me To The Hospital HOSPLP017	THE NIGHT IS MY FRIEND (12" EP)	12
92	XL XLLP 110	THE PRODIGY EXPERIENCE (2-LP)	60
94	XL XLLP 114	MUSIC FOR THE JILTED GENERATION (LP)	60
97	XL XLLP 121	THE FAT OF THE LAND (2-LP)	80
04	XL XLLP 183	ALWAYS OUTNUMBERED, NEVER OUTGUNNED (3-LP)	100
09	Take Me To The Hospital HOSPLP001	INVADERS MUST DIE (2-LP)	30
09	Take Me To The Hospital HOSPBOX001	INVADERS MUST DIE (Box set, CD/DVD/5x7")	30
15	Take Me To The Hospital HOSPLP005	THE DAY IS MY ENEMY (2-LP)	30
15	Take Me To The Hospital HOSPLP005	THE DAY IS MY ENEMY (2-LP as x 3 x 12", poster, print and download card)	35
18	Take Me To The Hospital HOSPLP 538426301	NO TOURISTS (2-LP, clear or clear violet)	20
18	Take Me To The Hospital 538426291	NO TOURISTS (2-LP)	20
21	XL Recordings – XL121LPE2	THE FAT OF THE LAND 2-LP, reissue, obi, orange vinyl	50

(see also Leeroy Thornhill)

PRODUCERS

80	Magic Moon MACH 4	Walk Right Back/All The Rage	15
80	Magic Moon MACH 1.S	On The Beach/Goin' Steady (die cut sleeve)	20
80	Edge EDGE 2	On The Shelf/Talking About My Baby (no p/s)	15

PRODUCT OF REASON

83	Tenuous Lynx LYNX 1	Man Of Your Dreams/These Days	15

PROFESSIONALS

80	Virgin VS 376	1-2-3/White Light White Heat/Baby I Don't Care (p/s, signed by Cook & Jones)	15
81	Virgin VS 426	Join The Professionals/Has Anybody Got An Alibi? (gatefold p/s)	7
81	Virgin VS 456	The Magnificent/Just Another Dream (p/s)	12
81	Virgin V 2220	I DIDN'T SEE IT COMING (LP)	15

(see also Sex Pistols, Greedies, Lightning Raiders, Steve Jones)

PROFESSIONAL UHURU DANCE BAND

71	Decca WAPS31	UHURU SPECIAL HI FI NUMBERS (LP)	35

PROFESSOR LONGHAIR

65	Sue WI 397	Baby Let Me Hold Your Hand/Looka' No Hair	40
78	Harvest HAR 5154	Mess Around/Tipitina	15
72	Speakeasy 10-78	NEW ORLEANS 88 (10" LP)	45
72	Atlantic K 40402	NEW ORLEANS PIANO (LP)	30
78	Harvest SHSP 4086	LIVE ON THE QUEEN MARY (LP)	30
80	Sonet SNTF 830	CRAWFISH SIESTA (LP)	15
83	Stateside SSL 6004	LIVE ON THE QUEEN MARY (LP, reissue)	18
81	JSP 1025	THE LONDON CONCERT (LP)	15

FRANK PROFFITT

66	Topic 12T 162	NORTH CAROLINA SONGS AND BALLADS (LP)	20

PROFIl

80	CBS S CBS 8574	Hey Music Man/Jour De Chance (p/s)	10

PROFILE (1)

65	Mercury MF 875	Haven't They Got Better Things To Do/Touch Of Your Hand	12
65	Mercury MF 981	Got To Find A Way/Don't Say Goodbye	12
69	Philips BF 1757	Politician Man/Where Is Love	8

(see also Voice)

PROFILE (2)

74	Surrey International SIT 5006I	Like It Like That/Easy Come Easy Go	8

PROJECTIVE VISION

94	Holistic AB 06	Close Encounter/Equilibrium (12")	40
94	Holistic AB 11	Apocalypse/Change (12")	90

PROJECT FEATURING JASMIN

90	Unyque UNQ 111T	Don't Be So Cruel/Understand(ing) (12")	12
91	Unyque UNQ 113T	Soul (Vocal)/(Club Remix)/No Pain No Gain (12")	15

PROLES

79	Rock Against Racism RAR 1	Stereo Love/Thought Crime/CONDEMNED: Soldier Boys/ Endless Revolution (p/s)	45
79	Small Wonder SMALL 23	Softground/SMK (p/s)	6

PROLETARIAT

85	Homestead HMS 037	Marketplace/Death Of a Headon (p/s)	8

PROMISE

69	NEMS 56-4129	Just For You/Nine To Five	100

PROPAGANDA

85	ZTT 12 ZTAS 2	Das Testaments Des Mabuse/Femme Fatale/The 9th Life (Of Dr. Mabuse) (12", white p/s, title sticker reads "13th Life New Mix")	15
85	ZTT PROP 1	Bejewelled (12", 1-sided, white label, stickered title sleeve, promo only)	12

(see also Act, Ralph Dorper, Claudia Brucken)

PROPERTY

MINT VALUE £

PROPERTY
70	Staple ST01	My Mind Sleeps/Calling You (some with p/s)	150

PROPHECY OF DOOM
89	Prophecy SRT 9KS 2178	Calculated Mind Rape/Hybrid Thought (p/s)	10
90	Deaf DEAF 02	ACKNOWLEDGE THE CONFUSION MASTER (LP, insert)	20
90	Strange Fruit SFPS 079	PEEL SESSIONS EP (12", p/s)	15

PROPHET
74	UK UK 64	Have Love Will Travel/Blues In B Sharp	30

MICHAEL PROPHET
79	Grove GMDM 17	Turn Me Loose/Praise You Jah Jah (12")	30
79	Grove GMDM 25	Warn Them Jah/Don't Interfere (12")	45
80	Greensleeves GRED 44	Help Them Please/WAILING SOULS : See Baba Joe (12", green vinyl)	30
80	Island/Grove Music 12WIP 6583	Fight to The Top (Discomix)/Love And Unity/Mash Down Rome (12")	35
80	Black Roots BR 004	My Lady/Lady Dub (12")	20
80	Love Linch LL 002	True Born African (with Soul Syndicate)/RANKING TOYAN: What A Bam Bam (12")	30
80	Love Linch LL 012	Struggle/80s Struggle (12", some on blue vinyl)	40
80s	WLN WLN 003	Rock Me Baby/Don't Throw Stone (12")	20
81	Greensleeves GRED 59	Gunman/Cassandra (12")	15
82	Greensleeves GRED 72	Here Comes The Bride/MYSTIC EYES: Bring The Kuchie Come	20
82	Greensleeves GRED 87	Boom Him Up Now/Trouble Nobody (12")	15
82	Greensleeves GRED 104	Just Talking/Thru Me (with Papa Dimes) (12")	15
90	Living Room LM 043	Hypocrites/Version (12", with Daddy Freddy)	12
90	Passion PE 6	Your Love (Michael Prophet Version)/Your Love (Ricky Tuff Version)/Acapella Version (12")	15
99	Blakamix BLK 030	Judgements/Dubments	15
80	Greensleeves GREL 18	RIGHTEOUS ARE THE CONQUEROR (LP)	25
80	Island ILPS 9606	SERIOUS REASONING (LP)	25
81	Greensleeves GRED 104	MICHAEL PROPHET (LP)	28

ORVAL PROPHET
63	London HLL 9729	Run Run Run/My Lois And Me	10

REX PROPHET
55	Brunswick OE 9144	CANADIAN PLOWBOY (EP)	10

PROPHETS
78	Grove Music GMDM 12	Give Thanks And Praise/Till I Kiss You (12")	40
79	Grove Music GMDM 4	Blessed Are The Meak (feat Trinity)/TOMMY MCCOOK: Stepping High (12", p/s)	25

(see also Yabby U)

PROPHETS (JAMAICA)
70	Big Shot BI 554	Crystal Blue Persuasion (Parts 1 & 2)	30
70	Big Shot BI 555	Tumble Time (Parts 1 & 2)	35
70	Big Shot BI 557	Revenge Of Eastwood Version One/Version Two	75
70	Jackpot JP 712	Let's Fall In Love/Purple Moon	45

(see also Lloyd & Prophets, Claudette, Lloyd & Claudette, Patrick & Lloyd)

PROPHETS (U.S.)
69	Mercury MF 1097	I Got The Fever/Soul Control	30
69	Mercury MF 1097	I Got The Fever/Soul Control (DJ copy)	50

(see also Creation [U.S.])

PROPHETS OF DOOM
80	Nonchalent N1	Apathy/1984 (1000 only, no p/s)	8

PROS & CONS
66	CBS 202341	Bend It/No Time	7

PROTECTORS
73	Live Wire SON 4004	Loretta/Jump The Sidewalk	15

PROTEGUE (& PRINCE BUSTER'S ALL STARS)
67	Blue Beat BB 398	Foul Dance/PRINCE BUSTER'S ALL STARS: This Is It	30

PROTEX
78	Good Vibrations GOT 6	Don't Ring Me Up/(Just Want) Your Attention/Listening In (wraparound p/s)	30
79	Rough Trade GOT 1	Don't Ring Me Up/(Just Want) Your Attention/Listening In (reissue, 1st pressing, text above telephone p/s)	10
79	Rough Trade GOT 1	Don't Ring Me Up/(Just Want) Your Attention/Listening In (reissue, 2nd pressing, text above telephone p/s)	8
79	Polydor 2059 124	I Can't Cope/Popularity (p/s)	25
79	Polydor 2059 167	I Can Only Dream/Heartache (p/s)	15
80	Polydor 2059 245	A Place In Your Heart/Jeepster (p/s)	15
01	Good Vibrations BIG 4	LISTENING IN (LP)	18

PROTON
80	Ballistic 12BP 264	We're Funkin'/Make Your Move (Instrumental Version)	40
81	Image IMA 1	Pay Up/Remixed Rhythm Track (12" as Proton Plus)	20
81	UK Champagne FUNK 4	Pay Up/Remixed Rhythm Track (as Proton Plus)	12

PROTOS
82	Airship AP 391	ONE DAY A NEW HORIZON (LP)	150

PROUDFOOT
73	Jam 33	Giant/Wanderer	7

PROVIDENCE
72	Threshold THS 9	EVER SENSE THE DAWN (LP, gatefold sleeve with insert)	40

PROWLER (1)
73	Parlophone R 5986	Pale Green (Hnmmmm) Driving Man/Jaywick Cowboy	30

PROWLER (2)
83	Pirate SS 226 S8	Forgotten Angels/Don't Let Go (p/s)	80
85	SRT SRT5KS/368	Alcatraz/So Lonely (p/s)	70

PRUNES

MINT VALUE £

PRUNES
70	Songbird SB 1023	Come A Little Closer/Come A Little Closer Version II	30

(see also Eric Donaldson, West Indians)

SNOOKY PRYOR
70	Flyright LP 100	SNOOKY PRYOR (LP)	15

RED PRYSOCK
59	Mercury AMT 1028	Chop Suey/Margie	20
58	Mercury MPL 6535	THE BEAT (LP)	50
58	Mercury MPL 6550	FRUIT BOOTS (LP)	40
56	Mercury MPT 7517	JUMP RED JUMP (10" LP)	40

PSEUDO EXISTORS
80	Dead Good DEAD 2	Pseudo Existence/Coming Up For Air/New Modern Warfare (rubber-stamped folded p/s, pink/white label)	60
80	Dead Good DEAD 2	Pseudo Existence/Coming Up For Air/New Modern Warfare (rubber-stamped folded p/s, later red/black label & stamped white sleeve)	35

PSEUDO 3
92	Music Madness MM001	Renk & Dirty/B-Line Stepper (12")	40

P.S. PERSONAL
83	New World NEW 1	Shoot Me Down/Shoot Me Down (no p/s)	25

PSYCHE
82	Burning World	Never Laugh/Psyche (p/s)	6

PSYCHEDELIC FURS
80	CBS 84084	THE PSYCHEDELIC FURS (LP, pink sleeve)	15
81	CBS SCBS 84892	TALK TALK TALK (LP)	15
82	CBS CBS85909	FOREVER NOW (LP)	15

(see also Unwanted)

PSYCHEOUT
00	Discord DISCORD 002	BOOM EP (12")	15
00	Discord DISCORD 003	WARP EP (12")	60
00	Discord DISCORD 004	TRAIN TRAX EP (12")	15
00	Discord DISCORD 005	SURGE EP (12")	10

PSYCHIC PHENOMENA
97	Lowlife LOW05	THE WHOLE CIRCUMFERENCE (12", EP)	15

PSYCHIC TV
82	Some Bizzare PTV 1	Just Drifting/Breakthrough (p/s)	15
82	Some Bizzare PTV 1T	Just Drifting/Just Drifting (Midnight) (12", p/s)	15
84	Temple TOPY 001	Unclean/Mirrors (12", p/s)	15
86	Temple TOPYS 009	Godstar/Godstar (BJ Mix)/Discopravity/Yes It's The B Side (double pack, gatefold p/s)	8
86	Temple TOPIC 009	Godstar/Godstar (California Mix) (12", picture disc)	15
86	Temple TOPYD 023	Good Vibrations/Interzone/Roman P/Hex-Sex/Godstar (Ugly Mix)/Je T'Aime (double pack, gatefold p/s)	6
86	Temple TOPYT 023	Roman P (Fireball Mix)/Interzone/Good Vibrations (Kundalini Mix)/Hex-Sex (Voodoo Mix) (12", p/s)	10
88	Temple TOPY 037	Tune In (Turn On To Thee Acide House) (12", p/s, as (Psychic TV/Jack The Tab)	10
88	DC DC 23	Superman/Jack The Tab (12", p/s, no artist credit on label)	15
89	Temple TOPY 048	Love, War, Riot/Eve Of Destruction (Vocoder Mixes) (12", p/s, including sticker)	10
82	Some Bizzare PSY 1	FORCE THE HAND OF CHANCE (LP, with bonus LP & double-sided poster, featuring Marc Almond)	80
82	Some Bizzare PSY 1	FORCE THE HAND OF CHANCE (LP, with poster)	35
83	CBS 25717	DREAMS LESS SWEET (LP, with inner sleeve, some with free 12" EP [XPR 1251])	35
83	CBS 25717	DREAMS LESS SWEET (LP, with inner sleeve)	25
84	Temple TOPY 003	PAGAN DAY (LP, picture disc, 999 copies)	40
84	Gramm GRAMM 23	THOSE WHO DO NOT (2-LP, 5000 copies)	30
85	Temple TOPY 004	THEMES 2 (LP)	25
85	Temple TOPY 008	THEMES 3 (LP)	25
85	Temple TOPY 010	MOUTH OF THE NIGHT (LP)	20
85	Temple TOPIC 010	MOUTH OF THE NIGHT (LP, picture disc)	25
86	Temple TOPIC 009	GODSTAR (LP, with picture disc)	15
86	Temple TOPY 014	LIVE IN PARIS (LP)	15
86	Temple TOPY 015	LIVE IN TOKYO (LP)	15
87	Temple TOPY 016	LIVE IN GLASGOW (LP)	15
87	Temple TOPY 018	LIVE IN HEAVEN (LP)	15
87	Temple TOPY 026	LIVE IN REYKJAUIK (LP)	15
87	Temple TOPY 027	LIVE EN SUISSE (LP)	15
87	Temple TOPY 028	LIVE IN TORONTO (LP)	15
87	Temple TOPY 029	LIVE IN GOTTINGEN (LP)	15
88	Temple TOPY 031	PSYCHIC TV (LP, picture disc)	15
88	Temple TOPY 032	ALBUM 10 (LP, picture disc)	15
88	Temple TOPY 038	ALLEGORY AND SELF (LP, blue vinyl)	15

(see also Throbbing Gristle)

PSYCHO'S MUM
89	Woronzow W 011	A SIBILANT SIN (LP, with insert)	15

PSYCOMETRIC
97	Acid Fever MDMA 9701	Piano Dreams/Funk Bits/The Kaison Ogle/DJ CYCLONE: Spare Parts/Meltdown/Chaos (12")	12

PSYKIS
95	Dee Jay DJX 025	Pretend (12" 1-sided promo)	20

PSYKYK VOLTS
79	Ellie Jay EJPS 9262	Totally Useless/Horror Story No. 5 (p/s)	20
79	MHG GHM 109	Totally Useless/Horror Story No. 5	35

PSYLONS

MINT VALUE £

PSYLONS
86	E Type ETYPE 1	The Mockery Of Decline/Clear Sky	10
87	Iron Lung IL 001	All The Things We Need (12", p/s)	15
90	Unsigned UN 001	No Choice/Surf Song (p/s)	8

PTOLOMY PSYCON
71	Hollick and Taylor HT/IPS 1306	LOOSE CAPACITOR (10" LP, 235 only, silkscreened front sleeve, printed back)	800

PUBLIC ENEMY
13	Vinyl Factory S714	Harder Than You Think (1-sided, Secret Seven, 100 only)	50
87	Def Jam 450482-1	YO BUM RUSH THE SHOW (LP, with lyric sheet)	20
88	Def Jam 462415-1	IT TAKES A NATION OF MILLIONS TO HOLD US BACK (LP, inner)	25
90	Def Jam 466281	FEAR OF A BLACK PLANET (LP, inner)	20
91	Def Jam 468751	APOCALYPSE 91 (2-LP, gatefold, inners)	20
94	Def Jam 523 362-1	MUSE SICK N HOUR MESS AGE (2-LP, gatefold)	20
05	Mercury 983 2545	POWER TO THE PEOPLE AND THE BEATS (box set, 5 x 12")	70

PUBLIC FOOT THE ROMAN
73	Sovereign SVNA 7259	PUBLIC FOOT THE ROMAN (LP, gatefold sleeve)	100

(see also Movies)

PUBLIC IMAGE LTD (PIL)
78	Virgin VS 228	Public Image/The Cowboy Song (foldout 'newspaper' p/s)	30
79	Virgin VS 29912	Memories/Another (12", p/s)	10
79	Virgin VS 274-12	Death Disco/And No Bird Do Sing (1/2 Mix)/Death Disco Megamix (12", p/s, 5,000 only)	15
81	Virgin VS 397-12	Flowers Of Romance (Exended Version)/Home Is Where The Heart Is (12", p/s)	12
87	Virgin VS 988	Seattle/Selfish Rubbish (box set with 7", badge, postcard & sew-on patch)	6
78	Virgin V2114	FIRST ISSUE (LP. 1st pressing, with colour inner sleeve and PiL on both labels, yellow sticker with SPOTS 007 and poster)	50
78	Virgin V2114	FIRST ISSUE (LP. 1st pressing, with colour inner sleeve and PiL on both labels)	30
79	Virgin V2114	FIRST ISSUE (LP, repressing with plain white inner sleeve)	15
79	Virgin METAL 1	METAL BOX (LP, 3 x 12" with circular paper dividers & inner sheet in round tin)	200
79	Virgin VD 2512	SECOND EDITION (standard issue, of Metal Box, 2-LP, gatefold)	30
80	Virgin V 2183	PARIS AU PRINTEMPS (LP)	15
82	Virgin V 2189	THE FLOWERS OF ROMANCE (LP)	20
83	Virgin VGD 3508	LIVE IN TOKYO (2-P)	20
84	Virgin V 2309	THIS IS WHAT YOU WANT...THIS IS WHAT YOU GET (LP)	25
86	Virgin V 2366	ALBUM (LP)	20
87	Virgin V 2455	HAPPY? (LP)	20
90	Virgin V 2644	THE GREATEST HITS SO FAR (2-LP)	20
92	Virgin V 2681	THAT WHAT IS NOT (LP)	40
12	PIL PIL 002 LP	THIS IS PIL (2-LP)	25

(see also Sex Pistols, Jah Wobble, Don Letts & Jah Wobble, Vivien Goldman, Cowboys International)

PUBLIC DISGRACE
82	Probe Plus PP2	TOXTETH EP	6

PUBLIC ZONE
77	Logo GO 104	Naive/Innocence (p/s)	6

GARY PUCKETT (& UNION GAP)
68	CBS 3714	Over You/If The Day Would Come	7
69	CBS 4122	Don't Give In To Him/Could I	7
69	CBS 4505	This Girl Is A Woman Now/His Other Woman	8
68	CBS (S) 63342	YOUNG GIRL (LP)	20
68	CBS (S) 63429	INCREDIBLE (LP)	20
70	CBS 63794	THE NEW GARY PUCKETT AND THE UNION GAP ALBUM (LP)	20

PUDDING
67	Decca F 12603	The Magic Bus/It's Too Late	70

TITO PUENTE
57	RCA RD 27002	LET'S CHA-CHA WITH PUENTE (LP)	15
58	RCA SF 5008	MUCHO PUENTE (LP)	15

PUFFIN CLUB
81	Big Nob NOB 001	Great Western Revival/Feel So Low/Anhedonia/Set A Table (no p/s, 50 only)	15

DUDU PUKWANA
74	Caroline C1504	IN THE TOWNSHIPS (LP, as Dudu Pukwana & Spear)	20
75	Caroline CA2005	FLUTE MUSIC (LP with Spear)	40
81	Jika ZL 1	SOUNDS ZILA (LP)	15
83	Jika ZL 2	LIFE IN BRACKNELL & WILLISAU (LP, featuring Dinise Saul)	25
86	Jika ZL 3	ZILA 86 (LP)	15

PULLED APART BY HORSES
10	Transgressive TRANS117X	PULLED APART BY HORSES (LP)	30

DWIGHT PULLEN
77	RM RMA 1024	Teen Age Bug/Sunglasses After Dark (reissue)	12

VERN PULLENS
72	Injun 107	Mama Don't Allow No Boppin'/Bop Crazy Baby	15
72	Injun 111	Bop Crazy Baby/Would You Be Happy	15

LEROY PULLINS
66	London HLR 10056	I'm A Nut/Knee Deep	12

PULLOVERS
80	Supermusic SUP 24/LYN 8613/4	Peter Pan Pill/Spare Part Surgery (p/s, some with kidney donor card)	20

PULP
SINGLES
83	Red Rhino RED 32	My Lighthouse (Remix)/Looking For Life (p/s)	100
83	Red Rhino RED 37	Everybody's Problem/There Was (p/s)	50

PULP MUSIC

MINT VALUE £

85	Fire BLAZE 5	Little Girl (With Blue Eyes)/Simultaneous/Blue Glow/The Will To Power (12", p/s)	25
85	Fire BLAZE 5	Little Girl (With Blue Eyes)/Simultaneous/Blue GLow/The Will To Power, 12" promo	40
86	Fire BLAZE 10	Dogs Are Everywhere/The Mark Of The Devil/97 Lovers/Aborigine/ Goodnight (12", p/s)	25
87	Fire BLAZE 17	They Suffocate At Night (Edited Version)/Tunnel (Cut Up Version) (p/s)	12
87	Fire BLAZE 17T	They Suffocate At Night (Uncut Version)/Tunnel (Full Length Version) (12", p/s)	15
87	Fire BLAZE 21T	Masters Of The Universe (Sanitised Version)/Manon/Silence (12", promo)	25
87	Fire BLAZE 21T	Masters Of The Universe (Sanitised Version)/Manon/Silence (12", p/s)	25
90	Fire BLAZE 44T	Is This House?/This House Is Condemned (12" promo, 1-sided)	25
90	Fire BLAZE 44T	My Legendary Girlfriend/Is This House?/This House Is Condemned (12", p/s)	10
91	Fire BLAZE 51T	Countdown/Death Goes To The Disco/Countdown (Radio Edit) (12", p/s)	10
92	Gift GIF 1	O.U. (Gone Gone)/Space/O.U. (Gone Gone) (Radio Edit) 12" promo & press sheet)	20
92	Caff CAFF 17	My Legendary Girlfriend/Sickly Grin/Back In L.A. (foldover p/s with insert in poly bag, 500 only)	100
92	Gift GIF 3	Babies/Styloroc (Nites Of Suburbia)/Sheffield : Sex City (12" promo with press sheet)	40
92	Gift GIF 3	Babies/Styloroc (Nites Of Suburbia)/Sheffield: Sex City (12", p/s)	30
93	Gift 7GIF6	Razzmatazz/Inside Susan/59 Lyndhurst Grove (p/s)	15
93	Gift GIF 6	Razzmatazz/Inside Susan : A Story In 3 Songs (Stacks/Inside Susan/59 Lyndhurst Grove) (12" promo with press sheet)	35
93	Gift GIF6	Razzmatazz/Stacks/Inside Susan/59 Lyndhurst Grove (12", p/s)	10
93	Island IS 567	Lipgloss/You're A Nightmare (p/s)	8
94	Island IS 595	THE SISTERS EP (gatefold, numbered)	18
94	Island 12 IS 595	THE SISTERS EP (12", p/s with print)	10
94	Island IS 674	Do You Remember The First Time?/Street Lites (p/s)	15
94	Island 12 IS 574	Do You Remember The First Time?/Street Lites/The Babysitter (12", p/s)	20
95	Island 12 IS 613	Common People/Underwear/Common People (Motiv8 Mix/Common People (Vocoda Mix) (12")	12
96	Island ISC 567	Lipgloss/You're A Nightmare (p/s, reissue, red vinyl)	20
96	Island ISC 574	Do You Remember The First Time/Street Lites (p/s, reissue, brown vinyl, p/s)	15
96	Island ISC 595	THE SISTERS EP (p/s, reissue, white vinyl)	10
96	Island ISC 613	Common People/Underwear (p/s, reissue, yellow vinyl)	60
96	Island ISC 620	Sorted For E's And Whizz/Miss-Shapes (p/s, reissue, blue vinyl)	30
96	Island 12 IS 620	Mis-Shapes/Sorted For E's & Wiz/P.T.A. (Parent Teacher Association)/Common People (Live At Glastonbury (12". p/s)	10
96	Island ISC 623	Disco 2000/Ansaphone (p/s, reissue, orange vinyl)	40
96	Island 12 IS 623	Disco 2000 (7" Mix)/Ansaphone/Disco 2000 (Motiv & Gimp Dub)/Disco 2000 (Motiv & Discoid Mix) (12")	15
96	Island ISC 632	Something Changed/Mile End (p/s, reissue pink vinyl)	30
96	Island (No Cat. No.)	SINGLES COLLECTION (7 x 7" boxed set, coloured vinyl)	100
97	Island IS 679	Help The Aged/Tomorrow Never Lies/Laughing Boy (p/s)	12
98	Island 12 ISX 695 DJ	This Is Hardcore/Ladies Man/The Professional/This Is Hardcore (End Of The Line Remix) (12", p/s. promo)	20

ALBUMS

84	Red Rhino REDLP 29	IT (mini-LP)	40
87	Fire FIRELP 5	FREAKS (LP)	25
92	Fire FIRE 11026	SEPARATIONS (LP)	40
93	Island ILPM 2076	INTRO (LP)	35
93	Fire FIRELP 5	FREAKS (LP, reissue, barcode on rear of sleeve)	15
94	Island ILPS 8025	HIS 'N' HERS (LP)	125
94	Fire FIRE LP 36	MASTERS OF THE UNIVERSE (PULP ON FIRE 1985-86)	35
95	Island ILPS 8041	DIFFERENT CLASS (LP, die-cut sleeve with 6 inserts)	250
95	Island ILPS 8041	DIFFERENT CLASS (LP, with 1 insert)	150
96	Nectar NTMLP 521	COUNTDOWN 1992-1983 (LP)	40
98	Island ILPSD 8066	THIS IS HARDCORE (2 x LP, gatefold, with insert)	150
99	Cooking Vinyl COOK CD 178	PULPED 93-92 (4-CD box set with booklet)	30
00	Simply Vinyl SVLP 166	DIFFERENT CLASS (LP, reissue 180gm vinyl)	35
01	Island ILPS 8110	WE LOVE LIFE (LP)	70
12	Fire FV223E	IT (mini-LP, reissue)	20

(see also Jarvis Cocker, Relaxed Muscle)

PULP MUSIC

79	Pulp Music PB 1	Low Flying Aircraft/Something Just Behind My Back/So Lo (blank labels, some numbered up to 2,000 & signed, with handmade sleeve)	25
79	Pulp Music PB 1	Low Flying Aircraft/Something Just Behind My Back/So Lo (blank labels, some numbered up to 2,000 & signed)	20

PULSAR

76	Decca SKL-R 5228	POLLEN (LP)	20
77	Decca TXS 119	STRANDS OF THE FUTURE (LP, gatefold sleeve)	25

PULSE (1)

70	Major Minor SMLP 64	PULSE (LP)	60

PULSE (2)

82	Tomato OK 1	Trouble With John/Red Day In Dallas	40

PULSEBEAT

83	A Love Bite ALB 1	Ride A White Swan/(Have) No Regrets	6

PUMPHOUSE GANG

77	Kitsch FAD 1	Motorcity Fantasy/Cocaine (p/s)	7
79	Splash SP 001	Spotlight/Lights Out (no p/s)	15
80	Splash SP 101	Judy Turn Out The Light/A Girl Like You	12

(see also Slush)

PUNCHERS

70	Punch PH 46	Sons Of Thunder (actually by Lee Perry & The Upsetters)/ Only If You Understand	25

(see also Upsetters, Chuck Jr)

PUNCHIN' JUDY

MINT VALUE £

PUNCHIN' JUDY
73 Transatlantic TRA 272   PUNCHIN' JUDY (LP, laminated front sleeve) 20
(see also Downliner Sect)

PUNCTURE
77 Small Wonder SMALL 1   Mucky Pup/Can't Rock'n'Roll (p/s) 50

PUNCTURED TOUGH GUY
85 Xcentric Noise NINIH 1   ACID RAINS EP 18

PUNISHMENT OF LUXURY
78 Small Wonder SMALL 8   Puppet Life/The Demon (p/s) 8
79 United Artists UP 36507   Engine Of Excess/Jellyfish (p/s) 6
79 United Artists UP 36537   Secrets/Brainbomb (p/s) 6
80 United Artists BP 317   Laughing Academy/Baby Don't Jump (p/s) 8
79 United Artists UAG 30258   LAUGHING ACADEMY (LP, with inner sleeve) 20

PUPILS
66 Wing WL 1150   A TRIBUTE TO THE ROLLING STONES (LP) 40
69 Fontana SFL 13087   A TRIBUTE TO THE ROLLING STONES (LP, reissue) 15
(see also Eyes)

PUPPETS
63 Pye 7N 15556   Poison Ivy/Everybody's Talking 50
64 Pye 7N 15625   Shake With Me/Three Boys Looking For Love (existence unconfirmed) 0
64 Pye 7N 15634   Baby Don't Cry/Shake With Me 60

DANNY PURCHES
55 Columbia SCM 5183   Mama/Just One More Time 8
58 Columbia DB 4129   The Shrine On The Second Floor/He 12

(BERNARD) PRETTY PURDIE
68 Direction 58-3301   Funky Donkey/Caravan 10
68 Direction 58-3628   Soul Clappin'/Blow Your Lid 10
71 Philips 6073 708   Good Livin' Good Lovin'/Day Dreaming 6
68 Direction 8-63290   SOUL DRUMS (LP) 40
71 Philips 6369 421   SOUL IS ... (LP) 25

PURE EVIL
73 Hybrid HB20   Never Trust A Woman/I See You Now 30

PURE GENIUS
95 Peer Pressure PEER 001   Undercover/Unbelievable (12") 20
96 Peer Pressure PEER 002   LAW OF THE LAND (12" EP) 20

PURE GOLD
69 President PT 250   Fairground/You've Gotta Give It Time 10

PURE HELL
78 Golden Sphinx GSX 002   These Boots Are Made For Walking/No Rules (p/s) 20

PURE LOVE & PLEASURE
70 Stateside SSL 5026   A RECORD OF PURE LOVE AND PLEASURE (LP) 30

PURE PRODUCT
79 Streets Ahead SA2   Rejection/Sugar Plum (p/s) 6

PURESSENCE
92 Damn Loud 2DM01   PETROL SKIN (EP, 1,000 only) 30
93 Damn Loud 2DM02   OFFSHORE (EP, 1,000 only) 35
96 Island ILPS 8946   PURESSENCE (LP) 30
98 Island ILPS 8064   ONLY FOREVER (LP) 25

PURE VIBES
98 PV 001   Murder Tune/Shake The Pressure/Got To Work (12") 30
98 PV 002   Shake The Pressure (Remix 1)/(Remix 2)/(Remix 3) (12", white label) 50

PURGE
69 Corn CP 101   The Mayor Of Simpleton Hall/The Knave 200
69 Corn CP 101   The Mayor Of Simpleton Hall/The Knave (without p/s) 90

JAMES & BOBBY PURIFY
66 Stateside SS 547   I'm Your Puppet/So Many Reasons 20
67 Stateside SS 595   Wish You Didn't Have To Go/You Can't Keep A Good Man Down 15
67 Stateside SS 2016   Shake A Tail Feather/Goodness Gracious 25
67 Stateside SS 2039   I Take What I Want/Sixteen Tons 12
67 Stateside SS 2049   Let Love Come Between Us/I Don't Want To Have To Wait 25
68 Stateside SS 2093   Do Unto Me/Everybody Needs Somebody 20
68 Bell BLL 1008   I Can't Remember/I Was Born To Lose Out 10
68 Bell BLL 1024   Help Yourself To All My Lovin'/Last Piece Of Love 10
69 Bell BLL 1043   Untie Me/We're Finally Gonna Make It 8
69 Bell BLL 1056   Let Love Come Between Us/Shake A Tail Feather 10
69 Bell BLL 1067   Do Unto Me/Wish You Didn't Have To Go 8
72 Mojo 2092 056   I'm Your Puppet/Wish You Didn't Have To Go 8
67 Stateside SL 10206   JAMES AND BOBBY PURIFY (LP) 60
67 Bell MBLL/SBLL 101   THE PURE SOUND OF THE PURIFYS (LP) 40

PURITAN GUITARS
80 Riverside Records   £100 In 15 Minutes/Making It (p/s, stamped white labels) 20

PURITY RING
11 Transparent TP 027   Ungirthed/Lofticries (p/s, 300 only) 15
12 4AD CAD 3218   SHRINES (LP, gatefold, teal-coloured vinyl) 18

ALTON PURNELL
70 Dixie DIX 4   TRAVELLING LIGHT (LP) 30

PURPLE ALGAE
95 Poor Person Prod. PPPR 7   ADRIFT ON A SEA OF SOUND (LP, handmade sleeve & 2 inserts, no'd, 500 only) 15

PURPLE DISCO MACHINE
17 Sweat It Out! SWEATA016V   SOULMATIC (2-LP) 70

PURPLE GANG

MINT VALUE £

21	Sweat It Out! SWEATSV020	EXOTICA (2-LP)	25

PURPLE GANG
67	Big T BIG 101	Granny Takes A Trip/Bootleg Whisky	15
68	Big T BIG 111	Kiss Me Goodnight Sally Green/Auntie Monica	7
68	Transatlantic TRA 174	THE PURPLE GANG STRIKES (LP)	60

PURPLE HAZE
85	S.R.S. SRS 6	Hear It On The Radio (p/s)	55

PURPLE HEARTS
79	Fiction FICS 003	Millions Like Us/Beat That! (p/s)	10
79	Fiction FICS 007	Frustration/Extraordinary Sensations (p/s)	10
80	Fiction FICS 9	Jimmy/What Am I Gonna Do (p/s)	10
80	Safari SAFE 30	My Life's A Jigsaw/The Guy Who Made Her A Star/Just To Please You (in foldout jigsaw p/s)	12
80	Safari SAFE 30	My Life's A Jigsaw/The Guy Who Made Her A Star/Just To Please You	8
82	Road Runner RR 1	Plane Crash/Scooby Doo/Gun Of Life (p/s)	12
86	UNICORN PHZ3	Friends Again/Head On Collision Time (p/s)	8
80	Fiction FIX 002/2383 568	BEAT THAT! (LP)	20

(see also Bob Manton, Rage)

PURPLE WINE
71	The Mental Health Council	It's My Mind/I'm Lonely/Friends (p/s)	100
71	NBR (No cat no)	PURPLE WINE (LP, plain white cover)	300

PURPLEMAN & PAPPA TULLO
83	Vista Sounds VSLP 4024	PURPLEMAN SAVES PAPPA TOLLO IN A DANCEHALL (LP)	40

PURSON
12	Rise Above B007929F6W	Rocking Horse/Twos And Ones (p/s, 1st press, black vinyl, 250 only)	8
12	Rise Above B007929F6W	Rocking Horse/Twos And Ones (p/s, 1st press, clear vinyl, 100 only)	12
12	Rise Above B007929F6W	Rocking Horse/Twos And Ones (p/s, 1st press, purple vinyl, 250 only)	8
13	Rise Above RISE7/173	The Contract/Blueprints Of The Dream (p/s, 200 on black vinyl)	10
13	Rise Above RISE7/173	The Contract/Blueprints Of The Dream (p/s, 100 on black vinyl)	15
13	Rise Above RISELP 152	THE CIRCLE & THE BLUE DOOR (LP. 'die hard' edition, 180 gram vinyl, A2 poster, patch and die-cut gatefold sleeve, 100 only)	50

PURSUIT OF COLOUR
84	Colour	LOVE PLAYS EGO: Can't Let You Go/Radomontade (b/w, p/s allegedly 50 copies only)	200

PUSSY (1)
69	Morgan Bluetown BT 5002	PUSSY PLAYS (LP)	1500
09	Morgan Bluetown BT 5002	PUSSY PLAYS (LP, reissue by Secret Records/Record Collector, 350 only with signed and numbered laminated insert)	40

(see also Angel Pavement, Fortes Mentum)

PUSSY (2)
72	Deram DM 368	Feline Woman/Ska Child	35

(see also Jerusalem. Gillan, Deep Purple)

PUSSYFOOT
66	Decca F 12474	Freeloader/Things That Still Remind Me	25
67	Decca F 12561	Mr Hyde/Hasty Words	30
67	Pye 7N 17395	Dee Dee Do Your Dance/Big Brown Eyes	30
68	Pye 7N 17520	Good Times/Till You Don't Want Me Anymore	25

(see also Rare Breed)

PUSSY GALORE
87	Vinyl Drip SUK 001	GROOVY HATE FUCK (LP)	25
87	Product Inc. 33PROD 19	RIGHT NOW (LP)	18
89	Product INCLP 1	DIAL M FOR MOTHERFUCKER (LP)	18
90	Rough Trade ROUGH 149	HISTORIA DE LA MUSICA ROCK (LP)	18

(see also Jon Spencer Blues Explosion)

ASHA PUTHLI
76	CBS 4623	The Devil Is Loose/Space Talk	10
73	CBS 65804	ASHA PUTHLI (LP)	20
75	CBS 80978	SHE LOVES TO HEAR THE MUSIC (LP)	15
76	CBS 81443	THE DEVIL IS LOOSE (LP)	30

PUTNEY BRIDGE
71	Chapter One CH 145	Take A Ride/Road To Purity	10

PUZZLE
69	Stateside SS 2146	Hey Medusa/Make The Children Happy	25
72	Jam JAM 1	Houla/Do You Feel The Pain	40
69	Stateside SSL 10285	PUZZLE (LP)	50

PVC 2
77	Zoom ZUM 2	Put You In The Picture/Pain/Deranged, Demented and Free (p/s)	12

(see also Midge Ure, Zones)o

PVRIS
16	(No label or cat. no.)	ACOUSTIC (10", p/s, white vinyl)	50

PYLON
80	Armageddon ARM 1	Cool/Dub/Driving School/Danger!! (10")	15

PYLONS
80	Hi Voltage HVVS 701	Marvel World/Spoof (p/s)	50

NATASHA PYNE
66	Polydor 56713	It's All In Your Head/I'm A Dreamer	15

PYRAMID
67	Deram DM 111	Summer Of Last Year/Summer Evening	50

(see also Fairport Convention, Ian Matthews)

PYRAMIDS (U.K.)
67	President PT 161	Train Tour To Rainbow City/John Chewey	20
68	President PT 177	Wedding In Peyton Place/Girls Girls Girls	10

PYRAMIDS (U.S.)

			MINT VALUE £
68	President PT 195	All Change On The Bakerloo Line/Playing Games	10
68	President PT 206	Mexican Moonlight/Mule	10
68	President PT 225	Tisko My Darling/Movement All Around	10
69	President PT 243	Do-Re-Mi/I'm Outnumbered	10
69	President PT 274	I'm A Man/Dragon Fly	10
69	JJ DB 1307	Stay With Him/Chicken Mary	150
70	Duke DU 80	Geronimo/Feel Alright	12
70	Trojan TR 7755	Telstar/Feel Alright	12
70	Trojan TR 7770	To Sir With Love/Reggae Shuffle	15
71	Trojan TR 7803	All For You/All For You Version	15
71	Creole CR 1003	Mosquito Bite/Mother's Bath	20
71	Creole 1006	Can't Leave Now/Teardrops	25
68	President PTL 1021	THE PYRAMIDS (LP)	100

(see also Equals, Little Grants & Eddie, Seven Letters, Bruce Ruffin)

PYRAMIDS (U.S.)

64	London HLU 9847	Penetration/Here Comes Marsha	50

PYTHAGORAS THEOREM

70	Pye 7N 17924	Give A Damn/London Bridge	12
70	Pye 7N 17990	Our House/Free Like Me	7

PYTHON LEE JACKSON

76	Young Blood YB 1077	The Blues/Cloud Nine	10
80	Young Blood YB 0089	In A Broken Dream/The Blues	6
80	Young Blood YEP 89	In A Broken Dream (mono)/In A Broken Dream (stereo)/The Blues/ Cloud Nine (EP, "Kelly Girl" Employment Agency advert on p/s)	10

(see also Rod Stewart)

Q

Q			
82	Cocteau COC 6	Playback/Music's Gone (p/s)	15

Q.A.X.

82	Vinyl Beat VB 001	Heart Alone/Does Me Good (p/s)	15
82	Vinyl Beat VB 002	Lightning Touch/Unconfirmed (p/s)	15
82	Vinyl Beat VB 003	Gimme Your Love/The Heat Of Love (p/s)	8

Q-CHASTIC

92	Rephlex 002EP	Q-CHASTIC EP (double pack, existence unconfirmed)	200

(see also Aphex Twin)

Q8

78	Flame FLM 018	Superband/Give A Little Love	10

Q.LAZZARUS

91	All Nations ANRS 001	Goodby Horses/White Lines (p/s)	100
91	All Nations 12ANRS 001	Goodby Horses/Goodby Horses (7" version)/White Lines (12", p/s)	150

QPR

67	Eyemark EMS 1008	QPR The Greatest/Supporters Support Us	45

Q-PROJECT

92	QTIP 001	FREESTYLE FANATIC EP (12", stamped white label, 4 untitled tracks)	39
93	Legend LEG 001	Return Of Q Project/Champion Sound/Night Moves (12")	20

QRUUX ADU XA

82	Shooting Star STAR 007	Shakin' All Over/Robotics (p/s, as K.A.D.)	15

QT'S

79	SRT SRTS/79/CUS 429	SAVAGE IN THE CITY EP	35

QUAD (1)

92	Kinetix KNT 008	INSTELLABRIATION TRILOGY PART II: UR Her Egg/Spirit Of Laurel Way (12")	15
93	Kinetix KNT 11	QUADRAVILLE EP (12")	15
94	Kinetix KNT 12	AQUAVILLE REMIXES (12")	15

QUAD (2)

97	Acme AC 8020LP	QUAD (LP, clear vinyl in printed clear PVC cover)	30
97	Prescription DRUG 3	Q (LP, hand-made sleeve, 99 copies only)	100

(see also Sun Dial)

QUADROPHONICS

75	Contempo 2054	Betcha If You Check It Out/Prove My Love To You	10

QUADS

79	Big Bear BB 23	There Must Be Thousands/You Gotta Jive	6
80s	Big Bear BB29	UFO/Astronaut's Journey (p/s)	10

CHRISTINE QUAITE

62	Oriole CB 1739	Guilty Eyes/Oh My!	20
62	Oriole CB 1772	Your Nose Is Gonna Grow/Our Last Chance	15
63	Oriole CB 1845	Mister Heartache/Whisper Wonderful Words	15
63	Oriole CB 1876	In The Middle Of The Floor/Tell Me Mama	60
63	Oriole CB 1921	I Believe In Love/Here She Comes	20
64	Oriole CB 1945	Mister Stuck Up/Will You Be The Same Tomorrow	15
65	Stateside SS 435	If You've Got A Heart/So Near So Far	20
66	Stateside SS 482	Long After Tonight Is All Over/I'm Hoping	50
66	Stateside SS 482	Long After Tonight Is All Over/I'm Hoping (DJ copy)	100

QUAKER CITY BOYS

59	London HLU 8796	Teasin'/Won't Y' Come Out, Mary Ann	15

QUAKERMAN

MINT VALUE £

QUAKERMAN
95	U Star US 005	QUAKERMAN EP (12")	20
01	U Star USR 008	Schlam Me (Work Mix)/U Star Mix)/(Work Dub) (12")	12

QUAKERS
65	Oriole CB 1992	I'm Ready/Down The Road A Piece	150
65	Studio 36 KSP 109/110	She's Alright/Talk To Me (only 50 pressed)	600

QUALITY DRIVEL
81	No Cure WHOOP 1	SUBLIMINAL CUTS EP (p/s)	35

QUANDO QUANGO
84	Factory FAC 102	Atom Rock (p/s)	6
85	Factory FAC 137	Genius/This Feeling (p/s)	6
85	Factory FACT 110	PIGS & BATTLESHIPS (LP)	18

QUANTIC
00	Breakin' Bread BNB 002	We Got Soul/Fresh Rhythm	25
01	Tru Thoughts TRU 014	Life In The Rain/Common Knowledge/Time Is The Enemy (12")	15
04	Tru Thoughts TRU 064	Don't Joke With A Hungry Man/(Instrumental Version)/Furthest Moment/Don't Joke With A Hungry Man (Acapella) (12", featuring Spanky Wilson)	35
01	Tru Thoughts TRU LP 016	THE 5TH EXOTIC (2-LP)	40
02	Tru Thoughts TRU LP 034	APRICOT MORNING (2-LP)	30
06	Tru Thoughts TRU LP 100	AN ANNOUNCEMENT TO MAKE (2xLP)	20

QUANTIC SOUL ORCHESTRA
01	Tru Thoughts TRU7 018	Super 8 (Part 1)/Super 8 (Part 2)	12
03	Tru Thoughts TRU7 051	Pushin' On/Pushin' On My Thing	8
03	Tru Thoughts TRU7 055	Babarabatiri/The Conspirator	10
03	Tru Thoughts TRU LP 029	STAMPEDE (LP)	30
05	Tru Thoughts TRU LP 074	PUSHIN' ON (LP)	30
07	Tru Thoughts TRU LP 139	TROPIDELICO (LP)	25

QUARRY
87	QP QP 001	Just Another Day/Promised Land	20

QUARRY MEN
58	'P.F. Phillips Kensington'	That'll Be The Day/In Spite Of All The Danger (78 rpm shellac acetate, handwritten labels, 1 copy only, owned by Paul McCartney)	200000
81	'Percy Philips, Kensington'	That'll Be The Day/In Spite Of All The Danger (78rpm, private pressing reproduction of 1958 demo disc, repro Parlophone co. sleeve, 25 only)	5000
81	'Percy Philips, Kensington'	That'll Be The Day/In Spite Of All The Danger (45rpm, private pressing reproduction of 1958 demo disc, repro Parlophone co. sleeve, 25 only)	5000

(see also Beatles, Trad Grads)

QUARTER NOTES
57	Parlophone R 4365	My Fantasy/Ten Minutes To Midnight	15

JOE QUARTERMAN & FREE SOUL
73	GSF GS 504	JOE QUARTERMAN & FREE SOUL (LP)	50

QUARTET
69	Decca F12974	Now/Will My Lady Come	8
70	Decca F13072	Mama Where Did You Fail/Joseph	10

QUARTZ (1)
77	Blyth Jex School	Witch Queen/Social Values (gatefold p/s)	7

QUARTZ (2)
77	Jet UP 36290	Sugar Rain/Street Fighting Lady/Mainline Riders	15
77	Jet UP 36317	Street Fighting Lady/Mainline Riders	12
80	Reddingtons R.R. DAN 1	Nantucket Sleighride/Wildfire (p/s, white or blue vinyl)	10
80	Jet SJET 189	Street Fighting Lady/Mainline Riders (p/s, reissue, demos £15)	8
80	Logo GOT 387	Satan's Serenade/Bloody Fool/Roll Over Beethoven (live) (12", p/s, blue vinyl)	20
80	Logo GOT 387	Satan's Serenade/Bloody Fool/Roll Over Beethoven (live) (12", p/s, red vinyl)	15
80	MCA MCA 642	Stoking The Fires Of Hell/Circles (p/s)	10
80	Logo MOGO 4007	LIVE QUARTZ (12" EP)	12
81	MCA MCA 661	Stand Up And Fight/Charlie Snow (p/s)	12
83	Heavy Metal HEAVY 17	Tell Me Why/Streetwalker (p/s)	7
77	Jet UAG 30081	QUARTZ (LP, with inner sleeve)	50
79	Jet JETLP 233	DELETED (LP, in sealed brown paper bag with insert. Reissue of 1st LP)	18
80	Reddingtons R.R. REDD 001	QUARTZ LIVE - COUNT DRACULA (LP, in b&w 'live' sleeve)	15
80	MCA MCF 3080	STAND UP AND FIGHT (LP, with lyric insert)	15
83	Heavy Metal HMRPD 9	AGAINST ALL ODDS (LP, picture disc)	20

(see also Black Sabbath, Copperfield, Bandy Legs)

QUASAR
82	Q QUA 1	FIRE IN THE SKY (LP, with insert)	20

(see also Solstice)

QUASI
98	Domino WIGLP 55	FEATURING "BIRDS" (LP)	20
99	Domino WIGLP 69	FIELD STUDIES (LP)	20

QUATERMASS (1)
70	Harvest SVHL 775	QUATERMASS (LP, gatefold sleeve, no EMI logo on label)	300
75	Harvest SHSM 2002	QUATERMASS (LP, reissue, different sleeve)	40

(see also Ian Gillan Band, Episode Six, Hard Stuff)

QUATERMASS (2)
97	Metropolitan MM 027	The Judgement (12", no p/s)	15

QUATOR
72	BBC RESL 6	Spy Trap/Playgirl	30

QUATRAIN
69	Polydor 583 743	QUATRAIN (LP)	60

SUZI QUATRO
72	Rak RAK 134	Rolling Stone/Brain Confusion (For All The Lonely People)	30

Finlay QUAYE

MINT VALUE £

73	Rak PSR 355	Primitive Love/Shakin' All Over (promo only)	30
87	Hackenbacker HACK 101	Am I Dreaming/Who Needs Chairs/Will You Take This Woman (only available at pantomime show)	10
73	SRAK 505	SUZI QUATRO (LP)	20
74	RAK SRAK 509	QUATRO (LP)	15

FINLAY QUAYE

97	Epic 488758	MAVERICK A STRIKE (LP, insert)	25

QUBISM

94	em:t 2294	QUBISM (CD, digipak)	50

QUE BONO

81	Naked BARE 1	Making Noise/Emelia	15

QUEEN
SINGLES

73	EMI EMI 2036	Keep Yourself Alive/Son And Daughter	40
74	EMI EMI 2121	Seven Seas Of Rhye/See What A Fool I've Been (later solid centre pressing)	40
74	EMI EMI 2229	Killer Queen/Flick Of The Wrist	6
75	EMI EMI 2256	Now I'm Here/Lily Of The Valley (push out centre)	8
75	EMI EMI 2256	Now I'm Here/Lily Of The Valley (later solid centre pressing)	35
75	EMI EMI 2375	Bohemian Rhapsody/I'm In Love With My Car (p/s; beware counterfeits with 'computer-scanned' logo)	35
75	EMI EMI 2375	Bohemian Rhapsody/I'm In Love With My Car (in company sleeve)	10
76	EMI EMI 2494	You're My Best Friend/'39 (solid centre)	30
76	EMI EMI 2565	Somebody To Love/White Man (p/s, push out centre, beware of counterfeit sleeves)	25
76	EMI EMI 2565	Somebody To Love/White Man (solid centre)	30
77	EMI EMI 2593	Tie Your Mother Down/You And I	8
77	EMI EMI 2623	QUEEN'S FIRST EP: Good Old Fashioned Lover Boy/Death On Two Legs/ Tenement Funster/White Queen (As It Began) (p/s)	10
77	EMI EMI 2708	We Are The Champions/We Will Rock You (p/s, push-out centre)	8
77	EMI EMI 2708	We Are The Champions/We Will Rock You (p/s, solid centre)	12
78	EMI EMI 2757	Spread Your Wings/Sheer Heart Attack (p/s, put-out centre)	8
78	EMI EMI 2757	Spread Your Wings/Sheer Heart Attack (p/s, solid centre)	15
78	EMI EMI 2870	Bicycle Race/Fat Bottomed Girls (p/s)	10
78	EMI EMI 2870	Bicycle Race/Fat Bottomed Girls (different p/s for export to Belgium)	200
79	EMI EMI 2910	Don't Stop Me Now/In Only Seven Days (p/s, push-out centre)	8
79	EMI EMI 2910	Don't Stop Me Now/In Only Seven Days (p/s, solid centre)	30
79	EMI EMI 2959	Love Of My Life (live)/Now I'm Here (live)	20
80	EMI EMI 5076	Play The Game/A Human Body (p/s, beige label with red 'EMI' logo or white label with large black 'Queen' logo)	6
80	EMI EMI 5102	Another One Bites The Dust/Dragon Attack (p/s)	8
82	EMI EMI 5293	Body Language/Life Is Real (Song For Lennon) (p/s, with Queen in black type on front of sleeve)	8
82	EMI EMI 5293	Body Language/Life Is Real (Song For Lennon) (p/s, with Queen in red type on front of sleeve)	80
82	EMI EMI 5316	Las Palabras De Amor (The Words Of Love)/Cool Cat (p/s)	8
82	EMI EMI 5325	Backchat/Staying Power (p/s)	10
82	EMI 12EMI 5325	Backchat (Extended)/Staying Power (12", p/s)	20
84	EMI 12QUEEN 1	Radio Ga Ga (Ext. Version)/Radio Ga Ga (Instrumental)/I Go Crazy (12", p/s)	10
84	EMI QUEEN 2	I Want To Break Free (Remix)/Machines (Back To Humans) ('Freddie' p/s, gold lettering)	10
84	EMI QUEEN 2	I Want To Break Free (Remix)/Machines (Back To Humans) ('Freddie' p/s, white lettering)	10
84	EMI QUEEN 2	I Want To Break Free (Remix)/Machines (Back To Humans) ('Brian' p/s, with gold lettering)	12
84	EMI QUEEN 2	I Want To Break Free (Remix)/Machines (Back To Humans) ('Roger' p/s, with gold lettering)	15
84	EMI QUEEN 2	I Want To Break Free (Remix)/Machines (Back To Humans) ('John' p/s, with gold lettering)	18
84	EMI 12QUEEN 2	I Want To Break Free (Extended Remix)/Machines (Back To Humans) (12", p/s, with red background with gold lettering)	20
84	EMI 12QUEEN 2	I Want To Break Free (Extended Remix)/Machines (Back To Humans) (12", p/s, with red background with black lettering)	12
84	EMI 12QUEEN 2	I Want To Break Free (Extended Remix)/Machines (Back To Humans) (12", p/s, with white background)	10
84	EMI QUEEN 3	It's A Hard Life/Is This The World We Created...? (p/s)	6
84	EMI QUEEN 3	It's A Hard Life/Is This The World We Created...? ('Roger Taylor' overprinted photo p/s)	20
84	EMI 12QUEEN 3	It's A Hard Life (Extended)/It's A Hard Life/ Is This The World We Created...? (12")	25
84	EMI 12QUEENP 3	It's A Hard Life/Is This The World We Created...? (12", picture disc)	20
84	EMI QUEEN 4	Hammer To Fall (Edit)/Tear It Up ('live' p/s, withdrawn)	100
84	EMI QUEEN 4	Hammer To Fall (Edit)/Tear It Up (red p/s)	6
84	EMI 12 QUEEN 4	Hammer To Fall (The Headbangers Mix)/Tear It Up (12", 'live' p/s, withdrawn)	150
84	EMI 12 QUEEN 4	Hammer To Fall (The Headbangers Mix)/Tear It Up (12", red p/s)	12
84	EMI QUEEN 5	Man On The Prowl/Keep Passing The Open Windows (unreleased, white label test pressings only)	150
84	EMI QUEEN 5	Thank God It's Christmas/Man On The Prowl/ Keep Passing The Open Windows (p/s)	8
84	EMI 12QUEEN 5	Thank God It's Christmas/Man On The Prowl (Extended Version)/ Keep Passing The Open Windows (Extended Version) (12", p/s)	10
84	EMI G 45 1	You're My Best Friend/Killer Queen (re-issue, Golden 45's series)	20
85	EMI QUEEN 6	One Vision (7" Mix)/Blurred Vision (p/s, with red lyric inner sleeve)	7
85	EMI 12QUEEN 6	One Vision (Extended Vision)/Blurred Vision (12", p/s, with red lyric inner sleeve)	12
85	EMI 12QUEEN 6	One Vision (Extended Vision)/Blurred Vision (12", p/s)	10
85	EMI 12QUEEN 6	One Vision (Extended Vision)/Blurred Vision (12", printed PVC sleeve & red inner)	30
86	EMI QUEEN 7	A Kind Of Magic (Ext. Version)/A Dozen Red Roses For My Darling (12", p/s)	12
86	EMI 12QUEENP7	A Kind Of Magic (Extended Version)/Don't Lose Your Head (Instrumental Version) (12", picture disc)	35

QUEEN

MINT VALUE £

Year	Catalogue	Description	Value
86	EMI QUEEN 8	Friends Will Be Friends/Seven Seas Of Rhye (p/s)	8
86	EMI QUEEN P8	Friends Will Be Friends/Seven Seas Of Rhye (picture disc)	40
86	EMI 12QUEEN 8	Friends Will Be Friends (Extended Version)/Friends Will Be Friends (7" Version)/Seven Seas Of Rhye (12", p/s)	10
86	EMI QUEEN 9	Who Wants To Live Forever/Killer Queen (p/s)	8
86	EMI 12QUEEN 9	Who Wants To Live Forever (7" Version)/(Album Version)/Killer Queen/ Who Wants To Live Forever (Piano Version) (12", p/s)	18
89	EMI QUEEN 10	I Want It All/Hang On In There (p/s)	8
89	Parlophone 12QUEEN 10	I Want It All (Single Version)/Hang On In There/ I Want It All (Album Version) (12", p/s)	12
89	Parlophone CDQUEEN 10	I Want It All (Album Version)/Hang On In There/I Want It All (Single Version) (CD, picture disc)	20
89	EMI QUEEN 11	Breakthru' (7" Mix)/Stealin' (p/s)	8
89	Parlophone QUEEN PD 11	Breakthru' (7" Mix)/Stealin' (shaped picture disc, 12" PVC sleeve with insert)	20
89	Parlophone QUEEN PD 11	Breakthru' (7" Mix)/Stealin' (uncut picture disc, 12" PVC sleeve with insert)	350
89	Parlophone QUEEN 12	The Invisible Man/Hijack My Heart (black vinyl, p/s)	8
89	Parlophone QUEEN X12	The Invisible Man/Hijack My Heart (clear vinyl, p/s)	12
89	Parlophone 12QUEEN 12	The Invisible Man (12" Version)/(7" Version)/Hijack My Heart (12", p/s)	12
89	Parlophone 12QUEENX12	The Invisible Man (12" Version)/The Invisible Man (7" Version)/ Hijack My Heart (12", clear vinyl, PVC sleeve with insert)	20
89	Parlophone CD QUEEN 12	The Invisible Man (12" Version)/Hijack My Heart/ The Invisible Man (Single Version) (CD)	30
89	Parlophone QUEEN 14	Scandal/My Life Has Been Saved (p/s)	10
89	Parlophone QUEEN P14	Scandal/My Life Has Been Saved (poster p/s)	20
89	Parlophone 12QUEEN 14	Scandal (12" Version)/Scandal (7" Version)/My Life Has Been Saved (12", p/s)	10
89	Parlophone 12QUEENS 14	Scandal (12" Version)/My Life Has Been Saved/Scandal (7" Version)/ (12", p/s, 1-sided, B-side etched with group's signatures)	25
89	Parlophone QUEEN 15	The Miracle/Stone Cold Crazy (live) (p/s)	10
89	Parlophone QUEEN H15	The Miracle/Stone Cold Crazy (live) (orange hologram p/s)	15
89	Parlophone QUEEN H15	The Miracle/Stone Cold Crazy (live) (proof sleeve with negative hologram p/s)	300
89	Parlophone 12QUEEN 15	The Miracle/Stone Cold Crazy (live)/My Melancholy Blues (live) (12", yellow p/s)	15
89	Parlophone 12QUEENP 15	The Miracle/Stone Cold Crazy (live)/My Melancholy Blues (live) (12", turquoise p/s with insert print)	20
89	Parlophone QUEENCD 15	The Miracle/Stone Cold Crazy (live)/My Melancholy Blues (live) (CD)	30
91	Parlophone QUEEN 16	Innuendo/Bijou (p/s)	8
91	Parlophone 12QUEEN 16	Innuendo (Explosive Version)/Under Pressure/Bijou (12", p/s)	18
91	Parlophone 12QUEEN PD16	Innuendo (Explosive Version)/Under Pressure/Bijou (12", picture disc, PVC sleeve with insert)	35
91	Parlophone QUEEN PD 17	I'm Going Slightly Mad/The Hitman (shaped picture disc with insert)	25
91	Parlophone QUEEN PD 17	I'm Going Slightly Mad/The Hitman (uncut picture disc with insert)	450
91	Parlophone 12QUEENG 17	I'm Going Slightly Mad/The Hitman/Lost Opportunity (12", gatefold p/s)	25
91	Parlophone QUEEN 18	Headlong/All God's People (p/s)	10
91	Parlophone 12QUEEN PD18	Headlong/All God's People/Mad The Swine (12", clear vinyl picture disc, with insert in PVC sleeve)	20
91	Parlophone QUEEN 19	The Show Must Go On/Keep Yourself Alive (p/s)	8
91	Parlophone 12QUEENSG 19	The Show Must Go On/Keep Yourself Alive/Queen Talks (12", 1-sided, B-side etched with group's signatures, gatefold p/s)	20
91	Parlophone QUEEN 19/20	The Show Must Go On/Bohemian Rhapsody (unissued, no p/s)	500
95	Parlophone QUEENLH 24	Let Me Live/Fat Bottomed Girls (Jukebox 45, black vinyl no p/s)	15
96	Parlophone QUEEN 23	Too Much Love Will Kill You/We Will Rock You/We Are The Champions (p/s, pink vinyl)	8
96	Parlophone QUEENPD 24	Let Me Live/Fat Bottomed Girls/Bicycle Race (picture disc with poster)	15
96	Parlophone 12QUEEN25	You Don't Fool Me (Remixes) 12"	10
97	Parlophone QUEENLH 26	No-One But You/We Will Rock You (Original 1977 version) (unreleased)	20
97	Parlophone QUEEN 26	No-One But You (Only The Good Die Young)/Princes Of The Universe/ We Will Rock You (Rick Rubin 'Ruined' Remix)/Gimme The Prize (Instrumental 'Eye' Remix) (Unissued 7")	175
97	Parlophone QUEENPD 27	No-One But You (Only The Good Die Young)/We Will Rock You (Rick Rubin 'Ruined' Remix)/Tie Your Mother Down/Gimme The Prize (Instrumental 'Eye' Remix) (picture disc)	6
98	Parlophone QUEEN PD28	Under Pressure (picture disc)	8
08	Parlophone 2370097	C-Lebrity/Fire And Water (picture disc, with Paul Rodgers)	15
11	Island 2765780	Stormtroopers In Stilettos/Stone Cold Crazy/Keep Yourself Alive (numbered picture disc in PVC sleeve, 2000 only)	15
15	Virgin/EMI 0602547500809	Bohemian Rhapsody/I'm In Love With My Car (12", p/s)	25
17	Virgin 0602557907667	We Are The Champions/We Will Rock You (12", p/s)	15
19	EMI 7735248	Bohemian Rhapsody/I'm In Love With My Car (reissue, purple/yellow vinyl, p/s)	20
21	EMI 0602435763033	Radio Ga Ga/I'm In Love With My Car (blue vinyl, Roger Taylor p/s, numbered)	100
21	EMI 0602435763040	We Will Rock You/Sail Away Sweet Sister (red vinyl, Brian May p/s, numbered)	250
21	EMI 602435763026	Spread Your Wings/One Year Of Love (green vinyl, John Deacon p/s, numbered)	100
21	EMI 602435763057	Somebody To Love/You Take My Breath Away (yellow vinyl, Freddie Mercury p/s, numbered)	125

SINGLES : 3" CD SINGLES

Year	Catalogue	Description	Value
80s	Parlophone	QUEEN : THE 3" SINGLES (gatefold wallet, card insert)	150

ALBUMS

Year	Catalogue	Description	Value
73	EMI EMC 3006	QUEEN (LP, 1st pressing with "KIP-HUGGYPOO KISSY" hand-etched into run out groove on side 1, laminated cover)	50
74	EMI EMA 767	QUEEN II (LP, laminated gatefold sleeve, lyric inner sleeve)	50
74	EMI EMA 767	QUEEN II (laminated gatefold sleeve, 2nd pressing, (P) 1974 below Trident logo on both sides)	15
74	EMI EMC 3061	SHEER HEART ATTACK (LP, laminated sleeve, inner lyric sleeve)	50
75	EMI EMTC 103	A NIGHT AT THE OPERA (LP, 1st pressing, embossed gatefold sleeve with cut corner inner, YAX 5063/4-2 "BLAIRS" in run-off)	70
75	EMI EMTC 103	A NIGHT AT THE OPERA (LP, later pressings, embossed gatefold sleeve with 'shaped' inner sleeve)	35
76	EMI EMTC 104	A DAY AT THE RACES (LP, gatefold, inner sleeve)	40

QUEEN

MINT VALUE £

Year	Cat. No.	Description	Value
77	EMI EMA 784	NEWS OF THE WORLD (LP, gatefold with lyric inner sleeve)	40
78	EMI EMA 788	JAZZ (LP, gatefold sleeve with attached poster, inner sleeve has band shot on one side and track listing on the other)	40
79	EMI EMSP 330	LIVE KILLERS (2-LP)	25
80	EMI EMA 795	THE GAME (LP, inner sleeve)	20
81	EMI EMTV30	GREATEST HITS (LP)	30
81	EMI EMTV 30	GREATEST HITS (LP, mispress, side 2 plays "Anne Murray's Greatest Hits")	50
82	EMI EMA 797	HOT SPACE (LP, inner)	20
82	EMI FA 3040	QUEEN (LP, 'fame' reissue)	15
84	Fame FA 4130991	QUEEN II (reissue, 'Fame' series)	15
85	EMI QB 1	THE COMPLETE WORKS (14-LP box set including "Complete Vision" LP of non-LP tracks, 2 booklets & map, numbered; 600 autographed)	1000
85	EMI QB 1	THE COMPLETE WORKS (14-LP box set including "Complete Vision" LP of non-LP tracks, 2 booklets & map, numbered)	300
86	EMI EU 3509	A KIND OF MAGIC (LP, gatefold)	20
86	EMI EU 3509	A KIND OF MAGIC ('Princes Of The Universe' proof sleeve; unreleased)	500
86	EMI EMC 3519	LIVE MAGIC (LP, gatefold)	15
89	Band Of Joy BOJLP 001	QUEEN AT THE BEEB (LP)	30
89	EMI PCSD 107	THE MIRACLE (LP, inner)	20
91	Parlophone PCSD 115	INNUENDO (LP, inner)	50
91	Parlophone PMTV 2	GREATEST HITS 2 (2-LP, embossed gatefold sleeve)	25
92	Parlophone PCSP 725	LIVE AT WEMBLEY (2-LP, gatefold sleeve)	150
92	Parlophone CDQTEL 0001	BOX OF TRIX (CD, box set, with video, book, poster, T-shirt, patch & badge)	60
92	Parlophone CQTEL 0001	BOX OF TRIX (cassette, box set, with video, book, poster, T-shirt, patch & badge)	50
95	Parlophone 724383608812	MADE IN HEAVEN (LP, stickered gatefold sleeve with inserts, ivory vinyl)	100
95	Parlophone 724383608812	MADE IN HEAVEN (LP, gatefold sleeve, black vinyl)	60
95	Parlophone QUEEN BOX 20	ULTIMATE QUEEN (20 x CD set, in numbered glazed box and numbered cardboard outer box, with Freddie hologram and 2 booklets)	450
97	EMI LPCENT 25	A NIGHT AT THE OPERA (LP, reissue, EMI 100 Centenary, stickered sleeve)	40
99	Parlophone 724352345211	GREATEST HITS III (2-LP with inners)	100
99	Parlophone 72433994621	A DAY AT THE RACES (LP, remaster, reissue, 180gm)	50
05	Parlophone 338 4781	A NIGHT AT THE OPERA (LP, reissue, half-speed remaster)	60
05	Parlophone 724386321114	QUEEN ON FIRE (3-LP box set)	75
09	EMI QUEENLP 1	QUEEN (LP, remastered)	18
09	EMI QUEENLP 2	QUEEN II (LP, remastered)	18
09	EMI QUEENLP 3	SHEER HEART ATTACK (LP, remastered)	18
09	EMI QUEEN 4	A NIGHT AT THE OPERA (LP, reissue)	20
09	EMI QUEEN 5	A DAY AT THE RACES (LP, reissue)	18
09	EMI QUEEN 6	NEWS OF THE WORLD (LP, reissue, remastered)	20
09	EMI QUEEN 10	HOT SPACE (LP, reissue, remastered)	20
09	EMI QUEEN 12	A KIND OF MAGIC (LP, reissue, remastered)	20
09	EMI 686644-1	ABSOLUTE GREATEST (3-LP box set)	90
10	EMI QUEEN 7	JAZZ (LP, reissue, remastered, poster)	25
15	EMI 00602547202642	QUEEN (LP, remastered, 180gm)	15
15	EMI 00602547288240	QUEEN II (LP, remastered, 180gm)	15
15	EMI 00602547202680	SHEER HEART ATTACK (LP, remastered, 180gm)	15
15	EMI 00602547202727	NEWS OF THE WORLD (LP, reissue, 180gm)	20
15	EMI 00602547202758	THE GAME (LP, reissue, remastered, 180gm)	20
17	EMI 0602567090441	NEWS OF THE WORLD (LP, Marvel X-Men edition, with alternative cover, art print, stickers sleeve, numbered, sold at 2017 London Comic Con and Queen online store, around 250 copies, 180gm)	1000
18	EMI 6781164	JAZZ (LP, reissue, picture disc, 1978 copies)	80
19	EMI 00602577626302	THE WORKS (LP, reissue, clear vinyl, HMV exclusive, stickered sleeve)	40
21	EMI 00602507489465	FLASH GORDON (LP, reissue, remastered, picture disc, 1980 copies)	60
21	EMI 00602438852925	QUEEN - THE GREATEST (2-LP, reissue, in slipcase)	50

PROMOS

Year	Cat. No.	Description	Value
73	EMI 2036	Keep Yourself Alive/Son And Daughter (demo copy, release date of (15.6.73) on label, different mix of A side to that later released)	500
73	EMI 2036	Keep Yourself Alive/Son And Daughter (second demo copy, release date of (6.7.73) on label)	250
73	EMI (no cat. no.)	QUEEN (LP, white label, EMI conference custom issue, die-cut sleeve, with outer envelope)	500
73	EMI (no cat. no.)	QUEEN (LP, white label, EMI conference custom issue, die-cut sleeve, without outer envelope)	400
74	EMI 2121	Seven Seas Of Rhye/See What A Fool I've Been (demo, with release date of (25.2.74) on label)	80
75	EMI 2256	Now I'm Here/Lily Of The Valley (demo, with release date (17.1.75) on label)	80
77	EMI 2593	Tie Your Mother Down/You And I (demo)	45
77	EMI SP SLP 241 A1U	We Will Rock You/We Are The Champions/Spread Your Wings (12", 1-sided)	1000
77	EMI 2623	QUEEN'S FIRST EP: Good Old Fashioned Lover Boy/Death On Two Legs/ Tenement Funster/White Queen (As It Began) (demo copy, p/s)	45
77	EMI 2708	We Will Rock You/We Will Rock You (demo, mispressing, We Are The Champions label on A side)	75
77	EMI 2708	We Are The Champions/We Will Rock You (demo)	40
77	EMI (no cat. no.)	NEWS OF THE WORLD (LP, box set, with factory sample sticker, 5 photos, bio, badge & demo copy of "We Are The Champions"/"We Will Rock You", 50 only)	1000
78	EMI EMI 2375	Bohemian Rhapsody/I'm In Love With My Car (EMI 'Queen's Award For Export' in-house edition, blue vinyl, Queen crest label, hand-numbered, purple p/s., with invites, matches, pen, ticket, menu, outer card sleeve, scarf & EMI goblets in card box)	5000
78	EMI EMI 2375	Bohemian Rhapsody/I'm In Love With My Car (EMI 'Queen's Award For Export' in-house edition, blue vinyl, Queen crest label, hand-numbered, purple p/s., with outer 'EMI International' carrying envelope)	4000
78	EMI EMI 2375	Bohemian Rhapsody/I'm In Love With My Car (EMI 'Queen's Award For Export' in-	3500

QUEEN LATIFAH

MINT VALUE £

		house edition, blue vinyl, Queen crest label, hand-numbered, purple p/s.	

(The blue vinyl 'Bohemian Rhapsody' was limited to 200 numbered copies)

78	EMI 2757	Spread Your Wings/Sheer Heart Attack (demo)	45
78	EMI 2870	Bicycle Race/Fat Bottomed Girls (demo)	45
79	EMI EMI 2910	Don't Stop Me Now/In Only Seven Days (demo in p/s)	35
79	EMI 2959	Love Of My Life (live)/Now I'm Here (live) (demo)	60
79	EMI 5001	Crazy Little Thing Called Love/We Will Rock You (live) (demo)	35
80	EMI 5022	Save Me/Let Me Entertain You (live) (demo)	35
80	EMI 5076	Play The Game/A Human Body (demo)	35
80	EMI 5102	Another One Bites The Dust/Dragon Attack (demo)	35
84	EMI QUEEN 1	Radio Ga Ga (Edit)/I Go Crazy ('video shoot' p/s, unreleased, proofs only)	750
84	EMI QUEENDJ 5	Man On The Prowl/Thank God It's Christmas	150
84	Flexi Ltd. (no cat. no.)	Excerpts From Their New Album 'The Works' (flexidisc sampler, p/s)	15
86	EMI 12 QUEEN 7	A Kind Of Magic/A Dozen Red Roses For My Darling (12" promo, white label with sticker)	40
86	EMI 12 QUEEN 7	A Kind Of Magic/A Kind Of Magic (12" promo, white label with sticker)	30
86	Parlophone EMCDV 2	THE HIGHLANDER SELECTION (CD Video, 50 only)	400
86	EMI/Channel 4 QUEEN 7	NETWORK QUEEN ('A Kind Of Magic' 7" housed in promotional fold-out sleeve that opens up to depict illustrated band playing to audience. 50 made to promote TV advertising for July 1986 Wembley Stadium concerts)	1000
89	Flexi Ltd. (no cat. no.)	A Message From Queen (flexidisc, 4th Fan Club Convention issue)	25
89	Parlophone CDPROMOQU 1	I Want It All (1-track CD promo)	40
89	Parlophone QUEEN 10	I Want It All/Hang On In There (p/s in promo gatefold p/s, press release, B&W photo)	80
89	Parlophone 12 QUEENX 12	The Invisible Man (12" Version)/The Invisible Man (7" Version)/ Hijack My Heart (12", clear vinyl test pressing with Queen logos within vinyl)	500
91	Parlophone (no cat. no.)	A SAMPLE OF MAGIC (CD, segued excerpts from "Greatest Hits 2")	60
91	EMI QUEEN DJ 16	Innuendo/Innuendo (12" promo, p/s)	30
91	Parlophone 12 QUEENDJ 18	Headlong/All God's People/Mad The Swine (12" promo)	25
91	Parlophone (no cat. no.)	HINTS OF INNUENDO (cassette, edits/out-takes sampler for "Innuendo")	30
91	EMI	INNUENDO (Promo boxed set with CD, cassette, calendar, folder, bio & photos)	60
91	Parlophone (no cat. no.)	EIGHT GOOD REASONS TO BUY GREATEST HITS 2 (cassette, segued excerpts)	30
94	EMI CD DIG 1	DIGITAL MASTER SAMPLER (CD, picture disc)	45
95	EMI QUEEN DJ95	Bohemian Rhapsody/I'm In Love With My Car (purple vinyl, hand numbered, p/s, Fan Club Convention issue, 2,000 only)	250
95	Parlophone QUEENDJ 22	A Winter's Tale/Thank God It's Christmas (jukebox issue, plain white sleeve, with jukebox strip)	10
95	Parlophone QUEENLHDJ 21	Heaven For Everyone (Album Version)/Heaven For Everyone (Single Version) (jukebox issue, plain white sleeve, with poster, fold-out card & jukebox strip)	20
96	Parlophone QUEENDJ 23	Too Much Love Will Kill You/We Are The Champions (jukebox issue, plain white sleeve, with jukebox strip)	10
96	Parlophone VIRGIN 1	Heaven For Everyone/Heaven For Everyone (12", white label, Virgin Radio 'Queen Day' competition prize, black 'Queen crest' p/s with handwritten details; mispressing with same tracks both sides, unreleased)	0
96	Parlophone VIRGIN 2	Heaven For Everyone (12", 1-sided, white labels, Virgin Radio 'Queen Day' competition prize, 'Queen crest' p/s w/ handwritten details, 15 copies only)	750
96	Parlophone VIRGIN 3	A Winter's Tale (12", 1-sided, white labels, Virgin Radio 'Queen Day' competition prize, 'Queen crest' p/s with handwritten details, 15 only)	750
96	Parlophone VIRGIN 4	Mother Love (12", 1-sided, white labels, Virgin Radio 'Queen Day' competition prize, 'Queen crest' p/s with handwritten details, 15 only)	750
96	Parlophone VIRGIN 5	Let Me Live (12", 1-sided, white labels, Virgin Radio 'Queen Day' competition prize, 'Queen crest' p/s with handwritten details, 15 only)	750
96	Parlophone VIRGIN 6	You Don't Fool Me (12", 1-sided, white labels, Virgin Radio 'Queen Day' competition prize, 'Queen crest' p/s with handwritten details, 15 only)	750
96	Parlophone VIRGIN 7	It's A Beautiful Day (12", 1-sided, white labels, Virgin Radio 'Queen Day' competition prize, 'Queen crest' p/s with handwritten details, 15 only)	750
96	Parlophone VIRGIN 8	I Was Born To Love You (12", 1-sided, white labels, Virgin Radio 'Queen Day' competition prize, 'Queen crest' p/s with handwritten details, 15 only)	750
96	Parlophone 12 RDJ 6446	You Don't Fool Me (Remixes) (12" promo, orange vinyl)	50
97	Parlophone CDQT 1	QUEEN ROCKS (CD, Brian May interview)	75
99	EMI QUEENWL 28	Under Pressure (Remixes) (with David Bowie) (12", white label, unreleased mix, promo only)	30

MISPRESSINGS

75	EMI EMI 2378	Bohemian Rhapsody/I'm In Love With My Car (2nd issue, with incorrect cat. no.)	12
78	EMI EMI 2870	Bicycle Race/Fat Bottomed Girls (p/s, B-side plays Crystal Gayle's 3 O'Clock In The Morning or Dollar track)	50
79	EMI EMI 2975	CLIFF RICHARD: We Don't Talk Anymore/Count Me Out (A-side plays "Bohemian Rhapsody")	12
79	EMI EMI 5001	Crazy Little Thing Called Love/We Will Rock You (live) (p/s, both sides play "We Will Rock You")	40
80	EMI EMI 5076	Play The Game/A Human Body (p/s, both sides play "A Human Body")	30
86	Parlophone RP 5452	BEATLES: Paperback Writer/Rain (picture disc, A-side plays Friends Will Be Friends)	75

(see also Freddie Mercury, Brian May, Roger Taylor, Larry Lurex, Cross, Immortals, Hilary Hilary, Eddie Howell, Man Friday & Jive Junior)

QUEEN LATIFAH

93	Motown 530 272 1	BLACK REIGN (LP)	45

QUEENS OF THE STONE AGE

00	Interscope 497 387-7	The Lost Art Of Keeping A Secret/Ode To Clarissa (p/s)	30
02	Interscope 497 812-7	No One Knows/Tension Head (Live From The Mean Fiddler) (p/s, grey vinyl)	30
03	Interscope 9810506	First It Giveth/The Most Exalted Potentate Of Love (red vinyl, p/s)	6
05	Interscope 988 354-2	In My Head/I Think I Lost My Headache (picture disc)	6
05	No label FUNMACHINE1	The Fun Machine Took A Shit And Died/Commentary (white label, signed)	20
11	Rekords REK 004	How To Handle A Rope (A Lesson In The Lariat)/Avon (p/s, 1000 only, numbered)	12
98	Roadrunner RR 8674-2	QUEENS OF THE STONE AGE (2-LP)	150
00	Interscope 490 683-1	X (LP, gatefold sleeve)	100
02	Interscope 493435-1	SONGS FOR THE DEAF (2-LP, gatefold)	150
05	Interscope 490 864-1	RATED R (LP reissue)	40

QUEENSRYCHE

MINT VALUE £

11	Music On Vinyl MOVLP 250	LULLABIES TO PARALYZE (2-LP, one side etched)	30
11	Music On Vinyl MOVLP 250	LULLABIES TO PARALYZE (2-LP, red vinyl, one side etched)	30
11	Rekords REK 001LP	QUEENS OF THE STONE AGE (2-LP reissue)	100
13	Matador OLE 1048-1	...LIKE CLOCKWORK (2-LP, blue sleeve)	30
13	Matador OLE 1048-1	...LIKE CLOCKWORK (2-LP, black artwork, 800 only)	40
13	Matador OLE 1040-0	...LIKE CLOCKWORK (2-LP, red sleeve, 180 gram edition, booklet)	35
17	Matador OLE 11251	VILLAINS (2-LP, 1 side etched)	25

QUEENSRYCHE
86	EMI America EAD 22	Gonna Get Close To You/Prophecy//Queen Of The Reich (live)/Deliverance (live) (double pack)	6
94	EMI MTL 1081	PROMISED LAND (LP, clear vinyl)	20

QUEERS
90	Shakin Street YEAH HUP 010	GROW UP (LP)	30

QUEL DOMAGE
84	Xcentric Noise SEVENTH 1	Bright Lights/Music For Serious And Solemn Occasions/Amendment (p/s)	7

QUEST
15	System SYSTM 011	Belly Of The Beast/EGOLESS: Dub Liberation (12")	30

? & THE MYSTERIANS
66	Cameo Parkway C 428	96 Tears/Midnight Hour	40
66	Cameo Parkway C 441	I Need Somebody/'8' Teen	45
67	Cameo Parkway C 467	Can't Get Enough Of You, Baby/Smokes	30
67	Cameo Parkway C 479	Girl (You Captivate Me)/Got To	25
67	Cameo Parkway C 496	Do Something To Me/Love Me Baby	25
76	London HLU 10534	96 Tears/'8' Teen	10

QUESTIONS (1)
68	Decca F 22740	We Got Love/Something Wonderful	35

QUESTIONS (2)
76	Look LK SP 6059	Sixty Nine/Mumbling Mosey	8

QUESTIONS (3)
79	Zoom ZUM 8	Can't Get Over You/Answers (p/s)	10

TOMMY QUICKLY (& REMO FOUR)
63	Piccadilly 7N 35137	Tip Of My Tongue/Heaven Only Knows (solo)	30
63	Piccadilly 7N 35151	Kiss Me Now/No Other Love	8
64	Piccadilly 7N 35167	Prove It/Haven't You Noticed	6
64	Piccadilly 7N 35183	You Might As Well Forget Him/It's As Simple As That	6
64	Pye 7N 15708	The Wild Side Of Life/Forget The Other Guy	6
64	Pye 7N 15748	Humpty Dumpty/I'll Go Crazy	8

(see also Remo Four)

QUICKSAND
70	Carnaby CNS 4015	Passing By/Cobblestones	15
73	Dawn DNS 1046	Time To Live/Empty Street, Empty Heart	10
73	Dawn DNLS 3056	HOME IS WHERE I BELONG (LP, gatefold sleeve, pink 'sun' label)	150

(see also Man)

QUICKSILVER MESSENGER SERVICE
68	Capitol (S)T 2904	QUICKSILVER MESSENGER SERVICE (LP, black label with rainbow rim)	80
69	Capitol E-(S)T 120	HAPPY TRAILS (LP)	35
70	Capitol E-ST 391	SHADY GROVE (LP)	20
70	Capitol EA-ST 498	JUST FOR LOVE (LP)	20
71	Capitol EA-ST 630	WHAT ABOUT ME? (LP)	15
72	Capitol E-SW 819	QUICKSILVER (LP)	15
83	Psycho PSYCHO 10	MAIDEN OF THE CANCER MOON (2-LP)	40

(see also Dino Valenti, Nicky Hopkins)

QUIET FIVE
65	Parlophone R 5273	When The Morning Sun Dries The Dew/Tomorrow I'll Be Gone (in p/s)	20
65	Parlophone R 5273	When The Morning Sun Dries The Dew/Tomorrow I'll Be Gone	10
65	Parlophone R 5302	Honeysuckle Rose/Let's Talk It Over	8
66	Parlophone R 5421	Homeward Bound/Ain't It Funny What Some Lovin' Can Do	18
66	Parlophone R 5470	I Am Waiting/What About The Time For Me	10
67	CBS 202586	Goodnight Sleep Tight/Just For Tonight	6

(see also Kris Ife, Richard Barnes)

QUIET SUN
75	Island HELP 19	MAINSTREAM (LP, black label with pink 'i' label)	40

(see also Phil Manzanera, Roxy Music)

QUIET WORLD
69	Dawn DNS 1001	Miss Whittington/There Is A Mountain (as Quiet World Of Lea & John)	40
70	Dawn DNS 1005	Children Of The World/Love Is Walking	40
70	Pye 7N 45005	Rest Comfortably/Gemima	12
71	Pye 7N 45074	Visitor/Sam	10
70	Dawn DNLS 3007	THE ROAD (LP)	200

(see also Steve Hackett, Genesis)

QUIK
67	Deram DM 121	Love Is A Beautiful Thing/Bert's Apple Crumble	150
67	Deram DM 139	King Of The World/My Girl	50
67	Deram DM 155	I Can't Sleep/Soul Full Of Sorrow	70
98	Klooks Kleek 60	Bert's Apple Crumble/THE SONICS: The Witch (re-issue)	10

(see also Meddy Evils)

QUILL (1)
79	Kite KR 10	LIVE (LP)	15

QUILL (2)
80	Kite KRS 10A	Love In A Jar/Time (no p/s)	18

QUILLER
75	BBC RESL 25	Quiller/General Direction 7

QUINCEHARMON
71	Columbia DB 8772	Suddenly The Whole World Is Mine/Strange Feeling 15
71	Columbia DB 8798	On The Buses/Don't Tell Me It's Over 10
72	Columbia DB8929	Sunshine City/Mr Sun 8

PAUL QUINCHETTE
57	Esquire 32-057	ON THE SUNNY SIDE (LP) 40

QUINCICASM
73	Saydisc SDL 249	QUINCICASM (LP) 50

ANTHONY QUINN
70	Capitol CL 15649	I Love You And You Love Me/Sometimes (I Just Can't Stand You) 8

MIKE QUINN
66	Fontana TF 761	Someone's Slipping Into My Mind/I Know What You Know 7
69	CBS 4506	Apple Pie/There's A Time 6

PAUL QUINN
92	Postcard DUBH 921	THE PHANTOMS AND THE ARCHETYPES (LP) 50

PAUL QUINN & EDWYN COLLINS
84	Swamplands SWX 1	Pale Blue Eyes/Pale Blues Eyes (Western)/Burro (12", original pressing with 'film' p/s, inner sleeve & yellow obi) 10

(see also Edwyn Collins, Orange Juice)

QUINTESSENCE
70	Island WIP 6075	Notting Hill Gate/Move Into The Light 7
71	Neon NE 1003	Sweet Jesus/You Never Stay The Same (in p/s) 15
71	Neon NE 1003	Sweet Jesus/You Never Stay The Same 6
69	Island ILPS 9110	IN BLISSFUL COMPANY (LP, gatefold, pink label with white 'i' logo, booklet) 100
70	Island ILPS 9128	QUINTESSENCE (LP, tri-fold sleeve, pink label with white 'i' logo) 80
71	Island ILPS 9143	DIVE DEEP (LP, inner sleeve, pink rim palm tree label) 60
72	RCA SF 8273	SELF (LP) 20
72	RCA SF 8317	INDWELLER (LP) 15

(see also Kala)

QUINTET MODERNE
87	Bead Records BEAD 26	IKKUNAN TAKANA (LP) 20

QUINTET OF HOT CLUB OF FRANCE
53	Decca LF 1139	SWING FROM PARIS (10" LP) 15

QUINTET OF THE YEAR
54	Vogue L.D.E. 087	JAZZ AT THE MASSAY HALL VOL. 3 (10" LP) 18

QUIRE
72	Polydor 2058 297	Strange One/Half Way Up The Hill 7

DARYL QUIST
63	Pye 7N 15538	Thanks To You/Keep Moving (in p/s) 10
64	Pye 7N 15656	See The Funny Little Clown/When She Comes To You 6
65	Decca F 12058	Put Away Your Teardrops/Across The Street (Is A Million Miles Away) 6

QUIVER
72	Warner Bros K 16165	Green Tree/I Might Stumble 6
71	Warner Bros K 46089	QUIVER (LP) 30

(see also Bridget St. John, Natural Gas, Sutherland Brothers, Village)

QUIZ
81	HCR 1	And The World/Call On You (no p/s) 12

QUODLING'S DELIGHT
76	Fanfare FR 2179	AMONG THE LEAVES SO GREEN (LP) 25

QUOTATIONS (U.K.)
64	Decca F 11907	Alright Baby/Love You All Over Again 25
68	CBS 3716	Cool It/Mark Of Her Head 35
69	CBS 4378	Hello Memories/Pretend 10

(see also Fleur De Lys, Johnny B. Great, Johnny Gustafson, Merseybeats, Johnny Goodison)

QUOTATIONS (U.S.)
61	HMV POP 975	Imagination/Ala-Men-Sy 80

QUOTING MARX
77	Full Stop PUNC 28	Opening And Closing/66 And 99 12

R

RAAW
78	Tempus TEM 111	Lili Twil/Just A Little Different (p/s) 15

RABBI JOSEPH GORDAN
85	Bam Caruso Intl. NRICO 30	Competition/Belief In Him (large centre hole, plain beige sleeve) 10

(see also Julian Cope)

RABBIT
73	Island ILPS 9238	BROKEN ARROWS (LP, gatefold sleeve, pink rim palm tree label) 18
74	Island ILPS 9289	DARK SALOON (LP) 15

(see also Free; Kossoff, Kirke, Tetsu & Rabbit)

RABBITS
79	Stortbeat BEAT 4	Kitchen Parties/Tonight (numbered p/s, 1000 only) 15

RABID
82	Fallout FALL 007	BLOODY ROAD TO GLORY (EP, with poster) 10

Michael RABIN

MINT VALUE £

MICHAEL RABIN
58	Columbia 33CX 1597	MENDELSSOHN VIOLIN CONCERTO (LP)	300
59	Capitol SP 8506	MOSAICS (LP, stereo)	700
60	Capitol SP 8510	THE MAGIC BOW (LP, stereo)	450
60	Capitol SP 8534	PAGANINI: CONCERTO NO 1 IN D MAJOR/WIENIAWSKI: CONCERTO NO.2 IN D MAJOR (LP, stereo)	300

MIKE RABIN (& DEMONS)
64	Columbia DB 7350	Head Over Heels/Leaving You (as Mike Rabin & Demons)	70
65	Polydor BM 56007	If I Were You/What Do You Do	25

RAC
92	Nucleus NUKE 001	Monsoon/Yogomotion (12")	30
92	Nucleus NUKE 004	Neo Rio/555/Choobes/Heaven (12")	40
93	Nucleus NUKE 005	Hula Hoops/ESP/Microtropics/Wavelength (12")	50

STEVE RACE
61	Parlophone R 4808	Crosstrap/Stop Look Listen	10

RACE FANS
68	Trojan TR 610	Bookie Man/UNIQUES: More Love	60
68	Trojan TR 637	Time Marches On/SILVERTONES: Party Night	80

YANK RACHELL TENNESSEE JUG BUSTERS
64	'77' LA 12-23	MANDOLIN BLUES (LP)	30

RACONTEURS
08	XL XLS 227	Steady As She Goes/Store Bought Bones (1st issue, 1,000 only, p/s Jack White to right of cover)	8
06	XL XLLP 196X	BROKEN BOY SOLDIERS (LP)	40
08	XL XLLP 359	CONSOLERS OF THE LONELY (2-LP)	50

(see also White Stripes)

BOGDAN RACZYNSKI
02	Rephlex BRCOM 2	Fnick You DJ (Flashulb Remix)/Kimi Mix 2 (Nautillis Remix)	25
99	Rephlex CAT 082 LP	BOKU MO WAKARAN (3-LP)	40
99	Rephlex CAT 085 LP	SAMURAI MATH BEATS (2-LP)	40
99	Rephlex CAT 089 LP	THINKING OF YOU (2-LP)	25
01	Rephlex CAT 115 CD	MYLOVEILOVE (LP, cherry red vinyl)	18
02	Rephlex CAT 120 LP	96 DRUM N BASS CLASSIXXX (2-LP)	20
07	Rephlex CAT 193 LP	ALRIGHT! (2-LP)	25

RADAR
83	House Of Wax WAX 1	Leave Her Alone/Reach For The Sky (p/s)	10

JIMMY RADCLIFFE
65	Stateside SS 374	Long After Tonight Is Over/What I Want I Can Never Have	35
65	Stateside SS 374	Long After Tonight Is Over/What I Want I Can Never Have (DJ copy)	150
16	Outta Sight OSV 157	Long After Tonight is Over/Long After Tonight Is Over (Italian) (reissue)	6

(see also Steve Karmen Big Band)

RADGE
79	Radge RAD 100	ABSOLUTELY...EP	8

RADHA KRISHNA
71	Columbia SCX 6462	RADHA KRISHNA (LP, composed & directed by John Mayer)	45

(see also John Mayer)

RADHA KRISHNA TEMPLE (LONDON)
69	Apple APPLE 15	Hare Krishna Mantra/Prayer To The Spiritual Masters (p/s, as Radha Krishna Temple [London], with insert)	30
69	Apple APPLE 15	Hare Krishna Mantra/Prayer To The Spiritual Masters (p/s, as Radha Krishna Temple [London], without insert)	20
69	Apple APPLE 15	Hare Krishna Mantra/Prayer To The Spiritual Masters (no p/s, as Radha Krishna Temple [London])	6
70	Apple APPLE 25	Govinda/Govinda Jai Jai (p/s)	30
70	Apple APPLE 25	Govinda/Govinda Jai Jai (in company sleeve)	12
71	Apple SAPCOR 18	THE RADHA KRISHNA TEMPLE (LP, gatefold sleeve, with insert)	50
71	Apple SAPCOR 18	THE RADHA KRISHNA TEMPLE (LP, gatefold sleeve, without insert)	40
93	Apple SAPCOR 18	THE RADHA KRISHNA TEMPLE (LP, reissue, gatefold sleeve with inner)	15

RADIANTS
64	Chess CRS 8002	Voice Your Choice/If I Only Had You	40
64	Chess CRS 8002	Voice Your Choice/If I Only Had You (DJ copy)	60
68	Chess CRS 8073	Hold On/I'm Glad I'm The Loser	20
68	Chess CRS 8073	Hold On/I'm Glad I'm The Loser (DJ copy)	50

(see also Maurice & Mac, Caston & Majors)

RADIATION
80	Martin's Mart 1X	Johnny/Last Day (no p/s)	15

RADIATORS (FROM SPACE)
77	Chiswick S 10	Television Screen/Love Detective (p/s, original issue has laminate sleeve)	10
78	Chiswick NS 24	Prison Bars/(Why Can't I Be A) Teenager In Love (unreleased, promo only white label in stamped white sleeve & loose printed labels)	40
79	Chiswick NS 45	Walkin' Home Alone Again/Try And Stop Me/The Hucklebuck (unreleased; white label test pressings exist with loose labels; as Radiators)	40
79	Chiswick CHIS 115	Kitty Ricketts/Ballad Of The Faithful Departed (company sleeve)	8
81	Chiswick CHIS 144	Song Of The Faithful Departed/They're Looting In The Town	10
77	Chiswick WIK 4	TV TUBE HEART (LP)	20

(see also Pogues)

RADICAL DANCE FACTION
80	Earth Zone EZ 001	BORDERLAND CASES (LP, 1st pressing with white picture sleeve)	20
80	Earth Zone EZ 001	BORDERLAND CASES (LP, 2nd pressing with black picture sleeve)	15
81	Earth Zone EZ 003	WATERLAND (LP)	15
91	Zone EZ3V	WASTELAND EARTH (LP)	15
95	Inna State 004DS4A	RAGAMUFFIN STATEMENT (LP)	35

RADICAL FACE

MINT VALUE £

RADICAL FACE
12 Bear Machine .... THE FAMILY TREE: THE ROOTS (LP, insert, some with art print) 100

RADICAL SOUND
95 Jungle Mania JM 6 .... Trigger 1/Trigger 2 (12") 40

RADICALS
84 Bluetrac BTR 003 .... Rum Tree/Racids In Dub (12") 50

MARK RADICE
72 Paramount PARA 3024 .... Hey My Love/Your Love Is Like Fire 8
72 Paramount PARA 3025 .... New Day/Take Me To The Park 6
72 Paramount SPFA 7004 .... MARK RADICE (LP) 20

RADIO GEMINI
74 Deroy DEROY 1064 .... THE RADIO GEMINI LP (LP) 40

RADIOACTIVE
77 Beeb BEEB 021 .... Ten Years After/All Time Needletime Loser (no p/s) 30

RADIO ACTORS
79 Charly CYS 1058 .... Nuclear Waste/Digital Love (p/s, reissue of Fast Breeder & Radio Actors single, 2 slightly different label designs) 20

(see also Fast Breeder & Radio Actors, Sting, Newcastle Big Band, Police, Gilli Smyth, Inner City Unit, Steve Hillage, Sphynx)

RADIO BIRDMAN
78 Sire 6078 617 .... What Gives/Anglo Girl Desire 20
78 Sire 9103 332 .... RADIOS APPEAR (LP, with inner sleeve) 35

RADIO CITY
80 Media Wave MW 001 .... Love And A Picture/She's A Radio (p/s) 200

RADIO DEPT
02 Rex REKD 30S .... Liebling/We Would Fall Against The Tide (die-cut Rex sleeve) 15
04 Rex REKD 41S .... Why Don't You Talk About It?/I Don't Need Love, I've Got My Band (p/s) 15
04 XL XLS 196 .... Where Damage Isn't Already Done/You And Me Then?/Peace Of Mind (p/s) 12
04 XL XLS 203 .... Ewan/Slottet/The Things That Went Wrong (p/s) 12
04 XL XLLP 177 .... LESSER MATTERS (LP) 50

RADIO DOOM
79 Private Pressing .... RADIO DOOM (LP, white sleeve 250 only) 50

RADIOHEAD
SINGLES
92 Parlophone TCR 6212 .... DRILL EP (Prove Yourself/Stupid Car/You/Thinking About You) (cassette, 3,000 only) 40
92 Parlophone 12R 6212 .... DRILL EP (Prove Yourself/Stupid Car/You/Thinking About You) (12", p/s, 3,000 only) 150
92 Parlophone CDR 6212 .... DRILL EP (Prove Yourself/Stupid Car/You/Thinking About You) (CD, 3,000 only) 80
92 Parlophone 12R 6078 .... Creep/Lurgee/Inside My Head/Million $ Question (12", p/s, 6,000 only) 40
93 Parlophone 12R 6333 .... Anyone Can Play Guitar/Faithless, The Wonder Boy/Coke Babies (12", p/s) 30
93 Parlophone 12R 6345 .... Pop Is Dead/Banana Co. (Acoustic)/Creep (live)/Ripcord (live) (12", g/fold p/s) 35
93 Parlophone RS 6359 .... Creep/Yes I Am/Blow Out (Remix)/Inside My Head (live) (p/s, clear vinyl) 20
93 Parlophone 12RG 6359 .... U.S. LIVE EP (Creep [Acoustic KROQ]/You [live]/Vegetable [live]/Killer Cars [live]) (12", numbered gatefold p/s) 15
94 Parlophone 12R 6394 .... My Iron Lung/Punchdrunk Lovesick Singalong/The Trickster/ Lewis (Mistreated) (12", numbered p/s) 25
95 Parlophone 12R 6405 .... Planet Telex/(remixes)/High & Dry (12", limited edition, numbered p/s) 12
95 Parlophone 8 83115 2 .... The Bends/My Iron Lung (Live At Forum)/Bones (Live At Forum) (CD, for export to Ireland, slimline jewel case) 35
95 Parlophone 8 83115 2 .... The Bends/My Iron Lung (Live At Forum)/Bones (Live At Forum) (CD, for export to Ireland, mispressed with "Planet Telex" instead of "The Bends" slimline jewel case) 40
96 Parlophone R 6419 .... Street Spirit (Fade Out)/Bishop's Robes (die-cut p/s, white vinyl) 20
96 Parlophone R 6419LH .... Street Spirit (Fade Out)/Bishop's Robes (jukebox issue, black vinyl) 15
97 Parlophone NODATA 01 .... Paranoid Android/Polyethelene (Parts 1 & 2) (blue vinyl, die-cut p/s) 20
97 Parlophone NODATALH 03 .... Karma Police (Album Version)/Lull (jukebox issue, black vinyl) 15
97 Parlophone 12NODATA 03 .... Karma Police/Meeting Up The Aisle/Climbing Up The Walls (Zero 7 Mix) (12", p/s) 30
97 Parlophone NODATALH 04 .... No Surprises/Palo Alto (jukebox issue, black vinyl) 12
97 Parlophone NODATALH 04 .... No Surprises/How I Made My Millions (jukebox 7") 12
98 Parlophone 12NODATA 04 .... No Surprises/Palo Alto (12", p/s) 25
01 Parlophone 12FHEIT 45103 .... Knives Out/Cuttooth/Life In A Glasshouse (Full Length Version) (12") 12
01 Parlophone 12FHEIT 45102 .... Pyramid Song/Fast Track/The Amazing Sounds Of Orgy (12", p/s) 10
03 Parlophone 12R 6213 .... Go To Sleep/I Am Citizen Insane/I Am A Wicked Child 10
11 XL TICK 02 .... Supercollider/The Butcher (12" p/s, 2000 only, some with reversed labels) 18
12 Young Turks YT 077 .... Bloom (Jamie XX Rework Pt. 3) (1-sided 12") 40
16 XL XLS791 .... Burn The Witch/Spectre (p/s, 2500 only) 30

ALBUMS
93 Parlophone PCS 7360 .... PABLO HONEY (LP, inner) 100
95 Parlophone PCS 7372 .... THE BENDS (LP, 1st pressing without pixelated 0% on black and white side of inner sleeve) 250
95 Parlophone PCS 7372 .... THE BENDS (LP, later pressings with pixelated 0% on black and white side of inner sleeve) 150
97 Parlophone NODATA 02 .... OK COMPUTER (2-LP, 1st pressing) 150
97 Parlophone NODATA 02 .... OK COMPUTER (2-LP, repressing on 180gm vinyl) 60
00 Parlophone LPKIDA .... KID A (2-LP 10") 50
01 Parlophone LPFHEIT 45101 .... AMNESIAC (2-LP, 10") 80
01 Parlophone 12FHEIT 45104 .... I MIGHT BE WRONG (mini-LP) 35
03 Parlophone 5848052 .... HAIL TO THE THIEF (CD, limited issue, with foldout map) 30
03 Parlophone 724358454314 .... HAIL TO THE THIEF (2-LP) 60
07 Parlophone 5.09995E+12 .... RADIOHEAD (Mail-order 4GB shaped USB stick, bespoke box, 7 albums as WAV files) 95
07 Xurbia Xendless Ltd X X001 ..... IN RAINBOWS (box set, 2 x CD, 2-LP, 2 booklets in presentation case) 100
07 XL Recordings XLLP 324 .... IN RAINBOWS (LP) 35
08 Parlophone 724385522918 .... OK COMPUTER (2-LP, reissue) 20
08 Parlophone 5099921b .... THE BEST OF (4-LP) 80

RADIO HEART

	210716		MINT VALUE £
09	Parlophone 584 5431	HAIL TO THE THIEF (2-LP, reissue, 180gm vinyl)	20
11	Ticker Tape/XL TICK 001S	THE KING OF LIMBS (2-10" clear vinyl LPs, with CD, newspaper, acid tab sheet, mail order only in sealed plastic bag)	60
11	Ticker Tape TICK001LP	THE KING OF LIMBS (LP, reissue)	18
11	Ticker Tape TICK 010	TKOL RMX 1234567 (Box set, 7 x 12")	80
17	XL XLLP790	A MOON SHAPED POOL (2-LP)	20
17	XL XLLP790X	A MOON SHAPED POOL (2-LP, white vinyl)	20
17	XL LLLPLLPLP 01	A MOON SHAPED POOL (2-LP, 2-CD with splice of original tape in hard case)	60
17	XL XLLP 868	OK COMPUTER - OKNOTOK (3-LP, blue vinyl)	25

PROMOS

92	EMI (no cat no)	Nothing Touches Me/Prove Yourself/I Can't (3-track internal EMI cassette)	300
92	Parlophone 12 R 6312	DRILL EP (White label promo in die cut sleeve)	80
92	Parlophone 12RDJ 6078	Creep/Lurgee/Inside My Head/Million Dollar Question (12", die-cut sleeve)	40
92	Parlophone CDRDJ 6078	Creep (Radio Version)/Lurgee/Inside My Head/Million Dollar Question (CD)	30
93	Parlophone CDRDJ 6345	Pop Is Dead/Banana Co. (live)/Creep (live)/Ripcord (live)	40
93	Parlophone CDRDJ 6359	Creep (CD, picture disc)	25
93	Parlophone 12RDJ 6369	Ripcord/Prove Yourself/Faithless, The Wonderboy/Stop Whispering (Album Version) (12", p/s)	40
93	Parlophone 12RDJ 6333	Anyone Can Play Guitar/Faithless, The Wonder Boy/Coke Babies (12", die-cut sleeve)	20
93	Parlophone (no cat. No.)	Stop Whispering (U.S. Version - Chris Sheldon Remix)/Creep (Acoustic)/Pop Is Dead/Inside My Head (Live) (CD)	30
94	Parlophone (no cat. no.)	PLANET TELEX: LFO & Hexidecimal mixes (12")	12
94	Parlophone 12RSDJ 6394	My Iron Lung/Lozenge Of Love/The Trickster/Punchdrunk Lovesick Singalong (12", die-cut red sleeve)	18
94	Parlophone 12RSDJ 6394	My Iron Lung/Lozenge Of Love/The Trickster/Punchdrunk Lovesick Singalong (12", die-cut blue sleeve)	18
94	Parlophone 12RSDJ 6394	My Iron Lung/Lewis (Mistreated)/Permanent Daylight/You Never Wash Up After Yourself (12" die-cut red sleeve)	15
94	Parlophone 12RSDJ 6394	My Iron Lung/Lewis (Mistreated)/Permanent Daylight/You Never Wash Up After Yourself (12" die-cut blue sleeve)	15
95	Parlophone 12RDJ 6405	CLUB MIX DJ: PLANET TELEX (Album version)/Hexadecimal Mix)/L.F.O DJ Mix)/Trashed Mix) (12")	12
95	Parlophone 12RDJ 6411	Fake Plastic Trees/India Rubber/How Can You Be Sure? (12", die-cut sleeve)	18
95	Parlophone 12RDJ 6145	Just/Planet Telex/Killer Cars (12", die-cut sleeve)	12
95	Parlophone 12RDJ 6145	Just/Planet Telex (Karma Sun Ra Mix)Killer Cars (Mogadon Version) (12")	15
95	Parlophone RHEAD US 1	JUST FOR COLLEGE: India Rubber/Maquiladora/How Can I Be Sure?/Just (CD)	70
96	Parlophone 12RDJ 6419	Street Spirit (Fade Out)/Talk Show Host/Bishop's Robes (12", promo-only)	18
97	Parlophone 724385522925	OK COMPUTER (Stickered jewel case, printed disc, mispressing plays Deep Purple's 'The Collection')	40
97	Parlophone (no cat. no.)	OK COMPUTER (Cassette, in customized jiffy bag)	35
97	Parlophone (no cat. no.)	OK COMPUTER (promo Aiwa personal stereo, glued-in cassette, two stickers)	120
97	Parlophone CDPP 005	OK COMPUTER (CD, numbered title sleeve)	35
97	Parlophone NODATA 02	OK COMPUTER (EPK, with CD & video in polystyrene case in jiffy bag)	70
98	Parlophone 12DATADJO3	Climbing Up The Walls (Zero 7 Mix)/(Fila Brazilia Mix) (1-sided 12", 200 only)	40
00	Parlophone 12KIDA 6	Idioteque (12", white label test pressing, p/s)	18
01	Parlophone AMNESIAC 01	4 SONGS FROM AMNESIAC: Pyramid Song/I Might Be Wrong/Packt Like Sardines In A Crushed Tin Box/Dollars & Cents (CD, card sleeve)	30
03	Parlophone 12RDJWL 6623	SKTTERBRAIN (Four Tet Mix)/REMYXOMOTOSIS (Super Collider Mix) (12", 100 only)	35

(see also Headless Chickens, On A Friday, Thom Yorke, Jonny Greenwood, Atoms For Peace)

RADIO HEART

87	GFM GFMG 109	Radio Heart/Radio Heart (Instrumental) (Uncut picture disc)	150
87	GFM GFMX 112	London Times/Rumous (Uncut picture disc)	150
87	NBR NBRL 1	RADIO HEART (LP, withdrawn)	15

(see also Gary Numan)

RADIO MOSCOW

87	Status RM 100	Hand Of Freedom (p/s)	8
91	Status RMLP 103	WORLD SERVICE (LP)	15
92	Status RMLP 104	GET A NEW LIFE (LP)	15

RADIO 9

90s	Enraptured RAPT 1031	Motorik/Fluid/Moving In Two Directions/Pianosong (10", 9 only)	15

RADIOPHONIC WORKSHOP

73	BBC RESL 13	Moonbase 3/World Of Dr. Who	20

(see also BBC Radiophonic Workshop)

RADIO RADIO

83	Radio RAD 101	Calling/Signed With A Star	20

RADIO STARS

77	Chiswick S9	Dirty Pictures/Sail Away (1st pressing with laminated sleeve, 1000 only)	7
77	Chiswick SW 17	STOP IT EP	6
78	Chiswick CWK 3001	HOLIDAY ALBUM (LP, with inner sleeve)	15

(see also John's Children, Andy Ellison, Trevor White)

RADIUM

81	Isotope 731	THROUGH THE SMOKE (EP)	125

RAELET(T)S

67	HMV POP 1591	One Hurt Deserves Another/One Room Paradise (as Raelets)	30

(see also Ray Charles, Merry Clayton)

GERRY RAFFERTY

71	Transatlantic TRA 241	CAN I HAVE MY MONEY BACK? (LP)	15

(see also Humblebums, Fifth Column)

RAG DOLLS (U.K.)

67	Columbia DB 8289	Never Had So Much Loving/Any Little Bit	10
68	Columbia DB 8378	My Old Man's A Groovy Old Man/They Didn't Believe Me	10

RAG DOLLS (U.S.)

MINT VALUE £

(see also Marionettes, Peanut, Katie Kissoon, Mac Kissoon)

RAG DOLLS (U.S.)
64	Cameo Parkway P 921	Society Girl/Ragen (with Caliente Combo)	35
65	Stateside SS 398	Dusty/Hey Hoagy	40

RAG RUBY RED
84	Rag RAG 001	Phantoms Of Fame/Sweet Banana	60

(see also Level 42)

RAGAMUFFIN
72	Decca F13312	Can I Have My Money Back/Fresh As A Daisy	12

RAGE (1)
80	Carrere CAR 159	Money/Thank That Woman (p/s)	8
80	Carrere CAR 159CT	Money/Thank That Woman (10", red vinyl, stickered clear sleeve)	12
81	Carrere CAR 182CT	Out Of Control (Extended Version)/Double Dealer (12", yellow vinyl, PVC sleeve)	15
83	Carrere CAR 304	Cry From A Hill (p/s)	10

(see also Nutz)

RAGE (2)
86	Diamond RAGE 1	Looking For You/Come On Now (p/s)	20
86	Diamond RAGE 112	Looking For You/Come On Now/Great Balls Of Fire/Hallelujah I Love Her So (12", unissued, test pressings only)	25

(see also Case, Long Tall Shorty, Purple Hearts, Chords)

RAGE AGAINST THE MACHINE
93	Epic 658 492-6	Killing In The Name/Clear The Lane/Darkness Of Greed (12" white vinyl, p/s)	25
93	Epic 659 258-6	Bullet In The Head (Remix)/Bullet In The Head/(Album Version) Settle For Nothing (live) (12", picture disc, p/s)	30
93	Epic 658 492-7	Killing In The Name/Clear The Lane/Darkness Of Greed (white vinyl, p/s)	12
96	Epic 663 152-7	Bulls On Parade/Hadda Be Playing On The Jukebox (red vinyl)	8
92	Epic EPC 72224	RAGE AGAINST THE MACHINE (LP)	100
92	Epic 47 22240	RAGE AGAINST THE MACHINE (LP, red vinyl, 12", tour edition)	200
96	Epic 481026	EVIL EMPIRE (LP, inner)	75
99	Simply Vinyl SVLP 069	RAGE AGAINST THE MACHINE (LP, reissue)	40
99	Epic 4919931000	THE BATTLE OF LOS ANGELES (LP)	70
00	Epic EPC 499921 1	RENEGADES (LP)	50

RAGGA TWINS
99	Shut Up And Dance SUADLP 0025	REGGAE OWES ME MONEY - 3 TRACK SAMPLER (12", stamped white labels)	40
91	Shut Up And Dance SUADLP 002	REGGAE OWES ME MONEY (LP)	20

RAGGAMUFFINS
67	London HLU 10134	Four Days Of Rain/It Wasn't Happening At All	15

RAGGED HEROES
83	Celtic CM 013	ANNUAL (LP)	25

RAGGED TROUSERS
75	EMI 2300	Mountain Child/Maybe I'm In Love	15

RAGING STORMS
62	London HLU 9556	The Dribble/Hound Dog	30

LOU RAGLAND
73	Warner Bros. K 16312	Since You Said You'd Be Mine/I Didn't Mean To Love You (DJ Copy)	80
73	Warner Bros K 16312	Since You Said You'd Be Mine/I Didn't Mean To Love You	50

BUNNY RAGS
80	Black Ark International BA 601	Let Love Touch Us Now/I Am I Said/THE FIGHTER: Freedom Fighter (12")	70

(see also Bunny & Ricky, Bunny Clarke)

RAH BAND
82	TNT RAH 1/RAH 2	Winter Love/Funk Me Down To Rio (82 Version)/Perfumed Garden (12")	10
83	TMT TMTT 5	Messages From The Stars (Long Wave Mix)/(Astro Mix)/(Short Wave Mix) (12", blue vinyl)	40
78	Ebony EBY 1001	THE CRUNCH AND BEYOND (LP)	15
81	DJM DJF 20573	RAH BAND (LP)	15
83	TMT RAH-1	GOING UP (LP)	20
84	S.O.U.N.D. SNDLP 60	UPPER CUTS (mini-LP)	15

(see also Richard Hewson Orchestra)

RAIDER OF THE LOST DUB
81	Island ILPS 9705	RAIDERS OF THE LOST DUB (LP) (withdrawn due to legal action)	40

RAIDERS
70	CBS 4801	Just Seventeen/Sorceress With Blue Eyes	10
70	CBS 5015	Gone Movin' On/Interlude (to Be Forgotten)	10
71	CBS 7474	Birds Of A Feather/The Turkey	7
72	CBS 7808	Country Wing/It's Hard Getting Up Today	7
72	CBS 8428	Song Seller/A Simple Song	10

(see also Paul Revere)

RAIME
10	Blackest Ever Black BLACKEST001	RAIME EP (12")	20
10	Blackest Ever Black BLACKEST002	If Anywhere Was Here He Would Know Where We Are/This Foundry (Regis Version) (12")	20
12	Blackest Ever Black BLACKESTLP001	QUARTER TURNS OVER A LIVING LINE (2-LP)	25

RAINBEAUS
60	Vogue V 9161	That's All I'm Asking Of You/Maybe It's Wrong	150

(RITCHIE BLACKMORE'S) RAINBOW
74	Oyster OYR 103	Man On The Silver Mountain/Snake Charmer (as Ritchie Blackmore's Rainbow)	8
78	Polydor 2066 968	L.A. Connection/Lady Of The Lake (p/s, initial pressing on red vinyl)	10

Chris RAINBOW

MINT VALUE £

83	Polydor POSPP 631	Street Of Dreams/Anybody There? (picture disc, 2000 only)	20
83	Polydor POSPP 654	Can't Let You Go/All Night Long (live) (guitar-shaped picture disc)	15
75	Oyster OYA 2001	RITCHIE BLACKMORE'S RAINBOW (LP, gatefold sleeve, as Ritchie Blackmore's Rainbow)	80
76	Polydor 2490 137	RAINBOW RISING (LP, gatefold)	30
77	Polydor 2808 010 010	RAINBOW ON STAGE (LP, music & interview disc, with insert, promo only)	100
79	Polydor POLD 5023	DOWN TO EARTH (LP, clear vinyl, with inner sleeve)	18
78	Polydor POLD 5002	LONG LIVE ROCK 'N' ROLL (LP, gatefold sleeve, insert)	15
83	Polydor POLD 5116	BENT OUT OF SHAPE (LP)	15

(see also Deep Purple, Elf, Dio, Graham Bonnet, Cozy Powell, Roger Glover, Wild Horses, Tony Carey)

CHRIS RAINBOW
81	EMI 5215-6	Body Music/Girl In Collision (p/s)	8
81	EMI 12EMI 5215	Body Music/Girl In Collision (12", p/s)	15

RAINBOW FAMILY
72	President PT 375	Travellin' Lady/My Father	60

RAINBOW FFOLLY
68	Parlophone R 5701	Go Girl/Drive My Car	70
67	Parlophone PMC/PCS 7050	SALLIES FFORTH (LP, laminated front, flipbacks, black/yellow label, "Sold in U.K..." text)	800

(see also Love Affair)

RAINBOW PEOPLE
68	Pye 7N 17582	Walk'll Do You Good/Dream Time	15
68	Pye 7N 17624	The Sailing Song/Rainbows	15
69	Pye 7N 17759	Living In A Dream World/Happy To See You Again	40

RAINBOWS
69	CBS 3995	Rainbows/Nobody But You	20
69	CBS 4568	New Day Dawning/Days And Nights	40

(see also Peeps, Martin Cure & Peeps)

RAINCHECKS
64	Solar SRP 104	Something About You/You're My Angel	20
65	R&B MRB 5002	How Are You Boy/Bye Bye Baby	40

RAINCOATS
79	Rough Trade RT 013	Adventures Close to Home/In Love/Fairytale In The Supermarket	25
82	Rough Trade RT 093	Running Away/No Ones Little Girl	25
83	Rough Trade RTT 153	Animal Rhapsody/Honey Mad Woman/No-Ones Little Girl (12")	18
95	Rough Trade R4047	Don't Be Mean/Vicious/I Keep Walking (p/s)	6
94	Blast First BFFP99	EXTENDED PLAY 10" EP	10
79	Rough Trade ROUGH 3	THE RAINCOATS (LP, with lyric booklet)	60
81	Rough Trade ROUGH 13	ODYSHAPE (LP)	40
83	Rough Trade ROUGH 66	MOVING (LP)	25
87	Femme FELP 4.00287J	THE RAINCOATS (LP, reissue, white vinyl)	15
95	Rough Trade R4031	LOOKING IN THE SHODOWS (LP)	30

(see also Slits)

RAINDANCE
87	Raindance X1S 121	RAINDANCE (LP)	40

RAINDROPS (U.K.)
59	Parlophone R 4559	Italian Style/Along Came Jones	10
60	Oriole CB 1544	Let's Make A Foursome/If I Had My Life To Live Over	7
60	Oriole CB 1555	Banjo Boy/Crazy Rhythm	10
61	Oriole CB 1595	Will You Love Me Tomorrow/Raindrops	10
62	Oriole CB 1707	Paintin' The Town With Teardrops/A Letter From Anne	7
67	CBS 202669	Foolman/Got To Find A Reason (credited to Raindrops '67)	10

(see also Jackie & Raindrops, Jackie Lee, Jacky, Emma Rede, Vince Hill)

RAINDROPS (U.S.)
63	London HL 9718	What A Guy/It's So Wonderful	25
63	London HL 9769	The Kind Of Boy You Can't Forget/Even Though You Can't Dance	30
64	London HL 9825	That Boy John/Hanky Panky	20
64	Fontana TF 463	The Book Of Love/I Won't Cry	25
64	London RE 1415	WHAT A GUY (EP)	125
64	London HA 8140	THE RAINDROPS (LP)	125

(see also Ellie Greenwich, Popsicles)

CLAIRE RAINE
68	Jolly JY 010	La-La-La/I Want You	20

LORRY RAINE
54	London HL 8043	You Broke My Broken Heart/I'm In Love With A Guy	25
55	London HL 8132	Love Me Tonight/What Would I Do	40

MA RAINEY
53	London AL 3502	MA RAINEY VOLUME 1 (10" LP)	25
55	London AL 3538	MA RAINEY VOLUME 2 (10" LP)	25
56	London AL 3558	MA RAINEY VOLUME 3 (10" LP)	25
50s	Ristic LP 13	MA RAINEY (10" LP)	25
50s	Ristic LP 19	MA RAINEY (10" LP)	25
62	Riverside RL 12-108	MA RAINEY SINGS THE BLUES (LP)	20
64	Riverside RLP 8807	MOTHER OF THE BLUES (LP, gatefold sleeve with booklet)	20

MA RAINEY & IDA COX
60	Jazz Collector JEL 12	THE FEMALE BLUES VOL. 1 (EP)	10

(see also Ida Cox, Tommy Ladnier)

MA RAINEY & PAPA CHARLIE JACKSON
50s	Poydras 11	Ma And Papa Poorhouse Blues/Big Feeling Blues	15

RAIN PARADE
83	Enigma BOB 4/LYN 15263	Sad Eyes Kill (3.16) (hard vinyl white label test pressing)	12

RAIN TREE CROW

			MINT VALUE £
83	Zippo ZING 001	EMERGENCY THIRD RAIL POWER TRIP (LP, gatefold)	18

RAIN TREE CROW
91	Virgin V2659	RAIN TREE CROW (LP)	50

(see also Japan)

MARVIN RAINWATER
55	MGM SP 1150	Tennessee Houn' Dog Yodel/Albino (Pink-Eyed) Stallion	50
56	MGM MGM 929	What Am I Supposed To Do/Why Did You Have To Go And Leave Me	25
57	MGM MGM 961	Gonna Find Me A Bluebird/So You Think You've Got	15
58	MGM MGM 974	Whole Lotta Woman/Baby, Don't Go	7
58	MGM MGM 980	I Dig You Baby/Two Fools In Love (B-side with Sister Patty)	6
58	MGM MGM 988	Dance Me Daddy/Because I'm A Dreamer (B-side with Sister Patty)	10
59	MGM MGM 1030	Half-Breed/A Song Of New Love	8
60	MGM MGM 1052	Nothin' Needs Nothin' (Like I Need You)/The Valley Of The Moon	10
61	London HLU 9447	Boo Hoo/I Can't Forget	80
58	MGM MGM-EP 647	MEET MARVIN RAINWATER (EP)	20
58	MGM MGM-EP 662	WHOLE LOTTA MARVIN (EP)	20
59	MGM MGM-EP 685	MARVIN RAINWATER SINGS (EP)	15
63	Ember EMB 4521	COUNTRY AND WESTERN FAVOURITES VOL. 2 (EP)	15
58	MGM MGM-D 152	SONGS BY MARVIN RAINWATER (10" LP)	60

(see also Connie Francis & Marvin Rainwater)

RAINY DAY
84	EMI EMI 5472	Painting Pictures/Welche Farbe Hat Der Sonnenschein (p/s)	12
84	Rough Trade ROUGH 70	RAINY DAY (LP)	25

RAINY DAZE
67	CBS 3200	What Do You Think/Autumn Leaves	18
67	Polydor 56731	That Acapulco Gold/In My Mind Lives A Forest	20
68	Polydor 56737	Blood Of Oblivion/Stop Sign	20
68	CBS 56731	THAT ACAPULCO GOLD (LP, unissued in U.K.)	0

RAINY DAYS
76	Seville SEV 1009	Party/Anything I Would Do For You	40

RAISINS
68	Major Major MM 540	Ain't That Lovin' You Baby/Stranger Things Have Happened	15
69	Major Minor MM 602	I Thank You/Don't Leave Me Like This	8
68	Major Minor MMLP 20	THE RAISINS (LP, also stereo SMLP 20)	30

(see also Coloured Raisins)

RAKES
04	Trash Aesthetics TA 702	22 Grand Job/Something Clicked And I Fell Off The Edge (Pink vinyl, insert and Fold-out sleeve. 480 only)	15
05	V2 VVR1032761	CAPTURE/RELEASE (LP)	30
07	V2 VVR1041851	TEN NEW MESSAGES (LP)	30

RALFI
75	Island USA 005	Wonderful Things/The Gambler	15

DON RALKE ORCHESTRA
60	Warner Brothers WB 2	77 Sunset Strip (as Big Sound Of Don Ralke)/PETE CANDOLI & HIS ORCHESTRA: 77 Sunset Strip Cha-Cha	6
60	Warner Bros. WM 4007/WS8007	BUT YOU NEVER HEARD GERSHWIN WITH BONGOS (LP)	15

RALLY ROUNDERS
64	Lyntone LYN 573/574	Bike Beat Part 1/Bike Beat Part 2 (actually by the Outlaws) (p/s, flexidisc)	50

(see also Outlaws)

RALPHAEL
84	Diddy Doll RM 04	Disco Lady/Dance To The Late Night Groove (12")	50
85	Simoon TC124	Disco Lady/Night Time Groove (p/s)	40
85	Simoon RM001	MIXED RHYTHM (LP)	80

BUCK RAM'S RAMROCKS
63	London HLU 9677	Benfica/Odd Man Theme	15

(see also Little Richard, Platters)

RAMA
69	Polydor 56328	God Created Love/Memory Of Love	6

RAMASES
71	Philips 6113 001	Ballroom/Muddy Water	25
71	Philips 6113 003	Jesus Come Back/Hello Mister	25
71	Vertigo 6360 046	SPACE HYMNS (LP, foldout poster sleeve, small swirl label)	350
71	Vertigo 6360 046	SPACE HYMNS (LP, foldout sleeve, later 'spaceship' label)	70
75	Vertigo 6360 115	GLASS TOP COFFIN (LP, die-cut gatefold sleeve, 'spaceship' label)	45

(see also 10cc, Ramases & Seleka, Ramases & Selket)

RAMASES & SELEKA
70	Major Minor MM 704	Love You/Gold Is The Ring	50

(see also Ramases)

RAMASES & SELKET
68	CBS 3717	Crazy One/Mind's Eye	80

(see also Ramases)

RAMATAM
72	Atlantic K 40415	RAMATAM (LP)	15

(see also Iron Butterfly)

EDDIE RAMBEAU
62	Stateside SS 116	Summertime Guy/Last Night Was My Last Night	10
64	Stateside SS 301	Come Closer/She's Smilin' At Me	8
65	Stateside SS 448	My Name Is Mud/I Just Need Your Love	8
66	Stateside SS 486	The Train/Yesterday's Newspapers	8
66	Stateside SS 501	I'm The Sky/I Just Need Your Love	7

RAMBLER

MINT VALUE £

	66	Stateside SS 561	The Clock/If I Were You ... 7

(see also Marcy Jo & Eddie Rambeau)

RAMBLER
	66	Pye 7N 17164	Love Minus Zero No Limit/An Bonnan Bui ... 7

(see also Johnny McEvoy)

RAMBLERS
	63	Decca F 11775	Dodge City/Just For Chicks ... 40

RAMBLETTES
	65	Brunswick 05932	Thinking Of You/On Back Street (DJ Copy) ... 35
	65	Brunswick 05932	Thinking Of You/On Back Street ... 20

RAMBLING SYD RUMPO
	67	Parlophone R 5638	The Ballad Of The Wogglers Moulie/Green Grow My Nadgers Oh! ... 6
	70	Starline SRS 5034	THE BEST OF RAMBLING SYD RUMPO (LP) ... 15

(see also Kenneth Williams)

SID RAMIN
	70	CBS 4813	Stiletto/Sugar In The Rain ... 20
	69	CBS 70062	STILETTO (LP, soundtrack) ... 30

LOUIE RAMIREZ
	67	Mercury 20113	IN THE HEART OF SPANISH HARLEM (LP) ... 25

RAM JAM BAND
	65	Columbia DB 7621	Shake Shake Senora/Akinla ... 25

(see also Geno Washington & Ram Jam Band, Ram John Holder, Ram Holder Brothers)

RAMLEH
	83	Broken Flag BF V4	THE HAND OF GLORY (EP, p/s) ... 30
	91	Shock SX 013	Slammers/Black Moby Dick (p/s, numbered, 500 only) ... 8
	92	Dying Earth DE 003	Loser Patrol/Tracers (p/s, numbered, 500 only, 1st 30 in red sleeve) ... 15
	92	Dying Earth DE 003	Loser Patrol/Tracers (p/s, numbered, 500 only) ... 8
	93	Dying Earth DE 007	Say Fuck/Slackjaw (wraparound p/s, numbered, 500 only) ... 8
	94	Format Supremacy 1 Of EACH	Welcome/Pristine Womankind (cardboard p/s, 500 only) ... 8
	82	Broken Flag BF 01	31/5/1962 - 1982 (cassette) ... 70
	83	Broken Flag BF V2	A RETURN TO SLAVERY (LP, with Libertarian Recordings) ... 30
	83	Broken Flag BF 07	LIVE McCARTHY (cassette) ... 50
	83	Broken Flag BF 20	LIVE NEW FORCE (cassette) ... 50
	83	Broken Flag BF 24	LIVE PHENOL (cassette) ... 50
	83	Broken Flag BF 25	LIVE PROSSNECK (cassette) ... 50
	83	Broken Flag BF 28	LIVE AT MORDEN TOWER (cassette) ... 50
	84	Broken Flag BF 37	104 WEEKS (cassette) ... 40
	84	Broken Flag BF 38	AS I HAVE WON (cassette) ... 40
	85	Broken Flag BF 40	AWAKE! (6 cassettes in lockable steel box with booklet) ... 400
	87	Broken Flag BF 59	HOLE IN THE HEART (cassette) ... 40

(see also Skullflower)

RAMMSTEIN
	04	Universal 9868673	Amerika/Wilder Wein (p/s) ... 50
	05	Universal 9870291	Keine Lust/Du Hast (Live) (p/s, clear vinyl) ... 40
	09	Spinefarm 2718498	Pussy (p/s,1-sided, limited edition blue vinyl) ... 30
	11	Spinefarm SPINE768292	Waidmanns Heil/Leibe Ist Fur Alle da (300 only) ... 80
	01	Motor 549 639-1	MUTTER (LP, gatefold) ... 60
	09	Universal 2721463	LIEBE IST FUR ALLE DA (2-LP, pink vinyl, gatefold) ... 80

RAMON & CRYSTALITES
	71	Songbird SB 1053	Golden Chickens/Stranger Version ... 80

DEE DEE RAMONE
	97	Blackout BLK 5000-7	I Am Seeing UFOs (featuring Joey Ramone)/Bad Horoscope (2,500 copies only) ... 8

DEE DEE RAMONE & ICLC
	94	World Service/Rough Trade RTD 157.1757.1	I HATE FREAKS LIKE YOU (LP, with inner) ... 30

(see also Ramones)

RAMONES
SINGLES
	76	Sire 6078 601	Blitzkrieg Bop/Havana Affair (in rare p/s) ... 200
	76	Sire 6078 601	Blitzkrieg Bop/Havana Affair ... 25
	77	Sire 6078 603	I Remember You/California Sun (live)/I Don't Wanna Walk Around With You (live) (p/s) .. 50
	77	Sire RAM 001 (6078 606)	Sheena Is A Punk Rocker/Commando/I Don't Care (12", with T-shirt offer on perforated centre of numbered p/s, 12,000 only) ... 30
	77	Sire RAM 001 (6078 606)	Sheena Is A Punk Rocker/Commando/I Don't Care (12", without T-shirt offer on perforated centre of numbered p/s, 12,000 only) ... 15
	77	Sire 6078 607	Swallow My Pride/Pinhead/Let's Dance (live) (p/s) ... 20
	77	Sire 6078 611	Rockaway Beach/Teenage Lobotomy/Beat On The Brat (p/s) ... 20
	77	Sire 6078 611	Rockaway Beach/Teenage Lobotomy/Beat On The Brat (12", p/s, with poster) ... 30
	77	Sire 6078 611	Rockaway Beach/Teenage Lobotomy/Beat On The Brat (12", p/s, without poster) ... 12
	78	Sire 6078 615	Do You Wanna Dance?/It's A Long Way Back To Germany/Cretin Hop (p/s) ... 18
	78	Sire (no cat. no.)	Questioning/Don't Come Close/Sedated/I Just Want To Have Something To Do (with p/s, promo only, with spoken intros by Joey Ramone) ... 45
	78	Sire (no cat. no.)	Questioning/Don't Come Close/Sedated/I Just Want To Have Something To Do (without p/s, promo only, with spoken intros by Joey Ramone) ... 15
	78	Sire SRE 1031	Don't Come Close/I Don't Want You (p/s, yellow vinyl) ... 15
	78	Sire SRE 1031	Don't Come Close/I Don't Want You (12", p/s, yellow or red vinyl, red vinyl lacks p/s) ... 10
	79	Sire SIR 4009	She's The One/I Wanna Be Sedated (p/s) ... 15
	79	Sire SIR 4021	Rock'n'Roll High School/Rockaway Beach (live)/Sheena Is A Punk Rocker (live) (p/s) ... 10
	80	RSO RSO 70 (2090 512)	I Wanna Be Sedated/The Return Of Jackie And Judy (p/s) ... 18
	80	Sire SREP 1	MELTDOWN WITH THE RAMONES: I Just Want To Have Something To Do/ Here Today	15

Michel RAMOS

MINT VALUE £

81	Sire SIR 4051	Gone Tomorrow/I Wanna Be Your Boyfriend/Questioningly (EP)	
81	Sire SIR 4051	We Want The Airwaves/You Sound Like You're Sick (p/s)	6
81	Sire SIR 4052	She's A Sensation/All Quiet On The Eastern Front (no p/s)	8
83	Sire W 9606	Time Has Come Today/Psycho Therapy (p/s)	15
83	Sire W 9606T	Time Has Come Today/Sheena Is A Punk Rocker/Teenage Lobotomy/ Rock'n'Roll Radio (12", p/s)	20
85	Beggars Banquet BEG 128D	Howling At The Moon//Smash You/ Chasing The Night/Street Fighting Man (double pack, gatefold sleeve)	8
85	Beggars Banquet BEG 140	Bonzo Goes To Bitburg/Go Home Ann (p/s)	7
86	Beggars Banquet BEG 157T	Somebody Put Something In My Drink/(You) Can't Say Anything Nice/ Something To Believe In (12", p/s, with promo poster)	15
86	Beggars Banquet BEG 167	Crummy Stuff/She Belongs To Me (p/s)	7
86	Beggars Banquet BEG 167T	Crummy Stuff/Something To Believe In/I Don't Want To Live This Life (12", p/s)	12
92	Chrysalis 0946 3 23917 66	Poison Heart/Chinese Rocks/Sheena Is A Punk Rocker (live)/Rockaway Beach (live) (12", yellow vinyl, p/s)	10

ALBUMS

76	Sire 9103 253	RAMONES (LP, with insert)	100
77	Sire 9103 254	RAMONES LEAVE HOME (LP, with "Carbona Not Glue" with inner sleeve)	40
77	Sire 9103 254	RAMONES LEAVE HOME (LP, repressing without "Carbona Not Glue")	35
77	Sire 9103 255	ROCKET TO RUSSIA (LP, with inner sleeve)	50
78	Sire SRK 6063	ROAD TO RUIN (LP, yellow vinyl, inner)	50
78	Sire SRK 6063	ROAD TO RUIN (LP)	30
79	Sire SRK 6077	END OF THE CENTURY (LP, inner)	30
79	Sire SRK2 6074	IT'S ALIVE (2-LP)	30
81	Sire SRK 3571	PLEASANT DREAMS (LP)	30
85	Beggars Banquet BEGA 59	TOO TOUGH TO DIE (LP)	25
86	Beggars Banquet BEGA 70	ANIMAL BOY (LP, picture inner sleeve and poster)	20
87	Beggars Banquet BEGA 89	HALFWAY TO SANITY (LP, inner)	35
89	Chrysalis CHR 1725	BRAIN DRAIN (LP, inner)	20
90	Beggar's Banquet	END OF THE DECADE (6 x 12" singles, box set with t-shirt, postcards & poster, 2,500 copies only)	50
91	Chysalis CHR 1901	LOCO LIVE (LP, inner)	40
92	Chrysalis 094632196019	MONDO BIZARRO (LP)	70
93	Chrysalis CHR 6052	ACID EATERS (LP)	100
95	Chrysalis 724383413614	ADIOS AMIGOS (LP)	80
04	Earmark 40033 1 P	LIVE : JANUARY 7 1978 PART ONE (LP, picture disc)	30

(see also Paley Brothers & Ramones, Holly & Joey, Dee Dee Ramone)

MICHEL RAMOS

55	London DEP 95013	PLAYING THE CLASSICS (EP, export)	20

RAMPENT

80	FMR 030 S80 CUS 804	Back Street Walker/Livin In The Past/Fight Back/No Friend Of Mine	100

RAM RAM GO GO SOUND

69	Halagala HG 26	Pep 77/USA Outcry	15

RAMRODS

65	United Artists UP 1113	Overdrive/Stalker	15

RAMRODS (U.S.)

61	London HLU 9282	Riders In The Sky/Zig Zag	6
61	London HLU 9355	Loch Lomond Rock/Take Me Back To My Boots And Saddle	20
61	London RE-U 1292	RIDERS IN THE SKY (EP)	70

BILL RAMSEY

62	Polydor NH 66812	Go Man Go/Rocking Mountain	12

LEE RAMSEY

96	Real Deal RD 001	RISE TO SHINE (EP)	12
96	Real Deal RD 002	RD STYLE (EP)	15

ANDREW RANCE

79	Trash TRA 1001	It Really Shouldn't Matter/Cold (no p/s)	14

RANCHERS

65	Cavern Sound IMSTL 2	An American Sailor At The Cavern/Sidetracked	25

RANCID

95	Out Of Step WOOS 8 S	Time Bomb/The War's End/Blast 'Em (p/s)	6
96	Epitaph 86464-7	Ruby Soho/That's Entertainment/Disorder And Disarray (p/s)	6
98	Epitaph 1005-7	Bloodclot/Endrine/Stop (p/s)	6
98	Epitaph 1009-7	Hooligans/Cash, Culture and Violence (Bass Drop Mix)/Things to Come (Dance hall Mix) (p/s)	6
00	Epitaph 1040-7	Let Me Go/Ben Zanotto/Dead And Fone (p/s)	6

ALAN RANDALL (& SHEP'S BANJO BOYS)

70	Domino 110	The Coventry City Song/Football Football	6

RANDALL AND ANDY C.

94	Ram RAMM 11	Sound Control/Feel It (12")	15

(see also Andy C)

ELLIOTT RANDALL

71	Polydor 2489 004	RANDALL'S ISLAND (LP)	20

FREDDY RANDALL & HIS BAND

58	Parlophone GEP 8715	CHICAGO JAZZ (EP)	10
58	Parlophone PMD 1046	DR JAZZ (LP)	20

TONY RANDALL & JACK KLUGMAN

73	Decca F 13439	You're So Vain/When Banana Skins Are Falling (I'll Come Sliding Back To You)	6
72	Decca Phase Four PFS 4277	THE ODD COUPLE SINGS (LP)	15

ALAN RANDALL

68	Electratone S1002	The Meditating Hindoo Man/Why Don't Women Like Me	15

Teddy RANDAZZO (& DAZZLERS)

MINT VALUE £

TEDDY RANDAZZO (& DAZZLERS)
59	HMV POP 578	It's Magic/Richer Than I	10
60	HMV POP 806	Journey To Love/Misery	10
61	HMV POP 866	Happy Ending/But You Broke My Heart	10
61	HMV POP 925	Let The Sunshine In/Broken Bell	10
62	HMV POP 1067	Dance To The Locomotion/Cottonfields (as Teddy Randazzo & Dazzlers)	15
63	HMV POP 1119	Echoes/It Wasn't A Dream	10
63	Pye International 7N 25181	Big Wide World/Be Sure, My Love	10
62	HMV CLP 1527	JOURNEY TO LOVE (LP, mono)	35
62	HMV CSD 1421	JOURNEY TO LOVE (LP, stereo)	40
63	HMV CLP 1601	TEDDY RANDAZZO TWISTS (LP, with Dazzlers)	90

(see also Three Chuckles)

LYNNE RANDELL
67	CBS 2847	Ciao Baby/Stranger In My Arms (DJ Copy)	250
67	CBS 2847	Ciao Baby/Stranger In My Arms	200
67	CBS 2927	That's A Hoe Down/I Need You Boy	30

RAN-DELLS
63	London HLU 9760	The Martian Hop/Forgive Me Darling (I Have Lied)	25

BARBARA RANDOLPH
67	Tamla Motown TMG 628	I Got A Feelin'/You Got Me Hurtin' All Over (DJ copy)	100
67	Tamla Motown TMG 628	I Got A Feelin'/You Got Me Hurtin' All Over	65
71	Tamla Motown TMG 788	I Got A Feelin'/You Got Me Hurtin' All Over (reissue)	10
79	Tamla Motown TMG 1133	Can I Get A Witness/You Got Me Hurtin' All Over/I Got A Feeling (reissue)	50

BOOTS RANDOLPH
62	London HLU 9567	Bluebird Of Happiness/Keep A Light In Your Window Tonight	6
63	London HLU 9685	Yakety Sax/I Really Don't Want To Know	10
63	London RE-U 1365	THE YAKETY SAX OF BOOTS RANDOLPH (EP)	15
63	London HA-U 8106	YAKETY SAX (LP)	25
66	London HA-U 8280	MORE YAKETY SAX (LP, as Boots Randolph & His Combo)	20

CHARLES RANDOLPH GREAN SOUND
69	London HLD 10283	Quintin's Theme/Number One At The Blue Whale	6

RANDY
96	Rugger Bugger SEEP 20	THE REST IS SILENCE (LP, printed inner sleeve)	25
99	Rugger Bugger SEEP 026	YOU CAN'T KEEP A GOOD BAND DOWN (LP, gatefold)	25

RANDY & RAINBOWS
63	Stateside SS 214	Denise/Come Back	50

RANDY'S ALLSTARS
70	Randy's RAN 500	I'm The One, You're The One/End Us	35
70	Randy's RAN 501	Pepper Pot (act. with Count Machuki)/The Same Things (B-side actually by Gaylads)	70
70	Randy's RAN 502	Dixie/Five Cents (B-side actually "A Lover's Question" by Winston Samuels)	10
70	Randy's RAN 505	Emperor Waltz/War	25
70	Randy's RAN 506	Blue Danube Waltz/Together (B-side actually by Delroy Wilson)	40
70	Randy's RAN 507	Bridge Over Troubled Water (actually by Lyrics)/Waterfall	12
71	Explosion EX 2052	Hold On Girl (actually by Lyrics)/Hold On Girl (Version)	12

(see also Impact Allstars, Lyrics, Dave Barker, Ethiopians, Jimmy London)

RANEE & RAJ
68	Fontana TF 920	Feel Like A Clown/Rainbow Land	20
68	Fontana TF 941	Don't Tell Me I Must Go/Razor Edge	20

SUE RANEY
57	Capitol CL 14757	The Careless Years/What's The Good Word, Mr. Bluebird	6
57	Capitol CL 14792	Please Hurry Home/Don't Take My Happiness	6
58	Capitol T 964	WHEN YOUR LOVER HAS GONE (LP)	15

WAYNE RANEY (STRING BAND)
54	Parlophone CSMP 20	Adam/The Roosters Are Crowing (export issue)	25
55	Parlophone DP 413	Mama (Don't You Remember When You Were Young)/Trying To Live Without You (78, export issue)	8
58	Parlophone GEP 8746	COUNTRY AND WESTERN (EP)	30

RANGLERS
68	Trend TRE 1007	You Never Said Goodbye/Step Down	60

ERNEST RANGLIN
62	Island WI 015	Harmonica Twist/Mitty Gritty (as Ernest Ranglin Orchestra)	40
63	Island WI 128	Exodus/ROBERT MARLEY: One Cup Of Coffee	300
66	Black Swan IEP 704	ERNEST RANGLIN & THE G.B.'s (EP, with p/s)	280
66	Black Swan IEP 704	ERNEST RANGLIN & THE G.B.'s (EP)	80
64	Island ILP 909	WRANGLIN' (LP)	180
64	Island ILP 915	REFLECTIONS (LP)	200
83	Vista Sounds	FROM KINGSTON J.A. TO MIAMI U.S.A. (LP)	80
96	Island Jamaica Jazz IJLP 4002	BELOW THE BASSLINE (LP)	150
97	Island Jamaica Jazz IJLP4004	MEMORIES OF BARBER MACK (LP)	35

(see also Owen Gray, Graham Bond)

KATNYA RANIERI
60	MGM 1088	The Torch/Kaniya	6

MASSIMO RANIERI
71	CBS 7207	Goodbye My Love/The Sun Shining Down On Me	12

BILLY RANKIN
83	A&M AM 172	Baby Come Back/Part Of The Scenery (p/s)	6

(see also Nazareth)

KENNY RANKIN
60	Brunswick 05845	As Sure As You're Born/Teasin' Heart	8
70	Mercury MF1128	Peaceful/The Dolphin	15

ROY RANKIN AND RAYMOND NAPTALI

MINT VALUE £

74	Little David	Carfish/Silver Morning	8

ROY RANKIN AND RAYMOND NAPTALI
81	KG Imperial KG 004	Go Deh In A Late Night Blues/Late Night Session/Babylon Policy/Peaceful Something (12", green vinyl)	25
81	KG Imperial KG 007	African Daughter/Disc Jockey In A 81 Style (12")	15
82	CF CFLP 001	LATE NIGHT SESSION (LP)	50

RANKING ANN
83	Rough Justice RJ 001	Kill The Police Bill/Rough Justice Dub (12")	20
85	Ariwa ARL SL 003	Something Fishy Going On/SANE INMATES: Whisper To A Roar	20
86	Ariwa ARI 7 55	Feminine Gender/Right To Fight	20
82	Ariwa ARILP 002	A SLICE OF ENGLISH TOAST (LP)	50
82	Ariwa ARILP 010	SOMETHING FISHY GOING ON (LP)	50

RANKING DREAD
78	Greensleeves GRE10	Dub Sister Dub It/Nine Months Belly	15
80	Art & Craft ACD 005	DISCO EP SHOWCASE: Honda Accord/Joe Grine Girl/Baby Mother/Nice Up The Lawn (12", miscredited, artist actually Ranking Joe)	15
80	Art & Craft AC006	DISCO EP SHOWCASE: My Liza/Same Thing/Hard Times Leave My Life/Jah Walk Through Galilee (12" green vinyl)	30
81	Greensleeves GRED 65	Fattie Boom Boom/SLY & ROBBIE : Dub Boom (12")	12
82	Greensleeves GRED 82	Shut Me Mouth/Shut Up Shut Up (Dub Version)	30
82	Greensleeves GRED 96	My Mammy/Mammy Mammy (12")	15
76	Burning Sounds BS 1025	GIRLS FIESTA (LP)	25
79	Burning Sounds BS 1037	KUNTA KINTE ROOTS (LP)	35
80	Freedom Sounds FSLP 001	LOTS OF LOVING (LP)	25
82	Silver Camel SCLP 002	RANKING DREAD IN DUB (LP)	40

RANKING IVAN
81	Discotex DT 10	Education/INSTIGATORS: Murder-Ration (12")	10
81	LJC LJC 01	Job Crisis/Red Eyed Gal (no p/s)	10

RANKING JOE
80	Art & Craft ACD 005	DISCO EP SHOWCASE (12", rd, green or gold vinyl, some copies miscredited to Ranking Dread)	15
78	Greensleeves GREL 2	WEAKHEART FADEAWAY (LP)	30
79	Student NWLP 009	ROUND THE WORLD (LP)	60
80	Greensleeves GREL 16	SATURDAY NIGHT JAMDOWN STYLE (LP)	25
81	Copasetic COPLPS 003	DISCO SKATE (LP, blue or black vinyl)	40

RANKING MANDEY
84	Hibiscus ED 006	Hard Times/Conflict & War (12", p/s)	50

PETER RANKING AND GENERAL LUCKY
82	Greensleeves GRED 98	Beverly Black/Walk And Talk (12")	18

RANKING ROCKER
80	Disco Mix DM 01	Give Jah The Glory/JAH I: Words Of Wisdom/RANKING ROCKER:Out Of The Ghetto/ Songs Of Jah (Disco Mix) (12")	40

RANKING TREVOR
78	Virgin Frontline FL1015	IN FINE STYLE (LP)	20

RANKING TREVOR AND TRINITY
78	Cha Cha CHALP 001	THREE PIECE CHICKEN AND CHIPS (LP, some copies on blue vinyl)	35

RANKING SUPERSTAR
80	Lord Koos KLP 1	REPATRIATION TIME (LP)	45

GAPPY RANKS
09	Peckings PT 1046	Jah Is My Everything/SOUL VENDORS: Version	8

RANSOME HEAD
71	York SYK 506	Sing/Wide Wide River	30

PETER RANSOME
72	York FYK 402	PETER RANSOME (LP, blue/silver label)	25

RAOUL & RUINED
84	Gutter Hearts GH 1	BITE BACK + BLUES (LP, fan-club only issue)	50

(see also Marc Almond)

RAPED
78	Parole KNIT 1	PRETTY PAEDOPHILES (EP)	20
78	Parole PURL 1	Cheap Night Out/Foreplay Playground (p/s, with ad sheet)	20
84	Iguana PILLAGED 1	PHILES AND SMILES (LP, official bootleg, with booklet)	50

(see also Cuddly Toys)

RAPEMAN
88	Fierce FRIGHT 031	Hated Chinee/Marmoset (p/s)	15

(see also Big Black)

JOHNNY RAPHAEL
58	Vogue V 9104	We're Only Young Once/The Lonely Road To Nowhere	50
58	Vogue V 9104	We're Only Young Once/The Lonely Road To Nowhere (78)	25

RAPHAEL (1)
67	Hispa Vox HXS 303	Please Speak To Me Of Love/While I Live	8
68	Columbia DB 8471	Ave Maria (Listen To Me)/Goin' Out Of My Head	6

RAPID DANCE
82	Resolute RO 1	Fragments Of Youth/Hidden So Well (p/s)	15

RAPIERS (1)
60s	Ilford Sound ILF 272	The Phantom Stage/Valencia	20

RAPIERS (2)
86	Off Beat NS 112A	The Closing Theme/Still I Cry	10
83	Red Door RA 001	THE RAPIERS VOL. 1 (EP)	18
84	Twang RA 002	THE RAPIERS VOL. 2 (EP)	12
85	Twang RA 003	THE RAPIERS VOL. 3 (EP)	12
86	Twang RA 004	THE RAPIERS VOL. 4 (EP)	12

Brian RAPKIN & KELVIN JONES

MINT VALUE £

91	Fury DEP 3018	THE RETURN OF THE RAPIERS (EP)	10
85	Off Beat WIK 40	STRAIGHT TO THE POINT (LP)	18
87	Off Beat WIK 67	1961 (LP)	18

BRIAN RAPKIN & KELVIN JONES
| 69 | MSR MID 1352 | DREAMS OF THE BEAST (LP) | 30 |

RARE AMBER
| 69 | Polydor BM 56309 | Malfunction Of The Engine/Blind Love | 30 |
| 69 | Polydor 583 046 | RARE AMBER (LP) | 250 |

RARE BIRD
70	Charisma CB 120	Sympathy/Devil's High Concern (in p/s)	15
70	Charisma CB 138	What You Want To Know/Hammerhead	10
72	Charisma CB 179	Sympathy/Devil's High Concern/What Do You Want To Know/Hammerhead (p/s)	10
74	Polydor SH 1041/2	Diamonds/BARCLAY JAMES HARVEST: Negative Earth (flexi, with Sounds)	10
69	Charisma CAS 1005	RARE BIRD (LP, laminated front sleeve, pink 'scroll label')	100
70	Charisma CAS 1011	AS YOUR MIND FLIES BY (LP, textured gatefold, pink 'scroll label')	75
72	Polydor 2442 101	EPIC FOREST (LP & poster, with bonus EP "Roadside Welcome"/Four Grey Walls/"You're Lost" [2814 011], p/s)	150
72	Polydor 2442 101	EPIC FOREST (LP, gatefold with free EP but no poster)	60
72	Polydor 2442 101	EPIC FOREST (LP with no poster or free EP)	30
73	Polydor 2383 211	SOMEBODY'S WATCHING (LP, gatefold sleeve)	20

(see also Fruit Machine)

RARE BREED
| 66 | Strike JH 316 | Beg, Borrow And Steal/Jeri's Theme | 30 |

(see also Ohio Express)

RARE EARTH
70	Rare Earth RES 114	(I Know) I'm Losing You/When Joanie Smiles	7
71	Rare Earth RES 104	Hey Big Brother/Under God's Light	8
71	Rare Earth RES 102	I Just Want To Celebrate/The Seed	6
70	Tamla Motown TMG 742	Get Ready/Magic Key	20
70	Tamla Motown STML 11165	GET READY (LP)	20
71	Tamla Motown STML 11180	ECOLOGY (LP)	20
71	Rare Earth SREA 4001	ONE WORLD (LP, textured gatefold sleeve)	18

RARE PLEASURE
| 76 | DJM DJS 10738 | Let Me Down Easy/Let Me Down Easy (Long Version) (Promo p/s) | 10 |
| 76 | DJM DJS 10738 | Let Me Down Easy/Let Me Down Easy (Long Version) | 7 |

HERMAN RAREBELL
| 81 | Harvest HAR 5215 | I'll Say Goodbye/Junk Funk | 10 |

RARE MOODS
| 86 | AGR AGR 5 | I've Got Love/Closer To Your Love (p/s) | 20 |
| 86 | AGR AGR T5 | I've Got Love/Closer To Your Love (12") | 50 |

RASALLA
| 76 | Kiss KISS 17 | Bosrah/Version (with The Spear) | 30 |

(see also Prince Alla, Yabby U)

RASCALS (1)
68	Atlantic 584 182	A Beautiful Morning/Rainy Day	8
68	Atlantic 584 210	People Got To Be Free/My World	8
69	Atlantic 584 255	Heaven/Baby I'm Blue	8
69	Atlantic 584 274	See/Away Away	8
69	Atlantic 584 292	Carry Me Back/Real Thing	7
70	Atlantic 584 307	Hold On/I Believe	8
70	Atlantic 2091 029	Glory, Glory/You Don't Know	6
71	CBS 7363	Love Me/Happy Song	6
71	CBS 7672	Lucky Day/Love Letter	6
68	Atlantic 587/588 098	ONCE UPON A DREAM (LP)	18

(see also Young Rascals)

RASCALS (2)
| 81 | Flexible FR 001 | UP TO MISCHIEF (sleeve back to front, no spine) | 80 |

RASCALS (3)
| 08 | Deltasonic DLTLP079 | RASCALIZE (LP) | 50 |

(EMPRESS) RASHEDA
87	Jah Shaka 862	Psalms 61 (Hear My Cry)/BLACK STEEL AND JAH SHAKA: Hear My Dub (12")	25
92	Rasheda Lioness RLM 001	Only Jah Worthy/Give Jah Praise (12")	30
95	Roots Music RRLP 011	HAIL H.I.M (LP)	30

RASI
| 83 | Yard Beat TB 001 | Jah Spoke To I/You Wan Tan Style | 25 |

RAS I
| 96 | Conscious Sounds DNC 1204 | Bad Boys/BUSH CHEMISTS: Dub//Exploitation/Bush Chemists: Dub (12") | 12 |

RAS IMRU
| 80 | Jah Shaka KMD001 | Marshall/SHAKA RYDIM SECTION : Warrior Style (12") | 60 |
| 85 | House Of Asha HA1LP | TRIBUTE TO SELASSE I (LP) | 25 |

RAS MIDAS
77	Black Swan WIP 6371	Kude A Bamba/Congo Dub	10
79	Tribesman TM 24	Natty Dread Surprise/Good Old Days Original (with I-Roy) (12")	60
79	Warrior WAR 138	Can't Stop Rasta Now/Rain And Fire (12")	20

RAS NATURAL
| 03 | Unity Sound US006 | Roar Like A Lion/Lion Chant/Version (10") | 20 |

RASPBERRY PIRATES
| 68 | Atlantic 584 230 | Looky Looky My Cookie's Gone/Good Morning Baby | 8 |

RASTAFARI
| 73 | Satril SAT8 | Funky City/In The Garden | 50 |

RATCHELL
MINT VALUE £

RATCHELL
72 MCA MUPS 455   RATCHELL (LP) 15
RATIO
70 Big Chief BC 102   Let There Be Peace In The World/Pharaoh's Walk 7
RATIONAL ANTHEM
86 Radio Humberside/HLS 001 THE NORTHERN TRAWL (LP) 50
ARMAN RATIP
70 Columbia SCX 6532   INTRODUCING THE ARMAN RATIP TRIO (LP) 100
73 Regal Zono. SLRZ 1038 THE SPY FROM ISTANBUL (LP, gatefold sleeve) 120
RATS (1)
64 Oak RGJ 145   Spoonful (1-sided, with foldout p/s) 400
64 Oak RGJ 145   Spoonful (1-sided) 250
65 Columbia DB 7483   Spoonful/I've Got My Eyes On You Baby 120
65 Columbia DB 7607   I Gotta See My Baby Everyday/Headin' Back (To New Orleans) 90
95 Tenth Planet TP 012   THE RISE AND FALL OF BERNIE GRIPPLESTONE & THE SPIDERS FROM HULL (LP, gatefold sleeve, 1,000 only) 20

(see also Beat Boys, Mark Peters)

RATS (2)
64 Oriole CB 1967   Parchman Farm/Every Day I Have The Blues 100
65 CBS 201740   Sack Of Woe/Gimme That Wine 100
RATS (3)
74 MAM MAM 113   Don't Let Go/Dragon Child 8
74 Goodear EAR. 101   Turtle Dove/Oxford Donna (with p/s) 40
74 Goodear EAR 101   Turtle Dove/Oxford Donna (without p/s) 15
74 Goodear EARLH 5003   FIRST (LP) 18

(see also World of Oz)

RATTLES
63 Philips BF 1277   The Stomp/Zip A Dee Doo Dah 20
64 Decca F 11873   Bye Bye Johnny/Roll Over Beethoven 25
64 Decca F 11936   Tell Me What I Can Do/Sunbeam At The Sky 25
65 Fontana TF 618   Come On And Sing/Candy To Me 25
66 Fontana TF 724   Say All Right/Love Of My Life 25
70 Decca F 23058   The Witch/Geraldine 6
71 Decca F 23119   You Can't Have Sunshine Everyday/Where Is The Friend 15
71 Decca FR 13243   The Devil's On The Loose/I Know You Don't Know 15
73 Decca FR 13390   Devils Son/What Do I Care 20
64 Decca DFE 8568   TEENBEAT FROM THE STAR CLUB HAMBURG (EP) 125
64 Philips BL 7614   TWIST AT THE STAR CLUB HAMBURG (LP) 100
67 Mercury MG 1127   GREATEST HITS (LP) 30
71 Decca SKL-R 5088   THE RATTLES (LP) 30

(see also Wonderland)

RATTLING THRONTONS
80 Beat Street BEAT 1   RATTLING THRONTONS EP 15
RAVE ONS
60s Sounds Good MT 103   She's A Spoon/Keep Wrong 120
CHRIS RAVEL & RAVERS
63 Decca F 11696   I Do/Don't You Dig This Kind Of Beat 20

(see also Chris Andrews)

RAVEN
80 Neat NEAT 06   Don't Need Your Money/Wiped Out (p/s) 8
81 Neat NEAT 11   Hard Ride/Crazy World (p/s) 6
82 Neat NEAT 1512   CRASH BANG WALLOP (Crash Bang Wallop/Firepower/Run Them Down/Rock Hard) (12" EP, mauve splattered vinyl) 15
86 WEA A 9453   Gimme Some Lovin' (no p/s) 8
81 Neat NEAT1001   ROCK UNTIL YOU DROP (LP + lyric insert) 20
83 Neat NEATP1001   ROCK UNTIL YOU DROP (reissue picture disc LP) 15
JON RAVEN
70s Broadside   HARVEST (LP, with book) 15
71 Argo ZFB 29   KATE OF COALBROOKDALE (LP, as Jon & Mike Raven with Jean Ward) ... 100
73 Trailer LER 2083   SONGS OF A CHANGING WORLD (LP, with Nic Jones & Tony Rose, red label with insert) ... 30
73 Broadside BRO 115   THE NAILMAKERS (LP, with Michael Totten) 15
75 Trailer LER 2083   SONGS OF A CHANGING WORLD (LP, 2nd pressing, with Nic Jones & Tony Rose, yellow label with insert) 20
75 Broadside BOR 116   BALLAD OF THE BLACK COUNTRY (LP) 15
76 Broadside BRO 117   HARVEST (LP) 50
81 Dingles DIN 319   REGAL SLIP (LP) 30

(see also Halliard, Black Country Three, John Kirkpatrick)

JON AND MICHAEL RAVEN
68 Broadside BOR 100   SONGS OF THE BLACK COUNTRY (LP) 40
MICHAEL RAVEN AND JOAN MILLS
70 Roman Head RH 021   A COLLECTION OF FOLKSONGS AND GUITAR MUSIC (LP, 99 copies only) ... 80
72 Folk Heritage FHR 047 DEATH AND THE LADY (LP) 400
74 Folk Heritage FHR 053 THE JOLLY MACHINE (LP) 50
74 Folk Heritage FHR 054 HYMN TO CHE GUEVARA (LP, 100 only) 500
MIKE RAVEN
66 Xtra 1046   GUITAR MAGIC (LP) 30
PAUL RAVEN (1)
61 Parlophone R 4812   Walk On Boy/All Grown Up 12
61 Parlophone R 4842   Tower Of Strength/Livin' The Blues 10
77 EMI NUT 2855   PAUL RAVEN (EP) 10

Paul RAVEN (2)

MINT VALUE £

PAUL RAVEN (2)
68	MCA MU 1024	Musical Man/Wait For Me	15
68	MCA MU1035	Soul Thing/We'll Go Where The World Can't	12

(see also Rubber Bucket)

SIMON RAVEN
66	Piccadilly 7N 35301	I Wonder If She Remembers Me/Sea Of Love	60

RAVENS ROCK GROUP
61	Pye International 7N 25077	The Ghoul Friend/Career Girl	20

RAVENS (2)
63	Oriole CB 1910	I Just Wanna Hear You Say/Send Me A Letter	30

RAVERS
69	Upsetter US 312	Babam Bam/UPSETTERS: Medical Operation	140

RAW DEAL (1)
78	Honky Tonk HTEP 44	Struck Down By Your Love/Rocky Rollin Road/Taking My Time/They're Red Hot (p/s)	12

RAW DEAL (2)
81	White Witch WIT 701	Out Of My Head/In The Mood (no p/s)	50
81	Neat NEAT 12	Lonewolf/Take The Sky (p/s)	10

RAW DEAL (3)
95	Mental Disorder MAD 666	THE LEGENDARY RAW DEAL (10" LP)	12

PETER RAWES
87	Official OFFA 5	Why Should I Ask Her To Stay?/Theme From Shark/Theme From Forever (with Jet Harris) (p/s)	6

(see also Jet Harris)

LOU RAWLS
65	Capitol CL 15398	Three O'Clock In The Morning/Nothing Really Feels The Same	10
66	Capitol CL 15465	Love Is A Hurtin' Thing/Memory Lane	10
67	Capitol CL 15488	You Can Bring Me All Your Heartaches/A Woman Who's A Woman	15
67	Capitol CL 15499	Dead End Street/Yes It Hurts Doesn't It	20
67	Capitol CL 15507	Show Business/When Loves Goes Wrong	25
67	Capitol CL 15515	Hard To Get Thing Called Love/(How Do You Say) I Don't Love You Anymore	10
67	Capitol CL 15522	Little Drummer Boy/Child With A Toy	8
68	Capitol CL 15533	My Ancestors/Evil Woman	8
68	Capitol CL 15548	You're Good For Me/Soul Serenade	10
68	Capitol CL 15560	Down Here On The Ground/I'm Satisfied	8
69	Capitol CL 15583	It's You/Sweet Charity	8
69	Capitol CL 15611	Your Good Thing (Is About To End)/Season Of The Witch	8
63	Capitol EAP-1 20646	LOST AND LOOKIN' (EP)	50
65	Capitol T 1824	BLACK AND BLUE (LP)	25
66	Capitol (S)T 2459	LIVE (LP)	20
67	Capitol (S)T 2566	SOULIN' (LP)	25
67	Capitol (S)T 2632	CARRYIN' ON! (LP)	20
68	Capitol (S)T 2864	FEELIN' GOOD (LP)	30
69	Capitol ST 2927	YOU'RE GOOD FOR ME (LP)	20
69	Capitol E-ST 215	THE WAY IT WAS THE WAY IT IS (LP)	20

RAW MATERIAL
69	Evolution E 2441	Time And Illusion/Bobo's Party	60
70	Evolution E 2445	Hi There Hallelujah/Days Of The Fighting Cock	50
70	Evolution E 24495	Traveller Man (Part 1)/Part 2	50
71	RCA Neon NE 1002	Ride On Pony/Religion	50
70	Evolution Z 1006	RAW MATERIAL (LP)	1000
71	RCA Neon NE 8	TIME IS (LP, gatefold sleeve)	1000

(see also Deep Feelings, Shoot)

RAW SILK
83	West End WEND 122	Just In Time/Just In Time And Space (Dub) (12")	12

ANNITA RAY
62	MGM 1177	Wouldn't It Be Lovely/I'm In Love With Jim	6

DANNY RAY
76	Doctor DR 01	Revolution Rock/Version	30

DANNY RAY & FALCONS
70	MCA MK 5037	Scorpion/I Love You Girl	10

DIANE RAY
63	Mercury AMT 1209	Please Don't Talk To The Lifeguard/That's All I Want From You	22

DON RAY
78	Polydor 2310610	THE GARDEN OF LOVE (LP)	20

FROGGIE RAY
71	Big BG 313	Uncle Charlie/Party Version	30
71	Big BG 314	Half Moon/RUPIE EDWARDS ALL STARS: Full Moon	20

(see also Hugh Roy Jr. U Roy Jr.)

JAMES RAY
62	Pye International 7N 25126	If You Gotta Make A Fool Of Somebody/It's Been A Drag	25
62	Pye International 7N 25147	Itty Bitty Pieces/You Remember The Face	20

JOHNNIE RAY
53	Columbia SCM 5015	Walkin' My Baby Back Home/The Lady Drinks Champagne (B-side with the Four Lads)	20
53	Columbia SCM 5033	Ma Says, Pa Says/A Full Time Job (with Doris Day)	20
53	Columbia SCM 5041	Whiskey And Gin/Tell The Lady I Said Goodbye	20
53	Columbia SCM 5074	Please Don't Talk About Me When I'm Gone/Coffee And Cigarettes (B-side with the Four Lads)	10
54	Columbia SCM 5111	Nobody's Sweetheart/I Can't Escape From You	10
54	Columbia SCM 5122	She Didn't Say Nothin' At All/I'm Just A Shadow Of Myself	10
57	Philips JK 1004	You Don't Owe Me A Thing/Look Homeward, Angel (jukebox issue)	10
57	Philips JK 1011	So Long/I Miss You So (jukebox issue)	10

RICARDO RAY

MINT VALUE £

57	Philips JK 1016	Yes, Tonight, Josephine/No Wedding Today (jukebox issue)	20
57	Philips JK 1025	Build Your Love (On A Strong Foundation)/Street Of Memories (jukebox issue)	10
57	Philips JK 1026	Up Above My Head, I Hear Music On The Air/Good Evening Friends/Memories (with Frankie Laine, jukebox issue only)	10
57	Philips JK 1033	Pink Sweater Angel/Texas Tambourine (jukebox issue)	30
59	Philips PB 952	You're All That I Live For/I'll Never Fall In Love Again	6
59	Philips PB 952	You're All That I Live For/I'll Never Fall In Love Again (78)	20
60	Philips PB 990	When It's Springtime In The Rockies/Wagon Wheels	6
60	Philips PB 1025	Before You/I'll Make You Mine	6
62	London HLG 9484	I Believe (with Timi Yuro)/TIMI YURO: Smile	15

(see also Timi Yuro)

RICARDO RAY
| 68 | Roulette RO 501 | Nitty Gritty/Mony Mony | 20 |

WADE RAY
| 63 | London HL 9700 | Burning Desire/Two Red Red Lips | 8 |

RAY & COLLUNEY
| 71 | Westwood WRS 001 | TYRANTS OF ENGLAND (LP) | 40 |

CHRIS(TINE) RAYBURN
63	Parlophone R 5098	Slow Loving Woman/Same Old Places	10
64	Parlophone R 5144	I've Cried My Last Tear/You Forgot To Say When	10
66	Parlophone R 5422	I Wanna Be In Love Again/Another Night Alone	10
68	Music Factory CUB 2	One Way Ticket/Photograph Of Love	20
69	Pye 7N 17679	Skip A Rope/Starlight (as Christine Rayburn)	10
66	Parlophone PCS7001	CHRIS RAYBURN (LP)	25

MARGIE RAYBURN
56	Capitol CL 14532	The Wedding Song/That's The Chance I've Got To Take	10
57	London HLU 8515	I'm Available/If You Were	25
58	London HLU 8648	I Would/Alright, But It Won't Be Easy	18

CLYDE RAY
| 57 | Columbia DB 3875 | Follow Me/Steady As A Rock | 10 |
| 58 | Columbia DB 4106 | Locked In The Arms Of Love/I'm Not Afraid Anymore | 10 |

ANTHONY RAYE
| 80 | Grapevine GRP 147 | Give Me One More Chance/Hold On To What You've Got | 8 |

SOL RAYE
| 63 | Oriole CB 1855 | Dear Michelle/I Love You Because | 10 |
| 67 | Deram DM 154 | While I'm Here/To Be With You | 12 |

RAYKO
| 11 | Autodiscotheque 7 | Inside Out/Sexy Lady (12") | 40 |

DANNY RAYMOND
| 71 | Big Shot BI 587 | Sister Big Stuff/BOY FRIDAY: Free Man | 20 |

LEE RAYMOND WITH COSTELLO SISTERS
| 55 | Brunswick 05438 | Foolishly Yours/Baby Darling | 10 |

MARK RAYMOND & CROWD
| 64 | Columbia DB 7308 | Girls/Remember Me To Julie | 15 |

TONY RAYMOND
59	Fontana H 213	Broken-Hearted Melody/This Earth Is Mine	8
62	Oriole CB 1708	Handful Of Songs/She'll Have To Go	8
62	Oriole CB 1777	The Infant King/Because Of You	6

IVOR RAYMONDE & HIS ORCHESTRA
| 65 | Mercury MF 866 | Feelin' Fruggy/Grotty | 12 |

JULIE RAYNE
59	HMV POP 665	Waltz Me Around/Love Where Can You Be?	10
60	HMV POP 785	Bim Bam Bom/One More Time	10
61	HMV POP 868	Green With Envy Purple With Passion/My First Romance	10
63	Windsor WPS 123	Faithfully/Free To Love	10
64	Windsor WPS 128	You Can't Come Back/Straight To Your Arms	10

LISA RAYNE
| 65 | Fontana TF 563 | Don't Ever Change/It Had To Be You | 10 |

MARTIN RAYNOR & SECRETS
| 65 | Columbia DB 7563 | Candy To Me/You're A Wonderful One | 60 |

(see also Secrets, Simon's Secrets, Clifford T. Ward)

MIKE RAYNOR & THE CONDORS
| 67 | Decca F22690 | Is She A Woman NOw/My Shy Serenade (export p/s) | 40 |

RAYS
| 57 | London HLU 8505 | Silhouettes/Daddy Cool | 25 |

RAZAR
| 78 | Polydor 2058 983 | Ascension Day/Ain't No Mystery (company sleeve) | 35 |
| 78 | Charisma CB 320 | Idle Rich/One Room Doom (p/s) | 10 |

(see also Third World War, Soho Jets, Nervous Germans)

RAZBERRY HOLIDAY BAND
| 89 | Caleche LIS 001 | Hangover Square/Promise | 20 |

RAZORCUTS
86	Subway Org. SUBWAY 5	Big Pink Cake/I'll Still Be There (foldover p/s with insert, poly bag, 2,000 only)	20
86	Subway Org. SUBWAY 8	Sorry To Embarrass You/Summer In Your Heart (p/s with insert, 2,000 only)	20
87	Sha La La BaBaBaBaBa 02	Sad Kaleidoscope/TALULAH GOSH: I Told You So (flexidisc p/s, 2,500 only)	12
80s	Caff CAFF 10	Sometimes I Worry About You/For Always/Sorry To Embarrass You/Music From The Big Pink (foldaround p/s with insert, 500 only)	20
88	Creation CRELP 026	STORYTELLER (LP)	25
89	Creation CRELP 045	THE WORLD KEEPS TURNING (LP)	25

(see also Cinematics, Red Chair Fadeaway)

RAZORLIGHT

MINT VALUE £

RAZORLIGHT
04	Vertigo 986 710-1	UP ALL NIGHT (LP, with free 7")..	40
06	Vertigo 17010901	RAZORLIGHT (LP)	40
09	Vertigo 17050004	SLIPWAY FIRES (LP)	18

RAZOR'S EDGE
66	Stateside SS 532	Let's Call It A Day, Girl/April	15

RAZZY
74	MCA 2006437	I Hate Hate/Singing Other Peoples Songs	8

CHRIS REA
74	Magnet MAG 10	So Much Love/Born To Lose (no p/s)	25

REACTA
79	Battery Operated WAC 1	Stop The World/SUS (p/s)	100

(see also Television Personalities)

REACTION (1)
68	President PT 208	That Man/Falling In Love With You	12

REACTION (2)
70	Columbia Blue Beat DB 119	Oh Me, Oh My/RECO: It's Love	20
70	Attack ATT 8022	You Yes You/CIMARONS: Be There	15

(see also Ezz Reco, Joe Higgs)

REACTION (3)
78	Island WIP 6437	I Can't Resist/I Am A Case (p/s)	20

(see also Talk Talk, Mark Hollis)

REACTION (4)
87	Waterloo Sunset RUSS 105	Make Up Your Mind/Four By Four	18

REACTORS
81	Slam! SSM 018	Travel Broadens The Mind/Dreams Without Sleep	30

PAT READER
60	Triumph RGM 1024	Ricky/Dear Daddy	60
62	Piccadilly 7N 35077	Cha Cha On The Moon/May Your Heart Stay Young Forever	40
63	Oriole CB 1903	Helpless/Lover's Lane	30

BERTICE READING
55	Parlophone R 4057	Songs From "Jazz Train" Parts 1 & 2 (with Edric Connor)	6
57	Decca F 10965	No Flowers By Request/September In The Rain	15
58	Parlophone R 4462	Rock Baby Rock/It's A Boy	60
58	Parlophone R 4487	My Big Best Shoes/No More In Life	10

REAL MACABRE
85	Push 2	White Horses/The Call (p/s)	7

REALISTICS
77	Epic 5439	Love Vibrations/The Magic That You Do	15
79	Bronze BRO 81	Pure Magic/Right From The Start	20

REALISTS
78	Stiff OFF 4	I've Got A Heart/Living in The City (p/s)	6
81	Eccentric YUR 1	Wonderland/Glad To Be Alive (1000 only, p/s)	7

REALITY FROM DREAM
75	(no label) CP 109	REALITY FROM DREAM (LP, private pressing)	150

REALITY (1)
67	Birchwood BW 01	Simple Skies/Ran Into The Forest	150

REALITY (2)
82	Subversive SUB	BLIND TO THE TRUTH (EP, foldout sleeve and insert)	10
84	Fight Back FIGHT 3	WHO KILLED THE GOLDEN GOOSE? (EP)	10

REALITY CONTROL
83	Volume VOL 7	THE REPRODUCTION OF HATE EP	8

REAL KIDS
78	Bronze BRO 54	All Kindsa Girls/Common At Noon (p/s)	8
78	Bronze BRON 509	REAL KIDS (LP)	22

REALLY FREE
78	Sya RFSM 002	New Day Dawning/Thank You Jesus	10

REALLY 3RDS
81	EJSP 9610	Everyday Everywhere/Daptapper (no p/s)	35

REALM
66	CBS 202044	Hard Time Loving You/Certain Kind Of Girl	35

(see also Earl Preston & Realms)

REAL McCOY
67	Fontana TF 794	Show Me How You Milk A Cow/I Paid For My Laughs	8
68	Target 7N 17669	Quick Joey Small/Happiness Is Love	20
68	Pye 7N 17618	I Get So Excited/Somebody's Taken Maria Away	8
69	Pye 7N 17669	Quick Joey Small/Happiness Is Love	8
69	Pye 7N 17704	Round The Gum Tree/I Will	8
69	Pye 7N 17772	Gitarzan/Anytime You Need Me	8
69	Pye 7N 17850	Many The Memories/She's Different, She's Beautiful	8
71	CBS 7165	I'll Give You Things/Baby, Go Home	8
70	Marble Arch MAL 1251	THIS IS THE REAL McCOY (LP)	20

(see also Tony Colton)

REALMS
70s	Summertime BUSS 11	Happiness Is Your Name/Happiest Dread	10

REAL THING
72	Bell BLL 1232	Vicious Circles Part 1/ Part 2	8
75	Pye 7N 25681	Stone Cold Love Affair/A Love That's Real (solid and push out centres) ...	25
81	Calibre CAB 109	I Believe In You/You're My Number One	30
81	Calibre CABL 109	I Believe In You (Extended Version)/You're My Number One (12")	30

REASONS
MINT VALUE £

77	Aye NSPH 20	4 FROM 8 (LP)	25
78	Pye NSPL 18587	STEP INTO OUR WORLD (LP)	15
79	Calibre CAB LP 1001	SAINTS OR SINNERS (LP)	15

(see also Chants)

REASONS
78	Island WIP 6467	Hard Day At The Office/Baby Bright Eyes (p/s)	30

REBEL
81	Bridge House BHS 2	Rocka Shocka/Drift Away (p/s)	12
86	Flying Pig REBS 1	Valentino/Lonely Traveller (p/s, with free single)	12

REBEL CHRISTENING
85	Clay 12 CLAY 44	TRIBAL EYE (12" EP, p/s)	12

REBEL REGULARS
81	Greensleeves GRED 48	Jah Love (with General Saint)/Irregular Dubs Part 1 and 2 (12")	35

REBEL ROUSERS
68	Fontana TF 973	Should I?/As I Look	200

(see also Cliff Bennett & Rebel Rousers, Soul Sounds)

REBELS
78	Rigid IS REB 1029	Suicide/The Leader Of The Rebellion	800

REBELS & ALLIES
79	Brixton Sound BS01234	BROKEN HEART (LP)	60

REBELS (JAMAICA)
70	Bullet BU 440	Nice Grind/SIDNEY ALL STARS: Nice Grind - Version	10
70	Trojan TR 7779	It's All In The Game (lead vocal Jimmy Riley)/Easy Come	15
76	Black Wax WAX 16	Rhodesia/Version	20

(see also The Pioneers)

REBELS (U.K.)
67	Page One POF 017	Hard To Love You/Call Me	40

REBOUNDS
64	Fontana TF 461	Help Me/The World Is Mine	25

REBS
58	Capitol CL 14932	Bunky/Renegade	15

RECKLESS
92	Pulse-8 12LOSE 24	Time To Make The Floor Burn (The Reckless Hypermix)/Take Me (Ruff Mix)/Take Me (Uplifting Piano Mix) (12", p/s)	25

RECO
69	Downtown DT 417	Quando Quando/Reg 'A' Jeg (as Reco & Rudies)	25
69	Jackpot JP 710	Memory Of Don Drummond/THE TOBIES: Resting	25
69	Treasure Isle TI 7052	The Lion Speaks/ANDY CAPP: Pop A Top	25
69	Pama ECO 14	RECO IN REGGAE LAND (LP)	120

(see also Reaction, Don Reco, Rico Rodriguez, Joe Monsano, Slim Smith, Laurel Aitken)

DON RECO
71	Big Shot BI 597	Waterloo Rock/LLOYD'S ALL STARS: Walls Soul	20

(see also Reco)

EZZ RECO & LAUNCHERS
64	Columbia DB 7217	King Of Kings/Blue Beat Dance	12
64	Columbia DB 7222	Little Girl/The Bluest Beat	7
64	Columbia DB 7290	Please Come Back/At A Party	7
64	Columbia SEG 8326	JAMAICA BLUE BEAT (EP)	25

(see also Reaction)

RECORD PLAYERS
78	Wreckord WRECK 001	DOUBLE C SIDE (EP, label also listed as Aerco AERO 1104)	8
80	Wreckord WRECK 002	Give An Inch/Squirming In The Vermin By The Bonny Banks Of Clyde/67/Parasite (p/s)	6

RECORDS
88	Waterfront WF 042	A SUNNY AFTERNOON IN WATERLOO (LP)	25

RECRUITS
83	RE1	THREE SQUEEZES EP (12", p/s)	30
89	SRT 9KS 1994 RE 2	See My Face/Dream Heaven Scene (p/s)	20

RECTIFY
88	Taffcore TAFF 001	20TH CENTURY EP (foldout p/s)	10

RED ALLIGATOR
69	Youngblood YB1004	Real Cool/Slow Down	18

(see Jimmy Powell)

RED BALUNE
78	MCCB 001	Capitalist Kid/Spider In Love (p/s)	12

DANNY RED
93	Abba Jahnoi AJ 001	Jah Is Here/Version (12")	18
95	Columbia 662157 6	BE GRATEFUL EP (12", p/s)	40

RED (1)
77	Electric WOT EP 1	RIDER IN THE SKY EP (p/s)	10

RED (2)
83	Jigsaw SAW 2	RED (LP, private pressing)	25

RED ALERT (1)
69	Total TL3	Witch Woman/Sabra	50

RED ALERT (2)
80	Guardian GM-RA/B 61	BORDER GUARDS (EP)	700
82	No Future OI 5	In Britain/Screaming At The Nation/Murder Missile (p/s)	10
82	No Future OI 33	Take No Prisoners/Empire Of Crime/Sell Out (p/s)	10
83	No Future OI 20	City Invasion/Negative Reaction (p/s)	8
83	No Future OI 27	THERE'S A GUITAR BURNING (12" EP)	15
83	No Future PUNK 5	WE'VE GOT THE POWER (LP)	15

RED ALERT (3)

MINT VALUE £

RED ALERT (3)
82	Steel City AJS7R	Run To Ground/Wild You (no p/s, some with hand-made 'Wildfire' stickers over band name)	20

(see also Next Band)

RED BEANS & RICE
80	Chiswick CHIS 124	That Driving Beat/Throw It In The Grass	15

REDBONE
70	CBS 5326	Maggie/New Blue Sermonette	6
70	CBS 64069	REDBONE (LP)	15
70	CBS 64198	POTLATCH (LP)	15
72	Epic EQ 30815	MESSAGE FROM A DRUM (LP, quadraphonic)	20

REDBRASS
78	Redgold RGR 101	REDBRASS EP	12
76	Riverside RR 2	SILENCE IS CONSENT (LP, insert)	20

REDCAPS
63	Decca F 11716	Shout/Little Things You Do	20
63	Decca F 11789	Talkin' 'Bout You/Come On Girl	15
64	Decca F 11903	Mighty Fine Girl/Funny Things	15

REDCELL
92	B12 B1205	REDCELL EP (12")	25
92	B12 B1205	REDCELL EP (12", purple vinyl)	80
92	B12 B1207	RETREAT FROM UNPLEASANT REALITIES EP (12")	40
92	B12 B1207	RETREAT FROM UNPLEASANT REALITIES EP (12", blue vinyl)	60
92	B12 B1207	RETREAT FROM UNPLEASANT REALITIES EP (12", red vinyl)	60
93	B12 B1208	INTERIM OUTERIM EP (12")	15
93	B12 B1208	INTERIM OUTERIM EP (12", white vinyl)	60
96	B12 B1215	Untitled (12", White label promo)	60

RED CHAIR FADEAWAY
89	Cosmic Eng. M. CTA 103	Let It Happen/Myra/Dragonfly/Grasshopper (12", p/s, 500 only)	15
90	Cosmic Eng. M. CTA 105	Mr Jones/Chimney Pots/Faraway Lights/Out Of The Grey (12", p/s, 450 only)	15
91	Waterbomb SPLAT 002	Never Remember/FUDGE: Girlwish (flexi, p/s)	12
91	Tangerine MM 10	CURIOUSER AND CURIOUSER (LP, foldaround sleeve with booklet, no'd)	20

(see also Razorcuts)

RED CLOUD
82	Echo STLP 1009	RED CLOUD IN DUB (LP)	30

RED CRAYOLA
78	Radar SAM 88	Pink Stainless Tail/13TH FLOOR ELEVATORS She Lives (In A Time Of Her Own) (promo)	15
78	Radar ADA 22	Wives In Orbit/Yik Yak (p/s, red vinyl)	7
78	Radar RAD 12	THE PARABLES OF ARABLE LAND (LP, stickered sleeve)	20
79	Radar RAD 18	SOLDIER TALK (LP)	15

FREDDIE REDD
58	Nixa NJL 19	GET HAPPY (LP)	200

GENE REDD & GLOBETROTTERS
59	Parlophone R 4584	Red River Valley Rock/Kentucky Home Rock	15

OTIS REDDING
SINGLES : SINGLES AND LPS
64	London HLK 9833	Pain In My Heart/Something Is Worrying Me	25
64	London HLK 9876	Come To Me/Don't Leave Me This Way	25
65	Atlantic AT 4024	Mr Pitiful/That's How Strong My Love Is	25
65	Sue WI 362	Shout Bamalama/Fat Girl	30
65	Atlantic AT 4029	I've Been Loving You Too Long/Winter Wonderland (unissued, demos only)	75
65	Atlantic AT 4039	Respect/I've Been Loving You Too Long	18
65	Atlantic AT 4050	My Girl/Down In The Valley	15
66	Atlantic AT 4080	(I Can't Get No) Satisfaction/Any Ole Way	12
66	Atlantic 584 019	My Lover's Prayer/Don't Mess With Cupid	12
66	Atlantic 584 030	I Can't Turn You Loose/Just One More Day	10
66	Atlantic 584 049	Fa-Fa-Fa-Fa-Fa (Sad Song)/Good To Me	10
67	Atlantic 584 070	Try A Little Tenderness/I'm Sick Y'all	10
67	Atlantic 584 091	Respect/These Arms Of Mine	8
67	Atlantic 584 092	My Girl/Mr Pitiful	8
67	Stax 601 005	Day Tripper/Shake (dark blue labels)	10
67	Stax 601 007	Let Me Come On Home/I Love You More Than Words Can Say (dark blue labels)	10
67	Stax 601 011	Shake (live)/634-5789 (live)	10
67	Stax 601 017	The Glory Of Love/I'm Coming Home	8
67	Stax 601 027	(I Can't Get No) Satisfaction/I've Been Loving You Too Long	8
68	Stax 601 031	(Sittin' On) The Dock Of The Bay/My Sweet Lorene	8
68	Stax 601 040	The Happy Song/Open The Door	8
68	Pye International 7N 25463	She's All Right/Gama Lama	10
68	Atlantic 584 199	Hard To Handle/Amen	8
68	Atlantic 584 220	Champagne And Wine/I've Got Dreams To Remember	10
68	Atlantic 584 234	Papa's Got A Brand New Bag/Direct Me	8
69	Atlantic 584 249	A Lover's Question/You Made A Man Out Of Me	10
69	Atco 226 001	Love Man/That's How Strong My Love Is	10
69	Atco 226 002	Free Me/Higher And Higher	8
69	Evolution E 2442	She's All Right/Tuff Enuff	15
70	Atco 226 012	Look At That Girl/That's A Good Idea	12
70	Atco 2091 020	Wonderful World/Security	8
05	Atco 002	Loving By The Pound/BENNY TROY: I Wanna Give You Tomorrow (promo, 500 only)	10
08	Kent Select CITY 008	Loving By The Pound/BARBARA AND THE BROWNS: I'm Gonna Start A War	10
66	Sue IEP 710	EARLY OTIS REDDING (EP)	100

Otis REDDING & CARLA THOMAS

MINT VALUE £

65	Atlantic ATL 5029	THE GREAT OTIS REDDING SINGS SOUL BALLADS (LP)	50
66	Atlantic ATL 5041	OTIS BLUE: OTIS REDDING SINGS SOUL (LP)	60
66	Atlantic 587 011	THE SOUL ALBUM (LP)	30
66	Atlantic 587 035	THE GREAT OTIS REDDING SINGS SOUL BALLADS (LP, reissue)	20
66	Atlantic 587/588 036	OTIS BLUE: OTIS REDDING SINGS SOUL (LP, reissue, mono/stereo)	35
67	Atlantic 587/588 050	COMPLETE AND UNBELIEVABLE: THE OTIS REDDING DICTIONARY OF SOUL (LP)	25
67	Atlantic 587 042	PAIN IN MY HEART (LP)	25
67	Stax VOLT 418	THE HISTORY OF OTIS REDDING (LP)	30
68	Stax 589 016	OTIS REDDING IN EUROPE (LP)	30
68	Stax 230 001/231 001	THE DOCK OF THE BAY (LP)	20
68	Atlantic 587/588 113	THE IMMORTAL OTIS REDDING (LP)	30
68	Atlantic 587/588 148	OTIS REDDING AT THE WHISKEY A GO GO, LOS ANGELES (LP)	25
69	Atco 228 001	THE HISTORY OF OTIS REDDING (LP, reissue)	15
69	Atco 228 025	LOVE MAN (LP)	30
70	Atlantic 2464 003	REMEMBERING (LP)	18
71	Atco 2400 018	TELL THE TRUTH (LP)	18
71	Reprise K 40430	LIVE AT THE MONTEREY INTERNATIONAL POP FESTIVAL (LP, shared with Jimi Hendrix)	30

OTIS REDDING & CARLA THOMAS

67	Stax 601 012	Tramp/Oooh Carla, Oooh Otis (with Carla Thomas)	8
67	Stax 601 021	Knock On Wood/Let Me Be Good To You	8
68	Stax 601 033	Lovey Dovey/New Year's Resolution	8
67	Stax 589 007	THE KING AND QUEEN OF SOUL	30

(see also Carla Thomas)

RED DIRT

70	Fontana STL 5540	RED DIRT (LP)	1750
10	Morgan Bluetown BT 5004	RED DIRT (LP, reissue, 500 only, with signed and numbered certificate)	25

RED DRAGON

86	Redman Intl. RED 4	Ease Off/ADMIRAL TIBET: New Tactics (12")	20

EMMA REDE

67	Columbia DB 8136	Just Like A Man/I Gotta Be With You (DJ copy)	40
67	Columbia DB 8136	Just Like A Man/I Gotta Be With You	20

(see also Jacky, Jackie Lee, Jackie & Raindrops, Raindrops)

TEDDY REDELL

60	London HLK 9140	Judy/Can't You See	60

RED FLY

70	Red Fly RF 01	Colour It Black/Scream It Out	30

REDGEE SEEBOE

74	Bug 38	Please Don't Bring Your Sister/Daphnies Brains	15

MICHAEL REDGRAVE & JULIET MILLS

61	Parlophone R 4804	No My Darling Daughter/Blimp's Blues	7

VANESSA REDGRAVE

64	Topic STOP 111	Hanging On A Tree/Where Have All The Flowers Gone (in title sleeve)	6

RED HARVEST

87	Quiet QS 019	Murder/Fifty Years/Burning Party (p/s)	20

RED HAWKES

66	ALP 595001	Friday Night/Lonely Boy	50

(see also Mark Five, Nazareth)

REDHEAD

73	UK UK R 38	We Ran And We Ran/Lookin' For You	8

RED HERRING

87	Crystal 717	Albert Road/Harbour Lights	30

RED HOT

91	Robin Hood RH 005	Letter To My Baby/Version (12")	15

RED HOT & BLUE

85	Northwood NOR 1	RED HOT & BLUE (LP)	25

RED HOT CHILI PEPPERS

85	EMI America EA 205	Hollywood (Africa)/Never Mind (p/s)	10
85	EMI America 12EA 205	Hollywood (Africa) (Remix)/Hollywood (Africa) (Dub Mix)/Never Mind (12", p/s)	12
89	EMI 12MT 70	KNOCK ME DOWN EP (12", p/s)	15
89	EMI 12MT 75	Higher Ground/Catholic Schoolgirls Rule (p/s)	10
90	EMI 12MTX 85	TASTE THE PAIN EP (12", push-out sleeve with inner)	12
90	EMI 10MTX 85	TASTE THE PAIN EP (square disc, numbered)	12
90	EMI 12MTG 88	Higher Ground/Catholic Schoolgirls Rule/None As Weird As Me (12", gatefold sleeve)	15
84	EMI USA MTL 1056	RED HOT CHILLI PEPPERS (LP)	30
87	EMI America AML 2125	UPLIFT MOFO PARTY PLAN (LP)	20
89	EMI America MTL 1046	MOTHERS MILK (LP)	20
91	Warner Bros. 7599 26681-1	BLOOD SUGAR SEX MAGIK (LP)	25
95	Warner Bros. 9362 457331	ONE HOT MINUTE (2-LP)	75
99	Warner Bros. 9362 47386-1	CALIFORNICATION (2-LP, 1st pressing with one small 'pressing' ring around centre hole)	100
01	Warner Bros. 9362-47386-1	CALIFORNICATION (2-LP 2nd pressing with two 'pressing' rings around centre hole)	50
02	Warner Bros. 9362-48140-1	BY THE WAY (2-LP)	40
02	Warner Bros. 9362854-1	GREATEST HITS (2-LP)	100
06	Warner Bros. 9362499961	STADIUM ARCADIUM (4xLP box set with foil outer & 2 booklets)	100
06	Warner Bros. 9362443911	STADIUM ARCADIUM (4xLP, standard edition)	50
11	Warner Bros. 9362-49564-1	I'M WITH YOU (2-LP)	45

(see also Atoms For Peace)

RED HOUSE PAINTERS

94	4AD BAD 4004	Shock Me/Sundays And Holidays/Three-Legged Cat/Shock Me (12", p/s)	40
92	4AD CAD 2014	DOWN COLOURFUL HILL (LP)	80

RED LETTERS

MINT VALUE £

93	4AD DAD 3008	RED HOUSE PAINTERS (2-LP, inner sleeves)	80
93	4AD CAD 3016	RED HOUSE PAINTERS (LP, different release from DAD 3008)	80
95	4A DADD 5005	OCEAN BEACH (LP, 2 x 10" with inner sleeves)	80
16	4AD RHP BOX 1	RED HOUSE PAINTERS (6-LP bronze vinyl box set)	150

RED LETTERS
79	Burning Bing CPS 025	Sacred Voices/Shot In The Dark/Science Has The Answer (folded p/s)	120

RED LIGHT
94	Black Tracks BT 001	Skylarking/Liquidator (12")	30
94	Red Light RL001	Coca Cola/Murder Tonight/Look Good (12")	25
94	Red Light RL003	Wow Yeh/The Burial (12")	25
94	Red Light RL003	Roots Rock/Fire (12")	15
95	Red Light RL005	Get Up/Sensi (12")	20
95	Red Light RL006	The Remix/Killer Sound Boy Nitty (12")	20
95	Red Light RL009	Hunt And Seek/Selekta (12")	30

RED LIGHTS
78	Free Range PF 5	Never Wanna Leave/Seventeen (p/s)	70

RED LINE EXPLOSION
71	Penny Farthing PEN 753	Sweet Talking Mother/Evil Woman	8

RED LONDON
83	Razor RZS 105	Sten Guns In Sunderland/This Is England/Soul Train/Revolution Times (p/s)	12
84	Razor RAZ 10	THIS IS ENGLAND (LP)	30

RED LORRY, YELLOW LORRY
82	Red Rhino RED 20	Beating My Head/I'm Still Waiting (p/s)	15
83	Red Rhino ED 39	He's Red/See The Fire (p/s)	7

RED MEAT
72	Worsley WR 1	She/My Mind Sleeps On (p/s)	50

RED MONEY
90	PF&G PFG 001	MY ERSTWHILE COMPANION EP	15

RED ONION JAZZ BABIES
60	Collector JE 19	RED ONION JAZZ BABIES (EP)	10

(see also Louis Armstrong)

JEAN REDPATH
66	Bounty BY 6004	LOVE LILT AND LAUGHTER (LP)	20

RED PYJAMAS
88	Ride SRT 8KS1750	Hands Off, Hands On, Lucinda Loves You/Lets Get Happy (p/s)	6

RED RAGE
80	Flicknife FLS 203	Total Control/I Give You This (p/s)	40

RED RIVER BAND
70	Banana BA 35	I'm Gonna Use What I've Got/Shame Shame	8

REDSKINS
82	CNT CNT 007	Lev Bronstein/The Peasant Army (p/s)	25
83	CNT CNT 016	Lean On Me!/Unionize! (p/s)	7

RED SNAPPER
96	Warp WARLP45	PRINCE BLIMEY (2-LP)	25
98	Warp WARLP56	MAKING BONES (2-LP)	25
00	Warp WARLP78	OUR AIM IS TO SATISFY RED SNAPPER (2-LP)	20

RED SQUARES
67	Columbia DB 8160	Mountain's High/Pity Me	20
67	Columbia DB 8257	True Love Story/Lollipop	12

RED STRIPE
80	Snotty Snail NELCOL 4	Inside Of Pain/Wogs Go Home/Trois Vielles Sacs Assises Lisant (hand stamped sleeve and insert)	100

RED TELEVISION
71	Brecht Times	RED TELEVISION (LP, private pressing with insert)	200

REDUCERS
78	Vibes XP 1/VR 001	Things Go Wrong/We Are Normal (p/s)	50
79	Vibes VR 003	Man With A Gun/Vengeance/Can't Stop Now (p/s)	50
80	EMI EMI 5028	Airways/Waiting For No One (p/s)	10

MIKE REDWAY
64	Oriole CB 1948	Many People/It's So Funny I Could Cry	8
65	CBS 202017	Magic Rocking Chair/When You Go	8
67	Deram DM 124	Have No Fear, Bond Is Here (Casino Royale)/My Poem For You	10
69	RCA 1873	Through The Eyes Of Love/Love Me	6

(see also Rod McKuen, Typhoons, Bud Ashton)

REDWOOD
79	SRT SRTS/79/CUS 582	Give The Indian Back His Land/Rock Of Ages (500 only, this price for 300 in p/s and insert)	35
79	SRT SRTS/79/CUS 582	Give The Indian Back His Land/Rock Of Ages (500 only, this price for 200 with no p/s)	15

REDWOODS
62	Columbia DB 4859	Please Mr Scientist/Where You Used To Be	25

DIZZY REECE QUINTET
56	Tempo A 140	Chorus/Basie Line	10
58	Tempo EXA 84	A VARIATION ON MONK (EP)	200
59	Tempo EXA 86	NOWHERE TO GO (EP, featuring Tubby Hayes)	200
59	Tempo EXA 89	ON THE SCENE (EP)	100
55	Tempo LAP 3	A NEW STAR... (10" LP)	250
57	Tempo TAP 9	PROGRESS REPORT (LP)	600
58	Esquire 32 185	ASIA MINOR (LP)	100
84	Jasmine JASM 2013	PROGRESS REPORT (LP, reissue)	20

(see also Victor Feldman, Ronnie Scott)

Bobby REED

MINT VALUE £

BOBBY REED
Shrine 114 — Caldonia Brown/Baby Don't Leave Me 6

CHUCK REED
57	Brunswick 05646	Whispering Heart/Another Love Has Ended	15
58	Columbia DB 4113	No School Tomorrow/Let's Put Our Hearts Together	30
62	Stateside SS 108	Just Plain Hurt/Talking No Trash	15

DEAN REED
59	Capitol CL 14986	The Search/Annabelle	10
59	Capitol CL 15030	I Kissed A Queen/A Pair Of Scissors (And A Pot Of Glue)	10

DENNY REED
| 61 | London HLK 9274 | A Teenager Feels It Too/Hot Water .... | 18 |

J REED
| 96 | Ugly UGM 005 | VIBE NATIONS EP (12") .... | 20 |

JERRY REED
58	Capitol CL 14851	Bessie Baby/Too Young To Be Blue	300
58	Capitol CL 14851	Bessie Baby/Too Young To Be Blue (78)	50
69	RCA SF 8006	ALABAMA WILD MAN (LP)	18

JIMMY REED
60	Top Rank JAR 333	Baby What You Want Me To Do/Caress Me Baby	20
60	Top Rank JAR 394	Found Love/Where Can You Be	20
60	Top Rank JAR 533	Hush-Hush/Going By The River	20
63	Stateside SS 205	Shame Shame Shame/Let's Get Together	22
64	Stateside SS 330	Shame Shame Shame/Let's Get Together (reissue)	12
66	Sue WI 4004	Odds And Ends/Going By The River Pt. II (B-side actually Pt. I)	40
67	HMV POP 1579	Two Ways To Skin A Cat/Got Nowhere To Go	40
64	Stateside SE 1016	BLUES OF JIMMY REED (EP)	30
64	Stateside SE 1026	I'M JIMMY REED (EP)	30
62	Stateside SL 10012	JIMMY REED AT CARNEGIE HALL (LP)	20
64	Stateside SL 10055	JUST JIMMY REED (LP)	30
64	Stateside SL 10069	SINGS THE BEST OF THE BLUES (LP)	20
64	Stateside SL 10086	PLAYS 12-STRING GUITAR BLUES (LP)	20
64	Stateside SL 10091	THE BOSS MAN OF THE BLUES (LP)	30
65	Fontana 688 514 ZL	THINGS AIN'T WHAT THEY USED TO BE (LP)	20
67	HMV CLP/CSD 3611	THE NEW JIMMY REED (LP)	20
68	Stateside S(S)L 10221	SOULIN' (LP)	35
69	Action ACLP 6011	DOWN IN VIRGINIA (LP)	60

JOE REED
| 71 | Dawn DNS 1012 | Ain't That A Shame/Follow Me .... | 6 |

LES REED
66	Fontana TF 765	Good King Went Ridiculous/Valley Of Kings	6
67	Deram DM 128	Imogene/Pay Off	10
69	Deram DM 244	Don't Linger With Your Finger On The Trigger/Big Drum	10

(see also Sounds of Les & Barry)

LOU REED
72	RCA RCA 2240	Walk And Talk It/Wild Child	15
72	RCA RCA 2303	Walk On The Wild Side/Perfect Day	6
73	RCA RCA 2318	Vicious/Satellite Of Love	7
73	MGM 2006 283	I'm Waiting For The Man/Run Run Run/Candy Says (with Velvet Underground)	10
74	RCA APBO 0221	Caroline Says (Parts 1 & 2)	7
72	RCA SF 8281	LOU REED (LP, laminated sleeve, orange label)	50
72	RCA LSP 4807	TRANSFORMER (LP, 1st pressing, laminated sleeve, orange labels)	100
73	RCA LSP 4807	TRANSFORMER (LP, 2nd pressing, non-laminated sleeve, orange labels)	40
73	RCA RS 1002	BERLIN (LP, orange labels with insert)	30
74	RCA APL1 0472	ROCK N ROLL ANIMAL (LP, gatefold)	20
74	RCA APL1 0611	SALLY CAN'T DANCE (LP, insert)	15
75	RCA CPL 2 1101	METAL MACHINE MUSIC (2-LP, U.S. import with U.K. sticker)	35
76	RCA RS 1035	CONEY ISLAND BABY (LP)	15
78	Arista SPART 1045	STREET HASSLE (LP, insert)	15
79	Arista SPART 1093	THE BELLS (LP)	15
80	Arista SPART 1131	GROWING UP IN PUBLIC (LP)	15
81	RCA Intl.INTS 5061	TRANSFORMER (LP, reissue, green labels)	20
82	RCA NL84780	THE BLUE MASK (LP)	15
89	Sire 925 829 1	NEW YORK (LP)	20
96	Warner Bros. 9362 46159-1	SET THE TWILIGHT REELING (LP, inner)	40

(see also Velvet Underground)

LULA REED
55	Parlophone CMSP 34	Troubles On Your Mind/Bump On A Log (export issue)	60
55	Parlophone DP 408	Troubles On Your Mind/Bump On A Log (78, export issue)	15

LULA REED & SYL JOHNSON
| 63 | Ember EMB EP 4535 | RHYTHM & BLUES BLUE BEAT STYLE (EP) .... | 70 |

LULA REED & FREDDIE KING
| 63 | Ember EMB 4536 | LULA REED AND FREDDIE KING (EP) .... | 60 |

(see also Freddie King)

OLIVER REED
61	Decca F 11390	The Wild One/Lonely For A Girl	15
62	Piccadilly 7N 35035	Sometimes/Ecstasy	15

(see also Joyce Blair)

TAWNY REED
65	Pye 7N 15935	Needle In A Haystack/I've Got A Feeling	50
66	Pye 7N 17078	You Can't Take It Away/My Heart Cries	30

Vivien REED

MINT VALUE £

VIVIEN REED
68	Direction 58-3574	I Wanna Be Free/Yours Until Tomorrow	8
71	Epic 7387	I Feel The Earth Move/Don't Close The Door On Me	6

WINSTON REED
72	Pama Supreme PS 365	Breakfast In Bed/RANNY WILLIAMS: Guitar Shuffle	7
73	Pama PM 863	Big Eight/RANNY WILLIAMS & CLASSICS: Big Eight - Version (some copies in p/s)	10

WINSTON REEDY
80	Music Scene MKS 6255	That Girl/GEORGE FAITH: Eternal Love (12")	18
82	SG SG 17	Daughter Of Zion/Zion Dub (12")	30
83	Carousel 12CAR 48	Dim The Light/Shower Of Rain (12")	20
84	Dep DEP 21	Ambition/Romantic Girl (12")	15

REEF
95	Sony Soho Square 480698 1	REPLENISH (LP, gatefold)	70
97	Sony 4869401	GLOW (LP)	25

VALA REEGAN & VALARONS
66	Atlantic 584 009	Fireman/Living In The Past	250
66	Atlantic 584 009	Fireman/Living In The Past (DJ copy)	300

REELS
79	Back Door 003	Prefab Hearts/Spot The Ridge	8

JUSTYN REES
70	Breakthrough HP 102	DOWN MY ROAD (LP)	35

TONY REES & COTTAGERS
75	Sonet SON 2059	Viva El Fulham/Rainbow	7

JAMES REESE AND THE PROGRESSIONS
15	Super Disco Edits SDE 14	Fool For Love No More/You Can Make It If You Try	8

DELLA REESE
57	London HL 7024	I Cried For You (Now It's Your Turn To Cry Over Me)/And That Reminds Me (export issue)	10
58	London HLJ 8687	You Gotta Love Everybody/I Wish	10
59	London HLJ 8814	Sermonette/Dreams End At Dawn	10
59	RCA RCA 1160	Not One Minute More/Soldier Won't You Marry Me	7
62	RCA 1306	Blow Out The Sun/I Love You So Much It Hurts	6
66	HMV POP 1553	It Was A Very Good Year/Solitary Woman	30
68	Stateside SS 2128	It Was A Very Good Year/I Had To Know My Way Around	20
72	Avco Embassy 6105 010	If It Feels Good, Do It/Good Lovin' (Makes It Right) (paper label)	10
74	People PEO 106	Who Is She And What Is She To You/If Loving You Is Wrong	6
59	London LTZ-J 15163	THE HISTORY OF THE BLUES (LP)	30
60	RCA RD 27167/SF 5057	DELLA (LP)	15
61	RCA RD 27208/SF 5091	DELLA DELLA CHA-CHA-CHA (LP)	18
62	RCA RD 27234/SF 5112	SPECIAL DELIVERY (LP)	20
63	RCA Victor RD/SF 7508	ON STAGE (LP)	15
68	Stateside SL 10261	I GOTTA BE ME...THIS TRIP OUT (LP)	35
74	People PLEO 7	LET ME IN YOUR LIFE (LP)	30

TONY REESE
59	London HLJ 8987	Just About This Time Tomorrow/Lesson In Love	20

DEL REEVES
65	United Artists UP 1092	Girl On The Billboard/Eyes Don't Come Crying To Me	7
66	United Artists UP 1122	Women Do Funny Things To Me/My Half Of Our Past	7
66	United Artists UP 1145	Gettin' Any Feed For Your Chickens/Plain As The Tears On My Face	7

EDDIE REEVES
62	London HL 9548	Cry Baby/Talk Talk	20

JIM REEVES

78s
59	RCA RCA 1144	Partners/I'm Beginning To Forget You	30
60	RCA RCA 1168	He'll Have To Go/In A Mansion Stands My Love	40

SINGLES
54	London HL 8014	Bimbo/Gipsy Heart	100
54	London HL 8030	Mexican Joe/I Could Cry (with Circle O Ranch Boys)	100
54	London HL 8055	Butterfly Love/It's Hard To Love Just One (with String Band)	100
54	London HL 8064	Echo Bonita/Then I'll Stop Loving You (with Louisiana Hayride Band)	100
54	London HL 8105	Padre Of Old San Antone/Mother Went A-Walkin'	60
55	London HL 8118	Penny Candy/I'll Follow You (with Louisiana Hayride Band)	60
55	London HLU 8185	Tahiti/Give Me One More Kiss	60
55	London HL 8159	Drinking Tequila/Red-Eyed And Rowdy	100

(The 45s listed above were Issued with gold label print on black labels.)

56	London HLU 8351	The Wilder Your Heart Beats, The Sweeter You Love/ Where Does A Broken Heart Go	50
57	RCA RCA 1005	Four Walls/I Know And You Know	10
58	RCA RCA 1074	Blue Boy/Theme Of Love	10
59	RCA RCA 1144	Partners/I'm Beginning To Forget You (triangular or round centre)	10

EPs
54	London RE-P 1015	THE BIMBO BOY (EP)	40
55	London RE-P 1033	THE BIMBO BOY VOL. 2 (EP)	40

REFARENDUM
69	RCA 1834	Love (Can Make You Happy)/Valley Of Love	8
70	RCA 1973	Lost and Found/Please Help Somebody	20

REFLECTION
68	Reflection RS 6001	Brave New Day/Lord I Believe (p/s)	60
68	Reflection RL 3015	THE PRESENT TENSE: SONGS OF SYDNEY CARTER (LP)	18

(see also Sounds Of Salvation)

REFLECTIONS A.O.B.

MINT VALUE £

REFLECTIONS A.O.B.
86	Keep KEEP 1 12	ONLY IN MY DREAMS EP (12")	40

REFLECTIONS (U.K.)
74	Purple PUR 124	Love And Affection/No More	10
75	Purple PUR 127	Moon Power/Little Star	10

REFLECTIONS (U.S.) (1)
64	Stateside SS 294	(Just Like) Romeo & Juliet/Can't You Tell By The Look In My Eyes	60
64	Stateside SS 294	(Just Like) Romeo & Juliet/Can't You Tell By The Look In My Eyes (DJ copy)	100
65	Stateside SS 406	Poor Man's Son/Comin' At You	30
74	Tamla Motown TMG 907	(Just Like) Romeo & Juliet/Can't You Tell By The Look In My Eyes (reissue)	15
77	ABC ABC 4181	Like Adam And Eve/AUGUST & DENEEN: We Go Together	15
65	Stateside SE 1034	POOR MAN'S SON (EP)	125

(see also The High and Mighty)

REFLECTIONS (U.S.) (2)
75	Capitol E-ST 11460	LOVE ON DELIVERY (LP)	15

REFLEX ACTION
80	Shock Rock SS 506	Spies/Recession	300

REFUGEE
74	Charisma CAS 1087	REFUGEE (LP, with lyric inner sleeve, large 'Mad Hatter' label)	20

(see also Nice, Yes)

REGAL DEWY
78	RCA XB 1032	Love Music/Where Would I Be Without Me	8

NORRIS REGAL
83	Sirion SRN 001	Struggle/Version (12")	40

REGAL ZONE
81	XS XS 1	FACTORY GIRL EP	10

JOAN REGAN
54	Decca F 10362	Wait For Me, Darling (with Johnston Brothers)/Two Kinds Of Tears (gold lettering)	20
54	Decca F 10362	Wait For Me, Darling (with Johnston Brothers)/Two Kinds Of Tears (silver lettering)	8
54	Decca F 10373	If I Give My Heart To You/Faded Flowers	8
54	Decca F 10397	This Ole House/Can This Be Love?	8
55	Decca F 10432	Prize Of Gold/When You're In Love	8
55	Decca F 10474	Open Up Your Heart And Let The Love In (with Rusty Regan)/ If You Learn To Love Each Other	8
55	Decca F 10505	Danger! Heartbreak Ahead/Don't Be Afraid Of Love	8
55	Decca F 10521	Just Say You Love Her/Nobody Danced With Me	8
55	Decca F 10598	The Shepherd Boy/The Rose And The Flame	8
56	Decca F 10659	Love And Marriage/Cross Of Gold (Croce Di Oro)	8
56	Decca F 10757	Sweet Heartaches/Second Fiddle (with Ted Heath)	7
57	Decca F 10871	Nearer To Me/Cross My Ever-Loving Heart	6
58	HMV POP 555	Love Like Ours/Take Me In Your Arms	6
60	Pye 7N 15310	One Of The Lucky Ones/My Thanks to You	15
66	CBS 202100	Don't Talk To Me About Love/I'm No Toy	20
66	CBS 202100	Don't Talk To Me About Love/I'm No Toy (DJ copy)	30
67	CBS 2657	No-One Beside Me/A Love So Fine	20
54	Decca LF 1182	THE GIRL NEXT DOOR (10" LP)	40
56	Decca LK 4153	JUST JOAN (LP)	100

RUSS REGAN
59	Capitol CL 15084	Adults Only/Just The Two Of Us	10

TOMMY REGAN
64	Colpix PX 725	I'll Never Stop Loving You/This Time I'm Losing You (DJ Copy)	125
64	Colpix PX 725	I'll Never Stop Loving You/This Time I'm Losing You	100

(see also Marcels)

REGENTS (U.K.) (1)
63	Oriole CB 1912	Bye Bye Johnny/Come Along	40

(see also Buddy Britten)

REGENTS (U.K.) (2)
66	CBS 202247	Words/Worryin' Kind	45

REGENTS (U.K.) (3)
79	Rialto TREB 111	7 Teen (Uncensored Version)/Hole In The Heart (p/s)	6

REGENTS (U.S.)
61	Columbia DB 4666	Barbara Ann/I'm So Lonely	30
61	Columbia DB 4694	Runaround/Laura My Darling	30

REGGAE BOYS
69	Amalgamated AMG 841	Me No Born Ya/The Wicked Must Survive	60
69	Amalgamated AMG 843	The Reggae Train/Dolly House On Fire	60
69	Gas GAS 135	Ba Ba/GLEN ADAMS: Power Cut	70
69	Unity UN 530	What You Gonna Do/HEDLEY BENNETT: Hot Coffee	110
70	Bullet BU 431	Pupa Live On Eye Top/Give Me Faith	40
70	Gas GAS 122	Phrases/Give Me Faith	50
70	Pressure Beat PR 5503	Walk By Day, Fly By Night/JOE GIBBS & DESTROYERS: Unknown Tongue	75

(see also Glen Adams, Alva Lewis, Upsetters)

REGGAE GEORGE
83	Greensleeves GRED 114	You'll Never Know/We Still Survive (12")	15

REGGAE GIRLS
69	Nu Beat NB024	Rescue Me/SOULMATES: Unity Is Strength	100

REGGAE REGULAR
77	Greensleeves GRE 001	Where Is Jah?/Jah Is Here	8
78	Greensleeves GRE 004	The Black Star Liner/It's Coming	6
78	Greensleeves GRED 2	The Black Star Liner/Where Is Jah? (12")	12

REGGAE STRINGS

MINT VALUE £

84	Greensleeves GREL 64	GHETTO ROCK (LP)	30

REGGAE STRINGS
73	Trojan TRLS 54	REGGAE STRINGS (LP)	20

(see also Horace Faith)

ELIS REGINA
69	Philis BF 1812	Zazueiro/Corrioa De Jangada	50
69	Philips SBL 7905	ELIS REGINA IN LONDON (LP)	100

REGULARS
81	Soundoff SOFFLP 001	I & I (LP, with band name on gold sticker on front of sleeve)	30

LOU REICHNER BAND
80	ESR Records S/80/CUS 733	Photograph/I Sit And Stare/The End Of The World/Out On The Streets (also listed as ESR 4, 300 only, with insert)	50
80	ESR Records S/80/CUS 733	Photograph/I Sit And Stare/The End Of The World/Out On The Streets (also listed as ESR 4, 300 only, without insert)	20

AL REID
69	Blue Cat BS 161	Vietcong/MAX ROMEO: Me Want Man	60
69	Blue Cat BS 163	Darling/MAX ROMEO: It's Not The Way	120

ALTYMAN REID
72	Green Door GD 4026	A Sugar/A Sugar Part Two (with Roy Shirley)	7

(see also Roy Shirley)

CARLTON REID
66	Ska Beat JB 254	Funny/Turn On The Lights	25
69	Blue Cat BS 162	Leave Me To Cry/Warning	125

DENNIS REID
77	Greensleeves GRE 6	Land Of The Rising Sun/DENNIS REID & REVOLUTIONARIES: Rising Sun Version	12
79	Discotheque PFL 2102	Living In The Slum/Prophet Shall Be Born (12")	60

DUKE REID (& HIS GROUP)
60	Blue Beat BB 24	Duke's Cookies (with His Group)/JIVING JUNIORS: I Wanna Love	25
62	Blue Beat BB 119	Twelve Minutes To Go (actually by Don Drummond)/ HORTENSE ELLIS: Midnight Train	30
63	Duke DK 1002	Pink Lane Shuffle (with His Group)/LAUREL AITKEN: Low Down Dirty Girl	20
67	Master's Time MT 003	Religious Service At Bond Street Gospel Hall/Religious Service At Bond Street Gospel Hall (Continued)	15
67	Trojan TR 001	Judge Sympathy (actually by Freedom Singers & Duke Reid All Stars)/ROLAND ALPHONSO: Never To Be Mine	50
60s	Doctor Bird DB 1028	True Confessions (actually by the Silvertones)/TOMMY McCCOOK : More Love	60
72	Duke Reid DR 2522	Hurt Parts 1 & 2 (actually by Eagles [Jamaica])	20
69	Trojan TTL 8	GOLDEN HITS (LP)	35

(see also Chuck & Darby, Derrick Morris, Stranger)

LEYROY REID
68	Blue Cat BS 125	The Fiddler/LOVELETTES: Shook	150
68	Blue Cat BS 127	Great Surprise/TEN(N)ORS: Khaki	65

(see also Nehemiah Reed)

MARC REID
66	CBS 202244	For No One/Lonely City Blues	15
67	CBS 202581	Magic Book/My World Turns Around	18
67	CBS 2950	We Should Live Together/Sale By Auction	15

NEHEMIAH REID('S ALL STARS)
68	Island WI 3102	Family War/Give Me That Love	40
70	Hot Shot HS 03	Hot Pepper/Seawave (as Nehemiah Reid's All Stars)	80
70	Torpedo TOR 23	Mafia/H.E.L.L. 5 (as Nehemiah Reid's All Stars)	150

(see also Leyroy Reid, Cynthia Richards)

P. REID
65	Ska Beat JB 197	Redeemed/Goodbye World	18

SANDRA REID
83	Sir George SG 004	Don't Tell Me Tell Her/Kaleidoscope (12")	75
83	Sir George SG 004	Don't Tell Me Tell Her/Kaleidoscope	25
83	Sir George SGLP 001	IF DREAMS WERE REAL (LP)	20
84	Sir George SGLP 004	FEEL SO GOOD (LP)	25

TERRY REID (& JAYWALKERS)
67	Columbia DB 8166	The Hand Don't Fit The Glove/This Time (as Terry Reid & Jaywalkers)	12
68	Columbia DB 8409	Better By Far/Fires Alive	20
69	Columbia PSRS 323	Superlungs (promo only, as "Terry Reid Is Superlungs")	25
69	Columbia SCX 6370	TERRY REID (LP, laminated front, flipbacks)	50
69	M. For Pleasure MFP 5220	THE MOST OF TERRY REID (LP, reissue of Terry Reid)	15
73	Atlantic K 40340	RIVER (LP, gatefold sleeve)	50
76	ABC ABCL 5162	SEED OF MEMORY (LP)	50
79	Capitol E-ST 11857	ROGUE WAVES (LP)	15
91	WEA 9031 74905 1	THE DRIVER (LP)	25

(see also Peter Jay & Jaywalkers)

REIGN
70	Regal Zonophone RZ 3028	Line Of Least Resistance/Natural Lovin' Man	90

(see also Yardbirds, Keith Relf, Renaissance, Armageddon, Illusion)

TOMMY REILLY
60	Philips PB 1094	Theme From "The Sundowners"/Down Under	7
63	Philips PB 1248	So Little Time/Moon Fire	6

REINCARNATE
82	Zipp REIN 001	Take It Or Leave It/Metal In Disguise	70

REINDEER SECTION
01	Bright Star BSR 14V	Y'ALL GET SCARED NOW, YA HEAR! (LP)	30
02	Bright Star BSR 19V	SON OF EVIL REINDEER (LP)	30

(see also Arab Strap, Belle & Sebastian, Snow Patrol, Mogwai, Teenage Fanclub, Idlewild)

REIVERS
MINT VALUE £

59	Top Rank JAR 244	Wee Magic Stane/The Wreck Of The John B	6
60	Top Rank JAR 283	Down In The Mines (Dark As Dungeon)/Govan Is A Busy Place	6

LOU REIZNER
69	Phillips	On Days Like This/Get A Bloomin' Move On	15

REJECTS
85	FM VHF 7	Back To The Start/Leave It (FM label house sleeve)	10
84	Heavy Metal HMR 22	QUIET STORM (LP)	15

(see also Cockney Rejects)

REJOICE!
69	Stateside S(S)L 5009	REJOICE! (LP)	20

RELATIVES
80	Smile SR 018	As A Child/Say Goodbye To Your Body	20

JANE RELF
71	Decca F 13231	Without A Song From You/Make My Time Pass By	30
70s	Findus SD/DS/7001	Gone Fishing/Gordon Jackson - Hints From The Findus Kitchen (p/s)	10

(see also Renaissance, Gordon Jackson)

KEITH RELF
66	Columbia DB 7920	Mr. Zero/Knowing	70
66	Columbia DB 8084	Shapes In My Mind/Blue Sands	100

(see also Yardbirds, Jim McCarty, Renaissance, Reign, Together, Armageddon)

RELOAD
92	Evolution EVO 01	RELOAD EP (12", plain sleeve)	20
92	Evolution EVO 02	AUTO RELOAD EP (12", with E 621)	35
92	Evolution EVO 03	RELOAD EP (12", 1-side credited to E 621)	40
93	Infonet INF 13	AUTO RELOAD EP VOLUME 2 (12", p/s)	10
93	Infonet INF 04LP	A COLLECTION OF SHORT STORIES (2-LP, with colour booklet)	50
93	Infonet INF 04LP	A COLLECTION OF SHORT STORIES (2-LP)	40

(see also Global Communications, Link, Mystic Institute)

RELUCTANT STEREOTYPES
79	Oval 1013	LULL EP (p/s)	7

R.E.M.
SINGLES
83	I.R.S. PFSX 1026	Talk About The Passion/Shaking Through/Carnival Of Sorts (Box Cars)/1,000,000 (12", p/s)	15
84	I.R.S. IRS 105	So. Central Rain (I'm Sorry)/King Of The Road (p/s)	10
84	I.R.S. IRSX 105	So. Central Rain (I'm Sorry)/Voice Of Harold/Pale Blue Eyes (12", p/s)	15
84	I.R.S. IRS 107	(Don't Go Back To) Rockville/Wolves (Lower) (p/s)	8
84	I.R.S. IRSX 107	(Don't Go Back To) Rockville/Wolves/9 - 9 (Live Version)/Gardening At Night (live) (12", p/s)	15
85	I.R.S. IRM 102	Can't Get There From Here/Bandwagon (p/s)	8
85	I.R.S. IRT 102	Can't Get There From Here (sleeve states 'Extended Mix', label states 'LP Version', but actually 3.39 edit)/Bandwagon/Burning Hell (12", p/s, with printed banner crediting unissued tracks)	10
85	I.R.S. IRM 105	Wendell Gee/Crazy (p/s)	6
85	I.R.S. IRMD 105	Wendell Gee/Crazy//Ages Of You/Burning Down (double pack)	10
85	I.R.S. IRT 105	Wendell Gee/Crazy/Driver 8 (live) (12", p/s)	10
86	I.R.S. IRMT 128	Superman/White Tornado/Femme Fatale (12", p/s)	12
86	I.R.S. DIRM 128	Superman/White Tornado/Femme Fatale (CD, unissued)	0
87	I.R.S. IRM 145	It's The End Of The World As We Know It (And I Feel Fine) (2.59 edit)/ This One Goes Out (live) (p/s, gold or metallic blue label)	8
87	I.R.S. IRM 146	The One I Love/Last Date (bronze label, glossy p/s; silver label, matt p/s)	8
88	I.R.S. IRM161	Finest Worksong/Time After Time Etc live (p/s)	8
88	I.R.S. DIRM 161	Finest Worksong (LP Version)/Time After Time, Etc. (live)/ It's The End Of The World As We Know It (And I Feel Fine) (CD, numbered stencilled 7" box, 5,000 only)	15
88	I.R.S. IRMT161	Finest Worksong Lengthy Club Mix/Other Mix/Time After Time Etc medley (12", p/s)	10
92	I.R.S. DIRM 180	It's The End Of The World As We Know It (And I Feel Fine)/Radio Free Europe (Hib-Tone Version) (gold or silver labels, p/s, with Album version of 'Radio Free Europe')	8

SINGLES : WARNER BROS SINGLES
89	Warner Bros W 2833W	Stand/Pop Song '89 (Acoustic) (stencil die-cut p/s)	10
89	Warner Bros W 2960B	Orange Crush/Ghost Riders ('The Green Package' box set with poster)	12
95	Warner Bros W0281X	Crush With Eyeliner (p/s, orange vinyl + calendar)	8
95	Warner Bros W0308X	Tongue/Instrumental (numbered tour booklet p/s)	6
95	Warner Bros W0290X	Strange Currencies/Strange Currencies Instrumental (p/s, Dayglo yellow/green vinyl + pin badge)	6
03	Warner Bros. W 624	Bad Day/Favourite Writer (p/s)	7
04	Warner Bros. W 654	Leaving New York/(Don't Go Back) To Rockville (live) (picture disc)	7
05	Warner Bros. W665	Electron Blue/What's The Frequency, Kenneth? (live) (limited edition sparkling blue vinyl, p/s)	7
08	Warner Bros. W807	Man Sized Wreath/Living Well Jesus Dog (clear vinyl, PVC stickered sleeve)	10

ALBUMS
83	IRS SP70604	MURMUR (LP, 1st pressing, with 'Original Sound recording made by IRS Inc')	30
84	IRS IRSA 7045	RECKONING (LP)	20
85	IRS MIRF 1003	FABLES OF THE RECONSTRUCTION/RECONSTRUCTION OF THE FABLES (LP)	20
86	IRS ILP 4653811	LIFE'S RICH PAGEANT (LP)	20
87	IRS SP70054	DEAD LETTER OFFICE (LP)	15
90	IRS 46588-2	THE COLLECTION (5-CD box set)	40
91	Warner Bros. WX404	OUT OF TIME (LP, with free 7")	40
91	Warner Bros. WX404	OUT OF TIME (LP, inner)	30
92	Warner Bros. 9362-45055-1 WX488	AUTOMATIC FOR THE PEOPLE (LP, 1st pressing with WMME in run out groove, inner)	60

REMARC

MINT VALUE £

Year	Label/Cat#	Title	Value
92	Warner Bros. 9362-45055-1 WX488	AUTOMATIC FOR THE PEOPLE (LP, 2nd pressing without WMME and B922353 in run out groove, inner)	40
94	Warner Bros. 9362-45740-1	MONSTER (LP)	80
96	Warner Bros. 9362-463210-1	NEW ADVENTURES IN HI-FI (2-LP, gatefold)	150
98	Warner Bros. 9362-47112-1	UP (2-LP)	150
01	Warner Bros. 9362 479461	REVEAL (LP)	100
03	Warners 9362 48381-1	IN TIME: THE BEST OF REM 1988-2003 (2-LP)	150
04	Warner Bros. 9362 48894-1	AROUND THE SUN (2-LP)	150
11	Warner Bros. 9362-49626-9	COLLAPSE INTO NOW (LP)	75
18	Craft 00888072067721	BEST OF REM AT THE BBC (2-LP, gatefold)	25
19	Craft 00888072067721	BINGO HAND JOB LIVE 1991 (2-LP)	30

PROMOS

Year	Label/Cat#	Title	Value
83	I.R.S. PFP 1017	Radio Free Europe/There She Goes Again (p/s, large 'A' on label)	50
83	I.R.S. PFP 1026	Talk About The Passion/Talk About The Passion (plain sleeve, promo only)	10
88	I.R.S. WIRM(T) 161 DL	Finest Worksong (Lengthy Club Mix)/Finest Worksong (Other Mix)/Time After Time Etc. (12" in 'media' p/s)	15
92	I.R.S. CDREM 92	THE ALTERNATIVE RADIO SAMPLER (CD, 7-track promo, includes unreleased version of 'Gardening At Night')	50
03	Warners PR 04359	THE BEST OF REM - IN TIME 1980-2003 (promo box set containing 18 1-track CDs each housed in individual card sleeve in flip top box)	40

FLEXIDISCS : FLEXIDISCS & OTHER RELEASES

Year	Label/Cat#	Title	Value
85	Bucketfull Of Brains BOB 5	Tighten Up (hard vinyl test pressing, 50 only)	50
92	Lyntone BOB 32	Academy Fight Song (live)/COAL PORTERS: Watching Blue Grass Burn (p/s, free with Bucketfull Of Brains magazine, double issue 39/40)	10
92	Lyntone BOB 32	Academy Fight Song (live)/COAL PORTERS: Watching Blue Grass Burn (white label test pressing)	20

(see also Syd Straw)

REMARC

Year	Label/Cat#	Title	Value
93	Dollar DOL 001	HELP ME (12", as Remarc!)	70
94	Dollar DOL 002	RICKY (12" with Lewi Cifer)	50
94	Dollar DOL 003	RICKY REMIXES (12")	30

REMA-REMA

Year	Label/Cat#	Title	Value
80	4AD BAD 5	WHEEL IN THE ROSES: Feedback Song/Rema-Ream/Instrumental/Fond Affections (12" EP, original pressing with blue labels)	40
80	4AD BAD 5	WHEEL IN THE ROSES: Feedback Song/Rema-Ream/Instrumental/Fond Affections (12" EP)	25

(see also Adam & The Ants, Mass, Models, Wolfgang Press)

REMEMBER THIS

Year	Label/Cat#	Title	Value
75	Penny Farthing PEN 862	Rock' N' Roll Revival/Over And Over Again	6

REMO FOUR

Year	Label/Cat#	Title	Value
64	Piccadilly 7N 35175	I Wish I Could Shimmy Like My Sister Kate/Peter Gunn	25
64	Piccadilly 7N 35186	Sally Go Round The Roses/I Know A Girl	25
67	Fontana TF 787	Live Like A Lady/Sing Hallelujah	70

(see also Tommy Quickly, Johnny Sandon, Gregory Phillips, Ashton Gardner & Dyke, Mike Hurst, George Harrison)

RENAISSANCE (U.K.)

Year	Label/Cat#	Title	Value
70	Island WIP 6079	Island/The Sea	15
78	Sire SRE 1022	Northern Lights/Opening Out (picture disc, export issue)	15
79	Sire SIR 4019	Jekyll And Hyde/Forever Changing (withdrawn)	15
69	Island ILPS 9114	RENAISSANCE (LP, gatefold, pink label with white 'i' logo)	30
71	Island HELP 27	ILLUSION (LP, withdrawn, export only, black labeil with pink 'i' logo)	50

(see also Keith Relf, Jane Relf, Yardbirds, Rupert's People, Reign)

RENAISSANCE (U.S.)

Year	Label/Cat#	Title	Value
68	Polydor BM 56736	Mary Jane (Get Off The Devil's Merry-Go-Round)/Daytime Lovers	35

RENAULTS

Year	Label/Cat#	Title	Value
60	Warner Bros WB 11	Meloncolie/Stella	7

DIANE RENAY

Year	Label/Cat#	Title	Value
64	Stateside SS 270	Navy Blue/Unbelievable Guy	15
64	Stateside SS 290	Kiss Me Sailor/Soft Spoken Guy	15
64	MGM MGM 1262	Watch Out Sally/Billy Blue Eyes	25
65	MGM MGM 1274	Troublemaker/I Had A Dream	25

(see also Laura Greene)

JOHN RENBOURN

Year	Label/Cat#	Title	Value
65	Transatlantic TRA 135	JOHN RENBOURN (LP, 1st pressing, purple/white label with 'Transatlantic' on top of label)	70
66	Transatlantic TRA 135	JOHN RENBOURN (LP, 2nd pressing, purple/white label with 'Transatlantic' on centre of label)	50
66	Transatlantic TRA 149	ANOTHER MONDAY (LP, 1st pressing without title and catalogue number on spine)	40
67	Transatlantic TRA 149	ANOTHER MONDAY (LP, 2nd pressing with title and catalogue number on spine)	30
68	Transatlantic TRA 167	SIR JOHN ALOT OF MERRIE ENGLANDE'S MUSICK THYNGE AND YE GREENE KNIGHT (LP)	30
70	Transatlantic TRA 224	THE LADY AND THE UNICORN (LP)	25
72	Transatlantic TRA 135	JOHN RENBOURN (LP, reissue, 'World globe' label)	15
72	Transatlantic TRA 149	ANOTHER MONDAY (LP, reissue, 'World globe' label)	15
72	Transatlantic TRA 167	SIR JOHN ALOT OF MERRIE ENGLANDE'S MUSICK THYNGE AND YE GREENE KNIGHT (LP, reissue. 'World globe' label)	15
72	Transatlantic TRA 247	FARO ANNIE (LP)	30
76	Transatlantic TRA 336	THE HERMIT (LP)	15
73	Transatlantic TRASAM 28	SO CLEAR - THE JOHN RENBOURN SAMPLER VOL. 2 (LP)	15
77	KPM KPM 1203	THE GUITAR OF JOHN RENBOURN (LP, plain generic green KPM sleeve)	35

(see also Pentangle, Bert Jansch & John Renbourn, Steve Tilston, Dorris Henderson)

JOHN RENBOURN'S SHIP OF FOOLS

Year	Label/Cat#	Title	Value
88	Run River 009	SHIP OF FOOLS (LP)	20

Don RENDELL

MINT VALUE £

DON RENDELL
55	Tempo A 108	Muskrat Ramble/Thames Walk	30
55	Tempo A 110	You Stepped Out Of A Dream/Slow Boat To China (78, as Don Rendell Quartet)	10
55	Tempo A 112	Didn't We/Dance Of The Ooblies (78, as Don Rendell Sextet)	10
55	Tempo A 114	From This Moment On/Blow Mr. Dexter (78, as Don Rendell Quartet)	10
54	Vogue EPV 1009	MUSIC IN THE MAKING VOL 1. (EP)	25
54	Vogue EPV 1034	MUSIC IN THE MAKING VOL 2 (EP)	25
55	Tempo EXA 11	DON RENDELL QUARTET (EP)	100
55	Tempo EXA 12	DON RENDELL SEXTET (EP)	100
55	Tempo EXA 16	DON RENDELL SEXTET/DAMIAN ROBINSON TRIO (EP, 2 tracks each)	50
55	Tempo EXA 20	DON RENDELL QUINTET (EP)	60
57	Pye Jazz NJE 1044	DOGGIN AROUND - DON RENDELL JAZZ SIX (EP)	50
58	Decca DFE 6501	PACKET OF BLUES (EP, as Don Rendell Jazz Six)	30
59	Decca DFE 6587	THE JAZZ COMMITTEE (EP, featuring Don Rendell)	100
54	Decca LK 4087	MODERN JAZZ AT THE FESTIVAL HALL (LP, also features Ken Moule Seven and Tony Crombie Orchestra)	70
54	Vogue LDE 050	MUSIC IN THE MAKING (10" LP)	100
55	Vogue LDE 144	DON RENDELL MEETS BOBBY JASPAR (10" LP)	125
55	Tempo LAP 1	MEET DON RENDELL (10" LP)	1000
56	Vogue LAE 12028	KENTON'S SIDEMEN (LP, featuring Don Rendell and Martial Solal)	150
56	Nixa NJL 4	TENORAMA (LP)	300
57	Nixa Jazz Today NJL 7	DON RENDELL PRESENTS THE JAZZ SIX (LP)	200
58	Decca LK 4265	PLAYTIME (LP, as Don Rendell Jazz 6)	200
62	Jazzland JLP 51	ROARIN' (LP, as Don Rendell New Jazz Quintet [with Graham Bond])	250
72	Columbia SCX 6491	SPACEWALK (LP, as Don Rendell Quintet)	150
75	Spotlite SPJ 501	LIVE AT THE AVGARDE GALLERY (LP, with the Joe Palin Trio)	20
76	Spotlite SPJ 502	JUST MUSIC (LP, as Don Rendell 5)	20
80	Spotlite SPJ 6315	EARTH MUSIC (LP, as Don Rendell 9)	30
80	Spotlite SPJ 516	SET 2 (LP)	20

(see also Frank Horrox)

DON RENDELL & IAN CARR QUINTET
65	Columbia 33SX 1733	SHADES OF BLUE (LP)	1000
66	Columbia S(C)X 6064	DUSK FIRE (LP, first pressing with blue label)	800
68	Columbia S(C)X 6064	DUSK FIRE (LP, reissue, silver/black Columbia label with EMI box logo)	350
68	Columbia SX 6214	PHASE III (LP, Mono)	400
68	Columbia SCX 6214	PHASE III (LP, Stereo)	400
69	Columbia SX 6316	LIVE (LP, Mono)	300
69	Columbia SCX 6315	LIVE (LP, Stereo)	300
69	Columbia SCX 6368	CHANGE IS (LP)	400
10	Stamford STAMLP1006	LIVE AT THE UNION (2-LP)	20
18	Jazzman JMANLP 106	THE COMPLETE LANSDOWNE RECORDINGS 1965 - 1969 (5-LP box set)	200
19	Jazzman JMANLP 107X	SHADES OF BLUE (LP, reissue, inner)	20
19	Jazzman JMANLP 108X	DUSK FIRE (LP, reissue, inner)	20
19	Jazzman JMANLP 109X	PHASE III (LP, reissue, inner)	20
19	Jazzman JMANLP 110X	LIVE (LP, reissue, inner)	20
19	Jazzman JMANLP 111X	CHANGE IS (LP, reissue, inner)	20

(see also Neil Ardley, Nucleus)

DON RENDELL QUARTET/JOE HARRIOT QUARTET
57	MGM MGM-EP 615	JAZZ BRITANNIA (EP, 2 tracks each)	60

(see also Joe Harriott)

DON RENDES
76	Neville King NK 3	Beware/Dun Beware	10

RENDESVIEW
71	Philron SP0019	It Shouldn't Have Happened/I'll Give You Love	100

RENE & HIS ALLIGATORS
66	Decca F 22324	She Broke My Heart/I Can Wait	18

GOOGIE RENE COMBO
60	London HLY 9056	Forever/Ez-zee	20
66	Atlantic AT 4076	Smokey Joe's La La/Needing You	30
66	Atlantic 584 015	Chica-Boo/Mercy Mercy (Too Much For The Soul)	10

HENRI RENE
55	HMV 7M 308	Enchantment/Crystal Chandelier (with Hugo Winterhalter Orchestra)	7
59	London HLP 8960	La Shabla (The Shovel)/Destiny (with His Orchestra & Chorus)	7

RENE & RENE
65	HMV POP 1468	Chantilly Lace/I'm Not The Only One	10
67	Island WIP 6001	Loving You Could Hurt Me So Much/Little Diamonds	8

RENE & ANGELA
80	Capitol E-ST 12077	RENE & ANGELA (LP)	30
81	Capitol EMS 1118	WALL TO WALL (LP)	25

RENEGADE (1)
73	Parlophone R 5981	Loving And Forgiving/Never Let Me Go	20
74	Dawn DNS 1067	A Little Rock 'N' Roll/My Revolution	25

RENEGADE (2)
80	White Witch WIT 1	LONELY ROAD (12" EP, with insert)	100

RENEGADES
66	Polydor BM 56508	Cadillac/Every Minute Of The Day	30
66	President PT 106	Thirteen Women/Walking Down The Street	200
67	Parlophone R 5592	Take A Message/Second Thoughts	25
68	Columbia DB 8383	No Man's Land/Sugar Loaf Mountain	25

RENIA

MINT VALUE £

RENIA
73 Transatlantic TRA 261 — FIRST OFFENDERS (LP) 30

DON RENNIE
56 Parlophone MSP 6218 — To Love, To Love Is Wonderful/One Girl - One Boy 7
56 Parlophone MSP 6237 — Who Are We?/Can You Find It In Your Heart? 7

DON RENO & RED SMILEY
58 Parlophone GEP 8777 — COUNTRY AND WESTERN (EP) 30

GERRY RENO
62 Decca F 11477 — Don't Ever Change/What Would You Do 8
62 Decca F 11516 — Who's Fooling You/Three Deadly Sins 8
63 Decca F 11774 — It Only Happens In The Movies/One Lonely Guy 15

GINETTE RENO
69 Decca F 22972 — Don't Let Me Be Misunderstood/Everything That I Am 8

PAUL RENO
63 Oriole CB 1872 — Lonely Little Girl/Angela 10

CHRIS RENSHAW & THE KEEPERS
73 Pye 7N 45185 — Banksie (A Tribute To Gordon Banks)/National (Health) Anthem (p/s) 6

ROBERT RENTAL
78 Regular ER 102 — Paralysis/A.C.C. (photocopied black & white foldover p/s) 30
78 Company/Regular RECO 2 — Paralysis/A.C.C. (reissue, card gatefold p/s) 20
80 Mute MUTE 010 — On Location/Double Heart (p/s) 15
79 Industrial IR 0007 — THE BRIDGE (LP, with Thomas Leer) 40
80 Rough Trade ROUGH 17 — ROBERT RENTAL AND THE NORMAL (LP, 1-sided, plain red sleeve) 25
(see also Thomas Leer)

REPARATA & DELRONS
65 Stateside SS 382 — Whenever A Teenager Cries/He's My Guy 30
65 Stateside SS 414 — Tommy/Momma Don't Allow 25
68 Bell BLL 1002 — Captain Of Your Ship/Toom Toom (Is A Little Boy) 15
68 RCA Victor RCA 1691 — I Can Hear The Rain/Always Waitin' 30
68 Bell BLL 1014 — Saturday Night Didn't Happen/Panic 50
68 Bell BLL 1014 — Saturday Night Didn't Happen/Panic (DJ copy) 60
68 Bell BLL 1021 — Weather Forecast/You Can't Change A Young Boy's Mind 20
76 Polydor 2058 688 — Jesabee Lancer (The Belly Dancer)/We Need You 7
76 Dart ART 2057 — Your Life Is Gone/Octopus Garden (credited to Reparata) 10
72 Avco 6467 250 — ROCK AND ROLL REVOLUTION (LP) 40

REPLACEMENTS
86 Sire W 8727 — Swingin' Party/Left Of The Dial 8
86 Sire W 8679 — Kiss Me On The Bus/Little Mascara (p/s) 8
87 Sire W 8297 — Alex Chilton/Election day (p/s) 20
87 Sire W8297 — THE REPLACEMENTS EP 15
84 Zippo ZONG 002 — LET IT BE (LP) 30
85 Sire 925330 — TIM (LP) 15
87 Sire 925557 — PLEASED TO MEET ME (LP) 20
89 What Goes On GOES ON 17 — SORRY MA, FORGOT TO TAKE OUT THE TRASH (LP, reissue) 30
88 What Goes On GOES ON 21 — HOOTENANNY (LP, reissue) 25
89 Sire 925831 — DON'T TELL A SOUL (LP) 15
89 What Goes On ON 20 — STINK (mini-LP) 18

REPORTERS (1)
81 GW1 — Scoop/NBZ (p/s) 40

REPORTERS (2)
81 Cloggtown CLOGGTOWN 1 — Office Staff/Cinema/Lady Luck (p/s) 20

REPS
80 Kingsway KMS 910 — Rebel/No More Yesterdays (p/s) 8

REPTILE RANCH
87 Z Block Z-1 — Don't Give The Lifeguard A Second Chance: WTB/Lifeguard (fold over p/s, 1000 only) 10

REPULSION
89 Necrosis NECRO 0002 — HORRIFIED (LP) 30

REQUIEM
80 Sacrificial SAC 001 — Angel Of Sin/Sacrificial Wanderer (no p/s) 80

RESCUE COMPANY NO 1
71 RAK 122 — Life's Too Short/Then I Think About You 10
72 Jam JAM 14 — I Want To Save You/Amanda 15
72 Jam JAM 27 — I Stand Alone/You Shouldn't Have Been So Nice 15
73 Jam JAM 45 — It's Only Words/Look Out 25
74 DJM DJS 309 — Esmerelda/As Long As You Want Me 10

RESERVE
88 Sha La La Ba Ba Ba-Ba Ba 006 — Wherever You Go/SIDDELEYS: The Sun Slid Down/Behind The Tower (flexi, foldover p/s) 10

RESIDENTS
80 Pre PRE 009 — THE COMMERCIAL SINGLE (p/s) 6
79 Virgin VR 3 — NIBBLES (LP, stickered sleeve, 5,000 only) 15
80 Pre PRE X2 — THE COMMERCIAL ALBUM (LP, 5,000 only, with incorrect song order) 15

RESISTANCE
81 Fontana KIT 1 — Survival Kit/Big Flame (p/s) 6

RESISTANCE 77
82 Riot City RIOT 18 — NOWHERE TO PLAY (EP) 18
84 Rot ASS 6 — Vive The Resistance 20
84 Rot ASS 14 — THOROUGHBRED MEN (LP) 80

RESISTORS
80 Break SMASH 1 — For Jeanie/Takeaway Love/End Of The Line (p/s) 35

REST
83	DT 027	That's It/Steal My Love	25

REST
79	Shooting Star SSR 1	Carnival/Small Town Rockers	7
80	Shooting Star SSR 2	Raga/My House (screen printed p/s)	10

RESTFULL ONES
70	Grade One GR 1	Turn To The Sun/She's Mine	50

JOHNNY RESTIVO
59	RCA RCA 1143	The Shape I'm In/Ya Ya (with triangular centre)	30
59	RCA RCA 1143	The Shape I'm In/Ya Ya (later round centre pressing)	15
59	RCA RCA 1159	I Like Girls/Dear Someone	15
59	RCA RCA 1159	I Like Girls/Dear Someone (78)	20
60	Ember EMB S 135	Look Here Now/Sweet Sweet Lovin'	15

RESTRICTED HOURS
79	Stevenage (no cat. no.)	Getting Things Done/Still Living Out The Car Crash/SYNDICATE: One Way Or Another/I Want To Be Somebody (white label, foldover p/s)	12

(see also Astronauts)

RETREADS
81	Eddi Osmo EO 101	Would You Listen Girl/One After 909/You Said You Knew (p/s, with mini-poster insert)	60

RETREAT FROM MOSCOW
80	Wicker Monkey WM 001/ MHMS 169/EJSP 9328	To The Night/Perception (p/s)	15

REUBEN
04	Extra Mile XMR001LP	RACECAR IS RACECAR BACKWARDS (LP)	150
05	Extra Mile XMR003LP	VERY FAST VERY DANGEROUS (LP)	50

REVELATION (JAMAICA)
70	Trojan TR 7727	Suffering/MEGATONS: Crazy Elephant	12

REVELATION (1)
78	Write Sounds WTS 1003	With You Boy/Dub You	10
78	Write Sounds WTS 1003	Jah Feelings/With You Boy (12")	20
78	Write Sounds WTS 1004	Jah Feelings/Dub Feelings	22
81	Kingdom KV 8013	Tonight/Fussin' And Fightin'	6
81	Kingdom KV 8013-12	Tonight/Fussin' And Fightin' (12")	10
78	Burning Sounds BS 1030	BOOK OF REVELATION (LP)	30
79	Burning Vibrations BV 1007	VARIATION ON A THEME (LP)	20

REVELATION (2)
80	Handshake HANDS 1	Feel It/When I Fall In Love	8

REVELATION (3)
91	Rise Above RISE 6	SALVATIONS ANSWER (LP, stickered sleeve)	30

REVELLERS
66	Columbia DB 8093	Believe, Believe/Love Is The Greatest Thing	7
67	Spin SP2002	Yasmin/When I Needed A Neighbour	12
67	Spin LP 1703	REVELLERS AGAIN (LP)	35

REVELLS
71	CBS 7050	Mind Party/Indian Ropeman	50

DIGGER REVELL'S DENVERMEN
63	Decca F 11657	Surfside/Lisa Marie	20

REVELS
59	Top Rank JAR 235	Midnight Stroll/Talking To My Heart	50

REVENGE (1)
78	Loony LOO 2	We're Not Gonna Take It/Pornography (glossy p/s, counterfeits have matt sleeve, and lack ridge around label)	200
78	Loony LOO 1	Our Generation/I Love Her Way (counterfeits lack ridge around label)	450

REVENGE (2)
80	Blood S/80/CUS 164	Don't Tell Me Lies/Gimme The Good Times	10

REVENGE (3)
89	Factyory FAC 247/7	7 Reasons/Jesus I Love You (white labels only)	30
90	Factory FACT 230	ONE TRUE PASSION (LP)	15

(see also Joy Division, New Order, Monaco)

REVERB
94	Ochre OCH 001	Pedal/Swift (Foldover p/s in poly bag)	10

PAUL REVERE & THE RAIDERS (FEATURING MARK LINDSAY)
61	Top Rank JAR 557	Like Long Hair/Sharon	20
65	Sue WI 344	Like Long Hair/Sharon (reissue)	30
65	CBS 202003	Steppin' Out/Blue Fox	10
66	CBS 202027	Just Like Me/B F D R F Blues	20
66	CBS 202205	Kicks/Shake It Up	15
66	CBS 202253	Hungry/There She Goes	10
66	CBS 202411	The Great Airplane Strike/In My Community	12
67	CBS 202502	Good Thing/Undecided Man	12
67	CBS 202610	Ups And Downs/Leslie	10
67	CBS 2737	Him Or Me - What's It Gonna Be?/The Legend Of Paul Revere	10
67	CBS 2919	I Had A Dream/Upon Your Leaving	6
67	CBS 3186	Mo'reen/Oh! To Be A Man	10
68	CBS 3310	Too Much Talk/Happening '68 (featuring Mark Lindsay)	20
68	CBS 3586	Don't Take It So Hard/Observation From Flight 285 (featuring Mark Lindsay)	8
68	CBS 3757	Cinderella Sunshine/Theme From It's Happening (featuring Mark Lindsay)	6
69	CBS 4025	Mr. Sun, Mr. Moon/With You (featuring Mark Lindsay)	6
69	CBS 4260	Let Me/I Don't Know (featuring Mark Lindsay)	7
69	CBS 4504	We Gotta All Get Up Together/Frankfurt Side Street (featuring Mark Lindsay)	6
76	Jay Boy BOY 108	Ain't Nothin' Wrong/ou're Really Sayin' Something	7
66	CBS (S)BPG 62406	JUST LIKE US (LP)	25

REVEREND W AWDRY

			MINT VALUE £
66	CBS (S)BPG 62797	MIDNIGHT RIDE (LP)	25
67	CBS (S)BPG 62963	GOOD THING (LP)	20
68	CBS (S)BPG 63095	REVOLUTION (LP)	20
69	CBS 63265	GOIN' TO MEMPHIS (LP, mono/stereo)	20
69	CBS 63649	HARD 'N' HEAVY (LP)	20

(see also Mark Lindsay, Raiders)

REVEREND W AWDRY
57	Chiltern C1000	Edwards Day Out/Edward And John (not in printed picture company sleeve)	10
67	Chiltern C1000	Edwards Day Out/Edward And John (in printed picture company sleeve)	20

REVIEW
80s	All The Madmen REV 1	England's Glory (stapled gatefold p/s with lyric insert)	10

REVILLOS
82	Superville SV 1001	She's Fallen In Love With A Monster Man/Mind Bending Cutie Doll (two different p/s, same front but different layout on rear)	10
82	Superville SV 2001	Bongo Brain/Hip City - You Were Meant For Me (p/s)	6
82	Aura AUS 135	Tell Him/Graveyard Groove (p/s)	6
96	Damaged Goods DAMGOOD 93	Jack The Ripper/A Yeah Yeah Yeah Yeah/Meet The Revillos (pink vinyl, p/s)	7
80	Snatzo/Dindisc DID X 3	REV UP (LP, green or pink titles)	25
82	Superville SV 4001	ATTACK! (LP, withdrawn)	40

(see also Rezillos)

REVOLUTION
66	Piccadilly 7N 35289	Hallelujah/Shades Of Blue	65

(see also Hellions, Luther Grosvenor, Traffic, Dave Mason & Cass Elliot, Spirit)

(THE) REVOLUTIONARIES
77	Sky Note SKY DD 002	Afro Rock Part 1/Afro Rock Part 2 (12")	85
77	Sky Note SKY 1002	El Bamba/Bamba In Dub	15
78	Island IPR 2024	Headache/Bellyache/Toothache/Headache (12")	30
78	Ballistic FORCE 2003	FATAL DUB (12" EP)	20
76	Trenchtown TRELP 001	REVOLUTIONARY DUB (LP, with the We The People Band)	60
78	Cha Cha CHALP 002	REACTION IN DUB (LP)	40
78	Cha Cha CHALP 005	JONKANOO DUB (LP)	30
79	Burning Vibrations BV 1002	DUTCH MAN DUB (LP)	30
79	Burning Vibrations BV 1004	GREEN BAY DUB (LP)	50
79	Burning Vibrations BV 1010	BURNING DUB (LP)	35
79	Trojan TRLS 169	OUTLAW DUB (LP)	25
82	Cha Cha CHALP 014	REVIVAL (LP)	40
07	Pressure Sounds PSLP 55	DRUM SOUND: MORE GEMS FROM THE CHANNEL ONE DUB ROOM 1974-1980 (2-LP)	20

REVOLUTIONARY ARMY OF INFANT JESUS
87	Probe Plus PROBE 12	THE GIFT OF TEARS (LP)	100

REVOLUTIONARY BLUES BAND
70	MCA MUP(S) 402	REVOLUTIONARY BLUES BAND (LP)	20

REVOLUTIONARY CORPS OF TEENAGE JESUS VS SUICIDE
96	Creeping Bent BENT 005	FRANKIE TEARDROP EP (Frankie Teardrop [126 b.p.m.]/U.S.A. '95/Frankie Teardrop [114 b.p.m.]/Womb 17) (12", p/s, 1,000 only)	10

(see also Suicide, Future Pilot A.KA.)

REVOLVER (1)
69	Young BLood YB 1006	Frisco Annie/Imaginations	20

REVOLVER (2)
78	Rockburgh ROCS 203	Silently Screaming/On The Run (p/s)	15
79	Rox ROX 10	One And One Is Two/Nobody I Know	8

REVOLVING PAINT DREAM
84	Creation CRE 002	Flowers In The Sky/In The Afternoon (foldaround p/s in poly bag)	20

(see also Laughing Apple, Primal Scream)

REVULSION
85	Radical Change RC 7	Ever Get The Feeling Of Utter... (12")	20

REX (MORRIS) & MINORS
60	Triumph RGM 1023	Chicken Sax/Snake Eyes	50

ROBERTA REX
68	Fontana TF 967	Joey/I Can Feel It	6

REXY
80	Alien ALIEN 12	(Don't) Turn Me Away/Rexy's Russian Blues	40
81	Alien ALIEN 19	Running Out Of Time/Alien/Funky Butt (12", p/s)	60
81	Alien ALIEN 17	In The Force/Johnny B. Goode (p/s)	25
81	Alien BEALIEN2	3 TRACKS FROM THE NEW REXY LP (flexi)	10
81	Alien BEALIEN2	RUNNING OUT OF TIME (LP)	100
16	Lucky Number LUCKY090LP	RUNNING OUT OF TIME (LP, reissue)	35

ALVINO REY
61	London HLD 9431	Original Mama Blues/Steel Guitar Rag	10
62	London HA-D 2414	ALVINO REY'S GREATEST HITS (LP)	20

CHICO REY & JET BAND
70	Pye 7N 17899	Stiletto/Midnight In Mexico	40

LITTLE BOBBY REY & HIS BAND
60	Top Rank JAR 525	Rockin' "J" Bells/Dance Of The New Year	8

REYNARD
76	Pilgrim/Grapevine GRA 102	FRESH FROM THE EARTH (LP)	40

DEBBIE REYNOLDS
55	MGM SP 1127	Carolina In The Morning/Never Mind The Noise In The Market (B-side as Debbie Reynolds' Naturals)	10
56	MGM SP 1155	(Love Is) The Tender Trap/Canoodlin' Rag	8
58	MGM MGM-EP 670	DEBBIE REYNOLDS (EP)	15

Donn REYNOLDS

MINT VALUE £

59	MGM MGM-EP 694	DELIGHTFUL DEBBIE REYNOLDS (EP)	12
60	MGM MGM-EP 725	FROM DEBBIE WITH LOVE (EP)	12
59	London HA-D 2200	DEBBIE (LP, mono)	20
59	London SAH-D 6051	DEBBIE (LP, stereo)	25
60	London HA-D 2294	AM I THAT EASY TO FORGET? (LP, mono)	20
60	London SAH-D 6106	AM I THAT EASY TO FORGET? (LP, stereo)	25
61	London HA-D 2326	FINE AND DANDY (LP)	20
63	London HA-D 8075	GREAT FOLK HITS (LP, mono)	20
63	London HA-D/SH-D 8075	GREAT FOLK HITS (LP, stereo)	25

(see also Naturals [U.S.])

DONN REYNOLDS
58	MGM MGM 996	Blue Eyes Crying In The Rain/Bella Belinda	6
58	Pye 7N 15122	Swing Low Sweet Chariot/Ramona	6
59	Pye NEP 24098	THE DONN REYNOLDS SONGBAG (EP)	10

ELI REYNOLDS
70	Punch PH 37	Mr Car Man/Chiney Man	20

JODY REYNOLDS
58	London HL 8651	Endless Sleep/Tight Capris	25

L J REYNOLDS
82	Capitol 260	Special Effects/Key To The World	20

TIMMY REYNOLDS
62	Ember EMB S 133	Lullaby Of Love/JEFF MILLS: Daddy's Home	70

REZILLOS
77	Sensible FAB 1	I Can't Stand My Baby/I Wanna Be Your Man (p/s, 15,000, 5,000 numbered)	35
77	Sensible FAB 1	I Can't Stand My Baby/I Wanna Be Your Man (p/s, 15,000, 10,000 unnumbered)	15
77	Sensible FAB 2	Flying Saucer Attack/(My Baby Does) Good Sculptures (p/s, unissued)	0
77	Sire 6078 612	Flying Saucer Attack/(My Baby Does) Good Sculptures (p/s)	12
78	Sire 6198 215	Cold Wars/William Mysterious Overture (unissued, picture sleeve only)	150
78	Sire SIR 4001	Top Of The Pops/20,000 Rezillos Under The Sea (p/s)	8
78	Sire SIR 4008	Destination Venus/Mystery Action (p/s)	6
79	Sire SIR 4014	Cold Wars (live)/Flying Saucer Attack (live)/Twist & Shout (live) (p/s)	12
79	Sensible FAB 1 (Mark 2)	Can't Stand My Baby/I Wanna Be Your Man (reissue, new p/s, run out groove reads "Come Back John Lennon")	7
79	Sensible FAB 1 (Mark 2)	Can't Stand My Baby/I Wanna Be Your Man (reissue, p/s, mispressing, B-side plays "(My Baby Does) Good Sculptures (live)", run-off groove reads "De-sire-able product?", 4,000 only)	6
78	Sire K 56530	CAN'T STAND THE REZILLOS (LP, with inner sleeve & postcard insert)	30
78	Sire SRK 6069	MISSION ACCOMPLISHED ... BUT THE BEAT GOES ON (LP, inner)	20

(see also Revillos, Shake, William Mysterious)

RHABSTALLION
81	Rhab RHAB 001	Day To Day/Breadline (p/s, with badge)	30
81	Rhab RHAB 001	Day To Day/Breadline (p/s)	20

RH FACTOR
03	Verve VERR01292-1	Poetry (DJ Spinna Remix)/(Album Version)/Forget Regret (Quantic Remix)/(Album Version) (12")	20
03	Verve 065 192-1	HARD GROOVE (2-LP)	150

(see also Roy Hargrove)

RHINOCEROS
69	Elektra EKSN 45051	Apricot Brandy/I Don't Want To Discuss It	10
69	Elektra EKSN 45058	I Will Serenade You/Belbuekul	7
70	Elektra EKSN 45080	Back Door/In A Little Room	6
70	Elektra 2101 009	Old Age/Let's Party	6
69	Elektra EKL 4030	RHINOCEROS (LP, orange label, also stereo EKS 74030)	20
69	Elektra EKL 4056	SATIN CHICKENS (LP, also stereo EKS 74056)	20
70	Elektra 2469 006	BETTER TIMES ARE COMING (LP, gatefold sleeve)	15

RHODA WITH THE SPECIAL A.K.A.
82	2-Tone CHS TT 18	The Boiler/Theme From The Boiler (paper labels)	8
82	2-Tone CHS TT 1218	The Boiler/Theme From The Boiler (12", p/s existence unconfirmed)	20

(see also Special A.K.A.)

JAN RHODE & HIS COOL CATS
60	Qualiton Offbeat PSP 7128	Come Back Baby/So Shy	8

PAT RHODEN
65	Ska Beat JB 195	Jezebel/You Can Hold My Hand	20
66	Blue Beat BB 360	Send Your Love/Make Believe	15
68	Trojan TR 606	Woman Is Greedy/Endlessly	10
70	Pama PM 811	Maybe The Next Time/Got To See You	8
70	Pama Supreme PS 298	Do What You Gotta Do/Crying Won't Help You	8
70	Mary Lyn ML 101	Time Is Tight/MILTON & DENZIL: I Like It Like That	20
73	Pama Supreme PS 378	Out Of Time/Put A Little Rain Into My Life	8

(see also Pat Riden, Pat & Marie, Denzil & Pat)

EMITT RHODES
71	Probe SPBA 6256	EMITT RHODES (LP, gatefold sleeve)	15
71	A&M AMLS 64254	AMERICAN DREAM (LP)	15

TODD RHODES ORCHESTRA
55	Parlophone MSP 6171	Specks/Silver Sunset	30

RHODESIANS
80	Period PER 001	Clock!!!/Postmortem (p/s)	15

RHUBARB RHUBARB
68	President PT 229	Rainmaker/Moneylender	160

GRUFF RHYS
06	Rough Trade RTRADS 375	Candylion/Colossal Smile (p/s, numbered)	8

RHYTHIM IS RHYTHIM

MINT VALUE £

11	Ovni OVNI 006	Y Baban Bach/Y Baban Back (instrumental) (tour 7", 300 only)	10
11	Ovni OVNI 008	ATHEIST XMAS EP (12")	15
12	Ovni OVNI 011	Gold Medal Winner/CATE LE BON: Time Could Change Your Mind (die-cut sleeve)	10
04	Placid Casual PLC10LP	YR ATAL GENHEDLAETH (LP)	25
11	Ovni OVNI 003	HOTEL SHAMPOO (LP)	20
14	Turnstile TS008LP	AMERICAN INTERIOR (LP, 12", CD, print, box set)	40

(see also Super Furry Animals)

RHYTHIM IS RHYTHIM
89	Jack Trax 12 J TRAX 11	Strings Of Life (Piano Mix)/(Exclusive Remix)/(Flam Boy Ant Mix)/MODEL 500: Off To Battle (Remix)/(Original Version)/Kaos (12")	12

(see also Model 500)

RHYTHM HAWKS
79	Redball RR 011	ZODIAC EP	25
81	Hot Rock HR45 009	No Chance/Clap Your Hands And Dance	30

RHYTHM METHODISTS
81	Methodisques MD 1	Don't Rely On Me/Cooler Relations (hand-made p/s)	12

RHYTHM ACES
61	Starlite ST45 061	A Thousand Teardrops/Wherever You May Go	20
61	Starlite ST45 066	Please Don't Go Away/Oh My Darling	20
62	Blue Beat BB 134	I'll Be There/DON DRUMMOND: Dewdrops	25
62	Island WI 032	C-H-R-I-S-T-M-A-S/TOP GRANT: A Christmas Drink	18

RHYTHM & BLUES INC.
65	Fontana TF 524	Louie Louie/Honey Don't	75

RHYTHM CATS
79	Tyger TYG 3	ROCK WITH THE RHYTHM CATS EP (1,000 only)	8

RHYTHMETTES
59	Coral Q 72358	Page From The Future/I'll Be With You In Apple Blossom Time	10

RHYTHM FORCE
72	Tropical AL 0013	Satta Call/Satta Version	10

RHYTHM INVENTION
92	Nucleus NUKE 002	Crunch (Original)/(Thank Goodness It's Saturday Mix)/Luvvly/Jubbly (12")	30

RHYTHM KINGS
63	Vocalion POP V 9212	Blue Soul/Exotic	30

RHYTHM OF LIFE
81	Rational RATE 6	Soon/Summertime (p/s; label also lists Rhythm RHYTHM 1)	10
82	Rational RATE 7	Uncle Sam/Portrait Of The Heart (p/s; label also lists Rhythm RHYTHM 2)	15

(see also Josef K, Paul Haig)

RHYTHM RULERS
70	Bullet BU 447	Second Pressure/Sammy Dead	35
70	Trojan TBL 132	MUDIES MOOD (LP)	50

(see also Lloyd Jones, U Roy Junior, Matadors, Winston Groovy, Pat, Winston Wright)

RHYZE
80	EPIC S EPC 13 8794	JUST HOW SWEET IS YOUR LOVE (LP)	20

RIBS
78	Aerco AERS 101	Man With No Brain/Long Time Coming (p/s)	25

RICARDOS
95	Raucous RAUC 023	RIVERSIDE ROCKABILLY EP	10
96	Raucous RAUC 026	Slinky/Sinful Woman/Let Me In	8

BOYD RICE & FRIENDS
81	Mute STUMM 4	BOYD RICE (LP)	30
90	New European BADVC 1969	MUSIC, MARTINIS AND MISANTHROPY (LP, with inner sleeve)	25

(see also Non, Death In June, Current 93)

MACK RICE
69	Atlantic 584 250	Love's A Mother Brother/Coal Man	12

TIM RICE & WEBBER GROUP
69	RCA RCA 1895	Come Back Richard (Your Country Needs You)/Roll On Over The Atlantic	8

(see also Tales Of Justine)

MANDY RICE-DAVIES
64	Ember EMB 4537	MANDY (EP)	40

BOB RICH
70	Mother MOT 1	Christas In My Pants/My Woman	8
73	Mother MOT 5	Filthy Rich/Navy Blue Blues	10

BOBBY RICH
03	Grapevine G2K 45 139	There's A Girl Somewhere For Me/I Can't Help Myself	7

BUDDY RICH
67	Fontana TF836	Norwegian Wood (This Bird Has Flown)/Monitor Theme	20

CHARLIE RICH
60	London HLU 9107	Lonely Weekends/Everything I Do Is Wrong	50
62	London HLS 9482	Just A Little Bit Sweet/It's Too Late	40
65	RCA RCA 1433	Too Many Teardrops/It's All Over Now	10
65	Philips BF 1432	Mohair Sam/I Washed My Hands In Muddy Water	10
67	London HLU 10104	Love Is After Me/Pass On By (silver-top label)	15
67	London HLU 10104	Love Is After Me/Pass On By (later boxed logo label)	10
67	London HLU 10104	Love Is After Me/Pass On By (DJ copy)	70
69	Mercury MF 1109	Mohair Sam/I Washed My Hands In Muddy Water (reissue)	10
65	RCA RD 7719	THAT'S RICH (LP)	40
66	Philips BL 7695	THE MANY NEW SIDES OF CHARLIE RICH (LP)	25

DAVE RICH
58	RCA RCA 1092	Burn On Love Fire/City Lights	15
66	Polydor BM 56113	Last Two People On Earth/I Just Wanna Dance	6

Johnny RICH

MINT VALUE £

JOHNNY RICH
| 64 | Mercury MF 836 | Dream On/Together | 6 |

LEWIS RICH
| 66 | Parlophone R 5434 | I Don't Want To Hear It Anymore/Shedding Tears | 15 |

SKETTO RICH
| 70 | Pama PM 806 | Hound Dog/Black Girl | 7 |

(see Buddy & Sketto, Ruddy & Sketto, Owen Gray)

TONY RICH
| 66 | Piccadilly 7N 35291 | Save Your Love/Don't Mention Your Name | 10 |
| 66 | Piccadilly 7N 35323 | It's All Up To You Now/See Saw | 15 |

(see also Tony Sheveton)

RICHARD
| 69 | Parlophone R 5754 | A Little Bit/Take Me | 15 |

RICHARD BROTHERS
| 63 | Island WI 060 | I Need A Girl/Desperate Lover | 15 |
| 63 | Island WI 109 | I Shall Wear A Crown/BABA BROOKS: Robin Hood | 20 |

(see also Joe White)

CLIFF RICHARD (& DRIFTERS/SHADOWS)

78s
58	Columbia DB 4178	Move It!/Schoolboy Crush	35
58	Columbia DB 4203	High Class Baby/My Feet Hit The Ground	30
59	Columbia DB 4249	Livin' Lovin' Doll/Steady With You	80
59	Columbia DB 4290	Mean Streak/Never Mind	80
59	Columbia DB 4306	Living Doll/Apron Strings	40

(The above 78s were credited to Cliff Richard & Drifters)

| 59 | Columbia DB 4351 | Travellin' Light/Dynamite (as Cliff Richard & Shadows) | 45 |
| 60 | Columbia DB 4398 | A Voice In The Wilderness/Don't Be Mad At Me (credited to Cliff Richard & Shadows) | 100 |

SINGLES : COLUMBIA
58	Columbia DB 4178	Move It!/Schoolboy Crush (green label)	20
58	Columbia DB 4178	Move It!/Schoolboy Crush (later pressing with black label)	10
58	Columbia DB 4203	High Class Baby/My Feet Hit The Ground (green label)	20
58	Columbia DB 4203	High Class Baby/My Feet Hit The Ground (later pressing with black label)	10
59	Columbia DB 4249	Livin' Lovin' Doll/Steady With You (green label)	30
59	Columbia DB 4249	Livin' Lovin' Doll/Steady With You (later pressing with black label)	10
59	Columbia DB 4290	Mean Streak/Never Mind (green label)	15
59	Columbia DB 4306	Living Doll/Apron Strings (later pressing with black label)	8
64	Columbia DB 7435	This Was My Special Day/I'm Feeling Oh So Lovely (withdrawn, credited to Cliff Richard, Audrey Bayley, Joan Palethorpe & Faye Fisher)	25
66	Columbia PSRS 304	Finders Keepers (promo only, 1-sided, with spoken intro by Simon Dee)	30

SINGLES : EMI SINGLES
73	EMI EMI 2022	Help It Along/Tomorrow Rising/The Days Of Love/Ashes To Ashes (in p/s)	6
74	EMI PSR 368	Nothing To Remind Me/The Learning (promo only)	40
75	EMI EMI 2344	Honky Tonk Angel/(Wouldn't You Know It) Got Myself A Girl (withdrawn)	15
79	EMI EMI 2975	We Don't Talk Anymore/Count Me Out (p/s, mispress, A-side plays Queen's "Bohemian Rhapsody")	12
84	EMI 5457	Ocean Deep/Baby You're Dynamite (p/s)	20

EXPORT SINGLES
| 63 | Columbia DC 758 | What'd I Say/Blue Moon | 150 |
| 65 | Columbia DC 762 | Angel/Razzle Dazzle | 50 |

EPs
59	Columbia SEG 7895	SERIOUS CHARGE (soundtrack)	30
59	Columbia SEG 7903	CLIFF NO. 1 (mono)	25
59	Columbia ESG 7754	CLIFF NO. 1 (stereo)	30
59	Columbia SEG 7910	CLIFF NO. 2 (mono)	20
59	Columbia ESG 7769	CLIFF NO. 2 (stereo)	25
59	Columbia SEG 7971	EXPRESSO BONGO (soundtrack, mono)	15
59	Columbia ESG 7783	EXPRESSO BONGO (soundtrack, stereo)	30
60	Columbia SEG 7979	CLIFF SINGS NO. 1 (mono)	25
60	Columbia ESG 7788	CLIFF SINGS NO. 1 (stereo)	30
60	Columbia SEG 7987	CLIFF SINGS NO. 2 (mono)	25
60	Columbia ESG 7794	CLIFF SINGS NO. 2 (stereo)	30
60	Columbia SEG 8005	CLIFF SINGS NO. 3 (mono)	25
60	Columbia ESG 7808	CLIFF SINGS NO. 3 (stereo)	30
60	Columbia SEG 8021	CLIFF SINGS NO. 4 (mono)	20
60	Columbia ESG 7816	CLIFF SINGS NO. 4 (stereo)	30
60	Columbia SEG 8050	CLIFF'S SILVER DISCS	20
60	Columbia SEG 8065	ME AND MY SHADOWS NO. 1 (mono)	25
60	Columbia ESG 7837	ME AND MY SHADOWS NO. 1 (stereo)	30
61	Columbia SEG 8071	ME AND MY SHADOWS NO. 2 (mono)	25
61	Columbia ESG 7481	ME AND MY SHADOWS NO. 2 (stereo)	30
61	Columbia SEG 8078	ME AND MY SHADOWS NO. 3 (mono)	25
61	Columbia ESG 7843	ME AND MY SHADOWS NO. 3 (stereo)	30
61	Columbia SEG 8105	LISTEN TO CLIFF NO. 1 (mono)	25
61	Columbia ESG 7858	LISTEN TO CLIFF NO. 1 (stereo)	30
61	Columbia SEG 8119	DREAM (mono)	15
61	Columbia ESG 7867	DREAM (stereo)	20
61	Columbia SEG 8126	LISTEN TO CLIFF NO. 2 (mono)	15
61	Columbia ESG 7870	LISTEN TO CLIFF NO. 2 (stereo)	20
62	Columbia SEG 8133	CLIFF'S HIT PARADE	20

Wendy RICHARD & DIANA BERRY

MINT VALUE £

Page	Catalogue	Title	Value
62	Columbia SEG 8151	CLIFF RICHARD	20
62	Columbia SEG 8159	HITS FROM 'THE YOUNG ONES'	20
62	Columbia SEG 8168	CLIFF RICHARD NO. 2	20

(The above EPs were originally issued with turquoise labels, later blue/black label copies are worth two-thirds these values.)

Page	Catalogue	Title	Value
62	Columbia SEG 8203	CLIFF'S HITS	20
63	Columbia SEG 8228	TIME FOR CLIFF AND THE SHADOWS (mono)	20
63	Columbia ESG 7887	TIME FOR CLIFF AND THE SHADOWS (stereo, turquoise label)	20
63	Columbia ESG 7887	TIME FOR CLIFF AND THE SHADOWS (stereo, blue/black label)	20
63	Columbia SEG 8246	HOLIDAY CARNIVAL (mono)	15
63	Columbia ESG 7892	HOLIDAY CARNIVAL (stereo)	20
63	Columbia SEG 8250	HITS FROM 'SUMMER HOLIDAY' (mono)	15
63	Columbia ESG 7896	HITS FROM 'SUMMER HOLIDAY' (stereo)	20
63	Columbia SEG 8263	MORE HITS FROM 'SUMMER HOLIDAY' (mono)	15
63	Columbia ESG 7898	MORE HITS FROM 'SUMMER HOLIDAY' (stereo)	20
63	Columbia SEG 8269	CLIFF'S LUCKY LIPS	20
63	Columbia SEG 8272	LOVE SONGS (mono)	20
63	Columbia ESG 7900	LOVE SONGS (stereo)	20
64	Columbia SEG 8290	WHEN IN FRANCE	20
64	Columbia SEG 8299	CLIFF SINGS 'DON'T TALK TO HIM'	15
64	Columbia SEG 8320	CLIFF'S PALLADIUM SUCCESSES	15
64	Columbia SEG 8338	WONDERFUL LIFE (mono)	10
64	Columbia ESG 7902	WONDERFUL LIFE (stereo)	15
64	Columbia SEG 8347	A FOREVER KIND OF LOVE	15
64	Columbia SEG 8354	WONDERFUL LIFE NO. 2 (mono)	12
64	Columbia ESG 7903	WONDERFUL LIFE NO. 2 (stereo)	15
64	Columbia SEG 8376	HITS FROM 'WONDERFUL LIFE' (mono)	12
64	Columbia ESG 7906	HITS FROM 'WONDERFUL LIFE' (stereo)	15
65	Columbia SEG 8384	WHY DON'T THEY UNDERSTAND?	15
65	Columbia SEG 8395	CLIFF'S HITS FROM 'ALADDIN AND HIS WONDERFUL LAMP'	10
65	Columbia SEG 8405	LOOK IN MY EYES, MARIA	15
65	Columbia SEG 8444	ANGEL	15
65	Columbia SEG 8450	TAKE FOUR	15
66	Columbia SEG 8474	WIND ME UP	15
66	Columbia SEG 8478	HITS FROM 'WHEN IN ROME'	15
66	Columbia SEG 8488	LOVE IS FOREVER	15
66	Columbia SEG 8510	THUNDERBIRDS ARE GO! (3 tracks by Cliff & Shadows, 1 solo)	50
66	Columbia SEG 8517	LA LA LA LA LA (1 track by Bruce Welch & Hank Marvin)	15
67	Columbia SEG 8527	CINDERELLA	40
67	Columbia SEG 8533	CAROL SINGERS	10
68	Columbia SEG 8540	CONGRATULATIONS	10

ALBUMS : COLUMBIA LPS

Page	Catalogue	Title	Value
59	Columbia 33SX 1147	CLIFF (green labels)	50
59	Columbia 33SX 1147	CLIFF (later blue/black labels)	20
59	Columbia 33SX 1192	CLIFF SINGS (green labels)	50
59	Columbia 33SX 1192	CLIFF SINGS (later blue/black labels)	20
60	Columbia 33SX 1261	ME AND MY SHADOWS (mono)	15
60	Columbia SCX 3330	ME AND MY SHADOWS (stereo)	25
61	Columbia SCX 3375	LISTEN TO CLIFF! (stereo)	15
61	Columbia 33SX 1368	21 TODAY (mono)	15
61	Columbia SCX 3409	21 TODAY (stereo)	15
62	Columbia 33SX 1431	32 MINUTES AND 17 SECONDS WITH... (mono)	15
62	Columbia 33SX 3436	32 MINUTES AND 17 SECONDS WITH...	15
66	Columbia SX 6079	FINDERS KEEPERS (soundtrack, with inner sleeve, mono)	15
66	Columbia SCX 6079	FINDERS KEEPERS (soundtrack, with inner sleeve, stereo)	20
67	Columbia S(C)X 6133	DON'T STOP ME NOW	15
67	Columbia JSX 6167	GOOD NEWS (export issue)	20

ALBUMS : OTHER LPS

Page	Catalogue	Title	Value
63	Elstree Extra Range	SUMMER HOLIDAY (2-LP, full soundtrack recording, 80 copies only)	400
64	Elstree Extra Range	WONDERFUL LIFE (2-LP, full soundtrack recording, 150 copies only)	250
64	EMI Regal SREG 1120	ME AND MY SHADOWS (export issue)	20

FLEXIDISCS : FLEXIDISCS & OTHER RELEASES

Page	Catalogue	Title	Value
98	Cruisin' The 50's CASB 007	Breathless/Lawdy Miss Clawdy (10" 78, p/s, with 6 inserts)	30

(see also Drifters [U.K.], Shadows, Olivia Newton-John, Sheila Walsh, Janet Jackson, Elton John, Grazina)

WENDY RICHARD & DIANA BERRY

Page	Catalogue	Title	Value
63	Decca F 11680	We Had A Dream/Keep 'Em Looking Around	15

(see also Mike Sarne)

RICHARD & GLEN

Page	Catalogue	Title	Value
72	Duke DU 141	Boat To Progress (Parts 1 & 2)	20

RICHARD & YOUNG LIONS

Page	Catalogue	Title	Value
66	Philips BF 1520	Open Up Your Door/Once Upon Your Smile	50

CYNTHIA RICHARDS

Page	Catalogue	Title	Value
69	Clandisc CLA 203	Foolish Fool/KING STITT: On The Street	25
70	Clandisc CLA 210	Conversation/DYNAMITES: Conversation Version II	20
70	Clandisc CLA 216	Can't Wait/Promises	12
70	Clandisc CLA 220	Foolish Fool/CLANCY & STITT: Dance Beat	12
71	Clandisc CLA 229	Stand By Your Man (actually by Merlene Webber)/DYNAMITES: Version 2	10
71	Big Shot BI 581	I'm Moving On/HIPPY BOYS: I'm Moving On - Version	10
71	Escort ERT 861	Love & Unity/MAYTONES: Wah Noh Dead	18

Johnny RICHARDS

MINT VALUE £

71	G.G. GG 4528	Place In My Heart/You've Got A Friend (act. Irving [Brown] & Cynthia Richards) 20
72	Pama Supreme PS 366	Mr Postman/SKIN, FLESH AND BONES: Version 10
73	Attack ATT 8047	Aily I/REID'S ALL STARS: Aily I - Version 10
70	Trojan TBL 123	FOOLISH FOOL (LP, actually Clancy Eccles productions compilation) 50

(see also Bobby Aitken, Lord Comic, Sir Lord Comic)

JOHNNY RICHARDS
| 59 | Esquire 32-076 | THE RITES OF DIABLO (LP) .... 25 |

KEITH RICHARDS
79	Rolling Stones RSR 102	Run Rudolph Run/The Harder They Come (p/s) 15
86	Arista ARIST 678P	Jumping Jack Flash/Integrity (with Aretha Franklin) (shaped pic disc & plinth) 12
89	Virgin VS 1179	Make No Mistake (Edit)/It Means A Lot (p/s) 6
88	Virgin KEITH 1234	Make No Mistake/Locked Away/Struggle/Big Enough (4 x 1-sided 7", "Talk Is Cheap" sampler box set, promo only) 90
88	Virgin 2-91047 A/B/C	TALK IS CHEAP (3 x 3" CDs in tin) 40
92	Virgin VUSLP 59	MAIN OFFENDER (LP, inner) 75

(see also Rolling Stones, Aranbee Pop Symphony Orchestra, Dirty Strangers, Screamin' Jay Hawkins)

LISA RICHARDS
| 65 | Vocalion VP 9244 | Mean Old World/Take A Chance .... 55 |
| 65 | Vocalion VP 9244 | Mean Old World/Take A Chance (DJ copy) .... 70 |

LLOYD RICHARDS
| 64 | Port-O-Jam PJ 4004 | Be Good/I Need You .... 25 |

ROY RICHARDS
66	Doctor Bird DB 1012	Contact/Maureen 20
66	Island WI 297	Green Collie/MARCIA GRIFFITHS: You No Good 40
66	Island WI 283	Double Trouble/FITSY & FREDDY: Why Did You Do It 25
66	Island WI 299	Western Standard Time/(JA) EAGLES: What An Agony 35
66	Island WI 3000	South Viet Nam/You Must Be Sorry (Vocal) 25
67	Island WI 3027	Rub-A-Dub/SHARKS: Baby Come Home 35
67	Tabernacle TS 1000	When I see Jesus/My Savior Come 25
67	Island WI 3037	Hopeful Village Ska/DELROY WILSON: Ungrateful Baby 45
67	Island WI 3050	Port-O-Jam/DELROY WILSON: Get Ready 60
67	Studio One SO 2020	Hanky Panky/ALTON ELLIS: I Am Still In Love 50
71	Fab FAB 17	Dirty People/D MAY: Where Have You Been (black label, promo only) 50
72	Fab 33	Vodoo/STRANGER COLE: Black Is Black (white label, no artist credits) 150

(see also Roland Alphonso, Lord Comic, Soul Vendors, Jackie Mittoo, Derrick Morgan, Righteous Flames)

RUSTY RICHARDS
| 60 | Top Rank JAR 297 | Middle Hand Road/Golden Moon (China Night) .... 7 |

TRUDY RICHARDS
57	Capitol CL 14728	Wishbone/Hangin' Around 10
57	Capitol CL 14744	Weaker Than Wise/I Want A Big Butter And Egg Man 6
58	Capitol CL 14857	Somebody Just Like You/The Night When Love Was Born 6
57	Capitol T 838	CRAZY IN LOVE (LP) 15

VIC RICHARDS
| 67 | Polydor 56163 | Jonathan Whatsit/Goodbye .... 70 |

WINSTON RICHARDS
| 67 | Rio R 124 | Studio Blitz/Don't Up .... 20 |

DEL RICHARDSON
| 73 | MCA MUPS 491 | PIECES OF A JIGSAW (LP, black/silver label) .... 200 |

(see also Osibisa, Sundae Times)

JOE 'GROUNDHOG' RICHARDSON
| 69 | Major Minor MM 632 | Take It Off/Blues To Take It Off .... 15 |

MARK RICHARDSON
| 65 | Stateside SS 440 | Baby, I'm Sorry/Blanket Fair .... 7 |
| 65 | Stateside SS 467 | See It My Way/Think .... 7 |

RICH FEVER
| 70 | Parlophone R5869 | Everything's Moving/King Of All The Kingdoms .... 15 |
| 71 | Parlophone R 5894 | Song Of A Sad Man/Island Dreams .... 12 |

RICH GYPSY
| 80 | Splash SP 016 | What Hit Me (no p/s) .... 25 |

TONY RICHIE
| 68 | Beacon BEA 114 | Anybody At The Party Seen Jenny/You Can't Win .... 40 |

RICH KIDS
78	EMI EMI 2803	Marching Men/Here Comes The Nice (p/s) 6
78	EMI 2848	Ghosts Of Princes Towers/Only Arsenic (company sleeve) 6
78	EMI EMC 3263	GHOSTS OF PRINCES IN TOWERS (LP) 18

(see also Sex Pistols, Ultravox, Spectres, Visage)

JONATHAN RICHMAN & MODERN LOVERS
75	United Artists UP 36006	Road Runner/It Will Stand (as Jonathan Richman) 7
77	Beserkley BSERK 9	ROCK 'N' ROLL WITH THE MODERN LOVERS (LP) 25
77	Beserkley BSERK 2	JONATHAN RICHMAN AND THE MODERN LOVERS (LP) 25
77	Beserkley BSERK 12	MODERN LOVERS LIVE (LP) 15
77	Beserkley BSERK 17	BACK IN YOUR LIFE (LP) 18
81	Mohawk LBOM 1	ORIGINAL (LP) 20
84	Rough Trade ROUGH 52	JONATHAN SINGS (LP) 15
85	Rough Trade ROUGH 72	ROCKIN' & ROMANCE (LP) 15
86	Rough Trade ROUGH 92	IT'S TIME FOR (LP) 20
88	Demon FIEND 106	MODERN LOVERS 88 (LP) 15
89	Special Delivery SPD 1024	JONATHAN RICHMAN (LP) 15
90	Special Delivery SPD 1037	JONATHAN GOES COUNTRY (LP) 15

RICH MIX

			MINT VALUE £
RICH MIX			
83	Satril 12 SAT 509	I Got The Love/Version (12")	15
RICHMOND			
73	Dart ART 2008	Candy Dora/Willow Farm	12
73	Dart ART 2025	Frightened/Breakfast	8
74	Dart ART 2044	Peaches/Work For My Baby	10
73	Dart ARTS 65371	FRIGHTENED (LP, textured sleeve, lyric insert)	30
BEN RICHMOND			
63	Piccadilly 7N 35092	Blue Bird/Bells All Started Ringing	6
63	Piccadilly 7N 35132	You Gotta Have Love/I Don't Care	6
FIONA RICHMOND			
73	Raymond PR 112	FRANKLY FIONA (LP)	50
JANET RICHMOND			
60	Top Rank JAR 288	You Got What It Takes/Not One Minute More	10
60	Top Rank JAR 378	June Bride/My One And Only Love	7
61	Top Rank JAR 536	Senora/I Need You	10
RICH PICKINGS			
69	Cresta CR 1	Time To Leave/Mind In Motion	200
73	Taylor Made TM 11	Jump To It/My Heroes Back (not sure if this is same group as above)	20
RICHUS FLAMES			
67	Fab FAB 17	Need To Be Loved/I Am Going Home	75
(see also Righteous Flames, Winston Jarrett)			
RICK & KEENS			
61	Mercury AMT 1150	Peanuts/I'll Be Home	50
RICK & SANDY			
65	Decca F 12196	Lost My Girl/I Can't Help It	40
65	Decca F 12311	Creation/In A 100 Years From Now	25
BERESFORD RICKETTS			
60	Starlite ST45 025	Cherry Baby/I Want To Know	30
60	Starlite ST45 029	Baby Baby/When I Woke Up	30
61	Starlite ST45 048	Hold Me Tight/Dream Girl (as Ricketts & Rowe)	30
62	Starlite ST45 079	I'm Going To Cry/Waiting For Me	30
62	Blue Beat BB 107	You Better Be Going/I've Been Walking (as Beresford Ricketts & Blue Beats)	22
63	Dice CC 12	Oh Jean/Rivers Of Tears (as Lauren Aitken's Group)	20
66	Blue Beat BB 350	Jailer Bring Me Water/Careless Love	22
RICKY & THE MUTATIONS			
83	Cool Ghoul COOL 003	Thatcher Rap (12")	15
RICKY BAILEY			
78	K&B KB 5525	Proud Mary/Proud Man	6
RICO (RODRIGUEZ)			
61	Blue Beat BB 56	Luke Lane Shuffle (as Rico Rodrigues & Buster's All Stars)/ BUSTER'S GROUP: Little Honey	25
62	Island WI 022	Rico Special (as Emanuel Rodrigues Orchestra; some copies may credit Reco & His Happy Orchestra)/BUNNY & SKITTER: A Little Mashin'	35
62	Planetone RC 1	London Here I Come/Midnight In Ethiopia	35
62	Planetone RC 4	Planet Rock/You Win	20
62	Planetone PT 35	Mighty As A Rose/MARVELLES: Tell All Those Girls	50
62	Planetone RC 5	Youth Boogie/Western Serenade (as Rico's Combo)	20
67	Fab FAB 12	Jingle Bells/Silent Night (with His Boys)	25
68	Pama PM 706	Soul Man/It's Not Unusual (as Reco Rodriguez)	45
68	Pama PM 715	Tender Foot Ska/Memories (as Reco Rodriguez)	25
69	Blue Cat BS 160	The Bullet/Rhythm In (as Reco Rodriguez & His Rhythm Aces)	35
69	Bullet BU 407	Tribute To Don Drummond/Japanese Invasion (as Rico Rodriquez)	100
71	Duke DU 96	Surprise Package (as Rico & Satch)/PETE JOHNSON: I'm Sorry	50
72	Count Shelly CS 013	Jungle Fever/UNKNOWN: River Jordan (white labels only)	60
77	Island WIP 6399	Africa/Afro-Dub	20
77	Island IPR 2006	Ska-Wars/Ramble (12")	20
78	Island IPR 2002	Dial Africa/Dub (12")	25
79	Island IPR 2016	Take 5/Sound Check (12")	20
80	Island IPR 2030	Children Of Sanchez/You Really Got Me/Midnight In Ethiopia (12")	45
80	2-Tone CHS TT 15	Sea Cruise/Carolina	25
82	2-Tone CHS TT 19	Jungle Music/Rasta Call You (paper label, 2-Tone sleeve, with Special A.K.A.)	25
82	2-Tone CHS TT 1219	Jungle Music/Rasta Call You/Easter Island (12", p/s, with Special A.K.A.)	20
69	Trojan TTL 12	BLOW YOUR HORN (LP, as Rico & Rudies)	50
78	Island ILPS 9485	MAN FROM WARREIKA (LP)	50
78	Ghetto Rockers PRE 1	WARREIKA DUB (LP, white label, white sleeve, beware of bootlegs)	80
81	2 Tone CHR TT 5005	THAT MAN IS FORWARD (LP)	50
82	2 Tone CHR TT5006	JAMA RICO (LP)	50
00	Simply Vinyl SVLP 187	MAN FROM WARREIKA (LP, reissue)	18
(see also Special A.K.A., Reco, Andy Capp, Don Reco, Prince Buster, Pioneers, Stranger, Marvels)			
RICOCHET			
80	Heavy Rock HER 1	Midas Light/Off The Rails (p/s)	150
RICOCHET KLASHNEKOFF			
02	Y n R YNR09	Daggo Mentality/Jankrowville (12")	12
RICOTTI & ALBUQUERQUE			
71	Pegasus PEG 2	FIRST WIND (LP)	50
(see also Frank Ricotti, Henry Lowther)			
FRANK RICOTTI QUARTET			
69	CBS 52668	OUR POINT OF VIEW (LP)	50
(see also Ricotti & Albuquerque, Chris Spedding)			

Nelson RIDDLE ORCHESTRA

MINT VALUE £

NELSON RIDDLE ORCHESTRA
55	Capitol CL 14241	Vera Cruz/You Won't Forget Me	6
55	Capitol CL 14262	The Pendulum Song/Brother John	6
56	Capitol CL 14510	Robin Hood/In Old Lisbon (Lisboa Antigua)	6
63	Capitol CL 15209	Supercar/The Dick Van Dyke Theme	8
66	Stateside SS 517	Batman Theme (from the T.V. series)/Nelson's Riddler	8
59	Capitol EAP 1034	JOHNNY CONCHO (EP)	10
62	MGM MGM-C 896	LOLITA (LP, soundtrack)	30
64	Reprise R 2021	ROBIN AND THE SEVEN HOODS (LP, soundtrack)	20
66	Stateside S(S)L 10279	BATMAN (LP, TV soundtrack)	50

RIDDLERS
66	Polydor BM 56716	Batman Theme/Weegie Walk	30

RIDE
89	Creation CRE 072T	RIDE EP (12")	25
90	Creation CRE 075T	PLAY EP (12")	25
90	Creation CRE 087T	FALL EP (12")	25
91	No Label	Like A Snowflake (7" sold at London ULU gig 19/12/91)	20
91	Creation CRE 100T	TODAY FOREVER EP (12" p/s)	20
92	Creation CRE 123T	Leave Them All Behind/Chrome Waves/Grasshopper (12", p/s)	20
92	Creation CRE 150P	Twisterella/Going Blank Again (promo)	15
92	Creation CRE 150T	Twisterella/Going Blank Again/Howard Hughes/Stampede (12")	12
94	Creation CRE 155TC	Birdman/Rolling Thunder No. 2/Let's Get Lost/Don't Let It Die (12", clear vinyl)	10
94	Creation CRE 184T	HOW DOES IT FEEL TO FEEL EP (12", p/s)	15
94	Creation CRE 189T	I DON'T KNOW WHERE IT COMES FROM EP (12", p/s)	15
94	Creation CRE 199T	BLACK NITE CRASH EP (12", p/s)	15
90	Creation CRELP 074	NOWHERE (LP, inner)	100
92	Creation CRELP 124	GOING BLANK AGAIN (LP as 2 x 45rpm 12", gatefold sleeve, lyric inner)	100
94	Creation CRELP 147	CARNIVAL OF LIGHT (2-LP, gatefold sleeve, lyric insert)	100
96	Creation CRELP 180	TARANTULA (LP)	100
01	Ignition IGN LP 14	OX4: THE BEST OF (2-LP)	40
12	Obscure Alternatives OAR 11081	GOING BLANK AGAIN (2-LP, reissue)	30
15	Ride RIDEMSC02LPX	NOWHERE (2-LP, reissue, gatefold, white/marbled vinyl, numbered, stickered sleeve)	100
15	Ride Music RIDEMSC06LP	OX4: THE BEST OF (2-LP, reissue, red vinyl)	25
17	Wichita WEBB510LP	WEATHER DIARIES (2-LP, purple vinyl, numbered)	25
17	Wichita WEBB510LP	WEATHER DIARIES (2-LP, black or clear vinyl copies)	20

(see also Motorcycle Ride, Andy Bell)

PAT RIDEN & BROTHER LLOYD'S ALL STARS
69	Mercury MF 1072	I Need Help/Let The Red Wine Flow (actually by Pat Rhoden)	6

(see also Pat Rhoden)

JACKIE RIDING & IMESON SOUND
66	Fab FAB 4	Don't Wanna Leave/The Wave	8

RIDJ XYLON
95	Roots Man Pro RMP 001	Black Consciousness/War Rumour Of War//NAPHTALI: Satan Disciples/Conscious Dub/Satan War Dub (12")	50

RIFF
64	Blue Beat BB 242	Oh What A Feeling/Primitive Man	70

RIFF-RAFF
73	RCA SF 8351	RIFF-RAFF (LP, with booklet)	45
73	RCA SF 8351	RIFF-RAFF (LP, without booklet)	25
74	RCA LPL1 5023	ORIGINAL MAN (LP)	30

RIFF RAFF
78	Chiswick SW 34	I WANNA BE A COSMONAUT (EP)	25
79	Albion DEL 6	Barking Park Lane/RUAN O' LOCHLAINN: Sweet Narcissis	15
80	Geezer GZ 2	Kitten/Fantocide (p/s)	8
80	Geezer GZ 3	Little Girls Know/She Don't Matter (p/s)	10
80	Geezer GZ 4	New Home Town/Richard (p/s)	6
80	Geezer GZ 3	Every Girl/You Shaped House (p/s)	10

RIFKIN
68	Page One POF 071	Continental Hesitation/We're Not Those People Any More	60

THE RIFLES
05	Blow Up BU 029	Peace And Quiet/Breakdown (die-cut Blow Up sleeve)	8
05	Xtra Mile XMR 007	When I'm Alone/ Holiday In The Sun (p/s)	7
05	Right Hook RHK 0017	Local Boy/Local Boy (Acoustic)	8
06	Red Ink 82876 85972 1	NO LOVE LOST (LP)	25
09	679 TRT 001	GREAT ESCAPE (2-LP)	40
15	Cooking Vinyl COOKLP 595	NONE THE WISER (LP)	20

ELEANOR RIGBY
85	Waterloo Sunset RUSS 101	I Want To Sleep With You/Till The End Of The Day (p/s with free condom and sticker)	15
85	Waterloo Sunset RUSS 101	I Want To Sleep With You/Till The End Of The Day	10
85	Waterloo Sunset RUSS 102	Take Another Shot Of My Heart/1995 (p/s, with story)	20
86	Waterloo Sunset RUSS 104	Kiss Me Quickly Its Christmas/Mad Xmas (p/s)	6
87	Waterloo Sunset RUSS 103	Over And Over/Last Night In Soho (p/s)	15
87	Waterloo Sunset RUSS 103T	Over And Over/Last Night In Soho (12", p/s)	20
97	Future Legend FLER 2	Love On The Phone/Play With Fire (p/s)	6
87	Waterloo Sunset WSR 001	CENSORSHIP (LP)	60
87	Waterloo Sunset WSR 001	CENSORSHIP (LP, with poster)	80
94	Future Legend FLEG 3	THE BEST OF ELEANOR RIGBY (LP, numbered)	25

JOHN L RIGBY & THE ALWOODLEY JETS
77	Petal PTL 020	HEAVEN CAN'T WAIT EP	10

Bram RIGG SET

MINT VALUE £

77	Petal PTL 020	Sleepwalkin/4/12 (500 only, no p/s)	15
77	Petal PTL 020	Sleepwalkin/4/12 (500 only, only a small number in this p/s)	50

BRAM RIGG SET
67	Stateside SS 2020	Take The Time Be Yourself/I Can Only Give You Everything	60

DIANA RIGG
72	RCA RCA 2178	Forget Yesterday/Sentimental Journey	20
02	Harkit HRKLP	DIANA RIGG SINGS (LP, test pressings only)	50

JACKIE RIGGS
56	London HLF 8244	The Great Pretender/His Gold Will Melt	40

RIGHT IDEA
70	Wastelands WL003	Memories/Strike Back	25

RIGHTEOUS BROTHERS
63	London HL 9743	Little Latin Lupe Lu/I'm So Lonely	12
63	London HL 9814	My Babe/Fee-Fi-Fidily-I-Oh	10
65	London HL 9975	Unchained Melody/Hung On You	6
65	London HL 10066	Just Once In My Life/The Blues	6
65	Pye International 7N 25297	Bring Your Love To Me/Try And Find Another Man	8
65	Pye International 7N 25304	Something's Got A Hold On Me/Night Owl	7
65	Pye Int. 7N 25323	Let The Good Times Roll/B Flat Blues	7
65	London HL 10011	Ebb Tide/(I Love You) For Sentimental Reasons	10
65	London HL 9962	Just Once In My Life/The Blues (withdrawn)	25
65	Pye International 7N 25358	Georgia On My Mind/My Tears Will Go Away	7
66	Verve VS 535	(You're My) Soul And Inspiration/B Side-Blues	7
66	Verve VS 537	He/He Will Break Your Heart	6
66	Sue WI 4018	You Can Have Her/Justine	20
66	London HL 10086	The White Cliffs Of Dover/Baby She's Mine	7
66	Verve VS 547	Island In The Sun/What Now My Love	8
67	Verve VS 560	Standing In The Middle Of No Place/Been So Nice	12
65	Pye Intl. NEP 44043	THE RIGHTEOUS BROTHERS (EP)	15
66	Verve VEP 5024	SOUL AND INSPIRATION (EP)	15
66	Verve VEP 5025	THE RIGHTEOUS BROTHERS (EP, reissue)	10
65	Pye Intl. NPL 28056	SOME BLUE-EYED SOUL (LP)	20
65	London HA 8226	YOU'VE LOST THAT LOVIN' FEELIN' (LP)	20
65	Pye Intl. NPL 28059	RIGHT NOW! (LP)	18
65	London HA 8245	JUST ONCE IN MY LIFE (LP)	15
66	London HA 8278	BACK TO BACK (LP)	15
66	Verve (S)VLP 9131	SOUL AND INSPIRATION (LP)	15
66	Sue ILP 937	IN ACTION! (LP)	40
68	Verve (S)VLP 9190	SOULED OUT (LP)	15
67	Verve VLP 9168	SAYIN SOMETHIN' (LP)	15

(see also Bill Medley, Bobby Hatfield)

RIGHTEOUS FLAMES
67	Fab FAB 18	Gimme Some Sign Girl/Let's Go To The Dance (B-side act. by Prince Buster)	250
67	Fab FAB 30	When A Girl Loves A Boy/DALTONS: Never Kiss You Again (gold & blue labels)	150
68	Coxsone CS 7061	You Don't Know/ROY RICHARDS & SOUL VENDORS: Summertime	500
71	High Note HS 052	Run To The Rock/GAYTONES: Run To The Rock Version	30
71	Nu Beat NB 083	Love And Emotion/Version	25
73	RCA Victor RCA 2353	Let The Music Play/True Born African	18
75	Grounation GRO 2026	Revolution/Version	25

(see also Richus Flames, Alton Ellis, Flames, Soul Vendors)

RIGHTEOUS HOMES (FLAMES)
68	Coxsone CS 7049	I Was Born To Be Loved(as Righteous Homes)/NORMA FRAZER: Heartaches	120
68	Blue Cat BS 112	Seven Letters (actually by Winston Jarrett)/SOUL VENDORS: To Sir With Love	100

RIGHTEOUS TWINS
69	Blue Cat BS 174	If I Could Hear My Master/Satan Can't Prevail	60

RIGOR MORTIS
73	Track 2094 107	Made In Japan/Hound Dog	8
73	Track 2406 106	RIGOR MORTIS SETS IN (LP, gatefold, inner sleeve)	20

(see John Entwistle, Who)

RIKKI & THE LAST DAYS OF EARTH
77	(own label)	Oundle 29/5/77 (1-sided) (Tracks are City Of The Damned/Dorian Grey)	60
77	DJM DJS 10814	City Of The Damned/Victimized (p/s)	10
78	DJM DJS 10822	Loaded/Street Fighting Man//City Of The Damned/Victimized (double pack)	7

J RILEY
68	Coxsone CS 7051	Great 68 Train/You Should Have Known	250

(see also Jimmy Riley)

RILEY ALL STARS/KING TUBBY
76	Concrete Jungle CJDPLP	CONCRETE JUNGLE DUB (LP, 300 pressed)	400

BILLY LEE RILEY
65	King KG 1015	I've Been Searchin'/Everybody's Twistin'	8
69	Stax STAX 120	Going Back To Memphis/Family Portrait	10
72	CBS 8182	I Got A Thing About You Baby/You Don't Love Me A.K.A Shimmy Shimmy Walk	7

(see also Megatons)

BOB RILEY
58	MGM MGM 977	The Midnight Line/Wanda Jean	50

DESMOND RILEY
69	Downtown DT 432	Tear Them/GEORGE LEE & RUDIES: Chaka Ground	50
69	Downtown DT 435	Tears On My Pillow/RUDIES: Man Pon Spot	20
69	Downtown DT 436	If I Had Wings/AUDREY: You'll Lose A Good Thing	100
69	Downtown DT 438	Out Your Fire/No Return	40

Howard RILEY (TRIO)

MINT VALUE £

69	Downtown DT 450	Skinhead, A Message To You/MUSIC DOCTORS: Going Strong	125
69	Downtown DT 454	If I Had Wings/AUDREY: You'll Lose A Good Thing (reissue)	20

HOWARD RILEY (TRIO)

68	Opportunity CP 2499	DISCUSSIONS (LP with insert, as Howard Riley Trio)	800
69	CBS 52669	ANGLE (LP)	50
70	CBS 64077	THE DAY WILL COME (LP)	60
71	Turtle TUR 301	FLIGHT (LP, gatefold sleeve)	150
75	Mosaic GCM 771	INTERTWINE (LP, solo)	15
76	Incus INCUS 13	SYNOPSIS (LP, as Howard Riley Trio with Tony Oxley & Barry Guy)	100
76	Mosaic GCM 781	SHAPED (LP, solo)	15
76	Cannon CNN 5967	SINGLENESS (LP, solo)	15
79	Spotlite	THE OTHER SIDE (LP)	15
81	View VS 020	DUALITY (LP, solo)	15
81	Impetus 38002	FACETS (box set, 3-LP with Barry Guy, John Stevens, Keith Tippett)	50
89	Falcon 1	SOLO 74 (cassette LP)	40

(see also Colosseum)

JEANNIE C. RILEY

68	Polydor 56748	Harper Valley P.T.A/Yesterday All Day Long Today	6
68	Polydor 56856	The Girl Most Likely/Scrapbook	6
69	Polydor 583 716	HARPER VALLEY P.T.A. (LP)	15

JIMI/JIMMY RILEY

71	Supreme SUP 217	Mount Zion (actually by Jimi Riley & Stranger Cole)/ ECCLE & NEVIL: All Over	20
75	Dip DL 5067	Ram Goat Liver/OMAR & MARSHA PERRY: Ram Goat Dub	20
76	Upsetter UP 101	Give Me A Love/UPSETTERS: Give Me A Dub	25
79	Attack TACK 1	Give Thanks And Praise/Feeling Is Believing (12")	30
78	Burning Sounds BS 1011	SHOWCASE (LP)	25
78	Burning Sounds BS 1029	MAJORITY RULE (LP)	35
79	Trojan TRLS 167	TELL THE YOUTHS THE TRUTH (LP)	20

(see also Martin Riley, Sensations, Uniques)

MARTIN RILEY

69	Gas GAS 114	Walking Proud/LLOYD CHARMERS: Why Baby	100
69	Punch PH 7	Trying To Be Free/I've Got It Bad	15
70	Camel CA 53	Catch This Sound/Suspense	15
70	Escort ES 823	It Grows (actually "It's Growing")/We Had A Good Thing Going	40
71	Camel CA 77	When Will We Be Paid/WILLIE FRANCIS: He's Got The Whole World In His Hands	8

(see also Jimmy Riley, Slim Smith, Slickers)

TERRY RILEY

71	CBS 64259	CHURCH OF ANTHRAX (LP, with John Cale, dark orange label)	35
71	CBS 64564	A RAINBOW IN CURVED AIR (LP)	20
71	CBS 64665	IN "C" (LP)	20
72	Shandar 83501/2	PERSIAN SURGERY DERVISHES (2-LP)	40
80	CBS 73929	SHRI CAMEL (LP, insert)	25
89	Edsel ED 314	IN C (LP, reissue)	20

(see also John Cale)

WINSTON RILEY

73	Techniques TE 922	Woman Don't You Go Astray/Travelling Man	15

(see also Techniques)

RILEY'S ALLSTARS

71	Banana BA 343	Glory Of Love (actually "Mystic Blue" by Hugh Hendricks & Buccaneers)/We'll Cry Together - Version	15

(see also Bobby Davis, Techniques)

RIMBARA

85	Cordelia	ON DRY LAND (LP, with free 7", 400 copies only)	30

RIMINGTON

73	Man MAM 95	In The Grip Of The Mullah/Dragon Child	20

SHANE RIMMER

59	Columbia DB 4293	(Roll Along) Wagon Train/A Touch Of Pink	8

RIMSHOTS

74	All Platinum 6 146 303	Who's Got The Monster (Inst.)/WHATNAUTS: Soul Walking (Inst.)	7
76	All Platinum 6146 314	Do What You Feel (Part 1)/(Part 2)	6
00	Sequel NEM LP 507	SOUL TRAIN (LP, reissue)	20

RIMSHOTS (1)

81	Spectro SPEC 101	At Night/Little Boys And Little Girls	15

RIMSHOTS (2)

82	Respond RESP 3	Sweet Talk/What's The Matter Baby (p/s)	6

RINGS

77	Chiswick S 14	I Wanna Be Free/Automobile (1st pressing in laminated p/s)	35
77	Chiswick S 14	I Wanna Be Free/Automobile (2nd pressing in non-laminated p/s)	20

(see also Maniacs, Twink)

RINGS & THINGS

68	Fontana TF 987	Strange Things Are Happening/To Me: To Me: To Me	200

RINKY DINKS

58	London HLE 8679	Early In The Morning/Now We're One (as Rinky-Dinks featuring Bobby Darin)	25
59	London HLE 8793	Mighty Mighty Man/You're Mine (as Bobby Darin with Rinky Dinks)	30

(see also Bobby Darin)

BOBBY RIO (U.S.)

63	Stateside SS 211	Don Diddley/I Got You	25

BOBBY RIO (& REVELLES)

65	Pye 7N 15790	Boy Meets Girl/Don't Break My Heart And Run Away	60
65	Pye 7N 15897	Everything In The Garden/When Love Was Young	50

RIO GRANDE

			MINT VALUE £
65	Pye 7N 15958	Value For Love/I'm Not Made Of Clay	50
66	Piccadilly 7N 35303	Ask The Lonely/Be Lonely Little Girl (solo)	25
66	Piccadilly 7N 35337	Angelica/Lovin' You (solo)	12

RIO GRANDE
71	RCA SF 8208	RIO GRANDE (LP)	15

RIO GRANDES
66	Pyramid PYR 6001	Soldiers Take Over/Moses	30

RIOT CLONE
82	Riot Clone RC 001	THERE'S NO GOVERNMENT LIKE NO GOVERNMENT (EP)	15
82	Riot Clone RC 002	DESTROY THE MYTH OF MUSICAL DESTRUCTION (EP)	12

RIOTOUS BROTHERS
80	Riotous RI 001	Vicki's Dancing/Operation Zero/Emotional Cripple (p/s)	25

RIOT ROCKERS
76	Box BOX 23A	Cast Iron Arm/Be Bop A Lula/Mystery Train/Mess Of Blues (no p/s)	60
78	Raw RAW 11	Tennessee Saturday Night/Some Kinda Earthquake (with 'fast' version of A side)	20
78	Raw RAW 11	Tennessee Saturday Night/Some Kinda Earthquake (with 'slow' version of A side)	15

RIOTS
65	Island WI 176	Telling Lies/Don't Leave Me (actually by Techniques)	60
65	Island WI 195	You Don't Know (actually by Techniques)/DON DRUMMOND & DRUMBAGO: Treasure Island	60
65	Island WI 197	I Am In Love/When You're Wrong (actually by Techniques)	55
65	Island WI 247	Yeah Yeah/BABA BROOKS: Virginia Ska	50

(see also Techniques)

RIOT SQUAD & MATUMBI
82	Extinguish EXT 004	Why Do You Make Me Wait/Paraphrase (12")	20

RIOT SQUAD (1)
65	Pye 7N 15752	Any Time/Jump	50
65	Pye 7N 15817	I Wanna Talk About My Baby/Gonna Make You Mine	60
65	Pye 7N 15869	Nevertheless/Not A Great Talker	60
66	Pye 7N 17041	Cry Cry Cry/How Is It Done	50
66	Pye 7N 17092	I Take It We're Through/Working Man	175
66	Pye 7N 17130	It's Never Too Late To Forgive/Try To Realise	50
67	Pye 7N 17237	Gotta Be A First Time/Bitter Sweet Love	60

(see also Graham Bonney, Jimi Hendrix Experience, Blue Aces)

RIOT SQUAD (2)
82	Rondelet ROUND 23	Fuck The Tories/Civil Destruction (p/s)	8
82	Rondelet ROUND 25	Riot In The City/Religion (p/s)	8
83	Rot ASS 1	DON'T BE DENIED (EP)	20
83	Rot ASS 2	I'm OK Fuck You/In The Future/Friday Night (p/s)	15
84	Rot ASS 13	NO POTENTIAL THREAT (LP, with free single [ASS3], stickered sleeve)	18

RIP CHORDS
78	Cells SELL 1	Ringing In The Streets/Music Is Peace/Artist/Television Television (p/s)	18

RIP CHORDS (U.S.)
63	CBS AAG 143	Here I Stand/Karen	25
63	CBS AAG 162	Gone/She Thinks I Still Care	20
64	CBS AAG 181	Hey Little Cobra/The Queen	30
64	CBS AAG 202	Three Window Coupe/Hot Rod USA	35
64	CBS BPG 62228	HEY LITTLE COBRA (LP)	100

(see also Terry Day, Terry Melcher)

RIPCORD
89	Raging Records RAGE 2	HARVEST HARDCORE (EP, foldout sleeve)	15
86	Raging RAGE 1	DAMAGE IS DONE (Flexi)	10
87	Manic Ears ACHE 005	DEFIANCE OF POWER (LP, with insert)	20
88	Raging RAGE 001	POETIC JUSTICE (LP, with inner)	15

MINNIE RIPERTON
74	Epic SEPC 80426	PERFECT ANGEL (LP)	30
75	Epic EPC 69142	ADVENTURES IN PARADISE (LP)	30
01	Stateside 7243 5 35127 1 2	LES FLEURS - THE MINNIE RIPPERTON ANTHOLOGY	30
02	Castle CMHLP 550	COME INTO MY GARDEN (LP, reissue, gatefold)	18

RIPLEY WAYFARERS
71	Tradition TSR 006	CHIPS AND BROWN SAUCE (LP, 500 only with front-laminated dark green and white flipback sleeve, title in blue)	30
73	Tradition TSR 006	CHIPS AND BROWN SAUCE (LP, reissue, plain green sleeve, title in black)	15

RIP 'N' LAN
71	Crab CRAB 64	In The Ghetto/Something Sweet	30

RIPPERS
68	Saga FID 21 42	HONESTLY (LP)	35

RIPPLE
78	Salsoul SSOL 105	The Beat Goes On/Facts Of Life	7
95	Charly CPLP 8193	RIPPLE (LP, reissue)	15

RIP RIG & PANIC
81	Virgin VZZ13	GOD (2 x 12")	15
82	Virgin V 2228	I AM COLD (2 x 12")	15
83	Virgin V 2268	ATTITUDE (LP)	15

RISAN
82	Saffron	Eastern Palace/Part 2	30

RISING FIRE
81	Cha Cha CHAD 45	You Lied/Free Blackman (12")	25

RISING HEAT
73	Firestone FS 02	My Magic Thimble/Evolution	25
75	Newbury N32	Drop The Act/Follow Me Home	40

RISING MOON

MINT VALUE £

RISING MOON
74   Theatre Projects 07691   RISING MOON (LP) 100
RISING SONS (U.K.)
68   Pye 7N 17554   Hold Me Just A Little While Longer/Fountain Of Love 10
RISING SONS (U.S.)
65   Stateside SS 426   You're My Girl/Try To Be A Man 35
RISING SUNS
72   Polydor 2121 49   Shay Laka Day/Happy Song 7
RISK (1)
79   Redball RR 023   Blazing Lights/Yesterday's Youth (no p/s) 8
RITA
69   Major Minor MM 653   Erotica/Sexologie 15
RITA (ALSTON)
69   Jackpot JP 718   Love Making/NAT COLE: My Love 20
(see also Rita Alston)
RITA & TIARAS
79   Destiny DS 1002   Gone With The Wind Is My Love/Wild Times (DJ copy with p/s) 18
09   Kent CITY 009   Gone With The Wind Is My Love/DORE STRINGS: Gone With The Wind Is My Love 8
TEX RITTER
56   Capitol CL 14581   The Wayward Wind/Gunsmoke 6
52   Capitol LC 6552   COWBOY FAVOURITES (10" LP) 20
BOB RITTERBUSH
59   Top Rank JAR 118   I Wish That You Were Mine/Darling Corey 7
RITUAL (1)
80   Mojo Funk MOD 1   Sore Lip/Non-Stop Boogie (p/s) 40
87   Warrior WR12 001   Sore Lip (Club Mix)/(Dub)/(Radio 7) (12") 10
RITUAL (2)
82   Red Flame RF 712   Mind Disease/Nine 8
RITUAL (3)
90   Romany RMY VI   Into The Night/Burning 10
RITZ
74   Dawn DNS 1070   Jenny Gentle/Why Love 20
(see also Paul Ryder & The Time Machine)
RIVAL SCHOOLS
02   Island 548936   UNITED BY FATE (LP) 20
13   Shop Radio Cast 022   FOUND (LP, green vinyl, UK pressing sold via band website) 20
RIVALS (1)
74   Decca F 13509   Speedway/Hoskins Still Rides 10
RIVALS (2)
78   Sound On Sound SOS 100   Skateboarding In The UK/Top Of The Pops 35
RIVALS (3)
80   Ace ACE 007   Future Rights/Flowers (p/s) 100
80   Oakwood/Ace ACE 011   Here Comes The Night/Both Sides (p/s) 40
RIVAL SAVAGES
80   Savage VC 1968   Get Some/Garden Of The Damned (fold-out p/s, dust sleeve stapled) 20
HECTOR RIVERA
67   Polydor 65728   At The Party/Do It To Me 60
89   Horace's HRH 003   Playing It Cool/I Want A Chance For Romance (reissue) 35
BLUE RIVERS & MAROONS
67   Columbia Blue Beat DB 103   Witchcraft Man/Searching For You Baby 30
68   Spectrum SP 105   Take It Or Leave It/I've Been Pushed Around 10
68   Columbia S(C)X 6192   BLUE BEAT IN MY SOUL (LP) 65
CLIFF RIVERS
63   London HLU 9739   True Lips/Marsha 40
DANNY RIVERS
60   Top Rank JAR 408   Hawk/I Got 40
60   Decca F 11294   Can't You Hear My Heart/I'm Waiting For Tomorrow 25
61   Decca F 11357   Once Upon A Time/My Baby's Gone Away (with Alexander Combo) 40
64   Decca F 11865   There Will Never Be Anyone Else/I Don't Think You Know How I Feel 25
62   HMV POP 1000   We're Gonna Dance/Movin' In (as Danny Rivers & River Men) 50
DEEK RIVERS
62   Oriole CB 1735   One Kiss/Outsider 25
JOHNNY RIVERS
61   Pye Intl. 7n 25118   Blue Skies/That Someone Should Be Me 10
64   Liberty LIB 66032   Memphis/It Won't Happen With Me 10
64   Liberty LIB 66056   Maybellene/Walk Myself n Home 10
64   Liberty LIB 66075   Mountain Of Love/Moody River 12
65   Liberty LIB 66087   Midnight Special/Cupid 12
65   Liberty LIB 66112   The Seventh Son/Un-Square Dance 8
65   Liberty LIB 12021   He Don't Love You Like I Love You/Where Have All The Flowers Gone 7
66   Liberty LIB 12023   Secret Agent Man/Tom Dooley 15
66   Liberty LIB 66144   Under Your Spell Again/Long Time Man 7
66   Liberty LIB 66175   I Washed My Hands In Muddy Water/Roogalator 15
66   Liberty LIB 66205   Poor Side Of Town/A Man Can Cry 12
67   Liberty LIB 66227   Baby I Need Your Loving/Getting Ready For Tomorrow 10
68   Liberty LIB 15078   Look To Your Soul/Something Strange 7
68   Liberty LBF 15163   Right Relations/A Better Life 7
69   Liberty LBF 15241   Muddy River/Resurrection 7
66   Liberty LEP 4049   MORE JOHNNY RIVERS (EP) 15
64   Liberty LBY 3031   AT THE WHISKY A GO-GO (LP) 20

Mavis RIVERS

MINT VALUE £

65	Liberty LBY 3036	HERE WE A GO-GO AGAIN (LP)	15
65	Liberty LBY 3064	RIVERS ROCKS THE FOLK (LP)	20
68	Liberty LBS 83040	REWIND (LP)	15

MAVIS RIVERS
63	Reprise RS 20115	Slightly Out Of Tune/Footsteps Of A Fool	30

ROYD RIVERS & CLIFF AUNGIER
65	Decca LK 4696	WANDERIN' (LP)	35

(see also Cliff Aungier)

TONY RIVERS & THE CASTAWAYS
63	Columbia DB 7135	Shake Shake Shake/Row Row Row	20
64	Columbia DB 7224	I Love The Way You Walk/I Love You	15
64	Columbia DB 7336	Life's Too Short/Tell On Me	15
65	Columbia DB 7448	She/Till We Get Home	15
65	Columbia DB 7536	Come Back/What To Do	15
66	Columbia DB 7971	God Only Knows/Charade	20
66	Parlophone R 5400	Nowhere Man/The Girl From New York City	25
66	Immediate IM 027	Girl Don't Tell Me/The Girl From Salt Lake City	50
68	Polydor 56245	I Can Guarantee Your Love/Pantomime	12

(see also Capability Brown, Grapefruit, Harmony Grass, Senators, Sugarbeats)

RIVIERAS
60	HMV POP 773	Blessing Of Love/Moonlight Cocktails	120

RIVIERAS (U.S.)
64	Pye International 7N 25237	California Sun/H B Goose Step	45

RIVINGTONS
62	Liberty LIB 55427	Papa Oom Mow Mow/Deep Water	50
63	Liberty LIB 55553	The Bird's The Word/I'm Losing My Grip	60
66	CBS 202088	Rose Growing In The Ruins/Tend To Business	75

RIVVITS
79	Alien AUX 1	Saturday Night At The Dance/Girl Next Door (p/s, with flexi)	10

R N B SPITFIRES
82	Mrs K GRC 143	Honeymaker/I Ain't Him (p/s)	8

FREDDIE ROACH
67	Transatlantic PR 7490	THE SOUL BOOK (LP)	40

MAX ROACH
60	Mercury MMC 14054	QUIET AS IT'S KEPT (LP)	20
62	HMV CLP 1522	PERC 'N' BITTER SUITE (LP)	15

MAX ROACH (& CLIFFORD BROWN GROUP)
58	Emarcy ERE 1572	MAX ROACH AND CLIFFORD BROWN (EP, withdrawn)	12
55	Vogue LDE 117	MAX ROACH & CLIFFORD BROWN IN CONCERT VOL. 1 (10" LP)	15
55	Vogue LDE 128	MAX ROACH & CLIFFORD BROWN IN CONCERT VOL. 2 (10" LP)	15
58	Emarcy EJL 1282	JAZZ IN THREE-QUARTER TIME (LP)	15
59	Emarcy MMB 12005	MAX ROACH, NEWPORT (LP, by Max Roach)	15
59	Emarcy MMB 12009	THE MAX ROACH FOUR PLUS FOUR (LP, by Max Roach)	15

(see also Clifford Brown)

ROAD
73	Rare Earth SRE 3006	ROAD (LP)	50

(see also Noel Redding)

ROADRUNNERS
65	Cavern Sound 2BSNL 7	PANTOMANIA (EP, with tracks by Chris Edwards & Clive Wood)	35

ROADSTER
81	Mayhem SRTS 81	Fantasy/45 MPH (p/s)	30

ROADSTERS
64	Stateside SS 293	Joy Ride/Drag	40

ROAMING DOG
72	Perfect PF 01	Sign Your Name/Eclipse	50

ROARING SIXTIES
66	Marmalade 598 001	We Love The Pirates/I'm Leaving Town	40

(see also Ivy League)

ROBAN'S SKIFFLE GROUP
61	Storyville A45 062	Careless Love/Frankie And Johnny (with p/s)	35
61	Storyville A45 062	Careless Love/Frankie And Johnny	18

E.G. ROBB
63	Columbia DB 7100	Stage To Cimarron/Jezebel	15

MARTY ROBBINS
SINGLES
57	Philips JK 1019	A White Sport Coat (And A Pink Carnation)/Grown-Up Tears (jukebox issue)	25
57	Philips PB 741	Please Don't Blame Me/Teen-Age Dream	10
58	Fontana H 128	Stairway Of Love/Just Married	8
58	Fontana H 150	Sittin' In A Tree House/She Was Only Seventeen	8
59	Fontana H 184	The Hanging Tree (from film)/The Blues Country Style	7
59	Fontana H 212	Cap And Gown/Last Night About This Time	7
59	Fontana H 229	Big Iron/Cool Water	6
59	Fontana H 233	El Paso/Running Gun	6
60	Fontana H 270	Ballad Of The Alamo/Five Brothers (in p/s)	10
63	CBS AAG 128	Ruby Ann/Won't You Forgive	6

EPs
59	Fontana TFE 17161	MARTY'S BIG HITS	12
61	Fontana TFE 17224	GUNFIGHTER	12

(see also Jordanaires)

Mel ROBBINS

MINT VALUE £

MEL ROBBINS
59 London HLM 8966 Save It/To Know You (initially pressing with triangular centre) 300
59 London HLM 8966 Save It/To Know You (later round centre) 100
59 London HLM 8966 Save It/To Know You (78) 40

SYLVIA ROBBINS
60 London HLJ 9118 Frankie And Johnny/Come Home 35

(see also Mickey & Sylvia)

ROBERT & REMOULDS
79 Black & White BW 1 X No. 1/Do Eyes Ever Meet? (p/s) 60

ANDY ROBERTS
70 RCA SF 8086 HOME GROWN (LP, laminated front sleeve, lyric insert) 100
71 Charisma CAS 1034 HOME GROWN (LP, reissue, different sleeve) 15
71 B&C HOME GROWN (LP, reissue) 20
71 Pegasus PEG 5 NINA AND THE DREAM TREE (LP) 80
73 Elektra K 42139 URBAN COWBOY (LP, with insert, 'butterfly' label) 20
73 Elektra K 42151 ANDY ROBERTS AND THE GREAT STAMPEDE (LP, gatefold sleeve) 15

(see also Clayton Squares, Liverpool Scene, Everyone, Plainsong, Mighty Baby)

BOB ROBERTS
70 Explosion EX 2021 Stick By Me/TOMMY McCOOK: The Designer 7

BOB ROBERTS (U.K.)
81 Solent SS 054 BREEZE FOR A BARGEMAN (LP) 15

HUGH ROBERTS
70 Explosion EX 2041 California Dreaming/One Woman (both sides actually by Lloyd Charmers) 12

J. ROBERTS
70 Bamboo BAM 30 Someday We'll Be Together/SOUND DIMENSION: Everyday People 20

JOHN ROBERTS
68 Sue WI 4042 Sockin' 1, 2, 3, 4/Sophisticated Funk 50
68 Action ACT 4511 I'll Forget You/Be My Baby 40

KEITH ROBERTS
72 Trailer LER 3031 PIER OF THE REALM (LP, red label) 15

KENNY ROBERTS (1)
57 Brunswick 05638 I'm Looking For The Bully Of The Town/Broken Teenage Heart 12

KENNY ROBERTS (2)
66 Pye 7N 17054 Run Like The Devil/Where Goes My Heart 50
66 Pye 7N 17054 Run Like The Devil/Where Goes My Heart (DJ copy) 75
65 Pye 7N 15882 Say, Do You Mean It/Since My Love Has Gone 15

(see also Kenny Damon)

KIM ROBERTS
64 Decca F 11813 I'll Prove It/For Loving Me This Way 65

PADDY ROBERTS
62 Decca F 11552 Merry Christmas You Suckers/Got 'n' Idea 6

RENEE ROBERTS
62 Oriole CB 1731 I Want To Love You/Aching Heart 10

ROCKY ROBERTS
67 Durium DRL 50026 SABATO SERA (LP) 30

STEVE ROBERTS
80s EXPLP 2002 DO YOU KNOW WHO I AM (LP) 15

(see also U.K.Subs)

DALE ROBERTSON
60 RCA SF 5064 PRESENTS HIS ALBUM OF WESTERN CLASSICS (LP) 20

DON ROBERTSON
50 London L 629 Gamblin' Fever/On The Hudson Bay Line (78, with Lou) 8
56 Capitol CL 14575 The Happy Whistler/You're Free To Go (B-side with Lou Dinning) 12

JIM ROBERTSON
55 MGM SPC 7 Pride Of My Heart/Walkin' And Talkin' With The Lord (export issue) 15

DAVE ROBIN
65 Eyemark EMS 1003 You I Don't Want To Share/Life's Too Short 6

EDE ROBIN
75 Crystal CR 7023 There Must Be A Love Somewhere/Soul Over Easy 8

RICHIE ROBIN
60 Top Rank JAR 262 Strange Dream/GERRY GRANAHAN: It Hurts 15

TINA ROBIN
57 Vogue Coral Q 72284 Over Somebody Else's Shoulder/Lady Fair 10
57 Vogue Coral Q 72294 Never In A Million Years/Ça C'est L'Amour 10
58 Coral Q 72309 Everyday/Believe Me) 20
58 Coral Q 72323 No School Tomorrow/Sugar Blues 20

ROGER ROBIN
95 Saxon SHF 004 Do Right/Tell Me (12") 20
98 Saxon SAX 065 Unity/Mix 2//My Medication/Version (12") 15

ROBIN HOODS
65 Mercury MF 865 Wait For The Dawn/Love You So 10

ROBINS
60 Vogue V 9168 Cherry Lips/Out Of The Picture 100
60 Vogue V 9173 Just Like That/Whole Lot Imagination 100

(see also H.B. Barnum)

JIMMY ROBINS
68 President PT 118 I Can't Please You/I Made It Over 150

ALVIN ROBINSON
64 Pye International 7N 25248 Something You Got/Searchin' 25
64 Red Bird RB 10010 Down Home Girl/Fever 30

Andy ROBINSON

			MINT VALUE £
66	Strike JH 307	You Brought My Heart Right Down To My Knees/Whatever You Had	20

ANDY ROBINSON
68	Philips SBL 7887	PATTERNS OF REALITY (LP, laminated sleeve, black/silver label)	30

BROTHER CLEOPHUS ROBINSON
57	Vogue EPV 1196	BROTHER CLEOPHUS ROBINSON (EP)	25

ROBINSON CREW
63	Decca F 11706	Taxi (Theme From TV Series)/Stormalong	7

(see also Lord Rockingham's XI)

DAVE ROBINSON
79	Bushays BFM 124	Ruby & Diamond (feat. Jah Thomas/Dub (12")	25

EDDIE ROBINSON
74	Myrrh MYR 1013	REFLECTIONS OF THE MAN INSIDE (LP)	15

FLOYD ROBINSON
59	RCA RCA 1146	Makin' Love/My Girl (initially with triangular centre)	8
60	RCA RCA 1179	I Believe In Love/Tattletale	10
60	RCA RD 27166	FLOYD ROBINSON (LP)	40

FREDDY ROBINSON
72	Stax 2325 085	AT THE DRIVE-IN (LP)	18

JACKEY ROBINSON
70	Punch PH 50	Heart Made Of Stone (actually by Jackie Bernard)/BOB TAYLOR: I May Never See My Baby Anymore	20

(see also Jackie Robinson, Pioneers)

JACKIE ROBINSON
68	Amalgamated AMG 819	Over And Over/Woman Of Samaria	45
68	Amalgamated AMG 824	Let The Little Girl Dance/DERRICK MORGAN: I Want To Go Home	40

(see also Pioneers)

JIM ROBINSON NEW ORLEANS BAND
61	Riverside RLP 369	NEW ORLEANS: THE LIVING LEGENDS (LP)	15
64	Riverside RLP 393	PLAYS SPIRITUAL AND BLUES (LP)	15

J.P. ROBINSON
72	Atlantic K 10149	George Jackson/Wall To Wall Love	10
72	Atlantic K 10209	What Can I Tell Her/Please Accept My Call	15

LLOYD ROBINSON
62	Blue Beat BB 122	Give Me A Chance/When You Walk	20
63	Blue Beat BB 159	I Need Your Love/You Told Me	30
69	Duke DU 5	Cuss Cuss/Lavender Blue	200
70	Camel CA 41	The Worm/NEVILLE HYNES: Afro (actually by Neville Hinds)	40
72	Green Door GD 4028	I Can't Forget/LLOYD AND THE NOW GENERATION: I Can't Forget - Version	6
77	Cactus CT 109	Rocky Road/Version	20
04	Trojan TJGSE014	Cuss Cuss/KING CANNON: Soul Special (reissue)	15

(see also Lloyd Clarke, Lloyd Charmers, Lloyd & Devon, Lloyd & Glen, Harry J. Allstars, Matadors, Melodians)

M. ROBINSON
64	Port-O-Jam PJ 4114	Who Are You/Follow You	15

MARTEL ROBINSON
75	Arrow AR 006	Sunny Soil/Sunny	15
78	Ray RALP 33	COOL SHADY TREE (LP)	20

PAUL ROBINSON
83	King City KCD 006	Come On Sister/Instrumental (12")	80

ROSCO ROBINSON
66	Pye International 7N 25385	That's Enough/One More Time	50
66	Pye International 7N 25385	That's Enough/One More Time (DJ copy)	100
72	Wand WN 27	That's Enough/One More Time (reissue)	10
73	Contempo C 16	We're Losing It Baby/We Got A Good Thing Going	8

SANDRA ROBINSON
85	Trojan TROT 9079	Sensi For Sale (Part 1)/TUFF TONES: Boogie Mix (Part 2)/SANDRA ROBINSON & TUFF TONES: Depression/DAN AMBRASSA: Life's Riddle/TUFF TONES: Boogie Mix (12")	20

SUGAR CHILE ROBINSON
53	Capitol LC 6586	CAPITOL PRESENTS SUGAR CHILE ROBINSON (10" LP)	40

TOM ROBINSON (BAND)
75	Chebel SRT/CUS 015	GLAD TO BE GAY (EP, as Bradford Gay Liberation Front, no p/s)	250
79	Deviant Wrecords DEVIATE 1	A Dyke's Gotta Do (What A Dyke's Gotta Do)/NOEL GREIG: Stand Together (All You Gay Women All You Gay Men) (die cut sleeve with sticker)	20
79	EMI EMI 2946	All Right All Night/Black Angel (withdrawn, demo-only)	8

(see also Cafe Society, Phantom, Billy Karloff [& Extremes])

ROBIN WANTS REVENGE
90	Jungle Jam JJR 102	ROBIN WANTS REVENGE EP (12")	40

CARSON ROBISON (& HIS PLEASANT VALLEY BOYS)
53	MGM SP 1004	Lady Round The Lady/Pokeberry Promenade	10
53	MGM SP 1024	Square Dance Jitterbug/Keep On Circlin' 'Round	18

RALPH ROBLES
69	London HA/SH 8285	TAKING OVER (LP)	20

ALEXANDER ROBOTNICK
84	Sire SAM 258	Problemes D'Amour (Aah Ooh Ah Mix)/Problemes D'Amour (Edit) (12" promo only)	40

ROBOTS AND HUMANOIDS
96	Alphaphone ALPHA 004	Indigo Octagon/Moment Of Truth/Inner Landscape/Paranoia (12")	20

(see also Cabaret Voltaire, Richard H. Kirk)

JEREMY ROBSON
63	Columbia SEG 8244	BLUES FOR THE LONELY (EP, with Michael Garrick and Shake Keane)	100

NICKY ROBSON
80	Scratch SCR 006	Stars/Eye To Eye (p/s)	20
80	Scratch SCRT 006	Stars (Extended)/Eye To Eye (12")	45

ROCAMARS

MINT VALUE £

(see also Gary Numan)

ROCAMARS
65	King KG 1031	All In Black Woman/Give Me Time	20

TONY ROCCO
62	Parlophone R 4886	Stalemate/Keep A Walking	15
62	Parlophone R 4946	Competition/Torture	15

HARRY ROCHE CONSTELLATION
67	CBS 202653	Casino Royale/In The Pad Of The Mountain King	10
67	CBS SBPG 63013	CASINO ROYALE (LP)	35
71	Studio Two TWO 340	SPINDRIFT (LP)	20
73	Pye Intl. NSPL 41024	SPIRAL (LP, laminated sleeve)	30
73	Pye QUAD 1022	SOMETIMES (LP, quadrophonic)	20

DICKIE ROCK & MIAMI SHOWBAND
64	Piccadilly 7N 35202	From The Candy Store/Twenty Flight Rock	7
64	Pye 7N 15729	Just For Old Times Sake/Me Not You	7
65	Pye 7N 15750	Round And Around/Little Baby	7
65	Pye 7N 15855	Every Step Of The Way/Rock And Roll Music	7
65	Pye 7N 17063	Come Back To Stay/Can't Make Up My Mind (p/s)	7

JOHNNY ROCK
55	Vogue VE170112	JOHNNY ROCK (EP)	40

PETE ROCK
98	RCA 74321619781	SOUL SURVIVOR (2-LP, inners)	25
01	BBE BBEBGLP 002	PETESTRUMENTALS (2-LP, gatefold)	20

PETE ROCK & C.L. SMOOTH
92	Elektra EKT 105	MECCA AND THE SOUL BROTHER (2-LP)	30
94	Elektra 7559-61661-1	THE MAIN INGREDIENT (2-LP)	20

ROCKABILLY REBS
79	SRTS 79 CUS 524	ROCKABILLY REBS (EP, no p/s)	100

ROCK-A-TEENS
59	Columbia DB 4361	Woo-Hoo/Untrue	40

ROCK BROTHERS
56	Parlophone MSP 6201	Dungaree Doll/Livin' It Up	90
56	Parlophone R 4119	Dungaree Doll/Livin' It Up (78)	30

ROCK CANDY
71	MCA MK 5069	Remember/Don't Put Me Down	6
72	MCA MK 5087	Some Fine Day/Magic Horse	8

ROCKERS ALL STARS
78	Rough Trade RT 002	Pablo Meets Mr. Bassie/Mr. Bassie Special	10

(see also Augustus Pablo)

ROCKERS HI-FI
96	Different Drummer 12 G 001	GOING UNDER (THE KRUDER & DORFMEISTER SESSIONS EP) (12" p/s)	12
95	4th & Broadway BRLPD 615	ROCKERS TO ROCKERS (2-LP)	30
96	Different Drummer LP 60016	MISH MASH (3-LP)	25

ROCKERS (1)
59	Oriole CB 1501	Get Cracking/Counter Melody	10

ROCKERS (2)
83	CBS TA 3929	We Are The Boys (Who Make All The Noise) (Extended Version)/Rockin' On Stage (12", p/s)	12
83	CBS A 3929	We Are The Boys (Who Make All The Noise)/Rockin' On Stage (p/s)	8

(see also Phil Lynott, Roy Wood, Status Quo)

ROCKET 88
81	Atlantic K 50776	ROCKET 88 (LP)	20

(see also Charlie Watts, Alexis Korner, Jack Bruce, Dick Heckstall-Smith)

ROCKET FROM THE CRYPT
93	Southern Studios PLIS 007	Glazed/Pressures/Cut It Loose (white label test pressing, 5-10 copies only)	30
95	Elemental ELM 32S	Born in 69/Ciao Patsy (p/s)	8
96	Elemental ELM 33S	Young Livers/Burning Army Men (p/s)	8
96	Dinked 1	Used/Lose Your Clown (in-store giveaway)	20
98	Elemental ELM 48S	Lipstick/Hot Heart (p/s)	6
98	Elemental ELM 49S	Break It Up/Turkish Revenge (p/s)	6
95	Elemental ELM 27LP	HOT CHARITY (LP)	15
08	One Little Indian ELM 50DMM	ROCKET FROM THE CRYPT (LP, 1000 only)	18
08	One Little indian ELM34DMM	SCREAM DRACULA SCREAM! (LP)	20

ROCKETS
60	Philips PB 982	Gibraltar Rock/Walkin' Home	20
60	Philips PB 982	Gibraltar Rock/Walkin' Home (78)	40
61	Zodiac ZR 0010	Warrior/Countdown	22

ROCKIN' BERRIES
63	Decca F 11698	Wah Wah Wah Woo/Rockin' Berry Stomp	25
63	Decca F 11760	Itty Bitty Pieces/The Twitch	20
64	Piccadilly 7N 35197	I Didn't Mean To Hurt You/You'd Better Come Home	10
64	Piccadilly 7N 35203	He's In Town/Flashback	6
65	Piccadilly 7N 35217	What The World's Come Over You/You Don't Know What To Do	6
65	Piccadilly 7N 35236	Poor Man's Son/Follow Me	6
65	Piccadilly 7N 35254	You're My Girl/Brother Bill	10
65	Piccadilly 7N 35270	The Water Is Over My Head/Doesn't Time Fly	10
67	Piccadilly 7N 35373	Sometimes/Needs To Be	6
67	Piccadilly 7N 35400	Smile/Breakfast At Sam's	6
67	Pye 7N 17411	Dawn (Go Away)/She's Not Like Any Girl	6

ROCKIN' DEVILS

			MINT VALUE £
68	Pye 7N 17519	Reach The Top/Pain	10
68	Pye 7N 17589	Mr. Blue/Land Of Love	10
73	Satril SAT 9	Day To Day/Big Louie's Birthday	10
75	Satril SAT 101	Lonely Summertime/Send Me No Letters	6
65	Piccadilly NEP 34039	I DIDN'T MEAN TO HURT YOU (EP)	35
65	Piccadilly NEP 34043	NEW FROM THE BERRIES (EP)	35
65	Piccadilly NEP 34045	HAPPY TO BE BLUE (EP)	50
78	Hollick & Taylor HT EPS 1561	5 FROM THE BERRIES (EP)	15
64	Piccadilly NPL 38013	IN TOWN (LP)	40
65	Piccadilly NPL 38022	LIFE IS JUST A BOWL OF BERRIES (LP)	40

(see also Jefferson)

ROCKIN' DEVILS
79	Hit Stuff HS 004	Apache/Bony Moronie/Give Me Muddy Water/Rumplestiltskin (no p/s)	30
79	HOT ROCK HS 007	GOT THEM BLUES (EP, red vinyl)	40
75	Hot Stuff HSL 001	BRING BACK ROCK'N' ROLL (LP)	50
75	Hot Stuff HSL 002	THAT OLD ROCK MUSIC'S HERE TO STAY (LP)	15
75	Hot Stuff HSL 003	WITH A LITTLE HELP FROM OUR FRIEND (LP)	20
76	Hot Stuff HSL 004	REMEMBER (LP)	70
77	HOT ROCK HSL 005	OFF MY ROCKER (LP)	40

ROCKIN' FOO
70	Stateside SS 2168	Rochester River/Stranger In The Attic	6
70	Stateside SSL 10303	ROCKIN' FOO (LP)	22

ROCKIN' HENRI & HAYSEEDS
63	Decca F 11700	Sally/Sweet Adeline	7

ROCKIN' HORSE
71	Philips 6006 156	The Biggest Gossip In Town/You Say	12
72	Philips 6006 200	Julian The Hooligan/Stayed Out Late Last Night	12
71	Philips 6308 075	YES IT IS (LP, laminated sleve, black/silver label)	150

(see also Jimmy Campbell, 23rd Turnoff, Kirkbys, Merseys)

ROCKIN' RAMRODS
66	Polydor BM 56512	Don't Fool With Fu Manchu/Tears Melt The Stone	25

ROCKIN' REBELS
63	Stateside SS 162	Wild Weekend/Wild Weekend Cha Cha	22
63	Stateside SS 187	Rockin' Crickets/Hully Gully Rock (both sides actually by Hot-Toddys)	20

(see also Hot-Toddys)

ROCKIN' R'S
59	London HL 8872	The Beat/Crazy Baby	40
59	London HL 8872	The Beat/Crazy Baby (78)	30

ROCKIN' SAINTS
60	Brunswick 05843	Cheat On Me, Baby/Half And Half	100

ROCKIN' SHADES
79	SRTS 79 CUS 404	LIVE AT CAISTER EP	20

ROCKIN' VICKERS
64	Decca F 11993	I Go Ape/Someone Like You (as Rocking Vickers)	40
66	CBS 202051	It's Alright/Stay By Me	55
66	CBS 202241	Dandy/I Don't Need Your Kind	40

(see also Motorhead)

ROCKING HORSE
71	Camel CA 75	Running Back Home/SOUL SYNDICATE BAND: Running Back - Version	15
72	Randy's RAN 522	Hard Time/Change Your Ways	10
73	Randy's RAN 535	I'm So Fed Up/I'm So Fed Up - Version	10
74	Pyramid PYR 7009	New Situation/New Version	8
74	Sydna SYD 5026	Be Thankful/Thankful Dub	15

ROCKING RICHARD AND WHISTLING VIC TEMPLAR
87	Hangman HANG 14 UP	PRESENT: TEA AND BACCY (LP)	15

ROCKITS
73	Mowest MW 3012	Livin' Without You/Love My Love	6
74	Mowest MW 3016	Gimme True Love/I'm Losing You	8

ROCK MACHINE
73	T.I.M.	THEMES (LP)	60

(see also Ugly Custard)

ROCK-OLGA
60	Ember EMB S 105	Red Sails In The Sunset/My Dixieland Doll (in p/s)	10

ROCKS
88	GOTELOAN GLP A1 88 TR	Human Music/Freedom	15

ROCKSLIDE
75	Reward MAG 004	Jump Bump Boogaloo/Roller Coaster	8

ROCKSTAR
76	MCA MCA 265	Mummy/Over The Hill	15

ROCKSTEADYS
67	Giant GN 2	Squeeze And Freeze/JUNIOR SMITH: I'm A Good Boy	35

ROCKSTONES
70	Trojan TR 7762	A.B.C. Reggae/BEVERLEY'S ALLSTARS: Be Yours	30
70	Summit SUM 8501	Everything Is Beautiful/BEVERLEY'S ALLSTARS: Give Up	10

(see also Gaylads)

ROCK TONE BAND
77	Militant ML 004	Burne Me Out/Version 1977	150

ROCK WORKSHOP
70	CBS 5046	You To Lose/Born In The City	6
70	CBS 64075	ROCK WORKSHOP (LP, orange label)	35

ROCKY FELLERS

MINT VALUE £

71	CBS 64394	THE VERY LAST TIME (LP, gatefold sleeve, orange label)	35

(see also Bob Downes, Alex Harvey)

ROCKY FELLERS
63	Stateside SS 175	Killer Joe/Lonely Treardrops	20
63	Stateside SS 212	Like The Big Guys Do/Great Big World	18
63	Pye International 7N 25225	Ching A Ling Baby/Hey Little Donkey	22

ROCKY HORROR SHOW
75	Ode ODS 66305	Science Fiction Double Feature/Time Warp	8
87	Ode RHVX 1	ROCKY HORROR BOX SET (4-LP box, with inserts, numbered)	20
87	Ode RHBXLP 1	ROCKY HORROR BOX SET (4-LP box, with different inserts to above)	20
90	Ode RHBXCD 1	THE ROCKY HORROR PICTURE ALBUMS (15th ANNIVERSARY) (4-CD, with booklet)	40

(see also Tim Curry, Meat Loaf, Original Soundtracks)

ROCOCO
73	Deram DM 375	Ultrastar/Wildfire	10
76	Mountain TOP 9	Follow That Car/Lucinda	6

ROD & CAROLYN
63	Pye 7N 15519	How Can You Tell/What About The Teardrops	6
63	Pye 7N 15565	Bye-Bye My Lover/To Be Alone	6
64	Pye 7N 15629	Young Love/Talk To Me	6
64	Pye 7N 15706	Love Is Where You Are/I've Got You On My Mind	6

GENE RODDENBERRY
76	CBS 4692	Star Trek Theme/Star Trek Philosophy	12

RODD-KEN & CAVALIERS
60	Triumph RGM 1001	Magic Wheel/Happy Valley	40

(see also Blue Men)

RODDY RADIATION & THE TEARJERKERS
80	Dodgy Demo Co	NOTHING LASTS FOREVER EP	25

(see also Specials)

TIM RODDY
82	Tiara 001	Frankly Fiona/Don't Turn The Light Out On Me	8

CLODA(GH) RODGERS
62	Decca F 11534	Believe Me I'm No Fool/End Of The Line	10
63	Decca F 11607	Sometime Kind Of Love/I See More Of Him	10
63	Decca F 11667	To Give My Love To You/I Only Live To Love You	10
64	Decca F 11812	Mister Heartache/Time	10
65	Columbia DB 7468	Wanting You/Johnny Come Home	8
66	Columbia DB 7926	Every Day Is Just The Same/You'll Come A Running	7
66	Columbia DB 8038	Stormy Weather/Lonely Room	8
68	RCA 1684	Room Full Of Roses/Play The Drame To The End	20
68	RCA 1748	Rhythm Of Love/River Of Tears	8
69	RCA 1891	Biljo/Spider	6
69	RCA SF 8033 / RD 8033	CLODAGH RODGERS (LP)	20
69	RCA SF 8071	MIDNIGHT CLODAGH (LP)	20
71	RCA SF 8180	RODGERS AND HEART (LP)	20
72	RCA SF 8271	IT'S DIFFERENT NOW (LP, gatefold)	15
73	RCA SF 8394	YOU ARE MY MUSIC (LP)	15
77	Polydor 2383473	SAVE ME (LP)	15

EILEEN RODGERS
58	Fontana H 136	Careful, Careful/I'm Alone Because I Love You	12
58	Fontana H 156	Treasure Of Your Love/Little Bit Bluer	12
61	London HLR 9271	Sailor (Your Home Is The Sea)/Wait Till Tomorrow	15

JEAN RODGERS
65	Columbia DB 7637	Take What I Have/Baby What You Gonna Do?	6

JIMMIE RODGERS (THE BLUE YODELLER)
58	HMV 7EG 8163	JIMMIE RODGERS (EP)	19
60	RCA RCX 1058	LEGENDARY JIMMIE RODGERS (EP)	10
59	RCA RD 27110	TRAIN WHISTLE BLUES (LP)	15
59	RCA RD 27138	NEVER NO MO' BLUES (JIMMIE RODGERS MEMORIAL ALBUM) (LP)	15
61	RCA RD 27203	MY ROUGH AND ROWDY WAYS (LP)	15
61	RCA RD 27241	JIMMIE THE KID (LP)	15
62	RCA RD 7505	COUNTRY MUSIC HALL OF FAME (LP)	15
63	RCA RD 7562	THE SHORT BUT BRILLIANT LIFE OF JIMMIE RODGERS (LP)	15
64	RCA RD 7644	MY TIME AIN'T LONG (LP)	15

JIMMIE RODGERS
57	Columbia DB 3986	Honeycomb/Their Hearts Were Full Of Spring (as Jimmy Rodgers)	10
57	Columbia DB 4052	Kisses Sweeter Than Wine/Better Loved You'll Never Be	8
58	Columbia DB 4078	Oh-Oh, I'm Falling In Love Again/The Long Hot Summer	8
58	Columbia DB 4130	Secretly/Make Me A Miracle	7
58	Columbia 33SX 1082	JIMMIE RODGERS (LP)	25
58	Columbia 33SX 1097	THE NUMBER ONE BALLADS (LP)	25

RODNEY & BRUNETTES
79	London/Bomp HLZ 10574	NEW YORK BLONDES featuring MADAME X: Little GTO/Holocaust On Sunset Boulevard(no p/s)	12

(see also Blondie, Debbie Harry)

RODNEY P (AKA RODDIE ROK)
01	Riddim Killah RK001	Murderer Style/Friction (12")	10
13	Tru Thoughts TRU 7274	Success/Live Up	25
02	Riddim Killah RKP04LP	THE FUTURE (LP, test pressing, version unreleased)	80
04	Riddim Killah RKP04LP	THE FUTURE (LP- Limited White Vinyl)	35

(see also London Posse)

RODS

MINT VALUE £

RODS
79	Rods ROD 1	Like A Mirror/Hear I Am	10

TOMMY ROE (& ROEMANS)
62	HMV POP 1060	Sheila/Save Your Kisses	7
62	HMV POP 1092	Susie Darlin'/Piddle De Pat	8
63	HMV POP 1117	Gonna Take A Chance/Don't Cry Donna	6
63	HMV POP 1174	Kiss And Run/What Makes The Blues (Want To Pick On Me)	7
63	HMV POP 1207	Everybody/There's A Great Day A-Coming	6
63	HMV POP 1259	Come On/There Will Be Better Years	6
64	HMV POP 1290	Be A Good Little Girl/Carol	6
64	HMV POP 1364	Little Miss Heartache/You Might As Well Forget Him	10
65	HMV POP 1368	Diane From Manchester Square/Part Girl	8
65	HMV POP 1469	Doesn't Anybody Know My Name/I'm A Rambler, I'm A Gambler	8
66	HMV POP 1539	Sweet Pea/Much More Love	10
69	Stateside SS 2152	Heather Honey/Money Is My Pay	8
63	HMV 7EG 8806	THE FOLK SINGER (EP)	15
63	HMV CLP 1614	SHEILA (LP)	40
64	HMV CLP 1704	EVERYBODY LIKES TOMMY ROE (LP)	20
65	HMV CLP 1860	BALLADS AND BEAT (LP)	20
69	Stateside S(S)L 10282	DIZZY (LP)	15

CE CE ROGERS
87	Atlantic SAM 502	Someday (Club MIx)/(Some Dub/)/Accainsttrumental) (12" promo)	25
89	WEA A 8852T	Forever (12" Extended Mix)/Forever (Club Mix)/Someday (12" Extended Mix) (12", no p/s)	10
89	Atlantic A 8852	Forever/Someday (p/s)	20

DANE ROGERS & NU BEATS
64	Pye 7N 15621	Mary Jane/Jeanette	10

DEAN ROGERS
60	Parlophone R 4732	End Of Time (as Dean Rogers & Hi-Fi's)/Keep The Miracle Going	10
61	Parlophone R 4835	Timber/High In A Misty Sky	20

(see also Sydney James)

ERIC ROGERS
63	Decca F 11585	The Iron Maiden/Fly-Wheel	7

JULIE ROGERS
64	Mercury 10023 MCE	JULIE ROGERS (EP)	10
65	Mercury 10028 MCE	THE SOUND OF JULIE (EP)	10
65	Mercury 20048 (S)MCL	THE SOUND OF JULIE (LP, mono/stereo)	20
66	Mercury 20086 (S)MCL	CONTRASTS (LP, mono/stereo)	20
67	Mercury 20100 (S)MCL	SONGS OF INSPIRATION (LP, mono/stereo)	15

LINCOLN ROGERS
73	Phoenix NIX 137	Let Love Come Between Us/She Looked At Me With Love	15

LYNNE ROGERS
65	RCA RCA 1479	Sometimes/I Shouldn't Care	7

MARK ROGERS & MARKSMEN
63	Parlophone R 5045	Bubble Pop/Hold It!	25

(see also Marksmen, Mark Wirtz)

PAUL ROGERS
61	HMV POP 872	Four An' Twenty Thousand Kisses/Free To Love	10
63	HMV POP 1121	Always/Joanie Don't Be Angry	10

PAULINE ROGERS
54	Columbia SCM 5106	Spinnin' The Blues/But Good	20

PIERCE ROGERS & OVERLANDERS
61	Parlophone R 4838	Do You Still Love Me?/That Someone	12

ROY ROGERS
55	HMV 7EG 8145	KING OF THE COWBOYS (EP)	10
55	HMV 7EG 8182	HAPPY TRAILS (EP)	10

SHORTY ROGERS & HIS ORCHESTRA
52	Capitol LC 6549	MODERN SOUNDS (10" LP, as Shorty Rogers & His Giants)	15
54	HMV DLP 1030	COOL AND CRAZY (10" LP, featuring Giants)	15
54	HMV DLP 1058	EIGHT SHORTY ROGERS' NUMBERS (10" LP)	15
56	Contemporary LDC 190	SHELLY MANNE, SHORTY ROGERS AND JIMMY GIUFFRE - THE THREE (10" LP, with Shelly Manne & Jimmy Giuffre)	18

(see also Boots Brown, Bud Shank, Shelly Manne, Jimmy Giuffre)

SIDNEY ROGERS
73	Techniques TE 923	Don't Throw Stones/Toughness	8
78	Ethnic Fight FTDD 4448	I Don't Want To End Up In Slavery/Mary And Bobby (12")	60
74	Ethnic Fight ETH 2214S	MIRACLE WORKER (LP)	30
75	Ethnic Fight EF 2222S	TIPPIN' IN (LP)	60

TIMMIE ROGERS
57	London HLU 8510	Back To School Again/I've Got A Dog Who Loves Me	60
57	London HLU 8510	Back To School Again/I've Got A Dog Who Loves Me (78)	20
58	London HLU 8601	Take Me To Your Leader/Fla-Ga-La-Pa	60
58	London HLU 8601	Take Me To Your Leader/Fla-Ga-La-Pa (78)	20

TRACY ROGERS
65	Polydor 56029	How Love Used To Be/When I Realise	7
65	Polydor 56037	Love Story/I Remember When I Loved You (p/s)	10
66	Polydor 56077	Baby/Through Thick And Thin	25
67	Polydor 56197	Back With You Baby/In The Morning	12

VERN ROGERS & HI-FI'S
62	Oriole CB 1785	That Ain't Right/Be Everything To Anyone You Love	20
63	Oriole CB 1826	He's New To You/Can't Complain	15

Diana ROGERSON

MINT VALUE £

63	Oriole CB 1885	I Will/One Way Love Affair	20
63	Oriole CB 1923	Anna/Pride	15

DIANA ROGERSON
85	United Dairies UD 017	THE INEVITABLE CHRYSTAL BELLE SCRODD RECORD (LP)	25
86	United Dairies UD 021	CHRYSTAL BELLE SCRODD: BELLE DE JOUR (LP)	25

(see also Nurse With Wound)

ROG & PIP
14	Rise Above Relics RARLP 013	OUR REVOLUTION (LP)	25

ROGUES (U.K.)
67	Decca F 12718	Memories Of Missy/And You Let Her Pass By	30

ROGUES (U.S.)
65	CBS 201731	Everyday/Rogers Reef	20

(see also Terry Day, Terry Melcher)

CHRIS ROHMANN
73	RCA Victor SF 8364	THE MAN I AM TODAY (LP)	22

ROKES
67	RCA RCA 1587	Let's Live For Today/Ride On	30
67	RCA RCA 1646	Hold My Hand/Regency Sue	50
68	RCA RCA 1694	When The Wind Arises/The Works Of Bartholemew	70

ROKKA
80	Rock Trax RT 01	Come Back/Touch & Go	10

BRIAN ROLAND SOUND
71	Ra 5007	Swing Low/Shake	10

CHERRY ROLAND
63	Decca F 11579	Handy Sandy/Stay As I Am	12
63	Decca F 11648	What A Guy/Just For Fun	12

(see also Cherry Rowland)

PAUL ROLAND
82	Aristocrat ARC 1389	Doctor Strange/Madelaine (p/s)	8
83	Aftermath AEP 12011	Blades Of Battenburg (Remix)/Captain Blood/Puppet Master/Cavalier (12", p/s)	10
86	Aftermath AEP 12013	Gabrielle/Berlin/Sword & Sorcery (p/s)	8
86	Imaginary MIRAGE 002	Demon In A Glass Case/In The Opium Den (oversized p/s)	7
87	Bam Caruso PABL 094	Alice's House/Go Down You Murderers/Happy Families/Jumbee (demo) (p/s)	8
80	Ace ACE 013	THE WEREWOLF OF LONDON (LP)	18

(see also Weird Strings, Midnight Rags, Beau Brummel)

WALTER ROLAND/GEORGIA SLIM
59	Jazz Collector JEL 2	THE MALE BLUES VOL. 1 (EP)	22

BARRY ROLFE
73	Philips 6006 331	Look The Business/Molly Molly	30
73	Philips 6006 348	Beam Me Aboard, Mr. Spock/Boadecia	8
74	Philips 6006 381	Going Up/Johnny Bo Jangle	6

ROLFE, GIFFORD & ANDREW MULLINS
72	Look REM 104	Tutankamun/Sad Eyes	10

PETER ROLFE
66	Strike JH 314	London/In The Middle Of Town	20

ROLLERS (1)
61	London HLG 9340	Continental Walk/I Want You So	18

ROLLERS (2)
79	Arista 259	Turn On The Radio/Washington's Birthday (p/s)	6

ROLLING STONES
SINGLES : DECCA SINGLES
63	Decca F 11675	Come On/I Want To Be Loved (demo copies £350)	50
63	Decca F 11742	Fortune Teller/Poison Ivy (solid centre, withdrawn)	1500
63	Decca F 11764	I Wanna Be Your Man/Stones (B-side mis-spelled)	35
63	Decca F 11764	I Wanna Be Your Man/Stoned	20
64	No Cat. No.	We Were Falling In Love (EMI disc acetate, unreleased single)	1000
64	Decca F 11845	Not Fade Away/Little By Little	12
64	Decca F 11934	It's All Over Now/Good Times, Bad Times	12
64	Decca F 12014	Little Red Rooster/Off The Hook	12

(The above singles were originally issued with "Recording first published..." text and wide label lettering.)

65	Decca F 12104	The Last Time/Play With Fire	15
65	Decca F 12220	(I Can't Get No) Satisfaction/The Spider And The Fly	15
65	Decca F 12263	Get Off Of My Cloud/The Singer Not The Song	15
66	Decca F 12331	19th Nervous Breakdown/As Tears Go By	10
66	Decca F 12395	Paint It, Black/Long Long While	15

(The above singles were originally issued with a round Decca logo; later boxed-logo pressings are worth £4 each.)

66	Decca F 12497	Have You Seen Your Mother, Baby, Standing In The Shadow?/ Who's Driving Your Plane..	15
67	Decca F 12546	Let's Spend The Night Together/Ruby Tuesday	12
67	Decca F 12654	We Love You/Dandelion	15
68	Decca F 12782	Jumping Jack Flash/Child Of The Moon	15
69	Decca F 12952	Honky Tonk Women/You Can't Always Get What You Want (in demo-only p/s)	70
69	Decca F 12952	Honky Tonk Women/You Can't Always Get What You Want	15
71	Decca F 13195	Street Fighting Man/Surprise Surprise/Everybody Needs Somebody To Love (33rpm maxi-single)	10
71	Decca F 13203	Street Fighting Man/Surprise Surprise (jukebox edition)	30
73	Decca F 13404	Sad Day/You Can't Always Get What You Want	20
74	Decca F 13517	Paint It Black/It's All Over Now (release cancelled, demo-only)	220
75	Decca F 13584	I Don't Know Why I Love You (credited to either 'Jagger/Richard/Taylor'/Try A Little Harder	20
75	Decca F 13584	I Don't Know Why I Love You (credited Stevie Wonder')/Try A Little Harder	15

ROLLING STONES

MINT VALUE £

Year	Catalogue	Description	Value
75	Decca F 13597	Out Of Time/Jiving Sister Fanny	8
76	Decca F 13635	Honky Tonk Women/Sympathy For The Devil	8
70s	Decca F 11934	It's All Over Now/Good Times, Bad Times (repressing, with stereo mix on A-side, [ZXDR instead of XDR matrix no.] boxed Decca logo)	8
87	Decca F 102	Jumping Jack Flash/Child Of The Moon (p/s, reissue)	8
87	Decca FX 102	Jumping Jack Flash/Child Of The Moon/Sympathy For The Devil (12", p/s, reissue)	20

SINGLES : ROLLING STONES LABEL SINGLES

Year	Catalogue	Description	Value
71	Rolling Stones RS 19100	Brown Sugar/Bitch/Let It Rock (in p/s)	50
71	Rolling Stones RS 19100	Brown Sugar/Bitch/Let It Rock	7
74	Rolling Stones RS 19114	It's Only Rock 'N' Roll/Through The Lonely Nights	6
78	R. Stones 12EMI 2802	Miss You (8.26)/Faraway Eyes (12", p/s, pink vinyl)	12
78	Rolling Stone 12EMI 2802	Miss You/Faraway Eyes (12", pink vinyl, p/s)	12
80	Rolling Stones RSR 105	Emotional Rescue/Down In The Hole (p/s)	6
81	Rolling Stones	Beast Of Burden/Everything Is Turning Gold (unreleased)	0
82	Rolling Stones 12RSR 111	Time Is On My Side (live)/Twenty Flight Rock (live)/ Under My Thumb (live) (12", p/s)	10
83	Rolling Stones 0-96978	Undercover Of The Night (Extended Version)/Feel On Baby (Instrumental) (12", p/s)	10
84	Rolling Stones SUGARP 1	Brown Sugar/Bitch (shaped picture disc)	30
93	Rolling Stone RS LH 1	Brown Sugar/Start Me Up (jukebox issue, no p/s)	15
93	Rolling Stone ORDER LH 1	Gimme Shelter (Live Version)/NEW MODEL ARMY FEATURING TOM JONES: Gimme Shelter (jukebox issue, no p/s)	15

SINGLES : CBS SINGLES

Year	Catalogue	Description	Value
86	CBS QTA 6864	Harlem Shuffle (N.Y. Mix)/(London Mix)/Had It With You (12", p/s)	10
89	CBS 655 193-7	Mixed Emotions/Fancyman Blues (p/s)	8
89	CBS 655 193-5	Mixed Emotions (7" Version)/Fancyman Blues/Tumbling Dice/Miss You (CD, picture disc, in circular tin with 'tongue' logo sticker)	35
89	CBS 655 214-2	Mixed Emotions (7" Version)/Fancyman Blues/Shattered/Waiting On A Friend (CD, picture disc, in circular tin with 'tongue' logo sticker)	35
89	CBS 655 422-2	Rock And A Hard Place (7" Version)/(Dance Mix)/(Bonus Beats Mix)/ Cook Cook Blues (CD, picture disc, card sleeve)	15
89	CBS 655 448-2	Rock And A Hard Place (7" Version)/Cook Cook Blues/It's Only Rock'n'Roll (But I Like It)/Rocks Off (3rd CD, picture disc, 7" box set with poster)	25
90	CBS 656 065-7	Almost Hear You Sigh/Wish I'd Never Met You (p/s)	8
90	CBS 656 065-5	Almost Hear You Sigh/Miss You/Waiting On A Friend/Wish I'd Never Met You (CD, in tin with 'Urban Jungle' sticker)	30
90	CBS 656 1227	Terrifying/Rock And A Hard Place (p/s)	8
91	CBS 656 756-7	Highwire/2000 Light Years Away (p/s)	8
91	CBS 656 892-6	Ruby Tuesday/Play With Fire (live)/You Can't Always Get What You Want (live)/Rock And A Hard Place (live) (12", p/s)	10

SINGLES : VIRGIN SINGLES

Year	Catalogue	Description	Value
94	Virgin VS 1503	Love Is Strong/The Storm (numbered p/s, 7,000 only)	10
94	Virgin VCS 1503	Love Is Strong/The Storm (injection moulded jukebox copy)	12
94	Virgin VS 1518	You Got Me Rocking/Jump On Top Of Me (numbered p/s, 7,000 only)	10
94	Virgin VS 1524	Out Of Tears/I'm Gonna Drive (numbered p/s, 7,000 only)	10
94	Virgin VSCDG 1524	Out Of Tears (Don Was Edit)/I'm Gonna Drive/So Young/The Storm/ Jump On Top Of Me (CD, digipak, numbered, 4,000 only, withdrawn)	250
94	Virgin VSP 1539	I Go Wild/I Go Wild (live) (numbered picture disc)	20
96	Virgin VS 1578	Wild Horses/Tumbling Dice/Gimme Shelter (unreleased)	0
96	Virgin VSCDT 1578	Wild Horses/Tumbling Dice/Gimme Shelter (CD, unreleased)	0
97	Virgin VST 1653	Anybody Seen My Baby? (LP Edit)/(Soul Solution Remix)/(Bonus Roll) (12", p/s)	15
97	Virgin VS 1653	Anybody Seen My Baby? (LP Edit)/(Soul Solution Remix Edit) (numbered picture disc, p/s, 7,500 only)	15
98	Virgin VSLH 1667	Saint Of Me/Radio Edit/Anyway You Look At It (injection moulded jukebox labels)	8
98	Virgin VSTTDT 1667	Saint Of Me (remixes)/Anybody Seen My Baby? (remixes) (12", double pack, stickered p/s)	15
98	Virgin VSTX 1667	Saint Of Me (remixes)/Anybody Seen My Baby? (remixes) (12", double pack, stickered p/s)	15
98	Virgin VSY 1700	Out Of Control (Album Radio Edit)/In Hand With Fluke Radio Edit (p/s)	10
98	Virgin VSY 1700	Out Of Control (Album Radio Edit)/(In Hand With Fluke Radio Edit)	10
02	Virgin VS 1838	Don't Stop (Edit)/New Rock Remix (red vinyl, numbered p/s)	12
05	Virgin VS 1905	Streets Of Love/Rough Justice (red vinyl, p/s)	10
05	Virgin VS 1907	Rain Fall Down (Will i Am Remix)/(Ashley Beedle's Heavy Vocal Re-Edit) (7", p/s)	10
06	Virgin VS 1914	Biggest Mistake/Hand Of Fate (red vinyl, p/s)	10

SINGLES : OTHER SINGLES

Year	Catalogue	Description	Value
72	Sound For Industry 107	Mick Jagger Introduces 'Exile On Main Street' (flexidisc free with NME, tracks by Curved Air and Fanny on other side)	15
74	Atlantic K 19107	Brown Sugar/Happy/Rocks Off (unissued)	300
02	Virgin VS1838	Don't Stop/New Rock Remix (Limited edition red vinyl, numbered)	12
03	Abkco 0602498106136	Sympathy For The Devil (Neptune's Radio Edit)/Original Version (p/s)	8
10	Universal 273 547-7	Plundered My Soul/All Down The Line (p/s)	10
11	Universal 0602527643410	Brown Sugar/Bitch/Let It Rock (Live At Leeds 13th March 1971) (p/s)	7
12	Universal 3723278	Doom And Gloom (Jeff Bhasker MIx) (10" 1-sided, other side etched, 1500 only)	10
15	Secret 7" S726	Dead Flowers (100 only, each with unique art sleeve)	200

SINGLES : SINGLES BOX SETS

Year	Catalogue	Description	Value
80	Decca STONE 1-12	SINGLE STONES (12-single box set)	60
80	Decca BROWSE 1	SINGLE STONES (in-store, 3 x 12-single box set [STONE 1-12], with poster & badge, also available via mail-order)	150

EXPORT SINGLES

Year	Catalogue	Description	Value
63	Decca AT 15005	I Wanna Be Your Man/Stoned	150
64	Decca AT 15006	Not Fade Away/Little By Little	150
64	Decca AT 15032	Come On/Tell Me (You're Coming Back)	150
64	Decca AT 15035	Empty Heart/Around And Around	175

ROLLING STONES

MINT VALUE £

65	Decca AT 15039	Time Is On My Side/Congratulations	175
65	Decca AT 15040	Little Red Rooster/Off The Hook	110
65	Decca AT 15043	(I Can't Get No) Satisfaction/The Under Assistant West Coast Promotional Man (p/s)	150
65	Decca F 12104	The Last Time/Play With Fire (with Dutch or Scandinavian p/s)	85
65	Decca F 12220	(I Can't Get No) Satisfaction/The Under Assistant West Coast Promotional Man (with p/s)	75
65	Decca F 12220	(I Can't Get No) Satisfaction/The Under Assistant West Coast Promotional Man	30
65	Decca F 22180	Heart Of Stone/What A Shame (in p/s)	140
65	Decca F 22180	Heart Of Stone/What A Shame	100
65	Decca F 22265	Get Off My Cloud/I'm Free	30
65	Decca F 22265	Get Off My Cloud/I'm Free (in p/s)	75
66	Decca F 12395	Paint It, Black/Long Long While (p/s)	50
66	Decca F 12331	19th Nervous Breakdown/As Tears Go By (with Dutch p/s)	50
67	Decca F 12546	Let's Spend The Night Together/Ruby Tuesday (p/s)	50
67	Decca F 12654	We Love You/Dandelion (p/s)	50
67	Decca F 22706	2,000 Light Years From Home/She's A Rainbow	50
68	Decca F 22825	Street Fighting Man (remix)/No Expectations (in p/s)	50
68	Decca F 22825	Street Fighting Man (remix)/No Expectations	30
69	Decca F 12952	Honky Tonk Women/You Can't Always Get What You Want (p/s)	50
71	Decca F 13195	Street Fighting Man/Surprise Surprise/Everybody Needs Somebody To Love (33rpm maxi-single, p/s)	40
71	Decca F 13126	Little Queenie/Love In Vain (in p/s)	55
71	Decca F 13126	Little Queenie/Love In Vain	20
71	Decca F 13204	Street Fighting Man/Everybody Needs Somebody To Love	20
71	Decca F 13204	Street Fighting Man/Everybody Needs Somebody To Love (in p/s)	40

EPs

64	Decca DFE 8560	THE ROLLING STONES (with unboxed Decca logo)	40
64	Decca DFE 8560	THE ROLLING STONES (later boxed Decca logo)	12
64	Decca DFE 8590	FIVE BY FIVE (with unboxed Decca logo)	40
64	Decca DFE 8590	FIVE BY FIVE (later boxed Decca logo)	12
65	Decca DFE 8620	GOT LIVE IF YOU WANT IT! (with unboxed Decca logo)	40
65	Decca DFE 8620	GOT LIVE IF YOU WANT IT! (later boxed Decca logo)	12
83	Decca DFEX 8560	THE ROLLING STONES (12", reissue)	12
83	Decca DFEX 8590	FIVE BY FIVE (12", reissue)	12
83	Decca DFEX 8620	GOT LIVE IF YOU WANT IT (12", reissue)	12

EPS : EXPORT EPS

64	Decca SDE 7260	ROLLING STONES	125
64	Decca SDE 7501	THE ROLLING STONES VOLUME 2	125
65	Decca DFE 8620	GOT LIVE IF YOU WANT IT! (red label, some with yellow titles on p/s)	125
65	Decca SDE 7502	GOT LIVE IF YOU WANT IT!	125
65	Decca SDE 7503	ROLLING STONES (with "Out Of Our Heads [U.K. version]" sleeve)	125

ALBUMS : DECCA ALBUMS

64	Decca LK 4605	ROLLING STONES (1st pressing, plays 2.52 version of "Tell Me"; Side 2 matrix: XARL 6272-1A)	1000
64	Decca LK 4605	ROLLING STONES (2nd pressing, plays 4.06 version of "Tell Me"; sleeves list "Mona")	350
64	Decca LK 4605	ROLLING STONES (2nd pressing, plays 4.06 version of "Tell Me"; more common, with sleeves that list "I Need You, Baby")	200
65	Decca LK 4661	ROLLING STONES NO. 2	200
65	Decca LK 4661	ROLLING STONES NO. 2 (with 'blind man' text pasted over on rear sleeve)	250
65	Decca LK 4733	OUT OF OUR HEADS (mono)	120
65	Decca SKL 4733	OUT OF OUR HEADS (stereo)	150

(The above LPs were simultaneously pressed with both flipback and non-flipback sleeves. Values are the same.)

66	Decca LK 4786	AFTERMATH (mono)	125
66	Decca SKL 4786	AFTERMATH (stereo)	150
66	Decca LK 4786	AFTERMATH (mono, front cover title has purple shadow)	250
66	Decca SKL 4786	AFTERMATH (stereo, front cover title is shadowed)	200
66	Decca TXL 101	BIG HITS (HIGH TIDE AND GREEN GRASS) (1st pressing, gatefold sleeve, with stapled 12" x 12" picture booklet, mono)	100
66	Decca TXS 101	BIG HITS (HIGH TIDE AND GREEN GRASS) (1st pressing, gatefold sleeve, with stapled 12" x 12" picture booklet, stereo)	100
66	Decca TXL/TXS 101	COULD YOU WALK ON THE WATER (unreleased, proof sleeves exist)	0
67	Decca TXS 101	BIG HITS (HIGH TIDE AND GREEN GRASS) (2nd pressing, gatefold sleeve, without booklet, stereo)	50
67	Decca TXL 101	BIG HITS (HIGH TIDE AND GREEN GRASS) (2nd pressing, gatefold sleeve, without booklet, mono)	30
67	Decca LK 4852	BETWEEN THE BUTTONS (mono)	175
67	Decca SKL 4852	BETWEEN THE BUTTONS (stereo)	150
67	Decca TXL 103	THEIR SATANIC MAJESTIES REQUEST (3-D gatefold sleeve with red inner, mono)	200
67	Decca TXS 103	THEIR SATANIC MAJESTIES REQUEST (3-D gatefold sleeve with red inner, stereo)	150
68	Decca LK 4955	BEGGARS BANQUET (gatefold sleeve, unboxed red label, with Stones Decca label insert, mono)	200
68	Decca SKL 4955	BEGGARS BANQUET (gatefold sleeve, unboxed blue Decca label, with Stones Decca label insert, stereo)	150
69	Decca LK 5019	THROUGH THE PAST, DARKLY (BIG HITS VOL. 2) (octagonal gatefold sleeve, mono)	80
69	Decca SKL 5019	THROUGH THE PAST, DARKLY (BIG HITS VOL. 2) (octagonal gatefold sleeve, stereo)	65
69	Decca LK 5025	LET IT BLEED (mono, red inner, with poster, with stickered sleeve)	400
69	Decca LK 5025	LET IT BLEED (mono, red inner, with poster, without stickered sleeve)	100
69	Decca SKL 5025	LET IT BLEED (stereo, blue inner, with poster, with stickered sleeve)	200
69	Decca SKL 5025	LET IT BLEED (stereo, blue inner, with poster, without stickered sleeve)	60
69	Decca TXL/TXS 103	THEIR SATANIC MAJESTIES REQUEST (2nd pressing, gatefold sleeve with red inner, stereo, stereo disc in stickered mono sleeve)	60

ROLLING STONES

MINT VALUE £

All of the above LPs were originally issued with Decca labels with a large-print logo without a box surrounding it; later pressings with smaller print & boxed logo are worth around two-thirds the value.)

Year	Cat. No.	Title	Value
69	Decca TXL/TXS 103	THEIR SATANIC MAJESTIES REQUEST (2nd pressing, gatefold sleeve with red inner, mono)	50
70	Decca SKL 5065	GET YER YA-YA'S OUT! (1st pressing with fully laminated sleeve front and back, with "sleeve printed in England" XZAL 10076 1W/XZAL 10077 1W. stereo)	80
70	Decca SKL 5065	GET YER YA-YA'S OUT! (2nd pressing with laminated front sleeve front and un-laminated rear sleeve with "sleeve printed in England by Clout & Baker Ltd.")	20
70	Decca TXS 101	BIG HITS (HIGH TIDE AND GREEN GRASS) (LP, reissue, green boxed Decca label, gatefold sleeve, with foldout insert, stereo only)	25
70s	Decca SKL 4733	OUT OF OUR HEADS (2nd pressing, light green sleeve, box Decca logo)	30
70	Decca SKL 5025	LET IT BLEED (LP, reissue, stereo only, no mono/stereo indicator hole on rear sleeve, poster and inner sleeve, boxed logo on label)	50
70	Decca SKL 4786	BEGGARS BANQUET (LP, reissue, laminated gatefold sleeve. small blue boxed Decca label, stereo)	30
70	Decca SKL 4852	BETWEEN THE BUTTONS (LP, reissue, blue boxed label, laminated sleeve)	25
71	Decca SKL 5084	STONE AGE	20
71	Decca SKL 5101	GIMME SHELTER	18
71	Decca NPS2	THEIR SATANIC MAJESTIES REQUEST (LP, gatefold, stereo reissue, boxed Decca logo)	25
73	Decca SKL 5165	GOLDEN B-SIDES (unreleased, test pressings only)	1000
73	Decca SKL 5173	NO STONE UNTURNED	20

(Except where noted, the above Decca LPs were originally issued with dark blue labels & laminated sleeves; later copies are worth two-thirds the value.)

Year	Cat. No.	Title	Value
75	Decca (no cat. no.)	THE HISTORY OF THE ROLLING STONES (3-LP box set; 3x12" pink label test pressings exist, no sleeves, matrices read: ZAL 12996/7, ZAL 12998/9 & ZAL 13000/1; release cancelled in favour of "Rolled Gold" 2-LP set)	1000
75	Decca SKL 5212	METAMORPHOSIS (dark blue label, matt sleeve)	20
75	Decca TXS 103	THEIR SATANIC MAJESTIES REQUEST (3rd pressing, 3-D matt gatefold sleeve, stereo only)	25
75	Decca ROST 3/4	LIVE STONES (2-LP, compilation, pink label test pressings only, follow-up to "Rolled Gold", unreleased)	500
79	Rolling Stones COC 69100	EXILE ON MAIN STREET (2-LP reissue, gatefold sleeve, inners)	40
80	Decca TAB 1	SOLID ROCK (LP)	20
83	Decca ROLL 1	THE FIRST EIGHT STUDIO ALBUMS (8-LP set, with 192-page book; wraparound card box, each LP has star printed on rear sleeve)	250

ALBUMS : EXPORT LPS

Year	Cat. No.	Title	Value
64	London LL 3402	12 X 5 (LP, for export with 'Congradulations' mis-print on rear of sleeve)	300
65	Decca SKL 4725	OUT OF OUR HEADS (with U.S. track listing & cover design, unboxed Decca label logo, stereo, withdrawn)	250
65	Decca LK 4725	OUT OF OUR HEADS (export, LP, with U.S. track listing & cover design, unboxed Decca label logo, mono, withdrawn)	200
66	Decca LK 4838	HAVE YOU SEEN YOUR MOTHER, LIVE (export LP, laminated sleeve & unboxed Decca label logo, mono)	200
66	Decca SKL 4838	HAVE YOU SEEN YOUR MOTHER, LIVE (export LP, laminated sleeve & unboxed Decca label logo, stereo)	250
67	Decca LK 4888	FLOWERS (export LP, mono, laminated sleeve, unboxed Decca label logo)	400
67	Decca SKL 4888	FLOWERS (export LP, stereo, laminated sleeve, unboxed Decca label logo)	250
70	Decca SKL 4786	AFTERMATH (export LP, white label, black print, supposedly for export)	25
70	Decca SKL 5065	GET YER YA-YA'S OUT! (export LP, white label, black print, supposedly for export)	20
70	Decca TXS 103	THEIR SATANIC MAJESTIES REQUEST (export LP, gatefold sleeve, white label, black print, supposedly for export)	25
72	Decca LK/SKL 4838	HAVE YOU SEEN YOUR MOTHER, LIVE (export LP, later pressing, boxed logo, laminated sleeve)	80
72	Decca LK/SKL 4888	FLOWERS (export LP, later pressing, laminated sleeve, boxed Decca label logo)	100

ALBUMS : ROLLING STONES LABEL LPS

Year	Cat. No.	Title	Value
71	Rolling Stones COC 59100	STICKY FINGERS ('big' zip sleeve with insert)	150
71	Rolling Stones COC 59100	STICKY FINGERS (zip sleeve with insert)	80
72	Rolling Stones COC 69100	EXILE ON MAIN STREET (2-LP, gatefold, with inners, postcard inserts)	200
72	Rolling Stones COC 69100	EXILE ON MAIN STREET (2-LP, with inners, TM next to Stones logo, without postcard inserts)	50
73	Rolling Stones COC 59101	GOAT'S HEAD SOUP (gatefold sleeve, with 2 inserts)	60
74	Rolling Stones COC 59103	IT'S ONLY ROCK 'N' ROLL (LP)	20
76	Rolling Stones COC 59106	BLACK AND BLUE (LP, gatefold)	20
78	Rolling Stones CUN 39108	SOME GIRLS (LP, die cut sleeve with uncensored inner cover, featuring Farrah Fawcett, Raquel Welch, Judy Garland and Marilyn Monroe)	35
78	Rolling Stones CUN 39108	SOME GIRLS (LP, die cut sleeve with censored inner cover, it is believed that those with the red 'Some Girls' title is the rarest with blue, green and yellow being more common)	20
80	Rolling Stones CUN 39111	EMOTIONAL RESCUE (LP with poster)	20
81	Rolling Stones CUN 39114	TATTOO YOU (LP)	20
82	Rolling Stones CUN 39115	STILL LIFE (AMERICAN CONCERT 1981) (LP)	15
82	Rolling Stones CUNP 39115	STILL LIFE (AMERICAN CONCERT 1981) (LP, picture disc, mispressed with wrong tracks)	150
82	Rolling Stones CUNP 39115	STILL LIFE (AMERICAN CONCERT 1981) (LP, picture disc)	25
83	Rolling Stones 1A 0641654361	UNDERCOVER (LP)	18
84	Rolling Stones 450196	EXILE ON MAIN STREET (2-LP, reissue in single sleeve)	20
91	Rolling Stones 4681351	FLASHPOINT (LP, stickered sleeve. 12 page booklet)	20
20	Rolling Stones 074 249-8	GOATS HEAD SOUP (LP, reissue, stickered sleeve, Carnaby Street edition, red vinyl)	150
20	Rolling Stones 3523970	STICKY FINGERS (LP, reissue, stickers sleeve, Carnaby Street edition, red vinyl)	150
21	Rolling Stones COC 59106	BLACK AND BLUE (LP, reissue, stickers sleeve, Carnaby Street edition, red vinyl)	50
21	Rolling Stones CUNS 39108	SOME GIRLS (LP, reissue, stickered sleeve, Carnaby Street edition, red vinyl)	50
21	Rolling Stones CUNS 39114	TATTOO YOU (LP, reissue, stickered sleeve, Carnaby Street edition, red vinyl)	60
21	Rolling Stones 355 867-4	BLUE & LONESOME (2-LP, stickered sleeve, Carnaby Street Edition, red vinyl)	50
21	Rolling Stones 352 731-1	HONK (3-LP, stickered sleeve, Carnaby Street Edition, red vinyl)	50
21	Rolling Stones 3594272	A BIGGER BANG - LIVE ON COPACABANA BEACH (3-LP, stickered sleeve, Carnaby Street Edition, splatter vinyl)	100

Audley ROLLINS

MINT VALUE £

ALBUMS : OTHER ALBUMS
77	CBS 450 208	LOVE YOU LIVE (2-LP)	25
83	R. Digest GROLA 119	THE GREAT YEARS (4-LP, box set)	25
86	CBS 86321	DIRTY WORK (LP, with inner)	25
89	CBS 465752	STEEL WHEELS (LP)	15
89	ABKCO 820900-1	ROLLING STONES SINGLES COLLECTION/LONDON YEARS (4-LP set)	45
89	CBS 466 918 2	COLLECTION 1971-1989 (15-CD box set, with bonus CD, 'Collector's Edition')	130
91	Sony 468 135-9/468 135-2	FLASHPOINT/INTERVIEW 1990 (2-CD pack, shrinkwrapped with tongue logo sticker, numbered)	40
94	Virgin V 2750	VOODOO LOUNGE (2-LP)	50
95	Virgin V 2801	STRIPPED (2-LP with inner sleeves)	80
97	Virgin V 2840	BRIDGES TO BABYLON (2-LP, with inner sleeves)	100
97	Virgin LPCENT 38	STICKY FINGERS (LP, reissue, 180gm vinyl, metal zipper)	60
02	Virgin CDVDXX2964	FORTY LICKS (Ltd edition CD box set)	35
10	Polydor 0602527147277	EMOTIONAL RESCUE (LP, reissue, 180gm)	20
10	Polydor 0602527147284	TATTOO YOU (LP, reissue, 180gm)	20
10	Eagle Rock ERELP 815	LADIES AND GENTLEMEN (2-LP)	20
10	Polydor 0602527147291	UNDERCOVER (LP, reissue 180gm)	18
10	Polydor 0602527147314	STEEL WHEELS (LP, reissue, 180gm)	20
10	Polydor 1602527147307	DIRTY WORK (LP, reissue, 180gm)	15
13	Eagle Vision ERDVLP 079	SWEET SUMMER SUN (3-LP, DVD foldout sleeve with inners)	40

PROMOS : PROMO SINGLES
72	Rolling Stones SAM 3	Excerpts From Exile On Main Street: All Down The Line/Rocks Off	400
72	Rolling Stones SAM 4	Excerpts From Exile On Main Street: Happy/Shine A Light	400
76	Rolling Stones RS 19121 DJ	Fool To Cry/Crazy Mama (7" promo, mono mix, edited down to 3.59, no 'phased' electric piano intro)	100
83	R. Stones RSR 112 (DJ)	Let's Spend The Night Together (live)/Start Me Up (live)	20
91	CBS A 026/B 027	Highwire/Sympathy For The Devil (live) (12")	15
93	EMI ORDERLH 1	Gimme Shelter (live) (1-sided jukebox issue)	20
93	Virgin STONES 1	JUMP BACK (EP)	25
98	Virgin VSTDJ 1667	Saint Of Me (Deep Dish Grunge Garage Remix) (Part 1)/(Part 2)/ (Grunge Garage Dub)/(Rolling Dub)/Anyone Seen My Baby? (Armand's Rolling Steelo Mix)/Anyone Seen My Baby? (Bonus Roll) (12" double pack, stickered sleeve)	20
98	Virgin VSTDJ 1700	Out Of Control (In Hand With Fluke)/(In Hand Full Version)/ (Bi-Polar's Fat Controller Mix)/(Bi-Polar At The Controls) (12")	10
98	Virgin VSP 1700	Out Of Control (Bi-Polar At The Controls)/(Bi-Polar Outer Version) (withdrawn brown label)	30
98	Virgin VSTDDJ 1700	Out Of Control (In Hand With Fluke Instrumental)/(In Hand Full Version)/ (Bi-Polar's Fat Controller Mix)/(Bi-Polar At The Controls) (12")	10
98	Virgin VSP 1700	Out Of Control (Bi-Polar At The Controls)/(Bi-Polar Outer Version) (withdrawn silver label)	15
00s	Virgin DEVIL 666	Sympathy For The Devil (Fatboy Slim Remix)/(Neptunes Remix)//(Full Phat Remix)/ (Original Version) (2x12", with press sheet)	20

PROMOS : PROMO LPS
69	Decca RSM. 1	PROMOTIONAL ALBUM (LP, U.K. disc in U.S. sleeve [lists RSD-1], 200 copies pressed [100 each for U.K. & U.S.], U.K. issues include a letter from Decca)	2000
86	CBS SAMP 1103	STONES ON CD - A RADIO SAMPLER (CD, poly sleeve)	200
89	CBS (no catalogue no.)	STEEL WHEELS - THE ALBUM OF THE TOUR (box set, with LP, CD, cassette and "Terrifying" 12", European tour dates & sticker)	150
89	CBS SAMPC 1347	SAY AHHH! (LP, promo-only compilation)	200
95	Virgin IVDG 2801	STRIPPED (2-CD, interview disc & album, fold-out digipak)	40
97	Virgin (no catalogue no.)	BRIDGES TO BABYLON (CD in promo box, with "Anybody Seen My Baby?" promo CD, press release, bottle opener, notebook and sheet of stamps, 200 only)	150
97	Virgin IVDG 2840	BRIDGES TO BABYLON INTERVIEW (2-CD, interview disc & album, fold-out digipak)	30
97	Virgin CDVDJ 2840	BRIDGES TO BABYLON (CD, with spoken word intros, 200 only)	70
99	Virgin CDIDJ 2880	NO SECURITY (3-CD [2 interview discs], foldout digipak)	45
90s	Virgin CDVDY 2964	FORTY LICKS (CD)	45

(see also Mick Jagger, Keith Richards, Pipes of Pan, Bill Wyman, Charlie Watts, Andrew Oldham, Bobbie Miller)

AUDLEY ROLLINS
72	Explosion EX 2062	Repatriation/HUGH ROY JUNIOR: Repatriation - Version	10
73	Attack ATT 8060	Without You In My World/It's Flowing (actually "It's Growing")	10
73	Harry J HJ 6654	What's Your Name/NOW GENERATION: What's Your Name - Version	6

(see also A. Boyne)

(HENRY) ROLLINS BAND
91	Vinyl Solution VS 30	Let There Be Rock/Carry Me Down (12", p/s, as Henry Rollins & Hard-Ons)	25
94	Imago 7432323057	LIAR (EP, poster p/s)	12
94	Imago 72787 21034-1	WEIGHT (LP, clear vinyl)	100

BIRD ROLLINS
72	Mojo 2092 049	Love Man From Carolina/She Needs Loving All The Time	10

SONNY ROLLINS
56	Esquire 20-050	SONNY ROLLINS QUARTET (10" LP)	65
57	Esquire 20-080	SONNY ROLLINS QUINTET (10" LP)	50
57	Esquire 32-025	SONNY ROLLINS PLUS FOUR (LP)	50
57	Esquire 32-035	PERSPECTIVES (LP, with Modern Jazz Quartet)	50
58	Esquire 32-038	WORKTIME (LP)	150
58	Esquire 32-045	SAXOPHONE COLOSSUS (LP, as Sonny Rollins Four)	200
58	Contemporary LAC 12118	WAY OUT WEST (LP)	70
58	Esquire 32-058	TENOR MADNESS (LP)	100
59	Esquire 32-075	ROLLINS PLAYS FOR BIRD (LP)	70
59	Esquire 32-085	TOUR-DE-FORCE (LP)	70
59	MGM MGM-C 776	SONNY ROLLINS AND THE BIG BRASS (LP)	20
60	Contemporary SCA 5013	SONNY ROLLINS AND THE CONTEMPORARY LEADERS (LP, stereo only)	20

ROLL MOVEMENT

			MINT VALUE £
61	Esquire 32-175	SONNY BOY (LP)	100
61	Riverside RLP 12-241	THE SOUND OF SONNY (LP)	25
62	Riverside RLP 12-258	FREEDOM SUITE (LP)	25
62	Esquire 32-155	MOVIN' OUT (LP)	50
62	RCA RD/SF 7504	THE BRIDGE (LP)	15
63	RCA RD/SF 7524	WHAT'S NEW (LP)	20
63	RCA RD/SF 7546	OUR MAN IN JAZZ (LP)	20
64	RCA RD/SF 7593	SONNY MEETS HAWK (LP, with Coleman Hawkins)	20
64	RCA RD/SF 7626	SONNY ROLLINS & CO. (LP)	20
65	RCA RD 7670	NOW'S THE TIME (LP)	20
65	Fontana FJL 124	BLOW! (LP)	25
66	HMV CLP 1915	ROLLINS ON IMPULSE (LP)	25
66	Stateside SL 10164	SAXOPHONE COLOSSUS (LP, reissue)	15
67	RCA RD/SF 7736	STANDARD SONNY ROLLINS (LP)	15
67	HMV CLP/CSD 3529	SONNY PLAYS ALFIE (LP)	15
67	HMV CLP/CSD 3610	EAST BROADWAY RUNDOWN (LP)	15

(see also Modern Jazz Quartet, Thelonious Monk, Clifford Brown, Coleman Hawkins)

ROLL MOVEMENT
67	Go AJ 11410	I'm Out On My Own/Just One Thing	35

ROLL-UPS
80	Bridgehouse BHS 6	Blackmail/Hold On (p/s)	15
79	Bridgehouse BHLP 004	LOW DIVES FOR HIGHBALLS (LP)	25

GLORIA ROMA
64	Decca F 12001	It Hurts Me So/I Didn't Know What Time It Was	8

ROMAN INDEX
81	123 Se 15V	Revolution/Burn Those Books (p/s)	20

MIMI ROMAN
61	Warner Bros WB 55	Johnny Will/Let It Be Me	8

MURRAY ROMAN
69	Track 613 007	YOU CAN'T BEAT PEOPLE UP AND HAVE THEM SAY I LOVE YOU (LP)	20
69	Track 613 015	A BLIND MAN'S MOVIE (LP)	20

TONY ROMAN
67	Stateside SS 2022	Shadows On A Foggy Day/Maggie	7

LYN ROMAN
67	Stateside SS2069	The Penthouse/Born To Lose	12

ROMANY
71	BEV SLP 1323	THE ROMANY (LP)	300

ROME STREETZ
20	Daupe! DM SP 057	JOYERIA (LP, as Rome Streetz x The Artivist, clear red vinyl, 100 only)	40
20	Daupe! DM SP 057	JOYERIA (LP, as Rome Streetz x The Artivist, splatter vinyl, 100 only)	40
20	Daupe! DM SP 057	JOYERIA (LP, as Rome Streetz x The Artivist, gold vinyl, 100 only)	60
20	Daupe! DM SP 057	JOYERIA (LP, as Rome Streetz x The Artivist, frosted clear vinyl, 80 only)	50
20	Daupe! DM SP 057	JOYERIA (LP, as Rome Streetz x The Artivist, black vinyl, 80 only)	40
20	Daupe! DM SP 057	JOYERIA (LP, as Rome Streetz x The Artivist, black vinyl, 20 only, with OBI strip)	100
20	Daupe! DM SP 064	NOISE KANDY 4 (LP, splatter vinyl, 100 only)	60
20	Daupe! DM SP 064	NOISE KANDY 4 (LP, silver vinyl, 150 only)	40
20	Daupe! DM SP 064	NOISE KANDY 4 (LP, black vinyl, 480 only)	40
20	Daupe! DM SP 064	NOISE KANDY 4 (LP, black vinyl, with OBI strip, 20 only)	100

MAX ROMEO
67	Caltone TONE 106	Don't Want To Let You Go/I Can't Do No More (as Romeo & the Emotions with Tommy McCook and the Supersonics)	70
68	Island WI 3104	Put Me In The Mood/My One Girl	100
68	Island WI 3111	Walk Into The Dawn/DAWN PENN: I'll Get You	200
68	Unity UN 503	Wet Dream/She's But A Little Girl	10
69	Blue Cat BS 161	We Want Man/AL REID: Vietcong	40
69	Blue Cat BS 163	It's Not The Way (as Maxie Romeo)/AL REID: Darling	120
69	Nu Beat NB 022	Blowing In The Wind/LARRY MARSHALL: Money Girl	60
69	Trojan TR 656	Sweet Chariot/Far Far Away (with Hippy Boys)	20
69	Unity UN 507	Belly Woman (actually by Derrick Morgan)/PAULETT & LOVERS: Please Stay	10
69	Unity UN 511	Twelfth Of Never (actually by Pat Kelly)/TARTONS: Solid As A Rock (actually by Tartans)	15
69	Unity UN 516	Wine Her Goosie/KING CANNON: Fireball	30
69	Unity UN 532	Mini-Skirt Vision/Far Far Away	25
70	Unity UN 544	Melting Pot/HIPPY BOYS: Death Rides A Horse	45
70	Unity UN 545	Clap Clap (with Hippy Boys)/You've Got Your Troubles	45
70	Unity UN 547	What A Cute Man/Buy You A Rainbow	35
70	Unity UN 560	Fish In The Pot/Feel It	30
71	Bullet BU 478	Mother Oh Mother/Dreams Of Passion (actually "Judgement Rock" by Charlie Ace)	10
71	Pama Supreme PS 328	Ginal Ship/UPSETTERS: Version 2	30
71	Pama Supreme PS 306	Let The Power Fall On I/The Raid	10
71	Pama Supreme PS 318	Don't You Weep/Weeping (Version)	10
71	Punch PH 73	Chie Chie Bud/Version	12
71	Unity UN 571	Macabee (Version)/SOUL SYNDICATE: Music Book	12
71	Camel CA 66	Black Equality/Suffering	20
71	Camel CA 82	The Coming Of Jah/Watch And Pray	10
71	Prince Buster PB 11	Words Sounds And Power/Version	18
72	Camel CA 85	Rasta Bandwagon/When Jah Speaks	10
72	Camel CA 86	Public Enemy Number One/How Long Must We Wait	30
72	Big BG 334	Are You Sure/RUPIE EDWARDS ALL STARS: Are You Sure - Version	6
72	Dynamic DYN 444	We Love Jamaica/SOUL RHYTHM: We Love Jamaica Version	8
72	G.G. GG 4535	Is It Really Over?/MAYTONES: Born To Be Loved	6

Victor ROMEO

MINT VALUE £

72	High Note Hs 058	Pray For Me (with Gaytones)/GAYTONES: Pray For Me - Version	10
72	Pama PM 836	Wet Dream/("Bang Bang Lulu" by Lloyd Tyrell)/("Birth Control" by Lloyd Tyrell)/ Sex Education by Classics) (Maxi-Single)	8
72	Pama Supreme PS 359	Are You Sure/CARL MASTERS: Va-Va-Voom	8
72	Prince Buster PB 11	River Jordan/Words Sound And Power	8
73	Magnet MA 032	Murder In The Place/Version	10
73	Pama Supreme PS 385	Everyman Aught To Know/Version	8
73	Unity UN 572	Rent Crisis/Version	8
75	Soul Food SF	Copie Duppy/DYNAMITES: Love Forever (white label only, as Tammie Lee, B-side actually by BIM SHERMAN)	70
76	Island WIP 6305	One Step Forward/One Step Dub	10
76	Island WIP 6330	Chase The Devil/UPSETTERS FEAT. PRINCE JAZZBO: Croaking Lizard	40
76	Mango MAN 1014	Fire Fe The Vatican/JAH LLOYD: Leggo	7
92	Jah Shaka SHAKA 930	Melt Away/Version	50
69	Pama PMLP 11	A DREAM (LP)	60
71	Pama PMP 2010	LET THE POWER FALL (LP)	50
75	Count Shelly CSLP 06	EVERY MAN OUGHT TO KNOW (LP)	60
76	Island ILPS 9392	WAR INA BABYLON (LP)	30
76	Tropical TSL 1000	REVELATION TIME (LP)	60
78	Mango MLPS 9503	RECONSTRUCTION (LP, blue rim)	30
92	Jah Shaka SHAKA 921	FAR I - CAPTAIN OF MY SHIP (LP)	30
95	Jah Shaka SHAKA 951	OUR RIGHTS (LP)	20
00	Simply Vinyl SVLP 250	OPEN THE IRON GATE 1973-77 (2-LP)	40

(see also Maxie & Glen, Henry & Lisa, Dennis Alcapone, George Meggie, David Isaacs)

VICTOR ROMEO
80	Local LR 3	Slacks And Sovereigns/DETONATORS: Working Dub (12")	6
80	Special Request LR 4	At The Club/DETONATORS: Lift Off (12")	15

(see also Detonators)

ROMEO Z
66	CBS 202645	Come Back Baby/Since My Baby Said Goodbye	30

ROMEO & EMOTIONS
67	Caltone TONE 106	Don't Want To Let You Go/I Can't Do No More	80

(see also Max Romeo)

CHAN ROMERO
59	Columbia DB 4341	The Hippy Hippy Shake/If I Had A Way	100
60	Columbia DB 4405	My Little Ruby/I Don't Care Now	200

ROMFORD STOMPERS
81	Rott ROTT 1	Dead Girls/MARY & KEN: Happy (stamped labels in stamped paper die-cut sleeve)	20

ROMI & JAZZ
90	Chrysalis CHSR 123545	One Love One World (Feel The Rhythm Mix)/One Love One World (Unity '90 Mix)/Love Crime (Sunrise Mix) (12", p/s)	12

RON AND MEL
65	Columbia DB 7469	In A Shabby Little Hut/I See Your Face	6

RONALD & RUBY
58	RCA RCA 1053	Lollipop/Fickle Baby	10

TERRY RONALD
91	MCA 1569	What The Child Needs/Overnight Dub	8

RONALD & LLOYD
74	Magnet MG 042	Back In My Arms/HEPTONES: Drifting Away	18

RONDELLS
58	London HLU 8716	Good Good/Dreamy (with Ned Jr.)	60
58	London HLU 8716	Good Good/Dreamy (with Ned Jr.) (78)	40

RONDELS
61	London HLU 9404	Back Beat No. 1/Shades Of Green	20

DON RONDO
57	London HLJ 8466	White Silver Sands/Stars Fell On Alabama	8
58	London HLJ 8567	What A Shame/Made For Each Other	10
58	London HLJ 8610	I've Got Bells On My Heart/School Dance	8
58	London HLJ 8641	Blonde Bombshell/Her Hair Was Yellow	6

GENE RONDO
68	Giant GN 39	Ben Nevis/Grey Lies	28
68	Jolly JY 004	Mary, Mary/Baby, Baby	25
69	Downtown DT 422	A Lover's Question/HERBIE GRAY & RUDIES: Blue Moon	20
69	Downtown DT 431	Sentimental Reasons/Then You Can Tell Me Goodbye	25
70	Downtown DT 459	Spreading Peace/MUSIC DOCTORS: Guitar Riff	20
72	Downtown DT 490	Wanna Be Like Daddy/STUDIO SOUND: A Little More	12
72	Count Shelly CS 005	Happy Birthday Sweet Sixteen/Meditation	25
73	Magnet MA 001	Prisoner Of Love/How Many Times Girl	8
73	Sir Collins SCMW 003	When I Give My Love/Overcome	20
73	Magnet MA 028	Oh Sweet Africa/This Is Love	18
73	Magnet MA 035	Valley Of Tears/He'll Break Your Heart	15
74	Queen Bee QB4	Rebel Woman/Version	45
77	Third World TW 52	Domestic Affair/Version	20
78	Burning Sounds BSD 007	Jah Jah Worker/MILITANT BARRY: Natty Dredd Supreme/Africa Is My Home/MILITANT BARRY: Sound Call Africa (12")	20
85	Roots Pool RP002	No One But You/SUGAR MINOTT: Children Of Africa	15
70	Trojan TBL 149	ON MY WAY (LP)	40
77	Venture VNLP 8862	MEMORIES (LP)	80

(see also Gene Pancho)

RONETTES
63	London HLU 9259	Be My Baby/Tedesco And Pitman	10

RONNIE & DEL AIRES

			MINT VALUE £
64	London HLU 9826	Baby I Love You/Miss Joan And Mr Sam	10
64	London HLU 9905	(The Best Part Of) Breakin' Up/Big Red	20
64	London HLU 9922	Do I Love You?/When I Saw You	20
64	London HLU 9931	(Walking) In The Rain/How Does It Feel?	18
65	London HLU 9952	Born To Be Together/Blues For Baby	20
65	London HLU 9976	Is This What I Get For Loving You?/You Baby	30
66	London HLU 10087	I Can Hear Music/When I Saw You (withdrawn)	100
69	London HLU 10240	Be My Baby/Baby I Love You	6
69	A&M AMS 748	You Came, You Saw, You Conquered/I Can Hear Music	8
75	Phil Spector Intl. 2010 009	I'm A Woman In Love/When I Saw You	10
77	Phil Spector Intl. 2010 017	I Wonder/Walking In The Rain	10
64	London HA-U 8212	PRESENTING THE FABULOUS RONETTES FEATURING VERONICA (LP, original pressing on plum label)	100
64	London HA-U 8212	PRESENTING THE FABULOUS RONETTES FEATURING VERONICA (LP, later pressing on black label)	50
65	Colpix PXL 486	THE RONETTES (LP)	80

(see also Ronnie Spector, Joey Dee & Starlighters)

RONNIE & DEL AIRES
| 64 | Coral Q 72473 | Drag/Wigglin' 'N' Wobblin' | 35 |

RONNIE & HI-LITES
| 62 | Pye International 7N 25104 | I Wish That We Were Married/Twistin' And Kissin' | 30 |

RONNIE & RAINBOWS
| 61 | London HL 9345 | Loose Ends/Sombrero | 25 |

RONNIE & ROY
| 59 | Capitol CL 15028 | Big Fat Sally/Here I Am | 150 |

RONNO
| 71 | Vertigo 6059 029 | Fourth Hour Of My Sleep/Powers Of Darkness | 65 |

(see also Mick Ronson)

RONNY
| 64 | Decca F 21908 | Oh! My Darling Caroline/Lu La Lu | 10 |

RONNY & THE DAYTONAS
64	Stateside SS 333	G.T.O./Hot Rod Baby	25
64	Stateside SS 367	California Bound/Hey Little Girl	25
65	Stateside SS 391	Bucket T/Little Rail Job	30
65	Stateside SS 432	Beach Boy/No Wheels	30
66	Stateside SS 484	Sandy/Sandy (Instrumental)	20

(see also Buzz & Bucky)

MICK RONSON
74	RCA APBO 0212	Love Me Tender/Only After Dark	6
74	RCA 11474 XSP	Love Me Tender/Slaughter On 10th Avenue (1-sided red or black interview flexidisc, included in press kits)	15
74	RCA LPBO 5022	Slaughter On 10th Avenue/Leave My Heart Alone	6
75	RCA RCA 2482	Billy Porter/Seven Days	6
74	RCA Victor APL1-0353	SLAUGHTER ON 10th AVENUE (LP)	20
74	RCA APL1-0681	PLAY DON'T WORRY (LP, laminated gatefold sleeve)	20
94	Epic EPC 474742 1	HEAVEN AND HULL (LP, picture disc)	50

(see also Ronno, David Bowie, Mott The Hoople, Slaughter & The Dogs, Ian Hunter)

ROOFTOP SINGERS
63	Fontana 271 700 TF	Walk Right In/Cool Water	6
63	Fontana 680 999 TL	WALK RIGHT IN (LP)	15
66	Fontana TFL 6065	RAINY RIVER (LP)	15

(see also Tarriers)

ROOGALATOR
| 76 | Stiff BUY 3 | WITH THE ROOGALATOR: All Aboard/Cincinnati Fatback (p/s, push-out centre) | 8 |
| 76 | Stiff BUY 3 | WITH THE ROOGALATOR: All Aboard/Cincinnati Fatback (p/s, 2nd pressing solid centre) | 6 |

ROOM FOR HUMANS
| 81 | Bandit BR 001 | Telephone Telephone/Girl Friend | 35 |

ROOM 10
| 65 | Decca F 12249 | I Love My Love/Going Back | 15 |

ROOM 13
| 82 | Woronzow W 002 | Murder Mystery/Need Some Dub (12", p/s) | 25 |

(see also Bevis Frond)

ROOM (1)
| 70 | Deram SML 1073 | PRE-FLIGHT (LP, non-laminated sleeve, white/red label) | 1200 |

ROOM (2)
| 80 | Box BOX 001 | Motion/Waiting Room (p/s) | 6 |

MARY ROOS
| 72 | CBS 7959 | Wake Me Early In The Morning/When You're Singing (Don't Forget) | 6 |

ROOSEVELT SINGERS
| 73 | Sioux SI 025 | Heavy Reggae/HONG GANG: Smoking Wild | 20 |

ROOT & JENNY JACKSON
| 70 | Beacon BEA 164 | Save Me/If I Didn't Love You | 40 |

(see also (Root and) Jenny Jackson)

ROOT BOYS
| 70 | Columbia Blue Beat DB 115 | Please Don't Stop The Wedding/Your Love, Your Love | 10 |

ROOTS MANUVA
95	Sound Of Money SNM006	Next Typa Motion/Raw Uncut (12")	25
99	Big Dada BD009	Juggle Tings Proper/Strange Behaviour (12")	12
01	Big Dada BD022/7	Witness (1 Hope)/(Walworth Rockers Dub)	20
01	Big Dada BD022	Witness/Son Of The Soil (12")	12
02	Ultimate Dilemma UDR050	Yellow Submarine (12" 1-sided p/s, Banksy artwork)	100

ROOTS MANUVA/MC SKEME

MINT VALUE £

05	Big Dada BD073P	Colossal Insight (Royskopp remix)	6
99	Big Dada BD010	BRAND NEW SECOND HAND (LP)	25
01	Big Dada BDLP032	RUN COME SAVE ME (LP)	20
02	Ultimate Dilemma UDR LP 019	BADMEANINGOOD VOL 2 (2-LP, Banksy artwork)	300
02	Big Dada BDLP040	DUB COME SAVE ME (LP)	20
05	Big Dada BD 072	AWFULLY DEEP (LP)	15

(see also IQ Procedure)

ROOTS MANUVA/MC SKEME
96	Wayward AHP01	Fever/Herbman Hustling/Life's Funny (12")	12

ROOTS RADICS
84	Kingdom KV 8032	Earsay/I'm Not A King	10
79	Form BB1004	OUTERNATIONAL RIDDIM (LP, with Revolutionaries)	30
82	Cha Cha CHALP 012	RADICFATION (LP)	50
82	Solid Groove SGL 102	RADICAL DUB SESSION (LP)	60

ROOTS (1)
78	Greensleeves GRE 7	Mash Down/Solja Man Skank	20

ROOTS (2)
93	Remedy RRLP 001	ORGANIX (2-LP)	40
94	Geffen GEF 24708	DO YOU WANT MORE?!!!??! (2-LP)	40
99	MCA MCA 11948	THINGS FALL APART (2-LP)	50
02	MCA MCA 112 996-1	PHRENOLOGY (2-LP)	50
04	Geffen 0602498624166	THE TIPPING POINT (2-LP)	60

ROOTS ROCKERS
83	Vista Sounds VSLP 4056	FE ME DUB AND DUBWISE SHOWER (2-LP)	25
83	Vista Sounds VSLP 4056	REGGAE MASTERPIECES IN DUB VOLUME 2 (LP)	25

RO RO
70	Parlophone R 5920	Here I Go Again/What You Gonna Do	20
72	Regal Zonophone RZ 3056	Goin' Round My Head/Down On The Road	10
73	Regal Zonophone RZ 3076	Blackbird/Feel It Coming	10
72	Regal Zono. SRZA 8510	MEET AT THE WATER (LP, textured gatefold sleeve, red/silver label)	300

ROSARIES
92	Sarah SARAH 623	FOREVER EP (p/s, insert)	25

RALPHI ROSARIO
89	Jack Trax JTX 1	You Used To Hold Me (Riviera Mix)/(89 Remix)/(Kehinny Jammin Jason Mix)/(Mickey Mixing Oliver Mix) (12")	10

ANDY ROSE
58	London HLU 8761	Lov-A Lov-A Love/Just Young	25

DAVID ROSE ORCHESTRA
60	MGM MGM 1110	Bonanza/Gloria's Theme From Butterfield 8	7
62	MGM MGM 1158	The Stripper/Ebb Tide	6

(see also Woody Herman)

DUSTY ROSE
55	London HLU 8162	The Birds And The Bees/It Makes Me So Mad	50
57	London RE-U 1078	COUNTRY SONGS (EP)	40

JOHNNY ROSE
60	Capitol CL 15166	Linda Lee/The Last One To Know	18

MICHAEL ROSE
76	Morpheus MOR 1008	Guess Who's Coming For Dinner/MORPHEUS PLAYERS: Straight To Rod's Head	15
77	Trojan Rockers TRO 9289	Key Of Keys/Version	10
77	Carib Gems CG 002	Observe Life/SKIN, FLESH & BONES: Version	40
79	Attack TACK 7	Born Free (with JAMMY)/DAD BROWN: Stand & Look (B-side actually by FANTELLS (12")	70

(see also Black Uhuru)

SAMANTHA ROSE
79	Empire EMPLP 902	IN PERSON (LP)	15
82	World International WRLP 701	TOGETHER IN LOVE (LP)	15

TIM ROSE
67	CBS 202631	Morning Dew/You're Slipping Away From Me	8
68	CBS 3277	I Got A Loneliness/Long Time Man	30
68	CBS 3478	I Guess It's Over/Hello Sunshine	6
68	CBS 3598	Long-Haired Boy/Looking At A Baby	6
69	CBS 4209	Roanoke/Baby You Turn Me On	6
70	CBS 2631	Morning Dew/You're Slipping Away From Me (reissue)	6
74	Dawn DN51085	You've Got To Hide Your Love Away/If I Were A Carpenter	8
67	CBS (S)BPG 63168	TIM ROSE (LP)	30
69	CBS 63636	THROUGH ROSE COLOURED GLASSES (LP)	30
71	Capitol ST 22673	LOVE - A KIND OF HATE STORY (LP)	30
74	Dawn DNLS 3062	TIM ROSE (LP)	18

TONY ROSE
70	Trailer LER 2013	YOUNG HUNTING (LP)	15
72	Trailer LER 2024	UNDER THE GREENWOOD TREE (LP)	15

ROSE COLOURED GLASS
71	President PT 338	Can't Find The Time/Mystic Touch	15

ROSE GARDEN
68	Atlantic 584 163	Next Plane To London/Flower Town	10

ROSEHIPS
87	Subway Organisation SUBWAY 10	Room In Your Heart/Thrilled To Bits/Dead End (foldaround p/s with insert in poly bag)	10
87	Subway Organisation SUBWAY 10T	Room In Your Heart/Middle Of Next Week/Thrilled To Bits/So Naive/ Just Another Girl/Dead End (12", p/s)	12

ROSEMARY'S CHILDREN

			MINT VALUE £
87	Subway Organisation SUBWAY 16	I Shouldn't Have To Say/Loophole/Wastin' My Time/All Mine/Sad As Sunday (p/s, with insert)	8
87	Subway Organisation SUBWAY 16T	I Shouldn't Have To Say/Loophole/Wastin' My Time/All Mine/Sad As Sunday (12", p/s with insert)	12
88	Sweet William BILLY 001	Ask Johnny Dee/FAT TULIPS: You Opened My Eyes (33rpm flexi, p/s w/insert)	12

ROSEMARY'S CHILDREN
| 86 | él GPO 012 | Southern Fields/Whatever Happened To Alice | 12 |
| 87 | Cherry Red MRED 077 | KINGS AND PRINCES EP (12", p/s) | 12 |

LEONARD ROSENMAN ORCHESTRA
| 57 | London HA-P 2040 | A TRIBUTE TO JAMES DEAN (LP) | 20 |

ROSE OF AVALANCHE
| 86 | Fire BLAZE 14 | Velveteen/Who Cares (p/s) | 6 |
| 89 | Avalanche AVE4T | A PEACE INSIDE (LP) | 20 |

ROSE OF VICTORY
| 83 | No Future Ol 24 | Suffragette City/Overdrive (p/s) | 12 |

(see also Blitz)

ROSES ARE RED
| 79 | Posthumous Petal PET 1 | Can't Understand/Your Love Is Like A Ballistic Missile (p/s) | 60 |

ROSE TATTOO
78	Carrere CAL 125	Bad Boy For Love/Tramp (p/s)	6
80	Repeal PRS 2724	Release Legalise/COL PATERSON: Bong On Aussie (500 only)	40
81	Mirage PR 405	Rock 'N' Roll Is King/Sidewalk Sally (12", promo only)	10

ROSEWATER
| 71 | Lost Dog L 001 | Sally Anne/Mind Your Head | 15 |

ROSIE (& ORIGINALS)
| 61 | London HLU 9266 | Angel Baby/Give Me Love (as Rosie & Originals) | 30 |
| 61 | Coral Q 72426 | Lonely Blue Nights/We'll Have A Chance | 40 |

ROSKO
| 70 | Trojan TR 7758 | Al Capone/Kaiser Bill | 10 |
| 70 | Philips 6009 070 | Grab The Rabbit/Mohammed Ben Ali | 15 |

(see also Emperor Rosko & Power Pack)

EMPEROR ROSKO & POWER PACK
| 69 | Polydor 56316 | Opposite Lock Parts 1 & 2 | 10 |
| 71 | B&C CB 148 | The Customs Man/Take It In Your Stride | 12 |

(see also Rosko, Power Pack, Pleasure Garden)

ANNIE ROSS
55	Decca F 10514	Mama (He Treats Your Daughter Mean)/The Fish	12
55	Decca F 10637	I Want You To Be My Baby (with Tony Crombie)/TONY CROMBIE & HIS ORCHESTRA: Three Little Words	6
56	Decca F 10680	Cry Me A River/Only You	10
63	Ember EMB S 182	Bye Bye Blues/A Lot Of Livin' To Do	10
72	Columbia DB 8912	Straight On Till Morning/God Bless The Child	10
57	Pye Jazz NJE 1035	NOCTURNE FOR VOCALIST (EP)	60
54	Esquire EP 1	WITH THE TEACHO WILTSHIRE GROUP (EP)	40
58	Pieces Of Eight PEP 604	WITH THE TONY CROMBIE FOURTET (EP)	12
64	Transatlantic TRAEP 112	GO TO THE WALL (EP)	15
57	Nixa Jazz NJT 504	ANNIE BY CANDLELIGHT (10" LP)	125
59	Vogue LAE 12203	ANNIE ROSS (LP, with Gerry Mulligan Quintet)	60
60	Vogue LAE 12233	A GASSER (LP, with Zoot Sims)	60
63	Ember NR 5008	A HANDFULL OF SONGS (LP)	75
63	Transatlantic TRA 107	LOGUERRHYTHMS (LP)	60
65	Golden Guinea GGL 0316	ANNIE BY CANDLELIGHT (LP, reissue)	50
66	Xtra XTRA 1049	ANNIE ROSS WITH THE TONY KINSEY QUINTET (LP)	60
71	Decca SKL 5099	YOU AND ME BABY (LP)	20

(see also Tony Crombie, Dave Lambert, Gerry Mulligan, Zoot Sims, Jack Parnell, Art Blakey, Quincy Jones)

DAVID ROSS
| 58 | Oriole CB 1416 | Pit-A-Patter Boom Boom/Everybody's Got A Girl But Tino (as Dave Ross) | 6 |

DIANA ROSS
70	Tamla Motown TMG 743	Reach Out And Touch (Somebody's Hand)/Dark Side Of The World	6
70	Tamla Motown TMG 751	Ain't No Mountain High Enough/Can't It Wait Until Tomorrow	6
71	Tamla Motown TMG 768	Remember Me/How About You	6
71	Tamla Motown TMG 781	I'm Still Waiting/Reach Out I'll Be There	6
71	Tamla Motown TMG 792	Surrender/I'm A Winner (green/white demo, stereo, has YTMG on label and etched into dead wax))	25
71	Tamla Motown TMG 792	Surrender/I'm A Winner (mono)	6
71	Tamla Motown TMG 792	Surrender/I'm A Winner (stereo)	10
79	Tamla Motown PSLP 304	Love Hangover/Touch Me In The Morning/Remember Me (12", promo)	30
70	Tamla Motown STML 11159	DIANA ROSS (LP)	15
91	EMI EMP 1023	THE FORCE BEHIND THE POWER (LP)	15
93	EMI ONE 1	ONE WOMAN (2-LP)	40

(see also Supremes)

DOCTOR (ISAIAH) ROSS
66	Blue Horizon LP 1	THE FLYING EAGLE (LP, 99 copies only)	1500
66	Xtra XTRA 1038	DOCTOR ROSS (LP, reissue of "The Flying Eagle")	40
66	Bounty BY 6020	CALL THE DOCTOR (LP)	60
72	Polydor 2460 169	LIVE AT MONTREUX (LP)	30
75	Big Bear BEAR 2	THE HARMONICA BOSS (LP)	25

ERROL ROSS
| 80 | Carrere CAR 149 | Round And Round In Circles/Reggae Music Of Today (p/s) | 6 |

GENE ROSS
| 58 | Parlophone R 4434 | Endless Sleep/The Only One | 25 |

Jack ROSS

MINT VALUE £

JACK ROSS
62 London HLD 9534 — Cinderella/Margarita 6

JACKIE ROSS
64 Pye International 7N 25259 — Selfish One/Everything But Love 60
64 Pye International 7N 25259 — Selfish One/Everything But Love (DJ copy) 100
64 Chess CRS 8003 — Jerk And Twine/New Lover 40
64 Chess CRS 8003 — Jerk And Twine/New Lover (DJ copy) 70

JOAN ROSS
70 Crab CRAB 61 — Band Of Gold/HAMMERS: Midnight Sunshine 50
(see also T.T. Ross, Silkie Davis)

JOE E. ROSS
64 Columbia 335X1710 — LOVE SONGS FROM A COP (LP) 18

RONNIE ROSS
58 Parlophone PMC 1079 — DOUBLE EVENT (LP) 125
61 Ember EMB 3323 — STOMPIN' WITH (LP) 100
65 Ember FA 2023 — THE SWINGIN' SOUNDS OF THE JAZZ MAKERS (LP, with Allan Ganley) 70
69 Fontana SFJL 915 — CLEOPATRA'S NEEDLE (LP) 250
(see also Bill Le Sage)

SONNY ROSS
71 Mojo 2093 001 — Alakazam/The Piper Must Be Paid 10

SPENCER ROSS
60 Philips PB 992 — Tracy's Theme/Thanksgiving Day Parade 6
60 London HLX 9141 — Theme Of A Lonely Evening/Bobby's Blues 7

T.T. ROSS (JOAN ROSS)
76 Lucky LY 6000 — No Charge/When I Was A Little Girl 7
76 Lucky LY 6014 — Baby Why/TOUGH GANG: Part 2 10
76 Lucky LY 6017 — Misty Blue/Version 10
76 House Of Eve 001 — Let The World Go Away/Part 2 8
76 House Of Eve 002 — Piece Of My Heart/Part 2 8
77 Lovers Rock CJ 622 — I Will/I Will Dub 10
76 Third World TWLP 201 — T.T. ROSS AND FRIENDS (LP) 30
77 Lovers Rock LP 005 — T.T. ROSS SHOWCASE (LP, no sleeve) 40

JOHN ROSSALL
75 Bell 1411 — I Was Only Dreaming/Every Night And Every Day 6
75 Bell 1428 — You'll Never know/Don't Beleive A Word 6

LEON ROSSELSON
62 Topic TOP 77 — SONGS FOR CITY SQUARES (EP) 15
66 BOUNTY BY 6029 — SONGS FOR SCEPTICAL CIRCLES (LP) 60
70 Acorn CF 206 — SONGS FOR SCEPTICAL CIRCLES (LP, reissue) 20
71 Trailer LER 3015 — THE WORD IS HUGGA MUGGA CHUGGA HUMBUGGA BOOM CHIT (LP, with Roy Bailey & Martin Carthy) 20
75 Acorn CF 249 — PALACES OF GOLD (LP) 18
75 Acorn CF 251 — THAT'S NOT THE WAY IT'S GOT TO BE (LP, with Roy Bailey) 18
(see also Three City Four, Roy Bailey)

NITA ROSSI
65 Piccadilly 7N 35258 — Every Little Day Now/Untrue Unfaithful 40
66 Piccadilly 7N 35307 — Here I Go Again/Something To Give 40
66 Piccadilly 7N 35307 — Here I Go Again/Something To Give (DJ copy) 70
66 Piccadilly 7N 35354 — The Daddy Christmas Song/Our Love Was Meant To Be 8
67 Piccadilly 7N 35384 — Misty Blue/Come Around 12
(see also Status Quo, Bernie Frost, Boz Frost, Mickey Jupp, Mitchell/Coe Mysteries)

JOHN HENRY ROSTILL
71 Columbia DB 8794 — Funny Old World/Green Apples 30
(see also Shadows)

STEVE ROSTnON
74 Sweet Folk & Country SFA 009 — NO STRANGER'S FACE (LP) 30

VINCENT ROSWELL
82 Water Mount MW 001 — Apple Of My Eye/Going To A Dance (12") 100

NINO ROTA
72 Paramount PARA 3023 — Love Theme Form "The Godfather"/The Godfather Waltz 6

ROTARY CONNECTION
68 Chess CRS 8072 — Soul Man/Ruby Tuesday 20
69 Chess CRS 8103 — The Weight/Respect 20
70 Chess CRS 8106 — Want You To Know/Memory Band 20
68 Chess CRL 4538 — ROTARY CONNECTION (LP) 30
69 Chess CRL(S) 4547 — ALADDIN (LP) 30
69 Chess CRLS 4551 — SONGS (LP) 30
71 Chess 6310105 — HEY LOVE (LP, as New Rotary Connection) 100

ROTATION
70 Polydor 2041-037 — Ra-Ta-Ta/Rotation 15

ROTEN ROSEN
87 Virgin VS 1031 — Itsy Bitsy Teenie Weenie Honolulu-Strand Bikini (German Version) Itsy Bitsy Teenie Weenie Honolulu-Strand Bikini (English Version) (p/s) 100
87 Virgin VST 1031 — Itsy Bitsy Teenie Weenie Honolulu-Strand Bikini (German Version) Itsy Bitsy Teenie Weenie Honolulu-Strand Bikini (English Version)/Agent X (12", p/s) 150

ROTHCHILDS
66 Decca F 12411 — You've Made Your Choice/It's Love 10
66 Decca F 12488 — Artificial City/I Let Her Go 15

LINDA ROTHWELL
73 Chapter One SCH 180 — Write Me A Letter/Tell Me 8

ROTOVATORS

MINT VALUE £

ROTOVATORS
78 Rotovator SRTS/78/CUS 143 Meat/East Coast Resort (hand folded and stapled p/s) 8

ROOTS TRUNKS AND BRANCHES
79 Splendor Heights WJWX 1945/2 Just The Way You Are/Chicken Disco (12") 20

ROTTEN TO THE CORE
73 Pye 7N 45257 Don't Let Me Wait Too Long/Let's Do It One More Time 10

ROUGE
78 SRT SRTSCUS 78104 Have You Seen Gene/Hard To Rock N Roll (no p/s) 75

ROUGH DIAMOND
90 Bedrock BR 1 Woman's Touch (p/s) 12

ROUGH ELEMENT
92 UAR UAR120020 The Elements/Breaking The Silence/Unbound Rage (remix) (EP) 35
94 UAR 003 Reflex Reaction/Criminal Behaviour (12") 15

ROUGH JUSTICE (1)
79 Croft TTS 7912 Black Knight (A Gothic Legend)/White Dove (200 only no p/s but all come with insert) 50

ROUGH JUSTICE (2)
82 Rough Justice RJ 001 MILLION TO ONE (EP, p/s) 200

ROUGH RIDERS
69 Jay Boy BOY 13 Boss/President House 30
74 Rare Earth RES 118 Hot California Beach/Do You See Me 20

ROULETTES
62 Pye 7N 15467 Hully Gully Slip 'N' Slide/La Bamba 15
63 Parlophone R 5072 Soon You'll Be Leaving Me/Tell Tale Tit 15
64 Parlophone R 5110 Bad Time/Can You Go 20
64 Parlophone R 5148 I'll Remember Tonight/You Don't Love Me 15
64 Parlophone R 5218 Stubborn Kind Of Fellow/Somebody 25
65 Parlophone R 5278 I Hope He Breaks Your Heart/Find Out The Truth 15
65 Parlophone R 5382 The Long Cigarette/Junk 25
66 Parlophone R 5419 The Tracks Of My Tears/Jackpot 20
66 Oak RGJ 205 I Can't Stop (1-sided, with p/s) 250
66 Oak RGJ 206 I Can't Stop (1-sided) 150
66 Parlophone R 5461 I Can't Stop/Yesterday, Today And Tomorrow 20
67 Fontana TF 822 Rhyme Boy, Rhyme/Airport People 40
67 Fontana TF 876 Help Me To Help Myself/To A Taxi Driver 20
65 Parlophone PMC 1257 STAKES AND CHIPS (LP, laminated front cover, flipbacks, black/yellow label with "Sold in the U.K..." text) 500

(see also Adam Faith, Unit 4 + 2, Argent)

ROUND ROBIN
64 London HLU 9908 Kick That Little Foot Sally Ann/Slauson Party 20
64 London HLU 9908 Kick That Little Foot Sally Ann/Slauson Party (DJ copy) 50

ROUNDHOUSE JUG BAND
61 Vintage Jazz Music VEP 10 ROUNDHOUSE JUG BAND EP (p/s) 150

(see also Cyril Davis)

ROUNDTABLE
69 Jay Boy BOY 18 Saturday Gigue/Scarborough Fair 20
69 Jay Boy JSL 2 SPINNING WHEEL (LP) 40

ROUNDTREE
79 Island IDJ 30 Discocide/Manhatten Fever (12" promo only) 10
82 Virgin VS 506 Hit On You/I Want To Spend A Moment With You (p/s) 8
79 Island ILPS 9527 ROLLER DISCO (LP) 20

CHARLIE ROUSE QUINTET
60 Riverside/Jazzland JLP19 TAKIN' CARE OF BUSINESS (LP) 15

ROUTERS
62 Warner Bros WB 77 Let's Go (Pony)/Mashy 10
63 Warner Bros WB 91 Make It Snappy/Half Time 10
63 Warner Bros WB 97 Stingray/Snap Happy 12
63 Warner Bros WB 108 Big Band/A Ooga 12
64 Warner Bros WB 139 Stamp And Shake/Ah Ya 12
63 Warner Bros WM/WS 8126 LET'S GO! WITH THE ROUTERS (LP, features Scott Walker) 40
64 Warner Bros WM/WS 8144 PLAY 1963'S GREAT INSTRUMENTALS (LP) 30
65 Warner Bros WM/WS 8162 CHARGE! (LP) 30

(see also Scott Walker)

ROVERS
55 Capitol CL 14283 Ichi-Bon Tami, Dachi/Why Oh-h (Why Do You Lie To Me?) 500
55 Capitol CL 14283 Ichi-Bon Tami, Dachi/Why Oh-h (Why Do You Lie To Me?) (78) 90

ROVING KIND
65 Decca F 12264 Ain't It True/Don't Tell Me The Time 8
66 Decca F 12381 Lies A Million/How Many Times 7

ROWAN BROTHERS
72 CBS 1125 All Together/Lady Of Laughter 20

ROWDIES
78 Birds Nest BN 109 A.C.A.B. (All Coppers Are Bastards)/Negative Malfunction/Free Zone 50
79 Teenage Depression TD 1/2 She's No Angel/Had Me A Real Good Time (p/s, different line-up) 8

(see also Boys, Lurkers, Steve Sharp & Cleancuts)

KEITH ROWE
77 Black Swan BS6 Groovy Situation/Groovy Dub (12") 40
77 Black Swan WIP 6205 Groovy Situation/Groovy Dub 20
81 Seven Leaves SLD 002 Groovy Situation/Groovy Dub (12") 40

(see also Keith & Tex)

Normie ROWE

MINT VALUE £

NORMIE ROWE
66	Polydor 56132	It's Not Easy/Mary Mary	15
66	Polydor 56144	Ain't Nobody Home/Ooh La La	6
67	Polydor 56159	Going Home/I Don't Care (Just Take Me There) (in p/s)	10
67	Polydor 56169	But I Know/Sunshine Secret	10

MAJOR ROWELY
65	Stateside SS 438	There's A Riot Going On/Do It The Right Way	15

JEFF ROWENA FIVE
61	Pye 7N 15328	Peanut Vendor/Bullfight	6
63	Oriloe CB 1310	Diddle De Dum (What Happens When Your Love Has Gone)/Lovely Watermelon	6
63	Oriole CB 1797	Dance Baby Dance/Love Me Once Again	10

CHERRY ROWLAND
63	Fontana TF 420	Nobody But Me/Boys	12
74	Decca F 13491	Here Is Where The Love Is/I Can Give You Back Yourself	6

(see also Cherry Roland)

JACKIE ROWLAND
72	Sioux SI 015	Indian Reservation/JUNIOR SMITH: I'm In A Dancing Mood	15
72	Sioux SI 022	Lonely Man/JOE MANSANO: The Trial Of Pama Dice	20

(see also Joe Higgs)

PAUL ROWLAND
84	Master Discs MD 01	Paradise/The Force (p/s)	80
84	Master Discs MDT 01	Paradise/The Force (12")	100

STEVE ROWLAND
67	Fontana TF 844	So Sad/I See Red	40

(see also Family Dogg)

JOHN ROWLES
68	MCA MUP 335	JOHN ROWLES (LP)	15

ROX
82	Teenteeze ROX 100	HOT LOVE IN THE CITY (Hot Love In The City/Do Ya Feel Like Lovin'/Love Ya Like A Diamond (EP)	25
83	Music For Nations MFN 11	VIOLENT BREED (LP, with innersleeve)	15

ROXY MUSIC
86	E.G. EGOX 26	Love Is The Drug/Let's Stick Together (12", p/s, promo only)	10
14	Secret 7" S720	Virginia Plain (100 only, each with unique art sleeve)	50
15	Universal 472 181 0	Ladytron (unreleased and unedited version)/The Numberer (Stereo remix by Steven Wilson) (10", p/s)	15
72	Island ILPS 9200	ROXY MUSIC (LP, 1st pressing, Matrixes ILPS 9200 A-1U GM 1/ILPS 9200 B-1U GR 1, matt gatefold sleeve with Basing Street London W11 address, pink rim palm tree label)	40
72	Island ILPS 9200	ROXY MUSIC (LP, 2nd pressing, Matrixes ILPS 9200 A-2U MR 1/ILPS 9200 B-3U GM 1, laminated gatefold sleeve with Basing Street London W11 address, pink rim palm tree label)	20
73	Island ILPS 9232	FOR YOUR PLEASURE (LP, 1st pressing, Matrixes ILPS 9232 A-1 LA 1/ILPS 9232 B-1 GDG 1, laminated gatefold sleeve with Basing Street London W11 address , pink rim/palm tree label)	40
73	Island ILPS 9252	STRANDED (LP, gatefold, pink rim, palm tree label)	20
74	Island ILPS 9303	COUNTRY LIFE (LP, inner, pink rim, palm tree label)	20
75	Island ILPS 9344	SIREN (LP)	15
81	Polydor/E.G. EGBS 001	THE FIRST SEVEN ALBUMS (7-LP box set plus insert)	100
90	EG EGLP 77	HEART STILL BEATING (2-LP)	50
95	VirginV 2791	MORE THAN THIS - THE BEST OF BRYAN FERRY AND ROXY MUSIC (2-LP)	100
97	Virgin LPCENT 37	ROXY MUSIC (LP, reissue)	25
20	Virgin 00602508553660	ROXY MUSIC (LP, reissue, clear vinyl, Steven Wilson remix)	20

(see also Brian Eno, Bryan Ferry, Andy Mackay, Phil Manzanera, Dumbelles, Fripp & Eno)

DEREK ROY
57	Oriole CB 1415	Derek Roy's All-Star Party (with Bob Monkhouse, Richard Murdoch, Jon Pertwee, Ted Ray & others)	8

(see also Jon Pertwee, Bob Monkhouse)

HUGH ROY/U ROY
70	Supreme SUP 211	Double Attack/Puzzle	20
70	Explosion EX 2040	Whisper A Little Prayer (actually by Audley Rollins)/ Rain A Fall (actually by Melanie)	15
70	Punch PH 34	Scandal/Son Of The Wise	15
70	Duke Reid DR 2509	Wake The Town/Big Boy And Teacher	20
70	Duke Reid DR 2510	Rule The Nation/NORA DEAN: Ay Ay Ay Ay	30
70	Duke Reid DR 2513	Wear You To The Ball (with John Holt)/EARL LINDO: The Ball	25
70	Duke Reid DR 2514	You'll Never Get Away/TOMMY McCOOK QUINTET: Rock Away	25
70	Duke Reid DR 2515	Version Galore/TOMMY McCOOK: Nehru	30
71	Duke Reid DR 2516	Testify/TOMMY McCOOK: Super Soul	35
71	Duke Reid DR 2517	Tom Drunk (with Hopeton Lewis)/TOMMY McCOOK: Wailing	40
71	Duke Reid DR 2518	True True/On The Beach	25
71	Duke Reid DR 2519	Flashing My Whip/Do It Right	18
71	Treasure Isle TI 7059	Drive Her Home (Parts 1 & 2) (with Hopeton Lewis)	15
71	Treasure Isle TI 7062	Behold/Way Back Home (with Tommy McCook)	18
71	Treasure Isle TI 7064	Everybody Bawlin'/Ain't That Loving You	18
71	Upsetter US 375	Earthquake/Suspicious Minds	30
71	Not On Label P001	Rhythim Land/Mr. Warner (with Upsetters)	45
71	Duke DU 105	Love I Tender/JOYA LANDIS: When The Lights Are Low	15
72	G.G. GG 4532	Way Down South/BILLY DYCE: Be My Guest	15
72	Dynamic DYN 448	Festival Wise/Festival Wise Part 2	15
72	Banana BA 367	Keep On Running/LARRY'S ALL STARS: Version	15
72	Grape GR 3026	On Top The Peak/TYPHOON ALLSTARS: Race Attack	15
72	Pama PM 835	Way Down South/BILLY DYCE: Be My Guest	15
72	Punch PH 104	Nannycrank (title actually "Nanny Skank")/PITTSBURG ALLSTARS: Scank Version	15

Hugh ROY JUNIOR

MINT VALUE £

72	Green Door GD 4034	Hudson Affair/KEITH HUDSON: Hot Stick - Version	40
72	Trojan TR 7884	Hat Trick/Wet Vision	10
73	Green Door GD 4052	King Tubby's Special/Here Come The Heartaches	12
73	Gayfeet GS 210	Hard Feeling/Regular Style	15
73	Duke DU 157	Higher The Mountain/OLD BOYS INC.: Version	10
73	Harry J. HJ 6651	Treasure Isle Skank/Words Of Wisdom	15
73	Lord Koos KOO 25	Call On I (with D. Wilson)/DJ Special	8
73	Black Ark BAR 101	006/Get Togther	70
75	Virgin VS 138	Runaway Girl/Chalice In The Palace	6
76	Soulfood SF 001	High Priest/London City Rock	25
71	Trojan TBL 161	VERSION GALORE (LP, as U Roy)	35
74	Attack ATLP 1006	U ROY (LP, as U Roy)	30
75	Virgin V2048	DREAD IN A BABYLON (LP, twin Virgin label)	30
76	Carib Gems CGLP 107	THE ORIGINATOR (LP, with Nuroy)	25
76	Virgin V2059	NATTY REBEL (LP)	20
77	Virgin V2092	RASTA AMBASSADOR (LP)	20
78	Virgin Frontline FL1018	VERSION GALORE (LP, reissue)	15
78	Virgin Frontline FL 1023	JAH SON OF AFRICA (LP, red vinyl)	20
78	Virgin Frontline FL 1023	JAH SON OF AFRICA (LP)	15
79	Virgin Frontline FLX 4004	WITH WORDS OF WISDOM (LP)	20
82	Trojan Records TRLS 211	RAVER'S PARTY (LP)	20
83	Virgin 1007	DREAD IN A BABYLON (LP, reissue, red/green labels)	20
02	Trojan TJALP 056	VERSION GALORE (LP, reissue, with barcode on rear)	15
07	Ariwa ARILP 207	OLD SCHOOL/NEW RULES (LP)	18

(see also Jeff Barnes, Melodians, Delroy Wilson)

HUGH ROY JUNIOR

71	Big BG 329	Papacito/RUPIE EDWARDS: I'm Gonna Live Some Life	12
72	Ashanti ASH 405	King Of The Road/ROOSEVELT ALL STARS: Version	8

I ROY

71	Moodisc MU 3509	Musical Pleasure/JO JO BENNETT: Hot Pop	20
71	Moodisc MU 3510	Heart Don't Leap (as I. Roy & Dennis Walks)/ DENNIS WALKS & MUDIE'S ALLSTARS: Snow Bird	15
71	Moodisc MU 3512	Let Me Tell You Boy (with Ebony Sisters)/MUDIE'S ALLSTARS: Version	20
71	Moodisc HM 104	The Drifter (with Dennis Walks)/JO JO BENNETT: Snowbird	22
72	Green Door GD 4030	Hot Bomb (with Jumpers)/JUMPERS: The Bomb	12
72	Soferno B SOF 001	No Money/Version	10
72	Green Door GD 4044	Make Love/STAGS: Tic Toc Bill	12
73	Pyramid PYR 7001	Tip From The Prince/Fat Beef Skank	22
73	Attack ATT 8050	Space Flight/JERRY LEWIS: Burning Wire	28
73	Downtown DT 503	Blackman's Time/High Jacking	30
73	Downtown DT 519	Clapper's Tail/Live And Learn	25
73	Duke DU 156	Buck And The Preacher/PETE WESTON ALLSTARS: Preacher - Version	15
73	Smash SMA 2337	The Magnificent Seven/Leggo Beast	15
73	Smash SMA 2338	Rose Of Sheron/Slip Out	15
73	Techniques TE 926	Pauper And The King/GREGORY ISAACS: Loving Pauper	20
73	Techniques TE 930	Monkey Fashion/Medley Mood	15
73	Ackee ACK 503	Great Great Great (with Ken Parker)/RUPIE EDWARDS ALLSTARS: Version	22
73	Ackee ACK 510	Sound Education/AUGUSTUS PABLO: Cinderella In Black	25
73	Harry J HJ-6655	Musical Drum Sound/NOW GENERATION: Musical Drum - Version	20
73	Pama PM 854	Cowtown Skank/AUGUSTUS PABLO: Cowtown Skank Version	20
73	Dip DL73 5006	Don't Get Weary Joe Frazier/Don't Get Weary	15
74	Atra ATRA 017	Yah Ma Ride/SWEET HARMONY: Mexican Rockin'	20
74	Ashanti ASH 412	Mood For Love (Parts 1 & 2)	10
75	Bullet BU 551	Step Right Up/ANDY'S ALLSTARS: Banjo Serenade	10
75	Lucky DL 5098	I Man Time/Version	12
75	Third World TW 015	Mr Benwood Dick/Mad Mad Hatter	8
75	Third World TW 85	New York City/CORNELL CAMPBELL: Blessed Are They	8
75	Student STU 1001	Jazz Bo Have Fe Run/Version	12
76	Dip DL 5107	Padlock/Lock And Key (copies also exist with Lucky label)	10
77	ATA ATA 1005	Roots Man/Observer Mix	10
77	Observer OB 002	Jamaican Girl/River Jordan/ OBSERVER IN FINE STYLE: First Cut/Second Cut (12", p/s)	40
78	Jungle Beat JBDC 805	Troubles/I Man (12" with CLARKIE BURNS/FREDDY CLARK)	100
78	GG's GG 011	Natty Get Ready/Version	10
79	Virgin Front Line FLS 124 12	Fire In A Wire/Hill And Gully (12")	15
70s	Nationwide NW 005	Tea Pot/Tea Cup	12
73	Trojan TRLS 63	PRESENTING I ROY (LP, original issue with "12 Neasden Lane" address and rough orange/white paper labels)	45
74	Trojan TRLS 71	HELL AND SORROW (LP, original issue with "12 Neasden Lane" address and rough orange/white paper labels)	35
74	Trojan TRLS 91	THE MANY MOODS OF I ROY (LP, original issue with "12 Neasden Lane" address and rough orange/white paper labels)	35
75	Grounation GROL 504	TRUTH & RIGHTS (LP)	25
76	Caroline CA 2011	CRISIS TIME (LP)	25
76	Klik 9020	DREAD BALDHEAD (LP)	45
77	Justice JUS LP 08	CAN'T CONQUER RASTA (LP)	30
77	Virgin V 2075	MUSICAL SHARK ATTACK (LP)	30
77	Virgin Frontline VF 1001	HEART OF A LION (LP)	20
78	Virgin Frontline FL 1028	TEN COMANDMENTS (LP)	15
78	Third World TWS 930	THE GODFATHER (LP)	25
79	Virgin Frontline FLD 6002	THE GENERAL (LP, with free dub LP SPIDER'S WEB)	30

Lee ROY

MINT VALUE £

79	Virgin Frontline FL 1033	WORLD ON FIRE (LP)	15
79	Virgin Frontline FLS 4001	CANCER (LP)	20
79	Virgin Frontline FLX 4001	CANCER DUB (LP)	20
97	Blood & Fire BAFLP 016	DON'T CHECK WITH ME NO LIGHTWEIGHT STUFF (1972-75) (LP)	20

(see also Keith Hudson & I Roy)

LEE ROY
65	Island WI 251	Oh Ee Baby/My Loving Baby Come Back	20

MAD ROY
70	Banana BA 324	Nanny Version (actually by Dennis Alcapone)/BIGGER D: Freedom Version	25
71	Banana BA 326	Home Version (actually by Dennis Alcapone)/SOUND DIMENSION: One Time	20
71	Banana BA 327	Universal Love/ROLAND ALPHONSO: Shelly Belly	20
71	Banana BA 328	Duppy Serenade/Sunshine Version (both sides actually by Dennis Alcapone)	20

(see also Horse Mouth)

ROY REDMOND
67	Warner Bros WB 2075	Good Day Sunshine/That Old Time Feeling	20

U ROY JUNIOR
72	Big BG 313	Uncle Charlie/Socialise	20
72	Duke Reid DR 2520	Rock To The Beat/Love Is Not A Gamble (both actually by Dennis Alcapone)	12
72	Attack ATT 8030	This Is A Pepper (as U Roy Junior)/JOHN HOLT: Justice	12
72	Sioux SI 024	The Wedding (as U Roy Junior)/LLOYD'S ALL STARS: Buttercup	8
73	Randy's RAN 532	Froggie (as U Roy Junior)/RHYTHM RULERS: Version	10
73	Techniques TE 928	Aunt Kereba (as U Roy Junior)/DON RECO: Waterloo Rock (B-side actually by Reco Rodriquez)	12

(see also Hugh Roy, Dennis Alcapone, Sir Harry, Shorty Perry, Heptones, Herman Chin-Loy)

BILLY JOE ROYAL
62	Oriole CB 1751	Never In A Hundred Years/We Haven't A Moment To Lose	20
65	CBS 201802	Down In The Boondocks/Oh! What A Night	15
65	CBS 201983	You Make Me Feel Like A Man/I've Got To Be Somebody	6
65	CBS 202009	I Knew You When/Steal Away	6
66	CBS 202052	It's A Good Time/Don't Wait Up For Me Mama	6
66	CBS 202087	Heart's Desire/Everbody's Gotta Cry	40
66	CBS 202087	Heart's Desire/Everbody's Gotta Cry (DJ copy)	75
66	CBS 202400	High On A Hilltop/I'm Gonna Get Right Tonight	6
66	Atlantic 584 002	Never In A Hundred Years/We Haven't A Moment To Lose (reissue)	7
67	CBS 202548	Yo Yo/We Tried	10
67	CBS 3044	Hush/Watching From The Bandstand	8
68	CBS 3644	Storybook Children/Just Between Me And You	8
68	CBS 3858	Gabriel/Movies In My Mind	7
69	CBS 4470	Cherry Hill Park/Helping Hand	7
71	CBS 7302	Tulsa/Pick Up The Pieces	7
72	CBS 7727	We Go Back/Colorado Rain	7
66	CBS BPG 62590	INTRODUCING BILLY JOE ROYAL (LP)	20

BOBBY ROYAL
63	HMV POP 1253	Big Big Star/Little Word Of Love	12
65	Decca F 12097	Within My Lonely Heart/When I Found You	10

ROBBIE ROYAL
65	Mercury MF 923	Only Me/I Don't Need You	8
65	Decca F 12097	Within My Lonely Heart/When I Found You	6

ROYAL BLOOD (1)
94	Phase One PRFLP001	ROYAL BLOOD (LP)	40

(see also Exiles Intact)

ROYAL BLOOD (2)
13	Black Mammoth BMR 001	Out Of The Black/Come One Over (p/s, 500 only)	40
14	Warners WEA 493	Come On Over/You Want Me	10
14	Black Mammoth/Warners Bros. WEA 491	Little Monster/Hole	10
14	Black Mammoth/Warner Bros. WEA 494	Figure It Out/Love & Leave It Alone	15
14	Black Mammoth/Warner Bros. WEA 495	Ten Tonne Skeleton/One Trick Pony	12
14	Warner Bros. 825646278541	ROYAL BLOOD (LP, white vinyl, 800 only sold via Rough Trade)	50
14	Black Mammoth 8256462785541	ROYAL BLOOD (LP, signed, 500 copies)	50
14	Black Mammoth 8256462785541	ROYAL BLOOD (LP, repressing, 100 only, numbered)	20

ROYAL BLUES
69	Pye 7N 17670	Mountain Of Love/Wishful Thinking	6
69	Pye 7N 17769	Proud Mary/Sunny Girl Friend	6

ROYALETTES
65	MGM MGM 1272	Poor Boy/Watch What Happens	15
65	MGM MGM 1279	It's Gonna Take A Miracle/Out Of Sight Out Of Mind	25
65	MGM MGM 1279	It's Gonna Take A Miracle/Out Of Sight Out Of Mind (DJ copy)	55
65	MGM MGM 1292	I Want To Meet Him/Never Again	18
66	MGM MGM 1302	You Bring Me Down/Only When You're Lonely	20
66	MGM MGM 1324	It's A Big Mistake/I Want To Meet Him	15
68	Big T BIG 106	River Of Tears/Something Wonderful	15
66	MGM MGM-C 8028	THE ELEGANT SOUND OF THE ROYALETTES (LP)	100

ROYAL FAMILY & THE POOR
82	Factory FAC 43	ART-DREAM DOMINATION EP (12", p/s)	15
84	Factory FACT 95	THE PROJECT - PHASE 1 OF THE TEMPLE OF THE 13TH TRIBE (LP, with booklet)	20
87	Gaia PHASE 3	IN THE SEA OF E (LP)	15

ROYAL GUARDSMEN

MINT VALUE £

ROYAL GUARDSMEN
67	Stateside SS 2010	The Return Of The Red Baron/Sweetmeats Slide	6
67	Stateside S(S)L 10202	SNOOPY VS THE RED BARON (LP)	20
68	London HA-P/SH-P 8351	THE RETURN OF THE RED BARON (LP)	15

ROYAL HOLIDAYS
58	London HLU 8722	Margaret/I'm Sorry (I Did You Wrong)	70
58	London HLU 8722	Margaret/I'm Sorry (I Did You Wrong) (78)	20

JAMES ROYAL (& HAWKS)
65	Parlophone R 5290	She's About A Mover/Black Cloud (as James Royal & Hawks)	25
65	Parlophone R 5383	Work Song/I Can't Stand It	35
67	CBS 202525	Call My Name/When It Comes To My Baby	20
67	CBS 2739	It's All In The Game/Green Days	7
68	CBS 3232	I Can't Stand It/Little Bit Of Rain (DJ copy)	125
68	CBS 3232	I Can't Stand It/Little Bit Of Rain	60
68	CBS 3450	Hey Little Boy/Thru' The Love (DJ Copy)	60
68	CBS 3450	Hey Little Boy/Thru' The Love	30
68	CBS 3624	A Woman Called Sorrow/Fire	20
69	CBS 3797	Time Hangs On My Mind/Anna-Lee	6
69	CBS 3915	House Of Jack/Which Way To Nowhere	30
69	CBS 4139	I've Something Bad On My Mind/She's Independent	6
69	CBS 4181	That Kind Of Girl/Will You Be Staying After Sunday	6
69	CBS 4463	Send Out Love/I've Lost You	30
70	CBS 5032	And Soon The Darkness/I'm Going Home	6
70	Carnaby CNS 4021	Carolina/Big Heat On The Loose	6
71	Carnaby 6151 002	Carolina/A Woman Called Sorrow	8
69	CBS 63780	CALL MY NAME (LP)	30
70	Carnaby CNLS 6008	ONE WAY (LP)	50
72	Carnaby 6302 011	THE LIGHT AND SHADE OF JAMES ROYAL (LP)	40

ROYAL RASSES
76	Neville King NK 01	Love The Way It Should Be/Dub The Way It Should Be	10
77	Neville King NK 4	Kingston 11/Dub Up Kingston	10
79	Ballistic 12 315	You Gotta Have Love (Jah Love)/Humanity (Love The Way It Should Be)/They Know Not Jah (12", clear vinyl)	12
79	Warrior BP 327	Ain't Nobody Here But Me/Kingston II (Ghetto Rock) (12")	80
79	Ballstic BP 327	Nobody Here But Me/Kingston II	12
79	Ballistic PRE 1	GOD SENT DUB (white label/plain sleeve) (LP)	130
79	Warrior WARLP 2002	HARDER NA RASS! (LP)	40
80	Ballistic LBR 1031	HARDER NA RASS! (LP)	20

ROYAL ROCKERS
60	Top Rank JAR 326	Jet II/Swinging Mambo	20

ROYALS
64	Blue Beat BB 259	Save Mama/Out De Fire	30
68	Amalgamated AMG 831	Never See Come See/CANNONBALL BRYAN TRIO: Jumping Jack	60
69	Trojan TR 662	Pick Out Me Eye/Think You Too Bad	60
69	Duke DU 29	Never Gonna Give You Up/Don't Mix Me Up	20
73	Dip DL 5016	Promised Land/Every Jamaican Is A Rebel	12
75	Mango MAN 1007	Peace And Love (Blacker Black)/Wigwam	15
79	Warrior WAR 143	Rising Sun/It's Real (Gone Sweet)	15
80	Warrior WAR 123	If You Want Good/When You Are Wrong (12")	20
77	Magnum DEAD 1004	PICK UP THE PIECES (LP)	25
78	Balistic UAS 30189	TEN YEARS AFTER (LP)	30
78	Ballistic UAG 30206	ISRAEL BE WISE (LP)	20
81	Kingdom KVLP 9006	MOVING ON (LP)	20

ROYAL TEENS
58	HMV POP 454	Short Shorts/Planet Rock	35
58	HMV POP 454	Short Shorts/Planet Rock (78)	20
59	Capitol CL 15068	Little Cricket/Believe Me	30

ROYALTONES
58	London HLJ 8744	Poor Boy/Wail!	15
58	London HLJ 8744	Poor Boy/Wail! (78)	20
61	London HLU 9296	Flamingo Express/Tacos	15
64	Stateside SS 309	Our Faded Love/Holy Smokes	10

ROYAL TRUX
95	Hut 12790	LIVE IN DENVER EP (10" promo)	12
93	Domino WIGLP 6	CATS & DOGS (LP)	15
95	Hut HUTLP 23	THANK YOU (LP, purple vinyl)	15
98	Domino WIGLP 45	ACCELERATOR (LP)	18
99	Domino WIGLP 68	VETERANS OF DISORDER (LP)	15

ROYALTY
69	CBS 4181	That Kind Of Girl/Will You Be Staying After Sunday	50
69	CBS 4498	Let's Ride/I Need Your Love	60

ROY & ANNETTE
63	R&B JB 107	My Baby/Go Your Ways	20

(see also Tommy McCook, Lester Sterling)

ROY & DUKE ALL STARS
68	Blue Cat BS 113	Pretty Blue Eyes Parts 1 & 2	110
68	Blue Cat BS 117	The Train (vocal)/Instrumental Version	80

(see also Roy Panton)

ROY & ENID
68	Coxsone CS 7063	Rocking Time/RALPH BLAKE: High Blood Pressure	100

ROY & JOE

MINT VALUE £

68	Coxsone CS 7069	He'll Have To Go/CARLTON & SHOES: Love Is A Treasure	120
69	Coxsone CS 7088	Reggae For Days/SOUND DIMENSION: Holy Moses	50

(see also Little Roys)

ROY & JOE

73	Camel CA 107	Rainy Weather/THE DEN BROTHERS: Version	10

ROY (PANTON) & MILLIE

62	Island WI 005	We'll Meet/ROLAND ALPHONSO: Back Beat (B-side act. with City Slickers)	25
63	Island WI 050	This World/Never Say Goodbye	20
63	Island WI 090	There'll Come A Day/I Don't Want You	20
63	Blue Beat BB 154	Over And Over/I'll Go (with Prince Buster All Stars)	20
64	Black Swan WI 409	Cherry I Love You/You're The Only One	30
64	Black Swan WI 410	Oh Merna/DON DRUMMOND: Dog War Bossa Nova	30
64	Black Swan WI 427	Oh Shirley/Marie	25

(see also Roy Panton, Millie [Small])

ROY (RICHARDS) & PAULETTE

63	Island WI 067	Have You Seen My Baby/Since You're Gone	25

ROY (PANTON) & YVONNE (HARRISON)

64	Blue Beat BB 258	Little Girl/No More	20
64	Black Swan WI 436	Two Roads/Join Together	20

(see also Roy Panton)

ROY (PANTON) & PATSY

62	Blue Beat BB 118	My Happy Home/In Your Arms Dear (with Hersang & His Combo)	25

(see also Roy Panton)

EARL ROYCE & OLYMPICS

64	Columbia DB 7433	Que Sera Sera/I Really Do	25
65	Parlophone R 5261	Guess Things Happen That Way/Sure To Fall (In Love With You)	25

ROYKSOPP

02	Wall Of Sound WALLLP 027	MELODY A.M. (2-LP, promo edition, 100 only - artwork by Banksy)	4000
02	Wall Of Sound WALLLP 027	MELODY A.M. (2-LP)	35
05	Wall Of Sound WALLLP035	THE UNDERSTANDING (2-LP)	30

ROYKSOPP & ROBYN

14	Dog Triumph DOG007V	DO IT AGAIN (LP, white vinyl)	35

ROY OF THE RAVERS

16	Acid Waxa ACIWAX 06	2 LATE 4 LOVE (12" EP, hand-stamped white sleeve with 'Roy of the Rovers' image, hand-stamped stamped white labels)	60

ROY'S BOYS

64	Columbia DB 7425	Do Wah Diddy Diddy-I'm Into Something Good-I Want To Hold Your Hand/ Oh! Pretty Woman-Have I The Right?-It's All Over Now	7

ROYSTON

79	Tuzmadoner TUZMADONER 001	Snake's Song/Gerald's Eyes//DIFFERENT EYES: Uncomfortable/Snake's Song (stapled photocopied cover, rubber-stamped labels)	100

LITA ROZA

53	Decca F 75082	(How Much Is) That Doggie In The Window/Tell Me We'll Meet Again (export issue)	20
54	Decca F 10240	Changing Partners/Just A Dream Or Two Ago (B-side with Stargazers)	10
54	Decca F 10269	Bell Bottom Blues (with Johnston Brothers)/Make Love To Me (both with Ted Heath Orchestra)	10
54	Decca F 10277	Young At Heart/Secret Love	10
54	Decca F 10393	Call Off The Wedding/The "Mama-Doll" Song	10
55	Decca F 10427	Heartbeat/Leave Me Alone	10
55	Decca F 10431	Let Me Go, Lover!/Make Yourself Comfortable	10
55	Decca F 10479	Tomorrow/Foolishly	8
55	Decca F 10536	Two Hearts, Two Kisses (Make One Love)/Keep Me In Mind	8
55	Decca F 10541	The Man In The Raincoat/Today And Ev'ry Day	8
55	Decca F 10611	Hey There/Hernando's Hideaway	8
56	Decca F 10679	Jimmy Unknown/The Rose Tattoo	8
56	Decca F 10728	Too Young To Go Steady/You're Not Alone	7
56	Decca F 10761	No Time For Tears/But Love Me (Love But Me)	7
56	Decca F 10792	Innismore/The Last Waltz	7
56	Decca F 10830	Hey! Jealous Lover/Julie	7
57	Decca F 10861	Lucky Lips/Tears Don't Care Who Cries Them	7
57	Decca F 10884	Tonight My Heart She Is Crying/Five Oranges, Four Apples	7
63	Ember EMB S 168	Mama (He Treats Your Daughter Mean)/(He's My) Dreamboat (as Lisa Rosa)	30
65	Columbia DB 7689	Keep Watch Over Him/Stranger Things Have Happened	30
57	Decca DFE 6386	LITA ROZA SELECTION (EP)	30
57	Decca DFE 6399	LITA ROZA (EP)	20
58	Decca DFE 6443	BETWEEN THE DEVIL AND THE DEEP BLUE SEA NO. 1 (EP)	20
54	Decca LF 1187	PRESENTING LITA ROZA (10" LP)	80
56	Decca LF 1243	LISTENING IN THE AFTER HOURS (10" LP)	100
57	Decca LK 4171	LOVE IS THE ANSWER (LP)	100
57	Decca LK 4218	BETWEEN THE DEVIL AND THE DEEP BLUE SEA (LP)	90
58	Pye Nixa NPL 18020	ME ON A CAROUSEL (LP, mono)	60
58	Pye Nixa NSPL 83003	ME ON A CAROUSEL (LP, stereo)	80
60	Pye NPL 18047	DRINKA LITA ROZA DAY (LP)	50
64	Ember NR 5009	LOVE SONGS FOR NIGHT PEOPLE (LP)	25

(see also Stargazers, Johnston Brothers)

ROZAA & WINE

76	Right On! 104	Disco Boogie Woman/Disco Boogie Woman Part 2	20

(see also David & Rozaa)

RT & B

79	Splendor Heights SH 1	Forward/Join Them (12")	20

Mister JACK RUANE ESQUIRE

MINT VALUE £

MISTER JACK RUANE ESQUIRE
68　Pye 7N 17529　　　　　　　　　Everybody Wants To Go To Heaven/Just For Fun 7

RUB-A-DUBS WITH DANDY
65　Blue Beat BB 304　　　　　　　Without Love/I Know 25
(see also Dandy)

RUBAIYATS
68　Action ACT 4516　　　　　　　Omar Khayam/Tomorrow 125

GIDEON JAH RUBBAAL
77　Greensleeves GRE 003　　　　Love Rasta/GIDEON JAH RUBBAAL ALL STARS: Rasta Version 8

RUBBER BAND
73　Youngblood YB 1052　　　　　Moonwalker/Wichita 6
69　Major Minor SMCP 5045　　　CREAM SONGBOOK (LP) 20
69　Major Minor SMCP 5048　　　HENDRIX SONGBOOK (LP) 20

RUBBER BOOTZ
67　Deram DM 134　　　　　　　　Joy Ride/Chicano 30

RUBBER BUCKET
69　MCA MK 5006　　　　　　　　We're All Living In One Place/Take Me Away 10
(see also Paul Raven)

JOHNNY RUBBISH
78　United Artists UP 36405　　　 Living In NW3 4JR/Other Side (p/s) 10

RUBIN
75　MCA MU 196　　　　　　　　　You've Been Away/Baby, You're My Everything 10
75　MCA MU 196　　　　　　　　　You've Been Away/Baby, You're My Everything (DJ copy) 20

RUBY
74　Chrysalis CHR 1061　　　　　RED CRYSTAL FANTASIES (LP, textured sleeve, green label) 20
(see also Procol Harum)

RUBY & GLORIA
71　Big Shot BI 583　　　　　　　Worried Over You/Worried Over You - Version 8
71　Black Swan BW 1409　　　　Talk To Me Baby/LLOYD'S ALL STARS: Talk To Me Baby - Version 8

RUBY & ROMANTICS
63　London HLR 9679　　　　　　Our Day Will Come/Moonlight And Music 10
63　London HLR 9734　　　　　　My Summer Love/Sweet Love And Sweet Forgiveness 10
63　London HLR 9771　　　　　　Hey There Lonely Boy/Not A Moment Too Soon 10
63　London HLR 9801　　　　　　Young Wings Can Fly/Day Dreaming 10
64　London HLR 9881　　　　　　Our Everlasting Love/Much Better Off Than I've Ever Been 15
64　London HLR 9916　　　　　　Baby Come Home/Every Day's A Holiday 15
64　London HLR 9935　　　　　　When You're Young And In Love/I Cry Alone 15
65　London HLR 9972　　　　　　Your Baby Doesn't Love You Anymore/We'll Meet Again 15
69　A&M AMS 750　　　　　　　　Hurting Each Other/Baby I Could Be So Good At Loving You 15
63　London RE-R 1389　　　　　　OUR DAY WILL COME (EP) 35
64　London RE-R 1427　　　　　　HEY THERE LONELY BOY (EP) 40
63　London HA-R 8078　　　　　　OUR DAY WILL COME (LP) 40
66　London HA-R 8282　　　　　　GREATEST HITS (LP) 30
(see also Danny Davis Orchestra)

RUBY RUSHTON
15　22a 006　　　　　　　　　　　TWO FOR JOY (LP) 30
17　22a 015　　　　　　　　　　　TRUDI'S SONGBOOK VOLUME 1 (LP) 30
17　22a 019　　　　　　　　　　　TRUDI'S SONGBOOK VOLUME 2 (LP) 20
(see also Tenderlonious)

RUDDY & SKETTO
71　Supreme SUP 218　　　　　　Every Night/Ethiopia 8
(see also Sketto Rich)

RUD(D)Y (GRANT) & SKETTO (RICH)
62　Dice CC 2　　　　　　　　　　Please Enid/ABC Boogie 12
62　Dice CC 5　　　　　　　　　　Summer Is Just Around The Corner/Nothing Like Time (as Ruddy & Sketto & Reco's All Stars) 25
62　Dice CC 7　　　　　　　　　　Little Schoolgirl/Hush Baby (as Ruddy & Sketto & Baron Twist & His Knights) 25
62　Dice CC 10　　　　　　　　　Mr Postman/Christmas Blues (as Rudy & Sketto with Laurel's Group) 25
63　Dice CC 16　　　　　　　　　Hold The Fire/Good Morning Mr Jones 25
63　Dice CC 19　　　　　　　　　Never Set You Free/Brothers And Sisters 20
63　Blue Beat BB 198　　　　　　Was It Me/Minna Don't Deceive Me 20
64　Blue Beat BB 208　　　　　　Show Me The Way To Go Home/Let Me Dream 20
64　Blue Beat BB 230　　　　　　Ten Thousand Miles From Home/I Need Someone (as Ruddy & Sketto) 25
64　Blue Beat BB 252　　　　　　I Love You/If Only Tomorrow 25
65　Blue Beat BB 297　　　　　　See What You Done/Heart's Desire (as Ruddy & Sketto) 20
65　Blue Beat BB 310　　　　　　Oh Dolly/You're Mine (as Ruddy & Sketto) 20
71　Supreme SUP 218　　　　　　Every Night/Ethiopia 8

RUDE AND DEADLY
95　Unity UNITY 002　　　　　　　Lightnin' and Tundra/Mash Dem Down (12") 40
95　No Smoking SMOKE 7　　　Give Me A Dub/Murder De Boy (12", as Rude And Deadly Vs. The Dogz) 25
97　Smokers Inc SINC 1200　　Give Me A Dubplate (97 Remix) (12", 1-sided, stamped white labels) 25
97　Smokers Inc SINC 1200　　Give Me A Dubplate (97 Remix)/Give Me A Dubplate (Original Mix) (12") 25

RUDE ASS TINKER
90s　Deathchant DEATH 30　　Imperial Break/Silk Ties (12", limited issue) 18
(see also Mu-Ziq, Tusken Raiders, U-Ziq)

RUDE BOYS (1)
67　Island WI 3088　　　　　　　Rock Steady Massachusetts/Going Home 30

RUDE BOYS (2)
89　Ska SKAT 002　　　　　　　RUDE BOY SHUFFLE EP (12") 15
(see also Oppressed)

RUDI
78	Good Vibrations GOT 1	Big Time/Number 1 (folded p/s, 3,000 only, push-put centre)	30
79	Good Vibrations GOT 1	Big Time/No. 1 (reissue p/s)	10
79	Good Vibrations GOT 12	I Spy/Genuine Reply/Sometimes/Ripped In Two (p/s)	30

RUDIES (FANATICS)
68	Blue Cat BS 107	7-11 (Parts 1 & 2)	180
68	Blue Cat BS 109	Cupid/RECO'S ALLSTARS: Wise Message	80
68	Nu Beat NB 001	Train To Vietnam/Skaville To Rainbow City	35
68	Nu Beat NB 005	Engine 59/My Girl	70
68	Fab FAB 46	I Wanna Go Home/La Mer	60
68	Fab FAB 70	Give Me The Rights/I Do Love You (as Rudies Fanatics)	25
68	Fab FAB 71	Mighty Meaty/Go (as Rudies Fanatics)	40
69	Doctor Bird DB 1302	Baby Face/News	35
69	JJ DB 1301	Sin Thing/What's Your Name	25
69	JJ DB 1302	Boss Sound/RECO & RUDIES: Peace	200
69	Fab FAB 104	Brixton Rocket/Rudie's Joy	500
70	Pama PM 789	Give Peace A Chance/She	15
70	Trojan TR 7798	Patches/The Split	40
71	Spinning Wheel SW 106	My Sweet Lord/Devil's Lead Soup	90

(see also Freddie Notes, Sonny, Binns & Rudies, Rico, Dandy, Owen & Dandy, Downtown All Stars, Desmond Riley)

RUDIMENTAL
13	The Vinyl Factory VF 084	HOME (3-LP)	60

RUDIMENTARY PENI
81	Outer Himalayan SRTS 81 CUS 1097	RUDIMENTARY PENI (EP, A4 foldout p/s with booklet)	30
81	Outer Himalayan BOOBOO 1	RUDIMENTARY PENI (EP, later 14" x 7" sleeve)	20
82	Crass 221984/2T	FARCE EP (Test pressing mispressed on 12" vinyl)	200
82	Crass 211984/2	FARCE (EP, initial pressing in 21" x 14" foldout black & white p/s)	20
97	Outer Himalayan BOOB 006	ECHOES OF ANGUISH (12", EP)	12
00	Outer Himalayan BOOB007	THE UNDERCLASS (EP, p/s)	30
04	Outer Himalayan BOOB008V	ARCHAIC EP (12")	40
04	Outer Himalayan BOOB008V	ARCHAIC EP (12", white vinyl)	25
08	Outer Himalayan BOOB009V	NO MORE PAIN EP (12", clear vinyl)	40
08	Outer Himalayan BOOB009V	NO MORE PAIN EP (12", grey/white vinyl)	20
83	Corpus Christi CHRIST ITS 6	DEATH CHURCH (LP, fold put poster sleeve)	40
87	Corpus Christi CHRIST IT'S 15	THE EPS OF RP (LP)	25
89	Corpus Christi BOOBOO 2	CACOPHONY (LP, with booklet)	40
95	Outer Himalayan BOOB005V	POPE ADRIAN 37th PSYCHRISTIC (LP, unreleased test pressing)	200

(see also Magits)

RUEFREX
80	Good Vibrations GOT 8	One By One/Cross The Line/Don't Panic (foldover p/s, 2 different designs)	15

RAY RUFF & CHECKMATES
64	London HLU 9889	I Took A Liking To You/A Fool Again	15

RUFF WITH THE SMOOTH
93	Basement BRSS 023	Art Of Intelligence/Sounds Superior (12")	15
94	Basement BRSS 037	Twisted Girl/Who's Loving Me (12")	10

(see also Jack Smooth)

RUFFIANS
71	Banana BA 359	Room Full Of Tears (actually by Sensations)/Black Soul (actually "Black And White - Version" by Riley's Allstars)	20

(see Al Brown, Sensations)

BRUCE RUFFIN
69	Songbird SB 1002	Long About Now/Come See About Me (as Bruce Ruffin & Temptations)	30
69	Trojan TR 7704	Dry Up Your Tears/BEVERLEY'S ALLSTARS: One Way Street	30
70	Trojan TR 7737	I'm The One/Who's Gonna Be Your Man?	20
70	Trojan TR 7776	Cecelia/BEVERLEY ALL STARS: Stand Up	10
70	Summit SUM 8509	O-o-h Child/Bitterness Of Life	18
71	Summit SUM 8516	Candida/Are You Ready	15
71	Trojan TR 7814	Rain/THE PYRAMIDS: Geronimo (B-side actually by Pyramids)	8
71	Trojan TR 7814	Rain/THE PYRAMIDS: Off Limits (B-side actually by Aquarians)	8
72	Trojan TRM 9000	Songs Of Peace/You Are The Best/We Can Make It	12
72	Rhino RNO 101	Mad About You/Save The People	6
73	Rhino RNO 114	Tickle Me/I Like Everything About You	6
71	Trojan TRL 23	RAIN (LP)	30

(see also Bruce Downer)

DAVID RUFFIN
69	Tamla Motown TMG 689	My Whole World Ended (The Moment You Left Me)/ I've Got To Find Myself A Brand New Baby (DJ Copy)	80
69	Tamla Motown TMG 689	My Whole World Ended (The Moment You Left Me)/ I've Got To Find Myself A Brand New Baby	20
69	Tamla Motown TMG 711	I've Lost Everything I've Ever Loved/We'll Have A Good Thing Going On (DJ Copy)	40
69	Tamla Motown TMG 711	I've Lost Everything I've Ever Loved/We'll Have A Good Thing Going On	15
75	Tamla Motown TMG 936	Take Me Clear From Here/Blood Donors Needed (Give All You Can)	10
76	Tamla Motown TMG 1022	Heavy Love/Me And Rock And Roll Are Here To Stay	6
75	Tamla Motown TMG 1017	Walk Away From Love/Love Can Be Hazardous To Your Health	10
76	Tamla Motown TMG 1036	Discover Me/Smiling Faces Sometimes	12
77	Tamla Motown TMG 1093	You're My Peace Of Mind/Rode By The Place (Where We Used To Stay)	15
77	Tamla Motown TMG 1078	I Can't Stop The Rain/My Whole World Ended (The Moment You Left Me)	15
69	T. Motown (S)TML 11118	MY WHOLE WORLD ENDED (LP, mono/stereo)	20
70	T. Motown (S)TML 11139	FEELIN' GOOD (LP)	30
73	Tamla Motown STML 11228	DAVID RUFFIN (LP)	20

Jimmy RUFFIN

			MINT VALUE £
75	Tamla Motown STML 11283	ME N ROCK AND ROLL ARE HERE TO STAY (LP)	15
77	Motown STML 12064	IN MY STRIDE (LP)	15

(see also Temptations)

JIMMY RUFFIN

66	Tamla Motown TMG 577	What Becomes Of The Broken-Hearted?/Baby I've Got It	18
66	Tamla Motown TMG 577	What Becomes Of The Broken-Hearted?/Baby I've Got It (DJ copy)	85
67	Tamla Motown TMG 593	I've Passed This Way Before/Tomorrow's Tears	20
67	Tamla Motown TMG 593	I've Passed This Way Before/Tomorrow's Tears (DJ copy)	20
67	Tamla Motown TMG 603	Gonna Give Her All The Love I Got/World So Wide, Nowhere To Hide (DJ copy)	60
67	Tamla Motown TMG 603	Gonna Give Her All The Love I Got/World So Wide, Nowhere To Hide	50
67	Tamla Motown TMG 617	Don't You Miss Me A Little Bit Baby/I Want Her Love	15
67	Tamla Motown TMG 617	Don't You Miss Me A Little Bit Baby/I Want Her Love (DJ copy)	40
68	Tamla Motown TMG 649	I'll Say Forever My Love/Everybody Needs Love	15
68	Tamla Motown TMG 649	I'll Say Forever My Love/Everybody Needs Love (DJ copy)	45
68	Tamla Motown TMG 664	Don't Let Him Take Your Love From Me/Lonely Lonely Man Am I	18
68	Tamla Motown TMG 664	Don't Let Him Take Your Love From Me/Lonely Lonely Man Am I (DJ copy)	30
69	Tamla Motown TMG 703	I've Passed This Way Before/Tomorrow's Tears	7
70	Tamla Motown TMG 726	Farewell Is A Lonely Sound/If You Let Me, I Know I Can	6
70	Tamla Motown TMG 740	I'll Say Forever My Love/Everybody Needs Love	6
70	Tamla Motown TMG 753	It's Wonderful (To Be Loved By You)/Maria (You Were The Only One)	6
71	Tamla Motown TMG 767	Let's Say Goodbye Tomorrow/Living In A world I Created For Myself	7
71	Tamla Motown TMG 784	On The Way Out (On The Way In)/Honey Come Back	12
67	Tamla Motown TML 11048	THE JIMMY RUFFIN WAY (LP, mono)	40
67	Tamla Motown STML 11048	THE JIMMY RUFFIN WAY (LP, stereo)	45
69	Tamla Motown TML 11106	RUFF 'N' READY (LP, mono)	35
69	Tamla Motown STML 11106	RUFF 'N' READY (LP, stereo)	30
70	Tamla Motown STML 11161	JIMMY RUFFIN ... FOREVER (LP)	20
73	Polydor 2383 240	JIMMY RUFFIN (LP)	20

(see also Council Collective)

JIMMY & DAVID RUFFIN

71	Tamla Motown STML 11176	I AM NOT MY BROTHER'S KEEPER (LP)	25

(see also David Ruffin, Temptations)

RUFFNECK

93	Represent REPREC 1	Radford(You Get Me)/You And Me (12")	25

RUFF SQWAD

03	Ruff Sqwad RUFF 1	Pied Piper/Stinging/Untitled (12" white label)	35
03	Ruff Sqwad RSQ 01	Tings In Boots/Instrumental/Raw To The Core (12" white label)	18
03	Ruff Sqwad RSQ 003	Misty Cold/Roots/Raw To The Core (Vocal) (12" white label)	35
04	Ruff Sqwad RSQ 004	Lethal Injection/Pied Piper (Slicks Vocal)/(Riko Vocal)/(Eskbar Vocal) (12" white label)	30
04	Ruff Sqwad RSQ 005	Pied Piper (Skepta Remix)/(Tinchy Stryda Vocal)/(Scratchy Vocal)/(Godsgift Vocal) (12" white label)	20
04	Ruff Sqwad RSQ 006	Misty Cold Remix/Pied Piper (Shifty Vocal)/Pied Piper (Stamina Vocal)/Pied Piper (All In One Vocal) (12" white label)	25
04	Ruff Sqwad RQ 007	Anna (Vocal)/Anna (Instrumental) (12" white label)	20
04	Ruff Sqwad RQ 007A	Love You Feel/Pied Piper (Instrumental)/Blaze (12" white label)	20

RUFFWOOD ARTS

72	Liverpool LS 1529	KNIGHTS AND VILLEINS (LP, with insert)	400

RUFIGE CRU

92	Reinforced RIVET 1220	Krisp Biscuit (Power)/Killa Muffin (The Band Dog Mix) (12", die-cut title sleeve with tracks and artist mispelt)	15
92	Reinforced RIVET 1224	Darkrider/Believe/Menace/Jim Skreech (12", p/s)	30
93	Reinforced RIVET 1244	Terminator II Remix/Fabio's Ghost (The Edit)/ Ghosts Of My Life/High Rollerz Ghostin' Out (12", promo only)	25

RUFIGE KRU

07	Exit EXIT 010	Is This Real/Is This Real (I'm Not Sure Remix) (12", p/s, yellow vinyl, poster)	25

RUFSTUFF

92	Lucky Spin LSR 01	Burn To The Spliff/Losing Control (12")	25

RUGBYS

69	Polydor 56781	You And I/Stay With Me	45
70	Polydor 56789	Wendegahl The Warlock/Light	20

PETE RUGOLO (& DIAMONDS)

60	Warner Bros WM 4001	BEHIND BRIGITTE BARDOT - COOL SOUNDS FROM HER HOT SCENES (LP, gatefold, also stereo WS 8001)	25

(see also Diamonds, Patti Page)

RULERS

66	Rio R 105	Don't Be A Rude Boy/Be Good	25
66	Rio R 107	Copasetic/Too Late	30
67	Rio R 132	Wrong 'em Boyo/Why Don't You Change	70
67	Rio R 135	Well Covered/CARL DAWKINS: Help Time	50
67	Rio R 138	Be Mine/CARL DAWKINS: Hot And Sticky	50
69	Trojan TR 696	Got To Be Free/Situation	50

RUMBLE

70	Warner Bros WB 8011	Rich Man, Poor Man/Let Me Down	30

RUMBLERS

63	London HLD 9684	Boss/I Don't Need You No More	20
65	King KG 1021	Soulful Jerk/Hey Did A Da Da	60
63	London RE-D 1396	BOSSOUNDS (EP)	100
63	London HA-D 8081	BOSSOUNDS (LP, mono)	90
63	London SH-D 8081	BOSSOUNDS (LP, stereo)	100

RUMOUR

79	Stiff RUM 1	Frozen Years/All Fall Down (promo in promo p/s)	6

RUMPLESTILTSKIN

MINT VALUE £

79	Stiff BUY 45 DJ	Emotional Traffic/Hard Enough To Show (1-sided promo, black vinyl)	10
79	Stiff BUY 45 DJ	Emotional Traffic/Hard Enough To Show (1-sided promo, blue vinyl)	7

(see also Graham Parker)

RUMPLESTILTSKIN
70	Bell BLL 1101	Squadron Leader Johnson/Rumplestiltskin	20
71	Bell BLL 1157	Wimoweh/Through My Looking Glass	6
70	Bell SBLL 130	RUMPLESTILTSKIN (LP, gatefold sleeve)	60

(see also Clem Cattini)

RUN 229
80	MM JR 7040S	Soho/Dance/In This Day And Age	40

RUNAWAYS
76	Mercury 6167 392	Cherry Bomb/Blackmail	15
77	Mercury 6167 493	Queens Of Noise/Born To Be Bad	10
77	Mercury 6167 587	School Days/Wasted (p/s)	12
79	Cherry Red CHERRY 8	Right Now/Black Leather (p/s)	12
76	Mercury 9100 029	THE RUNAWAYS (LP, with gatefold sleeve & lyric sheet; U.S. pressing, with cat. no. SRM 1 1090, in U.K. sleeve)	20
77	Mercury 9100 032	QUEENS OF NOISE (LP, with lyric sheet)	18
77	Mercury 9100 046	LIVE IN JAPAN (LP)	15
77	Mercury 9100 047	WAITIN' FOR THE NIGHT (LP)	15
79	Cherry Red ARED 38	AND NOW ... THE RUNAWAYS (LP, 1,000 copies each in yellow, red, blue & orange vinyl, numbered)	25

(see also Joan Jett, Lita Ford & Ozzy Osbourne)o

TODD RUNDGREN
72	Bearsville K 15502	I Saw The Light/Marlene	6
72	Bearsville K 65501	SOMETHING/ANYTHING (2-LP)	20
73	Bearsville K 45513	A WIZARD, A TRUE STAR (LP, gatefold)	15

(see also Utopia)

RUN DMC
84	4th & Broadway BRLP 506	RUN DMC (LP)	15

RUNESTAFF
85	FM VHF 5	Road To Ruin/Last Chances (p/s)	10
85	FM VHF 17	Do It!/Runestaff (no p/s)	6
85	Heavy Metal HMRLP 26	RUNESTAFF (LP)	15

RUNNER
79	Acrobat BAT 2	Run For Your Life/Gone Too Long	8
79	Acrobat ACRO1	RUNNER (LP, with inner)	15

RUNNERS
74	Ariel AR 11	Choose Me/Come Out Fighting	15

RUNNING DOGS (1)
80	Shooting Star SSR 1	Present Tense/Click Click Propaganda (no p/s)	7

RUNNING DOGS (2)
80	Shattered 1.5	EP (p/s)	10

RUNNING MAN
72	RCA Neon NE 11	THE RUNNING MAN (LP)	750

(see also Ray Russell Quartet, Rock Workshop)

RUNRIG
83	Ridge RRS 003	Loch Lomond/Tuireadh Iain Ruaida (p/s)	15
84	Simple SIM 4	Dance Called America/Na H Uain A's T-Earrach (p/s)	30
84	Simple 12 SIM 4	Dance Called America/Na H Uain A's T-Earrach/Ribhinn (12", p/s)	20
84	Simple SIM 8	Skye/Hey Mandu (p/s)	15
86	Ridge RRS 006	The Work Song/This Time Of Year (p/s)	10
86	Ridge RRS 007	Alba/Worker For The Wind (p/s)	12
88	Chrysalis CHS 3284	Protect And Survive/Hearts Of Olden Glory (live) (p/s)	6
88	Chrysalis CHS 12 3284	Protect And Survive/Hearts Of Olden Glory (live)/Protect And Survive (live) (12", p/s)	10
89	Chrysalis CHS 12T 3404	News From Heaven/Chi Mi'n Tir/The Times They Are A'Changing (12", picture disc)	20
89	Chrysalis CHS 3451	Every River/This Time Of Year (p/s)	6
90	Chrysalis CHSCD 1235941	CAPTURE THE HEART EP: Stepping Down The Glory Road/Satellite Flood/Harvest Moon/The Apple Came Down (12", p/s)	15
91	Chrysalis CHS 123805	FLOWER OF THE WEST EP (12", numbered box set, with poster, discography & sticker)	10
78	Neptune NA 105	RUNRIG PLAY GAELIC (LP)	20
79	Ridge RR 001	THE HIGHLAND CONNECTION (LP)	15
81	Ridge RR 002	RECOVERY (LP, with inner)	20

RUNS
80	Carrere CAR 139	Bun In The Oven/(Censored)(no p/s)	20

RUNT
71	Bearsville K 44505	RUNT (LP)	15
71	Bearsville K 44506	RUNT - THE BALLAD OF TODD RUNDGREN (LP)	15

(see also Todd Rundgren, Utopia, Nazz)

RUPERT'S PEOPLE
67	Columbia DB 8226	Reflections Of Charles Brown/Hold On	75

(this is the Fleur-De-Lys, they do not appear on the other 2 singles)

67	Columbia DB 8278	A Prologue To A Magic World/Dream In My Mind	100
68	Columbia DB 8362	I Can Show You/I've Got The Love	120
01	Circle CPW L103	THE MAGIC WORLD OF RUPERT'S PEOPLE (LP, with free 7")	30

(see also Renaissance, Fleur-De-Lys, Gun, Sweet Feeling)

RUPIE AND SIDY
70	Success RE 910	Return Of Herbert Spliffington/RUPIE EDWARDS ALL STARS: Young, Gifted And Black	40

RUSH (AUSTRALIA)
67	Decca F 12614	Happy/Once Again	20
67	Decca F 12635	Make Mine Music/Enjoy It	20

RUSH (Canada)

MINT VALUE £

RUSH (CANADA)
77	Mercury RUSH 7	Closer To The Heart/Bastille Day/Temples Of Syrinx (metallic blue label)	18
77	Mercury RUSH 7	Closer To The Heart/Bastille Day/Temples Of Syrinx (beige label)	8
78	Mercury RUSH 12	Closer To The Heart/Anthem/Bastille Day/Temples Of Syrinx (12", p/s)	10
80	Mercury RADIO 7	Spirit Of Radio/The Trees (p/s)	10
80	Mercury RADIO 12	Spirit Of Radio/The Trees/Working Man (12", p/s)	10
81	Mercury VITAL 7	Vital Signs/In The Mood (p/s)	8
81	Mercury EXIT 7	Tom Sawyer (live)/A Passage To Bangkok (live) (p/s)	6
82	Mercury RUSH 812	New World Man/Vital Signs (live)/Freewill (live) (12", p/s)	15
82	Mercury RUSH 10 PD	Countdown/New World Man (shaped picture disc)	15
82	Mercury RUSH 1012	Countdown/New World Man/Spirit Of Radio (live)/Interview Excerpts (12", p/s)	10
84	Vertigo RUSH 1110	The Body Electric/The Analog Kid/Distant Early Warning (10", p/s, red vinyl)	12
84	Vertigo RUSH 1112	The Body Electric/The Analog Kid/Distant Early Warning (12", p/s)	50
74	Mercury 9100 011	RUSH (LP, gatefold)	30
75	Mercury 9100 013	FLY BY NIGHT (LP, gatefold)	30
75	Mercury 9100 018	CARESS OF STEEL (LP, gatefold)	30
76	Mercury 9100 039	2112 (LP)	30
78	Mercury 9100 059	HEMISPHERES (LP, gatefold sleeve)	30
78	Mercury 9100 059	HEMISPHERES (LP, mispressing, both sides play Side 1)	60
80	Mercury 9100 071	PERMANENT WAVES (LP, with newspaper and lyric inner)	20
81	Mercury 6337 160	MOVING PICTURES (LP)	30
85	Vertigo VERHP 31	POWER WINDOWS (LP, picture disc, with discography on sleeve)	20
91	Atlantic 756782293-1	ROLL THE BONES (LP)	40
93	Atlantic 7567 82528-1	COUNTERPARTS (LP)	75
02	Atlantic 83531-1	VAPOR TRAILS (2-LP)	100
04	Atlantic 7567 83728 1	FEEDBACK (LP)	30

(see also McKenzie Doug & Bob, Max Webster Band)

ED RUSH
92	Primavera PRIM 001	Edrush/Fat Girl (12", as Edrush)	20
92	ER 007	I Wanna Stay In The Jungle/5AM/Touch Me/Keep On (12")	20
92	PSY 001	Look What They've Done/What If My Heart Stops?/Look What They've Done (Dub Mix) (12")	20
93	No U-Turn NUT 002	Bludclot Artattack/Bludclot Artattack (Dark Mix) (12")	20
94	Jet Star XCT 001	Selecta/Selecta (Remix) (12")	30
95	No U-Turn NUT 011	Gangsta Hardstep/The Force Is Electric (12")	12
95	No U-Turn NUT 012	Guncheck/The Force Is Electric (Remix) (12")	20
98	Virus VRS 001LP	WORMHOLE (5-LP, with Optical)	40

MERRILEE RUSH & TURNABOUTS
68	Bell BLL 1013	Angel Of The Morning/Reap What You Sow	6
68	Bell BLL 1026	That Kind Of Woman/Sunshine And Roses	6
69	Bell BLL 1041	Reach Out I'll Be There/Love Street	10
68	Bell MBLL/SBLL 109	MERRILEE RUSH (LP)	25

OTIS RUSH
66	Vocalion V-P 9260	Homework/I Have To Laugh	100
66	Vocalion V-P 9260	Homework/I Have To Laugh (DJ copy)	150
69	Blue Horizon 57-3159	All Your Love/Double Trouble	25
68	Blue Horizon 7-63222	THIS ONE'S A GOOD UN (LP)	90
69	Atlantic 588 188	MOURNING IN THE MORNING (LP)	40
70s	Atlantic K 40495	MOURNING IN THE MORNING (LP, reissue)	15
70	Python KM 3	GROANING THE BLUES (LP)	50
76	Delmark DS 63?	COLD DAY IN HELL (LP)	25

TOM RUSH
67	Elektra EKSN 45004	Who Do You Love/On The Road Again	8
67	Elektra EKSN 45015	On The Road Again/Love's Made A Fool Of You	8
68	Elektra EKSN 45025	No Regrets/Shadow Dream Song	7
68	Elektra EKSN 45032	Something In The Way She Moves/Rockport Sunday	8
66	Xtra XTRA 5024	BLUES, SONGS & BALLADS (LP)	30
66	Xtra XTRA 5053	I GOT A MIND TO RAMBLE (LP)	30
67	Elektra EKL 308	TAKE A LITTLE WALK WITH ME (LP, also stereo EKS 7308)	30
68	Elektra EKL 4018	THE CIRCLE GAME (also stereo EKS 74018) (LP, 1st issue black 'Elektra' on red label)	25
69	Elektra EKL 4062	CLASSIC RUSH (LP, red label, also stereo EKS 74062)	20

PATRICE RUSHEN
80	Elektra K 12414	Haven't You Heard/Keepin' Faith In Love (12")	20
82	Elektra K 13173T	Forget Me Nots/Haven't You Heard/Never Gonna Give You Up (Won't Let You Be) (12")	15
84	Elektra E 9702 (T)	Get Off (You Fascinate Me) (Dance Mix)/(Instrumental) (12")	20
77	Prestige PR 10101	SHOUT IT OUT (LP)	25
79	Elektra K 52190	PIZZAZZ (LP)	25
82	Elektra K 52352	STRAIGHT FROM THE HEART (LP)	20
84	Elektra 960 360-1	NOW (LP)	15
18	Strut STRUT205LP	REMIND ME (THE CLASSIC ELEKTRA RECORDINGS 1978-1984) (3-LP)	20

JIMMY RUSHING (WITH ADA MOORE & BUCK CLAYTON)
55	Vanguard PPT 12002	SINGS THE BLUES (10" LP)	30
57	Vanguard PPT 12016	SHOWCASE (10" LP)	30
57	Philips BBL 7105	CAT MEETS CHICK (LP, with Ada Moore & Buck Clayton)	15
57	Philips BBL 7166	THE JAZZ ODYSSEY OF JAMES RUSHING ESQ (LP, with Buck Clayton)	15
58	Vanguard PPL 11008	IF THIS AIN'T THE BLUES (LP)	15

(see also Count Basie, Dave Brubeck)

JIMMY RUSHING/CHAMPION JACK DUPREE
64	Ember CJS 800	TWO SHADES OF BLUE (LP, 1 side each)	30

(see also Champion Jack Dupree)

Barbara RUSKIN

MINT VALUE £

BARBARA RUSKIN
65	Piccadilly 7N 35224	Halfway To Paradise/I Can't Believe In Miracles	10
65	Piccadilly 7N 35246	You Can't Blame A Girl For Trying/No More To Fall	12
66	Piccadilly 7N 35274	Well How Does It Feel/Wishing Your Life Away	40
66	Piccadilly 7N 35296	Song Without End/Love Came Too Late	10
66	Piccadilly 7N 35328	Light Of Love/At Times Like These Mama	10
67	Parlophone R 5571	Take It Easy/Sunshowers	10
67	Parlophone R 5593	Euston Station/Hear That Telephone	10
67	Parlophone R 5642	Come Into My Arms Again/Just A Little While Longer	10
68	President PT 217	Pawnbroker Pawnbroker/Almost	25
69	President PT 238	Gentlemen Please/24th Of July	6
69	President PT 261	Hail Love/Lady Of Leisure	6
70	President PT 280	A Little Bit Of This (And A Little Bit Of That)/Where Are We	6
70	President PT 315	For The First Time In My Life/Merry-Go-Round	6
71	President PT 350	(I Wanna Be) Your Teddy Bear/It Really Doesn't Matter	6

ROGER RUSKIN SPEAR
74	United Artists UP 35683	On Her Doorstep Last Night/Frank The Ripper	12
74	United Artists UP 35721	I Love To Bumpity Bump/When Yuba Plays The Rhumba On The Tuba Down In Cuba	20
71	United Artists UP 35221	REBEL TROUSER: Trouser Freak/Trouser Press/Release Me/Drop Out (EP, without p/s)	10
71	United Artists UP 35221	REBEL TROUSER: Trouser Freak/Trouser Press/Release Me/Drop Out (EP, with p/s)	20
74	United Artists UAS 29568	UNUSUAL (LP)	20

(see also Bonzo Dog Doo-Dah Band, Topo D. Bill)

EDDIE RUSS
| 76 | Impact IMP 5 | Zauis/See The Light/Tea Leaves (12") | 150 |

LONNIE RUSS
| 62 | Fontana 267263 TF | Something Old Something New/My Wife Can't Cook | 7 |

THANE RUSSAL (& THREE)
66	CBS 202049	Security/Your Love Is Burning Me (in p/s)	300
66	CBS 202049	Security/Your Love Is Burning Me	150
66	CBS 202403	Drop Everything And Run/I Need You (solo)	150

RUSSANT
| 82 | Mach 1 MAGIC 003 | It Happened Then/Synthamation (no p/s) | 10 |

CHARLOTTE RUSSE
| 68 | Fontana BF1683 | Anyway The Wind Blows/High On A Roof Top | 25 |

ROLAND RUSSEL
| 68 | Nu Beat NB 019 | Rhythm Hips/RHYTHM FLAMES: Deltone Special | 50 |

ANDY RUSSELL
| 58 | RCA RCA 1076 | Seven Daughters/A Certain Smile | 6 |

ARTHUR RUSSELL
86	Rough Trade RT RTT184	Let's Go Swimming (Coastal Dub)/(Gulf Stream Dub)/(Puppy Surf Dub) (12" p/s)	30
96	Talkin Loud TLDJ 49	In The Light Of The Miracle (Untitled Mix 1)/In The Light Of The Miracle (Ponytail Club Mix Part 1 & 2) (12" white label)	120
11	Eclectic Avenue BEAR 006	JUSTIN HARRIS PRESENTS ARTHUR RUSSELL - MOON (12")	15
87	Rough Trade ROUGH 114	WORLD OF ECHO (LP)	20
04	Soul Jazz SJRLP 083	THE WORLD OF ARTHUR RUSSELL (3-LP, original 2004 pressing)	30

(see also Dinosaur L, Necessaries)

BOBBY RUSSELL
68	Bell BLL 1019	Dusty/I Made You This Way	6
68	Bell BLL 1034	1432 Franklin Pike Circle Hero/Let's Talk About It	6
69	Bell BLL 1050	Carlie/Ain't Society Great?	6

CONNIE RUSSELL
54	Capitol CL 14171	No One But You/One Arabian Night	10
54	Capitol CL 14197	Love Me/Papa's Puttin' The Pressure On	10
55	Capitol CL 14214	Foggy Night In San Francisco/This Is My Love	10
55	Capitol CL 14236	Ayuh, Ayuh/I'm Making Believe	15
55	Capitol CL 14246	Snow Dreams/Green Fire	6
55	Capitol CL 14268	Farewell, Farewell/The Magnificent Matador	6
57	Capitol CL 14676	All Of You/This Is My Love	6

DEVON RUSSELL
75	Third World TW 06	Race Track Riot/Rat And Bat (as D. Russell with A (Alphonse) Bailey)	40
75	Third World TW 07	Famine Time/Part 2 (as D. Russell)	15
82	Ethnic ETH 2237	Come A Me Girl/Gully Banking	20
91	CS Sweetest CSLP 2	DARKER THAN BLUE (LP)	18

DOROTHY RUSSELL
| 71 | Duke Reid DR 2524 | You're The One I Love/Version | 20 |

GEORGE RUSSELL
61	Riverside RLP 375	EZZ-THETICS (LP)	40
65	Polydor 583 705	AT BEETHOVEN HALL (PART 1) (LP)	18
65	Fontana 688 705 ZL	THE OUTER VIEW (LP. Stereo/mono)	50
71	Flying Dutchman FD10124	ELECTRONIC SONATA FOR SOULS (LP)	20

JANE RUSSELL
53	Columbia SCM 5043	Please Do It Again/Two Sleepy People (B-side with Bob Lowery)	15
56	Capitol CL 14590	If You Wanna See Mamie Tonight/Keep Your Eyes On The Hands	10
59	MGM MGM-EP 702	JANE RUSSELL (EP)	40

JANET RUSSELL
| 88 | Harbourtown HAR 003 | GATHERING THE FRAGMENTS (LP) | 20 |

JOHN RUSSELL/RICHARD COLDMAN
| 79 | Incus INCUS 31 | HOME COOKING/GUITAR SOLOS (LP, 1 side each) | 35 |

JOHNNY RUSSELL
| 60 | MGM MGM 1074 | Lonesome Boy/Baby Won't You Tell Me So | 10 |

Keith RUSSELL

MINT VALUE £

KEITH RUSSELL
65 Piccadilly 7N 35235 — People Get Ready/Paradise ... 10

KIT RUSSELL
73 Deram DM 399 — Peppers Last Stand/Shuffle Back ... 15

LEON RUSSELL
65 Dot DS 16771 — Everybody's Talkin' 'Bout The Young/It's Alright With Me ... 8
(see also Asylum Choir)

RAY RUSSELL QUARTET
68 CBS Realm 52586 — TURN CIRCLE (LP) ... 80
69 CBS Realm 52663 — DRAGON HILL (LP) ... 60
71 RCA SF 8214 — JUNE 11TH 1971 (LP) ... 50
71 CBS 64271 — RITES AND RITUALS (LP) ... 45
73 Black Lion BLP 12100 — SECRET ASYLUM (LP, gatefold) ... 30
77 DJM DJF 20506 — READY OR NOT (LP) ... 15
(see also Running Man, Chopyn)

IAN RUSSELL
70 Lucky LU 112 — Love Locked Out/The Worm Song ... 10

CHARLIE RUSSO
63 Stateside SS 165 — Preacherman/Teresa ... 8

WILLIAM RUSSO
63 Columbia 33SX 1508 — RUSSO IN LONDON (LP) ... 20
66 Columbia 33SX 1758 — STONEHENGE (LP, with the London Jazz Orchestra) ... 35

RUSTIKS
64 Decca F 11960 — What A Memory Can Do/Hello Anne ... 10
65 Decca F 12059 — I'm Not The Loving Kind/Can't You See ... 10

RUSTLERS
61 Pye 7N 15398 — High Strung/Matter Of Who ... 12

RUSTY & DOUG (KERSHAW)
59 Oriole CB 1510 — Hey Mae!/Why Don't You Love Me ... 100
59 Oriole CB 1510 — Hey Mae!/Why Don't You Love Me (78) ... 30
59 London HL 8972 — I Like You (Like This)/Dancing Shoes ... 30
59 London HL 8972 — I Like You (Like This)/Dancing Shoes (78) ... 30
62 Polydor NH 66970 — Hey Mae!/Sweet Thing ... 20
62 Fontana 267 238 TF — Cajun Joe (The Ballad Of The Bayou)/Sweet Sweet Girl To Me ... 15
(see also Doug Kershaw)

RUSTY HARNESS
70 Ember EMB S 283 — Ain't Gonna Get Married/Goodbye (in p/s) ... 10

RUSTY NAIL
60s Hi-Fi MEP 3093 — RUSTY NAIL (EP, in p/s) ... 100
60s Hi-Fi MEP 3093 — RUSTY NAIL (EP, no p/s) ... 40

RUTH
67 Columbia DB 8218 — Leaf In The Wind/Society's Child ... 7
68 Columbia DB 8386 — Cherish/Until It's Time For You To Go ... 7

RUTH & BEAUTY
72 Montagu MONT 3000 — 29 Days To Doomsday/Cutting The Traces ... 18

RUTHLESS RAP ASSASINS
87 White (Murdertone) AMC001 — We Don't Care/Kiss AMC (12", 500 pressed) ... 20

RUTLES
78 Warner Bros K 17180 — Let's Be Natural/Piggy In The Middle ... 6
78 Warner Bros WB K56459 — THE RUTLES (LP, gatefold, booklet and inner sleeve) ... 20
96 Virgin VUSLP 119 — ARCHAEOLOGY (LP, inner) ... 20
(see also Dirk & Stig, Neil Innes, Monty Python, Beach Boys, Patto)

RUTS (D.C.)
79 People Unite SJP 795 — In A Rut/H-Eyes (1,000 only, black-ringed label) ... 150
79 People Unite RUT 1 — In A Rut/H-Eyes (repressing) ... 10
79 Virgin VS 271 — Babylon's Burning/Society (p/s) ... 10
79 Virgin VS 285 — Something That I Said/Give Youth A Chance (p/s) ... 8
79 Virgin VS 298 — Jah War/I Ain't Sofisticated (p/s) ... 10
80 RSO RSO 71 — Babylon's Burning/XTC: Take This Town (p/s) ... 8
80 Virgin VS 327 — Staring At The Rude Boys/Love In Vain ... 8
83 Virgin VS 583-12 — 4-TRACK EP (12", p/s) ... 15
83 Bohemian BO 3 — Weak Heart/Militant (white label, with paper insert; as Ruts D.C., promo only) ... 15
83 Bohemian BO 4 — Stepping Bondage/Lobotomy/Rich Bitch (p/s) ... 15
86 Strange Fruit SFPS 011 — PEEL SESSIONS (12" EP) ... 12
79 Virgin V 2132 — THE CRACK (LP, stickered sleeve with "Pay no more than £3.99") ... 20
80 Virgin V 2188 — GRIN AND BEAR IT (LP, insert) ... 20
81 Virgin V 2193 — ANIMAL NOW (LP) ... 15
82 Bohemian BOLP 2 — RHYTHM COLLISION VOL 1 (LP) ... 22
87 Link LP 013 — LIVE AND LOUD (LP) ... 15
(see also Laurel Aitken, Typhoons, Pete Zear)

RU12
78 SRTS/78/CUS 131 — SHE'S GONE EP (no p/s, 500 only) ... 100

RYAN EXPRESS
74 Thor 1005 S — RYAN EXPRESS (LP, 200 only) ... 50

BARRY RYAN (& MAJORITY)
68 MGM MGM 1423 — Goodbye/I'm So Sad ... 10
68 MGM MGM 1442 — Eloise/Love I Almost Found You (as Barry Ryan & Majority) ... 8
69 Polydor 56348 — The Hunt/No Living Without Her ... 8
70 Polydor 56370 — Magical Spiel/Caroline ... 8

Cathy RYAN

MINT VALUE £

70	Polydor 2001 035	Kitsch/Give Me A Sign	8
71	Polydor 2001 154	It Is Written/Annabella	8
71	Poyldor 2001 256	Can't Let You Go/When I Was A Child (as Barry Ryan)	8
72	Polydor 2001 335	From My Head To My Toes/Alimony Money Blues	7
72	Polydor 2001 362	I'm Sorry Susan/L.A. Woman	7
75	Dawn DNS 1109	Do That/The Summers Over	12
76	Private Stock PVT 70	Where Were You/Making A Do	7
77	Private Stock PVT 87	Brother/Life's So Easy	7
69	MGM MGM-C(S) 8106	SINGS PAUL RYAN (LP)	30
69	Polydor 583 067	BARRY RYAN (LP)	25

(see also Paul & Barry Ryan)

CATHY RYAN
53	MGM SP 1051	Show Me The Way To Go Home/If I Had You	7

(see also Art Mooney)

KRIS RYAN (& QUESTIONS)
64	Mercury MF 818	Miss Ann/She Told Me Lies (as Kris Ryan & Questions)	10
64	Mercury MF 832	Don't Play That Song/If You Don't Come Back	10
64	Mercury MF 852	Marie Marie/I've Had Enough Of You Baby	10
65	Mercury MF 877	Tell Me How/She Belongs To Me	10
65	Mercury 10024 MCE	ON THE RIGHT TRACK (EP, as Kris Ryan & Questions)	40

MARION RYAN
58	Pye 7NSR 15157	The World Goes Around And Around/Please Don't Say Goodnight (stereo)	6
60	Columbia DB 4550	Somebody/It's You That I Love	6
68	Philips BF 1721	Better Use Your Head/The Seasons Change	30
57	Pye Nixa NEP 24041	THAT RYAN GIRL! (EP)	20
58	Pye NEP 24079	MARION RYAN HIT PARADE (EP)	20
59	Pye NPL 18030	A LADY LOVES! (LP, mono)	25
59	Pye NSPL 18030	A LADY LOVES! (LP, stereo)	30

(see also Ray Ellington, Gary Miller)

PAT RYAN
77	Folk Heritage FHR 094	LEABOY'S LASSIE (LP)	25

PAUL RYAN
72	Maple Annie MA 104	Born On A Beautiful Day/Come With Me	6
72	Maple Annie MA 107	Natural Gas/Hellow Hellow	6

PAUL & BARRY RYAN
65	Decca F 12260	Don't Bring Me Your Heartaches/To Remind You Of My Love	6
66	Decca F 12319	Have Pity On The Boy/There You Go	6
66	Decca F 12391	I Love Her/gotta Go Out To Work	6
66	Decca F 12445	I Love How You Love Me/Baby I'm Sorry	6
66	Decca F 12494	Have You Ever Loved Somebody?/I'll Tell You Later	6
66	Decca F 12520	Missy, Missy/Rainbow Weather	10
67	Decca F 12567	Keep It Out Of Sight/Who Told You?	8
67	Decca F 12633	Claire/I'll Make It Worth Your While	12
67	MGM 1354	Heartbreaker/Night Time	8
68	MGM 1385	Pictures Of Today/Madrigal	8
73	Polydor 2001488	Won't You Join Me/Glad To Know You	10
74	Polydor 2001511	Carry The Blues/Reincarnation Games	6
67	Decca LK 4878	THE RYANS - TWO OF A KIND (LP)	40
68	MGM MGM-C(S) 8081	PAUL AND BARRY RYAN (LP)	25

(see also Barry Ryan)

PETE RYAN BAND
82	Ebony EBON 4	Dolly Parton's Tits/Eva On My Mind	40

PHIL RYAN & CRESCENTS
64	Columbia DB 7406	Mary Don't You Weep/Yes I Will	8
65	Columbia DB 7574	Gypsy Woman/Be Honest With Yourself	20

LLOYD RYANS EXPRESS
77	Playback PBR 7003	Let There Be Drums/Listen To The Drummer	6
77	PVK SPVK 003	Hammer Head/Leo	6

BOBBY RYDELL
59	Top Rank JAR 181	Kissin' Time/You'll Never Tame Me	10
59	Top Rank JAR 181	Kissin' Time/You'll Never Tame Me (78)	25
59	Top Rank JAR 227	We Got Love/I Dig Girls	10
60	Columbia DB 4429	Wild One/Little Bitty Girl	6
60	Columbia DB 4471	Swingin' School/Ding-A-Ling	6
60	Columbia DB 4495	Volare/I'd Do It Again	6
60	Columbia DB 4545	Sway/Groovy Tonight	6
61	Columbia DB 4600	Good Time Baby/Cherie	6
61	Columbia DB 4651	Don't Be Afraid/That Old Black Magic	6
61	Columbia DB 4690	The Fish/The Third House	6
61	Columbia DB 4731	I Wanna Thank You/The Door To Paradise	6
62	Columbia DB 4785	I've Got Bonnie/Lose Her	6
62	Columbia DB 4858	I'll Never Dance Again/Gee, It's Wonderful	6
63	Cameo Parkway C 108	Forget Him/Hey Ev'rybody (in p/s)	10
63	Cameo Parkway C 108	Forget Him/Hey Ev'rybody	7
65	Capitol CL 1537	I Can't Say Goodbye/Two Is The Loneliest Number	6
60	Top Rank JKP 2059	LOVINGEST (EP)	25
63	Cameo Parkway CPE 551	SWAY WITH BOBBY RYDELL (EP)	15
63	Cameo Parkway CPE 553	BOBBY RYDELL (EP)	15
63	Summit LSE 2036	BEST OF BOBBY RYDELL (EP)	10
60	Columbia 33SX 1243	WILD ONE (LP)	40

RYDER

			MINT VALUE £
61	Columbia 33SX 1308	SINGS AND SWINGS (LP)	20
61	Columbia 33SX 1352	SALUTES "THE GREAT ONES" (LP)	20
62	Columbia 33SX 1425	RYDELL AT THE COPA (LP)	25
62	Cameo Parkway C 1019	ALL THE HITS (LP)	15
63	Cameo Parkway C 1040	ALL THE HITS VOL. 2 (LP)	15
63	Cameo Parkway C 1055	WILD (WOOD) DAYS (LP)	15
65	Capitol T 2281	SOMEBODY LOVES YOU (LP)	20

RYDER
74	Fly BUG 39	Ain't That Nice/Sugar Mama	10

FREDDIE RYDER
65	Mercury MF 864	To Get Your Love Back/A Little Thing Called Love	6
65	Mercury MF 879	Some Kind Of Wonderful/Slow Down	12
65	Mercury MF 935	Man Of The Moment/My Block	10
68	Columbia DB 8335	Shadows (I Can't See You)/Airport	6
68	Columbia DB 8427	Worst That Could Happen/World Of My Own	6

(see also Freddie Self, Trends)

MAL RYDER (& SPIRITS)
63	Decca F 11669	Cry Baby/Take Over (as Mal Ryder & Spirits)	25
64	Vocalion V 9219	See The Funny Little Clown/Slow Down	70
64	Piccadilly 7N 35209	Your Friend/Forget It (as Mal Ryder & Spirits)	40
65	Piccadilly 7N 35234	Lonely Room/Tell Your Friend	22

(see also Mal & Primitives)

MITCH RYDER (& DETROIT WHEELS)
66	Stateside SS 481	Jenny Take A Ride/Baby Jane	20
66	Stateside SS 498	Little Latin Lupe Lu/I Hope	20
66	Stateside SS 521	Breakout/I Need Help	50
66	Stateside SS 521	Breakout/I Need Help (DJ copy)	100
66	Stateside SS 549	Devil With A Blue Dress On (Medley)/I Had It Made	20
67	Stateside SS 596	Sock It To Me Baby/I Never Had It Better	20
67	Stateside SS 2023	Too Many Fish In The Sea/Three Little Fishes/One Grain Of Sand	25
67	Stateside SS 2037	Joy/I'd Rather Go To Jail (solo)	10
67	Stateside SS 2063	What Now My Love/Blessing In Disguise (solo)	25
68	Stateside SS 2075	You Are My Sunshine/Wild Child (solo)	7
68	Stateside SS 2096	Personality/Chantilly Lace/I Make A Fool Of Myself (solo)	7
69	Dot DOT 129	Sugar Bee/I Believe (There Must Be Someone)	8
66	Stateside SE 1039	RIDIN' (EP)	40
66	Stateside S(S)L 10178	TAKE A RIDE ... (LP)	40
67	Stateside S(S)L 10189	BREAKOUT. . . !! (LP)	30
67	Stateside S(S)L 10204	SOCK IT TO ME (LP)	25
68	Stateside S(S)L 10229	WHAT NOW MY LOVE (LP, solo)	30
69	Bell MBLL/SBLL 114	ALL MITCH RYDER HITS (LP)	25

(see also Detroit)

PAUL RYDER & TIME MACHINE
74	Penny Farthing PEN 834	Are You Ready/If You Ever Get To Heaven	8

STEVE RYDER
78	Jammy JRUJ 1	Ain't It Nice/Remember Me	50

TONY RYMOND
62	Oriole 1708	Handful Of Songs/She'll Have To Go	12

S

SABANOH 75
76	Sabanoh Sound SB75 103	Carry On/Arata Poison	10
77	Sabanoh Sound SB75 104	Arata (Part 1)/Atata (Part 2)	30
77	Sabanoh Sound SB75 106	Warn You Pikin/Salematu	10

DOV SABATO
71	Ember 307	Where You Lead/Leavin' Leavin'	7

SABICAS
70	Polyor 2482 023	ROCK ENCOUNTER (LP, with Joe Beck)	30

PARK SABLE & JUNGLE 'N' BEATS
64	Fontana TF 457	Never Be Blue/Rave On	40

SABOTAGE
80	Optimistic OPT 001	WHEN THE WAR IS OVER (EP)	18
80	Optimistic OPT 004	SUBTERFUGE (EP)	12

SABRE
83	Neat NEAT 23	Miracle Man/On The Loose (p/s)	8

SABREJETS
80	Blueport BLU 5	Voodoo Cave/At The Quayside (no p/s)	6

SABRES
66	Decca F 12528	Roly Poly/Will You Always Love Me?	30

(see also Peeps)

SABRES OF PARADISE
93	Sabres Of Paradise PT 001	United (Andrew Weatherall Mix) (12", p/s, actually remix of Throbbing Gristle's "United", 800 only)	25
93	Sabres Of Paradise PT 009	Smokebelch II (Entry)/(Exit) (12", red p/s)	12
93	Sabres Of Paradise PT 009R	Smokebelch II (David Holmes Mix)/(Flute Mix) (12", yellow p/s)	10

SACRE BLEU

MINT VALUE £

94	Sabres Of Paradise PT 014	Theme/Return Of Carter & Edge 6 (Original Mix) (12")	10
94	Sabres Of Paradise PT 014R	Theme (Underdog Vs Sabres)/(Version) (10" remix)	10
94	Warp WAP 50	Wilmot/Rumble Summons (12")	15
95	Warp WARP 62	Tow Truck/(mixes) (12")	10
96	Emissions SEO 11	Ysaebud (PVC sleeve, 1-sided, etched B-side, 1,000 only)	10
93	Warp WARPLP 16	SABRESONIC (2-LP, with unreleased 7", 5,000 only)	30

SACRE BLEU
80	Sacre Bleu SB-1	In This Mood/Somehow I Doubt It (p/s)	12

SACRED
93	Twilight 7R5010A	You're The Only One/Lost In Time	20

SACRED ALIEN
81	Greenwood GW 001	Spiritual Planet/Energy (stickered labels, in p/s)	30
81	Greenwood GW 001	Spiritual Planet/Energy (stickered labels)	10
83	Heighway Robbery SAD 001	Legends/VIRGIN: Sittin' In Front Row (gatefold p/s)	30

SACRILEGE
85	C.O.T.R. GURT 4	BEHIND THE REALMS OF MADNESS (6-track mini LP)	50
87	Under One Flag FLAG 15	WITHIN THE PROPHECY (LP)	15
90	Metalcore CORE 8	BEHIND THE REALMS OF MADNESS (Mini-LP, reissue)	20

SAD
72	Phoenix NIX 124	It Ain't Easy/Box	10

SAD AFFAIR
71	Lifelong LF 1	Coloured Rice/Strange Sky	30

SADDAR BAZAAR
98	Earworm WORM 13/WJ37	Crystalline/ELECTROSCOPE: Circus Heights/TRANSPARENT THING: Ahh (p/s, 1,500 in hand painted sleeve, 1st 176 embossed)	10
95	Delerium DELEC LP 034	THE CONFERENCE OF THE BIRDS (LP)	20

SADIE'S EXPRESSION
69	Plexium PXM 4	Deep In My Heart/My Way Of Living	10
70	Plexium PXM 13	Old Whitrehall Number/Annie Wagon	25

SADISTIC MIKA BAND
74	Harvest SHSP 4029	SADISTIC MIKA BAND (LP)	15
75	Harvest SHSP 4043	BLACK SHIP (LP)	15
75	Harvest SHSP 4049	HOT MENU (LP)	15

BARRINGTON SADLER
69	Clandisc CLA 204	Soul Power/Rub It Down	25

SAD LOVERS & GIANTS
81	Last Movement LM 003	CLE (EP)	35
83	Last Movement LM 005	Colourless Dream/Things We Never Did	20
87	Midnight DONG 31	Seven Kinds Of Sin/The Outsider/Ours To Kill (12", p/s)	10
87	Midnight DONG 34	White Russians/A Map Of My World/Life Under Glass (12", p/s)	10
88	Midnight DONG 36	Cow Boys (1988 Remix)/Lost In A Moment (1988 Remix)/The Best Film He Ever Made/Things We Never Did (Live) (12", p/s)	10
82	Midnight CHIME 01	EPIC GARDEN MUSIC (LP)	20
83	Midnight CHIME 03	FEEDING THE FLAME (LP)	15
84	Midnight CHIME 07	IN THE BREEZE (LP)	15
86	Midnight CHIME 22	TOTAL SOUND (LP)	15
87	Midnight CHIME 30	THE MIRROR TEST (LP)	15
90	Midnight CHIME 01.20 S	HEADLAND (LP)	15

SADONIANS
80	Freedom Sounds FSD 012	Goodbye My Love/Good Love	8
80	Freedom Sounds FSD 012	Goodbye My Love/Good Love (12")	10

SAD PEOPLE
69	Chapter One CH113	Lonely Man/Turn Around	15

SAD SOCIETY
87	X Cert	Contaminate/Nothing ever Changes	12

SAFARI SOUNDS
94	Droppin Science DS 004	DROPPIN SCIENCE VOLUME 04 (12")	15

SAFARIS (& PHANTOM BAND)
60	Top Rank JAR 424	Image Of A Girl/Four Steps To Love	50
60	Top Rank JAR 528	The Girl With The Story In Her Eyes/Summer Nights (with Phantom Band)	40

SAFE IN BED
85	SRT 5 KS 389	Days A Day/Going Quickly	10

SAFFIRE
76	Safari SFR 4	Lay You Boogy Down (Part One)/Lay Your Boogy Down (Part Two)	10

SAFFRON SUMMERFIELD
74	Mother Earth MUM 1001	SALISBURY PLAIN (LP)	60
76	Mother Earth MUM 1202	FANCY MEETING YOU HERE (LP)	50
76	Spectator	FANCY MEETING YOU HERE (LP, reissue)	20

SAFFRONS
73	Pye 7N 45235	Give Me Time/Baby Baby I Can't Let You Go	8

SA55
86	1966 EJSP 9868	Compromised/Love Is Blind (p/s)	80

SAFRON
71	RA 5005	Tune For A Vagabond/Ladies In Waiting	40

SAGA
83	Portrait XPS 186	Don't Be Late/Careful Where You Step (p/s)	6
72	Westwood WRS 017	SAGA (LP)	50
73	Westwood WRS 036	SWEET PEG O'DERBY (LP)	100

MIKE SAGAR (& CRESTERS)
60	HMV POP 819	Deep Feeling/You Know (as Mike Sagar & Cresters)	20
61	HMV POP 988	The Brothers Three/Set Me Free	10

SAGE

(see also Cresters, Richard Harding)

SAGE
80	Redball RR 032	GOING STRONG (LP)	45

SAGITTARIUS
67	CBS 2867	My World Fell Down/Libra	25
68	CBS 3276	Another Time/Virgo	25

(see also Glen Campbell)

SAHARA (1)
75	Dawn DNLS 3068	SUNRISE (LP)	35

SAHARA (2)
85	Elite DAZZ 38	Love So Fine/(Club Mix) (12")	15

DOUG SAHM
73	Atlantic K 40466	DOUG SAHM AND BAND (LP) (inc Dylan and Dr. John in his band)	18

(see also Sir Douglas Quintet)

ST. CHRISTOPHER
84	Bluegrass GM 001	Crystal Clear/My Fond Farewell (p/s)	10
86	Bluegrass GM 003	Go Ahead Cry/Charmelle (p/s)	8
89	Sarah SARAH 015	You Deserve More Than A Maybe/The Kind Of Girl/The Summer Of Love (foldaround p/s with poster in poly bag)	20
89	Sarah SARAH 20	All Of A Tremble/My Fortune/The Hummingbird	18
90	Sarah SARAH 34	Antoinette/Salvation (p/s, insert)	20
91	Sarah SARAH 46	Say Yes To Everything/It's Snowing On The Moon (p/s, insert)	20
90	Sarah SARAH 403	BACHARACH (10" LP)	20

CHERYL ST. CLAIR
66	CBS 202041	My Heart Is Not In It/We Want Love	15
66	Columbia DB 8077	What About Me/I'll Forget You Tonight	12

(see also Alison Wonder)

JERRY ST. CLAIR
69	Philips BF 1796	Summer Exodus/Mrs. Jensen Sits Alone	15

SAINT DAVIDS ROAD
69	Tangerine DP003	Let The Sun Come In/Mama Ain't Gonna Like What She Sees	15

SAINT ETIENNE
90	Heavenly HVN 2	Only Love Can Break Your Heart/Only Love Can Break Your Heart (Version) (p/s)	6
90	Heavenly HVN 212	Only Love Can Break Your Heart/Only Love Can Break Your Heart (Original Version) (12", p/s)	12
90	Heavenly HVN 412R	Kiss And Make Up (Midsummer Madness Remix)/Kiss And Make Up (Midsummer Dubness Mix) (12", p/s)	10
90	Heavenly HVN 4CD	Kiss And Make Up (7")/Kiss And Make Up (12")/Sky's Dead (CD)	10
91	Heavenly HVN 912R	Speedwell (Flying Mix)/Speedwell (Project Mix)/Nothing Can Stop Us (Instrumental)/3D Tiger (12", p/s)	10
92	Heavenly HVN 22	Live - Paris '92 (clear flexidisc, gig freebie, 1,000 only)	20
93	Heavenly HVN 2912	Hobart Paving/Who Do You Think You Are (12", p/s, mispressed with Hobart Paving & "Your Head My Voice" on both sides)	15
95	Heavenly HVN 41	XMAS '95: A Christmas Gift To You/Driving Home For Christmas/A Message In A Bottle (CD, signed fan club edition)	90
03	Mantra MNT 78	Soft Like Me/Gimp Crisis (p/s, limited edition)	8
91	Heavenly HVN LP1	FOXBASE ALPHA (LP)	25
93	Heavenly HVN 41	SO TOUGH (LP)	30
93	Heavenly HVNLP 6	YOU NEED A MESS OF HELP TO STAND ALONE (LP)	15
94	Heavenly HVMLP 8	TIGER BAY (LP)	30
95	Heavenly HVNLP 9CD	I LOVE TO PAINT (CD, fan club edition, 600 only)	40
95	Heavenly HVNCD 10	TOO YOUNG TO DIE (CD, with bonus CD "Too Young To Die - The Remix Album" [HVN LP 10CDR])	30
97	Heavenly HVN41-2	VALENTINES DAY (CD, EP fan club edition)	50
98	Fan Club SPCD 463	XMAS '98: I Don't Intend To Spend Christmas Without You/Kofi Annan (CD, fan club edition, in card sleeve)	40
98	Creation CRELP 225	GOOD HUMOR (LP, with free 10")	50
00	Mantra MNTLP 1018	SOUND OF WATER (LP)	40
00	Mantra MNSTET 1	BUILT ON SAND: RARITIES 1994-1999 (CD, fan club edition)	40
02	Mantra MNTLP 1033	FINISTERRE (LP)	30
03	Mantra HVN136CD	XMAS 2003 (CD, EP fan club issue)	30
05	Sanctuary SANLP 271	TALES FROM TURNPIKE HOUSE (LP)	25
08	Heavenly HVNLP 69	LONDON CONVERSATIONS - THE BEST OF ST. ETIENNE (2-LP)	20
08	Foreign Office FOREIGN OFFICE 004	BOXETTE (4-CD, 3000 only)	50
12	Heavenly HVMLP 92	WORDS AND MUSIC BY SAINT ETIENNE (LP)	35
17	Heavenly HVNLP 139	HOME COUNTIES (2-LP, hand-stickered sleeve)	30
17	Heavenly HVNLP 139 BUN	HOME COUNTIES (2-LP, CD and cassette)	30

(see also 50 Year Void, Sarah Cracknell, Lovecut D.B., Mike Vickers)

KIRK ST. JAMES
70	Pye 7N 25518	My Love Oh Linda/Tears I Cry	60

BARRY ST. JOHN
64	Decca F 11933	A Little Bit Of Soap/Thing Of The Past	20
64	Decca F 11975	Bread And Butter/Cry To Me	20
65	Decca F 12111	Mind How You Go/Don't You Feel Proud	20
65	Decca F 12145	Hey Boy/I've Been Crying	20
65	Columbia DB 7783	Come Away Melinda/Gotta Brand New Man	15
66	Columbia DB 7868	Everything I Touch Turns To Tears/Sounds Like My Baby	65
66	Columbia DB 7868	Everything I Touch Turns To Tears/Sounds Like My Baby (DJ copy)	80
68	Major Minor MM 587	Cry Like A Baby/Long And Lonely Night	15
69	Major Minor MM 604	By The Time I Get To Phoenix/Turn On Your Light	15
75	Bradleys BRAD 7507	I Won't Be A Party/Do Me Good	7

Bridget ST. JOHN

MINT VALUE £

69	M. Minor MMLP/SMLP 43	ACCORDING TO ST. JOHN (LP)	50

BRIDGET ST. JOHN
69	Dandelion K 4404	To B Without A Hitch/Autumn Lullaby	15
70	Warner Bros WB 8019	If You've Got Money/Yep	12
72	Polydor 2001 280	Fly High/There's A Place I Know/Suzanne (p/s)	12
72	Polydor 2001 361	Nice/Goodbye Baby Goodbye	8
73	MCA MUS 1203	Passing Thru'/The Road Was Lonely On My Own	10
69	Dandelion 63750	ASK ME NO QUESTIONS (LP, gatefold sleeve)	80
71	Dandelion DAN 8007	SONGS FOR THE GENTLE MAN (LP, gatefold sleeve)	100
71	Dandelion K 49007	SONGS FOR THE GENTLE MAN (LP, gatefold sleeve, with cat no K 49007)	30
72	Dandelion 2310 193	THANK YOU FOR... (LP, gatefold sleeve)	100
74	Chrysalis CHR 1062	JUMBLE QUEEN (LP)	40

(see also Kevin Ayers, Ron Geesin, Mike Oldfield, Quiver)

PAUL ST. JOHN
70	Pye 7N 45190	Flying Saucers Have Landed/Spaceship Love	150

TAMMY ST. JOHN
64	Pye 7N 15682	Boys/Hey Hey Hey Hey	15
65	Pye 7N 15762	He's The One For Me/I'm Tired Of Just Looking At You	15
65	Pye 7N 15948	Dark Shadows And Empty Hallways/I Mustn't Cry	15
66	Pye 7N 17042	Nobody Knows What's Goin' On (In My Mind But Me)/ Stay Together Young Lovers	50
66	Pye 7N 17042	Nobody Knows What's Goin' On (In My Mind But Me)/ Stay Together Young Lovers (DJ copy)	100
69	Tangerine DP 0007	Concerning Love/Sound Of Love	300

(see also Trends)

ST. LOUIS UNION
66	Decca F 12318	Girl/Respect	15
66	Decca F 12386	Behind The Door/English Tea	70
66	Decca F 12508	East Side Story/Think About Me	150

(see also Medicine Head)

SAINT ORCHESTRA
78	Pye 7N 46127	Return Of The Saint/Funko (p/s)	12

OLIVER ST. PATRICK & DIAMONDS
67	Trojan TR 005	I Want To Be Loved By You/Tulips	60

CRISPIAN ST. PETERS
65	Decca F 12080	At This Moment/Goodbye, You'll Forget Me	15
65	Decca F 12207	No No No/Three Goodbyes	15
66	Decca F 12359	The Pied Piper/Sweet Dawn My True Love	6
66	Decca F 12480	Changes/My Little Brown Eyes	15
66	Decca F 12525	But She's Untrue/Your Ever Changin' Mind	8
67	Decca F 12596	Almost Persuaded/You Have Gone	8
67	Decca F 12677	Free Spirit/I'm Always Crying	8
70	Decca F 13055	So Long/My Little Brown Eyes	10
74	Santa Ponsa PNS 17	Do Daddy Do/Every Time You Sinned	7
75	Route RT 18	Carolina/Samantha	7
67	Decca DFE 8678	ALMOST PERSUADED (EP)	55
66	Decca LK 4805	FOLLOW ME... (LP)	60
70	Square SQA 102	SIMPLY... CRISPIAN ST. PETERS (LP)	40

KIRBY ST. ROMAIN
63	Stateside SS 199	Summer's Comin'/Miss You So	10

SAINT STEVEN
69	Probe SPB 1005	OVER THE HILLS/THE BASTICH (LP)	75

ST. VALENTINE'S DAY MASSACRE
67	Fontana TF 883	Brother Can You Spare A Dime/Al's Party (with p/s)	150
67	Fontana TF 883	Brother Can You Spare A Dime/Al's Party	60

(see also Artwoods)

SAINTS (AUSTRALIA)
76	Power Exchange PX 242	I'm Stranded/No Time (p/s)	20
77	Power Exchange PXE 101	I'm Stranded/(STANLEY FRANK: 2 tracks) (p/s)	8
77	Harvest HAR 5123	Erotic Neurotic/One Way Street (with p/s)	150
77	Harvest HAR 5123	Erotic Neurotic/One Way Street	10
77	Harvest HAR 5130	This Perfect Day/L-I-E-S	6
77	Harvest 12 HAR 5130	This Perfect Day/L-I-E-S/Do The Robot (12", with 'disclaimer' stickered p/s)	10
77	Harvest HAR 5137	1, 2, 3, 4 (River Deep, Mountain High/Lipstick On Your Collar/One Way Street/Demolition Girl) (EP, double pack, gatefold sleeve)	15
78	Harvest HAR 5148	Know Your Product/Run Down (no p/s)	10
78	Harvest HAR 5166	Security/All Times Through Paradise (p/s)	12
77	Harvest SHSP 4065	I'M STRANDED (LP)	40
78	Harvest SHSP 4078	ETERNALLY YOURS (LP, with inner sleeve)	30
78	Harvest SHSP 4094	PREHISTORIC SOUNDS (LP)	25

SAINTS (JAMAICA)
66	Doctor Bird DB 1009	Brown Eyes/BABA BROOKS & HIS BAND: King Size	30
69	Big Shot BI 522	Windy Part One/Windy Part Two	25
73	Count Shelley CS 043	How Long/Feeling Good	20

SAINTS (U.K.)
63	Pye 7N 15548	Wipe Out/Midgets	25
63	Pye 7N 15582	Husky Team/Pigtails	25

(see also Tornados, Heinz)

SAINTS (U.K.)
64	MJB BEV 73/4	SAINTS (10" LP, private pressing)	300
64	MJB BEVLP 127/8	SAINTS ALIVE! (LP, private pressing)	300

Russ SAINTY (& NU NOTES)

MINT VALUE £

RUSS SAINTY (& NU NOTES)
- 60 Top Rank JAR 381   Happy-Go-Lucky-Me/Standing Around 10
- 60 Decca F 11270   Race With The Devil/Too Shy (solo) 20
- 61 Decca F 11325   Don't Believe Him, Donna/Your Other Love (solo) 10
- 62 HMV POP 1055   Keep Your Love Locked/I've Got A Girl (as Russ Sainty & Nu Notes) 10
- 62 HMV POP 1069   Send Me The Pillow That You Dream On/What Do You Know About That (solo) 10
- 63 HMV POP 1181   Unforgettable Love/The Twinkle In Your Eye (solo) 10

(see also Nu Notes)

KYU SAKAMOTO
- 63 HMV POP 1171   Sukiyaki/Anoko No Namae Wa Nantenkana 7
- 63 HMV POP 1211   China Nights/Benkyo No Cha Cha Cha 6
- 62 HMV CLP 1674   SUKIYAKI (LP) 40

RYUICHI SAKAMOTO
- 80 Island IPR 2048   Riot In Lagos/Iconic Storage (12", company sleeve) 10

(see also David Sylvian, Yellow Magic Orchestra)

(BOB) SAKER
- 68 Polydor BM 56231   Still Got You/Imagination (as Bob Saker) 30
- 68 Parlophone R 5740   Foggy Tuesday/Ooh Nana Na (as Bob Saker) 50
- 69 Parlophone R 5752   Hey Joe!/Christianity 15
- 71 CBS 7010   What A Beautiful World/City Of The Angels 6
- 71 CBS 7399   Even Though We Ain't Got Money/Wild Winds Are Blowing 6

SAL SALVADOR
- 55 KPL 105   SAL SALVADOR QUARTET (10" LP) 15

SALAMANDER
- 70 CBS 5102   Crystal Ball/Billy 15
- 71 Youngblood SSYB 14   THE TEN COMMANDMENTS (LP, gatefold poster sleeve) 400

(see also Onyx)

SALEM
- 82 Hilton FMR 056   Cold As Steel/Reach To Eternity 45

SALFORD JETS
- 78 WEA K 18008   Lookin' At The Squares/Dancing School (no p/s) 15
- 79 EMI INT 590   Manchester Boys/Last Bus (p/s) 20

SANDY SALISBURY
- 00 Poptones MC 5007   Do Unto Others/CURT BOETTCHER: That's The Way It's Gonna Be (numbered die-cut company sleeve) 6

SALIX ALBA
- 73 Columbiab R5990   I Can't Resist/Blue Sky 30

SALLY AND THE ALLEY CATS
- 64 Parlophone R 5183   Is It Something That I Said/You Forgot To Remember 15

SALLYANGIE
- 69 Big T BIG 126   Two Ships/Colours Of The World 100
- 72 Philips 6006 259   Child Of Allah/Lady Go Lightly 100
- 68 Transatlantic TRA 176   CHILDREN OF THE SUN (LP, gatefold sleeve, purple/white textured label) 80
- 78 Transatlantic TRA 176   CHILDREN OF THE SUN (LP, reissue, different single sleeve) 20

(see also Mike Oldfield, Sally Oldfield)

SALLYANNE
- 82 Galaxy GAL 002   Sex In The Movies/Oh Jackie (p/s) 8

DOUG SALMA & HIGHLANDERS
- 63 Philips BF 1279   Highland Fling/The Scavenger 10

SALMONTAILS
- 80 Oblivion OBL 001   SALMONTAILS (LP, with Dave Pegg) 20

SALOME
- 69 Page One POF 137   Vivo Cantando/Amigos Amigos 7

SALSOUL STRUT
- 96 Records Inc. no cat. no. Better Days/(Mixes) 12

SALT
- 78 Grapevine GRA 111   BEYOND A SONG (LP, with insert) 18

SALT & PEPPER
- 61 London HLU 9338   High Noon/Come Softly To Me 15

SALVATION (1)
- 69 United Artists UP 35048   Cinderella/The Village Shuck 15
- 69 United Artists UAS 29062 SALVATION (LP) 30

SALVATION (2)
- 83 Merciful Release MR 025   Girlsoul/Evelyn (p/s) 12
- 83 Merciful Release MRX 025 Girlsoul/Evelyn/Dust Up (12", p/s) 15
- 86 Batfish Inc. BF 103   Jessica's Crime/The Shining (p/s) 12

SAMMY SALVO
- 58 RCA RCA 1032   Oh Julie/Say Yeah 25
- 59 London HLP 8997   Afraid/Marble Heart 12

SAM
- 72 Pye 7N 45175   Johnny Rebel/He Loves Me, He Loves Me Not 6

SAM APPLE PIE
- 69 Decca F 22932   Tiger Man (King Of The Jungle)/Sometime Girl 20
- 72 DJM DJS 274   Call Me Boss/Old Tom 8
- 69 Decca LK-R 5005   SAM APPLE PIE (LP, mono, laminated front sleeve, unboxed logo label) 300
- 69 Decca SKL-R 5005   SAM APPLE PIE (LP, stereo, laminated sleeve, unboxed logo label) 250
- 73 DJM DJLPS 429   EAST 17 (LP) 30

SAM & BILL
- 66 Pye International 7N 25355 Fly Me To The Moon/Treat Me Right 15
- 67 Brunswick 05973   I Feel Like Cryin'/I'll Try 50
- 67 Brunswick 05973   I Feel Like Cryin'/I'll Try (DJ copy) 80

SAM & DAVE

SAM & DAVE

			MINT VALUE £
66	King KG 1041	No More Pain/You Ain't No Big Thing Baby	50
66	Atlantic AT 4066	You Don't Know Like I Know/Blame Me, Don't Blame My Heart	20
66	Atlantic 584 003	Hold On I'm A Comin'/I Got Everything I Need	10
66	Atlantic 584 047	If You Got The Loving (I Got The Time)/Said I Wasn't Gonna Tell Nobody	12
67	Atlantic 584 064	You Got Me Hummin'/Sleep Good Tonight	12
67	Atlantic 584 086	You Don't Know Like I Know/Blame Me, Don't Blame My Heart (reissue)	10
67	Stax 601 004	Soothe Me/Sweet Pains (initial dark blue label)	25
67	Stax 601 004	Soothe Me/Sweet Pains (later light blue label)	20
67	Stax 601 006	When Something Is Wrong With My Baby/A Small Portion Of Your Love (initial dark blue label)	10
67	Stax 601 006	When Something Is Wrong With My Baby/A Small Portion Of Your Love (later light blue label)	8
67	Stax 601 023	Soul Man/May I Baby	8
68	Stax 601 030	I Thank You/Wrap It Up	8
68	Atlantic 584 192	You Don't Know What You Mean To Me/This Is Your World	7
68	Atlantic 584 211	Can't You Find Another Way/Still Is The Night	7
68	Atlantic 584 228	Everybody's Got To Believe In Somebody/If I Didn't Have A Girl Like You	8
69	Atlantic 584 237	Soul Sister, Brown Sugar/Come On In	8
69	Atlantic 584 247	You Don't Know Like I Know/Hold On I'm A Comin'	7
69	Atlantic 584 303	Ooh, Ooh, Ooh/Holdin' On	8
70	Atlantic 584 324	Baby, Baby, Don't Stop Now/I'm Not An Indian Giver	8
66	King KGL 4001	SAM AND DAVE (LP)	75
66	Atlantic 587/588 045	HOLD ON, I'M A COMIN' (LP)	50
67	Stax 589 003	DOUBLE DYNAMITE (LP)	50
68	Stax 589 015	SOUL MEN (LP)	40
68	Major Minor MCP 5000	SAM AND DAVE (LP)	22
69	Atlantic 588 154	I THANK YOU (LP)	25
69	Atlantic 588 155	THE BEST OF SAM AND DAVE (LP)	18
69	Atlantic 587/588 181	DOUBLE TROUBLE (LP)	22
69	Atlantic 588 185	SOUL MEN (LP, reissue)	15

SAM & KITTY

80	Grapevine GRP 132	I've Got Something Good/Love Is The Greatest	10
80	Grapevine GRP 132	I've Got Something Good/Love Is The Greatest (DJ Copy)	20

SAMBA

17	System SYSTM 019	Kami/Hooves (with Sepia) (10")	30

SAME

79	Wessex WEX 267	Wild About You/Movements (p/s)	70
80	Blueprint BLU 2008	Movements/Wild About You (reissue with reversed sides & blue print on p/s)	30
80	Blueprint BLU 2008	Movements/Wild About You (reissue with reversed sides no p/s)	20

MIKE SAMMES SINGERS

68	Davjon DJ 1006	HYMNS A SWINGING (LP, with Ted Taylor Organisation)	30
06	Trunk JBH 109 LP	MUSIC FOR BISCUITS (LP, 750 only)	35

MICHAEL SAMMES SINGERS

59	Top Rank JAR 166	Upstairs And Downstairs/Ivor Raymonde - Mylene	6

SAMMY

72	Philips 6006 227	Goo Ger Woogie/Big Lovin' Woman	7
72	Philips 6308 136	SAMMY (LP, laminated sleeve, black/silver label)	40

(see also Ian Gillan, Audience, Episode Six, Quatermass, Roy Young Band, Stackridge, Ginhouse)

SAMPLES

80	Sample	VENDETTA (EP) (A4 fold-out sleeve, white labels, some stamped 'The Samples Cherry Red Records')	125
84	No Future OI 14	Dead Hero/Fire Around Round/Suspicion (p/s)	20

DAVE SAMPSON & HUNTERS

60	Columbia DB 4449	Sweet Dreams/It's Lonesome	20
60	Columbia DB 4502	If You Need Me/See You Around	15
61	Columbia DB 4597	Why The Chicken?/1999	12
61	Columbia DB 4625	Easy To Dream/That's All	12
62	Fontana H 361	Wide, Wide World/Since Sandy Moved Away (solo)	10
61	Columbia SEG 8095	DAVE (EP, mono)	40
61	Columbia ESG 7853	DAVE (EP, stereo)	30

(see also Hunters [U.K.])

TOMMY SAMPSON

58	Melodisc MEL 1411	Rockin'/Rock'n'Roll Those Big Brown Eyes (with His Strongmen)	22
58	Melodisc MEL 1411	Rockin'/Rock'n'Roll Those Big Brown Eyes (with His Strongmen) (78)	20
58	Parlophone R 4458	Lazy Train/Smooth Mood (as Tommy Sampson Orchestra)	7

SAMSON (1)

69	Instant INSP 004	ARE YOU SAMSON (LP)	100

(see also Strider)

SAMSON (2)

70	Parlophone R5867	Venus/Wool & Water	8

SAMSON (3)

78	Lightning GIL 547	Telephone/Leavin' You (p/s)	35
79	Lightning GIL 553	Mr. Rock'n'Roll/Drivin' Music (p/s)	35
79	Laser LAS 6	Mr. Rock'n'Roll (remix)/Primrose Shuffle	10
80	EMI EMI 5061	Vice Versa (Edit)/Hammerhead (p/s, withdrawn, 1,000 demos only)	40
80	Gem GEMS 34	Vice Versa (Edit)/Hammerhead (reissue, p/s, with sticker)	8
81	RCA RCA 67	Riding With The Angels (Edit)/Little Big Man (no p/s)	10
82	Polydor SAM 2	Red Skies/Young Idea (unissued, promo only)	18
83	Polydor PODJ 554	Red Skies (DJ Edit) (1-sided promo)	12
86	Capitol 12CLP 395	Vice Versa (Remix)/Losing My Grip (Remix) (12", picture disc)	15

SAM THE SHAM & THE PHARAOHS

			MINT VALUE £
79	Laser LAP 1	SURVIVORS (LP)	18
81	Gem GEMLP 113	SHOCK TACTICS (LP, release cancelled)	0
81	RCA LP 5031	SHOCK TACTICS (LP, with insert)	18
82	Polydor POLS 1077	BEFORE THE STORM (LP, with poster, stickered sleeve)	20
84	Polydor POLD 5132	DON'T GET MAD, GET EVEN (LP, with insert)	15
84	Polydor POLD 5132	DON'T GET MAD, GET EVEN (2-LP, white labels, 2 different mixes of same album, promo only)	60

(see also Bruce Dickinson, Iron Maiden, John McCoy, Tiger, Colin Towns, Thunderstick, Nicky Moore, Mammoth, Egypt)

SAM THE SHAM & THE PHARAOHS

65	MGM MGM 1269	Woolly Bully/Ain't Gonna Move	12
65	MGM MGM 1269	Woolly Bully/Ain't Gonna Move (DJ Copy)	50
65	MGM MGM 1278	Ju Ju Hand/Big City Lights	12
65	MGM MGM 1285	Ring Dang Doo/Don't Try It	12
66	MGM MGM 1298	Red Hot/Long Long Way	15
66	MGM MGM 1315	Li'l Red Riding Hood/Love Me Like Before	10
66	MGM MGM 1326	The Hair On My Chinny Chin Chin/The Out Crowd	8
66	MGM MGM 1331	How Do You Catch A Girl/The Love You Left Behind	10
67	MGM MGM 1337	Oh That's Bad No That's Good/Take What You Can Get	10
67	MGM MGM 1343	Black Sheep/My Day's Gonna Come	15
68	MGM MGM 1379	Yakety Yak/Let Our Lovelight Shine	10
69	MGM MGM 1473	Woolly Bully/Ring Dang Doo	6
66	MGM MGM-EP 794	RED HOT (EP)	60
65	MGM MGM-C 1007	WOOLY BULLY (LP)	40
66	MGM MGM-C(S) 8032	LI'L RED RIDING HOOD (LP)	30

LEROY SAMUEL (ACTUALLY LEROY SMART)

72	Punch PH 113	Trying To Wreck My Life/JOHN HOLT: Pride And Joy	12

(PHILLIP) SAMUEL THE FIRST

71	Summit SUM 8515	Sounds Of Babylon/BEVERLEY'S ALL STARS: Second Babylon Version	10

JERRY SAMUELS

56	HMV 7M 411	Puppy Love/The Chosen Few	15

(see also Napoleon XIV)

WINSTON SAMUELS

64	Columbia DB 7405	You Are The One/Angela	12
64	Rio R 26	Follow/I'm So Glad	12
64	Black Swan WI 419	Luck Will Come My Way/LLOYD BREVITT: One More Time	25
64	Black Swan WI 426	You Are The One/Gloria Love (B-side actually by Beltones)	15
65	Ska Beat JB 196	Be Prepared/Jericho Wall	18
65	Ska Beat JB 213	My Bride To Be/LLOYD PREVITT: Wayward Ska	25
65	Ska Beat JB 214	Never Again/My Angel	20
65	Ska Beat JB 238	What Have I Done/Broken Hearted	25
66	Ska Beat JB 241	Ups And Downs/Come What May	20
66	Ska Beat JB 244	Time Will Tell/I'm Sorry	20
67	Island WI 3051	The Greatest/FREDDIE & FITZY: Truth Hurts	50
67	Island WI 3053	I Won't Be Discouraged/FREDDIE & FITZIE: Why Did My Little Girl Cry	50
67	Fab FAB 21	Peace Of Mind/Shepherd Beng Beng (by Prince Buster & Teddy King, white labels only)	350
67	Fab FAB 14	Holding Out/To The Other Man	50
67	Fab FAB 28	Peace Of Mind/I'm Still Here	60
10	Randys THB 7002	Lick It Back/COUNT MACHUKI: Pepper Pot	30

SAMURAI (1)

68	United Artists UP 2242	Good Morning Starshine/Temple Of Gold	35
71	Greenwich GSLP 1003	SAMURAI (LP, gatefold sleeve, white/brown label)	250

SAMURAI (2)

85	Ebony EBON 25	Fires Of Hell/Dreams Of The World (no p/s)	12
84	Ebony EBON 24	SACRED BLADE (LP)	15

SAN FRANCISCO TKO'S

98	Kent 6T 14	Make Up Your Mind/PEGGY GAINES: When The Boy That You Love	25

SANCTUARY

87	Epic 460811	REFUGE DENIED (LP)	25

SAND

71	Philips 6006157	Soft Lady/Babylon	20

SANDALWOOD

76	Canon CNNS 33	Don't Let It Rain Today/In Dreams	25
71	S.R.T. 71136	CHANGELING (LP), hand pasted sleeve)	3000
20	Seelie Court SCLP 002	CHANGELING (LP, reissue)	20

SANDEENO

03	Wizkidz WK 011	Ah Mankind/Preaching the Board	12

ALEX SANDERS

70	A&M AMLS 984	A WITCH IS BORN (LP, foldout sleeve with warning sticker, withdrawn)	100

GARY SANDERS

66	Warner Bros WB 5676	Ain't No Beatle/Ain't I Good To You	12

PHARAOH SANDERS

66	ESP Disk/Fontana SFJL 931	PHARAOH SANDERS QUINTET (LP)	35
70	Impulse AS 9138	TAUHID (LP)	20
71	Probe SPB 1019	DEAF, DUMB AND BLIND (LP)	35
72	Impulse AS 9219	BLACK UNITY (LP)	35
72	Impulse AS 9227	LIVE AT THE EAST (LP)	35
73	Impulse 9233	WISDOM THROUGH MUSIC (LP)	30
74	Impulse 9254	VILLAGE OF PHARAOHS (LP)	30
74	Impulse 9261	ELEVATION (LP)	30

Ray SANDERS

MINT VALUE £

73	Impulse 9280	LOVE IN US ALL (LP)	35
78	Arista SPART 1051	LOVE WILL FIND A WAY (LP)	15
82	Jasmine JAS 53	THEMBI (LP)	18
13	Universal Sounds USLP 55	ELEVATION (2-LP, reissue)	35
15	Impulse AS 9181	KARMA (LP, reissue 180gm)	25

RAY SANDERS
60	London HLG 7106	A World So Full Of Love/A Little Bitty Tear (export issue)	12

TOMMY SANDERSON & SANDMEN
61	Ember EMB 131	Deadline/Candelglow	10
62	Ember EMB 152	Ding Dong Rag/Piano A-Go Go	10

CHRIS SANDFORD (& CORONETS)
64	Decca F 11842	You're Gonna Be My Girl/Don't Leave Me Now (with Coronets)	6
65	Fontana TF 633	I Wish They Wouldn't Always Say I Sound Like The Guy From The U.S.A. Blues/Little Man, Nobody Cares	7

SANDGATE
75	Dawn DWS 1114	A Thousand Years/Such A Sad Song	6

GERRY SANDON
96	Twangsville TW 001	JUST GERRY (EP)	10

JOHNNY SANDON (& REMO FOUR)
63	Pye 7N 15542	Lies/On The Horizon (as Johnny Sandon & Remo Four)	15
63	Pye 7N 15559	Magic Potion/Yes (as Johnny Sandon & Remo Four)	15
64	Pye 7N 15602	Sixteen Tons/The Blizzard	10
64	Pye 7N 15665	Donna Means Heartbreak/Some Kinda Wonderful	10
64	Pye 7N 15717	The Blizzard/(I'd Be A) Legend In My Time	10

(see also Remo Four)

HOPE SANDOVAL & WARM INTENTIONS
00	Rough Trade RTRADE S008	AT THE DOORWAY AGAIN EP (12")	25
01	Rough Trade RTRADELP 031	BAVARIAN FRUIT BREAD (LP)	100

(see also Mazzy Star)

SANDOZ
93	Touch TONE 4	DARK CONTINENT (12" EP)	30
94	Touch TO 23 12	INTENSELY RADIOACTIVE (LP as 2 x 12")	25
95	Touch TO 28 12	EVERY MAN GOT DREAMING (LP as 2 x 12")	25
02	Soul Jazz SJR LP 59	CHANT TO JAH: SANDOZ IN DUB (2-LP, reissue)	25
06	Soul Jazz SRR LP 130	LIVE IN THE EARTH: SANDOZ IN DUB (CHAPTER 2) (2-LP)	20
16	Mute SANDOZBX1	COLLECTED WORKS 1992-1994 (5-CD box set)	30

(see also Cabaret Voltaire, Electronic Eye, Richard H. Kirk, Sweet Exorcist)

SAND PEBBLES
67	Track 604 015	Love Power/Because Of Love	20
68	Toast TT 505	If You Didn't Hear Me The First Time/Flower Power	8
69	Track 604 028	Love Power/Because Of Love (reissue)	15

SANDPIPERS
66	Pye International 7N 25396	Louie Louie/Things We Said Today	8
68	A & M AMS 723	Quando M'Immamoro (A Man Without Love)/I'll Remember You	8
76	Satril SAT 111	For The Last Time/Down By The River	8

SANDRA
86	10 TENY 78-12	(I'll Never Be) Maria Magdalena/Party Games/Little Girl (12", picture disc)	15
86	10 TEN 113-12/TENY 78-12	In The Heat Of The Night/Heatwave (Instrumental)//(I'll Never Be) Maria Magdalena/Party Games/Little Girl (12", double pack, including picture disc, gatefold PVC sleeve)	20
89	Siren SRNCD 85	Everlasting Love/Stop For A Minute/Everlasting Love (Remix)/ (I'll Never Be) Maria Magdalena (CD)	50

SANDROSE
73	Polydor 2480 137	SANDROSE (LP)	275

SANDS (IRELAND)
69	Tribune TRS 122	Dance Dance Dance/The Cheater	20
69	Tribune TRS 129	Bubble Gum Music/Sherry	15
70	Major Minor MM 681	Venus/Cara Mia	10
69	Tribune	SAND DOIN'S (LP)	50
70s	Plough PLX 501	TIME OUT WITH THE SANDS (LP)	15

(see also Tony Kenny & Sands)

SANDS (U.K.)
67	Reaction 591 017	Mrs. Gillespie's Refrigerator/Listen To The Sky	400

(see also Sundragon)

CLIVE SANDS
69	S.N.B. 55-3955	Lo Mucho Que Te Quiro/Picture On The Wall	7
69	S.N.B. 55-4058	Hooked On A Feeling/Marie	7
69	S.N.B. 55-4231	Whitchi Tai Yo/In A Dream	12
69	CBS 4672	A Very Lonely Man/You Made Me What I Am	7

(see also Brothers Kane, Sarstedt Brothers, Wes Sands)

DAVEY SANDS & ESSEX
65	Decca F 12170	Please Me Mine/All The Time	20
67	CBS 202620	Advertising Girl/Without You I'm Nothing	25
71	Parlophone R5899	The Puppet Man/Oh What A Naughty Man	10

EVIE SANDS
65	Red Bird BC 118	Take Me For A Little While/Run Home To Mama	50
65	Red Bird BC 118	Take Me For A Little While/Run Home To Mama (DJ copy)	85
66	Cameo Parkway C 413	Picture Me Gone/It Makes Me Laugh	125
66	Cameo Parkway C 413	Picture Me Gone/It Makes Me Laugh (DJ copy)	200
68	A&M AMS 736	Shadow Of The Evening/Until It's Time For You To Go	10
69	A&M AMS 748	I'll Hold Out My Hand/One Fine Summer Morning	10
69	A&M AMS 760	Anyway That You Want Me/I'll Never Be Alone	10

Jodi(e) SANDS

			MINT VALUE £
75	Capitol CL 15818	You Brought The Woman Out In Me/Early Morning Sunshine	7

JODI(E) SANDS
57	London HL 8456	With All My Heart/More Than Only Friends (as Jodi Sands)	15
57	London HL 8530	Please Don't Tell Me (Sayonara)/If You're Not Completely Satisfied	12
58	Starlite ST45 005	All I Ask Of You/The Way I Love You	8
58	HMV POP 533	Someday (You'll Want Me To Want You)/Always In My Heart	8

SYLVIA SANDS
61	Columbia DB 4579	Autumn Tears/Steppin' Out With My Baby	8

TOMMY SANDS
57	Capitol CL 14695	Teen-Age Crush/Hep Dee Hootie (Cutie Wootie)	25
57	Capitol CL 14724	Ring-A-Ding-A-Ding/My Love Song	25
57	Capitol CL 14745	Goin' Steady/Ring My 'Phone	25
57	Capitol CL 14781	Let Me Be Loved/Fantastically Foolish	10
57	Capitol CL 14811	Man, Like Wow!/A Swingin' Romance	20
58	Capitol CL 14834	Sing, Boy, Sing/Crazy 'Cause I Love You	15
58	Capitol CL 14872	Hawaiian Rock/Teen-Age Doll	25
58	Capitol CL 14889	After The Senior Prom/Big Date	20
58	Capitol CL 14925	Blue Ribbon Baby/I Love You Because (as Tommy Sands & Raiders)	30
59	Capitol CL 14971	The Worryin' Kind/Bigger Than Texas	35
59	Capitol CL 15013	Is It Ever Gonna Happen/I Ain't Gettin' Rid Of You	30
59	Capitol CL 15047	Sinner Man/Bring Me Your Love	7
59	Capitol CL 15071	That's The Way I Am/I'll Be Seeing You	7
60	Capitol CL 15109	I Gotta Have You/You Hold The Future	7
60	Capitol CL 15143	The Old Oaken Bucket/These Are The Things You Are	7
61	Capitol CL 15219	Love In A Goldfish Bowl/I Love My Baby	7
63	HMV POP 1193	Connie/Young Man's Fancy	6
63	HMV POP 1247	Only 'Cause I'm Lonely/Cinderella	6
66	Liberty LIB 55842	The Statue/Lolita	45
66	Liberty LIB 55842	The Statue/Lolita (DJ copy)	85
57	Capitol EAP1 848	STEADY DATE WITH TOMMY SANDS PT. 1 (EP)	20
57	Capitol EAP2 848	STEADY DATE WITH TOMMY SANDS PT. 2 (EP)	20
57	Capitol EAP3 848	STEADY DATE WITH TOMMY SANDS PT. 3 (EP)	20
57	Capitol EAP1 851	TEENAGE CRUSH (EP)	20
59	Capitol EAP1 1081	SANDS STORM PART 1 (EP)	20
59	Capitol EAP2 1081	SANDS STORM PART 2 (EP)	20
59	Capitol EAP3 1081	SANDS STORM PART 3 (EP)	20
59	Capitol EAP1 1123	THIS THING CALLED LOVE (EP)	15
57	Capitol T 848	STEADY DATE WITH TOMMY SANDS (LP)	40
58	Capitol T 929	SING, BOY, SING (soundtrack) (LP)	40
59	Capitol T 1081	SANDS STORM! (LP)	80
59	Capitol T 1123	THIS THING CALLED LOVE (LP)	20
60	Capitol (S)T 1239	WHEN I'M THINKING OF YOU (LP, mono)	15
60	Capitol (S)T 1239	WHEN I'M THINKING OF YOU (LP, stereo)	15
61	Capitol T 1426	A DREAM WITH TOMMY SANDS (LP)	15

TONY SANDS & DRUMBEATS
60s	Studio 36 NSRS EP 1/22	Shame Shame Shame/I Got A Feeling	250

WES SANDS
63	Columbia DB 4996	There's Lots More Where This Came From/Three Cups	45

(see also Brothers Kane, Sarstedt Brothers, Clive Sands)

SANDS OF TIME
66	Pye 7N 17140	Where Did We Go Wrong/When I Look Back	10
67	Pye 7N 17236	One Day/Ev'ry Time We Say Goodbye	8

PAT SANDY
69	Attack ATT 8000	Gentle On My Mind/BIG L: Soulful	30

SANDY COAST
71	Polydor 2121 046	True Love/That's A Wonder	10
73	Polydor 2001 457	Blackboard Jungle Lady/Don't Get Me Wrong	7
69	Page One POLS 020	FROM THE STEREO WORKSHOP (LP)	350
69	Page One MORS 201	SHIPWRECK (LP)	300
73	Polydor 2310 277	STONEWALL (LP)	20

SAN FRANCISCO EARTHQUAKE
68	Mercury MF 1036	Fairy Tales Can Come True (Have You Heard About Lucy)/Su Su	10

SANG HUGH
73	Count Shelly CS 023	Rasta No Born Ya/MESSENGERS: Cherry Baby	8
73	Count Shelly CS 034	No Potion A Girl/The Way To Reason	8
75	Ethnic Fight EF 018	Last Call To Blackman/Black Track	15
76	Ethnic Fight EF 056	God's Children/ETHNIC FIGHT BAND: Dub In Blood Island	10

SAN REMO STRINGS
71	Tamla Motown TMG 795	Festival Time/All Turned On	12
71	Tamla Motown TMG 795	Festival Time/All Turned On (DJ copy)	30
72	Tamla Motown TMG 807	Reach Out, I'll Be There/Hungry For Love	10
72	Tamla Motown TMG 807	Reach Out, I'll Be There/Hungry For Love (DJ copy)	30
73	Tamla Motown STML 11216	SAN REMO STRINGS SWING (LP)	20

BOBBY SANSOM (& GIANTS)
63	Oriole CB 1837	There's A Place/Lucille (as Bobby Sansom & Giants)	20
63	Oriole CB 1888	Where Have You Been/Do You Promise (as Bobby Sansom & Giants)	18
70	Decca F 13104	Lady One And Only/Handbags And Gladrags	8
71	Decca F 13151	I Believe In Music/The Valley Of The Shadows Of Tears	8

MONGO SANTAMARIA
63	Riverside RIF 106909	Watermelon Man/Don't Bother Me No More	20

SANTANA

MINT VALUE £

65	CBS 201766	El Pussycat/Black Eyed Peas And Rice	20
69	Direction 58-4086	Cloud Nine/Son Of A Preacher Man	18
69	Direction 58-4430	Twenty Five Miles/El Tres	15
66	CBS SS 62123	HEY! LET'S PARTY (LP)	20
69	CBS S 233811	ALL STRUNG OUT (LP)	20
71	CBS 63904	WORKING ON A GROOVY THING (LP)	20
71	Atlantic 2400 140	MONGO'S WAY (LP)	20

SANTANA

70	CBS 5325	Black Magic Woman/Hope You're Feeling Better	10
69	CBS 63815	SANTANA (LP, laminated sleeve original, orange label)	30
70	CBS 64087	ABRAXAS (LP, orange label)	25
71	CBS 69015	SANTANA (III) (LP, gatefold sleeve, some stickered, orange label)	25
72	CBS CQ 30595	SANTANA (III) (LP, gatefold sleeve, quadrophonic)	40
72	CBS 65299	CARAVANSERAI (LP, gatefold sleeve, orange label)	20
73	CBS CQ 31610	CARAVANSERAI (LP, gatefold sleeve, quadrophonic)	25
74	CBS CQ 32445	WELCOME (LP, embossed gatefold sleeve, quadrophonic)	20
75	CBS CQ 30130	ABRAXAS (LP, gatefold sleeve, quadrophonic)	20
75	CBS Q 69081	GREATEST HITS (LP, quadrophonic)	15
75	CBS Q 69084	BORBOLETTA (LP, quadrophonic)	15
76	CBS Q 86005	AMIGOS (LP, quadrophonic)	15
85	CBS 69084	BORBOLETTA (LP, Nimbus Supercut, mail order only through Hi Fi Today magazine)	80
90	Thunderbolt THBL 079	LATIN TROPICAL (LP)	18
92	Polydor 513 197-1	MILAGRO (LP)	20
00	Arista 07822 19080-1	SUPERNATURAL (2-LP)	200
02	Arista 74321 97961-1	SHAMAN (2-LP)	100

CARLOS SANTANA & BUDDY MILES

| 73 | CBS CQ 31308 | CARLOS SANTANA & BUDDY MILES LIVE (LP, quadrophonic) | 15 |

(see also Santana, Buddy Miles, Mahavishnu Orchestra, John McLaughlin, John Lee Hooker)

SANTELLS
| 66 | Sue WI 4020 | So Fine/These Are Love | 25 |

GRANT SANTINO & THE FAMILY
| 79 | Polydor 2059 168 | L.O.V.E./Try Love | 20 |
| 79 | Polydor GS1 | L.O.V.E./Try Love (12", promo only) | 100 |

DAVID SANTO
| 68 | London HLK 10219 | Jingle Down A Hill/Rising Of Scorpio | 8 |

SANTO & JOHNNY
59	Pye International 7N 25037	Sleep Walk/All Night Diner	15
60	Parlophone R 4619	Tear Drop/The Long Walk Home	15
60	Parlophone R 4644	Caravan/Summertime	10
61	Pye International 7N 25111	Theme From Come September/Hopscotch	10
61	Parlophone R 4844	Bullseye!/Twistin' Bells	10
62	Parlophone R 4865	Birmingham/The Mouse	10
62	Stateside SS 110	Spanish Harlem/Stage To Cimarron	10
64	Stateside SS 253	Three Cabelleros/Manhattan Spiritual	10
64	Stateside SS 292	In The Still Of The Night/Song For Rosemary	10
60	Parlophone GEP 8806	SANTO AND JOHNNY NO. 1 (EP)	30
60	Parlophone GEP 8813	SANTO AND JOHNNY NO. 2 (EP)	30
64	Stateside S(S)L 1008	HAWAII (LP)	20

SAPODILLA PUNCH
| 69 | Mercury MF 112 | Hold On I'm Coming/Bach To Minor (DJ copy) | 20 |
| 69 | Mercury MF 1112 | Hold On I'm Coming/Bach To Minor | 8 |

SAPPHIRE
| 82 | Sapphire Rocks SRR 001 | Jealousy (p/s) | 200 |
| 72 | SRT SRT 72226 | SAPPHIRE (LP) | 200 |

SAPPHIRES
63	Stateside SS 223	Where Is Johnny Now/Your True Love	40
64	Stateside SS 267	Who Do You Love/Oh So Soon	65
65	HMV POP 1441	Gotta Have Your Love/Gee Baby I'm Sorry	180
65	HMV POP 1441	Gotta Have Your Love/Gee Baby I'm Sorry (DJ copy)	350
65	HMV POP 1461	Evil One/How Could I Say Goodbye	180
65	HMV POP 1461	Evil One/How Could I Say Goodbye (DJ copy)	300
72	Probe PRO 556	Gotta Have Your Love/Gee Baby I'm Sorry (reissue)	10
74	Probe PRO 609	Slow Fizz/Our Love Is Everywhere	10
78	ABC 4221	Gonna Be A Big Thing/EDDIE REGAN: Playin' Hide And Seek	8

SARABAND
| 73 | Folk Heritage FHR 050 | CLOSE TO IT ALL (LP) | 22 |

SARACEN
82	Nucleus SAR 1	No More Lonely Nights/Rock Of Ages (p/s, with patch)	8
82	Nucleus SAR 1	No More Lonely Nights/Rock Of Ages (p/s)	6
83	Neat NEAT 30	We Have Arrived/Face In The Crowd (p/s)	7
82	Nucleus MPGR 492	HEROES, SAINTS AND FOOLS (LP)	15

SARASOTA
| 96 | BIT Productions MIKE 004 | We're Gettin' Hot (1-sided 12") | 40 |
| 97 | BIT Productions MIKE 009 | Pleasure/We're Gettin' Hot (the Maximum Project Pumped Up Remix) (stickered white label 12") | 40 |

SARDONICUS
| 73 | Country Recording Service COUN 240 | Nympth/Evaporated Brain | 350 |

DON SARGENT
| 60 | Vogue Pop V 9160 | St. James' Infirmary/Gypsy Boots (triangular centre) | 300 |

SARI & SHALIMARS

SARI & SHALIMARS
68	United Artists UP 2235	It's So Lonely (Being Together)/You Walked Out On Me Before	30

DEREK SARJEANT
61	Oak RGJ 101	FOLK SONGS SUNG BY DEREK SARJEANT (EP)	20
61	Oak RGJ 103	SONGS WE LIKE TO SING (EP, with tracks by Lisa Turner & Mick Wells)	15
61	Oak RGJ 105	FOLK SONGS SUNG BY DEREK SARJEANT VOL. 2 (EP)	15
63	Oak RGJ 117	MAN OF KENT (EP)	18
61	Oak RGJ 7444	ENGLISH FOLK SONGS (EP)	20
61	Oak RGJ 7450	A SAILOR'S LIFE: SONGS OF THE SEA AND THE SHORE (EP)	20

MIKE SARNE
63	Parlophone R 5060	Please Don't Say/Now You've Moved	6
63	Parlophone R 5090	Hello Lover Boy/Baby I'm On My Way	6
64	Parlophone R 5129	Out And About/A Place To Go	6
64	Parlophone R 5170	Love Me Please/You've Got Something (as Mike Sarne & Le Roys)	12
63	Parlophone DP 558	Just Like Eddie/Slow Twistin' Round The Totem Pole (export issue)	50
63	Parlophone GEP 8879	MIKE SARNE HIT PARADE (EP)	15
62	Parlophone PMC 1187	COME OUTSIDE (LP)	25

(see also Wendy Richards, Le Roys, Billie Davis, Rod McKuen)

SAROFEEN & SMOKE
71	Pye International 7N 25556	Susan Jane/Tomorrow	15
71	Pye Intl. NSPL 28153	DO IT (LP)	40

SAROLTA
68	Island WIP 6035	Open Your Hands/L.O.V.E.	15
69	President PT248	I Am A Woman/Change Of Heart	10

SARR BAND
79	Calendar DAY 115	Double Action/Soul Tango	8
78	Calendar LDAY 115	Double Action/Magic Mandrake (12")	20
78	Calendar DAY 115	Magic Mandrake/Double Action	8
78	Calendar LDAY 115	Magic Mandrake/Double Action (12")	25

PETER SARSTEDT
68	Island WIP 6028	I Must Go On/Mary Jane	30
68	United Artists UP 2228	I Am A Cathedral/Blagged	10
69	United Artists UP 2262	Where Do You Go To (My Lovely)/Step Into The Candelight	10
69	United Artists UP 35021	Frozen Orange Juice/Arethusa Loser	15
69	United Artists UP 35041	As Though It Were A Movie/Take Off Your Clothes	8
69	United Artists UP 35075	Without Darkness (There's No Light)/Step Into The Candlelight	8

(see also Sarstedt Brothers, Brothers Kane, Peter Lincoln)

SARSTEDT BROTHERS
73	Regal Zonophone RZ 3081	Chinese Restaurant/Beloved Illusions	7
73	Regal Zono. SRZA 8516	WORLDS APART TOGETHER (LP, gatefold sleeve with booklet)	20

(see also Brothers Kane, Peter Sarstedt, Eden Kane, Clive Sands, Wes Sands)

DAN SARTAIN
09	Third Man TMR 011	Bohemian Grove/Atheist Funeral (100 only, luminous vinyl)	60

SAS
85	No Label SAS4	SUAVE AND SOPHISTICATED? (7" EP, fold-out sleeve)	25

SASPARELLA
69	Decca F 12892	Spooky/Come Inside	40

SASSAFRAS
73	Polydor 2383 245	EXPECTING COMPANY (LP)	15

SASSENACHS
64	Fontana TF 518	That Don't Worry Me/All Over You	30

SATAN
82	Guardian GRC 145	Kiss Of Death/Heads Will Roll (with p/s)	200
82	Guardian GRC 145	Kiss Of Death/Heads Will Roll	50
83	Roadrunner RR 9894	COURT IN THE ACT (LP, inner)	40
85	Neat NEAT 1012	COURT IN THE ACT (LP, reissue)	30

SATANIC MALFUNCTIONS
86	Teacore TEACORE 1	WHO WANTS THE WORLD EP (wraparound p/s)	15
89	Teacore TEA 3	REMEMBER EP (wraparound p/s)	12
88	Teacore TEA 2	HELLBOUND (LP, insert)	20
90	Teacore TEA 5	DISGRACE TO HUMANITY (LP, insert)	20

SATANIC RITES
81	Heavy Metal HEAVY 8	Live To Ride/Hit And Run (p/s)	12
85	Chub CHUBLP 001	WHICH WAY THE WIND BLOWS (LP)	25
87	Chub CHUBLP 002	NO USE CRYING (LP)	30

SATAN'S RATS
77	DJM DJS 10819	In My Love For You/Façade (p/s)	30
77	DJM DJS 10821	Year Of The Rats/Louise (p/s)	25
78	DJM DJS 10840	You Make Me Sick/Façade (p/s)	25
89	Overground OVER 01	Year Of The Rats/Louise (p/s, 600 yellow vinyl)	6
89	Overground OVER 01	Year Of The Rats/Louise (p/s, 400 white vinyl)	7
89	Overground OVER 01	Year Of The Rats/Louise (p/s, 25 gold vinyl, numbered test pressings)	15
89	Overground OVER 02	In My Love For You/Facade (p/s, 600 yellow vinyl)	12
89	Overground OVER 02	In My Love For You/Facade (p/s, 400 white vinyl)	12
89	Overground OVER 02	In My Love For You/Facade (p/s, 25 gold vinyl, numbered test pressings)	15
91	Overground OVER 14	You Make Me Sick/Louise (p/s, clear vinyl, 567 copies only)	7

YOUNG SATCH
70	Black Swan BW 1401	Bonga Bonga Bonga/HI-TALS: Ram Buck (4-prong centre)	45
70	Black Swan BW 1401	Bongo Bongo/BOYS: Ramba	12

(see also Rico & Satch, The Undivided)

Girl SATCHMO

MINT VALUE £

GIRL SATCHMO
61	Blue Beat BB 45	Satchmo's Mash Potato/Darling	20
62	Blue Beat BB 79	Twist Around Town/My New Honey (with Karl Rowe & Bluebeats)	20
63	Blue Beat BB 156	Don't Be Sad/Brother Joe (with Les Dawson Combo)	25
64	Blue Beat BB 227	Rhythm Of The New Beat/Blue Beat Chariot	30
69	Fab FAB 111	Take You For A Ride/I'm Coming Home	35
69	Trojan TR 676	Taken For A Ride/I'm Coming Home	20

(see also Pat Satchmo, Sugar & Dandy)

PAT SATCHMO
69	Punch PH 9	Hello Dolly/ERIC DONALSON: Never Get Away	200
69	Upsetter US 316	Hello Dolly/King Of The Trombone	120
70	Punch PH 24	Wonderful World/MEDITATORS: Purple Mast	50
70	Songbird SB 1039	A Handful Of Friends/CRYSTALITES: Handful - Version	25
72	Attack ATT 8024	What's Going On/LLOYD & CAREY: Tubby's In Full Swing	50

SATELLITES
83	Brickyard EOR 1	Vietnam/Lucy Is A Prostitute/I Fell In Love With A Lesbian (p/s)	10
83	Kamera ERA 016	NIGHTMARE EP	6
84	Brickyard	HERE IS TODAY'S NEWS (LP)	15

SATIN BELLS
68	Pye 7N 17531	Baby You're So Right For Me/When You're Ready	10
68	Pye 7N 17608	Da-Di-Da-Da/Oh No Oh Yes	6
69	Decca F 22937	I Stand Accused (Of Loving You)/Sweet Darlin'	20
70	Decca F 23044	The Power Of Love/Baby Come Back	6

(see also Three Bells)

SATIN STORM
91	Satin Storm SSP 201	Satin Storm 1999/Pleasurezone (inst)/Buzz/Feel The Spirit (12")	30
91	Satin Storm SSHC 1	See The Light/Call In The Hardcore/Kick Up A Sound Boy/Chill Out (12". As Satin Storm Dancers)	15
92	Satin Storm DJT DAPSS 1	Let's Get Together/Free Your Mind (12". Artist not credited on labels)	40
92	Satin Storm ST 01	Sweat/Can't Wait/Can't Take No More/Tekno/Satin Storm/EBGB (12")	20
92	Satin Storm SSHC 2	What About What I Need /Drop That Bass/House Of My Dreams/Ram It (12" Artist not credited on labels)	15
92	Satin Storm SSHC 3	Think I'm Going Out Of My Head/Unknown/What Do You Do? (12")	15
93	Satin Storm SSHC 4	Return Of The Blopblingers/Rough And Smooth & The Driven (12")	10
93	Satin Storm SSHC 5	Come On, Get Together/I'm A Technician/He's On It, All Night Long (12")	10

SATISFACTION (1)
71	Decca F 13129	Love It Is/Cold Summer	10
71	Decca F 13207	Don't Rag The Lady/Gregory Shan't	10
71	Decca SKL 5075	SATISFACTION (LP, laminated front sleeve, blue/silver boxed label)	50

(see also Mike Cotton Sound)

SATISFACTION (2)
79	Live & Love LAP 005	SATISFACTION IN DUB (LP)	40

SATISFIERS
57	Vogue Coral Q 72247	Where'll I Be Tomorrow Night?/Come Away, Love	12
57	Vogue Coral LVA 9068	THE SATISFIERS (LP)	20

LIZZARD SATTAI
76	Trojan TRLS 138	LIZZARD (LP)	30

LONNIE SATTIN
56	Capitol CL 14552	Trapped (In The Web Of Love)/Your Home Can Be A Castle	6

LON SATTON
74	CBS SCBS 2816	The Love I See In Your Eyes/Do You Need My Love	8

SATURNALIA
71	Matrix TRIX 1	MAGICAL LOVE (LP, picture disc with 3D labels, with booklet & ticket)	150
71	Matrix TRIX 1	MAGICAL LOVE (LP, allegedly some copies in laminated sleeve, picture disc with 3D labels, with booklet & ticket)	500
73	Matrix TRIX 1	MAGICAL LOVE (LP, picture disc, reissue)	25

(see also Horse)

SATYR
79	Stardust STAR 001	Love Slide Boogie/Problem In The City	10

SAUCERMAN
89	Fierce FRIGHT 035	I Will Be King/Sid James Rules (withdrawn)	25
80s	Fierce	WRESTLING (12", sampler, withdrawn)	12

(see also Kray Cherubs)

KEN SAUL
70	City Music	Warm Summer Rain/Pictures Framed in My Mind	80
71	Seashell SSLP 01	SONGS FOR A RAINY DAY (LP, 25 only, hand-made sleeve, hand-written labels)	750
73	SSLP 002	SEASHELLS (LP, hand-made sleeve, insert, 100 only)	750

(see also Stone Angel)

SAULT
19	Forever Living Originals FLO0002	5 (LP, 1st pressing, no 'FOREVER LIVING' in run out groove)	25
20	Forever Living Originals FLO0003	7 (LP)	20
20	Forever Living Originals FLO0003	7 (LP, repressing, blue vinyl)	30
20	Forever Living Originals FLO0005	UNTITLED (BLACK IS) (LP, red vinyl 300 only)	60
20	Forever Living Originals FLO0005	UNTITLED (BLACK IS) (LP, blue vinyl)	35
20	Forever Living Originals FLO0005	UNTITLED (BLACK IS) (LP, white vinyl 300 only)	60
20	Forever Living Originals FLO0006	UNTITLED (RISE) (LP)	50

SAUNA YOUTH

MINT VALUE £

(see also Cleo Sol)

SAUNA YOUTH
13	Static Shock SSR 17	False Jessi Ot II/Oh Joel (white vinyl, 150 only)	6
12	Faux Disex FAUX 016	DREAMLAND (LP)	18
15	Upset! The Rhythm UTR 017	DISTRACTIONS (LP)	15

JESSE SAUNDERS
| 15 | Trax TX 326 | Funk You Up (edit)/(Vocal)/(Club Mix)/Bonus Beats (12", reissue) | 10 |

LARRY SAUNDERS
| 74 | London HLU 10469 | On The Real Side/Let Me Be The Special One | 20 |
| 74 | London HLU 10469 | On The Real Side/Let Me Be The Special One (DJ copy) | 40 |

MAHALIA SAUNDERS
71	Moodisc HME 112	Down The Aisle/IAN ROBINSON: Three For One	18
71	Upsetter US 374	Pieces Of My Heart/UPSETTERS: Version	25
71	Pama Supreme PS 331	Peace Of My Heart/Right On The Tip Of My Tongue	20

KEVIN SAUNDERSON
| 88 | Kool Kat DJ 5 | Bounce Your Body To The Box (Mike 'Hitman' Wilson Acid Remix)/(Original Detroit Mix)/The Groove That Won't Stop (Detroit Special Mix)/Force Field (12") | 15 |

TUPPER SAUSSY
| 63 | London HAU 8127 | DISCOVER TUPPER SAUSSY (LP) | 15 |

LES SAUTERELLES
| 68 | Decca F 22824 | Heavenly Club/Dream Machine | 45 |

SAVAGE
| 82 | Ebony EBON 10 | Ain't No Fit Place/China Run | 8 |
| 83 | Ebony EBON 12 | LOOSE 'N' LETHAL (LP) | 25 |

EDNA SAVAGE
55	Parlophone MSP 6175	Stars Shine In Your Eyes/A Star Is Born	7
55	Parlophone MSP 6181	Candlelight/In The Wee Small Hours Of The Morning	7
55	Parlophone MSP 6189	Arrivederci Darling/Bella Notte	7
56	Parlophone MSP 6217	Tell Me, Tell Me, Tell Me That You Love Me/Please Hurry Home	7
56	Parlophone R 4226	My Prayer/Me 'n' You 'n' The Moon	7
56	Parlophone R 4253	Never Leave Me/Don't Ever Go (I Need You)	6
57	Parlophone R 4301	Me Head's In De Barrel/Five Iranges Four Apples	6
57	Parlophone R 4360	Let Me Be Loved/Diano Marina	6

(see also Michael Holliday)

JOAN SAVAGE
57	Columbia DB 3929	Five Oranges, Four Apples/Bamboozled	6
57	Columbia DB 3968	With All My Heart/Love Letters In The Sand	6
57	Columbia DB 4039	Shake Me, I Rattle/Lula Rock-A-Hula	20
58	Columbia DB 4159	Hello Happiness, Goodbye Blues/Left Right Out Of My Heart	6

SAVAGE PENCIL
| 88 | Blast First FU 3LP | PRESENTS ANGEL DUST: MUSIC FOR MOVIE BIKERS (LP, picture disc, 1,000 only) | 15 |

(see also Art Attacks, Kray Cherubs)

SAVAGE RESURRECTION
| 68 | Mercury MF 1027 | Thing In E/Fox Is Sick | 60 |
| 68 | Mercury SMCL 20123 | SAVAGE RESURRECTION (LP) | 175 |

SAVAGE ROSE
68	Polydor 184206	IN THE PLAIN (LP, red label)	40
69	Polydor 184316	TRAVELLIN' (LP, red label)	30
72	RCA Victor SF 8250	REFUGEE (LP, laminated front sleeve, orange label)	30
71	RCA Victor SF 8169	YOUR DAILY GIFT (LP, laminated front sleeve, orange label)	30

SAVAGES
| 63 | Decca DFE 8546 | EVERYBODY SURF! WITH THE SURFIN' SAVAGES (EP) | 200 |

(see also Soul Sounds, Screaming Lord Sutch, Circles, Tony Dangerfield & Thrills)

SAVANNA
| 82 | R&B RBS 209 | Never Let You Go/(Instrumental) | 8 |

JULIAN JAY SAVARIN
73	Lyntone LYN 3426	I Am You/Kizeesh (Corgi Books sampler)	50
73	Birth RAB 2	WAITERS ON THE DANCE (LP, textured sleeve with insert)	500
73	Birth RAB 2	WAITERS ON THE DANCE (LP, textured sleeve without insert)	300
87	Five Hours Back TOCK 002	WAITERS ON THE DANCE (LP, reissue)	40

(see also Julian's Treatment)

SAVES THE DAY
| 02 | B-Unique BUN021-7 | At Your Funeral/Ups And Downs (p/s) | 6 |

RONNIE SAVOY
| 61 | MGM MGM 1122 | And The Heavens Cried/Big Chain | 15 |
| 61 | MGM MGM 1131 | Bewitched/It's Gotta Be love | 10 |

SAVOY BROWN (BLUES BAND)
66	Purdah 45-3503	I Tried/Can't Quit You Baby (as Savoy Brown's Blues Band)	300
67	Decca F 12702	Taste And Try, Before You Buy/Someday People (as Savoy Brown Blues Band)	20
68	Decca F 12797	Walking By Myself/Vicksburg Blues	12
69	Decca F 12843	Train To Nowhere/Tolling Bells	15
69	Decca F 12978	I'm Tired/Stay With Me Baby	30
70	Decca F 13019	A Hard Way To Go/Waiting In The Bamboo Grove	15
70	Decca F 13098	Poor Girl/Master Hare	12
71	Decca F 13287	Tell Mama/Let It Rock	12
73	Decca F 13372	So Tired/The Saddest Feeling	7
73	Decca F 13431	Coming Down Your Way/I Can't Find You	7
67	Decca LK 4883	SHAKE DOWN (LP, mono, unboxed logo label)	200
67	Decca SKL 4883	SHAKE DOWN (LP, stereo, unboxed logo label)	150
68	Decca LK 4935	GETTING TO THE POINT (LP, mono, unboxed logo label)	150

SAVWINKLE AND TURNERHOPPER

MINT VALUE £

68	Decca SKL 4935	GETTING TO THE POINT (LP, stereo, unboxed logo label)	100
69	Decca SKL 4935	GETTING TO THE POINT (LP, second pressing, stereo, boxed logo)	25
69	Decca LK 4994	BLUE MATTER (LP, mono, unboxed logo label)	150
69	Decca SKL 4994	BLUE MATTER (LP, stereo, unboxed logo label)	75
69	Decca LK 5013	A STEP FURTHER (LP, mono, unboxed logo label)	150
69	Decca SKL 5013	A STEP FURTHER (LP, stereo, unboxed logo label)	70
70	Decca LK 5043	RAW SIENNA (LP, mono, laminated gatefold sleeve, boxed logo label)	150
70	Decca SKL 5043	RAW SIENNA (LP, stereo, laminated gatefold sleeve, boxed logo label)	75
70	Decca SKL 5066	LOOKING IN (LP, 1st pressing, dull laminated gatefold sleeve)	125
70	Decca SKL 5066	LOOKING IN (LP, 2nd pressing, glossy laminated gatefold sleeve)	50
71	Decca TXS 104	STREET CORNER TALKING (LP, gatefold sleeve)	60
72	Decca TXS 107	HELLBOUND TRAIN (LP, gatefold sleeve)	35
73	Decca SKL 5152	LION'S SHARE (LP)	15
73	Decca TXS 112	JACK THE TOAD (LP)	18

(see also Warren Philips & The Rockets, Chris Youlden, Stone's Masonry, Jackie Lynton, Foghat)

SAVWINKLE AND TURNERHOPPER
70	Pye 7N 17913	Your Mother Thinks I'm A Hoodlum/Dirtyin' My Thing	20

TOM SAWYER
69	CBS 4243	Cookbook/Gates	10

(see also Unit 4 + 2)

'ACE' DINNING SAX
59	Top Rank JAR 184	Mulholland Drive/My Love	15

SAX HAPPY
82	Take A Hammer TAH 001	Factory Song/Martian Spaceship	8

MIKE SAX & IDOLS
65	Mercury MF 886	My Little One/Come Back To Me	10

(see also Idols)

SAX MANIAX
82	Penthouse PEN 3	Never Gonna Lose Me/Let's Twist Again (p/s)	10
82	Penthouse PENT 1201	OVERSAXED (LP)	15

AL SAXON
58	Fontana H 164	The Day The Rains Came (Le Jour Ou La Pluie Viendra)/You're The Top-Cha	6
59	Fontana H 205	Only Sixteen/I'm All Right, Jack	7
59	Fontana H 222	Linda Lu/Heart Of Stone	7
61	Piccadilly 35002	Can You Keep A Secret/Promises	7
60	Fontana H 278	Blue-Eyed Boy/Don't Push Your Luck	10
61	Piccadilly 7N 35011	There I've Said It Again/You Came A Long Way From St. Louis	10
61	Piccadilly 7N 35021	Don't Get Around Much Anymore/Saturday Night	6
62	Piccadilly 7N 35036	Evil Eye/What More Can I Say	25
62	Parlophone R 4966	I Got A Girl/But I Do	7
63	Parlophone R 5016	The Man Who Broke The Bank At Monte Carlo/If You Want To Go To Dreamland	7
64	Mercury MF 801	Who Was That Girl?/All Night Long	7
64	Mercury MF 811	Another You/Hot And Bothered	7
68	President PT 183	Against The Wall/East Side 628	6
72	Phoenix NIX 125	Beautiful/Count To Ten	15
58	Fontana TFE 17014	THOSE YOU'VE NEVER HEARD (EP)	12

(see also Lana Sisters, Ella Stone & Moss)

SKY 'SUNLIGHT' SAXON
87	Fierce FRIGHT 009	Dog=God (p/s, with badge, piece of shirt, sugar 'skycubes' & inserts)	20
84	Psycho PSYCHO 29	STARRY EYED (LP, clear vinyl)	20

(see also Seeds)

SKY SAXON & THE NEW SEEDS
90s	Expression EXP 777-3	In Love With Life/Starry Ride/Queen/Tired Of Being Poor	6

SAXON (1)
63	Ace Of Clubs ACL 1173	MEET THE SAXONS (LP)	80

SAXON (2)
79	Carrere SAM 109	Big Teaser/Stallions Of The Highway (12", promo only)	10
79	Carrere CAR 118	Big Teaser/Stallions Of The Highway (p/s)	7
79	Carrere CAR 129	Backs To The Wall/Militia Guard (p/s)	7
80	Carrere CAR 165	Suzy Hold On/Judgement Day (live)	6
81	Carrere CAR 180P	And The Bands Played On/Hungry Years/Heavy Metal Thunder (7" picture disc)	6
83	Carrere CARP 284	Nightmare/Midas Touch (7" picture disc)	6
79	Carrere CAL 110	SAXON (LP)	15
80	Carrere CAL 115	WHEELS OF STEEL (LP)	15
80	Carrere CAL 120	STRONG ARM OF THE LAW (LP)	15
82	Carrere CAL 137	THE EAGLE HAS LANDED (LP)	15
82	Carrere CAL 137	THE EAGLE HAS LANDED (LP, picture disc)	15
83	Carrere CAL 147	THE POWER AND THE GLORY (LP, picture disc)	15
84	Carrere CAL 200	CRUSADER (LP, gatefold)	15
84	Carrere CALP 200	CRUSADER (LP, picture disc)	18
85	Parlophone SAXONP 2	INNOCENCE IS NO EXCUSE (LP, picture disc)	20
87	EMI EMS 1163	DENIM AND LEATHER (LP, blue vinyl reissue)	18
93	Warhammer WARLP 10	FOREVER FREE (LP)	80

LINDA SAXONE
64	Pye 7N 15624	Love Is A Many Splendoured Thing/The Other Side Of The Street	10
65	Polydor BM 56015	I've Got To Say No/Another Day Another Night	6
65	Polydor BM 56032	Only Last Night/Lucky Girl	6

SAXONS
65	Decca F 12179	Saxon War Cry/Click-Ete-Clack	60

(see also Tornados)

Johnny SAYLES

MINT VALUE £

JOHNNY SAYLES
66	Liberty LIB 12042	Deep Down In Your Heart/Anything For You	40
04	Soul City SC 160	I Can't Get Enough/Tell Me (Where I Stand)	8

RAT SCABIES
84	Paradiddle Music HIT 1	Let There Be Rats/Wiped Out/Drums Drums Drums (mail-order only, no p/s)	8

(see also Damned, Pete Zear)

SCABS
79	Clubland Records SJP 799	Amory Building/Leave Me Alone/Don't Just Sit There/U.R.E. (blue/black or red/black fold out 'envelope' p/s, 2 inserts)	40

SCAFFOLD
66	Parlophone R 5443	2 Day's Monday/3 Blind Jellyfish	10
66	Parlophone R 5548	Goodbat Nightman/A Long Strong Black Pudding	10
68	Parlophone R 5679	Do You Remember?/Carry On Krow	8
68	Parlophone R 5703	1-2-3/Today	6
69	Parlophone R 5784	Charity Bubbles/Goose	6
69	Parlophone R 5812	Gin Gan Goolie/Liver Birds	8
70	Parlophone R 5847	All The Way Up/Please - Sorry	8
70	Parlophone R 5866	Busdreams/If I Could Start All Over Again	8
71	Parlophone R 5922	Do The Albert/Commercial Break	8
74	Warner Bros K 16400	Liverpool Lou/Ten Years On After Strawberry Jam	6
68	Parlophone PMC/PCS 7051	SCAFFOLD ... - LIVE AT QUEEN ELIZABETH HALL (LP, black/yellow label with "Sold in U.K..." text)	40
69	Parlophone PMC/PCS 7077	L THE P (LP, black/yellow label with "Sold in U.K..." text)	30
73	Island ILPS 9234	FRESH LIVER (LP, gatefold sleeve, pink rim palm tree label)	20

(see also McGough-McGear, Roger McGough, Mike McGear, Liverpool Scene, Grimms, John Gorman)

BOZ SCAGGS
69	Atlantic 588 205	BOZ SCAGGS (LP)	30

(see also Steve Miller Band, Steve York's Camelo Pardalis)

SCALA TIMPANI
84	1066 Records ST 1	Winds Of Change/Destiny (no p/s)	10
85	Fire FIRE 3	Winds Of Change/Destiny (p/s)	6

HARVEY SCALES & 7 SOUND
67	Atlantic 584 146	Get Down/Love It Is	6

SCAMPS
59	London HLW 8827	Petite Fleur/Naomi	6

SCANDAL
79	Local LOC 1	Comic Book Hero/Casualty Of Love (p/s)	7

JOHNNY SCAR
85	Solomonic SM12 025	United Africa/Dub It In Africa (12")	200

SCARAB
80	Inferno HEADBANGER 1	Rock Night/Wicked Woman	30
84	Pharaoh PR-001	Poltergeist/Hell On Wheels (p/s)	50
03	Phoenix NWOBHM 7013	Rock Night/Wicked Woman (reissue, p/s, red vinyl 250 only, numbered)	15

SCARECROW
78	Spilt Milk SMFM 11278	SCARECROW (LP, numbered foldout sleeve with insert; beware of watermarked unnumbered copies)	150

SCARED OF THE DARK
86	Cottage Industry CIR 003	Give Me That Feeling/Summer Soul	20

SCARFACE (1)
75	DJM DJS 616	Dance To The Band/Tootsie Roll Baby	25

SCARFACE (2)
76	Concrete Jungle CJ 754	Blast Off/Blast Off 2	20

SCARLET ALIVE
82	Jive Alive JA001	THE TERMINAL JIVE AND SCARLET ALIVE EP (2 tracks on one side, p/s, insert)	15
82	S.R.R. SRR011	On Earth And In Heaven/Always (p/s)	15

SCARLET TRAIN
87	Nightshift NISHI 202	FIMBRIA (Mini-LP)	20

SCARLETS
64	Philips BF 1376	Let's Go/Tambourine Shake	6

CHARLES FRANCIS SCARRATT III
59	Felsted AF 113	Two Innocent Lovers/Lovemobile	6

SCARS
79	Fast Product FAST 8	Horrorshow/Adult-ery (p/s)	10
80	Pre PRE 005	Love Song/psychomodo (p/s)	15
81	Pre PRE 014	All About You/Author Author (p/s)	10
81	Pre PREX 5	AUTHOR! AUTHOR! (LP)	15

POLLY SCATTERGOOD
05	Ark 7ARK11	Glory Hallelujah/Throw Me A Hook Here (white vinyl, p/s)	8

SCATTEROCK
80	Rite Sound 010	Wonder Woman/Time	40

SCAVENGERZ DAUGHTER
91	SRT 91S2995	Eyes Of A Dead Man/Victim (no p/s)	15

SCENE (1)
80	Inferno BEAT 2	I've Had Enough/Show 'Em Now (p/s)	20

SCENE (2)
80	Hole In The Wall HS 1	Hey Girl/Reach The Top (p/s)	50

SCENE (3)
83	Diamond DIA 001	Looking For A Love/Let Me Know (p/s)	10
85	Diamond DIA 003	Something That You Said/Stop-Go (p/s)	7
85	Diamond DIA 007	Good Lovin'/2 Plus 2 (with p/s)	15

(see also Diplomats)

SCEPTRES
69	Spark SRL 1006	What's The Matter With Juliet/Something's Coming Along	30

SCHADEL
67	Parlophone R5554	Flower Shop Girl/Man In The Making	8
68	Pye 7N 17528	With The Sun In My Eyes/Goodbye Thimble Mill Lane	30
70	United Artists UAS 29114	SCHADEL NO.1 (LP, gatefold)	20

HAL SCHAEFER ORCHESTRA & CHORUS
58	London HLT 8692	March Of The Vikings/March Of The Parisian Bakers	7

JANEK SCHAEFER
99	Hot Air AIRMILE 72	Recorded Delivery: Evening 28/03/95/Morning 29/03/1995 (die cut sleeve, 600 only, red vinyl)	10

SCHEER
93	Son BUACD 293	Wish You Were Dead/Green Room Sex Kitten/Don't Know Why (p/s)	20
96	4AD CAD 6006	INFLICTION (LP)	15

SCHEME
82	No Label SS001	SCHEME SONGS (EP, 500 only, 2 inserts)	30
86	Scheme LP1	BLACK & WHITES (LP)	25

SCHEREZADE
82	Tombstone SRT TOM/S82 CUS 1	Seventeen/Million Years	12

HANK SCHIFNER
69	Liberty LBF15244	Long John/How Or When	15

LALO SCHIFRIN
66	MGM MGM 1329	Our Venetian Affair/Venice After Dark	12
68	Dot DOT 103	Mission: Impossible/Jim On The Move	25
74	20th Century BTC 2250	Ape Shuffle (Theme From 'Planet Of The Apes')/Escape From Tomorrow	25
74	Warner Bros K16233	Theme From Enter The Dragon/The Big Battle	10
77	CTI CTSP008	Theme From 'Most Wanted'/Roller Coaster	6
68	Dot (S)LPD 503	'MISSION: IMPOSSIBLE' - MUSIC FROM THE TV SERIES (LP, TV soundtrack)	40
69	Paramount SPFL 252	MORE 'MISSION: IMPOSSIBLE' (LP, TV soundtrack)	40

SCHIZO FUN ADDICT
07	Bracken fern 12	Dream Of The Portugal Keeper/Traditional/Jenny Says	12
08	Fruits De Mer CRUSTACIAN 01	Theme One/Ogden's Nut Gone Flake (p/s, coloured vinyl, 300 only)	40
14	Fruits De Mer Crustacean 48	Theme From Suspiria/In The Long Run/Back Of Her Car (p/s, black vinyl edition, 50 only)	10

SCHLEIMER K
81	Omega OMR 001	SCHLEIMER K (LP)	20
82	Glass GLASS 028	FUGUTIVE KIND (12" EP, p/s)	18
83	Lone WOlf LW 101	WOUNDED WOOD (LP)	40

SCHMETTERLINGE
77	Pye International 7N 25743	Boom Boom Boomerang/Mr Moneymaker's Music Show	10

TOBIAS SCHMIDT
96	Mosquito MSQ 06	THE FINGERPRINT EP (12", p/s)	15

ZAPPATTA SCHMIDT
70	President PT 318	You Got The Love/Someone In The Crowd	40
70	Torpedo TOR 28	Let's Do It Together/Hey Man. Why	25
71	President PTLS 1041	IT'S GONNA GET YOU (LP)	100

(see also Equals, Eddy Grant)

OLIVER LINDSEY SCHMITT
72	Private pressing	GRAFFENSTADDEN (LP)	30

WOLFGANG SCHMITT
69	RCA 1301	The Girl From the Monmouth County/Country Girl	6

EBERHARD SCHOENER
79	Harvest HAR 5196	Video Magic/Code Word Elvis (p/s)	8
79	Harvest SHSM 2030	VIDEO-FLASHBACK (LP)	20

(see also Police)

JOHN SCHOFIELD
84	Arista/Nimbus AN 3022	BAR TALK (LP, Nimbus Supercut, mail order only from Practical Hi-Fi magazine)	30

SCHOLARS
64	Stagesound SDE 29370/1	THE SCHOLARS (EP, no p/s)	15

SCHOOL TIES
81	School Ties SCF 01	No Future/Screw You	45
82	Quest S/82/Cus 1591	House Of The Rising Sun/Insanity (no p/s)	40

SCHOOLBOYS
69	Junior JR 113	Do It Now/Blame It On The Children	15

SCHOOL BOYS
63	Blue Beat BB 162	Little Boy Blue/PRINCE BUSTER: Money	40
63	Blue Beat BB 174	Little Dilly/The Joker (B-side actually by Prince Buster's Allstars)	40
64	Port-O-Jam PJ 4000	Dream Lover/I Want To Know	40

(see also Bill Gentles)

SCHOOLERS
69	Doctor Bird DB 1170	Ugly Man (actually by Scorchers)/Whip Cracker (actually by Vincent Gordon)	40

SCHOOLGIRL BITCH
78	Garage!/Aerco AERS 102	Abusing The Rules/Thinking For Yourself (spray-painted p/s)	200
78	Garage!/Aerco AERS 102	Abusing The Rules/Thinking For Yourself ('gasmask' p/s)	150
78	Garage!/Aerco AERS 102	Abusing The Rules/Thinking For Yourself ('queen' p/s)	100
78	Garage!/Aerco AERS 102	Abusing The Rules/Thinking For Yourself (no p/s)	40

SCHOOL GIRLS
63	Blue Beat BB 168	Love Another Love/Little Keithie	20
63	Blue Beat BB 185	Live Up To Justice/Keith My Darling	20

SCHOOL MEALS

			MINT VALUE £
64	Blue Beat BB 214	Sing And Shout/Last Time	20
64	Blue Beat BB 263	Never Let You Go/BUSTER'S ALL STARS: Supercharge	80

SCHOOL MEALS
78	Edible EAT 001	Headmaster (with insert, re-labelled Defendents)	25

SCHOOL OF CULTURE
91	White CS12 01	Detonate To Activate/Come On 33	30

DON SCHROEDER
62	Philips BF 3040033	Quicksand/My Kind Of Woman	10

JOHN SCHROEDER ORCHESTRA
65	Piccadilly 7N 35240	The Fugitive Theme/Don't Break The Heart Of Kimble (in p/s)	15
65	Piccadilly 7N 35240	The Fugitive Theme/Don't Break The Heart Of Kimble	6
65	Piccadilly 7N 35253	You've Lost That Lovin' Feeling/Funny How Love Can Be	6
65	Piccadilly 7N 35271	Agent 00 Soul/Night Rider	30
66	Piccadilly 7N 35285	Hungry For Love/Soul Destroyer	30
66	Piccadilly 7N 35319	On The Ball (Theme For The World)/The Britannia March	10
67	Piccadilly 7N 35362	Soul For Sale/Loving You Girl	30
69	Pye 7N 17862	The Virgin Soldiers' March/Sweet Soul Talk	12
71	Pye 7N 45108	One Way Glass/The Bird Has Flown	15
66	Piccadilly N(S)PL 38025	JOHN SCHROEDER'S WORKING IN THE SOULMINE (LP)	50
67	Piccadilly N(S)PL 38036	THE DOLLY CATCHER! (LP)	40
68	Marble Arch MAL 839	WORKING IN THE SOULMINE (LP, reissue)	20
71	Pye NSPL 18362	WITCHI-TAI-TO (LP, textured gatefold sleeve)	20
72	Polydor 2460 149	TV VIBRATIONS (LP)	15
71	Polydor 2460 134	DYLAN VIBRATIONS (LP)	15
71	Polydor 2460 135	PIANO VIBRATIONS (LP, with RIck Wakeman)	40
71	Marble Arch MAL 1381	YOU'VE MADE ME SO VERY HAPPY (LP)	30

IVY SCHULMAN & BOWTIES
57	London HLN 8372	Rock, Pretty Baby/BOWTIES: Ever Since I Can Remember	50

KLAUS SCHULZE
74	Caroline CA 2003	BLACK DANCE (LP, gatefold, black/white/red 'twin' label)	20
75	Caroline CA 2006	TIMEWIND (LP, gatefold)	20
76	Virgin V2064	MOONDAWN (LP, unissued)	0
77	Island ISPS 9461	MIRAGE (LP)	20

(see also Tangerine Dream) (Voices Of)

(VOICES OF) WALTER SCHUMANN
54	HMV 7M 229	Haunted House/I Only Have Eyes For You	8
55	HMV 7M 323	The Man From Laramie/Let Me Hear You Whisper	8

SCHUNGE
72	Regal Zonophone RZ 3066	Misty/Joseph Demanio	7
73	Regal Zonophone RZ 3077	Ballad Of A Simple Love/Enter The Violins	7
72	Regal Zono. SLRZ 1033	BALLAD OF A SIMPLE LOVE (LP, unlaminated front sleeve)	30
72	Regal Zono. SLRZ 1033	BALLAD OF A SIMPLE LOVE (LP, laminated front sleeve)	25

SCHWARTZENEGGER
94	Rugger Bugger SEEP 009	THE WAY THINGS ARE AND OTHER STORIES (LP)	20

SCIENCE POPTION
67	Columbia DB 8106	You've Got Me High/Back In Town	100

SCIENTIST
80	JB JBLP 004	INTRODUCING (LP)	75
80	Greensleeves GREL 13	HEAVYWEIGHT DUB CHAMPION (LP)	60
81	Starlight SLD 901	DUB LANDING (LP)	45
81	Greensleeves GREL 19	MEETS THE SPACE INVADERS (LP)	40
81	Kingdom KVL 9001	IN THE KINGDOM OF DUB (LP)	30
81	Greensleeves GREL 25	RIDS THE WORLD OF THE EVIL CURSE OF THE VAMPIRE (LP)	50
82	Greensleeves GREL 37	WINS THE WORLD CUP (LP)	40
82	Selena SLP 001	SCIENTIST MEETS THE ROOTS RADICS (LP)	50
82	Greensleeves GREL 46	ENCOUNTERS PAC MAN (LP)	50
82	Kingdom KVL 9011	HIGH PRIEST OF DUB (LP)	30
86	Kingdom KVC 6005	CRUCIAL CUTS VOLUME 2 (LP)	25
89	Tamoki Wambesi TWP 1022	INTERNATIONAL HEROES DUB (LP, with The Forces Of Music)	25
96	Blood & Fire BAFLP 007	DUB IN THE (ROOTS TRADITION) (LP)	15
08	Auralux LUXXLP 021	WORLD AT WAR (LP, reissue)	18

SCIENTIST & PRINCE JAMMY
82	Trojan TRLS 210	SCIENTIST & PRINCE JAMMY STRIKE BACK (LP)	40
97	Trojan TRLS 210	SCIENTIST & PRINCE JAMMY STRIKE BACK (LP, reissue)	15

SCIENTIST VERSUS PRINCE JAMMY
80	Greensleeves GRED 10	THE BIG SHOWDOWN 1980 (LP)	30
82	Starlight SLDLP 903	DUB LANDING VOLUME 2 (LP)	25

SCIENTIST V THE PROFESSOR
83	Kingdom KVL 9015	DUB DUEL AT KING TUBBY'S (LP)	35

SCIENTISTS (JAMAICA)
69	Amalgamated AMG 848	Professor In Action/SUPERSONICS: Reflections Of Don D	60

SCIENTISTS
85	Karbon KAR 007	You Only Live Twice/If It's The Last Thing I Do (p/s)	25
85	Karbon KAR 101 L	YOU GET WHAT YOU DESERVE (LP)	20
86	Karbon KAR 103 L	WEIRD LOVE (LP)	20
87	Karbon KAR 105 L	THE HUMAN JUKEBOX (LP)	20

SCISSOR FITS
79	Dubious DUB 1/SJP 793	TAUT? TENSE? ANGULAR? AND OTHER BRITISH RAIL SANDWICHES (EP, gatefold sleeve)	10
80	Tortch TOR 005	SOON AFTER DARK EP	10

SCONEHEADS

SCONEHEADS
81 Linden Sound LS 01 — GO BUCKSKIN (EP, 700 pressed) ... 30

SCOOP
80 Sharp POINT 1 — You Can Do It/Disco/My Friend Tony/Anonymity (p/s) ... 75

SCORCHED EARTH (1)
74 Youngblood YB1503 — On The Run/Can You Feel It ... 15
74 Philips 6006422 — On The Run/Super Woman Super Lover (p/s) ... 12

SCORCHED EARTH (2)
85 Carrere CAR 342 — Tomorrow Never Comes/Questions (promo only) ... 35
85 Carrere CART 342 — Tomorrow Never Comes/Questions/So Long/Where Do We Go From Here (12", initial black sleeve) ... 70
85 Carrere CART 342 — Tomorrow Never Comes/Questions/So Long/Where Do We Go From Here (12", later red sleeve with insert) ... 35

ERROL SCORCHER
78 Ballistic UAS 30198 — RASTAFIRE (LP, with the Revolutionaries) ... 25

SCORCHERS
69 Camel CA 17 — Hold On Tight/THE ROYALS: 100 Lbs Of Clay ... 80
69 Duke DU 26 — Hear Ya/VIBRATORS: Live Life ... 70
(see also Neville Hinds)

SCORE (1)
66 Decca F 12527 — Please Please Me/Beg Me ... 200

SCORN
92 Earache MOSH 54 — VAE SOLIS (2-LP) ... 20
95 Earache SCORN 001 — ELLIPSIS (5 x 12" box set) ... 18

SCORPIO
90 Intrigue IGE 9T — Power Struggle (Make It Mine)/SHADES OF BLACK: Mellow (909 Beats)/Mellow (808 Beats) (12") ... 10

SCORPIONS (GERMANY)
77 RCA PB 5556 — He's A Woman, She's A Man/Suspender Love ... 8
79 Harvest HAR 5185 — Is Anybody There?/Another Piece Of Meat (12", p/s) ... 10
91 Vertigo VERX 58 — Wind Of Change (12", white vinyl, 3-D sleeve) ... 12
75 RCA RS 1039 — IN TRANCE (LP, 'breast' sleeve) ... 20
76 RCA RS 1023 — FLY TO THE RAINBOW (LP) ... 20
76 RCA PPL 1-4225 — VIRGIN KILLER (LP, please note that 'banned; cover is German pressing not U.K.) ... 15
79 Harvest LP SHSP 4097 — LOVEDRIVE (LP) ... 20
80 Harvest SHSP 4113 — ANIMAL MAGNETISM (LP, inner sleeve) ... 15
82 H.M. Worldwide HMILP 2 — LONESOME CROW (LP, "castle" cover, clear vinyl) ... 20
82 H.M. Worldwide HMILP 2 — LONESOME CROW (LP, "castle" cover, black vinyl) ... 15
82 H.M. Worldwide HMIPD 2 — LONESOME CROW (LP, picture disc, re-issue) ... 15
82 Harvest SHVL 823 — BLACKOUT (LP, black or green print on label, inner sleeve) ... 15
88 Harvest SHSPP 4125 — SAVAGE AMUSEMENT (LP, picture disc, with lyric sheet) ... 15
93 Mercury 518 280-1 — FACE THE HEAT (LP) ... 25
(see also Group, UFO)

SCORPIONS (JAMAICA)
72 Green Door GD 4019 — Breaking Your Heart/IN CROWD BAND: Breaking Your Heart Version ... 6
(see also Bill Gentles)

SCORPIONS (U.K.)
61 Parlophone R 4740 — (Ghost) Riders In The Sky/Torquay ... 20
61 Parlophone R 4768 — Rockin' At The Phil/Scorpio ... 20
93 Sting SITTEP 1 — BACK TO THE TRACKS (EP) ... 12

COLIN SCOT
73 Warner Bros K 16330 — Call Me Mr Blue/It's Gonna Be Alright ... 7
71 United Artists UAG 29154 — COLIN SCOT WITH FRIENDS (LP, laminated gatefold sleeve, with Peter Hammill & Peter Gabriel) ... 25
(see also Peter Hammill, Peter Gabriel)

JOCK SCOT
80 Stiff MAX 1 — A Souvenir To Commemorate The Wedding Of Dave (Robinson) And Rosemary. Featuring the dulcet tones Of Jock Scot (Promo Only) ... 150

WINSTON SCOTLAND
72 Green Door GD 4027 — My (Girl) Little Filly/BUNNY BROWN: My Girl ... 12
72 Punch PH 100 — Butter Cup/RONALD WILSON: I Care ... 15
(see also Bunny Flip, Big Youth, Bongo Les, Lennox Brown, Dennis Alcapone)

SCOTS OF ST. JAMES
66 Go AJ 111404 — Gypsy/Tic Toc ... 200
67 Spot JW 1 — Timothy/Eiderdown Clown ... 350
(see also Hopscotch, Forever More, Five Day Rain)

ANDY SCOTT
75 RCA RCA 2629 — Lady Starlight/Where D'Ya Go (p/s) ... 12
83 Static TAK 10 — Krugerrands/Face (p/s) ... 8
84 Static TAK 24 — Let Her Dance/Suck It And See (p/s) ... 10
84 Static TAK 24-12 — Let Her Dance (Full Version)/(Instrumental)/Suck It And See (12", p/s) ... 10
84 Static TAK 31 — Invisible/Never Too Young (clear vinyl, stickered PVC sleeve) ... 12
84 Statik TAK 31-12 — Invisible (Single Version)/(Instrumental)/Invisible (Extended Version)/ Never Too Young (12", clear vinyl, stickered PVC sleeve) ... 12
(see also Sweet, Elastic Band, Mayfield's Mule)

ANITA SCOTT
61 Columbia DB 4623 — A Million And One Tears/Come On And Dance With Me ... 15

ARTIE SCOTT ORCHESTRA
70 Major Minor MM 670 — March Of The Skinheads/Love At First Sight ... 7

BILLY SCOTT
58 London HLU 8565 — You're The Greatest/That's Why I Was Born ... 20
60 Top Rank JAR 270 — Carole/Stairway To The Stairs ... 7

Bobby SCOTT (1)

MINT VALUE £

BOBBY SCOTT (1)
56	London HL 8254	Chain Gang/Shadrack	40
55	London Jazz LZ-N 14001	BOBBY SCOTT TRIO (10" LP)	15

BOBBY SCOTT (2)
70	Reflection RS2	Witness To A War/I Wish I Could Walk Away	6

BRUCE SCOTT
65	Mercury MF 857	I Made An Angel Cry/Don't Say Goodbye To Me	25
65	MGM MGM 1291	Once A Thief Twice A Thief/So Much To Live For	7

BUNNY SCOTT
75	2nd Tracs SK3	Come On Party/Azul Party	15
75	Upsetter UP 100	I Am I Said/Let Love Us Now (as Bunny Ruggs)	45
82	Seven Leaves SLD 01	What's The Use/I Never Had It So Good (12")	22
12	Black Swan THB 7019	Big May/NEVILLE GRANT: Sick And Tired (as Bunny 'Ruggs' Scott)	12
75	KLIK KLP 9004	TO LOVE SOMEBODY (LP)	60

(see also Bunny Clarke)

FREDDIE SCOTT
63	Colpix PX 692	Hey Girl/The Slide	35
63	Colpix PX 709	I Got A Woman/Brand New World	35
67	London HLZ 10103	Are You Lonely For Me/Where Were You	15
67	London HLZ 10123	Cry To Me/No One Could Ever Love You	15
67	London HLZ 10139	Am I Grooving You?/Never You Mind	10
67	London HLZ 10172	He Ain't Give You None/Run Joe	10
69	Roulette RO 509	Sugar Sunday/Johnny's Hill	6
71	Jay Boy BOY 34	Just Like A Flower/Spanish Harlem	10
72	Jay Boy BOY 59	Are You Lonely For Me Baby/The Woman Of My Love	10
72	Upfront UP 1	The Great If/Deep In The Night	10
71	Joy JOYS 215	ARE YOU LONELY FOR ME (LP)	25

GARRETT SCOTT
70	Mercury 6052 024	I'm Gonna Give You All My Love/Now That I Love You	15

GLORIA SCOTT
74	Casablanca CAS 152	Just As Long As We're Together/There Will Never Be Another	8

HAZEL SCOTT
53	Capitol LC 6607	LATE SHOW (10" LP)	20

JACK SCOTT (& CHANTONES)
58	London HLU 8626	My True Love/Leroy	10
58	London HLL 8765	With Your Love/Geraldine (as Jack Scott with Chantones)	15
59	London HLL 8804	Goodbye Baby/Save My Soul (as Jack Scott with Chantones)	15
59	London HL 7069	Goodbye Baby/Save My Soul (export issue)	20
59	London HLL 8851	I Never Felt Like This/Bella	20
59	London HLL 8912	The Way I Walk/Midgie (triangular or round centre)	25
59	London HLL 8970	There Comes A Time/Baby Marie (triangular or round centre)	25
60	Top Rank JAR 280	What In The World's Come Over You/Baby, Baby	6
60	Top Rank JAR 375	Burning Bridges/Oh, Little One	8
60	Top Rank JAR 419	Cool Water/It Only Happened Yesterday	10
60	Top Rank JAR 524	Patsy/Old Time Religion	10
61	Top Rank JAR 547	Is There Something On Your Mind/Found A Woman	10
61	Capitol CL 15200	A Little Feeling/Now That I	10
61	Capitol CL 15216	My Dream Come True/Strange Desire	10
62	Capitol CL 15236	Steps 1 And 2/One Of These Days	10
63	Capitol CL 15302	All I See Is Blue/Meo Myo	10
62	Capitol CL 15261	I Can't Hold Your Letters In My Arms/Sad Story	10
59	London RE-I 1205	MY TRUE LOVE (EP, initial triangular centre)	50
59	London RE-I 1205	MY TRUE LOVE (EP, later round centre)	25
61	Top Rank JKP 3002	WHAT IN THE WORLD'S COME OVER YOU (EP)	25
61	Top Rank JKP 3011	I REMEMBER HANK WILLIAMS (EP)	25
58	London HA-L 2156	JACK SCOTT (LP)	70
60	Top Rank BUY 034	I REMEMBER HANK WILLIAMS (LP)	40
60	Top Rank 25-024	WHAT IN THE WORLD'S COME OVER YOU (LP)	35
61	Top Rank 35-109	THE SPIRIT MOVES ME (LP)	30
64	Capitol T 2035	BURNING BRIDGES (LP, mono)	25
64	Capitol ST 2035	BURNING BRIDGES (LP, stereo)	30

JANET SCOTT & JACKIE RAE
60	Fontana TFE 17203	SWEET TALK (EP, also stereo STFE 8009)	12
60	Fontana TFL 5102	WE LOVE LIFE! (LP, also stereo STFL 533)	15

JILL SCOTT
00	Hidden Beach EPC 498625 1	WHO IS JILL SCOTT? - WORDS AND SOUNDS VOL. 1 (2-LP)	40
04	Hidden Beach EPC 517652 1	BEAUTIFULLY HUMAN - WORDS AND SOUND VOL. 2 (2-LP)	35

JIMMY SCOTT
68	Revolution REV 002	Ob-La-Di, Ob-La-Da/Story Part 2 - Allulo & Doh	40
70	Revolution Soul REVS 505	Doh (Ob-La-Di-Ob-Lh-Da Story Part 2/Allulo (Part 1) Note: "Ih" is how it is on the label	40
74	Deram DM 425	We All Need A Hero/Madeline	7

JOHN SCOTT
60	Parlophone R 4697	Hi-Flutin' Boogie/Peace Pipe	6
65	Parlophone R 5333	Sailing By/The Song Of The Cuckoo (as Johnny Scott)	8
65	Parlophone R 5380	A Study In Terror/Punjab	10
67	Polydor 56184	Rocket To The Moon Theme/The Long Duel Theme	15
68	Spark SRL 1008	Amsterdam Affair Theme/Kathleen	8
66	Columbia SX 6026	LONDON SWINGS (LP)	15
67	Columbia S(C)X 6149	COMMUNICATION (LP)	30

JOHNNY SCOTT
67	Columbia S(C)X 6149	COMMUNICATION (LP)	60
70	Fontana 6383 002	PURCELL VARIATIONS FOR FIVE (LP)	25
73	JSD JSD 100	JOHN SCOTT DEMONSTRATION RECORD (LP, beware, many warped)	80

JUDI SCOTT
68	Page One POF 066	Billy Sunshine/Happy Song	25

JUDY SCOTT
57	Brunswick 05687	The Game Of Love (A-One And A-Two)/With All My Heart	10
57	Brunswick 05704	Parlour Piano Theme/A Tender Word	8

JULIAN SCOTT
61	Columbia DB 4571	My Steady Date/So Tired	7

LINDA SCOTT (1)
61	Columbia DB 4692	Don't Bet Money, Honey/Starlight Starbright	12
61	Columbia DB 4748	I Don't Know Why/It's All Because	12
61	Columbia DB 4829	Count Every Star/Land Of Stars	12
62	Pye International 7N 25146	Never In A Million Years/Through The Summer	15
63	London HLR 9802	Let's Fall In Love/I Know It, You Know It	20
61	Columbia 33SX 1386	STARLIGHT, STARBRIGHT (LP)	60

LINDA SCOTT (2)
69	CBS 4528	The Composer/You Made A Fool Out Of Me (DJ copy)	25
69	CBS 4528	The Composer/You Made A Fool Out Of Me	15

MAUREEN SCOTT
63	HMV POP 1184	He's So Near/Ugly Bug Ball	6

MCBEAN SCOTT & CHAMPIONS
70	Jackpot JP 744	Top Of The World/LARRY LAWRENCE & CHAMPIONS: Everybody Reggae	15

MIKE SCOTT (1)
65	Mercury MF 906	I Am A Rock/I'm Gonna Be Somebody Someday	6

MIKE SCOTT (2)
95	Chrysalis CHR 6108	BRING 'EM ALL IN (LP, gatefold with inner)	60

(see also Waterboys)

NEIL SCOTT
61	Pye International 7N 25096	Bobby/I Haven't Found It With Another	8

NICKY SCOTT
67	Immediate IM 044	Big City/Everything's Gonna Be Alright	60
67	Immediate IM 045	Backstreet Girl/Chain Reaction	50
69	Pye 7N 17688	Honey Pie/No More Tomorrow	7

(see also Diane Ferraz & Nicky Scott)

PEGGY SCOTT & JO JO BENSON
68	Polydor 56745	Lover's Holiday/Here With Me	10
69	Polydor 56750	Pickin' Wild Mountain Berries/Pure Love And Pleasure	8
69	Polydor 56761	Soulshake/We Were Made For Each Other	10
69	Polydor 56773	We Got Our Own Bag/I Want To Love You Babe	8
69	Polydor 583 731	SOULSHAKE (LP)	25
70	Polydor 583 756	LOVER'S HEAVEN (LP)	25

ROBIN SCOTT
69	Head HDS 4003	The Sailor/Sound Of The Rain	40
69	Head HDLS 6003	WOMAN FROM THE WARM GRASS (LP, textured sleeve with insert, yellow/black label)	400
07	Sunbeam SBBLP 5009	WOMAN FROM THE WARM GRASS (LP, reissue)	15

(see also Mighty Baby, M)

RONNIE SCOTT
54	Esquire 10-335	Night And Day	10
56	Decca FJ 10712	Basie Talks/Flying Home (as Ronnie Scott Orchestra)	8
57	Tempo A 153	I'll Take Romance/Speak Low (as Ronnie Scott New Quintet)	35
55	Esquire EP 31	RONNIE SCOTT ORCHESTRA (EP)	20
55	Esquire EP 51	RONNIE SCOTT QUARTET (EP)	25
55	Esquire EP 61	RONNIE SCOTT ORCHESTRA (EP)	20
55	Esquire EP 65	RONNIE SCOTT QUINTET (EP)	25
56	Esquire EP 81	RONNIE SCOTT ORCHESTRA (EP)	25
56	Esquire EP 85	RONNIE SCOTT ORCHESTRA (EP)	30
56	Esquire EP 95	RONNIE SCOTT ORCHESTRA (EP)	25
56	Tempo EXA 45	RONNIE SCOTT BLOWS WITH THE DIZZY REECE QUARTET (EP)	100
52	Esquire 20-006	RONNIE SCOTT QUINTET (10" LP)	100
54	Esquire 32-001	THE RONNIE SCOTT JAZZ CLUB VOLUME 1 (LP)	50
54	Esquire 32-002	THE RONNIE SCOTT JAZZ CLUB VOLUME 2 (LP)	50
54	Esquire 32-003	THE RONNIE SCOTT JAZZ CLUB VOLUME 3 (LP)	50
54	Esquire 32-006	THE RONNIE SCOTT JAZZ CLUB VOLUME 4 (LP)	50
56	Decca LF 1261	AT THE ROYAL FESTIVAL HALL (10" LP)	50
57	Philips BBL 7153	PRESENTING THE RONNIE SCOTT SEXTET (LP)	100
66	Fontana TL 5332	THE NIGHT IS SCOTT AND YOU'RE SO SWINGABLE (LP)	45
69	CBS Realm Jazz 523661	LIVE AT RONNIE SCOTT'S (LP)	30
74	RCA Victor LPL1	SCOTT AT RONNIE'S (LP)	20
77	Pye NSPL 18542	SERIOUS GOLD (LP)	15

(see also Jazz Couriers, Tubby Hayes, Dizzy Reece)

SHARON SCOTT
96	Kent 6T 12	(Putting My Heart) Under Lock And Key/DEAN COURTNEY: Today Is My Day	35

SHIRLEY SCOTT
62	Esquire 32-186	HIP TWIST (LP)	25
66	Transatlantic PR 7205	HIP SOUL (LP)	18
67	Transatlantic PR 7338	BLUE FLAMES (LP, with Stanley Turrentine)	20

SIMON SCOTT (& LE ROYS)

MINT VALUE £

| 69 | Atlantic 588 175 | SOUL SONG (LP) | 15 |
| 71 | Chess 6310 109 | MYSTICAL LADY (LP) | 15 |

SIMON SCOTT (& LE ROYS)
64	Parlophone R 5164	Move It Baby/What Kind Of Woman (with Le Roys)	15
64	Parlophone R 5207	My Baby's Got Soul/MIdnight (with Le Roys)	12
65	Parlophone R 5298	Tell Him I'm Not Home (as Simon Scott & All Nite Workers)/Heart Cry	18
69	Polydor 56355	Brave New World/I'm The Universe	100

(see also Le Roys)

TERRY SCOTT
| 62 | Parlophone R 4967 | My Brother/Don't Light The Fire 'Til After Santa's Gone | 10 |
| 66 | Pye 7N 17193 | Juanita Banana/I Like Birds | 6 |

TOM SCOTT
| 77 | Epic EPC 5589 | Gotcha (Theme From 'Starsky & Hutch')/Smoothin' On Down | 12 |

RAMBLIN' TOMMY SCOTT
| 54 | Parlophone CMSP 15 | Ain't Love Grand/What Do You Know - I Love Her (export issue) | 20 |

TOMMY SCOTT
| 62 | Decca F 11474 | Angela/Did You (as Jay & Tommy Scott) | 6 |

TONY SCOTT
| 69 | Escort ES 805 | What Am I To Do/Bring Back That Smile | 60 |

SHEILA SCOTT WILKINGSON
| 68 | SNB 55-4124 | Down River/Quiet Man | 10 |

GIL SCOTT-HERON (& BRIAN JACKSON)
73	Philips 6073 705	Lady Day And John Coltrane/When You Are Who You Are (with Pretty Purdie & The Playboys)	20
78	Arista ARIST 169	The Bottle (live)/Hello Sunday, Hello Road	8
78	Arista ARIST 169	The Bottle (live)/Hello Sunday, Hello Road (12")	20
79	Inferno HEAT 23	The Bottle (Drunken Mix)/The Bottle (Sober Mix) (with Brian Jackson)	10
73	Philips 6369 415	PIECES OF A MAN (LP)	35
74	RCA SF 8428	THE REVOLUTION WILL NOT BE TELEVISED (LP)	25
75	Arista ARTY 106	FIRST MINUTES OF A NEW DAY (LP)	15
76	Arista DARTY 1	IT'S YOUR WORLD (LP, with Brian Jackson)	30

SCOTTY (DAVID SCOTT)
70	Songbird SB 1044	Sesame Street/CRYSTALITES: Version	30
71	Songbird SB 1049	Riddle I This/Musical Chariot	25
71	Songbird SB 1051	Jam Rock Style/Jam Rock Style Version (with Crystalites)	10
71	Songbird SB 1056	Penny For Your Song/CRYSTALITES: Version	15
72	Songbird SB 1080	Clean Race/CRYSTALITES: Version Train	30
72	Harry J. HJ 6642	Skank In Bed/BONGO HERMAN: African Breakfast	8
73	Count Shelley CS 036	Salvation Train/KEN PARKER: Message To Mary	20
71	Trojan TRL 33	SCHOOL DAYS (LP)	60
88	Trojan TRLS 264	UNBELIEVABLE SOUNDS (LP)	20

(see also Lloyd Charmers, Joe White, Federals)

SCRAPING FOETUS OFF THE WHEEL
| 81 | Womb WOMB-OYBL-2 | HOLE (LP, gatefold sleeve with lyrics, also listed as FDL 3) | 15 |

(see also Foetus,You've Got Foetus On Your Breath, Philip & His Foetus Vibrations, Foetus Inc, Foetus Uber Frisco)

SCRAPYARD
| 58 | Abbey APR 168 | RECIPRICAL RHUMBAS (LP, private press, 250 copies, with insert) | 200 |

SCRATCH ACID
| 86 | Fundamental HOLY 1 | SCRATCH ACID (Mini-LP) | 20 |
| 86 | Fundamental SAVE 12 | JUST KEEP EATING (LP) | 15 |

(see also Jesus Lizard)

SCRATCH PERVERTS
| 03 | Ultimate Dilemma UDR LP 021 | BADMEANINGOOD VOL 4 (2-LP, Banksy artwork) | 400 |

SCREAMER
| 75 | Arista ARISTA 18 | City Or Bust/We Got Hairs | 10 |

SCREAMING DEAD
82	Skull DEAD 1	Valley Of The Dead/Schoolgirl Junkie (p/s)	15
83	Skull DEAD 2	Paint It Black/Warriors (p/s)	18
83	No Future OI 25	NIGHT CREATURES EP (12")	20
84	Angel ANF 001	THE DANSE MACABRE COLLECTION EP (12")	10
85	Angel ANG 002	A DREAM OF YESTERDAY (12" EP, p/s)	10

DELTON SCREECHIE
77	Moa Anbessa MOA 0014	Jah Is My Light/Version	7
80	Kim KIM 18	My Black Girl/Diamond & Pearl/B DONALDSON & U BLACK : You Are Mine (12")	15
80	Moa Anbessa MA004	She Is My Woman/Woman Version (12")	15
81	Moa Anbessa Intl MALP 001	LIVING IN THE GHETTO (LP)	30
81	Moa Anbessa Intl MALP 002	SUFFERING IN THE GHETTO (LP)	50

SCREECHING WEASEL
| 88 | Wet Spots WETLP 005 | BOOGADA BOOGADA BOOGADA (LP) | 25 |
| 88 | What Goes On GOES ON 24 | SCREECHING WEASEL (LP, with insert) | 20 |

SCREEMER
| 76 | Bell Bell 1483 | Interplanetary Twist/Billy | 15 |

SCREEN
| 95 | Muzic W'out Control MWC 021 | I Wait For You (Sweep Sweep Mix)/I Wait For You (Radio Sweep Mix)/I Wait For You (Pink Noize Mix)/I Wait For You (T Rex Mix) (12', p/s) | 60 |

SCREEN GEMZ
| 79 | Inflatable IN 001 | I Just Can't Stand Cars/Teenage Teenage | 200 |

SCREEN IDOLS
| 79 | Cobra COB 2 | Blindman/Hit Me Where It Hurts (p/s) | 10 |

SCRITTI POLITTI

MINT VALUE £

SCRITTI POLITTI
78	St. Pancras SCRIT 1	Skank Bloc Bologna/Is And Ought Of The Western World/28.8.78 (photocopied stapled foldout p/s, hand-stamped white labels)	20
79	Rough Trade RT 027T	4 A SIDES: Doubt Beat/Confidences/Bibbly O'Tek/P.A.s (12" EP)	10
79	Rough Trade RT 034/St Pancras SCRIT 2	WORK IN PROGRESS : 2ND PEEL SESSION (7" EP p/s)	18
06	Rough Trade RTRADLP 270	WHITE BREAD BLACK BEER (LP)	35

SCROTUM POLES
79	Scrotum Poles ERECT 1	Revelation: Why Don't You Come Out Tonight?/Night Train/Pick The Cat's Eyes Out/Helicopter Honeymoon/Radio Tay (handwritten labels, 2 p/s designs, with insert)	120
79	Scrotum Poles ERECT 1	Revelation: Why Don't You Come Out Tonight?/Night Train/Pick The Cat's Eyes Out/Helicopter Honeymoon/Radio Tay (handwritten labels, 2 p/s designs, without insert) ...	100

SCRUBS
86	Anubis ANU 003	Battle (p/s)	15
87	Flicknife FLS 035	Time For You (p/s)	10

SCRUFF
78	Track 2094140	Get Out Of My Way/Rock N Roll Woman	6

SCRUGG
68	Pye 7N 17451	I Wish I Was Five/Everyone Can See	90
68	Pye 7N 17551	Lavender Popcorn/Sandwichboard Man	60
69	Pye 7N 17656	Will The Real Geraldine Please Stand Up/Only George	90

(see also Floribunda Rose, John T. Kongos)

IRENE SCRUGGS
50s	Poydras 80	You've Got What I Want/My Back To The Wall	8

DAVID SEA
07	Shotgun 101	Believe In Me/Let's Just Get Together	6

MR. JOHNNY SEA
60s	Fontana FJL 315	EVERYBODY'S FAVOURITE (LP)	15

SEA & CAKE
94	Rough Trade THRILL 021	SEA & CAKE (LP)	20
97	Thrill Jockey THRILL LP 039UK	THE FAWN (LP, gatefold)	18

(see also Tortoise)

SEA-DERS
67	Decca F 22576	Thanks A Lot/Undecidedly	80
67	Decca DFE-R 8674	THE SEA-DERS (EP, export issue)	250

(see also Cedars)

SEAHORSES
97	Geffen GEF 25134	DO IT YOURSELF (LP, inner)	100

(see also Stone Roses)

DAVE SEALEY
69	DJM DJS 210	Picking Up The Pieces/I Can't Go On Living Without You	6

PHIL SEAMEN
68	Verve (S)VLP 9220	PHIL SEAMEN NOW ... LIVE (LP)	200
68	Saga OPP 102	MEETS EDDIE GOMEZ (LP)	100
72	Decibel BSN 103	PHIL SEAMEN STORY (LP)	50
74	77 Records 77 SEU 12/53	PHIL ON DRUMS (LP)	50

SEA NYMPHS
91	Alphabet ALPH 016SP	Appealing To Venus/Tree Top High	8

SEARCH PARTY
70	Red Bull RB1	What Do You See Up There/Hidden Truth	35

SEARCHERS
SINGLES
63	Pye 7N 15533	Sweets For My Sweet/It's All Been A Dream	6
63	Philips BF 1274	Sweet Nuthins/What'd I Say	10
63	Pye 7N 15566	Sugar And Spice/Saints And Searchers (dark maroon label)	12
63	Pye 7N 15566	Sugar And Spice/Saints And Searchers (lighter pink label)	6
65	Pye 7N 15794	Goodbye My Love/Till I Met You	6
65	Pye 7N 15878	He's Got No Love/So Far Away	6
65	Pye 7N 15950	When I Get Home/I'm Never Coming Back	8
65	Pye 7N 15992	Take Me For What I'm Worth/Too Many Miles (in export p/s)	25
65	Pye 7N 15992	Take Me For What I'm Worth/Too Many Miles	8
66	Pye 7N 17094	Take It Or Leave It/Don't Hide It Away	10
66	Pye 7N 17170	Have You Ever Loved Somebody/It's Just The Way	12
67	Pye 7N 17225	Popcorn, Double Feature/Lovers	20
67	Pye 7N 17308	Western Union/I'll Cry Tomorrow	15
67	Pye 7N 17424	Secondhand Dealer/Crazy Dreams	80
68	Liberty LBF 15159	Umbrella Man/Over The Weekend	50
69	Liberty LBF 15340	Kinky Kathy Abernathy/Suzanna	50
71	RCA RCA 2057	Desdemona/The World Is Waiting For Tomorrow	15
71	RCA RCA 2139	Love Is Everywhere/And A Button	10
72	RCA RCA 2231	Sing Singer Sing/Come On Back To Me	10
72	RCA RCA 2248	Needles And Pins/When You Walk In The Room/Come On Back To Me	10
72	RCA RCA 2288	Vahevala/Madman	15
73	RCA RCA 2330	Solitaire/Spicks And Specks	6
79	Sire SIR 4026	Hearts In Her Eyes/Don't Hang On (p/s)	10
80	Sire SIR 4036	It's Too Late/This Kind Of Love Affair (p/s)	7
81	Sire SIR 4041	Love's Melody/Changing (p/s)	12
81	Sire SIR 4049	Another Night/Back To The War (p/s)	10
80s	Private pressing	Don't Make Promises	10
80s	Private pressing	Four Strong Winds	10

SEARGEANT SMILEY RAGS

MINT VALUE £

EPs
63	Pye NEP 24177	AIN'T GONNA KISS YA	12
63	Pye NEP 24183	SWEETS FOR MY SWEET (some copies with white & maroon label)	15
64	Pye NEP 24184	HUNGRY FOR LOVE	20
64	Pye NEP 24201	THE SEARCHERS PLAY THE SYSTEM	15
64	Pye NEP 24204	WHEN YOU WALK IN THE ROOM	20
65	Pye NEP 24218	BUMBLE BEE	20
65	Pye NEP 24222	SEARCHERS '65	30
65	Pye NEP 24228	FOUR BY FOUR	35
66	Pye NEP 24263	TAKE ME FOR WHAT I'M WORTH	100

ALBUMS
63	Pye NPL 18086	MEET THE SEARCHERS	50
63	Pye NPL 18089	SUGAR AND SPICE	25
64	Pye NPL 18092	IT'S THE SEARCHERS	25
65	Pye NPL 18111	SOUNDS LIKE SEARCHERS	40
65	Pye NPL 18120	TAKE ME FOR WHAT I'M WORTH	50

(see also Chris Curtis, Pasha)

SEARGEANT SMILEY RAGS
70	Decca F13088	Smoke Smoke/Hey Na I Think I Love You	12

SEARS
84	Bluurg FISH 9	IF ONLY... (LP)	15

SEASICK STEVE
07	Bronzerat BR 006	It's All Good/Thunderbird (p/s)	8

SEA STONE
80	Plankton PLANK 001	Summer Fever/Blow On By (p/s)	12
82	Plankton 02	AGAINST THE TIDE (EP, foldout sleeve)	40
78	Plankton PKN 101	MIRRORED DREAMS (LP, with insert)	80

SEATHROUGH
79	private pressing	LALA LAPLA (LP)	40

B.B. SEATON (HORACE SEATON)
63	Island WI 123	I'm So Glad/Tell Me	30
64	R&B JB 143	Hold On/LESTER STERLING: Peace And Love	40
72	Big BG 336	I Want Justice/RUPIE EDWARD'S ALL STARS: Justice (Version)	8
72	Bullet BU 514	I Miss My Schooldays/CONSCIOUS MINDS: School Days - Version	20
72	Camel CA 100	Lean On Me/U ROY: Black Heart	10
72	Pama PM 864	I Want Justice/RUPIE EDWARD'S ALL STARS: Justice - Version	20
73	Trojan TRLS 59	THIN LINE BETWEEN LOVE AND HATE (LP)	20
74	Caroline CA 2002	DANCING SHOES (LP)	20
75	Love LOV 01	GUN COURT DUB (LP, name not on sleeve or labels)	50

(see also Bibby, Winston & Bibby, Gaylads, Messengers)

SEA TRAIN
69	A&M AMLS 941	SEA TRAIN (LP)	30
71	Capitol EA-ST 659	SEA TRAIN (LP, gatefold)	20
72	Capitol EA-ST 829	MARBLEHEAD MESSENGER (LP, gatefold sleeve)	20
73	Warner Bros K 46222	WATCH (LP, gatefold)	20

(see also Blues Project, Old & In The Way)

SEA URCHINS
87	Kvatch KVATCH 001/	Clingfilm/GROOVE FARM: Baby Blue Marine (flexidisc, 1,000 only, 500 in p/s)	25
87	Sha La La Ba Ba Ba Ba 5	Summershine/ORCHIDS: From This Day (flexidisc, 2,500 only, 1,000 with p/s)	15
87	Sarah SARAH 001	Pristine Christine/Sullen Eyes/Everglades (foldaround p/s with 14" x 10" poster in poly bag, 1,600 only)	200
88	Sarah SARAH 008	Solace/Please Rain Fall (foldaround p/s in poly bag)	35
89	Fierce FRIGHT 032	30.10.88 (live) (1-sided, p/s)	10
91	Cheree CHEREE 15	Please Don't Cry/Time Is All I've Seen (die-cut company sleeve)	7
91	Cheree CHEREE 15T	Please Don't Cry/No Matter What/Time Is All I've Seen (12")	10
98	Sarah SARAH 33	A Morning Odyssey/Wild Grass Pictures	6
92	Sarah SARAH 609	STARDUST (LP)	70

JOHN SEBASTIAN
54	London HL 8029	Inca Dance/Foolish Waltz	20
55	London HL 8131	Stranger In Paradise/Autumn Leaves	15

JOHN (B.) SEBASTIAN
69	Kama Sutra 618 026	She's A Lady/The Room Nobody Lives In	6
70	Reprise RSLP 6379	JOHN B. SEBASTIAN (LP, gatefold sleeve)	20
71	Reprise K 44127	REAL LIVE JOHN SEBASTIAN (LP)	15

(see also Lovin' Spoonful, Even Dozen Jug Band)

SECESSION
80s	Siren SRN12 23	Michael (12", p/s)	12
83	Garden GAR 1	Betrayal/Reflections (p/s)	100
88	Siren SRNLP 11	A DARK ENCHANTMENT (LP, with inner)	40

SECOND CITY SOUND
65	Decca F 12310	Tchaikovsky One/Shadows	6
66	Decca F 12366	Greig One/In A Mist	6
66	Decca F 12406	Love's Funny/Tell Me Where I'm Going	6
69	Major Minor MM 600	The Dream Of Olwyn/A Touch Of Velvet, A Sting of Brass	10

SECOND COMING
71	Mercury 6338 030	SECOND COMING (LP)	50

SECOND HAND
72	Mushroom 50 MR 19	Funeral/Hangin' On An Eyelid	100
68	Polydor 583 045	REALITY (LP, early copies crediting band as Moving Finger)	300

SECOND IMAGE

MINT VALUE £

68	Polydor 583 045	REALITY (LP, later copies not crediting band as Moving Finger)	200
71	Mushroom MR 2006	DEATH MAY BE YOUR SANTA CLAUS (LP, 1st pressing, without "Funeral")	300
72	Mushroom MR 2006	DEATH MAY BE YOUR SANTA CLAUS (LP, 2nd pressing, with "Funeral")	150
07	Sunbeam SBRLP 5031	REALITY (LP, reissue)	20

(see also Andreas Thomopoulos, Fungus, Chillum, Vulcans)

SECOND IMAGE
| 85 | MCA MCF 3255 | STRANGE REFLECTIONS (LP) | 18 |
| 83 | Polydor POLS 1081 | SECOND IMAGE (LP) | 18 |

SECOND LAYER
79	Tortch TOR 001	FLESH AS PROPERTY (EP, white p/s, black printed labels)	30
80	Tortch TOR 006	State Of Emergency/I Need Noise/The Cutting Motion (p/s)	30
81	Tortch/Fresh FRESH 5	FLESH AS PROPERTY (EP, reissue, yellow p/s & white labels)	20
81	Cherry Red CHERRY 21	FLESH AS PROPERTY (EP, 2nd reissue, unreleased)	0
82	Cherry Red BRED 14	WORLD OF RUBBER (LP, with inner)	50

(see also Outsiders, Sound)

SECOND THOUGHTS
| 65 | Recorded Sound Studios RSL 1596 | Let's Stick Together/I'm Possessed | 300 |

(see also July, Nirvana)

SECONDARY MODERN
| 83 | Sorthern Sounds DJG 1 | Lucinda Dream/Boys Cry Too (p/s) | 60 |

SECOND OPINION
| 78 | Tash TASH 0035 | King Of The Raceway/Stormbird | 20 |

SECRET
| 77 | Arista ARIST 142 | The Young Ones/Handel A Vandel | 10 |
| 78 | Arista ARIST 173 | Do You Really Care?/I Wanna Car Like That | 15 |

SECRET AFFAIR
79	I-Spy SEE 1	Time For Action/Soho Strut (brown p/s, black print/paper labels)	10
79	I-Spy SEE 3	Let Your Heart Dance/Sorry Wrong Number (p/s, paper label)	6
80	I-Spy SEE 5	My World/So Cool (paper labels)	6
80	I-Spy SEE 8	Sound Of Confusion/Take It Or Leave It (p/s, paper labels)	6
81	I-Spy SEE 10	Do You Know?/Dance Master (keyhole company sleeve, paper labels)	6
82	I-Spy SEE 11	Lost In The Night (Mack The Knife)/The Big Beat (p/s)	8
79	I-Spy I SPY 1	GLORY BOYS (LP, with 2 inserts)	15
80	I-Spy I SPY 2	BEHIND CLOSED DOORS (LP, with inner sleeve)	15
82	I-Spy I SPY 3	BUSINESS AS USUAL (LP, stickered sleeve)	15

(see also New Hearts, Advertising, Innocents [U.K.])

SECRET OYSTER
| 74 | CBS 80489 | SEA SON (LP) | 15 |

SECRET SERVICE
| 79 | Sonet SON 2193 | Oh Susie/Give Me Your Love | 6 |

SECRET SHINE
91	Sarah SARAH 53	After Years/Snowfall Sorrow/Grey Skies (p/s)	20
92	Sarah SARAH 61	Honey Sweet/Secret Shine (p/s)	20
93	Sarah SARAH 71	Loveblind/Way Too High (p/s)	20
94	Sarah SARAH 89	GREATER THAN GOD EP (10" p/s)	60
93	Sarah SARAH 615	UNTOUCHED (LP)	70

SECRET SQUIRREL
92	Bogwoppa BOGWOPPA 05	E Drop/Come Rudeboy (12", handwritten white label, with AJ Flex)	60
92	Dance Bass DANCE BASS 01	Mu-Venom/DDT (12", stamped white label)	50
92	Dance Bass DANCE BASS 02	VOLUME 2 EP (12")	30
92	Dance Bass DANCE BASS 06	THE MAGIC FLUTE EP (12")	30

(See also Undercover Elephant and DJ Secret Squirrel)

SECRETS (U.K.)
66	CBS 202466	I Suppose/Such A Pity	40
67	CBS 202585	Infatuation/She's Dangerous	40
67	CBS 2818	I Intend To Please/I Think I Need The Cash	40

(see also Simon's Secrets, Clifford T. Ward, Martin Raynor & Secrets)

SECRETS (U.S)
| 64 | Philips BF 1298 | The Boy Next Door/Learnin' To Forget | 30 |
| 64 | Philips BF 1318 | Hey Big Boy/Other Side Of Town | 30 |

SECT (2)
86	Insect NASTY 1	A Free England/Never Go (p/s)	20
89	Damaged Goods YUBB 2	SUMMER GIRL EP, blue vinyl)	20
90	Damaged Goods YUBB 5	REMEMBERING EP (12")	15
90	Combat CR 001	PLAYING WITH FIRE EP (12")	15
87	Razor RAZ 27	THE VOICE OF REASON (LP)	15

SECTION
| 72 | RCA 2274 | Drowning In The Sea Of Love/Miss Me Just A Little BIt | 10 |

SECTION A
| 82 | Subversive SUB | TIME STANDS STILL EP | 15 |

SECTION 5
85	Oi OIR 002	WE WON'T CHANGE (LP)	20
87	Link LP 08	FOR THE LOVE OF OI! (LP)	20
88	Link LINK LP 031	STREET ROCK 'N' ROLL (LP)	15

SECTION 25
80	Factory FAC 18	Girls Don't Count/New Noise/Up To You (tracing paper p/s, produced by Ian Curtis and Rob Gretton)	35
80	Factory FAC 18	Girls Don't Count/New Noise Up To You (12", 3 different p/s depicting band members girlfriends, produced by Ian Curtis and Rob Gretton)	20
82	Factory FAC 66	The Beast/Sakura/Sakura (Matrixmix)/Trident (12")	10

Neil SEDAKA

MINT VALUE £

83	Factory FAC 68	Back To Wonder/Beating Heart (p/s)	10
84	Factory FAC 108	Looking From A Hilltop (Restructure)/(Megamix) (12")	10
81	Factory FACT 45	ALWAYS NOW (LP, in envelope/folder with poster)	60
81	Factory FACT 45	ALWAYS NOW (LP, in envelope/folder without poster)	40
84	Factory FACT 90	FROM THE HIP (LP, with inner)	35
86	Factory FACT 45c	ALWAYS NOW (reissue, cassette in box with insert)	100
86	Factory FACT 90c	FROM THE HIP (reissue, cassette in box with insert)	80
88	Factory FACT 160	LOVE & HATE (LP)	30
12	Factory FACT 90	FROM THE HIP (2-LP, reissue)	20

NEIL SEDAKA

59	RCA RCA 1099	The Diary/No Vacancy	20
59	RCA RCA 1115	I Go Ape/Moon Of Gold	15
59	RCA RCA 1130	You've Got To Learn Your Rhythm And Blues/Crying My Heart Out For You	15
59	London HLW 8961	Ring A Rockin'/Fly Don't Fly On Me	40

(The above 45s were originally issued with triangular centres; later round-centres are worth two-thirds these values.)

59	London HLW 8961	Ring A Rockin'/Fly Don't Fly On Me (78)	20
59	RCA RCA 1152	Oh! Carol/One Way Ticket (triangular centre)	12
59	RCA RCA 1152	Oh! Carol/One Way Ticket (78)	40
59	RCA RCA 1178	Stairway To Heaven/Forty Winks Away (78)	40
60	RCA RCA 1198	Run Samson Run/You Mean Everything To Me	10
60	RCA RCA 1198	Run Samson Run/You Mean Everything To Me (78)	40
62	Stateside SS 105	Oh Delilah/MARVELS: Neil's Twist	10
63	RCA RCA 1368	Bad Girl/Wait 'Til You See My Baby	15
65	RCA RCA 1475	World Through A Tear/High On A Mountain	6
59	RCA RCX 166	NEIL SEDAKA (EP)	20
60	RCA RCX 186	NEIL SEDAKA VOL. 2 (EP)	20
62	RCA RCX 212	NEIL SEDAKA VOL. 3 (EP)	15
59	RCA RD 27140	NEIL SEDAKA (LP)	40
60	RCA RD 27207	CIRCULATE (LP, mono)	20
60	RCA SF 5090	CIRCULATE (LP, stereo)	30

(see also Sam Cooke, Paul Anka, 10cc)

MIKE SEDGEWICK

71	President PT 348	Morning Has Broken/Pollution Song	8

(see also Adam Mike & Tim)

SEDITION 81

81	S81	Royal Command/Prat Music (p/s)	100

SEDUCER

83	Sticky SSR 0017	Call Your Name/Survivor (small number in p/s)	60
83	Sticky SSR 0017	Call Your Name/Survivor (no p/s)	20
84	Thunderbolt THBE 1007	Indecent Exposure/Down Down/No No Baby/DTs/Wild Joker (12", p/s)	25
85	Thunderbolt THBL 016	CAUGHT IN THE ACT (LP)	25
86	Stud STUDLP 2	'EADS DOWN - SEE YOU AT THE END (LP)	25

SEE SEE

08	Great Pop Supplement GPS 27	Up The Hill/Citadel Shuffle (p/s, 300 only)	12
10	Great Pop Supplement GPS 64	LATE MORNING LIGHT (LP, 250 only, black vinyl)	15
10	Great Pop Supplement GPS 64	LATE MORNING LIGHT (LP, 300 only, milk chocolate vinyl)	15

REDGIE SEEBOE

74	BUG 38	Please Don't Bring Your Sister/Daphne's Brains	10

RUDY SEEDORF

65	Island WI 189	One Million Stars/Mr. Blue	18

SEEDS

66	Vocalion VN 9277	Pushin' Too Hard/Try To Understand	60
66	Vocalion VN 9277	Pushin' Too Hard/Try To Understand (DJ copy)	100
67	Vocalion VN 9287	Can't Seem To Make You Mine/Daisy Mae	40
88	Bam Caruso OPRA 091	Pushin' Too Hard/Greener Day	15
67	Vocalion VAN 8062	A WEB OF SOUND (LP)	120
67	Vocalion VAN 8070	FUTURE (LP, mono)	50
67	Vocalion SAVN 8070	FUTURE (LP, stereo)	60
78	Sonet SNTF 746	THE SEEDS (LEGENDARY MASTER RECORDINGS) (LP)	15
88	Strange Things STRANGEP 1	EVIL HOODOO (LP, picture disc)	15

(see also Sky Saxon, Ya Ho Wa 13)

SEEDS OF THE EARTH

75	Contempo CS 2052	Planting Seeds/Brother Bad	20
75	Contempo CS 2073	Zion Plus/Phire	20

SEEDY GEES

77	Fairview SRTS FMR 006	Redancer/Peggy Sue/Drinking Their Lives Away/I'll Meet You At Midnight	30
80	SRTS/80/CUS 646	We Will Rock And Roll/Those Lonely Days/We Will Remember/We Will Dance Tonight	30

MIKE SEEGER

65	Fontana TFL 6039	MIKE SEEGER (LP)	15

(see also Peggy & Mike Seeger)

PEGGY SEEGER

57	Pye Jazz NJE 1043	ORIGINS OF SKIFFLE (EP)	20
57	Topic 7T 18	COME ALONG JOHN (EP, 33 rpm with 2 inserts, one hand-typed insert)	20
58	Topic TOP 18	COME ALONG JOHN (EP, 45 rpm reissue, with insert)	15
60	Topic TOP 38	SHINE LIKE A STAR (EP)	20
61	Topic TOP 72	TROUBLED LOVE (EP)	10
61	Topic TOP 73	EARLY IN THE SPRING (EP)	10
50s	Topic 10T 9	PEGGY SEEGER (10" LP)	20

Peggy SEEGER & GUY CARAWAN

MINT VALUE £

61	PRE 13005	THE BEST OF PEGGY SEEGER (LP)	15

(see also Al Lloyd)

PEGGY SEEGER & GUY CARAWAN
58	Nixa NPT 19029	WE SING AMERICA (10" LP)	30
58	HMV CLP 1174	AMERICA AT PLAY (LP)	20

(see also Guy Carawan)

PEGGY & MIKE SEEGER
68	Argo (Z)DA 80	PEGGY 'N' MIKE (LP)	15

(see also Ewan MacColl & Peggy Seeger, Mike Seeger)

PETE SEEGER
60	Top Rank TR 5020	Careless Love/LEON BIBB: Times Are Getting Hard (p/s)	10
59	Topic TOP 37	HOOTENANNY NEW YORK CITY (EP, with Sonny Terry)	15

(see also Big Bill Broonzy, Sonny Terry [& Brownie McGhee], Weavers)

PETE SEEGER & BIG BILL BROONZY
64	Xtra XTRA 1006	IN CONCERT - PETE SEEGER & BIG BILL BROONZY (LP)	20
66	Verve Folkways ST SVLP 506	IN CONCERT (LP, stereo, reissue)	15

(see also Big Bill Broonzy)

SEEKERS
65	Oriole CB 1935	With A Swag On My Shoulder/Myra	10
67	Columbia DB 8313	Emerald City/Music Of The World A Turnin'	10

SEEMON & MARIJKE
71	A&M AMLS 64309	SON OF AMERICA (LP)	30

SEFTONS
66	CBS 202491	I Can See Through You/Here Today	25

(see also Perishers)

VIVIENNE SEGAL & HAROLD LANG
54	Columbia SCM 5114	Den Of Iniquity/BARBARA ASHLEY: That Terrific Rainbow	7

TY SEGALL
12	Drag City DC530	TWINS (LP, gatefold)	18

BOB SEGER (SYSTEM)
68	Capitol CL 15574	Ramblin' Gamblin' Man/Tales Of Lucy Blue (as Bob Seger System)	15
70	Capitol CL 15642	Lucifer/Big River (as Bob Seger System)	20
72	Reprise K 44214	SMOKIN' O.P.'s (LP)	20

FLOYD LLOYD SEIVRIGHT
70	Big Shot BI 566	Freedom Sound/Last Love	8
82	Vista Sounds STLP 1016	BETTER TO LAUGH THAN CRY (LP)	15
83	Tropic TLPS 0023	SWEET LADY (LP)	15

SEIZE
81	Why Not? NOT 001	Grovelands Road/Why? (p/s)	18
82	Why Not? NOT 002	EVERYBODY DIES EP (p/s)	30

RICHARD SELANO
69	Jolly JY 019	All Of The Time/Broken Romance	40

SELECTED FOUR
71	Banana BA 351	Selection Train/SOUND DIMENSION: Version Train	25

SELECTER
79	2-Tone CHS TT 4	On My Radio/Too Much Pressure (paper label, company sleeve)	18
79	2-Tone CHS TT4	On My Radio/Too Much Pressure (sliver or blue plastic labels, company sleeve)	10
80	2-Tone CHS TT 8	Three Minute Hero/James Bond (paper labels, company sleeve)	20
80	2-Tone CHS TT 8	Three Minute Hero/James Bond (silver plastic label, company sleeve)	10
80	2-Tone CHS TT 10	Missing Words/Carry Go Bring Home (paper label, company sleeve)	20
80	2-Tone CMS TT10	Missing Words/Carry Go Bring Home (sliver plastic labels)	10
80	2-Tone CHS TT 10	Missing Words/Carry Go Bring Home (sliver plastic labels, 'Nissing Words' misprint)	8
80	Chrysalis CHS S1	The Whisper/Train To Skaville (paper labels)	6
80	Chrysalis CHS S12	Train To Skaville/The Whisper/Street Feeling (12". p/s) £8 80 Flexipop 001 Ready Mix Radio (1-sided clear vinyl flexidisc, with Flexipop magazine)	10
89	2-Tone TTP1	THE SPECIALS: Rudi, A Message To You/Ghost Town//SELECTER: On My Radio/ MADNESS: One Step Beyond (promo, 40 only)	200
80	2-Tone CDLTT 5002	TOO MUCH PRESSURE (LP)	25
81	Chrysalis CHR 1306	CELEBRATE THE BULLET (LP)	20

(see also Special A.K.A.)

FREDDIE SELF
64	Mercury MF 839	Don't Cry/Why Should I?	7

(see also Freddie Ryder, Trends)

RONNIE SELF
58	Philips PB 810	Bop-A-Lena/Ain't I A Dog (78)	200

SELF ABUSE
83	Radical Change RC 5	(I DON'T WANT TO BE A) SOLDIERS (EP)	18

SELF CONTROL
80	Dancing Sideways DS2 X	SELF CONTROL (EP)	10
81	Dancing Sideways DS 4X	Falling/Electricity (p/s)	6

BING SELFISH
83	El Frenzy NM008	SELFISH WORKS EP (12", p/s)	40

BROTHER JOHN SELLERS
56	Vanguard EPP 14002	BLUES AND SPIRITUALS (EP)	15
57	Columbia SEG 7740	BLUES AND SPIRITUALS (EP)	15
57	Decca DFE 6457	BROTHER JOHN SELLERS IN LONDON (EP)	15
56	Vanguard PPT 12008	BROTHER JOHN SELLERS SINGS BLUES AND FOLK SONGS (10" LP)	25
57	Vanguard PPT 12017	JACK OF DIAMONDS AND OTHER FOLK SONGS AND BLUES (10" LP)	25

PETER SELLERS (& SOPHIA LOREN)
65	Parlophone R 5393	A Hard Day's Night/Help!	7
66	United Artists UP 1152	After The Fox (as Peter Sellers & Hollies)/BURT BACHARACH: The Fox-Trot	35

SELOFANE

			MINT VALUE £
60	Parlophone PCS 3012	PETER AND SOPHIA (LP, with Sophia Loren, stereo)	15

SELOFANE
68	CBS 3413	Girl Called Fantasy/Happiness Is Love	15
68	CBS 3700	Shingle I.A.O./Chase The Face	30

SELWYN & JOHN
67	CBS 2708	Bogey Man/When God Gave Us Names	90

SEMA
82	Le Rey LR 06	THEME FROM HUNGER (EP)	60
82	Le Rey LR 04	NOTES FROM UNDERGROUND (LP)	150
83	Le Rey LR 101	EXTRACTS FROM ROSA SILBER (LP)	80
84	Le Rey LR 102	THREE SEASONS ONLY (LP)	60

SEMA 4
79	Pollen PBM 022	4 FROM SEMA 4 (EP, 2 different coloured sleeves, 500 only, numbered)	100
79	Pollen PBM 024	UP DOWN AROUND (EP, 1,000 only)	75

GEORGE SEMPER
18	Dynamite Cuts DYNAM7010	Pretty Lady/Universe/Extraterrestrial Search Contact Tones (reissue, p/s)	7

ARCHIE SEMPLE
60	Columbia 33SX 1240	JAZZ FOR YOUNG LOVERS (LP)	25
62	77 LP/10	THE ARCHIE SEMPLE QUARTET (10" LP, 100 only)	40
62	Columbia 33SX 1450	EASY LIVING (LP)	20
63	Columbia 33SX 1580	THE TWILIGHT COMETH (LP)	20
64	77 LEU 12/6	THE CLARINET OF ARCHIE SEMPLE (LP)	20

SENATE
67	Columbia DB 8110	I Can't Stop/Ain't As Sweet As You	60
68	United Artists (S)ULP 1180	THE SENATE SOCK IT TO YOU ONE MORE TIME (LP)	40

(see also Garnet Mimms)

SENATORS
64	Dial DSP 7001	She's A Mod/Lot About You	100
64	Oriole CB 1957	When Day Is Done/Breakdown	50
65	CBS 201768	The Tables Are Turning/Stop Wasting Time	30

(see also Tony Rivers & Castaways)

SENAY
15	Turkola TR-03	SENAY (LP, reissue)	20

SENDELICA
10	Fruits De Mer CRUSTACIAN 13	A NICE PAIR (gatefold p/s, green vinyl)	25

RAY SENDIT & HIS ROCKEY TEAM
57	Felsted SD 80052	Rocket 0869/Spike's Rock	8

SEND/RETURN
95	Emote MOTE 002	Alright/Not Bad/Reasonable/Fair (12")	80
95	Emote MOTE 003	Hair Of The Dog/Liquid Lunch/Nightcap (12")	80

(see also Mark Churcher)

SENSATION
73	Sticky STY 1	Everybody Wants It/Lady Put Me Down	8
73	Sticky STY 5	Black Eyed Woman/Baby	15

SENSATIONAL CREED
84	Beggars Banquet BEG 125	Nocturnal Operation/Down Periscope (p/s, reissue of Orbidöig single)	15
84	Beggars Banquet BEG 125T	Nocturnal Operation/Down Periscope/Voyage Of The Titanic (12", p/s, reissue of Orbidöig single)	25

(see also Orbidoig)

SENSATIONAL SPARES
83	Spare KF 001	No Time At All/The Windmill (no p/s)	40

SENSATIONS (JAMAICA)
67	Doctor Bird DB 1074	A Thing Called Soul/BOBBY LEE & SENSATIONS: I Was Born A Loser	65
67	Doctor Bird DB 1100	Right On Time/Lonely Lover	200
67	Doctor Bird DB 1102	Born To Love You/Your Sweet Love	85
68	Duke DU 2	Those Guys/I'll Never Fall In Love	80
68	Island WI 3110	Long Time Me No See You Girl/ROY SHIRLEY: Million Dollar Baby	200
69	Camel CA 31	The Warrior (actually by Johnny Osbourne & Sensations)/ JOHNNY ORGAN: Don Juan	60
70	Techniques TE 902	War Boat/Mr Blue	80
71	Duke DU 120	Remember/LARRY'S ALLSTARS: Madhouse	40
71	Duke DU 121	What Are You Doing Sunday/RUFFIANS: Sweet Dream	15

(see also Roy Shirley, Baba Dise, Winston Wright)

SENSATIONS (U.K.)
66	Decca F 12392	Look At My Baby/What A Wonderful Feeling	20
71	MCA MK 5078	Oh My Eli/Let's Get A Little Sentimental	30

SENSATIONS (FEATURING YVONNE) (U.S.)
61	Pye International 7N 25110	Music, Music, Music/A Part Of Me (as Sensations featuring Yvonne)	25
62	Pye International 7N 25128	Let Me In/Oh Yes I'll Be True	25

(see also Yvonne Baker)

SENSE OF VISION
84	Wipe 2	Dream/Destiny (p/s)	7

SEONA DANCING
83	London LON 22	More To Lose/You're On My Side (p/s)	18
83	London LONX 22	More To Lose (Extended Mix)/You're On My Side (12", p/s)	10
83	London LON 32	Bitter Heart/Tell Her (p/s)	18
83	London LONX 32	Bitter Heart/Tell Her (12", p/s)	12

SEPTIC DEATH
88	Pusmort PUS 00703	KICHIGAI EP (p/s)	7
85	Pusmort 0012-01D	NOW THAT I HAVE THE ATTENTION... (LP, with inner sleeve, 18 tracks)	15

SEPTIMUS
MINT VALUE £

SEPTIMUS
77 Pennine PSS 134 Ferrets/Do You Wanna Touch My Safety Pin? (no p/s) 100

SEPULTURA
94 Roadrunner RR2377-8 Refuse/Resist (12", die cut sleeve) 12
91 Roadracer RO 93281 ARISE (LP) 40
91 Roadracer RO 9328-8 ARISE (LP, picture disc) 35
94 Roadrunner RR 90000 0 CHAOS A.D. (CD, limited edition tin box; CD has embossed cover & different sleeve, Brazilian flag & 2 bonus tracks, "Policia" & "Inhuman Nature") 40

SEQUE
83 Storm STORM 1 3 On The Trot/Christine 12

SEQUENCE
84 CAMM CAMM 01 Child In The City/Theme (12") 35

SERCUS
90 SBS S.B.S. 91101 Signs Of Day/I Spy (no p/s) 10

SERENDIPITY
68 CBS 3733 Through With You/I'm Flying 130
69 CBS 4428 If I Could/Castles 60

SERENDIPITY SINGERS
64 Philips BF 1333 Don't Let The Rain Come Down (Crooked Little Man)/Freedom's Star 6

SERFS
69 Capitol E-ST 207 THE EARLY BIRD CAFE (LP) 18

SERGEANT PEPPER
83 Ariwa ARILP 006 JUDGEMENT DAY (LP) 25

WILL SERGEANT
78 (no label or cat. no.) WEIRD AS FISH (cassette, 7 copies only, each with a different cover) 150
82 WEA K 19238 Favourite Branches/RAVI SHANKAR & BILL LOVEDAY: Himalaya (p/s) 8
95 Ochre OCH 003 Cosmos/Venus In Flares (as GLIDE, p/s, orange vinyl) 7
(see also Echo & Bunnymen)

SERGIO & ESTIBALIZ
75 Epic S EPC 3187 Love Come Home/Tu Volveras 12

SERIES RED
85 Horizon RED 001 Don't Go/Hold Back Your Feelings (p/s) 35

SERIOUS DRINKING
83 Upright UP 5 Hangover/Don't Shoot Me Down/Baby I'm Dying A Death (p/s) 8
82 Upright YOURS 4 Love On The Terraces/Hypocrite/Bobby Moore Was Innocent (p/s) 10
84 Upright UP 8 Country Girl Became Drugs & Sex Punk/Go For The Burn 10
83 Upright UPLP 3 THE REVOLUTION STARTS AT CLOSING TIME (LP, with beer mat) 18

SERPENTINE
70 Decca F23001 Powerful Jim/I've Only Got Myself 20

JUAN MANUEL SERRAT
68 Philips BF 1654 She Gives Me Love (La La La)/La La La 6

BETTIE SERVEERT
92 Guernica GU 3 LP PALOMINE (LP, with free 7") 20

SERVICEMEN
00 Grapevine 116 Are You Angry/I Need A Helping Hand 15
01 Grapevine 136 I'll Stop Loving You/Sweet Magic 25

SESSION BOYS
70 Lynn L29 Looking To The Sun/Strike Back 20

SESSION MEN
80 LKJ 001 THE SESSION MEN : Solitude/ABU BAKE : Introducing Abu Baka/MICHAEL SMITH : Mi Cyaan Believe It/Roots (12") 25

CAMILO SESTO
72 Pye Intl. 7N 25589 To Be A Man/Now Is My Time (Yo Soy Asi) 40

BOLA SETE
76 Sonet SNTF 695 OCEAN (LP) 15

SETTERS
70 Duke DU 65 Paint Your Wagon/Organ Man (both sides actually by Hot Rod All Stars) 140
70 Trojan TR 7738 Virgin Soldier/Brixton Reggae Festival (both actually by Hot Rod All Stars) 60

SETTING SUN
68 Oak RGI 840 Ob La De Ob La Da/Boy Who Was Only One/Homeward Bound/Fascinating Rhythm 40

SETTLERS
65 Pye 7N 159645 Woman Called Freedom/I Know I'm Right 6
66 Pye 7N 17065 Nowhere Man/Call Again 7
67 Pye 7N 17375 Major To Minor/I Love 'Oo Kazoo ('Cos 'Oo Love Me) 6
70 Columbia DB 8695 Nessie The Monster/Jesus Met The Woman (At The Well) 6
71 York SYK 505 The Lightning Tree/Just This Side Of Nowhere 8
74 York YR 215 On Top Of The World/Let's Tell The World 6
64 Decca LK 4645 SING OUT (LP) 15
72 York FYK 405 LIGHTNING TREE (LP) 15

SEVEN AGES OF MAN
72 Rediffusion ZS 115 SEVEN AGES OF MAN (LP, yellow/black label) 40
(see also Madeline Bell, Gordon Beck)

SEVEN LETTERS/SYMARIP
69 Doctor Bird DB 1189 People Get Ready/The Fit (as Seven Letters) 65
69 Doctor Bird DB 1194 Please Stay/Special Beat (as Seven Letters) 70
69 Doctor Bird DB 1195 Flour Dumpling/Equality (as Seven Letters [Symarip]) 130
69 JJ DB 1206 Mama Me Want Girl/Sentry (as Seven Letters) 40
69 JJ DB 1207 Soul Crash/Throw Me Things (as Seven Letters) 100
69 Doctor Bird DB 1208 There Goes My Heart/Wish (as Seven Letters) 100
69 Doctor Bird DB 1209 Bam Bam Baji/Hold Him Joe (as Seven Letters [Symarip]) 90
69 Doctor Bird DB 1306 Fung Shore/Tomorrow At Sundown (as Symarip) 150

7 SECONDS

			MINT VALUE £
69	Treasure Isle TI 7050	Skinhead Moonstomp/Must Catch A Train (as Symarip)	30
70	Treasure Isle TI 7054	Parson Corner/Redeem (as Symarip)	30
70	Treasure Isle TI 7055	La Bella Jig/Holidays By The Sea (as Symarip)	25
70	Attack ATT 8013	I Am A Puppet/Vindication (as Symarip)	45
80	Trojan TRO 9062	Skinhead Moonstomp/Skinhead Jamboree (p/s)	10
70	Trojan TBL 102	SKINHEAD MOONSTOMP (LP, as Symarip)	80
80	Trojan TRLS 187	SKINHEAD MOONSTOMP (LP, reissue, blue label)	25
13	Sunspot SUNSPLP011	SKINHEAD MOONSTOMP (LP, reissue)	18

(see also Pyramids, Equals, Laurel Aitken)

7 SECONDS
82	Alt. Tentacles VIRUS 15	SKIN, BRAINS AND GUTS (EP, with insert)	12

SEVEN YEAR ITCH
81	Cargo CRS 007	I Wanna Make Ya/Oo Ya Ha	10

SEVENTEEN
80	Vendetta VD 001	Don't Let Go/Bank Holiday Weekend (p/s)	100

(see also Alarm)

SEVENTH ANGEL
90	Under One Flag FLAG 51	THE TORMENT (LP)	15
92	Under One Flag FLAG 65	LAMENT FOR THE WEARY (LP, inner)	20

7TH PLAIN
93	General Production GPR(X) 16	TO BE SURREAL EP (12")	70
94	General Production GPR(X) 19	ASTRA-NAUT EP (12")	30
94	General Prod. GPRLP03	THE 4 CORNERED ROOM (2-LP, poster)	30
94	General Prod. GPRLP08	MY YELLOW WISE RUG (2-LP, as Luke Slaters 7th Plain)	25
96	General Prod. GPRLP16	PLAYING WITH FOOLS (2-LP, test pressings only)	200

(see also Luke Slater)

SEVENTH SEAL
90	Mystic Red Corp MRC 8004	Sound Iration/Dub Seal (12")	50

SEVENTH SON
82	Rising Son FMR 067	Man In The Street/Immortal Hours (in original p/s with bass player obscured)	50
82	Rising Son FMR 067	Man In The Street/Immortal Hours (revised p/s with 'clearer' band photograph)	35
84	Rising Son SRT4KS 282	Metal To The Moon/Sound And Fury (in gatefold p/s)	60
84	Rising Son SRT4KS 282	Metal To The Moon/Sound And Fury	30
87	Music Factory MF 0043	Northern Boots/The Harder You Rock (p/s)	18
89	Rising Son SRT9KLS	What More Do You Want/Sister Strange/Bitter Ashes (12", p/s)	12
91	SRT 915 3116	Factory Girls/Last Band In Town	7

SEVENTH WAVE
89	SRT SRT9KS 2018	Tonight/Run (p/s)	20
74	Gull GULP 1001	THINGS TO COME (LP)	15
75	Gull GULP 1010	PSI-FI (LP)	18

(see also Second Hand, Fungus, Ken Elliott)

SEVENTH WONDER
80	Grapevine GRP 130	Captain Of My Ship/Pharaoh	10

SEVERE CARNAGE
90	White JC 002	The Struggle Continues/Back To Basics (12")	250

SEVERED HEAD
83	Plastic Canvas PC 002	Heavy Metal/Killin' The Kidz (p/s)	25

SEVERED HEADS
84	Ink INK 122	DEAD EYES OPENED (12" EP, p/s)	15
83	Ink INK 2	SINCE THE ACCIDENT (LP)	20
85	Ink INK 9	CITY SLAB HORROR (LP)	15
85	Ink INK 16D	CLIFFORD DARLING PLEASE DON'T LIVE IN THE PAST (2-LP)	20

SEVERINE
71	CBS 7230	Chance In Time/Nothing Bad Can Be This Good	8

DAVID SEVILLE & HIS ORCHESTRA (& THE CHIPMUNKS)
57	London HLU 8359	Armen's Theme/Carousel In Rome (initially gold label print)	20
58	London HLU 8619	Witch Doctor/Don't Whistle At Me Baby	6
64	Liberty 16170	All My Loving/Please Please Me	8

(see also Alfi & Harry)

ALEC SEWARD
56	Vogue LDE 165	CITY BLUES (10" LP)	40

SEX
00	Grapevine 113	It's You Baby (It's You)/It's You Baby (Extended)	15

SEX AIDS
83	Riot City RIOT 23	BACK ON THE PISS AGAIN (EP)	20

(see also Vice Squad)

SEX BEATLES
79	Charly CYS 1061	Well You Never/Fatal Fascination (p/s)	8

SEX GANG CHILDREN
82	Illuminated ILL 1112	Beasts (12", EP)	30

SEX PISTOLS
SINGLES
76	EMI 401	Anarchy In The U.K (4.01 longer version)/No Fun (Abbey Road 2-sided acetate, only 3 known to exist)	7000
76	EMI	Anarchy In The U.K. (3.36 version) (1-sided Abbey Road Acetate)	5000
76	EMI 2566	Anarchy In The U.K./I Wanna Be Me (2 x 1-sided white label test pressings, 4-pronge centre, MATRIXES EMI 2566 A1/EMI 2566B-2)	4000
76	EMI EMI 2566	Anarchy In The U.K./I Wanna Be Me (black p/s, with Chris Thomas production credit on B-side)	120

SEX PISTOLS

MINT VALUE £

Year	Label/Cat No.	Description	Value
76	EMI EMI 2566	Anarchy In The U.K./I Wanna Be Me ('Demo, not for sale'. Black p/s, Chris Thomas credit on both sides and with information slip)	300
76	EMI EMI 2566	Anarchy In The U.K./I Wanna Be Me (Dave Goodman production credit on B-side)	60
76	EMI EMI 2566	Anarchy In The U.K./I Wanna Be Me (Anarchy label on both sides)	150
77	(no label or cat. no.)	God Save The Queen/No Feeling (double sided 7" acetate on LTS - few copies pressed and used by Malcolm McLaren to get gigs and record deal)	10000
77	A&M AMS 2784	God Save The Queen/No Feeling (white label test pressing, A2/B1 Matrixes)	7000
77	A&M AMS 7284	God Save The Queen/No Feeling (withdrawn, in brown envelope with press release)	12000
77	A&M AMS 7284	God Save The Queen/No Feeling (withdrawn, without brown envelope and press release)	10000
77	Virgin VS 181	God Save The Queen/Did You No Wrong (white label test pressing VS 181 A1/B1 Matrixes)	2500
77	Virgin VS 181	God Save The Queen/Did You No Wrong (1st issue, with silver on blue sleeve and labels)	10
77	Virgin VS 181	God Save The Queen/Did You No Wrong (Plain blue no Queen's head sample sleeve - two known copies, Jamie Reid autograph added later to one)	1500
77	Virgin VS 181	God Save The Queen/Did You No Wrong (2nd issue, white on blue sleeve and labels)	8
77	Virgin VS 184 (not on acetate)	Pretty Vacant (1-sided acetate)	1000
77	Virgin VS 184	Pretty Vacant/No Fun (white label test pressing)	600
77	Virgin VS 184	Pretty Vacant/No Fun (p/s, blue white labels)	10
77	Virgin VS 184	Pretty Vacant/No Fun (p/s blue/white labels, with push-out centre)	30
77	Virgin VS 191	Holidays In The Sun/Satellite (withdrawn p/s)	40
77	Virgin/Lyntone LYN 3261	Lentilmas - A Seasonal Offering To You From Virgin Records (flexidisc, Xmas freebie to journalists; with Xmas card. It is believed that the Sex Pistols do not appear on this record)	1000
77	Virgin/Lyntone LYN 3261	Lentilmas - A Seasonal Offering To You From Virgin Records (flexidisc, Xmas freebie to journalists; without Xmas card. It is believed that the Sex Pistols do not appear on this record)	300
78	Virgin VS 184	Pretty Vacant/No Fun (p/s, repressing, green/red labels)	8
78	(No. Cat. No)	SID VICIOUS: My Way (1-sided Pye Studios Acetate)	700
78	VIrgin VS 220	No One Is Innocent/SID VICIOUS: My Way (p/s)	6
78	Virgin VS 220	No-One Is Innocent (mispress, plays Motors track)/SID VICIOUS: My Way (p/s)	35
78	Virgin VS 22012	The Biggest Blow (A Punk Prayer By Ronald Biggs)/(Interview)/SID VICIOUS: My Way (12", p/s [matrix: VS 22012A3], without interview [VS 22012 A1])	20
78	Virgin VS 22012	The Biggest Blow (A Punk Prayer By Ronald Biggs)/(Interview)/SID VICIOUS: My Way (12", p/s [matrix: VS 22012A3], with interview [VS 22012 A1])	10
78	(No label or cat no)	The Interview (recorded at Middlesborough Rock Garden August 1977, 7.30 minutes each side, 1000 pressed)	10
79	Virgin VS 240	Something Else/Friggin' In The Riggin' (p/s, black & white labels)	7
79	Virgin VS 256	Silly Thing/TENPOLE TUDOR: Who Killed Bambi (p/s)	6
79	Virgin VS 290	The Great Rock 'n' Roll Swindle/Rock Around The Clock (vocals by Tenpole Tudor) ('American Express' p/s)	6
79	Virgin VS 290	The Great Rock 'n' Roll Swindle (mispressing with 'lawyers' telephone conversation' track)/Rock Around The Clock ('American Express' p/s)	30
80	Virgin VS 339	(I'm Not Your) Stepping Stone/Pistols Propaganda (p/s, mispressing, B-side plays "Substitute")	25
80	Virgin VS 339	(I'm Not Your) Stepping Stone/Pistols Propaganda (p/s, mispressing, B-side plays Gillan track "No Laughing In Heaven")	30
80	Virgin SEX 1	PISTOLS PACK (6 x 7" in p/s; all in plastic wallet)	80
81	Virgin VS 443	Who Killed Bambi?/Rock Around The Clock (by Tenpole Tudor & Pistols, p/s)	10
85	Chaos DICK1	Submission/No Feelings (p/s, 5,000 only, blue vinyl)	7
85	Chaos DICK1	Submission/No Feelings (p/s, 5,000 only, pink vinyl)	15
85	Chaos SUB 1	Submission (12", 1-sided test pressing, die-cut sleeve, label has big red 'A')	30
85	Chaos	Pretty Vacant (unreleased, 20 copies only)	75
85	Chaos CARTEL 1	Submission (12" 1-track promo)	25
86	Archive 4 TOF 104	THE ORIGINAL SEX PISTOLS LIVE (4-track 12", p/s, blue vinyl)	12
88	Spiral Scratch SCRATCH 4	Pretty Vacant (Demo)/I Wanna Be Me (Demo) (with Spiral Scratch magazine, issue 4, B-side actually plays "Seventeen")	10
92	Virgin VS 1448	Pretty Vacant/No Feelings (p/s, Lady Di cover)	15
02	Virgin VS 1832	God Save The Queen/Did You No Wrong (reissue)	8
07	EMI EMI 2566	Anarchy In The U.K./I Wanna Be Me (180 gram repressing, p/s)	7
07	Virgin VS 181	God Save The Queen/Did You No Wrong (180 gram repressing, p/s)	7
07	Virgin VS 184	Pretty Vacant/No Fun (180 gram repressing, p/s)	7
07	Virgin VS 191	Holidays In The Sun/Satelitte (180 gram repressing, p/s)	7

ALBUMS

Year	Label/Cat No.	Description	Value
77	Virgin V 2086	NEVER MIND THE BOLLOCKS, HERE'S THE SEX PISTOLS (LP, 1st pressing with poster and free 'Submission' 7", 11 tracks listed on rear sleeve (no 'Submission'). Publishing credits '1977 Jones, Matlock, Cook & Rotten' except HOLIDAYS IN THE SUN (side 1) and BODIES (side 2) 'Jones, Cook, Rotten & Vicious')	100
77	Virgin V 2086	NEVER MIND THE BOLLOCKS, HERE'S THE SEX PISTOLS (LP, 1st pressing, poster and free 'Submission' 7", pink rear sleeve with no track listing, sources suggest as little as 1000 copies pressed with this sleeve, A1/B1 or A3/B2 matrixes. Publishing credits '1977 Jones, Matlock, Cook & Rotten' except HOLIDAYS IN THE SUN (side 1) and BODIES (side 2) 'Jones, Cook, Rotten & Vicious'))	150
77	Virgin V 2086	NEVER MIND THE BOLLOCKS, HERE'S THE SEX PISTOLS (LP, 2nd pressing with 12 tracks (no track listing on pink rear sleeve, 'Bodies' moved to side 1 and 'Submission' added to side 2. Publishing credits, 'Copyright control 1977, Jones, Matlock. Cook, Rotten' except HOLIDAYS IN THE SUN, BODIES & EMI 'Copyright Control 1977 Jones, Cook, Rotten, Vicious')	40
77	Virgin V 2086	NEVER MIND THE BOLLOCKS, HERE'S THE SEX PISTOLS (LP, 3rd pressing with 12 tracks and 12 tracks listed on pink rear sleeve,Publishing credits on 'EMI' changed from 'Jones, Matlock, Cook, Rotten' to 'Jones, Cook, Rotten, Vicious'.	30
77	Virgin V 2086	NEVER MIND THE BOLLOCKS, HERE'S THE SEX PISTOLS (LP, 3rd pressing with 12 tracks but 11 tracks listed on rear sleeve (no 'Submission'). Publishing credits, 'Copyright control 1977, Jones, Matlock. Cook, Rotten' except HOLIDAYS IN THE SUN, BODIES & EMI 'Copyright Control 1977 Jones, Cook, Rotten, Vicious')	25

Ann SEXTON

			MINT VALUE £
77	Virgin V 2086/SPOTS 001	NEVER MIND THE BOLLOCKS, HERE'S THE SEX PISTOLS (LP, pink rear sleeve, with no track listing, with poster & 1-sided single, "Submission" [VDJ 24], shrinkwrapped, with orange or green-stickered versions extremely rare)	1000
78	Virgin VP 2086	NEVER MIND THE BOLLOCKS, HERE'S THE SEX PISTOLS (LP, picture disc)	40
78	Virgin V 2086	NEVER MIND THE BOLLOCKS, HERE'S THE SEX PISTOLS (LP, 1st reissue. Green label side 1, red label on side 2 - Matlock credit returns on 'EMI', rear sleeve has 11 or 12 track listing)	15
79	Virgin VD 2510	THE GREAT ROCK 'N' ROLL SWINDLE (2-LP, 1st pressing with 23 tracks including "Watcha Gonna Do About It", with paper insert)	40
79	Virgin VD 2510	THE GREAT ROCK 'N' ROLL SWINDLE (2-LP, 2nd pressing with 24 tracks. "I Wanna Be Me" and "Who Killed Bambi?" replace "Watcha Gonna Do About It", with spoken overdubs on "God Save The Queen Symphony" 2 stickers on front and 1 on rear)	40
79	Virgin VD 2510	THE GREAT ROCK 'N' ROLL SWINDLE (2-LP, 2nd pressing with 24 tracks. "I Wanna Be Me" and "Who Killed Bambi?" replace "Watcha Gonna Do About It", with spoken overdubs on "God Save The Queen Symphony" 1 sticker on front)	20
79	Virgin V 2142	FLOGGING A DEAD HORSE (LP)	15
80	Factory FACT 30	THE HEYDAY (gold interview cassette in satin pouch with Xmas card)	50
80	Virgin V 2168	THE GREAT ROCK 'N' ROLL SWINDLE (LP, compilation with 2 stickers on front and free poster)	80
84	Virgin OVED 136	NEVER MIND THE BOLLOCKS, HERE'S THE SEX PISTOLS (LP, reissue, misprinted with 'Belsen Was A Gas' on rear of sleeve and 'Liar' printed twice)	15
85	Virgin OVED 136	NEVER MIND THE BOLLOCKS, HERE'S THE SEX PISTOLS (LP, reissue, misprinted with 'Belsen Was A Gas' on rear of sleeve)	18
92	Virgin V2702	KISS THIS (2-LP)	25
97	EMI LPCENT20	NEVER MIND THE BOLLOCKS, HERE'S THE SEX PISTOLS (LP, reissue, EMI 100 Centenary edition, stickered sleeve)	25
98	Virgin VP 2087	NEVER MIND THE BOLLOCKS, HERE'S THE SEX PISTOLS (LP, pink vinyl reissue, numbered on rear sleeve)	20
06	Castle CMQLP 1395	SPUNK (LP, yellow vinyl)	15
12	Universal SEXPISYP 1977	NEVER MIND THE BOLLOCKS, HERE'S THE SEX PISTOLS (2-LP, reissue yellow/pink vinyl, 1977 copies only, numbered)	35

(see also Public Image Ltd, Professionals, Rich Kids, Steve Jones, Cash Pussies, Spectres (UK))

ANN SEXTON

87	Charly CRB 1143	LOVE TRIALS (LP, reissue)	15
03	Soul Brother 1000001	ANTHOLOGY (LP)	25

TONY SEXTON

69	Camel CA 35	Nobody Knows/Somewhere (with Jr. English)	20
78	Fight FTDD 4429	My Heart Is Gone/VIN GORDON: Heartically/HIM & HER: Boneache/Pussy Galore (12")	15
78	Horse HOSS 153	Segregation/SUPER STAR: Segregation (Version)	25
78	Burning Sounds BSD 005	Desire (with Jah Son)/BOB DAVIS: World In My Arms (12")	20

SEXWITCH

15	Echo 538169301	SEXWITCH (LP)	40

(see also Bat For Lashes)

SEXY GIRLS

69	Fab FAB 100	Pon-Pon Song/LITTLE JOE & BUSTER'S ALLSTARS: Hy There (B-side actually by Melltones)	15
69	Dice CC 100	Pon-Pon Song/LITTLE JOE & BUSTER'S ALLSTARS: Hy There (B-side actually by Melltones) (reissue)	15

DENNY SEYTON & SABRES

64	Mercury MF 800	Tricky Dicky/Baby What You Want Me To Do	20
64	Mercury MF 814	Short Fat Fanny/Give Me Back My Heart	20
64	Mercury MF 824	The Way You Look Tonight/Hands Off	20
65	Parlophone R 5363	Just A Kiss/In The Flowers By The Trees (as Denny Seyton Group)	20
65	Wing WL 1032	IT'S THE GEAR (14 HITS) (LP)	30

SFW

78	Badarse SFW 1	True Life/The March (no p/s)	20

TONY SHABAZZ

79	Ethnic Fight FT DD 4436	Mr Fitzy/RUDDIE MOWATT: Public Enemy (12")	60

SHABBY TIGER

76	RCA Victor PL 25046	SHABBY TIGER (LP)	15

SHACK

88	Ghetto GTG B 1	Emergency/Liberation (p/s)	6
88	Ghetto GTG T 1	Emergency/Liberation/Faith (12", p/s)	12
89	Ghetto GTG T 2	High Rise Low Life/Who Killed Clayton Square?/High Rise Low Life (Bert Hardy Mix) (12", p/s)	10
88	Ghetto GHETT 1	ZILCH (LP, with free 12" distributed by Epic)	20
88	Ghetto GHETT 1	ZILCH (LP, later independent issue)	25
03	North Country NCLP 002	HERE'S TOM WITH THE WEATHER (LP)	25

(see also Pale Fountains, Michael Head & Strands)

SHADE JOEY & NIGHTOWLS

64	Parlophone R 5180	Bluebirds Over The Mountain/That's When I Need You Baby	90

SHADER

81	Piston Broke REDASH 1	Bad News Blues (no p/s)	100

SHADES

62	Starlite ST45 074	Weird Walk/Joe's Shuffle	20

SHADES (JAMAICA)

69	Gas GAS 119	Never Gonna Give You Up/Let Me Remind You (both actually by Techniques)	65

(see also Techniques)

SHADES OF BLUE (U.K.)

65	Parlophone R 5270	Voodoo Blues/Luceanne	50
65	Pye 7N 15982	Where Did All The Good Times Go/I Ain't No Use	15

SHADES OF BLUE (U.S.)

66	Sue WI 4022	Oh! How Happy/Little Orphan Boy	35

SHADES OF JOY

69	Fontana STL 5498	SHADES OF JOY (LP)	20

SHADES OF MACMURROUGH

MINT VALUE £

SHADES OF MACMURROUGH
73　Polydor 2908 007　　　　CRAIG RIVER (LP, red label, Irish pressing) 150

SHADES OF MORLEY BROWN
68　Mercury MF1054　　　　Silly Girl/Pretty Bluebird 120

SHADES (U.S.)
58　London HLX 8713　　　　Sun Glasses (with Knott Sisters)/KNOTT SISTERS: Undivided Attention 40

SHADES OF BLACK
90　Intrigue IGE 13T　　　　Make U Mine/2 Deep/C.O.D. (12") 12
90　Intrigue IGE 12T　　　　Play You A Song/Deeper Still/Shadows (12") 15
92　Intrigue IGE 25T　　　　CLASSIC CUTS 2 (12" EP) 15
92　Intrigue IGE 28T　　　　I Like It/Dream On (12") 10

SHADO
74　Montrose MON 1001　　　Evil City/Tell You I Know 60

JOHNNY SHADOW (& DANNY GAVAN)
63　Pye 7N 15506　　　　Golli Golli/I'm Coming Home To You (with Danny Gavan) (in p/s) 15
(see also Ivy League)

SHADOWBOYS
83　Pete Nik DFN 1A　　　　Waiting For Tomorrow/Out Of Reach (p/s) 10

SHADOWFAX
79　BFD SFX 100　　　　Really Into You/Spare Wheel Driver (no p/s, band name spelt as Shaddowfax on label) ... 50
80　Risky Discs RISK 1　　　The Russians Are Coming/Calling The Shots 25

SHADOWLANDS
86　Pharoah PR 002　　　　Cry From The Heart/Cold Nights (no p/s) 15

SHADOW RING
96　Dry Leaf DF 006　　　　Rats & Mice (lathe cut, 150 only) 20
93　Dry Leaf DF 001　　　　Don't Open The Window/The Heavy Foot Of The Lark 20
95　Dry Leaf DF 004　　　　Some Of Us/The Wallet Of Wasps 10
93　Dry Leaf DF 002　　　　CITY LIGHTS (LP) 70

SHADOWS (U.K.)
SINGLES
59　Columbia DB 4387　　　Saturday Dance/Lonesome Fella 40
59　Columbia DB 4387　　　Saturday Dance/Lonesome Fella (78) 150
60　Columbia DB 4484　　　Apache/Quartermaster's Stores (green label) 8
60　Columbia DB 4484　　　Apache/Quartermaster's Stores (later black label) 15
64　Columbia DB 7261　　　The Rise And Fall Of Flingel Bunt/It's A Man's World (mispressing with A-side on both sides) 8
64　Columbia DB 7342　　　Rhythm 'n' Greens/The Miracle 6
64　Columbia DB 7416　　　Genie With The Light Brown Lamp/Little Princess 7
65　Columbia DB 7476　　　Mary Anne/Chu-Chi 6
65　Columbia DB 7588　　　Stingray/Alice In Sunderland (in export p/s) 20
65　Columbia DB 7650　　　Don't Make My Baby Blue/My Grandfather's Clock (p/s) 20
65　Columbia DB 7769　　　The War Lord/I Wish I Could Shimmy Like My Sister Arthur 7
66　Columbia DB 7853　　　I Met A Girl/Late Night Set 10
66　Columbia DB 7952　　　A Place In The Sun/Will You Be There 10
66　Columbia DB 8034　　　The Dreams I Dream/Scotch On The Socks ('B' label demos worth £50) 35
67　Columbia PSR 305　　　Thunderbirds Are Go (1-sided advance promo) 60
67　Columbia DB 8170　　　Maroc 7/Bombay Duck 10
67　Columbia PSR 308　　　Maroc 7 (1-sided demo with spoken-word intro) 60
67　Columbia PSR 310　　　Chelsea Boot/Jigsaw (demo only) 80
67　Columbia DB 8264　　　Tomorrow's Cancelled/Somewhere 15
68　Columbia DB 8326　　　Running Out Of World/HANK MARVIN: London's Not Too Far 15
68　Columbia DB 8372　　　Dear Old Mrs. Bell/Trying To Forget The One You Love 15
69　Columbia DB 8628　　　Slaughter On Tenth Avenue/HANK MARVIN: Midnight Cowboy 15

EPs
61　Columbia SEG 8061　　　THE SHADOWS (mono) 10
61　Columbia ESG 7834　　　THE SHADOWS (stereo) 12
61　Columbia SEG 8094　　　THE SHADOWS TO THE FORE 10
62　Columbia SEG 8135　　　SPOTLIGHT ON THE SHADOWS 10
62　Columbia SEG 8148　　　THE SHADOWS NO. 2 (only some sleeves list "No. 2") 10
62　Columbia SEG 8166　　　THE SHADOWS NO. 3 10
62　Columbia SEG 8171　　　WONDERFUL LAND OF THE SHADOWS 10
(The above EPs were originally issued with turquoise labels; later blue/black label copies are worth two-thirds these values.)
62　Columbia SEG 8193　　　THE BOYS (mono) 10
62　Columbia ESG 7881　　　THE BOYS (stereo, turquoise labels) 10
62　Columbia ESG 7881　　　THE BOYS (stereo, later black/blue labels) 20
63　Columbia SEG 8218　　　OUT OF THE SHADOWS (mono) 10
63　Columbia ESG 7883　　　OUT OF THE SHADOWS (stereo, turquoise labels) 10
63　Columbia ESG 7883　　　OUT OF THE SHADOWS (stereo, black/blue labels) 15
63　Columbia SEG 8233　　　DANCE ON WITH THE SHADOWS 10
63　Columbia SEG 8249　　　OUT OF THE SHADOWS NO. 2 (mono) 10
63　Columbia ESG 7895　　　OUT OF THE SHADOWS NO. 2 (stereo ESG 7895) 15
63　Columbia SEG 8268　　　FOOT TAPPING WITH THE SHADOWS 10
63　Columbia SEG 8278　　　LOS SHADOWS (2 different sleeves) 10
63　Columbia SEG 8286　　　SHINDIG WITH THE SHADOWS 15
64　Columbia SEG 8321　　　THOSE BRILLIANT SHADOWS 15
64　Columbia SEG 8342　　　DANCE WITH THE SHADOWS 15
64　Columbia SEG 8362　　　RHYTHM AND GREENS (mono) 15
64　Columbia ESG 7904　　　RHYTHM AND GREENS (stereo) 20
64　Columbia SEG 8375　　　DANCE WITH THE SHADOWS NO. 2 15

SHADOWS (U.S.)

MINT VALUE £

65	Columbia SEG 8396	THEMES FROM "ALADDIN AND HIS WONDERFUL LAMP"	15
65	Columbia SEG 8408	DANCE WITH THE SHADOWS NO. 3	15
65	Columbia SEG 8445	ALICE IN SUNDERLAND	20
65	Columbia SEG 8459	THE SOUND OF THE SHADOWS	25
66	Columbia SEG 8473	THE SOUND OF THE SHADOWS NO. 2	25
66	Columbia SEG 8494	THE SOUND OF THE SHADOWS NO. 3	25
66	Columbia SEG 8500	THOSE TALENTED SHADOWS	22
66	Columbia SEG 8510	THUNDERBIRDS ARE GO! (with Cliff Richard)	50
67	Columbia SEG 8528	THE SHADOWS ON STAGE AND SCREEN	40

ALBUMS

61	Columbia 33SX 1374	THE SHADOWS (mono)	20
61	Columbia SCX 3414	THE SHADOWS (stereo)	30
62	Columbia 33SX 1458	OUT OF THE SHADOWS (mono)	15
62	Columbia SCX 3449	OUT OF THE SHADOWS (stereo)	20
63	Columbia 33SX 1522	GREATEST HITS (stereo SCX 1522)	15
64	Columbia 33SX 1619	DANCE WITH THE SHADOWS (mono)	15
64	Columbia SCX 3511	DANCE WITH THE SHADOWS (stereo)	22
65	Columbia 33SX 1736	THE SOUND OF THE SHADOWS (mono)	15
65	Columbia SCX 3554	THE SOUND OF THE SHADOWS (stereo)	20
65	Columbia 33SX 1791	MORE HITS! (stereo SCX 3578)	15
66	Columbia 33SX/SCX 6041	SHADOW MUSIC	15
67	Columbia S(C)X 6148	JIGSAW	15
67	Columbia S(C)X 6199	FROM HANK, BRUCE, BRIAN AND JOHN	15
68	Columbia SX 6282	ESTABLISHED 1958 (half by Cliff Richard, mono)	15
70	Columbia SCX 6420	SHADES OF ROCK	15
77	EMI EMTV 3	TWENTY GOLDEN GREATS (mispressing, side 2 plays Pink Floyd's "Animals")	30

(see also Cliff Richard, Drifters, Five Chesternuts, Hank Marvin, Marvin Welch & Farrar, Bruce Welch, John Henry Rostill, Brian Bennett, Jet Harris, Tony Meehan, Vipers Skiffle Group, Marty Wilde, Krew Kats, Interns, Strangers, Wasp, MacArthur Park, Thunder Company, Alan Hawkshaw)

SHADOWS (U.S.)

58	HMV POP 563	Jungle Fever/Under Stars Of Love	100
58	HMV POP 563	Jungle Fever/Under Stars Of Love (78)	50

SHADOWS OF KNIGHT

66	Atlantic AT 4085	Gloria/Dark Side	40
66	Atlantic 584 021	Oh Yeah/Light Bulb Blues	35
66	Atlantic 584 045	Bad Little Woman/Gospel Zone	30
67	Atlantic 584 136	Someone Like Me/Three For Love	35
69	Buddah 201 024	Shake/From Way Out To Way Under	30
79	Radar RAD 11	GLORIA (LP)	15
98	Sundazed LP 5024	GLORIA (LP, 180gm vinyl, insert)	18

SHADROCKS

67	Island WI 3061	Go Go Special/Count Down	12
68	Jay Boy BOY 2	There Is/Jigsaw	6

DOREEN SHAFFER

69	Unity UN 536	No Matter What/Walk Through This World	10
69	Unity UN 538	How Much Is That Doggy In The Window/As Long As He Needs Me	10
70	Pama SECO 31	FIRST LADY OF REGGAE (LP)	80

(see also Bob Marley/Wailers, Lloyd Clarke, Doreen & Jackie)

JOHN SHAFT

72	Downtown DT 488	Forever Music/BLOSSOM JOHNSON: The Boy I Love	6

BOBBY SHAFTO

66	Parlophone R 5403	Lonely Is As Lonely Does/The Same Old Room	15

SHAFTSBURY

80	O.K. OKA 001	THE LULL BEFORE THE STORM (LP, with insert)	15

SHAG

95	No Label or cat no	THE SHAG EP (stamped white labels, 250 only)	20

SHAG 'N' SKOOB

92	WINTER 3	SKOOBY CHEWNZ VOL. 1 EP (12")	40

SHAG NASTY

79	Shag Nasty SN 1	No Bullshit Just Rock 'n' Roll/Looking For A Love? (p/s)	40

SHAGRAT

90	Shagrat ORC 001	Amanda/Peppermint Flickstick (p/s, 500 only, autographed)	10
90	Shagrat ORC 001	Amanda/Peppermint Flickstick (p/s, 500 only, some autographed)	6

NADINE SHAH

13	Apollo AMB1314LP	LOVE YOUR MUM AND DAD (LP, with CD)	20
15	Apollo AMB1506LP	FAST FOOD (LP, red vinyl)	18

SHAKA FATMAN

80	Live And Love LAP 12	CONFRONTATION DUB - SHAKA (WARRIOR) VS. FATMAN (KILLER) (LP)	30

SHAKANE

70	UPC 110	Rhona/Find The Lady	15
72	Young Blood Int. YB 1004	Love Machine/Mr Jackson	6
76	United Artists UP 36087	Jenny/Gang Man	12

SHAKE (1)

79	Sire SIR 4016	Culture Shock/Dream On	10
79	Sire SIR 4016-10	Culture Shock/Glass House/Dream On/(But) Not Mine (10", p/s)	12

(see also Rezillos, TV 21)

SHAKE (2)

93	KMS UK8	CLUB SCAMS EP (12")	20

SHAKE APPEAL

87	Notown NO 2	Gimme Fever/Mexico City SOS (p/s)	10
88	Jericho JR 001	Amphetamine/ANYWAYS: Well Of Hurt (no p/s)	15

SHAKEDOWN

MINT VALUE £

SHAKEDOWN
78   Kricon KR0001 — F.B.I./Wish You Could See Me Now ... 7

SHAKEOUTS
65   Columbia DB 7613 — Every Little Once In A While/Well Who's That ... 60

SHAKER
94   Ugly Bird UBR 002 — Mooncat (Spear Vocal Mix)/Mooncat (Boneseys Hand) (12") ... 20

SHAKERS (U.K.)
63   Polydor NH 52158 — Money/Memphis Tennessee ... 25
63   Polydor NH 52213 — Hippy Hippy Shake/Dr. Feelgood ... 25
63   Polydor NH 66991 — Hippy Hippy Shake/Dr. Feelgood ... 25
63   Polydor NH 52258 — Money/Hippy Hippy Shake ... 25
63   Polydor NH 52272 — Whole Lotta Lovin'/I Can Tell ... 25
63   Polydor 237 139 — LET'S DO THE SLOP, TWIST, MADISON, HULLY GULLY WITH THE SHAKERS (LP) ... 70

(see also Kingsize Taylor & Dominoes)

SHAKERS (U.S.)
73   Probe PRO 582 — One Wonderful Moment/Love, Love, Love ... 7

SHAKES
83   S 83 CUS 1982 — Funeral Rites/I Kill God ... 30

CHRIS SHAKESPEARE GLOBE SHOW
69   Page One POF 113 — Ob-La-Di, Ob-La-Da/Tin Soldier ... 25

(see also Globe Show)

JOHN SHAKESPEARE
69   Decca F 12896 — Number One Theme/Fade Out (with p/s) ... 30
69   Decca F 12896 — Number One Theme/Fade Out ... 10

SHAKESPEARES
68   RCA Victor RCA 1695 — Something To Believe In/Burning My Fingers ... 70

(see also Fynn McCool)

SHAKE THE TREE
88   Brickworks — SHAKE THE TREE (LP) ... 30

SHAKEY VICK
69   Pye NPL 18276 — LITTLE WOMAN, YOU'RE SO SWEET (LP mono) ... 80
69   Pye NSPL 18276 — LITTLE WOMAN, YOU'RE SO SWEET (LP stereo, in mono sleeve with 'STEREO NSPL' sticker on rear) ... 50

SAM SHAM
69   Blue Cat BS 157 — Drumbago's Dead/SPARTERS: Song Of The Year ... 100

SHAM 69
77   Step Forward SF 4 — I Don't Wanna/Ulster/Red London (black & white photo p/s) ... 40
77   Step Forward SF 412 — I Don't Wanna/Ulster/Red London (12", black & white photo p/s) ... 20
77   Polydor (no cat. no.) — Song Of The Streets/Fanx (1-sided concert freebie, red brick-wall label; white label copies are counterfeits) ... 35
78   Polydor 2058 966 — Borstal Breakout/Hey Little Rich Boy (p/s, most with 2058 966, cat no correction sticker on rear) ... 20
78   Polydor 2059 023 — Angels With Dirty Faces/The Cockney Kids Are Innocent (p/s) ... 8
78   Polydor 2059 050 — If The Kids Are United/Sunday Morning Nightmare (p/s) ... 6
78   70s — What Have We Got? (1-sided gig only 45, 500 only) ... 30
79   Step Forward SF 412 — I Don't Wanna/Red London/Ulster (12" reissue, yellow p/s) ... 15
79   — Hersham Boys/Day Tripper (Original "Pye Studios" acetate for 'Hersham' single, release withdrawn as unable to clear copyright) ... 250
87   Legacy LGY 70 — Ban The Gun/Ban The Gun ... 15
78   Polydor 2383491 — TELL US THE TRUTH (LP) ... 25
78   Polydor POLD 5010 — THAT'S LIFE (LP, gatefold, with poster) ... 20
78   Polydor POLD 5010 — THAT'S LIFE (LP, gatefold, without poster) ... 15
79   Polydor POLD 5025 — THE ADVENTURES OF THE HERSHAM BOYS (LP, with 12" EP [2812 045], stickered sleeve) ... 20
79   Polydor POLD 5025 — THE ADVENTURES OF THE HERSHAM BOYS (LP, gatefold) ... 15
80   Polydor POLD 5033 — THE GAME (LP) ... 15
80   Polydor 2383 596 — THE FIRST, THE BEST AND THE LAST (LP, with live EP [RIOT 1/2816 028]) ... 18
86   Receiver RRLP 104 — ANGELS WITH DIRTY FACES - THE BEST OF SHAM 69 (LP) ... 20
87   Link LINK LP 04 — LIVE AND LOUD!! (LP, blue or black labels) ... 15
88   Link LINK LP 025 — LIVE AND LOUD!! VOLUME 2 (LP) ... 15
91   Limited Edition LTD EDN LP 5 — RARE AND UNRELEASED (LP) ... 15

(see also Jimmy Edwards, Framed, Wanderers)

SHAMBLES
75   RCA RCA 2533 — Hello Baby/Held Me Spellbound ... 50

(see also Mandrake Paddle Steramers, Prowler)

SHAME (1)
67   MGM MGM 1349 — Don't Go 'Way Little Girl/Dreams Don't Bother Me (with picture insert) ... 150
67   MGM MGM 1349 — Don't Go 'Way Little Girl/Dreams Don't Bother Me (without picture insert) ... 90

(see also Shy Limbs, King Crimson, Gods, Emerson Lake & Palmer)

SHAME (2)
16   Fnord FNORDSCR23 — The Lick/Gold Hole (die-cut sleeve) ... 20
17   Fnord FNORDSCR13INS — Tasteless/Visa Vulture (die-cut sleeve) ... 20
17   Vinyl Me — Gone Fisting/Donk (p/s) ... 30
18   Dead Oceans DOC 187 — ALL THE HITS (12" EP, p/s) ... 15
20   Dead Oceans (none) — Tinsel Gate - Playable Christmas Card 500 only ... 15
18   Dead Oceans DOC144 — SONGS OF PRAISE (LP) ... 20

SHAMEN
86   One Big Guitar OBG 003T — THEY MAY BE RIGHT ... BUT THEY'RE CERTAINLY WRONG (12" EP) ... 12
95   One Little Indian TPLP 52L — AXIS MUTATIS/ARBOR BONA ARBOR MALA (4-LP) ... 30
96   One Little Indian TPLP 082 — HEMPTON MANOR (3-LP) ... 30

(see also Stretchheads)

SHAMES

MINT VALUE £

SHAMES
66	CBS 202344	Sugar And Spice/Ben Franklin's Almanac	25
66	CBS 202450	I Wanna Meet You/We Could Be Happy	18
67	CBS 2704	Mr Unreliable/Georgia	12
67	CBS 2929	It Could Be We're In Love/I Was Lonely When	22
68	CBS 3820	Greenburg, Glickstein, Charles, David, Smith And Jones/Warm	15

(see also Isaac Guillory)

SHAMPOO
93	Icerink DAV 06	Blisters & Bruises/Paydirt/I Love Little Pussy (p/s, pink vinyl)	20

SHAMROCKS
65	Polydor BM 56503	La La La La La/And I Need You	20

WINSTON SHAN(D)
69	Bullet BU 399	Throw Me Corn/Darling Remember (B-side actually by Pat Edwards)	35
69	Bullet BU 411	Matilda (as Wilston Shan)/HARMONIANS: Come To Me	50
70	Moodisc MU 3505	I'll Run Away/Time Is The Master	60
72	Camel CA 88	Audrey (as Winston Shan)/So Nice (as Winston Shan)	20

TRISTRAM SHANDY
74	Tiffany 6121 505	Saccharine Sandie, Fingers 'N Thumbs/Mr. Blue	6

LISA SHANE
66	Pye 7N 17124	Come And Get Me/Big Wide World	6

SHANE & SHANE GANG
64	Pye 7N 15662	Whistle Stop/Who Wrote That Song	35

TONY SHANE
77	Pollen PBM 012	Bird Without Wings/Loneliest Band In Town (no p/s)	10

VALERIE SHANE
58	Philips PB 833	When The Boys Talk About Girls/Careful, Careful	8
58	Philips PB 879	Meet Me Tonight In Dreamland.One Billion Seven Million Thirty-Three	7
59	Philips PB 929	Make Love To Me/Baisez Moi	7

SHANES
65	Columbia DB 7601	I Don't Want Your Love/New Orleans	70

SHANE SISTERS
60	Ember EMB S 115	My Mommy Told Me/Presents On The Christmas Tree	7

SHANGAANS
65	Columbia DB 7551	Genzene (What Have I Done)/Yeh Girl	15
65	Columbia Studio 2 TWO 109	JUNGLE DRUMS (LP)	25

SHANGO
69	A&M AMS 754	Mama Lion/Ljuba Ljuba	6

SHANGRI-LAS
64	Red Bird RB 10008	Remember (Walking In The Sand)/It's Easier To Cry	10
64	Red Bird RB 10014	Leader Of The Pack/What Is Love?	10
65	Red Bird RB 10018	Give Him A Great Big Kiss/Twist And Shout	15
65	Red Bird RB 10025	Out In The Streets/The Boy	15
65	Red Bird RB 10030	Give Us Your Blessings/Heaven Only Knows	15
65	Red Bird RB 10036	Right Now And Not Later/Train From Kansas City	35
66	Red Bird RB 10043	I Can Never Go Home Anymore/Bulldog	15
66	Red Bird RB 10048	Long Live Our Love/Sophisticated Boom Boom	15
66	Red Bird RB 10053	He Cried/Dressed In Black	15
66	Red Bird RB 10068	Past, Present, And Future/Paradise	20
66	Philips 6051027	Train From Kansas City/Past Present And Future	10
67	Mercury MF 962	The Sweet Sound Of Summer/I'll Never Learn	15
67	Mercury MF 979	Take The Time/Footsteps On The Roof	15
65	Red Bird RB 40 002	THE SHANGRI-LAS (EP)	50
66	Red Bird RB 40 004	I CAN NEVER GO HOME ANYMORE (EP, unreleased)	0
65	Red Bird RB 20 101	THE SHANGRI-LAS - LEADER OF THE PACK (LP)	60
66	Mercury MCL 20096	GOLDEN HITS OF THE SHANGRI-LAS (LP)	20

BUD SHANK
56	Vogue V 2385	Shank's Pranks/Left Bank (with Shorty Rogers Quintet)	7
58	Vogue LAE 12041	THE BUD SHANK QUARTET FEATURING CLAUDE WILLIAMSON (LP)	30
59	Vogue LAE 12248	LATIN CONTRASTS (LP)	20

(see also Shorty Rogers)

ANANDA SHANKAR
69	Reprise RSLP 6398	ANANDA SHANKAR (JUMPING JACK FLASH) (LP)	80
71	Reprise K 44092	ANANDA SHANKAR (LP, reissue)	30

RAVI SHANKAR
72	Apple APPLE 37	Joi Bangla/Oh Bhaugowan/Raga Mishri-Jhinjhoti (p/s)	40
71	Mushroom 300 MR 8	FOUR RAGA MOODS (2-LP)	30
72	United Artists UAG 29379	AT THE WOODSTOCK FESTIVAL (LP, gatefold)	15
73	Apple SAPDO 1002	IN CONCERT - 1972 (2-LP, with Ali Akbar Khan, gatefold sleeve)	90

(see also Ali Akbar Khan, Will Sergeant)

BILL SHANKLY
70s	Technical TECLP 001A	SHANKS ON SOCCER (2-LP)	20

JOHNNY SHANLY
60	Columbia DB 4526	I Wonder/It Happens That Way	6

SHANNON
75	Magnet MAG 38	Come Back And Love Me/She's A High Flyer	10

(See also Marty Wilde)

DEAN SHANNON
60	HMV POP 820	Blinded With Love/Jezebel	25
62	HMV POP 1103	Ubangi Stomp/Blowing Wild	50

Del SHANNON

MINT VALUE £

DEL SHANNON
SINGLES
61	London HLX 9317	Runaway/Jody	6
61	London HLX 9317	Runaway/Jody (mispressed B-side, plays "The Snake" by Maximilian)	30
62	London HLX 9587	Cry Myself To Sleep/I'm Gonna Move On	8
63	London HLX 9761	Two Silhouettes/My Wild One	10
63	London HLU 9800	Sue's Gotta Be Mine/Since She's Gone	10
64	London HLU 9858	That's The Way Love Is/Time Of The Day	12
64	Stateside SS 269	Mary Jane/Stains On My Letter	10
64	Stateside SS 317	Handy Man/Give Her Lots Of Lovin'	10
64	Stateside SS 349	Do You Want To Dance/This Is All I Have To Give	10
64	Stateside SS 368	Keep Searching (We'll Follow The Sun)/Broken Promises	6
65	Stateside SS 395	Stranger In Town/Over You	12
65	Stateside SS 430	Break Up/Why Don't You Tell Him	12
65	Stateside SS 452	Move It On Over/She Still Remembers Tony	15
66	Stateside SS 494	I Can't Believe My Ears/I Wish I Wasn't Me Tonight	15
66	Liberty LIB 55866	The Big Hurt/I Got It Bad	10
66	Liberty LIB 55889	For A Little While/Hey Little Star	10
67	Liberty LIB 55939	She/What Makes You Run	10
67	Liberty LIB 10277	Mind Over Matter/Led Along	10
67	Liberty LBF 15020	Runaway/Show Me	10
68	Liberty LBF 15061	Thinkin' It Over/Runnin' On Back	10
68	Liberty LBF 15079	Gemini/Magical Musical Box	40
69	Stateside SS 8025	Comin' Back To Me/Sweet Mary Lou	10
70	Stateside SS 8040	Sister Isabelle/Colorado Rain	10

EPs
62	London RE-X 1332	RUNAWAY WITH DEL SHANNON	20
63	London RE-X 1346	DEL SHANNON NO. 2	20
63	London RE-X 1383	DEL'S OWN FAVOURITES	20
63	London RE-X 1387	FROM DEL TO YOU	20
67	Liberty LEP 2272	THE NEW DEL SHANNON	40
65	Stateside SE 1029	DEL SHANNON HITS	20

ALBUMS
61	London HA-X 2402	RUNAWAY WITH DEL SHANNON	30
63	London HA-X 8071	HATS OFF TO DEL SHANNON	30
63	London HA-X 8091	LITTLE TOWN FLIRT	30
65	Stateside SL 10115	HANDY MAN	40
65	Stateside SL 10130	DEL SHANNON SINGS HANK WILLIAMS	30
65	Stateside SL 10140	ONE THOUSAND SIX HUNDRED AND SIXTY-ONE SECONDS WITH DEL SHANNON	25
66	Liberty LBY 1320	THIS IS MY BAG (mono)	25
66	Liberty SLBY 1320	THIS IS MY BAG (stereo)	30
66	Liberty LBY 1335	TOTAL COMMITMENT (mono)	25
66	Liberty SLBY 1335	TOTAL COMMITMENT (stereo)	30
68	Liberty LBL/LBS 83114E	THE FURTHER ADVENTURES OF CHARLES WESTOVER	80

(see also Maximilian)

LINDA SHANNON
59	Parlophone R 4603	Goodbye Charlie/If You Only Knew	6

SHAPE
71	RCA RCA 2129	My Friend John/Yes	18

SHAPE OF THE RAIN
71	RCA Neon NE 1001	Woman/Wasting My Time	10
71	RCA Neon NE 7	RILEY, RILEY, WOOD & WAGGETT (LP, gatefold sleeve)	350

SHAPE & SIZES
66	Decca F 12441	A Little Lovin' Somethin'/Rain On My Face	10

SHAPES
79	Sofa SEAT 1/FRR 004	THE SHAPES (WOT'S FOR LUNCH, MUM?) (EP, no p/s, with insert)	20
79	Good Vibrations GOT 13	Blast Off/Airline Disasters (p/s)	15

HELEN SHAPIRO
SINGLES
63	Columbia DB 4966	Queen For Tonight/Daddy Couldn't Get Me One Of Those	7
63	Columbia DB 7130	Look Who It Is/Walking In My Dreams	10
64	Columbia DB 7190	Fever/Ole Father Time	25
64	Columbia DB 7266	Look Over Your Shoulder/You Won't Come Home	10
64	Columbia DB 7340	Shop Around/He Knows How To Love Me	150
64	Columbia DB 7395	I Wish I'd Never Loved You/I Was Only Kidding	10
65	Columbia DB 7517	Tomorrow Is Another Day/It's So Funny I Could Cry	10
65	Columbia DB 7587	Here In Your Arms/Only Once	10
65	Columbia DB 7690	Something Wonderful/Just A Line	10
66	Columbia DB 7810	Forget About The Bad Things/Wait A Little Longer	10
66	Columbia DB 8073	In My Calendar/Empty House	10
67	Columbia DB 8148	Make Me Belong To You/The Way Of The World	10
67	Columbia DB 8256	She Needs Company/Stop And You Will Become Aware	250
67	Columbia DB 8256	She Needs Company/Stop And You Will Become Aware (DJ copy)	300
68	Pye 7N 17600	You'll Get Me Loving You/Silly Boy (I Love You)	12
69	Pye 7N 17714	Today Has Been Cancelled/Face The Music	12
69	Pye 7N 17785	You've Guessed/Take Me For A While	20
70	Pye 7N 17893	Take Down A Note Miss Smith/Couldn't You See	10
70	Pye 7N 17975	Waiting On The Shores Of Nowhere/A Glass Of Wine	10

SHAPIROS

MINT VALUE £

EPs
61	Columbia ESG 7872	HELEN (stereo, 'smiling' or 'cross-armed' sleeve)	15
62	Columbia ESG 7880	A TEENAGER SINGS THE BLUES (stereo)	10

ALBUMS
62	Columbia SCX 3438	TOPS' WITH ME (stereo)	20
63	Columbia 33SX 1494	HELEN'S SIXTEEN (mono)	20
63	Columbia SCX 3470	HELEN'S SIXTEEN (stereo)	35
63	Columbia 33SX 1561	HELEN IN NASHVILLE	20
64	Columbia 33SX 1661	HELEN HITS OUT (mono)	20
64	Columbia SCX 3533	HELEN HITS OUT (stereo SCX 3533)	35

(see also Ella Stone & Moss)

SHAPIROS
79	Now Records N 702	Waitress/Isolde (no p/s, 1000 only)	20

SHARADES
64	Decca F 11811	Dumb Head/Boy Trouble	150

(see also Ladybirds, Breakaways)

BILLY SHA RAE
71	Action ACT 4602	Do It/Crying Clown	15

SHARK TABOO
82	Risque SRTS 82 CUS 1374	Crossfire/Dream Crumble	20

SHARKS (1)
68	RCA RCA 1776	Goodbye Lorene/Funkology	20

(see also Marcisa & Jeff, Roy Richards)

RALPH SHARON
53	Decca LF 1138	AUTUMN LEAVES (10" LP)	20
53	Lyragon AF 1	COCKTAIL TIME (10" LP)	15

SHARON AND MUSARRAT
81	Multitone MUT 1003	CHAL DISCO CHAL (LP)	20

SHARON TATE EXPERIENCE
13	Rise Above RISE7/175FREE	Christmas Killer/ADMIRAL SIR CLOUDESLEY SHOVEL: Blow Up The Xmas Tree 300 only: 100 white vinyl, 100 red vinyl and 100 green vinyl	80

(see also Uncle Acid and the Deadbeats)

BOBBY SHARP & OTHERS
65	Stateside SS 404	Blues For Mr. Charlie (Parts 1 & 2) (with Paul Sindap, Joe Lee Wilson & Little Butler)	20

DEE DEE SHARP
62	Columbia DB 4818	Mashed Potato Time/Set My Heart At Ease	25
62	Columbia DB 4874	Gravy (For My Mashed Potatoes)/Baby Cakes	25
62	Cameo Parkway C 230	Ride/Night	40
63	Cameo Parkway C 244	Do The Bird/Lover Boy	25
63	Cameo Parkway C 260	Rock Me In The Cradle Of Love/You'll Never Be Mine	20
63	Cameo Parkway C 274	Wild/Why Doncha Ask Me	20
65	Cameo Parkway C 375	I Really Love You/Standing In The Need Of Love	80
65	Cameo Parkway C 375	I Really Love You/Standing In The Need Of Love (DJ copy)	125
65	Cameo Parkway C 382	It's A Funny Situation/There Ain't Nothing I Wouldn't Do (demo-only)	150
66	Atlantic 584 056	My Best Friend's Man/Bye Bye Baby	20
69	Action ACT 4522	What Kind Of Lady/You're Gonna Miss Me	80
79	London HA-U 8514	CAMEO PARKWAY SESSIONS (LP)	25

(see also Chubby Checker & Dee Dee Sharp)

STEVE SHARP & THE CLEANCUTS
80	Happy Face MM 122	We Are The Mods/He Wants To Be A Mod	125

(see also Rowdies)

BERNARD SHARPE
66	Parlophone R 5519	Lost In Space/Jorrocks	10
67	Parlophone R 5611	The Other Side Of The Sky/Where Do We Go	15

RAY SHARPE
59	London HLW 8932	Linda Lu/Red Sails In The Sunset (triangular centre)	50
59	London HLW 8932	Linda Lu/Red Sails In The Sunset (round centre)	40
59	London HLW 8932	Linda Lu/Red Sails In The Sunset (78)	30
63	United Artists UP 1032	Hey Little Girl/Day You Left Me	15

ROCKY SHARPE & THE REPLAYS
82	Chiswick DICE 9	Heart/Mary (Won't You Marry Me) (withdrawn, approx. 100 only)	10

SHARPE & NUMAN
85	Polydor PODJ 722	Change Your Mind (p/s, 1-sided 7" DJ promo)	10
89	Polydor POPB 43	I'm On Automatic/No More Lies (New Version) (stickered poster sleeve)	6

(see also Gary Numan)

SHARPEES
66	Stateside SS 495	Tired Of Being Lonely/Just To Please You	75
66	Stateside SS 495	Tired Of Being Lonely/Just To Please You (DJ copy)	150
73	President PT 389	Do The 45/Make Up Your Mind	15
73	President PT 399	Tired Of Being Lonely/Just To Please You (reissue)	10

SHARPS
57	Vogue V 9086	Lock My Heart/Love Is Here To Stay	500
57	Vogue V 9086	Lock My Heart/Love Is Here To Stay (78)	100
58	Vogue V 9096	Shufflin'/What Will I Gain	500
58	Vogue V 9096	Shufflin'/What Will I Gain (78)	100

(see also Thurston Harris)

S-HATERS
81	Outer Himalayan OHR 02	Death Of A Vampire/Research (p/s)	30
82	Outer Himalayan OHR 005	STORIES AS COLD AS THE IRISH SEA (7" EP)	15

SHATTERED DOLLS

MINT VALUE £

SHATTERED DOLLS
80 Rox ROX 1 Lipstick Killer/Talk To Me/Valley Of The Dolls 1 & 2 20

SHAUN
78 Ice GUY19 Freedom/Hastings 8

MIKE SHAUN
63 Decca F 11733 So Lonely/Let's Fall In Love 15

ADRIAN SHAW
96 Woronzow W0027 TEA FOR THE HYDRA (LP, 299 copies only, in hand-finished sleeves) 15

(see also Hawkwind, Bevis Frond)

ALAN LEE SHAW
74 Alaska ALA 15 She Moans/Bolweevil 120

MARLENA SHAW
67 Chess CRS 8054 Mercy Mercy Mercy/Go Away Little Boy 12
76 United Artists UP 36125 It's Better Than Walking Out/Be For Real 8
76 Blue Note 36163 Love Has Gone Away/No Hiding Place 7
04 Jazzman JM 032 California Soul/Wade In The Water (1st pressing, black/light blue jukebox label) 10
76 Blue Note UAG 20006 JUST A MATTER OF TIME (LP) 15
77 CBS S CBS 81844 SWEET BEGINNINGS (LP) 15
79 CBS S CBS 83216 TAKE A BITE (LP) 15
00 Soul Brother LP SBPJ 2 ANTHOLOGY (2-LP) 20

NINA SHAW
68 CBS 3239 Woven In My Soul/Love So Fine (DJ copy) 150
68 CBS 3239 Woven In My Soul/Love So Fine 100
68 CBS 3556 From Now Till Then/Window Of My Mind 12
69 CBS 4227 One Fine Day/Somewhere In The World 12
84 Red Bus RBUS 90 Look At Me Now/Turkish Delight 8

RICKY SHAW
62 London HLU 9606 No Love But Your Love/Be Still, Be Still, My Own 8

SANDIE SHAW
SINGLES
64 Pye 7N 15671 As Long As You're Happy Baby/Ya-Ya-Da-Da 40
65 Pye 7N 15783 I'll Stop At Nothing/You Can't Blame Him 6
66 Pye 7N 17163 Run/Long Walk Home 8
66 Pye 7N 17212 Think Sometimes About Me/Hide All Emotion 10
67 Pye 7N 17239 I Don't Need Anything/Keep In Touch 10
67 Pye 7N 17346 Tonight In Tokyo/You've Been Seeing Her Again 6
68 Pye 7N 17504 Don't Run Away/Stop 10
68 Pye 7N 17564 Show Me/One More Lie 10
68 Pye 7N 17587 Together/Turn On The Sunshine 10
68 Pye 7N 17611 Those Were The Days/Make It Go 8
69 Pye 7N 17726 Think It All Over/Send Me A Letter 12
70 Pye 7N 17954 Wight Is Wight/That's The Way He's Made 10
70 Pye 7N 45040 Rose Garden/Maybe I'm Amazed 10
84 Rough Trade RT 130 Hand In Glove/I Don't Owe You Anything (white label test pressing) 100
84 Rough Trade RTT 130 Hand In Glove/I Don't Owe You Anything/Jeanne (12", p/s, with The Smiths) 10

EPs
64 Pye NEP 24208 (THERE'S) ALWAYS SOMETHING THERE TO REMIND ME 15
65 Pye NEP 24220 LONG LIVE LOVE 15
65 Pye NEP 24232 TALK ABOUT LOVE 15
65 Pye NEP 24234 SANDIE 15
66 Pye NEP 24236 MESSAGE UNDERSTOOD 15
66 Pye NEP 24247 TOMORROW 20
66 Pye NEP 24254 NOTHING COMES EASY 20
66 Pye NEP 24264 RUN WITH SANDIE SHAW 25
67 Pye NEP 24271 SANDIE SHAW IN FRENCH 25
67 Pye NEP 24273 SANDIE SHAW IN ITALIAN 25
67 Pye NEP 24281 TELL THE BOYS 25

ALBUMS
65 Pye NPL 18110 SANDIE 15
65 Pye NPL 18121 ME 15
69 Pye N(S)PL 18323 REVIEWING THE SITUATION 50

THOMAS SHAW
72 Xtra XTRA 1132 THOMAS SHAW (LP) 15

TIMMY SHAW & STERNPHONES
64 Pye International 7N 25239 Gonna Send You Back To Georgia/I'm A Lonely Guy 30

TREVOR SHAW
81 CMS PR 26 WHEELS IN MOTION (LP) 20

SHAZAM
83 ADSR 001 Let's Get Together/Memories 150

GEORGE SHEARING (QUINTET)
61 Capitol CL 15269 Baubles, Bangles And Beads/Cocktails For Two 6

(see also Peggy Lee)

DEL AARON SHEARS
79 Shearsongs SRTS/79/CUS 287 Keep A Little Marc In Your Heart/Beautiful Angel/Oh What A Lady (no sleeve) 8

GARY SHEARSTON
74 Charisma CB241 Without A Song/Aborigini 6

HENRY SHED
72 Stateside SS 2198 Bend Me Shape Me/Save The Last Dance For Me 6

SHED SEVEN

MINT VALUE £

SHED SEVEN
94	Polydor 523615-1	CHANGE GIVER (LP)	70
96	Polydor 531039-1	A MAXIMUM HIGH (LP, with booklet)	80
98	Polydor 557 359-1	LET IT RIDE (LP)	80

BOBBY SHEEN
66	Capitol CL 15455	Dr. Love/Sweet, Sweet Love	250
66	Capitol CL 15455	Dr. Love/Sweet, Sweet Love (DJ copies)	300
72	Capitol CL 15713	Dr. Love/Sweet, Sweet Love (reissue)	20
03	Atco 67855	Something New To Do/BEN E KING: I Can't Break The News To Myself	15

(see also Bob B. Soxx & Blue Jeans)

SHEEP (U.K.)
73	Myrrh MYR 1000	SHEEP (LP, with insert)	20

(see also Lonesome Stone)

SHEEP (U.S.)
66	Stateside SS 493	Hide And Seek/Twelve Months Later	30
69	Stateside SS 2147	Hide And Seek/HAWKS: The Grissle	12

SHEEPHOUSE
71	Decca 13229	Juicy Lucy/Part 2	100

SHEEPS HEAD BAY
71	Parlophone R5897	My Name Is In The Wind/The River Song	8

IREEN SHEER
74	Polydor 2041 533	Bye Bye I Love You/Roseberry Avenue	6
78	EMI 2796	Fire/Feuer ('Eurovision' p/s)	10

SHEER KHAN
84	SRT 4KS 140	Last Generation/Lady's Dance (p/s)	70
85	Mill	QUIET ENOUGH FOR LOVE (LP)	30

SHEFFIELDS
64	Pye 7N 15600	It Must Be Love/Say Girl	50
64	Pye 7N 15627	I Got My Mojo Working/Hey Hey Lover Boy	70
65	Pye 7N 15767	Bag's Groove (Skat Walking)/Plenty Of Love	75

SHEIKS (PORTUGAL)
66	Parlophone R 5500	Missing You/Tell Me Bird	15

SHEIKS (U.S.)
59	London HLW 9012	Très Chic/Little French Doll	10

SHEILA & JENNY
64	Ember EMB S 3202	When The Boy's Happy/Please Don't Break Her Heart (in p/s)	10
64	Ember EMB S 3202	When The Boy's Happy/Please Don't Break Her Heart	6

SHELBY
74	Santa Ponsa PNS 21	Dance With The Guitar Man/Jump Into The Fire	6
75	Route RT 02	Motorbike Girl/Cirrus	8

ALLEN SHELDON
70	Plexium PXM 14	Mirror Of My Mind/Old Windmill Tree	50

DOUG SHELDON
61	Decca F 11368	The Book Of Love/Play Me The Blues	10
61	Decca F 11398	Runaround Sue/Come With Me	10
61	Decca F 11416	Your Ma Said You Cried In Your Sleep/You're Only Fooling Yourself	10
62	Decca F 11433	My Kingdom For A Girl/You Never Had It So Good	10
62	Decca F 11463	A Big Big Baby/If You'd Be Mine	10
62	Decca F 11514	Lollipops And Roses/One Way To Say Goodbye	10
62	Decca F 11529	Live Now Pay Later/Me	15
63	Decca F 11564	I Saw Linda Yesterday/My Billy	8
63	Decca F 11654	Let's Make A Habit Of This/I Was Alone	10
63	Decca F 11790	Mickey's Monkey/Falling In Love With Love	10
65	Sue WI 332	Take It Like A Man/Lonely Boy	40
65	Pye 7N 17011	It's Because Of You/How Can I Tell Her?	7
63	Decca DFE 8527	HERE I STAND (EP)	50

SANDI SHELDON
76	Epic EPC 4186	You're Gonna Make Me Love You/Baby You're Mine	30
11	Outta Site OSV 031	You're Gonna Make Me Love You/Baby You're Mine (reissue)	8

SHELL
66	Columbia DB 8082	Goodbye Little Girl/Little Bit Of Lovin'	15

SHELLEY
64	Pye 7N 15711	I Will Be Wishing/Why Won't You Say (That You Love Me)	15
65	Pye 7N 15773	Stairway To A Star/I Heard A Whisper	10
65	Pye 7N 15913	Where Has Your Smile Gone/Paradise	10

LIZ SHELLEY
65	Brunswick 05940	Make Me Your Baby/You Made Me Hurt	10
66	Brunswick 05953	No More Love/I Can't Find You	10

PETE SHELLEY
82	Lyntone 10952/53	Qu'est-Ce Que C'est, Qu'est Que Ça (Dub)/ANIMAL MAGNET: More (hard vinyl test pressing, numbered, with info sheet/letter)	15
82	Lyntone 10952/53	Qu'est-Ce Que C'est, Qu'est Que Ça (Dub)/ANIMAL MAGNET: More (hard vinyl test pressing, numbered)	12
80	Groovy STP 2	SKY YEN (mini-LP)	18

(see also Buzzcocks, Free Agents, Tiller Boys)

SHELLS
61	London HLU 9288	Baby, Oh Baby/Angel Eyes	30
62	London HLU 9644	It's A Happy Holiday/Deep In My Heart	35

SHELLY
95	Sarah SARAH 98	Reproduction Is Pollution/Prejudice/Here (p/s)	12

ALAN SHELLY & MANU DIBANGO'S BROTHERS
69	Philips BF 1709	Lady Black Wife/Give Me Time	12

ANNE SHELTON
53	HMV 7M 164	Answer Me/The Bridge Of Sighs	10
54	HMV 7M 186	The Book/Why Does It Have To Be Me	10
54	HMV 7M 240	Goodnight, Well It's Time To Go/If I Give My Heart To You	10
54	HMV 7M 279	My Gypsy Heart/Teach Me Tonight	10
57	Philips JK 1012	Absent Friends/Seven Ages Of Man (Jukebox issue)	10
56	Decca DFE 6321	FOUR STANDARDS (EP)	10
52	Decca LF 1023	FAVOURITES (10" LP)	20

JO SHELTON
59	Top Rank JAR 124	Tread Softly (You're Stepping On My Heart)/More More More Romancing	6
59	Top Rank JAR 245	If There Are Stars In My Eyes/I Need Your Arms Around Me	6

ROSCOE SHELTON
65	Sue WI 354	Strain On My Heart/Question (A- & B-side labels reversed)	40

DEANNA SHENDEREY
65	Decca F 12090	Comin' Home Baby/I've Got That Feeling	100

SHENLEY (DUFFAS) & ANNETTE
61	Blue Beat BB 72	Million Dollar Baby/The First Time I Met You	20

SHENLEY (DUFFAS) & HYACINTH (BROWN)
66	Rio R 80	The World Is On A Wheel/ROY & CORNELL: Salvation	20

(see also Baba Brooks)

SHENLEY (DUFFAS) & (LITTLE) LUNAN
65	Rio R 52	Something On Your Mind/The Rain Came Tumbling Down	15

(see also Shenley Duffas)

SHEP & LIMELITES
61	Pye International 7N 25090	Daddy's Home/This I Know	60
61	Pye International 7N 25112	Ready For Your Love/You'll Be Sorry	100

DAVE SHEPHERD QUINTET
69	77 LEU 12/35	SHEPHERD'S DELIGHT (LP)	20

PAULINE SHEPHERD
57	Columbia DB 4010	Love Me To Pieces/Just Between You And Me	12

SHEPHERD BOYS (& GIRLS)
56	Columbia SCM 5282	Little Girls And Little Boys/Teenage Love (as Shepherd Boys & Girls)	8
56	Columbia DB 3816	Summer Sweetheart/Song For A Summer Night	6

ARCHIE SHEPP
66	HMV CLP/CSD 3524	FOUR FOR TRANE (LP)	35
66	HMV CLP/CSD 3561	ON THIS NIGHT (LP)	30
67	HMV CLP/CSD 3600	LIVE IN SAN FRANCISCO (LP)	35
67	Polydor 623 235	ARCHIE SHEPP AND THE NEW YORK CONTEMPORARY FIVE (LP)	30
67	Fontana 681 014 ZL	RUFUS (LP, with John Tchicai)	35
68	Impulse MIPL/SIPL 508	MAMA TOO TIGHT (LP)	35
68	Polydor 623 267	NEW YORK CONTEMPORARY FIVE VOL. 2 (LP)	25
69	Impulse MILP/SIPL 512	THE MAGIC OF JU-JU (LP)	30
69	Impulse MIPL/SIPL 516	THE WAY AHEAD (LP)	40

(see also John Coltrane)

SHEPPARDS
71	Jay Boy BOY 30	How Do You Like It/Stubborn Heart	40

SHEPHERD/SHEPPARD SISTERS
57	HMV POP 411	Alone (Why Must I Be Alone)/Congratulations To Someone	10
58	Mercury 7MT 196	Gettin' Ready For Freddy/Best Thing There Is (Is Love)(Sheppard Sisters)	15
58	Mercury 7MT 218	Eating Pizza/A Boy And A Girl (as Sheppard Sisters)	10
58	Mercury AMT 1005	Dancing Baby/Is It A Crime?	10
63	London HLK 9681	Don't Mention My Name/What Makes Little Girls Cry	20
63	London HLK 9758	Talk Is Cheap/Greatest Lover	15

SHEPPERTON FLAMES
69	Deram DM 257	Take Me For What I Am/Goodbye	20

(see also Mike Berry)

SHERE KHAN
69	Tepee TPR 1007	Little Louise/No Reason	200
71	UPC 110	Rhone/Find The Lady	60

SHERIDAN
70	Gemini GMS 001	Follow Me Follow/When Love Breaks Your Heart	15

(see also Sheridan-Price, Mike Sheridan & Night Riders, Mike Sheridan's Lot)

DANI SHERIDAN
66	Planet PLF 106	Guess I'm Dumb/Songs Of Love	50

LEE SHERIDAN
73	Deram DM 373	Sweet Tasting Candy Sugar/Big Louis' Gun	8

MIKE SHERIDAN & NIGHT RIDERS
63	Columbia DB 7141	Tell Me What'cha Gonna Do/No Other Guy	30
63	Columbia DB 7183	Please Mr. Postman/In Love	30
64	Columbia DB 7302	What A Sweet Thing That Was/Fabulous	25
65	Columbia DB 7462	Here I Stand/Lonely Weekends	25

(see also Roy Wood, Idle Race, Mike Sheridan's Lot, Sheridan-Price, Sight & Sound)

MIKE SHERIDAN'S LOT
65	Columbia DB 7677	Take My Hand/Make Them Understand	50
66	Columbia DB 7798	Don't Turn Your Back On Me, Babe/Stop, Look, Listen	50

(see also Roy Wood, Idle Race, Mike Sheridan & Night Riders, Sheridan-Price, Sight & Sound)

TONY SHERIDAN & THE BEAT BROTHERS
64	Polydor NH 52315	Jambalaya/Will You Still Love Me Tomorrow (with The Beat Brothers)	12

SHERIDAN-PRICE

MINT VALUE £

	64	Polydor NH 52927	Skinny Minny/You'd Better Move On (with The Beat Brothers) ... 12

(see also Bobby Patrick Big Six, Beat Brothers, Pete Best Four)

SHERIDAN-PRICE
70	Gemini GMS 009	Sometimes I Wonder (as Sheridan & Rick Price)/SHERIDAN: Lightning Never Strikes Twice ... 25
70	Gemini GME 1002	THIS IS TO CERTIFY THAT... (LP, gatefold sleeve) ... 40

(see also Rick Price, Mike Sheridan & Nightriders, Mike Sheridan's Lot, Idle Race, Sight & Sound, Sheridan)

SHERMAN
72	Pye 7N45131	If You Could Read My Mind/Find My Way Back Home ... 30

ALLAN SHERMAN
63	Warner Bros WB 106	Hello Muddah Hello Faddah/Rat Fink ... 6

BIM SHERMAN
77	Hawkeye HE 003	Ever Firm/GUSSIE ALLSTARS: Rigid ... 8
78	Yard International YI 1001	What Sweet You So/U BLACK: Pot A Bubble (12") ... 15
79	Hit Run DD6/7	Down In Jamtown (with Jah Lion)/TEEM ALL STARS: Version (12") ... 40
79	Hit Run HIT DD 11	Love Jah Only (with Jah Buzz)/CRYTUFF ALL STARS : Version (12") ... 40
79	Attack TACK 9	Lightning And Thunder/Why Don't You Come On? (12") ... 25
79	Savannah SUN 12-2	Golden Locks/Tribulation (12") ... 40
83	On-U Sound DP 10	Keep You Dancing (with Dub Syndicate)/Can't Stop Jumping (with Dub Syndicate and Dr. Pablo) (10", p/s) ... 60
77	Tribesman TM 007	LOVE FOREVER (LP) ... 100
84	Century CENTURY 100	CENTURY (LP, with Voluntary) ... 15
84	Century 200 C200	DANGER (LP) ... 30
86	RDL RDL 600	HAUNTING GROUND (LP) ... 20
87	RDL RDL 700	LOVER'S LEAP SHOWCASE (LP) ... 18
88	On U Sound 17	ACROSS THE RED SEA (LP) ... 20
88	RDL RDL 900	GHETTO DUB (LP) ... 25
92	Century CENTURY 900	GHETTO DUB (LP, reissue) ... 20

BOBBY SHERMAN
69	Pye Intl. 7N 25508	La La La (If I Had You)/Time ... 10
71	CBS 57468	Waiting At The Bust Stop/Runaway ... 12

JOE SHERMAN
58	Fontana H 129	Miraculous Music Box/Make Me Laugh ... 6
58	Fontana H 147	Buttermilk/Please Don't Say Goodnight ... 6

BILLY SHERRILL
61	Mercury AMT 1131	Like Making Love/Rules Of The Game ... 8

SHERRYS
62	London HLW 9625	Pop Pop Pop-Pie/Your Hand In Mine ... 20
63	London HL 9686	Let's Stomp Again/Slop Time ... 25
63	London RE 1363	DO THE POPEYE (EP) ... 70

SHERWOOD
86	Sherwood SRT6KL 901	RIDING THE RAINBOW (12" EP) ... 50

ADRIAN SHERWOOD
03	Real World LPRW 110	NEVER TRUST A HIPPY (2-LP) ... 40

BOBBY SHERWOOD
55	Vogue Coral Q 72097	The Kentuckian Song/Far Away Places ... 6

ROBERTA SHERWOOD
56	Brunswick 05572	Lazy River/This Train ... 10
63	Stateside SL 10039	ON STAGE (LP) ... 20

TONY SHERWOOD TRIO
60s	Zodiac ZR 010	Piano Boogie Twist/Tom Dooley ... 15

SHERWOODS (1)
61	Pye International 7N 25097	Nanette/El Scorpion ... 12

SHERWOODS (2)
64	Solar SRP 105	Memories/Some Other Time ... 8

SHE TRINITY
66	Columbia DB 7874	He Fought The Law/The Union Station Blues ... 20
66	Columbia DB 7943	Have I Sinned/Wild Flower ... 10
66	Columbia DB 7959	Wild Flower/The Man Who Took The Valise Off The Floor Of Grand Central Station At Noon ... 7
66	Columbia DB 7992	Yellow Submarine/Promise Me You'll Never Cry ... 20
67	CBS 2819	Across The Street/Over And Over Again ... 8
70	President PT 283	Hair/Climb That Tree ... 40

(see also Shotgun Express, Beryl Marsden, Gilded Cage)

SHEVELLES
63	Oriole CB 1915	Ooh Poo Pa Doo/Like I Love You ... 25

SHEVELLS
64	United Artists UP 1059	I Could Conquer The World/How Would You Like Me To Love You ... 30
65	United Artists UP 1076	Walking On The Edge Of The World/Not So Close ... 20
65	United Artists UP 1081	Watermelon Man/Taking Over Your Life ... 20
66	United Artists UP 1125	Come On Home/I Gotta Travel All Over ... 45
68	Polydor 56239	Big City Lights/Coffee Song ... 15

(see also Mike Stevens & Shevells)

TONY SHEVETON
62	Oriole CB 1705	Lullaby Of Love/I Have A Feeling ... 20
62	Oriole CB 1726	Lonely Heart/Foolish Doubts ... 20
62	Oriole CB 1766	Hey Little Girl/Kissing Date ... 25
63	Oriole CB 1788	Runaround Sue Is Getting Married/I Love The Girl Next Door ... 25
63	Oriole CB 1895	A Million Drums/Dance With Me ... 20
64	Oriole CB 1975	Excuses/Is It Me, Is It You? ... 18

(see also Tony Rich)

SHIDE & ACORN

MINT VALUE £

SHIDE & ACORN
73	Private pressing	UNDER THE TREE (LP)	400
94	Acme AC 8006LP	UNDER THE TREE (LP, reissue, 500 only, numbered)	15

(see also Jeremy Cahill)

SHIELA
71	Nu Beat NB 079	Only Heaven Knows/GRANT & RICHARDS: Freedom Psalm	7

TREVOR SHIELD
69	Harry J TR 664	The Moon Is Playing Tricks On Me/KING CANNON: Soul Special	60
69	Trojan TR 665	Please/JAY BOYS: Splendour Splash	40
72	Ashanti ASH 407	Rough Road/JAY BOYS: Rough The Road	18

(see also Beltones, Trevor (Shield, Joe White with Glenn & Trevor))

SHIELDS
58	London HLD 8706	You Cheated/That's The Way It's Gonna Be	30

KEITH SHIELDS
67	Decca F 12572	Hey Gyp (Dig The Slowness)/Deep Inside Your Mind	70
67	Decca F 12609	The Wonder Of You/Run, Run, Run	30
67	Decca F 12666	So Hard Livin' Without You/Baby Do You Love Me	30

(see also Marty Wilde [& Wildcats])

BRUSH SHIELS (IRELAND)
77	Hawk HASP 401	Love At Love Bleed/Better Than I Expected	8
77	Hawk HASP 419	Fight Your Heart Out/Coming Home	12

ALLAN SHIERS
74	Profle GMOR 003	THE MAN IN ME (LP)	40

SU SHIFRIN
76	EMI 2442	Over The Rainbow/When You Wish Upon A Star/Secrets	6
78	United Artists UP 36438	We Must Believe In Magic/All I Wanna Do In Life	6

SUSAN SHIFRIN
71	Decca F13145	To Love/25 Miles	30

SAHIB SHIHAB QUARTET
70	Youngblood SSYB 12	SEEDS (LP)	100

SHILLELAGH SISTERS
84	CBS A 4217	Give Me My Freedom/Teasin' Cheatin' Man (p/s)	8
84	CBS A 4684	Passion Fruit/These Boots Are Made For Walkin' (p/s)	15
84	CBS TA 4684	Passion Fruit/These Boots Are Made For Walkin'/Shout (12", p/s)	30
84	TA 4217	Give Me My Freedom (Club Mix)/Teasin' Cheatin' Man (12", p/s)	10

SHILLINGFORD MILL
71	Mam 28	Frightened/I Want To Know	12
71	Mam MAM 15	It's A Thing Called Love/Walking Along	6

SHINDIGS
65	Parlophone R 5316	One Little Letter/What You Gonna Do	35
65	Parlophone R 5377	A Little While Back/Why Say Goodbye	35

SHINDOGS
67	Fontana TF 790	Who Do You Think You Are/Yes, I'm Going Home	18

(see also Delaney & Bonnie, James Burton)

SHINE
74	Fontana 6007041	Candy Girl/I Wonder If Anything	10

JOHNNY SHINES
69	Blue Horizon (S) 7-63211	LAST NIGHT'S DREAM (LP, with Otis Spann, mono or stereo)	90
74	Xtra XTRA 1142	COUNTRY BLUES (LP)	25

DON SHINN (& THE SOUL AGENTS)
66	Polydor BM 56075	A Minor Explosion/Pits Of Darkness (with The Soul Agents)	70
69	Columbia S(C)X 6319	TEMPLES WITH PROPHETS (LP)	125
69	Columbia SCX 6355	DEPARTURES (LP)	150

(see also The Soul Agents)

SHINS
07	Sub Pop	Sea Legs/Strange Powers (p/s)	18

SHINY TWO SHINY
83	Red Flame RFB 29	Waiting For Us/Ritual Hate (p/s)	8

SHIP
72	Elektra K 42122	THE SHIP - A CONTEMPORARY FOLK JOURNEY (LP, gatefold sleeve)	35

SHIRALEE
67	Fontana TF 855	I'll Stay By Your Side/Penny Wren	20

SHIRELLES
58	Brunswick 05746	I Met Him On A Sunday/I Want You To Be My Boyfriend	70
58	Brunswick 05746	I Met Him On A Sunday/I Want You To Be My Boyfriend (78)	30
60	London HL 9233	Tonight's The Night/The Dance Is Over	20
60	Top Rank JAR 540	Will You Love Me Tomorrow/Boys	8
61	Top Rank JAR 549	Dedicated To The One I Love/Look-A-Here Baby	18
61	Top Rank JAR 567	Mama Said/Blue Holiday	15
61	Top Rank JAR 578	What A Sweet Thing That Was/A Thing Of The Past	12
61	Top Rank JAR 590	Big John/Twenty One	12
62	Top Rank JAR 601	Baby It's You/The Things I Want To Hear	20
62	HMV POP 1019	Soldier Boy/Love Is A Swingin' Thing	12
62	Stateside SS 119	Welcome Home Baby/Mama Here Comes The Bride	15
62	Stateside SS 152	Stop The Music/It's Love That Really Counts	18
63	Stateside SS 152	Everybody Loves A Lover/I Don't Think So	12
63	Stateside SS 181	Foolish Little Girl/Not For All The Money In The World	15
63	Stateside SS 213	Don't Say Goodnight And Mean Goodbye/I Didn't Mean To Hurt You	15
63	Stateside SS 232	What Does A Girl Do/Don't Let It Happen To Us	15
63	Pye International 7N 25229	It's A Mad, Mad, Mad, Mad World/31 Flavours	20

SHIRLEY

MINT VALUE £

Year	Label & Cat#	Title	Value
64	Pye International 7N 25233	Tonight You're Gonna Fall In Love With Me/20th Century Rock And Roll	20
64	Pye International 7N 25240	Sha La La/His Lips Get In The Way	15
64	Pye International 7N 25279	Maybe Tonight/Lost Love	15
65	Pye International 7N 25288	Are You Still My Baby/I Saw A Tear	12
66	Pye International 7N 25386	Shades Of Blue/When The Boys Talk About The Girls	12
67	Pye International 7N 25425	Too Much Of A Good Thing/Bright Shiny Colours	20
69	Mercury MF 1093	There's A Storm Going On In My Heart/Call Me (If You Want Me)	22
71	United Artists UP 35192	Take Me/Dedicated To The One I Love	10
75	Pye Disco Demand DDs 115	Last Minute Miracle/March	15
61	Top Rank JKP 3012	THE SHIRELLES SOUND FEATURING "WILL YOU LOVE ME TOMORROW" (EP)	100
61	Top Rank 35-115	THE SHIRELLES SING - TO TRUMPET AND STRINGS (LP)	100
62	Stateside SL 10006	BABY IT'S YOU (LP)	100
63	Stateside SL 10041	THE SHIRELLES' HITS (LP)	50
70	Wand WNS 4	ETERNALLY SOUL (LP, with King Curtis)	25
71	Wand WCS 1001	TONIGHT'S THE NIGHT (LP)	15

(see also Shirley & Shirelles, Shirley Alston)

SHIRLEY

74	London HLA 10477	I Hear Those Church Bells Ringing/Chapel Of Love/I Do Love You	7

DON SHIRLEY

56	London HA-A 2003	PIANO PERSPECTIVES (LP)	15
56	London HA-A 2004	TONAL EXPRESSIONS (LP)	15
57	London HAA 2046	IMPROVISATIONS (LP)	15
62	London HAA 2448	DROWN IN MY OWN TEARS (LP, also stereo [SAHA 6238])	15

ROY SHIRLEY

66	Ska Beat JB 253	Paradise/Calling (with Ken Boothe: uncredited)	30
66	Doctor Bird DB 1068	Hold Them/Be Good	30
67	Doctor Bird DB 1079	I'm The Winner/Sleeping Beauty	45
67	Doctor Bird DB 1088	Prophet/What To Do	40
67	Doctor Bird DB 1093	Music Field/LEE PERRY & DYNAMITES: Trial And Crosses	50
67	Doctor Bird DB 1108	Thank You/Touch Them	80
67	Caltone CAL 101	Get On The Ball/JOHNNY MOORE: Sound And Soul	60
67	Island WI 3070	People Rock Steady/I'm Trying To Find A Home (actually by Uniques)	90
67	Island WI 3071	Musical War/Soul Voice	100
67	Island WI 3120	Girlie/GLEN ADAMS: She's So Fine	80
68	Doctor Bird DB 1165	Hush A Bye/Musical Dinner	35
68	JJ DB 1168	Dance The Reggay/The Agreement	40
68	Giant GN 32	Dance Arena/The Musical Train	40
68	Giant GN 33	Warming Up The Scene/GLEN ADAMS: Lonely Girl	180
68	Island WI 3098	Thank You/Touch Them	45
68	Island WI 3108	Move All Day/Rolling Rolling	25
68	Island WI 3110	Million Dollar Baby/SENSATIONS: Long Time No See You Girl	200
68	Island WI 3118	Good Is Better Than Bad/Fantastic Lover	30
68	Island WI 3119	Facts Of Life/Lead Us Not Into Temptation (as Roy Shirley & Uniques; B-side actually by Roy Shirley & Slim Smith)	60
68	Island WI 3125	If I Did Know/Good Ambition (solid orange label, later brown labels worth £20)	40
68	Amalgamated AMG 815	The World Needs Love/Dance The Auna	25
68	Fab FAB 54	Think About The Future/Golden Festival	35
69	Duke DU 18	Life/I Like Your Smile	20
71	Nu Beat NB 090	Hold Them One/Two Three Four	10
72	Punch PH 108	A Sugar/ALTYMAN REID: A Sugar - Version	10
72	Punch PH 103	Don't Be A Loser/Jamaican Girl	15
73	Count Shelly CS 006	This World/Return To Me	8
74	Arrow AR 001	Welcome Home/What Am I Loving For	10
74	Leroy LYW 001	Don't Destroy The World/Golden Festival	8
74	Dip DL 5032	George Foreman Vs Muhammed Ali/DJ Race (white labels only)	20
75	R&J 001	Heart Breaking Jepsey/Version	7
74	Florence F001	HOLD THEM (LP, with the Undivided Band, plain sleeve only)	70
76	Trench Town TRELP 003	THE WINNER (LP)	15

(see also Val Bennett, Glen Adams, Shirley & Charmers, Sensations, Denzil, Errol & His Group, Ronsig, Stranger & Glady, Untouchables)

SUSAN SHIRLEY

70	Philips 6006 037	Really Into Somethin'/My Friend The Clown	30
71	Columbia DB 8787	True Love And Apple Pie/To Find Out (p/s)	15
71	Columbia DB 8835	Jealous Guy/Oh Yoko	6

SHIRLEY & CHARMERS

72	Bullet BU 502	Rum Rhythm/LLOYD CHARMERS: Rhythm (Version)	12

(see also Roy Shirley)

SHIRLEY & JOHNNY

64	Parlophone R 5149	I Don't Want To Know/It Must Be Love	7
69	Mercury MF 1074	Don't Make Me Over/Baby, Baby, Baby	7

SHIRLEY & LEE

56	Vogue V 9059	Let The Good Times Roll/Do You Mean To Hurt Me So	100
56	Vogue V 9059	Let The Good Times Roll/Do You Mean To Hurt Me So (78)	20
57	Vogue V 9063	I Feel Good/Now That It's Over	80
57	Vogue V 9063	I Feel Good/Now That It's Over (78)	20
57	Vogue V 9067	That's What I Wanna Do/When I Saw You	95
57	Vogue V 9067	That's What I Wanna Do/When I Saw You (78)	20
57	Vogue V 9072	Rock All Nite/Don't You Know I Love You	80
57	Vogue V 9072	Rock All Nite/Don't You Know I Love You (78)	20
57	Vogue V 9084	Rockin' With The Clock/The Flirt	80
57	Vogue V 9084	Rockin' With The Clock/The Flirt (78)	20

SHIRLEY & RUDE BOYS

MINT VALUE £

57	Vogue V 9088	I Want To Dance/Marry Me	60
57	Vogue V 9088	I Want To Dance/Marry Me (78)	20
57	Vogue V 9094	Feel So Good/You'd Be Thinking Of Me	60
57	Vogue V 9094	Feel So Good/You'd Be Thinking Of Me (78)	20
58	Vogue V 9103	I'll Thrill You/Love No One But You	85
58	Vogue V 9103	I'll Thrill You/Love No One But You (78)	30
58	Vogue V 9118	Everybody's Rockin'/Don't Leave Me Here To Cry	80
58	Vogue V 9118	Everybody's Rockin'/Don't Leave Me Here To Cry (78)	25
59	Vogue V 9129	All I Want To Do Is Cry/Come On And Have Your Fun	80
59	Vogue V 9129	All I Want To Do Is Cry/Come On And Have Your Fun (78)	25
59	Vogue V 9135	A Little Word/That's What I'll Do	60
59	Vogue V 9135	A Little Word/That's What I'll Do (78)	30
59	Vogue V 9137	I'll Do It/Lee's Dream	80

(The above 45s were originally issued with triangular centres; later round-centre issues are worth two-thirds of this value.)

| 59 | Vogue V 9137 | I'll Do It/Lee's Dream (78) | 30 |
| 59 | Vogue V 9156 | True Love/When Day Is Done | 60 |

(Later Vocalion pressings of the above 2 singles worth two-thirds of these values.)

59	Vogue V 9156	True Love/When Day Is Done (78)	40
60	London HLI 9186	I've Been Loved Before/Like You Used To Do	25
60	London HLI 9209	Let The Good Times Roll/Keep Loving Me	20
65	Island WI 257	Let The Good Times Roll/I'm Gone	20
57	Vogue VE 1-70101	ROCK 'N' ROLL (EP, triangular centre)	200
57	Vogue VE 1-70101	ROCK 'N' ROLL (EP, later round centre)	100
60	Vogue VE 1-70145	SHIRLEY AND LEE (EP)	150
71	Jay Boy JSX 2005	LET THE GOOD TIMES ROLL (LP)	20

SHIRLEY & RUDE BOYS
| 67 | Blue Beat BB 375 | Gently Set Me Free/BUSTER'S ALL STARS: Rock Steady | 200 |

SHIRLEY & SHIRELLES
69	Bell BLL 1049	Look What You've Done To My Heart/A Most Unusual Boy	12
69	Bell BLL 1065	Plaything/Looking Glass	6
72	Bell BLL 1251	Look What You've Done To My Heart/A Most Unusual Boy (reissue)	8

(see also Shirelles)

SHIRTS
| 78 | Harvest HAR 5165 | Tell Me Your Plans/Cyrinda | 6 |
| 78 | SHSP 4089 | THE SHIRTS (LP, blue vinyl) | 15 |

SHIVA (1)
| 72 | D'art ART 2017 | The Legend Of Tutankhamun/Valley Of The Kings | 10 |

SHIVA (2)
82	Heavy Metal HEAVY 13	Rock Lives On/Sympathy For The Devil (p/s)	20
82	Heavy Metal HEAVY 16	Angel Of Mons/Stranger Lands (p/s)	10
82	Heavy Metal HMRLP 6	FIREDANCE (LP)	20

BUNNY SHIVEL
| 67 | Capitol CL 15487 | You'll Never Find A Love Like Mine/The Slide | 20 |

SHOC CORRIDOR
82	Shout XW 203	A Blind Sign/Sargasso Sea/On Reflection (12")	10
84	Quiet QST 005	Fever/That Sinking Feeling (12")	12
83	Shout LX 003	EXPERIMENTS IN INCEST (LP)	45
84	Quiet QLP5	TRAIN OF EVENTS (LP)	25

SHOCK
80	Sidewalk PC 5290	Angel Face/R.E.R.B (12")	30
80	RCA DC 5290	Angel Face/R.E.R.B (12")	15
81	RCA RCAT 133	Dynamo Beat/Dream Games (12")	12

JOYCE SHOCK
58	Philips PB 824	Take Your Foot From The Door!/I've Got Bells On My Heart	6
58	Philips PB 872	Hoopa Hoola/You're Not Losing A Daughter, Mama	6
59	Philips PB 934	Personality/I Can't Love You Anymore	6
59	Philips PB 957	Cry, Baby, Cry/Dear Diary	6

SHOCKABILLY
| 84 | Rough Trade ROUGH 68 | COLOSSEUM (LP) | 15 |

SHOCK ABSORBERS
| 69 | Major Minor SMCP 5028 | GUITAR PARTY (LP) | 25 |

SHOCK HEADED PETERS
| 84 | él EL 1 | I, Blood Brother Be/Truth Has Come (p/s) | 7 |

(see also Lemon Kittens, Underneath, Karl Blake, Sol Invictus)

SHOCKING BLUE
69	Olga OLE 015	Send Me A Postcard/Harley Davidson (demo only)	60
70	Penny Farthing PEN 744	Sally Was A Good Old Girl/Long And Lonesome Road	6
70	Penny Farthing PELS 500	SHOCKING BLUE AT HOME (LP)	50
70	Penny Farthing PELS 510	SCORPIO'S DANCE (LP)	40

SHOCK TREATMENT (1)
| 80 | Skull SKR 2001 | The Mugger/Nuclear Warfare (p/s) | 200 |

SHOES (1)
| 67 | Polydor 56739 | Farewell In The Rain/What In The World Is Love | 7 |

SHOES (2)
| 79 | Sire SRK 6075 | BLACK VINYL SHOES (LP) | 20 |

SHOES FOR INDUSTRY
| 79 | Fried Egg EGG 001 | Laughbeat/Can't Help It (p/s) | 6 |
| 80 | Fried Egg FRY 1 | TALK LIKE A WHELK (LP) | 20 |

SHOESTRING BAND
| 73 | CBS SCBS 1284 | Thingumajig/Don't It Make You Feel Good | 6 |

SHOGUN MC

MINT VALUE £

86	Attack ATA 913	High In The Sky/When The Lights Go Down (p/s)	30
86	Attack ATA 006	SHOGUN (LP)	40

SHOGUN MC
| 89 | Blue Chip C22T | Ready For Action (12") | 15 |

TROY SHONDELL
61	London HLG 9432	This Time/Girl After Girl	8
62	Liberty LIB 55398	Island In The Sky/Tears From An Angel	15
63	London HL 9668	I Got A Woman/Some People Never Learn	12
64	London HAY 8128	MANY SIDES OF TROY SHONDELL (LP)	70

SHONDELLS
| 64 | Ember EMB S 191 | My Love/Don't Cry My Soldier Boy | 50 |

SHOO SHOO
| 77 | Pilot PT 1 | Clap Your Hands Louder/The Final Touch | 30 |

SHOOT
| 72 | EMI EMA 73 | ON THE FRONTIER (LP) | 25 |

(see also Manfred Mann Chapter 3, Yardbirds, Raw Material)

SHOOTING PARTY
| 88 | Lisson DOLER 9 | Safe In The Arms Of Love (Phil's Extra Beat Update)/Safe In The Arms Of Love (12") | 12 |

SHOP ASSISTANTS
85	Subway Organisation SUBWAY 1	All Day Long/All That Ever Mattered/It's Up To You/Switzerland (red foldaround hand-coloured p/s in poly bag)	12
85	Subway Organisation SUBWAY 1	All Day Long/All That Ever Mattered/It's Up To You/Switzerland (later blue foldaround hand-coloured p/s in poly bag)	6
86	Blue Guitar AZLP 2	SHOP ASSISTANTS (LP)	20

(see also Buba & Shop assistants)

DINAH SHORE
53	HMV 7M 119	Keep It A Secret/Bella Musica	8
53	HMV 7M 139	Sweet Thing/Three-Cornered Tune	8
54	HMV 7M 183	Changing Partners/Think	8
54	HMV 7M 221	This Must Be The Place/Come Back To My Arms	8
54	HMV 7M 236	Three Coins In The Fountain/Pakistan	8
54	HMV 7M 250	If I Give My Heart To You/Let Me Know	8
56	HMV 7M 352	Love And Marriage/Compare	8
57	RCA RCA 1003	The Cattle Call/Promises, Promises (Skip Redwine)	7
58	RCA RD 27072	HOLDING HANDS AT MIDNIGHT (LP)	15

BRIAN SHORT
| 71 | Transatlantic TRA 245 | ANYTHING FOR A LAUGH (LP, textured gatefold sleeve) | 30 |

(see also Black Cat Bones)

KEVIN SHORT
| 79 | EMI INT 574 | Punk Strut/Short Cut (no p/s, demos only) | 30 |

SHORT KUTS WITH EDDIE HARRISON
| 68 | United Artists UP 2233 | Your Eyes May Shine/Letting The Tears Tumbling Down | 40 |

SHORTCAKES
| 71 | Decca F13185 | I Can Try/Save Me | 10 |

ERROL SHORTER
| 81 | Greensleeves GRED 58 | Wild Inna Eighty-One Style/EEK A MOUSE : Wa Do Dem (12") | 10 |

WAYNE SHORTER
| 79 | Blue Note LBR 1021 | THE SOOTHSAYER (LP) | 15 |

SHORT FUSE
| 72 | Denby DB 316 | You Lied To Me/Circles | 50 |

SHORTWAVE (BAND)
| 77 | Crescent/Avada ARS 111 | GREATEST HATS (LP) | 20 |

SHORTY (THE PRESIDENT)
73	Ackee ACK 509	Aquarius Pressure/Halfway Tree Pressure (as Shorty The President)	30
73	Ackee ACK 517	Jelly-Belly-Nelly/Message Of Love (as Shorty)	12
75	Treble C CCC 03	Beast From The East/Version	10
76	Cactus CTLP	PRESENTING (LP)	30

(see also Shorty Perry)

SHORTY & THEM
| 64 | Fontana TF 460 | Pills Or Love's Labours Lost/Live Laugh And Love | 40 |

SHOT
| 86 | Affair FAIR 2 | Main Thing (Club Vocal)/(Dub Mix) (12") | 20 |

SHOTGUN EXPRESS
66	Columbia DB 8025	I Could Feel The Whole World Turn Round/Curtains	80
67	Columbia DB 8178	Funny 'Cos Neither Could I/Indian Thing	80
83	See For Miles CYM 2	I Could Feel The Whole World Turn Round/Curtains/Funny 'Cos Neither Could I/Indian Thing (10", p/s)	15

(see also Rod Stewart, Peter Bardens, Spencer Davis, Brian Auger, She Trinity, Beryl Marsden, Fleetwood Mac)

SHOTS
| 65 | Columbia DB 7713 | Keep A Hold Of What You've Got/She's A Liar | 70 |

(see also Smoke)

SHOUT (2)
| 92 | Entity SHOUT | Is It Ever Going To End (Remix 1)/Is It Ever Going To End (Remix 2)/Is It Ever Going To End (Remix 3)/Is It Ever Going To End (Radio Edit)/Is It Ever Going To End (Stiff Organ Mix)(12") | 60 |

SHOUTS
| 64 | React EA 001 | She Was My Baby/That's The Way It's Gonna Be | 50 |

(see also Gene Vincent)

THE SHOVE
81	Shove Off PBM033/S/81	Raise The Roof Tonite/Violence/Pigs/Nutters Of York (foldover p/s, 500 only)	40
81	Shove Off Records	ROUGH AND READY EP (with p/s)	25
81	Shove Off Records	ROUGH AND READY EP	15

SHOW STOPPERS
68	Beacon 3-100	Ain't Nothing But A House Party/What Can A Man Do (red swirly label)	15
68	Beacon 3-106	Shake Your Mini/Heartbreaker	40
68	MGM MGM 1436	Eeny Meeny/How Easy Your Heart Forgets Me	15
69	Beacon BEA 110	Don't Leave Me Standing In The Rain/Do You Need My Love	10
69	Beacon BEA 130	Just A Little Bit Of Lovin'/School Prom	15
69	Beacon BEA 100	Ain't Nothing But A House Party/What Can A Man Do (reissue, yellow label)	10
70	Beacon BEA 100	Ain't Nothing But A House Party/What Can A Man Do (reissue, green label)	8
71	Beacon BEA 177	Reach In The Goody Bag/How Do You Feel	10
71	Beacon BEA 3-182	Actions Speak Louder Than Words/ Pick Up Your Smile	20

SHOWBIZ KIDS
80	Top Secret CON 1	She Goes To Finos/I Don't Want To Discuss That (p/s)	40

(see also Toy Dolls)

SHOW BOYS
69	Gas GAS 129	People Are Wondering/Long Time	45

SHOWMEN
62	London HLP 9481	It Will Stand/Country Fool	60
62	London HLP 9571	The Wrong Girl/I Love You Can't You See	175
69	Pama PM 767	Action/What Would It Take	15

(see also Norman Johnson, General Johnson, Chairmen Of The Board)

SHOWTIMERS
64	HMV POP 1328	You Must Be Joking/Don't Say Goodbye	15

SHOX
80	Axis AXIS 4	No Turning Back/Lying Here (p/s)	18
80	Beggars Banquet BEG 33	No Turning Back/Lying Here (p/s, reissue)	8

SHPONGLE
00	Twisted TWST	DIVINE MOMENTS OF TRUTH (12", p/s)	15
99	Twisted TWSLP 4	ARE YOU SHPONGLED? (2-LP, 1st 1000, numbered with gold/silver writing)	150
01	Twisted TWSLP 13	TALES OF THE INEXPRESSABLE (2-LP)	125
03	Twisted TWSLP 23	REMIXED (2-LP)	70
05	Twisted TWSLP 28	NOTHING LASTS…BUT NOTHING IS LEFT (2-LP)	70
07	Twisted TWSLP 4	ARE YOU SHPONGLED? (2-LP reissue, clear sparkled vinyl)	40
08	Twisted TWSLP 13	TALES OF THE INEXPRESSABLE (2-LP, reissue clear sparkled vinyl)	40
10	Twisted TWSLP 36	INEFFABLE MYSTERIES FROM SHPONGLAND (2-LP)	35

SHRAPNEL
89	Words Of Warning WOW 6	Trivial Pursuit/Autumn/TOXIK EPHEX: Does Someone Have To Die/Life Is For Living split EP p/s)	10

MARK SHREEVE
83	Uniton U 021	ASSASSIN (LP)	15

SHRIEKBACK
81	Y T104	Working On The Ground/Nightwork (12", p/s)	12

DAVID SHRIGLEY
06	Contemporary Arts	Ding/Dong (p/s, 500 only)	20
06	Azuzi ALNLP16	FORCED TO SPEAK WITH OTHERS (LP)	20

SHRIMP TRACTOR
93	Shrimp Platters SPLAT 001	THE SHRIMP EP	10

SHRINK (1)
79	Oval AMS 7409	Valid Or Void/You Chauffeur Me (p/s)	6

SHRINK (2)
88	Chandarba GHAND 1	Around The World/Calling All Women	10

SHRUG
95	Private Pressing	THE YOGURTS VS YOGURT DEBATE (Demo cassette, glued sleeve)	80

(see also Snow Patrol)

SHUBERT
68	Fontana TF 942	Until The Rains Come/Let Your Love Go	20

SHUDDER TO THINK
91	Dischord	Vacation Brain (p/s, with insert)	12

SALMAN SHUKUR
77	Decca Headline HEAD 16	OUD (LP)	18

MORT SHUMAN
59	Decca F 11184	Turn Me Loose/I'm A Man (tri-centre)	80
59	Decca F 11184	Turn Me Loose/I'm A Man	60
59	Decca F 11184	Turn Me Loose/I'm A Man (78)	25
66	Fontana TF 685	Cry A Little/She Ain't Nothing But A Little Child	10
67	Immediate IM 048	Monday Monday/Little Children	20

SHUSHA
71	Tangent TGS 108	PERSIAN LOVE SONGS AND MYSTIC CHANTS (LP)	15

SHUTDOWNS
63	Colpix PX 11016	Four In The Floor/Beach Buggy	50

SHY LIMBS
69	CBS 4190	Reputation/Love	70
69	CBS 4624	Lady In Black/Trick Or Two	150

(see also Shame)

SHY ONES
63	Oriole CB 1848	Nightcap/Carry Me Back	20
64	Oriole CB 1924	La Route/Susanna	18

(see also Spotnicks)

SHY (1)
74	Deram DM417	Disney Girls (1957)/The Time That I Love You The Most	7

SHY (2)
83	Ebony EBON 15	ONCE BITTEN TWICE SHY (LP)	20

SHYSTER

MINT VALUE £

SHYSTER
68 Polydor 56202 — Tick Tock/That's A Hoe Down ... 220
(see also Fleur-De-Lys)

SHY TOTS
82 ST EP 1 — Gallery/Babble/English Industrial Estate (silk-screened cover) ... 25

SHYWOLF
82 MRS SW 001 — Lucretia/California Jam (p/s) ... 40

SIA
04 Go! Beat 986 610-1 — COLOUR THE SMALL ONE (LP) ... 40

LEROY SIBBLES & ROCKY ELLIS
68 Studio One SO 2042 — Love Me Girl/WRIGGLERS: Reel Up ... 80
79 Warrior Records WAR 133 — Ras-Tafari/MYSTIC EYES: Forward With Love/Dub (12") ... 30
(see also John Holt, King Rocky)

DON E SIBLEY & DIXIE PHOENIX
79 Hot Rock HR45-003 — Punk Bashing Boogie/Rock With The Devil ... 7

DUDLEY SIBLEY
67 Coxsone CS 7010 — Run Boy Run/Message Of Old (B-side actually by Joe Higgs & Ken Boothe) ... 70
67 Island WI 3034 — Gun Man/Monkey Speaks His Mind (B-side actually by Dinsdell Thorpe) ... 50
(see also Delroy & Sporty, King Sporty, Mr. Foundation)

SICK THINGS
83 Chaos CHS 3 — ANTI SOCIAL (EP) ... 25

SIDAN
72 Sain SAIN 27 — LLIWIAU (EP) ... 20
73 Sain SAIN 40 — AI CYMRO WYT TI? (EP) ... 20
75 Sain 1017 — TEULU YNCL SAM (LP, laminated front cover) ... 50

SID & JOE & MOHAWKS
70 Pama PM 800 — Down On The Corner/Who Is That Stranger ... 20
(see also Mohawks)

SIDDELEYS
87 Sha La La Ba Ba Ba 006 — Wherever You Go/RESERVE: The Sun Slid Down Behind The Tower (flexi with fanzines, p/s) ... 10
87 Medium Cool MC 005 — What Went Wrong This Time?/No Names/My Favourite Wet Wednesday Afternoon (p/s) ... 40
88 Sombrero THREE — Sunshine Thuggery/Are You Still Evil When You're Sleeping/Falling Off My Feet Again (12", p/s) ... 35

FRANK SIDEBOTTOM
86 Regal Zonophone 12Z41 — SCI-FI EP (12") ... 15
86 Regal Zonophone ZP41 — SCI-FI EP (picture disc) ... 15
86 Regal Zonophone Z41 — SCI-FI EP ... 8
88 In Tape IT 060 — 13:9:88 (LP) ... 15
(see also Freshies, Chris Sievey, Billy & Barry Belly)

SIDEKICKS
66 RCA RCA 1538 — Suspicions/Up On The Roof ... 20

SIDEWALK SOCIETY
10 Fruits De Mer Crustacean 14 — In The First Place/(Tell Me) Have You Ever Seen Me/Lazy Old Sun/Dandelion (folded p/s) ... 30

SIDNEY, GEORGE & JACKIE
71 Summit SUM 8528 — Lady Of My Complexion/No Sad Song ... 12
74 Attack ATT 8054 — At The Club/Reggae Fever ... 275
(see also Pioneers)

PAUL SIEBEL
70 Elektra EKS 74064 — WOODSMOKE AND ORANGES (LP) ... 20
71 Elektra EKS 74081 — JACK-KNIFE GYPSY (LP) ... 20

SIEGE
85 Siege THM 1 — Goddess Of Fire (no p/s) ... 18
90 Revolution — Infest/Drop Dead (p/s) ... 20

SIEGEL-SCHWALL BAND
68 Vanguard SVRL 19044 — SHAKE (LP) ... 20

CHRIS SIEVEY
79 Rabid TOSH 109 — Baiser/Last (p/s) ... 10
79 Razz RAZZXEP 1 — BAISER (33rpm EP, 2 tracks each by Sievey & Freshies, handwritten labels) ... 40
80 Razz RAZZ 9 — Last/Skip The Flight Jim (later promo edition, 50 copies only, hand-made sleeve, labels glued over original Rabid labels, please note that Skip The Flight Jim is actually Baiser) ... 200
80 Razz RAZZ 4 — My Tape's Gone/Moon Midsummer (with True Life Revealing Confessions Of Romance And Love fanzine) ... 10
81 Razz RAZZ 5 — Hey/FRESHIES: We're Like You (p/s) ... 6
82 Razz RAZZ 8 — RED INDIAN MUSIC (EP) ... 18
(see also Freshies, Frank Sidebottom, Billy & Barry Belly, Going Red?)

LABI SIFFRE
71 Pye Intl. 7N 25572 — It Must Be Love/To Find Love ... 6
70 Pye Intl. NSPL 28135 — LABI SIFFRE (LP) ... 15
71 Pye Intl. NSPL 28147 — THE SINGER AND THE SONG (LP, gatefold sleeve) ... 15
72 Pye Intl. NSPL 28163 — CRYING, LAUGHING, LOVING, LYING (LP, gatefold sleeve with lyric insert) ... 20
75 EMI EMC 3065 — REMEMBER MY SONG (LP) ... 150
98 EMI/Mr. Bongo MRBLP 011 — REMEMBER MY SONG (LP, reissue) ... 20

RON SIG
71 Camel CA 58 — 1970's/Version ... 30

SIGHT & SOUND
68 Fontana TF 927 — Ebenezer/Our Love (Is In The Pocket) ... 50
68 Fontana TF 982 — Alley Alley/Little Jack Monday ... 15
(see also Jefferson, Sheridan & Price, Mike Sheridan)

			MINT VALUE £
BUNNY SIGLER			
67	Cameo Parkway P 153	Let The Good Times Roll - Feel So Good/There's No Love Left	30
67	Cameo Parkway P 153	Let The Good Times Roll - Feel So Good/There's No Love Left (DJ copy)	60
76	Philadelphia SPIR 4935	Can't Believe That You Love Me/Woman, Woman	6
76	London HLU 10518	Let The Good Times Roll/Feel So Good	12
SIGNIFICANT ZEROS			
81	Dingy Roons DINGE ONE	Jungle/Stiff Citizens	20
SIGNS			
66	Decca F 12522	Ain't You Got A Heart/My Baby Comes To Me	40
SIGUE SIGUE SPUTNIK			
86	Parlophone PCSS 7305	FLAUNT IT (LP, box set with insert)	18

(see also Generation X, Sisters Of Mercy)

SIGUR RÓS			
99	Fat Cat 12FAT 036	Svefn-G-Englar (12" EP, custom sleeve 2,000 only)	20
00	Fat Cat 12FAT 039	NY BATTERI (mini-LP, 2,000 only)	25
04	EMI 5496916	BA BA TI KI DI DO (12" EP)	15
05	EMI 17571	Hoppipolla/Meo Bloonasir/Hafsol (12")	12
06	EMI EMI 673	Hoppipolla/Heysatan (numbered p/s, 3000 only)	10
06	EMI 12EM 687	SAEGOPUR (12" p/s)	15
07	EMI 736	Hljómalind/Staralfur (Live) (p/s)	6
12	EMI 10R 6860	Ekki Mukk/Kvistur (10" plays inside out)	12
00	Fat Cat FATLP 11	AGAETIS BYRJUN (2-LP)	90
03	Fat Cat FATLP 22	( ) (LP)	80
05	EMI 337 252 1	TAKK (2-LP, 10" special book edition)	120
05	EMI 337252	SIGUR RóS (2-LP, gatefold with inner sleeves and free 10")	60
07	EMI 5099951041991	HEIMA (Box set, CD, DVD, 116 page book)	120
09	Fat Cat FATLP 11X	AGAETIS BYRJUN (2-LP, reissue, 180 gm vinyl)	30
12	Krunk KRUNK7LP	INNI (3-LP, C-CD, DVD box set)	30
12	Parlophone 5099962355513	VALTARI (2-LP, CD, gatefold)	20
13	Parlophone 2564636943	VALTARI (2-LP, repressing)	20
13	Parlophone P 958 4341	HVARF/HEIM (2-LP, one green and one blue)	25
13	XL XLLP 606X	KVEIKUR (2-LP, 10" CD)	20
13	XL XLBY 606	KVEIKUR (8 x 12" and 1-sided 12" box set)	100
13	XL XLLP 606X	KVEIKUR (2-LP, hand printed alternative sleeve, 50 only)	120
18	XL XL918LP	ROUTE ONE (LP, reissue)	35
18	XL XL920LP	LIMINAL REMIXES (LP, reissue)	35

(see also Jonsi)

SILENT ECLIPSE			
92	White (Mendoza) MEN018	How Many Miles Back To London/MCs (12")	120
92	Mendoza MEN018	How Many Miles Back To London/MCs (12")	80
92	Dope Jams DJAM1	Take The Stage (3 Mixes, promo 12" only)	15

(see also Two Times Def)

SILENT MOVIES			
79	ESR Records ESR 1	Ain't No Van Gough/What Did Ya Say? (p/s)	40
SILENT NOISE			
79	Silent Noise/Easy ER 02	I've Been Hurt (Too Many Times Before)/Heart To Heart	75
SILENT ONES			
70	Pulse P1	When It Rains/Lost Dreams (p/s)	50
SILENT SCREAM			
84	Pure Motorised Instinct PMI 001	Handstands/Jagged Path (p/s)	25
SILENT WARRIORS			
80	Catfish CT1	Ride Of Death/Firefly	50
SILENT NIGHT			
83	Granny's Rockers S83/CVUS1847/UK	Cold Hearted Lady/Never Say It's Over (no p/s)	40
SILHOUETTE			
78	Wildfire WRL 23	RONDO EP (no p/s)	8
SILHOUETTES (JAMAICA)			
69	Sound System SSR 103	In Times Like These (act. by Lloyd Jackson & Groovers)/In Times Like These	70
SILHOUETTES (U.S.)			
58	Parlophone R 4407	Get A Job/I Am Lonely	100
58	Parlophone R 4407	Get A Job/I Am Lonely (78)	50
58	Parlophone R 4425	Headin' For The Poorhouse/Miss Thing	150
58	Parlophone R 4425	Headin' For The Poorhouse/Miss Thing (78)	80
SILICON TEENS			
79	Mute MUTE 003	Memphis Tennessee/Let's Dance (p/s, with poster)	10
80	Mute 008AX	Sunflight/Just Like Eddie (p/s)	6
80	Mute STUMM 2	MUSIC FOR PARTIES (LP)	6
SILKIE			
65	Fontana TF 556	Blood Red River/Close The Door Gently	6
65	Fontana TF 603	You've Got To Hide Your Love Away/City Winds	7
66	Fontana TF 709	Born To Be With You/So Sorry Now	6
65	Fontana TL 5256	THE SILKIE SING THE SONGS OF BOB DYLAN (LP)	20
SILK TIE			
73	Maple MP 004	Into The Night/Theresa	20
SILKY THREADS			
75	Waverley WAV 1	Jump To It/She Runs	40
JUDEE SILL			
71	Asylum AYM 502	Jesus Was A Cross Maker/The Phantom Cowboy	7
72	Asylum AYM 509	Enchanted Sky Machines/My Man On Love	6

John SILVA

			MINT VALUE £
72	Asylum SYLA 8751	JUDEE SILL (LP, gatefold sleeve)	40
73	Asylum SYL 9006	HEART FOOD (LP)	25

JOHN SILVA
79	Jayesque (no Cat No)	MAKE UP YOUR MIND (LP, as John Silva Sextet)	150
78	Jayesque SRT/SRTX/78/CUS 134	INN ATTENDANCE (LP)	80

SILVER EAGLE
67	MGM MGM 1345	Theodore/True As A Brand New Lie	30

SILVER (JAMAICA)
68	Jolly JY 006	Baby Oh Yeah/Rock Steady Is Here To Stay (as Silver & Magnets)	35
68	Jolly JY 012	Things/Sweet Lovin'	15
68	Jolly JY 017	I Need A Girl/Lost And Found	30
70	Columbia Blue Beat DB 117	Love Me Forever/Sugar, Sugar (B-side as Silver & Noreen)	70
71	Fab FAB 163	Change Has Got To Come/Magnet Stomp (as Silver & Magnets)	20

SILVER (U.S.)
76	Arista ARIST 79	Musician (It's Not An Easy Life)/Right On Time	6
76	Arista ARTY 144	SILVER (LP, U.S. disc & inner [AL 4076] in U.K. sleeve)	12

(see also Grateful Dead)

ANDEE SILVER
64	HMV POP 1297	Too Young To Go Steady/Sleeping Beauty	10
64	HMV POP 1344	The Boy I Used To Know/What Do You Do	10
66	Fontana TF 666	Only Your Love Can Save Me/Window Shopping	25
69	Decca F 22872	Go Now/You're Just What I Was Looking For Today	20
69	Decca F 22953	With A Little Love/Te Quiero (unreleased)	0
70	Decca F 23071	Love Me/You're Breaking My Heart (export issue)	10
70	Decca SKL-R 5059	A HANDFUL OF SILVER (LP)	50

EDDIE SILVER
58	Parlophone R 4439	Seven Steps To Love/Put A Ring On Her Finger	15
58	Parlophone R 4483	Rockin' Robin/The Ways Of A Woman In Love	20
58	Parlophone R 4483	Rockin' Robin/The Ways Of A Woman In Love (78)	20

HORACE SILVER QUINTET/TRIO
54	Vogue LDE 065	THE HORACE SILVER TRIO (10" LP)	20
69	Blue Note BST 84277	SERENADE TO A SOUL SISTER (LP)	25

LORRAINE SILVER
65	Pye 7N 15922	Lost Summer Love/I'll Know You'll Be There	100
65	Pye 7N 15922	Lost Summer Love/I'll Know You'll Be There (DJ copy)	150
66	Pye 7N 17055	The Happy Faces/When The Love Light Starts Shining Thru His Eyes	40
78	Casino Classics CC 2	Lost Summer Love/I Know You'll Be There	10

MIKE SILVER & MIKE BEASON
69	Fontana STL 5506	THE APPLICANT (LP)	25

SILVER APPLES
96	Enraptured RAPT 4507	Fractal Flow/Love Fingers (p/s)	6
97	Rocket Girl RGIRL 1	I Have Known Love/WINDY & CARL: Crazy In The Sun (p/s, green vinyl)	6

SILVER BIRCH
73	Brayford BRO 2	SILVER BIRCH (LP, private pressing)	150

SILVERBIRD
72	CBS 51279	I See The Writing On The Wall/The Summer's Gone (And I'm Alone)	8
73	CBS 51800	That's Why You Remember/You And Me	8

SILVER BULLET
91	Parlophone R 6290	Ruff Karnage/Never Authorise Apocalypse (p/s)	35
91	Parlophone PCS 7350	BRING DOWN THE WALLS NO LIMIT SQUAD RETURNS (LP)	15

SILVER BULLIT
72	Philips 6073808	Willpower Weak, Temptation Strong/Hittin' On You	15

SILVER BYKE
68	London HLZ 10200	I've Got Time/Who Needs Tomorrow	18

SILVERCHAIR
95	Columbia 662395 7	Tomorrow/Blind (live) (p/s)	10

SILVER DOLLAR
74	Shire SH 003	Frightened/Oh You Devil	30

SILVERHEAD
72	Purple PUR 104	Ace Supreme/Oh No No No	10
72	Purple PUR 110	Rolling With My Baby/In Your Eyes	10
73	Purple TPSA 7506	SILVERHEAD (LP, gatefold)	40
73	Purple TPSA 7511	SIXTEEN AND SAVAGED (LP, gatefold sleeve)	45

(see also Michael Des Barres, Blondie)

SILVER JEWS
96	Domino WIGLP 28	THE NATURAL BRIDGE (LP)	35
98	Domino WIGLP 56	AMERICAN WATER (LP)	35

SILVER MACHINE
78	Hillside HIL SP 5004	Take Me In Your Arms/You'll Always Be The One (no p/s)	50

SILVER MOUNTAIN
83	Road Runner RR 9884	SHAKIN' BRAINS (LP)	15

SILVERS
66	Polydor BM 56094	What A Way To Start A Day/Blue Blue Eyes	7

PHIL SILVERS
57	Fontana Fortune Z 4040	BUGLE CALLS FOR BIG BAND (LP)	15

SILVER SCREEN GIRLS
81	Siren SSG 1	Photographs/Silver Screen Girls (p/s)	15

SILVER SISTERS
60	Parlophone R 4669	Waiting For The Stars To Shine/When A Boy Meets A Girl	10

Dooley SILVERSPOON

MINT VALUE £

DOOLEY SILVERSPOON
76	Seville SEV 1022	Game Players/Believe In Me	8
75	Seville SEL 1	DOOLEY SILVERSPOON (LP)	15

SILVERSTARS
69	Trojan TR 646	Old Man Say/Promises	120

SILVER STARS STEEL BAND
63	Island ILP 904	THE SILVER STARS STEEL BAND (LP)	20

(see also Clancy Eccles)

SILVERTONES
66	Doctor Bird DB 1028	True Confession (with Duke Reid)/TOMMY McCOOK & SUPERSONICS: More Love	60
66	RYMSKA RA 105	True Confession/Honky Tonky Ska (with Granville Williams)	80
66	Doctor Bird DB 1041	It's Real (with Lynn Tait & Boys)/LYNN TAIT & BOYS: Storm Warning	50
67	Treasure Isle TI 7020	Cool Down/TOMMY McCOOK & SUPERSONICS: Shadow Of Your Smile	60
68	Treasure Isle TI 7027	In The Midnight Hour/TOMMY McCOOK & SUPERSONICS: Soul For Sale	25
68	Treasure Isle TI 7039	Old Man River/TOMMY McCOOK & SUPERSONICS: Our Man Flint	150
68	Treasure Isle TI 7042	Slow And Easy/TOMMY McCOOK & SUPERSONICS: Moving	80
69	Trojan TR 7705	Intensified Change/Marie	40
71	Clandisc CLA 234	Tear Drops Will Fall/DYNAMITES: Tear Drops - Version	15
73	Techniques TE 924	That's When It Hurts/I'll Take You Home	12
77	Trojan TRO 9013	African Dub/Version	35
77	Trojan TRO 9015	What A Situation/Version	15
71	Trojan TRLS 69	SILVER BULLETS (LP)	100

(see also Valentines, Tommy McCook, Vincent Gordon, Alton Ellis, Carl Bryon, Charmers)

SILVERWING
80	Mayhem SILVER 1	Rock'n'Roll Are Four-Letter Words/High Class Woman/Hot City Streets	7
82	Mayhem SILV 02	Sittin' Pretty/Teenage Love Affair (p/s)	8
82	Mayhem SILV 212	Sittin' Pretty/Teenage Love/Flashbomb Fever/Rock'n'Roll Mayhem (12")	10
82	Mayhem SILV 3	That's Entertainment/Flashbomb Fever (poster p/s)	8
83	Bullet BULP 1	ALIVE AND KICKING (LP)	15

(see also Pet Hate, Big Amongst Sheep)

VICTOR SILVESTER ORCHESTRA
66	Columbia DB 7900	The World Cup Waltz/The World Cup Cha Cha Cha	10

VICTOR SILVESTER & HIS ROCK 'N' ROLL RHYTHM
57	Columbia DB 3888	Rockin' Rhythm Roll/Society Rock	15
57	Columbia DB 3907	Alligator Roll/Off Beat Rock	15

TYRONE SIMEON
79	Burning Rockers BRD 010	Do Good In This Time/Do Good Dub (12")	15

SIMEONS
78	Freedom Sounds FSLP 002	DUB CONFERENCE IN LONDON (LP)	25

LEO SIMMO
66	Big Beat BB351	I Love Her So/It's Good To Be Seen	25

BEVERLEY SIMMON(D)S
68	Pama PM 716	Mr. Pitiful/That's How Strong My Love Is	15
73	Pama Supreme PS 380	You're Mine/What A Guy (as Beverley Simmonds)	8
69	Pama PMLP 1	PAYS TRIBUTE TO OTIS REDDING (LP)	50
69	Pama PMLP/PMSP 9	REMEMBER OTIS (LP)	30

(see also Little Beverly)

CHRIS SIMMONS
69	MCA MK 5009	Soraya/Gone Gone Gone	6

DESMOND SIMMONS
81	Dome 33.1	ALONE ON PENGUIN ISLAND (LP)	15

(JUMPIN') GENE SIMMONS
64	London HLU 9913	Haunted House/Hey, Hey Little Girl	20
64	London HLU 9933	The Jump/The Dodo	20

GENE SIMMONS
79	Casablanca CAN 134	Radioactive/When You Wish Upon A Star (p/s, red vinyl with mask, picture label, mispressed with black/red vinyl)	50
79	Casablanca CAN 134	Radioactive/When You Wish Upon A Star (p/s, red vinyl with mask, picture label)	20
79	Casablanca CAN 134	Radioactive/When You Wish Upon A Star (p/s, black vinyl)	8

(see also Kiss)

JEFF SIMMONS
69	Straight STS 1057	LUCILLE HAS MESSED UP MY MIND (LP)	80

(see also Frank Zappa)

LITTLE MAC SIMMONS
66	Outasite OSEP 1	BLUES FROM CHICAGO (EP, 99 copies only)	200

TONY SIMMONS
83	Record Shack SOHOT 2	I Can't Let You Go/I Can't Let You Go (Instrumental) (12" promo only)	150

JAGO SIMMS
68	Fontana TF 901	In Too Deep/Conventional Fella	45

JASON SIMMS & MUSIC THROUGH SIX
68	Domain D 5	It's Got To Be Mellow/MUSIC THROUGH SIX: Floppy Ears	20

(see also Music Through Six)

(ZOOT) SIMMS & (LLOYD) ROBINSON
62	Blue Beat BB 143	White Christmas/Searching	10

ZOOT SIMMS (JAMAICA)
63	Blue Beat BB 183	Press Along/PRINCE BUSTER ALLSTARS: 100 Ton Megaton (B-side actually "Mighty As A Rose" by Raymond Harper)	40
63	Blue Beat BB 193	Golden Pen/ERIC MORRIS: So You Shot Reds	45
64	Port-O-Jam PJ 4007	Please Don't Do It/Don't Do It (as Simms & [Lloyd] Robinson)	40
68	Blue Cat BS 118	Bye Bye Baby/AL & THRILLERS: Heart For Sale	150
69	Coxsone CS 7095	Tit For Tat/We Can Talk It Over (as Simms & Elmond)	80

SEIJA SIMOLA

MINT VALUE £

(see also Mr. Foundation, Alton Ellis)

SEIJA SIMOLA
78	Sonet SON 2145	Give Love A Chance/Little Smile (p/s)	12

SIMON
67	RCA Victor RCA 1609	I Like The Way/Little Tin Soldier	10
68	RCA Victor RCA 1668	Dream Seller/Sweet Reflections Of You	15
69	Plum PLS 002	Mrs Lillyco/There's No More You	40

JOE SIMON
66	London HLU 10057	Teenager's Prayer/Long Hot Summer	30
67	Monument MON 1004	My Special Prayer/Travelin' Man	10
68	Monument MON 1010	Nine Pound Steel/The Girl's Alright With Me	20
68	Monument MON 1014	No Sad Songs/Come On And Get It	10
68	Monument MON 1019	You Keep Me Hangin' On/What Makes A Man Feel Good	7
68	Monument MON 1025	Message From Maria/I Worry About You	7
69	Monument MON 1029	Looking Back/Standing In The Safety Zone	7
69	Monument MON 1032	The Chokin' Kind/Come On And Get It	7
70	Monument MON 1049	Yours Love/I Gotta Whole Lot Of Lovin'	25
70	Monument MON 1051	That's The Way I Want Our Love/When	15
71	Polydor 2066 066	Your Time To Cry/I Love You More (Than Anything)	8
74	Mojo 2093 030	Step By Step/Talk Don't Bother Me	6
67	Monument LMO/SMO 5005	SIMON PURE SOUL (LP)	18
68	Monument LMO/SMO 5017	NO SAD SONGS (LP)	18
69	Monument LMO/SMO 5026	SIMON SINGS (LP)	18
70	Monument LMO/SMO 5030	THE CHOKIN' KIND (LP)	18
70	Monument LMO/SMO 5033	BETTER THAN EVER (LP)	18

PAUL SIMON
65	CBS 201797	I Am A Rock/Leaves That Are Green	25
65	CBS (S) 62579	THE PAUL SIMON SONGBOOK (LP, mono, flipback sleeve)	25
65	CBS (S) 62579	THE PAUL SIMON SONGBOOK (LP, stereo, flipback sleeve)	30
72	CBS CQ 30750/Q 69007	PAUL SIMON (LP, quadrophonic)	20
74	CBS CQ 32280/Q 69035	THERE GOES RHYMIN' SIMON (LP, quadrophonic)	18
75	CBS Q 86001	STILL CRAZY AFTER ALL THESE YEARS (LP, quadrophonic)	18
85	Warner Bros. WB WX52	GRACELAND (LP, embossed stickered sleeve)	20

(see also Simon & Garfunkel, Jerry Landis, Tom & Jerry)

TONY SIMON
67	Track 604 012	Gimme A Little Sign/Never Too Much To Love	40

SIMON & GARFUNKEL
65	CBS 201977	The Sound Of Silence/We've Got A Groovy Thing Goin'	10
66	CBS 202045	Homeward Bound/Leaves That Are Green	10
66	CBS 202303	I Am A Rock/Flowers Never Bend With The Rainfall	10
66	CBS 202285	The Dangling Conversation/The Big Bright Green Pleasure Machine	15
66	CBS 202378	A Hazy Shade Of Winter/For Emily, Whenever I May Find Her	10
67	CBS 202608	At The Zoo/The 59th Street Bridge Song (Feelin' Groovy)	10
67	CBS 2911	Fakin' It/You Don't Know Where Your Interest Lies	20
68	CBS WB 728	The 59th Street Bridge Song (Feelin' Groovy)/TREMELOES: Here Comes My Baby (p/s, mail-order only with Pepsi Cola tokens)	7
69	CBS 4162	The Boxer/Baby Driver (p/s)	7
70	CBS 4916	Cecelia/The only Living Boy In New York	6
65	CBS EP 6053	WEDNESDAY MORNING 3AM (EP)	20
66	CBS EP 6074	I AM A ROCK (EP)	20
67	CBS EP 6360	FEELING GROOVY (EP)	20
68	CBS EP 6400	MRS ROBINSON (EP)	10
66	CBS (S)BPG 62690	THE SOUNDS OF SILENCE (LP, mono)	20
66	CBS (S)BPG 62690	THE SOUNDS OF SILENCE (LP, stereo)	35
66	CBS BPG 62860	PARSLEY, SAGE, ROSEMARY AND THYME (LP, mono, sleeve printed by 'Dawson Rossiter Limited')	25
66	CBS (S)BPG 62860	PARSLEY, SAGE, ROSEMARY AND THYME (LP, stereo)	35

(Originally issued with flipback sleeves & textured orange labels.)

67	Allegro ALL 836	SIMON AND GARFUNKEL (LP)	20
68	CBS 63101	BOOKENDS (LP, mono)	50
68	CBS 63101	BOOKENDS (LP, stereo, 1st issue, laminated front sleeve, textured orange labels, no 'stereo' on labels)	50
68	CBS 56301	BOOKENDS (LP, stereo, 2nd issue, laminated front sleeve, textured or smooth orange labels, 'stereo' on labels)	40
68	CBS (S) 70042	THE GRADUATE (LP, soundtrack, blue label, mono/stereo)	40
68	CBS (S) 63370	WEDNESDAY MORNING 3AM (LP, flipback sleeve, textured orange label, mono/stereo)	25
70	CBS S63699	BRIDGE OVER TROUBLED WATER (LP, 1st issue, laminated front sleeve, orange labels)	20
70	CBS S63699	BRIDGE OVER TROUBLED WATER (LP, 1st issue, matt front sleeve, orange labels)	15
72	CBS CQ 30995	BRIDGE OVER TROUBLED WATER (LP, quadrophonic)	30
72	CBS S69003	SIMON & GARFUNKEL'S GREATEST HITS (LP)	15

(see also Paul Simon, Art Garfunkel, Tom & Jerry)

NINA SIMONE
59	Parlophone R 4583	I Loves You Porgy/Love Me Or Leave Me	20
59	Pye International 7N 25029	Solitaire/Chilly Winds Don't Blow	10
63	Colpix PX 200	You Can Have Him/Return Home	10
64	Colpix PX 799	Exactly Like You/The Other Woman	10
65	Philips BF 1388	Don't Let Me Be Misunderstood/Monster	10
65	Philips BF 1415	I Put A Spell On You/Gimme Some	10
66	Philips BF 1465	Either Way I Lose/Break Down And Let It Out	15
69	RCA RCA 1903	Save Me/To Be Young Gifted And Black	15
78	CTI CTSP 14	Baltimore/Forget	30

SUGAR SIMONE

			MINT VALUE £
94	Mercury MER 403	Feeling Good/My Baby Just Cares For Me (live) (VW p/s)	40
02	Jazzman JM 023	Funkier Than A Mosquito/Save Me (jukebox centre)	15
61	Parlophone GEP 8844	MY BABY JUST CARES FOR ME (EP)	70
62	Parlophone GEP 8864	INTIMATE NINA SIMONE (EP)	25
64	Colpix PXE 303	FINE AND MELLOW (EP)	15
66	Colpix PXE 306	JUST SAY I LOVE HIM (EP)	15
66	Colpix PXE 307	I LOVE TO LOVE (EP)	15
65	Philips BE 12585	DON'T LET ME BE MISUNDERSTOOD (EP)	12
65	Philips BE 12589	STRANGE FRUIT (EP)	12
61	Pye Intl. NPL 28014	AT THE TOWN HALL (LP)	25
62	Pye Jazz NJL 36	FORBIDDEN FRUIT (LP)	25
64	Colpix PXL 419	FORBIDDEN FRUIT (LP, reissue)	15
64	Colpix PXL 421	NINA AT THE VILLAGE GATE (LP)	25
65	Colpix PXL 465	FOLKSY NINA (LP)	25
65	Fontana SFJL 954	TELL ME MORE (LP)	20
65	Philips BL 7662	BROADWAY . . . BLUES . . . BALLADS (LP)	20
65	Philips BL 7671	I PUT A SPELL ON YOU (LP)	50
65	Philips BL 7678	IN CONCERT (LP)	20
66	Philips BL 7683	PASTEL BLUES (LP)	30
66	Philips (S)BL 7722	LET IT ALL OUT (LP)	25
66	Philips (S)BL 7726	WILD IS THE WIND (LP)	30
67	Philips (S)BL 7764	HIGH PRIESTESS OF SOUL (LP)	25
67	RCA RD/SF 7883	SINGS THE BLUES (LP)	20
68	RCA RD/SF 7967	SILK AND SOUL (LP)	30
69	RCA Victor SF 7979	'NUFF SAID (LP)	30
69	RCA SF 8018	TO LOVE SOMEBODY (LP)	30
78	CTI 7084	BALTIMORE (LP, gatefold)	25

SUGAR SIMONE
68	Fab FAB 33	I Love My Baby/I'll Keep You Satisfied	18
66	Rainbow RAI 103	Is It Because/I Want To Know	20
67	Rainbow RAI 115	I Love My Baby/I'll Keep You Satisfied	8
67	Sue WI 4029	Suddenly/King Without A Throne	40
67	Go AJ 11409	It's Alright/Take It Easy	30
68	CBS 3250	The Vow/Spinning Wheel	18
69	Doctor Bird DB 1192	Black Is Gold/The Invitation	20
69	Doctor Bird DB 1193	The Squeeze Is On/Tell Me	25
69	Doctor Bird DB 1201	Come And Try/Don't Listen To What They Say	12
69	Fab FAB 106	Boom Biddy Boom/RUDIES: What Can I Do	10
69	Fab FAB 107	I Need A Witness/Johnny Dollar	10
69	Upfront UPF 1	Turns On The Heatwave/Crying Blues	10
70	Beacon BEA 156	Keep On Trying/Only The Lonely	7
70	Beacon BEA 174	Why Can't I Touch You/Gotta Get It Off My Mind	7
73	Smash SAM 2333	Rock And Cry/September	10
70	Up Front SUPF 1	ALIVE AND WELL (LP)	25

(see also Sugar & Dandy, Les Foster, Larry Foster & Soul Explosion, Lance Hannibal)

SIMON PLUG & GRIMES
70	Deram DM 296	Is This A Dream?/I'm Going Home	12

BESSA SIMONS
90	3rd Eye (No cat no)	BESSA (LP)	50

(see also Osibisa)

SIMON'S SECRETS
68	CBS 3406	Naughty Boy/Sympathy	35
68	CBS 3856	I Know What Her Name Is/Keeping My Head Above Water	40

(see also Secrets, Clifford T. Ward, Martin Raynor & Secrets)

SIMON SISTERS
64	London HLR 9893	Winkin', Cuddlebug' And Nod/So Glad I'm Here	20
65	London HLR 9984	Cuddlebug/No One To Talk My Trouble To	15

NIC SIMPER'S FANDANGO
83	Paro PAR 0S4	Just Another Day (In The Life Of A Fool)/Wish I'd Never Woke Up	6
79	Gull GULP 1033	SLIPSTREAMING (LP)	20

(see also Deep Purple, Warhorse)

NIGEL SIMPKINS
78	Waldo's SS 2	X.ENC EP (1500 only, numbered, these 100 with 'broken' USA bonus 7")	10

SIMPLE IMAGE
70	Carnaby CNS 4013	Spinning Spinning Spinning/Shy Boy	15

SIMPLE MINDS
79	Zoom ZUM 10	Life In A Day/Special View (p/s)	7
79	Zoom ZUM 11	Chelsea Girl/Garden Of Hate (p/s)	7
81	Virgin VS 451	Sweat In Bullet/20th Century Promised Land (original pressing, non-gatefold p/s)	30
88	Virgin VS 860/VS 817	All The Things She Said/Don't You Forget About Me (Live)//Alive And Kicking/Alive And Kicking (Intrumental) double single pack in PVC sleeve sealed by sticker that states "double pack 2 for the price of 1")	60
79	Zoom ZULP 1	LIFE IN A DAY (LP)	15
79	Zoom SPART 1109	REAL TO REAL CACOPHONY (LP)	15
80	Zoom SPART 1140	EMPIRES AND DANCE (LP)	15
95	Virgin V2760	GOOD NEWS FROM THE NEXT WORLD (LP)	80

(see also Johnny & Self Abusers)

SIMPLICITY PEOPLE
73	Grape GR 3062	Murderer/BIG YOUTH: The Killer	15
73	Harry J HJ 6649	Time Is Getting Harder/Hardest Version	6

Bill SIMPSON

MINT VALUE £

BILL SIMPSON
64	Piccadilly 7N 35179	I Love You For Sentimental Reasons/My Love Is Like A Red Red Rose (p/s)	8

DANNY SIMPSON
69	Trojan TR 653	Outa Sight/JOHN HOLT: I Want You Closer	30

DUDLEY SIMPSON ORCHESTRA
78	BBC RESL 58	Blake's 7/The Federation March (p/s)	8

DUDLEY SIMPSON & BRIAN HODGSON
73	Polydor 2383 210	IN A COVENT GARDEN (LP)	25

(See also BBC Radiophonic Workshop)

HOKE SIMPSON
58	HMV POP 442	I Finally Found You/Gi-Gi	8

JEANETTE SIMPSON
67	Giant GN 16	Rain/Whatcha Gonna Do About It	20
68	Giant GN 29	My Baby Just Cares For Me/Don't Let Me Cry No More (with Superboys)	100
68	Giant GN 35	Through Loving You/Send Me Some Lovin' (with Missions)	15

LEO SIMPSON
65	Blue Beat BB 351	I Love Her So/Good To Be Seen (as Leo Simmo)	18
73	Pyramid PYR 7004	Waxy Doodle/Go Away	6

(see also Lionel Simpson)

LIONEL SIMPSON
65	Ska Beat JB 205	Tell Me What You Want/Love Is A Game	20
65	Ska Beat JB 221	Red River Valley/Eight People	15
66	Ska Beat JB 233	Give Over/Never Before	15

(see also Leo Simpson)

MARTIN SIMPSON
76	Trailer LER 2099	GOLDEN VANITY (LP, yellow label)	20
86	Dambuster DAM 013	NOBODY'S FAULT BUT MINE (LP)	15

CHUCK SIMS
58	London HLR 8577	Little Pigeon/Life Isn't Long Enough	150
58	London HLR 8577	Little Pigeon/Life Isn't Long Enough (78)	60

FRANKIE LEE SIMS
71	Specialty SNTF 5004	LUCY MAE BLUES (LP)	15

JOAN SIMS
63	Parlophone R 5021	Oh Not Again Ken/Hurry Up Gran	7

KELLY SIMS
60	Top Rank JAR 321	Betrayed By Love/A Girl In Love	6

SIMS TWINS/VALENTINOS
68	Soul City SCM 001	THE VALENTINOS/THE SIMS TWINS (LP, 1 side each)	60

ZOOT SIMS
57	Esquire EP 183	ZOOT! (EP)	20
57	Esquire EP 204	ZOOT'S CASE (EP)	20
52	Esquire 20-002	ZOOT SIMS QUARTET/QUINTET (10" LP)	40
53	Esquire 20-010	ZOOT SIMS ALLSTARS (10" LP)	40
53	Esquire 20-018	ZOOT SIMS QUARTET/QUINTET (10" LP)	40
54	Vogue LDE 056	ZOOT SIMS GOES TO TOWN (10" LP)	200
55	Esquire 20-040	ZOOT SIMS QUARTET/QUINTET (10" LP)	60
56	Voge 12047	TONITE'S MUSIC TODAY (LP, with Bobby Brookmeyer)	30
57	Esquire 32-040	ZOOT SIMS SEPTET (LP)	60
58	HMV CLP 1165	GEORGE HANDY COMPOSITIONS (LP)	30
58	HMV CLP 1188	PLAYS FOUR ALTOS (LP)	40
61	Vogue LAE 12309	CHOICE (LP)	40
61	Fontana TFL 5176	ZOOT AT RONNIE SCOTT'S (LP)	200
61	Parlophone PMC 1169	DOWN HOME (LP)	80
62	Fontana (S)TFL 588	ZOOT AT RONNIE SCOTT'S (LP, reissue)	100
62	Fontana 886 151 TY	SOLO FOR ZOOT (LP, also mono [680 982 TL], £50)	200
65	Fontana FJL 123	COOKIN'! (LP)	150
60s	Xtra XTRA 5001	TROTTING! (LP)	15

(see also Sims-Wheeler Vintage Jazz Band)

FRANK SINATRA
53	Columbia SCM 5052	Birth Of The Blues/Why Try To Change Me Now?	20
53	Columbia SCM 5060	You Do Something To Me/Lover	25
53	Columbia SCM 5076	Santa Claus Is Comin' To Town/My Girl	25
54	Capitol CL 14064	Young-At-Heart/Take A Chance	15
54	Capitol CL 14120	Three Coins In The Fountain/I Could Have Told You	20
54	Capitol CL 14174	White Christmas/The Christmas Waltz	15
54	Capitol CL 14188	When I Stop Loving You/It Worries Me	15
55	Columbia SCM 5167	S'posin'/How Deep Is The Ocean	6

(Originally issued with triangular centre; later round-centre copies are worth half this value.)

54	Capitol LC 6654	SONGS FOR YOUNG LOVERS (10")	15
54	Capitol LC 6689	SWING EASY (10")	15
54	Philips BBR 8003	SING AND DANCE WITH FRANK SINATRA (10")	15
55	Capitol LC 6702	IN THE WEE SMALL HOURS VOL. 1 (10")	15
55	Capitol LC 6705	IN THE WEE SMALL HOURS VOL. 2 (10")	15
56	Capitol LCT 6106	SONGS FOR SWINGIN' LOVERS	15
56	Capitol LCT 6111	FRANK SINATRA CONDUCTS TONE POEMS OF COLOUR	15
62	Reprise R(9) 1006	SINATRA SINGS GREAT SONGS FROM GREAT BRITAIN (mono)	15
62	Reprise R(9) 1006	SINATRA SINGS GREAT SONGS FROM GREAT BRITAIN (stereo)	15
83	Mobile Fidelity SC 1	THE SINATRA COLLECTION (16-LPs in silver box, with Swing Easy LP unavailable elsewhere)	40
85	Capitol SINATRA 20	FRANK SINATRA: THE CAPITOL YEARS (20-LP, box set)	40

Nancy SINATRA

MINT VALUE £

(see also Nancy Sinatra, Count Basie, Tommy Dorsey, Dean Martin)

NANCY SINATRA

61	Reprise RS 20017	Cuff Links And Tie Clips/Not Just Your Friend (with p/s)	25
61	Reprise RS 20017	Cuff Links And Tie Clips/Not Just Your Friend	10
62	Reprise RS 20045	To Know Him Is To Love Him/Like I Do	12
63	Reprise RS 20144	I See The Moon/Put Your Head On My Shoulder	10
64	Reprise RS 20335	True Love/The Answer To Everything	10
65	Reprise RS 20407	So Long Babe/If He'd Loved Me	10
66	Reprise RS 20432	These Boots Are Made For Walkin'/The City Never Sleeps At Night	6
66	Reprise R 20461	How Does That Grab You Darlin'/I Move Around	7
66	Reprise RS 20491	Friday's Child/Hutchinson Jail	7
66	Reprise RS 20514	In Our Time/Leave My Dog Alone	7
67	Reprise RS 20527	Sugar Town/Summer Wine	8
67	Reprise RS 20559	Love Eyes/Coastin'	7
67	Reprise RS 20620	Lightning's Girl/Until It's Time For You To Go	8
69	Reprise RS 20869	The Highway Song/Are You Growing Tired Of My Love	7
77	Private Stock PVT 114	It's For My Dad/A Gentle Man Like You	7
66	Reprise REP 30069	RUN FOR YOUR LIFE (EP)	20
66	Reprise REP 30072	I MOVE AROUND (EP)	15
67	Reprise REP 30080	SORRY 'BOUT THAT (EP)	15
67	Reprise REP 30086	NASHVILLE NANCY (EP)	15
66	Reprise R 6202	BOOTS (LP)	25
66	Reprise R 6207	HOW DOES THAT GRAB YOU? (LP)	25
66	Reprise R(S)LP 6221	NANCY IN LONDON (LP)	25
67	Reprise RLP 6239	SUGAR (LP)	25
67	Reprise R(S)LP 6251	COUNTRY, MY WAY (LP)	20
68	Reprise R(S)LP 6277	MOVIN' WITH NANCY (LP)	20
69	Reprise RSLP 6333	NANCY (LP, flipback sleeve, laminated front)	20
73	RCA SF 8331	WOMAN (LP)	15

(see also Elvis Presley)

NANCY SINATRA & LEE HAZLEWOOD

67	Reprise RS 20629	Lady Bird/Sand	7
67	Reprise RS 23215	Some Velvet Morning/Tony Rome	8
71	Reprise K 14093	Did You Ever?/Back On The Road Again	6
67	Reprise REP 30083	JACKSON (EP)	15
68	Reprise R(S)LP 6273	NANCY & LEE (LP)	20
71	RCA Victor SF 8240	DID YOU EVER? (LP)	18

(see also Lee Hazlewood, Frank Sinatra)

JIMMY SINCLAIR

62	Wasp W005	To Prove My Love/Verona	12

JIMMY SINCLAIR & TRENTON SPENCE ORCHESTRA

61	Blue Beat BB 47	Verona/To Prove My Love	10

(see also Jimmy Sinclair)

PAUL SINCLAIR

76	Angen ANG 115	Jah Is My Saviour/Version	12
76	Third World TW 25	Naturalization/Version (as Paul Sinclaire)	40
78	Lovers Rock DYS 68	Perfidia (vocal)/Perfidia (instrumental)//GLEN ADAMS: Can't Hide Love/Blue Moon (instrumental) (12")	70

WINSTON SINCLAIR

69	Nu Beat NB 026	Another Heartache/Come On Little Girl	20

(see also Harmonisers)

BETTY SINCLAIRE

70	Torpedo TOR 19	Why Why Why/HOT ROD ALL STARS: Fistful Of Dollars	80

SINDELFINGEN

73	Deroy DER 035	ODGIPIG (LP, private pressing, with insert)	1000
90	Cenotaph CEN 111	ODGIPIG/TRIANGLE (2-LP, reissue with live album, 300 only)	40

TONY SINDEN

80	Piano PIANO 002	FUNCTIONAL ACTION PARTS 2 & 3 (LP)	25

SINE

77	CBS 82870	HAPPY IS THE ONLY WAY (LP)	20

(see also Cloud One, Bumblebee Unlimited)

NALA SINEPHRO

21	NTS NTSM2V	LIVE AT REAL WORLD STUDIOS (1-sided 12", stamped, p/s, 250 only)	60

SINES

82	Rave PE 001	Wishing My Life/She Knows	30

SINEWAVE

72	Chapter One SCH 172	Clochemerle/Star Trek	10

PETE SINFIELD

73	Manticore K 43501	STILL (LP, textured gatefold pink sleeve)	25
73	Manticore K 43501	STILL (LP, textured gatefold blue sleeve)	20

(see also Emerson Lake & Palmer, King Crimson)

SIN FX

80	Wombat S/80/CUS 616	STREET CREDIBILITY EP	8

SINGAPORE

79	SRTS/79/CUS 274	Launching/A Bird With No Wings	200

RAY SINGER

64	Ember EMB S 187	Tell Me Now/I'm Comin' Home	10
64	Ember EMB S 199	It's Gotta Be/Hey, Who?	10
65	Ember EMB S 215	I'm The Richest Man Alive/Pretty Little Rambling Rose (in p/s)	15
65	Ember EMB S 215	I'm The Richest Man Alive/Pretty Little Rambling Rose	10

SUSAN SINGER

MINT VALUE £

65	Fontana TF 621	You'll Come Crying To Me/Who Can I Talk To About You	10
67	Ember EMB S 231	What's Done Has Been Done/Won't It Be Fine	60
66	Ember EMB 3364	RAY SINGER (LP)	40

(see also Nirvana [U.K.])

SUSAN SINGER

62	Oriole CB 1703	Gee It's Great To Be Young/Hello First Love	20
62	Oriole CB 1741	Bobby's Loving Touch/Johnny Summertime	150
62	Oriole CB 1778	Love Me With All Your Heart/Autumn Leaves	20
63	Oriole CB 1802	Lock Your Heart Away/Answer To A Prayer	20
63	Oriole CB 1882	I Know (You Don't Love Me No More)/That Old Feeling	20

(see also Susan Holiday)

SINGER BLUE AND DUBATEERS

07	Dubateers DA 1007	Never Stop Praise Jah Jah/Jah Jah Dub/KENNY KNOTS & DUBATEERS: Show Dem/Rising Dub (10")	25

SINGERS & PLAYERS

82	On U Sound ON ULP5	WAR OF WORDS (LP)	25
82	On U Sound ON ULP11	REVENGE OF THE UNDERDOG (LP)	30
83	On U Sound ON ULP23	STAGGERING HEIGHTS (LP)	20
84	Trance TCLP4	LEAPS & BOUNDS (LP, white vinyl)	30
88	On U Sound ON ULP39	VACUUM BUMPING (LP)	20

SINGING BELLES

60	Top Rank JAR 350	The Empty Mailbox/Someone Loves You, Joe	6

SINGING DOGS

57	Pye NEP 24029	SINGING DOGS (EP)	10

SINGING KETTLES

74	Hadley HS 20	A Satisfied Mind/Little Boy Lost	15

SINGING LOINS

91	Hangman HANG 44 UP	SONGS FOR THE ORGAN (LP)	15
93	Hangman HANG 51 UP	STEAK AND GRAVY (LP)	15

(see also Billy Childish & Singing Loins)

SINGING POSTMAN

66	Parlophone R 5505	The Ladies Darts Team/Roundabout	7
67	Parlophone R 5584	Mind How You Go/Daddy's Trombone	7
67	Parlophone R 5632	Sound Barrier/Old North Walsham Line	7
64	Ralph Tuck Promotions Ltd. BEV EP 153	Come Along A Me/Moind Yer Hid Boy/Hev Yew Gotta Loight Boy/Miss From Diss (EP)	10
65	Ralph Tuck BEV EP 179	BBC SINGING POSTMAN (EP)	10
66	Parlophone PMC 7013	RECORDED DELIVERY (LP)	15

SINGING PRINCIPAL

73	Action ACT 4608	Thank You Baby/Women's Lib	75

SINGLE FACTOR

84	SF Records SINFAX 001	Fresh Upon Her Lips/I Think I'm Falling In Love (p/s, 2 inserts)	50

SINGLES

78	Sing SING 1	Adolf Hitler/Mercy (no p/s)	1000

MARGIE SINGLETON

60	Melodisc 45-1544	Angel Hands/The Eyes Of Love	15
62	Mercury AMT 1197	Magic Star/Only Your Shadow Knows	20
68	Fontana TL 5456	SINGS COUNTRY WITH SOUL (LP)	18

SINISTER DUCKS

83	Situation 2 SIT 25	Suicide: March Of The Sinister Ducks/Homicide: Old Gangsters Never (foldout p/s)	10

(see also Bauhaus)

SINITTA

83	Midas 12MID 3	Never Too Late (Special Extended US Mix)/Never Too Late (Instrumental) (12", p/s)	40

SINKING SHIPS

81	Recession REC S1	Dream/After The Rain (Live)	18

EARL SINK(S)

61	Warner Bros WB 38	Look For Me, I'll Be There/Super Market (as Earl Sink)	15
61	Warner Bros WB 51	Superstitious/Little Suzie Parker	20
63	Capitol CL 15210	Looking For Love/Raining On My Side Of Town (as Earl Sinks)	15

(see also Crickets, Sinx Mitchell)

SINNER

79	Whitetower AMC 705	Need Your Love/Beggar/God's In His Heaven (foldout p/s)	75

SINNERMAN & SARA

68	MGM 1450	Don't Think Twice It's Allright/Buffalo Boy	10
68	MGM MGM-C(S) 8099	SINNERMAN AND SARA (LP)	20

SINNERS

63	Columbia DB 7158	I Can't Stand It/If You Leave Me Now	10
64	Columbia DB 7295	It's So Exciting/Leave Him	10

(see also Linda Laine & Sinners)

SINS OF THE FLESH

90s	Plastic Head 014	In The Image Of Torture (12", p/s)	10

SIOUX

73	SRT SRT 73274	Prosmoe/Warlove/You're All I Need/Happiness In The Sky (EP)	75

SIOUXSIE AND THE BANSHEES

78	Polydor 2059 052	Hong Kong Garden/Voices (10,000 only in gatefold p/s; beige plastic, silver plastic, red plastic or red paper label)	20
79	Polydor POSP 9	The Staircase (Mystery)/20th Century Boy (thin paper p/s, very hard to find in mint)	6
79	Polydor POSP 59	Playground Twist/Pull To Bits (thin paper p/s, very hard to find in mint)	6
79	Polydor 2059 151	Mittageisen (Metal Postcard)/Love In A Void (p/s)	8
80	Polydor POSP 117	Happy House/Drop Dead (Celebration) (p/s)	6
80	Polydor POSP 205	Israel/Red Over White (picture label, gold die-cut sleeve)	6

SIR ALEC & HIS BOYS

MINT VALUE £

80	Polydor POSPX 205	Israel (Extended)/Red Over White (Extended) (12", a few with Made In England' credit, most with 'Made In France' credit)	12
80	Polydor POSP 249	Christine/Eve White, Eve Black (p/s)	8
81	Polydor POSP 309	Arabian Nights/Supernatural Thing (p/s)	6
82	Polydor POSPG 450	Fireworks/Coal Mind (foldout p/s, regular p/s copies worth £3)	6
83	Fan Club FILE 1	Head Cut/Running Town (freebie, p/s)	30
85	Wonderland SHE 8	Overground/Placebo Effect (p/s)	6
86	Wonderland SHEDP 10	Candyman/Lullaby (with free 2nd single, gatefold p/s, 2,000 only)	8
87	Wonderland SHEPK 4	The Passenger/Hall Of Mirrors/You're Lost Little Girl/Sea Breezes/This Town Ain't Big Enough For Both Of Us/Gun (3 X promo 7" in plain black sleeves in foldout stickered and printed PVC wallet, single cat. no's SHESP 1/2/3)	20
87	Wonderland SHEG 11	This Wheel's On Fire/Shooting Sun/Sleepwalking (On The High Wire)/She's Cracked (numbered double pack, gatefold p/s)	6
88	Spiral Scratch SCRATCH 2	An Interview With... (free with Spiral Scratch mag, 5,000 only)	6
78	Polydor POLD 5009	THE SCREAM (LP, with inner sleeve)	20
79	Polydor POLD 5009	THE SCREAM (LP, second pressing, no inner sleeve and 'fully laminated limited edition' in gold on sleeve)	15
79	Polydor POLD 5024	JOIN HANDS (LP, gatefold. with inner sleeve, stickered noting inclusion of 'Playground Twist'.)	18
81	Polydor POLD 5155	JUJU (LP, with inner)	15
81	Polydor POLS 1056	ONCE UPON A TIME : THE SINGLES (LP, 1st pressing with Siouxsie art print)	18
82	Polydor POLD 5064	A KISS IN THE DREAMHOUSE (LP, with inner sleeve)	15
87	Wonderland SHELP 4	THROUGH THE LOOKING GLASS (LP, die-cut sleeve)	15
87	Wonderland SHELP 4	THROUGH THE LOOKING GLASS (LP, mispressing, 1 side plays Jimi Hendrix's "War Heroes")	25
91	Polydor 847731 7	SUPERSTITION (LP)	25
92	Polydor 517160	TWICE UPON A TIME - THE SINGLES (2-LP)	80

(see also Cure, Glove)

SIR ALEC & HIS BOYS
67	Deram DM 116	I'm A Believer/Green Green Grass Of Home	8

SIR ALICK & PHRASER
82	Recommended/Black Noise 7 NO 5	In Search Of The Perfect Baby/PROLIFIKURDS: Nursery Crymes (printed p/s in PVC sleeve or standard p/s)	20

(see also Homosexuals)

SIR BEANZ OBE
12	B-Line Recordings BLN001	PAUSE TO DISCUSS (EP, white vinyl)	12

SIR CHING I
70	Spark SRL 1041	Hello Everyone/Hiawatha Mini Ha Ha Love	300

SIR (CLANCY) COLLINS (BAND)
68	Collins Downbeat CR 005	Sock It Softly (with Bob Stackie)/LESTER STERLING, SIR COLLINS & BAND: Three Wise Men	50
68	Collins Downbeat CR 0011	Collins And The Boys/Bob Stackie In Soho (both with Bob Stackie)	40
68	Collins Downbeat CR 0017	Soul Feelings/SIR COLLINS: Hello Stella	70
69	Duke DU 46	Black Panther/I Want To Be Loved	250
69	Duke DU 47	Black Diamonds (with Diamonds)/DIAMONDS: I Remember	60
69	Duke DU 55	Brother Moses/Funny Familiar Feeling (both with Earthquakes)	70
69	Duke DU 69	Pair Of Wings/I Can't Stop Loving	50
73	Sir Collins Musical Wheel SC 06	Gypsy Woman/I'm Free/Shakedown (Sir Collins with the Versatiles)	45
73	Sir Collins Musical Wheel SC 08	Big Teacher/COLLINS & HONEY BOY: Once I Was Lonely	30
73	Sir Collins Musical Wheel SC 07	Dr. Do Good/Can't Get No Satisfaction (with the Versatiles)	10
81	Sir Collins SC 001	NEW CROSS FIRE PAGE ONE (LP)	40

(see also Bob Stackie, Earthquakes, Collins Band, Owen Gray)

SIR COXSONE SOUND (LLOYD COXON)
75	Safari SFA 100	KING OF THE DUB ROCK (LP)	50
82	Regal RLP 001	KING OF THE DUB ROCK PART 2 (LP)	40

SIR D'S GROUP
61	Blue Beat BB 66	Hey Diddle Diddle (with K. Brown)/Pocket Money (with Mossman & Zeddze)	25

(see also Kent Brown & Rainbows)

SIR DOUGLAS QUINTET
65	London HLU 9964	She's About A Mover/We'll Take Our Last Walk Tonight	12
65	London HLU 9982	The Tracker/Blue Norther	12
65	London HLU 10001	The Story Of John Hardy/In Time	8
66	London HLU 10019	The Rains Came/Bacon Fat	8
69	Mercury MF 1079	Mendocino/I Wanna Be Your Mama Again	12
69	Mercury MF 1129	Dynamite Woman/Too Many Dociled Minds	8
69	London HLU 10248	She's About A Mover/The Rains Came (reissue)	6
65	London HA-U 8311	THE SIR DOUGLAS QUINTET (LP)	40
69	Mercury SMCL 20160	MENDOCINO (LP)	30
69	Mercury SMCL 20186	TOGETHER AFTER FIVE (LP)	30
75	Oval OVLM 5001	MENDOCINO (LP, with insert)	15

SIREN (1)
71	Dandelion DAN 7002	Strange Locomotion/I'm All Aching (label also lists K 19004)	6
69	Dandelion 63755	SIREN (LP, laminated front sleeve, black/red/silver labels)	60
71	Dandelion DAN 8001	STRANGE LOCOMOTION (LP, gatefold sleeve)	60
71	Dandelion DAN 8001	STRANGE LOCOMOTION (LP, with later label listing K 49001)	25

SIREN (2)
84	Distant Cousins DC4R	Deceiving Lies/American Girl (white or black sleeve)	10

SIR GIBBS
68	Amalgamated AMG 822	People Grudgeful/Pan Ya Machet (both sides actually by Pioneers)	65

SIR HARRY

MINT VALUE £

SIR HARRY
71	Duke DU 127	Last Call/ORGAN D: Hot Organ	15
72	Duke DU 136	Apples To Apples/DRUM BEAT ALL STARS: Good Life	15
72	Bullet BU 519	Mr. Parker's Daughter/U.ROY: On Top Of The Peak	18
72	Downtown DT 493	Meet The Boss/Musical Fight	40
73	Downtown DT 504	Apollo 17 (with Cables)/Uptown Rock	25

(see also Barbara Jones)

SIR HENRY (& HIS BUTLERS)
68	Columbia DB 8351	Camp/Pretty Style (as Sir Henry & His Butlers)	10
68	Columbia DB 8497	The Rolo Sensation (Camp)/Pretty Style (reissue, as Sir Henry & His Butlers)	10
70	Columbia DB 8740	Annie Got A Date/Like A Rose	8

SIR HORATIO
82	Rock Steady/666 Mix 1T	Abracadubra/Sommadub (12", plain sleeve)	15

(see also A Certain Ratio)

SIR LLOYD
71	Lion LEO 1	Mosi/Nursery Rhyme Version	20

SIR LORD COMIC
67	Doctor Bird DB 1019	Ska-ing West/MAYTALS: If You Act This Way	40
67	Doctor Bird DB 1070	The Great Wuga Wuga (with Cowboys)/THREE TOPS: Feel So Lonesome	45
70	Pressure Beat PR 5507	Jack Of My Trade/CYNTHIA RICHARDS: United We Stand	70

(see also Lord Comic)

SIR LORD COMIXX
96	Ugly FF 004	DANCETERIA (12")	30

SIRUS
91	White 002	THE ONE AND ONLY (EP)	75
93	SBP SBPR004	Clubland/Dett (12")	10
93	Go Boy GBR 001	LYRICAL JUICE EP (12")	40

SIR WASHINGTON
69	Star ST 1	Apollo 12/When You Kiss Me	40
70	Saga BC 100	Apollo 13/Space	40
70	Saga BC 102	Let There Be Peace in The World/THE RATIO: Pharoah's Walk	10

SISTA MARY
07	Roots Injection RI 10 003	Blindeye/Version/Dem Lost/Version (10")	25
08	Roots Injection RI 10 008	Hail Jah/RAS MUFFET: Version/Hail Jah/RAS MUFFET: Version (10")	15
10	Cultivators 001	Can't Fool I/ITAL THUNDER MEETS ECHO ROOTS: Can't Dub/DANN I LOCKS: Steppin/Steppin Dub (12")	35

SISTER
70	Camel CA 55	Feel It/MAYTONES: Serious	15
73	Camel CA 106	Every Day Is The Same Kind Of Thing/Sweat Of Your Brow	10

SISTER BEVERLEY
76	Concrete Jungle CJ 605	Rasta Woman/Rasta Dub (white labels only)	50
76	Rama (no cat no)	Rasta Woman/Rasta Woman Dub	30

SISTER CANDY
83	Vista Sounds VSLP 4026	BLACK CULTURE (LP)	20

SISTER RAIN
88	A Serene	BURT REYNOLDS (12", EP)	12

SISTERS
73	Bell BELL 1307	Kick Your Boots Off/Driving Me Home	15
74	Warner Brothers K 16245	There's A Raver Coming Home/Help The Music	8

SISTERS LOVE
70	A&M AMS 772	Forget It, I've Got It/Eye To Eye	8
70	A&M AMS 808	The Bigger Your Love/Piece Of My Heart	8
72	Tamla Motown TMG 828	Mr. Fix It Man/You've Got To Make Your Choice	10
73	Mowest MW 3009	I'm Learning To Trust My Man/Try It You'll Like It	20

SISTERS OF MERCY
80	Merciful Release MR 7	The Damage Done/Watch/Home Of The Hitmen (p/s, 1,000 only; beware of counterfeits without 'MR 7' matrix number)	500
82	CNT CNT 002	Body Electric/Adrenochrome (p/s)	200
82	Merciful Release MR 015	Alice/Floorshow (white background p/s)	30
84	Merciful Release/WEA	ALICE/TEMPLE OF LOVE/REPTILE HOUSE/BODY AND SOUL (4 x 12" box set, promo only)	750
84	Merciful Release MR 033	Walk Away/Poison Door (p/s, with flexidisc "Long Train" [SAM 218])	15
84	Merciful Release MR 033T	Walk Away/Poison Door/On The Wire (12", p/s, with flexi "Long Train")	15
85	Merciful Release MR 335	No Time To Cry/Blood Money (p/s)	6
88	Merciful Release MR 43TB	Dominion (Extended)/Untitled/Sandstorm/Emma (12", box set with poster)	15
93	Merciful Release MR59T	Under The Gun (Metropolis)/Alice (1993)/Under The Gun (Jutland Mix) (12", poster p/s)	15
85	Merciful Release MR337L	FIRST AND LAST AND ALWAYS (LP, gatefold)	15
87	Merciful Release MR441L	FLOODLANDS (LP)	15
90	Merciful Release MMR 449 L	VISION THING (LP)	15
92	East West 9031 76476-`	SOME GIRLS WANDER BY MISTAKE (2-LP)	25

(see also Mission, Ghost Dance, Dead Or Alive)

SITUATION
66	CBS 202392	Situation Now/Time	30

SIVUCA
74	Vanguard VSD 79237	SIVUCA (LP)	30

SIX OF ONE
64	Mercury MF 812	He's The One You Love/I Love My Little Girl	10

SIX TEASERS
89	Kent 6T 5	Doing The Hundred/WALLY COX: This Man Wants You	15

SIX MINUTE WAR

MINT VALUE £

SIX MINUTE WAR
80	(No label or cat no)	75P EP (7", fold-out p/s, 1st issue with 'soldier' sleeve)	15
80	(No label or cat no)	MORE SHORT SONGS (7" EP, fold-out p/s)	10
81	(No label or cat no)	SLIGHTLY LONGER SONGS (7" EP, fold-out, p/s)	10

SIXPENCE
67	London HLJ 10124	You're The Love/What To Do	10

EARL SIXTEEN
79	Cha Cha CHAD 16	The World Has Begun (with the Heptones)/Make Up Your Mind (12")	50
80	Sufferers Heights SUFF 007	African Tribesman/MIKEY DREAD: Butter Gainst Sun/Yoruba Dub (12")	35
81	DATC DCD 004	MR D.J./GILLY BUCHANAN: Ghetto Youths/DATC MUSIC STABLE : Dub (12")	25
81	Greensleeves GRED 64	Trials And Crosses/BARRY BROWN: Love Is What The World Wants (12")	20
92	Riz RIZ 004	Natural Roots/Version/Part 2/Dub (12")	40
81	Dread At The Controls DATCLP003	REGGAE SOUND (LP)	30
83	Vista VSLP 4023	SHINING STAR (LP)	30
93	Seven Leaves SLLP 08	PHOENIX OF PEACE (LP)	35

16B
95	Stronghouse STR12 008	TRAIL OF DREAMS (12" EP, die-cut sleeve)	20
95	Stronghouse STR12 009	NOWHERE (12" EP, die-cut sleeve)	12

SIX TEENS
56	London HLU 8345	A Casual Look/Teen Age Promise	250
56	London HLU 8345	A Casual Look/Teen Age Promise (78)	50

SIXTH COMM
87	Eyas Media EYAS 002	CONTENT WITH BLOOD/TURN OF THE WHEEL (LP, embossed, textured sleeve, 2,000 only)	20
87	Eyas Media EYAS 005	TASTE FOR FLESH (LP, 1st 2,000 in laminated, full-cover sleeve)	20
88	Eyas Media EYAS 006	FRUITS OF YGGDRASIL (LP, limited issue, 669 copies only)	25
90	Eyas Media EYAS 013	ASYLUM (LP)	15
90	Eyas Media EYAS 059	MORTHOGENISIS (LP)	20

65 DAYS OF STATIC
06	Monotreme MONO 21-7	Radio Protector/Asphalt & Trouble (p/s, 1500 only, 1000 with unique polaroid photos)	6

64 SPOONS
78	Bushbaby BBM 781	Ladies Don't Have Willies/Tails In The Sky (p/s)	35

67 PARK LANE
69	Toast TT516	I'm So Happy To Be With You/I Got Love	60

SIZE SEVEN GROUP
64	Rendevous HS 1/PR 5020	Crying My Heart Out/So How Come	20
65	Mercury MF 845	Where Do We Go From Here/Till I Die	10
65	Mercury MF 896	In Time/Walking Proud	10
65	Mercury MF 896	It's Got To Be Love/I Met Her In The Rain	8

SKA CHAMPIONS
65	Blue Beat BB 305	My Tears/Yesterday's Dreams	25

SKA CITY ROCKERS
80	Inferno BEAT 1	Time Is Tight/Roadrunner/You Don't Know Like I Know (p/s)	6
80	Inferno BEAT 1	Time Is Tight/Roadrunner/You Don't Know Like I Know (12", p/s)	10

SKA-DOWS
80	Cheapskate CHEAP 1	Apache/The Tune That Time Forgot (p/s)	7
80	Cheapskate CHEAP 4	Telstar/Yes Yes Yes (p/s)	8
81	Cheapskate CHEAP 25	Yes Yes Yes/Twice (p/s)	8
81	Penthouse PENT 7	Ska's On 45/Rhapsody In Buh (plain stickered sleeve)	6
81	Penthouse PENT 127	The Ska-Dows Live (Let's Twist Again/Everybody Knows It's Shocking/Aye-Ho - Kinky Reggae) (12", p/s)	12
81	Cheapskate CHEAP 36	Ska's On 45/Rhapsody In Buh (p/s, reissue)	6
82	Cheapskate SKATE 3	SKA'D FOR LIFE (LP)	15

SKA KINGS
64	Atlantic AT 4003	Jamaica Ska (actually by Keith Lynn & Ken Lazarus, & Byron Lee/Dragonaires)/Oil In My Lamp (actually by Eric Morris with Byron Lee & Dragonaires)	20
65	Parlophone R 5338	Bimbo/Ska'ville	10

SKANNA
92	White House WYHS 010	Intimidator/Jungle Rain/Cease Fire/Dreamin' (12")	20
93	White House WYHS 013	The Future/Nightstalker/Intimidator (Technoid Mix)/Exit The Lights (12")	50
93	Skanna 03	NIGHT STALKER EP (12")	50
93	Skanna 04	Until The Night Is Morning/Untitled (12")	50
93	Skanna 05	Heaven/Run To Me/This Way (12")	30
94	Skanna 07	The Greatest Thing (Summertime Mix)/The Greatest Thing/Heaven (Remix) (12")	12
94	Skanna 08	All You Wanted/The Greatest Thing (Criminal Minds Mix) (12")	15
96	Skanna 09	Find Me/Find Me (Classic Skanna Mix) (12")	20

(see also The Joker)

SKATALITES (JAMAICA)
65	Island WI 161	Trip To Mars/DOTTIE & BONNIE: Bunch Of Roses	45
64	Island WI 164	Good News/OWEN & LEON: The Fits Is On Me	25
65	Island WI 168	Guns Of Navarone (actually by Roland Alphonso & Studio One Orchestra)/Marcus Garvey (actually by Bongoman Byfield)	25
65	Island WI 175	Dragon Weapon/DESMOND DEKKER & FOUR ACES: It Was Only A Dream	80
65	Island WI 191	Dr. Kildare/Sucu Sucu	70
65	Island WI 207	Ball O' Fire/LINVAL SPENCER: Can't Go On	60
65	Island WI 226	Dick Tracy/RITA & SOULETTES: One More Chance	110
65	Island WI 228	Beardman Ska/BONNIE & RITA: Bless You	50
65	Island WI 244	Lucky Seven/JUSTIN HINDS & DOMINOES: Never Too Young	25
66	Island WI 260	Independent Anniversary Ska (I Should Have Known Better)/WAILERS: Jumbie Jamboree	100

SKATALITES (U.K.)

MINT VALUE £

65	Ska Beat JB 177	Latin Goes Ska/LORD TANAMO: Night Food Ska	60
65	Ska Beat JB 178	Silver Dollar/My Business	60
65	Ska Beat JB 182	Street Corner/DREAMLETS: Really Now	85
65	Ska Beat JB 206	Timothy/KING SCRATCH & DYNAMITES: Gumma	40
73	Trojan Maxi TRM 9008	Guns Of Navarone/Bonanza Ska/Napolean Solo	8
75	Tropical ALO64	Jumbo Malt/747 Dub (as Original Skatalites)	10
67	Studio One SOL 9006	SKA AUTHENTIC (LP)	450
03	Motion FASTLP 009	THE LEGENDARY SKATALITES IN DUB (LP, red vinyl)	25

(see also Justin Hinds, Deltas, Four Aces, Maytals, Jackie Opel, Joe White, Jackie Mittoo)

SKATALITES (U.K.)
| 68 | Decca F 12743 | Don't Knock It/I Know | 10 |
| 69 | Spark SRL 1034 | Cos You're The One I Love/Please Let Me Hide | 10 |

SKAVENGERS
| 80 | Identity Discs ID 001 | Party Girls/Go To Pieces/Happy | 10 |

SKAVILLE TRAIN
| 03 | Next Step RFDNX 4 | Jet 707/Darker Shot | 10 |

BOBBY SKEL
| 64 | London HLU 9942 | Kiss And Run/Say It Now | 15 |

SKELETAL FAMILY
83	Luggage RRP 00724	Trees/Just A Friend (foldout p/s)	25
86	Cave CAVE IN 1	Sharp Cheekbones In Black Clothing/Blood-Stained (p/s)	12
85	Red Rhino REDLP 57	FUTILE COMBAT (LP)	15

(see also Ghost Dance)

SKELETON CREW
| 87 | B BS 1 | BOOGIE-WOOGIE, SKIFFLE & BLUES (12" EP, p/s) | 15 |
| 88 | B BS 2 | House Of The Rising Sun/Hurricane Janine (white label promo only) | 15 |

(see also King Earl Boogie Band, Manfred Mann's Earth Band)

SKELLATON
| 94 | Viceroy GREEB028 | Bangers 'n' Mash (12") | 30 |

SKEPTIX
82	Zenon SKEP 001	Routine Machine/Curfew (p/s)	15
83	Zenon SKEP 002	Scarred For Life/Born To Lose/Peaceforce (p/s)	15
83	Zenon SKEP 003	RETURN TO HELL (EP)	15

SKERNE
| 81 | Guardian GRC 81 | BETTER LATE THAN NEVER (LP, private pressing) | 15 |

SKETTO
| 71 | Big Shot BI 596 | Know Your Friend/Three Sevens Version | 15 |

(, Ruddy and Sketto)

SKID
| 77 | Galaxy GY 118 | I Saw Her Standing There/Endless Sleep | 15 |

SKIDDO
| 79 | GTO GT 252 | A Touch Of The Sun/I'm Going On Me Holidays | 8 |

SKIDDY & DETROIT
| 72 | Grape GR 3030 | The Exile Song/BUNNY GALE: In The Burning Sun Joh-Ho | 35 |

ALAN SKIDMORE (QUINTET)
| 69 | Deram Nova SDN 11 | ONCE UPON A TIME (LP, Deram Nova on sleeve but has either Deram Nova or Decca Nova labels) | 250 |
| 71 | Philips 6308 041 | T.C.B. (LP) | 200 |

(see also John Mayall's Bluesbreakers, Brian Bennett, Centipede)

JIMMY SKIDMORE
| 72 | DJM DJSL 026 | SKID MARKS (LP) | 40 |

SKID ROW (IRELAND)
70	Song SO 002	New Places Old Faces/Misdemeanour Dream Felicity (Irish pressing)	100
70	Song SO003	Saturday Morning Man (Irish pressing)	25
70	CBS 4893	Sandie's Gone (Parts 1 & 2)	15
71	CBS 7181	Night Of The Warm Witch/Mr. Deluxe	15
70	CBS 63965	SKID (LP, orange label, red & blue sleeve)	60
71	CBS 64411	34 HOURS (LP, gatefold sleeve, orange label)	45
83	CBS 63964	SKID ROW (LP, different or alternative tracks)	15

(see also Gary Moore, Thin Lizzy, Peggy's Leg, UFO)

SKIDS
78	No Bad NB 1	Charles/Reasons/Test Tube Babies (p/s)	10
79	Virgin V 2116	SCARED TO DANCE (LP, blue vinyl, withdrawn)	500
79	Virgin V2116	SCARED TO DANCE (LP, embossed sleeve black vinyl)	15
79	Virgin V 2138	DAYS IN EUROPA (LP, with insert, 1st pressing with withdrawn cover featuring German 'gothic' lettering & 1936 Olympics picture)	15

(see also Big Country)

BJORN SKIFS
| 78 | EMI EMI 2785 | When The Night Comes/Don't Stop Now | 6 |
| 81 | EMI EMI 5172 | Haunted By A Dream/Fangad I En Drom | 8 |

SKILLETS
| 70 | Pantonic PAN 6303 | BOTH SIDES NOW (LP) | 15 |

SKIN
| 88 | Product Inc. 33 PROD 11 | SHAME, HUMILITY, REVENGE (LP, with inner) | 20 |

SKIN ALLEY
70	CBS 5045	Tell Me/Better Be Blind	20
72	Transatlantic BIG 506	You Got Me Danglin'/Skin Valley Serenade	8
72	Transatlantic BIG 511	In The Midnight Hour/Broken Eggs	8
73	Transatlantic BIG 514	If Only I Had The Time/Instrumental	10
69	CBS 63847	SKIN ALLEY (LP, laminated front sleeve, orange label)	150
70	CBS 64140	TO PAGHAM AND BEYOND (LP, gatefold sleeve, orange label)	60

			MINT VALUE £
72	Transatlantic TRA 260	TWO QUID DEAL (LP, laminated front with inner sleeve & poster)	50
73	Transatlantic TRA 273	SKIN TIGHT (LP)	25
75	Klik KLP 9007	BAG-O-WIRE (LP)	20

SKIN DEEP (1)
85	Enemy ENEMY 1	FOOTBALL VIOLENCE (EP)	250

SKIN DEEP (2)
88	Skank LP 103	MORE THAN SKIN DEEP (LP)	15

SKIN, FLESH & BONES
74	Pyramid PYR 7014	Butter Te Fish/Bammie And Fish	8
74	Opal PAL100	Man Come, Man Go/Guitar Rhythm	30
79	Love LPLV02	FIGHTING DUB (LP)	80

(see also Vincent Gordon, Cynthia Richards)

J SCOTT SKINNER
75	Topic 12T 280	STRATHSPEY KING (LP, blue label)	15

JIMMIE SKINNER
59	Mercury AMT 1030	Walkin' My Blues Away/Dark Hollow	15
59	Mercury AMT 1062	John Wesley Hardin/Misery Loves Company	10
64	London RE-B 1421	KENTUCKY COLONEL VOL. 1 (EP)	10
64	London RE-B 1422	KENTUCKY COLONEL VOL. 2 (EP)	10
64	London RE-B 1423	KENTUCKY COLONEL VOL. 3 (EP)	10

JIMMIE SKINNER/GEORGE JONES
59	Mercury ZEP 10012	COUNTRY AND WESTERN (EP, 2 tracks each)	10

SKINNYMAN
04	Low Life LOW 36LP	COUNCIL ESTATE OF MIND (LP)	60

SKIP BIFFERTY
67	RCA Victor RCA 1621	On Love/Cover Girl	30
67	RCA Victor RCA 1648	Happy Land/Reason To Live	40
68	RCA Victor RCA 1720	Man In Black/Mr. Money Man	55
68	RCA Victor RD/SF 7941	SKIP BIFFERTY (LP, black label)	400
68	RCA Victor RD/SF 7941	SKIP BIFFERTY (LP, later pressing with orange label)	200

(see also Chosen Few, Heavy Jelly, Griffin, Graham Bell, Arc, Bell & Arc, Every Which Way, Loving Awareness)

SKIP & FLIP
59	Top Rank JAR 156	It Was I/Lunch Hour	10
59	Top Rank JAR 248	Fancy Nancy/It Could Be	15
60	Top Rank JAR 358	Cherry Pie/(I'll Quit) Cryin' Over You	10

(see also Gary Paxton, Skip Battin, Hollywood Argyles)

SKI PATROL
80	Clever Metal VIN 1	Everything Is Temporary/Silent Screams (p/s)	10
80	Malicious Damage MD 2	Agent Orange/Driving (p/s, with insert)	12
81	Malicious Damage MD 3	Cut/Faith In Transition (p/s)	10

(see also Wall)

SKITZ
01	Ronin RDLP 2	COUNTRYMAN (LP)	15
02	Ultimate Dilemma UDR LP 018	BADMEANINGOOD VOL 1 (2-LP, Banksy artwork)	300

SKITZOFRENIK
81	Guardian GRC 120	USA/Lonely Road (p/s)	100

SAM SKLAIR
69	Pye 7N 25488	Zulu Warrior/Phata Phata	15

YANI SKORDALIDIS
75	Pinnacle P8413	Little Drummer Boy/Here Pussy Pussy	15

SKREAM
06	Big Apple BAM 007	Acid People/Get Mad/Who R Those Guys/Skunk Step (12")	25
06	Southside Dubstars DUBSTAR 008	SOUTHSIDE EP VOL 2 (12")	10
06	Tempa TEMPALP 008	SKREAM! (3-LP)	30
10	Tempa TEMPAL 016	OUTSIDE THE BOX (4-LP)	20

SKREWDRIVER
77	Chiswick S 11	You're So Dumb/Better Off Crazy (green p/s)	60
77	Chiswick S 11	You're So Dumb/Better Off Crazy (orange p/s)	50
77	Chiswick NS 11	You're So Dumb/Better Off Crazy (p/s, CBS repressing)	35
77	Chiswick NS 18	Anti-Social/19th Nervous Breakdown (p/s)	40
78	Chiswick NS 28	Streetfight/Unbeliever (unissued, Trident label)	300
80	TJM TJM 4	Built Up, Knocked Down/A Case Of Pride/Breakout (p/s)	25
82	Skrewdriver SKREW 1T	BACK WITH A BANG (12", p/s)	40
83	White Noise WN 1	White Power/Smash The I.R.A./Shove The Dove (p/s)	70
83	White Noise WN 2	Voice Of Britain/Sick Society (p/s)	50
77	Chiswick CH 3	ALL SKREWED UP (mini-LP, 12-track, 45rpm, 3 different colour sleeves)	100
77	Chiswick WIK 3	ALL SKREWED UP (LP, 15-track, 33rpm, unissued in U.K.; German-only)	100

SKROTEEZ
82	Skroteez SPILL 1	OVERSPILL (EP)	15

SKULLFLOWER
86	Broken Flag BF V9	BIRTHDEATH (12" EP)	80
89	Shock SX 001	(I Live) In The Bottomless Pit/Bo Diddley's Shitpump (foldaround p/s in poly bag, 500 only, 75 copies in 'burns victim' sleeve)	20
89	Shock SX 001	(I Live) In The Bottomless Pit/Bo Diddley's Shitpump (foldaround p/s in poly bag, 500 only)	12
90	Toe Jam FLUF 005	Rotten Sun/Spook Rise (p/s, numbered, 500 only)	15
92	Dying Artefact DE 002	Bad Alchemy/Blues For H.M. (p/s in poly bag, numbered, 500 only)	10
94	Freak Records RR 001	White Fang 2/Glassy Essence (wraparound sleeve, stamped label)	8
89	Shock SX 008	XAMAN (LP, 1000 only)	20

SKULLHEAD

MINT VALUE £

89	Broken Flag BFV 10	FORM DESTROYER (LP)	30
92	Headdirt HD 01	IIIRD GATEKEEPER (LP)	30

(see also Ramleh)

SKULLHEAD

87	United SKULL 1	WHITE WARRIOR (LP)	50
89	Counter Culture CCR1	Blame The Bosses/VIOLENT STORM: Celtic Warrior/Unemployed Voice (p/s)	10
89	United SKULL 2	ODIN'S LAW (LP)	20

SKULLS

89	Snake Skin SS 001	Graveyard Signal/Idols And Dolls (p/s, 300 only)	10

SKULL SNAPS

73	GSF GS 27	My Hang Up Is You/It's A New Day	60
18	Dynamite Cuts DYNAM7007	It's A New Day/Trespassing (reissue, p/s)	10
95	Charly CPLP 8094	SKULL SNAPS (LP, reissue, gatefold)	30

SKUNKS

78	Eel Pie EPS 001	Good From The Bad/Back Street Fightin' (2,000 only, die-cut 'swirl' sleeve)	12

(see also Craze, Hard Corps)

PATRICK SKY

65	Vanguard VSD 79179	PATRICK SKY (LP)	20
70	Vanguard SVRL 19254	A HARVEST OF GENTLE CLANG (LP)	20

SKY (1)

68	United Artists UP 2234	Air-O-Plane Ride/Weather Forecast	7
69	Decca F 12971	On Our Way/The Singer Is Singing His Song	7

(see also Knack)

SKYBIRD

74	Holyground HGS 118	SUMMER OF '73 (LP, 250 copies only)	60

SKYLARK

72	Capitol CL 15747	The Writings On The Wall/Wildflower	8

SKYLINERS

59	London HLB 8829	Since I Don't Have You/One Night, One Night	175
59	London HLB 8829	Since I Don't Have You/One Night, One Night (78)	50
59	London HLU 8924	This I Swear/Tomorrow	80
59	London HLU 8924	This I Swear/Tomorrow (78)	50
59	London HLU 8971	It Happened Today/Lonely Way	75
59	London HLU 8971	It Happened Today/Lonely Way (78)	60
60	Polydor NH 66951	Pennies From Heaven/I'll Be Seeing You	15
61	Pye International 7N 25091	I'll Close My Eyes/The Door Is Still Open	20

SKY PONY

70	Decca F 23082	Jubeldown/Chubby	8

SKYSOUNDS

66	Anglo TPMA 101/102	Two Timer/No Matter Where I Wander (private pressing)	10

SKYWHALE

77	Firebrand DM 013	THE WORLD AT MINDS END (LP)	50

SKYY

79	Salsoul SSLP 1516	SKYY (LP)	15
80	Salsoul SALP 231	SKYYPORT (LP)	15

(see also New York Skyy)

SLACK ALICE

74	Philips 6308 214	SLACK ALICE (LP)	20

(see also Sandra Alfred, Sandra Barry)

FREDDIE SLACK (& ORCHESTRA)

51	Capitol LC 6529	FREDDIE SLACK'S BOOGIE WOOGIE (10" LP)	35

(see also Ella Mae Morse & Freddie Slack)

SLADE

SINGLES

69	Fontana TF 1056	Wild Winds Are Blowing/One Way Hotel (credited to The Slade)	100
70	Fontana TF 1079	Shape Of Things To Come/C'mon C'mon	80
70	Polydor 2058 054	Know Who You Are/Dapple Rose	80
74	Polydor 2058 453	Everyday/Good Time Gals (misspressed with Hollies' The Air That I Breathe on A-side)	6
77	Barn 2014 106	Burning In The Heat Of Love/Ready Steady Kids	18
77	Barn 2014 114	My Baby Left Me; That's Alright/O.H.M.S. (p/s)	6
78	Barn 2014 121	Give Us A Goal/Daddio	8
78	Barn 2014 127	Rock'n'Roll Bolero/It's Alright By Me	15
79	Barn BARN 002	Ginny Ginny/Dizzy Mama (yellow vinyl only, with sticker)	10
79	Barn BARN 002	Ginny Ginny/Dizzy Mama (yellow vinyl only, without sticker)	8
79	Barn BARN 010	Sign Of The Times/Not Tonight Josephine	15
79	Barn BARN 011	Okey Cokey/My Baby's Got It	10
80	RSO RSO 051	Okey Cokey/My Baby's Got It (withdrawn reissue, existence unconfirmed)	0
80	S.O.T.B. SUPER 45 3	SIX OF THE BEST - NIGHT STARVATION (12" EP, die-cut sleeve)	15
80	Cheapskate CHEAP 5	ALIVE AT READING '80 (EP, die-cut sleeve)	7
80	Cheapskate CHEAP 11	Merry Xmas Everybody/Okey Cokey/Get Down And Get With It (as Slade & Reading Choir, some in die-cut p/s)	8
81	Cheapskate CHEAP 16	We'll Bring The House Down/Hold On To Your Hats (p/s)	7
81	Cheapskate CHEAP 21	Wheels Ain't Comin' Down/Not Tonight Josephine (p/s)	7
81	Cheapskate CHEAP 24	Knuckle Sandwich Nancy/I'm Mad (p/s)	10
81	RCA	Tak Me Bak 'Ome/Gudbuy T'Jane (12" EP, p/s)	10
82	RCA RCA 191	Ruby Red/Funk Punk And Junk (p/s)	10
82	Speed SPEED 201	Okey Cokey/Get Down And Get With It (no p/s)	8
85	Polydor POSPX 780	Merry Xmas Everybody/Don't Blame Me (12", p/s)	12
85	RCA PB 40449/PB 40549	Do You Believe In Miracles/My Oh My (Swing Version)//Santa Claus Is Coming To Town/Auld Lang Syne/You'll Never Walk Alone To Town/Auld Lang Syne/You'll Never Walk	15

Paul SLADE

MINT VALUE £

85	RCA PT 40450D	Alone .... Do You Believe In Miracles/My Oh My (Swing Version)/Time To Rock/Santa Claus Is Coming To Town/Auld Lang Syne/You'll Never Walk Alone (12", 'Slade Xmas' double pack, separate sleeves in gatefold PVC cover)	10
87	RCA PB 41147D	Still The Same/Gotta Go Home//The Roaring Silence/Don't Talk To Me About Love (21st anniversary double pack, gatefold p/s)	8
80s	Polydor 2058 422	Merry Xmas Everybody/Don't Blame Me (export p/s from various artist box set, green background, 4 individual photos)	15

ALBUMS : LPS

70	Polydor 2383 026	PLAY IT LOUD (LP, sleeve printed by E.J. Day)	40
70	Polydor 2383 026	PLAY IT LOUD (LP, later sleeve printed by Upton printers)	25
72	Polydor 2383 101	SLADE ALIVE (LP, gatefold sleeve)	20
72	Polydor 2383 163	SLAYED? (LP, laminated sleeve)	20
73	Polydor 2442 119	SLADEST (LP, gatefold sleeve with booklet)	25
73	Polydor 2383 261	OLD NEW BORROWED AND BLUE (LP, gatefold sleeve)	15
74	Polydor 2442 126	SLADE IN FLAME (LP, gatefold sleeve)	15
76	Polydor 2383 377	NOBODY'S FOOLS (LP, with inner sleeve)	25
77	Barn 2314 103	WHATEVER HAPPENED TO SLADE (LP, with lyric sheet)	20
78	Barn 2314 106	SLADE ALIVE VOLUME 2 (LP)	15
79	Barn NARB 003	RETURN TO BASE (LP)	40
81	Cheapskate SKATE 1	WE'LL BRING THE HOUSE DOWN (LP, insert)	15

PROMOS

72	Polydor 2814 008	Hear Me Calling/Get Down With It (33rpm sampler for "Slade Alive", 500 only)	125
74	Polydor 2058 492	The Bangin' Man/She Did It To Me (export p/s)	25
75	Polydor 2058 585	Thanks For The Memory (with altered lyrics)/Raining In My Champagne	25
77	Barn 2014 105	Gypsy Roadhog/Forest Full Of Needles (mono, DJ copy)	25
80	S.O.T.B. SUPER 3	Night Starvation/When I'm Dancing I Ain't Fightin'	45

FLEXIDISCS

72	Polydor/Sound For Industry SFI 122	The Whole World's Going Crazee/MIKE HUGG: Bonnie Charlie (33rpm with Music Scene magazine)	18
73	Lyntone LYN 2645	Slade talk to Melanie readers (with Melanie magazine)	15
74	Lyntone LYN 2797	Slade exclusive to all 19 readers (with 19 magazine)	15
75	Fan Club LYN 2645/2797	Slade talk to Melanie readers/Slade talk to 19 readers	10

(see also Ambrose Slade, Steve Brett, 'N Betweens, Vendors, Dummies, Jimmy Lea, China Dolls, Clout, Metal Gurus)

PAUL SLADE

69	Decca F12885	Odyssey/Sound Of Love	12
68	Decca F12840	Heaven Held/Remember Daphne	6

PRENTIS SLADE

61	Parlophone R 4850	I Can Tell/Looking For A Friend	6

SLADE BROTHERS

66	Pye 7N 17176	What A Crazy Life/For A Rainy Day	25
66	Pye 7N 17176	Peace In My Mind/Life's Great Race	60

SLAM CREEPERS

68	Olga OLE 009	Saturday/Hold It Baby	15

SLANES

65	Blue Beat BB 300	It Takes Time/LIGES: Have Mercy Baby (B-side actually by Frank Cosmo)	20

IVOR SLANEY ORCHESTRA

61	HMV POP 943	The Sir Francis Drake Theme/Midsummer Madness	6
64	HMV POP 1347	High Wire/Sacramento	10
66	Columbia DB 8020	Long Weekend/Eleven Up (as Slaney Strings)	8

SLAPP HAPPY

74	Virgin VS 105	Casablanca Moon/Slow Moon's Rose	15
75	Virgin VS 124	Johnny's Dead/Mr. Rainbow (p/s)	12
83	Half Cat HC 001	Everybody's Slimmin' (Even Men And Women!)/Blue-Eyed William (p/s)	15
72	Polydor 2310 204	SORT OF (LP, with German sleeve & insert)	500
74	Virgin V 2014	SLAPP HAPPY (LP, booklet insert)	40
75	Virgin V 2024	DESPERATE STRAIGHTS (LP, gatefold sleeve, with Henry Cow)	30
80	Recommended RR5	ACNALBASAC NOOM (LP, recorded 1973 with members of Faust)	40
81	Recommended RRS 5	SORT OF (LP, reissue)	40
98	V2 VVR1001661	CA VA (LP)	50

(see also Henry Cow, Peter Blegvad, Anthony Moore, Art Bears)

FELIX SLATKIN

60	London HLG 9256	Theme From "The Sundowners"/Gaythers Gone	7

SLAUGHTER (& THE DOGS)

77	Rabid TOSH 101	Cranked Up Really High/The Bitch (p/s, blue, red and later cream plastic labels)	20
77	Rabid TOSH 101	Cranked Up Really High/The Bitch (p/s, repressings with b&w paper label)	15
77	Decca FR 13723	Where Have All The Boot Boys Gone/You're A Bore (paper label)	8
77	Decca LF 13723	Where Have All The Boot Boys Gone/You're A Bore (12", p/s, 10,000 only)	12
77	Decca F 13743	Dame To Blame/Johnny T.	12
77	Decca F 13758	Quick Joey Small/Come On Back (promo with self sealing 'spit proof' sticker on PVC sleeve	75
78	Decca FR 13758	Quick Joey Small/Come On Back (with Mick Ronson)	6
79	TJM TJM 3	It's Alright/Edgar Allen Poe/Twist & Turn/UFO (12", p/s)	12
79	DJM DJS 10927	You're Ready Now/Runaway (p/s)	6
80	Decca FR	Where Have All The Boot Boys Gone/You're A Bore (reissue)	10
80	DJM DJS 10936	East Side Of Town/One By One (p/s, as Slaughter)	6
82	Thrush THRUSH 1	HALF ALIVE (12" EP)	10
88	Damaged Goods FNARR 1	Where Have All The Boot Boys Gone/You're A Bore/Johnny T. (p/s, 1,000 only: 500 on green vinyl, 500 on red vinyl)	15
78	Decca SKL 5292	DO IT DOG STYLE (LP)	30

(see also Studio Sweethearts, Ed Banger)

SLAVES

MINT VALUE £

SLAVES
13	Fonthill F002	Debbie Where's Your Car?/Okay/Not Ideal	25
13	Fonthill F002	Debbie Where's Your Car?/Okay/Not Ideal (gold vinyl)	35
14	Fonthill (No cat no)	Beauty Quest/Girl Fight x 15 (7" picture disc, tour issue)	20
15	Virgin 4714584	The Hunter/Hey (red vinyl)	12
13	Fonthill (No cat no)	SUGAR COATED BITTER TRUTH (LP, 300 only)	100
13	Fonthill (No cat no)	SUGAR COATED BITTER TRUTH (LP, 200 only, white vinyl)	110

FRANK SLAY & HIS ORCHESTRA
61	Top Rank JAR 599	Flying Circle/Cincinnati	8

SLAYER
84	Roadrunner RR 2444 2	HAUNTING THE CHAPEL (12" EP)	25
87	London LON 133	Criminally Insane/Aggressive Perfector (Remix) ('cross' p/s, on red vinyl with patch)	35
87	London LONX 133	Criminally Insane/Postmortem/Aggressive Perfector (Remix) (12", red vinyl, no p/s)	30
91	DEF DEFAP 912	Seasons In The Abyss/Aggressive Perfector (7" picture disc)	20
85	Roadrunner RR 9795	HELL AWAITS (LP)	20
87	Enigma 720151	LIVE UNDEAD (LP, picture disc)	25
86	London/Def Jam LONLP 34	REIGN IN BLOOD (LP, with inner)	25
87	London LONPP 34	REIGN IN BLOOD (LP, picture disc)	35
88	London/Def Jam LONLP 63	SOUTH OF HEAVEN (LP, stickered sleeve, inner)	30
90	Def American 846 871	SEASONS IN THE ABYSS (LP, with inner)	15
90	Metal Blade ZORRODM	SHOW NO MERCY (2-LP, reissue, poster)	30
91	Phonogram 510605-1	DECADE OF AGGRESSION (2-LP, booklet, 6,500 copies only)	25
98	American 491302 1	DIABOLUS IN MUSICA (2-LP, inners)	60
03	Universal B 00001519-02	SOUNDTRACK TO THE APOCALYPSE (4-CD set in 'ammo box' with backstage laminate, flag, bonus DVD in 'blood pack' and booklet)	35

SLEAFORD MODS
14	Fourth Dimension FDS 88	Mr Jolly Fucker/Tweet Tweet Tweet (p/s, 100 only, white vinyl, signed with badge)	75
14	Fourth Dimension FDS 88	Mr Jolly Fucker/Tweet Tweet Tweet (p/s, 100 only, red vinyl)	20
14	Fourth Dimension FDS 88	Mr Jolly Fucker/Tweet Tweet Tweet (p/s)	15
14	Fourth Dimension FDS 88	Mr Jolly Fucker/Tweet Tweet Tweet (p/s clear vinyl)	15
07	A52 Sounds A53CD001	SLEAFORD MODS (LP)	30
08	A52 Sounds A52CD002	THE MEKON (CD)	50
09	A52 Sounds A52CD003	THE ORIGINATOR (CD)	50
11	Deadly Beefburger A52CD004	S.P.E.C.T.R.E. (CD)	50
12	Deadly Beefburger DBRCD020	WANK (CD)	50
14	Harbinger HARBINGER 106	AUSTERITY DOGS (LP)	70
14	Harbinger HARBINGER 106	AUSTERITY DOGS (LP, repressing, clear vinyl)	18
15	Harbinger HARBINGER 121	DIVIDE AND EXIT (LP, red vinyl)	18
15	Harbinger HARBINGER 150	KEY MARKETS (LP)	20
17	Rough Trade RTRADLP 925	ENGLISH TAPAS (LP, red vinyl, insert, free 7" single)	35

SLEAZ BAND
74	Fontana 6007034	All I Want Is You/Midnight Band	15

SLEAZE
75	No Cat no	SLEAZE (LP, white label private pressing, 50 only, insert)	175

F. SLEDGE
67	Blue Beat BB 386	Red Eye Girl/Try To Love Again (actually by "Go On Girl"/"Giving You A Try Girl" by Freddie McKay & Buster's Group)	40

PERCY SLEDGE
66	Atlantic 584 001	When A Man Loves A Woman/Love Me Like You Mean It	8
66	Atlantic 584 034	Warm And Tender Love/Sugar Puddin'	7
66	Atlantic 584 055	Heart Of A Child/My Adorable One	10
67	Atlantic 584 071	It Tears Me Up/Oh, How Happy	10
67	Atlantic 584 080	Baby, Help Me/You've Lost That Something Wonderful	10
67	Atlantic 584 108	Out Of Left Field/It Can't Be Stopped	10
67	Atlantic 584 140	Pledging My Love/You Don't Miss Your Water	10
68	Atlantic 584 177	Take Time To Know Her/It's All Wrong But It's Alright	10
68	Atlantic 584 225	Come Softly To Me/You're All Around Me	10
69	Atlantic 584 264	Any Day Now/The Angels Listened In	10
69	Atlantic 584 286	Kind Woman/Woman Of The Night	8
69	Atlantic 584 300	True Love Travels On A Gravel Road/Faithful And True	8
72	Atlantic K 10144	Rainbow Road/Standing On The Mountain	6
72	Atlantic K 10165	Baby, Help Me/Warm And Tender Love/Take Time To Know Her	6
74	Capricorn 2089 009	I'll Be Your Everything/Walkin' In The Sun	6
67	Atlantic 587/588 048	WARM AND TENDER SOUL (LP)	20
67	Atlantic 587/588 081	THE PERCY SLEDGE WAY (LP)	20
68	Atlantic 587/588 015	WHEN A MAN LOVES A WOMAN (LP)	20
69	Atlantic 587/588 153	THE BEST OF PERCY SLEDGE (LP)	15

SLEDGEHAMMER
79	Slammer SRTS79CUS 395	Sledgehammer/Feel Good (with p/s)	20
79	Slammer SRTS79CUS 395	Sledgehammer/Feel Good	10
80	Slammer CELL 2	Living In Dreams/Fantasia (p/s)	10
80s	Slammer MRSB 2	In The Middle Of The Night	10
80	Valiant STRONG 1	Sledgehammer/Feel Good (p/s, reissue)	10
80	Valiant ROUND 2	Sledgehammer/Feel Good (p/s, 2nd reissue)	6
85	Illuminated ILL 33	In The Queue/Oxford City/1984 (shaped picture disc)	25
83	Illuminated JAMS 32	BLOOD ON THEIR HANDS (LP)	30
83	Illuminated JAMS 32	BLOOD ON THEIR HANDS (LP)	25
84	Mausoleum LUST 834950	SLEDGEHAMMER (LP, with free 12")	30

SLEEPER (2)
18	System SYSTM 022	Oram Mode/Level Up (12")	30

SLEEPERS
80	Bat FMR 034	Angel In A Raincoat/Endless/A Murder/TWBI	75

SLEEPING DOGS
82	Crass 221984/11	BEWARE SLEEPING DOGS (EP)	10

SLEEPWALKERS
59	Parlophone R 4580	Sleep Walk/Golden Mile	15

SLEEPY
68	CBS 3592	Love's Immortal Fire/Is It Really The Same	275
68	CBS 3838	Rosie Can't Fly/Mrs. Bailey's Barbecue And Grill	60
68	No Cat No	You'll See Me/Time Gone (White label test pressing)	250

(see also Grapefruit, Fynn McCool)

SLENDER LORIS
76	Reverence DM 70	I'm Only Heavy When You Get Me Down/A Week Of A Day	6

SLENDER PLENTY
67	Polydor BM 56189	Silver Tree Top School For Boys/I've Lost A Friend And Found A Lover	80

SLENDER THREAD
80	Rock MHMS 193	I See The Light/Where Is The Beat	30

JIMI SLEVIN
82	Claddagh CCF 7	FREEFLIGHT (LP)	45

(see also Peggy's Leg)

SLF
88	Warriors Dance WAF 005T	Show Me What You Got (Vocal)/(Acid Mix Pt. 1)/(Acid Mix Pt. 2) (12", p/s)	12
88	Warriors Dance WAAF 005	Show Me What You Got (Vocal)/Show Me What You Got (Acid Mix) (12")	12

GRACE SLICK
68	CBS 63476	CONSPICUOUS ONLY IN IT'S ABSENCE (LP, as Grace Slick And The Great Society)	40

SLICKERS
68	Blue Cat BS 133	Wala Wala/LESTER STERLING: Super Special	200
68	Blue Cat BS 134	Nana (actually by George Dekker)/MARTIN RILEY: I May Never See My Baby Anymore	85
69	Blue Cat BS 154	Frying Pan/RANFOLD WILLIAMS: Code It	140
69	Amalgamated AMG 852	Man Beware/Matty Matty	50
69	Amalgamated AMG 866	Money Raper/Man Beware	50
70	Bullet BU 449	Coolie Gal/BIGGIE: Bawling Baby	50
70	Trojan TR 7718	Run Fattie/Hoola Bulla (song actually "Bulla Man")	200
71	G.G. GG 4524	Oh My Baby/WINSTON WRIGHT: Change Of Love Version	6
71	Punch PH 59	Johnny Too Bad/Johnny Too Bad - Version	20
71	Dynamic DYN 406	Johnny Too Bad/ROLAND ALFONSO: Saucy Horde (act. by Roland Alphonso)	30
71	Dynamic DYN 419	You Can't Win/Don't Fight The Law	20
72	Explosion EX 2061	Bounce Me Johnny/Bounce Me 'Version' (actually "Say You")	12

(see also G.G. Allstars, Clancy Eccles, Viceroys)

SLIDE
80	Crash POW 4	Superman's Shoes/Meet Your New Neighbour (p/s)	50

SLIM & FREEDOM SINGERS
70	Banana BA 304	Do Dang Do (actually by Leroy Sibbles)/JACKIE MITTOO & SOUND DIMENSION: Hot Milk	60

SLIME
78	Toadstool GOOD 1	Controversial/Loony (p/s)	8

(see also Johnny Moped)

SLINT
91	Touch & Go T&GLP64	SPIDERLAND (LP)	18
93	Jennifer Hartman TG 138	TWEEZ (LP, reissue)	25

SLIPKNOT
00	Roadrunner RR 2090-7	Spit It Out/Surfacing (Live) (p/s, red vinyl)	12
00	Roadrunner RR 8655-6	SLIPKNOT (LP, picture disc)	15
01	Roadrunner 12 085641	IOWA (2-LP, gatefold, poster, mispressing on track 1 side 2)	25

SLIPMASTER J
92	Lucky Spin LSR 005	Symphonic (1-sided 12")	20
93	Dee Jay DJX 003	THE VISION EP (12")	20
94	Lucky Spin STU-3	Groundhog Day (12" 1-sided white label)	30
94	Lucky Spin STU 5	Groundhog Day Remix (12" 1-sided white label)	20

SLIQUE
89	ChampionCHAMP 12 212	Never Give Up (Vocal)/(Instrumental)/Cheating (Vocal)/(Instrumental) (12")	20

SLITS
79	Island WIP 6505	Typical Girls/I Heard It Through The Grapevine (p/s)	25
79	Island 12 WIP 6505	Typical Girls/I Heard It Through The Grapevine/Typical Girls (Brink Style)/Liebe And Romanize (12", p/s)	30
80	Rough Trade RT/Y 039	In The Beginning There Was Rhythm (1-sided promo)	15
80	Rough Trade RT 039/Y Y 1	In The Beginning There Was Rhythm/POP GROUP: Where There's A Will There's A Way (p/s)	18
80	Rough Trade/Y RT044/Y4	Man Next Door/Man Next Door (Version)	15
80	Human HUM 4	Animal Space/Animal Spacier (p/s)	12
81	CBS A1498	Earthbeat/Begin Again Rhythm	8
81	CBS A 131498	Earthbeat/Earthdub/Begin Again Rhythm (12", p/s)	12
06	Only Lovers Left Alive OLLA 0005	Slits Tradition/Number One Enemy/Kill Them With Love (p/s)	6
16	Island 4766321	I Heard It Through The Grapevine/Love Und Romance/Typical Girls/In The Beginning There Was Rhythm (Early Version) (10")	10
79	Island ILPS 9273	CUT (LP, laminated cover with inner sleeve)	100
80	Rough Trade/Y Y 3	BOOTLEG RETROSPECTIVE (LP, plain sleeve)	30
80	Basic 2	TYPICAL GIRLS LIVE IN CINCINNATI & SAN FRANCISCO USA (LP)	30

P.F. SLOAN

MINT VALUE £

81	CBS 85269	THE RETURN OF THE GIANT SLITS (LP, some with bonus 45 American Radio Interview/"Face Dub" [XPS 125])	40
81	CBS 85269	THE RETURN OF THE GIANT SLITS (LP)	20
88	Strange Fruit SFPS 021	THE PEEL SESSIONS (LP)	20
89	Strange Fruit SFPMA 207	DOUBLE PEEL SESSIONS (LP)	40
16	Island 4783700	CUT (LP, reissue, purple vinyl)	20

(see also Raincoats)

P.F. SLOAN

65	RCA Victor RCA 1482	Sins Of The Family/This Mornin'	12
67	RCA Victor RCA 1623	Sunflower Sunflower/The Man Behind The Red Balloon	12
72	Epic EPC 65179	RAISED ON RECORDS (LP, textured sleeve, lyric insert)	25
80s	Big Beat WIK 73	SONGS OF OTHER TIMES (LP, some tracks as Grass Roots)	25

(see also Grass Roots, Fantastic Baggys, Willie & Wheels)

SAMMI SLOAN

68	Columbia DB 8480	Yes I Would/Be His Girl	20

SLOANE SQUARE EAST

88	Hans Aid BMP 010	Hands Reach Out/Hand Reach Out (Remix) (p/s)	15

SLOWBONE

74	Rare Earth RES 119	Oh Man/Get What You're Given	6

(see also Roll Ups)

SLOWBONE & THE WONDERBOYS

74	Rare Earth RES 116	Tales Of A Crooked Man/Happy Birthday Sweet Sixteen	8

SLOW CLUB

07	Moshi Moshi	Because We're Dead/Sunday (500 only, p/s)	10
10	Moshi Moshi MOSHILP 29	YEAH SO (LP and CD, Record Store Day Release)	18
12	Moshi Moshi MOSHILP 41	PARADISE (LP, blue vinyl)	25

SLOWDIVE

17	Dead Oceans	Sugar For The Pill (Avalon Emerson's Gilden Escalation)/(Simon Scott Eurorack Remix) (12", p/s, signed, 20 only)	250
90	Creation CRE 093T	Slowdive/Avalyn 1/Avalyn 2	30
90	Creation CRE093T	SLOWDIVE EP	30
91	Creation CRE 098T	Morningrise/She Calls/Losing Today (12")	25
91	Creation CRE 112T	HOLDING OUR BREATH EP (12", numbered)	20
91	Creation CRE 112	Catch The Breeze/Shine (p/s, numbered)	15
91	Creation CRE 112T	Catch The Breeze/Golden Hair/Shine/Albatross (12")	10
93	Creation CRE 119T	OUTSIDE YOUR ROOM EP (12")	50
93	Creation CRE 157T	5 EP (12")	40
93	Creation CRE 157TR	5 EP (IN MIND REMIXES) (12", p/s)	10
19	Sonic Cathedral SCR 117	Golden Hair (Live) Part 1/Part 2 (p/s, gold vinyl)	80
91	Creation CRELP 094	JUST FOR A DAY (LP)	60
92	Creation CRE X101	BLUE DAY (LP)	80
93	Creation CRELP 139	SOUVLAKI (LP, picture inner sleeve)	200
95	Creation CRELP 168	PYGMALION (LP)	150
11	Music On Vinyl MOVLP354	JUST FOR A DAY (LP, reissue)	25
11	Music On Vinyl MOVLP202	SOUVAKI (LP, reissue)	25
12	Music On Vinyl MOVLP604	PYGMALION (LP, reissue)	25
12	Music On Vinyl MOVLP604	PYGMALION (LP, white vinyl, 1000 only)	25
15	Music On Vinyl MOVLP1380	BLUE DAY (LP, reissue)	20

(see also Mojave 3, Rachel Goswell, Neil Halstead, Eternal)

SLOW DOG

72	Parlophone R5942	Walking Through The Blue Grass/Ain't Never Going Home	30

SLOWGUNS

79	MPA SMP 088	TV Movie/American Heartbeat	15
80	Cult 45 CULT 001	Karma/The Time Is Right For Us	12

SLOWLOAD

71	MAM MAM 27	On The Road Again/Big Boobs Boogie	35

(see also Fruit Eating Bears)

SLOW MOTION

79	RK RK 1024	Christmas Charade/Maybe	40

SLOW READERS CLUB

13	(no label or cat. no.)	Forever In Your Debt/Days Like This Will Break Your Heart (p/s, 200 only)	50
18	Modern Sky MODERN036LPX	BUILD A TOWER (LP, red vinyl)	18
18	Modern Sky MODERN036LP	BUILD A TOWER (LP, different artwork, marigold and black swirl vinyl, insert signed by band)	50
18	(No label or cat. no.)	CAVALCADE: LIVE AT THE MET (LP, white vinyl, with marbled effect, printed set list, 500 only)	50

(see also Omerta)

SLOWTRAIN

80	Spirit SR 1	Ronnie/Just One Way	30

SLR CREW

88	SLR XPR1536	Bass Drum/Life's A Bitch (12")	50

SL TROOPERS

88	Global Rhythm GR001	Debut (Unarmed And Dangerous) (12", 500 pressed)	40
89	Music Of Life NOTE32	Movement (12")	12
91	Kold Sweat KSEP201	SYSTEMATIC TERROR (EP)	12

SLUSH

78	Ember EMB 5367	White Christmas/Rich Man (no p/s)	40

(See also Pumphouse Gang)

SLY ALICE

72	Sunday SUN 02	Drifting Away/The Games Over (p/s)	50

SLY & THE REVOLUTIONARIES

MINT VALUE £

SLY & THE REVOLUTIONARIES
80 Trojan TRLS 186 — BLACK ASH DUB (LP) 30

JOAN SMALL
56 Parlophone MSP 6219 — Change Of Heart/Come Next Spring 10
56 Parlophone R 4211 — Love Is A Stranger/Autumn Concerto 10
57 Parlophone R 4269 — Gonna Get Along Without You Now/You Can't Say I Love You To A Rock & Roll Tune 15
58 Parlophone R 4431 — Afraid/How Many Times (Can I Fall In Love) 10
60 Parlophone R 4622 — The Big Hurt/Ask Me To Go Steady 10

JOHN SMALL
70 G&W FAM 101 — Let's Ride/A Woman Who Can Shake My Mind 15

KAREN SMALL
66 Vocalion V 9281 — To Get You Back Again/That's Why I Cry 50

MARY SMALL
56 Vogue Coral 45-Q-72196 — Dino/None Of That Now 8

SMALLAGE
90 Jack Trax 7JTX 33 — Together (Club Edit)/Together (Dub) 10

DENIS SMALLEY
81 University Of East Anglia UEA 81063 — THE PULSE OF TIME (LP) 40

SMALL FACES
SINGLES
65 Decca F 12208 — Whatcha Gonna Do About It?/What's A Matter, Baby? 20
65 Decca F 12276 — I've Got Mine/It's Too Late 25
66 Decca F 12317 — Sha-La-La-La-Lee/Grow Your Own 10
66 Decca F 12393 — Hey Girl/Almost Grown 15
66 Decca F 12470 — All Or Nothing/Understanding (curved or boxed Decca logo) 12
66 Decca F 12500 — My Mind's Eye (alternate demo mix, matrix no. ends T1-1C)/I Can't Dance With You (withdrawn) 30
66 Decca F 12500 — My Mind's Eye (matrix no. ends T2-1C)/I Can't Dance With You 10
67 Decca F 12565 — I Can't Make It/Just Passing 25
67 Decca F 12565 — I Can't Make It/Just Passing (in export p/s) 60
67 Decca F 12619 — Patterns/E Too D (with export p/s) 140
67 Decca F 12619 — Patterns/E Too D 70
67 Immediate AS 1 — Small Faces (1-sided sampler for "Small Faces", promo only) 250
67 Immediate IM 050 — Here Comes The Nice/Talk To You 12
67 Immediate IM 057 — Itchycoo Park/I'm Only Dreaming 12
67 Immediate IM 062 — Tin Soldier/I Feel Much Better (in p/s) 80
67 Immediate IM 062 — Tin Soldier/I Feel Much Better 15
68 Immediate IM 064 — Lazy Sunday/Rollin' Over 12
68 Immediate IM 069 — The Universal/Donkey Rides, A Penny A Glass (lilac label) 12
68 Immediate IM 069 — The Universal/Donkey Rides, A Penny A Glass (later pink label) 8
69 Immediate IM 077 — Afterglow (Of Your Love)/Wham Bam, Thank You Mam (demos [perhaps some copies] have demo version of B-side) 60
69 Immediate IM 077 — Afterglow (Of Your Love)/Wham Bam, Thank You Mam (demos) 15
75 Immediate IM 064 — Lazy Sunday/Rollin' Over (p/s, reissue with white label) 8
80 Virgin VS 367 — Tin Soldier/Tin Soldier (live)/Rene 6
86 Archive 4 TOF 103 — Itchycoo Park/Lazy Sunday/Sha-La-La-La-Lee/Here Comes The Nice (12", p/s) 10

ALBUMS : LPS
66 Decca LK 4790 — SMALL FACES (original red label) 250
67 Decca LK 4879 — FROM THE BEGINNING (original red label) 280
67 Immediate IMLP 008 — SMALL FACES (mono) 250
67 Immediate IMSP 008 — SMALL FACES (stereo) 250
68 Immediate IMLP 012 — OGDENS' NUT GONE FLAKE (lilac label, circular foldout sleeve, mono) 250
68 Immediate IMSP 012 — OGDENS' NUT GONE FLAKE (lilac label, circular foldout sleeve, stereo) 150
68 Immediate IMLP 012 — OGDENS' NUT GONE FLAKE (pink label, circular foldout sleeve, mono) 120
68 Immediate IMSP 012 — OGDENS' NUT GONE FLAKE (pink label, circular foldout sleeve, stereo) 80
69 Decca LK 4790 — SMALL FACES (boxed Decca label) 50
69 Decca LK 4879 — FROM THE BEGINNING (boxed Decca label) 40
69 Immediate IMLP/IMSP 022 — IN MEMORIAM (export issue [German copies more common, £60]) 150
69 Immediate IMAL 01/02 — THE AUTUMN STONE (2-LP, gatefold sleeve) 80
75 Immediate/NEMS IML 1001 — OGDENS' NUT GONE FLAKE (reissue, round sleeve, white label) 40
76 NEMS AML 1008 — MAGIC MOMENTS 15
77 Immediate/NEMS IML 2001 — OGDENS' NUT GONE FLAKE (reissue, square sleeve) 15
77 Decca ROOTS 5 — ROCK ROOTS - THE DECCA SINGLES 15
78 Charly CR 300005 — OGDENS' NUT GONE FLAKE (export release, square sleeve) 15
78 Charly CR 300025 — THE SMALL FACES - LIVE U.K. 1969 (export release) 15
80 Virgin/Immediate V 2166 — SMALL FACES: BIG HITS (gatefold sleeve) 15
80 Virgin/Immediate V 2178 — FOR YOUR DELIGHT, THE DARLINGS OF WAPPING WHARF LAUNDERETTE 25
91 Castle CLACT 016 — OGDENS' NUT GONE FLAKE (CD, in round tin box with beer mats & booklet) 60
96 Deram 844583 — THE DECCA ANTHOLOGY 1965-1967 (2-LP) 25
97 Castle CLA 016 — OGDENS' NUT GONE FLAKE (reissue, round sleeve with obi) 15
01 Strange Fruit SFRSLP 087 — BBC SESSIONS (LP) 20

(see also Faces, Steve Marriott, Humble Pie, Jimmy Winston & His Reflections, Winston's Fumbs, Billy Nicholls, Kenney Jones)

SMALL FOUR
66 Pye 7N 17191 — One Up On Me/I'll Find Him 20

SMALL HOURS
80 Automatic K 17708 — The Kid/Business In Town/Midnight To Six/End Of The Night (p/s) 30
80 Automatic K 17708X — The Kid/Business In Town/Midnight To Six/End Of The Night (10", p/s) 20
81 Bridgehouse (No Cat No) — Denis/Denis Dub (white label promo only) 70

SMALL IN A BIG WAY

MINT VALUE £

SMALL IN A BIG WAY
84   Bedlam BLM 003   Katies Lips/Back To Zero (p/s) 8

SMALL WONDER
75   Dawn DNS 1094   Ordinary Boy/Ride A Black Sheep 18

GEORGE SMALLWOOD & MARSHMELLOW BAND
10   Jazzman JMANLP 031   JUST 4 YOU (2-LP) 18

SMALL WORLD
81   Whaam! WHAAM 003   Love Is Dead/Liberty (p/s) 100
83   Valid VC 001   First Impressions/Stupidity Street/Tomorrow Never Comes (p/s) 100

SMART
82   Complex CPX 001   This Time (p/s) 35

SMART ALEC
79   B&C BCS 20   Scooter Boys/Soho (p/s) 100

EVA SMART
76   Empire EMP 903   One Life to Live One Life To Love/One Life Version 20
76   Empire EMP 906   Someday (We'll Be Together)/Version 10
80   Empire EMPDC 310   Upside Down/In And Out 25

LEROY SMART
75   Third world TW 022   Get Smart/KING TUBBY & THE AGGROVATORS: Version 20
77   Conflict COND 2001   Jahovia/Dub (12") 30
78   Andinet AT 001   Zion/Version 25
78   Andinet AT 002   Faith/Version 25
78   Aries AR 003   It's A Long Time Now/Long Time Version 6
78   Write Sounds WTS 1001   Children Of The Getto/Version 8
78   Write Sounds WTS 001   What I Will Do/ROY SINCLAIR: Rite Mix/LEROY SMART: Jah Almighty (12") 25
79   Burning Sounds BDS 010   Find Your Destination/Jamaica In Peace (12") 15
79   Burning Sounds BDS 011   No One Remember Me/Don't Be Late (12") 15
70s   Aries ARI 002   Peace Is What We Want (with U. Brown)/Version (12", p/s) 30
80   Black Joy DH 803   Hooligan/Have Mercy (12") 12
82   Time One TR 0016   Money Is Comfort/If I Give My Love (12", with Barry Brown) 25
77   Conflict COLPD 2001   BALLISTIC AFFAIR (LP, gatefold, with free 12") 40
77   Dread Hot DHLP 1001   DREAD HOT IN AFRICA (LP) 40
77   Third World TWS 601   SUPER STAR (LP) 30
78   Burning Sounds BS 1004   DREAD HOT IN AFRICA (LP, reissue) 35
78   Burning Sounds BS 1005   IMPRESSIONS OF LEROY SMART (LP) 15
78   Burning Sounds BS 1008   JAH LOVES EVERYONE (LP, green vinyl) 35
78   Dread Hot DHLP 1004   IMPRESSIONS OF LEROY SMART (LP, reissue) 30
78   Burning Sounds BS 1009   PROPAGANDA (LP, clear vinyl) 25

LEROY SMART & BIG YOUTH
79   Dub Vendor DVD 01   Pride And Ambition (original style)/'79 Style (12") 60

SMART SYSTEMS
91   Jumpin' & Pumpin' 12TOT18   Tingler (Meltram Mix)/(Mingler Mix)/(State Side Swamp Mix (12" p/s) 10

SMASHING PUMPKINS
91   Hut   I Am One (1-sided blue flexidisc) 100
91   Caroline SMASH 1   Siva/Rhinoceros (no p/s, promo only) 80
91   Hut HUTT 6   Siva/Window Paine (12", p/s, 5,000) 30
92   Hut HUTT 10   LULL EP (Rhinoceros/Blue/Slunk/Bye June [Demo]) (12", p/s) 20
92   Hut HUTT 17   PEEL SESSIONS: Siva/A Girl Named Sandoz/Smiley (12" EP, p/s) 12
92   Hut HUTEN 18   I Am One/Terrapin (live)/Bullet Train To Osaka (10", p/s, 6,000 only) 20
92   Hut HUTT 18   I Am One/Plume/Starla (12", p/s) 12
93   Hut HUT 31   Cherub Rock/Purr Snickety (p/s, clear vinyl, numbered, 5,000 only) 20
93   Hut HUT 37   Today/Apathy's Last Kiss (p/s, red vinyl, 5,000 only) 12
93   Sub Pop SP 90   Tristessa/La Dolly Vita/Honeyspider (12", 5,000 only) 35
94   Hut HUT 43   Smile (Disarm/Siamese Dream) (stickered p/s, purple vinyl) 10
94   Hut SPBOX 1   SIAMESE SINGLES (Rocket/Never Let Me Down/Cherub Rock/Purr Snickety//Today/Apathy's Last Kiss/Smile [Disarm/Siamese Dream]) (4 x 7" box set, black vinyl, 6,000 only) 50
94   Hut HUTL 48   Rocket/Never Let Me Down (box set, salmon pink vinyl, 1,500 only) 40
95   Hut HUTTDJ 73   Zero (12", promo only) 12
98   Hut HUT 101   Ava Adore/Czarina (p/s, numbered) 6
91   Caroline CARLP 16   GISH (LP, 1st pressing, red label, inner) 40
91   Hut HUTL LP2   GISH (LP, inner) 25
93   Hut HUTLP11   SIAMESE DREAM (2-LP) 35
94   Hut HUTLPX 2   GISH (LP, reissue with inner) 30
95   Hut HUTDLP 30   MELLON COLLIE AND THE INFINITE SADNESS (3 x LP, 12 page booklet, numbered) 175
98   Hut HUTDLP 30   MELLON COLLIE AND THE INFINITE SADNESS (3 x LP, 12 page booklet, repressing and not numbered) 60
96   Hut HUTLP 41   PISCES ISCARIOT (LP, compilation) 30
96   Hut   THE AEROPLANE FLIES HIGH (5 x CD single box set with handle, lock & booklet) 50
00   HUTDLP 59   MACHINA/THE MACHINES OF GOD (2-LP) 35
12   Virgin 5099997855316   MELLON COLLIE AND THE INFINITE SADNESS (4 x LP, remastered repressing) 50
14   Virgin 6 02537 89926-5   ADORE (2-LP, reissue of 1998 LP not issued on vinyl in UK) 30
(see also Zwan)

ROY SMECK
54   Brunswick LA 8649   SONGS OF THE RANGE (10" LP) 15

PHILIP LLOYD SMEE & DONATO CINICOLO III
71   Deroy PLS 1   DAS LUNE/SYNTHI-A (LP, private pressing, handmade sleeve, 2 copies only) 500

SMILE
72   UNI UN 537   A Year Every Night/Southbound 10

SMILEY
72   Philips 6006 206   Penelope/I Know What I Want 15

Brett SMILEY

MINT VALUE £

(see also Creation)

BRETT SMILEY
Year	Label/Cat	Title	Value
74	Anchor ANC 70	Va Va Va Voom/Space Age (with p/s)	40
74	Anchor ANC 70	Va Va Va Voom/Space Age	25

SMILEY CULTURE
86	Top Notch TOP LP 001	THE ORIGINAL (LP)	15

SMILIN' JOE
54	London HL 8106	A.B.C.'s Parts 1 & 2 (78)	40

SMILING HARD
79	Survival SUR 5	Don't Call Us We'll Call You/Fire To The Galleon	8

SMIRKS
78	Beserkley BZZ17	OK UK/Streets (p/s)	8

SMITH
69	Stateside-Dunhill SS 8028	Baby It's You/I Don't Believe	6
70	Stateside-Dunhill SS 8042	Take A Look Around/Mojalesky Ridge	6
70	Stateside-Dunhill SS 8055	What Am I Gonna Do/Born In Boston	6
70	Probe PRO 508	Comin Back To Me/Minus Plus	25
73	Probe Goldies GFF 115	The Weight/Baby It's You	12
69	Stateside-Dunhill SSL 5016	A GROUP CALLED SMITH (LP)	25
70	Stateside-Dunhill SSL 5031	MINUS PLUS (LP)	25

SMITH (U.K.)
81	Rarn RARNS 1	Here Comes My Baby/Just Another Line/Too Late (p/s)	25

ADAM (ERIC) SMITH
62	Island WI 057	I Wonder Why/My Prayer	20

A.S.A.P. (ADRIAN SMITH & PROJECT)
89	EMI 12 EMPD 107	Silver And Gold/Blood Brothers (12", silver & gold vinyl)	10

(see also Iron Maiden, Urchin)

ALICE SMITH
06	BBE ASMITH 01	LOVE ENDEAVOUR (12", die-cut sleeve)	30

ARTHUR 'GUITAR BOOGIE' SMITH (& HIS CRACKERJACKS)
53	MGM SP 1008	Guitar Boogie/Be Bop Rag	25
53	MGM SP 1021	Five String Banjo Boogie/South	15
53	MGM SP 1039	Express Train Boogie/River Rag	15
54	MGM SP 1096	Oh, Baby Mine, I Get So Lonely/Outboard	15
54	MGM SP 1110	Redheaded Stranger/Texas Hop	20
54	MGM MGM-EP 510	ARTHUR 'GUITAR BOOGIE' SMITH AND HIS CRACKERJACKS (EP)	15
54	MGM MGM EPC 5	ARTHUR 'GUITAR BOOGIE' SMITH (EP, export issue)	15
59	MGM MGM-EP 695	ARTHUR 'GUITAR BOOGIE' SMITH AND HIS CRACKERJACKS (EP)	15
63	Stateside SE 1005	MISTER GUITAR (EP)	15
53	MGM MGM-D 111	FINGERS ON FIRE (10" LP)	20
54	MGM MGM-D 131	FOOLISH QUESTIONS (10" LP)	20

BEASLEY SMITH & HIS ORCHESTRA
56	London HLD 8235	Goodnight, Sweet Dreams/Parisian Rag	20
56	London HLD 8273	My Foolish Heart/Old Spinning Wheel	20

BETTY SMITH SKIFFLE GROUP
57	Tempo A 162	There's A Blue Ridge Round My Heart, Virginia/Double Shuffle	10

(see also Betty Smith Quintet)

BETTY SMITH QUINTET
57	Tempo A 163	Sweet Georgia Brown/Little White Lies	20
58	Decca F 10986	Hand Jive/Bewitched (as Betty Smith Group)	10
58	Decca F 11031	Will The Angels Play Their Harps For Me/Betty's Blues	10
59	Decca F 11124	Song Of India/Stormy Weather	10
57	Tempo EXA 74	BETTY SMITH QUINTET (EP)	30
57	Decca DFE 6446	BETTY SMITH QUINTET (EP)	30
58	Decca DFE 6547	BETTY SMITH GROUP (EP)	30

(see also Betty Smith Skiffle Group)

BRODERICK SMITH
72	Spark SRL 1087	Going Down To The End Of The World/She's Gone	8

CARL SMITH
56	Philips PB 572	Loose Talk/More Than Anything Else In The World (78)	7
59	Philips PB 943	Ten Thousand Drums/The Tall, Tall Gentlemen	8

CLARA SMITH & FLETCHER HENDERSON
61	Philips BBE 12491	BLUES BY CLARA SMITH 1926-1928 (EP)	10

DAVE SMITH & ASTRONAUTS
67	Columbia Blue Beat DB 104	A Lover Like You/Cup Of Love	15
67	Amusicon SLE 10	A Lover Like You/Cup Of Love	15

DAVE SMITH & JUDY DINNING
83	Rubber RUB 043	WAITING FOR THE CHANGE (LP)	20

DEREK SMITH TRIO
56	Pye Nixa NJE 1036	PIANO MOODS (EP)	80

DICK SMITH BAND
79	Smile SR 012	Body Heat/Motorway Madness (p/s)	75
80	Hol-O-Gram HOL 001	Way Of The World/Giving The Game Away (with p/s)	45
80	Hol-O-Gram HOL 001	Way Of The World/Giving The Game Away	25

EDDIE SMITH
55	Parlophone MSP 6186	Silver Star Stomp/Stumbling (as Eddie Smith & Chiefs)	15
60	Top Rank JAR 285	Upturn/Border Beat (as Eddie Smith & Hornets)	25

EDGEWOOD SMITH & FABULOUS TAILFEATHERS
67	Sue WI 4037	Ain't That Lovin'/Yeah	50

Effie SMITH

MINT VALUE £

EFFIE SMITH
66	Sue WI 4010	Dial That Telephone Parts 1 & 2	30

ELLIOTT SMITH
98	Domino RUG 074	Ballad Of Big Nothing/Some Song (p/s)	12
98	Dreamworks DRMS 22347	Waltz No. 2/Our Thing (p/s)	10
99	Dreamworks DRMS 7	Baby Britain/Waltz No. 1 (p/s)	30
00	Dreamworks 450 949-7	Son Of Sam/A Living Will	8
98	Domino REWIGLP 001	ELLIOTT SMITH (LP)	60
98	Domino REWIGLP 002	ROMAN CANDLE (LP)	60
98	Domino WIGLP 51	EITHER/OR (LP)	50
00	Geffen 533 867-2	FIGURE 8 (2-LP, with lyric insert)	30
04	Domino WIGLP 147	FROM A BASEMENT ON THE HILL (2-LP)	20
10	Domino WIGLP 265	AN INTRODUCTION TO (LP)	20
10	Domino REWIGLP1	ELLIOTT SMITH (LP, reissue)	20

ELSON SMITH
61	Fontana H 291	Flip Flop/Are You Ready For That	30

ERNIE SMITH
71	Duke DU 119	Bend Down/Heaven Help Us All	6
74	Attack ATT 8071	Duppy Gunman/Duppy Gunman Version	8

(LITTLE) GEORGE (HARMONICA) SMITH
65	Blue Horizon 45-1002	Blues In The Dark/Telephone Blues (as Little George Smith)	100
70	Blue Horizon 57-3170	Someday You're Gonna Learn/Before You Do Your Thing (as George Smith)	25
69	Liberty LBL/LBS 83218E	BLUES WITH FEELING - A TRIBUTE TO LITTLE WALTER (LP, with Chicago Blues Band)	60
70	Blue Horizon 7-63856	NO TIME TO JIVE (LP)	100
71	Deram SML 1082	ARKANSAS TRAP (LP)	60

(see also Bacon Fat)

GLORIA SMITH
59	London HLU 8903	Playmates/Don't Take Your Love From Me	18

GORDON SMITH
69	Blue Horizon 57-3156	Too Long/Funk Pedal	30
69	Blue Horizon S7-63211	LONG OVERDUE (LP, stereo)	100
69	Blue Horizon M7-63211	LONG OVERDUE (LP, mono)	150

(see also Kevin Coyne)

HAROLD SMITH'S MAJESTIC CHOIR
69	Chess CRS 8100	We Can All Walk A Little Bit Prouder/Why Am I Treated So Bad	8

HARVEY SMITH
75	Hankerchief Hanky 3	True Love/ End Of The World (p/s)	7

HOBART SMITH
69	Topic 12T187	THE OLD TIMEY RAP (LP)	20

HUEY 'PIANO' SMITH & THE CLOWNS
58	Columbia DB 4138	Don't You Just Know It/High Blood Pressure	85
58	Columbia DB 4138	Don't You Just Know It/High Blood Pressure (78)	50
60	Top Rank JAR 282	Don't You Just Know Kokomo/FRANKIE FORD: Cheatin' Woman	20
62	Top Rank JAR 614	Pop-Eye/Scald-Dog (as Huey Smith)	12
65	Sue WI 364	If It Ain't One Thing It's Another/Tu-Ber-Cu-Lucas And The Sinus Blues	25
65	Sue WI 380	Rockin' Pneumonia And The Boogie Woogie Flu (Parts 1 & 2)	25
78	Chiswick NS 43	Rockin' Pneumonia And The Boogie Woogie Flu (unissued)	0
82	Kent TOWN 502	Don't You Just Know It/MARY LOVE: Lay This Burden Down/DANNY MONDAY: Baby Without You	12
65	Sue ILP 917	ROCKIN' PNEUMONIA AND THE BOOGIE WOOGIE FLU (LP, titled "Havin' A Good Time" on labels)	40

(see also Frankie Ford, Lee Allen, Bobby Marchan, Robert Parker)

HURRICANE SMITH
71	Columbia DB 8785	Don't Let I Die/The Writer Sings His Songs	6
72	Columbia DB 8878	Oh Babe, What Would You Say/Getting To Know You	6
72	Columbia SCX 6510	DON'T LET IT DIE (LP)	15

IAN SMITH & INNER MIND
71	Bullet BU 490	Devil Woman/Nenn Street Rub	8

(see also Smithy All Stars)

JEFF SMITH
71	RAK RAK 120	Gypsy In My Blood/Going To A Party	25

JIMMY SMITH
62	HMV POP 1025	Walk On The Wild Side Parts 1 & 2 (blue label)	10
65	Verve VS 523	The Cat/Basin Street Blues	20
65	Verve VS 531	The Organ Grinder's Swing/I'll Close My Eyes	6
66	Verve VS 536	Got My Mojo Working Parts 1 & 2	10
66	Verve VS 540	I'm Your Hoochie-Coochie Man Parts 1 & 2	6
67	Verve VS 551	Cat In A Tree Parts 1 & 2	6
67	Verve VS 562	Mickey Mouse Parts 1 & 2	6
62	Verve CLP 1596/CSD 1462	BASHIN' THE UNPREDICTABLE (Verve label with HMV number)	25
63	Verve (S)VLP 9039	HOBO FLATS	25
64	Verve VLP 9057	ANY NUMBER CAN WIN	25
64	Verve VLP 9068	WHO'S AFRAID OF VIRGINIA WOOLF	15
64	Verve (S)VLP 9079	THE CAT	25
65	Verve (S)VLP 9093	MONSTER	25
66	Verve (S)VLP 9108	ORGAN GRINDER SWING	25
66	Verve (S)VLP 9123	GOT MY MOJO WORKING	25
66	Verve (S)VLP 9142	HOOCHIE COOCHIE MAN	25
67	Verve (S)VLP 9159	PETER & THE WOLF	15
67	Verve (S)VLP 9160	THE DYNAMIC DUO (with Wes Montgomery)	25

Joey SMITH & BABA BROOKS BAND

MINT VALUE £

67	Verve (S)VLP 9182	RESPECT	25
68	Verve (S)VLP 9218	STAY LOOSE	25
68	Verve (S)VLP 9227	LIVIN' IT UP	15
68	Verve (S)VLP 9231	CHRISTMAS COOKIN'	15
69	Verve (S)VLP 9241	FURTHER ADVENTURES OF JIMMY AND WES (with Wes Montgomery)	15
71	Verve 2304 020	I'M GON' GIT MYSELF TOGETHER	15
74	Verve 2304 167	PORTUGUESE SOUL	15

(see also Kenny Burrell)

JOEY SMITH & BABA BROOKS BAND
64	R&B JB 131	Maybe Once/Tell Me You're Mine	25

JORJA SMITH
18	FAMM JSLAFP01	LOST & FOUND (LP)	20

JUDI SMITH
65	Decca F 12132	Leaves Come Tumbling Down/Come My Way	15

JUNIOR SMITH
67	Giant GN 1	Cool Down Your Temper/I'm Groovin'	30
68	Giant GN 18	I'm Gonna Leave You Girl/I Love You, I Love You	30
68	Giant GN 25	Come Cure Me/I Want Your Lovin'	50
68	Gas GAS 132	Gimme Little/Trip To War Land	20
69	Crystal CR 7002	Put On The Pressure/I Don't Know	10
72	Sioux SI 019	Saturday Child/JUMBO STERLING: Hot Dog	20
72	Sioux SI 023	I Don't Know/JUMBO STERLING: My Sugar Ain't Sweet	100

(see also Stranger Cole, Derrick Morgan, Rocksteadys)

KATHY SMITH
70	Polydor 2310 081	SOME SONGS I'VE SAVED (LP)	60

KEELY SMITH (& LOUIS PRIMA)
59	London HLD 8984	If I Knew I'd Find You (I'd Climb The Highest Mountain)/Don't Let The Stars Get In Your Eyes	12
61	London RE-D 1269	YOU LOVERS (EP)	20
58	Capitol (S)T 914	I WISH YOU LOVE (LP, mono/stereo)	15
59	Capitol T 1160	HEY BOY! HEY GIRL! (LP, soundtrack, with Louis Prima)	25

(see also Louis Prima, Frank Sinatra)

KENDRA SMITH
95	4AD CAD 5006	FIVE WAYS OF DISAPPEARING (LP)	40

LONNIE SMITH
67	CBS 63146	FINGER LICKIN' GOOD (LP)	25
69	Blue Note BST 84313	TURNING POINT (LP)	25
69	Blue Note BST 84290	THINK (LP)	25
70	Blue Note BST 84326	MOVE YOUR HAND (LP)	30
70	Blue Note BST 84351	DRIVES (LP)	25
96	Blue Note 724383124916	MOVE YOUR HAND (LP, reissue)	20
97	Blue Note 724382996918	MOVE YOUR HAND (LP, reissue, repressing)	20

LONNIE LISTON SMITH (& THE COSMIC ECHOES)
75	RCA RCA 2568	Expansions (Parts 1 & 2) (& Cosmic Echoes)	15
79	RCA PB 9450	Expansions/A Chance For Peace	6
79	RCA PC 9450	Expansions/A Chance For Peace (12")	35
83	Bluebird BRT 4	Expansions/Voodoo Woman (12")	20
75	RCA SF 8434	EXPANSIONS (LP, with Cosmic Echoes)	20
76	RCA SF 8461	VISIONS OF A NEW WORLD (LP, gatefold)	20
76	RCA RS 1053	REFLECTIONS OF A GOLDEN DREAM (LP, with Cosmic Echoes)	20
77	RCA PL 11822	RENAISSANCE (LP, with Cosmic Echoes)	20
78	CBS 82837	LOVELAND (LP)	20
79	CBS S CBS 83809	A SONG FOR THE CHILDREN (LP)	15
80	CBS S CBS 84365	LOVE IS THE ANSWER (LP)	20

LORENZO SMITH
66	Outasite 45-503	(Too Much) Firewater/Count Down (99 copies only)	100

LOU SMITH
60	Top Rank JAR 520	Cruel Love/Close To My Heart	10

MARTHA SMITH
65	Pye 7N 15778	As I Watch You Walk Away/It Always Seems Like Summer	20
65	Pye 7N 15860	Love Means Nothing To You/The Song Is Love	7

MARVIN SMITH
66	Coral Q 72486	Time Stopped/Have More Time	50
66	Coral Q 72486	Time Stopped/Have More Time (DJ copy)	100

MEL SMITH
81	Mercury MEL 1	Mel Smith's Greatest Hits/Richard & Joey (p/s, with Roger Taylor)	15

MELODY SMITH
71	CBS CBS 7561	You Never Hear A Teardrop Fall/Rastus Ravel	10

MICK SMITH
76	Midas MFHR 078	SOMEBODY NOBODY KNOWS (LP)	30
77	Alida Star AS 771	WORDS AND MUSIC (LP)	30
79	Repercussion RR 1000	RAINDANCE (LP, as Mike Smith)	25

MIKE SMITH
85	Proto ENA 130	Medley (7" version)/Bits And Pieces (in p/s)	7
85	Proto ENAT 130	Medley (12" version)/Glad All Over (12", p/s)	12
90	Mooncrest MOON 1010	You Gotta Play Rock'N'Roll/Operator	6

(see also Dave Clark 5, Smith & D'Abo)

NR AND MRS SMITH AND MR DRAKE
84	Alphabet ALPH 005	tMR AND MRS SMITH AND MR DRAKE (cassette)	50

(see also Cardiac Arrest 1, Cardiacs)

O.C. (OCIE) SMITH

MINT VALUE £

O.C. (OCIE) SMITH
57	London HLA 8480	Lighthouse/Too Many (as Ocie Smith)	90
57	London HLA 8480	Lighthouse/Too Many (as Ocie Smith) (78)	60
68	CBS 3343	The Son Of Hickory Holler's Tramp/On A Clear Day You Can See Forever	8
68	CBS (S) 63147	THE DYNAMIC O.C. SMITH (LP)	20
68	CBS (S) 63362	HICKORY HOLLER REVISITED (LP)	15
69	CBS 63805	AT HOME (LP)	25

(see also Art Mooney)

OTELLO SMITH & TOBAGO BAD BOYS
68	Direction 8-63242	THE BIG ONES GO SKA (LP)	40

PATTI SMITH (GROUP)
76	Arista ARIST 47	Gloria (In Excelsis Deo) (Edit)/My Generation (p/s)	10
77	Arista ARIST 12135	Gloria (In Excelsis Deo)/My Generation (live) (12", Rough Trade copies in brown paper bag with titles in felt pen)	15
78	Arista ARIST 181	Because The Night/God Speed (p/s)	7
78	Sire 6078 614	Hey Joe (Version)/Piss Factory (p/s)	35
78	Arista ARIST 12197	Privilege (Set Me Free)/Ask The Angels/25th Floor (Live Version)/Babelfield (12", p/s)	10
88	Fierce FRIGHT 017	Brian Jones/Stockinged Feet/Jesus Christ (1-sided, white label)	15
75	Arista ARTY 122	HORSES (LP, 1st pressing, 'Horses' written in white, blue label)	40
76	Arista SPARTY 1001	RADIO ETHIOPIA (LP, as Patti Smith Group, with lyric insert)	25
78	Arista SPART 1043	EASTER (LP, lyric insert)	25
79	Arista SPART 1086	WAVE (LP, insert)	15
07	Columbia 88697094301	TWELVE (2-LP)	60

PAUL SMITH
65	Columbia DB 7636	Piccadilly Paper Boy/Yakety Yak	10

PETER SMITH
70s	Pilgrim JLPS 148P	FAITH, FOLK & CLARITY (LP, with Kinfolk)	18

RAY SMITH
60	London HL 9051	Rockin' Little Angel/That's All Right	50

ROY SMITH (JAMAICA)
70	Grape GR 3013	See Through Craze/TERRY CARL & DERRICK: I'm The One	30
70	Jackpot JP 723	The Wedding/Air Balloon	20

(see also Terry, Carl & Derrick)

SLIM SMITH (& THE UNIQUES)
66	Island WI 3023	I've Got Your Number/The New Boss	70
67	Coxsone CS 7016	Hip Hug/FREEDOM SINGERS: I Want Money	140
67	Coxsone CS 7034	Rougher Yet/I'll Never Let Go	150
67	Coxsone CS 7009	Mercy Mercy/JACKIE MITTOO: Baba Boom	135
68	Trojan TR 619	Watch This Sound/Out Of Love (as Slim Smith & Uniques)	45
69	Unity UN 504	Everybody Needs Love/JUNIOR SMITH: Come Back Girl	25
69	Unity UN 508	For Once In My Life/Burning Desire	25
69	Unity UN 510	Zip-A-Di-Do-Da/On Broadway	25
69	Unity UN 513	Let It Be Me/Love Makes Me Do Foolish Things (both with Paulette)	20
69	Unity UN 515	Somebody To Love/Confusion	40
69	Unity UN 520	Slipaway/Spanish Harlem	25
69	Unity UN 524	Sunny Side Of The Sea/A Place In The Sun	40
69	Unity UN 527	Blessed Are The Meek/Conversation	20
69	Unity UN 537	Keep That Light Shining On Me/Build My World Around You	20
69	Unity UN 539	Love Me Tender/This Feeling	30
69	Unity UN 542	Honey/There's A Light	30
69	Gas GAS 132	The Vow (& Doreen Shaeffer)/JAMES NEPHEW: Why Don't You Say	45
70	Gas GAS 150	What Kind Of Life/MARTIN RILEY: It's All In The Game	20
70	Unity UN 570	Jenny/The Race	30
70	S&S SC 001	Strong Love/Strange World	40
71	Supreme SUP 219	Stay/You're My Everything	12
71	Pama Supreme PS 334	Send Me Some Loving/I'm Lost	18
71	Camel CA 81	Spanish Harlem/Slip Away	25
71	Escort ERT 851	My Love Come True/This Feeling	75
71	Escort ERT 852	Life Keeps Turning/My Conversation	35
71	Escort ERT 859	My Girl/RECO: Plus One	40
71	Jackpot JP 779	Keep Walking/Will You Still Love Me Tomorrow	10
72	Jackpot JP 786	I Need Your Loving/You've Got What It Takes	15
72	Jackpot JP 788	Take Me Back/Where Do I Turn	12
72	Jackpot JP 789	Rain From The Sky/You're No Good	15
72	Jackpot JP 798	Closer Together/Blinded By Love	20
72	Jackpot JP 799	Turning Point/Money Lover	30
72	Dynamic DYN 428	Just A Dream/Send Me Some Loving	20
72	Pama PM 850	The Time Has Come/THE AGREVATORS: Version	15
72	Pama Supreme PS 373	A Place In The Sun/Stranger On The Shore	15
72	Camel CA 89	Take Me Back/Where Do I Turn	20
72	Explosion EX 2074	The Time Has Come/Blessed Is The Man	15
73	Explosion EX 2078	Stand Up And Fight/The Sunny Side Of The Sea	12
73	Green Door GD 4058	Let Me Love You/If It Don't Work Out	15
73	Bullet BU 523	A Place In The Sun/Burning Fire	35
69	Pama ECO 9	EVERYBODY NEEDS LOVE (LP)	60
72	Trojan TBL 186	JUST A DREAM (LP)	50
72	Trojan TBL 198	MEMORIAL (LP)	30
70s	Lord Koos KLP 1	SLIM SMITH (LP)	50
76	Angen ANGL 1	THE LATE AND GREAT (LP)	40
76	Pama PMLP 3242	JUST A DREAM (LP, reissue)	35

SLIM SMITH & THE FREEDOM SINGERS

MINT VALUE £

| 84 | Pama PMLP 3240 | TIME HAS COME (LP, actually a reissue of MEMORIAL) | 40 |

(see also Wonder Boy, Pioneers, Uniques, Roy Shirley, Ron Sig, Dakota Jim, Dennis Alcapone, David Isaacs, John Holt, (see also Wonder Boy, Pioneers, Uniques, Roy Shirley, Ron Sig, Dakota Jim, Dennis Alcapone, David Isaacs, John Holt,

SLIM SMITH & THE FREEDOM SINGERS
| 70 | Banana BA 304 | Do Dang Do/JACKIE MITTO: Hot Milk | 60 |

SOMETHIN' SMITH & THE REDHEADS
| 58 | Fontana H 154 | I Don't Want To Set The World On Fire/You Made Me Love You | 7 |
| 58 | Fontana TFR 6005 | PUT THE BLAME ON ME (10" LP) | 18 |

STUART SMITH
| 69 | Polydor 56336 | My Head Goes Around/Where Are You | 6 |

TAB SMITH & HIS ORCHESTRA
| 56 | Vogue V 2410 | Jump Time/Rock City | 15 |
| 59 | London HLM 8801 | Smoke Gets In Your Eyes/My Happiness Cha-Cha | 10 |

TERRY SMITH
| 69 | Philips (S)BL 7871 | FALL OUT (LP, laminated sleeve, black/silver label) | 125 |
| 77 | Lambert LAM 002 | TERRY SMITH AND TONY LEE TRIO (LP) | 20 |

(see also If)

TONI SMITH
| 83 | Malaco MAL 1213 | Ooh...I Like The Way It Feels/(Instrumental)/Funk Beats (12", p/s) | 35 |

TRIXIE SMITH
50s	Poydras 101	TRIXIE SMITH (10" EP, 45 rpm)	15
50s	Ristic 12	TRIXIE SMITH (10" EP, 45 rpm)	15
50s	Audubon AAE	TRIXIE SMITH (10" LP)	30

TRIXIE SMITH/MA RAINEY
| 64 | Jazz Collector JEL 22 | FEMALE BLUES VOL. 3 (EP, 2 tracks each) | 10 |

TRULY SMITH
66	Decca F 12373	My Smile Is Just A Frown Turned Upside Down/Love Is Me, Love Is You	25
67	Decca F 12645	I Wanna Go Back There Again/Window Cleaner	35
67	Decca F 12700	The Boy From Chelsea/Little Man With A Stick	20
68	MGM MGM 1431	This Is The First Time/Taking Time Off	20

VERDELLE SMITH
66	Capitol CL 15234	In My Room/Like A Man	18
66	Capitol CL 15456	Tar And Cement/A Piece Of The Sky	12
66	Capitol CL 15481	I Don't Need Anything/If You Can't Say Anything Nice	12
67	Capitol CL 15514	There's So Much Love Around Me/Baby Baby	12

WARREN SMITH
60	London HL 7101	I Don't Believe I'll Fall In Love/Cave-In (export issue)	25
61	London HLG 7110	Odds And Ends/A Whole Lot Of Nothin' (export issue)	25
64	Liberty LIB 55699	Blue Smoke/Judge And Jury	10

WAYNE SMITH
81	Black Joy DH 815	Life Is A Moment In Space/Ain't No Me Without You (12")	40
82	Black Joy DHB 17	Isim Rolie/Rose Marie (12", with Yellowman)	50
84	Greensleeves GRED 162	Come Along/Change Your Style (12")	30
85	Greensleeves GRED 169	Under Me Sleng Teng/MICHAEL BUCKLEY: Dance Gate (12")	30
85	Greensleeves GRED 183	Ickie All Over/TONTO IRIE: Life Story (12")	30
85	Tonos TON 006	Dancing Machine/PATRICK ANDY: Leave The Door (12")	30
85	Greensleeves GRED 177	Sleng Teng Mix Down Remix/PAD ANTHONY: Cry For Me (12")	20
86	Ras RAST 7021	No Puppy Love/Teach Me To Dance (12")	15
80s	Unity UN 019	My Sweet Love/TONTO IRIE: Murder Commit (12")	12
81	Black Joy BHLP 2005	YOUTHMAN SKANKING (LP)	50

WHISPERING SMITH
| 72 | Blue Horizon 2431 015 | OVER EASY (LP) | 120 |

ORVILLE SMITH
| 91 | Riz RIZ 001 | Leaving Rome/BOMBASTIC CREW: Repatriation Dub | 15 |

SMITH & MIGHTY
| 00 | Studio !K7 !K700LP | BASS IS MATERNAL (LP) | 22 |

SMITH & WESTON
| 73 | Decca F 13441 | A Shot Of Rhythm And Blues/Run Run Run | 15 |

SMITH BROTHERS (U.S.)
| 78 | Grapevine GRP 109 | There Can Be A Better Way/Payback's A Drag | 10 |

SMITHFIELD MARKET
| 73 | Gloucester GLS 0435 | LONDON IN 1665 (LP, private pressing, gatefold sleeve, existence unconfirmed) | 0 |
| 74 | Gloucester GLS 0443 | AFTER SHAKESPEARE (LP, private pressing, die-cut sleeve, with insert, existence unconfirmed) | 0 |

THE SMITHS
SINGLES
83	Rough Trade RT 131	Hand In Glove/Handsome Devil (p/s, original pressing with Manchester address on rear sleeve)	25
83	Rough Trade RT 131	Hand In Glove/Handsome Devil (p/s, second pressing with London address on rear label)	15
83	Rough Trade RT 131	Hand In Glove/Handsome Devil (p/s, third pressing with no address)	20
83	Rough Trade RT 131	Hand In Glove/Handsome Devil (later pressing with misprinted blue/negative p/s - beware of counterfeits!)	2000
83	Rough Trade RT 136	This Charming Man/Jeane (unreleased first pressing with Rough Trade/Capitol logo and solid centre, p/s with Manchester address on rear)	50
83	Rough Trade RT 136	This Charming Man/Jeane (Rough Trade/Capitol logo or reissued 'stamped' logo, p/s)	10
83	Rough Trade RTT 136	This Charming Man (Manchester)/This Charming Man (London)/Accept Yourself/Wonderful Woman (12", p/s; later pressing with band title on sleeve)	30
83	Rough Trade RTT 136	This Charming Man (Manchester)/This Charming Man (London)/Accept Yourself/Wonderful Woman (12", p/s)	15
83	Rough Trade RTT 136NY	This Charming Man (New York Vocal)/This Charming Man (New York Instrumental) (12", p/s)	15

The SMITHS

MINT VALUE £

Year	Catalogue	Description	Value
83	Rough Trade RTT 136NY	This Charming Man (New York Vocal)/This Charming Man (New York Instrumental) (12", p/s; later pressing with band title on sleeve)	50
84	Rough Trade RT 146	What Difference Does It Make?/Back To The Old House (Morrissey p/s)	10
84	Rough Trade RT 146	What Difference Does It Make?/Back To The Old House (Terence Stamp p/s)	10
84	Rough Trade RTT 146	What Difference Does It Make?/Back To The Old House/These Things Take Time (12", Morrissey or Terence Stamp p/s)	10
84	Rough Trade RTT 146	What Difference Does It Make?/Back To The Old House/These Things Take Time (Terence Stamp p/s, later pressing with band title on sleeve)	25
84	Rough Trade RT 156	Heaven Knows I'm Miserable Now/Suffer Little Children (p/s)	6
84	Rough Trade RT 156	Heaven Knows I'm Miserable Now/Suffer Little Children (late solid centre pressing, p/s)	40
84	Rough Trade RTT 156	Heaven Knows I'm Miserable Now/Girl Afraid/Suffer Little Children (12", p/s)	10
84	Rough Trade RTT 156	Heaven Knows I'm Miserable Now/Girl Afraid/Suffer Little Children (mispressed 12" with extended version)	50
84	Rough Trade RT 166	William, It Was Really Nothing/Please Please Please Let Me Get What I Want (original issue with green 'man on bed' p/s)	8
84	Rough Trade RTT 166	William, It Was Really Nothing/How Soon Is Now?/Please Please Please Let Me Get What I Want (12", original issue with green 'man on bed' p/s)	10
85	Rough Trade RT 176	How Soon Is Now?/Well I Wonder (p/s)	6
85	Rough Trade RTT 176	How Soon Is Now?/Well I Wonder/Oscillate Wildly (12", p/s)	10
85	Rough Trade RTT 181	Shakespeare's Sister/What She Said/Stretch Out And Wait (12", p/s, with yellow & blue discography inner)	10
85	Rough Trade RTT 181	Shakespeare's Sister/What She Said/Stretch Out And Wait (12", p/s, with misprinted red & green or magenta & green inner)	50
85	Rough Trade RT 186	That Joke Isn't Funny Anymore/Meat Is Murder (live) (p/s)	6
85	Rough Trade RTT 186	That Joke Isn't Funny Anymore/Nowhere Fast (live)/Stretch Out And Wait (live)/Shakespeare's Sister (live)/Meat Is Murder (live) (12", p/s)	10
85	Rough Trade RTT 191	The Boy With The Thorn In His Side/Rubber Ring/Asleep (12", p/s)	10
86	Rough Trade RTT 192	Bigmouth Strikes Again/Money Changes Everything/Unloveable (12", p/s, with or without sticker on sleeve)	10
86	Rough Trade RTT 193	Panic/Vicar In A Tutu (p/s, with square sheet of 'Hang The DJ' stickers)	25
86	Rough Trade RT 193	Panic/Vicar In A Tutu (p/s, with round sheet of 'Hang The DJ' stickers)	20
86	Rough Trade RTT 193	Panic/Vicar In A Tutu/The Draize Train (12", p/s, with 'Hang The DJ' stickers)	15
86	Rough Trade RTT 193	Panic/Vicar In A Tutu/The Draize Train (12", p/s, without 'Hang The DJ' stickers)	10
86	Rough Trade RT 194	Ask/Cemetry Gates (p/s)	6
86	Rough Trade RTT 194	Ask/Cemetry Gates/Golden Lights (12", p/s)	10
87	Rough Trade RT 195	Shoplifters Of The World Unite/Half A Person (p/s)	6
87	Rough Trade RTT 195	Shoplifters Of The World Unite/London/Half A Person (12", p/s; in carrier bag)	30
87	Rough Trade RTT 195	Shoplifters Of The World Unite/London/Half A Person (12", p/s, pink inner with RTT 195 in white in top right hand corner)	10
87	Rough Trade RTT 195	Shoplifters Of The World Unite/London/Half A Person (12", p/s, mispressing, A-side plays "You Just Haven't Earned It Yet Baby")	55
87	Rough Trade RTT 196	Sheila Take A Bow/Is It Really So Strange?/Sweet And Tender Hooligan (12", p/s)	10
87	Rough Trade RT 197	Girlfriend In A Coma/Work Is A Four Letter Word (grey p/s)	6
87	Rough Trade RT 197	Girlfriend In A Coma/Work Is A Four Letter Word (misprinted green p/s, incorrectly shows additional 12" track 'I Keep Mine Hidden' on reverse of sleeve)	500
87	Rough Trade RTT 197	Girlfriend In A Coma/Work Is A Four Letter Word/I Keep Mine Hidden (12", green p/s; some in grey p/s)	35
87	Rough Trade RT 198	I Started Something I Couldn't Finish/Pretty Girls Make Graves (Troy Tate demo) (p/s)	6
87	Rough Trade RTT 198	I Started Something I Couldn't Finish/Pretty Girls Make Graves (Troy Tate demo)/Some Girls Are Bigger Than Others (Live) (12", p/s)	10
87	Rough Trade RT 200	Last Night I Dreamt That Somebody Loved Me/Rusholme Ruffians (John Peel version) (p/s)	6
87	Rough Trade RTT 200	Last Night I Dreamt That Somebody Loved Me/Rusholme Ruffians (John Peel version)/Nowhere Fast (John Peel version) (12", p/s)	12
87	Rough Trade RT 166	William, It Was Really Nothing/How Soon Is Now? (reissue, Billie Whitelaw p/s)	22
87	Rough Trade RTT 166	William, It Was Really Nothing/How Soon Is Now?/Please Please Please Let Me Get What I Want (12", reissue, pale blue inner sleeve, cat no in top right hand corner in white, Billie Whitelaw p/s)	30
88	Rough Trade CAT 063	London (Live) (Square 1-sided black flexi, 33rpm free with The Catalogue magazine, reverse has reproduction of hand-written poem for 'Poppycocteau' by Morrissey)	10
92	WEA YZ0002	How Soon Is Now?/Hand In Glove (p/s, reissue)	15
92	WEA YZ0003	There Is A Light That Never Goes Out/Handsome Devil (live) (p/s)	50

SINGLES : CD REISSUE SINGLES

Year	Catalogue	Description	Value
88	Rough Trade RTT 166CD	William, It Was Really Nothing/How Soon Is Now?/Please Please Please Let Me Get What I Want	30
88	Rough Trade RTT 171CD	Barbarism Begins At Home/Shakespeare's Sister/Stretch Out And Wait	35
88	Rough Trade RTT 215CD	The Headmaster Ritual/Nowhere Fast (live)/Stretch Out And Wait (live)/Meat Is Murder (live) (withdrawn Viv Nicholson cover)	45

ALBUMS

Year	Catalogue	Description	Value
84	Rough Trade ROUGH 61	THE SMITHS (LP)	20
84	Rough Trade ROUGH 76	HATFUL OF HOLLOW (LP, original gatefold issue, with incorrect sleeve, no black dot appears between 'Accept Yourself' and 'Girl Afraid' on reverse of sleeve)	25
85	Rough Trade ROUGH 81	MEAT IS MURDER (LP, with lyric inner sleeve)	20
85	Rough Trade ROUGH CD 76	HATFUL OF HOLLOW (CD, original blue sleeve)	50
86	Rough Trade ROUGH 96	THE QUEEN IS DEAD (LP, gatefold, inner sleeve)	25
87	Rough Trade ROUGH 101	THE WORLD WON'T LISTEN (LP, inner)	25
87	Rough Trade ROUGH 106	STRANGEWAYS HERE WE COME (LP, embossed sleeve, inner)	20
87	Rough Trade ROUGH 255	LOUDER THAN BOMBS (2-LP, gatefold sleeve)	21
88	Rough Trade ROUGH 126	RANK (LP, gatefold sleeve, with inner, ltd. edition with poster and cover sticker denoting amended catalogue number)	30
88	Rough Trade ROUGH 126D	RANK (DAT)	50
93	WEA SMITHS 1	THE SMITHS (10" LP, reissue)	30
93	WEA SMITHS 2	HATFUL OF HOLLOW (2-LP, 10" reissue)	30
93	WEA SMITHS 3	MEAT IS MURDER (10" LP reissue)	30
93	WEA SMITHS 4	THE QUEEN IS DEAD (10" LP reissue)	30

The SMITHS

MINT VALUE £

93	WEA SMITHS 5	THE WORLD WON'T LISTEN (10" LP reissue)	30
93	WEA SMITHS 6	STRANGEWAYS, HERE WE COME (10" LP)	30
93	WEA SMITHS 7	RANK (10" 2-LP reissue)	35
92	Warner Bros. 4509 90327-1	BEST...1 (LP)	45

ALBUMS : BOXED SETS

95	WEA 2564 69320-7	SINGLES BOX (12 x 7" numbered, with badges and poster)	80
95	WEA 2564 69321-7	SINGLES BOX (12 x CD numbered)	45
11	Rhino 2564665906	COMPLETE (17 LP, 8 CD, 25 7" DVD & booklet)	350
11	Rhino 2564665908	COMPLETE (11 LP & booklet)	150

PROMOS : PROMOS & TEST PRESSINGS

83	Rough Trade RT 131	Hand In Glove (white label 1983 test pressing - approx. 5 only)	1500
83	N/A	3-Pack (Rough Trade promo cassette, promoting Hand In Glove and tracks by Zerra 1 and Influence)	100
83	Rough Trade RT 136	Reel Around The Fountain/Jeane (unissued, white label test pressings only - beware of counterfeits!)	1200
83	Rough Trade RT 136	This Charming Man (London Version) (rejected white label test pressing)	800
83	Rough Trade RT 136	This Charming Man (Manchester) (one-sided white label test pressing)	300
83	Rough Trade RTT 136NY	This Charming Man (New York vocal)/(New York Instrumental) (12" white label test pressing)	300
84	Rough Trade RT 146	What Difference Does It Make?/Back To The Old House (white label test pressing)	50
84	Rough Trade RTT 146	What Difference Does It Make?/Back To The Old House/These Things Take Time (12" white label test pressing)	100
84	Rough Trade R 61 DJ	Still Ill/You've Got Everything Now (test pressing)	200
84	Rough Trade RT 61 DJ	Still Ill/You've Got Everything Now (promo)	25
84	Rough Trade ROUGH 61	THE SMITHS (white label test pressing)	30
84	Rough Trade RT 131	Hand In Glove (one-sided white label 1984 test pressing)	100
84	Rough Trade RT 131	Hand In Glove/Handsome Devil (white label test pressing for 1984 repressing)	100
84	Rough Trade RT 156	Heaven Knows I'm Miserable Now/Suffer Little Children (one-sided test pressing)	200
84	Rough Trade RT 156	Heaven Knows I'm Miserable Now/Suffer Little Children (rejected white label test pressing with extended version)	800
84	Rough Trade RTT 156	Heaven Knows I'm Miserable Now/Girl Afraid/Suffer Little Children (rejected 12" white label test pressing with extended version)	800
84	Rough Trade RT 156	Heaven Knows I'm Miserable Now/Suffer Little Children (standard white label test pressing)	20
84	Rough Trade RTT 156	Heaven Knows I'm Miserable Now/Girl Afraid/Suffer Little Children (standard 12" white label test pressing)	200
84	Rough Trade RT 166	William, It Was Really Nothing/Please Please Please Let Me Get What I Want (white label test pressing)	20
84	Rough Trade RTT 166	William, It Was Really Nothing/How Soon Is Now?/Please Please Please Let Me Get What I Want (12" white label test pressing)	100
84	Rough Trade ROUGH 76	HATFUL OF HOLLOW (white label test pressing)	30
84	Copymasters	HATFUL OF HOLLOW (cassette, early version with unreleased tracks)	100
85	Rough Trade RTT 171	Barbarism Begins At Home (12", 2 different 1-sided white label test pressings)	500
85	Rough Trade RTT 171	Barbarism Begins At Home (12" one-sided, promo)	85
85	Rough Trade RTT 171	Barbarism Begins At Home (edited version)/(long version)	45
85	Rough Trade RTT 171	Barbarism Begins At Home (12", p/s, one-sided promo)	40
85	Rough Trade RT 176	How Soon Is Now?/Oscillate Wildly (white label test pressing with Oscillate Wildly instead of Well I Wonder on the B-side)	400
85	Rough Trade RTT 176	How Soon Is Now?/Well I Wonder/Oscillate Wildly (12" white label test pressing)	200
85	Rough Trade ROUGH 81	MEAT IS MURDER (white label test pressing)	300
85	Rough Trade RT 181	Shakespeare's Sister/What She Said (white label test pressing)	200
85	Rough Trade RT 186	Meat Is Murder/Nowhere Fast/Stretch Out And Wait (live EP, unissued, test pressings only)	1000
85	Rough Trade RT 186	Meat Is Murder/Nowhere Fast/Stretch Out And Wait (live EP, unissued, Mayking test pressings - beware of counterfeits!)	500
85	Rough Trade RTT 186	Meat Is Murder/William It Was Really Nothing/Nowhere Fast/Stretch Out And Wait /Miserable Lie (live 12" EP, unissued, test pressings only-beware of counterfeits!)	1000
85	Rough Trade RT 186	That Joke Isn't Funny Anymore/Meat Is Murder (live) (white label test pressing)	100
85	RT 186	That Joke Isn't Funny Anymore/Meat Is Murder (live) (Mayking test pressing)	300
85	Rough Trade RTT 191	The Boy With The Thorn In His Side/Rubber Ring/Asleep (white label test pressing)	20
86	Rough Trade RT 192	Bigmouth Strikes Again/Money Changes Everything (white label test pressing)	200
86	Rough Trade RT 192	Bigmouth Strikes Again/Money Changes Everything/Unloveable (12" white label test pressing)	30
86	Rough Trade ROUGH 96	THE QUEEN IS DEAD (white label test pressing)	150
86	Rough Trade ROUGH 96	THE QUEEN IS DEAD (Mayking test pressing)	300
86	Rough Trade RTT 193	Panic/Vicar In A Tutu/The Draize Train (12" white label test pressing with promo posters)	50
86	Rough Trade RT 194	Ask/Cemetry Gates (white label test pressing)	250
87	Rough Trade RTT 195	You Just Haven't Earned It Yet Baby/London/Half A Person (12", white label test pressing)	800
87	Rough Trade ROUGH 101	THE WORLD WON'T LISTEN (white label test pressing)	20
87	Rough Trade RT 196	Sheila Take A Bow/Is It Really So Strange? (white label test pressing)	200
87	Rough Trade ROUGH 255	LOUDER THAN BOMBS (2-LP, white label test pressings)	200
87	Rough Trade RT 197	Girlfriend In A Coma/Work Is A Four Letter Word (white label test pressing)	200
87	Rough Trade ROUGH 106	STRANGEWAYS, HERE WE COME (white label test pressing)	20
87	Rough Trade RT 198	I Started Something I Couldn't Finish/Pretty Girls Make Graves (Troy Tate demo) (white label test pressing)	200
87	Rough Trade RT 198	I Started Something I Couldn't Finish/Pretty Girls Make Graves (Mayking test pressing)	500
87	Rough Trade RT 166-B	How Soon Is Now? (1-sided white label test pressing for B-side of re-issued William, It Was Really Nothing 7")	200
88	Rough Trade ROUGH 126	RANK (white label test pressing; in misprinted sleeve, no cover star or title on sleeve, just states 'The Smiths')	200
88	Rough Trade ROUGH 126	RANK (white label test pressing)	20
06	Universal (No Cat. No)	THE SMITHS (2-CD Publishing sampler with 'The World Won't Listen' artwork on cover)	80

SMITH SISTERS

MINT VALUE £

(see also Morrissey, Sandie Shaw, The The, Electronic)

SMITH SISTERS
80	Union BB 1002	Sexy Eyes/Dub Version (12")	25

SMITHY ALL STARS
71	Hillcrest HCT 3	Witchfinder General/Deserted	80

(see also Ian Smith & Inner Mind)

SMOG
95	City Slang EFAD 49517	A Hit/Wine Stained Lips (p/s, yellow vinyl)	6
96	Domino RUG 45T	KICKING A COUPLE AROUND EP (12")	15
97	Domino RUG 58	Ex Con/Just Like Napoleon	6
95	City Slang 049521	WILD LOVE (LP)	20
97	Domino WIGLP 3	RED APPLE FALLS (LP)	18
99	Domino WIGLP 60	KNOCK KNOCK (LP)	25
00	Domino WIGLP 7	DONGS OF SEVOTION (2-LP)	20
01	Domino WIGLP 99	RAIN ON LENS (LP)	18
03	Domino WIGLP 127	SUPPER (LP)	20
05	Domino WIGLP 158	A RIVER AIN'T TOO MUCH TO LOVE (LP)	25

SMOKE DZA
19	Daupe! DM SP 051	PRIME LOCATION VOLUMES 1 & 2 (12", p/s, 80 copies)	40
19	Daupe! DM SP 051	PRIME LOCATION VOLUMES 1 & 2 (12", picture disc, 250 copies)	40
19	Daupe! DM SP 051	PRIME LOCATION VOLUMES 1 & 2 (12", p/s, red vinyl, 75 copies)	40
19	Daupe! DM SP 051	PRIME LOCATION VOLUMES 1 & 2 (12", green vinyl, 80 copies)	40
19	Daupe! DM SP 051	PRIME LOCATION VOLUMES 1 & 2 (12",p/s, with obi strip, 20 copies)	80

SMOKE (1)
67	Columbia DB 8115	My Friend Jack/We Can Take It	40
67	Columbia DB 8252	If The Weather's Sunny/I Would If I Could, But I Can't	35
67	Columbia DB 8252	If The Weather's Sunny/I Would If I Could, But I Can't (in export p/s)	80
67	Island WIP 6023	It Could Be Wonderful/Have Some More Tea	70
68	Island WIP 6031	Utterly Simple/Sydney Gill (unreleased)	0
71	Pageant SAM 101	Ride Ride Ride/Guy Fawkes	12
72	Regal Zonophone RZ 3071	Sugar Man/That's What I Want	25
74	Decca FR 13514	My Lullaby/Looking High	15
70s	Gull 128 301	IT'S SMOKE TIME (LP, reissue of German-only LP)	20
88	M. Blue Town MBT 5001	MY FRIEND JACK (LP)	15
12	M. Blue Town BT 5008	IT'S SMOKE TIME (LP, reissue with certificate)	15

(see also Shots)

SMOKE (2)
70	Revolution Pop REVP 1002	Dreams Of Dreams/My Birth	200

SMOKESTACK CRUMBLE
71	Dawn DNS 1013	Got A Bad Leg/Whiskey Macaroni	12

SMOKESTACK LIGHTNIN'
68	Bell BLL 1046	Light In My Window/Long Stemmed Eyes (John's Song)	15
69	Bell MBLL/SBLL 116	OFF THE WALL (LP)	40

SMOKEY BABE
62	77' LA 12-12	SMOKEY BABE AND HIS FRIENDS (LP)	25

SMOKEY CIRCLES
70	Carnaby CNLS 6006	THE SMOKEY CIRCLES ALBUM (LP, union jack flag label)	60

SMOKEY SMOTHERS
69	Polydor 623 239	THE DRIVING BLUES (LP)	50

SMOKIE
75	RAK SRAK 510	PASS IT AROUND (LP, name spelt as SMOKEY on cover)	15
75	RAK SRAK 517	CHANGING ALL THE TIME (LP)	15
76	RAK SRAK 520	MIDNIGHT CAFE (LP)	20
77	RAK SRAK 530	BRIGHT LIGHTS AND BACK ALLEYS (LP)	20
79	RAK SRAK 6757	THE OTHER SIDE OF THE ROAD (LP)	15
81	RAK SRAK 545	SOLID GROUND (LP)	15
82	RAK SRAK 546	STRANGERS IN PARADISE (LP)	18

SMOKIE & HIS SISTER
67	CBS 202605	Creators Of Rain/In Dreams Of Silent Seas	10

THE SMOKIN' MOJO FILTERS
95	Go! Discs GOD 136	Come Together/THE BEAUTIFUL SOUTH: A Minute's Silence/DODGY: Is It Me/BLACK GRAPE: In The Name Of The Father (Crown Of Thorns Mix) (7")	20

(See also Paul Weller, Oasis)

SMOKIN' ROADIE
83	Zone To Zone ZON 3	Midnight/Ripp Off (p/s)	30

SMOOTH BUT HAZZARDOUS
92	Basement BRSS 007	Smooth But Hazzardous/Made U Dance/Violent Headrush (12")	20
93	Sound Entity SENT 1200	We Are The Creator/Push Up The Levels (12")	40
93	Sound Entity SENT 1205	Made You Dance (Carl Cox Remix)/Push Up The Levels (SBH Remix)/Push Up The Levels (Originla Mix) (12")	15
94	Sinister SNS 003	Help Me/DMX Override (12")	10

JACK SMOOTH
91	Sound Entity SE 001	WAVEFORMS EP (12")	15
91	Sound Entity SE 03	Untitled/Untitled/Untitled/Untitled (12", white label, hand-written labels, some in stamped sleeve)	15
93	Sound Entity SENT 1201	Tell Me Something/Happy Nonsense (12", with Spencer T)	20
93	Sound Entity SENT 120220	HURTS EP (12", with Alex Reece)	40

(see also Ruff With The Smooth, DJ Chemistry Meets Jack Smooth)

SMUDGE
94	Domino WIGLP 7	MANILOW (LP, with free 7")	18

SMYLE
71	CBS 7225	Glory Glory/Will I Get Back Tomorrow	8

GILLI SMYTH & MOTHER GONG
78	Charly CRL 5007	MOTHER (LP, with insert)	15

(see also Gong)

DONALD SMYTHE
71	Punch PH 83	Where Love Goes/HURRICANES: You Can Run	380

GLORIA SMYTHE
60	Vogue V 9159	I'll Be Over After A While/Gee Baby Ain't I Good To You	10

SNAFU
74	WWA WWA 003	SNAFU (LP, gatefold sleeve)	18

(see also Whitesnake, Freedom)

SNAKEBITE
83	Astor ASTOR 1	Blow You Away/Thin Ice (no p/s)	25

SNAKEFINGER
80	Do It RIDE5	GREENER POSTURES (LP)	15

(see also The Residents, Chilli Willi)

SNAKEHIPS
75	Eden EDENLP 75	SNAKEHIPS ARNOLD AND THE KING OF BOOGIE (LP)	200

SNAKES
76	Dynamite DYR45006	Teenage Head/Lights Out (p/s)	8

(see also The Motors)

SNAPE
73	Transatlantic TRA 269	ACCIDENTALLY BORN IN NEW ORLEANS (LP)	22

(see also Alexis Korner)

SNAPPED ANKLES
12	Ears Have Eyes EHE 001	True Ecology (Shit Everywhere)/Nowhere/True Ecology (10", p/s)	20
15	Snapped Ankles (no Cat. No.)	I Want My Minutes Back/Instruminutel (p/s, white vinyl)	20
17	Leaf DOCK 66	THE BEST LIGHT IS THE LAST LIGHT (12" EP. p/s)	10

SNAPPERS (1)
59	Top Rank JAR 167	Big Bill/If There Were	18
59	Top Rank JAR 167	Big Bill/If There Were (78)	25

SNAPPERS (2)
67	CBS 2719	Upside Down Inside Out/Memories	40

SNATCH (1)
75	Polydor 2058619	For Always And Ever/Hunting Kind	12

SNATCH (2)
78	Lightning LIG 502	Stanley/I.R.T. (p/s)	10
78	Lightning LIG 505	All I Want/When I'm Bored ('foil' p/s)	10
80	Fetish FET 004	Shopping For Clothes/Joey/Red Army (12", die-cut p/s)	20

(see also Johnny Thunders, Judy Nylon)

SNATCH BACK
79	CSS CS 002	Eastern Lady/Cryin' To The Night (no p/s)	80

SNEAKER PIMPS
96	Clean Up CUP020LP	BECOMING X (LP)	50
99	Clean Up CUP040LP	SPLINTER (2-LP)	40
02	Tommy Boy TBV 1532	BLOODSPORT (2-LP, red vinyl)	30
08	Clean Up CUP020DMM	BECOMING X (2-LP, reissue, 1000 only, stickered sleeve)	25
08	Clean Up CUP040DMM	SPLINTER (2-LP, reissue, 1000 only, stickered sleeve)	25

SNEAKERS
77	Petal PTL 010	Link Lady/Vapour Trails (no p/s, 500 only)	150

SNEAKY PETES
60	Decca F 11199	Savage (Parts 1 & 2)	15

SNEEKERS
64	Columbia DB 7385	I Just Can't Get To Sleep/Bald Headed Woman	150

SNEEKY FEELINS
79	Warped W102	Private Mail/Only The Rain (p/s with insert)	50

DAVID SNELL
66	Decca SKL 4745	THE SUBTLE SOUND OF DAVID SNELL (LP)	15

LEN SNIDER
63	London HLU 9790	Everyone Knows/I'll Be Coming Home Tonight	8

SNIFF 'N' THE TEARS
79	Chiswick NS 40	Driver's Seat (cancelled, test pressings only, picture sleeve)	15

SNIFTERS
78	Lightning GIL 534	I Like Boys/Baby Punker	15

SNIPERS
81	Crass 321984/4	THREE PEACE SUITE (EP)	12

SNIVELLING SHITS
77	Ghetto Rockers PRE 2	Terminal Stupid/I Can't Come (p/s, 1st pressing of 500, paper labels/black print)	60
77	Ghetto Rockers PRE 2	Terminal Stupid/I Can't Come (p/s, 2nd pressing, plastic labels/juke box centre)	25
89	Damaged Goods FNARR 4	Isgodaman?/Terminal Stupid/I Can't Come (p/s)	20
89	Damaged Goods FNARR4B	Isgodaman?/Terminal Stupid/I Can't Come (box set with badge & inserts, pink vinyl in stamped plain white sleeve)	25

(see also Doctor Dark)

SNOBS
64	Decca F 11867	Buckle Shoe Stomp/Stand And Deliver	15

SNOOKY & MOODY
66	Blue Horizon 45-1003	Snooky And Moody's Blues/Telephone Blues (99 copies only)	150

HANK SNOW (& RAINBOW RANCH BOYS)
54	HMV 7MC 7	Why Do You Punish Me (For Loving You)/When Mexican Joe Meets Jole Blon (with	15

SNOW PATROL

MINT VALUE £

54	HMV 7MC 15	Spanish Fire Ball/Between Fire And Water (with Rainbow Ranch Boys) (export issue)............... Rainbow Ranch Boys) (export issue)...	15
54	HMV 7MC 24	My Arabian Baby/I Don't Hurt Anymore (with Rainbow Ranch Boys) (export issue)	15
54	HMV 7MC 25	My Religion's Not Old-Fashioned (But It's Real Genuine)/The Alphabet (with Rainbow Ranch Boys) (export issue)	15
54	HMV 7MC 31	Yellow Roses/Would You Mind (with Rainbow Ranch Boys) (export issue)......................	15
59	RCA RCA 1151	Old Shep/The Last Ride	10
59	RCA RCX 142	COUNTRY GUITAR NO. 7 (EP)	10
63	RCA RCX 7125	WHEN TRAGEDY STRUCK (EP)	10
64	RCA RCX 7154	THAT COUNTRY GENTLEMAN (EP)	12
59	RCA RD 27115	WHEN TRAGEDY STRUCK (LP)	15

SNOW PATROL

98	Jeepster JPR7 005	One Hundred Things You Should Have Done In Bed/My Last Girlfriend (p/s)	8
98	Jeepster JPR7 004	Little Hide/Sticky Teenage Twin (1,000 only, p/s)	18
98	Jeepster JPR7 007	Velocity Girl/Absolute Gravity (p/s)	8
03	Polydor 986712-1	Spitting Games/Wow (Acoustic) (white vinyl, p/s)	7
06	Fiction 0602517043985	Chasing Cars/Play Me Like You Own Hand (p/s, with inner p/s)	25
98	Jeepster JPRLP004	SONGS FOR POLAR BEARS (LP)	40
03	Polydor 9866073	FINAL STRAW (LP)	15
08	Fiction 1785268	A HUNDRED MILLION SUNS (2 x 12" 45 rpm, gatefold)	20
09	Fiction 272201-1	UP TO NOW (box set, 3-LP, CD, DVD)	50

(see also Shrug)

SNUFF

88	Deceptive	TWEET TWEET MY LOVELY (LP, with insert)	15

SNUFF CREW

17	I Love Acid ILA 015	I LOVE ACID 015 (12", hand-stamped and numbered, 303 only)	15

SNUGGY

71	Philips 6006138	Creole Jive/Jungle King...	12

(see also Jade Warrior)

RON SNYDER

63	Parlophone R 4993	Oh My Twisted Bach/Narcissus	6

SO WHAT!

86	No label or Cat. No.	It Is All Over/Now I Don't Want You Around (no p/s)	50
70	CBS 5005	Flowers/Tell Me Now	10

MIKE SOAR

72	Westwood WRS 014	OUR SIDE OF THE BRIDGE (LP)	400

S.O.B.

89	Rise Above RISE 002	THRASH NIGHT EP (p/s)	12

ERROL SOBERS

70	Beacon BEA 159	Sugar Shaker/You're In Love	12

(see also Bobby Bridger)

SOCIALITES

64	Warner Bros WB 148	Jive Jimmy/You're Losing Your Touch	40

SOCIAL SECURITY

78	Heartbeat PULSE 1	I Don't Want My Heart To Rule My Head/Stella's Got A Fella/Cider/Choc Ice (p/s)	30

SOCIETIE

67	Deram DM 162	Bird Has Flown/Breaking Down	60

SO CONFUSING AND SO VERY CLEAR

76	CFC 19776	SO CONFUSING AND SO VERY CLEAR (LP)	70

SOCRATES

72	Deram DM 362	Eating Momma's Cookin'/Dearest Agnes	15

SODS (1)

79	Tap TAP 1	Mopey Grape/Negative Positive (p/s)	30
79	Stortbeat SB 5	No Pictures Of Us/Plaything (p/s)...	40

SODS (2)

79	Step Forward SFLP 3	MINUTES TO GO (LP)	30

SOFERNO B

80	Soferno B SOLP 001	IN DUB (LP)	70

SOFT BOYS

77	Raw RAW 5	GIVE IT TO THE SOFT BOYS (EP, acetate with withdrawn track, Vyrna Knowl Is A Headbanger in place of "Ventilator")	200
77	Raw RAW 5	GIVE IT TO THE SOFT BOYS (EP)	20
78	Radar ADA 8	(I Want To Be An) Anglepoise Lamp/Fat Man's Son (p/s)	15
79	Raw RAW 37	GIVE IT TO THE SOFT BOYS (EP, unreleased reissue)	0
79	Raw RAW 41	Where Are The Prawns (unreleased)	0
80	Armageddon AS 005	I Wanna Destroy You/I'm An Old Pervert (Disco) (p/s)	10
81	Armageddon AS 029	Only The Stones Remain/The Asking Tree (p/s)	8
82	Bucketfull Of Brains BOB 1	Love Poisoning/When I Was A Kid (p/s, with Bucketfull Of Brains magazine)...........	15
82	Bucketfull Of Brains BOB 1	Love Poisoning/When I Was A Kid (p/s, without Bucketfull Of Brains magazine)	12
83	Midnight Music DING 4	He's A Reptile/Song No. 4 (p/s, 2 different designs)	8
89	Overground OVER 4	The Face Of Death/The Yodelling Hoover (p/s, 600 yellow viny or 400 white vinyl)...........	6
89	Overground OVER 4	The Face Of Death/The Yodelling Hoover (p/s, 15 gold test pressings)	15
85	Delorean SOFT 1P	WADING THROUGH A VENTILATOR (12" EP, picture disc)	10
79	Two Crabs CLAW 1001	A CAN OF BEES (LP, original issue, black & white labels)	30
80	Aura AUL 709	A CAN OF BEES (LP, reissue)	15
80	Armageddon ARM 1	UNDERWATER MOONLIGHT (LP)	50
83	M. Music CHIME 0002	INVISIBLE HITS (LP)	15
84	Two Crabs CLAW 1001	A CAN OF BEES (LP, 2nd reissue, black & red labels)	15
86	Living Cream MOIST 1	UNDERWATER MOONLIGHT (LP, reissue, different cover)	20
87	Glass Fish MOIST 4	LIVE AT THE PORTLAND ARMS (LP)	20

(see also Robyn Hitchcock)

SOFT CELL

MINT VALUE £

SOFT CELL
Year	Label/Cat	Title	Value
80	Big Frock ABF 1	MUTANT MOMENTS (EP, plain p/s with postcard; beware of counterfeits without postcard & in wraparound p/s!)	150
81	Some Bizzare HARD 1	A Man Can Get Lost/Memorabilia (p/s, 10,000 only)	10
81	Some Bizzare HARD 12	Memorabilia (Extended)/Persuasion (Extended) (12", p/s)	15
81	Some Bizzare BZS 212	Tainted Love/Where Did Our Love Go/Tainted Dub/Memorabilia (12", p/s, limited edition with 4 tracks)	10
81	Some Bizzare No Cat. No.	Metro Mr. X/B-MOVIE: Remembrance Day (white label test pressing)	60
82	Some Bizzare CELBX 1	THE 12" SINGLES (6 x 12" box set, with booklet)	50
84	Some Bizzare BZSR 2212	Down In The Subway (Remix)/Disease And Desire/Born To Lose (12", p/s)	18

(see also Marc Almond, Marc & Mambas, Anne Hogan)

SOFT ROCK
72	Philips 6308	INVENTION (LP)	15

SOFT DRINKS
82	Outer Himalayan OH 4	Pepsi Cola/Pop Stars In Their Pyjames (with booklet and sticker)	40

SOFTIES
78	Charly CYS 1047	KILLING TIME EP	6

(see also Captain Sensible)

MICK SOFTLEY
65	Immediate IM 014	I'm So Confused/She's My Girl	40
67	CBS 202469	Am I The Red One/That's Not My Kind Of Love	200
70	CBS 5130	Can You Hear Me Now/Time Machine	7
71	CBS 7337	Goin' Down The Road/Gypsy	7
72	CBS 8269	Lady Willow/From The Land Of The Crab	7
65	Columbia 33SX 1781	SONGS FOR SWINGIN' SURVIVORS (LP)	150
70	CBS 64098	SUNRISE (LP, gatefold sleeve)	80
71	CBS 64395	STREET SINGER (LP)	40
72	CBS 64841	ANY MOTHER DOESN'T GRUMBLE (LP)	40

SOFT MACHINE
67	Polydor 56151	Love Makes Sweet Music/Reelin' Feelin' Squeelin'	200
78	Harvest HAR 5155	Soft Space (Parts 1 & 2) (p/s)	8
69	Probe SPB 1002	THE SOFT MACHINE VOLUME TWO (LP, 1st pressing, black/silver label, laminated flipback sleeve)	80
69	Probe SPB 1002	THE SOFT MACHINE VOLUME TWO (LP, 2nd pressing, pink label, laminated flipback sleeve)	70
70	CBS 66246	THIRD (2-LP, gatefold)	50
71	CBS 64280	FOURTH (LP, embossed textured sleeve)	35
72	Probe GTSP 204	VOLUMES ONE AND TWO (2-LP, yellow labels)	25
72	CBS 64806	FIFTH (LP)	25
73	CBS 68214	SIX (2-LP, gatefold sleeve)	30
73	CBS 65799	SEVEN (LP, gatefold sleeve)	30
75	Harvest SHSP 4044	BUNDLES (LP, with inner sleeve)	30
76	Harvest SHSP 4056	SOFTS (LP)	25
77	Harvest SHTW 800	TRIPLE ECHO (3-LP, box set, with colour booklet)	60
78	Harvest SHSP 4083	ALIVE & WELL (LP)	20
78	ABC ABCD 602	THE COLLECTION (2-LP, this is One and Two from same stampers as the 1972 2-LP set VOLUMES ONE AND TWO)	20
81	EMI EMC 3348	LAND OF COCKAYNE (LP)	15
87	Big Beat WIKA 57	S0FT MACHINE (LP, reissue)	18
87	Big Beat WIKA 58	VOLUME TWO (LP, reissue)	18
88	Reckless RECKLP5	LIVE AT THE PROMS (LP)	15
88	Decal LIKD 35	THIRD (2-LP, reissue)	20

(see also Robert Wyatt, Kevin Ayers, Hugh Hopper, Elton Dean, Daevid Allen, Matching Mole, 'Igginbottom, Lyn Dobson)

SOFTNESS
80	Remedy RM 119	You Ain't My Lover/Locked Doors	30

SOFT SHOE
78	Aardvark AARD 1	FOR THOSE ALONE (LP, with insert)	100

SOFT TARGETS
83	Hard Labour HAL 1	Clive Steps South/Susan	8

SOFT TOUCH (1)
67	W+G WG 001	A Silent Life/Ellusive Face (Private Pressing)	300

SOFT TOUCH (2)
73	Acorn AC 04	Crazy Child/Down And Out	20

SOHEP
81	Merciful Release MR 3	So Much Fun/You Could Be So Nice Dear (p/s)	10

SOHO JETS
75	Polydor 2058 525	Hi Heel Tarzan/Night Flight	20
75	Polydor 2058 598	Denim Goddess/Smile	20

(see also Razar, Nervous Germans)

SOHO SKIFFLE GROUP
57	Melodisc EMP 7 72	SOHO SKIFFLE GROUP (EP)	75

CLEO SOL
20	Forever Living Originals FLO0004LP	ROSE IN THE DARK (LP)	30

(see also Sault)

SOL INVICTUS
90	Cerne 004	Abbatoirs Of Love/CURRENT 93: This Ain't The Summer Of Love (live in Japan, gig freebie, 93 with insert & gig ticket)	50
90	Cerne 004	Abbatoirs Of Love/CURRENT 93: This Ain't The Summer Of Love (live in Japan, gig freebie, [200 without insert])	25
91	Shock SX 016	See The Dove Fall/Somewhere In Europe (numbered foldover p/s in poly bag, 1,000 only)	15

SOLAR PLEXUS

MINT VALUE £

91	World Serpent WS7 002	Looking For Europe (1-sided, etched B-side, foldover sleeve in poly bag, 963 only)	15
89	SVL SVL 009	IN THE JAWS OF THE SERPENT (LP, with insert)	20
90	Tursa 001	TREES IN WINTER (LP)	30
90	Tursa 002	LEX TALIONIS (CD, special edit in leather wallet)	30
91	Tursa 003	KILLING TIDE (LP)	25
00	Tursa 026	EVE (picture disc, 1,000 only)	20
01	Tursa 029	HILL OF CROSSES (LP, 1,000 only, signed)	20

(see also Current 93, Death In June, Nurse With Wound, Karl Blake, Shock Headed Peters)

SOLAR PLEXUS
73	Polydor 2383 222	SOLAR PLEXUS (LP)	35

SOLDIER
82	Heavy Metal HEAVY 12	Sheralee/Force (p/s, with postcard)	35
82	Heavy Metal HEAVY 12	Sheralee/Force (p/s, without postcard)	25
04	Killer Metal KMRS 001	Murderous Night/I'm Taken In (red vinyl, 500 copies, numbered)	7

SOLDIER DOLLS
83	Scream 1	WHAT DO THEY KNOW? (EP)	15
84	Scream 2	A TASTE OF BLOOD (EP, red vinyl)	15

SOLDIERS OF FORTUNE
83	Total Darkness TD 1	Stars/Autonomia (fold-out p/s)	7

SOLENT
73	Decca F 13375	My World Fell Down/The Sound Of Summer's Over	10

SOLID BRITISH HAT BAND
71	Longman LG 0 582 56421 2	MISTER MONDAY AND OTHER SONGS FOR THE TEACHING OF ENGLISH (LP, with insert)	30
74	Longman LG 567	GOODBYE RAINBOW (LP, with insert)	30

SOLID GOLD CADILLAC
73	RCA SF 8311	SOLID GOLD CADILLAC (LP)	40
73	RCA SF 8365	BRAIN DAMAGE (LP)	50

(see also Battered Ornaments, Chris Spedding, Mike Westbrook)

SOLID GROOVE
94	Clockwork CLOCK 1	Work That Groove (Original Mix)/(Groove MIx)/Deep State/Technohouse (12")	15

SOLID N MIND
90	Liberty Grooves LIB001	An Original Break (12")	30
91	Liberty Grooves PPP001	Centre Stage/Woke With Nuthin' (Promo cassette)	50
91	Liberty Grooves LIB 002 1/2	Centre Stage/Woke With Nothin' (12")	15
92	Liberty Grooves LIB 003	Battle Tipped Rhyme (12")	18

SOLID ROCK BAND
78	Chapel Lane RWA 1	FOOTPRINTS ON THE WATER (LP, gatefold sleeve)	15

SOLID SPACE
82	In Phaze IP 011	SPACE MUSEUM (cassette)	150

SOLILOQUY
73	Lyntone LYN 2967	Father Moonshine/Asian Way/Lady Tarantula (50 only, no p/s)	300

SOLITAIRES
58	London HLM 8745	Walking Along/Please Kiss This Letter	130
58	London HLM 8745	Walking Along/Please Kiss This Letter (78)	60

JAKE SOLLO
78	Pye 7N 46131	Hot 'N' Spicy/Jacqueline (DJ Copy)	10
79	Pye 7N 46162	Say No More/Show Me How	8
79	Pye N 102	JAKE SOLLO (LP)	30

NORMAN SOLOMAN
81	Black Joy DH 816	Joy Bells Ringing/JAYS: Unity Call (12")	25

SOLSTICE (1)
84	Equinox EQRLP 001	SILENT DANCE (LP, gatefold sleeve)	18

SOLSTICE (2)
08	Iron Kodex IK 003	ONLY THE STRONG SURVIVE (2-LP with free 7")	20

SOLUTION
71	EMI 2023	Divergence/Fever	6
72	Decca SKL-R 5124	SOLUTION (LP)	25

SOME CHICKEN
77	Raw RAW 7	New Religion/Blood On The Wall (p/s)	20
78	Raw RAW 13	Arabian Daze/No. 7	15
78	Raw RAW 13	Arabian Daze/No. 7 (purple vinyl)	120

SOME OF MY BEST FRIENDS ARE CANADIAN
80	Bulge BLAST 4	Feeling Sheepish/Speaking Clock	20

SOMEONE'S BAND
70	Deram DM 313	Story/Give It To You	40
70	Deram SML 1068	SOMEONE'S BAND (LP)	600

SOMERVILLE GENTLEMAN'S BAND
80	Somerville PLR 026	FAR FROM HOME (LP, gatefold insert with sticker over 'Plant Life' logo)	25

JOANIE SOMMERS
60	Warner Bros WB 23	Be My Love/Why Don't You Do Right?	7
60	Warner Bros WB 31	Ruby-Duby-Du/Bob White	7
60	Warner Bros WB 44	One Boy/I'll Never Be Free	7
61	Warner Bros WB 71	Johnny Get Angry/Theme From A Summer Place	10
62	Warner Bros WB 85	Goodbye Joey/Bobby Is Bobby	7
63	Warner Bros WB 105	Little Girl Bad/Wishing Well	7
64	Warner Bros WB 78	When The Boys Get Together/Passing Strangers	7
65	Warner Bros WB 150	If You Love Him/I Think I'm Gonna Cry	15
13	Harkit HRKS 8431	Don't Pity Me/Johnny Get Angry (p/s)	15
60	Warner Bros WEP 6013	POSITIVELY THE MOST (EP, also stereo WSEP 2013)	20
61	Warner Bros WEP 6047	THE VOICE OF THE SIXTIES (EP, also stereo WSEP 2047)	15

SONAR NATION

MINT VALUE £

(see also Ed Byrnes)

SONAR NATION
| 92 | SRT 92 LS 3510 | Some Place Not Home/Master Plan/Hate Photo | 10 |

SONGSTERS
| 54 | London HL 8100 | Bahama Buggy Ride/It Isn't Right | 150 |

SON HOUSE
60s	Saydisc Roots SL 504	THE VOCAL INTENSITY OF SON HOUSE (LP)	40
66	CBS (S)BPG 62604	THE LEGENDARY FATHER OF FOLK BLUES (LP)	35
70	Liberty LBS 83391	JOHN THE REVELATOR (LP)	30

SON HOUSE/J.D. SHORT
| 69 | Xtra XTRA 1080 | DELTA BLUES (LP) | 20 |

SONIA
78	D Roy DRDD 006	Love Don't Live Here Any More/D ROY BAND: Version (12")	20
79	D Roy DRDD 18	Ooh Baby Baby/Back Street Dub (12")	12
79	Karn-Na KRN 002	Again (Suddenly You're Mine)/UNDIVIDED ROOTS: Version (12", purple vinyl)	12
81	S & S FERGY 001	Checking It Out/Version (12", with Creation Rebel)	20
80	Cha Cha CHAD 26	Easier To Love/That's The Way You Feel (12", with Earth & Stone)	15
79	D-Roy DRLP 1006	MAGIC LADY (LP)	60

SONIC BOOM
89	Silvertone ORET 11	Angel/(Extended Mix)/Help Me Please (Drum MIx) (12", p/s)	12
90	Silvertone SONIC 1	Octaves/Tremeloes (10", orange vinyl PVC sleeve, mail-order only)	18
91	Silvertone SONIC 2	(I Love You) To The Moon And Back/Capo Waltz (live) (gig freebie in black die-cut sleeve, promo only, 33rpm)	12
91	Silvertone SONIC 2	(I Love You) To The Moon And Back/Capo Waltz (live) (gig freebie in black die-cut sleeve, promo only, 33rpm, p/s later available separately)	8
90	Silvertone ORE ZLP 506	SPECTRUM (LP, gatefold rotatable plastic disc sleeve with inner)	40

(see also Spacemen 3, Spectrum)

SONIC YOUTH
86	Blast First BFFP 3	Flower/Halloween (12", p/s, some on yellow vinyl)	18
86	Blast First BFFP 3	Flower/Rewolf (12", p/s, censored version)	15
86	Blast First BFFP 3(B)	(Savage Pencil etch)/Halloween II (12", p/s, A-side engraved, 1st 100 signed)	65
86	Blast First BFFP 3(B)	(Savage Pencil etch)/Halloween II (12", p/s, A-side engraved)	40
86	Blast First BFFP 3X	Flower/Halloween/Satan Supermix (12", unreleased)	0
86	Blast First BFFP 7	Starpower (edit)/Bubblegum (12", some with badge & poster)	20
88	Fierce FRIGHT 015/016	Stick Me Donna Magick Momma/Making The Nature Scene (live) (p/s, 2 x 1-sided 7" with etched B-sides)	30
88	Fierce FRIGHT 015/016	Stick Me Donna Magick Momma/Making The Nature Scene (live) (p/s, single disc reissue)	12
98	Geffen GFS 22332	Sunday/Moist Vagina (p/s)	8
88	Catalogue CAT 064	Teenage Riot (square flexidisc sewn into 'The Catalogue' magazine)	15
89	Blast First BFFP 46	Touch Me I'm Sick/MUDHONEY: Halloween (12", p/s)	15
89	Blast First BFDJ1	Come And Smash Me Said The Boy With The Magic Penis/Magic Wand (die-cut company sleeve)	8
89	Blast First BFFP 48	Providence (stereo)/Providence (mono) (promo only)	6
91	DGC 21634	DIRTY BOOTS (12" EP)	15
92	Geffen DGCV 11	100% (10" EP, orange vinyl, numbered p/s)	10
92	Geffen DGCV 11	100% (10" EP, black vinyl promo)	30
92	Geffen DGCT 11	100% (12" EP, promo only, white label)	40
92	Geffen 7-19664 DJ	Personality Crisis/Dirty Boots (DJ promo only)	6
92	Geffen GFSV26	YOUTH AGAINST FASCISM (10" white vinyl EP, numbered p/s)	10
92	Geffen GFST 26	YOUTH AGAINST FASCISM EP (12", p/s)	10
00	Geffen SONIC 001	Free City Rhymes/Renegade Princess (7" promo p/s)	40
85	Blast First BFFP 1	BAD MOON RISING (LP, with lyric insert)	30
86	Blast First BFFP 4	EVOL (LP)	30
87	Blast First CHAT 1	SISTER INTERVIEW DISC (LP)	20
87	Blast First BFFP 20	SISTER (LP)	30
88	Blast First BFFP 34	DAYDREAM NATION (2-LP, 1st 1,000 with signed poster)	60
88	Blast First BFFP 34	DAYDREAM NATION (2-LP)	25
90	WEA 7599 24297-1	GOO (LP, with free 7")	25
90	WEA 7599 24297-1	GOO (LP)	20
92	Geffen GEF24485[2]	DIRTY (2-LP)	35
93	Geffen GEF424515	DAYDREAM NATION (2-LP, reissue, poster)	20
94	Geffen GEF 24632	EXPERIMENTAL JET SET, TRASH & NO STAR (LP, blue vinyl)	25
95	Geffen GEF24825	WASHING MACHINE (2-LP)	50
96	Blast First BFFP 113	CONFUSION IS SEX (LP, reissue)	15
98	Geffen GEF 25203	A THOUSAND LEAVES (2-LP)	25
00	Geffen 069400650 1	NYC GHOSTS & FLOWERS (LP)	20
09	Matador OLE 8721	BATTERY PARK NYC, JULY 4th 2008 (LP)	18
09	Matador OLE 829-1	THE ETERNAL (2-LP)	20

(see also Mudhoney)

SONNY
| 71 | Ackee ACK 127 | Love And Peace/LARRY & ALVIN: Throw Me Corn | 20 |

SONNY (& SONNY'S GROUP)
65	Atlantic AT 4038	Laugh At Me/Tony (as Sonny & Sonny's Group)	10
65	Atlantic AT 4060	The Revolution Kind/Georgia And John Quetzal (as Sonny & Sonny's Group)	10
67	Atlantic 584 131	I Told My Girl To Go Away/Misty Roses (solo)	6

(see also Sonny & Cher)

SONNY & CHER
64	Reprise R 20309	Baby Don't Go/Walkin' The Quetzal	8
65	Vocalion VL 9247	The Letter/Spring Fever (B-side by 'Sonny & Cher (Instrumental)')	15
66	Atlantic 584 018	Have I Stayed Too Long/Leave Me Be	6

SONNY & DAFFODILS

MINT VALUE £

66	Atlantic 584 040	Little Man/Monday	6
67	Atlantic 584 078	The Beat Goes On/Love Don't Come	6
67	Atlantic 584 110	Podunk/Beautiful Story	7
67	Atlantic 584 129	It's The Little Things/Plastic Man	7
68	Atlantic 584 162	Good Combination/You And Me	10
68	Atlantic 584 168	Circus/SONNY BONO: I Would Marry You Today	8
68	Atlantic 584 215	You Gotta Have A Thing Of Your Own/I Got You Babe	8
65	Reprise R 30056	CAESAR AND CLEO (EP, 2 tracks each by Sonny & Cher, Caesar & Cleo)	25

(see also Caesar & Cleo, Cher, Sonny, Date With Soul)

SONNY & DAFFODILS
63	Ember EMB EP 4538	SONNY & DAFFODILS (EP)	50

SONNY (BURKE) & YVONNE
64	Island WI 134	Life Without Fun/SONNY BURKE GROUP: Mount Vesuvius	25

(see also Sonny Burke)

SONNYJIM
18	Daupe! DM SP 034	DEATH BY MISADVENTURE (12", p/s, with Conway, red vinyl, 250 copies)	40
18	Daupe! DM SP 034	DEATH BY MISADVENTURE (12", p/s, with Conway, picture disc, 250 copies)	50
18	Daupe! DM SP 034	DEATH BY MISADVENTURE (12", p/s, with Conway, white vinyl, 250 copies)	40
18	Daupe! DM SP 034	DEATH BY MISADVENTURE (12", p/s, with Conway, 250 copies)	40
18	Daupe! DM SP 034	DEATH BY MISADVENTURE (12", p/s, with Conway, with obi strip, 20 copies)	150
16	Daupe! DM SP 014	MUD IN MY MALBEC (LP, with OBI strip, 20 only)	150
16	Daupe! DM SP 014	MUD IN MY MALBEC (LP, white vinyl, 100 only)	100
16	Daupe! DM SP 014	MUD IN MY MALBEC (LP, 120 only)	80

SON OF A GUN
75	RCA 2526	La Maison De L'Amour/All Smoke And No Fire	7

SON OF NOISE
91	Music Of Life NOTE53	Son Of Noise/Ill Justice (12")	15
91	Kold Sweat KS117	Master Of Menace/Milk In The Chocolate (12")	15
92	Kold Sweat KSEP207	NEGATIVE FORCES/THE MIGHTY SON/THE MISSION (EP)	12
92	Kold Sweat KSLP03	THE MIGHTY SON OF NOISE (LP)	20
95	Little Rascool MZE2711	ACCESS DENIED (LP)	15

(see also Hardnoise)

SON OF JOHN
86	Individual AIRS 104	People Shouting/Your Interpretation	8

SONS & LOVERS
67	Camp 602 002	Matters/Peaceful Is The River	6
68	Beacon BEA116	From Now On The Sunshine/How Could We Ever Get This Way	12

SONS OF ALBATROSS
75	Decca FR 13605	Africa/Ha-ri-ah	35

SONS OF CAIN
80	Loppylugs LOPPY 1	End Of Something/Kennedy Waltz (p/s)	10

SONS OF DEMENTED CHILDREN
87	Hatter MAD 003	Spoof Dealer/Busking (p/s, with insert)	18

SONS OF FRED
65	Columbia DB 7605	Sweet Love/I'll Be There	200
65	Parlophone R 5391	I, I, I (Want Your Lovin')/She Only Wants A Friend	100
66	Parlophone R 5415	Baby What Do You Want Me To Do/You Told Me	200

(see also Odyssey)

SONS OF GLORY
62	Columbia 33SX 1474	GOD GLORIFIES (LP)	25

SONS OF ISHMAEL
87	Manic Ears ACHE 10	PARIAH MARTYR DEMANDS A SACRIFICE (LP)	15

SONS OF JAH
75	Bullet BU 557	Nyah Chant/Rasta Waltz	20
78	Natty Congo NCDM 002	Anthem/WIJA LINDO: His Majesty's Authority (12")	30
78	Natty Congo NC 001	Save The Children/RANKING REUBEN: Psalm 72 (12")	20
78	Natty Congo NC 002	Israel/RANKING REUBEN: Dubsco (12")	20
79	Natty Congo PFUL 2301	Home To Zion/Woman (12")	40
82	Natty Congo NCDM 013	Breaking Down The Barriers/Barrier Dub (12")	20
78	Natty Congo PFULP 3501	BANKRUPT MORALITY (LP, with lyric sheet)	20
79	Natty Congo PFULP 3502	BURNING BLACK (LP)	30
80	Natty Congo PFULP 3505	REGGAE HIT SHOWCASE (LP)	70
82	Natty Congo NCLP 001	UNIVERSAL MESSAGE (LP)	25
82	Natty Congo NCLP 005	URBAN GUERILLA (LP, as Son Of Jah)	50
83	Natty Congo NCLP 002	WRITINGS ON THE WALL (LP, as Son of Jah)	30

SONS OF MAN
67	Oak RGJ 612	SONS OF MAN (EP, no p/s)	400

SONS OF NUBIA
90	White SON1	RAPS THE LAST MEANS (EP)	150

SONS OF PILTDOWN MEN
63	Pye International 7N 25206	Mad Goose/Be A Party	20

SONS OF SOUL
66	Doctor Bird DB 1037	Yeah Yeah Baby/So Ashamed	35

SONS OF MONKEYS
81	Slip 001	Me & Mr. Suzuki/DECADES BY NIGHT: Life Spiral	50

SONS OF ROBIN STONE
74	Atlantic K 10441	Got To Get You Back/Love Is Just Around The Corner	15
74	Atlantic K 10723	Got To Get You Back/Love Is Just Around The Corner	6

SONSONG
76	Zebra ZM 5761	SONSONG (LP)	30

SOPHIE
MINT VALUE £

SOPHIE
12	Huntleys and Palmers HP006	Nothing More To Say/Eeehhh (12", p/s)	60
13	Numbers NMBRS 26	Bipp/Elle (12", printed plastic sleeve)	20
14	Numbers NMBRS 34	Lemonade/Hard (12")	15
15	Numbers NMBRS 46	Msmsmsm/Vyzee (12")	35
15	Numbers NMBRS 47	L.O.V.E/Just Like We Never Said Goodbye (12")	30
18	Transgressive TRANS 368XX	OIL OF EVERY PEARL'S UN-INSIDES (LP, pink vinyl, 300 only)	200
18	Transgressive TRANS 368X	OIL OF EVERY PEARL'S UN-INSIDES (LP, red vinyl, with poster)	50

SOPHISTICATES
60s	Spectrum SPEEP 701	AT THE WOODVILLE (EP)	15

SOPHOMORES
60s	Seeco CELP 451	THE SOPHOMORES (LP)	30

SOPWITH CAMEL
86	Edsel ED 185	FRANTIC DESOLATION (LP, reissue)	20

SORE POINTS
81	Pointless SRTS 81 CUS 1113	Shop Born Sex/Never Gonna Go Outside At Any Point	25

SORE THROAT (1)
78	Hubcap SPIN 1	I Dunno/Complex	7

SORE THROAT (2)
88	Acid Rain ARRGHHH001	DEATH TO CAPITALIST HARDCORE EP	20
88	Meantime COX	UNHINDERED BY TALENT (LP, insert)	15
89	Manic Ears ACHE	INDESTROY (LP, with lyric poster, as SAW THROAT)	20
89	Earache MOSH 10	DISGRACE TO THE CORPSE OF SID (LP, insert)	15
80s	Manic Ears ACHE	NEVER MIND THE NAPALM HERE'S SORE THROAT (LP)	20

SORROWS
65	Piccadilly 7N 35219	I Don't Wanna Be Free/Come With Me	40
65	Piccadilly 7N 35230	Baby/Teenage Letter	50
65	Piccadilly 7N 35260	Take A Heart/We Should Get Along Fine	25
66	Piccadilly 7N 35277	You've Got What I Want/No, No, No (export p/s)	35
66	Piccadilly 7N 35277	You've Got What I Want/No, No, No	20
66	Piccadilly 7N 35309	Let The Live Live/Don't Sing No Sad Songs For Me	40
66	Piccadilly 7N 35336	Let Me In/How Love Used To Be	40
67	Piccadilly 7N 35385	Pink, Purple, Yellow And Red/My Gal	140
66	Piccadilly N(S)PL 38023	TAKE A HEART (LP, mono)	250
66	Piccadilly N(S)PL 38023	TAKE A HEART (LP, stereo)	350

(see also Don Fardon)

SORT SOL
81	4AD AD 101	Marble Station/Misguided (p/s)	8

S.O.U.L. (SOUNDS OF UNITY & LOVE)
72	Pye Intl. NSPL 28162	CAN YOU FEEL IT (LP)	80

HORATIO SOUL
68	Island WI 3132	Ten White Horses/Angela (Sweet Sweet)	8
69	Crystal CR 7006	Nobody's Gonna Sleep Tonight/Turn Around Baby	6

JIMMY SOUL
62	Stateside SS 103	Twistin' Matilda/I Can't Hold Out Any Longer	10
63	Stateside SS 178	If You Wanna Be Happy/Don't Release Me	20
64	Stateside SS 274	I Hate You Baby/Change Partners	10
64	Stateside SE 1010	IF YOU WANNA BE HAPPY (EP)	50

SHARON SOUL
65	Stateside SS 411	How Can I Get To You/Don't Say Goodbye Love	75
65	Stateside SS 411	How Can I Get To You/Don't Say Goodbye Love (DJ copy)	120
97	Connoisseurs GV105	Girl Crazy/BARBARA MERCER: Happiness Is Here	10

SOUL AGENTS
64	Pye 7N 15660	I Just Wanna Make Love To You/Mean Woman Blues	45
64	Pye 7N 15707	Seventh Son/Let's Make It Pretty Baby	75
65	Pye 7N 15768	Don't Break It Up/Gospel Train	70

(see also Loot, Don Shinn, Hookfoot)

SOUL AGENTS (JAMAICA)
67	Coxsone CS 7007	Get Ready It's Rocksteady/BOB & BELTONES: Smile Like An Angel (B-side actually by Bop & Beltones)	30
67	Coxsone CS 7018	For Your Education/SUMMERTAIRES: Tell Me	60
67	Coxsone CS 7027	Lecture/SOUL BOYS: Blood Pressure	65

SOUL BOYS
66	Rio R120	Rudie Get Wise/JACKIE OPEL: I Don't Want Her	60
67	Island WI 3052	Blood Pressure/RITA MARLEY: Come To Me	150

(see also Soul Agents [Jamaica])

SOUL BROTHERS
65	Mercury MF 916	Gotta Get A Good Thing Going/Good Lovin' Never Hurt	10
65	Decca F 12116	I Keep Ringing My Baby/I Can't Take It	18
65	Parlophone R 5321	I Can't Believe It/You Don't Want To Know	15

SOUL BROTHERS (JAMAICA)
65	Ska Beat JB 226	Train To Skaville/WAILERS: I Made A Mistake	200
66	Ska Beat JB 259	Bugaloo/I'll Come Back	100
66	Rio R 118	Crawfish/RITA MARLEY: You Lied	40
66	Rio R 121	Mr T.N.T./MARCIA GRIFFITHS: Mr Everything	50
66	Island WI 282	Green Moon/E Gal OK	30
66	Island WI 294	Ska-Bostello/DON DRUMMOND: Looking Through The Window	30
66	Island WI 296	Sound One/MARTINE: Grandfather's Clock (B-side actually by Emille Straker & Merrymen or Martinis)	50
66	Island WI 3013	More & More/DELROY WILSON: Dancing Mood	40
66	Island WI 3016	Mr Flint/Too Young To Love (B-side actually by Freddie McGregor)	40

SOUL BROTHERS SIX

MINT VALUE £

67	Island WI 3036	Sound Pressure/ETHIOPIANS: For You 30
67	Island WI 3039	Hi-Life/DELROY WILSON: Close To Me 50
67	Coxsone CS 7001	Take Ten/HUGH GODFREY: Deh Pon Dem 100
67	Coxsone CS 7020	Hey Windell/KEN BOOTHE: Home Home Home 40
67	Coxsone CS 7024	One Stop/TENNORS: Pressure And Slide 30
67	Studio One SO 2006	Hot And Cold/TERMITES: Mercy Mr. Percy 150
67	Studio One SO 2034	Hot Rod/GAYLADS: Africa (We Want To Go) 125
67	Island WI 3038	Sherry/SOUL JUNIOR : Out Of My Mind (Some list Bumps Oakley as the B-side) 100
67	Studio One SO 2016	Honey Pot/VICEROYS: Lose And Gain 60
70	Pressure Beat PR 5506	Pussy Catch A Fire (actually by Soul Twins)/DESTROYERS: Follow This Beat (B-side actually "Secret Weapon" by Ansell Collins) 15
67	Coxsone CSL 8001	HOT SHOT SKA (LP) 200
67	Coxsone CSL 8002	CARIB SOUL (LP) 250

(see also Earl Van Dyke & Soul Brothers, Soul Twins, Lee Perry, Tony Gregory, Ethiopians, Itals, Hortense & Delroy, Gaylads, Jennors, Derrick Morgan, Summertires, Delroy Wilson.)

SOUL BROTHERS SIX
67	Atlantic 584 118	Some Kind Of Wonderful/I'll Be Loving You 50
69	Atlantic 584 256	Some Kind Of Wonderful/Somebody Else Is Loving My Baby 25
72	Atlantic K 10204	Some Kind Of Wonderful/Check Yourself 10
74	Atlantic K 10471	Thank You Baby For Loving Me/Somebody Else Is Loving My Baby 8
00	Atlantic 45 2406	I'll Be Loving You/LITTLE ESTHER: Just Say Goodbye (reissue) 8

SOUL CAPSULE
01	Aspect ASC3	Law Of Grace/Meltdown/Meltdown (Dub) (12") 150

SOUL CATS
69	Camel CA 23	Keep It Moving/Your Sweet Love 30
69	Gas GAS 109	Choo Choo Train/The Load (actually "Swinging For Joy" by Count Ossie Band) 30
71	Hillcrest HCT 2	Reggay Got Soul (actually by Carl Bryan)/Land Of Love 10
70s	Junior JR 103	Reggay Got Soul (actually by Carl Bryan)/Land Of Love (reissue) 15

SOUL CITY ORCHESTRA
77	Rouge RMS 109	MEAT TICKET (LP) 40
78	De Wolfe DWS/LP 3387	RED LIGHT ZONE (LP) 20

SOUL CITY
62	Cameo Parkway P 103	Everybody Dance Now/Who Knows 100
62	Cameo Parkway P 103	Everybody Dance Now/Who Knows (DJ copy) 125

SOUL CITY EXECUTIVES
69	Soul City SC 109	Happy Chatter/Falling In Love 20

SOUL CLAN
68	Atlantic 584 202	Soul Meeting/That's How It Feels (in p/s) 15
68	Atlantic 584 202	Soul Meeting/That's How It Feels 8
68	Atlantic 587 127	SOUL MEETING (LP) 20

(see also Solomon Burke, Arthur Conley, Don Covay, Ben E. King, Joe Tex)

SOUL CONDOR
70	Polydor 2344002	CERTAIN LIONS & TIGERS (LP) 25

SOUL CONNECTION
88	Intrigue IGE 001T	Oh Ivy!/In (and Out Of) Love/Find The Time (To Play) (12") 15
88	Intrigue IGE 004T	Got To Find A Way/(Remix)/Groove And Move (12") 10
88	Intrigue IGE SC1	ROUGH & READY (LP) 30
90	Intrigue IGE SC2	RAW STREETSOUL (LP) 50

SOUL DEFENDERS
71	Banana BA 354	Way Back Home/SOUL REBELS: Stand For Your Rights 35
72	Ackee ACK 147	Sound Almighty/COUNT OSSIE: Meditation 20

(see also Eric Donaldson, Carey Johnson)

SOUL DESTROYERS
00	Stark Relaity STARK008	Blow Your Top Pt. 1/Blow Your Top Pt. 2 12

SOUL DIRECTIONS
70	Attack ATT 8011	Su Su Su/Better Hearing 200

SOUL DRIFTERS
07	Funk 45 FUNK45 037	Funky Soul Brother Part 1/Part 2 (reissue) 15

GEORGE SOULE
75	United Artists UP 35771	Get Involved/Everybody's Got A Song To Sing 8

SOUL ELECTRIX
96	Void VOID 004	Inside Fix/Drift (12") 12

SOULETTES
65	Ska Beat JB 204	Opportunity/DIZZY JOHNNY & STUDIO 1 ORCHESTRA: Sudden Destruction 50
70	Upsetter US 337	Let It Be/UPSETTERS: Big Dog Bloxie 30
71	Jackpot JP 766	My Desire/Bring It Up 25
71	Jackpot JP 767	All Of Your Loving/LLOYD CLARKE: Love Me 20
73	Attack ATT 8044	This World/Same Thing 12

(see also Rita Marley, Ken Boothe, Roland Alphonso, Uniques)

SOUL EXPLOSION
69	Downtown DT 455	Let's Try It Again/Gumption Rock 10
70	J-DAN JDN 4405	My Mother's Eyes/Gum Pot 12

SOUL FLAMES
68	Nu Beat NB 020	Mini Really Fit Dem/Soul Train 200

(see also Alton Ellis)

SOULFUL DYNAMICS
70	Decca F 23028	Madmoisselle Ninette/Monkey 6

SOULFUL STRINGS
67	Chess CRS 8068	Burning Spear/Within You, Without You 30
67	Chess CRS 8068	Burning Spear/Within You, Without You (DJ Copy) 50

SOUL GENERATION

MINT VALUE £

69	Chess CRS 8094	I Wish It Would Rain/Listen Here	10
69	Chess CRLS 4534	GROOVIN' WITH THE SOULFUL STRINGS (LP)	20

SOUL GENERATION
73	Sticky STY 2	Million Dollars/Sailing	8
79	Grapevine GRP 131	Hold On/The Lonely Sea	8
73	Sticky SBL 135	BEYOND BODY AND SOUL (LP)	25

SOUL KINGS
69	Blue Cat BS 169	The Magnificent Seven/RUPIE EDWARDS: Long Lost Love	60

SOUL LEADERS
67	Rio R 134	Pour On The Sauce/Beauty Is Only Skin Deep	40

SOUL LIFTERS
03	Funk 45 FUNK45 007	Hot Funky And Sweaty/Brothers And Sisters (reissue)	10

SOUL MAKERS
75	Island USA 2009	Missing You/Get What You Want	10

SOULMATES (JAMAICA)
69	Amalgamated AMG 836	Them A Laugh And A Ki Ki/The Hippys Are Here (B-side actually by Hippy Boys)	70
69	Amalgamated AMG 842	On The Move/Jump It Up (B-side actually by Viceroys)	70
69	Camel CA 33	Beware Of Bad Dogs/Short Cut (actually by Glen Adams)	50
70	Unity UN 555	Ten Cent/DOREEN SHAFFER: Stay With Me Forever	10

SOULMATES (U.K.)
65	Parlophone R 5334	Too Late To Say You're Sorry/Your Love	80
66	Parlophone R 5407	Bring Your Love Back Home (with Jet Set)/When Love Is Gone	15
66	Parlophone R 5506	Mood Melancholy/Sayin' Something	10
67	Parlophone R 5601	Is That You?/Time's Run Out	10

(see also Liza Strike)

SOUL MERCHANTS
67	President PT 166	Whole Lot Of Lovin'/Stormy Weather	10

SOUL OF THE CITY
77	Mandla MANDLA 002	CITY SOUL AND DIAGONAL STREET BLUES (LP)	60

SOUL ON DELIVERY
75	Decca F13601	Hustle/Crescent Boogie	10

SOULOSOPHY
71	Epic EPC 7203	Take Me To The Pilot/Friends And Lovers	10

SOUL PARTNERS
69	Pama PM 766	Walk On Judge/Lose The One You Love	20

SOUL PEOPLE
68	Island WIP 6040	Hummin'/Soul Drink	35

SOUL POTION
73	Contempo 2015	Circle Full Of Love/Soul Baby	6

SOUL PROPRIETORS
65	Concord CON STD 74	All/Lonely Separation (private pressing)	300

SOUL REBELS
72	Banana BA 374	Listen And Observe/What's Love	70
72	Count Shelly CS 001	Judgement Day Is Near/Solid As A Rock	25
72	Count Shelly CS 003	I'm The One Who Loves You/I ROY: War Zone	20

(see also Soul Defenders)

SOUL RHYTHMS
69	Bullet BU 404	Work Boy Work/CECIL THOMAS: Girl Lonesome Fever	25
69	High Note HS 013	National Lottery/Round Seven	30
69	Gas GAS 113	Soul Call/Musical Gate	70

(see also Hippy Boys, Max Romeo)

SOUL RUNNERS
67	Polydor 56732	Grits 'n' Cornbread/Spreading Honey	10

SOULSAVERS
12	V2 (no cat no)	Longest Day (7", 1-sided, Be side etched, 300 only)	8
07	V2 VVR1045531	IT'S NOT HOW FAR YOU FALL IT'S HOW YOU LAND (LP)	60

SOUL SEARCHERS
74	Sussex SXX 2	Blow Your Whistle (Parts 1 & 2)	8
10	Soul Brother SB 7004D	We The People/Think (reissue)	6
74	Sussex LPSX 4	SALT OF THE EARTH (LP)	25
06	Soul Brother SBCS 24	WE THE PEOPLE (LP, reissue)	15

SOUL SHACK
80	Record Shack GALD 003	Galactic Funk/(Instrumental) (12", white label only)	40

SOUL SISTERS (JAMAICA)
69	Amalgamated AMG 839	Wreck A Buddy/VERSATILES: Push It In	40

(see also Dennis Brown)

SOUL SISTERS (U.S.)
64	Sue WI 312	I Can't Stand It/Blueberry Hill	40
64	Sue WI 336	Loop De Loop/Long Gone	50
65	London HLC 9970	Foolish Dreamer/Good Time Tonight	60
65	London HLC 9970	Foolish Dreamer/Good Time Tonight (DJ copy)	100
72	United Artists UP 35388	Good Time Tonight/Some Soul Food	10
64	Sue ILP 913	THE SOUL SISTERS (LP)	150

SOUL SOUNDS
67	Columbia S(C)X 6158	SOUL SURVIVAL (LP)	40

(see also Savages, Rebel Rousers)

SOUL STIRRERS
69	Duke DU 25	Come See About Me/LLOYD CHARMERS: 5 To 5	60

(see also Sam Cooke)

SOUL SURVIVORS

MINT VALUE £

SOUL SURVIVORS
67	Stateside SS 2057	Expressway To Your Heart/Hey Gyp	30
68	Stateside SS 2094	Explosion (In Your Soul)/Dathon's Theme	18
69	Atlantic 584 275	Mama Soul/Tell Daddy	30

SOUL SYNDICATE
72	Green Door GD 4021	Riot (actually by Johnny Moore & Soul Syndicate)/Smoke Without Fire (actually by Keith Hudson)	30

(see also Rockin' Horse)

SOUL TONES
70	Pama PM 790	Dancing Time/BUNNY BARRETT: Love Locked Out	15

SOUL TOPS
67	Fab FAB 27	Baby I Got News/TEDDY KING & BUSTER'S ALL STARS: Mexican Divorce	120
68	Nu Beat NB002	Rain And Thunder/Swing Baby	60

SOUL TWINS (JAMAICA)
70	High Note HS 043	Little Suzie/Cherrie	25
72	Clandisc CLA 238	Don't Call Me Nigga/DYNAMITES: Joe Louis	35

SOUL TWINS (U.S.)
77	Grapevine GRP 101	Quick Change Artist/Give The Man A Chance	10

SOUL II SOUL
89	10 DIX 82	CLUB CLASSICS VOL 1. (LP)	15

SOUL VENDORS
67	Coxsone CS 07112	Honeypot/BUMPS OKALEY: Rag Doll (white label only)	400
67	Coxsone CS 7028	You Troubled Me/BOP & BELTONES: Love	80
67	Coxsone CS 7029	Fat Fish/MARCIA GRIFFITHS: Call To Me	150
67	Studio One SO 2018	Rocking Sweet Pea/JOE HIGGS: Change Of Plans	200
67	Studio One SO 2022	Cool Shade/RICHARD ACE: I Need You	120
67	Studio One SO 2028	Just A Bit Of Soul/ALTON ELLIS: I Am Just A Guy	120
67	Studio One SO 2031	Take Me/DELROY WILSON: I'm Not A King	60
67	Studio One SO 2032	Pe Da Pa/ERNEST WILSON: Money Worries	80
67	Studio One SO 2035	Pupa Lick/ETHIOPIANS: Leave My Business Alone	40
68	Studio One SO 2038	Psychedelic Rock/GAYLADS: I'm Free	500
68	Studio One SO 2043	Chinese Chicken/JACKIE MITTOO: Put It On	250
68	Studio One SO 2044	Happy Ogan (actually titled "Happy Organ")/INVADERS: Soulful Music	1200
68	Studio One SO 2048	Evening Time/RIGHTEOUS FLAMES: Ease Up	120
68	Studio One SO 2058	Frozen Soul/ERNEST WILSON: If I Were A Carpenter	200
68	Studio One SO 2066	Soul Joint/Soul Limbo	200
68	Studio One SO 2070	Captain Cojoe/JACKIE MITTOO: Drum Song	400
68	Coxsone CS 7037	Grooving Steady/ROY RICHARDS: Warm And Tender Ska	120
68	Coxsone CS 7038	Whipping The Prince (actually by Ed Hangle & Alton Ellis)/HEPTONES: If You Knew	100
68	Coxsone CS 7048	Last Waltz/HAMLINS: Sentimental Reasons	100
68	Coxsone CS 7057	Real Rock/AL CAMPBELL: Don't Run Away	220
68	Coxsone CS 7071	West Of The Sun/ALTON ELLIS: A Fool	150
69	Coxsone CS 7084	Six Figure/DENZIL LAING: Man Payaba	90
67	Coxsone CSL 8210	ON TOUR (LP)	350

(see also Dobby Dobson, Norma Fraser)

SOULWAX
04	Pias B060DLP	ANY MINUTE NOW (2-LP, inners)	20
05	PIAS PIASB 060	NITE VERSIONS (2-LP)	40
07	Parlophone 509995092471	MOST OF THE REMIXES WE'VE MADE... (2-LP)	20

SOUND
80	Korova KOW 10	Heyday/Brute Force (p/s)	8
81	Korova KOW 21	Sense Of Purpose/Point Of No Return (p/s)	8
79	Tortch TOR 003	PHYSICAL WORLD (EP)	35
79	Tortch TOR 008	THE SOUND (LP, possibly unissued)	0
80	Korova KODE 2	JEOPARDY (LP, with inner)	20
81	Korova KODE 5	FROM THE LIONS MOUTH (LP, gatefold)	35
82	Warner Bros. 240019	ALL FALL DOWN (LP)	20
85	Statik STAB 1	SHOCK OF DAYLIGHT (mini-LP)	15
85	Statik STATLP 24	HEAD & HEARTS (LP)	20
85	Statik STATDLP1	IN THE HOTHOUSE (2-LP, gatefold)	25

(see also Outsiders, Second Layer)

SOUND BARRIER
68	Beacon BEA 109	She Always Comes Back To Me/Groovin' Slow	100

SOUND CEREMONY
89	Celestial Sound SRT 8KF	You're Breaking My Heart (p/s)	10
79	Celestial Sound RWG 001	GUITAR STAR (LP)	20
79	Celestial Sound RWG 002	RON WARREN GANDERTON & SOUND CEREMONY (LP)	40
81	Celestial Sound RWG 003	PRECIOUS AS ENGLAND (LP)	20

SOUND DIMENSION
69	Coxsone CS 7083	Scorcia/CECIL & JACKIE: Breaking Up (B-side actually "Hold Me Baby" by Basil Daley)	50
69	Coxsone CS 7085	Soul Trombone (Suffering Stink)/LARRY & ALVIN: Your Cheating Heart	300
69	Coxsone CS 7090	Soulful Strut/Breaking Up	300
69	Coxsone CS 7093	More Scorchia (dredited to Sound Dimensions)/LENNIE HIBBERT: Village Soul	60
69	Coxsone CS 7097	Time Is Tight/BARRY LLEWELLYN: Sad Song	60
69	Bamboo BAM 5	Doctor Sappa Too/Soul Eruption (B-side actually by Roy Richards & Sound Dimension)	45
69	Bamboo BAM 7	Baby Face/GLADIATORS: Any Where	30
69	Bamboo BAM 9	Jamaica Rag/C. MARSHALL: I Need Your Loving	40
69	Bamboo BAM 13	Whoopy/NORMA FRAZER: Working (B-side actually by Marcia Griffiths)	120
69	Bamboo BAM 14	Black Onion/Bitter Blood	80
70	Bamboo BAM 18	Poison Ivy/BOB ANDY: Bonopart (actually by Al Senior)	50

SOUNDCARRIERS

MINT VALUE £

70	Bamboo BAM 50	Soul Food/BURNING SPEAR: Door Peeper	80
70	Banana BA 313	In The Summertime/In The Summertime - Version (actually by Winston Francis)	35
70	Supreme SUP 202	More Games/MR. FOUNDATION: Maga Dog (actually by Invaders)	60

(see also Brentford Road Allstars, Jackie Mittoo, Bob Andy, Horace Andy, John Holt, Larry Marshall, Irving Brown, Heptones, Freedom Singers, Winston Francis, Jerry Jones, Ethiopians, Cables, Alton Ellis, Gladiators, Ken Boothe, Soul Vendors)

SOUNDCARRIERS

09	Melodic MELO 059	HARMONIUM (2-LP, print, download card)	40
10	Melodic MELO 059	CELESTE (2-LP, gatefold)	40
13	The Great Pop Supplement GPS 103	THE OTHER WORLD OF THE SUONDCARRIERS (LP)	30
13	The Great Pop Supplement GPS 103	THE OTHER WORLD OF THE SUONDCARRIERS (LP, repressing, pink splatter vinyl)	25
14	Ghost Box GBX 020LP	ENTROPICALIA (LP)	20

SOUNDGARDEN

92	A&M AMY 723	Rusty Cage/Touch Me/Show Me (12", poster p/s, 5000 only)	15
96	A&M 5818457	Burden In My Hand/Karaoke (p/s, white vinyl, numbered, 5000 only)	15
89	A&M AMA 5252	LOUDER THAN LOVE (LP)	15
91	A&M 395 374-1	BADMOTORFINGER (LP, blue vinyl)	40
91	A&M 395 374 1	BADMOTORFINGER (LP)	18
96	A&M 540 558-1	DOWN ON THE UPSIDE (2-LP)	35
96	A&M 540 558-1	DOWN ON THE UPSIDE (2-LP, clear vinyl)	45
94	A&M 540215-1	SUPERUNKNOWN (2 x LP, clear, orange or blue vinyl, stickered, 2 lyric sheets)	60
11	A&M 80015268-01	LIVE ON I-5 (2-LP)	20

SOUND IRATION

89	Wau Mr. Modo MOWLP 001	IN DUB (LP)	35
89	Mystic Red Corp MRC 8888	Seventh Seal/Dub Seal (12")	30

SOUNDLAB

93	Lucky Spin LSR 009	VOLUME 1 EP (12")	20

SOUND NETWORK

65	Mercury MF 944	Watching/How About Now	25

SOUND OF JIMMY NICOL

65	Decca F 12107	Clementine/Bim Bam	25

(see also Jimmy Nicol)

SOUNDPROOF

71	Look LKSP511-301	Friday Every Friday/Lonely Boy Lonely Girl	100

SOUNDS AROUND

66	Piccadilly 7N 35345	What Does She Do?/Sad Subject	25
67	Piccadilly 7N 35396	Red White And You/One Of Two	25

(see also Peter & Wolves, John Pantry, Norman Conquest, Factory)

SOUNDS COMBINE

71	Escort ERT 862	African Museum/African Museum - Version	12

SOUNDS INCORPORATED

61	Parlophone R 4815	Mogambo/Emily	15
62	Decca F 11540	Sounds Like Locomotion/Taboo	8
63	Decca F 11590	Stop/Go	10
63	Decca F 11723	Order Of The Keys/Keep Moving	25
64	Columbia DB 7239	The Spartans/Detroit	7
64	Columbia DB 7321	Spanish Harlem/Rinky Dink	10
64	Columbia DB 7404	William Tell/Bullets	7
65	Columbia DB 7545	Time For You/Hall Of The Mountain King	7
65	Columbia DB 7676	My Little Red Book/Justice Neddi	10
65	Columbia DB 7737	On The Brink/I'm Comin' Thru	40
67	Polydor 56209	How Do You Feel/Dead As You Go	15
69	Decca 22883	Warmth Of The Sun/Apollo (export)	10
64	Columbia SEG 8360	TOP GEAR (EP)	25
64	Columbia 33SX 1659	SOUNDS INCORPORATED (LP, mono)	25
64	Columbia SCX 3531	SOUNDS INCORPORATED (LP, stereo)	30
65	EMI Regal SREG 1071	RINKY DINK (LP, export issue)	20
66	Studio Two TWO 144	SOUNDS INCORPORATED (LP)	20

(see also Jeff Beck, May Blitz, Boxer, Tony Newman)

SOUNDS NICE

69	Parlophone R 5797	Love At First Sight/Love You Too ('featuring Tim Mycroft')	8
69	Parlophone R 5821	Sleepless Night/Continental Exchange ('featuring Tim Mycroft')	6
69	Parlophone PMC/PCS 7089	LOVE AT FIRST SIGHT (LP)	25

(see also Third Ear Band, Chris Spedding, Clem Cattini Ork)

SOUNDS OF BOB ROGERS

67	CBS 3018	Among My Souveneirs/Dream With Me	20

SOUNDS OF JOHNNY HAWKSWORTH

66	Columbia DB 8059	Goal/"Goal - World Cup 1966" Theme	15

SOUNDS OF MODIFICATION

68	Stateside SL/SSL 10262	SOUNDS OF MODIFICATION (LP)	30

SOUNDS OF REFLECTION

68	Reflection RS6001SM	Brave New Day/Lord Of Believe (p/s)	50

SOUNDS OF SALVATION

74	Reflection RL 310	SOUNDS OF SALVATION (LP, with booklet)	90

(see also Reflection)

SOUNDS OF TIME

73	Columbia 9000	DANSE MACABRE (LP)	20

SOUNDS ORCHESTRAL

66	Piccadilly 7N 35284	Thunderball/Mr Kiss Kiss Bang Bang	10
68	Pye 7N 170507	When Love Has Gone/Fifth Avenue Breakdown	6

SOUNDS PROGRESSIVE

MINT VALUE £

65	Pye NPL 38016	THUNDERBALL - SOUNDS ORCHESTRAL MEET JAMES BOND (LP, in gatefold sleeve)	20
65	Pye NPL 38016	THUNDERBALL - SOUNDS ORCHESTRAL MEET JAMES BOND (LP)	30

SOUNDS PROGRESSIVE
70	Eyemark EMCL 1009S	KID JENSEN INTRODUCES SOUNDS PROGRESSIVE (LP)	40

SOUNDS SENSATIONAL
67	HMV POP 1584	Love In The Open Air/Night Cry	18

SOUND SCIENCE
91	Sound Entity SE 0002	HERT'Z SO GOOD EP (12")	15

SOUND SIXTY-SIX
66	Decca F 12323	Flight 4864/The Bouncer	12

SOUND STAGE ORCHESTRA
76	BBC RESL 30	Grandstand/Rugby Special	10

SOUND STYLISTICS
02	Bruton BRO 209	Get Ya Some/Down Home Style/The Players Theme	40
07	Bruton FSR LP018	PLAY DEEP FUNK (LP)	40

(see also James Taylor Quartet)

SOUND SYSTEM
65	Island WI 258	You Don't Know Like I Do/Take Me Serious	15

(see also Owen Gray)

SOUND VISION
70s	Key KL 007	IN CONCERT (LP, featuring Judy MacKenzie)	25

SOUP DRAGONS
86	Raw TV Products RTV 1	Hang Ten!/Slow Things Down (p/s, blue or red vinyl)	7
86	Raw TV Products RTV 2	Head Gone Astray/Girl In The World/So Sad I Feel (PVC sleeve, with poster)	8
86	Subway Organisation SUBWAY 4	THE SUN IS IN THE SKY (EP, unreleased, 1,000 only, foldaround p/s in poly bag)	15

(see also BMX Bandits, Future Pilot A.K.A.)

SOUP GREENS
65	Stateside SS 457	That's Too Bad/Like A Rolling Stone	70

SOUPHERBS
65	Oak RGJ 601	SOUPHERBS (LP)	350

SOURCE
86	Streetwave MKHAN 78	You Got The Love (featuring Candi Staton) (Extended)/(Radio Edit)/(Club Edit)/(House Acapella) (12")	15

SOURCE DIRECT
94	Odysee ODY 01	Future London/Shimmer (12")	20
95	Metalheadz MET H 016	A Made Up Sound/The Cult (12")	15
95	Source Direct SD 001	Fabric Of Space/Bliss (12")	20
95	Source Direct SD 002	Approach And Identity/Modem (12")	20
95	Source Direct SD 003	Snake Style/Exit 9 (12")	15

TIM SOUSTER
77	Transatlantic TRA 343	SW1T DR1MZ (LP)	20

APRIL SOUTH
81	Rockelly RKR 10781 EJSP 9319	Heroes Of The NIght/The Boys Are Out To Get Me (no p/s)	50
82	President PT 501	Heroes Of The NIght/The Boys Are Out To Get Me (p/s)	20

HARRY SOUTH ORCHESTRA
69	Philips BF 1770	Scarborough Fair/I'm Gonna Make You Love Me	25
75	EMI EMI 2252	The Sweeney (TV Theme) (Parts 1 & 2)	20
67	Mercury 20081 MCL	PRESENTING HARRY SOUTH (LP)	40

JOE SOUTH
62	Oriole CB 1752	Masquerade/I'm Sorry For You	20
63	MGM MGM 1206	Same Old Song/Standing Invitation	7
65	MGM MGM 1267	Concrete Jungle/Last One To Know	7
65	HMV POP 1474	I Want To Be Somebody/Deep Inside Me	7
68	Capitol CL 15535	Birds Of A Feather/It Got Away	6
69	Capitol CL 15579	Games People Play/Mirror Of Your Mind	6
69	Capitol CL 15608	Don't It Make You Want To Go Home/Heart's Desire	15

SOUTH COAST SKA STARS
80	Safari SAFE 27	South Coast Rumble/Head On (p/s)	8

(see also Ray Fenwick)

JERI SOUTHERN
54	Brunswick 05343	Remind Me/Little Boy Grown Tall	8
55	Brunswick 05367	The Man That Got Away/Speak Softly To Me	8
55	Brunswick 05490	An Occasional Man/It's D'Lovely	7
56	Brunswick 05529	Where Walks My True Love?/Don't Explain	10
57	Brunswick 05665	Fire Down Below/Smoke Gets In Your Eyes	8
55	Brunswick LA 8699	WARM (10" LP)	15
56	Brunswick LAT 8100	THE SOUTHERN STYLE (LP)	15

JOHNNY SOUTHERN & HIS WESTERN RHYTHM KINGS
57	Melodisc MEL 1413	We Will Make Love/Crazy Heart	10
57	Melodisc MEL 1434	She's Long, She's Tall/Lonesome Whistle	10

SOUTHERN SOUND
66	Columbia DB 7982	Just The Same As You/I Don't Wanna Go	300

SOUTHERN TONES
64	Jazz Collector JEN 10	WAITING FOR THE LORD (EP)	10

SOUTHERN COMFORT
71	Harvest HAR 5035	Willie Urricane/Berkshire Berk	10
71	Harvest HAR 5047	Morning Has Broken/Cosmic Jig	10
71	Harvest SHSP 4012	FROG CITY (LP, no EMI logo on label)	30
72	Harvest SHSP 799	SOUTHERN COMFORT (LP, gatefold, EMI logo on label)	50

SOUTHERN DEATH CULT

MINT VALUE £

| 72 Harvest SHSP 4021 | STIR DON'T SHAKE (LP, with EMI logo on label) | 25 |

(see also Matthews Southern Comfort)

SOUTHERN DEATH CULT
| 83 Situation 2 SIT 19 | Fatman/Moya (wraparound p/s) | 20 |

(see also Death Cult, Cult)

SOUTHLANDERS
55 Parlophone MSP 6182	Ain't That A Shame/Have You Ever Been Lonely	10
56 Parlophone MSP 6236	Hush-A-Bye Rock/The Wedding Of The Lucky Black Cat	10
58 Decca F 10982	Put A Light In The Window/Penny Loafers And Bobby Socks	10
58 Decca F 11032	I Wanna Jive Tonight/Torero	15
58 Decca F 11067	The Mole In A Hole/Choo-Choo-Choo-Choo Cha-Cha-Cha (tri-centre)	15
58 Decca F 11067	The Mole In A Hole/Choo-Choo-Choo-Choo Cha-Cha-Cha (tri-centre, repressing with solid centre)	7
58 Decca DFE 6508	THE SOUTHLANDERS NUMBER ONE (EP)	10

SOUTH REBELS
| 79 Red Hot! RH 1003 | THE SOUTH REBELS EP | 8 |

SOUTHSIDE JOHNNY & THE ASBURY JUKES
| 77 Epic EPC 5230 | Little Girl So Fine/I Ain't Got The Fever (withdrawn) | 20 |

SOUTHWEST F.O.B.
| 68 Stax STAX 107 | Smell Of Incense/Green Skies | 20 |

PHIL SOUTHWOOD
| 61 QRS 1-462 | D's Dilemma/Sister Sadie (in p/s) | 20 |
| 61 QRS 1-462 | D's Dilemma/Sister Sadie | 12 |

SOVEREIGNS
| 66 King KG 1050 | Bring Me Home Love/That's The Way Love Is | 15 |

RED SOVINE
| 56 Brunswick 05513 | Why Baby Why? (with Webb Pierce)/Sixteen Tons | 40 |
| 75 RCA 2738 | Teddy Bear/Daddy | 6 |

(see also Webb Pierce)

SOWELL RADICS
81 Attack TACK 24	Caution/Bali-Hi Special (12")	60
81 Attack TACK 27	Fight Fight Fight/Aces Rock (12")	40
81 Dread At The Controls DATC 006	All Nite Jammin/All Night Dubbin (12")	40
81 Big Youth Int. BYD 001	Love Is What She Wants/Love Dub (12")	35
82 SG SG 15	Wheel O' Matilda/Rub Dis Ya One Ya (12")	50

SOWERS WITH EILEEN GREAVES
| 69 Galliard GAL 4002 | SEEDS (LP) | 30 |

SO WHAT
| 70 CBS 5005 | Flowers/Tell Me Now | 20 |

BOB B. SOXX & THE BLUE JEANS
63 London HLU 9646	Zip-A-Dee-Doo-Dah/Flip And Nitty	20
63 London HLU 9694	Why Do Lovers Break Each Other's Heart?/Dr Kaplan's Office	25
63 London HLU 9754	Not Too Young To Get Married/Annette	20
69 London HLU 10243	Zip-A-Dee-Doo-Dah/Why Do Lovers Break Each Other's Heart?	7
63 London HA-U 8121	ZIP-A-DEE-DOO-DAH (LP)	100
75 Phil Spector Intl. 2307 004	BOB B. SOXX & THE BLUE JEANS (LP)	25

(see also Darlene Love, Bobby Sheen, Blossoms, Crystals, Phil Spector)

CATHERINE SPAAK
| 65 Fontana TL 5282 | NOI SIAMO I GIOVANI (LP) | 15 |

SPACE CADETS
| 96 Vinyl Japan JRLP 20 | ASTROBILLY ROCKIN (LP) | 20 |
| 00 Vinyl Japan JRLP 35 | CADETS A GO GO (LP) | 20 |

SPACE (1)
18 Electronic Sound ES 745	Magic Fly (Vince Clarke Rework)/REED & CAROLINE: Before (p/s)	8
77 Pye NSLP 28232	MAGIC FLY (LP)	15
78 Pye NSPH 28505	DELIVERANCE (LP)	20
79 Pye NSPH 28725	JUST BLUE (LP)	15
79 Pye NSPH 28725	JUST BLUE (LP, picture disc)	20

(see also Madeline Bell)

SPACE (2)
| 90 Space LP 1 | SPACE (LP) | 60 |
| 90 Space CD 1 | SPACE (CD, beware of counterfeits) | 40 |

(see also J.A.M.S., KLF, Timelords, Disco 2000, Angels One 5)

SPACE (3)
| 96 Gut GUT LP 1 | SPIDERS (LP) | 30 |

SPACE (4)
| 93 Hug HUG 1T | If It's Real/Lookin'/I'm Free (12", p/s with free 'fortune fish') | 12 |

SPACE ART
| 77 Arista AHAL 8001 | SPACE ART (LP) | 20 |

SPACED
| 92 Incite INC 1/123 | Deeper (Original Mix)/Deeper (Remix) (12", stickered white label) | 35 |
| 92 No Label PNI 001 | Deeper (Mix 1)/(Mix 2)/Mix 3) (12", white label) | 50 |

SPACEMEN
| 59 Top Rank JAR 228 | The Clouds/The Lonely Jet Pilot | 12 |

SPACEMEN 3
86 Glass GLAEP 105	Walkin' With Jesus (Sound Of Confusion)/Rollercoaster/Feel So Good (12" maxi-single, p/s, with numbered insert)	50
86 Glass GLAEP 105	Walkin' With Jesus (Sound Of Confusion)/Rollercoaster/Feel So Good (12" maxi-single, p/s, without numbered insert)	45
87 Glass GLAEP 108	Transparent Radiation/Ecstasy Symphony/Transparent Radiation (Flashback)/Things'll Never Be The Same/Starship (12" maxi-single, p/s)	40

SPACEPIMP

			MINT VALUE £
88	Glass GLASS 12054	Take Me To The Other Side/Soul 1/That's Just Fine (12", p/s, yellow label)	30
88	Fire BLAZE 29S	Revolution/Che (die-cut company sleeve)	6
88	Fire BLAZE 29T	Revolution/Che/May The Circle Be Unbroken (12")	12
89	Fire THREEBIE 3	THREEBIE 3: Starship/Revolution/Suicide/Repeater/Love Intro Theme (Xtacy) (12", mail-order only, numbered p/s)	20
89	Sniffin' Rock SR 008	When Tomorrow Hits (with Sniffin' Rock magazine)	15
89	Sniffin' Rock SR 008	When Tomorrow Hits (without Sniffin' Rock magazine)	10
89	Fire BLAZE 36S	Hypnotized/Just To See You Smile (Honey Pt 2) (die-cut company sleeve)	6
89	Fire BLAZE 36T	Hypnotized/Just To See You Smile (Honey Pt 2)/The World Is Dying (12", with poster)	18
89	Fire BLAZE 41T	Big City/Drive (12", p/s)	10
90	Fierce FRIGHT 042	Dreamweapon/Ecstasy In Slow Motion (12")	25
91	Fire BLAZE 41TR	Big City (Remix)/I Love You (Remix) (12", unissued, white label promo, 50 only)	60
91	Catalogue CAT 089	I Love You//Sometimes (2 x flexis, with The Catalogue magazine)	10
03	Earworm Gold EGS 01	Walking With Jesus/Take Me To The Other Side (Demo)/Walking With Jesus (Demo) (die-cut p/s, 'splatter' vinyl)	8
09	Great Pop Supplement GPS 50	Big City (demo)/WOODEN SHJIPS: I Believe It (red marbled vinyl, insert & sticker)	8
13	Great Pop Supplement GPS 100	SPECTRUM: Bo's Web/SPACEMEN 3: Why Couldn't I See/MGMT: Something To Do WIth Prince (withdrawn)	15
86	Glass GLALP 018	SOUND OF CONFUSION (LP)	50
87	Glass GLALP 026	THE PERFECT PRESCRIPTION (LP, gold/silver or bronze/silver sleeve)	50
88	Glass GLALP 030	PERFORMANCE (LP)	25
89	Fire FIRELP 16	PLAYING WITH FIRE (LP, embossed sleeve)	40
89	Fire REFIRE 5	SOUND OF CONFUSION (LP, reissue)	20
89	Fire REFIRE 6	THE PERFECT PRESCRIPTION (LP, reissue)	20
91	Fire FIRE LP 23	RECURRING (LP)	40
90	Fire REFIRE 11	PERFORMANCE (LP, reissue)	18
95	Space Age ORBIT 001	DREAMWEAPON (2-LP)	30
95	Space Age ORBIT 002LP	LIVE IN EUROPE 1989 (2-LP)	25
95	Fire FLIP DLP 003	TRANSLUSCENT FLASHBACKS (LP as 2 x 12")	30
99	Space Age ORBIT 011LP	PLAYING WITH FIRE (2-LP, reissue)	30
14	Fire FIRE 158	TRANSLUSCENT FLASHBACKS (3x12" box set)	40

(see also Sonic Boom, Spiritualized, Spectrum)

SPACEPIMP

95	Clear CLR 415	The Pimp/Spacechase/K9 Law (12", p/s, on clear vinyl)	25
95	Clear CLR 415	The Pimp/Spacechase/K9 Law (12", p/s)	20

SPACE TURKEYS

81	Tavern Sound	Fun With A Social Worker/Disco Not Disco (p/s)	15

SPAGHETTI HEAD

75	RCA RCA 2513	Big Noise From Winnetka/Funky Axe	30

(see also Clem Cattini Ork, Tornados)

SPAGHETTI JUNCTION

72	Columbia DB 8935	Work's Nice - If You Can Get It/Step Right Up	25

(see also Hank Marvin)

SPANIELS

71	Joy JOYS 197	THE SPANIELS (LP)	20

MUGGSY SPANIER & DIXIELAND/RAGTIME BAND

56	Tempo A 36	Tin Roof Blues/Muskrat Rumble	7

SPANISH BOYS

65	Blue Beat BB 331	I Am Alone/BUSTER'S ALL STARS: Vera Cruz	250

SPANISHTONIANS

67	Pyramid PYR 6009	Suffer Me Not/ROLAND ALPHONSO: Guantanamera Ska	30
67	Pyramid PYR 6018	Rudie Gets Plenty/ROLAND ALPHONSO: Sock It To Me	100

SPANISH TOWN SKABEATS

65	Blue Beat BB 315	Oh My Baby (actually by Charmers)/Stop That Train	600
65	Blue Beat BB 320	King Solomon/BUSTER'S ALLSTARS: Devil's Daffodil	60

SPANK CHANK BAND

17	Backatcha BK002	Outlaw/Buffalo Funk (reissue)	8

SPANKY & OUR GANG

67	Mercury MF 982	Sunday Will Never Be The Same/Distance	20
67	Mercury MF 999	Making Every Minute Count/If You Could Only Be Me	8
67	Mercury MF 1010	Lazy Day/It Ain't Necessarily Byrd Avenue	10
68	Mercury MF 1018	Sunday Mornin'/Echoes	8
68	Mercury MF 1023	Like To Get To Know You/Three Ways From Tomorrow	12
68	Mercury MF 1052	Give A Damn/The Swingin' Gate	10
69	Mercury MF 1123	And She's Mine/Leopard Skin Phone	7
76	Epic S EPC 3850	I Won't Brand You/When I Wanna	7
67	Mercury 20114 (S)MCL	SPANKY AND OUR GANG (LP)	30
68	Mercury 20121 SCML	LIKE TO GET TO KNOW YOU (LP)	30
69	Mercury 20150 SCML	ANYTHING YOU CHOOSE/WITHOUT RHYME OR REASON (LP)	30

(see also Mama & Papas)

OTIS SPANN

64	Decca F 11972	Stirs Me Up/Keep Your Hand Out Of My Pocket	25
68	Blue Horizon 57-3142	Bloody Murder/Can't Do Me No Good	15
69	Blue Horizon 57-3155	Walkin'/Temperature Is Rising (with Fleetwood Mac)	25
64	Decca LK 4615	THE BLUES OF OTIS SPANN (LP)	80
64	Storyville SLP 157	GOOD MORNING MR. BLUES (LP)	50
64	Storyville SLP 168	PIANO BLUES (LP, with Memphis Slim)	40
65	Decca LK 4661	BLUES NOW (LP)	65
66	Stateside SL 10169	THE BLUES NEVER DIE (LP)	35
67	HMV CLP/CSD 3609	BLUES ARE WHERE IT'S AT (LP)	35

SPANNER THRU MA BEATBOX

MINT VALUE £

67	Storyville 670 157	PORTRAITS IN BLUES VOL. 3 (LP, reissue of SLP 157)	15
67	Polydor 545 030	NOBODY KNOWS MY TROUBLES (LP)	35
67	Bounty BY 6037	NOBODY KNOWS MY TROUBLES (LP)	40
68	Stateside (S)SL 10255	BOTTOM OF THE BLUES (LP)	40
69	Chess CRLS 4556	FATHERS AND SONS (LP)	50
69	Blue Horizon S 7-63217	BIGGEST THING SINCE COLOSSUS (LP, with Fleetwood Mac)	100
69	Deram DML/SML 1036	CRACKED SPANNER HEAD (LP)	45
69	Python KM 4	RAISED IN MISSISSIPPI (LP, 99 copies only, with Robert Jnr. Lockwood)	90
70	Vanguard VSD 6514	CRYIN' TIME (LP)	20

(see also Fleetwood Mac, Memphis Slim, Johnny Shines, Lonnie Johnson)

SPANNER THRU MA BEATBOX

87	Earthly Delights EARTH 3	SPANNER THRU MA BEATBOX (LP)	15

SPARE PARTS

79	Random SP 100	She's A New Kind Of Girl/Paint It Black (p/s)	40

SPARKERS

69	Blue Cat BS 155	Dig It Up/DELROY WILSON: This Life Makes Me Wonder	200

(see also Samuel Edwards)

LOU SPARKES

69	Gayfeet GS 203	By The Time I Get To Phoenix/Lover Boy	30
70	Gayfeet GS 208	We Will Make Love/ROLAND ALPHONSO: Sticker	8

KRISTINE SPARKLE

74	Decca F 13485	Hokey Cokey/Baby I Love You	8
74	Decca 13515	Eight Days A Week/The Drum	8
74	Decca SKL 5192	IMAGE (LP)	15

SPARKLEHORSE

06	Parlophone R6714	Don't Take My Sunshine Away/Galvaston (p/s)	10
96	Parlophone 7243 8328 16 19	VIVADIXIESUBMARINETRANSMISSIONPILOT (LP)	100
98	Parlophone 49 6014 1	GOOD MORNING SPIDER (LP)	150

SPARKLES

74	Proteen PRO 1	THE SPARKLES EP (no ps)	25

SPARKS

72	Bearsville K 15505	Wonder Girl/(No More) Mr. Nice Guy	15
74	Bearsville K 15516	Girl From Germany/Beaver O'Lindy (brown or white label)	10
74	Island WIP 6211	Never Turn Your Back On Mother Earth/Alabamy Right (p/s)	6
75	Island WIP 6221	Something For The Girl With Everything/Marry Me (title sleeve)	6
75	Island WIP 6236	Get In The Swing/Profile (title sleeve)	6
75	Island WIP 6239	Looks, Looks, Looks/Pineapple (title sleeve)	6
75	Island WIP 6249	Looks, Looks, Looks/Pineapple (DJ copy in promo p/s)	12
76	Island WIP 6282	I Want To Hold Your Hand/England (withdrawn after 1 day)	25
77	Island WIP 6282	I Want To Hold Your Hand/Under The Table With Her (promo only)	20
77	Island WIP 6193	This Town Ain't Big Enough For The Both Of Us/Barbecutie (reissue, orange sunset label)	10
79	Island WIP 6532	This Town Ain't Big Enough For The Both Of Us/Looks, Looks, Looks	7
93	Finiflex FF 1004	National Crime Awareness Week (13 Minutes In Heaven)/National Crime Awareness Week (Perkins Playtime) (12", p/s)	20
94	Logic 7432 134461	When Do I Get To Sing My Way/(mixes) (12", doublepack, p/s)	12
73	Bearsville K 45210	A WOOFER IN TWEETERS CLOTHING (LP)	30
74	Island ILPS 9272	KIMONO MY HOUSE (LP, pink rim label, sleeve laminated both sides, A-2U/B-1U matrixes, inner)	50
74	Island ILPS 9312	PROPAGANDA (LP, inner, sticker on top right hand corner)	30
74	Bezarsville K45511	SPARKS (LP, reissue of original Halfnelson LP)	20
75	Island ILPS 9345	INDISCREET (LP, gatefold)	30
76	Island ILPS 9445	BIG BEAT (LP, with inner)	25
77	CBS 82284	INTRODUCING SPARKS (LP)	30
79	Virgin V 2115	NO. 1 IN HEAVEN (LP, with lyric inner sleeve)	40
79	Virgin V 2115	NO. 1 IN HEAVEN (LP, yellow vinyl with lyric inner sleeve)	45
80	Virgin V2137	TERMINAL JIVE (LP, inner sleeve)	30
81	Why Fi WHO 1	WHOMP THAT SUCKER (LP, inner sleeve)	30
86	Consolidated TOON LP 2	MUSIC THAT YOU CAN DANCE TO (LP)	20
04	Universal LBRV001	LIL' BEETHOVEN (LP)	150
06	Gut GUTLP 53	HELLO YOUNG LOVERS (LP, please note that pink vinyl edition is U.S. pressing)	80
09	Lil Beethoven LBRV4	THE SEDUCTION OF INGMAR BERGMAN (2-LP)	80
17	BMG 538279760	HIPPOPOTAMAS (2-LP, gatefold)	20

(see also Adrian Musey, Trevor White)

L. SPARKS

72	Big Shot BI 601	You Don't Care/TONY'S ALL STARS: Must Care (Version)	12
72	Pama PM 833	You Don't Care/TONY'S ALL STARS: Must Care (Version)	10

(see also Lloyd Parks, Termites)

SPARKY

72	UK UK 13	(Do You Remember) That Summertime Woman/You Gotta Have It Sometime	8

SPARKY AND THE INNER CITIZENS

76	Contempo CS2102	Golden Gate Get Down (Short version)Golden Gate Get Down (Long Version)	10

CANDY SPARLING

62	Piccadilly 7N 35046	When's He Gonna Kiss Me?/Lonely For You	15
63	Piccadilly 7N 35096	Can You Keep A Secret/Charm Bracelet	20

SPARROW (TRINIDAD)

60	Kalypso XX 10	Carnival Boycott/Gloria (with Lord Melody)	6
60s	Melodisc CAL 15	Leading Calypsonians/Love Is Everywhere	6

(see also Mighty Sparrow, King Sparrow)

SPARROW (U.S.)

66	CBS 202342	Tomorrow's Ship/Isn't It Strange	75

Jack SPARROW

(see also Steppenwolf)

JACK SPARROW
66	Doctor Bird DB 1005	Ice Water/ROLAND ALPHONSO: Ska-Culation	150
66	Doctor Bird DB 1027	More Ice Water/ROLAND ALPHONSO: Miss Ska-Culation	200

(see also Ethiopians)

SPARTA
80	Suspect SUS 1	Fast Lane/Fighting To Be Free (in p/s)	50
80	Suspect SUS 1	Fast Lane/Fighting To Be Free	18
81	Suspect SUS 2	Angel Of Death/Tonight (wraparound p/s)	25

(see also Ethiopians)

SPARTACUS R
79	Zara ZMRD 1	Mother Sucker/Stop Your Crying (12")	75
79	ZaraZMR 1001	My Love Is Gonna Getcha/(Try To Be More Like Our) Children	10
76	Zara ZMRL 101	WATCHING YOU GROW (LP, as Spartacus)	15
83	Zara ZMRLP 3	THIRD WORLD WAR (LP)	15
84	Zara ZMRLP 4	FREEDOM FIRST (LP)	15

(see also Osibisa)

SPARTANS
62	Stateside SS 117	Can You Waddle? (Parts 1 & 2)	12

SPARTAN WARRIOR
83	Guardian GRC 2164	STEEL 'N' CHAINS (LP)	20

SPASMS
80	Ellie Jay SAP 001	It Never Happens Like It Does On The Telly/Monday Morning (die cut p/s)	40

SPATTS
15	B-Line Recordings BLN015	Waiting For The Bomb/Chaos By Numbers (7" test pressing, never issued)	35

SPAZZTIC BLUR
87	Earache MOSH 5	BEFO DA AWBUM (LP)	15

ROGER RUSKIN SPEAR
72	United Artists UAG 29281	ELECTRIC SHOCKS (LP)	25

(see also Bonzo Dog [Doo Dah] Band)

SPECIAL DUTIES
81	Charnel H. SARCOPHAGI 2	Violent Society/Colchester Council (wraparound p/s)	30
82	Rondelet ROUND 15	VIOLENT SOCIETY (EP)	15
82	Rondelet ROUND 20	POLICE STATE (EP)	10
82	Rondelet ROUND 24	Bullshit Crass/You're Doing Yourself No Good (p/s)	12
83	Expulsion OUT 1	Punk Rocker/Too Much Talking (p/s)	12
82	Rondelet ABOUT 9	77 IN 82 (LP)	25
97	Captain Oi! AHOY LP 75	77 IN 82 (LP, blue vinyl reissue)	15

SPECIAL CLINIC
78	Penicillin POX 1	When The Going Gets Rough/Sumo Stomp (no p/s)	8

SPECIALS (THE SPECIAL A.K.A.)
79	2-Tone TT 1/TT 2	Gangsters (as The Special A.K.A.)/THE SELECTER: The Selecter (paper label, in stamped plain white sleeve; matrix numbers TT1-3 & TT2-1)	45
79	2-Tone TT 1/TT 2	Gangsters (as The Special A.K.A.)/THE SELECTER: The Selecter (paper label)	15
79	2-Tone TT 1/TT 2	Gangsters (as The Special A.K.A.)/THE SELECTER: The Selecter (paper label, die-cut 2-Tone sleeve, 2nd issue with Chrysalis CHS TT 1/2 matrix no.)	6
79	2-Tone CHS TT 5	Message To You Rudy/Nite Klub (paper label, company sleeve, as The Specials featuring Rico)	8
80	2-Tone CHS TT 7	THE SPECIAL A.K.A. LIVE (EP, paper label)	10
80	2-Tone CHS TT 11	Rat Race/Rude Boys Outa Jail (company sleeve, paper label, as The Specials)	8
80	2-Tone CHS TT 13	Stereotype/International Jet Set (company sleeve, paper label, as The Specials)	8
80	2-Tone CHS TT 16	Do Nothing/Maggie's Farm (laminated p/s, paper label, as The Specials)	8
81	2-Tone CHS TT 17	Ghost Town/Why/Friday Night Saturday Morning (paper labels p/s)	8
81	2-Tone CHS TT 1217	Ghost Town (6.02 Extended Version)/Why/Friday Night, Saturday Morning (12", p/s)	15
81	2-Tone CHS TT 17	Ghost Town/Why?/Friday Night Saturday Morning (later pressing with plastic moulded labels, p/s)	6
84	2-Tone CHS TT 27	What I Like Most About You Is Your Girlfriend/Can't Get A Break/War Crimes (The Crime Is Still The Same)/(Version) (double pack, as The Special A.K.A.)	8
84	2-Tone CHS TT 1227	What I Like Most About You Is Your Girlfriend/Can't Get A Break (12", poster p/s with free single)	10
89	2-Tone TTP1	THE SPECIALS: Rudi, A Message To You/Ghost Town//SELECTER: On My Radio/MADNESS: One Step Beyond (promo, 40 only)	200
91	2-Tone CHSTT 30	Ghost Town/Ghost Dub '91 (p/s)	20
91	2-Tone CHSTT 12 30	Ghost Town/Ghost Dub '91 (12", p/s)	30
14	2-Tone CHSTT27	Sock It To 'Em (Dub)/Rat Race (Dub) (2-Tone replica sleeve)	6
86	Strange Fruit SFPS 018	THE PEEL SESSIONS (EP)	10
79	2-Tone CDLTT 5001	SPECIALS (LP)	25
80	2-Tone CDLTT 5003	MORE SPECIALS (LP, with poster & bonus 7": Roddy Radiation & The Specials' "Braggin' And Tryin' Not To Lie"/Judge Roughneck's "Rude Buoys Outa Jail" [TT 999])	30
80	2-Tone CDL TT5003	MORE SPECIALS (LP)	15
81	2-Tone CDLTT5001-P	SPECIALS (LP, picture disc)	15
84	2 Tone CHRTT 5008	IN THE STUDIO (LP)	15
91	2 Tone CHRTT 5010	SINGLES (LP)	15
92	2 Tone CHR TT 5011	THE SPECIALS - LIVE AT THE MOONLIGHT CLUB (LP)	15
92	Receiver RRLP 161	LIVE - TOO MUCH TOO YOUNG (LP)	15
99	Chrysalis/Two-Tone 499 4701	SPECIALS (LP, reissue, barcode on sleeve)	30

(see also Selecter, Rhoda, Rico, Desmond Dekkar, Vegas)

SPECIAL TOUCH
89	TSR TSCRT 1	That Special Touch/Instrumental Version (12")	20
90	TSR TSCRT 3	You're So Good/Instrumental Version (12")	20
90	TSR TSCRT 3/4	You're So Good/GOLD IN THE SHADE: Shining Through (12")	50

SPECIFIK & PROJECT CEE

MINT VALUE £

91	TSR TSRCT 6	Our Love Goes/FORVER MORE: Ain't Easy/CRUIZE: Get Your Loving (12")	40
92	TSR TSCRT 7	I Want You/Dance Mix/FORVER MORE: Ain't Easy/LOLETA: Do You Really Love Me (12")	40
91	TSR TSCRLP 1	GARDEN OF LIFE (LP)	250

(see also Gold In The Shade)

SPECIFIK & PROJECT CEE
02	Core Level CLM 001	Where Your Mind Is	25
02	Sudden Debt SDR 004	RESURRECTING VIBES (EP)	12

SPECIFIK
16	B-Line Recordings BLN 021	EIGHTY3 (LP, splatter vinyl)	20

SPECIMEN
83	London LON 24	Returning From A Journey/Kiss Kiss Bang Bang (bat-shaped disc)	10

SPECKLED RED
60s	Storyville SEP 384	STORYVILLE BLUES ANTHOLOGY VOL. 4 (EP)	15
63	Esquire 32-190	THE DIRTY DOZENS (LP)	30
71	VJM LC 11	OH RED (LP)	20

PHIL SPECTOR
63	London HA-U 8141	A CHRISTMAS GIFT FOR YOU (LP, various artists, Spector as producer; plum label)	80
63	London HA-U 8141	A CHRISTMAS GIFT FOR YOU (LP, various artists, Spector as producer; later black label)	50
72	Apple APCOR 24	PHIL SPECTOR'S CHRISTMAS ALBUM (LP, reissue of London HA-U 8141)	25
74	Warner Bros K 59210	PHIL SPECTOR'S CHRISTMAS ALBUM (LP, 2nd reissue, with poster)	18
76	Phil Spector Intl. 2307 008	RARE MASTERS VOL. 1 (LP, various artists, Spector as producer)	20
76	Phil Spector Intl. 2307 009	RARE MASTERS VOL. 2 (LP, various artists, Spector as producer)	20
80	Phil Spector Intl. 2307 015	PHIL SPECTOR '74/'79 (LP, various artists, Spector as producer)	25
81	Phil Spector Intl. WOS 001	WALL OF SOUND (9-LP box set, various artists, Spector as producer)	60

(see also Ronettes, Crystals, Darlene Love, Bob B. Soxx & Blue Jeans, Teddy Bears)

RONNIE SPECTOR
71	Apple APPLE 33	Try Some, Buy Some/Tandoori Chicken (with p/s)	30
71	Apple APPLE 33	Try Some, Buy Some/Tandoori Chicken	10
77	Epic EPC 5185	Say Goodbye To Hollywood/Baby Please Don't Go (with E Street Band, p/s)	12
81	Red Shadow LP 002	SIREN (LP)	20

(see also Ronettes)

SPECTRES (IRELAND)
65	Lloyd Sound UED QU 1	The Facts Of Life/Whirlpool	300

SPECTRES (1)
66	Piccadilly 7N 35339	I (Who Have Nothing)/Neighbour, Neighbour (A label demo)	300
66	Piccadilly 7N 35339	I (Who Have Nothing)/Neighbour, Neighbour	350
66	Piccadilly 7N 35352	Hurdy Gurdy Man/LAticia (A label demo)	350
66	Piccadilly 7N 35352	Hurdy Gurdy Man/Laticia	400
67	Piccadilly 7N 35368	We Ain't Got Nothin' Yet/I Want It (A label demo)	400
67	Piccadilly 7N 35368	We Ain't Got Nothin' Yet/I Want It (beware bootlegs)	400

(see also Traffic Jam, Status Quo)

SPECTRES (2)
80	Direct Hit DH 1	This Strange Effect/Getting Away With Murder (p/s)	7

(see also Rich Kids)

SPECTRES (3)
13	Howling Owl HOWL 019	HUNGER EP (12", hand-made and numbered sleeve, 100 only)	40
13	Howling Owl HOWL 019	HUNGER EP (12" 2nd pressing with printed sleeve, 100 copies)	15
13	Howling Owl HOWL 024	Lump/THE NATURALS: Heat Death (10", lyric sheet, 100 only)	20
15	Howling Owl HOWL 043	Wonderful Christmas Time (lathe cut, 30 only)	30
15	Sonic Cathedral SCR 086	Stealed Scene/LORELLE MEETS THE OBSOLETE: The Sky Of All Places (365 copies)	15
15	Sonic Cathedral SCR 090LP	DYING (LP, grey vinyl)	25

SPECTRUM (1)
65	Columbia DB 7742	Little Girl/Asking You	10
67	RCA RCA 1589	Samantha's Mine/Saturday's Child	10
67	RCA RCA 1619	Portobello Road/Comes The Dawn	10
67	RCA RCA 1651	Headin' For A Heatwave/I Wanna Be Happy With You	10
68	RCA RCA 1700	London Bridge Is Coming Down/Tables And Chairs	10
68	RCA RCA 1753	Little Red Boat By The River/Forget Me Not	10
68	RCA RCA 1775	Ob-La-Di, Ob-La-Da/Music Soothes The Savage Beast	10
69	RCA RCA 1853	Free/The Tale Of Wally Toft	10
69	RCA RCA 1883	Glory/Nodnol	10
70	RCA RCA 1976	Portobello Road/Comes The Dawn (reissue)	10
69	RCA Intl. INTS 118	THE LIGHT IS DARK ENOUGH (LP)	30
00	Subway TRUMP 1	THE LIGHT IS DARK ENOUGH (LP, reissue)	20

SPECTRUM (2)
71	Parlophone R5908	I'll Be Gone/Launching Place	15

SPECTRUM (3)
79	Ellie Jay EJSP 9287	Walk On City/Strangers From Me/Blonde On Blue/Ruvid	40

SPECTRUM (4)
87	Phoenix Modernist THE 1	All Or Nothing (Contemporary Version)/All Or Nothing (Traditional Version) (12", p/s with 2 inserts & free 7", distributed by Nine Mile & Cartel)	10

(see also Steve Marriott, Chris Farlowe, P.P. Arnold, Creation)

SPECTRUM (5)
91	Silvertone SONIC 2	(I Love You)To The Moon And Back/Capo Waltz (Live) (die-cut p/s gig freebie)	8
91	Silvertone SONIC 2	(I Love You)To The Moon And Back/Capo Waltz (Live) (p/s, with Outer Limits fanzine)	25
92	Silvertone ORE 41	How Do You Satisfy Me/Don't Go (clear vinyl)	8
92	Silvertone ORE 41	How You Satisfy Me/Don't Go (Instrumental 2) (clear vinyl, printed plastic sleeve)	15
92	Silvertone ORE 44	True Love Will Find You In The End (Radio Mix)/My Life Spins Round Your Every Smile (Remix) (yellow vinyl, printed plastic sleeve)	8
93	Silvertone ORE 56	Indian Summer/Baby Don't You Worry (California Lullaby) (numbered p/s)	6

Chris SPEDDING

MINT VALUE £

93	Silvertone ORET 56	Indian Summer/Baby Don't You Worry (California Lullaby)/It's Alright/True Love Will Find You In The End (12", p/s)	10
94	Silvertone ORE P56	Soul Kiss Glide Divine/STEREOLAB: Tone Burst (demo)/Tempter (demo) (unrel., with colour photocopied wraparound p/s, 25 test pressings only)	150
94	Silvertone ORET 65	Undo The Taboo/In The Fullness Of Time/Turn The Tide (Sub Aqua)/Go To Sleep (12", p/s)	15
10	Great Pop Supplement GPS 54	Words May Shatter (with Tim "Love" Lee)/The Lonesome Death Of Johnny Ace (with Captain Memphis) (picture disc, printed plastic insert, PVC sleeve)	10
13	Great Pop Supplement GSP100	Bo's Web/SPACEMEN 3: Why Couldn't I See/MGMT: Something To Do WIth Prince (withdrawn)	20
92	Silvertone ORELP 518	SOUL KISS (GLIDE DIVINE) (LP, inner)	50
92	Silvertone OREZLP 518	SOUL KISS (GLIDE DIVINE) (LP, clear vinyl, printed double walled PVC sleeve containing liquid)	45
94	Silvertone ORELP 532	HIGHS, LOWS AND HEAVENLY BLOWS (LP)	80
97	Space Age ORBIT 008LP	FOREVER ALIEN (2-LP)	35
97	Space Age ORBIT 008LP	FOREVER ALIEN (2-LP, yellow vinyl)	40

(see also Spacemen 3, Sonic Boom)

CHRIS SPEDDING

70	Harvest HAR 5013	Rock'n'Roll Band/BATTERED ORNAMENTS: Goodbye We Loved You (Madly)	25
75	Island WIP 6225	My Bucket's Got A Hole In It/I Can't Boogie	8
76	RAK RAK 246	Pogo Dancing/Pose (p/s)	6
70	Harvest SHSP 4004	BACKWOOD PROGRESSION (LP, flipback sleeve no EMI logo on label)	60
72	Harvest SHSP 4017	THE ONLY LICK I KNOW (LP, laminated sleeve, with EMI logo on label)	40

(see also Sharks, Nucleus, Sounds Nice, Panhandle, Solid Gold Cadillac, Matthew Ellis, Vibrators, Battered Ornaments, IOFR)

SPEED (JAMAICA)

71	Bullet BU 477	There's A Train/Blue Moon	12

SPEED (1)

78	It IT 1	Big City/All Day And All The Night (in p/s)	40
78	It IT 1	Big City/All Day And All The Night	15

(see also Cobra, Tearjerkers)

SPEED (2)

80	Speed GJS 001	Man In The Street/Down The Road (p/s)	125

(see also Bruce Dickinson, Iron Maiden)

SPEEDBALL(S)

80	No Pap/Dirty Dick DD 1/2	No Survivors/Is Somebody There? (miscredited as 'Speedballs' on label, in withdrawn printed die-cut sleeve)	60
80	No Pap/Dirty Dick DD 1/2	No Survivors/Is Somebody There? (miscredited as 'Speedballs' on label)	25

SPELLBINDERS

66	CBS 202453	Help Me (Get Myself Back Together)/Danny Boy	40
66	CBS 202453	Help Me (Get Myself Back Together)/Danny Boy (DJ copy)	85
67	CBS 202622	Chain Reaction/For You	40
67	CBS 202622	Chain Reaction/For You (DJ copy)	75
67	CBS 2776	Since I Don't Have You/I Believe	8
69	Direction 58-3970	Help Me/Chain Reaction	15

SPELLING MISSTEAKS

79	Stortbeat BEAT 7	POPSTAR (EP)	50

BENNY SPELLMAN

62	London HLP 9570	Lipstick Traces/Fortune Teller	50
62	London HLP 9570	Lipstick Traces/Fortune Teller (DJ Copy)	100

BRUCE SPELMAN

69	Beacon BEA 112	Lady/Long Time Gone	8
72	Montagu MONT 3000	29 Years To Doomsday/Cutting The Traces	12
70	Beacon BES 3	YOU DON'T KNOW WHAT YOU'RE PADDLING IN (LP)	70
70	Montague MONS 1	YOU DON'T KNOW WHAT YOU'RE PADDLING IN (LP, different sleeve, blue/black label)	40

BARRINGTON SPENCE

76	Student STU 1005	Mash It Up/Straight To Radd Head	10
86	Camara CAM 002T	Hey Youthman/Version//K LEACOCK: Round And Round/Version (12")	30
88	Camara CAM 004T	Sons Of Far I/Far I Dub (12")	35
76	Trojan TRLS 117	SPEAK SOFTLY (LP)	20
76	Klik KLP 9014	TEARS ON MY PILLOW (LP)	25

JOHNNIE SPENCE

61	Parlophone R 4736	Wheels/First Romance	6
62	Parlophone R 4872	The Dr. Kildare Theme/The Midnight Theme	6

BRINDLEY D SPENCER

68	Domain D8	The Company I Keep/On A Day Like Today	10

DON SPENCER

62	HMV POP 1087	Fireball/I'm All Alone Again (blue or black labels)	10
63	HMV POP 1186	Busy Doing Nothing/The Joker	7
63	HMV POP 1205	Worried Mind/Give Give Give A Little	6
64	HMV POP 1306	Pride Is Such A Little Word/For Love (with Le Roys)	6
67	Talus TP1010	Uproar In The House/On The G.P.O Tower	20

(see also Le Roys)

DON SPENCER/XL5

63	HMV 7EG 8802	FIREBALL AND OTHER TITLES (EP, 2 tracks each)	50

EDDIE SPENCER

76	Power Exchange PX 207	If This Is Love (I'd Rather Be Lonely)/Power Of Love	25

JEREMY SPENCER (BAND)

70	Reprise RS 27002	Linda/Teenage Darling	10
70	Reprise RSLP 9002	JEREMY SPENCER (LP, label states K 44105 cat. no)	40
71	Reprise K 44105	JEREMY SPENCER (LP, reissue)	20

(see also Fleetwood Mac)

Jon SPENCER BLUES EXPLOSION

MINT VALUE £

JON SPENCER BLUES EXPLOSION
92	Clawfist 13	History Of Sex/Write A Song/Smoke Cigarettes (foldover p/s in poly bag)	8
94	Matador OLE 077	Afro/Relax Her (p/s)	6
91	Hut HUTLP 3	THE JON SPENCER BLUES EXPLOSION (LP)	18
96	Mute STUMM 132	NOW I GOT WORRY (LP)	20
98	Mute STUMM 156	ACME (LP, inner)	20

(see also Pussy Galore)

SONNY SPENCER
59	Parlophone R 4611	Oh Boy/Gilee	20

SPENCER & THE SAINTS
68	Tabernacle TS 1005	Something Within/When You Get To Heaven	8

VIC SPENCER
17	Daupe! DM SP 022	THE GHOST OF LIVING (LP, 180 copies)	70
17	Daupe! DM SP 022	THE GHOST OF LIVING (LP, purple vinyl, 100 copies)	100
17	Daupe! DM SP 022	THE GHOST OF LIVING (LP, orange vinyl, 100 copies)	100
17	Daupe! DM SP 022	THE GHOST OF LIVING (LP, with obi strip, 20 copies)	100
17	Daupe! DM SP 030	WHO THE F*** IS VIC SPENCER (LP, with Chris Crack, pink vinyl, 130 copies)	40
17	Daupe! DM SP 030	WHO THE F*** IS VIC SPENCER (LP, with Chris Crack, with OBI strip, 20 copies)	150
17	Daupe! DM SP 025	WHO THE F*** IS VIC SPENCER (LP, with Chris Crack, 230 copies)	40
18	Daupe! DM SP 030	SPENCER FOR HIGHER (LP, with SonnyJim, green vinyl, 125 copies)	50
18	Daupe! DM SP 030	SPENCER FOR HIGHER (LP, with SonnyJim, black vinyl, 125 copies)	50
18	Daupe! DM SP 030	SPENCER FOR HIGHER (LP, with SonnyJim, white vinyl, 125 copies)	40
18	Daupe! DM SP 030	SPENCER FOR HIGHER (LP, with SonnyJim, red vinyl, 125 copies)	40
18	Daupe! DM SP 030	SPENCER FOR HIGHER (LP, with SonnyJim, black vinyl, with OBI strip, 20 copies)	150
18	Daupe! DM SP 038	DUFFLE OF GEMS (2-LP)	40
18	Daupe! DM SP 038	DUFFLE OF GEMS (2-LP, picture disc)	40
18	Daupe! DM SP 038	DUFFLE OF GEMS (2-LP, purple vinyl)	30
18	Daupe! DM SP 038	DUFFLE OF GEMS (2-LP, with obi strip, 20 copies)	100

SPENCERS WASHBOARD KINGS
66	Pye 7N 17245	The Egg Plant That Ate Chicago/Somebody Stole My Gal	7
69	Parlophone R 5782	Pimlico/Ordinary People	15

SPERMICIDE
79	No Wonder NOW 3	Femme Prothèse/Belgique (p/s with lyrics)	30

SPG (SPECIAL PATROL GROUP)
80	Suspect ELO 1	Dracula/Christopher Columbus (p/s)	10

SPHERE
81	Cadillac SGE 1010	SPHERE (LP)	25

SPHERES
78	Sphere	FESTIVAL AND SUNS (LP, with insert)	25

(see also Jimmy Winston)

SPHERICAL OBJECTS
78	Object Music OM 01	The Kill/The Knot (p/s)	10
78	Object Music OM 04	Seventies Romance/Sweet Tooth (p/s)	10
78	Object Music PBJ 001	PAST & PARCEL (LP)	20
79	Object Music OBJ 004	ELLIPTICAL OPTIMISM (LP)	20

(see also Alternomen Unlimited, Noyes Brothers)

SPHYNKTA
83	Sultanic SUL 666	In The Shade Of The Gods/Jesus Bless My Upside-Down Cross (p/s, red vinyl, with 'devil' tattoo)	60
83	Sultanic SUL 999	Death And Violence/Ritual Slaughter (Of Your Daughter) (p/s, red vinyl)	40
84	Sultanic SUL 000	Spike Up My Sphynkta/No Pain No Gain (unissued)	100

SPHYNX
78	Charisma CDS 4011	XITINTODAY (LP, with booklet)	30
78	Charisma CDS 4011	XITINTODAY (LP, without booklet)	20

(see also Inner City Unit, Gong, Radio Actors)

SPICE GIRLS
96	Virgin V 2812	SPICE (LP, with glossy picture/lyric insert)	40
97	Virgin V 2850	SPICEWORLD (LP)	40

SPICE (U.K.)
68	United Artists UP 2246	What About The Music?/In Love	600

(see also Uriah Heep, Godz, Toe-Fat)

GEORGE SPICER
74	Topic 12T 235	BLACKBERRY FOLD (LP)	15

SPIDELLS
66	Sue WI 4019	Find Out What's Happening/That'll Make My Heart Break	50

SPIDER (1)
66	Decca F 12430	The Comedown Song/Blow Ya Mind	50

SPIDER (2)
77	Pennine PSS 136	Back To The Wall/Down And Out (p/s, 500 only, these 300 with p/s)	60
77	Pennine PSS 136	Back To The Wall/Down And Out (p/s, 500 only, these 200 without p/s)	30

SPIDER (3)
80	Alien ALIEN 14	Children Of The Street/Down 'N' Out (in p/s)	35
80	Alien ALIEN 14	Children Of The Street/Down 'N' Out	8
80	Alien ALIEN 16	College Luv/Born To Be Wild (in p/s)	35
80	Alien ALIEN 16	College Luv/Born To Be Wild	8

SPIDER & THE FLIES
07	Mute Irregulars IRREG 17	Metalurge/Desmond Leslie	15

(see also Horrors)

SPIDERS
66	Philips BF 1531	Sad Sunset/Hey Boy	40

SPIDERS (U.S.)

MINT VALUE £

SPIDERS (U.S.)
54	London HL 8086	I'm Slippin' In/I'm Searching (78)	65

SPIDERS FROM MARS
75	Pye 7N 45549	White Man Black Man/National Poll	6

(see also David Bowie, Kestrel, Mick Ronson)

BERND SPIER
65	Oriole CB 1987	A Million And One Times/Two Strangers	10

SPILL
92	Virgin VS 1141	Don't Wanna Know About Evil (7" Wireless Road Mix)/(Saspelofiska Dub Mix) (p/s)	12
92	Virgin VST 1141	Don't Wanna Know About Evil (Tumble Mix)/(Rumble Mix)/(Danny's Moto Mix)/(The Groovy Beats Mix) (12", p/s)	15

(see also Beth Orton)

SPINNERS (U.S.)
61	Columbia DB 4693	That's What Girls Are Made For/Heebie Jeebies	200
61	Columbia DB 4693	That's What Girls Are Made For/Heebie Jeebies (DJ copy)	250
65	Tamla Motown TMG 514	Sweet Thing/How Can I? (demo with 'Spinners' credit)	300
65	Tamla Motown TMG 514	Sweet Thing/How Can I? (demos with 'Detroit Spinners' credit)	250
65	Tamla Motown TMG 514	Sweet Thing/How Can I? (stock copies credited to 'Spinners')	400

(see also Detroit Spinners)

SPINNING JENNY
71	Midas MR004	SPINNING JENNY (LP)	70

SPINNING WHEEL
79	Private pressing	JACOB'S FLEECE (LP)	15

(see also Dragonsfire)

SPINNING WHEELS
75	Peter Dearden PD 205	SPINNING WHEELS (EP)	15

SPIRALS
58	Capitol CL 14958	The Rockin' Cow/Everybody Knows	15

SPIRAL SKY
93	Acme AC 8002LP	SPIRAL SKY (LP, numbered & sealed with insert, 500 only)	30
94	Acme 8002LP	SPIRAL SKY (LP, 2nd pressing numbered & sealed with insert, 300 only)	25

(see also Sun Dial, Ohr Musik)

SPIRAL STAIRCASE
68	CBS 3507	Baby What I Mean/Makin' Your Mind Up	25
69	CBS 4187	More Today Than Yesterday/Broken Hearted Man	50
69	CBS 4187	More Today Than Yesterday/Broken Hearted Man (DJ copy)	80
69	CBS 4524	No One For Me To Turn To/Sweet Little Thing	25

SPIRAL TRIBE
92	Big Life BLRT 79	Breach The Peace/Do ET/Seven/23 Minute Warning (12", p/s)	25
92	Big Life BLRT 85	Forward The Revolution/World Traveller Adventurer/Ragga Boom/Track 13 (criminal drug)(12", p/s)	25
92	Big Life BLRR 85	Forward The Revolution (the Youth remix) (1-sided, etched 12")	15
93	Butterfly BFLT 04	Sirius 23/Earthworm/Going All The Way/Predator (12", p/s, as Spiral Tribe Sound System)	20
93	Butterfly BFL LP 6	TECNO TERRA (2-LP)	50

SPIRAL VISIONS
82	SRTS 82 CUS 1450	Voices/Despair/Picture Portrait/Dance With Me	10

SPIRIT
68	CBS 3523	Uncle Jack/Mechanical World	15
69	CBS 3880	I Got A Line On You/She Smiles	25
69	CBS 4565	Dark Eyed Woman/New Dope In Town	12
70	CBS 4773	1984/Sweet Stella Baby	8
70	CBS 5149	Animal Zoo/Red Light Roll On	6
70	Epic SEPC 8083	Cadillac Cowboys/Darkness	6
68	CBS 63278	SPIRIT (LP, 1st pressing, stereo, laminated front cover, stereo sticker on rear, orange label)	35
68	CBS 63278	SPIRIT (LP, 1st pressing, mono, laminated front cover, orange label)	35
68	CBS 63523	THE FAMILY THAT PLAYS TOGETHER (LP, 1st pressing, mono, laminated front cover, orange label)	40
68	CBS 63523	THE FAMILY THAT PLAYS TOGETHER (LP, 1st pressing, stereo, laminated front cover, stereo sticker on rear, orange label)	25
69	CBS 63729	CLEAR (LP, laminated cover, orange label)	30
70	Epic EPC 64191	THE TWELVE DREAMS OF DR. SARDONICUS (LP, g/fold sleeve, yellow label)	20
72	Epic EPC 64507	FEED-BACK (LP, gatefold sleeve, yellow label)	15
75	Phonogram 6672 012	HIGHLIGHTS OF SPIRIT OF 76 (LP, promo)	20
81	Beggars Banquet BEGA 23	POTATOLAND (LP, with cartoon book)	15

(see also Kapt. Kopter & Fabulous Twirlybirds)

SPIRIT OF JOHN MORGAN
69	Carnaby CNS 4005	Ride On/Along Came John	10
71	RCA RCA 2085	Floating Opera Show/Never Let Go	10
69	Carnaby CNLS 6002	THE SPIRIT OF JOHN MORGAN (LP, union jack flag label)	200
70	Carnaby CNLS 6007	AGE MACHINE (LP, gatefold, union jack flag label)	150
71	Carnaby GOLD 6437 503	THE SPIRIT OF JOHN MORGAN (LP, reissue, 'crab' label logo)	50

(see also John Morgan)

SPIRIT OF MEMPHIS QUARTET
58	Parlophone PMD 1070	NEGRO SPIRITUALS (10" LP)	25
65	Vogue LAE 1033	NEGRO SPIRITUALS (LP, reissue)	15

SPIRIT OF PLAY
88	Release KIDS 1988	Children In Need/Children In Need (Instrumental) (with Paul McCartney) (in p/s)	50
88	Release KIDS 1988	Children In Need/Children In Need (Instrumental) (with Paul McCartney)	10

SPIRIT OF PROGRESS
71	Philips 6006089	Om Pa Pa/It's A Beautiful Day	35

SPIRITBORN
84	Spearhead	Pity The Unborn Child/Sing To The Lord	20

SPIRITUALIZED
90	Dedicated ZB 43783	Anyway That You Want Me/Step Into The Breeze (p/s)	15
90	Dedicated ZT 43784	Anyway That You Want Me (Extended)/Step Into The Breeze 1 & 2 (12", p/s)	20
90	Dedicated ZT 43780	Anyway That You Want Me (Remix)/Step Into The Breeze 1 & 2 (12", p/s)	20
91	Fierce FRIGHT 053	Feel So Sad/I Want You (gig freebie, no p/s, stamped plain white sleeve with date & venue details)	15
91	Dedicated SPIRT 001T	Feel So Sad (Rhapsodies)/(Glides And Chimes) (12", p/s)	12
91	Dedicated SPIRT 002	Run/I Want You (p/s, with luminous sleeve & clear luminous vinyl)	15
91	Dedicated SPIRT 002	Run/I Want You (p/s)	8
91	Dedicated SPIRT 002T	Run/Luminescence (Stay With Me)/I Want You/Effervescent (Chimes) (12", with luminous sleeve)	18
91	Dedicated SPIRT 002T	Run/Luminescence (Stay With Me)/I Want You/Effervescent (Chimes) (12")	10
91	Dedicated SPIRIT 003	Why Don't You Smile Now? (Edit)/Sway (clear vinyl, p/s)	10
91	Dedicated SPIRT 004	I Want You/You Know It's True (Instrumental)/100 Bars (Flashback) (p/s, mail-order with NME coupon only)	10
92	Dedicated SPIRIT 005	Medication/Smiles (p/s, red vinyl, 3000 only)	8
92	Dedicated SPIRT 005	Medication/Angel Sigh/Feel So Sad (white label test pressing, signed and inscribed by Jason Pierce in silver, limited availability through website)	25
92	Dedicated SPIRT 005T	Medication/Angel Sigh/Feel So Sad (12", p/s, with poster, 3000 only)	10
93	Dedicated SPIRT 006	Smiles (Live)/100 Bars (A Cappella) (7" flexidisc, fan-club only)	20
93	Greenpeace GR'NP'CE 001	Good Dope, Good Fun/MERCURY REV: 'Boys Peel Out (Live)' (gig 7", with booklet)	15
96	Dedicated SPIRT 101T	Pure Phase Tones For DJs (12")	15
92	Dedicated DEDLP 004S	LAZER GUIDED MELODIES (2-LP, limited Edition, with bonus 7" single 'Anyway That You Want Me'/'Why Don't You Smile Now?' [CWNN 7001])	
92	Dedicated DEDLP 004S	LAZER GUIDED MELODIES (2-LP, limited. Edition, without bonus 7" single)	40
93	Dedicated no cat. no.	SUMMER EUROPEAN 93 BOX (3-CD promo set, with ribbon and insert)	80
93	Dedicated DEDLP 008	FUCKED UP INSIDE (LP, mail-order only)	80
93	Dedicated DEDCD 008	FUCKED UP INSIDE (CD, mail-order only)	35
93	Dedicated DEDLP 017	PURE PHASE (2-LP 45rpm)	60
97	Dedicated DEDLP 034	LADIES AND GENTLEMEN WE ARE FLOATING IN SPACE (2-LP, limited issue)	150
97	Dedicated DEDCD 034S	LADIES AND GENTLEMEN WE ARE FLOATING IN SPACE (12 x 3" CDs, in blister packs in card box with insert, 1000 only, 200 with clear plastic backs)	80
97	Dedicated DEDCD 034S	LADIES AND GENTLEMEN WE ARE FLOATING IN SPACE (12 x 3" CDs, in blister packs in card box with insert, 1000)	50
97	Dedicated DEDCD 034P	LADIES AND GENTLEMEN WE ARE FLOATING IN SPACE (CD, 'Elvis version', given to Mercury Music Prize personnel, 50 copies only)	40
98	Deconstruction 74321662851	ROYAL ALBERT HALL (2-LP)	50
01	Spaceman OPM001LP	LET IT COME DOWN (2-LP, postcard)	40
03	Spaceman/Sanctuary OPM014LP/SANLP14	AMAZING GRACE (LP)	20
08	Sanctuary 1768732	SONGS IN A&E (2-LP, green vinyl)	25
08	Sanctuary 1768732	SONGS IN A&E (2-LP green vinyl, only availiable from Rough Trade)	30
12	Art Vinyl AVLP 11	LADIES AND GENTLEMEN WE ARE IN FLOATING IN SPACE (2-LP, reissue)	25

(see also Spacemen 3)

SPIROGYRA
72	Pegasus PGS 3	Dangerous Dave/Captain's Log	12
73	Polydor 2001-419	I Hear You're Going Nowhere/Old Boot Wine	35
71	B&C CAS 1042	ST. RADIGUND'S (LP, with lyric inner)	150
72	Pegasus PEG 13	OLD BOOT WINE (LP, textured sleeve)	250
73	Polydor 2310 246	BELLS, BOOTS AND SHAMBLES (LP)	800
14	Turning Round GYRALP5	SPIROGYRA 5 (LP)	40

SPITEFUL CHILD
83	Clubland SPJ 842	Voices In The Night/Is It Love	30
85	SRT SKJ 648	I Want To Hold You/Who's Crying Now	20

SPITERI
73	GM GML 1006	SPITERI (LP)	20

SPITFIRE (& BLACKFIRE BARMIES)
82	Carrere CAR 253	So You Want To Be A Rock'n'Roll Star/Spitfire Boogie	50

SPITFIRE BOYS
77	RK RK 1001	British Refugee/Mein Kampf (push-out centre)	75
77	RK RK 1001	British Refugee/Mein Kampf (reissue, solid centre, p/s)	60
79	Impeccable SRTS/79/CUS481	Funtime/Transendental Changing	35
83	RK RK 1001	British Refugee/Mein Kampf (2nd reissue to cash in on Frankie success p/s, no solid centre)	75

(see also Frankie Goes To Hollywood)

SPITTIN IMAGE
79	Wessex WEX 270	Baby Goodbye/(Wish I Could See A) UFO (no p/s)	15

SPITTIN MUSSELS
81	RAFOSM 1	Five Days A Week/Hold On Johnny (p/s)	35

SPITZBROOK
79	Ace SPIT 1	Stranger/Looking At You (p/s)	60

SPIV
73	Pye 7N 45293	Oh You Beautiful Child/Little Girl	120

SPIZZ (OIL/ENERGI)
79	Rough Trade RTSO 1	6000 Crazy/1989/Fibre (p/s)	8
79	Rough Trade RTSO 2	Cold City/Red And Black/Solarisation (Shun)/Platform 3 (as Spizz Oil) (p/s)	6
79	Rough Trade RTSO 3	Soldier Soldier/Virginia Plain (as Spizz Energi) (p/s)	6
79	Rough Trade RTSO 4	Where's Captain Kirk?/Amnesia (as Spizz Energi) (p/s)	6
20	Electronic Sound ES 761	Where's Captain Kirk?/Amnesia (p/s, reissue, green vinyl)	8
82	Rough Trade ROUGH501	SPIZZ HISTORY (LP)	20

S.P.K. (SEPPUKU/SURGICAL PENIS KLINIK)

MINT VALUE £

S.P.K. (SEPPUKU/SURGICAL PENIS KLINIK)
Year	Label/Cat	Title	Value
80	Industrial IR 0011	MEAT PROCESSING SECTION (Mekano/Slogun) (p/s, labels list "Slogan"/Factory, with insert, as Surgical Penis Klinik)	30
83	Side Effekts SER 003	Dekompositiones (12", p/s, as Seppuku)	20
81	Side Effekts SER 01	INFORMATION OVERLOAD UNIT (LP, 1st 1,000 with booklet)	70
81	Side Effekts SER 01	INFORMATION OVERLOAD UNIT (LP)	50
83	Walter Ulbright WULP 002	AUTO-DA-FE (LP)	20
86	Side Effekts SER 09	ZAMIA LEHMANNI (LP)	15
80s	Side Effekts SER 002	LEICHENSCHREI (LP)	30

SPLASH
Year	Label/Cat	Title	Value
95	Dee Jay DJX 022R	Babylon/Heaven (12")	10
95	Dee Jay DJX 022R2	Baylon Remixes (12")	10
95	Dee Jay DJX 022R2	Babylon Remixes 2 (12")	40

SPLAT!
Year	Label/Cat	Title	Value
83	Ron Johnson RON 1	Yeah The Dum Dum/Bookface/Biggles Bloodbath (p/s)	6

SPLINTER
Year	Label/Cat	Title	Value
74	Dark Horse AMS 7135	Costafine Town/Elly May	6
75	Dark Horse AMS 5501	Drink All Day/Haven't Got Time (withdrawn)	12
75	Dark Horse AMS 5502	China Light/Drink All Day	10
75	Dark Horse AMS 5503	Which Way Will I Get Home/Green Bus Line	8
76	Dark Horse AMS 5506	Half Way There/What Is It (If You Never Ever Tried It Yourself)	8
77	Dark Horse K 17009	Round And Round/I'll Bend For You	7
77	Dark Horse K 17116	New York City (Who Am I)/Baby Love	7
78	Barn BARN 4	Danger Zone/Swear To God	8
76	Dark Horse DH 2	SPLINTER (LP, promo only, plain white sleeve)	130

SPLIT BEAVER
Year	Label/Cat	Title	Value
81	Heavy Metal HEAVY 7	Savage/Hound Of Hell (with p/s)	25
81	Heavy Metal HEAVY 7	Savage/Hound Of Hell	8
82	Heavy Metal HMRLP 3	WHEN HELL WON'T HAVE YOU (LP, silver label)	18
82	Heavy Metal HMRLP 3	WHEN HELL WON'T HAVE YOU (LP, red label)	15

SPLITCROW
Year	Label/Cat	Title	Value
84	Guardian GRC 21	ROCKSTORM (LP)	15

SPLIT GENES
Year	Label/Cat	Title	Value
80	Sara Bee BN124	Somebody To Love/Submarine City (no p/s)	10

SPLIT IMAGE
Year	Label/Cat	Title	Value
82	Heroes ER 01	Now That We've Parted	25

SPLIT KNEE LOONS
Year	Label/Cat	Title	Value
81	Avatar AAA 111	THE SPECIAL COLLECTORS EP (p/s, brown vinyl, with badge)	10

(see also Gillan, Bernie Torme, John McCoy, Colin Towns)

SPLIT SCREENS
Year	Label/Cat	Title	Value
79	Rok ROK III/IV	Just Don't Try/JUST FRANK: You (die-cut company sleeve)	35

SPLODGENESSABOUNDS
Year	Label/Cat	Title	Value
80	Deram ROLF 1	Two Little Boys/Horse/Sox/Butterfly (p/s, with 'Splodge' boomerang)	15
81	Deram SML 1121	SPLODGENESSABOUNDS (LP)	15

SP MC
Year	Label/Cat	Title	Value
18	System SYSTM 020	Pondlife/R1 (10")	25

SPODE
Year	Label/Cat	Title	Value
71	Decca F 13142	Singalong Song/Cincinatti Woman	10

SPOILERS
Year	Label/Cat	Title	Value
72	London HLU 10399	Turbo Rock/Sad Man's Land	20

SPOKESMEN
Year	Label/Cat	Title	Value
65	Brunswick 05941	The Dawn Of Correction/For You Babe	12
65	Brunswick 05948	It Ain't Fair/Have Courage Be Careful	12
66	Brunswick 05950	Michelle/Better Days Are Yet To Come	8
66	Brunswick 05958	Today's The Day/Enchanté	8

SPONOOCH
Year	Label/Cat	Title	Value
79	EMI EMI 2941	Crime Buster/Laserdance (12", p/s)	50
79	EMI EMI 2941	Crime Buster/Laserdance (p/s)	10

SPONTANEOUS COMBUSTION
Year	Label/Cat	Title	Value
71	Harvest HAR 5046	Lonely Singer/200 Lives/Leaving	15
72	Harvest HAR 5060	Gay Time Night/Spaceship	30
73	Harvest HAR 5068	Sabre Dance/Sabre Dance	15
72	Harvest SHVL 801	SPONTANEOUS COMBUSTION (LP, with EMI logo on label)	125
72	Harvest SHVL 805	TRIAD (LP, with 3 inserts, with EMI logo on label)	100

(see also Time)

SPONTANEOUS MUSIC ENSEMBLE
Year	Label/Cat	Title	Value
66	Eyemark EMP L1002	CHALLENGE (LP)	450
68	Island ILP 979	KARYOBIN ... ARE THE IMAGINARY BIRDS SAID TO LIVE IN PARADISE (LP, pink label)	300
69	Marmalade 608 008	SPONTANEOUS MUSIC ENSEMBLE (LP)	100
70	A A001	FOR YOU TO SHARE (LP)	100
71	Tangent TNGS 107	SOURCE FROM AND TOWARDS (LP)	35
72	Marmalade 2384 009	SPONTANEOUS MUSIC ENSEMBLE (LP, reissue)	25
73	Emanem 303	FACE TO FACE (LP)	30
73	Tangent TNGS 118	SO WHAT DO YOU THINK (LP)	35
77	Incus INCUS 24	BIOSYSTEM (LP)	50
82	Affinity AFF 81	1 2 ALBERT AYLER (LP)	20

(see also Howard Riley Trio)

SPONTANEOUS MUSIC ORCHESTRA
Year	Label/Cat	Title	Value
75	A A003	+ = (LP)	75
81	Sweet Folk All SFA 112	SME + SMO IN CONCERT (LP)	50

SPOOKEY

MINT VALUE £

(see also Spontaneous Music Ensemble)

SPOOKEY
81	Satril HH 153	On The Rocks/Friends	15
81	Satril 12 HH 153	Friends/On The Rocks (12")	40

SPOOKY TOOTH
67	Island WIP 6022	Sunshine Help Me/Weird	25
68	Island WIP 6037	Love Really Changed Me/Luger's Grove	15
68	Island WIP 6046	The Weight/Do Right People	10
69	Island WIP 6048	Nobody There At All/ART: Room With A View (unissued, white labels only)	75
69	Island WIP 6060	Son Of Your Father/I've Got Enough Heartache	7
73	Island WIP 6168	All Sewn Up/As Long As The World Keeps Turning	6
68	Island ILP 980/ILPS 9080	IT'S ALL ABOUT (LP, 1st pressing pink 'eye' label)	150
70	Island ILP 980/ILPS 9080	IT'S ALL ABOUT (LP, 2nd pressing, pink label white 'i' logo)	50
69	Island ILPS 9098	SPOOKY TWO (LP, 1st pressing with pink 'eye' label, matrix numbers ILPS 9080 +A & +B stamped into dead wax. No 'Porky' or 'Pecko' in dead wax (unlike reissues), gatefold 'E.J.Day' sleeve)	100
69	Island ILPS 9098	SPOOKY TWO (LP, 2nd pressing with white 'i' on pink label, with Jimmy Miller production credit around a centimetre beneath SPOOKY TOOTH on label)	70
69	Island ILPS 9107	CEREMONY (LP, with Pierre Henry, pink label, gatefold sleeve)	100
70	Island ILPS 9098	SPOOKY TWO (LP, 3rd pressing with white 'i' on pink label, with Jimmy Miller production credit directly beneath SPOOKY TOOTH on label)	50
70	Island ILPS 9117	THE LAST PUFF (LP, pink label)	60
73	Island ILPS 9227	YOU BROKE MY HEART SO I BUSTED YOUR JAW (LP, gatefold sleeve, lyric insert, pink rim label)	30
73	Island ILPS 9255	WITNESS (LP, pink rim label)	30
74	Good Ear EARL 2001	THE MIRROR (LP)	25
74	Island ILPS 9292	THE MIRROR (LP, export issue)	25
77	Island ILP 980/ILPS 9080	IT'S ALL ABOUT (LP, repressing, palm tree label)	50

(see also Gary Wright, V.I.P.s, Art, Luther Grosvenor, Hellions, Revolution, State Of Mickey & Tommy, Mike Harrison)

SPOON FAZER
80	Project PROJECT 1	MUSIC 2 DANCE 2 (EP, p/s)	20
82	Illuminated ILL 912	Sunset/Ballad Of The Insectman/Flying Bodies/Fly On The Wall (12", p/s)	60

SPOONFUL
77	Bunbury DCS 340	Troubled Times/Country Blues (2 known copies in p/s)	300
77	Bunbury DCS 340	Troubled Times/Country Blues (no p/s)	50

SPORTS
80	Sire SRUK 6001	WHO LISTENS TO THE RADIO (LP)	15

SPORTS TEAM
18	Nice Swan NSWN 006	WINTER NETS (12" EP, p/s)	25
18	Nice Swan/Holm Front NSWN10/HF001	Margate/Kutcher (p/s)	15
18	(no label or cat. no.)	Liberal Friends/Stanton (p/s)	18
18	Holm Fron HF002	Get Along/Casper (p/s)	20

SPOTLIGHT
74	Globe GB 02	Find The Light/Emily Cries (p/s)	25

SPOTLIGHTERS
59	Vogue Pop V 9230	Please Be My Girlfriend/Whisper (with Bob Thompson & His Band)	500
59	Vogue Pop V 9230	Please Be My Girlfriend/Whisper (with Bob Thompson & His Band) (78)	100

SPOTLIGHTS
66	Philips BF 1485	Batman And Robin/Day Flower	20

SPOTNICKS
62	Oriole CB 1724	Orange Blossom Special/The Spotnicks Theme	10
62	Oriole CB 1755	Galloping Guitars/The Rocket Man	10
63	Oriole CB 1790	Hava Nagila/High Flyin' Scotsman	8
63	Oriole CB 1818	Just Listen To My Heart/Pony Express	10
63	Oriole CB 1844	Valentina/Save The Last Dance For Me/No Yaga Daga Blues	12
63	Oriole CB 1886	Anna/The Sailor's Hornpipe	12
64	Oriole CB 1953	Lovesick Blues/The Space Creatures	15
64	Oriole CB 1981	Donner Wetter/Shamus O'Toole	15
63	Oriole EP 7075	ON THE AIR (EP)	20
64	Oriole EP 7078	SPOTNICKS IN PARIS (EP)	20
64	Oriole EP 7079	SPOTNICKS AT THE OLYMPIA PARIS (EP)	20
63	Oriole PS 40036	OUT-A SPACE: THE SPOTNICKS IN LONDON (LP, mono)	25
63	Oriole SPS 40037	OUT-A SPACE: THE SPOTNICKS IN LONDON (LP, stereo)	35
64	Oriole PS 40054	THE SPOTNICKS IN SPAIN (LP)	30
65	Oriole PS 40064	THE SPOTNICKS IN BERLIN (LP)	30

(see also Bob Lander & Spotnicks, Shy Ones)

SPRATLEYS JAPS
18	(No label or cat no)	Her/Hands (lathe cut 7", clear vinyl, signed insert)	50

JACK SPRATT
69	Coxsone CS 7100	Give Me Your Love/LARRY & ALVIN: Magic Moments (B-side actually by Leroy Sibbles and Heptones)	200

SPREADEAGLE
72	Charisma BCP 7	Nightingal Lane/CAPABILITY BROWN: Liar (demo only in p/s)	10
72	Charisma CB 183	How Can We Be Lost/Nightmare (p/s, solid centre)	15
72	Charisma CB 183	How Can We Be Lost/Nightmare (four prong centre)	8
72	Charisma CAS 1055	THE PIECE OF PAPER (LP, pink 'scroll' label)	20

SPREDTHICK
78	An Actual ACT 003	SPREDTHICK (LP, with insert)	18

SPRIGUNS (OF TOLGUS)
76	Decca F 13676	Nothing Else To Do/Lord Lovell	20
77	Decca F 13739	White Witch/Time Will Pass	20

SPRING

			MINT VALUE £
75	Alida Star C'tage ASC7755	JACK WITH A FEATHER (LP, as Spriguns Of Tolgus)	1500
76	Decca SKL 5262	REVEL WEIRD & WILD (LP, with lyric insert)	275
77	Decca SKL 5286	TIME WILL PASS (LP, with lyric insert)	200
92	Kissing Spell KSLP 002	ROWDY DOWDY DAY (LP, reissue)	15

(see also Mandy Morton Band, Terra Cotta)

SPRING
71	RCA Neon NE 6	SPRING (LP, foldout sleeve, black inner sleeve)	1000

SPRING OFFENSIVE
81	SO 1	Cruising/Good To Be Back	35

SPRINGBOARD
69	Polydor 545007	SPRINGBOARD (LP)	100

DUSTY SPRINGFIELD
63	Philips BF 1292	I Only Want To Be With You/Once Upon A Time	6
64	Philips BF 1313	Stay Awhile/Something Special	6
64	Philips BF 1381	Oh Holy Child/SPRINGFIELDS: Jingle Bells (with p/s)	10
65	Philips BF 1418	In The Middle Of Nowhere/Baby Don't You Know	6
65	Philips BF 1430	Some Of Your Lovin'/I'll Love You For A While	6
66	Philips BF 1466	Little By Little/If It Hadn't Been For You	10
66	Philips BF 1482	You Don't Have To Say You Love Me/Every Ounce Of Strength	6
66	Philips BF 1502	Goin' Back/I'm Gonna Leave You	8
66	Philips BF 1510	All I See Is You/Go Ahead On (with p/s)	8
67	Philips BF 1577	Give Me Time/The Look Of Love	8
67	Philips BF 1608	What's It Gonna Be/Small Town Girl	25
68	Philips BF 1682	I Close My Eyes And Count To Ten/No Stranger Am I	6
68	Philips BF 1730	Son Of A Preacher Man/Just A Little Lovin' (Early In The Mornin')	15
69	Philips BF 1811	Am I The Same Girl/Earthbound Gypsy	20
69	Philips BF 1826	Brand New Me/Bad Case Of The Blues	10
70	Philips 6006 045	How Can I Be Sure/Spooky	50
72	Philips 6006 214	Yesterday When I Was Young/I Start Counting	6
73	Philips 6006 295	Who Gets Your Love/Of All The Things	6
74	Philips 6006 325	Learn To Say Goodbye/Easy Evil	6
74	Philips 6006 350	What's It Gonna Be/Bring Him Back	12
78	Mercury JUMBO 3	That'sThe Kind Of Love I've Got For You/That's The Kind Of Love I've Got For You (12", promo only)	40
79	Mercury DUSTY 412	Baby Blue (Disco Version)/Baby Blue (7" Version) (12")	10
15	Mercury 4720263	What's It Gonna Be/Spooky (p/s)	25
64	Philips BE 12560	I ONLY WANT TO BE WITH YOU (EP)	15
64	Philips BE 12564	DUSTY (EP)	15
65	Philips BE 12572	DUSTY IN NEW YORK (EP)	18
65	Philips BE 12579	MADEMOISELLE DUSTY (EP)	25
68	Philips BE 12605	IF YOU GO AWAY (EP)	18
72	Philips 6850751	STAR DUSTY (EP)	10
64	Philips BL 7594	A GIRL CALLED DUSTY (mono)	20
64	Philips SBL 7594	A GIRL CALLED DUSTY (stereo)	25
65	Philips RBL 1002	EVERYTHING'S COMING UP DUSTY (gatefold sleeve with booklet, mono)	25
65	Philips SRBL 1002	EVERYTHING'S COMING UP DUSTY (gatefold sleeve with booklet, stereo)	35
66	Philips BL 7737	GOLDEN HITS (LP, mono)	15
66	Philips SBL 7737	GOLDEN HITS (LP, stereo)	18
67	Philip BL 7820	WHERE AM I GOING? (LP, mono)	25
67	Philip SBL 7820	WHERE AM I GOING? (LP, stereo)	30
68	Philips (S)BL 7864	DUSTY... DEFINITELY (LP, stereo only)	25
69	Philips SBL 7889	DUSTY IN MEMPHIS (LP, stereo only)	60
70	Philips SBL 7927	FROM DUSTY... WITH LOVE (LP)	20
80	Philips PRICE 83	IN MEMPHIS PLUS (LP)	30
95	Columbia 478508 1	A VERY FINE LOVE (LP)	15

(see also Lana Sisters, Springfields, Tom Springfield, Pet Shop Boys)

TOM SPRINGFIELD (& HIS) ORCHESTRA
63	Philips BF 1294	The Moon Behind The Hill/The Londonderry Air	6
64	Philips BF 1331	Brazilian Shake/Brazilian Blues	6
69	Philips BF 1759	Theme From From The Troubleshooters/Homage To Spewdley Parsons (with p/s)	8
69	Philips BF 1759	Theme From From The Troubleshooters/Homage To Spewdley Parsons	6
68	Decca SKL 4967	SUN SONGS (LP)	80
69	Decca LK/SKL 5003	LOVE'S PHILOSOPHY BY... (LP, featuring Dusty Springfield)	30

(see also Springfields, Dusty Springfield)

SPRINGFIELD PARK
68	CBS 3775	Never An Everyday Thing/I Can See The Sun Shine	10

SPRINGFIELDS (1)
61	Philips PB 1145	Dear John/I Done What They Told Me To	6
61	Philips PB 1168	Breakaway/Good News	7
61	Philips PB 1178	Bambino/Star Of Hope (with p/s)	8
63	Philips BF 1263	Come On Home/Pit-A-Pat	6
64	Philips BF 1306	If I Was Down And Out/Maracabamba	6
61	Philips SBBE 9068	THE SPRINGFIELDS (EP, stereo)	12
62	Philips 433 622 BE	KINDA FOLKSY (EP)	10
62	Philips 433 623 BE	KINDA FOLKSY No. 2 (EP)	10
63	Philips 433 624 BE	KINDA FOLKSY No. 3 (EP)	12
63	Philips BBE 12538	HIT SOUNDS (EP)	12
63	Philips 433 643 BE	FOLK SONGS FROM THE HILLS (EP)	15
62	Philips BBL 7551	KINDA FOLKSY (LP, mono)	15
62	Philips SBBL 674	KINDA FOLKSY (LP, stereo)	15

SPRINGFIELDS (2)

MINT VALUE £

| 63 | Philips 632 304 BL | FOLK SONGS FROM THE HILLS (LP) .... 15 |

(see also Dusty Springfield, Lana Sisters, Tom Springfield, Mike Hurst)

SPRINGFIELDS (2)
88	Sarah SARAH 010	Sunflower/Clown/Are We Gonna Be Alright? (foldaround p/s with 14" x 10" poster in polyester bag; yellow p/s) 30
88	Sarah SARAH 010	Sunflower/Clown/Are We Gonna Be Alright? (foldaround p/s with 14" x 10" poster in polyester bag; later orange p/s) 18
91	Sarah SARAH 040	Wonder/Tomorrow Ends Today (p/s, with insert) 15

SPRING HEEL JACK
| 80 | Woodbine WSR 003 | 1960s Girl/How Many Colours (no p/s) .... 20 |

BRUCE SPRINGSTEEN
75	CBS A 3661	Born To Run/Meeting Across The River 15
76	CBS A 3940	Tenth Avenue Freeze-Out/She's The One 25
78	CBS A 6424	Prove It All Night/Factory 18
78	CBS A 6532	Badlands/Something In The Night 15
78	CBS A 6720	Promised Land/Streets Of Fire 65
80	CBS A 9309	Hungry Heart/Held Up Without A Gun (p/s, withdrawn first issue, black and white p/s, blue lettering) 25
80	CBS A 9309	Hungry Heart/Held Up Without A Gun 6
81	CBS A 9568	Sherry Darling/Independence Day (white label promo, 100 only 2 known copies with p/s listing 'Independence Day') 2500
81	CBS A 9568	Sherry Darling/Independence Day (white label promo, 100 only) 1500
81	CBS 9568	Sherry Darling/Be True (p/s) 15
81	CBS A 1179	The River/Independence Day (p/s) 15
81	CBS A 13-1179	The River/Born To Run/Rosalita (12", p/s, sleeves credit 'East Street Band') 15
81	CBS A 13-1179	The River/Born To Run/Rosalita (12", p/s) 12
81	CBS A 1557	Cadillac Ranch/Wreck On The Highway (p/s) 15
82	CBS A 2794	Atlantic City/Mansion On The Hill (p/s) 20
82	CBS A 2969	Open All Night/The Big Pay Back (p/s) 30
84	CBS WA 4436	Dancing In The Dark/Pink Cadillac (Cadillac-shaped picture disc) 20
84	CBS WA 4662	Cover Me/Jersey Girl (live) (Bruce-shaped picture disc with plinth) 25
84	CBS DA 4662/A 4436	Cover Me/Jersey Girl (live)//Dancing In The Dark/Pink Cadillac (shrinkable double pack, both 45s in p/s) 12
84	CBS DA 4662/A 7077	Cover Me/Jersey Girl (live)//Born To Run/Meeting Across The River (shrinkwrapped double pack, no p/s on 2nd 45) 12
84	CBS A 6561	I'm Going Down/Janey, Don't You Lose Heart (p/s) 7
85	CBS A 7077	Born To Run/Meeting Across The River (reissue, blue p/s, withdrawn) 25
85	CBS A 6342	I'm On Fire/Born In The U.S.A. (p/s, with competition postcard) 8
85	CBS WA 6342	I'm On Fire/Born In The U.S.A. (p/s, flag-shaped picture disc) 20
85	CBS BRUCE 1	BORN IN THE U.S.A. - THE 12" COLLECTION (4 x 12" & 7", box with poster) 20
86	CBS 650 193-0	War (live)/Merry Xmas Baby (live)//My Home Town (live)/Santa Claus Is Coming To Town (live) (shrinkwrapped double pack, both 45s in p/s) 10
87	CBS 650 381-6	Fire (live)/For You (live)/Born To Run (live)/No Surrender (live)/10th Avenue (live) Freeze-Out (live) (12", p/s) 12
87	CBS BRUCE B2	Born To Run/Spirit In The Night/Johnny 99/Because The Night (double pack box set) 8
87	CBS 651 141-0	Brilliant Disguise/Lucky Man (gatefold p/s, with discography) 6
87	CBS 651 295-0	Tunnel Of Love/Two For The Road (postcard-shaped picture disc) 15
88	CBS BRUCE Q4	Spare Parts/Cover Me (live)/Spare Parts (live)/I'm On Fire (live) (12", different p/s) 10
73	CBS 65480	GREETINGS FROM ASBURY PARK, N.J. (cutaway gatefold sleeve, orange label) 20
74	CBS 65780	THE WILD, THE INNOCENT AND THE E STREET SHUFFLE (orange label, yellow lettering on sleeve; with "Ashbury" mis-spelling on label) 20
75	CBS 69170	BORN TO RUN (with "John Landau" misprint on rear sleeve) 30
78	CBS 86061	DARKNESS ON THE EDGE OF TOWN (LP) 18
80	CBS 88510	THE RIVER (2-LP) 20
80	CBS 80959	BORN TO RUN (LP, reissue, half-speed master, 2 inserts) 20
82	CBS 25100	NEBRASKA (LP, inner) 20
84	CBS 86304	BORN IN THE U.S.A. (LP, inner, insert) 20
84	CBS 11-86304	BORN IN THE U.S.A. (picture disc) 30
87	CBS 460 270-0	TUNNEL OF LOVE (picture disc) 15
90	CBS LSP 980636 1	COLLECTED WORKS OF BRUCE SPRINGSTEEN (7 LP box set) 200
92	Sony 471 423-0	HUMAN TOUCH (picture disc) 15
92	Sony 471 424-0	LUCKY TOWN (picture disc, with side 1 on both sides) 75
92	Sony 471 424-0	LUCKY TOWN (picture disc) 15
92	Columbia 471423	LUCKY TOWN (LP) 15
93	Columbia 473860-1	IN CONCERT (2-LP, stickered sleeve) 40
95	Columbia 478555	GREATEST HITS (2-LP) 40
96	Columbia C 67484	THE GHOST OF TOM JOAD (LP) 100
02	Columbia COL 508000-1	THE RISING (2-LP) 125

(see also Roy Orbison)

SPRINGTIME
| 78 | Sonet SON 2143 | Mrs Caroline Robinson/Honey Bye Bye (p/s) .... 6 |

SPRINGWATER (1)
| 71 | Polydor 2058141 | I Will Return/Stone Cross .... 12 |
| 72 | Polydor 2058220 | Listen Everybody/Guiding Light .... 12 |

(see also Thurday's Children, Phil Cordell)

SPRINGWATER (2)
| 80 | Fabulous JC 2 | Sailing/Captain Of The Sea .... 6 |

SPRINGWELL
| 71 | London HLU 10345 | It's For You/Our Question .... 15 |

SPRONG & NYAH SHUFFLE
| 69 | Grape GR 3001 | Moonwalk/Think .... 30 |

Billy SPROUD & ROCK 'N' ROLL SIX

MINT VALUE £

BILLY SPROUD & ROCK 'N' ROLL SIX
57	Columbia DB 3893	Rock Mr. Piper/If You're So Smart (How Come You Ain't Rich)	25
57	Columbia DB 3893	Rock Mr. Piper/If You're So Smart (How Come You Ain't Rich) (78)	20

SPROUTS
58	RCA RCA 1031	Teen Billy Baby/Goodbye, She's Gone	35
58	RCA RCA 1031	Teen Billy Baby/Goodbye, She's Gone (78)	20

SPUD
75	Philips 9108 002	A SILK PURSE (LP)	20

SPUD AND THE FABS
80	Whitetower AMC 706	Your Place Or Mine (p/s)	25

THE SPUNKY ONION
74	Contempo CS2006	Cookie Man (Part 1)/Cookie Man (Part 2)	10

THE SPUNKY SPIDER
73	Phoenix S-NIX 143	You Won't Come/Perchance	80

SPUNKY ONIONS/GHETTOBETTIES
80	Temple Beat TR111	Split 7" (p/s)	25

WILD JIMMY SPURRILL
60s	XX MIN 717	NOBLE 'THIN MAN' WATTS AND WILD JIMMY SPURRILL (EP)	20

(see also Noble 'Thin Man' Watts, Guitar Crusher)

SPURS
88	Outback OUT 1	Soldier (p/s)	12

SPYROGYRA
79	Infinity (no cat. no.)	MORNING DANCE (LP, picture disc, in-house issue, top-flap poly sleeve, 50 copies)	50

SQUAD
79	Squad SQS 1	Red Alert/£8 A Week (in die cut p/s)	60
79	Squad SQS 1	Red Alert/£8 A Week	20
79	Squad SQS 2	Millionaire/Brockhill Boys (p/s)	40

SQUADRONAIRES
54	Decca F 10248	Coach Call Boogie/Donegal Cradle Song	10
54	Decca F 10274	Wolf On The Prowl/Mudhopper	7
57	Columbia DB 3882	Rock And Roll Boogie/Right Now, Right Now	10
53	Decca LF 1141	CONTRASTS IN JAZZ (10" LP)	15

SQUARE SET
71	Decca FR 13197	That's What I Want/Come On	80

SQUAREPUSHER
96	Rephlex CAT037LP	FEED ME WEIRD THINGS (2-LP)	30
97	Warp WARPLP50	HARD NORMAL DADDY (2-LP)	20
98	Warp WARPLP57	MUSIC IS ROTTED ONE NOTE (LP)	20
99	Warp WARPLP62	BUDAKHAN MINDPHONE (LP)	20
99	Warp WARLP72	SELECTION SIXTEEN (2x12", with 10")	20
99	Warp WARPLP85	GO PLASTIC (2-LP)	20
02	Warp WARPLP97	DO YOU KNOW SQUAREPUSHER? (LP)	20
04	Warp WARPLP117	ULTRAVISITOR (2-LP)	20
06	Warp WARPLP148X	HELLO EVERYTHING (3 x 12" plus bonus CD edition)	20
08	Warp WARLP148	JUST A SOUVENEIR (LP)	15

SQUARES (1)
78	Sire SIR 4003	No Fear/Nobodys Fool (p/s)	10
79	Sire SIR 4011	Stop Being A Boy/This Is Airebeat (p/s)	7

SQUARES (2)
91	Hangman HANG 45 UP	TRAPPED IN A SQUARE (LP)	15
93	Hangman HANG 52 UP	CURSE OF THE SQUARES (LP)	15

SQUEEK
72	Bronze BRO 130	Make Hay While The Sun Shines/L Amour D'un Apres Midi	20

SQUEELER
79	Hit H.I.T. 101	Jennifer Broadhurst/Menace/I Just Want To Be Me/Framed (7" no p/s)	100

SQUEEZE
77	BTM SBT 107	Take Me I'm Yours/No, Disco Kid, No (unreleased)	0
77	Deptford Fun City DFC 01	PACKET OF THREE (EP, red & blue photo p/s)	10
77	Deptford Fun City DFC 01	PACKET OF THREE (12" EP, plain pink die-cut sleeve, 500 only)	10
79	A&M AMS 7426	Cool For Cats/Model (p/s, brilliant pink vinyl, 5,000 only)	6
79	A&M AMS 7426	Cool For Cats/Model (p/s, red vinyl, 1,000 only)	7
81	A&M AMS 8166	Labelled With Love/Squabs On Forty Five (withdrawn p/s)	12
78	A&M AMLH 68465	SQUEEZE (LP)	15

SQUIBBY & REFLECTIONS
68	Direction 58-3453	Ragamuffin/For A Little While	7
68	Direction 58-3606	Loving You Has Made My Life Worthwhile/Better Off Without You	7
69	Direction 58-4073	You Got It/Come Back To Me	8

SQUIBS
81	Oily SLICK 1	On The Line (plain sleeve, with insert)	25
81	Oily SLICK 3	Parades/Out On The Town (p/s)	20

BILLY SQUIER
86	Capitol 12CL 433	Love Is The Hero (extended version with Freddie Mercury intro)/Learn How To Live (live) (12", p/s)	15

(see also Freddie Mercury, Roger Taylor)

SQUIRE
79	Rok ROK I/II	Get Ready To Go/COMING SHORTLY: Doing The Flail (company sleeve)	35
79	I-Spy SEE 2	Walking Down The King's Road/It's A Mod Mod Mod Mod World (company sleeve)	8
79	I-Spy SEE 4	The Face Of Youth Today/I Know A Girl (keyhole company sleeve, plastic labels)	6
80	Stage One STAGE 2	My Mind Goes Round In Circles/Does Stephanie Know? (p/s)	7
82	Hi-Lo HI 001	No Time Tomorrow/Don't Cry To Me (p/s)	7

Chris SQUIRE

MINT VALUE £

82	Hi-Lo HI 002	Girl On A Train/Every Trick In The Book (p/s)	7
83	Hi-Lo HI 004	Jesamine/When I Try, I Lie (p/s)	10
84	Hi-Lo HI 005/SFC 2	The Young Idea/It's Getting Better (Squire Fan Club issue)	10
94	Detour DR 020	The Place I Used To Live/Make Love To You/Over You (p/s, 900 only, 50 on white vinyl)	10
83	Hi-Lo LO 01	HITS FROM 3,000 YEARS AGO (LP)	18
83	Hi-Lo LO 02	GET SMART (LP, with poster)	15
85	Hi-Lo LO 03	THE SINGLES ALBUM (LP)	15

(see also Anthony Meynell)

CHRIS SQUIRE
75	Atlantic K 50203	FISH OUT OF WATER (LP, with inner sleeve & poster)	20

(see also Yes)

JOHN SQUIRE
02	North Country NCLP 001	TIME CHANGES EVERYTHING (2-LP)	35
04	North Country NCLP 003	MARSHALL'S HOUSE (LP)	30

(see also Stone Roses, Seahorses)

SQUIRES
69	MCA MU 1060	Funky Bayswater/Games People Play	20

ROSEMARY SQUIRES
56	Decca F 10685	Band Of Gold/Where You Are	10
58	HMV POP 462	Happy Is The Bride/Give Me The Simple Life	8
58	HMV POP 541	There Goes My Lover/Please Be Kind	8
64	HMV POP 1288	Bluesette/Nothing's Changed	8
56	MGM MGM-EP 640	MY LOVE IS A WANDERER (EP)	40
60	HMV 7EG 8588	ROSEMARY (EP)	40
63	HMV CLP 1669	EVERYTHINGS COMING UP ROSY (LP, mono)	400
63	HMV CSD 1508	EVERYTHINGS COMING UP ROSY (LP, stereo)	600
65	HMV CLP 1832	SOMETHING TO REMEMBER ME BY (LP, mono)	80
65	HMV CSD 1586	SOMETHING TO REMEMBER ME BY (LP, stereo)	120

S.R.C.
69	Capitol CL 15576	Black Sheep/Morning Mood	35
69	Capitol (S)T 2991	S.R.C. (LP)	80
69	Capitol E-(S)T 134	MILESTONES (LP)	70
70	Capitol E-(S)T 273	TRAVELLER'S TALE (LP)	70

(See also Streamliners with Joanne)

ROY ST. JOHN
76	Caroline CA 2008	DECLARE IMMIGRATION (LP)	15

STAA MARX
79	Cherry Red CHERRY 4	Crazy Weekend/P.V.S. Pleasant Valley Sunday (p/s)	6

ASHBURY STABBINS DUO
76	Bead Records BEAD 4	FIRE WITHOUT STICKS (LP)	50

STACCATOS
61	Parlophone R 4828	Main Line/Topaz	15
68	NEMS 3003	Why Care About Today/Cry To Me	25
68	Fontana TF 966	Butchers And Bakers/Imitations Of Love	30

STACCATOS (U.S.)
66	Capitol CL 15478	Let's Run Away/Face To Face (With Love)	7
67	Capitol CL 15505	Half Past Midnight/Weatherman	7

CLARENCE STACEY
59	Pye International 7N 25025	Just Your Love/Lonely Guy	35
59	Pye International 7N 25025	Just Your Love/Lonely Guy (78)	20

GWEN STACEY
65	RCA RCX 7166	INTRODUCING GWEN STACEY (EP)	150

STACK OF HEARTS
86	SOH SOH 001	Danger Zone/Searching For A Spirit (no p/s)	25

BOB STACKIE
68	Collins Downbeat CR 009	Grab It Hold It Feel It (with Sir Collins Band)/DAN SIMMONDS: Way Out Sound	50

(see also Sir Collins [Band], Owen Gray)

STACKRIDGE
72	MCA MKS 5091	Slark/Purple Spaceships Over Yatton	12
71	MCA MDKS 8002	STACKRIDGE (LP, gatefold sleeve, pink/orange 'dogbone' label)	40
72	MCA MKPS 2025	FRIENDLINESS (LP, blue/black 'hexagon' label)	20
74	MCA MCG 3501	THE MAN IN THE BOWLER HAT (LP, gatefold sleeve)	15
74	Rocket PIGL 11	EXTRAVAGANZA (LP, gatefold label)	15
76	MCA MCF 2747	DO THE STANLEY (LP)	15
76	Rocket ROLL 3	MR. MICK (LP)	15

STACKWADDY
70	Dandelion S 5119	Roadrunner/Kentucky	12
72	Dandelion 2001 331	You Really Got Me/Willie The Pimp	10
71	Dandelion DAN 8003	STACKWADDY (LP, gatefold sleeve with lyric insert)	175
71	Dandelion DAN 8003	STACKWADDY (LP, gatefold sleeve with lyric insert, as K 49003)	40
72	Dandelion 2310 231	BUGGER OFF! (LP)	175

STADIUM DOGS
77	Audiogenic A 17	Easy Beat/Android Rocker/Media Withdrawal (die-cut p/s)	10

JO STAFFORD
53	Columbia SCM 5011	Star Of Hope/Somebody	10
53	Columbia SCM 5012	It Is No Secret/He Bought My Soul At Calvary	15
53	Columbia SCM 5013	You Belong To Me/Jambalaya (On The Bayou)	50
53	Columbia SCM 5026	Keep It A Secret/Once To Every Heart	15
53	Columbia SCM 5046	Something To Remember You By/Blue Moon	15
53	Columbia SCM 5064	September In The Rain/JO STAFFORD & FRANKIE LAINE: Chow, Willy	15

Jo STAFFORD & FRANKIE LAINE

MINT VALUE £

57	Philips JK 1003	On London Bridge/Perfect Love (jukebox issue)	25
50	Capitol LC 6500	AMERICAN FOLK SONGS (10")	20
51	Capitol LC 6515	KISS ME KATE (10", with Gordon MacRae)	15
53	Capitol LC 6575	CAPITOL PRESENTS JO STAFFORD (10")	15
54	Capitol LC 6635	CAPITOL PRESENTS JO STAFFORD, VOL. 2 (10")	15
54	Columbia 33S 1024	AS YOU DESIRE ME (10")	15
56	Philips BBR 8076	THE VOICE OF YOUR CHOICE (10")	20
61	Philips BBL 7428	JO + JAZZ (also stereo SBBL 595)	25

(see also Tommy Dorsey)

JO STAFFORD & FRANKIE LAINE
53	Columbia SCM 5014	Settin' The Woods On Fire/Piece A-Puddin'	20
55	Philips BBR 8075	FLOATIN' DOWN TO COTTON TOWN (10" LP)	20

TERRY STAFFORD
63	Stateside SS 225	Heartache On The Way/You Left Me Here To Cry	15
64	London HLU 9871	Suspicion/Judy	10
64	London HLU 9902	I'll Touch A Star/Playing With Fire	10
64	London HLU 9923	Follow The Rainbow/Are You A Fool Like Me	12
64	London RE-U 1436	SUSPICION (EP)	40
64	London HA-U 8200	SUSPICION (LP)	60

STAG MARKS BAND
81	Double Image SRTS 81 CUS 1223	Ain't No Fun On The Dole/Story Of My Life	20

STAGEFRIGHT
85	STN STN 1	Strangers In The Night/Heartless/Rock City (no p/s)	150

ROSS STAGG
74	Dawn DNS 1059	I'll Never Be A Star (But I Might)/Oh Captain	6

STAIFFI ET SES MUSTAFA'S
59	Pye Intl. 7N 25057	Mustafa Cha Cha Oriental/Zoubida Cha Cha Oriental	10

STAINED GLASS
74	Sweet Folk & C. SFA 019	OPEN ROAD (LP)	200

GREG STAINER
97	VIP 003	ORIGINAL FLAVA EP (12")	25

STAINS
79	Redball RR 020	Emotional Pills/Believer/Bored (p/s)	100

STAIRS
92	Imaginary MIRAGE 029	Weed Bus (12", unissued, test pressings only, proof p/s)	40

STAIRSTEPS
71	Buddah 2011 092	Stay Close To Me/I Made A Mistake	8
75	Dark Horse AMS 5505	From Us To You/Time (in USA p/s)	10
75	Dark Horse AMS 5505	From Us To You/Time	8
76	Dark Horse AMS 5507	Pasado/Throwin' Stones Atcha	10
71	Buddah 2359 021	STEP BY STEP BY STEP (LP)	20
71	Buddah 2365 015	STAY CLOSE TO ME (LP)	20
72	Buddah 2365 016	THE STAIRSTEPS (LP)	20
76	Dark Horse AMLH 22004	2ND RESSURECTION (LP)	20

(see also Five Stairsteps)

STAKKA AND SKYNET
00	Underfire UDFR 016	Knight Lore/Global Report (12")	10
01	Underfire UDFRLPS 04	CLOCKWORK SAMPLER EP: Decoy/Side Effects (Kemal and Rob Data Remix)/9000 series/Side Effects (Teebee Remix) (2 x 12", stickered, die-cut sleeve)	20
01	Underfire UDRFRLP 04	CLOCKWORK (LP, 5 discs)	40

STALAG 17
85	Mortarhate MORT 14	THE TRUTH WILL BE HEARD (12", split EP with TOXIC WASTE)	15

STALLION
75	Flyright FLY 45 003	Skinny Kid/Cobra	45

STAMFORD BRIDGE
70	Penny Farthing PEN 715	Chelsea/Ossie	12
71	Penny Farthing PELS 515	FIRST DAY OF YOUR LIFE (LP)	25

STAMINA
92	Wax FLX 2052-1	Onslaught (flexi, in card sleeve)	20

TERRY STAMP
75	A&M AMLH 68329	FAT STICKS (LP, with lyric insert)	100

(see also Third World War)

STAMPEDE
82	Polydor POSP 507	Days Of Wine And Roses/Photographs (p/s)	12
82	Polydor POSP 507	Photographs/Days Of Wine And Roses (A-side switched, no p/s)	30
82	Polydor POSPX 507	Days Of Wine And Roses/Movin' On/Photographs/Missing You (12", p/s)	20
83	Polydor POSP 592	The Other Side/The Runner (p/s)	10
82	Polydor ROCK 1	OFFICIAL BOOTLEG (LP)	15
83	Polydor POLS 1083	HURRICANE TOWN (LP)	15

STAMPEDERS
71	Stateside SS2197	Devil You/Giant In The Streets	8
72	Regal Zonophone RZ 3069	Johnny Lightning/Today's The Beginning Of The Rest Of Your Life	6
73	Regal Zonophone RZ 3079	Oh My Lady/No Destination	6
73	Regal Zonophone RZ3085	Ride In The Wind/Running Wild	20
72	Regal Zono. SLRZ 1032	THE STAMPEDERS (LP)	40
74	Regal Zono. SLRZ 1039	FROM THE FIRE (LP)	50

JOE STAMPLEY
73	Dot DOT 145	Soul Song/Not Too Long Ago	10

JEAN STANBACK
69	Deep Soul DS 9101	I Still Love You/If I Ever Needed Love	50

STANDELLS

MINT VALUE £

STANDELLS
- 64 Liberty LIB 55722 — I'll Go Crazy/Help Yourself 35
- 66 Capitol CL 15446 — Dirty Water/Rari 50
- 65 Liberty LBY 1243 — THE STANDELLS IN PERSON AT P.J.'s (LP) 60

STANDING OVATION
- 92 Kold Sweat KS126 — Shadows Of Mayhem (12") 15

STANDING FLAT
- 79 MUN 001 — FASCINATION EP (p/s) 15

JOHNNY STANDLEY
- 56 Capitol EAP 1020 — IT'S IN THE BOX (EP) 10

STANDS
- 04 Echo ECHLP 50 — ALL YEARS LEAVING (LP) 30
- 05 Echo ECHLP 60 — HORSE FABULOUS (LP) 30

PAUL STANLEY
- 79 Casablanca CAN 140 — Hold Me Touch Me/Goodbye (p/s, purple vinyl with mask & picture label, most with mispressed B-side: "Love In Chains") 25

(see also Kiss)

PETE STANLEY & ROGER KNOWLES
- 75 Xtra TRANS 1146 — PICKING AND SINGING (LP) 25

PETE STANLEY & WIZZ JONES
- 65 Columbia DB 7776 — The Ballad Of Hollis Brown/Riff Minor 20
- 66 Columbia SX 6083 — SIXTEEN TONS OF BLUEGRASS (LP) 60

(see also Wizz Jones)

STANLEY AND THE TURBINES
- 83 GG GGLP 0029 — BIG BAMBOO (LP) 15

VIV(IAN) STANSHALL
- 70 Liberty LBF 15309 — Labio-Dental Fricative/Paper Round (with Sean Head Show Band featuring Eric Clapton) 40
- 71 Fly BUG 4 — Suspicion (with Gargantuan Chums)/Blind Date (with biG GRunt) 15
- 74 Warner Bros K 16424 — Lakonga/Baba Tunde 20
- 76 Harvest HAR 5114 — Young Ones/Are You Havin' Any Fun/Question 15
- 80 Charisma CB 373 — Terry Keeps His Clips On/King Cripple (p/s) 6
- 74 Warner Bros K 56052 — MEN OPENING UMBRELLAS AHEAD (LP, with inner) 70
- 78 Charisma CAS 1139 — SIR HENRY AT RAWLINSON END (LP, soundtrack, with insert) 25
- 81 Charisma CAS 1153 — TEDDY BOYS DON'T KNIT (LP) 25
- 84 Demon Verbals VERB 1 — SIR HENRY AT NDIDDI'S KRAAL (LP) 25

(see also Bonzo Dog [Doo Dah] Band, Grimms)

STAPLE SINGERS
- 64 Riverside 106902 RIF — Hammer And Nails/Glory Land 10
- 67 Columbia DB 8292 — For What It's Worth/Are You Sure? 30
- 69 Soul City SC 117 — For What It's Worth/Are You Sure? (reissue) 18
- 62 Riverside REP 3220 — THE SAVIOUR IS BORN (EP) 15
- 63 Stateside SL 10015 — SWING LOW (LP) 30
- 63 Riverside RLP 3501 — HAMMER AND NAILS (LP) 25
- 65 Fontana 688 515 ZL — UNCLOUDY DAY (LP) 20
- 66 Columbia SX 6023 — FREEDOM HIGHWAY (LP) 20
- 69 Stax (S)XATS 1004 — SOUL FOLK IN ACTION (LP) 15
- 69 Stax SXATS 1018 — WE'LL GET OVER (LP) 15
- 73 Stax 2325 103 — BE WHAT YOU ARE (LP) 20
- 80 Stax STM 7009 — BRAND NEW DAY (LP) 15

STUART A STAPLES
- 05 Beggars Banquet BBQLP 242 — LUCKY DOG RECORDINGS (LP) 40

(see also Asphalt RIbbons, Tindersticks)

CYRIL STAPLETON & HIS ORCHESTRA
- 55 Decca F 10456 — Tango Mambo/Mexican Madness 8
- 55 Decca F 10470 — Fanfare Boogie/Time After Time 6
- 55 Decca F 10488 — Elephant Tango/Gabrielle 6
- 55 Decca F 10559 — Blue Star (The "Medic" Theme) (with Julie Dawn)/Honey Babe (with Gordon Langhorn).. 10
- 56 Decca F 10703 — The Italian Theme/Come Next Spring 6
- 56 Decca F 10735 — The Happy Whistler (with Desmond Lane)/Tiger Tango 6
- 56 Decca F 10793 — Highway Patrol/Maids Of Madrid 6
- 57 Decca F 10912 — Forgotten Dreams/It's Not For Me To Say 7
- 62 Decca F 11443 — Afrikaan Beat/My Sad Girl 6
- 69 Pye 7N 17807 — Department S (Theme)/W. Somerset Maugham TV Theme (in p/s) 10

(see also Gordon Langhorn, Desmond Lane)

JULIE STAPLETON
- 91 V4Visions VIS 0612T — Wheres Your Love Gone (Remix)/(New York Mix)/Just Dreaming (12", p/s) 15

STEVEN STAPLETON & DAVID TIBET
- 91 United Dairies UD 037 — THE SADNESS OF THINGS/THE GRAVE AND BEAUTIFUL NAME OF SADNESS (LP, one side each) 35

(see also Current 93, Nurse With Wound, Tibet & Stapleton)

STA-PREST
- 80 Avatar AAA 103 — Schooldays/Tomorrow (p/s) 75

STAR
- 73 Bradley BRAD 315 — Children Of the Sun/Your Day Will Come 12

STAR SPANGLES
- 02 Capitol R 6593 — Which Of The Two Of Us Is Gonna Burn This House Down/Stain Glass Shoes (p/s) 10

STAR WITH PETER COLLINS
- 60s SRT/Custom 10 — Give It Up/Wake Up 10

STARBOUND
- 77 Star Bound SB 01 — CHANGES (LP) 20

STARBUCK

MINT VALUE £

STARBUCK
73	RCA RCA 2350	Wouldn't You Like It/Manana	8
73	Bradleys BRAD 312	Do You Like Boys?/You Never Wanna Rock 'N' Roll	15
74	Bradleys BRAD 7411	Heart Throb/Ricochet	8

(see also Mandrake Paddle Steamer, Shambles)

STARCROST
19	Jazzman JMANLP 114	STARCROST (LP)	20

STARFIGHTERS
80	Motor City MCR 105	I'm Falling/Heaven And Hell (in p/s)	40
80	Motor City MCR 105	I'm Falling/Heaven And Hell	7
81	Jive JIV 003	Alley Cat Blues/Don't Touch Me (p/s)	7
81	Jive JIVET 003	Alley Cat Blues/Don't Touch Me (12", p/s)	15
81	Jive JIVET 6	Power Crazy/I Want You (p/s)	6
81	Jive HOP 200	STARFIGHTERS (LP, with inner)	22

STARGARD
95	Noid ROR 1	Wear It Out (Re-Edit)/EL COCO: Commotion (Re-Edit Version 1)/Version 2) (12")	12

STARGAZERS
54	Decca F 10213	I See The Moon/Eh Cumpari	25
54	Decca F 10259	The Happy Wanderer/Till We Two Are One	15
54	Decca F 10379	365 Kisses/I Need You Now	6
54	Decca F 10412	Rose Of The Wildwood/Come The Morning	6
55	Decca F 10437	Somebody/(My Baby Don't Love Me) No More (& Sonny Farrar Banjo Band)	10
55	Decca F 10523	The Crazy Otto Rag/Hey, Mr. Banjo	10
55	Decca F 10594	Close The Door/I've Got Four Big Brothers	12
55	Decca F 10626	Twenty Tiny Fingers/An Old Beer Bottle	10
56	Decca F 10696	Zambesi/When The Swallows Say Goodbye	10
56	Decca F 10731	Hot Diggity (Dog Ziggity Boom)/Rockin' And Rollin'	10
56	Decca F 10775	She Loves To Rock/John Jacob Jingleheimer Smith	10
60	Palette PG 9003	Three Beautiful Words/Manhattan Spiritual	6
56	Decca DFE 6341	THE STARGAZERS (EP)	10
56	Decca DFE 6362	ROCKIN' AND ROLLIN' (EP)	10
54	Decca LF 1186	PRESENTING THE STARGAZERS (10" LP)	20
59	Decca LK 4309	SOUTH OF THE BORDER (LP)	20

(see also Roy Smith & Stargazers, Lita Roza, Dickie Valentine)

STARJETS
78	Epic S EPC 6902	Here She Comes Again/Watch Out	8
79	Epic S EPC 6968/7123	It Really Doesn't Matter/Schooldays//Run With The Pack/Watch Out (double pack, die-cut sleeves, promo only)	15
79	Epic S EPC 7417	Ten Years/One More Word (Manchester gig issue, stamped white labels)	12
79	Epic S EPC 7986	Schooldays/What A Life (p/s)	6
79	Epic EPC 83534	GOD BLESS STARJETS (LP)	15

STARLAND VOCAL GROUP
76	RCA RCA 2716	Afternoon Delight/Starland (as Starland Vocal Band)	6

STARLITES
73	Downtown DT 502	You're A Wanted Man/G.G. ALL STARS: Back To Dubwise	7
74	Big Shot BI 629	Mama Dee Part One/Mama Dee Part Two	8
75	Bullet BU 554	Healing In The Barnyard/G.G. ALL STARS: Version	6
68	Philips BF 1725	Good Morning Mr Milkman/Don't Break My Heart Again	12

(see also Bellfield)

CHUKKI STARR
98	Ariwa AWM 002	The Almighty One/MAD PROFESSOR: Version	10
98	Saxon SAX 064	Mark A De Beast/(Version)//Youth Dem Anthem/Youth Dem Anthem (Mix 2) (12")	25
98	Ariwa ARI 147	GHETTO YOUTHS (LP)	20

CINDY STARR
68	Columbia Blue Beat DB 107	Pain Of Love/Hippy Ska (as Cindy Starr & Rude Boys)	20
68	Columbia Blue Beat DB 110	The Way I Do/Sad Movies (Make Me Cry) (as Cindy Starr & Mopeds)	15

(see also Mopeds, Teardrops)

EDWIN STARR
66	Polydor BM 56702	Stop Her On Sight (S.O.S.)/I Have Faith In You (demo)	500
66	Polydor BM 56702	Stop Her On Sight (S.O.S.)/I Have Faith In You	25
66	Polydor BM 56717	Headline News/Harlem	20
67	Polydor BM 56726	It's My Turn Now/Girls Are Getting Prettier	25
68	Polydor BM 56753	Stop Her On Sight (S.O.S.)/Headline News (reissue)	10
67	Tamla Motown TMG 630	I Want My Baby Back/Gonna Keep On Tryin' Till I Win	30
67	Tamla Motown TMG 630	I Want My Baby Back/Gonna Keep On Tryin' Till I Win (DJ copy)	50
68	Tamla Motown TMG 646	I Am The Man For You Baby/My Weakness Is You	30
68	Tamla Motown TMG 646	I Am The Man For You Baby/My Weakness Is You (DJ copy)	90
68	Tamla Motown TMG 672	25 Miles/Mighty Good Lovin'	12
68	Tamla Motown TMG 672	25 Miles/Mighty Good Lovin' (DJ copy)	45
69	Tamla Motown TMG 692	Way Over There/If My Heart Could Tell The Story	20
69	Tamla Motown TMG 692	Way Over There/If My Heart Could Tell The Story (DJ copy)	50
69	Tamla Motown TMG 720	Oh How Happy/O, O, O, Baby (demos only, unissued, with Blinky)	375
70	Tamla Motown TMG 725	Time/Running Back And Forth	20
70	Tamla Motown TMG 754	War/He Who Picks A Rose	7
71	Tamla Motown TMG 764	Stop The War Now!/Gonna Keep On Tryin' Till I Win	8
71	Tamla Motown TMG 790	Agent Double 0 Soul/Back Street	12
71	Tamla Motown TMG 790	Agent Double 0 Soul/Back Street (DJ copy)	40
72	Tamla Motown TMG 810	Funky Music Sho' Nuff Turns Me On/Cloud Nine	8
73	Tamla Motown TMG 875	You've Got My Soul On Fire/Love The Lonely People's Prayer	20
73	Tamla Motown TMG 930	Ain't It Hell Up In Harlem/Who's Right Or Wrong	8

Frank STARR

MINT VALUE £

75	Bradleys BRAD 7520	Stay With Me/I'll Never Forget You	15
75	Bradleys BRAD 7531	Pain/Party	10
76	GTO GT 65	Accident/Eavesdropper	8
70s	Tamla Motown TMG 905	Stop Her On Sight/Headline News (reissue)	6
70s	Tamla Motown TMG 1028	Time/Running Back And Forth (reissue)	10
69	Tamla Motown STML 11094	SOUL MASTER (LP, mono)	35
69	Tamla Motown STML 11094	SOUL MASTER (LP, stereo)	40
69	Tamla Motown TML 11115	25 MILES (LP, mono)	30
69	Tamla Motown STML 11115	25 MILES (LP, stereo)	25
70	Tamla Motown (S)TML 11131	JUST WE TWO (LP, as Edwin Starr & Blinky)	25
70	Tamla Motown STML 11171	WAR AND PEACE (LP)	20
72	Tamla Motown STML 11199	INVOLVED (LP)	20
72	Tamla Motown STML 11209	THE HITS OF EDWIN STARR (LP)	15
74	Tamla Motown STML 11260	HELL UP IN HARLEM (LP, soundtrack)	15

(see also Blinky & Edwin Starr, Holidays)

FRANK STARR

62	London HLU 9545	Little Bitty Feeling/Lost In A Dream	12

FREDDIE STARR & MIDNIGHTERS

63	Decca F 11663	Who Told You?/Peter Gunn Locomotion	20
63	Decca F 11786	It's Shaking Time/Baby Blue	20
64	Decca F 12009	Never Cry On Someone's Shoulder/Just Keep On Dreaming	40

(see also Howie Casey & Seniors)

JIMMY STARR

58	London HL 8731	It's Only Make Believe/Ooh Crazy	30

KAY STARR

54	Capitol CL 14151	Am I A Toy Or A Treasure?/Fortune In Dreams	20
54	Capitol CL 14167	Fool, Fool, Fool/Allez-Vous En	20
55	HMV 7M 300	If Anyone Finds This, I Love You/Turn Right	0
55	HMV 7M 307	Foolishly Yours/For Better Or Worse	10
55	HMV 7M 315	Where, What Or When?/Good And Lonesome	10
56	HMV 7M 371	Rock And Roll Waltz/I've Changed My Mind 1,000 Times	20
56	HMV 7M 420	Second Fiddle/Love Ain't Right	10
57	HMV POP 345	A Little Loneliness/Touch And Go	8
57	HMV POP 357	Jamie Boy/The Things I Never Had	8
58	RCA RCA 1065	Stroll Me/Rockin' Chair	6
60	Capitol CL 15105	Riders In The Sky/Night Train	7
60	Capitol CL 15137	Wheel Of Fortune/If You Love Me (Really Love Me)	12
53	Capitol LC 6574	CAPITOL PRESENTS KAY STARR (10")	25
54	Capitol LC 6630	THE KAY STARR STYLE (10")	20
56	Capitol LC 6835	THE HITS OF KAY STARR (10")	20
57	Capitol T 580	IN A BLUE MOOD	20
57	London HA-U 2039	SWINGING WITH THE STARR	20
58	RCA RD 27056	BLUE STARR	20

LUCILLE STARR

64	London HL 9900	The French Song/Sit Down And Write A Letter To Me	12

LUCKY STARR

62	Parlophone R 4963	I've Been Everywhere/Wrong	7

MAXINE STARR

63	London HLU 9712	The Wishing Star/Sailor Boy	8

RANDY STARR

57	London HL 8443	After School/Heaven High (Man So Low)	30
58	Felsted AF 106	Pink Lemonade/Count On Me	15
60	Top Rank JAR 264	Workin' On The Santa Fe/You're Growing Up	7

RINGO STARR

71	Apple R 5898	It Don't Come Easy/Early 1970 (p/s, B-side with Ringo or George Harrison production credit)	6
72	Apple R 5944	Back Off Boogaloo/Blindman (p/s, blue label)	6
73	Apple R 5992	Photograph/Down And Out (p/s)	6
75	Apple R 6004	Snookeroo/Oo-wee (stock EMI, not Apple sleeve)	12
76	Apple R 6011	Oh My My/No No Song (not in die-cut apple sleeve)	20
76	Polydor 2001 694	A Dose Of Rock 'N' Roll/Cryin'	20
76	Polydor 2001 695	You Don't Know Me At All/Cryin' (unissued in U.K., Europe only)	0
76	Polydor 2001 699	Hey Baby/Lady Gaye	15
77	Polydor 2001 734	Drowning In The Sea Of Love/Just A Dream	50
78	Polydor 2001 782	Lipstick Traces/Old Time Relovin' (unissued in U.K., Europe only)	0
78	Polydor 2001 795	Tonight/Heart On My Sleeve	120
72	R.O.R. ROR 2001	Steel (1-sided promo-only interview disc for 'Ringo Or Robin' reception at Liberty's department store; available for 1 week only, p/s)	1000
74	Parlophone PSR 374	Interview By Bob Mercer With Ringo For The Salesmen and Uxbridge Road/Only You (promo only)	500
70s	Apple R 5944	Back Off Boogaloo/Blindman (green apple label)	150
84	Apple G45 13	It Don't Come Easy/Back Off Boogaloo (P/s EMI Golden 45s series)	20
70	Apple PCS 7101	SENTIMENTAL JOURNEY (LP)	30
70	Apple TD-PCS 7101	SENTIMENTAL JOURNEY (reel-to-reel tape, jewel case)	20
70	Parlophone PPCS 7101	SENTIMENTAL JOURNEY (LP, export edition, black/silver label, 'Parlophone' and 'EMI' boxed logos)	250
70	Apple PAS 10002	BEAUCOUPS OF BLUES (LP, gatefold sleeve)	40
73	Apple PCTC 252	RINGO (LP, gatefold with 12" x 12" booklet)	15
74	Apple PCS 7168	GOODNIGHT VIENNA (LP, with inner)	15
74	Apple PCS 7170	BLAST FROM YOUR PAST (LP, with inner)	15

STELLA STARR

			MINT VALUE £
76	Polydor 2302-040	ROTOGRAVURE (LP, gatefold with inner)	15
78	Polydor 2310-599B	BAD BOY (LP, with inner)	15
78	Polydor 2480 429	SCOUSE THE MOUSE (LP, with Adam Faith, Donald Pleasance etc.; with stickered sleeve & printed [not photocopied] competition insert)	100
78	Polydor 2480 429	SCOUSE THE MOUSE (LP, with Adam Faith, Donald Pleasance etc.; without stickered sleeve & printed [not photocopied] competition insert)	50
90	EMI EMS 1375	RINGO STARR AND HIS ALL STARR BAND (LP)	35

(see also Beatles, Harry Nilsson, Billy Connolly & Chris Tummings, Traveling Wilburys)

STELLA STARR
67	Piccadilly 7N 35366	Bring Him Back/Say It	50
67	Piccadilly 7N 35366	Bring Him Back/Say It (DJ copy)	80

TONY STARR
64	Decca F 11847	I'll Take A Rocket To The Moon/Next Train Leaving	60

STARR BOUNDS
75	Horse HOSS 95	Heavenly (Parts 1 & 2)	8

(see also Starbound)

STARRY EYED
76	CBS 4805	Saturday/Believe	6

STARRY EYED & LAUGHING
74	CBS 80450	STARRY EYED & LAUGHING (LP)	15

STARSAILOR
01	Chrysalis 7243 535350 1 8	LOVE IS HERE (LP)	30

STARSHIP
77	Scratch SCH 01	Vampire For Your Love/You Can Dance/Hey Girl/Never Thought I'd See The Day	15

STARSHIP ORCHESTRA
80	CBS 84558	CELESTIAL SKY (LP)	20

STARS OF HEAVEN
85	Hotwire HWS 853	Clothes Of Pride/All About You (beige or black label, with p/s)	8
85	Hotwire HWS 853	Clothes Of Pride/All About You (beige or black label)	6

STARVATION ARMY
83	Linden Sounds LS004	Stranger In My Room/Walrus Is Dead (no p/s)	30

STASIS
92	B12 B1211	Point Of No Return (12", 300 only on silver vinyl)	60
93	B12 B1211	Point Of No Return (12")	40
93	Likemind 01	Likemind 01 (12", 3 Nuron tracks on B-side) (12")	80
93	Peacefrog PF 013	Circuit Funk (12")	35
93	Time Is Right TIT 005	Disco 4000 (Witness To The Future)/So-Lar/Vannannans Answer (Feat. Nuron) (12")	60
94	Peacefrog PF 028	INSPIRATION (2-LP)	50
96	Peacefrog PF 046	FROMTHEOLDTOTHENEW (2-LP)	35

(see also Nuron)

STATEN ISLAND FERRY
69	Major Minor MM 643	Candy Bar/Charlie Chan	20

STATE OF GRACE
81	Flamingo FM 18	Walking Rhythm/Version	8
83	PRT 12P266	Touching The Times/Instrumental Mix (12")	60

STATE OF MICKEY & TOMMY
67	Mercury MF 996	With Love From One To Five/I Know What I Will Do	150
67	Mercury MF 1009	Frisco Bay/Nobody Knows Where You've Been	150

(see also Spooky Tooth, Nero & Gladiators)

STATESMEN
63	Fontana TF 432	I've Just Fallen In Love/It's All Happening	8
63	Decca F11687	Look Around/I'm Wondering	8
63	Studio Republic	FIVE PLUS ONE (LP, private pressing)	100

STATE TROOPER
85	Neat 5212	SHE GOT THE LOOK (12" EP)	10

STATIC (1)
67	Page One POF 039	When You Went Away/Let Me Tell You	7

STATIC (2)
81	Eeyo EEYO 1	Voice On The Line/Stealin' (no p/s, 1,000 only)	15

(see also White Lightning)

(THE) STATICS
80	Mercury MER 41	Turn The Radio On/Over Now (as Static)	20
81	Carrere CAR 186	Turn The Radio On/Last Night In Chinatown	6

STATION SKIFFLE GROUP
58	Esquire EP 161	STATION SKIFFLE GROUP (EP)	50

(see also Jimmy Miller)

STATION 360
84	SRT STA 360	Optimist/Stars	30

STATISTICS
79	Tyger TYG 4	Dumb/Home Movies (p/s)	8

STATLER BROTHERS
65	CBS 201976	Flowers On The Wall/Billy Christian	8
66	CBS BPG 62713	FLOWERS ON THE WALL (LP)	15

(see also Johnny Cash)

CANDI STATON
69	Capitol CL 15601	I'd Rather Be An Old Man's Sweetheart/For You	10
69	Capitol CL 15620	Heart On A String/I'm Just A Prisoner	10
70	Capitol CL 15646	Sweet Feeling/Evidence	8
70	Capitol CL 15620	I'm Just A Prisoner/Heart On A String	6
70	Capitol CL 15658	Stand By Your Man/How Can I Put Out The Flame (When You Keep The Fire Burning)	8
75	United Artists UP 35823	Love Chain/I'm Gonna Hold On	6

Dakota STATON

MINT VALUE £

76	Warner Bros. SAM 60	Young Hearts Run Free/I Know (12" promo only)	200
70	Capitol ST 21631	I'M JUST A PRISONER (LP)	80
76	Warner Bros. K56259	YOUNG HEARTS RUN FREE (LP)	15

DAKOTA STATON

55	Capitol CL 14314	Don't Leave Me Now/A Little You	12
55	Capitol CL 14339	I Never Dreamt/Abracadabra	12
58	Capitol CL 14931	A Foggy Day/My Funny Valentine	7

STATUES

| 60 | London HLG 9192 | Blue Velvet/Keep The Hall Burning | 45 |

STATUS QUO

SINGLES : PYE SINGLES

68	Pye 7N 17449	Pictures Of Matchstick Men/Gentleman Joe's Sidewalk Café (75c Minimum)(blue label, full B-side title, push-out centre)	10
68	Pye 7N 17449	Pictures Of Matchstick Men/Gentleman Joe's Sidewalk Café (75c Minimum)(blue label, full B-side title, solid centre)	12
68	Pye 7N 17449	Pictures Of Matchstick Men/Gentleman Joe's Sidewalk Café (blue label, shortened B-side title, push-out centre)	10
68	Pye 7N 17449	Pictures Of Matchstick Men/Gentleman Joe's Sidewalk Café (blue label, shortened B-side title, push-out centre)	12
68	Pye 7N 17497	Black Veils Of Melancholy/To Be Free (1st pressing, plain black text on blue label, push-out centre)	35
68	Pye 7N 17497	Black Veils Of Melancholy/To Be Free (1st pressing, plain black text on blue label, solid centre)	50
68	Pye 7N 17497	Black Veils Of Melancholy/To Be Free (2nd pressing, blue label with black Pye banner, push-out centre)	30
68	Pye 7N 17581	Ice In The Sun/When My Mind Is Not Live (blue label, push-out centre)	8
68	Pye 7N 17581	Ice In The Sun/When My Mind Is Not Live (blue label, solid centre)	12
68	Pye 7N 17650	Technicolor Dreams/Paradise Flat	800
69	Pye 7N 17665	Make Me Stay A Bit Longer/Aunt Nellie (blue label, push-out centre)	25
69	Pye 7N 17665	Make Me Stay A Bit Longer/Aunt Nellie (blue label, solid centre)	40
69	Pye 7N 17728	Are You Growing Tired Of My Love/So Ends Another Life (blue label, push-out centre)	25
69	Pye 7N 17728	Are You Growing Tired Of My Love/So Ends Another Life (blue label, solid centre)	35
69	Pye 7N 17825	The Price Of Love/Little Miss Nothing (blue label push-out centre)	30
69	Pye 7N 17825	The Price Of Love/Little Miss Nothing (blue label solid centre)	50
70	Pye 7N 17907	Down The Dustpipe/Face Without A Soul (blue label, push-out centre))	6
70	Pye 7N 17907	Down The Dustpipe/Face Without A Soul (blue label, solid centre)	8
70	Pye 7N 17998	In My Chair/Gerdundula (blue label, push-out centre with p/s)	50
70	Pye 7N 17998	In My Chair/Gerdundula (blue label solid centre, no p/s)	20
71	Pye 7N 45077	Tune To The Music/Good Thinking (blue label, push-out centre)	20
71	Pye 7N 45077	Tune To The Music/Good Thinking (blue label, solid centre)	50
73	Pye 7N 45229	Mean Girl/Everything (blue labels, solid centre)	10
73	Pye 7N 45253	Gerdundula/Lakky Lady (red/pink label, with black text, solid centre)	15
73	Pye 7N 45253	Gerdundula/Lakky Lady (red/pink label, with silver text, solid centre)	15
77	Pye BD 103	Down The Dustpipe/Mean Girl/In My Chair/Gerdundula (12", generic sleeve, reissued on PRT)	10
79	Pye Flashbacks FBS 2	Pictures Of Matchstick Men/Down The Dustpipe (yellow vinyl, p/s)	6
79	Pye QUO 1/SFI 434	In My Chair (flexi, concert freebie, with Record Mirror Quo special)	10
78	Pye 7N 46096	Mean Girl/In My Chair (red/pink label, push-out centre or solid centre)	6

SINGLES : VERTIGO SINGLES

72	Vertigo 6059 071	Paper Plane/Softer Ride (swirl label, solid centre)	6
74	Vertigo 6059 101	Break The Rules/Lonely Night (mispressed, B-side labels on both sides)	7
76	Vertigo 6059 153	Wild Side Of Life/All Through The Night (brown plastic labels)	6
77	Vertigo 6059 184	Rockin' All Over The World/Ring Of A Change (p/s, with small poster)	15
82	Vertigo QUO 9	Jealousy/Calling The Shots (unreleased in U.K./ Irish promos only)	150
83	Vertigo QUO 1414	Marguerita Time/Resurrection//Caroline/Joanne (double pack, stickered gatefold p/s)	10
84	Vertigo QUO 15	Too Close To The Ground/I Wonder Why (release cancelled)	0
85	Vertigo QUO 17	Naughty Girl (actually "Dreamin' ") (unreleased)	0
86	Vertigo QUOPD 18	Rollin' Home/Lonely (uncut picture disc)	175
86	Vertigo QUODP 19	Red Sky/Don't Give It Up//Rockin' All Over The World/Whatever You Want (double pack, gatefold p/s)	6
86	Vertigo QUOPB 191	Red Sky/Don't Give It Up/The Milton Keynes Medley (12", 'Wembley Souvenir Pack', poster p/s)	15
86	Vertigo QUO 20	In The Army Now/Heartburn (stickered p/s, with sew-on patch, shrinkwrapped)	10
86	Vertigo QUOPD 20	In The Army Now/Heartburn (picture disc)	15
86	Vertigo QUODP 20	In The Army Now/Heartburn//Marguerita Time/What You're Proposing (double pack, gatefold p/s)	6
86	Vertigo QUOP 21	Dreamin'/Long-Legged Girls (p/s, with foldout poster/calendar)	6
88	Vertigo QUO 2512	Burning Bridges (On And Off And On Again) (Extended Version)/Whatever You Want/Marguerita Time (12", mispressing also including 7" edit)	10
89	Vertigo 080 630-2	Burning Bridges (On And Off And On Again) (Extended Version)/Whatever You Want (Extended Version)/Marguerita Time/Who Gets The Love?/Burning Bridges (Video) (CD Video)	0
90	Vertigo QUO 2812	The Anniversary Waltz/The Power Of Rock/Perfect Remedy (12", p/s, mispress, B-side plays "Little Lady" (live) & exclusive "Paper Plane" re-recording)	45
90	Vertigo QUO 2812	The Anniversary Waltz/The Power Of Rock/Perfect Remedy (12", p/s, mispress, A-side plays "The Power Of Rock [Full Version]")	45
91	Vertigo QUO 31	Fakin' The Blues (Edit)/Heavy Daze (p/s, swirl label, release cancelled, approximately 25 copies only)	1500
91	Vertigo QUO 3112	Fakin' The Blues (Edit)/Fakin' The Blues (Album Version)/Heavy Daze/Better Times (12", swirl label, p/s, cancelled, approx. 25 copies only)	1500
91	Vertigo QUOCD 31	Fakin' The Blues (Edit)/Fakin' The Blues (Album Version)/Heavy Daze/Better Times (CD, unissued, 2,000 later sent out by fan club, no inlay)	40
91	Vertigo STATUS 30	Can't Give You More/(Radio Edit)/Dead In The Water (swirl label, stickered stock p/s)	80
92	Vertigo QUO 3212	Rock 'Til You Drop/Medley/Forty-Five Hundred Times (12", p/s, mispressing, omits	15

STATUS QUO

MINT VALUE £

92	Vertigo QUOCD 32	"Forty-Five Hundred Times").. Rock 'Til You Drop/Medley/Forty-Five Hundred Times (CD in no'd guitar-shaped case).....	12

SINGLES : OTHER SINGLES

75	Lyntone LYN 3154/5	Down Down/Break The Rules (Smiths Crisps flexidisc, with 'Smiths' p/s)..........................	15
80s	Lyntone QUO 1-4	Interview picture discs (4-single pack)...	20
99	From The Makers Of... FTMOCD1	FAKIN' THE BLUES (MILLENNIUM EDITION) (CD, fanclub mail order-only edition, hand-no'd exclusive p/s, contains unreleased Vertigo CD [QUOCD 31])	50

ALBUMS : LPS

68	Pye NPL 18220	PICTURESQUE MATCHSTICKABLE MESSAGES (mono)	200
68	Pye NSPL 18220	PICTURESQUE MATCHSTICKABLE MESSAGES (stereo)	175
69	Pye NPL 18301	SPARE PARTS (blue label, mono)..	175
69	Pye NSPL 18301	SPARE PARTS (blue label, stereo)...	150
69	Marble Arch MAL 1193	STATUS QUO-TATIONS (mono)	30
69	Marble Arch MAL(S) 1193	STATUS QUO-TATIONS (stereo, most copies exported)	50
70	Pye NSPL 18344	MA KELLY'S GREASY SPOON (1st pressing, blue labels with poster).........................	150
70	Pye NSPL 18344	MA KELLY'S GREASY SPOON (1st pressing, blue labels, no poster)...........................	30
70	Pye NSPL 18344	MA KELLY'S GREASY SPOON (2nd pressing, blue labels with black banner on top of label)..	25
71	Pye NSPL 18371	DOG OF TWO HEAD (gatefold sleeve, blue labels)...	40
71	Pye NSLP 18371	DOG OF TWO HEAD (gatefold sleeve, repressing, turquoise labels)	20
71	Pye NSLP 18371	DOG OF TWO HEAD (gatefold sleeve, repressing, black & white labels)	30
72	Vertigo 6360 082	PILEDRIVER (swirl label, gatefold sleeve)	30
73	Vertigo 6360 098	HELLO! (spaceship label, with inner sleeve & poster)..	20
74	Vertigo 9102 001	QUO (with poster/lyric sheet)	15
74	Record Club ACB 00217	QUO (Audio Club of Britain Record Club' issue ACB 00217 on labels, spine and rear sleeve)	25
74	Vertigo ACB 00217/9102 001	QUO (hybrid issue with ACB 00217 on spine and 9102 001 on rear sleeve and labels)	30
79	Pye NPSL18607	JUST FOR THE RECORD (red vinyl)	15
79	Pye NSLP 18607	JUST FOR THE RECORD (repressing, black vinyl, black and white labels)	20
82	Phonogram PRO BX 1	FROM THE MAKERS OF... (3-LP, with inserts in round metal tin, some numbered)	20
83	Vertigo VERH 10	BACK TO BACK (in-store promo copies with poster insert)	15
85	PRT Flashbacks FBLP 8082	NANANA	15
87	PRT PYL 6020	PICTURESQUE MATCHSTICKABLE MESSAGES (LP, reissue)	20
87	PRT PYL 6024	QUOTATIONS VOLUME ONE - THE EARLY YEARS	15
87	PRT PYL 6025	QUOTATIONS VOLUME TWO - FLIPSIDES, ALTERNATIVES AND ODDITIES	18
88	PRT PYX 4007	FROM THE BEGINNING (picture disc)...	25
90	Essential! ESBLP 136	THE EARLY WORKS (5-LP box set with book)	30
91	Baktabak LINT 5003	INTROSPECTIVE (clear vinyl, 6 Pye-era tracks & interview)	30
91	Vertigo 51 341-1	ROCK 'TILL YOU DROP (swirl label)	25
92	Polydor 517 367-1	LIVE ALIVE QUO (with inner sleeve)...	40
94	Polydor 523 607-1	THIRSTY WORK (with inner sleeve)	100
04	Earmark EAR 42032	SPARE PARTS (180gm reissue, stickered PVC wallet sleeve)	40
04	Earmark EAR 42033	MA KELLY'S GREASY SPOON (180gm reissue stickered PVC wallet sleeve)	40
04	Earmark EAR 42046	PICTURESQUE MATCHSTICKABLE MESSAGES (LP, reissue, in stickered PVC wallet)	40
04	Earmark EAR 42035	DOG OF TWO HEADS (180gm reissue, stickered PVC wallet sleeve)	40
07	Fourth Chord QUOLP 001	IN SEARCH OF THE FOURTH CHORD (LP, gatefold sleeve).....................................	25
11	Fourth Chord QUOBS002	QUID PRO QUO (2-LP, gatefold, mail order only)	40
12	Music On Vinyl MOVLP 229	HELLO! (180gm reissue, lyrical insert, in stickered PVC sleeve)..................................	25
13	Fourth Chord QUOCD010	BULA QUO (box set, LP, 2-CD, 7-inch, poster, 5 postcards, flight ticket. Mail-order only) ...	50
13	Demon DEMREC 17	IN SEARCH OF THE FOURTH CHORD (180gm picture disc, numbered stickered PVC sleeve. 500 only, mail-oder only)...	25
13	Demon DEMREC 18	QUID PRO QUO (180gm picture disc, numbered stickered PVC wallet sleeve, Mail-order only)	25
14	Mercury 3739863	TOKYO QUO (gatefold, insert)	20

ALBUMS : CDS

01	From The Makers Of ... FTMOCD2	FTMO LIVE! NO.1 (fanclub mail-order only, soundchecks & interviews).......................	30

PROMOS : PROMO ONLY SINGLES

68	Pye 7N 17449	Pictures Of Matchstick Men/Gentleman Joe's Sidewalk Café (75c Minimum) ('A' label)....	60
68	Pye 7N 17497	Black Veils Of Melancholy/To Be Free ('A' label)...	70
68	Pye 7N 17581	Ice In The Sun/When My Mind Is Not Live ('A' label)	60
68	Pye 7N 17650	Technicolor Dreams/Paradise Flat('A' label)..	700
69	Pye 7N 17665	Make Me Stay A Bit Longer/Aunt Nellie ('A' label)	70
69	Pye 7N 17728	Are You Growing Tired Of My Love/So Ends Another Life ('A' label)...........................	70
69	Pye 7N 17825	The Price Of Love/Little Miss Nothing ('A' label)..	70
70	Pye 7N 17907	Down The Dustpipe/Face Without A Soul ('A' label)	60
70	Pye 7N 17998	In My Chair/Gerdundula ('A' label)	60
71	Pye 7N 45077	Tune To The Music/Good Thinking ('A' label)	60
72	Phonogram DJ 005	Roadhouse Blues/BLACK SABBATH: Children Of The Grave (100 copies only)	500
72	Vertigo 6059 071	Paper Plane/Softer Ride ('A' label)	45
73	Pye 7N 45229	Mean Girl/Everything ('A' label)	50
73	Pye 7N 45253	Gerdundula/Lakky Lady ('A' label)	40
75	Lyntone LYN 3154	Down Down (Smiths Crisps 1-sided gold flexidisc test pressing, plays Bye Bye Baby by Bay City Rollers)	25
75	Lyntone LYN 3155	Break The Rules (Smiths Crisps 1-sided gold flexidisc test pressing, plays Bye Bye Baby by Bay City Rollers)	25
79	Pye 7P 103	In My Chair/Gerdundula ('A' label)	20
81	Vertigo QUO JB 6	Rock 'N' Roll/Hold You Back (jukebox issue, B-side at 33rpm)	10
86	Vertigo QUODJ 2112	Dreamin' (Wet Mix)/Long-Legged Girls/The Quo Xmas Cake Mix (12")	15
88	Vertigo QUOLP 99	Ain't Complaining (12" promo, 1-sided)	30

STAVELY MAKEPEACE

MINT VALUE £

88	Vertigo QUODJ 2212	Ain't Complaining (Extended)/That's Alright/Lean Machine (12")...	10
88	Vertigo QUODJ 25	Burning Bridges (On & Off & On Again)/Burning Bridges (On & Off & On Again)...	12
90	Vertigo (no cat. no.)	The Power Of Rock (Album Version)/(Single Edit)/Perfect Remedy (12" white label)...	100
91	Vertigo QUO DJ 30	Can't Give You More/Dead In The Water (swirl label)...	20

PROMOS : PROMO ONLY ALBUMS & ALBUM SAMPLERS

82	Phonogram PRO BX 1	FROM THE MAKERS OF... (3-LP, 20 copies in bronze tin for in-house use)...	300
86	Vertigo MADDOX 18	IN THE ARMY NOW (LP, 4-track sampler, includes unreleased version of Dreamin')...	50
88	Vertigo QUOLP 99	AIN'T COMPLAINING (LP, 4-track one-sided sampler)...	25
88	Vertigo	AIN'T COMPLAINING (box set containing LP sampler [QUOLP 99], cassette, 1-track video, photo & press sheet)...	70
88	Music & Media MM 1221	INTERVIEW (LP, uncut test pressing for unreleased saw-shaped picture disc)...	50
89	Vertigo 842 077-9	LITTLE DREAMER (CD, card p/s, 4-track sampler for PERFECT REMEDY album)...	40
90	Phonogram (no cat. no.)	ROCKING ALL OVER THE YEARS SNIPPETS (cassette, titles inlay)...	20
90	Vertigo 846 797-2	ROCKING ALL OVER THE YEARS (CD, in Butlin's party pack containing Kiss Me Quo baseball cap, stick of Status Quo rock, and selection of party poppers, streamers, whistle, trumpet, silver Quo balloons & pack of condoms, all with "Anniversary Waltz" stickers)...	75
02	Sanctuary CMRCD 490	SWEDISH RADIO SESSIONS (CD-R, titles insert, commercial release cancelled)...	50

(see also Spectres, Traffic Jam, Rossi & Frost, Andy Bown, Partners In Crime, Rockers, John Du Cann, Manchester United Football Squad, Marietta, Stretch, Jimmy Sweep)

STAVELY MAKEPEACE

69	Pyramid PYR 6072	(I Want To Love You Like A) Mad Dog/Greasy Haired Woman...	8
70	Pyramid PYR 6082	Tarzan Harvey/Reggae Denny (unissued, test pressings exist)...	6
77	Unigram U6312	Baby Blue Eyes/Big Bad Baby Blonde...	8

(see also Lieutenant Pigeon, Shel Naylor)

STAVERTON BRIDGE

76	Saydisc SDL 266	STAVERTON BRIDGE (LP, with lyrics)...	30

STEAK CATS

93	April 10 Records TEN 1	The Steak Song/Dead Real Soon/Fluffy's Lament/My Name Is Miguel (12")...	12
96	April 10 Records TEN 4	Last Night In A Porn Stars Bed I Became A Man/From Behind (12" 200 only)...	15
97	April 10 LP1	THE RISE OF ROSCOE (LP)...	15

STEAM MACHINE

72	Capitol CL15746	You Make It Move/I Can't Help It...	8

STEAMHAMMER

69	CBS 4141	Junior's Wailing/Windmill...	25
69	CBS 4496	Autumn Song/Blues For Passing People...	18
71	Reflection HRS 9	Junior's Wailing/You'll Never Know...	12
68	CBS (S) 63611	STEAMHAMMER (LP)...	100
70	CBS (S) 63694	STEAMHAMMER MK. II (LP)...	100
70	B&C CAS 1024	MOUNTAINS (LP, stickered gatefold sleeve)...	50
70	Reflection REFL 1	STEAMHAMMER (LP, reissue, different sleeve)...	50
71	Reflection REFL 12	STEAMHAMMER MK. II (LP, reissue)...	40

(see also Armageddon, Rod Stewart)

STEAM-SHOVEL

68	Trojan/Big Bear TR 635	Rudi, The Red Nosed Reindeer/White Christmas...	7
68	Decca F 22863	Rudi, The Red Nosed Reindeer/White Christmas (export issue)...	12

(see also Locomotive)

STEEL

81	Neat NEAT 14	Rock Out/All Systems Go (p/s)...	10

STEEL AN' SKIN

79	Steel An Skin SS01	Reggae Is Here Again/Fire In Soweto/Afro Punk Reggae (Dub) (12", p/s)...	70
85	Cougar (no cat. no.)	STEEL AN' SKIN (LP)...	20

GARY STEEL SOUND

72	Zel-La JHEPM 131	Go Go Girl/I've Got A Feeling Coming On...	25

BETTE ANNE STEELE

55	Capitol CL 14315	Barricade/Give Me A Little Kiss Will Ya, Huh?...	8

DORIS STEELE

59	Oriole CB 1468	Why Must I?/Never Again...	6

JAN STEELE & JOHN CAGE

76	Obscure OBS 5	VOICES AND INSTRUMENTS (LP)...	20

SONDRA & JON STEELE

55	Parlophone MSP 6166	I'm Crazy With Love/Fill My Heart With Happiness...	8

TOMMY STEELE (& THE STEELMEN)

56	Decca F 10795	Rock With The Caveman/Rock Around The Town (with The Steelmen)...	25
56	Decca F 10808	Doomsday Rock/Elevator Rock...	30
56	Decca F 10819	Singing The Blues/Rebel Rock (with The Steelmen)...	20
57	Decca F 10849	Knee Deep In The Blues/Teenage Party (with The Steelmen)...	10
56	Decca DFE 6388	YOUNG LOVE (EP)...	10
56	Decca DFE 6389	SINGING THE BLUES (EP)...	10

(The above 2 EPs were originally issued with triangular centres; later round-centre reissues are worth two-thirds this value)

58	Decca DFE 6551	C'MON LET'S GO (EP)...	10
57	Decca LF 1287	THE TOMMY STEELE STAGE SHOW (10")...	15
57	Decca LF 1288	THE TOMMY STEELE STORY (10")...	15

STEELERS

70	Direction 58-4675	Get It From The Bottom/I'm Sorry...	10

STEELEYE SPAN

71	B&C CB 164	Rave On/Reels/Female Drummer (p/s)...	7
72	Pegasus PGS 6	JIGS AND REELS (maxi-single, with p/s)...	10
72	Pegasus PGS 6	JIGS AND REELS (maxi-single)...	6
70	RCA SF 8113	HARK! THE VILLAGE WAIT (LP, with lyric insert)...	40
71	B&C CAS 1029	PLEASE TO SEE THE KING (LP, in 'hessian' textured sleeve, insert)...	35

STEEL MILL

			MINT VALUE £
71	Pegasus PEG 9	TEN MAN MOP, OR MR. RESERVOIR BUTLER RIDES AGAIN (LP, gatefold sleeve, initially with 8-page booklet)	50
72	Chrysalis CHR 1008	BELOW THE SALT (LP, gatefold, green label)	18

(see also Maddy Prior, Tim Hart & Maddy Prior, Gay & Terry Woods, Ashley Hutchings, Fairport Convention, Martin Carthy, Bob Johnson & Pete Knight)

STEEL MILL

71	Penny Farthing PEN 770	Green Eyed God/Zang Will	15
72	Penny Farthing PEN 783	Get On The Line/Summer's Child	20
75	Penny Farthing PEN 894	Green Eyed God/Zang Will (reissue)	15
75	Penny Farthing PELS 549	GREEN EYED GOD (LP, reissue, green sleeve. Original released in Germany in 1972 in black sleeve)	750
11	Rise Above Relics RARLP 008	JEWELS OF THE FOREST (2-LP, 3 x 7" with booklet, 280 copies)	50
11	Rise Above Relics RARLP 008	JEWELS OF THE FOREST (2-LP, green, clear or blue vinyl, booklet - 300 copies of each)	30
11	Rise Above Relics RARLP 008	JEWELS OF THE FOREST (2-LP, with booklet)	20

STEEL PULSE

76	Concrete Jungle CJ 602	Kibudu Mansatta Abuku/Version	70
77	Anchor ANC 1046	Nyah Luv/Luv Nyah (p/s, copies on Tempus TEM 105 are worth 12)	7
78	Island IPR 2013	Ku Klux Klan/Bun Dem (12")	10
80	PSLP 321	STEEL PULSE DUB (12", white labels only)	50

STEELY DAN

73	Probe PRO 587	Reelin' In The Years/Only A Fool	7
74	Probe PRO 622	Rikki Don't Lose That Number/Any Major Dude Will Tell You (gatefold sleeve, 1974 'Spacemen' tour logo)	50
82	MCA MCAT 786	FM EP	25
85	MCA MCAT 852	Reelin' In The Years/Rikki Don't Lose That Number/Do It Again/Haitian Divorce (12", p/s)	20
73	Probe SPB 1062	CAN'T BUY A THRILL (LP, original, with 'pink' label)	25
77	ABC ABCL5225	AJA (LP, gatefold, inner)	15
82	MCA MCF 3165	GOLD (LP, with free EP [MSAMT 21])	20
03	Reprise 9362 48435 1	EVERYTHING MUST GO (LP)	100

(see also Donald Fagen)

WOUT STEENHUIS

70	Stereo2Stereo TWO 283	BIRD IN THE PARK (LP, features cover of Hum Dono)	25

STEEPLECHASE

71	Polydor 2489 001	LADY BRIGHT (LP)	15

(see also Dean Parrish)

STEERPIKE

68	(no label credit) ADM 417	STEERPIKE (LP, private pressing)	550

STEFAN

73	Stax 2025 153	Holy Cow/Take It Like It Comes	6

BILL STEGMEYER & HIS ORCHESTRA

54	London HL 8078	On The Waterfront (From The Film)/We Just Couldn't Say Good-Bye	20

LOU STEIN

57	London HLZ 8419	Almost Paradise/Soft Sands	20
58	Mercury 7MT 226	Who Slammed The Door/Got A Match?	8

STEINWAYS

85	Kent TOWN 106	You've Been Leading Me On/JOHNNY CASWELL: You Don't Love Me No More	20

MIKE STEIPHENSON

73	Pye 7N 25577	Rainbows/Dreams	15

STELLA

82	President PT 504	Si Tu Aimes Ma Musique/If You Do Like My Music (p/s)	7

STENCH

82	Sticky PEEL OFF 5	MORAL DEBAUCHERY: Raspberry Cripple/Nonces/Adoption	15

MALCOLM STENT

70s	Starline SWL 2002	GO AND PLAY UP YOUR OWN END (LP)	15

STEPASIDE

80	Gale GALELP 01	SIT DOWN AND RELAPSE (LP)	20

STEPHEN

74	Antic K 11513	Right On Running Man/Epitath	8

LEIGH STEPHENS

69	Philips SBL 7897	RED WEATHER (LP)	70
71	Charisma CAS 1040	AND A CAST OF THOUSANDS (LP)	40

(see also Blue Cheer)

STEPPENWOLF

68	RCA RCA 1679	Sookie Sookie/Take What You Need	15
68	RCA RCA 1735	Born To Be Wild/Everybody's Next One	15
68	Stateside-Dunhill SS 8003	Magic Carpet Ride/Sookie Sookie	15
69	Stateside-Dunhill SS 8013	Rock Me/Jupiter Child	7
69	Stateside-Dunhill SS 8017	Born To Be Wild/Everybody's Next One (reissue)	8
69	Stateside-Dunhill SS 8027	Magic Carpet Ride/Sookie Sookie (reissue)	6
70	Stateside-Dunhill SS 8035	Monster/Move Over	6
70	Stateside-Dunhill SS 8038	The Pusher/Your Wall's Too High	6
70	Stateside-Dunhill SS 8049	Hey Lawdy Mama/Twisted	6
70	Stateside-Dunhill SS 8056	Screaming Night Hog/Spiritual Fantasy	6
70	Probe PRO 510	Who Needs Ya/Earschplittenloudenboomer	6
71	Probe PRO 525	Snowblind Friend/Hippo Stomp	6
71	Probe PRO 534	Ride With Me/For Madmen Only	6
71	Probe PRO 544	For Ladies Only/Sparkle Eyes	6
74	CBS MUM 2679	Straight Shootin' Woman/Justice Don't Be Slow	6
75	CBS MUM 3147	Smokey Factory Blues/A Fool's Fantasy	6
75	CBS MUM 3470	Caroline (Are You Ready)/Angel Drawers	6

STEPPES

MINT VALUE £

68	RCA RD/SF 7974	STEPPENWOLF (LP, 1st pressing, mono, band name in blue)	150
68	RCA RD/SF 7974	STEPPENWOLF (LP, repressing, stereo)	80
68	Stateside SL 5003	STEPPENWOLF THE SECOND (LP, mono)	70
69	Stateside (S)SL 5003	STEPPENWOLF THE SECOND (LP, stereo)	40
69	Stateside SL 5011	AT YOUR BIRTHDAY PARTY (LP, mono)	40
69	Stateside(S)SL 5011	AT YOUR BIRTHDAY PARTY (LP, stereo)	35
69	Stateside (S)SL 5015	EARLY STEPPENWOLF (LP)	15
69	Stateside (S)SL 10276	CANDY (LP, soundtrack, 2 tracks by Steppenwolf, 1 track by Byrds)	30
70	Stateside-Dunhill SSL 5020	STEPPENWOLF (reissue)	15
70	Stateside-Dunhill SSL 5021	MONSTER (LP, gatefold sleeve)	18
70	Stateside-Dunhill SSL 5029	STEPPENWOLF 'LIVE' (LP, gatefold sleeve)	20
70	Probe SPBA 6254	STEPPENWOLF 7 (LP)	15
71	Probe SPBA 6260	FOR LADIES ONLY (LP)	15

(see also John Kay)

STEPPES

79	South Circular SGS 108	The Beat Drill/FIFTY FANTASTICS: God's Got Religion (p/s, white label)	10

(see also Fifty Fantastics, Disco Zombies)

STEPPING TALK

79	Eustone/Rough Trade TO1	Alice In Sunderland/Health And Safety/Common Problems/John Turtles (p/s, with stamped inner)	15

STEREOLAB

91	Duophonic DS 45-01	SUPER 45: The Light That Will Cease To Fail/Au Grand Jour/Brittle/Au Grand Jour! (10" EP, with insert, mail-order, sold at gigs and some record shops 40 with hand-painted p/s, in poly bag)	175
91	Duophonic DS 45-01	SUPER 45: The Light That Will Cease To Fail/Au Grand Jour/Brittle/Au Grand Jour! (10" EP, with insert, mail-order, sold at gigs and some record shops)	100
91	Duophonic DS 45-01	SUPER 45: The Light That Will Cease To Fail/Au Grand Jour/Brittle/Au Grand Jour! (25 test pressings, 10" cut into 12" discs)	175
91	Too Pure PURE 4	SUPER ELECTRIC: Super-Electric/High Expectation/The Way Will Be Opening/Contact (10" EP, with red and yellow sleeve, w/insert)	10
91	Duophonic DS 45-02	STUNNING DEBUT ALBUM: Doubt/Clanger (20 black test pressings withdrawn due to pressing fault/warping, different cut of both tracks)	100
91	Duophonic DS 45-02	STUNNING DEBUT ALBUM: Doubt/Clanger (p/s, mail-order, sold at gigs and some Record shops gatefold p/s with insert in poly bag; mulit coloured vinyl, unknown quantity but probably over 200)	150
91	Duophonic DS 45-02	STUNNING DEBUT ALBUM: Doubt/Clanger (p/s, mail-order, gigs and some record Shops, gatefold p/s with insert in poly bag; 985 copies on clear vinyl)	60
92	Duophonic DS 45-04	Harmonium/Farfisa (p/s, mail-order, gigs and some record shops 1,306 copies on transparent amber vinyl, with insert & fluorescent sticker)	35
93	Duophonic DS45-05/06	SHIMMIES IN SUPER 8 (2 x 7", green and white vinyl, foldout sleeve with inserts)	25
92	Too Pure PURE 14	Low Fi/Varoom!/Laissez-Faire/Elektro (He Held The World In His Iron Grip) (10", p/s, clear vinyl, 2,000 only, numbered)	25
93	Sub Pop SP107/283	Lo Boob Oscillator/Tempter (clear vinyl, p/s with US address on back cover)	6
93	Sub Pop SP107/283	Lo Boob Oscillator/Tempter (clear vinyl, p/s with German address on back cover)	6
93	Spacewatch FLX 2107	Ronco Symphony (demo)/Seeming And The Meaning (demo)/SUBMARINER: Lyricist Downer (clear vinyl flexi comes with Spacewatch fanzine in sleeve)	12
93	Duophonic D-UHF-D 01	Jenny Ondioline/Fruition/Golden Ball/French Disko (10", p/s)	12
93	Duophonic D-UHF-D 01	Jenny Ondioline (Part 1)/Golden Ball (Studio) (10", factory custom pressings; 3 on 'thick' clear vinyl, later endorsed & signed by band; no p/s)	220
93	Duophonic D-UHF-D 01	Jenny Ondioline (Part 1)/Golden Ball (Studio) (10", factory custom pressings; 5 copies on multicoloured vinyl; 25 on 'thin' clear vinyl, no p/s)	80
93	Clawfist 20	CRUMB DUCK (10" EP, shared with Nurse With Wound; 37 with hand-drawn p/s (Gain/Sadier only)	120
93	Clawfist 20	CRUMB DUCK (10" EP, shared with Nurse With Wound; 1,450 regular p/s)	20
93	Duophonic D-UHF-D 03	French Disko/Jenny Ondioline ('teaser' single, p/s, 1,500 only, with hand printed sleeves)	50
93	Duophonic D-UHF-D 03	French Disko/Jenny Ondioline ('teaser' single, p/s, 1,500 only, regular printed sleeves)	15
94	Duophonic D-UHF-D 04S	Ping Pong/Moogie Wonderland (p/s, 2,150 on pink vinyl)	10
94	Duophonic D-UHF-D 04S	Ping Pong/Moogie Wonderland (p/s, 3,322 on green vinyl)	10
94	Silvertone	Tone Burst (demo)/Tempter (demo)/SPECTRUM: Soul Kiss Glide Divine (unreleased, with colour photocopied wraparound p/s, 25 test pressings only)	150
94	Duophonic D-UHF-07	Wow And Flutter/Heavy Denim (3,000 only with hand-painted p/s)	18
95	Wurlitzer Jukebox WJ 3	The Eclipse/Yes Sir! I Can Moogie/CAT'S MIAOW: Shoot The Moon (flexidisc, 1,000 only with insert and info sheet)	18
95	Duophonic Super 45s DS 45-10	Long Hair Of Death/YO LA TENGO: Evanescent Psychic Pez Drop (gig single, fluorescent yellow vinyl, plain white stickered card sleeve, 3,000 only)	12
95	Independent Project IP 060	Blue Milk/One Thousand Miles An Hour/Aluminum Tune (set of 4 singles all With same tracks in different coloured vinyl and different sets of gatefold sleeve. American Import. Singles worth £10 each)	50
96	Duophonic D-UHF-D 10S	Cybele's Reverie/Brigitte (p/s, with insert)	6
96	Duophonic D-UHF-D 10	Cybele's Reverie/Les Yper Yper Sound/Brigitte/Young Lungs(25 black vinyl test pressing and 102 cut into 12" disc)	25
96	Duophonic D-UHF-D 10	Cybele's Reverie/Les Yper Yper Sound/Brigitte/Young Lungs(10", p/s, 2,000 only)	12
96	Lissy's LISS 15	You Used To Call Me Sadness/FUXA: Skyhigh (p/s, 400 on white vinyl)	10
96	Lissy's LISS 15	You Used To Call Me Sadness/FUXA: Skyhigh (p/s, 1,500 on black vinyl)	8
96	Duophonic D-UHF-D 12	Speedy Car/TORTOISE: Yaus (gig freebie, blue vinyl, p/s, 3,000 only)	10
96	Duophonic D-UHF-D 12	Speedy Car/TORTOISE: Yaus (orange vinyl export issue, p/s, 3,000 only)	15
96	Duophonic D-UHF-D 15	Metronomic Underground (Wagon Christ Mix)/Percolations (12", plain red sleeve, 2,500 only)	12
97	Duophonic DS 4517	Splitting The Atom (Parts 1 & 2) (with Sonic Boom)/Monkey Brain (p/s, 2,500 only)	10
97	Duophonic D-UHF-D 18	Iron Man/The Incredible He Woman (red vinyl, p/s, gig single, 2,000 only)	6
97	Duophonic Super 45s DS 3311	Simple Headphone Mind/NURSE WITH WOUND: Trippin' With The Birds (12", 5,000 copies)	10
97	Duophonic Super 45s DS 3311	Simple Headphone Mind/NURSE WITH WOUND: Trippin' With The Birds (12", 1,000 copies on yellow vinyl, in sealed foil sleeve)	20
97	Duophonic Super 45s CD	Simple Headphone Mind/NURSE WITH WOUND: Trippin' With The Birds (CD, sealed foil	30

STEREOLAB & BRIGITTE FONTAINE

MINT VALUE £

		3311	sleeve, 1,000 only) ....
99	Duophonic D-UHF-D24	THE UNDERGROUND IS COMING: The Super-It/Monkey Jelly/Fried Monkey Eggs (Instrumental)/Fried Monkey Eggs (Vocal) (p/s) 10
01	Duophonic D-UHF 026	Captain Easychord (12") 12
01	Duophonic DS 45 30	Free Witch And No Bra Queen/Speck Voice (p/s, tour single) 10
04	Duophonic D-UHF-D 30S	Rose, My Pocket Brain!/Banana Monster Ne Repond Plus/University Microfilms International (p/s, tour single, 500 only) 15
06	Duophonic DS 45 38	Solar Throw Away/Jump Drive Shut Out (p/s, tour single) 12
92	Too Pure PURELP 11	PENG! (LP, inner sleeve, insert) 20
93	Duophonic D-UHF-D 02	TRANSIENT RANDOM NOISE-BURSTS WITH ANNOUNCEMENTS (2-LP, with inner sleeves, poor playing-quality gold vinyl, with stickered sleeve, 1,500 only, numbered) 70
93	Duophonic D-UHF-D 02	TRANSIENT RANDOM NOISE-BURSTS WITH ANNOUNCEMENTS (2-LP, inners, black vinyl) 25
94	Duophonic D-UHF-D 05	MARS AUDIAC QUINTET (2-LP, without single) 30
95	Duophonic D-UHF-D 05X	MARS AUDIAC QUINTET (2-LP, gatefold sleeve, 1st 1,000 copies with bonus coloured vinyl single "Klang Tone"/"Ulan Bator" [D-UHF-06]) 55
95	Duophonic D-UHF-D 08	MUSIC FOR THE AMORPHOUS BODY STUDY CENTRE (40 black vinyl test pressings 10" sides cut into 12" discs) 80
95	Duophonic D-UHF-D 08	MUSIC FOR THE AMORPHOUS BODY STUDY CENTRE (10" LP, 3,000 only, insert) 20
95	Duophonic D-UHF-CD 08	MUSIC FOR THE AMORPHOUS BODY STUDY CENTRE (CD, first issue with white cover & "1st edition" printed on disc available at Charles Long art exhibition; reissue has yellow sleeve) 40
95	Duophonic D-UHF LP 09	REFRIED ECTOPLASM - SWITCHED ON VOL 2 LP, orange vinyl, card insert) 30
96	United Dairies UD 059	CRUMB DUCK (LP, shared with Nurse With Wound (2 extra tracks, reissue of Clawfist EP, 50 copies on pink vinyl) 70
96	United Dairies UD 059	CRUMB DUCK (LP, shared with Nurse With Wound (2 extra tracks, reissue of Clawfist EP, 500 on fluorescent green vinyl) 40
96	Duophonic UHF D-UHF-D11	EMPEROR TOMATO KETCHUP (2-LP, yellow glitter vinyl, gatefold sleeve) 80
96	Duophonic DUHFD11	EMPEROR TOMATO KETCHUP (2-LP, black vinyl) 50
97	Duophonic D-UHF-D 17	DOTS & LOOPS (2-LP, one green, one white vinyl) 50
98	Drag City CD 159	ALUMINIUM TUNES - SWITCHED ON VOL. 3 (3 x LP) 40
99	Duophonic D-UHF-D 23	COBRA & PHASES GROUP PLAY VOLTAGE IN THE MILKY NIGHT (2-LP) 40
00	Duophonic D-UHF-D 25	THE FIRST OF THE MICROBE HUNTERS (2-LP) 35
01	Duophonic D-UHF-D 27	SOUND-DUST (2-LP, hand-numbered, screenprinted heavy card sleeve, inners, 1200 only) 50
01	Duophonic D-UHF-D 27	SOUND-DUST (2-LP, inners, 1800 only) 40
04	Duophonic D-UHF-D 29	MARGERINE ECLIPSE (2-LP, 3500 only) 35
06	(No Cat. No.)	FAB FOUR SUTURE (LP as 6 x 7" hand-stamped box) 20
06	Duophonic D-UHF-D 31	SERENE VELOCITY: A STEREOLAB ANTHOLOGY (2-LP, numbered sticker on sleeve, inners) 25
08	4AD CAD 2815	CHEMICAL CHORDS (2-LP) 25
10	Duophonic D-UHF D32	NOT MUSIC (LP, clear vinyl) 18

(see also McCarthy, Spectrum, Mouse On Mars, Cavern Of Anti Matter)

STEREOLAB & BRIGITTE FONTAINE

90s	Duophonic Super 45s DS 45-25	Caliméro/MONADE: Cache Cache (white vinyl, p/s) 8

STEREO MC'S

89	4th & Broadway BRLP 532	33 45 78 (LP) 15
90	4th & Broadway 211 094	SUPERNATURAL (LP) 15
92	4th & Broadway 512 743 1	CONNECTED (LP) 20
01	Island ILPST 8106	DEEP DOWN AND DIRTY (3-LP) 50

STEREOPHONICS

96	V2 SPH 1	Looks Like Chaplin/More Life In A Tramp's Vest (p/s, 500 only) 40
96	V2 SPHD 1	Looks Like Chaplin/More Life In A Tramp's Vest/Raymond's Shops (CD) 30
96	V2 SPH 2	Local Boy In The Photograph/Too Many Sandwiches (p/s, 2,000 only) 12
97	V2 SPH 4	More Life In A Tramp's Vest/Raymond's Shop (p/s) 8
99	V2 no catalogue number	PERFORMANCE AND COCKTAILS (7 x 10" box set, with booklet and CD, promo mail order only) 30
99	V2 VVR 500 6777	Pick A Part That's New/Nice To Be Out (Demo) (p/s) 6
97	V2 VVR 1000 431	WORD GETS AROUND (LP, gatefold sleeve) 60
97	V2 VVR 1000 431	WORD GETS AROUND (LP, with bonus 12") 65
99	V2 VVR1004499	PERFORMANCE AND COCKTAILS (LP, gatefold) 50
01	V2 VVR1015831	JUST ENOUGH EDUCATION TO PERFORM (2-LP, gatefold) 40
03	V2 VVR 1021901	YOU GOTTA GO THERE TO COME BACK (2-LP) 20
05	V2 VVR 1031051	LANGUAGE. SEX. VIOLENCE. OTHER? (LP) 30
06	V2 VVR 1038091	LIVE FROM DAKOTA (2-LP) 40
07	V2 VVR 1048561	PULL THE PIN (LP) 40

STEREOS

61	MGM MGM 1143	I Really Love You/Please Come Back To Me 50
61	MGM MGM 1149	The Big Knock/Sweet Water 30
66	MGM MGM 1328	Sweet Water/The Big Knock (reissue) 7

STEREOTYPES (1)

79	Hinterland/SRT no cat. no.	THE STEREOTYPES EP (no p/s) 800
13	Hinterland (No Cat. No.)	THE STEREOTYPES EP (reissue, no p/s, signed insert, 350 only) 15

STEREOTYPES (2)

80	Art Theft AT 001	Calling All The Shots/Lovers Of The Future (p/s) 8

DEAN STERLING & TEENBEATS

61	Pye 7N 15345	Send Me A Girl/Lost Love 12

FITZROY STERLING

68	Gas GAS 102	Got To Play It Cool/Jezebel 20
70	Bullet BU 422	That's My Life/Queen Of Hearts 15
70	Bullet BU 438	Freedom Street/FITZROY ALL STARS: Freedom Street Version 15
71	Escort ERT 858	Girl Tell Me What To Do/Be Careful 8

Lester STERLING (& HIS GROUP)

MINT VALUE £

LESTER STERLING (& HIS GROUP)

63	Island WI 121	Clean The City/Long Walk Home (B-side actually by Charmers)	20
63	R&B JB 111	Air Raid Shelter/ROY & ANNETTE: I Mean It	25
63	R&B JB 115	Gravy Cool/WINSTON & BIBBY: Lover Lover Man	50
64	R&B JB 143	Peace And Love/HORACE SEATON: Hold On	40
64	R&B JB 150	Hot Cargo/MAYTALS: Marching On	45
64	R&B JB 155	Baskin' Hop (as Lester Sterling & His Group)/MAYTALS: Shining Light	25
64	R&B JB 172	Indian Summer (as Lester Sterling & His Group)/STRANGER & PATSY: I'll Forgive You	35
66	Doctor Bird DB 1057	Inez (with Tommy McCook & Supersonics)/GLORIA CRAWFORD: Sad Movies	40
67	Doctor Bird DB 1107	Soul Voyage/ALVA LEWIS: Revelation	60
67	Collins Downbeat CR 001	Sir Collins Special/Lester Sterling '67	60
68	Coxsone CS 7080	Afrikkaan Beat/PARAGONS: My Satisfaction	150
68	Blue Cat BS 116	Zigaloo/Wiser Than Solomon	150
68	Unity UN 502	Bangarang (with Stranger Cole)/STRANGER COLE: If We Should Ever Meet	25
69	Unity UN 505	Reggie On Broadway (this is what it states on label)/CLIQUE: Love Can Be Wonderful	25
69	Unity UN 509	Spoogy/TOMMY McCOOK: Monkey Fiddle	20
69	Unity UN 512	Regina/Bright As A Rose	15
69	Unity UN 517	1,000 Tons Of Megaton/KING CANNON: Five Card Stud (white labels only)	50
69	Unity UN 518	Man About Town/Man At The Door (white labels only)	40
69	Unity UN 531	Lonesome Feeling/Bright As A Rose	25
69	Big Shot BI 507	Forest Gate Rock/RAVING RAVERS: Rock Rock And Cry	45
69	Gas GAS 103	Reggae In The Wind/SOUL SET: Try Me One More Time (B-side actually by Stranger & Gladdy)	40
70	Unity UN 562	Slip Up/DAVE BARKER: On Broadway	35
71	Nu Beat NB 095	Iron Side Part 1/COXSON'S ALL STARS: Iron Side Part 2	25
71	Ocean CNBU 96	War Is Not The Answer Part 2/Iron Side Part 2 (promo only)	15
72	Ashanti ASH 409	Iron Sound Part 1/COXSON'S ALL STARS: Iron Sound Part 2	6
72	Ashanti ASH 410	War Is Not The Answer/COXSON'S ALL STARS: Version	18
69	Pama SECO 15	BANGARANG (LP)	100

(see also Mister Versatile, Bobby Aitken, Eric Morris, Sir Collins Band, Slickers, Uniques)

NINA STERN

65	Pye 7N 15823	Take It From Me/Please Come Back To Me	8

STEROID KIDDIES

79	Steroid/Grundinga SK 001	THE KIDDIES EP	55

STEROID MAXIMUS

90s	Big Cat ABB 28	QUILOMBO (LP)	20

STEROIDS

78	Radar ADA 11	In The Colonies/Sha La La Loo Ley (p/s)	6

STEVE 'N' BONNIE

72	Young Blood YB 1033	Brief Encounter/Don't/Lady	6
73	Sovereign SOV123	Me 'N' My Soul/A Screw Called Kirk	8
72	Young Blood SSYB 16	BRIEF ENCOUNTER (LP)	18

STEVE & STEVIE

68	Toast TT510	Merry-Go-Round/Remains To Be Seen	15
68	Toast TLP 2	STEVE AND STEVIE (LP)	30

(see also Tin Tin, Fut)

APRIL STEVENS

53	Parlophone MSP 6060	C'est Si Bon/Soft Warm Lips	10
54	Parlophone MSP 6088	How Could Red Riding Hood (Have Been…)/You Said You'd Do It	10
67	MGM MGM 1366	Falling In Love Again/Wanting You	100
67	MGM MGM 1366	Falling In Love Again/Wanting You (DJ copy)	200
76	MGM 2006 586	Wanting You/Falling In Love Again (reissue)	6

(see also Nino Tempo & April Stevens)

CAT STEVENS

66	Deram DM 110	Matthew And Son/Granny	7
67	Deram DM 156	Kitty/Blackness Of The Night	10
68	Deram DM 178	Lovely City/Image Of Hell	7
68	Deram DM 211	Here Comes My Wife/It's A Supa (Dupa) Life	7
69	Deram DM 260	Where Are You/The View From The Top	7
70	Island WIP 6086	Lady D'Arbanville/Time/Fill My Eyes (in p/s)	8
67	Deram DML/SML 1004	MATTHEW AND SON (LP)	25
67	Deram DML/SML 1018	NEW MASTERS (LP)	25
67	Deram	CATS AND DOGS (LP, unreleased, test pressings only)	30
70	Island ILPS 9118	MONA BONE JAKON (LP, inner, pink label with white 'i' logo)	120
70	Island ILPS 9135	TEA FOR THE TILLERMAN (LP, gatefold, pink label, with white 'i' logo)	70
71	Island ILPS 9135	TEA FOR THE TILLERMAN (LP, reissue, pink rim labels)	20
73	Island ILPS 5924	FOREIGNER (LP, insert)	15

CHUCK STEVENS

57	Columbia DB 3883	Take A Walk/The Way I Do	7
57	Columbia DB 3938	My London/Couldn't Care More	7

CONNIE STEVENS

60	Warner Bros WB 3	Sixteen Reasons (with Don Ralke)/Little Sister (with Buddy Cole Trio)	8
60	Warner Bros WB 17	Too Young To Go Steady/A Little Kiss Is A Kiss, Is A Kiss	8
60	Warner Bros WB 25	Apollo/Why Do I Cry For Joey	8
61	Warner Bros WB 41	And This Is Mine/Make-Believe Lover	8
61	Warner Bros WB 47	The Greenwood Tree/If You Don't, Somebody Else Will	8
62	Warner Bros WB 63	Why'd You Wanna Make Me Cry/Just One Kiss	10
62	Warner Bros WB 73	Mr. Songwriter/I Couldn't Say No	7
64	Warner Bros WB 128	They're Jealous Of Me/A Girl Never Knows	7
60	Warner Bros WEP 6007	CONNIE STEVENS AS CRICKET (EP, mono)	10

Dean STEVENS

			MINT VALUE £
60	Warner Bros WSEP 2007	CONNIE STEVENS AS CRICKET (EP, stereo)	12
63	Warners WEP 6105	CONNIE STEVENS AS CRICKET NO. 2 (EP, mono)	10
63	Warners WSE 6105	CONNIE STEVENS AS CRICKET NO. 2 (EP, stereo)	12
63	Warners WEP 6112	CONNIE STEVENS AS CRICKET NO. 3 (EP, mono)	10
63	Warners WSE 6112	CONNIE STEVENS AS CRICKET NO. 3 (EP, stereo)	12
62	Warner Bros WM 4060	CONNIE (LP, mono)	15
62	Warner Bros WS 8061	CONNIE (LP, stereo)	25
63	Warner Bros WM/WS 8111	THE HANK WILLIAMS SONG BOOK (LP)	15

(see also Edward Byrnes)

DEAN STEVENS
62	Philips 326540 BF	Sad And Lonely/I've Just Heard	10
64	Philips BF 1300	Only 'Cause I'm Lonely/Love Me Like I Love You	8
63	Philips 326580	Let Me Show You How/High On The Hill Of Hope	8

DODIE STEVENS
59	London HLD 8834	Pink Shoe Laces/Coming Of Age	10
60	London HLD 9174	No/A-Tisket A-Tasket	6
61	London HLD 9280	Yes, I'm Lonesome Tonight/Too Young	10
63	London HLP 9672	Don't Send Me Roses/Daddy Couldn't Get Me One Of Those	10
64	Liberty LIB 83	I Wore Out Our Record/You Don't Have To Prove A Thing	8

JERRY STEVENS
66	CBS 2831	You Make My Life Worthwhile/So This Is Love	6

JIMMY STEVENS
66	Fontana TF 721	I Love You/Wharf 130	7

JOHN STEVENS AWAY
76	Vertigo 6059140	Anni Part 1/Anni Part 2	8
76	Vertigo 6360 131	JOHN STEVEN'S AWAY (LP)	20
76	Vertigo 6360 135	SOMEWHERE IN BETWEEN (LP)	20
78	Spotlite SPJ 508	NO FEAR! (LP)	30
78	Spotlite SPJ 513	APPLICATION INTERACTION AND... (LP)	30
82	Affinity AFF 101	FREEBOP (LP)	20
84	Affinity AYF 130	THE LIFE OF RILEY (LP, as John Steven's Solkus)	30

JOHNNY STEVENS & BLUE BEATS
64	Blue Beat BB 229	Shame/Ball And Chain	20

JOHNNY STEVENS & LES DAWSON SYNDICATE
62	Melodisc M 1586	Last Chicken In The Shop/Oh Yeah (some in p/s)	10

KIRK STEVENS
57	Decca F 10863	Once/This Silver Madonna	8

MARY STEVENS
16	Backatcha BK015	Find Your Love (Remix)/Find Your Love	7

MEIC STEVENS
65	Decca F 12174	Did I Dream/I Saw A Field (as Mike Stevens)	40
70	Warner Bros WB 8007	Ballad Of Old Joe Blind/Blue Sleep	15
70	Wren WSP 2005	Nid Oes Un Gwydr Ffenestr/Rhywbeth Gwell I Ddod	40
78	YM SP 01	DIC PENDERYN EP (THEATR YR YMYLON Theatrical soundtrack)	50
68	Wren WRE 1045	MIKE STEVENS (EP, p/s)	50
68	Wren WRE 1053	RHIF 2 (EP, p/s)	50
69	Wren WRE 1073	MWG (EP, p/s)	50
70	Newyddion Da ND1	MEIC STEVENS (EP, p/s)	100
70	Sain SAIN 004	Y BRAWN HOUDINI (EP, p/s)	50
71	Wren WRE 1107	BYW YN Y WLAD (EP, p/s)	50
71	Sain SAIN 13	DIONCH YN FAWR (EP, p/s)	50
70	Warner Brothers WS 3005	OUTLANDER (LP, with insert)	300
72	Wren WRL 536	GWYMON (LP)	300
77	Sain SAIN 1065	GOG (LP)	120
79	Tic Toc no cat. no.	CANAEON CYNNAR (LP, private pressing)	220
82	Sain SAIN 1239	NOS DU NOS DA (LP)	50
83	Sain SAIN 1312	LAPIS LAZULI (LP, lyric insert)	50
86	Timeless TIME 705	TIMELESS (LP, reissue, 500 only)	20

(see also Gary Farr)

MICK STEVENS
79	Spaceward SRS 030	THE ENGLISHMAN (LP, insert)	40
71	Deroy (no cat. no.)	SEE THE MORNING (LP, private pressing)	400
75	Deroy (no cat. no.)	NO SAVAGE WORD (LP, private pressing)	300

MIKE STEVENS
66	Pye 7N 17243	Cathy's Clown/Go-Go Train	60
68	Polydor 56269	Guaranteed To Drive You Wild/Hog-Tied	12

(see also Shevells)

MORT STEVENS & HIS ORCHESTRA
70	Capitol CL 15655	Hawaii Five-O Theme/McGarrett's Theme	10

PROFESSOR NOALL STEVENS
80	No label or cat no	The People's Anthem/The People's Anthem (p/s, inserts)	8

RAY STEVENS
58	Capitol CL 14881	Chickie-Chickie Wah Wah/Crying Goodbye	10
61	Mercury AMT 1158	Jeremiah Peabody's Polyunsaturated Quick Dissolving Fast Acting Pleasant Tasting Green And Purple Pills/Teen Years	7
62	Mercury AMT 1184	Ahab The Arab/It's Been So Long	10
63	Mercury AMT 1207	Harry The Hairy Ape/Little Stone Statue	7
66	London HLU 10016	Party People/ABC	10
68	Monument MON 1022	Mr Businessman/Face The Music	8

Ricky STEVENS

MINT VALUE £

RICKY STEVENS
61	Columbia DB 4739	I Cried For You/I Am	7
62	Columbia DB 4778	Forever/Now, It's All Over	10
63	Columbia DB 4981	My Mother's Eyes/I'll Get By	10
62	Columbia SEG 8172	I CRIED FOR YOU (EP)	40

SHAKIN' STEVENS (& SUNSETS)
70	Parlophone R 5860	Spirit Of Woodstock/Down On The Farm	60
72	Polydor 2058 213	Sweet Little Rock'n'Roller/White Lightning	50
74	Emerald MD 1176	Honey Honey/Holey Moley 2001	25
76	Mooncrest MOON 51	Jungle Rock/Girl In Red	10
77	Track 2094 134	Never/You Always Hurt The One You Love	10
77	Track 2094 136	Somebody Touched Me/Way Down Yonder In New Orleans (in p/s)	10
77	Track 2094 136	Somebody Touched Me/Way Down Yonder In New Orleans	6
78	Track 2094 141	Justine/Wait And See	10
78	Epic SEPC 6567	Treat Her Right/I Don't Want No Other Baby	8
79	Epic SEPC 6845	Endless Sleep/Fire	8
79	Epic SEPC 7235	Spooky/I Don't Want No Other Baby	20
80	Epic SEPC 8090	Hot Dog/Apron Strings	6
80	Epic SEPC 8573	Hey Mae/I Guess I Was A Fool (in p/s)	50
80	Epic SEPC 8573	Hey Mae/I Guess I Was A Fool	10
80	Epic SEPC 9064	Shooting Gallery/Make It Right Tonight (p/s)	6
90	Epic SHAKY P13	Pink Champagne/Rockin' The Night Away (picture disc)	40
70	Parlophone PCS 7112	A LEGEND (LP)	80
71	CBS 52901	I'M NO J.D. (LP)	40
72	Contour 2870 152	ROCKIN' AND SHAKIN' (LP)	15
73	Emerald GES 1121	SHAKIN' STEVENS AND THE SUNSETS (LP)	15
78	Track 2406 011	SHAKIN' STEVENS (LP, with insert)	15
80	Epic EPC 84547	MARIE MARIE (LP, withdrawn)	18

TERRI STEVENS
59	Felsted AF 126	Adonis/Vieni, Vieni	6

RICHARD STEVENSEN
70	Pye 7N 45004	The Day That You Came Back/The Gates Of Me	8
70	Pye NSPL 18358	GATES OF ME (LP, textured sleeve)	25

MICKEY STEVENSON
72	Ember EMBS 320	Here I Am/Joe Poor Loves Daphne Elizabeth Richard	6
72	Ember NR 5063	HERE I AM (LP)	20

N A STEVENSON AND THE 4 ACES
73	Injun 103	Boogie Woogie Country Girl/Pins & Needles	10

STEVIE'S BUZZ
96	Nice no cat. no.	Autumn Stone/P.P. & THE PRIMES: Understanding (promo only, large centre)	8

(see also P.P. Arnold, Buzzcocks, Primal Scream)

AL STEWART
66	Decca F 12467	The Elf/Turn To Earth	70
67	CBS 3034	Bedsitter Images/Swiss Cottage Manoeuvres	12
70	CBS 4843	Electric Los Angeles Sunset/My Enemies Have Sweet Voices	8
70	CBS 5351	The News From Spain/Elvaston Place	15
72	CBS 7763	You Don't Even Know Me/I'm Falling	6
72	CBS 7992	Amsterdam/Songs Out Of Clay	6
73	CBS SCBS 1791	Terminal Eyes/Last Day Of June 1934	10
67	CBS (S)BPG 63087	BEDSITTER IMAGES (LP)	125
69	CBS (S) 63460	LOVE CHRONICLES (LP, gatefold sleeve)	25
70	CBS 63848	ZERO SHE FLIES (LP, gatefold sleeve)	22
70	CBS 64023	FIRST ALBUM (BEDSITTER IMAGES) (LP, remixed reissue, different track listing)	25
72	CBS 64730	ORANGE (LP)	20

(see also Jimmy Page)

BILLY STEWART
62	Pye International 7N 25164	Reap What You Sow/Fat Boy	15
63	Pye International 7N 25222	Strange Feeling/Sugar And Spice	15
65	Chess CRS 8009	I Do Love You/Keep Loving	10
65	Chess CRS 8017	Sitting In The Park/Once Again	10
66	Chess CRS 8028	Because I Love You/Mountains Of Love	10
66	Chess CRS 8038	Love Me/Why Am I Lonely	10
66	Chess CRS 8040	Summertime/To Love To Love	15
66	Chess CRS 8045	Secret Love/Look Back And Smile	10
66	Chess CRS 8050	Ole Man River/Every Day I Have The Blues	10
67	Chess CRS 8067	Cross My Heart/Why (Do I Love You So)	10
69	Chess CRS 8092	Summertime/I Do Love You	15
72	Chess 6145 017	Sitting In The Park/Summertime	8
65	Chess CRE 6010	IN CROWD (EP, with Ramsey Lewis Trio, et al)	30
67	Chess CRE 6024	I DO LOVE YOU (EP)	30
66	Chess CRL 4523	UNBELIEVABLE (LP)	30

BOB STEWART
55	MGM SP 1114	It's A Woman's World/I Went Out Of My Way	6

BRIDIE STEWART
75	Affection AFF 1	Can't Let You Go/(Version)	75
75	Affection AFF 003	Sugar Me Baby/Didn't Mean To Hurt You Baby	80
82	SS SSMD 12	Keep An Eye On You/Aquastrumental (12")	30

DELANO STEWART
68	Doctor Bird DB 1138	That's Life/Tell Me Baby	50
68	High Note HS 004	Let's Have Some Fun/Dance With Me	30

Graham STEWART SEVEN

MINT VALUE £

69	High Note HS 014	Rocking Sensation/GAYSTERS: One Look	350
70	High Note HS 027	Got To Come Back/Don't Believe In Him	20
70	High Note HS 034	Hallelujah/I Wish It Could Last	10
70	High Hote HS 039	Wherever I Lay My Hat/Don't Believe Him (B-side actually by Gladstone Anderson & Gaytones)	20
70	High Note HS 041	Stay A Little Bit Longer/Stay A Little Bit Longer (Version II) (B-side actually by Gladstone Anderson & Gaytones)	20
70	Trojan TBL 138	STAY A LITTLE BIT LONGER (LP)	75

(see also Winston Stewart, Gaylads, Patsy Todd)

GRAHAM STEWART SEVEN
59	Tempo EXA 91	GRAHAM STEWART SEVEN (EP)	10

(DAVE) STEWART & HARRISON
70	Multicord MULT SH 1	GIRL (EP)	15

(see also Longdancer, Eurythmics)

JAMES STEWART & HENRY FONDA
70	Stateside SS 2179	Rolling Stone/Theme From Cheyenne Social Club	8

JOHN STEWART
69	Capitol CL 15589	July, You're A Woman/Shackles And Chains	8

(see also Kingston Trio, Cumberland Three, Scott Engel)

JOHNNY STEWART
58	HMV POP 480	Wishing For Your Love/Promise Me	7

PAUL STEWART (MOVEMENT)
67	Decca F12577	Saturday Mornin Man/Too Too Good (in export p/s)	50
66	Philips BF 1513	Queen Boadicea/Talkin'	7
67	Decca F 12577	Saturday Morning Man/Too Too Good (as Paul Stewart Movement)	15

(see also Hamilton & [Hamilton] Movement)

RAPHAEL STEWART & HOT TOPS
71	Punch PH 71	Put Your Sweet Lips/JUSTINS: Stand By Me	10

REX STEWART'S LONDON FIVE
55	Tempo EXA 8	REX STEWART'S LONDON FIVE (EP)	15

ROD STEWART
64	Decca F 11996	Good Morning Little Schoolgirl/I'm Gonna Move To The Outskirts Of Town	180
65	Columbia DB 7766	The Day Will Come/Why Does It Go On?	150
66	Columbia DB 7892	Shake/I Just Got Some	200
68	Immediate IM 060	Little Miss Understood/So Much To Say	100
70	Vertigo 6086 002	It's All Over Now/Jo's Lament	15
72	Phonogram DJ004	Twisting The Night Away (EP 1-track on 4 track promo 7" also featuring Chuck Berry, Diane Davidson and the Stylistics)	20
77	Riva RIVA 1	You're Insane/You're Insane (DJ copy, 500 only)	25
78	Riva RIVA 9	Sailing/Stone Cold Sober(HMS Ark Royal Commemorative issue, blue vinyl, p/s)	150
70	Vertigo VO 4	AN OLD RAINCOAT WON'T EVER LET YOU DOWN (gatefold sleeve, large swirl label, original pressing with 'Philips' credit on label)	125
70	Vertigo VO 4	AN OLD RAINCOAT WON'T EVER LET YOU DOWN (gatefold sleeve, 2nd pressing, large swirl label, later pressing without 'Philips' credit on label)	45
70	Vertigo 6360 500	GASOLINE ALLEY (LP, 1st pressing, gatefold sleeve, large swirl label)	100
71	Vertigo 6360 500	GASOLINE ALLEY (LP, 2nd pressing, gatefold sleeve, small swirl label)	45
71	Mercury 6338 063	EVERY PICTURE TELLS A STORY (black label, with poster)	30
71	Vertigo VO 4	AN OLD RAINCOAT WON'T EVER LET YOU DOWN (gatefold sleeve, 3rd pressing, with small 'swirl' and 'Vertigo' above centre hole, title all on one line)	25
72	Vertigo VO 4	AN OLD RAINCOAT WON'T EVER LET YOU DOWN (gatefold sleeve, 4th pressing, small 'swirl' and 'Vertigo' above centre hole but title on two lines)	25

(see also Jeff Beck, Shotgun Express, Faces, Python Lee Jackson, Long John Baldry, Steamhammer, Ted Wood)

ROMAN STEWART
72	Songbird SB 1075	Changing Times (with Dave)/CRYSTALITES: Changing Times Version	18
73	Downtown DT 518	Try Me/BIG YOUTH: Rhythm Style	15
73	Techniques TE 932	Tonight I'm Staying Here (& Tennors)/Lady Love (& Tennors)	8
75	Morpheus MOR 1	In The Chapel/E MCLEAN: You Pick Me Up	50
75	Torpedo TOR 39	Loving ArmsVersion	8
79	GGS 049	Don't Get Jumpy/GG ALL STARS: Dub Cut (12")	25
78	Pirate PIR 002	Herbalist/Version (12", various coloured vinyl)	35
78	Strong Like Sampson SLSD 06	Mr. Officer/Ain't Too Proud To Beg (12")	40
79	Thompson & Koots TK002	Rice & Peas/Breaking Up (12", with Linval Thompson)	40
80	D-Roy DRDD 25	What You Wanna Do/REVOLUTIONARIES: Rockers Delight (12")	15

SANDY STEWART
58	London HLE 8683	A Certain Smile/Kiss Me Richard	10

TINGA STEWART
71	Songbird SB 1048	Hear That Train/CRYSTALITES: Hear That Train - Version	12
72	Tropical AL 0018	A Brand New Me/BROWNS ALL STARS: Nice Version	6
74	Dragon DRA 1025	The Message/Dub	25
84	Londisc LDLP 003	KEY TO YOUR HEART (LP)	15

WINSTON STEWART
64	R&B JB 147	But I Do/MAYTALS: Four Seasons	35
64	Port-O-Jam PJ 4002	All Of My Life/How Many Times	30
65	Ska Beat JB 225	You Made Me Cry/CHECKMATES: Invisible Ska	40

(see also Andy & Clyde, Gaylads, Delano Stewart, Winston & Tonettes)

WYNN STEWART
60	London HL 7087	Wishful Thinking/Uncle Tom Got Caught (export issue)	20

STEWPOT & SAVE THE CHILDREN FUND CHOIR
68	MGM 1448	I Like My Toys/Myrtles Birthday	20

J.E. STICK & DRUMBAGO
61	Blue Beat BB 64	Boss Gill/COUNT OSSIE : Cassavuba	20

STICKERS (2)

MINT VALUE £

STICKERS (2)
79	Reliable GUM 1	Shake Me/Kids Stuff (p/s)	6

STICKLEBACKS
87	Dub House KS 1292	All You Get/It's For You	20

STICK SHIFTS
80	Chiswick CHIS 118	Automobile/Parramatta Road (3 different p/s)	12

STIFF LITTLE FINGERS
78	Rigid Digits SRD-1	Suspect Device/Wasted Life (hand-made p/s, 500 only, red label with catalogue number on right-hand side)	200
78	Rigid Digits SRD-1	Suspect Device/Wasted Life (re-pressing, different machine-cut p/s, various colour labels/yellow labels)	45
78	Rough Trade RT 004	78 R.P.M./Alternative Ulster (p/s, A & B-sides reversed)	20
78	Rough Trade RT 004	Alternative Ulster/78 R.P.M. (p/s)	15
78	Rough Trade RT 006	Suspect Device/Wasted Life (reissue)	8
79	Chrysalis CHS 2368	Straw Dogs/You Can't Say Crap On The Radio (p/s)	7
81	SLFDJ1	Just Fade Away/Go For It (DJ promo)	10
82	Chrysalis CHSDJ 2580	Listen/Two Guitars Clash (p/s, jukebox issue)	12
89	Virgin SLFDJ1	St. Patrix, The Wild Rover/Johnny Was (DJ promo, unreleased as 7")	12
89	Link 1203	THE LAST TIME (EP)	10
86	Strange Fruit SFPS 004	PEEL SESSIONS (12")	12
79	Rough Trade ROUGH 1	INFLAMMABLE MATERIAL (LP, with inner)	20
80	Chrysalis CHR 1270	NOBODY'S HEROES (LP, inner)	18
80	Chrysalis CHR 1300	HANX! (LP)	20
82	Chrysalis CHR 1400	NOW THEN... (LP, inner and poster)	18
89	Limited Edition LTD EDT LP 3	LIVE IN SWEDEN (LP)	15

(see also Billy Karloff & Extremes)

STIFF LIZARD
87	Compass MRC 003	The Spy/Swings And Roundabouts (p/s)	8

STIFFS
79	Dork UR 1	Standard English/S.C. Rip/Brookside Riot Squad (die-cut sleeve)	25
79	Dork UR 2	Inside Out/Kids On the Street (die cut sleeve or later Zonophone Z3 p/s)	20
80	Zonophone Z 14	Volume Control/Nothing To Lose (p/s)	15
80	Stiff BUY 86	Goodbye My Love/Magic Roundabout (p/s)	10
85	Dork UR 7(12)	The Young Guitars/Yer Under Attack (12", red p/s)	10

STILETTOS
80	Ariola ARO 200	This Is The Way/Who Can It Be (p/s)	20

STILL COOL
79	Hit Run HITDD 22	Insane Love/Stereo Version '79 (12")	25

STILL LIFE (1)
68	Columbia DB 8245	What Did We Miss/My Kingdom Cannot Lose	100
71	Vertigo 6360 026	STILL LIFE (LP, gatefold sleeve, large swirl label)	750

(see also Jon, Titus Groan)

STEPHEN STILLS
70	Atlantic 2401 004	STEPHEN STILLS (LP)	35
71	Atlantic 2401 104	STEPHEN STILLS 2 (LP, gatefold sleeve)	25
73	Atlantic K 40440	DOWN THE ROAD (LP)	15
75	CBS 69146	STILLS LP, inner)	15
08	Rhino 8122799297	JUST ROLL TAPE (LP, 180gm vinyl)	15

(see also Buffalo Springfield, Al Kooper Mike Bloomfield & Stephen Stills, Crosby Stills Nash & Young, Manassas, Stills-Young Band)

STILLS-YOUNG BAND
76	Reprise K 54081	LONG MAY YOU RUN (LP)	15

(see also Stephen Stills, Manassas, Neil Young, Buffalo Springfield, Crosby Stills Nash & Young)

STING
82	A&M PARTY 1	Need Your Love So Bad/PAULINE BLACK : No Woman, No Cry (Promo)	10
85	A&M DREAMP 1	THE DREAM OF THE BLUE TURTLES (LP, picture disc, die-cut sleeve, insert)	15
93	A&M 540 075-1	TEN SUMMONERS TALES (LP, insert)	40
94	A&M 540 307-1	FIELDS OF GOLD - THE BEST OF STING 1984 - 1994 (2-LP)	100
96	A&M 540 486-1	MERCURY FALLING (LP)	40

(see also Police, Last Exit, [Fast Breeder &] Radio Actors, Newcastle Big Band)

STINGERS
72	Upsetter US 395	Preacher Man/UPSETTERS: Version	40
72	Explosion EX 2075	Forward Up/UPSETTERS: Forward	35

STING-RAYS
82	Big Beat SW 82	Dinosaurs/Math Of Trend/Another Cup Of Coffee/You're Gonna Miss Me (white label test pressing, 100 Club gig freebie, 80 only)	20
87	Kaleidoscope Sound 7KS 102	Behind The Beyond/Perverted Justice (p/s)	10
87	Kaleidoscope Sound KSLP 1	CRYPTIC AND COFFEE TIME (LP)	15
87	Big Beat WIK 61	THE ESSENTIAL EARLY STING-RAY RECORDINGS 1982 TO 1985 (LP)	15
87	Raucous FASTBUCK 1	LIVE & RAW (10")	15

STINGRAYS (1)
80	Earache SRTS./80/CUS 809	Still In Love WIth You/Wasting Your Time/Couldn't Get It Right/Walking Down London Street (EP)	25

STINGRAYS (2)
80	Fried Egg EGG 006	Countdown/Exceptions Action	40
82	Rocket XPRES 78	Radiator Rock/Slap Bass Boogie (die cut sleeve)	8
81	Circus CIRC 0003	Never Do/Satellites	20

STINKY TOYS
77	Polydor 2056 630	Boozy Creed/Driver Blues (p/s)	10
77	Polydor 2393 174	STINKY TOYS (LP)	20

STIR
87	Spoonin SPOON 01	CHEEKY MONKEY (12", EP)	20

(peter) LEE STIRLING (& BRUISERS)

MINT VALUE £

(PETER) LEE STIRLING (& BRUISERS)
63	Columbia DB 4992	My Heart Commands Me/Welcome Stranger (as Lee Stirling & Bruisers)	7
63	Parlophone R 5063	I Could If I Wanted To/Right From The Start (as Lee Stirling & Bruisers)	7
64	Parlophone R 5112	Now That I've Found You/I Believe (as Peter Lee Stirling & Bruisers)	7
64	Parlophone R 5158	Sad, Lonely And Blue/I'm Looking For Someone To Love (as Peter Lee Stirling & Bruisers)	10
64	Parlophone R 5198	Everything Will Be Alright/You'll Be Mine (as Peter Lee Stirling & Bruisers)	10
66	Decca F 12433	The Sweet And Tender Hold Of Your Love/Everybody Needs A Someone	7
66	Decca F 12535	Oh What A Fool/I'm Sportin' A New Baby	7
67	Decca F 12628	You Don't Live Twice/8.35 On The Dot	25
67	Decca F 12674	Goodbye Thimblemill Lane/Hey Conductor	12
69	MCA MU 1093	Big Sam/Mr. Average Man	6

(see also Bruisers, Hungry Wolf)

GARY STITES
59	London HLL 8881	Lonely For You/Shine That Ring	25
59	London HLL 9003	Starry Eyed/Without Your Love	20
60	London HLL 9082	Lawdy, Miss Clawdy/Don't Wanna Say Goodbye	25

SONNY STITT
53	Esquire 20-013	SONNY STITT-BUD POWELL QUARTET (10" LP)	20
58	Esquire 32-049	S.P.J. JAZZ (LP, with Bud Powell & J.J. Johnson)	20
58	Columbia Clef 33CX 10114	NEW YORK JAZZ (LP)	20
59	Esquire 32-078	STITT'S BITS (LP)	20
59	HMV CLP 1280	ONLY THE BLUES (LP)	20
60	HMV CLP 1384	SONNY STITT WITH THE OSCAR PETERSON TRIO (LP)	20
61	HMV CLP 1420	BLOWS THE BLUES (LP, mono)	20
61	HMV CSD 1341	BLOWS THE BLUES (LP, stereo)	20
64	Chess CRL 4503	MY MAIN MAN (LP)	15
67	Marble Arch MAL 753	SONNY STITT (LP)	15

(see also J.J. Johnson)

TESSA STIVAR
83	Smash TESS 001	My Jealousy/Thin Air (p/s)	10

CLIFF ST LEWIS
74	Cactus CT 18	That Train/Commandment Rock	10
80	King Cliff KC 102	Dready Daya/Mever Met A Girl As Sweet As You (12")	12
80	King Cliff KC 103	Versatility/Give Me Your Love	10
80	King Cliff KCLP 104	VERSATILITY 7 IN MANY MOODS (LP)	30

STOAT
78	City NIK 3	Up To You/Loving A Killer (p/s)	7

STOCKER, GREENWOOD & FRIENDS
79	Changes CR1400	BILLY + NINE (LP)	25

(see also Slack Alice)

KARLHEINZ STOCKHAUSEN
65	CBS S72647	MIKROPHONIE I/MIKROPHONIE II (LP)	20
67	CBS 77209	COMPLETE PIANO MUSIC (2-LP, box set)	40
67	Vox STABY 615	PROZESSION (LP)	15
69	Vox VS 3184	STOCKHAUSEN (LP)	15
70	Deutsche Grammophon 2543003	STIMMUNG (LP)	20
74	Open University OP 15	TWENTIETH CENTURY MUSIC (LP)	25
75	Deutsche Grammophon 2530 582	PROZESSION (LP, reissue)	20

STOCK, HAUSEN & WALKMAN
96	Hot Air QRM SP 101	ORGAN TRANSPLANTS (EP)	10
97	Hot Air SPME 2	Buy Me/Sue Me (500 only on pink vinyl)	10
97	Hot Air SPME 2	Buy Me/Sue Me (300 on clear vinyl)	12
97	Hot Air SPME 2	Buy Me/Sue Me (200 on light blue vinyl)	15
99	Hot Air AIRMILE 76	HANG UPS EP (die-cut cover)	8
99	Hot Air ALERT 01	Alert/Crash (500 only)	20
98	Hot Air QRM LP 010	OH MY BAG! (LP, clear vinyl, 300 only)	15
96	Hot Air QRM LP 101	ORGAN TRANSPLANTS VOL 1. (LP)	15
00	Hot Air QRM LP 000	ORGAN TRANSPLANTS VOL 2. (LP)	18

(see also Dummy Run)

STOCKHOLM MONSTERS
81	Factory FAC 41	Fairytales/Death Is Slowly (p/s)	15
82	Factory FAC 58	Happy Ever After/Soft Babies (p/s)	15
84	Factory FAC 107	All At Once (p/s)	10
84	Factory FACT 80	ALMA MATER (LP)	20

STOCKING TOPS
68	Toast TT 500	You're Never Gonna Get My Lovin'/You Don't Know What Love Is All About	18
68	CBS 3407	I Don't Ever Wanna Be Kicked By You/The World We Live In Is A Lonely Place	15

(see also Sue & Sunny, Sue & Sunshine, Myrtelles)

STOICS
68	RCA RCA 1745	Earth, Fire, Air And Water/Search Of The Sea	30

STOKES
65	London HLU 9955	Whipped Cream/Pie Crust	15

SIMON STOKES & NIGHTHAWKS
70	Elektra EKSN 45082	Voodoo Woman/Can't Stop Now	20

JOOP STOKKERMANS
71	Gemini GM 2017	THE MAGIC OF THE ARP SYNTHESISER (LP)	20

STOLEN POWER
81	Hornsey Rising POWER EP 1	The Wheel Is Turning/Family Snapshot/Sick And Tired/Little White Lies (p/s)	30

STOLEN PROPERTY

MINT VALUE £

STOLEN PROPERTY
75 Live Wire SON 4012   Low Rider/Black Jack 8

STOLEN YOUTH
76 Sunday SUN 1   Wheels In Motion/Kick The Door Down 30

RHET STOLLER (& HIS ECHOES)
60 Decca F 11271   Walk Don't Run/All Rhet 12
60 Decca F 11302   Chariot/Night Theme 10
63 Decca F 11738   Countdown/Over The Steppes (as Rhet Stoller & His Echoes) 12
64 Melodisc MEL 1595   Beat That/Treble Gold + One 15
64 Windsor PS 119   Caravan/Short Cut 20
64 Windsor PS 130   Ricochet/Knockout 20
66 Columbia DB 8013   Uncrowned King/Surf Ride (unissued, demos only) 20
67 Coronet EC 101   THE INCREDIBLE RHET STOLLER (LP) 25

STOLLERS TEAM
72 Decca F13280   Sapporo/Mean 12

JACKIE STOLLINGS (& NASHVILLE BOYS)
62 Starlite ST45 092   Footsteps Of A Fool/And Then I Knew (B-side with Nashville Boys) 6

(See also Jess Conrad)

MORRIS STOLOFF (& COLUMBIA PICTURES ORCHESTRA)
56 Brunswick 05553   Moonglow/Theme From "Picnic" 7
61 Warner Bros WB 48   Fanny/Panisse And Son 6

STOMPERS
62 Fontana H 385   Quarter To Four Stomp (Surf Stompin')/Foolish One 50

ALEXANDER STONE
70 Gemini GMS 003   I Try To Make You Good/Man In A Suitcase 10

ANGIE STONE
99 Arista 74321 72775   BLACK DIAMOND (2-LP) 35

CISSY STONE
76 Decca 13646   Gone But Not Forgotten/Part Of The Band 12

CLIFFIE STONE & HIS ORCHESTRA
55 Capitol CL 14330   Barracuda/The Popcorn Song (with Billy Strange & Speedy West) 100
55 Capitol CL 14330   Barracuda/The Popcorn Song (with Billy Strange & Speedy West) (78) 20
59 Capitol T 1080   THE PARTY'S ON ME (LP) 15

(see also Jeanne Gayle, Billy Strange)

DAVID STONE
68 Reynold R 1   Trust Me/Evil Child 20

DAVINA STONE
82 Ariwa ARI 1004   Love Power/Love On A Two Way Street (12") 30

ELLA STONE & MOSS
70s Phoenix SNIX 128   The Prophet/Now Or Never 6

(see also Helen Shapiro, Al Saxon)

GEORGE STONE
65 Stateside SS 479   Hole In The Wall/My Beat 20

KIRBY STONE QUARTET/FOUR
56 Vogue Coral Q 72129   Honey Hush/Lassus Trombone 15
63 Warner Bros WB 118   Washington Square/Blue Guitar 7

MARK STONE
58 London HLR 8543   Ever Since I Met Lucy/The Stroll 70
58 London HLR 8543   Ever Since I Met Lucy/The Stroll (78) 30

ROB STONE
68 Delta DT 3941   Sorry Suzanna/Peace Of Mind 20

SLY (& FAMILY) STONE
68 Columbia DB 8369   Dance To The Music/Let Me Hear It From You 100
68 Columbia DB 8369   Dance To The Music/Let Me Hear It From You (DJ copy) 150
68 Direction 58-3568   Dance To The Music/Let Me Hear It From You (reissue) 8
68 Direction 58-3707   M'Lady/Life 8
69 Direction 58-3938   Everyday People/Sing A Simple Song 8
69 Direction 58-4279   Stand!/I Want To Take You Higher 8
69 Direction 58-4471   Hot Fun In The Summertime/Fun 10
70 Direction 58-4782   Thank You (Falettinme Be Mice Elf Agin)/Everybody Is A Star 8
70 CBS 5054   I Want To Take You Higher/You Can Make It If You Try 6
68 Direction 8-63412   DANCE TO THE MUSIC (LP) 25
68 Direction 8-63461   M'LADY (LP) 20
69 Direction 8-63655   STAND! (LP, CBS sleeve with Direction label) 20
71 Epic S EPC 64613   THERE'S A RIOT GOING ON (LP, gatefold, yellow labels) 30
70 Epic 462524   GREATEST HITS (LP) 15
73 Epic EPC 69030   FRESH (LP, gatefold, inners, yellow labels) 30
86 Edsel ZED 165   THERE'S A RIOT GOING ON (LP, reissue) 18
87 Edsel XED 232   FRESH (LP, reissue) 18
99 Epic SVLP 125   BEST OF SLY AND THE FAMILY STONE (LP) 20

(see also Little Sisters)

STONE ANGEL
75 SSLP 04   STONE ANGEL (LP, private pressing, blue/silver label) 400
94 Acme AC 8008 LP   STONE ANGEL (LP, reissue, 500 only) 15

(see also Ken Saul)

STONE CROSS
72 Access ACC 3   Light Up The Sun/At My Funeral 35

STONEFIELD TRAMP
74 Acorn/Tramp CF 247   DREAMING (LP) 300

(see also Terry Friend, Rob Van Spyk)

STONE GRAPHICS

MINT VALUE £

STONE GRAPHICS
68	Parlophone R 5735	A Tale Of Long Ago/Travelling Man	8

STONEGROUND
71	Warner Bros K 46087	STONEGROUND (LP)	20
71	Warner Bros K 53999	FAMILY ALBUM (LP)	20

STONEGROUND BAND
70s	Nut	SUNSTRUCK!! (LP, stickered sleeve)	30

HARRY STONEHAM
76	One UP OU 2127	I FEEL GOOD, I FEEL FUNKY (LP)	15

HARRY STONEHAM & JOHNNY EYDEN
67	Tepee TPRLP 100	TWO GUYS TO FOLLOW (LP, mono [70s reissues credited soley to Harry Stoneham £15])	20

STONEHENGE MEN
62	HMV POP 981	Big Feet/Pinto	30

STONEHOUSE
71	RCA SF 8197	STONEHOUSE CREEK (LP, laminated front sleeve, orange label)	200

STONEPILLOW
69	Decca PFS 4163	ELEAZAR'S CIRCUS (LP, stereo, laminated front to sleeve)	15

STONE PONEYS
67	Capitol CL 15523	Different Drum/I've Got To Know	10

STONE ROSES

SINGLES
85	Thin Line THIN 001	So Young/Tell Me (12", p/s, 1,200 only; beware of counterfeits!)	120
87	Black/Revolver 12 REV 36	Sally Cinnamon/Here It Comes/All Across The Sand (12", 'Printed In England' on rear p/s & no barcode, "All Across The Sands" listed on label; different mixes of 2 tracks to later reissue - increasingly difficult to find original)	30
88	Silvertone ORE 1	Elephant Stone/The Hardest Thing In The World (catalogue number in black print on rear of p/s)	8
88	Silvertone ORET 1	Elephant Stone (4.48)/Elephant Stone (7" Version) (3.00)/Full Fathom Five/The Hardest Thing In The World (12", p/s, cat. no. in black print on rear of p/s) (unique recording of Full Fathom Five on original pressing)	25
89	Silvertone ORE 2	Made Of Stone/Going Down (p/s, cat. no. in black print on rear of p/s)	7
89	Silvertone ORET 2	Made Of Stone/Going Down/Guernica (12", p/s, catalogue number in black print on rear of p/s)	18
89	Silvertone OREX 6	She Bangs The Drums/Standing Here (p/s, with postcard, 3,000 only)	8
89	Silvertone OREZ 6	She Bangs The Drums/Mersey Paradise/Standing Here (12", p/s with colour print (I Wanna Be Adored cover), 5,000 only)	15
89	Silvertone ORE 13	What The World Is Waiting For/Fools Gold 4.15 (paper label, with postcard stickered p/s credits "What The World Is Waiting For")	8
89	Silvertone ORET 13	What The World Is Waiting For/Fools Gold 9.23 (12", stickered p/s credits What The World Is Waiting For, with print)	15
89	Black/Revolver 12 REV 36	Sally Cinnamon/Here It Comes/All Across The Sand (12" 'Printed in W Germany' on rear p/s – barcode)	10
89	Black/Revolver REV 36	Sally Cinnamon/Here It Comes (p/s)	6
90	Silvertone ORE 1	Elephant Stone (7" Version)/The Hardest Thing In The World (catalogue number in red print on rear of p/s)	8
90	Silvertone ORE 2	Made Of Stone/Going Down (p/s, cat. no. in blue print on rear of p/s)	6
90	Fierce FRIGHT 044	SPIKE ISLAND EP (fan interviews, P.A. announcements & fireworks, with cigarette, badge, bag of grass & banana sweet)	18
90	Silvertone OREZ 13	Fools Gold (The Top Won Mix!)/Fools Gold (The Bottom Won Mix!) (12")	12
91	Silvertone ORE 31	I Wanna Be Adored (3.28)/Where Angels Play (p/s)	6
91	Silvertone ORET 31	I Wanna Be Adored (4.52)/Where Angels Play/Sally Cinnamon (live at the Hacienda) (12" p/s)	10
91	Silvertone OREZ 31	I Wanna Be Adored (4.52)/Where Angels Play/Sally Cinnamon (live at the Hacienda) (12", stickered p/s with print)	18
92	Silvertone ORE 35	Waterfall (7" Version 3.31)/One Love (7" Version 3.40) (p/s)	6
92	Silvertone OREZT 35	Waterfall (12" Version 5.23)/One Love (Adrian Sherwood 12" Version 7.10) (12", p/s with print)	12
92	Silvertone ORE 40	I Am The Resurrection (Pan And Scan Radio Version)/I Am The Resurrection (Highly Resurrected Dub) (p/s)	6
92	Silvertone ORET 40	I Am The Resurrection (Extended 19:9 Ratio Club Mix)/(Original LP Version)/Fools Gold (Bottom Won Mix) (12", with print)	20
92	Silvertone ORET 40	I Am The Resurrection (Extended 19:9 Ratio Club Mix)/(Original LP Version)/Fools Gold (Bottom Won Mix) (12", without print)	15
92	Black/Revolver 12REV 36	Sally Cinnamon/All Across The Sands/Here It Comes (12" reissue, barcode on sleeve)	10
92	Silvertone SRBX 2	12" SINGLES COLLECTION (10 x 12" singles box set, numbered 1,000 only)	150
92	Silvertone SRBX 1	COMPACT DISC SINGLES COLLECTION (8 x CD singles box set, 1,000 only)	35
95	Geffen GFST 87	Ten Storey Love Song/Moses/Ride On (12", stickered/numbered p/s)	10
95	Geffen GFST 22060	Begging You (Album Version)/(Chic Mix)/(Cox's Ultimatum Mix)/(Stone Corporation Vox) (12" p/s with art print)	10
09	Silvertone 88697574727	THE 7" SINGLES COLLECTION (5 x 7" box set)	30

ALBUMS : LPS
89	Silvertone ORE LP 502	THE STONE ROSES (LP, original pressing, embossed sleeve with gold lettering)	40
89	Silvertone ORE LP 502	THE STONE ROSES (LP, original pressing, not embossed gold lettering)	25
91	Silvertone OREZ LP 502	THE STONE ROSES (2-LP, reissue, numbered gatefold sleeve with silver lettering)	25
92	Silvertone ORE LP 521	TURNS INTO STONE (LP, original pressing)	30
94	Geffen GEF 24503	SECOND COMING (2-LP, original pressing, gatefold)	35
95	Silvertone ORE LP 535	THE COMPLETE STONE ROSES (2-LP)	25
96	Garage Flower GARAGE LP 1	GARAGE FLOWER (LP, with print)	40
96	Garage Flower GARAGE LP 1	GARAGE FLOWER (LP, without print)	25
99	Geffen/Simply Vinyl SVLP 111	SECOND COMING (2-LP, limited edition, gatefold, heavy duty 180g vinyl)	20
09	Silvertone 88697430302	THE STONES ROSES (Box set, 3-CD, LP, 2x12", DVD, memory stick)	80
10	Silvertone Sony/BMG 88697694171	THE STONE ROSES (LP, 1000 only, numbered, 2010 Record Store day release with 6 art prints)	30

STONE'S MASONRY

MINT VALUE £

PROMOS
85	Thin Line THIN 001	So Young/Tell Me (12" promo (pale) pink label test press) 100 pressed (in Cartel sleeve with press pack)	400
85	Thin Line THIN 001	So Young/Tell Me (12" promo (pale) pink label test pressing, 100 pressed, this price without press pack)	250
89	Silvertone ORE DJ 6	She Bangs The Drums (7" promo)	12
89	Silvertone ORE DJ T 13	Fools Gold 9.53/ What The World Is Waiting For (12" promo, b-side white label)	20
89	Silvertone ORE DJ 13	Fools Gold 4.15/ What The World Is Waiting For (7" promo)	12
90	Silvertone ORE DJ T 17	One Love/Something's Burning (12" promo, b-side white label)	12
90	Silvertone ORE DJ 17	One Love (7" edit) /Something's Burning (7" edit) (7" promo)	12
92	Silvertone ORE T DJ 34	Waterfall (12" Version 5.23)/One Love (Adrian Sherwood 12" Version 7.10) (12" promo)	15
90	Silvertone STONE ONE	Fools Gold (A Guy Called Gerald Remix)/Elephant Stone (DJ Mix) (12", white label) this is actually a bootleg recording by Hard Tymez Productions	15

(see also Ian Brown, Seahorses)

STONE'S MASONRY
66	Purdah 45-3504	Flapjacks/Hot Rock (99 copies only)	200

(see also Action, Mighty Baby)

STONE TEMPLE PILOTS
92	Atlantic 7567824	CORE (LP)	40
94	Atlantic 82607	PURPLE - 12 GRACIOUS MELODIES (LP, purple vinyl)	40

STONE THE CROWS
70	Polydor 2425 017	STONE THE CROWS (LP)	80
70	Polydor 2425 042	ODE TO JOHN LAW (LP, gatefold sleeve)	60
71	Polydor 2425 071	TEENAGE LICKS (LP, gatefold sleeve)	60
72	Polydor 2391 043	ONTINUOUS PERFORMANCE (LP)	20

(see also White Trash)

STONEY BROOK PEOPLE
69	CBS 4538	Easy To Be Hard/There's Tomorrow	30

STONEY & MEAT LOAF
71	Rare Earth RES 103	What You See Is What You Get/The Way You Do The Things You Do	12
79	Prodigal PROD 10	What You See Is What You Get/The Way You Do The Things You Do (reissue)	8
72	Rare Earth SRE 3005	STONEY AND MEAT LOAF (LP)	25
79	Prodigal PDL 2010	MEAT LOAF (FEATURING STONEY & MEAT LOAF) (LP, revised reissue of "Stoney And Meat Loaf" with different tracks)	15

(see also Meat Loaf)

STOOGES
05	Elektra 8122732137	I Wanna Be Your Dog/Real Cool TIme (reissue)	8
69	Elektra EKS 74051	THE STOOGES (LP, red label)	250
70	Elektra 2410 009	FUN HOUSE (LP, red label)	300
73	CBS 65586	RAW POWER (LP, as Iggy & Stooges, no name on front cover, plain orange label, with inner sleeve)	100
77	Elektra K 42032	THE STOOGES (LP, reissue, 'butterfly' label)	20
77	Elektra K 42051	FUN HOUSE (LP, reissue, 'butterfly' label)	20
99	Elektra 7559624421	NO FUN (LP, as The Stooges featuring Iggy Pop)	15
05	Elektra 8122 73237 1	THE STOOGES (2-LP, reissue, gatefold)	25
05	Elektra 8122 73238 1	FUN HOUSE (2-LP, reissue, gatefold)	25

(see also Iggy Pop)

STOP THE TRAIN
83	Stranded S83 CUS 1908	Suspicions/Empty Rooms	10

STOPOUTS
78	Skeleton LYN 5912	Strange Thoughts/Just For You And Me (p/s)	15

STOREY SISTERS
58	London HLU 8571	Bad Motorcycle/Sweet Daddy	50
58	London HLU 8571	Bad Motorcycle/Sweet Daddy (78)	25

STORM
85	Silent SILENT 1	Malice In Wonderland/Malice In Wonderland (Edit)/Doctor Storm (12", p/s)	25

STORM/CUTMASTER SWIFT
91	White SOLID001	Playing The Field/Live In Spain (12")	70

STORM/MIGHTY ETHNICZ
91	Bite It! BITE 3	You're Out There (12")	10

BILLY STORM
59	Philips PB 916	I've Come Of Age/This Is Always	10
60	London HLK 9236	Sure As You're Born/In The Chapel In The Moonlight	10

DANNY STORM (& STROLLERS)
62	Piccadilly 7N 35025	Honest I Do/Sad But True (in p/s)	10
62	Piccadilly 7N 35025	Honest I Do/Sad But True	7
62	Piccadilly 7N 35053	Just You/I Told You So	10
62	Piccadilly 7N 35091	I Just Can't Fool My Heart/Thinking Of You	12
63	Piccadilly 7N 35143	Say You Do/Let The Sunshine In (as Danny Storm & Strollers)	15

GALE STORM
56	London HLD 8222	I Hear You Knocking/Never Leave Me	50
56	London HLD 8232	Memories Are Made Of This/A Teen-Age Prayer	30
56	London HLD 8283	Ivory Tower/I Ain't Gonna Worry	25
56	London HLD 8286	Why Do Fools Fall In Love/I Walk Alone	20
56	London HL 7008	Why Do Fools Fall In Love/I Walk Alone (export issue)	20
56	London HLD 8311	Don't Be That Way (Please Listen To Me)/Tell Me Why	25
56	London HLD 8329	A Heart Without A Sweetheart/Now Is The Hour	15
57	London HLD 8393	Lucky Lips/On Treasure Island	30
57	London HLD 8413	Orange Blossoms/My Heart Belongs To You	15
57	London HLD 8424	Dark Moon/A Little Too Late	15

Rory STORM & HURRICANES

MINT VALUE £

58	London HLD 8570	Love Theme From "Farewell To Arms"/I Get That Feeling	10
58	London HLD 8632	You/Angry	10
56	London HB-D 1056	PRESENTING GALE STORM (10" LP)	40
58	London HA-D 2104	SENTIMENTAL ME (LP)	30

RORY STORM & HURRICANES
63	Oriole CB 1858	Dr. Feelgood/I Can Tell	45
64	Parlophone R 5197	America/Since You Broke My Heart	25

(see also Keef Hartley, Paddy Klaus & Gibson)

STORMBOYS
84	Guardian GRC 360	Wasted On Me/Instrumental Remix (p/s)	8

STORMCHILD
82	Serpent S001	Rockin'Steady/Last Night (hand folded sleeve, white label, 50 only)	1000

ROBB STORME (& WHISPERS)
60	Decca F 11282	1000, 900 And When/I Don't Need Your Love Anymore	6
61	Decca F 11313	Music/Five Minutes More (as Robb Storme & Whispers)	6
61	Decca F 11388	Transistor Sister/Earth Angel	12
63	Pye 7N 15515	Sixteen Years Ago Tonight/Surprise Surprise	7
63	Piccadilly 7N 35133	Happens Ev'ryday/Surprise Surprise	6
63	Piccadilly 7N 35160	To Know Her Is To Love Her/Bu Bop A Lu Bop A Lie	6
65	Pye 7N 15819	Love Is Strange/Shy Guy	10
65	Columbia DB 7756	Where Is My Girl?/Double Oh Seven (as Robb Storme & Whispers)	10
66	Columbia DB 7993	Here Today/Don't Cry (as Robb Storme Group)	20
62	Decca DFE 6200	WHEELS (EP)	100

STORMER
78	Ring O' 2017 113	My Home Town/Shake It Baby (in promo p/s)	70
78	Ring O' 2017 113	My Home Town/Shake It Baby	40

STORM QUEEN
82	Real Fire RF001	Come Silent The Night/Raising The Roof (1st press, red labels no p/s)	400
82	Real Fire RF001	Come Silent To The World/Raising The Roof (2nd press, black labels with correct spelling for A-side)	275

STORMRIDER
77	Crossover CS 7701	Mr Supercool/Sister Bring Down (no p/s)	30

STORMTROOPER (1)
78	Solent SS 047	I'm A Mess/It's Not Me (in stamped plain sleeve with insert)	30
78	Solent SS 047	I'm A Mess/It's Not Me	12

STORMTROOPER (2)
80	Heartbeat BEAT 1	Pride Before A Fall/Still Comin' Home (p/s)	25

STORMY PETREL
71	CBS 7271	Hello Hello Hello/The Light Of Day	10

STORYTELLER (1)
70	Transatlantic TRA 220	STORYTELLER (LP, gatefold sleeve, white/lilav label, 't' logo)	60
71	Transatlantic TRA 232	MORE PAGES (LP, textured sleeve)	35

(see also Johnny Neal & Starliners, Terry Durham, Other Two, Andy Bown)

STORYTELLER (2)
79	Alladin MDS 1002	Just Another Cloud In The Sky/Weatherman	20

STORYTELLER (3)
85	Storyteller ZELSP 438	Mystery Girl (p/s)	50

LALLY STOTT
71	Philips 6025029	Jakaranda/Love Is Free Love Is Blind	8
71	Philips 6323 006	CHIRPY CHIRPY CHEEP CHEEP (LP)	15

WALLY STOTT ORCHESTRA/CHORUS
60	Pye 7N 15271	The Unforgiven/Mr. Lucky	6

DAVID STOUGHTON
68	Elektra EKS 74034	TRANSFORMER (LP)	40

STOWAWAYS
79	Supermusic SUP 27	I Wanna Be Me/My Friends/You'll Tie Me Down (p/s)	25

STP 23
89	Wau! Mr. Modo WMS 001R	Let Jimi Take Over/Let Jimi Take Over (Remix By Youth) (12", p/s)	10

STRAFE FÜR REBELLION
80s	Touch TO 6	SANTA MARIA (LP, with inner)	15

STRAIGHT EIGHT
78	Eel Pie EPS 003	Modern Times/Tell Me If You Wanna Bleed (p/s)	10
80	Logo DEAL 1	I'm Sorry/Satisfied (p/s)	6
82	Logo GO 416	Tomorrow/Faded Stars/You Are What You Are (with p/s)	10
82	Logo GO 416	Tomorrow/Faded Stars/You Are What You Are	8
79	Eel Pie EPRP 001	NO NOISE FROM HERE (LP)	15

STRAIGHT UP
80	Rok XX/XIX	One Out All Out/JUSTIN CASE: T.V. (die-cut company sleeve)	40

STRAIGHT CORNERS
80	SRTS/80/CUS 809	Legal Executive/Berlin Wall (p/s)	25

STRAIGHT SHOOTER BAND
83	Magic MR 001	Blueman/Flag Of Freedom (p/s)	20

STRAIGHTSHOOTER
79	Strolling Bone S 79 CUS 398	Straightshooter/She's So Fine (no p/s)	120

NICK STRAKER
83	Pinnacle PIN 100T	Turn Me Down/We Can Still Be Friends (12")	15

PETER STRAKER
74	RCA LPBO 5011	From The Underworld/Love Motion	8
77	EMI EMI 2700	Ragtime Piano Joe/Saddest Clown	10

STRAND
80	Yob YOB 001	Here Today Gone Tomorrow/Changing World/POSITIVE SIGNALS: Media Man/Only For A	15

Pauline STRAND

MINT VALUE £

Day (split EP, p/s) ....

PAULINE STRAND
68   Carousel CR3   Love Me Always/The End Of Me 25
STRANDSMEN
67   Philips BF 1572   I Know/Stay Close To Me 10
JOHN STRANG
68   No label or cat no   THE MASTERPIECE (LP, 50 only, white labels in finished sleeve) 400
BILLY STRANGE (& CHALLENGERS)
61   London HLG 9321   Where Your Arms Used To Be/Sadness Done Come 6
64   Vocalion V-N 9228   The James Bond Theme/007 Theme 15
64   Vocalion V-N 9231   Goldfinger/"Munsters" Theme 10
66   Vocalion V-N 9257   Thunderball/"Ninth Man" Theme 10
66   Vocalion V-N 9259   Get Smart/Run Spy, Run 15
67   Vocalion V-N 9289   A Few Dollars More Theme/You Only Live Twice 10
63   Vocalion VA/SVN 8022   12-STRING GUITAR (LP) 15
64   Vocalion VAN 8026   MR GUITAR (LP) 15
64   Vocalion VAN/SAVN 8032   THE JAMES BOND THEME (LP) 20
65   Vocalion VAN/SAVN 8038   GOLDFINGER (LP) 20
65   Vocalion VAN/SAVN 8042   ENGLISH HITS OF '65 (LP) 15
65   Vocalion VAN/SAVN 8045   STRANGE PLAYS THE HITS (LP) 15
(see also Cliffie Stone)
STRANGE BROTHERS SHOW
70   Polydor 2001-116   Right On/Shakey Jakes 15
STRANGE BUT TRUE
91   SBT 001   Blair Peach/Stephanie 10
GILES STRANGE
66   Stateside SS 570   Watch The People Dance/You're Goin' Up To The Bottom (DJ Copy) 100
66   Stateside SS 570   Watch The People Dance/You're Goin' Up To The Bottom 80
STEVE STRANGE
82   Palace PALACE 1   In The Year 2525/Strange Connexions (white label, unreleased) 30
82   Palace PALACE 1   In The Year 2525/Strange Connexions (p/s, available separately) 20
(see also Visage)
STRANGE CRUISE
86   EMI 12EMI 5549   Rebel Blue Rocker/Love Addiction (12", p/s) 10
86   EMI EMC 3513   STRANGE CRUISE (LP) 18
STRANGE DAYS (1)
75   Retreat RTL 6005   NINE PARTS TO THE WIND (LP, lyric inner sleeve, blue label) 25
STRANGE DAYS (2)
83   Powerstation OHM 1   Within These Walls/Swimming Into The Doctor 15
STRANGE FOX
70   Parlophone R5876   Bring It On HOme/Time And Tide 30
73   Parlophone R5978   Rock 'N' Roll Band/Tamarin Girl 15
STRANGE FRUIT
71   Village Thing VTSX 1001   Cut Across Shorty/Shake That Thing 25
STRANGELOVE
94   Food FOODLP 11   TIME FOR THE REST OF YOUR LIFE (2-LP, numbered) 40
96   Food FOODLP 15   LOVE AND OTHER DEMONS (LP, with 12 page booklet) 40
97   Food FOODLPD 24   STRANGELOVE (2-LP) 40
STRANGELOVES
65   Stateside SS 446   I Want Candy/It's About My Baby 25
65   Immediate IM 007   Cara-Lin/Roll On Mississippi 30
66   London HLZ 10020   Night Time/Rhythm Of Love 50
66   London HLZ 10063   Hand Jive/I Gotta Dance 12
69   London HLZ 10238   Honey Do/I Wanna Do It 15
(see also Beach-Nuts)
STRANGE MOVEMENTS
79   Good Vibrations GOT 5   Dancing In The Ghetto/Amuse Yourself (foldout p/s) 25
STRANGER (COLE)
63   Blue Beat BB 165   Rough And Tough (with Duke Reid Band)/DUKE REID BAND: The Mood I Am In 40
63   Blue Beat BB 195   Miss Reamer/RICO & HIS BLUES BAND: Blues From The Hills 20
(see also Stranger Cole)
STRANGER (COLE) & GLADY (ANDERSON)
67   Island WI 3128   Love Me Today/Over Again 100
68   Amalgamated AMG 806   Seeing Is Knowing/ROY SHIRLEY: Music Is The Key 40
71   Clandisc CLA 230   Tomorrow (as Stranger & Gladdy)/DYNAMITES: Tomorrow Version 10
71   Supreme SUP 227   My Application (as Stranger & Gladdy)/TADDY & DIAMONDS: Oh No, My Baby 25
73   Count Shelley CS 015   Don't Give Up The Fight (as Stranger & Gladdy)/TIDALS: Stand Firm 10
73   Dragon DRA 1014   Conqueror/Conqueror (Instrumental Version) 20
(see also Stranger Cole, Gladdy & Followers, Gladstone Anderson, Gladdy & Stranger, Charlie Kelly)
STRANGER (COLE) & HORTENSE (ELLIS)
74   Count Shelley CS 049   Mocking Bird/Corra Bella Baby 6
STRANGER (COLE) & KEN (BOOTHE)
63   R&B JB 120   Thick In Love/All Your Friends 30
(see also Stranger Cole, Ken Boothe)
STRANGER (COLE) & PATSY (TODD)
63   Blue Beat BB 171   When I Call Your Name/Take My Heart (with Duke Reid All Stars) 25
63   Island WI 113   Senor And Senorita/DON DRUMMOND: Snowboy 35
64   Island WI 141   Oh Oh I Need You/DON DRUMMOND: J.F.K.'s Memory 35
64   Island WI 144   Tom, Dick And Harry/We Two, Happy People 20
64   Island WI 152   Yeah Yeah Baby/BABA BROOKS: Boat Ride 25

STRANGERS (with Mike Shannon)

MINT VALUE £

64	Island WI 160	Miss B/Thing Come To Those Who Wait	20
65	Black Swan WI 462	Hey Little Girl/CORNELL CAMBELL: Make Hay	40
66	Rio R 81	Give Me One More Chance/Fire In Cornfield	18
66	Doctor Bird DB 1050	Give Me The Right/Tonight	30
67	Doctor Bird DB 1084	Tell It To Me/Your Photograph	120
67	Doctor Bird DB 1087	Down The Trainlines/Sing And Pray	40
69	Escort ES 807	My Love/SWEET CONFUSION: Windsor Castle	28
69	Escort ES 811	Why Did You/Do You Remember	12

(see also Stranger Cole, Patsy)

STRANGERS (WITH MIKE SHANNON)

64	Philips BF 1335	One And One Is Two/Time And The River (as Strangers with Mike Shannon)	40
64	Philips BF 1378	Do You Or Don't You/What Can I Do	8

(see also Shadows)

STRANGERS

67	Pye 7N 17240	Look Out (Here Comes Tomorrow)/Mary Mary	40
67	Pye 7N 17351	You Didn't Have To Be So Nice/Daytime Turns To Night	15
68	Pye 7N 17585	I'm On An Island/Step Inside	20

STRANGER THAN FICTION

79	Ellie Jay EJSP 9301	Into The Void/Darkness (p/s)	25
87	Constitution CON 3T	Prelude/Is She In Love With Love/The Realization (12", p/s)	25

STRANGE STONE

77	Own label DER 1399	STRANGE STONE (LP, private pressing, numbered sleeve with insert, 255 only)	400

STRANGE U

13	Eglo EGLP 025	SCARLET JUNGLE EP	50
14	White Label STRANGEU 01	EP 2040 (EP)	35
14	Y n R YNR 062	Dolph Lundgren/Instrumental (gig-only 7" with JEHST)	50
17	High Focus HFRLP 056	#LP4080 (2-LP)	35

STRANGEWAYS

78	Real ARE 2	Show Her you Care/You're On Your Own (p/s)	20
79	Real ARE 7	Wasting Time/All The Sounds Of Fear (p/s)	30

STRANGLERS

SINGLES

77	United Artists UP 36211	(Get A) Grip (On Yourself)/London Lady (card p/s)	12
77	United Artists UP 36248	Peaches/Go Buddy Go ('group' p/s with 'blackmail' lettering, withdrawn)	800
77	United Artists UP 36248	Peaches/Go Buddy Go ('peach' p/s)	12
77	United Artists UP 36277	Something Better Change/Straighten Out (p/s)	8
77	United Artists UP 36300	No More Heroes/In The Shadows (p/s, 'wreath' label)	8
80	United Artists 12-BP 344	Bear Cage (Extended)/Shah Shah A Go Go (Extended) (12", p/s)	10
84	Epic A 4738	Skin Deep/Here And There ('skin-feel' p/s, with 'Skin Deep' tattoo, 10,000 only)	6
84	Epic EPC GA 4921	No Mercy/In One Door/Hot Club (Riot Mix)/Head On The Line (gatefold)	6
86	Epic SOLAR D1	Always The Sun/Norman Normal//Nice In Nice/Since You Went Away (double pack, shrinker & stickered)	8
86	Epic HUGE D1	Big In America/Dry Day//Always The Sun/Norman Normal (double pack, shrinkwrapped & stickered)	8
88	Epic VICE 1	All Day And All Of The Night/¡Viva Vlad! ('Monica Coughlan' p/s, withdrawn sold via fan club)	12
90	Epic TEARS T1	96 Tears/Instead Of This/Poisonality (12" p/s with 'paint set')	15
14	Parophone RSD14TS	Peaches/Go Buddy Go (reissue, 'group' p/s with 'blackmail' lettering, green vinyl)	10

ALBUMS : LPS

77	United Artists UAG 30045	STRANGLERS IV - RATTUS NORVEGICUS (LP, 10,000 with 7" Choosey Susie/"Peasant In The Big Shitty" (Live At The Nashville, 12/76) [FREE 3, orange p/s,"What Do You Expect..." in run-off groove], some with sticker)	50
77	United Artists UAG 30045	STRANGLERS IV - RATTUS NORVEGICUS (LP)	20
77	United Artists UAG 30200	NO MORE HEROES (LP, inner)	15
78	United Artists UAK 30222	BLACK AND WHITE (LP, 75,000 with white vinyl 7" "Walk On By"/"Tits"/"Mean To Me [FREE 9, black die-cut sleeve & card insert], mispressed on blue or beige vinyl)	65
78	United Artists UAK 30222	BLACK AND WHITE (LP, 75,000 with white vinyl 7" "Walk On By"/"Tits"/"Mean To Me [FREE 9, black die-cut sleeve & card insert])	18
79	United Artists UAG 30262	THE RAVEN (LP, 20,000 with 3-D cover, cartoon on inner sleeve)	20
82	Liberty LBG 30353	THE COLLECTION '77-82 (LP, withdrawn plastic logo sleeve)	25
83	Epic EPC 25237	FELINE (LP, with bonus 1-sided 7" "Aural Sculpture" [XPS 167])	15
92	United Artists SPEAKDLP 101	EARLY YEARS 74-75-76 RARE LIVE & UNRELEASED (2-LP, orange/green vinyl)	25
95	When! WEL LP 001	ABOUT TIME (LP, numbered)	30

PROMOS : FREEBIES, PROMOS & MISCELLANEA

75	(no cat no)	My Young Dreams/Wasted (existence unconfirmed)	150
77	United Artists FREE 4	Peaches (radio version)/Go Buddy Go (promo only, p/s)	750
77	United Artists FREE 4	Peaches (radio version)/Go Buddy Go (promo only, no p/s)	150
77	United Artists UP 36262	Mony Mony/Mean To Me (p/s, as Celia And The Mutations)	7
77	United Artists UP 36211	(Get A) Grip (On Yourself)/London Lady (double A label demo)	25
77	United Artists UP 36277	Something Better Change/Straighten Out	25
77	United Artists FREE 8	No More Heroes (1-sided radio edit, promo only)	150
77	United Artists UP 36300	No More Heroes (1-sided, misprinted "No More Stheroes")	25
77	United Artists UP 36300	No More Heroes/In The Shadows (p/s, stamped, misprinted "No More Stheroes")	25
78	United Artists UP 36248	Peaches/Go Buddy Go (p/s, mispressing, B-side plays Buzzcocks' "Oh Shit")	75
78	United Artists UP 36300	Walk On By (Promo Edit)/Old Codger/Tank	25
78	United Artists FREE 9	Walk On By/Mean To Me/Tits (EP [free with LP U.A. UAK 30222], mispressing, black die-cut sleeve & card insert, blue/clear vinyl)	30
78	United Artists FREE 9	Walk On By/Mean To Me/Tits (EP [free with LP U.A. UAK 30222], mispressing, black die-cut sleeve & card insert, pink/clear vinyl)	15
78	United Artists UP 36350	5 Minutes/Rok It To Me Moon (A label demo)	15
78	United Artists UP 36379	Nice N Sleazy/Shut Up (A label demo)	12

STRAPS

MINT VALUE £

78	United Artists UP 36379	Nice 'N' Sleazy/Shut Up (p/s, mispressing, B-side plays tracks by other artist)	30
79	United Artists PB 308	Duchess/Fools Rush Out (A label demo)	10
79	United Artists PB 318	Nuclear Device (The Wizard Of Aus)/Yellowcake UF 6 (A label demo)	10
79	United Artists UA STR 1 DJ	Don't Bring Harry/HUGH CORNWELL: Wired (45rpm, promo only)	20
79	United Artists (no cat. no.)	Two Sunspots (unreleased)	30
79	United Artists UAG 30262	THE RAVEN (LP, mispressing, 2nd side plays country & western [B-side matrix: UAK 30263])	25
80	Stranglers Info Service SIS 001	Tomorrow Was The Hereafter/Bring On The Nubiles (Cocktail Version) (numbered p/s, label has "Nublies")	15
81	Liberty BP 393	Just Like Nothing On Earth/Maninwhite (p/s, mispressing, plays A-side both sides)	20
82	Epic EPC A2893	The European Female (In Celebration Of)/(Promo Edit)	10
82	Liberty BP 410	La Folie (Promo Edit)/Waltzinblack	10
82	Liberty LBG 30353	THE COLLECTION '77-82 (LP, Stranglers' own concept sleeve, unissued)	0
82	United Artists BP 407	Golden Brown/Love 30 (B-side plays "Everybody Salsa")	20

STRAPS

80	Donut DONUT 1	Just Can't Take Anymore/New Age (p/s)	8
82	Donut DONUT 3	Brixton/No Liquor (p/s)	12
83	Cyclops CYC 2	THE STRAPS ALBUM (LP)	15

(see also Public Image Ltd.)

STRATEGY

82	Ebony EBON 7	Technical Overflow/Astral Planes (in p/s)	60
82	Ebony EBON 7	Technical Overflow/Astral Planes	50

STRATE JACKET

80	Wessex WEX 269	You're A Hit/Too Soon Too Young (stamped plain sleeve)	15

STRATUS

85	Steel Trax STEEL 31001	THROWING SHAPES (LP)	18

(see also Grand Prix, Uriah Heep, Iron Maiden, Praying Mantis)

STRAWBERRY ALARM CLOCK

67	Pye International 7N 25436	Incense And Peppermints/The Birdman Of Alkatrash	30
68	Pye International 7N 25446	Tomorrow/Birds In My Tree	20
68	Pye International 7N 25456	Sit With The Guru/Pretty Song From Psych-Out	20
69	MCA MU 1080	Good Morning Starshine/Me And The Township	10
68	NPL 28106	INCENSE AND PEPPERMINTS (LP, mono)	200
68	Pye Intl. NSPL 28106	INCENSE AND PEPPERMINTS (LP, stereo)	150

STRAWBERRY CHILDREN

67	Liberty LBF 15012	Love Years Coming/One Stands Here	35

(see also Jim Webb)

STRAWBERRY JAM

69	Pye 7N 17711	Per-Son-Al-Ly/This Is To A Girl	10

STRAWBERRY PARK

82	Sonet 2245	Summer Is A Coming/Beach Party (in p/s)	8
82	Sonet 2245	Summer Is A Coming/Beach Party	7

STRAWBERRY SMELL

97	Detour DR 053	Penelope Bloomington/Kangeroo In My Garden (p/s, blue vinyl, 100 only)	6

STRAWBERRY SWITCHBLADE

85	Korova KODE 11	STRAWBERRY SWITCHBLADE (LP, with bonus 7" "Trees And Flowers", mispressed with some tracks playing twice & others out of order)	15

(see also Poems)

STRAWBS

68	A&M AMS 725	Oh How She Changed/Or Am I Dreaming	30
68	A&M AMS 738	The Man Who Called Himself Jesus/Poor Jimmy Wilson	8
70	A&M AMS 791	Forever/Another Day	10
71	A&M AMS 837	Witchwood/Keep The Devil Outside/We'll Meet Again Sometime (live) (withdrawn)	30
71	A&M AMS 874	Benedictus/Keep The Devil Outside	6
69	private pressing	STRAWBERRY MUSIC SAMPLER NO. 1 (LP, publisher's sampler, 100 only)	500
69	A&M AMLS 936	STRAWBS (LP; disc inserted in middle of sleeve)	50
69	A&M AMLS 936	STRAWBS (LP; disc inserted at edge of sleeve)	30
70	A&M AMLS 970	DRAGONFLY (LP, textured sleeve, lyric insert, mustard label)	40
70	A&M AMLS 994	JUST A COLLECTION OF ANTIQUES AND CURIOS (LP, laminated gatefold sleeve, mustard label; 2 different rear sleeves)	20
71	A&M AMLH 64304	FROM THE WITCHWOOD (LP, gatefold sleeve)	40
72	A&M AMLH 68078	GRAVE NEW WORLD (LP, triple gatefold sleeve, with 12-page booklet)	15
73	Hallmark SHM 813	ALL OUR OWN WORK (LP, with Sandy Denny)	20
74	A&M AMLH 63607	HERO AND HEROINE (LP, inner)	15
74	A&M AMLH 68277	GHOSTS (LP, inner)	15

(see also Dave Cousins, Sandy Denny, Fire, Foggy, Monks, Davey & Morris, Hudson-Ford, Yes, Rick Wakeman)

STRAW DOGS

81	(No label) DOG 001	Black Leather/Don't Need You/We Ain't Dead (Yet)/All The Lads (some with xeroxed sleeve)	80

STRAY

70	Transatlantic PROMO 1	Only What You Make It/Time Machine	50
72	Big T BIG 141	Our Song/Mama's Coming Home	8
73	Transatlantic BIG 12	Hallelujah/Brand New Day	7
70	Transatlantic TRA 216	STRAY (LP, die-cut gatefold sleeve, white/lilac 't' logo label)	50
71	Transatlantic TRA 233	SUICIDE (LP, textured sleeve, white/lilac 't' logo label)	40
71	Transatlantic TRA 248	SATURDAY MORNING PICTURES (LP, gatefold sleeve)	25
73	Transatlantic TRA 268	MUDANZAS (LP, gatefold sleeve)	25
74	Transatlantic TRA 281	MOVE IT (LP, die-cut sleeve with inner)	15
75	Dawn DNLS 3066	STAND UP AND BE COUNTED (LP, lyric insert, pink 'sun' label)	15

STRAY DOG

74	Manticore K 13508	Junkyard Angel/World Winds	6

STREAK

			MINT VALUE £
73	Manticore K 43506	STRAY DOG (LP, textured sleeve, insert)	20
74	Manticore K 53504	WHILE YOU'RE DOWN THERE (LP)	20

(see also Emerson Lake & Palmer)

STREAK
72	A&M AME 602	Gonna Have A Good Time/Be Your Ryder/Hard Times (In New York City) (promo, b side plays at 33 rpm)	40
72	A&M AMS 7012	Gonna Have A Good Time/Be Your Ryder	15
73	Deram DM 376	Bang Bang Bullet/Black Jack Man	15

STREAKERS
74	Dawn DNS 1066	Turn Me Down/Wake Up Sunshine	15

STREET BIZARRE
79	Monarch MON 05	Normal Life/Nervous Exhaustion	150

GARY STREET & FAIRWAYS
68	Domain D 2	Flipperty Flop/Hold Me Closer	20

(see also Fairways)

JOHN STREET & INMATES OF NO. 12
67	Deram DM 147	Keep A Little Love/My Kind Of Luck	10

JUDY STREET
78	Grapevine GRP 106	What/You Turn Me On	10
78	Grapevine GRP 106	What/You Turn Me On (DJ Copy)	15
82	Soul Stop SS 3003	What/HI-FLY: Theme For A Dream	15
13	Outta Sight OSV 088	What/TINA MASON: What	10

STREET LEGAL
84	Weird Brothers SLW 1	Rollin' On/Mississippi Moonshine (p/s, initially with sticker over typo error in sleeve)	150
84	Weird Brothers SLW 1	Rollin' On/Mississippi Moonshine (p/s, without sticker)	150

STREETFIGHTER
82	J.R. JR 7049S	CRAZY DREAM (EP)	40

STREETFIGHTER (U.K.)
81	Streetfighter 749	STREETFIGHTER (12" EP)	25

STREET PEOPLE (1)
70	Stateside SS 2163	Jennifer Tomkins/All Night Long	10

STREET PEOPLE (2)
79	Ellie Jay EJSP 9276	PERSONAL VALUES EP (500 only, p/s)	75

STREETS
02	Locked On 679003TLP	ORIGINAL PIRATE MATERIAL (2-LP)	20
04	679 679LD70LP	A GRAND DON'T COME FOR FREE (2-LP)	25

STREET SERVICE
90	I Like It ILIT 01	JUST FOR YOU (LP)	18

STREET SPIRITS
77	Storm SR 020	Street Strutting Punks/All Right/Excitement In The Air/Makin Me Sore (no p/s)	15

STREETWALKERS
76	Vertigo 9102 010	RED CARD (LP, red vinyl with inner sleeve, numbered, 'spaceship' label)	15

(see also Hummingbird, Nicko McBrain)

TEXAS' BILL STRENGTH
55	Capitol CL 14357	Cry, Cry, Cry/The Yellow Rose Of Texas	8

STRESS (2)
91	Eternal YZ 550	Flowers In The Rain/Flowers In The Rain (p/s)	6
85	Adventures In Reality ARR 14	THE BIG WHEEL (LP, with insert)	40

STRETCH
75	Anchor ANCL 2014	ELASTIQUE (LP)	15
76	Anchor ANCL 2016	YOU CAN'T BEAT YOUR BRAIN FOR ENTERTAINMENT (LP)	15
77	Anchor ANCL 2023	LIFE BLOOD (LP)	15
78	Hot Wax HW 1	FORGET THE PAST (LP)	30

(see also Elmer Gantry, Kirby, Status Quo, Clifford Davis, Legs, Curved Air)

STRETCHHEADS
88	Moksha SOMALP2	FIVE FINGERS FOUR (LP)	20

DAVID STRETTON
68	Plum PL 4	Windmills/Haunted Staircase	20

WILLIAM R. STRICKLAND
69	Deram DML/SML 1041	WILLIAM R. STRICKLAND IS ONLY THE NAME (LP)	20

STRIDER
73	GM GML 1002	EXPOSED (LP, gatefold sleeve)	30
74	GM GML 1012	MISUNDERSTOOD (LP)	20

(see also Samson)

STRIFE
77	Outlaw OUT 1	School/Go/Feel So Good (p/s)	10
75	Chrysalis 1063	RUSH (LP)	15
78	Gull GULP 1029	BACK TO THUNDER (LP, on green vinyl with poster)	18

STRIKE
80	Shock SRS 504	Teenage Rebel/Radio Songs (p/s, Irish issue but imported into U.K.)	150

LIZA STRIKE
68	Parlophone R 5725	All's Quiet On West 23rd/Mr Daddy-Man	15

(see also Liza & Jet Set, Soulmates, Vice Versa)

STRIKER BLUE
76	Bootlegger 596	Get On Down/Loyalty To The Board	75

STRIKERS BAGTHORPE & CHILDREN OF SELSTON BAGTHORPE PRIMARY SCHOOL CHOIR
78	Eagle EGL 003	Good Old Charlie/Forest Fire	8

STRING-A-LONGS
61	London HLU 9354	Panic Button/Brass Buttons	6
61	London HLU 9394	Should I/Take A Minute	7

STRING CHEESE

MINT VALUE £

61	London HLU 9452	Scottie/Ming Bird	6
62	London HLD 9535	Sunday/Twistwatch	10
62	London HLD 9588	Spinning My Wheels/My Blue Heaven	8
63	London HLD 9652	Matilda/Replica	12
61	London RE-U 1322	THE STRING-A-LONGS (EP)	25
63	London RE-D 1350	THE STRING-A-LONGS (EP)	25
63	London RE-D 1398	STRINGALONG WITH THE STRING-A-LONGS (EP)	30
63	London HA-D 8054	THE STRING-A-LONGS (LP, mono)	40
63	London SH-D 8054	THE STRING-A-LONGS (LP, stereo)	40
69	London HAU/SHU 8371	WIDE WORLD HITS (LP)	25

STRING CHEESE
72	RCA SF 8222	STRING CHEESE (LP)	20

STRING DRIVEN THING
70	Concord CON 7	Another Night/Say What You Like	15
70	Concord CON 1001	STRING DRIVEN THING (LP, 100 only)	300
72	Charisma CAS 1062	STRING DRIVEN THING (LP, gatefold, insert,large 'Mad Hatter' label)	40
73	Charisma CAS 1070	THE MACHINE THAT CRIED (LP, gatefold sleeve, large 'Mad Hatter' label)	40
74	Charisma CAS 1097	PLEASE MIND YOUR HEAD (LP, lyric sheet, small 'Mad Hatter' label)	15
76	Charisma CAS 1112	KEEP YOUR 'AND ON IT (LP, insert)	15

STRIPES
82	Ellie Jay EJSP 9808/PINK01	One Step Ahead/Canteen Girls (no p/s)	100

STRIPES OF GLORY
62	Vogue V 9194	The Denial/O' Send The Fire	18

SYLVIA STRIPLIN
86	Music Of Love MOLS 8	Give Me Your Love/Will You Ever Pass This Way Again/Look Towards The Sky (12")	20
94	Expansion EXAPAND 47	You Can't Turn Me Away/INGRAM: Mi Sabrina Tecuana (12")	15
10	Universal Sounds US LP 34	GIVE ME YOUR LOVE (2-LP, reissue)	35

STROBE
82	SRR 1	MANDARIN LADY EP	10

ARTHUR 2 STROKE
79	Anti Pop AP 1	The Wundersea World Of Jacques Cousteau/NOISE TOYS: Pocket Money (p/s)	7

STROKES
80	Translobe Earways CD 1	I Am A Plastic Carrier Bag/Watcha (Whatcha) Gonna Do (p/s)	10

(THE) STROKES
01	Rough Trade RTRADES 010	The Modern Age/Last Nite (with barcode 2000 only)	25
01	Rough Trade RTRADES 023	Hard To Explain/New York City Cops (p/s, 2000 only)	8
01	Rough Trade RTRADES 041	Last Nite/When It Started (p/s)	12
02	Rough Trade RTRADES 063	Someday/Alone Together/Is This It (p/s, yellow vinyl)	10
03	Rough Trade RTRADES 140	12.51/The Way It Is (p/s, red vinyl)	6
03	Rough Trade RTRADES 155	Reptillia/Modern Girls & Old Fashioned Men (p/s)	7
06	Rough Trade RTRADES 305	Heart In A Cage/I'll Try Anything Once (p/s)	6
06	Rough Trade RTRADES 312	You Only Live Twice/Mercy Me (The Ecology) (p/s. sticker)	7
01	Rough Trade RTRADELP 030	IS THIS IT? (LP, 'STERLING' stamped in run-out groove)	80
03	Rough Trade RTRADELP 130	ROOM ON FIRE (LP)	18
06	Rough Trade RTRADELP 330	FIRST IMPRESSIONS OF EARTH (LP)	15

STROLLERS
58	Vogue V 9113	Jumping With Symphony Sid/Swinging Yellow Rose Of Texas	10
58	Vogue V 9124	Little Bitty Pretty One/Flute Cha-Lypso	10
61	London HLL 9336	Come On Over/There's No One But You	40

BARRETT STRONG
60	London HLU 9088	Money (That's What I Want)/Oh I Apologise	80
73	Epic S EPC 1778	Stand Up And Cheer For The Preacher/Instrumental	10
76	Capitol CL 15864	Man Up In The Sky/Gonna Make It Right	40

STRUGGLE
80s	Regal RD 013	No Stronger Love/Bad Boy (12", with ENFORCER)	20

JOE STRUMMER
88	Epic TRASH 1	Trash City/Theme From Permanent Record (p/s)	8
86	CBS A 7244	Love Kills/Dum Dum Club (p/s)	10
89	Epic STRUMG1	Gangsterville/Jewellers And Bums/Passport To Detroit (gatefold)	10
89	Epic STRUM 2	Island Hopping/15th Brigade (p/s)	8
89	Epic STRUM E2	Island Hopping/Cholo Vest/Mango Street/Baby O Boogie (12", all tracks on A side, B side etched, die-cut sleeve)	12
03	Hellcat 1149-7	Redemption Song/Arms Aloft/Junco Partner (Live) (with the Mescaleros, picture disc, stickered polythene sleeve)	18
87	Virgin V 2497	WALKER (LP, soundtrack)	25
89	EPIC 465347	EARTHQUAKE WEATHER (LP, with inner)	25
99	Mercury 546 654	ROCK ART AND THE X-RAY STYLE (LP, with the Mescaleros)	100
01	Hellcat 0440-1	GLOBAL A GO GO (2-LP, with the Mescaleros)	80
03	Hellcat 0454-1	STREETCORE (LP, gatefold, with the Mescaleros)	100
12	Hellcat 05251	FRIDAY 15TH NOVEMBER 2002 ACTON TOWN HALL. LONDON (2-LP, numbered)	60
12	Hellcat HELL 20523	STREETCORE (LP, with CD, reissue, gatefold, with the Mescaleros)	40
17	Hellcat 05251	FRIDAY 15TH NOVEMBER 2002 ACTON TOWN HALL. LONDON (2-LP, reissue, 500 copies)	100
18	Ignition IGNLP 53X	JOE STRUMMER 001 (3-LP and 12")	50
18	Ignition IGNLP 53 BOX	JOE STRUMMER 001 (3-LP, 12", 2-CD, cassette, screen print, 2 art prints, sticker, badge and replica driving license)	100

(see also The Clash)

STRUTT
76	Brunswick BR 35	Time Moves On/Front Row Romeo	7
76	Brunswick BRLS 3021	TIME MOVES ON (LP)	25

STRYDER
80	Quartz QS 010	Forcin' Thru'/Settle Down	50

STRYPES

MINT VALUE £

STRYPES
12   Heavy Soul ROR033HS20   YOUNG GIFTED AND BLUE EP (p/s) 10

GLEN STUART
60s   Honey Hit TB 126   Make Me An Angel/Walking To Heaven (with p/s) 7

GLEN STUART & CLANSMEN
59   Pye 7N 15232   Weepy Willow/Della Darling 6

SHAWN STUART
74   Epic SEPC 2496   It's All Because Of You/Wise Old Man 8

FRANKIE STUBBS
90s   Sounds Of Subterrania S09   SECOND HAND SUIT (10" EP) 20
95   Rugger Bugger DUMP 025   UNHINGED (EP) 15
(see also Leatherface)

NAT STUCKEY
67   Pye International 7N 25403   Sweet Thang/Paralyze My Mind 6
69   RCA RCA 1890   Cut Across Shorty/Understand, Little Man 7

STUD
70   Deram SML-R 1084   STUD (LP, laminated front sleeve, white/red label with small logo) 175
(see also Taste, Blossom Toes, Eric Burdon & Animals)

STUDD PUMP
71   Penny Farthing PEN 757   Spare The Children/Floatin' 8

STUDIO G'S
70   LPSG 100   BETA GROUP (LP, library edition) 150
96   Tenth Planet TP 023   BEAT GROUP (LP, 600 only) 20

STUDIO ONE ALLSTARS
67   Island WI 3038   Sherry (actually by Bumps Oakley)/Out Of My Mind (actually by Soul Junior) 100

STUDIO PRESSURE
93   Certificate 18 CERT 1803   Jump/Don't Worry/Know Yourself (12") 35
93   Certificate 18 CERT 1804   Jump MK II/Presha/Test 1/Junglistics Pt 1 (12") 40
94   Photek PTK 01   FORM & FUNCTION VOL 1 (12") 12
94   Photek PTK 03   Touching Down...Planet Photek/The Physical (12") 12
94   Certificate 18 CERT 1808   Relics/Presha III (12") 20
(see also System X (Ex))

STUDIO SIX
66   Polydor 56131   When I See My Baby/Don't Tell Lies 15
67   Polydor 56162   Bless My Soul (I've Been And Gone And Done It)/People Say 10
67   Polydor 56174   Times Were When/I Can't Sleep 10
67   Polydor 56219   Strawberry Window/Falling Leaves 40
69   Polydor 56361   Bless My Soul/People Say 10

STUDIO SOUND
72   Downtown DT 489   Give Me Some More/Some More Version 50

STUDIO SWEETHEARTS
79   DJM DJS 10915   I Believe/It Isn't Me (p/s) 20
(see also Cult, Slaughter & Dogs)

STUDIO 2
95   Jet Star FJD 002   Dirty Games/Who Bless Jah? (12", stamped white labels) 50

STUD LEATHER
73   Dart ART 2024   Cut Loose/Emma Louise 100

STIKKI STUFF
81   Carrere CAR 206   School/The Wiggle 10
81   Floppy Discs FLO 1   School/The Wiggle (12") 15
81   Carrere CAR 206T   School/The Wiggle (12", reissue) 18

STUKAS
77   Chiswick NS 21   Klean Living Kids/Oh Little Girl (p/s) 10
77   Sonet SON 2134   I Like Sport/I'll Send You A Postcard/Dead Lazy (p/s) 8
78   Sonet SON 2159   Wash Machine Boogie/Motorbike 10

STUMPY
74   Dawn DNS 1080   Make Me A Superman/Keep It Coming 6

STUPIDS
85   Children Of Rev. COR 3   VIOLENT NUN (EP, some mispressed) 20
86   C.O.R. GURT 15   RETARD PICNIC (LP, 2 inserts) 20
88   C.O.R. GURT 9   PERUVIAN VACATION (LP, blue cover, lyric sheet) 15
88   Vinyl Solution SOL 2   JESUS MEETS THE STUPIDS (LP, insert with free 7") 15

STURGEON ROW
79   RhopeySRTS 79 CUS 262   FRICTION EP (with insert) 60

ST VINCENT
07   Beggars Banquet BBQ 406   Now Now/All My Stars Aligned (p/s) 12
07   Beggars Banquet BBQ 410   Jesus Saves I Spend/These Days (p/s) 12
09   4AD AD 2918   Actor Out Of Work/Bicycle (p/s) 12
12   4AD AD 3211   Krokodil/Grot (die-cut sleeve, red vinyl) 25
15   Secret 7& S727   Digital Witness (100 only, each with unique art sleeve) 45
07   Beggars Banquet BBQLP 239   MARRY ME (LP) 15
09   4AD CAD 2919   ACTOR (LP) 18
11   4AD CAD 3123   STRANGE MERCY (LP) 20

STYLE COUNCIL
89   Polydor TSCB 17   Promised Land (Juan Atkins Mix)/Can You Still Love Me? (7", stickered box set with numbered 7" in p/s & poster) 20
89   Polydor TSC 18   Sure Is Sure/Love Of The World (unissued, acetates may exist) 0
83   Polydor 815 277 1   INTRODUCING THE STYLE COUNCIL (LP) 15
84   Polydor TSCLP 1   CAFE BLEU (LP) 15
85   Polydor TSCLP 2   OUR FAVOURITE SHOP (LP, gatefold) 20

86	Polydor TSCLP 3	HOME AND ABROAD (LP)	20
87	Polydor TSCLP 4	THE COST OF LOVING (2-LP)	35
87	Polydor TSCLP 4	THE COST OF LOVING (LP)	15
88	Polydor TSCLP 5	CONFESSIONS OF A POP GROUP (LP)	20
88	Polydor	CONFESSIONS OF A POP GROUP (box set, VHS & cassette;some with promo CD [CPGCD 1])	50
88	Polydor	CONFESSIONS OF A POP GROUP (box set, VHS & cassette;some without promo CD [CPGCD 1])	40
89	Polydor TSCTV 1	THE SINGULAR ADVENTURES OF (LP)	15
89	polydor 557 789 2	THE COMPLETE ADVENTURES OF THE STYLE COUNCIL (Box set, 5-CD, booklet)	60
98	Polydor TSCLP 6	MODERNISM: A NEW DECADE (LP, promo only)	80
98	Polydor TSCLP 6	MODERNISM: A NEW DECADE (LP, 2 x 12" set, promo only)	100
00	Polydor 549135-1	GREATEST HITS (2-LP)	50
17	Polydor TSCLP 006	MODERNISM: A NEW DECADE (LP, reissue, yellow vinyl)	20
20	Polydor 089 415 2	LONG HOT SUMMERS - THE STORY OF THE STYLE COUNCIL (3-LP, pink, blue and orange vinyl)	45

(see also Council Collective, Paul Weller, Jam, Merton Parkas, King Truman)

STYLE X
81	Rygel RYGI 12	No Secret Affair (Instrumental)/No Secret Affair (Vocal) (12", no p/s)	80

(see also Cloud (2))

STYLISTICS
71	Avco 6466 008	THE STYLISTICS (LP)	15

STYLOS
64	Liberty LBS 10173	Head Over Heels/Bye Bye, Baby, Bye Bye	100

STYMULATORS
79	Pennine PSS 150	If You Gotta Make A Fool Of Somebody/Make A Fool Dub (no p/s)	10

POLY STYRENE
86	Awesome AOR 7	Gods And Goddesses: Trick Of The Witch/Paramatma (p/s)	7
80	United Artists UAG 30290	TRANSLUCENCE (LP, with lyric inner)	20
11	Future Noise FN 1	GENERATION INDIGO (LP)	18

(see also X-Ray Spex, Mari Elliott)

STYVAR MANOR
70	Polydor 2058034	Just Dropped In/That's What I Need Most Of All	40

DANNY SUAREZ
97	Groove Yard GYARD 15A	LIFE IN THE EAST VILLAGE EP (12")	20

SUBCULTURE
83	Essential ESS 002	Loud & Clear/Rogue Trooper/University City (p/s)	30

SUBDUED HUBBUB
70	Ra RALP 6005	SUBDUED HUBBUB (LP)	15

SUBHUMANS
82	Spiderleg SDL 7	Religious Wars/Love Is.../Work Experience/It's Gonna Get Worse (p/s)	8
82	Spiderleg SPIDL 5	Big City/Reason For Existence/Cancer/Peroxide (p/s)	10
83	Bluurg XEP 2	Big City/Reason For Existence/Cancer/Peroxide (repressing, p/s)	6
81	Spider Leg SDL 3	DEMOLITION WAR (EP, gatefold p/s with "Pay no more than 85p" rubber stamped on front cover)	15
82	Spiderleg SDL9	THE DAY THE COUNTRY DIED (LP, gatefold, original pressing with "Pay no more than £3.25" on front cover)	15
83	Bluurg FISH 5	TIME FLIES...BUT AEROPLANES CRASH (LP, insert)	20
83	Bluurg Fish 8	FROM THE CRADLE TO THE GRAVE (LP, gatefold, original pressing with "Pay no more than £3.50" on front cover)	15
85	Bluurg Fish VIG 1 T	20:20 SPLIT VISION (LP, with insert and has 'Pay no more than £3.50' on front sleeve)	15
85	Bluurg FISH 12	WORDS APART (LP)	15

SUBITA AND EMPHASIS
81	Crazy Plane SP 004	Once In A Blue Moon/Dub (no p/s)	8

SUBLIME
97	MCA MCS 48045	What I Got (Super No Mofo Edit)/RIvers Of Babylon p/s, yellow vinyl)	8

SUBMARINER
93	Spacewatch FLX 2107	Lyricist Downer/Seeming And The Meaning (demo)/STEREOLAB:Ronco Symphony (demo) (clear vinyl flexi with paper strip insert)	25

SUBMARINES
87	Head HEAD 4	Grey Skies Blue/I Saw The Children (p/s)	6

SUB MURIS
83	Dog Rock SD104	Honesty/Open Doors (p/s)	10

SUBS
78	Stiff OFF 1	Gimme Your Heart/Party Clothes (p/s)	8

(see also Larry Wallis)

SUBSTITUTE
79	Ignition IR 2	The One/Look Sharp (in p/s)	35
79	Ignition IR 2	The One/Look Sharp	20

(see also Vibrators)

SUB SUB
90s	Ten TENX 373	Space Face/Ecto-Jam-Sub (12", die-cut sleeve)	35
90s	Robs Records 12ROB 07	Coast/Inside Of This/Past/Inside Out (12", p/s)	10
90s	Robs Records 7ROB 9	Ain't No Love/Parkside Mix (p/s)	8
90s	Robs Records 7ROB 19	Respect (Radio Edit)/(Dasliva-McCready Mix)	8

(see also Doves)

SUBURBAN KNIGHTS
03	Peacefrog PFG025	MY SOL DARK DIRECTION (3-LP)	25

SUBURBAN STUDS
77	Pogo POG 001/LYN 44845	No Faith/Questions (no p/s, 'with horns' version)	35
77	Pogo POG 001/LYN 44845	No Faith/Questions (p/s)	6
78	Pogo POG 002	I Hate School/Young Power (p/s)	15

SUBWAYS

			MINT VALUE £
78	Pogo POW 001	SLAM (LP)	25

SUBWAYS
04	Private Pressing	DEMO (CD, sold at gigs, p/s)	30
04	Transgressive 58241H1	1 am/I Want To Hear What You Gotta Say/You Got Me (500 only, p/s)	10
05	Infectious 25646248	YOUNG FOR ETERNITY (LP, 2x10")	30
11	Cooking VInyl COOK 549	MONEY & CELEBRITY (LP, red vinyl)	25

SUBWAY SECT
78	Braik BRS 01	Nobody's Scared/Don't Split It (p/s)	30
78	Braik BRS 01	Nobody's Scared/Don't Split It (no p/s)	12
79	Rough Trade RT 007	Ambition/A Different Story (initially in yellow text p/s)	10
79	Rough Trade RT 007	Ambition/A Different Story (later orange text p/s)	8

(see also Vic Godard [& Subway Sect])

NIKKI SUDDEN
86	Glass GLAEP 102	PIN YOUR HEAR TO ME (12" EP, with Dave Kusworth & The Jacobites)	10
86	Creation CRE 033	Jangle Town/The Last Bandit (p/s)	8
82	ABSTRACT ABT 003	WAITING ON EGYPT (LP)	25
83	Flicknife SHARP 110	THE BIBLE BELT (LP)	18
84	Glass GLALP 008	JACOBITES (LP, with Dave Kusworth)	15
91	UFO UFO 4	THE JEWEL THIEF (LP)	15

(see also Swell Maps, Last Bandits, Jeremy Gluck)

(A) SUDDEN SWAY
80	Chant CHANT 1	Jane's Third Party/Don't Go (p/s, as A Sudden Sway)	15
81	Chant CHANT 2/EJSP 9692	TO YOU, WITH REGARD (12" EP, with insert)	20
84	Chant CHANT 3	The Traffic Tax Scheme (12" with badge & inserts in folder)	12
86	WEA BYN 8B	Spacemate (2 x 12" box set with stickers, info sheets, 2 booklets & poster)	12

SUDETEN CRECHE
| 83 | Illuminated ILL 1712 | Kindergarten/Dance (instrumental Version)/Dance/Asylums in Beirut (12", p/s) | 25 |

SUE & MARY
| 62 | Decca F 11517 | Traitor In Disguise/I Love You (Oh Yes I Do) | 7 |

SUE & SUNNY
65	Columbia DB 7748	Every Ounce Of Strength/So Remember	15
67	Columbia DB 8099	You Can't By-Pass Love/I Like Your Style	25
68	CBS 3874	The Show Must Go On/Little black Book	20
68	Island WIP 6043	Set Me Free/NIRVANA ORCHESTRA: City Of The South	25
69	CBS 4567	Let Us Break Bread/Stop Messing About With My Heart	10
70	CBS 4757	You Devil, Cotton-Eyed Joe/Night In The City	10
70	Deram DM 318	Ain't That Telling You People/Didn't I Blow Your Mind	10
71	Deram DM 328	Freedom/Break Up	10
71	Reflection HRS 10	Let Us Break Bread Together/Michael From Mountains	6
72	Deram DM 355	I'm Gonna Make You Love Me/High On The Thought Of You	10
70	CBS 63740	SUE AND SUNNY (LP)	20
70	Reflection REFL 4	SUE AND SUNNY (LP, reissue)	20

(see also Sue & Sunshine, Myrtelles, Stockingtops, Brotherhood Of Man)

SUE & SUNSHINE
| 64 | Columbia DB 7409 | A Little Love/If You See Me Crying | 10 |
| 65 | Columbia DB 7533 | We're In Love/Don't Look Behind | 7 |

(see also Sue & Sunny, Myrtelles, Stockingtops)

SUEDE
91	RML RML 001	Be My God/Art (12", unissued, white label copies only, MPO pressings, no p/s; counterfeits have off-white labels and no MPO etchings)	150
92	Nude NUD 1 S	The Drowners (Radio Edit)/To The Birds (p/s, 1,000 copies only)	18
92	Nude NUD 3 T	Metal Mickey/Where Pigs Don't Fly/He's Dead (12", test pressing, plain sleeve)	30
93	Nude NUD 4T	Animal Nitrate/Painted People/The Big Time (12", p/s)	10
94	Nude NUD 9T	Stay Together/The Living Dead/My Dark Star (12" numbered gatefold p/s)	10
94	Nude NUD 10 S	We Are The Pigs/Killing Of A Flash Boy (numbered gatefold p/s)	6
94	Nude NUD 11 T	The Wild Ones/Eno's Introducing The Band/Asda Town (12", photo insert, p/s)	10
96	Nude NUD 21S	Trash/Europe Is Our Playground (p/s, mail order only)	15
97	Nude NUD 24 S	Saturday Night/Beautiful Ones (double pack, p/s, mail-order only)	10
13	Warner Bros. SUEDE 9313	Barriers/Animal Nitrate	6
04	S.I.S. SIS4CD	SEE YOU IN THE NEXT LIFE (CD, fan club farewell, 2000 copies)	50
11	Edsel DROWN 1	The Drowners (Demo)/To The Birds (Demo) (p/s, Record Store Day release)	18
93	Nude NUDE 1LP	SUEDE (LP, with inner sleeve; with carrier bag from Chain With No Name stores)	50
93	Nude NUDE 1LP	SUEDE (LP, with inner sleeve)	45
94	Nude NUDE 3	DOG MAN STAR (LP, with poster)	100
96	Nude 4851212	COMING UP (LP, with inner sleeve)	50
99	Nude NUDE 14LP	HEAD MUSIC (2-LP)	60
13	Warner Bros. SUEDEBS X001	BLOODSPORTS (LP, CD, booklet & 7", hardback book)	50
13	Demon SUEDEBOX 1	THE VINYL COLLECTION (10-LP box set)	120
14	Demon SUEDEBOX 003	7" SINGLES (24 x 7" box set)	70
14	Demon INSATIABLE 1	SUEDE (LP, reissue, download card)	15
14	Demon INSATIABLE 3	COMING UP (LP, reissue, mispressing, side 1 plays side 2 of Avicci LP)	20
14	Demon INSATIABLE 3	COMING UP (LP, reissue, download card)	15
14	Demon INSATIABLE 5	A NEW MORNING (LP, reissue, download card)	15
14	Demon INSATIABLE 7	SCI-FI LULLABIES (3-LP, reissue, download card)	20
15	Demon INSATIABLE 9	DOG MAN STAR 20th ANNIVERSARY LIVE ROYAL ALBERT HALL (2-LP)	25
15	Demon SUEDEBOX 006	DOG MAN STAR 20th ANNIVERSARY LIVE ROYAL ALBERT HALL (4-LP, 2CD)	30

(see also Elastica, Tears)

SUEDE CROCODILES
| 83 | No Strings NOSP 2 | Pleasant Dreams/Stop The Rain | 75 |

SUFFERER SOUND

MINT VALUE £

SUFFERER SOUND
78	Tempus TEMD 2	I A Sufferer/National Front (12")	12

SUFJAN STEVENS
15	Asthmatic Kitty AKR 271	Exploding Whale/Fourth Of July (PPD Remix) (UK tour edition)	25
05	Rough Trade RTRADLP 250	COME ON FEEL THE ILLINOISE (2-LP)	30

SUGAR & SPICE (JAMAICA)
73	Stop Points DL 021	Indeed I Love You/Version	10

SUGAR MINOTT
79	Warrior WAR 124	Never Too Young/DON CARLOS: Hey Little Girl (12")	10
79	Sufferers Heights SUFF 002	Hard Time Pressure (with Captain Sinbad)/Dub On The Pressure (12")	30
80	Strong Like Sampson SLSD 014	Half Of Love/AL CAMPBELL: Jah Shine On Me (12")	25
81	SMP 101	Play Me Nah Play/Version (12", white label only)	200
83	PCJ PCJ 001	Can't Stop Jah Music/PCJ: Nah Stop Jah Music (12")	50
83	SMP SMP 003	Come Again/BERTIE AT THE CONTROLS: Dubbing A Storm At Omega Studio (12")	150
84	Black Roots BR 181264	Now We Know/Row Fast (12")	50
84	Black Roots LML 201284	Herbman Hustling/TAXI GANG: Hustling Dub (12")	20
77	Studio One PSOL001	LIVE LOVING (LP)	50
79	United Artists UAG 30310	GIVE THE PEOPLE (LP)	20
79	Island ILPS 9591	BLACK ROOTS (LP)	20
79	Trojan TRLS 173	GHETTO-OLOGY (LP)	30
79	Warrior WARLP20	BITTER SWEET (LP)	25
80	Black Roots BRLP 3000	AFRICAN GIRL (LP)	25
70s	Uptempo UT 1	SHOWCASE (10" mini LP, no ps)	40
82	Black Roots BRLP 001	MEET THE PEOPLE IN A LOVER DUBBER STYLE (LP)	35

SUGAR SHACK
68	Tribune TRS 112	Sunshine Of Your Love/Morning Dew	25

SUGAR (1)
69	CBS 4226	It Was Yesterday Today/11AM Tuesday Morning Taxi	40

SUGAR (2)
92	Creation CRELP 129	COPPER BLUE (LP, lyric inner)	25
93	Creation CRELP 153	BEASTER (mini-LP)	15
94	Creation CRELP 172	FILE UNDER EASY LISTENING (LP)	25

(see also Bob Mould, Husker Du)

SUGAR (SIMONE) & DANDY (LIVINGSTONE)
63	Carnival CV 7006	One Man Went To Mow/Cryin'	8
64	Carnival CV 7009	Oh Dear What Can The Matter Be/Tra La La	8
64	Carnival CV 7015	What A Life/Time And Tide	8
64	Carnival CV 7016	I'm Not Crying Now/Blues Got A Hold On Me	8
65	Carnival CV 7023	Let's Ska/Only Heaven Knows	8
65	Carnival CV 7024	I'm Into Something Good/Crazy For You	8
65	Carnival CV 7027	Think Of The Good Times/Girl Come See	8
65	Carnival CV 7029	I Want To Be Your Lover/I Don't Know What I'm Going To Do Now	7
66	Blue Beat BB 367	Meditation (as Jetliners)/GIRL SATCHMO & JET LINERS: Nature Of Love	15
67	Page One POF 044	Let's Ska/Only Heaven Knows	8
64	Carnival CX 1000	THE SKA'S THE LIMIT (LP)	40
67	Page One FOR 006	THE SKA'S THE LIMIT (LP, reissue)	20

(see also Sugar Simone)

SUGAR & PEE WEE
58	Vogue Pop V 9112	One, Two, Let's Rock/Just A Few Little Words	500
58	Vogue Pop V 9112	One, Two, Let's Rock/Just A Few Little Words (78)	100

SUGAR & SPICE
69	London HLU 10259	Cruel War/Not To Return	10

SUGAR BEARS
72	Philips 6073 812	You Are The One/Someone Like You	10

SUGARBEATS
66	Polydor BM 56069	I Just Stand Here/The Ballad Of Ole Betsy	20
66	Polydor BM 56120	Alice Designs/Sunny Day Girl	20

(see also Tony Rivers & Castaways)

SUGARCUBES
87	One Little Indian 7z TP 7	Birthday/Birthday (Icelandic) (p/s)	6
88	One Little Indian 12TP 11L	BIRTHDAY CHRISTMAS MIX (12" EP, double groove, with Jesus & Mary Chain)	12
89	House Of Dolls HOD 010	Dark Disco/HOST: Homelands/MURRUMBRIDGE WHALERS: Giving Away To Trains/SHARK TABOO: Tinsel Town (live) (no p/s, with House Of Dolls mag)	6
89	One Little Indian OLI26TP7	Regina/Hot Meat/Hey/Regina (Propellor vs Jet) (with poster)	6
92	One Little Indian OLI104TP12	Birthday (Justin Robertson 12" Mix)/Tommy D Dub Mix/Christmas Eve Mix/Original 7" Mix/Tommy D 12" Mix/Justin Robertson Dub/Christmas Day Mix/Demo (12")	10
90	One Little Indian TP BOX 2	7.8 (8 x 7" box set)	25
90	One Little Indian TP BOX 1	12.11 (11 x 12" box set)	40
90	One Little Indian TP BOX 3	CD.6 (6 x CD box set)	45
08	One Little Indian 950TP7BOX	BOX SET (8 x 7")	25
88	One Little Indian TPLP 5	LIFE'S TOO GOOD (LP, green/blue/yellow/orange/pink sleeve)	20
89	One Little Indian TPLP 15SP	HERE TODAY, TOMORROW NEXT WEEK! (LP, silver vinyl, gatefold sleeve with sticker & inner)	20
89	One Little Indian TPLP 15L	SYKURMOLARNIR ILLUR ARFUR! (LP, as Sykurmolarnir, gatefold sleeve)	15
92	One Little Indian TPLP40	IT'S IT (2-LP)	30
92	One Little Indian TP LP 30	STICK AROUND FOR JOY (LP)	25

(see also Bjork, Kukl)

SUGAR DEE & THE OFFBEAT POSSE
89	YND YDD 0137	Danger/Having A Party (12")	25

SUGAR LOAF

MINT VALUE £

SUGAR LOAF
70	RCA INTS 1113	SOUL STRUTTING (LP)	30

SUGARLOAF
70	Liberty LBF 15401	Green-Eyed Lady/West Of Tomorrow	12
71	Liberty LBS 83415	SUGARLOAF (LP)	15
75	Polydor 2310 394	DON'T CALL US, WE'LL CALL YOU (LP, with Jerry Corbetto)	15

SUGAR LUMPS
69	Jay Boy BOY 16	Sugar Sugar/Can't We Be Friends	20
70	Jay Boy BOY 20	Satan's People/Shame Shame	20

SUGARPLUMS
70	Fab FAB 160	Red River Reggae/Too Much	20

SUGAR SHOPPE
68	Capitol CL 15555	Skip-A-Long Sam/Let The Truth Come Out	20

SUGGESTIVE MOTION
83	Bodie BR 101	Loving You/In Your Mind	10

SUGARGLIDERS
92	Sarah SARAH 63	Letter From A Lifeboat/Strong/What We Had Hoped (p/s, insert)	18
92	Sarah SARAH 67	Seventeen/Aloha Street/Fruitloopin' (p/s, insert)	18
93	Sarah SARAH 72	Ahprahan/Corn Circles/Theme From Boxville (p/s, insert)	25
93	Sarah SARAH 77	Trumpet Play/Unkind/Beloved (p/s, insert)	25
93	Sarah SARAH 83	Will We Ever Learn?/Dolly/Reinventing Penicillin (p/s, insert)	25
93	Sarah SARAH 86	Top 40 Sculpture/90 Days Of Moths And Rust/Yr. Jacket (p/s, insert)	25
94	Sarah SARAH 619	WE'RE ALL TRYING TO GET THERE (LP)	50

SUICIDAL TENDENCIES
87	Virgin VS 967-12	Possessed To Skate/Human Guinea Pig/Two Wrongs Don't Make A Right (12", picture disc)	15
88	Virgin VST 1039	Institutionalised/War Inside My Head/Cyco (12", p/s)	15
87	Virgin V 2495	SUICIDAL TENDENCIES (LP, with poster)	18
88	Virgin V 2551	HOW WILL I LAUGH TOMORROW WHEN I CAN'T EVEN SMILE TODAY? (LP)	15

SUICIDE
78	Bronze BRO 57	Cheree/I Remember (p/s, A label promo)	70
78	Red Star/Bronze BRO 57	Cheree/I Remember (p/s)	25
78	Red Star/Bronze 12 BRO 57	Cheree/I Remember (12", 'limited edition', p/s)	20
79	Island WIP 6543	Dream Baby Dream/Radiation (A label promo)	40
79	Island WIP 6543	Dream Baby Dream/Radiation (p/s)	40
79	Island 12 WIP 6543	Dream Baby Dream (Long Version)/Radiation (12", p/s)	40
86	Demon D 1046	Cheree/I Remember (promo only)	20
88	Chapter 22 12 CHAP 36	Surrender/Rain Of Ruin (12", die cut p/s)	18
22	Electronic Sound ES785	Ghost Rider/Frankie Teardrop (First Mix) (p/s, red vinyl)	12
89	Chapter 22 12CHAP 42	SUICIDE (12", unissued)	0
77	Red Star/Bronze BRON 508	SUICIDE (LP)	60
78	Red Star FRANKIE 1	24 MINUTES OVER BRUSSELS (LP, official bootleg, 1,000 only, no p/s)	100
80	Ze/Island ILPS 7007	SUICIDE: ALAN VEGA/MARTIN REV (LP, with printed inner sleeve)	50
86	Demon FIEND 74	SUICIDE (LP, reissue, with incorrect Rocket U.S.A and Ghost Rider running order on side 1)	40
86	Demon FIEND 74	SUICIDE (LP, reissue, tracks in correct order)	25
88	Chapter 22 CHAP LP 35	A WAY OF LIFE (LP)	40
98	Blast First BFFP 133 1/2	SUICIDE (2-LP, reissue)	30
99	Blast First BFFP 162	THE SECOND ALBUM + FIRST REHEARSAL TAPES (2-LP, with insert)	40
02	Blast First BFFP 168	AMERICAN SUPREME (2-LP)	60
08	Blast First Petite PTYT 011	LIVE 1977 - 1978 (6-CD box set, booklet)	40
19	Mute SUICIDELP01	SUICIDE (LP, reissue, with booklet, art print and com come with badge)	15

(see also Alan Vega)

SUICIDE TWINS
86	Lick LICLP 9	SILVER MISSILES AND NIGHTINGALES (LP)	15

BIG JIM SULLIVAN
61	Decca F 11387	You Don't Know What You've Got/Hot Hiss Of Steam (as Big Jim Sullivan Combo)	12
65	Mercury MF 928	She Walks Through The Fair/Don't Know What I'm Doing (as Jim Sullivan Sound)	25
73	MAM MAM 100	Out Of The Question/Alone Again	6
67	Mercury SML 30001	SITAR BEAT (LP)	40
74	Retreat RTA 4001	BIG JIM'S BACK (LP, gatefold sleeve, blue/green label)	15

(see also Maureeny Wishfull, Brian Bennett, Tiger)

JOE SULLIVAN
56	London HA-U 2011	NEW SOLOS BY AN OLD MASTER (LP, thin card sleeve with no spine)	15

MAXINE SULLIVAN
54	Parlophone MSP 6086	Boogie Woogie Maxine/Piper In The Glen (with Vic Ash)	15

PETER SULLY
70	Pye 7N 17935	Row Row Row/Everybodys Talkin' About The War	8
68	Polydor 56291	My Idea/Evil Woman (as Pete Sully And The Orchard)	35

SULTANS OF PING (F.C.)
91	Divine ATHY 01	Where's Me Jumper/I Said I Am I Said (p/s)	20
91	Divine ATHY 01T	Where's Me Jumper/I Said I Am I Said/Turnip Fish (12")	15
93	Rhythm King 472495-1	CASUAL SEX IN THE CINEPLEX (LP, inner)	25
94	Rhythm King 4747161	TEENAGE DRUG (LP)	30
96	Rhythm King ATHY 05 LP	GOOD YEAR FOR TROUBLE (LP)	30

YMA SUMAC
53	Capitol LC 6522	VOICE OF THE XTABAY (10" LP)	15
54	Capitol LC 6609	LEGEND OF THE SUN VIRGIN (10" LP)	15
59	Capitol T 1169	FUEGO DEL ANDE (LP)	15
72	London HLU/SHU 8431	MIRACLES (LP)	15

Hubert SUMLIN

MINT VALUE £

HUBERT SUMLIN
65 Blue Horizon 45-1000 — Across The Board/Sumlin Boogie (99 copies only) 150
(see also Howlin' Wolf)

DONNA SUMMER
74 People PEO 115 — The Hostage/Let's Work Together Now 7
82 Casablanca FEEL 12 — I Feel Love (Mega Mix)/I Feel Love (Mega Edit) (12", reissue) 15
75 GTO GTLP 008 — LOVE TO LOVE YOU BABY (LP) 15
(see also Donna Gaines, John Barry)

SUMMERHILL
69 Polydor 583 746 — SUMMERHILL (LP) 40

BOB(BY) SUMMERS
59 Capitol CL 15063 — Rattle Rhythm/Excitement (as Bob Summers) 12
60 Capitol CL 15130 — Little Brown Jug/Twelfth Street Rag (as Bobby Summers) 7

JOHN SUMMERS
65 Pye 15918 — Don't Fool Yourself/Looking In Windows 30
66 Pye 7N 17081 — That's A Magic Moment/One A Day 10

SUMMER SET
66 Columbia DB 8004 — Farmer's Daughter/Papa-Oom-Mow-Mow 40
66 Columbia DB 8004 — Farmer's Daughter/What Are You Gonna Do (2nd issue with different B-side) 40
67 Columbia DB 8215 — Overnight Changes/It's A Dream 120
(see also Candy Choir)

SUMMERTAIR GIRLS
66 Ska Beat JB 258 — My Heart Cries Out/SOUL BROTHERS: James Bond Girl 60
(see also Jackie Mittoo, Soul Agents)

SUMMER WINE
73 Philips 6006 288 — Living Right Next Door To An Angel/Sound Of Summer's Over 7
(see also Tony Rivers)

SUMMIT UP
89 Soundworx SOX 101 — Watch The Sun Light Up Your Face/I Don't Mind (The Nude MIx) p/s 50

SUMO GIANTS
81 Metro 88 ELECS 1 — Tower Of Babel/Foolish Things (p/s with insert) 12

SUN ALSO RISES
70 Village Thing VTS 2 — THE SUN ALSO RISES (LP, with insert) 100

SUN DIAL
90 UFO 45 001T — Exploding In Your Mind/Otherside/Slow Motion (12", 1-sided, p/s) 15
91 Tangerine TANGERINE 111 — Exploding In Your Mind (Colour Mix)/Otherside/Slow Motion (12", unreleased, 80 white label test pressings only) 30
90 Tangerine TAN 11145 — Exploding In Your Mind/Other Side 50
91 UFO PF 2 — Fireball/Only A Northern Song ('Pre-Flight' 7", promo only) 20
91 UFO UFO 45002 T — OVERSPILL EP (12", orange vinyl) 10
92 UFO UFO 45008 T — FAZER EP (12") 10
90 Tangerine MM 07 — OTHER WAY OUT (LP, with insert, signed in silver ink) 50
90 Tangerine MM 07 — OTHER WAY OUT (LP, with insert) 30
91 UFO UFO 1LP — OTHER WAY OUT (LP, reissue in gatefold sleeve) 15
92 UFO UFO 8 — REFLECTER (LP, with free 1-sided 7", Let It Go (live), TEX-4) 20
92 UFO UFO 8 — REFLECTER (LP, clear vinyl) 20
93 Beggars Banquet BBQLP 138 — LIBERTINE (LP, with poster) 18
94 Acme AC 8001 — RETURN JOURNEY (LP, official bootleg; 200 promos with inserts) 40
94 Acme AC 8001 — RETURN JOURNEY (LP, official bootleg; 500 numbered commercial copies) 30
95 Acme AC 8011 — ACID YANTRA (LP, gatefold sleeve, some purple vinyl) 25
96 Acme AC 8015 — LIVE DRUG (LP, red vinyl) 15
02 Ace Of Discs ACE 001 — WILD BUG (LP) 15
05 Third Eye TESLP 1001 — OTHER WAY IN (LP) 15
(see also Modern Art, Spiral Sky, Quad)

SUN SINGERS
72 UK UK 12 — You Were On My Mind/Sunshine 8

SUNBIRD
70 Phillips 6011070 — Brother Bird/Love Of The Free 18
(see also Nirvana)

SUNCHARIOT
72 Decca F13317 — Rosemarie/Do You Wanna Know 15
73 Decca F13407 — Firewater/The Only Girl I Knew 10

SUNDAE TIMES
68 President PT 203 — Baby Don't Cry/Aba-Aba 25
68 President PT 219 — Jack Boy/I Don't Want Nobody 25
70 President PT 285 — Live Today/Take Me Higher Baby 25
70 Joy JOYS 159 — US COLOURED KIDS (LP, laminated front sleeve, flipbacks) 150
(see also Osibisa, Crosyby Stills Nash & Young, One)

SUNDANCE
73 Decca TXS 111 — RAIN STEAM SPEED (LP, with insert) 20
74 Decca SKL 5183 — CHUFFER (LP) 18

SUNDAY AFTERNOONS
70s Longman — SUNDAY AFTERNOONS (LP) 90

SUNDAYS
89 Rough Trade RTX 218 — Can't Be Sure/I Kicked A Boy (export issue, brown p/s) 6
89 Rough Trade RTTX 218 — Can't Be Sure/I Kicked A Boy/Don't Tell Your Mother (12", export issue, brown p/s) 10
90 Catalogue CAT 076 — I Won (square flexidisc with The Catalogue magazine) 10
90 Rough Trade ROUGH 148 — READING WRITING AND ARITHMATIC (LP) 30
90 Rough Trade ROUGH 148P — READING, WRITING AND ARITHMETIC (LP, picture disc, stickered sleeve) 25
92 Parlophone PCSD 121 — BLIND (LP) 70

SUNDOWNERS

			MINT VALUE £
97	Parlophone 724382121216	STATIC AND SILENCE (LP)	70

SUNDOWNERS
63	Piccadilly 7N 35142	Baby Baby/House Of The Rising Sun	8
64	Piccadilly 7N 35162	Come On In/Shot Of Rhythm And Blues	8
65	Parlophone R 5243	Where Am I/Gonna Make The Future Bright	8
68	Columbia DB 8239	Dr. J. Wallace-Brown/Love Is In The Air	15
68	Spark SRL 1016	Gloria The Bosom Show/Don't Look Back	8

SUNDOWN PLAYBOYS
72	Apple APPLE 44	Saturday Nite Special/Valse De Soleil Couche (in p/s)	35
72	Apple APPLE 44	Saturday Nite Special/Valse De Soleil Couche	10
72	Apple APPLE 44	Saturday Nite Special/Valse De Soleil Couche (10", 78rpm, pink-patterned die-cut sleeve)	300

SUNDRAGON (1)
68	MGM MGM 1380	Green Tambourine/I Need All The Friends I Can Get	12
68	MGM MGM 1391	Blueberry Blue/Far Away Mountain	12
68	MGM MGM 1458	Five White Horses/Look At The Sun	30
68	MGM MGM-C(S) 8090	GREEN TAMBOURINE (LP, yellow/black 'lion' label)	175

(see also Sands)

SUNDRAGON (2)
03	Y n R YNR014	The Path/Watching (12")	12

SUNFIGHTER
76	EMI EMI 2493	Drag Race Queen/Riding On Your Star	15
76	EMI EMI 2553	Such A Lovely Night/Don't Get Me Wrong	10

(see also Chris Rainbow)

SUNFLAYRE
70	Realm RM 1	The Passing Dream/Rich Woman (private pressing)	300

SUNFOREST
70	Deram Nova DN 7	SOUND OF SUNFOREST (LP, mono, laminated front sleeve)	400
70	Deram Nova SDN 7	SOUND OF SUNFOREST (LP, stereo, laminated front sleeve)	300

SUNGLASSES AFTER DARK
84	Anagram ANA 20	Morbid Silence/Let's Go	10

SUNHOUSE
98	Independiente ISOM 4LP	CRAZY ON THE WEEKEND (LP)	70

SUNN O)))
04	Anti-Mosh 444	Candlewolff Ov Thee Golden Chalice (12")	35
03	Dirtier Promotions DPROMLP52	VOID (2-LP, 150 on green vinyl)	45
03	Dirtier Promotions DPROMLP52	VOID (2-LP, 850 on black vinyl)	25
13	Southern Lord SUNN 50	BLACK ONE (2-LP, reissue)	20

SUNNY & HI-JUMPERS
65	Carnival CV 7022	Tarry Till You're Better/Dance Til You're Better	6
65	Carnival CV 7025	Going To Damascus/Sweet Potatoes	6

SUNNY & THE SUNGLOWS/SUNLINERS
63	London HL 9792	Talk To Me (as Sunny & the Sunglows)/Every Week, Every Month, Every Year (as Sunny & the Sunliners)	25

SUNNYLAND SLIM
65	77' LA 12-23	CHICAGO BLUES SESSION (LP, with Little Brother Montgomery)	30
65	Storyville SLP 169	I DONE YOU WRONG (LP)	20
69	Liberty LBS 83237	SLIM'S GOT THIS THING GOIN' ON (LP)	30
69	Blue Horizon 7-63213	MIDNIGHT JUMP (LP, mono)	100
69	Blue Horizon S7-63213	MIDNIGHT JUMP (LP, stereo)	70

SUNNYSIDERS
55	London HL 8135	Hey! Mr. Banjo/Zoom, Zoom, Zoom	50
55	London HL 8160	Oh Me Oh My Oh/(Let's Gather Round) The Parlour Piano	30
55	London HLU 8180	Banjo Woogie/She Didn't Even Say Goodbye	30
55	London HLU 8202	I Love You Fair Dinkum/Stay On The Sunny Side	25
56	London HLU 8246	Doesn't He Love Me/Humdinger	30

SUN PALACE
83	Passion PASH 12 8	Winning/Rude Movements (12", p/s)	40

SUN RA
74	Decca F 13542	Can We Change/Don't Go (Demos only)	30

(This artist has no link to the legendary Sun Ra)

SUN RA ARKESTRA
85	MT 1	Nuclear War/IAN DURY: Fuck Off Noddy (white label, 500 only)	50
82	Y 1 RA	NUCLEAR WAR (12" EP)	50
10	Jazzman JM 079	THE WORLD IS NOT MY HOME (3 x clear vinyl 7", numbered)	35
69	Fontana STL 5514	HELIOCENTRIC WORLDS VOL. 1 (LP)	100
69	Fontana STL 5499	HELIOCENTRIC WORLDS VOL. 2 (LP)	100
68	Delmark DL 411	JAZZ BY SUN RA VOL 1. (LP, U.K. pressed record in American sleeve)	40
71	Black Lion BLP 30103	PICTURES OF INFINITY - IN CONCERT (LP)	40
71	Byg 529 341	THE SOLAR MYTH APPROACH VOL. 2 (LP)	40
71	Polydor 2460 106	PICTURES OF INFINITY (LP)	40
78	Affinity AFF 10	S-M APPROACH (LP, with Solar-Myth Ark)	25
79	Cobra COB 37001	FATE IN A PLEASANT MOOD (LP)	35
80	Y Y 19	STRANGE CELESTIAL ROAD (LP)	40
81	Recommended RR 11	NUITS DE LA FOUNDATION MAEGHT VOL 1 (LP, plays at 45rpm, pasted front cover)	30
81	Recommended RR 11	NUITS DE LA FOUNDATION MAEGHT VOL 1 (LP, plays at 45rpm, silk-screened sleeve)	60
85	Saturn/Recommended SRRRD1	COSMO SUN CONNECTION (LP, pasted cover)	300
88	Leo LR 154	LOVE IN OUTER SPACE (LP)	25

SUNRAY

MINT VALUE £

89	Blast First BFFP 42	OUT THERE A MINUTE (LP)	25
90	Blast First BFFP 60	SUN RA & MYTH SCIENCE ARKESTRA (3 x 10", box set, with insert)	40
04	Art Yard ARTYARDLP 001	DISCO 3000 (LP, reissue)	20
04	Art Yard ARTYARDLP 002	MEDIA DREAMS (LP, reissue)	30
05	Art Yard ARTYARDLP 003	SLEEPING BEAUTY (LP, reissue)	20
05	Art Yard ARTYARDLP 005	ON JUPITER (LP, reissue)	25

SUNRAY
00	Earworm WORM 68	Music For The Dreammachine (Phase One) (Sonic Boom Remix)(1-sided 12", clear vinyl)	10

SUNRAYS
65	Capitol CL 15416	I Live For The Sun/Bye, Baby, Bye	15
66	Capitol CL 15433	Andrea/You Don't Phase Me	15

SUNRISE
76	Grapevine GRA 105	BEFORE MY EYES (LP)	30

SUN SET
67	Polydor BM 56193	East Baby/You Can Ride My Rainbow	20

SUNSETS
61	Ember EMB S 125	Cry Of The Wild Goose/Manhunt	15

SUNSHINE COMPANY
67	Liberty LBF 15008	Happy/Blue May	12
67	Liberty LBF 15034	Back On The Street Again/A Year Of Janie's Time	10
68	Liberty LBF 15060	Look Here Comes The Sun/It's Sunday	8
68	Liberty LBF 15149	On A Beautiful Day/To Put Up With You	10
68	Liberty LBL/LBS 83120	THE SUNSHINE COMPANY (LP)	35
69	Liberty LBL/LBS 83159	SUNSHINE AND SHADOWS (LP)	35

SUNSHINE KID
73	RCA RCA 2413	My Linda/Get Your Rocks Off Baby	25

MR. SUNSHINE
56	MGM SP 1160	Along The China Coast/MRS. SUNSHINE: Two Car Garage	7

SUNSHINE POWER
89	Sing A Song SASM 1	It's Too Late (Vocal)/It's Too Late (Instrumental)/It's Too Late (Accapella) (12")	15

SUNSHINE (1)
72	Warner Brothers K 46169	SUNSHINE (LP, gatefold sleeve)	15

(see also Pretty Things)

SUNSHINE (2)
81	B's KNEES S 81 CUS 948	Double Dealin/(Instrumental Version)	10

SUNSHINE THEATRE
71	Harp SP1004	Mountain/I Want	400

SUNSTROKE
78	Hot Stuff HS 004	HERE COMES THE TRAIN EP	20

SUNTREADER
73	Island HELP 13	ZIN ZIN (LP, insert sleeve, black label, pink 'i' logo)	15

SUPER 8
95	García POUM 001	Billy The Kid/It Doesn't Matter/How Can I Understand The Flies? ('hairloss' p/s, 500 only, 37 sold, 35 returned for refund, the rest believed burned)	25

SUPER TONES
70	Banana BA 312	Freedom Blues/First Time I Met You	50

SUPERBOYS
68	Giant GN 22	Ain't That A Shame/Do It Right Now	30
68	Giant GN 31	You're Hurtin' Me/Funky Soul	30

(see also Dandy & Superboys, Little Sal)

SUPER CAT
88	Blue Trac BTRD 020	Nuff Man Dead Ya/ABC (12")	30

SUPERCHARGE
76	Virgin VS 145	Lonely And In Love/Give It The Nasty	6
78	Virgin VS 20212	I Think I'm Gonna Fall In Love/Long Version (12")	10

SUPERCHUNK
95	City Slang EFA 049261	HERE'S WHERE THE STRINGS COME IN (LP, insert)	20

SUPER COMBO
75	Rokel RKL 5001	Woko/Afro Funk	15

SUPERFLY
79	Firebrand DM 1021	Disco Crazy/Superfly	8

SUPER FURRY ANIMALS
95	SFAP1	Frisbee (12" promo, 1-sided, unreleased intended debut single. Not on a label)	25
96	Creation CRE 222	Hometown Unicorn/Don't Be A Fool Billy (p/s)	6
98	Creation CRE 288	Ice Hockey Hair/Smokin' (stickered p/s, limited edition)	6
00	Placid Casual PLC02	Ysbediau Heulog/Charge (White vinyl in PVC sleeve, 3000 only)	9
95	Ankst ANKST 057	LLANFAIRPWLLGWYNGYLLGOGERYCHWYRNDROBWLLANTYSILIOGOGOGOCHYNYGOFOD (IN SPACE) (EP) (1st issue/2nd issue, same cat no)	10
95	Ankst ANKST 62	MOOG DROOG EP (EP, 1st issue, p/s)	10
96	Creation CRELP 190	FUZZY LOGIC (LP, with insert)	100
97	Creation CRELP 214	RADIATOR (2-LP)	100
98	Creation CRELP 228	OUT SPACED (LP)	100
99	Creation CRELP 242	GUERRILLA (LP, gatefold, pop up sleeve)	100
00	Placid Casual PLC03LP	MWNG (LP, ltd white vinyl, p/s PVC sleeve. 2000 copies)	80
01	Sony/Epic 5024131	RINGS AROUND THE WORLD (2-LP, side 3 plays from inside out, with free 7" white label 7")	200
03	Epic 5123751	PHANTOM POWER (2-LP etched vinyl with insert, 3000 copies)	50
04	Placid Casual PL07CD	PHANTOM PHORCE (2-LP ltd version with bonus 'Slow Life' EP disc, fold-out packaging. 3000 copies)	25
05	Epic 5176711	SONGBOOK - THE SINGLES VOLUME ONE (2x12" pop up gatefold sleeve)	35

SUPERGRASS

MINT VALUE £

05	Sony 5205011	LOVE KRAFT (2-LP, gatefold)	50
15	Domino REWIGLP98X	MWNG (3-LP, reissue, white vinyl)	25

(see also Gruff Rhys)

SUPERGRASS

94	Backbeat BEAT 4	Caught By The Fuzz/Strange Ones (hand-stamped labels, 1,000 only, later re-pressed)	30
94	Backbeat BEAT 6	Mansize Rooster/Sitting Up Straight (luminous green vinyl, printed green cardboard sleeve, 500 only)	10
97	Parlophone GRASS 9497	THE SINGLES 1994-1997 (8 x 7" black vinyl, 'grass'-covered box set, with signed & numbered insert, promo only)	30
95	Parlophone PCSX 7373	I SHOULD COCO (LP, with inner & bonus single "Stone Free"/"Odd?" [PCSS 7373])	70
97	Parlophone 724385522819	IN IT FOR THE MONEY (LP)	60
99	Parlophone 5220561	SUPERGRASS (LP, with poster)	70
02	Parlophone 724354180019	LIFE ON OTHER PLANETS (LP)	40
04	EMI 5789941	SUPERGRASS IS 10 : BEST OF 94-04 (2 x 10" LP, clear vinyl, gatefold)	40
05	Parlophone 333 334-1	ROAD TO ROUEN (LP)	35
08	Parlophone 519 7341	DIAMOND HOO HA (LP)	20

(see also Jennifers, Hot Rats)

SUPERIMPOSERS

05	Little League LL 704	Seeing Is Believing/Shadows	75

SUPERMARKET

92	Icerink DAVO 4 12	SUPERMARKET (12")	12

(see also Felt, Denim, Go-Kart Mozart)

SUPERMATIX

81	MC 4	BAD TIMING EP (p/s)	20

SUPER$HIT666

00	Infernal INFERNAL003LP	SUPER$HIT666 (10" LP, with inner sleeve, purple vinyl)	70
00	Infernal INFERNAL 003LP	SUPER$HIT666 (10" LP, with inner sleeve, black vinyl)	50

(see also Backyard Babies, Hellacopters, Wildhearts)

SUPERSISTER

72	Polydor 2001 379	No Tree Will Grow/She Was Naked	12
71	Dandelion 2310 146	TO THE HIGHEST BIDDER (LP, gatefold sleeve)	125
71	Polydor 2419 030	SUPER STARSHINE 3 (LP)	40
72	Polydor 2419 061	PRESENT FROM NANCY (LP)	40
73	Polydor 2480 153	PUDDING & YESTERDAY (LP)	50
73	Polydor 2925 021	ISKANDER (LP, gatefold sleeve with lyric sheet)	25

SUPERTRAMP

70	A&M AMLS 981	SUPERTRAMP (LP, laminated sleeve, brown label)	50
71	A&M AMLH 64306	INDELIBLY STAMPED (LP, gatefold sleeve, brown label)	50
74	A&M AMLS 68258	CRIME OF THE CENTURY (LP, lyric inner, 'McNeil Press Ltd' printing credit)	15
84	A&M AMLK63708	BREAKFAST IN AMERICA (LP, Nimbus Supercut mail order only through Practical Hi Fi magazine)	80

SUPPORTERS

70	RCA 1972	Sing Your Own Team/On The Ball	10

(DIANA ROSS &) SUPREMES

64	Stateside SS 257	When The Lovelight Starts Shining Thru' His Eyes/Standing At The Crossroads Of Love	50
64	Stateside SS 257	When The Lovelight Starts Shining Thru' His Eyes/Standing At The Crossroads Of Love (DJ copy)	100

(Credited to Supremes.)

64	Stateside SS 327	Where Did Our Love Go/He Means The World To Me	12
64	Stateside SS 327	Where Did Our Love Go/He Means The World To Me (DJ copy)	100
64	Stateside SS 350	Baby Love/Ask Any Girl	12
64	Stateside SS 350	Baby Love/Ask Any Girl (DJ copy)	100
65	Stateside SS 376	Come See About Me/(You're Gone But) Always In My Heart	12
65	Stateside SS 376	Come See About Me/(You're Gone But) Always In My Heart (DJ copy)	100
65	Tamla Motown TMG 501	Stop! In The Name Of Love/I'm In Love Again	12
65	Tamla Motown TMG 501	Stop! In The Name Of Love/I'm In Love Again (DJ copy)	100
65	Tamla Motown TMG 516	Back In My Arms Again/Whisper You Love Me Boy	25
65	Tamla Motown TMG 516	Back In My Arms Again/Whisper You Love Me Boy (DJ copy)	85
65	Tamla Motown TMG 527	Nothing But Heartaches/He Holds His Own	25
65	Tamla Motown TMG 527	Nothing But Heartaches/He Holds His Own (DJ copy)	85
65	Tamla Motown TMG 543	I Hear A Symphony/Who Could Ever Doubt My Love	20
65	Tamla Motown TMG 543	I Hear A Symphony/Who Could Ever Doubt My Love (DJ copy)	75
66	Tamla Motown TMG 548	My World Is Empty Without You/Everything Is Good About You	25
66	Tamla Motown TMG 548	My World Is Empty Without You/Everything Is Good About You (DJ copy)	75
66	Tamla Motown TMG 560	Love Is Like An Itching In My Heart/He's All I Got	50
66	Tamla Motown TMG 560	Love Is Like An Itching In My Heart/He's All I Got (DJ copy)	150
66	Tamla Motown TMG 575	You Can't Hurry Love/Put Yourself In My Place	15
66	Tamla Motown TMG 575	You Can't Hurry Love/Put Yourself In My Place (DJ copy)	70
66	Tamla Motown TMG 585	You Keep Me Hangin' On/Remove This Doubt	15
66	Tamla Motown TMG 585	You Keep Me Hangin' On/Remove This Doubt (DJ copy)	60
67	Tamla Motown TMG 597	Love Is Here And Now You're Gone/There's No Stopping Us Now	12
67	Tamla Motown TMG 597	Love Is Here And Now You're Gone/There's No Stopping Us Now (DJ copy)	70
67	Tamla Motown TMG 607	The Happening/All I Know About You	12
67	Tamla Motown TMG 607	The Happening/All I Know About You (DJ copy)	75

(The above 45s are credited to the Supremes.)

67	Tamla Motown TMG 616	Reflections/Going Down For The Third Time	12
67	Tamla Motown TMG 616	Reflections/Going Down For The Third Time (DJ copy)	60
67	Tamla Motown TMG 632	In And Out Of Love/I Guess I'll Always Love You	12
67	Tamla Motown TMG 632	In And Out Of Love/I Guess I'll Always Love You (DJ copy)	40
68	Tamla Motown TMG 650	Forever Came Today/Time Changes Things	12
68	Tamla Motown TMG 650	Forever Came Today/Time Changes Things (DJ copy)	40

SUPREMES & FOUR TOPS

MINT VALUE £

Year	Label/Cat#	Title	Value
68	Tamla Motown TMG 662	Some Things You Never Get Used To/You've Been So Wonderful To Me	10
68	Tamla Motown TMG 662	Some Things You Never Get Used To/You've Been So Wonderful To Me (DJ copy)	40
68	Tamla Motown TMG 677	Love Child/Will This Be The Day?	10
68	Tamla Motown TMG 677	Love Child/Will This Be The Day? (DJ copy)	40
68	Tamla Motown PSRS 317	Love Child (special Royal Command Performance promo sent to journalists with Ken East "talking invite" with Love Child playing in the background)	70
69	Tamla Motown TMG 695	I'm Living In Shame/I'm So Glad I Got Somebody (Like You Around)	10
69	Tamla Motown TMG 695	I'm Living In Shame/I'm So Glad I Got Somebody (Like You Around) (DJ copy)	40
69	Tamla Motown TMG 704	No Matter What Sign You Are/The Young Folks	8
69	Tamla Motown TMG 704	No Matter What Sign You Are/The Young Folks (DJ copy)	35
69	Tamla Motown TMG 721	Someday We'll Be Together/He's My Sunny Boy	7
69	Tamla Motown TMG 721	Someday We'll Be Together/He's My Sunny Boy (DJ copy)	35

(The above 45s are credited to Diana Ross & Supremes.)

Year	Label/Cat#	Title	Value
70	Tamla Motown TMG 735	Up The Ladder To The Roof/Bill, When Are You Coming Back	7
70	Tamla Motown TMG 735	Up The Ladder To The Roof/Bill, When Are You Coming Back (DJ copy)	30
70	Tamla Motown TMG 747	Everybody's Got The Right To Love/But I Love You More	8
70	Tamla Motown TMG 747	Everybody's Got The Right To Love/But I Love You More (DJ copy)	25
70	Tamla Motown TMG 760	Stoned Love/Shine On Me	6
71	Tamla Motown TMG 760	Stoned Love/Shine On Me (DJ copy)	30
71	Tamla Motown TMG 782	Nathan Jones/Happy (Is A Bumpy Road)	7
71	Tamla Motown TMG 782	Nathan Jones/Happy (Is A Bumpy Road) (DJ copy)	30

(The above 45s are credited to the Supremes and do not feature Diana Ross)

Year	Label/Cat#	Title	Value
65	Tamla Motown TME 2008	THE SUPREMES HITS (EP, with flipback sleeve & push-out centre)	30
65	Tamla Motown TME 2008	THE SUPREMES HITS (EP)	35
66	Tamla Motown TME 2011	SHAKE (EP)	75
64	Stateside SL 10109	MEET THE SUPREMES (Stateside in green writing)	50
65	Tamla Motown TML 11002	WITH LOVE - FROM US TO YOU (mono)	60
65	Tamla Motown TML 11012	WE REMEMBER SAM COOKE	50
65	Tamla Motown TML 11018	THE SUPREMES SING COUNTRY, WESTERN AND POP	50
65	Tamla Motown TML 11020	MORE HITS BY THE SUPREMES	35
66	T. Motown TML 11026	THE SUPREMES AT THE COPA (mono)	25
66	T. Motown STML 11026	THE SUPREMES AT THE COPA (stereo)	30
66	T. Motown TML 11028	I HEAR A SYMPHONY (mono)	25
66	T. Motown STML 11028	I HEAR A SYMPHONY (stereo)	30
66	T. Motown TML 11039	SUPREMES A-GO GO (mono)	25
66	T. Motown STML 11039	SUPREMES A-GO GO (stereo)	35
67	T. Motown TML 11047	THE SUPREMES SING MOTOWN (mono)	25
67	T. Motown STML 11047	THE SUPREMES SING MOTOWN (stereo)	30
67	T. Motown TML 11054	THE SUPREMES SING RODGERS AND HART (mono)	20
67	T. Motown STML 11054	THE SUPREMES SING RODGERS AND HART (stereo)	22

(The LPs listed above are credited to the Supremes, with flipback sleeves.)

Year	Label/Cat#	Title	Value
68	T. Motown (S)TML 11063	GREATEST HITS (stereo/mono, original pressing with flipback laminated sleeve)	15
68	T. Motown (S)TML 11070	'LIVE' AT LONDON'S TALK OF THE TOWN (mono/stereo)	15
68	T. Motown (S)TML 11073	REFLECTIONS (mono/stereo)	25
69	T. Motown TML 11088	SING & PERFORM FUNNY GIRL (mono)	20
69	T. Motown STML 11088	SING & PERFORM FUNNY GIRL (stereo)	18
69	T. Motown TML 11095	LOVE CHILD (mono)	25
69	T. Motown STML 11095	LOVE CHILD (stereo)	20
69	T. Motown TML 11114	LET THE SUNSHINE IN (mono)	25
69	T. Motown STML 11114	LET THE SUNSHINE IN (stereo)	22
70	T. Motown TML 11137	CREAM OF THE CROP (mono)	20
70	T. Motown STML 11137	CREAM OF THE CROP (stereo)	18

(The above LPs are credited to Diana Ross & Supremes. Originally issued with flipback sleeves; later pressings are worth two-third of these values.)

Year	Label/Cat#	Title	Value
70	T. Motown STML 11157	RIGHT ON (as Supremes)	20
70	T. Motown STML 11175	NEW WAYS BUT LOVE STAYS	20
71	T. Motown STML 11189	TOUCH (LP, as Supremes)	15
72	T. Motown STML 11210	FLOY JOY	15
73	T. Motown STML 11222	PRODUCED AND ARRANGED BY JIMMY WEBB (LP, as Supremes)	15
75	T. Motown STML 11293	THE SUPREMES	15
76	T. Motown STML 12047	MARY, SCHERRIE & SUSAYE	15

(see also Primettes, Diana Ross, Temptations, Four Tops, Florence Ballard, Mary Wilson)

SUPREMES & FOUR TOPS

Year	Label/Cat#	Title	Value
71	T. Motown STML 11179	THE SUPREMES AND THE FOUR TOPS - MAGNIFICENT 7 (LP)	15

DIANA ROSS & THE SUPREMES & THE TEMPTATIONS

Year	Label/Cat#	Title	Value
69	Tamla Motown TMG 685	I'm Gonna Make You Love Me/A Place In The Sun	6
69	Tamla Motown TMG 709	I Second That Emotion/The Way You Do The Things You Do	7
70	Tamla Motown TMG 730	Why (Must We Fall In Love)/Uptight (Everything Is Alright)	8
69	T. Motown TML 11096	DIANA ROSS & THE SUPREMES JOIN THE TEMPTATIONS (LP, mono)	20
69	T. Motown STML 11096	DIANA ROSS & THE SUPREMES JOIN THE TEMPTATIONS (LP, stereo)	18
69	T. Motown (S)TML 11110	THE ORIGINAL SOUNDTRACK FROM TCB (LP, gatefold laminated sleeve)	15
70	T. Motown TML 11122	TOGETHER (LP, flipback sleeve, mono)	18
70	T. Motown STML 11122	TOGETHER (LP, flipback sleeve, stereo)	15

SUPREME WARRIOR

Year	Label/Cat#	Title	Value
83	Supreme Warrior SW001	Treading The Tightrope/Mad & Cynical	50

ADAM SURF & PEBBLE BEACH BAND

Year	Label/Cat#	Title	Value
76	Paladin PAL 3	Fun Fun Fun/Blue Surf	10

SURFACE

Year	Label/Cat#	Title	Value
83	Salsoul SAL 104	Falling In Love/Instrumental	15
83	Salsoul SALT 104	Falling In Love/Instrumental (12")	20
83	Salsoul SALT 104/XD 01291	Falling In Love (1-sided 12")	15

SURFACE TENSION

MINT VALUE £

15	Salsoul SALT 104	Falling In Love/Instrumental (12", reissue)	15

SURFACE TENSION
83	Spiv 2TS	Rotation/Don't Let Them/Traffic Accident (p/s)	15

SURFARIS
63	London HLD 9751	Wipe Out/Surfer Joe	10
63	Brunswick 05894	Waikiki Run/Point Panic	15
64	Brunswick 05902	Scatter Shield/Bat Man	15
66	Dot DS 26756	Wipe Out/Surfer Joe (reissue)	10
63	London RE-D 1405	WIPE OUT (EP)	35
63	London HA-D 8110	WIPE OUT (LP)	40
63	Brunswick LAT 8561	THE SURFARIS PLAY (LP, mono)	30
63	Brunswick STA 8561	THE SURFARIS PLAY (LP, stereo)	40
64	Brunswick LAT 8567	HIT CITY '64 (LP, mono)	30
64	Brunswick STA 8567	HIT CITY '64 (LP, stereo)	40
64	Brunswick LAT 8582	FUN CITY (LP)	30
65	Brunswick LAT 8605	HIT CITY '65 (LP)	40
65	Brunswick LAT 8631	IT AIN'T ME BABE (LP, mono)	35
65	Brunswick STA 8631	IT AIN'T ME BABE (LP, stereo)	40
66	Dot DLP 3535	WIPE OUT (LP, reissue)	25
87	MCA MCL 1842	WIPE OUT - THE SINGLES ALBUM 1963-1967 (LP, withdrawn)	20

SURFERS
59	Vogue V 9147	Mambo Jambo/ALAN KALANI: A Touch Of Pink	10

LES SURFS
64	RCA RCA 1432	Just For The Boy/Stop	10
65	RCA RCA 1461	Go Your Way/Chained To A Memory	7
67	Fontana TF 832	When I Tell You (That I Love You)/I Want To Be Free	6

SURGEON
96	Downwards DNLP1	COMMUNICATIONS (LP as 2 x 12")	18
97	Tresor 74321 47314 1	BASICTONALVOCABULARY (LP as 2 x 12")	18

SURGEONS
79	Surgery S-100	Sid Never Did It/Breaking Rocks On Riker's Island	50

SURGICAL SUPPORTS
81	Industrious Youth CONSTRUCT 2	WITHDRAWN FOR DISPOSAL EP	30

JOHN SURMAN (TRIO)
69	Deram DM 224	Obeah Wedding/Can't Stop The Carnival	40
68	Deram DML/SML 1030	JOHN SURMAN (LP)	100
69	Deram DML-R/SML-R 1045	HOW MANY CLOUDS CAN YOU SEE? (LP)	100
70	Futura GER 12	ALORS! (LP)	45
71	Dawn DNLS 3006	THE TRIO (LP, with Stu Martin, poster)	70
71	Dawn DNLS 3018	WHERE FORTUNE SMILES (LP, with insert, with John McLaughlin, Karl Berger, Stu Martin & Dave Holland)	40
71	Dawn DNLS 3022	CONFLAGRATION (LP)	60
71	Deram SML 1094	TALES OF THE ALGONQUIN (LP, with John Warren)	100
72	Island HELP 10	WESTERING HOME (LP)	20
73	Island ILPS 9237	MORNING GLORY (LP)	20
79	Ogun OG 259	BY CONTRACT (LP)	18

(see also Morning Glory, Trio, Mike Westbook, John McLaughlin, Alan Skidmore/Mike Osborne/John Surman)

SURPLUS STOCK
79	Outatune OUT 7911	Spiv/Vips (p/s)	7

SURPRISES
79	Dead Dog DEAD 01	Jeremy Thorpe Is Innocent/Flying Attack/Little Sir Echo (p/s)	35

SURPRISE SISTERS
76	Good Earth GD1	Seashore/La Booga Rooga	8

SURVIVE
16	HoloDeck HD015LP	HDO15 (LP. marbled grey vinyl)	20
16	Relapse RR7349	RR7349 (LP. green vinyl)	20

SURVIVOR
78	Southern SSM 1	PASTICHE EP	6

SURVIVORS (1)
65	Rio R 55	Take Charge/Ska-Ology	25
65	Rio R 70	Rawhide Ska/OWEN GRAY: Girl I Want You	35

SURVIVORS (2)
79	Capitol PSR 436	Pamela Jean/After The Game (Credits the Beach Boys on p/s, Survivors on disc)	10

(see also The Beach Boys)

SURVIVORS (3)
79	Tribesman TM 22	Angel Of Love/Fashion Rock (12")	15

SUSHI
99	Ariwa ARI 187	Peace And Harmony/MAD PROFESSOR: Aahha (12")	15

SUSIE (1)
71	Decca F 13217	I Feel The Earth Move/We Are All The Same	20

SUSIE (2)
76	King Cliff KC 001	Love As Been Good/Version	25

SUSPECT
71	Decca FR 13218	Mariooka/Belinda	20

SUSPEKT
93	Union Hall UH002	Under Suspicion (12")	12

SUSSED (1)
79	Shoestring LACE 002	I Like You/Tango/The Perv (p/s)	15
80	Graduate GRAD 7	I've Got Me A Parka/Myself, Myself And I Repeated (p/s, paper labels; later reissued [1986] with silver labels)	6

SUSSED (2)

MINT VALUE £

86	Fusion FU 001	Harlem Spirit/Part Two	12

(SCREAMING) LORD SUTCH (& THE SAVAGES)

61	HMV POP 953	Till The Following Night/Good Golly Miss Molly	30
63	Decca F 11598	Jack The Ripper/Don't You Just Know It	15
63	Decca F 11747	I'm A Hog For You/Monster In Black Tights	15
64	Oriole CB 1944	She's Fallen In Love With A Monster Man/Bye Bye Baby	50
64	Oriole CB 1962	Dracula's Daughter/Come Back Baby	80
65	CBS 201767	The Train Kept A-Rollin'/Honey Hush (as Lord Sutch)	50
66	CBS 202080	The Cheat/Black And Hairy	50
70	Atlantic 584 321	Cause I Love You/Thumping Beat	15
70	Atlantic 2091 006	Cause I Love You/Thumping Beat (reissue)	6
70	Atlantic 2091 017	Election Fever/Rock The Election	10
72	Atlantic K 10221	Gotta Keep A-Rockin'/Flashing Lights/Hands Of Jack The Ripper	10
76	SRT SRTS 76361	Monster Ball/Rang-Tang-A-Lang	8
76	SRT SRTS 76375	I Drink To Your Health Marie (Parts 1 & 2)	8
77	Decca F 13697	Jack The Ripper/I'm A Hog For You	6
80	Ace SW 70	All Black A Hairy/London Rocker/Oh Well	8
89	Invitation KORNER 001	Creepy Christmas Party/Rap Up Christmas (no p/s)	10
81	Ridgemount RMR 45 010	LOONABILLY (EP, p/s, with bonus "Loon Party" single)	10
70	Atlantic 2400 008	LORD SUTCH AND HIS HEAVY FRIENDS (LP)	25
72	Atlantic K 40313	HANDS OF JACK THE RIPPER (LP, as Lord Sutch & Heavy Friends)	25
81	Ace MAD 1	THE METEORS MEET SCREAMING LORD SUTCH (mini-LP, 1 side each, stickered cartoon print on plain grey card sleeve, 1,000 only)	100
82	Ace CHA 65	ROCK A HORROR (LP, gatefold)	15

(see also Savages, Meteors, Led Zeppelin, Cliff Bennett & Rebel Rousers, Circles, Nero & Gladiators, Neil Christian & Crusaders)

SUTCLIFFE JUGEND

82	Come Org. WDC 883030	WE SPIT ON THEIR GRAVES (10 x cassette box)	150
82	Come Org. WDC 883028	CAMPAIGN (cassette, beware of Japanese bootlegs)	75

ROGER SUTCLIFFE

76	Look LKLP 6038RS	DEATH LETTER (LP)	30

SUTHERLAND BROTHERS BAND

71	Island ILPS 9181	THE SUTHERLAND BROTHERS BAND (LP, blue inner)	15

SUZANNE

77	Ring O' 2017 108	Born On Hallowe'en/Like No One Else (in promo p/s)	25
77	Ring O' 2017 108	Born On Hallowe'en/Like No One Else	12
78	Ring O' 2017 111	You Really Got A Hold On Me/You Could Be Right This Time	10
78	Ring O' 2017 115	single (unreleased)	0
78	Ring O' 2320 105	SUZANNE (LP, unreleased)	0

SUZI & BIG DEE IRWIN

66	Polydor BM 65715	Ain't That Lovin' You Baby/I Can't Get Over You	15

(see also Big Dee Irwin)

PAT SUZUKI

60	RCA RCA 1171	I Enjoy Being A Girl/Sunday	7

SUZY & THE RED STRIPES

77	A&M AMS 7461	Seaside Woman/B-side To The Seaside (yellow vinyl, die-cut p/s)	10
79	A&M AMSP 7461	Seaside Woman/B-side To The Seaside (yellow vinyl, die-cut p/s, in box set with badge & 10 'saucy' mini-postcards)	40
80	A&M AMS 7548	Seaside Woman/B-side To The Seaside (reissue, cartoon p/s, as Linda McCartney alias Suzy & Red Stripes)	10
80	A&M AMSP 7548	Seaside Woman/B-side To The Seaside (12", as Linda McCartney alias Suzy & Red Stripes)	12
86	EMI EMI 5572	Seaside Woman/B-side To The Seaside (p/s)	6
86	EMI 12EMI 5572	Seaside Woman/B-side To The Seaside (12", p/s)	10

(see also Paul McCartney [& Wings])

SVENSK

67	Page One POF 036	Dream Magazine/Getting Old	25
67	Page One POF 050	You/All I Have To Do Is Dream	18

(see also Jason Paul)

SWALLOWS WITH SONNY THOMPSON

52	Vogue V 2136	Roll, Roll Pretty Baby/It Ain't The Meat (78)	50

(see also Sonny Thompson & His Rhythm & Blues Band)

SWAMP DOGG

72	Mojo 2916 014	TOTAL DESTRUCTION TO YOUR MIND (LP)	20
73	President PTLS 1	GAG A MAGGOT (LP)	15

(see also Jerry Williams, Brooks & Jerry)

SWAMP CHILDREN

82	Factory FACT 70	SWAMP CHILDREN (LP)	20

SWAMPTALK

79	Ace 004	SWAMPTALK EP (p/s)	8

SWAN ARCADE

73	Trailer LER 2032	SWAN ARCADE (LP)	20
84	Fellside FE 037	TOGETHER FOREVER (LP)	18

SWANEE RIVER BOYS

54	Parlophone CMSP 7	Do You Believe/Gloryland Boogie (export issue)	15

BETTYE SWANN

67	CBS 2942	Make Me Yours/I Will Not Cry	70
67	CBS 2942	Make Me Yours/I Will Not Cry (DJ copy)	100
67	CBS 2942	Make Me Yours/I Will Not Cry (DJ copy in p/s)	150
69	Capitol CL 15586	Don't Touch Me/(My Heart Is) Closed For The Season	30
72	Atlantic K 10174	Victim Of A Foolish Heart/Cold Day In Hell	10

SWANS (1)

MINT VALUE £

72	Atlantic K 10273	Today I Started Loving You Again/I'd Rather Go Blind	6
73	Mojo 2092 059	Make Me Yours/I Will Not Cry (reissue)	6
75	Atlantic K 10622	Doing It For The One I Love/All The Way In Or All The Way Out	6
03	Atlantic 69530	Kiss My Love Goodbye/MAJOR HARRIS: Loving You Is Mellow	8
04	Honest Jons HJRLP 8	BETTYE SWANN (2-LP)	40

(see also Sam Dees & Bettye Swann)

SWANS (1)
63	Stateside SS 224	He's Mine/You Better Be A Good Girl Now	40
64	Cameo Parkway C 302	The Boy With The Beatle Hair/Please Hurry Home	40

SWANS (2)
84	K.422 KDE112	YOUNG GOD (12" EP)	18
86	K.422/Some Bizzare KDE 312	A Screw (Holy Money)/Blackmail/A Screw (12", p/s)	10
88	Product Inc. 12PROD 23	Love Will Tear Us Apart (Red Version)/Trust Me/Love Will Tear Us Apart (Black Version)/Our Love Lies (12", black vinyl, p/s)	15
88	Product Inc. PROD 23	Love Will Tear Us Apart/Trust Me (red vinyl, 750 only, p/s)	10
84	K. 422/Some Bizzare KCC 1	COP (LP, with inner)	50
86	K. 422/Some Bizzare KCC 2	GREED (LP, with inner)	25
86	K. 422/Some Bizzare KCC 3	HOLY MONEY (LP)	18
87	Product Inc. 33PROD 17	CHILDREN OF GOD (2-LP)	50
86	No label BURN ONE	PUBLIC CASTRATION IS A GOOD IDEA (2-LP)	30
87	Young God LOVE 1	FEEL GOOD NOW (2-LP, with poster)	35
89	MCA MCG 6047	THE BURNING WORLD (LP, with lyric inner)	18
90	Young God	FILTH (LP, U.K. reissue, 500 only, numbered)	30
91	Young God YGLP 3	WHITE LIGHT FROM THE MOUTH OF INFAMY (LP)	75
92	Young God YGLP 5	LOVE OF LIFE (LP, insert)	40
94	Young God YGLP 9	THE GREAT ANNIHILATOR (2-LP)	125
95	Young God YGLP 004	BODY TO BODY, JOB TO JOB (LP)	30
95	Young God YGLP 005B	LOVE OF LIFE (LP, in box)	80

BENRICE SWANSON
65	Chess CRS 8008	Lying Awake/Baby I'm Yours	30
65	Chess CRS 8008	Lying Awake/Baby I'm Yours (DJ copy)	50

DAVE SWARBRICK
67	Bounty BYI 6030	RAGS, REELS AND AIRS (LP, with Martin Carthy & Diz Disley)	40
67	Polydor Special 236 514	RAGS, REELS AND AIRS (LP, reissue, with Martin Carthy & Diz Disley)	25

(see also Martin Carthy & Dave Swarbrick, Fairport Convention,Young Tradition, Vashti Bunyan, Ian Campbell)

SWARBRIGG (PLUS TWO)
75	MCA MCA 179	That's What Friends Are For/Love Is	6

SWEAT
80	Double D DDLP	NO MORE RUNNING (LP, insert)	20

ROSALYN SWEAT & PARAGONS
73	Duke DU 160	Blackbird Singing/Always	25

(see also Paragons)

SWE-DANES
61	Warner Bros WEP 6017	THE SWE-DANES (EP; mono)	10
61	Warner Bros SWEP 2017	THE SWE-DANES (EP; stereo)	15

(see also Alice Babsi)

SWEDEN THROUGH THE AGES
86	Snappy SW 001	IT HELPS TO CRY EP (12", p/s)	12

SWEDISH MODERN JAZZ GROUP
61	Tempo TAP 31	SAX APPEAL (LP)	200

SWEENEY'S MEN
67	Pye 7N 17312	Old Maid In The Garrett/Derby Ram	10
68	Pye 7N 17459	Waxies Dargle/Old Woman In Cotton	10
69	Transatlantic TRASP 19	Sullivan's John/Rattlin' Roarin' Willy	8
68	Transatlantic TRA 170	SWEENEY'S MEN (LP)	90
69	Transatlantic TRA 200	THE TRACKS OF SWEENEY (LP)	90
76	Transatlantic TRASAM 37	SWEENEY'S MEN (LP, reissue)	20
77	Transatlantic TRASAM 40	THE TRACKS OF SWEENEY (LP, reissue)	18

(see also Gay & Terry Woods, Dr. Strangely Strange)

SWEENY BEAN
72	Sonet SON 2028	Rock 'N' Roll Wedding/Overcoat	10

JIM SWEENY
58	Philips PB 811	The Midnight Hour/Till The Right One Comes Along	20

SWEENY TODD
70s	London L2616	Shut Up/Wastin' Time	10
76	London HLU 10540	Roxy Roller/Rue De Chance	12

JIMMY SWEEP
81	Tamarin TAM 3	London Town/Bridgetown Girls (written, produced by & feat. Alan Lancaster)	10
82	PRT 7P 233	London Town/Bridgetown Girls (reissue)	8

(see also Status Quo)

SWEET
68	Fontana TF 958	Slow Motion/It's Lonely Out There	400
69	Parlophone R 5803	The Lollipop Man/Time	100
70	Parlophone R 5826	All You'll Ever Get From Me/The Juicer	40
70	Parlophone R 5848	Get On The Line/Mr. McGallagher	70
71	RCA RCA 2051	Funny Funny/You're Not Wrong For Loving Me	10
71	RCA RCA 2087	Co Co/Done Me Wrong, All Right	10
71	Parlophone R 5902	All You'll Ever Get From Me/The Juicer (reissue)	15
73	RCA RCA 2403	Ballroom Blitz/Rock & Roll Disgrace (mispressed at wrong speed, 49rpm; matrix: 2403-A-1E)	15

SWEET AIR

MINT VALUE £

Year	Label/Cat	Title	Value
77	RCA PB 5011	Fever Of Love/A Distinct Lack Of Ancient	6
77	RCA PB 5046	Stairway To The Stars/Why Don't You Do It To Me	8
78	Polydor POSP 5	California Nights/Show Me The Way (unreleased)	0
79	Polydor POSP 36	Call Me/Why Don't You	7
79	Polydor POSP 73	Big Apple Waltz/Why Don't You	20
80	RCA PE 5226	Fox On The Run/Hellraiser/Ballroom Blitz/Blockbuster (EP, p/s)	15
80	Polydor POSP 131	Give That Lady Some Respect/Tall Girls	7
80	Polydor POSP 160	Sixties Man/Oh Yeah	15
80	Polydor POSP 160	Sixties Man/Oh Yeah (mispressing, B-side plays "Tall Girls")	20
84	Anagram ANA 27	The Sixteens/Action (p/s)	10
85	Anagram ANA 29	Sweet 2th - The Wig Wam-Willy Mix/The Teen Action Mix (p/s)	8
71	RCA SF 8288	FUNNY HOW SWEET CO-CO CAN BE (LP)	80
74	RCA LPL 15039	SWEET FANNY ADAMS (LP)	80
74	RCA LPL 15080	DESOLATION BOULEVARD (LP, gatefold sleeve)	60
75	RCA SPC 0001	STRUNG UP (2-LP)	50
76	RCA RS 1036	GIVE US A WINK (LP)	20
77	RCA PL 25072	OFF THE RECORD (LP, gatefold, with inner sleeve)	18
78	Polydor POLD5001	LEVEL HEADED (LP)	20
79	Polydor POLD 5022	CUT ABOVE THE REST (LP, with inner sleeve)	18
80	Polydor POLS 1021	WATER'S EDGE (LP)	25
82	Polydor 2311 1179	IDENTITY CRISIS (LP)	22
84	Anagram GRAM 16	SWEET SIXTEEN (LP)	15
84	Anagram P GRAM 16	SWEET SIXTEEN (LP, picture disc)	25

(see also Brian Connolly, Mayfield's Mule, Elastic Band, Andy Scott)

SWEET AIR
70	Chime CH 1	Pictures In A Puddle/Sally Finne	200

SWEET AS CANDY
71	Stem ST 3	At The Bus Stop/The Missing Keys	20

SWEET BRIAR
70	Access ACC 314	The Liar/Choose Me/Sunworshipper (p/s)	40

SWEET HENRY
71	Paramount PARA 3017	Falling In Love With Baby/Love Is Two	8

SWEET PEA
70	Tribual TR 1	Run To The Forest/I'm In My Bad Books	20

SWEET CHARIOT
69	MCA MK 5010	Heavenly Road/Wish I Were A Child	8
73	Columbia DB 8999	When I'm A Kid/Mozart '73	8
70s	T.O.G. SCEP 001	Angelina/Young At Heart/America	8
72	De Wolfe DWLP 3230	SWEET CHARIOT & FRIENDS (LP, library issue only)	40

SWEET CHARLES
88	Urban URB 15	Yes It's You/LYN COLLINS: Rock Me Again And Again And Again and Again	25

SWEET CONFUSION
69	Escort ES 809	Elizabeth Serenade/Don At Rest	40
69	Escort ES 812	Hotter Scorcher/Conquer Lion	30

(see also Stranger & Patsy)

SWEETCORN
71	Pye 7N45047	We Can Work Together/Carpet Ride	15

SWEET CREAM
78	Ember EMBS 368	I Don't Know What I'd Do/Skunk Funk	8

SWEETEST ACHE
90	Sarah SARAH 36	If I Could Shine/Here Comes The Ocean (p/s, insert)	25
90	Sarah SARAH 39	Tell Me How It Feels/Heaven-Scented World (p/s, insert)	25
91	Sarah SARAH 47	Everlasting/Sickening (p/s, insert)	25
91	Sarah SARAH 608	JAGUAR (LP)	50

SWEET FEELING
67	Columbia DB 8195	All So Long Ago/Charles Brown	200

(see also Rupert's People)

SWEETHEARTS
65	Blue Beat BB 389	Sit Down And Cry (actually with Clinton & Rufus)/PRINCE BUSTER: Ghost Dance	80

HARRY SWEETING
68	Coxsone CSL 8012	FROM JAMAICA WITH LOVE (LP)	100

SWEET INSPIRATIONS
67	Atlantic 584 117	Why (Am I Treated So Bad)/I Don't Want To Go On Without You	10
67	Atlantic 584 132	Let It Be Me/When Something Is Wrong With My Baby	10
68	Atlantic 584 167	Sweet Inspiration/I'm Blue	10
68	Atlantic 584 233	What The World Needs Now Is Love/You Really Didn't Mean It	10
69	Atlantic 584 241	Sweet Inspiration/I'm Blue	6
69	Atlantic 584 279	Sweets For My Sweet/Get A Little Order	6
70	Atlantic 584 312	(Gotta Find) A Brand New Lover (Parts 1 & 2)	6
68	Atlantic 587/588 090	THE SWEET INSPIRATIONS (LP)	25
69	Atlantic 587/588 137	WHAT THE WORLD NEEDS NOW IS LOVE (LP)	25
69	Atlantic 587/588 194	SWEETS FOR MY SWEET (LP)	20
70	Atlantic 2465 003	SWEET SWEET SOUL (LP)	20
79	RSO RSS 12	HOT BUTTERFLY (LP)	15
20	Reel RMLP 6139LE	THE SWEET INSPIRATIONS (LP, reissue, 500 only, numbered)	20

(see also Cissy Houston)

SWEET JESUS
91	Chapter 22 CHAP 63	Cat Thing/Honey Loving Honey/Peach/Baby Blue (12" EP)	10

SWEET LIFE
71	Ra 5008	Hold Back The Horses/Shadow Clock	10

SWEET LITTLE BUNTY

MINT VALUE £

SWEET LITTLE BUNTY
75	Ackee ACK 540	I (Who Have Nothing)/Oh Me Oh My	6

SWEET PAIN
69	Mercury 20146 SMCL	SWEET PAIN (LP, laminated gatefold, black/silver label)	175

(see also Dick Heckstall-Smith)

SWEET PLUM
69	Middle Earth MDS 103	Lazy Day/Let No Man Steal Your Thyme	30
70	Middle Earth MDS 105	Set The Wheels In Motion/Catch A Cloud	30

SWEET REACTION
72	Satril SAT 5	Come Back My Dream/Call Me Maria	10

SWEET REVENGE
80s	SRS SRS 15	Feel The Bullets Bite/Inside Your Head	125

SWEET SAVAGE
81	Park PRK 1001	Take No Prisoners/Killing Time (p/s, red and yellow label)	60
81	Park PRK 1001	Take No Prisoners/Killing Time (p/s, black and yellow label)	40
80s	Crashed CAR 48	Straight Through The Heart/Teaser (no p/s)	150
80s	private pressing	The Raid/Prosecutors Of Greed (possibly unreleased)	50

(see also Dio, Whitesnake)

SWEETSHOP
68	Parlophone R 5707	Barefoot And Tiptoe/Lead The Way	30

(see also Mark Wirtz)

SWEET SLAG
71	President PTLS 1042	TRACKING WITH CLOSE-UPS (LP)	160

SWEET THURSDAY
69	Polydor 2310 051	SWEET THURSDAY (LP)	25

(see also Nicky Hopkins, Mark-Almond)

SWEETWATER
72	Polydor 2058 239	Uncle Tom/Apple Pie	10

SWEGAS
70	Trend 6099 001	What You Gonna Do/There Is Nothing In It	10
71	Trend 6480 002	CHILD OF LIGHT (LP, gatefold sleeve)	50

SWELL
92	Mean MEAN LP 002	...WELL? (LP, marble vinyl)	15

SWELL MAPS
78	Rather GEAR ONE	Read About Seymour/Ripped And Torn/Black Velvet (p/s)	35
79	Rough Trade RT 010/Rather GEAR ONE MK. 2	Read About Seymour/Ripped And Torn/Black Velvet (p/s, reissue, different back sleeve)	15
79	R. Trade RT 012/GEAR 3	Dresden Style/Mystery Track/Ammunition Train/Full Moon (Dub) (p/s)	25
79	R. Trade RT 021/GEAR 6	Real Shocks/English Verse/Monlogues (p/s, 2 different colours)	25
79	R. Trade RT 036/GEAR 7	Let's Build A Car/Big Maz In The Country/...Then Poland (p/s)	15
81	Rough Trade RT 012/Rather GEAR 3	Dresden Style (new vocal)/Ammunition Train/Full Moon (Dub) (p/s, reissue, different back sleeve)	10
79	Rough Trade ROUGH 2/Rather TROY 1	A TRIP TO MARINEVILLE (LP, with inner sleeve, with bonus EP in die-cut sleeve [Rather GEAR FIVE])	45
79	Rough Trade ROUGH 2/Rather TROY 1	A TRIP TO MARINEVILLE (LP, with inner sleeve, without bonus EP in die-cut sleeve [Rather GEAR FIVE])	30
80	Rough Trade ROUGH 15	SWELL MAPS IN 'JANE FROM OCCUPIED EUROPE' (LP)	35
81	Rough Trade ROUGH 21	WHATEVER HAPPENS NEXT... (2-LP)	20
84	Rough Trade ROUGH 41	SWELL MAPS IN 'COLLISION TIME' (LP)	15
89	Mute MAPS 1	A TRIP TO MARINEVILLE (LP, reissue)	15
89	Mute MPAS 2	SWELL MAPS IN 'JANE FROM OCCUPIED EUROPE' (LP, reissue)	15

(see also Cult Figures, Nikki Sudden, Steve Treatment,, Metrophase, Last Bandits)

SWERVEDRIVER
91	Creation CREF 009	Surf Twang/Deep Twang (p/s)	6
91	Creation CRE 079T	SON OF MUSTANG FORD EP (12")	10
91	Creation CRE 088T	RAVE DOWN EP (12")	10
91	Creation CRELP 093	RAISE (LP, with free 7")	35
91	Creation CRELP 093	RAISE (LP, without free 7")	20
93	Creation CRELP 143	MEZCAL HEAD (LP)	70
95	Creation CRELP 157	EJECTOR SEAT RESERVATION (LP, with free 7")	70
95	Creation CRELP 157	EJECTOR SEAT RESERVATION (LP, without free 7")	60
98	Sonic Waves SWD 099LP	99TH DREAM (LP)	30

ANTHONY SWETE
69	RCA RCA 1905	Backfield in Motion/Soul Deep	8

JONATHAN SWIFT
71	CBS 64412	INTROVERT (LP, side opening gatefold, nude cover)	20
72	CBS 64751	SONGS (LP, with lyric insert)	15

TUFTY SWIFT
77	Free Reed FRR 017	HOW TO MAKE A BAKEWELL TART (LP, with booklet)	25
85	Shark SHARK 04	YOU'LL NEVER DIE FOR LOVE (LP, private pressing)	15

SWIM DEEP
12	Chess Club 88725478887	Honey/Orange County	10
13	Chess Club CC 052	The Sea/Down By The Seaside	8
13	Chess Club CCLP 02	WHERE THE HEAVEN ARE WE (LP & 7" signed)	40

SWINDLEFOLK
69	Deroy	SWINDLED (LP, private pressing)	75
70	Deroy	A-ROVIN' (LP, private pressing)	75
71	CAM 311	DUSK TO DAWN (LP, white label, hand-mae sleeves)	150

RAY SWINFIELD
68	Morgan MR 107P	ONE FOR RAY (LP)	45

SWINGERS
MINT VALUE £

SWINGERS
60	Vogue V 9158	Love Makes The World Go Round/Jackie	15
67	Blue Beat BB 379	Simpleton/FRANCIS: Warn The People	75

SWINGING BLUE JEANS
63	HMV POP 1170	It's Too Late Now/Think Of Me	12
63	HMV POP 1206	Do You Know/Angie	15
64	HMV POP 1327	Promise You'll Tell Her/It's So Right	7
64	HMV POP 1375	It Isn't There/One Of These Days	7
65	HMV POP 1409	Make Me Know You're Mine/I've Got A Girl	10
65	HMV POP 1477	Crazy 'Bout My Baby/Good Lovin'	8
66	HMV POP 1501	Don't Make Me Over/What Can I Do Today	8
66	HMV POP 1533	Sandy/I'm Gonna Have You	15
66	HMV POP 1564	Rumours, Gossip, Words Untrue/Now The Summer's Gone	15
67	HMV POP 1596	Tremblin'/Something's Coming Along	18
67	HMV POP 1605	Don't Go Out Into The Rain/One Woman Man	18
64	HMV 7EG 8850	SHAKE WITH THE SWINGING BLUE JEANS (EP)	40
64	HMV 7EG 8868	YOU'RE NO GOOD MISS MOLLY (EP)	40
64	HMV CLP 1802	BLUE JEANS A' SWINGING (LP, mono)	60
64	HMV CSD 1570	BLUE JEANS A' SWINGING (LP, stereo)	75
64	Regal SREG 1073	TUTTI FRUTTI (LP, export issue)	50
67	MFP MFP 1163	SWINGING BLUE JEANS (LP, reissue of HMV CLP 1802)	15
74	Dart BULL 1001	BRAND NEW AND FADED (LP)	18

(see also Ray Ennis & Blue Jeans, Blue Jeans, Escorts)

SWINGING CATS
80	Two Tone CHS TT 14	Mantovani/Away (paper label, company sleeve)	15
80	Two Tone CHS TT 14	Mantovani/Away (silver plastic label, company sleeve)	25

SWINGIN' MEDALLIONS
66	Philips BF 1500	Double Shot Of My Baby's Love/Here It Comes Again	10
66	Philips BF 1515	She Drives Me Out Of My Mind/You Gotta Have Faith	10

SWINGING SAPERLIPOPETTE
79	Kitty 7	Little Claw/I'm Not A Teddy Bear	30

SWINGING SOUL MACHINE
69	Polydor 56760	Spooky's Day Off/Nobody Wants You	15

(see also Machine)

SWISS MOVEMENT
00	Grapevine 118	I Wish Our Love Would Last Forever/One In A Million	10

SWITCH 7
80	Noisy HISS 1	You Win/Credit Cards (no p/s)	25

SWORDEDGE
80	Swordedge 001	SWORDEDGE (LP)	250

SWORD OF JAH MOUTH
81	Metro PBLP 001	INVASION (LP)	80

SWORN LORD
90	Davy G DG003	The Vengeance Is Mine (12")	150

SWR
15	Something In Construction	Close The Damn/Electric Scales (12", signed)	12

DAMNED 04

(see also Happy Mondays)

SWS
88	DTI MAC2	Boys From The Bec/Our Rhymes Are Fly (12")	10
90	Cue TCUE003	Overture/Empirical Expansions/Info Nation/Leaf In The Wind	10

SWV
92	RCA 07863 66074 1	IT'S ABOUT TIME (LP)	80

SYDNEY (CROOKS) ALL STARS
70	Bullet BU 436	The Return Of Batman/In Action	30
70	Bullet BU 437	Outer Space/Full Moon	40

(see also Pioneers, Junior English, Sammy Morgan)

JOHN SYKES
82	MCA MCA 792	Please Don't Leave Me/(Instrumental) (with Phil Lynott, in p/s)	35
82	MCA MCA 792	Please Don't Leave Me/(Instrumental) (with Phil Lynott)	10

(see also Thin Lizzy, Phil Lynott, Tygers Of Pan Tang, Whitesnake)

SYKES & MEDINA
69	CBS 4529	Everything's Fine Fine Fine/I Can Feel The Thickness	10

ROOSEVELT SYKES
56	Vogue V 2389	Fine And Brown/Too Hot To Hold	75
56	Vogue V 2389	Fine And Brown/Too Hot To Hold (78)	30
56	Vogue V 2393	Walkin' This Boogie/Security Blues	75
56	Vogue V 2393	Walkin' This Boogie/Security Blues (78)	30
66	Delmark DJB 2	BACK TO THE BLUES (EP)	30
62	Encore ENC 183	BIG MAN OF THE BLUES (LP)	25
61	Columbia 33SX 1343	FACE TO FACE WITH THE BLUES (LP)	30
62	Columbia 33SX 1422	THE HONEYDRIPPER (LP, with Alexis Korner)	60
65	Bluesville BVLP 1006	THE RETURN OF ROOSEVELT SYKES (LP)	25
67	77' 77LEU 12-50	BLUES FROM BAR ROOMS (LP)	30
67	Riverside RLP 8819	MR SYKES' BLUES 1929-1932 (LP)	22
67	Ember EMB 3391	ROOSEVELT SYKES SINGS THE BLUES (LP)	20
71	Barclay 920 294	THE HONEYDRIPPERS' DUKE'S MIXTURE (LP)	15
70s	Delmark DL 607	HARD DRIVIN' BLUES (LP, blue label)	15

(see also Robert Pete Williams)

SYKO & CARIBS

MINT VALUE £

SYKO & CARIBS
64 Blue Beat BB 213   Do The Dog/Jenny 20
64 Blue Beat BB 223   Big Boy/Sugar Baby 15

SYKO & MAK
92 PM PMT 002   MURDA EP (12") 10
92 PM PMT 004   HOMICIDE EP (12") 20

SYLTE SISTERS
63 London HLU 9753   Summer Magic/Well It's Summertime 15

SYLVAN
65 Columbia DB 7674   We Don't Belong/Life's Colours Have Gone 15

GOOD PAUL SYLVAN
70 Polydor 2001 090   Ophelia/Stop Making A Fool Of Me 6

C. SYLVESTER & PLANETS
64 Blue Beat BB 206   Going South/LITTLE JOYCE: Oh Daddy 12

ROLAND SYLVESTER
64 Carnival CV 7018   Grandfather's Clock/SANDRA MURRAY: Nervous 6

SYLVESTER'S JUKE BOX
73 CBS 8419   Juke Box/It's Because 50

SYLVIA
67 Fontana TF 884   Make Me A Woman/Without Your Love 10
68 Fontana TF 932   Down Hill/A Few Sweet Moments Of Love 10

SYLVIA (U.S.)
68 Soul City SC 103   I Can't Help It/It's A Good Life 20
75 London HLU 10415   Pillow Talk/My Thing 7

DAVID SYLVIAN
84 Virgin V 2290   BRILLIANT TREES (LP) 20
86 Virgin VDL 1   GONE TO EARTH (2-LP, gatefold) 20
87 Virgin V2471   SECRETS OF THE BEEHIVE (LP) 35
89 Virgin DSCD 1   WEATHERBOX (5-CD box set, with poster & booklet) 100
04 Samadhisound SOUNDLP 1   BLEMISH (LP, gatefold sleeve, featuring Derek Bailey, 2000 only, extra track: Trauma) 100
10 Samadhisound SOUND LP 2 MANAFON (2-LP, 180gm vinyl, gatefold) 75
18 Virgin 671 524-6   DEAD BEES ON A CAKE (2-LP, white vinyl, stickered sleeve) 40

(See also Japan, Virginia Astley)

DAVID SYLVIAN & ROBERT FRIPP
93 Virgin SYLLP 1   DARSHAN (Mini-LP) 15
93 Virgin V2712   THE FIRST DAY (2-LP, inners) 50

DAVID SYLVIAN AND HOLGER CZUKAY
88 Venture VE 11   PLIGHT AND PREMONITION (LP) 30
89 Venture VE 49   FLUX AND MUTABILITY (LP) 20

(see also David Sylvian, Can, Japan)

SYLVIN & GLENROY
70 Torpedo TOR 25   What You Gonna Do 'Bout It/KEN JONES: Sad Mood 40

SYMBOL
79 Art & Craft AC 001   Motherless Children/RANKING CARETAKER: Take It Away (12") 40
79 Kebra Nagast KH 04   Black Man's Word/Mr. Oppressor (12") 15

SYMBOLICS
76 Angen ANG 119   Tell Them Jah Jah/Version 8

SYMBOLS
65 Columbia DB 7459   One Fine Girl/Don't Go 10
65 Columbia DB 7664   You're My Girl/Why Do Fools Fall In Love 10
66 President PT 104   See You In September/To Make You Smile Again 8
66 President PT 113   Canadian Sunset/The Gentle Art Of Loving 6
67 President PT 128   You'd Better Get Used To Missing Her/Hideaway 6
67 President PT 144   Bye Bye Baby/The Things You Do To Me 10
67 President PT 173   (The Best Part Of) Breaking Up/Again 10
68 President PT 190   Lovely Way To Say Goodnight/Pretty City 18
68 President PT 216   Do I Love You/Schoolgirl 20
72 CBS 7725   No No No/Woman 8
75 Crystal CR 7021   Sound Of Sunset (Instrumental)/Canadian Sunset (Vocal Recording) 6
68 President PTL 1018   THE BEST PART OF THE SYMBOLS (LP) 25

(see also Johnny Milton & Condors)

SYMON & PI
68 Parlophone R 5662   Sha La La La Lee/Baby Baby 25
68 Parlophone R 5719   Got To See The Sunrise/Love Is Happening To Me 12

SYMPHONICS
73 Polydor 2058 341   Heaven Must Have Sent You/Using Me 15

SYMPHONIC SLAM
76 A&M AMLH 69023   SYMPHONIC SLAM (LP) 20

PAT SYMS
64 Oriole CB 1971   It's Got To Be You Or No One/Lost 7

SYLVIA SYMS
58 Brunswick 05771   The Night They Invented Champagne/The Nature Of Things 6

SYN
67 Deram DM 130   Created By Clive/Grounded 120
67 Deram DM 145   14-Hour Technicolour Dream/Flowerman 120

(see also Syndicats, Yes, Peter Banks)

SYNANTHESIA
69 RCA SF 8058   SYNANTHESIA (LP) 400

SYNCHROMESH
80 Rok ROK XI/XII   October Friday/E.F. BAND: Another Day Gone (company die-cut sleeve) 40

SYNDICATE OF SOUND

MINT VALUE £

SYNDICATE OF SOUND
66	Stateside SS 523	Little Girl/You	35
66	Stateside SS 538	Rumours/The Upper Hand	18
66	Stateside S(S)L 10185	LITTLE GIRL (LP)	50

SYNDICATE (1)
79	Stevenage/Rock Against Racism	One Way Or Another/I Want To Be Somebody/RESTRICTED HOURS: Getting Things Done/Still Living Out The Car Crash (white label, foldover p/s)	12

(see also Astronauts)

SYNDICATE (2)
81	EMI 12EMI 5182	Dance You To The Ground/Step On The Gas (12")	35

SYNDICATS
64	Columbia DB 7238	Maybellene/True To Me	150
65	Columbia DB 7441	Howlin' For My Baby/What To Do	250
65	Columbia DB 7686	On The Horizon/Crawdaddy Simone	650
65	Columbia DB 7686	On The Horizon/Crawdaddy Simone (demos)	450

(see also Peter Banks, Ray Fenwick, Syn, Tomorrow, Yes)

SYNTHETIC DREAMS
81	Logical Step LOGIC 02	Obsessions/U+500 (p/s)	15
82	Logical Step LOGIC 03	Sulphate Suicide/Voices (p/s)	10

SYNYX
82	Reality Attack RAF 1	BLACK DEATH (EP, fold out sleeve, plain white labels)	20

SYRUP
70	Amity OTS 501	Gentlemen Joe's Sidewalk Café/Love Is Love	10

SYSTEM OF A DOWN
99	Columbia/American	Sugar/War (live)	30
01	Columbia 672634 7	Chop Suey!/Johnny (clear vinyl)	8
01	Columbia 5015241	TOXICITY (LP)	30

SYSTEM ROOTS
17	System SYSTM 017	Step On It/Step on It (Dub)/Sweet Harmony (12", p/s)	15

SYSTEM (1)
77	Tash	THE OTHER SIDE OF TIME (LP, 250 copies only)	110

SYSTEM (2)
82	Spiderleg SDL 11	THE WARFARE (EP)	12
82	Spiderleg SDL 11	THE SYSTEM IS MURDER (EP)	10

SYSTEM X (EX)
94	3rd Eye EYE 001	MINDGAMES EP (12")	20
94	3rd Eye EYE 002	SOMETHING OF REAL EXISTENCE EP (12", white label, various coloured vinyl)	20
94	3rd Eye EYE 004	SOMETHING OF INTELLEGENT EXISTENCE EP (12")	25

(see also Studio Pressure)

SYZYGY
85	Taptag TAP 3	LADY IN GREY (mini-LP)	20

(see also Blackthorn)

S/Z
83	East Jazz Records 1	S/Z (LP)	25

GABOR SZABO
66	HMV CLP 3614	JAZZ RAGA (LP)	25
67	Impulse MILP 506	THE SORCERER (LP, mono)	30
69	Fontana STL 5489	BACCHANAL (LP)	40

LEO SZILARD
80	KIK 3	Stranger/On Comes The Night	10

T

ANDY T
82	221984/05	WEARY OF THE FLESH (EP)	15

(see also Crass)

ERROL T. & ROOSEVELT ALL STARS
72	Ashanti ASH 406	Jamaica Born And Bred/Version	7

JAMIE T.
05	Pacemaker PANICSDJ 001	So Lonely Was The Ballad/Back In The Game (p/s, 500 only)	15
06	Pacemaker PANICS 002	Salvador/Livin With Betty (p/s)	10
06	Virgin VS 1921	If You Got The Money/A New England (gatefold p/s)	8
07	Virgin 0094637885512	PANIC PREVENTION (LP)	60
09	Virgin V3059	KINGS AND QUEENS (LP)	40

T. & UNKNOWN
80	Carrere CAR 142	My Generation/Woodstock Rock (p/s)	12

PHILIP TABANE & MALOMBO
88	Kijima BIG 002	MALOMBO (LP)	40

TABLE
77	Virgin VS 176	Do The Standing Still/Magical Melon Of The Tropics (p/s)	8
78	Chiswick NS 28	Sex Cells/The Road Of Lyfe (p/s)	7

TABLE TOPPERS
62	Starlite ST45 069	Rocking Mountain Dew/My Wild Irish Rose Rock	20

CHARLIE TABOR
63	Island WI 061	Blue Atlantic/Red Lion Madison	20

June TABOR

MINT VALUE £

JUNE TABOR
86	Strange Fruit SFPS 015	THE PEEL SESSIONS (12" EP)	15
76	Topic 12TS 298	AIRS AND GRACES (LP)	15
77	Topic 12TS 360	ASHES AND DIAMONDS (LP)	15
05	Topic TSECD 4003	ALWAYS (4-CD box set, booklet)	20

TAC-TIX
88	R.E. Good GSM 188	Whisper On The Street/R.E. Good (p/s)	15

TAD & SMALL FRY
62	London HLU 9542	Checkered Continental Pants/Pretty Blue Jean Baby	15

TADPOLE
73	More MR2	Follow The Rain/Suzy Jones	15

TADPOLES
69	High Note HS 032	Rasta/Like Dirt	25

TAFARI & PAUL FOX
90	Cause N Effect CE 007	Jah Jah Bless Mandela/Version	20
90	Cause N Effect CE12 007	Jah Jah Bless Mandela/Version (12")	25

TAG
75	Philips 6006 477	Off Down The Road/Guitar Love	15

TAGES
66	Columbia DB 8019	Crazy 'Bout My Baby/In My Dreams	15
66	HMV POP 1515	So Many Girls/I'm Mad	50
67	Parlophone R 5640	Treat Me Like A Lady/Wanting	15
68	Parlophone R 5702	There's A Blind Man Playin' Fiddle In The Street/Like A Woman	15
68	MGM MGM 1443	Halcyon Days/I Read You Like An Open Book	20

(see also Blond)

BLIND JOE TAGGART
52	Tempo R 55	Religion Is Something Within You/Mother's Love (78)	20
55	Jazz Collector L 129	Religion Is Something Within You/Mother's Love (78, reissue)	15

TAGMEMICS
80	Index INDEX 003	Chimneys/(Do The) Big Baby/Take Your Brain Out For A Walk (p/s, with insert)	15

(see also Art Attacks)

TAICONDEROGA
69	Beacon BEA 143	Whichi Tai To/Speakin' My Mind	70

JACQUELINE TAIEB
68	Fontana TF 952	Tonight I'm Going Home/7 A.M.	150

LYN(N) TAIT(T) (& THE JETS)
66	Doctor Bird DB 1006	Vilma's Jump Up (as Lyn Taitt & The Comets)/GLEN MILLER & HONEYBOY MARTIN: Dad Is Home	25
66	Doctor Bird DB 1047	Spanish Eyes (with Tommy McCook)/STRANGER & HORTENSE: Loving Wine	50
67	Island WI 3066	Something Stupid/Blue Tuesday (as Lyn Tait & the Jets)	35
67	Island WI 3075	I Don't Want To Make You Cry/Nice Time (as Lyn Taitt & the Jets)	250
68	Island WI 3139	Napoleon Solo/Pressure And Slide (as Lyn Taitt & the Jets)	70
68	Amalgamated AMG 810	El Casino Royale/Dee's Special (as Lynn Taitt & the Jets)	35
68	Pama PM 723	Soul Food/Music Flames (as Lyn Tait & the Jets)	40
68	Island ILP 969	SOUNDS ROCK STEADY (LP, as Lyn Taitt & the Jets)	250
68	Big Shot BBTL 4002	GLAD SOUNDS (LP, as Lynn Taitt & the Jets)	150

(see also Mike Thompson Jnr, ALton Ellis, Ken Boothe, Baba Brooks)

PAULETTE TAJAH
93	Discotex DTLP 15	HAPPY MEMORIES VOL. 5 (LP)	15

YUKIHIRIO TAKAHASHI
82	Alfa 86393	NEUROMANTIC (LP)	15

(see also Yellow Magic Orchestra)

TAKE FIVE
60s	D.S.C.A (no cat. no.)	MY GIRL (EP, oversized p/s; Dundee Students Charity Appeal record)	100

TAKE IT
79	Fresh Hold TRI	Man Made World/Taking Sides/How It Is (p/s)	40
80	Fresh Hold FHR 1	Twenty Lines/Armchairs/Friends And Relations (foldout p/s with insert)	20

TAKE THAT
91	Dance U.K. DUK 2	Do What U Like/Waiting Around (p/s)	15
91	Dance U.K. 12DUK 2	Do What U Like (Club Mix)/Do What U Like (Radio Mix)/Waiting Around (12", p/s; most with wrong tracks listed on sleeve)	25

(see also Robbie Williams)

TAKE 3
84	Elite DAZZ 32	Music & Time/Music & Time (extended version) (12")	15

TAKERS
64	Pye 7N 15690	If You Don't Come Back/Think	25

(see also Undertakers, Jackie Lomax)

TAKO
08	Ambassador's Reception ABR 002	My Kind Of Woman/Flotation Dance/Space Fever/Data Transfer (12")	15

TALAN
89	Talan SRT 9KS 2208	Spellbinder/Underground Madness (p/s)	20

TALBOT BROTHERS
59	Melodisc MEL 1507	Bloodshot Eyes/She's Got Freckles	15
60s	Melodisc CAL 20	Bloodshot Eyes/She's Got Freckles (reissue)	6

ZIGGY TALENT
55	Brunswick 05506	Cheek To Cheek (Cha Cha)/Bozooki Blues	7

TALES
73	MAM 93	Someone Like You/Rockin' Suzanna	15

TALES OF JUSTINE
67	HMV POP 1614	Albert/Monday Morning (in p/s)	180

TALISKER

MINT VALUE £

| 67 | HMV POP 1614 | Albert/Monday Morning | 60 |
| 97 | Tenth Planet TP 034 | PETALS FROM A SUNFLOWER (LP, gatefold sleeve, numbered, 1,000 only) | 30 |

TALISKER
| 75 | Caroline CA 1513 | DREAMING OF GLENISLA (LP) | 25 |

TALISMAN (1)
| 73 | Argo ZDA 161 | STEPPING STONES (LP) | 12 |

TALISMAN (2)
| 81 | Recreational SPORT 22 | Wicked Dem/Run Come Girl (12", p/s) | 10 |
| 84 | Embryo CELA 1T | TAKIN THE STRAIN (LP) | 15 |

TALISMEN
| 65 | Stateside SS 408 | Masters Of War/Casting My Spell | 70 |

TALKBACK
| 83 | Cottage S 83 CUS 1991 | Pleasure/Everyday | 10 |

TALKIES
| 81 | Hook HK1 | I Fell In Love Last Night/Foreign Legion (p/s) | 20 |

TALKING HEADS
77	Sire 6078 604	Love Goes To Building On Fire/New Feeling (p/s)	7
77	Sire SAM 87	Love Goes To Building On Fire/New Feeling (limited edition, in p/s)	12
77	Sire SAM 87	Love Goes To Building On Fire/New Feeling	10
77	Sire 6078 610	Psycho Killer/I Wish You Wouldn't Say That (p/s)	10
77	Sire 6078 610	Psycho Killer/Psycho Killer (Acoustic)/I Wish You Wouldn't Say That (12", p/s)	12
78	Sire 6078 620	Pulled Up/Don't Worry About The Government (p/s)	10
79	Sire SIR 4004	Take Me To The River/Found A Job (p/s)	10
79	Sire SIR 4004/SAM 87	Take Me To The River/Found A Job//Love Goes To Building On Fire/ Psycho Killer (double pack, gatefold p/s)	15
79	Sire SIR 4027	Life During Wartime (live version)/Electric Guitar (p/s)	12
80	Sire SIR 4033	I Zimbra/Paper (p/s)	10
80	Sire SIR 4040	Cities/Cities (live) (p/s)	7
80	Sire SIR 4040T	Cities/Cities (live)/Artists Only (live) (12", p/s)	10
80	Sire SIR 4050	Houses In Motion (Special Re-Mixed Version)/Air (p/s)	8
80	Sire SIR 4050T	Houses In Motion/Air/Houses In Motion (Live) (12")	10
85	EMI 12EMID 5520	Lady Don't Mind/Give Me Back My Name//Slippery People (live)/This Must Be The Place (Naive Melody) (live) (12", p/s, double pack)	10
77	Sire SR6036	TALKING HEADS : 77 (LP, inner)	25
78	Sire SR 6036	TALKING HEADS : 77 (LP, repressing with STRAWBERRY in run out groove, inner)	15
78	Sire K 56531	MORE SONGS ABOUT BUILDING AND FOOD (LP, stickered sleeve, inner)	20
79	Sire K 56707	FEAR OF MUSIC (LP, textured sleeve with free single "Psycho Killer"/"New Feeling" [SAM 108])	30
79	Sire SRK6076	FEAR OF MUSIC (LP, textured sleeve, without free 7", inner)	20
80	Sire SRK 6095	REMAIN IN LIGHT (LP, inner and insert)	20
82	Sire SIRK 66112	THE NAME OF THIS BAND IS TALKING HEADS (2-LP)	20
83	EMI 9237711	SPEAKING IN TONGUES (LP, clear vinyl in special cover)	30
83	Sire 92 3883 1	SPEAKING IN TONGUES (LP)	20
84	EMI 0642402431	STOP MAKING SENSE (LP, inner, booklet)	15
85	EMI 2403521	LITTLE CREATURES (LP, inner)	20
86	Sire EU3511	TRUE STORIES (LP, inner)	20
88	Sire EMD 1005	NAKED (LP, inner and insert)	20
99	EMI 4994711	STOP MAKING SENSE (2-LP, reissue)	20

TALK TALK
84	EMI EMID 5433	THE TALK TALK DEMOS (double pack, poster p/s [EMI 5433 & PSR 467])	10
86	EMI 12EMID 5540	Life's What You Make It (Extended)/It's Getting Late In The Evening// It's My Life/Does Caroline Know? (12", p/s, double pack)	15
86	EMI EMIP 5551	Living In Another World/For What It's Worth (shaped picture disc)	15
91	Verve TALKD1/2/3	After The Flood/Myrrhman// New Grass/Stump//Ascension Day/5.09 (3-CD, in die-cut box)	40
82	EMI EMC 3413	THE PARTY'S OVER (LP)	15
84	EMI EMC 240021	IT'S MY LIFE (LP)	15
86	EMI EMC 3506	THE COLOUR OF SPRING (LP, inner)	20
88	Parlophone PCSD 105	SPIRIT OF EDEN (LP)	40
91	Polydor 847 717-1	LAUGHING STOCK (LP)	100
91	Parlophone PCSD 109	HISTORY REVISITED - THE REMIXES (LP)	25
97	EMI LPCENT 14	THE COLOUR OF SPRING (LP, reissue, EMI 100 Centenary, stickered sleeve)	30
90	EMI PCSD 109	NATURAL HISTORY - THE BEST OF TALK TALK (LP)	18
00	Simply Vinyl SVLP 224	IT'S MY LIFE (LP, reissue 180gm vinyl)	20
12	Parlophone PCSDX105	SPIRIT OF EDEN (LP, reissue, with CD)	15
12	Back To Black 533764	LAUGHING STOCK (LP, reissue 180gm)	25

(see also Reaction)

TOM TALL
55	London HL 8150	Are You Mine/Boom Boom Boomerang (as Ginny Wright & Tom Tall)	20
55	London HLU 8216	Give Me A Chance/Remembering You	40
56	London HLU 8231	Underway/Goldie Jo Malone	40
57	London HLU 8429	Don't You Know/If You Know What I Know (with Ruckus Taylor)	40
55	London RE-U 1035	COUNTRY SONGS VOL. 2 (EP, as Tom Tall & Ginny Wright)	25

(see also Ginny Wright)

TALL BOYS
| 82 | Big Beat NS 79 | Island Of Lost Souls/Another Half Hour Till Sunrise (p/s) | 8 |
| 85 | Big Beat NS 107 | Final Kick/Interceptor (p/s) | 6 |

(see also Meteors)

TALMY/STONE BAND
| 62 | Decca F 11543 | Madison Time/Madison Time (A-side with Alan Freeman) | 10 |

TALULAH GOSH

MINT VALUE £

TALULAH GOSH
86	53rd & 3rd AGARR 4	Beatnik Boy/My Best Friend (p/s)	8
86	53rd & 3rd AGARR 4/5T	Beatnik Boy/My Best Friend/Steaming Train/Just A Dream (12", p/s)	15
88	53rd & 3rd AGARR 14	Bringing Up Baby/The Girl With The Strawberry Hair (p/s)	6
87	53rd & 3rd AGAS 004	ROCK LEGENDS VOL. 69 (LP, clear vinyl)	20
91	Sarah 064	THEY'VE SCOFFED THE LOT (LP)	40

(see also Heavenly, Amelia Fletcher)

TAMANGOES
79	Grapevine GRP 122	I Really Love You/You've Been Gone So Long	30

TAME DOLL
76	Hopscotch HP 7	I Don't Give A Damn/You	20

TAMEN
72	Flake FL 1	Sweet Loretta, Make No Mistakes/Drifting (p/s)	50

TAMINDAY
73	Dile DL3	Dear Lisa/Break The Chain	30

TAMING THE OUTBACK
86	Black Sun BS 1	Blue Heart/Fire	15

JAMES TAMLIN
65	Columbia DB 7438	Is There Time/Main Line Central Station	20
65	Columbia DB 7577	Yes I Have/Now There Are Two	10

TAMLINS
79	Deb Music DEB 007	Still Water/AUGUSTUS PABLO: Spirit Of Umoja (12")	20
80	Taxi RIC 110	Baltimore/Laying Beside You	10
76	State ETAT 9	BLACK BEAUTY (LP)	15

TAMPA RED
64	RCA RCX 7160	R & B VOL. 3 (EP)	25
60s	Memory TR 1	TAMPA RED (LP)	35

TAMPA RED/GEORGIA TOM
59	Jazz Collector JEL 3	THE MALE BLUES VOLUME 2 (EP)	20

TAMS
63	Stateside SS 146	Untie Me/Disillusioned	30
63	HMV POP 1254	What Kind Of Fool Do You Think I Am/Laugh It Off	20
64	HMV POP 1298	It's All Right, You're Just In Love/You Lied To Your Daddy	18
64	HMV POP 1331	Hey Girl Don't Bother Me/Take Away	150
64	HMV POP 1331	Hey Girl Don't Bother Me/Take Away (DJ copy)	200
65	HMV POP 1464	Concrete Jungle/Till The End Of Time	15
69	Stateside SS 2123	Be Young, Be Foolish, Be Happy/That Same Old Song	15
70	Capitol CL 15650	Too Much Foolin' Around/How Long Love	15
75	ABC ABC 4020	Hey Girl Don't Bother Me/Be Young, Be Foolish, Be Happy	8
68	Stateside (S)SL 10258	A LITTLE MORE SOUL (LP)	40
70	Stateside SSL 10304	BE YOUNG, BE FOOLISH, BE HAPPY (LP)	25

TANAMO
63	Island WI 108	Come Down/I Am Holding On (actually by Lord Tanamo)	30

TANDOORI CASSETTE
83	IKA IKA 001	Angel Talk/Third World Brief Case (p/s, 5,000 only)	20

(see also Nazareth, Alex Harvey, Tear Gas, Stone The Crows)

SHARON TANDY
65	Mercury MF 898	Love Makes The World Go Round/By My Side	30
65	Pye 7N 15806	Now That You've Gone/Hurtin' Me	40
65	Pye 7N 15939	I've Found Love/Perhaps Not Forever	15
67	Atlantic 584 098	Toe Hold/I Can't Get Over It	20
67	Atlantic 584 124	Stay With Me/Hold On	60
67	Atlantic 584 137	Our Day Will Come/Look And Find	20
68	Atlantic 584 166	Fool On The Hill/For No One	20
68	Atlantic 584 181	Love Is Not A Simple Affair/Hurry Hurry Choo-Choo	40
68	Atlantic 584 194	You've Gotta Believe It/Border Town	20
68	Atlantic 584 214	The Way She Looks At You/He'll Hurt Me	30
68	Atlantic 584 219	Hold On/Daughter Of The Sun	100
69	Atlantic 584 242	Gotta Get Enough Time/Somebody Speaks Your Name	80

(see also Fleur-De-Lys, Tony & Tandy)

NORMA TANEGA
66	Stateside SS 496	Walkin' My Cat Named Dog/I'm The Sky	6
66	Stateside SS 520	A Street That Rhymes At Six A.M./Treat Me Right	8
66	Stateside S(S)L 10182	WALKIN' MY CAT NAMED DOG (LP)	20

TANGENT
80	President PT483	Atlantica/Living In The City	15

TANGERINE DREAM
74	Virgin PR 214	Phaedra (Edit)/Mysterious Semblance At The Strand Of Nightmares (promo)	30
76	Virgin VDJ 17	Stratosfear/The Big Sleep In Search Of Hades (promo only)	25
77	MCA PSR 413	Betrayal (Sorceror Theme)/Search (promo only)	25
81	Virgin VS 444	Chronozon/Network 23 (p/s)	8
84	Jive Electro P 74	Warsaw In The Sun/Polish Dance (map-shaped picture disc)	15
84	Jive Electro T 74	Warsaw In The Sun (Parts 1 & 2)/Polish Dance/Rare Bird (12", p/s)	12
85	Jive JIVE 101	Streethawk/Tear Garden (p/s)	15
85	Jive Electro T 101	STREETHAWK (12" EP)	20
87	Jive Electro 143	Tyger/21st Century Common Man II (p/s)	6
87	Jive Electro T 143	Tyger/Tyger (7" Version)/21st Century Common Man II (12", p/s)	10
74	Virgin V2010	PHAEDRA (LP, copies with A1U/B2U matrixes and catalogue number misprinted with catalogue number on top left hand of gatefold sleeve instead of rear)	20
74	Polydor Super 2383 297	ATEM (LP)	20

TANGERINE PEEL

MINT VALUE £

75	Virgin V2025	RUBYCON (LP, gatefold sleeve)	15
75	Polydor Super 2383 314	ALPHA CENTAURI (LP)	20
76	Virgin V2503	ZEIT (2-LP, reissue)	25
76	Virgin V2068	STRATOSPHERE (LP, green "mirror" girl label, 'Robor Limited' sleeve)	15
76	Virgin V 2044	RICOCHET (LP, original copies with incorrect matrix numbers VS 2044 A1/B1 with "S" scratched out)	15
78	Virgin V2111	FORCE MAJEURE (LP, clear vinyl, textured stickered sleeve)	15
80	Virgin VBOX 2	TANGERINE DREAM '70-80 (4-LP box set)	40
80	Virgin TCVX 2	TANGERINE DREAM '70-80 (4-cassette box set)	25
81	Virgin V 2212	EXIT (LP, 1st 1,000 with poster)	15
84	MCA MCF 3233	FIRESTARTER (LP, soundtrack)	15
84	Jive Electro HIPX 22	POLAND - THE WARSAW CONCERT (2-LP, picture disc)	25
85	Heavy Metal HMXD 29	FLASHPOINT (CD, soundtrack; playable CD [most copies faulty])	40
86	Jive Electro TANG 1	IN THE BEGINNING (6-LP box set, with booklet)	30
90	Virgin TD AK 11	TANGERINE DREAM (3-CD, 'Collector's Edition' box set)	20
03	Virgin 724359612829	TANGENTS 1973 - 1983 (5-CD box set with booklet)	20

(see also Edgar Froese, Klaus Schulze)

TANGERINE PEEL

67	United Artists UP 1193	Every Christian Lion-Hearted Man Will Show You/Trapped	30
68	CBS 3402	Solid Gold Mountain/Light Across The River	130
68	CBS 3676	Talking To No One/Wishing Tree	20
69	MGM MGM 1470	Never Say Never Again/A Thousand Miles Away	15
69	MGM MGM 1487	Play Me A Sad Song And I'll Dance/Wish You Could Be Here With Me	15
70	RCA RCA 1936	Move Into My World/In Between	6
70	RCA RCA 1990	Soft Delights/Thinking Of Me	6
70	RCA RCA 2036	What Am I To Do?/Don't Let Me Be Misunderstood	6
70	RCA LSA 3002	SOFT DELIGHTS (LP)	40

TANGLE BROTHERS

85	Tangle TB 001	Jessica/Hopes A Stranger (p/s with insert)	12

TANGO

92	Formation FORM 12004	THE IMPACT EP (12", p/s)	25
93	F Project WHITE 024	Future Followers/Time Bomb (12")	20

TANGO & DOM

92	Double Vision DV 001	My Mind Is Going/Got To Release (12")	40

TANGO PROJECT

92	White 004	Project 1/Untitled (12", white label test pressing)	100

TANK (1)

73	Polydor 2058391	Fast Train/The World's An Apple	20
72	Bumble GE 105	Heads I Win, Tails You Lose/Burgundy, Port And Red Wine	20

TANK (2)

81	Kamaflage KAM 1	Don't Walk Away/Shellshock/Hammer On (p/s, with cover mounted patch)	10
81	Kamaflage KAM 1	Don't Walk Away/Shellshock/Hammer On (p/s)	8
82	Kamaflage KAM 3	Turn Your Head Around/Steppin' On A Landmine (p/s)	15
82	Kamaflage KAMLP 1	FILTH HOUNDS OF HADES (LP, 1st pressing, with black & yellow sleeve)	15
82	Kamaflage KAMLP 1	FILTH HOUNDS OF HADES (LP, 2nd pressing, with bonus p/s 7" Don't Walk Away (live)/"The Snake" [KAM F1])	15
83	Music For Nations MFN 3P	THIS MEANS WAR (LP, picture disc)	20

(see also Damned)

PHIL TANNER

68	EDF SSLP 1005	PHIL TANNER (LP, with lyric book)	25

TAN TAN

81	Maccabees MPCLP TT1	MUSICAL NOSTALGIA FOR TODAY (LP)	40

TANTARA

86	President PT 543	I.D.O/Rumours	40
86	President PT 12-543	I.D.O/Rumours (12")	100

TANTARA BLADE

88	King Dice	Seven Shades Of Shame/This Car Has Crushed (p/s)	50

TANTONES

57	Vogue V 9085	So Afraid/Tell Me	500
57	Vogue V 9085	So Afraid/Tell Me (78)	100

TANZ DER YOUTH

78	Radar ADA 19	I'm Sorry, I'm Sorry/Delay (p/s)	6

(see also Brian James, Damned)

TAO JONES INDEX

97	RCA 512541	Pallas Athena (live)/V-2 Schneider (live) (12", p/s)	12

(see also David Bowie)

TAPESTRY (1)

67	London HLZ 10138	Carnaby Street/Taming Of The Shrew	30
68	NEMS 56-3679	Like The Sun/Florence	20
69	NEMS 5639-64	Heart & Soul/Who Wants Happiness	60

TAPESTRY (2)

73	Rosemount ROS EP 1	Oh Mountain/Till We Meet/Fire And Rain	30

TAPE WAVES

13	Box Bedroom BBR 3	DRIFTING EP (p/s, numbered, insert, 100 only)	20

DEMETRISS TAPP

64	Coral Q 72470	Lipstick Paint A Smile On Me/If You Find Love	40

TARA

70	Polydor 2062009	Happy/The Love Of A Woman	15

TARANTULA

70	A&M AMLS 959	TARANTULA (LP)	15

Jimmy TARBUCK

MINT VALUE £

JIMMY TARBUCK
65 Immediate IM 018   Someday/(We're) Wastin' Time 7

TARHEEL SLIM & LITTLE ANN
65 Sue WI 390   You Make Me Feel So Good/Got To Keep On Lovin' You 40

TARIKA BLUE
19 Dynamite Cuts DYNAM7045/Truth Is The Key/You'll Be With Me/Love It/Charlie (reissue, 2 x 7", p/s) 10
46
01 Soul Brother LP SCBS 11   ...THE VERY BEST OF (LP) 20

TARNEY BAND, ALAN
78 A&M AMS 7339   Takin Me Back/Set The Minstrel Free 6

DAVE TARRIDA
99 Mosquito MSQ 013   PLAYING THE GAME (12" EP) 10

TARRIERS
56 London HLN 8340   Cindy, Oh Cindy/Only If You Praise The Lord (gold label lettering, as Vince Martin & Tarriers) 15
56 London HLN 8340   Cindy, Oh Cindy/Only If You Praise The Lord (silver label lettering, as Vince Martin & Tarriers) 7
57 Columbia DB 3891   The Banana Boat Song/No Hidin Place 10
57 Columbia 33S 1115   THE TARRIERS (10" LP) 15
62 London STA 8525   A LIVE PERFORMANCE AT THE BITTER END (LP) 15
(see also Vince Martin, Rooftop Singers)

TARTAN HORDE
75 United Artists UP 35891   Bay City Rollers, We Love You/Rollers Theme 15
(see also Nick Lowe, Rat Scabies, Roogalator)

TARTANS
67 Island WI 3058   Dance All Night/What Can I Do 50
68 Caltone TONE 115   Awake The Town (with Lynn Taitt's Band)/LYNN TAITT & JETS: The Brush 70
68 Caltone TONE 117   Coming On Strong/It's Alright (with Tommy McCook's Band) 80
71 Escort ERT 843   A Day Will Come/ROBI'S All STARS: Version 15
(see also Devon & Tartans, Kaddo Strings, Max Romeo, Derrick Morgan)

TARTS
81 If You Can't Take A Joke JOKE1   Tie Me Kangeroo Down/Gene Queenie 100

TASAVALLAN PRESIDENTTI
73 Sonet SNTF 636   LAMBERTLAND (LP) 30
74 Sonet SNTF 658   MILKY WAY MOSES (LP, with insert) 30

TASKFORCE
00 White(Lowlife)grafpromo1   Graf Da Bus Up (12" - One sided, 500 pressed) 15
00 White(Lowlife)no matrix   Wha Blow (12", 1-Sided white label, 200 only) 15
00 Lowlife LOW10   VOICE OF THE GREAT OUTDOORS (EP, 2000 only p/s) 40
01 Rehab RHB001   A LIFE WITHOUT INSTRUCTIONS (EP) 15
02 White no matrix   Graf Da Bus Up/Wha Blow (2 Mixes of A side, 12") 12
06 White WS01   The Bitches (3 versions) (12", 500 only) 10
99 K'Boro KBR1005   NEW MIC ORDER (LP) 40
03 MFTC MFTC 02   MUSIC FROM THE CORNER VOL 2 (2-LP) 50

TASSELS
59 London HL 8885   To A Soldier Boy/The Boy For Me 100
59 London HL 8885   To A Soldier Boy/The Boy For Me (78) 40
59 Top Rank JAR 229   To A Young Lover/My Guy And I 30

TASSILLI PLAYERS
95 Universal Egg WWLP 011   WONDERFUL WORLD OF WEED IN DUB (LP) 20

TASTE
68 Major Minor MM 560   Blister On The Moon/Born On The Wrong Side Of Time 125
69 Polydor 56313   Born On The Wrong Side Of Time/Same Old Story 40
70 Major Minor MM 718   Born On The Wrong Side Of Time/Blister On The Moon 40
69 Polydor 583 042   TASTE (LP, laminated sleeve) 100
70 Polydor 583 083   ON THE BOARDS (LP, textured sleeve) 80
71 Polydor 2310 082   LIVE TASTE (LP) 15
72 Polydor 2383 120   TASTE - LIVE AT THE ISLE OF WIGHT (LP) 60
(see also Rory Gallagher, Stud)

TASTE OF HONEY
69 Original Rim RIM 11   Goody Goody Gum Drops/Sunshine Rainbows 12

TASTY
77 DJM DJS 10751   Just A Little Too Much/You're A Heartbreaker (Promo p/s) 8

BUDDY TATE
58 Felsted FAJ 7004   SWINGING LIKE TATE (LP) 30

GRADY TATE
69 Fontana STL 5490   WINDMILLS OF MY MIND (LP) 15

HOWARD TATE
66 Verve VS 541   Ain't Nobody Home/How Come My Bulldog Won't Bark 15
67 Verve VS 549   Look At Granny Run Run/Half A Man 20
67 Verve VS 552   Get It While You Can/Glad I Knew Better 15
67 Verve VS 555   Baby I Love You/How Blue Can You Get 25
67 Verve VS 556   I Learned It All The Hard Way/Part Time Love 15
68 Verve VS 565   Stop/Shoot 'Em All Down 15
68 Verve VS 571   Night Owl/Every Day I Have The Blues 20
70 Major Minor MM 696   My Soul's Got A Hole In It/It's Too Late 10
67 Verve (S)VLP 9179   GET IT WHILE YOU CAN (LP) 70

SNUKY TATE
80 ZE/Island 12WIP4785   He's The Groove (Extended)/He's The Groove Part 2 (12", p/s) 10

TOMMY TATE

			MINT VALUE £
66	Columbia DB 8046	Big Blue Diamonds/A Lover's Reward	75
66	Columbia DB 8046	Big Blue Diamonds/A Lover's Reward (DJ Copy)	125
03	Grapevine G2K 45 137	Do You Think There's A Chance/If You Gotta Love Somebody	8

JACQUES TATI
58	Fontana TFE 17175	MY UNCLE (EP)	12

TATTY OLLITY
79	Tatty TR 101	Punktuation/Never Swat A Fly (p/s)	30

ART TATUM
53	Capitol LC 6625	OUT OF NOWHERE (10" LP)	15
54	Vogue LDE 081	ART TATUM "JUST JAZZ" (10" LP)	15
55	Vogue Coral LRA 10011	THE ART TATUM TRIO (10" LP)	15
55	Columbia Clef 33CX 10005	THE GENIUS OF ART TATUM (LP)	15
55	Capitol LC 6638	ART TATUM ENCORES (10" LP)	15
56	Columbia Clef 33CX 10053	THE GENIUS OF ART TATUM (NO. 2) (LP)	15
57	Columbia Clef 33C 9033	THE GENIUS OF ART TATUM (NO. 3) (10" LP)	15
57	Columbia Clef 33C 9039	PRESENTING THE ART TATUM TRIO (10" LP)	15
57	Vogue Coral LVA 9047	HERE'S ART TATUM (LP)	15
58	Columbia Clef 33CX 10115	ART TATUM (LP)	15
59	Columbia Clef 33CX 10137	ART TATUM-BEN WEBSTER QUARTET (LP)	20
60	Top Rank 35/067	ART TATUM DISCOVERIES (LP)	15

BERNIE TAUPIN
71	DJM DJLPS 415	TAUPIN (LP, textured gatefold sleeve with booklet)	50
71	DJM DJLPS 415	TAUPIN (LP, textured gatefold sleeve without booklet)	20

TAVASCO
00	Grapevine 106	Love Is Trying To Get A Hold Of Me/(Radio Edit)	10

JOHN TAVENER
70	Apple SAPCOR 15	THE WHALE (LP, gatefold sleeve)	40
71	Apple SAPCOR 20	CELTIC REQUIEM (LP, gatefold sleeve, with insert & 'Apple' inner sleeve)	80
77	Ring O' 2320 104	THE WHALE (LP, reissue, different single sleeve)	45
92	Apple SAPCOR 15	THE WHALE (LP, 2nd reissue, gatefold sleeve with inner sleeve)	25
93	Apple SAPCOR 20	CELTIC REQUIEM (LP, reissue, gatefold sleeve with inner sleeve)	25

CYRIL TAWNEY
62	HMV 7EG 8738	BABY LIE EASY (EP)	10
69	Polydor 236 577	THE OUTLANDISH KNIGHT (LP)	20
70	Argo ZFB 4	SINGS CHILDREN'S SONGS FROM DEVON AND CORNWALL (LP)	15
70	Argo ZFB 9	A MAYFLOWER GARLAND (LP)	20

TAX DODGERS
93	TAX 2	Ragamuffin Bizness/Flying High (12", stamped white label)	20
94	TAX IT	Hot Off D Press/Rebel Without Applause (Two Mixes) (12", stamped white labels)	20

TAX LOSS
79	Logo GO 355	Going My Way/THEME FROM THERE IS NO CONSPIRACY (stamped die cut seeve)	10

TAXMAN
84	Senator SEN 001	Bionic Tonic/Video Crazy (white label)	35
88	Stush STU 002	Tina/Version/Vocal Version (12")	30
93	Sir George SO 945	Well Armed And Dangerous/She Keeps Running Away (12")	30

ALLAN TAYLOR
71	Liberty LBF 15447	Sometimes/Song For Kathy	6
73	United Artists UP 35541	My Father's Room/Always You	6
71	Liberty LBS 83483	SOMETIMES (LP, gatefold sleeve)	50
72	United Artists UAS 29275	THE LADY (LP)	50
73	United Artists UAG 29468	THE AMERICAN ALBUM (LP, gatefold sleeve)	20

(see also Fairport Convention)

ARTHUR TAYLOR
59	Esquire 32149	TAYLOR'S TENNORS (LP)	150

AUSTIN TAYLOR
60	Top Rank JAR 511	Push Push/A Heart That's True	20

BARRY TAYLOR
70	Destiny DS 01	Tiger Woman/I'll Shoot The Lights (p/s)	20

BILLY TAYLOR (TRIO)
57	Esquire EP 115	MAMBO! (EP)	15
57	Esquire EP 169	THE MOON IN CONCERT (EP)	20
54	Felsted EDL 87009	JAZZ AT STORYVILLE (10" LP)	35
54	Esquire 20-053	AT THE TOWN HALL 1954 (LP)	30
54	Esquire 32-010	A TOUCH OF TAYLOR (LP)	30
57	HMV DLP 1181	MY FAIR LADY LOVES JAZZ (10" LP)	20
60	Vogue LAE 12192	TAYLOR MADE PIANO (LP)	20

BOBBY TAYLOR
64	Columbia DB 7282	Temptation/Mod Bod	15

BOBBY TAYLOR (& VANCOUVERS)
68	Tamla Motown TMG 654	Does Your Mama Know About Me/Fading Away (with Vancouvers)	50
73	Epic EPC 1720	I Can't Quit Your Love/Queen Of The Ghetto (solo)	8
69	Tamla Motown (S)TML 11093	BOBBY TAYLOR AND THE VANCOUVERS (LP, mono/stereo)	60
70	Tamla Motown (S)TML 11125	TAYLOR MADE SOUL (LP, stereo, solo)	140

BRYAN TAYLOR
61	Piccadilly 7N 35018	The Donkey's Tale/Let It Snow On Christmas Day	25

CECIL TAYLOR
60	Contemporary LAC12216	LOOKING AHEAD! (LP)	35
77	Blue Note BNS 40023	UNIT STRUCTURES (LP, reissue)	20

Cecil TAYLOR JAZZ UNIT

MINT VALUE £

88	Leo LR 152	CHINAMPAS (LP)	15
88	Leo LR 162	TZOTZIL MUMMERS TZOTZIL (LP)	15
88	Leo LR 404/405	LIVE IN BOLOGNA (2-LP)	25
88	Leo LR 408/409	LIVE IN VIENNA (2-LP)	25

CECIL TAYLOR JAZZ UNIT
62	Fontana SFJL 926	NEFERTITI, THE BEAUTIFUL ONE HAS COME (LP)	40

CHIP TAYLOR
62	Warner Bros WB 82	Here I Am/I Love You But I Know	6
73	Buddah 2318 074	GASOLINE (LP)	25
74	Warner Bros K 56032	CHIP TAYLOR'S LAST CHANCE (LP)	15

(see also Wes Voigt)

DEBBIE TAYLOR
76	Arista ARISTA 50	I Don't Wanna Leave You/Just Don't Pay	30

DUFFY TAYLOR BLUES
69	Page One POF 130	You Wrecked My Life/I'll Be There	12

ELIZABETH TAYLOR
63	Colpix PXL 459	IN LONDON (LP, TV soundtrack, music by John Barry, mono)	30
63	Colpix PXL 459	IN LONDON (LP, TV soundtrack, music by John Barry, stereo)	35

(see also John Barry)

FELICE TAYLOR
67	President PT 155	I Feel Love Comin' On/BOB KEENE ORCHESTRA: Comin' On Again	8
68	President PT 193	Captured By Your Love/I Can Feel Your Love (Coming Down On Me)	7

TED TAYLOR FOUR
58	Oriole CB 1464	Son Of Honky Tonk/Farrago	12
60	Oriole CB 1573	M.1./You Are My Sunshine	7
61	Oriole CB 1574	Fried Onions/Yellow Rock Of Texas	10
61	Oriole CB 1628	Cat's Eyes/Canyon	10
61	Oriole CB 1630	Flyover/Haunted Pad	10
62	Oriole CB 1713	Jericho/Everytime We Say Goodbye	15
62	Oriole CB 1767	Surfrider/Spotlight	15

GEOFF TAYLOR
55	Esquire EP 55	GEOFF TAYLOR SEXTET (EP)	10
57	Esquire EP 105	GEOFF TAYLOR ALL STARS (EP)	10
55	Esquire 20-060	GEOFF TAYLOR ALL STARS (10" LP)	50

GLORIA TAYLOR
70	Polydor BM 56788	You Gotta Pay The Price/Loving You And Being Loved By You	15

HOUND DOG TAYLOR
66	Outasite 45-504	Christine/Alley Music (99 copies only)	100

JAMES TAYLOR
70	Apple APPLE 32	Carolina In My Mind/Something's Wrong	20
68	Apple APCOR 3	JAMES TAYLOR (LP, gatefold sleeve, black inner, orange cover lettering, mono)	40
68	Apple SAPCOR 3	JAMES TAYLOR (LP, gatefold sleeve, black inner, orange cover lettering, stereo)	25
70	Apple SAPCOR 3	JAMES TAYLOR (LP, 2nd issue, gatefold sleeve, 'Apple' inner sleeve, black cover lettering)	25
70	Warner Bros WS 1843	SWEET BABY JAMES (LP, orange label, later green label)	20
71	Warner Bros WS 2561	MUD SLIDE SLIM AND THE BLUE HORIZON (LP, g/fold sleeve, green label)	18
72	Warner Bros K 46243	SWEET BABY JAMES (LP, reissue, green label)	15
91	Apple SAPCOR 3	JAMES TAYLOR (LP, reissue, gatefold sleeve)	18

JAMES TAYLOR QUARTET
95	Acid Jazz JAZID 124S	Whole Lotta Love (white label, withdrawn)	50
96	Acid Jazz JAZID 139	Creation (10", p/s, misspressed with Hungarian porn music on A-side)	35
87	Re-Elect Pres. REAGAN 2D	MISSION: IMPOSSIBLE (mini-LP, with film dialogue, 500 only)	30

(see also Prisoners, Daggermen, New Jersey Kings, Sound Stylistics)

JEREMY TAYLOR
62	Decca F 11502	Ag Pleez Daddy/Jo'burg Talking Blues	8
66	Decca LK 4731	ALWAYS SOMETHING NEW (LP)	30
68	Fontana (S)TL 5475	HIS SONGS (LP)	20
69	Fontana (S)TL 5523	MORE OF HIS SONGS (LP)	20
72	Galliard GAL 4018	PIECE OF GROUND (LP)	15

JOHN TAYLOR
71	Turtle TUR 302	PAUSE AND THINK AGAIN (LP)	400

JOHNNIE TAYLOR
67	Stax 601 003	Ain't That Lovin' You/Outside Love (dark blue label)	50
67	Stax 601 003	Ain't That Lovin' You/Outside Love (light blue label)	30
68	Stax STAX 106	Who's Makin' Love/I'm Trying	8
69	Stax STAX 114	Take Care Of Your Homework/Hold On This Time	8
69	Stax STAX 122	(I Wanna) Testify/I Had To Fight With Love	10
69	Stax STAX 129	I Could Never Be President/It's Amazing	8
70	Stax STAX 141	Love Bones/Separation Line	8
70	Stax STAX 150	Steal Away/Friday Night	20
70	Stax STAX 156	I Am Somebody (Parts 1 & 2)	8
71	Stax 2025 021	Jody's Got Your Girl And Gone/A Fool Like Me	8
73	Stax 2025 083	Standing In For Jody/Shackin' Up	8
73	Stax 2025 194	I Believe In Love/Love Depression	8
75	Stax STXS 2021	It's September/Just One Moment	8
75	Stax STXS 2025	Friday Night/I Ain't Particular	10
76	CBS 4886	Disco Lady/Somebody's Gettin' It (blue vinyl)	8
67	Stax 589 008	WANTED, ONE SOUL SINGER (LP)	50
69	Stax (S)XATS 1006	WHO'S MAKING LOVE (LP)	20
69	Stax 228 008	LOOKING FOR JOHNNIE TAYLOR (LP)	25

(little) JOHNNY TAYLOR

MINT VALUE £

69	Stax SXATS 1024	THE J.T. PHILOSOPHY CONTINUES (LP)	25
70	Soul City SCB 2	ROOTS OF JOHNNIE TAYLOR (LP)	75

(LITTLE) JOHNNY TAYLOR

65	Vocalion V 9234	Part Time Love/Somewhere Down The Line	50
65	Vocalion V 9234	Part Time Love/Somewhere Down The Line (DJ copy)	75
66	Vocalion VP 9264	One More Chance/Looking At The Future	40
72	Mojo 2092 033	Everybody Knows About My Good Thing (Parts 1 & 2)	8
72	Mojo 2092 044	It's My Fault Darling/There's Something On Your Mind	8
65	Vocalion VA-F 8031	LITTLE JOHNNY TAYLOR (LP)	100
72	Mojo 2916 015	EVERYBODY KNOWS ABOUT MY GOOD THING (LP)	30
73	Contempo COLP 1003	OPEN HOUSE AT MY HOUSE (LP)	15
74	Contempo CLP 502	SUPER TAYLORS (LP, with Ted Taylor)	15

JOSEPH TAYLOR

72	Leader LEA 4050	UNTO BRIGG FAIR (LP, gatefold sleeve with booklet)	20

KAREN TAYLOR AND IAN SHAW

78	Granny GRAN 001	FRIENDS... (LP)	40

KINGSIZE TAYLOR (& DOMINOS)

64	Polydor NH 66990	Memphis Tennessee/Money (reissue of Shakers single)	30
64	Polydor NH 66991	Hippy Hippy Shake/Dr. Feelgood (reissue of Shakers single)	30
64	Decca F 11874	Stupidity/Bad Boy	50
64	Decca F 11935	Somebody's Always Trying/Looking For My Baby (solo)	150
65	Polydor BM 56152	Thinkin'/Let Me Love You	40
63	Polydor EPH21 628	TWIST AND SHAKE (EP, manufactured in Germany)	110
64	Decca DFE 8569	TEENBEAT 2 - FROM THE STAR CLUB, HAMBURG (EP)	130

(see also Shakers, Paddy Klaus & Gibson)

LINDA TAYLOR

82	Groove Production GPLP 31	TAYLOR MADE (LP)	20

MICK TAYLOR

65	CBS 201770	London Town/Hoboin'.	40

MIKE TAYLOR

65	Columbia SX 6042	PENDULUM (LP)	1500
67	Columbia SX 6137	TRIO (LP)	1500
07	Trunk JBH 016 LP	MIKE TAYLOR REMEMBERED (LP)	35

(see also Jack Bruce)

NEVILLE TAYLOR (& CUTTERS)

58	Parlophone R 4447	House Of Bamboo/Mercy, Mercy, Percy (solo)	40
58	Parlophone R 4447	House Of Bamboo/Mercy, Mercy, Percy (solo) (78)	20
58	Parlophone R 4476	Tears On My Pillow/I Don't Want To Set The World On Fire (solo)	20
58	Parlophone R 4493	A Baby Lay Sleeping/The Miracle Of Christmas (solo)	10
59	Parlophone R 4524	Crazy Little Daisy/The First Words Of Love (solo)	20
60	Oriole CB 1546	Dance With Dolly/Free Passes	20
60	Embassy WB 373	It Ain't Necessarily So/BOBBIE BRITTON: Woman Is A Sometime Love	6
60s	Honey Hit TB 127	Joshua Fit The Battle Of Jericho/It's Me, It's Me, It's Me, My Love (in p/s)	6

(see also Bobbie Britton)

PEGGY TAYLOR

60	Top Rank JAR 421	(Don't You Come Home!) Bill Bailey/So Similar	7

R. DEAN TAYLOR

68	Tamla Motown TMG 656	Gotta See Jane/Don't Fool Around	10
71	Tamla Motown TMG 763	Indiana Wants Me/Love's Your Name	10
71	Tamla Motown TMG 786	Ain't It A Sad Thing/Backstreet (unissued)	0
71	Rare Earth RES 101	Ain't It A Sad Thing/Back Street (has TMG 786 matrix in run-out groove)	15
74	Tamla Motown TMG 896	There's A Ghost In My House/Let's Go Somewhere (DJ Copy)	25
71	Tamla Motown STML 11185	INDIANA WANTS ME (LP)	18

ROD TAYLOR

78	Little Lute HITDD 311	If Jah Should Come Now/Africa Be Free/PRINCE HAMMER: Maccabee Bible (12")	30
78	Freedom Sounds FS 004	Ethiopian King/Version	20
78	Freedom Sounds FSD 004	Ethiopian King/PHILIP FRAZER: Come Ethiopians (12")	40
79	Hit Run DD 16	No One Can Tell I About Jah/ERROL HOLT : Yes Yes Yes (12")	60
79	Lovelinch LL05	True History (Disco Mix Version)/Scientist Vex Version (12")	15
80	Strong Like Sampson SLSD 011	Jah Is Calling/Inside Right (12")	20
81	Unity UP 003	Moving Out Ever/Version (12", with Ranking Dread)	20
82	Dread At The Controls DATCD 015	Sun Moon and Stars/BLAKKA STAR: Rubber Dub Rock/ROOF RADICS: Hand Cuff Dub (12")	15
78	Hit Run APLP 9031	IF JAH SHOULD COME NOW (LP)	50
80	Greensleeves GREL 17	WHERE IS YOUR LOVE MANKIND? (LP, green vinyl)	22

ROD TAYLOR & MIKEY DREAD & KING TUBBY

79	Sufferers Heights SUFF 006	Behold Him/Parrot Jungle/His Majesty/Dread All The Way (12")	30

ROGER TAYLOR

77	EMI EMI 2679	I Wanna Testify/Turn On The TV (demo copies £40)	30
81	EMI EMI 5200	My Country (Edit)/Fun In Space (p/s)	20
84	EMI EMI 5478	Man On Fire/Killing Time (p/s)	10
84	EMI 12 EMI 5478	Man On Fire (Extended)/Killing Time (12", p/s)	25
84	EMI EMI 5490	Strange Frontier/I Cry For You (Remix) (p/s)	15
84	EMI 12 EMI 5490	Strange Frontier (Extended)/I Cry For You (Extended Remix)/ Two Sharp Pencils (Get Bad) (12", p/s)	20
94	Parlophone 12RC 6379	Nazis 1994 (Single Version)/(Radio Mix)/(Makita Mix - Extended)/ (Big Science Mix) (12" clear vinyl, numbered insert in PVC sleeve)	10
94	Parlophone NAZIS 1	Nazis 1994 (Radio Mix)/Nazis 1944 (Kick Mix) (12", black vinyl, p/s, promo only)	15
94	Parlophone NAZIS 3	Nazis 1994 (Radio Mix)/(Kick Mix)/(Big Science Mix)/(Makita Mix) (12", black vinyl, promo only)	15

Rosemarie TAYLOR

MINT VALUE £

94	Parlophone NAZIS 4	Nazis 1994 (Schindler's Mix)/(Big Science Mix)/(Makita Mix - Extended) (12", black vinyl, p/s, promo only)	10
94	Parlophone 12RDJ 6379	Nazis 1994 (Schindler's Mix)/(Big Science Mix)/(Makita Mix - Extended) (12", white label DJ promo)	30
93	Parlophone PCSD 157	HAPPINESS? (LP, numbered)	60
93	Parlophone PCSD 157	HAPPINESS? (LP, un-numbered)	80
98	Parlophone 4967241	ELECTRIC FIRE (LP, orange vinyl)	80

(see also Queen, Cross, Hilary Hilary, Ian Hunter, Fox, Kansas, Mel Smith, Billy Squier)

ROSEMARIE TAYLOR
75	JD 2009	TAYLORMAID (LP, private pressing with insert)	200

ROY TAYLOR BAND
70	Bun BUN 009	Shake Me/Tidy Place In Me	10

SAM ('THE MAN') TAYLOR
54	MGM SP 1106	Please Be Kind/This Can't Be Love (as Sam 'The Man' Taylor & Cat Men)	30
56	MGM MGM-EP 531	SAM TAYLOR ORCHESTRA (EP)	35

(see also Claude Cloud)

TAYLOR SHARP & TAYLOR
70	CBS 5197	The Look Of Love/Mr Snow	15

TYRONE TAYLOR
75	Torpedo TOR 48	Move Up Blackman/Version	15
76	Island WIP 6275	Extra Extra/Life Turning Table	8
77	Observer OBMM 1000	Soul On Fire (Gregory Isaacs)/Saturday Night (Christine)/Christine (12")	40

VERNON TAYLOR
59	London HLS 8905	Today Is A Blue Day/Breeze (unreleased)	0
60	London HLS 9025	Mystery Train/Sweet And Easy To Love	100

VIC TAYLOR
67	Treasure Isle TI 7021	Heartaches/When It Comes To Loving You I'm Alright (B-side actually "Loving Pauper" by Dobby Dobson)	80
71	Trojan TRLS 38	DOES IT HIS WAY (LP)	20

(see also Tommy McCook)

VINCE TAYLOR (& HIS PLAYBOYS)
58	Parlophone R 4505	Right Behind You Baby/I Like Love (solo)	80
58	Parlophone R 4505	Right Behind You Baby/I Like Love (solo) (78)	40
59	Parlophone R 4539	Brand New Cadillac/Pledging My Love	70
60	Palette PG 9001	I'll Be Your Hero/Jet Black Machine	25
61	Palette PG 9020	Move Over Tiger/What'cha Gonna Do	25
97	Cruisin' 50 CASB 006	Brand New Cadillac/Right Behind You Baby (78, 300 only)	30

VINCENT TAYLOR
80	Live & Love LLDIS 115	Can't Seem To Forget You/Living A Lie (12")	50
80	Live & Love LLDIS 117	Got To Have You/TAYLOR PLAYERS: Got You Version (12")	30

WALTER TAYLOR
50s	Poydras 2	Thirty-Eight And Plus/Diamond Ring Blues	8

TAYLOR MAIDS
55	Capitol CL 14322	Po-Go Stick/Theme From "I Am A Camera" (Why Do I)	12

T-BONES
64	Columbia DB 7401	How Many More Times/I'm A Lover Not A Fighter	60
65	Columbia DB 7489	Won't You Give Him (One More Chance)/Hamish's Express Relief	35

(see also Gary Farr & T-Bones, Kevin Westlake)

T-BOYS
80	Nems BSS 104	Bus Song/Mary Jane	30
81	Almost Animal AA001	One Way Street/Factory Girl	20

JOHN TCHKAI
66	Fontana 881014/681 014ZL	RUFUS (LP, with ARCHIE SHEPP)	20

TDS MOB
10	Diggers With Gratitude DWG 006	THE DOPE COMMITTEE (EP, 75 only, burgundy vinyl)	45
10	Diggers With Gratitude DWG 006	THE DOPE COMMITTEE (EP, 275 only, black vinyl)	25
10	Diggers With Gratitude DWG 007	THE BOSTON CLASSICS (EP, 75 only, white vinyl)	35
10	Diggers With Gratitude DWG 007	THE BOSTON CLASSICS (EP)	12

TEA
75	Philips 6305 238	TEA (LP)	15

TEA & SYMPHONY
69	Harvest HAR 5005	Boredom/Armchair Theatre	20
69	Harvest SHVL 761	AN ASYLUM FOR THE MUSICALLY INSANE (LP, laminated gatefold sleeve. The name of the band appears above the "Harvest" logo. Those with "An Asylum For The Musically Insane" above the Harvest Logo are Dutch pressings from 1969)	400
70	Harvest SHVL 785	JO SAGO (LP, gatefold sleeve no EMI logo on label)	700

TEACH YOURSELF TURNTABLISM
04	Pedestrian	TUTORITOOL - INTERACTIVE TURNTABLISM TUTORIAL (LP, gatefold with inserts and inner sleeves, 1000 only)	25

TEACHERS PET
80	TP 001	Missing Person/Tug Of Love (p/s)	40

TEACHO & HIS STUDENTS
58	Felsted AF 104	Rock-et/Stop	60
58	Felsted AF 104	Rock-et/Stop (78)	30

TEA COMPANY
68	Mercury SMCL 20127	COME AND HAVE SOME TEA WITH THE TEA COMPANY (LP)	50

ANTHONY TEAGUE
62	Decca F 11548	Like I Don't Love You/My Guardian Angel	7

TEAM DOKUS
MINT VALUE £

TEAM DOKUS
94	Tenth Planet TP 007	TEAM DOKUS (LP, numbered, 500 only)	25

TEAM 23
81	Race RB 002	Whatever Moves You/Move Into The Rhythm	10

TEAMWORKS
89	Wau! Mr. Modo WMS 014T	Never Leave/Version/Rockfort Rock/Version (12")	15
89	Wau! Mr. Modo MOWLP 003	TEAMWORKS PRESENTS RUDY LEE AND STEPPER (LP)	20

TEA PARTY
94	Chrysalis CHR 6072	SPLENDOR SOILS (LP)	150
95	Chrysalis CHR 6108	THE EDGES OF TWILIGHT (LP)	150

TEARDROP EXPLODES
79	Zoo CAGE 003	Sleeping Gas/Camera Camera/Kirkby Workers' Dream Fades (red p/s)	20
79	Zoo CAGE 003	Sleeping Gas/Camera Camera/Kirkby Workers' Dream Fades (blue p/s)	15
79	Zoo CAGE 005	Bouncing Babies/All I Am Is Loving You (p/s)	10
80	Zoo CAGE 008	Treason (It's Just A Story)/Read It In Books (in blue & green p/s)	15
80	Zoo CAGE 008	Treason (It's Just A Story)/Read It In Books	6
80	Mercury TEAR 2	Reward/Strange House In The Snow (p/s, limited pressing with paper labels not moulded plastic, textured sleeve)	6
81	Mercury TEAR 4	Ha Ha I'm Drowning/Poppies In The Field (in withdrawn p/s, limited pressing with paper labels not moulded plastic)	15
81	Mercury TEAR 44	Ha Ha I'm Drowning/Poppies In The Field/Bouncing Babies/Read It In Books (double pack, gatefold p/s, limited pressing with paper labels not moulded plastic)	6
81	Mercury TEAR 44	Ha Ha I'm Drowning/Poppies In The Field/Bouncing Babies/Read It In Books (double pack, withdrawn gatefold p/s)	40
81	Mercury TEAR 5	Passionate Friend/Christ Versus Warhol (p/s, limited pressing with paper labels not moulded plastic)	6
81	Mercury TEAR 6	Colours Fly Away/Window Shopping For A New Crown Of Thorns (p/s & insert, limited pressing with paper labels not moulded plastic)	6
82	Mercury TEAR 7G	Tiny Children/Rachael Built A Steamboat (gatefold p/s, paper labels)	6
83	Mercury TEAR 88	You Disappear From View/Suffocate//Ouch Monkey's/Soft Enough For You/ The In-Psychlopedia (double pack, gatefold p/s, limited pressing with paper labels not moulded plastic)	6
89	Fontana DROP 112	Serious Danger/Sleeping Gas/Seven Views Of Jerusalem (p/s)	6
80	Mercury 6359 035	KILIMANJARO (LP, 1st pressing, light blue labels, 'group photo' on cover & inner sleeve)	20
80	Mercury 6359 035	KILIMANJARO (LP, 2nd pressing, dark blue labels)	15
81	Mercury 6359056	WILDER (LP)	15
90	Mercury 8424391	EVERYBODY WANTS TO SHAG THE TEARDROP EXPLODES (LP, with inner)	15
90	Document DLP 4	PIANO (LP)	15

(see also Julian Cope)

TEARDROPS (JAMAICA)
72	Fab FAB 187	Let Me Be Free/Version (white labels only)	40
71	Ackee ACK 126	Let Me Be Free/CINDY STARR: Sentimental Girl	15
71	Big Shot BI 582	Two In One/LAURIE'S ALL STARS: Rock-A-Boogie	20

TEARDROPS (1)
78	Bent BIGB 3	IN AND OUT OF FASHION (12" EP, foldout p/s in poly bag)	18
79	TJM TJM 9	Seeing Double/Teardrops And Heartaches (p/s)	20
80s	Illuminated JAMS 2	FINAL VINYL (LP)	15

TEARDROPS (2)
93	Kent 6T 9	Here Comes The Lonliness/CHUBBY CHECKER: You Can't Lose Something You've Never Had	10

TEAR GAS
70	Famous SFMA 5751	PIGGY GO-GETTER (LP, textured gtefold sleeve)	100
71	Regal Zono. SLRZ 1021	TEAR GAS (LP)	300

(see also Alex Harvey, Tandoori Cassette)

TEARJERKERS
80	Back Door DOOR 1	Murder Mystery/Heart On The Line (die cut p/s with insert)	8

(see also Speed)

THE TEARS
05	Independiente ISOM49LP	HERE COME THE TEARS (LP, numbered)	30

(see also Suede)

TEARS FOR FEARS
81	Mercury IDEA 1	Suffer The Children/Wino (p/s, original issue with light labels)	8
81	Mercury IDEA 12	Suffer The Children (Remix)/Wino/Suffer The Children (Instrumental) (12", p/s)	15
82	Mercury IDEA 33	Mad World/Mad World (World Remix)//Suffer The Children/ Ideas As Opiates (double pack)	20
82	Mercury IDEA 4	Change/The Conflict (poster p/s)	7
82	Mercury IDEA 4	Change/The Conflict (withdrawn 'fishing net' sleeve)	50
82	Mercury IDEA 412	Change/The Conflict (12" withdrawn 'fishing net' sleeve)	100
83	Mercury IDEA R/B 5	Pale Shelter/We Are Broken (p/s, red or blue vinyl)	15
83	Mercury IDEAG 5	Pale Shelter/We Are Broken (p/s, translucent green vinyl)	10
83	Mercury IDEAS 6	(The) Way You Are/The Marauders//Change (Live)/Start Of The Breakdown (live) (shrinkwrapped double pack)	10
84	Mercury IDEA 7	Mother's Talk/Empire Building (clear vinyl picture disc)	20
15	Mercury 0600753579046	Shout (Extended Version)/Everybody Wants To Rule The World (Extended Version) (12", withdrawn)	60
83	Mercury MERS 17	THE HURTING (LP, inner)	15
89	Mercury MERH 58	SONGS FROM THE BIG CHAIR (LP)	15
89	Fontana 838 730 1	THE SEEDS OF LOVE (LP)	15
92	Fontana 510 939 1	TEARS ROLL DOWN (LP)	40
93	Mercury 514875 1	ELEMENTAL (LP)	150
14	Mercury 4700591	SONGS FROM THE BIG CHAIR (2014 STEREO MIX) (LP, reissue)	80
17	Virgin EMI V 3197	RULE THE WORLD (2-LP)	20

(see also Graduate)

TEARS ON THE CONSOLE

MINT VALUE £

TEARS ON THE CONSOLE
75	Holyground HG 120	TEARS ON THE CONSOLE (LP, with booklet, 120 demo copies only)	150
90	Magic Mixture MM 3	TEARS ON THE CONSOLE (LP, reissue, 425 only, with insert)	20

TEASER
89	LTW 9KS 2049	Here Tonight (p/s)	20

TEA SET (1)
66	King KG 1048	Join The Tea Set/Ready Steady Go!	25

TEA SET (2)
79	Waldo's Beat PS 006	Parry Thomas/Tri-X Pan (gatefold p/s with poster 'mystery' envelope)	10
78	Waldo's Beat Series 003	CUPS AND SAUCERS (EP, with stapled lyric book sleeve)	20
80	Demon D 1009	South Pacific/The Preacher (foldout p/s with inserts)	10

TECHNIQUES (JAMAICA)
65	Island WI 231	Little Did You Know/DON DRUMMOND: Cool Smoke	60
67	Treasure Isle TI 7001	You Don't Care (with Tommy McCook & Supersonics Band)/ TOMMY McCOOK & SUPERSONICS BAND: Down On Bond Street	50
67	Treasure Isle TI 7019	Queen Majesty/Fighting For The Right	55
67	Treasure Isle TI 7026	Love Is Not A Gamble/Bad-Minded People	40
68	Treasure Isle TI 7031	My Girl/Drink Wine (with Tommy McCook & Supersonics)	30
68	Treasure Isle TI 7038	Devoted/Bless You (with Tommy McCook & Supersonics)	35
68	Treasure Isle TI 7040	It's You I Love/Travelling Man (with Tommy McCook & Supersonics)	60
68	Duke DU 1	I Wish It Would Rain/There Comes A Time	60
69	Duke DU 6	A Man Of My Word/The Time Has Come	70
69	Duke DU 22	What Am I To Do/You're My Everything	60
69	Duke DU 60	Where Were You/Just One Smile	25
69	Camel CA 10	Who You Gonna Run To/Hi There (B-side act. "Look Who's Back" by Carl Bryan)	60
69	Camel CA 19	Everywhere Everyone/Find Yourself Another Fool	35
70	Treasure Isle TI 7054	He Who Keepeth His Mouth/One Day (act. by Johnny Osborne & Sensations)	25
70	Techniques TE 904	Lonely Man/I Feel Alive	10
70	Techniques TE 906	Feel A Little Better (actually by Techniques Allstars)/You'll Get Left	10
70	Big Shot BI 536	He Who Keepeth His Mouth/One Day (act. by Johnny Osborne & Sensations)	15
71	Banana BA 350	Since I Lost You/RILEY'S ALLSTARS: Version	15

(see also Techniques All Stars, Riots, Tommy McCook, Mighty Avengers, Gaylads, Rad Bryan)

TECHNIQUES (U.S.)
58	Columbia DB 4207	Hey! Little Girl/In A Round About Way	45

TECHNIQUES ALL STARS
70	Big Shot BI 543	Come Back Darling/Move Over (actually by Johnny Osborne & Sensations)	30
70	Big Shot BI 545	Elfrego Bacca (actually by Dave Barker)/TECHNIQUES: Iron Joe (B-side actually by Techniques All Stars)	35
70	Techniques TE 900	Something Tender/CANNONBALL: Bewitch	35
70	Trojan TR 7728	Eldora/TECHNIQUES: If It's Not True (B-side actually by Techniques All Stars)	20

(see also Dennis Alcapone, Ansell Collins)

TECHNO POP
79	Fairview SRTS 79424	Paint It Black/What Are You	7

TECHNOSAURUS
93	Invention TBH 1	YOU GAVE ME NOTHING EP (12", stamped white labels)	25

TED
74	Epic SPEC 3126	Gonna Make You My Angel/Can't Stop The Train	8

TEDDIE & THE TIGERS
67	Spin SP 2004	Hold On I'm Comin'/First Love Never Dies	30

TEDDY
71	Upsetter US 353	Elusion/UPSETTERS: Big John Wayne	25

TEDDY & THE CONQUERORS
71	High Note HS 053	Homebound/GAYTONES: Homebound Chapter 3	10

TEDDY & THE TWILIGHTS
63	Stateside SS 167	I'm Just Your Clown/Bikini Bimbo	22

TEDDY BEARS
58	London HL 8733	To Know Him Is To Love Him/Don't You Worry, My Little Pet	8
59	London HLP 8836	I Don't Need You Anymore/Oh Why	15
59	London HLP 8889	You Said Goodbye/If You Only Knew	20
59	London HA-P 2183	THE TEDDY BEARS SING! (LP)	200

(see also Phil Spector, Carol Connors)

WILLIE TEE
67	Atlantic 584 116	Thank You John/Walking Up A One-Way Street	35
71	Mojo 2092 025	Thank You John/Walking Up A One-Way Street/Teasin' You	8
02	Grapevine G2K 45 128	I'm Having So Much Fun/First Taste Of Hurt	8
03	Grapevine G2K 45 142	Teasing You Again/Teasing You	8
17	Super Disco Edits SDE 23	Don't Get Caught/Instrumental Version	10

TEEGARDEN & VAN WINKLE
70	Pye 7N 25535	God, Love And Rock And Roll/Work Me Tomorrow	6
69	Atco 228028	BUT ANYHOW (LP)	15

TEENAGE FANCLUB
90	Paperhouse PAPER 003	Everything Flows/Primary Education/Speeeder (1,500 only, die-cut p/s)	20
90	Paperhouse PAPER 005	The Ballad Of John And Yoko (p/s, 1-sided, 5,000 only, 2nd side engraved)	6
91	Strange Fruit SFPS 081	PEEL SESSIONS (12")	12
95	Creation CRE 216	TEENAGE FANCLUB HAVE LOST IT EP (7", p/s)	20
03	Poolride POOLS 5	Did I Say/The Cabbage (p/s, 500 only)	6
90	Paperhouse PAPLP 004	A CATHOLIC EDUCATION (LP, gatefold sleeve)	30
91	Creation CRELP 096	THE KING (LP, available for 1 week only, sprayed plain sleeve)	40
91	Creation CRELP 106	BANDWAGONESQUE (LP, with inner)	40
93	Creation CRELP 144	THIRTEEN (LP)	40
95	Creation CRELP 137L	GRAND PRIX (LP, with free 7")	80

TEENAGE FILMSTARS

MINT VALUE £

95	Creation CRELP 137L	GRAND PRIX (LP, without free 7").. 60
97	Creation CRELP 196	SONGS FROM NORTHERN BRITAIN (LP) 80
00	Columbia 5006221	HOWDY! (LP) 50
03	Poolside POOLS 3LP	FOUR THOUSAND SEVEN HUNDRED AND SIXTY-SIX SECONDS - A SHORT CUT TO TEENAGE FANCLUB (2-LP) 60
05	Pema PEMA 002LP	MAN-MADE (LP) 25
10	Pema PEMA 007LP	SHADOWS (LP) 20

(see also Boy Hairdressers, BMX Bandits, Clouds, Eugenius)

TEENAGE FILMSTARS

79	Clockwork COR 002	(There's A) Cloud Over Liverpool/Sometimes Good Guys Don't Follow Trends (1st 150 with foldout p/s).. 150
79	Clockwork COR 002	(There's A) Cloud Over Liverpool/Sometimes Good Guys Don't Follow Trends................. 25
80	Wessex WEX 275	The Odd Man Out/I Apologise 25
80	Blueprint BLU 2013	The Odd Man Out/I Apologise (reissue, p/s) 20
80	Fab Listening FL 1	I Helped Patrick McGoohan Escape/We're Not Sorry (p/s)... 15

(see also Television Personalities, Times, O Level)

TEENAGERS

| 57 | RCA RCX 102 | THE TEENAGERS (EP) .... 60 |

TEENBEATS

79	Safari SAFE 17	I Can't Control Myself/I'll Never Win (p/s) 8
79	Safari SAFE 19	Strength Of The Nation/I'm Gone Tomorrow (in p/s) 15
79	Safari SAFE 19	Strength Of The Nation/I'm Gone Tomorrow 6

TEEN BEATS (U.S.)

| 60 | Top Rank JAR 342 | The Slop Beat/Califf Boogie (featuring Don Rivers & Califfs) .... 25 |

TEEN QUEENS

| 65 | R&B MRB 5000 | Eddie My Love/Just Goofed .... 30 |

TEE SET (2)

| 70 | Major Minor MM 666 | Ma Belle Amie/Angels Coming .... 8 |
| 70 | Columbia SCX 6419 | MA BELLE AMIE (LP) .... 15 |

TEETH OF THE SEA

10	Rocket LAUNCH 035	HYPNOTICON EP (12", 500 only) 10
15	God Unknown GOD 003	Up With People/ONEIDA: The Shah Arrives At The Checkpoint (7", 300 only) 12
09	Rocket LAUNCH 031	ORPHANED BY THE OCEAN (LP, orange vinyl) 18
10	Rocket LAUNCH 040	YOUR MERCY (LP) 18
13	Rocket LAUNCH 059 LP	MASTER (LP, magenta vinyl) 15
14	Rocket LAUNCH 064 LP	A FIELD IN ENGLAND RE-IMAGINED (LP, white vinyl, 200 only) 20

TEK 9

91	Reinforced RIVET 1205	KINGDOM OF DUB EP (12") 10
92	Reinforced RIVET 1229	JUST A DREAM EP (12") 20
92	Reinforced RIVET 1229R	JUST A DREAM EP (Remixes) (12") 10
93	Reinforced RIVET 1238	THE RETURN OF TEK 9 EP (12") 15
93	Reinforced RIVET 1238R	THE RETURN OF TEK 9 (Rpt) (12") 10
93	Reinforced RIVET 1253	BREAKIN' THE SOUND BARRIERS EP (12") 15
94	Reinforced RIVET 1262	KILLING TIME EP (10") 12
94	Reinforced RIVET 1269	JUS' A LIKKLE SUMTIN' EP (2x12") 25

TELEGENTS

| 81 | Gent GEN 1 | Get Out/Telephone Romance (p/s) .... 15 |
| 82 | Gent GEN 2 | Seen It Before/TV Gents (p/s) .... 15 |

TELEMAN

| 15 | Speedy Wunderground SW011 | Strange Combinations/(Mr Dan's Strange Dubby Nations) .... 25 |

TELESCOPE

| 77 | Pentagon PENT 5 | Bye Bye (ain't Nice)/A Personal Message From Telescope To You .... 10 |

TELESCOPES

88	Cheree CHEREE 1	Forever Close Your Eyes/LOOP: Soundhead (33rpm flexi, p/s, 1,000 only) 10
89	Cheree CHEREE 2	Kick The Wall/This Is The Last Of What's Coming Now (numbered re-pressing, 500 only, red wraparound p/s) 8
89	What Goes On WHAT GOES ON 32	TASTE (LP, inner) 18
90	Fierce FRIGHT 039	TRADE MARK OF QUALITY (LP) 15
92	Creation CRELP 079	TELESCOPES (LP, with booklet) 18

TELEVISION

77	Elektra K 12252	Marquee Moon Parts 1 & 2 10
79	Ork/WEA NYC 1T	Little Johnny Jewel Parts 1 & 2/Little Johnny Jewel (live) (12", p/s) 15
77	Elektra K52046	MARQUEE MOON (LP, 1st pressing with quotation marks around title) 50
77	Elektra K52046	MARQUEE MOON (LP, second pressing with no quotation marks around title) 30
78	Elektra K52072	ADVENTURE (LP, red vinyl, insert).. 18
78	Elektra K52072	ADVENTURE (LP, black vinyl) 15

(see also Neon Boys)

TELEVISION PERSONALITIES

78	Teen '78 SRTS/CUS/77/089	14th Floor/Oxford Street W1 (1st issue as TEEN '78, 'Teen 78' p/s - (b&w, a few red or blue ones have surfaced) some with TELEVISION PERSONALITIES added later in pen, or on reversed sleeve) 400
78	Teen '78 SRTS/CUS/77/089	14th Floor/Oxford Street (2nd issue, 'four pictures' p/s, TEEN '78 on labels)................ 300
78	Teen '78 SRTS/CUS/77/089	14th Floor/Oxford Street (3rd issue, 'Santa p/s', TEEN '78 on labels) 250
78	Teen '78 SRTS/CUS/77/089	14th Floor/Oxford Street (4th issue, no p/s, in brown die-cut sleeve handwritten by band members)... 75
78	Kings Road Records LYN 5976/5977	WHERE'S BILL GRUNDY NOW? (EP, 1st issue, 'Headless Man' p/s. Band name in upper case on front, no track list. Back of foldout features details of EP's pressing and printing. White labels, many hand stamped or handwritten. Matrix no's LYN-5976 and LYN-5977) . 75
78	Kings Road LYN 5976/7	WHERE'S BILL GRUNDY NOW? (EP, 2nd issue, 'Black Square' p/s with photo of Beatles on back. No track details. White labels, many hand stamped or handwritten. Matrix no's LYN-5976 and LYN-5977) 60

TELEX

MINT VALUE £

78	Kings Road LYN 5976/7	WHERE'S BILL GRUNDY NOW? (EP, 3rd issue, 'Shane MacGowan' p/s, picture of Shane on front, reproduction of letter from Garry Bushell on back. White labels, many hand stamped or handwritten. Matrix no's LYN-5976 and LYN-5977)	50
79	Rough Trade RT 033	WHERE'S BILL GRUNDY NOW? (EP, reissue, 2nd 'Headless Man' p/s, band name in upper/lower case, track titles on front cover. George & Ringo pics and 'Kings Road Records' address on back. RT 033 added to matrixes, printed labels (two variants) or rarer stamped labels)	30
80	Rough Trade RT 051	Smashing Time/King & Country (test pressing, white label and sleeve with handwritten information)	35
80	Rough Trade RT 051	Smashing Time/King & Country (p/s)	25
81	Rough Trade RT 063	I Know Where Syd Barrett Lives/Arthur The Gardener (p/s)	25
82	Whaam! WHAAM 4	Three Wishes/Geoffrey Ingram/And Don't The Kids Just Love It (p/s, 2 different sleeve designs with either a picture of Dan Treacy or picture of three children on back, White, red or green paper. 2,000 only)	35
82	Creation Artefact 002/ Lyntone LYN 13546	Biff Bang Pow!/A Picture Of Dorian Gray (1-sided flexidisc, with Communication Blur fanzine)	25
82	Creation Artefact 002/ Lyntone LYN 13546	Biff Bang Pow!/A Picture Of Dorian Gray (1-sided flexidisc, without Communication Blur fanzine)	18
83	Rough Trade RT 109	A Sense Of Belonging/Paradise Estate (p/s)	20
86	Dreamworld DREAM 4	How I Learned To Love The Bomb/Then God Snaps His Fingers/Now You're Just Being Ridiculous (12", p/s, 3,700 only)	18
86	Dreamworld DREAM 007	How I Learnt To Love The Bomb/Grocer's Daughter/Girl Called Charity (Test pressings with handwritten labels)	30
86	Dreamworld DREAM 10	How I Learned To Love The Bomb/Grocer's Daughter/Girl Called Charity (7", reissue, p/s, 1,000 only)	20
87	Dreamworld DREAM 13(T)	Privilege/Me And My Desires (unreleased)	0
89	Overground OVER 03	14th Floor/Oxford Street W1 (numbered new p/s, 600 yellow vinyl)	10
89	Overground OVER 03	14th Floor/Oxford Street W1 (numbered new p/s, 400 white vinyl)	10
89	Overground OVER 03	14th Floor/Oxford Street W1 (numbered new p/s, 1,000 black vinyl)	8
89	Caff CAFF 5	I Still Believe In Magic/Respectable (p/s, in poly bag, 500 only)	35
89	Caff CAFF 5	I Still Believe In Magic/Respectable (p/s, 500 only)	25
90	Overground OVER 13	I Know Where Syd Barrett Lives/Arthur The Gardener (reissue, p/s, 2000 only)	10
90	Overground OVER 15	The Prettiest Girl In The World/If That's What Love Is/Look Back In Anger (Alternative Version)/Silly Girl (Alternative Version) (withdrawn,100 test pressings only)	50
90	Overground OVER 20	Three Wishes/Geoffrey Ingram/And Don't The Kids Just Love It (new p/s, reissue)	10
91	Clawfist XPIG 8	Your Class/BMX BANDITS : Somebody To Share My Life With	12
92	Seminal Twang TWANG 15	We Will Be Your Gurus/Miro/An Exhibition By Jane/Love Is Better Than War (p/s)	7
92	Overground OVER 25	PART TIME PUNKS 4 Track EP (reissue of WHERE'S BILL GRUNDY NOW? EP)	18
92	Overground OVER 23	Smashing Time/King And Country/Three Cheers For Simon (p/s, reissue)	12
92	Overground OVER 27	My Favourite Films/The Dream Inspires/Happy All The TIme ('Ten Years Ahead Of It's Time' version) (p/s)	10
94	Overground OVER 34	A Sense Of Belonging/Baby's Turning Blue (p/s)	8
94	Overground OVER 38	The Prettiest Girl In the World/Miracles Take Longer/It That's What Love Is/Apples And Oranges (p/s)	10
81	Rough Trade ROUGH 24	AND DON'T THE KIDS JUST LOVE IT (LP, 1st 1,000 with insert)	120
81	Rough Trade ROUGH 24	AND DON'T THE KIDS JUST LOVE IT (LP, no insert)	80
81	Whaam! WHAAM 3	MUMMY YOUR NOT WATCHING ME (LP, 3,500 only, 1st 1,000 with insert)	100
81	Whaam! WHAAM 3	MUMMY YOUR NOT WATCHING ME (LP, 3,500 only, 2,500 without insert)	80
82	Whaam! BIG 5	THEY COULD HAVE BEEN BIGGER THAN THE BEATLES (LP, 2,500 only, hand-drawn or hand-painted sleeve, some with blue 'Wham' sticker)	120
83	Whaam! BIG 10	TURN ON … TUNE IN (LP, unreleased)	0
85	Illuminated JAMS 37	THE PAINTED WORD (LP, with company inner sleeve)	60
86	Dreamworld BIG DREAM 2	THEY COULD HAVE BEEN BIGGER THAN THE BEATLES (LP, reissue, new sleeve with insert)	30
86	Dreamworld BIG DREAM 4	MUMMY YOUR NOT WATCHING ME (LP, reissue, new sleeve with insert)	30
87	Dreamworld BIG DREAM 6	PRIVILEGE (LP, unreleased)	0
90	Fire LP 21	PRIVILEGE (LP, insert)	25
90	Fire REFIRE 7	AND DON'T THE KIDS JUST LOVE IT (LP, 2nd reissue, with inner)	35
90	Fire REFIRE 8	MUMMY YOUR NOT WATCHING ME (LP, 2nd reissue, with inner)	30
90	Fire REFIRE 9	THEY COULD HAVE BEEN BIGGER THAN THE BEATLES (LP, 2nd reissue, with inner)	30
90	Fire REFIRE 10	THE PAINTED WORD (LP, reissue with inner)	25
91	Overground OVER 21	CAMPING IN FRANCE (LP)	18
92	Fire FIRE LP 32	CLOSER TO GOD (2-LP, gatefold sleeve)	25
95	Overground OVER 41	I WAS A MOD BEFORE YOU WAS A MOD (LP, with inset)	35
96	Overground OVER 52	PAISLEY SHIRTS AND MINI SKIRTS (LP, with insert)	40

(see also Teenage Filmstars, Times, O Level, Missing Scientists, Reacta, Dry Rib, Slaughter, Gifted Children)

TELEX

79	Sire SRK 6072	LOOKING FOR ST. TROPEZ (LP, with lyric inner sleeve)	15
80	Sire SRK 6090	NEUROVISION (LP)	18
82	Interdisc INTO 1	BIRDS AND BEES (LP)	15

SYLVIA TELLA

96	Saxon SAX 047	Brothers And Sisters/Version/Jamaica Land/Jamaica Land (mix II) (12")	30
81	Sarge SRL 1005	SPELL (LP)	20

TELLERS

74	Pyramid PYR 7011	No Work, No Pay/Version	6
74	Dragon DRA 1031	A Ya It Deh/Attit Dub	6

TELSTARS

62	Oriole CB 1754	I Went A' Walkin'/A Rose And A Thorn	20

TEMPERANCE SEVEN

63	Parlophone R 5070	From Russia With Love/P.C.Q/Please Charleston Quietly	7

(see also Ted Wood)

TEMPEST (1)

85	Magnet PEST 1	Always The Same/Love In The Wintertime (p/s)	50
85	Magnet 10PEST 1	Always The Same/The Physical Act (10")	25

TEMPEST (2)

MINT VALUE £

85	Magnet PEST 2	Bluebelle/I Want To Live (p/s)	50
85	Magnet 10PEST 2	Bluebelle/I Want To Live (10")	25
86	Magnet LAZY 1	Lazy Sunday/You've Always Got Something To Say (p/s)	15
86	Magnet PEST 3	Didn't We Have A Nice Time?/The Physical Act	50

TEMPEST (2)
| 73 | Bronze ILPS 9220 | TEMPEST (LP, foldover cover with lyric inner sleeve) | 80 |
| 74 | Bronze ILPS 9267 | LIVING IN FEAR (LP, die-cut cover with inner sleeve) | 70 |

(see also Colosseum, Patto)

BOBBY TEMPEST
| 59 | Decca F 11125 | Love Or Leave/Don't Leave Me | 12 |

KATE TEMPEST
| 13 | Speedy Wunderground SW005 | Hot Night Cold Spaceship/(Mr Dan's Monday Morning Remix) | 20 |
| 14 | Speedy Wunderground SW009 | Guts/(Mr Dan's Baloon Dub) (with Loyle Carner) | 40 |

BOB TEMPLE
| 57 | Parlophone R 4264 | Come Back, Come Back/Vim Vam Vamoose | 80 |

GERRY TEMPLE
61	HMV POP 823	No More Tomorrows/So Nice To Walk You Home	40
61	HMV POP 939	Seventeen Come Sunday/Tell You What I'll Do	30
63	HMV POP 1114	Angel Face/Since You Went Away	45
68	RCA Victor RCA 1670	Lovin' Up A Storm/Everything I Do is Wrong	20

RICHARD TEMPLE
70	Jay Boy BOY 31	That Beatin' Rhythm/Could It Be	15
70	Jay Boy BOY 31	That Beatin' Rhythm/Could It Be (DJ copy)	30
76	Contempo CS 9040	That Beatin' Rhythm/Could It Be (reissue)	15

SHIRLEY TEMPLE
| 59 | Top Rank JKR 8003 | I REMEMBER (EP) | 20 |
| 63 | Music For Pleasure MFP 1141 | LITTLE MISS WONDERFUL (LP) | 15 |

TEMPLEAIRES
| 60s | Vogue V 2421 | He Spoke/What Will Heaven Have In Store For Me | 20 |

TEMPLE OF LIFE
| 91 | T Life 001 | EDP/Relax Your Soul/Slayer/Trancetone (12", stamped white labels) | 50 |

TEMPLE OF THE DOG
92	A&M AM 0091	Hunger Strike/All Night Thing (picture disc)	20
92	A&M AMY 0091	Hunger Strike/Your Saviour/All Night Thing (12", p/s, with poster)	15
91	A&M 395350-1	TEMPLE OF THE DOG (LP)	50

(see also Pearl Jam)

TEMPLE ROW
| 72 | Polydor 2058254 | King & Queen/One Of A Million Faces | 50 |
| 73 | Polydor 2058-329 | Walk The World Away/Mystery Man | 8 |

TEMPLES
13	Heavenly HVN 250	Shelter Song/Prisms (die-cut sleeve)	50
13	Heavenly HVN 261	Colours To Life/Ankh (10" white vinyl, 300 only)	15
13	Heavenly HVN 267	Keep In The Dark/Jewel Of Mine Eye (die-cut sleeve)	10
14	Heavenly HVNLP 100	SUN STRUCTURES (LP, orange vinyl)	60

TEMPLE SONGS
| 13 | Box Bedroom BBR 4 | ATONAL NOISE EP (p/s, insert, numbered, 100 only) | 20 |

TEMPLETON TWINS
| 70 | Liberty LBF 15379 | Hey Jude/Macarthur Park | 6 |

NINO TEMPO
57	London HLU 8387	Tempo's Tempo/June's Blues (as Nino Tempo & His Band)	200
57	London HLU 8387	Tempo's Tempo/June's Blues (as Nino Tempo & His Band) (78)	50
73	A&M 7089	Sister James/Clair De Luna (In Jazz) (as Nino Tempo & 5th Avenue)	6
58	London HB-U 1075	ROCK 'N' ROLL BEACH PARTY (10" LP)	125

(see also Nino Tempo & April Stevens, April Stevenso)

NINO TEMPO & APRIL STEVENS
62	London HLK 9580	Sweet And Lovely/TOP NOTES: Twist And Shout	15
69	London HLU 10245	All Strung Out/My Old Flame	8
64	London HA-K 8168	NINO TEMPO AND APRIL STEVENS - DEEP PURPLE (LP)	20
64	Atlantic AL 5006	SING THE GREAT SONGS (LP, mono)	15
64	Atlantic SAL 5006	SING THE GREAT SONGS (LP, stereo)	18
66	Atlantic	HEY BABY (LP)	15
67	London HA-U/SH-U 8314	ALL STRUNG OUT (LP)	20

(see also Nino Tempo, April Stevens)

TEMPOS (1)
| 59 | Pye International 7N 25026 | See You In September/Bless You My Love | 100 |
| 59 | Pye International 7N 25026 | See You In September/Bless You My Love (78) | 40 |

TEMPOS (2)
| 00 | Goldmine SG 0202 | (Countdown) Here I Come/FREDDIE CHAVEZ: They'll Never Know | 8 |
| 00 | Soul City SC 147 | A Little Togetherness/Countdown Here I Come | 8 |

TEMPREES
| 72 | Stax 2325 083 | LOVEMEN (LP) | 30 |
| 74 | Stax STX 1040 | 3 (LP) | 15 |

TEMPTATIONS (1)
| 60 | Top Rank JAR 384 | Barbara/Someday | 30 |

TEMPTATIONS (2)

SINGLES
| 64 | Stateside SS 278 | The Way You Do The Things You Do/Just Let Me Know | 70 |
| 64 | Stateside SS 278 | The Way You Do The Things You Do/Just Let Me Know (DJ copy) | 120 |

TEMPTATIONS (2)

MINT VALUE £

Year	Label & Cat No	Title	Value
64	Stateside SS 319	I'll Be In Trouble/The Girl's Alright With Me	80
64	Stateside SS 319	I'll Be In Trouble/The Girl's Alright With Me (DJ copy)	120
64	Stateside SS 348	Girl (Why You Wanna Make Me Blue)/Baby Baby I Need You	80
64	Stateside SS 348	Girl (Why You Wanna Make Me Blue)/Baby Baby I Need You (DJ copy)	240
65	Stateside SS 378	My Girl/(Talking 'Bout) Nobody But My Baby	45
65	Stateside SS 378	My Girl/(Talking 'Bout) Nobody But My Baby (DJ copy)	150
65	Tamla Motown TMG 504	It's Growing/What Love Has Joined Together	40
65	Tamla Motown TMG 504	It's Growing/What Love Has Joined Together (DJ copy)	100
65	Tamla Motown TMG 526	Since I Lost My Baby/You've Got To Earn It	50
65	Tamla Motown TMG 526	Since I Lost My Baby/You've Got To Earn It (DJ copy)	200
65	Tamla Motown TMG 541	My Baby/Don't Look Back	45
65	Tamla Motown TMG 541	My Baby/Don't Look Back (DJ copy)	100
66	Tamla Motown TMG 557	Get Ready/Fading Away	30
66	Tamla Motown TMG 557	Get Ready/Fading Away (DJ copy)	100
66	Tamla Motown TMG 565	Ain't Too Proud To Beg/You'll Lose A Precious Love (spelt "Previous")	30
66	Tamla Motown TMG 565	Ain't Too Proud To Beg/You'll Lose A Precious Love (spelt "Previous") (DJ copy)	130
66	Tamla Motown TMG 578	Beauty Is Only Skin Deep/You're Not An Ordinary Girl (DJ copy)	140
66	Tamla Motown TMG 578	Beauty Is Only Skin Deep/You're Not An Ordinary Girl	30
66	Tamla Motown TMG 587	(I Know) I'm Losing You/Little Miss Sweetness	25
66	Tamla Motown TMG 587	(I Know) I'm Losing You/Little Miss Sweetness (DJ copy)	80
67	Tamla Motown TMG 610	All I Need/Sorry Is A Sorry Word	20
67	Tamla Motown TMG 610	All I Need/Sorry Is A Sorry Word (DJ copy)	60
67	Tamla Motown TMG 620	You're My Everything/I've Been Good To You	20
67	Tamla Motown TMG 620	You're My Everything/I've Been Good To You (DJ copy)	50
67	Tamla Motown TMG 633	(Loneliness Made Me Realise) It's You That I Need/I Want A Love I Can See	40
67	Tamla Motown TMG 633	(Loneliness Made Me Realise) It's You That I Need/I Want A Love I Can See (DJ copy)	45
68	Tamla Motown TMG 641	I Wish It Would Rain/I Truly, Truly Believe	20
68	Tamla Motown TMG 641	I Wish It Would Rain/I Truly, Truly Believe (DJ copy)	30
68	Tamla Motown TMG 658	I Could Never Love Another (After Loving You)/Gonna Give Her All The Love I've Got	15
68	Tamla Motown TMG 658	I Could Never Love Another (After Loving You)/Gonna Give Her All The Love I've Got (DJ copy)	30
68	Tamla Motown TMG 671	Why Did You Leave Me Darling/How Can I Forget	15
68	Tamla Motown TMG 671	Why Did You Leave Me Darling/How Can I Forget (DJ copy)	30
69	Tamla Motown TMG 688	Get Ready/My Girl	7
69	Tamla Motown TMG 688	Get Ready/My Girl (DJ copy)	30
69	Tamla Motown TMG 699	Ain't Too Proud To Beg/Fading Away	7
69	Tamla Motown TMG 699	Ain't Too Proud To Beg/Fading Away (DJ copy)	25
69	Tamla Motown TMG 707	Cloud Nine/Why Did She Have To Leave Me (Why Did She Have To Go)	7
69	Tamla Motown TMG 707	Cloud Nine/Why Did She Have To Leave Me (Why Did She Have To Go) (DJ copy)	25
69	Tamla Motown TMG 716	Runaway Child, Running Wild/I Need Your Lovin'	8
70	Tamla Motown TMG 722	I Can't Get Next To You/Running Away (Ain't Gonna Help You)	7
70	Tamla Motown TMG 749	Ball Of Confusion (That's What The World Is Today)/It's Summer	7
70	Tamla Motown TMG 741	Psychedelic Shack/That's The Way Love Is	6
71	Tamla Motown TMG 773	Just My Imagination (Running Away With Me)/You Make Your Own Heaven And Hell Right Here On Earth	6
71	Tamla Motown TMG 783	It's Summer/Unite The World (Ungena Za Ulimwengu)	6
71	Tamla Motown TMG 783	Unite The World (Ungena Za Ulimwengu)/It's Summer (reissue)	8
72	Tamla Motown TMG 800	Superstar/Gonna Keep Tryin' Till I Win Your Love	8
72	Tamla Motown TMG 808	Take A Look Around/Smooth Sailing (From Now On)	6
72	Tamla Motown TMG 832	Smiling Faces Sometimes/Mother Nature	8
83	Tamla Motown TMG 1320	Papa Was A Rolling Stone/FOUR TOPS: Medley	35

EPs

Year	Label & Cat No	Title	Value
65	Tamla Motown TME 2004	THE TEMPTATIONS (EP)	50
66	Tamla Motown TME 2010	IT'S THE TEMPTATIONS	40

ALBUMS : LPS

Year	Label & Cat No	Title	Value
65	Tamla Motown TML 11009	MEET THE TEMPTATIONS	200
65	Tamla Motown TML 11016	SING SMOKEY	60
66	Tamla Motown TML 11023	THE TEMPTIN' TEMPTATIONS (mono)	45
66	Tamla Motown STML 11023	THE TEMPTIN' TEMPTATIONS (stereo)	55
66	Tamla Motown TML 11035	GETTIN' READY (mono)	40
66	Tamla Motown STML 11035	GETTIN' READY (stereo)	50
67	Tamla Motown STML 11057	WITH A LOT O'SOUL (stereo)	40
67	Tamla Motown STML 11053	THE TEMPTATIONS LIVE! (stereo)	25
67	Tamla Motown STML 11042	GREATEST HITS (stereo)	25
67	Tamla Motown TML 11042	GREATEST HITS (mono)	20
67	Tamla Motown TML 11053	TEMPTATIONS LIVE! (mono)	20
67	Tamla Motown TML 11057	WITH A LOT O'SOUL (mono)	35
68	Tamla Motown TML 11068	IN A MELLOW MOOD (mono)	30
68	Tamla Motown STML 11068	IN A MELLOW MOOD (stereo)	35
68	Tamla Motown TML 11079	WISH IT WOULD RAIN (LP, mono)	30
68	Tamla Motown STML 11079	WISH IT WOULD RAIN (LP, stereo)	35
68	Tamla Motown (S)TML 11079	THE TEMPTATIONS WISH IT COULD RAIN	40
69	Tamla Motown TML 11104	THE TEMPTATIONS LIVE AT THE COPA (mono)	30
69	Tamla Motown STML 11104	THE TEMPTATIONS LIVE AT THE COPA (stereo)	25
69	Tamla Motown (S)TML 11109	CLOUD NINE (mono/stereo)	30
70	Tamla Motown STML 11141	'LIVE' AT LONDON'S TALK OF THE TOWN (stereo, mono unconfirmed)	20
70	Tamla Motown TML 11133	PUZZLE PEOPLE (mono)	25
70	Tamla Motown STML 11133	PUZZLE PEOPLE (stereo)	22

70	Tamla Motown STML 11147	PSYCHEDELIC SHACK	25
70	Tamla Motown STML 11170	GREATEST HITS Vol. 2	15
71	Tamla Motown STML 11184	THE SKY'S THE LIMIT	15
72	Tamla Motown STML 11202	SOLID ROCK	15
72	Tamla Motown STML 11218	ALL DIRECTIONS	15
73	Tamla Motown STML 11229	MASTERPIECE	15

(see also David Ruffin, Diana Ross)

TEMPUS FUGIT
69	Philips BF 1802	Come Alive/Emphasis On Love	60

(see also Jensens)

10CC
72	UK UK 22	Johnny Don't Do It/4% Of Something	6
74	UK UK 57	The Worst Band In The World/18 Carat Man Of Means	6
73	UK UKAL 1005	10cc (LP)	20
74	UK UKAL 1007	SHEET MUSIC (LP)	20
75	Mercury 9102501	HOW DARE YOU (LP, gatefold)	20
77	Mercury 9102 502	DECEPTIVE BENDS (LP)	20
95	Avex AVEXLP	MIRROR MIRROR (LP)	100
12	Mercury 5340276	TENOLOGY (4-CD box set)	40

(see also Godley & Creme, Graham Gouldman, Lol, Mindbenders, Mockingbirds, Hotlegs, Whirlwinds, Tristar Airbus, Yellow Bellow Room Boom, Nick Mason & Rick Fenn, Frabjoy & Runcible Spoon, Manchester Mob, Ramases, Festival)

TENASTELIN
86	Vibes Sounds VS 001	Commercial Bwoy/Burial Tonight (12")	25
89	Wau! Mr. Modo MWS 011T	Jah Equity/Jah Equity (Version) (12")	50
89	Wau! Mr. Modo MWS 015T	King Of Kings/Give Thanks And Praise (12")	50
90	Black Legacy BL002	Urban Ghetto Youth/Run Away Mengistu (12")	50
90	Conscious Sounds DPS 102	Can't Touch Jah/CENTRY: Version	40
00	Jah Tubbys JT 7005	Look After Yourself/DISCIPLES RHYTHM SECTION: Dub Yourself	20
89	Wai! Mr. Modo MOWLP 002	WICKED INVENTION (LP)	50
92	Conscious Sounds DNC 001	SUN AND MOON (LP, as Tena Stelin Meets Centry)	35

(see also Iration Steppas and Tena Stelin)

TENDER TONES
69	Crab CRAB 38	Devil Woman/Nobody Cares	70

TENDER TOUCH
73	Hot Lead HL 7	Scarlet Ribbons/Your Tender Touch	8

TENDERLONIOUS
13	22a 001	TENDERLONIOUS/AL DOBSON (12" split EP, 200 only, 1st pressing)	15
14	Sounds Of The Universe SOTU 009	Caramel/Something Different (Vocal)/Something Different (Inst.) (12" with print)	15
17	22a 014	SV Disco/Shakedown (p/s, 300 only some hand-coloured)	20
18	22a 020	Yusef's Groove/Maria (p/s, 300 only, with 22arkestra)	12
16	22a 012	ON FLUTE (mini-LP)	20
17	22a 017	8RICK CI7Y (LP, with Dennis Ayler)	20
18	22a 022	THE SHAKEDOWN (2-LP, limited edition, hand-stamped labels, numbered with print)	40

(see also Ruby Rushton)

TEN FEET
66	RCA RCA 1544	Got Everything But Love/Factory Worker	100
67	CBS 3045	Shoot On Sight/Losing Game	120

TEN FEET FIVE
65	Fontana TF 578	Baby's Back In Town/Send Me No More Lovin'	45

(see also Troggs)

TEN FOOT BONELESS
88	Fierce FRIGHT 027	Powerslide/Duane Peters Is God (12", yellow or white p/s, with inner)	12

(see also Pooh Sticks)

TENNENT & MORRISON
72	Polydor 2383 152	TENNENT & MORRISON (LP, with lyric insert)	150

(see also Joe Soap)

TENNIS SHOES
78	Bonaparte BONE 3	(Do The) Medium Wave/Rolf Is Stranger Than Richard/So Large (p/s)	15

TENNORS
68	JJ DB 1152	Massie Massa/CLIVE ALLSTARS: San Sebastian	75
68	Doctor Bird DB 1175	Sufferer (Make It)/Little Things	70
68	Island WI 3133	Ride Your Donkey/I've Got To Get You Off My Mind	25
68	Island WI 3140	Copy Me Donkey (as Tenors)/The Stage (B-side actually by Ronnie Davis)	40
68	Island WI 3156	Grampa/ROMEO STEWART: While I Was Walking	40
68	Blue Cat BS 127	Khaki/LEYROY REID: Great Surprise (Pound Get A Blow)	85
68	Big Shot BI 501	Reggae Girl/CLIVE ALLSTARS: Donkey Trot	80
68	Fab FAB 41	Ride You Donkey/Cleopatra (as Tenners)	25
68	Fab FAB 50	Let Go Yah Donkey/ROMEO STEWART: While I Was Walking	40
69	Big Shot BI 514	You're No Good/Do The Reggae	60
69	Big Shot BI 517	Another Scorcher/My Baby	85
69	Duke Reid DR 2502	Hopeful Village/TOMMY McCOOK: The Village	20
69	Bullet BU 406	Greatest Scorcher/Making Love (white labels only)	100
69	Bullet BU 406	Festival Knocks/Making Love	60
69	Crab CRAB 26	Baff Boom/Feel Bad	50
69	Crab CRAB 29	True Brothers/Sign Of The Time	50
69	Crab CRAB 36	I Want Everything/Cherry	75
73	Explosion EX 2079	Weather Report/Weather Report - Version	20
73	Pyramid PYR 7000	Money Never Built A Mountain/My World	20

(see also Jennors, Prince Buster, Soul Brothers)

Jimi TENOR

MINT VALUE £

JIMI TENOR
97	Warp WARPLP 48	INTERVISION (2-LP)	20
99	Warp WARLP 60	ORGANISM (LP)	15

TENOR SAW
84	SKD SKD 092	Bad Bwoy/Dub (12")	18
85	Kings & Lion KLJJ 003	Tidal Wave/Punkin Belly (12")	40
86	Uptempo TU 012	Golden Hen/Golden Dun (12")	10
87	Blue Mountain BMD 034	Come Me Just A Come (Version)/SLY & ROBBIE: Version/Come Me Just A Come (Club Version)/SLY & ROBBIE: Version (12")	30
84	Hawkeye HLD 0012	CLASH (LP, with Coco Tea)	18
86	Uptempo UTLP 04	TENOR SAW MEETS DON ANGELO (LP)	25
94	Black Roots BR 002LP	WITH LOTS OF SIGNS (LP)	30

10,000 MANIACS
84	Reflex RE 1	My Mother The War (Remix)/Planned Obsolescence/National Education Week (12", p/s)	20
84	Press P 2010	HUMAN CONFLICT 5 (12" EP, gatefold p/s)	30
84	Press P 3001 LP	SECRETS OF THE I-CHING (LP, with insert)	25
84	Press P 3001 LP	SECRETS OF THE I-CHING (LP, with insert; later re-pressing in different 'Chinese Chicken' sleeve, some with insert)	15
87	Elektra EKT 41	IN MY TRIBE (LP, inner with free 7")	20
89	Elektra EKT57W	BLIND MAN'S ZOO (LP, with print)	15

10000 RUSSOS
15	Fuzz Club FC23V12	10000 RUSSOS (LP, white vinyl)	20
15	Fuzz Club FC23V12	10000 RUSSOS (LP, black & white vinyl, 100 only)	35

TEN WHEEL DRIVE (WITH GENYA RAVAN)
69	Polydor 583 577	CONSTRUCTION NO. 1 (LP)	20
70	Polydor 2425 002	BRIEF REPLIES (LP, with Genya Ravan)	20
71	Polydor 2425 065	PECULIAR FRIENDS (LP, with Genya Ravan)	20

(see also Goldie [& Gingerbreads])

TEN YEARS AFTER
68	Deram DM 176	Portable People/The Sounds	20
68	Deram DM 221	Hear Me Calling/I'm Going Home	8
70	Deram DM 299	Love Like A Man/Love Like A Man	6
71	Deram XDR 48532	She Lies In The Morning/Sweet Little Sixteen (demo only)	15
67	Deram DML 1015	TEN YEARS AFTER (LP, mono)	100
67	Deram SML 1015	TEN YEARS AFTER (LP, stereo)	80
68	Deram DML 1023	UNDEAD (LP, mono)	80
68	Deram SML 1023	UNDEAD (LP, stereo)	60
69	Deram DML 1029	STONEDHENGE (LP, gatefold sleeve, mono)	70
69	Deram SML 1029	STONEDHENGE (LP, laminated gatefold sleeve, stereo)	50
69	Deram DML/SML 1052	SSSSH! (LP, gatefold sleeve, mono/stereo)	60
70	Deram DML 1065	CRICKLEWOOD GREEN (LP, gatefold sleeve, with 'Alvin Lee' poster, mono)	100
70	Deram SML 1065	CRICKLEWOOD GREEN (LP, gatefold sleeve, with 'Alvin Lee' poster, stereo)	50
71	Deram SML 1078	WATT (LP, gatefold sleeve, with poster)	70
71	Chrysalis CHR 1001	A SPACE IN TIME (LP, 1st pressing with 'manufactures and distributed by Island Records Basing St' on top)	50
72	Deram SML 1096	ALVIN LEE AND COMPANY (LP)	15
72	Chrysalis CHR 1009	ROCK & ROLL MUSIC TO THE WORLD (gatefold sleeve)	18
78	Deram SML 1023	UNDEAD (LP, reissue)	15
74	Chrysalis CHR 1060	POSITIVE VIBRATIONS (LP)	15
80	Chrysalis CHR 1001	WATT (LP, reissue, single sleeve)	20

(see also Alvin Lee, Chick Churchill)

WAYNE TENYUE
82	Red Nail RN 0035	Murderous Time/THE DUB BAND: Life Sentence (12")	10

TEREA
11	Jazzman JMANLP 040	TEREA (LP, reissue)	40

TERMINAL
80	Cargo CRS 0081	Hold On/We're Only Human (in p/s)	100
82	Termite TERM 2	Am I Doing It Right/I Don't Mind/Turn Around And Don't Make Me Laugh (p/s)	20

TERMINAL BEACH
82	TB SRTS 82	Love On Auto/Dark Words (p/s)	50

TERMINAL CHEESECAKE
88	Wiiija WIIIJIT1	BLADDERSACK EP (12", p/s)	15
88	Wiiija WIIIJLP1	JOHNNY TOWN-MOUSE (LP)	20
89	Wiiija WIIIJLP3	V.C.L. (LP)	15
90	Pathological PATH 3	ANGELS IN PIGTAILS (LP)	25
92	World Serpent WSLP 001	PEARLESQUE KINGS OF THE JEWMOST (LP)	20
93	Jackass JAK 3	GATEAU D-ESPACE (mini-LP)	20
94	Jackass JAK 8	KING OF ALL SPACEHEADS (2-LP, golden vinyl, 1000 only, 500 with free live 12")	35
94	Jackass JAK 8	KING OF ALL SPACEHEADS (2-LP, golden vinyl, 1000 only, without 12")	30

TERMINAL FUN
82	Projected Image PRIM 4	Great Moments/Twist And Survive	10

TERMINAL JIVE
82	Jive Alive JA001	THE TERMINAL JIVE AND SCARLET ALIVE EP (2 tracks on one side, p/s)	15

TERMINAL SPECTATORS
82	Tiny Chariot CAT 002	Another Day Another Dream/Reach For The Sky	60

TERMITES
65	Oriole CB 1989	Tell Me/I Found My Place	40
65	CBS 201761	Every Day Every Day/No-One In The Whole Wide World	20

TERMITES (JAMAICA)
67	Coxsone CS01/02	Hold Down Rudie/JOE HIGGS AND THE WAILERS: Keep Cool (white label only)	80

Pete TERRACE

MINT VALUE £

67	Studio One SO 2006	Mercy Mr. Percy/SOUL BROTHERS: Hot And Cold	150
67	Studio One SO 2029	It Takes Two To Make Love/Beach Boy	100
67	Coxsone CS 7008	Sign Up/DELROY WILSON: Troubled Man	80
67	Coxsone CS 7025	Do It Right Now/SUMMERTAIRES: Stay (B-side actually by Gaylads)	85
68	Studio One SO 2040	Mr D.J. (actually by Delroy Wilson)/Tripe Girl (actually by Heptones)	110
68	Coxsone CS 7039	Mama Didn't Know/I Made A Mistake	375
68	Pama PM 729	Push It Up/Two Of A Kind (B-side act. by Clancy Eccles & Cynthia Richards)	90
68	Pama PM 738	Show Me The Way/What Can I Do	75
68	Trojan TR 634	Love Up Kiss Up/TOMMY McCOOK : Regay	120
69	Nu Beat NB 017	Push Push/Girls (actually by Hi Tones)	60
67	Studio One SOL 9003	DO THE ROCK STEADY (LP)	500

(see also L. Sparks, Ken Boothe, Upsetters)

PETE TERRACE

67	Pye International 7N 25427	At The Party/No! No! No!	30
67	Pye International 7N 25440	Shotgun Boo-Ga-Loo/I'm Gonna Make It	40
67	Pye Intl. NPL 28102	BOOGALOO (LP)	50

TERRA COTTA

78	Terra Cotta TC 001	To Be Near You (p/s, with insert)	15

(see also Spriguns)

TERRAIN

83	Terrain Musak TS 001	Who's To Blame?/Vacation (no p/s)	150

TERRAPLANE (1)

70	Saturn R4	TERRAPLANE (LP, 2 inserts)	200

TERRAPLANE (2)

85	Epic 26439	BLACK AND WHITE (LP)	15

(see also Thunder, Nuthin' Fancy)

LLOYD TERRELL

68	Island WI 3158	My Argument (as Lloyd & Johnny Melody)/JOHNNY MELODY: Foey Man (B-side actually by George Dekker)	300
68	Pama PM 710	Bang Bang Lulu/MRS MILLER: I Never Knew	10
68	Pama PM 740	How Come (actually by Lee Perry)/MRS MILLER: Oh My Lover	15
69	Pama PM 752	Lulu Returns/MRS MILLER: I Feel The Music	15
69	Nu Beat NB 023	Mr Rhya/After Dark	18
70	Pama PM 792	Birth Control/VAL BENNET: Return To Peace	18
70	Bullet BU 434	Exposure/Baby Huey	18
70	Bullet BU 443	Oh Me Oh My/I Did It	25
71	Escort ERT 855	One Woman/CHARMERS: What Should I Do (act. by Dave Barker & Charmers)	12
72	Bullet BU 508	Oily Sounds/Oily Version (as Lloyd Tyrell)	8
73	Pama PM 863	Big Eight/JUNIOR BYLES: Auntie Lu Lu	10
73	Pama PM 863	Big Eight/Lightning Stick (withdrawn)	70

(see also Charmers, Lloyd Charmers, Lloyd & Johnny, Lloyd & Ken, Lloydie & Lowbites)

TAMMI TERRELL

66	Tamla Motown TMG 561	Come On And See Me/Baby Don'tcha Worry (DJ copy)	200
66	Tamla Motown TMG 561	Come On And See Me/Baby Don'tcha Worry	120
69	T. Motown (S)TML 11103	THE IRRESISTIBLE TAMMI TERRELL (LP, mono/stereo)	100

(see also Marvin Gaye & Tammi Terrell)

TAMMI TERRELL/CHUCK JACKSON

69	Marble Arch MAL 1110	THE EARLY SHOW (LP)	20

(see also Chuck Jackson)

PHIL TERRELL

94	Kent 6T 10	Love Has Passed Me By/VIC & JOHN: Why Did She Lie	35

TERRIBLE LIZARD

81	Head Bang HB 1	Bang Your Head/(Instrumental Version)	7

TERRORIZER

89	Earach MOSH 16	WORLD DOWNFALL (LP, with inner)	30

TERRORVISION

92	Total Vegas 12VEGAS 1	THRIVE EP (12" EP)	12
92	Total Vegas ATVRLP 1	FORMALDEHYDE (LP, 14 tracks, green vinyl, 500 only, stickered sleeve)	40
93	Total Vegas VEGASLPS 1	FORMALDEHYDE (reissue LP, 12 tracks, 1,000 copies with 12-page booklet, stickered sleeve & lyric inner)	20
93	Total Vegas BOOT 1	LIVE AT THE DON VALLEY STADIUM (CD, picture disc, 250 promo copies only)	30
94	Total Vegas VEGASLP 2	HOW TO MAKE FRIENDS AND INFLUENCE PEOPLE (LP, gatefold)	15
96	Total Vegas VEGASLP 3	REGULAR URBAN SURVIVORS (LP)	18

TERRY

66	Fontana TF 751	Spilt Milk/The Way That I Remember Him	10

TERRY, CARL & DERRICK

69	Grape GR 3012	True Love/ROY SMITH: Another Saturday Night	80

DEWEY TERRY

73	Tumbleweed TW 3502	CHIEF (LP)	18

(see also Don & Dewey, Don Harris, Harvey Mandel)

GORDON TERRY

57	London REA 1098	COUNTRY CLAMBAKE (EP)	20

KARL TERRY & THE BRUISERS

78	ROX 008	Haunted House/Stick It In Your Pipe	6

PAT TERRY (GROUP)

70s	Myrrh MYR 1031	PAT TERRY GROUP (LP)	18

SONNY TERRY (TRIO)

53	Parlophone MSP 6017	Hootin' Blues/TOMMY REILLY: Bop! Goes The Weasel	35
56	Vogue EPV 1095	SONNY TERRY (EP)	50
55	Vogue LDE 137	FOLK BLUES (10" LP)	40
55	Vogue LDE 165	CITY BLUES (10" LP)	40

Sonny TERRY & BROWNIE McGHEE

MINT VALUE £

58	Melodisc MLP 516	WHOOPIN' THE BLUES (10" LP)	40
58	Topic 10T 30	HARMONICA BLUES (10" LP)	40
65	Topic 12T 30	HARMONICA BLUES (12" LP, reissue)	35
66	Xtra XTRA 5025	SONNY'S STORY (LP)	25
69	Ember CW 136	BLIND SONNY TERRY & WOODY GUTHRIE (LP)	15
69	Xtra XTRA 1064	SONNY TERRY (LP)	15
60s	Mainstream MSL 1037	GOING DOWN SLOW (LP, with BROWNIE McGHEE & PEPPERMINT HARRIS)	18
70	Xtra XTRA 1099	BLUES FROM EVERYWHERE (LP)	15
71	Xtra XTRA 1110	ON THE ROAD (LP, with J.C. Burris)	15

(see also Woody Guthrie)

SONNY TERRY & BROWNIE McGHEE

60	Columbia DB 4433	Talking Harmonica Blues/Rockin' And Whoopin'	35
64	Oriole CB 1946	Dissatisfied Woman/SONNY TERRY: Goin' Down Slow	20
50s	Melodisc EPM7 83	ME AND SONNY (EP)	25
58	Pye Jazz NJE 1060	THE BLUEST (EP)	10
59	Pye Jazz NJE 1073	SONNY TERRY & BROWNIE McGHEE & CHRIS BARBER'S JAZZ BAND (EP)	10
59	Pye Jazz NJE 1074	TERRY AND McGHEE IN LONDON PT. 1 (EP)	15
59	Topic TOP 37	HOOTENANNY NEW YORK CITY (EP, with Pete Seeger)	15
61	Top Rank JKP 3007	WORK-PLAY-FAITH-FUN-SONGS (EP)	15
64	Ember EP 4562	SONNY TERRY AND BROWNIE McGHEE (EP)	20
64	Topic TOP 121	R AND B FROM S AND B (EP)	15
64	Realm REP 4002	PAWNSHOP BLUES (EP)	15
64	Vocalion EPV 1274	SONNY TERRY AND BROWNIE McGHEE (EP)	20
65	Vocalion EPV 1279	I SHALL NOT BE MOVED (EP)	20
58	Topic 12T 29	BROWNIE McGHEE AND SONNY TERRY (LP)	30
58	Pye Nixa Jazz NJT 515	SONNY, BROWNIE AND CHRIS (10" LP, with Chris Barber)	45
58	Pye Nixa Jazz NJL 18	SONNY TERRY AND BROWNIE McGHEE IN LONDON (LP)	30
58	London Jazz LTZ-C 15144	BACK COUNTRY BLUES (LP)	50
60	Columbia 33SX 1223	BLUES IS MY COMPANION (LP)	50
61	World Record Club 7379	SONNY TERRY AND BROWNIE McGHEE (LP)	20
61	Vogue LAE 12247	BLUES IS A STORY (LP, mono)	30
61	Vogue SEA 5014	BLUES IS A STORY (LP, stereo)	40
63	Vogue LAE 12266	DOWN SOUTH SUMMIT MEETIN' (LP)	25
63	CBS 52165	BACK COUNTRY BLUES (LP)	25
64	Xtra XTRA 1004	BIG BILL BROONZY/SONNY TERRY/BROWNIE McGHEE (LP)	30
64	Vogue LAE 552	BROWNIE McGHEE AND SONNY TERRY (LP)	30
64	Realm RM 165	BACK COUNTRY BLUES (LP)	15
64	Stateside SL 10076	BLUES HOOT (LP, some tracks by Lightnin' Hopkins)	40
64	Fontana 688 006ZL	LIVIN' WITH THE BLUES (LP)	30
66	Philips BL 7675	AT THE BUNK HOUSE (LP)	20
66	Verve VLP 5010	GUITAR HIGHWAY (LP, mono)	20
66	Verve SVLP 5010	GUITAR HIGHWAY (LP, stereo)	25
66	Fontana TL 5289	HOMETOWN BLUES (LP)	20
69	Capitol T 20906	WHOOPIN' THE BLUES (LP)	20
69	Stateside SSL 10291	LONG WAY FROM HOME (LP)	15
70	Fontana SFJL 979	WHERE THE BLUES BEGAN (LP)	20
73	Mainstream MSL 1019	HOMETOWN BLUES (LP, gatefold sleeve)	15

(see also Brownie McGhee, Chris Barber, Pete Seeger, Big Bill Broonzy, Lightnin' Hopkins, Big Joe Turner)

SUSAN TERRY
62	Piccadilly 7N 35026	Along Came Love/Looking For A Boy	15

TERRY & JERRY
65	R&B MRB 5009	People Are Doing It Every Day/Mama Julie	22

TERRY SISTERS
57	Parlophone R 4364	It's The Same Old Jazz/Broken Promises	6
58	Parlophone R 4509	Sweet Thing (Tell Me That You Love Me)/You Forgot To Remember	6

TESCO BOMBERS
82	Y Y14	Hernando's Hideaway/Break The Ice At Parties/Girl From Ipanema (p/s)	10

(see also Homosexuals)

TEST DEPARTMENT
83	Some Bizzare TEST 112	Compulsion/Pulsations (12", p/s)	10
87	Some Bizzare 12MOP 13	Victory (12", p/s)	10
80s	Media City CMC 1	Gododdin (12", p/s, Welsh gig freebie with Brith Gof)	10
90	Mop MOP 5T	Jihad/(Desert Mix)/(Oil Mix) (12", p/s)	12
93	Mop MOP 8T	Bang On It/(Tao Systems Mix)/(TC Ruff House Remix) (12", die-cut p/s)	10
85	Test TEST 33	BEATING THE RETREAT (LP, box set)	18

TESTCARD F
83	Backs NCH 004	Bandwagon Tango/Unfamiliar Rooms (p/s)	10
83	Backs NCH 10	Third Stroke/If Only It Wasn't (p/s)	10

TETRACK
77	Hawkeye HE 006	Let's Get Started/PABLO EXPERIENCE: Go it	18
78	Greensleeves GRE 8	Only Jah Knows/ROCKERS ALL STARS: Jah Jah Dub	20
78	Rockers APD 2	Love And Unity/JAH LEVI & JAH BULL: Two The Hard Way/JUNIOR DAN: Jah Foundation (12")	45
89	Greensleeves GREL 121	LET'S GET STARTED (LP)	20

ALAN TEW ORCHESTRA
76	Epic EPC 4676	The Sweeney/The Prowler	15
67	Decca Phase 4 PFS 4120	THIS IS MY SCENE (LP)	40
72	CBS 64665	LET'S FLY (LP)	25

JOE TEX
65	Atlantic AT 4015	Hold What You've Got/Fresh Out Of Tears	22

TEXANS

MINT VALUE £

65	Atlantic AT 4021	You Better Get It/You Got What It Takes	20
65	Sue WI 370	Yum Yum Yum/You Little Baby Face Thing	40
65	Atlantic AT 4027	A Woman Can Change A Man/Don't Let Your Left Hand Know	15
65	Atlantic AT 4045	I Want To (Do Everything For You)/Funny Bone	15
65	Atlantic AT 4058	A Sweet Woman Like You/Close Your Door	15
66	Atlantic AT 4081	The Love You Save/If Sugar Was As Sweet As You	15
66	Atlantic 584 016	S.Y.S.L.J.F.M. (Letter Song)/I'm A Man	10
66	Atlantic 584 035	You Better Believe It/I Believe I'm Gonna Make It	25
67	Atlantic 584 068	Papa Was Too/The Truest Woman In The World	10
67	Atlantic 584 096	Hold What You've Got/A Sweet Woman Like You	10
67	Atlantic 584 102	Show Me/Woman Sees A Hard Time (When Her Man Is Gone)	15
67	Atlantic 584 119	Woman Like That, Yeah/I'm Going And Get It	10
67	Atlantic 584 144	Skinny Legs And All/Watch The One (That Brings The Bad News)	10
68	Atlantic 584 171	Men Are Getting Scarce/You're Gonna Thank Me Woman	10
68	Atlantic 584 212	Go Home And Do It/Keep The One You Got	10
69	Atlantic 584 296	We Can't Sit Down Now/It Ain't Sanitary	10
70	Atlantic 584 318	You're Alright Ray Charles/Everything Happens On Time	10
71	Mercury 6052 067	I Knew Him/Bad Feet	6
72	Mercury 6052 111	Give The Baby Anything/Takin' A Chance	6
72	Mercury 6052 129	I Got 'Cha/Mother Prayer	6
72	Mercury 6052 156	You Said A Bad Word/It Ain't Gonna Work Baby	6
03	Soul Food EAT SF001	I Wanna Be Free/Under Your Powerful Love	8
65	Atlantic ATL 5043	THE NEW BOSS (LP)	40
66	Atlantic ATL 587 009	THE LOVE YOU SAVE (LP)	35
67	Atlantic 587 053	I'VE GOT TO DO A LITTLE BETTER (LP)	25
67	Atlantic 587/588 059	THE NEW BOSS (LP, reissue)	15
67	London HA-U 8334	THE BEST OF JOE TEX (LP)	40
67	Atlantic 587/588 079	GREATEST HITS (LP)	15
68	Atlantic 587/588 104	LIVE AND LIVELY (LP)	25
68	Atlantic 587/588 118	SOUL COUNTRY (LP)	20
69	Atlantic 587/588 130	YOU BETTER GET IT (LP)	20
69	Atlantic 588 193	BUYING A BOOK (LP)	15
77	EPIC EPC 81931	BUMPS AND BRUISES (LP)	15

(see also Soul Clan)

TEXANS
| 64 | Columbia DB 7242 | Being With You/Wondrous Look Of Love | 6 |

TEXTONES
| 87 | Enigma 3268-1 | CEDAR CREEK (LP) | 18 |

TEXTOR SINGERS
| 54 | Capitol CL 14211 | Sobbin' Women/Remember Me | 10 |

RUDY THACKER & STRINGBEANS
| 62 | Starlite ST45 087 | The Ballad Of Johnny Horton/Tomorrow Is My Last Day | 10 |

JAKE THACKRAY
| 67 | Columbia SCX 6178 | LAST WILL AND TESTAMENT (LP) | 15 |

THAMESIDERS/DAVY GRAHAM
| 63 | Decca DFE 8538 | FROM A LONDON HOOTENANNY (EP, 2 tracks each) | 50 |

(see also Davy Graham)

THANES OF CAWDOR
| 87 | DDT DISPLP11 | THANES OF CAWDOR (LP) | 18 |

SISTER ROSETTA THARPE
60	MGM MGM 1072	If I Can Help Somebody/Take My Hand, Precious Lord	6
58	Brunswick OE 9284	GOSPEL SONGS No. 2 (EP)	12
57	Mercury MPL 6529	GOSPEL TRAIN (LP)	25
59	Brunswick LAT 8290	GOSPEL TRAIN (LP)	20
61	Mercury MMC 14057	THE GOSPEL TRUTH (LP)	20
63	Society SOC 900	HOT HOT HOT (LP)	15
65	Ember NR 5023	SPIRITUALS IN RHYTHM (LP)	20

(see also Little Richard)

THAT CORPORATE FEELING
| 84 | Platform SOUL XX1 | The Rain Has Gone/Industrial Backlash (die-cut Corporate Feeling sleeve) | 50 |

THATCHER ON ACID
| 88 | Rugger Bugger SEEP 1 | THATCHER ON ACID (LP) | 15 |

T.H.C. ROLLER
| 94 | Poor Person Prod. PPPR 4 | CHAPTER IN THE LIFE OF T.H.C. ROLLER (LP, handmade sleeve with insert & king-size rolling papers, numbered, 500 only) | 20 |
| 94 | Poor Person Prod. | THIS MUST BE THE JOINT (LP, 500 only) | 70 |

THEATRE OF HATE
80	S.S. SS 3	Original Sin/Legion (p/s)	10
81	Burning Rome BRR 1	Rebel Without A Brain/My Own Invention (p/s, mispress with 2 B-side labels)	8
81	Burning Rome BRR 1	Rebel Without A Brain/My Own Invention (p/s)	6
85	Bliss TOH 1EP	The Wake/Love Is A Ghost/Poppies/Legion (EP, 33rpm, with T-shirt in stickered pack, sealed)	10
82	Burning Rome TOH 1	WESTWORLD (LP)	15

(see also Pack, Spear Of Destiny, Cult, Crisis)

THEE
| 65 | Decca F 12163 | Each And Every Day/There You Go! | 40 |

THEE HEADCOATEES
| 92 | Damaged Goods DAMGOOD 4 | Davey Crockett (Gabba Hey)/Young Blood (p/s, yellow vinyl, 2000 only) | 12 |
| 97 | Vinyl Japan ASKLP 65 | BOSTIK HAZE (LP) | 15 |

THEE HEADCOATEES/THE HEADCOATS

MINT VALUE £

THEE HEADCOATEES/THE HEADCOATS
92	Damaged Goods DAMGOOD 1	Headcoat Girl/THEE HEADCOATS: Lakota Woman (p/s, different coloured sleeves & vinyl)	8
93	Twist TWIST 5	Strychnine/THEE HEADCOATS: Branded (p/s, different sleeve colours exist)	8
95	Damaged Goods DAMGOOD 63	Johnny Jack!/THEE HEADCOATS: Sufference Wharf (p/s)	6
98	Damaged Goods DAMGOOD 155	Jackie Chan Does Kung Fu/THEE HEADCOATS: The Rise And Fall Of A Double (p/s)	8

(see also Mickey & Ludella, Delmonas)

THEE HYPNOTICS
88	Hipsville HIP 1	Love In A Different Vein/All Night Long (p/s)	6
90	Situation 2 SITU 28	COME DOWN HEAVY (LP)	18

HANS THEESINK
80	Kettle KOP 7	LATE LAST NIGHT (LP)	25

THE FOR CARNATION
00	Domino WIGLP 77	THE FOR CARNATION (LP, insert)	80

BOB THEIL
82	Private (no cat. no.)	SO FAR (LP, private pressing)	250

LLANS THELWELL & HIS CELESTIALS
66	Island WI 262	Choo Choo Ska/Lonely Night (B-side vocal: Busty Brown)	60

THEM
64	Decca F 11973	Don't Start Crying Now/One Two Brown Eyes	80
64	Decca F 12018	Baby Please Don't Go/Gloria	12
65	Decca F 12094	Here Comes The Night/All For Myself	10
65	Decca F 12175	One More Time/How Long Baby?	10
65	Decca F 12215	(It Won't Hurt) Half As Much/I'm Gonna Dress In Black	10
65	Decca F 12281	Mystic Eyes/If You And I Could Be As Two	15
65	Decca F 12355	Call My Name/Bring 'Em On In	20
66	Decca F 12403	Richard Cory/Don't You Know?	20
67	Major Minor MM 509	Gloria/Friday's Child	20
67	Major Minor MM 513	The Story Of Them (Parts 1 & 2)	25
73	Deram DM 394	Gloria/Baby Please Don't Go (reissue)	8
65	Decca DFE 8612	THEM (EP, unboxed decca logo)	150
65	Decca DFE 8612	THEM (EP, export-only 'band-on-ladder' p/s)	500
65	Decca LK 4700	(THE ANGRY YOUNG) THEM (LP, original label, with flipback sleeve, 1st sleeve with only Tommy Scott credited as producer)	200
65	Decca LK 4700	(THE ANGRY YOUNG) THEM (LP, original label, with flipback sleeve, 2nd sleeve with Bert Berns and Dick Rowe added to production credits)	120
65	Parrot PA 61005	THEM (LP, mono, export only, UK pressed issue of 1st LP, in US sleeve)	150
66	Decca LK 4751	THEM AGAIN (LP, original label, with flipback sleeve)	200
66	Decca LK 4751	THEM AGAIN (LP, unboxed Decca labels, flipback sleeve)	150
69	Decca LK 4700	(THE ANGRY YOUNG) THEM (LP, re-pressing, red label, boxed Decca logo)	50
70	Decca LK 4751	THEM AGAIN (LP, re-pressing, red label, boxed Decca logo)	60
70	Decca PA 86	THE WORLD OF THEM (LP, original issue, mono)	25
70	Decca (S) PA 86	THE WORLD OF THEM (LP, original issue, stereo)	15
73	Deram DPM 3001/2	THEM - FEATURING VAN MORRISON LEAD SINGER (2-LP, gatefold sleeve)	25
78	Sonet SNTF 738	BELFAST GYPSIES (LP, features Them without Van Morrison)	25
76	Decca ROOTS 3	ROCK ROOTS (LP)	15

(see also Van Morrison, Trader Horne, Taste, Belfast Gypsies, Moses K. & Prophets, Peter Barden, Jackie McCauley)

THEME
82	Creed CR 001	Sacred/Conflict	6

JOHN THEMIS
83	Coda CODS 1	Goblins In Sherwood/Post Hypnotic Suggestions (p/s)	6

THE PURIST
16	Daupe! DM SP 011	ROSES ARE RED...SO IS BLOOD (10", red vinyl, p/s, with Westside Gunn, 100 only)	300
15	Daupe! DM SP 097	PYREX SCHOLAR (LP, clear vinyl)	80

THERAPY
72	CBS 69017	ALMANAC (LP, gatefold sleeve with inside centre opening)	25
73	Indigo IRS 5124	ONE NIGHT STAND (LP, private pressing)	15

THERAPY?
90	Multifuckingnational MFN 1	Meat Abstract/Punishment Kisses (p/s, labels on wrong sides, 1,000 only)	30
92	A&M (no cat. no.)	TEETHGRINDER (12", double pack, white labels in presentation pack)	30
92	A&M THX 1	Have A Merry Fucking Christmas: Teenage Kicks/With Or Without You (Xmas gig freebie)	18
92	Wiiija WIJ 11	PLEASURE DEATH (mini-LP, 10 white labels)	35
94	A&M 540196-1	TROUBLEGUM (LP, green vinyl)	50
95	A&M 540379-1	INFERNAL LOVE (LP, red vinyl)	30
98	A&M 582548-7	SEMI-DETATCHED (LP, as 6 x 7" box set)	30

THERMOMETERS
80	Fokker FEP 100	20th Century Girl/Newtown Refugees/Stole Your Drugs (in oversized p/s)	30
80	Fokker FEP 100	20th Century Girl/Newtown Refugees/Stole Your Drugs (p/s)	20

THESE IMMORTAL SOULS
87	Mute STUMM 48	GET LOST (DON'T LIE) (LP)	20
92	Mute STUMM 98	I'M NEVER GONNA DIE AGAIN (LP)	30

(see also the Birthday Party)

THE THE
80	4AD AD 10	Controversial Subject/Black And White (p/s)	30
81	Some Bizzare BZS 4	Cold Spell Ahead/Hot Ice (p/s)	25
86	Epic TRUTH Q3	Infected/Infected (Energy Mix)/Disturbed (12", uncensored 'wank' p/s)	15
82	private cassette	PORNOGRAPHY OF DESPAIR (LP, unreleased, cassettes exist)	0
83	Epic EPC 25525	SOUL MINING (LP, with inner sleeve, initially with 12" single Perfect/"Soup Of Mixed Emotions"/"Fruit Of The Heart")	75

Rare Record Price Guide 2024

THEY MUST BE RUSSIANS

MINT VALUE £

86	Epic EPC 26770	INFECTED (LP, with poster & inner, 1st 25,000 with 'torture' sleeve)	20
86	Epic EPC 26770	INFECTED (LP, with poster & inner)	15
89	Epic 463319 1	MIND BOMB (LP)	20
93	Epic 472468-1	DUSK (LP)	150
94	Epic 4781390	HANKY PANKY (LP as 2 x 10")	35

(see also Matt Johnson, Gadgets)

THEY MUST BE RUSSIANS

79	Gramme/Lyntone LYN 6526/27	Psycho Analysis/JOE 9T AND THE THUNDERBIRDS: Psycho Analysis (p/s, stamped white label)	15
79	RVS 001	THEY MUST BE RUSSIANS 4-TRACK EP (p/s)	15
80	Fresh FRESH 18	Don't Try To Cure Yourself/The Truth About Kanga Pants/Air To Breathe (p/s)	8
80	No label	Nagasaki's Children/Nellie The Elephant/Circus/I Want To Hold You Now (mail-order only, p/s with poster insert)	10
83	First Floor FF2	THEY MUST BE RUSSIANS (LP)	15

(see also Joe 9T & Thunderbirds)

MOR THIAM
| 16 | Jazzman JMANLP 091 | DINI SAFARRAR (DRUMS OF FIRE) (LP, reissue, numbered, download card) | 35 |

THICK AS THIEVES
| 01 | Noid NOIDLP 004 | THICK AS THIEVES (2-LP) | 20 |

THICK PIGEON
| 84 | Factory FACT 85 | TOO CRAZY COWBOYS (LP) | 40 |

THIEVES LIKE US
| 80 | Earlobe ELS 1 | Mind Made/Strike Out (p/s) | 8 |

THIN END OF THE WEDGE
| 81 | Jungle JR 051S | Lights Are On Green/I'm Not Dead Yet (in p/s) | 30 |
| 81 | Jungle JR 051S | Lights Are On Green/I'm Not Dead Yet | 12 |

(see also Damascus)

FRODE THINGNAES QUINTET
| 78 | BBC AIR 800037 | SOAPY CROW (LP) | 35 |

THINGS
| 80 | Imperial IP 4301 | Pieces Of You/Lost Love (p/s) | 10 |

(see also Buzzcocks)

THINGS FALL APART
| 72 | President PT378 | Bye Bye My Rose/Manna | 20 |

THINGS TO COME
| 72 | Regal Zonophone RZ 3058 | Buildin' Me Up/Ain't Love Good | 8 |

THIN ICE
| 88 | Blag It SJP 858 | Freedom Road (p/s) | 40 |

THIN LIZZY
SINGLES
70	Parlophone DIP 513	The Farmer/I Need You (Irish only, as Thin Lizzie)	1000
71	Decca F 13208	NEW DAY (EP, 33rpm, gatefold p/s)	300
71	Decca F 13208	NEW DAY (EP, 33rpm, without p/s)	100
72	Decca F 13355	Whiskey In The Jar/Black Boys On The Corner	8
72	Decca F 13355	Whiskey In The Jar/Black Boys On The Corner (demos in p/s)	30
73	Decca F 13402	Randolph's Tango/Broken Dreams (2 versions of A-side: matrices ZDR 53384 & ZCPDR 53312)	15
74	Decca F 13507	Little Darlin'/Buffalo Gal	8
74	Vertigo 6059 111	Philomena/Sha La La	8
75	Vertigo 6059 124	Rosalie/Halfcaste	6
75	Vertigo 6059 129	Wild One/For Those Who Love To Die	8
76	Vertigo 6059 150	Jailbreak/Running Back	25
77	Vertigo 6059 177	Dancing In The Moonlight/Bad Reputation (p/s)	10
78	Decca F 13748	Whiskey In The Jar/Vagabond Of The Western World/Sitamoia (p/s)	8
79	Vertigo LIZZY 3	Waiting For An Alibi/With Love (p/s, with cartoon lyric sheet)	8
70s	Vertigo DJ 016	It's Only Money/JANNE SCHAFFER: Dr Abraham (promo only, no p/s)	200
82	Vertigo LIZZY 10	Hollywood (Down On Your Luck) (10", p/s, 1-sided, existence unconfirmed)	0

ALBUMS
71	Decca SKL 5082	THIN LIZZY (dark blue/silver label, early copies with laminated sleeve)	100
71	Decca SKL 5082	THIN LIZZY (dark blue/silver label, later pressing with matt sleeve)	35
72	Decca TXS 108	SHADES OF A BLUE ORPHANAGE (1st pressing, gatefold sleeve, green label)	75
72	Decca TXLS 108	SHADES OF A BLUE ORPHANAGE (2nd pressing, gatefold sleeve, blue label)	60
73	Decca SKL 5170	VAGABONDS OF THE WESTERN WORLD (dark blue/silver label, with lyric insert)	40
73	Decca SKL 5170	VAGABONDS OF THE WESTERN WORLD (dark blue/silver label, without insert)	20
74	Vertigo 6360 116	NIGHT LIFE (LP, 'spaceship' label)	15
75	Vertigo 6360 121	FIGHTING (LP, 'spaceship' label)	15
76	Vertigo 9102 008	JAILBREAK (LP, die-cut sleeve, 'spaceship' label)	30
76	Vertigo 9102 012	JOHNNY THE FOX (LP, inner sleeve, 'spaceship' label)	15
78	Vertigo 9199 645	LIVE & DANGEROUS (2-LP, inners)	25
83	Vertigo VERL 3	THUNDER AND LIGHTNING (with free 12")	18
92	Windsong WINLP024	BBC RADIO 1 LIVE IN CONCERT (2-LP emerald green vinyl)	70

(see also Phil Lynott, Wild Horses, Phenomena, Eric Bell Band, Greedies, John Sykes, Gary Moore)

THIN YOGHURTS
| 80 | Lowther Street Runner YOG 1 | Girl On The Bus/Drink Problem (p/s) | 25 |

THIRD & FOURTH GENERATION
| 72 | Punch PH 91 | Rudies Medley (actually by Peter Tosh & Soulmates)/Rude Boy - Version | 10 |

(see also Peter Tosh)

3RD ARMY
| 81 | No 2 | March Of 10,000 Soldiers/All Set To Go (no p/s) | 25 |

THIRD DIMENSION

			MINT VALUE £
81	Elite DAZZ 10	March Of 10,000 Soldiers (All Set To Go)/Step One (12")	50
81	Elite DAZZ 09	Step One/POWERLINE: Watching You (12")	80

THIRD DIMENSION
| 70 | Unity UN 566 | Peace And Love/Peace And Love - Version | 6 |

THIRD EAR BAND
69	Harvest SHVL 756	ALCHEMY (LP, with "Sold in U.K…" label text on 4 lines)	125
69	Harvest SHVL 756	ALCHEMY (LP, later pressing without "Sold in U.K…" label text)	50
70	Harvest SHSP 773	THIRD EAR BAND: ELEMENTS (LP, no EMI logo on label)	60
72	Harvest SHSP 4019	MUSIC FROM MACBETH (LP, EMI logo on label)	50
76	Harvest SHSM 2007	EXPERIENCES (LP)	20
82	GI WAX 2	ALCHEMY (LP, reissue, single sleeve)	18
88	Dropout DO 1999	ALCHEMY (LP, reissue)	15
90	BGO BGOLP 89	THIRD EAR BAND (LP, reissue)	18
90	Beat Goes On BGOLP 61	MUSIC FROM MACBETH (LP, reissue)	15

(see also High Tide, Sounds Nice)

THIRD EYE BAND
| 82 | Scarlet Quest 01 | Pass Myself/May The Circle Remain Unbroken (p/s) | 80 |

THIRD MEN
| 79 | SCHOOL 1 | You're So Fashionable/The Robot Age (p/s) | 20 |

THIRD QUADRANT
| 82 | Rock Cottage (no cat. no.) | SEEING YOURSELF AS YOU REALLY ARE (LP, private pressing, wraparound sleeve with handwritten insert, blank white label) | 40 |

3RD RAIL
| 92 | Delirious DELIS 5 | Look No Further/123 Break/Stand By For Fast Beats/Drop (KZ1 Remix) (12") | 40 |

THIRD RAIL
| 67 | Columbia DB 8274 | Run, Run, Run/No Return | 30 |

THIRD WORLD
| 71 | CBS 7182 | Miracles/Baby Boeing | 6 |

THIRD WORLD ALL STARS
| 75 | Third World TWLP 103 | REBEL ROCK (LP) | 25 |

THIRD WORLD WAR
71	Fly BUG 7	Ascension Day/Teddy Teeth Goes Sailing (p/s)	8
71	Fly BUG 11	A Little Bit Of Urban Rock/Working Class Man	6
71	Fly FLY 4	THIRD WORLD WAR (LP, with lyric insert)	80
71	Fly FLY 4	THIRD WORLD WAR (LP, without lyric insert)	50
72	Track 2406 108	THIRD WORLD WAR II (LP)	80

(see also Terry Stamp)

THIRD GUITAR
| 05 | Funk 45 FUNK45 025 | Baby Don't Cry/SOUL PLEASERS: Baby Don't Cry (reissue) | 25 |

THIRD TIME AROUND
| 74 | Contemp CS 2076 | Soon Everything Is Going To Be Alright (Inst.)/(Vocal) | 6 |

13 AMP
| 75 | Power Exchange PX 114 | Need A Woman/Can You Feel The Music | 15 |

THIRTEEN AT MIDNIGHT
| 82 | Pure PURE 1 | Other Passengers/Other Passengers (p/s) | 12 |

THIRTEEN SENSES
| 02 | Private Pressing | NO OTHER LIFE IS ATTRACTIVE EP (CD) | 35 |
| 04 | Vertigo 981633-4 | Thru The Glass/No Other Life Is Attractive (1,500 only p/s) | 8 |

13TH CHIME
81	Ellie Jay Records EJSP 9700	Cuts Of Love/Coffin Maker (foldout p/s)	50
82	13th Chime THC 1	Cursed/Dug Up (p/s)	40
82	13th Chime THC 2	Fire/Hide And Seek/Sally Ditch (p/s, 1,000 only)	25

13TH FLOOR
| 17 | Blue Candle BL 55056 | 13TH FLOOR (LP, reissue) | 15 |

13TH FLOOR ELEVATORS
78	Radar SAM 88	She Lives (In A Time Of Her Own)/RED CRAYOLA: Pink Stainless Tail (promo)	15
78	Radar ADA 13	You're Gonna Miss Me/Tried To Hide (green vinyl)	10
78	Radar RAD 13	THE PSYCHEDELIC SOUNDS OF … (LP)	30
79	Radar RAD 15	EASTER EVERYWHERE (LP)	30
89	Decal LIK 28	EASTER EVERYWHERE (LP, reissue)	20
88	Decal LIK 19	THE PSYCHEDELIC SOUNDS OF… (LP, reissue)	30
92	Xgarely/Decal LIKP 003	THE PSYCHEDELIC SOUNDS OF… (LP, picture disc)	15
92	Decal LIKP002	LIVE (LP, picture disc with poster)	15
01	Get Back GET 594	EASTER EVERYWHERE (LP, reissue)	20
11	Charly 113L	BULL OF THE WOODS (2-LP, reissue, gatefold)	20
11	International/Charly IA16	MUSIC OF THE SPHERES (Box set, 8-LP, 1 10" EP, booklet, 3-D prints)	200

(see also Roky Erickson, Red Crayola)

13TH HOUR
| 81 | Time And Motion SMT 2009 | Stereo Smiles/Inner Stu | 20 |

38 SPESH
19	Daupe! DM SP 050	A BULLET FOR EVERY HEATHEN (LP, with Big Ghost Ltd, 230 copies)	40
19	Daupe! DM SP 050	A BULLET FOR EVERY HEATHEN (LP, with Big Ghost Ltd, red vinyl, 200 copies)	40
19	Daupe! DM SP 050	A BULLET FOR EVERY HEATHEN (LP, with Big Ghost Ltd, white vinyl, 200 copies)	40
19	Daupe! DM SP 050	A BULLET FOR EVERY HEATHEN (LP, with Big Ghost Ltd, splatter vinyl, 100 copies)	60
19	Daupe! DM SP 050	A BULLET FOR EVERY HEATHEN (LP, with Big Ghost Ltd, with obi strip, 20 copies)	150

(see also El Camino)

31ST OF FEBRUARY
| 69 | Vanguard (S)VRL 19045 | THE 31ST OF FEBRUARY (LP) | 90 |

39 CLOCKS
| 83 | Flicknife SHARP 109 | BLADES IN YOUR MASQUERADE (LP) | 15 |

32nd TURN-OFF

MINT VALUE £

32ND TURN-OFF
69   Jay Boy JSL 1   32ND TURN OFF (LP, textured sleeve, brown/black label) 150
(see also Equals)

30 SECONDS TO MARS
07   Virgin 00946354474 77   The Kill/Attack (live) (picture disc, PVC stickered sleeve) 15
08   Virgin VUS 340   From Yesterday (red vinyl, 1-side etched) 15

THIS DRIFTIN'S GOTTA STOP
75   private pressing   THIS DRIFTIN'S GOTTA STOP (LP) 30

THIS ETERNAL WAITING
86   I Live In Hell BURN 2   The Prize/Love And Live Tombs 20

THIS HEAT
80   Piano THIS 1201   Health And Efficiency/Graphic/Varispeed (12", p/s with insert) 25
79   Piano THIS 1   THIS HEAT (LP) 60
81   Rough Trade ROUGH 26   DECEIT (LP, 1st pressing) 45
88   These HEAT 1   THIS HEAT (reissue) 30
88   These HEAT 1   DECEIT (reissue) 30
98   These 12/6   REPEAT/HEALTH AND EFFICIENCY (2 x 12") 20
99   These HEAT 10   MADE AVAILABLE: PEEL SESSIONS (LP) 50
06   This Is LC 02677   OUT OF COLD STORAGE (6-CD box set) 40
(see also Gareth Williams, Charles Hayward, Camberwell Now)

THIS KIND
67   MJB SP 112   Dirty City/I've Got It 200

THIS MORTAL COIL
83   4AD AD 310   Song To The Siren/16 Days (Reprise) (p/s) 8
83   4AD BAD 310   16 Days/Gathering Dust/Song To The Siren/16 Days (reprise) (12", p/s) 15
84   4AD AD 410   Kangaroo/It'll End In Tears (p/s, 2 different designs & label colours, 2,500 of each) 8
86   4AD BAD 608   Come Here My Love/Drugs (10", p/s with inner sleeve) 10
84   4AD CAD 411   IT'LL END IN TEARS (LP, inners) 20
86   4AD DAD 609   FILIGREE AND SHADOW (2-LP, inners) 25
91   4AD DAD 1005   BLOOD (2-LP, with inners) 35
(see also Cocteau Twins, Modern English, Cindytalk)

THIS 'N' THAT
66   Mercury MF 938   Someday/Loving You 20
67   Strike JH 310   Get Down With It/I Care About You 10
(see also Cleo)

THIS PERFECT DAY
83   No Friction NFR 001   The Garden/The Time Of Your Life 80

MABI THOBEJANE
97   M.E.L.T. 2000 BWLP096   MADIBA (LP) 15

B.J. THOMAS
66   Hickory 45-1395   Never Tell/Billy & Sue 15
66   Pye International 7N 25374   Mama/Wendy 10
69   Wand WN 1   Raindrops Keep Falling On My Head/Never Had It So Good 6

CARLA THOMAS
61   London HLK 9310   Gee Whiz/For You 20
61   London HLK 9359   A Love Of My Own/Promises 15
62   London HLK 9618   I'll Bring It On Home To You/I Can't Take It 15
64   Atlantic AT 4005   I've Got No Time To Lose/A Boy Named Tom 18
66   Atlantic AT 4074   Comfort Me/I'm For You 12
66   Atlantic 584 011   Let Me Be Good To You/Another Night Without My Man 10
66   Atlantic 584 042   B-A-B-Y/What Have You Got To Offer Me 10
67   Stax 601 002   Something Good (Is Going To Happen To You)/It's Starting To Grow 10
67   Stax 601 008   When Tomorrow Comes/Unchanging Love (dark blue label) 15
67   Stax 601 008   When Tomorrow Comes/Unchanging Love (later light blue label) 8
68   Stax 601 032   Pick Up The Pieces/Separation 10
68   Stax STAX 103   Where Do I Go/I've Fallen In Love 8
69   Stax STAX 112   I Like What You're Doing To Me/Strung Out 8
69   Stax STAX 131   Unyielding/I've Fallen In Love 6
72   Stax 2025 082   Love Means/You've Got A Cushion To Fall On 6
91   Kent 6T 7   I'll Never Stop Loving/Prophets Band/Peaches Baby 60
91   Horace's HRH 007   I'll Never Stop Loving You/BARBARA LEWIS: The Stars 40
67   Stax 589 004   CARLA THOMAS (LP) 35
67   Stax 589 012   THE QUEEN ALONE (LP) 20
69   Stax SXATS 1019   MEMPHIS QUEEN (LP) 40
71   Stax 2362 023   LOVE MEANS ...(LP) 20
(see also Otis Redding & Carla Thomas)

CHARLIE THOMAS (& DRIFTERS)
75   EMI International INT 506   I'm Gonna Take You Home/Run, Run, Roadrunner 8
76   EMI Int. 520   A Midsummer Night In Harlem/Lonely Drifter Don't Cry 10

CLAUDETTE THOMAS
68   Caltone TONE 116   Roses Are Red My Love/YVONNE HARRISON: Near To You 80

CREEPY JOHN THOMAS
69   RCA RCA 1912   Ride A Rainbow/Moon And Eyes Song 15
69   RCA SF 8061   CREEPY JOHN THOMAS (LP, laminated front sleeve) 300
(see also Paul Kossoff, Edgar Broughton Band)

DON THOMAS
76   DJM DJS 670   Come On Train Parts 1 & 2 (Promos in p/s) 20
76   DJM DJS 10670   Come On Train Parts 1 & 2 (second pressing) 10

GENE THOMAS
64   United Artists UP 1047   Baby's Gone/Stand By Love 20

Hersal THOMAS

MINT VALUE £

HERSAL THOMAS
50	Parlophone R 3261	Suitcase Blues/Hersal Blues (78)	35

IRMA THOMAS
64	Liberty LIB 66013	Breakaway/Wish Someone Would Care	25
64	Liberty LIB 66041	Anyone Who Knows What Love Is (Will Understand)/Time Is On My Side	20
65	Liberty LIB 66080	He's My Guy/True True Love	20
65	Liberty LIB 66095	Some Things You Never Get Used To/You Don't Miss A Good Thing (Until It's Gone)	20
65	Sue WI 372	Don't Mess With My Man/Set Me Free	40
65	Liberty LIB 66106	I'm Gonna Cry Till My Tears Run Dry/ Nobody Wants To Hear Nobody's Troubles	20
66	Liberty LIB 66137	Take A Look/What Are You Trying To Do	75
66	Liberty LIB 66137	Take A Look/What Are You Trying To Do (DJ copy)	125
66	Liberty LIB 66178	It's A Man's-Woman's World	20
72	Atlantic K 10167	Full Time Woman/She's Taking My Part	6
72	United Artists UP 35284	Time Is On My Side/Anyone Who Knows What Love Is (Will Understand) (reissue)	8
65	Liberty LEP 4035	TIME IS ON MY SIDE (EP)	100
68	Minit MLL/MLS 40004E	TAKE A LOOK (LP)	75
76	Island HELP 29	LIVE (LP)	15
81	Charly CRB 1020	IN BETWEEN TEARS (LP, reissue, different cover from US original)	15
83	Kent 010	TIME IS ON MY SIDE (LP)	15
19	Reel RMLP 4579LE	IN BETWEEN TEARS (LP, reissue, 500 only, white vinyl)	15

JAMES 'CREOLE' THOMAS
18	22a 021	OMAS SEXTET (LP)	40

JAMO THOMAS & HIS PARTY BROTHERS ORCHESTRA
66	Polydor BM 56709	I Spy (For The FBI)/Snake Hip Mama	15
69	Polydor 56755	I Spy (For The FBI)/Snake Hip Mama (reissue)	8
69	Chess CRS 8098	I'll Be Your Fool/Jamo Soul	20
71	Mojo 2092 013	I Spy (For The FBI)/Snake Hip Mama (2nd reissue)	8

JIMMY THOMAS
69	Parlophone R 5773	The Beautiful Night/Above A Whisper (withdrawn)	300
69	Parlophone R 5773	The Beautiful Night/Above A Whisper (withdrawn; DJ copy)	250
69	Spark SRL1035	(We Ain't Looking For) No Trouble/Springtime	200
70	Spark SRL 1040	White Dove/You Don't Have To Say Goodbye	12
72	Jay Boy BOY 67	Where There's A Will/Just Tryin' To Please You	6
75	20th Century BTC 1002	Beautiful Night/I Can't Live My Life Without You	6
81	Osceola OSC 1	Hang Right On In There Part 1/Driving Wheel (12. p/s)	20
73	Contempo COLP 1002	ABYSS (LP)	25

JOE THOMAS
72	People PLE 015	JOY OF COOKIN' (LP)	15

KID THOMAS/EMANUEL BAND
64	'77' LA 12/26	VICTORY WALK (LP, with Barry Martyn's Band)	30

LEON THOMAS
73	Philips 6369 417	BLUES & SOULFUL TRUTH (LP)	30

NICKY THOMAS
70	Amalgamated AMG 863	Danzella/JOE GIBBS ALLSTARS: Kingstonians Reggae	25
70	Trojan TR 7750	Love Of The Common People/DESTROYERS: Compass	15
70	Trojan TR 7796	God Bless The Children/Red Eye	12
71	Trojan TR 7807	If I Had A Hammer/Lonely Feelin'	10
71	Trojan TR 7830	Tell It Like It Is/B.B.C.	10
70	Trojan TBL 143	LOVE OF THE COMMON PEOPLE (LP)	20
72	Trojan TRLS 25	TELL IT LIKE IT IS (LP)	25

(see also Joe Gibbs)

PAT THOMAS (1)
62	MGM 1194	Home In The Meadow/Where There's Love There's Hope	6
62	MGM 1234	Stranger On The Shore/C'est Si Bon	6

PAT THOMAS (2)
80	Pan African PAR 003	1980 (LP)	70
80	Pan African PAR 006	SWEETER THAN HONEY, CALYPSO MAHUNO AND HIGH LIFE CELEBRATION (LP, with Ebo Taylor)	100
80	Nakasi NAK 004	MPAEBO (LP)	100
84	Earthworks/Rough Trade ERT 1001	IN ACTION VOLUME 2 (LP, reissue)	15
85	Jap JAP 0101	ASANTEMAN (LP)	20

PETER THOMAS SOUND ORCHESTRA
68	Poydor 184171	ORGANIC (LP)	35
70	Polydor 2418 074	CHARIOTS OF THE GODS (LP)	35

ROD THOMAS
72	Fly BUG 19	Timothy Jones/Arthur Smith	7

RUDDY THOMAS
78	Lightning LIG 526	Loving Pauper/TRINITY: Judgement Time	8
79	DEB DEB 015	Dry Up Your Tears/Rat Trap (12")	25
80s	Shuttle SH 005	Bless You/The Right Time (12")	15

RUDY THOMAS
83	Mobiliser MMLP 34	VERY BEST OF (LP)	15

RUFUS THOMAS
63	London HLK 9799	Walking The Dog/Fine And Mellow	25
64	London HLK 9850	Can Your Monkey Do The Dog/I Want To Get Married	15
64	London HLK 9884	Somebody Stole My Dog/I Want To Be Loved	15
64	Atlantic AT 4009	Jump Back/All Night Worker	18
66	Atlantic 584 029	Willy Nilly/Sho' Gonna Mess Him Up	12
67	Atlantic 584 089	Jump Back/Walking The Dog	10

Sybil THOMAS

MINT VALUE £

67	Stax 601 013	Greasy Spoon/Sophisticated Sissy	8
68	Stax 601 028	Down Ta My House/Steady Holding On	8
68	Stax 601 037	The Memphis Train/I Think I Made A Boo-Boo	15
68	Stax STAX 105	Funky Mississippi/So Hard To Get Along With	6
70	Stax STAX 144	Do The Funky Chicken/Turn Your Damper Down	8
71	Stax 2025 060	The Breakdown (Parts 1 & 2)	6
71	Stax 2025 080	Do The Funky Penguin (Parts 1 & 2)	6
64	Atlantic AET 6001	DO THE DOG (EP)	50
65	Atlantic AET 6011	JUMP BACK WITH RUFUS (EP)	50
64	London HA-K 8183	WALKING THE DOG (LP)	80
70	Stax SXATS 1033	FUNKY CHICKEN (LP)	35
71	Stax 2363 001	FUNKY CHICKEN (LP, reissue)	15
71	Stax 2362 010	DOING THE PUSH AND PULL LIVE AT P.J.'s (LP)	25
72	Stax 2362 028	DID YOU HEAR ME? (LP)	25
74	Stax STX 1004	CROWN PRINCE OF DANCE (LP)	30
02	Stax SX2 135	THE FUNKIEST MAN (2-LP)	20

SYBIL THOMAS

83	West End WEND 124	Rescue Me (Vocal)/(Instrumental) (12")	10
83	West End WEND 4	Recue Me (Vocal)/(Instrumental)	8

TERRY-THOMAS ESQUIRE

56	Decca F 10804	A Sweet Old Fashioned Boy (with Rock 'N' Roll Rotters)/Lay Down Your Arms	12
61	Decca LK 4398	STRICTLY T-T (LP)	40

TIM THOMAS

66	Polydor BM 56052	Walking/Fever	8
71	Decca F13235	Silver Morning/Gravy Train	10

TIMMY THOMAS

73	Mojo 2956 002	WHY CAN'T WE LIVE TOGETHER (LP)	20

VAUGHAN THOMAS

70	Page One POF 167	Need You Girl/Come Together	12
70	Page One POF 178	Is This What I Get For Loving You Baby/Since You've Been Mine	10
71	DJM DJS 238	I Wanna Be Famous Like My Dad/Love	15
72	Jam JAM 9	Gotta Be You, Gotta Be Me/Woman	6
72	Jam JAM 26	Giant/Good Old Sam	6
72	Jam JAL 101	VAUGHAN THOMAS (LP, textured sleeve, white/red/black label)	40

WAYNE THOMAS

67	Coral Q 72491	I've Never Known A Lady/My Life's Gonna Change	6

ANDREAS THOMOPOULOS

70	Mushroom 100 MR 1	SONGS OF THE STREET (LP)	80
71	Mushroom 150 MR 4	BORN OUT OF THE TEARS OF THE SUN (LP)	90

(see also Secondhand)

BOBBY THOMPSON

69	Columbia Blue Beat DB 113	That's How Strong My Love Is/Trouble In Town	15
69	Jolly JY 001	That's How Strong My Love Is/Trouble In The Town	50

(see also Dandy)

CARROLL THOMPSON

83	Carousel 7CA	Honis I Do/Give Me A Chance	6
81	Carib Gems CGLP 15	HOPELESSLY IN LOVE (LP)	25
93	Ariwa ARILP 077	THE OTHER SIDE OF LOVE (LP)	15

CHERYLE THOMPSON

64	Stateside SS 291	Teardrops/Black Night	30

CHRIS THOMPSON

73	Village Thing VTS 21	CHRIS THOMPSON (LP, allegedly 101 sold and 899 destroyed, 'Shorewood Packaging Ltd.' printer credit)	250

COLIN THOMPSON

80	Fellside FE 021	THREE KNIGHTS (LP)	15

DONNEY THOMPSON

79	Third World TWDIS 20	Rocking Time/PAGET KING: Close Encounter (12")	60

EDDIE THOMPSON

55	Jazz Today JTE 101	THE FABULOUS EDDIE THOMPSON (EP)	60
57	Nixa NJE 1030	PIANO MOODS VOLUME 6 (EP)	60
60	Ember EMB 3303	PIANO MOODS (LP)	100
60	Tempo TAP 24	HIS MASTER'S JAZZ (LP)	250
69	77 LEU 12/39	BY MYSELF (LP)	40

EVERAND THOMPSON

78	Ultra PFU 1005	Babylon Hustle Me/Babylon Version	75

HANK THOMPSON (& BRAZOS VALLEY BOYS)

60	Capitol CL 15114	A Six Pack To Go/What Made Her Change	10

JACKIE THOMPSON

69	Direction 58-4521	Bad Women A Dime A Dozen/Games People Play	6

JOHNNY THOMPSON & ONE-EYED JACKS

65	Ember EMB S 206	For Us There'll Be No Tomorrow/Soul Chant (in p/s)	20
65	Ember EMB S 206	For Us There'll Be No Tomorrow/Soul Chant	6

KAY THOMPSON

56	London HLA 8268	Eloise/Just One Of Those Things	40

LEROY THOMPSON

78	Noel DN 005	Hard Times Criminal Times/Since You Left Me & Gone (12")	30

LINCOLN THOMPSON

80	God Sent GDIS 1	One Common Need/Food Clothing And Shelter (12", with the Rasses)	60

LINVAL THOMPSON

75	Ackee ACK 541	Kung Fu (Vocal)/Kung Fu (Instrumental)	10

Lucky THOMPSON

MINT VALUE £

Year	Label & Cat#	Title	Value
75	Action ACT 103	Natty Dread Girl/AGGROVATORS: Natty Dread Girl (Version)	10
75	Attack ATT 8101	Don't Cut Off Your Dreadlocks/KING TUBBYS: Version	10
75	Faith FA 010	Girl You Got To Run/Run Come Feel	8
75	Faith FA 018	Jah Redder Than Red/Version	8
78	Attack ATT 8135	I Love Marijuana/Jamaican Calley (Version)	15
78	Star PTP 1007	If I Follow My Heart/THOMPSON ALL STARS: Rocking version (12")	20
79	Burning Rockers BRD 003	Follow My Heart/THOMPSON ALL STARS: Rockers Version (12")	20
79	Burning Sounds BSD 023	Rocking Vibration/Natty Dread (12')	20
79	Burning Sounds BSD 031	Bound To Surrender/Dub Version (12")	20
79	Greensleeves GRED 12	I Never Run I Never Hide/REVOLUTIONARIES: Natty Dread Style (12")	12
79	GG's GG 056	Mad Dog (with Ranking Trevor)/REVOLUTIONARIES: Kevin At The Controls (12")	30
79	Greensleeves GRED 024	One More Chance/Long Time Me Na Rub You In A Dance (12", with Trinity)	20
79	D-Roy DRDD 16	She Is Mad At Me/Stop Your War (12")	30
80	Attack TACK 19	Here With Me/ROOTS RADICS BAND: Come On Baby Dub Style (12")	15
80	Attack TACK 22	Pop No Style/SCIENTIST: Second Hand Girl (12")	20
80	Black Joy DH 804	Brown Skin Girl/RANKING TREVOR: Brown Skin Girl Rub A Dub (12")	15
80	Strong Like Sampson SLSD 04	Mr Boss Man (with Trevor Ranking)/BARNABOUS: Stop Push Me Around (12")	20
80	Strong Like Sampson SLSD 016	Curfew/PAPPA TULLO: Morning Curfew (12")	20
80	Strong Like... SLSD 012	I'm Sorry/My Little Honey (12")	10
81	Cha Cha CHAD 29	Gambler/Everyday Rain (with WAYNE WADE, 12", blue vinyl)	20
82	A1 A1 004	Poor People (with U Brown)/Reggae Dub (12")	12
84	M&M MM06	Back To Africa/Jungle Man Skank	8
76	Third World TWLP 010	DON'T CUT OFF YOUR DREADLOCKS (LP)	30
78	Trojan TRLS 151	I LOVE MARIJUANA (LP)	35
78	Burning Sounds BSD 1014	LOVE IS THE QUESTION (LP)	25
78	Burning Sounds BS 1027	ROCKING VIBRATION (LP)	40
79	Burning Sounds BS 1035	I LOVE JAH (LP)	35
79	Trojan TRLS 153	NEGREA LOVE DUB (LP)	25
80	Burning Rockers BR 1006LP	FOLLOW MY HEART (LP)	30
82	Greensleeves GREL 33	LOOK HOW ME SEXY (LP)	18
83	Greensleeves GREL 51	BABY FATHER (LP)	18
94	Trojan TRLS 153	NEGREA LOVE DUB (LP, reissue)	18
96	Trojan TRLS 151	I LOVE MARIJUANA (LP, reissue)	15
00	Blood & Fire SVLP 294	RIDE ON DREADLOCKS (2-LP)	25

(see also Bunny Lion)

LUCKY THOMPSON
| 56 | Vogue V 2388 | But Not For Me/East Of The Sun | 10 |

MIKE THOMPSON JNR.
| 67 | Island WI 3090 | Rocksteady Wedding/Flower Pot Bloomers (both with Lyn Taitt & Jets) | 25 |

MOLLIE THOMPSON
| 66 | Asteroid JH 101 | SONG NOTES SINGS FROM WORLDS AFAR (LP, private pressing) | 40 |

OWEN THOMPSON
| 72 | Camel CA 103 | Must I Be Blue/Version | 8 |

PETER THOMPSON & NTH DEGREE
| 65 | Fontana TF 656 | For Me It's All Over/The Way You Used To Do | 20 |

RICHARD THOMPSON
72	Island ILPS 9197	HENRY THE HUMAN FLY (LP, 'pink rim palm tree' label)	25
83	Hannibal HNBL 1313	HAND OF KINDNESS (LP)	15
84	Hannibal HNBL 1316	SMALL TOWN ROMANCE (LP)	15
91	Capitol 0547957131	RUMOR AND SIGH (LP)	40
93	Capitol 07777 81492 1 7	MIRROR BLUE (LP)	80
03	Diverse DIV 004DLP	THE OLD KIT BAG (2-LP)	40
05	Diverse DIV009LP	FRONT PARLOUR BALLADS (LP)	35
07	Diverse DIV011DLP	SWEET WARRIOR (2-LP)	60
10	Proper PRPLP064	DREAM ATTIC (2-LP)	25

RICHARD & LINDA THOMPSON
73	Island ILPS 9266	I WANT TO SEE THE BRIGHT LIGHTS TONIGHT (LP, palm tree pink rim label)	35
74	Island ILPS 9305	HOKEY POKEY (LP, blue rim palm tree label with lyric inner sleeve)	25
75	Island ILPS 9348	POUR DOWN LIKE SILVER (LP, 'palm tree' label with lyrics)	20
75	Island	OFFICIAL LIVE TOUR 1975 (LP, unreleased, test pressings may exist)	100
76	Island ILPS 9266	I WANT TO SEE THE BRIGHT LIGHTS TONIGHT (LP, repressing, blue rim)	18
76	Island ICD 8	GUITAR/VOCAL (2-LP, gatefold sleeve, blue rim/palm tree label)	25
78	Island ILPS 9266	I WANT TO SEE THE BRIGHT LIGHTS TONIGHT (LP, repressing, dark blue label)	15

(see also Fairport Convention, Richard Thompson, Sandy Denny, Marc Ellington, Nick Drake, Gary Farr, Paul McNeill & Linda Peters)

ROBERT THOMPSON
| 75 | Pinnacle P 8408 | I Look At The Sun/You Can't See Me | 12 |

ROY THOMPSON
| 67 | Columbia DB 8108 | Sookie Sookie/Love You Say | 30 |

SIR CHARLES THOMPSON
| 53 | Vogue LDE 032 | SIR CHARLES THOMPSON'S ALL STARS WITH CHARLIE PARKER (10" LP) | 20 |
| 56 | Vanguard PPT 12011 | AND HIS BAND FEATURING COLEMAN HAWKINS (10" LP) | 15 |

SONNY THOMPSON & HIS RHYTHM & BLUES BAND
| 60 | Starlite ST45 008 | Screamin' Boogie/The Fish | 250 |
| 56 | Parlophone GEP 8562 | SONNY THOMPSON INSTRUMENTALS (EP, as Sonny Thompson Orchestra) | 40 |

(see also Claude Cloud & Thunderclaps)

SUE THOMPSON
| 61 | Polydor NH 66967 | Sad Movies/Throwing Kisses | 10 |
| 62 | Fontana 267 244TF | James (Hold The Ladder Steady)/My Hero | 7 |

Sue THOMPSON & BOB LUMAN

MINT VALUE £

63	Fontana 267 262TF	Willie Can/Too Much In Love 7
65	Hickory 45-1284	Paper Tiger/Mama Don't Cry At My Wedding 7
65	Hickory 45-1328	It's Break Up Time/Afraid 8
65	Hickory 45-1340	Just Kiss Me/Sweet Hunk Of Misery 8
65	Hickory 45-1359	I'm Looking For A World/Walkin' My Baby 6
65	Hickory 45-1381	What Should I Do/After The Heartache 10
67	London HLE 10142	Ferris Wheel/Don't Forget To Cry 7
72	London HLE 1040	How I Love Them Old Songs/That's Just Too Much 7
73	London HLE 10440	Oh, Johnny, Oh Johnny, Oh/Just Pain Country 7
65	Hickory LPE 1507	INTRODUCING KRIS JENSEN AND SUE THOMPSON (EP, 2 tracks each) 15
64	Hickory LPM 102	PAPER TIGER (LP) 25

(see also Kris Jensen)

SUE THOMPSON & BOB LUMAN
| 63 | Polydor NH 66989 | I Like Your Kind Of Love/Too Hot To Dance .... 10 |

(see also Bob Luman)

THOMPSON TWINS
80	Dirty Discs RANK 1	Squares And Triangles/Could Be Her...Could Be You (p/s, different colours) 35
80	Latent LATE 1	She's In Love With Mystery/Fast Food/Food Style 8
85	Arista TWINS 128	Roll Over (Again)/Fools In Paradise (Extended) (12", p/s, withdrawn) 80
81	T Records TELP 1	A PRODUCT OF... (LP) 15

GUNILLA THORN
| 63 | HMV POP 1239 | Merry-Go-Round/Go On Then .... 90 |

TRACEY THORN
| 82 | Cherry Red MRED 35 | A DISTANT SHORE (LP) .... 20 |
| 07 | Virgin V 3030 | OUT OF THE WOODS (LP) .... 70 |

(see also Marine Girls, Everything But The Girl)

DAVID THORNE
62	Stateside SS 141	The Alley Cat Song/The Moon Was Yellow 6
63	Stateside SS 190	One More Fool, One More Broken Heart/Don't Let It Get Away 6
64	Stateside SE 1020	WHAT WILL I TELL MY HEART (EP) 25
63	Stateside SL 10036	THE ALLEY CAT SONGSTER (LP) 35

KEN THORNE ORCHESTRA
| 68 | United Artists ULP 1201 | INSPECTOR CLOUSEAU (LP, soundtrack) .... 30 |
| 69 | Stateside S(S)L 10271 | THE TOUCHABLES (LP, with Nirvana, Wynder K. Frog, et al.) .... 50 |

WOODY THORNE
| 62 | Vogue Pop V 9202 | Sadie Lou/Teenagers In Love .... 400 |

LEEROY THORNHILL
| 95 | LP 001 | LOWRISE (12" EP white label) .... 30 |

(see also The Prodigy)

CLAUDE THORNHILL & HIS ORCHESTRA
54	London HL 8042	Pussy-Footin'/Adios 40
54	London RE-P 1009	CLAUDE THORNHILL GOES MODERN (EP) 20
54	London H-ABP 1019	CLAUDE THORNHILL GOES MODERN (10" LP) 20
54	London H-ABP 1021	DREAM MUSIC (10" LP) 20

THORNS OF AFFLICTION
| 81 | Cargo CRS 001 | Panic Stricken/Eyes Of The Dead .... 10 |

WILLIE MAE 'BIG MAMA' THORNTON
54	Vogue V 2284	Hound Dog/Mischievous Boogie (78) (as Willie Mae 'Big Mama' Thornton) 80
65	Sue WI 345	Tom Cat/Monkey In The Barn (as Willie Mae Thornton) 250
69	Mercury SMCL 20176	STRONGER THAN DIRT (LP) 40
78	Vanguard VPC 40001	MAMA'S PRIDE (LP) 25

EDDIE THORNTON OUTFIT
| 69 | Instant IN 003 | Baby Be My Gal/SONNY BURKE OUTFIT: All You .... 120 |

CLIFFORD THORNTON
| 76 | JCOA/Virgin J2004 | GARDENS OF HARLEM (LP, with Jazz Composers Orchestra) .... 15 |

PETER THOROGOOD
| 68 | Pye 7N 17597 | Haunted/If No One Sang .... 100 |

BILLY THORPE & AZTECS
| 65 | Parlophone R 5381 | Twilight Time/Over The Rainbow .... 7 |

THOR'S HAMMER
66	Parlophone DP 565	Once/A Memory (export issue) 200
66	Parlophone DP 567	If You Knew/Love Enough (export issue) 185
66	Parlophone CGEP 62	THOR'S HAMMER (EP, export issue, gatefold p/s, with bonus 45 "If You Knew"/"Love Enough" [CGEP 62]) 1200

LINDA THORSON
68	Ember EMB S 257	Here I Am/Better Than Losing You (p/s) 40
68	Ember EMB S 257	Here I Am/Better Than Losing You 15
70	Ember EMBS 284	Wishful Thinking/You Will Want Me 20
70	Ember LT 1	Bad Time To Stop Loving Me/Pick Up My Heart (promo) 25

THOSE ATTRACTIVE MAGNETS
| 83 | Tavern AD MAG 10 | Nightlife/Love Chimes (p/s) .... 70 |

THOSE HELICOPTERS
| 79 | Cargo CRS 011 | SOUTH COAST TOWNS EP .... 8 |
| 80 | State Of The Art STATE 1 | Shark/Eskimo (p/s) .... 6 |

THOSE INTRINSIC INTELLECTUALS
| 80 | Fault Line CPS 040 | Do The Executive/Radio Iceland (fold out p/s in printed bag, insert) .... 12 |

THOSE NAUGHTY LUMPS
| 79 | Zoo CAGE 002 | Iggy Pop's Jacket/Pure And Innocent (foldout p/s) .... 6 |

THOSE DANCING DAYS
| 08 | Wichita WEBB 184LP | IN OUR SPACE HERE SUITS (LP) .... 20 |

THOUGHT POLICE

MINT VALUE £

THOUGHT POLICE
79   Wessex WEX 263   Mr Sad/You Tell Me Lies/Pictures (p/s) 30

THOUGHTS
66   Planet PLF 118   All Night Stand/Memory Of Your Love 100
(see also Tiffany [& Thoughts], Paul Dean & Soul Savages)

THOUGHTS & WORDS
69   Liberty LBF 15187   Morning Sky/Give Me A Reason 10
69   Liberty LBL 83224   THOUGHTS & WORDS (LP) 35

THOUGHTS OF DES COX
69   Morgan MR 4S   Isn't It Nice/It's All Very Strange 12

THREADBARE CONSORT
80s   private pressing   WEARING THIN (LP) 15

THREADS
86   Unicorn PHZ 2   Step Back/UNDERGROUND ARROWS: Backbeat Of Life (p/s) 10

THREADS OF LIFE
72   Alco ALC 530   THREADS OF LIFE (LP, actually by Alco) 800

THREAT
80   One Web 001 WEB   Lullaby In C/High Cost Of Living 75

THREATS
82   Rondelet ROUND 22   GO TO HELL (EP) 15
82   Rondelet ROUND 29   Politicians & Ministers/Writing's On The Wall/Deep End Depression (p/s) 20
82   Rondelet ROUND 1229   POLITICIANS & MINISTERS (12" EP) 18

THREE BARRY SISTERS
59   Decca F 11099   Little Boy Blue/My Sweetie's Coming To Call 10
59   Decca F 11118   Tall Paul/Till Then 7
(see also Barry Sisters)

THREE BELLS
60   Pye 7N 15252   Steady Date/In Between (Wishing I Was Sweet Sixteen) 8
61   Pye 7N 15335   You/Melody Of Love 8
64   Columbia DB 7399   Softly In The Night/He Doesn't Love Me 10
65   Columbia DB 7570   Someone To Love/Over And Over Again 7
66   Columbia DB 7980   Cry No More/He Doesn't Want You 15
(see also Satin Bells)

THREE CAPS
66   Atlantic 584 004   Cool Jerk/Hello Stranger 15
66   Atlantic 584 043   I Got To Handle It/Zig-Zagging 12
69   Atlantic 584 251   Cool Jerk/Hello Stranger 10
(see also Capitols)

THREE CHUCKLES
55   HMV 7M 292   Runaround/At Last You Understand 40
56   HMV 7M 333   Still Thinking Of You/Times Two I Love You 35
57   HMV POP 292   We're Gonna Rock Tonight/Want You Give Me A Chance 80
57   HMV POP 292   We're Gonna Rock Tonight/Want You Give Me A Chance (78) 25
(see also Teddy Randazzo)

THREE CITY FOUR
65   Decca LK 4705   THREE CITY FOUR (LP) 150
67   CBS 63039   SMOKE AND DUST WHERE THE HEART SHOULD HAVE BEEN (LP) 100
(see also Martin Carthy, Leon Rosselson)

THREE COINS
70   Sugar SU 106   Come And Do The Right Thing/It's So Long 20

THREE DANCERS
87   Dilletante Disques 007   Seventeen/It Doesn't Matter (p/s) 40

3D PRODUCTION
80   Third Kind TKS 001   Riot/Riot (Rearrage) 40

THREE DEGREES
65   Stateside SS 413   Gee Baby I'm Sorry/Do What You're Supposed To Do 60
65   Stateside SS 459   Close Your Eyes/Gotta Draw The Line 70
65   Stateside SS 459   Close Your Eyes/Gotta Draw The Line (DJ copy) 100
71   Mojo 2092 001   Maybe/There's So Much Love Around Me 6
71   Mojo 2092 002   You're The One/Rose Garden 6
71   Mojo 2092 009   There's So Much Love Around Me/Maybe (reissue) 6
71   Mojo 2092 009   There's So Much Love Around Me/Yours (different B-side) 6
75   Pye International 7N 25671 Sugar On Sunday/Maybe 6
71   Mojo 2916 002   THE THREE DEGREES (LP) 25

THREE DOG NIGHT
69   Stateside SS 8041   It's For You/Feelin' Alright 6
69   Stateside SS 8030   Eli's Coming/Circle For A Landing 6
69   Stateside-Dunhill SS 8008 Nobody/It's For You 6
70   Stateside-Dunhill SS 8052 Mama Told Me Not To Come/Rock And Roll Widow 7
71   Probe PRO 523   Joy To The World/I Can Hear You Calling 6
71   Probe PRO 536   Liar/Can't Get Enough Of It 6
69   Stateside-Dun. (S)SL 5006 THREE DOG NIGHT (LP) 15
(see also Danny Hutton)

THREE DOLLS
57   MGM MGM 958   The Living End/The Octopus Song 10

THREE GOOD REASONS
65   Mercury MF 883   Build Your Love/Don't Leave Me Now 10
65   Mercury MF 899   Nowhere Man/Wire Wheels 18
65   Mercury MF 929   The Moment Of Truth/Funny Kind Of Loving 10

THREE JOHNS

MINT VALUE £

THREE JOHNS
- 82 CNT CNT 003   English White Boy Engineer/Secret Agent (p/s) 8
- 83 CNT CNT 011   Pink Headed Bug/Lucy In The Rain (p/s) 7

THREE KAYES (SISTERS)
- 56 HMV 7M 401   Ivory Tower/Mister Cuckoo (Sing Your Song) 12
- 56 HMV POP 251   Lay Down Your Arms/First Row Balcony (as Three Kaye Sisters) 10

(see also Kaye Sisters, Frankie Vaughan)

THREE LITTLE PIGGIES
- 88 Mrs Slocombe   FRIVILOUS FROLICS (mini-LP) 50
- 89 Mrs Slocombe MSD2   Clarke's Commandos/Ain't He Happy/Uncle Chris (p/s) 80

THREE MAN ARMY
- 72 Pegasus PGS 1   What's Your Name/Travellin' 10
- 71 Pegasus PEG 3   A THIRD OF A LIFETIME (LP, gatefold) 80
- 74 Reprise K 54201   THREE MAN ARMY TWO (LP) 30

(see also Gun, Baker Gurvitz Army, Andy Newman, Spooky Tooth)

3 MINUTES
- 80 Rocket XPRES 40   Automatic Kids/Future Fun (p/s) 8

THREE PARTY SPLIT
- 79 B&C BCS 16   Dubious Parentage/Kandidate (p/s) 20
- 79 B&C BCS 19   Insane/Totally Insane (unissued, 1 known copy) 350

THREE PEOPLE
- 66 Decca F 12473   Have You Ever Been There/Good Times 10
- 66 Decca F 12514   Suspicions/Easy Man To Find 10
- 67 Decca F 12581   Got To Find A Reason/Simple Thing Would Be For You To Start Loving Me 10

(see also John Bromley)

THREE PIECES
- 75 Fantasy FTC 116   I Need You Girl/Short'nin' Bread (Demo) 30
- 75 Fantasy FTC 116   I Need You Girl/Short'nin' Bread (unissued) 50
- 09 Fryers FRY 007   I Need You Girl/If Only I Could Prove To You (reissue) 25
- 95 BGP BDPD 1097   VIBES OF TRUTH (LP, reissue) 20

3 PM
- 91 Alma Vale ALMA 1   Out Of Control (12") 15
- 91 Alma Vale ALMA 2   ST.P/3PM/Lynx (12") 20
- 92 Busted Loop 3   Better Late Than Never (12") 15

THREE QUARTERS
- 65 Columbia DB 7467   People Will Talk/Love Come A-Tricklin' Down 15
- 65 Columbia DB 7576   The Pleasure Girls/Little People 6

THREE SOUNDS
- 68 Liberty LBF 15062   Makin' Bread Again/Still I'm Sad 8

3 THIEVES AND A LIAR
- 92 3 Thieves And A Liar 3TAL   In The House/I Get A Chill/You Bring Me Joy/Tonight (12") 25

THREE TONES
- 70 Bamboo BAM 32   Good Ways/Everything We Do 180

THREE TOPS
- 67 Doctor Bird DB 1101   Miserable Friday/This World Has A Feeling 50
- 67 Studio One SO 2023   Moving To Progress/Love And Inspiration 80
- 67 Trojan TR 003   It's Raining/Sound Of Music (Treetops on label) 40
- 67 Treasure Isle TI 7008   Do It Right/You Should Have Known 30
- 68 Coxsone CS 7033   A Man Of Chances(as Tree Tops)/HORTENSE ELLIS: A Groovy Kind Of Love 300
- 71 Fab FAB 16   Down At The Boneyard/ALF AND TEEP: Freedom, Justice And Equality (promo only, black label) 100
- 73 Bullet BU 527   Take Time Out/Just Like A Log 20

(see also Dion Cameron & Three Tops, Sir Lord Comic, King Rocky)

THREE WISE MEN
- 83 Virgin VS 642   Thanks For Christmas/Countdown To Christmas Partytime (p/s) 10

(see also XTC)

THREE'S A CROWD
- 66 Fontana TF 673   Look Around The Corner/Living In A Dream 20

(see also Embers, Writing On The Wall)

THRESHOLD OF PLEASURE
- 68 Decca F12785   Rain Rain Rain/He Could Never Love You Like I Do 40

THRILLERS
- 68 Blue Cat BS 128   The Last Dance/DELTA CATS: Unworthy Baby 500

(see also Phil Pratt)

THRILLING WONDER STORIES
- 83 Made In Space MIS 2001   Two Way Video/Computer Mix 10

PERCY 'THRILLS' THRILLINGTON
- 77 Regal Zono. EMI 2594   Uncle Albert - Admiral Halsey/Eat At Home 100
- 77 Regal Zono. EMC 3175   THRILLINGTON (LP, with inner sleeve) 200
- 77 Regal Zono. TC-EMC 3175   THRILLINGTON (cassette) 25

(see also Paul McCartney)

THRILLS (1)
- 66 Capitol CL 15469   No One/What Can Go Wrong 100
- 66 Capitol CL 15469   No One/What Can Go Wrong (DJ copy) 200

THRILLS (2)
- 03 Virgin VSDJ 1855   Last Night I Dreamt That Somebody Loved Me (1-sided gig issue, p/s, 500 only) 10
- 03 Virgin V 2975   SO MUCH FOR THE CITY (LP) 30

THROBBING GRISTLE
- 78 Industrial IR 0003   United/Zyklon B Zombie (p/s) 20
- 78 Industrial IR 0003/U   United/Zyklon B Zombie (p/s, white or clear vinyl, 1,000 only of each) 25
- 80 Industrial IR 0003   United/Zyklon B Zombie (longer version) (p/s, reissue, 'Memorial Issue' scratched in   15

THROWING MUSES

MINT VALUE £

80	Industrial IR 0013	Subhuman/Something Came Over Me (in polythene camouflage bag)	20
80	Industrial IR 0015	Adrenalin/Distant Dreams (Part Two) (in polythene camouflage bag)	20
81	Fetish FET 006	Discipline (live, Berlin)/Discipline (live, Manchester) (12", p/s)	20
77	Industrial IR 0002	SECOND ANNUAL REPORT (LP, 785 only, white hand-made sleeve, 'Nothing short of a total war' sticker on inner sleeve, xerox strip, 'technical note' strip & 2 or 3 TG stickers)	250
78	Industrial IR 0004	D.O.A. THE THIRD AND FINAL REPORT (LP, 1st 1,000 with calendar & postcard)	100
78	Industrial IR 0004	D.O.A. THE THIRD AND FINAL REPORT (LP)	25
78	Fetish FET 2001	SECOND ANNUAL REPORT (LP, 2,000 only, T.G. 'lightning flash' sleeve, with questionnaire & insert, "Coom" mispelling)	40
79	Fetish FET 2001	SECOND ANNUAL REPORT (LP, reissue, glossy sleeve with inserts, with correct "Coum" spelling)	15
79	Industrial IR 0004	D.O.A. THE THIRD AND FINAL REPORT (LP, re-pressing, 1,000 only, banded as 16 equal length tracks)	60
79	Industrial IR 0008	20 JAZZ FUNK GREATS (LP, 5,000 only, 1st 2,000 with b&w poster)	80
79	Industrial IR 0008	20 JAZZ FUNK GREATS (LP, 5,000 only)	40
80	Industrial IR 0009	HEATHEN EARTH (LP, gatefold sleeve, 785 on blue vinyl)	100
80	Industrial IR 0009	HEATHEN EARTH (LP, gatefold sleeve)	25
81	Fetish FET 2001	SECOND ANNUAL REPORT (LP, backwards version, 1st 2,000 in T.G. 'flash' sleeve)	40
81	Fetish FET 2001	SECOND ANNUAL REPORT (LP, backwards version, later issue in black & white sleeve)	15
81	Fetish FX 1	A BOXED SET (5-LP box set with 28-page booklet & badge, 5,000 only)	150
82	Death 01	MUSIC FROM THE DEATH FACTORY, MAY '79 (LP, 50 only)	350
82	Power Focus 001	ASSUME POWER FOCUS (LP, 500 only, numbered)	90
82	T.G. 33033	LIVE AT THE DEATH FACTORY, MAY '79 (LP, reissue picture disc, 1,355 only)	40
82	Karnage/Illuminated KILL 1	THEE PSYCHICK SACRIFICE (2-LP)	30
83	Mute MIR 001	THE SECOND ANNUAL REPORT (LP, reissue)	20
83	Mute MIR 002	D.O.A. THE THIRD AND FINAL REPORT (LP, reissue)	20
83	Mute MIR 003	20 JAZZ FUNK GREATS (LP, reissue)	20
83	Mute MIR004	HEATHEN EARTH (LP, reissue)	20
84	Illuminated JAMS 35	IN THE SHADOW OF THE SUN (LP, soundtrack)	20
84	Illuminated JAMS 39	THE INDUSTRIAL RECORDS STORY 1976-1981 (LP)	35
84	Casual Abandon CAS 1J	ONCE UPON A TIME (LP)	15
84	Mental Decay 01-1	SPECIAL TREATMENT (LP)	15
80s	Sprut 001	VERY FRIENDLY - THE FIRST ANNUAL REPORT OF T.G. (LP)	25
80s	Industrial IRC 1-IRC 24	24 HOURS (box set of cassettes with total of 24 hours playing time; every set is unique)	300
03	Grey Area	TG+ (10-CD box set with metal cards)	70

(see also Psychic TV, Coil, Sabres Of Paradise)

THROWING MUSES

86	4AD CAD 607	THROWING MUSES (LP)	15
87	4AD MAD 706	THE FAT SKIER (LP)	15
88	4AD CAD 802	HOUSE TORNADO (LP)	15
89	4AD CAD 901	HUNKPAPA (LP, lyric inner)	15
91	4AD CAD 1002	THE REAL RAMONA (LP, inner)	20
93	4AD CADD 2013	RED HEAVEN (LP, with free live Kristin Hersh LP)	40
95	4AD CAD 5002	UNIVERSITY (LP)	40
96	4AD CAD 6014	LIMBO (LP)	40

(see also Belly, Kristin Hersh)

THE THRUST

80	Ellie Jay EJSP 9341	THE THRUST EP	100

THUG LIFE

94	Interscope 6544 92360-1	VOLUME 1 (LP, inner)	100

THUNDER

90	EMI EMPD 126	Dirty Love/Fired Up (uncut picture disc with insert in PVC sleeve)	15
90	EMI EMS 137	Back Street Symphony/No Way Out Of The Wilderness (box set with postcards, some also with badge)	6

(see also Terraplane, Nuthin' Fancy)

JOHNNY THUNDER

63	Stateside SS 149	Loop De Loop/Don't Be Ashamed	10
63	Stateside SS 168	Rock-A-Bye My Darling/The Rosy Dance	10
63	Stateside SS 200	Jailer, Bring Me Water/Outlaw	15
63	Stateside SS 229	Hey Child/Everybody Likes To Dance With Johnny	10
64	Stateside SS 337	More, More, More Love, Love, Love/Shout It To The World	10
65	Stateside SS 370	Send Her To Me/Everybody Likes To Dance With Johnny	20
65	Stateside SS 454	Dear John I'm Going To Leave You/Suzie-Q	10
65	Stateside SS 476	Everybody Do The Sloopy/Beautiful	10
66	Stateside SS 499	My Prayer/A Broken Heart	10
63	Stateside SL 10029	LOOP DE LOOP (LP)	75

JOHNNY THUNDER & RUBY WINTERS

67	Stateside SS 2005	Make Love To Me/Teach Me Tonight	15

THUNDERBIRDS

66	Polydor 56710	Your Ma Said You Cried (In Your Sleep Last Night)/Before It's Too Late	70

(see also Chris Farlowe & Thunderbirds)

THUNDERBIRDS (AUSTRALIA)

61	Oriole CB 1610	Wild Weekend/Rat Race	20
61	Oriole CB 1625	New Orleans Beat/Delilah Jones	20

THUNDERBIRDS (U.S.)

55	London HL 8146	Ayuh, Ayuh/Blueberries	70

(see also Bert Convy & Thunderbirds, Midnighters)

THUNDERBOLTS

62	Decca F 11522	Fugitive/Feelin' In A Mood	15

THUNDERBOYS

MINT VALUE £

THUNDERBOYS
80   Recent EJSP 9339   Fashion/Someone Like You (p/s) 40

THUNDERCLAP NEWMAN
69   Track 604031   Something In The Air/Wilhemina 6
70   Track 2094 002   Wild Country/Hollywood 7
70   Track 2094 003   The Reason/Stormy Petrel 7
79   Track 2095 002   Wild Country/Hollywood (reissue, p/s) 8
70   Track 2406 003   HOLLYWOOD DREAM (LP, gatefold sleeve, lyric insert) 100
70   Track 2406 003   HOLLYWOOD DREAM (LP, gatefold sleeve, without lyric insert) 30
(see also Stone The Crows, One In A Million, Paul McCartney & Wings, Speedy Keen, Andy Newman)

THUNDER COMPANY
70   Columbia DB 8706   Ridin' On The Gravy Train (5.03)/Bubble Drum 40
70   Columbia DB 8706   Ridin' On The Gravy Train (2.35 Edit)/Bubble Drum (demo only) 50
(see also Brian Bennett, Shadows)

THUNDERHEAD
93   Thunderhead TH 01   Lost In Time/Untitled (12") 20

THUNDERMUG
73   London HLZ 10411   Africa/Will They Ever 6
72   Axe AXS 502   STRIKES (LP) 15

JOHNNY THUNDERS (& THE HEARTBREAKERS)
78   Real ARE 1   Dead Or Alive/Downtown (p/s) 20
78   Real ARE 3   You Can't Put Your Arms Around A Memory (Edit)/Hurtin' (p/s) 15
78   Real ARE 3T   You Can't Put Your Arms Around A Memory/Hurtin' (12", p/s, blue or pink vinyl, die-cut
                                         company sleeve) 15
83   Jungle JUNG 5   VINTAGE '77 (12" EP) 12
14   Remarquable RBL 1   REAL TIMES EP (10", pink or blue vinyl, poster insert) 20
77   Real RAL 1   SO ALONE (LP, with inner sleeve) 30
86   Jungle JT BOX 1   ALBUM COLLECTION (3-LP & 12" box set with poster and badge) 30
(see also New York Dolls, Heartbreakers)

SAM THUNDER
84   Bullet BULP 5   MANOUEVRES (LP, picture disc) 18

THUNDERSTICK
83   Thunderbolt THBE 1002   FEEL LIKE ROCK'N'ROLL (12" EP, p/s, with patch) 12
(see also Samson, Gillan)

THURSDAY'S CHILDREN
66   Piccadilly 7N 35276   Just You/You Don't Believe Me 25
66   Piccadilly 7N 35306   Crawfish/Come Softly To Me 15
(see also Phil Cordell)

BOBBY THURSTON
81   Epic EPC A1301   Very Last Drop/Life Is What You Make It 20
81   Epic EPC A 13 1301   Very Last Drop/Life Is What You Make It (12") 20
01   Expansion Special Reserve
     EXSR7-4   Just Ask Me/Treat Me The Same Way (reissue) 20
80   Epic EPC 82257   YOU GOT WHAT IT TAKES (LP) 15
81   Epic EPC 85070   MAIN ATTRACTION (LP) 15
88   HI Hut HH 1135   SWEETEST PIECE OF THE PIE (LP) 50
01   Expansion EXLM 8   SWEETEST PIECE OF THE PIE (LP, reissue) 30

THYRDS
64   Oak RGJ 133   Hide 'N' Seek/I've Got My Mojo Working 300
64   Decca F 12010   Hide 'N' Seek/No Time Like The Present 60

TIAMAT
90   CMFT CMFT 6   SUMERIAN CRY (LP) 40
90   Metalcore CORE 9   SUMERIAN CRY (LP, reissue) 30

TIARAS
63   Warner Bros WB 92   You Told Me/I'm Gonna Forget You 15

TIBET & STAPLETON
96   United Dairies UDOR 1   MUSICALISCHE KÜRBS HÜTTE (LP, clear vinyl, with insert) 30
(see also Current 93, Steven Stapleton & David Tibet)o

TICH - TED TAYLOR FOUR WITH CORONA KIDS
65   Oriole CB 1980   Santa Bring Me Ringo/Santa's Got Such A Terrible Cold 10
(see also Ted Taylor)

TICKAWINDA
79   Pennine PSS 153   ROSEMARY LANE (LP) 800

KATHRYN TICKELL
84   Saydisc SDL 343   ON KIELDER SIDE (LP) 20

TICKETS
79   Bridgehouse BHS 3   I'll Be Your Pin Up/Guess I Have To Sit Alone (p/s) 6
(see also Wasted Youth)

TICKLE
67   Regal Zonophone RZ 3004   Subway (Smokey Pokey World)/Good Evening 500
(see also Junior's Eyes, Outsider, Bunch Of Fives)

TIC TAC TOE
92   Tic Tac Toe TTT 456   456/Ephemerol (12", stamped white label) 30
92   Tic Tac Toe TTT 457   456/(Remix)/Ephemerol (Mickey Finn Remix) (12") 10

TIDAL WAVE
69   Decca F 22973   With Tears In My Eyes/We Wanna Know 10

TIDBITS
71   Fly BUG 12   Jean Harlow/Vietnam/Six O'Clock Blues (p/s) 8

PETER TIERNEY & NIGHTHAWKS
65   Fontana TF 547   Oh How I Need You/That's Too Bad (p/s) 15

Roy TIERNEY

MINT VALUE £

ROY TIERNEY
61	Philips BF 1159	Cupid/The Lonely One (in p/s)	15
61	Philips BF 1159	Cupid/The Lonely One	7
61	Philips BF 1194	Just Out Of Reach (Of My Two Empty Arms)/Casanova	10

TIERNEY'S FUGITIVES
65	Decca F 12247	Did You Want To Run Away?/Morning Mist	25

TIFFANIES
67	Chess CRS 8059	It's Got To Be A Great Song/He's Good For Me	100
67	Chess CRS 8059	It's Got To Be A Great Song/He's Good For Me (DJ copy)	150

TIFFANY (WITH THOUGHTS)
65	Parlophone R 5311	I Know/Am I Dreaming	20
66	Parlophone R 5439	Find Out What's Happening/Baby Don't Look Down (as Tiffany with Thoughts)	50

(see also Thoughts)

TIFFANY SHADE
68	Fontana (S)TL 5469	TIFFANY SHADE (LP)	100

JIMMY & LOUISE TIG
69	Deep Soul DS 9205	A Love That Never Grows Cold/Who Can I Turn To	40

TIGER
75	United Artists UP 35848	I Am An Animal/Stop That Machine	20
76	Retreat RTL 6006	TIGER (LP, with lyric inner sleeve)	15
76	EMI EMC3153	GOIN' DOWN LAUGHING (LP, lyric inner sleeve)	15

(see also Hackensack, Samson, Brinsley Schwarz, Big Jim Sullivan, Nicky Moore Band)

TIGER ASHBY
80	T&A Records TA 1	Jet Free/Burning Cross (p/s)	20

TIGER (JAMAICA)
70	New Beat NB 052	Soul Of Africa/Dallas Texas	20
70	New Beat NB 064	Musical Scorcher/Three Dogs Night	20
71	Camel CA 70	Guilty/United We Stand	15
71	New Beat NB 075	African Beat/Black Man Land	15
71	New Beat NB 088	Have You Ever Been Hurt/Our Day Will Come	10

(see also Laurel Aitken)

TIGER LILY
75	Gull GULS 12	Monkey Jive/Ain't Misbehavin'	10
77	Gull GULS 54	Monkey Jive/Ain't Misbehavin' (reissue, p/s)	15

(see also Ultravox)

TIGERMOTH
84	Rogue FMSL 2006	TIGERMOTH (LP)	15

TIGERS (2)
79	Strike STING 1	Savage Music/Jack It Up	8
79	Strike KIK 1	Kidding Stops/Big Expense, Small Income (p/s)	8

TIGER TAILS
80	Snotty Snails NELCO 2	Words Without Conviction/Norman/Fashion Fool (p/s)	20

TIGHT LIKE THAT
72	Village Thing VTS 12	HOKUM (LP)	40

TIGHTS
78	Cherry Red CHERRY 1	Bad Hearts/It Cracked (p/s)	25
78	Cherry Red CHERRY 2	Howard Hughes/China's Eternal (p/s)	15

TIKKI, TAKI, SUZI, LIES
70	UPC UPC 102	Welcome To My House/I Believe In Love	8
70	UPC UPC 109	Ba-Da-Da-Dum/Dream Stealer	25

JOHN TILBURY
75	Decca HEAD 9	MR JOHN CAGES PREPARED PIANO (LP)	25

TILLER BOYS
79	New Hormones ORG 3	Big Noise From The Jungle/Slaves And Pyramids/What Me Worry? (p/s)	6

(see also Buzzcocks, Pete Shelley)

TILLERMEN
71	Duke DU 109	Be Loving To Me/Judgement Rock	25

(see also Greyhound)

DEREK JOHN TILLEY
70	Decca F 13043	Sunny Day/Living For Love	30

BERTHA TILLMAN
62	Oriole CB 1746	Oh, My Angel/Lovin' Time	80

JOHNNY TILLOTSON
59	London HLA 8930	True True Happiness/Love Is Blind	30
60	London HLA 9048	Why Do I Love You So/Never Let Me Go	20
60	London HLA 9101	Earth Angel/Pledging My Love	30
61	London HLA 9275	Jimmy's Girl/His True Love Said Goodbye	10
61	London HLA 9412	Without You/Cutie Pie	15
62	London HLA 9514	Dreamy Eyes/Much Beyond Compare	6
62	London HLA 9550	It Keeps Right On A-Hurtin'/She Gave Sweet Love To Me	8
62	London HLA 9598	Send Me The Pillow You Dream On/What'll I Do	7
62	London HLA 9642	I Can't Help It/I'm So Lonesome I Could Cry	7
63	London HLA 9695	Out Of My Mind/Judy, Judy, Judy	7
63	London HLA 9811	Funny How Time Slips Away/A Very Good Year For Girls	7
63	MGM MGM 1214	Talk Back Trembling Lips/Another You	7
63	MGM MGM 1225	Worried Guy/Please Don't Go Away	6
63	MGM MGM 1235	I'm Watching My Watch/I Rise, I Fall	6
64	MGM MGM 1247	Suffering From A Heartache/Worry	6
64	MGM MGM 1252	She Understands Me/Tomorrow	8
64	MGM MGM 1266	Angel/Little Boy	7

TILSLEY ORCHESTRA

MINT VALUE £

65	MGM MGM 1275	Then I'll Count Again/One's Yours, One's Mine	8
65	MGM MGM 1281	Heartaches By The Number/Your Memory Comes Along	8
65	MGM MGM 1290	Our World/(Wait 'Til You See) My Gidget	8
66	MGM MGM 1300	Hello Enemy/I Never Loved You Anyway	8
66	MGM MGM 1311	Me Myself And I/Country Boy, Country Boy	8
66	MGM MGM 1319	No Love At All/What Am I Gonna Do	8
68	MGM MGM 1393	Cabaret/If I Were A Rich Man	8
62	London RE-A 1345	JOHNNY TILLOTSON (EP)	35
63	London RE-A 1388	J.T. (EP)	35
63	MGM MGM-EP 788	JOHNNY TILLOTSON (EP)	20
64	MGM MGM-EP 790	JOHNNY TILLOTSON'S HIT PARADE (EP)	20
61	London HA-A 2431	JOHNNY TILLOTSON'S BEST (LP)	30
62	London HA-A 8019	IT KEEPS RIGHT ON A-HURTIN' (LP)	25
64	MGM MGM-C 972	ALONE WITH YOU (LP)	20
65	MGM C/CS 1002	SHE UNDERSTANDS ME (LP)	20
65	MGM MGM-C(S) 8005	JOHNNY TILLOTSON SINGS OUR WORLD (LP)	20
66	MGM MGM-C(S) 8025	NO LOVE AT ALL (LP)	20

TILSLEY ORCHESTRA

66	Fontana TF 783	Thunderbirds Theme/Theme From "The Power Game"	20
67	Polydor 56150	Mr. Aitch Theme/Cotton Reed	8
67	Fontana (S)TL 5211	TOP T.V. THEMES (LP)	20

(see also Electric Banana)

STEVE TILSTON

71	Village Thing VTS 5	AN ACOUSTIC CONFUSION (LP)	35
72	Transatlantic TRA 252	COLLECTION (LP, textured gatefold sleeve)	18
77	Cornucopia CR 1	SONGS FROM THE DRESS REHEARSAL (LP, with Rupert Hine/John Renbourn)	25
83	TM PROP 4	IN FOR A PENNY IN FOR A POUND (LP, with Peter Bardens)	15

TIMBER

71	Elektra K 12022	Bring America Home/Splinters From Timber	6
72	Elektra K 12042	Outlaw/Song For Two Signs	6

TIMBER TIMBRE

11	Full Time Hobby FTH 114LP	CREEP ON CREEPING ON (LP)	18
14	Full Time Hobby FTH 189LP	HOT DREAMS (LP, white vinyl repressing)	25

TIME

65	Pye 7N 17019	Take A Bit Of Notice/Every Now And Then	60
66	Pye 7N 17146	The First Time I Saw The Sunshine/Annabel	30

TIME

75	B.U.K. BULP 2005	TIME (LP)	60

(see also Spontaneous Combustion)

T.I.M.E. (TRUST IN MEN EVERYWHERE)

69	Liberty LBF 15082	Take Me Along/Make It Alright	10
68	Liberty LBL/LBS 83144	T.I.M.E. (LP)	50
69	Liberty LBL/LBS 83232	SMOOTH BALL (LP)	70

TIME MACHINE (2)

78	Rip Off RIP 6	NEVER MET SUZI EP	40

TIME UK

83	Red Bus TIM 123	The Cabaret/Remember Days (gatefold p/s)	10

(see also the Jam)

TIMEBOX

67	Piccadilly 7N 35369	I'll Always Love You/Save Your Love	100
67	Piccadilly 7N 35379	Soul Sauce/I Wish I Could Jerk Like My Uncle Cyril	200
67	Deram DM 153	Walking Through The Streets Of My Mind/Don't Make Promises	25
68	Deram DM 194	Beggin'/A Woman That's Waiting	60
68	Deram DM 219	Girl Don't Make Me Wait/Gone Is The Sad Man	35
69	Deram DM 246	Baked Jam Roll In Your Eye/Poor Little Heartbreaker	30
69	Deram DM 271	Yellow Van/You've Got The Chance	30

(see also Bo Street Runners, [Mike] Patto, V.I.Ps)

TIMECOP1983

19	Timeslave TSR58	JOURNEYS (2-LP, pink vinyl)	40
18	Timeslave TSR45	NIGHT DRIVE (2-LP, purple vinyl, 500 only)	70
19	Timeslave TSR45	NIGHT DRIVE (2-LP, repressing blue/black splatter, 500 only)	50
20	Timeslave TSR45	NIGHT DRIVE (2-LP, repressing clear/purple splatter vinyl, 500 only)	40
20	Timeslave TSR73	LOVERS PART 1 AND 2 (2-LP, blue/white and blue/pink splatter)	60
21	Timeslave TSR73	LOVERS PART 1 AND 2 (2-LP, repressing, pink/blue split vinyl)	30
21	Timeslave TSR71	REFLECTIONS (2-LP)	50

TIME CRYSTALS

91	Talisman TAL 1	The Fool/Geve Me Back What's Mine	10

TIMELORDS

88	KLF 003GG	Gary In The Tardis (Radio)/(Minimal) (white label promo, 500 only)	15
88	KLF 003GG	Gary In The Tardis (Radio)/(Minimal) (12", p/s)	10
88	KLF 003P	Doctorin' The Tardis (Radio)/(Minimal) (car-shaped picture disc)	15
88	KLF 003R	Doctorin' The Tardis (Radio)/Doctorin' The Tardis (Minimal)/ Gary Glitter Joins The JAMs (12", 4,000 only, this price for those in full 'Gary Glitter' p/s)	30

(see also Angels One 5, KLF, Disco 2000, JAMs, Bill Drummond, Orb, Space)

TIME MACHINE (1)

72	Play PLAY 41	Railroad/Going Down Down Down	30

TIMEPIECE

70	Dolphin 4759	Hitchin To Miami/Mad Dan The Romeo Man	8

TIMES (1)

65	EMI 7ES 24	Ooh Wee/Shepherd Blues/Suzie/Running And Hiding (EP, demo only)	70

TIMES (2)

			MINT VALUE £
66	Columbia DB 7804	Think About The Times/Tomorrow Night	35
66	Columbia DB 7904	(She Can't Replace) The Love We Knew/Reconciled	35
68	Pye 7N 17647	What's Made Milwaukee Famous/Follw The Times	10
70	Parlophone R 5855	Looking Thru' The Eyes Of A Beautiful Girl/Flyin' High Feelin' Low	10

TIMES (2)

81	Whaam! WHAAM 2	Red With Purple Flashes/Biff! Bang! Pow! (p/s)	100
82	Art Pop POP 49	I Helped Patrick McGoohan Escape/The Theme From "Danger Man" (p/s)	20
82	Art Pop POP 50	Here Come The Holidays (Voici Les Vacances)/Three Cheers For The Sun (A-side as Joni Dee & Times, p/s, with 'Times' sticker)	18
82	Art Pop POP 50	Here Come The Holidays (Voici Les Vacances)/Three Cheers For The Sun (A-side as Joni Dee & Times, p/s)	12
84	Art Pop POP 46	Boys Brigade/Power Is Forever (p/s)	7
84	Art Pop POP 45	Blue Fire/Where The Blue Begins (p/s)	6
90	Caff CAFF 13	Extase/BIFF BANG POW!: Sleep (p/s, with insert)	20
85	Art Pop 43DOZ	BOYS ABOUT TOWN (12", EP)	10
81	Whaam! BIG 1	POP GOES ART (LP, hand-sprayed sleeve)	60
82	Art Pop ART 20	POP GOES ART! (LP, reissue, hand-sprayed sleeve, with magazine cuttings taped to plain white cover)	35
82	Art Pop ART 20	POP GOES ART! (LP, reissue, hand-sprayed sleeve, without magazine cuttings taped to plain white cover)	25
83	Art Pop ART 19	THIS IS LONDON (LP, white label with blue print)	35
83	Art Pop ART 19	THIS IS LONDON (LP, black label with white print)	18
83	Art Pop No. 1	I HELPED PATRICK McGOOHAN ESCAPE (mini-LP)	18
86	Art Pop ART 16	UP AGAINST IT (LP)	25
86	Art Pop ART 15	ENJOY! (LP, gatefold sleeve)	15
90	Art Pop ART 20	POP GOES ART (LP, 'hand-painted' picture disc reissue, signed)	15
91	Creation CRELP 091	PURE (LP)	15
92	Creation CRELP 123	AT THE ASTRADOME LUNAVILLE (LP)	15
93	Creation CRELP 137	ALTERNATIVE COMMERCIAL CROSSOVER (LP, with inner)	15

(see also Television Personalities, Teenage Filmstars, O Level, Biff Bang Pow!, L'Orange Mechanik)

BOBBY TIMMONS

61	Riverside RLP 334	SOUL TIME (LP, with Art Blakey, also stereo [RLP 9334])	20
60	Riverside 12-317	THIS HERE IS (LP)	20

TIMON

68	Pye 7N 17451	Bitter Thoughts Of Little Jane/Ramblin' Boy	100
70	Threshold TH 3	And Now She Says She's Young/I'm Just A Travelling Man	8

(see also Tymon Dogg)

TIMONEERS

76	WHM WHM 1919	ROASTED LIVE (LP)	20

AL TIMOTHY & HIS BAND

55	Decca F 10558	Gruntin' Blues/You Mad Man!	10

TIM TAM & TURN ONS

67	Island WIP 6007	Wait A Minute/Ophelia	50

TINA

61	Piccadilly 7N 35022	What I Want For Christmas (Is Six More Years)/My Brother Wants A Doll For Christmas	6

TINA & MEXICANS

68	Pye 7N 17525	One Love Two/Longing To Hold You	8

TINARIWEN

08	Independiente ISOM 65LP	AMAN IMAN (2-LP)	50
09	Independiente ISOM78LP	IMIDIWAN: COMPANIONS (LP)	35

TINDERBOX (1)

68	Polydor 56296	Farewell Britannia/Rainsong	60

TINDERBOX (2)

74	Cannon CAN 2	Inside A Dream/Sad N Lonely	60

TINDERSTICKS

92	Tippy Toe 1	Patchwork/Milky Teeth (p/s, hand-coloured inner sleeve & insert; 1,000 only, numbered in positive or negative figures [from -500 to 500])	60
93	Tippy Toe/Ché TIPPY-CHE 2	Marbles/Joe Stumble/For Those.../Benn (10", p/s, stickered PVC sleeve, inner sleeve & insert, 2,000 only)	25
93	Rough Trade 45rev16	A Marriage Made In Heaven/A Marriage Made In Heaven (Instrumental) ('singles club' release, p/s, 5,000 only)	10
93	Domino RUG 006	UNWIRED EP: Feeling Relatively Good/Rotweilers And Mace/She/Kooks (EP, numbered p/s; 1 copy in 10 with 'Domino' stamp, 1,500 only)	12
93	This Way Up WAY 1811	City Sickness/Untitled/The Bullring (p/s, 1,500 only)	12
93	Clawfist XPIG 21	We Have All The Time In The World/GALLON DRUNK: Known Not Wanted ('singles club' release, p/s, 1,400 only)	12
93	Tippy Toe 003	LIVE IN BERLIN: Raindrops/Tyed (in stamped brown paper bag, mail-order/tour release, 1,500 only)	20
94	This Way Up WAY 2811	Kathleen/Summat Moon/Sweet, Sweet Man/E Type Joe (33 rpm 7", 5000 only)	8
95	Sub Pop SP 297	THE SMOOTH SOUND OF TINDERSTICKS: Here/Harry's Dilemma (p/s, 3,000 only)	10
95	This Way Up 2888	KATHLEEN (10")	10
97	This Way Up WAY 6122	Bathtime/Paco's Theme/Shadow / Manalow (12", p/s)	12
08	Lucky Dog LD 05	What Are You Fighting For? (one-sided 7", die cut sleeve, 200 only)	15
93	This Way Up 518306	TINDERSTICKS (1st album) (2-LP, first 1000 with 4 postcards)	100
93	This Way Up 518306	TINDERSTICKS (1st album) (2-LP, without postcards)	60
93	This Way Up 518308-1	TINDERSTICKS (1st album) (2-LP reissue, green vinyl)	50
95	This Way Up THIS 1.1	TINDERSTICKS (2nd album) (LP, with free 7")	100
94	This Way Up WAY 3288	LIVE IN AMSTERDAM (10" LP, brown sleeve)	40
95	This Way Up	THE BLOOMSBURY THEATRE 12/3/95 (LP, 2-10" LP)	30
96	This Way Up 5243002	NENETTE ET BONI (LP)	40
97	This Way Up 5243441	CURTAINS (2xLP)	120
98	Island ILPS 8074	DONKEYS 92-97 (LP)	80

TING TINGS

			MINT VALUE £
99	Simply Vinyl SVLP 112	SIMPLE PLEASURE (LP)	120
01	Beggars Banquet BBQLP 222	CAN OUR LOVE... (LP, gatefold)	40
01	Beggars Banquet BBQLP 225	TROUBLE EVERY DAY (LP, soundtrack, with booklet)	30
03	Beggars Banquet BBQLP 232	WAITING FOR THE MOON (LP)	35
08	Beggars Banquet BBQLP 259	HUNGRY SAW (LP)	35
10	4AD CAD 3X02	FALLING DOWN A MOUNTAIN (LP)	15
10	This Way Up 518 306 1	TINDERSTICKS (2-LP, reissue of 1st LP)	30
11	Moving Vinyl MOVLP 371	THE HUNGRY SAW (LP)	20
13	Moving Vinyl MOVLP 712	TINDERSTICKS (2-LP, reissue of 2nd LP, blue vinyl)	25

(see also Asphalt Ribbons, Stuart A. Staples)

TING TINGS
07	Switchflicker SWALF 11	That's Not My Name/Great DJ (p/s)	12
07	No label or cat no	Fruit Machine/Impacilla Carpisung (4 x 100 7" given away at 4 live shows, customized blank sleeve)	25
08	Columbia – 88697318871	WE STARTED NOTHING (LP, red vinyl)	20

TINGA (STEWART) & ERNIE (WILSON)
69	Explosion EX 2009	She's Gone/Old Old Song	100

TIN KAN
79	White Dove WD103A	A Thousand Miles Of White/Girl I'd Never Let You Down	10

TINKERBELL'S FAIRYDUST
67	Decca F 12705	Lazy Day/In My Magic Garden	70
68	Decca F 12778	Twenty Ten/Walking My Baby	80
69	Decca F 12865	Sheila's Back In Town/Follow Me Follow	100
69	Decca LK/SKL 5028	TINKERBELL'S FAIRYDUST (LP, unreleased; finished copies in laminated front sleeve with mono/stereo 'peephole' on rear, machine etched matrix number, blue/silver label with large unboxed Decca logo)	8000
69	Decca LK/SKL 5028	TINKERBELL'S FAIRYDUST (LP, unreleased; test pressings in sleeve)	2000

TIN MACHINE
89	EMI USA MTPD 76	Prisoner Of Love/Baby Can Dance (Live) (picture disc)	15
89	EMI USA MTPD 73	Maggies Farm (Live)/Tin Machine (picture disc)	15
89	EMI America MTLS 1044	TIN MACHINE (LP)	20
91	Victory 828 272-1	TIN MACHINE II (LP)	40

(see also David Bowie)

BABS TINO
62	London HLR 9589	Forgive Me/If I Didn't Love You So Much	30
63	London RE-R 1377	FORGIVE ME (EP)	100

TINOPENERS
79	Logo GO 375	Set Me Free/I'm Not Your Type	150

TIN PAN SKIFFLE GROUP
57	Nestles NR 06	Poor Howard (1-sided card flexi 78)	12

TINS
79	Quest BR 001	There Is No Steel/Working For The Corporation	20

TINSLEY
71	Pye 7N45057	My Brother Mary/Situation Vacant	6

MICK TINSLEY
67	Decca F 12544	Let It Be Me/How're You Gonna Tell Me	6

(see also Hedgehoppers Anonymous)

TIN SOLDIERS
82	Spanking SPANK2	Tin Soldiers/Cuckoo In The Nest (p/s)	10
93	Detour DR 002	A New Beat/Girlfriend/Get Up And Go! (p/s, insert 1,000, only 100 on clear vinyl)	12

TINTERN ABBEY
67	Deram DM 164	Beeside/Vacuum Cleaner	1000

TIN TIN
69	Polydor 56332	Only Ladies Play Croquet/He Wants To Be A Star	10
70	Polydor 2058 023	Toast And Marmalade For Tea/Manhattan Woman	12
70	Polydor 2058 076	Come On Over Again/Back To Winona	10
71	Polydor 2001 146	Shana/Rocky Mountain	10
71	Polydor 2058 114	Is That The Way/Swans In That Canal	10
72	Polydor 2058 232	Toast And Marmalade For Tea/Cavalry's Coming/Ships On The Starboard	10
72	Polydor 2058 238	Talking Turkey/Cavalry's Coming	10
69	Polydor 2384 011	TIN TIN (LP)	25
72	Polydor 2382 080	ASTRAL TAXI (LP)	20

(see also Steve & Stevie)

TINY TIM
68	Reprise RS 20769	Hello Hello/The Other Side	10
68	Reprise RSLP 6292	GOD BLESS TINY TIM (LP)	20
69	Reprise RSLP 6323	TINY TIM'S SECOND ALBUM (LP)	20
69	Reprise RSLP 6351	FOR ALL MY LITTLE FRIENDS (LP)	20

TINY TOPSY (& CHARMS)
58	Parlophone R 4397	Come On, Come On, Come On/A Ring Around My Finger (with Charms)	80
58	Parlophone R 4397	Come On, Come On, Come On/A Ring Around My Finger (with Charms) (78)	25
58	Parlophone R 4427	You Shocked Me/Waterproof Eyes (solo)	100
58	Parlophone R 4427	You Shocked Me/Waterproof Eyes (solo) (78)	25
61	Pye International 7N 25104	After Marriage Blues/Working On Me Baby (solo)	30

TINY VIPERS
15	Box Bedroom Rebels BBR10	Ambience 3 (p/s, with CD, 250 copies, numbered)	12

DIMITRI TIOMKIN
54	Vogue Coral Q 2016	The High And The Mighty/Dial M For Murder	15

KEITH TIPPETT
69	Polydor 2384 004	YOU ARE HERE, I AM THERE (LP)	100
71	Vertigo 6360 024	DEDICATED TO YOU BUT YOU WEREN'T LISTENING (LP, gatefold sleeve, large swirl	175

Julie TIPPETTS

			MINT VALUE £
		label)	
72	RCA SF 8290	BLUEPRINT (LP)	75
76	Steam SJ 104	TNT (LP, with Stan Tracey)	15
77	Vinyl VS 101	WARM SPIRITS, COOL SPIRITS (LP)	15
78	Ogun OGD 003/4	FRAMES (2-LP)	30
78	Ogun OGUN 003/004	ARK (2-LP)	35

(see also Centipede, King Crimson, Ovary Lodge, Nicra)

JULIE TIPPETTS
76	Utopia UTS 601	SUNSET GLOW (LP)	22

(see also Julie Driscoll, Brian Auger, Centipede, Keith Tippett, Elton Dean, Ninesense, Mark Charig)

TIPPIE & THE CLOVERS
63	Stateside SS 160	My Heart Said/Bossa Nova Baby	25

LESTER TIPTON
80	Grapevine GRP 138	This Won't Change/MASQUERADERS: How	20
98	Goldmine GS 203	Time Won't Change/AL WILLIAMS: I Am Nothing	6

TIP TOPS
63	Cameo Parkway P 868	He's Braggin'/Oo-Kook-A-Boo	35

TÍR NA NOG
72	Chrysalis CHS 2001	The Lady I Love/Heidi	7
73	Chrysalis CHS 2016	Strong In The sun/The Mountain And I	6
71	Chrysalis ILPS 9153	TÍR NA NOG (LP, laminated gatefold sleeve)	25
72	Chrysalis CHR 1006	A TEAR AND A SMILE (LP, gatefold sleeve)	20
73	Chrysalis CHR 1047	STRONG IN THE SUN (LP)	15

TITAN
80	Wild Dog DOG 26	East Wind West Wind/Losing The Fight	200
83	After Hours AFT 09	Imaginary Lady/Tooty Flutey	30

TITANIC
72	CBS 8185	Rain 2,000/Blond	20
71	CBS 64104	TITANIC (LP)	20
72	CBS 64791	SEA WOLF (LP, gatefold sleeve)	20
73	CBS 65661	EAGLE ROCK (LP, gatefold sleeve)	15

TITANS
58	London HLU 8609	Don't You Just Know It/Can It Be	80
58	London HLU 8609	Don't You Just Know It/Can It Be (78)	35

TITUS GROAN
70	Dawn DNX 2503	Open The Door Homer/Woman Of The World/Liverpool (p/s)	20
70	Dawn DNLS 3012	TITUS GROAN (LP, gatefold sleeve)	350

CAL TJADER
65	Verve VS 529	Soul Sauce/Naked City Theme	50
65	Verve VS 529	Soul Sauce/Naked City Theme (DJ copy)	80
58	Vocalion LAE 556	RITMO CALIENTE (LP, as Cal Tjader Quintet)	20
60	Vocalion LAE 560	THE WEST SIDE STORY (LP)	15
62	HMV/Verve CLP 1587	IN A LATIN BAG (LP, as Cal Tjader Sextet, also stereo [CSD 1454])	15
65	Vocalion LAE-F 599	GREATEST HITS (LP)	15
65	Verve (S)VLP 9136	SOUL BIRD: WHIFFENPOOF (LP)	15
66	Verve (S)VLP 9155	SOUL BURST (LP)	15
68	Verve (S)VLP 9192	THE BEST OF CAL TJADER (LP)	15
68	Verve (S)VLP 9215	HIP VIBRATIONS (LP)	20
61	Vogue SEA 568	CONCERT BY THE SEA (LP)	15

TLC
94	La Face 73008 26009-1	CRAZYSEXYCOOL (LP)	35

TMR
92	Pirate Club PCR 001	Pirate Toon (Moose Mix)/Pirate Toon (Pirate Excursion)/Pirate Toon (Pirate Dub) (12", white stamped label)	60

T.N.T.
72	Jam JAM 4	Big Trouble (Part One)/Big Trouble (Part Two)	40

TNT
84	Neat NEAT 39	Back On The Road/Rockin' The Night (p/s)	12

TOAD
72	RCA Victor SF 8241	TOAD (LP)	200

TOAD THE WET SPROCKET
79	Sprockets BRS 004	Pete's Punk Song/Feel It (fold out p/s)	45
80	Sprockets BRS 008	Reaching For The Sky/One Glass Of Whiskey (foldout stapled p/s)	70

TOAST
70	CBS 4768	Flowers Never Bend With The Rainfall/Summer Of Miranda	10

TOASTERS
87	Unicorn PHZA-5	POOL SHARK (LP)	18
90	Unicorn PHZA-60	FRANKENSKA (LP)	15

TOBA
81	Connection CON 8101	Make Your Mind Up/Don't Take It (12")	30
82	Connection CONT 8203	Moving Up/Moving Up (Instrumental) (12", red or blue vinyl)	30

AMON TOBIN
19	Electronic Sound ES 752	On A Hilltop Sat The Moon/ONLY CHILD TYRANT: King Of Kong (p/s)	10
97	Ninja Tune ZEN 29	BRICOLAGE (2-LP, gatefold sleeve)	35
97	Ninja Tune ZEN 29	BRICOLAGE (2-LP, single sleeve)	20
98	Ninja Tune ZEN 36	PERMUTATION (2-LP)	35
00	Ninja Tune ZEN 48	SUPERMODIFIED (2-LP)	40
02	Ninja Tune ZEN 70	OUT FROM OUT WHERE (2-LP)	25
05	Ninja Tune ZEN 100	CHAOS THEORY (2-LP)	50
11	Ninja Tune ZEN 171	CHAOS THEORY REMIXED (2-LP)	100

			MINT VALUE £
15	Nina Tune ZEN 12387	DARK JOVIAN (2 x 12" etched on sides A and D, perspex box)	40

TOBRUK
83	Neat NEAT 32	Wild On The Run/The Show Must Go On (p/s)	8
85	Parlophone 12R 6093	Falling/Like Lightning/Under The Gun (12", p/s)	10
85	Parlophone R 6101	On The Rebound/Poor Girl (p/s)	10
88	FM WKFMLP 105	PLEASURE AND PAIN (LP)	15

TOBY JUG
69	Toby Toons TLP 01	GREASY QUIFF (LP, with insert, 50 only)	15

TOBY TWIRL
68	Decca F 12728	Harry Faversham/Back In Time	30
68	Decca F 12804	Toffee Apple Sunday/Romeo And Juliet 1968	400
69	Decca F 12867	Movin' In/Utopia Daydream	40

(see also Shades Of Blue)

TODAY'S WITNESS
72	Emblem JDR 345	TODAY'S WITNESS (LP)	35

ART & DOTTY TODD
58	London HLB 8620	Chanson D'Amour (Song Of Love)/Along The Trail With You	18
59	London HLN 8838	Straight As An Arrow/Stand There, Mountain	18

DIANE TODD
58	Decca F 10993	It's A Wonderful Thing To Be Loved/You Are My Favourite Dream	8

GARY TODD & ROGER TURNER
79	Incus INCUS 79	SUNDAY BEST (LP)	50

NICK TODD
57	London HLD 8500	Plaything/The Honey Song	40
58	London HLD 8537	At The Hop/I Do	15
59	London HLD 8902	Tiger/Twice As Nice	30

PATSY TODD
66	Doctor Bird DB 1086	Pata Pata Rocky Steady (with Count Ossie)/COUNT OSSIE: Nyah Bongo	60
68	High Note HS 007	Fire In Your Wire/AL & VIBRATORS: Move Up Calypso	15
69	High Note HS 012	We Were Lovers/Give Me A Chance (B-side with Delano Stewart)	75

(see also Patsy, Stranger & Patsy, Derrick & Patsy)

SHARKEY TODD & MONSTERS
59	Parlophone R 4536	Cool Gool/The Horror Show	25
59	Parlophone R 4536	Cool Gool/The Horror Show (78)	20

(see also Wally Whyton, Vipers [Skiffle Group])

TONY TODD
83	Crash CRA 504	You're Breaking My Heart/Waiting For Love	12

WILF TODD COMBO
64	Blue Beat BB 240	He Took Her Away/Have You Ever Been Lonely	12

WILF TODD & HIS MUSIC
66	Oak WT 101	WILF TODD AND HIS MUSIC (LP)	15

TOE-FAT
70	Parlophone R 5829	Working Nights/Bad Side Of The Moon	15
72	Chapter One SCH 175	Brand New Band/Can't Live Without You	10
70	Parlophone PCS 7097	TOE-FAT (LP, black/silver label with boxed logo)	175
70	Regal Zono. SLRZ 1015	TOE-FAT TWO (LP, red/silver label)	175

(see also Uriah Heep, Glass Menagerie)

TOGETHER (1)
68	Columbia DB 8491	Henry's Coming Home/Love Mum And Dad	70
69	Aurora 4278	Memories Of Melinda/Good Morning World	50

(see also Keith Relf)

TOGETHER (2)
90	Thumbs Up Magic GH 001	Hardcore Uproar (12", white label)	250
91	Thumbs Up Magic TUM002	The Luv Bug (12")	70
92	Thumbs Up Magic GH003	The House Sound Vol 2/Coming On Strong (12", with CYBERTEC)	60

TOGGERY FIVE
64	Parlophone R 5175	Bye Bye Bird/I'm Gonna Jump	50
65	Parlophone R 5249	I'd Much Rather Be With The Boys/It's So Easy	50

TOKALON
81	EDM Champagne BUBL 701	Coming To Get You/Dance Version	10

TOKENS
61	Parlophone R 4790	Tonight I Fell In Love/I Love My Baby	30
62	RCA RCA 1313	I'll Do My Crying Tomorrow/Dream Angel Goodnight	10
62	RCA RCA 1322	Wishing/A Bird Flies Out Of Sight	6
64	Fontana TF 500	He's In Town/Oh Kathy	10
62	RCA RD 27256	THE LION SLEEPS TONIGHT (LP, mono)	30
62	RCA SF 5128	THE LION SLEEPS TONIGHT (LP, stereo)	35
62	RCA RD 7535	WE THE TOKENS SING FOLK (LP)	18

(see also We Ugly Dogs, Cross Country)

TOK-IO-ROSE
84	TOK 001	Bad Girls/Desperate Situation (p/s)	40

TOKYO BLADE
83	Powerstation OHM 2	Powergame/Death On Main Street (p/s)	8
85	Powerstation LEG 1T	THE CAVE SESSIONS (12" EP)	15
85	Tokyo Blade TBR 1	BLACKHEARTS AND JADED SPADES (LP, gatefold sleeve)	15

TOKYO ROSE
83	Guardian GRC 270	Dry Your Eyes/This Is Tokyo Rose (p/s)	40

ISRAEL 'POPPER STOPPER' TOLBERT
70	Stax STAX 157	Big Leg Woman/I Got Love	7
71	Stax 2362 020	POPPER STOPPER (LP)	25

TOLL

MINT VALUE £

TOLL
86 Broken Flag BF V7 CHRIST KNOWS (LP, featuring Tim Gane) 20
(see also Ramleh, McCarthy)

JUKKA TOLONEN
74 Sonet STNF 652 TOLONOEN! (LP, laminated front cover).. 15

TOM & JERRIO
65 HMV POP 1435 Boo-Ga-Loo/Boomerang 30

TOM & JERRY (CARTOON CHARACTERS)
58 MGM MGM-EP 688 JOHANN MOUSE (EP) 15

TOM & JERRY (1)
59 Gala GSP 806 Baby Talk/PAUL SHELDON: Thank You Pretty Baby (picture labels) 45
63 Pye International 7N 25202 I'm Lonesome/Looking At You 95
(see also Simon & Garfunkel)

TOM AND JERRY
92 Tom And Jerry SHELL 001 The One Reason/The Second Reason (12") 80
92 Tom And Jerry SHELL 002 We Can Be Free/For The Gold Teeth/Baby Don't Shout/Physics (12") 90
93 Tom And Jerry SHELL 003 Papillon Love Song/A Patch Of Blue/B.O.S Realting/Cat Got Your Tongue (12") 70
93 Tom And Jerry SHELL 004 Let Your Spirit Rise/Programme 205/Strings & Me/Mousetrap (Dangerous) (12") 60
93 Tom And Jerry SHELL 005 Scooby's Dreaming/Neatly Dealt Wid/Nine Lives (Mind Out Tube Mice)/Yamming Snacks Like Shaggy (12") 60
93 Tom And Jerry SHELL 006 All Alone Wid Dog Face/Laughing Like Muttley/Sun On My Head/Escape (12") 60
93 Tom And Jerry SHELL 007 IT COMES A DIME A DOZEN EP (12") 80
94 Tom And Jerry SHELL 008 Dancer/Thriller/Maxi(Mun) Style/I Wanna Say (Yeah) (12") 40
94 Tom And Jerry SHELL 009 Still Lets Me Down/Luv & Run/Maxi(mun) Style Remix/Airfreshner/For Your Sampling Pleasure (12") 60
94 Tom And Jerry SHELL 010 It's All Over/Who Kan Draw/Say Goodbye Broke My Heart/Max(imum) Booty Style Part III (12") 40
94 Tom And Jerry SHELL 011 On & On/Follow Da Massive/Till The Morning/Tom & Jerry/Tom & Jerry (12") 40
95 Tom And Jerry SHELL 012 Maxi(Mum) Style (Nasty Jungle Remix)/All Of My.../The Joker Played (12") 30

TOM & MICK
69 Olga OLE 014 Somebody's Taken Maria Away/Pandemonium 15

TOMANGOES
79 Grapevine GRP 122 I Really Love You/You've Been Gone So Long (reissue) 25

ROLO TOMASSI
07 Danger! Laser! Phaser! Razor! DLPR 003 ROLO TOMASSI (EP, 1000 only, blue vinyl) 20
08 Hassle HOFF055LP HYSTERICS (LP) 20
10 Holy Roar HRR046V COSMOLOGY (LP, 100 on blue translucent or 100 on red translucent vinyl) 25

TOM CATS
61 Starlite ST45 054 Tom Tom Cat/Big Brother 25

GARY TOMS EMPIRE
75 Epic S EPC 3611 Drive My Car/Love Me Right 12

TOMITA
77 RCA Red Seal RL1 1919 THE TOMITA PLANETS SUITE (LP, withdrawn after 1 day) 15

LEE TOMLIN
66 CBS 202455 Sweet Sweet Lovin'/Save Me (DJ copy).. 150
66 CBS 202455 Sweet Sweet Lovin'/Save Me 75

ALAN TOMLINSON
81 Bead Records BEAD 17 STILL OUTSIDE (LP) 25

ALBERT TOMLINSON
68 Giant GN 28 Don't Wait For Me/LLOYD EVANS: Losing You 300

LOUIS TOMLINSON
20 78 Productions 19075814461 WALLS (LP, picture disc) 45

ROY TOMLINSON
68 Coxsone CS 7056 I Stand For I/MARTIN: I Second That Emotion (actually by Martin Riley) 150

TOMMI & THE SPELLBINDERS
76 Target TQT 107 I Can't Get Away From You/Love Bandit 10

TOMMY (MCCOOK) & UPSETTERS
69 Trojan TR 7717 Lock Jaw (vocal by Dave Barker)/YARDBROOMS: My Desire 20
(see also Tommy McCook, Upsetters)

TOMORROW
67 Parlophone R 5597 My White Bicycle/Claramont Lake 70
67 Parlophone R 5627 Revolution/Three Jolly Little Dwarfs 70
69 Parlophone R 5813 My White Bicycle/Claramont Lake (reissue) 50
68 Parlophone PMC TOMORROW (LP, mono, yellow/black label with "Sold in U.K..." text) 500
68 Parlophone PCS 7042 TOMORROW (LP, stereo, yellow/black label with "Sold in U.K..." text) 450
76 Harvest SHSM 2010 TOMORROW (LP, reissue) 30
86 Decal LIK 2 TOMORROW (LP, reissue) 15
(see also Keith West, Steve Howe, Twink, Four + One, In Crowd, Syndicats, Aquarian Age, Fairies)

TOMORROW COME SOME DAY
69 SNB 97 TOMORROW COME SOME DAY (LP).. 900
(see also Ithaca, Friends, Agincourt, Alice Through The Looking Glass, BBC Radiophonic Workshop/Peter Howell)

TOMORROW'S CHILDREN (JAMAICA)
67 Island WI 3073 Bang Bang Rock Steady/Rain Rock Steady (some w/same label on both sides) 600

TOMORROW'S PEOPLE
17 Melodies Int. MEL 005 OPEN SOUL (LP) 15

TOMPALL & GLASER BROTHERS
68 MGM MGM-C 8082 THROUGH THE EYES OF LOVE (LP) 25

TOM TOM CLUB
81 Island ILPS 9686 TOM TOM CLUB (LP) 20
(see also Talking Heads)

TONE DEAF & THE IDIOTS

MINT VALUE £

TONE DEAF & THE IDIOTS
79	Lyntone BLI 1/Angel BL 12	Why Does Politics Turn Men Into Toads/Repatriate The National Front (flexi)	15

ELEANOR TONER
65	Decca F 12119	All Cried Out/A Hundred Guitars	8
65	Decca F 12192	Will You Still Love Me Tomorrow/Between The Window And The Phone	15
65	Decca F 12267	Danny Boy/It Hurts So Much (To See You Go)	6
66	Decca F 12454	Black Rose/Time To Spare Darling	6

TONES ON TAIL
82	4AD BAD 203	A Bigger Splash/Means Of Escape/Copper/Instrumental (12", p/s)	20
82	Beggars Banquet BEG 85T	There's Only One!/Now We Lustre (12", p/s)	12
84	Beggars Banquet BEG 109T	Lions/Go! (Club Mix) (12", p/s red vinyl)	10
84	Beggars Banquet BEGA 51	POP (LP)	20

(see also Bauhaus, Love & Rockets, Daniel Ash)

TONETTES
62	Island WI 064	Love That Is Real/Pretty Baby	12

(see also Marlene Webber, Lyrics, Don Drummond)

OSCAR TONEY JR.
67	Stateside SS 2033	For Your Precious Love/Ain't That True Love	20
67	Stateside SS 2033	For Your Precious Love/Ain't That True Love (DJ Copy)	50
67	Stateside SS 2046	Turn On Your Love Light/Any Day Now	20
67	Stateside SS 2061	You Can Lead Your Woman To The Altar/Unlucky Guy	20
68	Bell BLL 1003	Without Love There Is Nothing/Love That Never Grows Cold	10
68	Bell BLL 1011	No Sad Songs/Never Get Enough Of Your Love	10
69	Bell BLL 1057	Down In Texas/Just For You	10
72	Capricorn K 17505	Thank You, Honey Chile/I Do What You Wish	6
73	Contempo C 6	Kentucky Bluebird (A Message To Martha)/Everything I Own	6
73	Contempo CS2075	Chicken Heads/Everybody's Needed	15
74	Contempo CS 2002	Is It Because I'm Black/Make It Easy On Yourself	10
75	Contempo CS 2043	I've Been Loving You Too Long/For Your Precious Love	6
67	Stateside (S)SL 10211	FOR YOUR PRECIOUS LOVE (LP)	40

TONGUE & GROOVE
69	Fontana STL 5528	TONGUE & GROOVE (LP)	45

(see also Charlatans)

TONIGHT
78	TDS 1	Drummerman/Stroll On By (p/s)	8

(see also Andy Arthurs, Celia & Mutations)

TERRY TONIK
80	Posh TOFF 1	Just A Little Mod/Smashed And Blocked (with die-cut p/s)	150
80	Posh TOFF 1	Just A Little Mod/Smashed And Blocked (with promo A4 booklet)	70
80	Posh TOFF 1	Just A Little Mod/Smashed And Blocked	30

TONTO
74	Polydor 2383 308	IT'S ABOUT TIME (LP, insert, poster)	20

(see also Tonto's Expanding Head Band)

TONTON (MACOUTE)
72	RCA 2190	Summer Of Our Love/Greyhound Lady (as Tonton)	20
71	RCA Neon NE 4	TONTON MACOUTE (LP, gatefold sleeve, black inner)	300

TONTO'S EXPANDING HEAD BAND
71	Atlantic 2400 150	ZERO TIME (LP, gatefold sleeve)	25

(see also Tonto)

TONTRIX
79	Townton 1TON	Shell Shocked/Slipping Into Life (p/s)	7

TONY & DENNIS
67	Trojan TR 002	Folk Song/TOMMY McCOOK & SUPERSONICS: Starry Night	35

TONY FIELD
66	Pye 7N 17020	Dale Ann/Dial My Number	10

TONY & GRADUATES
60s	Hit HIT 13	The Statue	50
68	Pye 7N 17578	I Wanna Live/Angel	10
66	Pye 7N 17077	Just My Baby And Me/Another You	10

TONY & HIPPY BOYS
69	Gas GAS 121	Janet/HARMONIANS: Believe Me (states 'Beleive' on label)	35

TONY & HOWARD WITH DICTATORS
65	Oriole CB 307	Just In Case/Walk Right Out Of The Blues	30

TONY & HOWIE
72	Banana BA 371	Fun It Up/Fun Version	100

TONY & JOE
58	London HLN 8694	The Freeze/Gonna Get A Little Kissin' Tonight	40
58	London HLN 8694	The Freeze/Gonna Get A Little Kissin' Tonight (78)	25

TONY (TOMAS) & LOUISE
62	Island WI 059	Ups And Downs/TONY TOMAS: Brixton Lewisham	12

(see also Tony Washington)

TONY & TANDY
69	Atlantic 584 262	Two Can Make It Together/The Bitter And The Sweet (with Fleur De Lys)	20
71	Atlantic 2091 075	Two Can Make It TogetherSHARON TANDY: /Look And Find	8

(see also Sharon Tandy, Fleur De Lys)

TONY & THE VELVETS
63	Decca F 11637	Sunday/One More Once	10

TONY & TYRONE
70	Ember EMBS 290	Everyday Fun/Whip Your Loving On Me (p/s)	10
75	Atlantic K10217	Please Operator/Apple Of My Eye	8

TONY, CARO & JOHN

MINT VALUE £

TONY, CARO & JOHN
72	private pressing	ALL ON THE FIRST DAY (LP, with insert)	300

TONY & CHAMPIONS
70	Duke DU 90	Eye For An Eye/CHAMPIONS: Broke My Heart - Version	20

(see also Errol & Champions, Domino Johnson)

TONY'S ALLSTARS
72	Green Door GD 4041	Rub Up A Daughter/DENNIS ALCAPONE: Daughter Version	15
72	Bullet BU 509	Dub Up A Daughter (as Prince Tony's Allstars)/ DENNIS ALCAPONE: Daughter Version	8
73	Downtown DT 508	You Don't Say/DENNIS ALCAPONE: Version	12

TONY'S DEFENDERS
66	Columbia DB 7850	Yes I Do/It's Easy To Say Hello	35
66	Columbia DB 7996	Since I Lost You Baby/Waiting For A Call From You	35

TOO FUNK
95	Ferox FER 008	THE RETURN OF TOO FUNK (12" EP)	15

TOOL
94	Zoo-RCA 74321 19432-1	Prison Sex (LP Version)/Prison Sex (Edit Version)/Opiate (Live)/Undertow (Live) (12", grey vinyl)	30

TOOLS
79	Oily SLICK 2	Gotta Make Some Money Somehow/TV Eyes (p/s)	8

(see also Leisure Research)

TOOMORROW
70	RCA RCA 1978	You're My Baby Now/Goin' Back (in custom RCA sleeve)	60
70	Decca F 13070	I Could Never Live Without Your Love/Roll Like A River	60
70	RCA LSA 3008	TOOMORROW (LP, soundtrack, with insert)	125

(see also Olivia Newton-John)

TOO MUCH
78	Lightning GIL 513	Who You Wanna Be/Another Time Another Place (in p/s)	35
78	Lightning GIL 513	Who You Wanna Be/Another Time Another Place	10
78	Lightning GIL 552	Kick Me One More TIme//Be Mine/It's Only For Me (gatefold p/s)	30

DAVID TOOP
75	Obscure OBS 4	NEW AND REDISCOVERED MUSICAL INSTRUMENTS (LP, with Max Eastley & Brian Eno)	25
79	Quartz 003	WOUNDS (LP, with Paul Burwell)	30

(see also Brian Eno)

TOOTS (ACTUALLY LEE PERRY)
70	Upsetter US 327	Do You Like It/UPSETTERS: Touch Of Fire	60

TOO TUFF
88	Unyque UNQ 4T	Is This Hard Enuf?/90% Funk 10% Rhymes Or What Can You Do/Why Am I Waiting (12", p/s)	10

TOPO D. BILL
70	Charisma CB 116	Witchi Tai To/Jam (in p/s)	20
70	Charisma CB 116	Witchi Tai To/Jam	7

(see also Bonzo Dog [Doo Dah] Band, Roger Ruskin Spear)

TOPPERS
57	Brunswick 05678	Stash Pandowski (She's Not Very Much Good For Pretty)/Pots And Pans	6

TOPPICKS
78	Basilick BVK 001	Can't Let You Go/Version	10

TOP TOPHAM
69	Blue Horizon 57-3167	Christmas Cracker/Cracking Up Over Christmas	25
70	Blue Horizon 7-63857	ASCENSION HEIGHTS (LP)	120

(see also Fox, Yardbirds)

TORA TORA
80	Mancunian Metal TT 5000	Red Sun Setting/Highway (Shooting Like A Bullet) (p/s)	15
80	Tora TT 5001	Don't Want To Let You Go/Sorry I Broke Your Heart	40

TORCH
82	Ted TED 1	I Need Rock/Unknown (no p/s)	35

STEVE TORCH
79	Redball RR 005	Live In Fear/Smoke Your Own (p/s)	10

(see also Gillan, Split Knee Loons, Girl)

(BERNIE) TORMÉ (BAND)
78	Jet JET 126	I'm Not Ready/Free (p/s, as Bernie Tormé Band, orange vinyl)	6
70s	Peter Collins PC 1	The Hunter/Soul Sister	8
80	Island WIP 6586	The Beat/I Want/Bony Maronie (p/s, pink vinyl, promos on black vinyl)	8
81	Fresh FRESH 7	All Day And All Of The Night/What's Next (p/s, also listed as Parole PURL 5)	12

MEL TORME (& MEL-TONES)
SINGLES
56	Vogue Coral Q 72150	Mountain Greenery/Jeepers Creepers	15
56	London HLN 8305	Lulu's Back In Town/The Lady Is A Tramp	10
56	London HLN 8322	Lullaby Of Birdland/I Love To Watch The Moonlight	7
62	London HLK 9643	Comin' Home Baby/Right Now	30
62	London HLK 9643	Comin' Home Baby/Right Now (DJ copy)	40
66	CBS 202065	(You Got) The Power Of Love/Dominique's Discotheque	8

EPs
58	Philips BBE 12181	TORME MEETS THE BRITISH (EP)	12

ALBUMS
57	Philips BBL 7205	TORME MEETS THE BRITISH	20
63	London HA-K/SH-K 8021	MEL TORME AT THE RED HILL (with Jimmy Wisner Trio, mono/stereo)	15
63	London HA-K 8065	COMIN' HOME BABY	25

TORNADOS
62	Decca F 11449	Love And Fury/Popeye Twist	15
63	Decca F 11562	Globetrotter/Locomotion With Me (some B-sides credit "Locomotion With You")	6

Mitchell TOROK

MINT VALUE £

63	Decca F 11606	Robot/Life On Venus	8
63	Decca F 11662	The Ice Cream Man/Theme From "The Scales Of Justice"	8
63	Decca F 11745	Dragonfly/Hymn For Teenagers	12
64	Decca F 11838	Hot Pot/Joystick	10
64	Decca F 11889	Monte Carlo/Blue Blue Beat	20
64	Decca F 11946	Exodus/Blackpool Rock	20
65	Columbia DB 7455	Granada/Ragunboneman	25
65	Columbia DB 7589	Early Bird/Stompin' Through The Rye (as Tornados '65)	25
65	Columbia DB 7687	Stingray/Aqua Marina	40
66	Columbia DB 7856	Pop-Art Goes Mozart/Too Much In Love To Hear	30
66	Columbia DB 7984	Is That A Ship I Hear/Do You Come Here Often	40
62	Decca DFE 8510	THE SOUNDS OF THE TORNADOS (EP)	15
62	Decca DFE 8511	TELSTAR (EP)	15
63	Decca DFE 8521	MORE SOUNDS FROM THE TORNADOS (EP)	20
63	Decca DFE 8533	TORNADO ROCK (EP)	25
63	Decca LK 4552	AWAY FROM IT ALL (LP)	50
63	London LL 3279	TELSTAR - THE SOUND OF THE TORNADOS (LP, export copy, UK pressed LP in US sleeve)	50

(see also Heinz, Billy Fury, Clem Cattini Ork, Saints, Original Tornados, Roger LaVern & Microns, Saxons, George Bellamy, Gemini, Roger La Vern & Microns)

MITCHELL TOROK

54	London HL 8004	Caribbean/Weep Away (with Louisiana Hayride Band) (gold tri label)	40
54	London HL 8004	Caribbean/Weep Away (with Louisiana Hayride Band) (round centre)	20
54	London HL 8048	Hootchy Kootchy Henry (From Hawaii)/Gigolo	50
54	London HL 8083	The Haunting Waterfall/Dancerette (with Louisiana Hayride Band)	50
55	Brunswick 05423	The World Keeps Turning Around/A Peasant's Guitar	15
56	Brunswick 05586	When Mexico Gave Up The Rhumba/I Wish I Was A Little Bit Younger	25
56	Brunswick 05626	Red Light, Green Light (with Tulane Sisters)/Havana Huddle	25
57	Brunswick 05642	Drink Up And Go Home/Take This Heart	15
57	Brunswick 05657	Pledge Of Love/What's Behind That Strange Door	15
57	Brunswick 05718	Two Words (True Love)/You're Tempting Me (with Anita Kerr Quartet)	10
60	London HLW 9130	Pink Chiffon/What You Don't Know (Won't Hurt You)	12
54	London RE-P 1014	LOUISIANA HAYRIDE (EP, with Louisiana Hayride Band)	20
60	London HA-W 2279	CARIBBEAN (LP)	30

STEFANO TOROSSI

19	Dynamite Cuts DYNAM7054/Running Fast/Fearing Much/Feeling Tense/Walking In The Dark (reissue, 2 x 7", p/s)		12
76	Conroy BMLP 143	FEELINGS (LP)	500

MICHELLE TORR
66	Fontana TF 676	Only Tears Are Left For Me/I Love That Man	15

DONALD TORR
69	CBS 4383	My Cherie Amour/Never Will I Be	20
70	CBS 4769	Way Of The World/Green Green Yesterday	10

GEORGE TORRENCE & NATURALS
68	London HLZ 10181	Lickin' Stick/So Long Goodbye	15
71	Jay Boy BOY 48	Lickin' Stick/So Long Goodbye (reissue)	6

CLARE TORRY
67	Fontana TF 852	The Music Attracts Me/It Takes One To Make The Other Cry (as Claire Terry)	6
67	Fontana TF 878	Unsure Feelings/The End Of A Lifetime (as Claire Terry)	6
69	Decca F 12945	Love For Living/Love Tomorrow, Love Today (as Clare Torry)	6

TORTOISE
95	Soul Static SOUL 7	Why We Fight/Whitewater (p/s)	8
96	Duophonic D-UHF-D 12	Yaus/STEREOLAB: Speedy Car (gig freebie, blue vinyl, p/s, 3,000 only)	15
96	Duophonic D-UHF-D 12	Yaus/STEREOLAB: Speedy Car (orange vinyl export issue, p/s, 3,000 only)	15
01	Duophonic Super 45s DS 33 09	Gamera/Cliff Dweller Society (12", 1500 on red vinyl, 1500 on clear vinyl, 1500 on black vinyl)	15
01	Duophonic Super 45s DS 33 09	Gamera/Cliff Dweller Society (12", 1000 on fluorescent yellow vinyl)	20
96	City Slang EFA 04971	RHYTHMS, RESOLUTIONS & CLUSTERS (LP, clear vinyl)	30
98	City Slang EFA 08705-1	TNT (2-LP, gatefold sleeve)	40
00	Warp WARPLP 81	STANDARDS (LP)	20

(see also Sea & Cake)

TORTURE
81	Wildebeest WILD 1	Last Post/Lucky/Finding My Way Home	50

TOSH
82	Bicycle MP 1003	ONE MORE FOR THE ROAD (LP)	100

PETER TOSH
70	No label T 1023	No Sympathy (with The Wailers)/Boy Named Tom (actually Soulettes) (white label only)	65
71	Bullet BU 486	Maga Dog/THIRD & FOURTH GENERATION: Bull Dog	15
72	Pressure Beat PR 5559	Them A Fe Get A Beatin' (as Peter Touch)/THIRD & FOURTH GENERATION: Version	25
79	Rolling Stones RSR 103	I'm The Toughest/Toughest Version (p/s)	8
76	Virgin V 2061	LEGALIZE IT (LP)	15
77	Virgin V 2081	EQUAL RIGHTS (LP, red "mirror" girl sleeve)	15

(see also Peter Touch, Bob Marley & Wailers, Cat & Nicky Campbell, Glen Adams)

TOTAL CHAOS
81	Slam! SSM 026	There Are No Russians In Afghanistan/Primitive Feeling/Revolution Part 10 (p/s, lyric insert, original copies have "50p" on front)	20
82	Volume VOL 1	There Are No Russians In Afghanistan/Primitive Feeling/Revolution Part 10 (p/s, reissue)	8
83	Volume VOL 2	Factory Man/Brixton Prison/She Don't Care/Die (p/s)	7
83	Volume VOLT 6	FIELDS AND BOMBS EP (12")	15

TOTAL CONTRAST

MINT VALUE £

TOTAL CONTRAST
84 Total Contrast TCR 2   Next Time I'll Know Better/Sunshine (12") 35

TOTAL FIASCO
89 White TF001   See How They Run/Method To The Madness 75
(see also Killa Instinct)

TOTAL OUTPUT AND KILLERHERTZ
92 FX FXUKT 11   Acid Mind/Monolithic/Analog Xpression/Digital Kiss (12") 12
(see also Killerhertz)

TOTAL SCIENCE
96 Void VOID 004   Combined Science/Sands Of Time (12") 12
97 Void VOID 007   AEROSPACE EP (12") 10

TOTALLY OUTTA HAND BAND
78 Kilgaron KIL 1   Teenage Revolution/Too Much Trouble By Far (p/s) 8

TO THE FINLAND STATION
81 Melodia   DOMINO THEORY (7" EP) 6

TOTNAMITES
61 Oriole CB 1615   Danny Boy/The Spurs Song 15

TOTO
84 Polydor 422 8237-2   DUNE (LP, soundtrack, 1 track by Brian Eno) 15

TOTS
74 Philips 6006 408   Please Yourself/Time To Go Home (p/s) 7

TINA TOTT
69 Pye 7N 17823   Take Away The Emptiness Too/Burning In The Background Of My Mind 30

TOTTENHAM HOTSPUR F.C.
67 Columbia SEG 8532   THE SPURS GO MARCHING ON: SINGALONG SPURS (EP) 20
(see also Terry Venables)

PETER TOUCH
65 Island WI 211   Hoot Nanny Hoot (actually by Peter Tosh & Wailers)/ BOB MARLEY: Do You Remember
                                    (actually Peter Tosh & Wailers) 160
65 Island WI 215   Shame And Scandal (with Wailers)/WAILERS: The Jerk 100
67 Island WI 3042   I Am The Toughest (actually by Peter Tosh & Wailers)/ MARCIA GRIFFITHS: No Faith 75
67 Coxsone CS 7012   Dancing Time/Treat Me Good 120
69 Jackpot JP 706   The Crimson Pirate/Moon Duck 45
69 Unity UN 525   Return Of A Capone/LENEX BROWN : Q Club 30
69 Unity 529   Sun Valley/Headley Bennett - Drums Of Fu Man Chu 40
(see also Peter Tosh, Bop & The Beltone, Glen Adams)

TOUCH (1)
69 Deram DM 243   Miss Teach/We Feel Fine 12
69 Deram DML/SML 1033   THIS IS TOUCH (LP, with poster) 200
69 Deram DML/SML 1033   THIS IS TOUCH (LP, without poster) 100
(see also Don & Goodtimes, Kingsmen)

TOUCH (2)
80 Ariola ARO 243   Don't You Know What Love Is/My Life Depends On You (in p/s) 20
80 Ariola ARO 243   Don't You Know What Love Is/My Life Depends On You 6
80 Ariola ARO 250   Love Don't Fail Me Now (p/s) 6

TOUCH (3)
81 Record Corner EJSP 9750   Keep On/Keep On Remixin' (12") 20
81 Elite DAZZ 11   Keep On/Keep On Remixin' (12") 15
82 Elite DAZZ 14-7   Love Something Special/Keep On 20
82 Elite DAZZ 14   Love Something Special/Love Speciality (12") 15

TOUCHDOWN
83 Record Shack SHACK 12   Ease Your Mind (Remix)/Aquadance (12") 20

TOUCHED
84 Ebony EBON 27   Dream Girl/We'll Fight Back 10

TOUCH OF CLASS
76 GTO GTLP 024   I'M IN HEAVEN (LP) 15

TOUCHSTONE
72 MAS 9   MUSIC FROM PANDORAS BOX (LP, white label) 2000

TOUGH CROWD
18 Tough Crowd TC001   TOUGH CROWD (LP) 30

ALI FARKA TOURE
87 World Circuit WCB 007   ALI FARKA TOURE (LP) 30
90 World Circuit WCB 017   THE RIVER (LP) 80
94 World Circuit WCB 040   TALKING TIMBUKTU (LP, with Ry Cooder) 50

TOURS
79 Tours T 1   Language School/Foreign Girls (paper p/s) 20
79 Tours T 1   Language School/Foreign Girls (printed PVC sleeve) 12
79 Virgin VS 307   Tourist Information/You Knew (p/s) 8

AL TOUSAN
61 London HLU 9211   Naomi/Indinna (some copies miscredited to 'Al Pousan') 8
(see also Allen Toussaint)

ALLEN TOUSSAINT
69 Soul City SC 119   We The People/Tequila 25
72 Reprise K 14200   Soul Sister/She Once Belonged To Me 6
72 Reprise K 44202   LIFE, LOVE AND FAITH (LP) 22
75 Reprise K 54201   SOUTHERN NIGHTS (LP) 30
85 Kent KENT 036   FROM A WHISPER TO A SCREAM (LP) 15
85 Edsel ED 155   SOUTHERN LIGHTS (LP, reissue) 15
(see also Al Tousan)

CALINE & OLIVER TOUSSAINT
78 Epic S EPC 6334   The Gardens Of Monaco/Les Jardins De Monaco 12

Roberta TOVEY

MINT VALUE £

ROBERTA TOVEY
65	Polydor BM 56021	Who's Who/Not So Old (in p/s)	45
65	Polydor BM 56021	Who's Who/Not So Old	25

TOWER OF POWER
73	Reprise K 16278	So Very Hard To Go/Clean Slate	8
73	Reprise K 16211	You're Still A Young Man/Skating On Thin Ice	8
75	Reprise K 16543	It's Not The Crime/Only So Much Time On The Ground	8
75	Warner Bros. K 56088	URBAN RENEWAL (LP)	15

JOHN TOWERS
67	CBS 2943	Seasons Song/It's Spring Again	10

JOHNNY TOWERS
62	Philips 326554 BF	The Lonely Man Theme/There's No Place Like Rome	8
63	Philips 326570 BF	This Kind Of Love/My First Romance	7

COLIN TOWNS
78	Virgin VS 204	Full Circle (Main Theme)/Olivia (p/s)	10
80	MCA MCA 643	Breakdown/Working Man (p/s)	15

(see also Gillan, Samson, Split Knee Loons)

TOWNSEL SISTERS
60	Polydor NH 66954	Will I Ever/I Know	12

ED TOWNSEND (& TOWNSMEN)
58	Capitol CL 14867	For Your Love/Over And Over Again	10
58	Capitol CL 14927	When I Grow Too Old To Dream/You Are My Everything	10
59	Capitol CL 14976	Richer Than I/Getting By Without You	7
59	Capitol CL 15020	Don't Ever Leave Me/Lover Come Back To Me	7
59	Capitol CL 15072	This Little Love Of Mine/Hold On	7
60	Capitol CL 15141	Don't Get Around Much Anymore/Do Nothin' Till You Hear	7
60	Warner Bros WB 21	Stay With Me (A Little While Longer)/I Love Everything About You	40
59	Capitol EAP1 1091	ED TOWNSEND (EP)	20
59	Capitol T 1140	NEW IN TOWN (LP)	25
76	Curtom K 56180	NOW (LP)	20

JOHN TOWNSEND
70s	Sweet Folk All SFA 002	NO MUCKING ABOUT (LP)	18

PETE TOWNSHEND
82	Eva-Tone 623827XS	My Generation/Pinball Wizard (U.S. square flexidisc sewn into U.K. copies of Richard Barnes' Maximum R&B book; with book)	20
72	Track 2408 201	WHO CAME FIRST (LP, gatefold sleeve with poster)	25
72	Track 2408 201	WHO CAME FIRST (LP, laminated gatefold sleeve without poster)	15

(see also The Who, Meher Baba, Billy Nicholls, Elton John)

PETE TOWNSHEND & RONNIE LANE
77	Polydor 2058 944	Street In The City/RONNIE LANE: Annie (limited issue)	20
77	Polydor 2058 944	Street In The City/RONNIE LANE: Annie (12", p/s)	12

(see also Who, Ronnie Lane)

TOXIC
92	D-Zone DANCE 26	Simple Warnin' (Ruffneck Mix)/Simple Warnin' (Riffist Mix)/Simple Warnin' (Hi Power Version)Kik The Break (12", company sleeve)	60

TOXIC REASONS
84	T-REASON HANG 1	God Bless America/Can't Get Away/Destroyer (p/s)	6
84	Alt. Tentacles VIRUS 42	KILL BY REMOTE CONTROL (LP)	15

TOXIK EPHEX
89	Words Of Warning WOW 6	Does Someone Have To Die/Life Is For Living/SHRAPNEL: Trivial Pursuit/Autumn Split EP p/s	10
89	One Up	THE ADVENTURES OF NOBBY PORTHOLE - THE COCK OF THE NORTH (LP)	20

TOYAN
81	Greensleeves GREL 20	HOW THE WEST WAS WON (LP)	25
83	Vista STLP 1023	MURDER (LP, as Toyan with Tippa Lee)	45
83	Upfront UPFLP 11	DJ DADDY (LP)	15

TOY DOLLS
81	GBH SSM 005	Tommy Kowey's Car/She Goes To Finos (500 only)	200
81	GBH GRC 104	TOY DOLLS EP: Tommy Kowey's Car/She's A Working Ticket/Everybody Jitterbug/Teenager In Love/I've Got Asthma (yellow paper p/s, with insert)	60
82	Zonophone Z 31	Everybody Jitterbug/(She's A) Working Ticket (p/s)	30
83	Volume VOL 3	Nellie The Elephant/Dig That Groove Baby (p/s)	15
83	Volume VOL 5	Cheerio And Toodle Pip/H.O. (p/s)	10
83	Volume VOL 7	Alfie From The Bronx/Hanky Panky (p/s)	10
84	Volume VOL 10	We're Mad/Deirdre's A Slag (p/s)	6
84	Volume VOLT 10	We're Mad/Deirdre's A Slag/Rupert The Bear (12", p/s)	10
85	Volume VOL 17	James Bond (Lives Down Our Street)/Olga... I cannot! (p/s)	8
86	Volume VOL 21	Geordie's Gone To Jail/Idle Gossip (p/s)	8
82	WOWLP 1	THE TOY DOLLS ALBUM (LP)	20
84	Volume VOLP 1	DIG THAT GROOVE, BABY (LP)	20
85	Volume VOLP 2	A FAR OUT DISC (LP)	15
86	Volume VOLP 3	IDLE GOSSIP (LP)	20
94	Toy Dolls NIT 2	TEN YEARS OF TOYS (LP, with inner)	20

(see also Showbiz Kids)

TOY DOLLS (U.S.)
63	London HLN 9647	Little Tin Soldier/Fly Away	30

TOYS
79	SRT SRTS/79/CUS 345	My Mind Wanders/The Girl On My Wall/Toytime/I'd Do Anything For You (p/s)	20
79	Toy TOYS 2	STILL DANCING (EP, hand-stamped white label, foldaround p/s)	100

TOYS
80	Red Bus RBUS 54	Go To The Police/Breakdown	50

TOYS (U.S.)

MINT VALUE £

TOYS (U.S.)
Year	Cat No	Title	Value
65	Stateside SS 460	A Lover's Concerto/This Night	8
66	Stateside SS 483	Attack/See How They Run	8
66	Stateside SS 502	May My Heart Be Cast Into Stone/On Backstreet	20
66	Stateside SS 519	Silver Spoon/Can't Get Enough Of You Baby	22
66	Stateside SS 539	Baby Toys/Happy Birthday Broken Heart	10
67	Philips BF 1563	Ciao Baby/I Got Carried Away	10
67	Philips BF 1581	My Love Sonata/I Close My Eyes	10
69	Bell BLL 1053	A Lover's Concerto/Baby Toys	7
66	Stateside SL 10275	THE TOYS SING "A LOVER'S CONCERTO" AND "ATTACK" (LP, mono)	40
66	Stateside SSL 10275	THE TOYS SING "A LOVER'S CONCERTO" AND "ATTACK" (LP, stereo)	50

TOYSHOP
69	Polydor 56317	Say Goodbye To Yesterday/Send My Love To Lucy	12

T.P.I.
79	SRT SRTS 79 CUS 489	She's Too Clever For Me/You Rool Me (no p/s, 1000 only)	90

TRACE (1)
74	Vertigo 6360 852	TRACE (LP)	25
75	Vertigo 6413 080	BIRDS (LP)	25

(see also Curved Air)

TRACE (2)
95	Lucky Spin LSR 019	Lost Entity Remix/Jazz Primitives (12")	40

TRACER
83	Mouse Hole TRA 1	CHANNELLED AGGRESSION EP (p/s)	125

MARK TRACEY
62	Parlophone R 4944	Caravan Of Lonely Men/Never Ending (with John Barry & His Orchestra)	10

STAN TRACEY
58	Vogue LA 160130	STAN TRACEY SHOWCASE (LP)	70
59	Vogue LA 160155	LITTLE KLUNK (LP, as Stan Tracey Trio)	130
65	Columbia 33SX 1774	JAZZ SUITE (LP, as Stan Tracey Quartet, also stereo SCX 3589)	100
66	Columbia S(C)X 6051	ALICE IN JAZZLAND (LP, as Stan Tracey Big Band)	40
67	Columbia S(C)X 6124	STAN TRACEY... IN PERSON (LP)	40
68	Columbia S(C)X 6205	WITH LOVE FROM JAZZ (LP)	50
69	Ace Of Clubs ACL 1259	LITTLE KLUNK (LP, reissue)	30
69	Columbia S(C)X 6320	WE LOVE YOU MADLY (LP, as Stan Tracey Big Brass)	50
69	Columbia SCX 6358	THE LATIN AMERICAN CAPER (LP, with Big Brass & Woodwind)	40
70	Columbia SCX 6385	FREE AN' ONE (LP, as Stan Tracey Quartet)	70
70	Columbia SCX 6413	SEVEN AGES OF MAN (LP, as Stan Tracey Big Band)	35
72	Columbia SCX 6485	PERSPECTIVES (LP as Stan Tracey Trio)	40
74	Cadillac SGC 1003	ALONE AT WIGMORE HALL (LP)	15

(see also New Departures Quartet, Mike Osborne, Neil Ardley, Laurie Johnson)

ZEN TRACEY
62	Decca F 11492	Shamrocker (Phil The Fluter's Ball)/Two By Two	8

TRACK
66	Columbia DB 7987	Why Do Fools Fall In Love?/Cry To Me	18

TRACK 4
82	Track 4 TR4 001	Mr Charisma (p/s, with insert)	100

TRACTOR (1)
72	Dandelion 2001 282	Stone Glory/Marie/As You Say	15
78	UK UK 93	Roll The Dice/Vicious Circle	8
81	Cargo CRS 002	No More Rock & Roll/Northern City	10
72	Dandelion 2310 217	TRACTOR (LP)	300
83	Thunderbolt THBL 002	TRACTOR (LP, reissue)	20

(see also Way We Live)

TRACTOR (2)
77	Cargo CRS 002	No More Rock 'N' Roll/Northern City	15

TRACY
66	Columbia DB 7802	Don't Hold It Against Me/These Four Walls	8
69	Columbia DB 8569	Life's Like That/Let Me Love You	7
69	Columbia DB 8637	Follow Me/A City Called Soul	12
71	Columbia DB 8750	Rock Me In The Cradle/Strange Love	10

ARTHUR TRACY
67	Decca F 12656	Marta/Wanderer	6

GRANT TRACY & SUNSETS
61	Ember EMB S 126	Say When/Please Baby Please	20
61	Ember EMB S 130	Pretend/Love Me	20
62	Ember EMB S 148	The Great Matchmaker/Tears Came Rolling Down	20
62	Ember EMB S 155	Taming Tigers/The Painted Smile	20
63	Decca F 11741	Everybody Shake/Turn The Lights Down, Jenny	20
64	Ember EMB 3352	TEENBEAT (LP)	80

(see also Pete Dello, Honeybus)

WENDALL TRACY
58	London HLM 8664	Who's To Know/Corrigidor Rock	15

TRADER
79	Bos	Back Street Trader/Love On The Run (p/s)	15

TRADER HORNE
69	Pye 7N 17846	Morning Way/Sheena	40
70	Dawn DNS 1003	Here Comes The Rain/Goodbye Mercy Kelly	40
70	Dawn DNLS 3003	MORNING WAY (LP, gatefold, with photo & insert)	300
70	Dawn DNLS 3003	MORNING WAY (LP, gatefold, without photo & insert)	150

(see also Them, Fairport Convention, Jackie McAuley)

TRADEWINDS

MINT VALUE £

TRADEWINDS
59	RCA RCA 1141	Crossroads/Furry Murray	20
59	RCA RCA 1141	Crossroads/Furry Murray (78)	25

TRADE WINDS
65	Red Bird RB 10020	New York Is A Lonely Town/Club Seventeen	22
66	Kama Sutra KAS 202	Mind Excursion/Little Susan's Dreaming	20

TRAD GRADS (WITH LEN, HERB, KIKO & RICHARD)
61	Decca F 11403	Runnin' Shoes/Rag-Day Jazz-Band Ball	8

(see also Quarry Men)

TRADITION
76	Venture VEN 7705	Movin On/Movin Rocker	10
77	Venture VNLP 8877	MOVIN' ON (LP)	25
77	Venture CUT 6	IN DUB (LP)	60
78	RCA PL 25169	TELL YOUR FRIENDS ABOUT DUB (LP)	20
78	RAC PL 25186	ALTERNATIVE ROUTES (LP)	30
80	Venture CUT 9	CAPTAIN GANJA AND THE SPACE PATROL (LP)	200
80	Venture CUT 10	PARTY DISCO (LP, blue vinyl, no sleeve)	250

TRAFFIC
67	Island WIP 6002	Paper Sun/Giving To You (in p/s)	12
67	Island WIP 6017	Hole In My Shoe/Smiling Phases (in p/s)	12
67	Island WIP 6025	Here We Go Round The Mulberry Bush/Coloured Rain (1st 100,000 in p/s)	15
67	Island WIP 6025	Here We Go Round The Mulberry Bush/Coloured Rain	12
68	Island WIP 6030	No Face, No Name, No Number/Roamin' In The Gloamin' With 40,000 Headmen	12
68	Island WIP 6041	You Can All Join In/Withering Tree (unissued in U.K.)	0
68	Island WIP 6041	Feelin' Alright/Withering Tree	10
68	Island WIP 6050	Medicated Goo/Shanghai Noodle Factory	10
71	Island No Cat No	Welcome To The Canteen (promo 7" with blank labels in mini LP sleeve)	40
71	Island TIM 1	Gimme Some Lovin Part One (live)/Gimme Some Lovin Part Two (live) (p/s, white label only)	25
74	Island WIP 6207	Walking In The Wind/Walking In The Wind (Instrumental)	10
67	Island ILP 961	MR FANTASY (LP, gatefold sleeve internal flipbacks, 1st pressing pink label with black 'circle' logo, mono)	300
67	Island ILPS 9061	MR FANTASY (LP, gatefold sleeve internal flipbacks, 1st pressing pink label with black 'circle' logo, stereo)	250
68	Island ILPS 9081T	TRAFFIC (LP, gatefold sleeve with stapled-in booklet; pink label with black 'circle' logo)	150
68	Island ILPS 9081T	TRAFFIC (LP, gatefold sleeve with stapled-in booklet; pink rim label with 'palm tree' logo)	20
69	Island ILP(S) 9097	LAST EXIT (LP, pink label with black/red 'eyeball' logo)	150
70	Island ILPS 9070	LAST EXIT (LP, 2nd pressing pink 'i' label)	60
74	Island ILP(S) 9097	LAST EXIT (LP, pink rim label with 'palm tree' logo)	20
69	Island ILP(S) 9112	THE BEST OF TRAFFIC (LP, 1st pressings with pink "I" label)	30
69	Island ILPS 9061	MR. FANTASY (LP, 2nd pressing, stereo, pink 'i' label)	150
70	Island ILPS 9081	MR. FANTASY (LP, 3rd pressing, pink rim label with 'palm tree' logo)	20
70	Island ILPS 9116	JOHN BARLEYCORN MUST DIE (LP, gatefold sleeve, 1st pressings with pink "i" label)	50
71	Island ILPS 9142	LIVE - NOVEMBER '70 (LP, unreleased, may exist as test pressing)	0
71	Island ILPS 9166	WELCOME TO THE CANTEEN (LP, 'sniped' spine edges, pink rim palm tree label)	40
71	Island ILPS 9180	THE LOW SPARK OF THE... (LP, laminated sleeve, pink rim/palm tree label)	20
73	Island ILPS 9224	SHOOT OUT AT THE FANTASY FACTORY (LP, pink rim/palm tree label)	15
74	Island ILPS 9273	WHEN THE EAGLE FLIES (LP, 1st pressing. Hand etched MATRIXES: ILPS 9273 A-1U GT 1 STERLING/ILPS 9273 B-1U AM 2 STERLING)	25

(see also Spencer Davis Group, Stevie Winwood, Revolution, Hellions, Dave Mason, Gordon Jackson)

TRAFFIC JAM
67	Piccadilly 7N 35386	Almost But Not Quite There/Wait Just A Minute (demo copy)	400
67	Piccadilly 7N 35386	Almost But Not Quite There/Wait Just A Minute	500

(see also Status Quo, Spectres)

JIM TRAGAS
72	Buddah 2011 157	White Buffalo/Mama Took Me From The Jungle	6

TRAGEDY
10	Diggers With Gratitude DWG 009	THE BLACK RAGE DEMOS (EP, 75 only, red vinyl)	60
10	Diggers With Gratitude DWG 009	THE BLACK RAGE DEMOS (EP, 175 only, black vinyl)	30

TRAGICIAN
79	Look LKSP 6411	The Wild The Scared And The Timid/Traces Of Impact (numbered gatefold p/s)	35

PHIL TRAINER
77	Splash CP17	Carousel/Rose Coloured Sky	8
73	BASF BAG 22 29107-3	TRAINER (LP, gatefold)	35

(see also Trees)

TRAIN SET
80s	Play Hard DEC 11	She's Gone (12", p/s)	35
89	Play Hard DEC 17	Hold On (12", p/s)	35

TRAINSPOTTERS
79	Arista ARIST 290	High Rise/Rock N Roll Hall Of Fame (p/s)	10
79	Arista ARIST 320	Unfaithful/Hiring The Hall	15

TRAITOR
81	Airship APP 377	That's Life/Stone Cold Sober	100

TRAITOR'S GATE
85	Bullet BOLT 12	DEVIL TAKES THE HIGH ROAD (EP)	10

TRAITS
67	Pye International 7N 25404	Harlem Shuffle/Strange Lips (Start Ole Memories)	35

(see also Roy Head)

Alan TRAJAN

MINT VALUE £

ALAN TRAJAN
69 MCA MK 5002   Speak To Me, Clarissa/This Might Be My Last Number 50
69 MCA MKPS 2000   FIRM ROOTS (LP, laminated front sleeve) 120

TRAMLINE
68 Island ILPS 9088   SOMEWHERE DOWN THE LINE (LP, pink label black/orange circle) 200
69 Island ILPS 9095   MOVES OF VEGETABLE CENTURIES (LP, pink label) 200

(see also Whitesnake)

BOBBY LEE TRAMMELL
64 Sue WI 326   New Dance In France/Carolyn 40

TRAMMY (RON WILSON)
72 Techniques TE 920   Horns Of Paradise/TECHNIQUES ALL STARS: Grass Root 30

TRAMP
69 Young Blood SBY 4   Vietnam Rose/Each Day 12
74 Spark SRL 1107   Put A Record On/You've Gotta Move 8
69 Music Man SMLS 603   TRAMP (LP, laminated front, flipbacks, white/black label) 150
73 Spark Replay SRLM 2001 TRAMP (LP, reissue) 30
74 Spark SRLP 112   PUT A RECORD ON (LP) 30

(see also Dave Kelly, Jo-Ann Kelly, Brunning Hall Sunflower Blues Band, Fleetwood Mac)o

TRAMWAY
91 Sarah SARAH 52   Technical College/Balla (p/s, insert) 20
91 Sarah SRH 43   Maritime City/Boathouse/Star (p/s, with insert) 20

TRANE
71 BBC RESL 5   Wagoner's Walk/Jenny's Song/Ragged Bird/Mansion Of Cards (p/s) 15

TRANQUILITY
72 Epic EPC 64729   TRANQUILITY (LP, yellow label) 20
72 Epic EPC 65418   SILVER (LP, lyric insert, yellow label) 15

TRANS AM
95 Thrill Jockey THRILL 024 TRANS AM (LP) 15

TRANSATLANTICS
65 Fontana TF 593   Many Things From Your Window/I Tried To Forget 35
65 Fontana TF 638   Stand Up And Fight Like A Man/But I Know 20
65 Mercury MF 948   Don't Fight It/Look Before You Leap 50
65 King KG 1033   Run For Your Life/It's All Over 15
66 King KG 1040   Louie Go Home/Find Yourself Another Guy 30

TRANSCRIPT CARRIERS
92 Transcript Carriers TC999 ALL FEAR IS BONDAGE (EP) 40

TRANSIENT WAVES
98 Fat Cat 12FAT 011   Born With A Body And Fucked In The Heads/(2 Lone Swordsmen Mix)/(Skye [Stasis] Mix) (12", custom embossed sleeve) 10

TRANSISTORS
81 Open Circuit   RIOT SQUAD (EP) 20

TRANSIT
09 Third Man TMR 012   Come On And Ride/After Party (100 only, luminous vinyl) 40

TRANSMISSION
84 PMP PMP 001   Reaching Out/Bouncing Ball/Take It Easy/Mystery Lady (12", p/s) 60

TRANSMITTERS
78 Ebony EYE 11   Party/0.5 Alive (p/s) 15
78 Ebony EBY 1002   24 HOURS (LP) 15

TRANSPARENT ILLUSION
81 Vortex VEX 001/002   Vortex/Nuclear Release (p/s) 150
82 Vortex VEX 5   Guilty Rich Men (p/s) 10
81 Vortex VEX 3   STILL HUMAN (LP) 150
82 Vortex VEX 4   CHAGRIN RECEIVER (LP) 20

TRANSPORTER
70s Mother Truck MT 1   Kids On The Run/Intoxicating 6

TRANSVOLTA
79 Pinnacle PIN 3   Disco Computer/You're Disco 8
79 Pinnacle PIN 3 12   Disco Computer/You're Disco (12") 30

TERRY TRANZ & THE VESTITES
81 Go Round TOUCH 1   State Hand Out/We Had It Here (2 different white or yellow home-made sleeves) 150

BOUBACAR TRAORE
90 Sterns 1032   MARIAMA (LP) 40

TRAPEZE
69 Threshold TH 2   Send Me No More Letters/Another Day 10
72 Threshold TH 11   Coast To Coast/Your Love Is Alright 10
75 Warner Bros K 16606   Sunny Side Of The Street/Monkey 8
79 Aura AUS 114   Don't Ask Me How I Know/Take Good Care (p/s) 15
80 Aura AUS 116   Running Away/Don't Break My Heart (p/s) 15
69 Threshold THS 2   TRAPEZE (LP, gatefold sleeve) 90
70 Threshold THS 4   MEDUSA (LP) 70
73 Threshold THS 8   YOU ARE THE MUSIC ... WE'RE JUST THE BAND (LP) 20
74 Warner Bros K 56064   HOT WIRE (LP) 15
81 Aura AUL 717   LIVE IN TEXAS ... DEAD ARMADILLOS (LP) 15

(see also Finders Keepers, Montanas, Deep Purple, Glenn Hughes, Judas Priest, Whitesnake)

TRASH TOWN
85 Course CORS 1   Unlucky Numbers/Down 18

TRASH (1)
69 Apple APPLE 6   Road To Nowhere/Illusions (initial copies as White Trash) 200
69 Apple APPLE 6   Road To Nowhere/Illusions (later copies as Trash) 70
69 Apple APPLE 17   Golden Slumbers - Carry That Weight/Trash Can 30

(see also Poets, Pathfinders)

TRASH (2)

MINT VALUE £

TRASH (2)
77	Polydor 2058 939	Priorities/Look (p/s)	6
78	Polydor 2059 - 013	N-n-e-r-v-o-u-s/Page 3 (p/s)	8

TRASHCAN SINATRAS
89	Go! Discs GODX 34	Obscurity Knocks/The Best Man's Fall/Drunken Chorus/Who's He? (12", p/s)	12
90	Go! Discs GOD 41	Only Tongue/Useless Begins With You/Tonight You Belong To Me (p/s)	6
90	Go! Discs GODX 41	Only Tongue/Useless Begins With You/Tonight You Belong To Me (12", p/s)	10
90	Go! Discs GOD 46	Circling The Circumference/My Mistake (p/s)	8
90	Go! Discs GODX 46	Circling The Circumference/My Mistake/White Horses (12", p/s)	12
92	Go! Discs EXTCS1	Senses Working Overtime/For The Meantime (12", promo, numbered)	25
93	Go! Discs GOD 100	I've Seen Everything/Houseproud/I'm The One Who Fainted (p/s)	6
96	Go! Discs GOD 141	The Main Attraction/Stainless Stephen/Charles Atlas/Jane's Estranged (p/s)	8
96	Go! Discs GOD 151	How Can I Apply?/Save Me (p/s)	6
96	Go! Discs GOD 157	To Sir, With Love/Claw/A Boy And A Girl/You Only Live Twice (p/s)	8
90	Go! Discs 828 2011	CAKE (LP)	35
93	Go! Discs 824 408-1	I'VE SEEN EVERYTHING (LP)	150
96	Go! Discs 828 696-1	A HAPPY POCKET (LP)	100

TRASHMEN
64	Stateside SS 255	Surfin' Bird/King Of The Surf	35
64	Stateside SS 276	Bird Dance Beat/A-Bone	35

TRAVELING WILBURYS
88	Warner Bros W 7732W	Handle With Care/Margarita (gatefold p/s with sticker, sealed)	10
88	Warner Bros W 7732TE	Handle With Care (Extended)/Margarita (10", p/s)	10
89	Warner Bros W 7637TW	End Of The Line (Extended)/Congratulations (12", p/s, with sheet of stickers)	10
91	Warner Bros W 0019	Wilbury Twist/New Blue Moon (Instrumental) (p/s)	6
91	Warner Bros W 0018W	Wilbury Twist/New Blue Moon (Instrumental) (card p/s with 4 postcards)	8
88	Warner Bros WX 224W	VOLUME ONE (LP, some with stickered sleeve & sticker inserts)	20

(see also George Harrison, Bob Dylan, Roy Orbison, Tom Petty)

TRAVELLERS
77	Paradise PDS 001	Jah Give Us The World (feat. U Brown)/Girl I Left Behind (12", p/s)	15
77	Paradise PDL 002	BLACK BLACK MINDS (LP)	80
05	Pressure Sounds PSLP 49	BLACK BLACK MINDS (2-LP, reissue)	30

MARY TRAVERS
72	Warner Bros K 16191	Morning Glory/That's Enough For Me	7

(See also Peter, Paul & Mary)

PAT TRAVERS
76	Polydor SFI 221/2814 040	Makes No Difference (1-sided flexidisc, promo only, black & white p/s)	10

(see also Nicko McBrain)

MERLE TRAVIS
53	Capitol CL45 13985	Gamblers Guitar/Shut Up And Drink Your Beer	35
56	Capitol EAP1 032	MERLE TRAVIS GUITAR (EP)	10
57	Capitol EAP2 650	MERLE TRAVIS GUITAR NO. 2 (EP)	10
59	Capitol EAP1 891	BACK HOME (EP)	10
63	Capitol EAP1 1391	WALKIN' THE STRINGS (EP)	10

(see also Brown's Ferry Four)

PAUL TRAVIS
75	A&M AMLS 68290	RETURN OF THE NATIVE (LP, with lyric inner)	15

(see also Travis)

TRAVIS (1)
73	A&M AMS 7081	Band Of Heroes/Out In The Country	8
73	A&M AMLS 68120	SHINE ON ME (LP)	50

(see also Paul Travis)

TRAVIS (2)
96	Red Telephone Box PHONE 001	All I Want Do Is Rock/Line Is Fine/Funny Thing (10", numbered, stickered p/s, 750 only)	30
97	Independiente ISOM 1LP	GOOD FEELING (LP, inner)	50
99	Independiente ISOM 9 LP	THE MAN WHO (LP, with bonus remix 12")	100
99	Independiente ISOM 9 LP	THE MAN WHO (LP)	50
01	Independiente ISOM 25 LP	THE INVISIBLE BAND (LP, with free 7")	40
03	Independiente ISOM 40LP	12 MEMORIES (LP)	25
07	Epic ISOM 67LP	THE BOY WITH NO NAME (LP, and free 7")	50
08	Red Telephone Box PHONE 004V	ODE TO J SMITH (LP)	30

TRAVIS & BOB
59	Pye International 7N 25018	Tell Him No/We're Too Young	15
61	Mercury AMT 1142	Baby Stay Close To Me/Give Your Love To Me	7

TRAX
74	Fresh Air 6121 108	Wasn't It Nice/Black Boy	6
74	Fresh Air 6121 117	Number One Lover/Hounds	6
79	Lonely LONESOME ONE	HOME EP	20

TRAX FOUR
66	Ace Of Clubs S/ACL 1216	WINGDING PARTY!!! (LP, mono/stereo)	55

JACK TRAYLOR & STEELWIND
73	Grunt FTR 0194	CHILD OF NATURE (LP)	20

TREASURE BOY
67	Trojan TR 010	Love Is A Treasure (actually by Freddie McKay)/TOMMY McCOOK: Zazuka	35

TREATMENT
81	Private Pressing	Stamp Out Mutants/Doncha Know (p/s)	15
87	Number NUMB 001	Feeling Like A Ghost/Rowing Boat	8
89	Number TAO 1	LIVE (LP)	18
93	Delerium DELEC 026	CIPHER CAPUT (LP, insert)	20

Steve TREATMENT

MINT VALUE £

STEVE TREATMENT
78	Rather GEAR 2	A SIDED 45 EP (p/s)	20
79	Backbone ZBHIT 1	Heaven Knows (Juvenile Wrecks)/Step Inside A Worn Out Shoe (fold-out p/s)	20
79	Backbone ZBHIT 2	CHANGE OF PLAN EP (p/s)	20

TREBLETONES
61	Butlin CP 2424	Butlin Holiday/Butlin Holiday	8
63	Oriole CB 1838	In Real Life/Dream Of A Lifetime	12

TREDEGAR
86	Aries CEP 0001	Duma/The Jester (p/s)	75
86	Aries CEP LP 001	TREDEGAR (LP, gatefold sleeve, embossed)	18

(see also Budgie)

HERBERT BEERBOHM TREE
65	OMY 69	KEEP THOSE DOGS AWAY (EP)	25

TREES
70	CBS 5078	Nothing Special/Epitaph	25
70	CBS 63837	THE GARDEN OF JANE DELAWNEY (LP)	350
71	CBS 64168	ON THE SHORE (LP)	400
87	Decal LIK 12	ON THE SHORE (LP, reissue)	15
87	Decal LIK 15	THE GARDEN OF JANE DELAWNEY (LP, reissue)	30
06	Sunbeam SBR2LP 5056	THE GARDEN OF JANE DELAWNEY (2-LP, reissue, 180gm vinyl, booklet)	20
08	Sunbeam SBR2LP 5057	ON THE SHORE (2-LP, reissue, 180gm vinyl, booklet)	30

(see also Casablanca, Juliet Lawson, Trainer)

TREETOPS
67	Parlophone R 5628	Don't Worry Baby/I Remember	15
68	Parlophone R 5669	California My Way/Carry On Living	12
70	Columbia DB 8727	Mississippi Valley/Man Is A Man	12
71	Columbia DB 8799	Without The One You Love/So Here I Go Again	15
73	Columbia DB 9013	Gypsey/Life Is Getting Better	15

TREKKAS
65	Planet PLF 105	Please Go/I Put A Spell On You	150

TREM
83	AM 251	My Robotic Friend/Colour Vision (p/s, 1000 only)	25

TREMBLING BLUE STARS
96	Shinkansen SHINKANSEN 1	Abba On The Jukebox/She's Always There (p/s, 1,000 only)	8

TREMELOES
66	Decca F 12423	Blessed/The Right Time	20
66	CBS 202242	Good Day Sunshine/What A State I'm In	15
67	CBS 202519	Here Comes My Baby/Gentlemen Of Pleasure	6
67	CBS 2723	Silence Is Golden/Let Your Hair Hang Down (p/s)	6
67	CBS 2930	Even The Bad Times Are Good/Jenny's Alright (p/s)	6
67	CBS 3043	Be Mine/Suddenly Winter	10
68	CBS 3234	Suddenly You Love Me/As You Are	6
68	CBS 2889	Helule Helule/Girl From Nowhere	6
68	CBS 3680	My Little Lady/All The World To Me	6
68	CBS 3873	I Shall Be Released/I Miss My Baby	7
69	CBS 4065	Hello World/Up Down All Around	7
68	CBS Special Products WB 728	Here Comes My Baby/SIMON & GARFUNKEL: The 59th Street Bridge Song (p/s, mail-order only with Pepsi Cola tokens)	6
70	CBS 4815	By The Way/Breakheart Motel	8
70	CBS 5139	Me And My Life/Try Me	6
71	CBS 7294	Hello Buddy/My Woman	8
72	Epic EPC 5S 1019	Blue Suede Tie/Yodel Ay	8
75	DJM DJS 406	Be Boppin' Boogle/Ascot Cowboys	7
68	CBS EP 6402	MY LITTLE LADY (EP)	18
67	CBS (S)BPG 63017	HERE COME THE TREMELOES (LP)	18
68	CBS (S)BPG 63138	THE TREMELOES: CHIP, RICK, ALAN AND DAVE (LP)	18
69	CBS 63547	THE TREMELOES 'LIVE' IN CABARET (LP)	15
70	CBS 64242	MASTER (LP)	15

(see also Brian Poole & Tremeloes)

TREMORS
79	Redball RR 0002	Modern World/Smashed Reality (p/s)	15

TREND (1)
67	Page One POF 004	Boyfriends And Girlfriends/Shoot On Sight	80

TREND (2)
70	Trendy TREND 1	Teenage Crush/Cool Johnny (with press sheet)	50
70	Trendy TREND 1	Teenage Crush/Cool Johnny	40

TREND (3)
80	MCA MCA 583	Polly And Wendy/Family Way (p/s)	20
80	MCA MCA 629	This Dance Hall Must Have A Back Way Out/Fiction, Love & Romance (p/s)	15

TRENDS
63	Piccadilly 7N 35171	All My Loving/Sweet Little Miss Love	15
64	Pye 7N 15644	You're A Wonderful One/The Way You Do The Things You Do	20

(see also Tammy St. John, Freddie Self, Freddie Ryder)

TRENDSETTERS
64	Silver Phoenix 1001	You Don't Care/My Heart Goes	65

TRENDSETTERS
60s	Oak RGJ 999	AT THE HOTEL DE FRANCE (EP)	30

TRENDSETTERS LTD
64	Parlophone R 5118	In A Big Way/Lucky Date	20
64	Parlophone R 5161	Hello Josephine/Move On Over	20

TRENIERS

MINT VALUE £

| 64 | Parlophone R 5191 | Go Away/Lollipops And Roses | 15 |
| 65 | Parlophone R 5324 | You Sure Got A Funny Way Of Showing Your Love/I'm Coming Home | 12 |

(see also King Crimson, Giles Giles & Fripp, Brain)

TRENIERS
58	Coral Q 72319	Ooh-La-La/Pennies From Heaven	25
58	Fontana H 137	Go! Go! Go!/Get Out Of The Car (featuring Don Hill, Alto Sax)	100
59	London HLD 8858	When Your Hair Has Turned To Silver/Never, Never	40
59	London HLD 8858	When Your Hair Has Turned To Silver/Never, Never (78)	25

BARBARA TRENT
| 07 | Funk 45 035 | Heart Break Hotel/RICHI CORBIN TRIO: A Woman Was Made For A Man | 10 |

JACKIE TRENT
61	Oriole CB 1711	Pick Up The Pieces/In Your Heart	15
62	Oriole CB 1749	The One Who Really Loves You/Your Conscience Or Your Heart	40
63	Piccadilly 7N 35121	Melancholy Me/So Did I	15
64	Piccadilly 7N 35165	If You Love Me/Only One Such As You	40
65	Pye 7N 15865	When Summertime Is Over/To Show I Love Him	6
65	Pye 7N 15949	It's All In The Way You Look At Life/Time After Time	6
66	Pye 7N 17047	You Baby/Send Her Away (DJ Copy)	40
66	Pye 7N 17047	You Baby/Send Her Away	30
66	Pye 7N 17082	Love Is Me Love Is You/This Time	6
66	Pye 7N 17158	If You Ever Leave Me/There Goes My Love, There Goes My Life	6
67	Pye 7N 17249	Open Your Heart/Love Can Give	15
67	Pye 7N 17323	Your Love Is Everywhere/It's Not Easy Loving You	6
67	Pye 7N 17415	That's You/Stop Me And Buy One	6
67	Pye 7N 17437	Bye Bye Love (German Version)/Alles Okay (Send Her Away)	6
69	Pye 7N 17693	I'll Be There/Close To You	10
78	Casino Classics CC 4	You Baby/Send Her Away/FAMILY AFFAIR: Love Hustle	6
65	Pye NEP 4225	WHERE ARE YOU NOW (EP)	15
65	Pye NPL 18125	THE MAGIC OF JACKIE TRENT (LP)	25
67	Pye NPL 18173	ONCE MORE WITH FEELING (LP)	15
67	Pye NSPL 18201	STOP ME AND BUY ONE (LP)	20
69	Pye NSPL 18315	THE LOOK OF LOVE (LP)	20

JACKIE TRENT & TONY HATCH
67	Pye 7N 17300	The Two Of Us/I'll Be With You	6
74	Pye 7N 45392	Together/Going Our Own Sweet Way	6
75	Pye 7N 45490	Mr And Mrs (Be Nice To Each Other)/Positive Thinking	7
68	Pye NPL 18214	THE TWO OF US (LP)	20
68	Pye NSPL 18229	LIVE FOR LOVE (LP)	20
68	Pye NSPL 18304	TOGETHER AGAIN (LP)	15
74	Pye NSPL 18422	OPPOSITE YOUR SMILE (LP)	15

TRESPASS
79	Trial CASE 1	One Of These Days/Bloody Moon (p/s)	25
80	Trial CASE 2	Jealousy/Live It Up! (p/s)	18
81	Trial CASE 3	Bright Lights/The Duel/Man And Machine (p/s)	20

TREVER T
| 98 | First Handed FHR 005 | Loving You/On Me Mind Body And Soul Mix/Exclusive/On Me Mellow Mix (12") | 40 |

TREVOR (SHIELD)
64	Blue Beat BB 228	Down In Virginia/Hey Little Schoolgirl (with Caribs)	25
68	Blue Cat BS 129	Tender Arms (with Joe White & Glen Brown)/DERMOTT LYNCH: Something Is Worrying Me	100
68	Blue Cat BS 130	Pretty Girl (with Joe White & Glen Brown)/DERMOTT LYNCH: You Went Away	500
69	Blue Cat BS 153	Everyday Is Like A Holiday/Have You Time (by Trevor & Maytones)	200

TREVOR & KEITH
| 70 | Punch PH 41 | The Ark/MINNA BOYS: False Reador (actually titled "Got To Move") | 7 |

(see also Carl Bryan)

ANDREYA TRIANA
| 10 | Ninja Tune ZEN 155 | LOST WHERE I BELONG (LP) | 30 |

TRIARCHY
79	SRT/79/CUS 599	Save The Khan/Juliet's Tomb (in p/s, 1,000 only)	80
79	SRT/79/CUS 599	Save The Khan/Juliet's Tomb (1,000 only)	30
79	Direct NEON 1	Save The Khan/Juliet's Tomb (reissue, p/s)	35
80	Direct NEON 2	Metal Messiah/Sweet Alcohol/Hell Hound On My Trail (in p/s)	70
80	Direct NEON 2	Metal Messiah/Sweet Alcohol/Hell Hound On My Trail	30

TRIBAN
69	Cambrian CSP 707	Leaving On A Jet Plane/Night In The City	6
69	Cambrian MCT 592	TRIBAN (LP)	15
72	Cambrian MCT 218	RAINMAKER (LP, laminated cover)	18

TONY TRIBE
| 69 | Downtown DT 419 | Red Red Wine/RECO & RUDIES: Blues (some miscredited to Tony Tripe) | 30 |
| 69 | Downtown DT 439 | Gonna Give You All The Love/HERBIE GREY: Why Wait | 30 |

TRIBE (U.K.) (1)
| 66 | Planet PLF 108 | The Gamma Goochie/I'm Leavin' | 100 |
| 67 | RCA RCA 1592 | Love Is A Beautiful Thing/Steel Guitar | 25 |

TRIBE (U.K.) (2)
| 75 | BB BB003 | Africa (Part 1)/Africa (Part 2) | 30 |

TRIBE (U.S.)
| 66 | Polydor 56210 | Dancin' To The Beat Of My Heart/Woofin' | 70 |

TRIBESMAN
| 79 | Boa BOA 102-12 | Finsbury Park/The Tribe (12", p/s) | 30 |
| 80 | Direct ROS001-12 | Sunburst/Lion (Concrete Jungle) (12", p/s) | 20 |

TRIBUTE

MINT VALUE £

80	Direct ROS 001	Sunburst/Lion (Concrete Jungle)	10
12	Reggae Archive RARC001V	The Tribe/Dub/Finsbury Park/Dub (12", reissue)	20
78	Promo 1	WONDER WOLF (mini-LP, promo only, white sleeve)	25
79	Boa BOA 001	STREET LEVEL (LP)	20

TRIBUTE
73	Jam JAM 48	Bobby Charlton/City Summer	12

TRICKS
70	CBS 4867	Wham! Bam! Ala Cazam!/Lucy Brown	8

TRICKY
95	4th & Broadway BRLP 610	MAXINQUAYE (LP, gatefold, inner)	50
96	4th & Broadway BRLP 623	PRE-MILLENIUM TENSION (LP)	50
98	Island ILPSD 8071	ANGELS WITH DIRTY FACES (2-LP, numbered on rear)	60
99	Island ILPS 8087	JUXTAPOSE (LP, with DJ Muggs and Grease)	40
01	Anti 6596-1	BLOWBACK (LP)	40
03	Anti 6648-1	VULNERABLE (LP, gatefold)	20
08	Domino WIGLP 195	KNOWLE WEST BOY (LP)	15
10	Domino WIGLP 256	MIXED RACE (LP)	25

TRICKY DISCO
91	Warp WAP 11	HOUSEFLY EP (12")	10

TRI-CORE
92	Underground UNR 001T	BELFAST SAYS EP (12")	80

TRIDENT
84	SRT TRI 1	Destiny/Power Of The Trident	50

(see also Filthy Rich)

TRIFFIDS (1)
63	Columbia DB 7084	Lookin Around/She's No Longer Your Girl	12

TRIFFIDS (2)
11	Domino REWIGCD 72X	COME RIDE WITH ME...WIDE OPEN ROAD (10-CD box set)	70

TRIFLE
69	United Artists UP 2270	All Together Now/Got My Thing	10
70	Dawn DNS 1008	Old-Fashioned Prayer Meeting/Dirty Old Town	10
71	Dawn DNLS 3017	FIRST MEETING (LP, textured gatefold sleeve)	150

(see also George Bean)

TRILOGY
71	Mercury 6338 034	I'M BEGINNING TO FEEL IT (LP)	20

TOMMY TRINDER & THE GANG
59	Fontana H 204	La Plume De Ma Tante/On The Sunny Side Of The Street	10

TRINIDAD ALL STARS
59	Parlophone GEP 8625	TRINIDAD ALL STARS STEEL BAND (EP)	50
56	Parlophone DP 524	Trouble In Arima/Stone Cold Dead In De Market (78, export issue)	12

TRINIDAD OIL COMPANY
77	Harvest SHSP 4070	THE CALENDAR SONG (LP)	20

TRINITY
77	Burning Sounds BS 011	Natty Tired To Carry Load/Dubwise	10
77	Caribbean CBN 314	Natty On De Banking/Banking Dub	8
77	Carib Gems CG 005	Three Meals A Day/Version	8
77	Conflict CON 303	Up-Town Girl/PRINCE JAMMY & AGGROVATORS: Channel One A Boy	10
78	Grove Music GM 7	Jesus Dread/Yabby U Sound	12
79	Attack TACK 2	Follow My Heart/Pope Paul Dead And Gone (12")	30
70s	Burning Vibrations BVD 002	Roots Man Party/Healing The Nation (12", with Mystic EMP Group)	20
80	Spectrum SP 01	Jamaican People A Nice People/Heaven And Hell/LLOYD CLARKE SPARROW: The Young Ones (12")	35
79	Burning Sounds BDS 012	SHOWCASE EP (12")	20
77	Magnum DERD 1003	UPTOWN GIRL (LP)	20
79	Trojan TRLS 170	ROCK IN THE GHETTO (LP)	20
81	JB JBLP 006	FULL HOUSE (LP)	20
83	Vista Sounds VSLP 4009	SIDE KIKS (LP, reissue of Uptown Girl)	15
00	Blood & Fire/Simply Vinyl SVLP 284	SHANTY TOWN DETERMINATION (2-LP)	25

TRINITY HOUSE
77	Profile GMOR 146	FLASHBACK THROUGH HISTORY (LP, private pressing, with insert)	40

TRIO
71	Dawn DNLS 3022	CONFLAGRATION (LP)	60
76	Dawn DNLS 3072	LIVE AT WOODSTOCK TOWN HALL (LP, with Stu Martin)	25

(see also John Surnam)

TRIPLETS
69	President PT 245	When Lovers Say Goodbye/You Won't See Me Leaving	10

TRIPPERS
66	Pye International 7N 25388	Dance With Me/Keep A-Knockin'	20

TRIPTI DAS
67	Flowers FL 001	Kat Put Li {Puppet On A String)/Lagta Mahi Dil	20

TRISHA
65	CBS 201800	The Darkness Of My Night/Confusion	8

TRISTAR AIRBUS
72	RCA RCA 2170	Travellin' Man/Willie Morgan On The Wing	10

(see also Wimple Winch, 10cc, Hotlegs)

TRITONS
73	Bradley BAR 24	I Can't Get Not Satisfaction/Drifter	50

TRIUMVIRAT
74	Harvest SHSP 4030	ILLUSION ON A DOUBLE DIMPLE (LP, 1st pressing normal green label)	15
75	Harvest SHSP 4048	SPARTACUS (LP)	15

TRIXIE'S BIG RED MOTORBIKE

MINT VALUE £

82	Chew CH 9271	A Splash Of Red/Invisible Boyfriend (white label, stapled foldover p/s)	15
82	Ram RAM 51	TRIXIE'S BIG RED MOTORBIKE (EP, plain sleeve with stapled strip)	10
84	Lobby Ludd L 100001	Norman And Narcissus/In Timbuktu (p/s)	10
84	Lobby Ludd L 100002	A Splash Of Red/Invisible Boyfriend (reissue, different p/s)	8
95	Accident DENT 1	THE INTIMATE SOUND OF... (LP, handmade sleeve, numbered)	40
95	Accident DENT 1	THE INTIMATE SOUND OF... (LP, green vinyl, 500 only)	25

TRIXONS

69	Major Minor MM 665	Just Another Song/Sunny Side Sam	15

MARCUS TRO

65	Ember EMB S 203	Tell Me/What's The Matter Little Girl (in p/s)	18
65	Ember EMB S 203	Tell Me/What's The Matter Little Girl	10
65	Ember EMB 3365	INTRODUCING MARCUS TRO (LP)	40

TROBWLL

79	Buwch Hapus MW 1	TAITH (EP)	40

TROGGS

SINGLES

66	CBS 202038	Lost Girl/The Yella In Me	50
66	Fontana TF 689	Wild Thing/From Home	8
66	Fontana TF 717	With A Girl Like You/I Want You	7
66	Page One POF 001	I Can't Control Myself/Gonna Make You	7
66	Page One POF 010	Any Way That You Want Me/6-5-4-3-2-1	7
67	Page One POF 015	Give It To Me/You're Lyin'	7
67	Page One POF 022	My Lady/Girl In Black (withdrawn)	50
67	Page One POF 022	Night Of The Long Grass/Girl In Black	7
67	Page One POF 030	Hi Hi Hazel/As I Ride By	8
67	Page One POF 040	Love Is All Around/When Will The Rain Come	6
68	Page One POF 056	Little Girl/Maybe The Madman?	7
68	Page One POF 064	Surprise Surprise/Marbles And Some Gum?	10
68	Page One POF 082	You Can Cry If You Want To/There's Something About You	10
68	Page One POF 092	Hip Hip Hooray/Say Darlin'!	8
69	Page One POF 114	Evil Woman/Sweet Madeline	8
69	Page One POF 126	Wild Thing/I Can't Control Myself	6
70	Page One POF 164	Easy Lovin'/Give Me Something	8
70	Page One POF 171	Lover/Come Now	8
70	Page One POF 182	The Raver/You	10
71	DJM DJM 248	Lazy Weekend/Let's Pull Together	6
72	Pye 7N 45147	Everything's Funny/Feels Like A Woman	7
73	Pye 7N 45244	Listen To The Man/Queen Of Sorrow	7
73	Pye 7N 45295	Strange Movies/I'm On Fire	15
75	Penny Farthing PEN 861	Good Vibrations/Push It Up To Me	6
78	Raw RAW 25	Just A Little Too Much/The True Troggs Tapes (p/s)	6
67	Page One POE 001	TROGGS TOPS (EP)	20
67	Page One POE 002	TROGGS TOPS VOLUME TWO (EP)	40
67	Page One	TRACK A TROGG (EP, unreleased)	0

ALBUMS

66	Fontana TL 5355	FROM NOWHERE - THE TROGGS (LP, mono)	70
66	Fontana STL 5355	FROM NOWHERE - THE TROGGS (LP, stereo)	80
66	Page One POL 001	TROGGLODYNAMITE (LP, mono)	70
66	Page One POLS 001	TROGGLODYNAMITE (LP, stereo)	90
67	Page One FOR 001	THE BEST OF THE TROGGS (LP)	30
67	Page One POL 003	CELLOPHANE (LP, mono)	80
67	Page One POLS 003	CELLOPHANE (LP, stereo)	90
68	Page One POL 1	THE TROGGS ON TOUR (LP, export issue)	150
68	Page One FOR 007	THE BEST OF THE TROGGS VOLUME TWO (LP)	35
68	Page One POL(S) 012	MIXED BAG (LP)	150
69	Page One POS 602	TROGGLOMANIA (LP)	40
70	DJM Silverline DJML 009	CONTRASTS (LP, original issue)	15
76	Penny Farthing PELS 551	THE TROGG TAPES (LP)	20

(see also Reg Presley, Chris Britton, Ronnie Bond, Ten Feet Five)

CHUCK TROIS & AMAZING MAZE

68	Action ACT 4517	Call On You/Woodsman	25

TROJAN

88	GI GILP 444	THE MARCH IS ON (LP)	18

TROJANS (1)

58	Decca F 11065	Man I'm Gonna Be/Make It Up	15

TROJANS (2)

89	Gaz's LPGAZ 002	ALA-SKA (LP)	15
95	Gaz's LPGAZ 012	STACK-A-DUB (2-LP)	20

TROLL BROTHERS

73	SRT SRT 73316	You Turn Me On/Turn Out The Lights (p/s)	10

TRONICS (1)

61	Fontana H 348	Cantina/Pickin' & Stompin'	18

TRONICS (2)

78	Tronics T 001	Suzie (actually "Suzie's Vibrator")/Favourite Girls (plain sleeve with inserts)	25
79	Tronics T 002	Time Off/Goodbye (p/s)	12
81	Alien ALIEN 18	Shark Fucks/Time Off (p/s, with insert)	25
83	Red Rhino RED 3	Wild Cat Rock/Tonight (p/s)	8
81	Alien BALIEN 3	LOVE BACKED BY FORCE (LP)	25

TROOPERS

MINT VALUE £

(see also Les Zarjaz)

TROOPERS
57	Vogue V 9087	Get Out/My Resolution	700
57	Vogue V 9087	Get Out/My Resolution (78)	150

TROOPS FOR TOMORROW
82	Rhythmic RMNS 1	Songs Of Joy And Faith/Prisoner (p/s)	15

TROPIC SHADOWS
72	Big Shot BI 603	Our Anniversary/Anniversary (Version)	15

TROPICAL BREEZE
80	Silver Camel SC 001	So Naive/FORCE 7: Naivity (12")	20
81	Daddy Kool DKR 126	You're The One/One + One Dub (12")	30

ARCHIBALD TROTT
64	Black Swan WI 407	Get Together/Just Because	40

(see also Baba Brooks)

TROUBADORS DU ROI BAUDOUIN
69	Philips BF 1732	Sanctus (Missa Luba)/Kyrie (p/s)	8

TROUBADORS/TROUBADOUR SINGERS
57	London HLR 8469	Fascination/Midnight In Athens	8
58	London HLR 8541	The Lights Of Paris/The Flaming Rose	12

(see also Jane Morgan)

TROUBLE
88	Justice JTT002	I Get Hype/I Guess It's Dope (12")	20

BOBBY TROUP
55	Capitol CL 14219	Julie Is Her Name/Instead Of You	12
54	Capitol LC 6660	BOBBY TROUP (10" LP)	20

BOB TROW QUARTET
54	London HL 8082	Soft Squeeze Baby/I Went Along For The Ride	40

ROBIN TROWER
73	Chrysalis CHR 1039	TWICE REMOVED FROM YESTERDAY (LP)	15
74	Chrysalis CHR 1057	BRIDGE OF SIGHS (LP)	15

(see also Paramounts, Procol Harum)

TROY
80s	Love Linch LL 022	Love & Harmony/Land Of Love (12")	20

BENNY TROY
05	Atco 002	I Wanna Give You Tomorrow/OTIS REDDING: Loving By The Pound (promo, 500 only)	10

DORIS TROY
63	London HLK 9749	Just One Look/Bossa Nova Blues	35
64	Atlantic AT 4011	What'cha Gonna Do About It/Tomorrow Is Another Day	25
65	Atlantic AT 4020	One More Chance/Please Little Angel	18
65	Atlantic AT 4032	Heartaches/You'd Better Stop	18
65	Cameo Parkway C 101	I'll Do Anything (He Wants Me To)/But I Love Him	150
65	Cameo Parkway C 101	I'll Do Anything (He Wants Me To)/But I Love Him (DJ copy)	200
68	Atlantic 584 148	Just One Look/What'cha Gonna Do About It	12
68	Toast TT 507	I'll Do Anything (Anything He Wants Me To)/Heartaches	15
70	Apple APPLE 24	Ain't That Cute/Vaya Con Dios (with p/s)	22
70	Apple APPLE 24	Ain't That Cute/Vaya Con Dios	10
70	Apple APPLE 28	Jacob's Ladder/Get Back	15
71	Mojo 2092 011	I'll Do Anything (He Wants Me To)/But I Love Him (reissue)	15
73	Mojo 2092 062	Baby I Love You/To My Father's House	6
74	People PEO 112	Stretchin' Out/Don't Tell Your Mama	6
18	Super Disco Edits SDE 40	What'cha Gonna Do/You Got Me Baby (12")	20
65	Atlantic AET 6007	WATCHA GONNA DO ABOUT IT (EP)	100
70	Apple SAPCOR 13	DORIS TROY (LP)	80
73	Mojo 2956 001	THE RAINBOW TESTAMENT (LP, with Gospel Truth)	35
74	Polydor 2464 001	JUST ONE LOOK (LP)	30
74	People PLEO 12	STRETCHIN' OUT (LP)	20
92	Apple SAPCOR 13	DORIS TROY (LP, reissue, gatefold sleeve with bonus 12" [SAPCOR 132])	35

TROY & THUNDERBIRDS
61	London HL 9476	Twistle/Take Ten	15

WILLIAM TRUCKAWAY
69	Reprise RS 20842	Bluegreens On The Wing/Besides Yourself	15
71	Reprise K 44165	BREAKAWAY (LP, with lyric insert)	20

TRUE ADVENTURE
74	Decca F 13528	Where The Roxy Use To Be/Outlaw Love	15

TRUE FEELINGS
81	Amber EM001	Love Me Love Me/Love Me Love Me Disco (12")	200

TRUE IMAGE
02	Grapevine G2K 45 105	I'm Not Over You Yet/I'm Not Over You Yet (Extended)	20

TRUE SPIRITED
70	Wren WR 1	Over And Over/Pollution	30

TRUE STYLE
91	Liberty Grooves LIB002	CODES OF CONDUCT (EP)	15

FRED TRUEMAN
69	NEMS 56-4293	Red Is Red/A Million Times A Day	6

TRUFFLE
72	JAM 8	Poco Poco/Julie's Place	6
81	Chesnut NUT 6	Round Tower/If You Really Want (p/s)	100

TRUK
71	CBS 57201	Winters Coming On/You	15

Jonny TRUNK

MINT VALUE £

JONNY TRUNK
01	Trunk TTT 001	The Snow It Melts/Scooby Don't (7", 300 only)	25
01	Trunk TTT 002	Sister Woo/Mr Hand (300 only)	15
03	Trunk TTT 004	Dead Soon/Dead Mouse Blues (7", 400 only)	15
11	Ghost Box GBX706	ANIMATION AND INTERPRETATION EP (p/s)	20
04	Trunk JBH 008 LP	THE INSIDE OUTSIDE (LP, 500 only)	30

TRUTH (1)
65	Pye 7N 15923	Baby Don't You Know/Come On Home	20
65	Pye 7N 15998	Who's Wrong/She's A Roller	25
66	Pye 7N 17035	Girl/Jailer Bring Me Water	8
66	Pye 7N 17095	I Go To Sleep/Baby You've Got It	30
66	Deram DM 105	Jingle Jangle/Hey Gyp (Dig The Slowness)	100
67	Decca F 12582	Walk Away Renee/Fly Away Bird	20
68	Decca F 22764	Seuno/Old Ma Brown	60

TRUTH & BEAUTY
74	Rak RAK 181	Tuff Little Surfer Boy/Touch-a Touch-a Touch Me	25

TRUTH CLUB
80	Le Rey LR 01	Sleight/FOTE: Looking For Lost Toy	20

TRUTH OF TRUTHS
71	Oak OR 1001	TRUTH OF TRUTHS (LP)	25

TRUTH (2)
83	WEA TRUTH 1F	Confusion/Me And My Girl//Love A Go Go/From The Heart (p/s, doublepack)	8

TRUTH (3)
92	Funky Groove FUNKY 4	The End/Calm Down/Newlands/Emotional/The Start (12")	250

TRUTH, FACT & CORRECT
76	Black Wax WAX 18	Babylon Deh Pon Fire/Jungle Fever (with LYN 3754 etching in run-out groove)	45

TRUX
82	Trux TRX 01	Bad Luck (no p/s)	200

TANIA TSANAKLIDOU
78	EMI EMI 2797	Charlie Chaplin (English)/Charlie Chaplin (Greek)	12

T.S.O.L.
82	Alt. Tentacles VIRUS 10	WEATHERED STATUES (EP)	10
81	Frontier FLP 1004	DANCE WITH ME (LP)	18

T34
81	Spaceward DIV 1	Computer Dating/Mind Your Own Business	20
83	Galaxy GAL 007	Rock On/Looking After Me (Looking After You) (p/s)	20

T2
70	Decca SKL 5050	IT'LL ALL WORK OUT IN BOOMLAND (LP, blue/silver label/boxed logo)	300

(see also Flies, Cross & Ross)

ERNEST TUBB (& HIS TEXAS TROUBADORS)
50	Decca BM 31206	The Blues/Half A Mind (Export Issue)	15
56	Brunswick 05527	Thirty Days/Answer The Phone (triangular centre)	30
56	Brunswick 05587	So Doggone Lonesome/If I Never Have Anything Else	20
50s	Decca BM 31214	What Am I Living For/Goodbye Sunshine, Hello Blues (export issue)	15
56	Brunswick LA 8736	JIMMIE RODGERS SONGS (10" LP)	30

(see also Red Foley & Ernest Tubb)

JUSTIN TUBB
67	RCA Victor RCA 1585	But Wait There's More/The Second Thing I'm Gonna Do	6
64	RCA RCX 7133	JUSTIN TUBB (EP)	30

TUBES
79	A&M AMS 7423	Prime Time (promo box of 7 different coloured vinyl editions & picture disc)	30

TUBEWAY ARMY
78	Beggars Banquet BEG 5	That's Too Bad/Oh! I Didn't Say (p/s)	10
78	Beggars Banquet BEG 8	Bombers/O.D. Receiver/Blue Eyes (p/s)	10
79	Beggars Banquet BEG 17T	Down In The Park/Do You Need The Service?/I Nearly Married A Human 2 (12", p/s)	25
79	Beggars Banquet BEG 17T	Down In The Park/Do You Need The Service?/I Nearly Married A Human 2 (12", p/s, sleeve misprint with Leif Garrett's Feel The Need LP image overprinted on both sides)	100
79	Beggars Banquet BEG 18	Are "Friends" Electric?/We Are So Fragile (p/s original semi-transparent sleeve)	18
79	Beggars Banquet BACK 2	That's Too Bad/Oh! I Didn't Say/Bombers/Blue Eyes/O.D. Receiver (double pack, gatefold p/s, mispressed 2nd disc omits "O.D. Receiver")	15
83	Beggars Banquet BEG 92E	TUBEWAY ARMY VOL. 1 (12" EP, with "That's Too Bad [Alternate Mix]", yellow vinyl)	10
85	Beggars Banquet BEG 123 E	1978-1979 VOL. 2 (12", blue vinyl, p/s)	10
85	Beggars Banquet BEG 124E	1978-1979 VOL. 3 (12", red vinyl, p/s)	10
78	Beggars Banquet BEGA 4	TUBEWAY ARMY (LP, blue vinyl, gatefold stickered sleeve, some with badge)	70
78	Beggars Banquet BEGA 4	TUBEWAY ARMY (LP, blue vinyl, gatefold stickered sleeve)	60
79	Beggars Banquet BEGA 7	REPLICAS (LP, with large black & white poster)	25
79	Beggars Banquet BEGA 7	REPLICAS (LP, inner)	18
79	Beggars Banquet BEGA 4	TUBEWAY ARMY (LP, reissue, 'head' sleeve, inner)	15
79	Beggars Banquet BEGA 4	TUBEWAY ARMY (LP, reissue, mispressing, plays The Pleasure Principle on side 2)	100
08	VIN 180 LP 002	REPLICAS (LP, (LP, pressed on 180 gram vinyl, numbered with 8" x 6" print)	18
10	Vinyl 180 VIN180LP026	TUBEWAY ARMY (LP, blue vinyl reissue)	18
15	Beggars Banquet BBQ LP 7	REPLICAS (LP, reissue, orange vinyl, 600 only, sold at gigs)	40

(see also Gary Numan, Paul Gardiner)

TUBEWAY PATROL
81	Carrere CAR 218	Do Eyes Ever Meet/No Time (no p/s)	18

TUBILAH DOG
96	S04	IN SEARCH OF PLAICE (LP, gatefold with poster)	20

TUB-THUMPER
74	Alaska ALA 18	Kick Out The Jams/Kahoutec	25

TUCHWOOD
72	Polydor 2058233	Freedom For The Stallion/Morning Light	8

Bessie TUCKER

MINT VALUE £

BESSIE TUCKER
55 HMV 7EG 8085   BLUES BY BESSIE (EP) 20

BILLY JOE TUCKER
61 London HLD 9455   Boogie Woogie Bill/Mail Train 60

CY TUCKER
63 Fontana TF 424   My Prayer/High School Dance 8
64 Fontana TF 470   Let Me Call You Sweetheart/I Apologise 7

TERRY TUCKER'S ORANGE CLOCKWORK
70 Warner Brothers K16337   Overture To The Sun Part 1/Overture To The Sun Part II 10

TOMMY TUCKER
64 Pye International 7N 25238   Hi-Heel Sneakers/I Don't Want 'Cha 20
64 Pye International 7N 25246   Long Tall Shorty/Mo' Shorty 25
64 London HLU 9932   Oh! What A Feeling/Wine Bottles 40
69 Chess CRS 8086   Hi-Heel Sneakers/I Don't Want 'Cha (reissue) 15
64 Pye Intl. NEP 44027   HI HEEL SNEAKERS (EP) 50

WINSTON TUCKER
73 Explosion EX 2083   I'm A Believer/You'll Be Mine 7
(see also Winston Groovy)

TUCKY BUZZARD
73 Purple PUR 113   Gold Medallions/Fast Bluesy Woman 7
77 Purple PUR 134   Gold Medallions/Superboy Rock 'N' Roller '73' 7
71 Capitol E-ST 864   WARM SLASH (LP, laminated front sleeve, flipbacks) 60
73 Purple TPSA 7510   ALRIGHT ON THE NIGHT (LP, laminated gatefold sleeve) 25
73 Purple TPSA 7512   BUZZARD (LP) 20

HENRY TUDOR
67 Decca F12574   How Many Times/Another Name From Nowhere 25

TUDOR LODGE
71 Vertigo 6059 044   The Lady's Changing Home/Back To The Good Times We Had 75
71 Vertigo 6360 043   TUDOR LODGE (LP, foldout textured sleeve, swirl label) 1750
88 Zap! ZAP 4   TUDOR LODGE (LP, reissue) 25

TUDOR MINSTRELS
66 Decca F 12536   Love In The Open Air/A Theme From "The Family Way" 22

TUDORS
83 Stiff BUY 172   Tied Up With Joe Cool/Cry Baby Cry (p/s) 7

TUESDAY
72 Pye 7N 45194   Big Mister Little Man/Sewing Machine 20

TUESDAY'S CHILDREN
66 Columbia DB 7978   When You Walk In The Sand/High And Drifting 20
66 Columbia DB 8018   High On A Hill/Summer Leaves Me With A Sigh 22
67 King KG 1051   A Strange Light From The East/That'll Be The Day 30
67 Pye 7N 17406   Baby's Gone/Guess I'm Losin' You 15
68 Pye 7N 17474   In The Valley Of The Shadow Of Love/Ain't You Got A Heart 12
68 Mercury MF 1063   She/Bright-Eyed Apples 20
(see also Warm Sounds)

T.U.F.F.
80s SONO 001   We've Got A Hot One (Speed Mix) (unreleased, white label promos only) 10
(see also Hard Corps)

TUFF GONG ALLSTARS
72 Punch PH 114   You Should Have Known Better (actually by The Wailing Souls)/Known Better 20
(see also Wailing Souls)

TUFF LITTLE UNIT
91 Warp WAP 12   Join The Future/Master Plan (12") 15

TONY TUFF
79 Niagra NIADD 101   Ease Up Oppressor/JAH THOMAS: Answer The Phone (12") 15
79 King Sounds GMDM 26   You Wrong/TOMMY McCOOK: Sensimena (12") 25
80 Art & Craft 003   Look Ya/TONY TUFF & JAH STITCH: Rumours Of War (12") 35
80 Cha Cha CHAD 11   Deliver Me/Africa We Want To Go (12") 20
80 Grove ILPS 9619   TONY TUFF (LP) 30

SHANE TUFF
82 Roots Man Pro RMP 002   Can't Take No More/Yearning For Some Loving 40

NANA TUFFOUR
79 GAB 001   HIGHLIFE ROMANCE (LP) 80

TULIPS
74 Explosion EX 2091   Mocking Bird/DES ALL STARS: Version 7

LEE TULLY
57 London HL 8363   Around The World With Elwood Pretzel (Parts 1 & 2) (gold print label) 100
57 London HL 8363   Around The World With Elwood Pretzel (Parts 1 & 2) (silver print label) 60
57 London HL 8363   Around The World With Elwood Pretzel (Parts 1 & 2) (78) 25

TUMBLACK
79 Island 12XWIP 6500   Caraiba (1-sided 12" promo) 30
79 Island 12XWIP 6500   Caraiba/Invocation (12", p/s) 50

TUMBLEWEEDS
70 Phoenix NIX 111   Making My Way Back To Louisiana/I Guess I'd Better Go 10

TUNDRA
70s Greenwich Village GVR 208   THE KENTISH SONGSTER (LP) 15
78 Sweet Folk & C. SFA 078   A KENTISH GARLAND (LP, gatefold sleeve) 25
81 Greenwich Village GVR 218   SONGS FROM GREENWICH (LP, gatefold sleeve) 15

TUNE ROCKERS
58 London HLT 8717   The Green Mosquito/Warm Up 20

TUNEWEAVERS

TUNEWEAVERS
57   London HL 8503 — Happy Happy Birthday Baby/PAUL GAYTEN: Yo, Yo, Walk 80
(see also Paul Gayten)

TUNJI WITH CHRIS MCGREGOR
60s Jika 001 — Ko Gbele Oko/Lisabi Egba 8

TUNNEL RUNNERS
80   Sonic International SI 4282 — Plastic Land/Drug (numbered p/s) 80

TUNNELVISION
81   Factory FAC 39 — Watching The Hydroplanes/Morbid Fear (1st pressing, clear vinyl) 12
81   Factory FAC 39 — Watching The Hydroplanes/Morbid Fear (later pressing, black vinyl) 8

TUNNG
04   Static Caravan VAN 72 — Tales From Black/Pool Beneath The Pond (500 only) 15
05   Static Caravan VAN 73 — Maypole Song/Suprize Me 44 (100 lathe cut only, p/s) 30
05   Static Caravan VAN 88 — MOTHER'S DAUGHTERS AND OTHER SONGS (LP, 300 only - withdrawn) 50
06   Full Time Hobby FTH019LP — COMMENTS ON THE INNER CHORUS (LP, inner, poster) 20
06   Static Caravan VAN 88V — MOTHER'S DAUGHTERS AND OTHER SONGS (LP, reissue, clear vinyl) 20
07   Full Time Hobby FTH040LP — GOOD ARROWS (LP) 15

K.T. TUNSTALL
04   Outcaste OUT 56 — Throw Me A Rope/Black & White (500 only) 8
04   Relentless REL 12 — FALSE ALARM EP (2 x 7") 10
05   Relentless LPREL06 — EYE TO THE TELESCOPE (LP) 50

TURBO
80   Cargo CRS 004 — STALLION (EP, p/s) 100
82   Turbo CUS 1261 — Charged For Glory/Race For The Dawn 8

TURGID TOOL
01   Stand STAND 11 — Terror In A Turgid Tool!/Stand Up For England (pop-up p/s) 8

TURNBULL & ARKWRIGHT
72   Peacock PEA 501 — Smuggling Man/Misty Roses 15

BRUCE TURNER
54   Columbia SCMC 9 — Falling Leaves/I Wished On The Moon (export issue) 6
60   Melodisc MEL 1551 — Nuages/My Guy's Come Back 6
60s CRD 1000 — Jamaica Jump/Big Noise From Winetka 10
63   77 EP/EU 1 — LIVING JAZZ (EP) 10

CHUCK TURNER
87   Stereo One STO 003 — Youthman Struggling/FUNNY WONDER: Jollification (12") 70
87   Live & Love LLD 44 — We Rule The Dance/We Rule The Dub (12") 30
88   Live & Love LALP 21 — ONE THE HARD WAY (LP) 20

DENNIS TURNER
62   London HL 9537 — Lover Please/How Many Times 25

FRANK TURNER
09   Xtra Mile — Reasons Not To Be An Idiot/Thunder Road (p/s, 300 only, each with hand-written reason not to be an idiot by Frank Turner) 30

GORDON TURNER
70   Charisma CAS 1009 — MEDITATION (LP, 1st pressing laminated 'landscape' sleeve) 40
70   Charisma CAS 1009 — MEDITATION (LP, 2nd pressing non laminated 'blue room' sleeve) 20

IKE TURNER
72   United Artists UP 35411 — Lawdy Miss Clawdy/Tacks In My Shoes/Soppin' Molasses (with Family Vibes) 6
60s Ember EMB 3395 — IKE TURNER ROCKS THE BLUES (LP) 50
72   United Artists UAG 29362 — BLUES ROOTS (LP) 30
75   DJM DJSLM 2010 — FUNKY MULE (LP) 15
(see also Ike & Tina Turner)

IKE & TINA TURNER
SINGLES
60   London HLU 9226 — A Fool In Love/The Way You Love Me 20
61   London HLU 9451 — It's Gonna Work Out Fine/Won't You Forgive Me 20
64   Sue WI 306 — Gonna Work Out Fine/Won't You Forgive Me (reissue) 20
64   Sue WI 322 — The Argument/Poor Fool 20
64   Sue WI 350 — I Can't Believe What You Say/My Baby Now 40
65   Warner Bros WB 153 — Finger Poppin'/Ooh Poo Pah Doo 25
65   Sue WI 376 — Please, Please, Please/Am I A Fool In Love 40
66   London HLU 10046 — River Deep - Mountain High/I'll Keep You Happy 8
66   Warner Bros WB 5753 — Tell Her I'm Not Home/Finger Poppin' 20
66   HMV POP 1544 — Anything You Wasn't Born With/Beauty Is Just Skin Deep 30
66   London HLU 10083 — A Love Like Yours (Don't Come Knockin' Every Day)/Hold On Baby 18
66   Stateside SS 551 — Goodbye, So Long/Hurt Is All You Gave Me 18
66   Warner Bros WB 5766 — Somebody (Somewhere) Needs You/(I'll Do Anything) Just To Be With You 100
66   Warner Bros WB 5766 — Somebody (Somewhere) Needs You/(I'll Do Anything) Just To Be With You (DJ copy) 120
67   HMV POP 1583 — I'm Hooked/Dust My Broom 70
67   HMV POP 1583 — I'm Hooked/Dust My Broom (DJ copy) 120
67   London HLU 10155 — I'll Never Need More Than This/Save The Last Dance For Me 20
68   London HLU 10189 — So Fine/So Blue Over You 10
68   London HLU 10217 — We Need An Understanding/It Sho' Ain't Me 15
69   Minit MLF 11016 — I'm Gonna Do All I Can/You've Got Too Many Ties That Bind 15
69   London HLU 10267 — I'll Never Need More Than This/A Love Like Yours 8
69   Liberty LBF 15223 — Crazy 'Bout You Baby/I've Been Lovin' You Too Long 10
70   Liberty LBF 15303 — Come Together/Honky Tonky Women 6
70   A&M AMS 783 — Make 'Em Wait/Everyday I Have To Cry 8
70   Harvest HAR 5018 — The Hunter/Bold Soul Sister 8
71   Liberty LBF 15432 — Proud Mary/Funkier Than A Mosquito's Tweeter 15
71   A&M AMS 829 — River Deep - Mountain High/Oh Baby 6

Jesse LEE TURNER

MINT VALUE £

EPs
64	Sue IEP 706	THE SOUL OF IKE AND TINA TURNER	200
65	Warner Bros WEP 619	THE IKE AND TINA TURNER SHOW	60
66	Warner Bros WEP 620	SOMEBODY NEEDS YOU	70
83	Sue ENS 1	SUE SESSIONS	15

ALBUMS
65	Warner Bros WM 8170	THE IKE AND TINA TURNER SHOW	60
65	London HA-C 8248	THE GREATEST HITS OF IKE & TINA TURNER	60
66	Ember EMB 3368	THE IKE AND TINA TURNER REVUE	40
66	Warner Bros W 1579	THE IKE AND TINA TURNER SHOW	40
66	London HA-U/SH-U 8298	RIVER DEEP MOUNTAIN HIGH	40
67	Warner Bros WB 5904	THE IKE AND TINA TURNER SHOW VOL. 2	35
69	London HA-U/SH-U 8370	SO FINE (with Fontella Bass)	30
69	Liberty LBS 83241	OUTTA SEASON	22
69	Minit MLS 40014	IN PERSON	25
69	Warner Bros ES 1810	GREATEST HITS	20
70	Liberty LBS 83350	COME TOGETHER	20
70	Harvest SHSP 4001	THE HUNTER	120
71	Liberty LBS 83455	WORKIN' TOGETHER	20
71	Liberty LBS 83468/9	LIVE IN PARIS	15
71	Capitol E-ST 571	HER MAN...HIS WOMAN	15
71	United Artists UAD 60005/6	WHAT YOU HEAR IS WHAT YOU GET	15
84	Kent KENT 014	THE SOUL OF IKE AND TINA (LP)	20

(see also Ike Turner, Ikettes)

JESSE LEE TURNER
59	London HLL 8785	The Little Space Girl/Shake, Baby, Shake	60
59	London HLL 8785	The Little Space Girl/Shake, Baby, Shake (78)	30
60	London HLP 9108	I'm The Little Space Girl's Father/Valley Of Lost Soldiers	20
60	Top Rank JAR 303	That's My Girl/Teenage Misery	20
60	Top Rank JAR 516	Do I Worry (Yes I Do)/All Right, Be That Way	7
62	Vogue V 9201	The Voice Changing Song/All You Gotta Do Is Ask	7

(see also Pete Johnson, Meade Lux Lewis, Pete Johnson, Albert Ammons, Sonny Terry & Brownie McGhee)

(BIG) JOE TURNER
51	Parlophone DP 265	Roll 'Em Pete/Goin' Away Blues (with Pete Johnson) (78, export only)	60
56	London HLE 8301	Corrine Corrina/Morning, Noon And Night (triangular or centre)	350
56	London HLE 8301	Corrine Corrina/Morning, Noon And Night (round centre)	100
56	London HLE 8301	Corrine Corrina/Morning, Noon And Night (78)	40
56	London HLE 8332	Boogie Woogie Country Girl/The Chicken And The Hawk	600
56	London HLE 8332	Boogie Woogie Country Girl/The Chicken And The Hawk (78)	45
57	London HLE 8357	Lipstick, Powder And Paint/Rock A While (gold label label print)	350
57	London HLE 8357	Lipstick, Powder And Paint/Rock A While (silver label print)	175
57	London HLE 8357	Lipstick, Powder And Paint/Rock A While (78)	40
60	London HLE 9055	Honey Hush/Tomorrow Night	60
60	London HLK 9119	My Little Honey Dripper/Chains Of Love	50
65	Atlantic AT 4026	Midnight Cannonball/Baby I Still Want You	20
57	London REE 1111	PRESENTING JOE TURNER (EP, initially tri-centre)	250
57	London REE 1111	PRESENTING JOE TURNER (EP, later round centre)	150
57	London Jazz LTZ-K 15053	BOSS OF THE BLUES (LP, mono)	80
57	London Jazz SAH-K 6123	BOSS OF THE BLUES (LP, stereo)	90
59	London HA-E 2173	ROCKIN' THE BLUES (LP)	120
60	London Jazz LTZ-K 15205	BIG JOE RIDES AGAIN (LP, mono)	75
60	London Jazz SAH-K 6123	BIG JOE RIDES AGAIN (LP, stereo)	80
60	London HA-E 2231	BIG JOE IS HERE (LP)	80
64	Realm RM 207	JOE TURNER SINGS THE BLUES VOL. 1 (LP)	20
64	Realm RM 229	JOE TURNER SINGS THE BLUES VOL. 2 (LP)	20
65	Fontana 688 802 ZL	JUMPIN' THE BLUES (LP)	25
67	Atlantic Special 590 006	BOSS OF THE BLUES (LP)	18
68	Stateside (S)SL 10226	SINGING THE BLUES (LP)	18
70	Philips SBL 7911	THE REAL BOSS OF THE BLUES (LP)	15

JOE TURNER/RUTH BROWN
56	London REE 1047	KING AND QUEEN OF R&B (EP, 2 tracks each)	150

(see also Ruth Brown, Big Joe Turner)

JOE TURNER & PETE JOHNSON GROUP
56	Emarcy ERE 1500	JOE TURNER & PETE JOHNSON GROUP (EP)	30

(see also Pete Johnson, Big Joe Turner)

MEL TURNER (& BANDITS)
61	Melodisc MEL 1580	Let Me Hold Your Hand/I'll Be With You In Apple Blossom Time (with Bandits)	20
62	Columbia DB 4791	Daddy Cool/Swing Low Sweet Chariot (with Bandits)	25
63	Columbia DB 4963	Don't Cry/I Need	10
63	Columbia DB 7076	I Can't Stand Up Alone/Doing The Ton (with Mohicans)	15
63	Carnival CV 7003	Mohican Crawl/White Christmas	10
66	Island WI 276	Welcome Home Little Darlin'/C'est L'Amour	40
64	Carnival CV 1005	The Hermit And The Rosetree/What's The Matter With Me	10

SAMMY TURNER
59	London HLX 8918	Lavender Blue (Dilly, Dilly)/Sweet Annie Laurie	10
59	London HLX 8963	Always/Symphony	15
59	London HLX 8963	Always/Symphony (78)	20
60	London HLX 9062	Paradise/I'd Be A Fool Again	15
62	London HLX 9488	Raincoat In The River/Falling	25

Spyder TURNER

MINT VALUE £

60	London HA-X 2246	LAVENDER BLUE MOODS (LP)	60

SPYDER TURNER
67	MGM MGM 1332	Stand By Me/You're Good Enough For Me	20
74	Kwanza K 19502	Since I Don't Have You/Happy Days	8

TITUS TURNER
60	London HLU 9024	We Told You Not To Marry/Taking Care Of Business	25
61	Oriole CB 1611	Pony Train/Bla Bla Cha Cha Cha	20
61	Parlophone R 4746	Sound-Off/Me And My Lonely Telephone	25
61	Blue Beat BB 32	Miss Rubberneck Jones/Way Down Yonder	18

TURNING POINT
77	Gull GULP 1022	CREATURES OF THE NIGHT (LP)	20
78	Gull GULP 1027	SILENT PROMISE (LP)	15

TURNPIKE
74	Fontana 6007032	Big Machine/Lazer Thereza	10

TURNSTYLE
68	Pye 7N 17653	Riding A Wave/Trot	325

TURQUOISE
68	Decca F 12756	53 Summer Street/Tales Of Flossie Fillett	70
68	Decca F 12842	Woodstock/Saynia	100

TURQUOISE DAYS
84	Disques Strategie STRAT XX1	Grey Skies/Blurred (p/s, 1000 only)	80

STANLEY TURRENTINE
66	Fontana TL 5300	TIGER TAIL (LP)	20
72	CTI CTL2	SUGAR (LP, gatefold)	20
97	Blue Note 7243 8 29908 1 9	EASY WALKER (LP, reissue)	18

(see also Milt Jackson & Stanley Turrentine)

HENRY TURTLE
72	Columbia DB 8859	Do You Believe/You Turned Your Back And Walked Away	30
73	Bell 1318	When Eleanor Comes Around/One Of A Million Faces	8

TURTLES
65	Pye International 7N 25320	It Ain't Me Babe/Almost There	20
66	Pye International 7N 25341	Let Me Be/Your Ma Said You Cried (In Your Sleep Last Night)	15
66	Immediate IM 031	You Baby/Wanderin' Kind	25
66	London HLU 10095	Can I Get To Know You Better/Like The Seasons	10
67	Pye International 7N 25421	Let Me Be/Almost There	8
67	London HLU 10153	You Know What I Mean/Rugs Of Woods And Flowers	8
67	London HLU 10168	She's My Girl/Chicken Little Was Right	12
68	London HLU 10184	Sound Asleep/Umbassa The Dragon	10
68	London HLU 10207	The Story Of Rock And Roll/Can't You Hear The Cows	10
69	London HLU 10251	You Showed Me/Buzz-Saw	12
69	London HLU 10279	You Don't Have To Walk In The Rain/Come Over	12
69	London HLU 10291	Love In The City/Bachelor Mother	7
67	Pye Intl. NEP 44089	IT AIN'T ME BABE (EP)	45
67	London HA-U 8330	HAPPY TOGETHER (LP)	20
68	London HA-U/SH-U 8376	THE TURTLES PRESENT THE BATTLE OF THE BANDS (LP)	20

(see also Flo & Eddie, Frank Zappa)

GEOFF TURTON
68	Pye 7N 17483	Don't You Believe It/I've Got To Tell Her	10

RITA TUSHINGHAM & LYNN REDGRAVE
68	Stateside SS 2081	Smashing Time/Waiting For My Friend	10

TUSKEN RAIDERS
99	Planet Mu ZIQ 003	BANTHA TRAX VOL. 2 EP (12", p/s)	12

TUSS
07	Rephlex CAT 190EP	CONFEDERATION TROUGH EP	30
07	Rephlex CAT 189	RUSHUP EDGE (3-LP)	60

(see also Aphex Twin, Polygon Window, Caustic Window)

TUTCH
80	Gargoyle GRGL 773	The Battle/You Don't Care/Round And Round	60

TU-TONES
59	London HLW 8904	Still In Love WIth You/Saccharin Sally	125
59	London HLW 8904	Still In Love WIth You/Saccharin Sally (78)	30

WESLEY & MARILYN TUTTLE
55	Capitol CL 14291	Jim, Johnny And Jonas/Say You Do	10

TUXEDO
85	Rushmore RR/TX/238	Take It Easy/Set Me Free (p/s)	35

TUXEDOMOON
80	PREX 4	DESIRE (LP, with art print insert)	20
82	Operation Twilight OPT 1	DIVINE (LP)	20
91	LTM LTM 2303	THE GHOST SONATA (LP)	25

TV ON THE RADIO
04	4AD AD 2421	Staring At The Sun/Freeway/On A Train	6
04	4AD AD 2606	Wolf Like Me/Snakes & Martyrs	10
06	4AD RTCM2	Province (with David Bowie, 200 only, green vinyl)	40
09	Parlophone LCO 299	TV ON THE RADIO : Heroes/DAVID BOWIE : Heroes	40
04	4AD CAD 2470	DESPERATE YOUTH, BLOODTHIRSTY BABES (LP, with free 12")	20
04	4AD CAD 2470	DESPERATE YOUTH, BLOODTHIRSTY BABES (LP)	15
06	4AD CAD 2607	RETURN TO COOKIE MOUNTAIN (LP)	18
08	4AD CAD 2821	DEAR SCIENCE (2-LP, white vinyl)	15

T.V. PRODUCTO
79	Limited Edition TAKE 3	Nowhere's Safe/Jumping Off Walls/PRAMS: Me/Modern Man (folded p/s)	12

T.V. & TRIBESMEN

MINT VALUE £

(see also Mission)

T.V. & TRIBESMEN
66 Pye International 7N 25375   Barefootin'/Fat Man 20

TV 21
80 Powbeat AAARGH! 1   Playing With Fire/Shattered By It All (foldout p/s) 12
80 Powbeat AAARGH! 2   Ambition/Ticking Away/This Is Zero (foldout p/s) 15
81 Demon D 1004   On The Run/End Of A Dream (p/s) 8
82 Deram ATV 21   All Join Hands/A Journey Up The Zambezi (And Back) (p/s) 8

(see also DNV, Shake)

TWELFTH NIGHT (1)
73 Acorn CF 239   TWELFTH NIGHT (EP) 70

TWELFTH NIGHT (2)
80 Twelfth Night TN 001   THE FIRST 7" ALBUM ("The Cunning Man"/"Für Helene") (p/s) 30

TWELVE CUBIC FEET
82 Namedrop NR2   STRAIGHT OUT OF THE FRIDGE (10" EP, with Bumper Booklet) 40

20TH CENTURY FOX ORCHESTRA
65 Stateside SS422   Those Magnificent Men In Their Flying Machines/Arizona 15

(see also Ron Goodwin)

25 RIFLES
79 25 Rifles TFR 1   World War 3/Revolution Blues/Hey Little/Dance 'Bout Now (12") 20

25 VIEWS OF WORTHING
77 Worthings LYN 4423/4424   RAT BRAIN INCISION EP 10

21 GUNS
81 Shack SHA001   21 Guns/Ambition (p/s) 8

22ND STREET
72 Polydor 2058 212   Sunny Sleeps Late/Home 8

23RD TURNOFF
67 Deram DM 150   Michael Angelo/Leave Me Here 90

(see also Kirkbys, Jimmy Campbell, Rockin' Horse)

23 JEWELS
79 Temporary TEMP 1   You Don't Know Me/Playing Bogart (white labels, plain sleeve with photocopied insert) . 20
80 Temporary TEMP 2   WELTSCHMERZ A GO-GO! (EP, white label) 12
81 Let's Call It Temporary TEMP 3   I'll Pay For This/Down To Minimum (p/s) 15

23 SKIDOO
81 Pineapple PULP 23   Ethics/Another Baby's Face (p/s) 8
81 Fetish FE 10   Last Words/Version (promo only) 12
81 Fetish FE 11   The Gospel Comes To New Guinea/Last Words (12", p/s) 15
82 Fetish FP 20   Tearing Up The Plans/Just Like Everybody/Gregouka (12", p/s) 10
85 Illuminated ILL 2812   Coup/Version (In The Palace) (12", p/s) 10
82 Fetish FM 2008   SEVEN SONGS (mini-LP) 20
83 Operation Twilight OPT 23   THE CULLING IS COMING (LP) 20
84 Illuminated JAM 40   URBAN GAMELAN (LP) 20

(see also Current 93)

24 CARAT BLACK
94 Stax SXD 090   GHETTO: MISFORTUNES WEALTH (LP, reissue) 20

24 HOUR EXPERIENCE
94 Nice N Ripe NNR 018   PART ONE: DUB ESSENTIALS (12") 15
94 Nice N Ripe NN R017   PART TWO: MORE DUB ESSENTIALS EP (12", 1st pressing red/black labels) 30
97 Nice N Ripe NNR 017   PART TWO: MORE DUB ESSENTIALS EP (12", 2nd pressing green labels) 20

TWICE AS MUCH
66 Immediate IM 033   Sittin' On A Fence/Baby I Want You 6
66 Immediate IM 036   Step Out Of Line/Simplified 12
66 Immediate IM 039   True Story/You're So Good 18
67 Immediate IM 042   Crystal Ball/Why Don't They All Go Away And Leave Me Alone 18
66 Immediate IMLP 007   OWN UP (LP, mono) 90
66 Immediate IMSP 007   OWN UP (LP, stereo) 100
69 Immediate IMCP 013   THAT'S ALL (LP) 60

TWICE AS NICE
74 CAE TAN 1   Going Places/Follow Me Around/Have You Been Along Way 20
74 Tan 002   Thoughts Of You/Dan Dare Rides Again/Hometown 20

TWIGGY
67 Ember EMB S 239   Beautiful Dreams/I Need Your Hand In Mine (in p/s) 20
67 Ember EMB S 239   Beautiful Dreams/I Need Your Hand In Mine 10
67 Ember EMB S 244   When I Think Of You/Over And Over (in p/s) 20
67 Ember EMB S 244   When I Think Of You/Over And Over 10
72 Ember SE 8012   TWIGGY & THE GIRLFRIENDS (LP) 20

TWIGGY & ANNE
66 Columbia DB 7799   Some Do, Some Don't/With Open Arms 6

CALVIN TWILIGHT
79 President PT 477   Harmony/Isabelle Blue 20
80 Norwood NR 2003 S 80 CUS 803   Night Time In The City/Lovely Lady Smile 20

TWILIGHT PASSION
88 Hard Records COMM 2   MEG 1 (12" EP p/s) 25

TWILIGHT ZONERS
79 ZIP/Dining Out ZEROZERO1   ZERO ZERO ONE (Hospital/The Wrap/Twister/The Film)(EP, various silk-screened in red & hand-coloured p/s, signed & numbered) 75
80 ZIP/Dining Out ZIP 002   Brighton Rock/Diversion (p/s) 6

(see also Occult Chemistry)

TWILIGHTS (Australia)

MINT VALUE £

TWILIGHTS (AUSTRALIA)
66	Columbia DB 8065	Needle In A Haystack/I Don't Know Where The Wind Will Blow Me	30
67	Columbia DB 8125	What's Wrong With The Way I Live/It's Dark	20
68	Columbia DB 8396	Cathy, Come Home/The Way They Play	30

TWILIGHTS (U.S.)
65	London HLU 9992	Take What I Got/She's There	25

TWIN FREAKS
05	Grazw GRAZ011	Rinse The Rain/What's That You're Doing? (12", promo, 200 only)	50
05	Parlophone 311 3001	TWIN FREAKS (2-LP, gatefold)	40

(see also Beatles, Paul McCartney/Wings, Fireman)

TWINK (& FAIRIES)
78	Chiswick SWT 26	Do It '77/Psychedelic Punkeroo/Enter The Diamonds (12", p/s, with Fairies)	12
86	Twink TWK 2	SPACE LOVER (EP)	12
70	Polydor 2343 032	THINK PINK (LP, with pink lyric insert)	350
70	Polydor 2343 032	THINK PINK (LP, without pink lyric insert)	200
70	Polydor 2343 032	THINK PINK (LP, red vinyl with pink lyric insert)	400
91	Twink LP 2	ODDS & BEGINNINGS (LP, with insert, numbered & signed, some on red vinyl, 1,500 only)	15
97	Twink LP4	THINK PINK (LP, reissue, 1000 only)	25

(see also Pretty Things, Pink Fairies, Fairies, Tomorrow, Aquarian Age, Rings, Mick Farren, Magic Muscle)

TWINKLE (RIPLEY)
64	Decca F 12013	Terry/The Boy Of My Dreams	6
65	Decca F 12076	Golden Lights/Ain't Nobody Home But Me	10
65	Decca F 12139	Tommy/So Sad	12
65	Decca F 12219	Poor Old Johnny/I Need Your Hand In Mine	15
65	Decca F 12305	The End Of The World/Take Me To The Dance	15
66	Decca F 12464	What Am I Doing Here With You?/Now I Have You	15
69	Instant IN 005	Micky/Darby And Joan	15
74	Bradleys BRAD 7418	Days/Caroline (as Twinkle Ripley) (p/s)	15
74	Bradleys BRAD 7418	Days/Caroline (as Twinkle Ripley)	7
82	EMI 5278	I'm A Believer/For Sale (p/s)	15
65	Decca DFE 8621	TWINKLE - A LONELY SINGING DOLL (EP)	60

(see also Silkie Davis)

TWINKLE BROTHERS
70	Jackpot JP 731	Shu Be Du/All My Enemies Beware	8
70	Jackpot JP 740	Miss World/Take What You've Got	15
70	Jackpot JP 741	Sweet Young Thing/Grandma	8
71	Jackpot JP 768	Do Your Own Thing/BOY WONDER: They Talk About Love	10
71	Green Door GD 4007	Miss Labba Labba/The Best Is Yet To Come	10
71	Big Shot BI 593	You Took Me By Suprise/You Took Me By Suprise - Version (both sides actually by Tony Brevitt)	15
71	Big Shot BI 600	It's Not Who You Know/I Need Someone	8
73	Camel CA 105	Room Full All Full/Version	12
73	Count Shelley CS 31	Mother Whiney/JACKIE BROWN: Fight My Way	6
73	Camel CA 106	Room Full All Full/Version	12
73	Pama PM 876	Village Ram/Push It Inna	10
75	Faith FA 022	Mother And Wife/GENE RONDO: Impossible Dream	6
77	Carib Gems CG 009	Jah Army/Dub The Wicked	10
79	Virgin Front Line FLS 119 12	Keep On Trying/King Pharoah (12")	12
79	Virgin Front Line FLS 123 12	Jahoviah/Free Africa (12")	35
80	Virgin Front Line FLS 127 12	Never Get Burned/Jah Kingdom Come (12" white label)	30
81	Twinkle TW 1/12	Rasta Pon Top/It Gwine Dread (12")	15
81	Twinkle A 621	Robot/Don't Turn Your Back On Jah (12")	35
81	Twinkle NG 643	Africa For The Africans/Stomach Sick (12")	10
83	Twinkle NG 369	Let Jah In/Don't Jump The Fence (12")	30
86	Jah Shaka SHAKA 855	Faith Can Move Mountain/Mob Fury (12")	25
91	Twinkle NG 100	Ethiopia Is Calling/COLOUR RED: Ethiopia Here I Come (12")	18
92	Twinkle NG 106	The Reality Of Jah Kingdom/Twinkle Brothers	20
92	Twinkle NG107	Constipated People/Version	10
92	Jah Shaka	Africa/Version (tracks not printed on labels)	20
92	Jah Shaka	Rasta Surface/Version (tracks not printed on labels)	20
92	Jah Shaka 855	Faith Can Move Mountains/Mob Fury (12")	15
75	Grounation GROL 506	RASTA PON TOP (LP)	35
76	Carib Gems CGLP 1001	DO YOUR OWN THING (LP)	60
78	Front Line FCL 5001	LOVE (10" LP)	15
80	Virgin V2169	COUNTRYMEN (LP)	20
82	Twinkle NG 500	UNDERGROUND (LP)	15
82	Twinkle NNG 741	DUB MASSACRE (INNA MURDER STYLE) (LP)	15
83	Twinkle NG 502	DUB MASSACRE PART TWO (LP)	15
84	Twinkle NG 501	BURDEN BEARER (LP)	20
85	Twinkle NGLP 505	DUB MASSACRE PART THREE (LP)	15
89	Twinkle NG 515	DUB MASSACRE PART FOUR (LP)	15

(see also Busty Brown, Sammy Jones)

TWINN CONNEXION
16	Super Disco Edits SDE 17	Don't Fight The Love/Don't Fight The Love	20

TWINS
73	Downtown DT 511	Rastafari Ruler/TYRONE TAYLOR: Yesterday	8

TWINSET
67	Decca F 12629	Tremblin'/Sneakin' Up On You	25

TWIN-TONES

MINT VALUE £

TWIN-TONES
58	RCA RCA 1040	Jo Ann/Before You Go	50

TWIN TUNES QUINTET
58	RCA RCA 1046	The Love Nest/Baby Lover	12

TWIST & SHOUT
79	Wessex WEX 268	Bounce Back/As It Happens (p/s)	20

TWIST (1)
79	Polydor 2059 156	This Is Your Life/Life's A Commercial Break (p/s)	10
79	Polydor POSP 84	Ads/Rebound	10
79	Polydor 2383 552	THIS IS YOUR LIFE (LP)	20

TWISTED ACE
81	Heavy Metal HEAVY 9	Firebird/I Won't Surrender (in p/s)	12

TWISTED SISTER
82	Secret SHH 137-12	RUFF CUTS (12" EP, p/s)	10

TWISTED NERVE
82	Playlist PLAY 3	CAUGHT IN SESSION EP (poster p/s)	15
83	Criminal Damage CRI 102	Five Minutes Of Fame/Strange Sensation	8
83	Criminal Damage CRI 103	EYES YOU CAN DROWN IN EP	20
84	Nerve NERVE 1	SEANCE (Mini-LP)	25

TWISTERS
60	Capitol CL 15167	Turn The Page/Dancing Little Clown	8
62	Aral/Windsor PSA 106	Peppermint Twist Time/Silly Chilli	12

TWISTING FERRARIS
80	Round TF 001	Our Favourite Photograph/Lipsticks (p/s)	12

CONWAY TWITTY

78s
57	Mercury MT 173	Shake It Up/Maybe Baby	30
59	MGM MGM 1029	Mona Lisa/Heavenly	20
59	MGM MGM 1047	Rosaleena/Halfway To Heaven	30

SINGLES
58	MGM MGM 992	It's Only Make Believe/I'll Try	10
59	MGM MGM 1003	The Story Of My Love/Make Me Know You're Mine	10
59	MGM MGM 1016	Hey Little Lucy! (Don'tcha Put No Lipstick On)/ When I'm Not With You	10
59	MGM MGM 1029	Mona Lisa/Heavenly	6
59	MGM MGM 1047	Rosaleena/Halfway To Heaven	6
60	MGM MGM 1056	Lonely Blue Boy/My One And Only You	10
60	MGM MGM 1066	What Am I Living For/The Hurt In My Heart	10
60	MGM MGM 1082	Is A Blue Bird Blue/She's Mine	15
60	MGM MGM 1095	What A Dream/Tell Me One More Time	6
60	MGM MGM 1108	Whole Lotta Shakin' Goin' On/The Flame	12
61	MGM MGM 1118	C'est Si Bon/Don't You Dare Let Me Down	12
61	MGM MGM 1129	The Next Kiss/Man Alone	6
61	MGM MGM 1137	It's Drivin' Me Wild/Sweet Sorry	10
62	MGM MGM 1152	Tower Of Tears/Portrait Of A Fool	12
62	MGM MGM 1170	Comfy An' Cozy/Unchained Melody	10
62	MGM MGM 1187	I Hope I Think I Wish/The Pick Up	12
63	MGM MGM 1201	Handy Man/Little Piece Of My Heart	10
63	MGM MGM 1209	She Ain't No Angel/Got My Mojo Workin'	12
63	HMV POP 1258	Go On And Cry/She Loves Me	8

EPs
58	MGM MGM-EP 684	IT'S ONLY MAKE BELIEVE	30
59	MGM MGM-EP 698	HEY LITTLE LUCY	50
60	MGM MGM-EP 719	SATURDAY NIGHT WITH CONWAY TWITTY	50
60	Mercury ZEP 10069	I NEED YOUR LOVIN'	100
60	MGM MGM-EP 738	IS A BLUEBIRD BLUE?	40
61	MGM MGM-EP 752	THE ROCK 'N' ROLL STORY	50

ALBUMS
59	MGM MGM-C 781	CONWAY TWITTY SINGS	100
60	MGM MGM-C 801	SATURDAY NIGHT WITH CONWAY TWITTY	100
60	MGM MGM-C 829	LONELY BLUE BOY	100
63	MGM MGM-C 950	R AND B '63	50
68	MCA MUP(S) 342	HERE'S CONWAY TWITTY (AND HIS LONELY BLUE BOYS)	18
68	MGM C/CS 8100	THE ROCK AND ROLL STORY	40
69	MCA MUPS 363	NEXT IN LINE	15

TWIZZLE & HOT ROD ALLSTARS
70	Torpedo TOR 3	Jook Jook/The Graduate	100

TWO
84	Reflex 12 RE 7	2 x 2 (12" EP)	20
83	Future FL3	DREAMING SPIRES (LP)	25

TWO & A HALF
66	CBS 202248	Midnight Swim/Faith	10
66	CBS 202404	Questions/In Harmony	8
67	CBS 202526	The Walls Are High/Love You	8
67	Decca F 22672	Suburban Early Morning Station/Just Couldn't Believe My Ears	15
67	Decca F 22715	I Don't Need To Tell You/Christmas Will Be Round Again	18

TWO DARK TROOPERS
92	Basement BRSS 020	I Wanna Be Your Lover/Darkcore (12")	10

(see also Chemical, DJ Mayhem)

TWO FINGERED APPROACH
82	Virus 026	World War Album/Society Hooked/Family Traditions (p/s. 500 only)	60

TWO FOR THE ROAD
70s	Pastiche BJ 2929	TWO FOR THE ROAD (LP)	20

TWO KINGS
65	Island WI 240	Rolling Stone/SUFFERER: Tomorrow Morning (B-side act. by Frank Cosmo)	18
65	Island WI 249	Hit You Let You Feel It/Honey I Love You (both sides actually by Fugitives)	18

TWO MAN SOUND
74	Spark SRL 118	Amadeo/Somebody Is Ready To Love You	8
78	Miracle M12	Que Tal America/Brazil O Brazil (12")	15

TWO MINDS CRACK
84	Sedition EDIT 2	Enemies Of Promise/The Stealer (p/s)	6

TWO MUCH
67	Fontana TF 858	Wonderland Of Love/Mister Money	7
68	Fontana TF 900	It's A Hip Hip Hippy World/Stay In My World	10

TWO-NINETEEN (2.19) SKIFFLE GROUP
57	Esquire 10-512	Where Can I Go?/Roll The Union On (78)	20
57	Esquire 10-515	This Little Light Of Mine/Union Maid (78)	20
57	Esquire EP 126	TWO-NINETEEN SKIFFLE GROUP (EP)	40
57	Esquire EP 146	TWO-NINETEEN SKIFFLE GROUP (EP)	50
58	Esquire EP 176	TWO-NINETEEN SKIFFLE GROUP (EP)	50
58	Esquire EP 196	TWO-NINETEEN SKIFFLE GROUP (EP)	60

TWO OF CLUBS
64	Columbia DB 7371	The Angels Must Have Made You/True Love Is Here	15

TWO OF EACH
67	Decca F 12626	Every Single Day/I'm Glad I Got You	12
68	Pye 7N 17555	The Summer Of Our Love/Saturday Morning	12

TWO PEOPLE (1)
76	Bright Spot BS 009	Time Is Precious/Jump Higher	15

TWO PEOPLE (2)
86	Polydor POSP 818	Mouth Of An Angel/Let's Raise Murder (p/s)	20
85	Polydor POSP 741	This Is The Shirt/Sister Sister (p/s)	6

2 SLICES OF JAM
92	White Label	Pressing On Ya Mind/Beat Like This (12" white label)	60

TWO SPARKS
72	Moodisc HM 113	Run Away Girl/When We Were Young	8

(see also Carl Bryan, Winston Wright)

2 THE TOP
89	Rhyme & Reason 12RNR2	The Rhythm I Give Em (12")	10
90	President PT12590	Score To Settle/The Matter At Hand (12")	30

(see also Kinetic Effect)

2001
91	B12 B1202	SPACE AGE EP (12", white label promo)	60
91	B12 B1202	SPACE AGE EP (12", orange marbled vinyl, 300 only)	40
92	B12 B1202	SPACE AGE EP (12", black vinyl)	35

2 3
78	Fast Products FAST 2	Where To Now?/All Time Low (p/s)	15

TWO TIMES DEF
92	Mendoza MEN016	First And Last (Vocal)/First And Last (Instrumental)/First And Last (Alternative Mix) (12", stamped white labels)	150

(see also Silent Eclipse)

TWO TONE COMMITTEE
91	Precinct PREC002	Beings From A Word Stuck Surface (12")	35
98	Dope On Plastic 12 DOP 006	Submission (12" EP)	15

2 BAD MICE
91	Moving Shadow SHADOW 3	2 Bad Mice/No Respect (12")	20
92	Moving Shadow SHADOW 14	HOLD IT DOWN EP (12", p/s)	20

TWO DOOR CINEMA CLUB
12	Kitsume LP 046	BEACON (LP, red vinyl, CD)	40

2-X-TREME
92	Empire E 001	X-TREMITY EP (12", white label stamped in red, beware of represses!)	50

2562
08	Tectonic TEC 021	AERIAL (2-LP)	25

2 KILOS ?
90	Radioactive Lamb (No Cat. No)	MOHAMED'S MIND (12" EP, later red/white labels)	15
90	Radioactive Lamb (No Cat. No)	MOHAMED'S MIND (12", EP, 1st pressing, red/white labels, 150 only)	30
91	Radioactive Lamb RAL 002	VISIONS OF PARADISE (12" EP, purple/white labels, blue vinyl 150 only)	25
91	Radioactive Lamb RAL 002	VISIONS OF PARADISE (12" EP, purple/white labels)	15
91	Radioactive Lamb RAL 003	UNTITLED EP (12")	20
92	Radioactive Lamb RAL 005	THE NO SELL OUT EP (12", p/s)	40

2 MEN AND A MAN
91	ZMAM XX1	Untitled/Untitled (12", white label only)	25

2 PAC
95	Death Row DRWJB 3	California Love (Short Radio Edit)/(Short Remix Edit) (Jukebox pressing)	40
95	Interscope 6544 92399-1	ME AGAINST THE WORLD (2-LP)	100
97	Interscope HIP 195	R U STILL DOWN? (REMEMBER ME) (3-LP)	50
98	Jive HIP 200	ME AGAINST THE WORLD (2-LP, reissue, stickers sleeve)	100
01	Jive HIP 197	STRICTLY FOR MY N.I.G.G.A.Z.. (2-LP, reissue)	50

TWO'S COMPANY

			MINT VALUE £
02	Interscope 497 070 1	BETTER DAYZ (4-LP)	40
02	Simply Vinyl S 12	ALL EYEZ ON ME (3-LP, reissue)	30

TWO'S COMPANY
76	Thor 1009 S	TWO'S COMPANY (LP, 200 only)	50

TYDE
02	Rough Trade RTRADES 056	Blood Brothers/Play It As It Lays (p/s)	6

ARLYNE TYE
59	London HLL 8825	The Universe/Who Is The One	25

TYGERS OF PAN TANG
79	Neat NEAT 03	Don't Touch Me There/Burning Up/Bad Times (first pressing of around 1,000 in slightly oversized p/s giving it a 'home made' feel)	25
79	Neat NEAT 03	Don't Touch Me There/Burning Up/Bad Times (p/s)	12
80	MCA MCA 582	Don't Touch Me There/Burning Up/Bad Times (p/s, reissue)	10
81	MCA MCA 672	Hellbound/Bad Times//Bad Times/Don't Take Nothin' ('The Audition Tapes' double pack)	6
81	MCA MCAT 723	Don't Stop By/Slave To Freedom (12", p/s)	12
81	MCA MCA 755	Love Don't Stay/Paradise Drive (p/s)	8
81	MCA MCA 759	Do It Good/Slip Away (no p/s)	30
82	MCA MCA 777	Rendezvous/Life Of Crime (white vinyl, p/s)	6
82	MCA MCA 790	Paris By Air/Love's A Lie (standard p/s with earring)	10
82	MCA MCAT 798	Making Tracks (Extended Remix)/What You Saying (12", p/s)	10
80	MCA MCF 3075	WILD CAT (LP, with lyric insert)	18
81	MCA MCF 3104	SPELLBOUND (LP, with poster)	18
81	MCA MCF 3123	CRAZY NIGHTS (LP, stickered sleeve, insert, with bonus 12")	22
81	MCA MCF 3123	CRAZY NIGHTS (LP, stickered sleeve, insert)	15
85	MFN MFN 50	THE WRECK AGE (LP, lyric sleeve)	15
86	Neat 1037	FIRST KILL (LP, with inner)	15

(see also John Sykes)

TYLA GANG
76	Stiff BUY 4	Styrofoam/Texas Chainsaw Massacre Boogie (push-out centre, die-cut ' stamped' white sleeve)	10
76	Stiff BUY 4	Styrofoam/Texas Chainsaw Massacre Boogie (push-out centre, plain die-cut white sleeve)	6

(see also Ducks Deluxe)

BIG 'T' TYLER
57	Vogue V 9079	King Kong/Sadie Green	200
57	Vogue V 9079	King Kong/Sadie Green (78)	100

RED TYLER
56	Parlophone MSP 6215	Fool 'Em Devil/Stardust	18
60	Top Rank JAR 306	Junk Village/Happy Sax	12

T. TEXAS TYLER
59	Parlophone GEP 8788	COUNTRY ROUND-UP (EP)	30
67	London HA-B 8322	MAN WITH A MILLION FRIENDS (LP)	25

TERRY TYLER
61	Pye International 7N 25119	A Thousand Feet Below/Answer Me	15

TOBY TYLER
64	Emidisc no cat. no.	The Road I'm On (Gloria)/Blowin' In The Wind (acetate, 1 copy only)	3000
89	Archive Jive TOBY 1	The Road I'm On (Gloria) (mail-order issue, numbered p/s, 1-sided, 1,500 only)	15

(see also Marc Bolan)

TYMES
63	Cameo Parkway P 871	So Much In Love/Roscoe James McClain	10
63	Cameo Parkway P 884	Wonderful Wonderful/Come With Me To The Sea (in p/s)	25
63	Cameo Parkway P 884	Wonderful Wonderful/Come With Me To The Sea	10
64	Cameo Parkway P 891	Somewhere/View From My Window	15
64	Cameo Parkway P 908	To Each His Own/Wonderland Of Love	15
64	Cameo Parkway P 919	The Magic Of Our Summer Love/With All My Heart	15
64	Cameo Parkway P 924	Here She Comes/Malibu	100
64	Cameo Parkway P 924	Here She Comes/Malibu (DJ copy)	200
68	Direction 58-3903	People/For Love Of Ivy	6
69	Direction 58-4450	If You Love Me Baby/Find My Way	10
71	CBS 7250	Someone To Watch Over Me/She's Gone (featuring George Williams)	8
63	Cameo Parkway P 7032	SO MUCH IN LOVE (LP)	70
69	Direction 8-63558	PEOPLE (LP, mono or stereo)	25
78	London HAU 8516	CAMEO PARKWAY SESSIONS (LP)	25

MCCOY TYNER
70s	Impulse IMPL 8043	INCEPTION (LP)	15
76	Impulse IMPL 8010	LIVE AT NEWPORT (LP, reissue)	15
77	Blue Note 84275	TENDER MOMENTS (LP, reissue)	15

TYPE O NEGATIVE
92	Roadrunner RO 9174	THE ORIGIN OF THE FECES (NOT LIVE AT BRIGHTON BEACH) (LP)	70
91	Roadrunner RO 9313-1	SLOW DEEP AND HARD (LP)	40
93	Roadrunner RR 9100-1	BLOODY KISSES (2-LP)	125
96	Roadrunner RR 8874-1	OCTOBER RUST (2-LP)	100

TYPHOONS (1)
63	Embassy WB 589	Surf City/I Want To Stay Here	7
65	Embassy WB 677	Tired Of Waiting For You/Baby Please Don't Go	7
65	Embassy WEP 1115	Hard Day's Night/And I Love Her/I Should Have Known Better/Tell Me Why (EP)	10
65	Embassy WT 2006	Ticket To Ride/Here Comes The Night/I'll Be There/I Can't Explain (EP)	15

(see also Bud Ashton, Ray Pilgrim, Mike Redway)

TYRANNOSAURUS REX
68	Regal Zonophone RZ 3008	Debora/Child Star (with promo only p/s)	400

TYRANT

MINT VALUE £

68	Regal Zonophone RZ 3008	Debora/Child Star (with promo only p/s, with insert)	500
68	Regal Zonophone RZ 3008	Debora/Child Star (demo copy as above, but without promo only p/s)	375
68	Regal Zonophone RZ 3008	Debora/Child Star	35
68	Regal Zonophone RZ 3011	One Inch Rock/Salamanda Palaganda (promo only p/s)	375
68	Regal Zonophone RZ 3011	One Inch Rock/Salamanda Palaganda (promo only p/s, with insert)	425
68	Regal Zonophone RZ 3011	One Inch Rock/Salamanda Palaganda	40
69	Regal Zonophone RZ 3016	Pewter Suitor/Warlord Of The Royal Crocodiles	70
69	Regal Zonophone RZ 3022	King Of The Rumbling Spires/Do You Remember (with promo only p/s)	450
69	Regal Zonophone RZ 3022	King Of The Rumbling Spires/Do You Remember (demo, without promo only p/s)	400
69	Regal Zonophone RZ 3022	King Of The Rumbling Spires/Do You Remember	40
70	Regal Zonophone RZ 3025	By The Light Of A Magical Moon/Find A Little Wood	50
91	Tyrannosaurus Rex TYR 1	Sleepy Maurice/1968 Radio Promos (Tyrannosaurus Rex Appreciation Society release, 2,000 only, p/s with card insert)	8
68	Regal Zonophone LRZ 1003	MY PEOPLE WERE FAIR AND HAD SKY IN THEIR HAIR BUT NOW THEY'RE CONTENT TO WEAR STARS ON THEIR BROWS (LP, mono, with lyric sheet & manuscript)	100
68	Regal Zonophone LRZ 1003	MY PEOPLE WERE FAIR AND HAD SKY IN THEIR HAIR BUT NOW THEY'RE CONTENT TO WEAR STARS ON THEIR BROWS (LP, mono)	50
68	Regal Zonophone SLRZ 1003	MY PEOPLE WERE FAIR AND HAD SKY IN THEIR HAIR BUT NOW THEY'RE CONTENT TO WEAR STARS ON THEIR BROWS (LP, stereo, with lyric sheet & manuscript)	60
68	Regal Zonophone SLRZ 1003	MY PEOPLE WERE FAIR AND HAD SKY IN THEIR HAIR BUT NOW THEY'RE CONTENT TO WEAR STARS ON THEIR BROWS (LP, stereo)	20
68	Regal Zonophone TA-LRZ 1003	MY PEOPLE WERE FAIR AND HAD SKY IN THEIR HAIR BUT NOW THEY'RE CONTENT TO WEAR STARS ON THEIR BROWS (reel-to-reel tape, mono)	35
68	Regal Zonophone LRZ 1005	PROPHETS, SEERS AND SAGES, THE ANGELS OF THE AGES (LP, with lyric sheet, textured sleeve, mono)	100
68	Regal Zonophone SLRZ 1005	PROPHETS, SEERS AND SAGES, THE ANGELS OF THE AGES (LP, with lyric sheet, textured sleeve, stereo)	80
69	R. Zonophone LRZ 1007	UNICORN (LP, gatefold sleeve, original with blue/silver label, mono)	120
69	R. Zonophone LRZ 1007	UNICORN (LP, gatefold sleeve, later issue with red/silver label mono)	60
70	R. Zonophone SLRZ 1007	UNICORN (LP, gatefold sleeve, original with blue/silver label, stereo)	100
70	R. Zonophone SLRZ 1007	UNICORN (LP, gatefold sleeve, later issue with red/silver label, stereo)	30
70	R. Zonophone SLRZ 1013	A BEARD OF STARS (LP, with lyric sheet)	60
70	R. Zonophone SLRZ 1013	A BEARD OF STARS (LP, without lyric sheet)	30

(see also Marc Bolan/T. Rex, John's Children, Dib Cochran & Earwigs, Shagrat)

TYRANT
83	SRTS 83 CUS 2046	Hold Back The Lightning/Eyes Of A Stranger	400

TYRONE & CARR
72	Jam JAM 7	I Want To Give You My Everything/I'm Still In Love With You	8
73	Jam JAM 36	Love Me Love You/Take Me With You	30
75	DJM DJS 349	Love Me Love You/Take Me With You	30

GORDON TYRRALL
78	Hill & Dale HD 002	FAREWELL TO FOGGY HILLS (LP)	18

TYSONDOG
83	Neat NEAT 33	Eat The Rich/Dead Meat (p/s)	10
85	Neat NEAT 46	Shoot To Kill/Hammerhead (p/s)	10
85	Neat NEAT 4612	Shoot To Kill/Hammerhead/Changeling/Back To The Bullet (12", p/s)	15
86	Neat NEAT 56	School's Out/Don't Let The Bastards Grind You Down (p/s)	12
86	Neat NEAT 1031	CRIMES OF INSANITY (LP, with inner)	18
84	Neat NEAT 1017	BEWARE OF THE DOG (LP, with insert)	20

TYTAN
82	Kamaflage KAM 6	Blind Men And Fools/The Ballad Of Edward Case (p/s)	18
82	Kamaflage KAMA 6	Blind Men And Fools/The Ballad Of Edward Case (12", p/s)	20
85	Metal Masters METALP 105	ROUGH JUSTICE (LP)	22

(see also Angel Witch)

TZUKE & PAXO
76	Good Earth GD 12	These Are The Laws/It's Only Fantasies	15

U

U BLACK
78	Hit Run HIT 621	Wicked Are To Blame/Dub (12")	20
77	Third World TWS 926	WESTBOUND THING A SWING (LP)	40

U BROWN
77	Third World TWS 909	LONDON ROCK (LP)	30
78	Live & Love LALP 002	REVELATION TIME (LP)	30

UBIK
90	Zoom ZOOM 003	NON STOP TECHNO EP (12")	20
91	Zoom ZOOM 006	SYSTEM OVERLOAD EP (12")	10
92	Zoom ZOOM LP1	JUST ADD PEOPLE (LP)	40

U.F.O.
70	Beacon BEA 161	Shake It About/Evil	40
70	Beacon BEA 165	Come Away Melinda/Unidentified Flying Object	30
70	Beacon BEA 172	Boogie For George/Treacle People (with postcard)	35
70	Beacon BEA 172	Boogie For George/Treacle People	25
71	Beacon BEA 181	Prince Kajuku/The Coming Of Prince Kajuku	25
73	Chrysalis CHS 2024	Give Her The Gun/Sweet Little Thing (unreleased in U.K.)	0
74	Chrysalis CHS 2040	Doctor Doctor/Lipstick Traces	12

Leslie UGGAMS

MINT VALUE £

75	Chrysalis CHS 2072	Shoot Shoot/Love Lost Love (unissued)	0
77	Chrysalis CHS 2146	Alone Again Or/Electric Phase	10
77	Chrysalis CHS 2178	Gettin' Ready/Lights Out (unissued)	0
78	Chrysalis CHS 2241	Only You Can Rock Me/Cherry/Rock Bottom (p/s, red vinyl, with frisbee offer)	8
78	Chrysalis CHS 2241	Only You Can Rock Me/Cherry/Rock Bottom (p/, with frisbee offer)	6
79	Chrysalis CHS 2287	Doctor Doctor (live)/On With The Action (live)/Try Me (p/s, clear vinyl)	6
79	Chrysalis CHS 2287	Doctor Doctor (live)/On With The Action (live)/Try Me (p/s, mauve vinyl)	10
83	Lyntone LYN 12821	Blinded By A Lie (edit)/Diesel In The Dust (edit)/When It's Time To Rock (edit) (flexidisc with Metal Fury magazine, issue 12)	10
70	Beacon BEAS 12	U.F.O. 1 (LP)	150
72	Beacon BEAS 19	U.F.O. 2 - FLYING (ONE HOUR SPACE ROCK) (LP, 1st pressing, white label, with inner lyric sleeve)	200
72	Beacon BEAS 19	U.F.O. 2 - FLYING (ONE HOUR SPACE ROCK) (LP, 2nd pressing, orange label)	80
74	Chrysalis CHS 1059	PHENOMENON (LP, misprinted green label, matt sleeve)	15
76	Chrysalis CHR 1103	NO HEAVY PETTING (LP, 1st pressing, green labels, A1/B1 matrixes)	20
77	Chrysalis CHR 1127	LIGHTS OUT (LP, 1st pressing, etched matrix numbers CHR1127 A/B, TML-S stamped into dead wax on both sides, green label wih red text on outer rim, 'Chrysalis Records Ltd, Printed in U.K,' on spine)	20

(see also Michael Schenker Group)

LESLIE UGGAMS

59	Philips BBL 7370	THE EYES OF GOD (LP)	12

UGLY CUSTARD

70	Kaleidoscope KAL 100	UGLY CUSTARD (LP)	150

(see also Hungry Wolf, Alan Parker, Rock Machine)

UGLYS

65	Pye 7N 15858	Wake Up My Mind/Ugly Blues	30
65	Pye 7N 15968	It's Alright/A Friend	20
66	Pye 7N 17027	A Good Idea/A Quiet Explosion	30
66	Pye 7N 17178	End Of The Season/Can't Recall Her Name	40
67	CBS 2933	And The Squire Blew His Horn/Real Good Girl	50
69	MGM MGM 1465	I See The Light/Mary Cilento (6 demo copies only, pink/silver labels)	1500

(see also Steve Gibbons, Balls, Lemon Tree, Move, Trevor Burton)

U.K. BONDS

65	Polydor BM 56061	The World Is Watching Us/I Said Goodbye To The Blues	10
66	Polydor BM 56112	Anything You Do Is Alright/The Last Thing I Ever Do	20

U.K. DECAY

79	Plastic PLAS 001	U.K. Decay/Car Crash/PNEUMONIA: Exhibition/Coming Attack (folded p/s)	25
80	Fresh FRESH 012	For My Country/Unwind (p/s)	10
81	Fresh FRESH 26	Unexpected Guest/Dresden (foldout p/s)	6
82	C. Christi CHRIST ITS 1	Rising From The Dread/Testament/Werewolf/Jerusalem Over (The White Cliffs Of Dover) (12", p/s with insert)	12
81	Fresh LP5	FOR MADMEN ONLY (LP)	18
80s	UK Decay DKLP1	FOR MADMEN ONLY (LP)	25
13	Rainbow City LP 1606	NEW HOPE FOR THE DEAD (LP)	15

UK PLAYERS

82	A&M AMLH 68544	NO WAY OUT (LP)	30

U.K. SUBS

78	City NIK 5	C.I.D./Live In A Car/B.I.C. (p/s, 1st pressing, red green or orange vinyl, "FOR STRONGER PAIN RELIEF" and "KEEP AWAY FROM CHILDREN" in run out grooves)	40
78	City NIK 5	C.I.D./Live In A Car/B.I.C. (p/s, 1st pressing, yellow vinyl, "FOR STRONGER PAIN RELIEF" and "KEEP AWAY FROM CHILDREN" in run out grooves)	100
78	City NIK 5	C.I.D./Live In A Car/B.I.C. (p/s, 2nd pressing, clear, blue orange and green vinyl, "A PORKY PRIME CUT" in side 1 run out groove)	25
78	City NIK 5	C.I.D./Live In A Car/B.I.C. (p/s, 3rd pressing, blue or black vinyl)	10
79	Gem GEMS 5	Stranglehold/World War/Rockers (p/s, red vinyl)	8
82	Ramkup CAC 2	Party In Paris (1-sided fan club single, no p/s, 500 only)	30
84	Gem FALL 12024	SPELL EP (12")	10
11	Time & Matter T&M 005	Product Supply/Rare Disease/Embryo (p/s, 250 only, signed, white vinyl)	40
15	Time & Matter T&M 018	AMOEBA SOUNDS EP	25
15	Captain Oi! AHOY 704	THE PEEL SESSIONS VOL 1 (7" EP 250 on white and 250 on yellow vinyl)	25
15	Captain Oi! AHOY 705	THE PEEL SESSIONS VOL 2 (7" EP, 250 on green and 250 on white vinyl)	25
16	Captain Oi! AHOY 706	THE PEEL SESSIONS VOL 3 (7" EP 250 on red and 250 on white vinyl)	25
16	Demon DEMRECBOX 09	THE GEM SINGLES (8 x 7" box set)	35
18	Punkerama 2020 218	Endangered Species/Lie Down And Die (splatter pink and vinyl with silver flecks)	15
79	Gem GEMLP 100	ANOTHER KIND OF BLUES (LP, blue vinyl, with inner sleeve)	20
80	Gem GEMLP 106	BRAND NEW AGE (LP, clear vinyl, with insert)	15
80	Gem GEMLP 111	CRASH COURSE LIVE (LP, purple vinyl, 15,000 with export 12" [GEMEP 1])	15
80	Gem GEMLP 111	CRASH COURSE LIVE (LP, clear vinyl)	15
80	Stiff Records MAIL 1	LIVE KICKS (LP, brown card inner sleeve, mail order only)	15
81	Gem GEMLP 112	DIMINISHED RESPONSIBILITY (LP, red vinyl with inner sleeve)	15
82	Abstract AABT 300	RECORDED '79-'81 (LP, blue vinyl with free stencil)	15
82	Abstract AABT 300	RECORDED '79-'81 (LP, red vinyl)	15
82	Abstract AABT 800	THE SINGLES 78-82 (LP, blue vinyl)	15
83	Scarlett FALLLP 018	FLOOD OF LIES (LP)	15
85	RFB LP 1	HUNTINGTON BEACH (LP)	15
97	Fallout LP 053	PEEL SESSIONS 1978-79 (LP)	50
11	Captain Oi! AHOYLP 310	WORK IN PROGRESS (LP, red vinyl)	40
15	Captain Oi! AHOYLP 317	YELLOW LEADER (LP, yellow vinyl, clear yellow flexi and CD)	150
16	Demon DEMREC118	THE GEM SINGLES (LP, green vinyl)	15

(see also Urban Dogs, Charlie Harper & Captain Sensible)

ANYAOGU UKONU & HIS AFRO-CALYPSOIANS

56	London HA-U 2019	AFRO U.S.A (LP)	30

U.K.S
64	HMV POP 1310	Ever Faithful, Ever True/Your Love Is All I Want	25
64	HMV POP 1357	I Will Never Let You Go/I Know	25

TRACEY ULLMAN
83	Stiff BUY DJ 195	Move Over Darling/Bobby's Girl (pink promo, "A" label)	15
85	Stiff BUY DJ 232	Shattered/Alone (light blue promo "A" label)	6

JAMES 'BLOOD' ULMER
80	Rough Trade ROUGH 16	ARE YOU GLAD TO BE IN AMERICA? (LP)	15

PETER ULRICH
90	Corner Stone PTD-001	Taqaharu's Leaving/Evocation (12")	10

ULTERIOR MOTIVES
79	Motive Music MMR 1	Another Lover (p/s)	30

ULTIMATE PAINTING
14	Trouble In Mind TIM 081LP	ULTIMATE PAINTING (LP, pink vinyl)	25
15	Trouble In Mind TIM 096LP	GREEN LANES (LP, marbled vinly)	20

ULTIMATE SPINACH
68	MGM MGM-C(S) 8071	ULTIMATE SPINACH (LP)	175
68	MGM MGM-C(S) 8094	BEHOLD AND SEE (LP)	175

ULTRAFOX
71	Deram DM339	Nine By Nine/Stomping At Decca	6

ULTRAFUNK
75	Contempo CS 2020	Sweet F.A./Use Me	7
75	Contempo CLP 509	ULTRAFUNK (LP)	50
77	Contempo CLP 601	MEAT HEAT (LP)	40

ULTRA HIGH FREQUENCY
73	Pye International 7N 25628	We're On The Right Track/We're On The Right Track (version)	6

ULTRAMAGNETIC MCS
89	FFRR FFR 22	Give The Drummer Some - Vocal Rermix/Moe Luv's Theme - Vocal Remix (p/s)	150
92	FFRR FYHU 3458	FUNK YOUR HEAD UP (LP)	20

ULTRAMARINE
91	Brainiak BRAINK 21LP	EVERY MAN AND WOMAN IS A STAR (2-LP)	20

ULTRA VIOLENT
83	Riot City RIOT 25	CRIME FOR REVENGE (EP)	20

ULTRA VIVID SCENE
89	4AD BAD 906	Mercy Seat/Codeine/H Like In Heaven/Mercy Seat (LP Version) (12", uncut p/s [most copies die-cut])	22
89	4AD AD 908	Something To Eat/H Like In Heaven (freebie, 1,000 only)	10
90	4AD AD 0016	Special One/Kind Of Drag	7
90	4AD UVS 1	Staring At The Sun/Three Stars (12", promo only)	10
92	4AD UVS 2	Medicating Angels/Mirror To Mirror (12", promo only)	10
88	4AD CAD 809	ULTRA VIVID SCENE (LP)	20
90	4ad CAD 0005	JOY 1967-1990 (LP)	15
92	4AD CAD 2017	REV (LP)	20

ULTRAVOX
77	Island IDJ-18	Dangerous Rhythm/My Sex/The Wild The Beautiful And The Damned (12" promo)	15
77	Island WIP 6375	Dangerous Rhythm/My Sex (initially no p/s)	6
77	Island WIP 6375	Dangerous Rhythm/My Sex (reissue, later pressing with p/s)	7
77	Island WIP 6392	Young Savage/Slip Away (p/s)	8
77	Island WIP 6404	Rockwrock/Hiroshima Mon Amour (p/s)	12
77	Island WIP 6417	Quirks/Modern Love (no p/s, most given away with LP Ha! Ha! Ha!)	6
78	Island WIP 6459	Quiet Men/Cross Fade (p/s)	6
78	Island 12WIP 6459	Quiet Men/Cross Fade (12", p/s, white vinyl)	10
80	Chrysalis CHS 2441	Sleepwalk/Waiting (clear vinyl)	10
20	Electronic Sound ES 768	Herr X/Alles Klar (p/s, clear vinyl)	20
77	Island ILPS 9449	ULTRAVOX (LP, gatefold sleeve)	25
77	Island ILPS 9505	HA! HA! HA! (LP, with 7" "Quirks"/"Modern Love" [WIP 6417] & inner sleeve)	35
77	Island ILPS 9505	HA! HA! HA! (LP, without free single)	20
78	Island ILPS 9555	SYSTEMS OF ROMANCE (LP, with inner sleeve)	25
80	Chrysalis CHR 1296	VIENNA (LP)	15
13	Chrysalis CHRS 1296	VIENNA (LP, reissue, white vinyl, lyric inner, stickered sleeve, 500 only)	20

(see also Tiger Lily, John Foxx, Midge Ure, Helden)

UMPS & DUMPS
80	Topic 12TS 416	THE MOON'S IN A FIT (LP)	15

UNANIMITY
69	Clementswood CC127	Loner/All Right	50

UNANIMOUS DECISION
92	Kold Sweat KSEP211	RAP SINGS THE BLUES (EP)	10
93	Kold Sweat KSMEP 301X	IT AIN'T CLEVER (DOUBLE PACK EP) (12")	12

UNAUTHORISED VERSION
69	CBS 4135	Hey Jude/Girl In A Bus Queue	20

UNCLE DAVID
70	Westbrook WK2	Magic Mirror/You've Lost Me	40

UNCLE DOG
72	Signpost SG 4253	OLD HAT (LP)	200

(see also Carol Grimes)

UNCLE FUNKENSTEIN
08	Jazzman JMANLP 023	TOGETHER AGAIN (LP, reissue)	35

UNCLE PO
78	Beeb BEEB 23	Use My Friends/15 Minutes	25

UNCLE SAM

MINT VALUE £

UNCLE SAM
78	Ariola ARO 116	Oh Pretty Woman/Do It For Love	6

UNCLE 22
92	U No Dat HN 08	Wonderful Life/Love Me Once/Calling All Cars (12")	10
93	Ram RAMM 008	SPICE OF LIFE EP: 6 Million Ways To Die (DJ Hype Remix)/6 Million Ways To Die (Uncle 22 Mix) (12")	20
93	Pure Energy PE 003	SUPER MARIO EP: Super Mario (In Darkness)/Take You High/Love Me Twice/Dark Forces (12")	10
93	Pure Energy PE 004	Choose One (Part 1)/Choose One (Part 2)/Crazy Kid (12", with Navigator)	15

UNCOMMUNITY
85	Black Dwarf BDBG 1	Brutality Of Fact/Wall Of Sleep (Soundtrack)/The Price Of Your Entry Is Sin (card sleeve, 525 only, numbered, hand-painted labels, with insert)	25

(see also McCarthy)

UNCOOL DANCEBAND
79	Polydor PB 30	Let Me Be Your Boyfriend/Heads I Win (no p/s)	100
81	Polydor POSP 253	Jacqueline/No. 17 (no p/s)	20

UNDEAD
82	Riot City RIOT 7	It's Corruption/Undead (p/s)	7
82	Stiff TEES 7	NINE TOES LATER EP	12
82	Riot City RIOT 15	VIOLENT VISIONS (EP)	10
84	City 006	KILLING OF REALITY (LP, lyric insert)	35

UNDERCOVER ELEPHANT & SECRET SQUIRREL
92	Dance Bass DANCE BASS 03	VOLUME 3 EP (12", stamped white label)	30

(see also Secret Squirrel)

UNDERDOG
79	Dor Rock DRO1/01	Life At 21/Blue Water, White Death (no p/s)	200

UNDERDOGS
83	Riot City RIOT 26	EAST OF DACHAU (EP)	12

UNDERGROUND
69	Major Minor SMCP 5014	BEAT PARTY (LP)	30

(see also Madeline Bell)

UNDERGROUND EVOLUTION
96	Ugly UGM 008	WALK ON WATER (12")	18

UNDERGROUNDS
72	High Note HS 061	Skavito/Savito	15

UNDERGROUND SET
70	Pantonic PAN 6302	UNDERGROUND SET (LP, laminated front sleeve, red/black label)	70

UNDERGROUND SUNSHINE
69	Fontana TF 1049	Birthday/All I Want Is You	10

UNDERGROUND WITH STYLE
92	UAR UAR001	Lyrics Of A Gangster/Unbound Rage/Words Of Reality (EP)	40

UNDERGROUND ZERO
84	Underground UNDER 001	Seven Light Years/Canes Venatici (12")	15

UNDERNEATH
86	él ACME 9	LUNATIC DAWN OF THE DISMANTLER (LP)	20

(see also Karl Blake, Shock Headed Peters, Lemon Kittens)

UNDERTAKERS
63	Pye 7N 15543	Everybody Loves A Lover/Mashed Potatoes	25
63	Pye 7N 15562	What About Us/Money	25
64	Pye 7N 15607	Just A Little Bit/Stupidity	30

(see also 'Takers, Jackie Lomax)

UNDER THE SUN
79	Redball RR 010	UNDER THE SUN (LP)	45

UNDER THE GUN
85	Under The Gun UTG1	Dance Of The Samurai/Traitor (fold-out sleeve)	15

UNDER THE SKIN
75	Scotty SC 01	Shake It Girl/Lose The Image	20

UNDERTONES
78	Good Vibrations GOT 4	TEENAGE KICKS (EP, white poster p/s)	100
78	Good Vibrations GOT 4	TEENAGE KICKS (EP, pink/yellow/blue p/s)	70
78	Sire SIR 4007 PRO	Teenage Kicks/True Confessions (specially mastered promo, no p/s)	12
79	Sire SIR 4010	Get Over You/Really Really/She Can Only say No ('She Can Only...' not listed on p/s)	8
79	Sire SIR 4015	Jimmy Jimmy/Mars Bars (green vinyl, printed PVC sleeve & insert)	8
79	Sire SIR 4022	Here Comes The Summer/One Way Love/Top 20 (p/s)	6
79	Sire SIR 4022	Here Comes The Summer/One Way Love/Top 20 (mispressing, A side plays Tubeway Army's Are Friends Electric?)	60
79	No label	CRACKS 90 MANAGEMENT EP: Teenage Kicks/Get Over You/Jimmy Jimmy/ Here Comes The Summer (promo-only, numbered with typed insert, 250 only)	60
80	Sire SAM 120	HYPNOTIZED APPETIZER (6-track promn 12" EP b/w custom sleeve)	40
83	Ardeck 12 ARDS 11	The Love Parade/Like That/You're Welcome/Crises Of Mine/ Family Entertainment (12", p/s)	10
83	Ardeck ARDS 12	Got To Have You Back/Turning Blue (p/s)	8
83	Ardeck ARDS 13	Chains Of Love/Window Shopping For New Clothes (p/s)	10
05	Sanctuary SAN07370	TEENAGE KICKS EP (reissue, numbered)	12
16	Salvo SALVOSV 013	My Perfect Cousin/Hard Luck (Again)/I Don't Wanna See You Again (magnet p/s, red vinyl, reissue)	20
79	Sire SRK 6071	UNDERTONES (LP, black & white cover, without "Teenage Kicks" & "Get Over You" & different version of "Here Comes The Summer" to reissue, inner)	30
80	Sire SRK 6088	HYPNOTISED (LP, with cardboard mobile)	15
83	Ardeck ARD 104	THE SIN OF PRIDE (LP, mispressing with different tracks: Bittersweet & "Stand So Close")	40
83	EMI SP8311RS	ALL WRAPPED UP (LP, with free LP)	15
94	Dojo DOJOLP 192	HYPNOTISED (10" LP, numbered, 500 only)	15

UNDERWORLD

			MINT VALUE £
94	Dojo DOJOLP 193	POSITIVE TOUCH (10" LP, numbered, 500 only)	15
94	Dojo DOJOLP 194	THE SIN OF PRIDE (10" LP, numbered, 500 only)	15

(see also Feargal Sharkey)

UNDERWORLD

92	Tomato PLUM 2001	Mother Earth/Mother Earth (FM Mix)/The Hump/The Hump (Groove Without A Doubt Mix) (12", p/s)	50
93	Boys Own BOIX 13	Mmm... Skyscraper I Love You/Mmm... Skyscraper I Love You (Telegraph 6.11.92)/Mmm... Skyscraper I Love You (Jam Scraper) (12", p/s)	20
93	Boys Own Collect 002	Rez/Cowgirl (12", company sleeve)	10
93	Boys Own Collect 002P	Rez/Cowgirl (12", glossy pink sleeve, pink vinyl, white label)	20
94	Junior Boys Own JBO 19	Dark & Long (Dark Train Mix)/(Burts Mix) (12", p/s)	15
15	Secret 7" S728	Something Slippy (Nuxx) (100 only, each with unique art sleeve)	25
18	Electronic Sound ES 41	Puppies/Twenty Three Blue (p/s)	15
93	Junior Boy's Own JBOLP1	DUBNOBASSWITHMYHEADMAN (2-LP)	25
96	Junior Boy's Own LOC 187	SECOND TOUGHEST IN THE INFANTS (2-LP, gatefold)	30
98	Simply Vinyl S160217	DUBNOBASSWITHMYHEADMAN (2-LP, reissue)	25
98	Junior Boy's Own JBO1005431	BEACOUP FISH (2-LP, gatefold)	20
02	Junior Boy's Own JBO 1020102	A HUNDRED DAYS OFF (2-LP, gatefold, inners)	25

(see also Lemon Interrupt)

UNDISPUTED TRUTH

71	Tamla Motown TMG 776	Save My Love For A Rainy Day/Since I Lost You	12
71	Parlophone TMG 776	Save My Love For A Rainy Day/Since I Lost You (mispress on Parlophone)	60
71	Tamla Motown TMG 789	Smiling Faces Sometimes/You Got The Love I Need	18
72	Tamla Motown TMG 818	Superstar/Ain't No Sun Since You've Been Gone	10
74	Tamla Motown TMG 897	Help Yourself/What It Is	8
76	Warner Bros K 16804	You + Me = Love Parts 1 & 2	8
76	Warner Bros K 16804	You + Me = Love Parts 1 & 2 (12")	10
72	Tamla Motown STMA 8004	FACE TO FACE WITH THE TRUTH (LP)	30
72	Tamla Motown STML 11197	THE UNDISPUTED TRUTH (LP)	30
73	Tamla Motown STML 11240	THE LAW OF THE LAND (LP)	30
75	Tamla Motown STML 11277	DOWN TO EARTH (LP)	20
75	Tamla Motown STMA 8023	COSMIC TRUTH (LP)	20
75	Tamla Motown STML 12009	HIGHER THAN HIGH (LP)	20
76	Whitfield K 56289	METHOD TO THE MADNESS (LP)	20
79	Whitfield K 56497	SMOKIN (LP)	20

UNEXPLORED BEATS

95	Unexplored Beats UXB 001	Skool Beats/Inner Life (12")	30

(see also Black Dog)

UNFORGETTABLES

75	Angen ANG 108	Many A Call/Chosen Dub	8

CHARLIE UNGRY

80	Charlie Ungry CU 001	House On Chester Road/Pleacher/Who Is My Killer	60

UNICORN (1)

70	Hollick & Taylor HT 1258	Going Home/Another World	300

UNICORN (2)

71	Transatlantic BIG 138	P.F. Sloan/Going Back Home	6
72	Transatlantic BIG 509	Cosmic Kid/All We Really Want To Do	6
71	Transatlantic TRA 238	UPHILL ALL THE WAY (LP, gatefold, plastic inner)	35
74	Charisma CAS 1092	BLUE PINE TREES (LP, small 'Mad Hatter' logo)	20
76	Harvest SHSP 4054	TOO MANY CROOKS (LP, inner sleeve, EMI logo on label)	15

UNIFICS

68	London HLR 10231	Court Of Love/Which One Should I Choose	10

UNION EXPRESS

73	Decca F 13408	Do You Love Me/Alligator Fix	12
71	Decca F 13230	Ring A Ring A Rosies/Emily Knows	10

UNIQUE (1)

83	Prelude TA 3707	What I Got Is What You Need/What I Got Is What You Need (Instrumental) (12")	10

UNIQUE (2)

08	Diggers With Gratitude DWG 003	THE DIE HARD (EP)	120

UNIQUES (FEATURING JOE STAMPLEY) (U.S)

65	Pye International 7N 25303	Not Too Long Ago/Fast Way Of Living	30
65	Pye International 7N 25303	Not Too Long Ago/Fast Way Of Living (DJ copy)	50
66	Pye Intl. NPL 28094	UNIQUELY YOURS (LP)	120

UNIQUES (JAMAICA)

67	Collins Downbeat CR 002	Dry The Water/I'm A Fool For You	65
67	Island WI 3070	People Rock Steady/I'm Trying To Find A Home (credited to Roy Shirley)	140
67	Island WI 3084	Gypsy Woman/KEN ROSS: Wall Flower	130
67	Island WI 3086	Let Me Go Girl/SOULETTES: Dum Dum	60
68	Island WI 3087	Never Let Me Go/DON LEE: Lee's Special	40
68	Island WI 3106	Speak No Evil/GLEN ADAMS: That New Girl	65
68	Island WI 3107	Lesson Of Love/DELROY WILSON: Til I Die	80
68	Island WI 3114	Build My World Around You/LLOYD CLARKE: I'll Never Change	70
68	Island WI 3117	Give Me Some More Of Your Loving/VAL BENNETT: Lovell's Special	60
68	Island WI 3122	My Conversation/SLIM SMITH: Love One Another	70
68	Island WI 3123	The Beatitude/KEITH BLAKE: Time On The River (actually "Time & The River")	80
68	Island WI 3145	Girl Of My Dreams/LESTER STERLING: Tribute To King Scratch	75
68	Trojan TR 619	Watch This Sound/Out Of Love	40
68	Trojan TR 645	A-Yuh/Just A Mirage	120

UNIT 4 + 2

MINT VALUE £

68	Blue Cat BS 126	Girls Like Dirt/ALVA LEWIS: She Is Leaving	80
69	Gas GAS 117	Too Proud To Beg/Love And Devotion	40
69	Nu Beat NB 034	Crimson And Clover/What A Situation	75
69	Nu Beat NB 037	I'll Make You Love Me/Lover's Prayer	50
69	Unity UN 527	The Beatitude/My Conversation	45
69	Trojan TRL 15	ABSOLUTELY THE UNIQUES (LP)	150
79	Plant PLAN 10002	GIVE THANKS (LP)	30
78	Third World TWS 935	UNIQUE SHOWCASE VOLUME ONE (LP)	35

(see also Slim Smith, Melodians, Lloyd Charmers, Tommy McCook)

UNIT 4 + 2

64	Decca F 11821	The Green Fields/Swing Down Chariot	15
64	Decca F 11994	Sorrow And Pain/The Lonely Valley	12
65	Decca F 12071	Concrete And Clay/When I Fall In Love	6
65	Decca F 12144	(You've) Never Been In Love Like This Before/Tell Somebody You Know	8
65	Decca F 12211	Hark/Stop Wasting Your Time	7
65	Decca F 12299	You've Got To Be Cruel To Be Kind/I Won't Let You Down	7
66	Decca F 12333	Baby Never Say Goodbye/Rainy Day	12
66	Decca F 12398	For A Moment/Fables	12
66	Decca F 12509	I Was Only Playing Games/I've Seen The Light	10
67	Fontana TF 834	Too Fast, Too Slow/Booby Trap	20
67	Fontana TF 840	Butterfly/A Place To Go	15
67	Fontana TF 891	Loving Takes A Little Understanding/Would You Believe What I Say? (as Unit)	200
68	Fontana TF 931	You Ain't Goin' Nowhere/So You Want To Be A Blues Player	15
69	Fontana TF 990	I Will/3.30	50
65	Decca DFE 8619	UNIT 4 + 2 (EP)	60
65	Decca LK 4697	UNIT 4 + 2 - 1st ALBUM (LP)	60
69	Fontana SFL 13213	UNIT 4 + 2 (LP)	50
76	Decca REM 6	REMEMBERING (LP)	15

(see also Roulettes, Tom Sawyer, Capability Brown, Argent)

UNIT 19

67	Unit 19 19 1006	GI Blues/Sleep Perchance To Dream	15

UNIT 1

94	Creative Wax CW 102	Theme/Your Mind/Arden (12")	15
94	Creative Wax CW 104	Atlantic Drama/Love Me (12")	15

UNITED FUTURE ORGANISATION

94	Talkin Loud 518 166-1	UNITED FUTURE ORGANISATION (2-LP)	20
96	Talkin Loud 534 587-1	3RD PERSPECTIVE (2-LP, with free 12")	20
99	Brownswood PHJR-10003/4	BON VOYAGE (2-LP)	20

UNITED SONS OF AMERICA

71	Mercury 6338 036	GREETINGS FROM THE U.S. OF A. (LP)	18

UNITED SOUNDS OF LONDON

94	USL USL 6	Making Love/Making Dub (12")	15

UNITED STATES DOUBLE QUARTET

67	Stateside SS 590	Life Is Groovy/Split	20
67	BT Puppy BTS 45524	Life Is Groovy/Split (reissue)	15

(see also Tokens, Kirby Stone 4)

UNITED STATES OF AMERICA

68	CBS 3745	Garden Of Earthly Delights/Love Song For The Dead Che	15
68	CBS (S) 63340	UNITED STATES OF AMERICA (LP, laminated cover, mono/stereo)	60
87	Edsel ED 233	UNITED STATES OF AMERICA (LP, reissue)	15

UNITY ALL STARS

75	Nice N 001	Africa/BIG DREAD & UNITY ALL STARS: Africa Is Our Home	25

UNITY AND FIRE

88	Delicious WGO 101	I Know A Girl/Nothing Brings You Nothing (p/s)	100

UNIVERSAL ENERGY

77	Harvest HAR 5138	Universal Energy/Christmas For Space	6
77	Harvest SHSP 4075	UNIVERSAL ENERGY (LP)	20

UNIVERSAL INDICATOR

92	Rephlex TB-303	1-BLUE (12")	35
92	Rephlex TR-606	2-RED (12")	35
93	Rephlex MC-202	3-YELLOW (12")	30
95	Rephlex SH-101	4-GREEN (7", 10" + 12" in bag, all green vinyl)	100

(see also Kosmik Kommando)

UNIVERSAL ROBOT BAND

84	Streetwave MKHAN 48	Barely Breaking Even (85 Club MIx)/Barely Breaking Even (Edit)/Barely Breaking Even (Instrumental) (12")	30

UNIVERSALS (1)

67	Page One POF 032	I Can't Find You/Hey You	200
67	Page One POF 049	Green Veined Orchid/While The Cat's Away	35

(see also Chris Lamb & Universals, Gidian, Lace, Gary Walker & Rain, Plastic Penny)

UNIVERSALS (2)

06	Funk 45 FUNK45 031	New Generation/The Way A Girl Should Be (reissue)	30

UNIVERSE

84	MBT U1107	Every Single Night/(Instrumental)	15
84	MBT U1112	Every Single Night/(Instrumental) (12")	20

U.N.K.L.E.

95	Mo Wax MW 028	THE TIME HAS COME EP (2 x 12" EP, picture disc)	15
98	Mo Wax MW 085DJ	PSYENCE FICTION SURVIVAL KIT (promo, 12" in pop-up gatefold p/s, 5" vinyl single in envelope, bag of stickers, press release, all in box mailer, 700 only)	35
98	Mo Wax 085	PSYENCE FICTION (2-LP)	25
98	Mo Wax 085	PSYENCE FICTION (2-LP, hardcover gatefold sleeve with booklet)	40

UNKNOWNS

MINT VALUE £

03	Mo Wax MWU 001	NEVER NEVER LAND (3-LP, picture discs, gatefold sleeve, foldout inserts)	20
07	Surrender ALL SURR LPXX	WAR STORIES (4x12", gatefold sleeve in slipcase with book)	25
10	Surrender ALL SURR 017 LP	WHERE DID THE NIGHT FALL (3-LP box set with two books)	250
11	Vinyl Factory VF 029	THE HERETIC'S GATE SCORE (with Doug Foster) (1-sided LP, orange vinyl, sleeve signed and numbered by James Lavelle and Doug Foster, 100 only)	120

(see also DJ Shadow)

UNKNOWNS
66	London HLU 10082	Melody For An Unknown Girl/Peith's Song	7

UNLEASHED
03	Century Media 77544-0	AND WE SHALL TRIUMPH IN VICTORY (Numbered box set with 6 picture discs LPs and booklet, 2000 only)	60

UNLIMITED TOUCH
80	epic A 13 1454	I Hear Music In The Streets/In The Middle (12")	12
83	Prelude PRL 25294	YES, WE'RE READY (LP)	15

UNLIMITED SOURCE
82	Source SM003	Down In The Cellar/Lemonade/Nicola Nicola (12")	60

UN PROJET
81	Rygel RY2	Ki-Ak/Un Projet (p/s)	15

UNREST
92	Guernica GU1 LP	IMPERIAL F.F.R.R. (LP, with free 7")	15
93	4AD CAD 3012	PERFECT TEETH (LP)	15

UNSEEN TERROR
87	Earache MOSH 4	HUMAN ERROR (LP, inner)	15

UNTAMED YOUTH
79	Hardcore HAR 001	Untamed Youth/Runnin' Wild (p/s, 1,000 only)	15

UNTAMED (1)
64	Decca F 12045	So Long/Just Wait	70
65	Parlophone R 5258	Once Upon A Time/I'm Asking You	100
65	Stateside SS 431	I'll Go Crazy/My Baby Is Gone	70
66	Planet PLF 103	It's Not True/Gimme Gimme Some Shade	100

(see also Lindsay Muir's Untamed)

UNTOUCHABLES
80	Fried Egg EGG 2	Keep On Walking/Keep Your Distance (p/s)	8

UNTOUCHABLES (JAMAICA)
68	Blue Cat BS 137	Prisoner In Love/EDWARD RAPHAEL: True Love	70
68	Trojan TR 613	Tighten Up/ROY SHIRLEY: Good Ambition	40
70	Upsetter US 345	Same Thing All Over/UPSETTERS: It's Over	40
70	Upsetter US 350	Knock On Wood/UPSETTERS: Tight Spot (featured Dave Barker - uncredited)	200
71	Bullet BU 460	Can't Reach You/CARL DAWKINS: Natural Woman	22
73	Bread BR 1113	Pay For The Wicked/Pay For The Wicked - Version (actually titled "Pray For The Wicked')	30
79	Sagittarius SUS 10	Help Us Jah/Sea Of Love (12")	20
03	Trojan TGSe 008	Tighten Up/ROY SHIRLEY: Good Ambition (reissue)	18

(see also Inspirations, Dave Barker, Leroy Reid)

UNWANTED
77	Raw RAW 6	Withdrawal/1978/Bleak Outlook (p/s)	40
77	Raw RAWT 6	Withdrawal/1978/Bleak Outlook (12", reissue)	20
78	Raw RAW 15	Secret Police/These Boots Are Made For Walking (p/s)	20
78	Raw RAW 30	Memory Man/Guns Of Love (unissued)	0
85	Delorian No One	SECRET PAST (LP)	15

(see also Psychedelic Furs)

UPBEATS
58	London HLU 8688	Just Like In The Movies/My Foolish Heart	25
59	Pye International 7N 25016	You're The One I Care For/Keep Cool Crazy Heart	15
59	Pye International 7N 25028	Teenie Weenie Bikini/Satin Shoes	15

PHIL UPCHURCH COMBO
61	HMV POP 899	You Can't Sit Down Parts 1 & 2	35
66	Sue WI 4005	You Can't Sit Down Parts 1 & 2 (reissue)	30
66	Sue WI 4017	Nothing But Soul/Evad	40
72	Blue Thumb ILPS 9219	DARKNESS, DARKNESS (LP)	20

UPCOMING WILLOWS
65	Island WI 182	Jonestown Special/SHENLEY DUFFAS: La La La	40
65	Island WI 184	Red China/SHENLEY DUFFAS: You Are Mine	50

(see also Shenley Duffas)

UPFRONT RUDIES
92	Krazy Fly Recz RUDIE 9	REAL SKILLS (EP)	10

UPP
75	Epic EPC 80625	UPP (LP)	15

(see also Clark-Hutchinson)

UPRISING
79	Tribesman TM 11	Come On Over/Try Me Girl (12")	18

UPROAR
82	Beat The System RAW 1	Rebel Youth/No More War/Fallen Angel/Victims (p/s)	12
83	Lightbeat RAW 2	DIE FOR ME (EP)	12
83	Volume VOL 9	NOTHING CAN STOP YOU (EP)	10
80s	Beat The System BTSLP 1	AND THE LORD SAID LET THERE BE UPROAR (LP)	30

UPSETTERS (1)
65	Island WI 223	Country Girl/Strange Country (both sides actually by Ossie & Upsetters)	35
65	Rio R 70	Walk Down The Aisle/So Bad	40
66	Doctor Bird DB 1034	Wildcat/I Love You So	40

(see also Ossie & Upsetters, Dave Barker)

UPSETTERS (2)

MINT VALUE £

Year	Label	Title	Value
69	Duke DU 11	Eight For Eight/Stand By Me (B-side actually by Inspirations)	55
69	Camel CA 13	Taste Of Killing/My Mob	75
69	Punch PH 18	Return Of The Ugly/I've Caught You	30
69	Punch PH 19	Dry Acid/REGGAE BOYS: Selassie	60
69	Punch PH 21	Clint Eastwood/Lenox Mood	20
69	Upsetter US 300	Eight For Eight/You Know What I Mean (B-side actually by Inspirations)	40
69	Upsetter UP 301	Return Of Django/Dollar In The Teeth	15
69	Upsetter US 303	Ten To Twelve/LEE PERRY: People Funny Fi True	50
69	Upsetter US 305	Farmers In The Den/BUSTY BROWN : To Love Somebody	65
69	Upsetter US 307	Night Doctor/TERMITES: I'll Be Waiting	40
69	Upsetter US 309	Kiddyo/Endlessly (both sides actually by Silvertones)	25
69	Upsetter US 310	Man From MI5/WEST INDIANS: Oh Lord	55
69	Upsetter US 313	Live Injection/BLEECHERS: Everything For Fun	40
70	Upsetter US 317	Vampire/BLEECHERS: Check Him Out (early copies with B-side listed as UPSETTERS worth £80)	45
69	Upsetter US 315	Cold Sweat/Pound Get A Blow (B-side actually by Bleechers)	60
70	Upsetter US 318	Soulful I/MILTON HENRY: Bread And Butter	40
70	Upsetter US 321	Drugs And Poison/Stranger On The Shore	30
70	Upsetter US 325	Kill Them All/Soul Walk	45
70	Upsetter US 326	Bronco Ol' Man River/One Punch	30
70	Upsetter US 331	Shocks A Mighty/DAVE BARKER: Set Me Free	25
70	Upsetter US 332	Na Na Hey Hey/Pick Folk Kinkiest	35
70	Upsetter US 333	Granny Show/Version	30
70	Upsetter US 334	Fire Fire/Jumper	75
70	Upsetter US 335	The Pillow/Grooving	25
70	Upsetter US 336	Self Control/The Pill	22
70	Upsetter US 338	Fresh Up/Toothaches	60
70	Upsetter US 339	The Thanks We Get/Hurry Up	40
70	Upsetter US 342	Dreamland/Version Of Cup (possibly unreleased)	45
70	Upsetter US 343	Sipreano/Ferry Boat	65
70	Upsetter US 346	Bigger Joke/Return Of The Vampire	60
70	Upsetter US 349	Upsetting Station (actually plays "Did Your Grave" by Bob Marley & Wailers/UPSETTERS: Justice (Instrumental)	40
70	Upsetter US 352	Heart And Soul/Zig Zag	70
70	Spinning Wheel SW 100	Haunted House/Double Wheel (beware of reissues with darker purple on labels)	160
70	Spinning Wheel SW 101	The Miser/CHUCK JUNIOR: Do It Madly	50
70	Spinning Wheel SW 102	The Chokin' Kind/CHUCK JUNIOR: Penny Wise	150
70	Spinning Wheel SW 103	Land Of Kinks/O'NEIL HALL: This Man	110
70	Trojan TR 7748	Family Man/Mellow Mood	30
70	Trojan TR 7749	Capo/Mama Look	45
70	Punch PH 27	The Result/Feel The Spirit	80
71	Bullet BU 461	All Combine Parts 1 & 2	18
71	Upsetter US 361	Capasetic (actually "Copasetic" by Lord Comic)/All Africans (actually "Don't Cross The Nation" by Little Roy)	25
71	Upsetter US 365	Earthquake/JUNIOR BYLES: Palace Called Africa	30
71	Upsetter US 370	Dark Moon/DAVID ISAACS: You'll Be Sorry	25
72	Upsetter US 387	Festival Da-Da/JUNIOR BYLES: Version	25
72	Upsetter US 393	Crummy People/BIG YOUTH: Moving - Version	35
72	Upsetter US 394	Water Pump Parts 1 & 2	15
73	Upsetter US 396	Puss See Hole/WINSTON GROOVY: Want To Be Loved	15
73	Upsetter US 397	Jungle Lion/Freak Out Skank	120
73	Upsetter US 398	Cow Thief Skank (with Charlie Ace)/7 3/4 Skank	45
73	Downtown DT 499	Black Ipa/Ipa Skank	35
73	Downtown DT 506	Sunshine Showdown/Sunshine Version	40
73	Downtown DT 512	Tighten Up Skank/Mid-East Rock (vocals by Dillinger)	125
73	Downtown DT 513	Bucky Skank/Yucky Skank	70
74	Count Shelly CS 052	San-San/OSBOURNE GRAHAM: Baby Don't Go	15
74	Dip DL 5031	Enter The Dragon/JOY WHITE: Lady Lady	15
74	Dip DL 5032	Rebels Train/Rebels Dub	25
75	Dip DL 5054	Cane River Rock/Riverside Rock	35
75	Dip DL 5056	I Man Free/King Burnett: Version	35
75	Dip DL 5073	Key Card/Domino Game	20
75	Angen ANG 107	Stay Dread/Kingdom Of Dub	25
75	Attack ATT 8090	Kiss Me Neck/Da Ba Day	35
78	Island IPR 2010	Close Together/Dreadlocks In The Moonlight (12" as UPSETTER REVIEW featuring JUNIOR MURVIN)	20
69	Pama Special PSP 1014	CLINT EASTWOOD (LP)	100
69	Trojan TTL 13	THE UPSETTER (LP)	50
69	Trojan TRL 19	THE RETURN OF DJANGO (LP, orange/white label)	80
70	Trojan TTL 28	SCRATCH THE UPSETTER AGAIN (LP)	55
70	Trojan TBL 119	THE GOOD, THE BAD AND THE UPSETTERS (LP)	55
70	Trojan TBL 125	EASTWOOD RIDES AGAIN (LP)	120
70	Pama SECO 24	THE MANY MOODS OF THE UPSETTERS (LP)	100
74	Trojan TRLS 70	DOUBLE SEVEN (LP, black sticker on rear cover showing song titles and marketed by B & C Records	75
75	DIP DLPD 6002	RETURN OF WAX (LP, label says "Upsetters" in red print, plain sleeve)	300
76	Island ILPS 9417	SUPER APE (LP)	65
90	Trojan PERRY 3	BUILD THE ARK (3-LP box set)	40
99	Simply Vinyl SVLP 098	SUPER APE (LP, reissue, 180gm vinyl)	20

(see also Lee Perry, Ossie & Upsetters, Hippy Boys, Bob Marley/Wailers, Family Man, Tommy McCook, Max Romeo, Melodians, Lord Creator, Dennis

UPSETTING BROTHERS

MINT VALUE £

Alcapone)

UPSETTING BROTHERS
71   Supreme SUP 229   Not You Baby/DREAD LOCK ALL-STARS: Baby (Version) 12

CHARLES UPTON
65   Ralph Tuck EP CU 01   SINGS (EP) 10

UPTOWNERS
64   London HLU 9877   If'n/Search Is Over 15

URBAN CLEARWAY (1)
70   Torpedo TOR 21   Open Up Wide Parts 1 & 2 20

URBAN CLEARWAY (2)
82   Bandit X 82 CUS 1609   Lost Memories/You've Always Known (12", p/s) 100

URBAN DISTURBANCE
79   Rok ROK V/VI   Wild Boys In Cortinas/V.I.P.s: Can't Let You Go (die-cut sleeve) 25

URBAN DOGS
88   Fallout FALL LP 12   URBAN DOGS (LP) 18
(see Hanoi Rocks, U.K. Subs, Vibrators)

URBAN MYTHS
98   Urban Myths MYTH 1   Lose You/Lose You (Dub)//Makin' Me Feel/No Man (12") 20

URBAN SHAKEDOWN
82   Respond RESP5   Wolves/Rap The Wolf 10

URBAN TRIBE
92   Sub Assertive CUE 6   THE UNKNOWN EP (12", white label) 20

URCHIN
77   DJM DJS 10776   Black Leather Fantasy/Rock & Roll Woman (in promo p/s) 275
77   DJM DJS 10776   Black Leather Fantasy/Rock & Roll Woman (no p/s) 100
78   DJM DJS 10850   She's A Roller/Long Time No Woman (in promo p/s) 275
79   DJM DJS 10850   She's A Roller/Long Time No Woman (no p/s) 100
(see also Iron Maiden)

URCHINS
66   Polydor BM 56145   I Made Her That Way/Twas On A Night Like This 10

URGE
81   Consumer Discks CD 0861 Revolting Boy/Revolve (p/s) 10

URGENT CRUNCH
81   NYECK NECK 1   Listen To Silence/Trust (p/s) 30

URIAH HEEP
71   Bronze WIP 6111   Look At Yourself/Simon The Bullet Freak 7
72   Bronze WIP 6126   The Wizard/Gypsy 6
72   Bronze WIP 6140   Easy Livin'/Why 6
73   Bronze BRO 7   Stealin'/Sunshine 6
76   Bronze BRODJ 1   One Way Or Another/Misty Eyes (promo only p/s, 750 copies) 20
77   Bronze BRO 47   Free Me/Masquerade (p/s) 6
83   Bronze BROG 168   Stay On Top/Playing For Time//Gypsy/Easy Livin'/Sweet Lorraine/Stealin' (double pack, gatefold p/s) 7
70   Vertigo 6360 006   VERY 'EAVY... VERY 'UMBLE (1st pressing, LP, gatefold sleeve, large swirl label. Matrixes: 1Y//1 420 113//2Y//1 420 111) 400
71   Vertigo 6360 028   SALISBURY (LP, gatefold sleeve, large swirl label) 400
71   Vertigo 6360 006   VERY 'EAVY... VERY 'UMBLE (2nd pressing, LP, reissue, Matrix 1Y//1 420 1 1 9/2Y//1 420 111) 80
71   Bronze ILPS 9152   SALISBURY (LP, reissue, with 'Howards Printers (Slough) Ltd' printers credit) ... 30
71   Bronze ILPS 9169   LOOK AT YOURSELF (LP, 'mirror' sleeve, inner sleeve) 250
72   Bronze ILPS 9193   DEMONS AND WIZARDS (LP, gatefold, lyric inner) 80
72   Island ILPS 9213   THE MAGICIAN'S BIRTHDAY (LP, gatefold with inner sleeve, abandoned Island pressing with pink rim palm tree label, with 'Bronze' records hand-written half-paste on label) ... 200
72   Bronze ILPS 9213   MAGICIAN'S BIRTHDAY (LP, gatefold with inner sleeve) 75
72   Vertigo 6360 006   VERY 'EAVY... VERY 'UMBLE (3rd pressing, LP, gatefold sleeve, small 'swirl' and 'Vertigo' above centre label) 30
72   Bronze ILPS 9142   VERY 'EAVY... VERY 'UMBLE (LP, reissue, sleeve printed by 'Howards Printers (Slough) Ltd') 25
73   Bronze ILPS 9245   SWEET FREEDOM (LP, gatefold with extra page) 150
73   Bronze ISLD 1   LIVE (2-LP, laminated gatefold sleeve with booklet and inners) 20
74   Island ILPS 9142   VERY 'EAVY... VERY 'UMBLE (LP, reissue, pink rim palm tree label) 20
74   Bronze ILPS 9280   WONDERWORLD (LP, inner) 20
75   Bronze ILPS 9335   RETURN TO FANTASY (LP, gatefold sleeve) 50
76   Bronze ILPS 9384   HIGH AND MIGHTY (LP) 50
77   Bronze ILPS 9193   DEMONS AND WIZARDS (LP, reissue, no insert) 20
77   Bronze BRON 504   INNOCENT VICTIM (LP) 15
77   Bronze ILPS 9483   FIREFLY (LP) 60
78   Bronze BRNA 512   FALLEN ANGEL (LP, gatefold) 25
80   Bronze BRONX 524   CONQUEST (LP) 30
91   Legacy LLP 37   DIFFERENT WORLD (LP) 40
97   Castle ORR LP 003   DEMONS AND WIZARDS (LP, reissue, insert) 18
95   HTD LP 33   SEA OF LIGHT (2-LP, with inner) 35
(see also Gods, Head Machine, Natural Gas, Spice, King Crimson, John Lawton, Grand Prix, Stratus)

RENE URTREGER
56   Felsted ESD 3027   SALUTE TO BUD POWELL (EP) 15
56   Felsted EDL 87020   PLAYS BUD POWELL (10" LP) 30

URUSEI YATSURA
95   Modern Ind. MIR 001   Pampered Adolescent/BLISTERS: A Dull Thought In Itself (burgundy vinyl, p/s, 500 only) ... 6
95   Love Train PUBE 08   Kernel/Teendream (p/s, 1,000 only) 6

US FOLK
65   Eyemark EMS 1001   Funny Old World/Dives 8

U.S. T-BONES

MINT VALUE £

U.S. T-BONES
65	Liberty LIB 55836	No Matter What Shape/Feelin' Fine	12
66	Liberty LIB 55867	Sippin'n'Chippin'/Moment Of Softness	15
66	Liberty LIB 55951	The Proper Thing To Do/Tee-Hee-Hee	15

US (1)
70s	Jeff Wayne Music SD 015	You're OK With Us/Tomorrow (p/s, promo for Johnson Wax)	10

(see also David Essex, Randells)

US (2)
67	Polydor 56179	Barefoot In The Park/Four's A Crowd	8

US & THEM
11	Fruits De Mer Crustacean 20	Summerisle Songs From The Wicker Man (1st press, white vinyl, folded white p/s, insert)	20
11	Fruits De Mer Crustacean 20	Summerisle Songs From The Wicker Man (Repressing, orange/yellow vinyl, folded p/s, insert)	15

USELESS UNICORN
74	Horny HORN 11	RUBBER HORN (LP, gatefold sleeve, with pop-up horn)	15

USERS
77	Raw RAW 1	Sick Of You/(I'm) In Love With Today (p/s, numbered on rear, 2500 only)	30
77	Raw RAW 1	Sick Of You/(I'm) In Love With Today (p/s, 2nd pressing, 5000 copies)	15
77	Raw RAWT 1	Sick Of You/(I'm) In Love With Today (12", no p/s)	15
78	Warped WARP 1	Warped 45: Kicks In Style/Dead On Arrival (p/s, 5,000 only, numbered sleeve, some un-numbered)	30
06	Damaged Goods DAMGOOD 139	Sick Of You/(I'm) In Love With Today (p/s, reissue)	8
17	Love Child	Now That It's Over/Listen (black vinyl with poster)	10

PETER USTINOV
53	Parlophone MSP 6012	Mock Mozart (with Anthony Hopkins, Harpsichord)/Phoney Folk-Lore	8

UT
87	Blast First BFFP 12	EARLY LIVE LIFE (LP)	15
87	Blast First BFFP 17	IN GUT'S HOUSE (LP, 2 x 12")	15

UTICA
76	Concrete Jungle CJ 603	Over The River/Cross Over	10

UTOMICA
93	Pro-One PRONE 9T	Rok A Bye/Rok A Bye (12", stamped or hand-written white label)	50
93	Pro-One PRONE 11T	Pumpkin/Pumpkin (12", white stamped label)	15

UTOPIA (GERMANY)
73	United Artists UAG 29438	UTOPIA (LP)	35

(see also Amon Duull)

UTOPIA (U.S.)
82	Epic XPS 166	Infrared And Ultra Violet/Forgotten But Not Gone/Private Heaven/Princess Of The Universe/Chapter And Verse (EP)	12
82	Epic EPC 25207	UTOPIA (LP, with free 5-track EP)	20

(see also Todd Rundgren)

UTTER COWBOYS
83	Denbeat GO 001	Saturday Night Games/Keys To Your Heart	8

U-TURN
81	Epigram 001	U-TURN EP (detergent shaped sleeve)	20

U2
SINGLES : SINGLES: IRISH PRESSINGS

79	CBS 7951	U2: THREE (Out Of Control/Stories For The Boys/Boy-Girl) (p/s, black vinyl) (CBS 'Sunburst Label' with UK TM NoB81 809) on label (1st Pressing)	150
79	CBS 7951	U2: THREE (Out Of Control/Stories For The Boys/Boy-Girl) (p/s, black vinyl)	50
80	CBS 7951	U2: THREE (Out Of Control/Stories For The Boys/Boy-Girl) (p/s, orange vinyl)	150
80	CBS 7951	U2: THREE (Out Of Control/Stories For The Boys/Boy-Girl) (p/s, white vinyl)	300
80	CBS 7951	U2: THREE (Out Of Control/Stories For The Boys/Boy-Girl) (p/s, yellow vinyl)	100
80	CBS 7951	U2: THREE (Out Of Control/Stories For The Boys/Boy-Girl) (p/s, brown vinyl mispressing, fewer than 50 copies exist)	1000
80	CBS 8306	Another Day/Twilight (Demo Version) (p/s, yellow vinyl)	80
80	CBS 8306	Another Day/Twilight (Demo Version) (p/s, orange vinyl)	150
80	CBS 8306	Another Day/Twilight (Demo Version) (p/s, white vinyl)	350
80	CBS 8306	Another Day/Twilight (Demo Version) (p/s, black vinyl, with postcard designed by Bono)	200
80	CBS 8306	Another Day/Twilight (Demo Version) (p/s, black vinyl, without postcard designed by Bono)	40
80	CBS 8687	11 O'Clock Tick Tock/Touch (p/s, yellow vinyl)	60
80	CBS 8687	11 O'Clock Tick Tock/Touch (p/s, orange vinyl)	150
80	CBS 9065	I Will Follow/Boy-Girl (live) (p/s, yellow vinyl)	50
80	CBS 9065	I Will Follow/Boy-Girl (live) (p/s, orange vinyl)	100
80	CBS 9065	I Will Follow/Boy-Girl (live) (p/s, white vinyl)	300
80	CBS 9065	I Will Follow/Boy-Girl (live) (p/s, brown vinyl, fewer than 50 copies)	1500
81	CBS 12-7951	U2: THREE (12" EP, with numbered sticker, orange CBS sleeve, 1,000 only)	2000
81	CBS 12-7951	U2: THREE (12" EP, reissue, die-cut CBS sleeve)	60
81	CBS 12-7951	U2: THREE (12" EP, 2nd reissue, plain black sleeve, slightly different labels)	40
82	CBS PAC 1	4 U2 PLAY (4 x 7", each in p/s, black vinyl)	120
82	CBS PAC 1	4 U2 PLAY (4 x 7", each in p/s, yellow vinyl)	300
82	CBS PAC 1	4 U2 PLAY (4 x 7", each in p/s, orange vinyl)	600
82	CBS PAC 1	4 U2 PLAY (4 x 7", each in p/s, white vinyl)	1000
85	CBS 40-7951	U2: THREE (cassette, reissue)	50
80s	CBS PAC 2	PAC 2 (4 x 7" with p/s in plastic wallet)	60
80s	CBS PAC 3	PAC 3 (4 x 7" with p/s in plastic wallet)	50

SINGLES : SINGLES: UK PRESSINGS

80	Island WIP 6601	11 O'Clock Tick Tock/Touch (p/s)	25

U2

MINT VALUE £

80	Island WIP 6630	A Day Without Me/Things To Make And Do (p/s)	20
80	Island WIP 6656	I Will Follow/Boy-Girl (live) (p/s)	15
81	Island WIP 6679	Fire/J. Swallo (p/s)	6
81	Island UWIP 6679	Fire/J. Swallo//11 O'Clock Tick Tock (live)/The Ocean (live)/Cry (live)/ The Electric Co. (live) (double pack, single p/s)	10
81	Island WIP 6733	Gloria/I Will Follow (live) (p/s)	10
82	Island WIP 6770	A Celebration/Trash, Trampoline And The Party Girl (p/s)	10
83	Island UWIP 6848	New Year's Day/Treasure (Whatever Happened To Pete The Chop)// Fire (live)/I Threw A Brick Through A Window (live)/A Day Without Me (live) (double pack, single p/s, black inners)	10
83	Island ISD 109	Two Hearts Beat As One/Endless Deep//New Year's Day (U.S.A. Remix)/ Two Hearts Beat As One (U.S.A. Remix) (p/s, double pack)	10
84	Island ISP 202	Pride (In The Name Of Love)/Boomerang 2 (Vocal) (picture disc)	20
84	Island ISD 202	Pride (In The Name Of Love)/4th Of July/Boomerang I (Instrumental)/ Boomerang 2 (Vocal) (double pack, gatefold p/s)	6
85	Island ISP 220	The Unforgettable Fire/A Sort Of Homecoming (live) (Uncut, logo-shaped pic disc)	600
84	Island 12ISX 202	Pride (In The Name Of Love)/Boomerang I/Boomerang 2/ 11 O'Clock Tick Tock/Touch (Full Length Version) (12", blue p/s)	10
85	Island ISD 220	The Unforgettable Fire/A Sort Of Homecoming (live)/Love Comes Tumbling/ Sixty Seconds In Kingdom Come/The Three Sunrises (double pack, gatefold p/s)	6
85	Island ISP 220	The Unforgettable Fire/A Sort Of Homecoming (live) (logo-shaped pic disc)	45
87	Island 12IS 340	Where The Streets Have No Name/Race Against Time/Silver And Gold/ The Sweetest Thing (12", p/s with "Silver And Gold" lyric insert)	15
88	Island U2 PK 1	THE JOSHUA TREE SINGLES (4 x 7"s in PVC wallet with 'obi' band)	40
89	Island CIDP 411	When Love Comes To Town/Dancing Barefoot/When Love Comes To Town (Live From The Kingdom Mix) (with BB King)/God Part II (The Hard Metal Dance Mix) (CD picture disc)	15
89	Island ISB 422	All I Want Is You (Edit)/Unchained Melody (in numbered tin box)	18
89	Island 12 ISB 422	All I Want Is You (Full Version)/Unchained Melody/Everlasting Love (12", p/s, box set with 4 prints)	15
89	Island CIDP 422	All I Want Is You (4.14)/Unchained Melody/Everlasting Love/ All I Want Is You (Full Version) (CD, picture disc)	15
91	Island 12IS 509	Mysterious Ways (4.04)/(Solar Plexus Extended Club Mix 7.01)/ (Apollo 440 Magic Hour Remix)/(Tabla Motown Remix)/(Solar Plexus Club Mix) (12" p/s, withdrawn)	15
92	Island 12IS 525	Even Better Than The Real Thing/Salomé/Where Did It All Go Wrong/ Lady With The Spinning Head (UVI) (Extended Dance Mix) (12" with giant 'Zoo TV' poster)	20
95	Atlantic A 7131	Hold Me, Thrill Me, Kiss Me, Kill Me/ELLIOTT GOLDENTHAL: Themes From Batman Forever (p/s, red vinyl, B-side miscredited to U2)	8
97	Island 12IST649	Discothèque (Howie B Hairy B Mix)/Discothèque (Hexidecimal Mix)// Discothèque (DM Deep Extended Club Mix)/Discothèque (DM Deep Beats Mix)/Discothèque (DM Tec Radio Mix)/Discotheque (DM Deep Instrumental Mix)/Discothèque (Single Version)/Discothèque (David	12
97	Island 12IS 684	Mofo (Mother's Mix)/Mofo (House Flavour Mix)/Mofo (Romin Mix)/Mofo (Phunk Force Mix)/Mofo (Black Hole Dub) (12", die-cut p/s, 2,000 only)	10
10	Mercury 2739289	Soon/Soon (p/s, red vinyl)	12
17	Third Man TMR 522	The Blackout/Jacknife Lee Remix (12", black and white vinyl)	150

ALBUMS

80	Island ILPS 9646	BOY (LP)	20
81	Island ILPS 9680	OCTOBER (LP)	20
83	Island PILPS 9733	WAR (LP, picture disc, beware of counterfeits with ILPS cat. no.)	100
85	Island CID 112	WAR (CD, pink cover lettering, no bar code)	25
85	Island CID 102	THE UNFORGETTABLE FIRE (CD, no bar code)	30
87	Island U2 6	THE JOSHUA TREE (LP, gatefold, insert)	25
88	Island U27	RATTLE AND HUM (LP)	18
91	Island U2-8	ACHTUNG BABY (LP, inner sleeve, lyric insert, 10 art prints)	50
93	Island U2-9	ZOOROPA (LP, inner sleeve, lyric insert)	80
97	Island U2 10	POP (2-LP, gatefold sleeve, insert, stickered sleeve)	70
98	Island U2 11	THE BEST OF 1980-1990 (2-LP, gatefold sleeve)	80
00	Island U2 12	ALL THAT YOU CAN'T LEAVE BEHIND (LP, with booklet)	70
02	Island U2 13	THE BEST OF 1990-2000 (2-LP, gatefold)	50
04	Island U2 14	HOW TO DISMANTLE AN ATOMIC BOMB (LP, with booklet)	50
09	Island 1796038	NO LINE ON THE HORIZON (2-LP)	30
06	Island U2 18	18 SINGLES (2-LP)	40
11	Mercury 00602527788333	ACHTUNG BABY (20th anniversary box set, 6-CD, 4-DVD, 2-LP, 5 x 7" and booklet)	200
11	Mercury 602527788272	ACHTUNG BABY (20th anniversary edition, 2-LP, 2 x blue vinyl 12", booklet)	150
15	Island B0022855-01	SONGS OF INNOCENCE (2-LP, 5000, numbered, RSD release)	80

PROMOS : PROMOS - SINGLES

80	Island WIP 6601	11 O'Clock Tick Tock/Touch (p/s, 'A' label)	50
80	Island WIP 6630	A Day Without Me/Things To Make And Do (p/s, 'A' label)	50
80	Island WIP 6656 DJ	I Will Follow (Special Edited DJ Version) (1-sided, company sleeve)	80
81	WIP 6679	Fire (Radio Edit) (1-sided, p/s)	70
81	WIP 6733	Gloria (Radio Edit) (1-sided, p/s)	60
84	Island U2 2	Wire/Bad/The Unforgettable Fire (12", black die-cut sleeve)	70
87	Island ISJ 319	With Or Without You/Walk To The Water (jukebox issue, solid centre)	10
87	Island ISJ 328	I Still Haven't Found What I'm Looking For/Spanish Eyes (jukebox issue, solid centre)	20
87	Island ISJ 328	I Still Haven't Found What I'm Looking For/Spanish Eyes (jukebox issue, large centre hole)	10
87	Island ISJB 340	Where The Streets Have No Name/Silver And Gold (jukebox issue, large centre hole)	10
88	Island 12ISX 400	Desire (9.23 Hollywood Remix) (12", 1-sided, custom black p/s, 800 only)	25
88	Island U2V 7	EXCERPTS FROM RATTLE AND HUM (In God's Country [live]/Hawkmoon 269/ Bad [live]/God Part II/With Or Without You [live]) (CD, card gatefold sleeve)	70
88	Island IS 319	With Or Without You/Luminous Times (Hold Onto Love)/Walk To The Water/ With Or Without You (Video) (CD Video, withdrawn, less than 100 copies)	350
89	Island 12 ISX 411	U2 3D DANCE MIXES: When Love Comes To Town (Live From The Kingdom Dance Mix)/God Part II (Hard Metal Dance Club Mix)/Desire (Hollywood Remix 5.23) (12" EP p/25	

U2

MINT VALUE £

90	Island RHB 1	Night And Day (Twilight Remix)/Steel String Mix) (12", p/s, numbered, 4,000 copies only)	50
91	Island U2-3	OCTOBER 1991: I Will Follow/Pride (In The Name Of Love)/God Part II/ Where The Streets Have No Name) (CD EP, 250 only)	400
92	Island 12IS 550DJ	Salomé (Zooromancer Remix 8.02)/Can't Help Falling In Love (Mystery Train Dub 8.20) (12", black die-cut sleeve, 1,000 only)	70
92	Island REAL 1	Even Better Than The Real Thing (The Perfecto Mix)/Even Better Than The Real Thing (Trance Mix)/Even Better Than The Real Thing (Sexy Dub Mix) (12", black die-cut sleeve with title sticker)	10
92	Island REAL 2DJ	Even Better Than The Real Thing (The Perfecto Mix-Radio Edit) (2-sided radio promo, some with p/s)	40
92	Island REAL 2DJ	Even Better Than The Real Thing (The Perfecto Mix-Radio Edit) (2-sided radio promo, some with p/s)	15
93	Island NUMJB 1	Numb (2-sided jukebox issue, large centre hole)	10
93	Island NUMCD 1	Numb (CD, 1-track, with lyric inner, 250 only)	80
93	Island 12LEM DJ 1	Lemon (Bad Yard Club)/(Momo Beats)/(Version Dub)/(Serious Def Dub)// (Perfecto Mix)/(Trance Mix) (12", double pack, p/s, 1,000 only, numbered with press sheets)	60
93	Island LEMCD 1	Lemon (Radio Edit) (CD, 1-track, with lyric inner)	30
95	Island 12 MELON 1	MELON (Salomé [Zooromancer Remix]/Lemon [Bad Yard Club Mix]/ Numb [The Soul Assassins Mix]/Numb [Gimme Some More Dignity Mix]) (12" EP, 800 only)	20
97	Island ISD(X) 649 D(J)	Discothèque (Howie B Hairy B Mix)/Discothèque (Hexidecimal Mix)// Discothèque (DM Deep Extended Club Mix)/Discotheque (DM Deep Beats Mix)/Discotheque (DM Tec Radio Mix)/Discotheque (DM Deep Instrumental Mix)/Discotheque (Single Version)/Discotheque (David	25
97	Island ISJB 649	Discotheque/Holy Joe (jukebox issue, large centre hole)	8
97	Island ISJB 658	Staring At The Sun/North And South Of The River (jukebox issue, large centre hole)	8
97	Island 12IS 658DJ	Staring At The Sun (Monster Truck Mix)/Staring At The Sun (Lab Rat Mix)/ Staring At The Sun (Sad Bastard's Mix) (12", p/s)	20
97	Island ISJB 664	Last Night On Earth (Single Mix)/Last Night On Earth (First Night In Hell Remix) (jukebox issue, large centre hole)	10
97	Island 12IS 664DJ	Last Night On Earth (First Night In Hell Remix)/Happiness Is A Warm Gun (The Gun Mix)/Pop Muzik (Pop Mart Mix)/Happiness Is A Warm Gun (The Danny Sabre Mix)/ (12" p/s)	20
97	Island MUZIK 1	Pop Muzik (Pop Mart Mix - Radio Edit) (CD, 1-track, picture disc, jewel case, 250 only)	100
97	Island MART 1	Pop Muzik (Pop Mart Mix)/Last Night On Earth (First Night In Hell Mix) (12", plain black die cut sleeve)	70
97	Island ISJB 673	Please/Where The Streets Have No Name (live) (jukebox issue, large centre hole)	10
97	Island ISJB 684	If God Will Send His Angels (Single Vesion)/Sunday Bloody Sunday (live from Sarajevo) (jukebox issue, large centre hole)	15
97	Island 12MOFO 1	Mofo (Phunk Force Mix)/Mofo (Black Hole Dub)/Mofo (Romin Remix) (12", orange label, orange & silver die-cut title sleeve)	15
97	Island 12MOFO 2	Mofo (Mother's Mix)/Mofo (House Flavor Mix) (12", pink label, pink & silver die-cut title sleeve, 250 only)	15
97	Island 12MOFO 3	Mofo (Explicit Mix) (12", 1-sided, stamped white label, plain black die-cut sleeve, 200 only)	50
97	Island MOFOCD 1	Mofo (Album Version) (CD, 1-track, card sleeve, export issue [to Mexico])	80
97	Island MOFOCD 2	Mofo (Phunk Force Mix) (CD, 1-track, jewel case, export issue [to Mexico])	60
98	Island CIDDJ 727	Sweetest Thing/Twilight (Live)/An Cat Dubh (Live)/Stories For Boys Out Of Control (Live) (CD, die-cut sleeve)	50
00	Island GROUND 1	The Ground Beneath Her Feet (1-sided promo)	100
01	Island 12ISD 780	Beautiful Day (Quincy & Sonance Mix)/(The Perfecto Mix)/(David Holmes Remix)/Elevation (The Vandit Club Mix)/(Influx Remix)/(Escalation Mix)/Quincy & Sonance Remix) (2x12", p/s, inners)	15
00	Island 12 BEAUT 1	Beautiful Day (Quincey & Sonance Mix) (1-sided 12", in black die-cut title sleeve)	15
01	Island ISJB770	Stuck In A Moment You Can't Get Out Of/Big Girls Are Best (UK jukebox promo 7" with large centre)	10
01	Island 12 ELE 1	Elevation (Escalation Mix)/Elevation (Influx Mix) (12", red custom p/s, 250 only)	25
01	Island 12 ELE 2	Elevation (Paul Vandyk Remix)/Elevation (The Vandit Club Mix) (12", blue custom p/s, 250 only, exclusive mixes)	10
02	Island 12REMIX U2 13	U2 REMIXES FROM THE 1990S (2 x 12" sampler, black inner sleeves, silver outer sleeve)	20
02	Island CID 808	Electrical Storm (William Orbit Mix)/New York (Nice Mix)/New York (Nasty Mix)/ Bad (Live)/Where The Streets Have No Name (2-CD + DVD set in limited issue collectors' wallet, mail order only)	40
03	Island 12 Sun U2	Staring At The Sun (Brothers In Rhythm Club Mix)/Staring At The Sun (Brothers In Rhythm Ambient Mix) (12", black die-cut custom sleeve)	15
04	Island U2PRO2	Vertigo (Jacknife Lee 7" mix) (7" vinyl promo, picture sleeve. Matt/gloss finish)	50
04	Island 10IS878DJ	Vertigo (Jacknife Lee 7" mix)/Vertigo (Jacknife Lee 10" mix) 10" vinyl p/s	20
04	Island CID878/X878/V878	Vertigo (CD1, CD2 & DVD set in wallet issued by U2.Com)	50
05	Island CID886/X/V	Sometimes You Can't Make It On Your Own (CD1, CD2 & DVD set in wallet, issued by U2.com)	25
05	Island CID890/X/V	City Of Blinding Lights (CD1, CD2 & DVD set in wallet via u2.com)	20
05	Island CID906/X/V	All Because Of You (CD1, CD2 & DVD set in wallet in wallet via u2.com)	20

PROMOS : PROMOS - ALBUMS

83	Island U2 1	UNDER A BLOOD RED SKY - A DIALOGUE WITH U2 LIVE (LP, custom sleeve, with cue sheet, numbered, 1,000 only)	75
87	Island U2-6	THE JOSHUA TREE (CD, LP & cassette in black/gold 'pizza' box set)	250
87	Island U2 6-1 - U2 6-5	THE JOSHUA TREE COLLECTION Red Hill Mining Town/Where The Streets Have No Name//Trip Through Your Wires/Running To Stand Still//I Still Haven't Found What I'm Looking For/One Tree Hill//Exit/Mothers Of The Disappeared//In God's Country/Bullet The Blue Sky	500
87	Island U2 6-1 - U2 6-5	THE JOSHUA TREE COLLECTION (5 x 7" black box set, with U2 6-1 mispressed with "Red Hill Mining Town" both sides, less than 50 copies)	1000
87	Island U2CLP 1	THE U2 TALKIE: A CONVERSATION WITH LARRY, BONO, ADAM & THE EDGE (LP, music & interview with Dave Fanning for "The Joshua Tree")	30
87	Island BOU2 1	CASSETTE SAMPLER (cassette, 17-track instore 'best of' compilation)	30
88	Island U2-7	RATTLE AND HUM (CD, LP & cassette in flight case with leather tag, 250 only)	1000
89	Island U2 2DI	U2 2 DATE (LP, 8-track hits compilation)	25

U.V. POP

MINT VALUE £

91	Island U2-8	ACHTUNG BABY (CD, cassette in 'User's Kit', including map/poster, torch, key ring, spanner & screwdriver in printed green nylon kit bag)	500
91	Island CIDDJ U2-8	ACHTUNG (graphics CD, in jewel case marked "promo only - not for sale")	100
95	Island MELONCD 1	MELON (REMIXES FOR PROPAGANDA) (CD, 9-track compilation, card sleeve, fan club issue, 20,000 only; sealed with Propaganda No. 21)	50
97	Island CID U2 10	POP (CD, in large cube-shaped picture box set, with prismatic pen & custom notepad)	200
97	Island POP 1	U2 TALK POP (CD, interview with Dave Fanning, card sleeve)	50
97	Island POP 2	U2 TALK POP (CD, interview with Dave Fanning, card sleeve, same tracks as POP 1)	50
97	Island POP 3	U2 TALK POP (CD, interview with Dave Fanning, card sleeve, same track as POP 1)	50
98	Island CIDDU211	THE BEST OF THE 'B' SIDES 1980-1990 (2-CD, discs marked 'A' and 'B', in card sleeves with gold slipcase)	50
98	Island BXU2 11	THE 'BEST OF' COLLECTION 1980-1990 (14 x 7" singles, 2-CDs, 16-page booklet, in gold box, 2000 copies only)	250
00	Island CID U212	ALL THAT YOU CAN'T LEAVE BEHIND (promo pack, with 1-track CD Beautiful Day [BEAUT CD 1] in blue picture slipcase, booklet, window sticker, video tape, "playback" invitation, in laminated picture bag with rope handles; with signed print)	600
00	Island CID U212	ALL THAT YOU CAN'T LEAVE BEHIND (promo pack, with 1-track CD Beautiful Day [BEAUT CD 1] in blue picture slipcase, booklet, window sticker, video tape, "playback" invitation, in laminated picture bag with rope handles; without signed print)	200
00	Island HASTACD 1	HASTA LA VISTA BABY! LIVE FROM MEXICO CITY (CD, fan-club only p/s)	50
02	Island CIDDJ U2 13	THE BEST OF THE B-SIDES OF 1990-2000 (2-CD set card sleeves in card wallet)	30
02	Island BX U2 13	THE BEST OF COLLECTION 1990-2000 (15 x 7", with 2 CDs & 16-page booklet in silver fliptop card box)	200
02	Island REMIXCD U2 13	REMIXES FROM THE 90S (2 x 12", promo p/s card wallet)	20
05	Island UCOMV1	U2 COMMUNICATION (CD & DVD fan club issue)	30
06	Island U2.COM2	U2 ZOO TV LIVE (2xCD & poster in card sleeve & outer card slipcase Issued to U2.com subscribers only)	50
07	Island U2.COM3	U2 GO HOME - LIVE FROM SLANE CASTLE (2xCD issued to u2.com subscribers only)	30
08	Island	U23D (Promo CD, audio press kit, DVD box)	35

(see also The Edge, Passengers)

U.V. POP

82	Pax PAX 9	Just A Game/No Songs Tomorrow (p/s)	30
85	Flow Motion FM 007	Anyone For Me/Hands To Me	30
85	Flow Motion FM 12/007	ANYONE FOR ME (12" EP)	35
85	Native NTV4	SERIOUS EP (12")	20
86	Extra EXTRA T001	MUSIC TO YEAH TO EP (12")	30
83	Flow Motion FM 004	NO SONGS TOMORROW (LP)	40
86	Extra EXTRA LP1	BENDY BABY MAN (LP)	50

UWANDILE
87	Mother Africa MALP 01	APARTHEID (LP)	60

UXB
80	Crazy Plane SP 002	Crazy Today/Mister Fix It (p/s)	100

UZI
70	Beacon BEA 152	Morning Train/Where Were You Last Night	30

U-ZIQ
93	Rephlex CAT 018	Bluff Limbo (remixes) (2 x 12", 800 only)	20
17	Revoke REVOKE 003	PTHAGONAL EP (12") (100 only, white label)	40
93	Rephlex CAT 013	TANGO N VECTIF (2-LP)	20
97	Planet Mu PULP 5	LUNATIC HARNESS (2-LP)	20

(see also Mike & Rich)

V

DONNA V
96	Fashion FAD 153	Prophecy Revealing (Natural Mix)/Mystic Mix/GENERALY LEVY : Inna We Culture/Remember Yu Roots (12")	35

VACELS
65	Pye International 7N 25330	Can You Please Crawl Out Your Window/I'm Just A Poor Boy	35

VAGABONDS
64	Island ILP 916	PRESENTING THE FABULOUS VAGABONDS (LP)	300

(see also Jimmy James & Vagabonds, Jamaica's Own Vagabonds)

VAGINA DENTATA ORGAN
83	WSNS 001	VAGINA DENTATA ORGAN PRESENTS: MUSIC FOR HASHASINS, IN MEMORIAM OF HASSAN-I-SABBAH (LP, 500 copies)	50
84	WSNS 002	THE LAST SUPPER, THE REVEREND JIM JONES IN PERSON (LP, picture disc, 912 numbered, with transcript)	90
84	WSNS 002	THE LAST SUPPER, THE REVEREND JIM JONES IN PERSON (LP, picture disc, 912 numbered, without transcript)	80
84	WSNS 003	THE PAGAN DRUMS OF CALANDA (LP, picture disc, 12 copies adorned with 'real' blood and handpainted)	300
84	WSNS 003	THE PAGAN DRUMS OF CALANDA (LP, picture disc, 30 copies adorned with 'real' blood but not handpainted)	150
84	WSNS 003	THE PAGAN DRUMS OF CALANDA (LP, picture disc, adorned with 'fake blood')	100
84	WSNS 003	THE PAGAN DRUMS OF CALANDA (LP, 900 'bloodless' copies)	50
86	WSNS 004	COLD MEAT/EROS & THANATOS (LP picture disc, 4 copies with 1 black side with Elvis image missing)	150
86	WSNS 004	COLD MEAT/EROS & THANATOS (LP picture disc, 12 copies with hand drawings and personal dedications)	300
86	WSNS 004	COLD MEAT/EROS & THANATOS (LP picture disc, no drawings or dedications)	50
87	Temple TOPY 012	MUSIC FOR THE HASHISHINS (LP)	25

VAGRANTS

MINT VALUE £

	87	Temple TPY 013	THE LAST SUPPER (LP) 25

VAGRANTS
66 Fontana TF 703   I Can't Make A Friend/Young Blues 60

VAIN AIMS
80 We Practice In a Gang WPG 1   You/Count (fold over stapled sleeves) 50
80 We Practice In a Gang WPG 1   You/Count (with hand-made p/s) 100

VALADIERS
63 Oriole CBA 1809   I Found A Girl/You'll Be Sorry Someday 1000
63 Oriole CBA 1809   I Found A Girl/You'll Be Sorry Someday (DJ copy) 1000

RICKY VALANCE
60 Columbia DB 4543   Movin' Away/Lipstick On Your Lips 8
61 Columbia DB 4586   Jimmy's Girl/Only The Young 8
61 Columbia DB 4592   Why Can't We/Fisherboy 8
61 Columbia DB 4680   Bobby/I Want To Fall In Love 10
61 Columbia DB 4725   I Never Had A Chance/It's Not True 10
62 Columbia DB 4787   Try To Forget Her/At Times Like These 10
62 Columbia DB 4864   Don't Play No. 9/Till The Final Curtain Falls 10
65 Decca F 12129   Six Boys/Face The Crowd 10
76 Valley VLY 001   RICKY VALANCE (EP, no p/s) 25
78 Tank BBS 324   RAINBOW (LP) 40

(see also Jason Merryweather)

RITCHIE VALENS
58 Pye International 7N 25000   Come On Let's Go/Dooby Dooby Wah 150
58 Pye International 7N 25000   Come On Let's Go/Dooby Dooby Wah (78) 80
59 London HL 8803   Donna/La Bamba 30
59 London HL 8803   Donna/La Bamba (78) 80
59 London HL 7068   Donna/La Bamba (export issue) 30
59 London HL 8886   That's My Little Suzie/Bluebirds Over The Mountains (tri centre) 40
59 London HL 8886   That's My Little Suzie/Bluebirds Over The Mountains (round centre) 30
59 London HL 8886   That's My Little Suzie/Bluebirds Over The Mountains (78) 80
62 London HL 9494   La Bamba/Ooh, My Head 20
59 London RE 1232   RITCHIE VALENS (EP, initial pressing with triangular centre) 200
59 London RE 1232   RITCHIE VALENS (EP, later round centre) 150
61 London HA 2390   RITCHIE (LP) 150
64 London HA 8196   HIS GREATEST HITS (LP) 50
67 President PTL 1001   I REMEMBER RITCHIE VALENS (LP) 20

DINO VALENTI
68 CBS 65715   DINO (LP) 45

(see also Quicksilver Messenger Service)

VALENTINE
72 Track 2094104   Time/Leader Of The Band 6

BILLY VALENTINE
55 Capitol CL 14320   It's A Sin/Your Love Has Got Me (Reelin' And Rockin') 10

DICKIE VALENTINE (& STARGAZERS)
SINGLES
54 Decca F 10346   Endless/I Could Have Told You 30
54 Decca F 10394   The Finger Of Suspicion (with Stargazers)/ Who's Afraid (Not I, Not I, Not I) 20
54 Decca F 10415   Mister Sandman/Runaround 40
55 Decca F 10430   A Blossom Fell/I Want You All To Myself (Just You) 15
55 Decca F 10484   Ma Cherie Amie/Lucky Waltz 10
55 Decca F 10493   I Wonder/You Too Can Be A Dreamer 10
55 Decca F 10517   Hello Mrs. Jones (Is Mary There?)/Lazy Gondolier 10
55 Decca F 10549   No Such Luck/The Engagement Waltz 10
55 Decca F 10628   Christmas Alphabet/Where Are You Tonight? 20
55 Decca F 10645   The Old Pi-Anna Rag/First Love 15
55 Decca F 10667   Dreams Can Tell A Lie/Song Of The Trees 7
56 Decca F 10714   The Voice/The Best Way To Hold A Girl 7
56 Decca F 10753   My Impossible Castle/When You Came Along 7
56 Decca F 10766   Day Dreams/Give Me A Carriage With Eight White Horses 8
56 Decca F 10798   Christmas Island/The Hand Of Friendship 15
56 Decca F 10820   Dickie Valentine's Rock 'N' Roll Party Medley (Parts 1 & 2) 10

JACK VALENTINE
55 MGM SPC 8   Dressing Up My Heart/Song Of The Bandit (export issue) 12

VALENTINE GUINNESS
80 RAK RAK 308   (Hey Hey) C.J.T./When Mandy Calls 35

VALENTINES (JAMAICA)
67 Doctor Bird DB 1065   Blam Blam Fever/BABA BROOKS: The Scratch 100

VALENTINES (U.S.)
60 Ember EMB S 123   Hey Ruby/That's How I Feel 90

ANNA VALENTINO
57 London HLD 8421   Calypso Joe/You're Mine 30

DANNY VALENTINO
59 MGM MGM 1049   Stampede/(You Gotta Be A) Music Man 30
60 MGM MGM 1067   Biology/A Million Tears 20
60 MGM MGM 1109   Pictures From The Past/'Till The End Of Forever 15

MARK VALENTINO
63 Stateside SS 148   The Push And Kick/Walking Alone 25
63 Stateside SS 186   Do It/Hey You're Looking Good 15

VALENTINOS

MINT VALUE £

63	Stateside SS 233	Jivin' At The Drive In/Part Time Job	25

VALENTINOS

68	Soul City SC 106	It's All Over Now/Tired Of Livin' In The Country	25
68	Stateside SS 2137	Tired Of Being Nobody/The Death Of Love	18
71	Polydor 2058 090	Don't Raise Up Your Hands In Anger/Stand Up And Be Counted	10
68	Soul City SCM 001	THE VALENTINOS/THE SIMS TWINS (LP, with Sims Twins)	70

(see also Bobby Womack)

VALERIE (THE ROCK 'N' ROLL YOUNGSTER)

56	Columbia DB 3832	Tonight You Belong To Me/The Man Who Owns The Sunshine	20

VALERIE AND THE WEEK OF WONDERS

83	Soon Come VA 01	Too Late/Helpless (hand made p/s)	20

DANA VALERY

64	Decca F 11881	This Is My Prayer/Would I Love You Again/T'en Va Pas	7
64	Decca F 11977	I Wake Up Crying/Never Let Go	12
65	Decca F12134	She Doesn't Love You (Half As Much As Me)/We're Gonna Be Happy	6
13	Outta Sight OSV 105	You Don't Know Where Your Interest Lie/You Don't Know Where Your Interest Lie (reissue)	6

VALHALLA (1)

81	Asgard ASG 69151	Lightning In The Sky/These Sunday Nights	300

VALHALLA (2)

82	Neat NEAT 22	Coming Home/Through With You	10
84	Neat NEAT 36	Still in Love With You/Jack	8

JOE VALINO (& GOSPELAIRES)

57	HMV POP 283	The Garden Of Eden/Caravan	25
58	London HLT 8705	God's Little Acre/I'm Happy With What I've Got (with Gospelaires)	15

VALJEAN (AT THE PIANO)

62	London HLL 9203	Till There Was You/The Eighteenth Variation	6

VALKYRIES

64	Parlophone R 5123	Rip It Up/What's Your Name?	40

DIORIS VALLADARES ORCHESTRA

64	Island IEP 703	AUTHENTIC MERINGUE (EP)	12
64	Island ILP 910	LET'S GO LATIN (LP, withdrawn)	60

MARCOS VALLE

68	Verve VLP 9206	SAMBA '68 (LP)	30
95	Mr. Bongo MRBLP003	THE ESSENTIAL MARCOS VALLE (LP)	20
95	Mr. Bongo MRBLP007	THE ESSENTIAL MARCOS VALLE VOL 2 (LP)	20
97	Far Out FARO 022	NOVA BOSSA NOVA (LP)	25

VALLEY FORGE

86	Revue REV 0312	FROM ACROSS THE SEE (12" EP, p/s)	20

VALLEY OF ACHOR

75	Dovetail DOVE 18	A DOOR OF HOPE (LP, gatefold sleeve)	15

(see also Wine Of Lebanon)

FRANKIE VALLI

66	Philips BF 1467	(You're Gonna) Hurt Yourself/VALLI BOYS: Night Hawk	10
66	Philips BF 1512	You're Ready Now/Cry For Me	10
66	Philips BF 1529	The Proud One/Ivy	10
67	Philips BF 1556	Beggin'/Dody	10
67	Philips BF 1580	Can't Take My Eyes Off You/The Trouble With Me	7
67	Philips BF 1603	I Make A Fool Of Myself/September Rain	7
68	Philips BF 1634	To Give (The Reason I Live)/Watch Where You Walk	7
69	Philips BF 1795	The Girl I'll Never Know/A Face Without A Name	6
70	Philips 320 226 BF	You're Ready Now/Cry For Me (reissue)	10
67	Philips (S)BL 7814	SOLO (LP)	25
69	Philips SBL 7856	TIMELESS (LP)	20
77	Private Stock PVLP 1029	LADY PUT THE LIGHT OUT (LP, withdrawn)	40

FRANKIE VALLI & THE FOUR SEASONS

71	Warner Bros K 16107	Whatever You Say/Sleeping Man (withdrawn, 300 only)	45
72	Tamla Motown TMG 819	You're A Song/Sun Country	10
72	Mowest MW 3002	The Night/When The Morning Comes	75
73	Mowest MW 3003	Walk On, Don't Look Back/Touch The Rainchild	8
72	Mowest MWSA 5501	CHAMELEON (LP)	20

(see also Four Seasons, Wonder Who)

JUNE VALLI

54	HMV 7M 245	I Understand (Just How You Feel)/Old Shoes And A Bag Of Rice	7
54	HMV 7M 259	Tell Me, Tell Me/Boy Wanted	7
55	HMV 7M 284	Wrong, Wrong, Wrong/Ole Pappy Time	7
56	HMV 7M 347	Por Favor (Please)/The Things They Say	7
59	Mercury AMT 1034	The Answer To A Maiden's Prayer/In His Arms	6
59	Mercury AMT 1048	An Anonymous Letter/Bygones	6
61	Mercury AMT 1130	I Guess Things Happen That Way/Tell Him For Me	7

TONY VALOR SOUNDS

77	Brunswick BRBS 5003	GOTTA GET IT (LP)	15

ANTON VALOTTI

75	Rouge RMS 106	BLACKOUT (LP)	80

VALUES

66	Ember EMB S 211	Return To Me/That's The Way (with p/s)	80
66	Ember EMB S 211	Return To Me/That's The Way	50

HUBERT THOMAS VALVERDE & THE HTS

68	S n B 55 3922	Genevieve/We Don't Care	25

VALVERDE BROTHERS

MINT VALUE £

VALVERDE BROTHERS
69 CBS 4519 — River Of My Mind/I Wanna Love You 20

VALVES
77 Zoom ZUM 1 — Robot Love/For Adolfs Only (p/s) 12
77 Zoom ZUM 3 — Tarzan Of The Kings Road/Ain't No Surf In Portobello (p/s) 12
79 Albion DEL 3 — I Don't Mean Nothing At All/Linda Vindalco (p/s) 12

VAL & V'S
67 CBS 2780 — Do It Again A Little Bit Slower/For A Rainy Day 20
67 CBS 2956 — I Like The Way/With This Theme 20
68 CBS 3316 — This Little Girl/Dreamer 15

VAMP
68 Atlantic 584 213 — Floatin'/Thinkin' Too Much 100
69 Atlantic 584 263 — Green Pea/Wake Up And Tell Me (withdrawn) 150

(see also Viv Prince, Clark-Hutchinson)

VAMPIRE WEEKEND
07 XL XLS 299 — Mansard Roof/Ladies Of Cambridge 8
08 XL XLS 399 — The Kids Don't Stand a Chance /(Chromeo Remix) (white vinyl) 15
10 XL 1779816 — White Sky/White Sky (Basement Jaxx Remix) (white vinyl) 10
13 XL XLS 601 — Diane Young/Step (hand-printed sleeve, hand stamped labels) 6
08 XL XLLP 318 — VAMPIRE WEEKEND (LP) 15
13 XL XLLP 556 — MODERN VAMPIRES OF THE CITY (LP, hand-printed alternative sleeve, 50 only) 70
13 XL XLLP 556 — MODERN VAMPIRES OF THE CITY (LP, CD and poster) 18

VAMPIRES (1)
59 Parlophone R 4599 — Swinging Ghosts/Clap Trap 20

VAMPIRES (2)
68 Pye 7N 17553 — Do You Wanna Dance/My Girl 20

VAMPIRES (3)
82 Next NEX 702 — Harry's House/Mystery And Madness (p/s) 10

VAMPS
79 Dental DK 001 — She Exudes Sexuality/Love Letters/I Only Saw You (p/s, red vinyl, 1000 only, hand-made p/s) 25

VAN DER GRAAF GENERATOR

SINGLES
69 Polydor 56758 — People You Were Going To/Firebrand 750
70 Charisma CB 122 — Refugees/The Boat Of Millions Of Years (three prong centre) ... 45
73 Charisma CB 175 — Theme One/W (with p/s, "D.J. sample not for sale") 50
72 Charisma CB 175 — Theme One/W (with p/s, solid centre) 30
76 Charisma CB 297 — Wondering/Meurglys III 8
76 Charisma PRO 002 — Wondering (Song)/Wondering (Heroics) (promo only) 25
11 Esoteric VDGS 101 — Highly Strung/Elsewhere (die-cut sleeve) 6

ALBUMS
69 Mercury SMCL 20177 — THE AEROSOL GREY MACHINE (LP, unreleased, finished gatefold sleeve only) 750
70 Charisma CAS 1007 — THE LEAST WE CAN DO IS WAVE TO EACH OTHER (LP, pink 'scroll' label, original mix, matrices read: CAS 1007 A/B, gatefold sleeve, with poster) 400
70 Charisma CAS 1007 — THE LEAST WE CAN DO IS WAVE TO EACH OTHER (LP, pink 'scroll' label, original mix, matrices read: CAS 1007 A/B, gatefold sleeve, without poster) 60
70 Charisma CAS 1007 — THE LEAST WE CAN DO IS WAVE TO EACH OTHER (LP, pink 'scroll' label, remix, matrices read: CAS 1007 A+G/B+G, gatefold sleeve; with poster) 150
70 Charisma CAS 1007 — THE LEAST WE CAN DO IS WAVE TO EACH OTHER (LP, pink 'scroll' label, remix, matrices read: CAS 1007 A+G/B+G, gatefold sleeve; without poster) 50
70 Charisma CAS 1027 — H TO HE, WHO AM THE ONLY ONE (LP, pink label, gatefold sleeve) 150
70 Charisma CAS 1027 — H TO HE, WHO AM THE ONLY ONE (LP, reissue 'Mad Hatter' label) 30
71 Charisma CAS 1051 — PAWN HEARTS (LP, gatefold sleeve, pink 'scroll' label, with insert) 100
71 Charisma CAS 1051 — PAWN HEARTS (LP, gatefold sleeve, pink 'scroll' label, without insert) 35
72 Charisma CS 2 — 1968-71 (LP, pink label) 25
75 Charisma CAS 1109 — GODBLUFF (LP, with inner sleeve) 15
76 Charisma CAS 1116 — STILL LIFE (LP, small 'Mad Hatter' logo) 15
76 Charisma CAS 1120 — WORLD RECORD (LP) 15
76 Charisma CAS 1007 — THE LEAST WE CAN DO IS WAVE TO EACH OTHER (LP, gatefold reissue, 'Mad hatter' label) 18
77 Charisma CAS 1131 — THE QUIET ZONE/THE PLEASURE ZONE (LP, as Van Der Graaf) 18
78 Charisma CVLP 101 — VITAL (2-LP) 20
00 Virgin VDGGBOX 1 — THE BOX (4-CD box set) 20
12 Back On Black PCV004LP — THE LEAST WE CAN DO IS WAVE TO EACH OTHER (2-LP, reissue) 20
12 Back On Black PCV005LP — H TO HE AM THE ONLY ONE (2-LP, reissue) 25
12 Back On Black PCV006LP — PAWN HEARTS (2-LP, reissue) 20
12 Back On Black PCV007LP — GODBLUFF (2-LP, reissue) 20
12 Esoteric EANTLP 1003 — ALT (LP) 15
15 Esoteric EANTPL 1044 — MERLIN ATHOS (LP) 15
16 Esoteric EANTLP 1062 — DO NOT DISTURB (LP) 15

(see also Peter Hammill, Long Hello, Juicy Lucy, Misunderstood, David Jackson)

HARRY VANDA
69 Polydor 56357 — I Love Marie/Gonna Make It 10

(see also Easybeats)

LEE VANDERBILT
74 Bell 1384 — It's Dawn Again/Pick Up Your Troubles 15

GREG VANDIKE
79 Cloned CLONE 1 — All Of The Girls/Clone (p/s) 7

MAMIE VAN DOREN
58 Capitol CL 14850 — Something To Dream About/I Fell In Love (promos in p/s) 40
58 Capitol CL 14850 — Something To Dream About/I Fell In Love 25

Linda VAN DYCK

MINT VALUE £

LINDA VAN DYCK
69	Gemini GMS 004	The Seduction Song/Unlock My door	12

VANDYKE & BAMBIS
64	Piccadilly 7N 35180	Doin' The Mod/All I Want Is You	50

EARL VAN DYKE (& SOUL BROTHERS)
64	Stateside SS 357	Soul Stomp/Hot 'N' Tot (DJ copy)	200
64	Stateside SS 357	Soul Stomp/Hot 'N' Tot	125
65	Tamla Motown TMG 506	All For You/Too Many Fish In The Sea (as Earl Van Dyke & Soul Brothers)(DJ copy)	175
65	Tamla Motown TMG 506	All For You/Too Many Fish In The Sea (as Earl Van Dyke & Soul Brothers)	125
70	Tamla Motown TMG 759	Six By Six/All For You (matt black label, later shiny)	12
72	Tamla Motown TMG 814	I Can't Help Myself/How Sweet It Is (To Be Loved By You) (& Soul Brothers)	10
65	Tamla Motown TML 11014	THAT MOTOWN SOUND (LP)	120

LEROY VAN DYKE
65	Warner Bros WB 5650	It's All Over Now Baby Blue/Just A State Of Mind	8
66	Warner Bros WB 5807	You Couldn't Get My Love Back/Fool Such As I	8
67	Warner Bros WB 5777	Almost Persuaded/Less Of Me	10
62	Mercury MMC 14101	WALK ON BY (LP)	30
63	Mercury MMC 14118	MOVIN' VAN DYKE (LP)	30

VAN DYKES
66	Stateside SS 504	No Man Is An Island/I Won't Hold It Against You	25
66	Stateside SS 504	No Man Is An Island/I Won't Hold It Against You (DJ Copy)	40
66	Stateside SS 530	I've Gotta Go On Without You/What Will I Do	25

LON & DERREK VAN EATON
73	Apple APPLE 46	Warm Woman/More Than Words (in p/s)	125
73	Apple APPLE 46	Warm Woman/More Than Words	60
73	Apple SAPCOR 25	BROTHER (LP, gatefold sleeve, with insert)	100
73	Apple SAPCOR 25	BROTHER (LP, gatefold sleeve, without insert)	60

NICK VAN EEDE
78	Barn 201 4128	Rock'n'Roll Fool/Ounce Of Sense	6
79	Barn BARN 003	All Or Nothing/Hold On To Your Heart	7
79	Barn BARN 008	I Only Want To Be Number One/Dicing	60

(see also Drivers)

VANGELIS
75	RCA RS 1025	HEAVEN AND HELL (LP, gatefold sleeve)	15
76	Polydor 2489 113	L'APOCALYPSE DES ANIMAUX (LP, TV soundtrack)	18
15	Warner Bros. 0825646122110	BLADE RUNNER (LP, red or black vinyl)	35

(see also Aphrodite's Child, Forminx, Cosmic Baby)

ILA VAN
74	Pye Intl. DDS 108	Can't Help Loving Dat Man/I've Got The Feeling	8

CHERRY VANILLA
77	RCA PB 5053	The Punk/Foxy Bitch (title sleeve)	8
79	RCA PL 25217	VENUS DE VINYL (LP)	15

VANILLA FUDGE
67	Atlantic 584 123	You Keep Me Hanging On/Take Me For A Little While	10
67	Atlantic 584 139	(Illusions Of My Childhood) Eleanor Rigby (Parts 1 & 2)	8
68	Atlantic 584 179	Where Is My Mind?/The Look Of Love	12
69	Atlantic 584 257	Shotgun/Good Good Lovin'	7
69	Atlantic 584 276	Some Velvet Morning/Thoughts	12
67	Atlantic 587/588 086	VANILLA FUDGE (LP, red & plum label)	75
68	Atlantic 587 100	THE BEAT GOES ON (LP, mono)	40
68	Atlantic 588 100	THE BEAT GOES ON (LP, stereo)	40
68	Atlantic 587 110	RENAISSANCE (LP, mono)	45
68	Atlantic 588 110	RENAISSANCE (LP, stereo)	40
69	Atco 228 020	NEAR THE BEGINNING (LP)	25
70	Atco 228 029	ROCK 'N' ROLL (LP)	25

(see also Beck Bogert & Appice, Cactus)

VANITY FARE
68	Page One POF 075	I Live For The Sun/On The Other Side Of Life	10
68	Page One POF 100	Summer Morning/Betty Carter	7
69	Page One POF 117	Highway Of Dreams/Waiting For The Downfall	7
69	Page One POF 142	Early In The Morning/You Made Me Love You	7
69	Page One POF 158	Hitchin' A Ride/Man Child	10
70	Page One POF 170	Come Tomorrow/Megowd (Something Tells Me)	12
70	Page One PDF 180	Carolina's Coming Home/On Your Own	8
71	DJM DJS 234	Where Did All The Good Times Go/Stand	6
71	DJM DJS 250	Better By Far/Rock 'N Roll Band	6
71	DJM DJS 526	Our Own Way Of Living/Nowhere To Go	6
72	Philips 6006237	I'm In Love With The World/At The End Of The Pier	6
69	Page One POLS 010	THE SUN, THE WIND AND OTHER THINGS (LP)	45
70	DJM DJSL 001	COMING HOME (LP)	20

(see also Avengers)

VANITY 6
82	Warner Bros. 57 023	VANITY 6 (LP)	15

TEDDY VANN (ORCHESTRA)
60	London HLU 9097	Cindy/I'm Waiting	25
61	Philips PB 1160	The Lonely Crowd/I Was Born to Love You	6

ORNELLA VANONI
67	Decca F 22703	Only Two Can Play/Can I?	10

Dave VAN RONK

DAVE VAN RONK
65 Stateside SL 10153   INSIDE (LP) 30

ROB VAN SPYK
74 Acorn CF 241   FOLLOW THE SUN (LP) 75
(see also Stonefield Tramp)

TOWNES VAN ZANDT
99 Exile EX 7013   Riding The Range/Dirty Old Town (p/s, 2000 only) 6
69 RCA SF 8040   OUR MOTHER THE MOUNTAIN (LP) 30
73 United Artists UAS 29442 THE LATE GREAT TOWNES VAN ZANDT (LP, gatefold sleeve) 30
87 Heartland HLD 003   AT MY WINDOW (LP) 15
88 Decal LIK 32   TOWNES VAN ZANDT (LP, reissue) 20
88 Decal LIK 25   DELTA MOMMA BLUES (LP, reissue) 20
89 Decal LIK 59   FLYIN' SHOES (LP, reissue) 15

VAPORS
80 United Artists UAG 30300 NEW CLEAR DAYS (LP) 15

PETER VARDAS
59 Top Rank JAR 173   He Threw A Stone/Checkerboard Love 6

VARDI AND HIS ORCHESTRA
62 London 45 HLR 9518   Theme From Ballad Of A Soldier/Exodus - Main Theme 15

VARDIS
79 Redball RR 017   100 MPH (EP) 150
80 Castle CQUEL 2/100MPH   Out Of The Way/If I Were King 7
81 Logo VAR3   Silver Machine/Come On (7", die cut p/s) 6
81 Logo VAR4   All You'll Ever Need/If I Were King/Jumping Jack Flash (p/s) 6

VARIATION
72 Warner Bros K 16233   Snowbird/Nebula 6

VARIATIONS
65 Immediate IM 019   The Man With All The Toys/She'll Know I'm Sorry 35
69 Major Minor MM 638   Crimson And Clover/She Couldn't Dance 20

VARIATIONS (U.S.)
75 UK USA 10   Sayin' It And Doin' It Pts I & II 8

VARICOSE VEINS
78 Warped WARP 1   INCREDIBLE (EP, mail-order only, 200 only, beware of counterfeits) .. 80
(see also Orange Disaster)

VARIOUS ARTISTS
81 Not On Label – VA 1   SOLO ALBUM (LP) 20

LYN VARNADO
05 Hayley HR 002   Ain't That Something/Wash And Wear Love 10

SYLVIE VARTAN
65 RCA Victor RCA 1490   One More Day/I Made My Choice 75
65 RCA Victor RCA 1495   Another Heart/Think About You 12
79 RCA PB 1578   I Don't Want The Night To End/Distant Shores (p/s, coloured vinyl) 6
65 RCA Victor RCX 7165   SYLVIE VARTAN (EP) 200

VARUKERS
81 Tempest/Inferno HELL 1 Protest And Survive/No Scapegoat (p/s) 10
83 Riot City RIOT 27   Die For Your Government/All Systems Fail (p/s) 7
83 Riot City RIOT 29   Led To The Slaughter/The End Is Nigh (p/s) 10
83 Riot City RIOT 31   ANOTHER RELIGION ANOTHER WAR (12" EP) 15
84 Rot ASS 16   MASSACRED MILLIONS (12" EP) 20
83 Riot City RIOT 005   BLOODSUCKERS (LP, with inner) 20
84 Attack ATTACK 001   PREPARE FOR THE ATTACK (LP, 1000 only) 18
85 Liberate 1   ONE STRUGGLE ONE FIGHT (LP) 15
87 Rot DUTCH 001   LIVE IN HOLLAND (LP) 15

VASALINES
92 Avalanche ONLYLP 013   ALL THE STUFF AND MORE (LP) 15

VASELINE TIGERS
80 Dance DANCE 513   I'm A Golliwog/Back In The Square (Again) 18

VASELINES
87 53rd & 3rd AGARR 10   Son Of A Gun/Rory Rides Away/You Think You're A Man (12", die-cut sleeve) 25
88 53rd & 3rd AGARR 17   Dying For It/Molly's Lips (p/s) 20
88 53rd & 3rd AGARR 17T   Dying For It/Molly's Lips/Teenage Superstars/Jesus Wants Me For A Sunbeam (12", p/s) 15
90 53rd & 3rd AGAS 7   DUM DUM (LP) 30
98 Avalanche ONLY LP 013P ALL THE STUFF AND MORE (LP, picture disc) 15
14 Rosary RMUSIC1LPX   V FOR VASELINES (LP, red vinyl, 2-CD, signed, with poster) 20
(see also Pastels, BMX Bandits)

VASHTI
65 Decca F 12157   Some Things Just Stick In Your Mind/I Want To Be Alone 80
66 Columbia DB 7917   Train Song/Love Song 60
(see also Vashti Bunyan)

VASTIK
82 Lynx SSM 030   Running Out Of Time/Teenage Dream (no p/s) 6

FITZ VAUGHAN BRYAN ORCHESTRA
60 Melodisc 45/1560   Evening News/Hold Up Your Head And Smile 60
(see also Kendrick Patrick, Lord Creator)

FRANKIE VAUGHAN
53 HMV 7M 167   Istanbul (Not Constantinople)/Cloud Lucky Seven 20
54 HMV 7M 182   The Cuff Of My Shirt/Heartless 10
54 HMV 7M 252   My Son, My Son/Cinnamon Sinner (Selling Lollipop Lies) 10
54 HMV 7M 270   Happy Days And Lonely Nights/Danger Signs 10

Malcolm VAUGHAN

MINT VALUE £

55	HMV 7M 298	Too Many Heartaches/Unsuspecting Heart	10
57	Philips JK 1002	Garden Of Eden/Priscilla (jukebox issue)	10
57	Philips JK 1014	What's Behind That Strange Door/Cold, Cold Shower (jukebox issue)	10
57	Philips JK 1022	These Dangerous Years/Isn't This A Lovely Evening (jukebox issue)	10
57	Philips JK 1030	Gotta Have Something In The Bank, Frank/Single (with Kaye Sisters, jukebox issue)	10
57	Philips JK 1035	Kisses Sweeter Than Wine/Rock-A-Chicka (jukebox issue)	15
57	Philips PB 775	Kisses Sweeter Than Wine/Rock-A-Chicka	10

(see also Kaye Sisters, Marilyn Monroe)

MALCOLM VAUGHAN

56	HMV 7M 338	With Your Love/Small Talk	15
56	HMV 7M 389	Only You (And You Alone)/I'll Be Near To You	7
56	HMV POP 250	St. Therese Of The Roses/Love Me As Though There Were No Tomorrow	10
57	HMV POP 303	The World Is Mine/Now	7
57	HMV POP 325	Chapel Of The Roses/Guardian Angel	7
59	HMV CLP 1284	HELLO MALCOLM VAUGHAN (LP)	15

SARAH VAUGHAN
SINGLES

58	Mercury 7MT 198	My Darling, My Darling/Bewitched	10
58	Mercury 7MT 212	Padre/Spin Little Bottle	10
58	Mercury 7MT 222	Too Much, Too Soon/What's So Bad About It	10
59	Mercury AMT 1010	Everything I Do/I Ain't Hurtin'	8
59	Mercury AMT 1029	Cool Baby/Are You Certain?	6
59	Mercury AMT 1044	Careless/Separate Ways	7
59	Mercury AMT 1057	Broken-Hearted Melody/Misty	10
59	Mercury AMT 1080	You're My Baby/Eternally	6
59	Mercury AMT 1087	Don't Look At Me That Way/Sweet Affections	10
60	Columbia DB 4491	Ooh! What A Day/My Dear Little Sweetheart	10
60	Columbia DB 4511	If I Were A Bell/Teach Me Tonight (with Count Basie & Joe Williams)	6
74	Mainstream MSS 355	I Need You Now (More Than Ever Before)/Do Away With April	15

ALBUMS

55	Oriole/Mercury MG 26005	IMAGES (10")	20
55	Mercury MG 25188	THE DIVINE SARAH	15
56	London HB-U 1049	SARAH VAUGHAN SINGS (10", with John Kirby & His Orchestra)	20
56	Emarcy EJL 100	IN THE LAND OF HI FI (10")	15
56	Philips BBL 7082	SARAH VAUGHAN	15
56	Mercury MPT 7503	MAKE YOURSELF COMFORTABLE (10")	20
57	Mercury MPT 7518	IMAGES (10", reissue)	15
57	Emarcy EJL 1258	SASSY	15
57	Mercury MPL 6522	SINGS GREAT SONGS FROM HIT SHOWS PART 1	15
57	Philips BBL 7165	LINGER AWHILE	15
57	Mercury MPL 6523	SINGS GREAT SONGS FROM HIT SHOWS PART 2	15
57	Mercury MPL 6525	SINGS GEORGE GERSHWIN VOL. 1	15
57	Mercury MPL 6527	SINGS GEORGE GERSHWIN VOL. 2	15
58	Mercury MPL 6532	WONDERFUL SARAH	15
58	Emarcy EJL 1273	SWINGIN' EASY	15
58	Mercury MPL 6540	IN ROMANTIC MOOD	15
58	Mercury MPL 6542	AT MISTER KELLY'S	15
59	Mercury MMC 14001	AFTER HOURS AT THE LONDON HOUSE	15
59	Mercury MMC 14011	VAUGHAN AND VIOLINS (also stereo CMS 18003)	15

BILLY VAUGHN (& HIS ORCHESTRA)

55	London HL 8112	Melody Of Love/Joy Ride (gold label print)	15
55	London HLD 8205	The Shifting Whispering Sands (Parts 1 & 2) (with Ken Nordine) (gold print)	15
56	London HLD 8238	Theme From 'The Threepenny Opera'/I'd Give A Million Tomorrows (gold label print, later with silver label print)	20
56	London HLD 8319	When The Lilac Blooms Again/Autumn Concerto (gold label print)	20
56	London HLD 8342	Petticoats From Portugal/La La Colette (gold label print)	20
57	London HLD 8417	The Ship That Never Sailed/Little Boy Blue (with Ken Nordine)	10
57	London HLD 8511	Johnny Tremain/Naughty Annetta (as Billy Vaughn's Orchestra & Chorus)	10
57	London HLD 8522	Raunchy/Sail Along Silvery Moon	15
58	London HLD 8612	Tumbling Tumbleweeds/Trying	8

(see also Hilltoppers, Ken Nordine)

MORRIS VAUGHN

69	Fontana TF 1031	My Love Keeps Growing/Make It Look Good	30

VBW

80	Heaven International	VBW EP (no p/s)	40

V.D.U.'S

79	Thin Sliced	Don't Cry For Me/Little White Lie/Holiday Romances (p/s)	30

(see also Boys Wonder)

VECO 19

90	Irdial Discs VCO 1	Eep!/Eep!/Hardhead (12")	50

VED BUENS ENDE

95	Misanthropy AMAZON 006	WRITTEN IN WATERS (2-LP, marbled purple vinyl)	60

CHUCK VEDDER

59	London HL 8951	Spanky Boy/Arriba	30
59	London HL 8951	Spanky Boy/Arriba (78)	20

BOBBY VEE
SINGLES

60	London HLG 9179	Devil Or Angel/Since I Met You, Baby	20
61	London HLG 9459	Love's Made A Fool Of You/Susie-Q	8

			MINT VALUE £
67	Liberty LBF 15016	Come Back When You Grow Up/Let The Four Winds Blow	6
67	Liberty LIB 15042	Beautiful People/I May Be Gone	6
68	Liberty LBF 15058	Maybe Just Today/You're A Big Girl Now	6
68	Liberty LBF 15096	Medley, My Girl - Hey Girl/Take Good Care Of My Baby	7
68	Liberty LBF 15134	Do What You Gotta' Do/Thank You	7
69	Liberty LBF 15178	(I'm Into Looking For) Someone To Love Me/Sunrise Highway	7
69	Liberty LBF 15234	I'm Gonna Make It Up To You/Let's Call It A Day	8
69	Liberty LBF 15305	Electric Trains And You/In And Out Of Love	8
70	Liberty LBF 15420	Sweet Sweetheart/Rock 'N Roll Music And You	8

EPs

61	London RE-G 1278	BOBBY VEE NO. 1	15
61	London RE-G 1299	BOBBY VEE NO. 2	15
61	London RE-G 1308	BOBBY VEE NO. 3	15
61	London RE-G 1323	BOBBY VEE NO. 4	20
61	London RE-G 1324	HITS OF THE ROCKIN' 50's	30
62	Liberty LEP 2053	SINCERELY	15
63	Liberty LEP 2084	JUST FOR FUN (2 tracks by Bobby Vee, 2 by Crickets)	15
63	Liberty LEP 2089	A FOREVER KIND OF LOVE	15
63	Liberty LEP 2102	BOBBY VEE'S BIGGEST HITS (mono)	12
63	Liberty SLEP 2102	BOBBY VEE'S BIGGEST HITS (stereo)	12
63	Liberty LEP 2116	BOBBY VEE MEETS THE CRICKETS (mono)	10
63	Liberty SLEP 2116	BOBBY VEE MEETS THE CRICKETS (stereo)	10
64	Liberty LEP 2149	BOBBY VEE MEETS THE CRICKETS VOL. 2	10
64	Liberty LEP 2181	NEW SOUNDS	25
65	Liberty LEP 2212	BOBBY VEE MEETS THE VENTURES (with Ventures)	25

ALBUMS

61	London HA-G 2320	BOBBY VEE SINGS YOUR FAVOURITES	45
61	London HA-G 2352	BOBBY VEE (mono)	20
61	London SAH-G 6152	BOBBY VEE (stereo)	25
61	London HA-G 2374	WITH STRINGS AND THINGS (mono)	15
61	London SAH-G 6174	WITH STRINGS AND THINGS (stereo)	25
61	London HA-G 2406	SINGS HITS OF THE ROCKIN' 50s (mono)	30
61	London SAH-G 6206	SINGS HITS OF THE ROCKIN' 50s (stereo)	35
61	London HA-G 2428	TAKE GOOD CARE OF MY BABY (mono)	20
61	London SAH-G 6224	TAKE GOOD CARE OF MY BABY (stereo)	25
63	Liberty LBY 1147	BOBBY VEE MEETS THE VENTURES (with Ventures, mono)	15
63	Liberty SLBY 1147	BOBBY VEE MEETS THE VENTURES (with Ventures, stereo)	20

(see also Crickets, Ventures)

ALAN VEGA

81	Celluloid WIP 6744	Jukebox Babe/Lonely (p/s)	6
81	Celluloid 12WIP 6744	Jukebox Babe/Lonely (12", p/s)	10
88	Sniffin' Rock SR 009	WACKO WARRIOR/(track by African Headcharge) (with Sniffin' Rock fanzine No. 12)	8
81	Ze/Island ILPS 9692	COLLISION DRIVE (LP)	15

(see also Suicide, Future Pilot AKA Alan Vega)

TATA VEGA

79	Motown TMG 1157	If Love Must Go/Come In Heaven (Earth Is Calling) Part 2	6
80	Motown TMG 1219	You Keep Me Hanging On/You Better Watch Out	10
81	Motown TMG 1230	Love Your Neighbour/There's Love In The World	8
81	Motown STML 12138	GIVIN ALL MY LOVE (LP)	20

VEGAS

92	RCA 743211104418	VEGAS (LP)	30

(see also Eurythmics, Fun Boy Three, Specials)

VEINS

80	Redball RR 3	Complete Control Rock 'n' Roll/Champagne	25

VEJTABLES

65	Pye International 7N 25539	I Still Love You/Anything	50

VEKTORS

81	Little Black EJSP 9662	Yesterday's Dream/Razor Smile/I Don't Know Why (300 only, no p/s)	35

RUTH VELDON

66	Decca F12436	A Most Peculiar Man/Show Me The Way Back To My World	15

MARTHA VELEZ

69	London HLK 10266	It Takes A Lot To Laugh/Come Here Sweet Man	10
69	London HLK 10280	Tell Mama/Swamp Man	25
69	London HLK 10280	Tell Mama/Swamp Man (DJ Copy)	40
72	Blue Horizon 2096 010	Boogie Kitchen/Two Bridges	20
69	London HA-K/SH-K 8395	FIENDS AND ANGELS (LP)	70
70	Blue Horizon 7-63867	FIENDS AND ANGELS AGAIN (LP)	100
76	Sire 9103 252	ESCAPE FROM BABYLON (LP)	20

VELLUM STAIRS

89	Marker JUNE 1002	Jamie's Coming Back/Writing On The Wall (p/s)	25
90	Marker JUNE 1003	You're Always Guilty/Karin Mist (p/s)	20

VELOURS

67	MGM 2006 603	I'm Gonna Change/Don't Pity Me	10

(see also Fantastics)

VELVELETTES

64	Stateside SS 361	Needle In A Haystack/Should I Tell Them? (DJ Copy)	100
64	Stateside SS 361	Needle In A Haystack/Should I Tell Them?	45
65	Stateside SS 387	He Was Really Sayin' Something/Throw A Farewell Kiss (DJ Copy)	125
65	Stateside SS 387	He Was Really Sayin' Something/Throw A Farewell Kiss	65

VELVET CUSHION

MINT VALUE £

65	Tamla Motown TMG 521	Lonely Lonely Girl Am I/I'm The Exception To The Rule (DJ Copy)	300
65	Tamla Motown TMG 521	Lonely Lonely Girl Am I/I'm The Exception To The Rule	175
66	Tamla Motown TMG 580	These Things Will Keep Me Loving You/Since You've Been Loving Me (DJ Copy)	100
66	Tamla Motown TMG 580	These Things Will Keep Me Loving You/Since You've Been Loving Me	55
67	Tamla Motown TMG 595	He Was Really Sayin' Something/Needle In A Haystack	30
71	Tamla Motown TMG 780	These Things Will Keep Me Loving You/Since You've Been Loving Me (reissue)	12
72	Tamla Motown TMG 806	Needle In A Haystack/I'm The Exception To The Rule	8
90	Motorcity MOTCLP 43	ONE DOOR CLOSES (LP)	15

VELVET CUSHION
| 71 | Sky SKY 3 | Lost In The Maze/It's All Over Me | 100 |

VELVET GLOVE
| 74 | Fresh Air 6370 502 | SWEET WAS MY ROSE (LP, laminated sleeve, lyric insert) | 15 |

VELVET HUSH
| 68 | Oak RGJ 648 | Broken Heart/Lover Please | 300 |

(see also Factory [Oak label])

VELVET MIST
| 70 | Tank BSS 103 | Rock N Roll Band/Bye Bye Johnny (with booklet) | 60 |

VELVET OPERA
69	CBS 4189	Anna Dance Square/Don't You Realize	10
70	CBS 4802	Black Jack Davy/Statesboro' Blues	10
70	Spark SRL 1045	She Keeps Giving Me These Feelings/There's A Hole In My Pocket	7
69	CBS 63692	RIDE A HUSTLER'S DREAM (LP)	100

(see also Elmer Gantry's Velvet Opera, Stretch, Hudson-Ford, Johnny Joyce)

VELVET SHADOWS
| 77 | Horse HOSS 148 | Wailing Of Black People/Dubbin n Wailin | 20 |

VELVETS
61	London HLU 9328	That Lucky Old Sun/Time And Time Again	25
61	London HLU 9372	Tonight (Could Be The Night)/Spring Fever	35
61	London HLU 9444	Laugh/Lana	45
61	London RE-U 1297	VELVETS (EP)	100

VEL-VETS
| 74 | Disco Demand DDS 109 | I Got To Find Me Somebody/What Now My Love | 10 |

VELVETTES
| 64 | Mercury MF 802 | He's The One I Want/That Little Boy Of Mine (in p/s) | 25 |
| 64 | Mercury MF 802 | He's The One I Want/That Little Boy Of Mine | 20 |

VELVETT FOGG
69	Pye 7N 17673	Telstar '69/Owed To The Dip	25
69	Pye NSPL 18272	VELVETT FOGG (LP, laminated sleeve; beware of non-laminated counterfeits)	250
89	See For miles SEE 259	VELVETT FOG (LP, reissue)	20

(see also Ghost)

VELVET UNDERGROUND
SINGLES
71	Atlantic 2091 088	Who Loves The Sun/Sweet Jane	70
73	MGM 2006 283	I'm Waiting For The Man/Run Run Run/Candy Says (as Lou Reed & Velvet Underground)	15
73	Atlantic K 10339	Sweet Jane/Rock And Roll (as Velvet Underground featuring Lou Reed)	15
82	Polydor POSPX 603	Heroin/Venus In Furs/I'm Waiting For The Man (12", p/s)	10
12	Atlantic 8122797366	Sweet Jane/Rock And Roll (reissue in p/s)	8

ALBUMS
67	Verve VLP 9184	THE VELVET UNDERGROUND AND NICO (LP, single sleeve, 'non-banana' cover, mono)	300
67	Verve SVLP 9184	THE VELVET UNDERGROUND AND NICO (LP, single sleeve, 'non-banana' cover, stereo)	200
68	Verve 2315 056	THE VELVET UNDERGROUND AND NICO (LP, UK pressing in stickered US peelable banana gatefold censored sleeve, stereo)	250
68	Verve VLP 9201	WHITE LIGHT WHITE HEAT (LP, 'skull' sleeve, mono)	250
68	Verve SVLP 9201	WHITE LIGHT WHITE HEAT (LP, 'skull' sleeve, stereo)	150
69	MGM MGM-CS 8108	THE VELVET UNDERGROUND (LP, 'Val Valentin mix', flapped laminated sleeve, with horizontal split of Lou Reed picture on rear sleeve)	200
71	MGM/Verve Super 2315 056	THE VELVET UNDERGROUND AND NICO (LP, reissue stereo, UK LP in US Verve stereo V6 5008 sleeve with peelable banana on front cover, UK sticker on back cover with 2315 056 covering US catalogue number, "Marketed by Polydor")	80
71	Atlantic 2400 111	LOADED (LP)	70
71	MGM 2315 056	THE VELVET UNDERGROUND AND NICO (LP, reissue, gatefold sleeve)	25
71	MGM Select 2353 022	THE VELVET UNDERGROUND (LP, reissue, gatefold sleeve)	35
71	MGM Select 2353 024	WHITE LIGHT WHITE HEAT (LP, reissue)	25
72	MGM Select 2683 006	ANDY WARHOL'S VELVET UNDERGROUND (2-LP)	30
72	Atlantic K 30022	LIVE AT MAX'S KANSAS CITY (LP)	25
73	Polydor 2383 180	SQUEEZE (LP)	40
77	Warner Bros. K40113	LOADED (LP, reissue)	20
84	Polydor SPELP 73	WHITE LIGHT WHITE HEAT (LP, reissue, different sleeve)	15
84	Polydor SPELP 20	THE VELVET UNDERGROUND AND NICO (LP, reissue)	15
85	Polydor POLD 5167	VU (LP)	18
86	Polydor VUBOX 1	THE VELVET UNDERGROUND BOX SET (5-LP box set, with booklet)	40
86	Verve POLD 5208	ANOTHER VIEW (LP)	15
95	Polydor 527887	PEEL SLOWLY AND SEE (5-CD box set)	35
99	Simply Vinyl SVLP 090	THE VELVET UNDERGROUND AND NICO (LP, reissue)	20
00	Simply Vinyl SVLP 200	WHITE LIGHT/WHITE HEAT (LP, reissue)	15
12	Polydor B001764901	SCEPTER STUDIO SESSIONS (LP)	20

(see also Lou Reed, Nico, John Cale)

VENDETTA
| 88 | Plaza PZA 042 | Don't Let The World Drag You Under/Don't Let The World Drag You Under Pt.2 (p/s) | 6 |

VENDORS

MINT VALUE £

VENDORS
64 Domino Studios (no cat. no.) Don't Leave Me Now/Twilight Time/Take Your Time/Peace Pipe (acetate, private pressing, 12 copies only) 500

(see also 'N Betweens, Slade)

VENGERS
63 Oriole CB 1879 Shake And Clap/Shakedown 25

VENIGMAS
79 Graduate GRAD 2 Red Revenge/Turn The Lights Out (p/s) 10

VENOM
81	Neat NEAT 08	In League With Satan/Live Like An Angel, Die Like An Devil (p/s)	35
82	Neat NEAT 13	Bloodlust/In Nomine Satanas (p/s)	30
82	Neat NEAT 13	Bloodlust/In Nomine Satanas (purple vinyl)	80
83	Neat NEAT 27	Die Hard/Acid Queen (p/s, with poster)	25
83	Neat NEAT 27	Die Hard/Acid Queen (p/s)	15
83	Megaforce LOM 1/NEAT 27	Die Hard/Acid Queen (picture disc, export issue, 1,000 only)	25
84	Neat NEAT 38	Warhead/Lady Lust (p/s)	12
84	Neat NEATP 38	Warhead/Lady Lust (p/s, mauve vinyl)	20
84	Neat NEAT 3812	Warhead/Lady Lust/Gates Of Hell (12", p/s)	18
85	Neat NEATP 43	Manitou/Woman (picture disc)	18
85	Neat NEATSHAPE 43	Manitou/Woman (shaped picture disc)	20
85	Neat NEAT 4312	Manitou/Woman/Dead Of Night (12", p/s)	18
85	Neat NEATS 47	Nightmare/Satanarchist (shaped picture disc)	25
85	Neat NEAT 4712	Nightmare/Satanarchist/F.O.A.D./Warhead (live) (12", 'face' p/s)	20
85	Neat NEAT 4712	Nightmare/Satanarchist/F.O.A.D./Warhead (live) (12", p/s, withdrawn)	25
85	Neat NEATSP 4712	Nightmare/Satanarchist/F.O.A.D./Warhead (live) (12", picture disc, withdrawn) ..	40
06	Castle CMWSE 1333	Antechrist/Metal Black (p/s, signed by band)	10
85	Neat 5312	HELL AT HAMMERSMITH EP (Witching Hour/Teacher's Pet/Poison) (12", 10,000 only)	25
81	Neat 1002	WELCOME TO HELL (LP, 1st issue, with poster and lyric insert)	30
82	Neat 1005	BLACK METAL (LP, 1st issue, textured sleeve, with poster, on coloured vinyl)	35
82	Neat 1005	BLACK METAL (LP, 1st issue, textured sleeve, with poster, silver/red/green or blue labels)	40
82	Neat NEAT 1005	BLACK METAL (LP, picture disc)	30
82	Neat NEAT 1005	BLACK METAL (LP, green marbled vinyl)	400
83	Neat NEATP 1002	WELCOME TO HELL (LP, reissue, purple vinyl)	50
84	Neat NEAT 1015	AT WAR WITH SATAN (LP, textured sleeve, 1st 19,000 with poster)	20
84	Neat NEAT 1015	AT WAR WITH SATAN (LP, textured sleeve)	15
85	Neat NEATP 1005	BLACK METAL (LP, reissue, picture disc)	40
85	Neat NEATSP 1015	AT WAR WITH SATAN (LP, picture disc)	40
85	Neat NEATP 1024	POSSESSED (LP, picture disc)	20
85	Neat NEAT 1024	POSSESSED (LP, inner, blue vinyl)	20
86	Demon APKPD 12	OBSCENE MATERIAL (LP, picture disc)	20
86	Raw Power RAWLP 001	FROM HELL TO THE UNKNOWN (2-LP)	20
86	A.P. APK 12	OFFICIAL BOOTLEG (LP, picture disc)	15
89	Under One Flag FLAG 36P	PRIME EVIL (LP, numbered picture disc, stickered clear sleeve)	20

CAROL VENTURA
65	Stateside SS 466	Please Somebody Help Me/The Old Lady Of Threadneedle Street	20
65	Stateside SL 10246	CAROL! (LP)	20
66	Stateside S(S)L 10180	I LOVE TO SING (LP)	20

CHARLIE VENTURA
55 Vogue Coral Q 72048 I Love You/Intermezzo 7

DAVE VENTURA
64	Mercury MF 805	The Hurt Stays In The Heart/Is A Redbird Red?	8
64	Mercury MF 827	I Forgot What It Was Like/I'll Never Love Again	7

DAVE VENTURA & THE ORBITS
63 Hardy Records 001 Yo Yo Twist/Yo Yo Twist Story (Flexi) 10

TOBY VENTURA
63 Decca F 11581 If My Heart Were A Storybook/Vagabond 40

VENTURES
SINGLES
60	Top Rank JAR 417	Walk Don't Run/Home	10
60	London HLG 9232	Perfidia/No Trespassing	8
61	London HLG 9292	Ram-Bunk-Shush/Lonely Heart	10
61	London HLG 9344	Lullaby Of The Leaves/Ginchy	10
61	London HLG 9411	Theme From 'Silver City'/Bluer Than Blue	10
61	London HLG 9465	Blue Moon/Wailin'	15
61	London HLG 7113	Lady Of Spain/Blue Moon (export issue)	30
62	Liberty LIB 60	Lolita Ya-Ya/Lucille	8
62	Liberty LIB 67	The 2,000 Pound Bee Parts 1 & 2	12
63	Liberty LIB 68	El Cumbanchero/Skip To M'Limbo	8
63	Liberty LIB 78	The Ninth Wave/Damaged Goods	10
64	Liberty LIB 91	Journey To The Stars/Walkin' With Pluto	10
64	Liberty LIB 96	Walk Don't Run '64/The Cruel Sea	12
64	Liberty LIB 10142	Penetration/Solar Race	10
65	Liberty LIB 300	Slaughter On Tenth Avenue/Rap City	10
65	Liberty LIB 303	Diamond Head/Lonely Girl	10
65	Liberty LIB 306	The Swingin' Creeper/Pedal Pusher	10
65	Liberty LIB 308	The Stranger/Bird Rockers	10
65	Liberty LIB 10219	Sleigh Ride/White Christmas	10
66	Liberty LIB 316	Secret Agent Man/007-11	15
67	Liberty LIB 10266	Theme From The Wild Angels/High And Dry	10

VENUS IN FURS

MINT VALUE £

67	Liberty LIB 55967	Strawberry Fields Forever/Endless Dream	10
68	Liberty LBF 15075	Flights Of Fantasy/Pandora's Box	15
70	Liberty LBF 15221	Hawaii Five-O - Theme/Higher Than Thou	15
71	United Artists UP 36316	Theme From 'Shaft'/Tight Fit	7
77	United Artists UP 36223	Starsky And Hutch/Charlie's Angels	7

EPs

61	London REG 1279	THE VENTURES	20
61	London REG 1283	THE VENTURES (export issue)	20
61	London REG 1288	RAM-BUNK-SHUSH!	20
62	London REG 1326	ANOTHER SMASH	20
62	London REG 1328	COLOURFUL VENTURES	20
62	Liberty LEP 2058	TWIST WITH THE VENTURES	20
62	Liberty LEP 2131	SMASH HITS	20
63	Liberty LEP 2104	THE VENTURES PLAY TELSTAR AND LONELY BULL	20
64	Liberty LEP 2174	THE VENTURES PLAY COUNTRY GREATS	20
65	Liberty LEP 2212	BOBBY VEE MEETS THE VENTURES (with Bobby Vee)	25
66	Liberty LEP 2250	SECRET AGENT MEN	25

ALBUMS

61	London HA-G 2340	THE VENTURES (mono)	30
61	London SAH-G 6143	THE VENTURES (stereo)	40
61	London HA-G 2376	ANOTHER SMASH (mono)	20
61	London SAH-G 6209	ANOTHER SMASH (stereo)	30
61	London HA-G 2409	THE COLOURFUL VENTURES (mono)	20
61	London SAH-G 6209	THE COLOURFUL VENTURES (stereo)	30
62	Liberty LBY 1002	WALK DON'T RUN	25
62	London HA-G 2429	TWIST WITH THE VENTURES (mono)	20
62	London SAH-G 6225	TWIST WITH THE VENTURES (stereo)	30
62	Liberty LBY 1072	TWIST PARTY	20
63	Liberty (S)LBY 1110	GOING TO THE VENTURES DANCE PARTY! (mono)	20
63	Liberty (S)LBY 1110	GOING TO THE VENTURES DANCE PARTY! (stereo)	30
63	Liberty (S)LBY 1147	BOBBY VEE MEETS THE VENTURES (with Bobby Vee, mono)	20
63	Liberty (S)LBY 1147	BOBBY VEE MEETS THE VENTURES (with Bobby Vee, stereo)	25
63	Liberty (S)LBY 1150	SURFING (mono)	22
63	Liberty (S)LBY 1150	SURFING (stereo)	30
64	Liberty (S)LBY 1169	LET'S GO! (mono)	18
64	Liberty (S)LBY 1169	LET'S GO! (stereo)	25
64	Liberty (S)LBY 1189	THE VENTURES IN SPACE (mono)	22
64	Liberty (S)LBY 1189	THE VENTURES IN SPACE (stereo)	30
65	Liberty (S)LBY 1228	WALK DON'T RUN - VOL. 2 (mono)	22
65	Liberty (S)LBY 1228	WALK DON'T RUN - VOL. 2 (stereo)	30
65	Liberty (S)LBY 1252	KNOCK ME OUT (mono)	20
65	Liberty (S)LBY 1252	KNOCK ME OUT (stereo)	20
65	Liberty (S)LBY 1270	ON STAGE (mono)	20
65	Liberty (S)LBY 1270	ON STAGE (stereo)	20
66	Liberty (S)LBY 1274	VENTURES A-GO GO (mono)	18
66	Liberty (S)LBY 1274	VENTURES A-GO GO (stereo)	20
66	Liberty (S)LBY 1285	THE VENTURES' CHRISTMAS ALBUM (mono)	20
66	Liberty (S)LBY 1285	THE VENTURES' CHRISTMAS ALBUM (stereo)	30
66	Liberty (S)LBY 1297	WHERE THE ACTION IS! (mono)	15
66	Liberty (S)LBY 1297	WHERE THE ACTION IS! (stereo)	18
66	Liberty (S)LBY 1323	GO WITH THE VENTURES (mono)	15
66	Liberty (S)LBY 1323	GO WITH THE VENTURES (stereo)	18
67	Liberty (S)LBY 1345	GUITAR FREAKOUT (mono)	15
67	Liberty (S)LBY 1345	GUITAR FREAKOUT (stereo)	18
67	Liberty (S)LBY 1372	SUPER PSYCHEDELICS (mono)	15
67	Liberty (S)LBY 1372	SUPER PSYCHEDELICS (stereo)	18

(see also New Ventures, Bobby Vee, Nokie Edwards)

VENUS IN FURS

83	Movement MOVEMENT 001	EXTENDED PLAY (p/s)	18
85	Backs 12CH 105	MOMENTO MORI EP (12", p/s)	15
86	Backs 12CH 107	LOVE LIES EP (12", p/s)	10
84	MOVEMENT 002LP	PLATONIC LOVE AND OTHER STORIES (LP)	15
85	Backs NCH MLP 6	STRIP (LP)	15
89	Backs NCH LP 16	MEGALOMANIA (LP)	20
90	Backs NCH LP 17	THE SPEED OF A PUN (LP)	20

VENUS & RAZORBLADES

77	Spark SRL 1153	I Wanna Be Where The Boys Are/Dogfood (numbered p/s)	8
78	Spark SRL 1159	Workin' Girl/Midnight	8

BILLY VERA

68	Atlantic 584 196	With Pen In Hand/Good Morning Blues	10

BILLY VERA & JUDY CLAY

68	Atlantic 584 169	Country Girl City Man/Let It Be Me	7
68	Atlantic 584 164	Storybook Children/Really Together	8
69	Atlantic 584 293	Reaching For The Moon/Tell It Like It Is	8
68	Atlantic 588 158	THE STORYBOOK CHILDREN (LP)	20

(see also Judy Clay)

JOHN VERITY BAND

74	Probe SPB 1087	JOHN VERITY BAND (LP)	35

(see also Argent)

Tim VERLANDER

MINT VALUE £

TIM VERLANDER
72 Midas MR 007 .... TIM VERLANDER (LP, with booklet) 40

VERMILION
78 Illegal ILM 0010 .... Angry Young Women/Nymphomania/Wild Boys (p/s) 18
79 Illegal ILS 0015 .... I Like Motorcycles/The Letter (p/s) 10
(see also Menace)

VERNON VERMONT
67 CBM CBM 02 .... Too Late/Come Back 30

VERN & ALVIN
69 Blue Cat BS 167 .... Everybody Reggae/Another Fool 120
69 Big Shot BI 525 .... Old Man Dead/G.G. RHYTHM SECTION: Reggae Me 70
(see also Maytones)

VERN & SON
71 G.G. GG 4523 .... Little Boy Blue/TYPHOON ALL STARS: Little Boy Blue - Version 8
(see also Maytones)

LARRY VERNE
60 London HLN 9194 .... Mr. Custer/Okeefenokee Two Step 8
61 London HLN 9263 .... Mr. Livingstone/Roller Coaster 7

LYN VERNON
60 Top Rank JAR 323 .... Woodchoppers Ball/Caravan 7

MIKE VERNON
72 Blue Horizon 2096 007 .... Let's Try It Again/Little Southern Country Girl 25
71 Blue Horizon 2931 003 .... BRING IT BACK HOME (LP, textured sleeve with insert) 250
71 Blue Horizon 2931 003 .... BRING IT BACK HOME (LP, textured sleeve without insert) 175

VERNON & THE G.I.S
77 Creeper VGI 001 .... G.I. Bop/Jim Dandy (no p/s) 25
77 Creeper VGI 002 .... Be-Boppin' Baby/Jungle Rock (no p/s) 20
78 Creeper VGI 005/6 .... Follow Me/Better Get Rockin' (no p/s) 20
78 Creeper VGI 007/008 .... Brand New Lover/All Night Long 20
79 Billy Goat BILL 004 .... Ghost Train Boogie/(I'm A) Teddy Boy 6
80 Billy Goat BILL 006 .... I Wanna Be A Ted/Banjo Baby (p/s) 7

VERNONS GIRLS
58 Parlophone R 4497 .... Lost And Found/White Bucks And Saddle Shoes 25
59 Parlophone R 4532 .... Jealous Heart/Now Is The Month Of Maying 20
59 Parlophone R 4596 .... Don't Look Now But/Who Are They To Say? 20
60 Parlophone R 4624 .... We Like Boys/Boy Meets Girl 15
60 Parlophone R 4654 .... Madison Time (with Jimmy Saville)/The Oo-We 15
61 Parlophone R 4734 .... Ten Little Lonely Boys/Anniversary Song 10
61 Parlophone R 4832 .... Let's Get Together/No Message 10
62 Decca F 11450 .... Lover Please/You Know What I Mean 7
62 Decca F 11495 .... The Loco-motion/Don't Wanna Go 10
62 Decca F 11549 .... Funny All Over/See For Yourself 10
63 Decca F 11629 .... Do The Bird/I'm Gonna Let My Hair Down 10
63 Decca F 11685 .... He'll Never Come Back/Stay-At-Home 10
63 Decca F 11781 .... Tomorrow Is Another Day/Why Why Why 20
64 Decca F 11807 .... We Love The Beatles/Hey Lover Boy 10
64 Decca F 11887 .... Only You Can Do It/Stupid Little Girl 18
64 Decca F 12021 .... It's A Sin To Tell A Lie/Don't Say Goodbye 10
62 Decca DFE 8506 .... THE VERNONS GIRLS (EP) 40
58 Parlophone PMC 1052 .... THE VERNONS GIRLS (LP) 50
(see also Krimson Kake, Fran & Alan, Wilde Three, Lee Francis, Samantha Jones, Breakaways)

LILI VERONA
54 HMV 7MC 13 .... Massa Johnny/Hoggin' In The Cocoa (export issue) 15
56 Melodisc MEL 1383 .... French Lesson/Pica Now (78, with Gulf Stream Calypso Boys) 10
59 HMV DLP 1202 .... JAMAICA SINGS (10" LP) 22

VERONICA FALLS
10 Trouble DUDE 016 .... Fell In Love In A Graveyard/Stephen (hand-printed sleeve, 300 only) 20
11 Bella Union BELLAU 310 .... SIX COVERS (12" EP, 300 only) 20
14 Beach Head VF 004 .... Nobody There/I Need You Around (numbered, 300 only) 25
11 Bella Union BELLAV301W .... VERONICA FALLS (LP, white vinyl, CD) 30
13 Bella Union BELLACD383P .... WAITING FOR SOMETHING TO HAPPEN (LP, CD) 20

VERSA
06 Versa VER 01 .... Da VersAtile EP (12") 30
12 Smokin' Sessions SMOKE 015 ...... 5AM (12") 40
12 On The Edge OTE 018 .... SHADOW MOVEMENT EP (12") 10
15 System SYSTM008 .... Rainfall in Dub/Road To Righteousness (10") 40
16 System SYSTM 014 .... Dub Of Existence/Memories Of The East 15

VERSA & ROWL
12 Smokin' Sessions SMOKE 017 ...... LUNAR EP (12") 12
12 Smokin' Sessions SMOKE 020 ...... JUPITER EP (12") 25
16 Zam Zam ZAMZAM 43 .... A Midsummer Night's Dub/Trimorphic 12

VERSATILE NEWTS
80 Shanghai No. 2 .... Newtrition/Blimp (p/s, stamped white label) 60
(see also Felt)

VERSATILES (JAMAICA)
68 Island WI 3142 .... Teardrops Falling/Someone To Love 60
68 Amalgamated AMG 802 .... Just Can't Win/LEADERS: Sometimes I Sit Down Down And Cry 60
68 Crab CRAB 1 .... Children Get Ready/Someone To Love 70

VERSATILITY

MINT VALUE £

69	Amalgamated AMG 854	Lu Lu Bell/Long Long Time	100
69	Big Shot BI 520	Worries/VAL BENNETT: Hound Dog Special	450
69	Crab CRAB 5	Spread Your Bed/Worries A Yard	180
70	Nu Beat NB 060	Pick My Pocket/FREEDOM SINGERS: Freedom	30
71	Nu Beat NB 076	Give It To Me/TIGER: With Hot	30
74	Dip DL 5039	Cutting Rasor (as Versatiles)/UPSETTERS: Black Belt Jones	45
74	No Label TSL EDT 1210/1211	Thanks We Get/Ungrateful Skank	65

(see also Pioneers, Soul Sisters, Junior Byles)

VERSATILITY

75	President PT 435	Tequila Madness/B Side Blues	10

VERTICAL HOLD

80	Vertical Hold VH 001	Rubber Cross/Injustice (p/s)	40
84	Vertical Hold VH 002	Angel Dust/Four Years/Dub Years (p/s, insert)	15
85	Vertical Hold VH 003	Bio-Hazard/The War That Time Won (p/s)	15

VERVE

92	Hut HUTT 12	All In The Mind/Man Called Sun/One Way To Go (12" promo, white label)	10
92	Hut HUTT 16	She's A Superstar/Feel (12" promo, white label)	10
92	Hut HUT 16	She's A Superstar (Edit)/Feel (p/s)	10
92	Hut HUTEN 21	GRAVITY GRAVE EP (Gravity Grave [Edit]/Endless Life/ She's A Superstar [Live at Clapham Grand]) (10", p/s)	15
93	Hut HUTEN 29	Blue/Twilight/Where The Geese Go/No Come Down (10", p/s)	10
93	Hut HUT 35	Slide Away/Make It 'Til Monday (pink vinyl, p/s)	10
93	(no label) FLEXI 1	Make It 'Til Monday (Glastonbury '93) (clear vinyl stickered flexi with magazine)	12
95	Hut HUT 54	This Is Music/Let The Damage Begin (purple vinyl, p/s)	8
95	Hut HUT 55	On Your Own/I See The Door (green vinyl, p/s)	8
95	Hut HUT 55	On Your Own/I See The Door (green vinyl, p/s, mispressing, B-side plays 'Friends' by Daryll-Ann)	6
97	Hut HUTLH 82	Bitter Sweet Symphony/So Sister (Jukebox issue)	6
97	Hut HUTLH 88	The Drugs Don't Work/The Drugs Don't Work (Original Demo) (Jukebox issue)	6
98	Hut HUTTX 100	SINGLES (Box set, 4 x 12")	25
93	Hut HUTLP 3	A STORM IN HEAVEN (LP, gatefold)	80
93	Jolly Roger JOLLY ROGER 2	VOYAGER 1 (LP, official bootleg, blue vinyl, 1,000 only)	100
95	Hut HUTLP 27	A NORTHERN SOUL (2-LP, mirrored sleeve)	100
97	Hut HUTLPX 45	URBAN HYMNS (2-LP, with inner sleeves, printed outer mailer, 5,000 only)	100
97	Hut HUTLPX 45	URBAN HYMNS (2-LP)	70
08	Parlophone 82075 2355841	FORTH (LP)	15
16	Virgin 00602547865380	A STORM IN HEAVEN (LP, reissue)	15
16	Virgin 4786539	A NORTHERN SOUL (LP, reissue)	15
16	Virgin EMI 4787014	URBAN HYMNS (2-LP, reissue)	20

(see also Richard Ashcroft)

VERY THINGS

83	Corpus Christi CHRISTIT's 2	The Gong Man/The Colours Are Speaking To Me (poster p/s)	10
84	Reflex LEX 3	THE BUSHES SCREAM WHILE MY DADDY PRUNES (LP)	15
93	Fire REFIRELP 13	IT'S A DRUG, IT'S A DRUG (LP)	15

VETS

79	SRT SRTS 79 CUS 513	Flies/Contrix (wrap around p/s)	50
80	Deckchair DECK 80/001	World In Action/GO ATTIC: Waiting For Fashion (fold-around p/s)	25

VEX

84	Fight Back FIGHT 1	SANCTUARY (12" EP, with insert)	50

ROD VEY

80	Rip Off RIP 13	Metal Love/Silicone City (die-cut sleeve)	25

VHF (1)

80	Lion PAW 1	Heart Of Stone (no p/s)	40

VHF (2)

81	Distil DIST 81	First Impressions/First Impressions (no p/s, many labels signed)	35
81	Pennine	1st IMPRESSIONS (LP)	90

LUKE VIBERT

98	Mo Wax MW 072 LP	BIG SOUP (2-LP, inners)	20

DANNY VIBES

00	Jah Tubbys JT 006	Want No Wickedness/Want No Dub	20

VIBRASONIC

95	Yep! YEPLP 01	VIBRASONIC (LP)	15

VIBRATIONS

61	Pye International 7N 25251	The Watusi/Wallflower	25
64	London HLK 9875	My Girl Sloopy/Daddy Woo Woo	20
66	Columbia DB 7895	Canadian Sunset/The Story Of A Starry Night	25
67	Columbia DB 8175	Pick Me/You Better Beware	30
67	Columbia DB 8318	Talkin' 'Bout Love/One Mint Julep	25
68	Direction 58-3511	Love In Them There Hills/Remember The Rain	15
67	Columbia SX 6206	NEW VIBRATIONS (LP)	75
69	Direction 8-63244	GREATEST HITS (LP)	30
72	RCA SF 8254	THE VIBRATIONS (LP)	20

(see also Jayhawks)

VIBRATORS

76	RAK RAK 245	We Vibrate/Whips And Furs	15
76	RAK RAK 246	Pogo Dancing/The Pose (as Vibrators with Chris Spedding)	10
77	RAK RAK 253	Bad Times/No Heart (unreleased, this price is for acetates, of which 2 copies exist)	200
77	Epic EPC 5302	Baby Baby/Into The Future (p/s)	10
77	Epic S PEC 5565	London Girls (studio)/London Girls (live) (promo only no p/s)	10
77	Epic EPC 5565	London Girls/Stiff Little Fingers (live) (p/s)	10

VIBRATORS (Jamaica)

MINT VALUE £

78	Epic SEPC 6137	Automatic Lover/Destroy (p/s)	7
78	Epic SEPC 6393	Judy Says (Knock You On The Head)/Pure Mania (p/s)	10
80	Rat Race RAT 2	Gimme Some Lovin'/Power Cry (live) (p/s, in slightly different colours)	7
77	Epic EPC 82097	PURE MANIA (LP)	30
78	Epic EPC 82495	V2 (LP, with inner lyric sleeve)	30
82	Anagram GRAM 002	GUILTY (LP)	15

(see also Boyfriends, Chris Spedding, Nazis Against Fascism, Substitute, Urban Dogs)

VIBRATORS (JAMAICA)

66	Doctor Bird DB 1036	Sloop John B/Amour	45

(see also Al & Vibrators, Wilbert Francis & Vibrators)

VIBRAVOID

09	Fruits De Mer Crustacean 07	KRAUT ROCK SENSATION EP (1st pressing, 300 copies on marbled blue vinyl)	45
09	Fruits De Mer Crustacean 07	KRAUT ROCK SENSATION EP (repressing, 300 copies on clear red vinyl)	35
10	Fruits De Mer Crustacean 10	WHAT COLOUR IS PINK EP (p/s, insert, 300 only, pink vinyl)	30

VIBRONICS

98	Deep Root ROOT 002	Jah Light, Jah Love/Dub	25
04	Jah Tubbys JT 10021	Terror/African Stone (10")	20

VIC & JOHN

94	Kent 6T 10	Why Did She Lie/PHIL TERRELL: Love Has Passed Me By	35

VICE CREEMS

78	Tiger GRRRR 1	Won't You Be My Girl?/01-01-212 (gatefold p/s)	30
79	Zig Zag ZZ22 001	Danger Love/Like A Tiger (p/s)	25

VICE VERSA

80	Neutron NT 001/PX 1092	MUSIC 4 (EP, poster p/s)	30

(see also Liza Strike)

VICEROYS

67	Island WI 3095	Lip And Tongue/DAWN PENN: When I'm Gonna Be Free	125
67	Coxsone CS 7031	Magadown/RICHARD ACE: Don't Let The Sun Catch You Crying	150
67	Studio One SO 2016	Lose And Gain (as Voiceroys)/SOUL BROTHERS: Honey Pot	130
67	Studio One SO 2025	Shake Up/NORMA FRASER: Telling Me Lies	75
68	Studio One SO 2064	Last Night/Ya Ho	250
68	Blue Cat BS 121	Fat Fish/OCTAVES: You're Gonna Lose	750
69	Punch PH 3	Jump In A Fire/Give To Get (as Voiceroys)	85
69	Crab CRAB 12	Work It/You Mean So Much To Me (B-side actually by Paragons)	60
73	Harry J. HJ 6658	Chucky (Parts 1 & 2)	7
74	Harry J. HJ 6669	Wheel & Jig (Parts 1 & 2)	8
76	Angen ANG 112	Marcus Marcus Garvey/Change Your Style	8
79	Music Hawk MH 01	Can't Stop Us/ROD TAYLOR: Jah Jah Calling (12")	40
84	Greensleeves GRED 146	New Clothes/New Clothes Rhythm/Bubblers Version (12")	15
12	Taxi TX 002	Heart Made Of Stone/SLY & ROBBIE: Heart Made Of Rock Dub (12" reissue)	12
82	Trojan TRLS 206	WE MUST UNITE (LP)	45
83	Csa CSLP 5	BRETHEREN AND SISTREN (LP)	50
84	Greensleeves GREL 57	CHANCERY LANE (LP)	15

(see also Richard Ace, Interns [Jamaica], Derrick Morgan, Vincent Gordon, Hub, Truth, Fact & Correct)

VICEROYS (U.K.)

70	Bullet BU 441	Chariot Coming/SYDNEY ALLSTARS: Stackata	25
70	Bullet BU 444	Power Control/SLICKERS: Dip Dip	25
70	Bullet BU 450	Come On Over/SYDNEY ALLSTARS: Version	20
70	Bullet BU 453	Fancy Clothes/BIGGIE: Jack And Jill	20
71	Bullet BU 470	Rebel Nyah/Feel The Spirit	20

VICE SQUAD

80	Riot City RIOT 1	Last Rockers/Living On Dreams/Latex Love (p/s, with poster)	15
81	Riot City RIOT 2	Resurrection/Young Blood/Hurricane (p/s)	6
80s	Vice Squad Fan Club	EVIL (EP, flexidisc)	12
81	Riot City ZEM 103	NO CAUSE FOR CONCERN (LP)	15
82	EMI ZEM 104	STAND STRONG STAND PROUD (LP, with inner)	15
84	Anagram GRAM 14	SHOT AWAY (LP)	15

(see also Sex Aids)

SID VICIOUS

79	Virgin V 2144	SID SINGS (LP, picture inner, with poster)	45
79	Virgin V 2144	SID SINGS (LP, picture inner, without poster)	15

(see also Sex Pistols)

MIKE VICKERS (ORCHESTRA)

65	Columbia DB 7657	On The Brink/The Puff Adder (as Mike Vickers & Orchestra)	50
65	Columbia DB 7657	On The Brink/The Puff Adder (as Mike Vickers & Orchestra) (DJ Copy)	100
66	Columbia DB 7825	Eleventy One/The Inkling	20
66	Columbia DB 7906	Morgan - A Suitable Case For Treatment/Gorilla Of My Dreams (as Mike Vickers Orchestra)	20
67	Columbia DB 8171	Air On A G-String/Proper Charles (as Mike Vickers Orchestra)	10
67	Columbia DB 8281	Captain Scarlet And The Mysterons/Kettle Of Fish	30
90s	Emidisc EMIDISC 101	On The Brink/SAINT ETIENNE: Emidisc Theme (promo only)	10
19	Electronic Sound ES 749	The Adding Machine/Elastic Band (p/s)	6
68	Columbia S(C)X 6180	I WISH I WERE A GROUP AGAIN (LP)	45

(see also Manfred Mann)

MACK VICKERY

60	Top Rank JAR 420	Fantasy/Hawaiian Stroll	12

VICKY

67	Philips BF 1565	Colours Of Love (Love Is Blue)/Who Can Tell	15
67	Philips BF 1599	Sunshine Boy/Tell Me	10
68	Philips BF 1631	Dance With Me Until Tomorrow/Give Me Your Hand	10

VICKY & JERRY

MINT VALUE £

VICKY & JERRY
60 HMV POP 715   Don't Cry/A Year Ago Tonight 20

VICTIM
78 Good Vibrations GOT 2   Strange Things By Night/Mixed Up World (wraparound p/s) 15
79 TJM TJM 13   THE VICTIM (EP, unreleased) 0
79 TJM TJM 14   Why Are Fire Engines Red/I Need You (p/s) 30
80 TJM TJM 15   The Teen Age/Junior Criminals/Hung On To Yourself (p/s) 25
80 Illuminated ILL 1   The Teen Age/Junior Criminals/Hung On To Yourself (p/s, reissue) 15

VICTIMIZE
79 I.M.E. IME 1   Baby Buyer/Hi Rising Failure (folded p/s) 70
80 I.M.E. IME 2   Where Did the Money Go/Innocence (p/s, some on white labels) 80

VICTIMS OF CHANCE
70 Stable SLE 8004   VICTIMS OF CHANCE (LP) 125

VICTIMS OF CIRCUMSTANCE
80s Double Vision DV 1   Very Little Glory/OPPOSITION: Wires (p/s) 10

VICTIMS OF PLEASURE
80 P.A.M. VOP 1   When You're Young/If I Was/Sporting Pastimes (p/s) 10

VICTIMS OF VICTIMISATION
87 Death DEAD 2   Kill Or Be Killed/As A Doornail (p/s) 18

TONY VICTOR
62 Decca F 11459   Dear One/There Was A Time 25
63 Decca F 11626   Thinking Of You/Hokey Cokey 12
63 Decca F 11708   In The Still Of The Night/Money 12

VICTORIA
71 Atlantic 2091 084   Tule's Blues/Helplessly Hoping 6
71 Atlantic 2400 176   VICTORIA (LP) 30
71 Atlantic 2466 008   SECRET OF THE BLOOM (LP) 45

VICTORIANS
64 Liberty LIB 55693   Oh What A Night For Love/Happy Birthday Blue 25

VICTORS (1)
65 Oriole CB 1984   Take This Old Hammer/Answer's No 15

VICTORS (2)
69 High Note HS 019   Reggae Buddy/Easy Squeeze 65
69 Studio One SO 2077   Things A-Come To Bump (A-side actually by BASES/LYRICS: Old Man Say 70
71 Escort ERT 846   Me A Tell Yuh/LLOYD'S ALL-STARS: More Echoe 45

VICTORY
82 Rods HOT 3   TAKING THE FIGHT (LP, with lyric insert) 60
(see also Keith Howard)

VIDELS
60 London HLI 9153   Mister Lonely/I'll Forget You 60

VIDEOS
81 Guardian GRC 85   Deo/Beautiful People/Him Or Me 15

VIDEO 2000
79 Philips (no cat no)   On The Move/On The Move (p/s) 10

VIENNA PHILHARMONIC ORCHESTRA
71 Decca F 13259   The Onedin Line Theme/Sable Dance 6

VIETNAM ALL STARS (ACTUALLY PRINCE BUSTER WITH UNKNOWN VOCALIST)
66 Rio R 109   The Toughest/ERROL DUNKLEY : Love Me Forever 100

VIETNAMESE ROSE
82 aaron B ROSE 1   Curtains You/Tinker Tailor 15

VIGILANTES
61 Pye International 7N 25082 Eclipse/Man In Space 20

VIGRASS & OSBORNE
72 UNI UNS 544   Men Of Learning/Forever Autumn 10
72 Uni UDLS 501   QUEUES (LP, gatefold) 40

(PAUL) VIGRASS
68 RCA RCA 1755   New Man/Curly 10
69 RCA RCA 1800   Suzie/Funky Piano Joe (as Vigrass) 8
69 RCA RCA 1857   Free Lorry Ride/Flying 15
70 RCA RCA 1911   Stop/Like It Never Was 8

VIKINGS (JAMAICA)
63 Island WI 035   Maggie Don't Leave Me/Henchmen (both actually with Victor Wong) 20
63 Island WI 065   Hallelujah/Helpin' Ages (actually by Maytals) 12
63 Island WI 075   Six And Seven Books Of Moses/Zacions (actually by Maytals) 25
63 Island WI 101   Never Grow Old/Irene (actually by Maytals) 30
63 Island WI 107   Just Got To Be/You Make Me Do (actually by Maytals) 20
63 Island WI 117   Fever/Cheer Up (actually by Maytals) 30
64 Island WI 167   Daddy/It's You (actually by Maytals) 20
64 Black Swan WI 423   Down By The Riverside/This Way 30
64 Black Swan WI 428   Treat Me Bad/Sitting On Top 25
64 Black Swan WI 430   Come Into My Parlour/I Am In Love 20
(see also Maytals, Flames [Jamaica], Bonnie & Skitto)

VIKINGS
66 Alp 595 011   Bad News Feeling/What Can I Do 30

VIKINGS INTERNATIONAL
70s Penthouse   VOLUME 1 (LP) 350

KURT VILE
15 Matador   B'lieve I'm Goin' Down (1-side etched, 100 only) 8
13 Matador OLE 998-0   WALKIN ON A PRETTY DAZE (2-LP, blue vinyl with stickers) 20
18 Matador OLE 1146-2   BOTTLE IT IN (2-LP, orange/yellow sunburst edition with stickers) 40

VILENESS
VILENESS
90 Noisome STENCH 3   March Of The Vile/Sex Is Vile (12", vile-scented p/s) 10
VILLAGE
69 Head HDS 4002   Man In The Moon/Long Time Coming 75
(see also Peter Bardens, Quiver)
VILLAGE SOUL CHOIR
70 Direction 58-4969   Catwalk/Country Walk 8
VILLAGERS
88 Hole In One HOLEIN 1   Marie/Don't Try (p/s, 500 only) 35
VILLAGERS/PARCEL OF ROGUES
73 Deroy (no cat. no.)   PARCEL OF FOLK (LP, private pressing, with insert) 100
CATERINA VILLALBA
60 Ember EMB S 104   Quando La Luna/Amore Fantastico (p/s) 6
NICK VILLARD
62 Pye 7N 15418   High Noon/Sail Ho 10
VILLIERS & GOLD
68 Polydor 56235   Of All The Young Girls/This East 20
RAE VINCE & VINCENTS
64 Piccadilly 7N 35211   One Fine Day/Little Girl, I'm Sad 10
GENE VINCENT (& BLUE CAPS)
78s
56 Capitol CL 14628   Race With The Devil/Gonna Back Up, Baby 25
57 Capitol CL 14681   Jumps, Giggles And Shouts/Wedding Bells (Are Breaking Up That Old Gang Of Mine) 30
57 Capitol CL 14693   Crazy Legs/Important Words 30
57 Capitol CL 14722   Bi-I-Bickey-Bi, Bo-Bo-Go/Five Days, Five Days 30
57 Capitol CL 14763   Lotta Lovin'/Wear My Ring 25
57 Capitol CL 14808   Dance To The Bop/I Got It 25
58 Capitol CL 14830   Walkin' Home From School/I Got A Baby 35
59 Capitol CL 15053   Right Now/The Night Is So Lonely 150
SINGLES
56 Capitol CL 14599   Be-Bop-A-Lula/Woman Love 40
56 Capitol CL 14628   Race With The Devil/Gonna Back Up, Baby 100
56 Capitol CL 14637   Bluejean Bop/Who Slapped John? 60
57 Capitol CL 14681   Jumps, Giggles And Shouts/Wedding Bells (Are Breaking Up That Old Gang Of Mine)
                                        (promo copy in p/s) 125
57 Capitol CL 14681   Jumps, Giggles And Shouts/Wedding Bells (Are Breaking Up That Old Gang Of Mine) 100
57 Capitol CL 14693   Crazy Legs/Important Words (in p/s) 75
57 Capitol CL 14693   Crazy Legs/Important Words 50
57 Capitol CL 14722   Bi-I-Bickey-Bi, Bo-Bo-Go/Five Days, Five Days (in p/s) 150
57 Capitol CL 14722   Bi-I-Bickey-Bi, Bo-Bo-Go/Five Days, Five Days 75
57 Capitol CL 14763   Lotta Lovin'/Wear My Ring 50
57 Capitol CL 14808   Dance To The Bop/I Got It 50
58 Capitol CL 14830   Walkin' Home From School/I Got A Baby (in p/s) 70
58 Capitol CL 14830   Walkin' Home From School/I Got A Baby 50
58 Capitol CL 14868   Baby Blue/True To You 40
58 Capitol CL 14908   Rocky Road Blues/Yes I Love You, Baby 40
58 Capitol CL 14935   Git It/Little Lover 40
59 Capitol CL 14974   Say Mama/Be Bop Boogie Boy 30
59 Capitol CL 15000   Who's Pushin' Your Swing/Over The Rainbow 20
59 Capitol CL 15035   Summertime/Frankie And Johnnie 25
59 Capitol CL 15053   Right Now/The Night Is So Lonely 20
59 Capitol CL 15099   Wild Cat/Right Here On Earth 15
60 Capitol CL 15115   My Heart/I've Got To Get You Yet 15
(Credited to Gene Vincent & Blue Caps.)
60 Capitol CL 15136   Pistol Packin' Mama (as Gene Vincent & Beat Boys)/Weeping Willow 15
60 Capitol CL 15169   Anna-Annabelle/Ac-Cent-Tchu-Ate The Positive 15
61 Capitol CL 15179   Maybe/Jezebel 15
61 Capitol CL 15185   If You Want My Lovin'/Mister Loneliness 15
61 Capitol CL 15202   She She Little Sheila/Hot Dollar 15
61 Capitol CL 15215   I'm Going Home (To See My Baby)/Love Of A Man 15
61 Capitol CL 15231   Unchained Melody/Brand New Beat (with The Blue Caps) 15
62 Capitol CL 15243   Lucky Star/Baby Don't Believe Him (with Dave Burgess Band) 18
62 Capitol CL 15264   Be-Bop-A-Lula/The King Of Fools (with Charles Blackwell Orchestra) 15
63 Capitol CL 15290   Held For Questioning/You're Still In My Heart (with Charles Blackwell Orch.) 15
63 Capitol CL 15307   Rip It Up/High Blood Pressure (unissued, demo copies only) 250
63 Capitol CL 15307   Crazy Beat/High Blood Pressure 40
63 Columbia DB 7174   Temptation Baby/Where Have You Been All My Life 20
64 Columbia DB 7218   Humpity Dumpity/A Love 'Em And Leave 'Em Kinda Guy 20
64 Columbia DB 7293   La-Den-Da Den-Da-Da/The Beginning Of The End 20
64 Columbia DB 7343   Private Detective/You Are My Sunshine (as Gene Vincent & Shouts) 20
66 London HLH 10079   Bird Doggin'/Ain't That Too Much 30
66 London HLH 10099   Lonely Street/I've Got My Eyes On You 30
68 Capitol CL 15546   Be-Bop-A-Lula/Say Mama 15
69 Dandelion S 4596   Be-Bop-A-Lula '69/Ruby Baby 10
70 Dandelion S 4974   White Lightning/Scarlet Ribbons (For Her Hair) 10
71 Kama Sutra 2013 018   The Day The World Turned Blue/High On Life (some with large centre) 10
73 Spark SRL 1091   Story Of The Rockers/Pickin' Poppies (push-out or solid centre) 10
87 Nighttracks SFNT 001   Nighttracks (Distant Drums/Be-Bop-A-Lula) (p/s, promo only with insert) 10

EPs

			MINT VALUE £
58	Capitol EAP 1-985	HOT ROD GANG	75
59	Capitol EAP 1-1059	A GENE VINCENT RECORD DATE	75
60	Capitol EAP 3-1059	A GENE VINCENT RECORD DATE PART 3	80
61	Capitol EAP 1-20173	IF YOU WANT MY LOVIN'	80
62	Capitol EAP 1-20354	RACE WITH THE DEVIL	80
63	Capitol EAP 1-20461	TRUE TO YOU	80
64	Capitol EAP 1-20453	THE CRAZY BEAT OF GENE VINCENT NO. 1	80
64	Capitol EAP 2-20453	THE CRAZY BEAT OF GENE VINCENT NO. 2	80
64	Capitol EAP 3-20453	THE CRAZY BEAT OF GENE VINCENT NO. 3	80
69	EMIdisc (no cat. no.)	LIVE & ROCKIN'! (fan club issue, mail-order, 99 only)	250
79	Rollin' Danny RD 1	RAINY DAY SUNSHINE (L.A. 1969 demos, 500 only)	12

ALBUMS : LPS

56	Capitol T 764	BLUEJEAN BOP! (original pressing with turquoise labels)	130
56	Capitol T 764	BLUEJEAN BOP! (later pressing with rainbow labels)	60
57	Capitol T 811	GENE VINCENT AND THE BLUECAPS (turquoise label)	125
57	Capitol T 811	GENE VINCENT AND THE BLUECAPS (rainbow label)	60
58	Capitol T 970	GENE VINCENT ROCKS! & THE BLUECAPS ROLL (turquoise label)	130
58	Capitol T 970	GENE VINCENT ROCKS! & THE BLUECAPS ROLL (later rainbow label)	60
59	Capitol T 1059	A GENE VINCENT RECORD DATE	70
59	Capitol T 1207	SOUNDS LIKE GENE VINCENT	70
60	Capitol T 1342	CRAZY TIMES! (mono)	60
60	Capitol ST 1342	CRAZY TIMES! (stereo)	70
63	Capitol T 20453	THE CRAZY BEAT OF GENE VINCENT	65
64	Columbia 33SX 1646	SHAKIN' UP A STORM (as Gene Vincent & The Shouts)	60
67	London HA-H 8333	GENE VINCENT	50
67	Capitol T 20957	THE BEST OF GENE VINCENT ('rainbow' label; reissue with pink label £12)	20
68	Capitol ST 21144	THE BEST OF GENE VINCENT VOL. 2 ('rainbow' label; reissue with pink label £12)	20
70	Dandelion 63754	I'M BACK AND I'M PROUD (gatefold sleeve)	30
71	Kama Sutra 2316 005	THE DAY THE WORLD TURNED BLUE	20
71	Kama Sutra 2316 009	IF YOU COULD ONLY SEE ME TODAY	20
87	Charly BOX 108	GENE VINCENT: THE CAPITOL YEARS '56-'63 (10-LP box set with 36-page booklet; later remastered and reissued with slimmer box, 1989)	50
90	EMI CDGV 1	THE GENE VINCENT BOX SET (Complete Capitol & Columbia Recordings, 1956-64) (6-CD set)	20

RORY VINCENT

73	Columbia SCXA 9254	SINGS THE MUSIC OF WLODEK GULGOWSKI (LP)	20

CAROLE VINCI

78	EMI EMI 2801	Vivre/Souffire Et Sourire	12

JOEY VINE

65	Immediate IM 017	Down And Out/The Out Of Towner	30

VINEGAR JOE

72	Island ILPS 9183	VINEGAR JOE (LP)	30
72	Island ILPS 9214	ROCK 'N ROLL GYPSIES (LP, gatefold sleeve)	25
73	Island ILPS 9262	SIX STAR GENERAL (LP, gatefold sleeve, inner)	25

(see also Dada, Elkie Brooks)

VINES (1)

02	Heavenly HVNLP 36	HIGHLY EVOLVED (LP)	25
04	Capitol 724358433814	WINNING DAYS (LP)	20
06	Heavenly HVNLP 56	VISION VALLEY (LP)	25

VINES (2)

04	Goldmine G2K 45 146	After The Rain/So Be It	6

VINEYARD

74	Decca F13518	Ghost Train/Unicorns & Minotaurs	8

LEROY VINNEGAR

63	Contemporary LAC 570	LEROY WALKS AGAIN! (LP)	30

EDDIE 'MR. CLEANHEAD' VINSON

64	Riverside RLP 3302	BACK DOOR BLUES (LP)	40
72	Philips 6369 406	THE ORIGINAL CLEANHEAD (LP)	18

(see also Wynonie Harris)

V. VINSTRICK & J.J. ALLSTARS

68	Doctor Bird DB 1167	Love Is Not A Game/CINDERELLA: The Way I See You	65

IAN VINT

62	Columbia DB 7514	Long Lonely Nights/Satin	7
64	Columbia 33SX 1649	TELL ME WHY (LP)	25

BOBBY VINTON

61	Fontana H 307	Little Lonely One/Corrine Corrina	10
62	London HLU 9592	I Love You The Way You Are/CHUCK & JOHNNY: You Are My Girl	10
63	Columbia DB 7110	Blue Velvet/Is There A Place	10
64	Columbia DB 7422	Mr Lonely/The Bell That Couldn't Jingle	15
62	Columbia SEG 8212	YOUNG IN HEART (EP)	20
64	Columbia SEG 8363	SONGS OF CHRISTMAS (EP)	25
63	Columbia 33SX 1517	SINGS THE BIG ONES (LP)	25
62	Columbia 33SX1465	ROSES ARE RED (LP)	25
63	Columbia 33SX 1566	BLUE ON BLUE (LP)	25
63	Columbia 33SX 1611	MY HEART BELONGS TO ONLY YOU (LP)	25
65	Columbia 33SX1725	LAUGHING ON THE OUTSIDE (LP)	25

MATT VINYL

77	Housewife's Choice	Useless Tasks (p/s)	8

VIOLATORS

MINT VALUE £

VIOLATORS
82	No Future OI 9	Gangland/Fugitive (p/s, with insert)	20
82	No Future OI 19	Summer Of '81/Live Fast Die Young (p/s)	20
83	No Future FS 2	Life On The Red Line/Crossing The Sangsara (p/s)	6
83	No Future OI 26	DIE WITH DIGNITY EP (12")	50

VIOLENT CIRCUIT
85	Circuit 1	Vision Of Love/All Our Fatal Charms/Of Dust	8

VIOLENT FEMMES
83	Rough Trade ROUGH 55	VIOLENT FEMMES (LP)	30
84	Slash SLAP 1	HALLOWED GROUND (LP)	15

VIOLENTS
63	HMV POP 1130	Alpen Ros/Ghia	18

VIOLENT THIMBLE
67	Polydor 56217	Gentle People Parts 1 & 2	15

VIPERS (SKIFFLE GROUP)
56	Parlophone R 4238	Ain't You Glad/Pick A Bale Of Cotton	20
57	Parlophone R 4261	Don't You Rock Me Daddy-O/10,000 Years Ago	20
57	Parlophone R 4286	Jim Dandy/Hi Liley, Liley Lo	15
57	Parlophone R 4289	The Cumberland Gap/Maggie May	15
57	Parlophone R 4308	Streamline Train/Railroad Steam Boat	15
57	Parlophone R 4351	Homing Bird/Pay Me My Money Down	15
57	Parlophone R 4371	Skiffle Party Medley Parts 1 & 2	15
58	Parlophone R 4393	Baby Why?/No Other Baby (as Vipers)	15
58	Parlophone R 4435	Make Ready For Love/Nothing Will Ever Change (My Love For You)(as Vipers)	15
58	Parlophone R 4484	Summertime Blues/Liverpool Blues (as Vipers)	35
58	Parlophone R 4484	Summertime Blues/Liverpool Blues (as Vipers) (78)	20
57	Parlophone GEP 8615	SKIFFLE MUSIC VOL. 1 (EP)	20
57	Parlophone GEP 8626	SKIFFLE MUSIC VOL. 2 (EP)	20
57	Parlophone GEP 8655	SKIFFLING ALONG WITH THE VIPERS (EP)	20
57	Parlophone PMD 1050	COFFEE BAR SESSION (10" LP)	60

(see also Jet Harris & Tony Meehan, Shadows, Wally Whyton, Sharkey Todd & Monsters)

VIPERS
78	Mulligan LUNS 718	I've Got You/No Such Thing (p/s)	10

VIPPS
66	CBS 202031	Wintertime/Anyone	80

(see also VIPS)

VIPS
64	RCA RCA 1427	Don't Keep Shouting At Me/She's So Good	100
66	Island WI 3003	I Wanna Be Free/Don't Let It Go	50
67	Island WIP 6005	Straight Down To The Bottom/In A Dream	80

(see also Vipps, Art, Spooky Tooth, Felder's Orioles, Timebox, Patto, Baron & His Pounding Piano, Keith Emerson)

V.I.P.S
78	Bust SOL 3	MUSIC FOR FUNSTERS (EP)	20
79	Rok ROK V/VI	Can't Let You Go/URBAN DISTURBANCE: Wild Boys In Cortinas	25
80	Gem GEMS 25	Causing Complications/Run Run Belinda/Love Is A Golden Word (p/s)	6
80	Gem GEMS 43	I Need Somebody To Love (Could It Be You?)/One More Chance// Stuttgart Special/Who Knows/Janine (double pack, stickered p/s)	8
81	Gem GEMS 47	Things Aren't What They Used To Be/I Thought You Were My Friend (p/s)	6

(see also Mood Six, Jed Dmochowski)

VIRGIL BROTHERS
69	Parlophone R 5787	Temptation 'Bout To Get Me/Look Away	15
69	Parlophone R 5802	Good Love/When You Walk Away	6

VIRGIN DANCE
84	Spartan SP10	Desire/Make Love (p/s)	8

VIRGINIANS
63	Pye International 7N 25175	Limbo Baby/Greenback Dollar	10

VIRGINIA TREE
75	Minstrel 0001	FRESH OUT (LP)	50

(see also Shirley Kent, Ghost)

VIRGINIA WOLF
86	Atlantic A 9459	Waiting For Your Love/Take A Chance (p/s)	10

VIRGINIA WOLVES
66	Stateside SS 563	Stay/B.L.T.	50
66	Stateside SS 563	Stay/B.L.T. (DJ copy)	100

VIRGIN PRUNES
81	Baby BABY 001	TWENTY TENS (EP)	15
81	Rough Trade RT 072	Moments Of Mine (Despite Straight Lines)/In The Greylight/War/Moments Of Mine (Despite Straight Lines) (1st issue in blue p/s with insert)	15
81	Rough Trade RT 072	Moments Of Mine (Despite Straight Lines)/In The Greylight/War/Moments Of Mine (Despite Straight Lines) (later issue in black p/s without insert)	10
81	Rough Trade RT 89	A New Form Of Beauty 1; Sandpaper Lullaby/Sleep Fantasy Dreams (p/s)	15
82	Rough Trade TI COPY 007	A New Form Of Beauty 4:Din Glorious (cassette)	25
82	Rough Trade RT 106	Pagan Lovesong/Dave-id Is Dead (p/s)	8
82	Rough Trade 12 RT 106	Pagan Lovesong (Vibe Akimbo)/Pagan Lovesong/Dave-id Is Dead (12", p/s)	10
82	Rough Trade ROUGH 49	...IF IF DIE, I DIE (LP)	15
87	Baby BABY 011	HERESIE (10", double pack, gatefold p/s, 1st 1,000 on clear vinyl)	15
87	Baby BABY 011	HERESIE (10", double pack, gatefold p/s)	10

(see also Gavin Friday)

VIRGIN SLEEP
67	Deram DM 146	Love/Halliford House	70
68	Deram DM 173	Secret/Comes A Time	80

VIRGO

MINT VALUE £

VIRGO
89	Radical RADICAL 1	DO YOU KNOW WHO YOU ARE? (12" EP p/s)	20
89	Radical Records VIRG01	VIRGO (LP)	35

VIRTUE
85	Other OTH 1	We Stand To Fight/High Treason (p/s)	20

VIRTUES (JAMAICA)
65	Island WI 196	Your Wife And Mother/Amen (actually with Ambassadors)	40
68	Doctor Bird DB 1164	High Tide/RUPIE EDWARDS & VIRTUES: Burning Love	60
68	Doctor Bird DB 1166	Sweet Nanny/RUPIE EDWARDS : Falling In Love	70

(see also Lloyd & Devon)

VIRTUES (U.S.)
59	HMV POP 621	Guitar Boogie Shuffle/Guitar In Orbit	15
59	HMV POP 637	Flippin' In/Shufflin' Along	15

FRANK VIRTUOSO ROCKETS
58	Melodisc MEL 1386	Rollin' And A-Rockin'/Rock - Good Bye Mambo (red label, tri centre, export issue)	30
58	Melodisc MEL 1386	Rollin' And Rockin'/Toodle-Oo Kangaroo (green label, round centre)	15

VISAGE
79	Radar ADA 48	Tar/Frequency 7 (p/s)	15
81	Polydor POSPX 194	Fade To Grey/The Steps (12", p/s)	15
81	Polydor POSPX 236	Mind Of A Toy (Dance Mix)/We Move (Dance Mix)/Frequency 7 (Dance Mix) (12", p/s)	10
82	Polydor POSPX 523	Pleasure Boys (Dance Mix)/The Anvil (Dance Mix) (12", 800 only)	10
82	Polydor POSPV 523	Der Amboss/The Anvil (Mix) (12", stickered plain black sleeve & labels, promo only)	10

(see also Rich Kids, Steve Strange, Strange Cruise, Midge Ure, Ultravox)

TONY VISCONTI
74	Regal Zonophone RZ 3089	I Remember Brooklyn/Sitting In A Field Of Heather	20

(see also Dib Cochran & Earwigs)

VISCOUNTS
60	Pye 7N 15249	That's All Right/Rockin' Little Angel	6
60	Pye 7N 15287	Shortnin' Bread/Fee-Fi-Fo-Fum	7
61	Pye 7N 15323	Money Is The Root Of All Evil/One-Armed Bandit	6
61	Pye 7N 15344	Banned In Boston/Moonlight Promises	6
61	Pye 7N 15356	Joe Sweeney/Honey Come On And Dance With Me	6
61	Pye 7N 15379	Who Put The Bomp (In The Bomp Bomp Bomp)/What Am I saying	10
61	Pye 7N 15414	Mama's Doing The Twist/I'm Going - But I'll Be Back	7
62	Pye 7N 15431	One Of The Guys/Dear Mary Brown	6
62	Pye 7N 15445	Everybody's Got a Ya Ya/A Lot of Livin' To Do	8
63	Pye 7N 15479	That Stranger Used To Be My Girl/Silent Night	6
63	Pye 7N 15510	Don't Let Me Cross Over/I'm Coming Home	7
63	Pye 7N 15336	It's You/I'll Never Get over You	8
63	Columbia DB 7146	I Don't Care What People Say/Roll On Little Darlin'	6
60	Pye NEP 24132	VISCOUNTS' HIT PARADE (EP)	20

VISCOUNTS (U.S.)
59	Top Rank JAR 254	Harlem Nocturne/Dig	15
60	Top Rank JAR 388	The Touch (Le Grisbi)/Chug-A-Lug	15
60	Top Rank JAR 502	Night Train/Summertime	18
64	Columbia DB 7253	Where Do You Belong/Kiss Me	8
61	Top Rank JKP 3005	VISCOUNTS ROCK (EP)	35

VISION
86	PRT 7P 366	Who's That Stranger/Breakdown	10

VISIONS
69	Grape GR 3009	Captain Hook/The Girl	100

(see also King Horror)

VISIONS IN WINTER
84	VIW SRT4KS 226	The Calling/Secret Garden	10

VISITORS (1)
78	NRG SRTS/NRG 002	Take It Or Leave It/No Compromise	25
79	Deep Heat DEEP ONE	Electric Heat/Moth/One Line (p/s)	40
80	Departure RAPTURE 1	Empty Rooms/The Orcadian Visitors (foldover p/s)	15

VISITORS (2)
87	Sha La La BA BA BA BA 8	Goldmining/MAGIC SHOP: It's True (flexidisc, p/s, free with Simply Thrilled & other fanzines. With magazine)	10

VITAL
81	Cosmic Enterprises KK001	Real Life/Sinking Ships (p/s)	12

VITAL DISORDERS
81	Lowther International VD 1	PRAMS EP: Snatcher/Tough TImes/'Prams (6 different p/s variations)	20
82	Vital Disorders VD2	Zombie/Wargames (p/s)	10
83	Vital Disorders VD3	Some People/Christmas Island Calypso (p/s)	15

VITAL DUB
77	Virgin V 2055	WELL CHARGED (LP, green two virgins label)	20

VITAL FORCE
87	Buce BUCE 1	Roll The Dice/Poor Little Rich Boy (no p/s)	25

VITAL ORGANS
82	Airship AP 594	Radio Active/Glastonbury (p/s)	15

VITAL REMAINS
92	Deaf DEAF 9	LET US PRAY (LP)	25

VITAL SIGNS
83	Powerstation PS 1	Tradiing In Guilt/Miracles	80

VITAMIN B12
00	Private Press (No Cat. No.)	VITAMIN B12 (2-LP, 99 copies only)	20

Miroslav VITOUS

MINT VALUE £

MIROSLAV VITOUS
79   Warner Bros. K 17448 T   New York City/Basic Laws (12") 40
76   Warner Bros. K56219   MAGIC SHEPHERD (LP) 15

VIVEK
07   On The Edge OTE 001   Natural Mystic/Sunshine (12") 18
13   System SYSTM 001   Asteroids/Over My Head/Over My Head (Om Unit Remix) (12") 40
13   System SYSTM 003   Mantra/Show Me/Soundman VIP/Asteroids VIP (2 x 12") 30
15   System SYSTM 009   Square Up/Slippin' (12") 35
18   System SYSTM 010   94/Namaste (10") 18

AMOR VIVI
70   Big Shot BI 534   Dirty Dog/Round And Round The Moon 8

VLADO & ISOLDA
84   Ariola 106 500   Ciao Amore (English)/Ciao Amore (Croatian) 10

V-NECK
95   Emote MOTE 004   Auto/Quasi/Semi/Uni (12") 60
96   Emote MOTE 005   Woh Yeh/Burning The Toast/Woh Yeh (Version)/Dubbing The Toast (12") 20
97   Emote MOTE 006   At The Door (Remix)/(Original)/Red Eye Dub (12" as V Neck vs Zion Train) 40

CRISTIAN VOGEL
94   Ferox FER 004   NARCO SYNTHESIS EP (12", plain sleeve) 25
94   Mosquito MSQ 01   WE EQUATE MACHINES WITH FUNKINESS EP (12", custom sleeve) 25
95   Mosquito MSQ 03   ARTISTS IN CHARGE OF EXPERT SYSTEMS EP (12", custom sleeve) 20
95   Solid SOL 002   DEFUNKT EP (12". Three untitled tracks) 20
96   Solid SOL 004   The Visit/Spoke/Small Dogs (12") 30
(see also Blue Arsed Fly)

VOGUES (U.K.)
66   Columbia DB 7985   Younger Girl/Lies 18
(see also Llan)

VOGUES (U.S.)
65   London HLU 9996   You're The One/Some Words 20
66   London HLU 10014   Five O'Clock World/Nothing To Offer You 20
66   King KG 1035   Magic Town/Humpty Dumpty 25
68   Reprise RS 20766   My Special Angel/I Keep It Hid 6
68   Reprise RS 20686   Turn Around Look At Me/Then 6
69   Reprise RS 20788   Till/I Will 6
69   London HLG 10247   Five O'Clock World/You're The One 15
69   Reprise RS 20820   Earth Angel/P.S. I Love You 6
69   Reprise RS 23366   No, Not Much/You Were Too Good To Me 6
66   King KGL 4003   MEET THE VOGUES (LP) 45
66   King KGL 4006   FIVE O'CLOCK WORLD (LP) 40
69   Reprise RSLP 6314   TURN AROUND, LOOK AT ME (LP) 20
69   Reprise RSLP 6326   TILL (LP) 15

VOICE
66   Mercury MF 905   Train To Disaster/Truth 250
(see also Karl Stuart & Profile, Profile, Miller Anderson)

VOICE OF PROGRESS
82   Negus Roots NERLP 003   MINI BUS DRIVER (LP) 30

VOICE OF THE PUPPETS
80   IS/VP/1044   I Don't Want To Know/You're All I Wanted (And A Car) (poster p/s) 300

STEVE VOICE
79   EMI RB 102   UFO/Radio Blue 6

VOICES IN LATIN
68   Morgan MR 104P   VOICE IN LATIN (LP) 60

VOID
82   Hole In Space VOID 1   Into The Void/I Want You (no p/s) 40

STERLING VOID
88   FFRR FFR 21   Runaway Girl/It's All right (die-cut sleeve) 8
89   DJ International/CBS   IT'S ALL RIGHT (LP) 18
      4661461

VOIDS
66   Polydor BM 56073   Come On Out/I'm In A Fix 120

WES VOIGHT
59   Parlophone R 4586   I'm Movin' In/I'm Ready To Go Steady 80
(see also Chip Taylor)

VOIZ
77   Pilgrim/Grapevine GRA 110   BOANERGES (LP, with insert) 25

HOWARD VOKES COUNTRY BOYS
62   Starlite STEP 27   HOWARD VOKES COUNTRY BOYS (EP) 15
63   Starlite STEP 37   MOUNTAIN GUITAR (EP) 15

VOLCANOS
61   Philips PB 1098   Ruby Duby Du/Redhead 20
61   Philips PB 1113   Tightrope/Great Imposter 20
62   Philips PB 1246   Polaris/Scotch Mist 20
60   Philips BBE 12432   THE VOLCANOS (EP) 100

VOLTZ
82   Airship PP 580   KNIGHT'S FALL (LP) 70

VOLUMES
62   Fontana 270 109TF   I Love You/Dreams 80
63   London HL 9733   Sandra/Teenage Paradise 75

VOLUNTEERS (1)
63   Parlophone R 5088   Farther Along/Little David 8

VON TRAP FAMILY

MINT VALUE £

(see also Karol Keyes)
VON TRAP FAMILY
80 Woronzow W 001 — Brand New Thrill/Dreaming/No Reflexes (p/s, 500 only) 40

(see also Bevis Frond)
ERIC VON SCHMIDT
68 Transatlantic PR 7384 — ERIC SINGS VON SCHMIDT (LP) 80

VON SUDENFED
07 Domino WIGLP 190 — TROMATIC REFLEXXIONS (2-LP) 25

(see also The Fall, Mouse On Mars)
VONTASTICS
66 Chess CRS 8043 — Day Tripper/My Baby 25
67 Stateside SS 2002 — Lady Love/When My Baby Comes Back Home 65
67 Stateside SS 2002 — Lady Love/When My Baby Comes Back Home (DJ Copy) 85

VOOMINS
65 Polydor 56001 — If You Don't Come Back/March Of The Voomins 35

VOXPOPPERS
58 Mercury 7MT 202 — The Last Drag/Wishing For Your Love 30
58 Mercury 7MT 202 — The Last Drag/Wishing For Your Love (78) 25
58 Mercury MEP 9533 — VOXPOPPERS (EP) 150

VOYAGER (1)
85 Fighting Cock — Run Away Heart/Don't Hold Back (p/s) 15

VOYAGER (2)
95 Lucky Spin LSR 018 — PART 1: Knowledge/Haunted (12") 25
95 Lucky Spin INT 002 — PART 2: Eastern Promise/Voyager (12") 15

V2
78 Bent SMALL BENT 1 — Speed Freak/Nothing To Do/That's It (800 only, later reissued on red vinyl) 40
78 Bent SMALL BENT 1 — Speed Freak/Nothing To Do/That's It (red vinyl reissue) 15
79 TJM TJM 1 — Man In The Box/When The World Isn't There (12", p/s) 20
79 TJM TJM 6 — Is Anybody Out There? (unissued) 0
70s Groove ZOE 1 — Gee Whiz It's You/Face In The Crowd (p/s, stamped white labels) 30

VULCAN
73 Epic SEPC 1763 — Much To Young/Action Man 6

VULCANS
72 Big Shot BI 612 — Dr. Spock/Joe Kidd 10
73 Big Shot BI 615 — Red Herring/Vulcanised 10
72 Trojan TR 7863 — Star Trek/Back A Yard 20
73 Trojan TRLS 53 — STAR TREK (LP) 70

VULCAN'S HAMMER
73 Brown BVH 1 — TRUE HEARTS AND SOUND BOTTOMS (LP, with insert) 450

VULTURES
79 Rubber Connection SP 522 — Time Let's Go/Is This A Man (p/s, with insert & sticker) 15

VYLLIES
86 Fun After All FAA 103 — Ahia/The Sky Is Full Of Stitches (p/s) 8
86 Fun After All AFTER 2 — LILTH (LP) 25

W

PHIL WACHSMANN
85 Bead Records BEAD 23 — WRITING IN WATER (LP) 20

PHILIPP WACHSMANN, RICHARD BESWICK & TONY WREN
77 Bead Records BEAD 7 — SPARKS OF THE DESIRE MAGNETO (LP, with insert) 30

WACKERS (1)
63 Oriole CB 1902 — I Wonder Why/Why Can't It Happen To Me 25
64 Piccadilly 7N 35195 — Love Or Money/Hooka Tooka 15
64 Piccadilly 7N 35210 — The Girl Who Wanted Fame/You're Forgetting 15

ADAM WADE
61 HMV POP 843 — Take Good Care Of Her/Sleepy Time Gal 10
63 Columbia DB 4986 — Don't Let Me Cross Over/Rain From The Skies 70
60 HMV 7EG 8620 — AND THEN CAME ADAM (EP) 15
64 Columbia SEG 8316 — FOUR FILM SONGS (EP) 15
61 HMV CLP 1451 — ADAM AND EVENING (LP) 30

CLIFF WADE
69 Morgan Bluetown BT 1S — You've Never Been To My House/Sister 30

JOHNNY WADE
60 HMV POP 757 — Funny Thing/Shadow Love 8

WAYNE WADE
75 Mango MAN 1005 — Black Is Our Colour/PROPHETS ALLSTARS: Upsetters Vengeance 20
77 Grove Music GMDM 2 — Happy Go Lucky Girl/PRINCE POMPADO: Jamaican Girl/WAYNE WADE: I Kissed A Rose (12", p/s) 10
79 Cha Cha CHAD 34 — Tell Me What Going On/WAILING SOULS: Rudeboy Say Him Bad (12") 30
80 Pirate PIR 003 — African Monica/Down In Iran (12", yellow vinyl) 35
81 Greensleeves GRED 52 — Poor And Humble/BUNNY LIE LIE: Babylonian (12") 35
78 Grove Music GMLP 3 — DANCING TIME (LP) 30

WELLINGTON WADE
63 Oriole CB 1857 — Let's Turkey Trot/It Ain't Necessarily So 40

(see also Ian & Zodiacs)

WADSWORTH MANSION

MINT VALUE £

WADSWORTH MANSION
71 A&M AMS 842   Sweet Mary/What's On Tonight 6

WAGADU
77 Rokel SD RK01   Sweet Mother/Aki Special (12", as Wagadu Gu) 15
79 Rokel ROK 12   Freetown Calypso/Easy Dancin'.. 25

WAGES OF SIN
70 CBS 4971   West Virginia/Hey Hey Hey (Well I'm On My Way) 10

ADRIAN WAGNER
74 Atlantic K 50082   DISTANCES BETWEEN US (LP, with Robert Calvert)... 22
(see also Robert Calvert)

ROBERT WAGNER
57 London HLU 8491   Almost Eighteen/So Young 10

CHUCK WAGON
79 A&M AMS 7450   Rock 'n' Roll Won't Go Away/The Spy In My Face (p/s, black vinyl)................. 10
79 A&M AMS 7450   Rock 'n' Roll Won't Go Away/The Spy In My Face (p/s, purple vinyl)............... 15
(see also Dickies)

WAGON CHRIST
94 Rising High RSN LP 18   PHAT LAB. NIGHTMARE (2-LP) 40
95 Rising High RSN LP 30   THROBBING POUCH (2-LP) 30
98 Personal/Virgin V2863   TALLY HO! (2-LP).. 30

PORTER WAGONER
64 RCA Victor RCX 7157   A LITTLE SLICE OF LIFE (EP) 10
64 RCA Victor RCX 7158   Y'ALL COME (EP) 10

WAHIB
82 Hits From Heaven HIT 1   Brings On The Tears/Grey Blues.. 15

WAIKIKIS
61 Palette PG 9025   Hawaii Tattoo/Waikiki Welcome 7
65 Pye Intl. 7N 26286   Hawaii Tattoo/Waikiki Welcome (reissue) 12

BUNNY WAILER
76 Island WIP 6347   Dream Land/Dream Land Dub 10
76 Island BUNNY 1   Blackheart Man/Amagideon (12").. 28
77 Island IPR 2003   Get Up Stand Up/This Train (12") 20
78 Island IPR 2015   Love Fire/Love's Version (12").. 15
78 Island IPR 2025   Roots, Radics, Rockers and Reggae/Fig Tree/Armagideon (12")................... 25
81 Solomonic SM 01   Rise & Shine/Riding 35
81 Solomonic SM07   Rise & Shine/Solomonic Dub (12") 50
82 Solomonic BWD 017   Collie Man/Trouble On The Road 12
83 Solomonic SM 018   Boderation/THE SOLOMONIC PLAYERS - Badder ridim (12")....................... 25
76 Island ILPS 9415   BLACKHEART MAN (LP, gatefold) 30
80 Island ISLP 9629   SINGS THE WAILERS (LP).. 18
81 Solomic SMDUBLP 002   DUB DISCO VOL. 2 (LP) 18

WAILERS (U.S.)
59 London HL 8958   Tall Cool One/Road-Runner 25
59 London HL 8958   Tall Cool One/Road-Runner (78)... 30
59 London HL 8994   Mau-Mau/Dirty Robber 150
59 London HL 8994   Mau-Mau/Dirty Robber (78) 70
64 London HL 9892   Tall Cool One/Road-Runner (reissue)... 10

WAILING SOULS
70 Banana BA 305   Row Fisherman Row/Thou Shalt Not Steal 60
70 Banana BA 307   Back Out/Pack Your Things.. 50
71 Banana BA 335   Walk Walk Walk/KING SPORTY: Love Me - Version (B-side actually by Denis Alcapone) 60
71 Green Door GD 4014   Harbour Shark/Harbour Shark - Version 25
76 Conflict 301   Back Out/Dub 12
78 Greensleeves GRED 1   War/Jah Give Us Life (12") 20
80 Greensleeves GRED 043   Kingdom Rise Kingdom Fall/A Day Will Come (12").. 35
80 Taxi IPR 2044   Old Broom/Bredda Gravilicious/Sweet Sugar Plum (12") 25
81 Cha Cha CHAD 34   Rudeboy Say Him Bad/WAYNE WADE: Tell Me What Going On (12") 30
81 Greensleeves GRED 51   Who No Waan Come/AL CAMPBELL: Unfaithful Children (12")..................... 35
81 Cha Cha CHAD 32   Penny I Love You/EARL SIXTEEN: Black Man Time (12")................................ 25
81 Cha Cha CHAD 51   Grabbing And Running/Dub 25
82 Greensleeves GRED 111   They Don't Know Jah/Sticky Stay (12")... 30
82 Upfront UPF 001   Take We Back (feat Ranking Trevor)/RANKING TREVOR: Yard Oh (12").... 15
82 Upfront UPF 004   Take A Taste/JOHNNY RINGO: Don't Know Much (12")................................. 15
83 Greensleeves GRED 115   Bounce Back/Sweetie (12") 15
83 Greensleeves GRED 125   Water Pumpee/Shall Up (12") 18
84 Greensleeves GRED 152   War Deh Round A Shop John/Peace And Love Shall Reign (12") 30
79 Island ILPS 9523   WILD SUSPENSE (LP) 20
81 Greensleeves GREL 21   FIRE HOUSE ROCK (LP) 25
83 Greensleeves GREL 47   INCHPINCHERS (LP) 20
(see also Denis Alcapone, Tuff Gong All Stars)

CHERRY WAINER
58 Pye 7N 15161   Itchy Twitchy Feeling/Cerveza 10
59 Pye 7N 15197   The Happy Organ/Spanish Marching Song... 7
59 Pye 7N 15217   The Song Of Lotus Lee/Iced Coffee 6
59 Top Rank JAR 253   I'll Walk The Line/Saturday Night In Tia Juana 8
60 Columbia DB 4528   Happy Like A Bell (Ding Dong)/Money (That's What I Want)......................... 20
63 Honey Hit TB 128   Sleepwalk/Red River Rock (with Red Price Combo, with p/s).......................... 10
59 Pye NEP 24099   CHERRY WAINER (EP) 15
60 Top Rank BUY 042   WALTZES IN SPRINGTIME (LP).. 15
(see also Red Price Combo)

Phil WAINMAN

MINT VALUE £

PHIL WAINMAN
65	Columbia DB 7615	Hear Me A Drummer Man/Hear His Drums	30
68	Fontana TF 978	Going Going Gone/Hey Paradiddle	300

LOUDON WAINWRIGHT III
71	Atlantic 2400 103	ALBUM I (LP)	22
72	Atlantic K 40272	ALBUM II (LP)	15
79	Radar RAD 24	A LIVE ONE (LP)	15

WAITING FOR THE SUN
78	Profile GMOR 167	WAITING FOR THE SUN (LP, private pressing)	35

(see also After The Fire)

WAITRESSES
81	Ze Records WIP 6821	Christmas Wrapping/Hangover (stock copy promo, in bespoke Ze records paper wrapping)	15

TOM WAITS
79	Asylum K 12347	Somewhere/Red Shoes By The Drugstore	8
86	Island ISD 260	In The Neighbourhood/Singapore//Tango Till They're Sore/Rain Dogs (double pack, p/s)	8
85	Island 12IS 260	In The Neighbourhood/Singapore//Tango Till They're Sore/Rain Dogs (12")	15
73	Asylum SYM 9007	CLOSING TIME (LP, with insert)	30
74	Asylum SYM 9012	THE HEART OF SATURDAY NIGHT (LP)	30
75	Asylum SYSP 903	NIGHTHAWKS AT THE DINER (2-LP, gatefold sleeve)	25
76	Asylum K 53030	CLOSING TIME (LP, reissue)	20
76	Asylum K 53035	THE HEART OF SATURDAY NIGHT (LP, 'door' label)	30
77	Asylum K 53050	SMALL CHANGE (LP, 'sky' label)	30
77	Asylum K 53068	FOREIGN AFFAIRS (LP, with inner sleeve)	30
79	Asylum K 53088	BLUE VALENTINE (LP, gatefold sleeve)	30
80	Asylum K 52252	HEARTATTACK AND VINE (LP, with inner sleeve)	20
81	Elektra K 52316	BOUNCED CHEQUES (LP)	20
82	Island ILPS 9762	SWORDFISHTROMBONES (LP, inner 'blue' Island sleeve)	25
83	Island TW1	A CONVERSATION WITH TOM WAITS (LP promo interview disc)	40
84	Asylum 960321-1	ASYLUM YEARS (2-LP)	20
85	Island ILPS 9803	RAIN DOGS (LP)	30
85	Island ILPM 9762	SWORDFISHTROMBONES (LP, repressing, white 'palm tree' label, generic Island inner)	15
86	Island ITW 3	FRANK'S WILD YEARS (LP, gatefold)	30
88	Island ITW4	BIG TIME (LP)	25
91	Island 212370	NIGHT ON EARTH (LP)	35
92	Island ILPS 9993	BONE MACHINE (LP)	80
93	Island ILPS 8021	BLACK RIDER (LP, with inner)	80

(see also Roy Orbison)

WAKE (1)
69	Pye 7N 17813	Angelina/So Happy	15
70	Carnaby CNS 4010	Live Today Little Girl/Days Of Emptiness	15
70	Carnaby CNS 4014	Boys In The Band/To Make You Happy	12
70	Carnaby CNS 4016	Noah/To Make You Happy	12
71	Carnaby 6151 001	Linda/Got My Eyes On You	12
70	Carnaby CNLS 6005	23.59 (LP, union jack flag label)	250

(see also Rubettes)

WAKE (2)
82	Scan SCN 01	On Our Honeymoon/Give Up (p/s in bag)	25
84	Scan 45/Factory FAC 88	Talk About The Past/Everybody Works So Hard (p/s)	7
84	Scan 45/Factory FAC 8812	Talk About The Past/Everybody Works So Hard (12", p/s)	12
85	Factory FAC 113	Of The Matter/Of The Matter (p/s)	10
87	Factory FAC12 178	Something No-one Else Can Bring/Gruesome Castle	20
89	Sarah SARAH 21	Crush The Flowers/Carbrain (p/s, with postcard)	20
93	Sarah SARAH 48	Major John/Lousy Pop Group (p/s)	20
83	Factory FACT 60	HARMONY (LP)	20
85	Factory FACT 130	HERE COMES EVERYBODY (LP)	40
90	Sarah SARAH 602	MAKE IT LOUD (LP)	40
94	Sarah SARAH 618	TIDAL WAVE OF HYPE (LP)	60
12	Captured CT-152	HERE COMES EVERYBODY (2-LP box set, booklet and badge)	40

JIMMY WAKELY
56	Vogue Coral Q 72125	Are You Mine? (with Ruth Ross)/Yellow Roses	15
56	Brunswick 05542	Are You Satisfied? (with Gloria Wood)/Mississippi Dreamboat	15
56	Brunswick 05563	Folsom Prison Blues/That's What The Lord Can Do	20
57	Brunswick LAT 8179	SANTA FE TRAIL (LP)	20

(see also Karen Chandler, Bob Hope, Margaret Whiting)

RICK WAKEMAN (BAND)
75	A&M AMS 7206	Love's Dream/Orpheus' Song	6
75	A&M/Lyntone LYN 3176/7	Wagner's Dream/Love's Dream/Count Your Blessings (with 2 tracks by Roger Daltrey, flexidisc with 19 magazine)	10
80	WEA K 18354	The Spider/Danielle (some with p/s, 2,000 only)	8
71	Polydor 2460 135	PIANO VIBRATIONS (LP, with John Schroeder Orchestra)	100
74	A&M QU-84361	THE SIX WIVES OF HENRY VIII (LP, gatefold sleeve, quadrophonic mix)	18
73	A&M AMLH 64361	THE SIX WIVES OF HENRY VIII (LP, gatefold sleeve)	15
89	A&M RWCD 20	RICK WAKEMAN: 20TH ANNIVERSARY (4-CD box set, 1,000 only)	40

(see also Strawbs, Yes, Dib Cochran & Earwigs, Steve Howe, Jon Anderson)

CONRAD WALDRON
81	Red Stripe SON 2233	you Love's A Voodoo/RED STRIPE BAND: The Heat Is On	20

LARRINGTON WALKER
77	United Artists UP34210	Joy/Trust In Me	25

WALHAM GREEN EAST WAPPING CARPET CLEANING RODENT & BOGGIT EXTERMINATING

Anna WALKER & CROWNETTES

MINT VALUE £

ASSOCIATION
68	Columbia DB 8426	Sorry Mr. Green/Death Of A Kind	250

ANNA WALKER & CROWNETTES
69	Pama PM 768	You Don't Know/Billy Joe	10

BILLY WALKER (U.S.)
60	Philips PB 1001	Forever/Changed My Mind	6
66	London HLU 10060	Million And One/Close To Linda	7

BOOTS WALKER
69	London HLP 10265	No One Knows/Geraldine	15

CLINT WALKER
60	Warner Bros WEP 6006	INSPIRATION (EP, mono)	12
60	Warner Bros WSEP 2006	INSPIRATION (EP, stereo)	15

DAVID WALKER
68	RCA RCA 1664	Ring The Changes/Keep A Little Love	125

(see also Paradox)

GARY WALKER (& RAIN)
66	CBS 202036	You Don't Love Me/Get It Right	20
66	CBS 202081	Twinkie-Lee/She Makes Me Feel Better	10
68	Polydor 56237	Spooky/I Can't Stand To Lose You (as Gary Walker & Rain)	20
69	Philips BF 1740	Come In You'll Get Pneumonia/Francis (as Gary Walker & Rain)	60
74	United Artists UP 35742	Hello How Are You/Fran	7
66	CBS EPS 5742	HERE'S GARY (EP)	45

(see also Walker Brothers, Paul & Ritchie & Cryin' Shames, Badfinger, Universals)

HOWARD WALKER & BEACHCOMBERS
70	Decca F12997	Eat Me/Love Will Find A Way	15

JACKIE WALKER
58	London HLP 8588	Oh Lonesome Me/Only Teenagers Allowed	250
58	London HLP 8588	Oh Lonesome Me/Only Teenagers Allowed (78)	60

JERRY JEFF WALKER
68	Atlantic 584 200	Mr Bojangles/Round And Round	8
68	Atco 228 006	MR BOJANGLES (LP)	20
71	Atlantic 2466 007	BEIN' FREE (LP)	18

JOHN WALKER
67	Philips BF 1593	Anabella/You Don't Understand Me	8
67	Philips BF 1612	If I Promise/I See Love In You	7
68	Philips BF 1655	I'll Be Your Baby Tonight/Open The Door Homer	7
68	Philips BF 1676	Kentucky Woman/I Cried All The Way Home	8
68	Philips BF 1724	Woman/A Dream	6
69	Philips BF 1758	Yesterday's Sunshine/Little One	6
69	Carnaby CNS 4004	Everywhere Under The Sun/Traces Of Tomorrow	6
70	Carnaby CNS 4009	True Grit/Sun Comes Up	7
70	Carnaby CNS 4012	Cottonfields/Jamie	7
70	Carnaby CNS 4017	Over And Over Again/Sun Comes Up	7
67	Philips (S)BL 7829	IF YOU GO AWAY (LP)	25
69	Carnaby CNLS 6001	THIS IS JOHN WALKER (LP)	25

(see also Walker Brothers, John & Scott Walker, Johnny & Judy)

JOHN & SCOTT WALKER
66	Philips BE 12597	SOLO JOHN - SOLO SCOTT (EP, 2 tracks each)	10

(see also Walker Brothers, Scott Walker, John Walker, Scott Engel)

JUNIOR WALKER & ALL STARS
65	Tamla Motown TMG 509	Shotgun/Hot'Cha	45
65	Tamla Motown TMG 509	Shotgun/Hot'Cha (DJ copy)	100
65	Tamla Motown TMG 520	Do The Boomerang/Tune Up	70
65	Tamla Motown TMG 520	Do The Boomerang/Tune Up (DJ copy)	150
65	Tamla Motown TMG 529	Shake And Fingerpop/Cleo's Back	50
65	Tamla Motown TMG 529	Shake And Fingerpop/Cleo's Back (DJ copy)	80
66	Tamla Motown TMG 550	Cleo's Mood/Baby You Know It Ain't Right	45
66	Tamla Motown TMG 550	Cleo's Mood/Baby You Know It Ain't Right (DJ copy)	80
66	Tamla Motown TMG 559	Road Runner/Shoot Your Shot	30
66	Tamla Motown TMG 559	Road Runner/Shoot Your Shot (DJ copy)	100
66	Tamla Motown TMG 571	How Sweet It Is (To Be Loved By You)/Nothing But Soul	25
66	Tamla Motown TMG 571	How Sweet It Is (To Be Loved By You)/Nothing But Soul (DJ copy)	60
67	Tamla Motown TMG 571	How Sweet It Is (To Be Loved By You)/Nothing But Soul (later pressing)	7
66	Tamla Motown TMG 586	Money (That's What I Want) Parts 1& 2	30
66	Tamla Motown TMG 586	Money (That's What I Want) Parts 1& 2 (DJ copy)	55
67	Tamla Motown TMG 596	Pucker Up Buttercup/Any Way You Wanna	30
67	Tamla Motown TMG 596	Pucker Up Buttercup/Any Way You Wanna (DJ copy)	60
68	Tamla Motown TMG 637	Come See About Me/Sweet Soul	18
68	Tamla Motown TMG 637	Come See About Me/Sweet Soul (DJ copy)	70
68	Tamla Motown TMG 667	Hip City Parts 1 & 2	25
68	Tamla Motown TMG 667	Hip City Parts 1 & 2 (DJ copy)	40
69	Tamla Motown TMG 682	Home Cookin'/Mutiny	20
69	Tamla Motown TMG 682	Home Cookin'/Mutiny (DJ copy)	30
69	Tamla Motown TMG 691	Road Runner/Shotgun	7
69	Tamla Motown TMG 691	Road Runner/Shotgun (DJ copy)	30
69	Tamla Motown TMG 712	What Does It Take (To Win Your Love)/Brainwasher	8
70	Tamla Motown TMG 727	These Eyes/I've Got To Find A Way To Win Maria Back	12
70	Tamla Motown TMG 727	These Eyes/I've Got To Find A Way To Win Maria Back (DJ copy)	30
70	Tamla Motown TMG 750	Do You See My Love (For You Growing)/Groove And Move	8
70	Tamla Motown TMG 750	Do You See My Love (For You Growing)/Groove And Move (DJ Copy)	30

Karl WALKER & ALLSTARS

MINT VALUE £

72	Tamla Motown TMG 824	Walk In The Night/Right On Brothers And Sisters/ Gotta Hold On To This Feeling (maxi-single)	8
73	Tamla Motown TMG 840	Take Me Girl, I'm Ready/I Don't Want To Do Wrong	8
73	Tamla Motown TMG 857	Way Back Home (Vocal)/Way Back Home (Instrumental)	10
73	Tamla Motown TMG 857	Way Back Home (Vocal)/Way Back Home (Instrumental)/Country Boy (reissue)	20
73	Tamla Motown TMG 872	Holly Holy/Peace And Understanding (Is Hard To Find)	6
74	Tamla Motown TMG 889	Don't Blame The Children/Soul Clappin'	6
74	Tamla Motown TMG 894	Gotta Hold On To This Feeling/I Ain't Going Nowhere	10
74	Tamla Motown TMG 894	Gotta Hold On To This Feeling/I Ain't Going Nowhere (DJ copy)	25
76	Tamla Motown TMG 1027	I'm So Glad/Dancin' Like They Do On Soul Train (as Jr. Walker)	8
66	Tamla Motown TME 2013	SHAKE AND FINGERPOP (EP)	55
65	Tamla Motown TML 11017	SHOTGUN (LP)	55
66	T. Motown TML 11029	SOUL SESSION (LP, mono)	50
66	T. Motown STML 11029	SOUL SESSION (LP, stereo)	60
66	T. Motown TML 11038	ROAD RUNNER (LP, mono)	35
66	T. Motown STML 11038	ROAD RUNNER (LP, stereo)	45
69	T. Motown TML 11097	HOME COOKIN' (LP, mono)	30
69	T. Motown STML 11097	HOME COOKIN' (LP, stereo)	25
69	T. Motown (S)TML 11120	JUNIOR WALKER'S GREATEST HITS (LP, original with flipback sleeve)	15
70	T. Motown (S)TML 11140	THESE EYES (LP)	25
70	T. Motown STML 11152	LIVE (LP)	20
70	T. Motown STML 11167	A GASSSSSSSSSS! (LP)	20
72	T. Motown STML 11198	RAINBOW FUNK (LP)	20
72	T. Motown STML 11211	MOODY JR. (LP)	18
76	T. Motown STML 12018	HOT SHOT (by Jr. Walker)	10
76	T. Motown STML 12033	SAX APPEAL (by Jr. Walker)	10
76	Motown STML 12048	WHOPPER BOPPER SHOW STOPPER (by Jr. Walker)	10

KARL WALKER & ALLSTARS

66	Rymska RA 103	One Minute To Zero/Don't Come Back (both sides actually featuring Tommy McCook & Supersonics)	45

(see also Ernel Braham)

ROB WALKER

71	Upsetter US 366	Run Up Your Mouth (actually by Stranger Cole)/UPSETTERS: Mouth Version	20
71	Jackpot JP 761	Hear My Heart/Puppet On A String	15

(see also Stranger Cole, Tommy McCook)

RONNIE WALKER

69	Stateside SS 2151	It's A Good Feeling/Precious	30
69	Stateside SS 2151	It's A Good Feeling/Precious (DJ Copy)	50
75	Polydor 2066 578	Magic's In The Air/Just Can't Say Hello	8

SCOTT WALKER

67	Philips BF 1628	Jackie/The Plague	6
68	Philips BF 1662	Joanna/Always Coming Back To You	6
69	Philips BF 1793	Lights of Cincinnati/Two Weeks Since You've Gone	6
71	Philips 6006 168	I Still See You/My Way Home	6
73	Philips 6006 311	The Me I Never Knew/This Way Mary	6
73	CBS 1795	A Woman Left Lonely/Where Love Has Died	7
74	CBS 2521	Delta Dawn/We Had It All	7
66	Liberty LEP 2261	SCOTT ENGEL (WALKER) (EP)	35
67	Philips SBL 7816	SCOTT (LP, stereo)	30
67	Philips BL 7816	SCOTT (LP, mono)	40
68	Philips BL 7840	SCOTT 2 (LP, mono, with signed portrait)	40
68	Philips BL 7840	SCOTT 2 (LP, mono, without signed portrait)	20
68	Philips SBL 7840	SCOTT 2 (LP, stereo, with signed portrait)	40
68	Philips SBL 7840	SCOTT 2 (LP, stereo, without signed portrait)	20
68	Ember EMB LP 3393	LOOKING BACK WITH SCOTT WALKER (LP, mono or stereo)	30
69	Philips SBL 7882	SCOTT 3 (LP, gatefold sleeve)	50
69	Philips SBL 7900	SCOTT WALKER SINGS SONGS FROM HIS TV SERIES (LP)	18
69	Philips SBL 7910	THE BEST OF SCOTT WALKER VOL. 1 (LP)	18
69	Philips SBL 7913	SCOTT 4 (LP)	60
70	Philips 6308 035	'TIL THE BAND COMES IN (LP)	50
72	Philips 6308 127	THE MOVIEGOER (LP)	25
73	Philips 6308 148	ANY DAY NOW (LP)	30
73	CBS 65725	STRETCH (LP)	20
73	Philips 6850 013	THE ROMANTIC SCOTT WALKER (LP, Audio Club issue)	20
73	Philips 6856 022	TERRIFIC (LP, Audio Club issue, reissue of "Scott 2" with different tracks)	40
74	CBS 80254	WE HAD IT ALL (LP)	20
81	Zoo ZOO 2	FIRE ESCAPE IN THE SKY - THE GODLIKE GENIUS OF SCOTT WALKER (LP)	40
81	Philips 6359 090	SINGS JACQUES BREL (LP)	15
84	Virgin V2303	CLIMATE OF HUNTER (LP, inner)	25
90	Phonogram 824832	BOY CHILD - BEST OF 1967 - 1970 (LP)	18
95	Fontana 526859-1	TILT (LP, limited edition)	70
06	4AD DRIFT 1	THE DRIFT (2-LP, 500 promo copies with 24 page booklet)	60
12	4AD CAD 3220	BISH BOSCH (2-LP, CD)	20
14	4AD CAD 3428	SOUSED (2-LP with SUNN O))))	30

(see also Scott Engel, Scott Engel & John Stewart, John & Scott Walker, Walker Brothers, Routers)

STEWART WALKER

98	Mosquito MSQ 012	ARTIFICIAL MUSIC FOR ARTIFICIAL PEOPLE (12" EP)	15

SYLFORD WALKER

75	Locks LOX 9	Burn Babylon/Burn Version	40
79	Art & Craft AC 002	Book Of The Old Testament/JAH STITCH: Jah Speak Unto Moses (12")	30

T-bone WALKER

MINT VALUE £

80	Art & Craft ACD002	I Love You (feat. Jah Stitch)/Version (12")	20
88	Greensleeves GREL 119	LAMBS BREAD (LP)	40

(see also Glen Brown)

T-BONE WALKER

54	London HL 8087	The Hustle Is On/Baby Broke My Heart (78)	40
65	Liberty LIB 12018	Party Girl/Here In The Dark	25
63	London REP 1404	TRAVELLIN' BLUES (EP)	40
54	Capitol LC 6681	CLASSICS IN JAZZ (10" LP)	40
63	Capitol T 1958	T-BONE WALKER (LP)	50
65	Liberty LBY 3047	SINGS THE BLUES (LP)	50
66	Liberty LBY 3057	SINGING THE BLUES (LP)	40
68	MCA MUPS 331	THE TRUTH (LP)	20
68	Stateside S(S)L 10223	STORMY MONDAY BLUES (LP)	25
69	Stateside S(S)L 10265	FUNKY TOWN (LP)	25
74	Atlantic K 40131	T-BONE BLUES (LP)	15

WENDY WALKER (1)

63	Decca F 11573	Window Shopping/Ain't A Boy In The World	8
63	Decca F 11671	Boys Will Be Happy/Casanova	8

WENDY WALKER (2)

92	Sir George SG 103	We've Got One/(Version)/JUNIOR DANGEROUS: Slow Talk (12")	10

DEE WALKER

82	Arts Network DEE 1	DIAL 'L' FOR LOVE (mini-LP)	30

WALKER BROTHERS

65	Philips BF 1401	Pretty Girls Everywhere/Doin' The Jerk	15
65	Philips BF 1409	Love Her/The Seventh Dawn	10
65	Philips BF 1428	Make It Easy On Yourself/But I Do	6
65	Philips BF 1454	My Ship Is Coming In/You're All Around Me	6
66	Philips BF 1473	The Sun Ain't Gonna Shine Anymore/After The Lights Go Out	6
66	Philips BF 1497	(Baby) You Don't Have To Tell Me/My Love Is Growing	8
66	Philips BF 1514	Another Tear Falls/The Saddest Night In The World	8
66	Philips BF 1537	Deadlier Than The Male/Archangel	8
67	Philips BF 1548	Stay With Me Baby/Turn Out The Moon	8
67	Philips BF 1576	Walking In The Rain/Baby Make It The Last Time	8
76	GTO GT 67	Lines/First Day	6
77	GTO GT 78	We're All Alone/Have You Seen My Baby	6
66	Philips BE 12596	I NEED YOU (EP)	15
67	Philips BE 12603	THE WALKER BROTHERS (EP, probably unreleased)	0
65	Philips BL 7691	TAKE IT EASY WITH THE WALKER BROTHERS (LP)	18
66	Philips BL 7732	PORTRAIT (LP, with photo insert, mono)	20
66	Philips SBL 7732	PORTRAIT (LP, with photo insert, stereo)	30
67	Philips (S)BL 7770	IMAGES (LP)	20
78	GTO GTLP 033	NITE FLIGHTS (LP, gatefold sleeve)	80

(see also Scott Walker, Scott Engel, John Walker, John & Scott Walker, Gary Walker [& Rain], Routers)

WALKERS

79	Walker WAK 1/2	NOTES FOR THE HOPELESSLY BORED EP	6

TREVOR WALKERS

82	Mutual Life MU 002	They'll Never Get Away/Version (12", blue vinyl)	20

WALKIE TALKIES

79	Sire SIR 4023	Rich And Nasty/Summer In Russia (p/s)	6

(see also Pauline Murray & Invisible Girls, Mission)

WALKING FLOORS

80s	My Death Telephone TEL 1	No Next Time/Removal (foldover p/s)	8

DENNIS WALKS

68	Amalgamated AMG 816	Having A Party/GROOVERS: Day By Day	85
68	Blue Cat BS 144	Belly Lick/DRUMBAGO & BLENDERS: The Game Song	400
69	Bullet BU 402	Heart Don't Leap/CLARENDONIANS: I Am Sorry	350
69	Bullet BU 408	Love Of My Life/Under The Shady Tree	38
69	Crab CRAB 10	The Drifter/G.G. GROSSETT: Run Girl Run	100
71	Moodisc HM 101	Time Will Tell/Under The Shady Tree	20
74	Magnet MG 062	Don't Play That Song/Version	6
82	Greensleeves GREL 77	Roast Fish And Cornbread/Wicked She Wicked (12", with Billy Boyo)	20

(see also I Roy)

SHELTON WALKS

73	Bullet BU 550	No Money No Friend/BOB MAC ALL STARS: Money Dub	12
74	Dip DL 5026	One Of Us Will Weep/KING EDWARDS ALL STARS: Version	22

WALL

80	Fresh FRESHLP 2	PERSONAL TROUBLES AND PUBLIC ISSUES (LP)	15
80	Fresh FRESHLP 2	PERSONAL TROUBLES AND PUBLIC ISSUES LP, with insert, withdrawn "Crass style" stencil lettered sleeve)	30

(see also Ski Patrol)

MAX WALL

77	Stiff BUY 12	England's Glory/Dream Tobacco (glossy or matt p/s)	7

REM WALL & HIS GREEN VALLEY BOYS

60	Top Rank JAR 324	Heartsick And Blue/One More Time	10

ERROL WALLACE

69	Escort ES 817	Bandit/ASTON BORROT: Family Man Mood (actually by Aston "Family Man" Barrett)	40

GIG WALLACE & HIS ORCHESTRA

60	Philips PB 981	Rockin' On The Railroad/Show Me The Way To Go Home	10

JERRY WALLACE

58	London HL 8719	With This Ring/How The Time Flies	40

Mike WALLACE

MINT VALUE £

58	London HL 7062	With This Ring/How The Time Flies (export issue)	30
59	London HLH 8943	Primrose Lane/By Your Side	10
60	London HLH 9040	Little Coco Palm/Mission Bell Blues	6
60	London HLH 9110	You're Singing Our Love Song To Somebody Else/King Of The Mountain	6
60	London HLH 9177	Swingin' Down The Lane/Teardrop In The Rain	7
62	London HLH 9630	Shutters And Boards/Am I That Easy To Forget	8

MIKE WALLACE
70	Major Minor D570	Daffodil/Early Morning Bird	12
70	Polydor 2058065	Natural High/Mandrin	50

SIPPIE WALLACE
67	Storyville 671 198	SIPPIE WALLACE SINGS THE BLUES (LP)	15

WALLACE BROTHERS
64	Sue WI 334	Precious Words/You're Mine	40
65	Sue WI 355	Lover's Prayer/Love Me Like I Love You	40
67	Sue WI 4036	I'll Step Aside/Hold My Heart For A While	40
67	Sue ILP 950	SOUL CONNECTION (LP)	250

WALLACE COLLECTION
69	Parlophone R 5764	Daydream/Baby I Don't Mind	12
69	Parlophone R 5793	Fly Me To The Earth/Love	25
70	Parlophone R 5844	Serenade/Walk On Out	10

GORDON (WALLER)
68	Columbia DB 8337	Rosecrans Boulevard/Red, Cream And Velvet	20
68	Columbia DB 8440	Every Day/Because Of A Woman	10
68	Columbia DB 8518	Weeping Analeah/The Seventh Hour	10
69	Bell BLL 1059	I Was A Boy When You Needed A Man/Lady In The Window	7
70	Bell BLL 1106	You're Gonna Hurt Yourself/Sunshine	7
72	Vertigo 6360 069	GORDON (LP, as Gordon, single sleeve, small swirl label)	1000

(see also Peter & Gordon)

GEORGE WALLINGTON
56	Columbia Clef 33C9035	THE WORK SHOP OF GEORGE WALLINGTON TRIO (10" LP)	60
57	Esquire 32-132	NEW YORK SCENE (LP)	150

BOB WALLIS & HIS STORYVILLE JAZZMEN
57	77 EP 10	NEW ORLEANS JAM SESSION VOLUME 1 (EP)	15
59	77 Records 77LE 12/2	THE RAVING SOUNDS OF BOB WALLIS (LP)	20

LARRY WALLIS
77	Stiff BUY 22	Police Car/On Parole (with p/s)	10

(see also Pink Fairies, Subs, Deviants, Shagrat, Peter Wyngarde, Motorhead)

SHANI WALLIS
60	Philips PB 1019	Sixteen Reasons (Why I Love You)/Forever Forever	6
63	Decca F11632	My Heart Cries For You/All Over Again	20
60	Philips BBE 12337	SHANI! (EP)	10

WALL OF SLEEP
95	Woronzow WOO 24	WALL OF SLEEP (LP, with insert)	12

WALL STREET DIVERSION
68	Concord CON 006	She's Mine/Joey The Lipstick Collector	25

WALLY BROTHERS
74	Explosion EX 2090	The Man Who Sold The World/Version	40

WALRUS
70	Deram DM 308	Who Can I Trust?/Tomorrow Never Comes	20
71	Deram DM 323	Never Let My Body Touch Ground/Why?	20
71	Deram SML 1072	WALRUS (LP)	300

JAMES WALSH GYPSY BAND
79	RCA PB 11403	Cuz It's You Girl/Bring Yourself Together	50
79	RCA PB 11403	Cuz It's You Girl/Bring Yourself Together (DJ copy)	100

JOHNNY WALSH
61	Warner Bros. WB 40	Girl Machine/Beautiful Obsession	10

BURT WALTERS
68	Trojan TR 636	Honey Love/KING CANNONBALL BRYAN: Thunderstorm	65

(see also Lee 'Scratch' Perry)

JULIE WALTERS
82	Deaville STL 7	Toy Boys/Bad Loser	6

DAVE WALTON
66	CBS 202057	Love Ain't What It Used To Be/Tell Me A Lie	8
66	CBS 202098	Every Window In The City/I've Left The Troubled Ground	15
67	CBS 202508	After You There Can Be Nothing/Can I Get It From You	30

(see also The First Gear)

TRAVIS WAMMACK
65	Atlantic AT 4017	Scratchy/Fire Fly	50
65	Atlantic AT 4017	Scratchy/Fire Fly (DJ copy)	100
72	United Artists UP 35412	Whatever Turns You On/Slip Away	6
73	United Artists UP 35468	So Good/Darling, You're All That I Need	6

WAND
97	Deconstruction 74321 51222 1	Happiness/Happiness (12")	10

WANDERER
59	Top Rank JAR 183	The Happy Hobo/True True Happiness	6

WANDERERS
81	Polydor POSP 239	Ready To Snap/Beyond The Law	25
81	Polydor POSP 284	The Times They Are A'Changin'/Little Bit Frightening	15
81	Polydor POLS 1028	ONLY LOVERS LEFT (LP)	30

WANDERERS (Jamaica)

MINT VALUE £

(see also Lords Of The New Church, Stiv Bators, Dead Boys, Sham 69)

WANDERERS (JAMAICA)
69	Trojan TR 7721	Wiggle Waggle/Jaga Jaga War	300

WANDERERS (U.S.)
60	MGM MGM 1102	I Could Make You Mine/I Need You More	50
61	MGM MGM 1169	As Time Goes By/There Is No Greater Love	20
64	United Artists UP 1020	Run Run Senorita/After He Breaks Your Heart	30

(see also Ray Pollard)

MATT WAND & LAURENCE LANE
97	Hot Air VIBRO1	Good Vibrations 1RPM/Good Vibrations 2RPM (300 only, replica Capitol label)	10

(see also Stock, Hausen and Walkman)

HANK WANGFORD
80	Cow Pie PIE 02	Cowboys Stay On Longer/Whiskey On	15

WANGLERS
79	Matchbox Classics MC 5	KICKIN' OUT FOR THE COAST (EP, white label, yellow or red stickered foldover p/s)	10

WANNADIES
95	Indolent DIELP 002	BE A GIRL (LP)	30
96	Indolent DIELP 008S	BAGSY ME (LP with free 7")	30

DEXTER WANSEL
85	Streetwave SWAVE 9	Life On Mars/WILLIE BOBO: Always There (12")	25

WAR
71	Liberty LBF 15443	Sun Oh Son/Lonely Feelin'	6
71	United Artists UP 35281	All Day Music/Get Down	6
74	United Artists UP 35623	Me And Baby Brother/In Your Eyes	8
80	MCA MCAT 557	The World Is A Ghetto (Special Disco Mix)/I'll Take Care Of You (12". p/s)	25
71	Liberty LBG 83478	WAR (LP)	20
72	United Artists UAS 29269	ALL DAY MUSIC (LP)	15
73	United Artists UAS 29400	THE WORLD IS A GHETTO (LP)	20
73	United Artists UAG 29521	DELIVER THE WORD (LP)	15
75	United Artists ILPS 9378	WHY CAN'T WE BE FRIENDS (LP, with poster)	15

(see also Eric Burdon & War)

BILLY WARD & HIS DOMINOES
53	Parlophone R 3789	Don't Thank Me/Rags To Riches (78)	40
54	Parlophone MSP 6112	Three Coins In The Fountain/Lonesome Road	150
54	Parlophone MSP 6112	Three Coins In The Fountain/Lonesome Road (78)	25
56	Brunswick 05599	St. Therese Of The Roses/Home Is Where You Hang Your Heart	40
57	Brunswick 05656	Evermore/Half A Love (Is Better Than None)	30
57	London HLU 8465	Stardust/Lucinda	20
57	London HLU 8502	Deep Purple/Do It Again	20
58	London HLU 8634	Jennie Lee/Music, Maestro, Please	20
59	London HLU 8883	Please Don't Say 'No'/Behave, Hula Girl	20
58	London REU 1114	BILLY WARD & HIS DOMINOES (EP)	100
58	Parlophone PMD 1061	BILLY WARD & HIS DOMINOES FEATURING CLYDE McPHATTER (10" LP)	600
58	London HA-U 2116	YOURS FOREVER (LP)	60

(see also Dominoes, Clyde McPhatter, Jackie Wilson)

CHRISTIAN WARD
66	Decca F 12339	The Face Of Empty Me/Girl I Used To Know	35

CLARA WARD & HER SINGERS
65	Stateside SS 474	Gonna Build A Mountain/God Bless The Child	10

CLIFFORD T. WARD
72	Dandelion 2001 327	Carrie/Sidetrack	12
72	Dandelion 2001 382	Coathanger/Rayne	10
73	Charisma CB 205	Home Thoughts From Abroad/Gaye	7
73	Charisma CB 212	Wherewithal/Thinking Of Something To Do	7
74	Charisma CB 233	Jayne/Maybe I'm Right	7
75	Charisma CB 248	Jigsaw Girl/Cellophane	7
75	Philips 6006 490	No More Rock'n'Roll/Gandalf	7
76	Philips 6006 542	Ocean Of Love/Tomorrow Night	7
77	Mercury 6007 132	Up In The World/Not Waving, Drowning (Revisited)	7
77	Mercury 6007 149	I Got Lost Tonight/Detriment (p/s)	7
77	Mercury LUV 1	Someone I Know/If I Had Known (gatefold p/s)	8
80	WEA K 18294	Convertible/Taking The Long Way Round	7
81	WEA K 18426	The Best Is Yet To Come/Lost Again	7
81	WEA K 18486	Contrary/Climate Of Her Favour	7
84	Philips 880 550 7	Messenger/Where Do Angels Really Come From (p/s)	8
86	Tembo TML 114	Cricket/Computer	10
86	Tembo TML 123	Sometime Next Year/Turbo (p/s)	8
72	Dandelion 2310 216	SINGER SONGWRITER (LP)	25
75	Charisma CAS 1098	ESCALATOR (LP)	15

(see also Secrets, Simon's Secrets, Martin Raynor & Secrets)

DALE WARD
64	London HLD 9835	Oh Julie/Letter From Sherry	20

DOUGLAS WARD
71	Forward FS1001	FROM AN ELEVATED PLATFORM (LP)	20

JONATHAN WARD
67	Eyemark EMS 1009	Fools Paradise/One Step At A Time	30

ROBIN WARD
63	London HLD 9821	Wonderful Summer/Dream Boy	25

SAM WARD
98	Goldmine Soul Supply GS	Sister Lee/THE PROFESSIONALS: That's Why I Love You	8

		MINT VALUE £

TERRY WARD WITH BUMBLIES
65   Fontana TF 558   Gotta Tell/When I Come To You 10

SHEELAGH WARDE
59   Top Rank JAR 131   Let Mr. Maguire Sit Down/The Golden Jubilee 7

WARDENS
79   SNU PEAS TIC 001   Last Like This/Do So Well (with insert).. 50

WARDS OF COURT
67   Deram DM 127   All Night Girl/How Could Say One Thing 70

WARD SINGERS
56   London Jazz EZ-C 19024   THE FAMOUS WARD SINGERS (EP) 20
56   London Jazz LZ-C 14013   THE FAMOUS WARD SINGERS (10" LP) 25

WARD 34
79   Woof Woof WOOF 1   Religion For The 70s/Disco Limbo (p/s) 20

LEON WARE
77   Motown STML 12050   MUSICAL MASSAGE (LP) 25
99   Expansion EXLPM 5   INSIDE OF LOVE (LP, reissue) 15
01   Elektra 7559-62728-1   LEON WARE (LP, reissue) 15

WARFARE
83   Neat (No. cat. no.)   This Machine Kills/Burn Down The Kings Road (white label) 20
84   Neat NEAT 45-12   Two Tribes/Hell/Blown To Bits (12") 12
84   Neat NEAT 49-12   TOTAL DEATH (12", EP) 15
84   Neat NEAT 1021   PURE FILTH (LP) 15

WARHOLS
87   Zoot WAR 001   Fear Of Falling/Other Side 20

WARHORSE
71   Vertigo 6059 027   St. Louis/No Chance 20
70   Vertigo 6360 015   WARHORSE (LP, large swirl label, gatefold sleeve) 300
72   Vertigo 6360 066   RED SEA (LP, small swirl label, gatefold sleeve) 400
84   Thunderbolt THBL 010   RED SEA (LP, reissue, red vinyl) 18
84   Thunderbolt THBL 010   RED SEA (LP, reissue) 15
14   Repertoire V110   WARHORSE (LP, reissue) 15
14   Repertoire V111   RED SEA (LP, reissue) 15

(see also Deep Purple, Nic Simper's Fandango)

RAY WARLEIGH
69   Philips (S)BL 7881   RAY WARLEIGH'S FIRST ALBUM (LP) 40

(see also John Mayall's Blues Breakers, Alexis Korner)

OZZIE WARLOCK & WIZARDS
59   HMV POP 635   Juke Box Fury/Wow! 12

(see also Tony Osbourne)

WARM
79   Warm AWMR 2007   007 (Shanty Town)/Just To Stay Ahead (promo only) 12
79   MHG GHM 208/PF 9002   Tired Of Waiting For You/Tired Dub 12

WARM HANDS
72   Access ACC 2   Disappear/My God I Love You 25

WARM AIR
70   Linette LT 1   Sugar Cane/Don't Dream 8

JOHNNY WARMAN
78   Ring O' 2017 112   Head On Collision/London's Burning/Mind Games (in p/s) 20
78   Ring O' 2017 112   Head On Collision/London's Burning/Mind Games 15

WARM DUST
71   Trend 6099 002   It's A Beautiful Day/Worm Dance 15
70   Trend TNLS 700   AND IT CAME TO PASS (2-LP, gatefold sleeve, grey label) 200
71   Trend 6480 001   PEACE FOR OUR TIME (LP, gatefold sleeve, grey label) 70

WARM GOLD
60s   Hurls 008   A TASTE OF CORNWALL (EP) 25

KEITH WARMINGTON
83   Right Track S83CUS1710 RTR 029   Evening Song/Sentimental 10

WARM JETS (1)
78   Bridgehouse BHS 1   Sticky Jack/Shell Shock (p/s, some with sides reversed & small extra labels) 8

WARM JETS (2)
96   Island 524 354-1   FUTURE SIGNS (LP) 25

WARM SENSATION
69   Columbia DB 8568   I'll Be Proud Of You/The Clown 25

(see also Ivy League)

WARM SOUNDS
67   Immediate IM 058   Sticks And Stones/Angeline 20
67   Deram DM 120   The Birds And Bees/Doo-Dah 15
68   Deram DM 174   Nite Is A-Comin'/Smeta Mergaty 50

(see also Denny Gerrard, Tuesday's Children, Open Road)

FLORENCE WARNER
73   Epic EPC 1626   For No Good Reason/Remember 6
75   Epic EPC 3817   Anyway I Love You/Dreamer 6
74   Epic EPC 80077   FLORENCE WARNER (LP) 18

HERB & BETTY WARNER
59   Felsted AF 114   Slowly/'BUGS' BOWER GROUP: Slowly 7

JACK WARNER
71   President PT 360   You Have Got The Gear/ Somebody Asked Me 15
68   MFP MFP 1278   YER CAN'T 'ELP LAUGHIN' (LP) 15

Kai WARNER'S ORIENTAL EXPRESS

MINT VALUE £

KAI WARNER'S ORIENTAL EXPRESS
77	Power Exchange PX 244	Fly Butterfly/Funky Harem	6

WARP NINE
75	Stax STXS 2030	Theme From 'Star Trek'/Para Song One	6

FRAN WARREN
59	MGM MGM 1008	Shame/As Long As You Believe Me	10

GUY WARREN OF GHANA
59	Brunswick 05791	Monkies And Butterflies/An African's Prayer (with Rod Saunders)	6
57	Brunswick LAJ 8237	AFRICA SPEAKS - AMERICA ANSWERS (LP)	35
64	Columbia 33SX 1584	EMERGENT DRUMS (LP)	100
69	Columbia SCX 6340	AFRO-JAZZ (LP, as Guy Warren Of Ghana)	150
72	Regal Zono. SLRZ 1031	THE AFRICAN SOUNDS OF GUY WARREN OF GHANA (LP)	100

WARREN G
94	Violator 314 523 335-1	REGULATE...G FUNK ERA (LP)	25

WARRIÖR
80	Rambert RAM ONE	Don't Let It Show/The Lord's Prayer/Silver Lady (10", p/s)	120
80	Goodwood GM 12326	TROUBLE MAKER (LP)	150

WARRIOR (1)
72	Eden LP 27	INVASION! (LP, private pressing, plain white sleeve & label, some handwritten, 100 only)	160
80	Rainbow RSL 132	LET BATTLE COMMENCE (LP, private pressing, 500 only)	100

WARRIOR (2)
82	Neat NEAT 20	Dead When It Comes To Love/Kansas City/Stab In The Back	10
84	Warrior WOO 2	Breakout/Dragon Slayer/Take Your Chance (paper sleeve)	55
83	Warrior WOO 1	FOR EUROPE ONLY (mini-LP)	20

WARRIORS (1)
64	Decca F 11926	Don't Make Me Blue/You Came Along	40

(see also Hans Christian, Jon Anderson)

WARRIORS (2)
79	Object OM 07	Martial Time/Martial Law (p/s)	15

WARRIORS (3)
82	Ensign ENVY 6001	BEHIND THE MASK (LP)	25

WARSAW PAKT
78	Island PAKT 1	Safe And Warm/Sick And Tired (with stamped sleeve)	30
78	Island PAKT 1	Safe And Warm/Sick And Tired	18
77	Island ILPS 9515	NEEDLE TIME (LP, numbered stamped mailer p/s, with insert)	30

WARWICK
75	RAK RAK 211	Let's Get The Party Going/How Does It Feel	15

DEE DEE WARWICK
65	Mercury MF 860	Do It With All Your Heart/Happiness	20
65	Mercury MF 867	We're Doin' Fine/You Don't Know	20
65	Mercury MF 890	Gotta Get Hold Of Myself/Another Lonely Saturday	20
66	Mercury MF 909	A Lover's Chant/Worth Every Tear I Cry	150
65	Mercury MF 937	I Want To Be With You/Alfie	18
65	Mercury MF 953	Yours Till Tomorrow/I'm Gonna Make You Love Me	15
67	Mercury MF 974	When Love Slips Away/House Of Gold	40
68	Mercury MF 1061	I'll Be Better Off (Without You)/Monday, Monday	20
69	Mercury MF 1084	Foolish Heart/Thank God	10
69	Mercury MF 1125	That's Not Love/It's Not Fair	10
70	Atlantic 2091 011	She Didn't Know (She Kept On Talking)/Make Love To Me	8
70	Atlantic 2091 037	If This Was The Last Song/I'm Only Human	6
71	Atlantic 2091 057	Cold Night In Georgia/Searching	6
71	Atlantic 2091 092	Suspicious Minds/I'm Glad I'm A Woman	15
75	Private Stock PVT 13	Get Out Of My Life/Funny How We Change Places	30
66	Mercury 10036 MCE	WE'RE DOING FINE (EP)	80
71	Atco	TURNIN' AROUND (LP)	30

DIONNE WARWICK
SINGLES
63	Stateside SS 157	Don't Make Me Over/I Smiled Yesterday	22
63	Stateside SS 157	Don't Make Me Over/I Smiled Yesterday (DJ Copy)	50
63	Stateside SS 191	This Empty Place/Wishin' And Hopin'	22
63	Pye International 7N 25223	Please Let Him Love Me/Make The Music Play	8
64	Pye International 7N 25234	Anyone Who Had A Heart/The Love Of A Boy	10
64	Pye International 7N 25241	Walk On By/Any Old Time Of Day	6
64	Pye International 7N 25256	You'll Never Get To Heaven/A House Is Not A Home	8
64	Pye International 7N 25265	Reach Out For Me/How Many Days Of Sadness	8
65	Pye International 7N 25290	You Can Have Him/Don't Say I Didn't Tell You	8
65	Pye International 7N 25302	Who Can I Turn To/That's Not The Answer	6
65	Pye International 7N 25310	(Here I Go Again) Looking With My Eyes/Only The Strong, Only The Brave	6
65	Pye International 7N 25316	Here I Am/They Long To Be Close To You	6
65	Pye International 7N 25338	Are You There (With Another Girl)/If I Ever Make You Cry	6
66	Pye International 7N 25357	In Between The Heartaches/Long Day, Short Night	6
66	Pye International 7N 25368	A Message To Michael/Here Where There Is Love	6
66	Pye International 7N 25378	Trains And Boats And Planes/Don't Go Breaking My Heart	6
66	Pye International 7N 25395	Another Night/Go With Love	6
67	Pye International 7N 25424	Alfie/The Beginning Of Loneliness	6
67	Pye International 7N 25428	The Windows Of The World/Walk Little Dolly	6
67	Pye International 7N 25435	I Say A Little Prayer/Window Wishin'	7
68	Pye International 7N 25445	(Theme From) The Valley Of The Dolls/Zip-A-Dee-Doo-Dah	8
76	Warner Bros SAM 61	Track Of The Cat/LIVERPOOL EXPRESS: You Are My Love (12", promo only)	15

WASHBOARD RHYTHM KINGS

MINT VALUE £

ALBUMS
64	Pye Intl. NPL 28037	PRESENTING DIONNE WARWICK	20
64	Pye Intl. NPL 28046	MAKE WAY FOR DIONNE WARWICK	15
65	Pye Intl. NPL 28055	THE SENSITIVE SOUND OF DIONNE WARWICK	15
66	Pye Intl. NPL 28071	HERE I AM	15
68	Pye Intl. N(S)PL 28114	VALLEY OF THE DOLLS (LP)	15
73	Warner Bros. K46186	JUST BEING MYSELF (LP, credited to Dionne Warwicke)	18

WASHBOARD RHYTHM KINGS
56	HMV 7EG 8101	WASHBOARD RHYTHM KINGS (EP)	15

WASHBOARD SAM
72	RCA RD 8274	FEELING LOWDOWN (LP, with Big Bill Broonzy & Memphis Slim)	15

(see also Big Bill Broonzy, Memphis Slim)

LALOMIE WASHBURN
77	Parachute RRL 2002	MY MUSIC IS HOT (LP)	20

ALBERT WASHINGTON & KINGS
67	President PT 137	Doggin' Me Around/A Woman Is A Funny Thing	10
68	President PT 182	I'm The Man/These Arms Of Mine	50
68	President PT 227	Woman Love/Bring It On Up	10
69	President PT 242	Turn On The Bright Lights/Lonely Mountain	10
73	President PT 391	Rome, GA/Telling All Your Friends	10
03	Kent TOWN 118	I'm The Man/DOROTHY WILLIAMS: The Well's Gone Dry	6

BABY WASHINGTON
64	Sue WI 302	That's How Heartaches Are Made/Doodlin'	50
64	Sue WI 321	I Can't Wait Until I See My Baby/Who's Gonna Take Care Of Me	50
65	London HLC 9987	Only Those In Love/Ballad Of Bobby Dawn	25
68	United Artists UP 2247	Get A Hold Of Yourself/Hurt So Bad	15
69	Atlantic 584 299	I Don't Know/I Can't Afford To Lose Him	15
70	Atlantic 584 316	Breakfast In Bed/What Becomes Of A Broken Heart	15
73	People PEO 105	Just Can't Get You Out Of My Mind/You're Just A Dream	10
74	People PEO 107	I've Got To Break Away/Can't Get Over You	10
66	London HA-C 8260	THAT'S HOW HEARTACHES ARE MADE (LP)	50
66	London HA-C 8292	ONLY THOSE IN LOVE (LP)	50
68	United Artists SULP 1217	WITH YOU IN MIND (LP)	40

BABY WASHINGTON & DON GARDNER
74	People PLEO 13	LAY A LITTLE LOVIN' ON ME (LP)	20

(see also Don Gardner & Dee Dee Ford)

DELROY WASHINGTON
73	Count Shelly CS 033	Lonely Street/ANTROY ALL STARS: Antroy All Stars	12
73	Sir Christopher KOO 022	Papa Was A Rolling Stone (as D. Washington)/KEITH HUDSON: Fight Fight	60
77	Virgin VDJ 22	Give All The Praise To Jah/Stand Up And Be Happy (12")	15
78	Burning Sounds BSD 006	Memories (with Jah Son)/EVERARD THOMPSON & SUPERSTAR: Rasta Roots (12")	15
76	Virgin V 2060	I-SUS (LP, with insert)	20
77	Virgin V 2088	RASTA (LP)	20

(see also Carl Dawkins)

DINAH WASHINGTON
59	Mercury AMT 1051	What A Diff'rence A Day Made/Come On Home	10
61	Mercury AMT 1162	September In The Rain/Wake The Town And Tell The People	10
62	Mercury AMT 1170	Tears And Laughter/If I Should Lose You	6
62	Mercury AMT 1176	Dream/Such A Night	8
63	Columbia DB 7049	Soulville/Let Me Be The First To Know	25
56	Emarcy EJT 501	AFTER HOURS WITH MISS D. (10" LP)	30
57	Emarcy EJL 1255	DINAH (LP)	25
57	Mercury MPL 6519	SINGS THE BEST IN BLUES (LP)	15
59	Top Rank RX 3006	THE BLUES (LP, with Betty Roche)	15
60	Mercury MMC 14030	WHAT A DIFF'RENCE A DAY MADE (LP)	15
60	Mercury MMC 14048	THE UNFORGETTABLE DINAH WASHINGTON (LP)	15
61	Mercury MMC 14063	I CONCENTRATE ON YOU (LP, mono)	18
61	Mercury CMS 18043	I CONCENTRATE ON YOU (LP, stereo)	20
61	Mercury MMC 14107	SEPTEMBER IN THE RAIN (LP)	12

(see also Brook Benton & Dinah Washington)

ELLA WASHINGTON
69	Monument MON 1030	He Called Me Baby/You're Gonna Cry, Cry, Cry	20

GENO WASHINGTON & RAM JAM BAND
66	Piccadilly 7N 35312	Water/Understanding	10
66	Piccadilly 7N 35329	Hi! Hi! Hazel/Beach Bash	12
66	Piccadilly 7N 35346	Que Sera Sera/All I Need	12
66	Piccadilly 7N 35359	Michael/Hold On To My Love	15
67	Piccadilly 7N 35392	She Shot A Hole In My Soul/I've Been Hurt By Love	15
67	Piccadilly 7N 35403	Tell It Like It Is/Girl I Want To Marry	8
67	Pye 7N 17425	Different Strokes/You Got Me Hummin'	7
68	Pye 7N 17570	I Can't Quit Her/Put Out The Fire Baby	7
68	Pye 7N 17649	I Can't Let You Go/Bring It To Me Baby	10
69	Pye 7N 17745	My Little Chickadee/Seven Eleven	7
71	Pye 7N 45019	Alison Please/Each And Every Part Me	7
71	Pye 7N 45085	Feeling So Good/Would You Believe My Little Chickadee	6
66	Piccadilly NEP 34054	HI (EP)	25
68	Pye NEP 24293	DIFFERENT STROKES (EP)	20
68	Pye NEP 24302	SMALL PACKAGE OF HIPSTERS (EP)	20
66	Piccadilly NPL 38026	HAND CLAPPIN', FOOT STOMPIN', FUNKY-BUTT . . . LIVE! (LP)	20

Jerry WASHINGTON

			MINT VALUE £
67	Piccadilly N(S)PL 38032	HIPSTERS, FLIPSTERS, FINGER-POPPIN' DADDIES! (LP)	20
68	Piccadilly N(S)PL 38029	SHAKE A TAIL FEATHER! (LP)	15
68	Pye N(S)PL 18219	LIVE! - RUNNING WILD (LP)	15

(see also Ram Jam Band, Ram John Holder, Ram Holder Brothers, Dave Greenslade)

JERRY WASHINGTON
06	Jazzman JM 12 007	STONY ISLAND BAND: Stony Island Band/Don't Waste My Time (12" reissue)	20
75	Contempo CLP 517	RIGHT HERE IS WHERE YOU BELONG (LP)	35

GROVER WASHINGTON JR
71	Kid KU 03	INNER CITY BLUES (LP)	18
75	Kudu KU 20	MR MAGIC (LP)	18

KAMASI WASHINGTON
15	Brainfeeder BF 050	THE EPIC (3-LP, box set)	35

KENNETH WASHINGTON (& CHRIS BARBER BAND)
67	CBS 202494	If I Had A Ticket/They Kicked Him Out Of Heaven (with Chris Barber & T-Bones)	10

(see also Chris Barber)

NORMAN T. WASHINGTON
68	Pama PM 730	Same Thing All Over/You've Been Cheating	10
68	Pama PM 741	Tip Toe/Don't Hang Around	25
69	Pama PM 749	Jumping Jack Flash/Spinning	30
69	Punch PH 11	Oh Happy Day/Spinning	10
70	Gas GAS 159	It's Christmas Time Again/If I Could See You	10
70	Punch PH 26	Sweeter Than Honey/1,000 Pearls	10
70	Punch PH 31	Last Goodbye/Mother's Pride	10

SHERI WASHINGTON & BAND
57	Vogue V 9070	I Got Plenty/Ain't I Talkin' To You Baby	500
57	Vogue V 9070	I Got Plenty/Ain't I Talkin' To You Baby (78)	100

SISTER ERNESTINE B. WASHINGTON
55	Melodisc EPM 7-52	SISTER ERNESTINE WASHINGTON (EP)	20

TONY WASHINGTON (& HIS D.C.S
63	React EA 002	Crying Man/Please Mr. DJ	20
63	Island WI 068	Something Gotta Be Done/TONY & LOUISE: I Have Said	20
64	Sue WI 327	Show Me How (To Milk A Cow)/Boof Ska	50
64	Fontana TF 478	Surely You Love Me/Man To Man	15
65	Black Swan WI 459	But I Do/Night Train (as Tony Washington & His D.C.s)	25
65	Black Swan WI 460	Dilly Dilly/Night Train (as Tony Washington & His D.C.s)	25

(see also Tony & Louise)

WASHINGTON D.C.S
64	Ember EMB S 190	Kisses Sweeter Than Wine/Where Did You Go	15
66	CBS 202226	32nd Floor/Whole Lot More	15
67	CBS 202464	Seek And Find/I Love Gerald Chevin The Great (in p/s)	70
67	CBS 202464	Seek and Find/I Love Gerald Chevin The Great (no p/s)	50
69	Domain D 9	I've Done It All Wrong/Anytime	30

(see also Dave Clark Five, Freedom)

WASHINGTON FLYER
79	EMI 2926	Bufflao Bill/Star Dance	15

WASHINGTON FLYERS
74	Dawn DNS 1076	Another Saturday Morning/The Comets Are Coming	6

WASP
75	EMI EMI 2253	Melissa/Little Miss Bristol	20

(see also Brian Bennett, Shadows)

W.A.S.P.
84	Music For Nations PKUT 109	Animal (Fuck Like A Beast)/Show No Mercy (shaped picture disc, pig's head or codpiece designs)	20
84	Music For Nations 12KUT 109	Animal (Fuck Like A Beast)/Show No Mercy (12", gold vinyl, U.K. issue pressed in France)	35
84	Music For Nations 12KUT 109	Animal (Fuck Like A Beast)/Show No Mercy (12", white, vinyl, U.K. issue pressed in France)	15
84	Music For Nations 12KUT 109	Animal (Fuck Like A Beast)/Show No Mercy (12", clear vinyl, U.K. issue pressed in France)	20
84	Music For Nations 12KUT 109	Animal (Fuck Like A Beast)/Show No Mercy (12", red vinyl, U.K. issue pressed in France)	15
89	Capitol ESTPD 2087	THE HEADLESS CHILDREN (LP, picture disc)	15
92	Parlophone PCSDS 118	CRIMSON IDOL (LP, red vinyl, inner)	50
95	RAW LP 103	STILL NOT BLACK ENOUGH (LP, 3000 only)	80

WASPS
77	4-Play FOUR 001	Teenage Treats/She Made More Magic (p/s)	25
77	NEMS NES 115	Can't Wait 'Til '78/MEAN STREET: Bunch Of Stiffs (p/s)	18
78	RCA PB 5137	Rubber Cars/This Time (p/s)	10

WASTE
86	Morterhate MORT 21	NOT JUST SOMETHING TO BE SUNG (EP, foldout p/s)	25

WASTED YOUTH
81	Bridge House BHS 12	Rebecca's Room/Things Never Seem The Same (p/s)	6
82	Bridge House BHFNEE 1	Caveman (1-sided, limited issue)	8
80	Bridge House BHLP006	WILD AND WANDERING (LP)	15
82	Bridge House BHLP007	THE BEGINNING OF THE END (LP, with free 'Caveman 7", 5000 only)	15

WASTELAND
79	Ellie Jay/Disaster EJSP 9261	WANT NOT EP (p/s, 2,000 only)	30
80	Invicta INV 014	Friends, Romans, Countrymen/Leave Me Alone (p/s, 1,000 only)	30

WATCH COMMITTEE
68	Philips BF 1695	Throw Another Penny In The Well/Now I Think The Other Way	6

WATCHMAKERS

MINT VALUE £

WATCHMAKERS
14   Box Bedroom Rebels BBR13   WATCHMAKERS (p/s, inserts, 150 only, numbered) 20

WATERBOYS
85   Ensign ENGL 5   THIS IS THE SEA (LP) 15
11   Proper PRPLP 081   AN APPOINTMENT WITH MR YEATS (2-LP) 25

WATERFALL
76   Bob FRR 001   FLIGHT OF THE DAY (LP, private pressing) 100
79   Avada AVA 104   THREE BIRDS (LP, with insert) 22
81   Gun Dog GUN 003LP   BENEATH THE STARS (LP, private pressing) 22

WATER FOR A THIRSTY LAND
74   MRA P 100   WATER FOR A THIRSTY LAND (LP, with insert) 22

SHEILA WATERHOUSE
71   Canvas CV 037   Let Go Of The Chain/Love Me 20

WATER INTO WINE BAND
73   Myrrh MYR 1004   HILL CLIMBING FOR BEGINNERS (LP, brown cover, with insert) 150
73   Myrrh MYR 1004   HILL CLIMBING FOR BEGINNERS (LP, white cover, with insert) 100
76   CJT 002   HARVEST TIME (LP, private pressing, 500 copies) 100

WATER PISTOLS
76   State STATE 38   Gimme That Punk Junk/Soft Punk (p/s, with insert) 10

WATERPROOF CANDLE
68   RCA RCA 1717   Electrically Heated Child/Saturday Morning Repentance 15

FREDDIE WATERS
75   Mint CHEW 2   Groovin On My Baby's Love/Kung Fu & You Too 20

MUDDY WATERS
53   Vogue V 2101   Walkin' Blues/Rollin' Stone Blues (78) 80
54   Vogue V 2273   Hello Little Girl/Long Distance Call (78) 80
55   Vogue V 2372   Honey Bee/Too Young To Know (78) 80
65   Chess CRS 8001   My John The Conquer Root/Short Dress Woman 20
65   Chess CRS 8019   I Got A Rich Man's Woman/My Dog Can't Bark 20
69   Chess CRS 8083   Let's Spend The Night Together/I'm A Man 25
69   Python PKM 04   Country Boy/All Night Long (99 copies only) 85
55   Vogue EPV 1046   MUDDY WATERS WITH LITTLE WALTER (EP) 150
56   London RU-E 1060   MISSISSIPPI BLUES (EP) 175
63   Pye Intl. NEP 44010   MUDDY WATERS (EP) 40
65   Chess CRE 6006   I'M READY (EP) 50
66   Chess CRE 6022   THE REAL FOLK BLUES VOL. 4 (EP) 45
59   London Jazz LJZ-M 15192   THE BEST OF MUDDY WATERS (LP) 100
61   Pye Jazz NJL 34   AT NEWPORT (LP) 75
64   Pye Intl. NPL 28038   MUDDY WATERS - FOLK SINGER (LP) 60
64   Pye Intl. NPL 28040   THE BEST OF MUDDY WATERS (LP) 60
64   Pye Intl. NPL 28048   MUDDY SINGS BIG BILL (LP) 35
65   Chess CRL 4513   AT NEWPORT (LP, reissue) 40
66   Chess CRL 4515   THE REAL FOLK BLUES (LP) 35
67   Chess CRL 4525   MUDDY, BRASS AND THE BLUES (LP) 35
67   Chess CRL 4529   SUPER BLUES (LP, with Little Walter & Bo Diddley) 40
68   Chess CRL 4537   THE SUPER SUPER BLUES BAND (LP, with Howlin' Wolf & Bo Diddley) 50
68   Bounty BY 6031   DOWN ON STOVALL'S PLANTATION (LP) 30
69   Chess CRL 4542   ELECTRIC MUD (LP) 40
69   Chess CRL 4553   AFTER THE RAIN (LP) 20
69   Chess CRL 4556   FATHERS AND SONS (LP) 30
69   Polydor 236 574   BLUES MAN (LP) 25
69   Python PLP 12   MUDDY WATERS (LP, 99 copies only) 80
69   Python PLP 18   MUDDY WATERS VOLUME 2 (LP, 99 copies only) 80
69   Python PLP 19   MUDDY WATERS VOLUME 3 (LP, 99 copies only) 80
70   Syndicate Chapter SC 002   GOOD NEWS (LP) 15
70   Sunnyland KS 100   VINTAGE MUDDY WATERS (LP, gatefold sleeve with inserts, 99 copies only) 30
71   Chess 6671 001   McKINLEY MORGANFIELD AKA MUDDY WATERS (LP) 20
72   Black Bear LP 901   RARE LIVE RECORDINGS VOL. 1 (LP) 15
72   Black Bear LP 902   RARE LIVE RECORDINGS VOL. 2 (LP) 15
72   Black Bear LP 903   RARE LIVE RECORDINGS VOL. 3 (LP) 15
72   Chess 6310 121   THE LONDON SESSIONS (LP) 15
77   Blue Sky SKY 81853   HARD AGAIN (LP) 15

(see also Little Walter, Howlin' Wolf, Bo Diddley, Luther 'Georgia Boy Snake' Johnson)

ROGER WATERS
84   Harvest HAR 5230   5.06 AM (Every Stranger's Eyes)/4.39 AM (For The First Time Today) (p/s) 15
87   EMI EM 6   Radio Waves/Going To Live In L.A. (Demo) (p/s) 6
87   EMI EM 20   Sunset Strip/Money (live) (withdrawn) 200
70   Harvest SHSP 4008   MUSIC FROM THE FILM "THE BODY" (LP, with Ron Geesin, green labels, with Waters/Geesin photos) 50
70   Harvest SHSP 4008   MUSIC FROM THE FILM "THE BODY" (LP, with Ron Geesin, black labels) 15
83   Harvest SHVL 240105   THE PROS AND CONS OF HITCHHIKING (LP, gatefold) 25
87   EMI KAOS DJ 1   RADIO KAOS (LP, 'banded' radio promo, custom sleeve) 75
87   EMI KAOS 1   RADIO KAOS (LP, inner, poster, stickered sleeve) 25
92   Mercury 468761   AMUSED TO DEATH (2-LP) 150

(see also Pink Floyd, Ron Geesin)

LAL WATERSON & OLIVER KNIGHT
10   Three Black Feathers TBFLP 004   ONCE IN A BLUE MOON (LP, reissue) 18

LAL & MIKE WATERSON
72   Trailer LES 2076   BRIGHT PHOEBUS (LP, original pressing, red/black label) 100

Lal AND NORMA WATERSON

MINT VALUE £

73	Trailer LER 2076	BRIGHT PHOEBUS (LP, second pressing, yellow label)	35
82	Highway	BRIGHT PHOEBUS (LP, reissue)	20

LAL AND NORMA WATERSON
77	Topic 12T5331	A TRUE HEARTED GIRL (LP)	20

(see also Watersons)

MIKE WATERSON
77	Topic 12TS 332	MIKE WATERSON (LP)	20

(see also Waterson, Lal & Mike Waterson)

WATERSONS
65	Topic 12T 125	NEW VOICES (LP, blue label, with Harry Boardman & Maureen Craik)	18
65	Topic 12T 136	FROST AND FIRE (LP, blue label)	20
66	Topic 12T 142	WATERSONS (LP, blue label)	20
66	Topic 12T 167	A YORKSHIRE GARLAND (LP, blue label)	18
60s	Topic TS 346	THE WATERSONS SOUND (LP)	15

WATER WORLD
13	Box Bedroom BBR 1	Dead EP (p/s, numbered, 100 only)	10

GEORGE WATKINS
69	NEMS 56-3861	The Fly/Barrer Boy Blues	7

LOVELACE WATKINS
67	Fontana TF879	I Apologie Baby/You Can't Stop Love	300

DOC WATSON
64	Fontana TFL 6045	DOC WATSON (LP)	22
65	Fontana TFL 6055	DOC WATSON & SON (LP)	20
72	Vanguard VSD 9/10	ON STAGE (2-LP)	20

EARL WATSON
61	Ember EMB S 129	Nightmare/That Old Black Magic	10

JOHN L. WATSON (& HUMMELFLUGS)
64	Pye 7N 15746	Looking For Love/Dance With You	12
65	Piccadilly 7N 35233	Standing By/I'll Make It Worth Your While	10
70	Deram DM-R 285	A Mother's Love/Might As Well Be Gone (solo)	12
70	Deram SML 1061	WHITE HOT BLUE BLACK (LP)	40

(see also Web)

JOHNNY WATSON & KAMPAI KINGS
60	Oriole CB 1532	Moshi, Moshi, Anone!/ABDULLA & HIS LITTLE BAND: Fatima's Theme (78)	30

PAULA WATSON
63	Oriole 45-CV1785	Love Me Forever/Tell All The World About You	20

BEN WATT
81	Cherry Red CHERRY 25	Can't/Aubade/Tower Of Silence (p/s)	8
82	Cherry Red 12CHERRY 36	SUMMER INTO WINTER (12" EP, with Robert Wyatt, p/s)	10
83	Cherry Red BRED 40	NORTH MARINE DRIVE (LP)	20

(see also Everything But The Girl)

TOMMY WATT
57	Parlophone GEP 8660	TOMMY WATT AND HIS ORCHESTRA (EP)	10
57	Parlophone R 4377	Overdrive/The Little Hut	8
60	Parlophone R 4704	Les Cigale De St. Tropez/The Night We Got The Bird	6

ANDY WATTS & COBRA
77	Nebula PSS 008	Anna/I Don't Wanna Fight (no p/s)	35

BARI WATTS
80	Banazz BANAZZ 1	Move On Down/Rock 'N' Roll Romance (stamped die-cut sleeve, 500 only)	20

CHARLIE WATTS
86	CBS 450 253-1	LIVE AT FULHAM TOWN HALL (LP, as Charlie Watts & His Orchestra, with insert)	15
91	UFO UFO CD	FROM ONE CHARLIE (CD box set with book & Charlie Parker photo, signed)	40
91	UFO UFO 2 LP	FROM ONE CHARLIE (10" LP, box set with book & Charlie Parker photo, signed)	50
91	UFO UFO 2 LP	FROM ONE CHARLIE (10" LP, box set with book & Charlie Parker photo, unsigned)	20

(see also Rolling Stones, People Band, Rocket 88)

NOBLE 'THIN MAN' WATTS (& HIS BAND)
57	London HLU 8627	Hard Times (The Slop)/Midnight Flight (with His Rhythm Sparks)	75
57	London HLU 8627	Hard Times (The Slop)/Midnight Flight (with His Rhythm Sparks) (78)	20
64	Sue WI 347	Noble's Theme/JUNE BATEMAN: I Don't Wanna	70
79	Flyright 547	BLAST OFF (LP, mono)	20

(see also Wild Jimmy Spurrill)

QUEENIE WATTS
66	Columbia SX 6047	QUEEN HIGH (LP)	30

TREVOR WATTS
78	Ogun OG 526	CYNOSURE (LP)	20

WAT TYLER
83	2-Lone DUMP 016	Operation Ivy & Don Brennan/Rude Girl (1-sided, wraparound p/s)	8

WATUSI WARRIORS
59	London HL 8866	Wa-Chi-Bam-Ba/Kalahari	15

ASHANTI WAUGH
80	Attack TACK 20	Babylon Wrong/BARRY BROWN: Cool Pun Yu Corner (12")	25

WAVEMAKER
75	Polydor 2383 331 15	WHERE ARE WE CAPTAIN? (LP)	15

WAVES
75	Stretch STR5	You Lose Out Girl/Hide Away	20

WAVING AT TRAINS
88	Gash 111	WAVING AT TRAINS (EP)	60

(see also Playing At Trains)

WAX DOCTOR
92	Basement BRSS 011	A New Direction/Herbal Tekno/Protplasm (12")	15

WAX DOLL

MINT VALUE £

93	Basement BRSS 018	Another Direction/The Stalker (12")	10
93	Basement BRSS 027	New Direction (93 Remix)/What's Goin' On (12", with Jack Smooth)	15
93	Basement BRSS 030	Unfriendly/Rock To The Groove (12", with Jack Smooth)	12

(see also Kev Bird)

WAX DOLL
76	Homer HM 009	Shout Loud/My Oh My	30

VALERIE WAY
72	Ra EP 7003	VALERIE WAY (EP)	12

NANCY WAYBURN
65	Warner Bros WB 5646	The World Goes On Without Me/Listen To My Heart	15

OTIS WAYGOOD BAND
77	Decca F13744	Sweet Soul Syncopation/Who Is Your Friend? (p/s)	12
77	Decca 13688	Get It Started/Red Hot Passion	30
78	Decca F 13760	Everything I Am/Then You Can Tell Me Goodbye	10

WAYGOOD ELLIS
67	Polydor 56729	I Like What I'm Trying To Do/Hey Lover	50

(see also Fleur-De-Lys)

ALVIS WAYNE
63	Starlite ST45 104	Don't Mean Maybe, Baby/I'd Rather Be With You	400
73	Injun 113	I Gottum/Lay Your Head On My Shoulder	10

BOBBY WAYNE
65	Pye International 7N 25315	Ballad Of A Teenage Queen/River Man	10

CARL WAYNE (& VIKINGS)
64	Pye 7N 15702	What's A Matter Baby/Your Loving Ways (as Carl Wayne & Vikings)	50
65	Pye 7N 15824	This Is Love/You Could Be Fun (as Carl Wayne & Vikings)	40
70	RCA RCA 2032	Maybe God's Got Something Up His Sleeve/Rosanna	6
72	RCA RCA 2257	Take My Hands For A While/Sweet Seasons	7
75	Polydor 2058 527	Way Back In The Fifties/Candy (You Know That I'm In Love With You)	6
77	Target TGT 125	A Little Give, A Little Take/Home Lovin' Man	6
77	DJM DJS Weeken 10797	Hi Summer/My Girl And Me	6
72	RCA SF 8239	CARL WAYNE (LP)	20

(see also Move, Ace Kefford Stand, Cheetahs, Acid Gallery, Keith Powell [& Valets])

CHRIS WAYNE & ECHOES
60	Decca F 11231	Lonely/Counting Girls	15

JEFF WAYNE
69	Columbia S(C)X 6330	TWO CITIES (LP, soundtrack)	35

(see also Ran-Dells)

JERRY WAYNE
60	Vogue V 9169	Half-Hearted Love/Ten Thousand Miles	25

JOHN WAYNE
73	RCA PL 13484	AMERICA, WHY I LOVE HER (LP)	15

PAT WAYNE (& BEACHCOMBERS)
63	Columbia DB 7121	Go Back To Daddy/Jambalaya	20
63	Columbia DB 7182	Roll Over Beethoven/Is It Love?	25
64	Columbia DB 7262	Bye Bye Johnny/Strictly For The Birds	25
64	Columbia DB 7417	Brand New Man/Nobody's Child	20
65	Columbia DB 7603	Come Dance With Me/I Don't Want To Cry (solo)	12
65	Columbia DB 7739	My Friend/Tomorrow Mine (solo)	10
66	Columbia DB 7944	The Night Is Over/Hombre (solo)	12

RICK WAYNE
93	Sunjam SR 0014	Our Younger Years/PICK A POW: Time Hard (12")	30
94	Pathway To Freedom R+R 002	Almighty Father/Bad Behaviour (12")	80
02	One Studio OS4	Magnify/Version	20
02	One Studio OS5	If It Weren't For Jah/Version	20

RICK(Y) WAYNE (& OFF-BEATS)
60	Triumph RGM 1009	Chick A'Roo/Don't Pick On Me (with Fabulous Flee-Rakkers)	50
60	Pye 7N 15289	Make Way Baby/Goodness Knows (as Ricky Wayne & Off-Beats)	45
65	Oriole CB 306	Say You're Gonna Be My Own/It's A Crying Shame (as Rick Wayne)	20
65	CBS 201764	In My Imagination/Don't Ever Share Your Love (as Rick Wayne)	15

(see also [Fabulous] Flee-Rekkers)

TERRY WAYNE
57	Columbia DB 4002	Matchbox/Your True Love	25
57	Columbia DB 4035	Plaything/Slim Jim Tie	25
58	Columbia DB 4067	All Mama's Children/Forgive Me	25
58	Columbia DB 4112	Oh! Lonesome Me/There's Only One You	20
58	Columbia DB 4205	Little Brother/Where My Baby Goes	18
59	Columbia DB 4312	Brooklyn Bridge/She's Mine	20
58	Columbia SEG 7758	TERRIFIC (EP)	80

THOMAS WAYNE
59	London HLU 8846	Tragedy/Saturday Date	20
59	London HLU 8846	Tragedy/Saturday Date (78)	25
59	London HL 7075	Tragedy/Saturday Date (export issue)	20

WAYS & MEANS
66	Columbia DB 7907	Little Deuce Coupe/The Little Old Lady From Pasadena	25
66	Pye 7N 17217	Sea Of Faces/Make The Radio A Little Louder	25
68	Trend TRE 1005	Breaking Up A Dream/She	60

WAY WE LIVE
71	Dandelion DAN 8004	A CANDLE FOR JUDITH (LP, gatefold sleeve, label and sleeve DAN 8004)	250
71	Dandelion DAN 8004	A CANDLE FOR JUDITH (LP, gatefold sleeve, as K 49004)	125

WAZMO NARIZ

(see also Tractor, Beau)

WAZMO NARIZ
78 Stiff BUY 33   Tele-tele-phone/Wacker Drive (blue label, push-out centre) 8

WE'RE ONLY HUMAN
82 VC VC 002   I Wouldn't Treat A Dog/Hold Your Head Up High (no p/s, 500 only) 40

WEAK LINK
74 Slowgun SLO 341   Let's Rock/The Way Is Hard 12

WEAPON
80 Weapon WEAP 1   It's A Mad Mad World/Set The Stage Alight (p/s) 30
81 Virgin WEAPONE   It's A Mad Mad World/Set The Stage Alight (12", p/s, reissue) 40

(see also Wildfire)

WEASELSNOUT
72 Weaselsnout WUS 140   UNSUNG LIES (LP, private pressing) 500

WEATHER
69 Philips BF 1734   Look In My Eyes/Running Forward 35
69 Philips BF 1819   Jamboree Special/Two Peculiar People 10

WEATHER REPORT
85 Nimbus 80027   MYSTERIOUS TRAVELLER (LP, Nimbus Supercut, mail order only through Practical Hi Fi magazine) 60

ALFIE WEATHERBY
58 Columbia DC 729   49 Juke Boxes/Why Am I Crying? (78, export issue) 20

OSCAR WEATHERS
72 Mojo 2092 006   The Spoiler/You Want To Play 15

VIVIAN WEATHERS
78 Virgin Frontline FL 1025 BAD WEATHER (LP) 15

DENNIS WEAVER
77 DJM DJS 10758   Devil In My Arms/Flat Bed Truck (p/s, promo) 8

JANE WEAVER V DOVES
98 Manchester MANC 9   Seven Day Smile/ANDY VOTEL & JANE WEAVER: Gutter Girl (p/s) 6

(see also Doves)

WEAVERS
59 Top Rank JAR 120   Wild Goose Grasses/Meet The Johnson Boys 6

(see also Pete Seeger)

WEB (1)
68 Deram DM 201   Hatton Mill Morning/Conscience 25
68 Deram DM 217   Baby Won't You Leave Me Alone/McVernon Street 25
69 Deram DM 253   Monday To Friday/Harold Dubbleyew 25
68 Deram DML 1025   FULLY INTERLOCKING (LP, mono) 100
68 Deram SML 1025   FULLY INTERLOCKING (LP, stereo) 120
70 Deram DAL-R 1058   THERAPHOSA BLONDI (LP, mono) 200
70 Deram SML-R 1058   THERAPHOSA BLONDI (LP, stereo) 125
70 Polydor 2383 024   I SPIDER (LP, gatefold sleeve, red label) 500

(see also John L. Watson [& Hummelflugs], Samurai, Greenslade)

WEB (2)
96 Fat Cat 12FAT 001   EVA EP (12", plain sleeve) 20

BARRY WEBB (O.P.M.C)
70 Decca F 23012   Live For Tomorrow Harry James/At The Hop 8

DEAN WEBB
59 Parlophone R 4549   Warm Your Heart/Hey Miss Fannie 50
59 Parlophone R 4587   The Rough And The Smooth/Streamline Baby 50

DON WEBB
60 Coral Q 72385   Little Ditty Baby/I'll Be Back Home 100

GEORGE WEBB DIXIELANDERS
56 Decca DFE 6351   AND HIS DIXIELANDERS (EP) 10
50s Melodisc EPM7 70   THE GEORGE WEBB DIXIELANDERS (EP) 10

JANET WEBB
71 Polydor 2058-131   I Cried For You/Mama (p/s) 10

JILLA WEBB
56 MGM SP 1180   You Gotta Love Me Now/What Do You Think It Does To Me? 10

JIMMY WEBB
68 CBS 3672   I Keep It Hid/I Need You (as Jim Webb) 25
71 Reprise RS 20978   P.F. Sloan/Psalm One-Five-O 10
68 CBS (S) 63335   JIM WEBB SINGS JIM WEBB (LP, as Jim Webb, laminated front cover) 25
71 Reprise RSLP 6421   WORDS AND MUSIC (LP, with insert) 20
72 Reprise K 44134   AND SO ON (LP) 15
72 Reprise K 44173   LETTERS (LP) 15
77 Atlantic K 50370   EL MIRAGE (LP, with inner sleeve) 15

(see also Strawberry Children, Glen Campbell)

JOHNNY WEBB
56 Columbia DB 3805   Dig/Glendora 10
60s Melodisc MEL 1617   Travelin' Man/Hold Back The Town (with p/s) 12

(see also June Laverick)

PETA WEBB
73 Topic 12TS 223   I HAVE WANDERED IN EXILE (LP, blue label) 35

(see also Oak)

PETA WEBB & PETE COOPER
86 Heart   HEART IS TRUE (LP) 15

ROGER WEBB (& HIS TRIO)
67 RCA 1599   A Man And His Woman/The Spiderman 30
71 Columbia DB 8803   Strange Report/Summer Fancy 12
82 Chandos SBR 102   The Gentle Touch/Arthur's Theme 6

			MINT VALUE £
84	Chips CH 104	Hammer House Of Horror/Cover Theme (p/s)	12
64	Parlophone PMC 1233	JOHN, PAUL AND ALL THAT JAZZ (LP)	18

SKEETER WEBB
55	Parlophone CMSP 32	Was It A Bad Dream/Your Secret's Not A Secret Anymore (export issue)	15

SONNY WEBB & CASCADES
64	Oriole CB 1873	You've Got Everything/Border Of The Blues	45
64	Polydor NH 52158	You've Got Everything/Border Of The Blues (reissue)	15

A J WEBBER
80	Gundog GUN 002	OF THIS LAND (LP)	30

MARLENE WEBBER
70	Bamboo BAM 33	My Baby/BRENTFORD ALLSTARS: You Gonna Hold Me (Version)	40
71	Ackee ACK 120	Natengula/Natengula-Kera (as Merlin Webber)	18
71	Ackee ACK 122	Cumbaya/Hail-Hi Freedom (as Merlin Webber)	15
71	Smash SMA 2322	Hard Life/COLLINS ALL STARS: Version Life (as Merlene Webber)	50
71	Trojan TR 7815	Stand By Your Man/CLANCY ECCLES: Credit Squeeze	12
76	Jama JALP 004	ONCE YOU HIT THE ROAD LP	30

(see also Webber Sisters, Tonettes)

WEBBER SISTERS
67	Island WI 3109	My World/ALVA LEWIS: Lonely Still	60

(see also Delroy Wilson)

WEBBY JAY
79	Awawak DD 008	In The Rain/Rain Unlimited (12")	20

WEBS
68	London HLU 10188	This Thing Called Love/Tomorrow	25

WEBSPINNERS
73	Buddah 2011 150	Spider Man - Theme/Goin' 'Cross Town	6

BEN WEBSTER
55	Columbia CLEF 33CX 10014	MUSIC FOR LOVERS (LP)	20
57	Vogue Coral 10021	TENOR SAX STYLIST (10" LP)	40
59	Columbia 33CX 10122	SOULVILLE (LP)	25
59	HMV CLP 1336	BEN WEBSTER AND ASSOCIATES (LP)	30
60	HMV CLP 1412	BEN WEBSTER MEETS OSCAR PETERSON (LP)	30
60	HMV CLP 1437	THE SOUL OF BEN WEBSTER (LP)	25
64	HMV CLP 1896	SEE YOU AT THE FAIR (LP)	20
65	Fontana FJL 126	INTIMATE! (LP)	20
67	Fontana FJL 316	BIG BEN TIME! (LP)	20
69	Ember CJS 822	BEN WEBSTER AT EASE (LP)	15
69	EMI SCX 6389	FOR THE GUV'NOR (LP)	20

CHASE WEBSTER
64	Hickory 45-1283	Life Can Have Meaning/Where Is Your Heart	6

DEENA WEBSTER
68	Parlophone R 5699	You're Losing/Wish You Were Here	25
68	Parlophone R 5721	Your Heart Is Free Just Like The Wind/Queen Merka And Me	25
68	Parlophone R 5738	Scarborough Fair/The Water Is Wide	25
69	Parlophone R 5798	Joey/It's Alright With Me	25
68	Parlophone PMC/PCS 7052	TUESDAY'S CHILD (LP)	200
14	Record Collector RCLP011	TUESDAY'S CHILD (LP, reissue)	30

WEDDING PRESENT
85	Reception REC 001	Go Out And Get 'Em Boy/(The Moment Before) Everything's Spoiled Again (p/s, 500 only, with poster & badge)	40
85	Reception REC 001	Go Out And Get 'Em Boy/(The Moment Before) Everything's Spoiled Again (p/s, 500 only, without poster & badge)	30
85	City Slang CSL 001	Go Out And Get 'Em Boy/(The Moment Before) Everything's Spoiled Again (reissue, different foldout p/s, 1,000 only)	15
86	Reception REC 002	Once More/At The Edge Of The Sea (p/s, 3,500 only)	8
86	Reception REC 003	This Boy Can Wait/You Should Always Keep In Touch With Your Friends (p/s, matrix numbers: 003 A2 & 003 B1)	6
87	Reception REC 005	My Favourite Dress/Every Mother's Son/Never Said (p/s, white vinyl, 3,000 only, 2,000 of which free with "George Best" LP)	6
87	Reception	A Million Miles/What Did Your Last Servant Die Of? (DJ promo, 200 only)	25
88	Reception REC 010X	Davni Chasy/Katrusya (promo only)	6
89	M'night Music DONG 39 CD	Pourquoi Es Tu Devenue Si Raisonable? (CD, unreleased)	0
89	RCA	Davni Chasy/Katrusya (promo only)	12
90	RCA PB 43403	Brassneck/Don't Talk, Just Kiss (custom hand-painted p/s, 3,000 only)	40
92	RCA PB 45185	Blue Eyes/Cattle And Cane (p/s)	7
92	RCA PB 45183	Go Go Dancer/Don't Cry No Tears (p/s)	6
92	RCA PB 45181	Three/Think That It Might (p/s)	6
92	RCA PB 45311	Silver Shorts/Falling (p/s)	6
92	RCA PB 45313	Come Play With Me/Pleasant Valley Sunday (p/s)	6
92	RCA No Cat. No.	HIT PARADE (12 x 7" in custom box)	40
87	Reception LEEDS 1	GEORGE BEST (LP, 2,000 only with white vinyl 7": My Favourite Dress/ Every Mother's Son/Never Said [REC 005] & inner sleeve; later with bonus black vinyl 7" or 12" edition, £10)	40
87	Reception LEEDS 1	GEORGE BEST (LP)	30
88	Reception LEEDS 2	TOMMY (LP, 1,000 signed by band, with poster & inner sleeve)	20
89	RCA PL74302	BIZARRO (LP)	15
91	RCA PL 75012	SEAMONSTERS (LP, inner)	20
92	BMG PL75183	HIT PARADE 1 (LP)	30
94	RCA 8014524-044-1	WATUSI (LP, inner)	40
96	Cooking Vinyl COOK 099	SATURNALIA (LP, 2 x 10")	30
08	Vibrant VIBLP01	EL REY (LP)	30
10	Cooking Vinyl 900915	GEORGE BEST (2-LP, reissue)	30

WEDGE

MINT VALUE £

12	Vinyl 180 VIN180LP039	BIZARRO (LP, reissue)	30
11	Vinyl 180 VIN180LP044	SEAMONSTERS (LP, reissue)	30
12	Vinyl 180 VIN180LP035	BIZARRO (LP, reissue, as 3 x 10")	35
12	Vinyl 180 VIN180LP045	SEAMONSTERS (LP, reissue as 3 x 10")	40
14	Demon DEMREC40X	GEORGE BEST (LP, reissue, red vinyl)	30
15	Scopitones TONE 020	TAKE FOUNTAIN (2-LP)	20

WEDGE
69	Midas MD3904	Sleep Child/Fly Away	25

WEDGWOODS
64	Pye 7N 15642	September In The Rain/Gone Gone Away	12
65	Pye 7N 15846	Peace/Summer Love	10
68	Columbia DB 8459	Red Sky At Night/When Day Is Done	15

WEE CHERUBS
84	Bogaten	Dreaming /Waiting For My Man (p/s, 400 only)	175

WEE THREE
73	People PEO 104	Get On Board/Get On Board (Instrumental)	8

BUDDY WEED & HIS ORCHESTRA
57	Vogue V 9075	The Kent Song/For Love	25

BERT WEEDON
56	Parlophone MSP 6242	The Boy With The Magic Guitar/Flannel-Foot	20
57	Parlophone R 4256	Theme From ITV's '$64,000 Question'/Twilight Time	20
57	Parlophone R 4315	The Jolly Gigolo/Soho Fair	20
57	Parlophone R 4381	Play That Big Guitar/Quiet, Quiet, Ssh!	10
58	Parlophone R 4446	Big Note Blues/Rippling Tango	10
60	Top Rank JAR 517	Sorry Robbie/Easy Beat	8
61	Top Rank JAR 537	Ginchy/Yearning	6
61	Top Rank JAR 559	Mr. Guitar/Eclipse	8
56	Esquire EP 56	WAXING THE WINNERS (EP)	25
59	Selmer Amplifiers	DEMONSTRATION RECORD WITH DAVID GELL (EP, with mailer)	20
60	Top Rank BUY 026	KINGSIZE GUITAR (LP)	20
61	Top Rank 35/101	HONKY TONK GUITAR (LP)	20

(see also George Chisholm, Craig Douglas)

WEEDS
86	In Tape IT 34	China Doll/Crazy Face (p/s)	12

WEEKENDERS
94	Blow Up (Blow UP BU 001)	All Grown Up/House Husband (mail-order only)	10

WEEKND
13	Republic 602537512935	KISS LAND (2-LP)	20
15	Republic 0602547264756	HOUSE OF BALLOONS (2-LP)	30
15	Republic 0602547264930	THURSDAY (2-LP)	50
15	Republic 0602547261472	ECHOES OF SILENCE (2-LP)	50
17	Republic 0602557227512	STARBOY (2-LP, red vinyl)	30
20	Republic 00602507395711	BEAUTY BEHIND THE MADNESS (2-LP, yellow/black splatter vinyl)	40

WEEN
93	August RUST 002 LP	PURE GUAVA (2-LP)	40
94	Flying Nun FN 31	CHOCOLATE & CHEESE (2-LP with free 7")	40
95	Flying Nun FN 322	THE POD (2-LP, reissue)	30
96	Flying Nun FN 386	12 GOLDEN COUNTRY GREATS (LP)	40
97	Mushroom MUSH 3LP	THE MOLLUSK (LP, inner)	50
00	Mushroom MUSH 69LP	WHITE PEPPER (LP)	25
03	Sanctuary 0607684591	QUEBEC (2-LP)	35
06	Schnitzel SRLP 125525	LIVE IN TORONTO CANADA FEATURING THE SHIT CREEK BOYS (2-LP, reissue white vinyl)	25
07	Schnitzel SRLP 1255211	LA CUCARACHA (LP)	20

WEENY BOPPER
72	Pye 45203	David, Donny & Michael/Won't You Smile For Me	8

WEEPING MESSERSCHMITTS
86	Upright UPT 17	NOTHING YET (12" EP, p/s)	15

WEEZER
94	Geffen GFS 85	Undone: The Sweater Song/Mykel And Carli/Susanne/Holiday (blue vinyl, p/s)	20
95	Geffen GFS 88	Buddy Holly/Jamie (p/s)	18
95	Geffen GFSV 95	Say It Ain't So (Remix)/No One Else (Live & Acoustic)/Jamie (10", p/s)	10
96	Geffen GFS 22167	El Scorcho/You Gave Your Love To Me Softly (p/s)	10
01	Geffen 497567-7	Hash Pipe/Teenage Victory Song (p/s)	10
01	Geffen 497616-7	Island In The Sun/Always (p/s, yellow vinyl)	10
02	Geffen 497771-7	Keep Fishin'/Photograph (live) (p/s)	8
95	Geffen GEF 24629	WEEZER (LP)	50
96	Geffen 425007-1	PINKERTON (LP)	40
02	Geffen DGC 25007	PINKERTON (LP, reissue)	20

WE FIVE
65	Pye International 7N 25314	You Were On My Mind/Small World	12
66	Pye International 7N 25346	Let's Get Together/Cast Your Fate To The Wind	20
66	Pye Intl. NEP 44056	LET'S GET TOGETHER (EP)	60
65	Pye Intl. NPL 28067	YOU WERE ON MY MIND (LP)	60

WE 4
69	Major Minor MM 593	Candy Floss Man/Perry Park	6

FRANK WEIR & HIS ORCHESTRA
54	Decca F 10271	The Happy Wanderer/From Your Lips	15
60	Oriole CB 1559	Caribbean Honeymoon/Farewell My Love	10
62	Philips 326560 BF	Manhunt/Chant Of The Jungle	6
55	Decca DFE 6226	THE HAPPY WANDERER (EP)	10

Norris WEIR (& JAMAICANS)

MINT VALUE £

(see also Bill Darnell, Vera Lynn, Janie Marden)

NORRIS WEIR (& JAMAICANS)
70	Duke DU 85	Hard On Me (with Jamaicans)/TOMMY COWAN & JAMAICANS: Please Stop The Wedding	12
74	Dragon DRA 1030	Reggay Revolution/Version	12
75	Horse HOSS 81	Dr. Honey/Honey Dub	8

(see also Jamaicans)

WEIRD STRINGS
80	Velvet Moon VM 1	Oscar Mobile/Ancient Square (foldover p/s)	10
80	Ace ACE 009	Criminal Cage/Mi££ionaire (p/s)	8

(see also Paul Roland, Midnight Rags)o

KLAUS WEISS
17	Trunk JBH 063 LP	TIME SIGNALS (LP, reissue)	18

BRUCE WELCH
74	EMI EMI 2141	Please Mr. Please/Song Of Yesterday	35

(see also Marvin, Welch & Farrar; Shadows, Cliff Richard)

ED WELCH
71	United Artists UP35284	Clowns/The Bird Song	10
71	United Artists UAS 29248	CLOWNS (LP, with inner)	15

ELIZABETH WELCH
80	Industrial IR 0012	Stormy Weather/You're Blase (p/s)	8

HONEE WELCH
69	London HLU 10288	I'm Gonna Try/It's My Girl	7

KEN & MITZIE WELCH
62	London RE-R 1275	A PIANO, ICE BOX AND BED (EP)	15

LENNY WELCH
60	London HLA 9094	You Don't Know Me/I Need Someone	6
62	London HLA 9601	Taste Of Honey/Old Cathedral	6
63	London HLA 9810	Since I Fell For You/Are You Sincere	6
64	London HLA 9880	Ebb Tide/Congratulations Baby	6
64	London HLR 9910	If You See My Love/Father Sebastian	6
65	London HLR 9981	Darling Take Me Back/Time After Time	15
65	London HLR 9991	Two Different Worlds/I Was There	8
65	London HLR 10010	Run To My Lovin' Arms/Coronet Blue	20
66	London HLR 10031	Rags To Riches/I Want You To Worry	10
66	London HA-R/SH-R 8267	TWO DIFFERENT WORLDS (LP)	25
66	London HA-R 8290	RAGS TO RICHES (LP)	30

TIM WELCH
60	Columbia DB 4529	Weak In The Knees/A Boy And A Girl In Love	7

WELD OF LIQUOR
95	Weld Record WELD 05	We Are The Weld/For Manze's Sake (vinegar-scented p/s)	10

WELFARE STATE
78	Look LKLP 6347	WELFARE STATE SONGS (LP, with insert)	60

LAWRENCE WELK ORCHESTRA
64	Dot DS 16697	The 'Addams Family' Theme/Apples And Bananas	10

WELL WISHERS
73	Pendant PEN 1	Find Mister Jameson/Weird	40

PAUL WELLER

SINGLES
92	Go! Discs GOD 86	Uh Huh Oh Yeh/Fly On The Wall (7"; paper or plastic labels)	6
92	Go! Discs GOD 91	Above Clouds/Everything Has A Price To Pay (7"; paper or plastic labels)	6
93	Go! Discs GOD 102	Sunflower/Bull-Rush-Magic Bus (Live at RAH 10.92) (7")	6
93	Go! Discs GOD 104	Wild Wood/Ends Of The Earth (7")	6
93	Go! Discs GODT 104	Wild Wood/Ends Of The Earth (10", numbered with poster)	10
93	Matrix: WELLER+F1	The Loved (blank clear flexi with The Big Issue mag)	12
05	V2 VVR 5030597	Early Morning Rain/Come Together (7", red vinyl, die-cut sleeve, 4,000 only)	6
09	Universal (No cat no)	7 & 3 Is The Striker's Name (one sided 7", screen printed sleeve, 1000 only)	50
10	V2	Aim High (Aim Higher)/Pieces Of A Dream (Dreams In Pieces)/Aim High (The Higher Aim)/Aim High (Like Water Needs A Flower) All The Amorphous Androgymous remixes (10", p/s, 500 only for 2010 Record Store Day)	25
13	Virgin VFW 1	Flame-Out!/The Olde Original 'twin Virgins' label)	12
14	Virgin RSD14PW	Brand New Toys/Landslide ('two Virgins' label, white vinyl, stickered die-cut sleeve)	20

ALBUMS
92	Go! Discs 828 343-1	PAUL WELLER (LP, gatefold sleeve, stapled-in lyric booklet)	60
93	Go! Discs 828 435-1	WILD WOOD (LP, gatefold sleeve with 'obi' band & poster)	150
94	Go! Discs 828 513-1	WILD WOOD (LP, gatefold sleeve with 'obi' band & poster; reissue with extra track 'Hung Up', 'second edition' on label of side 2)	75
94	Go! Discs 828 561-1	LIVE WOOD (2-LP, single sleeve with picture inners)	150
95	Go! Discs 828 619-1	STANLEY ROAD (LP, gatefold sleeve with Excerpts booklet)	80
95	Go! Discs 850 070-7	STANLEY ROAD (6 x 7" singles in 7" box)	90
97	Island ILPS 8058	HEAVY SOUL (LP, gatefold sleeve with picture inner and insert)	80
97	Island CID 8058	HEAVY SOUL ("unofficial" wooden box set, 1,000 only, incl.: hinged wooden box, numbered certificate, promo CD, 5 postcards, CD booklet, promo 7", 5 guitar plectrums & polo shirt)	175
98	Island ILPSD 8080	MODERN CLASSICS - THE GREATEST HITS (2-LP, gatefold sleeve with picture inners & insert)	50
98	Island IBX 8080	MODERN CLASSICS (box set, numbered 4 x 7" + 16-page photo book & colour print)	60
00	Island ILPS 8093	HELIOCENTRIC (LP, with foldout poster)	200
01	Independiente ISOM26LP	DAYS OF SPEED (2-LP, gatefold sleeve with pic inners)	250
02	Independiente ISOM33LP	ILLUMINATION (LP, rounded corners, gatefold sleeve with picture inner & booklet)	200
03	Universal 0635271	FLY ON THE WALL (3-LP, stickered sleeve)	175

Paul WELLER MOVEMENT

MINT VALUE £

04	V2 VVR 1026902	STUDIO 150 (CD, autographed for competition)	30
04	V2 VVR 1026901	STUDIO 150 (LP, 2,000 only, with inner sleeve)	250
05	V2 VVR 1033201	AS IS NOW (2-LP, gatefold, inners, print)	150
06	V2 VVR 1039391	CATCH FLAME (2-LP, gatefold, 2 inners, free 7")	150
08	Island 176935	22 DREAMS (2-LP, gatefold, booklet, with Island 'pink eye' logo)	150
08	Universal 5313274	AT THE BBC (3-LP)	100
10	Island 2732868	WAKE UP THE NATION (LP, flipback sleeve, inserts)	100
14	Virgin V 3127	MORE MODERN CLASSICS (2-LP)	35
15	Vinyl Factory VVR798608	SONIK KICKS (LP)	35
15	Parlophone 0825646030354	SATURNS PATTERN (LP, clear vinyl)	30
17	Parlophone 0190295866020	MUSIC FROM THE FILM JAWBONE (LP)	20
17	Parlophone 0190295845261	A KIND REVOLUTION (LP)	25
17	Parlophone 0190295830588	A KIND REVOLUTION (LP as 5 x 10")	30
18	Parlophone 0190295635987	TRUE MEANINGS (2-LP)	30
19	Parlophone 0190295494018	OTHER ASPECTS (3-LP, DVD)	40
19	Parlophone 0190295846428	A KIND REVOLUTION (LP, reissue, blue vinyl, numbered, 50 only, stickered sleeve)	400
20	Polydor 00602508598579	ON SUNSET (2-LP)	20
20	Polydor 0880415	ON SUNSET (LP, picture disc)	25
21	Polydor 3556636	FAT POP (3-LP, box set)	100
21	Polydor 3554122	FAT POP (LP, red, yellow or orange vinyl)	20

PROMOS

91	Freedom High FHP 1	Into Tomorrow/Here's A New Thing (7", white label promo, 1991)	25
91	Freedom High FHPT 1	Into Tomorrow/Here's A New Thing/That Spiritual Feeling/Into Tomorrow (8-Track Demo) (12", white label promo, 1991)	35
92	Echantillon (no cat. no.)	Uh Huh Oh Yeh/Arrival Time/Fly On The Wall/ Always There To Fool You (12", yellow label test pressing)	50
92	Go! Discs KOSX 1	Kosmos (12", 1-sided)	25
92	Go! Discs GOXDJ 102	Kosmos (12", printed label)	25
93	Go! Discs GOPRO 102	Sunflower (12")	12
93	Go! Discs GOTDJ 104	Wild Wood/Ends Of The Earth (10")	20
93	Go! Discs GOXDJ 111	Hung Up/Foot Of The Mountain (Live Royal Albert Hall 23.11.93)/The Loved/ Kosmos (Lynch Mob Bonus Beats) (12", printed white labels)	10
94	Go! Discs PNME 1	Shadow Of The Sun (Live at Wolverhampton Civic Hall 9.3.94)/ Sunflower (Lynch Mob Dub Edit)/Wild Wood (Sheared Wood - Remixed by Portishead with A. Utley) (white label promo for NME cover mount)	35
95	Go! Discs LYNCH 1	Lynch Mob Beats (12", stamped 1-sided white label, 500 only)	60
95	Go! Discs SPLINT 1	Walk On Gilded Splinters (12", white label test pressing, 1-sided, 1995)	70
95	Go! Discs (no cat. no.)	CD SAMPLER (CD, given away in queue for 100 Club gig, 200 only)	45
95	Disctronics matrix: WELLERSPEC 01	OUR PRICE PAUL WELLER SPECIAL (CD, in-store album, no inlay, PVC outer)	60
96	Go! Discs PWRT 1	PEACOCK SUIT (CD, 7-track, picture disc in cloth bag)	25
97	Island HEAVY 1	Heavy Soul (Pt 1)/Heavy Soul (Pt 2) (7", Island sleeve)	50
97	Island PWICD 1	HEAVY SOUL (box set: interview CD, EPK, 5 cards & insert)	45
97	Southern Songs WELLER 1	LIVE... FROM THE ROOF OF THE HAYWARD GALLERY (LP, finished sleeve, white labels)	30
97	Island KINGS 1	KINGS ROAD (CD sampler, 350 only)	45
98	Island 12IS 711DJ	Brand New Start/Right Underneath It (12")	12
99	Island 12IS 734DJ	Wild Wood (The Sheared Wood Remix)/Science (Lynch Mob Remix with Psychonauts) (12", white label, only 130 copies mailed out)	18
99	Island INTCD 3	IN CONVERSATION (interview CD, gatefold card p/s)	30
00	Island HELIO-1	Heliocentric (Two Lone Swordsmen 4UR Mix)/Heliocentric (Original Version)/There's No Drinking After You're Dead (Noonday Underground Mix) (12" white label)	30
01	Independiente DOSB 1	DAYS OF SPEED SELECTIONS (3-CD set, card outer sleeve with CDs in individual card inners)	50
03	Universal CUFF 1	BUTTON DOWNS (LP, promo-only vinyl edition of third disc of cover versions from Fly On The Wall)	35
05	V2 VVR 5033488P	From The Floorboards Up (7", white label test pressing, stamped white sleeve)	25
05	V2 VVR 1033202P	SINGLES BOX (box set, mail-order only, houses all As Is Now 7"s; priced without singles)	20
05	Universal STAN 1	STANLEY ROAD - 10TH ANNIVERSARY EP (7")	10

(see also Jam, Style Council, Smokin' Mojo Filters, Andy Lewis & Paul Weller, Paul Weller Movement, Noonday Underground)

PAUL WELLER MOVEMENT

91	Freedom High FHP 1	Into Tomorrow/Here's A New Thing (7", with or without 'Paul Weller Movement' printed on label)	8
91	Freedom High FHPT 1	Into Tomorrow/Here's A New Thing/That Spiritual Feeling/Into Tomorrow (8-Track Demo) (12")	12

PAUL WELLER & THE RAKES

05	V2 FP01	Shine On/Ausland Mission (Promo, given out at Fred Perry party)	45

ORSON WELLES

59	Top Rank TR 5001	The Courtroom Scene From The Film 'Compulsion' (both sides) (in p/s)	12
84	Splash SP 29	I Know What It Is To Be Young (But You Don't Know What It Is To Be Old)/Love Is A Lovely Word (p/s)	8

NICK WELLINGS & SECTION

77	The Label TLR 011	You Better Move On/Punk Funk	6

WELLINGTON

74	Concord CON 029	Alright I'll See You Tonight/How Would You Like To Rock With Me	8
74	Concord CON 031	Catch Us If You Can/Superstar	8

BOBBY WELLINS

78	Vortex VS1	LIVE JUBILATION (LP)	40
78	Vortex VS2	DREAMS ARE FREE (LP)	40

BOBBY WELLS

68	Beacon 3-102	Let's Copp A Groove/Recipe For Love (yellow label)	30
68	Beacon 3-102	Let's Copp A Groove/Recipe For Love (white label)	20
68	Beacon 3-102	Let's Copp A Groove/Recipe For Love (green label)	15

Brian WELLS

MINT VALUE £

79	Grapevine GRP 124	Be's That Way Sometimes/Recipe For Love	10

BRIAN WELLS

72	Spark SRL 1082	Paper Party/Just A Summer High	6

COBY WELLS

67	Decca F 12560	My Feet Ache/Venus De Milo	12

HOUSTON WELLS (& MARKSMEN)

62	Parlophone R 4955	This Song Is Just For You/Paradise	10
62	Parlophone R 4980	Shutters And Boards/North Wind	10
63	Parlophone R 5031	Only The Heartaches/Can't Stop Pretending	8
63	Parlophone R 5069	Blowing Wild (The Ballad Of Black Gold)/Crazy Dreams	10
64	Parlophone R 5099	Anna Marie/Moon Watch Over My Baby	10
64	Parlophone R 5141	Galway Bay/Livin' Alone (as Houston Wells & Outlaws)	10
65	Parlophone R 5226	Blue Of The Night/Coming Home (solo)	7
68	CBS 3572	Teach Me Little Children/Does My Ring Hurt Your Finger	6
63	Parlophone GEP 8878	JUST FOR YOU (EP)	50
63	Parlophone GEP 8914	RAMONA (EP)	60
64	Parlophone PMC 1215	WESTERN STYLE (LP)	50

(see also Marksmen, Outlaws)

JEAN WELLS

71	Mojo 2092 023	After Loving You/Puttin' The Best On The Outside	20
70	Sonet SNTF 606	WORLD! HERE COMES JEAN WELLS (LP)	50

JOHNNY WELLS (1)

59	Columbia DB 4377	Lonely Moon/The One And Only One	50

JOHNNY WELLS (2)

67	Parlophone R 5559	Guess I'm Dumb/Wondering Why	40

JUNIOR WELLS

66	Delmark DS 9612	Hoodoo Man Blues (blue label)	30
66	Delmark DS 628	Southside Blues Jam (blue label)	20
68	Mercury MF 1056	Girl You Lit My Fire/It's A Man Down There	15
66	Delmark DJB 1	BLUES WITH A BEAT (EP)	35
68	Fontana (S)TFL 6084	IT'S MY LIFE BABY (LP)	40
68	Vanguard SVRL 19011	COMING AT YOU (LP, also stereo, VSD 79262)	30
68	Vanguard SVRL 19028	IT'S MY LIFE BABY (LP, reissue)	25
68	Mercury SMCL 20130	YOU'RE TUFF ENOUGH (LP)	45
71	Delmark DS 628	SOUTHSIDE BLUES JAM (LP)	22
75	Delmark DS 635	JUNIOR WELLS ON TAP (LP)	15

(see also Buddy Guy)

KITTY WELLS

55	Brunswick OE 9149	KITTY SINGS (EP)	12

MARY WELLS

62	Oriole CBA 1762	You Beat Me To The Punch/Old Love	70
63	Oriole CBA 1796	Two Lovers/Operator	50
63	Oriole CBA 1829	Laughing Boy/Two Wrongs Don't Make A Right	50
63	Oriole CBA 1847	Your Old Standby/What Love Has Joined Together	50
63	Stateside SS 242	You Lost The Sweetest Boy/What's Easy For Two Is So Hard For One	25
63	Stateside SS 242	You Lost The Sweetest Boy/What's Easy For Two Is So Hard For One (DJ Copy)	100
64	Stateside SS 288	My Guy/Oh Little Boy (What Did You Do To Me)	12
64	Stateside SS 288	My Guy/Oh Little Boy (DJ Copy)	100
64	Stateside SS 316	Once Upon A Time (with Marvin Gaye)/What's The Matter With You, Baby	40
64	Stateside SS 316	Once Upon A Time (with Marvin Gaye)/What's The Matter With You, Baby (DJ Copy)	85
65	Stateside SS 372	Ain't It The Truth/Stop Takin' Me For Granted	30
65	Stateside SS 372	Ain't It The Truth/Stop Takin' Me For Granted (DJ Copy)	50
65	Stateside SS 396	Use Your Head/Everlovin' Boy	30
65	Stateside SS 396	Use Your Head/Everlovin' Boy (DJ Copy)	50
65	Stateside SS 415	Never Never Leave Me/Why Don't You Let Yourself Go	20
65	Stateside SS 415	Never Never Leave Me/Why Don't You Let Yourself Go (DJ Copy)	50
65	Stateside SS 439	He's A Lover/I'm Learnin'	25
65	Stateside SS 439	He's A Lover/I'm Learnin' (DJ Copy)	50
65	Stateside SS 463	Me Without You/I'm Sorry	25
65	Stateside SS 463	Me Without You/I'm Sorry (DJ Copy)	50
68	Stateside SS 2111	The Doctor/Two Lovers' History	20
66	Atlantic AT 4067	Dear Lover/Can't You See (You're Losing Me)	50
66	Atlantic 584 054	Me And My Baby/Such A Sweet Thing	20
67	Atlantic 584 104	(Hey You) Set My Soul On Fire/Coming Home	18
70	Direction 58-4816	Dig The Way I Feel/Love Shooting Bandit	15
72	Atlantic K 10254	Dear Lover/Can't You See (You're Losing Me) (reissue)	10
65	Tamla Motown TME 2007	MARY WELLS (EP)	100
63	Oriole PS 40045	TWO LOVERS (LP)	80
63	Oriole PS 40051	BYE BYE BABY (LP)	90
64	Stateside SL 10095	SINGS MY GUY (LP)	70
64	Stateside SL 10133	MARY WELLS (LP)	80
65	Tamla Motown TML 11006	MY BABY JUST CARES FOR ME (LP)	55
66	Stateside S(S)L 10171	LOVE SONGS TO THE BEATLES (LP)	50
66	Tamla Motown TML 11032	GREATEST HITS (LP)	35
68	Stateside S(S)L 10266	SERVIN' UP SOME SOUL (LP)	50
68	Atlantic 587 049	THE TWO SIDES OF MARY WELLS (LP)	30
69	Tamla Motown (S)TML 11102	VINTAGE STOCK (LP, unissued)	0

(see also Marvin Gaye)

Alex WELSH & DIXIELANDERS

MINT VALUE £

ALEX WELSH & DIXIELANDERS
61	Columbia DB 4686	Tansy/Memphis March	10
55	Decca DFE 6254	DIXIELANDERS AT THE RFH (EP)	10

WENDY & LEMMY
82	Bronze BRO 151	Stand By Your Man/No Class/Masterplan (p/s)	15

(see also Motorhead)

WE'RE TIRED
77	Deadline DEADS 8	My Life's On The Line/Against All Odds (p/s)	20
77	Deadline DEADS 11	Guide Me Through Hell/Time Is Against Me (p/s)	25
78	Deadline DEADS 15	Over The Edge/Anal Retentive (p/s, as We're Tired & We're Proud)	8
77	Deadline DEADLP 2	FIND THE PRICE IN TIME (LP)	50

WERE ONLY HUMAN
83	VC Records VC002	Hold Your Head Up High/I Wouldn't Treat A Dog Like Me (no p/s)	200

WERLWINDS
61	Columbia DB 4650	Winding It Up/Dig Deep	22

BRIAN WESKE
62	Oriole CB 1723	In The Midst Of The Crowd/All Mine Alone	15
62	Oriole CB 1776	24 Hours In A Day/Where Does The Clown Go	15

FRED WESLEY & J.B.S
80	RSO RSO 67	Houseparty/I Make Music (12", solo)	10
74	Polydor 2391 125	DAMN RIGHT, I AM SOMEBODY (LP, with J.B.s)	25
74	Polydor 2391 161	BREAKIN' BREAD (LP, with J.B.s)	20

(see also James Brown, J.B.s)

WES MINSTER FIVE
64	Carnival CV 7017	Shakin' The Blues/Railroad Blues	50
65	Carnival CV 7019	Sticks And Stones/Mickey's Monkey	50

(see also Maynell Wilson, Dave Greenslade)

WESS
73	Pye 7N 25607	Harmony/There's Gonna Be A Revolution	15
77	Pinnacle 8450	Good Time/Carrie	15

FRANK WESS
54	Atlantic Golden Bell ATL LP1	FRANK WESS QUINTET (10" LP)	30

ADAM 'BATMAN' WEST
76	Target TGT 111	Batman And Robin/The Story Of Batman	7

DODIE WEST
64	Decca F 12046	Goin' Out Of My Head/Is He Feeling Blue	15
65	Piccadilly 7N 35239	In The Deep Of The Night/Rovin' Boy (in p/s)	30
65	Piccadilly 7N 35239	In The Deep Of The Night/Rovin' Boy	20
65	Piccadilly 7N 35261	Thinking Of You/And Love Will Come	8
66	Piccadilly 7N 35287	Make The World Go Away/Who Does He Think He Is	8
68	Philips BF 1698	Living In Limbo/Birdie Told Me	7

HARRY & JEANIE WEST
60	Melodisc EPM 7-111	SOUTHERN MOUNTAIN FOLK SONGS (LP)	15

HEDY WEST
65	Topic 12T 117	OLD TIMES AND HARD TIMES (LP)	20
66	Topic 12T 146	PRETTY SARO (LP)	20
67	Topic 12T 163	BALLADS (LP, with Bill Clifton)	20
67	Fontana STL 5432	SERVES'EM FINE (LP)	20

KEITH WEST
67	Parlophone R 5623	Excerpt From "A Teenage Opera"/MARK WIRTZ ORCHESTRA: Theme From "A Teenage Opera"	8
67	Parlophone R 5651	Sam (From "A Teenage Opera')/MARK WIRTZ'S MOOD MOSAIC: Thimble Full Of Puzzles (promos in art sleeve)	30
67	Parlophone R 5651	Sam (From "A Teenage Opera')/MARK WIRTZ'S MOOD MOSAIC: Thimble Full Of Puzzles	12
68	Parlophone R 5713	On A Saturday/The Kid Was A Killer	65
72	Parlophone R 5957	Excerpt From "A Teenage Opera"/Sam (From "A Teenage Opera")	7
73	Deram DM 402	Riding For A Fall/Days About To Rain	7
74	Deram DM 410	Havin' Someone/Know There's No Livin' Without You	7

(see also Tomorrow, Four + One, In Crowd, Mark Wirtz)

LESLIE WEST('S MOUNTAIN)
69	Bell BLL 1078	Dreams Of Milk And Honey/Wheels On Fire (as Leslie West's Mountain)	20
69	Bell SBLL 126	MOUNTAIN (LP, as Leslie West's Mountain)	40
75	RCA RS 1009	THE GREAT FATSBY (LP)	20

(see also Jolliver Arkansas, Mountain, West Bruce & Laing)

MAE WEST
67	Stateside SS 2021	Twist And Shout/Day Tripper	15
73	MGM 2006 203	Great Balls Of Fire/Men	15
56	Brunswick LAT 8082	THE FABULOUS MAE WEST (LP)	40
67	Stateside (S)SL 10197	WAY OUT WEST (LP)	20
73	Polydor 2315 207	GREAT BALLS OF FIRE (LP)	15

TABBY WEST
58	Capitol CL 14861	All That I Want/If You Promise Not To Tell	10

MIKE WESTBROOK (CONCERT BAND)
69	Deram DM 234	A Life Of Its Own/Can't Get It Out Of My Mind	20
70	Deram DM 286	Requiem/Hooray	20
70	Deram DM 311	Original Peter/Magic Garden (with Norma Winstone)	200
67	Deram DML 1013	CELEBRATION (LP, as Mike Westbrook Concert Band)	100
68	Deram DML/SML 1031	RELEASE (LP)	100
69	Deram SML 1047	MARCHING SONG VOL. 1 (LP)	125
69	Deram SML 1048	MARCHING SONG VOL. 2 (LP)	125
70	Deram SML 1069	LOVE SONGS (LP, as Mike Westbrook Concert Band with Norma Winstone)	150

WEST, BRUCE & LAING

MINT VALUE £

71	RCA SER 5612	TYGER: A CELEBRATION OF WILLIAM BLAKE (LP, with insert)	100
72	RCA Neon NE 10	MIKE WESTBROOK'S METROPOLIS (LP, gatefold sleeve)	100
72	Cadillac SGC 1001	LIVE (LP, private pressing)	25
75	RCA SF 8433	CITADEL/ROOM 315 (2-LP, with John Surman)	30
75	Transatlantic TRA 323	LOVE/DREAM & VARIATIONS (LP)	20
76	Transatlantic TRA 312	PLAYS FOR THE RECORD (LP, as Mike Westwood's Brass Band)	18
78	Original ORA 001	GOOSE SAUCE (LP)	18
78	Original ORA 002	PIANO (LP)	18
79	RCA PL 25252	MAMA CHICAGO (LP)	18
80	Original ORA 203	WESTBROOK BLAKE (LP)	25
82	Original ORA 309	THE CORTEGE (LP)	25
83	Westbrook LWN 1	A LITTLE WESTBROOK MUSIC (LP)	25

(see also Solid Gold Cadillac, John Surman, Norma Winstone)

WEST, BRUCE & LAING
73	RSO 2090 113	Dirty Shoes/Backfire	6

(see also Jack Bruce, Leslie West, Mountain)

WEST COAST CONSORTIUM
67	Pye 7N 17352	Some Other Someday/Looking Back	20
68	Pye 7N 17482	Colour Sergeant Lillywhite/Lady From Baltimore	45

(see also Consortium)

WEST COAST DELEGATION
67	Deram DM 113	Reach The Top/Mr. Personality Man	20

WEST COAST KNACK
67	Capitol CL 15497	I'm Aware/Time Waits For No One	20

WEST COAST POP ART EXPERIMENTAL BAND
68	Reprise RSLP 6298	A CHILD'S GUIDE TO GOOD AND EVIL (LP)	250

JOHNNY WESTERN
60	Philips PB 1030	The Ballad Of Paladin/The Guns Of Rio Muerto (B-side with Richard Boone)	7

WESTERNAIRES
75	Ra EP 7010	WESTERNAIRES EP	8

WEST FIVE
65	HMV POP 1396	Congratulations/She Mine	40
65	HMV POP 1428	Someone Ain't Right/Just Like Romeo And Juliet	35
66	HMV POP 1513	If It Don't Work Out/Back To Square One	20

(see also Ferris Wheel)

WEST INDIANS
68	Doctor Bird DB 1121	Right On Time/Hokey Pokey	60
68	Doctor Bird DB 1127	Falling In Love/I Mean It	140
69	Camel CA 16	Strange Whisperings/CARL DAWKINS: Hard To Handle	55
71	Dynamic DYN 413	Never Gonna Give You Up/REBELLIOUS SUBJECTS: Never Give Up	10

(see also Eric Donaldson, Prunes, Kilowatts, Upsetters)

CLIVE WESTLAKE
68	Fontana TF 940	199 Days/From The Beginning To The End	6

JILL WESTLAKE
58	Columbia DB 4132	Sharin'/Over And Over Again	12

KEVIN WESTLAKE & GARY FARR
68	Marmalade 598 007	Everyday/Green	20

(see also Gary Farr & T-Bones, T-Bones, Blossom Toes, B.B. Blunder)

WESTLAND STEAMBOAT
70	CBS	Born Under A Bad Sign/Missouri Train	10

MALCOLM WESTLEIGHS BAND
73	Coysti CT 11	High Again/Delta Lady (p/s)	20

WESTMORELITES
70	Clandisc CLA 217	Zion/CLANCY ECCLES & DYNAMITES: Revival	12
71	Fab FAB 16	Longing To Hold You/JACKIE BERNARD: Torture And Flames (promo only, black label)	70

(see also Minstrels)

GLEN WESTON
67	Columbia DB8253	Pattern People/In The Still Of The night	20

KIM WESTON
64	Stateside SS 359	A Little More Love/Go Ahead And Laugh (DJ copy)	150
64	Stateside SS 359	A Little More Love/Go Ahead And Laugh	100
65	Tamla Motown TMG 511	I'm Still Loving You/Just Loving You (DJ copy)	300
65	Tamla Motown TMG 511	I'm Still Loving You/Just Loving You	180
65	Tamla Motown TMG 538	Take Me In Your Arms (Rock Me A Little While)/Don't Compare Me With Her (DJ copy)	100
65	Tamla Motown TMG 538	Take Me In Your Arms (Rock Me A Little While)/Don't Compare Me With Her	80
66	Tamla Motown TMG 554	Helpless/A Love Like Yours (DJ Copy)	400
66	Tamla Motown TMG 554	Helpless/A Love Like Yours	100
67	MGM MGM 1338	I Got What You Need/Someone Like You	30
67	MGM MGM 1357	That's Groovy/Land Of Tomorrow	30
68	MGM MGM 1382	Nobody/You're Just The Kind Of Guy (DJ copy)	50
68	MGM MGM 1382	Nobody/You're Just The Kind Of Guy	20
69	Major Minor MM 619	From Both Sides Now/We Try Harder	6
70	Major Minor MM 683	Danger, Heartbreak Dead Ahead/I'll Be Thinking	12
80	Tamla Motown TMG 1000	Do Like I Do/MARVELETTES: Finders Keepers, Losers Weepers	100
65	Tamla Motown TME 2005	KIM WESTON (EP)	110
66	Tamla Motown TME 2015	ROCK ME A LITTLE WHILE (EP)	450
67	MGM MGM-C(S) 8055	FOR THE FIRST TIME (LP)	50
71	Stax 2362 021	KIM KIM KIM (LP)	30

(see also Marvin Gaye & Kim Weston)

Mark WESTON & THE TWO PART TARIFF

MINT VALUE £

MARK WESTON & THE TWO PART TARIFF
69	Tepee TPR 1006	Standing At The Bus Stop/Portrait On The Blackboard	40

PETE WESTON
70	Gas GAS 146	Something Sweet/BIM & BAM: Love Letters	12
70	Punch PH 28	In The Mood (& His Band) (credited to Pete Western)/ASTON BARRETT: Slide Mongoose	15
72	Ashanti ASH 402	Pup'n Temper/PETE'S ALL STARS: Version 2	8

(see also I Roy)

RANDY WESTON TRIO
55	London H-APB1040	RANDY WESTON PLAYS COLE PORTER IN A MODERN MOOD (10" LP)	20
55	London HB-U1046	THE RANDY WESTON TRIO (10" LP with Art Blakey)	20
56	London HA-U 2018	GET HAPPY WITH THE RANDY WESTON TRIO (LP)	20
73	CTI CTL 12	BLUE MOSES (LP)	18

WEST ONE
88	Que Q 9	California '69/Eurotrash (gig freebie, white label)	12

WEST POINT
70	Decca F 13050	Don't Know Why/Take What You Want	8

WEST POINT SUPERNATURAL
67	Reaction 591 013	Time Will Tell/Night Train	20

WESTSIDE GUNN
16	Daupe! DM SP 011	ROSES ARE RED...SO IS BLOOD (10", red vinyl, p/s, with The Purist, 100 only)	300
16	Daupe! DM SP 016	GRISELDA GHOST (12", p/s, 250 copies, with Conway)	300
16	Daupe! DM SP 016	GRISELDA GHOST (12", p/s, aqua marine vinyl, 150 copies, with Conway)	400
16	Daupe! DM SP 016	GRISELDA GHOST (12", p/s, with obi strip, 20 copies only)	500
16	Daupe! DM SP 017	HALL & NASH (12", p/s, 230 only, with Conway)	250
16	Daupe! DM SP 017	HALL & NASH (12", p/s, liquor coloured vinyl, 150 only, with Conway)	300
16	Daupe! DM SP 017	HALL & NASH (12", p/s, 20 only, with Conway)	500
17	Daupe! DM SP 019	THERE'S GOD AND THERE'S FLYGOD, PRAISE BOTH (12", p/s, 230 only)	150
17	Daupe! DM SP 019	THERE'S GOD AND THERE'S FLYGOD, PRAISE BOTH (12", p/s, gold vinyl, 150 only)	200
17	Daupe! DM SP 019	THERE'S GOD AND THERE'S FLYGOD, PRAISE BOTH (12", p/s, with obi strip, 150 only)	250
17	Daupe! DM SP 028	HITLER WEARS HERMES I (12", p/s,187 copies)	200
17	Daupe! DM SP 028	HITLER WEARS HERMES I (12", p/s,cherry red vinyl, 187 copies)	200
17	Daupe! DM SP 028	HITLER WEARS HERMES I (12", p/s, orange vinyl, 187 copies)	200
17	Daupe! DM SP 028	HITLER WEARS HERMES I (12", p/s, gold vinyl, 187 copies)	150
17	Daupe! DM SP 028	HITLER WEARS HERMES I (12", p/s, with obi strip, 20 copies)	250
17	Daupe! DM SP 029	WESTSIDE DOOM (12", p/s, with MF Doom, 300 copies)	100
17	Daupe! DM SP 029	WESTSIDE DOOM (12", p/s, with MF Doom, purple vinyl, 300 copies)	100
17	Daupe! DM SP 029	WESTSIDE DOOM (12", p/s, with MF Doom, yellow vinyl, 300 copies)	100
17	Daupe! DM SP 029	WESTSIDE DOOM (12", p/s, with MF Doom, picture disc, 300 copies)	200
17	Daupe! DM SP 029	WESTSIDE DOOM (12", p/s, with MF Doom, with obi strip, 20 copies)	300
16	Daupe! DM SP 012	FLYGOD (2-LP, 230 copies)	400
15	Daupe! DM SP 008	HITLER WEARS HERMES II (LP, numbered, 150 copies)	300
15	Daupe! DM SP 008	HITLER WEARS HERMES II (LP, numbered, clear red vinyl 100 copies)	500
15	Daupe! DM SP 008	HITLER WEARS HERMES II (LP, with obi strip, 20 copies)	400
15	Daupe! DM SP 010	HITLER WEARS HERMES III (LP, numbered, white vinyl 100 copies)	500
15	Daupe! DM SP 010	HITLER WEARS HERMES III (LP, numbered, black vinyl, 150 copies)	250
15	Daupe! DM SP 010	HITLER WEARS HERMES III (LP, with obi strip, 20 copies)	400
17	Daupe! DM SP 020	HITLER WEARS HERMES IV (LP, 230 copies)	200
17	Daupe! DM SP 020	HITLER WEARS HERMES IV (LP, clear vinyl, 125 copies)	300
17	Daupe! DM SP 020	HITLER WEARS HERMES IV (LP, red vinyl, 150 copies)	300
17	Daupe! DM SP 020	HITLER WEARS HERMES IV (LP, with obi strip, 20 copies)	300
17	Daupe! DM SP 024	HITLER ON STEROIDS (LP as 2 x 12", with Green Lantern, 250 copies	300
17	Daupe! DM SP 024	HITLER ON STEROIDS (LP as 2 x 12", with Green Lantern, red vinyl, 125 copies)	250
17	Daupe! DM SP 024	HITLER ON STEROIDS (LP as 2 x 12", with Green Lantern, green vinyl, 125 copies)	250
17	Daupe! DM SP 024	HITLER ON STEROIDS (LP as 2 x 12", with Green Lantern, with obi strip, 20 copies)	400
18	Daupe! DM SP 031	HITLER WEARS HERMES V (LP, 250 copies)	150
18	Daupe! DM SP 031	HITLER WEARS HERMES V (LP, pink vinyl, 250 copies)	150
18	Daupe! DM SP 031	HITLER WEARS HERMES V (LP, yellow vinyl, 250 copies)	150
18	Daupe! DM SP 031	HITLER WEARS HERMES V (LP, picture disc, 250 copies)	150
18	Daupe! DM SP 031	HITLER WEARS HERMES V (LP, with obi strip, 20 copies)	250
18	Daupe! DM SP 036	CHRIS BENOIT (2-LP, splatter vinyl, 375 copies)	150
18	Daupe! DM SP 036	CHRIS BENOIT (2-LP, clear vinyl, 375 copies)	150
18	Daupe! DM SP 036	CHRIS BENOIT (2-LP, with obi strip, 20 copies)	200
18	Daupe! DM SP 036	GOD IS THE GREATEST (2-LP, 375 copies)	100
18	Daupe! DM SP 036	GOD IS THE GREATEST (2-LP, clear vinyl, 375 copies)	100
18	Daupe! DM SP 036	GOD IS THE GREATEST (2-LP, ruby red vinyl, 375 copies)	100
18	Daupe! DM SP 036	GOD IS THE GREATEST (2-LP, mustard vinyl, 375 copies)	100
18	Daupe! DM SP 036	GOD IS THE GREATEST (2-LP, cream vinyl, 375 copies)	100
18	Daupe! DM SP 036	GOD IS THE GREATEST (2-LP, with obi strip, 20 copies)	200
18	Daupe! DM SP 036	SUPREME BLIENTELE (2-LP, clear vinyl, 375 copies)	100
18	Daupe! DM SP 036	SUPREME BLIENTELE (2-LP, 375 copies)	100
18	Daupe! DM SP 036	SUPREME BLIENTELE (2-LP, red vinyl, 375 copies)	100
18	Daupe! DM SP 036	SUPREME BLIENTELE (2-LP, with obi strip, 20 copies)	200
18	Daupe! DM SP 040	HITLER WEARS HERMES VI (LP, red vinyl, two different covers)	100
18	Daupe! DM SP 040	HITLER WEARS HERMES VI (LP, two different covers)	100
18	Daupe! DM SP 040	HITLER WEARS HERMES VI (LP, picture disc, two different covers)	100
18	Daupe! DM SP 040	HITLER WEARS HERMES VI (LP, with obi strip, two different covers, 20 of each)	250
19	Daupe! DM SP 047	FOURTH ROPE (2-LP, 250 copies)	150
19	Daupe! DM SP 047	FOURTH ROPE (2-LP, yellow vinyl, 250 copies)	150
19	Daupe! DM SP 047	FOURTH ROPE (2-LP, red vinyl, 250 copies)	150

WESTVIEW

			MINT VALUE £
19	Daupe! DM SP 047	FOURTH ROPE (2-LP, with obi strip, 20 copies)	200
19	Daupe! DM SP 053	HITLER WEARS HERMES VII (LP)	100
19	Daupe! DM SP 053	HITLER WEARS HERMES VII (LP, yellow vinyl, 333 copies)	100
19	Daupe! DM SP 053	HITLER WEARS HERMES VII (LP, blue vinyl, 333 copies)	120
19	Daupe! DM SP 053	HITLER WEARS HERMES VII (LP, red vinyl, 300 copies)	100
19	Daupe! DM SP 053	HITLER WEARS HERMES VII (LP, picture disc, 300 copies)	150
19	Daupe! DM SP 053	HITLER WEARS HERMES VII (LP, splatter vinyl,100 copies)	200
19	Daupe! DM SP 053	HITLER WEARS HERMES VII (LP, with obi strip, 20 copies)	300
20	Daupe! DM SP 056	FLYEST NIG@@ IN CHARGE - MIXTAPE VOL 1 (2-LP, 380 copies)	40
20	Daupe! DM SP 056	FLYEST NIG@@ IN CHARGE - MIXTAPE VOL 1 (2-LP, white vinyl, 333 copies)	40
20	Daupe! DM SP 056	FLYEST NIG@@ IN CHARGE - MIXTAPE VOL 1 (2-LP, aquamarine vinyl, 333 copies)	40
20	Daupe! DM SP 056	FLYEST NIG@@ IN CHARGE - MIXTAPE VOL 1 (2-LP, orange vinyl, 333 copies)	40
20	Daupe! DM SP 056	FLYEST NIG@@ IN CHARGE - MIXTAPE VOL 1 (2-LP, splatter, 100 copies)	50
20	Daupe! DM SP 056	FLYEST NIG@@ IN CHARGE - MIXTAPE VOL 1 (2-LP, with obi strip, 20 copies)	100
20	Daupe! DM SP 060	PRAY FOR PARIS (LP)	150
20	Daupe! DM SP 060	PRAY FOR PARIS (LP, gold vinyl)	150
20	Daupe! DM SP 060	PRAY FOR PARIS (LP, white vinyl)	150
20	Daupe! DM SP 060	PRAY FOR PARIS (LP, French tricolour vinyl, 200 copies)	250
20	Daupe! DM SP 060	PRAY FOR PARIS (LP, splatter vinyl, 100 copies)	250
20	Daupe! DM SP 060	PRAY FOR PARIS (LP, with obi strip, 20 copies)	300

WESTVIEW
67	Tenby TB1	She's A Witch/Time Passes Slowly	40

WESTWIND
70	Penny Farthing PEN 737	Love Is A Funny Sort Of Thing/Breakout	8
70	Penny Farthing PELS 505	LOVE IS (LP)	225

WE TALKIES
66	CBS 202245	I Wanna Walk In Your Sun/I Order You	6

WE THE PEOPLE
66	London HLH 10089	He Doesn't Go About It Right/You Burn Me Up And Down	125

WE THREE TRIO
65	London HLA 9966	Baby The Rain Must Fall/Shine For Me	8
67	Fontana TL 5308	THE WE THREE TRIO (LP)	15

WET LEG
20	Domino RUG 1232	Chaise Lounge/Chaise Lounge (demo) (p/s)	35

WET WILLIE
71	Atlantic 2091155	Dirty Leg/Rock And Roll Band	8
71	Atlantic 2400162	WET WILLIE (LP)	20

WE UGLY DOGS
67	BT Puppy BTS 45537	First Spring Rain/Poor Man	12

(see also Tokens)

WE WERE PROMISED JETPACKS
09	Fat Cat FATLP 72	THESE FOUR WALLS (LP)	40
11	Fat Cat FATLP 97	IN THE PIT OF THE STOMACH (LP)	20
14	Fat Cat FATLP 127	UNRAVELLING (LP)	18

WHALE FEATHERS
71	Blue Horizon 2431 009	WHALE FEATHERS (LP)	175

WHALES
68	CBS 3766	Come Down Little Bird/Beachcomber	20
69	CBS 4126	Tell It To The Rain/Girl, Hey Girl	15

WHAM!
86	Epic WHAM 2	THE FINAL (2-LP box, picture discs, with sealed T-shirt, calendar, pencil, note-pad and numbered certificate)	80

(see also George Michael, Pepsi & Shirley)

WHAT
79	Humber HREP 45	What Is The Cure?/Anything Goes/East Coast Kids	40

WHAT IS OIL
83	Oof Potato BEAT 1	HUMAN SUFFERING EP (p/s)	40

WHAT THE CURTAINS
84	Rideaux WTC 0042	Crime Of Passion/Words (Can't Tell)	20

WHAT TO WEAR
80	Basic And Typical BAT 1	CASUAL BUT SMART (EP)	25

PEETIE WHEATSTRAW
69	Matchbox SDR 191	THE DEVIL'S SON IN LAW (LP)	25
69	Matchbox SDR 192	THE HIGH SHERIFF FROM HELL (LP)	25
74	Flyright LP 111	1930-36 (LP)	15

KENNY WHEELER
68	Fontana STL 5494	WINDMILL TILTER (LP)	150
77	Incus 10	SONG FOR SOMEONE (LP)	60

(see also Johnny Dankworth, Elton Dean)

WHEELER ST JAMES & JAMES
72	RCA 2233	My Impersonal Life/Lovely To See You	20

WHEELS OF TIME
67	Spin SP 62008	1984/So Long (not in company sleeves)	90
67	Spin SP 62008	1984/So Long (in company sleeve)	100

WHEELS (1)
65	Columbia DB 7682	Gloria/Don't You Know	120
66	Columbia DB 7827	Bad Little Woman/Road Block (mispressing, demos & a few issues play "Call My Name" on B-side)	150
66	Columbia DB 7827	Bad Little Woman/Road Block	375
66	Columbia DB 7981	Kicks/Call My Name	120

(see also James Brothers, Demick & Armstrong)

WHEELS (2)

MINT VALUE £

WHEELS (2)
71	Decca F13268	Take Me Home Country Roads/She Don't Mean It	30

WHICHWHAT
69	Beacon BEA 127	Gimme Gimme Good Lovin'/Wonderland Of Love	25
69	Beacon BEA 131	Why Do Lovers Break Each Other's Heart/When I See Her Smile	6
69	Beacon BEA 133	In The Year 2525/Parting	15
69	Beacon BEA 144	I Wanna Be Free/It's All Over Again	25
70	Beacon BEA 169	Vietnam Rose/Shame And Solution	6
70	Beacon BEAS 14	WHICHWHAT'S FIRST (LP)	50

OSCAR WHIFLEY
68	Dolphin DOS6	Tommy Jones/Creeque Alley (as The Oscar Whifley Sound)	8

WHIP
71	Mother MOT 6	Julie Ivory Towers/MUFF & BANKHOUSE ASSEMBLY: Funky Shoot Out	10
71	CBS 7242	I Never Win/Papa's On The Bottles Again	10

WHIRL
89	Sound Of Spasm 2	Bizarre Love Triangle/CROCODILE RIDE: Shimmer (1-sided flexi-disc, foldover p/s In poly bag with fanzine)	10

WHIRLWIND
78	Chiswick NS 25	Hang Loose/Together Forever (p/s)	10
78	Chiswick NS 42	I Only Wish (That I'd Been Told)/Ducktails (unissued)	0
78	Chiswick CHIS 103	I Only Wish (That I'd Been Told)/Ducktails (p/s)	10
79	Chiswick CHIS 117	You Got Class/Losing To You (unissued in U.K.; France-only)	0
79	Lyntone (No Cat. No)	On Wheels (flexi, originally promo for Isle Of Man TT races, repackaged in picture sleeve with 2 inserts for 1979 Earls Court Concert)	50
80	Chiswick CHIS 122	Heaven Knows/Cruisin' Around (p/s)	10
80	Chiswick CHIS 127	Stayin' Out All Night/Running Wild (unissued; p/s only)	0
80	Chiswick PSR 447	Midnight Blue/Honey Hush/Such A Fool/Stayin' Out All Night (promo only)	8
78	Chiswick WIK 7	BLOWIN' UP A STORM (LP, with 2 extra tracks)	15
80	Chiswick CWK 3012	MIDNIGHT BLUE (LP)	15

WHIRLWIND D
12	Tru-Tone TTR004	WD40 (12" EP)	10
13	Tru-Tone TTR005	BRISTOL BUILT (12" EP)	10
14	B-Line Recordings BLN011	Time Waits/One, Two	7
14	Tru-Tone TTR 007	Gain My Perspective/Run Fast (with Phill Most Chill & Mr Fantastic 12" test pressings only)	40
15	Tru-Tone TTR 008	B-Line Business/Battle Tip 2015	8
14	B-Line Recordings BLN 006	NOMANSLAND (LP)	15
16	B-Line Recordings BLI 001	THE OTHER SIDE OF NOMANSLANDS (LP, 100 only)	20

WHIRLWIND D/MR THING/AGENT FINC & SPECIFIK
14	Tru-Tone TTR 006	Broadway (12", test pressings only)	35

WHIRLWINDS
64	HMV POP 1301	Look At Me/Baby Not Like You	50

(see also Mockingbirds, Graham Gouldman, 10cc)

NANCY WHISKEY (& HER SKIFFLERS)
57	Oriole CB 1394	He's Solid Gone/Ella Speed (as Nancy Whiskey & Her Skifflers)	20
58	Oriole CB 1452	Hillside In Scotland/I Know Where I'm Goin'	10
59	Oriole CB 1485	The Old Grey Goose/Johnny Blue	10
57	Topic 7T 10	NANCY WHISKEY SINGS (7" LP)	25
57	Oriole MG 10018	THE INTOXICATING MISS WHISKEY (10" LP, with Chas McDevitt Skiffle Group)	30

(see also Chas McDevitt Skiffle Group)

WHISTLE
73	York YR 201	The Party Must Be Over/Hideaway	20
74	York YR 209	When The Lights Go Out On Broadway/Lincoln Lullabies	20

WHISTLER (1)
71	Deram SML 1083	HO-HUM (LP)	250

WHISTLER (2)
74	Capricorn CAP 2	I'm Running Out Of Time/Dear Diary	15

WHISTLING WILLIE
68	Duke DU 8	Penny Reel/Soul Tonic	20

(see also Neville)

SHARON WHITBREAD & FRED
72	RA RALP 6011	SPICE OF LIFE (LP)	25

IAN WHITCOMB
65	Capitol CL 15382	This Sporting Life/Fizz	6
65	Capitol CL 15395	You Turn Me On/Poor But Honest	10
65	Capitol CL 15418	N-N-Nervous!/The End	6
66	Capitol CL 15431	Good Hard Rock/High Blood Pressure	6
66	Stateside SS 573	Where Did Robinson Crusoe Go With Friday/Poor Little Bird	6
73	Ember NR 5065	YOU TURN ME ON (LP, with Jimmy Page & John Paul Jones)	40

ANDY WHITE
85	Stiff BUY DJ 234	Religious Persuasion (Light blue promo "A" label)	7

BARRY WHITE
67	President PT 139	All In The Run Of A Day/Don't Take Your Love From Me	30

BERGEN WHITE
76	Private Stock PVT 69	Duke Of Earl/She Won't Let You Down	7

BRIAN WHITE & MAGNA JAZZ BAND
62	HMV CLP 1534	BRIAN WHITE AND THE MAGNA JAZZ BAND (LP)	80

BUKKA WHITE
66	Fontana 688 804 ZL	SKY SONGS (LP, with Big Willie)	40
66	CBS Realm 52629	BUKKA WHITE (LP)	40
69	Blue Horizon 7-63229	MEMPHIS HOT SHOTS (LP)	80

Chalky WHITE

MINT VALUE £

CHALKY WHITE
83 So So SOS 019   One Shot/Israelites (p/s) 12

CHRIS WHITE
76 Charisma CB 272   Spanish Wine/She's Only Dancing 8
76 Charisma CB 282   Natural Rhythm/Another Little Miracle 7
76 Charisma CB 294   Don't Look Down/Summertime Summertime 8
77 Charisma CB 303   Don't Worry Baby/Child Of The Sun 15
76 Charisma CAS 1118   MOUTH MUSIC (LP)... 15
(see also Joyce's Angels)

CHRISTINE WHITE
77 Golden Age GAM 02   You'll Lose A Good Thing/Caught By Love 6
77 Golden Age GAM 13   You've Got To Come Back/Love Me Boy 6
77 Black Jack BJLP 001   PURE LOVE (LP) 25

DANNY WHITE
67 Sue WI 4031   Keep My Woman Home/I'm Dedicating My Life 75

DUKE WHITE
63 Island WI 084   It's Over/Forever 15
64 Black Swan WI 442   Be Wise/BABA BROOKS: Musical Workshop 40
65 Black Swan WI 444   Sow Good Seeds/BABA BROOKS BAND: Bus Strike 40

ED WHITE (THE SOUNDS OF)
61 Pye 7N 15320   Coral Reef/Tropical Blue (mono) 8
61 Pye 7N SR15320   Coral Reef/Tropical Blue (stereo) 20

GEORGIA WHITE
54 Vocalion V 1038   Was I Drunk?/Moonshine Blues (78) 20

IAN WHITE
70 private pressing   IAN WHITE (LP) 20

JACK WHITE
09 Third Man TMR 013   Fly Farm Blues (luminous one-sided Halloween cover, 100-only) 120
21 Third Man TMR 748   Taking Me Back/Taking Me Back (Gently) (p/s, tri-colour vinyl) 100
(see also White Stripes, Raconteurs, Dead Weather)

JAMES WHITE
79 Ze ZE 3303   OFF WHITE (LP, as James White & The Blacks) 20
82 Animal CHR 1401   SAX MANIAC (LP, as James White & The Blacks) 20

JAY WHITE
56 London RE-F 1045   FAR-AWAY PLACES VOL. 1 (EP) 15

JEANETTE WHITE
69 A&M AMS 761   Music/No Sunshine 30
69 A&M AMS 761   Music/No Sunshine (Yellow DJ copy or brown label) 75

JOE WHITE
64 R&B JB 137   Sinners (as Joe White & Maytals)/ROLAND ALPHONSO: King Solomon 40
64 Ska Beat JB 180   Punch You Down (with Chuck)/TOMMY McCOOK: Cotton Tree 45
64 Island WI 145   When Are You Young/Wanna Go Home 25
64 Island WI 159   Hog In A Co Co/SKATALITES: Sandy Gully 30
64 Island WI 166   Downtown Girl/RICHARD BROS.: You Are My Sunshine (B-side is actually "Cool Smoke" by Don Drummond) 40
65 Island WI 201   Low-Minded People (as Chuck & Joe White)/Irene 20
66 Doctor Bird DB 1001   Every Night (with Chuck)/BABA BROOKS & HIS BAND: First Session 30
66 Doctor Bird DB 1024   My Love For You/SAMMY ISMAY & BABA BROOKS BAND: Cocktails For Two 25
66 Doctor Bird DB 1043   So Close (as Joe White & Della)/BABA BROOKS & HIS BAND: Eighth Games 25
67 Doctor Bird DB 1069   Rudies All Around/Bad Man 100
67 Doctor Bird DB 1080   Lovely Nights/I Need You 20
67 Doctor Bird DB 1090   I Need A Woman/Hot Hops 50
68 Blue Cat BS 108   Way Of Life (with Glen Brown & Trevor Shield/I'm So Proud 175
68 Blue Cat BS 119   Try A Little Tenderness/LYN TAITT & CARL BRYAN: Tender Arms 250
68 Blue Cat BS 130   Pretty Girl (with Glen Brown & Trevor Shield)/DERMOTT LYNCH: You Went Away 100
69 Sugar ESS 102   My Guiding Star/If I Needed Someone 70
70 Sugar SU 103   Yesterday/I Am Free 160
70 Trojan TR 7742   So Much Love/Maybe Now 20
70 Trojan TR 7768   I'm Going To Get There/RUPIE EDWARDS ALLSTARS: Kinky Funky Reggae 12
70 Big BG 301   This Is The Time/The Other Day 10
71 Big BG 309   Baby I Care/Ain't Misbehavin' 20
72 Dynamic DYN 440   Kenyata/RECORDING BAND: Version 35
73 Gayfeet GS 202   If It Don't Work Out/BABA BROOKS BAND: Ki Salaboca 15
73 Harry J. HJ 6648   Joe White (Mrs. Jones)/Joe White (Mrs. Jones) - Version (song actually titled "Me And Mrs Jones") 10
77 Ultra PFU 1002   Give And Take (On Both Sides)/Roots Dub 60
79 Splendor Heights SH 2   Forward To Zion/Only The Strong/Join Them/Are You Leavine Me (12" as Joe White Band) 60
77 Trench Town TRELP 002   LOVE FOR EVERY FAMILY (LP) 140
70s Magnet MGT 006   SINCE THE OTHER DAY (LP) 50
(see also Chuck, Rue Lloyd)

JOHN WHITE
78 Obscure OBS 8   MACHINE MUSIC (split LP with Gavin Bryers) 20

JOSH & BEVERLEY WHITE
64 Realm REP 4003   BEVERLEY & JOSH WHITE JNR (EP) 12

JOY WHITE
75 Attack ATT 8093   Dread Out De/Dread Dub 25
75 Love LOV 0010   Check You Daughter/NIght Life 10
79 Tribesman TM 25   Always Together (with Jerry Baxter)/Dubbing To Sir Coxsone Sound (12") 20
79 Fight FDD 4438   The First Cut Is The Deepest/ITALS : Rougher Yet (12") 20
78 Hawkeye HLP 002   SENTIMENTAL REASONS (LP) 30

K.C. WHITE

MINT VALUE £

K.C. WHITE
72	Dynamic DYN 434	Man No Dead/Man No Dead - Version	8
73	Green Door GD 4056	First Cut Is The Deepest/No Good Girl	20
73	Technique TE 929	Anywhere But Nowhere/Bush In Session	20

KITTY WHITE
54	London HL 8202	Jesse James/Scratch My Back (B-side with Dave Howard)	200
54	London HL 8202	Jesse James/Scratch My Back (78, B-side with Dave Howard)	20

LENNY WHITE
83	Elektra ED 4921	My Turn To Love You (Special Mix)/(Dub Version) (12")	12
75	Atlantic K 50213	VENUSIAN SUMMER (LP)	15

LOUISA JANE WHITE
69	Philips BF 1810	When The Battle Is Over/Blue Ribbons	30
70	Philips BF 1834	How Does It Feel/Truth In My Tears	100

SHEILA WHITE
66	CBS 202465	Misfit/Switch Off The Night	15

TAM WHITE
67	Decca F 12711	World Without You/Someone You Should Know (unreleased)	0
68	Decca F 12723	Dancing Out Of My Heart/I'll Stay Loving You	10
68	Decca F 12849	Waiting Till The Night Comes Around/Girl Watcher	15
69	Deram DM 261	That Old Sweet Roll/Don't Make Promises	25
70	Middle Earth MDS 104	Lewis Carroll/Future Thoughts	50
70	Middle Earth MDLS 304	TAM WHITE (LP)	100

(see also Boston Dexters)

TERRY WHITE & TERRIERS
59	Decca F 11133	Rock Around The Mailbags/Blackout	80
59	Decca F 11133	Rock Around The Mailbags/Blackout (78)	20

THOMAS WHITE
79	Hit Run HD 12	Ivory Girl/KEITH FRANCIS: Prejudice Country (12")	50

TONY JOE WHITE
68	Monument MON 1024	Soul Francisco/Whompt Out On You	8
69	Monument MON 1031	Polk Salad Annie/Aspen Colorado	15
69	Monument MON 1036	Willie And Laura Mae Jones/Baby Scratch My Back	10
68	Monument LMO/SMO 5027	BLACK AND WHITE (LP)	15
70	Monument LMO/SMO 5035	TONY JOE WHITE CONTINUED (LP)	15
70	Monument SMO 5043	TONY JOE (LP)	15
71	Warner Bros WS 1900	TONY JOE WHITE (LP)	18
72	Warner Bros K 46147	THE TRAIN I'M ON (LP)	15
73	Warner Bros K 46229	HOME-MADE ICE CREAM (LP)	15

TREVOR WHITE
76	Island WIP 6291	Crazy Kids/Movin' In The Right Direction (with p/s)	20
76	Island WIP 6291	Crazy Kids/Movin' In The Right Direction	8

(see also Sparks, Radio Stars)

WHITE CAR
81	Friday FRI 13	Cinema Girl/Channel One (p/s)	25

WHITE DOOR
83	Clay CLAY 23	Love Breakdown/Breakdown (Instrumental)	6
84	Clay 37	Flame In My Heart/Behind The White Door (p/s)	6

WHITE DUCK
72	Uni UN 541	Billy Goat/Really	8
73	Uni UN 555	Honey, You'll Be Alright/Carry Love	8
72	Uni UNLS 123	WHITE DUCK (LP)	22
73	Uni UNLS 129	IN SEASON (LP)	22

WHITE FEATHER
83	No No N.N001	Summer Days/Golden Haze/Feathered Girl (no p/s)	15

RICK WHITEFIELD
71	Horse HOSS 10	Hey Mama/Ride Baby Ride	6

WHITEFIRE
78	Whitefire 98DB 001	SUZANNE (EP)	40

WHITE HART
79	Tradition TSR 033	IN SEARCH OF REWARD (LP)	50

WHITE HEAT (1)
79	Valium VAL 01	Nervous Breakdown/Sammy Sez (gatefold p/s)	25
80	Valium VAL 02	Finished With The Fashions/Ordinary Joe (p/s, with insert)	20
81	Valium VAL 03	City Beat/It's No Use (Young Ones) (p/s)	15
81	Valium VALP 101	IN THE ZERO HOUR (LP)	25

WHITE HEAT (2)
84	RSR 007	Soldier Of Fortune/Lovemaker	75
84	Rock Shop RSR 007	WHITE HEAT (LP)	25

WHITE HORN
75	Philips 6006 440	Making It Funky/Mama Said	8

WHITEHOUSE
90	Sue Lawley SLS 002	Still Going Strong/Ankles And Wrists	15
01	SLA-003	Cruise (Force The Truth)/Instrumental Version (12")	20
02	SLA-004	Wriggle Like A Fucking Eel/Instrumental Version (12")	18
80	Come Org. WDC 881004	BIRTHDEATH EXPERIENCE (LP, first pressing pink labels, 850 copies)	150
80	Come Org. WDC 881005	TOTAL SEX (LP, 400 on green vinyl)	120
80	Come Org. WDC 881005	TOTAL SEX (LP, 800 on black vinyl)	80
80	Come Org. WDC 883005	TOTAL SEX (cassette)	75
80	Come Org. WDC 883003	ULTRASADISM (cassette)	60
81	Come Org. WDC 881010	DEDICATED TO PETER KÜRTEN, SADIST AND MASS SLAYER (LP, some on coloured vinyl)	120

WHITE LIES

MINT VALUE £

80	Come Org. WDC 881007	some in custom sleeve)...	
80	Come Org. WDC 881007	ERECTOR (LP, different coloured vinyls)	100
81	Come Org. WDC 881013	BÜCHENWALD (LP, clear vinyl)	120
81	WDC 883013	BUCHENWALD (cassette)	60
81	Come Org. WDC 881017	NEW BRITAIN (LP, with insert)	125
82	Come Org. WDC 881027	PSYCHOPATHIA SEXUALIS (LP, clear vinyl, black is bootleg)	200
82	Come Org. WDC 883020	LIVE ACTION 1 (cassette)	45
83	Come Org. WDC 883027	PSYCHOPATHIA SEXUALIS (cassette)	70
83	Come Org. WDC 883033	RIGHT TO KILL - DEDICATED TO DENNIS ANDREW NEILSEN (LP, & inserts)	120
83	Come Org. WDC 883044048	USA I - V (5 cassettes documenting 1983 USA tour, pice for each)	45
85	Come Org. WDC	GREAT WHITE DEATH (LP)	80

(Many Whitehouse LP's were issued in customised white card sleeves & were later available in a generic 'Peter Kürten' sleeve, originally used for the 2nd pressing of the 'Peter Kürten' LP. This latter design was also used for counterfeits. There may also be coloured vinyl variations which are worth the same)

80s	Come Org. WDC	150 MURDEROUS PASSIONS (LP, with Nurse With Wound)	75
80s	United Dairies UD 009	150 MURDEROUS PASSIONS (LP, with Nurse With Wound, reissue)	40
80s	United Dairies UD 009	150 MURDEROUS PASSIONS (LP, with Nurse With Wound, export issue, sealed in black vinyl)	125
80s	Susan Lawley 1	CREAM OF THE SECOND COMING (2-LP)	45
91	Susan Lawley SL 002	THANK YOUR LUCKY STARS (LP)	30
92	Susan Lawley SL 003	TWICE IS NOT ENOUGH (LP)	30

(see also Come, Nurse With Wound, New Order, Skullflower, Konstruktivits)

WHITE LIES
08	Fiction 1795718	To Lose My Life (6 x 7" box set with signed print)	40

WHITE LIGHT
74	Scotia SCO/LP 4791	PARABLE (LP)	300

WHITE LIGHTNING
84	Wild Party PP 1000	This Poison Fountain/Hypocrite (no p/s, 1,000 only)	50
90	Workshop JOB LP 2	AS MIDNIGHT APPROACHES (LP, with inner)	18

(see also Static)

WHITE LINING
70	Parlophone R 5868	Back In The Sun/Mon Amour	20

WHITE MULE
70	UNI UNS 523	Looking Through Cat's Eyes/Hundred Franc Blues	15

WHITE NOISE
75	Virgin VDJ 2	An Extract From White Noise 2 (promo only)	20
69	Island ILPS 9099	AN ELECTRIC STORM (LP, pink label black/orange circle logo)	150
69	Island ILPS 9099	WHITE NOISE (LP, repressing pink label with white 'i' logo)	50
75	Virgin V 2032	WHITE NOISE 2 (LP)	15
08	Island 5313 125	AN ELECTRIC STORM (LP, reissue, pink rim palm tree label)	18

(see also BBC Radiophonic Workshop)

WHITE ON BLACK
74	Saydisc SDL 251	WHITE ON BLACK (LP, fully laminated sleeve)	30

WHITE PLAINS
70	Deram DM 280	My Baby Loves Lovin'/Show Me Your Hand	7
70	Deram DM 291	I've Got You On My Mind/Today I Killed A Man I Didn't Know	8
70	Deram DM 315	Julie Do Ya Love Me/I Need Your Everlasting Love	7
71	Deram DM 333	When You Are A King/The World Gets Better With Love	8
71	Deram DM 340	Gonna Miss Here Mississippi/I'll Go Blind	7
71	Deram DM 348	I Con't Stop/Julie Anne	7
73	Deram DM 371	Step Into A Dream/Look To See	8
73	Deram DM 388	Does Anybody Know Where My Baby Is/Just For A Change	10
70	Deram SML 1067	WHITE PLAINS (LP, laminated cover)	30
71	Deram SML 1092	WHEN YOU ARE A KING (LP)	25

(see also Edison Lighthouse, David & Jonathan, Kestrels, Brotherhood Of Man, Peter's Faces, Carter-Lewis & Southerners, Ivy League)

WHITE RABBIT
69	NEMS 56-4165	Ain't That Something/I'll Do The Rest	8

WHITE RUSSIA
80	Trivia TRIV 01	Valentine/Clothes (p/s)	40

WHITESNAKE
78	EMI International INEP 751	SNAKEBITE (EP, white vinyl, p/s; later black vinyl with no p/s)	15
78	EMI International INT 568	Lie Down/Don't Mess With Me	6
79	EMI International INT 578	The Time Is Right For Love/Come On (live)	6
82	Liberty BP 418	Love An' Affection/Victim Of Love (withdrawn)	35
78	EMI Intl. INS 3022	TROUBLE (LP, grey or pink inner sleeve)	20
82	Liberty LBGP 30354	SAINTS AN' SINNERS (LP, picture disc)	18
84	Liberty LBGP 240 000 0	SLIDE IT IN (LP, picture disc, U.S. mixes)	18
87	EMI EMCP 3528	WHITESNAKE 1987 (LP, picture disc)	18
89	EMI EMCDJ 1013	SLIP OF THE TONGUE (LP, with track by track interview, promo only)	20

(see also David Coverdale, Deep Purple, Rainbow, Roger Glover, Jon Lord, Phenomena, Cozy Powell, Young & Moody Band, Company, Snafu, Bogdan, Gogmagog, Tramline, National Health)

WHITE SOLES
76	Satril SAT 104	Beside You/Never Say Die	10

WHITE SPIRIT
80	Neat NEAT 05	Back To The Grind/Cheetah (p/s)	10
81	MCA MCA 638	Midnight Chaser/Suffragettes (p/s)	30
81	MCA MCA 652	High Upon High/No Reprieve/Arthur Guitar	15
80	MCA MCF 3079	WHITE SPIRIT (LP, with lyric insert)	18

(see also Gillan, Iron Maiden)

WHITE SS
78	White SS CIA 72	Mercy Killing/I'm Not One (live) (p/s)	25

WHITE STRIPES

WHITE STRIPES
			MINT VALUE £
01	XL XLS 139	Hotel Yorba (Live At The Hotel Yorba)/Rated X (p/s, 4000 only)	6
02	XL XLS 142	Fell In Love With A Girl/I Just Don't Know What To Do With Myself (p/s, 5000 only)	12
02	XL XLS 148	Dead Leaves And The Dirty Ground/Stop Breaking Down (Live) (p/s, 5000 only)	6
02	XL/MOJO no cat. no.	Red Death At 6:14 (1-sided, promo only, red vinyl, numbered label, 3000 only, mail order only via Mojo magazine, with letter)	25
02	XL XLS 162	Merry Christmas From The White Stripes: Candy Cane Children/The Reading Of The Story Of The Magi/The Singing Of Silent Night (1000 only, p/s)	8
03	XL LP 162 DJ	Seven Nation Army/In The Cold, Cold Night (p/s, ELEPHANT SAMPLER)	10
03	XL XLS 162	Seven Nation Army/Good To Me (p/s)	15
03	XL no cat. no.	Seven Nation Army (1-sided 12" promo, stamped white label, no p/s)	25
04	XL XLS 181	There's No Home For You Here/I Fought Piranhas/Let's Build A Home (die-cut sleeve)	15
05	XL (no. cat. No.)	DENIAL TWIST (10 x printed/stickered CD's in different artwork card wallets. One given away at each night of UK autumn tour. Each CD blank - 10 downloads were availiable online only, this price for complete set)	200
07	XL XL 277	Rag And Bone (with etched B-side of Jack and Meg's faces given away free with copies of NME, gatefold sleeve)	6
01	XL XLLP 150	DE STIJL (LP)	25
01	XL XLLP151	WHITE BLOOD CELLS (LP, red vinyl, insert)	60
01	XL XLLP 151	WHITE BLOOD CELLS (LP)	30
01	XL XLLP 149	WHITE STRIPES (LP)	25
01	XL XLPD149	WHITE STRIPES (LP, picture disc)	18
03	XL XLLP 162	ELEPHANT (2-LP, promo, custom sleeve, 500 only)	100
05	XL XLLP 191 P	GET BEHIND ME SATAN (300 copies pressed for U.K.2-LP promo, different p/s)	200
07	XL XLLP271	ICKY THUMP (2-LP, red/white vinyl)	30

(see also Raconteurs)

WHITE TRASH
69	Apple APPLE 6	Road To Nowhere/Illusions (early copies as White Trash)	200
69	Apple APPLE 6	Road To Nowhere/Illusions (later copies as Trash)	60

(see also Trash, Poets, Stone The Crows)

WHITE ZOMBIE
89	Caroline CAROL 1457	God Of Thunder/Love Razor/Disaster Blaster 2 (12", withdrawn)	15

DAVID WHITFIELD
54	Decca F 10242	The Book/Heartless	10
54	Decca F 10327	Carla Mia/Love, Tears And Kisses	15
54	Decca F 10355	Smile/When Or Where	8
54	Decca F 10399	Santa Natale(Merry Christmas)/Adeste Fideles (O Come All Ye Faithful)	8
56	Decca F 10690	My September Love/The Rudder And The Rock	10
57	Decca F 10833	The Adoration Waltz/If I Lost You	10

WILBUR WHITFIELD
57	Vogue V 9078	P.B. Baby/The One I Love	600
57	Vogue V 9078	P.B. Baby/The One I Love (78)	150

(see also Little Wilbur & Pleasers)

LEONARD WHITING
65	Pye 7N 15943	The Piper/That's What Mama Says	40

MARGARET WHITING
55	Capitol CL 14213	My Own True Love (Tara's Theme)/Can This Be Love (triangular centre)	12
55	Capitol CL 14242	Heat Wave/Come Rain Or Shine (triangular centre)	12
55	Capitol CL 14307	Stowaway/All I Want Is All There Is And Then Some (triangular centre)	12
55	Capitol CL 14348	A Man/Mama's Pearls (triangular centre)	12
55	Capitol CL 14375	Lover, Lover/I Kiss You A Million Times (triangular centre)	12
56	Capitol CL 14527	I Love A Mystery/Bidin' My Time	10
56	Capitol CL 14591	Old Enough/Day In - Day Out	8
56	Capitol CL 14647	True Love/Haunting Love	8
57	Capitol CL 14685	The Money Tree/Maybe I Love Him	8
57	London HLD 8451	Kill Me With Kisses/Speak For Yourself, John	10
58	London HLD 8562	I Can't Help (If I'm Still In Love With You)/That's Why I Was Born	10
58	London HLD 8662	Hot Spell/I'm So Lonesome I Could Cry	10
66	London HLD 10078	Nothing Lasts Forever/The Wheel Of Hurt	10
68	London HLU 10196	Faithfully/Am I Losing You	6
53	Capitol LC 6585	CAPITOL PRESENTS MARGARET WHITING (10" LP)	15
56	Capitol LC 6811	MARGARET WHITING (10" LP)	15
58	London HA-D 2109	GOIN' PLACES (LP)	15
61	London HA-D 2321	JUST A DREAM (LP)	20

(see also Jimmy Wakely, Bob Hope, Dean Martin)

RAY WHITLEY
65	HMV POP 1473	I've Been Hurt/There Is One Boy	150
65	HMV POP 1473	I've Been Hurt/There Is One Boy (DJ copy)	250

BOBBY WHITLOCK
72	CBS 65109	BOBBY WHITLOCK (LP)	30
73	CBS 65301	RAW VELVET (LP)	20

(see also Derek & Dominoes)

SLIM WHITMAN
SINGLES
54	London L 1149	Indian Love Call/China Doll	20
54	London HL 1149	Indian Love Call/China Doll (re-pressing with different prefix)	15
54	London L 1214	There's A Rainbow In Every Teardrop/Danny Boy	20
54	London HL 1214	There's A Rainbow In Every Teardrop/Danny Boy (re-pressing)	15
54	London L 1226	North Wind/Darlin' Don't Cry	30
54	London HL 1226	North Wind/Darlin' Don't Cry (re-pressing with different prefix)	30
54	London HL 8018	Stairway To Heaven/Lord, Help Me To Be As Thou	30

			MINT VALUE £
54	London HL 8039	Secret Love/Why	30
54	London HL 8061	Rose Marie/We Stood At The Altar	15
54	London HL 8080	Beautiful Dreamer/Ride Away	15
54	London HL 8091	The Singing Hills/I Hate To See You Cry	15
55	London HL 8125	When I Grow Too Old To Dream/Cattle Call	12
55	London HL 8141	Haunted Hungry Heart/Roll On, Silvery Moon	10
55	London HLU 8167	I'll Never Stop Loving You/I'll Never Take You Back Again	10
55	London HLU 8196	Song Of The Wild/You Have My Heart	10
56	London HLU 8230	Tumbling Tumbleweeds/Tell Me	10
56	London HLU 8252	I'm A Fool/My Heart Is Broken In Three	10
56	London HLU 8287	Serenade/I Talk To The Waves	10
56	London HLU 8327	Dear Mary/Whiffenpoof Song	10
56	London HLU 8350	I'm Casting My Lasso Towards The Sky/There's A Love Knot In My Lariat	10
57	London HLP 8403	I'll Take You Home Again Kathleen/Careless Love	10

(The above 45's were originally issued with gold label print & tri-centres; later round-centre and/or silver label print copies are worth half these values.)

57	London HLP 8416	Curtain Of Tears/Smoke Signals (silver label print)	6
57	London HLP 8420	Gone/An Amateur In Love (gold label print)	15
59	London HLP 8896	What Kind Of God (Do You Think You Are)/A Tree In The Meadow (unissued)	0

EPs

54	London RE-P 1006	SLIM WHITMAN AND HIS SINGING GUITAR (at least 8 different colour sleeves, with matt finish & various label designs)	12
66	Liberty LEP 4046	A SATISFIED MIND	10

ALBUMS

54	London H-APB 1015	SLIM WHITMAN & HIS SINGING GUITAR (10", gold label print)	40
54	London H-APB 1015	SLIM WHITMAN & HIS SINGING GUITAR (10", silver label print)	25
56	London HA-U 2015	SLIM WHITMAN & HIS SINGING GUITAR VOL. 2	30
59	London HA-P 2139	SLIM WHITMAN SINGS	20
59	London HA-P 2199	SLIM WHITMAN SINGS VOL. 2	20
61	London HA-P 2392	JUST CALL ME LONESOME	20
60	London HA-P 2343	SLIM WHITMAN	18
62	London HA-P 2443	SLIM WHITMAN SINGS VOL. 3 (Mono)	18
62	London HA-P 2443	SLIM WHITMAN SINGS VOL. 3 (also stereo SAH-P 6232)	20

MARVA WHITNEY

70	Polydor 2001 036	This Girl's In Love With You/He's The One	8
69	Polydor 583 767	IT'S MY THING (LP)	75

(see also James Brown)

JAKI WHITREN

83	Living LRS 111	International Times/Inner Fire (p/s)	20
83	Living 12 LR1	International Times/Dub Version (12", p/s)	40
73	Epic EPC 65645	RAW BUT TENDER (LP, with insert)	45
83	Living LR1	INTERNATIONAL TIMES (LP, with John Cartwright)	100

TIM WHITSETT

64	Sue WI 318	Macks By The Tracks/Shine	45

TIM WHITSETT/STICKS HERMAN

60s	Range JRE 7002	RHYTHM & BLUES (EP)	30

PAUL WHITSUN JONES & WALLAS EATON & HOLLAND

65	Oriole CB 1991	Shake It Baby/Instant Marriage	20

WHITSUNTIDE EASTER

77	Pilgrim/Grapevine GRA 109	NEXT TIME YOU PLAY A WRONG NOTE...MAKE IT A SHORT ONE (LP, gatefold sleeve)	100

ROGER WHITTAKER (& COMPANIONS)

62	Fontana 267 217TF	Steel Men/After The Laughter	6

TOMMY WHITTLE (& HIS QUARTET)

57	HMV 45 POP 379	The Finisher/Cabin In The Sky	25
55	Esquire EP 37	TOMMY WHITTLE QUINTET (EP)	40
56	Esquire EP 37	TOMMY WHITTLE QUINTET (EP)	40
58	HMV 7EG 8325	TOMMY WHITTLE QUARTET (EP)	100
54	Esquire 20-028	WAXING WITH WHITTLE (LP)	50
55	Esquire 20-048	TOMMY WHITTLE QUINTET (LP)	60
56	Esquire 20-061	SPOTLIGHTING TOMMY WHITTLE (LP)	90
56	Esquire 20-068	LULLABY & RHYTHM (LP)	100
60	Tempo TAP 27	NEW HORIZONS (LP)	1000
60s	Ember EMB 3305	EASY LISTENING (LP)	75
67	Masquerade MQ 2000	SAX FOR DREAMERS (LP)	100
77	Jam 648	WHY NOT? (LP)	20
82	Tee Jay 101	THE NEARNESS OF YOU (LP)	20
88	Esquire 334	MORE WAXING WITH WHITTLE (LP, reissue)	20

WHIZZ KIDS

79	Dead Good DEAD SIX	P.A.Y.E./99% Proof/National Assistance/Cheek To Cheek (p/s, with insert)	20
80	Ovation OVS 1213	Suspect No. 1/Coma Life (p/s)	10

THE WHO

SINGLES

65	Brunswick 05926	I Can't Explain/Bald Headed Woman	40
65	Brunswick 05935	Anyway Anyhow Anywhere/Daddy Rolling Stone	35
65	Brunswick 05944	My Generation/Shout And Shimmy	20
66	Brunswick 05951	Circles/Instant Party Mixture (unreleased)	0
66	Reaction 591 001	Substitute/Circles (temporarily withdrawn)	40
66	Reaction 591 001	Substitute/Instant Party (temporarily withdrawn)	30
66	Brunswick 05956	The Kids Are Alright/The Ox (existence unconfirmed)	0

The WHO

MINT VALUE £

Year	Catalogue	Title	Value
66	Brunswick 05956	A Legal Matter/Instant Party	50
66	Reaction 591 001	Substitute/WHO ORCHESTRA: Waltz For A Pig (B-side actually by Graham Bond Organisation)	25
66	Brunswick 05965	The Kids Are Alright/The Ox	60
66	Brunswick 05968	La-La-La-Lies/The Good's Gone	70
66	Reaction 591 004	I'm A Boy/In The City	12
66	Reaction 591 010	Happy Jack/I've Been Away	12
67	Track 604 002	Pictures Of Lily/Doctor, Doctor	12
67	Track 604 006	The Last Time/Under My Thumb	65
67	Track 604 011	I Can See For Miles/Someone's Coming	15
68	Track 604 023	Dogs/Call Me Lightning	25
68	Track 604 024	Magic Bus/Dr. Jekyll And Mr Hyde	12
69	Track 604 027	Pinball Wizard/Dogs Part Two	12
70	Track 604 036	The Seeker/Here For More	10
70	Track 2094 002	Summertime Blues/Heaven And Hell	10
70	Track 2094 004	See Me, Feel Me/Overture From 'Tommy' (withdrawn)	40
71	Track 2094 009	Won't Get Fooled Again/Don't Know Myself (p/s, large centre)	25
71	Track 2094 009	Won't Get Fooled Again/Don't Know Myself (p/s, with middle)	35
73	Track 2094 115	5.15/Water	7
75	Polydor 2001 561	Overture/See Me Feel Me/Listening To You (from "Tommy" soundtrack, p/s)	10
78	Polydor Who 1 DJ	Who Are You/Had Enough (DJ copy in brown paper bag with 'Who Promotional Copy' stamped on outside)	30
79	Polydor WHO 2	Long Live Rock/I'm The Face/My Wife (withdrawn, blank run-off groove)	6
80	Polydor WHO 3	5.15/I'm One (p/s)	6
82	Polydor WHOPX 6	Athena/A Man Is A Man/Won't Get Fooled Again (12", picture disc, mispressing, plays "Why Did I Fall For That")	15
88	Polydor POSP 907	My Generation/Substitute (p/s)	6
88	Olydor POSPX 907	My Generation/Substitute/Baba O'Riley/Behind Blue Eyes (12", p/s)	12
88	Polydor POSPX 917	Won't Get Fooled Again/Boney Moronie/Dancing In The Street/Mary-Anne With The Shaky Hand (12", p/s)	15
88	Polydor POSP 917	Won't Get Fooled Again/Boney Moronie (p/s)	8
90	Virgin VS 1259	Join Together/I Can See Fore Miles/Behind Blue Eyes (p/s)	8
90	Virgin VST 1259	Join Together/Christmas/I Can See For Miles/Behind Blue Eyes (12", p/s)	12
98	Polydor 8939187	My Generation/Pinball Wizard (live) (p/s, yellow vinyl)	8
04	Polydor 9866447	THE FIRST SINGLES BOX (12 x 7" box set with booklet)	75
06	Polydor 1702801	WIRE & GLASS: SIX SONGS FROM A MINI OPERA (12", p/s)	12
13	Universal 3716687	MUSIC FOR LOSING CEREMONY OF THE LONDON 2012 OLYMPIC GAMES (12", p/s)	50
15	Polydor 4713989	THE BRUNSWICK SINGLES 1965-1966 (box set, 8 x 7"	45
15	Polydor 4724720	THE REACTION SINGLES 1966 (Box set, 5 x 7")	35
16	Polydor 4765358	THE POLYDOR SINGLES (box set, 15 x 7")	60

EXPORT SINGLES

Year	Catalogue	Title	Value
66	Brunswick 05956	A Legal Matter/Instant Party (with Scandinavian p/s)	150
68	Decca AD 1001	My Generation/Shout And Shimmy	100
68	Decca AD 1001	My Generation/Shout And Shimmy (in p/s)	200
68	Decca AD 1002	A Legal Matter/Instant Party	100
72	Track 2094 102	Join Together/Baby Don't You Do It (p/s, for Spain with 'special Londres import' on front and 'Imported by Polydor S.A.' on rear)	25

EPs

Year	Catalogue	Title	Value
66	Reaction 592 001	READY STEADY WHO	90
70	Track 2252 001	EXCERPTS FROM "TOMMY" (33rpm)	25
83	Reaction WHO 7	READY STEADY WHO (reissue)	20

ALBUMS

Year	Catalogue	Title	Value
65	Brunswick LAT 8616	MY GENERATION (laminated front sleeve, black/silver label)	600
66	Reaction 593 002	A QUICK ONE (laminated sleeve, blue/silver label)	200
67	Track 612 002	THE WHO SELL OUT (LP, mono)	200
67	Track 613 002	THE WHO SELL OUT (LP, stereo)	150
67	Track 612 002	THE WHO SELL OUT (mono, 500 with stickered sleeve & poster)	800
67	Track 613 002	THE WHO SELL OUT (stereo, 500 with stickered sleeve & poster)	800
68	Track 612 006	DIRECT HITS (mono)	40
68	Track 613 006	DIRECT HITS (stereo)	50
69	Track 613 013/014	TOMMY (2-LP, 1st issue fold-out laminated gatefold sleeve made by E.J. Day, A1/B1/A1/B1 matrixes, "double album" on labels with and must not have catalogue number under 'ST33' on the right side (as this is a later pressing) with numbered 12-page booklet)	150
69	Track 613 013/014	TOMMY (2-LP, 2nd issue fold-out matt gatefold sleeve, no "double album" on labels with 12-page booklet, un-numbered)	40
70	Track 2406 001	LIVE AT LEEDS (1st issue with BLACK stamp on front, foldout sleeve with 12 inserts including poster)	250
70	Track 2406 001	LIVE AT LEEDS (with BLUE or RED stamp on front, foldout sleeve with 12 inserts including poster stating 'Tuesdays At The Marquee')	80
70	Track 2406 001	LIVE AT LEEDS (with BLUE or RED stamp on front, foldout sleeve with 12 inserts including poster stating 'Live At Leeds', A1/B1 matrix')	50
70	Track 2406 001	LIVE AT LEEDS (second pressing, BLUE or RED stamp on front, foldout sleeve with 12 inserts including poster stating 'Live At Leeds', A3/B3 matrix')	40
70	Track 2407 008	BACKTRACK 8: A QUICK ONE (mono budget reissue)	25
70	Track 2407 009	BACKTRACK 9: SELL OUT (stereo budget reissue)	30
70	Track 2407 014	BACKTRACK 14: THE OX	20
70	Track 2856 001	WHO DID IT? (mail-order only, withdrawn)	600
71	Track 2408 102	WHO'S NEXT (1st pressing with poly-lined inner sleeve with black and white Polydor artist photos on front and "HEAD HUNTERS - GET A HEAD" on rear. MATRIX: 2408 102 A1/B2) Pleated end spines)	50
71	Track 2408 102	WHO'S NEXT (later pressing, MATRIX: 2408 102 A4/B3)	25
71	Track 2406 006	MEATY, BEATY, BIG AND BOUNCY (gatefold sleeve)	30

The WHO

MINT VALUE £

71	Track 2406 006	MEATY, BEATY, BIG AND BOUNCY (gatefold sleeve, mispressed, plays "The Seeker" instead of "Magic Bus")	40
72	Track 2406 007	TOMMY PART ONE	20
72	Track 2406 008	TOMMY PART TWO (with lyric sheet)	20
73	Track 2406 110	QUADROPHENIA (2-LP, original with 22-page photo booklet, matt labels)	60
73	Track 613013/613014	TOMMY (2-LP, reissue)	20
74	Track ACB 254	ODDS AND SODS (LP)	45
74	Track 2406 116	ODDS AND SODS (cut-away braille sleeve, with poster & lyric sheet)	40
74	Track 2409209/10	A QUICK ONE/THE WHO SELL OUT (2-LP, reissue, E.J. Day printing credit)	70
75	Polydor 2490 129	THE WHO BY NUMBERS (LP, numbered)	20
76	Polydor 2478091	THE STORY OF THE WHO (2-LP, booklet)	25
78	Polydor WHOD 5004	WHO ARE YOU (LP)	20
79	Polydor 2488 739	THE KIDS ARE ALRIGHT (2-LP, booklet and inner sleeves)	30
80	Virgin V 2179	MY GENERATION (reissue)	25
80	Polydor 2683 084	LIVE AT LEEDS/WHO ARE YOU (2-LP)	20
81	Polydor 2675 216	PHASES (9-LP box set, stickered cover)	150
81	Polydor	FACE DANCES (Promo boxed set with poster and bio of artists, numbered Peter Blake print, 300 only)	200
81	Polydor WHOD 5037	FACE DANCES (LP, inner, poster)	20
82	Polydor De Luxe WHOD 5066	IT'S HARD (LP)	15
83	Polydor Mid Price SPELP 60	LIVE AT LEEDS (2-LP, reissue)	20
83	Polydor SPELT 49	WHO'S NEXT LP, reissue)	20
83	Polydor SPLEP 9	RARITIES VOL 1 1966-1968 (LP)	15
83	Polydor SPLEP 10	RARITIES VOL 2 1970-1973 (LP)	15
84	MCA Who 1	WHO'S LAST (2-LP)	20
84	Polydor WHOH 17	THE SINGLES (LP)	20
85	Polydor Impression IMDP 4	THE WHO COLLECTION (2-LP)	20
88	Polydor SPELT 114	A QUICK ONE (LP, reissue)	25
88	Polydor SPELT 115	THE WHO SELL OUT (LP, reissue)	20
88	Polydor SVLP 201	TOMMY (2-LP, reissue)	20
88	Polydor WTV 1	WHO'S BETTER WHO'S BEST (LP)	20
88	Polydor 8375571	WHO'S MISSING (LP)	20
88	Polydor 8375581	TWO'S MISSING (LP)	20
90	Virgin VDT 201	JOIN TOGETHER (3-LP, inner sleeves)	40
99	Simply Vinyl SVLP 088	WHO'S NEXT (LP, reissue, 180gm)	30
00	Polydor 5477271	BBC SESSIONS (2-LP)	25
01	Polydor 8310741	QUADROPHENIA (2-LP, reissue, 22 page book, 180gm)	20
02	Polydor 11398111	MY GENERATION (2-LP, reissue, first stereo remix with bonus tracks)	40
03	Polydor 076 176-1	WHO'S NEXT (3-LP, reissue)	40
03	Polydor 8117151	THE WHO BY NUMBERS (LP, reissue)	20
04	Polydor 8357281	A QUICK ONE (LP, reissue)	20
08	Polydor 0042281365119	WHO'S NEXT (LP, reissue)	25
11	Polydor 2780405	QUADROPHENIA (2-LP, reissue, 22 page book, 180gm)	20
11	Back On Black RCV 065LP	LIVE AT THE ISLE OF WIGHT FESTIVAL (3-LP)	40
12	Polydor 3715573	THE STUDIO ALBUMS (13-LP box set)	200
12	Eagle VV 3 LP 006	LIVE AT THE ISLE OF WIGHT FESTIVAL (3-LP, blue or white vinyl)	30
13	Polydor 3715751	ENDLESS WIRE (2-LP)	25
13	Universal 00600753271278	WHO'S NEXT (LP, reissue, picture disc)	35
15	Polydor 3715603	MY GENERATION (LP, reissue)	20
15	Polydor 3715608	A QUICK ONE (LP, reissue)	15
15	Poyldor 3715609	THE WHO SELL OUT (LP, reissue)	20
15	Polydor 3715749	TOMMY (2-LP, reissue, 180gm)	25
15	Polydor 3715630	WHO ARE YOU (LP, reissue, 180gm)	20
15	Polydor 3715627	THE WHO BY NUMBERS (LP, reissue)	20
15	Polydor 5780504	QUADROPHENIA (2-LP, reissue,180gm)	25
16	Polydor 0600753698075	LIVE AT LEEDS (3-LP, entire concert)	50
17	Polydor 5372747	MY GENERATION (3-LP reissue)	30
17	Polydor 5774830	LIVE AT LEEDS (LP, reissue)	20
17	Polydor 5774828	MEATY, BEATY, BIG AND BOUNCY (LP, reissue)	25
17	Eagle ER 416812	TOMMY LIVE AT THE ALBERT HALL (3-LP)	25
18	Polydor 3715614	WHO'S NEXT (LP, reissue, blue vinyl)	15
18	Polydor 6713232	THE KIDS ARE ALRIGHT (2-LP, reissue, red and blue vinyl)	40
18	Polydor 6744480	LIVE AT FILLMORE EAST 1968 (2-LP)	25
19	Polydor WHO 7748605	WHO (LP as 2 x 12" on blue/white vinyl , with red 10")	35
19	Polydor WHO 08249751921	WHO (LP, with additional Bonus Hits LP on cream vinyl, HMV exclusive)	20
20	Polydor 7712462	ODDS AND SODS (2-LP, red and yellow vinyl, bonus tracks, half-speed remaster)	40

PROMOS : DEMO SINGLES

65	Brunswick 05926	I Can't Explain/Bald Headed Woman (demo, red label)	500
65	Brunswick 05935	Anyway Anyhow Anywhere/Daddy Rolling Stone (demo, red label)	400
65	Brunswick 05944	My Generation/Shout And Shimmy (demo, red label)	450
66	Brunswick 05956	A Legal Matter/Instant Party (demo, red label)	400
66	Brunswick 05965	The Kids Are Alright/The Ox (demo, red label)	400
66	Brunswick 05968	La-La-La-Lies/The Good's Gone (demo, red label)	400
69	Track PRO 1	The Acid Queen/We're Not Gonna Take It (existence unconfirmed)	0
69	Track PRO 2	Go To The Mirror!/Sally Simpson	80
69	Track PRO 3	I'm Free/1921	80
69	Track PRO 4	Christmas/Overture	80
78	Polydor WHO 1 DJ 3	Who Are You (Edited Version) (single sided promo)	75
82	Polydor WHOX 6A2420	Emindence Front/Athena/Dangerous)12", promo, stamped white sleeve large 1 and 2 on labels)	50

WHO THE HELL DOES JANE SMITH THINK SHE IS

MINT VALUE £

84	MCA MCA 927	Twist & Shout/I Can't Explain (p/s)	7
96	Polydor WHO 1	My Generation (Love To Infinity's Regeneration Mix)/(Aphrodisiac Mix)/(Deep Love Mix)/(Deep Love Instrumental (12", promo)	10

(see also High Numbers, Pete Townshend, Roger Daltrey, John Entwistle, Keith Moon, Kenney Jones, Graham Bond Organisation, Rigor Mortis, McEnroe & Cash)

WHO THE HELL DOES JANE SMITH THINK SHE IS
87	Influx FUX 1	Use/Imagination (p/s)	25
87	Influx FUX 1T	Use/Imagination (12", p/s)	60

WI & HDEA
93	Hype! VEN 001	VENTURE F.M. PRESENTS SUMMER RUSH EP (12", stamped white label)	20

WICHITA FALL
69	Liberty LBS 83208	LIFE IS BUT A DREAM (LP)	25

WICHITA TRAIN WHISTLE
68	Dot DOT 111	Don't Cry Now/Tapioca Tundra (unissued)	0
68	Dot (S)LPD 516	MICHAEL NESMITH PRESENTS THE WICHITA TRAIN WHISTLE SINGS (LP)	40

(see also Michael Nesmith)

WICKY WACKY
90	EMI WACKY PROMO 1	Let's Get Down (6 mixes, promo only, 300 copies)	50

(see also Cabaret Voltaire)

WIDERVISION
80	Widermusic 001	People/Truant (p/s)	25

WIDOWMAKER
76	Jet JET 766	On The Road/Pin A Rose On Me	7
77	United Artists UAG 30038	TOO LATE TO CRY (LP, gatefold sleeve)	15

(see also Luther Grosvenor, Steve Ellis, Huw Lloyd Langton)

DAVID WIGG
66	CBS 202233	Life Is Complicated/Turning Around	10

TREVOR WIGGAN
75	Not on label	Beg You Not To Go/JAH MAN: Please Stay	100

WIGGANS
61	Blue Beat BB 29	Rock Baby/Let's Sing The Blues	25

PERCY WIGGINS
67	Atlantic 584 113	Book Of Memories/Can't Find Nobody (To Take Your Place)	10

SPENCER WIGGINS
67	Stateside SS 2024	Uptight Good Woman/Anything You Do Is Alright	25
70	Pama PM 794	I'm A Poor Man's Son/That's How Much I Love You	25

WIGWAM
76	Virgin V2051	LUCKY GOLDEN STRIPES AND STARPOSE (LP, "mirror" girl label, lyric insert, embossed sleeve)	20
75	Virgin V 2035	NUCLEAR NIGHTCLUB (LP)	25

LEO WIJNKAMP JR
75	Kicking Mule SNKF 108	RAGS TO RICHES (LP)	25
79	Kicking Mule SNKF 156	RETURN OF DR. HACKENBUSH (LP)	25

WIKKYD VIKKER
83	Boogie FUR 0235	Black Of The Night/Release (no p/s)	120

JACK WILCE
69	Elektra EKSN 45068	Apple Pie, Mother & The Flag/Ballad Of Baby Browning	10

WILCO
04	Nonesuch 7559 79851	I'm A Wheel/Kicking Television (p/s)	6
11	dBpm 87162-7	I Might/I Love My Label (p/s, silver vinyl)	6
11	dBpm 87181-1	SPEAK INTO THE ROSE (10" red vinyl, Record Store Day release)	10
97	Reprise 9362 46236-1	BEING THERE (2-LP)	40
99	Reprise 9362 47282-1	SUMMERTEETH (2-LP)	40
04	Nonesuch 76492-1	A GHOST IS BORN (2-LP)	25

WILD BEASTS (1)
79	Warped BEND 1	LIFE IS A BUM EP (folded p/s)	10

WILD ANGELS
68	Major Minor MM 569	Nervous Breakdown/Watch The Wheels Go Round	25
69	B&C CB 114	Buzz Buzz/Please Don't Touch	12
70	B&C CB 123	Sally-Ann/Wrong Number, Try Again	12
71	B&C CB 145	Three Nights A Week/Time To Kill	8
72	Decca F 13308	Jo-Jo Ann/My Way	7
72	Decca F 13356	Beauty School Dropout/Midnight Rider	7
73	Decca F 13374	Running Bear/Sussin'	6
73	Decca F 13412	Greased Lightning/Born To Hand-Jive/Beauty School Dropout	6
73	Decca F 13456	Clap Your Hands And Stamp Your Feet/Wild Angels Rock'n'Roll	8
70	B&C BCM 101	LIVE AT THE REVOLUTION (LP)	15
70	B&C BCM 102	RED HOT'N'ROCKIN' (LP)	15

WILD BOYS
78	Ring Piece CUS 886	Last One Of The Boys/We're Only Monsters	400

WILD BUNCH
84	Ariwa ARILP 15	THE WILD BUNCH (LP)	20

WILDCATS (1)
59	London HLT 8787	Gazachstahagen/Billy's Cha Cha	25

WILD COUNTRY
70	Trafalgar TRAF 01	Silent Village/Too Bad	65

JACK WILD(E)
69	Elektra EKSN 45068	Apple Pie Mother And The Flag/Ballad Of Baby Browning	6
70	Capitol CL 15635	Picture Of You/Some Beautiful	7
71	Buddah 2011-19	Punch & Judy/Takin It Easy	10

Marty WILDE (& WILDCATS)

MINT VALUE £

MARTY WILDE (& WILDCATS)

78s
58	Philips PB 781	Love Bug Crawl/Afraid Of Love	30
58	Philips PB 804	Sing, Boy, Sing/Oh-Oh, I'm Falling In Love Again (with Wildcats)	25
59	Philips PB 902	Donna/Love-a, Love-a, Love-a	25
59	Philips PB 926	A Teenager In Love/Danny	30
59	Philips PB 959	Sea Of Love/Teenage Tears	40
59	Philips PB 972	It's Been Nice/Bad Boy	40
60	Philips PB 1002	Johnny Rocco/My Heart And I	50

SINGLES
57	Philips JK 1028	Honeycomb/Wild Cat (as Marty Wilde & Wildcats) (jukebox issue)	50
58	Philips PB 804	Sing, Boy, Sing/Oh-Oh, I'm Falling In Love Again (with Wildcats)	40
58	Philips PB 835	Endless Sleep/Her Hair Was Yellow (as Marty Wilde & Wildcats)	15
58	Philips PB 850	My Lucky Love/Misery's Child (as Marty Wilde & Wildcats)	12
58	Philips PB 875	No One Knows/The Fire Of Love	15
59	Philips PB 902	Donna/Love-a, Love-a, Love-a	10
59	Philips PB 926	A Teenager In Love/Danny	10
59	Philips PB 959	Sea Of Love/Teenage Tears	10
59	Philips PB 972	Bad Boy/It's Been Nice	10
60	Philips PB 1002	Johnny Rocco/My Heart And I	10
60	Philips PB 1022	The Fight/Johnny At The Crossroads	10
60	Philips PB 1037	I Wanna Be Loved By You/Angry	6
60	Philips PB 1078	Little Girl/Your Seventeenth Spring	6
61	Philips PB 1101	Rubber Ball/Like Makin' Love	6
61	Philips PB 1121	When Does It Get To Be Love/Your Loving Touch	7
61	Philips PB 1161	Hide And Seek/Crazy Dream	15
61	Philips PB 1191	Tomorrow's Clown/The Hellions	12
61	Philips PB 1206	Come Running/Ev'ryone	12
62	Philips PB 1240	Jezebel/Don't Run Away	10
62	Philips 326 546BF	Ever Since You Said Goodbye/Send Me The Pillow You Dream On	10
63	Columbia DB 4980	Lonely Avenue/Brand New Love	10
63	Philips 326 579BF	No! Dance With Me/Little Miss Happiness	7
63	Columbia DB 7145	Save Your Love For Me/Bless My Broken Heart	10
64	Columbia DB 7198	When Day Is Done/I Can't Help The Way I Feel	10
64	Columbia DB 7285	Kiss Me/My, What A Woman	10
64	Decca F 11979	The Mexican Boy/Your Kind Of Love	12

EPs
57	Philips BBE 12164	PRESENTING MARTY WILDE	30
58	Philips BBE 12200	MORE OF MARTY	30
59	Philips BBE 12327	SEA OF LOVE	30
60	Philips BBE 12385	VERSATILE MR. WILDE	25
60	Philips BBE 12422	MARTY WILDE FAVOURITES	25
62	Philips BBE 12517	COME RUNNING	25
63	Philips BE 433 638	MARTY	25

ALBUMS
59	Philips BBL 7342	WILDE ABOUT MARTY	50
60	Philips BBL 7380	MARTY WILDE SHOWCASE	35
60	Philips BBL 7385	THE VERSATILE MR. WILDE (mono)	30
60	Philips SBBL 570	THE VERSATILE MR. WILDE (stereo)	35

(see also Wilde Three, Brian Bennett, Shadows, Keith Shields, Capricorn, Deke Leonard)

OLIVER WILDE
15	Howling Owl HOWL 042	Yuletide (with EBU, 1-sided lathe cut, 30 only)	25
13	Howling Owl HOWL 022	AN INTRODUCTION TO UNNATURAL LIGHTYEARS (LP, 1st pressing, white vinyl, 250 only, insert)	30

RICKY WILDE
73	UK 28	April Love/Round And Round	6
74	UK 59	Mrs Malinski/Cassette Blues	6
74	UK 63	Round And Round/Teen Wave	6
74	UK UK 70	I Wanna Go To A Disco/I Wanna Go To A Disco (double A sided promo)	10

WILDER BROTHERS
57	HMV POP 365	I Want You/Teenage Angel	250
57	HMV POP 365	I Want You/Teenage Angel (78)	50

WILDERNESS ROAD
74	Dawn DNLS 3057	WILDERNESS ROAD (LP, unissued)	0

WILDERVISION
80	Wildermusic WDR 1	People/Truant	10

WILDE THREE
65	Decca F 12131	Since You've Gone/Just As Long	75
65	Decca F 12232	I Cried/Well Who's That?	75

(see also Marty Wilde, Justin Hayward, Vernons Girls)

WILDFIRE (1)
84	Mausoleum GUTS 8403	Nothing Lasts Forever/Blood Money	8
83	Mausoleum SKUL 8307	BRUTE FORCE AND IGNORANCE (LP)	25
83	Mausoleum SKUL 8338	SUMMER LIGHTNING (LP, with insert)	15

(see also Weapon)

GINGER WILDHEART
12	(No label or Cat. No)	555% (3-LP, red, white and blue vinyl, tri-fold sleeve, inners. Pledge mail order only)	50
14	(No label or Cat. No)	ALBION (2-LP, gatefold sleeve. Pledge mail order only)	40
15	GASSLP 001	YEAR OF THE FANCLUB (2-LP, clear glitter vinyl, gatefold and innder. Pledge mail-order	40

WILDHEARTS

MINT VALUE £

only) ....

(see also Wildhearts, Super$hit666, Jason & the Scorchers)

WILDHEARTS
SINGLES

92	East West YZ 669T	MONDO AKIMBO A-GO-GO (12" EP, with inner sleeve)	35
92	East West YZ 669TX	MONDO AKIMBO A-GO-GO (12" EP, white vinyl, with inner sleeve, advance copies with artwork postcard & press sheet)	60
92	East West YZ 669TX	MONDO AKIMBO A-GO-GO (12" EP, white vinyl, with inner sleeve)	50
92	East West YZ 669CD	MONDO AKIMBO A-GO-GO (CD EP)	40
93	East West YZ 773	Greetings From Shitsville/The Bullshit Goes On (p/s, brown vinyl, with insert)	12
94	East West YZ 794	Caffeine Bomb/Girlfriend Clothes (p/s, green vinyl, with insert)	8
94	East West YZ 828TE	Suckerpunch/Beautiful Thing You/Two-Way Idiot Mirror/29 x The Pain (10", p/s, 1-sided, etched)	12
94	East West YZ 874TEX	If Life Is Like A Lovebank I Want An Overdraft/Geordie In Wonderland/ Hate The World Day/Fire Up (10", gatefold sleeve with banknote)	10
95	East West YZ 923TEX	I Wanna Go Where The People Go/Shandy Bang/Can't Do Right For Doing Wrong/Give The Girl A Gun (10", p/s)	10
95	East West YZ 976TEX	Just In Lust/Mindslide/Friend For Five Minutes/S.I.N (In Sin) (10", p/s)	10
04	(no label or cat no)	Vanilla Radio/Stormy In The North, Karma In The South (CD-R, p/s in DVD case, sold at gigs)	40
07	Round ROUND 011S-7	The New Flesh/(Radio Edit)/Unbroken (p/s, white vinyl)	8

ALBUMS

92	East West 4509-91202-1	DON'T BE HAPPY... JUST WORRY (LP, as 2 x 12", with inner sleeves)	40
93	East West 4509-93287-1	EARTH VS THE WILDHEARTS (LP, with exclusive uncredited track)	100
94	East West 4509-99039-2	FISHING FOR LUCKIES (CD, 6-track mini-album, fan club/mail-order only)	40
95	East West 0630-10404-1	P.H.U.Q. (LP, gatefold sleeve)	80
95	East West 0630-12850-1	FISHING FOR MORE LUCKIES (LP, reissue, with 3 extra tracks Underkill, "Saddened" & "I Wanna Go Where The People Go [Early Version]", unreleased, most copies destroyed)	400
95	East West 0630-12850-2	FISHING FOR MORE LUCKIES (LP, reissue, with 3 extra tracks Underkill, "Saddened" & "I Wanna Go Where The People Go [Early Version]")	35
96	Round 0630-14888-1	FISHING FOR LUCKIES (2-LP, reissue, gatefold, Side 3 exclusive to vinyl)	50
97	Mushroom MUSH13LP	ENDLESS, NAMELESS (LP, inner sleeve)	50
98	Kuro Neko KNEKLP3	ANARCHIC AIRWAVES - THE WiLDHEARTS AT THE BBC (2-LP, 200 mail-order copies only - 1000 copies made but 800 destroyed)	60
99	Kuro Neko KNEK3LTD	ANARCHIC AIRWAVES - THE WiLDHEARTS AT THE BBC (2-CD, with bonus disc "THE REST OF READING")	30
98	Kuro Neko KNEK4LB	LANDMINES & PANTOMIMES - THE LAST OF THE WiLDHEARTS...? (CD in square stickered metal tin with insert, 1000 copies only)	45
03	Gut GUTLP25	THE WILDHEARTS MUST BE DESTROYED (LP, gatefold sleeve)	40
04	Gut GUTLP32	THE WILDHEARTS STRIKE BACK (2 x LP, gatefold)	50
08	Round ROUND010LP	THE WILDHEARTS (2 x LP, white vinyl, photo insert, 1,000 only)	40
16	Round RRRLP001	NEVER OUTDRUNK, NEVER OUTSUNG - PHUQ LIVE (2-LP, purple vinyl with bonus CD, gatefold sleeve/inners. Pledge mail-order only)	50
16	Round RRRLP001	NEVER OUTDRUNK, NEVER OUTSUNG - PHUQ LIVE (2-LP, yellow vinyl vinyl, reissue with bonus CD, gatefold sleeve/inners. Pledge mail-order only)	25

(see also Backyard Babies, Energetic Krusher, Honeycrack, Jellys,, Super$hit666, Yo-Yo's)

WILD HORSES

80	EMI EMI 5078	Fly Away/Blackmail (p/s, white vinyl; black vinyl demos £15)	6
81	EMI EMC 3368	STAND YOUR GROUND (LP, with inner sleeve)	15

(see also Thin Lizzy, Motorhead, Rainbow, Dio)

WILD MAGNOLIAS

75	Barclay 80 529	THE WILD MAGNOLIAS 1 (LP, gatefold sleeve)	20
75	Barclay 90 033	THEY CALL US WILD (LP, gatefold sleeve)	20

WILD OATS

63	Oak RGJ 117	WILD OATS (EP)	750
95	Tenth Planet TP 013	LIVE AT LEISTON (LP, numbered)	20
16	Big Beat HIQLP 044	THE WILD OATS (10" LP, reissue of original EP)	15

WILD ONES (U.K.)

64	Fontana TF 468	Bowie Man/Purple Pill Eater	75

WILD ONES (U.S)

65	United Artsts ULP 1119	THE ARTHUR SOUND (LP)	40

WILD ORKID

94	Lucky Spin LSR 014	The Magic In You/Orkid (12")	30

WILD PUSSY

88	Metallion	MECHANARCH (12", EP, wih insert)	100

WILD SILK

68	Polydor 56256	Poor Man/Stop Crying	10
69	Columbia DB 8534	(Visions In A) Plaster Sky/Toymaker	30
69	Columbia DB 8611	Help Me/Crimson And Gold	20

WILD SWANS

82	Zoo CAGE 009	The Revolutionary Spirit/God Forbid (unissued, stamped white label)	12
82	Zoo CAGE 009	The Revolutionary Spirit/God Forbid (12", p/s)	10
82	Zoo CAGE 009	The Revolutionary Spirit/God Forbid (12", p/s, with 'The Lament Of Icarus' painting in top right of front sleeve, withdrawn)	15

(see also Care)

WILD THING

69	Elektra EKSN 45076	Old Lady/Next To Me	6
70	Elektra EKS 74059	PARTYIN' (LP)	18

WILD TURKEY

72	Chrysalis CHR 1002	BATTLE HYMN (LP, gatefold sleeve)	40
73	Chrysalis CHR 1010	TURKEY (LP, gatefold sleeve)	20

(see also Babe Ruth, Jethro Tull, Man, Gary Pickford-Hopkins, Whitesnake)

WILD UNCERTAINTY

MINT VALUE £

WILD UNCERTAINTY
66   Planet PLF 120   A Man With Money/Broken Truth 100

WILD & WANDERING
86   Iguana VYK 14   2,000 LIGHT ALES FROM HOME (12" EP, with insert) 25

(see also Pop Will Eat Itself)

WILDWEEDS
67   Chess CRS 8065   It Was Fun While It Lasted/Sorrow's Anthem 20

WILDY
76   Paladin PAL 12   No Smokin'/All The Children 10

WILEY
03   XL Recordings XLLP 178   TREDDIN ON THIN ICE (2-LP) 25
07   Big Dada BD 104   PLAYTIME IS OVER (2-LP) 25

WILFRED
70   Parlophone R5836   Candle In The Wind/Between The Lines 15

WILFRED & MILLICENT
65   Island WI 190   The Vow/I'll Never Believe In You 12

(see also Jackie [Edwards] & Millie [Small])

MIKE WILHELM
76   Zigzag/United Artists ZZ 1   MIKE WILHELM (LP, sold via Zigzag magazine) 45

(see also Charlatans, Flamin' Groovies)

JOHN BUCK WILKIN
70   LBF 15375   Apartment Twenty-One/Boy Of The Country 6

ROBERT WILKINS
60s   Piedmont PLP 13261   REV ROBERT WILKINS (LP) 20
70   Spokane SPL 1002   BEFORE THE REVERENCE (LP) 40

C.T WILKINSON
76   DJM DJS 668   My Happiness/Monday Coming Up 8

WILLARDS LEAP
77   Wren CW 71010   ADIEU, JOHN BARLEYCORN 20

E WILLIAM
67   Polydor 56181   Lazy Life/Crazy How love Slips Away 50

AL WILLIAMS
80   Grapevine GRP 136   I Am Nothing/Brand New Love 35
05   Grapevine G2K 45-162   Try Then/LPTs: Try Me (Instrumental) 20

ANDY WILLIAMS
56   London HLA 8284   Walk Hand In Hand/Not Any More 30
56   London HLA 8315   Canadian Sunset/High Upon A Mountain (gold label print) 40
56   London HLA 8315   Canadian Sunset/High Upon A Mountain (silver label print) 15
56   London HL 7013   Canadian Sunset/High Upon A Mountain (export issue) 20
56   London HLA 8360   Baby Doll (From The Film)/Since I've Found My Baby (gold print) 35
56   London HLA 8360   Baby Doll (From The Film)/Since I've Found My Baby (silver print) 15
57   London HLA 8399   Butterfly/It Doesn't Take Very Long 15
57   London HLA 8437   I Like Your Kind Of Love/Stop Teasin' Me 10
57   London HLA 8487   Lips Of Wine/Straight From My Heart 10
58   London HLA 8587   Are You Sincere/Be Mine Tonight 10
58   London HL 7034   Are You Sincere/Be Mine Tonight (export issue) 10
58   London HLA 8710   Promise Me, Love/Your Hand, Your Heart, Your Love 10
59   London HLA 8784   Hawaiian Wedding Song/House Of Bamboo 10
59   London HLA 8957   Lonely Street/Summer Love 7
59   London HLA 9018   The Village Of St. Bernadette/I'm So Lonesome I Could Cry 6
67   CBS 3104   Holly/God Only Knows (B-side is Beach Boys cover) 7
57   London RE-A 1088   ANDY WILLIAMS' BIG HITS (EP) 12
57   London RE-A 1102   ANDY WILLIAMS' BIG HITS No. 2 (EP) 12
57   London HA-A 2054   ANDY WILLIAMS SINGS STEVE ALLEN (LP) 20
58   London HA-A 2113   ANDY WILLIAMS SINGS RODGERS AND HAMMERSTEIN (LP) 20
59   London HA-A 2203   TWO TIME WINNERS (LP) 20

AUDREY WILLIAMS
56   MGM SP 1179   Ain't Nothing Gonna Be All Right No How/Livin' It Up And Havin' A Ball 25

(see also Hank Williams)

BIG JOE WILLIAMS
57   Jazz Collector JEN 3   A MAN SINGS THE BLUES (EP) 10
57   Jazz Collector JEN 4   A MAN SINGS THE BLUES VOLUME 2 (EP) 10
67   Delmark DJB 4   ON THE HIGHWAY (EP) 15
63   Esquire 32-191   BLUES ON HIGHWAY 51 (LP) 40
63   '77' LA 12-19   PINEY WOODS BLUES (LP) 30
64   CBS BPG 63813   CLASSIC DELTA BLUES (LP) 20
64   Storyville SLP 158   PORTRAITS IN BLUES VOLUME 4 (LP) 20
64   Storyville SLP 163   PORTRAITS IN BLUES VOLUME 7 (LP) 20
65   Fontana 688 800 ZL   TOUGH TIMES (LP) 25
66   Xtra XTRA 1033   BIG JOE WILLIAMS (LP) 30
66   Bounty BY 6018   BACK TO THE COUNTRY (LP) 40
66   Society SOC 1020   BIG JOE, SONNY, BROWNIE, LIGHTNIN' (LP, with Lightnin' Hopkins, Sonny Terry & Brownie McGhee) 15
69   Storyville 618 011   DON'T YOU LEAVE ME HERE (LP) 20
69   Liberty LBL/LBS 83207   HAND ME DOWN MY OLD WALKING STICK (LP) 20
69   Xtra XTRA 5059   LIVE AT FOLK CITY (LP) 15
70   RCA Intl. INTS 1087   CRAWLIN' KING SNAKE (LP) 18
72   Delmark DS 627   NINE STRING GUITAR (LP) 15

(see also Poor Joe Williams)

Billy WILLIAMS (QUARTET)

MINT VALUE £

BILLY WILLIAMS (QUARTET)
54	Vogue Coral Q 2012	Sh'Boom/Whenever Wherever	15
54	Vogue Coral Q 2039	The Honeydripper/Love Me (as Billy Williams Quartet)	40
56	Vogue Coral Q 72149	A Crazy Little Palace/Cry Baby (as Billy Williams Quartet)	40
56	Vogue Coral Q 72180	Pray/You'll Reach Your Star	18
57	Vogue Coral Q 72222	Follow Me/Shame, Shame, Shame (as Billy Williams Quartet)	20
57	Vogue Coral Q 72241	Butterfly/The Pied Piper	20
57	Vogue Coral Q 72266	I'm Gonna Sit Right Down And Write A Letter/Date With The Blues	20
57	Vogue Coral Q 72295	Got A Date With An Angel/The Lord Will Understand	30
58	Coral Q 72303	Don't Let Go/Baby, Baby (as Billy Williams Quartet)	30
58	Coral Q 72316	Steppin' Out Tonight/There I've Said It Again (as Billy Williams Quartet)	30
58	Coral Q 72331	I'll Get By/It's Prayin' Time	15
59	Coral Q 72359	Nola/Tied To The Strings Of Your Heart	10
59	Coral Q 72369	Goodnight Irene/Red Hot Love	20
59	Coral Q 72377	Telephone Conversation/Go To Sleep, Go To Sleep, Go To Sleep (with Barbara McNair)	15
60	Coral Q 72402	I Cried For You/Lover Of All Lovers	10
58	Coral LVA 9092	BILLY WILLIAMS	90
60	Coral LVA 9120	HALF SWEET HALF BEAT	20
61	Coral LVA 9139	THE BILLY WILLIAMS REVUE	20

(see also Barbara McNair)

BOBBY WILLIAMS
68	Action ACT 4509	Baby I Need Your Love/Try It Again	50
73	Contempo C 17	Let's Jam/You're My Baby	8

CAROL WILLIAMS
76	Salsoul SZ 2021	Love Is You/Just Feel	20
76	Salsoul SLS 5506	LECTRIC LADY (LP)	15

CHRIS WILLIAMS & HIS MONSTERS
59	Columbia DB 4383	The Monster/The Eton Boating Song	25
60	Triumph RGM 1003	Kicking Around/Midnight Rocker (unissued; white label demo copies only)	250

CINDY WILLIAMS
67	Parlophone R 5648	They Talk About Us/Did He Call Today Mama	8

CLARENCE WILLIAMS (& HIS WASHBOARD BAND)
54	Columbia SCM 5134	High Society/Left All Alone With The Blues	20
54	London AL 3526	CLARENCE WILLIAMS AND HIS ORCHESTRA (10" LP)	20
55	Columbia 33S 1067	BACK ROOM SPECIAL (10" LP)	20
57	London AL 3561	CLARENCE WILLIAMS AND HIS ORCHESTRA VOL. 2 (10" LP)	20

CLIVE WILLIAMS
69	Rock Steady Rev. REVR 6	Take Good Care Of My Baby/RICO: In Loving Memory Of Don Drummond	25

DAN WILLIAMS & HIS ORCHESTRA
55	London CAY 110	Donkey City/SHAW PARK CALYPSO BAND: Take Her To Jamaica	10

DANNY WILLIAMS
59	HMV POP 624	Tall A Tree/I Look At You	7
59	HMV POP 655	So High - So Low/My Own True Love	7
59	HMV POP 703	Youthful Years/It Doesn't Matter	7
60	HMV POP 803	A Million To One/Call Me A Dreamer	6
63	HMV POP 1112	My Own True Love/Who Can Say?	8
63	HMV POP 1150	More/Rhapsody	6
63	HMV POP 1172	The Wild Wind/Once Upon A Time	8
63	HMV POP 1203	A Day Without You/Secret Love	6
63	HMV POP 1236	How Do You Keep From Crying?/Now The Day Is Over	6
63	HMV POP 1263	White On White/After You	8
64	HMV POP 1305	Today/Lonely In A Crowd	6
64	HMV POP 1325	The Seventh Dawn/The World Around Me	6
64	HMV POP 1372	Forget Her, Forget Her/Lollipops And Roses	30
65	HMV POP 1410	Go Away/Masquerade	30
66	HMV POP 1506	I've Got To Find That Girl Again/Throw A Little Lovin' My Way	30
67	Deram DM 149	Never My Love/Whose Little Girl Are You (with inverted matrix)	30
67	Deram DM 149	Never My Love/Whose Little Girl Are You (re-pressing with matrix correct way up)	10
62	HMV 7EG 8748	HITS OF DANNY WILLIAMS (EP)	15
62	HMV 7EG 8763	DANNY WILLIAMS SWINGS WITH TONY OSBORNE (EP)	10
63	HMV 7EG 8800	THE DAYS OF WINE AND ROSES AND OTHER FILM FAVOURITES (EP)	10
61	HMV CLP 1458	DANNY (LP, mono)	25
61	HMV CSD 1369	DANNY (LP, stereo)	20
61	HMV CLP 1521	MOON RIVER AND OTHER TITLES (LP)	20
62	HMV CSD 1471	SWINGING FOR YOU (LP, stereo)	15
66	HMV CLP/CSD 3523	ONLY LOVE (LP)	20
67	Deram DML 1017	DANNY WILLIAMS (LP)	20

DELROY WILLIAMS
71	Trojan TR 7813	Down In The Boondocks/Baby Make It	7
76	Treble C CCC 013	Red, Green And Gold (In My Garden)/Let's Be People	12

EDWARD WILLIAMS
09	Trunk JBH 034	LIFE ON EARTH (LP, 750 only)	20

ESTHER WILLIAMS
81	RCA RCA 78	I'll Be Your Pleasure/Make It With You	6
81	RCA RCAT 78	I'll Be Your Pleasure (Larry Levan Remix)/Make It With You (12")	10
81	RCA RCAT LP 5039	INSIDE OF ME (LP)	20

GARETH WILLIAMS
12	Blackest Ever Black BLACKEST009	FLAMING TUNES (LP, inner, insert)	50

(see also This Heat)

George WILLIAMS

MINT VALUE £

GEORGE WILLIAMS
69	Bullet BU 405	No Business Of Yours/Mast It Up (actually titled "Mash It Up")	35
77	Lovers Rock LRD 01	Reggae Woman/No One Takes The Place Of You (12")	20

GEORGE WILLIAMS & HIS ORCHESTRA
55	Vogue Coral Q 72053	The Rompin' Stomper/Knock-Out Choo-Choo	8
56	HMV DLP 1140	RHYTHM WAS HIS BUSINESS (10" LP)	15

GINGER WILLIAMS
74	Paradise PR 01	I Can't Resist Your Tenderness/Little Boy	12
77	B&B BBLP 1001	STRANGE WORLD (LP, purple vinyl)	30
80	B&B BBLP 1111	COOL LOVING (LP, lilac vinyl)	25

GRANVILLE WILLIAMS ORCHESTRA
67	Island WI 3062	Hi-Life/More	12
67	Island ILP 971	HI-LIFE (LP)	60

(see also Silvertones)

HANK WILLIAMS (& HIS DRIFTING COWBOYS)

78s
56	MGM MGM 889	The First Fall Of Snow/Someday You'll Call My Name (withdrawn)	0

SINGLES
53	MGM SP 1016	I'll Never Get Out Of This World Alive/I Could Never Be Ashamed Of You (as Hank Williams & His Drifting Cowboys)	50
53	MGM SP 1034	Kaw-Liga/Take These Chains From My Heart (& His Drifting Cowboys)	50
53	MGM SP 1049	Ramblin' Man/I Won't Be Home No More	40
53	MGM SP 1048	My Bucket's Got A Hole In It/Let's Turn Back The Years	40
54	MGM SP 1067	Weary Blues (From Waitin')/I Can't Escape From You	40
54	MGM SP 1085	There'll Be No Teardrops Tonight/Crazy Heart	40
54	MGM SP 1102	I'm Satisfied With You/I Ain't Got Nothin' But Time	40
56	MGM SP 1163	The First Fall Of Snow/Someday You'll Call My Name (unreleased)	0
56	MGM MGM 921	There's No Room In My Heart (For The Blues)/I Wish I Had A Nickel	30
56	MGM MGM 931	Blue Love (In My Heart)/Singing Waterfall	30
57	MGM MGM 942	Low Down Blues/My Sweet Love Ain't Around	30
57	MGM MGM 957	Rootie Tootie/Lonesome Whistle	30
57	MGM MGM 966	Leave Me Alone With The Blues/With Tears In My Eyes	30

EPs
54	MGM MGM-EP 512	HANK WILLIAMS AND HIS DRIFTING COWBOYS (company sleeve)	25
54	MGM EPC 7	HANK WILLIAMS (export issue)	30
55	MGM MGM-EP 551	JUST WAITIN' (as Luke The Drifter, company sleeve)	20
55	MGM MGM-EP 551	JUST WAITIN' (as Luke The Drifter, later issue with p/s)	30
56	MGM MGM-EP 569	I SAW THE LIGHT (No. 1) (company sleeve)	15
56	MGM MGM-EP 569	I SAW THE LIGHT (No. 1) (later issue with p/s)	20
57	MGM MGM-EP 582	HONKY TONKIN'	20
57	MGM MGM-EP 608	I SAW THE LIGHT (No. 2)	20
57	MGM MGM-EP 614	HONKY TONK BLUES	20
58	MGM MGM-EP 639	SONGS FOR A BROKEN HEART (No. 1)	20
58	MGM MGM-EP 649	SONGS FOR A BROKEN HEART (No. 2)	20
58	MGM MGM-EP 675	HANK'S LAMENTS	20
60	MGM MGM-EP 710	THE UNFORGETTABLE HANK WILLIAMS	20
60	MGM MGM-EP 726	THE UNFORGETTABLE HANK WILLIAMS (No. 2)	20
60	MGM MGM-EP 732	THE UNFORGETTABLE HANK WILLIAMS (No. 3)	20
61	MGM MGM-EP 757	HANK WILLIAMS FAVOURITES	20
63	MGM MGM-EP 770	THE AUTHENTIC SOUND OF THE COUNTRY HITS	20

ALBUMS
52	MGM MGM-D 105	HANK WILLIAMS SINGS (10" LP, company sleeve)	40
53	MGM MGM-D 105	HANK WILLIAMS SINGS (10" LP, later issue in p/s)	50
53	MGM MGM-D 119	HANK WILLIAMS AS LUKE THE DRIFTER (10" LP, company sleeve)	30
53	MGM MGM-D 119	HANK WILLIAMS AS LUKE THE DRIFTER (10" LP, later issue in p/s)	40
55	MGM MGM-D 137	HANK WILLIAMS MEMORIAL ALBUM (10")	30
56	MGM MGM-D 144	MOANIN' THE BLUES (10")	40
58	MGM MGM-D 150	SING ME A BLUE SONG (10")	40
58	MGM MGM-D 154	THE IMMORTAL HANK WILLIAMS (10")	30
59	MGM MGM-C 784	THE UNFORGETTABLE HANK WILLIAMS	20
60	MGM MGM-C 811	THE LONESOME SOUND OF HANK WILLIAMS	30
60	MGM MGM-C 834	WAIT FOR THE LIGHT TO SHINE	20
62	MGM MGM-C 893	ON STAGE	20
63	MGM MGM-C 956	THE SPIRIT OF HANK WILLIAMS	20
66	MGM MGM-C 8019	MAY YOU NEVER BE ALONE	15
66	MGM MGM-C 8020	IN MEMORY OF HANK WILLIAMS	15
66	MGM MGM-C 8021	I'M BLUE INSIDE	20
66	MGM MGM-C 8022	LUKE THE DRIFTER	15
66	MGM MGM-C 8023	THE MANY MOODS OF HANK WILLIAMS	15
67	MGM MGM-C(S) 8031	THE LEGEND LIVES ANEW	15
67	MGM MGM-C(S) 8038	MORE HANK WILLIAMS AND STRINGS	15
67	MGM MGM-C 8040	LOVE SONGS, COMEDY AND HYMNS	15
79	World Records SM 551-556	THE LEGENDARY HANK WILLIAMS (6-LP box set)	20

(see also Audrey Williams)

HANK WILLIAMS JR.
63	MGM MGM 1223	Long Gone Lonesome Blues/Doesn't Anybody Know My Name	6

(see also Connie Francis)

JEANETTE WILLIAMS
69	Action ACT 4534	Stuff/You Gotta Come Through	15

(little) JERRY WILLIAMS

MINT VALUE £

70	Action ACT 4557	Hound Dog/I Can Feel A Heartbreak	12

(see also Swamp Dogg, Brooks & Jerry)

(LITTLE) JERRY WILLIAMS

65	Cameo Parkway C 100	Baby You're My Everything/Just What Do You Plan To Do About It	85
65	Cameo Parkway C 100	Baby You're My Everything/Just What Do You Plan To Do About It (DJ copy)	120
74	Pye Disco Demand DDS 102	If You Ask Me/Yvonne (as Jerry Williams)	8

JIMMY WILLIAMS

65	Atlantic AT 4042	Walking On Air/I'm So Lost	25

JOE WILLIAMS

56	London HB-C 1065	JOE WILLIAMS SINGS (10" LP)	20
57	HMV CLP 1109	THE GREATEST (LP)	15
58	Columbia 33SX 1087	A MAN AIN'T SUPPOSED TO CRY (LP)	20
60	Columbia SCX 3308	JOE WILLIAMS SINGS ABOUT YOU (LP, stereo)	15
60	Columbia SCX 3325	THAT KIND OF WOMAN (LP, stereo)	15
61	Columbia SX 1392	TOGETHER (LP, with Harry "Sweets" Edison, also stereo SCX 3421)	15

(see also Count Basie)

JOHN WILLIAMS

67	Columbia DB 8128	She's That Kind Of Woman/My Ways Are Set	15
67	Columbia DB 8251	Flowers In Your Hair/Can't Find Time For Anything Now	10
67	Columbia SX 6169	JOHN WILLIAMS (LP)	100

(see also Maureeny Wishfull)

JOHN WILLIAMS

84	Island IS 155	Paul McCartney's Theme From 'The Honorary Consul'/Clara's Theme (p/s)	7

JOHN WILLIAMS ORCHESTRA (U.S.)

66	Stateside S(S)L 10237	HOW TO STEAL A MILLION (LP, soundtrack)	25
83	MCA MCA 70000	E.T. – THE EXTRA TERRESTRIAL (LP, soundtrack, box set with booklet & poster)	30
83	MCA CAC 70000	E.T. – THE EXTRA TERRESTRIAL (cassette, soundtrack box set with booklet & poster)	30

JOHNNY WILLIAMS

74	Polydor 2001 596	You're Something Kinda Mellow/You Make Me Want To Last Forever	25

KENNETH WILLIAMS

67	Decca LK 4856	ON PLEASURE BENT (LP)	15

(see also Rambling Syd Rumpo)

LARRY WILLIAMS

57	London HLN 8472	Short Fat Fannie/High School Dance	40
58	London HLN 8532	Bony Moronie/You Bug Me Baby	20
58	London HLU 8604	Dizzy Miss Lizzy/Slow Down	25
58	London HLU 8604	Dizzy Miss Lizzy/Slow Down (78)	25
59	London HLU 8844	She Said "Yeah"/Bad Boy (silver top label)	30
59	London HLU 8844	She Said "Yeah"/Bad Boy (78)	30
60	London HLU 8911	I Can't Stop Loving You/Steal A Little Kiss	30
60	London HLU 8911	I Can't Stop Loving You/Steal A Little Kiss (78)	50
60	London HLM 9053	Baby, Baby/Get Ready	30
65	Sue WI 371	Strange/Call On Me	40
65	Sue WI 381	Turn On Your Lovelight/Dizzy Miss Lizzy	40
68	MGM MGM 1447	Shake Your Body Girl/Love, I Can't Seem To Find It	20
59	London RE-U 1213	LARRY WILLIAMS (EP)	100
65	Sue ILP 922	LARRY WILLIAMS ON STAGE (LP)	80
70s	Specialty SNTF 5025	SLOW DOWN (LP)	20
70s	Speciality SNTF 5008	ORIGINAL HITS (LP)	20

LARRY WILLIAMS & JOHNNY 'GUITAR' WATSON

65	Decca F 12151	Sweet Little Baby/Slow Down	20
67	Columbia DB 8140	Mercy, Mercy, Mercy/A Quitter Never Wins	60
67	Columbia DB 8140	Mercy, Mercy, Mercy/A Quitter Never Wins (DJ copy)	175
76	Epic EPC 4421	Too Late/Two For The Price Of One	20
65	Decca LK 4691	THE LARRY WILLIAMS SHOW (LP, with Stormsville Shakers)	80

(see also Philip Goodhand-Tait [& Stormville Shakers])

LENNY WILLIAMS

78	ABC 4239	Midnight Girl/Cause I Love You	15

LEW WILLIAMS

50s	London (no cat. no.)	Cat Talk (1-sided, orange label demo-only)	50

LLOYD WILLIAMS

66	Doctor Bird DB 1051	Sad World/TOMMY McCOOK'S BAND: A Little Bit Of Heaven	30
68	Treasure Isle TI 7029	Funky Beat/Goodbye Baby	22
68	Doctor Bird DB 1135	Wonderful World (with Tommy McCook)/TOMMY McCOOK SUPERSONICS: Mad Mad World	35
70	Bamboo BAM 41	I'm In Love With You/Little Girl	60

LORETTA WILLIAMS

66	Atlantic 584 032	Baby Cakes/I'm Missing You	50

LUCINDA WILLIAMS

89	Rough Trade 130	LUCINDA WILLIAMS (LP, with inner lyric bag)	20

LUTHER WILLIAMS ORCHESTRA

61	Melodisc MLP 12-125	TROPICAL RHYTHMS OF JAMAICA (LP)	15

MARY LOU WILLIAMS

64	Sue WI 311	Chuck-a-Lunk Jug (Parts 1 & 2)	25
53	Vogue LDE 022	PLAYS IN LONDON (10" LP)	20
54	Esquire 20-026	PIANO PANORAMA (10" LP)	20
55	Felsted EDL 87012	IN PARIS (10" LP)	20

MASON WILLIAMS

68	Warner Bros WB 7190	Classical Gas/Long Time Blues	6

Maurice WILLIAMS (& ZODIACS)

MINT VALUE £

MAURICE WILLIAMS (& ZODIACS)
60	Top Rank JAR 526	Stay/Do You Believe (as Maurice Williams & Zodiacs)	15
61	Top Rank JAR 550	I Remember/Always	20
61	Top Rank JAR 563	Come Along/Do I	20
61	Top Rank JKP 3006	STAY WITH MAURICE WILLIAMS & THE ZODIACS (EP)	100

(see also Gladiolas)

MIKE WILLIAMS
66	Atlantic 584 027	Lonely Soldier/If This Isn't Love	25

MOON WILLIAMS
73	DJM DJS10283	Forever Kind Of Love/All For You (DJ Copy)	200
74	DJM DJS 299	Excuse Me (For The Strange Things I Do)/Can't Live Without You	18

OTIS WILLIAMS & HIS CHARMS
55	Parlophone CMSP 36	Ivory Tower/In Paradise (export issue)	300
56	Parlophone MSP 6239	Ivory Tower/In Paradise	400
56	Parlophone R 4210	One Night Only/It's All Over	300
56	Parlophone R 4210	One Night Only/It's All Over (78)	25
57	Parlophone R 4293	Walkin' After Midnight/I'm Waiting Just For You	300
57	Parlophone R 4293	Walkin' After Midnight/I'm Waiting Just For You (78)	50
58	Parlophone R 4495	The Secret/Don't Wake Up The Kids	100
58	Parlophone R 4495	The Secret/Don't Wake Up The Kids (78)	70
62	Parlophone R 4860	The Secret/Two Hearts	60

(see also Charms)

PAUL WILLIAMS
70s	Parry Music Library PML 168	AQUARIUS (LP)	18

PAUL WILLIAMS BIG ROLL BAND/SET
64	Columbia DB 7421	Gin House/Rockin' Chair (as Paul Williams Big Roll Band)	20
65	Columbia DB 7768	The Many Faces Of Love/Jumpback (as Paul Williams & Zoot Money Band)	30
68	Decca F 12844	My Sly Sadie/Stop The Wedding (as Paul Williams Set)	15

(see also Zoot Money's Big Roll Band, John Mayall's Bluesbreakers, Alan Price [Set], Juicy Lucy)

PAUL WILLIAMS (1)
73	Sonet SNTF 654	IN MEMORY OF ROBERT JOHNSON (LP)	15

PAUL WILLIAMS (2)
74	A&M AMS 7125	That's What Friends Are For/Born To Fly	8
74	A&M AMLS 63653	PHANTOM OF THE PARADISE (LP, soundtrack)	20

PAULINE WILLIAMS
73	Explosion EX 2084	My Island/My Island (Version)	7

POOR JOE WILLIAMS
60	Collector JEN 3	A MAN SINGS THE BLUES (EP)	10
60	Collector JEN 4	A MAN SINGS THE BLUES VOL. 2 (EP)	10

(see also Big Joe Williams)

RANNY/RONNY WILLIAMS
69	Bullet BU 426	Summer Place (with Hippy Boys)/Big Boy	30
69	Gas GAS 120	Throw Me Corn (as Ronny Williams)/HIPPY BOYS: Temptation	45
69	Unity UN 526	Pepper Seed/Ambitious Beggar	40
70	Punch PH 32	Smile/Musical I.D.	20

(see also Winston Reed, Ranny Bop)

RITA WILLIAMS
58	Oriole CB 1417	Looking For Someone To Love/Love Me Forever	10
70	Gemini GMS 011	You're Nearer/With Love From Amsterdam	6

ROBBIE WILLIAMS
98	Chrysalis/HMV HMV 78	Millennium/ROYAL ALBERT HALL ORCHESTRA: Nimrod, Enigma Variations Op. 36 (78rpm, promo only, 1,000 only, numbered p/s)	25
98	Chrysalis CDPP 080	I'VE BEEN EXPECTING YOU (metal case with album CD, interview disc in digipak, EPK video in p/s, gold press release and photos)	70
01	Chrysalis 7243 536826 1 3	SWING WHEN YOU'RE WINNING (LP)	20
02	Chrysalis 7243 54399 41-1	ESCAPOLOGY (2-LP)	30
04	Chrysalis 7243 8668191	GREATEST HITS (2-LP)	20

(see also Take That)

ROBERT WILLIAMS
90	Blast First FU8	CHROME, FIRE AND SMOKE (2-LP, picture disc, 1000 only)	25

ROBERT PETE WILLIAMS
63	'77' LA 12-17	THOSE PRISON BLUES (LP)	35
70s	Blues Beacon 1932 101ST	SUGAR FARM (LP)	25
72	Saydisc AMS 2002	ROBERT PETE WILLIAMS (LP)	18

ROBERT PETE WILLIAMS/ROOSEVELT SYKES
67	'77' LEU 12-50	BLUES FROM THE BOTTOM (LP)	25

(see also Roosevelt Sykes)

ROCKMORE WILLIAMS
73	Mooncrest Moon 15	Lady Rock/Junkyard Blues	10

RODIGAN V WILLIAMS
79	Exclusive/Ethnic Fight EFLP 60-11-13	ROCKERS ARENA (LP)	50

ROGER WILLIAMS
55	London HLU 8214	Autumn Leaves/Take Care	10
56	London HLU 8341	Two Different Worlds (with Jane Morgan)/I'll Always Walk With You	8
57	London HLU 8379	Anastasia/A Serenade For Joy	6
58	London HLR 8643	Indiscreet/Young And Warm And Wonderful (silver top with tri-centre)	10

(see also Jane Morgan)

ROY WILLIAMS TRINITY
73	Hillside HIL LP 1013	A TOUCH OF CLASS (LP)	15
79	Hillside HIL LP 1016	GOOD NEWS IN TOWN (LP)	45

Sam WILLIAMS

MINT VALUE £

SAM WILLIAMS
78	Grapevine GRP 116	Love Slipped Thru' My Fingers/TOWANDA BARNES: You Don't Mean It	35

SHINA WILLIAMS
84	Earthworks/Rough Trade ET 003	Agboju Logun/Gboro Mi Ro (12", die-cut sleeve)	50

SID WILLIAMS
77	ATA ATA 1001	Don't Play That Rock 'N' Roll/Time To Spare	8

SIL WILLIAMS
69	Wolf WM 04	Reggae Moon Rising/People Get Ready	10

SMITTY WILLIAMS
62	MGM MGM 1167	The Cure/Oh Seymour	7

SONNY WILLIAMS
59	London HLD 8931	Bye Bye Baby Goodbye/Lucky Linda	45
59	London HLD 8931	Bye Bye Baby Goodbye/Lucky Linda (78)	20

SPARKIE WILLIAMS
58	Parlophone R 4475	Sparkie Williams/Sparkie the Fiddle	7

SYLVAN WILLIAMS
69	Big Shot BI 532	Sweeter Than Honey/Son Of Reggae	45
69	Big Shot BI 533	This Old Man/When Morning Comes	50

TEX WILLIAMS
54	Brunswick 05327	River Of No Return/Dawn In The Meadow	10
54	Brunswick 05341	This Ole House (with Rex Allen)/They Were Doin' The Mambo	12
55	Brunswick 05393	Money/If You'd Believe Me	10
57	Brunswick 05684	Talkin' To The Blues/Every Night (with Anita Kerr Singers)	6
60	Top Rank JAR 330	The Keeper Of Boothill/Bummin' Around	6

(see also Roberta Lee, Rex Allen)

TOMMY WILLIAMS
76	Free Reed FRR 008	SPRINGTIME IN BATTERSEA (LP, gatefold sleeve)	18

TONY WILLIAMS
61	Reprise RS 20019	Sleepless Nights/Mandolino Mandolino	10
61	Reprise RS 20030	My Prayer/Miracle	10
63	Philips BF 1282	How Come/When I Had You	100
60	Mercury MMC 14027	A GIRL IS A GIRL IS A GIRL (LP)	40
61	Reprise R 6001	SINGS HIS GREATEST HITS (LP, mono)	20
61	Reprise ST R9 6006	SINGS HIS GREATEST HITS (LP, stereo)	30

(see also Platters, Linda Hayes)

TONY WILLIAMS' LIFETIME
69	Polydor 583 574	EMERGENCY! (2-LP, gatefold sleeve)	50
70	Polydor 2425 019	TURN IT OVER (LP)	25
71	Polydor 2425 065	EGO (LP, textured gatefold sleeve)	35

(see also Lifetime, John McLaughlin)

WILLIE WILLIAMS, JACKIE MITTOO & MARSHAL COUSINS
79	Ziggy FDP 001	Rocking Universally/JACKIE MITTOO & BONGO GENE: Universal rock (12")	30

WILLYWILLIE/WILLI WILLIAMS
81	Black Roots BR0017	Come Make We Rally/YABBY YOU: Thirty Pieces Of Silver (12")	80
83	WLN WLN 004	Repatriation/Come Along/Armagideon Time/Justice Tonight (12")	25
92	Jah Shaka No Cat No	Stand Up/Version	50
92	Jah Shaka SHAKA 922	NATTY WITH A CAUSE (LP)	22
05	Blood & Fire BAFLP 048	MESSENGER MAN (2-LP, reissue)	35

WINSTON WILLIAMS
70	Jackpot JP 733	D.J.'s Choice/SLIM SMITH: Can't Do Without It (B-side actually titled "Lesson/Story Of Love" by Uniques)	30
70	Jackpot JP 743	The People's Choice/BOBBY JAMES: Let Me Go Girl	40
71	Jackpot JP 757	Love Version/SLIM SMITH: Ball Of Confusion	30

HARVEY WILLIAMS
94	Sarah SARAH 406	REBELLION (10" LP)	15

BOBBY WILLIAMSON
54	HMV 7MC 26	Sh-Boom/Love March (export issue)	20

MARK WILLIAMSON
70s	Myrrh MYR 1154	MISSING IN ACTION (LP)	15

ROBIN WILLIAMSON
72	Island HELP 2	MYRRH (LP, textured sleeve, black label with pink 'i' logo, lyric inner sleeve)	35

(see also Incredible String Band, Vashti Bunyan)

SONNY BOY WILLIAMSON (I)
69	Matchbox SDR 169	SONNY BOY AND HIS PALS (LP)	30
70	RCA Intl. INTS 1088	BLUEBIRD BLUES (LP)	15

SONNY BOY WILLIAMSON (I)/BIG BILL BROONZY
65	RCA Victor RD 7685	BIG BILL BROONZY/SONNY BOY WILLIAMSON (LP)	30

SONNY BOY WILLIAMSON (II)
63	Pye International 7N 25191	Help Me/Bye Bye Bird	25
64	Pye International 7N 25268	Lonesome Cabin/The Goat	20
65	Sue WI 365	No Nights By Myself/Boppin' With Sonny Boy	40
66	Chess CRS 8030	Bring It On Home/Down Child	20
66	Blue Horizon 45-1008	From The Bottom/Empty Bedroom	80
64	Pye Intl. NEP 44037	SONNY BOY WILLIAMSON (EP)	25
65	Chess CRE 6001	HELP ME (EP)	25
66	Chess CRE 6013	IN MEMORIAM (EP)	35
66	Chess CRE 6018	REAL FOLK BLUES VOL. 2 (EP)	30
64	Pye Intl. NPL 28036	DOWN AND OUT BLUES (LP)	60
64	Storyville SLP 158	PORTRAITS IN BLUES, VOL. 4 (LP)	40
65	Chess CRL 4510	IN MEMORIAM (LP)	50

Sonny BOY WILLIAMSON (II) & YARDBIRDS

MINT VALUE £

66	Storyville SLP 170	THE BLUES OF SONNY BOY WILLIAMSON (LP)	22
66	Fontana 670 158	PORTRAITS IN BLUES, VOL. 4 (LP, reissue)	30
67	Storyville 671 170	THE BLUES OF SONNY BOY WILLIAMSON (LP, reissue)	25
68	Marmalade 607/608 004	DON'T SEND ME NO FLOWERS (LP, with Brian Auger & Jimmy Page)	80
74	Rarity RLP 1	THE LAST SESSIONS - 1963 (LP)	25

(see also Ottilie Patterson)

SONNY BOY WILLIAMSON (II) & YARDBIRDS

65	Fontana TL 5277	SONNY BOY WILLIAMSON & THE YARDBIRDS (LP)	175
68	Fontana SFJL 960	SONNY BOY WILLIAMSON & THE YARDBIRDS (LP, reissue, different sleeve)	30
71	Philips 6435 011	SONNY BOY WILLIAMSON & THE YARDBIRDS (LP, 2nd reissue)	18

(see also Yardbirds, Brian Auger)

STU WILLIAMSON

| 56 | London Jazz LZ-N 14290 | SAPPHIRE (10" LP) | 20 |

WILLIE AND THE RED RUBBER BAND

| 69 | RCA 1842 | Mary Jane/Chicky Chicky Boom Boom | 12 |

WILLIE (FRANCIS) & LLOYD (LINDSAY)

| 71 | Camel CA 80 | Marcus Is Alive/GLADIATORS: Freedom Train | 25 |

(see also Willie Francis)

WILLIE & WHEELS

| 77 | ABC ABC 4184 | Skateboard Craze/Do What You Did (p/s, label states "illie & The Wheels") | 10 |

(see also P.F. Sloan, Grass Roots, Fantastic Baggys')

DORIS WILLINGHAM

| 69 | Jay Boy BOY 1 | You Can't Do That/Lost Again | 15 |

CHUCK WILLIS

57	London HLE 8444	C.C. Rider/Ease The Pain	80
57	London HLE 8444	C.C. Rider/Ease The Pain (78)	30
57	London HLE 8489	That Train Has Gone/Love Me Cherry	80
57	London HLE 8489	That Train Has Gone/Love Me Cherry (78)	20
58	London HLE 8595	Betty And Dupree/My Crying Eyes	80
58	London HLE 8595	Betty And Dupree/My Crying Eyes (78)	20
58	London HLE 8635	What Am I Living For/Hang Up My Rock And Roll Shoes	50
58	London HLE 8635	What Am I Living For/Hang Up My Rock And Roll Shoes (78)	25
58	London HL 7039	What Am I Living For/Hang Up My Rock And Roll Shoes (export issue)	30
59	London HLE 8818	My Life/Thunder And Lightning	45
59	London HLE 8818	My Life/Thunder And Lightning (78)	30
59	Fontana TFE 17138	CHUCK WILLIS WAILS (EP)	300
65	Atlantic ATL 5003	I REMEMBER CHUCK WILLIS (LP)	80
69	Atlantic 588 145	I REMEMBER CHUCK WILLIS (LP, reissue)	20

DOUG WILLIS

| 97 | Z Records ZEDD 12029 | Get Your Own (12") | 10 |

HAL WILLIS

| 68 | President PT 197 | The Lumberjack/Klondike Mike | 12 |

LARRY WILLIS

| 74 | People PLEO 2 | INNER CRISIS (LP) | 20 |

LLOYD WILLIS

| 70 | Pressure Beat PR 5502 | Mad Rooster (Parts 1 & 2)/NINEY & THE DESTROYERS: As Far As I Can See | 15 |

(see also Dynamic Gang, Urie Aldridge)

RALPH WILLIS

| 61 | Esquire EP 241 | RALPH WILLIS (EP) | 40 |

SLIM WILLIS

| 65 | R&B MRB 5004 | Running Around/No Feeling For You | 30 |

WILL-O-BEES

| 67 | CBS 3263 | It's Not Easy/Looking Glass | 15 |

WILLOWS

| 56 | London HLU 8290 | Church Bells May Ring/Baby Tell Me | 600 |
| 56 | London HLU 8290 | Church Bells May Ring/Baby Tell Me (78) | 80 |

(see also Tony Middleton)

BOB WILLS WITH TOMMY DUNCAN

| 60 | London HL 7102 | Heart To Heart Talk/What's The Matter With The Mill (export issue) | 20 |

MICK WILLS

| 88 | Woronzow WOO 9 | FERN HILL (LP) | 15 |

VIOLA WILLS

68	President PT 108	Lost Without The Love Of My Guy/I Got Love	15
68	President PT 150	Together Forever/Don't Kiss Me Hello And Mean Goodbye	10
68	President PT 152	I've Got To Have All Of You/Night Scene	8
68	President PT 154	You're Out Of My Mind/Any Time	8

WILMER & DUKES

| 68 | Action ACT 4500 | Give Me One More Chance/Get It | 10 |

FRANKIE WILMOTT

| 86 | Musical Ambassador MAD 005 | Give Me No Rock (Sensemilla)/ANDY TOSH: Lick A Shot (12") | 50 |
| 87 | Music House MH1 | I Won't Give Up/I Won't Give Up (version) (12") | 15 |

SUE WILSHAW

| 69 | SNB 55-3957 | Empty Sunday/My My My | 15 |

ADA WILSON

| 79 | Ellie Jay EJSP 9288 | In The Quiet Of My Room/I'm In Control Here (p/s) | 12 |
| 80 | Barn BARN 012 | In The Quiet Of My Room/I'm In Control Here (reissue, no p/s) | 6 |

(see also Strangeways)

AL WILSON

| 68 | Liberty LBF 15044 | Do What You Gotta Do/Now I Know What Love Is | 20 |
| 68 | Liberty LBF 15121 | The Snake/Who Could Be Lovin' You | 20 |

Bobby WILSON

MINT VALUE £

69	Liberty LBF 15236	Shake Me Wake Me/I Stand Accused	8
69	Liberty LBF 15257	Lodi/By The Time I Get To Phoenix	8
75	Bell BLL 1436	The Snake/Willoughby Brook	10
02	Soul City	The Snake/Now I Know What Love Is	12
12	Outta Sight OSV-078	The Snake/Show And Tell (reissue)	7
69	Liberty LBS 83173	SEARCHING FOR THE DOLPHINS (LP)	20

BOBBY WILSON
| 14 | Soul Brother SB7015D | Don't Shut Me Out/Deeper And Deeper (jukebox centre) | 7 |

BRIAN WILSON
66	Capitol CL 15438	Caroline, No/Summer Means New Love	50
88	Sire W 7814 B	LOVE AND MERCY (7" box set, with interview and postcards, limited edition)	40
98	Giant/Mojo 74321 58760 2	INTERVIEW/IMAGINATION (promo CD, with Peter Buck)	40
04	Nonesuch 7559-79869-7	Wonderful/Wind Chimes (three different coloured vinyl - blue, yellow,green)	18
04	Nonesuch 7559-79885-7	Good Vibrations/Our Prayer/Good Vibrations (live)(p/s) (Ltd edition)	10
05	Nonesuch 7559-798957	Our Prayer (Freeform Reform) (10" one sided clear vinyl in clear plastic sleeve)	12

(see also Beach Boys, Date With Soul, American Spring)

BRIAN WILSON & MIKE LOVE
| 67 | Capitol CL 15513 | Gettin' Hungry/Devoted To You (as Brian Wilson & Mike Love) | 30 |

CASSANDRA WILSON
93	Blue Note F671007	BLUE LIGHT 'TIL DAWN (LP)	40
96	Blue Note 72438 37183 1 3	NEW MOON DAUGHTER (2-LP)	80
99	Blue Note 602537813735	TRAVELLING MILES (2-LP)	30
03	Blue Note 7243 58186017	GLAMOURED (2-LP)	20

CLIVE WILSON
| 64 | R&B JB 144 | Mango Tree/Midnight In Chicago | 20 |

COLIN WILSON
| 75 | Tabitha TAB 101 | CLOUDBURST (LP) | 30 |

DELROY WILSON
63	Island WI 097	Naughty People/I Shall Not Remove	25
63	Island WI 103	One, Two, Three/Back Biter	20
63	Island WI 116	You Bend My Love/Can't You See	30
63	R&B JB 108	Lion Of Judah/Joe Liges	30
63	R&B JB 128	Prince Pharoah/Don't Believe Him	25
63	R&B JB 132	Squeeze Your Toe/Sugar Pie	30
64	Black Swan WI 405	Spit In The Sky/Voodoo Man	25
64	Black Swan WI 420	Goodbye/Treat Me Right	40
64	R&B JB 148	Lover Mouth/Every Mouth Must Be Fed	30
64	R&B JB 168	Sammy Dead/CYNTHIA & ARCHIE: Every Beat	25
65	Island WI 205	Pick Up The Pieces/Oppression	55
66	Doctor Bird DB 1022	Give Me A Chance/(It's) Impossible	35
66	Island WI 3013	Dancing Mood/SOUL BROTHERS: More And More	40
67	Island WI 3033	Riding For A Fall/Got To Change Your Ways	75
67	Island WI 3037	Ungrateful Baby/ROY RICHARDS: Hopeful Village Ska	45
67	Island WI 3039	Close To Me/SOUL BROTHERS: Hi-Life	50
67	Island WI 3050	Get Ready/ROY RICHARDS: Port-O-Jam	60
67	Studio One SO 2009	Won't You Come Home Baby/PETER & HORTENSE: I've Been Lonely	70
67	Studio One SO 2014	Mother Word/HEPTONES: Fatty Fatty	30
67	Studio One SO 2019	Never Conquer/Run For Your Life	80
67	Studio One SO 2031	I'm Not A King/HEPTONES: Take Me (B-side actually by Soul Vendors)	60
68	Island WI 3099	This Old Heart Of Mine/GLEN ADAMS: Grab A Girl	70
68	Island WI 3127	Once Upon A Time/I Want To Love You (B-side actually with Stranger Cole)	80
68	Coxsone CS 7064	True Believer/MARSHALL WILLIAMS: College Girl	100
68	Studio One SO 2040	Mr. D.J./HEPTONES: Tripe Girl(both sides credited to Termites)	110
68	Studio One SO 2046	Rain From The Skies/How Can I Love Someone	75
68	Studio One SO 2057	Feel Good All Over/I Like The Way You Walk	85
69	Studio One SO 2074	Easy Snappin'/WEBBER SISTERS: Come On	50
69	High Note HS 011	Put Yourself In My Place/It Hurts	45
69	High Note HS 015	I'm The One Who Loves You/AFROTONES: If I'm In A Corner	40
69	High Note HS 022	Your Number One/I've Tried My Best	40
69	High Note HS 028	Good To Me/What Do You Want Me To Do	25
69	Camel CA 15	Sad Mood (actually by Ken Parker)/STRANGER COLE: Give It To Me	70
70	Trojan TR 7740	Show Me The Way/BEVERLEY'S ALLSTARS: Version	45
70	Trojan TR 7769	Gave You My Love/BEVERLEY'S ALLSTARS: Version	50
70	Summit SUM 8503	Got To Get Away/BEVERLEY'S ALLSTARS: Version	25
70	Unity UN 559	Drink Wine, Everybody/Someone To Call My Own	35
71	Smash SMA 2317	I Am Trying/COLLINS ALLSTARS: Version	30
71	Smash SMA 2318	Satisfaction/Satisfaction Version (B-side with Alton Ellis)	40
71	Smash SMA 2323	What It Was/LLOYD CLARKE: Chicken Thief	50
71	Jackpot JP 763	Better Must Come/BUNNY LEE'S ALLSTARS: Better Must Come - Version	10
71	Jackpot JP 769	Cool Operator/I'm Yours	15
71	Jackpot JP 770	Try Again/AGGROVATORS: Try Again - Version	10
71	Jackpot JP 780	Keep Your Love Strong/Nice To Be Near	15
71	Jackpot JP 781	Peace And Love/JEFF BARNES: Who's Your Brother	15
71	Banana BA 333	Just Because Of You/I Love You Madly	60
72	Banana BA 367	You Keep On Running (& U Roy)/LARRY'S ALL STARS: Running Version	18
72	Bullet BU 520	Hear Come The Heartaches (actually "Here Come The Heartaches")/ You'll Be Sorry	18
72	Jackpot JP 792	Who Cares/HUGH ROY JUNIOR: Who Cares - Version	15
72	Jackpot JP 795	The Same Old Song/Stay By Me	12
72	Jackpot JP 804	Cheer Up/Loving You	15

Dennis WILSON (& RUMBO)

MINT VALUE £

Year	Label/Cat	Title	Value
72	Fab FAB 32A/FAB34A	Your Love Is Amazing/KING SPORTY: A Year Full Of Sunday	35
72	Spur SP 2	Adis Ababa/KEITH HUDSON: Rudie Hot Stuff	50
73	Downtown DT 501	Pretty Girl/JOE GIBBS & PROFESSIONALS: Face Girl	12
73	Grape GR 3038	Can I Change My Mind/Just Because	12
73	Green Door GD 4060	Ain't That Peculiar/What Is Man	30
73	Smash SMA 2336	Trying To Wreck My Life/Live And Learn	20
73	Count Shelley CS 024	Never Give Up/I ROY: Problem Of Life	12
73	Count Shelley CS 047	Dum Dum/HORACE ANDY: Rasta Saw Them Coming	10
74	Faith FA 006	Love Got Me Doing Things/PHIL PRATT ALL STARS: Version	6
74	Harry J. HJ 6667	What Happen To The Youth Of Today/Baby Don't Do It	12
75	Fab FAB 266	Dancing Mood/Version	20
75	Attack ATT 8111	Seven Letters/Version	10
75	Attack ATT 8120	Honey Child/Time Is Running Out	8
76	Black Wax WAX 20	Mother Nature/CHANNEL ONE: Natural Version	10
76	Third World TW03	Chueekey Rock/You're No Good	25
77	Tribesman TM 002	What Is Man/Version	40
78	Burning Sounds BSD 017	All In This Together/Because I Am Black (12")	25
78	Burning Sounds BSD 018	Love Got Me Doing Things/Go Away Little Girl (12")	25
79	Cha Cha CHAD 10	Money Love/I Want To Love You (12")	20
79	E & J EJD1	Sharing The Night Together/I Won't Take You Back (12")	10
84	Greensleeves GRED 157	Dancing Mood/TETRACK: Trappers (12")	12
88	Conqueror LD 045	I Have Been In Love/NAGGO MORRIS AND THE HEPTONES: You Want To Get I Out (12")	50
64	R&B JBL 1112	I SHALL NOT REMOVE (LP, beware of Jamiacan copies in U.K. sleeves)	600
68	Coxsone CSL 8016	GOOD ALL OVER (LP)	200
72	Trojan TRLS 44	BETTER MUST COME (LP)	40
73	Big Shot BILP 102	CAPTIVITY (LP)	40
73	Warwick WLP 01	LIVE AS ONE (LP, white label only, includes track by Alton Ellis)	150
77	Eji EJI 1001	MR. COOL OPERATOR (LP)	30
78	Third World TWD 001	20 GOLDEN HITS (2-LP)	50
78	Charmers LP 1	SARGE (LP)	18
78	Burning Sounds BS 1020	LOVERS ROCK (LP)	20
79	Groundnation GROL 501	FOR I AND I (LP)	30
82	Black Music BMLP 803	GO AWAY DREAM (LP)	20

(see also Hortense & Delroy, Joe Liges, Roy Richards, Soul Brothers, Dennis Alcapone, Stranger Cole, Uniques, Soul Vendors)

DENNIS WILSON (& RUMBO)

Year	Label/Cat	Title	Value
70	Stateside SS 2184	Sound Of Free/Lady (as Dennis Wilson & Rumbo)	70
77	Caribou CRB 5663	River Song/Farewell My Friend	15
77	Caribou CRB 81272	PACIFIC OCEAN BLUE (LP, gatefold sleeve, lyric insert, on blue vinyl)	50
77	Caribou CRB 81272	PACIFIC OCEAN BLUE (LP, gatefold sleeve, lyric insert)	40

(see also Beach Boys)

DENNIS WILSON

Year	Label/Cat	Title	Value
57	Donegall DON 1005	TRANSATLANTIC (LP)	20
67	Envoy VOS 3111	DENNIS PLUS 3 (10" LP)	35

THE DIERDRE WILSON TABAC

Year	Label/Cat	Title	Value
69	RCA RCA 1880	Get Back/Angel Baby	15

DOYLE WILSON WITH JIMMY LACEY & BAND

Year	Label/Cat	Title	Value
58	Vogue Pop V 9117	Hey-Hey/You're The One For Me	600
58	Vogue Pop V 9117	Hey-Hey/You're The One For Me (7)	150

EDDIE WILSON (1)

Year	Label/Cat	Title	Value
62	Oriole CB 1780	Dankeschoen-Bitteschoen-Wiederschoen/Rheinlaender Waltz	8

EDDIE WILSON (2)

Year	Label/Cat	Title	Value
69	Action ACT 4536	Shing-A-Ling Stroll/Don't Kick The Teenager Around	25
70	Action ACT 4555	Get Out On The Street/Must Be Love	20

ERNEST ('SOUL') WILSON

Year	Label/Cat	Title	Value
67	Studio One SO 2032	Money Worries/SOUL VENDORS: Pe Da Pa	80
68	Studio One SO 2058	If I Were A Carpenter/SOUL VENDORS: Frozen Soul	200
68	Coxsone CS 7044	Storybook Children (as Ernest 'Soul' Wilson)/LITTLE FREDDIE: After Laughter (B-side actually by Freddie McGregor)	80
68	Coxsone CS 7059	Undying Love/SOUL VENDORS: Tropic Isle	100
69	Amalgamated AMG 837	Private Number (A-side miscredit to Ernest Jones/GLEN ADAMS: She's So Fine	50
69	Crab CRAB 9	Private Number/Another Chance	40
69	Crab CRAB 17	Freedom Train/STRANGER COLE: You Should Never Have To Come	45
69	Crab CRAB 21	Just Once In My Life (with Freddy)/GLEN ADAMS: Mighty Organ	75
70	Crab CRAB 45	Sentimental Man/It's A Lie	30
70	Unity UN 564	Love Makes The World Go Round/Love (Instrumental Version)	30
71	Gas GAS 168	What You Gonna Do About it/DOBBY DOBSON: Halfway To Paradise	60
71	Jackpot JP 765	Let Them Talk/The Truth Hurts	8
76	Fab FAB 280	Storybook Children/SOUND DIMENSION: Version	12
78	Cha Cha CC 001	I Know Myself/REVOLUTIONARIES: I Know Myself Dub	25
86	Natty Congo NCLP 006	LOVE REVOLUTION (LP)	20

(see also Tinga & Ernest, Clarendonians, Freddy & Fitzie)

FLICK WILSON

Year	Label/Cat	Title	Value
77	Ultra PFU 1003	Keep The Troubles Down/Saturday Night Shubin (12")	20
77	Ultra PFU 1001	Rocking Chair/Selassie Shuffle	8
80	Greensleeves/Cool Rockers GRED 37	Slavemaster/Pretty Blue Eyes (12")	40

FRANK WILSON

Year	Label/Cat	Title	Value
79	Tamla Motown TMG 1170	Do I Love You (Indeed I Do)/Sweeter As The Days Go By	100
79	Tamla Motown TMG 1170	Do I Love You (Indeed I Do)/Sweeter As The Days Go By (DJ copy, p/s)	200
04	Tamla Motown 982 153 0	Do I Love You (Indeed I Do)/CHRIS CLARK: Do I Love You (Indeed I Do) (die-cut p/s)	25

Frank WILSON & CAVALIERS

MINT VALUE £

18	Outta Sight SEV 001	Do I Love You (Indeed I Do)/Sweeter As The Days Go By (reissue)	15

FRANK WILSON & CAVALIERS

64	Fontana TF 505	Last Kiss/That's How Much I Love You	12

GARLAND WILSON

53	HMV 7M 122	Just You, Just Me/Sweet Georgia Brown	6

GARY WILSON

80	Sour Grape SG 115	Movie Queen/Movie Queen (p/s)	6

JACK WILSON QUARTET

64	London HA-K/SH-K 8170	THE JACK WILSON QUARTET (LP, featuring Roy Ayers)	20
66	Vocalion LAE-L 603	RAMBLIN' (LP)	20

(see also Roy Ayers)

JACKIE WILSON

78s

58	Coral Q 72347	Lonely Teardrops/In The Blue Of The Evening	40
59	Coral Q 72366	That's Why/Love Is All	40
59	Coral Q 72372	I'll Be Satisfied/Ask	50
59	Coral Q 72380	You Better Know It/Never Go Away	75
59	Coral Q 72384	Talk That Talk/Only You, Only Me	80

SINGLES

57	Vogue Coral Q 72290	Reet Petite/By The Light Of The Silvery Moon	25
57	Coral Q 72290	Reet Petite/By The Light Of The Silvery Moon (2nd pressing)	15
58	Coral Q 72306	To Be Loved/Come Back To Me	25
58	Coral Q 72332	I'm Wanderin'/As Long As I Live	25
58	Coral Q 72338	We Have Love/Singing A Song	22
58	Coral Q 72347	Lonely Teardrops/In The Blue Of The Evening	25
59	Coral Q 72366	That's Why/Love Is All	20
59	Coral Q 72366	That's Why/Love Is All (mispressing, B-side plays "You Better Know It")	15
59	Coral Q 72372	I'll Be Satisfied/Ask	15
59	Coral Q 72380	You Better Know It/Never Go Away	15
59	Coral Q 72384	Talk That Talk/Only You, Only Me	15
60	Coral Q 72393	Doggin' Around/The Magic Of Love	15
60	Coral Q 72407	A Woman, A Lover, A Friend/(You Were Made For) All My Love	15
60	Coral Q 72412	Alone At Last/Am I The Man	25
61	Coral Q 72421	The Tear Of The Year/My Empty Arms (withdrawn B-side, demos only)	65
61	Coral Q 72424	The Tear Of The Year/Your One And Only Love	15
61	Coral Q 72430	Please Tell Me Why/(So Many) Cute Little Girls	15
61	Coral Q 72434	I'm Comin' On Back To You/Lonely Life	15
61	Coral Q 72439	You Don't Know What It Means/Years From Now	15
61	Coral Q 72444	The Way I Am/My Heart Belongs To Only You	15
62	Coral Q 72450	The Greatest Hurt/There'll Be No Next Time	15
62	Coral Q 72453	Sing (And Tell The Blues So Long)/I Found Love (B-side with Linda Hopkins)	15
62	Coral Q 72454	I Just Can't Help It/My Tale Of Woe	15
63	Coral Q 72460	Baby Workout/What Good Am I Without You	15
63	Coral Q 72464	Shake A Hand/Say I Do (as Jackie Wilson & Linda Hopkins)	15
63	Coral Q 72465	Shake! Shake! Shake!/He's A Fool	15
63	Coral Q 72467	Baby Get It/The New Breed	15
64	Coral Q 72474	Big Boss Line/Be My Girl	15
64	Coral Q 72476	Squeeze Her - Tease Her (But Love Her)/Give Me Back My Heart	15
65	Coral Q 72480	Yes Indeed!/When The Saints Go Marching In (with Linda Hopkins)	18
65	Coral Q 72481	No Pity (In The Naked City)/I'm So Lonely	20
65	Coral Q 72481	No Pity (In The Naked City)/I'm So Lonely (DJ copy)	45
65	Coral Q 72482	I Believe I'll Love On/Lonely Teardrops	15
66	Coral Q 72484	To Make A Big Man Cry/Be My Love	20
66	Coral Q 72484	To Make A Big Man Cry/Be My Love (DJ copy)	45
66	Coral Q 72487	Whispers/The Fairest Of Them All	40
66	Coral Q 72487	Whispers/The Fairest Of Them All (DJ copy)	85
67	Coral Q 72493	(Your Love Keeps Lifting Me) Higher And Higher/I'm The One To Do It	20
67	Coral Q 72493	(Your Love Keeps Lifting Me) Higher And Higher/I'm The One To Do It (DJ copy)	85
67	Coral Q 72496	Since You Showed Me How To Be Happy/The Who-Who Song	30
67	Coral Q 72496	Since You Showed Me How To Be Happy/The Who-Who Song (DJ copy)	75
68	MCA MU 1014	For Your Precious Love/Uptight (Everything's Alright) (with Count Basie)	10
68	Decca AD 1008	For Your Precious Love/Uptight (Everything's Alright) (export issue)	25
69	MCA Soul Bag BAG 2	(Your Love Keeps Lifting Me) Higher And Higher/Whispers (Gettin' Louder)	10
69	MCA Soul Bag BAG 7	Since You Showed Me How To Be Happy/Chain Gang	10
69	MCA MU 1104	Since You Showed Me How To Be Happy/The Who-Who Song (reissue)	10
69	MCA MU 1105	Helpless/Do It The Right Way	10
70	MCA MU 1131	(Your Love Keeps Lifting Me) Higher And Higher/Whispers (Gettin' Louder) (reissue)	6
72	MCA MU 1160	I Get The Sweetest Feeling/Soul Galore	6
73	Brunswick BR 3	Beautiful Day/What'cha Gonna Do About Love	20
77	Brunswick BR 43	It Only Happens When I Look At You/Just As Soon As The Feeling's Over (DJ Copy)	150
77	Brunswick BR 43	It Only Happens When I Look At You/Just As Soon As The Feeling's Over	100
80s	Kent Town 101	I Don't Want To Lose You/ADAM'S APPLES: Don't Take It Out On This World	12

EPs

59	Coral FEP 2016	JACKIE WILSON (triangular centre)	100
59	Coral FEP 2016	JACKIE WILSON (round centre)	70
60	Coral FEP 2043	THE DYNAMIC JACKIE WILSON (triangular centre)	100
60	Coral FEP 2043	THE DYNAMIC JACKIE WILSON (round centre)	70

Jackie WILSON/CLYDE MCPHATTER

MINT VALUE £

ALBUMS

58	Coral LVA 9087	HE'S SO FINE	150
59	Coral LVA 9108	LONELY TEARDROPS	150
60	Coral LVA 9121	SO MUCH	110
60	Coral LVA 9130	JACKIE SINGS THE BLUES	125
60	Coral LVA 9135	MY GOLDEN FAVOURITES	90
61	Coral LVA 9144	A WOMAN, A LOVER, A FRIEND	100
61	Coral LVA 9148	YOU AIN'T HEARD NOTHIN' YET	85
62	Coral LVA 9151	BY SPECIAL REQUEST (mono)	75
62	Coral SVL 3018	BY SPECIAL REQUEST (stereo)	90
62	Coral LVA 9202	BODY AND SOUL	65
63	Coral LVA 9209	JACKIE WILSON AT THE COPA (mono)	70
63	Coral SVL 9209	JACKIE (stereo)	80
63	Coral LVA 9214	THE WORLD'S GREATEST MELODIES (mono)	55
63	Coral SVL 9214	THE WORLD'S GREATEST MELODIES (stereo)	65
66	Coral LVA 9231	SPOTLIGHT ON JACKIE WILSON	70
66	Coral LVA 9232	SOUL GALORE (mono)	70
66	Coral SVL 9232	SOUL GALORE (stereo)	80
67	Coral LVA 9235	WHISPERS	75
68	MCA MUP(S) 304	HIGHER AND HIGHER	20
68	MCA MUP(S) 333	TWO MUCH (with Count Basie & His Orchestra)	20
69	MCA MUPS 361	I GET THE SWEETEST FEELING	20
70	MCA MUPS 405	DO YOUR THING	25
73	Brunswick BRLS 3001	YOU GOT ME WALKIN'	25

(see also Billy Ward & Dominoes, Clyde McPhatter, Count Basie, Chi-Lites, Linda Hopkins)

JACKIE WILSON/CLYDE MCPHATTER

62	Ember JBS 705	Tenderly/CLYDE McPHATTER: Harbour Lights	250
62	Ember NR 5001	MEET BILLY WARD & THE DOMINOES (LP, 1 side each)	200

(see also Clyde McPhatter)

JOANNE WILSON

81	Red Stripe 2222	Gotta Have You Back/Part 2	12

JOE WILSON

71	Pye International 7N 25550	Sweetness/When A Man Cries	10

JONATHAN WILSON

13	074186	FANFARE	0

JR. WILSON

89	Blue Trac BTRD 035	Speak Softly (with T. Sparks and Mystic Man)/CONROY SMITH: Problems (12")	40

MARTY WILSON & STRAT-O-LITES

58	Brunswick 05750	Hey! Eula/Hedge-Hopper	20

MARY WILSON

79	Motown TMG 1177	Pick Up The Pieces/You're The Light That Guides My Way	10
87	Nightmare MARES 39	Don't Get Mad Get Even/(Instrumental Version) (p/s)	8

(see also Supremes)

MAYNELL WILSON (ACTUALLY WILSON MAYNELL) & WESTMINSTER FIVE

64	Carnival CV 7014	Hey Hey Johnny/Baby	10
67	CBM CBM 001	Motown Feeling/Mean Ole World (with p/s)	20
67	CBM CBM 001	Motown Feeling/Mean Ole World	10

(see also Wes[t]minster Five)

MURRY WILSON

67	Capitol CL 15525	Plumber's Tune/Love Won't Wait	8
67	Capitol (S)T 2819	THE MANY MOODS OF MURRY WILSON (LP)	20

(see also Beach Boys)

NANCY WILSON

64	Capitol CL 15352	(You Don't Know) How Glad I Am/Never Less Than Yesterday	10
65	Capitol CL 15378	Don't Come Running Back To Me/Love Has Many Faces	10
65	Capitol CL 15412	Where Does That Leave Me/Gentle Is My Love	25
66	Capitol CL 15443	Power Of Love/Rain Sometimes	15
66	Capitol CL 15466	You've Got Your Troubles/Uptight (Everything's Alright)	20
67	Capitol CL 15508	Don't Look Over Your Shoulder/Mercy, Mercy, Mercy	15
68	Capitol CL 15536	You Don't Know Me/Ode To Billie Joe	10
68	Capitol CL 15547	Face It Girl It's Over/The End Of Our Love	40
68	Capitol CL 15547	Face It Girl It's Over/The End Of Our Love (DJ copy)	80
74	Capitol CL 15796	Streetrunner/Ocean Of Love	8
77	Capitol CL 15547	End Of Our Love/Face It Girl, It's Over (white logo, reissue)	12
62	Capitol EAP1 20604	SECOND TIME AROUND (EP)	10
64	Capitol EAP4 2082	TODAY, TOMORROW, FOREVER (EP)	10
62	Capitol (S)T 1767	HELLO YOUNG LOVERS (LP, mono/stereo)	18
63	Capitol (S)T 1828	BROADWAY - MY LOVE (LP, mono/stereo)	18
63	Capitol (S)T 1934	HOLLYWOOD - MY WAY (LP, mono/stereo)	18
63	Capitol (S)T 2012	YESTERDAY'S LOVE SONGS (LP, mono/stereo)	18
64	Capitol (S)T 2082	TODAY, TOMORROW, FOREVER (LP)	18
65	Capitol (S)T 2136	THE NANCY WILSON SHOW (LP)	18
65	Capitol (S)T 2155	HOW GLAD I AM (LP)	18
65	Capitol (S)T 2321	TODAY- MY WAY (LP)	18
65	Capitol (S)T 2351	GENTLE IS MY LOVE (LP)	18
66	Capitol (S)T 2433	FROM BROADWAY WITH LOVE (LP)	18
66	Capitol (S)T 2495	A TOUCH OF TODAY (LP)	30
66	Capitol (S)T 2555	TENDER LOVING CARE (LP)	20
67	Capitol (S)T 2634	NANCY - NATURALLY (LP)	20

Nancy WILSON & CANNONBALL ADDERLEY

MINT VALUE £

NANCY WILSON & CANNONBALL ADDERLEY
62	Capitol ST 1657	NANCY WILSON & CANNONBALL ADDERLEY (LP, stereo)	15

(see also Cannonball Adderley)

PEANUTS WILSON
58	Coral Q 72302	Cast Iron Arm/You've Got Love	500
58	Coral Q 72302	Cast Iron Arm/You've Got Love (78)	150
76	MCA MCA 240	Cast Iron Arm/DON WOODY: Barking Up The Wrong Tree	6

PHIL WILSON
89	Caff CAFF 3	Better Days/You Won't Speak (p/s, with insert, handwritten label)	12

(see also June Brides)

REUBEN WILSON (1)
76	Chess 6078 700	Got To Get Your Own Parts 1 & 2	60
97	Blue Note 7243 8 29906 1 1	BLUE MODE (LP, reissue)	15

REUBEN WILSON (2)
19	Dynamite Cuts DYNAM7024	Got To Get Your Own/Tight Money (p/s)	10

ROB WILSON BAND
90	Metro Music MMI 6	The Girl In the Polka-Dot Dress/The Greatest Crime/King Of The Blues (p/s)	20

RON WILSON
68	Island WI 3112	Dred Saras/DAVID BROWN: All My Life	70

(see also Winston Scotland, Douglas Brothers)

SHARK WILSON & BASEMENT HEATERS
71	Ashanti ASH 400	Make It Reggae/Version	40

SMILEY WILSON
60	London HLG 9066	Running Bear/Long As Little Birds Fly	50

TOMY WILSON
64	Decca F12033	Yes I Do/Lost Without You	10

TONY WILSON
67	Columbia DB 8153	Can't Waste A Good Thing/What Did I Do?	30
69	Bell BLL 1081	Baby, I Love, Love I Love You/Come Back To My Lonely World	6

(see also Hot Chocolate)

TREVOR WILSON
65	Ska Beat JB 207	You Couldn't Believe/You Told Me You Care	50

STEVEN WILSON
09	Kscope KSCOPE 804	Harmony Korine (edit)/The 78 (p/s, 1000 only)	10
09	Kscope KSCOPE 804	Harmony Korine (edit)/The 78 (p/s, red vinyl, 1000 only)	10
09	Kscope KSCOPE 804	Harmony Korine (edit)/The 78 (p/s, white vinyl, 1000 only)	10
09	Kscope KSCOPE 809	NSRGNTS RMXS (12" EP, p/s, 1000 only)	10
11	Kscope LOTSCOPE 001	Stone Age Dinosaurs/OCEANZIZE: Fear (white vinyl, p/s, 2000 only)	12
13	Kscope KSCOPE 838	Luminol/The Watchmaker (12" picture disc)	18
16	Kscope KSCOPE 710	Happiness III/Space Oddity (Live) (p/s)	8
05	Tonefloat TF 22	UNRELEASED ELECTRONIC MUSIC (2-LP, white vinyl)	45
05	Tonefloat TF 22	UNRELEASED ELECTRONIC MUSIC (2-LP)	40
09	Tonefloat TF 50	INSURGENTES (Box set, 4 x 10", 1000 only)	250
09	Kscope KSCOPE 808	INSURGENTES (2-LP, gatefold sleeve, 2000 only)	40
10	Tonefloat TF 107	TAPE EXPERIMENTS 1985-6 (2-LP)	35
11	Kscope KSCOPE 818	GRACE FOR DROWNING (2-LP)	20
12	Kscope KSCOPE 827	CATALOGUE/PRESERVE/AMASS (LP)	15
13	Kscope KSCOPE 240	THE RAVEN THAT REFUSED TO SING AND OTHER STORIES (2-LP)	20
15	Kscope KSCOPE 875	HAND. CANNOT. ERASE (2-LP)	20
15	Tonefloat TF 22	UNRELEASED ELECTRONIC MUSIC (2-LP, reissue)	20
17	Caroline Int. CAROL 016LPB	TO THE BONE (2-LP, white vinyl)	25

(see also Porcupine Tree, No Man)

GABY WILTON & CHARLIE ACE
72	Bullet BU 511	Babylon Falling/CHARLIE ACE: Make It Love	8

JOHNNY WILTSHIRE & HIS TREBLETONES
59	Oriole CB 1494	If The Shoe Fits/Cha Cha Choo Choo	10

WIMPLE WINCH
66	Fontana TF 686	What's Been Done/I Really Love You	350
66	Fontana TF 718	Save My Soul/Everybody's Worried 'Bout Tomorrow	500
67	Fontana TF 781	Rumble On Mersey Square South/Typical British Workmanship	300
67	Fontana TF 781	Rumble On Mersey Square South/Typical British Workmanship (mispressing, B-side plays "Atmospheres")	600
88	Bam Caruso OPRA 45	Save My Soul/NIRVANA: Black Flower (jukebox issue, die-cut sleeve)	12
91	Bam Caruso KIRI 108	THE PSYCHEDELIC YEARS VOLUME 2 (LP)	20

(see also Just Four Men, Four Just Men, Pacific Drift, Tristar Airbus)o

WIMPS
79	Sniff Records SNORT 1	Hamburger Radio/New Girl At School/Modern Girl (numbered p/s)	10
79	Sniff Records SNORT 2	At The Discoteque/Blind Minds/Gonna Lose (p/s)	10

WIN
87	Swamplands	UH! TEARS BABY (CD)	30

LEM WINCHESTER & BENNY GOLSON
59	Esquire 32-142	WINCHESTER SPECIAL (LP)	25
61	Esquire 32-172	ANOTHER OPUS (LP)	15

KAI WINDING
65	Verve VS 512	Comin' Home Baby/More	15
55	London LTZ-N 15003	K AND J.J. (LP, with J.J. Johnson Quintet)	15
59	Philips SBBL 515	TROMBONES (LP)	18
61	Parlophone PMC 1138	SLIDE RULE (LP, with J.J. Johnson Quintet)	20
63	Verve VLP 9049	SOUL SURFIN' (LP)	30

(see also Dizzy Gillespie, J.J. Johnson Quintet)

WIND IN THE WILLOWS

MINT VALUE £

WIND IN THE WILLOWS
68	Capitol CL 15561	Moments Spent/Friendly Lion	25
68	Capitol ST 2956	WIND IN THE WILLOWS (LP)	30

(see also Debbie Harry, Blondie)

WINDMILL
70	MCA MK 5024	Such Sweet Sorrow/I Can Fly	10

WINDMILLS
88	S.T.S. 2	The Day Dawned On Me/Dolphins (p/s)	20
90	Wasteful SRT 90s 2734	Nothing At All/Secrets (p/s)	20

BARRY WINDOW
69	BAF BAF 7	I Thank You/End Of Our Road	50

WINDOWS (1)
72	Polydor 2058 206	How Do You Do/Nobody's Baby	18

WINDOWS (2)
78	Skeleton SKL 008	Re-Arrange/Over Dub (p/s)	15
81	Skeleton SKULP 2	UPPERS ON DOWNERS (LP, with inserts)	40

(see also Mutants)

BARBARA WINDSOR
61	HMV POP 883	Ten Gallon Hat/Funny Face	7
62	HMV POP 1104	It Has Better Be A Wonderful Life/ I'm Not That Sort Of Girl (with Harry Fowler & Kenny Lynch)	7
63	HMV POP 1128	Sparrows Can't Sing/On Mother Kelly's Doorstep	7
67	Parlophone R 5629	Don't Dig Twiggy/Swinging London	7
70	UPC UPC 101	When I Was A Child/What A Right Carry On	12
72	Decca F 13323	Grin And Bare It/Cheeky Sorta' Bird	7

WINDY & CARL
95	Enraptured RAPT 4501	Emerald/Fragments Of Time And Space (500 in hand-painted p/s)	12
95	Enraptured RAPT 4501	Emerald/Fragments Of Time And Space (300 in tracing paper sleeve)	10
96	Enraptured RAPT 4509	Christmas Song/GRIMBLE GRUMBLE: Odyssey And Oracle (no'd p/s, coloured vinyl, 350 only)	20

WINDY CORNER
73	Deroy DER 977	THE HOUSE AT WINDY CORNER (LP, private pressing)	300

AMY WINEHOUSE
03	Island 12 IS 830 DJ	Stronger Than Me (Curtis Lynch Jnr Vocal Remix)/(Curtis Lynch Jnr Dub Remix) (12" Promo)	30
03	Island 12 IS 830	Stronger Than Me (Album Version(Curtis Lynch Jnr Remix featuring Blackout Ja and Isha Sesay)/(Harmonic 33 Remix)/Acapella Version) (12")	15
03	Island 12 ISX 840 DJ	Take The Box (Seiji's Buggin' Mix)/(Seiji's Buggin' Rub)/(The Headquarters MIx) (Promo 12")	18
04	Island 12 IS 840	Take The Box (Seiji's Buggin' Mix)/(The Headquarters MIx)/(Acapella) (12")	10
03	Island 12 IS 840 DJ	In My Bed (1-sided promo 12")	12
03	Island ISX 852 DJ	In My Bed (Bass Gangsta Mix)/(CJ Mix)/(Full Length Version) (Promo 12")	18
03	Island 12 IS 852 DJ	In My Bed (Bugz In The Attic Vocal Mix)/(Bugz In The Attic Dub)/(Full Length Version) (Promo 12")	18
04	Island 12 IS 852	In My Bed (Bugz In The Attic Vocal Mix)/You Sent Me Flying/In My Bed (Bad Gangsta)/In My Bed (Radio Edit) (12")	10
03	Island 12 IS 865 DJ	Pumps (MJ Cole Remix)/Pumps (Mylo Remix)/Pumps (Promo 12")	18
04	Island IS 865	Pumps (MJ Cole Remix)/Mylo Remix)/(Album Version) (12")	10
06	Island 3789621 0 1	Rehab - Amy Vs Pharoahe (Promo 12" stickered white label)	10
06	Island AMY 12 PRO 1	Rehab (Hot Chip Remix)/(Hot Chip Instrumental)/(Desert Eagle Discs Remix)/(Desert Eagle Discs Instrumental) (Promo 12")	25
05	Universal Island AMY 12PRO 1	Rehab (Hot Chip Remix)/(Hot Chip Instrumental)/(DED Instrumental)/(Original Version) (promo 12")	10
06	AMY/AMX 12 PRO	Love Is A Losing Game (Moody Boyz Dubstep Remix)/(Moody Boyz Dubland Version) (Promo 12", 300 only)	25
06	Island AMY 7 PRO 2	Love Is A Losing Game/(Moody Boys Dubstep Remix) promo 12", 300 only	40
06	Island AMYLPPRO 1	Back To Black (The Rumble Strips Remix)/Back To Black (p/s, clear vinyl promo)	20
07	Island 1732327	Back To Black (Steve Mac Vocal 6:12)/(Steve Mac Smack Dub 6:15)/(Original Version 4:00)/(Mushtaq Vocal Remix 4.03) (12")	8
07	Island 1732326	Back To Black/Back To Black (Rumble Strips Remix) (p/s, white vinyl)	6
07	Island 1744792	Tears Dry On Their Own/Tears Dry On Their Own (NYPC's Fucked MIx) (p/s, clear vinyl)	15
03	Universal Island FRANK LP 3	FRANK (ALBUM SAMPLER) EP (promo 12", p/s)	20
03	Island 9812918	FRANK (LP)	20
07	Island 1735948	FRANK - REMIXES (2 x 12", gatefold)	15
07	Island/Universal 1734128	BACK TO BLACK (LP, inner)	20
08	Island ILPS 8148	FRANK (LP, reissue, 180gm includes free download, sealed, stickered)	20

WINE OF LEBANON
76	Dovetail DOVE 46	WINE OF LEBANON (LP)	20

WINNERS (1)
73	Ensign EN 39	Sing Your Song/Have We Finished?	45

WINNERS (2)
79	Ariola ARPD 144	Get Ready For The Future/Music (12")	15

PETE WINSLOW & KING SIZE BRASS
73	BBC 103S	GIRL ON THE TESTCARD (LP)	20

WINSTON
74	York YR 212	I Wanna Let Anna Go/Brother Jim	15
60s	Holyground	WINSTON SINGS (EP)	10
73	Bradley BRAD 306	Mona/Rockerdile (p/s)	20

WINSTON (RICHARDS) & BIBBIE (B.B. SEATON)
63	R&B JB 115	Lover Man/LESTER STIRLING: Gravy Cool	50

WINSTON (FRANCIS) & CECIL (LOCKE)
70	Banana BA 306	United We Stand/SOUND DIMENSION: Sweet Message	25

WINSTON & ERROL

MINT VALUE £

WINSTON & ERROL
64	Blue Beat BB 272	Fay Is Gone/MONARCHS : Sadler	10
71	Punch PH 74	There Is A Land/Goodnight My Love	18

WINSTON & FAY
64	Blue Beat BB 272	Fay Is Gone (Winston & Errol)/MONARCHS: Sauce And Tea	22

WINSTON & GEORGE
66	Pyramid PYR 6002	Denham Town/Keep The Pressure On	35
12	Pyramid THB 7021	Denham Town/THE RIO GRANDES: Soldiers Take Over	20

JIMMY WINSTON (& HIS REFLECTIONS)
66	Decca F 12410	Sorry She's Mine/It's Not What You Do (But The Way That You Do It)	300
76	Nems NEMS 12	Sun In The Morning/Just Wanna Smile (solo)	8

(see also Small Faces, Winston's Fumbs, Spheres)

WINSTON (GROOVY) & PAT (RHODEN)
68	Trojan TR 605	Pony Ride/Baby You Send Me	15
71	Bullet BU 475	The Same Thing For Breakfast/Sweeter Than Honey	12

(see also Winston Tucker)

WINSTON (RICHARDS) & TONETTES
65	Ska Beat JB 225	You Make Me Cry/CHECKMATES: Invisible Ska	40

WINSTON & ROY
62	Blue Beat BB 80	Babylon Gone/COUNT OSSIE ON AFRICAN DRUMS: First Gone	35

WINSTON & RUPERT
70	Bullet BU 425	Come By Here/Somebody	50
70	Moodisc HM 106	Musically Beat/Let Me Tell You Girl	85

(see also Eternals)

ERIC WINSTONE (& HIS) ORCHESTRA
64	Pye 7N 15603	Dr. Who Theme/Pony Express	18

NORMA WINSTONE
72	Argo ZDA 148	EDGE OF TIME (LP)	300

(see also Mike Westbrook, Michael Garrick)

WINSTONS
69	Pye International 7N 25493	Colour In Father/Amen, Brother	20
69	Pye International 7N 25500	Love Of The Common People/Wheel Of Fortune	7

WINSTON'S FUMBS
67	RCA RCA 1612	Real Crazy Apartment/Snow White	600

(see also Small Faces, Jimmy Winston & His Reflections, Yes, Spheres, Federals)

WINSTONS & M-SQUAD
71	Green Door GD 4003	Carroll Street/Carroll Street - Version (B-side act. by Ansel Collins/M-Squad)	10

EDGAR WINTER (GROUP)
70	CBS 64083	ENTRANCE (LP, as Edgar Winter)	15
71	CBS 64298	EDGAR WINTER'S WHITE TRASH (LP)	15

JOHNNY WINTER
69	CBS 4386	I'm Yours And I'm Hers/I'll Drown In My Tears	6
69	Liberty LBF 15219	Rollin' And Tumblin'/Bad Luck And Trouble	7
70	CBS 4794	Johnny B. Goode/I'm Not Sure	6
69	CBS 63619	JOHNNY WINTER (LP)	25
69	Liberty LBL/LBS 83240E	THE PROGRESSIVE BLUES EXPERIMENT (LP)	25
70	Buddah 2359 011	FIRST WINTER (LP)	20
70	CBS 64117	JOHNNY WINTER AND... (LP)	15
74	CBS CQ 32188/Q 65484	STILL ALIVE AND WELL (LP, quadrophonic)	15

DON WINTERS
60	Brunswick 05827	Someday Baby/That's All I Need	15

LIZ WINTERS & BOB CORT SKIFFLE GROUP
57	Decca F 10878	Freight Train/Love Is Strange	20
57	Decca F 10899	Maggie May/Jessamine	20
57	Decca DFE 6409	LIZ WINTERS AND BOB CORT (EP)	25

(see also Bob Cort Skiffle Group)

LOIS WINTERS
56	London HLD 8266	Japanese Farewell Song/JAN GARBER & HIS ORCHESTRA: My Dear	35

RON WINTERS
63	Colpix PX 11022	Snow Girl/In The Middle Of The Morning	20

RUBY WINTERS
68	Stateside SS 2090	I Want Action/Better	150
68	Stateside SS 2090	I Want Action/Better (DJ copy)	200

WYOMA WINTERS
54	HMV 7M 222	Where Can I Go Without You?/Won't You Give A Repeat Performance	7
54	HMV 7M 260	Toy Balloon/Shish Kebab	7

WINTERS REIGN
84	Scoff DTO33	Save It/Keep Trying	8
87	Link LOPL 501	THE BEIGNNING (LP, with free 7")	15

STEVIE WINWOOD
77	Island WIP 6394	Time Is Running Out/Penultimate Zone (12", pre-release sleeve)	20
87	Island SW 1/2/3	BACK IN THE HIGH LIFE (3 x 7" set, each in p/s, promo only)	20
87	Island	CHRONICLES (5 x 7" box set, promo, 500 only)	30

(see also Winwood Kabaka Amoa, Anglos, Spencer Davis Group, Traffic, Blind Faith.)

WINWOOD/KABAKA/AMAO
73	Island HELP 14	AIYE-KETA THIRD WORLD (LP)	15

(see also Stevie WInwood)

WIPEOUT
82	M&L MNL 2/ACE 37	Baby Please Don't Go/Two-O-Five/Crawdaddy/Should A' Known Better (p/s)	15
83	Out OUT 1A/B1	NO SWEAT (LP)	15

WIPEOUT

MINT VALUE £

WIPEOUT
90s	Deluxe DELUX 002	Snowflake/Confusion Bee (12")	10

WIPERS
84	Psycho PSYCHO 22	IS THIS REAL? (LP, with lyric insert)	20
84	Psycho PSYCHO 23	YOUTH OF AMERICA (LP)	20

WIRE
77	Harvest HAR 5144	Mannequin/Feeling Called Love/12XU (p/s)	100
77	Harvest HAR 5144	Mannequin/Feeling Called Love/12XU (no p/s)	30
78	Harvest HAR 5151	I Am The Fly/Ex-Lion Tamer (p/s)	80
78	Harvest HAR 5151	I Am The Fly/Ex-Lion Tamer (no p/s)	30
78	Harvest HAR 5161	Dot Dash/Options R (p/s)	50
78	Harvest HAR 5161	Dot Dash/Options R (no p/s)	20
79	Harvest HAR 5172	Outdoor Miner/Practice Makes Perfect (p/s, white vinyl)	50
79	Harvest HAR 5172	Outdoor Miner/Practice Makes Perfect (p/s)	20
79	Harvest HAR 5187	A Question Of Degree/Former Airline (p/s)	40
79	Harvest HAR 5192	Map Ref 41° N 93° W/Go Ahead (p/s)	40
79	Harvest SPSLP 299	154 (12", p/s, white label sampler with insert & press release; beware of counterfeits)	35
81	Rough Trade RT 079	Our Swimmer/Midnight Bahnhof Cafe (p/s)	25
83	Rough Trade RTT 123	Crazy About Love/Second Length (Our Swimmer)/Catapult 30 (12", p/s, 2 different sleeve colours)	20
86	Mute 12 MUTE 53	SNAKEDRILL (12" EP, p/s)	15
87	Mute 7 MUTE 57	Ahead/Feed Me (p/s)	8
87	Mute 12 MUTE 57	AHEAD (12" EP, p/s)	10
88	Mute 12 MUTE 67	KIDNEY BINGOS (12" EP, p/s)	12
88	Mute MUTE 84	Silk Skin Paws/German Shepherds (p/s)	6
88	Mute 12 MUTE 84	SILK SKIN PAWS (12" EP, p/s)	10
89	Mute MUTE 87	Eardrum Buzz/The Offer (p/s, clear vinyl, withdrawn)	30
89	Mute MUTE 87	Eardrum Buzz/The Offer (p/s)	6
89	Mute 12 MUTE 87	EARDRUM BUZZ (12", EP. p/s)	12
89	Mute 12 MUTE 98	IN VIVO (12" EP, p/s)	10
95	Touch TONE 5	THE FIRST LAST NUMBER (12" EP. p/s as Wir30)	15
01	Pink Flag VPF 3	Twelve Times You/X U Version (white labels, clear bag sealed with sticker)	6
77	Harvest SHSP 4076	PINK FLAG (LP, with lyric inner)	80
78	Harvest SHSP 4093	CHAIRS MISSING (LP, 1st 10,000 with lilac lyric inner sleeve)	80
79	Harvest SHSP 4105	154 (LP, with inner lyric sleeve & bonus 7" EP: "Song 2"/"Get Down [Parts I & II]"/"Let's Panic"/"Later"/"Small Electric Piece" [PSR 444])	100
79	Harvest SHSP 4105	154 (LP, without 7")	50
84	Rough Trade ROUGH 29	DOCUMENT AND EYEWITNESS (LP, with free 12" EP [ROUGH 2912])	30
86	Pin Label PINKY 7	WIRE PLAY POP (mini-LP)	15
86	Dojo DOJOLP 36	IN THE PINK (LP)	15
87	Mute STUMM 42	THE IDEAL COPY (LP)	15
87	Harvest SHSP 4076	PINK FLAG (LP, reissue, black label)	30
87	Harvest SHSP 4093	CHAIRS MISSING (LP, reissue)	30
87	Harvest SHSP 4105	154 (LP, reissue, barcoded on rear sleeve)	30
88	Mute STUMM 54	A BELL IS A CUP UNTIL IT IS STRUCK (LP)	20
89	Mute STUMM 66	IBTABA (LP)	20
89	Harvest SHSP 4127	ON RETURNING (LP)	30
89	Strange Fruit SFRLP 108	PEEL SESSIONS (LP)	15
90	Mute STUMM 80	MANSCAPE (LP)	18
91	Mute STUMM 74	THE DRILL (LP)	20
91	Mute 7 STUMM 74	THE DRILL (3-LP and 7" box set, numbered)	50
91	Mute STUMM 87	WIR (LP, as Wir, die-cut sleeve)	20
93	Mute STUMM 116	1985-1990 (2-LP)	40
96	WMO 4LP	TURNS AND STROKES (LP)	40
03	PF456REDUX	PF456 REDUX (LP)	35
08	Pink Flag PF 17 LP	OBJECT 47 (LP, with free 12")	50
11	Pink Flag PF 18 LP	RED BARKED TREE (LP)	20
18	Pink Flag PFS 1-9	NINE SEVENS (box set with 9 x 7" singles)	70

(see also Dome, Cupol, Colin Newman, Snakes, P'O, Bruce Gilbert, Gilbert & Lewis, Duet Emmo)

WIRE DOLL
71	Milestone MS 2	To The Sun/Terry I Love You	15

NICKY WIRE
06	Red Ink ENOLAT 001	Break My Heart Slowly/Casual Glam	6

(see also Manic Street Preachers)

MARK WIRTZ (ORCHESTRA & CHORUS)
68	Parlophone R 5668	(He's Our Dear Old) Weatherman (From "A Teenage Opera")/Possum's Dance	30
68	Parlophone R 5683	Mrs. Raven/Knickerbocker Glory	25
69	CBS 4306	My Daddie Is A Baddie/I Love You Because	15
69	CBS 4539	Caroline/Goody, Goody, Goody	18
64	World Record Club T 452	TEN AGAIN (LP, by Belle Gonzalez & Russ Loader, Wirtz as producer)	30

(see also Mood Mosaic, Keith West, Sweet Shop, Philwit & Pegasus, Mark Rogers & Marksmen, Belle Gonzalez, Russ Loader, Zion De Gallier, Elmer Hockett's Hurdy Gurdy, Steve Flynn, Fickle Finger, Matchmaker)

BOBBY WISDOM
07	Kent TOWN 126	Handwriting On The Wall/MORRIS CHESTNUT: Too Darm Soulful (reissue)	6

NORMAN WISDOM
56	Columbia SCM 5222	Two Rivers/Boy Meets Girl (with Ruby Murray)	10
57	Columbia DB 3864	Up In The World/Me And My Imagination	10
57	Columbia DB 3903	The Wisdom Of A Fool/Happy Ending	10
61	Columbia SCD 2160	Narcissus (The Laughing Record)/I Don't 'Arf Love You (with Joyce Grenfell)	6
61	Columbia DB 4601	If You Believe In Me/Yer Gotta Get Aht	6

WISE BLOOD

MINT VALUE £

64	Columbia DB 7352	The Joker/Who Can I Turn To	6
56	Columbia SEG 7612	NORMAN WISDOM (EP)	10
57	Columbia SEG 7687	NORMAN AND RUBY (EP, with Ruby Murray)	10
58	Columbia SEG 7856	NORMAN WISDOM (EP)	10
59	Top Rank JKP 2052	FOLLOW A STAR (EP)	10

(see also Ruby Murray)

WISE BLOOD

85	Wise 1-12	Motorslug/Death Rape 2000 (12", p/s)	12
86	Wise 2-12	Someone Drowned In My Pool/Stumbo (12", p/s)	12
91	Wise 003	DISHDIRT (LP, with sticker)	15

(see also Foetus)

WISE BOYS

60	Parlophone R 4693	Why, Why, Why/My Fortune	10

WISE GUYS

60	Top Rank JAR 271	(Little Girl) Big Noise/As Long As I Have You	10

MAC WISEMAN

55	London HLD 8174	The Kentuckian Song/Wabash Cannon Ball	30
56	London HLD 8226	My Little Home In Tennessee/I Haven't Got The Right To Love You	30
56	London HLD 8259	Fireball Mail/When The Roses Bloom Again	40
57	London HLD 8412	Step It Up And Go/Sundown	400
57	London HL 8412	Step It Up And Go/Sundown (78)	40
59	London HL 7084	Jimmy Brown The Newsboy/I've Got No Use For Woman (export issue)	20
56	London RE-D 1056	SONGS FROM THE HILLS (EP)	20
58	London RE-D 1147	SONGS FROM THE HILLS VOL. 2 (EP)	20
60	London RE-D 1242	SONGS FROM THE HILLS VOL. 3 (EP)	20
56	London HB-D 1052	SONGS FROM THE HILLS (10" LP)	30
60	London HA-D 2217	GREAT FOLK BALLADS (LP)	20

TREVOR WISHART

78	York YES 7	RED BIRD: A POLITICAL PRISONER'S DREAM (LP, with insert)	40
79	private pressing	BEACH SINGULARITY AND MENAGERIE (LP, with insert)	20

WISHBONE ASH

70	MCA MK 5061	Blind Eye/Queen Of Torture	8
72	MCA MKS 5097	No Easy Road/Blowin' Free	6
75	MCA MCA 176	Silver Shoes/Persephone	6
76	MCA/SFI 263	Outward Bound/Runaway/Mother Of Pearl/You Rescue Me (flexidisc, with "New England" tour programme)	12
81	MCA MCA 726	Get Ready/Kicks On The Street (p/s, with patch)	8
70	MCA MKPS 2014	WISHBONE ASH (LP, gatefold sleeve, red/pink 'dogbone' label)	150
70	MCA MDKS 2014	WISHBONE ASH (LP, blue/black labels)	60
71	MCA MDKS 8004	PILGRIMAGE (LP, gatefold sleeve, purple/red 'dogbone' label)	150
71	MCA MDKS 8004	PILGRIMAGE (LP, blue/black labels)	50
72	MCA MDKS 8006	ARGUS (LP, gatefold sleeve, black/blue 'hexagon' label)	150
73	MCA MDKS 8011	WISHBONE FOUR (LP, gatefold sleeve, black label, with poster & lyrics)	40
73	MCA MKPS 2014	WISHBONE ASH (LP, reissue, black labels)	30
73	MCA MDKS 8005	ARGUS (LP reissue, black labels)	30
73	MCA ULD 2	LIVE DATES (2-LP, gatefold sleeve, pink label)	25
74	MCA MCF 2585	THERE'S THE RUB (LP)	15
76	MCA MCG 3523	NEW ENGLAND (LP)	15
78	MCA MCG 3528	NO SMOKE WITHOUT FIRE (LP, with stickered sleeve & inner, with bonus live single "Come In From The Rain"/"Lorelei" [PSR 431])	15
80	MCA MCG 4012	LIVE DATES II (LP, textured gatefold sleeve, with live bonus LP)	15
85	Neat NEAT 1027	RAW TO THE BONE (LP)	18
18	Madfish SMABX1065	THE VINTAGE YEARS 1970 - 1991 (box set, 30 x CD, booklet, posters, signed photos and 7" flexi)	200

(see also Home, Big Daisy)

WISHFUL THINKING

66	Decca F 12438	Turning Round/V.I.P.	20
66	Decca F 12499	Step By Step/Looking Around	7
67	Decca F 12598	Count To Ten/Hang Around Girl	8
67	Decca F 12627	Peanuts/Cherry Cherry	12
67	Decca F 22673	Meet The Sun/Easier Said Than Loving You	10
68	Decca F 22742	Alone/Vegetables (export issue)	10
68	Decca F 12760	It's So Easy/I Want You Girl	15
72	B&C CB 169	Lu La Le Lu/We're Gonna Change All This	7
72	B&C CB 184	Clear White Light/Hiroshima	10
67	Decca SKL 4900	LIVE VOL. 1 (LP)	50
71	Charisma CAS 1038	HIROSHIMA (LP)	25

WISHING STONES

86	Head HEAD 2	Beat Girl/Two Steps Take Me Back (p/s)	6

(see also The Loft)

WITCHCRAFT

06	Rise Above RISE 7/089	If Crimson Was Your Colour/I Know You Killed Someone... (P/s, clear, red, green or black vinyl)	10
04	Rise Above RISELP 47	WITCHCRAFT (LP)	25
04	Rise Above RISEPD 47	WITCHCRAFT (LP, picture disc)	30
07	Rise Above RISELP 103	THE ALCHEMIST (LP, blue vinyl, 25 only)	120
07	Rise Above RISELP 103	THE ALCHEMIST (LP, green, clear, purple or suitably gold vinyl)	20

WITCHDOCTOR AND THE SPIRIT

85	Zella ZEL SPS 427	Carry On/Version (no p/s)	25

WITCHES BREW

80s	Pussy PU 016	Angeline (p/s)	20

WITCHFINDER GENERAL

MINT VALUE £

WITCHFINDER GENERAL
81	Heavy Metal HEAVY 6	Burning A Sinner/Satan's Children (p/s)	60
82	Heavy Metal 12HM 17	Soviet Invasion/Rabies/R.I.P. (live) (12", p/s)	35
83	Heavy Metal HEAVY 21	Music/Last Chance (p/s)	12
82	Heavy Metal HMRLP 8	DEATH PENALTY (LP, red, blue or clear vinyl, with inner)	30
82	Heavy Metal HMRPD 8	DEATH PENALTY (LP, picture disc)	18
83	Heavy Metal HMRLP 13	FRIENDS OF HELL (LP, red, silver or clear vinyl)	20
83	Heavy Metal HMRPD 13	FRIENDS OF HELL (LP, picture disc)	18

WITCHFYNDE
79	Rondelet ROUND 1	Give 'Em Hell/Getting' Heavy (p/s)	6
83	Expulsion OUT 3	I'd Rather Go Wild/Cry Wolf (p/s)	20
80	Rondelet ABOUT 1	GIVE 'EM HELL (LP)	25
80	Rondelet ABOUT 2	STAGE FRIGHT (LP)	15
83	Expulsion PEXIT 5	CLOAK AND DAGGER (LP, picture disc)	18
84	Mausoleum SKULL 8352	LORDS OF SIN (LP, gatefold sleeve, with bonus 12" [Cloak & Dagger/ I'd Rather Go Wild/ Moon Magic/Give 'Em Hell])	15

WITCHING HOUR
92	Succubus WITCHEP1	HOURGLASS EP (12")	30

BILL WITHERS
87	CBS 650992 6	Lovely Day/Lean On Me/Lovely Night For Dancing (12", p/s)	20
72	A&M AMLS 68107	STILL BILL (LP, gatefold)	30
71	Sussex LPSX 3	JUST AS I AM (LP)	40
81	CBS 85049	GREATEST HITS (LP)	18
77	CBS 82265	MENAGERIE (LP)	15

BRIAN WITHERS
66	RCA RCA 1536	For No One/Here There And Everywhere	8

WIZ WITHERS
85	Wizbang WW01	Rock N Roll Singer/Isn't It The Lost Time	10

JIMMY WITHERSPOON

78s
54	Parlophone R 3914	It/Highway To Happiness	20
54	Parlophone R 3951	Oh Boy/I Done Told You	20
54	Vogue V 2261	Failing By Degrees/New Orleans Woman	20
54	Vogue V 2295	Who's Been Jivin' With You/Rain, Rain, Rain	20
56	Vogue V 2060	Big Fine Girl/No Rollin' Blues	20
56	Vogue V 2356	Jump, Children/Take Me Back Baby	20

SINGLES
54	Parlophone MSP 6125	It/Highway To Happiness	100
54	Parlophone MSP 6142	Oh Boy/I Done Told You	100
56	Vogue V 2060	Big Fine Girl/No Rollin' Blues	75
62	Vogue V 2420	When The Lights Go Out/All That's Good	75
64	Stateside SS 304	Evenin'/Money Is Getting Cheaper	15
64	Stateside SS 325	I Will Never Marry/I'm Coming Down With The Blues	15
64	Stateside SS 362	You're Next/Happy Blues	15
65	Stateside SS 429	Come Walk With Me/Oh How I Love You	15
65	Stateside SS 461	Love Me Right/Make My Heart Smile Again	15
66	Stateside SS 503	If There Wasn't Any You/I Never Thought I'd See The Day	15
66	Verve VS 538	It's All Over But The Crying/If I Could Have You Back Again	8
67	Verve VS 553	Past Forty Blues/My Baby's Quit Me	6

EPs
61	Vogue EPV 1269	JIMMY WITHERSPOON AT MONTEREY	30
61	Vogue EPV 1270	JIMMY WITHERSPOON AT MONTEREY No. 2	30
64	Vocalion EPVH 1278	JIMMY WITHERSPOON	20
65	Vocalion EPVH 1284	OUTSKIRTS OF TOWN	20
66	Vocalion VEH 170158	FEELING THE SPIRIT VOL. 1	20
66	Vocalion VEH 170159	FEELING THE SPIRIT VOL. 2	20

ALBUMS
59	London Jazz LTZ-K 15150	NEW ORLEANS BLUES (with Wilbur de Paris)	40
60	Vogue LAE 12218	SINGIN' THE BLUES	40
61	Vogue LAE 12253	AT THE RENAISSANCE (with Gerry Mulligan)	35
64	Stateside SL 10088	EVENIN' BLUES	35
65	Stateside SL 10105	BLUES AROUND THE CLOCK	40
65	Fontana 688 005 ZL	THERE'S GOOD ROCKIN' TONIGHT	30
65	Stateside SL 10114	SOME OF MY BEST FRIENDS ARE BLUES	25
65	Stateside SL 10139	BLUE SPOON	22
65	Vogue VRL 3005	JIMMY WITHERSPOON IN PERSON	22
66	Ember EMB 3369	JIMMY WITHERSPOON	20
67	Fontana (S)TL 5382	'SPOON SINGS AND SWINGS	25
67	Verve (S)VLP 9156	BLUE POINT OF VIEW	18
67	Transatlantic PR 7300	EVENIN' BLUES (reissue)	18
68	Transatlantic PR 7356	SOME OF MY BEST FRIENDS ARE THE BLUES (reissue)	15
68	Stateside (S)SL 10232	LIVE	20
68	Verve (S)VLP 9181	BLUES IS NOW (with Brother Jack McDuff)	15
68	Verve (S)VLP 9216	SPOONFUL OF SOUL	18
68	Transatlantic PR 7418	SPOON IN LONDON	15
68	Transatlantic PR 7475	BLUES FOR EASY LIVERS	15
69	Stateside SSL 10289	THE BLUES SINGER	18
69	Polydor Intl. 623 256	BACK DOOR BLUES	20

Jimmy WITHERSPOON/HELEN HUMES

MINT VALUE £

71	Probe SPB 1031	HANDBAGS AND GLADRAGS 15

(see also Eric Burdon & Jimmy Witherspoon, Brother Jack McDuff)

JIMMY WITHERSPOON/HELEN HUMES
60 Vogue EPV 1198 — RHYTHM AND BLUES CONCERT (EP, 2 tracks each) 80

(see also Helen Humes)

BITTER WITHY
69 Nevis NEVIS R005 — SAMPLER (LP) 20

WITNESSES
60s Herald ELR 1076 — THE WITNESSES (EP) 70

D WITTER
78 D-Roy DRLP 1001 — MAWAMBA DUB (WARRIOR) (LP) 70

(See also World Sound & Power Band)

WIZARD'S CONVENTION
76 RCA RS 1085 — WIZARD'S CONVENTION (LP, with insert) 15

(see also Deep Purple, Roger Glover, Jon Lord, David Coverdale, Ray Fenwick, Glenn Hughes, ELP, Hardin & York)

WIZZ
85 Jah Life — MR. SUNSHINE (LP) 40

WIZZARD
73 Harvest SHSP 4025 — WIZZARD BREW (LP, with lyric insert) 15
74 Warner Bros. K 56029 — INTRODUCING EDDY AND THE FALCONS (LP, gatefold with poster) 25

(see also Roy Wood, Balls, Idle Race, Grunt Futtock)

WJW & ROOTS TRUNKS & BRANCHES
79 Splendour Heights WJWX 1945 — THE WEAK WILL BE STRONG (LP) 25

WKGB
79 Fetish FET 002 — Non-Stop/Ultra Marine (p/s) 8

W.L.S.
77 Cancer CAND 001 — Dub Punk/Simply Funky (12") 15

JEZZ WODROFFE
80 Graduate GRAD LP 1 — OPPOSITE DIRECTIONS (LP) 50

CHARLES WOLCOTT
60 MGM 1115 — Leatherjacket Cowboy/Ruby Duby Do 15

DARRYL WAY'S WOLF
73 Deram DM 378 — Wolf/Spring Fever 8
73 Deram DM 395 — A Bunch Of Fives/Five In The Morning 8
73 Deram DM 401 — Two Sisters/Go Down 8
73 Deram SDL 14 — CANIS LUPUS (LP, as Darryl Way's Wolf, gatefold sleeve) 18
73 Deram SML 1104 — SATURATION POINT (LP, laminated sleeve, as Darryl Way's Wolf) 15
74 Deram SML 1116 — NIGHT MUSIC (LP) 18

(see also Curved Air, King Crimson, Marillion)

WOLF
81 Gremlin GREM 72 — See Them Running/Creatures Of The Night (no p/s) 75
84 Mausoleum 8323 — EDGE OF THE WORLD (LP) 18

WOLF
82 Chrysalis CHS 2592 — Head Contact/Rock'n'Roll (p/s, clear vinyl, with sticker) 15
82 Chrysalis CHS 2592 — Head Contact/Rock'n'Roll (p/s, clear vinyl, without sticker) 6

PATRICK WOLF
02 Faith & Industry FAI 001 — THE PATRICK WOLF EP: Bloodbeat/Empress/A Boy Like Me/Pumpkin Soup (12") 50

HENRY WOLFF AND NANCY HENNINGS
72 Island HELP 3 — TIBETAN BELLS (LP, black label with pink "i") 15

WOLFGANG
70 Bell BLL 1120 — Sandman/You 12

WOLFGANG PRESS
83 4AD (no cat. no.) — Kings Of Soul (Crowned Mix)/(De-Throned Mix)/(7" Mix) (12", same both sides, promo only, 50 copies pressed) 15
95 4AD CAD 4016 — FUNKY LITTLE DEMONS (LP) 20

(see also Mass, Models)

WOLFMAN
04 Rough Trade RTRADS177 — For Lovers/Back From The Dead (with Pete Doherty, p/s) 10

WOLFRILLA
71 Concord CON 015 — Song For Jimi/Come Tomorrow 7

WOLVES
64 Pye 7N 15676 — Journey Into Dreams/What Do You Mean 20
64 Pye 7N 15733 — Now/This Year Next Year 30
65 Pye 7N 17013 — At The Club/Distant Dreams 35
66 Parlophone R 5511 — Lust For Life/My Baby Loves Them 70

BOBBY WOMACK
68 Minit MLF 11001 — Broadway Walk/Somebody Special 8
68 Minit MLF 11005 — What Is This?/What You Gonna Do 15
68 Minit MLF 11010 — Fly Me To The Moon/Take Me 8
69 Minit MLF 11012 — California Dreamin'/Baby You Oughta Think It Over 10
72 United Artists UP 35339 — That's The Way I Feel About 'Cha/Come, L'Amore 7
73 United Artists UP 35456 — I Can Understand It/Harry Hippie (in p/s) 12
73 United Artists UP 35456 — I Can Understand It/Harry Hippie 8
73 United Artists UP 35512 — Across 110th Street/Hang On In There (as Bobby Womack & Peace) ... 25
73 United Artists UP 35565 — Nobody Wants You When You're Down And Out/I'm Through Trying To Prove My Love For You 6
74 Jay Boy BOY 75 — What Is This?/I Wonder 20
75 United Artists UP 35859 — Check It Out/Interlude No. 2 6
76 United Artists UP 36042 — Where There's A Will There's A Way/Everything's Gonna Be Alright 6
76 United Artists UP 36098 — Daylight/Trust Me 8

WOMB

MINT VALUE £

77	CBS 4827	Home Is Where The Heart Is/We've Only Just Begun	30
77	CBS 4827	Home Is Where The Heart Is/We've Only Just Begun (DJ Copy)	75
79	Arista ARIST 284	How Could You Break My Heart/I Honestly Love You	15
82	Tamla Motown TMG1267	So Many Sides of You/Just My Imagination (7", p/s)	30
87	Arista RIS 17	How Could You Break My Heart/Give It Up (p/s)	20
87	Arista RIST 17	How Could You Break My Heart/Give It Up/Mr. D.J. Don't Stop The Music (12", p/s)	15
71	United Artists UAS 29306	COMMUNICATION (LP)	15
72	United Artists UAS 29365	UNDERSTANDING (LP)	15
72	United Artists UAS 29451	ACROSS 110TH STREET (LP, soundtrack, with J.J. Johnson)	20
73	United Artists UAG 29456	FACTS OF LIFE (LP, gatefold)	15
79	Arista ARTY 165	ROADS OF LIFE (LP)	20

(see also Valentinos, Ted Wood)

WOMB

| 69 | Dot DLP 25933 | WOMB (LP) | 25 |
| 70 | Dot DLP 25959 | OVERDUB (LP) | 30 |

WOMBATS

| 06 | Kids KIDS 005 | Lost In The Post/Patricia The Stripper (in stickered mailer, 500 only) | 10 |
| 07 | No Label | Moving To New York/Happily Screwed/The Barman's Fault/Ba Ba Song (EP) | 15 |

WOMENFOLK

64	RCA RCA 1439	Turn Around/One Man's Hand	8
64	RCA LSP 2919/SF 7671	NEVER UNDERESTIMATE THE POWER OF WOMENFOLK (LP)	15
65	RCA RD 7704	AT THE HUNGRY I (LP)	15

ALISON WONDER

| 70 | Columbia DB 8667 | Once More With Feeling/Black Paper Roses | 6 |

(see also Cheryl St. Clair)

(LITTLE) STEVIE WONDER

63	Oriole CBA 1853	Fingertips (Parts 1 & 2)	40
63	Oriole CBA 1853	Fingertips (Parts 1 & 2) (DJ copy)	85
63	Stateside SS 238	Workout, Stevie, Workout/Monkey Talk	50
63	Stateside SS 238	Workout, Stevie, Workout/Monkey Talk (DJ copy)	100
64	Stateside SS 285	Castles In The Sand/Thank You (For Loving Me All The Way)	80
64	Stateside SS 285	Castles In The Sand/Thank You (For Loving Me All The Way) (DJ copy)	100
64	Stateside SS 323	Hey, Harmonica Man/This Little Girl	55
64	Stateside SS 323	Hey, Harmonica Man/This Little Girl (DJ copy)	85

(The above 45's are credited to Little Stevie Wonder.)

65	Tamla Motown TMG 505	Kiss Me Baby/Tears In Vain	50
65	Tamla Motown TMG 505	Kiss Me Baby/Tears In Vain (DJ copy)	100
65	Tamla Motown TMG 532	High-Heel Sneakers/Music Talk	40
65	Tamla Motown TMG 532	High-Heel Sneakers/Music Talk (DJ copy)	100
66	Tamla Motown TMG 545	Uptight (Everything's Alright)/Purple Raindrops	25
66	Tamla Motown TMG 545	Uptight (Everything's Alright)/Purple Raindrops (DJ cop)	200
66	Tamla Motown TMG 558	Nothing's Too Good For My Baby/With A Child's Heart	45
66	Tamla Motown TMG 558	Nothing's Too Good For My Baby/With A Child's Heart (DJ copy)	150
66	Tamla Motown TMG 570	Blowin' In The Wind/Ain't That Asking For Trouble	25
66	Tamla Motown TMG 570	Blowin' In The Wind/Ain't That Asking For Trouble (DJ copy)	75
66	Tamla Motown TMG 588	A Place In The Sun/Sylvia	20
66	Tamla Motown TMG 588	A Place In The Sun/Sylvia (DJ copy)	50
67	Tamla Motown TMG 602	Travelin' Man/Hey Love	18
67	Tamla Motown TMG 602	Travelin' Man/Hey Love (DJ copy)	50
67	Tamla Motown TMG 613	I Was Made To Love Her/Hold Me	10
67	Tamla Motown TMG 613	I Was Made To Love Her/Hold Me (DJ copy)	40
67	Tamla Motown TMG 626	I'm Wondering/Every Time I See You I Go Wild	12
67	Tamla Motown TMG 626	I'm Wondering/Every Time I See You I Go Wild (DJ copy)	40
68	Tamla Motown TMG 653	Shoo-Be-Doo-Be-Doo-Da-Day/Why Don't You Lead Me To Love	12
68	Tamla Motown TMG 653	Shoo-Be-Doo-Be-Doo-Da-Day/Why Don't You Lead Me To Love (DJ copy)	30
68	Tamla Motown TMG 666	You Met Your Match/My Girl	15
68	Tamla Motown TMG 666	You Met Your Match/My Girl (DJ copy)	35
68	Tamla Motown TMG 679	For Once In My Life/Angie Girl	6
68	Tamla Motown TMG 679	For Once In My Life/Angie Girl (DJ Copy)	30
69	Tamla Motown TMG 690	My Cherie Amour/I Don't Know Why I Love You	6
69	Tamla Motown TMG 690	My Cherie Amour/I Don't Know Why I Love You (DJ copy)	25
69	Tamla Motown TMG 717	Yester-Me, Yester-You, Yesterday/I'd Be A Fool Right Now	6
69	Tamla Motown TMG 717	Yester-Me, Yester-You, Yesterday/I'd Be A Fool Right Now (DJ copy)	25
70	Tamla Motown TMG 731	Never Had A Dream Come True/Somebody Knows, Somebody Cares	7
70	Tamla Motown TMG 731	Never Had A Dream Come True/Somebody Knows, Somebody Cares (DJ copy)	25
70	Tamla Motown TMG 744	Signed, Sealed, Delivered, I'm Yours/I'm More Than Happy (I'm Satisfied)	6
70	Tamla Motown TMG 744	Signed, Sealed, Delivered, I'm Yours/I'm More Than Happy (I'm Satisfied) (DJ copy)	25
70	Tamla Motown TMG 757	Heaven Help Us All/I Gotta Have A Song	6
70	Tamla Motown TMG 757	Heaven Help Us All/I Gotta Have A Song (DJ copy)	20
71	Tamla Motown TMG 772	We Can Work It Out/Don't Wonder Why (in p/s)	30
71	Tamla Motown TMG 772	We Can Work It Out/Don't Wonder Why	6
71	Tamla Motown TMG 772	We Can Work It Out/Don't Wonder Why (DJ copy)	25
71	Tamla Motown TMG 779	Never Dreamed You'd Leave Me In Summer/If You Really Love Me	8
71	Tamla Motown TMG 779	Never Dreamed You'd Leave Me In Summer/If You Really Love Me (DJ copy)	25
72	Tamla Motown TMG 798	If You Really Love Me/Think Of Me As Your Soldier	7
64	Stateside SE 1014	I CALL IT PRETTY MUSIC BUT THE OLD PEOPLE CALL IT THE BLUES (EP)	120

(Credited to Little Stevie Wonder.)

| 65 | Tamla Motown TME 2006 | LITTLE STEVIE WONDER (EP) | 90 |
| 63 | Oriole PS 40049 | TRIBUTE TO UNCLE RAY (LP) | 325 |

WONDER WHO

			MINT VALUE £
63	Oriole PS 40050	THE TWELVE-YEAR-OLD GENIUS - LIVE (LP)	110
64	Stateside SL 10078	THE JAZZ SOUL OF LITTLE STEVIE WONDER (LP)	150

(The above LP's are Credited to Little Stevie Wonder.)

65	Stateside SL 10108	HEY, HARMONICA MAN (LP)	150

(Originally came with flipback sleeves)

66	Tamla Motown TML 11036	UPTIGHT (EVERYTHING'S ALRIGHT) (LP, mono)	35
66	T. Motown TMG STML 11036	UPTIGHT (EVERYTHING'S ALRIGHT) (LP, stereo)	45
67	Tamla Motown TML 11045	DOWN TO EARTH (LP, mono)	30
67	Tamla Motown STML 11045	DOWN TO EARTH (LP, stereo)	40
68	Tamla Motown STML 11059	I WAS MADE TO LOVE HER (LP, stereo)	25
68	Tamla Motown TML 11059	I WAS MADE TO LOVE HER (LP, mono)	20
68	T. Motown (S)TML 11075	GREATEST HITS (LP, mono/stereo)	15
68	Tamla Motown (S)TML 11085	SOMEDAY AT CHRISTMAS (LP, mono/stereo)	35
69	Tamla Motown (S)TML 11098	FOR ONCE IN MY LIFE (LP, mono/stereo)	20
69	Tamla Motown (S)TML 11128	MY CHERIE AMOUR (LP, mono/stereo)	18

(The LP's listed above originally came with flipback sleeves.)

70	T. Motown STML 11150	STEVIE WONDER LIVE	15
70	Tamla Motown STML 11169	SIGNED SEALED AND DELIVERED	15
71	Tamla Motown STML 11183	WHERE I'M COMING FROM (LP)	15
72	Tamla Motown STMA 8002	MUSIC OF MY MIND (LP)	15
73	Tamla Motown STMA 8007	TALKING BOOK (LP, gatefold)	15
73	Tamla Motown STMA 8011	INNERVISIONS (LP, gatefold)	15
74	Tamla Motown STMA 8019	FULFILLINGNESS FIRST FINALE (LP, gatefold)	15
76	Tamla Motown STML 60021	SONGS IN THE KEY OF LIFE (2-LP, with free 7")	20
79	Tamla Motown TMSP 6009	THE SECRET LIFE OF PLANTS (2-LP)	20
05	Tamla Motown 12 MOW 13	A TIME 2 LOVE (LP)	15

WONDER WHO

65	Philips BF 1440	Don't Think Twice, It's Alright/Sassy	20
66	Philips BF 1504	On The Good Ship Lollipop/You're Nobody Till Somebody Loves You	10
67	Philips BF 1600	Lonesome Road/FOUR SEASONS: Around And Around	20

(see also Four Seasons, Frankie Valli)

WONDER BOY

69	Jackpot JP 703	Sweeten My Coffee (actually by Slim Smith)/MISTER MILLER: Cherry Pink	25
69	Jackpot JP 705	Love Power (actually by Slim Smith)/LITTLE BOY BLUE: Since You Are Gone	35
71	Jackpot JP 764	Just For A Day/He Ain't Heavy (actually by Pat Kelly)	12
75	Ackee ACK 546	Pressure Parts 1 & 2	6

(see also Slim Smith)

GIRL WONDER

66	Doctor Bird DB 1015	Mommy Out Of The Light/Cutting Wood	25

WONDERLAND

68	Polydor 56539	Poochy/Moscow	15

ALICE WONDERLAND

63	London HLU 9783	He's Mine/Cha Linde	20

WONDERS OF YOUTH

71	Alert AL 2	Down And Out Man/Terry	25
72	Fly FL 2	Jump Over My Head/Say Hello	40

WONDER STUFF

87	Far Out GONE ONE	It's Not True.../A Wonderful Day/Like A Merry-Go-Round/Down Here (EP, p/s)	40
89	House Of Dolls HOD 011	Who Wants To Be The Disco King? (King Of Disco Megamix)/PRUDES: Christmas/SANDKINGS: Colourblind/WORLD MUSIC: Stop Playing With My Heart (no p/s, free with House Of Dolls magazine)	6
93	Polydor 519 8941	CONSTRUCTION FOR THE MODERN IDIOT (LP)	30

(see also Vic Reeves)

ROYCE WONG

65	Blue Beat BB 301	Everything's Gonna Be Alright/Hang Your Head And Cry	20

WONKY ALICE

92	Pomona POM 004	SIRIUS EP (12", p/s)	12

WOOB

94	Em:t	WOOB 1194 (CD)	40
95	Em:t	WOOB 4495 (CD)	40

ANITA WOOD

62	London HLS 9585	I'll Wait Forever/I Can't Show You How I Feel	25
64	Sue WI 328	Dream Baby/This Happened Before	40

BOBBY WOOD

64	Pye International 7N 25264	I'm A Fool For Loving You/My Heart Went Boing! Boing! Boing!	15

BRENTON WOOD

67	Philips BF 1579	Oogum Boogum Song/I Like The Way You Love Me	8
67	Liberty LBF 15021	Gimme Little Sign/I Think You Got Your Fools Mixed Up	8
68	Liberty LBF 15065	Baby You Got It/Catch You On The Rebound	8
68	Liberty LBF 15103	Some Got It, Some Don't/Me And You	8
70	Pye International 7N 25522	Great Big Bundle Of Love/Can You Dig It	15
67	Liberty LBL/LBS 83088E	GIMME A LITTLE SIGN (LP)	20

CHUCK WOOD

67	Big T BIG 104	Seven Days Too Long/Soul Shing-A-Ling	20
67	Big T BIG 104	Seven Days Too Long/Soul Shing-A-Ling (DJ Copy)	50
68	Big T BIG 107	I've Got My Movelight Shining/Baby You Win	10
75	Pye Disco Demand DDS 111	Seven Days Too Long/WIGANS'S CHOSEN FEW: Footsee (in p/s)	10
13	Outta Sight OSV 103	Dance, Dance, Dance. Seven Days Too Long (reissue)	6

Del WOOD

MINT VALUE £

DEL WOOD
54	London HL 8036	Ragtime Annie/Backroom Polka	50
54	London RE-P 1007	RAGTIME PIANO (EP)	15

RONNIE WOOD
92	Continuum 12210-2	Show Me/Breathe On Me (CD, with Ronnie Wood print, signed & numbered, in black card case tied with ribbon, 600 only)	50

(see also Faces, Rolling Stones, Jeff Beck, Ted Wood)

ROY WOOD
73	Harvest SHVL 803	BOULDERS (LP, textured sleeve with EMI logo on label)	25
76	Harvest SHDW 408	THE ROY WOOD STORY (LP)	15

(see also Wizzard, Gerry Levine & Avengers, Mike Sheridan, Danny King['s Mayfair Set], Move, ELO, Renaissance [UK], Rockers, Birds)

TED WOOD
76	Penny Farthing PEN 891	Am I Blue/Shine (B-side features Rod Stewart, Ronnie Wood, Gary Glitter & Bobby Womack)	8

(see also Temperance Seven)

WOOD CHILDREN
88	Cat & Mouse ABB 05	Happens Everyday/2 Red Buses	8

WOODEN HORSE
72	York SYK 526	Pick Up The Pieces/Wake Me In The Morning	20
73	York SYK 543	Wooden Horses/Typewriter And Guitar	20
72	York FYK 403	WOODEN HORSE (LP)	350
73	York FYK 413	WOODEN HORSE II (LP, withdrawn, with sleeve, blue/silver label)	900
73	York FYK 413	WOODEN HORSE II (LP, withdrawn, without sleeve, blue/silver label)	500

(see also Fox)

WOODEN O & GUESTS
69	Middle Earth MDLS 301	A HANDFUL OF PLEASANT DELITES (LP)	150

(see also 'Middle Earth Sampler' in Various Artists section)

WOODEN SHJIPS
09	Great Pop Supplement GPS 50	I Believe It/SPACEMEN 3: Big City (demo) (red marbled vinyl, insert & sticker)	15

GEORGE WOODHOUSE
79	Milestone M 001	Thanks/HOPETON JURNER: Living In The Ghetto (12")	150

KEN WOODMAN & HIS PICCADILLY BRASS
66	Strike JLH 101	THAT'S NICE (LP)	40

WOODMARK
83	Ooze S83 CUS 1692	When You're Gone/Life Is Cruel	20

WOODPECKERS
64	Decca F 11835	The Woodpecker/You Can't Sit Down	10
65	Oriole CB 311	Hey Little Girl/What's Your Name	20

STANLEY WOODRUFF & U.S. TRIO
70	Ember EMB S 288	If I Let You/Will You Still Love Me Tomorrow	7

BILLY WOODS
04	Soul City SC 155	Let Me Make You Happy/That Was The Love That Was	6

CAROL WOODS
70	Ember EMB S 288	If I Let You/Will You Still Love Me Tomorrow (p/s)	10
72	Ember NR 5059	OUT OF THE WOODS (LP)	40

CORA WOODS
56	Parlophone DP 505	Rocks In Your Head/I Don't Want To Cry (export 78)	10

DONALD WOODS & EARL PALMER BAND
58	Vogue V 9107	Memories Of An Angel/That Much Of Your Love	650
58	Vogue V 9107	Memories Of An Angel/That Much Of Your Love (78)	150

GAY & TERRY WOODS
77	Polydor 2058 810	Save The Last Dance For Me/One More Time	10
78	Rockburgh ROCS 202	We Can Work This One Out/Piece Of Summer (p/s)	10
75	Polydor 2383 322	BACKWOODS (LP)	50
76	Polydor 2383 375	THE TIME IS RIGHT (LP, with lyric insert)	60
76	Polydor 2383 406	RENOWNED (LP, with lyric insert)	50
78	Rockburgh ROC 104	TENDER HOOKS (LP, with lyric insert)	20

(see also Woods Band, Gay Woods, Steeleye Span, Sweeney's Men)

JIMMY WOODS
63	Contemporary LAC 571	CONFLICT (LP)	20

NICK WOODS
62	London HLU 9621	Ballad Of Billy Budd/Don't Let Me Down	8

PEGGY WOODS
88	Kent 6T 4	Love Is Gonna Get You/ZZ: You Just Cheat And Lie	20

PHIL WOODS
57	Esquire EP 168	THE YOUNG IDEAS (EP)	12
55	Esquire 20-055	NEW JAZZ QUINTET (10" LP)	50
57	Esquire 32-020	WOODLORE (LP)	80

TONY WOODS
71	Spiral DIT 2	I'm Only A Man/Blues	6

TED WOODS
71	Spiral DIT 2	I'm Only A Man/Blues	10

TERRY WOODS
81	Chiswick CHIS 244	Tennessee Stud/I Don't Know About Love	30

WOODS BAND
71	Greenwich GSLP 1004	THE WOODS BAND (LP, gatefold sleeve)	150
77	Rockburgh CREST 29	THE WOODS BAND (LP, reissue in different sleeve)	20

(see also Gay & Terry Woods)

WOODWARD BROTHERS
86	Debut DEBTX 3010	You Set Me Up/Physical Attraction/You Set Me Up (Dub Version) (12")	12

MAGGIE WOODWARD
59	Vogue V 9148	Ali Bama/Zulu Warrior	15
59	Vogue V 9148	Ali Bama/Zulu Warrior (78)	20

WOODY KERN
69	Pye 7N 17672	Biography/Tell You I'm Gone (demo)	100
69	Pye NSPL 18273	THE AWFUL DISCLOSURES OF MARIA MONK (LP)	150

WOOL
69	Stateside SS2153	Love Love Love Love Love/If They Left Us Alone Now	25

BRIAN WOOLEY
58	Esquire EP 170	BRIAN WOOLEY'S JAZZMEN (EP)	10
58	Esquire EP 190	WILD 'N WOOLEY (EP)	10

SHEB WOOLEY
51	MGM MGM 439	Hoot Owl Boogie/Country Kisses (78)	20
55	MGM SP 1130	38-24-35/I Flipped	25
55	MGM SPC 5	Hill Billy Mambo/I Go Outa My Mind (export issue)	30
58	MGM MGM 981	The Purple People Eater/I Can't Believe You're Mine	15
58	MGM MGM 981	The Purple People Eater/Recipe For Love (2nd pressing, different B-side)	10
58	MGM MGM 997	Santa And The Purple People Eater/Star Of Love)	6
59	MGM MGM 1017	Sweet Chile/More	8
60	MGM MGM 1081	Luke The Spook/My Only Treasure	7
61	MGM MGM 1132	The Wayward Wind/Bars Across The Windows	6
61	MGM MGM 1147	That's My Pa/Meet Mr. Lonely	7
62	MGM MGM 1162	Laughing The Blues/Somebody Please	7
56	MGM MGM-EP 540	JEST PLAIN, WILD AND WOOLEY (EP)	40
61	MGM MGM-C 859	SONGS FROM THE DAY OF RAWHIDE (LP)	20
62	MGM MGM-C 903	THAT'S MY MA AND THAT'S MY PA (LP)	20

CHARLIE WOOLFE
68	NEMS 56-3675	Dance Dance Dance/Home	35

(see also At Last The 1958 Rock & Roll Show)

WOOLIES
67	RCA RCA 1602	Who Do You Love?/Hey Girl	50

JOHN WOOLLEY & JUST BORN
71	Decca 23134	Ruby Baby/Make Love Not War	10

WOOLLY
72	RCA 2297	Golden Golden/Sugar Daddy Song	20

WOOLLY FISH
70	Plexium PXM 16	Way You Like It/Sound Of Thick	15

BRENDA WOOTTON
68	Pipers VRC 1	JOHN THE FISH (LP)	20

JIMMY WORK
56	London HLD 8270	When She Said "You All"/There's Only One You	60
56	London HLD 8270	When She Said "You All"/There's Only One You (78)	20
56	London HLD 8308	You've Gotta Heart Like A Merry-Go-Round/Blind Heart	45
56	London HLD 8308	You've Gotta Heart Like A Merry-Go-Round/Blind Heart (78)	20
55	London RE-D 1039	COUNTRY SONGS - WORK STYLE (EP)	30

WORKING MEN'S CLUB
19	Melodic MELO 120	Bad Blood/Suburban Heights (p/s)	15
19	Heavenly HVN 520	Teeth/Teeth (Instrumental) (p/s)	15
20	Heavenly HVNLP199RAW	WORKING MEN'S CLUB (LP, 300 only, hand-sprayed sleeve, poster, patch, hand-stamped)	70

WORLD
70	Liberty LBF 15402	Angelina/Come Out Into The Open	10
70	Liberty LBG 83219	LUCKY PLANET (LP, textured gatefold sleeve)	50

(see also Neil Innes, Bonzo Dog [Doo-Dah] Band)

WORLD COLUMN
76	Capitol CL 15852	So Is The Sun/It's Not Right	10
76	Capitol CL 15852	So Is The Sun/It's Not Right (DJ Copy)	15

WORLD OF OZ
68	Deram DM 187	The Muffin Man/Peter's Birthday (Black And White Rainbows)	15
68	Deram DM 205	King Croesus/Jack	15
69	Deram DM 233	Willow's Harp/Like A Tear	25
69	Deram DML/SML 1034	THE WORLD OF OZ (LP)	120

(see also David Kubinec)

WORLD SOUND & POWER BAND
80	D Roy DRLP 1006	MAWAMBA DUB (WARRIOR) CHAPTER TWO (LP)	55

(See also D Witter)

WORLD VISION QUARTET
63	Herald HSR 2518	Dry Bones/You Ain't Got Nothin'	8

WORMS
78	Ice GUY 21	London Bus (I Can't Take My Eyes Off You/Okay At Christmas (500 only)	50

BIMBI WORRICK
69	Polydor 56321	Long Time Comin'/Tomorrow Is My Day	8

WORRYING KYNDE
67	Piccadilly 7N 35370	Call Out The Name/Got The Blame	80

WORTH
72	CBS 7728	Don't Say You Don't/Polecat Alley	10

JOHNNY WORTH
57	Columbia DB 3962	Let's Go/Just Because	6
60	Oriole CB 1545	Nightmare/Hold Me, Thrill Me, Kiss Me	75

MARION WORTH
60	London HL 7089	Are You Willing, Willie/This Heart Of Mine (export issue)	25

Stan WORTH ORCHESTRA

MINT VALUE £

60	London HL 7097	That's My Kind Of Love/I Lost Johnny (export issue)	25

STAN WORTH ORCHESTRA
63	London HLU 9703	Roman Holiday/Wiggle Wobble Walkers	8

TONY WORTH
69	Cleo CL 3194	Why Not Love Me/Dream	20

WOULD-BE-GOODS
87	El GPO 28	Fruit Paradise/The Hanging Gardens Of Reigate (p/s)	10
88	El GPO 39	The Camera Loves Me/Cecil Beaton's Diary (p/s)	15
88	El ACME 14	THE CAMERA LOVES ME (LP)	20

WOVEN WEB
72	Shell SH2	High On Life/Lost Inside The Well	40

WRANGLER
14	MemeTune MEME14VA01	LA SPARK (LP)	15
16	MemeTune MEME14VA04	WHITE GLUE (LP)	15

(see also Cabaret Voltaire, Stephen Mallinder)

WRANGLERS
64	Parlophone R 5263	Liza Jane/It Just Won't Work	70

(see also Kenny Bernard, Kenny & Wranglers)

LINK WRAY (& HIS RAY MEN)
58	London HLA 8623	Rumble/The Swag (as Link Wray & His Ray Men)	50
58	London HLA 8623	Rumble/The Swag (as Link Wray & His Ray Men) (78)	30
63	Stateside SS 217	Jack The Ripper/The Black Widow	30
64	Stateside SS 256	The Sweeper/Weekend	20
65	Stateside SS 397	Good Rockin' Tonight/I'll Do Anything For You	20
71	Polydor 2066 120	Fire And Brimstone/Jukebox Mama	6
73	Polydor 2066 320	Lawdy Miss Clawdy/Shine The Light	6
73	Virgin VS 103	I'm So Glad, I'm So Proud/Shawnee Tribe	6
76	Virgin VS 142	I Know You're Leaving Me Now/Quicksand	6
64	Stateside SE 1015	MR. GUITAR (EP, sleeve credits Link Ray)	100
71	Polydor 2489 029	LINK WRAY (LP)	40
71	Union Pacific UP 002	THERE'S GOOD ROCKIN' TONIGHT (LP)	25
73	Virgin V 2006	BEANS & FATBACK (LP)	20
73	Polydor 2391063	BE WHAT YOU WANT TO (LP)	15
74	Polydor 2391 128	THE LINK WRAY RUMBLE (LP)	15
88	Hangman HANG 31 UP	64 (THE SWAN DEMOS) (LP)	30
88	Hangman HANG 33 UP	JACK THE RIPPER (LP)	30

(see also Robert Gordon with Link Wray)

RAY WRAY QUARTET
62	Salvo SLO 1808	When Your Lover Has Gone/A Song Is Born	20

WRECKERS
64	Granta GR 7EP 1010	THE WRECKERS' SOUND (EP)	120

WRECKLESS ERIC
77	Stiff BUY 16	Whole Wide World/Semaphore Signals (p/s, push-out centre)	10
78	Stiff BUY 25	Reconnez Cherie/Rags And Tatters ("Factory sample" sticker on label)	10
78	Stiff BUY 25	Reconnez Cherie/Rags And Tatters (p/s)	6
78	Stiff BUY 34	Take The Cash (K.A.S.H)/Girlfriend (die-cut company sleeve)	6
78	Stiff BUY 40	Crying, Waiting, Hoping/I Wish It Would Rain (p/s)	6
78	Stiff SEEZ 6	WRECKLESS ERIC (LP)	15
78	Stiff SEEZ 9	THE WONDERFUL WORLD OF... (LP, picture disc in LP sleeve)	15
93	Hangman HANG 50 UP	THE DONOVAN OF TRASH (LP)	18

(see also Len Bright Combo)

JENNY WREN
66	Fontana TF 672	Chasing My Dreams All Over Town/A Thought Of You	250
66	Fontana TF 772	The Merry-Go-Round (Is Slowing You Down)/Take A Walk Bobby	15

WRENS
96	Grass GROW 10021	SECAUCUS (LP)	150
06	BB 0031	THE MEADOWLANDS (2-LP, gatefold)	100

WRETCHED
81	Wretched Music GRC 102	DNR/Souls In Torment (500 only)	50

WRIGGLERS
68	Giant GN 26	The Cooler/You Cannot Know	400
68	Blue Cat BS 106	Get Right/If I Did Look	120

BETTY WRIGHT
68	Atlantic 584 216	Girls Can't Do What The Guys Do/Sweet Lovin' Daddy	15
72	Atlantic K 10143	Clean Up Woman/I'll Love You Forever	15
72	Atlantic K 40364	I LOVE THE WAY YOU LOVE (LP)	20
74	RCA SF 8408	DANGER - HIGH VOLTAGE (LP)	20
76	RCA RS 1063	EXPLOSION (LP)	20
77	T.K. XL 14053	THIS TIME FOR REAL (LP)	20

BILLY WRIGHT
61	Parlophone R 4852	Sing Song For Kicks Part 1/Part 2	10

CHARLES WRIGHT & WATTS 103RD STREET RHYTHM BAND
69	Warner Bros WB 7250	Do Your Thing/A Dance, A Kiss And A Song	8
69	Warner Bros WB 7298	Till You Get Enough/Light My Fire	8
70	Warner Bros WB 7365	Love Land/Sorry Charlie	8
70	Warner Bros WB 7417	Express Yourself/Living On Borrowed Time	20
72	Jay Boy BOY 71	Spreadin' Honey/Charley (as Watts 103rd Street Rhythm Band)	10
70	Warner Bros 1864	EXPRESS YOURSELF (LP)	30

DALE WRIGHT
58	London HLD 8573	She's Neat/Say That You Care (as Dale Wright & Rock-Its)	175

Earl WRIGHT

MINT VALUE £

58	London HLD 8573	She's Neat/Say That You Care (as Dale Wright & Rock-Its) (78)	40
59	Pye International 7N 25022	That's Show Biz/That's My Gal (as Dale Wright & Wright Guys)	80
59	Pye International 7N 25022	That's Show Biz/That's My Gal (as Dale Wright & Wright Guys) (78)	50

EARL WRIGHT
| 75 | Capitol CL 15825 | Thumb A Ride/Like A Rolling Stone | 8 |
| 75 | Capitol CL 15825 | Thumb A Ride/Like A Rolling Stone (DJ Copy) | 15 |

GARY WRIGHT('S WONDERWHEEL)
72	A&M AMS 888	I know/Tonight It's Right	12
71	A&M AMLS 2004	EXTRACTIONS (LP, poster sleeve)	30
72	A&M AMLS 64296	FOOTPRINT (LP)	18
72	A&M AMLH 64362	RING OF CHANGES (LP, as Wright's Wonderwheel; unissued, test pressings only)	50

(see also Spooky Tooth, Magic Christians, Thomas F. Browne)

GEORGE WRIGHT/NEVILLE MITCHELL
| 82 | Kingdom KV 8026 | GEORGE WRIGHT - You Are The One I Love/ROOTS RADICS - I Done It Dub/NEVILL MITCHELL - Get Out Of Hand/ROOTS RADICS - Hand Made Dub | 25 |

GINNY WRIGHT (& TOM TALL)
55	London HL 8119	Indian Moon/Your Eyes Feasted Upon Her (solo)	50
55	London HL 8150	Are You Mine?/Boom Boom Boomerang (with Tom Tall)	30
55	London RE-U 1035	COUNTRY SONGS VOL. 2 (EP, with Tom Tall)	30

(see also T. Tommy Cutrer & Ginny Wright, Tom Tall)

MILTON WRIGHT & TERRA SHIRMA STRINGS
| 07 | Jazzman JM12.011 | Keep It Up/The Silence That You Keep (12", p/s) | 15 |
| 08 | Jazzman JMANLP 025 | SPACED (LP, reissue) | 30 |

NAT WRIGHT
| 59 | HMV POP 629 | Anything/For You My Love | 75 |

OTIS WRIGHT
69	High Note HS 033	Man Of Galilee/Take Up The Cross	6
67	Doctor Bird DLM 5005	PEACE PERFECT PEACE (LP)	50
67	Doctor Bird DLM 5006	IT WILL SOON BE DONE (LP)	50
69	High Note BSL5003	SACRED SONGS (LP)	30
60s	Coxsone TLP 1001	OVER IN GLORYLAND (LP)	50
73	Tabernacle BSLP 5021	SOUL STIRRING GOSPEL SONGS (LP)	40

O.V. WRIGHT
65	Vocalion VP 9249	You're Gonna Make Me Cry/Monkey Dog	20
66	Vocalion VP 9255	Poor Boy/I'm In Your Corner	20
66	Vocalion VP 9272	Gone For Good/How Long Baby	20
67	London HLZ 10137	8 Men 4 Women/Fed Up With The Blues	15
68	Sue WI 4043	What About You/What Did You Tell This Girl Of Mine	50
68	Action ACT 4505	Oh Baby Mine/Working Your Game	15
69	Action ACT 4527	I Want Everyone To Know/I'm Gonna Forget About You	15
65	Vocalion VEP 170165	CAN'T FIND TRUE LOVE (EP)	100
68	Island ILP 975	8 MEN, 4 WOMEN (LP)	120

OWEN WRIGHT
| 70 | Banana BA 310 | Wala Wala (actually by Burning Spear)/JERRY & FREEDOM SINGERS: Got To Be Sure (B-side actually by Horace Andy) | 80 |

RICHARD WRIGHT
| 78 | Harvest SHVL 818 | WET DREAM (LP, gatefold stickered sleeve) | 25 |

(see also Pink Floyd)

RITA WRIGHT
68	Tamla Motown TMG 643	I Can't Give Back The Love I Feel For You/Something On My Mind	25
68	Tamla Motown TMG 643	I Can't Give Back The Love I Feel For You/Something On My Mind (DJ copy)	40
71	Tamla Motown TMG 791	I Can't Give Back The Love I Feel For You/Something On My Mind (reissue)	10
78	Jet UP 36382	Love Is All You Need/Touch Me, Take Me	100

RUBEN WRIGHT
| 66 | Capitol CL 15460 | Hey Girl/I'm Walking Out On You | 35 |
| 66 | Capitol CL 15460 | Hey Girl/I'm Walking Out On You (DJ copy) | 75 |

RUBY WRIGHT
53	Parlophone MSP 6025	Till I Waltz Again With You/When I Gave You My Love (with Charlie Gore)	20
54	Parlophone MSP 6073	Bimbo/Boy, You Got Yourself A Gal	25
54	Parlophone MSP 6133	Santa's Little Sleigh Bells/Toodle-oo To You	10
55	Parlophone MSP 6150	What Have They Told You?/I Had The Funniest Feeling	15
56	Parlophone MSP 6209	I Fall In Love With You Ev'ry Day/Do You Believe?	15
59	Parlophone GEP 8785	THE THREE STARS GIRL (EP)	30

SAMUEL E. WRIGHT
| 73 | Paramount PARA 3035 | There's Something Funny Going On/300 Pounds Of Hunger | 15 |

SANDRA WRIGHT
| 89 | Demon FIEND 138 | WOUNDED WOMAN (LP) | 150 |

SEAN WRIGHT
78	Ellie Jay EJSP 8624	Strange Situation/Silent Dreams (1st issue, 50 with folded p/s some with insert)	30
81	Media PR 001	Strange Situation/Silent Dreams (2nd issue, p/s as Media but new labels are pasted over records from 1st pressing)	15
82	Heavy Leather	Strange Situation/Silent Dreams (3rd issue, p/s new labels are pasted over records from 1st pressing)	12

STEVE WRIGHT
| 59 | London HLW 8991 | Wild, Wild, Woman/Love You | 200 |
| 59 | London HLW 8991 | Wild, Wild, Woman/Love You (78) | 100 |

STEVEN WRIGHT
| 93 | Reggae On Top ROT 001 | Vision Of Jah/Dub Versions (12") | 25 |

STEVIE WRIGHT
| 74 | Polydor 2121246 | Evie - Let Your Hair Down/Evie | 8 |
| 74 | Polydor 2480 249 | HARD ROAD (LP) | 20 |

Syreeta WRIGHT

MINT VALUE £

SYREETA WRIGHT
72   Mowest MWS 7001   SYREETA (LP) 25

WINSTON WRIGHT
69   Camel CA 32   Power Pack/TWO SPARKS: Throwing Stones.. 80
69   Explosion EX 2003   Barefoot Brigade/Slippery (with the Crystalites)... 75
69   Trojan TR 7701   Moonlight Groover/SENSATIONS: Everyday Is Just A Holiday... 60
69   Trojan TR 7715   Moon Invader (with Tommy McCook)/RADCLIFF RUFFIN: You Got To Love Me 50
70   Trojan TR 7775   Meshwire (with Tommy McCook)/BARONS: Darling Please Return................................... 45
70   Explosion EX 2011   Flight 404/LLOYD & ROBIN: Gawling Come Down (B-side actually Higher Than The Highest Mountain by Monty Morris) 35
70   Explosion EX 2015   Funny Girl/Funny Girl Version II... 25
70   Duke DU 62   Poppy Cock (with J.J. All Stars)/CARL DAWKINS: This World And Me (B-side actually "Satisfaction")... 30
70   Bamboo BAM 60   Reggae Feet/DON DRUMMOND: Royal Flush (B-side act. titled "The Rocket")................ 35
70   High Note HS 040   Soul Pressure/Seed You Sow (with Gaytones).. 30
70   Moodisc MU 3501   Musically Red (with Maudie's Allstars; actually also with Count Sticky)/ RHYTHM RULERS: Bratah 150
70   G.G. GG 4504   It's Been A Long Time/PAULETTE & GEE: Feel It More And More 15
70   Techniques TE 907   Top Secret/Crazy Rhythm 85
71   Upsetter US 378   Example (with 3rd & 4th Generation)/UPSETTER: Version 25
71   Duke DU 111   Silhouettes/That Did It 20
71   Camel CA 71   Silhouettes/That Did It 20
71   Green Door GD 4011   Heads Or Tails/THE ROASTERS: Raunchy... 6
77   Third World TWS 923   JUMP THE FENCE (LP) 20

(see also Ethiopians, John Holt, J.J. Allstars, Slickers)

ZACHARIAH WRIGHT
70s Bamboo BAM 403   Lumumba Limbo/Green, Red and Gold 10

WRIGHTSOUND
75   Peacock AT 842   Dance Apache/Jelly 18

BERNARD WRIGLEY
76   Transatlantic TRA 327   SONGS, STORIES AND ELEPHANTS (LP) 12

WRIGLEYS
69   Page One POF 118   A Little Bit/Come Down Little Bird 10

WRIT
66   Decca F 12385   Did You Ever Have To Make Up Your Mind/Solid Golden Teardrops 20

WRITING ON THE WALL
69   Middle Earth MDS 101   Child On A Crossing/Lucifer Corpus 60
73   Pye 7N 45251   Man Of Renown/Buffalo 20
69   Middle Earth MDLS 303   THE POWER OF THE PICTS (LP, textured sleeve) 400
95   Pie & Mash PAM 003   RARITIES FROM THE MIDDLE EARTH (LP, 500 copies only) 15
95   Tenth Planet TP 017   CRACKS IN THE ILLUSION OF LIFE (LP, gatefold sleeve) 18
96   Tenth Planet TP 018   BURGHLEY ROAD (LP, 1,000 copies only) 18

(see also 'Middle Earth Sampler' in Various Artists; Three's A Crowd)

WRONG TITLE
75   Primary 01   My Oh My/A Time Forgotten (p/s) 10

W12 SPOTS
70s Shepherds Bush SB 1   Sid Never Did/COSMIC PUNKS: 99 Years 12

HENRY WU/JEEN BASSA
14   22a 002   HENRY WU/JEAN BASSA (12" split EP, 1st pressing red stamped labels)......................... 15

WUGGERY
98   Wuggery WUG 1   Wuggery Muggery/Wugwats Weekend (p/s) 8

WURZEL
87   GWR GWR 4   Bess/People Say I'm Crazy (p/s) 8
87   GWR GWT 4   Bess/People Say I'm Crazy/Midnight In London/E.S.P. (12", p/s) 15

(see also Motorhead)

WURZELS
77   EMI EMI 2686   One For The Bristol City/Cheddar Cheese (p/s)... 6
05   Rough Trade RTRADS302   Remember Me/I Am A Cider Drinker (British Sea Power) (7" ltd ed. 1,966 copies) 10

JOHNNY WYATT
68   President PT 109   This Thing Called Love/To Whom It May Concern (DJ Copy)... 50
68   President PT 109   This Thing Called Love/To Whom It May Concern (horizontal) 30
68   President PT 109   This Thing Called Love/To Whom It May Concern (vertical artist credit) 10

ROBERT WYATT
77   Virgin VS 115   Yesterday Man/Sonia 6
81   Rough Trade RT 081   Grass/Trade Union/Dishari (p/s) 8
82   Rough Trade RT 115   Shipbuilding/Memories of You (This 7" came in 4 different multi-fold art sleeves. Most common are 'Blanket' and 'Rope' covers, 'Metal Rings' and 'Hot Coals' are less common) .. 6
97   Hannibal TRDSC 010   Free Will And Testament/The Sight Of The Wind 6
87   Strange Fruit SFPS 037   PEEL SESSIONS (12") 15
70   CBS 64189   THE END OF AN EAR (LP) 40
74   Virgin V 2017   ROCK BOTTOM (LP, 1st pressing, coloured "girl and dragon" labels) 40
75   Virgin V 2034   RUTH IS STRANGER THAN RICHARD (LP) 40
82   Rough Trade ROUGH 35   NOTHING CAN STOP US (LP, early pressing without "Shipbuilding", insert)..................... 20
81   Virgin VGD 3505   ROCK BOTTOM/RUTH IS STRANGER THAN RICHARD (2-LP reissue) 35
85   Rough Trade ROUGH 69   OLD ROTTENHAT (LP, gatefold) 20
91   Rough Trade R2741   DONDESTAN (LP) 30
07   Domino WIGLP 202   COMICOPERA (2-LP) 20
08   Domino REWIGLP 47   CUCKOOLAND (2-LP) 20
08   Domino REWIGLP 45   SHLEEP (2-LP) 20

(see also Soft Machine, Matching Mole, Centipede, Ben Watt)

Richard ('POPCORN') WYLIE

MINT VALUE £

RICHARD ('POPCORN') WYLIE
63	Columbia DB 7012	Brand New Man/So Much Love In My Heart (as Richard Wylie)	40
77	Grapevine GRP 100	Rosemary What Happened (Parts 1 & 2) (as Richard 'Popcorn' Wylie)	8

BILL WYMAN
74	Rolling Stones RS 19115	White Lightning/Pussy	7
83	Ripple (no cat. no.)	DIGITAL DREAMS (LP, soundtrack, promo only)	50

(see also Rolling Stones)

WYNDER K. FROG
66	Island WI 280	Turn On Your Lovelight/Zooming	30
66	Island WI 3011	Sunshine Superman/Blues For A Frog	30
67	Island WIP 6006	Green Door/Dancing Frog	45
67	Island WIP 6014	I Am A Man/Shook Shimmy & Shake	55
68	Island WIP 6044	Jumping Jack Flash/Baldy	35
67	Island ILP 944	SUNSHINE SUPERFROG (LP, white label, mono)	100
67	Island ILPS 9044	SUNSHINE SUPERFROG (LP, white label, stereo)	125
68	Island ILP 982/ILPS 9082	OUT OF THE FRYING PAN (LP, pink label. orange/black circle)	75

(see also Keef Hartley Band, Miller Anderson, Fair Weather, Grease Band)

KES WYNDHAM
71	Pye 7N 45082	Honey Call Me Home/Broken Bicycle	10

WYNDRUSH
72	Wealden WS 116	LET IT SHINE (LP)	300

PETER WYNGARDE
70	RCA Victor RCA 1967	La Ronde De L'Amour/The Way I Cry Over You	30
70	RCA Victor PW 1	Commits Rape/The Way I Cry Over You (LP sampler, promo only)	45
70	RCA Victor SF 8087	PETER WYNGARDE (LP, gatefold sleeve)	50

(see also Larry Wallis, Tyrannosaurus Rex)

PETER WYNNE
59	Parlophone R 4597	Twilight Time/Chapel Of Dreams	7
60	Parlophone R 4668	Ask Anyone In Love/I Need You Close Again	6
60	Parlophone R 4705	Our Concerto/Your lover	6

SANDY WYNNS
65	Fontana TF 550	Touch Of Venus/Lovers' Quarrel	300

MARK WYNTER
60	Decca F 11263	Image Of A Girl/Glory Of Love	7
60	Decca F 11279	Kickin' Up The Leaves/That's What I Thought	10
62	Decca F 11467	Angel Talk/I Love Her Still	6
63	Pye 7N 15511	Aladdin's Lamp/It Can Happen Any Day	6
63	Pye 7N 15525	Shy Girl/Because Of You	6
63	Pye 7N 15554	Running To You/Don't Cry	6
66	Pye 7N 17122	We'll Sing In The Sunshine/Pencil And Paper	8
60	Decca DFE 6674	MARK TIME (EP)	12
63	Pye NEP 24176	IT'S MARK TIME (EP)	10
64	Pye NEP 24185	WYNTER TIME (EP)	10
61	Decca LK 4409	THE WARMTH OF WYNTER (LP)	25
65	Ace Of Clubs ACL 1141	MARK WYNTER (LP)	15

(see also Joe Brown & Mark Wynter)

GAIL WYNTERS
67	London HLE 10144	Snap Your Fingers/Find Myself A New Love	12

WYOMING
72	MAM MAMR 76	Seven Days/Two Faced Woman	12

X

X
80	Slash Records UK SR-104	LOS ANGELES (LP, with insert)	18
81	Slash/Rough Trade SR 107	WILD GIFT (LP)	15

NATHALIE XAVIER
81	People Unite PU NAT 1	Atomic Energy/Set Me Free (12")	40

X-CALIBURS
65	CBS 201805	We Will Love/Swing That Chariot	10
65	Mercury MF 941	You'll Find Out/That's What Happens (possibly as Xcalibres)	10

X-CELLS
81	Snotty Snail NEL COL 4	Freedom Man/SCHIZOID: Nowhere To Go (p/s)	20

X CERTIFICATE
73	Spark SRL 1096	Don't Stick Stickers On My Paper Knickers/Come Home Baby	6

X-CERTS
78	Zama	Feeling The Groove (p/s)	15
81	Recreational PLAY 1	Together/Untogether (p/s, with lyric insert)	6

XCLUSIV
82	Le Maitre KA 100 12	Fools Are Friendly/Insrumental (12")	50
82	Le Maitre KA 100	Fools Are Friendly/Insrumental (p/s)	30
82	Le Maitre KA 101	Cest La Vie/Instrumental	20

X-COLLECTOR
83	So So SOSO 027	T.V. Set/Christine	25

X-DREAMYSTS
78	Good Vibrations GOT 5	Right Way Home/Dance Away Love (p/s)	15

X-E-CUTORS

MINT VALUE £

79	Polydor 2059 129	Bad News/Money Talks (p/s)	10
80	Polydor 2059 235	I Don't Wanna Go/Silly Games (p/s)	10
80	Polydor 2059 252	Stay The Way You Are/Race Against Time (p/s)	10
80	Polydor	XDREAMYSTS (LP)	25

X-E-CUTORS
79	Rok ROK 13/14	Too Far To Look Inside My Head/X-FILMS: After My Blood (die-cut co. sleeve)	15

XERO
83	Brickyard XERO 1	Oh Baby/Hold On (2-track issue, p/s, Moon Williams on vocals)	15
83	Brickyard XERO 1	Oh Baby/Hold On/Lone Wolf (3-track limited issue, p/s)	8
83	Brickyard XERO 1T	Oh Baby/Hold On/Lone Wolf (12", plain card sleeve with sticker, withdrawn)	15

(see also Bruce Dickinson, Iron Maiden)

X-FILMS
79	Rok ROK XIII/XIV	After My Blood/X-E-CUTORS: Too Far To Look Inside My Head (die-cut co. sleeve)	15

XILES
64	Xiles 80-XIL-1	THE XILES (EP, home-made p/s)	40
65	Xiles XIL 004	Our Love Will Never End/The Only People In This World	25

XIT
72	Rare Earth SREA 4002	PLIGHT OF THE RED MAN (LP)	15

XL5
63	HMV POP 1148	XL5 (Zero G)/Caviare	20
63	HMV 7EG 8802	FIREBALL AND OTHER TITLES (EP, 2 tracks by Don Spencer)	50

XL5'S
80	Fourplay FOUR 004	Fireball/Misirlou	8

X-MAL DEUTSCHLAND
83	4AD AD 311	Incubus Succubus II/Vito (12" p/s, with "Vito" listed as A-side)	10
83	4AD CAD 302	FETISCH (LP, inner)	20
84	4AD CAD 197	TOCSIN (LP)	20
87	Xile XMAL P1	VIVA (LP)	20

X-MEN (1)
84	Creation CRE 006	Do The Ghost/Talk (foldaround p/s in bag, orange/blue or yellow/green p/s)	8
85	Creation CRE 013	Spiral Girl/Bad Girl (foldaround p/s in polyester bag)	8

X-MEN (2)
91	Mutant 12 MUTATE 1	Mutants (By Wolverine)/Mutants (By Storm) (12")	30
91	Mutant 12 MUTATE 2	Childs Play (Mix 1)/(Mix 2)/Read Your Mind (12")	35
91	Mutant 12 MUTATE 3	Breakout/Phase 2 (12")	20
92	Mutant 12 MUTATE 7	Return Of A Simple Song/Make It So (12")	10
92	Mutant 12 MUTATE 9	Make It So (Vocal)/Ragga Dub (12")	12

X-O-DUS
79	Factory FAC 11	English Black Boys/See Them A-Come (12", dark-grey textured p/s, later light grey p/s)	20

XPERTS
80	XP001	Race/Beat Me	15

XPOZEZ
81	Retaliation FIGHT 1	SYSTEMS KILL EP (photocopied sleeve with insert stating that if you want a proper sleeve to send the band a SAE)	60
82	Red Rhino RED 15	1,000 Marching Feet/Terminal Case (p/s)	7
83	Sexual Phonograph SPH 2	(Be My) New York Doll/It's All Been Done Before (p/s)	7
84	Retaliation/Bearded Viking FIGHT 2	BURNOUT YOUTH EP (folded poster p/s with lyrics and photos)	10
85	Children Of The Revolution COR 2	FORCEFED THE TRUTH DRUG (EP)	10

X PRESS
75	A Rover AR 03	Tell Me Baby/High Road	8
74	Magnet MA 011	Tenderness/Black Ivory (4 different coloured labels)	10

X-PRESS
80	Express 1	Junked Up Judy/Stop Start (p/s)	90

X PROJECT
92	X Project XPROJECT 1	Walking In The Air (Mix 1)/(Mix 2)/(Mix 3)/(Mix 4) (12", stamped white label)	40
00	Congo Natty LION 5	Jah Sunshine/Dubplate Mix (12")	15

XPUPILS
81	Skool SKREP 0001	MONTPELLIER NEWS EP	50

X-RAY SPEX
77	Virgin VS 189	Oh Bondage, Up Yours/I Am A Cliche (p/s, with large 'A' to denote promo copy, blue labelsl, A-1 Matrix with 'original' mix)	75
77	Virgin VS 189	Oh Bondage, Up Yours/I Am A Cliche (in p/s, A-1 matrix, 'original' mix)	60
77	Virgin VS 189	Oh Bondage, Up Yours/I Am A Cliche (in p/s, A-2 matrix, 'second' mix)	40
77	Virgin VS 189	Oh Bondage, Up Yours/I Am A Cliche	10
77	Virgin VS 189-12	Oh Bondage, Up Yours/I Am A Cliche (12", company sleeve)	20
78	EMI International INT 553	The Day The World Turned Day-Glo/Lama Poseur (p/s, 15,000 orange vinyl)	15
78	Virgin VS 189	Oh Bondage, Up Yours/I Am A Cliche (p/s, reissue, green/red labels)	8
78	EMI International INT 563	Identity/Let's Submerge (p/s, on pink vinyl)	15
79	EMI International INT 583	Highly Inflammable/Warrior In Woolworths (p/s, on red vinyl)	8
78	EMI International INS 3023	GERM FREE ADOLESCENTS (LP laminated sleeve, with lyric inner sleeve)	40
91	Receiver RRLP 145	OBSESSED WITH YOU - THE EARLY YEARS (LP)	30
91	Receiver RRLP 140	LIVE AT THE ROXY CLUB (LP)	18
01	Earmark 640005	GERM FREE ADOLESCENTS (LP, reissue, clear vinyl)	15

(see also Poly Styrene, Essential Logic)

X-RAYS
59	London HLR 8805	Chinchilla/Out Of Control	35
59	London HLR 8805	Chinchilla/Out Of Control (78)	20

XS DISCHARGE
80	G. Marxist COMMINIQUE 3	Across The Border/Frustration (p/s)	15

XS ENERGY

MINT VALUE £

80	Groucho Marxist WH 3	Life's A Wank (p/s)	20

XS ENERGY
78	World WRECK 1	Eighteen/Jenny's Alright/Horrorscope! (numbered foldover yellow or green p/s, stamped white labels)	40
79	Dead Good DEAD 1	Eighteen/Jenny's Alright/Horrorscope! (reissue, 'National Souvenir Issue', different foldover p/s, stamped white labels)	10
79	Dead Good DEAD 1	Eighteen/Jenny's Alright/Horrorscope! (stamped white sleeve & yellow printed labels)	10
79	Dead Good DEAD 3	Use You/Imaginary (p/s)	15

XTC
77	Virgin VS 188	Science Friction/She's So Square (unreleased, in picture sleeve)	3000
77	Virgin VS 188	Science Friction/She's So Square (unreleased, no picture sleeve)	150
78	Virgin VS 201	Statue Of Liberty/Hang On To The Night (p/s)	8
78	Virgin VS 209	This Is Pop?/Heatwave (p/s)	8
78	Virgin VS 231	Are You Receiving Me/Instant Tunes (p/s)	8
79	Virgin VS 259	Life Begins At The Hop/Homo Safari (30,000 clear vinyl, PVC sleeve & insert)	8
80	Virgin VS 365	Generals And Majors/Don't Lose Your Temper//Smokeless Zone/ The Somnambulist (double pack)	6
81	Virgin VS 372	Towers Of London/Set Myself On Fire (live)//Battery Brides (live)/ Scissor Man (double pack)	6
81	RSO RSO 71	Take This Town/RUTS: Babylon's Burning (p/s)	6
82	Virgin VS 490	No Thugs In Our House/Chain Of Command/Limelight/ Over Rusty Water (9" die-cut gatefold p/s)	6
92	Virgin VS 1426	Wrapped In Grey (p/s, withdrawn, 2,000 only)	30
92	Virgin VSCDT 1426	WRAPPED IN GREY (CD EP, withdrawn, 2,000 only)	40
78	Virgin V 2095	WHITE MUSIC (LP, with black inner sleeve)	20
78	Virgin V 2108	GO 2 (LP, with insert, 1st 15,000 with bonus 12" EP: "Go +")	25
79	Virgin V 2129	DRUMS AND WIRES (LP, with gatefold insert, 1st 15,000 with free 7": Chain Of Command/"Limelight" [VDJ 30])	25
80	Virgin V 2173	BLACK SEA (LP, with green paper outer sleeve & lyric insert)	25
82	Virgin V 2223	ENGLISH SETTLEMENT (2-LP)	30
83	Virgin V 2264	MUMMER (LP)	25
84	Virgin V 2251	WAXWORKS (LP, with bonus LP, "Beeswax")	25
84	Virgin V 2325	THE BIG EXPRESS (LP, circular sleeve & lyric inner)	25
86	Virgin V 2399	SKYLARKING (LP)	25
89	Virgin V 2381	ORANGES & LEMONS (2-LP)	30
92	Virgin V 2699	NONSUCH (2-LP)	70
99	Cooking Vinyl COOK 172	APPLE VENUS (LP, inner)	100
99	Cooking Vinyl COOK 188	HOMESPUN (LP)	40
00	Cooking Vinyl COOK 194	WASP STAR (2-LP, gatefold, inners)	60
01	Idea IDEA 004	HOMEGROWN (2-LP)	80
10	Ape House APELP044D	SKYLARKING (2-LP, reissue, hardbound book edition)	100
10	Ape House APELP044D	SKYLARKING (2-LP, reissue)	40
16	Ape House APELPD105	ENGLISH SETTLEMENT (2-LP, reissue, box set with CD and booklet)	45

(see also Mr Partridge, Barry Andrews, Three Wise Men, Dukes Of Stratosphere Colonel)

XTRACT
83	Pax PAX 10	Blame It On The Youth/War Heroes/Iron Lady/Boys In Blue (p/s)	25

XTRAVERTS
78	Spike SRTS SP 001	Blank Generation/A-Lad-In-Sane (p/s)	90
78	Rising Sun RS 1	Police State/PLASTIC PEOPLE: Demolition (p/s, multi-coloured vinyl)	60
81	Xtraverts XTRA 001	Speed/1984 (white labels, 'photo' foldout poster p/s)	35
81	Xtraverts XTRA 001	Speed/1984 (white labels, 'no photo' foldout poster p/s)	50
97	Bin Liner RUBBISH LP 001	SO MUCH HATE (LP)	20

XTREME
80	Xtreme IS/X/1045	The Tramp/The Latest Craze (For Alison)	40

XX
09	Young Turks YT 023	Crystalised/Hot Like Fire (p/s)	8
10	Young Turks YT 041	Do You Mind?/Hot Like Fire/Teardrops/Blood Red Moon (die-cut p/s with 3 inner p/s, tour issue)	20
09	Young Turks YT031LP	XX (LP, CD, poster)	25
13	Young Turks YT104	XX (11 x 7", box set)	40
10	Young Turks YT031LP	XX (LP, 12", etched, 3 prints, 500 only)	50
13	Young Turks YT105	COEXIST (11 x 7", box set)	35

XY LOVE
84	Moonboule BOULE 1	Whistle And They'll Come/Cinnamon Girl	20

Y

YABBY U/YABBY YOU/YABBY YOUTH
78	Prophets PHTS 2337	King Pharaoh Plague On The Land/Babylon Kingdom Fall (12")	30
78	Grove Music GMDM 6	Jah Vengeance/Free Africa (12", as Vivian "Yabby U" Jackson with Trinity)	50
79	Grove Music GMDM 18	Babylon A Fall/TONY TUFF - Falling Babylon (12")	40
79	Grove Music GMDM 24	Lady Lady/Stop Your Quarelling (12", B-side with Tommy McCook)	30
76	Lucky PD LPYU	RAM-A-DAM (LP, white sleeve with separate cover sheet)	250
76	Prophets VJ 8124	KING TUBBY'SPROPHECY OF DUB (LP, green label, plain sleeve)	300
77	Grove Music GMLP 001	DELIVER ME FROM MY ENEMIES (LP, credited to The Yabby You Vibration on sleeve)	60
77	Grove Music GMLP 004	BEWARE DUB (LP)	150
78	Nationwide PRO 001	CHANT DOWN BABYLON KINGDOM (LP)	120

YACHTS

MINT VALUE £

78	RAMA/EVE PD LP YU	RAM-A-DAM (LP, reissue of Lucky PD LPYU)	200
80	Grove/Island ILPS 9615	JAH JAH WAY (LP)	40
82	WLN WNLP001	YABBY YOU MEETS SLY 'N' ROBBIE (LP, with Tommy McCook)	20
84	Greensleeves GREL 86	COLLECTION (LP)	30
97	Blood & Fire BAFLP 021	JESUS DREAD 1972 - 1977 (4-LP)	50

(see also Vivian Jackson & the Prophets)

YACHTS
77	Stiff BUY 19	Suffice To Say/Freedom (Is A Heady Wine)	6
78	Radar ADA 23	Look Back In Love (Not In Anger)/I Can't Stay Long (p/s, blue vinyl)	6
80	Radar RAD 27	YACHTS WITHOUT RADAR (LP, die-cut sleeve)	15

(see also Big In Japan)

YADS
| 92 | Fairfields YAD 2 | Yippee For Shtonk/It's There, You Mong (p/s) | 7 |

YA HO WA 13
| 83 | Psycho PSYCHO 2 | GOLDEN SUNRISE (LP, 319 copies only, different coloured vinyl) | 60 |

(see also Seeds)

YAKS
| 65 | Decca F 12115 | Yakety Yak/Back In '57 | 15 |

YAMASUKI
| 05 | Finders Keepers FKR 002LP | LE MONDE FABULEUX DES (LP, insert) | 35 |

YAMASUKIS
| 71 | Dandelion DAN 7004 | Yamasuki/Aieada (p/s) | 15 |

YAMI BOLO
| 86 | Greensleeves GREL 140 | JAH JAH MADE THEM ALL (LP) | 25 |

YANA
56	HMV POP 252	Climb Up The Wall/If You Don't Love Me	20
57	HMV POP 340	Mr. Wonderful/Too Close For Comfort	8
58	HMV POP 481	I Need You/I Miss You Mama	7
58	HMV POP 546	Papa And Mama/In The Morning	7

YANCEY
| 79 | Octane WS 302 | Standing Waiting/Woman (no p/s) | 20 |
| 79 | Hammer HS 302 | Standing Waiting/Woman (reissue) | 8 |

JIMMY YANCEY
54	HMV 7EG 8062	JIMMY YANCEY (EP)	20
55	HMV 7EG 8083	JIMMY YANCEY (EP)	20
58	Vogue EPV 1203	YANCEY'S PIANO (EP)	20
54	London AL 3525	JIMMY YANCEY - A LOST RECORDING DATE (10" LP)	25
56	Vogue LDE 166	JAZZ IMMORTALS VOLUME 2 (10" LP)	30
68	Atlantic 590 018	LOWDOWN DIRTY BLUES (LP)	15

MAMA YANCEY/DON EWELL
| 57 | Tempo LAP 7 | MAMA YANCEY-DON EWELL (10" LP) | 30 |

ZALMAN YANOVSKY
67	Kama Sutra KAS 209	As Long As You're Here/Ereh Er'uoy Sa Gnol Sa (unreleased)	0
67	Pye International 7N 25438	As Long As You're Here/Ereh Er'uoy Sa Gnol Sa	8
71	Kama Sutra 2316 003	ALIVE AND WELL IN ARGENTINA (LP)	18

(see also Mugwumps, Lovin' Spoonful)

GLENN YARBOROUGH
| 65 | RCA 1449 | Baby The Rain Must Fall/I've Been To Town | 7 |
| 66 | RCA 1555 | Everybody's Rich But Us/Walk On Little Baby | 6 |

YARD ACT
20	Zen FC FC 002S	The Trappers Pelts/Fixer Upper (p/s, numbered)	30
20	Zen FC FC 002S	The Trappers Pelts/Fixer Upper (yellow print p/s, numbered)	45
20	Zen FC FC 002S	The Trappers Pelts/Fixer Upper (red print p/s, numbered)	45
21	Zen FC FC 004S	Peanuts/Dark Days (silver p/s)	20
21	Zen FC FC 004S	Peanuts/Dark Days (peanut coloured p/s, peanut coloured vinyl, insert and sticker)	35
21	Zen FC FC 004S	Peanuts/Dark Days (green p/s, peanut coloured vinyl, insert and sticker)	40
21	Zen FC FC 004S	Peanuts/Dark Days (red p/s, peanut coloured vinyl, insert and sticker)	40
21	Zen FC FC 004S	Peanuts/Dark Days (yellow p/s, peanut coloured vinyl, insert and sticker)	40

YARDBIRDS
64	Columbia DB 7283	I Wish You Would/A Certain Girl	40
64	Columbia DB 7391	Good Morning Little Schoolgirl/I Ain't Got You	40
65	Columbia DB 7499	For Your Love/Got To Hurry	10
65	Columbia DB 7594	Heart Full Of Soul/Steeled Blues	10
65	Columbia DB 7706	Evil Hearted You/Still I'm Sad (some copies with A-side miscredited to Samwell-Smith & McCartney)	7
66	Columbia DB 7848	Shapes Of Things/You're A Better Man Than I	7
66	Columbia DB 7848	Shapes Of Things/Still I'm Sad (mispressing)	45
66	Columbia DB 7928	Over, Under, Sideways, Down/Jeff's Boogie	15
66	Columbia DB 8024	Happenings Ten Years Time Ago/Psycho Daisies	35
67	Columbia DB 8165	Little Games/Puzzles	35
64	Columbia SEG 8421	FIVE YARDBIRDS (EP)	100
67	Columbia SEG 8521	OVER UNDER SIDEWAYS DOWN (EP)	225
64	Columbia 33SX 1677	FIVE LIVE YARDBIRDS (LP, 1st pressing, blue/black label, flipback sleeve)	250
69	Columbia 33SX 1677	FIVE LIVE YARDBIRDS (LP, 2nd pressing, black/silver label, flipback sleeve)	25
60s	Columbia TA SX 6063	FIVE LIVE YARDBIRDS (reel-to-reel tape)	20
66	Columbia SCXC 28	HAVING A RAVE UP WITH THE YARDBIRDS (LP, export issue)	200
66	Columbia SX 6063	THE YARDBIRDS (LP, 1st pressing, blue/black label, flipback sleeve, mono)	70
66	Columbia SCX 6063	THE YARDBIRDS (LP, 1st pressing, blue/black label, flipback sleeve, stereo)	60
69	Columbia S(C) X 6063	THE YARDBIRDS (LP, 2nd pressing, black/silver label, flipback sleeve)	25
70	Columbia S(C)X 6063	THE YARDBIRDS (LP, 3rd pressing, black/silver label, non-flipback sleeve; misprinted	20

Per YARROH

			MINT VALUE £
		without front cover illustration)	
70	Columbia S(C)X 6063	THE YARDBIRDS (LP, 3rd pressing, black/silver label, non-flipback sleeve)	20
84	Charly BOX 104	SHAPES OF THINGS (LP, box set)	50

(see also Eric Clapton, Jeff Beck, Jimmy Page, Keith Relf, Reign, Sonny Boy Williamson & Yardbirds, Shoot)

PER YARROH
88	HMV PY 1	Laughing Inside/Laughing Inside (p/s, promo only; actually by Roy Harper)	7

(see also Roy Harper)

TOM YATES
67	CBS BPG 63094	SECOND CITY SPIRITUAL (LP, as Thomas Yates)	100
72	President PTLS 1053	LOVE COMES WELL ARMED (LP, with booklet)	30
77	Satril SATL 4007	SONG OF THE SHIMMERING WAY (LP, with insert)	20

TOMMY YATES
65	Pye 7N 15980	Rattle Of A Toy/Long Time Gone	10

YA-YA
83	Buzz BUZZ 2	What Can I Say/Maybe Tomorrow	6

Y BLEW
67	Qualiton QSP 7001	Maes 'B'/Beth Sy'n Dod Rhyngom Ni (p/s)	50

Y DILFOR
73	Westwood WSR 002	Y DILFOR (LP)	30

YE ASCOYNE D'ASCOYNES
92	Hangman GIBBET 1	JUST THE BIGGEST THING (EP)	8

(see also Dentists, Claim)

YEAH YEAH YEAHS
01	Wichita WEBB 029T	YEAH YEAH YEAHS EP: Bang/Mystery Girl/Art Star/Miles Away/Our Time (12", p/s)	10
03	Polydor 981 141-4	Maps/Countdown/Miles Away (p/s)	10
07	Polydor 1741099	IS IS EP (2 x 7")	15
03	Dress Up 0760611	FEVER TO TELL (LP picture disc with bonus track 'Poor Song')	60
06	Polydor 985 295-6	SHOW YOUR BONES (LP)	15
09	Polydor 2702576	IT'S BLITZ! (LP)	15

YEAR ONE
69	Major Minor MM 660	Eli's Comin'/Will You Be Staying After Sunday	12

YEARS
79	Tuff Going TGF 123	TUFF GOING EP (p/s, 500 only)	80

(see also Chameleons, Sun And The Moon)

SAM YEBOAH
88	Asona ARLP 016	MEBA FIE (LP)	15

YEH YEH
85	Berlin BRS 001	You Will Pay/7 Bells (1st pressing in grey p/s)	15
86	TMA BRS 001	You Will Pay/7 Bells (later pressing in colour p/s)	10

YELLO
81	Do It DUN 11	Bimbo/I.T. Splash (p/s)	6
82	Do It DUNIT 13	Bostich/Downtown Samba/She's Got A Gun/Daily Disco (12", p/s)	10
82	Do It DUNIT 23	Pinball Cha Cha/Smile On You (12", p/s)	12
83	Stiff DBUY 191	Lost Again/Base For Alec//Let Me Cry/She's Got A Gun (double pack)	6
86	Mercury MERDP 218	Goldrush/She's Got A Gun (live at Palladium N.Y.)//I Love You/ Desire (double pack, unreleased)	0
81	Do It RIDE 4	SOLID PLEASURE (LP)	20
81	Do It RIDE 8	CLARO QUE SI! (LP)	20
83	Stiff SEEZ 48	YOU GOTTA SAY YES TO ANOTHER EXCESS (LP, with bonus white label 12": "I Love You"/"Lost Again"/"You Gotta Say To Another Excess [Remix]"Pumping Velvet")	15
85	Vertigo 822 820-1	STELLA (LP)	20
87	Mercury MERH 100	ONE SECOND (LP, with bonus 12" in p/s: "Call It Love (Trego Snare Version 2)"/"Santiago [live at Roxy New York]")	20
87	Mercury MERH 100	ONE SECOND (LP)	18
88	Mercury 836 778-1	FLAG (LP, HMV competition issue, 100 only)	40
91	Mercury 848 791-1	BABY (LP)	50
94	Mercury 522 496-1	ZEBRA (LP)	125
95	Urban 527 603-1	HANDS ON YELLO (2-LP)	60
97	Mercury 534 353-1	POCKET UNIVERSE (2-LP)	150

(see also Associates)

YELLOW
70	CBS 4869	Roll It Down The Hill/Living A Lie	50

YELLOW BALLOON
67	Stateside SS 2008	Yellow Balloon/Noollab Wolley	20
68	Stateside SS 2124	Stained Glass Window/Can't Get Enough Of Your Love	20

YELLOW BELLOW ROOM BOOM
68	CBS 3205	Seeing Things Green/Easy Life	30

(see also 10cc, Frabjoy & Runcible Spoon)

YELLOW BIRD
74	Magnet MAG 16	Attack Attack/Right On	12

YELLOW MAGIC ORCHESTRA
79	A&M AMLH68506	YELLOW MAGIC ORCHESTRA (LP)	20
80	A&M AMSP 7502	FIRECRACKER (LP, clear plastic sleeve, yellow vinyl)	15
81	A&M AMLH 64853	BGM (LP)	15
82	Alfa ALF 85664	SOLID STATE SURVIVOR (LP)	15

(see also Ruichi Sakamoto, Yukihiro Takahashi)

YELLOW PAGES
68	Page One POF 090	Here Comes Jane/Ring-A-Ding	25

(see also Mirage)

YELLOW PAYGES
70	UNI UNS 516	Follow The Bouncing Ball/Little Woman	8

YELLOW 6
			MINT VALUE £
90s	Enraptured RAPTLP 36	OVERTONE (2-LP, clear vinyl, numbered, handprinted sleeve, 300 only)	20

YELLOW TAXI
70	President PT 296	Anna Laura Lee/Mary Ann	15

YELLOWMAN
82	Greensleeves GREL 36	MISTER YELLOWMAN (LP)	15
82	Arrival ALP 004	FOR YOUR EYES ONLY (LP, as Yellowman And Fathead)	15
82	Greensleeves GREL 44	BAD BOY SKANKING (LP, as Yellowman and Fathead)	18
82	Greensleeves GREL 49	THE YELLOW, THE PURPLE AND THE NANCY (LP, with Fathead, Purpleman and Sister Nancy)	15
84	Pama PMLP 3215	OPERATION RADICATION (10" LP)	20
84	Greensleeves GREL 57	ZUNGGUZUNGGUGUZUNGGUNZENG!!! (LP)	18
84	Arrival ARLP 013	UNDER ME FAT THING (LP)	15

YELLOWSTONE & VOICE
72	Parlophone R5965	Philosopher/The Flying Dutchman	12
72	Regal Zono. SRZA 8511	YELLOWSTONE & VOICE (LP)	20

YEMM & YEMEN
66	Columbia DB 8022	Black Is The Night/Do Blondes Really Have More Fun?	35

YEOW
82	Patch YEOW 001	Prepare Yourself/Energy (12")	25

YES
69	Atlantic 584 280	Sweetness/Something's Coming	60
69	Atlantic 584 298	Looking Around/Everydays (unreleased; demos may exist)	175
70	Atlantic 584 323	Time And A Word/The Prophet	150
70	Atlantic 2091 004	Sweet Dreams/Dear Father	45
71	Atlantic 2814 003	I've Seen All Good People (a) Your Move/Starship Trooper (a) Life Seeker (promo only)	75
72	6-A1/-B1	Siberian Khatru/And You And I (white label promo)	50
77	Atlantic K 10985	Going For The One/Parallels (unreleased, copies may exist)	60
77	Atlantic K 10985T	Going For The One (Extended)/Parallels (12", unreleased, copies may exist)	40
70s	Lyntone LYN 2535	Interview/Five Songs (flexidisc or vinyl, with 80-page Yes songbook)	70
70s	Lyntone LYN 2535	Interview/Five Songs (flexidisc or vinyl)	35
69	Atlantic 588 190	YES (LP, gatefold, red/plum label with lyric insert)	175
70	Atlantic 2400 006	TIME AND A WORD (LP, red/plum label, with lyric insert)	150
71	Atlantic 2400 101	THE YES ALBUM (LP, red/plum label, gatefold sleeve)	150
71	Atlantic 2401 019	FRAGILE (LP, red/plum label, gatefold sleeve with booklet)	125
72	Atlantic K 50012	CLOSE TO THE EDGE (LP, 1st pressing with A1/B1 matrix numbers, no "W" logo at 3 O'clock, textured sleeve inside and outside, green inner sleeve, darker with lyric insert)	70
73	Atlantic K 60045	YESSONGS (3-LP, wide spine, 'book opening' gatefold sleeve printed by 'Robor Ltd' , no 'W' logo on labels, outline 'Yes' on inner sleeves, all matrixes end in '1')	25
73	Atlantic K 80001	TALES FROM TOPOGRAPHIC OCEANS (2-LP)	25
74	Atlantic K 50096	RELAYER (LP, gatefold sleeve)	30
77	Atlantic DSK 50379	GOING FOR THE ONE (LP, as 3 x 12" singles, promo only)	100
77	Atlantic K 50379	GOING FOR THE ONE (LP)	18
80	Atlantic K 50842	CLASSIC YES (LP, with bonus 7" "Roundabout"/"Your Move" [SAM 141])	15
80	Atlantic K 50842	CLASSIC YES (LP, promo, with different sleeve)	30

(see also Jon Anderson, Hans Christian, Syn, Syndicats, Winston's Fumbs, Warriors, Federals, Peter Banks, Flash, Asia, Rick Wakeman, Steve Howe, Refugee, Chris Squire)

JOHN YLVISAKER
68	Avantgarde AV 107	COOL LIVIN' (LP)	75

YOBS
77	NEMS NES 114	Run Rudolph Run/The Worm Song (p/s)	15
78	Yob YOB 79	Silent Night/Stille Nacht (p/s)	7
81	Safari YULE 1	Rub-A-Dum-Dum/Another Christmas (p/s)	7
82	Fresh FRESH 41	Yobs On 45/The Ballad Of Warrington (p/s)	7

(see also Boys)

MAHARISHI MAHESH YOGI
67	Liberty LBS 83075E	MAHARISHI MAHESH YOGI (LP)	25

SUSUMU YOKOTA
99	Leaf BAY 9	IMAGE 1983-1998 (LP)	15
00	Leaf BAY 13	SAKURA (2-LP)	25

YO LA TENGO
95	Duophonic Super 45s DS 45-10	Evanescent Psychic Pez Drop/STEREOLAB: Long Hair Of Death (gig single, fluorescent yellow vinyl,	40
96	Earworm WORM 4	Blue - Green Arrow/Watching The Sun Set On Johnny Carson (2,000 only, 100 in handmade p/s)	12
96	Earworm WORM 4	Blue - Green Arrow/Watching The Sun Set On Johnny Carson (2,000 only)	8
87	What Goes On GOES ON13	NEW WAVE HOT DOGS (LP)	20
87	Shigaku SHIGLP 2	RIDE THE TIGER (LP)	30
89	What Goes On GOES ON28	PRESIDENT YO LA TENGO (LP)	20

YOLANDA
60	Triumph RGM 1007	With This Kiss/Don't Tell Me Not To Love You	40

(see also Kenny Graham & His Satellites)

STEVE YORK'S CAMELO PARDALIS
73	Virgin V 2003	MANOR LIVE (LP)	20

(see also Elkie Brooks, Boz Scaggs, Lol Coxhill, Graham Bond, Mike Patto)

NOLA YORK
67	Philips BF 1558	I Can Hear You Calling/Clown Face	6
68	Philips BF 1714	Ciao Baby/We'll Get To Heaven	6

(see also Bow Bells)

PETE YORK PERCUSSION BAND
73	Decca TXS 109	PERCUSSION BAND (LP, with Ian Paice, gatefold sleeve)	50

Rusty YORK

MINT VALUE £

(see also Spencer Davis Group, Hardin & York, Deep Purple)

RUSTY YORK
| 58 | Parlophone R 4398 | Peggy Sue/Shake 'Em Up Baby (unissued, demos only) | 1500 |

(see also Bonnie Lou & Rusty York)

YORK BROTHERS
54	Parlophone CMSP 5	Why Don't You Open The Door?/You're My Every Dream Come True (export issue)	20
54	Parlophone CMSP 22	Strange Town/Three O'Clock Blues (export issue)	20
58	Parlophone GEP 8736	COUNTRY AND WESTERN (EP)	40
58	Parlophone GEP 8753	COUNTRY AND WESTERN NO. 2 (EP)	40

THOM YORKE
07	XL XLT 238P	Harrowdown Hill/The Drunkk Machine/Jetstream, (12" promo)	10
08	XL XLT 335	Eraser Rmxs 1 (12", 2000 only)	15
08	XL XLT 336	Eraser Rmxs 2 (12", 2000 only)	15
08	XL XLT 337	Eraser Rmxs 3 (12", 2000 only)	15
09	_Xurbia _Xendless XX002	Feelingpulledapartbyhorses/Thehollowearth (12", 8000 only)	10
09	Mezzotint 6015665427	All For The Best/MARK MULCAHY: Ciao My Shining Star	6
11	Text 10	Ego/Mirror (12", with Burial and Four Tet, black labels on both sides)	18
06	XL XLLP 200	THE ERASER (LP, 3D effect on embossed sleeve)	30
15	Landgrab GRAB 001	TOMORROW'S MODERN BOXES (LP, white vinyl in resealable printed bag)	20

(see also Radiohead, Atoms for Peace)

YO3
| 94 | General Production GENPX 22 | DEEP SLEEP (12" EP) | 30 |
| 94 | General Production GPRLP 05 | BITTER SWEET (2-LP) | 30 |

YOU
| 80 | Ram RAMYOU2 | THE NIGHT AND MUSIC (EP) | 20 |

YOU KNOW WHO GROUP
| 65 | London HLR 9947 | Roses Are Red My Love/Playboy | 20 |

YOU BAND
| 84 | Guardian GRC 84 | Jonathan Oracle/Disco Inferno (p/s) | 20 |

CHRIS YOULDEN
73	Deram DM 377	Nowhere Road/Standing On The Corner	12
73	Deram SML 1099	NOWHERE ROAD (LP, lyric insert)	60
74	Deram SML 1112	CITY CHILD (LP)	50

BARRY YOUNG
| 65 | Dot DS 16756 | One Has My Name (The Other Has My Heart)/Show Me The Way | 10 |

BILLY YOUNG
| 72 | Atlantic K 10277 | The Sloopy/Same Old Thing Again | 8 |
| 72 | Jay Boy BOY 55 | I'm Available/Sweet Woman | 8 |

BILLY YOUNG/LIZZIE MILES
| 56 | HMV 7EG 8178 | THE BLUES THEY SANG (EP, with Jelly Roll Morton) | 20 |

BRETT YOUNG (& GHOST SQUAD)
| 63 | Pye 7N 15578 | Guess What/It Just Happened | 12 |
| 64 | Pye 7N 15641 | Never Again/You Can't Fool Me (as Brett Young & Ghost Squad) | 12 |

COLIN YOUNG
| 71 | Trend 6099 005 | Anytime At All/You're No Good | 8 |

DARREN YOUNG
| 63 | Parlophone R 4919 | My Tears Will Turn To Laughter/I've Just Fallen For Someone | 20 |

(see also Johnny Gentle)

DESI YOUNG
| 70 | Pressure Beat PB 5504 | News Flash/JOE GIBBS & DESTROYERS: News Flash - Version | 25 |
| 72 | Blue Mountain BM 1017 | Don't Know Why I Love You/BONGO HERMAN: Skank | 8 |

(see also Desi Roots)

EDDY YOUNG
| 71 | Beacon BEA 178 | A Little On The Heavy Side/Give'Em A Hand | 12 |

FARON YOUNG
55	Capitol CL 14336	Live Fast, Love Hard, Die Young/Forgive Me, Dear	30
56	Capitol CL 14574	If You Ain't Lovin' (You Ain't Livin')/All Right	20
56	Capitol CL 14655	I've Got 5 Dollars And It's Saturday Night/You're Still Mine	30
57	Capitol CL 14735	The Shrine Of St. Cecilia/He Was There	8
57	Capitol CL 14762	Love Has Finally Come My Way/Moonlight Mountain	8
57	Capitol CL 14793	Honey Stop! (And Think Of Me)/Vacation's Over	8
58	Capitol CL 14822	Snowball/The Locket	6
58	Capitol CL 14860	I Can't Dance/Rosalie (Is Gonna Get Married)	8
58	Capitol CL 14891	Every Time I'm Kissing You/Alone With You	6
59	Capitol CL 14975	Last Night At A Party/A Long Time Ago	8
59	Capitol CL 15050	I Hear You Talkin'/Country Girl	25

GEORGIE YOUNG & ROCKIN' BOCS
| 58 | London HLU 8748 | Nine More Miles/The Sneak | 15 |

HARRY YOUNG
| 65 | Dot DS 16756 | Show Me The Way/One Has My Name | 10 |

YOUNG JESSIE
| 58 | London HLE 8544 | Shuffle In The Gravel/Make Believe | 300 |
| 58 | London HLE 8544 | Shuffle In The Gravel/Make Believe (78) | 50 |

JIMMY YOUNG
54	Decca F 10232	A Baby Cried/Remember Me	10
54	Decca F 10406	Give Me Your Word/Lonely Nightingale	10
55	Decca F 10444	These Are The Things We'll Share/Don't Go To Strangers	8
55	Decca F 10483	If Anyone Finds This, I Love You/The Sand And The Sea	8
55	Decca F 10502	Unchained Melody/Help Me Forget	15

Joe E. YOUNG & TONIKS

MINT VALUE £

55	Decca F 10597	The Man From Laramie/No Arms Can Ever Hold You	15
55	Decca F 10640	Someone On Your Mind/I Look At You	15
56	Decca F 10694	Chain Gang/Capri In May	10
56	Decca F 10736	Rich Man, Poor Man/The Wayward Wind	10
56	Decca F 10774	More/I'm Gonna Steal You Away	10
57	Decca F 10875	Round And Round/Walkin' After Midnight	6

JOE E. YOUNG & TONIKS
68	Toast TT 502	Life Time Of Lovin'/Flower In My Hand	20
69	Toast TT 514	Good Day Sunshine/Life Time Of Lovin'	20
68	Toast (S)TLP 1	SOUL BUSTER! (LP)	40

JOHNNIE YOUNG
| 67 | Polydor 56199 | Every Christian/Epitath To Mr Simon Sir | 20 |
| 67 | Polydor 56186 | Craise Finton Kirk/I Am The World | 20 |

JOHNNY YOUNG
67	Decca F 22548	Step Back/Cara Lyn (as Johnny Young & Kompany)	15
67	Decca F 22636	Lady/Good Evening Girl	10
68	RCA RCA 1826	Always Thinking Of You/Dreaming Country (as Johnny Young Four)	10
70	Blue Horizon 7-63852	FAT MANDOLIN (LP)	90

KAREN YOUNG
65	Mercury MF 943	I'm Yours, You're Mine/Are You Kidding	8
65	Pye 7N 15956	We'll Start The Party Again/Wonderful Summer	8
68	Major Minor MM 584	Too Much Of A Good Thing/You Better Sit Down	50
70	Major Minor MM 691	One Tin Soldier/Que Sera Sera (B-side arranged by Paul McCartney)	12
69	M. Minor MMLP/SMLP 66	SINGS NOBODY'S CHILD AND 13 OTHER GREAT SONGS (LP)	20

KATHY YOUNG & INNOCENTS
| 61 | Top Rank JAR 534 | A Thousand Stars/Eddie My Darling | 40 |
| 61 | Top Rank JAR 554 | Happy Birthday Blues/Someone To Love | 30 |

(see also Innocents)

K.G. YOUNG
| 69 | CBS 4302 | Spider/Spider Woogie 9th Movement | 30 |

LEON YOUNG STRINGS
| 64 | Pye 7N 15646 | This Boy/Glad All Over | 40 |

LESTER YOUNG (QUINTET)
56	Vogue V 2362	New Lester Leaps In/She's Funny That Way	6
56	Vogue V 2384	You're Driving Me Crazy/East Of The Sun	6
56	Vogue EPV 1127	LESTER YOUNG (EP)	10
53	Mercury MG 25015	KANSAS CITY 7/THE LESTER YOUNG QUARTET (LP, 1 side each)	30
55	Felsted EDL 87014	BATTLE OF THE SAXES (10" LP)	35
55	Columbia Clef 33C 9001	LESTER YOUNG WITH THE OSCAR PETERSON TRIO (10" LP)	40
56	Columbia Clef 33C 9015	LESTER YOUNG (10" LP)	40
56	Columbia Clef 33CX 10031	THE PRESIDENT, LESTER YOUNG (LP)	40
56	Columbia Clef 33CX 10054	THE JAZZ GIANTS '56 (LP)	40
57	Columbia Clef 33CX 10070	PRES (LP)	40
58	London Jazz LTZ-C 15132	BLUE LESTER (LP)	40
59	HMV CLP 1302	PRES AND TEDDY (LP, with Teddy Wilson)	25

(see also Count Basie, Coleman Hawkins & Lester Young)

LLOYD YOUNG
72	Bullet BU 500	Bread And Butter/SHALIMAR ALLSTARS: Version	15
72	Green Door GD 4037	Shalimar Special/G. MAHTANI ALLSTARS: Version	20
72	Techniques TE 917	High Explosion/ANSELL COLLINS: Version	20

(see also Carey & Lloyd)

YOUNG LOVE
| 80 | Flair FLA 001 | Doing It The English Way/Easy To Do It (p/s) | 40 |

YOUNG MARBLE GIANTS
80	Rough Trade RT 043	Final Day/Radio Silents/Cakewalking/Colossal Youth (p/s)	10
81	Rough Trade RT 059	TESTCARD (EP)	20
80	Rough Trade ROUGH 8	COLOSSAL YOUTH (LP)	50
83	Rough Trade ROUGH 57	NIPPED IN THE BUD (LP, compilation LP with The Gist and Weekend but features 9 Young Marble Giants tracks)	20
84	Rough Trade ROUGHL8	COLOSSAL YOUTH (LP, reissue)	15
07	Domino REWIGLP 32	COLOSSAL YOUTH (LP, reissue)	18

YOUNG MC
| 88 | Delicious Vinyl BRW 120 | KNOW HOW (12", EP) | 20 |

MIGHTY JOE YOUNG
| 69 | Parlophone 5794 | Why Don't You Follow Me/By My Side | 25 |
| 72 | Delmark DS 629 | BLUES WITH A TOUCH OF SOUL (LP, blue label) | 22 |

NEIL YOUNG
69	Reprise RS 23405	The Loner/Everybody Knows This Is Nowhere	25
70	Reprise RS 20861	Oh Lonesome Me (Long Version)/Sugar Mountain	30
70	Reprise RS 23462	Down By The River (edit)/Cinnamon Girl (alternate mix)	12
70	Reprise RS 20958	Only Love Can Break Your Heart/Birds	15
71	Reprise RS 23488	When You Dance I Can Really Love/After The Goldrush	10
72	Reprise K 14167	Old Man/The Needle And The Damage Done	6
73	Reprise SAM 15	Don't Be Denied/Love In Mind/Last Dance (p/s, 1-sided, promo only sampler for "Time Fades Away" LP)	30
74	Reprise K 14350	Southern Man/Till The Morning Comes/After The Goldrush/Heart Of Gold (special sleeve)	20
74	Reprise K 14360	Walk On/For The Turnstiles	20
76	Reprise K 14431	Don't Cry No Tears/Stupid Girl	6
80	Reprise K 14509	Captain Kennedy/Stayin' Power	10
69	Reprise RSLP 6317	NEIL YOUNG (LP, with name on front of sleeve)	80

Ralph YOUNG

Year	Label & Cat No	Title	MINT VALUE £
69	Reprise RSLP 6317	NEIL YOUNG (LP, without name on front of sleeve)	100
69	Reprise RSLP 6349	EVERYBODY KNOWS THIS IS NOWHERE (LP)	100
70	Reprise RSLP 6383	AFTER THE GOLDRUSH (LP, gatefold sleeve with lyric insert)	60
71	Reprise K 44059	NEIL YOUNG (LP, reissue)	20
71	Reprise K 44073	EVERYBODY KNOWS THIS IS NOWHERE (LP, reissue)	20
71	Reprise K 44088	AFTER THE GOLDRUSH (LP, reissue, gatefold sleeve with lyric insert)	25
72	Reprise K 54005	HARVEST (LP, thick cardboard gatefold sleeve with insert)	60
72	Reprise K 64015	JOURNEY THROUGH THE PAST (2-LP, soundtrack, fold-out sleeve & inners)	40
73	Reprise K 54010	TIME FADES AWAY (LP, with lyric insert)	40
74	Reprise K 54014	ON THE BEACH (LP, with inner sleeve)	70
75	Reprise K 54040	TONIGHT'S THE NIGHT (LP, gatefold sleeve with inner sleeve & insert)	25
75	Reprise K 54057	ZUMA (LP, with inner sleeve & lyric insert)	35
77	Reprise K 54088	AMERICAN STARS AND BARS (LP, with inner sleeve)	18
77	Reprise K 64037	DECADE (3-LP)	40
78	Reprise K 54099	COMES A TIME (LP)	18
79	Reprise K 54105	RUST NEVER SLEEPS (LP, with inner sleeve & lyric insert)	20
79	Reprise K 64041	LIVE RUST (2-LP, with inner sleeves)	30
80	Reprise K 54109	HAWKS & DOVES (LP, with inner sleeve)	15
82	Geffen GEF 25019	TRANS (LP, inner)	15
85	Geffen GEF 26377	OLD WAYS (LP, inner sleeve)	15
89	Reprise WX257	FREEDOM (LP)	18
90	Geffen WX 374	RAGGED GLORY (LP, inner, with Crazy Horse)	50
92	Reprise 9362450571	HARVEST MOON (LP)	80
92	Reprise 7599 26671-1	WELD (2-LP with Crazy Horse)	60
93	Geffen GEF24252	LUCKY THIRTEEN (LP)	80
93	Reprise 9362-45310-1	UNPLUGGED (LP)	100
94	Reprise 9362-45749-1	SLEEPS WITH ANGELS (2-LP, with Crazy Horse)	100
95	Reprise 9362 45934-1	MIRROR BALL (2-LP, with PEARL JAM)	80
96	Vapor 9362-46171-1	DEAD MAN (2-LP)	150
96	Reprise 9362461711	BROKEN ARROW (2-LP, with Crazy Horse)	100
97	Reprise 9362466521	YEAR OF THE HORSE (2-LP, with Crazy Horse)	100
00	Reprise 9362480361	ROAD ROCK (2-LP, insert)	100
00	Reprise 9362473051	SILVER & GOLD (LP)	20
02	Vapor 9362481111	ARE YOU PASSIONATE? (2-LP)	50
03	Vapor 486992	GREENDALE (3-LP box set with green 7", booklet)	175
06	Reprise 444991	LIVE AT THE FILLMORE EAST (LP, 180gm vinyl)	20
12	Reprise 9362457491	PSYCHEDELIC PILL (3-LP, as Neil Young and Crazy Horse)	30
15	Reprise 9362492611	BLUENOTE CAFE (4-LP)	40
16	Reprise 9362492045	OFFICIAL RELEASE SERIES 8.5-13 (5-LP box set)	50

(see also Buffalo Springfield, Crosby Stills Nash & Young, Stills-Young Band, Crazy Horse)

RALPH YOUNG

55	Brunswick 05466	The Man From Laramie/The Bible Tells Me So	7

(see also Jack Pleis)

ROBERT YOUNG

71	CBS 7350	Rosemary Blue/When Time Began	7

ROGER YOUNG

66	Columbia DB 7869	Sweet, Sweet Morning/Whatcha Gonna Give Me?	60
66	Columbia DB 8092	No Address/It's Been Nice	250

ROY YOUNG (BAND)

59	Fontana H 200	Just Keep It Up/Big Fat Mama	25
59	Fontana H 215	Hey Little Girl/Just Ask Your Heart	20
60	Fontana H 237	I Hardly Know Me/Gilee	20
60	Fontana H 247	Taboo/I'm In Love	15
61	Fontana H 290	You Were Meant For Me/Plenty Of Love (as Roy Young & Hunters)	10
61	Ember EMB S 128	Four And Twenty Thousand Kisses/Late Last Evening	12
71	MCA MKS 5071	Wild Country Wine/New Sun New Horizon (p/s)	8
70	RCA SF 8161	ROY YOUNG BAND (LP)	20

ROY YOUNG

73	MCA MUS 1214	Dig A Hole/I'm A Loner	12

SUSANNAH YOUNG

67	Philips BL 7728	SWEETEST SOUNDS (LP)	15

TED YOUNG

71	Ra 5006	The Day They Gave Our Fish Away/Romany	8

TERRY YOUNG

61	Pye 7N 15321	Maverick/Partners	7
61	Pye 7N 15353	Someone New/Now Forever And A Day	12
62	Pye 7N 15416	Joe's Been A-Gittin' There/They Took John Away	6

TOMMIE YOUNG

73	Contempo C 12	Everybody's Got A Little Devil In Their Soul/Do You Still Feel The Same Way	10
73	Contempo C 23	She Don't Have To See You/That's All Part Of Loving Him	10
74	Contempo CLP 501	DO YOU STILL FEEL THE SAME WAY (LP)	50

VICKI YOUNG

55	Capitol CL 14228	Hearts Of Stone/Tweedlee Dee (triangular centre)	40
55	Capitol CL 14281	Live Fast, Love Hard, Die Young/Zoom, Zoom, Zoom (triangular centre)	25
56	Capitol CL 14528	Steel Guitar/Bye Bye For Just A While	12
56	Capitol CL 14653	Spanish Main/Tell Me In Your Own Sweet Way (with Joe 'Fingers' Carr)	12
56	Capitol EAP1 593	VICKI YOUNG (EP)	35

(see also Joe 'Fingers' Carr)

YOUNG AL CAPONE

71	Green Door GD 4012	Girl Called Clover/Girl Called Clover (Version)	25

YOUNG BLOOD

MINT VALUE £

YOUNG BLOOD
68	Pye 7N 17495	Green Light/Don't Leave Me In The Dark	25
68	Pye 7N 17588	Just How Loud/Masquerade	20
68	Pye 7N 17627	Bang-Shang-A-Lang/I Can't Stop	20
69	Pye 7N 17696	The Continuing Story Of Bungalow Bill/I Will	20

(see also Cozy Powell, Ace Kefford Stand, Big Bertha)

YOUNG BLOOD
84	Landslide LAND 1	FIRST BLOOD (12" EP, p/s)	18

YOUNGBLOODS
69	RCA RCA 1821	Darkness, Darkness/On Sir Francis Drake	10
69	RCA RCA 1877	Get Together/Beautiful	10
69	RCA SF 8026	ELEPHANT MOUNTAIN (LP)	22
70	Warner Bros WS 1878	ROCK FESTIVAL (LP)	15

YOUNG BROTHERS
68	MCA MU 1042	I've Always Wanted Love/Mirror Mirror	15

YOUNG BUCKS
77	Blueport BLU 1	Get Your Feet Back On The Ground/Cold, Cold Morning (p/s)	6

YOUNG DISCIPLES
91	Talkin Loud 510097	ROAD TO FREEDOM (LP, inner)	15

YOUNG EARTH
70	Priory PR3	Silent Eyes/Death To Eliza	50

COLE YOUNGER
74	ABC ABC 4009	Don't Stop/Call Me	10
77	Magnet MAG 112	She's Not My Lover/Don't Use Me	12
80	Ariola AHA 555	Candy/I'd Rather Be Me	6

YOUNG FATHERS
15	Big Dada BD 264Z	Soon Come Soon/Everyguy	6

YOUNGFOLK
68	President PT 136	Lonely Girl/Joey	20

YOUNG FOLK
72	Midas MR 001	RIBBLE VALLEY DREAM (LP)	50

YOUNG FREDDIE
70	Camel CA 38	Drink And Gamble/LENNOX BROWN & HUE ROY: King Of The Road	25

(see also Freddie McGregor)

YOUNG GENTS
67	M&G 01	Lift Up Your Body/Evening Star	30

YOUNG GROWLER & CALYPSO RHYTHM KINGS
66	Columbia DB 7870	Amy The Sunbather/Sweet Trinidad	7
66	Columbia DB 7958	V For Victory/Be Nice To Women (in 'Test Match' p/s)	12
66	Columbia DB 7958	V For Victory/Be Nice To Women	7
66	Columbia SEG 8502	V FOR VICTORY (EP)	12

YOUNG-HOLT TRIO
67	Coral Q 72489	Wack Wack/This Little Light Of Mine	15
67	Coral Q 72489	Wack Wack/This Little Light Of Mine (DJ copy)	40

YOUNG-HOLT UNLIMITED
73	Contempo COLP-R 1004	PLAYS SUPERFLY (LP)	15
69	MCA MUP(S) 368	SOULFUL STRUT (LP)	20

(see also Ramsey Lewis Trio)

YOUNG IDEA
66	Columbia DB 7961	The World's Been Good To Me/It Can't Be	10
67	Columbia DB 8205	With A Little Help From My Friends/Colours Of Darkness	12
67	Columbia DB 8284	Mister Lovin' Luggage Man/Room With A View	8
68	Music For Pleasure MFP 1225	WITH A LITTLE HELP FROM MY FRIENDS (LP)	20

YOUNG LIONS
78	Discovery D-DISC 001	Take Five (12", p/s)	30

YOUNG ONES (1)
63	Decca F 11705	How Do I Tell You/Baby That's It	8

YOUNG ONES (2)
78	Virgin VS 205	Rock 'N' Roll Radio/Little Bit Of Loving (p/s)	6

YOUNG RASCALS
65	Atlantic AT 4059	I Ain't Gonna Eat My Heart Out Anymore/Slow Down	15
66	Atlantic AT 4082	Good Lovin'/Mustang Sally	15
66	Atlantic 584 024	You Better Run/Love Is A Beautiful Thing	18
66	Atlantic 584 050	Come On Up/What Is The Reason	18
66	Atlantic 584 067	Too Many Fish In The Sea/No Love To Give	15
67	Atlantic 584 081	I've Been Lonely Too Long/If You Knew	15
67	Atlantic 584 085	I Ain't Gonna Eat My Heart Out Anymore/Good Lovin'	12
67	Atlantic 584 111	Groovin'/Sueno	12
67	Atlantic 584 128	A Girl Like You/It's Love	12
67	Atlantic 584 138	How Can I Be Sure/I Don't Love You Anymore	7
68	Atlantic 584 161	It's Wonderful/Of Course	10
66	Atlantic 587/588 012	THE YOUNG RASCALS (LP)	30
67	Atlantic 587/588 060	COLLECTIONS (LP)	20
67	Atlantic 587/588 074	GROOVIN' (LP)	25

(see also Rascals, Joey Dee & Starlighters)

RICHARD YOUNGS
88	No Fans NFR01	ADVENT (LP)	25

YOUNG SISTERS
62	London HLU 9610	Casanova Brown/My Guy	25

YOUNG SOULS
69	Amalgamated AMG 844	Why Did You Leave/Main A Wail	100

YOUNG TRADITION
74	Argo AFW 115	The Shepherd's Hymn/The Boar's Head Carol	6
68	Transatlantic TRAEP 164	CHICKEN ON A RAFT (EP)	25
66	Transatlantic TRA 142	THE YOUNG TRADITION (LP)	22
67	Transatlantic TRA 155	SO CHEERFULLY ROUND (LP)	18
68	Transatlantic TRA 172	GALLERIES (LP, with Dave Swarbrick)	18

(see also Dave Swarbrick, Peter Bellamy)

YOUNG TURKS
66	CBS 202353	Duel At Diablo/Our Lady From Maxim's	12

YOUNG WORLD SINGERS
64	Brunswick 05916	Ringo For President/A Boy Like That	6

YOUR HERO
79	Mirimar MIR 69	The Dictator/KALEIDOSCOPE: Snoggin' At The Roxy (no p/s, 500 only)	8

YOUR OLD DROOG
17	Daupe! DM SP 021	LOOSEYS (12", p/s, 200 only)	35
17	Daupe! DM SP 021	LOOSEYS (12", p/s, smoked vinyl, 100 only)	40
17	Daupe! DM SP 021	LOOSEYS (12", p/s, with obi strip, 20 only)	100
14	Chopped Herring CHDR00GLP01	YOUR OLD DROOG (2-LP)	35
14	Chopped Herring CHDR00GLP01	YOUR OLD DROOG (2-LP, clear, red or yellow vinyl, 75 copies of each)	50

JOHNNY YOUTH
69	Grape GR 3002	Darling It Won't/HIP CITY BOYS: Moon Train	50

YOUTH (1)
66	Polydor 56121	As Long As There Is Your Love/Your One And Only Love	20

YOUTH (2)
69	Deram DM 226	Meadow Of My Love/Love Me Or Leave Me	20

YOU'VE GOT FOETUS ON YOUR BREATH
81	Self Immolation WOMB 07	Wash It All Off/333 (p/s)	8
80s	Self Immolation	Tell Me, What Is The Bane Of Your Life?	10
81	Self Imm. WOMB OYBL-1	DEAF (LP)	25
81	Self Imm. WOMB OYBL-2	ACHE (LP)	25

(see also Foetus etc., Philip & His Foetus Vibrations, Scraping Foetus Off The Wheel)

LES YPER SOUND
67	Fontana TF 880	Too Fortiche/Psyche Rock	60

(see also Pierre Henry)

YR HWNTWS
82	Loco LOCO 1001	YR HWNTWS (LP)	80

YR AWR
71	Wren WRE 1096	RHIF 2 (EP)	10

Y TRWYNAU COCH
70s	Record. Sqwar RSROC 1	WASTOD AR Y TU FAS (BANANAS) (EP, around 1,000 only)	50
78	Record. Sqwar RSROC 002	Merched Dan 15 (I Often Think Of Girls Under 15)/Byw Ar Arian Fy Rhieni/ Mynd I'r Capel Mewn Levis/Ail Ddechre (around 1,000 only)	50
80	Record. Coch RCTC 3	Methu Dawnsio/CRACH: Putain Rhad (multifold p/s)	20
81	Sain SAIN 92	Paqn Fo Cyrff Yn Cwrdd/Beth Am Take Away/Camera Yn Y Gornel (p/s)	50
80s	Record. Coch OCHR 2198	RHEDEG RHAG Y TORPIDOS (LP)	30

JOHNNY YUKON
60	Top Rank JAR 347	Made To Be Loved/Magnolia	7

YUM YUMS
13	Outta Sight OSV 985	Gonna Be A Big Thing/Looky Looky (What I Got) (reissue)	10

YUNX
97	Void VOID 007	BILLODYSSEY EP (12")	10

TIMI YURO
61	London HLG 9403	Hurt/I Apologise	20
62	London HLG 9484	Smile/I Believe (B-side with Johnnie Ray)	15
62	Liberty LIB 55410	Let Me Call You Sweetheart/Satan Never Sleeps	10
62	Liberty LIB 55469	What's-A-Matter Baby (Is It Hurting You)/Thirteenth Hour	30
63	Liberty LIB 55519	The Love Of A Boy/I Ain't Gonna Cry No More	30
63	Liberty LIB 55519	The Love Of A Boy/I Ain't Gonna Cry No More (DJ Copy)	60
63	Liberty LIB 55587	Make The World Go Away/Look Down	12
64	Liberty LIB 10177	Hurt/Be Anything (But Be Mine)	10
64	Mercury MF 826	If/I'm Afraid The Masquerade Is Over	20
65	Mercury MF 848	You Can Have Him/Could This Be Magic	12
65	Mercury MF 859	Get Out Of My Life/Can't Stop Running Away	60
66	Mercury MF 978	Cuttin' In/Why Not Now	6
68	Liberty LBF 15092	Something Bad On My Mind/Wrong	30
68	Liberty LIB 15142	I Must Have Been Out Of My Mind/Interlude	25
68	Liberty LIB 15182	It'll Never Be Over For Me/As Long As There Is You	1500
19	Expansion EXUMG03	As Long As There Is You/It'll Never Be Over For Me (reissue)	10
65	Liberty LEP 2214	TIMI YURO: SOUL! (EP)	30
66	Liberty LEP 2252	MAKE THE WORLD GO AWAY (EP)	25
62	London HA-G 2415	TIMI YURO (LP)	75
62	Liberty LBY 1042	SOUL! (LP)	35
63	Liberty LBY 1154	WHAT'S-A-MATTER BABY (LP, mono)	25
63	Liberty SLBY 1154	WHAT'S-A-MATTER BABY (LP, stereo)	30
64	Liberty LBY 1192	MAKE THE WORLD GO AWAY (LP)	25
64	Mercury 20032 MCL	THE AMAZING TIMI YURO (LP)	22
65	Liberty LBY 1247	HURT (LP)	30

ZABANDIS

MINT VALUE £

66	Liberty LBY 1275	LET ME CALL YOU SWEETHEART (LP, mono)	20
66	Liberty SLBY 1275	LET ME CALL YOU SWEETHEART (LP, stereo)	30
66	Liberty (S)LBY 1290	THE BEST OF TIMI YURO (LP)	20
68	Liberty LBL/LBS 83115	GREAT PERFORMANCES (LP)	15
68	Liberty LBL/LBS 83128	TIMI IN THE BEGINNING (LP)	20
69	Liberty LBS 83198E	SOMETHING BAD ON MY MIND (LP)	50
69	Mercury SMWL 21010	TALENTED TIMI (LP)	15

(see also Johnnie Ray)

Z

ZABANDIS
82	True Vision TRV 001	Jah Jah Say/Things Are Getting Harder (12")	200

JOHN ZACHERLE
58	London HLU 8599	Dinner With Drac Part 1/Dinner With Drac - Conclusion	20

(see also Dave Appell & Applejacks)

ZAFTIG MADEL
84	Shine SHTUP 3	Dori Duz/Curvy 'N' Creamy (p/s)	6

ZAGADA
79	AJ B ZA001	THE ZAGADA AND FANS EP (12", p/s)	30
79	AJB AJB 1004	SPECIAL (LP)	80

ZAGER & EVANS
69	RCA SF 8056	2525 (LP)	20

ZAKARRIAS
71	Deram SML 1091	ZAKARRIAS (LP, white/red label, small logo)	1000

ZAKATEK
73	Bell 1289	I Gotcha Now/So Good To You	7

IWO ZALUSKI
73	Hobbiton HOB 103	LEGEND OF THE SAFFRON SORCERESS (EP, insert)	150
69	John Hassell Records HAS LP 2026	BRANDYBUCK AND THE ELECTRIC ZEON BAND (LP, as Iwo Zaluski and the Cardinal Newman School)	500
69	John Hassell Records HAS LP MAS 701	THE WORLD OF MY DREAMS (LP)	100
74	Hobbiton HOB 104	THE REMARKABLE EARTH MAKING MACHINE (LP)	150
75	Hobbiton HOB 105	TALES OF TOLKIEN HIGHLIGHTS (LP)	150
77	Hobbiton HOB 107	A LIFE IN THE WEEK OF A DAY (LP)	150

GEORGE ZAMBETAS & THE GROUP TEN PLAYERS
66	Pye 7N 17180	Moussaka/Monlight Over The Acropolis (p/s)	6

ZANADU
82	SMT 14	Let's See You Rockin'/Nutbush City Limits	10

ALEX ZANETIS
71	Moodisc HM 102	Guilty/JOLLY BOYS: Do Fe Do (actually both by Jolly Boys)	8

TOMMY ZANG
59	HMV POP 611	Break The Chain/I'll Put A String On Your Finger	10
62	Polydor NH 66955	I'm Gonna Slip You Offa My Mind/Every Hour, Every Day	10
62	Polydor NH 66957	Hey, Good Lookin'/With Love (For You)	20
62	Polydor NH 66960	Take These Chains From My Heart/Truly, Truly	10
62	Polydor NH 66977	I Can't Hold Your Letters (In My Arms)/She's Getting Married	10
62	Polydor NH 66980	Just Call My Name/I Love You Because	10

WILLY ZANGO
73	Jam JAM 58	Hot Rod/Goom	8
74	DJM DJS 312	Hot Rod/The Voice Of Melody	7

ZANTI MISFITZ
82	Clay 9	Kidz Songs/Alice Liddle's Bad Trip (p/s)	10

FRANK ZAPPA/MOTHERS OF INVENTION
SINGLES
66	Verve VS 545	It Can't Happen Here/How Could I Be Such A Fool (as Mothers Of Invention)	60
67	Verve VS 557	Big Leg Emma/Why Don't You Do Me Right (as Mothers Of Invention)	60
71	Reprise K 14100	Tears Began To Fall/Junier Mintz Boogie (as Mothers Of Invention)	40
71	United Artists UP 35319	What Will This Evening Bring Me This Morning?/Daddy, Daddy, Daddy	35
74	Discreet K 19201	Cosmic Debris/Uncle Remus	10
74	Discreet K 19202	Don't Eat The Yellow Snow/Camarillo Brillo	10
80	CBS 7950	Joe's Garage/Catholic Girls	6
80	CBS 7950	Joe's Garage/BOB DYLAN: When You Gonna Wake Up (mispressing)	30
80	CBS 8652	I Don't Wanna Get Drafted/Ancient Armaments (p/s)	6
81	CBS A 1622	You Are What You Is/Harder Than Your Husband (p/s)	6
81	CBS A 12-1622	You Are What You Is/Pink Napkins/Harder Than Your Husband/Soup 'N Old Clothes (12", picture disc)	15
81	CBS XPS 147	Shut Up 'N' Play Yer Guitar/Variation On The C. Santana Secret (p/s), issued free with "Ship Arriving Too Late To Save A Drowning Witch" LP)	6
82	CBS A 2412	Valley Girl/Teenage Prostitute (p/s)	6
84	EMI EMI 5499	Baby Take Your Teeth Out/Stevie's Spanking (p/s)	8

ALBUMS : VERVE ORIGINALS
66	Verve VLP 9154	FREAK OUT! (as Mothers Of Invention, mono, single disc)	150
66	Verve SVLP 9154	FREAK OUT! (as Mothers Of Invention, stereo, single disc)	100
67	Verve VLP 9174	ABSOLUTELY FREE (as Mothers Of Invention, mono)	150

ZAPPO

			MINT VALUE £
67	Verve SVLP 9174	ABSOLUTELY FREE (as Mothers Of Invention, stereo)	100
68	Verve VLP 9199	WE'RE ONLY IN IT FOR THE MONEY (as Mothers Of Invention, gatefold sleeve, mono)	150
68	Verve SVLP 9199	WE'RE ONLY IN IT FOR THE MONEY (as Mothers Of Invention, gatefold sleeve, stereo)	100
68	Verve VLP 9223	LUMPY GRAVY (gatefold sleeve, mono)	150
68	Verve SVLP 9223	LUMPY GRAVY (gatefold sleeve, stereo)	100
69	Verve VLP 9237	CRUISING WITH RUBEN AND THE JETS (as Mothers Of Invention, mono)	150
69	Verve SVLP 9237	CRUISING WITH RUBEN AND THE JETS (as Mothers Of Invention, stereo)	100
69	Verve VLP 9239	MOTHERMANIA - THE BEST OF THE MOTHERS (as Mothers Of Invention, mono)	70
69	Verve SVLP 9239	MOTHERMANIA - THE BEST OF THE MOTHERS (as Mothers Of Invention, stereo)	30

ALBUMS : VERVE REISSUES

71	Verve/Polydor 2683 004	FREAK OUT (2-LP)	30
72	Verve/Polydor 2317 034	WE'RE ONLY IN IT FOR THE MONEY (gatefold sleeve)	30
72	Verve/Polydor 2317 035	ABSOLUTELY FREE (gatefold sleeve)	25
72	Verve/Polydor 2317 046	LUMPY GRAVY (gatefold sleeve)	30
72	Verve/Polydor 2317 047	MOTHERMANIA - THE BEST OF THE MOTHERS	25
73	Verve/Polydor 2352 017	MOTHERMANIA - THE BEST OF THE MOTHERS (2nd reissue)	25
73	Verve/Polydor 2317 069	CRUISIN' WITH RUBEN AND THE JETS (gatefold sleeve)	25
75	Verve/Polydor 2352 057	ROCK FLASHBACKS (LP)	15

ALBUMS : ORIGINAL REPRISE/WARNER/DISCREET ISSUES

70	Reprise RSLP 6356	HOT RATS (1st pressing, pink, gold & green 'riverboat' label, gatefold sleeve)	75
70	Reprise RSLP 6356	HOT RATS (2nd pressing, tan 'riverboat' label, gatefold sleeve)	35
70	Reprise RSLP 6370	BURNT WEENY SANDWICH (as Mothers Of Invention, 1st pressing, pink, gold & green 'riverboat' label, gatefold sleeve)	80
70	Reprise RSLP 2028	WEASELS RIPPED MY FLESH (as Mothers Of Invention, tan 'riverboat' label)	40
70	Reprise RSLP 2030	CHUNGA'S REVENGE (tan 'riverboat' label, green gatefold sleeve)	45
70	Reprise RSLP 2030	CHUNGA'S REVENGE (tan 'riverboat' label, red gatefold sleeve)	20
71	Reprise K 44150	FILLMORE EAST, JUNE 1971 (as Mothers Of Invention)	15

(First pressings issued without Warner Bros logo on label or sleeve; copies with Warners logos are post-1975 pressings worth £6-£8 each.)

71	Reprise K 44078	HOT RATS (tan 'riverboat' label, gatefold sleeve)	25
71	Reprise K 44083	BURNT WEENY SANDWICH (tan 'riverboat' label)	20
71	Reprise K 44019	WEASELS RIPPED MY FLESH (tan 'riverboat' label)	20
71	Reprise K 44020	CHUNGA'S REVENGE (tan 'riverboat' label, gatefold sleeve)	15

(Issued without Warner Bros logo on label or sleeve; post-1975 pressings with logos are worth £6-£8 each.)

72	Reprise K 44179	JUST ANOTHER BAND FROM L.A. (as Mothers Of Invention, gatefold sleeve)	20
72	Reprise K 44203	WAKA/JAWAKA (HOT RATS)	15
72	Reprise K 44209	THE GRAND WAZOO (gatefold sleeve)	20
73	DiscReet K 41000	OVER-NITE SENSATION (as Mothers Of Invention, gatefold sleeve)	15
74	DiscReet K 59201	APOSTROPHE (') (no lyric insert)	15

(First pressings issued without Warner Bros logo on label or sleeve; copies with Warners logos are post-1975 pressings worth £6-£8 each.)

75	DiscReet K 59207	ONE SIZE FITS ALL (as Mothers Of Invention, gatefold sleeve)	15

(First pressings issued without Warner Bros logo on label or sleeve; copies with Warners logos are post-1975 pressings worth £8-£12 each.)

76	Warner Bros K 56298	ZOOT ALLURES (LP)	15
77	DiscReet K 69204	ZAPPA IN NEW YORK (LIVE) (2-LP, with & without reference to Punky's Whips)	20
77	DiscReet K 69204	ZAPPA IN NEW YORK (LIVE) (2-LP, "Punky's Whips" listed on sleeve but not on label or LP)	20
77	DiscReet K 69204	ZAPPA IN NEW YORK (LIVE) (2-LP, 1st pressing plays "Punky's Whips", listed on sleeve and on label)	150
78	DiscReet K 59210	STUDIO TAN	15
78	DiscReet K 59211	SLEEP DIRT	15
78	DiscReet K 59212	ORCHESTRAL FAVORITES	15

ALBUMS : CBS/EMI/OTHER LABELS

69	Transatlantic TRA 197	UNCLE MEAT (2-LP, as Mothers Of Invention)	80
71	United Artists UDF 50003	200 MOTELS (2-LP, with booklet & poster, as Frank Zappa & Mothers Of Invention)	40
79	CBS 86101	JOE'S GARAGE ACT 1 (gatefold sleeve, lyric insert)	20
81	CBS 66368	SHUT UP 'N' PLAY YER GUITAR (3-LP box set, with inner sleeves)	25
82	CBS 85804	SHIP ARRIVING TOO LATE TO SAVE A DROWNING WITCH (LP, with bonus 7" Shut Up 'N' Play Yer Guitar/"Variation On The C. Santana Secret" [XPS 147])	20
84	EMI EL 2701531	BOULEZ CONDUCTS ZAPPA: 'THE PERFECT STRANGER'	15
84	EMI EJ2702561	FRANCESCO ZAPPA (with inner sleeve)	15
84	EMI 2402943	THING-FISH (3-LP, box set, with libretto)	20
84	EMI EMC 3500	THE MAN FROM UTOPIA	15
84	EMI FZAP1	JOE'S GARAGE ACTS 1, 2 & 3 (3-LP, box set, inner sleeves only, with libretti)	25
84	EMI no cat. no.	SHUT UP 'N' PLAY YER GUITAR (3-LP, box set, with inner sleeves)	25
86	EMI EN 3521	JAZZ FROM HELL	15
86	EMI EC 3507	FRANK ZAPPA MEETS THE MOTHERS OF PREVENTION (European version)	15
95	Simply Vinyl SLVP 0024	WEASELS RIPPED MY FLESH (180gm vinyl)	20
95	Simply Vinyl SLVP 0025	BURNT WEENY SANDWICH (gatefold sleeve, 180gm vinyl)	20

ALBUMS : ZAPPA LABEL

80s	Zappa Records ZAPPA 5	LONDON SYMPHONY ORCHESTRA VOLUME II	15
90	Zappa Records ZAPPA 20	JOE'S GARAGE ACTS 1, 2 & 3 (3-LP, box set, original sleeves, with libretti)	30
91	Zappa Records ZAPPA 35	BURNT WEENY SANDWICH (gatefold sleeve)	15
91	Zappa Records ZAPPA 42	SHIP ARRIVING TOO LATE TO SAVE A DROWNING WITCH	15
92	Zappa Records ZAPPA 39	ROXY AND ELSEWHERE (2-LP, as Mothers Of Invention, gatefold lyric sleeve)	20

(see also Flo & Eddie, Jeff Simmons, Wild Man Fischer, Captain Beefheart, John Lennon, Geronimo Black)

ZAPPO

73	Magnet MAG 2	Rock And Roll Crazy/Right On!	8

ZAP POW

72	Harry J HJ 6650	Lottery Spin/Lottery Spin - Version	8
73	Trojan TR 7741	This Is Reggae Music/Break Down The Barriers	7

MINT VALUE £

73	Blue Mountain BM 1027	This Is Reggae Music/Break Down The Barriers	6
74	Island WIP 6181	This Is Reggae Music/Break Down The Barriers	6
76	Vulcan VUL 1010	Jungle Beat/Rock Your Bones	8
78	Island IPR 2028	Roots Man Reggae/Let's Fall In Love (12")	12
76	Vulcan VULP 004	NOW (LP)	15

ZARACK
99	All Tone AT 020	Look Into My Eyes/My Eyes	45

LES ZARJAZ
85	Creation CRE 014	One Charming Nyte/My Baby Owns A Fallout Zone (foldover p/s, poly bag)	8

(see also Tronics)

LENA ZAVARONI
80	Galaxy GY 177	Will he Kiss Me Tonight/Dream Come True (no p/s)	100
77	Galaxy GAL 6012	PRESENTING LENA ZAVARONI (LP)	30
82	BBC REB 443	HOLD TIGHT, IT'S LENA (LP)	40

PETE ZEAR
80	(no label) matrix: 22-1	Tomorrow's World/Fast Food (stamped white label, with insert, numbered)	12

(see also Ruts, Rat Scabies)

ZEBEDEE
71	Decca F13144	So Long Marianne/She Couldn't Make Gravy	30

ZEEBRA
79	Jungle JR 7038S	Anytime/Sign Your Name/Lux Gud/Night (no p/s)	25

ZEITGEIST
80	Enchaine ENC 1	Shake-Rake/Sniper (p/s)	6

ZEN
68	Philips BF 1746	Hair/Aquarius	20

ZENITH
86	ZENITH 5001	Heavy Heavy Heart (p/s)	75

SI ZENTNER ORCHESTRA
64	Liberty LIB 10169	The James Bond Theme/Bond's 007 Theme	7
63	Liberty LBY 1164	RHYTHM PLUS BLUES (LP)	15

ZEPHYR
70	Probe SPB 1006	ZEPHYR (LP)	60

(see also Tommy Bolin)

ZEPHYRS
63	Decca F 11647	What's All That About/Oriental Dream	40
64	Columbia DB 7199	I Can Tell/Sweet Little Baby	50
64	Columbia DB 7324	A Little Bit Of Soap/No Message	35
64	Columbia DB 7410	Wonder What I'm Gonna Do/Let Me Love You Baby	35
65	Columbia DB 7481	She's Lost You/There's Something About You	35
65	Columbia DB 7571	I Just Can't Take It/She Laughed	35

EARL ZERO
78	Studio 16 WE 401	Rough And Tough/PRINCE JAZZBO: Suffer Must Live (12")	30
79	Sufferers Height SUF004	Please Officer/AUGUSTUS PABLO: In Moonlight City (12")	50
79	Greensleeves GRED 23	City Of The Wicked/Rightous Works (12")	40
79	Student STU 007	IN THE RIGHT WAY (LP)	80

ZERO FIVE
65	Columbia DB 7751	Dusty/Just Like A Girl	6

ZERO LE CRECHE
84	Flicknife FLS 029	Last Year's Wife/Women Say (p/s)	15
84	Flicknife FLST 029	Last Year's Wife/Women Say/Fall To Dust (p/s)	25
85	Cherry Red CHERRY 87	Falling/Beyond Westworld (p/s)	10
85	Cherry Red 12 CHERRY 87	Falling/Beyond Westworld/Terminal Tracks (12", p/s)	15

ZERO 7
00	Ultimate Dilemma UDR	EP VOL. 1 (12")	18
00	Ultimate Dilemma UDR 040	EP VOL. 2 (12")	18
01	Ultimate Dilemma UDRLP	SIMPLE THINGS (2-LP)	80
04	Ultimate Dilemma 5050467 0987 1 8	WHEN IT FALLS (2-LP)	60
06	Ultimate Dilemma 5015011 2857 1 4	THE GARDEN (2-LP, gatefold, inners)	80
15	Warner Bros. 0825646132751	SIMPLE THINGS (2-LP, reissue, 180gm vinyl, download card)	20

ZERO TWENTY ONE
81	UK UK 201	Pop Song (p/s)	100

ZERO ZERO
79	Interference INT 00	Chinese Boys/Coup De Ville Dawn (p/s, 1000 only)	8

ZEROS
77	Small Wonder SMALL 2	Hungry/Radio Fun	20
79	Rok ROK XV/XVI	What's Wrong With A Pop Group/ACTION REPLAY: Decisions (die-cut co. sleeve)	20

021
82	UK POP 0201	The Pop Song/Aversion! (p/s)	40

MONICA ZETTERLUND
58	Columbia DB 4246	There's No You/Don't Be That Way	15
59	Columbia SEG 8015	SWEDISH SWEET (EP)	60
58	Columbia 33CSX 20	SWEDISH SENSATION (LP, export only)	200
64	Philips BL 7647	MAKE MINE SWEDISH STYLE (LP)	100

Z'EV
82	Fetish FE 13	Wipeout!/Element L. (p/s)	10
88	Coercion COERCIONLP 001	THE INVISIBLE MAN (LP)	25

ZIMM & DEE DEE
71	Green Door GD 4006	You've Got A Friend (actually by Winston Francis & Donna Hinds)/GROOVERS: Cheep	7

Tucker ZIMMERMAN

MINT VALUE £

(see also Winston Francis)

TUCKER ZIMMERMAN
69	Regal Zonophone RZ 3020	The Red Wind/Moondog	25
69	Regal Zono. (S)LRZ 1010	TEN SONGS BY TUCKER ZIMMERMAN (LP)	120
72	Village Thing VTS 13	TUCKER ZIMMERMANN (LP)	70

PETER ZINOVIEFF
70	3M/Lyntone LYN 2443	A Lollipop For Papa (1-sided with book)	50
70	3M/Lyntone LYN 2443	A Lollipop For Papa (1-sided without book)	30

ZION TRAIN
99	Universal Egg WWLP030	LOVE REVOLUTIONARIES (2-LP)	25

ZIOR
71	Nepentha 6129 002	Za Za Za Zilda/She's A Bad Bad Woman	25
71	Nepentha 6129 003	Cat's Eyes/I Really Do	20
71	Nepentha 6437 005	ZIOR (LP, gatefold sleeve)	500

(see also Monument, Cardboard Orchestra)

RB ZIPPER
76	Alaska ALA 2004	Cruisin With The Fonz/Superstream	6
77	Alaska ALA 2006	Come On Marriane/Lamplight Lady	8

ZIPPER (1)
74	Youngblood YB 170	Streak Up And Down/Funk 74	30

ZIPPER (2)
79	Spanking SRTS/79/CUS 278 SPANK 1	The Life Of Riley/Treat Me Pretty	10

ZIPPERS
64	Hickory 45-1252	My Sailor Boy/Pretend You're Still Mine	15

ZIPPS
79	Rip Off RIP 12	Friends/Don't Tell The Detectives (die cut p/s)	60

ZIPS
79	Black Gold ZIPS1	Take Me Down/Don't Be Pushed Around/I'm In Love Over and Over (500 only with A4 insert & 2 stickers)	150
80	Tenement Tunes TEN 01	Radioactivity/I'm Not Impressed (p/s)	30

ZIPZ
80	Voyage VOY 14	As I Pass You By/Tonight (p/s)	10

ZNR
81	Recommended RR 7	BARRICADE 3 (LP)	18

ZODIAC
68	Elektra EKL 4009	COSMIC SOUNDS (LP, also stereo EKS 74009)	70

ZODIACS
57	Oriole CB 1383	Why Don't They Understand/The Game Of Love	18
58	Oriole CB 1432	The Yum-Yum Song/Secrets	10

ZOMBIES
64	Decca F 11940	She's Not There/You Make Me Feel Good	15
64	Decca F 12004	Leave Me Be/Woman	15
65	Decca F 12072	Tell Her No/What More Can I Do	15
65	Decca F 12125	She's Coming Home/I Must Move	15
65	Decca F 12225	Whenever You're Ready/I Love You	15
65	Decca F 12296	Is This The Dream/Don't Go Away	25
66	Decca F 12322	Remember You/Just Out Of Reach	25
66	Decca F 12426	Indication/How We Were Before	35
66	Decca F 12495	Gotta Get A Hold Of Myself/The Way I Feel Inside	40
67	Decca F 12584	Goin' Out Of My Head/She Does Everything For Me	50
68	Decca F 12798	I Love You/The Way I Feel Inside	15
67	CBS 2960	Friends Of Mine/Beechwood Park	60
67	CBS 3087	Care Of Cell 44/Maybe After He's Gone	50
68	CBS 3380	Time Of The Season/I'll Call You Mine	60
73	Epic EPC 3380	Time Of The Season/I'll Call You Mine (reissue)	8
65	Decca DFE 8598	THE ZOMBIES (EP)	125
10	Big Beat LTDEP 003	ZOMBIES R&B (EP)	10
10	Big Beat LTDEP 006	ZOMBIES 66 (EP)	10
10	Big Beat LTDEP 007	TIME OF THE SEASON (EP)	12
10	Big Beat LTDEP 008	ZOMBIES ON THE BBC (EP)	10
65	Decca LK 4679	BEGIN HERE (LP)	500
65	RCA RD 7791	BUNNY LAKE IS MISSING (LP, soundtrack)	65
68	CBS BPG 63280	ODESSEY AND ORACLE (LP, mono)	900
68	CBS SBPG 63280	ODESSEY AND ORACLE (LP, stereo)	700
70	Decca SPA 95	THE WORLD OF THE ZOMBIES (LP)	18
73	Epic EPC 65728	TIME OF THE ZOMBIES (2-LP)	40
76	Decca ROOTS 2	ROCK ROOTS (LP)	15
86	Decca DOA 4	BEGIN HERE (LP, reissue, silver labels)	20
15	Repertoire V 102 M	ODESSEY AND ORACLE (LP, reissue, mono half-speed master)	30

(see also Unit Four Plus Two, Argent, Neil MacArthur, Colin Blunstone)

ZOO
70	Major Minor SMLP 74	ZOO (LP)	50
71	Barclay 521172	ZOO (LP)	30

ZOO BOUTIQUE
82	Lightbeat LIGHT 006	Forgive And Forget/Happy Families (p/s, clear vinyl)	6

ZOOKIE
77	DJM DJS 10796	Judie Judie Hold On/I Couldn't Be You	8
78	DJM DJS 10866	Bubbles/Don't Rock Me	8

(see also Tzuke & Paxo)

ZOOM CLUB

MINT VALUE £

ZOOM CLUB
80	Happy Face MM 130	I Can't Compete/It's Not Fair (no p/s)	100

ZOOM LENS
80	Negative NEG 1	Side To Side/Running In Mazes (blue vinyl, p/s)	25
84	Negative NEG 2	Welcome To China/Waxworks (p/s)	25

ZOOT ALORS
79	Decca FR 13874	Send Me A Postcard/It's A Crime	40

ZORKIE TWINS
80	Skeleton SKL 006	Mr. Simpson/From Now On (p/s)	15

JOHN ZORN
86	Nonesuch 979 139-1	THE BIG GUNDOWN (LP, gatefold)	20
87	Nonesuch 979 172-1	SPILLANE (LP)	20
89	Nonesuch 960844-1	SPY VS SPY (LP)	20
89	Nonesuch 7559 792381	NAKED CITY (LP)	40

ZORRO
79	Bridgehouse BHEP 1	'Arrods Don't Sell 'Em/Soldier Boy/Starflight (with p/s)	30
79	Bridgehouse BHEP 1	'Arrods Don't Sell 'Em/Soldier Boy/Starflight	10

ZOSKIA
84	All The Madmen MAD 8	Rape/Thank You (p/s)	8
85	Temple TOPY 005	Be Like Me (12", p/s, transparent vinyl)	12

ZOSKIA MEETS SUGARDOG
84	Temple TOPYS 021	J.G. /`That's Heavy Baby	10

ZOUNDS
81	Crass 4219844/3	Can't Cheat Karma/War/Subvert (gatefold paper p/s, with poster)	15
81	Rough Trade RT 069	Demystification/Great White Hunter (p/s)	10
82	Rough Trade RT 094	Dancing/True Love (p/s)	8
82	Not So Brave NSB 001	LA VACHE QUI RIT (EP, with poster)	12
82	Rough Trade RT 098	More Trouble Coming Every Day/Knife (p/s)	8
82	Rough Trade ROUGH 31	THE CURSE OF ZOUNDS (LP, inner)	20

ZOVIET-FRANCE
82	Red Rhino RED 12	ZOVIET-FRANCE (12" EP, printed hessian sleeve)	60
12	Altvinyl AV040/ AV041.AV042	7.10/12 (box set of one clear vinyl 7", one clear vinyl 10" and one clear vinyl 12", 250 only)	50
83	Red Rhino RED 23	NORSCHE (LP)	35
84	Red Rhino RED 40	MOHNOMISCHE (LP, 1st pressing with silver/dark green labels)	80
84	Red Rhino RED 40	MOHNOMISCHE (LP, 2nd pressing with light green/dark green labels)	40
84	Red Rhino REDLP 45	EOSTRE (LP)	50
85	Singing Ringing	POPULAR SOVIET SONGS AND YOUTH MUSIC (2-cassette)	40
86	Red Rhino RED 67	MISFITS, LOONY TUNES AND SQUALID CRIMINALS (LP)	35
87	Red Rhino RED 68	A FLOCK OF ROTATIONS (LP)	40
88	Red Rhino RED 91	SHOUTING AT THE GROUND (2-LP)	40
90	Charm CHARRMLP 14	LOOK INTO ME (LP, 45rpm)	40

ZOWLAS
67	Amusicon SLE 12	Honest I Do/Gonna Love My Baby	12

ZUGZWANG
95	Aphelion AHP 001	Euphonic/Arrest/Focussed/Bermuda (12")	40
96	Aphelion AHP 002	MiiA/The Ticket/Tastes Like A Peach/Brighton Terrace SW2/Wireless (12")	30

ZUIDERZEE
66	CBS 202062	(You're My) Soul And Inspiration/Please Don't Call Me	10
66	CBS 202235	Peace Of Mind/Provocative Child	10

TAPPA ZUKIE
75	Locks LOX 8	Judge I O' Lord/LLOYDIE SLIM AND KING TUBBY: State Dub	20
75	Attack ATT 8110	Natty Dread Don't Cry (as Topper Zukie)/TOMMY McCOOK : The Meducia	8
77	New Star DNEW 1	What's Yours/Make Faith (12", as Tappa Zukie & Knowledge)	25
77	Achilles ACHILLES 54	Liberation Struggle/Double Struggle	10
78	Music Of The Most High MER 602	Viego/Archie The Rednose Reindeer (p/s)	8
73	Count Shelly CSLP 04	MAN A WARRIOR (LP)	60
76	Stars (No. Cat. No.)	TAPPA ZUKIE IN DUB (LP)	100
76	KLIK 9022	M.P.L.A. (LP)	20
78	Virgin Frontline FL1006	M.P.L.A. (LP, reissue)	20
78	Virgin Frontline FL1009	PEACE IN THE GHETTO (LP)	20
79	Virgin Frontline FL1029	TAPPA ZUKIE IN DUB (LP)	20
79	Virgin Frontline FL1032	TAPPER ROOTS LP)	15

(see also Honey Boy, Alton Ellis & Dennis Alcapone)

ZULEMA
75	RCA SF 8419	ZULEMA (LP)	15

ZULU
77	Big Bear BB9	Red Red Libanon/Okavanga Swamp	15

ZULU WARRIORS
89	Wau! Mr. Modo MOWLP 004	WARRIOR DUB (LP)	20

ZUM ZEAUX
70s	Black Pig PUG1	WOLF AT THE DOOR (LP)	40

ZUTONS
04	Deltasonic DLTLP019	WHO KILLED...THE ZUTONS (LP, with 3D glasses)	40
06	Deltasonic DLTLP040	TIRED OF HANGING AROUND (LP)	20

ZWAN
03	Reprise 9362-48436-1	MARY STAR OF THE SEA (2-LP)	50

(see also Smashing Pumpkins)

ZYGOAT
74	Polydor 2383 270	ELECTROPHON (LP)	20

			MINT VALUE £
ZZ			
88	Kent 6T3	PEGGY WOODS: Love Is Gonna Get You/ZZ: You Just Cheat And Lie	20
ZZEBRA			
74	Polydor 2058 446	Zardoz/Amusofi	20
75	Polydor 2058 579	Mr. J/Put The Light On Me	6
74	Polydor 2383 296	ZZEBRA (LP)	15
75	Polydor 2383 326	PANIC (LP, with insert)	18
(see also John McCoy, Gillan)			
ZZ TOP			
72	London HLU 10376	Francene/Down Brownie	15
74	London HLU 10458	Beer Drinkers And Hell Raisers/La Grange	12
75	London HLU 10475	La Grange/Just Got Paid	10
75	London HLU 10495	Tush/Blue Jean Blues	10
76	London HLU 10538	It's Only Love/Asleep In The Desert	8
77	London HLU 10547	Arrested For Driving While Blind/Neighbour, Neighbour	8
77	London HLU 10547	Arrested For Driving While Blind/Neighbour, Neighbour (mispressing, B-side plays Ray Charles' "I Can See Clearly Now")	12
80	Warner Bros K 17576	I Thank You/A Fool For Your Stockings (p/s)	7
85	Warner Bros W 2001F	Sleeping Bag/Party On The Patio//Sharp Dressed Man/I Got The Fix (p/s, sealed, stickered double pack)	10
86	Warner Bros W 2003FP	Rough Boy/Delirious (shaped pic-disc, part 3 of interlocking set, shrinkwrapped with bonus 12")	30
86	Warner Bros W 2003FP	Rough Boy/Delirious (shaped pic-disc, part 3 of interlocking set)	20
11	Warner Bros/Reprise 527517-7	Just Got Paid/MASTODON: Just Got Paid (yellow vinyl, jukebox centre)	6
71	London PS 584	ZZ TOP (LP, with inner sleeve)	60
72	London SH-U 8433	RIO GRANDE MUD (LP, original issue)	75
73	London SH-U 8459	TRES HOMBRES (LP, original issue)	50
75	London SH-U 8482	FANDANGO! (LP, original issue)	40
76	London LDU 1	TEJAS (LP, original foldout sleeve)	40
83	Warner Bros W 3774	ELIMINATOR (LP, with bonus stickered p/s 12" "Legs [Metal Mix]")	15
83	Warner Bros W3774P	ELIMINATOR (LP, picture disc)	20

Various Artists

VARIOUS ARTISTS EPs 50s/60s
(alphabetical by title)

A

62	MGM MGMEP 768	A VERY PRIVATE AFFAIR (includes Brigitte Bardot: Sidonie)	60

B

64	Fontana TFE 18010	BLOWIN' IN THE WIND (withdrawn; Bob Dylan/Joan Baez/Pete Seeger)	100
64	Pye Intl. NEP 44029	THE BLUES VOL. 1 PT. 1 (John Lee Hooker/Muddy Waters/Sonny Boy Williamson/Jimmy Witherspoon)	35
60	Pye Intl. NEP 44035	THE BLUES VOL. 1 PT. 2 (Howling Wolf/Buddy Guy/Little Walter/Muddy Waters)	25
66	Chess CRE 6011	THE BLUES VOL. 2 PT. 1 (Otis Rush/Chuck Berry/John Lee Hooker/ Little Walter)	25
64	Pye Intl. NEP 44038	BLUES FESTIVAL (Sugar Pie De Santo/Willie Dixon/Sonny Boy Williamson/ Howlin' Wolf)	30
63	Columbia SEG 8226	BLUES ON PARADE NO. 1 (Jimmy Cotton/Brownie McGhee/ Roosevelt Sykes/Sonny Terry)	25
56	HMV 7EG 8178	THE BLUES THEY SANG (Lizzie Miles/Billy Young & Jelly Roll Morton)	20

C

60s	Heritage 105	THE COUNTRY BLUES (99 only)	80

D

60s	XX MIN 706	DARK MUDDY BOTTOM (Jimmy Slim/Good Jelly Bess/Lightning Leon/ Little Red Walters/ Willie B.)	20
50s	Poydras 102	DEPRESSION BLUES	25
63	Decca DFE 8520	DISCS-A-GO GO (Karl Denver/Billy Fury/Jet Harris/Vernons Girls)	50
60s	Jan & Dil JR 450	DOWN HOME BLUES - SIXTIES STYLE (Lightning Leon/Jerry McCain/ Little Red Walters)	30
59	Fontana TFE 17146	DRUMBEAT (Lana Sisters/Adam Faith/Bob Miller & Millermen/ Sylvia Sands/Roy Young)	40

E

65	Edinburgh S.C. ESC 02	EDINBURGH STUDENTS CHARITIES APPEAL (33rpm, die-cut paper p/s; Athenians/ Avengers/Ray & Archie Fisher/Lynn & Kathy)	50
66	Edinburgh S.C. ESC 03	EDINBURGH STUDENTS CHARITIES APPEAL (33rpm, Athenians/Gear System/Old Bailey's Jazz Advocates)	60

F

64	Pye Intl. NEP 44030	FESTIVAL OF THE BLUES NO. 1 (Willie Dixon/Buddy Guy/Muddy Waters/ Sonny Boy Williamson)	20
63	Decca DFE 8538	FROM A LONDON HOOTENANNY (Davy Graham/Thamesiders)	25

G

G

Year	Label/Cat	Title	Value £
67		Down with the Game 202	
67		Down with the Game 203	
60s	XX MIN 707	GOD DON'T LIKE IT (99 only)	40
66	Pye Intl. NEP 45054	GOD DON'T LIKE IT VOLUME 2 (99 only)	40
63	London RE-U 1393	GOING TO CALIFORNIA (Little Sonny Willis/Eddie Williams)	15
59	Mercury ZEP 10010	THE GREATEST ON STAGE (Maxine Brown/Chuck Jackson/Shirelles/Dionne Warwick)	25
		GROUP OF GOODIES (Marcie Blane/Kokomo/Bill Black's Combo/Ernie Maresca)	50
		GROUPS GALORE (Del Vikings/Mark IV/Diamonds/Hi-Liters)	70

H

Year	Label/Cat	Title	Value £
66	Pye NEP 24242	THE HITMAKERS VOL. 2 (Chuck Berry/Kinks/Sue Thompson/Shangri-La's)	30
66	Pye Intl. NEP 44065	HITMAKERS INTERNATIONAL (Fontella Bass/James Brown/Petula Clark/Lovin' Spoonful)	25
62	Mercury ZEP 10133	HITSVILLE! (Brook Benton/Crew Cuts/Phil Philips/Diamonds)	30
59	Coral FEP 2034	HITSVILLE VOL. 1 (Buddy Holly/McGuire Sisters/Betty Madigan/Billy Williams)	60
59	Coral FEP 2035	HITSVILLE VOL. 2 (Lennon Sisters/Art Lund/Teresa Brewer/Jackie Wilson)	50
65	Tamla Motown TME 2001	HITSVILLE U.S.A. NO. 1 (Marvin Gaye/Brenda Holloway/Carolyn Crawford/Eddie Holland)	110
66	Post War Blues 100	HOBOS AND DRIFTERS	50

I

Year	Label/Cat	Title	Value £
65	Chess CRE 6010	IN CROWD (Radiants/Ramsey Lewis Trio/Little Milton/Billy Stewart)	30

J

Year	Label/Cat	Title	Value £
59	Decca DFE 6587	THE JAZZ COMMITTEE (featuring Don Rendell)	100

K

Year	Label/Cat	Title	Value £
63	Lyntone LYN 347/348	KEELE RAG RECORD (flexidisc; Rhythm Unlimited & Halettes/Keele Quintet)	18
64	Lyntone LYN 508/509	KEELE RAG RECORD NO. 2 (flexidisc; Escorts/Lance Harvey & Kingpins/Keele Row; some in die-cut sleeve)	35
65	Lyntone LYN 765/766	KEELE RAG RECORD (flexidisc; Bob Wilson/Changing Times/Lance Harvey & Kingpins/Incas)	40
61	RCA Victor RCX 203	KINGS OF THE BLUES VOL. 2 (Jazz Gillum/Big Maceo/Washboard Sam/Sonny Boy Williamson)	20
61	RCA Victor RCX 204	KINGS OF THE BLUES VOL. 3 (Arthur Big Boy Crudup/Furry Lewis/Poor Joe Williams)	25
66	Holyground HG 111	THE LAST THING ON MY MIND (EP, 99 copies only)	80
60	Philips BBE 12414/	LET'S MAKE LOVE - FILM SOUNDTRACK (Yves Montand/Marilyn Monroe/Frankie Vaughan; stereo)	25
63	Embassy WEP 1104	LIVERPOOL BEAT (Typhoons/Mike Redway/Ray Pilgrim/Bobby Stevens)	10
57	London RE-P 1096	LONDON HIT PARADE NO. 2 (Fats Domino/Slim Whitman/Ken Copeland/Roy Brown)	40
58	London RE-P 1137	LONDON TOPPERS NO. 3 (export issue; Slim Whitman/Fats Domino/Ricky Nelson/Ernie Freeman)	20

M

Year	Label/Cat	Title	Value £
59	Jazz Collector JEL 2	THE MALE BLUES VOL. 1 (Georgia Slim/Walter Roland)	25
59	Jazz Collector JEL 4	THE MALE BLUES VOL. 3 (Blind Blake/Ramblin' Thomas)	25
59	Jazz Collector JEL 5	THE MALE BLUES VOL. 4 (Tall Tom/Pinewood Tom)	25
59	Jazz Collector JEL 8	THE MALE BLUES VOL. 5 (Blind Lemon Jefferson/Buddy Boy Hawkins)	20
60	Jazz Collector JEL 10	THE MALE BLUES VOL. 6 (Hound Head Henry/Frankie Jaxon)	20
60	Jazz Collector JEL 13	THE MALE BLUES VOL. 7 (Blind Lemon Jefferson/Ed Bell)	20
61	Jazz Collector JEL 24	THE MALE BLUES VOL. 8 (Blind Lemon Jefferson/Leadbelly)	20
69	Middle Earth MDE 201	MIDDLE EARTH SAMPLER (WRITING ON THE WALL: Aries/WOODEN O: Overture/ARCADIUM: Poor Lady) (promo only, 33rpm, no p/s)	80
60s	Jan & Dil TR 451	MORE DOWN HOME BLUES (Good Jelly Boss/Juke Boy Bonner/Papa Lightfoot/Snooky Prior)	30

N

Year	Label/Cat	Title	Value £
56	Vogue EPV 1106	NEGRO SPIRITUALS (Original Five Blind Boys/Sensational Nightingales)	18
64	Vocalion EPVP 1271	NEGRO SPIRITUALS (Dixie Hummingbirds/Sensational Nightingales)	18
64	Vocalion EPVP 1276	NEGRO SPIRITUALS (Five Blind Boys/Spirits Of Memphis)	18
66	Tamla Motown TME 2014	NEW FACES FROM HITSVILLE (Jimmy Ruffin/Chris Clark & Lewis Sisters/Tammi Terrell/Monitors)	350

O

Year	Label/Cat	Title	Value £
65	Columbia SEG 8413	ON THE SCENE (Downliners Sect/Animals/Cherokees/Cheynes/Georgie Fame/Yardbirds)	150
63	MGM MGM-EP 787	ORIGINAL HITS (Tommy Edwards/Johnny Ferguson/Jimmy Jones/Conway Twitty)	30
63	London RE-K 1390	THE ORIGINAL HITS (Drifters/Ritchie Barrett/Coasters/Ben E. King)	40
65	Atlantic AET 6006	ORIGINAL HITS VOL. 2 (Barbara Lewis/Coasters/Solomon Burke/Drifters)	40
62	Ember EMB 4522	ORIGINAL RHYTHM AND BLUES HITS (Jesse Belvin/Ray Charles/Linda Hayes/Jimmy McCracklin/Johnny Moore Blazers)	75
55	Pye Jazz NJE 1043	ORIGINS OF SKIFFLE (Isla Cameron/Guy Carawan/Peggy Seeger)	20

R

Year	Label/Cat	Title	Value £
67	Action ACT 002 EP	RAG GOES MAD AT THE MOJO (33rpm; Joe Cocker's Blues Band/Tangerine Ayr Band/Pitiful Souls/Delroy Good Good Band)	50
56	Vogue EPV 1113	RHYTHM AND BLUES (Dominoes/Swallows)	300
63	Stateside SE 1008	RHYTHM AND BLUES (Jimmy Reed/John Lee Hooker)	40
64	Stateside SE 1009	R&B CHARTMAKERS (Martha/Vandellas/Miracles/Marvin Gaye/Marvelettes)	100
64	Stateside SE 1018	R&B CHARTMAKERS NO. 2 (Miracles/Kim Weston/Supremes/Marvelettes)	125
64	Stateside SE 1022	R&B CHARTMAKERS NO. 3 (Marvin Gaye/Darnells/Eddie Holland/Martha & Vandellas)	125
64	Stateside SE 1025	R&B CHARTMAKERS NO. 4 (Supremes/Eddie Holland/Temptations/Contours)	120
60	Vogue EPV 1198	RHYTHM AND BLUES CONCERT (Helen Humes/Jimmy Witherspoon)	80

S

			MINT VALUE £
64	Pye Intl. NEP 44021	RHYTHM AND BLUES SHOWCASE VOL. 1 (Don & Bob/Dale Hawkins/ Clarence Henry/ Larry Williams)	30
64	Pye Intl. NEP 44022	RHYTHM AND BLUES SHOWCASE VOL. 2 (Jimmy McCracklin/ Muddy Waters/Little Walter/Howlin' Wolf)	30
57	Vogue VE 170211	ROCK AND ROLL (Mister Google Eyes August/Louis Jones Rock & Roll Band/Walter Price Rock & Roll Band/Clarence Gatemouth Brown)	80
60	Top Rank JKP 2060	RUSHING FOR PERCUSSION (Preston Epps/Sandy Nelson)	20

S

60s	S.A.U.C.C. PR 5262	ST. ANDREWS UNIVERSITY CHARITIES CAMPAIGN (20th Century Sounds/ Steve Hall & Roosters/Black Ring; no p/s)	35
64	Lyntone LYN 738/739	SHEFFIELD UNIVERSITY RAG RECORD (flexidisc; Vantennas/Dave Allen Band/ Addy Street Five/Los Caribos; die-cut sleeve)	40
55	Columbia SEG 7528	SHOUT FOR JOY (Pete Johnson/Albert Ammons/Meade Lux Lewis)	30
63	London RE-P 1403	SINGING THE BLUES (Ernie K-Doe/Showmen/Jesse Hill/Chris Kenner)	60
65	Keele Rag/Lyntone	SOUNDS OF SAVILE (flexidisc; Hipster Image/London Apprentices/ Tom & Brennie; some in die-cut title sleeve)	60
60	Mercury ZEP 10088	SURPRISE PACKAGE (Ben Hewitt/Diamonds)	50
59	Top Rank JKR 8007	SWEET BEAT (Lee Allen Band/Fred Parris/Cindy Mann/Mellokings)	30

T

63	Oriole EP 7080	TAKE SIX (Mark Peters' Silhouettes/Ian & Zodiacs/Faron's Flamingos/Earl Preston & T.T.s/Rory Storm & Hurricanes/Sonny Wade & Cascades)	25
59	Mercury ZEP 10015	TEAR IT UP (Boyd Bennett Orchestra/Red Prysock/Hi-Liters)	25
57	Mercury MEP 9522	TEEN-AGE ROCK (Red Prysock/Rusty Draper/Chuck Miller/Crew Cuts)	25
58	RCA RCX 111	TEENAGE TOPS (Ray Peterson/Jimmy Dell/Marlin Greene/Barry De Vorzon)	20
64	Ember EMB 4540	TEEN SCENE '64 (Dave Clark Five/Ray Singer/Washington D.C.s)	20
65	Century 21 MA 105	T.V. CENTURY 21 THEMES (David Graham/Sylvia Anderson/Peter Dyneley/ Barry Gray Orchestra/Gary Miller/Eric Winstone Orchestra)	15
64	Decca DFE 8585	T.V. THEMES (Andrew Oldham Orchestra/Ted Heath Music/Ron Grainer Music/Cyril Stapleton Orchestra)	25
62	Starlite STEP 31	TWIST OFF (Wayne Farmer/Medallions/Charles Perrywell/Piano Slim/Teenbeats/Dellos)	30
62	Starlite STEP 29	TWIST ON (Mighty Trojans/Dee Dee Gaudet/Dixie Lee/ Percy & The Rocking Aces)	20

W

69	Apple CT 1	WALLS ICE CREAM PRESENTS (Mary Hopkin/Iveys/Jackie Lomax/ James Taylor; with p/s)	50
65	Liberty LEP 4036	WE SING THE BLUES (Jesse Hill/Ernie K. Doe/Aaron Neville/Benny Spellman)	65
64	Fontana TFE 18009	WITH GOD ON OUR SIDE (withdrawn; Bob Dylan/Joan Baez/Pete Seeger)	100
66	Chess CRE 6009	WITH THE BLUES (Eddie Boyd Blues Combo/Buddy Guy)	40

Y

64	Fontana TFE 18011	YE PLAYBOYS AND PLAYGIRLS (withdrawn; Bob Dylan/Joan Baez/ Pete Seeger)	100
68	Chess CRE 6026	YOUR CHESS REQUESTS (Fontella Bass/Tony Clarke/Mitty Collier/ Billy Stewart)	40

VARIOUS ARTISTS SINGLES & EPs 70s/80s/90s/00s

A

87	London SAM 4	ADONIS: No Way Back (Club Mix)/ADONIS : No Way Back (Mix)/HERCULES: 7 Ways To Jack/MR. FINGERS: Can You Feel It (12", Promo only)	30
09	Anjunabeats ANJEP 002	ANJUNABEATS EP 002 (12", p/s)	35
91	ART 1	APPLIED RHYTHMIC TECHNOLOGY (12" EP)	25
98	Twisted Nerve TN 003	ALL OAR NOTHING (10", p/s; Badly Drawn Boy/Mum & Dad/Dakota Oak/ Sirconical/ Andy Votel)	15
84	Relegated	ARISTOCRAP (p/s; Pulex Irritans/Seventh Plague/Vendetta)	10
80	Deleted DEP 002	ANGST IN MY PANTS (2x7", fold-out numbered sleeve, Instant Automatons/Door & The Window/Mic Woods/Midnight Circus/012/Digital Dinosaurs/Missing Persons, etc)	50

B

83	Secret SHH 138	BACK ON THE STREET (p/s; Skin Disease/Angela Rippon's Bum/Venom/ Strike/East End Badoes)	12
87	Other OTH 6	BATTLEAXE (p/s; Black Riders/Holosade/Kes/Teacher's Pet)	30
78	Good Vibrations GOT 7	BATTLE OF THE BANDS (double pack, no'd p/s; Idiots/Rudi/Outcasts/Spider)	25
95	Ka-boom KA-BOOM 1	BIG BOLLOCKED BONFIRE BLOW-UP (Hood, et al.)	12
80	Vinyl Drip DRIP 001	BLACKPOOL ROX (p/s; Membranes/Section 25/Syntax/Kenneth Turner Set)	10
79	Skeleton SKL 002	THE BLANK TAPES VOL. 1 (folded p/s; Attempted Moustache/Junk Act/ Geisha Girls/ Zorkie Twins)	10
81	Secret SHH 126	BOLLOCKS TO CHRISTMAS (p/s; Business/4-Skins/Gonads/Max Splodge)	30
80s	Secret	BRITANNIA WAIVES THE RULES (12", p/s; Exploited/Chron Gen/Infa Riot)	12
80	Crass 421984/5	BULLSHIT DETECTOR (12", p/s; A.P.F. Brigade/Alternative/Amebix/ Clockwork Criminals/ Counter Attack/Crass/Frenzy Battalion/Fuck The CIA)	0

C

15	Universal 00600753574263	CAPITOL NORTHERN SOUL 7S BOX (7 x 7" box set)	80
15	Universal 00600753592380	CHESS NORTHERN SOUL (7 x 7" box set)	100
16	Universal 535 923-8	CHESS NORTHERN SOUL VOLUME 2 (7 x 7" box set)	60
98	Twisted Nerve TNXMS 1	CHRISTMAS STOCKING FILLER (Badly Drawn Boy/Dakota Oak/Sirconical/Mum & Dad/Elbow) (green vinyl in green wraparound sleeve or red vinyl in red sl.)	25
80s	No Future	A COUNTRY FIT FOR HEROES (12", p/s)	12
80s	No Future	A COUNTRY FIT FOR HEROES VOL. 2 (12", p/s)	20
94	Fierce Panda NING 02	CRAZED AND CONFUSED (p/s; Supergrass/Ash et al.)	12
15	Cherry Red CRCREBOX 18	CREATION ARTIFACT - THE FIRST TEN SINGLES	25
80	Newtown NTP 1	CRIME DECK: Arms Race/BASIC UNIT: Ladder//BEAT NECESSITY: Just Fine/STORY SO FAR: Radiated (p/s)	100

D

MINT VALUE £

07	Cultivated Electronics CE 001	CULTIVATED ELECTRONICS EP 001 (12:)	30
08	Cultivated Electronics CE 002	CULTIVATED ELECTRONICS EP 002 (12:)	50
08	Cultivated Electronics CE 003	CULTIVATED ELECTRONICS EP 003 (12:)	20

D

71	Dandelion DS 7001	DANDELION (die-cut sleeve; Principal Edwards Magic Theatre/Stackwaddy/ Siren/The Way We Live)	15
92	Delirious DELIS 6	DELIRIOUS PRIME CUTS VOL. 1 (12"; The Moog/Hardcore Rhythm Team/Justice And Mercy)	40
01	Trunk WWW 1	DIRTY FAN MAIL (7", white vinyl)	20
15	Disco Haman DISCOHAMAN 02	DISCO HAMAN 2 (12")	35
17	Disco Haman DISCOHAMAN 03	DISCO HAMAN 3 (12")	15
18	Disco Haman DISCOHAMAN 04	DISCO HAMAN 4 (12")	15
19	Disco Haman DISCOHAMAN 05	DISCO HAMAN 5 (12")	15
12	Fruits De Mer Crustacean 22	DO NOT ADJUST YOUR SET EP (purple vinyl)	15

E

79	Fast Products FAST 9B	EARCOM 2 (12", p/s; Joy Division/Thursdays/Basczax)	50
99	Lowlife LOW8	EASTER ISLAND (EP, 750 only)	15
10	Fruits De Mer Crustacean 15	EDDIE COCHRAN INSTRUMENTALS EP	25
97	Fat Cat 12FAT 003	8. 8.5, 9 (12", custom sleeve)	10
80	Newtown Products NTP 1	SIMPLE APPROACH TO NEWTOWN PRODUCTS (p/s)	200
96	Mo' Wax MWEX 001-010	EXCURSIONS (10 x 12", box set; the Prunes/IO/Olde Scottish/David Caron/DJ Solo & DJ Aura/Midnight Funk Assoc./Stasis/Solo feat. JT/Twig Bud/DJ Shadow)	30
99	AI AI 001	EXPERIMENTS IN COLOUR (12"; Normal/Cell/Fil)	20

F

19	Electronic Sound ES 754	A FACTORY ASSEMBLY (2 x 7", A Certain Ration/Durutti Column/Minny Pops/Section 25. p/s)	25
78	Factory FAC 2	A FACTORY SAMPLE (double pack, p/s, in plastic bag, with 5 stickers; Joy Division/ Cabaret Voltaire/Durutti Column/John Dowie)	400
04	Firecracker FIREC001	FIRECRACKER EP 1 (10")	40
05	Firecracker FIREC002	FIRECRACKER EP 1 (10")	20
95	555 5X555	5x555 (5x7" box set; Boyracer/Mike Nichols And His Excellency/Amy Linton & Stewart Anderson/Father/Hood)	30
91	Fontana FONT 1	THE FONTANA SINGLES BOX SET VOLUME 1 - HITS AND RARITIES (12-single box set, with 12 inserts)	30
91	Fontana FONT 2	THE FONTANA SINGLES BOX SET VOLUME 2 - HITS AND RARITIES (12-single box set, with 12 inserts)	30
79	Heartbeat PULSE 4	4 ALTERNATIVES (p/s; 48 Hours/Joe Public/Numbers/X-Certs)	15
80	Con (no cat. no.)	THE FOUR EPs (cassette; Mark Perry et al.)	15
96	Ché CHE 059	4 TRACK 3 BAND TOUR EP (p/s, Mogwai/Urusei Yatsura/Backwater, 50 only)	25
96	Mosquito MSQ 05	FRESH AS YOU FUCKIN' LIKE (12"; Paul Hannah/Russ Gabriel/Steve Patton/ Cristian Vogel/Si Begg)	15
11	Fruits De Mer Crustacean 16	THE FRUITS DE MER ANNUAL 2011 (2x7")	30
11	Fruits De Mer Crustacean 23	THE FRUITS DE MER ANNUAL 2012 (2x7", p/s)	30

G

72	Chess 6145 011	GENESIS - THE BEGINNINGS OF ROCK	10
83	Mouth MOUTH 1	G-FORCE (Shady Deal/Dead Loss/Blythe Rocket/Egypt)	20
70	Ra 5002	GOOD TIDINGS OF GREAT JOY (Faraway Folk, Torbay Quartet and Indiana Highway)	15
81	Thin Face JIM 1	GOT MY GOAT EP	35
70	Village Thing VTSX 1000	THE GREAT WHITE DAP (Wizz Jones/Sun Also Rises/Ian A. Anderson/Pigsty Hill Light Orchestra)	20

H

15	Hamas House HAMANHOUSE 01	HAMAN HOUSE 1 (12", p/s)	40
17	Hamas House HAMANHOUSE 02	HAMAN HOUSE 2 (12", p/s)	15
17	Hamas House HAMANHOUSE 03	HAMAN HOUSE 3 (12", p/s)	15
19	Hamas House HAMANHOUSE 04	HAMAN HOUSE 4 (12", p/s)	30
20	Hamas House HAMANHOUSE 05	HAMAN HOUSE 5 (12", p/s)	15
06	Trojan TJBX 330	HAUNTED HOUSE - SKINHEAD SEVENS BOXSET (8 x 7")	55
80	Groucho Marxist	HA! HA! FUNNY POLIS (PAISLEY ROCKS AGAINST RACISM) (p/s; Defiant Pose/Fegs/Urban Enemies/XS Discharge)	20
71	Abreaction ABR 001	HART ROCK (Brass Alley/Yellow/Trilogy/Lucas Tyson) (no p/s)	20

I

78	Radar SAM 88	INTERNATIONAL ARTISTS (13th Floor Elevators/Red Crayola/ Lost & Found/Golden Dawn; Red Crayola Hope & Anchor gig freebie	0
74	Galbraith POT 1	It's A Gas/Put In A Potterton (features 'The Goodies' on B-side)	6

L

11	Sanctuary	LUCKY SEVENS (7 x 7" box set of Trojan reissues, insert)	40
79	Decca FR 13864	THE LONDON BOYS (p/s; David Bowie/Small Faces/Birds/Dobie Gray)	10

M

MINT VALUE £

71	Track 2094 011	MAXI TRACK RECORD (John's Children/Crazy World Of Arthur Brown/ Thunderclap Newman/Jimi Hendrix; withdrawn blue sleeve crediting	0
71	Track 2094 011	MAXI TRACK RECORD (John's Children/Crazy World Of Arthur Brown/ Thunderclap Newman/Jimi Hendrix; red & white sleeve with press pack,	0
80	Paul Panic PANIC 001	MELL SQUARE MUSICK (1000 only, white labels, p/s, 50 came with inserts)	50
97	Begg. Banquet Random 2.1	METAL (12", red vinyl promo, die-cut sleeve, 1200 only; Robert Armani)	10
19	Mighty Force MFACID001	MF ACID 1 (12", limited to 123 copies)	20
19	Mighty Force MFACID002	MF ACID 2 (12", limited to 123 copies)	20
90	Mickey Rourke's Fridge MRF2	MICKEY ROURKE'S FRIDGE PRESENTS EP	50
97	V/VM VVMT4	MISSINGTOE & WHINE (EP, 500 only)	15
99	Twisted Nerve TN 009	MODERN MUSIC FOR MOTORCYCLES (10" EP, some on yellow vinyl; Dakota Oak/Alfie/ Sirconical & Andy Votel/Mum & Dad/Badly Drawn Boy)	15
95	Fierce Panda NING 15	MORTAL WOMBAT (double pack, p/s; Super Furry Animals/Baby Bird/ Panda/Mexican Pets/Harvey's Rabbit/Spare Snare)	10
13	Universal 534 542 5	MOTOWN 7s BOX: RARE AND UNRELEASED VINYL (7 x 7" box set)	200
14	Universal 535 056-2	MOTOWN 7s BOX: RARE AND UNRELEASED VINYL VOLUME 2 (7 x 7" box set)	100
16	Universal 536 953-7	MOTOWN 7s BOX: RARE AND UNRELEASED VINYL VOLUME 3 (7 x 7" box set)	60
17	Universal 537 482-5	MOTOWN 7s BOX: RARE AND UNRELEASED VINYL VOLUME 4 (7 x 7" box set)	50
80	EMI 12EMI 5074	MUTHA'S PRIDE (12", p/s; Wildfire/Quartz/White Spirit/Baby Jane)	20

N

98	Lowlife LOW6	98 Series Vol. 1 (EP)	15
98	Lowlife LOW7	98 Series Vol. 2 (EP)	15
80	Neutron NT 003	1980! THE FIRST FIFTEEN MINUTES EP (gatefold p/s with inserts; Vice Versa/Clock DVA/ I'm So Hollow/Stunt Kites)	25

O

82	Neat NEAT 25	ONE TAKE NO DUBS (12", p/s; Black Rose/Hellanbach/Alien/Avenger)	12

P

92	Art 2.1	THE PHILOSOPHY OF SOUND AND MACHINES EP 1 (12")	30
92	Art 2.1	THE PHILOSOPHY OF SOUND AND MACHINES EP 2 (12")	30
80s	A&M A&M PARTY 1/2/3/4/5/6	THE PARTY PARTY PACK (6 x 7", with picture sleeves, in PVC outer sleeve; Sting/Pauline Black/Dave Edmunds/Midge Ure/Modern Romance/Bad Manners)	20
80	L'Aventure SNS 001	THE POTENT HUMAN EP (p/s, different coloured sleeves)	30
97	V/VM VVMT4	PRIVILEGED FRAMES FOR REFERENCE (12" EP, p/s, 450 only)	15

R

93	Raptor RAP 1	RAPTOR PRESENTS . . . (12", p/s, 500 only; Ash/Buttlip/Marrow Bone/Fat)	40
10	Rave Wars RW1	RAVE WARS (p/s, red vinyl with random Star Wars figure)	40
12	Rave Wars RW2	RAVE WARS II - THE HARDCORE STRIKES BACK (p/s, blue vinyl with Star Wars figure)	50
14	Rave Wars RW3	RAVE WARS III (p/s, black or orange vinyl, with Star Wars figure)	40
91	Ptolemaic Terrascope POT 8	RED FLIPPER (no p/s, Nurse With Wound/The Underworlde/Caravan Of Dreams)	20
83	Consett Music Project RD 1	ROCK AND DOLE (Obnoxious Tartus/Decade Waltz/Task Force/Hot Banana)	25

S

80	Sonic Int. S14283	SEX, VIOLENCE & ETERNAL TRUTH (Lost Boys/What To Wear/The Venom/The Dodos, oversized poster sleeve, 4 A5 inserts, 250 only, stickered white labels, stamped plain white inner sleeve)	125
94	Fierce Panda/	SHAGGING IN THE STREETS (double pack, wraparound p/s in poly bag, 1,000 only; SMASH/Blessed Ethel/Mantaray/Done Lying Down)	12
95	Enraptured RAPT 4502	SILVER APPLES TRIBUTE (10", 12 in hand-drawn sleeve; Windy & Carl/Scaredycat/Third Eye Foundation/Flowchart/Sabine	30
79	Groucho Marxist WH 1	SPECTACULAR COMMODITY (p/s; Mental Errors/Mod Cons/ Poems/Sneex/XS Discharge)	10
14	Stateside 535 414-5	STATESIDE 7S (7 x 7" box set)	40
70s	Stiff BUY 1-10	STIFF BOX SET NO. 1 (10 x 7" box set)	35
70s	Stiff BUY 11-20	STIFF BOX SET NO. 2 (10 x 7" box set)	35
71	Ra EP 7002	STRICTLY FOR THE BIRDS	12
73	Nice DCL 773	SUBBUTEO SOUND EP	12
01	Edel 0128655ERESA	SUBSTITUTE EP : THE SONGS OF THE WHO (white vinyl, promo)	60

T

90s	Enraptured RAPT 4513	TERRASCOPE/TERRASTOCK (Bevis Frond/Damon & Naomi/Flying Saucer Attack/Silver Apples)	12
83	White Noise WN 3	THIS IS WHITE NOISE (p/s; Skrewdriver/Brutal Attack/Die Hards/A.B.H.)	60
02	Warner Bros 50466 13441	TOP-DECK SKA 45'S BOX (8 x 7"s, coloured vinyl in cardboard box)	25
82	Total Noise TOT 1	TOTAL NOISE # 1 (Business/Blitz/Dead Generation/Gonads)	10

U

80s	Fierce FRIGHT/SFTRI 28	AN UNHOLY MONTAGE (200 only [100 U.K./100 U.S.], coloured vinyl with numbered insert)	25
96	V/VM VVMT1	UPLINK DATA TRANSMISSIONS (12" EP, with 'data sheets', 250 only)	20

V

79	Pink BRS 002/INK 1000	THE VOXHALL TRACKS - LUTON (Klips/Para-Noia/Tee Vees/Friction (multifold p/s, 1000 only)	50

W

98	Goldmine GS1000X	WIGAN CASINO 25th ANNIVERSARY BOX SET (10 x 7")	60
80	Fuck Off FEP 001	WEIRD NOISE (p/s, white labels; Danny & Dressmakers/The Door & The Window/Instant	10

Y

			MINT VALUE £
77	MPL MPL 1	Automatons/012/Sell-Outs).. WE'VE MOVED! (Wings/Gene Vincent/Frank Sinatra et al., promo only excerpts sampler, with press pack)	350
84	Rather/Seventeen	WHAT A NICE WAY TO TURN SEVENTEEN NO. 2 (p/s; Swell Maps & others; with magazine)	12

Y

80s	Wonderful World Of WOW 1	YOU ARE NOT ALONE (p/s, with insert; Oi Polloi/Hex/Stalag 17/Symbol Of Freedom)	15

UNTITLED EPs & SINGLES 50s-00s

60s	Coxsone SCE 1	(no p/s, 33rpm; Gaylads/Hugh Godfrey/Glen & Dave/Roy Richards/ Cables/Richard Ace)	85
69	De Wolfe	(Lemon Dips, et al.)	75
94	Kennel Club VTDOG 10	(Strangelove/Tindersticks/God Machine/Breed (10", numbered, 1,500 only, free with Purr magazine issue 2)	10
98	Fat Cat 12FAT 008	REMIXES (12", custom sleeve; remixes of Fat Cat 12FAT 003 by Autechre et al.)	12
94	Kennel Club VTDOG 10	TINDERSTICKS: Girl On Death Row/STRANGELOVE: Wolf's Story/GOD MACHINE: The Devil Song/BREED: Diamonds Are Forever (10", numbered p/s, free with	15
96	SKAM MASK 1	UNTITLED (12", custom sleeve, 100 only; Freeform/Funkstorung/Boards Of Canada/ Jega)	150
97	SKAM MASK 2	UNTITLED (12", custom sleeve, 350 only; Hellinterface/Funkstorung/Bola/ Jega/Intron)	75

VARIOUS ARTISTS LPs & COMPILATIONS
(alphabetical by title)

A

88	Woronzow WOO 6	ACID JAM (with insert)	18
88	Serious DRUG 1	ACID TRAX	15
88	Serious DRUG 2	ACID TRAX VOL 2	20
88	Needle DRUG 3	ACID TRAX VOL 3	15
88	Warriors Dance WAF 006	ACID TRAX AND WARRIORS DANCE	15
89	Popdy POPDY 101	(0222) A COMPILATION OF CARDIFF BANDS (LP)	80
69	Action ACLP 6005	ACTION PACKED SOUL	50
70s	Jem JEM	A DEAL A DAY	25
96	Ferox FERLP 1	ADVENTURES IN TECHNO SOUL (2-LP; Too Funk/Paul Hannah/Carl Craig et al.)	30
85	United Dairies UD 012	AN AFFLICTED MAN'S MUSICAL BOX (3 different editions, 1st in gatefold sleeve)	75
75	Leader LEE 4056	A FINE HUNTING DAY - SONGS OF THE HOLME VALLEY BEAGLES (with book)	15
70	Pama PMP 2004	AFRICAN MELODY	90
71	Trojan TBL 166	AFRICA'S BLOOD (Lee Perry, et al.) (orange/white label)	40
98	Harmless HURTLP016	AFRICAKFUNK (2-LP)	30
77	Tartone TTL 101	AFRO AND REGGAE HITS	35
64	Decca LK 4606	AFTER SUNSET	150
66	Stateside SL 10172	AN ALBUM FULL OF SOUL	50
69	Key KL 002	ALIVE!	20
70	Talisman STAL 5013	ALL FOLK TOGETHER	20
84	Whaam! BIG 8	ALL FOR ART... AND ART FOR ALL	30
83	Neat NEAT 102A/B	ALL HELL LET LOOSE	20
76	Count Shelly CSLP 08	ALL STAR	30
61	Blue Beat BBLP 801	ALL STARS - JAMAICAN BLUES	300
70s	Rare Records 2	AMERICAN FOLK BLUES FESTIVAL 1962	25
64	Fontana TL 5204	AMERICAN FOLK BLUES FESTIVAL 1963	25
65	Fontana TL 5225	AMERICAN FOLK BLUES FESTIVAL 1964	25
66	Fontana TL 5286	AMERICAN FOLK BLUES FESTIVAL 1965	25
66	Fontana (S)TL 5389	AMERICAN FOLK BLUES FESTIVAL 1966 (mono/stereo)	22
70	CBS 63912	AMERICAN FOLK BLUES FESTIVAL 1969	20
80s	Pleasantly Surprised PS 2	THE ANGELS ARE COMING (2-cassette, with booklet)	25
83	No Future MPUNK 8	ANGELS WITH DIRTY FACES	18
60s	77' 77LA 12/13	ANGOLA PRISON SPIRITUALS	18
69	Immediate IMAL 03/04	ANTHOLOGY OF BRITISH BLUES VOLUME 1 (2-LP, gatefold sleeve)	30
69	Immediate IMAL 05/06	ANTHOLOGY OF BRITISH BLUES VOLUME 2 (2-LP, gatefold sleeve)	30
10	Fruits De Mer Crustacean 11	A PHASE WE'RE GOING THROUGH (300-500 only, light/dark grey vinyl)	35
10	Fruits De Mer Crustacean 11	A PHASE WE'RE GOING THROUGH (scarce coloured vinyl pressings)	150
64	London HA-K/SH-K 8174	APOLLO SATURDAY NIGHT (mono/stereo)	60
91	Delerium DELP 005D	A PSYCHEDELIC PSAUNA (2-LP)	30
92	Warp WARP LP 6	ARTIFICIAL INTELLIGENCE I	60
94	Warp WARLP LP 23	ARTIFICIAL INTELLIGENCE II (with 12")	60
94	Warp WARLP LP 23	ARTIFICIAL INTELLIGENCE II (without 12")	50
69	Atlantic 587/588 180	ATLANTIC BLOCKBUSTERS	20
65	Atlantic ATL 5020	ATLANTIC DISCOTHEQUE	40
64	Decca LK 4597	AT THE CAVERN	80
70	Beacon SBEAB 9	AUTHENTIC CHICAGO BLUES	20
57	London WB 91034	AUTHENTIC CARIBBEAN CALYPSOS (10" LP)	30
64	Stateside SL 10107	AUTHENTIC SKA	70
64	Stateside SL 10068	AUTHENTIC R & B	40
79	Heartbeat HB 1	AVON CALLING - THE BRISTOL COMPILATION (with poster)	25
95	Ministry Of Sound/AWOL LP 1	A.W.O.L: A WAY OF LIFE (3-LP, stickered sleeve)	40
80	K-Tel NE 1100	AXE ATTACK (early copies with demo of Iron Maiden's "Running Free")	15
74	Deroy DER 1052	AYRSHIRE FOLK (LP, private pressing)	70

B

MINT VALUE £

B

90	Warriors Dance WAFLP 4	BACK TO PRISON	20
70	Track 2407 001	BACKTRACK ONE	25
70	Track 2407003	BACKTRACK THREE	15
70	Track 2407004	BACKTRACK FOUR	15
70	Track 2407005	BACKTRACK FIVE	15
70	Track 2407 006	BACKTRACK SIX	15
54	London AL 3535	BACKWOODS BLUES (10")	50
73	Incus INCUS 11	BALANCE (Ian Brighton, et al.)	60
62	Fontana 688 200 ZL	BALLIN'	18
68	Pama PMLP 4	BANG BANG LULU	45
69	Pama Economy ECO7	BANGARANG (LP)	60
73	BBC/Roundabout 17	BANG ON A DRUM	18
60	Melodisc 12-115	BANJO BREAKDOWN	15
59	Fontana TFR 6018	BARRELHOUSE, BOOGIE WOOGIE AND BLUES (10")	20
58	Vogue Coral LRA 10022	BARRELHOUSE PIANO (10" LP)	20
59	Vogue Coral LRA 10023	BARRELHOUSE PIANO VOLUME 2 (10" LP)	20
95	Sarah SARAH 359	BATTERY POINT (LP)	100
98	Trunk BARKED 3	THE BATTLE OF BOSWORTH (LP)	15
64	Melodisc MLP 12-192	BATTLE OF THE GIANTS	20
53	MGM MGM-D 115	A BATTLE OF JAZZ: HOT VERSUS COOL (10")	30
71	BBC REC 118	BBC's FOLK ON TWO PRESENTS NORTHUMBRIAN FOLK	15
69	Beacon BEAB 1	BEACON BRINGS IT TO YOU	18
84	Well Suspect SUSS 1	THE BEAT GENERATION AND THE ANGRY YOUNG MEN	20
86	Mercury WILD 1	BEAT RUNS WILD (Wet Wet Wet et al.)	25
84	Xcentric ODDUMPTEENTH	BEATING THE MEAT	30
82	X-centric Noise 2	BEAT THE MEAT (cassette LP, insert)	50
87	Pink PINKY 15	BEAUTY (McCarthy et al.)	12
68	Elektra EUK 262	BEGIN HERE (also stereo EUKS 7262)	20
78	Rip Off ROLP 1	BELFAST ROCKS	35
68	Bell MBLL 102	BELL'S CELLAR OF SOUL VOLUME 1	30
69	Bell MBLL 107	BELL'S CELLAR OF SOUL VOLUME 2	30
69	Bell MBLL 117	BELL'S CELLAR OF SOUL VOLUME 3	30
69	Bell MBLL/SBLL 111	THE BEST FROM BELL	20
69	Bell MBLL/SBLL 124	THE BEST FROM BELL VOLUME 2	20
78	Stiff ODD 2	BE STIFF '78 (TOUR '78 OFFICIAL RELEASE) (promo only, Stiff artists performing Devo's Be Stiff - some sold by mail order)	18
78	Stiff DEAL 1	BE STIFF ROUTE '78 (with 16-page booklet & biographies, etc.)	15
12	BBE 173 CLP 1	BEST OF DISCO DEMANDS (2-LP)	20
12	BBE 173 CLP 2	BEST OF DISCO DEMANDS 2 (2-LP)	20
96	Universal Sounds US LP 2	BEST OF BLACK JAZZ RECORDS (2-LP)	25
69	Pama SECO 18	THE BEST OF CAMEL - AN OASIS OF SOUND	350
92	Chrysalis CHR TT 5012	BEST OF 2 TONE (LP)	40
83	Statik STATLP 14	THE BEST OF YOUR SECRET'S SAFE WITH US (This LP came with a free 7". The tracks were 'Sub Dub' by Sun Ya and on Side Two 'The Fools by Anthony Lindo. Cat. number was STAT26A/26B)	20
86	Plastic Head PLASLP 008	BEYOND THE FENCE BEGINS THE SKY (LP)	40
82	Open Door OD 001	BEYOND THE RIVER (LP, some with booklet)	15
73	Attack ATLP 1011	BIG BAMBOO	30
60	Fontana TFL 5080	THE BIG BEAT!	55
85	Big Beat WIKM39	BIG BEAT BEACH PARTY	15
78	Giorno GPS	BIG EGO	20
64	Capitol ST 2146	BIG SOUNDS OF THE DRAGS Vol 2	12
72	CBS 64844	THE BIG SUR FESTIVAL	18
73	Rhino SRNN 7002	BIG 12 - REGGAE STEADY GO VOL. 2	18
70	Pama SECO 32	BIRTH CONTROL	40
70	Matchbox SDX 207/8	BLACK DIAMOND EXPRESS TO HELL (2-LP)	25
80	Form BB 1003	BLACK MAGIC DUB (LP)	100
58	HMV CLP 1167	BLACK SLACKS AND BOBBY SOCKS (LP)	150
70	Ember SE 8009	BLACK SOUL EXPLOSION	18
70	CBS 52796	BLACK WHITES AND BLUES	20
10	Balkan BV 03	BLUE (with free CD)	30
68	Coxsone CSP 1	BLUE BEAT SPECIAL	60
92	Blue Note B1 99106	BLUE BREAK BEATS (2-LP)	20
93	Blue Note B1 89907	BLUE BREAK BEATS VOLUME TWO (2-LP)	20
96	Blue Note B1 54360	BLUE BREAK BEATS VOLUME THREE (2-LP)	20
98	Blue Note 724349402713	BLUE BREAK BEATS VOLUME FOUR (2-LP)	30
96	Blue Note B1 54357	BLUE JUICE (2-LP)	20
62	Columbia 33SX 1417	THE BLUES	60
66	London HA-S 8265	THE BLUES CAME DOWN FROM MEMPHIS	80
73	Flyright LP 504	BLUES CAME TO CHAPEL HILL	15
71	Python PLP-KM 17	BLUES - CHICAGO STYLE (LP)	45
60	Philips BBL 7369	BLUES FELL THIS MORNING	40
79	Look LK LP 6400	BLUES FOR SUZY	30
69	Chess CRLS 4558	BLUES FROM BIG BILL'S COPACABANA	35
69	Python PLP 6	BLUES FROM CHICAGO (99 copies only)	80
70	Python PLP 9	BLUES FROM CHICAGO VOL. 2 (99 copies only)	80
71	Python PLP 15	BLUES FROM CHICAGO VOL. 3 (99 copies only)	80
60s	Heritage 1004	BLUES FROM MAXWELL STREET (with insert, 99 copies only)	100

Year	Label/Cat	Title	Mint Value £
71	Python PLP 21	BLUES FROM THE WINDY CITY (99 copies only)	80
63	Stateside SL 10076	BLUES HOOT (Lightning Hopkins)	35
57	Pye Nixa NJL 8	(ALAN LOMAX PRESENTS) BLUES IN THE MISSISSIPPI NIGHT	35
60s	Sunflower (no cat. no.)	BLUES IS MY COMPANION (99 copies only)	34
60s	Sunflower (no cat. no.)	BLUES KEEP FALLING (99 copies only)	80
69	Blue Horizon 7-66227	BLUES JAM AT CHESS (2-LP)	60
67	Saydisc Match. SDM 142	BLUES LIKE SHOWERS OF RAIN	70
68	Saydisc Match. SDM 167	BLUES LIKE SHOWERS OF RAIN VOLUME 2	70
65	Decca LK 4681	BLUES NOW	60
72	Blues Obscurities BOV 1	BLUES OBSCURITIES VOL. 1: SOUTHERN BLUES/DARK MUDDY BOTTOM (plain cover with photocopied inserts)	40
72	Blues Obscurities BOV 2	BLUES OBSCURITIES VOL. 2: LONESOME HARMONICA	25
72	Blues Obscurities BOV 3	BLUES OBSCURITIES VOL. 3: WEST COAST BLUES	25
72	Blues Obscurities BOV 4	BLUES OBSCURITIES VOL. 4: ONE RAINY MORNING	25
72	Blues Obscurities BOV 5	BLUES OBSCURITIES VOL. 5: SOMETHING'S GONE WRONG	25
72	Blues Obscurities BOV 6	BLUES OBSCURITIES VOL. 6: COMING BACK HOME	25
72	Blues Obscurities BOV 7	BLUES OBSCURITIES VOL. 7	25
72	Blues Obscurities BOV 8	BLUES OBSCURITIES VOL. 8	25
72	Blues Obscurities BOV 9	BLUES OBSCURITIES VOL. 9	25
72	Blues Obscurities BOV 10	BLUES OBSCURITIES VOL. 10	25
74	London HA-U 8454	BLUES OBSCURITIES VOL. 1: DARK MUDDY BOTTOM (reissue)	15
74	London HA-U 8455	BLUES OBSCURITIES VOL. 2: LONESOME HARMONICA (reissue)	15
69	Highway 51 H 102	BLUES PEOPLE	40
68	Kokomo K 1001	A BLUES POTPOURRI (99 copies only)	60
71	Rarities (Tony's Records)	BLUES RARITIES VOL. 1 (2-LP)	25
69	Atlantic Special 590 019	THE BLUES ROLL ON (reissue of "Southern Folk Heritage: The Blues Roll On")	15
69	Poppy PYM 11001	BLUES ROOTS VOLUME ONE	25
66	Decca LK 4748	BLUES SOUTHSIDE CHICAGO	55
71	Python PLP 16	BLUES TODAY - SOUTHERN STYLE (99 copies only)	40
12	Belter 001	BONEHEAD CRUNCHERS VOLUME 1 (300 only)	40
12	Belter 002	BONEHEAD CRUNCHERS VOLUME 2 (300 only)	30
13	Belter 003	BONEHEAD CRUNCHERS VOLUME 3 (300 only)	25
13	Belter 004	BONEHEAD CRUNCHERS VOLUME 4 (300 only)	20
13	Belter 005	BONEHEAD CRUNCHERS VOLUME 5 (300 only)	20
09	BBE 142CLP	THE BOOGIE BACK (2-LP)	40
55	London AL 3544	BOOGIE WOOGIE WITH THE BLUES (10")	25
69	Pama SECO 17	BOSS REGGAE	200
74	Eron 002	BOTH SIDES OF THE DOWNS (with insert)	25
80	Aardvark STEAL 2	BOUQUET OF STEEL (blue vinyl with 27-page booklet)	15
81	Bristol Recorder BR 002	THE BRISTOL RECORDER VOL. 2 (with magazine booklet)	15
68	Island ILP 966/ILPS 9066	BRITISH BLUE-EYED SOUL	75
67	T. Motown TML 11059	BRITISH MOTOWN CHARTBUSTERS (mono, flipback sleeve)	20
69	T. Motown STML 11055	BRITISH MOTOWN CHARTBUSTERS (stereo reissue, flipback sleeve)	20
68	T. Motown (S)TML 11082	BRITISH MOTOWN CHARTBUSTERS VOL. 2 (mono/stereo, flipback sleeve)	18
83	Royal Records JBLP 306	BRITISH MUSIC SCENE (LP)	80
70	Trojan TBL 106	BRIXTON CAT	50
64	Decca LK 4598	BRUM BEAT	85
64	Dial DLP 1	BRUM BEAT	50
79	Big Bear BRUM 1	BRUM BEAT - LIVE AT THE BARREL ORGAN (2-LP, with inserts)	20
80	MCA MCF 3074	BRUTE FORCE	20
69	Pama Economy SECO 18	BULLET : A WORLD OF REGGAE, SKA, ROCK STEADY, BLUE BEAT (LP)	200
81	Crass 421984/4	BULLSHIT DETECTOR 1	20
82	Crass 221984/3	BULLSHIT DETECTOR 2 (2-LP)	20
82	Crass 221984/3	BULLSHIT DETECTIVE 2 (2-LP)	15
83	Crass	BULLSHIT DETECTIVE 3	15
66	Decca LK 4734	BUMPER BUNDLE 16 HITS	25
77	Stiff SEEZ 2	A BUNCH OF STIFF RECORDS	15
79	Cherry Red ARED 2	BUSINESS UNUSUAL (with Zig Zag small labels catalogue)	30
81	Autumn AU 2	BUSTED AT OZ	20
84	Dambusters DAM 003	BUTTONS AND BOWS VOLUME 1 (2-LP)	30
84	Dambusters DAM 006	BUTTONS AND BOWS VOLUME 2 (2-LP)	30

C

50s	Melodisc MLP 507	CALYPSO CARNIVAL (10" LP)	18
72	Topic 12TS 219	CANNY NEWCASSEL (with booklet, blue label)	20
67	Bounty BY 6035	CAN'T KEEP FROM CRYING (TOPICAL BLUES ON THE DEATH OF PRESIDENT KENNEDY)	12
91	Horace's HRH 102	CAPITAL SOUL - THE SOUND OF D.C. 1965/66	20
77	Carib Gems CGDD 301	CARIB GEMS DISCO DISC	25
50s	Parlophone CPMD 13	CARIBBEAN CALYPSO (10" LP, export issue)	25
07	Jazzman JMAN018LP	CAROLINA FUNK (2-LP)	30
81	Secret SEC 2	CARRY ON OI!	15
73	Nottingham Festival FEST 2	CASTLE ROCK	50
78	Nice NICE 1	CATCH A WAVE (2 x 10", gatefold sleeve)	30
80	Island IRSP7	CATCH THIS BEAT	20
90	Cerne CERNE 001/002/003	THE CERNE BOX SET (3-LP box set; Nurse With Wound/ Current 93/Sol Invictus; with 3 inserts)	125
60s	Columbia	CHARTBUSTERS USA	45
64	Chess CRL 4004	CHESS STORY VOL. 1	25
65	Chess CRL 4516	CHESS STORY VOL. 2	25
68	Sunflower ET 1401	THE CHICAGO HOUSE BANDS (99 copies only)	40

D

MINT VALUE £

Year	Label/Cat	Title	Value
69	Kokomo K 1005	CHICAGO SESSIONS VOLUME 1 (99 copies only)	50
80	Relics LSD 1	CHOCOLATE SOUP FOR DIABETICS VOL. 1	15
81	Relics ACID 1	CHOCOLATE SOUP FOR DIABETICS VOL. 2 (gatefold sleeve)	15
84	MCA CHUNK 1	CHUNKS OF FUNK	20
73	United Artists UDX 205/6	CHRISTMAS AT THE PATTI (2 x 10", gatefold sleeve)	22
68	Chess CRLS 4541	CHRISTMAS DEDICATION	25
63	London HA-U 8141	A CHRISTMAS GIFT FOR YOU (plum label)	80
78	Incus INCUS 33	CIRCADIAN RHYTHM	50
80s	White Elephant RIOCH 1	CITY WALLS - A SOUTHAMPTON COMPILATION (with insert)	12
94	Mastercuts CUTSLP 20	CLASSIC HOUSE MASTERCUTS VOLUME 1 (2-LP)	20
94	Mastercuts CUTSLP 22	CLASSIC HOUSE MASTERCUTS VOLUME 2 (2-LP)	20
13	Trunk JBH 049 LP	CLASSROOM PROJECTS (LP)	20
85	Pusmort 0012-02	CLEANSE THE BACTERIA	20
90s	Distronics ITCD 3	THE CLOSING PARTY - IN THE CITY LIVE UNSIGNED (CD)	50
99	Strut STRUTLP 001	CLUB AFRICA (2-LP)	20
72	Trojan TBL178	CLUB REGGAE 3	25
70	Trojan TTL 54	CLUB ROCK STEADY	25
68	W.I.R.L. ILP 965	CLUB ROCK STEADY '68	70
67	W.I.R.L. ILP 948	CLUB SKA '67	50
67	W.I.R.L. ILP 956	CLUB SKA '67 VOL. 2	60
70	Trojan TTL 48	CLUB SKA VOLUME ONE	30
70	Trojan TTL 51	CLUB SKA VOLUME TWO (Existence unconfirmed)	30
68	Island ILP 964	CLUB SOUL	50
84	Kent 022	CLUB SOUL	15
67	Elektra EUK 253	A COLD WIND BLOWS	15
65	T. Motown TML 11001	A COLLECTION OF 16 TAMLA MOTOWN HITS	25
67	T. Motown TML 11043	A COLLECTION OF 16 ORIGINAL BIG HITS VOL. 4	35
67	T. Motown TML 11050	A COLLECTION OF 16 ORIGINAL BIG HITS VOL. 5	35
68	T. Motown (S)TML 11074	A COLLECTION OF 16 ORIGINAL BIG HITS VOL. 6 (mono/stereo)	20
69	T. Motown (S)TML 11092	A COLLECTION OF 16 ORIGINAL BIG HITS VOL. 7 - THE MOTOWN SOUND	25
70	T. Motown (S)TML 11130	A COLLECTION OF 16 ORIGINAL BIG HITS VOL. 8	20
86	Color Disc COLORS 4	COLOR SUPPLEMENT (400 only)	15
93	2-Tone CDCHRTT 5013	THE COMPACT 2-TONE STORY (4-CD, box set with book)	40
76	Incus INCUS 21	COMPANY 1	40
77	Incus INCUS 29	COMPANY 6	40
77	Incus INCUS 30	COMPANY 7	40
82	Starforce COMP 1	COMPILATION 1	20
72	Apple STCX 3385	THE CONCERT FOR BANGLA DESH (3-LP box set, orange inside with BMI/ASCAP label credits, with booklet, featuring Bob Dylan)	75
64	Decca LK 4664	CONVERSATION WITH THE BLUES	70
57	Tempo TAP 10	COOL MUSIC FOR A HOT NIGHT - MOOD MUSIC IN THE MODERN MANNER	150
72	Wicksteed WCKLP 02	CORBY CATCHMENT AREA (private pressing)	200
81	No Future OI 3	COUNTRY FIT FOR HEROES	15
82	No Future 12 OI 23	COUNTRY FIT FOR HEROES 2	18
69	Pama ECO 2	CRAB - BIGGEST HITS	150
80	Rabid/Absurd LAST 1	THE CRAP STOPS HERE	25
60	Fontana TFL 5103	THE CREAM OF 'TAKE IT FROM HERE' (also stereo SFL 534)	12
74	Eron 005	CRYPTADIA	15
79	Trojan TRLS 180	CREATION ROCKERS 1	18
79	Trojan TRLS 181	CREATION ROCKERS 2	20
79	Trojan TRLS 183	CREATION ROCKERS 3	18
79	Trojan TRLS 183	CREATION ROCKERS 4	15
79	Trojan TRLS 184	CREATION ROCKERS 5	15

D

Year	Label/Cat	Title	Value
81	Two Tone CHRTT 5004	DANCE CRAZE (with poster)	20
68	H. Note/B. Shot BSLP 5002	DANCING DOWN ORANGE STREET	150
84	Kent KENT 026	DANCING 'TIL DAWN	15
76	Dark Horse DH 1 (DHSAM 1)	DARK HORSE RECORDS '76 (promo only sampler, stickered sleeve & inner)	40
86	EMI EQ 5003	DAVE CLARK'S TIME (2-LP, with brochure and lyric inner, some with hologram)	30
00	Nuphonic NUX 136LP	DAVID MANCUSO PRESENTS THE LOFT VOL. 1 (4 x 12" with booklet)	100
00	Nuphonic NUX 154LP	DAVID MANCUSO PRESENTS THE LOFT VOL. 2 (4 x 12")	100
79	Dead Good DEAD 4	DEAD GOOD'S DEAD GOODS (unissued)	0
78	Virgin VD 2508	DEAD ON ARRIVAL (glow-in-the-dark vinyl with poster, export copies to US have "EXPACK 001" sticker on sleeve))	20
66	Highway 51 H 100	DECADE OF THE BLUES - THE 1950's (99 copies only)	75
66	Highway 51 H 104	DECADE OF THE BLUES - THE 1950's VOLUME 2 (99 copies only)	50
70	Polydor 2673 001	DEEP OVERGROUND POP	20
70	Stax SXATS 1037	THE DEEP SOUL OF STAX	22
71	Flyright LP 102	DEEP SOUTH COUNTRY BLUES	12
83	Insane 1001	DEMOLITION BLUES (featuring the Oppressed/Decesed and Epidemic)	25
86	Decal LIK 9	DERAM DAYZE	15
68	Deram SML 1027	THE DERAM GOLDEN POPS SAMPLER	80
67	Island ILP 955	DERRICK HARRIOTT'S ROCK (SKA) STEADY PARTY	500
72	Trojan TTL 54	DERRICK HARRIOTT'S ROCKSTEADY PARTY (reissue - existence unconfirmed)	50
85	Yangki 01	DEVASTATE TO LIBERATE	15
89	Blast First BFDJ 1	DEVIL'S JUKEBOX (10 x 7" in numbered box, with booklet, 3,000 only)	20
87	Manic Ears ACHE 3	DIGGING IN WATER (LP, featuring Disorder/Chaos UK/Oi Polloi..)	15
74	DIP DLP 5026	D.I.P. PRESENTS THE UPSETTER (Lee Perry et al.)	175
69	Minit MLL/MLS 40089	DIRT BLUES	25

			MINT VALUE £
01	Trunk DFM 001 LP	DIRTY FAN MAIL (LP)	20
70	BBC REC 65M	DISC A DAWN	20
11	BBE BB E 172 CLP	DISCO LOVE 2 (2-LP)	20
13	BBE 224 CLP	DISCO LOVE 3 (2-LP)	20
15	BBE 319 CLP	DISCO LOVE 4 (2-LP)	20
67	Island ILP 943	DOCTOR SOUL	90
82	BBC 2-LP-22001	DOCTOR WHO COLLECTOR'S EDITION (2-LP, with poster)	30
80s	Pleasantly Surprised PS 12	DOCUMENT (cassette)	18
84	Hope Springs HOP 1	DON'T LET THE HOPE CLOSE DOWN	15
70	Python PLP	DOWNHOME BLUES (99 copies only)	90
94	React REACT LP 55	DOPE ON PLASTIC! (2-LP)	20
94	React REACT LP 65	DOPE ON PLASTIC 2 (2-LP)	20
96	React REACT LP 073	DOPE ON PLASTIC 3 (2-LP)	20
96	React REACT LP 97	DOPE ON PLASTIC 4 (3-LP)	20
98	React REACT LP 118	DOPE ON PLASTIC 5 (4-LP)	20
99	React REACT LP 147	DOPE ON PLASTIC 6 (4-LP)	20
00	React REACT LP 169	DOPE ON PLASTIC 7 (3-LP)	20
01	React REACT LP 195	DOPE ON PLASTIC 8 (3-LP)	20
70	Python PLP 14	DOWNHOME BLUES VOLUME 2 (99 copies only)	90
71	Python PLP 22	DOWNHOME BLUES VOLUME 3 (99 copies only)	90
87	No label or cat no	DOUBLE EXPOSURE (2-LP)	50
67	Down With The Game 200	DOWN WITH THE GAME VOLUME 1 (99 copies only)	40
67	Down With The Game 201	DOWN WITH THE GAME VOLUME 2 (99 copies only)	40
68	Down With The Game 203	DOWN WITH THE GAME VOLUME 3 (99 copies only)	40
68	Down With The Game 204	DOWN WITH THE GAME VOLUME 4 (99 copies only)	40
68	Down With The Game 205	DOWN WITH THE GAME VOLUME 5 (99 copies only)	40
68	Down With The Game 206	DOWN WITH THE GAME VOLUME 6 (99 copies only)	40
67	Island ILP 954	DR. KITCH	60
76	Live and Love LALP 05	DREAD LOCKS IN JAMAICA	30
85	Capitol EG 26 0573 1-4	DREAM BABIES	15
83	International INTEL 4	DREAM SEQUENCE 2-LP)	100
59	Parlophone PMC 1101	DRUMBEAT (Adam Faith et al.)	30
68	Island ILP 976	THE DUKE AND THE PEACOCK	150
69	Trojan TTL 8	DUKE REID'S GOLDEN HITS	50
67	Island ILP 958	DUKE REID'S ROCK STEADY	400
70	Trojan TTL 53	DUKE REID'S ROCK STEADY (reissue, existence unconfirmed)	30

E

79	Fast FAST 9A	EARCOM 1	30
70	Middle Earth MDLS 20	EARTHED	75
80	Dead Good GOOD 1	EAST (with inner & stickered sleeve)	25
81	Nothing Shaking SHAK 1	EAST OF CROYDON (with booklet)	25
73	Southern Sound SD 200	EAST VERNON BLUES	30
63	Decca LK 4546	EDINBURGH FOLK FESTIVAL VOLUME 1	30
63	Decca LK 4563	EDINBURGH FOLK FESTIVAL VOLUME 2	30
75	Island/Transatlantic	ELECTRIC MUSE - THE STORY OF FOLK INTO ROCK (4-LP box set with booklet)	40
64	Turnabout TV340465	ELECTRONIC MUSIC	25
73	YES 2-4	ELECTRONIC MUSIC FROM YORK (3-LP, box set, with insert)	250
85	Push PUSH 001	ELEGANCE, CHARM AND DEADLY DANGER	25
10	Universal Sound USLP 38	ELEKTRONISCHE MUSIK AUS KOLN (2-LP)	20
80s	Master BBSLP 007	ELEMENTALS	20
77	EMI PSPL 209	EMI INTRODUCES THE NEW BRONZE AGE (LP)	20
92	Sarah SARAH 628	ENGINE COMMON	70
83	Psycho PSYCHO 1	ENDLESS JOURNEY VOL. 1 (numbered)	20
83	Psycho PSYCHO 3	ENDLESS JOURNEY VOL. 2 (numbered)	15
83	Psycho PSYCHO 19	ENDLESS JOURNEY VOL. 3 (numbered)	15
88	MEK MEK 006	THE ENGLISH REBELS (with insert)	20
84	Street Sounds HBOX 1	ESSENTIAL ELECTRO (9 LP box set, 5000 only)	100
72	Blue Horizon 2683 007	THE EXCELLO STORY (2-LP)	120
68	Amal. AMGLP 2002	EXPLOSIVE ROCKSTEADY	85
87	Rot ASS 100	THE END OF AN ERA (LP)	15

F

80	Factory FACT 24	A FACTORY QUARTET (2-LP, featuring Durutti Column, Kevin Hewick, Blurt & Royal Family And The Poor)	20
76	Lightning LIP 2	FAREWELL TO THE ROXY (LP)	20
73	Count Shelly CSLP 03	FEELING HIGH VOL 1	45
68	Zeus CF 201	FESTIVAL AT TOWERSEY	50
63	Pye Intl. NPL 28033	FESTIVAL OF THE BLUES	30
65	Sue ILP 920	50 MINUTES & 24 SECONDS OF RECORDED DYNAMITE!	100

(Each of the above 10 LPs came with blue labels and a booklet.)

85	L.A.Y.L.A.H. LAY 10	THE FIGHT IS ON (Nurse With Wound, Organum, et al.)	30
72	Warner Bros K 66013	FILLMORE: THE LAST DAYS (3-LP box set with poster & booklet)	35
88	Re-Elect The President NIXON 4	THE FINAL COUNTDOWN (LP)	25
60	HMV CLP 1358/CSD 1298	FINGS AIN'T WOT THEY USED TO BE	20

(Each of the above 10 LPs came with blue labels and a booklet.)

69	Music Man	FIREPOINT - A COLLECTION OF FOLK BLUES	100
73	Spark SRLM 2003	FIREPOINT - A COLLECTION OF FOLK BLUES (reissue)	30

(Each of the above 10 LPs came with blue labels and a booklet.)

G

			MINT VALUE £
95	Dub Jockey DJLP 005	FIRST BOOK OF DUB CHANTS (no sleeve)	50
71	CBS 66311	THE FIRST GREAT ROCK FESTIVALS OF THE 70s: ISLE OF WIGHT AND ATLANTA (3-LP)	30
73	Spaceward EDENLP 53	THE FIRST LAME BUNNY ALBUM (LP, fold out sleeve)	400
57	Esquire 20-089	THE FIRST NATIONAL SKIFFLE CONTEST (10")	80
56	Mercury MPT 7512	FIRST ROCK 'N' ROLL PARTY (10")	130

(Each of the above 10 LPs came with blue labels and a booklet.)

89	Confection LC 7871	FLAIR: THE OTHER WORLD OF BRITISH FOOTBALL (2-LP)	20
84	Kent KENT 017	FOOT STOMPERS	15
83	Kent KENT 007	FOR DANCERS ONLY	15
78	Trailer LER 2015	FLYDE ACOUSTIC	15
64	Blue Beat BBLP 803	FLY FLYING SKA	400
69	Atlantic 588 184	FLYING HIGH (record club edition)	15
76	Flams/Wounded WR 1068	FOLK AT THE CHEQUERS (private pressing)	15
73	Counterpoint CPT 3994	FOLK FROM McTAVISH'S KITCHENS	30
73	Windmill WMD	FOLK HERITAGE	30
73	Nottingham Festival FEST 1	FOLK NOTTINGHAM STYLE	200
65	Decca LK 4783	FOLK NOW	25

(Each of the above 10 LPs came with blue labels and a booklet.)

66	Folkscene FSP 001	FOLK SCENE (LP, private pressing)	100
73	Eron ERON 001	FOLK IN SANDWICH (LP)	40
69	Topic	THE FOLK SONGS OF BRITAIN VOLS. 1-10 (10 x LP box set)	80
57	HMV DLP 1143	FOLK SONG TODAY (SONGS AND BALLADS OF ENGLAND AND SCOTLAND) (10")	25
71	Nicro K 220971	FOLK UPSTAIRS	80
83	Greensleeves GREL 60	FORWARD	20
92	Sarah SARAH 583	FOUNTAIN ISLAND	70
65	Decca LK 4695	FOURTEEN - THE LORD'S TAVERNERS' ALBUM	25
70	Bamboo BLP 205	FREEDOM SOUNDS	60
72	Trojan TRL 51	FROM BAM BAM TO CHERRY OH BABY	20
81	Alternative ALT 007A	FROM BROMLEY WITH LOVE (LP)	120
70	Liberty LBS 83278	FROM THE VAULTS	15
83	New European BADVC 666	FROM TORTURE TO CONSCIENCE (with insert)	80
71	Cutty Wren	FROST LANE	50
89	Sub Pop DAMP 104	FUCK ME, I'M RICH!	15
89	Unrest UNREST 14	FULL FORCE VOL. 3	15
70	Trojan TBL 137	FUNKY CHICKEN	25
70	Bamboo BLP 206	FUNKY REGGAE	75
76	Burning Sounds BS 1024	FUNNY FEELING (LP)	30
82	Come Org. WDC 881021	FÜR ILSE KOCH (some on red vinyl)	120
70	RCA Victor SF 8118	49 GREEK STREET (LP, featuring Synanthesia, Nadia Cattouse, Tin Angel & Keith Christmas)	70
03	Trunk JBH 004 LP	FLEXI SEX (LP)	30
06	Trunk JBH 018 LP	FUZZY FELT FOLK (LP)	60
06	Trunk JBH 018 LP	FUZZY FELT FOLK (LP, 100 with fuzzy felt inserts)	80

G

95	Sarah SARAH 530	GAOL FERRY BRIDGE	80
69	Pama ECO 4	GAS - GREATEST HITS	160
66	Doctor Bird DSL 5001	GAYFEET (Jamaican sleeve and UK pressed LP)	400
84	Kent KENT 021	GEMS	15
55	HMV DLP 1039	GENE NORMAN PRESENTS JUST JAZZ (10")	20
72	Chess 6641 047	GENESIS - THE BEGINNINGS OF ROCK (4-LP box set with booklet)	60
73	Chess 6641 125	GENESIS - MEMPHIS TO CHICAGO (4-LP box set with booklet)	60
75	Chess 6641 174	GENESIS - SWEET HOME CHICAGO (4-LP box set with booklet)	60
69	Kokomo K 1004	GEORGIA GUITARS 1927-1938 (99 copies only)	60
67	Coxsone CSL 8007	GET READY ROCK STEADY	200
02	Soundway SNDWLP001	GHANA SOUNDZ - AFRO-BEAT, FUNK AND FUSION IN THE 70s (2-LP)	25
69	Pama SECO 20	A GIFT FROM PAMA	60
80s	Sarah	GLASS ARCADE (The Field Mice/The Sea Urchins, et al.)	50
72	Revelation REV 1/2/3	GLASTONBURY FAYRE REVELATIONS - A MUSICAL ANTHOLOGY (3-LP, poster sleeve with booklets, pyramid & printed polythene bag)	200
66	Columbia SX 6062	GO!	70
95	Lissy's LISS 5	GODZ IS NOT A PUT ON (500 only, in hand-pressed sleeve; some with free 7")	30
70	Python LP 1	GOIN' BACK TO CHICAGO (99 copies only)	80
60s	Heritage 1003	GOING TO CALIFORNIA (99 copies only)	80
69	Oliver & Boyd SBN 05 002118/9	THE GOLDEN BIRD (2-LP)	30
64	Columbia 33SX 1664	GOLDEN GOODIES VOL. 1	60
64	Columbia 33SX 1672	GOLDEN GOODIES VOL. 2	60
69	Roulette RCP 1000	GOLDEN GOODIES VOL. 1	20
69	Roulette RCP 1001	GOLDEN GOODIES VOL. 2	20
68	Allegro ALL885	GOLDEN HITS OF SOUL	20
57	Capitol T 830	THE GOLD RECORD (blue label)	10
03	Dust To Digital DTD 01	GOODBYE BABYLON (6-CD box set)	60
75	Eron 004	GOOD FOLK OF KENT (with insert)	40
65	Atlantic ATL 5004	GOOD OLD FIFTIES	55
68	Elek. EUK 260/EUKS 7260	GOOD TIME MUSIC (U.K. version of "What's Shakin' ", gold or red label)	40
72	CBS 67234	GOSPEL SOUND (2-LP)	20
59	Brunswick LAT 8290	GOSPEL TRAIN	20
73	United Artists UDX 203/4	GREASY TRUCKERS PARTY (2-LP, gatefold sleeve)	20
54	London AL 3530	THE GREAT BLUES SINGERS (10")	45

H

MINT VALUE £

70	Trojan TBL 111	GREATER JAMAICA - MOONWALK REGGAE	60
64	Stateside SL 10075	THE GREATEST GOSPEL SONGS OF OUR TIME	25
67	Doctor Bird DLM 5009	GREATEST JAMAICAN BEAT	200
70	Transatlantic TRASAM 17	GREAT SCOTS SAMPLER	20
70	Transatlantic TRASAM 21	GREAT SCOTS SAMPLER VOL. 2	20
54	HMV DLP 1054	GREAT TRUMPET SOLOISTS (10")	20
10	Balkan BV 02	GREEN (with free CD)	20
85	Crashed METALPS 107	GREEN METAL	30
83	Anagram KILO 1	GRIME OF THE CENTURY (6-LP, box set)	50
71	Bamboo BDLP 215	GROOVING WITH BAMBOO	70
69	Direction 8-63452	GROOVY BABY	15
63	Realm RM 149	GROUP BEAT '63	40
63	London HA-U 8086	GROUP OF GOODIES	55
78	Virgin VCL 5001	GUILLOTINE (10" mini-LP, with inner sleeve)	18
71	Sunnyland KS 102	GULF COAST BLUES (99 copies only)	40
69	Trojan TTL 16	GUNS OF NAVARONE	35
84	Fashion FAD LP 001	GREAT BRITISH MCS	15
79	Bead Records BEAD 15	GROUPS IN FRONT OF PEOPLE (LP)	25
79	Bead Records BEAD 15	GROUPS IN FRONT OF PEOPLE 2 (LP)	25
76	Cactus CTLP 115	GUSSIE PRESENTS THE RIGHT TRACKS	20
69	Liberty LBX 3	GUTBUCKET	25
68	Island ILP 977	GUY STEVENS' TESTAMENT OF ROCK AND ROLL	60
71	Wand WCS 1002	THE GUYS WITH SOUL	20

H

80	Hackney Music Coll LP1	HACKNEY MUSIC COLLECTIVE	25
88	Hangman HANG 22-UP	HANGMAN SAMPLER	20
88	HandMade (no cat. no.)	HANDMADE FILMS MUSIC - THE 10TH ANNIVERSARY (CD, promo only)	100
85	Anagram GRAM 23	HANG 11 (MUTANT SURF PUNKS)	20
78	Black Symbol BS 004	HANDSWORTH EXPLOSION VOL 1 (LP)	80
68	Immediate IMLYIN 2	HAPPY TO BE PART OF THE INDUSTRY OF HUMAN HAPPINESS	18
88	Strange Fruit SFRLP 101	HARDCORE HOLOCAUST	15
90	Strange Fruit SFRLP 113	HARCORE HOLOCAUST 2	20
88	BPM BPLP2	HARDCORE ONE (LP)	25
87	Music Scene MKSLP 11416	HARDER THAN THE REST (LP)	40
74	Decca DPA 3009/10	HARD UP HEROES 1963-68 (2-LP, gatefold sleeve)	20
99	Harvest 724352119820	HARVEST FESTIVAL (5-CD box set)	20
69	Harvest SPSLP 118	HARVEST SAMPLER OF THE INITIAL FOUR JUNE RELEASES (promo only)	300
84	Rot ASS 18	HAVE AROTTEN CHRISTMAS (LP)	25
71	Sunnyland KS 101	HAVIN' A GOOD TIME - CHICAGO BLUES ANTHOLOGY (99 copies only)	50
12	Fruits De Mer CRUSTACEAN 26	HEAD MUSIC (2-LP, 850 only, gatefold sleeve, 1 LP yellow and one LP purple vinyl)	25
71	Vertigo 6360 045	HEADS TOGETHER, FIRST ROUND (gatefold sleeve, swirl label)	18
94	Mo' Wax MWLP 026	HEADZ: A SOUNDTRACK OF EXPERIMENTAL BEATHEAD JAMS (3-LP)	25
96	Mo' Wax MW 061LP	HEADZ VOLUME 2A (4-LP)	40
08	Jonny JBH 025 LP	HEAR O ISRAEL (LP)	20
81	Red Stripe SNTF 856	THE HEAT IS ON	40
90	Imaginary ILLUSION 016	HEAVEN AND HELL VOLUME 1: A TRIBUTE TO THE VELVET UNDERGROUND	70
81	Heavy Metal HMR LP 1	HEAVY METAL HEROES	30
82	Heavy Metal HMR LP 7	HEAVY METAL HEROES VOLUME 2	25
84	Heavy Metal HMR LP 24	HEAVY METAL RECORDS (blue, clear & white vinyl, round sleeve)	15
68	Trojan TRL 6	HERE COMES THE DUKE	40
85	Rock 'N' Dole RDR 2	HEROES	15
80s	Temps Modernes LTMV:XI	HEURES SANS SOLEIL	20
69	Pama PSP 1002	HEY BOY HEY GIRL	60
59	Parlophone PMD 1085	HIGHWAY TO HEAVEN (10")	20
88	Westside HOUSEBX 1	THE HISTORY OF HITS - THE HISTORY OF HOUSE RECORDS (box set, 14-LPs, numbered)	120
52	Capitol LC 6508	THE HISTORY OF JAZZ - THE SOLID SOUTH	20
69	Bamboo BDLP 203	HISTORY OF SKA VOLUME ONE	200
87	Fanfare/PWL HFCD 2	HIT FACTORY - THE BEST OF STOCK, AITKEN & WATERMAN VOL. 2 (CD, with exclusive mix of Kylie Minogue's "I Should Be So Lucky", etc)	30
64	Pye NPL 18108	THE HITMAKERS	20
65	Tamla Motown TML 11073	HITSVILLE U.S.A.	35
67	Stax 589 005	HIT THE ROAD STAX	30
81	United Dairies UD 05	HOISTING THE BLACK FLAG	35
74	Melodisc 12-216	HONEYS	75
60s	Riverside RLP 8806	HONKY TONK TRAIN (with booklet)	10
84	Kent KENT 023	HOT CHILLS AND COLD THRILLS	15
71	Pama PMP 2006	HOT NUMBERS	40
71	Pama PMP 2009	HOT NUMBERS VOLUME TWO	40
77	WEA M 100	HOT PLATTER CORDON BLEU (available via Melody Maker)	20
70	Trojan TBL 128	HOT SHOTS OF REGGAE	40
72	Hot Wax SHW 5008	HOT WAX GREATEST HITS	15
69	Track 613 016	THE HOUSE THAT TRACK BUILT (gatefold sleeve)	30
80	Stark ST1	HOUSEHOLD SHOCKS	40
69	Blue Horizon PR 45/46	HOW BLUE CAN WE GET (2-LP, gatefold sleeve with insert)	40
82	Native NAT 001	HUNDREDS AND THOUSANDS	45

I

69	Liberty LBL/LBS 83252	I ASKED FOR WATER ... AND SHE GAVE ME GASOLINE	80

J

			MINT VALUE £
88	Idea IDEALP 003	IDEA COMPENDIUM (LP)	35
81	TJM TJML 1	IDENTITY PARADE (LP)	15
02	Universal 0647491	IMPRESSED (2-LP, Gilles Peterson compilation)	35
02	Universal 982 197 0	IMPRESSED 2 (2-LP, Gilles Peterson compilation)	25
88	Bam Caruso MARX 085	ILLUSIONS FROM THE CRACKLING VOID	15
90s	Dig The Fuzz DIG 013	ILLUSIONS OF ALICE IN BLACK (650 only, with booklet)	20
69	Immediate IMLYIN 1	IMMEDIATE LETS YOU IN	20
70	Highway 51 H-104	I'M YOUR COUNTRY MAN (99 copies only)	40
95	Dig The Fuzz DIG 001	INCREDIBLE SOUND SHOW STORIES VOL 1: THE TECHNICOLOUR MILKSHAKE (LP)	20
96	Dig The Fuzz DIG 004	INCREDIBLE SOUND SHOW STORIES VOL 2: WHEN THE TANGERINE STRIKES TWELVE (LP, gatefold sleeve, orange vinyl)	20
96	Dig The Fuzz DIG 007	INCREDIBLE SOUND SHOW STORIES VOL 3: 200 FEEL DEEP IN A PURPLE IDEA (LP)	20
96	Dig The Fuzz DIG 008	INCREDIBLE SOUND SHOW STORIES VOL 4: A TRIP ON THE MAGIC FLYING MACHINE (LP)	20
96	Dig The Fuzz DIG 009	INCREDIBLE SOUND SHOW STORIES VOL. 5: YELLOW STREET BOUTIQUE (LP)	20
97	Dig The Fuzz DIG 010	INCREDIBLE SOUND SHOW STORIES VOL. 6: PLASTIC & OTHER RUBBERS OF LIFE (LP)	20
97	Dig THe Fuzz DIG 013	INCREDIBLE SOUND SHOW STORIES VOL. 7: ILLUSIONS OF ALICE IN BLACK (LP, with booklet)	20
99	Dig The Fuzz DIG 016	INCREDIBLE SOUND SHOW STORIES: VOL. 8: PROFESSOR POTTS PORNOGRAPHIC PROJECTOR (LP, with booklet)	30
99	Dig The Fuzz DIG 036	INCREDIBLE SOUND SHOW STORIES VOL. 9: CLAP HANDS DADDY COME HOME! (LP, booklet)	20
99	Dig THe Fuzz DIG 039	INCREDIBLE SOUND SHOW STIRIES VOL. 10: A HIDDEN SECRET GARDEN FOUND (LP, booklet)	20
99	Dig The Fuzz DIG 033	INCREDIBLE SOUND SHOW STORIES: VOL. 11: CRIMSON VALLET CREATURES IN YOUR ZOO (LP, with booklet)	20
01	Dig THe Fuzz DIG 043	INCREDIBLE SOUND SHOW STORIES VOL. 12: FUZZ PUDDING FACTORY (LP)	15
01	Buzz With Fuzz FUZZLP 3301	INCREDIBLE SOUND SHOW STORIES VOL. 13: FAR AWAY ROUNDABOUT (LP, 500 only)	15
00	Dig THe Fuzz DIG 042	INCREDIBLE SOUND SHOW SPORIES VOL. 14: CANDY COLOURED DAYDREAMS (LP, with gatefold insert)	20
03	Dig THe Fuzz DIG 046	INCREDIBLE SOUND SHOW STORIES VOL. 16 : SECOND GLANCE THROUGH THE LOOKING GLANCE (LP)	20
02	Dig THe Fuzz DIG 045	INCREDIBLE SOUND SHOW STORIES VOL. 17 CLAP HANDS DADDY COME HOME1 PART 2 (LP, with inner sleeve, 400 only)	20
66	CBS/Denson Shoes	THE IN CROWD (shoe offer compilation)	25
69	Trojan TTL 15	INDEPENDENT JAMAICA	50
79	Object Music OBJ 002	INDISCRETE MUSIC - DUBIOUS COLLABORATION (500 only)	15
84	Illuminated JAMS 39	THE INDUSTRIAL RECORDS STORY 1976-1981	35
84	United Dairies UD 015	IN FRACTURED SILENCE	35
69	T. Motown (S)TML 11264	IN LOVING MEMORY (TRIBUTE TO MRS LOUCYE G. WAKEFIELD)	55
70	Blue Horizon PR 37	IN OUR OWN WAY (OLDIES BUT GOODIES)	20
84	People Unite PU 104	IN PROGRESS	150
70	Ember EMB 34111	IN REGGAE TIME	15
90	Warriors Dance WAFLP 3	INTERNATIONAL SMOKE SIGNAL	35
83	Future FUTURE 1	INVISIBLE FRAME	18
66	Ember FA 2034	IRELAND'S GREATEST SOUNDS: FIVE TOP GROUPS FROM BELFAST'S MARITIME CLUB	70
79	Rationale RATE 8	IRRATIONALE (cassette, in bag with booklet)	20
79	K Block	IS THE WAR OVER?	25
61	Oriole MG 20046	IT'S ALL HAPPENING HERE	35
85	Kent KENT 046	IT'S TORTURE	15
84	Sain 002	IT'S UNHEARD OF	150

J

69	Amalgamated CSP 3	JACKPOT OF HITS	50
74	Atra ALP 001	JAH GUIDE - JAMAICA'S GREATEST HITS	45
71	Ashanti SHAN 102	JAMAICAN FOLK SINGERS	20
07	Soul Jazzz SJR LP 171	JAMAICA FUNK (2-LP)	30
68	Blue Cat BCL 1	JAMAICAN MEMORIES	150
64	Atlantic 587 075	JAMAICA SKA (colour 'Dancers' sleeve)	100
67	Atlantic 587 075	JAMAICA SKA (reissue, orange sleeve)	40
60s	Wirl WHIRL 1	JAMAICA'S AMBASSADORS OF SONG	100
60s	Melodisc MLP 12-158	JAMAICA'S GREATEST	40
56	Tempo TAP 5	JAZZ AT THE FLAMINGO	250
68	Columbia SLJS 1	JAZZ EXPLOSION	25
72	Decca ECS 2114	JAZZ IN BRITAIN 1968-1969	50
84	Streetsounds MUSIC 1	JAZZ JUICE	25
85	Streetsounds SOUND 1	JAZZ JUICE (reissue)	20
85	Natalie LIE 1	JOBS FOR THE BOYS	15
77	Decca DPA 3035/3036	THE JOE MEEK STORY (2-LP)	30
69	BBC REC 52S	JOHN PEEL PRESENTS TOP GEAR	40
70	BBC REC 68M	JOHN PEEL'S ARCHIVE THINGS	35
60	HMV CLP 1327	A JUG OF PUNCH (also issued as XLP 50003)	20
81	Eric's ERICS 008	JUKEBOX AT ERIC'S	20
76	RCA RS 1066	JUMPING AT THE GO GO	18
64	R&B/Ska Beat JBL 1111	JUMP JAMAICA WAY	650
69	RCA Intl. INT 1014	JUST A LITTLE BIT OF SOUL	22
75	Count Shelly CSLP 7	JUST BETWEEN (nude cover)	100
79	Kick KK 1	JUST FOR KICKS	35

K

11	Fruits De Mer Crustacian 21	KEEP OFF THE GRASS (2-LP)	20
56	Vogue LAE 12028	KENTON'S SIDEMEN (Don Rendell, et al.)	150

L

81	White Witch	KENT ROCKS (200 only, white cover)	180
54	HMV DLP 1048	KEYBOARD KINGS OF JAZZ (10")	20
72	Key	KEY COLLECTION (with insert)	15
82	Kik KIKLP 01	KIKROCK VOLUME ONE	35
70	Trojan TBL 140	KING SIZE REGGAE	35
72	Sioux SLX 7502	KING OF THE ROAD	30

L

79	Cherry Red A RED 4	LABELS UNLIMITED (LP with inner)	15
83	Fetish FR 2011	THE LAST TESTAMENT (with inner, stickered sleeve)	18
87	Other OTH 10	LAST WARRIOR	18
68	Island ILP 986	LEAPING WITH MR LEE (by Bunny Lee All Stars)	400
80	Atra ATRA LP 1003	THE LEGEND (Augustus Pablo et al.)	30
03	Ai AILP 004	LEISURE (100 copies only)	15
99	Jazzman 1	LE JAZZBEAT!	20
66	Blue Horizon LP 2	LET ME TELL YOU ABOUT THE BLUES (99 copies only)	1000
84	Cult 1	LET'S GET PISSED IT'S CHRISTMAS	15
66	Neshoba N 11	LET'S GO DOWN SOUTH (99 copies only)	50
58	Brunswick LAT 8271	LET'S HAVE A PARTY	30
81	Alt. Tentacles VIRUS 4	LET THEM EAT JELLYBEANS (with lyric poster)	20
80s	Third Mind/Abstract	LIFE AT THE TOP	20
85	Riot City CITY 019	LIFE'S A RIOT WITH RIOT CITY RECORDS	20
80	BUN 01	LIVE AT BUNJIES (gatefold sleeve with insert)	30
77	NEMS NEL 6013	LIVE AT THE VORTEX	15
65	Fontana TL 5240	LIVE AT THE WHISKEY A-GO-GO	40
68	Big Shot BBTL 4000	LIVE IT UP	150
64	Embassy WLP 6065	LIVERPOOL BEAT	15
65	Ember NR 5028	LIVERPOOL TODAY - LIVE AT THE CAVERN	40
08	Honest Jons HJRLP 33	LIVING IS HARD - WEST AFRICAN MUSIC IN BRITAIN 1927-29 (2-LP)	20
70	Trojan TBL 135	LOCH NESS MONSTER	50
98	Simply Vinyl SVLP 089	LOCK, STOCK AND TWO SMOKING BARRELS (2-LP)	100
87	4AD CAD 703D	LONELY IS AN EYESORE (cardboard pack with book)	40
87	4AD CADX 703	LONELY IS AN EYESORE (CD, LP & cassette, in wooden box with etching, screen print & video, 100 only)	1000
71	Count Shelly SSLP 03	LOOK BEFORE YOU LEAP	60
91	Holyground HG 121	LOOSE ROUTES (2-LP, gatefold foldover sleeve)	30
78	Love Bird LB 430	LOVE AFFAIR	30
69	Pama PSP 1001	THE LOVELY DOZEN	60
96	Earth EARTHLP 001	LTJ BUKEM PRESENTS EARTH VOLUME 1 (5 LP box set, stickered box, 5 picture sleeves,5000 only)	35
97	Earth EARTHLP 002	LTJ BUKEM PRESENTS EARTH VOLUME 2 (5 LP box set, 5 picture sleeves)	25
98	Good Looking EARTH LP 003	LTJ BUKEM PRESENTS EARTH VOLUME 3 (5 LP box set)	25

M

76	Cornish Legend CLM 1	MADE IN CORNWALL (with insert)	60
02	Honest Jons HJRLP1	MALI MUSIC (2-LP, poster)	25
03	Peckings PTI 001	MAMA PECKINGS AND THE DUTCHESS	30
79	Object Music OBJ 003	A MANCHESTER COLLECTION	25
70	Trojan TBL 129	MAN FROM CAROLINA	30
70	CBS 52798	MA RAINEY AND THE CLASSIC BLUES SINGERS	20
69	Marmalade 643 314	MARMALADE - 100% PROOF	15
72	Village Thing VTSAM 16	MATCHBOX DAYS	25
68	President PTL 1002	MAR-V-LUS SOUND OF R&B AND SOUL MUSIC	40
60s	Wudwink ISMF 107	MARY'S FOLK	200
96	Skam MASK 100	MASK 100 (100 only)	250
97	Skam MASK 200	MASK 200 (LP, 200 only)	150
98	Skam MASK 300	MASK 300 (LP, 300 only)	50
98	Skam MASK 400	MASK 400 (LP, 400 only)	40
99	Skam MASK 500	MASK 500 (LP, 500 only, includes remix of Bowie's Ashes To Ashes)	80
69	Liberty LBL/LBS 83190	ME AND THE DEVIL	75
88	Hangman HANG 15-UP	THE MEDWAY POETS (LP)	20
87	Hangman HANG 4 UP	MEDWAY POWER HOUSE 1	20
87	Hangman HANG 8 UP	MEDWAY POWER HOUSE 2	20
88	Hangman HANG 17 UP	MEDWAY POWER HOUSE 3	25
69	T. Motown (S)TML 11126	MERRY CHRISTMAS FROM MOTOWN (mono/stereo)	40
10	Universal Sounds USLP5	MESSAGE FROM THE TRIBE (2-LP, reissue)	30
80	BBC REH 397	METAL EXPLOSION	20
80	EMI EMC 3318	METAL FOR MUTHAS	20
97	Metalheadz METBOX 001	METALHEADZ (5 discs in circular tin, booklet)	30
87	Other OTH 9	METAL WARRIOR	50
66	Atlantic 587 021	MIDNIGHT SOUL	20
80	Pipe PIPE 2	MINIATURES (with poster insert, 500 only)	18
80	Pipe PIPE 2	MINIATURES (cassette with mini-booklet insert, 100 only)	30
71	Trojan TBL 174	MISS LABBA LABBA	30
60s	Bounty BY 6025	MODERN CHICAGO BLUES	30
56	Tempo TAP 2	MODERN JAZZ SCENE 1956	100
79	Bridge House BHLP 003	MODS MAYDAY '79 (original issue)	20
01	EMI 5 35078 2	MOJO PRESENTS ACID DROPS, SPACEDUST AND FLYING SAUCERS (4-CD box set)	40
70	Trojan TTL 31	MOONLIGHT GROOVER	35
62	HMV CLP 1583	MORE OF YOUR FAVOURITE TV AND RADIO THEMES	20

N

			MINT VALUE £
67	Atlantic 587088	MORE MIDNIGHT SOUL	15
65	private pressing	MORE SINGING AT THE COUNT HOUSE	150
72	Island HELP 5	MORRIS ON (black label with pink 'i')	20
80	Conventional CON 013	MOTHER OF A PUNK (cassette)	12
86	Iguana VYK LP 11	MOTOR CITY 9 (with booklet)	15
65	Tamla Motown TML 11007	THE MOTORTOWN REVUE LIVE	80
66	Tamla Motown TML 11027	THE MOTORTOWN REVUE IN PARIS	70
70	Tamla Motown (S)TML 11127	THE MOTORTOWN REVUE LIVE (mono/stereo)	20
74	Tamla Motown STML 11270	MOTOWN CHARTBUSTERS VOL. 9 (green vinyl)	15
66	Tamla Motown TML 11030	MOTOWN MAGIC	35
68	Tamla Motown TML 11064	MOTOWN MEMORIES (flipback sleeve)	60
68	Tamla Motown TML 11077	MOTOWN MEMORIES VOL. 2	60
70	Tamla Motown STML 11143	MOTOWN MEMORIES VOL. 3	50
72	Tamla Motown TMSP 1130	THE MOTOWN STORY (5-LP box set)	20
83	Tamla Motown TMSP 6019	THE MOTOWN STORY - THE FIRST 25 YEARS (box set)	20
77	Mountain PSLP 200	MOUNTAIN ROCKS INTO '77 (Mountain label sampler, promo only)	20
84	Kent 013	MOVING ON UP	15
83	Showcase SHOWC 1	MUSIC BIZ SHOWCASE '83	50
71	Mushroom 100 MR 16	THE MUSHROOM FOLK SAMPLER	40
57	Brunswick LAT 8201	MUSIC FOR THE BOYFRIEND - HE REALLY DIGS ROCK'N'ROLL	100
57	Brunswick LAT 8202	MUSIC FOR THE BOYFRIEND - HE REALLY DIGS JAZZ	30
57	Brunswick LAT 8205	MUSIC FOR THE BOYFRIEND - THE FEMININE TOUCH	35
67	Argo RG 533	MUSIC FROM THE FAR NORTH (with foldout inner)	15
15	Balkan BV 16	MUTANT CITY ACID	25
15	Balkan BV 17	MUTANT CITY ACID 2	20
16	Balkan BV 19	MUTANT CITY ACID 3	20
17	Balkan BV 22	MUTANT CITY ACID 4	18
81	Ze ISSP 4001	MUTANT DISCO (3 x 12" box set, numbered, 2,000 only)	20
04	Ze ZEREC LP02-2	MUTANT DISCO VOLUME 2 (2-LP)	20
05	Ze ZEREC LP 14	MUTANT DISCO VOLUME 3 (2-LP)	20
77	EMI NUT 4	MY GENERATION	15
89	Hangman HANG 35 UP	MEDWAY POWERHOUSE (LP)	30

N

71	Eden LP 43	NAPTON FOLK CLUB (private pressing, 100 only)	35
69	Bamboo BLP 201	NATURAL REGGAE VOLUME ONE	60
70	Bamboo BLP 204	NATURAL REGGAE VOLUME TWO	100
81	4AD CAD 117	NATURES MORTES - STILL LIVES (export issue)	60
85	Musique Brut BRV 002	NECROPOLIS, AMPHIBIANS AND REPTILES: THE MUSIC OF ADOLF WOLFLI	20
71	RCA NEON 1	NEON PROMOTIONAL ALBUM	150
83	Pax PAX 14	NEVER MIND THE GONADS - HERE'S THE TESTICLES	15
87	Broken Flag BF V8	NEVER SAY WHEN	40
77	Vertigo 6300 902	NEW WAVE	20
79	Planet PR 003	NEW WAVE FROM THE HEART	70
69	Blue Horizon 7-63210	THE 1968 MEMPHIS COUNTRY BLUES FESTIVAL	25
81	NMX	NMX: LIVE AT SHEFFIELD (cassette)	20
68	Spark SRLM 107	NO INTRODUCTION	30
69	Trojan TTL 14	NO MORE HEARTACHES	35
70	Polydor 545 017	NON STOP SOUL	30
69	Regal Starline SRS 5013	NO ONE'S GONNA CHANGE OUR WORLD	18
89	Manic Ears ACHE 017	NORTH ATLANTIC NOISE ATTACK (2-LP, insert)	20
14	Harmless HURTBOX 007	NORTHERN SOUL: THE SOUNDTRACK (box set 14 x 7")	80
14	Harmless NTHSOULLP01	NORTHERN SOUL: THE SOUNDTRACK (2-LP)	30
60	Fontana TFL 5123	NOTHIN' BUT THE BLUES (gatefold sleeve)	60
71	CBS 66278	NOTHING BUT THE BLUES (2-LP, Blue Horizon pressings may also exist (£75))	60
79	Giorno GPS	THE NOVA CONVENTION	20
70	Decca Nova SPA 72	NOVA SAMPLER	20
70s	Warm PFLP 201	NOVA-VAGA	15
84	Virgin/EMI CDP 26 0408 2	NOW THAT'S WHAT I CALL MUSIC 4 (CD)	200
86	Virgin/EMI CDNOW 8	NOW THAT'S WHAT I CALL MUSIC 8 (CD)	35
87	Virgin/EMI CDNOW 9	NOW THAT'S WHAT I CALL MUSIC 9 (CD)	35
92	EMI NOW 21	NOW THAT'S WHAT I CALL MUSIC 21 (2-LP)	40
92	EMI NOW 22	NOW THAT'S WHAT I CALL MUSIC 22 (2-LP)	40
92	EMI NOW 23	NOW THAT'S WHAT I CALL MUSIC 23 (2-LP)	35
93	EMI NOW 24	NOW THAT'S WHAT I CALL MUSIC 24 (2-LP)	40
93	EMI NOW 25	NOW THAT'S WHAT I CALL MUSIC 25 (2-LP)	40
93	EMI NOW 26	NOW THAT'S WHAT I CALL MUSIC 26 (2-LP)	40
94	EMI NOW 27	NOW THAT'S WHAT I CALL MUSIC 27 (2-LP)	40
94	EMI NOW 28	NOW THAT'S WHAT I CALL MUSIC 28 (2-LP)	40
94	EMI NOW 29	NOW THAT'S WHAT I CALL MUSIC 29 (2-LP)	50
95	EMI NOW 30	NOW THAT'S WHAT I CALL MUSIC 30 (2-LP)	50
95	EMI NOW 31	NOW THAT'S WHAT I CALL MUSIC 31 (2-LP)	50
95	EMI NOW 32	NOW THAT'S WHAT I CALL MUSIC 32 (2-LP)	70
96	EMI NOW 33	NOW THAT'S WHAT I CALL MUSIC 33 (2-LP)	80
96	EMI NOW 34	NOW THAT'S WHAT I CALL MUSIC 34 (2-LP)	80
96	EMI NOW 35	NOW THAT'S WHAT I CALL MUSIC 35 (2-LP)	100
69	Pama ECO 6	NU BEAT - GREATEST HITS	100
73	Elektra K 62012	NUGGETS (Original Artyfacts From The First Psychedelic Era 1965-1968) (2-LP, gatefold sleeve)	45

			MINT VALUE £
86	Numa NUMA 1004	NUMA RECORDS YEAR 1 (with bonus Italian 12" "My Dying Machine")	15
81	Guardian Records	N E 1 (LP)	40

O

69	Liberty LBS 83234	OAKLAND BLUES	30
79	Rok ROK LP 001	ODD BODS, MODS AND SODS	75
85	Micro MIC 15001	OFFERING OF ISCA (LP, features 2 tracks by Circuit 7)	100
58	Parlophone PMC 1072	OH BOY!	40
78	Raw RAWLP 2	OH NO IT'S MORE FROM RAW (Users/Killjoys et al.)	20
80	EMI ZIT 1	OI! - THE ALBUM (initially mail-order only from Sounds magazine)	30
87	Link LP 23	OI! GLORIOUS OI!	15
84	Syndicate SYNLP 4	OI! OF SEX	15
83	Secret SEC 5	OI! OI! THAT'S YER LOT	15
60s	Melodisc MS 4	OLDIES BUT GOODIES	65
64	Stateside SL 10094	OLDIES R & B	70
06	Peckings PTI LP 003	OLD SKOOL YOUNG BLOOD (2-LP)	40
69	Transatlantic XTRA 1076	O LIVERPOOL WE LOVE YOU (Stan Kelly/Bill Shankley/Jimmy Tarbuck et al.)	40
68	Big Shot BBTL 4001	ONCE MORE	130
69	Marmalade 643 314	100% PROOF	15
99	Universal MCD 60066	1-2-3-4 PUNK AND NEW WAVE 1976 - 1979 (5-CD box set)	30
86	Stateside/EMI SSL 6002	ONE MINIT AT A TIME	18
73	Charisma CLASS 3	ONE MORE CHANCE	20
63	Columbia 33SX 1536	ONE NIGHT STAND	40
63	Stateside SL 10065	ON STAGE LIVE!	65
69	Atco 228 009/010	ON STAGE - LIVE (2-LP)	25
84	Sane SANE 003	ON THE STREET (LP)	35
83	Kent KENT 006	ON THE SOUL SIDE	15
64	Columbia 33SX 1662	ON THE SCENE	90
84	Kent KENT 20	ON THE UP BEAT	15
10	Balkan BV 05	ORANGE (with free CD)	20
95	Tip TIPLP 2	ORANGE COMPILATION (2-LP)	20
64	Rio RLP 1	THE ORIGINAL COOL JAMAICAN SKA	150
70	Mercury SMCL 20182	ORIGINAL GOLDEN HITS OF THE GREAT BLUES SINGERS	20
60	London HA-G 2308	THE ORIGINAL HITS	30
61	London HA-G 2339	THE ORIGINAL HITS VOL. 2	30
64	Vocalion VA 8017	ORIGINAL SURFIN' HITS	65
62	London HA-U 2404	OUR SIGNIFICANT HITS	70
83	Peninsula	OUT OF THE UNKNOWN	70
13	Z ZEDDLP 028	OVERDOSE OF THE HOLY GHOST (2-LP)	60

P

70	Golden Guinea GGL 0451	PADDY IS DEAD AND THE KIDS KNOW IT (LP)	150
65	Blue Beat BBLP 804	PAIN IN MY BELLY	300
67	Island ILP 945	PAKISTANI SOUL SESSION	75
90	Factory FACT 400	PALATINE - THE FACTORY STORY (4-LP)	150
85	LIL LP2	PARKSIDE STEELWORKS	60
73	Charisma CAS 1078	THE PARLOUR SONG BOOK (LP)	15
68	Studio One SOL 9009	PARTY TIME IN JAMAICA	300
88	On U Sound 37	PAY IT ALL BACK VOL 1	15
88	On U Sound 42	PAY IT ALL BACK VOL 2 (with booklet)	20
77	CollinsMusic CM001 BLP	PEACE AND LOVE	50
66	Decca LK 4824	PENTHOUSE MAGAZINE PRESENTS THE BEDSIDE BOND	40
83	Psycho PSYCHO 6	THE PERFUMED GARDEN	20
84	Psycho PSYCHO 15	THE PERFUMED GARDEN II	20
81	Cherry Red BRED 15	PERSPECTIVES AND DISTORTION (gatefold sleeve)	15
86	Streetsounds PHST 1986	THE PHILADELPHIA YEARS (14-LP box set)	80
92	Art ART2 CD	THE PHILOSOPHY OF SOUND AND MACHINE (CD compilation)	60
72	Apple APCOR 24	PHIL SPECTOR'S CHRISTMAS ALBUM (reissue of "A Christmas Gift For You")	30
75	Warner Bros K 59010	PHIL SPECTOR'S CHRISTMAS ALBUM (2nd reissue, some with poster)	18
80	Phil Spector Intl. 2307 015	PHIL SPECTOR '74/'79	25
67	Riverside RLP 8809	PIANO BLUES 1927-1933	20
60	HMV CLP 1362/XLP 50044	A PINCH OF SALT - BRITISH SEA SONGS OLD AND NEW	30
53	London AL 3506	PIONEERS OF BOOGIE WOOGIE (10")	40
54	London AL 3537	PIONEERS OF BOOGIE WOOGIE VOLUME TWO (10")	40
98	Just Say JUSTLP 001-3	THE PIONEERS OF HOUSE MUSIC - CHICAGO REUNION (2-LP)	20
80	Incus INCUS 37	PISA 1980: IMPROVISOR'S SYMPOSIUM	50
13	RCLP 009	PLANKTON - A FRUITS DE MER COMPILATION (LP, gatefold with free 7")	20
81	P. Surprised KLARK 002	PLEASANTLY SURPRISED - AN HOUR OF ELOQUENT SOUNDS (cassette)	20
71	Argo ZPR 264/5	POETRY AND JAZZ IN CONCERT 250	15
89	Link LINK LP 095	POP OI!	20
68	Polydor 236 517/8/9	POP PARTY! (3-LP in box)	20
65	Post War Blues PWB 1	POST WAR BLUES: CHICAGO (99 copies only)	45
66	Post War Blues PWB 2	POST WAR BLUES: MEMPHIS ON DOWN (99 copies only)	45
67	Post War Blues PWB 3	POST WAR BLUES: EASTERN AND GULF COAST STATES (99 copies only)	45
68	Post War Blues PWB 4	POST WAR BLUES: TEXAS (99 copies only)	45
68	Post War Blues PWB 5	POST WAR BLUES: DETROIT (99 copies only)	45
60s	Post War Blues PWB 6	POST WAR BLUES: WEST COAST (99 copies only)	45
60s	Post War Blues PWB 7	POST WAR BLUES: THE DEEP SOUTH (99 copies only)	45
69	Python PWBC 1	POST WAR COLLECTOR SERIES VOL. 1 (99 copies only)	80

Q

			MINT VALUE £
80	4AD BAD 11	PRESAGES (mini-LP, green/pink or brown sleeve)	15
79	Preseli PRE 001	PRESELI FOLK (private pressing with insert)	30
77	Uptempo UTLP 001	PRESENTING THE POSSE	30
70	Kokomo K 1006	PRE-WAR TEXAS BLUES (99 copies only)	45
87	A&M AMA 3906	PRINCE'S TRUST 10TH ANNIVERSARY BIRTHDAY PARTY (2-LP, some stickered, with Paul McCartney 7": "Long Tall Sally"/"I Saw Her Standing There")	20
90	Intrigue IGE LP4	PRODUCED BY NEMESIS VOL III	18
90	United Dairies UD 134	PSILOTRIPITAKA (3-LP [UD 01, 03 & 04], with bonus LP "Registered Nurse" [UD 00], 1,000 only, some possibly in leather bag)	400
90	United Dairies UD 134CD	PSILOTRIPITAKA (3-CD [UD 01, 03 & 04], with bonus CD "Registered Nurse" [UD 00CD], 1,000 only, 30 in 'leather bondage bag')	400
81	Abstract AABT 100	PUNK AND DISORDERLY (red vinyl)	20
82	Anagram GRAM 001	PUNK AND DISORDERLY 2 (blue vinyl)	20
82	Anagram GRAM 005	PUNK AND DISORDERLY 2 (Multi-coloured vinyl)	20
82	Pax 7	PUNK DEAD?...NAH MATE	20
91	Sink Below SINK 2	PUNK'S NOT DREAD (LP, with inner)	15
65	Sue ILP 919	PURE BLUES VOLUME ONE	60
83	Guardian GRC 2162	PURE OVERKILL	18
85	Color Disc COLORS 2	PURPLE TWILIGHT (400 only)	20
68	Island ILP 978	PUT IT ON, IT'S ROCK STEADY	40
71	Pye PSA 6	PYE SALES SAMPLER (sampler for Pye & Dawn releases; 99 copies only, with release sheet)	20

Q

68	Stateside S(S)L 10209	A QUARTET OF SOUL	50
70	Trojan TBL 136	QUEEN OF THE WORLD	120
82	Quest BRA 002	THE QUEST TAPES	75

R

07	Mikili AFRO 1	RARE AFRO & CARIBBEAN FUNK	20
07	Mikili AFRO 2	RARE AFRO & CARIBBEAN FUNK VOL 2	20
76	Grounation GROL 509	RAS CLAAT DUB	50
69	United Artists (S)UX 1214	RAVE	25
73	Attack ATLP 1012	RAVE ON BROTHER	35
67	Ace Of Clubs ACL 1220	RAW BLUES (also stereo SCL 1220)	10
77	Raw RAWLP 1	RAW DEAL (black & white sleeve & red/blue label)	25
64	Decca LK 4577	READY, STEADY, GO!	45
68	Pama PMLP 3	READY STEADY GO ROCKSTEADY	70
64	Decca LK 4634	READY, STEADY, WIN	75
65	Stateside SL 10112	THE REAL R & B	40
89	Intrigue IGE LP1	THE REBEL PRESENTS	30
95	4th & Broadway BRLPD 617	THE REBIRTH OF COOL PHIVE (2-LP)	40
82	Recommended 104	RECOMMENDED SAMPLER	15
79	Destiny DS 10001	THE RECORD COLLECTOR	20
81	Recorder BR 003	RECORDER THREE	20
70	CBS 52797	RECORDING THE BLUES	22
12	Balkan BV 01	RED (with CD)	30
65	Red Bird RB 20-102	RED BIRD GOLDIES	50
69	Trojan TTL 11	RED RED WINE	30
70	Downtown TBL 116	RED RED WINE VOLUME 2	35
69	Trojan TBLS 105	REGGAE CHARTBUSTERS	20
70	Pama Economy ECO 34	REGGAE FOR DAYS (LP)	150
68	Big Shot BIL 3000	REGGAE GIRL	200
69	Pama ECO 3	REGGAE HITS '69 VOL. 1	35
69	Pama ECO 11	REGGAE HITS '69 VOL. 2	50
69	Pama PTP 1001	REGGAE HIT THE TOWN	50
68	Studio One SOL 9007	REGGAE IN THE GRASS	150
71	Trojan TBL 181	REGGAE JAMAICA	20
71	Trojan TBL 193	REGGAE JAMAICA VOL. 2	20
71	Bamboo BDLP 208	REGGAEMATIC SOUNDS	100
70	Trojan TBL 144	REGGAE MOVEMENT	20
72	Trojan TBL 189	REGGAE POWER VOL 2	45
72	Trojan TBL176	REGGAE REGGAE VOL 2	45
69	Coxsone CSP 2	REGGAE SPECIAL	50
71	Pama 2001	REGGAE SPECTACULAR WITH STRINGS	25
70	Trojan TBL 151	REGGAE STEADY GO VOL 1	18
73	Rhino SRNN 7001	REGGAE STEADY GO	18
73	Trojan TRLS 54	REGGAE STRINGS	30
74	Trojan TRLS 92	REGGAE STRINGS VOL 2	18
68	Coxsone CSL 8017	REGGAE TIME	150
72	Ashanti ANB 201	REGGAE TIME	25
71	Pama PMP 2012	REGGAE TO REGGAE	50
69	Pama PSP 1004	REGGAE TO UK WITH LOVE	225
76	Third World TWLP 107	REGGAE VARIOUS ARTISTS	70
86	Rot HELL 36	RELIGION AS HELL (LP)	20
80s	Ré 0101	RE RECORDS QUARTERLY VOL. No. 1 (with book)	15
01	Trunk/Second Coming SEC 001	RESURRECTION: THE AMPLIFIED BIBLE OF HEAVENLY GROOVES (LP)	20
72	Count Shelly CSLP 01	RETURN TO ME REGGAE	30
73	Count Shelly CSLP 02	RETURN TO ME REGGAE 2	40
64	Decca LK 4616	RHYTHM AND BLUES	80

S

Year	Label/Cat#	Title	MINT VALUE £
64	Mercury MCL 20019	RHYTHM AND BLUES PARTY	40
73	Tamla Motown STML 11232	RIC TIC RELICS	20
68	Coxsone CSL 8015	RIDE ME DONKEY	150
69	Trojan TTL 18	RIDE YOUR DONKEY	40
85	Kent KENT 039	RIGHT BACK WHERE WE STARTED FROM	15
03	Dig The Fuzz DIG048	RIOT OF THE AMPHETAMINE GENERATION (400 copies only, with booklet)	40
82	Riot City ASSEMBLY 1	RIOTOUS ASSEMBLY (red vinyl)	18
61	London HA-A 2338	ROCK-A-HITS	40
57	London HB-C 1067	ROCK 'N' ROLL (10")	40
59	London HA-E 2180	ROCK AND ROLL FOREVER	40
58	Decca LF 1300	ROCKIN' AT THE '2 I'S' (10")	30
69	Decca LK 5002	ROCK STEADY	30
69	Pama PMLP 7	ROCK STEADY COOL	100
68	Coxsone CSL 8013	ROCK STEADY COXSONE STYLE	175
67	Studio One SOL 9000	ROCK STEADY SKA	200
80	Guardian GRC 80	ROKSNAX	50
83	Cha Cha CHALP 016	ROOTS AND CULTURE	25
10	Fruits De Mer Crustacean 18	ROQUETING THROUGH SPACE (LP and free 7")	40
84	Rot ASS 15	ROT IN HELL (LP)	25
82	Guardian GRC 130	ROXCALIBUR	70
77	Harvest SHSP 4069	THE ROXY LONDON W.C.2 (JAN - APR 77) (with inner bag)	25
94	Mo' Wax MWLP 003	ROYALTIES OVERDUE (2-LP, coloured vinyl)	60
84	Bam Caruso KIRI 024	RUBBLE 1: THE PSYCHEDELIC SNARL (with 8-page insert; first 2000 with inner sleeve and lightshow labels)	20
86	Bam Caruso KIRI 025	RUBBLE 2: POP-SIKE PIPE DREAMS (with inner sleeve)	20
86	Bam Caruso KIRI 026	RUBBLE 3: NIGHTMARES IN WONDERLAND (with inner sleeve)	20
86	Bam Caruso KIRI 027	RUBBLE 4: THE 49 MINUTE TECHNICOLOUR DREAM (some with 4-page insert; first 2000 with inner sleeve and lightshow labels)	20
86	Bam Caruso KIRI 044	RUBBLE 5: THE ELECTRIC CRAYON SET (with inner sleeve)	15
86	Bam Caruso KIRI 049	RUBBLE 6: THE CLOUDS HAVE GROOVY FACES (with inner sleeve)	15
87	Bam Caruso KIRI 050	RUBBLE 7: PICTURES IN THE SKY (with inner sleeve)	15
88	Bam Caruso KIRI 051	RUBBLE 8: ALL THE COLOURS OF DARKNESS	15
87	Bam Caruso KIRI 065	RUBBLE 9: FROM THE HOUSE OF LORDS (1000 copies only)	18
87	Bam Caruso KIRI 079	RUBBLE 9: PLASTIC WILDERNESS	15
88	Bam Caruso KIRI 098	RUBBLE 10: PROFESSOR JORDAN'S MAGIC SOUND SHOW (with inner sleeve)	15
86	Bam Caruso KIRI 069	RUBBLE 11: ADVENTURES IN THE MIST (with inner sleeve)	20
86	Bam Caruso KIRI 070	RUBBLE 12: STAIRCASE TO NOWHERE (with inner sleeve)	20
86	Bam Caruso KIRI 102	RUBBLE 13: FREAK BEAT FANTOMS	20
88	Bam Caruso KIRI 106	RUBBLE 14: THE MAGIC ROCKING HORSE (with inner sleeve)	20
91	Bam Caruso KIRI 084	RUBBLE 15: 5000 SECONDS OVER TOYLAND	20
91	Bam Caruso KIRI 096	RUBBLE 16: GLASS ORCHID AFTERMATH	15
91	Bam Caruso KIRI 099	RUBBLE 17: A TRIP IN A PAINTED WORLD	20
92	Bam Caruso KIRI 101	RUBBLE 18: RAINBOW THYME WINDERS (unreleased, 25 test pressings only)	200
92	Bam Caruso KIRI 109	RUBBLE 19: EIDERDOWN MINDFOG (unreleased, 25 test pressings only)	200
90s	Bam Caruso KIRI 110	RUBBLE 20: THRICE UPON A TIME - NOTHING IS REAL (unreleased)	0
91	Ruff Kut RCLP001	RUFF KUT	145
81	Naive 002	RUPERT PREACHING AT A PICNIC (LP)	100
74	Cactus CTLP 104	RUPIE'S GEMS	30
76	Cactus CTLP 119	RUPIES GEMS CHAPTER II	40
69	Xtra XTRA 1035	RURAL BLUES (2-LP)	25

S

Year	Label/Cat#	Title	MINT VALUE £
81	Adult Entertainments ADD 1LP	SAD DAY WE LEFT THE CROFT	50
70	Transworld SPLP 101	SAMANTHA PROMOTIONS (orange cover, private pressing, a few with poster)	600
70	Transworld SPLP 102	SAMANTHA PROMOTIONS (purple cover, private pressing, a few with poster)	600
78	Live And Love LAP 005	SATISFACTION IN DUB	50
60	Parlophone PMC 1130	SATURDAY CLUB	30
64	Decca LK 4583	SATURDAY CLUB	25
67	Atlantic Special 590 007	SATURDAY NIGHT AT THE APOLLO (reissue of "Apollo Saturday Night")	20
81	Suspect SU S3	SCENE OF THE CRIME	60
81	Treble Chants ASN 1	SCALING TRIANGLES (Petticoats/Sole Sisters/Sub Versa)	60
65	Columbia 33SX 1730	SCENE '65	125
69	Bamboo BDLP 202	A SCORCHA FROM BAMBOO	80
95	Blue Eyed Dog VTDOG 12	SEARCH AND DISOBEY (2-LP, 10")	20
81	Airship AP 342	SEASIDE ROCK (2-LP, with insert)	20
81	Come Org. WDC 881008	THE SECOND COMING (various coloured vinyls)	50
87	Cherry Red BRED 74	SEEDS I: POP (TV Personalities/Marine Girls, et al.)	20
68	Elektra EUK 261	SELECT ELEKTRA (also stereo EUKS 7261)	30
73	Lord Koos KLP 3	SEND REQUEST	60
80	Kathedral KATH 1	SENT FROM COVENTRY (with booklet)	15
84	Glass GLALP7	SHADOW AND SUBSTANCE	15
88	Sarah SARAH 587	SHADOW FACTORY (The Sea Urchins/14 Iced Bears, et al.)	40
74	Eron 003	SHEPWAY FOLK (with insert)	30
84	Kent KENT 015	SHOES	15
81	9 Danke 9DANKE	SHOOT THE HOSTAGES (screenprint sleeve, stapled, multiple inserts)	150
86	GI GILP 999	SHOOTING FROM THE HIP	20
78	Virgin VCL 5003	SHORT CIRCUIT - LIVE AT THE ELECTRIC CIRCUS (10"; orange, yellow or blue vinyl)	120
78	Virgin VCL 5003	SHORT CIRCUIT - LIVE AT THE ELECTRIC CIRCUS (10"; black vinyl with free John Dowie EP [VED 1004])	20

S

			MINT VALUE £
90	Horaces HRH 101	SHRINE - THE RAREST SOUL LABEL	20
12	Robot Elephant RER 013	SID CHIP SOUNDS - THE MUSIC OF THE COMMODORE 64 (2-LP)	50
84	Only A Revolution ONLY 2	SIGNAL TO NOISE SET	40
66	Chess CRL 4519	SING A SONG OF SOUL	40
73	Sir Collins SCMW 001	SIR COLLINS MUSIC WHEEL CHAPTER 1	50
57	Parlophone PMC 1047	SIX-FIVE SPECIAL	50
72	Trojan TBL 191	16 DYNAMIC REGGAE HITS	18
73	Trojan TBL 209	16 DYNAMIC HITS 2	20
71	Pama PMP 2015	16 DYNAMIC REGGAE HITS	40
66	Island ILP 930	SKA AT THE JAMAICA PLAYBOY CLUB (gatefold sleeve)	250
67	Coxsone CSL 8003	SKA-A-GO-GO	200
66	Doctor Bird DLM 5000	SKA-BOO-DA-BA	400
60s	Page One FOR 006	SKA'S THE LIMIT (copies on Carnival label CX 1000, worth £80)	50
68	Ace Of Clubs ACL 1250	SKIFFLE	30
81	RSB 1	THE SNOOPIES ALBUM (THE LAST REMAINS OF A RICHMOND VENUE) (numbered, with booklet, 1,000 only)	20
60s	Solar	THE SOLAR BOX SET	40
71	Bamboo BDLP 212	SOLID GOLD	50
66	Atlantic ATL 5048	SOLID GOLD SOUL	20
67	Atlantic 587 058	SOLID GOLD SOUL VOL. 2	20
75	Disco Demand DDLP 5002	SOLID SOUL SENSATIONS	18
72	South. Preservation SPR 1	SOME COLD RAINY DAY	15
65	Lestar LLP 101	SOME FOLK IN LEICESTER (private pressing)	20
13	RCLP 010	SOMETHING IN THE WATER (LP, gatefold)	30
13	RCLP 010	SOMETHING IN THE WATER (LP, gatefold, clear vinyl band edition, 100 only)	50
84	Adventures In Reality ARR 017	SOMETHING STIRS	15
70	Pama PMP 2003	SOMETHING SWEET THE LADY	150
69	Liberty LBX 4	SON OF GUTBUCKET	20
76	Harvest SHSM 2012	SON OF MORRIS ON	18
83	Syndicate SYNLP 3	SON OF OI!!	15
12	Fruits De Mer Crustacean 25	SORROW'S CHILDREN	25
84	Kent KENT 011	SOUL CLASS OF '66	15
69	Direction (S)PR 28	SOUL DIRECTION	25
69	Page One POS 608	SOULED AGAIN	20
69	Polydor 584 163	SOUL FEVER	20
60s	Minit MLL 40011E	SOUL FOOD	40
69	Soul City SCB 1	SOUL FROM THE CITY	45
70	Specialty SPE 6606	SOUL FROM THE VAULTS	15
70	Polydor 583 757	SOUL GOLD	18
68	Trojan TRL 3	SOUL OF JAMAICA	50
86	None	SOUL OF HARINGAY	100
68	Polydor Special 236 213	SOUL PARTY	20
69	Pama PMLP 8	SOUL SAUCE	70
69	Polydor 236 554	SOUL SELLER	18
69	United Artists UAL 29018	SOUL SENSATION	15
85	Kent KENT 041	SOUL SERENADE	15
66	Stateside SL 10186	SOUL SIXTEEN	45
66	Sue ILP 934	SOUL '66	60
67	CBS BPG 62965	SOUL SOUNDS	25
67	HMV CLP 3619	SOUL SOUNDS OF THE 60s	45
98	BBE BBELP 013	SOUL SPECTRUM (2-LP)	40
67	Stateside SL 10203	SOUL SUPPLY	50
69	Atlantic 218005	SOUL TOGETHER	15
73	Trojan TRLS 74	SOUL TO SOUL DJ CHOICE	20
65	Pye Intl. NPL 28061	THE SOUND OF BACHARACH	20
95	EMI EMI 8322 801	THE SOUND GALLERY	25
15	DJ International DJISX1001	SOUND OF DJ INTERNATIONAL (3-LP)	20
19	Pikes PIKESLP002	THE SOUND OF MERCURY RISING (2-LP, compiled by DJ Harvey)	30
68	President PTL 1008	THE SOUND OF SOUL	30
79	Grapevine GRAL 1001	SOUND OF THE GRAPEVINE	20
69	Cambridge University Press	SOUNDS AND SILENCE	75
64	Stateside SL 10077	THE SOUND OF THE R&B HITS	65
70	Sentinel SENS 1001	SOUNDS LIKE WEST CORNWALL	20
09	Finders Keepers FK023LLP	THE SOUNDS OF WONDER (2-LP)	25
09	Finders Keepers FK023LLP	THE SOUNDS OF WONDER (2-LP, limited edition 100 only different sleeve)	40
69	London HAK 8405	SOUTHERN COMFORT	125
83	Spectrum ASPEC 001	SOUTHERN COMFORT	75
80s	Spectrum ASPEC 003	SOUTHERN COMFORT 3	50
70	Saydisc RL 328	SOUTHERN SANCTIFIED SINGERS (insert)	20
71	Python PLP 10	SOUTHSIDE CHICAGO (99 copies only)	80
58	Tempo TAP 17	SPEAK LOW - MORE MUSIC IN THE MODERN MANNER	400
69	BAF BAF001	SPECIAL BAF SOUNDS VOL. 1	30
18	Trunk JBH070LP	SPIDER-JAZZ (splatter vinyl)	30
13	Rongorongo RORO LP1	SPIKY DREAD ISSUE ONE	15
73	Tempo TMP 9001	SPIN A MAGIC TUNE	20
82	WEA K 58415	A SPLASH OF COLOUR	15
62	Liberty LBY 1001	THE STARS OF LIBERTY	30
57	Decca LF 1299	STARS OF THE 6.5 SPECIAL (10")	50
84	Broken Flag BF V5	STATEMENT	40

T

MINT VALUE £

85	Statik POL 274	STATIK COMPILATION ONE (2-LP)	20
69	Stax XATS 1007	STAX SOUL EXPLOSION	18
70s	Stax STXH 5004	THE STAX STORY (VOL. 1)	20
70s	Stax STXH 5005	THE STAX STORY (VOL. 1)	15
67	Stax 589 010	THE STAX/VOLT SHOW VOL. 1	20
67	Stax 589 011	THE STAX/VOLT SHOW VOL. 2	20
07	Step Forward CMXBX 1509	STEP FORWARD - I WANNA PUNK ROCK - SINGLES COLLECTION (10x7")	25
94	Tenth Planet TP 010	THE STORY OF OAK RECORDS	25
70	Pama PMP 2002	STRAIGHTEN UP	70
71	Pama PMP 2007	STRAIGHTEN UP VOLUME TWO	40
71	Pama PMP 2014	STRAIGHTEN UP VOLUME THREE	40
72	Pama PMP 2017	STRAIGHTEN UP VOLUME FOUR	30
00	BBE BBELP 031	STRANGE GAMES & FUNKY THINGS III (3 x 12")	35
77	Beggars Banquet BEGA 1	STREETS	15
80s	Streetsounds	STREETSOUND ELECTRO (box set)	70
79	Open Eye OE LP 501	STREET TO STREET - A LIVERPOOL ALBUM	30
81	Decca SKIN 1	STRENGTH THROUGH OI!	50
85	Wonderful World WOWLP 3	STRENGTH THROUGH OI! (reissue)	20
86	Sub Pop SP 0010	SUB POP 100	20
83	Sane SANE 001	SUBTLE HINTS	100
81	Chick CHR 001	SUBWAY (clear vinyl)	15
73	Vertigo 6499 386	SUCK IT AND SEE (2-LP, spaceship label)	20
98	Sorted SRLP 04	SUCTION PRINTS (handpainted or wraparound sleeve)	35
65	Sue ILP 919	SUE SAMPLER RECORD FOR CLUBS (promo, no sleeve, typed labels with detail sheet)	120
65	London HA-C 8239	THE SUE STORY	60
65	Sue ILP 925	THE SUE STORY!	55
69	United Artists UAS 29028	THE SUE STORY (reissue)	18
66	Sue ILP 933	THE SUE STORY VOL. 2	55
66	Sue ILP 938	THE SUE STORY VOL. 3	55
76	Giorno GPS	SUGAR, ALCOHOL & MEAT	20
82	CBS 22139	SUMMER MEANS FUN (2-LP)	20
75	Island ISS 1	SUMMER '75 (promo-only sampler)	15
66	Reprise R 5031	THE SUMMIT	30
02	Sun FBUBX 002	SUN RECORD COMPANY 50 GOLDEN YEARS 1952-2002 (8-CD + 7")	40
86	Sun/Charly BOX 105	SUN RECORDS: THE BLUES YEARS (9-LP box with booklet)	40
81	Sunset Gun	SUNSET GUN (cassette with Sunset Gun fanzine)	15
68	Ember NR 5038	SUNSTROKE	20
73	Philips 6369 416	SUPER BLACK BLUES	20
68	Pye Intl. NPL 28107	SUPER SOUL	25
96	Trunk BARKED 1 LP	THE SUPER SOUNDS OF BOSWORTH (promo cassette, 50 only)	50
68	Chess SRL 4537	SUPER SUPER BLUES BAND	25
74	People PLEO 24	SUPER SWEET SOUL	15
64	Vocalion VA 8018	SURF BATTLE	60
86	Capitol EMS 1180	SURF CITY/DRAG CITY	25
88	Decal LIK 39	SURFERS STOMP	25
73	Pye/Disques Vogue HEN 1	SURPRISE PARTIE TOUS LES JEUNES	18
71	Blue Horizon 7-66263	SWAMP BLUES (2-LP)	75
68	Stateside S(S)L 10243	SWEET SOUL SOUNDS	50
68	Coxsone CSL 8018	SWING EASY	125
58	Tempo TAP 21	SWINGIN' THE BLUES (with Victor Fedman, Tubby Hayes, Don Rendell, Ronnie Scott & Dizzy Reece)	250
93	Tenth Planet TP 002	SYDE TRYPS ONE (numbered, 500 only, with insert)	40
93	Tenth Planet TP 004	SYDE TRYPS TWO ... FROM THERE TO UNCERTAINTY (numbered, 500 only, with insert)	30
93	Tenth Planet TP 006	SYDE TRYPS THREE (numbered, 500 only, with insert)	30
94	Tenth Planet TP 008	SYDE TRYPS FOUR (numbered, 500 only, with insert)	60
95	Tenth Planet TP 020	SYDE TRYPS VOLUME 5 (numbered, 500 only, insert)	25
96	Tenth Planet TP 024	SYDE TRYPS SIX (numbered, gatefold sleeve, 1,000 only)	30
01	Tenth Planet TP 052	SYDE TRYPS VOLUME SEVEN (numbered, 1000 only, insert)	20
82	EBONY 2 S82 CUS 1362	SYNTHETIC ROMANCE (LP)	450
15	System SYSTM 004	SYSTEM SOUND EP (4 x 10" BOX SET)	50
78	BBC REC 303	SCRAPBOOK OF 1977 (LP)	15
96	Trunk BARKED 1	THE SUPER SOUNDS OF BOSWORTH (LP, 3000 copies)	30
96	Trunk BARKED 2	THE SUPER SOUNDS OF BOSWORTH 2 (LP, 1000 only with track 1 missing on side 2 due to pressing fault)	50

T

72	Rubber RUB 001	TAKE OFF YOUR HEAD AND LISTEN	15
78	Grapevine GRAL 1000	TALK OF THE GRAPEVINE	25
85	Kent KENT 045	TEAR IN MY EYES	30
58	Capitol T 1009	TEENAGE ROCK (turquoise or 'rainbow' label)	40
90	Sarah SARAH 376	TEMPLE CLOUD - A SARAH COMPILATION (LP)	45
56	Nixa Jazz Today NJL 4	TENORAMA	300
02	Jazzman JMANLP 006	TEXAS FUNK (2-LP)	30
69	Highway 51 H 103	TEXAS-LOUISIANA BLUES (99 copies only)	60
82	No Future PUNK 9	THERE IS NO FUTURE	18
72	Dandelion 2485 021	THERE IS SOME FUN GOING FORWARD (with poster)	18
82	Big Beat NED 3	THESE CATS AIN'T NOTHING BUT TRASH	20
69	Action ACLP 6009	THESE KIND OF BLUES VOL. 1	80
81	TTFTC 001	THE THING FROM THE CRYPT (I NEARLY DIED LAUGHING)	50
87	Kent KENT 066	THINK SMART SOUL STRINGS	15

Year	Label/Cat#	Title	MINT VALUE £
57	Tempo TAP 11	THIRD BRITISH FESTIVAL OF JAZZ	50
80s	Come Org. WDC 881221	33 FÜR ILSE KOCH (some on red vinyl)	70
68	Minit MLL/MLS 40002	THIRTY-THREE MINITS OF BLUES AND SOUL	45
83	2-Tone CHR TT 5007	THIS ARE 2-TONE (with free poster, green or pink sleeve)	30
64	Island ILP 910	THIS IS BLUE BEAT (unreleased, white labels may exist)	250
76	Loma/Warners K 56265	THIS IS LOMA VOL. 1	20
76	Loma/Warners K 56266	THIS IS LOMA VOL. 2	20
76	Loma/Warners K 56267	THIS IS LOMA VOL. 3	20
76	Loma/Warners K 56268	THIS IS LOMA VOL. 4	20
76	Loma/Warners K 56269	THIS IS LOMA VOL. 5	20
76	Loma/Warners K 56270	THIS IS LOMA VOL. 6	20
63	Oriole PS 40047	THIS IS MERSEYBEAT VOL. 1	50
63	Oriole PS 40048	THIS IS MERSEYBEAT VOL. 2	50
80	Grapevine GRAL 1002	THIS IS NORTHERN SOUL	30
86	OI OIR 004	THIS IS OI!	15
69	Pama PSP 1003	THIS IS REGGAE	30
71	Pama PMP 2005	THIS IS REGGAE VOLUME TWO	30
71	Pama PMP 2008	THIS IS REGGAE VOLUME THREE	40
72	Pama PMP 2016	THIS IS REGGAE VOLUME FOUR	30
69	Island IWP 3	THIS IS SUE!	25
63	RCA RD/SF 7608	THE THREE GREAT GUYS (Paul Anka, Sam Cooke & Neil Sedaka)	15
70	Saydisc Matchbox SDR182	THOSE CAKEWALKIN' BABIES FROM HOME	22
66	Allegro ALL 807	THUNDERBALL AND OTHER SECRET AGENT THEMES	15
69	Trojan TTL 7	TIGHTEN UP VOLUME TWO (pink Island label with different track listing & sleeve)	40
82	Mobile Suit SUIT 1	TOKYO MOBILE MUSIC 1 (LP)	20
92	Too Pure SFRLP 119	TOO PURE - THE PEEL SESSIONS (LP, limited issue, custom sleeve)	20
64	Golden Guinea GGL 0277	TOP 10 HITS, ORIGINAL ARTISTS	15
72	Studio 2 TWO 391	TOP TV THEMES AND COMMERCIALS	30
66	Topic TPS 205	TOPIC SAMPLER No. 7 - SEA SONGS & SHANTIES (blue label)	10
56	Tempo TAP 4	TOP TRUMPETS	250
82	Zoo ZOO 4	TO THE SHORES OF LAKE PLACID (gatefold sleeve with 4-page booklet)	18
92	Trojan TRLS 304	TOUGHER THAN TOUGH	18
60s	Fishers Music	TRANSAFRICK MUSICMAKERS	25
77	Free Reed FRRD 021/022	THE TRANSPORTS (2-LP, with book)	60
76	Eron 006	TRAVELLING FOLK (with insert)	25
61	77' LA 12-2	A TREASURY OF FIELD RECORDINGS VOLUME 1	35
61	77' LA 12-3	A TREASURY OF FIELD RECORDINGS VOLUME 2	35
84	Parlophone CAV 1	TRIBUTE TO THE CAVERN (LP)	40
69	Key KL 003	A TRIBUTE TO YOUTH PRAISE	20
80	Skeleton SKL LP 1	A TRIP TO THE DENTIST (with insert)	15
61	Parlophone PMC 1139	TRIPLE TREAT	25
03	Trojan TRBLP 003	TROJAN ROCKSTEADY BOX (3-LP)	100
74	Trojan TDRLP1	THE TROJAN SOUND (LP)	15
71	Trojan TALL 1	TROJAN STORY (3xLP in fold-over sleeve)	40
80	Trojan TALL 100	TROJAN STORY (3-LP)	30
82	Trojan TALL 200	TROJAN STORY VOLUME 2 (BOX SET)	60
89	Warriors Dance WAFLP 2	THE TUFFEST OF THE TUFFEST	30
74	Melodisc 12-193	12 BIG HITS- SOUNDS OF YOUNG JAMAICA	60
74	Melodisc 12-217	12 CARAT GOLD	35
76	Lucky LYLP 5204	TWELVE TRIBES OF ISRAEL (LP)	200
73	Trojan TRLS 81	20 EXPLOSIVE REGGAE HITS	18
65	Ember EMB 3359	25 YEARS OF RHYTHM & BLUES HITS	30
89	WEA 241 690-1	TWIST & SHOUT - 12 ATLANTIC TRACKS PRODUCED BY PHIL SPECTOR (gatefold sleeve)	35
63	Philips BL 7578	TWIST AT THE STAR-CLUB, HAMBURG	50
82	Beat The System BTSLP 1	TOTAL ANARCHY (LP)	15
89	2-TONE CHR TT 5009	THE 2 TONE STORY (2-LP)	30

U

Year	Label/Cat#	Title	MINT VALUE £
68	BBC REC 28M	ULSTER'S FLOWERY VALE	15
69	Island ILP 993/ILPS 9293	THE UNFOLDING OF THE BOOK OF LIFE VOL. 1	45
72	Nevis NEV R 007	UNITY CREATES STRENGTH	25
69	Pama ECO 7	UNITY'S GREATEST HITS	110
88	Unicorn PHZA 17	UNSUNG HEROES (red vinyl)	15
80	Safari UPP 1	UPPERS ON THE SOUTH DOWNS (original issue without Purple Hearts)	15
68	Atlantic 588 122	UPTOWN SOUL	20
72	Village Thing VTSAM 15	US	20

V

Year	Label/Cat#	Title	MINT VALUE £
78	Attrix RB 03	VAULTAGE '78 (TWO SIDES OF BRIGHTON) (originally hand-screened sleeve, later with insert)	20
80	Attrix RB 11LP	VAULTAGE 80	15
71	Trojan TBL 175	VERSION GALORE VOLUME TWO	15
73	Trojan TBL 200	VERSION GALORE VERSION THREE	30
72	Trojan TBL 182	VERSION TO VERSION	18
70	Vertigo 6499 407/8	VERTIGO ANNUAL 1970 (2-LP, set no.: 6657 001)	30
10	Balkan BV 06	VIOLET (with free CD)	20

W

Year	Label/Cat#	Title	MINT VALUE £
70s	Object Music OBJ 007	WAITING ROOM	15
85	Psycho PSYCHO 35	THE WAKING DREAM	15

			MINT VALUE £
64	Pye Intl. NPL 28041	WALKING BY MYSELF	40
64	Pye Intl. NPL 28044	WALKING THE BLUES	35
81	Phil Spector Intl. WOS 001	WALL OF SOUND (9-LP box set)	60
03	Soul Brother LP SBPJ 14	WANTS LIST (2-LP)	30
05	Soul Brother LP SBPJ 27	WANTS LIST 2 (2-LP)	30
09	Warp WARP 20	WARP 20 (5 x 10", 5-CD, booklet, box set)	150
79	A&M AMLH 64761	THE WARRIORS	20
98	Warp WAP 100	WE ARE REASONABLE PEOPLE (3-LP)	30
78	Bridgehouse BHLP 001	A WEEKEND AT THE BRIDGEHOUSE E16 (with bonus 12" EP)	30
81	Romans In Britain NERO 1	WELCOME TO NORWICH A FINE CITY (LP)	70
87	Streetsounds WTND 1	WEST END STORY (2-LP)	20
93	West End 110651	WEST END STORY VOL 1	20
93	West End 110691	WEST END STORY VOL 2	20
93	West End 110941	WEST END STORY VOL 3	20
84	Rot ASS 4	WET DREAMS (LP)	20
70	Harry J TTL 34	WHAT AM I TO DO	40
68	Elektra EKS 7304	WHAT'S SHAKIN' (reissue of "Good Time Music")	10
80	S & T	WHERE THE HELL IS LEICESTER? (with bonus single & booklet)	25
86	Sunrise A40 111M	WHERE WOULD YOU RATHER BE TONIGHT?	25
83	Kamera KAM 14	THE WHIP (with insert)	20
79	London Bomp DHS-Z 3	WHO PUT THE BOMP? (2-LP, gatefold sleeve)	25
70	Trojan TBL 134	WHO YOU GONNA RUN TO	50
72	private pressing	WHOLLY GRAIL	25
98	Trunk BARKED 3CP	THE WICKER MAN (promo cassette, 50 only)	30
81	Cherry Red BRED 24	WILD PAARTY SOUNDS VOLUME 1	20
91	Cherry Red BRED 24	WILD PAARTY SOUNDS VOLUME 1 (reissue)	25
66	Dot DLP 3535	WIPE OUT	25
76	RCA RS 1085	WIZARD'S CONVENTION (with insert)	12
67	RCA Victor RD 7840	WOMEN OF THE BLUES	20
81	Glass GLASS 010	THE WONDERFUL WORLD OF GLASS	15
96	Magna Carta MA 9010/2	WORKING MAN	15
63	London HA-P 8099	A WORLD OF BLUES	25
85	Radical Change RCLP 4	WORDS WORTH SHOUTING (insert)	15
78	Yuk NE 1023	THE WORLD'S WORST RECORD SHOW (multi-coloured vinyl)	20
89	Woronzow WOO 10	WORONZOID (2-LP)	20

Y

10	Balkan BV 04	YELLOW (with free CD)	15
85	Cathexis/Pleasantly Surprised PS 014	YOU BET WE'VE GOT SOMETHING AGAINST YOU	15
70	Trojan TBL 142	YOU CAN'T WINE	65
69	Trojan TTL 9	YOU LEFT ME STANDING	40
84	Peninsula PENCV 1002	YOUNG BLOOD (LP)	50
69	Youngblood SBYB 1	YOUNGBLOOD VOL. 1	15
71	Youngblood SBYB4	YOUNBLOOD VOL. 2	18
70	Pama ECO 35	YOUNG GIFTED AND BLACK	175
71	Bamboo BDLPS 211	YOUR JAMAICAN GIRL	50
82	Statik STATLP 7	YOUR SECRET'S SAFE WITH US (2-LP)	20

Z

91	Document ZBOX 1	ZOO: THE COMPLETE WORKS (Box set 3-LP, 12", 1,000 only)	60
84	Zulu ZULU 6	THE ZULU COMPILATION	20

FILM & TV SOUNDTRACK LPs
(alphabetical by title, composers/artists in brackets)
(Only the first issue of soundtracks by the Beatles and Elvis Presley are listed below: for later repressings see their entries)

A

73	United Artists UAS 29451	ACROSS 110TH STREET (J.J. Johnson & Bobby Womack)	15
62	RCA RD 7512	ADVISE AND CONSENT (Jerry Fielding)	15
13	Rook RFV 002	A FIELD IN ENGLAND (2-LP, white vinyl, poster, blade of grass)	100
67	United Artists (S)ULP 1172	AFRICA ADDIO (Riz Ortolani/Jimmy Roselli)	20
66	United Artists (S)ULP 1151	AFTER THE FOX (Burt Bacharach/Hollies)	25
64	Parlophone PMC 1230	A HARD DAY'S NIGHT (Beatles) (LP, mono, 1st pressing, with The Parlophone Co. Ltd label rim copy & "Sold In The UK..." text)	100
64	Parlophone PCS 3058	A HARD DAY'S NIGHT (Beatles) (LP, stereo, 1st pressing, with "The Parlophone Co. Ltd" label rim copy & "Sold In The UK..." text; stereo, with mid-sized "stereo"	250
56	Nixa NPT 19010	ALEXANDER THE GREAT (Mario Nascimbene) (10"; beware of counterfeits)	40
69	MGM CS 8112	ALFRED THE GREAT (Ray Leppard)	100
61	Fontana TFL 591	ALL NIGHT LONG (LP, mono, Dave Brubeck, Tubby Hayes, Johnny Dankworth et al.)	30
61	Fontana STFL 591	ALL NIGHT LONG (LP, stereo, Dave Brubeck, Tubby Hayes, Johnny Dankworth et al.)	20
65	Reprise R 6151	AMERICANIZATION OF EMILY (Johnny Mandel)	20
65	RCA RD 7732	THE AMOROUS ADVENTURES OF MOLL FLANDERS (John Addison)	35
57	Brunswick LAT 8175	ANASTASIA (Alfred Newman)	15
60	Philips SBBL 514	ANATOMY OF A MURDER (Duke Ellington)	25
76	BBC REB 236	ANGELS AND 15 OTHER BBC TV THEMES (Alan Parker, et al.)	15
72	Polydor 2383 109	ANTONY AND CLEOPATRA (John Scott) (foldout sleeve)	20
60	London HA-T 2287	THE APARTMENT (Adolph Deutsch)	18

B

			MINT VALUE £
79	Elektra K 62025	APOCALYPSE NOW (2-LP, music & dialogue)	20
69	CBS 70054	APRIL FOOLS (Marvin Hamlisch)	15
66	RCA Victor RD 7817	ARABESQUE (Henry Mancini)	15
66	Fontana FJL 135	L'ASCENSEUR POUR L'ECHAFAUD/FEMME DISPARAISSANTE (Miles Davis/Art Blakey [1 side each])	30
54	HMV DLPC 1	AS LONG AS THEY'RE HAPPY (Jack Buchanan) (10")	50
67	Pye NPL 18198	AT LAST THE 1948 SHOW (TV soundtrack)	25
67	Marble Arch MAL 695	THE AVENGERS AND OTHER FAVOURITES (Laurie Johnson)	35

B

66	Fontana TL 5306	BABY, THE RAIN MUST FALL (Elmer Bernstein)	15
62	Pye Intl. NPL 28020	BARABBAS (Mario Nascimbene)	15
68	Stateside (S)SL 10260	BARBARELLA (Bob Crewe/Charles Fox)	75
67	London HA-D 8337	BAREFOOT IN THE PARK (Neal Hefti)	15
66	Stateside S(S)L 10179	BATMAN (Nelson Riddle) (TV show music)	50
13	Silva SILLP 1316	BATMAN BEGINS (2-LP, 500 only)	30
66	Warner Bros W 1617	BATTLE OF THE BULGE (Benjamin Frankel)	25
60	Columbia 33SX 1225	BEAT GIRL (John Barry/Adam Faith)	40
57	London HAP 2056	BEAU JAMES (Joseph Lilley)	25
64	RCA Victor RD 7679	BECKET (dialogue only)	15
68	Decca LK 4923	BEDAZZLED (LP, mono, Peter Cook/Dudley Moore)	100
70	Island ILPS 9140	BE GLAD FOR THE SONG HAS NO ENDING (Incredible String Band)	15
15	Finders Keepers FKR79L	BELLADONNA (leather sleeve)	40
60	Capitol W/SW 1435	BELLS ARE RINGING (André Previn) (mono/stereo)	15
60	MGM MGM-C(S) 802	BEN HUR (Miklos Rozsa) (box set with hardback book; mono/stereo)	15
70	Stateside SSL 10311	BEYOND THE VALLEY OF THE DOLLS (Stu Phillips/Strawberry Alarm Clock)	70
68	MGM MGM-C(S) 8066	BIGGEST BUNDLE OF THEM ALL (Riz Ortolani/Eric Burdon)	20
69	United Artists (S)ULP 1228	THE BIG GUNDOWN (Ennio Morricone)	15
67	United Artists (S)ULP 1183	BILLION DOLLAR BRAIN (Richard Rodney Bennett)	30
73	Polydor 2490 117	BLACK CAESAR (James Brown)	35
	Cinephile CINLP004	THE BLACK WINDMILL	30
72	Pye NSPL 18376	BLOOMFIELD	15
66	MGM MGM-C(S) 8039	BLOW-UP (Herbie Hancock/Yardbirds)	80
68	Dot (S)LPD 508	BLUE (Manos Hadjidakis)	30
61	RCA RD 27238	BLUE HAWAII (Elvis Presley) (black/silver label, mono)	15
61	RCA SF 5115	BLUE HAWAII (Elvis Presley) (black/silver label, stereo)	20
87	Thats Entertainment TER 1127	BLUE VELVET (Angelo Badalamenti)	15
62	RCA RD 7520	BONANZA (L.Greene, M. Langdon)	20
69	MCA MUPS 360	BOOM! (John Barry/Georgie Fame)	60
68	Warner Bros W 1742	BONNIE AND CLYDE (Charles Strouse)	20
70	Paramount SPFL 263	BORSALINO (Claude Bolling)	15
58	RCA RD 27054	BOTH ENDS OF THE CANDLE (Gogi Grant)	15
57	Brunswick LAT 8193	BOY ON A DOLPHIN (Hugo Friedhoffer)	30
71	Capitol E-SW 621	THE BUGALOOS (LP)	30
72	Bell BELLS 209	THE BURGLARS (Ennio Morricone)	30
66	RCA RD 7791	BUNNY LAKE IS MISSING (Paul Glass/Zombies)	65
65	Liberty LBY 1246	BURKE'S LAW (Herschel/Burke/Gilbert) (TV series music)	15
63	RCA Victor SF 7580	BYE BYE BIRDIE (musical) (Charles Strouse; stereo)	15
80	Chrysalis CHR 1234	BABYLON (blue/white label)	20
05	Trunk JBH 016LP/PD	BOD: WORDS & MUSIC (LP 1-sided picture disc)	20
07	Trunk JBH 023 LP	BLOOD ON SATAN'S CLAW (LP, 500 only)	40

C

66	RCA Victor RD 7820	CALIFORNIA HOLIDAY (Elvis Presley) (black/red dot labels, mono)	20
66	RCA Victor SF 7820	CALIFORNIA HOLIDAY (Elvis Presley) (black/red dot labels, stereo)	30
69	Stateside (S)SL 10276	CANDY (Dave Grusin/Steppenwolf, et al.)	30
69	MCA MUPS 380	CAN HEIRONYMUS MERKIN EVER FORGET MERCY HUMPPE AND FIND TRUE HAPPINESS? (Anthony Newley)	30
60	Delyse DL 3057/DLS 6057	CAPTAIN HORATIO HORNBLOWER (Robert Farnon) (mono)	30
76	United Artists UA 30033	CARRIE (Pino Donaggio)	40
67	RCA Victor RD/SF 7874	CASINO ROYALE (Burt Bacharach/Herb Alpert/Dusty Springfield) (mono/stereo	30
66	United Artists (S)ULP 1140	CAST A GIANT SHADOW (Elmer Bernstein/Vince Hill)	18
65	Columbia SX 1756	CATCH US IF YOU CAN (Dave Clark Five)	30
62	Warner Bros WS 8177	THE CHAPMAN REPORT (Leonard Rosenman)	15
63	RCA SF 7620	CHARADE (Henry Mancini)	20
63	MGM MGM-C 969	THE CHARGE IS MURDER (John Green)	20
68	United Artists SULP 1189	THE CHARGE OF THE LIGHT BRIGADE (John Addison/Manfred Mann)	18
66	CBS (S)BPG 62665	THE CHASE (John Barry) (mono) (stereo copy is £30)	20
69	Polydor 583 736	CHE! (Lalo Schifrin)	15
67	Fontana TL 5417	CHIMES AT MIDNIGHT (Angelo Lavagnino)	30
74	ABC ABCL 5068	CHINATOWN (Jerry Goldsmith)	20
68	RCA Victor RD/SF 7917	CLAMBAKE (Elvis Presley) (black/red dot labels, mono/stereo)	20
01	Trunk SOUP 001LP	THE CLANGERS (Vernon Elliot) (TV soundtrack, with knitted sleeve, 26 only)	150
01	Trunk SOUP 001LP	THE CLANGERS (Vernon Elliot) (TV soundtrack, without knitted sleeve)	30
63	Stateside S(S)SL 10044	CLEOPATRA (Alex North)	15
65	Fontana (S)TL 5259	THE COLLECTOR (Maurice Jarre)	30
67	MGM MGM-C(S) 8058	THE COMEDIANS (Laurence Rosenthal)	15
72	Pye NSPL 18389	CONCERTO FOR HARRY - SOMETHING TO HIDE (Roy Budd)	25
75	Polydor 2383 350	CONFESSIONS OF A POP PERFORMER (Three's A Crowd/Ed Welch)	30

D

MINT VALUE £

71	Philips 6332 033	CONTINENTAL CIRCUS (Gong)	20
62	Parlophone PMC 1194	THE COOL MIKADO (John Barry Seven/Frankie Howerd, et al.)	25
70	United Artists UAS 29119	COTTON COMES TO HARLEM (Galt McDermott)	30
67	Brunswick AXA 4544	COUNTESS FROM HONG KONG (Charles Chaplin) (with booklet)	15
70	Capitol E-ST 640	CROMWELL (Frank Cordell)	15
70	Word WST 5550	THE CROSS & THE SWITCHBLADE (Ralph Carmichael)	25
77	EMI EMA 782	CROSS OF IRON (Ernest Gold) (gatefold sleeve)	15
80	CBS 70182	CRUISING (John Hiatt/Willy DeVille/Germs)	25
73	Buddah 2318 091	CURTIS IN CHICAGO (Curtis Mayfield/Impressions/Jerry Butler, Gene Chandler, Leroy Hutson) (TV soundtrack, gatefold sleeve)	15
68	Stateside (S)SL 10222	CUSTER OF THE WEST (Bernardo Segall)	20

D

62	Fontana TFL 5184	DANGEROUS FRIENDSHIPS (Art Blakey, et. al.)	25
63	MGM MGM-C 952	DAVID AND LISA (Mark Lawrence/Victor Feldman All Stars)	15
04	Trunk JBH 011 LP	DAWN OF THE DEAD (LP, 500 only)	30
67	Stateside (S)SL 10217	THE DAY THE FISH CAME OUT (Mikis Theodorakis)	30
18	Laced LMLP 020	DEAD CELLS (2-LP, orange and violet vinyl)	80
68	Stateside (S)SL 10263	DEADFALL (John Barry/Shirley Bassey)	20
73	Columbia SCX 6550	DEAF SMITH AND JOHNNY EARS (Daniele Patucchi)	35
74	CBS 80546	DEATH WISH (Herbie Hancock)	15
68	Stateside (S)SL 10259	DECLINE AND FALL... OF A BIRDWATCHER (Ron Goodwin)	125
55	MGM MGM-C 755	DEEP IN MY HEART (Howard Keel/Vic Damone, et al.)	15
00	Trunk/Bonk XXX 1 LP	DEEP THROAT (LP)	20
58	London HA-D 2111	DESIRE UNDER THE ELMS (Elmer Bernstein)	20
63	Colpix PXL 440	DIAMOND HEAD (John Williams)	15
76	Pye Intl. NSPL 28219	DIAMOND MERCENARIES (Georges Garvarentz)	15
76	Bradley BRADS 8002	DIAMONDS (Roy Budd)	50
71	United Artists UAS 29216	DIAMONDS ARE FOREVER (John Barry/Shirley Bassey)	20
59	Top Rank RX 3016	THE DIARY OF ANNE FRANK (Alfred Newman)	30
83	Ripple (no cat. no.)	DIGITAL DREAMS (Bill Wyman) (promo only)	50
68	MGM MGM-C(S) 8048	DIRTY DOZEN (Frank de Vol/Trini Lopez) (yellow label)	18
67	CBS S 63189	DR. FAUSTUS (Mario Nascimbene)	75
65	United Artists ULP 1097	DOCTOR NO (Monty Norman) (mono)	50
65	United Artists (S)ULP 1097	DOCTOR NO (Monty Norman) (stereo)	100
62	Columbia 33SX 1446	DON'T KNOCK THE TWIST (Chubby Checker/Gene Chandler, et al.)	25
18	Laced (no Cat no)	DOOM (ORIGINAL GAME SOUNDTRACK) (2-LP, red vinyl)	40
67	RCA Victor SF 7892	DOUBLE TROUBLE (Elvis Presley) (black/red dot labels, stereo) (Mono version RD7892 = £15)	20
12	Death Waltz DW 004	DONNIE DARKO (Michael Andrews: blue/black vinyl, lithograph, 100 only)	50
12	Death Waltz DW 004	DONNIE DARKO (Michael Andrews: blue vinyl, lithograph, 300 only)	30
12	Death Waltz DW 004	DONNIE DARKO (Michael Andrews: standard black vinyl, poster)	15
74	Enterprise ENTF 3003	DON'T LOOK NOW (Pino Donaggio)	40
69	Capitol EST 672	THE DOUBLE DECKERS (TV soundtrack)	30
87	Crammed MTM 14	DOWN BY LAW (John Lurie)	20
70	President PTLS 1068	DRAKE'S DREAM (Paul Jones)	20
12	Invada INV106LP	DRIVE	40
59	Parlophone PMCL 1101	DRUMBEAT (Adam Faith/John Barry Seven, et al.)	50
58	Decca LF 1308	THE DUKE WORE JEANS (Tommy Steele) (10")	15

E

58	HMV DLP 1088	EDDIE FOY AND THE SEVEN LITTLE FOYS (10", Bob Hope/James Cagney)	30
54	Brunswick LAT 8040	THE EGYPTIAN (Alfred Newman)	25
67	Columbia S(C)X 6155	EL DORADO (Nelson Riddle)	25
63	Colpix PXL 459	ELIZABETH TAYLOR IN LONDON (John Barry) (mono/stereo)	20
69	RCA Victor RD 8011	ELVIS ("TV Special", mono)	15
74	Warner Bros K 56084	EMMANUELLE (Pierre Bachelet)	15
57	Vogue Coral LVA 9063	END AS A MAN (Kenyon Hopkins)	30
74	Warner Bros K 46275	ENTER THE DRAGON (Lalo Schifrin)	40
84	Alt. Ten. VIRUS 30	ERASERHEAD (Fats Waller/Peter Ivers/et al.) (with insert)	40
81	That's Entertainment TER 1011	ESCAPE FROM NEW YORK (John Carpenter and Alan Howarth)	25
12	Death Waltz DW 0002	ESCAPE FROM NEW YORK (poster, inner, orange/green vinyl, 100 only)	40
76	EMI EMC 3148	ESCAPE FROM THE DARK (Ron Goodwin)	15
63	Parlophone PMC 1198	THE ESTABLISHMENT (Peter Cook, et al.)	20
83	MCA MCA 70000	E.T. - THE EXTRA TERRESTRIAL (John Williams) (box set, with booklet & poster)	30
83	MCA CAC 70000	E.T. - THE EXTRA TERRESTRIAL (John Williams) (cassette, box set, with booklet & poster)	15
67	Brunswick LAT 8678	AN EVENING WITH BORIS KARLOFF AND FRIENDS	30
97	London 828 939-1	EVENT HORIZON (featuring Orbital)	25
87	That's Entertainment TER 1142	EVIL DEAD II (Joseph Lo Duca)	45
74	Warner Bros K 56071	THE EXORCIST (Jack Nitzsche, et al.)	20
72	Deram SML 1095	EXTREMES (Tony Klinger & Michael Lyons)	100

F

57	Capitol LCT 6139	A FACE IN THE CROWD (Tom Glazer) (10")	20
64	CBS (S)BPG 62277	FALL OF THE ROMAN EMPIRE (Dimitri Tiomkin)	20
67	Decca LK 4847	THE FAMILY WAY (Paul McCartney/George Martin) (mono)	70
67	Decca SKL 4847	THE FAMILY WAY (LP, stereo, soundtrack)	90
60	Top Rank 30/003/4/5	FANTASIA (various classical pieces) (3-LP, with book)	30

G

			MINT VALUE £
58	Capitol LCT 6162	A FAREWELL TO ARMS (Mario Nascimbene)	15
67	MGM MGM-C(S) 8053	FAR FROM THE MADDING CROWD (Richard Rodney Bennett)	20
68	London HA-U/SH-U 8358	THE FASTEST GUITAR ALIVE (Roy Orbison)	20
67	Stateside S(S)L 10213	FATHOM (Johnny Dankworth)	40
73	Pye NSPL 18398	FEAR IS THE KEY (Roy Budd)	50
70	United Artists UAS 29118	FELLINI-SATYRICON (Nino Rota)	15
65	Columbia 33SX 1693	FERRY CROSS THE MERSEY (Gerry & Pacemakers/Cilla Black/Fourmost) (also stereo SCX 3544 = £35)	25
99	Restless Records 74321716431	FIGHT CLUB (2-LP)	80
01	Simply Vinyl SLVP 161	FIGHT CLUB (2-LP, reissue)	50
63	CBS SBPG 62148	55 DAYS AT PEKING (Dimitri Tiomkin/Andy Williams)	18
66	Columbia SX 6079	FINDERS KEEPERS (Cliff Richard) (with inner sleeve, mono) (stereo SCX 6079 = £15)	15
57	Brunswick LAT 8194	FIRE DOWN BELOW (Arthur Benjamin)	25
67	RCA Victor RD/SF 7875	A FISTFUL OF DOLLARS (Ennio Morricone)	20
72	United Artists UAS 29345	A FISTFUL OF DYNAMITE (Ennio Morricone)	40
65	RCA Victor RD 7723	FLAMING STAR AND SUMMER KISSES (Elvis Presley) (mono only, black labels)	50
85	Heavy Metal HMXD 29	FLASHPOINT (Tangerine Dream) (CD, playable [most copies faulty])	50
61	Golden Guinea GGL 0092	THE FLINTSTONES (TV soundtrack)	20
62	Brunswick LAT 8392	FLOWER DRUM SONG (Nancy Kwan, et al.) (also stereo STA 3054)	15
64	Ace Of Clubs ACL 1166	FLYING CLIPPER (Riz Ortolani)	15
13	Death Waltz DW03.5	THE FOG (black vinyl)	40
13	Death Waltz DW03.5	THE FOG (splatter vinyl)	30
73	York BYK 715	FOLLYFOOT (LP)	20
65	Ember NR 5029	FOUR IN THE MORNING (John Barry) (mono)	35
74	T. Motown STML 11269	FOXY BROWN (Willie Hutch)	40
66	RCA Victor RD 7793	FRANKIE AND JOHNNY (Elvis Presley) (black/red dot labels, mono) (Stereo SF 7793 = £30)	20
94	FREE LP FRE4	FREE D	80
64	Fontana TL 5208	FREEDOM ROAD (Madeleine Bell, et al.) (TV production)	15
63	United Artists (S)ULP 1052	FROM RUSSIA WITH LOVE (John Barry/Matt Monroe) (mono/stereo)	25
60	London HA-T 2257	THE FUGITIVE KIND (Kenyon Hopkins)	30
67	RCA RD 7860	FUNERAL IN BERLIN (Konrad Elfers/Puppets)	20
63	RCA Victor RD/SF 7609	FUN IN ACAPULCO (Elvis Presley) (black/silver label, mono. (stereo = £35)	20

G

70	Stateside SOSL 10091	THE GAMES (Francis Lai)	200
65	Liberty (S)LBY 1261	GENGHIS KHAN (Dusan Radic) (mono/stereo)	20
56	Vogue Coral LVA 9003	GENTLEMEN MARRY BRUNETTES (Robert Farnon)	30
53	MGM MGM-D 116	GENTLEMEN PREFER BLONDES (Marilyn Monroe, et al.) (10")	75
65	Mercury 20061 MCL	GENTLE RAIN (Luis Bonfa & Deodato)	15
99	Cinephile CINLP001	GET CARTER (LP, gatefold)	25
70	RCA SF 8137	GETTING STRAIGHT (Ronald Stein)	20
57	Capitol LCT 6122	GIANT (Dimitri Tiomkin)	15
60	RCA RD 27192	G.I. BLUES (Elvis Presley) (black/silver label, mono) (stereo SF 5078 = £25)	15
66	MGM MGM-C(S) 8034	GIRL FROM U.N.C.L.E. (Jerry Goldsmith & Teddy Randazzo)	40
65	RCA Victor RD 7714	GIRL HAPPY (Elvis Presley) (black/red dot labels, mono) (stereo SF 7714 = £30)	20
68	Polydor 583 714	GIRL ON A MOTORCYCLE (Les Reed)	40
63	RCA Victor RD 7534	GIRLS! GIRLS! GIRLS! (Elvis Presley) (black/silver label, mono) (Stereo SF 7534 = £35)	15
66	United Artists SULP 1120	THE GLORY GUYS (Riz Ortolani)	30
72	Paramount SPFA 7003	THE GODFATHER (Nino Rota) (gatefold sleeve)	15
75	ABC ABCL 5128	THE GODFATHER - PART 2 (Nino Rota) (gatefold sleeve)	15
58	London HA-T 2125	GOD'S LITTLE ACRE (Elmer Bernstein)	20
72	Mother MO 4001	GOLD (MC5/David McWilliams, et al.)	35
73	United Artists UAS 29576	THE GOLDEN VOYAGE OF SINBAD (Miklos Rozsa)	15
64	United Artists ULP 1076	GOLDFINGER (John Barry/Shirley Bassey) (mono) (Stereo, SULP 1076 = £30)	15
64	Decca LK 4673	GONKS GO BEAT (Lulu/Nashville Teens/Graham Bond, et al.)	100
68	United Artists (S)ULP 1197	THE GOOD, THE BAD AND THE UGLY (Ennio Morricone)	15
69	Warner Bros W(S) 1786	GOODBYE COLUMBUS (Charles Fox/Association)	18
70	DJM DJLPS 408	GOODBYE GEMINI (Christopher Gunning/Peddlers/Jackie Lee)	50
63	United Artists (S)ULP 1041	THE GREAT ESCAPE (Elmer Bernstein) (mono/stereo)	15
71	Pye NSPL 18373	GREAT SONGS AND THEMES FROM GREAT FILMS (Roy Budd)	40
75	MCA MCF 2707	THE GREAT WALDO PEPPER (Henry Mancini)	15
68	United Artists SULP 1220	GREAT WESTERN FILM THEMES (Various Artists)	15
70	Polydor 2384 021	GROUPIE GIRL (Opal Butterfly/English Rose, et al.)	40
09	Trunk JBH 032 LP	G SPOTS (LP)	20
67	RCA RD/SF 7899	GUNN (Henry Mancini)	18

H

20	Varese Sarabande VSD00026	HACKERS (2-LP, reissue, original release was CD-only)	40
65	United Artists SULP 1106	THE HALLELUJAH TRAIL (Elmer Bernstein)	15
75	Contour 2870 437	THE HANGED MAN (Bullet) (TV soundtrack)	40
68	United Artists SULP 1204	HANG 'EM HIGH (Dominic Frontiere) (stereo/mono)	20
69	United Artists SULP 1231	HANNIBAL BROOKS (Francis Lai)	30
70	United Artists UAS 29084	THE HAPPY ENDING (Michel Legrand)	20
56	Philips BBL 7100	HAPPY HOLIDAY (Jo Stafford)	15
65	RCA Victor RD 7767	HAREM HOLIDAY (Elvis Presley) (black/red dot labels, mono) (stereo SF 7767 = £25)	20
65	Warner Bros W 1599	HARLOW (Neal Hefti)	15
80s	PRT/Chips CHILP 1	HAWK THE SLAYER (Harry Robertson) (gatefold sleeve)	15
68	RCA RD/SF 8051	HEAD (Monkees) (mono) Stereo = £60)	90

I

			MINT VALUE £
72	Reprise K 44168	THE HEIST (Quincy Jones/Little Richard)	15
74	Tamla Motown STML 11260	HELL UP IN HARLEM (Edwin Starr)	15
65	Parlophone PMC 1255	HELP! (Beatles) (1st pressing, with "The Gramophone Co. Ltd" & "Sold In The UK..." label text; mono, with "mono" in outline type on front cover)	100
65	Parlophone PCS 3071	HELP! (Beatles) (1st pressing, with "The Gramophone Co. Ltd" & "Sold In The UK..." label text; stereo, with "stereo" in outline type on front cover)	150
67	United Artists ULP 1186	HERE WE GO ROUND THE MULBERRY BUSH (Spencer Davis/Traffic/Andy Ellison) (mono) (stereo SULP 1186 = £35)	40
59	Capitol T 1160	HEY BOY! HEY GIRL! (Louis Prima/Keely Smith, et al.)	25
62	Columbia 33SX 1421	HEY, LET'S TWIST (Joey Dee, et al.)	20
83	A&R FILM 001	HIGH ROAD TO CHINA (John Barry)	15
70	Columbia SCX 6443	HIS LAND (Cliff Richard/Cliff Barrows)	15
67	United Artists ULP 1161	THE HONEY POT (John Addison)	15
59	London HA-T 2197	THE HORSE SOLDIERS (David Buttolph)	15
16	Laced (no Cat no)	HOTLINE MIAMI (3-LP, red, black and yellow vinyl)	200
59	Philips BBL 7292	HOUSEBOAT (George Duning)	25
87	Silva Screen FILM 041	HOW TO GET AHEAD IN ADVERTISING/WITHNAIL & I	20
65	United Artists (S)ULP 1098	HOW TO MURDER YOUR WIFE (Neal Hefti)	15
72	Atlantic K 40371	HOW TO STEAL A DIAMOND IN FOUR UNEASY LESSONS (Quincy Jones)	15
66	Stateside S(S)L 10187	HOW TO STEAL A MILLION (John Williams)	25
67	RCA Victor RD/SF 7877	HURRY SUNDOWN (Hugo Montenegro)	20

I

70	United Artists UAS 29044	IF IT'S TUESDAY THIS MUST BE BELGIUM (Walter Scharf)	15
67	Brunswick LAT/STA 8689	I'LL NEVER FORGET WHAT'S 'ISNAME (Francis Lai)	50
65	United Artists ULP 1105	I'LL TAKE SWEDEN (Bob Hope/Frankie Avalon, et al.)	15
68	RCA Victor RD/SF 7931	IN COLD BLOOD (Quincy Jones)	20
65	RCA RD 7707	IN HARM'S WAY (Jerry Goldsmith)	25
67	Stateside S(S)L 10207	IN LIKE FLINT (Jerry Goldsmith)	50
68	United Artists ULP 1201	INSPECTOR CLOUSEAU (Ken Thorne)	20
69	RCA Victor RD/SF 7990	INTERLUDE (Georges Delarue/Timi Yuro)	15
62	Colpix PXL 427	THE INTERNS (Leith Stevens)	18
67	United Artists (S)ULP 1181	IN THE HEAT OF THE NIGHT (Quincy Jones/Ray Charles)	25
65	CBS BPG 62530	THE IPCRESS FILE (John Barry) (mono only)	150
84	Illuminated JAMS 35	IN THE SHADOW OF THE SUN (Throbbing Gristle)	20
66	CBS (S)BPG 62843	IS PARIS BURNING? (Maurice Jarre)	18
69	Paramount SPFL 256	THE ITALIAN JOB (Quincy Jones/Matt Monro)	75
63	RCA Victor RD 7565	IT HAPPENED AT THE WORLD'S FAIR (Elvis Presley) (black/silver label, mono) (stereo SF 7565 = £35)	18
63	Columbia 33SX 1537	IT'S ALL HAPPENING (Tommy Steele/Shane Fenton, et al.) (also stereo SCX 3486)	15
63	United Artists (S)ULP 1053	IT'S A MAD MAD MAD MAD WORLD (Ernest Gold)	15
65	Decca LK 4677	I'VE GOTTA HORSE (Billy Fury/Bachelors, et al.)	40
71	CBS 70083	I WALK THE LINE (Johnny Cash)	15
07	Trunk JBH 027 LP	IVOR THE ENGINE & POGLES WOOD (LP)	15

J

57	Capitol LCT 6140	THE JAMES DEAN STORY (Leith Stevens)	25
54	Brunswick LA 8671	JAZZ THEMES FROM "THE WILD ONE" (Leith Stevens) (10")	30
62	HMV CLP 1582	JESSICA (Mario Nascimbene)	15
77	Pye NSPH 28504	JESUS OF NAZARETH (Maurice Jarre) (gatefold sleeve)	15
71	Mercury 6338 029	JOE (Bobby Scott/Jenny Butler)	20
64	United Artists ULP 1060	JOHNNY COOL (Billy May/Sammy Davis Jr.)	25
72	Reprise K 64015	JOURNEY THROUGH THE PAST (Neil Young) (2-LP, fold-out cover with inner sleeves)	40
77	Polydor/EG 2302 079	JUBILEE (Adam & Ants/Brian Eno, et al.)	20
61	HMV CLP 1545	JUDGEMENT AT NUREMBURG (Ernest Gold)	15
67	Fontana (S)TL 5317	JULIET OF THE SPIRITS (Nino Rota)	30
63	Decca LK 4524	JUST FOR FUN (Tornados/Karl Denver, et al.)	25
64	Decca LK 4620	JUST FOR YOU (Applejacks/Merseybeats, et al.)	40
70	Monument LMO/SMO 5031	JUSTINE (Jerry Goldsmith)	20

K

71	MGM 2315 019	KELLY'S HEROES (Lalo Schifrin/Mike Curb)	25
01	Trunk KES 001 LP	KES (LP - 1-sided)	40
66	United Artists (S)ULP 1139	KHARTOUM (Frank Cordell)	30
72	Polydor 2383 102	KIDNAPPED (Roy Budd/Mary Hopkin)	25
58	RCA RD 27088	KING CREOLE (Elvis Presley) (black/silver labels)	40
76	Reprise K 54090	KING KONG (John Barry) (with poster)	15
61	MGM MGM-CS 6043	KING OF KINGS (Miklos Rozsa)	20
58	Capitol LCT 6165	KINGS GO FORTH (Elmer Bernstein)	15
66	Fontana (S)TL 5302	KING RAT (John Barry)	18
64	RCA Victor RD 7645	KISSIN' COUSINS (Elvis Presley) (black/red dot labels, mono) (stereo SF 7645 = £30)	18
64	MGM MGM-C 753	KISS ME KATE (Howard Keel, et al.)	15
65	United Artists ULP 1104	THE KNACK (AND HOW TO GET IT) (John Barry)	80
74	Warner Bros K 46271	KUNG FU (TV soundtrack) (with inner sleeve) (Jim Helms)	20

L

61	RCA RD 27202	LA DOLCE VITA (Nino Rota) (gatefold sleeve)	50
63	Ace Of Hearts AH 70	THE LADY AND THE TRAMP (Peggy Lee)	20
69	Stateside S(S)L 10267	LADY IN CEMENT (Hugo Montenegro)	40
71	United Artists UAS 29120	THE LANDLORD (Al Kooper)	20
00	DC DC 33LP	LA PLANETE SAUVAGE (LP, reissue)	30

M

MINT VALUE £

Year	Catalogue	Title	Value
72	MGM 2315 072	THE LAST RUN (Jerry Goldsmith/Steve Lawrence)	25
73	United Artists UAS 29440	LAST TANGO IN PARIS (Gato Barbieri)	15
71	Probe SPB 1027	THE LAST VALLEY (John Barry) (mono, with insert) (stereo = £20)	15
85	United Artists 86002	LEGEND (Jerry Goldsmith)	25
74	Warner Bros K 56085	THE LEGEND OF THE 7 GOLDEN VAMPIRES (James Bernard/Peter Cushing)	18
64	Stateside S(S)L 10058	THE LEOPARD (Nino Rota)	30
70	Apple PXS 1	LET IT BE (Beatles) (LP box set, 1st pressing, dark green label, red Apple logo on LP rear sleeve & white inner, with Get Back book housed in black card tray ['PXS1'] not listed on package)	800
70	Apple PCS 7096	LET IT BE (Beatles) (2nd pressing, green Apple logo on rear sleeve, plain white inner)	40
60	Philips BBL 7414/SBBL 592	LET'S MAKE LOVE (Marilyn Monroe/Yves Montand/Frankie Vaughan)	40
64	Columbia SX 1626	LILIES OF THE FIELD (Jerry Goldsmith)	20
66	MGM MGM-CS 8029	THE LIQUIDATOR (Lalo Schifrin/Shirley Bassey)	40
73	United Artists UAS 29475	LIVE AND LET DIE (George Martin/Wings) (gatefold sleeve)	25
76	MGM 2315 376	LOGAN'S RUN (Jerry Goldsmith)	20
62	MGM MGM-C 896	LOLITA (Nelson Riddle)	30
67	Polydor 583 014	LONG DUEL (Patrick John Scott/Vince Hill)	20
63	Stateside S(S)L 10045	THE LONGEST DAY (dialogue only)	15
83	CES CES 1001	THE LONG GOOD FRIDAY (Francis Monkman) (numbered sleeve with insert, black label print, 2,000 only)	50
83	CES CES 1001	THE LONG GOOD FRIDAY (Francis Monkman) (re-pressing, with insert, blue label print, 500 only)	40
84	CES CES 1001	THE LONG GOOD FRIDAY (Francis Monkman) (3rd pressing, with insert, blue label print, 5,000 only)	40
89	Silva Screen FILM 020	THE LONG GOOD FRIDAY (Francis Monkman) (reissue)	20
70	CBS 70073	LOOT (Keith Mansfield/Steve Ellis)	40
65	Colpix PXL 521	LORD JIM (Bronislau Kaper)	15
69	Uni UNLS 103	LOST MAN (Quincy Jones)	25
70	CBS 70067	LOVE CIRCLE (Ennio Morricone)	50
57	RCA RC 24001	LOVING YOU (Elvis Presley) (10", silver spot label)	75

M

Year	Catalogue	Title	Value
73	Tamla Motown STMA 8003	THE MACK (Willie Hutch)	35
69	Warner Bros WS 1805	THE MADWOMAN OF CHAILLOT (Michael Lewis)	15
70	Pye Intl. NSPL 28133	THE MAGIC CHRISTIAN (Ken Thorne/Badfinger, et al.)	40
54	Brunswick LAT 8045	MAGNIFICENT OBSESSION (Frank Skinner)	20
65	MGM MGM-C 995	THE MAGNIFICENT SHOWMAN (Dimitri Tiomkin)	25
76	Atlantic K 50308	MAHONEY'S LAST STAND (Ronnie Lane & Ron Wood)	15
63	Ace Of Clubs ACL 1135	MAIGRET (Ron Grainer) (TV series music)	15
66	CBS SBPG 62525	MAJOR DUNDEE (Daniele Amfitheatrof/Mitch Miller)	15
11	Finders Keepers FKRO40LP	MALA MORSKA (ZDENEK LISKA) (foil/red wax edition)	30
59	Top Rank 35/043	MAN FROM INTERPOL (Tony Crombie) (TV series music)	25
66	RCA Victor RD 7758	THE MAN FROM U.N.C.L.E. (Hugo Montenegro)	40
13	Death Waltz DW 014	MANIAC (flesh coloured vinyl)	20
13	Death Waltz DW 014	MANIAC (silver vinyl)	30
64	Stateside S(S)L 10087	MAN IN THE MIDDLE (Lionel Bart & John Barry)	30
56	Brunswick LAT 8101	THE MAN WITH THE GOLDEN ARM (Elmer Bernstein)	20
74	United Artists UAS 29671	THE MAN WITH THE GOLDEN GUN (John Barry/Lulu)	15
63	Stateside S(S)L 10048	MARILYN (Marilyn Monroe) (mono/stereo)	40
72	MCA MUPS 441	MARY QUEEN OF SCOTS (John Barry)	20
70	United Artists UAS 29122	MASTER OF THE ISLANDS (Henry Mancini)	15
69	Philips SBL 7876	MAYERLING (Francis Lai)	20
64	United Artists SULP 1059	McLINTOCK (Frank De Vol)	35
80	Polydor POLD 5034	McVICAR (Roger Daltrey) (some on clear vinyl)	15
71	Polydor 2383 043	MELODY (Bee Gees, Richard Hewson, et al.)	15
57	London HA-P 2076	MEN IN WAR (Elmer Bernstein)	15
69	Bell BELL 6053	MERRY CHRISTMAS (David Frost/Billy Taylor)	20
65	MGM MGM-C 8001	MICKEY ONE (Stan Getz & Eddie Sauter) (with booklet, mono) (stereo MGM-CS 8001 = £25)	20
66	Mercury 20072 (S)MCL	MIRAGE (Quincy Jones)	25
61	HMV CLP 1481	THE MISFITS (Alex North)	25
68	Dot (S)LPD 503	MISSION: IMPOSSIBLE - MUSIC FROM THE TV SERIES (Lalo Schifrin)	40
54	Mercury 25181	MISS SADIE THOMPSON (George Duning) (10")	30
66	Fontana TL 5347	MODESTY BLAISE (Johnny Dankworth)	40
70	Paramount SPFL 259	THE MOLLY MAGUIRES (Henry Mancini)	15
80	BBC REB 384	MONKEY (Godiego) (TV soundtrack)	25
69	Paramount SPFL 255	MONTE CARLO OR BUST! (Ron Goodwin)	25
79	United Artists UAG 30247	MOONRAKER (John Barry/Shirley Bassey)	15
69	Columbia SCX 6346	MORE (Pink Floyd) (laminated flipback sleeve, 'couple facing west' photo on green-tinted rear sleeve)	100
70s	Columbia SCX 6346	MORE (Pink Floyd) (laminated non-flipback sleeve, 'couple facing west' photo on black-tinted rear sleeve)	80
70s	Columbia SCX 6346	MORE (Pink Floyd) (laminated non-flipback sleeve, 'couple facing east' photo on black-tinted rear sleeve)	70
69	Paramount SPFL 252	MORE 'MISSION: IMPOSSIBLE' (Lalo Schifrin)	40
60	MGM MGM-C(S) 857	MORE MUSIC FROM BEN-HUR (Miklos Rozsa)	15
66	RCA Victor RD 7832	MORE MUSIC FROM 'THE MAN FROM U.N.C.L.E.' (Hugo Montenegro)	45
62	MGM	MORE MUSIC FROM 'MUTINY ON THE BOUNTY' (Bronislau Kaper)	20
68	MGM CS8063	MORE THAN A MIRACLE (Piero Piccioni)	15
67	RCA RD 7847	MURDERERS' ROW (Lalo Schifrin)	50
80	Unicorn Kachana KPM 7009	MUSIC FROM THE AVENGERS, THE NEW AVENGERS AND THE PROFESSIONALS	20
70	Harvest SHSP 4008	MUSIC FROM THE BODY (Ron Geesin & Roger Waters) (photos/green labels)	50

N

MINT VALUE £

90	Warner Bros. 7599 26316-1	MUSIC FROM TWIN PEAKS	40
62	MGM MGM-CS 6060	MUTINY ON THE BOUNTY (Bronislau Kaper)	20
85	Cloud Nine CN 4002	MYSTERIOUS ISLAND (Bernard Herrman)	15

N

70	United Artists UAS 29108	NED KELLY (Shel Silverstein/Mick Jagger/Waylon Jennings)	30
72	Bell BELLS 202	NICHOLAS AND ALEXANDRA (Richard Rodney Bennet)	15
67	RCA RD 7848	NIGHT OF THE GENERALS (Maurice Jarre)	30
65	MGM MGM-C 994	NIGHT OF THE IGUANA (Benjamin Frankel)	15
69	United Artists (S)ULP 1235	THE NIGHT THEY RAIDED MINSKY'S (Charles Strouse)	20
62	Decca LK 4527	NINE HOURS TO RAMA (Malcolm Arnold)	50
68	Dot (S)LPD 507	NO WAY TO TREAT A LADY (American Breed)	20

O

72	Harvest SHSP 4020	OBSCURED BY CLOUDS (Pink Floyd) (rounded sleeve)	75
76	Phase 4 Stereo PF5 4381	OBSESSION (Bernard Herrman)	15
83	A&M 394 967-2	OCTOPUSSY (John Barry) (CD, withdrawn)	75
68	Dot (S)LPD 514	THE ODD COUPLE (Neal Hefti)	15
60	London HA-T 2220	ODDS AGAINST TOMORROW (John Lewis)	20
57	Brunswick LAT 8226	OMAR KHAYYAM/THE MOUNTAIN (Victor Young/Daniele Amfitheatrof)	30
75	Fantasy FTA 3004	ONE FLEW OVER THE CUCKOO'S NEST (Jack Nitzsche) (gatefold sleeve)	15
69	United Artists UAS 29020	ON HER MAJESTY'S SECRET SERVICE (John Barry) (foldout sleeve)	25
70	Fontana SFJL 950	ORFEU NEGRO (BLACK ORPHEUS) (Luis Bonfa/Antonio Carlos Jobim)	15
69	RCA SF 8014	OTLEY (Stanley Myers/Don Partridge)	25
66	Stateside S(S)L 10174	OUR MAN FLINT (Jerry Goldsmith)	30
76	Warner Bros K 56286	THE OUTLAW JOSEY WALES (Jerry Fielding)	25

P

63	Warner Bros WM 8141	PALM SPRINGS WEEKEND (Frank Perkins)	20
66	RCA Victor SF 7810	PARADISE, HAWAIIAN STYLE (Elvis Presley) (black/red dot labels, mono) (stereo SF 7810 = £30)	20
61	HMV CLP 1499	PARIS BLUES (Duke Ellington)	20
61	Warner Bros WS 8044	PARRISH (Max Steiner/George Greely)	20
65	Mercury 20063 SML	THE PAWNBROKER (Quincy Jones)	30
66	Philips (S)BL 7782	THE PEKING MEDALLION (Georges Garvarentz/Dusty Springfield)	20
67	Ember NR 5040	THE PENTHOUSE (John Hawksworth)	40
71	Pye NSPL 18365	PERCY (Kinks)	50
70	Warner Bros WS 2554	PERFORMANCE (First pressing, orange label, Mick Jagger/Jack Nitzsche/Randy Newman, et al.)	40
70	Warner Bros WS 2554	PERFORMANCE (Second pressing, green label, Mick Jagger/Jack Nitzsche/Randy Newman, et al.)	35
59	RCA RD 27123/SF 5033	PETER GUNN (Henry Mancini)	15
79	Gem GEM 102	PHANTASM (Fred Myrow & Malcolm Seagrave)	60
56	Brunswick LAT 8120	PICNIC (George Duning)	20
68	Philips SBL 7858	PLAYTIME (Jacques Tati, Yan Tatore, Leo Petit)	35
70	Paramount SPFL 258	POOKIE (Fred Karlin/Sandpipers)	15
57	Capitol LCT 6141	THE PRIDE AND THE PASSION (Georges Antheil)	15
86	Bam Caruso WEBA 066	THE PRISONER (Ron Grainer, et al.) (fan club issue, gatefold sleeve with inner sleeve, booklet, membership form, map & poster)	40
67	HMV CLP/CSD 3623	PRIVILEGE (Paul Jones & Mike Leander)	40
69	RCA SF 8072	THE PRODUCERS (John Morris)	15
69	United Artists UAS 29005	A PROFESSIONAL GUN (Ennio Morricone)	25
67	RCA Victor RD/SF 7876	THE PROFESSIONALS (Maurice Jarre)	50
60	Contemporary LAC 12293	THE PROPER TIME (Shelly Manne)	15
68	Stateside S(S)L 10248	PRUDENCE AND THE PILL (Bernard Ebbinghouse)	25
75	Unicorn RHS 336	PSYCHO (Bernard Herrmann)	20
03	Trunk JBH002LP	PSYCHOMANIA	60

Q

| 71 | Sonet SNTF 622 | QUIET DAYS IN CLICHY (Country Joe McDonald) | 15 |
| 66 | CBS (S)BPG 62869 | THE QUILLER MEMORANDUM (John Barry/Matt Monro) (mono/stereo) | 25 |

R

71	Reprise K 44159	RAINBOW BRIDGE (Jimi Hendrix) (matt gatefold sleeve, 'steamboat' label)	20
75	Dart ARTS 65376	RANSOM (Jerry Goldsmith)	40
60	London HAD 2288	THE RAT RACE (Sam Butera & The Witnesses)	25
67	United Artists (S)ULP 1184	RED AND BLUE (Vanessa Redgrave)	40
72	Paramount SPFL 275	THE RED TENT (Ennio Morricone)	15
75	RCA Red Seal RS 1010	THE RETURN OF THE PINK PANTHER (Henry Mancini)	15
69	United Artists ULP 29069	REVOLUTION (Quicksilver Messenger Service/Steve Miller, et al.)	20
70	United Artists UAS 29137	RIDER IN THE RAIN (Francis Lai)	25
68	MGM MGM-C(S) 8079	THE RISE AND FALL OF THE THIRD REICH (Lalo Schifrin)	20
53	Brunswick LA 8578	ROAD TO BALI (Bob Hope, Bing Crosby) (10")	30
62	Decca LKR 4427	THE ROAD TO HONG KONG (Robert Farnon/Bob Hope & Bing Crosby)	20
54	Brunswick LAT 8031	THE ROBE	15
67	Decca LK/SKL 4892	ROBBERY (Johnny Keating/Jackie Lee)	30
64	Reprise R 2021	ROBIN AND THE SEVEN HOODS (Nelson Riddle)	20
61	RCA RD 27233	ROCCO AND HIS BROTHERS (Nino Rota)	20
57	Mercury MPT 7527	ROCK ALL NIGHT (Platters, Norah Hayes, et al.) (10")	125
67	Polydor 583 013	JULES VERNE'S ROCKET TO THE MOON (John Scott)	100
57	Brunswick LAT 8162	ROCK, PRETTY BABY (Henry Mancini/Rod McKuen)	80

S

			MINT VALUE £
87	Ode RHVX 1	ROCKY HORROR BOX SET (Richard O'Brien) (4-LP box, with inserts, numbered)	20
87	Ode RHBXLP 1	ROCKY HORROR BOX SET (Richard O'Brien) (4-LP box, with different inserts to above)	20
83	Ode OSVP 78332	THE ROCKY HORROR PICTURE SHOW ALBUM (picture disc)	15
90	Ode RHBXCD 1	THE ROCKY HORROR PICTURE SHOW - 15TH ANNIVERSARY (Richard O'Brien, et al.) (4-CD box)	40
68	Dot (S)LPD 519	ROSEMARY'S BABY (Kryzstophe Komeda)	50
65	Parlophone PMC 1262	ROTTEN TO THE CORE (New Jazz Voices)	20
64	RCA Victor RD 7678	ROUSTABOUT (Elvis Presley) (black/red dot labels, mono) (stereo SF 7678 = £25)	15
64	Capitol (S)T 1771	ROUTE 66 AND OTHER GREAT T.V. THEMES (Nelson Riddle) (TV show)	15
18	Laced LMLP014	RUINER (2-LP, red and black vinyl)	80
66	United Artists ULP 1147	THE RUSSIANS ARE COMING THE RUSSIANS ARE COMING (Johnny Mandel)	15

S

72	RCA SF 8211	SACCO AND VANZETTI (Ennio Morricone/Joan Baez)	20
53	Brunswick LA 8604	SALOMÉ (George Duning) (10")	30
68	United Artists SULP 1202	SALT AND PEPPER (Johnny Dankworth/Sammy Davis Jr)	15
65	Mercury MCL 20065	THE SANDPIPER (Johnny Mandel)	15
78	Polydor 2480 429	SCOUSE THE MOUSE (Ringo Starr/Adam Faith, et al.) (some w/stickered sleeve & printed [not photocopied] competition insert)	100
78	Polydor 3194 429	SCOUSE THE MOUSE (Ringo Starr/Adam Faith, et al.) (cassette)	30
62	Reprise R 2013	SERGEANTS 3 (Billy May)	20
73	Paramount SPFL 296	SERPICO (Mikis Theodorakis)	26
64	United Artists ULP 1072	THE 7th DAWN (Riz Ortolani)	15
74	United Artists UAS 29763	THE SEVENTH VOYAGE OF SINBAD (Bernard Hermann)	20
16	Laced LMLP007	SHADOW WARRIOR 2 (12", picture disc)	35
73	Probe SPB 1077	SHAFT IN AFRICA (Johnny Pate/Four Tops)	40
72	MGM 2315 115	SHAFT'S BIG SCORE! (Gordon Parks/O.C. Smith/Isaac Hayes)	35
66	CBS BPG 62755	SHAKESPEARE WALLAH (Satyajit Ray)	15
68	Philips SBL 7867	SHALAKO (Robert Farnon)	15
80	Warner Bros K 56827	THE SHINING (Bela Bartok et al.)	25
12	Trunk RSD 001	THE SHUTTERED ROOM (9 copies only, stamped white labels, inserts, stamped white sleeve)	300
12	Trunk RSD 001	THE SHUTTERED ROOM (25 copies only, stamped white labels, inserts, screenprinted brown sleeve)	400
70	Stateside SSL 10307	THE SICILIAN CLAN (Ennio Morricone)	40
12	Rook RFV 001	SIGHTSEERS SESSIONS (45rpm red vinyl LP, poster, 150 only)	100
72	MCA MUPS 458	SILENT RUNNING (Pete Schikele/Joan Baez)	20
66	RCA RD 7792	THE SILENCERS (Elmer Bernstein/Vikki Carr)	30
58	Capitol T 929	SING, BOY, SING (Tommy Sands)	50
78	Charisma CAS 1139	SIR HENRY AT RAWLINSON END (Vivian Stanshall) (with insert)	20
16	Laced 302 067 410 1	65DAYSOFSTATIC (2-LP)	35
16	Laced LMLP004X	65DAYSOFSTATIC (4-LP)	100
64	United Artists ULP 1071	633 SQUADRON (Ron Goodwin)	20
69	RCA SF 8010	SKIDOO (Nilsson)	20
73	Polydor 2391 084	SLAUGHTER'S BIG RIP-OFF (James Brown)	30
66	Mercury MCL 20080	THE SLENDER THREAD (Quincy Jones)	20
69	NEMS 6-70059	THE SMASHING BIRD I USED TO KNOW (Bobby Richards)	20
68	Stateside S(S)L 10224	SMASHING TIME (John Addison)	30
73	PRT FBLP 8085	SMIKE	15
56	Pye Disneyland DPL 39003	SNOW WHITE AND THE SEVEN DWARFS (Disney Orchestra)	30
70	Pye NSPL 18348	SOLDIER BLUE AND OTHER THEMES (Roy Budd)	40
60	London HA-T 2221	SOLOMON AND SHEBA (Mario Nascimbene)	75
59	Capitol LCT 6180	SOME CAME RUNNING (Elmer Bernstein)	15
59	London HA-T 2176	SOME LIKE IT HOT (Marilyn Monroe) (also stereo SAH-T 6040 = £60)	30
67	RCA RD 7845	SONGS FROM THE SWINGER (Marty Paich/Ann-Margret)	50
74	Rapple/RCA APL1-0220	SON OF DRACULA (Ringo Starr/Harry Nilsson, fold-out sleeve)	15
69	RCA Victor SF 8024	THE SOUTHERN STAR (Matt Monro/Georges Garvarentz)	15
58	London HA-D 2079	SPANISH AFFAIR (Daniele Amfitheatrof)	20
61	Brunswick LAT 8363	SPARTACUS (Alex North) (gatefold sleeve)	20
68	RCA Victor SF 7957	SPEEDWAY (Elvis Presley/Nancy Sinatra) (black/red dot labels, mono) (stereo SF 7957 = £25)	30
53	Capitol CCL 7505	SPELLBOUND/THE RED HOUSE (Miklos Rosza) (10")	25
66	RCA RD 7787	THE SPY WHO CAME IN FROM THE COLD (Sol Kaplan)	20
68	CBS 62919	THE SPY WITH THE COLD NOSE (Riz Ortolani)	35
66	Fontana TL 5354	STAGECOACH (Jerry Goldsmith)	25
77	20th C. BTD 541	STAR WARS (John Williams) (2-LP, with insert and poster)	20
69	CBS 70062	STILETTO (Sid Ramin)	30
52	Capitol LC 6542	A STREET CAR NAMED DESIRE (Alex North) (10")	35
63	Elstree Extra Range	SUMMER HOLIDAY (2-LP, full soundtrack recording, 80 copies only)	400
63	Columbia SCX 3462	SUMMER HOLIDAY (Cliff Richard) (first pressing, stereo, with inner sleeve, with green labels)	25
57	London HA-R 2077	THE SUN ALSO RISES (Hugo Friedhofer)	25
55	HMV DLP 1104	SUN VALLEY SERENADE (Glenn Miller)	15
62	Golden Guinea GGL 0106	SUPERCAR - FLIGHT OF FANCY (Barry Gray/Edwin Astley)	50
72	Buddah 2318 065	SUPERFLY (Curtis Mayfield) (gatefold sleeve)	20
73	Buddah 2318 087	SUPER FLY T.N.T. (Osibisa)	15
64	Stateside SL 10089	SURF PARTY (Astronauts, Routers, et al.)	50
79	EMI EMC 3222	SUSPIRIA (Goblin)	40
57	Brunswick LAT 8195	SWEET SMELL OF SUCCESS (Elmer Bernstein)	20
68	Stateside S(S)L 10250	THE SWEET RIDE (Pete Rugolo/Dusty Springfield)	15
68	CBS 70043	THE SWIMMER (Marvin Hamlisch)	25

			MINT VALUE £
65	MGM MGM-C 8012	THE SWINGIN' SET (Dave Clark Five/Animals, et al.)	30
66	Mercury 20057 SMCL	SYLVIA (David Raksin)	15
16	Laced (no Cat no)	SYMPHONIC FANTASIES TOKYO: MUSIC FROM SQUARE ENIX (3-LP)	60

T

70	Pye NSPL 18353	TAKE A GIRL LIKE YOU (Stanley Myers/Foundations)	30
01	Simply Vinyl SVLP 358	THE TAKING OF PELHAM ONE TWO THREE	40
57	Vogue Coral LVA 9070	TAMMY/INTERLUDE (Frank Skinner/Debbie Reynolds) (1 film per side)	30
63	United Artists ULP 1025	TARAS BULBA (Franz Waxman)	25
76	Arista ARTY 132	TAXI DRIVER (Bernard Herrman)	30
71	RCA Victor SF 8162	THAT'S THE WAY IT IS (Elvis Presley) (glossy or matt sleeve)	15
63	Parlophone PMC 1197	THAT WAS THE WEEK THAT WAS (Millicent Martin, et al.) (also stereo PCS 3040)	15
59	Coral LVA 9102	THEMES FROM HORROR MOVIES (Dick Jacobs)	15
73	Elektra K 46239	THE THIEF WHO CAME TO DINNER (Henry Mancini)	15
82	MCA MCF 3148	THE THING (Ennio Morricone)	30
70	United Artists UAS 29128	THEY CALL ME MISTER TIBBS (Quincy Jones)	60
69	Philips SBL 7898	THEY CAME TO ROB LAS VEGAS (Georges Gavarentz)	40
70	Stateside SSL 10305	THEY SHOOT HORSES, DON'T THEY? (John Green)	15
66	Verve VLP 9147	THIS PROPERTY IS CONDEMNED (Kenyon Hopkins)	35
68	United Artists SULP 1218	THE THOMAS CROWN AFFAIR (Michel Legrand/Noel Harrison)	35
70	Sunset SLS 50519	THE THOMAS CROWN AFFAIR (Michel Legrand, reissue)	20
65	Stateside SL 10136	THOSE MAGNIFICENT MEN IN THEIR FLYING MACHINES (Ron Goodwin)	20
54	Capitol LC 6665	THREE SAILORS AND A GIRL (Gordon MacRae, et al.) (10")	30
61	Golden Guinea GGL 0065	THREE WORLDS OF GULLIVER (Bernard Herrmann)	20
85	Cloud Nine CN 4003	THREE WORLDS OF GULLIVER (Bernard Herrmann) (reissue)	15
65	United Artists (S)ULP 1110	THUNDERBALL (John Barry) (mono/stereo)	35
67	United Artists (S)ULP 1159	THUNDERBIRDS ARE GO! (Barry Gray/Cliff Richard & Shadows) (mono) (stereo = £120)	100
66	NPL 18154	TILL DEATH US DO PART (Warren Mitchell et al.)	15
69	Polydor 583 717	TILL DEATH DO US PART (Wilfred Burns)	15
63	MGM MGM-C 934	TO KILL A MOCKINGBIRD (Elmer Bernstein)	20
06	Trunk JBH 017 LP	THE TOMORROW PEOPLE (LP)	40
59	MGM MGM-C 772	TOM THUMB (Russ Tamblyn)	15
68	Instant INLP 002	TONITE LET'S ALL MAKE LOVE IN LONDON (Pink Floyd/Chris Farlowe, et al.)	100
70	RCA LSA 3008	TOOMORROW (with insert)	125
67	Fontana (S)TL 5446	TO SIR, WITH LOVE (Ron Grainer/ Lulu/Mindbenders)	35
69	Stateside S(S)L 10271	THE TOUCHABLES (Ken Thorne/Nirvana/Wynder K. Frog, et al.)	35
66	Polydor 582 004	THE TRAP (Ron Goodwin)	40
96	EMI EMC 3789	TRAINSPOTTING (2-LP)	80
67	United Artists ULP 1176	TRIPLE CROSS (Georges Garvarentz/Tony Allen)	25
82	CBS 70223	TRON (Wendy Carlos/Journey)	15
73	T. Motown STML 11225	TROUBLE MAN (Marvin Gaye)	20
03	XL XLLP 161	28 DAYS LATER	100
01	Factory FAC 401	24 HOUR PARTY PEOPLE (12" promo, Joy Division/New Order/Happy Mondays)	40
69	Polydor 583 728	TWISTED NERVE/LES BICYCLETES DE BELSIZE (Les Reed/Barry Mason, Bernard Herrman)	80
69	Columbia S(C)X 6330	TWO CITIES (Jeff Wayne)	30
67	RCA RD/SF 7891	TWO FOR THE ROAD (Henry Mancini)	15
63	United Artists ULP 1027	TWO FOR THE SEESAW (André Previn)	15
71	United Artists UDF 50003	200 MOTELS (Frank Zappa) (2-LP, with booklet & poster)	40
70	MCA MKPS 2013	TWO MULES FOR SISTER SARA (Ennio Morricone)	30
62	Columbia 33SX 1482	TWO TICKETS TO PARIS (Joey Dee)	20

U

04	Trunk JBHO10LP	UFO (500 black/500 clear vinyl)	50
60	London HA-T 2258	THE UNFORGIVEN (Dimitri Tiomkin)	18
68	Fontana (S)TL 5460	UP THE JUNCTION (Manfred Mann)	50
70	Fontana 6852 005	UP THE JUNCTION (Manfred Mann) (reissue)	25
69	Stax (S)XATS 1005	UPTIGHT (Booker T & MGs)	15

V

73	Philips 6303 075	THE VALACHI PAPERS (Riz Ortolani)	25
11	Finders Keepers FKRO48LP	VALERIE AND HER WEEK OF WONDERS (lubos Fiser)	20
68	Stateside (S)SL 10228	VALLEY OF THE DOLLS (André Previn/John Williams)	20
71	London SH-U 8420	VANISHING POINT (Delaney & Bonnie/Sam & Dave, et al.)	20
82	MGM 2315 437	VICTOR, VICTORIA (Henry Mancini)	15
63	Colpix PXL 516	THE VICTORS (Sol Kaplan/Frank Sinatra)	15
58	London HAT 2118	THE VIKINGS (Mario Nascimbene)	20
68	Dot (S)LPD 515	VILLA RIDES (Maurice Jarre)	15
63	MGM MGM-C 951/CS 6074	THE VIPs (Miklos Rozsa)	20
66	United Artists (S)ULP 1126	VIVA MARIA! (Georges Delerue) (mono/stereo)	30

W

60	Mercury MMC 14033	WAGON TRAIN (Stanley Wilson, et al.)	25
62	MGM MGM-C 891	WALK ON THE WILD SIDE (Elmer Bernstein)	15
66	Brunswick STA 8636	THE WAR LORD (Jerome Moross)	35
78	Satril SATL 4009	THE WATER MARGIN (Godiego) (TV soundtrack)	20
67	Virtuoso TPLS 13010	WELLES RAISES KANE (Bernard Herrman)	30
64	Piccadilly N(S)PL 38011	WHAT A CRAZY WORLD (Joe Brown/Susan Maughan/Marty Wilde; mono/stereo)	22
66	RCA SF 7818	WHAT DID YOU DO IN THE WAR, DADDY? (Henry Mancini)	15
65	United Artists ULP 1096	WHAT'S NEW PUSSYCAT? (Burt Bacharach/Tom Jones/Manfred Mann, et al.)	20

Y

			Mint Value £
66	MGM MGM-C(S) 8006	WHEN THE BOYS MEET THE GIRLS (Connie Francis/Herman's Hermits) (mono/stereo)	15
69	MGM MGM-C(S) 8102	WHERE EAGLES DARE (Ron Goodwin)	20
66	United Artists (S)ULP 1166	WHIPLASH WILLIE (André Previn)	15
67	United Artists (S)ULP 1168	THE WHISPERERS (John Barry)	40
67	Warner Bros W 1656	WHO'S AFRAID OF VIRGINIA WOOLF? (Alex North)	25
98	Trunk BARKED 4	THE WICKER MAN (Giovanni) (1st pressing, black vinyl)	75
98	Trunk BARKED 4	THE WICKER MAN (Giovanni) (2nd pressing, red vinyl with inserts)	90
90	London 845128	WILD AT HEART	20
57	London HA-N 2023	WILD BILL HICKOCK AND JINGLES ON THE SANTA FE TRAIL (TV s/track)	18
69	Warner Bros WS 1814	THE WILD BUNCH (Jerry Fielding) (orange label original)	25
71	Warner Bros K 46035	THE WILD BUNCH (Jerry Fielding) (reissue)	15
78	A&M AMLH 64730	THE WILD GEESE (Roy Budd/Joan Armatrading)	15
68	Capitol (S)T 5099	WILD IN THE STREETS (Les Baxter/Gurus) (original issue, black label, rainbow rim)	25
71	MGM 2315 062	WILD ROVERS (Jerry Goldsmith)	20
83	Chrysalis CHR 1453	WILD STYLE (various artists)	20
71	Paramount SPFL 274	WILLY WONKA AND THE CHOCOLATE FACTORY (Leslie Bricusse)	25
75	Arista ARTY 111	THE WIND AND THE LION (Jerry Goldsmith)	15
87	Filmtrax MOMENT 110	WITHNAIL AND I (David Dundas)	40
57	MGM MGM-C 757	THE WIZARD OF OZ (Judy Garland, et al.)	40
67	Capitol (S)T 2800	WOMAN TIMES SEVEN (Riz Ortolani)	18
64	Elstree Extra Range	WONDERFUL LIFE (2-LP, full soundtrack recording, 150 copies only)	250
68	Apple (S)APCOR 1	WONDERWALL MUSIC (George Harrison) (with insert & black inner sleeve, mono/stereo)	250
60	RCA RD 27198	THE WORLD OF SUZIE WONG (George Duning)	15
57	Brunswick LAT 8174	WRITTEN ON THE WIND/FOUR GIRLS IN TOWN (Frank Skinner)	25

Y

69	Apple PMC 7070	YELLOW SUBMARINE (Beatles) (1st pressing, laminated flipback sleeve with red lines above & below rear liner note & black inner; with "Sold In The UK..." label text, mono	300
69	Apple PCS 7070	YELLOW SUBMARINE (Beatles) (1st pressing, laminated flipback sleeve with red lines above & below rear liner note & black inner; with "Sold In The UK..." label text, stereo)	150
17	Laced LMLP008	YOOKA LAYLEE (2-LP, green and purple vinyl)	60
69	CBS (S) 70045	YOU ARE WHAT YOU EAT (Tiny Tim/Electric Flag, et al.)	18
79	MCA MCF 2804	YOUNGBLOOD (War)	15
66	Philips (S)BL 7792	YOUNG GIRLS OF ROCHEFORT (Michel Legrand)	25
57	Brunswick LAT 8252	THE YOUNG LIONS (Hugo Friedhofer)	35
61	Columbia 33SX 1384	THE YOUNG ONES (Cliff Richard) (with inner sleeve, also stereo SCX 3397 = £30)	15
67	United Artists (S)ULP 1271	YOU ONLY LIVE TWICE (John Barry/Nancy Sinatra)	15
65	MGM MGM-CS 6081	YOUR CHEATIN' HEART (Hank Williams Jr.)	15
67	Kama Sutra KLP 402	YOU'RE A BIG BOY NOW (Lovin' Spoonful)	18

Z

70	MGM MGM CS 8120	ZABRISKIE POINT (Pink Floyd/Jerry Garcia/Kaleidoscope, et al.)	30
69	Philips 600-287	ZITA	40
12	Death Waltz DW001	ZOMBIE 2 (clear splatter vinyl)	25
12	Death Waltz DW001	ZOMBIE 2 (red vinyl)	15
64	Ember NR 5012	ZULU (John Barry) (yellow/orange label, flipback sleeve)	20

A-Z MUSIC LIBRARY LPs

At one point in time little was known about the mysterious and often forgotten sub genre of music known as library, or rather non-commercial music pressed just for use in film, TV and radio. Thankfully, the internet has allowed light to be shined into the darkest nooks and crannies of this genre and labels like Trunk have reissued many wonderful examples of this music. Since the mid 1990s collecting interest has peaked, dropped away and is now well on the rise again, as are prices for some of the rarer and more important pieces. Collectors either favour early recordings by famous artists such as Jimmy Page or Tubby Hayes or those of a more funky persuasion that can be mined for breakbeats. Original pressing numbers and distribution still remain mysterious, although most people guestimate that 500 to 1,000 copies for each library pressing is about the average, especially as we move towards the mid 1970s. Older and larger music companies such as De Wolfe originally issued recordings on ten inch (throughout the late 1960s) in incredibly short runs - maybe only 200 - 300 copies, and if these recordings proved commercially successful they were repressed later on twelve inch. Obviously the original smaller pressings are more desirable. But still pressing numbers and habits remain shrouded in mystery. It has to be noted that many international and desirable labels distributed their library recordings over here and these do turn up from time to time, however we only list original UK pressings in this price guide. Also, it is worth noting that for libraries such as Chappell and Conroy, not all LPs have titles, they simply list the artist names and track titles. In these cases we have just put own the LP catalogue numbers. One final note, all library records are still the property of the libraries companies that issued them and they can, at any time, ask for them back. Like promos for pop and rock artists this is all a little unlikely, but you have been warned.

AMPHONIC

71	AMPS LP 101	BIG BAND SOUNDS OF TODAY (OTTO KELLER BAND)	15
72	AMPS LP 102	THE ALL ELECTRIC STEAM RADIO BAND	30
72	AMPS LP 103	HAVE BAND - WILL TRAVEL	20
72	AMPS LP 104	MORTIMERS PEOPLE	15
72	AMPS LP 105	THE OTTO KELLER ORCHESTRA	20

APOLLO SOUND

Page	Cat#	Title	Mint Value £
73	AMPSLP1001	MOODSETTER/PACESETTER	30
73	AMPS 1001	SMALL GROUP + SYNTHESISER (JAMES CLARK SOUNDS)	35
73	AMPS 1002	SCENE SETTER	40
73	AMPS 1003	DYNAMIC RHYTHMS	20
73	AMPS 1004	MORTIMERS PEOPLE	20
73	AMPS 1005	ACTION!	30
73	AMPS 1006	SMOOTH THEMES/SWINGING PERCUSSION	20
74	AMPS 107	THE HAPPY BEAT	15
74	AMPS 108	SUPER SOUNDS UNLIMITED	60
74	AMPS 109	START THE DAY RIGHT	18
74	AMPS 110	IN A QUIET MOOD	18
74	AMPS 111	THE LONDON LIFE	35
75	AMPS 112	SPECIAL ASSIGNMENT	70
74	AMPS 113	MELODY ALL THE WAY	20
75	AMPS 114	SOUNDS 80	60
76	AMPS 115	DIMENSIONS IN SOUND	25
76	AMPS 116	SYD DALE SPECIAL (MUNICH CONCERT POP ORCHESTRA)	15
76	AMPS 117	IT'S ALL IN THE BEAT (MUNICH CONCERT POP ORCHESTRA)	25
76	AMPS 118	PICTURES IN SOUND	45
77	AMPS 119	MELLOW MOODS	20
77	AMPS 120	WHERE THE ACTION IS	30
78	AMPS 121	MOOGERAMA (PADDY KINGSLAND)	35
78	AMPS 122	KEYBOARD COLLECTION	18
79	AMPS 123	NIGHT BIRD (Keith Mansfield)	125
79	AMPS 124	ONCE MORE FROM THE TOP (THE DOUBLE DOZEN ORCHESTRA)	20
80	AMPS 125	LET ME CALL YOU SWINGER (THE DOUBLE DOZEN ORCHESTRA)	20
80	AMPS 126	JUMP TO IT (NOAH'S PEOPLE)	20
80	AMPS 009	WOTTA LOTTA BRASS	20
80	AMPS 1010	SHADES OF GRAY (STEVE GRAY ORCHESTRA)	40
80	AMPS 1011	METROPOLIS NOW (DICK WALTER)	30
81	AMPS 127	IT'S A COLOURFUL WORLD	20
81	AMPS 1012	KEEPING IT LOOSE	20
81	AVF 1	SOUND STAGE I	30
81	AVF 1	MUSIC ACTION (SOUND STAGE 1) (different sleeve)	30
81	AVF 2	SOUND STAGE 2	20
81	AVF 3	SOUND STAGE 3	25
83	AMPS 129	DANCE DATE (THE DOUBLE DOZEN ORCHESTRA)	20
83	AMPS 128	SCENE IN MANHATTAN	20
81	AVF 4	SOUND STAGE 4	20
81	AVF 5	SOUND STAGE 5	18
81	AVF 6	SOUND STAGE 6	20
82	AVF 7	SOUND STAGE 7	30
82	AVF 8	SOUND STAGE 8	15
82	Sound Stage 9	SOUND STAGE 9	20
83	AVF 10	SOUND STAGE 10	15
83	AVF 11	SOUND STAGE 11	18
83	AVF 12	SOUND STAGE 12	20
83	AVF 13	SOUND STAGE 13	20
83	AVF 14	SOUND STAGE 14	18
83	AVF 15	SOUND STAGE 15	15
83	AVF 16	SOUND STAGE 16	15
87	AVF 57	SOUND STAGE 57: OFFICE HOURS	40

APOLLO SOUND

Page	Cat#	Title	Mint Value £
67	APP APS 1001	MEDITATIONS FOR BRASS/SUITE FOR BRASS INSTRUMENTS (WESTMINSTER BRASS ENSEMBLE) (10")	20
68	APP 5001	INSTRUMENTAL POPS NO. 1	15
68	APP 5002	INSTRUMENTAL POPS NO. 2	20
68	App 5003	INSTRUMENTAL POPS NO. 3	20
69	App 5004	INSTRUMENTAL POPS NO. 4	20
69	APP 5007	MELODY AND RHYTHM 1 (JOHN FOX ORCHESTRA/DAVID LINDUP SOUND)	40
69	APP 5008	MELODY AND RHYTHM 2 (LEM ARCON AND HIS ORCHESTRA/DAVID LINDUP SOUND)	25
70	APP 5009	MELODY AND RHYTHM 3	25
71	APP 5010	MELODY AND RHYTHM 4 (BUXTON ORR SOUND/LEM ARCON AND HIS BAND)	40
71	APP 5011	MELODY AND RHYTHM 5 (REG TILSLEY AND HIS MUSIC)	20
71	APP 5012	DENGA (ROBIN JONES AND HIS QUINTET, blue label)	40
71	APP 5012	DENGA (ROBIN JONES AND HIS QUINTET, yellow label)	30
71	APP 5013	COLOURS IN RHYTHM VOLUME 1 (WILF TODD/PETER BALDING)	40
71	APP 5014	MELODY AND RHYTHM 6 (JOSE PRIVSEK)	40
71	APP 5015	JAZZ IN LANDSCAPE (JOHN PORTER TRIO)	20
71	APP5016	EL MAJA (ROBIN JONES SEVEN, blue label)	125
72	APP 5017	INSTRUMENTAL GROUPS 1 (MOJMIR SEPE)	20
72	APP 5017	INSTRUMENTAL GROUPS 2 (SIMON GALE MUSIC)	20
72	APP 5019	INSTRUMENTAL GROUPS 3 (JURE ROBEZNIK)	25
72	APP 5020	SIMPLE MELODY 1 (BORIS KOVACIC)	25
73	APP 5021	COLOURS IN RHYTHM 2 (KARL HEINZ LOGES MUSIC/MARTIN GOLDSTEIN PLAYERS)	30
73	APP 5022	COLOURS IN RHYTHM 3 (SIMON GALE MUSIC/DICK HUNTER FIVE)	20
73	APP 5023	MELODY AND RHYTHM 7 (DICK HUNTER FIVE/GORDON LANGFORD GROUP)	50
74	APP 5024	COLOURS IN RHYTHM 4 (PETER HUGHES QUINTET/TED NORD SOUND)	60
74	APP 5025	MELODY AND RHYTHM 8 (BUDAPEST RADIO ORCHESTRA/GORDON LANGFORD GROUP)	20

BACKGROUND MUSIC

MINT VALUE £

75	APP 5026	COLOURS IN RHYTHM 5 (BUDAPEST RADIO ORCHESTRA/REG TILSLEY GROUP)	60
75	APP 5027	MELODY AND RHYTHM 9 (JUDD PROCTER SEXTET/POLISH RADIO ORCHESTRA)	30
75	APP 5028	COLOURS IN RHYTHM 6 (REG TILSLEY SOUND/POLISH RADIO ORCHESTRA)	50
75	APP 5029	PERSPECTIVES (IAN HENRY TRIO)	25
76	APP 5030	MELODY AND RHYTHM 10 (POLISH RADIO ORCHESTRA/PETER SANDER PLAYERS)	80
77	APP 5031	COLOURS IN RHYTHM 7 (REG TILSLEY PLAYERS/POLISH RADIO ORCHESTRA)	40
77	APP 5032	MELODY AND RHYTHM 11 (POLISH RADIO ORCHESTRA/PETER SANDER GROUP)	20
77	APP 5033	MELODY AND RHYTHM 12 (BUDAPEST RADIO ORCHESTRA/POLISH RADIO ORCHESTRA)	40
77	APP 5034	MELODY AND RHYTHM 13 (POLISH RADIO ORCHESTRA/PETER SANDER PLAYERS)	30
78	APP 5035	MELODY AND RHYTHM 14 (BUDAPEST RADIO ORCHESTRA/POLISH RADIO ORCHESTRA)	40
78	APP 5036	COLOURS IN RHYTHM 8 (BUDAPEST RADIO ORCHESTRA/POLISH RADIO ORCHESTRA)	35
80	APP 5037	MELODY AND RHYTHM 15 (KENNETH B. JONES/POLISH RADIO ORCHESTRA)	30
80	APP 5038	HIS AND HERS (PETER SANDERS/JACQUELINE BINNS ENSEMBLE)	20

BACKGROUND MUSIC

68	Audio BMP 137	SCARLATTI SOUNDS	15
71	Audio BMP 138	HORNS IN RHYTHM/ON THE CLASSICAL BEAT	20
71	Audio BMP 139	STRINGS GO POP/BRASS & STRING BAG	100

BOSWORTH

66	BLP 102	ELECTRONIC MUSIC (VACLAV NELHYBEL, 10" LP)	80
69	BLP 103	THE MELODY MEN AND THE SWING MEN (HAROLD GELLAR SOUND) (10")	20
69	BLP 104	TIJUANA SOUND/ATONAL JAZZ STRUCTURES (HEINZ HOTTER/JAZZ ARCHITECTS) (10")	25
69	BLP 105	EBBINGHOUSE SOUND/IN A SWINGING MOOD (BERNARD EBBINGHOUSE/ERWIN LEHN ORCHESTRA) (10")	20
69	BLP 106	A MODERN SOUND (ERWIN LEHN DANCE ORCHESTRA) (10")	20
69	BLP 107	A MUSICAL MELANGE (EDWIN LEHN ORCHESTRA) (10")	20
68	BLP 108	MODERN DRAMATICS (ERWIN LEHN ORCHESTRA/KENNY SALMON MODERN JAZZ GROUP (10")	20
69	BLP 109	MODERN RHYTHM (10")	20
69	BLP 110	MODERN INDUSTRIALS (CONTINENTAL THEATRE ORCHESTRA/CONTEMPORARY MUSIC GROUP)	20
69	BLP 116	INDUSTRIAL ROCK/SOUNDS OF THE METROPOLIS (10")	20
69	BLP 111	ACHIEVEMENT/BRIGHT MOVEMENT (CONTINENTAL THEATRE ORCHESTRA) (10")	20
69	BLP 112	ROUND THE WORLD/MELODY AND RHYTHM (10")	20
69	BLP 117	ORCHESTRAL POTPOURRI (INTERNATIONAL ORCHESTRA)	30
70	BLP 118	MODERN DRAMATICS/DRUMS AND PERCUSSION (SEVENTY SOUNDS GROUP/SPERIE KARAS) (10")	25
70	BLP 119	JAZZ POTPOURRI/THE JOLLY JOKERS	25
70	BLP 120	HARD AND FAST/MELLOW MOODS (SYDNEY DALE ORCHESTRA)	25
71	BLP 121	MISCELLANEA (KURT EDELHAGEN ORCHESTRA) (10")	25
71	BLP 122	DRAMATIC MELODIES AND SIMPLE MELODIES (SYD DALE)	25
71	BLP 123	FIVE INVENTIONS FOR FLUTE AND SIX PERSPECTIVES FOR STRINGS (DERRICK MASON)	30
71	BLP 124	ROMANTIC STRINGS AND A PIANO AND DRAMATIC SOUNDS	30
72	BLP 125	THE BIG BAND SOUND AND ORCHESTRAL SOUNDS (KURT EDELHAGEN ORCHESTRA)	30
72	BLP 126	RHYTHMIC MOODS (KURT EDELHAGEN ORCHESTRA) (10")	35
72	BLP 127	IN A QUIET MOOD/HAPPY BEAT (10")	20
73	BLP 130	SOUNDS ELECTRIC AND FLUGAL SOUNDS/KEYBOARD PLUS AND MODERN MELODY	25
73	BLP 131	HENRY'S HAPPY SOUND/LINKS ELECTRIC/EASY LISTENING/MODERN MOVEMENT	20
73	BLP 132	VISIONS/CLASSICA A LA MODE/FOUR PERIOD PIECES	25
73	BLP 133	DRAMATICS ELECTRONIC (FRANK GARTNER)	35
73	BLP 134	DRAMATIC DIVERSIONS/ROMANTIC RELAXATION/GENTLE MOVEMENT	35
74	BLP 135	MOVEMENT IN RHYTHM/RHYTHM AT RANDOM	80
74	BLP 136	BRASSY AND RHYTHMIC	30
74	BLP 137	FLUTES, GUITARS AND KEYBOARDS (ANTHONY MAWER)	30
74	BLP 138	WALTZ, SHUFFLE AND SWING/LATIN AMERICA TIME/SWING TO A MELODY	20
75	BLP 139	SEVEN SHADES OF SOUND (SEVEN SHADOWS)	40
75	BLP 140	BIG AND BRASSY/LIGHT AND EASY	20
75	BLP 141	AMERICA '76	100
75	BLP 142	LET'S GO SOLO/ROCK BEAT/DRUMS & PERCUSSION	60
75	BLP 143	MUSICAL COCKTAIL 1 & 2/MUSICAL FLASHES	100
76	BLP 144	THE GENTLE TOUCH/BRIGHT AND BRASSY	20
76	BLP 145	HARD AND FAST/MELLOW MOODS/MISCELLANEOUS MOODS	20
76	BLP 146	ROMANTIC STRINGS/DRAMATIC SOUNDS/SIMPLE MELODIES/DRAMATIC MELODIES	30
76	BLP 147	BIG BAND SOUNDS/ORCHESTRAL SOUNDS/RHYTHMIC MOODS/IN A QUIET MOOD	20
77	BLP 148	SOFT SWEET AND SWING	40
77	BLP 149	THE '77 SOUND/MUSICAL COCKTAILS (NO.3)	30
77	BLP 150	MUSICAL CONCEPTIONS/MORE MUSICAL CONCEPTIONS	40
77	BLP 151	MUSICAL COCTAIL NO. 4	100

BRUTON

78	BRN 1	HERITAGE/PARONAMA	20
78	BRE 1	PLAYTIME	15
78	BRL 1	AUTURBINE (1st pressing, white textured sleeve)	40
78	BRF 1	COMEDY SITUATIONS/COMEDY SYNTHESIZER	20
78	BRA 1	FANFARES, LINKS, BRIDGES, STINGS	15
78	BRQ 1	CONFLICT/WAR OF NERVES	20
78	BRM 1	MENACE	40
78	BRR 1	FRANCE	15
78	BRG 1	SPORTS STADIUM	15
78	BRB 1	JINGLES VOL. 1	15
78	BRK 1	DRIVING FORCE	50
78	BRI 1	TERRESTRIAL JOURNEY	40

BRUTON

MINT VALUE £

78	BRS 1	PALAIS DE DANCE/DEAR OLD DIXIELAND	15
78	BRC 1	HARP	15
78	BRP 1	BAROQUE ENSEMBLE	15
78	BRJ 1	GREAT EXPECTATIONS	20
78	BRD 1	FOUR SEASONS/COUNTRY LIFE	15
78	BRO 1	PALM COURT	15
78	BRH 1	ROCK CITY	40
78	BRC 2	HARPSICHORD	15
78	BRH 2	HEAVY ROCK	40
78	BRR 2	WESTERN MUSIC	15
78	BRP 2	BAROQUE	15
78	BRM 2	ABSTRACTIONS IN TIME	40
78	BRR 2	WESTERN MUSIC	15
78	BRJ 2	DRAMA MONTAGE	80
78	BRD 2	GOLDEN PLAINS	40
78	BRI 2	TEMPUS FUGIT	60
78	BRK 2	HIGH ADVENTURE	70
78	BRS 2	SWING WITH THE BIG BANDS	15
78	BRL 2	INDUSTRIAL POWER	25
78	BRG 2	CONTEMPORARY ORCHESTRAL	15
78	BRN 2	IMPRESSIVE SCENES	20
78	BRB 2	JINGLES VOL. 2	15
78	BRC 3	CLASSICAL GUITAR	15
78	BRH 3	ROCK 'N' ROLL	15
78	BRR 3	GREECE/CENTRAL EUROPE	15
78	BRD 3	LITTLE CREATURES	20
78	BRI 3	CITY OF THE FUTURE SUITE/EQUINOX	30
78	BRJ 3	IMPORTANT PROJECT/WONDERS OF THE WORLD/ENDEAVOUR	20
78	BRN 3	PROGRESS	20
78	BRG 3	COUNTRY BOUND	15
78	BRI 10	FANTASIA	80
78	BRP 3	MASTERWORKS/IMPRESSIONS	15
78	BRM 3	DARKSIDE	60
78	BRH 4	DISCO HAPPENING	40
78	BRR 4	THE ORIENT	15
78	BRG 4	GOOD TIMES	15
78	BRM 4	FEAR	40
78	BRR 5	IRELAND	15
78	BRR 6	COUNTRY & WESTERN	15
78	BRR 7	INDIA/ARABIA	15
78	BRJ 8	DRAMA MONTAGE VOLUME 2	75
78	BRN 8	EXPANDING HORIZONS	20
78	BRJ 12	WILDLIFE	50
78	BRD 8	TONE POEMS	40
78	BRG 6	SUNNY SIDE	100
79	BRI 6	FRONTIERS OF SCIENCE	120
78	BRJ 9	WEB OF INTRIGUE	40
79	BRJ 4	THRILLER/SUITE OF THE HURRICANE/SHARK OF THE SUITE	25
79	BRJ 7	LIFE OF ADVENTURE/VIDEO TECHNIQUES	20
79	BHR 5	LIGHT MY FIRE	70
79	BRK 4	DRAMATIC ACTION	30
79	BRI 4	ENERGISM	40
79	BRK 5	CONTEMPORARY ACTION	40
79	BRS 3	SMALL BAND JAZZ	20
79	BRK 5	CONTEMPORARY MOTION	40
79	BRD 10	RELAX	40
79	BRK 3	SPEED FEVER	35
79	BRL 4	FUTURAMA	40
79	BRE 3	KIDS AND CARTOONS	20
79	BRG 7	SPREAD YOUR WINGS	30
80	BRI 8	KINETICS/VISION	40
80	BRD 13	SERENITY	40
80	BRM 5	HOUSE OF HORROR	25
80	BRL 6	UNDERGROOVE	40
80	BRH 10	BLOW OUT	20
80	BRI 12	GYROSCOPE	60
80	BRI 9	SUSPENSIONS/GALAXY	50
80	BRI 11	THE VIDEO AGE	50
81	BRM 6	BUILDING TENSION	40
81	Bruton BRM 8	WATCHFUL EYE	45
81	BRL 7	MUSIC MACHINE	60
81	BRJ 22	INTERPOL	100
81	BRJ 24	EARTH	40
81	BRM 9	SURVIVAL	40
82	BRI 21	TOMORROW'S WORLD	70
82	BRI 22	MUSIC BEDS	50
83	BRJ 25	ESPIONAGE	30
83	BRM 11	STRANGE	25
84	BRI 23	FORCEFIELD	30

CHAPPELL

			MINT VALUE £
84	BRK 9	HIGH TENSION	30
85	BRM 13	STRING TENSION	30
84	BRR 18	EAST MEETS WEST	70

(The first 50 Bruton LPs were issued simultaneously in April 1978)

CHAPPELL

66	LPC 712-717	VARIOUS ARTISTS	25
66	LPC 781-885	VARIOUS ARTISTS	20
66	LPC 861-866	VARIOUS ARTISTS	30
68	LPC 1005-1009	VARIOUS ARTISTS	20
70	CIS 5003	INDUSTRIAL SOUNDS VOL 2	25
70	CIS 5007	LIGHT ATMOSPHERE VOL 2	40
70	CIS 5008	MUSIC FOR DRAMA VOL 1	30
70	CIS 5009	MUSIC FOR DRAMA VOL 2	25
70	CIS 5013	DANCE MUSIC VOL 1 (NIGHT CLUB)	20
70	CIS 5023	JAZZ (SMALL GROUP)	30
70	CIS 5024	MUSIC FOR DRAMA VOL 3	30
70	672-677	672-677	25
70	678-682	678-682	20
70	LPC 1032	THE EIFFEL TOWER	50
70	LPC 1034	OLE JENSEN AND HIS MUSIC	30
70	LPC 1036	PAUL DUPONT AND HIS ORCHESTRA	50
70	LPC 1038	OLE JENSEN AND HIS MUSIC	30
70	LPC 1039	OLE JENSEN AND HIS MUSIC	30
71	LPC 1040	OLE JENSEN AND HIS MUSIC	15
70	LPC 1042	JOHN CACAVAS/PAUL DUPONT	20
70	LPC 1043	ROGER ROGER	20
70	LPC 1044	OLE JENSEN AND HIS MUSIC	25
70	LPC 1045	LEE MASON AND HIS ORCHESTRA	200
70	LPC 1047	OLE JENSEN AND HIS MUSIC	30
70	LPC 1049	OLE JENSEN AND HIS MUSIC	20
72	LPC 1051	LEE MASON AND HIS ORCHESTRA	75
72	LPC 1052	MARK DUVAL AND HIS MUSIC	60
72	LPC 1053	POP SOUNDS	40
73	LPC 1055	ELECTRONIC MUSIC	35
73	LPC 1056	MARK DUVAL AND HIS MUSIC	50
73	LPC 1058	MARK DUVAL AND HIS MUSIC	35
73	LPC 1059	LEE MASON AND HIS ORCHESTRA	80
73	LPC 1060	ROBERT FARNON	15
73	LPC 1062	PAUL DUPONT AND HIS ORCHESTRA	30
73	LPC 1063	THE RED BRICKS	50
73	LPC 1065	MARK DUVAL AND HIS ORCHESTRA - RHYTHM N BRASS	100
73	LPC 1066	MUSIC BY ROGER ROGER	30
73	LPC 1068	POP SOUNDS - MAD DOG	40
73	LPC 1069	MARK DUVAL AND HIS MUSIC - LIGHT AND BRIGHT	40
74	LPC 1070	MARK DUVAL AND HIS MUSIC - BRASS AND RHYTHMS	100
74	LPC 1071	MARK DUVAL AND HIS MUSIC - SOFT AND SWEET	40
74	LPC 1075	MARK DUVAL AND HIS MUSIC - LIGHT AND BRIGHT	20
74	LPC 1076	MARK DUVAL AND HIS MUSIC - BRASS AND RHYTHMS	100
74	LPC 1077	MARK DUVAL AND HIS MUSIC - SOFT AND SWEET	30
75	LPC 1082	ELECTRONIC MUSIC/SYNTHESIZER EFFECTS	25
77	LPC 1085	MARK DUVAL AND HIS ORCHESTRA	30
77	LPC 1086	ZOUCHE ORCHESTRA - A HUNK OF FUNK	25
77	LPC 1087	PAUL DUPONT AND HIS ORCHESTRA - TAPESTRY	60
77	LPC 1088	PAUL REY - ZAP! KAPOW!!	20
79	LPC 1090	BECKETT & HOWARD - NICE AND MEAN	20
79	LPC 1091	SUGAR AND SPICE	40
79	LPC 1092	REPERTOIRE EVOCATEUR	15

CHAPPELL INTERNATIONAL

73	CAL 4001	HAPPY MUSIC/COMEDY MUSIC	20
73	CAL 4002	MOOG SYNTHESISER MUSIC	40
73	CAL 4004	SOUNDS ELECTRONIC	50
73	CAL 4005	MUSIC FOR DRAMA	40
74	CAL 4006	HAPPY AND SWEET MUSIC/GOLDEN OLDIES	15
73	CAL 4007	SMALL GROUP SOUNDS	25
73	CAL 4008	BAND MUSIC	15
73	CAL 4009	THE SOUND OF STRINGS	40
74	CAL 4010	MUSIC BY ROGER ROGER	30
74	CAL 4012	NATIONAL FLAVOURS	15
74	CAL 4011	ORCHESTRAL SOUNDS	15
74	CAL 4013	SMALL GROUP SOUNDS	200
74	CAL 4015	MUSIC FOR DRAMA (ORCHESTRAL)	40
74	CAL 4015	MUSIC FOR DRAMA (SMALL GROUPS)	45
74	CAL 4016	LIGHT AND SWEET	15
74	CAL 4017	BAND MUSIC	15

CONROY

70	BMLP 070	UNTITLED	15
70	BMLP 071	UNTITLED	20
70	BMLP 072	ELEKTRONIC PERCUSSION POINTS	30
70	BMLP 073	UNTITLED	15

CONROY EUROBEATS SERIES

MINT VALUE £

70	BMLP 074	THEME SETS	40
70	BMLP 075	THEME SETS	20
70	BMLP 076	THEME SETS	15
70	BMLP 077	THEME SETS	15
70	BMLP 078	DOUBLE CROSS	20
70	BMLP 079	CAPITAL CITIES	15
70	BMLP 080	ELECTROSCOPE	30
71	BMLP 085	MODERN MOVEMENTS	35
72	BMLP 086	RHYTHMIC UNDERSCORES	25
71	BMLP 089	LARRY ROBBIN'S PERCUSSION	50
71	BMLP 090	LARRY ROBBIN'S PERCUSSION/UNDERDRAMA	40
71	BMLP 090A	LARRY ROBBIN'S PERCUSSION/UNDERDRAMA (repressing with different - full orange - cover)	40
71	BMLP 091	HARP QUARTET	20
72	BMLP 092	LONDON'S UNDERGROUND	75
72	BMLP 092	LONDON'S UNDERGROUND (repressing with full orange cover)	50
72	BMLP 093	LARRY ROBBIN'S SPORTSTUDIO BAND	50
72	BMLP 093A	LARRY ROBBIN'S SPORTSTUDIO BAND (repressing with full orange sleeve)	80
72	BMLP 094	INDUSTRIAL OPENINGS AND ENDINGS	20
72	BMLP 095	MOOD MOVEMENTS	20
72	BMLP 097	MOOD MOVEMENTS - AFRO PATTERNS	80
72	BMLP 098	MODERN MOVEMENT - PERCUSSIVE MOMENT	30
72	BMLP 099	BRIGHT HAPPY BEAT/GENTLE LYRICAL BEAT	30
73	BMLP 101	HAPPY MOOG	25
73	BMLP 102	DYNAMIC DRUMS PLUS	50
73	BMLP 103	LARRY ROBBIN'S CLAP TRAP DRUMS/DRUM BAND	40
73	BMLP 104	MODERATE BEAT MOVEMENTS	30
73	BMLP 107	MODERN MOVEMENT - ACTION TRACKS	30
74	BMLP 112	WILDLIFE - THEME SETS	15
74	BMLP 113	WAY IN WAY OUT	25
74	BMLP 114	SOFT SOUNDS AND GENTLE MOVEMENTS	40
75	BMLP 115	LONDON'S UNDERGROUND 2	40
75	BMLP 117	KLAUS WEISS SOUNDS AND PERCUSSION	100
75	BMLP 118	WALT ROCKMAN MOOG MOODS	18
75	BMLP 121	BACKGROUND ACTION	200
75	BMLP 122	MULTI TRACKS	80
75	BMLP 123	ELECTRONIC SOUNDS - ORGAN SOUNDS	30
75	BMLP 124	DRAMATIC TEMPI	100
75	BMLP 125	ALL KINDS OF MACHINES	60
75	BMLP 126	HANS EHRLINGER SWINGING BAROQUE BRASS	20
75	BMLP 128	CHROMOZONES	50
75	BMLP 129	PANORAMIC SRINGS - SOFT SOUNDS	25
75	BMLP 131	ON THE ROAD	40
75	BMLP 132	SOUNDS FUNKY	60
75	BMLP 133	MODERN MIXTURE	40
76	BMLP 133	PERCUSSION PLUS VOLS 3 AND 4	18
75	BMLP 143	FEELINGS	500
75	BMLP 144	LIGHT ACTIVITY/DRAMATIC	25
75	BMLP 145	NEW DIMENSION	80
75	BMLP 150	DRAMA TENSION	40
76	BMLP 158	PSYCHOSES SUITE	30
76	BMLP 162	ACTION AND ACTIVITY	40
76	BMLP 163	SPAGE AGE	30
76	BMLP 167	BRASSBOUND BACKGROUND	35
76	BMLP 176	MOVING PERCUSSION	40
77	BMLP 177	DRAMATIC ACTION - DRAMATIC SOUNDS	40

CONROY EUROBEATS SERIES

73	EURO 1	SILLY SYNTHESISERS	30
73	EURO 2	ETHNIC SONGS AND DANCES/INDIA - A THEME SET	60
73	EURO 3	MODERN BAROQUE	30
73	EURO 4	ROMANTIC BACKGROUNDS	50
73	EURO 5	DRAMATIC BACKGROUNDS	100
73	EURO 6	SOLO INSTRUMENTS	20
73	EURO 7	GOING WEST - TWO GUITARS	20
73	EURO 8	CLASSICAL VIEW/NEW TESTAMENT	20
73	EURO 9	THEMES AND BACKGROUNDS/TWO MOODS	20
73	EURO 10	WORLD AT WORK	150
73	EURO 11	COLLA VOCE	100

DE WOLFE

64	DW/LP 2824	YOUNG WORLD (10")	30
64	DW/LP 2853	GUITARS IN MOTION (10")	15
65	DW/LP 2890	ILLUSTRATIONS NO 4 (10")	20
65	DEW/LP 2918	ILLUSTRATIONS NO 5 (10")	30
65	DW/LP 2922	POWER PROJECT (10")	30
66	DW/LP 2949	BAND 8 (10")	60
66	DW/LP 2950	HIGH SPEED JAZZ (10")	40
66	DW/LP 2966	MIND ON THE RUN (10")	200
66	DW/LP 2968	JOURNEY INTO SOUND (10")	40
66	DW/LP 2969	AN EYE FOR AN EYE (10")	60

DE WOLFE

			MINT VALUE £
66	DW/LP 2973	ABSTRACTIONS OF THE INDUSTRIAL NORTH (10")	250
66	DW/LP 2974	THE WILD ONE (10") - (features Jimmy Page)	150
66	DW/LP 2975	TOWN BEAT (10")	80
66	DW/LP 2981	ON THE TOWN (10")	20
66	DW/LP 2987	CONTINENT SEVEN (10")	25
66	DWLP 2990	YOUNG BEAT (10")	20
67	DL/LP 3019	THE NEW BREED (10")	80
67	DW/LP 3022	CHECKPOINT (10")	20
67	DW/LP 3023	THE SWINGING CITY (10")	25
67	DW/LP 3024	SILK ORGANDIE (10")	20
67	DW/LP 3029	POLARIS (10")	60
67	DW/LP 3030	LUNAR PROBE (10")	80
67	DW/LP 3032	THE MUSIC OF REG TILSLEY (10")	20
67	DW/LP 3033	CHAPTER TWO - BEAT GROUP (10")	25
67	DW/LP 3036	ARCTIC LIFE (10")	18
67	DW/LP 3040	ELECTRIC BANANA (10")	150
67	DW/LP 3046	YOUNG FRIENDS (10" LP)	20
67	DW/LP 3049	Z PATROL	30
67	DW/LP 3063	ASSIGNEMENT LONDON	50
67	DW/LP 3066	DON'T LOSE YOUR COOL (10")	200
68	DW/LP 3069	MORE ELECTRIC BANANA (10")	200
68	DW/LP 3070	BIG CITY STORY	20
68	DW/LP 3084	ELECTROSHAKE (10" LP)	70
68	DW/LP 3097	ON THE BUTTON (10")	20
68	DW/LP 3088	QUIETLY WITH JOHAN (10")	20
69	DW/LP 3108	QUINTET OF MODERN JAZZ	25
69	DW/LP 3110	TIME OUT TO LISTEN	50
69	DW/LP3114	WHO'S GONN BUY (THE LEMON DIPS) (10")	150
69	DW/LP 3115	JOHNNY HAWKSWORTH'S CARIBBEAN SOUND	35
69	DW/LP 3116	BEST OF JOHNNY HAWKSWORTH	20
69	DW/LP 3119	TOOTH FOR A TOOTH	40
69	DW/LP 3123	EVEN MORE ELECTRIC BANANA	100
69	DW/LP 3127	AMBER TURNING MAUVE	18
69	DW/LP 3131	MOSAIC	20
69	DW/LP 3135	ELECTROSHAKE No. 2	40
69	DW/LP 3136	POP SOUNDS BY THE COOL	100
69	DW/LP 3141	NEW DECADE	20
69	DW/LP 3149	A DAY IN THE LIFE OF	30
70	DW/LP 3154	HEAVY GRAVY	25
70	DW/LP 3174	THEME AND VARIATION	20
71	DW/LP 3182	VOCAL PATTERNS	150
71	DW/LP 3185	BUMPER BUNDLE	20
71	DW/LP 3193	ILLINOIS	20
71	DW/LP 3199	ATOMIC BUTTERFLY	35
71	DW/LP 3200	SING ME A SONG	35
71	DW/LP 3201	ELECTROBEDS VOL. 1	20
71	DW/LP 3205	PINK SAUCE	25
71	DW/LP 3208	ELECTROBEDS VOL. 2	20
71	DW/LP 3212	MOONSHADE	80
71	DW/LP 3214	ANGLO AMERICAN JAZZ	100
71	DW/LP 3215	CULT AND COLOUR	20
71	DW/LP 3219	ALTERNATIVES	40
71	DW/LP 3220	AFRO-ROCK	250
71	DW/LP 3224	LITTLE BOSSA	40
72	DW/LP 3225	FORMULA	40
72	DW/LP 3227	VOCAL SHADES AND TONES	200
72	DW/LP 3228	PROTOTYPE	80
72	DW/LP 3229	FREE AS AIR	50
72	DW/LP 3230	SWEET CHARIOT AND FRIEND	30
72	DW/LP 3238	9-10-OUT	35
72	DW/LP 3243	HOGAN, THE HAWK AND DORTY JOHN CROWN	80
72	DW/LP 3247	THE ART OF THE SYNTHESISER	50
72	DW/LP 3255	TILSLEY ORCHESTRAL NO. 10	80
72	DW/LP 3258	GREAT DAY	80
72	DW/LP 3259	HERE AND THERE	20
73	DW/LP 3260	MUSIC FOR TUNED PERCUSSION	25
73	DW/LP 3262	BLACK PEARL	100
73	DW/LP 3263	OUTPUT	40
73	DW/LP 3265	BRASS GAME	30
73	DW/LP 3271	SYNTHESISER CONTACT	40
73	DW/LP 3275	HEAVY TRUCKIN'	50
73	DW/LP 3284	HOT LICKS	60
73	DW/LP 3285	BIG BEAT	300
74	DWS/LP 3276	METROPOLIS	20
74	DW/LP 3278	HOT ICE	100
74	DWS/LP 3291	ELECTRIC BIRD	40
74	DWS/LP 3292	DARK MYSTERY	30
75	DWS/LP 3298	SOUL SARABANDE	25
75	DWS/LP 3300	SPINECHILLER	25

DE WOLFE "IN EDITIONS" SERIES

MINT VALUE £

Page	Cat No	Title	Value
75	DWS/LP 3302	AWAKENING	30
75	DWS/LP 3304	SOUNDS UNUSUAL	40
75	DWS/LP 3312	LIKE A FRIEND	25
75	DWS/LP 3314	GO LIGHTLY	25
75	DWS/LP 3315	DANGEROUS CONNECTION	80
74	DW/LP 3318	HARD HITTER	150
75	DW/LP 3319	METAL SUNRISE	60
75	DWS/LP 3321	GOOD COMPANY	35
75	DWS/LP 3322	DREAM KINGDOM	60
75	DWS/LP 3323	SLICED ORANGE	60
75	DWS/LP 3324	BITE HARD	80
76	DWS/LP 3327	STRETCH	25
76	DWS/LP 3328	RHYMES	200
76	DW/LP 3331	RUBBER RIFF	40
76	DWS/LP 3336	DISCO QUEEN	30
76	DWS/LP 3338	WINGS	40
77	DWS/LP 3340	THE WORLD OF PERCUSSION AND TUNED PERCUSSION	25
77	DWS/LP 3351	8 DAYS A WEEK	40
77	DWS/LP 3352	OPTIMUM	40
77	DWS/LP 3358	CONNECTION	35
77	DWS/LP 3363	NATURAL BREAK	15
78	DWS/LP 3374	SCHIZO	20
78	DWS/LP 3378	KALEIDOSCOPE	40
78	DWS/LP 3380	GUN BARREL HIGHWAY	15
78	DWS/LP 3381	THE RETURN OF ELECTRIC BANANA	50
78	DW/LP 3385	FOREST OF EVIL	60
78	DWS/LP 3387	RED LIGHT ZONE	30
78	DW/LP 3392	MEAN AND DIRTY	200
78	DWS/LP 3393	SLIPSTREAM	20
78	DWS/LP 3394	BADLY BRUISED, SLIGHTLY STONED	50
79	DWS/LP 3397	FURTHER EXPLORATION OF THE ART OF THE SYNTHESISER	30
79	DWS/LP 3398	TUMBLING DICE	25
79	DWS/LP 3399	HUBBLE BUBBLE	30
79	DWS/LP 3405	MEETING POINT	20
79	DWS/LP 3414	PUSH BUTTON	70
79	DWS/LP 3416	GROOVE TUBE	30
80	DWS/LP 3412	POWER SOURCE	20
80	DWS/LP 3421	BACKING TRACKS	20
80	DWSLP 3428	IN MOTION	200
80	DWSLP 3429	GUN MAN	30
80	DWSLP 3435	THE PROFESSIONALS	35
80	DWSLP 3437	SUNNY JIM	20
80	DWSLP 3438	MOVING ON THROUGH	20
80	DWSLP 3445	SPACE DRIVE	40
81	DWSLP 3457	SOUND WAVES PART 2	30
81	DWSLP 3468	THE SHADOW	35
81	DW/LP 3469	FOREST OF EVIL PART 2	60
82	DW/LP 3465	FEELING ALAVE	25
82	DWSLP 3481	HIGH CLIMBER	30
82	DWSLP 3482	ELECTRA	15
82	DWSLP 3483	DELTA	40
82	DWSLP 3485	MELODIOUS THUNK	25
82	DWSLP 3487	PIUSSYFOOTING	30
82	DWSLP 3491	OXYGEN	30
83	DWSLP 3502	FLASHPOINT	30
83	DWSLP 3504	MILLENNIUM	30
83	DWSLP 3509	BACKING TRACKS VOLUME 2	30
84	DWSLP 3525	BACKING TRACK VOLUME 3	30
86	DWSLP 3566	SILICON VALLEY	15

DE WOLFE "IN EDITIONS" SERIES

76	Timing 14	CRADLE OF TIME	50

DAY & HUNTER

68	FDH LP 1018	DIPLOMATIC IMMUNITY	70
68	FDH LP 1019	SPECTRUM OF COLOUR	20
68	FDH LP 1020	PROGRESSIONS	20
68	FDH LP 1023	PROECTIONS	20

HARMONIC

68	CBW 616	SHAKIN' AND SOULIN'	40
68	CBW 617	NEAR DRAMATIC	30
69	CBW 622	SUITE IN BEAT AND SUITE IN BLUES	20
68	CBD 609	BEAT!	25
68	CBO 613	INDUSTRIAL ESPIONAGE SUITE	150
68	CBG 610	SWINGING SINGERS	20
68	CBL 618	FONTEYNS FOLK JAZZ	20
69	CBL 621	MORE BEAT	40
69	CBW 598	RONNIE ROSS PLAYS (NO 1)	200
70	CBW 628	BEAT DRAMA	30
71	CBO 640	STUDIES IN DRAMA	20
71	CBW 637	DRAMA IN RHYTHM	50

HUDSON

			MINT VALUE £
72	CBO 654	CITY VISIT	40
73	CBO 665	WEIGHTY AND SOLID	40
71	CBW 639	PSYCHO SOUL AND DRAMATIC ORCHESTRAL SUITE	100
72	CBW 659	STUDIES FOR GUITAR AND DRAMA BEAT	40
72	CBW 660	THEMES IN BEAT	100
72	CBJ 674	SYNTHETICS	40
76	CBJ 670	SYNTHETRONICS	70
76	CBD 671	A GOOD MUSIC	25
76	CBG 672	MODERN DRAMATIC ACTIONS	40
76	CBG 674	UNDERSCORES	20

HUDSON

71	HMC LP 501	ROCKING TEMPO (PETER MERRICK)	15
71	HMC LP 502	INVENTION (PAUL KASS)	15
71	HMC LP 503	SIT BACK	20
71	HMC LP 504	CLASSICAL COLOURS (REG TILSLEY)	15
72	HMC LP 505	FRIENDLY FACE (P RENO)	20
72	HMC LP 506	MINDBINDER (PETER MERRICK)	50
72	HMC LP 507	DRAMATURGY/COSMOGONY (PAUL LEMEL)	40
74	HMC LP 508	THIS IS BRASS (J. TROMBEY)	15
74	HMC LP 509	EMPTY HORIZONS (PIERRE ARVAY)	40
74	HMC LP 510	CHICKEN WIRE AND HEN'S NEXT	20
74	HMC LP 511	HOT BREATH (PETER RENO/REG TILSLEY)	40
74	HMC LP 512	PRESTIGE LINE (NICK INGMAN/GRAHAM PRESKETT)	30
75	HMC LP 513	BLOOD ON THE FLOWERS (PRESTON JAMES)	80
76	HMC LP 514	STEPPING QUICK (R WALE)	15
76	HMC LP 516	CLASSICAL INTERLUDE (SIMON PARK)	15
76	HMC LP 517	DECISIVE ACTION (KEITH PAPWORTH)	50
79	HMC LP 518	DIMPLES (SOHO JAZZ GROUP)	20
79	HMC LP 519	NETWORK (COMPLEX STUDIO GROUP)	15
79	HMC LP 521	WORK IN - WALK OUT	20
79	HMC LP 523	BLUEPRINT (TAKE SIX)	50
80	HMC LP 524	DAWN OF MAN	15
80	HMC LP 525	BLACK SUN	20
81	HMC LP 528	CHAMPAGNE COCKTAIL	15
81	HMC LP 527	HEADLINE	20
81	HMC LP 529	VIEWPOINT	15
82	HMC LP 530	WHODUNNIT?	15
82	HMC LP 531	AWAYDAY (PETER FENN)	15
82	HMC LP 532	ACROSS THE BOARD (TREVOR BROWN)	15
82	HMC LP 533	SUNNY SIDE UP (TAKE SIX)	15
82	HMC LP 534	SLAVE DRIVER (BLUE STEEL)	15
83	HMC LP 535	PRIDE OF THE TOWN (KEITH PAPWORTH)	15
83	HMC LP 536	SWINGS AND ROUNDABOUTS	15
83	HMC LP 537	MIXED SELLS (ASTRAL SOUNDS)	15
83	HMC LP 538	PORTRAITS IN SOUND	15
83	HMC LP 539	JONAH SYMPHONIA	15

JW THEME MUSIC

70	JW 401	BOB DOWNES NEW SOUNDS FOR FLUTE, PERCUSSION AND SYNTHESISER	125
72	JW 402	ELECTRONIA/HAIR RAISERS	40
73	JW 403	BE DAZZED/MAKE RHYTHM	40
74	JW 404	FACES OF FUNK	40
74	JW 405	TUNE IN - DROP OUT	60
74	JW 406	STRINGS GO POP/BRASS & STRING BAG	100
74	Jw 407	MILITARY BAND/BRASS BAND	15
74	JW 408	HORNS IN RHYTHM - ON THE CLASSICAL BEAT	15
76	JW 409	SOFT SELL	15
76	JW 410	ELECTRIC STRINGMOBILE	30
76	JW 411	EASY COME, EASY GO	18
76	JW 412	RENT A MOOD	60
77	JW 413	EL PIANO	30
77	JW 414	FLAVOUR OF THE MONTH	60
77	JW 415	SWINGS AND ROUNDABOUTS	20
78	JW 416	ALL THE ARABIAS	30
78	JW 417	IDENTI-KIT	15
79	JW 418	WIDE REPERCUSSIONS	15
79	JW 419	PHOTO-FIT	20
79	JW 420	TRADEWINDS	20
79	JW 421	RHYTHM AND BRASS	20
80	JW 422	ELECTRIC LIGHT	35
80	JW 423	KEYBOARD HARMONY	15

KPM

66	KPM 1001	THE MOOD MODERN	20
66	KPM 1002	THE SOUNDS OF SYD DALE	50
66	KPM 1003	THE BACKGROUNDS	15
66	KPM 1004	COLOURED STRINGS	30
66	KPM 1004	SACRED MUSIC	35
66	KPM 1006	LIGHT INTIMATIONS 1	20
66	KPM 1007	LIGHT INTIMATIONS 2	25
66	KPM 1008	A DISTINCTIVE APPROACH	20

KPM

			MINT VALUE £
66	KPM 1009	ACCENT ON PERCUSSION	30
66	KPM 1010	HAPPY FAMILIES	25
66	KPM 1011	ORIGINAL APPLICATION OF THE AUGMENTED STRING QUARTET	15
66	KPM 1012	LIGHTWEIGHT BACKGROUNDS	25
67	KPM 1013	HARP SOLOS	15
67	KPM 1014	ALL THAT JAZZ	40
67	KPM 1015	THE SOUND OF POP	50
67	KPM 1016	PLEASURE SPECTACLE	20
67	KPM 1017	IMPACT AND ACTION	40
67	KPM 1018	TENSION AND SUSPENSE	30
67	KPM 1019	COMEDY	15
67	KPM 1020	TWENTIETH CENTURY PORTRAIT	15
68	KPM 1021	LIGHT JAZZ FEELING	30
68	KPM 1022	SUITE FOR HORN, WOODWIND AND STRINGS	15
68	KPM 1024	SERIAL STRUCTURES	15
68	KPM 1066	PROCESS AND PRESTIGE/FOURTH DIMENSION	20
68	KPM 1024	IT'S ABOUT TIME	20
68	KPM 1026	ORCHESTRAL KALEIDOSCOPE	25
68	KPM 1027	SOUL ORGAN SHOWCASE	75
68	KPM 1028	MINIATURE MOODS	15
68	KPM 1029	COLOURS IN RHYTHM	40
68	KPM 1030	BAR PIANO	15
68	KPM 1031	MUSIC OF THE NATIONS - ARABIC/ASIAN/ORIENTAL	40
68	KPM 1032	JAZZ ORCHESTRAL	30
68	KPM 1033	MASQUERADE	15
68	KPM 1035	UNDERSCORE	80
68	KPM 1036	GENTLE SOUNDS	15
68	KPM 1037	FLAMBOYANT THEMES	60
68	KPM 1038	FLAMBOYANT THEMES VOL. 2	60
68	KPM 1039	LIGHT INTIMATIONS 3	15
68	KPM 1040	THEME SUITES VOL. 2	18
69	KPM 1041	FLAMBOYANT THEMES VOL. 3	30
69	KPM 1042	JAZZ GRAPHICS/SPY SET	50
69	KPM 1043	BEAT INCIDENTAL	80
69	KPM 1044	THE BIG BEAT (Mohawks & Alan Hawkshaw)	200
69	KPM 1045	CHILDREN AND ANIMATION	30
69	KPM 1046	SOUNDS IN PERCUSSION	30
69	KPM 1043	SINGLE INSTRUMENTS VOL 1 - PERCUSSION	40
69	KPM 1048	TWO HARPSICHORD/TWO ELIZABETHAN SUITES	20
66	KPM/ACW1	MUSIC FOR YOUR MOVIES	20
68	KPM INT 001	JAZZ CONVENTION VOLUME I	80
68	KPM INT 002	JAZZ CONVENTION VOLUME II	175
68	KPM INT 004	JAZZ CONVENTION VOLUME III	200
69	KPM 1051	LIGHT INTIMATIONS VOL. IV	20
69	KPM 1049	CHORUS AND ORCHESTRA (SYD DALE)	100
69	KPM 1050	NATURE STUDY	15
69	KPM 1052	CHRISTMAS PARTY	15
69	KPM 1053	NATIVE AFRICA	25
69	KPM 1054	NATIVE AFRICA	30
70	KPM 1055	DRAMATIC BACKGROUND	40
70	KPM 1056	UNDERSCORE VOL. 2	50
70	KPM 1057	SCENE SETTERS - FANFARES AND PUNCTUATIONS	20
70	KPM 1058	GENTLE SOUNDS VOL. 2	30
70	KPM 1059	GENTLE SOUNDS VOL. 3	30
70	KPM 1060	OPEN AIR	20
69	KPM 1061	IMPACT AND ACTION VOL. 2	50
70	KPM 1062	ON THE LIGHTER SIDE	25
70	KPM 1063	CONTEMPORARY COLOUR	40
70	KPM 1064	HAPPY NOVELTIES	15
70	KPM 1065	FLAMBOYANT THEMES VOL. 4	40
70	KPM 1067	THE BIG BEAT VOL. 2	200
70	KPM 1068	THE HERITAGE OF MAN/TEXTURES FOR STRING QUINTET, KEYBOARD AND PERCUSSION	18
70	KPM 1069	THE CONTEMPORARY ORCHESTRA/INTERFUSIONS	15
70	KPM 1070	BUGALOO IN BRAZIL	100
70	KPM 1071	THE BRAZILIAN SUITE	150
70	KPM 1072	THE GUITAR FAMILY	15
70	KPM 1073	CONTEMPORARY GUITAR	15
70	KPM 19074	MARCHES FOR ANY OCCASION	15
70	KPM 1075	MUSIC IN A SERIOUS VEIN/MUSIC IN A LIGHTER VEIN	20
70	KPM 1076	SPEED AND EXCITEMENT	80
70	KPM 1077	PROGRESSIVE POP	80
70	KPM 1078	SWEET GROOVE	30
71	KPM 1083	PIANO COCKTAIL	15
71	KPM 1079	BEAT INDUSTRIAL	50
71	KPM 1080	BEAT INCIDENTAL	50
71	KPM 1080	FLUTE FOR MODERNS	60
71	KPM 1081	CARTOON CAPERS	20
71	KPM 1082	THE BRASS FAMILY	15
71	KPM 1085	ELECTRONIC MUSIC	50

KPM

Page	Cat. No.	Title	Mint Value £
72	KPM 1084	MEDITERRANEAN INTRIGUE/MARTENOT	60
71	KPM 1086	MUSIC FOR A YOUNG GENERATION	60
71	KPM 1087	TECHNICAL STANDPOINT/SPICE OF LIFE	30
71	KPM 1088	BASS GUITAR AND PERCUSSION	80
71	KPM 1089	BASS GUITAR AND PERCUSSION - VOLUME 2	60
71	KPM 1090	BASS GUITAR AND PERCUSSION - VOLUME 3	30
71	KPM 1091	VIBRAPHONE JAZZ QUARTET	25
71	KPM 1092	TODAYS ACHIEVEMENTS/TOPICAL EVENTS	20
71	KPM 1093	THE WORLD OF JOHNNY SCOTT	15
71	KPM 1094	ACCENT ON PERCUSSION/CONSTRUCTION IN JAZZ	50
71	KPM 1095	THEME SUITES/MUSTANG	60
71	KPM 1097	JAZZROCK	60
72	KPM 1098	PROGRESS AND PRESTIGE VOLUME 2	18
72	KPM 1099	OPEN AIR - VOLUME 2	15
72	KPM 1100	THE BIG SCREEN	20
72	KPM 1101	A MOOG FOR ALL REASONS	30
72	KPM 1102	ELECTROSOUND	80
72	KPM 1103	ELECTROMUSIC	30
72	KPM 1104	ELECTROSONIC	75
72	KPM 1105	MEDIEVAL MUSIC	15
72	KPM 1106	WOODWIND AND HARPSICHORD	15
72	KPM 1107	HARPSICHORD OLD AND NEW	15
72	KPM 1108	THE SOLO HARP	15
72	KPM 1109	THE MAGIC OF BOUCHETY	20
72	KPM 1110	LIFE IS FOR LIVING	30
72	KPM 1111	BRASS PLUS MOOG	50
72	KPM 1112	THE RHYTHM OF MODERN LIFE/VAUDEVILLE	15
72	KPM 1113	PERCUSSION WORKSHOP	20
73	KPM 1118	THE HUMAN TOUCH	25
73	KPM 1119	LOOK ON THE BRIGHT SIDE	20
73	KPM1120	DAYBREAK	40
73	KPM 1121	FUSION - CONTEMPORARY STYLES IN ELECTRO-POP	80
73	KPM 1122	MOVE WITH THE TIMES	60
73	KPM 1123	FRIENDLY FACES	40
73	KPM 1173	HAPPY RAINBOWS	25
73	KPM 1124	BIG BUSINESS	80
73	KPM 1125	VOICES IN HARMONY	200
73	KPM 1126	SUMMER SONGBIRDS	60
73	KPM 1128	COUNTERPOINT IN RHYTHM	40
73	KPM 1129	THE CONTEMPORARY HARP	20
73	KPM 1130	AFRO ROCK	200
73	KPM 1131	TRENDSETTERS	50
73	KPM 1132	SYNTHESIS	100
73	KPM 1133	ANIMATION PLAYTIME	15
74	KPM 1134	CHILDOOD	15
74	KPM 1135	DISCOTHEQUE	30
74	KPM 1136	INDUSTRIAL PANORAMA	100
74	KPM 1137	GREAT EXPECTATIONS	35
74	KPM 1138	GATHERING CROWDS	20
74	KPM 1139	HAPPY HEARTS	20
74	KPM 1140	SOFT HORIZONS	18
74	KPM 1141	IMAGES	125
74	KPM 1142	WOODWIND	15
74	KPM 1143	SUSPENDED WOODWIND	30
74	KPM 1151	COME DANCING	15
74	KPM 1152	SOUND ODYSSEY	20
74	KPM 1153	ELECTRONIC LIGHT ORCHESTRA	20
74	KPM 1154	ELECTROSOUND VOLUME 2	60
74	KPM 1155	A MOOG FOR MORE REASONS	30
75	KPM 1156	METROPOLIS	70
75	KPM 1157	THE HUNTER/ADVENTURE SUITE	100
75	KPM 1158	FLAMBOYANT THEMES VOL. 5	20
75	KPM 1159	THE PLEASURES OF LIFE	60
75	KPM 1160	FRIENDS AND LOVERS	50
75	KPM 1161	INDUSTRY VOL 1	50
75	KPM 1162	INDUSTRY VOL 2	40
75	KPM 1163	ROCK SPECTRUM	50
75	KPM 1164	LOONY TUNES	15
75	KPM 1165	A JAZZ INCLINATION	40
75	KPM 1166	PIANO VIBERATIONS	75
75	KPM 1167	OUTDOOR LIFE	18
75	KPM 1168	DRAMATIC ACTION	100
75	KPM 1169	ARP ODYSSEY	30
75	KPM 1170	SOUNDS OF THE TIME	75
75	KPM 1171	IMPACT AND ACTION	60
76	KPM 1172	VISUAL IMPACT	100
76	KPM 1173	SOLID GOLD	40
76	KPM 1174	AMUSEMENT	50
76	KPM 1175	LOVES THEMES	40

PEER INTERNATIONAL

MINT VALUE £

76	KPM 1176	CHARTBUSTERS	18
76	KPM 1177	HOT WAX	80
76	KPM 1178	CARICATURE	20
76	KPM 1179	ORCHESTRAL CONTRASTS	25
76	KPM 1180	TENDER EMOTIONS	30
76	KPM 1181	SILVER BAND	15
76	KPM 1182	TRADITIONAL FOLK MUSIC OF GREAT BRITAIN AND FRANCE	15
77	KPM 1183	MIDDLE EAST SUITE/INDIA	40
77	KPM 1184	GEMINI SUITE	20
77	KPM 1185	THE STRING FAMILY	15
77	KPM 1187	THE NATURE OF WOODWIND	15
77	KPM 1188	CONTEMPO	100
77	KPM 1189	DISTINCTIVE THEMES/RACE TO ACHIEVEMENT	150
77	KPM 1190	VIVID UNDERSCORES	75
77	KPM 1191	LANDSCAPES/THINGS TO COME/NEW INNOVATIONS SUITE	15
77	KPM 1192	THE ROAD FORWARD	100
77	KPM 1193	CLASSICAL SYNTHESIZER/STAINED GLASS WINDOWS	18
77	KPM 1194	BIG CITY SUITE/JINGLE JANGLE JINGLES	60
77	KPM 1195	MUSIC SUITES VOL. 1	20
77	KPM 1196	ROCK ON	50
77	KPM 1197	INDUSTRY VOL 3	20
77	KPM 1198	THE LIGHTER SIDE/LIFE OF LEISURE	25
77	KPM 1199	THE CLASSICAL HARP	20
77	KPM 1120	DAYBREAK	40
77	KPM 1214	PULSE OF THE CITY	15

PEER INTERNATIONAL

69	PIL 9001	THE GOOD WORD	25
70	PIL 9002	PACE-SETTER	20
70	PIL 9003	STRING SCENE	20
70	PIL 9004	SOUL OF A CITY	40
70	PIL 9005	INTER RELATION	30
70	PIL 9006	MY THING	150
70	PIL 9007	SOUND OF MEXICO	18
71	PIL 9008	COMBUSTION	30
71	PIL 9009	BIG HAMMER	100
71	PIL 9010	DELMA	15
71	PIL 9011	THE WORLD OVER	15
71	PIL 9012	NO WAITING	20
72	PIL 9013	MINDBENDER	500
72	PIL 9014	ZENITH	30
72	PIL 9015	SUN SEEKER	20
72	PIL 9016	GEMINI	35
73	PIL 9017	CONTRASTS IN JAZZ VOL 1	15
73	PIL 9018	CONTRASTS IN JAZZ VOL 2	25
73	PIL 9019	CONTRASTS IN JAZZ VOL 3	35
73	PIL 9021	FLIP TOP	30
73	PIL 9023	REGGAE FOR REAL	250
74	PIL 9024	CONFRONTATION	25
74	PIL 9025	SWEET SURPRISE	20
74	PIL 9026	SOLAR FLARES	350
74	PIL 9027	ELECTRIC BAZAAR	150
75	PIL 9028	SCOOP!	200
76	PIL 9029	FIVE PLUS FOUR	200
76	PIL 9030	FREE DIMENSION	20
76	PIL 9032	TRENDY	15
76	PIL 9034	EARTH SHAKER	70
76	PIL 9035	TIME OF YOUR LIFE	20
76	PIL 9036	ROCK ALLEGRO	20
77	PIL 9037	HIT MAN	100
77	PIL 9038	HANGOVER	100
78	PIL 9039	LOST STAR	200
79	PIL 9040	POINT BLANK	40
80	PIL 9042	PRETTY POSE	20
80	PIL 9043	WORKFORCE	60
80	PIL 9042	CENTRAL PARK	15

PROGRAMME MUSIC

73	Programme PM 001	BEATS & BALLADS	25
73	Programme PM 002	CONTRASTS	30
74	Programme PM 003	SHADES OF ROCK	25
74	Programme PM 004	FACES OF FUNK	30
74	Programme PM 005	HARMONY GRASS/REGGAE	25
74	Programme PM 006	DESIGN IN BRASS AND SILVER	20
75	Programme PM 007	STRICTLY FOR THE BIRDS AND STRAIGHT DOWN THE MIDDLE	25
75	Programme PM 008	ON THE SIDE OF THE ANGELS	35
75	Programme PM 011	MUSIC TO VARNISH OWLS BY	100
75	Programme PM 009	FURTHER FACES	40
75	Programme PM 010	MORE THAN SOMEWHAT!	25
75	Programme PM 012	LIGHT AND SHADE	25
75	Programme PM 013	SHEER ENJOYMENT	25

REGENCY LINE

			MINT VALUE £
75	Programme PM 014	A HUNDRED AND ONE GUITARS	20
76	Programme PM 015	DOUBLE EXPOSURE	40
77	Programme PM 016	ROCK REFLECTIONS	15
77	Programme PM 017	GUITAR BREAK	18
77	Programme PM 019	MEDIUM - RARE	40
78	Programme PM 020	HARD CORE...SOFT CENTRE	18
78	Programme PM 022	CHOICE MORSELS	25
78	Programme PM 023	TAKE YOUR PICK!	15
79	Programme PM 024	LUCKY NUMBERS	18
79	Programme PM 025	HEY DISCO!	120
79	Programme PM 026	SUPERTRAX	20

REGENCY LINE

75	RL 1001	LIGHT BACKGROUND VOL 1	20
75	RL 1002	THEMES	30
75	RL 1003	ROCK	30
75	RL 1004	BOLIVIAN CARNIVAL	40
75	RL 1005	LATIN POP	30
75	RL 1006	MUSIQUE MEDIEVALE	15
75	RL 1007	HARPSICHORD	20
75	RL1008	SYNTHESIZER SPOTS	30
75	RL 1009	HARMONICA	18
75	RL 1010	HEAVY ROCK	60
75	RL 1011	WESTERN MUSIC	15
75	RL 1012	FESTIVAL OF BRASS	15
75	RL 1013	DRAMATIC MOODS	40
75	RL 1014	LIGHT BACKGROUND VOL II	15
75	RL 1015	THEMES VOL II	35
75	RL 1016	SAMPLER	15
75	RL 1017	FLUTE AND SAX	30
75	RL 1018	PLAYTIME	20
76	RL1019	THE DETECTIVES	40
76	RL 1020	BITS 'N' PIECES	20
76	RL1021	ROCKIN IN RHYTHM	50
76	RL1022	HAPPY HOLIDAY	60
76	RL 1023	STRANGE!!!	20
76	RL 1024	GRECIAN ADVENTURE/GYPSY	15
76	RL 1025	ROCK 'N' ROLL	15
76	RL 1026	SPORT	15
76	RL1027	LATE NIGHT MUSIC	30
76	RL1028	DISCO HAPPENING	40
77	RL 1029	PALM COURT	15
77	RL 1030	NEWS!!!	15
77	RL 1031	CLASSICAL GUITAR	15
77	RL 1033	HAPPY GUITAR	15
77	RL 1034	CHINESE	15
77	RL 1036	TENSION UNLIMITED	80

ROUGE MUSIC

75	RMS LP 101	SKYBOAT	25
75	RMS LP 102	SWEET SOUL	30
75	RMS LP 103	INTERLACE	30
75	RMS LP 104	THE KING AND THE CLOWN	30
75	RMS 105	HI-FLY	30
75	RMS LP 106	BLACKOUT	150
76	RMS LP 107	RETURN TO BASE	15
76	RMS LP 108	COBRA	40
77	RMS LP 109	MEAL TICKET	60
77	RMS LP 110	MUSIC REPORT	60
77	RMS LP 111	KITES	20
77	RMS LP 112	LET THE MUSIC PLAY	20
78	RMS LP 113	HARD AS ROCK	20
79	RMS LP 114	SOFT AND TENDER	15
78	RMS LP 115	DO IT	25
78	RMS LP 116	FADED JEANS	15
78	RMS LP 117	ALL ABOUT THE SEA	15
78	RMS LP 118	DISCOS LIKE THIS	40
79	RMS LP 119	PULSES	30
79	RMS LP 120	CANDOUR	20
79	RMS LP 121	FRIDAY GIRL	25
79	RMS LP 122	ROBOT DANCER	40
80	RMS LP 124	COUNTRY GRASS	15
81	RMS LP 125	MAKING TRACKS	15
81	RMS LP 126	PATTERNS	50
81	RMS LP 127	DANCING GRASS	15
81	RMS LP 128	IMPETUS	15
81	RMS LP 129	PLAY ON	20
81	RMS LP 130	GLASS HEAD	25
81	RMS LP 131	SPERDOUP	35
81	RMS LP 132	SLICED APPLE	30
81	RMS LP 133	PIPSQUEEK	15

SOUNDS OF NOW

MINT VALUE £

81	RMS LP 134	WHISPER TO THE MOON	15
81	RMS LP 135	HISTORY OF JAZZ	15
82	RMS LP 136	TELETEXT	35
82	RMS LP 137	VOYAGE OF DISCOVERY	15
82	RMS LP 138	MOVEMENT	25
82	RMS LP 140	INSTANT REGGAE	18
82	RMS LP 141	HERCULES	15
82	RMS LP 142	RED KITE	40
82	RMS LP 143	NEW AGE	15
82	RMS LP 144	REMEMBER	15
82	RMS LP 145	DRUMATICS	20
83	RMS LP 147	CUTAWAY	20
83	RMS LP 148	SOLARIUM	20
83	RMS LP 149	SOME SHUFFLIN'	15
83	RMS LP 150	BASS MOODS VOL 1	20
83	RMS LP 151	BASS MOODS VOL 2	20
83	RMS LP 152	UNDERCOVER	30
84	RMS LP 153	TOMORROW, TODAY	18
84	RMS LP 154	SNEAKING UP	18
84	RMS LP 157	BREAKDANCE	20
84	RMS LP 158	TOPSY TURVY	15
85	RMS LP 159	AHEAD OF THE FIELD	15
85	RMS LP 160	NEW OUTLOOK	15
86	RMS LP 161	REFLEX	15
86	RMS LP 162	REFLEX (REMIXES)	15
85	RMS LP 165	SOUND ON SOUND	15
86	RMS LP 168	AUDIOTRONICS	15
86	RMS LP 170	REGGAE INVASION	30
86	RMS LP 169	HIGHLIGHTS	15
87	RMS LP 173	PACW AGE	15
87	RMS LP 175	CHANGING SEASONS	25
87	RMS LP 178	KINETICS	20

SOUNDS OF NOW
71	Sounds Of Now 1	SOUNDS OF NOW (ERIC SIDAY)	50
71	Sounds Of Now 2	SOUNDS OF NOW 2 (ERIC SIDAY)	75
72	Sounds Of Now 3	SOUNDS OF NOW 2 (PAUL DUNLAP)	100

SOUTHERN MUSIC
66	MQLP 19	ELECTRONIC MUSIC	20
68	MQLP 27	THE SCOTTMEN	20
70	MQLP 47	JAZZ BEAT/JAZZ BEAT BOSSA NOVA	30
71	MQLP 32	JAZZ DRAMATIC	30
72	MQLP 38	ELECTRONIC MUSIC	75
72	MQLP 39	AFRO SPOOKY	200
73	MQLP 40	ELECTRONIC MUSIC	30
78	MQLP 48	Electronic Music	75
78	MQLP 51	EXOTICA	30

STANDARD
70	ESL 196	NATIONAL BALKAN ENSEMBLE	20
74	ESL 127	ELECTRONIC MUSIC	70
75	ESL 133	ENCORE ELECTRONIC	40
69	ESL 103	SOLO GUITAR (Michael Chapman)	60
00	ESL 104	ELECTRONIC MUSIC	100

STUDIO G
70	LPSG 1001	BEAT GROUP	80
70	LPSG 1002	BIG JAZZ AND BIG BEAT	25
70	LPSG 1003	LIGHT JAZZ	25
70	LPSG 1004	ANIMALS AND CHILDREN	20
70	LPSG 1005	SCENIC AND ROMANCE	20
70	LPSG 1006	DESCRIPTIVE SUITES VOLUME 1	20
70	LPSG 1007	INDUSTRIAL AND WAR	20
70	LPSG 1008	DRAMATIC AND HORROR VOLUME 1	30
70	LPSG 1009	ELECTRONIC AGE	70
70	LPSG 1010	LOCATIONS AND COMEDY VOLUME 1	15
70	LPSG 1011	PERIOD MUSIC AND SOLO INSTRUMENTS	15
70	LPSG 1012	NATIONAL	15
74	LPSG 2001	DISCO BEAT	40
74	LPSG 2002	COOL BEAT	60
74	LPSG 2003	LIGHT MOVEMENT VOLUME 2	15
74	LPSG 2004	ANIMALS AND CHILDREN VOLUME 2	20
74	LPSG 2005	SCENIC AND ROMANCE VOLUME 2	20
74	LPSG 2006	DESCRIPTIVE	15
74	LPSG 2007	INDUSTRIAL AND WAR VOLUME 2	15
74	LPSG 2008	DRAMA AND HORROR VOLUME 2	20
74	LPSG 2009	AVANT GARDE	75
74	LPSG 2010	LOCATIONS AND COMEDY VOLUME 2	15
74	LPSG 2011	PERIOD MUSIC VOLUME 2	15
74	LPSG 2012	NATIONAL - VOLUME 2	15
76	LPSG 3001	POP SPECTRUM VOLUME 3	40
76	LPSG 3002	BEAT UNDERSCORE	80

STUDIO ONE

			MINT VALUE £
76	LPSG 3003	THEMATIC MUSIC VOLUME 3	15
76	LPSG 3004	ANIMALS AND CHILDREN VOLUME 3	15
78	LPSG 3005	TRAVEL AND ROMANCE VOLUME 3	15
78	LPSG 3006	MUSIC FOR STRINGS	15
78	LPSG 3007	RHYTHM - INDUSTRIAL UNDERSCORE - VOLUME 3	250
78	LPSG 3008	DRAMA AND HORROR VOLUME 3	40
78	LPSG 3009	MUSIC FOR SYNTHESIZERS	40
78	LPSG 3010	LOCATIONS AND COMEDY VOLUME 3	15
78	LPSG 3012	MUSIC OF THE MIDDLE EAST	25
79	LPSG 4001	ACTION DISCO	60
81	LPSG 4002	IMAGES	40
81	LPSG 4003	TITLE MUSIC	15
80	LPSG 4004	ABSTRACTS	40
82	LPSG 4005	NATURES WORLD	40
82	LPSG 4008	JAZZ FUNK ROAD	15

STUDIO ONE

71	SO7	MAURICE POP	15
73	SO14	PIERRE LAVIN POP BAND	30

SYLVESTER MUSIC

67	SMC/LP501	JAZZ WAVES (10")	25
67	SMC/LP502	VOICES IN THE WIND (10")	30
67	SMC/LP503	STRIPTEASE (10")	15
67	SMC/LP504	AQUAPLANE (10")	20
67	SMC/LP505	ZENITH (10")	30
67	SMC/LP506	TUTTI FLUTTI (10")	20
67	SMC/LP507	GO (10")	20
68	SMC/LP508	KIKI (10")	20
68	SMC/LP509	CONTEMPORARY ARTS (10")	15
68	SMC/LP510	EMBARGO (10")	20
68	SMC/LP511	RHYTHM FOR URSULA (10")	20
68	SMC/LP512	EXCHANGES (10")	20
68	SMC/LP513	SILHOUETTES	20
68	SMC/LP514	HEMISPHERE (10")	15
68	SMC/LP515	AND SO ON... (10")	20
68	SMC/LP516	RACING TEMPO (10")	15
68	SMC/LP517	PHILOSOPHALE (10")	20
68	SMC/LP518	IMAGES MUSICALES NO 1	15
69	SMC/LP519	CHATEAU (10")	15
69	SMX/LP520	PLAQUES TORNANTES (10")	50
69	SMC/LP521	PRAELUDIUM (10")	15
69	SMC/LP522	THE MUSIC OF ERIC TOWREN	15
70	SMC/LP523	PICTURES OF CHILDREN	20
70	SMC/LP524	ACTION	20
70	SMC/LP525	JAZZ FOR ACTION	35
71	SMC/LP526	POST COMBUSTION	25
71	SMC/LP527	BLUE CYLINDER	30
71	SMC/LP528	CHRONORADIAL	20
71	SMC/LP529	ULTRA POP-UP	60
71	SMC/LP530	MOODS AND MARCHES	15
71	SMC/LP531	RAGGERS	35
71	SMC/LP532	BEFORE OR AFTER	40
71	SMC/LP533	FILIGREE	15
72	SMC/LP534	LIFE STORY	20
72	SMC/LP535	STROLL THROUGH BRAZIL	15
72	SMC/LP536	PATCHWORK ORCHESTRA VOLUME ONE	25
72	SMC/LP537	PATCHWORK ORCHESTRA VOLUME TWO	25
72	SMC/LP538	PATCHWORK ORCHESTRA VOLUME THREE	40
72	SMC/LP539	PATCHWORK ORCHESTRA VOLUME FOUR	25
72	SMC/LP541	COMMERCIAL SOUNDS	20
72	SMC/LP542	CITY IN TERROR	20
74	SMCS/LP544	AQUASUN	30
79	SMCS/LP555	CHARADE	30
80	SMCS/LP556	TINTED GLASS	30
81	SMCS/LP557	BRIGHT AND SHINING	50

THEMES INTERNATIONAL

73	TIM 1001	THE LIGHTER TOUCH	20
70	TIM 1002	NEW BLOOD	80
70	TIM 1003	MAIN THEMES AND SIG TUNES	30
73	TIM 1006	THE ROMANTIC MOOD	20
73	TIM 1007	LIGHT ACTIVITY	20
73	TIM 1008	DRAMATIC ACTION	40
73	TIM 1009	HAPPY PASTIMES	20
73	TIM 1011	THE ROCK MACHINE	50
74	TIM 1012	SYNTHESIZER AND PERCUSSION	100
74	TIM 1013	BREATH OF DANGER	60
74	TIM 1014	FREEDOM ROAD	35
74	TIM 1015	MYSTERY MOVIE	100
76	TIM 1017	ROCK COMEDY	30
75	TIM 1018	THE ALL AMERICAN POWERHOUSE	100

THEMES INTERNATIONAL

MINT VALUE £

76	TIM 1019	JE T'AIME	70
76	TIM 1020	PAN AMERICAN TRAVELOGUE	70
76	TIM 1021	THE VOICE OF SOUL	175
76	TIM 1022	THE SOUND OF SOUL	100
76	TIM 1023	PULSE OF EVENTS	80
76	TIM 1024	DRAMA SUITE VOL 1	100
76	TIM 1025	DRAMA SUITE PART II	200
77	TIM 1026	THINGS TO COME	35
77	TIM 1027	CONTEMPORARY CONTRASTS	35
79	TIM 1029	PERCUSSION SPECTRUM	40
78	TIM 1030	LISTEN TO L.A.	35
78	TIM 1031	HAVE SOUND WILL TRAVEL	30
78	TIM 1032	STREET PICTURES	25
78	TIM 1033	KEYTRONICS	30
78	TIM 1034	WISH YOU WERE HERE	20
81	TIM 1037	STREET LEVEL	30
82	TIM 1040	NIGHT SENSATIONS	20

TAX SCAM RECORDS

Back in the late 70s there was a legal loophole that was exploited in America where the potential sales of a record could be legally offset against costs. This led to the formation of a number of 'tax scam' labels where albums were recorded and pressed up in small numbers with the sole intention of avoiding tax. There was, as you might imagine, much more to the process than that but the key thing was to make it look as if the record had been released in order to generate the tax loss that could lead to a profit for the company or investors concerned. As far as we know most of these labels were confined to America but it appears that Ebonite Records was a label that licensed material to the U.K.. This label then pressed records up with a view to selling them in the normal legal fashion. These records were, however, all released at once as an advert in Melody Maker in 1978 suggests. There were over 80 titles. The advert stated "the most extensive collection of hit product to hit the world." This was somewhat far from the truth as many of the records - that ranged from jazz standards to pop covers - were very poor as the musicians involved (all working under a number of made-up names) recorded, in some instances, some awful cover versions that - for some reason - went on for several minutes or more in order that the record could be classed as an LP - even though they were marketed as 12" singles. indeed. It is probably true to suggest that it was quantity rather than quality that was the order of the day as some records have different artist titles but it is obvious from the playing - and in some cases awful singing - that they were recorded by the same people at the same session and then spread over different releases. Of course, some of the musicians involved were very good and turned out slabs of funk/disco/soul that is now sought after and collectable. There are some absolute killers out there and some of the excellent records put out by Ebonite in the U.K. testify to this. The Returners 12" is a case in point whereas others are so bad that is is not even funny. This list is not exhaustive as some records were named in that 1978 advert that have, as far as we know, not surfaced - as yet. These artists have mouth watering names like Blind Faith, Midshipmen, The Bodybuilders, Cabaret, The Short People, The Astronomers, Wrecking Havok and The Earth City Rockers etc.. If you find any of them or know of any other examples of tax related records pressed for the U.K. please let us know. Finally, although the ultra collectable DISCO FOX LP was listed in that Melody Maker advert we have yet to see a UK pressing. Those that have surfaced so far have been US pressings.

78	Ebonite EE001	VOYAGE: Watermelon Man/Maiden Voyage (33rpm 12")	20
78	Ebonite EE003	LOVE MAKERS: Gloria/What's Going On (33rpm 12")	60
78	Ebonite EE004	AFTER TIME: Itchy Fingers/When Your Lovers Gone/Time After Time/Love For Sale (33rpm 12")	25
78	Ebonite EE005	BLUESERS: All Blues/Blues In G (33rpm 12")	20
78	Ebonite EE007	MISTY TIME: Laura/Now's The Time//Misty (33rpm 12")	18
78	Ebonite EE009	ANYTIME: Do It Any Way You Want To Do It/The World Is A Ghetto (33rpm 12")	40
78	Ebonite EE010	JOGGERS: Killer Joe/Milestones/The Nearness Of You (33rpm 12")	20
78	Ebonite EE011	RELATIVITY: Bad Luck/Peace Song/Low Down (33rpm 12")	30
78	Ebonite EE012	LUMBERJACKS: Lady Bird/Blue Train/Forest Flower (33rpm 12")	20
78	Ebonite EE019	SOMEBODY: Meditations/There Will Never Be Another You/Everybody Loves Somebody (33rpm 12")	15
78	Ebonite EE027	CLASS ACT: When The Lights Are Low/The Strut/Stairway To The Stars (33rpn 12")	15
78	Ebonite EE028	FINDERS: You'll Never Find/Blues In C/Breezin (33rpm 12")	15
78	Ebonite EE030	SECRET SERVICE: Maiden Voyage/Secret Love/Bongo Bop (33rpm 12")	15
78	Ebonite EE034	RINGS AND THINGS: My Favourite Things/Rhythm-A-Ning (33rpm 12")	10
78	Ebonite EE033	ENGINEERS: Long Train Running/Silly Love Songs/ Donna Lee (33rpm 12")	12
78	Ebonite EE037	QUIZMASTERS: If You Want Me To Stay/Fever (33rpm 12")	30
78	Ebonite EE038	LADY MAKERS: Ain't No Sunshine When She's Gone/East Of The Sun/Mr Luckt (33rpm 12")	35
78	Ebonite EE043	BARTENDERS: I Love Everything About You/Love Hangover (33rpm 12")	20
78	Ebonite EE044	STAR RIDERS: Stella By Starlight/Blooz/Cute/It's Yours/Take The A Train (33rpm 12")	15
78	Ebonite EE050	ENGLISH MUSTARD: English Mustard/I Don't Know (33rpm 12")	15
78	Ebonite EE055	PEPPER SHAKERS: Fever/Shake Your Booty (33rpm 12")	30
78	Ebonite EE056	SENTIMENTALISTS: Getting Sentimental Over You/Poincianna/Love Walked In (33rpm 12")	15
78	Ebonite EE065	MICRONIZERS: Tangerine/Mercy Mercy (33rpm 12")	20
78	Ebonite EE067	G MEN: Somewhere In The Night/You'd Be So Nice To Come Home To/Godfathers Theme/Blues In G (33rpm 12")	20
78	Ebonite EE069	AMOURIZERS: Our Love Is Here To Stay/Naima (33rpm 12")	18
78	Ebonite EE072	BUTCHERMEN: Mack The Knife And Other Ditties/Jazzy Rock/Changing Moods (33rpm	20

THEMES INTERNATIONAL

MINT VALUE £

78	Ebonite EE074	STOMPERS: Killing Me Softtly/Stomping at The Savoy (33rpm 12")...... [cont.] 12")......	15
78	Ebonite EE077	THE RETURNERS: It Seems That Way/Long Road Back/Here We Go (33rpm 12")......	50
78	Ebonite EE080	CITY OF ANGELS: Angel Eyes/Au Preavauve/Living For The City (33rpm 12")......	15
78	Ebonite EE083	WINTER SUN: Baby It's Cold Outside/Sunny Moon For Two/Colors (33rpm 12")......	15
78	Ebonite EE086	AFFIRMATIVES: Getting The Prize/This Masquerade (33rpm 12")......	20
78	Ebonite EE088	LITTLE SUNFLOWER: Little Sunflower/Hang Up Your Hangups (33rpm 12")......	40
78	Ebonite EE089	WARLOCKS: Witchcraft/Impressions (33rpm 12")......	30
78	Ebonite EE090	WINEMAKERS: I'm Gonna Love You A Little Bit More/Heard It Through The GrapevineGhetto (33rpm 12")......	25
78	Ebonite EE092	UMBRELLISTICS: Ease On Down The Road/Here's That Rainy Day/Sunny (33rpm 12")......	15
78	Ebonite EE093	BEATFINDERS: Samba De Orpheo/Walking In Rhythm/Sway (33rpm 12")......	25
78	Ebonite EE096	MARKSMEN: Watermelon Man/Disco Queen (33rpm 12")......	35
78	Ebonite EE104	PERSUASIVE JAZZ: Nicole/Polynesian/Pretty Elizabeth Jane (33rpm 12" in Persuasive Jazz sleeve)......	40
78	Ebonite EE108	DESTRUCTORS: Sunshine/The Ghetto (33rpm 12")......	15
78	Ebonite EE115	GROOVERS: Do You Like It/Groovin (33rpm, 12")......	40
78	Ebonite EE142	TRAILBLAZER: Don't Want To Be The Lone Ranger/Sing A Song/Walk On By (33rpm 12")	10
78	Ebonite EE142	FLOORWARD: Let's Groove/Dance To The Music (33rpm 12")......	10
78	Ebonite EE148	CHAMELEONS: Chameleon/Sure Is unky/Foot Stompin Music (33rpm 12")......	20
78	Ebonite EE166	LOVE MAGIC: Isn't She Lovely/Superstition (33rpm, 12")......	15
78	Ebonite EE169	SKY LAW: That's The Way Of The World/Kalimba (33rpm 12")......	30
78	Ebonite EE171	FORAGERS: What's Going On/Grapevine/You're All I Need (33rpm 12")......	18
78	Ebonite EE178	CYMBALISM: Mercury 49/Mr Tambourine Man/Feel Like Making Love (33rpm 12")......	10
78	Ebonite EE173	SONGSTERS: I'm Gonna Love You A Little Bit More/Sing A Song (33rpm 12")......	25
78	Ebonite EE172	MOUNTAIN WOMAN: Ain't No Mountain High Enough/Super Woman (33rpm 12")......	15
78	Ebonite EE 177	SECRET RAINBOW: April In Paris/Secret Love/Somewhere Over The Rainbow (33rpm 12")......	15
78	Ebonite EE179	PSYCHOSIS: Amalgamation/I Mean You/Tenor Madness (33rpm 12")......	15
78	Ebonite EE181	SEVEN COLOURS: Summertime/Canadian Sunset/Girl Talk (33rpm 12")......	15
78	Ebonite EE524	INVERTERS: Colours/Nobody Loves You When You're Down And Out (33rpm 12")......	15
78	Ebonite EE520	CALENDARS: Like A Rolling Stone/Taxman/Last TIme (33rpm 12")......	15
78	Ebonite EE544	MEASURING STICK: I Love Music/How Long Has This Been Going On (33rpm 12")......	25
78	Ebonite EE595	JOG WALKERS: Walking To New Orleans/Life In The Jungle Boogie/California Dreaming (33rpm 12")......	15
78	Ebonite EE605	SANDSTORM: Season Of The Witch/All Along The Watch Tower/Take FIve (33rpm 12")	15
78	Ebonite EE 1009	THE WORKING MAN: Coming Home/Georgia (33rpm 12")......	15
78	Ebonite EE1016	HEY MEN: Hey Joe/Crossroads (33rpm, 12")......	15
78	Ebonite EE 1001	ESCHALOT: Love Love You/Come On Up (33rpm 12")......	15
78	Ebonite EE 5017	INSPECTOR GENERALS: (33rpm 12")......	15
78	Ebonite EE 5021	POLARIZATION: (LP, die cut sleeve)......	15
78	Ebonite EE 7010	THE INVISIBLE CHASE: Red House Blues/Catch The Wind/I Want You (33rpm 12")......	18

RECORD COLLECTOR'S
GRADING SYSTEM

In order to assist everyone who buys and sells rare discs, *Record Collector* magazine has originated a set of standards for the condition of second-hand records, cassettes and CDs. Anyone buying or selling records through the magazine must use our conditions to state what amount of wear and tear the disc, its sleeve and/or contents have been subject to. The seven standard condition categories, and a description of what each one means, are listed below:

MINT: The record itself is in brand new condition with no surface marks or deterioration in sound quality. The cover and any extra items such as the lyric sheet, booklet or poster are in perfect condition. Records advertised as Sealed or Unplayed should be Mint.

EXCELLENT: The record shows some signs of having been played, but there is very little lessening in sound quality. The cover and packaging might have slight wear and/or creasing.

VERY GOOD: The record has obviously been played many times, but displays no major deterioration in sound quality, despite noticeable surface marks and the occasional light scratch. Normal wear and tear on the cover or extra items, without any major defects, is acceptable.

GOOD: The record has been played so much that the sound quality has noticeably deteriorated, perhaps with some distortion and mild scratches. The cover and contents suffer from folding, scuffing of edges, spine splits, discoloration, etc.

FAIR: The record is still just playable but has not been cared for properly and displays considerable surface noise; it may even jump. The cover and contents will be torn, stained and/or defaced.

POOR: The record will not play properly due to scratches, bad surface noise, etc. The cover and contents will be badly damaged or partly missing.

BAD: The record is unplayable or might even be broken, and is only of use as a collection-filler.

CDs & CASSETTES: As a general rule, CDs and cassettes either play perfectly — in which case they are in Mint condition — or they don't, in which case their value is minimal. Cassette tape is liable to deteriorate with age, even if it remains unplayed, so care should be taken when buying old tapes. CDs are difficult to grade visually: they can look perfect but actually be faulty, while in other cases they may appear damaged but still play perfectly. Cassette and CD inlays and booklets should be graded in the same way as record covers and sleeves. In general, the plastic containers for cassettes and CDs can easily be replaced if they are broken or scratched, but card covers and digipaks are subject to the same wear as record sleeves.

RECORD COLLECTOR'S
GRADING READY RECKONER

This Ready Reckoner will help you work out the value of a record in any condition. For example, if you see a disc which is valued at £10 in Mint condition, but which you consider to be in only Very Good condition, then you can consult the Ready Reckoner and find out the appropriate price for the record — in this case, £5. As very few collectors are interested in records in Poor or Bad condition, we consider that any disc worth less than £10 in Mint condition is effectively worthless in Poor or Bad condition.

MINT	EX	VG	Good	Fair	Poor	Bad
1,000	800	500	300	150	80	25
500	400	250	150	75	40	12
300	240	150	90	45	25	8
250	200	125	75	38	20	6
200	160	100	60	30	15	5
150	120	75	45	25	13	4
125	100	60	38	18	12	3
100	80	50	30	15	8	2.50
75	60	35	22	10	6	2
50	40	25	15	8	4	1.50
40	32	20	12	6	3	1
30	25	15	9	4.50	2.50	—
25	20	12	7.50	3.50	2	—
22	18	11	6.50	3	1.75	—
20	16	10	6	2.50	1.50	—
15	12	8	4.50	2	1	—
12	10	6	3.50	1.75	0.75	—
10	8	5	3	1.50	—	—
8	6	4	2.50	1	—	—
7	5	3.50	2	0.75	—	—
6	4.50	3	1.75	—	—	—
5	4	2.50	1.50	—	—	—
4	3.25	2	1.25	—	—	—
3	2.50	1.50	1	—	—	—
2	1.75	1	—	—	—	—

RECORD COLLECTOR BACK ISSUES

**For digital copies please go to
www.pocketmags.com/record-collector-magazine/issues.
Digital back issues are now available from issue 408 onwards on iOS,
Android or Amazon.**

THE HOME OF VINYL

Visit www.recordcollectormag.com
To order an extensive range of back issues

Record Collector Presents . . . Genesis is a new, one-off magazine that celebrates the storied career of Genesis. Looking solely at the work of the group (as their solo releases are another magazine in itself!), *RC* follows them from their early days recording for Decca in 60s London to their current – and possibly final – world tour. There's everything a Genesis collector needs to know, including a brand-new updated UK discography, an in-depth look at their international rarities and memorabilia. Steve Hackett speaks extensively about his time with the group in a new interview; honorary Genesis member Richard Macphail has written an introduction and ex-members John Silver and Anthony Phillips contribute, too. Writer Joanne Harris (of *Chocolat* fame) tells of her love for the group. With box-fresh appraisals of all the group's studio and live albums, and assessments of singles and compilations, there's no trick in this tale – we know what you like!

Available now from: shop.recordcollectormag.com

Record Collector Presents… Black Sabbath is essential reading for those of you who like it heavy. We've asked Bill Ward questions from fans; Tony Iommi has written an exclusive foreword; Geezer Butler talks bass, lyrics... and football?!; and we've spoken exclusively to Sharon Osbourne about her collection of Sabbath and Ozzy memorabilia. And that's just for starters, you'll also find a career-spanning guide to the rarest UK and international releases; an in-depth UK discography; new features covering every studio album; an early look at the new *Sabotage* box set; hardcore fans show us their amazing collections; a look at Ozzy's solo years; classic features from the *RC* archive; an inside look at the huge *Home Of Metal* exhibition that took place in Birmingham in 2019; and much more.

Available now from: shop.recordcollectormag.com

The latest in *RC*'s series of special editions will thrill fans of the explosive rockers, one of the most successful (and most collectable) British bands of all time. With fantastic features and interviews from the *RC* archive, newly commissioned pieces from some of the best music writers out there, and in-depth looks at their most sought-after records and memorabilia, it'll resonate with rock lovers of every g-g-generation.

Available now from: shop.recordcollectormag.com

Record Collector Presents The Kinks is a one-off special edition celebrating one of the most significant – and collectable – British bands of all time. Featuring exclusive new interviews with Ray Davies, Dave Davies and Mick Avory; in-depth new pieces on their classic studio albums of the 60s and 70s; features on their most in-demand worldwide releases and a comprehensive UK discography; an appreciation of Ray Davies' solo albums and extra-curricular activities; an interview with the man behind their official fanclub; profiles of some dedicated followers; classic interviews with the band, and much more. Kinks fans will be in paradise.

Available now from: shop.recordcollectormag.com

An indispensable guide to the 100 most valuable UK prog pressings out there.

Know your 'Igginbottom from your Cressida? This *RC* special's for you – our experts delve deep into the world of 70s prog, telling the stories behind some of the most forward-thinking music of the time, from private pressings to *The Dark Side Of The Moon*. With a foreword from Steve Hackett and interviews with many of the musicians behind the albums, and much more.

Available now from: shop.recordcollectormag.com